BUTTERWORTHS INSURANCE LAW HANDBOOK

Eleventh edition

Consultant Editor
ANDREW BARTON MA (Cantab)

Counsel, Allen & Overy LLP Insurance Group

LexisNexis®

Members of the LexisNexis Group worldwide

United Kingdom	LexisNexis, a Division of Reed Elsevier (UK) Ltd, Halsbury House, 35 Chancery Lane, London, WC2A 1EL, and London House, 20-22 East London Street, Edinburgh EH7 4BQ
Australia	LexisNexis Butterworths, Chatswood, New South Wales
Austria	LexisNexis Verlag ARD Orac GmbH & Co KG, Vienna
Benelux	LexisNexis Benelux, Amsterdam
Canada	LexisNexis Canada, Markham, Ontario
China	LexisNexis China, Beijing and Shanghai
France	LexisNexis SA, Paris
Germany	LexisNexis Deutschland GmbH, Munster
Hong Kong	LexisNexis Hong Kong, Hong Kong
India	LexisNexis India, New Delhi
Italy	Giuffrè Editore, Milan
Japan	LexisNexis Japan, Tokyo
Malaysia	Malayan Law Journal Sdn Bhd, Kuala Lumpur
New Zealand	LexisNexis NZ Ltd, Wellington
Poland	Wydawnictwo Prawnicze LexisNexis Sp, Warsaw
Singapore	LexisNexis Singapore, Singapore
South Africa	LexisNexis Butterworths, Durban
USA	LexisNexis, Dayton, Ohio

Published by LexisNexis

A CIP Catalogue record for this book is available from the British Library.

ISBN 978 1 4057 4997 8

Printed in the UK by CPI William Clowes, Beccles, NR34 7TL

Visit LexisNexis Butterworths at www.lexisnexis.co.uk

PREFACE

This, the Eleventh edition of Butterworths Insurance Law Handbook, is the second edition which I have had the privilege of editing. One of the legacies of the hard work of my predecessor editors is that the Handbook has grown to become a wide-ranging and extremely comprehensive collection of insurance-related materials, which now includes not only insurance statutes and regulations, but also extensive material from the Financial Services Authority Handbook, EU legislation and ABI guidance and codes of practice.

Whilst the vast majority of this material is now available online, I remain a firm believer in the value of this work. As a long-time user of the Handbook, I can personally vouch for the usefulness of having an up-to-date hard copy which can be thrown into a briefcase or kept ready at one's elbow during meetings. It is surprising how often I find myself reaching for this book, even when at my desk where the information is only a few clicks away. There is nothing quite like a hard copy when serious concentration is needed. Old habits die hard (and I know I am not alone in this regard).

Regular updating is, of course, crucial to allow practitioners to continue to rely on the Handbook and this Eleventh edition continues the annual updating cycle first established by the last edition. Whilst there have been relatively few entirely new pieces of legislation, there have been the usual myriad tweaks and changes to existing statutes and regulations and LexisNexis have been hard at work ensuring that all the material is current. Not least among these are the changes to FSMA to give effect to the Acquisitions Directive in the UK, and the final text of the Solvency II Directive, as adopted by the European Council in November 2009.

As in previous editions, we have included the vast majority of the FSA Handbook which is relevant to the insurance industry including for the first time the "permitted links" section from the Conduct of Business Sourcebook (COBS).

As always, feedback from users to me (at Allen & Overy) or to LexisNexis is welcome. On the presumption that LexisNexis ask me to continue in the editorial chair, I will do my best to include requests where I think they will be of general interest.

I would like to thank the LexisNexis team whose primary task it is to keep the existing material up-to-date - this Handbook is what it is largely due to their skill and professionalism. It has been a pleasure to work with them.

I have also been assisted by several of my colleagues here at Allen & Overy (they know who they are), for which I am extremely grateful. I would like to thank in particular Tove Webster and Kate McInerney, colleagues of mine in the Insurance Group, whose help and suggestions have been invaluable in finalising the contents of this edition.

The law reflected in the Eleventh edition is that in force on 22nd February 2010.

ANDREW BARTON

Allen & Overy LLP

Publisher's Note

The Third Parties (Rights Against Insurers) Act 2010 received Royal Assent on 25 March 2010 as this book was being prepared for press. The Act is not yet in force and will repeal and replace the Third Parties (Rights Against Insurers) Act 1930, as from a day to be appointed. The Act also amends the Road Traffic Act 1988, s 153, and the Merchant Shipping Act 1995, s 165, as from a day to be appointed. The full text of the Act can be found on www.opsi.gov.uk or www.lexisnexis.com/uk/legal.

CONTENTS

Preface ... *page v*

PART I FINANCIAL SERVICES AND MARKETS LEGISLATION

A. Financial Services and Markets Act 2000, ss 1–39, 40–71, 104–142, 144–158, 165–194, 195, 196–232, 234, 234A, 314–410, 412, 413–424, 425–433, Schs 1–3, 5–7, 12–15, 17, 18, Pt II, para 16, Sch 21 ... **[1]**

B. Financial Services and Markets Act 2000 Statutory Instruments

Financial Services and Markets Act 2000 (Regulated Activities) Order 2001, SI 2001/544, arts 1–4, 10–25A, 25D, 26–44, 52–53A, 54–60A, 64–69, 72–73, 75, 82, 86, 92–96, Schs 1, 4 ... **[501]**

Financial Services and Markets Act 2000 (Carrying on Regulated Activities by Way of Business) Order 2001, SI 2001/1177, arts 1–3A, 4 ... **[591]**

Financial Services and Markets Act 2000 (Exemption) Order 2001, SI 2001/1201 ... **[595A]**

Financial Services and Markets Act 2000 (Appointed Representatives) Regulations 2001, SI 2001/1217 ... **[596]**

Financial Services and Markets Act 2000 (Professions) (Non-exempt Activities) Order 2001, SI 2001/1227, arts 1–6B, 7, 8 ... **[599]**

Financial Services and Markets Act 2000 (Compensation Scheme: Electing Participants) Regulations 2001, SI 2001/1783 ... **[611]**

Financial Services and Markets Act 2000 (Rights of Action) Regulations 2001, SI 2001/2256 ... **[618]**

Financial Services and Markets Act 2000 (Meaning of "Policy" and "Policyholder") Order 2001, SI 2001/2361 ... **[625]**

Financial Services and Markets Act 2000 (Variation of Threshold Conditions) Order 2001, SI 2001/2507 ... **[628]**

Financial Services and Markets Act 2000 (Gaming Contracts) Order 2001, SI 2001/2510 ... **[631]**

Financial Services and Markets Act 2000 (EEA Passport Rights) Regulations 2001, SI 2001/2511, regs 1–3, 6–8, 10, 13–21 ... **[633]**

Financial Services and Markets Act 2000 (Communications by Auditors) Regulations 2001, SI 2001/2587 ... **[649]**

Financial Services and Markets Act 2000 (Mutual Societies) Order 2001, SI 2001/2617 ... **[651]**

Financial Services and Markets Act 2000 (Insolvency) (Definition of "Insurer") Order 2001, SI 2001/2634 ... **[668]**

Financial Services and Markets Act 2000 (Law Applicable to Contracts of Insurance) Regulations 2001, SI 2001/2635 ... **[670]**

Financial Services and Markets Act 2000 (Control of Business Transfers) (Requirements on Applicants) Regulations 2001, SI 2001/3625 ... **[820]**

Financial Services and Markets Act 2000 (Control of Transfers of Business Done at Lloyd's) Order 2001, SI 2001/3626 ... **[826]**

Financial Services and Markets Act 2000 (Misleading Statements and Practices) Order 2001, SI 2001/3645, arts 1–3 ... **[838]**

Financial Services and Markets Act 2000 (Scope of Permission Notices) Order 2001, SI 2001/3771 ... **[848]**

Financial Services and Markets Act 2000 (Administration Orders Relating to Insurers) Order 2002, SI 2002/1242 ... **[852]**

Financial Services and Markets Act 2000 (Fourth Motor Insurance Directive) Regulations 2002, SI 2002/2706 ... **[857]**

Financial Services and Markets Act 2000 (Communications by Actuaries) Regulations 2003, SI 2003/1294 . . . . **[859]**
Financial Services and Markets Act 2000 (Transitional Provisions) (Complaints Relating to General Insurance and Mortgages) Order 2004, SI 2004/454 . . . . **[914]**
Financial Services and Markets Act 2000 (Stakeholder Products) Regulations 2004, SI 2004/2738, regs 1–3, 5–9 . . . . **[951]**
Financial Services and Markets Act 2000 (Financial Promotion) Order 2005, SI 2005/1529, arts 1, 2, 4–21, 24–39, 45, 47–52, 57, 61, 72, 73, Sch 1, Pt 1, paras 2–8, 11, Pt 2, paras 13, 24, 27, 28, Schs 2, 5 . . . . **[966]**
Financial Services and Markets Act 2000 (Controllers) (Exemption) Order 2009, SI 2009/774 . . . . **[1026]**
Financial Services and Markets Act 2000 (Law Applicable to Contracts of Insurance) Regulations 2009, SI 2009/3075 . . . . **[1032]**

PART II FINANCIAL SERVICES AUTHORITY HANDBOOK MATERIALS

Glossary . . . . **[2001]**
Principles for Businesses (PRIN) . . . . **[2002]**
Senior Management Arrangements, Systems and Controls (SYSC) . . . . . . **[2012]**
Threshold Conditions (COND) . . . . **[2025]**
Statements of Principle and Code of Practice for Approved Persons (APER) **[2034]**
Fit and Proper Test for Approved Persons (FIT) . . . . **[2045]**
General Provisions (GEN), Chapter 6 . . . . **[2054]**
General Prudential sourcebook (GENPRU) . . . . **[2055]**
Prudential sourcebook for Insurers (INSPRU) . . . . **[2065]**
Prudential sourcebook for Mortgage and Home Finance Firms, and Insurance Intermediaries (MIPRU) . . . . **[2081]**
Interim Prudential sourcebook: Insurers (IPRU(INS)) . . . . **[2093]**
Conduct of Business sourcebook (COBS), Chapters 7, 20, 21 . . . . **[2110A]**
Insurance: New Conduct of Business sourcebook (ICOBS) . . . . **[2111]**
Client Assets (CASS) . . . . **[2126]**
Training and Competence (TC) . . . . **[2141]**
Supervision (SUP) . . . . **[2154]**
Compensation (COMP) . . . . **[2184]**
Professional Firms (PROF) . . . . **[2205]**
Service companies (SERV) . . . . **[2219]**
Enforcement Guide (EG) . . . . **[2219A]**
Perimeter Guidance Manual (PERG), Chapters 2, 5, 6, 8.17A . . . . **[2220]**
Responsibilities of Providers and Distributors for the Fair Treatment of Customers (RPPD) . . . . **[2224]**
Unfair Contract Terms Regulatory Guide (UNFCOG) . . . . **[2225]**

PART III STATUTES

Life Assurance Act 1774 . . . . **[3001]**
Fires Prevention (Metropolis) Act 1774, ss 83, 86 . . . . **[3005]**
Policies of Assurance Act 1867 . . . . **[3009]**
Lloyd's Act 1871 . . . . **[3019]**
Married Women's Property Act 1882, s 11, 26, 27 . . . . **[3040]**
Life Assurance Companies (Payment into Court) Act 1896 . . . . **[3043]**
Marine Insurance Act 1906 . . . . **[3048]**
Marine Insurance (Gambling Policies) Act 1909 . . . . **[3141]**
Lloyd's Act 1911 . . . . **[3143]**
Third Parties (Rights Against Insurers) Act 1930 . . . . **[3155]**
Restriction of Advertisement (War Risks Insurance) Act 1939 . . . . **[3161]**
Lloyd's Act 1951 . . . . **[3167]**

Marine and Aviation Insurance (War Risks) Act 1952 . . . . **[3173]**
Nuclear Installations Act 1965, ss 19, 30 . . . . **[3182]**
Misrepresentation Act 1967 . . . . **[3184]**
Employers' Liability (Compulsory Insurance) Act 1969 . . . . **[3189]**
Local Government Act 1972, ss 140, 140A–140C, 274 . . . . **[3196]**
Insurance Companies Amendment Act 1973, ss 50, 51, 57 . . . . **[3201]**
Solicitors Act 1974, ss 37, 90 . . . . **[3315]**
Unfair Contract Terms Act 1977 . . . . **[3317]**
Lloyd's Act 1982 . . . . **[3352]**
Companies Act 1985, ss 255, 255A, 264–268, 279, 747, Schs 9A, 11 . . . . **[3376]**
Outer Space Act 1986, ss 1–5, 15 . . . . **[3391]**
Road Traffic Act 1988, ss 143–154, 157–162, 197, Sch 2A . . . . **[3397]**
Transport and Works Act 1992, ss 46, 72 . . . . **[3541]**
Reinsurance (Acts of Terrorism) Act 1993 . . . . **[3543]**
Finance Act 1994, ss 48–56, 59–74, 257(1), 259, Schs 6A, 7, 7A . . . . **[3548]**
British Waterways Act 1995, ss 1, 17, Sch 2, Pt I . . . . **[3597]**
Merchant Shipping Act 1995, ss 163–165, 181, 192A, 316, Sch 5A . . . . . **[3600]**
Disability Discrimination Act 1995, ss 19, 70 . . . . **[3608]**
Employment Rights Act 1996, ss 203, 245 . . . . **[3610]**
Finance Act 1997, ss 24, 29, 114 . . . . **[3612]**
Data Protection Act 1998, ss 1–8, 10–29, 31, 33, 34–54, 55–58, 60, 61, 64–68, 70–75, Schs 1–4, Sch 5, Pt I, paras 4(6), 6, 7, Sch 6, Sch 7, paras 1, 5–7, 10, 11, Sch 8, Pts I–III, V, Schs 9, 10, Sch 14, paras 1–19 . . . . **[3615]**
Access to Justice Act 1999, ss 29, 30, 110 . . . . **[3643]**
Contracts (Rights of Third Parties) Act 1999, ss 1–8, 10 . . . . **[3646]**
Electronic Communications Act 2000 . . . . **[3655]**
Health and Social Care (Community Health and Standards) Act 2003, ss 164, 202, 203 . . . . **[3663]**
Companies Act 2006, ss 232–235, 843, 1165, 1298–1300, Sch 10, Pt 2, para 17 . . . . **[3666]**

PART IV STATUTORY INSTRUMENTS

Industrial Assurance (Individual Transfer) Regulations 1928, SR & O 1928/580 . . . . **[4001]**
Industrial Assurance (Premium Receipt Books) Regulations 1948, SI 1948/2770 . . . . **[4006]**
Motor Vehicles (International Motor Insurance Card) Regulations 1971, SI 1971/792 . . . . **[4012]**
Motor Vehicles (Third Party Risks) Regulations 1972, SI 1972/1217 . . . . . **[4020]**
Motor Vehicles (Compulsory Insurance) (No 2) Regulations 1973, SI 1973/2143 . . . . **[4034]**
Motor Vehicles (Third-Party Risks Deposits) Regulations 1992, SI 1992/1284 . . . . **[4042]**
Insurance Accounts Directive (Miscellaneous Insurance Undertakings) Regulations 1993, SI 1993/3245 . . . . **[4067]**
Insurance Premium Tax Regulations 1994, SI 1994/1774 . . . . **[4075]**
Companies (Summary Financial Statement) Regulations 1995, SI 1995/2092, regs 10, 10A, Schs 3, 3A . . . . **[4132]**
Life Assurance and Other Policies (Keeping of Information and Duties of Insurers) Regulations 1997, SI 1997/265 . . . . **[4158]**
Oil Pollution (Compulsory Insurance) Regulations 1997, SI 1997/1820 . . . **[4167]**
Merchant Shipping (Compulsory Insurance: Ships Receiving Trans-shipped Fish) Regulations 1998, SI 1998/209 . . . . **[4170]**
Employers' Liability (Compulsory Insurance) Regulations 1998, SI 1998/2573 . . . . **[4180]**
Unfair Terms in Consumer Contracts Regulations 1999, SI 1999/2083 . . . **[4193]**

Insurers (Winding Up Rules) 2001, SI 2001/3635 . . . . [4212]
European Communities (Rights against Insurers) Regulations 2002, SI 2002/3061 . . . . [4247]
Motor Vehicles (Compulsory Insurance) (Information Centre and Compensation Body) Regulations 2003, SI 2003/37 . . . . [4250]
Insurers (Reorganisation and Winding Up) Regulations 2004, SI 2004/353 [4270]
Financial Services (Distance Marketing) Regulations 2004, SI 2004/2095, regs 1–13, 15–23, 29, Schs 1, 2 . . . . [4321]
Insurance Accounts Directive (Lloyd's Syndicate and Aggregate Accounts) Regulations 2004, SI 2004/3219 . . . . [4347]
Insurers (Winding-Up) Rules (Northern Ireland) 2005, SR 2005/399 . . . . . [4365]
Insurers (Reorganisation and Winding Up (Lloyd's) Regulations 2005, SI 2005/1998 . . . . [4398]
Companies (Summary Financial Statement) Regulations 2008, SI 2008/374, reg 11(4), (7), Schs 3, 6 . . . . [4446]
Large and Medium-sized Companies and Groups (Accounts and Reports) Regulations 2008, SI 2008/410, reg 6, Sch 3, Sch 6, Pts 1, 3, Schs 9, 10 [4449]
Insurance Accounts Directive (Miscellaneous Insurance Undertakings) Regulations 2008, SI 2008/565 . . . . [4459]
Consumer Protection from Unfair Trading Regulations 2008, SI 2008/1277, regs 1–18, Sch 1 . . . . [4475]
Insurance Accounts Directive (Lloyd's Syndicate and Aggregate Accounts) Regulations 2008, SI 2008/1950 . . . . [4494]
Legislative Reform (Lloyd's) Order 2008, SI 2008/3001, arts 1, 2, 6 . . . . . [4531]
Mutual Societies (Transfers) Order 2009, SI 2009/509 . . . . [4534]

PART V OTHER MATERIALS

A. Professional Indemnity of Solicitors

Solicitors (Scotland) Professional Indemnity Insurance Rules 2005 . . . . . . [5001]
Solicitors' Indemnity (Enactment) Rules 2007 . . . . [5002]
Solicitors (Scotland) Professional Indemnity Insurance Contingency Fund Rules 2007 . . . . [5009]
Indemnity Insurance Disclosure Guidelines (9 December 2008) . . . . [5009A]
Solicitors' Indemnity Insurance Rules 2009 . . . . [5010]

B. Motor Insurers' Bureau Agreements

A. Compensation of victims of untraced drivers (14 February 2003) . . . . [5021]

B. Compensation of victims of uninsured drivers (13 August 1999) . . . . [5030]

C. Association of British Insurers Statements, Codes and Guidelines

General Insurance Codes and Guidance Notes

ABI Statement of Principles for Trade Credit Insurance (April 2009) . . . . [5041]
ABI Good Practice Guide: Ensuring Positive Customer Experiences of Buying Insurance Online (April 2009) . . . . [5042]

Life and Savings Codes and Guidance Notes

ABI With-profits Bonds Best Practice Guide (revised 11 December 2002) . [5043]
ABI Mortgage Endowment Policy Reviews Code of Practice (1 June 2004) and *Guidance for Insurers* complying with the ABI Code of Practice . . . . . . [5044]
ABI Guide of Good Practice for Unit Linked Funds (1 June 2006) . . . . . [5046]
ABI Guide to the ICA Process for Insurers (2 February 2007) . . . . [5050]
ABI Good Practice Guide: Improving customers' retirement experiences (July 2008) . . . . [5055]

Health and Protection Codes and Guidance Notes

ABI Statement of Best Practice for Income Protection Insurance (August 2003 and amended as at 14 January 2005) . . . . [5060]
ABI and HM Government Concordat and Moratorium on Genetics and Insurance (March 2005) . . . . [5077]
ABI Statement of Best Practice for Critical Illness Insurance cover (12 April 2006) . . . . [5078]
ABI Statement of Best Practice for the selling of Private Medical Insurance Cover (October 2007) . . . . [5088]
ABI Code of Practice for Genetic Tests (June 2008) . . . . [5092]
ABI Statement of Best Practice for HIV and Insurance (July 2008) . . . . . . [5097]
Medical information and insurance Joint guidelines from the British Medical Association and the Association of British Insurers (July 2008) . . . . [5109]
ABI Code of Practice: Managing Claims for Individual and Group Life, Critical Illness and Income Protection Insurance Products (January 2009) [5124]

Other

ABI Statement of Recommended Practice on Accounting for Insurance Business (SORP) (December 2005 as amended in December 2006) . . . . [5126]
ABI Guidelines on the instruction and use of private investigators and tracing agents (5 July 2007) . . . . [5135]
ABI/Government Statement on Flooding and Insurance for England (July 2008) . . . . [5141]
ABI/Scottish Government Joint Statement on the Provision of Flood Insurance (December 2008) . . . . [5145]

D. Code of Practice for Tracing Employers' Liability Insurance Policies [5148]

PART VI EUROPEAN MATERIALS

A. General

Treaty on the Functioning of the European Union (formerly Treaty of Rome), arts 56–66, 101 . . . . [6001]
Council Directive (71/86/EEC) on harmonisation of the basic provisions in respect of guarantees for short-term transactions (political risks) with public buyers or with private buyers . . . . [6014]
Council Regulation (2155/91/EEC) EEC and Swiss Confederation Agreement–Joint Committee Regulations . . . . [6021]
Council Decision (91/370/EEC) EEC and Swiss Confederation Agreement on Non-Life Insurance (Conclusion) . . . . [6025]
Council Directive (91/371/EEC) EEC and Swiss Confederation Agreement on Non-Life Insurance (Implementation) . . . . [6091]
Council Directive (91/675/EEC) on setting up a European Insurance and Occupational Pensions Committee . . . . [6095]
European Parliament and Council Regulation (593/2008/EC) on the law applicable to contractual obligations (Rome I) . . . . [6098AA]

B. Regulation and Solvency

Council Regulation (1534/91/EEC) on the application of Article 85(3) of the Treaty to Certain Insurance Practices . . . . [6099]
European Parliament and Council Directive (98/78/EC) on the supplementary supervision of insurance and reinsurance undertakings in an insurance or reinsurance group . . . . [6107]
European Parliament and Council Directive (2002/13/EC) amending Council Directive 73/239/EEC as regards solvency margin requirements for non-life

insurance undertakings . . . . [6125]

Commission Regulation (358/2003/EC) on the application of Article 81(3) of the Treaty to certain categories of agreements, decisions and concerted practices in the insurance sector . . . . [6130]
Commission Decision (2009/79/EC) establishing the Committee of European Insurance and Occupational Pensions Supervisors . . . . [6144]
European Parliament and Council Directive (2009/138/EC) on the taking-up and pursuit of the business of Insurance and Reinsurance (Solvency II) . . [6153]

C. Accounting

Council Directive (91/674/EEC) on the annual accounts and consolidated accounts of insurance undertakings . . . . [6482]

D. Life

European Parliament and Council Directive (2002/83/EC) concerning life assurance . . . . [6556]

E. Non-Life

First Council Directive (73/239/EEC) on the coordination of laws, Regulations and administrative provisions relating to the taking-up and pursuit of the business of direct insurance other than life assurance (First Non-Life Co-ordination Directive) . . . . [6643]
Council Directive (73/240/EEC) abolishing restrictions on freedom of establishment in the business of direct insurance other than life assurance (Non-Life Insurance Establishment Directive) . . . . [6693]
Council Directive (78/473/EEC) on the coordination of laws, regulations and administrative provisions relating to Community co-insurance (Co-Insurance Directive) . . . . [6701]
Council Directive (84/641/EEC) amending, particularly as regards tourist assistance, the First Directive (73/239/EEC) on the coordination of laws, regulations and administrative provisions relating to the taking-up and pursuit of the business of direct insurance other than life assurance (Tourist Insurance Directive) . . . . [6714]
Council Directive (87/344/EEC) on the coordination of laws, regulations and administrative expenses insurance (Legal Expenses Insurance Directive) [6722]
Second Council Directive (88/357/EEC) on the coordination of laws, regulations and administrative provisions relating to direct insurance other than life assurance and laying down provisions to facilitate the effective exercise of freedom to provide services and amending Directive 73/239/EEC (Second Non-Life Co-ordination Directive) . . . . [6734]
Council Directive (92/49/EEC) on the coordination of laws, regulations and administrative provisions relating to direct insurance other than life assurance and amending Directives 73/239/EEC and 88/357/EEC (Third Non-Life Insurance Directive) . . . . [6760]

F. Insurance Mediation

European Parliament and Council Directive (2002/92/EC) on insurance mediation . . . . [6800]

G. Motor Insurance

Council Directive (90/618/EEC) amending, particularly as regards motor vehicle liability insurance, Directive 73/239/EEC and Directive 88/357/EEC which concern the coordination of laws, regulations and administrative provisions relating to direct insurance other than life assurance (Directive on Freedom of Motor Insurance Services) . . . . [6848]

European Parliament and Council Directive (2009/103/EC) relating to insurance against civil liability in respect of the use of motor vehicles, and the enforcement of the obligation to insure against such liability . . . . [6853]

H. Reinsurance

Council Directive (64/225/EEC) on the abolition of restrictions on freedom of establishment and freedom to provide services in respect of reinsurance and retrocession . . . . [6866]
European Parliament and Council Directive (2005/68/EC) on reinsurance and amending Council Directives 73/239/EEC, 92/49/EEC as well as Directives 98/78/EC and 2002/83/EC . . . . [6872]

I. Winding Up

Council Directive (2001/17/EC) on the reorganisation and winding-up of insurance undertakings . . . . [6937]

Alphabetical list

ABI and HM Government Concordat and Moratorium on Genetics and Insurance (March 2005) . . . . [5077]
ABI Code of Practice for Genetic Tests (June 2008) . . . . [5092]
ABI Code of Practice: Managing Claims for Individual and Group Life, Critical Illness and Income Protection Insurance Products (January 2009) [5124]
ABI Good Practice Guide: Ensuring Positive Customer Experiences of Buying Insurance Online (April 2009) . . . . [5042]
ABI Good Practice Guide: Improving customers' retirement experiences (July 2008) . . . . [5055]
ABI/Government Statement on Flooding and Insurance for England (July 2008) . . . . [5141]
ABI Guide of Good Practice for Unit Linked Funds (1 June 2006) . . . . . [5046]
ABI Guide to the ICA Process for Insurers (2 February 2007) . . . . [5050]
ABI Guidelines on the instruction and use of private investigators and tracing agents (5 July 2007) . . . . [5135]
ABI Mortgage Endowment Policy Reviews Code of Practice (1 June 2004) and Guidance for Insurers complying with the ABI Code of Practice . . . . . . [5044]
ABI/Scottish Government Joint Statement on the Provision of Flood Insurance (December 2008) . . . . [5145]
ABI Statement of Best Practice for Critical Illness Insurance cover (12 April 2006) . . . . [5078]
ABI Statement of Best Practice for HIV and Insurance (July 2008) . . . . . . [5097]
ABI Statement of Best Practice for Income Protection Insurance (August 2003 and amended as at 14 January 2005) . . . . [5060]
ABI Statement of Best Practice for the selling of Private Medical Insurance Cover (October 2007) . . . . [5088]
ABI Statement of Principles for Trade Credit Insurance (April 2009) . . . . [5041]
ABI Statement of Recommended Practice on Accounting for Insurance Business (SORP) (December 2005 as amended in December 2006) . . . . [5126]
ABI With-profits Bonds Best Practice Guide (revised 11 December 2002) . [5043]
Access to Justice Act 1999, ss 29, 30, 110 . . . . [3643]
British Waterways Act 1995, ss 1, 17, Sch 2, Pt I . . . . [3597]
Client Assets (CASS) . . . . [2126]
Code of Practice for Tracing Employers' Liability Insurance Policies [5148]
Co-Insurance Directive (Council Directive (78/473/EEC) on the coordination of laws, regulations and administrative provisions relating to Community co-insurance) . . . . [6701]

Commission Decision (2009/79/EC) establishing the Committee of European Insurance and Occupational Pensions Supervisors . . . . **[6144]**
Commission Regulation (358/2003/EC) on the application of Article 81(3) of the Treaty to certain categories of agreements, decisions and concerted practices in the insurance sector . . . . **[6130]**
Companies (Summary Financial Statement) Regulations 1995, SI 1995/2092, regs 10, 10A, Schs 3, 3A . . . . **[4132]**
Companies (Summary Financial Statement) Regulations 2008, SI 2008/374, reg 11(4), (7), Schs 3, 6 . . . . **[4446]**
Companies Act 1985, ss 255, 255A, 264–268, 279, 747, Schs 9A, 11 . . . . **[3376]**
Companies Act 2006, ss 232–235, 843, 1165, 1298–1300, Sch 10, Pt 2, para 17 . . . . **[3666]**
Compensation (COMP) . . . . **[2184]**
Compensation of victims of uninsured drivers (13 August 1999) . . . . **[5030]**
Compensation of victims of untraced drivers (14 February 2003) . . . . **[5021]**
Conduct of Business sourcebook (COBS), Chapters 7, 20, 21 . . . . **[2110A]**
Consumer Protection from Unfair Trading Regulations 2008, SI 2008/1277, regs 1–18, Sch 1 . . . . **[4475]**
Contracts (Rights of Third Parties) Act 1999, ss 1–8, 10 . . . . **[3646]**
Council Decision (91/370/EEC) EEC and Swiss Confederation Agreement on Non-Life Insurance (Conclusion) . . . . **[6025]**
Council Directive (64/225/EEC) on the abolition of restrictions on freedom of establishment and freedom to provide services in respect of reinsurance and retrocession . . . . **[6866]**
Council Directive (71/86/EEC) on harmonisation of the basic provisions in respect of guarantees for short-term transactions (political risks) with public buyers or with private buyers . . . . **[6014]**
Council Directive (73/240/EEC) abolishing restrictions on freedom of establishment in the business of direct insurance other than life assurance (Non-Life Insurance Establishment Directive) . . . . **[6693]**
Council Directive (78/473/EEC) on the coordination of laws, regulations and administrative provisions relating to Community co-insurance (Co-Insurance Directive) . . . . **[6701]**
Council Directive (84/641/EEC) amending, particularly as regards tourist assistance, the First Directive (73/239/EEC) on the coordination of laws, regulations and administrative provisions relating to the taking-up and pursuit of the business of direct insurance other than life assurance (Tourist Insurance Directive) . . . . **[6714]**
Council Directive (87/344/EEC) on the coordination of laws, regulations and administrative expenses insurance (Legal Expenses Insurance Directive) **[6722]**
Council Directive (90/618/EEC) amending, particularly as regards motor vehicle liability insurance, Directive 73/239/EEC and Directive 88/357/EEC which concern the coordination of laws, regulations and administrative provisions relating to direct insurance other than life assurance (Directive on Freedom of Motor Insurance Services) . . . . **[6848]**
Council Directive (91/371/EEC) EEC and Swiss Confederation Agreement on Non-Life Insurance (Implementation) . . . . **[6091]**
Council Directive (91/674/EEC) on the annual accounts and consolidated accounts of insurance undertakings . . . . **[6482]**
Council Directive (91/675/EEC) on setting up a European Insurance and Occupational Pensions Committee . . . . **[6095]**
Council Directive (92/49/EEC) on the coordination of laws, regulations and administrative provisions relating to direct insurance other than life assurance and amending Directives 73/239/EEC and 88/357/EEC (Third Non-Life Insurance Directive) . . . . **[6760]**
Council Directive (2001/17/EC) on the reorganisation and winding-up of insurance undertakings . . . . **[6937]**
Council Regulation (1534/91/EEC) on the application of Article 85(3) of the Treaty to Certain Insurance Practices . . . . **[6099]**

Council Regulation (2155/91/EEC) EEC and Swiss Confederation Agreement–Joint Committee Regulations . . . . . [6021]
Data Protection Act 1998, ss 1–8, 10–29, 31, 33, 34–54, 55–58, 60, 61, 64–68, 70–75, Schs 1–4, Sch 5, Pt I, paras 4(6), 6, 7, Sch 6, Sch 7, paras 1, 5–7, 10, 11, Sch 8, Pts I–III, V, Schs 9, 10, Sch 14, paras 1–19 . . . . . [3615]
Directive on Freedom of Motor Insurance Services (Council Directive (90/618/EEC) amending, particularly as regards motor vehicle liability insurance, Directive 73/239/EEC and Directive 88/357/EEC which concern the coordination of laws, regulations and administrative provisions relating to direct insurance other than life assurance) . . . . . [6848]
Disability Discrimination Act 1995, ss 19, 70 . . . . . [3608]
Electronic Communications Act 2000 . . . . . [3655]
Employers' Liability (Compulsory Insurance) Act 1969 . . . . . [3189]
Employers' Liability (Compulsory Insurance) Regulations 1998, SI 1998/2573 . . . . . [4180]
Employment Rights Act 1996, ss 203, 245 . . . . . [3610]
Enforcement Guide (EG) . . . . . [2219A]
European Communities (Rights against Insurers) Regulations 2002, SI 2002/3061 . . . . . [4247]
European Parliament and Council Directive (98/78/EC) on the supplementary supervision of insurance and reinsurance undertakings in an insurance or reinsurance group . . . . . [6107]
European Parliament and Council Directive (2002/13/EC) amending Council Directive 73/239/EEC as regards solvency margin requirements for non-life insurance undertakings . . . . . [6125]
European Parliament and Council Directive (2002/83/EC) concerning life assurance . . . . . [6556]
European Parliament and Council Directive (2002/92/EC) on insurance mediation . . . . . [6800]
European Parliament and Council Directive (2005/68/EC) on reinsurance and amending Council Directives 73/239/EEC, 92/49/EEC as well as Directives 98/78/EC and 2002/83/EC . . . . . [6872]
European Parliament and Council Directive (2009/103/EC) relating to insurance against civil liability in respect of the use of motor vehicles, and the enforcement of the obligation to insure against such liability . . . . . [6853]
European Parliament and Council Directive (2009/138/EC) on the taking-up and pursuit of the business of Insurance and Reinsurance (Solvency II) . [6153]
European Parliament and Council Regulation (593/2008/EC) on the law applicable to contractual obligations (Rome I) . . . . . [6098AA]
Finance Act 1994, ss 48–56, 59–74, 257(1), 259, Schs 6A, 7, 7A . . . . . [3548]
Finance Act 1997, ss 24, 29, 114 . . . . . [3612]
Financial Services (Distance Marketing) Regulations 2004, SI 2004/2095, regs 1–13, 15–23, 29, Schs 1, 2 . . . . . [4321]
Financial Services and Markets Act 2000 (Administration Orders Relating to Insurers) Order 2002, SI 2002/1242 . . . . . [852]
Financial Services and Markets Act 2000 (Appointed Representatives) Regulations 2001, SI 2001/1217 . . . . . [596]
Financial Services and Markets Act 2000 (Carrying on Regulated Activities by Way of Business) Order 2001, SI 2001/1177, arts 1–3A, 4 . . . . . [591]
Financial Services and Markets Act 2000 (Communications by Actuaries) Regulations 2003, SI 2003/1294 . . . . . [859]
Financial Services and Markets Act 2000 (Communications by Auditors) Regulations 2001, SI 2001/2587 . . . . . [649]
Financial Services and Markets Act 2000 (Compensation Scheme: Electing Participants) Regulations 2001, SI 2001/1783 . . . . . [611]
Financial Services and Markets Act 2000 (Control of Business Transfers) (Requirements on Applicants) Regulations 2001, SI 2001/3625 . . . . . [820]

Financial Services and Markets Act 2000 (Control of Transfers of Business Done at Lloyd's) Order 2001, SI 2001/3626 . . . . **[826]**
Financial Services and Markets Act 2000 (Controllers) (Exemption) Order 2009, SI 2009/774 . . . . **[1026]**
Financial Services and Markets Act 2000 (EEA Passport Rights) Regulations 2001, SI 2001/2511, regs 1–3, 6–8, 10, 13–21 . . . . **[633]**
Financial Services and Markets Act 2000 (Exemption) Order 2001, SI 2001/1201 . . . . **[595A]**
Financial Services and Markets Act 2000 (Financial Promotion) Order 2005, SI 2005/1529, arts 1, 2, 4–21, 24–39, 45, 47–52, 57, 61, 72, 73, Sch 1, Pt 1, paras 2–8, 11, Pt 2, paras 13, 24, 27, 28, Schs 2, 5 . . . . **[966]**
Financial Services and Markets Act 2000 (Fourth Motor Insurance Directive) Regulations 2002, SI 2002/2706 . . . . **[857]**
Financial Services and Markets Act 2000 (Gaming Contracts) Order 2001, SI 2001/2510 . . . . **[631]**
Financial Services and Markets Act 2000 (Insolvency) (Definition of "Insurer") Order 2001, SI 2001/2634 . . . . **[668]**
Financial Services and Markets Act 2000 (Law Applicable to Contracts of Insurance) Regulations 2001, SI 2001/2635 . . . . **[670]**
Financial Services and Markets Act 2000 (Law Applicable to Contracts of Insurance) Regulations 2009, SI 2009/3075 . . . . **[1032]**
Financial Services and Markets Act 2000 (Meaning of "Policy" and "Policyholder") Order 2001, SI 2001/2361 . . . . **[625]**
Financial Services and Markets Act 2000 (Misleading Statements and Practices) Order 2001, SI 2001/3645, arts 1–3 . . . . **[838]**
Financial Services and Markets Act 2000 (Mutual Societies) Order 2001, SI 2001/2617 . . . . **[651]**
Financial Services and Markets Act 2000 (Professions) (Non-exempt Activities) Order 2001, SI 2001/1227, arts 1–6B, 7, 8 . . . . **[599]**
Financial Services and Markets Act 2000 (Regulated Activities) Order 2001, SI 2001/544, arts 1–4, 10–25A, 25D, 26–44, 52–53A, 54–60A, 64–69, 72–73, 75, 82, 86, 92–96, Schs 1, 4 . . . . **[501]**
Financial Services and Markets Act 2000 (Rights of Action) Regulations 2001, SI 2001/2256 . . . . **[618]**
Financial Services and Markets Act 2000 (Scope of Permission Notices) Order 2001, SI 2001/3771 . . . . **[848]**
Financial Services and Markets Act 2000 (Stakeholder Products) Regulations 2004, SI 2004/2738, regs 1–3, 5–9 . . . . **[951]**
Financial Services and Markets Act 2000 (Transitional Provisions) (Complaints Relating to General Insurance and Mortgages) Order 2004, SI 2004/454 . . . . **[914]**
Financial Services and Markets Act 2000 (Variation of Threshold Conditions) Order 2001, SI 2001/2507 . . . . **[628]**
Financial Services and Markets Act 2000, ss 1–39, 40–71, 104–142, 144–158, 165–194, 195, 196–232, 234, 234A, 314–410, 412, 413–424, 425–433, Schs 1–3, 5–7, 12–15, 17, 18, Pt II, para 16, Sch 21 **[1]**
Fires Prevention (Metropolis) Act 1774, ss 83, 86 . . . . **[3005]**
First Council Directive (73/239/EEC) on the coordination of laws, Regulations and administrative provisions relating to the taking-up and pursuit of the business of direct insurance other than life assurance (First Non-Life Coordination Directive) . . . . **[6643]**
Fit and Proper Test for Approved Persons (FIT) . . . . **[2045]**
General Provisions (GEN), Chapter 6 . . . . **[2054]**
General Prudential sourcebook (GENPRU) . . . . **[2055]**
Glossary . . . . **[2001]**
Health and Social Care (Community Health and Standards) Act 2003, ss 164, 202, 203 . . . . **[3663]**
Indemnity Insurance Disclosure Guidelines . . . . **[5020]**

Industrial Assurance (Individual Transfer) Regulations 1928, SR & O 1928/580 . . . . **[4001]**
Industrial Assurance (Premium Receipt Books) Regulations 1948, SI 1948/2770 . . . . **[4006]**
Insurance Accounts Directive (Lloyd's Syndicate and Aggregate Accounts) Regulations 2008, SI 2008/1950 . . . . **[4494]**
Insurance Accounts Directive (Lloyd's Syndicate and Aggregate Accounts) Regulations 2004, SI 2004/3219 . . . . **[4347]**
Insurance Accounts Directive (Miscellaneous Insurance Undertakings) Regulations 1993, SI 1993/3245 . . . . **[4067]**
Insurance Accounts Directive (Miscellaneous Insurance Undertakings) Regulations 2008, SI 2008/565 . . . . **[4459]**
Insurance Companies Amendment Act 1973, ss 50, 51, 57 . . . . **[3201]**
Insurance Premium Tax Regulations 1994, SI 1994/1774 . . . . **[4075]**
Insurance: New Conduct of Business sourcebook (ICOBS) . . . . **[2111]**
Insurers (Reorganisation and Winding Up (Lloyd's) Regulations 2005, SI 2005/1998 . . . . **[4398]**
Insurers (Reorganisation and Winding Up) Regulations 2004, SI 2004/353 **[4270]**
Insurers (Winding Up Rules) 2001, SI 2001/3635 . . . . **[4212]**
Insurers (Winding-Up) Rules (Northern Ireland) 2005, SR 2005/399 . . . . . **[4365]**
Interim Prudential sourcebook: Insurers (IPRU(INS)) . . . . **[2093]**
Large and Medium-sized Companies and Groups (Accounts and Reports) Regulations 2008, SI 2008/410, reg 6, Sch 3, Sch 6, Pts 1, 3, Schs 9, 10 **[4449]**
Legal Expenses Insurance Directive (Council Directive (87/344/EEC) on the coordination of laws, regulations and administrative expenses insurance) **[6722]**
Legislative Reform (Lloyd's) Order 2008, SI 2008/3001, arts 1, 2, 6 . . . . . **[4531]**
Life Assurance Act 1774 . . . . **[3001]**
Life Assurance and Other Policies (Keeping of Information and Duties of Insurers) Regulations 1997, SI 1997/265 . . . . **[4158]**
Life Assurance Companies (Payment into Court) Act 1896 . . . . **[3043]**
Lloyd's Act 1871 . . . . **[3019]**
Lloyd's Act 1911 . . . . **[3143]**
Lloyd's Act 1951 . . . . **[3167]**
Lloyd's Act 1982 . . . . **[3352]**
Local Government Act 1972, ss 140, 140A–140C, 274 . . . . **[3196]**
Marine and Aviation Insurance (War Risks) Act 1952 . . . . **[3173]**
Marine Insurance (Gambling Policies) Act 1909 . . . . **[3141]**
Marine Insurance Act 1906 . . . . **[3048]**
Married Women's Property Act 1882, s 11, 26, 27 . . . . **[3040]**
Medical information and insurance Joint guidelines from the British Medical Association and the Association of British Insurers (July 2008) . . . . . . **[5109]**
Merchant Shipping (Compulsory Insurance: Ships Receiving Trans-shipped Fish) Regulations 1998, SI 1998/209 . . . . **[4170]**
Merchant Shipping Act 1995, ss 163–165, 181, 192A, 316, Sch 5A . . . . . **[3600]**
Misrepresentation Act 1967 . . . . **[3184]**
Motor Vehicles (Compulsory Insurance) (Information Centre and Compensation Body) Regulations 2003, SI 2003/37 . . . . **[4250]**
Motor Vehicles (Compulsory Insurance) (No 2) Regulations 1973, SI 1973/2143 . . . . **[4034]**
Motor Vehicles (International Motor Insurance Card) Regulations 1971, SI 1971/792 . . . . **[4012]**
Motor Vehicles (Third Party Risks) Regulations 1972, SI 1972/1217 . . . . . **[4020]**
Motor Vehicles (Third-Party Risks Deposits) Regulations 1992, SI 1992/1284 . . . . **[4042]**
Mutual Societies (Transfers) Order 2009, SI 2009/509 . . . . **[4534]**
Non-Life Insurance Establishment Directive (Council Directive (73/240/EEC) abolishing restrictions on freedom of establishment in the business of direct insurance other than life assurance) . . . . **[6693]**

Nuclear Installations Act 1965, ss 19, 30 . . . [3182]
Oil Pollution (Compulsory Insurance) Regulations 1997, SI 1997/1820 . . . [4167]
Outer Space Act 1986, ss 1–5, 15 . . . [3391]
Perimeter Guidance Manual (PERG), Chapters 2, 5, 6, 8.17A . . . [2220]
Policies of Assurance Act 1867 . . . [3009]
Principles for Businesses (PRIN) . . . [2002]
Professional Firms (PROF) . . . [2205]
Prudential sourcebook for Insurers (INSPRU) . . . [2065]
Prudential sourcebook for Mortgage and Home Finance Firms, and Insurance Intermediaries (MIPRU) . . . [2081]
Reinsurance (Acts of Terrorism) Act 1993 . . . [3543]
Responsibilities of Providers and Distributors for the Fair Treatment of Customers (RPPD) . . . [2224]
Restriction of Advertisement (War Risks Insurance) Act 1939 . . . [3161]
Road Traffic Act 1988, ss 143–154, 157–162, 197, Sch 2A . . . [3397]
Rome I (European Parliament and Council Regulation (593/2008/EC) on the law applicable to contractual obligations) . . . [6098AA]
Second Council Directive (88/357/EEC) on the coordination of laws, regulations and administrative provisions relating to direct insurance other than life assurance and laying down provisions to facilitate the effective exercise of freedom to provide services and amending Directive 73/239/EEC (Second Non-Life Co-ordination Directive) . . . [6734]
Senior Management Arrangements, Systems and Controls (SYSC) . . . [2012]
Service companies (SERV) . . . [2219]
Solicitors (Scotland) Professional Indemnity Insurance Contingency Fund Rules 2007 . . . [5009]
Solicitors (Scotland) Professional Indemnity Insurance Rules 2005 . . . [5001]
Solicitors Act 1974, ss 37, 90 . . . [3315]
Solicitors' Indemnity (Enactment) Rules 2007 . . . [5002]
Solicitors' Indemnity Insurance Rules 2009 . . . [5010]
Solvency II (European Parliament and Council Directive (2009/138/EC) on the taking-up and pursuit of the business of Insurance and Reinsurance) . . . [6153]
Statements of Principle and Code of Practice for Approved Persons (APER) [2034]
Supervision (SUP) . . . [2154]
Third Non-Life Insurance Directive (Council Directive (92/49/EEC) on the coordination of laws, regulations and administrative provisions relating to direct insurance other than life assurance and amending Directives 73/239/EEC and 88/357/EEC) . . . [6760]
Third Parties (Rights Against Insurers) Act 1930 . . . [3155]
Threshold Conditions (COND) . . . [2025]
Tourist Insurance Directive (Council Directive (84/641/EEC) amending, particularly as regards tourist assistance, the First Directive (73/239/EEC) on the coordination of laws, regulations and administrative provisions relating to the taking-up and pursuit of the business of direct insurance other than life assurance) . . . [6714]
Training and Competence (TC) . . . [2141]
Transport and Works Act 1992, ss 46, 72 . . . [3541]
Treaty on the Functioning of the European Union (formerly Treaty of Rome), arts 56–66, 101 . . . [6001]
Unfair Contract Terms Act 1977 . . . [3317]
Unfair Contract Terms Regulatory Guide (UNFCOG) . . . [2225]
Unfair Terms in Consumer Contracts Regulations 1999, SI 1999/2083 . . . [4193]

Index *p 3177*

PART I
FINANCIAL SERVICES AND MARKETS LEGISLATION

A. FSMA 2000

FINANCIAL SERVICES AND MARKETS ACT 2000

(2000 c 8)

ARRANGEMENT OF SECTIONS

PART I
THE REGULATOR

1 The Financial Services Authority . . . [1]

The Authority's general duties

2 The Authority's general duties . . . [2]

The regulatory objectives

3 Market confidence . . . [3]
4 Public awareness . . . [4]
5 The protection of consumers . . . [5]
6 The reduction of financial crime . . . [6]

Corporate governance

7 Duty of Authority to follow principles of good governance . . . [7]

Arrangements for consulting practitioners and consumers

8 The Authority's general duty to consult . . . [8]
9 The Practitioner Panel . . . [9]
10 The Consumer Panel . . . [10]
11 Duty to consider representations by the Panels . . . [11]

Reviews

12 Reviews . . . [12]
13 Right to obtain documents and information . . . [13]

Inquiries

14 Cases in which the Treasury may arrange independent inquiries . . . [14]
15 Power to appoint person to hold an inquiry . . . [15]
16 Powers of appointed person and procedure . . . [16]
17 Conclusion of inquiry . . . [17]
18 Obstruction and contempt . . . [18]

PART II
REGULATED AND PROHIBITED ACTIVITIES

The general prohibition

19 The general prohibition . . . [19]

Requirement for permission

20 Authorised persons acting without permission . . . [20]

Financial promotion

21 Restrictions on financial promotion . . . [21]

Regulated activities

22 The classes of activity and categories of investment . . . [22]

Offences

23 Contravention of the general prohibition . . . [23]
24 False claims to be authorised or exempt . . . [24]
25 Contravention of section 21 . . . [25]

Enforceability of agreements

26 Agreements made by unauthorised persons . . . [26]
27 Agreements made through unauthorised persons . . . [27]
28 Agreements made unenforceable by section 26 or 27 . . . [28]
29 Accepting deposits in breach of general prohibition . . . [29]
30 Enforceability of agreements resulting from unlawful communications . . . [30]

PART III
AUTHORISATION AND EXEMPTION

Authorisation

31 Authorised persons . . . [31]

32 Partnerships and unincorporated associations . . . [32]

Ending of authorisation

33 Withdrawal of authorisation by the Authority . . . [33]
34 EEA firms . . . [34]
35 Treaty firms . . . [35]
36 Persons authorised as a result of paragraph 1(1) of Schedule 5 . . . [36]

Exercise of EEA rights by UK firms

37 Exercise of EEA rights by UK firms . . . [37]

Exemption

38 Exemption orders . . . [38]
39 Exemption of appointed representatives . . . [39]

PART IV
PERMISSION TO CARRY ON REGULATED ACTIVITIES

Application for permission

40 Application for permission . . . [40]
41 The threshold conditions . . . [41]

Permission

42 Giving permission . . . [42]
43 Imposition of requirements . . . [43]

Variation and cancellation of Part IV permission

44 Variation etc at request of authorised person . . . [44]
45 Variation etc on the Authority's own initiative . . . [45]
46 Variation of permission on acquisition of control . . . [46]
47 Exercise of power in support of overseas regulator . . . [47]
48 Prohibitions and restrictions . . . [48]

Connected persons

49 Persons connected with an applicant . . . [49]

Additional permissions

50 Authority's duty to consider other permissions etc . . . [50]

Procedure

51 Applications under this Part . . . [51]
52 Determination of applications . . . [52]
53 Exercise of own-initiative power: procedure . . . [53]
54 Cancellation of Part IV permission: procedure . . . [54]

References to the Tribunal

55 Right to refer matters to the Tribunal . . . [55]

PART V
PERFORMANCE OF REGULATED ACTIVITIES

Prohibition orders

56 Prohibition orders . . . [56]
57 Prohibition orders: procedure and right to refer to Tribunal . . . [57]
58 Applications relating to prohibitions: procedure and right to refer to Tribunal . . . [58]

Approval

59 Approval for particular arrangements . . . [59]
60 Applications for approval . . . [60]
61 Determination of applications . . . [61]
62 Applications for approval: procedure and right to refer to Tribunal . . . [62]
63 Withdrawal of approval . . . [63]

Conduct

64 Conduct: statements and codes . . . [64]
65 Statements and codes: procedure . . . [65]
66 Disciplinary powers . . . [66]
67 Disciplinary measures: procedure and right to refer to Tribunal . . . [67]
68 Publication . . . [68]
69 Statement of policy . . . [69]
70 Statements of policy: procedure . . . [70]

Breach of statutory duty

71 Actions for damages . . . [71]

PART VII
CONTROL OF BUSINESS TRANSFERS

104 Control of business transfers . . . [72]

105 Insurance business transfer schemes [73]
106 Banking business transfer schemes [74]
106A Reclaim fund business transfer scheme [74A]
107 Application for order sanctioning transfer scheme [75]
108 Requirements on applicants [76]
109 Scheme reports [77]
110 Right to participate in proceedings [78]
111 Sanction of the court for business transfer schemes [79]
112 Effect of order sanctioning business transfer scheme [80]
112A Rights to terminate etc [80A]
113 Appointment of actuary in relation to reduction of benefits [81]
114 Rights of certain policyholders [82]
114A Notice of transfer of reinsurance contracts [82A]

Business transfers outside the United Kingdom

115 Certificates for purposes of insurance business transfers overseas [83]
116 Effect of insurance business transfers authorised in other EEA States [84]

Modifications

117 Power to modify this Part [85]

PART VIII
PENALTIES FOR MARKET ABUSE

Market abuse

118 Market abuse [86]
118A Supplementary provision about certain behaviour [87]
118B Insiders [88]
118C Inside information [89]

The code

119 The code [90]
120 Provisions included in the Authority's code by reference to the City Code [91]
121 Codes: procedure [92]
122 Effect of the code [93]

Power to impose penalties

123 Power to impose penalties in cases of market abuse [94]

Statement of policy

124 Statement of policy [95]
125 Statement of policy: procedure [96]

Procedure

126 Warning notices [97]
127 Decision notices and right to refer to Tribunal [98]

Miscellaneous

128 Suspension of investigations [99]
129 Power of court to impose penalty in cases of market abuse [100]
130 Guidance [101]
130A Interpretation and supplementary provision [102]
131 Effect on transactions [103]
131A Protected disclosures [104]

PART IX
HEARINGS AND APPEALS

132 The Financial Services and Markets Tribunal [105]
133 Proceedings before Tribunal: general provision [106]
133A Proceedings before Tribunal: decision and supervisory notices, etc [106A]
133B Offences [106B]

Legal assistance before the Tribunal

134 Legal assistance scheme [107]
135 Provisions of the legal assistance scheme [108]
136 Funding of the legal assistance scheme [109]

Appeals

137 Appeal on a point of law [110]

PART X
RULES AND GUIDANCE

CHAPTER I
RULE-MAKING POWERS

138 General rule-making power [111]
139 Miscellaneous ancillary matters [112]

140 Restriction on managers of authorised unit trust schemes [113]
141 Insurance business rules [114]
142 Insurance business: regulations supplementing Authority's rules [115]

Specific rules

144 Price stabilising rules [117]
145 Financial promotion rules [118]
146 Money laundering rules [119]
147 Control of information rules [120]

Modification or waiver

148 Modification or waiver of rules [121]

Contravention of rules

149 Evidential provisions [122]
150 Actions for damages [123]
151 Limits on effect of contravening rules [124]

Procedural provisions

152 Notification of rules to the Treasury [125]
153 Rule-making instruments [126]
154 Verification of rules [127]
155 Consultation [128]
156 General supplementary powers [129]

CHAPTER II
GUIDANCE

157 Guidance [130]
158 Notification of guidance to the Treasury [131]

PART XI
INFORMATION GATHERING AND INVESTIGATIONS

Powers to gather information

165 Authority's power to require information [132]
166 Reports by skilled persons [133]

Appointment of investigators

167 Appointment of persons to carry out general investigations [134]
168 Appointment of persons to carry out investigations in particular cases [135]

Assistance to overseas regulators

169 Investigations etc in support of overseas regulator [136]

Conduct of investigations

170 Investigations: general [137]
171 Powers of persons appointed under section 167 [138]
172 Additional power of persons appointed as a result of section 168(1) or (4) [139]
173 Powers of persons appointed as a result of section 168(2) [140]
174 Admissibility of statements made to investigators [141]
175 Information and documents: supplemental provisions [142]
176 Entry of premises under warrant [143]

Offences

177 Offences [144]

PART XII
CONTROL OVER AUTHORISED PERSONS

Notices of acquisitions of control over UK authorised persons

178 Obligation to notify the Authority: acquisitions of control [145]
179 Requirements for section 178 notices [146]
180 Acknowledgment of receipt [147]

Acquiring control and other changes of holding

181 Acquiring control [148]
182 Increasing control [149]
183 Reducing or ceasing to have control [150]
184 Disregarded holdings [151]

Assessment procedure

185 Assessment: general [152]
186 Assessment criteria [153]
187 Approval with conditions [154]
188 Assessment: consultation with EC competent authorities [155]
189 Assessment: Procedure [156]
190 Requests for further information [157]

191 Duration of approval . . . [158]

Enforcement procedures

191A Objection by the Authority . . . [158A]
191B Restriction notices . . . [158B]
191C Orders for sale of shares . . . [158C]

Notice of reductions of control of UK authorised persons

191D Obligation to notify the Authority: dispositions of control . . . [158D]
191E Requirements for notices under section 191D . . . [158E]

Offences

191F Offences under this Part . . . [158F]

Interpretation

191G Interpretation . . . [158G]

Miscellaneous

192 Power to change definitions of control etc . . . [159]

PART XIII
INCOMING FIRMS: INTERVENTION BY AUTHORITY

Interpretation

193 Interpretation of this Part . . . [160]
194 General grounds on which power of intervention is exercisable . . . [161]
195 Exercise of power in support of overseas regulator . . . [162]
196 The power of intervention . . . [163]

Exercise of power of intervention

197 Procedure on exercise of power of intervention . . . [164]
198 Power to apply to court for injunction in respect of certain overseas insurance companies . . . [165]
199 Additional procedure for EEA firms in certain cases . . . [166]

Supplemental

200 Rescission and variation of requirements . . . [167]
201 Effect of certain requirements on other persons . . . [168]
202 Contravention of requirement imposed under this Part . . . [169]

Powers of Director General of Fair Trading

203 Power to prohibit the carrying on of Consumer Credit Act business . . . [170]
204 Power to restrict the carrying on of Consumer Credit Act business . . . [171]

PART XIV
DISCIPLINARY MEASURES

205 Public censure . . . [172]
206 Financial penalties . . . [173]
207 Proposal to take disciplinary measures . . . [174]
208 Decision notice . . . [175]
209 Publication . . . [176]
210 Statements of policy . . . [177]
211 Statements of policy: procedure . . . [178]

PART XV
THE FINANCIAL SERVICES COMPENSATION SCHEME

The scheme manager

212 The scheme manager . . . [179]

The scheme

213 The compensation scheme . . . [180]

Provisions of the scheme

214 General . . . [181]
214A *Contingency funding* . . . [181A]
214B Contribution to costs of special resolution regime . . . [181B]
215 Rights of the scheme in relevant person's insolvency . . . [182]
216 Continuity of long-term insurance policies . . . [183]
217 Insurers in financial difficulties . . . [184]

Annual report

218 Annual report . . . [185]

Information and documents

218A Authority's power to require information . . . [185A]
219 Scheme manager's power to require information . . . [186]
220 Scheme manager's power to inspect information held by liquidator etc . . . [187]

221 Powers of court where information required . . . . . [188]

Miscellaneous

221A Delegation of functions . . . . . [188A]
222 Statutory immunity . . . . . [189]
223 Management expenses . . . . . [190]
223A Investing in National Loans Fund . . . . . [190A]
223B Borrowing from National Loans Fund . . . . . [190B]
223C Payments in error . . . . . [190C]
224 Scheme manager's power to inspect documents held by Official Receiver etc . . . . . [191]
224A Functions under the Banking Act 2009 . . . . . [191A]

PART XVI
THE OMBUDSMAN SCHEME

The scheme

225 The scheme and the scheme operator . . . . . [192]
226 Compulsory jurisdiction . . . . . [193]
226A Consumer credit jurisdiction . . . . . [193A]
227 Voluntary jurisdiction . . . . . [194]

Determination of complaints

228 Determination under the compulsory jurisdiction . . . . . [195]
229 Awards . . . . . [196]
230 Costs . . . . . [197]

Information

231 Ombudsman's power to require information . . . . . [198]
232 Powers of court where information required . . . . . [199]

Funding

234 Industry funding . . . . . [200]
234A Funding by consumer credit licensees etc . . . . . [200A]

PART XIX
LLOYD'S

General

314 Authority's general duty . . . . . [201]

The Society

315 The Society: authorisation and permission . . . . . [202]

Power to apply Act to Lloyd's underwriting

316 Direction by Authority . . . . . [203]
317 The core provisions . . . . . [204]
318 Exercise of powers through Council . . . . . [205]
319 Consultation . . . . . [206]

Former underwriting members

320 Former underwriting members . . . . . [207]
321 Requirements imposed under section 320 . . . . . [208]
322 Rules applicable to former underwriting members . . . . . [209]

Transfers of business done at Lloyd's

323 Transfer schemes . . . . . [210]

Supplemental

324 Interpretation of this Part . . . . . [211]

PART XX
PROVISION OF FINANCIAL SERVICES BY MEMBERS OF THE PROFESSIONS

325 Authority's general duty . . . . . [212]
326 Designation of professional bodies . . . . . [213]
327 Exemption from the general prohibition . . . . . [214]
328 Directions in relation to the general prohibition . . . . . [215]
329 Orders in relation to the general prohibition . . . . . [216]
330 Consultation . . . . . [217]
331 Procedure on making or varying orders under section 329 . . . . . [218]
332 Rules in relation to persons to whom the general prohibition does not apply . . . . . [219]
333 False claims to be a person to whom the general prohibition does not apply . . . . . [220]

PART XXI
MUTUAL SOCIETIES

Friendly societies

334 The Friendly Societies Commission . . . . . [221]
335 The Registry of Friendly Societies . . . . . [222]

Building societies

336 The Building Societies Commission [223]
337 The Building Societies Investor Protection Board [224]

Industrial and provident societies and credit unions

338 Industrial and provident societies and credit unions [225]

Supplemental

339 Supplemental provisions [226]

PART XXII
AUDITORS AND ACTUARIES

Appointment

340 Appointment [227]

Information

341 Access to books etc [228]
342 Information given by auditor or actuary to the Authority [229]
343 Information given by auditor or actuary to the Authority: persons with close links [230]
344 Duty of auditor or actuary resigning etc to give notice [231]

Disqualification

345 Disqualification [232]

Offence

346 Provision of false or misleading information to auditor or actuary [233]

PART XXIII
PUBLIC RECORD, DISCLOSURE OF INFORMATION AND CO-OPERATION

The public record

347 The record of authorised persons etc [234]

Disclosure of information

348 Restrictions on disclosure of confidential information by Authority etc [235]
349 Exceptions from section 348 [236]
350 Disclosure of information by the Inland Revenue [237]
351 Competition information [238]
352 Offences [239]
353 Removal of other restrictions on disclosure [240]

Co-operation

354 Authority's duty to co-operate with others [241]

PART XXIV
INSOLVENCY

Interpretation

355 Interpretation of this Part [242]

Voluntary arrangements

356 Authority's powers to participate in proceedings: company voluntary arrangements [243]
357 Authority's powers to participate in proceedings: individual voluntary arrangements [244]
358 Authority's powers to participate in proceedings: trust deeds for creditors in Scotland [245]

Administration orders

359 Administration order [246]
360 Insurers [247]
361 Administrator's duty to report to Authority [248]
362 Authority's powers to participate in proceedings [249]
362A Administrator appointed by company or directors [250]

Receivership

363 Authority's powers to participate in proceedings [251]
364 Receiver's duty to report to Authority [252]

Voluntary winding up

365 Authority's powers to participate in proceedings [253]
366 Insurers effecting or carrying out long-term contracts of insurance [254]

Winding up by the court

367 Winding-up petitions [255]
368 Winding-up petitions: EEA and Treaty firms [256]
369 Insurers: service of petition etc on Authority [257]
369A Reclaim funds: service of petition etc on Authority [257A]
370 Liquidator's duty to report to Authority [258]

371 Authority's powers to participate in proceedings [259]

Bankruptcy

372 Petitions [260]
373 Insolvency practitioner's duty to report to Authority [261]
374 Authority's powers to participate in proceedings [262]

Provisions against debt avoidance

375 Authority's right to apply for an order [263]

Supplemental provisions concerning insurers

376 Continuation of contracts of long-term insurance where insurer in liquidation [264]
377 Reducing the value of contracts instead of winding up [265]
378 Treatment of assets on winding up [266]
379 Winding-up rules [267]

PART XXV
INJUNCTIONS AND RESTITUTION

Injunctions

380 Injunctions [268]
381 Injunctions in cases of market abuse [269]

Restitution orders

382 Restitution orders [270]
383 Restitution orders in cases of market abuse [271]

Restitution required by Authority

384 Power of Authority to require restitution [272]
385 Warning notices [273]
386 Decision notices [274]

PART XXVI
NOTICES

Warning notices

387 Warning notices [275]

Decision notices

388 Decision notices [276]

Conclusion of proceedings

389 Notices of discontinuance [277]
390 Final notices [278]

Publication

391 Publication [279]

Third party rights and access to evidence

392 Application of sections 393 and 394 [280]
393 Third party rights [281]
394 Access to Authority material [282]

The Authority's procedures

395 The Authority's procedures [283]
396 Statements under section 395: consultation [284]

PART XXVII
OFFENCES

Miscellaneous offences

397 Misleading statements and practices [285]
398 Misleading the Authority: residual cases [286]
399 Misleading the Director General of Fair Trading [287]

Bodies corporate and partnerships

400 Offences by bodies corporate etc [288]

Institution of proceedings

401 Proceedings for offences [289]
402 Power of the Authority to institute proceedings for certain other offences [290]
403 *Jurisdiction and procedure in respect of offences* [291]

PART XXVIII
MISCELLANEOUS

Schemes for reviewing past business

404 Schemes for reviewing past business [292]

Third countries

405 Directions [293]
406 Interpretation of section 405 [294]
407 Consequences of a direction under section 405 [295]
408 EFTA firms [296]
409 Gibraltar [297]

International obligations

410 International obligations [298]

Gaming contracts

412 Gaming contracts [299]

Limitation on powers to require documents

413 Protected items [300]

Service of notices

414 Service of notices [301]

Jurisdiction

415 Jurisdiction in civil proceedings [302]

Removal of certain unnecessary provisions

416 Provisions relating to industrial assurance and certain other enactments [303]

PART XXIX
INTERPRETATION

417 Definitions [304]
418 Carrying on regulated activities in the United Kingdom [305]
419 Carrying on regulated activities by way of business [306]
420 Parent and subsidiary undertaking [307]
421 Group [308]
421A Meaning of "participating interest" [308A]
422 Controller [309]
422A Disregarded holdings [309A]
423 Manager [310]
424 Insurance [311]
425 Expressions relating to authorisation elsewhere in the single market [312]

PART XXX
SUPPLEMENTAL

426 Consequential and supplementary provision [313]
427 Transitional provisions [314]
428 Regulations and orders [315]
429 Parliamentary control of statutory instruments [316]
430 Extent [317]
431 Commencement [318]
432 Minor and consequential amendments, transitional provisions and repeals [319]
433 Short title [320]

SCHEDULES:

Schedule 1—The Financial Services Authority
Part I—General [321]
Part II—Status [322]
Part III—Penalties and Fees [323]
Part IV—Miscellaneous [324]
Schedule 2—Regulated Activities
Part I—Regulated Activities: General [325]
Part 1A—Regulated Activities: Reclaim Funds [325A]
Part II—Investments [326]
Part III—Supplemental Provisions [327]
Schedule 3—EEA Passport Rights
Part I—Defined Terms [328]
Part II—Exercise of Passport Rights by EEA Firms [329]
Part III—Exercise of Passport Rights by UK Firms [330]
Schedule 5—Persons Concerned in Collective Investment Schemes [331]
Schedule 6—Threshold Conditions
Part I—Part IV Permission [332]
Part II—Authorisation [333]
Part III—Additional Conditions [334]
Schedule 7—The Authority as Competent Authority for Part VI [335]
Schedule 12—Transfer Schemes: Certificates
Part I—Insurance Business Transfer Schemes [336]
Part II—Banking Business Transfer Schemes [337]
Part 2A—Reclaim Fund Business Transfer Schemes [337A]
Part III—Insurance Business Transfers Effected Outside the United Kingdom [338]

Schedule 13—The Financial Services and Markets Tribunal
Part I—General . . . . . [339]
Part II—The Tribunal . . . . . [340]
Part III—Constitution of Tribunal . . . . . [341]
Part IV—Tribunal Procedure . . . . . [342]
Schedule 14—Role of the Competition Commission . . . . . [343]
Schedule 15—Information and Investigations: Connected Persons
Part I—Rules for Specific Bodies . . . . . [344]
Part II—Additional Rules . . . . . [345]
Schedule 17—The Ombudsman Scheme
Part I—General . . . . . [346]
Part II—The Scheme Operator . . . . . [347]
Part III—The Compulsory Jurisdiction . . . . . [348]
Part 3A—The Consumer Credit Jurisdiction . . . . . [348A]
Part IV—The Voluntary Jurisdiction . . . . . [349]
Schedule 18—Mutuals
Part II—Friendly Societies: Subsidiaries and Controlled Bodies . . . . . [350]
Schedule 21—Transitional Provisions and Savings . . . . . [351]

An Act to make provision about the regulation of financial services and markets; to provide for the transfer of certain statutory functions relating to building societies, friendly societies, industrial and provident societies and certain other mutual societies; and for connected purposes

14 June 2000

NOTES

Limited liability partnerships. The provisions of this Act relating to companies and partnerships are applied with modifications to limited liability partnerships: see the Limited Liability Partnerships Regulations 2001, SI 2001/1090.

Transitional provisions and savings. A number of instruments have been made under this Act making transitional provisions and savings. These instruments are listed under the note "Orders under this section" to s 426 at **[313]**.

Transfer of functions: mutual societies. The Financial Services and Markets Act 2000 (Mutual Societies) Order 2001, SI 2001/2617, art 4(2) at **[654]** transfers to the Financial Services Authority certain functions which, immediately before 1 December 2001, were functions of: (a) the Chief Registrar of friendly societies, assistant registrars of friendly societies or the central office of the registry of friendly societies; (b) the Friendly Societies Commission; or (c) the Building Societies Commission. Sch 2 to the 2001 Order at **[667]** makes provisions concerning the application of this Act in relation to functions transferred (or to be transferred) to the Authority by the said art 4(2).

PART I
THE REGULATOR

[1]

1 The Financial Services Authority

(1) The body corporate known as the Financial Services Authority ("the Authority") is to have the functions conferred on it by or under this Act.

(2) The Authority must comply with the requirements as to its constitution set out in Schedule 1.

(3) Schedule 1 also makes provision about the status of the Authority and the exercise of certain of its functions.

[(4) Section 249 of the Banking Act 2009 provides for references to functions of the Authority (whether generally or under this Act) to include references to functions conferred on the Authority by that Act (subject to any order under that section).]

NOTES

Sub-s (4): added by the Banking Act 2009, s 249(4).

The Authority's general duties

[2]

2 The Authority's general duties

(1) In discharging its general functions the Authority must, so far as is reasonably possible, act in a way—

- (a) which is compatible with the regulatory objectives; and
- (b) which the Authority considers most appropriate for the purpose of meeting those objectives.

(2) The regulatory objectives are—

- (a) market confidence;
- (b) public awareness;

(c) the protection of consumers; and
(d) the reduction of financial crime.

(3) In discharging its general functions the Authority must have regard to—
(a) the need to use its resources in the most efficient and economic way;
(b) the responsibilities of those who manage the affairs of authorised persons;
(c) the principle that a burden or restriction which is imposed on a person, or on the carrying on of an activity, should be proportionate to the benefits, considered in general terms, which are expected to result from the imposition of that burden or restriction;
(d) the desirability of facilitating innovation in connection with regulated activities;
(e) the international character of financial services and markets and the desirability of maintaining the competitive position of the United Kingdom;
(f) the need to minimise the adverse effects on competition that may arise from anything done in the discharge of those functions;
(g) the desirability of facilitating competition between those who are subject to any form of regulation by the Authority.

(4) The Authority's general functions are—
(a) its function of making rules under this Act (considered as a whole);
(b) its function of preparing and issuing codes under this Act (considered as a whole);
(c) its functions in relation to the giving of general guidance (considered as a whole); and
(d) its function of determining the general policy and principles by reference to which it performs particular functions.

(5) "General guidance" has the meaning given in section 158(5).

The regulatory objectives

[3]

3 Market confidence

(1) The market confidence objective is: maintaining confidence in the financial system.

(2) "The financial system" means the financial system operating in the United Kingdom and includes—
(a) financial markets and exchanges;
(b) regulated activities; and
(c) other activities connected with financial markets and exchanges.

[4]

4 Public awareness

(1) The public awareness objective is: promoting public understanding of the financial system.

(2) It includes, in particular—
(a) promoting awareness of the benefits and risks associated with different kinds of investment or other financial dealing; and
(b) the provision of appropriate information and advice.

(3) "The financial system" has the same meaning as in section 3.

[5]

5 The protection of consumers

(1) The protection of consumers objective is: securing the appropriate degree of protection for consumers.

(2) In considering what degree of protection may be appropriate, the Authority must have regard to—
(a) the differing degrees of risk involved in different kinds of investment or other transaction;
(b) the differing degrees of experience and expertise that different consumers may have in relation to different kinds of regulated activity;
(c) the needs that consumers may have for advice and accurate information; and
(d) the general principle that consumers should take responsibility for their decisions.

(3) "Consumers" means persons—
(a) who are consumers for the purposes of section 138; or
(b) who, in relation to regulated activities carried on otherwise than by authorised persons, would be consumers for those purposes if the activities were carried on by authorised persons.

[6]

6 The reduction of financial crime

(1) The reduction of financial crime objective is: reducing the extent to which it is possible for a business carried on—

(a) by a regulated person, or
(b) in contravention of the general prohibition,

to be used for a purpose connected with financial crime.

(2) In considering that objective the Authority must, in particular, have regard to the desirability of—

(a) regulated persons being aware of the risk of their businesses being used in connection with the commission of financial crime;
(b) regulated persons taking appropriate measures (in relation to their administration and employment practices, the conduct of transactions by them and otherwise) to prevent financial crime, facilitate its detection and monitor its incidence;
(c) regulated persons devoting adequate resources to the matters mentioned in paragraph (b).

(3) "Financial crime" includes any offence involving—

(a) fraud or dishonesty;
(b) misconduct in, or misuse of information relating to, a financial market; or
(c) handling the proceeds of crime.

(4) "Offence" includes an act or omission which would be an offence if it had taken place in the United Kingdom.

(5) "Regulated person" means an authorised person, a recognised investment exchange or a recognised clearing house.

Corporate governance

[7]
7 Duty of Authority to follow principles of good governance

In managing its affairs, the Authority must have regard to such generally accepted principles of good corporate governance as it is reasonable to regard as applicable to it.

Arrangements for consulting practitioners and consumers

[8]
8 The Authority's general duty to consult

The Authority must make and maintain effective arrangements for consulting practitioners and consumers on the extent to which its general policies and practices are consistent with its general duties under section 2.

[9]
9 The Practitioner Panel

(1) Arrangements under section 8 must include the establishment and maintenance of a panel of persons (to be known as "the Practitioner Panel") to represent the interests of practitioners.

(2) The Authority must appoint one of the members of the Practitioner Panel to be its chairman.

(3) The Treasury's approval is required for the appointment or dismissal of the chairman.

(4) The Authority must have regard to any representations made to it by the Practitioner Panel.

(5) The Authority must appoint to the Practitioner Panel such—

(a) individuals who are authorised persons,
(b) persons representing authorised persons,
(c) persons representing recognised investment exchanges, and
(d) persons representing recognised clearing houses,

as it considers appropriate.

[10]
10 The Consumer Panel

(1) Arrangements under section 8 must include the establishment and maintenance of a panel of persons (to be known as "the Consumer Panel") to represent the interests of consumers.

(2) The Authority must appoint one of the members of the Consumer Panel to be its chairman.

(3) The Treasury's approval is required for the appointment or dismissal of the chairman.

(4) The Authority must have regard to any representations made to it by the Consumer Panel.

(5) The Authority must appoint to the Consumer Panel such consumers, or persons representing the interests of consumers, as it considers appropriate.

[(5A) The Secretary of State may direct the Authority to appoint as a member of the Consumer Panel a person specified by the Secretary of State who—

(a) is a non-executive member of the National Consumer Council, and
(b) is nominated for the purposes of this subsection by the National Consumer Council after consultation with the Authority.

(5B) Only one person may, at any time, be a member of the Consumer Panel appointed in accordance with a direction under subsection (5A); but that does not prevent the Authority appointing as a member of the Consumer Panel any person who is also a member of the National Consumer Council.

(5C) A person appointed in accordance with a direction under subsection (5A) ceases to be a member of the Panel on ceasing to be a non-executive member of the National Consumer Council.]

(6) The Authority must secure that the membership of the Consumer Panel is such as to give a fair degree of representation to those who are using, or are or may be contemplating using, services otherwise than in connection with businesses carried on by them.

(7) "Consumers" means persons, other than authorised persons—

(a) who are consumers for the purposes of section 138; or

(b) who, in relation to regulated activities carried on otherwise than by authorised persons, would be consumers for those purposes if the activities were carried on by authorised persons.

NOTES

Sub-ss (5A)–(5C): inserted by the Consumers, Estate Agents and Redress Act 2007, s 39.

[11]

11 Duty to consider representations by the Panels

(1) This section applies to a representation made, in accordance with arrangements made under section 8, by the Practitioner Panel or by the Consumer Panel.

(2) The Authority must consider the representation.

(3) If the Authority disagrees with a view expressed, or proposal made, in the representation, it must give the Panel a statement in writing of its reasons for disagreeing.

Reviews

[12]

12 Reviews

(1) The Treasury may appoint an independent person to conduct a review of the economy, efficiency and effectiveness with which the Authority has used its resources in discharging its functions.

(2) A review may be limited by the Treasury to such functions of the Authority (however described) as the Treasury may specify in appointing the person to conduct it.

(3) A review is not to be concerned with the merits of the Authority's general policy or principles in pursuing regulatory objectives or in exercising functions under Part VI.

(4) On completion of a review, the person conducting it must make a written report to the Treasury—

(a) setting out the result of the review; and

(b) making such recommendations (if any) as he considers appropriate.

(5) A copy of the report must be—

(a) laid before each House of Parliament; and

(b) published in such manner as the Treasury consider appropriate.

(6) Any expenses reasonably incurred in the conduct of a review are to be met by the Treasury out of money provided by Parliament.

(7) "Independent" means appearing to the Treasury to be independent of the Authority.

[13]

13 Right to obtain documents and information

(1) A person conducting a review under section 12—

(a) has a right of access at any reasonable time to all such documents as he may reasonably require for purposes of the review; and

(b) may require any person holding or accountable for any such document to provide such information and explanation as are reasonably necessary for that purpose.

(2) Subsection (1) applies only to documents in the custody or under the control of the Authority.

(3) An obligation imposed on a person as a result of the exercise of powers conferred by subsection (1) is enforceable by injunction or, in Scotland, by an order for specific performance under section 45 of the Court of Session Act 1988.

Inquiries

[14]
14 Cases in which the Treasury may arrange independent inquiries
(1) This section applies in two cases.
(2) The first is where it appears to the Treasury that—
(a) events have occurred in relation to—
(i) a collective investment scheme, or
(ii) a person who is, or was at the time of the events, carrying on a regulated activity (whether or not as an authorised person),
which posed or could have posed a grave risk to the financial system or caused or risked causing significant damage to the interests of consumers; and
(b) those events might not have occurred, or the risk or damage might have been reduced, but for a serious failure in—
(i) the system established by this Act[, or by any previous statutory provision,] for the regulation of such schemes or of such persons and their activities; or
(ii) the operation of that system.
(3) The second is where it appears to the Treasury that—
(a) events have occurred in relation to listed securities or an issuer of listed securities which caused or could have caused significant damage to holders of listed securities; and
(b) those events might not have occurred [in—
(i) the regulatory system established by Part 6 or by any previous statutory provision concerned with the official listing of securities; or
(ii) the operation of that system.]
(4) If the Treasury consider that it is in the public interest that there should be an independent inquiry into the events and the circumstances surrounding them, they may arrange for an inquiry to be held under section 15.
(5) "Consumers" means persons—
(a) who are consumers for the purposes of section 138; or
(b) who, in relation to regulated activities carried on otherwise than by authorised persons, would be consumers for those purposes if the activities were carried on by authorised persons.
[(5A) "Event" does not include any event occurring before 1st December 2001 (but no such limitation applies to the reference in subsection (4) to surrounding circumstances).]
(6) "The financial system" has the same meaning as in section 3.
(7) "Listed securities" means anything which has been admitted to the official list under Part VI.

NOTES
Sub-s (2): words in square brackets inserted by the Inquiries Act 2005, s 46(1), (2).
Sub-s (3): words in square brackets substituted by the Inquiries Act 2005, s 46(1), (3).
Sub-s (5A): inserted by the Inquiries Act 2005, s 46(1), (4).

[15]
15 Power to appoint person to hold an inquiry
(1) If the Treasury decide to arrange for an inquiry to be held under this section, they may appoint such person as they consider appropriate to hold the inquiry.
(2) The Treasury may, by a direction to the appointed person, control—
(a) the scope of the inquiry;
(b) the period during which the inquiry is to be held;
(c) the conduct of the inquiry; and
(d) the making of reports.
(3) A direction may, in particular—
(a) confine the inquiry to particular matters;
(b) extend the inquiry to additional matters;
(c) require the appointed person to discontinue the inquiry or to take only such steps as are specified in the direction;
(d) require the appointed person to make such interim reports as are so specified.

[16]
16 Powers of appointed person and procedure
(1) The person appointed to hold an inquiry under section 15 may—
(a) obtain such information from such persons and in such manner as he thinks fit;
(b) make such inquiries as he thinks fit; and
(c) determine the procedure to be followed in connection with the inquiry.

(2) The appointed person may require any person who, in his opinion, is able to provide any information, or produce any document, which is relevant to the inquiry to provide any such information or produce any such document.

(3) For the purposes of an inquiry, the appointed person has the same powers as the court in respect of the attendance and examination of witnesses (including the examination of witnesses abroad) and in respect of the production of documents.

(4) "Court" means—

(a) the High Court; or

(b) in Scotland, the Court of Session.

[17]

17 Conclusion of inquiry

(1) On completion of an inquiry under section 15, the person holding the inquiry must make a written report to the Treasury—

(a) setting out the result of the inquiry; and

(b) making such recommendations (if any) as he considers appropriate.

(2) The Treasury may publish the whole, or any part, of the report and may do so in such manner as they consider appropriate.

(3) Subsection (4) applies if the Treasury propose to publish a report but consider that it contains material—

(a) which relates to the affairs of a particular person whose interests would, in the opinion of the Treasury, be seriously prejudiced by publication of the material; or

(b) the disclosure of which would be incompatible with an international obligation of the United Kingdom.

(4) The Treasury must ensure that the material is removed before publication.

(5) The Treasury must lay before each House of Parliament a copy of any report or part of a report published under subsection (2).

(6) Any expenses reasonably incurred in holding an inquiry are to be met by the Treasury out of money provided by Parliament.

[18]

18 Obstruction and contempt

(1) If a person ("A")—

(a) fails to comply with a requirement imposed on him by a person holding an inquiry under section 15, or

(b) otherwise obstructs such an inquiry,

the person holding the inquiry may certify the matter to the High Court (or, in Scotland, the Court of Session).

(2) The court may enquire into the matter.

(3) If, after hearing—

(a) any witnesses who may be produced against or on behalf of A, and

(b) any statement made by or on behalf of A,

the court is satisfied that A would have been in contempt of court if the inquiry had been proceedings before the court, it may deal with him as if he were in contempt.

PART II
REGULATED AND PROHIBITED ACTIVITIES

The general prohibition

[19]

19 The general prohibition

(1) No person may carry on a regulated activity in the United Kingdom, or purport to do so, unless he is—

(a) an authorised person; or

(b) an exempt person.

(2) The prohibition is referred to in this Act as the general prohibition.

Requirement for permission

[20]

20 Authorised persons acting without permission

(1) If an authorised person carries on a regulated activity in the United Kingdom, or purports to do so, otherwise than in accordance with permission—

(a) given to him by the Authority under Part IV, or

(b) resulting from any other provision of this Act,

he is to be taken to have contravened a requirement imposed on him by the Authority under this Act.

(2) The contravention does not—

(a) make a person guilty of an offence;

(b) make any transaction void or unenforceable; or

(c) (subject to subsection (3)) give rise to any right of action for breach of statutory duty.

(3) In prescribed cases the contravention is actionable at the suit of a person who suffers loss as a result of the contravention, subject to the defences and other incidents applying to actions for breach of statutory duty.

NOTES

For transitional provisions in relation to persons with an interim permission see: the Financial Services and Markets Act 2000 (Transitional Provisions) (Mortgages) Order 2004, SI 2004/2615, arts 1(3), 2, 5, Schedule, paras 1, 2; the Financial Services and Markets Act 2000 (Transitional Provisions) (General Insurance Intermediaries) Order 2004, SI 2004/3351, arts 1(3), 2, 5, Schedule, paras 1, 2; the Financial Services and Markets Act 2000 (Regulated Activities) (Amendment) Order 2006, SI 2006/1969, art 7, Schedule, paras 1, 2; the Financial Services and Markets Act 2000 (Regulated Activities) (Amendment) (No 2) Order 2006, SI 2006/2383, art 40, Schedule, paras 1, 2; the Financial Services and Markets Act 2000 (Regulated Activities) (Amendment) Order 2009, SI 2009/1342, art 34, Schedule, paras 1, 2.

Regulations: the Financial Services and Markets Act 2000 (Rights of Action) Regulations 2001, SI 2001/2256 at **[618]**.

Financial promotion

[21]

21 Restrictions on financial promotion

(1) A person ("A") must not, in the course of business, communicate an invitation or inducement to engage in investment activity.

(2) But subsection (1) does not apply if—

(a) A is an authorised person; or

(b) the content of the communication is approved for the purposes of this section by an authorised person.

(3) In the case of a communication originating outside the United Kingdom, subsection (1) applies only if the communication is capable of having an effect in the United Kingdom.

(4) The Treasury may by order specify circumstances in which a person is to be regarded for the purposes of subsection (1) as—

(a) acting in the course of business;

(b) not acting in the course of business.

(5) The Treasury may by order specify circumstances (which may include compliance with financial promotion rules) in which subsection (1) does not apply.

(6) An order under subsection (5) may, in particular, provide that subsection (1) does not apply in relation to communications—

(a) of a specified description;

(b) originating in a specified country or territory outside the United Kingdom;

(c) originating in a country or territory which falls within a specified description of country or territory outside the United Kingdom; or

(d) originating outside the United Kingdom.

(7) The Treasury may by order repeal subsection (3).

(8) "Engaging in investment activity" means—

(a) entering or offering to enter into an agreement the making or performance of which by either party constitutes a controlled activity; or

(b) exercising any rights conferred by a controlled investment to acquire, dispose of, underwrite or convert a controlled investment.

(9) An activity is a controlled activity if—

(a) it is an activity of a specified kind or one which falls within a specified class of activity; and

(b) it relates to an investment of a specified kind, or to one which falls within a specified class of investment.

(10) An investment is a controlled investment if it is an investment of a specified kind or one which falls within a specified class of investment.

(11) Schedule 2 (except paragraph 26) applies for the purposes of subsections (9) and (10) with references to section 22 being read as references to each of those subsections.

(12) Nothing in Schedule 2, as applied by subsection (11), limits the powers conferred by subsection (9) or (10).

(13) "Communicate" includes causing a communication to be made.

(14) "Investment" includes any asset, right or interest.
(15) "Specified" means specified in an order made by the Treasury.

NOTES

For transitional provisions in relation to a person with an interim permission not being treated as an authorised person for the purposes of sub-ss (1), (2) above see: the Financial Services and Markets Act 2000 (Transitional Provisions) (Mortgages) Order 2004, SI 2004/2615, arts 1(3), 2, 5, Schedule, paras 4, 6; the Financial Services and Markets Act 2000 (Transitional Provisions) (General Insurance Intermediaries) Order 2004, SI 2004/3351, arts 1(3), 2, 5, Schedule, paras 4, 6; the Financial Services and Markets Act 2000 (Regulated Activities) (Amendment) Order 2006, SI 2006/1969, art 7, Schedule, paras 4, 6; the Financial Services and Markets Act 2000 (Regulated Activities) (Amendment) (No 2) Order 2006, SI 2006/2383, art 40, Schedule, paras 4, 6; the Financial Services and Markets Act 2000 (Regulated Activities) (Amendment) Order 2009, SI 2009/1342, art 34, Schedule, paras 4, 6.

Orders: the Financial Services and Markets Act 2000 (Miscellaneous Provisions) Order 2001, SI 2001/3650; the Financial Services and Markets Act 2000 (Financial Promotion) Order 2005, SI 2005/1529 at **[966]**.

Regulated activities

[22]

22 The classes of activity and categories of investment

(1) An activity is a regulated activity for the purposes of this Act if it is an activity of a specified kind which is carried on by way of business and—
- (a) relates to an investment of a specified kind; or
- (b) in the case of an activity of a kind which is also specified for the purposes of this paragraph, is carried on in relation to property of any kind.

(2) Schedule 2 makes provision supplementing this section.
(3) Nothing in Schedule 2 limits the powers conferred by subsection (1).
(4) "Investment" includes any asset, right or interest.
(5) "Specified" means specified in an order made by the Treasury.

NOTES

Orders: the Financial Services and Markets Act 2000 (Regulated Activities) Order 2001, SI 2001/544 at **[501]**.

Offences

[23]

23 Contravention of the general prohibition

(1) A person who contravenes the general prohibition is guilty of an offence and liable—
- (a) on summary conviction, to imprisonment for a term not exceeding six months or a fine not exceeding the statutory maximum, or both;
- (b) on conviction on indictment, to imprisonment for a term not exceeding two years or a fine, or both.

(2) In this Act "an authorisation offence" means an offence under this section.
(3) In proceedings for an authorisation offence it is a defence for the accused to show that he took all reasonable precautions and exercised all due diligence to avoid committing the offence.

[24]

24 False claims to be authorised or exempt

(1) A person who is neither an authorised person nor, in relation to the regulated activity in question, an exempt person is guilty of an offence if he—
- (a) describes himself (in whatever terms) as an authorised person;
- (b) describes himself (in whatever terms) as an exempt person in relation to the regulated activity; or
- (c) behaves, or otherwise holds himself out, in a manner which indicates (or which is reasonably likely to be understood as indicating) that he is—
    - (i) an authorised person; or
    - (ii) an exempt person in relation to the regulated activity.

(2) In proceedings for an offence under this section it is a defence for the accused to show that he took all reasonable precautions and exercised all due diligence to avoid committing the offence.
(3) A person guilty of an offence under this section is liable on summary conviction to imprisonment for a term not exceeding six months or a fine not exceeding level 5 on the standard scale, or both.
(4) But where the conduct constituting the offence involved or included the public display of any material, the maximum fine for the offence is level 5 on the standard scale multiplied by the number of days for which the display continued.

[25]
25 Contravention of section 21

(1) A person who contravenes section 21(1) is guilty of an offence and liable—
- (a) on summary conviction, to imprisonment for a term not exceeding six months or a fine not exceeding the statutory maximum, or both;
- (b) on conviction on indictment, to imprisonment for a term not exceeding two years or a fine, or both.

(2) In proceedings for an offence under this section it is a defence for the accused to show—
- (a) that he believed on reasonable grounds that the content of the communication was prepared, or approved for the purposes of section 21, by an authorised person; or
- (b) that he took all reasonable precautions and exercised all due diligence to avoid committing the offence.

Enforceability of agreements

[26]
26 Agreements made by unauthorised persons

(1) An agreement made by a person in the course of carrying on a regulated activity in contravention of the general prohibition is unenforceable against the other party.

(2) The other party is entitled to recover—
- (a) any money or other property paid or transferred by him under the agreement; and
- (b) compensation for any loss sustained by him as a result of having parted with it.

(3) "Agreement" means an agreement—
- (a) made after this section comes into force; and
- (b) the making or performance of which constitutes, or is part of, the regulated activity in question.

(4) This section does not apply if the regulated activity is accepting deposits.

[27]
27 Agreements made through unauthorised persons

(1) An agreement made by an authorised person ("the provider")—
- (a) in the course of carrying on a regulated activity (not in contravention of the general prohibition), but
- (b) in consequence of something said or done by another person ("the third party") in the course of a regulated activity carried on by the third party in contravention of the general prohibition,

is unenforceable against the other party.

(2) The other party is entitled to recover—
- (a) any money or other property paid or transferred by him under the agreement; and
- (b) compensation for any loss sustained by him as a result of having parted with it.

(3) "Agreement" means an agreement—
- (a) made after this section comes into force; and
- (b) the making or performance of which constitutes, or is part of, the regulated activity in question carried on by the provider.

(4) This section does not apply if the regulated activity is accepting deposits.

[28]
28 Agreements made unenforceable by section 26 or 27

(1) This section applies to an agreement which is unenforceable because of section 26 or 27.

(2) The amount of compensation recoverable as a result of that section is—
- (a) the amount agreed by the parties; or
- (b) on the application of either party, the amount determined by the court.

(3) If the court is satisfied that it is just and equitable in the circumstances of the case, it may allow—
- (a) the agreement to be enforced; or
- (b) money and property paid or transferred under the agreement to be retained.

(4) In considering whether to allow the agreement to be enforced or (as the case may be) the money or property paid or transferred under the agreement to be retained the court must—
- (a) if the case arises as a result of section 26, have regard to the issue mentioned in subsection (5); or
- (b) if the case arises as a result of section 27, have regard to the issue mentioned in subsection (6).

(5) The issue is whether the person carrying on the regulated activity concerned reasonably believed that he was not contravening the general prohibition by making the agreement.

(6) The issue is whether the provider knew that the third party was (in carrying on the regulated activity) contravening the general prohibition.

(7) If the person against whom the agreement is unenforceable—

(a) elects not to perform the agreement, or

(b) as a result of this section, recovers money paid or other property transferred by him under the agreement,

he must repay any money and return any other property received by him under the agreement.

(8) If property transferred under the agreement has passed to a third party, a reference in section 26 or 27 or this section to that property is to be read as a reference to its value at the time of its transfer under the agreement.

(9) The commission of an authorisation offence does not make the agreement concerned illegal or invalid to any greater extent than is provided by section 26 or 27.

[29]

29 Accepting deposits in breach of general prohibition

(1) This section applies to an agreement between a person ("the depositor") and another person ("the deposit-taker") made in the course of the carrying on by the deposit-taker of accepting deposits in contravention of the general prohibition.

(2) If the depositor is not entitled under the agreement to recover without delay any money deposited by him, he may apply to the court for an order directing the deposit-taker to return the money to him.

(3) The court need not make such an order if it is satisfied that it would not be just and equitable for the money deposited to be returned, having regard to the issue mentioned in subsection (4).

(4) The issue is whether the deposit-taker reasonably believed that he was not contravening the general prohibition by making the agreement.

(5) "Agreement" means an agreement—

(a) made after this section comes into force; and

(b) the making or performance of which constitutes, or is part of, accepting deposits.

[30]

30 Enforceability of agreements resulting from unlawful communications

(1) In this section—

"unlawful communication" means a communication in relation to which there has been a contravention of section 21(1);

"controlled agreement" means an agreement the making or performance of which by either party constitutes a controlled activity for the purposes of that section; and

"controlled investment" has the same meaning as in section 21.

(2) If in consequence of an unlawful communication a person enters as a customer into a controlled agreement, it is unenforceable against him and he is entitled to recover—

(a) any money or other property paid or transferred by him under the agreement; and

(b) compensation for any loss sustained by him as a result of having parted with it.

(3) If in consequence of an unlawful communication a person exercises any rights conferred by a controlled investment, no obligation to which he is subject as a result of exercising them is enforceable against him and he is entitled to recover—

(a) any money or other property paid or transferred by him under the obligation; and

(b) compensation for any loss sustained by him as a result of having parted with it.

(4) But the court may allow—

(a) the agreement or obligation to be enforced, or

(b) money or property paid or transferred under the agreement or obligation to be retained,

if it is satisfied that it is just and equitable in the circumstances of the case.

(5) In considering whether to allow the agreement or obligation to be enforced or (as the case may be) the money or property paid or transferred under the agreement to be retained the court must have regard to the issues mentioned in subsections (6) and (7).

(6) If the applicant made the unlawful communication, the issue is whether he reasonably believed that he was not making such a communication.

(7) If the applicant did not make the unlawful communication, the issue is whether he knew that the agreement was entered into in consequence of such a communication.

(8) "Applicant" means the person seeking to enforce the agreement or obligation or retain the money or property paid or transferred.

(9) Any reference to making a communication includes causing a communication to be made.

(10) The amount of compensation recoverable as a result of subsection (2) or (3) is—

(a) the amount agreed between the parties; or

(b) on the application of either party, the amount determined by the court.

(11) If a person elects not to perform an agreement or an obligation which (by virtue of subsection (2) or (3)) is unenforceable against him, he must repay any money and return any other property received by him under the agreement.

(12) If (by virtue of subsection (2) or (3)) a person recovers money paid or property transferred by him under an agreement or obligation, he must repay any money and return any other property received by him as a result of exercising the rights in question.

(13) If any property required to be returned under this section has passed to a third party, references to that property are to be read as references to its value at the time of its receipt by the person required to return it.

PART III
AUTHORISATION AND EXEMPTION

Authorisation

[31]

31 Authorised persons

(1) The following persons are authorised for the purposes of this Act—

(a) a person who has a Part IV permission to carry on one or more regulated activities;

(b) an EEA firm qualifying for authorisation under Schedule 3;

(c) a Treaty firm qualifying for authorisation under Schedule 4;

(d) a person who is otherwise authorised by a provision of, or made under, this Act.

(2) In this Act "authorised person" means a person who is authorised for the purposes of this Act.

[32]

32 Partnerships and unincorporated associations

(1) If a firm is authorised—

(a) it is authorised to carry on the regulated activities concerned in the name of the firm; and

(b) its authorisation is not affected by any change in its membership.

(2) If an authorised firm is dissolved, its authorisation continues to have effect in relation to any [individual or] firm which succeeds to the business of the dissolved firm.

[(3) For the purposes of this section, an individual or firm is to be regarded as succeeding to the business of a dissolved firm only if succession is to the whole or substantially the whole of the business of the former firm.]

(4) "Firm" means—

(a) a partnership; or

(b) an unincorporated association of persons.

(5) "Partnership" does not include a partnership which is constituted under the law of any place outside the United Kingdom and is a body corporate.

NOTES

Sub-s (2): words in square brackets inserted by the Regulatory Reform (Financial Services and Markets Act 2000) Order 2007, SI 2007/1973, arts 2, 3(a).

Sub-s (3): substituted by SI 2007/1973, arts 2, 3(b).

Ending of authorisation

[33]

33 Withdrawal of authorisation by the Authority

(1) This section applies if—

(a) an authorised person's Part IV permission is cancelled; and

(b) as a result, there is no regulated activity for which he has permission.

(2) The Authority must give a direction withdrawing that person's status as an authorised person.

[34]

34 EEA firms

(1) An EEA firm ceases to qualify for authorisation under Part II of Schedule 3 if it ceases to be an EEA firm as a result of—

(a) having its EEA authorisation withdrawn; or

(b) ceasing to have an EEA right in circumstances in which EEA authorisation is not required.

(2) At the request of an EEA firm, the Authority may give a direction cancelling its authorisation under Part II of Schedule 3.

(3) If an EEA firm has a Part IV permission, it does not cease to be an authorised person merely because it ceases to qualify for authorisation under Part II of Schedule 3.

[35]
35 Treaty firms
(1) A Treaty firm ceases to qualify for authorisation under Schedule 4 if its home State authorisation is withdrawn.
(2) At the request of a Treaty firm, the Authority may give a direction cancelling its Schedule 4 authorisation.
(3) If a Treaty firm has a Part IV permission, it does not cease to be an authorised person merely because it ceases to qualify for authorisation under Schedule 4.

[36]
36 Persons authorised as a result of paragraph 1(1) of Schedule 5
(1) At the request of a person authorised as a result of paragraph 1(1) of Schedule 5, the Authority may give a direction cancelling his authorisation as such a person.
(2) If a person authorised as a result of paragraph 1(1) of Schedule 5 has a Part IV permission, he does not cease to be an authorised person merely because he ceases to be a person so authorised.

Exercise of EEA rights by UK firms

[37]
37 Exercise of EEA rights by UK firms
Part III of Schedule 3 makes provision in relation to the exercise outside the United Kingdom of EEA rights by UK firms.

Exemption

[38]
38 Exemption orders
(1) The Treasury may by order ("an exemption order") provide for—
(a) specified persons, or
(b) persons falling within a specified class,
to be exempt from the general prohibition.
(2) But a person cannot be an exempt person as a result of an exemption order if he has a Part IV permission.
(3) An exemption order may provide for an exemption to have effect—
(a) in respect of all regulated activities;
(b) in respect of one or more specified regulated activities;
(c) only in specified circumstances;
(d) only in relation to specified functions;
(e) subject to conditions.
(4) "Specified" means specified by the exemption order.

NOTES
For the disapplication of a person's interim permission for the purposes of sub-s (2) above see: the Financial Services and Markets Act 2000 (Transitional Provisions) (Mortgages) Order 2004, SI 2004/2615, arts 1(3), 2, 5, Schedule, paras 1, 3; the Financial Services and Markets Act 2000 (Transitional Provisions) (General Insurance Intermediaries) Order 2004, SI 2004/3351, arts 1(3), 2, 5, Schedule, paras 1, 3; the Financial Services and Markets Act 2000 (Regulated Activities) (Amendment) Order 2006, SI 2006/1969, art 7, Schedule, paras 1, 3(a); the Financial Services and Markets Act 2000 (Regulated Activities) (Amendment) (No 2) Order 2006, SI 2006/2383, art 40, Schedule, paras 1, 3(a); the Financial Services and Markets Act 2000 (Regulated Activities) (Amendment) Order 2009, SI 2009/1342, art 34, Schedule, paras 1, 3(a).
Orders: the Financial Services and Markets Act 2000 (Exemption) Order 2001, SI 2001/1201 at **[595A]**.

[39]
39 Exemption of appointed representatives
(1) If a person (other than an authorised person)—
(a) is a party to a contract with an authorised person ("his principal") which—
(i) permits or requires him to carry on business of a prescribed description, and
(ii) complies with such requirements as may be prescribed, and
(b) is someone for whose activities in carrying on the whole or part of that business his principal has accepted responsibility in writing,
he is exempt from the general prohibition in relation to any regulated activity comprised in the carrying on of that business for which his principal has accepted responsibility.
[(1A) But a person is not exempt as a result of subsection (1)—
(a) if his principal is an investment firm or a credit institution, and
(b) so far as the business for which his principal has accepted responsibility is investment services business,
unless he is entered on the applicable register.

(1B) The "applicable register" is—

(a) in the case of a person established in an EEA State (other than the United Kingdom) which permits investment firms authorised by the competent authority of that State to appoint tied agents, the register of tied agents maintained in that State pursuant to Article 23 of the markets in financial instruments directive;

(b) in the case of a person established in an EEA State which does not permit investment firms authorised as mentioned in paragraph (a) to appoint tied agents—

(i) if his principal has his relevant office in the United Kingdom, the record maintained by the Authority by virtue of section 347(1)(ha), and

(ii) if his principal is established in an EEA State (other than the United Kingdom) which permits investment firms authorised by the competent authority of the State to appoint tied agents, the register of tied agents maintained by that State pursuant to Article 23 of the markets in financial instruments directive; and

(c) in any other case, the record maintained by the Authority by virtue of section 347(1)(ha).]

(2) A person who is exempt as a result of subsection (1) is referred to in this Act as an appointed representative.

(3) The principal of an appointed representative is responsible, to the same extent as if he had expressly permitted it, for anything done or omitted by the representative in carrying on the business for which he has accepted responsibility.

(4) In determining whether an authorised person has complied with a provision contained in or made under this Act, [or with a provision contained in any directly applicable Community regulation made under the markets in financial instruments directive,] anything which a relevant person has done or omitted as respects business for which the authorised person has accepted responsibility is to be treated as having been done or omitted by the authorised person.

(5) "Relevant person" means a person who at the material time is or was an appointed representative by virtue of being a party to a contract with the authorised person.

(6) Nothing in subsection (4) is to cause the knowledge or intentions of an appointed representative to be attributed to his principal for the purpose of determining whether the principal has committed an offence, unless in all the circumstances it is reasonable for them to be attributed to him.

[(7) A person carries on "investment services business" if—

(a) the business includes providing services or carrying on activities of the kind mentioned in Article 4.1.25 of the markets in financial instruments directive, and

(b) as a result of providing such services or carrying on such activities he is a tied agent or would be if he were established in an EEA State.

(8) In this section—

"competent authority" has the meaning given in Article 4.1.22 of the markets in financial instruments directive;

"credit institution" means—

(a) a credit institution authorised under the banking consolidation directive, or

(b) an institution which would satisfy the requirements for authorisation as a credit institution under that directive if it had its relevant office in an EEA State;

"relevant office" means—

(a) in relation to a body corporate, its registered office or, if it has no registered office, its head office, and

(b) in relation to a person other than a body corporate, the person's head office.]

NOTES

Sub-ss (1A), (1B): inserted by the Financial Services and Markets Act 2000 (Markets in Financial Instruments) Regulations 2007, SI 2007/126, reg 3(5), Sch 5, paras 1, 2(a), subject to transitional provisions in reg 9 thereof.

Sub-s (4): words in square brackets inserted by SI 2007/126, reg 3(5), Sch 5, paras 1, 2(b), subject to transitional provisions in reg 9 thereof.

Sub-ss (7), (8): added by SI 2007/126, reg 3(5), Sch 5, paras 1, 2(c), subject to transitional provisions in reg 9 thereof.

Regulations: the Financial Services and Markets Act 2000 (Appointed Representatives) Regulations 2001, SI 2001/1217 at **[596]**.

39A *(Outside the scope of this work.)*

PART IV
PERMISSION TO CARRY ON REGULATED ACTIVITIES

Application for permission

[40]
40 Application for permission
(1) An application for permission to carry on one or more regulated activities may be made to the Authority by—
(a) an individual;
(b) a body corporate;
(c) a partnership; or
(d) an unincorporated association.
(2) An authorised person may not apply for permission under this section if he has a permission—
(a) given to him by the Authority under this Part, or
(b) having effect as if so given,
which is in force.
(3) An EEA firm may not apply for permission under this section to carry on a regulated activity which it is, or would be, entitled to carry on in exercise of an EEA right, whether through a United Kingdom branch or by providing services in the United Kingdom.
(4) A permission given by the Authority under this Part or having effect as if so given is referred to in this Act as "a Part IV permission".

NOTES
For the disapplication of a person's interim permission for the purposes of sub-s (2) above see: the Financial Services and Markets Act 2000 (Transitional Provisions) (Mortgages) Order 2004, SI 2004/2615, arts 1(3), 2, 5, Schedule, paras 1, 3; the Financial Services and Markets Act 2000 (Transitional Provisions) (General Insurance Intermediaries) Order 2004, SI 2004/3351, arts 1(3), 2, 5, Schedule, paras 1, 3; the Financial Services and Markets Act 2000 (Regulated Activities) (Amendment) Order 2006, SI 2006/1969, art 7, Schedule, paras 1, 3(b); the Financial Services and Markets Act 2000 (Regulated Activities) (Amendment) (No 2) Order 2006, SI 2006/2383, art 40, Schedule, paras 1, 3(b); the Financial Services and Markets Act 2000 (Regulated Activities) (Amendment) Order 2009, SI 2009/1342, art 34, Schedule, paras 1, 3(b).

[41]
41 The threshold conditions
(1) "The threshold conditions", in relation to a regulated activity, means the conditions set out in Schedule 6.
(2) In giving or varying permission, or imposing or varying any requirement, under this Part the Authority must ensure that the person concerned will satisfy, and continue to satisfy, the threshold conditions in relation to all of the regulated activities for which he has or will have permission.
(3) But the duty imposed by subsection (2) does not prevent the Authority, having due regard to that duty, from taking such steps as it considers are necessary, in relation to a particular authorised person, in order to secure its regulatory objective of the protection of consumers.

Permission

[42]
42 Giving permission
(1) "The applicant" means an applicant for permission under section 40.
(2) The Authority may give permission for the applicant to carry on the regulated activity or activities to which his application relates or such of them as may be specified in the permission.
(3) If the applicant—
(a) in relation to a particular regulated activity, is exempt from the general prohibition as a result of section 39(1) or an order made under section 38(1), but
(b) has applied for permission in relation to another regulated activity,
the application is to be treated as relating to all the regulated activities which, if permission is given, he will carry on.
(4) If the applicant—
(a) in relation to a particular regulated activity, is exempt from the general prohibition as a result of section 285(2) or (3), but
(b) has applied for permission in relation to another regulated activity,
the application is to be treated as relating only to that other regulated activity.
(5) If the applicant—
(a) is a person to whom, in relation to a particular regulated activity, the general prohibition does not apply as a result of Part XIX, but
(b) has applied for permission in relation to another regulated activity,

the application is to be treated as relating only to that other regulated activity.
(6) If it gives permission, the Authority must specify the permitted regulated activity or activities, described in such manner as the Authority considers appropriate.
(7) The Authority may—
 (a) incorporate in the description of a regulated activity such limitations (for example as to circumstances in which the activity may, or may not, be carried on) as it considers appropriate;
 (b) specify a narrower or wider description of regulated activity than that to which the application relates;
 (c) give permission for the carrying on of a regulated activity which is not included among those to which the application relates.

NOTES

For the disapplication of a person's interim permission for the purposes this section see: the Financial Services and Markets Act 2000 (Transitional Provisions) (Mortgages) Order 2004, SI 2004/2615, arts 1(3), 2, 5, Schedule, paras 1, 3; the Financial Services and Markets Act 2000 (Transitional Provisions) (General Insurance Intermediaries) Order 2004, SI 2004/3351, arts 1(3), 2, 5, Schedule, paras 1, 3; the Financial Services and Markets Act 2000 (Regulated Activities) (Amendment) Order 2006, SI 2006/1969, art 7, Schedule, paras 1, 3(c), 7; the Financial Services and Markets Act 2000 (Regulated Activities) (Amendment) (No 2) Order 2006, SI 2006/2383, art 40, Schedule, paras 1, 3(c), 7; the Financial Services and Markets Act 2000 (Regulated Activities) (Amendment) Order 2009, SI 2009/1342, art 34, Schedule, paras 1, 3(c), 7.

[43]

43 Imposition of requirements

(1) A Part IV permission may include such requirements as the Authority considers appropriate.
(2) A requirement may, in particular, be imposed—
 (a) so as to require the person concerned to take specified action; or
 (b) so as to require him to refrain from taking specified action.
(3) A requirement may extend to activities which are not regulated activities.
(4) A requirement may be imposed by reference to the person's relationship with—
 (a) his group; or
 (b) other members of his group.
(5) A requirement expires at the end of such period as the Authority may specify in the permission.
(6) But subsection (5) does not affect the Authority's powers under section 44 or 45.

NOTES

For the disapplication of a person's interim permission for the purposes of this section see: the Financial Services and Markets Act 2000 (Transitional Provisions) (Mortgages) Order 2004, SI 2004/2615, arts 1(3), 2, 5, Schedule, paras 1, 3; the Financial Services and Markets Act 2000 (Transitional Provisions) (General Insurance Intermediaries) Order 2004, SI 2004/3351, arts 1(3), 2, 5, Schedule, paras 1, 3; the Financial Services and Markets Act 2000 (Regulated Activities) (Amendment) Order 2006, SI 2006/1969, art 7, Schedule, paras 1, 3(d); the Financial Services and Markets Act 2000 (Regulated Activities) (Amendment) (No 2) Order 2006, SI 2006/2383, art 40, Schedule, paras 1, 3(d); the Financial Services and Markets Act 2000 (Regulated Activities) (Amendment) Order 2009, SI 2009/1342, art 34, Schedule, paras 1, 3(d).

Variation and cancellation of Part IV permission

[44]

44 Variation etc at request of authorised person

(1) The Authority may, on the application of an authorised person with a Part IV permission, vary the permission by—
 (a) adding a regulated activity to those for which it gives permission;
 (b) removing a regulated activity from those for which it gives permission;
 (c) varying the description of a regulated activity for which it gives permission;
 (d) cancelling a requirement imposed under section 43; or
 (e) varying such a requirement.
(2) The Authority may, on the application of an authorised person with a Part IV permission, cancel the permission.
(3) The Authority may refuse an application under this section if it appears to it—
 (a) that the interests of consumers, or potential consumers, would be adversely affected if the application were to be granted; and
 (b) that it is desirable in the interests of consumers, or potential consumers, for the application to be refused.
(4) If, as a result of a variation of a Part IV permission under this section, there are no longer any regulated activities for which the authorised person concerned has permission, the Authority must, once it is satisfied that it is no longer necessary to keep the permission in force, cancel it.

(5) The Authority's power to vary a Part IV permission under this section extends to including any provision in the permission as varied that could be included if a fresh permission were being given in response to an application under section 40.

NOTES

For the disapplication of a person's interim permission for the purposes of sub-ss (1), (4), (5) above see: the Financial Services and Markets Act 2000 (Transitional Provisions) (Mortgages) Order 2004, SI 2004/2615, arts 1(3), 2, 5, Schedule, paras 1, 3; the Financial Services and Markets Act 2000 (Transitional Provisions) (General Insurance Intermediaries) Order 2004, SI 2004/3351, arts 1(3), 2, 5, Schedule, paras 1, 3; the Financial Services and Markets Act 2000 (Regulated Activities) (Amendment) Order 2006, SI 2006/1969, art 7, Schedule, paras 1, 3(e); the Financial Services and Markets Act 2000 (Regulated Activities) (Amendment) (No 2) Order 2006, SI 2006/2383, art 40, Schedule, paras 1, 3(e); the Financial Services and Markets Act 2000 (Regulated Activities) (Amendment) Order 2009, SI 2009/1342, art 34, Schedule, paras 1, 3(e).

[45]

45 Variation etc on the Authority's own initiative

(1) The Authority may exercise its power under this section in relation to an authorised person if it appears to it that—

(a) he is failing, or is likely to fail, to satisfy the threshold conditions;

(b) he has failed, during a period of at least 12 months, to carry on a regulated activity for which he has a Part IV permission; or

(c) it is desirable to exercise that power in order to protect the interests of consumers or potential consumers [(whether of the services of the authorised person or of the services of other authorised persons)].

(2) The Authority's power under this section is the power to vary a Part IV permission in any of the ways mentioned in section 44(1) or to cancel it.

[(2A) Without prejudice to the generality of subsections (1) and (2), the Authority may, in relation to an authorised person who is an investment firm, exercise its power under this section to cancel the Part IV permission of the firm if it appears to it that—

(a) the firm has failed, during a period of at least six months, to carry on a regulated activity which is an investment service or activity for which it has a Part IV permission;

(b) the firm obtained the Part IV permission by making a false statement or by other irregular means;

(c) the firm no longer satisfies the requirements for authorisation pursuant to Chapter I of Title II of the markets in financial instruments directive, or pursuant to or contained in any Community legislation made under that Chapter, in relation to a regulated activity which is an investment service or activity for which it has a Part IV permission; or

(d) the firm has seriously and systematically infringed the operating conditions pursuant to Chapter II of Title II of the markets in financial instruments directive, or pursuant to or contained in any Community legislation made under that Chapter, in relation to a regulated activity which is an investment service or activity for which it has a Part IV permission.

(2B) For the purposes of subsection (2A) a regulated activity is an investment service or activity if it falls within the definition of "investment services and activities" in section 417(1).]

(3) If, as a result of a variation of a Part IV permission under this section, there are no longer any regulated activities for which the authorised person concerned has permission, the Authority must, once it is satisfied that it is no longer necessary to keep the permission in force, cancel it.

(4) The Authority's power to vary a Part IV permission under this section extends to including any provision in the permission as varied that could be included if a fresh permission were being given in response to an application under section 40.

(5) The Authority's power under this section is referred to in this Part as its own-initiative power.

NOTES

Sub-s (1): words in square brackets in para (c) added by the Banking Act 2009, s 248.

Sub-ss (2A), (2B): inserted by the Financial Services and Markets Act 2000 (Markets in Financial Instruments) Regulations 2007, SI 2007/126, reg 3(5), Sch 5, paras 1, 4.

For the disapplication of a person's interim permission for the purposes of sub-sg (1)(b) above see: the Financial Services and Markets Act 2000 (Regulated Activities) (Amendment) Order 2009, SI 2009/1342, artg 34, Schedule, parasg 1, 3(f).

[46]

46 Variation of permission on acquisition of control

(1) This section applies if it appears to the Authority that—

(a) a person has acquired control over a UK authorised person who has a Part IV permission; but

(b) there are no grounds for exercising its own-initiative power.

(2) If it appears to the Authority that the likely effect of the acquisition of control on the authorised person, or on any of its activities, is uncertain the Authority may vary the authorised person's permission by—

(a) imposing a requirement of a kind that could be imposed under section 43 on giving permission; or

(b) varying a requirement included in the authorised person's permission under that section.

(3) Any reference to a person having acquired control is to be read in accordance with Part XII.

[47]

47 Exercise of power in support of overseas regulator

(1) The Authority's own-initiative power may be exercised in respect of an authorised person at the request of, or for the purpose of assisting, a regulator who is—

(a) outside the United Kingdom; and

(b) of a prescribed kind.

(2) Subsection (1) applies whether or not the Authority has powers which are exercisable in relation to the authorised person by virtue of any provision of Part XIII.

(3) If a request to the Authority for the exercise of its own-initiative power has been made by a regulator who is—

(a) outside the United Kingdom,

(b) of a prescribed kind, and

(c) acting in pursuance of provisions of a prescribed kind,

the Authority must, in deciding whether or not to exercise that power in response to the request, consider whether it is necessary to do so in order to comply with a Community obligation.

(4) In deciding in any case in which the Authority does not consider that the exercise of its own-initiative power is necessary in order to comply with a Community obligation, it may take into account in particular—

(a) whether in the country or territory of the regulator concerned, corresponding assistance would be given to a United Kingdom regulatory authority;

(b) whether the case concerns the breach of a law, or other requirement, which has no close parallel in the United Kingdom or involves the assertion of a jurisdiction not recognised by the United Kingdom;

(c) the seriousness of the case and its importance to persons in the United Kingdom;

(d) whether it is otherwise appropriate in the public interest to give the assistance sought.

(5) The Authority may decide not to exercise its own-initiative power, in response to a request, unless the regulator concerned undertakes to make such contribution towards the cost of its exercise as the Authority considers appropriate.

(6) Subsection (5) does not apply if the Authority decides that it is necessary for it to exercise its own-initiative power in order to comply with a Community obligation.

(7) In subsections (4) and (5) "request" means a request of a kind mentioned in subsection (1).

NOTES

Regulations: the Financial Services and Markets Act 2000 (Own-initiative Power) (Overseas Regulators) Regulations 2001, SI 2001/2639.

[48]

48 Prohibitions and restrictions

(1) This section applies if the Authority—

(a) on giving a person a Part IV permission, imposes an assets requirement on him; or

(b) varies an authorised person's Part IV permission so as to alter an assets requirement imposed on him or impose such a requirement on him.

(2) A person on whom an assets requirement is imposed is referred to in this section as "A".

(3) "Assets requirement" means a requirement under section 43—

(a) prohibiting the disposal of, or other dealing with, any of A's assets (whether in the United Kingdom or elsewhere) or restricting such disposals or dealings; or

(b) that all or any of A's assets, or all or any assets belonging to consumers but held by A or to his order, must be transferred to and held by a trustee approved by the Authority.

(4) If the Authority—

(a) imposes a requirement of the kind mentioned in subsection (3)(a), and

(b) gives notice of the requirement to any institution with whom A keeps an account,

the notice has the effects mentioned in subsection (5).

(5) Those effects are that—

(a) the institution does not act in breach of any contract with A if, having been instructed by A (or on his behalf) to transfer any sum or otherwise make any payment out of

A's account, it refuses to do so in the reasonably held belief that complying with the instruction would be incompatible with the requirement; and

(b) if the institution complies with such an instruction, it is liable to pay to the Authority an amount equal to the amount transferred from, or otherwise paid out of, A's account in contravention of the requirement.

(6) If the Authority imposes a requirement of the kind mentioned in subsection (3)(b), no assets held by a person as trustee in accordance with the requirement may, while the requirement is in force, be released or dealt with except with the consent of the Authority.

(7) If, while a requirement of the kind mentioned in subsection (3)(b) is in force, A creates a charge over any assets of his held in accordance with the requirement, the charge is (to the extent that it confers security over the assets) void against the liquidator and any of A's creditors.

(8) Assets held by a person as trustee ("T") are to be taken to be held by T in accordance with a requirement mentioned in subsection (3)(b) only if—

(a) A has given T written notice that those assets are to be held by T in accordance with the requirement; or

(b) they are assets into which assets to which paragraph (a) applies have been transposed by T on the instructions of A.

(9) A person who contravenes subsection (6) is guilty of an offence and liable on summary conviction to a fine not exceeding level 5 on the standard scale.

(10) "Charge" includes a mortgage (or in Scotland a security over property).

(11) Subsections (6) and (8) do not affect any equitable interest or remedy in favour of a person who is a beneficiary of a trust as a result of a requirement of the kind mentioned in subsection (3)(b).

Connected persons

[49]

49 Persons connected with an applicant

(1) In considering—

(a) an application for a Part IV permission, or

(b) whether to vary or cancel a Part IV permission,

the Authority may have regard to any person appearing to it to be, or likely to be, in a relationship with the applicant or person given permission which is relevant.

(2) Before—

(a) giving permission in response to an application made by a person who is connected with an EEA firm [(other than an EEA firm falling within paragraph 5(e) of Schedule 3 (insurance and reinsurance intermediaries))], or

[(b) varying any permission given by the Authority to such a person, where the effect of the variation is to grant permission for the purposes of a single market directive other than the one for the purposes of which the existing permission was granted,]

the Authority must consult the firm's home state regulator.

[(2A) But subsection (2) does not apply to the extent that the permission relates to—

(a) an insurance mediation activity (within the meaning given by paragraph 2(5) of Schedule 6); or

(b) a regulated activity involving a regulated mortgage contract[, a regulated home reversion plan *or a regulated home purchase plan*].]

(3) A person ("A") is connected with an EEA firm if—

(a) A is a subsidiary undertaking of the firm; or

(b) A is a subsidiary undertaking of a parent undertaking of the firm.

[(4) In subsection (2A)(b) "regulated mortgage contract", "regulated home reversion plan", "regulated home purchase plan" and "regulated sale and rent back agreement" shall be construed in accordance with—

(a) section 22;

(b) any relevant order under that section; and

(c) Schedule 2.]

NOTES

Sub-s (2): words in square brackets in para (a) inserted by the Financial Services and Markets Act 2000 (Regulated Activities) (Amendment) (No 2) Order 2003, SI 2003/1476, art 20(1), (2); para (b) substituted by the Regulatory Reform (Financial Services and Markets Act 2000) Order 2007, SI 2007/1973, arts 2, 4.

Sub-s (2A): inserted by the Financial Services and Markets Act 2000 (Regulated Activities) Order 2001, SI 2001/544, art 97 (as inserted by the Financial Services and Markets Act 2000 (Regulated Activities) (Amendment) Order 2004, SI 2004/1610, art 3); words in square brackets in para (b) inserted by the Financial Services and Markets Act 2000 (Regulated Activities) (Amendment) (No 2) Order 2006, SI 2006/2383, art 28, subject to transitional provisions in arts 37–39 thereof; for the words in italics in para (b) there are substituted the words ", a regulated home purchase plan or a regulated sale and rent back agreement" by the Financial Services and Markets Act 2000 (Regulated Activities) (Amendment) Order 2009, SI 2009/1342, art 25(a), as from 1 July 2009 (for certain purposes) and 30 June 2010 (for remaining purposes) (for the full commencement details and for transitional provisions etc see arts 1, 32–34 of that Order).

Sub-s (4): added by SI 2009/1342, art 25(b), as from the same dates and for the same purposes as noted above.

Additional permissions

[50]

50 Authority's duty to consider other permissions etc

(1) "Additional Part IV permission" means a Part IV permission which is in force in relation to an EEA firm, a Treaty firm or a person authorised as a result of paragraph 1(1) of Schedule 5.

(2) If the Authority is considering whether, and if so how, to exercise its own-initiative power under this Part in relation to an additional Part IV permission, it must take into account—

(a) the home State authorisation of the authorised person concerned;

(b) any relevant directive; and

(c) relevant provisions of the Treaty.

Procedure

[51]

51 Applications under this Part

(1) An application for a Part IV permission must—

(a) contain a statement of the regulated activity or regulated activities which the applicant proposes to carry on and for which he wishes to have permission; and

(b) give the address of a place in the United Kingdom for service on the applicant of any notice or other document which is required or authorised to be served on him under this Act.

(2) An application for the variation of a Part IV permission must contain a statement—

(a) of the desired variation; and

(b) of the regulated activity or regulated activities which the applicant proposes to carry on if his permission is varied.

(3) Any application under this Part must—

(a) be made in such manner as the Authority may direct; and

(b) contain, or be accompanied by, such other information as the Authority may reasonably require.

(4) At any time after receiving an application and before determining it, the Authority may require the applicant to provide it with such further information as it reasonably considers necessary to enable it to determine the application.

(5) Different directions may be given, and different requirements imposed, in relation to different applications or categories of application.

(6) The Authority may require an applicant to provide information which he is required to provide under this section in such form, or to verify it in such a way, as the Authority may direct.

[52]

52 Determination of applications

(1) An application under this Part must be determined by the Authority before the end of the period of six months beginning with the date on which it received the completed application.

(2) The Authority may determine an incomplete application if it considers it appropriate to do so; and it must in any event determine such an application within twelve months beginning with the date on which it received the application.

(3) The applicant may withdraw his application, by giving the Authority written notice, at any time before the Authority determines it.

(4) If the Authority grants an application for, or for variation of, a Part IV permission, it must give the applicant written notice.

(5) The notice must state the date from which the permission, or the variation, has effect.

(6) If the Authority proposes—

(a) to give a Part IV permission but to exercise its power under section 42(7)(a) or (b) or 43(1), or

(b) to vary a Part IV permission on the application of an authorised person but to exercise its power under any of those provisions (as a result of section 44(5)),

it must give the applicant a warning notice.

(7) If the Authority proposes to refuse an application made under this Part, it must (unless subsection (8) applies) give the applicant a warning notice.

(8) This subsection applies if it appears to the Authority that—
- (a) the applicant is an EEA firm; and
- (b) the application is made with a view to carrying on a regulated activity in a manner in which the applicant is, or would be, entitled to carry on that activity in the exercise of an EEA right whether through a United Kingdom branch or by providing services in the United Kingdom.

(9) If the Authority decides—
- (a) to give a Part IV permission but to exercise its power under section 42(7)(a) or (b) or 43(1),
- (b) to vary a Part IV permission on the application of an authorised person but to exercise its power under any of those provisions (as a result of section 44(5)), or
- (c) to refuse an application under this Part,

it must give the applicant a decision notice.

NOTES

For the disapplication of a person's interim permission for the purposes of this section, see the Financial Services and Markets Act 2000 (Regulated Activities) (Amendment) Order 2009, SI 2009/1342, art 34, Schedule, paras 1, 3(g).

[53]

53 Exercise of own-initiative power: procedure

(1) This section applies to an exercise of the Authority's own-initiative power to vary an authorised person's Part IV permission.

(2) A variation takes effect—
- (a) immediately, if the notice given under subsection (4) states that that is the case;
- (b) on such date as may be specified in the notice; or
- (c) if no date is specified in the notice, when the matter to which the notice relates is no longer open to review.

(3) A variation may be expressed to take effect immediately (or on a specified date) only if the Authority, having regard to the ground on which it is exercising its own-initiative power, reasonably considers that it is necessary for the variation to take effect immediately (or on that date).

(4) If the Authority proposes to vary the Part IV permission, or varies it with immediate effect, it must give the authorised person written notice.

(5) The notice must—
- (a) give details of the variation;
- (b) state the Authority's reasons for the variation and for its determination as to when the variation takes effect;
- (c) inform the authorised person that he may make representations to the Authority within such period as may be specified in the notice (whether or not he has referred the matter to the Tribunal);
- (d) inform him of when the variation takes effect; and
- (e) inform him of his right to refer the matter to the Tribunal.

(6) The Authority may extend the period allowed under the notice for making representations.

(7) If, having considered any representations made by the authorised person, the Authority decides—
- (a) to vary the permission in the way proposed, or
- (b) if the permission has been varied, not to rescind the variation,

it must give him written notice.

(8) If, having considered any representations made by the authorised person, the Authority decides—
- (a) not to vary the permission in the way proposed,
- (b) to vary the permission in a different way, or
- (c) to rescind a variation which has effect,

it must give him written notice.

(9) A notice given under subsection (7) must inform the authorised person of his right to refer the matter to the Tribunal.

(10) A notice under subsection (8)(b) must comply with subsection (5).

(11) If a notice informs a person of his right to refer a matter to the Tribunal, it must give an indication of the procedure on such a reference.

(12) For the purposes of subsection (2)(c), whether a matter is open to review is to be determined in accordance with section 391(8).

NOTES

For the disapplication of a person's interim permission for the purposes of this section, see the Financial Services and Markets Act 2000 (Regulated Activities) (Amendment) Order 2009, SI 2009/1342, art 34, Schedule, paras 1, 3(h).

[54]

54 Cancellation of Part IV permission: procedure

(1) If the Authority proposes to cancel an authorised person's Part IV permission otherwise than at his request, it must give him a warning notice.

(2) If the Authority decides to cancel an authorised person's Part IV permission otherwise than at his request, it must give him a decision notice.

NOTES

For the disapplication of a person's interim permission for the purposes of this section, see the Financial Services and Markets Act 2000 (Regulated Activities) (Amendment) Order 2009, SI 2009/1342, art 34, Schedule, paras 1, 3(i).

References to the Tribunal

[55]

55 Right to refer matters to the Tribunal

(1) An applicant who is aggrieved by the determination of an application made under this Part may refer the matter to the Tribunal.

(2) An authorised person who is aggrieved by the exercise of the Authority's own-initiative power may refer the matter to the Tribunal.

NOTES

For the disapplication of a person's interim permission for the purposes of this section, see the Financial Services and Markets Act 2000 (Regulated Activities) (Amendment) Order 2009, SI 2009/1342, art 34, Schedule, paras 1, 3(j).

PART V
PERFORMANCE OF REGULATED ACTIVITIES

Prohibition orders

[56]

56 Prohibition orders

(1) Subsection (2) applies if it appears to the Authority that an individual is not a fit and proper person to perform functions in relation to a regulated activity carried on by an authorised person.

(2) The Authority may make an order ("a prohibition order") prohibiting the individual from performing a specified function, any function falling within a specified description or any function.

(3) A prohibition order may relate to—

(a) a specified regulated activity, any regulated activity falling within a specified description or all regulated activities;

(b) authorised persons generally or any person within a specified class of authorised person.

(4) An individual who performs or agrees to perform a function in breach of a prohibition order is guilty of an offence and liable on summary conviction to a fine not exceeding level 5 on the standard scale.

(5) In proceedings for an offence under subsection (4) it is a defence for the accused to show that he took all reasonable precautions and exercised all due diligence to avoid committing the offence.

(6) An authorised person must take reasonable care to ensure that no function of his, in relation to the carrying on of a regulated activity, is performed by a person who is prohibited from performing that function by a prohibition order.

(7) The Authority may, on the application of the individual named in a prohibition order, vary or revoke it.

(8) This section applies to the performance of functions in relation to a regulated activity carried on by—

(a) a person who is an exempt person in relation to that activity, and

(b) a person to whom, as a result of Part XX, the general prohibition does not apply in relation to that activity,

as it applies to the performance of functions in relation to a regulated activity carried on by an authorised person.

(9) "Specified" means specified in the prohibition order.

[57]
57 Prohibition orders: procedure and right to refer to Tribunal
(1) If the Authority proposes to make a prohibition order it must give the individual concerned a warning notice.
(2) The warning notice must set out the terms of the prohibition.
(3) If the Authority decides to make a prohibition order it must give the individual concerned a decision notice.
(4) The decision notice must—
- (a) name the individual to whom the prohibition order applies;
- (b) set out the terms of the order; and
- (c) be given to the individual named in the order.

(5) A person against whom a decision to make a prohibition order is made may refer the matter to the Tribunal.

[58]
58 Applications relating to prohibitions: procedure and right to refer to Tribunal
(1) This section applies to an application for the variation or revocation of a prohibition order.
(2) If the Authority decides to grant the application, it must give the applicant written notice of its decision.
(3) If the Authority proposes to refuse the application, it must give the applicant a warning notice.
(4) If the Authority decides to refuse the application, it must give the applicant a decision notice.
(5) If the Authority gives the applicant a decision notice, he may refer the matter to the Tribunal.

Approval

[59]
59 Approval for particular arrangements
(1) An authorised person ("A") must take reasonable care to ensure that no person performs a controlled function under an arrangement entered into by A in relation to the carrying on by A of a regulated activity, unless the Authority approves the performance by that person of the controlled function to which the arrangement relates.
(2) An authorised person ("A") must take reasonable care to ensure that no person performs a controlled function under an arrangement entered into by a contractor of A in relation to the carrying on by A of a regulated activity, unless the Authority approves the performance by that person of the controlled function to which the arrangement relates.
(3) "Controlled function" means a function of a description specified in rules.
(4) The Authority may specify a description of function under subsection (3) only if, in relation to the carrying on of a regulated activity by an authorised person, it is satisfied that the first, second or third condition is met.
(5) The first condition is that the function is likely to enable the person responsible for its performance to exercise a significant influence on the conduct of the authorised person's affairs, so far as relating to the regulated activity.
(6) The second condition is that the function will involve the person performing it in dealing with customers of the authorised person in a manner substantially connected with the carrying on of the regulated activity.
(7) The third condition is that the function will involve the person performing it in dealing with property of customers of the authorised person in a manner substantially connected with the carrying on of the regulated activity.
(8) Neither subsection (1) nor subsection (2) applies to an arrangement which allows a person to perform a function if the question of whether he is a fit and proper person to perform the function is reserved under any of the single market directives to an authority in a country or territory outside the United Kingdom.
(9) In determining whether the first condition is met, the Authority may take into account the likely consequences of a failure to discharge that function properly.
(10) "Arrangement"—
- (a) means any kind of arrangement for the performance of a function of A which is entered into by A or any contractor of his with another person; and
- (b) includes, in particular, that other person's appointment to an office, his becoming a partner or his employment (whether under a contract of service or otherwise).

(11) "Customer", in relation to an authorised person, means a person who is using, or who is or may be contemplating using, any of the services provided by the authorised person.

NOTES

For the disapplication of a person's interim permission for the purposes of this section, see the Financial Services and Markets Act 2000 (Regulated Activities) (Amendment) Order 2009, SI 2009/1342, art 34, Schedule, paras 1, 3(k).

[60]

60 Applications for approval

(1) An application for the Authority's approval under section 59 may be made by the authorised person concerned.

(2) The application must—

(a) be made in such manner as the Authority may direct; and

(b) contain, or be accompanied by, such information as the Authority may reasonably require.

(3) At any time after receiving the application and before determining it, the Authority may require the applicant to provide it with such further information as it reasonably considers necessary to enable it to determine the application.

(4) The Authority may require an applicant to present information which he is required to give under this section in such form, or to verify it in such a way, as the Authority may direct.

(5) Different directions may be given, and different requirements imposed, in relation to different applications or categories of application.

(6) "The authorised person concerned" includes a person who has applied for permission under Part IV and will be the authorised person concerned if permission is given.

NOTES

In relation to applications for approval by EEA firms, see the Financial Services and Markets Act 2000 (EEA Passport Rights) Regulations 2001, SI 2001/2511, reg 10 at **[639]**.

For the disapplication of a person's interim permission for the purposes of this section, see the Financial Services and Markets Act 2000 (Regulated Activities) (Amendment) Order 2009, SI 2009/1342, art 34, Schedule, paras 1, 3(l).

[61]

61 Determination of applications

(1) The Authority may grant an application made under section 60 only if it is satisfied that the person in respect of whom the application is made ("the candidate") is a fit and proper person to perform the function to which the application relates.

(2) In deciding that question, the Authority may have regard (among other things) to whether the candidate, or any person who may perform a function on his behalf—

(a) has obtained a qualification,

(b) has undergone, or is undergoing, training, or

(c) possesses a level of competence,

required by general rules in relation to persons performing functions of the kind to which the application relates.

(3) The Authority must, before the end of the period of three months beginning with the date on which it receives an application made under section 60 ("the period for consideration"), determine whether—

(a) to grant the application; or

(b) to give a warning notice under section 62(2).

(4) If the Authority imposes a requirement under section 60(3), the period for consideration stops running on the day on which the requirement is imposed but starts running again—

(a) on the day on which the required information is received by the Authority; or

(b) if the information is not provided on a single day, on the last of the days on which it is received by the Authority.

(5) A person who makes an application under section 60 may withdraw his application by giving written notice to the Authority at any time before the Authority determines it, but only with the consent of—

(a) the candidate; and

(b) the person by whom the candidate is to be retained to perform the function concerned, if not the applicant.

NOTES

For the disapplication of a person's interim permission for the purposes of this section, see the Financial Services and Markets Act 2000 (Regulated Activities) (Amendment) Order 2009, SI 2009/1342, art 34, Schedule, paras 1, 3(m).

[62]

62 Applications for approval: procedure and right to refer to Tribunal

(1) If the Authority decides to grant an application made under section 60 ("an application"), it must give written notice of its decision to each of the interested parties.

(2) If the Authority proposes to refuse an application, it must give a warning notice to each of the interested parties.

(3) If the Authority decides to refuse an application, it must give a decision notice to each of the interested parties.

(4) If the Authority decides to refuse an application, each of the interested parties may refer the matter to the Tribunal.

(5) "The interested parties", in relation to an application, are—

(a) the applicant;

(b) the person in respect of whom the application is made ("A"); and

(c) the person by whom A's services are to be retained, if not the applicant.

NOTES

For the disapplication of a person's interim permission for the purposes of this section, see the Financial Services and Markets Act 2000 (Regulated Activities) (Amendment) Order 2009, SI 2009/1342, art 34, Schedule, paras 1, 3(n).

[63]

63 Withdrawal of approval

(1) The Authority may withdraw an approval given under section 59 if it considers that the person in respect of whom it was given is not a fit and proper person to perform the function to which the approval relates.

(2) When considering whether to withdraw its approval, the Authority may take into account any matter which it could take into account if it were considering an application made under section 60 in respect of the performance of the function to which the approval relates.

(3) If the Authority proposes to withdraw its approval, it must give each of the interested parties a warning notice.

(4) If the Authority decides to withdraw its approval, it must give each of the interested parties a decision notice.

(5) If the Authority decides to withdraw its approval, each of the interested parties may refer the matter to the Tribunal.

(6) "The interested parties", in relation to an approval, are—

(a) the person on whose application it was given ("A");

(b) the person in respect of whom it was given ("B"); and

(c) the person by whom B's services are retained, if not A.

NOTES

For the disapplication of a person's interim permission for the purposes of this section, see the Financial Services and Markets Act 2000 (Regulated Activities) (Amendment) Order 2009, SI 2009/1342, art 34, Schedule, paras 1, 3(o).

Conduct

[64]

64 Conduct: statements and codes

(1) The Authority may issue statements of principle with respect to the conduct expected of approved persons.

(2) If the Authority issues a statement of principle under subsection (1), it must also issue a code of practice for the purpose of helping to determine whether or not a person's conduct complies with the statement of principle.

(3) A code issued under subsection (2) may specify—

(a) descriptions of conduct which, in the opinion of the Authority, comply with a statement of principle;

(b) descriptions of conduct which, in the opinion of the Authority, do not comply with a statement of principle;

(c) factors which, in the opinion of the Authority, are to be taken into account in determining whether or not a person's conduct complies with a statement of principle.

(4) The Authority may at any time alter or replace a statement or code issued under this section.

(5) If a statement or code is altered or replaced, the altered or replacement statement or code must be issued by the Authority.

(6) A statement or code issued under this section must be published by the Authority in the way appearing to the Authority to be best calculated to bring it to the attention of the public.

(7) A code published under this section and in force at the time when any particular conduct takes place may be relied on so far as it tends to establish whether or not that conduct complies with a statement of principle.
(8) Failure to comply with a statement of principle under this section does not of itself give rise to any right of action by persons affected or affect the validity of any transaction.
(9) A person is not to be taken to have failed to comply with a statement of principle if he shows that, at the time of the alleged failure, it or its associated code of practice had not been published.
(10) The Authority must, without delay, give the Treasury a copy of any statement or code which it publishes under this section.
(11) The power under this section to issue statements of principle and codes of practice—
 (a) includes power to make different provision in relation to persons, cases or circumstances of different descriptions; and
 (b) is to be treated for the purposes of section 2(4)(a) as part of the Authority's rule-making functions.
(12) The Authority may charge a reasonable fee for providing a person with a copy of a statement or code published under this section.
(13) "Approved person" means a person in relation to whom the Authority has given its approval under section 59.

[65]
65 Statements and codes: procedure
(1) Before issuing a statement or code under section 64, the Authority must publish a draft of it in the way appearing to the Authority to be best calculated to bring it to the attention of the public.
(2) The draft must be accompanied by—
 (a) a cost benefit analysis; and
 (b) notice that representations about the proposal may be made to the Authority within a specified time.
(3) Before issuing the proposed statement or code, the Authority must have regard to any representations made to it in accordance with subsection (2)(b).
(4) If the Authority issues the proposed statement or code it must publish an account, in general terms, of—
 (a) the representations made to it in accordance with subsection (2)(b); and
 (b) its response to them.
(5) If the statement or code differs from the draft published under subsection (1) in a way which is, in the opinion of the Authority, significant—
 (a) the Authority must (in addition to complying with subsection (4)) publish details of the difference; and
 (b) those details must be accompanied by a cost benefit analysis.
(6) Neither subsection (2)(a) nor subsection (5)(b) applies if the Authority considers—
 (a) that, making the appropriate comparison, there will be no increase in costs; or
 (b) that, making that comparison, there will be an increase in costs but the increase will be of minimal significance.
(7) Subsections (1) to (6) do not apply if the Authority considers that the delay involved in complying with them would prejudice the interests of consumers.
(8) A statement or code must state that it is issued under section 64.
(9) The Authority may charge a reasonable fee for providing a copy of a draft published under subsection (1).
(10) This section also applies to a proposal to alter or replace a statement or code.
(11) "Cost benefit analysis" means an estimate of the costs together with an analysis of the benefits that will arise—
 (a) if the proposed statement or code is issued; or
 (b) if subsection (5)(b) applies, from the statement or code that has been issued.
(12) "The appropriate comparison" means—
 (a) in relation to subsection (2)(a), a comparison between the overall position if the statement or code is issued and the overall position if it is not issued;
 (b) in relation to subsection (5)(b), a comparison between the overall position after the issuing of the statement or code and the overall position before it was issued.

NOTES
Disapplication: this section is disapplied in relation to a rule, guidance, statement or code made by the Authority which applies only to persons with an interim permission or an interim approval (or only to a class of such persons), by the Financial Services and Markets Act 2000 (Transitional Provisions) (Mortgages) Order 2004, SI 2004/2615, arts 1(3), 2, 3, 4(2); the Financial Services and Markets Act 2000 (Transitional Provisions) (General Insurance Intermediaries) Order 2004, SI 2004/3351, art 4 at **[962]**; the Financial Services

and Markets Act 2000 (Regulated Activities) (Amendment) Order 2006, SI 2006/1969, art 6(2); the Financial Services and Markets Act 2000 (Regulated Activities) (Amendment) Order 2009, SI 2009/1342, art 33(2).

[66]

66 Disciplinary powers

(1) The Authority may take action against a person under this section if—

(a) it appears to the Authority that he is guilty of misconduct; and

(b) the Authority is satisfied that it is appropriate in all the circumstances to take action against him.

(2) A person is guilty of misconduct if, while an approved person—

(a) he has failed to comply with a statement of principle issued under section 64; or

(b) he has been knowingly concerned in a contravention by the relevant authorised person of a requirement imposed on that authorised person by or under this Act [or by any directly applicable Community regulation made under the markets in financial instruments directive].

(3) If the Authority is entitled to take action under this section against a person, it may—

(a) impose a penalty on him of such amount as it considers appropriate; or

(b) publish a statement of his misconduct.

(4) The Authority may not take action under this section after the end of the period of two years beginning with the first day on which the Authority knew of the misconduct, unless proceedings in respect of it against the person concerned were begun before the end of that period.

(5) For the purposes of subsection (4)—

(a) the Authority is to be treated as knowing of misconduct if it has information from which the misconduct can reasonably be inferred; and

(b) proceedings against a person in respect of misconduct are to be treated as begun when a warning notice is given to him under section 67(1).

(6) "Approved person" has the same meaning as in section 64.

(7) "Relevant authorised person", in relation to an approved person, means the person on whose application approval under section 59 was given.

NOTES

Sub-s (2): words in square brackets inserted by the Financial Services and Markets Act 2000 (Markets in Financial Instruments) Regulations 2007, SI 2007/126, reg 3(5), Sch 5, paras 1, 5.

Modification: this section and ss 67–70 are applied with modifications in respect of the Financial Services Authority's functions under the Payment Services Regulations 2009, SI 2009/209, by SI 2009/209, reg 95, Sch 5, Pt 1, para 1., and in respect of the Financial Services Authority's functions under the Cross-Border Payments in Euro Regulations 2010, SI 2010/89, by SI 2010/89, reg 19, Schedule, Pt 1, para 1.

[67]

67 Disciplinary measures: procedure and right to refer to Tribunal

(1) If the Authority proposes to take action against a person under section 66, it must give him a warning notice.

(2) A warning notice about a proposal to impose a penalty must state the amount of the penalty.

(3) A warning notice about a proposal to publish a statement must set out the terms of the statement.

(4) If the Authority decides to take action against a person under section 66, it must give him a decision notice.

(5) A decision notice about the imposition of a penalty must state the amount of the penalty.

(6) A decision notice about the publication of a statement must set out the terms of the statement.

(7) If the Authority decides to take action against a person under section 66, he may refer the matter to the Tribunal.

NOTES

Modification: see the note to s 66 at **[66]**.

[68]

68 Publication

After a statement under section 66 is published, the Authority must send a copy of it to the person concerned and to any person to whom a copy of the decision notice was given.

NOTES

Modification: see the note to s 66 at **[66]**.

[69]
69 Statement of policy
(1) The Authority must prepare and issue a statement of its policy with respect to—
(a) the imposition of penalties under section 66; and
(b) the amount of penalties under that section.
(2) The Authority's policy in determining what the amount of a penalty should be must include having regard to—
(a) the seriousness of the misconduct in question in relation to the nature of the principle or requirement concerned;
(b) the extent to which that misconduct was deliberate or reckless; and
(c) whether the person on whom the penalty is to be imposed is an individual.
(3) The Authority may at any time alter or replace a statement issued under this section.
(4) If a statement issued under this section is altered or replaced, the Authority must issue the altered or replacement statement.
(5) The Authority must, without delay, give the Treasury a copy of any statement which it publishes under this section.
(6) A statement issued under this section must be published by the Authority in the way appearing to the Authority to be best calculated to bring it to the attention of the public.
(7) The Authority may charge a reasonable fee for providing a person with a copy of the statement.
(8) In exercising, or deciding whether to exercise, its power under section 66 in the case of any particular misconduct, the Authority must have regard to any statement of policy published under this section and in force at the time when the misconduct in question occurred.

NOTES
Modification: see the note to s 66 at **[66]**.

[70]
70 Statements of policy: procedure
(1) Before issuing a statement under section 69, the Authority must publish a draft of the proposed statement in the way appearing to the Authority to be best calculated to bring it to the attention of the public.
(2) The draft must be accompanied by notice that representations about the proposal may be made to the Authority within a specified time.
(3) Before issuing the proposed statement, the Authority must have regard to any representations made to it in accordance with subsection (2).
(4) If the Authority issues the proposed statement it must publish an account, in general terms, of—
(a) the representations made to it in accordance with subsection (2); and
(b) its response to them.
(5) If the statement differs from the draft published under subsection (1) in a way which is, in the opinion of the Authority, significant, the Authority must (in addition to complying with subsection (4)) publish details of the difference.
(6) The Authority may charge a reasonable fee for providing a person with a copy of a draft published under subsection (1).
(7) This section also applies to a proposal to alter or replace a statement.

NOTES
Modification: see the note to s 66 at **[66]**.

Breach of statutory duty

[71]
71 Actions for damages
(1) A contravention of section 56(6) or 59(1) or (2) is actionable at the suit of a private person who suffers loss as a result of the contravention, subject to the defences and other incidents applying to actions for breach of statutory duty.
(2) In prescribed cases, a contravention of that kind which would be actionable at the suit of a private person is actionable at the suit of a person who is not a private person, subject to the defences and other incidents applying to actions for breach of statutory duty.
(3) "Private person" has such meaning as may be prescribed.

NOTES

Regulations: the Financial Services and Markets Act 2000 (Rights of Action) Regulations 2001, SI 2001/2256 at **[618]**.

72–103 (*(Pt VI) outside the scope of this work.*)

PART VII
CONTROL OF BUSINESS TRANSFERS

[72]
104 Control of business transfers

No insurance business transfer scheme or banking business transfer scheme is to have effect unless an order has been made in relation to it under section 111(1).

NOTES

Commencement: 1 December 2001 (for the purpose of insurance business transfer schemes); to be appointed (remaining purposes).

[73]
105 Insurance business transfer schemes

(1) A scheme is an insurance business transfer scheme if it—
(a) satisfies one of the conditions set out in subsection (2);
(b) results in the business transferred being carried on from an establishment of the transferee in an EEA State; and
(c) is not an excluded scheme.

(2) The conditions are that—
(a) the whole or part of the business carried on in one or more member States by a UK authorised person who has permission to effect or carry out contracts of insurance ("the authorised person concerned") is to be transferred to another body ("the transferee");
(b) the whole or part of the business, so far as it consists of reinsurance, carried on in the United Kingdom through an establishment there by an EEA firm [falling within paragraph 5(d) of Schedule 3 and qualifying for authorisation under that Schedule] ("the authorised person concerned") is to be transferred to another body ("the transferee");
(c) the whole or part of the business carried on in the United Kingdom by an authorised person who is neither a UK authorised person nor an EEA firm but who has permission to effect or carry out contracts of insurance ("the authorised person concerned") is to be transferred to another body ("the transferee").

(3) A scheme is an excluded scheme for the purposes of this section if it falls within any of the following cases:

CASE 1

Where the authorised person concerned is a friendly society.

CASE 2

Where—
(a) the authorised person concerned is a UK authorised person;
[(aa) the authorised person concerned is not a reinsurance undertaking (within the meaning of Article 2.1(c) of the reinsurance directive);]
(b) the business to be transferred under the scheme is business which consists of the effecting or carrying out of contracts of reinsurance in one or more EEA States other than the United Kingdom; and
(c) the scheme has been approved by a court in an EEA State other than the United Kingdom or by the host state regulator.

CASE 3

Where—
(a) the authorised person concerned is a UK authorised person;
(b) the business to be transferred under the scheme is carried on in one or more countries or territories (none of which is an EEA State) and does not include policies of insurance . . . against risks arising in an EEA State; and
(c) the scheme has been approved by a court in a country or territory other than an EEA State or by the authority responsible for the supervision of that business in a country or territory in which it is carried on.

CASE 4

Where[—

(a) the business to be transferred under the scheme is the whole of the business of the authorised person concerned;]

(b) all the policyholders are controllers of the firm or of firms within the same group as the firm which is the transferee, and

[(c)] all of the policyholders who will be affected by the transfer have consented to it.

[CASE 5

Where—

(a) the business of the authorised person concerned consists solely of the effecting or carrying out of contracts of reinsurance;

(b) the business to be transferred is the whole or part of that business;

(c) the scheme does not fall within Case 4;

(d) all of the policyholders who will be affected by the transfer have consented to it; and

(e) a certificate has been obtained under paragraph 2 of Schedule 12 in relation to the proposed transfer.]

(4) The parties to a scheme which falls within Case 2, [3, 4 or 5] may apply to the court for an order sanctioning the scheme as if it were an insurance business transfer scheme.

[(5) If the scheme involves a compromise or arrangement falling within Part 27 of the Companies Act 2006 (mergers and divisions of public companies), the provisions of that Part (and Part 26 of that Act) apply accordingly but this does not affect the operation of this Part in relation to the scheme.]

(8) "UK authorised person" means a body which is an authorised person and which—

(a) is incorporated in the United Kingdom; or

(b) is an unincorporated association formed under the law of any part of the United Kingdom.

(9) "Establishment" means, in relation to a person, his head office or a branch of his.

NOTES

Sub-s (2): words in square brackets in para (b) substituted by the Reinsurance Directive Regulations 2007, SI 2007/3253, reg 2(1), Sch 1, paras 1, 2(1)(a).

Sub-s (3): Case 2, para (aa) inserted, words omitted from Case 3 repealed, words in square brackets in Case 4 substituted and Case 5 inserted by SI 2007/3253, reg 2(1), Sch 1, paras 1, 2(1)(b)–(e).

Sub-s (4): words in square brackets substituted by SI 2007/3253, reg 2(1), Sch 1, paras 1, 2(1)(f).

Sub-s (5): substituted for original sub-ss (5)–(7) by the Companies Act 2006 (Consequential Amendments etc) Order 2008, SI 2008/948, art 3(1)(b), (6), Sch 1, Pt 2, para 211(1).

[74]

106 Banking business transfer schemes

(1) A scheme is a banking business transfer scheme if it—

(a) satisfies one of the conditions set out in subsection (2);

(b) is one under which the whole or part of the business to be transferred includes the accepting of deposits; and

(c) is not an excluded scheme.

(2) The conditions are that—

(a) the whole or part of the business carried on by a UK authorised person who has permission to accept deposits ("the authorised person concerned") is to be transferred to another body ("the transferee");

(b) the whole or part of the business carried on in the United Kingdom by an authorised person who is not a UK authorised person but who has permission to accept deposits ("the authorised person concerned") is to be transferred to another body which will carry it on in the United Kingdom ("the transferee").

(3) A scheme is an excluded scheme for the purposes of this section if—

(a) the authorised person concerned is a building society or a credit union; or

[(b) the scheme is a compromise or arrangement to which Part 27 of the Companies Act 2006 (mergers and divisions of public companies) applies.]

(4) For the purposes of subsection (2)(a) it is immaterial whether or not the business to be transferred is carried on in the United Kingdom.

(5) "UK authorised person" has the same meaning as in section 105.

(6) "Building society" has the meaning given in the Building Societies Act 1986.

(7) "Credit union" means a credit union within the meaning of—

(a) the Credit Unions Act 1979;

(b) the Credit Unions (Northern Ireland) Order 1985.

NOTES

Sub-s (3): para (b) substituted by the Companies Act 2006 (Consequential Amendments etc) Order 2008, SI 2008/948, arts 3(1)(b), (6), Sch 1, Pt 2, para 211(2).

[74A]

[106A Banking business transfer schemes

(1) A scheme is a reclaim fund business transfer scheme if, under the scheme, the whole or part of the business carried on by a reclaim fund is to be transferred to one or more other reclaim funds.

(2) "Reclaim fund" has the meaning given by section 5(1) of the Dormant Bank and Building Society Accounts Act 2008.]

NOTES

Commencement: 12 March 2009.

Inserted by the Dormant Bank and Building Society Accounts Act 2008, s 15, Sch 2, para 2.

[75]

107 Application for order sanctioning transfer scheme

(1) An application may be made to the court for an order sanctioning an insurance business transfer scheme[, a banking business transfer scheme or a reclaim fund business transfer scheme].

(2) An application may be made by—

- (a) the authorised person concerned;
- (b) the transferee; or
- (c) both.

(3) The application must be made—

- (a) if the authorised person concerned and the transferee are registered or have their head offices in the same jurisdiction, to the court in that jurisdiction;
- (b) if the authorised person concerned and the transferee are registered or have their head offices in different jurisdictions, to the court in either jurisdiction;
- (c) if the transferee is not registered in the United Kingdom and does not have his head office there, to the court which has jurisdiction in relation to the authorised person concerned.

(4) "Court" means—

- (a) the High Court; or
- (b) in Scotland, the Court of Session.

NOTES

Sub-s (1): words in square brackets substituted by the Dormant Bank and Building Society Accounts Act 2008, s 15, Sch 2, para 3.

[76]

108 Requirements on applicants

(1) The Treasury may by regulations impose requirements on applicants under section 107.

(2) The court may not determine an application under that section if the applicant has failed to comply with a prescribed requirement.

(3) The regulations may, in particular, include provision—

- (a) as to the persons to whom, and periods within which, notice of an application must be given;
- (b) enabling the court to waive a requirement of the regulations in prescribed circumstances.

NOTES

Regulations: the Financial Services and Markets Act 2000 (Control of Business Transfers) (Requirements on Applicants) Regulations 2001, SI 2001/3625 at **[820]**.

[77]

109 Scheme reports

(1) An application under section 107 in respect of an insurance business transfer scheme must be accompanied by a report on the terms of the scheme ("a scheme report").

(2) A scheme report may be made only by a person—

- (a) appearing to the Authority to have the skills necessary to enable him to make a proper report; and
- (b) nominated or approved for the purpose by the Authority.

(3) A scheme report must be made in a form approved by the Authority.

[78]
110 Right to participate in proceedings
On an application under section 107, the following are also entitled to be heard—
(a) the Authority, and
(b) any person (including an employee of the authorised person concerned or of the transferee) who alleges that he would be adversely affected by the carrying out of the scheme.

[79]
111 Sanction of the court for business transfer schemes
(1) This section sets out the conditions which must be satisfied before the court may make an order under this section sanctioning an insurance business transfer scheme[, a banking business transfer scheme or a reclaim fund business transfer scheme].
(2) The court must be satisfied that—
(a) [in the case of an insurance business transfer scheme or a banking business transfer scheme,] the appropriate certificates have been obtained (as to which see Parts I and II of Schedule 12);
[(aa) in the case of a reclaim fund business transfer scheme, the appropriate certificate has been obtained (as to which see Part 2A of that Schedule);]
(b) the transferee has the authorisation required (if any) to enable the business, or part, which is to be transferred to be carried on in the place to which it is to be transferred (or will have it before the scheme takes effect).
(3) The court must consider that, in all the circumstances of the case, it is appropriate to sanction the scheme.

NOTES
Sub-s (1): words square brackets substituted by the Dormant Bank and Building Society Accounts Act 2008, s 15, Sch 2, para 4(1), (2).
Sub-s (2): words in square brackets in para (a) and the whole of para (aa) inserted by the Dormant Bank and Building Society Accounts Act 2008, s 15, Sch 2, para 4(1), (3).

[80]
112 Effect of order sanctioning business transfer scheme
(1) If the court makes an order under section 111(1), it may by that or any subsequent order make such provision (if any) as it thinks fit—
(a) for the transfer to the transferee of the whole or any part of the undertaking concerned and of any property or liabilities of the authorised person concerned;
(b) for the allotment or appropriation by the transferee of any shares, debentures, policies or other similar interests in the transferee which under the scheme are to be allotted or appropriated to or for any other person;
(c) for the continuation by (or against) the transferee of any pending legal proceedings by (or against) the authorised person concerned;
(d) with respect to such incidental, consequential and supplementary matters as are, in its opinion, necessary to secure that the scheme is fully and effectively carried out.
(2) An order under subsection (1)(a) may—
(a) transfer property or liabilities whether or not the authorised person concerned otherwise has the capacity to effect the transfer in question;
(b) make provision in relation to property which was held by the authorised person concerned as trustee;
(c) make provision as to future or contingent rights or liabilities of the authorised person concerned, including provision as to the construction of instruments (including wills) under which such rights or liabilities may arise;
(d) make provision as to the consequences of the transfer in relation to any [occupational pension scheme (within the meaning of section 150(5) of the Finance Act 2004)] operated by or on behalf of the authorised person concerned.
[(2A) Subsection (2)(a) is to be taken to include power to make provision in an order—
(a) for the transfer of property or liabilities which would not otherwise be capable of being transferred or assigned;
(b) for a transfer of property or liabilities to take effect as if there were—
(i) no such requirement to obtain a person's consent or concurrence, and
(ii) no such contravention, liability or interference with any interest or right, as there would otherwise be (in the case of a transfer apart from this section) by reason of any provision falling within subsection (2B).

(2B) A provision falls within this subsection to the extent that it has effect (whether under an enactment or agreement or otherwise) in relation to the terms on which the authorised person concerned is entitled to the property or subject to the liabilities in question.
(2C) Nothing in subsection (2A) or (2B) is to be read as limiting the scope of subsection (1).]
(3) If an order under subsection (1) makes provision for the transfer of property or liabilities—
 (a) the property is transferred to and vests in, and
 (b) the liabilities are transferred to and become liabilities of,
the transferee as a result of the order.
(4) But if any property or liability included in the order is governed by the law of any country or territory outside the United Kingdom, the order may require the authorised person concerned, if the transferee so requires, to take all necessary steps for securing that the transfer to the transferee of the property or liability is fully effective under the law of that country or territory.
(5) Property transferred as the result of an order under subsection (1) may, if the court so directs, vest in the transferee free from any charge which is (as a result of the scheme) to cease to have effect.
(6) An order under subsection (1) which makes provision for the transfer of property is to be treated as an instrument of transfer for the purposes of [section 770(1) of the Companies Act 2006] and any other enactment requiring the delivery of an instrument of transfer for the registration of property.
(7) . . .
(8) If the court makes an order under section 111(1) in relation to an insurance business transfer scheme, it may by that or any subsequent order make such provision (if any) as it thinks fit—
 (a) for dealing with the interests of any person who, within such time and in such manner as the court may direct, objects to the scheme;
 (b) for the dissolution, without winding up, of the authorised person concerned;
 (c) for the reduction, on such terms and subject to such conditions (if any) as it thinks fit, of the benefits payable under—
  (i) any description of policy, or
  (ii) policies generally,
 entered into by the authorised person concerned and transferred as a result of the scheme.
(9) If, in the case of an insurance business transfer scheme, the authorised person concerned is not an EEA firm, it is immaterial for the purposes of subsection (1)(a), (c) or (d) or subsection (2), [(2A),] (3) or (4) that the law applicable to any of the contracts of insurance included in the transfer is the law of an EEA State other than the United Kingdom.
(10) The transferee must, if an insurance or banking business transfer scheme is sanctioned by the court, deposit two office copies of the order made under subsection (1) with the Authority within 10 days of the making of the order.
(11) But the Authority may extend that period.
(12) "Property" includes property, rights and powers of any description.
(13) "Liabilities" includes duties.
(14) "Shares" and "debentures" have the same meaning as in [the Companies Acts (see sections 540 and 738 of the Companies Act 2006).]
(15) "Charge" includes a mortgage (or, in Scotland, a security over property).

NOTES

Sub-s (2): words in square brackets substituted by the Taxation of Pension Schemes (Consequential Amendments) Order 2006, SI 2006/745, art 17.

Sub-ss (2A)–(2C): inserted by the Financial Services and Markets Act 2000 (Amendments to Part 7) Regulations 2008, SI 2008/1468, reg 2(1).

Sub-ss (6), (14): words in square brackets substituted by the Companies Act 2006 (Consequential Amendments etc) Order 2008, SI 2008/948, arts 3(1)(b), 6, Sch 1, Pt 2, para 211(3)(a), (c), subject to savings in arts 11, 12 thereof.

Sub-s (7): repealed by SI 2008/948, art 3(1)(b), (2), Sch 1, Pt 2, para 211(3)(b), Sch 2, subject to savings in arts 11, 12 thereof.

Sub-s (9): number in square brackets inserted by SI 2008/1468, reg 2(2).

[80A]

[112A Rights to terminate etc

(1) Subsection (2) applies where (apart from that subsection) a person would be entitled, in consequence of anything done or likely to be done by or under this Part in connection with an insurance business transfer scheme or a banking business transfer scheme—
 (a) to terminate, modify, acquire or claim an interest or right; or
 (b) to treat an interest or right as terminated or modified.

(2) The entitlement—

(a) is not enforceable in relation to that interest or right until after an order has been made under section 112(1) in relation to the scheme; and

(b) is then enforceable in relation to that interest or right only insofar as the order contains provision to that effect.

(3) Nothing in subsection (1) or (2) is to be read as limiting the scope of section 112(1).]

NOTES

Commencement: 30 June 2008.

Inserted by the Financial Services and Markets Act 2000 (Amendments to Part 7) Regulations 2008, SI 2008/1468, reg 2(3).

[81]

113 Appointment of actuary in relation to reduction of benefits

(1) This section applies if an order has been made under section 111(1).

(2) The court making the order may, on the application of the Authority, appoint an independent actuary—

(a) to investigate the business transferred under the scheme; and

(b) to report to the Authority on any reduction in the benefits payable under policies entered into by the authorised person concerned that, in the opinion of the actuary, ought to be made.

[82]

114 Rights of certain policyholders

(1) This section applies in relation to an insurance business transfer scheme if—

(a) the authorised person concerned is an authorised person other than an EEA firm qualifying for authorisation under Schedule 3;

(b) the court has made an order under section 111 in relation to the scheme; and

(c) an EEA State other than the United Kingdom is, as regards any policy included in the transfer which evidences a contract of insurance [(other than a contract of reinsurance)], the State of the commitment or the EEA State in which the risk is situated ("the EEA State concerned").

(2) The court must direct that notice of the making of the order, or the execution of any instrument, giving effect to the transfer must be published by the transferee in the EEA State concerned.

(3) A notice under subsection (2) must specify such period as the court may direct as the period during which the policyholder may exercise any right which he has to cancel the policy.

(4) The order or instrument mentioned in subsection (2) does not bind the policyholder if—

(a) the notice required under that subsection is not published; or

(b) the policyholder cancels the policy during the period specified in the notice given under that subsection.

(5) The law of the EEA State concerned governs—

(a) whether the policyholder has a right to cancel the policy; and

(b) the conditions, if any, subject to which any such right may be exercised.

(6) Paragraph 6 of Schedule 12 applies for the purposes of this section as it applies for the purposes of that Schedule.

NOTES

Sub-s (1): words in square brackets in para (c) inserted by the Reinsurance Directive Regulations 2007, SI 2007/3253, reg 2(1), Sch 1, paras 1, 2(2).

[82A]

[114A Notice of transfer of reinsurance contracts

(1) This section applies in relation to an insurance business transfer scheme if—

(a) the authorised person concerned is an authorised person other than an EEA firm qualifying for authorisation under Schedule 3;

(b) the court has made an order under section 111 in relation to the scheme; and

(c) an EEA State other than the United Kingdom is, as regards any policy included in the transfer which evidences a contract of reinsurance, the State in which the establishment of the policyholder to which the policy relates is situated at the date when the contract was entered into ("the EEA State concerned").

(2) The court may direct that notice of the making of the order, or the execution of any instrument, giving effect to the transfer must be published by the transferee in the EEA State concerned.]

NOTES

Commencement: 10 December 2007.

Inserted by the Reinsurance Directive Regulations 2007, SI 2007/3253, reg 2(1), Sch 1, paras 1, 2(3).

Business transfers outside the United Kingdom

[83]

115 Certificates for purposes of insurance business transfers overseas

Part III of Schedule 12 makes provision about certificates which the Authority may issue in relation to insurance business transfers taking place outside the United Kingdom.

[84]

116 Effect of insurance business transfers authorised in other EEA States

(1) This section applies if, as a result of an authorised transfer, an EEA firm falling within paragraph 5(d) [or (da)] of Schedule 3 transfers to another body all its rights and obligations under any UK policies.

[(2) This section also applies if, as a result of an authorised transfer, any of the following transfers to another body all its rights and obligations under any UK policies—

(a) an undertaking authorised in an EEA State other than the United Kingdom under Article 51 of the life assurance consolidation directive;

(b) an undertaking authorised in an EEA State other than the United Kingdom under Article 23 of the first non-life insurance directive;

(c) an undertaking, whose head office is not within the EEA, authorised under the law of an EEA State other than the United Kingdom to carry out reinsurance activities in its territory (as mentioned in Article 49 of the reinsurance directive).]

(3) If appropriate notice of the execution of an instrument giving effect to the transfer is published, the instrument has the effect in law—

(a) of transferring to the transferee all the transferor's rights and obligations under the UK policies to which the instrument applies, and

(b) if the instrument so provides, of securing the continuation by or against the transferee of any legal proceedings by or against the transferor which relate to those rights and obligations.

(4) No agreement or consent is required before subsection (3) has the effects mentioned.

(5) "Authorised transfer" means—

(a) in subsection (1), a transfer authorised in the home State of the EEA firm in accordance with—

[(i) Article 14 of the life assurance consolidation directive; . . .]

(ii) Article 12 of the third non-life directive; [or]

[(iii) Article 18 of the reinsurance directive; and]

(b) in subsection (2), a transfer authorised in an EEA State other than the United Kingdom in accordance with—

[(i) Article 53 of the life assurance consolidation directive; . . .]

(ii) Article 28a of the first non-life directive [or

(iii) the provisions in the law of that EEA State which provide for the authorisation of transfers of all or part of a portfolio of contracts of an undertaking authorised to carry out reinsurance activities in its territory (as mentioned in Article 49 of the reinsurance directive).]

[(6) "UK policy" means—

(a) in the case of an authorised transfer within the meaning of paragraph (a)(i) or (ii) or (b)(i) or (ii) of subsection (5), a policy evidencing a contract of insurance (other than a contract of reinsurance) to which the applicable law is the law of a part of the United Kingdom;

(b) in the case of an authorised transfer within the meaning of paragraph (a)(iii) or (b)(iii) of that subsection, a policy evidencing a contract of reinsurance to which the applicable law is the law of a part of the United Kingdom.]

(7) "Appropriate notice" means—

(a) if the UK policy evidences a contract of insurance in relation to which an EEA State other than the United Kingdom is the State of the commitment, notice given in accordance with the law of that State;

(b) if the UK policy evidences a contract of insurance where the risk is situated in an EEA State other than the United Kingdom, notice given in accordance with the law of that EEA State;

(c) in any other case, notice given in accordance with the applicable law.

(8) Paragraph 6 of Schedule 12 applies for the purposes of this section as it applies for the purposes of that Schedule.

NOTES

Sub-s (1): words in square brackets inserted by the Reinsurance Directive Regulations 2007, SI 2007/3253, reg 2(1), Sch 1, paras 1, 2(4)(a).

Sub-s (2): substituted by SI 2007/3253, reg 2(1), Sch 1, paras 1, 2(4)(b).

Sub-s (5): paras (a)(i), (b)(i) substituted by the Life Assurance Consolidation Directive (Consequential Amendments) Regulations 2004, SI 2004/3379, reg 6(1), (2)(b), (c); words omitted from paras (a)(i), (b)(i) repealed, word in square brackets in para (a)(ii) substituted, and paras (a)(iii), (b)(iii) and word preceding it inserted by SI 2007/3253, reg 2(1), Sch 1, paras 1, 2(4)(c).

Sub-s (6): substituted by SI 2007/3253, reg 2(1), Sch 1, paras 1, 2(4)(d).

Modifications

[85]

117 Power to modify this Part

The Treasury may by regulations—

(a) provide for prescribed provisions of this Part to have effect in relation to prescribed cases with such modifications as may be prescribed;

(b) make such amendments to any provision of this Part as they consider appropriate for the more effective operation of that or any other provision of this Part.

NOTES

Regulations: the Financial Services and Markets Act 2000 (Motor Insurance) Regulations 2007, SI 2007/2403.

PART VIII
PENALTIES FOR MARKET ABUSE

Market abuse

[86]

[118 Market abuse

(1) For the purposes of this Act, market abuse is behaviour (whether by one person alone or by two or more persons jointly or in concert) which—

(a) occurs in relation to—

(i) qualifying investments admitted to trading on a prescribed market,

(ii) qualifying investments in respect of which a request for admission to trading on such a market has been made, or

(iii) in the case of subsection (2) or (3) behaviour, investments which are related investments in relation to such qualifying investments, and

(b) falls within any one or more of the types of behaviour set out in subsections (2) to (8).

(2) The first type of behaviour is where an insider deals, or attempts to deal, in a qualifying investment or related investment on the basis of inside information relating to the investment in question.

(3) The second is where an insider discloses inside information to another person otherwise than in the proper course of the exercise of his employment, profession or duties.

(4) The third is where the behaviour (not falling within subsection (2) or (3))—

(a) is based on information which is not generally available to those using the market but which, if available to a regular user of the market, would be, or would be likely to be, regarded by him as relevant when deciding the terms on which transactions in qualifying investments should be effected, and

(b) is likely to be regarded by a regular user of the market as a failure on the part of the person concerned to observe the standard of behaviour reasonably expected of a person in his position in relation to the market.

(5) The fourth is where the behaviour consists of effecting transactions or orders to trade (otherwise than for legitimate reasons and in conformity with accepted market practices on the relevant market) which—

(a) give, or are likely to give, a false or misleading impression as to the supply of, or demand for, or as to the price of, one or more qualifying investments, or

(b) secure the price of one or more such investments at an abnormal or artificial level.

(6) The fifth is where the behaviour consists of effecting transactions or orders to trade which employ fictitious devices or any other form of deception or contrivance.

(7) The sixth is where the behaviour consists of the dissemination of information by any means which gives, or is likely to give, a false or misleading impression as to a qualifying investment by a person who knew or could reasonably be expected to have known that the information was false or misleading.

(8) The seventh is where the behaviour (not falling within subsection (5), (6) or (7))—

(a) is likely to give a regular user of the market a false or misleading impression as to the supply of, demand for or price or value of, qualifying investments, or

(b) would be, or would be likely to be, regarded by a regular user of the market as behaviour that would distort, or would be likely to distort, the market in such an investment,

and the behaviour is likely to be regarded by a regular user of the market as a failure on the part of the person concerned to observe the standard of behaviour reasonably expected of a person in his position in relation to the market.

(9) Subsections (4) and (8) and the definition of "regular user" in section 130A(3) cease to have effect on [31 December 2011] and subsection (1)(b) is then to be read as no longer referring to those subsections.]

NOTES

Commencement: 1 July 2005.

Substituted, together with ss 118A–118C for original s 118, by the Financial Services and Markets Act 2000 (Market Abuse) Regulations 2005, SI 2005/381, reg 5, Sch 2, para 1.

Sub-s (9): words in square brackets substituted by the Financial Services and Markets Act 2000 (Market Abuse) Regulations 2009, SI 2009/3128, reg 2(1), (2).

[87]

[118A Supplementary provision about certain behaviour

(1) Behaviour is to be taken into account for the purposes of this Part only if it occurs—

(a) in the United Kingdom, or

(b) in relation to—

(i) qualifying investments which are admitted to trading on a prescribed market situated in, or operating in, the United Kingdom,

(ii) qualifying investments for which a request for admission to trading on such a prescribed market has been made, or

(iii) in the case of section 118(2) and (3), investments which are related investments in relation to such qualifying investments.

(2) For the purposes of subsection (1), as it applies in relation to section 118(4) and (8), a prescribed market accessible electronically in the United Kingdom is to be treated as operating in the United Kingdom.

(3) For the purposes of section 118(4) and (8), the behaviour that is to be regarded as occurring in relation to qualifying investments includes behaviour which—

(a) occurs in relation to anything that is the subject matter, or whose price or value is expressed by reference to the price or value of the qualifying investments, or

(b) occurs in relation to investments (whether or not they are qualifying investments) whose subject matter is the qualifying investments.

(4) For the purposes of section 118(7), the dissemination of information by a person acting in the capacity of a journalist is to be assessed taking into account the codes governing his profession unless he derives, directly or indirectly, any advantage or profits from the dissemination of the information.

(5) Behaviour does not amount to market abuse for the purposes of this Act if—

(a) it conforms with a rule which includes a provision to the effect that behaviour conforming with the rule does not amount to market abuse,

(b) it conforms with the relevant provisions of Commission Regulation (EC) No 2273/2003 of 22 December 2003 implementing Directive 2003/6/EC of the European Parliament and of the Council as regards exemptions for buy-back programmes and stabilisation of financial instruments, or

(c) it is done by a person acting on behalf of a public authority in pursuit of monetary policies or policies with respect to exchange rates or the management of public debt or foreign exchange reserves.

(6) Subsections (2) and (3) cease to have effect on [31 December 2011].]

NOTES

Commencement: 1 July 2005.

Substituted as noted to s 118 at **[86]**.

Sub-s (6): words in square brackets substituted by the Financial Services and Markets Act 2000 (Market Abuse) Regulations 2009, SI 2009/3128, reg 2(1), (3).

Commission Regulation (EC) No 2273/2003: OJ L336, 23.12.2003, p 33.
Directive 2003/6/EC of the European Parliament and of the Council: OJ L96, 12.4.2003, p 16.

[88]
[118B Insiders
For the purposes of this Part an insider is any person who has inside information—
- (a) as a result of his membership of an administrative, management or supervisory body of an issuer of qualifying investments,
- (b) as a result of his holding in the capital of an issuer of qualifying investments,
- (c) as a result of having access to the information through the exercise of his employment, profession or duties,
- (d) as a result of his criminal activities, or
- (e) which he has obtained by other means and which he knows, or could reasonably be expected to know, is inside information.]

NOTES
Commencement: 1 July 2005.
Substituted as noted to s 118 at **[86]**.

[89]
[118C Inside information
(1) This section defines "inside information" for the purposes of this Part.
(2) In relation to qualifying investments, or related investments, which are not commodity derivatives, inside information is information of a precise nature which—
- (a) is not generally available,
- (b) relates, directly or indirectly, to one or more issuers of the qualifying investments or to one or more of the qualifying investments, and
- (c) would, if generally available, be likely to have a significant effect on the price of the qualifying investments or on the price of related investments.

(3) In relation to qualifying investments or related investments which are commodity derivatives, inside information is information of a precise nature which—
- (a) is not generally available,
- (b) relates, directly or indirectly, to one or more such derivatives, and
- (c) users of markets on which the derivatives are traded would expect to receive in accordance with any accepted market practices on those markets.

(4) In relation to a person charged with the execution of orders concerning any qualifying investments or related investments, inside information includes information conveyed by a client and related to the client's pending orders which—
- (a) is of a precise nature,
- (b) is not generally available,
- (c) relates, directly or indirectly, to one or more issuers of qualifying investments or to one or more qualifying investments, and
- (d) would, if generally available, be likely to have a significant effect on the price of those qualifying investments or the price of related investments.

(5) Information is precise if it—
- (a) indicates circumstances that exist or may reasonably be expected to come into existence or an event that has occurred or may reasonably be expected to occur, and
- (b) is specific enough to enable a conclusion to be drawn as to the possible effect of those circumstances or that event on the price of qualifying investments or related investments.

(6) Information would be likely to have a significant effect on price if and only if it is information of a kind which a reasonable investor would be likely to use as part of the basis of his investment decisions.
(7) For the purposes of subsection (3)(c), users of markets on which investments in commodity derivatives are traded are to be treated as expecting to receive information relating directly or indirectly to one or more such derivatives in accordance with any accepted market practices, which is—
- (a) routinely made available to the users of those markets, or
- (b) required to be disclosed in accordance with any statutory provision, market rules, or contracts or customs on the relevant underlying commodity market or commodity derivatives market.

(8) Information which can be obtained by research or analysis conducted by, or on behalf of, users of a market is to be regarded, for the purposes of this Part, as being generally available to them.]

NOTES

Commencement: 1 July 2005.
Substituted as noted to s 118 at **[86]**.

The code

[90]
119 The code

(1) The Authority must prepare and issue a code containing such provisions as the Authority considers will give appropriate guidance to those determining whether or not behaviour amounts to market abuse.

(2) The code may among other things specify—

(a) descriptions of behaviour that, in the opinion of the Authority, amount to market abuse;
(b) descriptions of behaviour that, in the opinion of the Authority, do not amount to market abuse;
(c) factors that, in the opinion of the Authority, are to be taken into account in determining whether or not behaviour amounts to market abuse;
[(d) descriptions of behaviour that are accepted market practices in relation to one or more specified markets;
(e) descriptions of behaviour that are not accepted market practices in relation to one or more specified markets.]

[(2A) In determining, for the purposes of subsections (2)(d) and (2)(e) or otherwise, what are and what are not accepted market practices, the Authority must have regard to the factors and procedures laid down in Articles 2 and 3 respectively of Commission Directive 2004/72/EC of 29 April 2004 implementing Directive 2003/6/EC of the European Parliament and of the Council.]

(3) The code may make different provision in relation to persons, cases or circumstances of different descriptions.

(4) The Authority may at any time alter or replace the code.

(5) If the code is altered or replaced, the altered or replacement code must be issued by the Authority.

(6) A code issued under this section must be published by the Authority in the way appearing to the Authority to be best calculated to bring it to the attention of the public.

(7) The Authority must, without delay, give the Treasury a copy of any code published under this section.

(8) The Authority may charge a reasonable fee for providing a person with a copy of the code.

NOTES

Sub-s (2): paras (d), (e) added by the Financial Services and Markets Act 2000 (Market Abuse) Regulations 2005, SI 2005/381, reg 5, Sch 2, para 2(1), (2).
Sub-s (2A): inserted by SI 2005/381, reg 5, Sch 2, para 2(1), (3).
Commission Directive 2004/72/EC: OJ L162, 30.4.2004, p 70.
Directive 2003/6/EC of the European Parliament and of the Council: OJ L96, 12.4.2003, p 16.

[91]
120 Provisions included in the Authority's code by reference to the City Code

(1) The Authority may include in a code issued by it under section 119 ("the Authority's code") provision to the effect that in its opinion behaviour conforming with the City Code—

(a) does not amount to market abuse;
(b) does not amount to market abuse in specified circumstances; or
(c) does not amount to market abuse if engaged in by a specified description of person.

(2) But the Treasury's approval is required before any such provision may be included in the Authority's code.

(3) If the Authority's code includes provision of a kind authorised by subsection (1), the Authority must keep itself informed of the way in which the Panel on Takeovers and Mergers interprets and administers the relevant provisions of the City Code.

(4) "City Code" means the City Code on Takeovers and Mergers issued by the Panel as it has effect at the time when the behaviour occurs.

(5) "Specified" means specified in the Authority's code.

[92]
121 Codes: procedure

(1) Before issuing a code under section 119, the Authority must publish a draft of the proposed code in the way appearing to the Authority to be best calculated to bring it to the attention of the public.

(2) The draft must be accompanied by—
(a) a cost benefit analysis; and
(b) notice that representations about the proposal may be made to the Authority within a specified time.
(3) Before issuing the proposed code, the Authority must have regard to any representations made to it in accordance with subsection (2)(b).
(4) If the Authority issues the proposed code it must publish an account, in general terms, of—
(a) the representations made to it in accordance with subsection (2)(b); and
(b) its response to them.
(5) If the code differs from the draft published under subsection (1) in a way which is, in the opinion of the Authority, significant—
(a) the Authority must (in addition to complying with subsection (4)) publish details of the difference; and
(b) those details must be accompanied by a cost benefit analysis.
(6) Subsections (1) to (5) do not apply if the Authority considers that there is an urgent need to publish the code.
(7) Neither subsection (2)(a) nor subsection (5)(b) applies if the Authority considers—
(a) that, making the appropriate comparison, there will be no increase in costs; or
(b) that, making that comparison, there will be an increase in costs but the increase will be of minimal significance.
(8) The Authority may charge a reasonable fee for providing a person with a copy of a draft published under subsection (1).
(9) This section also applies to a proposal to alter or replace a code.
(10) "Cost benefit analysis" means an estimate of the costs together with an analysis of the benefits that will arise—
(a) if the proposed code is issued; or
(b) if subsection (5)(b) applies, from the code that has been issued.
(11) "The appropriate comparison" means—
(a) in relation to subsection (2)(a), a comparison between the overall position if the code is issued and the overall position if it is not issued;
(b) in relation to subsection (5)(b), a comparison between the overall position after the issuing of the code and the overall position before it was issued.

[93]
122 Effect of the code
(1) If a person behaves in a way which is described (in the code in force under section 119 at the time of the behaviour) as behaviour that, in the Authority's opinion, does not amount to market abuse that behaviour of his is to be taken, for the purposes of this Act, as not amounting to market abuse.
(2) Otherwise, the code in force under section 119 at the time when particular behaviour occurs may be relied on so far as it indicates whether or not that behaviour should be taken to amount to market abuse.

Power to impose penalties

[94]
123 Power to impose penalties in cases of market abuse
(1) If the Authority is satisfied that a person ("A")—
(a) is or has engaged in market abuse, or
(b) by taking or refraining from taking any action has required or encouraged another person or persons to engage in behaviour which, if engaged in by A, would amount to market abuse,

it may impose on him a penalty of such amount as it considers appropriate.
(2) But the Authority may not impose a penalty on a person if, having considered any representations made to it in response to a warning notice, there are reasonable grounds for it to be satisfied that—
(a) he believed, on reasonable grounds, that his behaviour did not fall within paragraph (a) or (b) of subsection (1), or
(b) he took all reasonable precautions and exercised all due diligence to avoid behaving in a way which fell within paragraph (a) or (b) of that subsection.
(3) If the Authority is entitled to impose a penalty on a person under this section it may, instead of imposing a penalty on him, publish a statement to the effect that he has engaged in market abuse.

Statement of policy

[95]
124 Statement of policy

(1) The Authority must prepare and issue a statement of its policy with respect to—
- (a) the imposition of penalties under section 123; and
- (b) the amount of penalties under that section.

(2) The Authority's policy in determining what the amount of a penalty should be must include having regard to—
- (a) whether the behaviour in respect of which the penalty is to be imposed had an adverse effect on the market in question and, if it did, how serious that effect was;
- (b) the extent to which that behaviour was deliberate or reckless; and
- (c) whether the person on whom the penalty is to be imposed is an individual.

(3) A statement issued under this section must include an indication of the circumstances in which the Authority is to be expected to regard a person as—
- (a) having a reasonable belief that his behaviour did not amount to market abuse; or
- (b) having taken reasonable precautions and exercised due diligence to avoid engaging in market abuse.

(4) The Authority may at any time alter or replace a statement issued under this section.

(5) If a statement issued under this section is altered or replaced, the Authority must issue the altered or replacement statement.

(6) In exercising, or deciding whether to exercise, its power under section 123 in the case of any particular behaviour, the Authority must have regard to any statement published under this section and in force at the time when the behaviour concerned occurred.

(7) A statement issued under this section must be published by the Authority in the way appearing to the Authority to be best calculated to bring it to the attention of the public.

(8) The Authority may charge a reasonable fee for providing a person with a copy of a statement published under this section.

(9) The Authority must, without delay, give the Treasury a copy of any statement which it publishes under this section.

[96]
125 Statement of policy: procedure

(1) Before issuing a statement of policy under section 124, the Authority must publish a draft of the proposed statement in the way appearing to the Authority to be best calculated to bring it to the attention of the public.

(2) The draft must be accompanied by notice that representations about the proposal may be made to the Authority within a specified time.

(3) Before issuing the proposed statement, the Authority must have regard to any representations made to it in accordance with subsection (2).

(4) If the Authority issues the proposed statement it must publish an account, in general terms, of—
- (a) the representations made to it in accordance with subsection (2); and
- (b) its response to them.

(5) If the statement differs from the draft published under subsection (1) in a way which is, in the opinion of the Authority, significant, the Authority must (in addition to complying with subsection (4)) publish details of the difference.

(6) The Authority may charge a reasonable fee for providing a person with a copy of a draft published under subsection (1).

(7) This section also applies to a proposal to alter or replace a statement.

Procedure

[97]
126 Warning notices

(1) If the Authority proposes to take action against a person under section 123, it must give him a warning notice.

(2) A warning notice about a proposal to impose a penalty must state the amount of the proposed penalty.

(3) A warning notice about a proposal to publish a statement must set out the terms of the proposed statement.

[98]
127 Decision notices and right to refer to Tribunal
(1) If the Authority decides to take action against a person under section 123, it must give him a decision notice.
(2) A decision notice about the imposition of a penalty must state the amount of the penalty.
(3) A decision notice about the publication of a statement must set out the terms of the statement.
(4) If the Authority decides to take action against a person under section 123, that person may refer the matter to the Tribunal.

Miscellaneous

[99]
128 Suspension of investigations
(1) If the Authority considers it desirable or expedient because of the exercise or possible exercise of a power relating to market abuse, it may direct a recognised investment exchange or recognised clearing house—
(a) to terminate, suspend or limit the scope of any inquiry which the exchange or clearing house is conducting under its rules; or
(b) not to conduct an inquiry which the exchange or clearing house proposes to conduct under its rules.
(2) A direction under this section—
(a) must be given to the exchange or clearing house concerned by notice in writing; and
(b) is enforceable, on the application of the Authority, by injunction or, in Scotland, by an order under section 45 of the Court of Session Act 1988.
(3) The Authority's powers relating to market abuse are its powers—
(a) to impose penalties under section 123; or
(b) to appoint a person to conduct an investigation under section 168 in a case falling within subsection (2)(d) of that section.

[100]
129 Power of court to impose penalty in cases of market abuse
(1) The Authority may on an application to the court under section 381 or 383 request the court to consider whether the circumstances are such that a penalty should be imposed on the person to whom the application relates.
(2) The court may, if it considers it appropriate, make an order requiring the person concerned to pay to the Authority a penalty of such amount as it considers appropriate.

[101]
130 Guidance
(1) The Treasury may from time to time issue written guidance for the purpose of helping relevant authorities to determine the action to be taken in cases where behaviour occurs which is behaviour—
(a) with respect to which the power in section 123 appears to be exercisable; and
(b) which appears to involve the commission of an offence under section 397 of this Act or Part V of the Criminal Justice Act 1993 (insider dealing).
(2) The Treasury must obtain the consent of the Attorney General and the Secretary of State before issuing any guidance under this section.
(3) In this section "relevant authorities"—
(a) in relation to England and Wales, means the Secretary of State, the Authority, the Director of the Serious Fraud Office and the Director of Public Prosecutions;
(b) in relation to Northern Ireland, means the Secretary of State, the Authority, the Director of the Serious Fraud Office and the Director of Public Prosecutions for Northern Ireland.
(4) Subsections (1) to (3) do not apply to Scotland.
(5) In relation to Scotland, the Lord Advocate may from time to time, after consultation with the Treasury, issue written guidance for the purpose of helping the Authority to determine the action to be taken in cases where behaviour mentioned in subsection (1) occurs.

[102]
[130A Interpretation and supplementary provision
(1) The Treasury may by order specify (whether by name or description)—
(a) the markets which are prescribed markets for the purposes of specified provisions of this Part, and
(b) the investments that are qualifying investments in relation to the prescribed markets.
(2) An order may prescribe different investments or descriptions of investment in relation to different markets or descriptions of market.

(3) In this Part—

"accepted market practices" means practices that are reasonably expected in the financial market or markets in question and are accepted by the Authority or, in the case of a market situated in another EEA State, the competent authority of that EEA State within the meaning of Directive 2003/6/EC of the European Parliament and of the Council of 28 January 2003 on insider dealing and market manipulation (market abuse),

"behaviour" includes action or inaction,

"dealing", in relation to an investment, means acquiring or disposing of the investment whether as principal or agent or directly or indirectly, and includes agreeing to acquire or dispose of the investment, and entering into and bringing to an end a contract creating it,

"investment" is to be read with section 22 and Schedule 2,

"regular user", in relation to a particular market, means a reasonable person who regularly deals on that market in investments of the kind in question,

"related investment", in relation to a qualifying investment, means an investment whose price or value depends on the price or value of the qualifying investment.]

NOTES

Commencement: 1 July 2005.

Inserted by the Financial Services and Markets Act 2000 (Market Abuse) Regulations 2005, SI 2005/381, reg 5, Sch 2, para 3.

Directive 2003/6/EC of the European Parliament and of the Council: OJ L96, 12.4.2003, p 16.

[103]

131 Effect on transactions

The imposition of a penalty under this Part does not make any transaction void or unenforceable.

[104]

[131A Protected disclosures

(1) A disclosure which satisfies the following three conditions is not to be taken to breach any restriction on the disclosure of information (however imposed).

(2) The first condition is that the information or other matter—

(a) causes the person making the disclosure (the discloser) to know or suspect, or

(b) gives him reasonable grounds for knowing or suspecting, that another person has engaged in market abuse.

(3) The second condition is that the information or other matter disclosed came to the discloser in the course of his trade, profession, business or employment.

(4) The third condition is that the disclosure is made to the Authority or to a nominated officer as soon as is practicable after the information or other matter comes to the discloser.

(5) A disclosure to a nominated officer is a disclosure which is made to a person nominated by the discloser's employer to receive disclosures under this section, and is made in the course of the discloser's employment and in accordance with the procedure established by the employer for the purpose.

(6) For the purposes of this section, references to a person's employer include any body, association or organisation (including a voluntary organisation) in connection with whose activities the person exercises a function (whether or not for gain or reward) and references to employment must be construed accordingly.]

NOTES

Commencement: 1 July 2005.

Inserted by the Financial Services and Markets Act 2000 (Market Abuse) Regulations 2005, SI 2005/381, reg 5, Sch 2, para 4.

PART IX
HEARINGS AND APPEALS

NOTES

Modification: this Part is applied with modifications in respect of references to the Tribunal made under various instruments: see the Money Laundering Regulations 2007, SI 2007/2157, reg 44(4), (8), Sch 5, Pt 1, para 2; the Transfer of Funds (Information on the Payer) Regulations 2007, SI 2007/3298, reg 13(3), Sch 2, para 1; the Northern Rock plc Compensation Scheme Order 2008, SI 2008/718, art 2, Schedule, Pt 5, paras 15–18; the Bradford & Bingley plc Compensation Scheme Order 2008, SI 2008/3249, art 2, Schedule, Pt 5, paras 14–17; the Payment Services Regulations 2009, SI 2009/209, reg 95, Sch 5, Pt 1, para 2; the Dunfermline Building Society Independent Valuer Order 2009, SI 2009/1810, arts 14(1)(a), 15–18; and the Cross-Border Payments in Euro Regulations 2010, SI 2010/89, reg 19, Schedule, Pt 2, paras 7, 8.

[105]

132 The Financial Services and Markets Tribunal

(1) For the purposes of this Act, there is to be a tribunal known as the Financial Services and Markets Tribunal (but referred to in this Act as "the Tribunal").

(2) The Tribunal is to have the functions conferred on it by or under this Act.

(3) The Lord Chancellor may by rules make such provision as appears to him to be necessary or expedient in respect of the conduct of proceedings before the Tribunal.

(4) Schedule 13 is to have effect as respects the Tribunal and its proceedings (but does not limit the Lord Chancellor's powers under this section).

NOTES

Repealed by the Transfer of Tribunal Functions Order 2010, SI 2010/22, art 5(1), Sch 2, paras 43, 44, as from 6 April 2010, subject to transitional and saving provisions in art 5(4) thereof and Sch 5 thereto.

Rules: the Financial Services and Markets Tribunal Rules 2001, SI 2001/2476.

[106]

[133 Proceedings before Tribunal: general provision

(1) This section applies in the case of a reference or appeal to the Tribunal (whether made under this or any other Act) in respect of—

(a) a decision of the Authority;

(b) a decision of the Bank of England; or

(c) a decision of a person relating to the assessment of any compensation or consideration under the Banking (Special Provisions) Act 2008 or the Banking Act 2009.

(2) In this section—

"relevant decision" means a decision mentioned in subsection (1)(a), (b) or (c); and

"the decision-maker", in relation to a relevant decision, means the person who made the relevant decision.

(3) Tribunal Procedure Rules may make provision for the suspension of a relevant decision which has taken effect, pending determination of the reference or appeal.

(4) The Tribunal may consider any evidence relating to the subject-matter of the reference or appeal, whether or not it was available to the decision-maker at the material time.

(5) The Tribunal must determine what (if any) is the appropriate action for the decision-maker to take in relation to the matter referred or appealed to it.

(6) On determining the reference or appeal, the Tribunal must remit the matter to the decision-maker with such directions (if any) as the Tribunal considers appropriate for giving effect to its determination.

(7) The decision-maker must act in accordance with the determination of, and any direction given by, the Tribunal.

(8) An order of the Tribunal may be enforced—

(a) as if it were an order of a county court; or

(b) in Scotland, as if it were an order of the Court of Session.]

NOTES

Commencement: 6 April 2010.

Substituted, together with ss 133A, 133B, by the Transfer of Tribunal Functions Order 2010, SI 2010/22, art 5(1), Sch 2, paras 43, 45, as from 6 April 2010, subject to transitional and saving provisions in art 5(4) thereof and Sch 5 thereto. Section 133 originally read as follows:

"133 Proceedings: general provision

(1) A reference to the Tribunal under this Act must be made before the end of—

(a) the period of 28 days beginning with the date on which the decision notice or supervisory notice in question is given; or

(b) such other period as may be specified in rules made under section 132.

(2) Subject to rules made under section 132, the Tribunal may allow a reference to be made after the end of that period.

(3) On a reference the Tribunal may consider any evidence relating to the subject-matter of the reference, whether or not it was available to the Authority at the material time.

(4) On a reference the Tribunal must determine what (if any) is the appropriate action for the Authority to take in relation to the matter referred to it.

(5) On determining a reference, the Tribunal must remit the matter to the Authority with such directions (if any) as the Tribunal considers appropriate for giving effect to its determination.

(6) In determining a reference made as a result of a decision notice, the Tribunal may not direct the Authority to take action which the Authority would not, as a result of section 388(2), have had power to take when giving the decision notice.

(7) In determining a reference made as a result of a supervisory notice, the Tribunal may not direct the Authority to take action which would have otherwise required the giving of a decision notice.

(8) The Tribunal may, on determining a reference, make recommendations as to the Authority's regulating provisions or its procedures.

(9) The Authority must not take the action specified in a decision notice—

(a) during the period within which the matter to which the decision notice relates may be referred to the Tribunal; and
(b) if the matter is so referred, until the reference, and any appeal against the Tribunal's determination, has been finally disposed of.

(10) The Authority must act in accordance with the determination of, and any direction given by, the Tribunal.

(11) An order of the Tribunal may be enforced—
(a) as if it were an order of a county court; or
(b) in Scotland, as if it were an order of the Court of Session.

(12) "Supervisory notice" has the same meaning as in section 395.".

[106A]

[133A Proceedings before Tribunal: decision and supervisory notices, etc

(1) In determining a reference made (whether under this or any other Act) as a result of a decision notice given by the Authority, the Tribunal may not direct the Authority to take action which the Authority would not, as a result of section 388(2), have had power to take when giving the notice.

(2) In determining a reference made as a result of a supervisory notice given by the Authority, the Tribunal may not direct the Authority to take action which would have otherwise required the giving of a decision notice.

(3) In subsection (2) "supervisory notice" has the same meaning as in section 395.

(4) The Authority must not take the action specified in a decision notice—
(a) during the period within which the matter to which the notice relates may be referred to the Tribunal (whether under this or any other Act); and
(b) if the matter is so referred, until the reference, and any appeal against the Tribunal's determination, has been finally disposed of.

(5) The Tribunal may, on determining a reference (whether made under this or any other Act) in respect of a decision of the Authority, make recommendations as to the Authority's regulating provisions or its procedures.]

NOTES

Commencement: 6 April 2010.
Substituted as noted to s 133 at **[106]**.

[106B]

[133B Offences

(1) This section applies in the case of proceedings before the Tribunal in respect of—
(a) a decision of the Authority;
(b) a decision of the Bank of England; or
(c) a decision of a person relating to the assessment of any compensation or consideration under the Banking (Special Provisions) Act 2008 or the Banking Act 2009.

(2) A person is guilty of an offence if that person, without reasonable excuse—
(a) refuses or fails—
 (i) to attend following the issue of a summons by the Tribunal; or
 (ii) to give evidence; or
(b) alters, suppresses, conceals or destroys, or refuses to produce a document which he may be required to produce for the purposes of proceedings before the Tribunal.

(3) A person guilty of an offence under subsection (2)(a) is liable on summary conviction to a fine not exceeding level 5 on the standard scale.

(4) A person guilty of an offence under subsection (2)(b) is liable—
(a) on summary conviction, to a fine not exceeding the statutory maximum;
(b) on conviction on indictment, to imprisonment for a term not exceeding two years or a fine or both.]

NOTES

Commencement: 6 April 2010.
Substituted as noted to s 133 at **[106]**.

Legal assistance before the Tribunal

[107]

134 Legal assistance scheme

(1) The Lord Chancellor may by regulations establish a scheme governing the provision of legal assistance in connection with proceedings before the Tribunal.

(2) If the Lord Chancellor establishes a scheme under subsection (1), it must provide that a person is eligible for assistance only if—

(a) he falls within subsection (3); and

(b) he fulfils such other criteria (if any) as may be prescribed as a result of section 135(1)(d).

(3) A person falls within this subsection if he is an individual who has referred a matter to the Tribunal under section 127(4).

(4) In this Part of this Act "the legal assistance scheme" means any scheme in force under subsection (1).

NOTES

Regulations: the Financial Services and Markets Tribunal (Legal Assistance) Regulations 2001, SI 2001/3632; the Financial Services and Markets Tribunal (Legal Assistance Scheme—Costs) Regulations 2001, SI 2001/3633.

[108]

135 Provisions of the legal assistance scheme

(1) The legal assistance scheme may, in particular, make provision as to—

(a) the kinds of legal assistance that may be provided;

(b) the persons by whom legal assistance may be provided;

(c) the manner in which applications for legal assistance are to be made;

(d) the criteria on which eligibility for legal assistance is to be determined;

(e) the persons or bodies by whom applications are to be determined;

(f) appeals against refusals of applications;

(g) the revocation or variation of decisions;

(h) its administration and the enforcement of its provisions.

(2) Legal assistance under the legal assistance scheme may be provided subject to conditions or restrictions, including conditions as to the making of contributions by the person to whom it is provided.

[109]

136 Funding of the legal assistance scheme

(1) The Authority must pay to the Lord Chancellor such sums at such times as he may, from time to time, determine in respect of the anticipated or actual cost of legal assistance provided in connection with proceedings before the Tribunal under the legal assistance scheme.

(2) In order to enable it to pay any sum which it is obliged to pay under subsection (1), the Authority must make rules requiring the payment to it by authorised persons or any class of authorised person of specified amounts or amounts calculated in a specified way.

(3) Sums received by the Lord Chancellor under subsection (1) must be paid into the Consolidated Fund.

(4) The Lord Chancellor must, out of money provided by Parliament fund the cost of legal assistance provided in connection with proceedings before the Tribunal under the legal assistance scheme.

(5) Subsection (6) applies if, as respects a period determined by the Lord Chancellor, the amount paid to him under subsection (1) as respects that period exceeds the amount he has expended in that period under subsection (4).

(6) The Lord Chancellor must—

(a) repay, out of money provided by Parliament, the excess to the Authority; or

(b) take the excess into account on the next occasion on which he makes a determination under subsection (1).

(7) The Authority must make provision for any sum repaid to it under subsection (6)(a)—

(a) to be distributed among—

(i) the authorised persons on whom a levy was imposed in the period in question as a result of rules made under subsection (2); or

(ii) such of those persons as it may determine;

(b) to be applied in order to reduce any amounts which those persons, or such of them as it may determine, are or will be liable to pay to the Authority, whether under rules made under subsection (2) or otherwise; or

(c) to be partly so distributed and partly so applied.

(8) If the Authority considers that it is not practicable to deal with any part of a sum repaid to it under subsection (6)(a) in accordance with provision made by it as a result of subsection (7), it may, with the consent the Lord Chancellor, apply or dispose of that part of that sum in such manner as it considers appropriate.

(9) "Specified" means specified in the rules.

NOTES

Cross-heading repealed by the Transfer of Tribunal Functions Order 2010, SI 2010/22, art 5(1), Sch 2, paras 43, 46, as from 6 April 2010, subject to transitional and saving provisions in art 5(4) thereof and Sch 5 thereto.

Appeals

[110]

137 Appeal on a point of law

(1) A party to a reference to the Tribunal may with permission appeal—

(a) to the Court of Appeal, or

(b) in Scotland, to the Court of Session,

on a point of law arising from a decision of the Tribunal disposing of the reference.

(2) "Permission" means permission given by the Tribunal or by the Court of Appeal or (in Scotland) the Court of Session.

(3) If, on an appeal under subsection (1), the court considers that the decision of the Tribunal was wrong in law, it may—

(a) remit the matter to the Tribunal for rehearing and determination by it; or

(b) itself make a determination.

(4) An appeal may not be brought from a decision of the Court of Appeal under subsection (3) except with the leave of—

(a) the Court of Appeal; or

[(b) the Supreme Court.]

(5) An appeal lies, with the leave of the Court of Session or the [Supreme Court], from any decision of the Court of Session under this section, and such leave may be given on such terms as to costs, expenses or otherwise as the Court of Session or the [Supreme Court] may determine.

(6) Rules made under section 132 may make provision for regulating or prescribing any matters incidental to or consequential on an appeal under this section.

NOTES

Repealed by the Transfer of Tribunal Functions Order 2010, SI 2010/22, art 5(1), Sch 2, paras 43, 46, as from 6 April 2010, subject to transitional and saving provisions in art 5(4) thereof and Sch 5 thereto.

Sub-s (4): para (b) substituted by the Constitutional Reform Act 2005, s 40(4), Sch 9, Pt 1, para 70(a).

Sub-s (5): words in square brackets substituted by the Constitutional Reform Act 2005, s 40(4), Sch 9, Pt 1, para 70(b).

PART X
RULES AND GUIDANCE

CHAPTER I
RULE-MAKING POWERS

[111]

138 General rule-making power

(1) The Authority may make such rules applying to authorised persons—

(a) with respect to the carrying on by them of regulated activities, or

(b) with respect to the carrying on by them of activities which are not regulated activities,

as appear to it to be necessary or expedient for the purpose of protecting the interests of consumers.

[(1A) The Authority may also make such rules applying to authorised persons who are investment firms or credit institutions, with respect to the provision by them of a relevant ancillary service, as appear to the Authority to be necessary or expedient for the purpose of protecting the interests of consumers.

(1B) "Credit institution" means—

(a) a credit institution authorised under the banking consolidation directive, or

(b) an institution which would satisfy the requirements for authorisation as a credit institution under that directive if it had its registered office (or if it does not have a registered office, its head office) in an EEA State.

(1C) "Relevant ancillary service" means any service of a kind mentioned in Section B of Annex I to the markets in financial instruments directive the provision of which does not involve the carrying on of a regulated activity.]

(2) Rules made under this section are referred to in this Act as the Authority's general rules.

(3) The Authority's power to make general rules is not limited by any other power which it has to make regulating provisions.

(4) The Authority's general rules may make provision applying to authorised persons even though there is no relationship between the authorised persons to whom the rules will apply and the persons whose interests will be protected by the rules.
(5) General rules may contain requirements which take into account, in the case of an authorised person who is a member of a group, any activity of another member of the group.
(6) General rules may not—
(a) make provision prohibiting an EEA firm from carrying on, or holding itself out as carrying on, any activity which it has permission conferred by Part II of Schedule 3 to carry on in the United Kingdom;
(b) make provision, as respects an EEA firm, about any matter responsibility for which is, under any of the single market directives, reserved to the firm's home state regulator.
(7) "Consumers" means persons—
(a) who use, have used, or are or may be contemplating using, any of the services provided by—
(i) authorised persons in carrying on regulated activities; . . .
[(ia) authorised persons who are investment firms or credit institutions in providing a relevant ancillary service; or]
(ii) persons acting as appointed representatives;
(b) who have rights or interests which are derived from, or are otherwise attributable to, the use of any such services by other persons; or
(c) who have rights or interests which may be adversely affected by the use of any such services by persons acting on their behalf or in a fiduciary capacity in relation to them.
(8) If an authorised person is carrying on a regulated activity in his capacity as a trustee, the persons who are, have been or may be beneficiaries of the trust are to be treated as persons who use, have used or are or may be contemplating using services provided by the authorised person in his carrying on of that activity.
(9) For the purposes of subsection (7) a person who deals with an authorised person in the course of the authorised person's carrying on of a regulated activity is to be treated as using services provided by the authorised person in carrying on those activities.

NOTES

Sub-ss (1A)–(1C): inserted by the Financial Services and Markets Act 2000 (Markets in Financial Instruments) (Modification of Powers) Regulations 2006, SI 2006/2975, regs 2, 3(a), subject to transitional provisions in reg 14 thereof.

Sub-s (7): word omitted from para (a)(i) repealed and para (a)(ia) inserted by SI 2006/2975, regs 2, 3(b), subject to transitional provisions in reg 14 thereof.

Modification: sub-ss (1), (1A) are modified by the Northern Rock plc Transfer Order 2008, SI 2008/432, art 15(1), the Bradford & Bingley plc Transfer of Securities and Property etc Order 2008, SI 2008/2546, art 37(1), the Heritable Bank plc Transfer of Certain Rights and Liabilities Order 2008, SI 2008/2644, arts 2, 27(1), the Transfer of Rights and Liabilities to ING Order 2008, SI 2008/2666, arts 2, 18(1), the Kaupthing Singer & Friedlander Limited Transfer of Certain Rights and Liabilities Order 2008, SI 2008/2674, arts 2, 29(1), the Amendments to Law (Resolution of Dunfermline Building Society) Order 2009, SI 2009/814, art 9(1), the Northern Rock plc Transfer Order 2009, SI 2009/3226, art 20(1).

[112]

139 Miscellaneous ancillary matters

(1) Rules relating to the handling of money held by an authorised person in specified circumstances ("clients' money") may—
(a) make provision which results in that clients' money being held on trust in accordance with the rules;
(b) treat two or more accounts as a single account for specified purposes (which may include the distribution of money held in the accounts);
(c) authorise the retention by the authorised person of interest accruing on the clients' money; and
(d) make provision as to the distribution of such interest which is not to be retained by him.
(2) An institution with which an account is kept in pursuance of rules relating to the handling of clients' money does not incur any liability as constructive trustee if money is wrongfully paid from the account, unless the institution permits the payment—
(a) with knowledge that it is wrongful; or
(b) having deliberately failed to make enquiries in circumstances in which a reasonable and honest person would have done so.
(3) In the application of subsection (1) to Scotland, the reference to money being held on trust is to be read as a reference to its being held as agent for the person who is entitled to call for it to be paid over to him or to be paid on his direction or to have it otherwise credited to him.
(4) Rules may—

(a) confer rights on persons to rescind agreements with, or withdraw offers to, authorised persons within a specified period; and
(b) make provision, in respect of authorised persons and persons exercising those rights, for the restitution of property and the making or recovery of payments where those rights are exercised.

(5) "Rules" means general rules.
(6) "Specified" means specified in the rules.

[113]
140 Restriction on managers of [certain collective investment schemes]
[(1) The Authority may make rules prohibiting an authorised person who has permission to act as—
(a) the manager of an authorised unit trust scheme, or
(b) the management company of an authorised UCITS open-ended investment company,
from carrying on a specified activity.]
(2) Such rules may specify an activity which is not a regulated activity.
[(3) In this section—
(a) "authorised UCITS open-ended investment company" means an authorised open-ended investment company to which the UCITS directive applies; and
(b) "management company" has the meaning given by Article 1a.2 of the UCITS directive.]

NOTES
Section heading: words in square brackets substituted by the Collective Investment Schemes (Miscellaneous Amendments) Regulations 2003, SI 2003/2066, reg 5(a).
Sub-s (1): substituted by SI 2003/2066, reg 5(b).
Sub-s (3): added by SI 2003/2066, reg 5(c).

[114]
141 Insurance business rules
(1) The Authority may make rules prohibiting an authorised person who has permission to effect or carry out contracts of insurance from carrying on a specified activity.
(2) Such rules may specify an activity which is not a regulated activity.
(3) The Authority may make rules in relation to contracts entered into by an authorised person in the course of carrying on business which consists of the effecting or carrying out of contracts of long-term insurance.
(4) Such rules may, in particular—
(a) restrict the descriptions of property or indices of the value of property by reference to which the benefits under such contracts may be determined;
(b) make provision, in the interests of the protection of policyholders, for the substitution of one description of property, or index of value, by reference to which the benefits under a contract are to be determined for another such description of property or index.
(5) Rules made under this section are referred to in this Act as insurance business rules.

[115]–[116]
142 Insurance business: regulations supplementing Authority's rules
(1) The Treasury may make regulations for the purpose of preventing a person who is not an authorised person but who—
(a) is a parent undertaking of an authorised person who has permission to effect or carry out contracts of insurance, and
(b) falls within a prescribed class,
from doing anything to lessen the effectiveness of asset identification rules.
(2) "Asset identification rules" means rules made by the Authority which require an authorised person who has permission to effect or carry out contracts of insurance to identify assets which belong to him and which are maintained in respect of a particular aspect of his business.
(3) The regulations may, in particular, include provision—
(a) prohibiting the payment of dividends;
(b) prohibiting the creation of charges;
(c) making charges created in contravention of the regulations void.
(4) The Treasury may by regulations provide that, in prescribed circumstances, charges created in contravention of asset identification rules are void.
(5) A person who contravenes regulations under subsection (1) is guilty of an offence and liable on summary conviction to a fine not exceeding level 5 on the standard scale.
(6) "Charges" includes mortgages (or in Scotland securities over property).

143 (*Repealed by the Companies Act 2006, ss 964(1), (2), 1295, Sch 16.*)

Specific rules

[117]

144 Price stabilising rules

(1) The Authority may make rules ("price stabilising rules") as to—

(a) the circumstances and manner in which,

(b) the conditions subject to which, and

(c) the time when or the period during which,

action may be taken for the purpose of stabilising the price of investments of specified kinds.

(2) Price stabilising rules—

(a) are to be made so as to apply only to authorised persons;

(b) may make different provision in relation to different kinds of investment.

(3) The Authority may make rules which, for the purposes of section 397(5)(b), treat a person who acts or engages in conduct—

(a) for the purpose of stabilising the price of investments, and

(b) in conformity with such provisions corresponding to price stabilising rules and made by a body or authority outside the United Kingdom as may be specified in the rules under this subsection,

as acting, or engaging in that conduct, for that purpose and in conformity with price stabilising rules.

(4) The Treasury may by order impose limitations on the power to make rules under this section.

(5) Such an order may, in particular—

(a) specify the kinds of investment in relation to which price stabilising rules may make provision;

(b) specify the kinds of investment in relation to which rules made under subsection (3) may make provision;

(c) provide for price stabilising rules to make provision for action to be taken for the purpose of stabilising the price of investments only in such circumstances as the order may specify;

(d) provide for price stabilising rules to make provision for action to be taken for that purpose only at such times or during such periods as the order may specify.

(6) If provisions specified in rules made under subsection (3) are altered, the rules continue to apply to those provisions as altered, but only if before the alteration the Authority has notified the body or authority concerned (and has not withdrawn its notification) that it is satisfied with its consultation procedures.

[(7) "Consultation procedures" means procedures designed to provide an opportunity for persons likely to be affected by alterations to those provisions to make representations about proposed alterations to any of those provisions.]

NOTES

Sub-s (7): substituted by the Companies Act 2006, s 964(1), (3).

[118]

145 Financial promotion rules

(1) The Authority may make rules applying to authorised persons about the communication by them, or their approval of the communication by others, of invitations or inducements—

(a) to engage in investment activity; or

(b) to participate in a collective investment scheme.

(2) Rules under this section may, in particular, make provision about the form and content of communications.

(3) Subsection (1) applies only to communications which—

(a) if made by a person other than an authorised person, without the approval of an authorised person, would contravene section 21(1);

(b) may be made by an authorised person without contravening section 238(1).

[(3A) But subsection (3) does not prevent the Authority from making rules under subsection (1) in relation to a communication that would not contravene section 21(1) if made by a person other than an authorised person, without the approval of an authorised person, if the conditions set out in subsection (3B) are satisfied.

(3B) Those conditions are—

(a) that the communication would not contravene subsection (1) of section 21 because it is a communication to which that subsection does not apply as a result of an order under subsection (5) of that section;

(b) that the Authority considers that any of the requirements of—

(i) paragraphs 1 to 8 of Article 19 of the markets in financial instruments directive; or
(ii) any implementing measure made under paragraph 10 of that Article,
apply to the communication; and
(c) that the Authority considers that the rules are necessary to secure that the communication satisfies such of the requirements mentioned in paragraph (b) as the Authority considers apply to the communication.]

(4) "Engage in investment activity" has the same meaning as in section 21.

(5) The Treasury may by order impose limitations on the power to make rules under this section.

NOTES

Sub-ss (3A), (3B): inserted by the Financial Services and Markets Act 2000 (Markets in Financial Instruments) (Modification of Powers) Regulations 2006, SI 2006/2975, regs 2, 4, subject to transitional provisions in reg 14 thereof.

[119]

146 Money laundering rules

The Authority may make rules in relation to the prevention and detection of money laundering in connection with the carrying on of regulated activities by authorised persons.

[120]

147 Control of information rules

(1) The Authority may make rules ("control of information rules") about the disclosure and use of information held by an authorised person ("A").

(2) Control of information rules may—
(a) require the withholding of information which A would otherwise have to disclose to a person ("B") for or with whom A does business in the course of carrying on any regulated or other activity;
(b) specify circumstances in which A may withhold information which he would otherwise have to disclose to B;
(c) require A not to use for the benefit of B information A holds which A would otherwise have to use in that way;
(d) specify circumstances in which A may decide not to use for the benefit of B information A holds which A would otherwise have to use in that way.

Modification or waiver

[121]

148 Modification or waiver of rules

(1) . . .

[(2) The Authority may, on the application or with the consent of a person who is subject to rules made by the Authority, direct that all or any of those rules (other than rules made under section 247 (trust scheme rules) or section 248 (scheme particulars rules))—
(a) are not to apply to that person; or
(b) are to apply to him with such modifications as may be specified in the direction.]

(3) An application must be made in such manner as the Authority may direct.

(4) The Authority may not give a direction unless it is satisfied that—
(a) compliance by the . . . person with the rules, or with the rules as unmodified, would be unduly burdensome or would not achieve the purpose for which the rules were made; and
(b) the direction would not result in undue risk to persons whose interests the rules are intended to protect.

(5) A direction may be given subject to conditions.

(6) Unless it is satisfied that it is inappropriate or unnecessary to do so, a direction must be published by the Authority in such a way as it thinks most suitable for bringing the direction to the attention of—
(a) those likely to be affected by it; and
(b) others who may be likely to make an application for a similar direction.

(7) In deciding whether it is satisfied as mentioned in subsection (6), the Authority must—
(a) take into account whether the direction relates to a rule contravention of which is actionable in accordance with section 150;
(b) consider whether its publication would prejudice, to an unreasonable degree, the commercial interests of the . . . person concerned or any other member of his immediate group; and
(c) consider whether its publication would be contrary to an international obligation of the United Kingdom.

(8) For the purposes of paragraphs (b) and (c) of subsection (7), the Authority must consider whether it would be possible to publish the direction without either of the consequences mentioned in those paragraphs by publishing it without disclosing the identity of the . . . person concerned.
(9) The Authority may—
(a) revoke a direction; or
(b) vary it on the application, or with the consent, of the . . . person to whom it relates.
(10) "Direction" means a direction under subsection (2).
(11) "Immediate group", in relation to [a person] ("A"), means—
(a) A;
(b) a parent undertaking of A;
(c) a subsidiary undertaking of A;
(d) a subsidiary undertaking of a parent undertaking of A;
(e) a parent undertaking of a subsidiary undertaking of A.

NOTES

Sub-s (1): repealed by the Regulatory Reform (Financial Services and Markets Act 2000) Order 2007, SI 2007/1973, arts 2, 10(a).

Sub-s (2): substituted by SI 2007/1973, arts 2, 10(b).

Sub-ss (4), (7)–(9): words omitted repealed by SI 2007/1973, arts 2, 10(c).

Sub-s (11): words in square brackets substituted by SI 2007/1973, arts 2, 10(d).

Modification: sub-ss (3)–(9), (11) above have effect, with certain modifications, in relation to a direction by the Financial Services Authority under the Open-Ended Investment Companies Regulations 2001, SI 2001/1228, reg 7(1), (2), to modify or waive the application of any rules made by the Authority under reg 6 of the 2001 Regulations, as they have effect in relation to a direction under sub-s (2) above; see SI 2001/1228, reg 7(3), (4).

Application: see the Heritable Bank plc Transfer of Certain Rights and Liabilities Order 2008, SI 2008/2644, arts 2, 27(2), the Transfer of Rights and Liabilities to ING Order 2008, SI 2008/2666, arts 2, 18(2), the Kaupthing Singer & Friedlander Limited Transfer of Certain Rights and Liabilities Order 2008, SI 2008/2674, arts 2, 29(2), the Amendments to Law (Resolution of Dunfermline Building Society) Order 2009, SI 2009/814, art 9(2)–(5), and the Northern Rock plc Transfer Order 2009, SI 2009/3226, art 20(2)–(4).

Disapplication: see the Capital Requirements Regulations 2006, SI 2006/3221, reg 8, the Heritable Bank plc Transfer of Certain Rights and Liabilities Order 2008, SI 2008/2644, arts 2, 27(3), the Transfer of Rights and Liabilities to ING Order 2008, SI 2008/2666, arts 2, 18(3), and the Kaupthing Singer & Friedlander Limited Transfer of Certain Rights and Liabilities Order 2008, SI 2008/2674, arts 2, 29(3).

Contravention of rules

[122]
149 Evidential provisions
(1) If a particular rule so provides, contravention of the rule does not give rise to any of the consequences provided for by other provisions of this Act.
(2) A rule which so provides must also provide—
(a) that contravention may be relied on as tending to establish contravention of such other rule as may be specified; or
(b) that compliance may be relied on as tending to establish compliance with such other rule as may be specified.
(3) A rule may include the provision mentioned in subsection (1) only if the Authority considers that it is appropriate for it also to include the provision required by subsection (2).

[123]
150 Actions for damages
(1) A contravention by an authorised person of a rule is actionable at the suit of a private person who suffers loss as a result of the contravention, subject to the defences and other incidents applying to actions for breach of statutory duty.
(2) If rules so provide, subsection (1) does not apply to contravention of a specified provision of those rules.
(3) In prescribed cases, a contravention of a rule which would be actionable at the suit of a private person is actionable at the suit of a person who is not a private person, subject to the defences and other incidents applying to actions for breach of statutory duty.
(4) In subsections (1) and (3) "rule" does not include—
(a) [Part 6 rules]; or
(b) a rule requiring an authorised person to have or maintain financial resources.
(5) "Private person" has such meaning as may be prescribed.

NOTES

Sub-s (4): words in square brackets substituted by the Financial Services and Markets Act 2000 (Market Abuse) Regulations 2005, SI 2005/381, reg 6.

Regulations: the Financial Services and Markets Act 2000 (Rights of Action) Regulations 2001, SI 2001/2256 at **[618]**; the Financial Services and Markets Act 2000 (Fourth Motor Insurance Directive) Regulations 2002, SI 2002/2706 at **[857]**.

[124]
151 Limits on effect of contravening rules

(1) A person is not guilty of an offence by reason of a contravention of a rule made by the Authority.

(2) No such contravention makes any transaction void or unenforceable.

Procedural provisions

[125]
152 Notification of rules to the Treasury

(1) If the Authority makes any rules, it must give a copy to the Treasury without delay.

(2) If the Authority alters or revokes any rules, it must give written notice to the Treasury without delay.

(3) Notice of an alteration must include details of the alteration.

[126]
153 Rule-making instruments

(1) Any power conferred on the Authority to make rules is exercisable in writing.

(2) An instrument by which rules are made by the Authority ("a rule-making instrument") must specify the provision under which the rules are made.

(3) To the extent to which a rule-making instrument does not comply with subsection (2), it is void.

(4) A rule-making instrument must be published by the Authority in the way appearing to the Authority to be best calculated to bring it to the attention of the public.

(5) The Authority may charge a reasonable fee for providing a person with a copy of a rule-making instrument.

(6) A person is not to be taken to have contravened any rule made by the Authority if he shows that at the time of the alleged contravention the rule-making instrument concerned had not been made available in accordance with this section.

[127]
154 Verification of rules

(1) The production of a printed copy of a rule-making instrument purporting to be made by the Authority—

- (a) on which is endorsed a certificate signed by a member of the Authority's staff authorised by it for that purpose, and
- (b) which contains the required statements,

is evidence (or in Scotland sufficient evidence) of the facts stated in the certificate.

(2) The required statements are—

- (a) that the instrument was made by the Authority;
- (b) that the copy is a true copy of the instrument; and
- (c) that on a specified date the instrument was made available to the public in accordance with section 153(4).

(3) A certificate purporting to be signed as mentioned in subsection (1) is to be taken to have been properly signed unless the contrary is shown.

(4) A person who wishes in any legal proceedings to rely on a rule-making instrument may require the Authority to endorse a copy of the instrument with a certificate of the kind mentioned in subsection (1).

[128]
155 Consultation

(1) If the Authority proposes to make any rules, it must publish a draft of the proposed rules in the way appearing to it to be best calculated to bring them to the attention of the public.

(2) The draft must be accompanied by—

- (a) a cost benefit analysis;
- (b) an explanation of the purpose of the proposed rules;
- (c) an explanation of the Authority's reasons for believing that making the proposed rules is compatible with its general duties under section 2; and
- (d) notice that representations about the proposals may be made to the Authority within a specified time.

(3) In the case of a proposal to make rules under a provision mentioned in subsection (9), the draft must also be accompanied by details of the expected expenditure by reference to which the proposal is made.
(4) Before making the proposed rules, the Authority must have regard to any representations made to it in accordance with subsection (2)(d).
(5) If the Authority makes the proposed rules, it must publish an account, in general terms, of—
  (a) the representations made to it in accordance with subsection (2)(d); and
  (b) its response to them.
(6) If the rules differ from the draft published under subsection (1) in a way which is, in the opinion of the Authority, significant—
  (a) the Authority must (in addition to complying with subsection (5)) publish details of the difference; and
  (b) those details must be accompanied by a cost benefit analysis.
(7) Subsections (1) to (6) do not apply if the Authority considers that the delay involved in complying with them would be prejudicial to the interests of consumers.
(8) Neither subsection (2)(a) nor subsection (6)(b) applies if the Authority considers—
  (a) that, making the appropriate comparison, there will be no increase in costs; or
  (b) that, making that comparison, there will be an increase in costs but the increase will be of minimal significance.
(9) Neither subsection (2)(a) nor subsection (6)(b) requires a cost benefit analysis to be carried out in relation to rules made under—
  (a) section 136(2);
  (b) subsection (1) of section 213 as a result of subsection (4) of that section;
  (c) section 234;
  (d) paragraph 17 of Schedule 1.
(10) "Cost benefit analysis" means an estimate of the costs together with an analysis of the benefits that will arise—
  (a) if the proposed rules are made; or
  (b) if subsection (6) applies, from the rules that have been made.
(11) "The appropriate comparison" means—
  (a) in relation to subsection (2)(a), a comparison between the overall position if the rules are made and the overall position if they are not made;
  (b) in relation to subsection (6)(b), a comparison between the overall position after the making of the rules and the overall position before they were made.
(12) The Authority may charge a reasonable fee for providing a person with a copy of a draft published under subsection (1).

NOTES

Modification: sub-s (7) is modified by the Northern Rock plc Transfer Order 2008, SI 2008/432, art 6(1), the Bradford & Bingley plc Transfer of Securities and Property etc Order 2008, SI 2008/2546, art 38(1), the Heritable Bank plc Transfer of Certain Rights and Liabilities Order 2008, SI 2008/2644, arts 2, 28(1), the Transfer of Rights and Liabilities to ING Order 2008, SI 2008/2666, arts 2, 19(1) and the Kaupthing Singer & Friedlander Limited Transfer of Certain Rights and Liabilities Order 2008, SI 2008/2674, arts 2, 30(1), the Amendments to Law (Resolution of Dunfermline Building Society) Order 2009, SI 2009/814, art 10(1), and the Northern Rock plc Transfer Order, SI 2009/3226, art 21(1).

Disapplication: this section is disapplied by the Financial Services and Markets Act 2000 (Transitional Provisions) (Mortgages) Order 2004, SI 2004/2615, arts 1(3), 2, 3, 4(2), the Financial Services and Markets Act 2000 (Transitional Provisions) (General Insurance Intermediaries) Order 2004, SI 2004/3351, the Financial Services and Markets Act 2000 (Regulated Activities) (Amendment) Order 2006, SI 2006/1969, art 6(2), the Compensation Act 2006 (Contribution for Mesothelioma Claims) Regulations 2006, SI 2006/3259, reg 4, and the Financial Services and Markets Act 2000 (Regulated Activities) (Amendment) Order 2009, SI 2009/1342, art 33(2).

[129]

156 General supplementary powers

(1) Rules made by the Authority may make different provision for different cases and may, in particular, make different provision in respect of different descriptions of authorised person, activity or investment.
(2) Rules made by the Authority may contain such incidental, supplemental, consequential and transitional provision as the Authority considers appropriate.

CHAPTER II
GUIDANCE

[130]

157 Guidance

(1) The Authority may give guidance consisting of such information and advice as it considers appropriate—

(a) with respect to the operation of this Act and of any rules made under it;
(b) with respect to any matters relating to functions of the Authority;
(c) for the purpose of meeting the regulatory objectives;
(d) with respect to any other matters about which it appears to the Authority to be desirable to give information or advice.

(2) The Authority may give financial or other assistance to persons giving information or advice of a kind which the Authority could give under this section.

(3) If the Authority proposes to give guidance to regulated persons generally, or to a class of regulated person, in relation to rules to which those persons are subject, [subsections (1), (2)(d) and (4) of section 155 apply to the proposed guidance as they apply to proposed rules, unless the Authority considers that the delay in complying with them would be prejudicial to the interests of consumers].

(4) The Authority may—

(a) publish its guidance;
(b) offer copies of its published guidance for sale at a reasonable price; and
(c) if it gives guidance in response to a request made by any person, make a reasonable charge for that guidance.

(5) In this Chapter [(except in section 158A)], references to guidance given by the Authority include references to any recommendation made by the Authority to persons generally, to regulated persons generally or to any class of regulated person.

(6) "Regulated person" means any—

(a) authorised person;
(b) person who is otherwise subject to rules made by the Authority.

NOTES

Sub-s (3): words in square brackets substituted by the Regulatory Reform (Financial Services and Markets Act 2000) Order 2007, SI 2007/1973, arts 2, 13.

Sub-s (5): words in square brackets inserted by the Financial Services and Markets Act 2000 (Markets in Financial Instruments) (Modification of Powers) Regulations 2006, SI 2006/2975, regs 2, 5.

Modification: this section is modified by the Northern Rock plc Transfer Order 2008, SI 2008/432, art 16(2), the Bradford & Bingley plc Transfer of Securities and Property etc Order 2008, SI 2008/2546, art 38(2), the Heritable Bank plc Transfer of Certain Rights and Liabilities Order 2008, SI 2008/2644, arts 2, 28(2), the Transfer of Rights and Liabilities to ING Order 2008, SI 2008/2666, arts 2, 19(2), the Kaupthing Singer & Friedlander Limited Transfer of Certain Rights and Liabilities Order 2008, SI 2008/2674, arts 2, 30(2), the Amendments to Law (Resolution of Dunfermline Building Society) Order 2009, SI 2009/814, art 10(2), and the Northern Rock plc Transfer Order, SI 2009/3226, art 21(2).

Disapplication: sub-s (3) above is disapplied by the Financial Services and Markets Act 2000 (Transitional Provisions) (Mortgages) Order 2004, SI 2004/2615, arts 1(3), 2, 3, 4(2), the Financial Services and Markets Act 2000 (Transitional Provisions) (General Insurance Intermediaries) Order 2004, SI 2004/3351, art 4, the Financial Services and Markets Act 2000 (Regulated Activities) (Amendment) Order 2006, SI 2006/1969, art 6(2), the Compensation Act 2006 (Contribution for Mesothelioma Claims) Regulations 2006, SI 2006/3259, reg 4, and the Financial Services and Markets Act 2000 (Regulated Activities) (Amendment) Order 2009, SI 2009/1342, art 33(2).

[131]

158 Notification of guidance to the Treasury

(1) On giving any general guidance, the Authority must give the Treasury a copy of the guidance without delay.

(2) If the Authority alters any of its general guidance, it must give written notice to the Treasury without delay.

(3) The notice must include details of the alteration.

(4) If the Authority revokes any of its general guidance, it must give written notice to the Treasury without delay.

(5) "General guidance" means guidance given by the Authority under section 157 which is—

(a) given to persons generally, to regulated persons generally or to a class of regulated person;
(b) intended to have continuing effect; and
(c) given in writing or other legible form.

(6) "Regulated person" has the same meaning as in section 157.

158A–164 *(S 158A, ss 159–164 (Ch III) outside the scope of this work.)*

PART XI
INFORMATION GATHERING AND INVESTIGATIONS

NOTES

Modification: this Part is applied, with modifications, in respect of the Financial Services Authority's functions under the Payment Services Regulations 2009, SI 2009/209, by SI 2009/209, reg 95, Sch 5, Pt 1, para 3, and in respect of the Financial Services Authority's functions under the Cross-Border Payments in Euro Regulations 2010, SI 2010/89, by SI 2010/89, reg 19, Schedule, Pt 1, para 2.

Powers to gather information

[132]

165 Authority's power to require information

(1) The Authority may, by notice in writing given to an authorised person, require him—

(a) to provide specified information or information of a specified description; or

(b) to produce specified documents or documents of a specified description.

(2) The information or documents must be provided or produced—

(a) before the end of such reasonable period as may be specified; and

(b) at such place as may be specified.

(3) An officer who has written authorisation from the Authority to do so may require an authorised person without delay—

(a) to provide the officer with specified information or information of a specified description; or

(b) to produce to him specified documents or documents of a specified description.

(4) This section applies only to information and documents reasonably required in connection with the exercise by the Authority of functions conferred on it by or under this Act.

(5) The Authority may require any information provided under this section to be provided in such form as it may reasonably require.

(6) The Authority may require—

(a) any information provided, whether in a document or otherwise, to be verified in such manner, or

(b) any document produced to be authenticated in such manner, as it may reasonably require.

(7) The powers conferred by subsections (1) and (3) may also be exercised to impose requirements on—

(a) a person who is connected with an authorised person;

(b) an operator, trustee or depositary of a scheme recognised under section 270 or 272 who is not an authorised person;

(c) a recognised investment exchange or recognised clearing house.

(8) "Authorised person" includes a person who was at any time an authorised person but who has ceased to be an authorised person.

(9) "Officer" means an officer of the Authority and includes a member of the Authority's staff or an agent of the Authority.

(10) "Specified" means—

(a) in subsections (1) and (2), specified in the notice; and

(b) in subsection (3), specified in the authorisation.

(11) For the purposes of this section, a person is connected with an authorised person ("A") if he is or has at any relevant time been—

(a) a member of A's group;

(b) a controller of A;

(c) any other member of a partnership of which A is a member; or

(d) in relation to A, a person mentioned in Part I of Schedule 15.

NOTES

Application: this section and s 166 are applied, with modifications, by the Regulated Covered Bonds Regulations 2008, SI 2008/346, reg 46, Schedule, Pt 1, paras 3, 4.

[133]

166 Reports by skilled persons

(1) The Authority may, by notice in writing given to a person to whom subsection (2) applies, require him to provide the Authority with a report on any matter about which the Authority has required or could require the provision of information or production of documents under section 165.

(2) This subsection applies to—
  (a) an authorised person ("A"),
  (b) any other member of A's group,
  (c) a partnership of which A is a member, or
  (d) a person who has at any relevant time been a person falling within paragraph (a), (b) or (c),

who is, or was at the relevant time, carrying on a business.
(3) The Authority may require the report to be in such form as may be specified in the notice.
(4) The person appointed to make a report required by subsection (1) must be a person—
  (a) nominated or approved by the Authority; and
  (b) appearing to the Authority to have the skills necessary to make a report on the matter concerned.

(5) It is the duty of any person who is providing (or who at any time has provided) services to a person to whom subsection (2) applies in relation to a matter on which a report is required under subsection (1) to give a person appointed to provide such a report all such assistance as the appointed person may reasonably require.
(6) The obligation imposed by subsection (5) is enforceable, on the application of the Authority, by an injunction or, in Scotland, by an order for specific performance under section 45 of the Court of Session Act 1988.

NOTES
Application: see the note to s 165 at **[132]**.

Appointment of investigators

[134]
167 Appointment of persons to carry out general investigations
(1) If it appears to the Authority or the Secretary of State ("the investigating authority") that there is good reason for doing so, the investigating authority may appoint one or more competent persons to conduct an investigation on its behalf into—
  (a) the nature, conduct or state of the business of [a recognised investment exchange or] an authorised person or of an appointed representative;
  (b) a particular aspect of that business; or
  (c) the ownership or control of [a recognised investment exchange or] an authorised person.

(2) If a person appointed under subsection (1) thinks it necessary for the purposes of his investigation, he may also investigate the business of a person who is or has at any relevant time been—
  (a) a member of the group of which the person under investigation ("A") is part; or
  (b) a partnership of which A is a member.

(3) If a person appointed under subsection (1) decides to investigate the business of any person under subsection (2) he must give that person written notice of his decision.
(4) The power conferred by this section may be exercised in relation to a former authorised person (or appointed representative) but only in relation to—
  (a) business carried on at any time when he was an authorised person (or appointed representative); or
  (b) the ownership or control of a former authorised person at any time when he was an authorised person.

(5) "Business" includes any part of a business even if it does not consist of carrying on regulated activities.
[(6) References in subsection (1) to a recognised investment exchange do not include references to an overseas investment exchange (as defined by section 313(1)).]

NOTES
Sub-s (1): words in square brackets in paras (a), (c) inserted by the Financial Services and Markets Act 2000 (Markets in Financial Instruments) Regulations 2007, SI 2007/126, reg 3(5), Sch 5, paras 1, 7(a).
Sub-s (6): added by SI 2007/126, reg 3(5), Sch 5, paras 1, 7(b).

[135]
168 Appointment of persons to carry out investigations in particular cases
(1) Subsection (3) applies if it appears to an investigating authority that there are circumstances suggesting that—
  (a) a person may have contravened any regulation made under section 142; or
  (b) a person may be guilty of an offence under section 177, 191, 346 or 398(1) or under Schedule 4.

(2) Subsection (3) also applies if it appears to an investigating authority that there are circumstances suggesting that—

(a) an offence under section 24(1) or 397 or under Part V of the Criminal Justice Act 1993 may have been committed;

(b) there may have been a breach of the general prohibition;

(c) there may have been a contravention of section 21 or 238; or

(d) market abuse may have taken place.

(3) The investigating authority may appoint one or more competent persons to conduct an investigation on its behalf.

(4) Subsection (5) applies if it appears to the Authority that there are circumstances suggesting that—

(a) a person may have contravened section 20;

(b) a person may be guilty of an offence under prescribed regulations relating to money laundering;

[(ba) a person may be guilty of an offence under Schedule 7 to the Counter-Terrorism Act 2008 (terrorist financing or money laundering);]

(c) an authorised person may have contravened a rule made by the Authority;

(d) an individual may not be a fit and proper person to perform functions in relation to a regulated activity carried on by an authorised or exempt person;

(e) an individual may have performed or agreed to perform a function in breach of a prohibition order;

(f) an authorised or exempt person may have failed to comply with section 56(6);

(g) an authorised person may have failed to comply with section 59(1) or (2);

(h) a person in relation to whom the Authority has given its approval under section 59 may not be a fit and proper person to perform the function to which that approval relates;

. . .

(i) a person may be guilty of misconduct for the purposes of section 66[; or

(j) a person may have contravened any provision made by or under this Act for the purpose of implementing the markets in financial instruments directive or by any directly applicable Community regulation made under that directive].

(5) The Authority may appoint one or more competent persons to conduct an investigation on its behalf.

(6) "Investigating authority" means the Authority or the Secretary of State.

NOTES

Sub-s (4): para (ba) inserted by the Counter-Terrorism Act 2008, s 62, Sch 7, Pt 7, para 33(3); word omitted from para (h) repealed, and para (j) and word immediately preceding it inserted by the Financial Services and Markets Act 2000 (Markets in Financial Instruments) Regulations 2007, SI 2007/126, reg 3(5), Sch 5, paras 1, 8.

Regulations: the Money Laundering Regulations 2007, SI 2007/2157; the Transfer of Funds (Information on the Payer) Regulations 2007, SI 2007/3298.

Assistance to overseas regulators

[136]

169 Investigations etc in support of overseas regulator

(1) At the request of an overseas regulator, the Authority may—

(a) exercise the power conferred by section 165; or

(b) appoint one or more competent persons to investigate any matter.

(2) An investigator has the same powers as an investigator appointed under section 168(3) (as a result of subsection (1) of that section).

(3) If the request has been made by a competent authority in pursuance of any Community obligation the Authority must, in deciding whether or not to exercise its investigative power, consider whether its exercise is necessary to comply with any such obligation.

(4) In deciding whether or not to exercise its investigative power, the Authority may take into account in particular—

(a) whether in the country or territory of the overseas regulator concerned, corresponding assistance would be given to a United Kingdom regulatory authority;

(b) whether the case concerns the breach of a law, or other requirement, which has no close parallel in the United Kingdom or involves the assertion of a jurisdiction not recognised by the United Kingdom;

(c) the seriousness of the case and its importance to persons in the United Kingdom;

(d) whether it is otherwise appropriate in the public interest to give the assistance sought.

(5) The Authority may decide that it will not exercise its investigative power unless the overseas regulator undertakes to make such contribution towards the cost of its exercise as the Authority considers appropriate.
(6) Subsections (4) and (5) do not apply if the Authority considers that the exercise of its investigative power is necessary to comply with a Community obligation.
(7) If the Authority has appointed an investigator in response to a request from an overseas regulator, it may direct the investigator to permit a representative of that regulator to attend, and take part in, any interview conducted for the purposes of the investigation.
(8) A direction under subsection (7) is not to be given unless the Authority is satisfied that any information obtained by an overseas regulator as a result of the interview will be subject to safeguards equivalent to those contained in Part XXIII.
(9) The Authority must prepare a statement of its policy with respect to the conduct of interviews in relation to which a direction under subsection (7) has been given.
(10) The statement requires the approval of the Treasury.
(11) If the Treasury approve the statement, the Authority must publish it.
(12) No direction may be given under subsection (7) before the statement has been published.
(13) "Overseas regulator" has the same meaning as in section 195.
(14) "Investigative power" means one of the powers mentioned in subsection (1).
(15) "Investigator" means a person appointed under subsection (1)(b).

Conduct of investigations

[137]

170 Investigations: general

(1) This section applies if an investigating authority appoints one or more competent persons ("investigators") under section 167 or 168(3) or (5) to conduct an investigation on its behalf.
(2) The investigating authority must give written notice of the appointment of an investigator to the person who is the subject of the investigation ("the person under investigation").
(3) Subsections (2) and (9) do not apply if—
- (a) the investigator is appointed as a result of section 168(1) or (4) and the investigating authority believes that the notice required by subsection (2) or (9) would be likely to result in the investigation being frustrated; or
- (b) the investigator is appointed as a result of subsection (2) of section 168.

(4) A notice under subsection (2) must—
- (a) specify the provisions under which, and as a result of which, the investigator was appointed; and
- (b) state the reason for his appointment.

(5) Nothing prevents the investigating authority from appointing a person who is a member of its staff as an investigator.
(6) An investigator must make a report of his investigation to the investigating authority.
(7) The investigating authority may, by a direction to an investigator, control—
- (a) the scope of the investigation;
- (b) the period during which the investigation is to be conducted;
- (c) the conduct of the investigation; and
- (d) the reporting of the investigation.

(8) A direction may, in particular—
- (a) confine the investigation to particular matters;
- (b) extend the investigation to additional matters;
- (c) require the investigator to discontinue the investigation or to take only such steps as are specified in the direction;
- (d) require the investigator to make such interim reports as are so specified.

(9) If there is a change in the scope or conduct of the investigation and, in the opinion of the investigating authority, the person subject to investigation is likely to be significantly prejudiced by not being made aware of it, that person must be given written notice of the change.
(10) "Investigating authority", in relation to an investigator, means—
- (a) the Authority, if the Authority appointed him;
- (b) the Secretary of State, if the Secretary of State appointed him.

[138]

171 Powers of persons appointed under section 167

(1) An investigator may require the person who is the subject of the investigation ("the person under investigation") or any person connected with the person under investigation—
- (a) to attend before the investigator at a specified time and place and answer questions; or
- (b) otherwise to provide such information as the investigator may require.

(2) An investigator may also require any person to produce at a specified time and place any specified documents or documents of a specified description.
(3) A requirement under subsection (1) or (2) may be imposed only so far as the investigator concerned reasonably considers the question, provision of information or production of the document to be relevant to the purposes of the investigation.
[(3A) Where the investigation relates to a recognised investment exchange, an investigator has the additional powers conferred by sections 172 and 173 (and for this purpose references in those sections to an investigator are to be read accordingly).]
(4) For the purposes of this section and section 172, a person is connected with the person under investigation ("A") if he is or has at any relevant time been—
(a) a member of A's group;
(b) a controller of A;
(c) a partnership of which A is a member; or
(d) in relation to A, a person mentioned in Part I or II of Schedule 15.
(5) "Investigator" means a person conducting an investigation under section 167.
(6) "Specified" means specified in a notice in writing.
[(7) The reference in subsection (3A) to a recognised investment exchange does not include a reference to an overseas investment exchange (as defined by section 313(1)).]

NOTES
Sub-ss (3A), (7): inserted by the Financial Services and Markets Act 2000 (Markets in Financial Instruments) Regulations 2007, SI 2007/126, reg 3(5), Sch 5, paras 1, 9.

[139]
172 Additional power of persons appointed as a result of section 168(1) or (4)
(1) An investigator has the powers conferred by section 171.
(2) An investigator may also require a person who is neither the subject of the investigation ("the person under investigation") nor a person connected with the person under investigation—
(a) to attend before the investigator at a specified time and place and answer questions; or
(b) otherwise to provide such information as the investigator may require for the purposes of the investigation.
(3) A requirement may only be imposed under subsection (2) if the investigator is satisfied that the requirement is necessary or expedient for the purposes of the investigation.
(4) "Investigator" means a person appointed as a result of subsection (1) or (4) of section 168.
(5) "Specified" means specified in a notice in writing.

[140]
173 Powers of persons appointed as a result of section 168(2)
(1) Subsections (2) to (4) apply if an investigator considers that any person ("A") is or may be able to give information which is or may be relevant to the investigation.
(2) The investigator may require A—
(a) to attend before him at a specified time and place and answer questions; or
(b) otherwise to provide such information as he may require for the purposes of the investigation.
(3) The investigator may also require A to produce at a specified time and place any specified documents or documents of a specified description which appear to the investigator to relate to any matter relevant to the investigation.
(4) The investigator may also otherwise require A to give him all assistance in connection with the investigation which A is reasonably able to give.
(5) "Investigator" means a person appointed under subsection (3) of section 168 (as a result of subsection (2) of that section).

[141]
174 Admissibility of statements made to investigators
(1) A statement made to an investigator by a person in compliance with an information requirement is admissible in evidence in any proceedings, so long as it also complies with any requirements governing the admissibility of evidence in the circumstances in question.
(2) But in criminal proceedings in which that person is charged with an offence to which this subsection applies or in proceedings in relation to action to be taken against that person under section 123—
(a) no evidence relating to the statement may be adduced, and
(b) no question relating to it may be asked,
by or on behalf of the prosecution or (as the case may be) the Authority, unless evidence relating to it is adduced, or a question relating to it is asked, in the proceedings by or on behalf of that person.

(3) Subsection (2) applies to any offence other than one—
(a) under section 177(4) or 398;
(b) under section 5 of the Perjury Act 1911 (false statements made otherwise than on oath);
(c) under section 44(2) of the Criminal Law (Consolidation) (Scotland) Act 1995 (false statements made otherwise than on oath); or
(d) under Article 10 of the Perjury (Northern Ireland) Order 1979.
(4) "Investigator" means a person appointed under section 167 or 168(3) or (5).
(5) "Information requirement" means a requirement imposed by an investigator under section 171, 172, 173 or 175.

[142]
175 Information and documents: supplemental provisions
(1) If the Authority or an investigator has power under this Part to require a person to produce a document but it appears that the document is in the possession of a third person, that power may be exercised in relation to the third person.
(2) If a document is produced in response to a requirement imposed under this Part, the person to whom it is produced may—
(a) take copies or extracts from the document; or
(b) require the person producing the document, or any relevant person, to provide an explanation of the document.
(3) If a person who is required under this Part to produce a document fails to do so, the Authority or an investigator may require him to state, to the best of his knowledge and belief, where the document is.
(4) A lawyer may be required under this Part to furnish the name and address of his client.
(5) No person may be required under this Part to disclose information or produce a document in respect of which he owes an obligation of confidence by virtue of carrying on the business of banking unless—
(a) he is the person under investigation or a member of that person's group;
(b) the person to whom the obligation of confidence is owed is the person under investigation or a member of that person's group;
(c) the person to whom the obligation of confidence is owed consents to the disclosure or production; or
(d) the imposing on him of a requirement with respect to such information or document has been specifically authorised by the investigating authority.
(6) If a person claims a lien on a document, its production under this Part does not affect the lien.
(7) "Relevant person", in relation to a person who is required to produce a document, means a person who—
(a) has been or is or is proposed to be a director or controller of that person;
(b) has been or is an auditor of that person;
(c) has been or is an actuary, accountant or lawyer appointed or instructed by that person; or
(d) has been or is an employee of that person.
(8) "Investigator" means a person appointed under section 167 or 168(3) or (5).

NOTES

Open-ended investment companies: sub-ss (2)–(4), (6) above have effect as if the Open-Ended Investment Companies Regulations 2001, SI 2001/1228, reg 30 was contained in Pt XI (ss 165–177 and Sch 15) of this Act; see reg 30(6) of the 2001 Regulations.

[143]
176 Entry of premises under warrant
(1) A justice of the peace may issue a warrant under this section if satisfied on information on oath given by or on behalf of the Secretary of State, the Authority or an investigator that there are reasonable grounds for believing that the first, second or third set of conditions is satisfied.
(2) The first set of conditions is—
(a) that a person on whom an information requirement has been imposed has failed (wholly or in part) to comply with it; and
(b) that on the premises specified in the warrant—
(i) there are documents which have been required; or
(ii) there is information which has been required.
(3) The second set of conditions is—
(a) that the premises specified in the warrant are premises of an authorised person or an appointed representative;

(b) that there are on the premises documents or information in relation to which an information requirement could be imposed; and
(c) that if such a requirement were to be imposed—
(i) it would not be complied with; or
(ii) the documents or information to which it related would be removed, tampered with or destroyed.

(4) The third set of conditions is—
(a) that an offence mentioned in section 168 for which the maximum sentence on conviction on indictment is two years or more has been (or is being) committed by any person;
(b) that there are on the premises specified in the warrant documents or information relevant to whether that offence has been (or is being) committed;
(c) that an information requirement could be imposed in relation to those documents or information; and
(d) that if such a requirement were to be imposed—
(i) it would not be complied with; or
(ii) the documents or information to which it related would be removed, tampered with or destroyed.

(5) A warrant under this section shall authorise a constable—
(a) to enter the premises specified in the warrant;
(b) to search the premises and take possession of any documents or information appearing to be documents or information of a kind in respect of which a warrant under this section was issued ("the relevant kind") or to take, in relation to any such documents or information, any other steps which may appear to be necessary for preserving them or preventing interference with them;
(c) to take copies of, or extracts from, any documents or information appearing to be of the relevant kind;
(d) to require any person on the premises to provide an explanation of any document or information appearing to be of the relevant kind or to state where it may be found; and
(e) to use such force as may be reasonably necessary.

(6) In England and Wales, sections 15(5) to (8) and section 16 of the Police and Criminal Evidence Act 1984 (execution of search warrants and safeguards) apply to warrants issued under this section.

(7) In Northern Ireland, Articles 17(5) to (8) and 18 of the Police and Criminal Evidence (Northern Ireland) Order 1989 apply to warrants issued under this section.

(8) Any document of which possession is taken under this section may be retained—
(a) for a period of three months; or
(b) if within that period proceedings to which the document is relevant are commenced against any person for any criminal offence, until the conclusion of those proceedings.

(9) In the application of this section to Scotland—
(a) for the references to a justice of the peace substitute references to a justice of the peace or a sheriff; and
(b) for the references to information on oath substitute references to evidence on oath.

(10) "Investigator" means a person appointed under section 167 or 168(3) or (5).

(11) "Information requirement" means a requirement imposed—
(a) by the Authority under section [87C, 87J,] 165 or 175; or
(b) by an investigator under section 171, 172, 173 or 175.

NOTES

Sub-s (11): words in square brackets inserted by the Prospectus Regulations 2005, SI 2005/1433, reg 2(1), Sch 1, para 12.

Modification: sub-ss (1)–(9) above are modified in relation to open-ended investment companies by the Open-Ended Investment Companies Regulations 2001, SI 2001/1228, reg 30.

Offences

[144]

177 Offences

(1) If a person other than the investigator ("the defaulter") fails to comply with a requirement imposed on him under this Part the person imposing the requirement may certify that fact in writing to the court.

(2) If the court is satisfied that the defaulter failed without reasonable excuse to comply with the requirement, it may deal with the defaulter (and in the case of a body corporate, any director or officer) as if he were in contempt[; and "officer", in relation to a limited liability partnership, means a member of the limited liability partnership].

(3) A person who knows or suspects that an investigation is being or is likely to be conducted under this Part is guilty of an offence if—

(a) he falsifies, conceals, destroys or otherwise disposes of a document which he knows or suspects is or would be relevant to such an investigation, or

(b) he causes or permits the falsification, concealment, destruction or disposal of such a document,

unless he shows that he had no intention of concealing facts disclosed by the documents from the investigator.

(4) A person who, in purported compliance with a requirement imposed on him under this Part—

(a) provides information which he knows to be false or misleading in a material particular, or

(b) recklessly provides information which is false or misleading in a material particular,

is guilty of an offence.

(5) A person guilty of an offence under subsection (3) or (4) is liable—

(a) on summary conviction, to imprisonment for a term not exceeding six months or a fine not exceeding the statutory maximum, or both;

(b) on conviction on indictment, to imprisonment for a term not exceeding two years or a fine, or both.

(6) Any person who intentionally obstructs the exercise of any rights conferred by a warrant under section 176 is guilty of an offence and liable on summary conviction to imprisonment for a term not exceeding *three months* or a fine not exceeding level 5 on the standard scale, or both.

(7) "Court" means—

(a) the High Court;

(b) in Scotland, the Court of Session.

NOTES

Sub-s (2): words in square brackets inserted by the Limited Liability Partnerships Regulations 2001, SI 2001/1090, reg 9, Sch 5, para 21.

Sub-s (6): for the words in italics there are substituted the words "51 weeks" by the Criminal Justice Act 2003, s 280(2), (3), Sch 26, para 54(1), (2), as from a day to be appointed.

Open-ended investment companies: this section has effect as if the Open-Ended Investment Companies Regulations 2001, SI 2001/1228, reg 30 was contained in Pt XI (ss 165–177 and Sch 15) of this Act; see reg 30(6) of the 2001 Regulations.

PART XII
CONTROL OVER AUTHORISED PERSONS

[Notices of acquisitions of control over UK authorised persons

[145]

178 Obligation to notify the Authority: acquisitions of control

(1) A person who decides to acquire or increase control over a UK authorised person must give the Authority notice in writing before making the acquisition.

(2) For the purposes of calculations relating to this section, the holding of shares or voting power by a person ("A1") includes any shares or voting power held by another ("A2") if A1 and A2 are acting in concert.

(3) In this Part, a notice given under this section is a "section 178 notice" and a person giving notice is a "section 178 notice-giver".]

NOTES

Commencement: 21 March 2009.

Sections 178–191G were substituted (for the original ss 178–191) by the Financial Services and Markets Act 2000 (Controllers) Regulations 2009, SI 2009/534, reg 3, Sch 1, subject to transitional provisions in reg 8 thereof which provides that Part XII of this Act, as it stood immediately before 21 March 2009, applies in respect of any notification submitted to the FSA under those provisions before that date.

[146]

[179 Requirements for section 178 notices

(1) A section 178 notice must be in such form, include such information and be accompanied by such documents as the Authority may reasonably require.

(2) The Authority must publish a list of its requirements as to the form, information and accompanying documents for a section 178 notice.

(3) The Authority may impose different requirements for different cases and may vary or waive requirements in particular cases.]

NOTES

Commencement: 21 March 2009.

Substituted as noted to s 178 at [145].

[147]
[180 Acknowledgment of receipt
(1) The Authority must acknowledge receipt of a completed section 178 notice in writing before the end of the second working day following receipt.
(2) If the Authority receives an incomplete section 178 notice it must inform the section 178 notice-giver as soon as reasonably practicable.]

NOTES
Commencement: 21 March 2009.
Substituted as noted to s 178 at [145].

[Acquiring control and other changes of holding

[148]
181 Acquiring control
(1) For the purposes of this Part, a person ("A") acquires control over a UK authorised person ("B") if any of the cases in subsection (2) begin to apply.
(2) The cases are where A holds—
(a) 10% or more of the shares in B or in a parent undertaking of B ("P");
(b) 10% or more of the voting power in B or P; or
(c) shares or voting power in B or P as a result of which A is able to exercise significant influence over the management of B.]

NOTES
Commencement: 21 March 2009.
Substituted as noted to s 178 at [145].

[149]
[182 Increasing control
(1) For the purposes of this Part, a person ("A") increases control over a UK authorised person ("B") whenever—
(a) the percentage of shares which A holds in B or in a parent undertaking of B ("P") increases by any of the steps mentioned in subsection (2);
(b) the percentage of voting power A holds in B or P increases by any of the steps mentioned in subsection (2); or
(c) A becomes a parent undertaking of B.
(2) The steps are—
(a) from less than 20% to 20% or more;
(b) from less than 30% to 30% or more;
(c) from less than 50% to 50% or more.]

NOTES
Commencement: 21 March 2009.
Substituted as noted to s 178 at [145].

[150]
[183 Reducing or ceasing to have control
(1) For the purposes of this Part, a person ("A") reduces control over a UK authorised person ("B") whenever—
(a) the percentage of shares which A holds in B or in a parent undertaking of B ("P") decreases by any of the steps mentioned in subsection (2);
(b) the percentage of voting power which A holds in B or P decreases by any of the steps mentioned in subsection (2); or
(c) A ceases to be a parent undertaking of B.
(2) The steps are—
(a) from 50% or more to less than 50%;
(b) from 30% or more to less than 30%;
(c) from 20% or more to less than 20%.
(3) For the purposes of this Part, a person ("A") ceases to have control over a UK authorised person ("B") if A ceases to be in the position of holding—
(a) 10% or more of the shares in B or in a parent undertaking of B ("P");
(b) 10% or more of the voting power in B or P; or

(c) shares or voting power in B or P as a result of which A is able to exercise significant influence over the management of B.]

NOTES

Commencement: 21 March 2009.
Substituted as noted to s 178 at **[145]**.

[151]

[184 Disregarded holdings

(1) For the purposes of sections 181 to 183, shares and voting power that a person holds in a UK authorised person ("B") or in a parent undertaking of B ("P") are disregarded in the following circumstances.

(2) Shares held only for the purposes of clearing and settling within a short settlement cycle are disregarded.

(3) Shares held by a custodian or its nominee in a custodian capacity are disregarded, provided that the custodian or nominee is only able to exercise voting power represented by the shares in accordance with instructions given in writing.

(4) Shares representing no more than 5% of the total voting power in B or P held by an investment firm are disregarded, provided that it—

(a) holds the shares in the capacity of a market maker (as defined in article 4.1(8) of the markets in financial instruments directive);

(b) is authorised by its home state regulator under the markets in financial instruments directive; and

(c) neither intervenes in the management of B or P nor exerts any influence on B or P to buy the shares or back the share price.

(5) Shares held by a credit institution or investment firm in its trading book are disregarded, provided that—

(a) the shares represent no more than 5% of the total voting power in B or P; and

(b) the credit institution or investment firm ensures that the voting power is not used to intervene in the management of B or P.

(6) Shares held by a credit institution or an investment firm are disregarded, provided that—

(a) the shares are held as a result of performing the investment services and activities of—

(i) underwriting a share issue; or

(ii) placing shares on a firm commitment basis in accordance with Annex I, section A.6 of the markets in financial instruments directive; and

(b) the credit institution or investment firm—

(i) does not exercise voting power represented by the shares or otherwise intervene in the management of the issuer; and

(ii) retains the holding for a period of less than one year.

(7) Where a management company (as defined in Article 1a.2 of the UCITS directive) and its parent undertaking both hold shares or voting power, each may disregard holdings of the other, provided that each exercises its voting power independently of the other.

(8) But subsection (7) does not apply if the management company—

(a) manages holdings for its parent undertaking or an undertaking in respect of which the parent undertaking is a controller;

(b) has no discretion as to the exercise of the voting power attached to such holdings; and

(c) may only exercise the voting power in relation to such holdings under direct or indirect instruction from—

(i) the parent undertaking; or

(ii) an undertaking in respect of which of the parent undertaking is a controller.

(9) Where an investment firm and its parent undertaking both hold shares or voting power, the parent undertaking may disregard holdings managed by the investment firm on a client by client basis and the investment firm may disregard holdings of the parent undertaking, provided that the investment firm—

(a) has permission to provide portfolio management;

(b) exercises its voting power independently from the parent undertaking; and

(c) may only exercise the voting power under instructions given in writing, or has appropriate mechanisms in place for ensuring that individual portfolio management services are conducted independently of any other services.]

NOTES

Commencement: 21 March 2009.
Substituted as noted to s 178 at **[145]**.

[Assessment procedure

[152]
185 Assessment: general
(1) Where the Authority receives a section 178 notice, it must—
(a) determine whether to approve the acquisition to which it relates unconditionally; or
(b) propose to—
(i) approve the acquisition subject to conditions (see section 187); or
(ii) object to the acquisition.
(2) The Authority must—
(a) consider the suitability of the section 178 notice-giver and the financial soundness of the acquisition in order to ensure the sound and prudent management of the UK authorised person;
(b) have regard to the likely influence that the section 178 notice-giver will have on the UK authorised person; and
(c) disregard the economic needs of the market.
(3) The Authority may only object to an acquisition—
(a) if there are reasonable grounds for doing so on the basis of the matters set out in section 186; or
(b) if the information provided by the section 178 notice-giver is incomplete.]

NOTES
Commencement: 21 March 2009.
Substituted as noted to s 178 at **[145]**.

[153]
[186 Assessment criteria
The matters specified in section 185(3)(a) are—
(a) the reputation of the section 178 notice-giver;
(b) the reputation and experience of any person who will direct the business of the UK authorised person as a result of the proposed acquisition;
(c) the financial soundness of the section 178 notice-giver, in particular in relation to the type of business that the UK authorised person pursues or envisages pursuing;
(d) whether the UK authorised person will be able to comply with its prudential requirements (including the threshold conditions in relation to all of the regulated activities for which it has or will have permission);
(e) if the UK authorised person is to become part of a group as a result of the acquisition, whether that group has a structure which makes it possible to—
(i) exercise effective supervision;
(ii) exchange information among regulators; and
(iii) determine the allocation of responsibility among regulators; and
(f) whether there are reasonable grounds to suspect that in connection with the proposed acquisition—
(i) money laundering or terrorist financing (within the meaning of Article 1 of Directive 2005/60/EC of the European Parliament and of the Council of 26th October 2005 on the prevention of the use of the financial system for the purpose of money laundering and terrorist financing) is being or has been committed or attempted; or
(ii) the risk of such activity could increase.]

NOTES
Commencement: 21 March 2009.
Substituted as noted to s 178 at **[145]**.

[154]
[187 Approval with conditions
(1) The Authority may impose conditions on its approval of an acquisition.
(2) The Authority may only impose conditions where, if it did not impose those conditions, it would propose to object to the acquisition.
(3) The Authority may not impose conditions requiring a particular level of holding to be acquired.
(4) The Authority may vary or cancel the conditions.]

NOTES
Commencement: 21 March 2009.

Part I FSMA Legislation

Substituted as noted to s 178 at **[145]**.

[155]

[188 Assessment: consultation with EC competent authorities

(1) The Authority must consult any appropriate home state regulator before making a determination under section 185 and, in doing so, must comply with such requirements as to consultation as may be prescribed.

(2) Where the Authority makes a determination under section 185, it must indicate any views or reservations received from any home state regulator it consults in accordance with subsection (1).

(3) The Authority must cooperate with any equivalent consultation by a host state regulator in relation to a UK authorised person.

(4) In order to comply with an obligation under subsection (1) or (3), the Authority must provide the regulator with—

(a) any relevant information that it requests; and

(b) any information that the Authority considers that it needs.]

NOTES

Commencement: 21 March 2009.

Substituted as noted to s 178 at **[145]**.

Regulations: the Financial Services and Markets Act 2000 (Consultation with Competent Authorities) Regulations 2001, SI 2001/2509; the Financial Conglomerates and Other Financial Groups Regulations 2004, SI 2004/1862. Note that these Regulations were originally made under ss 183 and 188 of this Act (prior to the substitution of those sections as noted above). These Regulations now have effect under this section and s 191A post. Note also that the following amending Regulations were also made under the original ss 183, 188, ie, the Collective Investment Schemes (Miscellaneous Amendments) Regulations 2003, SI 2003/2066; the Financial Services and Markets Act 2000 (Reinsurance Directive) Regulations 2007, SI 2007/3255.

[156]

[189 Assessment: Procedure

(1) The Authority must act under section 185 within a period of 60 working days beginning with the day on which the Authority acknowledges receipt of the section 178 notice ("the assessment period").

(2) The assessment period may be interrupted, no more than once, in accordance with section 190.

(3) The Authority must inform the section 178 notice-giver in writing of—

(a) the duration of the assessment period;

(b) its expiry date; and

(c) any change to the expiry date by virtue of section 190.

(4) The Authority must, within two working days of acting under section 185 (and in any event no later than the expiry date of the assessment period)—

(a) notify the section 178 notice-giver that it has determined to approve the acquisition unconditionally; or

(b) give a warning notice stating that it proposes to—

(i) approve the acquisition subject to conditions; or

(ii) object to the acquisition.

(5) Where the Authority gives a warning notice stating that it proposes to approve the acquisition subject to conditions—

(a) it must, in the warning notice, specify those conditions; and

(b) the conditions take effect as interim conditions.

(6) The Authority is treated as having approved the acquisition if, at the expiry of the assessment period, it has neither—

(a) given notice under subsection (4); nor

(b) informed the section 178 notice-giver that the section 178 notice is incomplete.

(7) If the Authority decides to approve an acquisition subject to conditions or to object to an acquisition it must give the section 178 notice-giver a decision notice.

(8) Following receipt of a decision notice under this section, the section 178 notice-giver may refer the Authority's decision to the Tribunal.]

NOTES

Commencement: 21 March 2009.

Substituted as noted to s 178 at **[145]**.

[157]

[190 Requests for further information

(1) The Authority may, no later than the 50th working day of the assessment period, in writing ask the section 178 notice-giver to provide any further information necessary to complete its assessment.

(2) On the first occasion that the Authority asks for further information, the assessment period is interrupted from the date of the request until the date the Authority receives the requested information ("the interruption period").

(3) But the interruption period may not exceed 20 working days, unless subsection (4) applies.

(4) The interruption period may not exceed 30 working days if the notice-giver—

- (a) is situated or regulated outside the European Community; or
- (b) is not subject to supervision under—
  - (i) the UCITS directive;
  - (ii) the insurance directives;
  - (iii) the markets in financial instruments directive;
  - (iv) the reinsurance directive; or
  - (v) the banking consolidation directive.

(5) The Authority may make further requests for information (but a further request does not result in a further interruption of the assessment period).

(6) The Authority must acknowledge in writing receipt of further information before the end of the second working day following receipt.]

NOTES

Commencement: 21 March 2009.
Substituted as noted to s 178 at **[145]**.

[158]

[191 Duration of approval

(1) Approval of an acquisition (whether granted unconditionally or subject to conditions) is effective for such period as the Authority may specify in writing.

(2) Where the Authority has specified a period under subsection (1), it may extend the period.

(3) Where the Authority has not specified a period, the approval is effective for one year beginning with the date—

- (a) of the notice given under section 189(4)(a) or (b)(i);
- (b) on which the Authority is treated as having given approval under section 189(6); or
- (c) of a decision on a reference to the Tribunal which results in the person receiving approval.]

NOTES

Commencement: 21 March 2009.
Substituted as noted to s 178 at **[145]**.

[Enforcement procedures

[158A]

191A Objection by the Authority

(1) The Authority may object to a person's control over a UK authorised person in any of the circumstances specified in subsection (2).

(2) The circumstances are that the Authority reasonably believes that—

- (a) the person acquired or increased control without giving notice under section 178(1) in circumstances where notice was required;
- (b) the person is in breach of a condition imposed under section 187; or
- (c) there are grounds for objecting to control on the basis of the matters in section 186.

(3) The Authority—

- (a) must take into account whether influence exercised by the person is likely to operate to the detriment of the sound and prudent management of the UK authorised person; and
- (b) may take into account whether the person has co-operated with any information requests made or requirements imposed by the Authority.

(4) If the Authority proposes to object to a person's control over a UK authorised person, it must give that person a warning notice.

(5) The Authority must consult any appropriate home state regulator before giving a warning notice under this section and, in doing so, must comply with such requirements as to consultation as may be prescribed.

(6) If the Authority decides to object to a person's control over a UK authorised person, it must give that person a decision notice.
(7) A person to whom the Authority gives a decision notice under this section may refer the matter to the Tribunal.]

NOTES
Commencement: 21 March 2009.
Substituted as noted to s 178 at **[145]**.
Regulations: see the note to s 188 at **[155]**.

[158B]
[191B Restriction notices
(1) The Authority may give notice in writing (a "restriction notice") to a person in the following circumstances.
(2) The circumstances are that—
(a) the person has control over a UK authorised person by virtue of holding shares or voting power; and
(b) in relation to the shares or voting power, the Authority has given the person a warning notice or a decision notice under section 189 or 191A or a final notice which confirms a decision notice given under section 189 or 191A.
(3) In a restriction notice, the Authority may direct that shares or voting power to which the notice relates are, until further notice, subject to one or more of the following restrictions—
(a) except by court order, an agreement to transfer or a transfer of any such shares or voting power or, in the case of unissued shares, any agreement to transfer or transfer of the right to be issued with them, is void;
(b) no voting power is to be exercisable;
(c) no further shares are to be issued in pursuance of any right of the holder of any such shares or voting power or in pursuance of any offer made to their holder;
(d) except in a liquidation, no payment is to be made of any sums due from the body corporate on any such shares, whether in respect of capital or otherwise.
(4) A restriction notice takes effect—
(a) immediately; or
(b) on such date as may be specified in the notice.
(5) A restriction notice does not extinguish rights which would be enjoyable but for the notice.
(6) A copy of the restriction notice must be served on—
(a) the UK authorised person in question; and
(b) in the case of shares or voting power held in a parent undertaking of a UK authorised person, the parent undertaking.
(7) A person to whom the Authority gives a restriction notice may refer the matter to the Tribunal.]

NOTES
Commencement: 21 March 2009.
Substituted as noted to s 178 at **[145]**.

[158C]
[191C Orders for sale of shares
(1) The court may, on the application of the Authority, order the sale of shares or the disposition of voting power in the following circumstances.
(2) The circumstances are that—
(a) a person has control over a UK authorised person by virtue of holding the shares or voting power; and
(b) the acquisition or continued holding of the shares or voting power by that person is in contravention of a final notice which confirms a decision notice given under section 189 or section 191A.
(3) Where the court orders the sale of shares or disposition of voting power it may—
(a) if a restriction notice has been given in relation to the shares or voting power, order that the restrictions cease to apply; and
(b) make any further order.
(4) Where the court makes an order under this section, it must take into account the level of holding that the person would have been entitled to acquire, or to continue to hold, without contravening the final notice.

(5) If shares are sold or voting power disposed of in pursuance of an order under this section, any proceeds, less the costs of the sale or disposition, must be paid into court for the benefit of the persons beneficially interested in them; and any such person may apply to the court for payment of a whole or part of the proceeds.
(6) The jurisdiction conferred by this section may be exercised by the High Court and the Court of Session.]

NOTES

Commencement: 21 March 2009.
Substituted as noted to s 178 at **[145]**.

[Notice of reductions of control of UK authorised persons

[158D]
191D Obligation to notify the Authority: dispositions of control

(1) A person who decides to reduce or cease to have control over a UK authorised person must give the Authority notice in writing before making the disposition.
(2) For the purposes of calculations relating to this section, the holding of shares or voting power by a person ("A1") includes any shares or voting power held by another ("A2") if A1 and A2 are acting in concert.]

NOTES

Commencement: 21 March 2009.
Substituted as noted to s 178 at **[145]**.

[158E]
[191E Requirements for notices under section 191D

(1) A notice under section 191D must be in such form, include such information and be accompanied by such documents as the Authority may reasonably require.
(2) The Authority must publish a list of its requirements as to the form, information and accompanying documents for a notice under section 191D.
(3) The Authority may impose different requirements for different cases and may vary or waive requirements in particular cases.]

NOTES

Commencement: 21 March 2009.
Substituted as noted to s 178 at **[145]**.

[Offences

[158F]
191F Offences under this Part

(1) A person who fails to comply with an obligation to notify the Authority under section 178(1) or 191D(1) is guilty of an offence.
(2) A person who gives notice to the Authority under section 178(1) and makes the acquisition to which the notice relates before the expiry date of the assessment period is guilty of an offence unless the Authority has approved the acquisition or given a warning notice under section 189(4)(b)(i).
(3) A person who contravenes an interim condition in a warning notice given under section 189(4)(b)(i) or a condition in a decision notice given under section 189(7) or a final notice which confirms a decision notice under that section is guilty of an offence.
(4) A person who makes an acquisition in contravention of a warning notice given under section 189(4)(b)(ii) or a decision notice given under section 189(7) or a final notice which confirms a decision notice under that section is guilty of an offence.
(5) A person who makes an acquisition after the Authority's approval for the acquisition has ceased to be effective by virtue of section 191 is guilty of an offence.
(6) A person who provides information to the Authority which is false in a material particular is guilty of an offence.
(7) A person who breaches a direction contained in a restriction notice given under section 191B is guilty of an offence.
(8) A person guilty of an offence under subsection (1) to (3) or (5) to (7) is liable—
- (a) on summary conviction to a fine not exceeding the statutory maximum; or
- (b) on conviction on indictment, to a fine.

(9) A person guilty of an offence under subsection (4) is liable—
- (a) on summary conviction, to a fine not exceeding the statutory maximum; or

(b) on conviction on indictment, to imprisonment for a term not exceeding two years or a fine, or both.]

NOTES

Commencement: 21 March 2009.

Substituted as noted to s 178 at **[145]**.

[Interpretation

[158G]

191G Interpretation

(1) In this Part—

"acquisition" means the acquisition of control or of an increase in control over a UK authorised person;

"credit institution" means—

(a) a credit institution authorised under the banking consolidation directive; or

(b) an institution which would satisfy the requirements for authorisation as a credit institution under that directive if it had its registered office (or if it does not have a registered office, its head office) in an EEA State;

"shares" has the same meaning as in section 422;

"UK authorised person" means an authorised person who—

(a) is a body incorporated in, or an unincorporated association formed under the law of, any part of the United Kingdom; and

(b) is not a person authorised as a result of paragraph 1 of Schedule 5; and

"voting power" has the same meaning as in section 422.

(2) For the purposes of this Part, a "working day" is a day other than—

(a) a Saturday or a Sunday; or

(b) a day which is a bank holiday in England and Wales under the Banking and Financial Dealings Act 1971.]

NOTES

Commencement: 21 March 2009.

Substituted as noted to s 178 at **[145]**.

Miscellaneous

[159]

192 Power to change definitions of control etc

The Treasury may by order—

(a) provide for exemptions from the obligations to notify imposed by sections 178 and [191D];

(b) amend section [181] by varying, or removing, any of the cases in which a person is treated as [acquiring] control over a UK authorised person or by adding a case;

(c) amend section [182] by varying, or removing, any of the cases in which a person is treated as increasing control over a UK authorised person or by adding a case;

(d) amend section [183] by varying, or removing, any of the cases in which a person is treated as [reducing or ceasing to have] control over a UK authorised person or by adding a case;

(e) amend section 422 by varying, or removing, any of the cases in which a person is treated as being a controller of a person or by adding a case.

NOTES

Words and figures in square brackets substituted by the Financial Services and Markets Act 2000 (Controllers) Regulations 2009, SI 2009/534, reg 4.

Orders: the Financial Services and Markets Act 2000 (Controllers) (Exemption) Order 2009, SI 2009/774 at **[1026]**.

PART XIII
INCOMING FIRMS: INTERVENTION BY AUTHORITY

Interpretation

[160]

193 Interpretation of this Part

(1) In this Part—

"additional procedure" means the procedure described in section 199;

"incoming firm" means—
(a) an EEA firm which is exercising, or has exercised, its right to carry on a regulated activity in the United Kingdom in accordance with Schedule 3; or
(b) a Treaty firm which is exercising, or has exercised, its right to carry on a regulated activity in the United Kingdom in accordance with Schedule 4; and

"power of intervention" means the power conferred on the Authority by section 196.

(2) In relation to an incoming firm which is an EEA firm, expressions used in this Part and in Schedule 3 have the same meaning in this Part as they have in that Schedule.

[161]
194 General grounds on which power of intervention is exercisable
(1) The Authority may exercise its power of intervention in respect of an incoming firm if it appears to it that—
(a) the firm has contravened, or is likely to contravene, a requirement which is imposed on it by or under this Act (in a case where the Authority is responsible for enforcing compliance in the United Kingdom);
(b) the firm has, in purported compliance with any requirement imposed by or under this Act, knowingly or recklessly given the Authority information which is false or misleading in a material particular; or
(c) it is desirable to exercise the power in order to protect the interests of actual or potential customers.

(2) Subsection (3) applies to an incoming EEA firm falling within sub-paragraph (a) or (b) of paragraph 5 of Schedule 3 which is exercising an EEA right to carry on any Consumer Credit Act business in the United Kingdom.
(3) The Authority may exercise its power of intervention in respect of the firm if [the Office of Fair Trading] has informed the Authority that—
(a) the firm,
(b) any of the firm's employees, agents or associates (whether past or present), or
(c) if the firm is a body corporate, a controller of the firm or an associate of such a controller,

has done any of the things specified in paragraphs [(a) to (e) of section 25(2A)] of the Consumer Credit Act 1974.
(4) "Associate", "Consumer Credit Act business" and "controller" have the same meaning as in section 203.

NOTES
Sub-s (3): words in first pair of square brackets substituted by the Enterprise Act 2002, s 278(1), Sch 25, para 40(1), (6); words in second pair of square brackets substituted by the Consumer Credit Act 2006, s 33(7).

194A *(Outside the scope of this work.)*

[162]
195 Exercise of power in support of overseas regulator
(1) The Authority may exercise its power of intervention in respect of an incoming firm at the request of, or for the purpose of assisting, an overseas regulator.
(2) Subsection (1) applies whether or not the Authority's power of intervention is also exercisable as a result of section 194.
(3) "An overseas regulator" means an authority in a country or territory outside the United Kingdom—
(a) which is a home state regulator; or
(b) which exercises any function of a kind mentioned in subsection (4).

(4) The functions are—
(a) a function corresponding to any function of the Authority under this Act;
(b) a function corresponding to any function exercised by the competent authority under Part VI . . . ;
(c) a function corresponding to any function exercised by the Secretary of State under [the Companies Acts (as defined in section 2 of the Companies Act 2006)];
(d) a function in connection with—
 (i) the investigation of conduct of the kind prohibited by Part V of the Criminal *Justice Act 1993* (insider dealing); or
 (ii) the enforcement of rules (whether or not having the force of law) relating to such conduct;
(e) a function prescribed by regulations made for the purposes of this subsection which, in the opinion of the Treasury, relates to companies or financial services.

(5) If—

(a) a request to the Authority for the exercise of its power of intervention has been made by a home state regulator in pursuance of a Community obligation, or

(b) a home state regulator has notified the Authority that an EEA firm's EEA authorisation has been withdrawn,

the Authority must, in deciding whether or not to exercise its power of intervention, consider whether exercising it is necessary in order to comply with a Community obligation.

(6) In deciding in any case in which the Authority does not consider that the exercise of its power of intervention is necessary in order to comply with a Community obligation, it may take into account in particular—

(a) whether in the country or territory of the overseas regulator concerned, corresponding assistance would be given to a United Kingdom regulatory authority;

(b) whether the case concerns the breach of a law, or other requirement, which has no close parallel in the United Kingdom or involves the assertion of a jurisdiction not recognised by the United Kingdom;

(c) the seriousness of the case and its importance to persons in the United Kingdom;

(d) whether it is otherwise appropriate in the public interest to give the assistance sought.

(7) The Authority may decide not to exercise its power of intervention, in response to a request, unless the regulator concerned undertakes to make such contribution to the cost of its exercise as the Authority considers appropriate.

(8) Subsection (7) does not apply if the Authority decides that it is necessary for it to exercise its power of intervention in order to comply with a Community obligation.

NOTES

Sub-s (4): words omitted from para (b) repealed by the Prospectus Regulations 2005, SI 2005/1433, reg 2(1), Sch 1, para 13; words in square brackets in para (c) substituted by the Companies Act 2006 (Commencement No 3, Consequential Amendments, Transitional Provisions and Savings) Order 2007, SI 2007/2194, art 10(1), (2), Sch 4, Pt 3, para 92, subject to savings in art 12 thereof.

195A *(Outside the scope of this work.)*

[163]

196 The power of intervention

If the Authority is entitled to exercise its power of intervention in respect of an incoming firm under this Part, it may impose any requirement in relation to the firm which it could impose if—

(a) the firm's permission was a Part IV permission; and

(b) the Authority was entitled to exercise its power under that Part to vary that permission.

Exercise of power of intervention

[164]

197 Procedure on exercise of power of intervention

(1) A requirement takes effect—

(a) immediately, if the notice given under subsection (3) states that that is the case;

(b) on such date as may be specified in the notice; or

(c) if no date is specified in the notice, when the matter to which it relates is no longer open to review.

(2) A requirement may be expressed to take effect immediately (or on a specified date) only if the Authority, having regard to the ground on which it is exercising its power of intervention, considers that it is necessary for the requirement to take effect immediately (or on that date).

(3) If the Authority proposes to impose a requirement under section 196 on an incoming firm, or imposes such a requirement with immediate effect, it must give the firm written notice.

(4) The notice must—

(a) give details of the requirement;

(b) inform the firm of when the requirement takes effect;

(c) state the Authority's reasons for imposing the requirement and for its determination as to when the requirement takes effect;

(d) inform the firm that it may make representations to the Authority within such period as may be specified in the notice (whether or not it has referred the matter to the Tribunal); and

(e) inform it of its right to refer the matter to the Tribunal.

(5) The Authority may extend the period allowed under the notice for making representations.

(6) If, having considered any representations made by the firm, the Authority decides—

(a) to impose the requirement proposed, or

(b) if it has been imposed, not to rescind the requirement,

it must give it written notice.
(7) If, having considered any representations made by the firm, the Authority decides—
(a) not to impose the requirement proposed,
(b) to impose a different requirement from that proposed, or
(c) to rescind a requirement which has effect,
it must give it written notice.
(8) A notice given under subsection (6) must inform the firm of its right to refer the matter to the Tribunal.
(9) A notice under subsection (7)(b) must comply with subsection (4).
(10) If a notice informs a person of his right to refer a matter to the Tribunal, it must give an indication of the procedure on such a reference.

[165]
198 Power to apply to court for injunction in respect of certain overseas insurance companies
(1) This section applies if the Authority has received a request made in respect of an incoming EEA firm in accordance with—
(a) Article 20.5 of the first non-life insurance directive; . . .
[(b) Article 37.5 of the life assurance consolidation directive][; or
(c) Article 42.4 of the reinsurance directive].
(2) The court may, on an application made to it by the Authority with respect to the firm, grant an injunction restraining (or in Scotland an interdict prohibiting) the firm disposing of or otherwise dealing with any of its assets.
(3) If the court grants an injunction, it may by subsequent orders make provision for such incidental, consequential and supplementary matters as it considers necessary to enable the Authority to perform any of its functions under this Act.
(4) "The court" means—
(a) the High Court; or
(b) in Scotland, the Court of Session.

NOTES
Sub-s (1): word omitted from para (a) repealed and para (c), together with word preceding it, inserted by the Reinsurance Directive Regulations 2007, SI 2007/3253, reg 2(1), Sch 1, paras 1, 3; para (b) substituted by the Life Assurance Consolidation Directive (Consequential Amendments) Regulations 2004, SI 2004/3379, reg 6(1), (3).

[166]
199 Additional procedure for EEA firms in certain cases
(1) This section applies if it appears to the Authority that its power of intervention is exercisable in relation to an EEA firm exercising EEA rights in the United Kingdom ("an incoming EEA firm") in respect of the contravention of a relevant requirement.
(2) A requirement is relevant if—
(a) it is imposed by the Authority under this Act; and
[(b) as respects its contravention, the single market directive in question provides that a procedure of the kind set out in the following provisions of this section (so far as they are relevant in the firm's case) is to apply.]
(3) The Authority must, in writing, require the firm to remedy the situation.
[(3A) If the firm falls within paragraph 5(da) of Schedule 3, the Authority must at the same time as it gives notice to the firm under subsection (3) refer its findings to the firm's home state regulator.
(3B) Subsections (4) to (8) apply to an incoming EEA firm other than a firm falling within paragraph 5(da) of Schedule 3.]
(4) If the firm fails to comply with the requirement under subsection (3) within a reasonable time, the Authority must give a notice to that effect to the firm's home state regulator requesting it—
(a) to take all appropriate measures for the purpose of ensuring that the firm remedies the situation which has given rise to the notice; and
(b) to inform the Authority of the measures it proposes to take or has taken or the reasons for not taking such measures.
(5) Except as mentioned in subsection (6), the Authority may not exercise its power of intervention [before informing the firm's home state regulator and] unless satisfied—
(a) that the firm's home state regulator has failed or refused to take measures for the purpose mentioned in subsection (4)(a); or
(b) that the measures taken by the home state regulator have proved inadequate for that purpose.

(6) If the Authority decides that it should exercise its power of intervention in respect of the incoming EEA firm as a matter of urgency in order to protect the interests of consumers, it may exercise that power—

(a) before complying with subsections (3) and (4); or

(b) where it has complied with those subsections, before it is satisfied as mentioned in subsection (5).

(7) In such a case the Authority must at the earliest opportunity inform the firm's home state regulator and the Commission.

(8) If—

(a) the Authority has (by virtue of subsection (6)) exercised its power of intervention before complying with subsections (3) and (4) or before it is satisfied as mentioned in subsection (5), and

(b) the Commission decides under any of the single market directives [(other than the markets in financial instruments directive)] that the Authority must rescind or vary any requirement imposed in the exercise of its power of intervention,

the Authority must in accordance with the decision rescind or vary the requirement.

[(9) In the case of a firm falling within paragraph 5(da) of Schedule 3, the Authority may not exercise its power of intervention before informing the firm's home state regulator and unless satisfied—

(a) that the firm's home state regulator has failed or refused to take all appropriate measures for the purpose of ensuring that the firm remedies the situation which gave rise to the notice under subsection (3); or

(b) that the measures taken by the home state regulator have proved inadequate for that purpose.]

NOTES

Sub-s (2): para (b) substituted by the Reinsurance Directive Regulations 2007, SI 2007/3253, reg 2(1), Sch 1, paras 1, 4(a).

Sub-ss (3A), (3B): inserted by SI 2007/3253, reg 2(1), Sch 1, paras 1, 4(b).

Sub-s (5): words in square brackets inserted by SI 2007/3253, reg 2(1), Sch 1, paras 1, 4(c).

Sub-s (8): words in square brackets in para (b) inserted by the Financial Services and Markets Act 2000 (Markets in Financial Instruments) Regulations 2007, SI 2007/126, reg 3(1), Sch 1, paras 1, 4.

Sub-s (9): added by SI 2007/3253, reg 2(1), Sch 1, paras 1, 4(d).

Supplemental

[167]

200 Rescission and variation of requirements

(1) The Authority may rescind or vary a requirement imposed in exercise of its power of intervention on its own initiative or on the application of the person subject to the requirement.

(2) The power of the Authority on its own initiative to rescind a requirement is exercisable by written notice given by the Authority to the person concerned, which takes effect on the date specified in the notice.

(3) Section 197 applies to the exercise of the power of the Authority on its own initiative to vary a requirement as it applies to the imposition of a requirement.

(4) If the Authority proposes to refuse an application for the variation or rescission of a requirement, it must give the applicant a warning notice.

(5) If the Authority decides to refuse an application for the variation or rescission of a requirement—

(a) the Authority must give the applicant a decision notice; and

(b) that person may refer the matter to the Tribunal.

[168]

201 Effect of certain requirements on other persons

If the Authority, in exercising its power of intervention, imposes on an incoming firm a requirement of a kind mentioned in subsection (3) of section 48, the requirement has the same effect in relation to the firm as it would have in relation to an authorised person if it had been imposed on the authorised person by the Authority acting under section 45.

[169]

202 Contravention of requirement imposed under this Part

(1) Contravention of a requirement imposed by the Authority under this Part does not—

(a) make a person guilty of an offence;

(b) make any transaction void or unenforceable; or

(c) (subject to subsection (2)) give rise to any right of action for breach of statutory duty.

(2) In prescribed cases the contravention is actionable at the suit of a person who suffers loss as a result of the contravention, subject to the defences and other incidents applying to actions for breach of statutory duty.

NOTES

Regulations: the Financial Services and Markets Act 2000 (Rights of Action) Regulations 2001, SI 2001/2256 at **[618]**.

Powers of [Office of Fair Trading]

NOTES

Cross-heading: words in square brackets substituted by the Enterprise Act 2002, s 278(1), Sch 25, para 40(1), (7).

[170]

203 Power to prohibit the carrying on of Consumer Credit Act business

(1) If it appears to [the Office of Fair Trading ("the OFT")] that subsection (4) has been, or is likely to be, contravened as respects a consumer credit EEA firm, [it] may by written notice given to the firm impose on the firm a consumer credit prohibition.

(2) If it appears to the [OFT] that a restriction imposed under section 204 on an EEA consumer credit firm has not been complied with, [it] may by written notice given to the firm impose a consumer credit prohibition.

(3) "Consumer credit prohibition" means a prohibition on carrying on, or purporting to carry on, in the United Kingdom any Consumer Credit Act business which consists of or includes carrying on one or more listed activities.

(4) This subsection is contravened as respects a firm if—

(a) the firm or any of its employees, agents or associates (whether past or present), or

(b) if the firm is a body corporate, any controller of the firm or an associate of any such controller,

does any of the things specified in paragraphs [(a) to (e) of section 25(2A)] of the Consumer Credit Act 1974.

(5) A consumer credit prohibition may be absolute or may be imposed—

(a) for such period,

(b) until the occurrence of such event, or

(c) until such conditions are complied with,

as may be specified in the notice given under subsection (1) or (2).

(6) Any period, event or condition so specified may be varied by the [OFT] on the application of the firm concerned.

(7) A consumer credit prohibition may be withdrawn by written notice served by the [OFT] on the firm concerned, and any such notice takes effect on such date as is specified in the notice.

(8) Schedule 16 has effect as respects consumer credit prohibitions and restrictions under section 204.

(9) A firm contravening a prohibition under this section is guilty of an offence and liable—

(a) on summary conviction, to a fine not exceeding the statutory maximum;

(b) on conviction on indictment, to a fine.

(10) In this section and section 204—

"a consumer credit EEA firm" means an EEA firm falling within any of paragraphs (a) to (c) of paragraph 5 of Schedule 3 whose EEA authorisation covers any Consumer Credit Act business;

"Consumer Credit Act business" means consumer credit business, consumer hire business or ancillary credit business;

"consumer credit business", "consumer hire business" and "ancillary credit business" have the same meaning as in the Consumer Credit Act 1974;

"listed activity" means an activity listed in [Annex 1 to the banking consolidation directive] or the Annex to the investment services directive;

"associate" has the same meaning as in section [25(2A)] of the Consumer Credit Act 1974;

"controller" has the meaning given by section 189(1) of that Act.

NOTES

Sub-ss (1), (2): words in square brackets substituted by the Enterprise Act 2002, s 278(1), Sch 25, para 40(1), (7).

Sub-s (4): words in square brackets substituted by the Consumer Credit Act 2006, s 33(7).

Sub-ss (6), (7): words in square brackets substituted by the Enterprise Act 2002, s 278(1), Sch 25, para 40(1), (7).

Sub-s (10): words in square brackets in definition "listed activity" substituted by the Banking Consolidation Directive (Consequential Amendments) Regulations 2000, SI 2000/2952, reg 8(1), (2); number in square brackets in definition "associate" substituted by the Consumer Credit Act 2006, s 33(8).

Application: this section and s 204 are applied in relation to EEA authorised payment institutions exercising passport rights in the United Kingdom under the Payment Services Regulations 2009, SI 2009/209, by SI 2009/209, reg 26(1), (3).

[171]
204 Power to restrict the carrying on of Consumer Credit Act business

(1) In this section "restriction" means a direction that a consumer credit EEA firm may not carry on in the United Kingdom, otherwise than in accordance with such condition or conditions as may be specified in the direction, any Consumer Credit Act business which—

(a) consists of or includes carrying on any listed activity; and

(b) is specified in the direction.

(2) If it appears to the [OFT] that the situation as respects a consumer credit EEA firm is such that the powers conferred by section 203(1) are exercisable, the [OFT] may, instead of imposing a prohibition, impose such restriction as appears to [it] desirable.

(3) A restriction—

(a) may be withdrawn, or

(b) may be varied with the agreement of the firm concerned,

by written notice served by the [OFT] on the firm, and any such notice takes effect on such date as is specified in the notice.

(4) A firm contravening a restriction is guilty of an offence and liable—

(a) on summary conviction, to a fine not exceeding the statutory maximum;

(b) on conviction on indictment, to a fine.

NOTES

Sub-ss (2), (3): words in square brackets substituted by the Enterprise Act 2002, s 278(1), Sch 25, para 40(1), (8).

Application: see the note to s 203 at **[170]**.

PART XIV
DISCIPLINARY MEASURES

[172]
205 Public censure

If the Authority considers that an authorised person has contravened a requirement imposed on him by or under this Act, [or by any directly applicable Community regulation made under the markets in financial instruments directive,] the Authority may publish a statement to that effect.

NOTES

Words in square brackets inserted by the Financial Services and Markets Act 2000 (Markets in Financial Instruments) Regulations 2007, SI 2007/126, reg 3(5), Sch 5, paras 1, 10.

[173]
206 Financial penalties

(1) If the Authority considers that an authorised person has contravened a requirement imposed on him by or under this Act, [or by any directly applicable Community regulation made under the markets in financial instruments directive,] it may impose on him a penalty, in respect of the contravention, of such amount as it considers appropriate.

(2) The Authority may not in respect of any contravention both require a person to pay a penalty under this section and withdraw his authorisation under section 33.

(3) A penalty under this section is payable to the Authority.

NOTES

Sub-s (1): words in square brackets inserted by the Financial Services and Markets Act 2000 (Markets in Financial Instruments) Regulations 2007, SI 2007/126, reg 3(5), Sch 5, paras 1, 11.

[174]
207 Proposal to take disciplinary measures

(1) If the Authority proposes—

(a) to publish a statement in respect of an authorised person (under section 205), or

(b) to impose a penalty on an authorised person (under section 206), it must give the authorised person a warning notice.

(2) A warning notice about a proposal to publish a statement must set out the terms of the statement.

(3) A warning notice about a proposal to impose a penalty, must state the amount of the penalty.

[175]
208 Decision notice
(1) If the Authority decides—
(a) to publish a statement under section 205 (whether or not in the terms proposed), or
(b) to impose a penalty under section 206 (whether or not of the amount proposed),
it must without delay give the authorised person concerned a decision notice.
(2) In the case of a statement, the decision notice must set out the terms of the statement.
(3) In the case of a penalty, the decision notice must state the amount of the penalty.
(4) If the Authority decides to—
(a) publish a statement in respect of an authorised person under section 205, or
(b) impose a penalty on an authorised person under section 206,
the authorised person may refer the matter to the Tribunal.

[176]
209 Publication
After a statement under section 205 is published, the Authority must send a copy of it to the authorised person and to any person on whom a copy of the decision notice was given under section 393(4).

[177]
210 Statements of policy
(1) The Authority must prepare and issue a statement of its policy with respect to—
(a) the imposition of penalties under this Part; and
(b) the amount of penalties under this Part.
(2) The Authority's policy in determining what the amount of a penalty should be must include having regard to—
(a) the seriousness of the contravention in question in relation to the nature of the requirement contravened;
(b) the extent to which that contravention was deliberate or reckless; and
(c) whether the person on whom the penalty is to be imposed is an individual.
(3) The Authority may at any time alter or replace a statement issued under this section.
(4) If a statement issued under this section is altered or replaced, the Authority must issue the altered or replacement statement.
(5) The Authority must, without delay, give the Treasury a copy of any statement which it publishes under this section.
(6) A statement issued under this section must be published by the Authority in the way appearing to the Authority to be best calculated to bring it to the attention of the public.
(7) In exercising, or deciding whether to exercise, its power under section 206 in the case of any particular contravention, the Authority must have regard to any statement published under this section and in force at the time when the contravention in question occurred.
(8) The Authority may charge a reasonable fee for providing a person with a copy of the statement.

NOTES
Application: this section and s 211 are applied in relation to the imposition of penalties under the Regulated Covered Bonds Regulations 2008, SI 2008/346, by SI 2008/346, reg 36.
Modification: this section and s 211 are applied with modifications in respect of the Financial Services Authority's functions under the Cross-Border Payments in Euro Regulations 2010, SI 2010/89, by SI 2010/89, reg 19, Schedule, Pt 1, para 3.

---

[178]
211 Statements of policy: procedure
(1) Before issuing a statement under section 210, the Authority must publish a draft of the proposed statement in the way appearing to the Authority to be best calculated to bring it to the attention of the public.
(2) The draft must be accompanied by notice that representations about the proposal may be made to the Authority within a specified time.
(3) Before issuing the proposed statement, the Authority must have regard to any representations made to it in accordance with subsection (2).
(4) If the Authority issues the proposed statement it must publish an account, in general terms, of—
(a) the representations made to it in accordance with subsection (2); and
(b) its response to them.

(5) If the statement differs from the draft published under subsection (1) in a way which is, in the opinion of the Authority, significant, the Authority must (in addition to complying with subsection (4)) publish details of the difference.
(6) The Authority may charge a reasonable fee for providing a person with a copy of a draft published under subsection (1).
(7) This section also applies to a proposal to alter or replace a statement.

NOTES

Application: see the note to s 210 at **[177]**.
Modification: see the note to s 210 at **[177]**.

PART XV
THE FINANCIAL SERVICES COMPENSATION SCHEME

The scheme manager

[179]
212 The scheme manager

(1) The Authority must establish a body corporate ("the scheme manager") to exercise the functions conferred on the scheme manager by or under this Part.
(2) The Authority must take such steps as are necessary to ensure that the scheme manager is, at all times, capable of exercising those functions.
(3) The constitution of the scheme manager must provide for it to have—
- (a) a chairman; and
- (b) a board (which must include the chairman) whose members are the scheme manager's directors.

(4) The chairman and other members of the board must be persons appointed, and liable to removal from office, by the Authority (acting, in the case of the chairman, with the approval of the Treasury).
(5) But the terms of their appointment (and in particular those governing removal from office) must be such as to secure their independence from the Authority in the operation of the compensation scheme.
(6) The scheme manager is not to be regarded as exercising functions on behalf of the Crown.
(7) The scheme manager's board members, officers and staff are not to be regarded as Crown servants.

The scheme

[180]
213 The compensation scheme

(1) The Authority must by rules establish a scheme for compensating persons in cases where relevant persons are unable, or are likely to be unable, to satisfy claims against them.
(2) The rules are to be known as the Financial Services Compensation Scheme (but are referred to in this Act as "the compensation scheme").
(3) The compensation scheme must, in particular, provide for the scheme manager—
- (a) to assess and pay compensation, in accordance with the scheme, to claimants in respect of claims made in connection with regulated activities carried on (whether or not with permission) by relevant persons; and
- (b) to have power to impose levies on authorised persons, or any class of authorised person, for the purpose of meeting its expenses (including in particular expenses incurred, or expected to be incurred, in paying compensation, borrowing or insuring risks).

(4) The compensation scheme may provide for the scheme manager to have power to impose levies on authorised persons, or any class of authorised person, for the purpose of recovering the cost (whenever incurred) of establishing the scheme.
(5) In making any provision of the scheme by virtue of subsection (3)(b), the Authority must take account of the desirability of ensuring that the amount of the levies imposed on a particular class of authorised person reflects, so far as practicable, the amount of the claims made, or likely to be made, in respect of that class of person.
(6) An amount payable to the scheme manager as a result of any provision of the scheme made by virtue of subsection (3)(b) or (4) may be recovered as a debt due to the scheme manager.
(7) Sections 214 to 217 make further provision about the scheme but are not to be taken as limiting the power conferred on the Authority by subsection (1) [(except where limitations are expressly stated)].
(8) In those sections "specified" means specified in the scheme.
(9) In this Part (except in sections 219, 220 or 224) "relevant person" means a person who was—

(a) an authorised person at the time the act or omission giving rise to the claim against him took place; or

(b) an appointed representative at that time.

(10) But a person who, at that time—

(a) qualified for authorisation under Schedule 3, and

(b) fell within a prescribed category,

is not to be regarded as a relevant person in relation to any activities for which he had permission as a result of any provision of, or made under, that Schedule unless he had elected to participate in the scheme in relation to those activities at that time.

NOTES

Sub-s (7): words in square brackets added by the Banking Act 2009, s 170(2), as from a day to be appointed.

Disapplication: sub-s (3)(a) above is disapplied to a person who is a relevant person only by virtue of his having interim permission, by the Financial Services and Markets Act 2000 (Regulated Activities) (Amendment) Order 2006, SI 2006/1969, art 7, Schedule, paras 4, 8, and the Financial Services and Markets Act 2000 (Regulated Activities) (Amendment) (No 2) Order 2006, SI 2006/2383, art 40, Schedule, para 8, and the Financial Services and Markets Act 2000 (Regulated Activities) (Amendment) Order 2009, SI 2009/1342, art 34, Schedule, paras 4, 7.

Regulations: the Financial Services and Markets Act 2000 (Compensation Scheme: Electing Participants) Regulations 2001, SI 2001/1783 at **[611]**.

Provisions of the scheme

[181]

214 General

(1) The compensation scheme may, in particular, make provision—

(a) as to the circumstances in which a relevant person is to be taken (for the purposes of the scheme) to be unable, or likely to be unable, to satisfy claims made against him;

(b) for the establishment of different funds for meeting different kinds of claim;

(c) for the imposition of different levies in different cases;

(d) limiting the levy payable by a person in respect of a specified period;

(e) for repayment of the whole or part of a levy in specified circumstances;

(f) for a claim to be entertained only if it is made by a specified kind of claimant;

(g) for a claim to be entertained only if it falls within a specified kind of claim;

(h) as to the procedure to be followed in making a claim;

(i) for the making of interim payments before a claim is finally determined;

(j) limiting the amount payable on a claim to a specified maximum amount or a maximum amount calculated in a specified manner;

(k) for payment to be made, in specified circumstances, to a person other than the claimant.

[(1A) Rules by virtue of subsection (1)(h) may, in particular, allow the scheme manager to treat persons who are or may be entitled to claim under the scheme as if they had done so.

(1B) A reference in any enactment or instrument to a claim or claimant under this Part includes a reference to a deemed claim or claimant in accordance with subsection (1A).

(1C) Rules by virtue of subsection (1)(j) may, in particular, allow, or be subject to rules which allow, the scheme manager to settle a class of claim by payment of sums fixed without reference to, or by modification of, the normal rules for calculation of maximum entitlement for individual claims.]

(2) Different provision may be made with respect to different kinds of claim.

(3) The scheme may provide for the determination and regulation of matters relating to the scheme by the scheme manager.

(4) The scheme, or particular provisions of the scheme, may be made so as to apply only in relation to—

(a) activities carried on,

(b) claimants,

(c) matters arising, or

(d) events occurring,

in specified territories, areas or localities.

(5) The scheme may provide for a person who—

(a) qualifies for authorisation under Schedule 3, and

(b) falls within a prescribed category,

to elect to participate in the scheme in relation to some or all of the activities for which he has permission as a result of any provision of, or made under, that Schedule.

(6) The scheme may provide for the scheme manager to have power—

(a) in specified circumstances,

(b) but only if the scheme manager is satisfied that the claimant is entitled to receive a payment in respect of his claim—
(i) under a scheme which is comparable to the compensation scheme, or
(ii) as the result of a guarantee given by a government or other authority,

to make a full payment of compensation to the claimant and recover the whole or part of the amount of that payment from the other scheme or under that guarantee.

NOTES

Sub-ss (1A)–(1C): inserted by the Banking Act 2009, s 174(1).

Regulations: the Financial Services and Markets Act 2000 (Compensation Scheme: Electing Participants) Regulations 2001, SI 2001/1783 at **[611]**.

[181A]

[214A Contingency funding

(1) The Treasury may make regulations ("contingency fund regulations") permitting the scheme manager to impose levies under section 213 for the purpose of maintaining contingency funds from which possible expenses may be paid.

(2) Contingency fund regulations may make provision about the establishment and management of contingency funds; in particular, the regulations may make provision about—
(a) the number and size of funds;
(b) the circumstances and timing of their establishment;
(c) the classes of person from whom contributions to the funds may be levied;
(d) the amount and timing of payments into and out of funds (which may include provision for different levies for different classes of person);
(e) refunds;
(f) the ways in which funds' contents may be invested (including (i) the extent of reliance on section 223A, and (ii) the application of investment income);
(g) the purposes for which funds may be applied, but only so as to determine whether a fund is to be used (i) for the payment of compensation, (ii) for the purposes of co-operating with a bank liquidator in accordance with section 99 of the Banking Act 2009, or (iii) for contributions under section 214B;
(h) procedures to be followed in connection with funds, including the keeping of records and the provision of information.

(3) The compensation scheme may include provision about contingency funds provided that it is not inconsistent with contingency fund regulations.]

NOTES

Commencement: to be appointed.

Inserted by the Banking Act 2009, s 170(1), as from a day to be appointed.

[181B]

[214B Contribution to costs of special resolution regime

(1) This section applies where—
(a) a stabilisation power under Part 1 of the Banking Act 2009 has been exercised in respect of a bank, building society or credit union (within the meaning of that Part), and
(b) the Treasury think that the bank, building society or credit union was, or but for the exercise of the stabilisation power would have become, unable to satisfy claims against it.

(2) Where this section applies—
(a) the Treasury may require the scheme manager to make payments in connection with the exercise of the stabilisation power, and
(b) payments shall be treated as expenditure under the scheme for all purposes (including levies, contingency funds and borrowing).

(3) The Treasury shall make regulations—
(a) specifying what expenses the scheme manager may be required to incur under subsection (2),
(b) providing for independent verification of the nature and amount of expenses incurred in connection with the exercise of the stabilisation power (which may include provision about appointment and payment of an auditor), and
(c) providing for the method by which amounts to be paid are to be determined.

(4) The regulations must ensure that payments required do not exceed the amount of compensation that would have been payable under the scheme if the stabilisation power had not been exercised and the bank had been unable to satisfy claims against it; and for that purpose the amount of compensation that would have been payable does not include—

(a) amounts that would have been likely, at the time when the stabilisation power was exercised, to be recovered by the scheme from the bank, or
(b) any compensation actually paid to an eligible depositor of the bank.

(5) The regulations must provide for the appointment of an independent valuer (who may be the person appointed as valuer under section 54 of the Banking Act 2009 in respect of the exercise of the stabilisation power) to calculate the amounts referred to in subsection (4)(a); and the regulations—
(a) must provide for the valuer to be appointed by the Treasury or by a person designated by the Treasury,
(b) must include provision enabling the valuer to reconsider a decision,
(c) must provide a right of appeal to a court or tribunal,
(d) must provide for payment of the valuer,
(e) may replicate or apply a provision of section 54 or 55, and
(f) may apply or include any provision that is or could be made under that section.

(6) Payments required to be made by the scheme by virtue of section 61 of the Banking Act 2009 (special resolution regime: compensation) shall be treated for the purposes of subsection (4) as if required to be made under this section.

(7) The regulations may include provision for payments (including payments under those provisions of the Banking Act 2009) to be made—
(a) before verification in accordance with subsection (3)(b), and
(b) before the calculation of the limit imposed by subsection (4), by reference to estimates of that limit and subject to any necessary later adjustment.

(8) The regulations may include provision—
(a) about timing;
(b) about procedures to be followed;
(c) for discretionary functions to be exercised by a specified body or by persons of a specified class;
(d) about the resolution of disputes (which may include provision conferring jurisdiction on a court or tribunal).

(9) The compensation scheme may include provision about payments under and levies in connection with this section, provided that it is not inconsistent with this section or regulations under it.]

NOTES

Commencement: 17 February 2009 (for the purpose of enabling subordinate legislation or codes of practice to be made); 21 February 2009 (otherwise).

Inserted by the Banking Act 2009, s 171(1).

Regulations: the Financial Services and Markets Act 2000 (Contribution to Costs of Special Resolution Regime) Regulations 2009, SI 2009/807.

---

[182]

[215 Rights of the scheme in insolvency]

[(1) The compensation scheme may make provision—
(a) about the effect of a payment of compensation under the scheme on rights or obligations arising out of matters in connection with which the compensation was paid;
(b) giving the scheme manager a right of recovery in respect of those rights or obligations.]

(2) Such a right of recovery conferred by the scheme does not, in the event of [a person's insolvency], exceed such right (if any) as the claimant would have had in that event.

(3) If a person other than the scheme manager [makes an administration application under Schedule B1 to the 1986 Act or [Schedule B1 to] the 1989 Order] in relation to a company or partnership which is a relevant person, the scheme manager has the same rights as are conferred on the Authority by section 362.

[(3A) In subsection (3) the reference to making an administration application includes a reference to—
(a) appointing an administrator under paragraph 14 or 22 of Schedule B1 to the 1986 Act [or paragraph 15 or 23 of Schedule B1 to the 1989 Order], or
(b) *filing with the court* a copy of notice of intention to appoint an administrator under [any] of those paragraphs.]

(4) If a person other than the scheme manager presents a petition for the winding up of a body which is a relevant person, the scheme manager has the same rights as are conferred on the Authority by section 371.

(5) If a person other than the scheme manager presents a bankruptcy petition to the court in relation to an individual who, or an entity which, is a relevant person, the scheme manager has the same rights as are conferred on the Authority by section 374.

(6) Insolvency rules may be made for the purpose of integrating any procedure for which provision is made as a result of subsection (1) into the general procedure on the administration of a company or partnership or on a winding-up, bankruptcy or sequestration.

(7) "Bankruptcy petition" means a petition to the court—

(a) under section 264 of the 1986 Act or Article 238 of the 1989 Order for a bankruptcy order to be made against an individual;

(b) under section 5 of the 1985 Act for the sequestration of the estate of an individual; or

(c) under section 6 of the 1985 Act for the sequestration of the estate belonging to or held for or jointly by the members of an entity mentioned in subsection (1) of that section.

(8) "Insolvency rules" are—

(a) for England and Wales, rules made under sections 411 and 412 of the 1986 Act;

(b) for Scotland, rules made by order by the Treasury, after consultation with the Scottish Ministers, for the purposes of this section; and

(c) for Northern Ireland, rules made under Article 359 of the 1989 Order and section 55 of the Judicature (Northern Ireland) Act 1978.

(9) "The 1985 Act", "the 1986 Act", "the 1989 Order" and "court" have the same meaning as in Part XXIV.

NOTES

Section heading: substituted by the Banking Act 2009, s 175(1), (4).

Sub-s (1): substituted by the Banking Act 2009, s 175(1), (2).

Sub-s (2): words in square brackets substituted by the Banking Act 2009, s 175(1), (3).

Sub-s (3): words in first (outer) pair of square brackets substituted by the Enterprise Act 2002, s 248(3), Sch 17, paras 53, 54(1), (2); words in second (inner) pair of square brackets substituted by the Insolvency (Northern Ireland) Order 2005, SI 2005/1455, art 3(3), Sch 2, paras 56, 57(1), (2).

Sub-s (3A): inserted by the Enterprise Act 2002, s 248(3), Sch 17, paras 53, 54(1), (3); words in square brackets in para (a) inserted and word in square brackets in para (b) substituted by SI 2005/1455, art 3(3), Sch 2, paras 56, 57(1), (3).

Modification: this section is applied, with modifications, in relation to liquidation and administration by the Banking Act 2009 (Parts 2 and 3 Consequential Amendments) Order 2009, SI 2009/317, art 5(1), (2).

[183]

216 Continuity of long-term insurance policies

(1) The compensation scheme may, in particular, include provision requiring the scheme manager to make arrangements for securing continuity of insurance for policyholders, or policyholders of a specified class, of relevant long-term insurers.

(2) "Relevant long-term insurers" means relevant persons who—

(a) have permission to effect or carry out contracts of long-term insurance; and

(b) are unable, or likely to be unable, to satisfy claims made against them.

(3) The scheme may provide for the scheme manager to take such measures as appear to him to be appropriate—

(a) for securing or facilitating the transfer of a relevant long-term insurer's business so far as it consists of the carrying out of contracts of long-term insurance, or of any part of that business, to another authorised person;

(b) for securing the issue by another authorised person to the policyholders concerned of policies in substitution for their existing policies.

(4) The scheme may also provide for the scheme manager to make payments to the policyholders concerned—

(a) during any period while he is seeking to make arrangements mentioned in subsection (1);

(b) if it appears to him that it is not reasonably practicable to make such arrangements.

(5) A provision of the scheme made by virtue of section 213(3)(b) may include power to impose levies for the purpose of meeting expenses of the scheme manager incurred in—

(a) taking measures as a result of any provision of the scheme made by virtue of subsection (3);

(b) making payments as a result of any such provision made by virtue of subsection (4).

[184]

217 Insurers in financial difficulties

(1) The compensation scheme may, in particular, include provision for the scheme manager to have power to take measures for safeguarding policyholders, or policyholders of a specified class, of relevant insurers.

(2) "Relevant insurers" means relevant persons who—
(a) have permission to effect or carry out contracts of insurance; and
(b) are in financial difficulties.
(3) The measures may include such measures as the scheme manager considers appropriate for—
(a) securing or facilitating the transfer of a relevant insurer's business so far as it consists of the carrying out of contracts of insurance, or of any part of that business, to another authorised person;
(b) giving assistance to the relevant insurer to enable it to continue to effect or carry out contracts of insurance.
(4) The scheme may provide—
(a) that if measures of a kind mentioned in subsection (3)(a) are to be taken, they should be on terms appearing to the scheme manager to be appropriate, including terms reducing, or deferring payment of, any of the things to which any of those who are eligible policyholders in relation to the relevant insurer are entitled in their capacity as such;
(b) that if measures of a kind mentioned in subsection (3)(b) are to be taken, they should be conditional on the reduction of, or the deferment of the payment of, the things to which any of those who are eligible policyholders in relation to the relevant insurer are entitled in their capacity as such;
(c) for ensuring that measures of a kind mentioned in subsection (3)(b) do not benefit to any material extent persons who were members of a relevant insurer when it began to be in financial difficulties or who had any responsibility for, or who may have profited from, the circumstances giving rise to its financial difficulties, except in specified circumstances;
(d) for requiring the scheme manager to be satisfied that any measures he proposes to take are likely to cost less than it would cost to pay compensation under the scheme if the relevant insurer became unable, or likely to be unable, to satisfy claims made against him.
(5) The scheme may provide for the Authority to have power—
(a) to give such assistance to the scheme manager as it considers appropriate for assisting the scheme manager to determine what measures are practicable or desirable in the case of a particular relevant insurer;
(b) to impose constraints on the taking of measures by the scheme manager in the case of a particular relevant insurer;
(c) to require the scheme manager to provide it with information about any particular measures which the scheme manager is proposing to take.
(6) The scheme may include provision for the scheme manager to have power—
(a) to make interim payments in respect of eligible policyholders of a relevant insurer;
(b) to indemnify any person making payments to eligible policyholders of a relevant insurer.
(7) A provision of the scheme made by virtue of section 213(3)(b) may include power to impose levies for the purpose of meeting expenses of the scheme manager incurred in—
(a) taking measures as a result of any provision of the scheme made by virtue of subsection (1);
(b) making payments or giving indemnities as a result of any such provision made by virtue of subsection (6).
(8) "Financial difficulties" and "eligible policyholders" have such meanings as may be specified.

Annual report

[185]
218 Annual report
(1) At least once a year, the scheme manager must make a report to the Authority [and the Treasury] on the discharge of its functions.
(2) The report must—
(a) include a statement setting out the value of each of the funds established by the compensation scheme; and
(b) comply with any requirements specified in rules made by the Authority [or in contingency fund regulations].
(3) The scheme manager must publish each report in the way it considers appropriate.

NOTES
Sub-s (1): words in square brackets inserted by the Banking Act 2009, s 170(3)(a), as from a day to be appointed.
Sub-s (2): words in square brackets added by the Banking Act 2009, s 170(3)(b), as from a day to be appointed.

Information and documents

[185A]

[218A Authority's power to require information

(1) The Authority may make rules enabling the Authority to require authorised persons to provide information, which may then be made available to the scheme manager by the Authority.

(2) A requirement may be imposed only if the Authority thinks the information is of a kind that may be of use to the scheme manager in connection with functions in respect of the scheme.

(3) A requirement under this section may apply—

(a) to authorised persons generally or only to specified persons or classes of person;

(b) to the provision of information at specified periods, in connection with specified events or in other ways.

(4) In addition to requirements under this section, a notice under section 165 may relate to information or documents which the Authority thinks are reasonably required by the scheme manager in connection with the performance of functions in respect of the scheme; and section 165(4) is subject to this subsection.

(5) Rules under subsection (1) shall be prepared, made and treated in the same way as (and may be combined with) the Authority's general rules.]

NOTES

Commencement: 17 February 2009 (for the purpose of enabling subordinate legislation or codes of practice to be made); 21 February 2009 (otherwise).

Inserted by the Banking Act 2009, s 176(1).

[186]

219 Scheme manager's power to require information

(1) The scheme manager may, by notice in writing [require a person]—

(a) to provide specified information or information of a specified description; or

(b) to produce specified documents or documents of a specified description.

[(1A) A requirement may be imposed only—

(a) on a person (P) against whom a claim has been made under the scheme,

(b) on a person (P) who is unable or likely to be unable to satisfy claims under the scheme against P,

(c) on a person ("the Third Party") whom the scheme manager thinks was knowingly involved in matters giving rise to a claim against another person (P) under the scheme, or

(d) on a person ("the Third Party") whom the scheme manager thinks was knowingly involved in matters giving rise to the actual or likely inability of another person (P) to satisfy claims under the scheme.

(1B) For the purposes of subsection (1A)(b) and (d) whether P is unable or likely to be unable to satisfy claims shall be determined in accordance with provision to be made by the scheme (which may, in particular—

(a) apply or replicate, with or without modifications, a provision of an enactment;

(b) confer discretion on a specified person).]

(2) The information or documents must be provided or produced—

(a) before the end of such reasonable period as may be specified; and

(b) in the case of information, in such manner or form as may be specified.

(3) This section applies only to information and documents the provision or production of which the scheme manager considers [to be necessary (or likely to be necessary) for the fair determination of claims which have been or may be made against P].

[(3A) Where a stabilisation power under Part 1 of the Banking Act 2009 has been exercised in respect of a bank, the scheme manager may by notice in writing require the bank or the Bank of England to provide information that the scheme manager requires for the purpose of applying regulations under section 214B(3) above.]

(4) If a document is produced in response to a requirement imposed under this section, the scheme manager may—

(a) take copies or extracts from the document; or

(b) require the person producing the document to provide an explanation of the document.

(5) If a person who is required under this section to produce a document fails to do so, the scheme manager may require the person to state, to the best of his knowledge and belief, where the document is.

(6) If [P] is insolvent, no requirement may be imposed under this section on a person to whom section 220 or 224 applies.

(7) If a person claims a lien on a document, its production under this Part does not affect the lien.

(8) . . .
(9) "Specified" means specified in the notice given under subsection (1).
(10) . . .

NOTES
Sub-ss (1), (3): words in square brackets substituted by the Banking Act 2009, s 176(2), (3), (5).
Sub-ss (1A), (1B), (3A): inserted by the Banking Act 2009, s 176(2), (4), (6).
Sub-s (6): reference in square brackets substituted by the Banking Act 2009, s 176(2), (7).
Sub-ss (8), (10): repealed by the Banking Act 2009, s 176(2), (8), (9).

[187]
220 Scheme manager's power to inspect information held by liquidator etc
(1) For the purpose of assisting the scheme manager to discharge its functions in relation to a claim made in respect of an insolvent relevant person, a person to whom this section applies must permit a person authorised by the scheme manager to inspect relevant documents.
(2) A person inspecting a document under this section may take copies of, or extracts from, the document.
(3) This section applies to—
- (a) the administrative receiver, administrator, liquidator[, bank liquidator][, building society liquidator] or trustee in bankruptcy of an insolvent relevant person;
- (b) the permanent trustee, within the meaning of the Bankruptcy (Scotland) Act 1985, on the estate of an insolvent relevant person.

(4) This section does not apply to a liquidator, administrator or trustee in bankruptcy who is—
- (a) the Official Receiver;
- (b) the Official Receiver for Northern Ireland; or
- (c) the Accountant in Bankruptcy.

(5) "Relevant person" has the same meaning as in section 224.

NOTES
Sub-s (3): words in first pair of square brackets inserted by the Banking Act 2009, s 123(3); words in second pair of square brackets inserted by the Building Societies (Insolvency and Special Administration) Order 2009, SI 2009/805, art 15.

[188]
221 Powers of court where information required
(1) If a person ("the defaulter")—
- (a) fails to comply with a requirement imposed under section 219, or
- (b) fails to permit documents to be inspected under section 220,

the scheme manager may certify that fact in writing to the court and the court may enquire into the case.
(2) If the court is satisfied that the defaulter failed without reasonable excuse to comply with the requirement (or to permit the documents to be inspected), it may deal with the defaulter (and, in the case of a body corporate, any director or officer) as if he were in contempt[; and "officer", in relation to a limited liability partnership, means a member of the limited liability partnership].
(3) "Court" means—
- (a) the High Court;
- (b) in Scotland, the Court of Session.

NOTES
Sub-s (2): words in square brackets added by the Limited Liability Partnerships Regulations 2001, SI 2001/1090, reg 9, Sch 5, para 21.

Miscellaneous

[188A]
[221A Delegation of functions
(1) The scheme manager may arrange for any of its functions to be discharged on its behalf by another person (a "scheme agent").
(2) Before entering into arrangements the scheme manager must be satisfied that the scheme agent—
- (a) is competent to discharge the function, and
- (b) has been given sufficient directions to enable the agent to take any decisions required in the course of exercising the function in accordance with policy determined by the scheme manager.

(3) Arrangements may include provision for payments to be made by the scheme manager to the scheme agent (which payments are management expenses of the scheme manager).]

NOTES

Commencement: 17 February 2009 (for the purpose of enabling subordinate legislation or codes of practice to be made); 21 February 2009 (otherwise).

Inserted by the Banking Act 2009, s 179(1).

[189]

222 Statutory immunity

(1) Neither the scheme manager nor any person who is, or is acting as, its board member, officer[, scheme agent] or member of staff is to be liable in damages for anything done or omitted in the discharge, or purported discharge, of the scheme manager's functions.

(2) Subsection (1) does not apply—

(a) if the act or omission is shown to have been in bad faith; or

(b) so as to prevent an award of damages made in respect of an act or omission on the ground that the act or omission was unlawful as a result of section 6(1) of the Human Rights Act 1998.

NOTES

Sub-s (1): words in square brackets inserted by the Banking Act 2009, s 179(2).

[190]

223 Management expenses

(1) The amount which the scheme manager may recover, from the sums levied under the scheme, as management expenses attributable to a particular period may not exceed such amount as may be fixed by the scheme as the limit applicable to that period.

(2) In calculating the amount of any levy to be imposed by the scheme manager, no amount may be included to reflect management expenses unless the limit mentioned in subsection (1) has been fixed by the scheme.

(3) "Management expenses" means expenses incurred, or expected to be incurred, by the scheme manager in connection with its functions under this Act other than those incurred—

(a) in paying compensation;

(b) as a result of any provision of the scheme made by virtue of section 216(3) or (4) or 217(1) or (6)[;

(c) under section 214B.]

NOTES

Sub-s (3): words in square brackets added by the Banking Act 2009, s 171(2).

[190A]

[223A Investing in National Loans Fund

(1) Sums levied for the purpose of maintaining a contingency fund may be paid to the Treasury.

(2) The Treasury may receive sums under subsection (1) and may set terms and conditions of receipts.

(3) Sums received shall be treated as if raised under section 12 of the National Loans Act 1968 (and shall therefore be invested as part of the National Loans Fund).

(4) Interest accruing on the invested sums may be credited to the contingency fund (subject to any terms and conditions set under subsection (2)).

(5) The Treasury shall comply with any request of the scheme manager to arrange for the return of sums for the purpose of making payments out of a contingency fund (subject to any terms and conditions set under subsection (2)).]

NOTES

Commencement: to be appointed.

Inserted by the Banking Act 2009, s 172, as from a day to be appointed.

[190B]

[223B Borrowing from National Loans Fund

(1) The scheme manager may request a loan from the National Loans Fund for the purpose of funding expenses incurred or expected to be incurred under the scheme.

(2) The Treasury may arrange for money to be paid out of the National Loans Fund in pursuance of a request under subsection (1).

(3) The Treasury shall determine—

(a) the rate of interest on a loan, and

(b) other terms and conditions.

(4) The Treasury may make regulations—

(a) about the amounts that may be borrowed under this section;
(b) permitting the scheme manager to impose levies under section 213 for the purpose of meeting expenses in connection with loans under this section (and the regulations may have effect despite any provision of this Act);
(c) about the classes of person on whom those levies may be imposed;
(d) about the amounts and timing of those levies.

(5) The compensation scheme may include provision about borrowing under this section provided that it is not inconsistent with regulations under this section.]

NOTES

Commencement: 17 February (for the purpose of enabling subordinate legislation or codes of practice to be made); 21 February 2009 (otherwise).

Inserted by the Banking Act 2009, s 173.

[190C]
[223C Payments in error

(1) Payments made by the scheme manager in error may be provided for in setting a levy by virtue of section 213, 214A, 214B or 223B.

(2) This section does not apply to payments made in bad faith.]

NOTES

Commencement: 17 February (for the purpose of enabling subordinate legislation or codes of practice to be made); 21 February 2009 (otherwise).

Inserted by the Banking Act 2009, s 177.

[191]
224 Scheme manager's power to inspect documents held by Official Receiver etc

(1) If, as a result of the insolvency or bankruptcy of a relevant person, any documents have come into the possession of a person to whom this section applies, he must permit any person authorised by the scheme manager to inspect the documents for the purpose of establishing—
(a) the identity of persons to whom the scheme manager may be liable to make a payment in accordance with the compensation scheme; or
(b) the amount of any payment which the scheme manager may be liable to make.

(2) A person inspecting a document under this section may take copies or extracts from the document.

(3) In this section "relevant person" means a person who was—
(a) an authorised person at the time the act or omission which may give rise to the liability mentioned in subsection (1)(a) took place; or
(b) an appointed representative at that time.

(4) But a person who, at that time—
(a) qualified for authorisation under Schedule 3, and
(b) fell within a prescribed category,

is not to be regarded as a relevant person for the purposes of this section in relation to any activities for which he had permission as a result of any provision of, or made under, that Schedule unless he had elected to participate in the scheme in relation to those activities at that time.

(5) This section applies to—
(a) the Official Receiver;
(b) the Official Receiver for Northern Ireland; and
(c) the Accountant in Bankruptcy.

NOTES

Regulations: the Financial Services and Markets Act 2000 (Compensation Scheme: Electing Participants) Regulations 2001, SI 2001/1783 at **[611]**.

[191A]
[224A Functions under the Banking Act 2009

A reference in this Part to functions of the scheme manager (including a reference to functions conferred by or under this Part) includes a reference to functions conferred by or under the Banking Act 2009.]

NOTES

Commencement: 17 February 2009 (for the purpose of enabling subordinate legislation or codes of practice to be made); 21 February 2009 (otherwise).

Inserted by the Banking Act 2009, s 180.

PART XVI
THE OMBUDSMAN SCHEME

NOTES

Application: this Part of this Act applies as if persons who fall within the Payment Services Regulations 2009, SI 2009/209, reg 122(1) or 123(1) were payment service providers within the meaning of those Regulations; see SI 2009/209, reg 125.

The scheme

[192]

225 The scheme and the scheme operator

(1) This Part provides for a scheme under which certain disputes may be resolved quickly and with minimum formality by an independent person.

(2) The scheme is to be administered by a body corporate ("the scheme operator").

(3) The scheme is to be operated under a name chosen by the scheme operator but is referred to in this Act as "the ombudsman scheme".

(4) Schedule 17 makes provision in connection with the ombudsman scheme and the scheme operator.

[193]

226 Compulsory jurisdiction

(1) A complaint which relates to an act or omission of a person ("the respondent") in carrying on an activity to which compulsory jurisdiction rules apply is to be dealt with under the ombudsman scheme if the conditions mentioned in subsection (2) are satisfied.

(2) The conditions are that—

(a) the complainant is eligible and wishes to have the complaint dealt with under the scheme;

(b) the respondent was an authorised person[, or a payment service provider within the meaning of the Payment Services Regulations 2009,] at the time of the act or omission to which the complaint relates; and

(c) the act or omission to which the complaint relates occurred at a time when compulsory jurisdiction rules were in force in relation to the activity in question.

(3) "Compulsory jurisdiction rules" means rules—

(a) made by the Authority for the purposes of this section; and

(b) specifying the activities to which they apply.

(4) Only activities which are regulated activities, or which could be made regulated activities by an order under section 22, may be specified.

(5) Activities may be specified by reference to specified categories (however described).

(6) A complainant is eligible, in relation to the compulsory jurisdiction of the ombudsman scheme, if he falls within a class of person specified in the rules as eligible.

(7) The rules—

(a) may include provision for persons other than individuals to be eligible; but

(b) may not provide for authorised persons to be eligible except in specified circumstances or in relation to complaints of a specified kind.

(8) The jurisdiction of the scheme which results from this section is referred to in this Act as the "compulsory jurisdiction".

NOTES

Sub-s (2): words in square brackets in para (b) inserted by the Payment Services Regulations 2009, SI 2009/209, reg 126, Sch 6, Pt 1, para 1(1)(a).

[193A]

[226A Consumer credit jurisdiction

(1) A complaint which relates to an act or omission of a person ("the respondent") is to be dealt with under the ombudsman scheme if the conditions mentioned in subsection (2) are satisfied.

(2) The conditions are that—

(a) the complainant is eligible and wishes to have the complaint dealt with under the scheme;

(b) the complaint falls within a description specified in consumer credit rules;

(c) at the time of the act or omission the respondent was the licensee under a standard licence or was authorised to carry on an activity by virtue of section 34A of the Consumer Credit Act 1974;

(d) the act or omission occurred in the course of a business being carried on by the respondent which was of a type mentioned in subsection (3);

(e) at the time of the act or omission that type of business was specified in an order made by the Secretary of State; and
(f) the complaint cannot be dealt with under the compulsory jurisdiction.

(3) The types of business referred to in subsection (2)(d) are—
(a) a consumer credit business;
(b) a consumer hire business;
(c) a business so far as it comprises or relates to credit brokerage;
(d) a business so far as it comprises or relates to debt-adjusting;
(e) a business so far as it comprises or relates to debt-counselling;
(f) a business so far as it comprises or relates to debt-collecting;
(g) a business so far as it comprises or relates to debt administration;
(h) a business so far as it comprises or relates to the provision of credit information services;
(i) a business so far as it comprises or relates to the operation of a credit reference agency.

(4) A complainant is eligible if—
(a) he is—
(i) an individual; or
(ii) a surety in relation to a security provided to the respondent in connection with the business mentioned in subsection (2)(d); and
(b) he falls within a class of person specified in consumer credit rules.

(5) The approval of the Treasury is required for an order under subsection (2)(e).
(6) The jurisdiction of the scheme which results from this section is referred to in this Act as the "consumer credit jurisdiction".
(7) In this Act "consumer credit rules" means rules made by the scheme operator with the approval of the Authority for the purposes of the consumer credit jurisdiction.
(8) Consumer credit rules under this section may make different provision for different cases.
(9) Expressions used in the Consumer Credit Act 1974 have the same meaning in this section as they have in that Act.]

NOTES

Commencement: 16 June 2006.

Inserted by the Consumer Credit Act 2006, s 59(1), subject to transitional provisions in s 69(1) of, and Sch 3, paras 1, 29 to, that Act.

Orders: the Financial Services and Markets Act 2000 (Ombudsman Scheme) (Consumer Credit Jurisdiction) Order 2007, SI 2007/383.

---

[194]

227 Voluntary jurisdiction

(1) A complaint which relates to an act or omission of a person ("the respondent") in carrying on an activity to which voluntary jurisdiction rules apply is to be dealt with under the ombudsman scheme if the conditions mentioned in subsection (2) are satisfied.

(2) The conditions are that—
(a) the complainant is eligible and wishes to have the complaint dealt with under the scheme;
(b) at the time of the act or omission to which the complaint relates, the respondent was participating in the scheme;
(c) at the time when the complaint is referred under the scheme, the respondent has not withdrawn from the scheme in accordance with its provisions;
(d) the act or omission to which the complaint relates occurred at a time when voluntary jurisdiction rules were in force in relation to the activity in question; and
(e) the complaint cannot be dealt with under the compulsory jurisdiction [or the consumer credit jurisdiction].

(3) "Voluntary jurisdiction rules" means rules—
(a) made by the scheme operator for the purposes of this section; and
(b) specifying the activities to which they apply.

(4) The only activities which may be specified in the rules are activities which are, or could be, specified in compulsory jurisdiction rules.
(5) Activities may be specified by reference to specified categories (however described).
(6) The rules require the Authority's approval.
(7) A complainant is eligible, in relation to the voluntary jurisdiction of the ombudsman scheme, if he falls within a class of person specified in the rules as eligible.
(8) The rules may include provision for persons other than individuals to be eligible.

(9) A person qualifies for participation in the ombudsman scheme if he falls within a class of person specified in the rules in relation to the activity in question.
(10) Provision may be made in the rules for persons other than authorised persons to participate in the ombudsman scheme.
(11) The rules may make different provision in relation to complaints arising from different activities.
(12) The jurisdiction of the scheme which results from this section is referred to in this Act as the "voluntary jurisdiction".
(13) In such circumstances as may be specified in voluntary jurisdiction rules, a complaint—
(a) which relates to an act or omission occurring at a time before the rules came into force, and
(b) which could have been dealt with under a scheme which has to any extent been replaced by the voluntary jurisdiction,

is to be dealt with under the ombudsman scheme even though paragraph (b) or (d) of subsection (2) would otherwise prevent that.
(14) In such circumstances as may be specified in voluntary jurisdiction rules, a complaint is to be dealt with under the ombudsman scheme even though—
(a) paragraph (b) or (d) of subsection (2) would otherwise prevent that, and
(b) the complaint is not brought within the scheme as a result of subsection (13),

but only if the respondent has agreed that complaints of that kind were to be dealt with under the scheme.

NOTES

Sub-s (2): words in square brackets in para (e) inserted by the Consumer Credit Act 2006, s 61(2).

Determination of complaints

[195]
228 Determination under the compulsory jurisdiction
(1) This section applies only in relation to the compulsory jurisdiction [and to the consumer credit jurisdiction].
(2) A complaint is to be determined by reference to what is, in the opinion of the ombudsman, fair and reasonable in all the circumstances of the case.
(3) When the ombudsman has determined a complaint he must give a written statement of his determination to the respondent and to the complainant.
(4) The statement must—
(a) give the ombudsman's reasons for his determination;
(b) be signed by him; and
(c) require the complainant to notify him in writing, before a date specified in the statement, whether he accepts or rejects the determination.

(5) If the complainant notifies the ombudsman that he accepts the determination, it is binding on the respondent and the complainant and final.
(6) If, by the specified date, the complainant has not notified the ombudsman of his acceptance or rejection of the determination he is to be treated as having rejected it.
(7) The ombudsman must notify the respondent of the outcome.
(8) A copy of the determination on which appears a certificate signed by an ombudsman is evidence (or in Scotland sufficient evidence) that the determination was made under the scheme.
(9) Such a certificate purporting to be signed by an ombudsman is to be taken to have been duly signed unless the contrary is shown.

NOTES

Sub-s (1): words in square brackets inserted by the Consumer Credit Act 2006, s 61(3).

[196]
229 Awards
(1) This section applies only in relation to the compulsory jurisdiction [and to the consumer credit jurisdiction].
(2) If a complaint which has been dealt with under the scheme is determined in favour of the complainant, the determination may include—
(a) an award against the respondent of such amount as the ombudsman considers fair compensation for loss or damage (of a kind falling within subsection (3)) suffered by the complainant ("a money award");

(b) a direction that the respondent take such steps in relation to the complainant as the ombudsman considers just and appropriate (whether or not a court could order those steps to be taken).

(3) A money award may compensate for—

(a) financial loss; or

(b) any other loss, or any damage, of a specified kind.

(4) The Authority may specify [for the purposes of the compulsory jurisdiction] the maximum amount which may be regarded as fair compensation for a particular kind of loss or damage specified under subsection (3)(b).

[(4A) The scheme operator may specify for the purposes of the consumer credit jurisdiction the maximum amount which may be regarded as fair compensation for a particular kind of loss or damage specified under subsection (3)(b).]

(5) A money award may not exceed the monetary limit; but the ombudsman may, if he considers that fair compensation requires payment of a larger amount, recommend that the respondent pay the complainant the balance.

(6) The monetary limit is such amount as may be specified.

(7) Different amounts may be specified in relation to different kinds of complaint.

(8) A money award—

(a) may provide for the amount payable under the award to bear interest at a rate and as from a date specified in the award; and

(b) is enforceable by the complainant in accordance with Part III of Schedule 17 [or (as the case may be) Part 3A of that Schedule].

(9) Compliance with a direction under subsection (2)(b)—

(a) is enforceable by an injunction; or

(b) in Scotland, is enforceable by an order under section 45 of the Court of Session Act 1988.

(10) Only the complainant may bring proceedings for an injunction or proceedings for an order.

[(11) "Specified" means—

(a) for the purposes of the compulsory jurisdiction, specified in compulsory jurisdiction rules;

(b) for the purposes of the consumer credit jurisdiction, specified in consumer credit rules.

(12) Consumer credit rules under this section may make different provision for different cases.]

NOTES

Sub-ss (1), (4): words in square brackets inserted by the Consumer Credit Act 2006, s 61(3), (4).
Sub-s (4A): inserted by the Consumer Credit Act 2006, s 61(5).
Sub-s (8): words in square brackets in para (b) inserted by the Consumer Credit Act 2006, s 61(6).
Sub-ss (11), (12): substituted, for original sub-s (11), by the Consumer Credit Act 2006, s 61(7).

[197]

230 Costs

(1) The scheme operator may by rules ("costs rules") provide for an ombudsman to have power, on determining a complaint under the compulsory jurisdiction [or the consumer credit jurisdiction], to award costs in accordance with the provisions of the rules.

(2) Costs rules require the approval of the Authority.

(3) Costs rules may not provide for the making of an award against the complainant in respect of the respondent's costs.

(4) But they may provide for the making of an award against the complainant in favour of the scheme operator, for the purpose of providing a contribution to resources deployed in dealing with the complaint, if in the opinion of the ombudsman—

(a) the complainant's conduct was improper or unreasonable; or

(b) the complainant was responsible for an unreasonable delay.

(5) Costs rules may authorise an ombudsman making an award in accordance with the rules to order that the amount payable under the award bears interest at a rate and as from a date specified in the order.

(6) An amount due under an award made in favour of the scheme operator is recoverable as a debt due to the scheme operator.

(7) Any other award made against the respondent is to be treated as a money award for the purposes of paragraph 16 of Schedule 17 [or (as the case may be) paragraph 16D of that Schedule].

NOTES

Sub-ss (1), (7): words in square brackets inserted by the Consumer Credit Act 2006, s 61(8).

Information

[198]

231 Ombudsman's power to require information

(1) An ombudsman may, by notice in writing given to a party to a complaint, require that party—

(a) to provide specified information or information of a specified description; or

(b) to produce specified documents or documents of a specified description.

(2) The information or documents must be provided or produced—

(a) before the end of such reasonable period as may be specified; and

(b) in the case of information, in such manner or form as may be specified.

(3) This section applies only to information and documents the production of which the ombudsman considers necessary for the determination of the complaint.

(4) If a document is produced in response to a requirement imposed under this section, the ombudsman may—

(a) take copies or extracts from the document; or

(b) require the person producing the document to provide an explanation of the document.

(5) If a person who is required under this section to produce a document fails to do so, the ombudsman may require him to state, to the best of his knowledge and belief, where the document is.

(6) If a person claims a lien on a document, its production under this Part does not affect the lien.

(7) "Specified" means specified in the notice given under subsection (1).

[199]

232 Powers of court where information required

(1) If a person ("the defaulter") fails to comply with a requirement imposed under section 231, the ombudsman may certify that fact in writing to the court and the court may enquire into the case.

(2) If the court is satisfied that the defaulter failed without reasonable excuse to comply with the requirement, it may deal with the defaulter (and, in the case of a body corporate, any director or officer) as if he were in contempt[; and "officer", in relation to a limited liability partnership, means a member of the limited liability partnership].

(3) "Court" means—

(a) the High Court;

(b) in Scotland, the Court of Session.

NOTES

Sub-s (2): words in square brackets added by the Limited Liability Partnerships Regulations 2001, SI 2001/1090, reg 9, Sch 5, para 21.

233 (*Inserts the Data Protection Act 1998, s 31(4A) at* **[3642AA]**.)

Funding

[200]

234 Industry funding

(1) For the purpose of funding—

(a) the establishment of the ombudsman scheme (whenever any relevant expense is incurred), and

(b) its operation in relation to the compulsory jurisdiction,

the Authority may make rules requiring the payment to it or to the scheme operator, by authorised persons or any class of authorised person [or any payment service provider within the meaning of the Payment Services Regulations 2009] of specified amounts (or amounts calculated in a specified way).

(2) "Specified" means specified in the rules.

NOTES

Sub-s (1): words in square brackets inserted by the Payment Services Regulations 2009, SI 2009/209, reg 126, Sch 6, Pt 1, para 1(1)(b).

[200A]

[234A Funding by consumer credit licensees etc

(1) For the purpose of funding—

(a) the establishment of the ombudsman scheme so far as it relates to the consumer credit jurisdiction (whenever any relevant expense is incurred), and

(b) its operation in relation to the consumer credit jurisdiction,

the scheme operator may from time to time with the approval of the Authority determine a sum which is to be raised by way of contributions under this section.

(2) A sum determined under subsection (1) may include a component to cover the costs of the collection of contributions to that sum ("collection costs") under this section.
(3) The scheme operator must notify the OFT of every determination under subsection (1).
(4) The OFT must give general notice of every determination so notified.
(5) The OFT may by general notice impose requirements on—
(a) licensees to whom this section applies, or
(b) persons who make applications to which this section applies,
to pay contributions to the OFT for the purpose of raising sums determined under subsection (1).
(6) The amount of the contribution payable by a person under such a requirement—
(a) shall be the amount specified in or determined under the general notice; and
(b) shall be paid before the end of the period or at the time so specified or determined.
(7) A general notice under subsection (5) may—
(a) impose requirements only on descriptions of licensees or applicants specified in the notice;
(b) provide for exceptions from any requirement imposed on a description of licensees or applicants;
(c) impose different requirements on different descriptions of licensees or applicants;
(d) make provision for refunds in specified circumstances.
(8) Contributions received by the OFT must be paid to the scheme operator.
(9) As soon as practicable after the end of—
(a) each financial year of the scheme operator, or
(b) if the OFT and the scheme operator agree that this paragraph is to apply instead of paragraph (a) for the time being, each period agreed by them,
the scheme operator must pay to the OFT an amount representing the extent to which collection costs are covered in accordance with subsection (2) by the total amount of the contributions paid by the OFT to it during the year or (as the case may be) the agreed period.
(10) Amounts received by the OFT from the scheme operator are to be retained by it for the purpose of meeting its costs.
(11) The Secretary of State may by order provide that the functions of the OFT under this section are for the time being to be carried out by the scheme operator.
(12) An order under subsection (11) may provide that while the order is in force this section shall have effect subject to such modifications as may be set out in the order.
(13) The licensees to whom this section applies are licensees under standard licences which cover to any extent the carrying on of a type of business specified in an order under section 226A(2)(e).
(14) The applications to which this section applies are applications for—
(a) standard licences covering to any extent the carrying on of a business of such a type;
(b) the renewal of standard licences on terms covering to any extent the carrying on of a business of such a type.
(15) Expressions used in the Consumer Credit Act 1974 have the same meaning in this section as they have in that Act.]

NOTES
Commencement: 16 June 2006.
Inserted by the Consumer Credit Act 2006, s 60.

235–313D (*(Pts XVII–XVIIIA) outside the scope of this work.*)

PART XIX
LLOYD'S

General

[201]
314 Authority's general duty
(1) The Authority must keep itself informed about—
(a) the way in which the Council supervises and regulates the market at Lloyd's; and
(b) the way in which regulated activities are being carried on in that market.
(2) The Authority must keep under review the desirability of exercising—
(a) any of its powers under this Part;
(b) any powers which it has in relation to the Society as a result of section 315.

The Society

[202]

315 The Society: authorisation and permission

(1) The Society is an authorised person.

(2) The Society has permission to carry on a regulated activity of any of the following kinds—

(a) arranging deals in contracts of insurance written at Lloyd's ("the basic market activity");

(b) arranging deals in participation in Lloyd's syndicates ("the secondary market activity"); and

(c) an activity carried on in connection with, or for the purposes of, the basic or secondary market activity.

(3) For the purposes of Part IV, the Society's permission is to be treated as if it had been given on an application for permission under that Part.

(4) The power conferred on the Authority by section 45 may be exercised in anticipation of the coming into force of the Society's permission (or at any other time).

(5) The Society is not subject to any requirement of this Act concerning the registered office of a body corporate.

Power to apply Act to Lloyd's underwriting

[203]

316 Direction by Authority

(1) The general prohibition or (if the general prohibition is not applied under this section) a core provision applies to the carrying on of an insurance market activity by—

(a) a member of the Society, or

(b) the members of the Society taken together,

only if the Authority so directs.

(2) A direction given under subsection (1) which applies a core provision is referred to in this Part as "an insurance market direction".

(3) In subsection (1)—

"core provision" means a provision of this Act mentioned in section 317; and

"insurance market activity" means a regulated activity relating to contracts of insurance written at Lloyd's.

(4) In deciding whether to give a direction under subsection (1), the Authority must have particular regard to—

(a) the interests of policyholders and potential policyholders;

(b) any failure by the Society to satisfy an obligation to which it is subject as a result of a provision of the law of another EEA State which—

(i) gives effect to any of the insurance directives; and

(ii) is applicable to an activity carried on in that State by a person to whom this section applies;

(c) the need to ensure the effective exercise of the functions which the Authority has in relation to the Society as a result of section 315.

(5) A direction under subsection (1) must be in writing.

(6) A direction under subsection (1) applying the general prohibition may apply it in relation to different classes of person.

(7) An insurance market direction—

(a) must specify each core provision, class of person and kind of activity to which it applies;

(b) may apply different provisions in relation to different classes of person and different kinds of activity.

(8) A direction under subsection (1) has effect from the date specified in it, which may not be earlier than the date on which it is made.

(9) A direction under subsection (1) must be published in the way appearing to the Authority to be best calculated to bring it to the attention of the public.

(10) The Authority may charge a reasonable fee for providing a person with a copy of the direction.

(11) The Authority must, without delay, give the Treasury a copy of any direction which it gives under this section.

[204]

317 The core provisions

(1) The core provisions are Parts V, X, XI, XII, XIV, XV, XVI, XXII and XXIV, sections 384 to 386 and Part XXVI.

(2) References in an applied core provision to an authorised person are (where necessary) to be read as references to a person in the class to which the insurance market direction applies.
(3) An insurance market direction may provide that a core provision is to have effect, in relation to persons to whom the provision is applied by the direction, with modifications.

[205]
318 Exercise of powers through Council
(1) The Authority may give a direction under this subsection to the Council or to the Society (acting through the Council) or to both.
(2) A direction under subsection (1) is one given to the body concerned—
 (a) in relation to the exercise of its powers generally with a view to achieving, or in support of, a specified objective; or
 (b) in relation to the exercise of a specified power which it has, whether in a specified manner or with a view to achieving, or in support of, a specified objective.
(3) "Specified" means specified in the direction.
(4) A direction under subsection (1) may be given—
 (a) instead of giving a direction under section 316(1); or
 (b) if the Authority considers it necessary or expedient to do so, at the same time as, or following, the giving of such a direction.
(5) A direction may also be given under subsection (1) in respect of underwriting agents as if they were among the persons mentioned in section 316(1).
(6) A direction under this section—
 (a) does not, at any time, prevent the exercise by the Authority of any of its powers;
 (b) must be in writing.
(7) A direction under subsection (1) must be published in the way appearing to the Authority to be best calculated to bring it to the attention of the public.
(8) The Authority may charge a reasonable fee for providing a person with a copy of the direction.
(9) The Authority must, without delay, give the Treasury a copy of any direction which it gives under this section.

[206]
319 Consultation
(1) Before giving a direction under section 316 or 318, the Authority must publish a draft of the proposed direction.
(2) The draft must be accompanied by—
 (a) a cost benefit analysis; and
 (b) notice that representations about the proposed direction may be made to the Authority within a specified time.
(3) Before giving the proposed direction, the Authority must have regard to any representations made to it in accordance with subsection (2)(b).
(4) If the Authority gives the proposed direction it must publish an account, in general terms, of—
 (a) the representations made to it in accordance with subsection (2)(b); and
 (b) its response to them.
(5) If the direction differs from the draft published under subsection (1) in a way which is, in the opinion of the Authority, significant—
 (a) the Authority must (in addition to complying with subsection (4)) publish details of the difference; and
 (b) those details must be accompanied by a cost benefit analysis.
(6) Subsections (1) to (5) do not apply if the Authority considers that the delay involved in complying with them would be prejudicial to the interests of consumers.
(7) Neither subsection (2)(a) nor subsection (5)(b) applies if the Authority considers—
 (a) that, making the appropriate comparison, there will be no increase in costs; or
 (b) that, making that comparison, there will be an increase in costs but the increase will be of minimal significance.
(8) The Authority may charge a reasonable fee for providing a person with a copy of a draft published under subsection (1).
(9) When the Authority is required to publish a document under this section it must do so in the way appearing to it to be best calculated to bring it to the attention of the public.
(10) "Cost benefit analysis" means an estimate of the costs together with an analysis of the benefits that will arise—
 (a) if the proposed direction is given; or
 (b) if subsection (5)(b) applies, from the direction that has been given.
(11) "The appropriate comparison" means—

(a) in relation to subsection (2)(a), a comparison between the overall position if the direction is given and the overall position if it is not given;
(b) in relation to subsection (5)(b), a comparison between the overall position after the giving of the direction and the overall position before it was given.

Former underwriting members

[207]
320 Former underwriting members
(1) A former underwriting member may carry out each contract of insurance that he has underwritten at Lloyd's whether or not he is an authorised person.
(2) If he is an authorised person, any Part IV permission that he has does not extend to his activities in carrying out any of those contracts.
(3) The Authority may impose on a former underwriting member such requirements as appear to it to be appropriate for the purpose of protecting policyholders against the risk that he may not be able to meet his liabilities.
(4) A person on whom a requirement is imposed may refer the matter to the Tribunal.

[208]
321 Requirements imposed under section 320
(1) A requirement imposed under section 320 takes effect—
(a) immediately, if the notice given under subsection (2) states that that is the case;
(b) in any other case, on such date as may be specified in that notice.
(2) If the Authority proposes to impose a requirement on a former underwriting member ("A") under section 320, or imposes such a requirement on him which takes effect immediately, it must give him written notice.
(3) The notice must—
(a) give details of the requirement;
(b) state the Authority's reasons for imposing it;
(c) inform A that he may make representations to the Authority within such period as may be specified in the notice (whether or not he has referred the matter to the Tribunal);
(d) inform him of the date on which the requirement took effect or will take effect; and
(e) inform him of his right to refer the matter to the Tribunal.
(4) The Authority may extend the period allowed under the notice for making representations.
(5) If, having considered any representations made by A, the Authority decides—
(a) to impose the proposed requirement, or
(b) if it has been imposed, not to revoke it,
it must give him written notice.
(6) If the Authority decides—
(a) not to impose a proposed requirement, or
(b) to revoke a requirement that has been imposed,
it must give A written notice.
(7) If the Authority decides to grant an application by A for the variation or revocation of a requirement, it must give him written notice of its decision.
(8) If the Authority proposes to refuse an application by A for the variation or revocation of a requirement it must give him a warning notice.
(9) If the Authority, having considered any representations made in response to the warning notice, decides to refuse the application, it must give A a decision notice.
(10) A notice given under—
(a) subsection (5), or
(b) subsection (9) in the case of a decision to refuse the application,
must inform A of his right to refer the matter to the Tribunal.
(11) If the Authority decides to refuse an application for a variation or revocation of the requirement, the applicant may refer the matter to the Tribunal.
(12) If a notice informs a person of his right to refer a matter to the Tribunal, it must give an indication of the procedure on such a reference.

[209]
322 Rules applicable to former underwriting members
(1) The Authority may make rules imposing such requirements on persons to whom the rules apply as appear to it to be appropriate for protecting policyholders against the risk that those persons may not be able to meet their liabilities.
(2) The rules may apply to—
(a) former underwriting members generally; or

(b) to a class of former underwriting member specified in them.

(3) Section 319 applies to the making of proposed rules under this section as it applies to the giving of a proposed direction under section 316.

(4) Part X (except sections 152 to 154) does not apply to rules made under this section.

Transfers of business done at Lloyd's

[210]

323 Transfer schemes

The Treasury may by order provide for the application of any provision of Part VII (with or without modification) in relation to schemes for the transfer of the whole or any part of the business carried on by one or more [underwriting members of the Society or by one or more persons who have ceased to be such a member (whether before, on or after 24th December 1996)].

NOTES

Words in square brackets substituted by the Financial Services and Markets Act 2000 (Amendment of section 323) Regulations 2008, SI 2008/1469, reg 2.

Orders: the Financial Services and Markets Act 2000 (Control of Transfers of Business Done at Lloyd's) Order 2001, SI 2001/3626 at **[826]**.

Supplemental

[211]

324 Interpretation of this Part

(1) In this Part—

"arranging deals", in relation to the investments to which this Part applies, has the same meaning as in paragraph 3 of Schedule 2;

"former underwriting member" means a person ceasing to be an underwriting member of the Society on, or at any time after, 24 December 1996; and

"participation in Lloyd's syndicates", in relation to the secondary market activity, means the investment described in sub-paragraph (1) of paragraph 21 of Schedule 2.

(2) A term used in this Part which is defined in Lloyd's Act 1982 has the same meaning as in that Act.

PART XX

PROVISION OF FINANCIAL SERVICES BY MEMBERS OF THE PROFESSIONS

[212]

325 Authority's general duty

(1) The Authority must keep itself informed about—

(a) the way in which designated professional bodies supervise and regulate the carrying on of exempt regulated activities by members of the professions in relation to which they are established;

(b) the way in which such members are carrying on exempt regulated activities.

(2) In this Part—

"exempt regulated activities" means regulated activities which may, as a result of this Part, be carried on by members of a profession which is supervised and regulated by a designated professional body without breaching the general prohibition; and

"members", in relation to a profession, means persons who are entitled to practise the profession in question and, in practising it, are subject to the rules of the body designated in relation to that profession, whether or not they are members of that body.

(3) The Authority must keep under review the desirability of exercising any of its powers under this Part.

(4) Each designated professional body must co-operate with the Authority, by the sharing of information and in other ways, in order to enable the Authority to perform its functions under this Part.

[213]

326 Designation of professional bodies

(1) The Treasury may by order designate bodies for the purposes of this Part.

(2) A body designated under subsection (1) is referred to in this Part as a designated professional body.

(3) The Treasury may designate a body under subsection (1) only if they are satisfied that—

(a) the basic condition, and

(b) one or more of the additional conditions,

are met in relation to it.

(4) The basic condition is that the body has rules applicable to the carrying on by members of the profession in relation to which it is established of regulated activities which, if the body were to be designated, would be exempt regulated activities.

(5) The additional conditions are that—

(a) the body has power under any enactment to regulate the practice of the profession;

(b) being a member of the profession is a requirement under any enactment for the exercise of particular functions or the holding of a particular office;

(c) the body has been recognised for the purpose of any enactment other than this Act and the recognition has not been withdrawn;

(d) the body is established in an EEA State other than the United Kingdom and in that State—

(i) the body has power corresponding to that mentioned in paragraph (a);

(ii) there is a requirement in relation to the body corresponding to that mentioned in paragraph (b); or

(iii) the body is recognised in a manner corresponding to that mentioned in paragraph (c).

(6) "Enactment" includes an Act of the Scottish Parliament, Northern Ireland legislation and subordinate legislation (whether made under an Act, an Act of the Scottish Parliament or Northern Ireland legislation).

(7) "Recognised" means recognised by—

(a) a Minister of the Crown;

(b) the Scottish Ministers;

(c) a Northern Ireland Minister;

(d) a Northern Ireland department or its head.

NOTES

Orders: the Financial Services and Markets Act 2000 (Designated Professional Bodies) Order 2001, SI 2001/1226.

[214]

327 Exemption from the general prohibition

(1) The general prohibition does not apply to the carrying on of a regulated activity by a person ("P") if—

(a) the conditions set out in subsections (2) to (7) are satisfied; and

(b) there is not in force—

(i) a direction under section 328, or

(ii) an order under section 329,

which prevents this subsection from applying to the carrying on of that activity by him.

(2) P must be—

(a) a member of a profession; or

(b) controlled or managed by one or more such members.

(3) P must not receive from a person other than his client any pecuniary reward or other advantage, for which he does not account to his client, arising out of his carrying on of any of the activities.

(4) The manner of the provision by P of any service in the course of carrying on the activities must be incidental to the provision by him of professional services.

(5) P must not carry on, or hold himself out as carrying on, a regulated activity other than—

(a) one which rules made as a result of section 332(3) allow him to carry on; or

(b) one in relation to which he is an exempt person.

(6) The activities must not be of a description, or relate to an investment of a description, specified in an order made by the Treasury for the purposes of this subsection.

(7) The activities must be the only regulated activities carried on by P (other than regulated activities in relation to which he is an exempt person).

(8) "Professional services" means services—

(a) which do not constitute carrying on a regulated activity, and

(b) the provision of which is supervised and regulated by a designated professional body.

NOTES

Orders: the Financial Services and Markets Act 2000 (Professions) (Non-Exempt Activities) Order 2001, SI 2001/1227 at **[599]**; the Financial Services and Markets Act 2000 (Miscellaneous Provisions) Order 2001, SI 2001/3650.

[215]
328 Directions in relation to the general prohibition
(1) The Authority may direct that section 327(1) is not to apply to the extent specified in the direction.
(2) A direction under subsection (1)—
(a) must be in writing;
(b) may be given in relation to different classes of person or different descriptions of regulated activity.
(3) A direction under subsection (1) must be published in the way appearing to the Authority to be best calculated to bring it to the attention of the public.
(4) The Authority may charge a reasonable fee for providing a person with a copy of the direction.
(5) The Authority must, without delay, give the Treasury a copy of any direction which it gives under this section.
[(6) The Authority may exercise the power conferred by subsection (1) only if it is satisfied either—
(a) that it is desirable to do so in order to protect the interests of clients; or
(b) that it is necessary to do so in order to comply with a Community obligation imposed by the insurance mediation directive.]
(7) In considering whether it is [satisfied of the matter specified in subsection (6)(a)], the Authority must have regard amongst other things to the effectiveness of any arrangements made by any designated professional body—
(a) for securing compliance with rules made under section 332(1);
(b) for dealing with complaints against its members in relation to the carrying on by them of exempt regulated activities;
(c) in order to offer redress to clients who suffer, or claim to have suffered, loss as a result of misconduct by its members in their carrying on of exempt regulated activities;
(d) for co-operating with the Authority under section 325(4).
(8) In this Part "clients" means—
(a) persons who use, have used or are or may be contemplating using, any of the services provided by a member of a profession in the course of carrying on exempt regulated activities;
(b) persons who have rights or interests which are derived from, or otherwise attributable to, the use of any such services by other persons; or
(c) persons who have rights or interests which may be adversely affected by the use of any such services by persons acting on their behalf or in a fiduciary capacity in relation to them.
(9) If a member of a profession is carrying on an exempt regulated activity in his capacity as a trustee, the persons who are, have been or may be beneficiaries of the trust are to be treated as persons who use, have used or are or may be contemplating using services provided by that person in his carrying on of that activity.

NOTES
Sub-s (6): substituted by the Insurance Mediation Directive (Miscellaneous Amendments) Regulations 2003, SI 2003/1473, reg 9(a).
Sub-s (7): words in square brackets substituted by SI 2003/1473, reg 9(b).

[216]
329 Orders in relation to the general prohibition
(1) Subsection (2) applies if it appears to the Authority that a person to whom, as a result of section 327(1), the general prohibition does not apply is not a fit and proper person to carry on regulated activities in accordance with that section.
(2) The Authority may make an order disapplying section 327(1) in relation to that person to the extent specified in the order.
(3) The Authority may, on the application of the person named in an order under subsection (1), vary or revoke it.
(4) "Specified" means specified in the order.
(5) If a partnership is named in an order under this section, the order is not affected by any change in its membership.
(6) If a partnership named in an order under this section is dissolved, the order continues to have effect in relation to any partnership which succeeds to the business of the dissolved partnership.
(7) For the purposes of subsection (6), a partnership is to be regarded as succeeding to the business of another partnership only if—

(a) the members of the resulting partnership are substantially the same as those of the former partnership; and
(b) succession is to the whole or substantially the whole of the business of the former partnership.

[217]
330 Consultation
(1) Before giving a direction under section 328(1), the Authority must publish a draft of the proposed direction.
(2) The draft must be accompanied by—
(a) a cost benefit analysis; and
(b) notice that representations about the proposed direction may be made to the Authority within a specified time.
(3) Before giving the proposed direction, the Authority must have regard to any representations made to it in accordance with subsection (2)(b).
(4) If the Authority gives the proposed direction it must publish an account, in general terms, of—
(a) the representations made to it in accordance with subsection (2)(b); and
(b) its response to them.
(5) If the direction differs from the draft published under subsection (1) in a way which is, in the opinion of the Authority, significant—
(a) the Authority must (in addition to complying with subsection (4)) publish details of the difference; and
(b) those details must be accompanied by a cost benefit analysis.
(6) Subsections (1) to (5) do not apply if the Authority considers that the delay involved in complying with them would prejudice the interests of consumers.
(7) Neither subsection (2)(a) nor subsection (5)(b) applies if the Authority considers—
(a) that, making the appropriate comparison, there will be no increase in costs; or
(b) that, making that comparison, there will be an increase in costs but the increase will be of minimal significance.
(8) The Authority may charge a reasonable fee for providing a person with a copy of a draft published under subsection (1).
(9) When the Authority is required to publish a document under this section it must do so in the way appearing to it to be best calculated to bring it to the attention of the public.
(10) "Cost benefit analysis" means an estimate of the costs together with an analysis of the benefits that will arise—
(a) if the proposed direction is given; or
(b) if subsection (5)(b) applies, from the direction that has been given.
(11) "The appropriate comparison" means—
(a) in relation to subsection (2)(a), a comparison between the overall position if the direction is given and the overall position if it is not given;
(b) in relation to subsection (5)(b), a comparison between the overall position after the giving of the direction and the overall position before it was given.

[218]
331 Procedure on making or varying orders under section 329
(1) If the Authority proposes to make an order under section 329, it must give the person concerned a warning notice.
(2) The warning notice must set out the terms of the proposed order.
(3) If the Authority decides to make an order under section 329, it must give the person concerned a decision notice.
(4) The decision notice must—
(a) name the person to whom the order applies;
(b) set out the terms of the order; and
(c) be given to the person named in the order.
(5) Subsections (6) to (8) apply to an application for the variation or revocation of an order under section 329.
(6) If the Authority decides to grant the application, it must give the applicant written notice of its decision.
(7) If the Authority proposes to refuse the application, it must give the applicant a warning notice.
(8) If the Authority decides to refuse the application, it must give the applicant a decision notice.
(9) A person—
(a) against whom the Authority have decided to make an order under section 329, or

(b) whose application for the variation or revocation of such an order the Authority had decided to refuse,

may refer the matter to the Tribunal.

(10) The Authority may not make an order under section 329 unless—

(a) the period within which the decision to make to the order may be referred to the Tribunal has expired and no such reference has been made; or

(b) if such a reference has been made, the reference has been determined.

[219]

332 Rules in relation to persons to whom the general prohibition does not apply

(1) The Authority may make rules applicable to persons to whom, as a result of section 327(1), the general prohibition does not apply.

(2) The power conferred by subsection (1) is to be exercised for the purpose of ensuring that clients are aware that such persons are not authorised persons.

(3) A designated professional body must make rules—

(a) applicable to members of the profession in relation to which it is established who are not authorised persons; and

(b) governing the carrying on by those members of regulated activities (other than regulated activities in relation to which they are exempt persons).

(4) Rules made in compliance with subsection (3) must be designed to secure that, in providing a particular professional service to a particular client, the member carries on only regulated activities which arise out of, or are complementary to, the provision by him of that service to that client.

(5) Rules made by a designated professional body under subsection (3) require the approval of the Authority.

[220]

333 False claims to be a person to whom the general prohibition does not apply

(1) A person who—

(a) describes himself (in whatever terms) as a person to whom the general prohibition does not apply, in relation to a particular regulated activity, as a result of this Part, or

(b) behaves, or otherwise holds himself out, in a manner which indicates (or which is reasonably likely to be understood as indicating) that he is such a person,

is guilty of an offence if he is not such a person.

(2) In proceedings for an offence under this section it is a defence for the accused to show that he took all reasonable precautions and exercised all due diligence to avoid committing the offence.

(3) A person guilty of an offence under this section is liable on summary conviction to imprisonment for a term not exceeding six months or a fine not exceeding level 5 on the standard scale, or both.

(4) But where the conduct constituting the offence involved or included the public display of any material, the maximum fine for the offence is level 5 on the standard scale multiplied by the number of days for which the display continued.

PART XXI
MUTUAL SOCIETIES

Friendly societies

[221]

334 The Friendly Societies Commission

(1) The Treasury may by order provide—

(a) for any functions of the Friendly Societies Commission to be transferred to the Authority;

(b) for any functions of the Friendly Societies Commission which have not been, or are not being, transferred to the Authority to be transferred to the Treasury.

(2) If the Treasury consider it appropriate to do so, they may by order provide for the Friendly Societies Commission to cease to exist on a day specified in or determined in accordance with the order.

(3) The enactments relating to friendly societies which are mentioned in Part I of Schedule 18 are amended as set out in that Part.

(4) Part II of Schedule 18—

(a) removes certain restrictions on the ability of incorporated friendly societies to form subsidiaries and control corporate bodies; and

(b) makes connected amendments.

NOTES

Orders: the Financial Services and Markets Act 2000 (Mutual Societies) Order 2001, SI 2001/2617 at **[651]**.

[222]

335 The Registry of Friendly Societies

(1) The Treasury may by order provide—

(a) for any functions of the Chief Registrar of Friendly Societies, or of an assistant registrar of friendly societies for the central registration area, to be transferred to the Authority;

(b) for any of their functions which have not been, or are not being, transferred to the Authority to be transferred to the Treasury.

(2) The Treasury may by order provide—

(a) for any functions of the central office of the registry of friendly societies to be transferred to the Authority;

(b) for any functions of that office which have not been, or are not being, transferred to the Authority to be transferred to the Treasury.

(3) The Treasury may by order provide—

(a) for any functions of the assistant registrar of friendly societies for Scotland to be transferred to the Authority;

(b) for any functions of the assistant registrar which have not been, or are not being, transferred to the Authority to be transferred to the Treasury.

(4) If the Treasury consider it appropriate to do so, they may by order provide for—

(a) the office of Chief Registrar of Friendly Societies,

(b) the office of assistant registrar of friendly societies for the central registration area,

(c) the central office, or

(d) the office of assistant registrar of friendly societies for Scotland,

to cease to exist on a day specified in or determined in accordance with the order.

NOTES

Orders: the Financial Services and Markets Act 2000 (Mutual Societies) Order 2001, SI 2001/2617 at **[651]**.

Building societies

[223]

336 The Building Societies Commission

(1) The Treasury may by order provide—

(a) for any functions of the Building Societies Commission to be transferred to the Authority;

(b) for any functions of the Building Societies Commission which have not been, or are not being, transferred to the Authority to be transferred to the Treasury.

(2) If the Treasury consider it appropriate to do so, they may by order provide for the Building Societies Commission to cease to exist on a day specified in or determined in accordance with the order.

(3) The enactments relating to building societies which are mentioned in Part III of Schedule 18 are amended as set out in that Part.

NOTES

Orders: the Financial Services and Markets Act 2000 (Mutual Societies) Order 2001, SI 2001/2617 at **[651]**.

[224]

337 The Building Societies Investor Protection Board

The Treasury may by order provide for the Building Societies Investor Protection Board to cease to exist on a day specified in or determined in accordance with the order.

NOTES

Orders: the Financial Services and Markets Act 2000 (Mutual Societies) Order 2001, SI 2001/2617 at **[651]**.

Industrial and provident societies and credit unions

[225]

338 Industrial and provident societies and credit unions

(1) The Treasury may by order provide for the transfer to the Authority of any functions conferred by—

(a) the Industrial and Provident Societies Act 1965;

(b) the Industrial and Provident Societies Act 1967;

(c) the Friendly and Industrial and Provident Societies Act 1968;
(d) the Industrial and Provident Societies Act 1975;
(e) the Industrial and Provident Societies Act 1978;
(f) the Credit Unions Act 1979.

(2) The Treasury may by order provide for the transfer to the Treasury of any functions under those enactments which have not been, or are not being, transferred to the Authority.

(3) The enactments relating to industrial and provident societies which are mentioned in Part IV of Schedule 18 are amended as set out in that Part.

(4) The enactments relating to credit unions which are mentioned in Part V of Schedule 18 are amended as set out in that Part.

NOTES

Orders: the Financial Services and Markets Act 2000 (Mutual Societies) Order 2001, SI 2001/2617 at **[651]**.

Supplemental

[226]

339 Supplemental provisions

(1) The additional powers conferred by section 428 on a person making an order under this Act include power for the Treasury, when making an order under section 334, 335, 336 or 338 which transfers functions, to include provision—
(a) for the transfer of any functions of a member of the body, or servant or agent of the body or person, whose functions are transferred by the order;
(b) for the transfer of any property, rights or liabilities held, enjoyed or incurred by any person in connection with transferred functions;
(c) for the carrying on and completion by or under the authority of the person to whom functions are transferred of any proceedings, investigations or other matters commenced, before the order takes effect, by or under the authority of the person from whom the functions are transferred;
(d) amending any enactment relating to transferred functions in connection with their exercise by, or under the authority of, the person to whom they are transferred;
(e) for the substitution of the person to whom functions are transferred for the person from whom they are transferred, in any instrument, contract or legal proceedings made or begun before the order takes effect.

(2) The additional powers conferred by section 428 on a person making an order under this Act include power for the Treasury, when making an order under section 334(2), 335(4), 336(2) or 337, to include provision—
(a) for the transfer of any property, rights or liabilities held, enjoyed or incurred by any person in connection with the office or body which ceases to have effect as a result of the order;
(b) for the carrying on and completion by or under the authority of such person as may be specified in the order of any proceedings, investigations or other matters commenced, before the order takes effect, by or under the authority of the person whose office, or the body which, ceases to exist as a result of the order;
(c) amending any enactment which makes provision with respect to that office or body;
(d) for the substitution of the Authority, the Treasury or such other body as may be specified in the order in any instrument, contract or legal proceedings made or begun before the order takes effect.

(3) On or after the making of an order under any of sections 334 to 338 ("the original order"), the Treasury may by order make any incidental, supplemental, consequential or transitional provision which they had power to include in the original order.

(4) A certificate issued by the Treasury that property vested in a person immediately before an order under this Part takes effect has been transferred as a result of the order is conclusive evidence of the transfer.

(5) Subsections (1) and (2) are not to be read as affecting in any way the powers conferred by section 428.

NOTES

Orders: the Financial Services and Markets Act 2000 (Mutual Societies) Order 2001, SI 2001/2617 at **[651]**; the Financial Services and Markets Act 2000 (Transitional Provisions, Repeals and Savings) (Financial Services Compensation Scheme) Order 2001, SI 2001/2967; the Financial Services and Markets Act 2000 (Consequential Amendments and Savings) (Industrial Assurance) Order 2001, SI 2001/3647.

PART XXII
AUDITORS AND ACTUARIES
Appointment

[227]
340 Appointment
(1) Rules may require an authorised person, or an authorised person falling within a specified class—
(a) to appoint an auditor, or
(b) to appoint an actuary,
if he is not already under an obligation to do so imposed by another enactment.
(2) Rules may require an authorised person, or an authorised person falling within a specified class—
(a) to produce periodic financial reports; and
(b) to have them reported on by an auditor or an actuary.
(3) Rules may impose such other duties on auditors of, or actuaries acting for, authorised persons as may be specified.
(4) Rules under subsection (1) may make provision—
(a) specifying the manner in which and time within which an auditor or actuary is to be appointed;
(b) requiring the Authority to be notified of an appointment;
(c) enabling the Authority to make an appointment if no appointment has been made or notified;
(d) as to remuneration;
(e) as to the term of office, removal and resignation of an auditor or actuary.
(5) An auditor or actuary appointed as a result of rules under subsection (1), or on whom duties are imposed by rules under subsection (3)—
(a) must act in accordance with such provision as may be made by rules; and
(b) is to have such powers in connection with the discharge of his functions as may be provided by rules.
(6) In subsections (1) to (3) "auditor" or "actuary" means an auditor, or actuary, who satisfies such requirements as to qualifications, experience and other matters (if any) as may be specified.
(7) "Specified" means specified in rules.

Information

[228]
341 Access to books etc
(1) An appointed auditor of, or an appointed actuary acting for, an authorised person—
(a) has a right of access at all times to the authorised person's books, accounts and vouchers; and
(b) is entitled to require from the authorised person's officers such information and explanations as he reasonably considers necessary for the performance of his duties as auditor or actuary.
(2) "Appointed" means appointed under or as a result of this Act.

NOTES
Modification: this section and ss 342–346 are applied, with modifications, in respect of the Financial Services Authority's functions under the Payment Services Regulations 2009, SI 2009/209; see SI 2009/209, reg 95, Sch 5, Pt 1, para 4.

[229]
342 Information given by auditor or actuary to the Authority
(1) This section applies to a person who is, or has been, an auditor of an authorised person appointed under or as a result of a statutory provision.
(2) This section also applies to a person who is, or has been, an actuary acting for an authorised person and appointed under or as a result of a statutory provision.
(3) An auditor or actuary does not contravene any duty to which he is subject merely because he gives to the Authority—
(a) information on a matter of which he has, or had, become aware in his capacity as auditor of, or actuary acting for, the authorised person, or
(b) his opinion on such a matter,
if he is acting in good faith and he reasonably believes that the information or opinion is relevant to any functions of the Authority.

(4) Subsection (3) applies whether or not the auditor or actuary is responding to a request from the Authority.
(5) The Treasury may make regulations prescribing circumstances in which an auditor or actuary must communicate matters to the Authority as mentioned in subsection (3).
(6) It is the duty of an auditor or actuary to whom any such regulations apply to communicate a matter to the Authority in the circumstances prescribed by the regulations.
(7) The matters to be communicated to the Authority in accordance with the regulations may include matters relating to persons other than the authorised person concerned.

NOTES

Modification: see the note to s 341 at **[228]**.

Regulations: the Financial Services and Markets Act 2000 (Communications by Auditors) Regulations 2001, SI 2001/2587 at **[649]**; the Financial Services and Markets Act 2000 (Communications by Actuaries) Regulations 2003, SI 2003/1294 at **[859]**.

[230]

343 Information given by auditor or actuary to the Authority: persons with close links

(1) This section applies to a person who—
- (a) is, or has been, an auditor of an authorised person appointed under or as a result of a statutory provision; and
- (b) is, or has been, an auditor of a person ("CL") who has close links with the authorised person.

(2) This section also applies to a person who—
- (a) is, or has been, an actuary acting for an authorised person and appointed under or as a result of a statutory provision; and
- (b) is, or has been, an actuary acting for a person ("CL") who has close links with the authorised person.

(3) An auditor or actuary does not contravene any duty to which he is subject merely because he gives to the Authority—
- (a) information on a matter concerning the authorised person of which he has, or had, become aware in his capacity as auditor of, or actuary acting for, CL, or
- (b) his opinion on such a matter,

if he is acting in good faith and he reasonably believes that the information or opinion is relevant to any functions of the Authority.
(4) Subsection (3) applies whether or not the auditor or actuary is responding to a request from the Authority.
(5) The Treasury may make regulations prescribing circumstances in which an auditor or actuary must communicate matters to the Authority as mentioned in subsection (3).
(6) It is the duty of an auditor or actuary to whom any such regulations apply to communicate a matter to the Authority in the circumstances prescribed by the regulations.
(7) The matters to be communicated to the Authority in accordance with the regulations may include matters relating to persons other than the authorised person concerned.
(8) CL has close links with the authorised person concerned ("A") if CL is—
- (a) a parent undertaking of A;
- (b) a subsidiary undertaking of A;
- (c) a parent undertaking of a subsidiary undertaking of A; or
- (d) a subsidiary undertaking of a parent undertaking of A.

(9) "Subsidiary undertaking" includes all the instances mentioned in Article 1(1) and (2) of the Seventh Company Law Directive in which an entity may be a subsidiary of an undertaking.

NOTES

Modification: see the note to s 341 at **[228]**.

Regulations: the Financial Services and Markets Act 2000 (Communications by Auditors) Regulations 2001, SI 2001/2587 at **[649]**; the Financial Services and Markets Act 2000 (Communications by Actuaries) Regulations 2003, SI 2003/1294 at **[859]**.

[231]

344 Duty of auditor or actuary resigning etc to give notice

(1) This section applies to an auditor or actuary to whom section 342 applies.
(2) He must without delay notify the Authority if he—
- (a) is removed from office by an authorised person;
- (b) resigns before the expiry of his term of office with such a person; or
- (c) is not re-appointed by such a person.

(3) If he ceases to be an auditor of, or actuary acting for, such a person, he must without delay notify the Authority—

(a) of any matter connected with his so ceasing which he thinks ought to be drawn to the Authority's attention; or

(b) that there is no such matter.

NOTES

Modification: see the note to s 341 at **[228]**.

Disqualification

[232]

345 Disqualification

(1) If it appears to the Authority that an auditor or actuary to whom section 342 applies has failed to comply with a duty imposed on him under this Act, it may disqualify him from being the auditor of, or (as the case may be) from acting as an actuary for, any authorised person or any particular class of authorised person.

(2) If the Authority proposes to disqualify a person under this section it must give him a warning notice.

(3) If it decides to disqualify him it must give him a decision notice.

(4) The Authority may remove any disqualification imposed under this section if satisfied that the disqualified person will in future comply with the duty in question.

(5) A person who has been disqualified under this section may refer the matter to the Tribunal.

NOTES

Modification: see the note to s 341 at **[228]**.

Offence

[233]

346 Provision of false or misleading information to auditor or actuary

(1) An authorised person who knowingly or recklessly gives an appointed auditor or actuary information which is false or misleading in a material particular is guilty of an offence and liable—

(a) on summary conviction, to imprisonment for a term not exceeding six months or a fine not exceeding the statutory maximum, or both;

(b) on conviction on indictment, to imprisonment for a term not exceeding two years or a fine, or both.

(2) Subsection (1) applies equally to an officer, controller or manager of an authorised person.

(3) "Appointed" means appointed under or as a result of this Act.

NOTES

Modification: see the note to s 341 at **[228]**.

PART XXIII
PUBLIC RECORD, DISCLOSURE OF INFORMATION AND CO-OPERATION

The public record

[234]

347 The record of authorised persons etc

(1) The Authority must maintain a record of every—

(a) person who appears to the Authority to be an authorised person;

(b) authorised unit trust scheme;

(c) authorised open-ended investment company;

(d) recognised scheme;

(e) recognised investment exchange;

(f) recognised clearing house;

(g) individual to whom a prohibition order relates;

(h) approved person; . . .

[(ha) person to whom subsection (2A) applies; and]

(i) person falling within such other class (if any) as the Authority may determine.

(2) The record must include such information as the Authority considers appropriate and at least the following information—

(a) in the case of a person appearing to the Authority to be an authorised person—

(i) information as to the services which he holds himself out as able to provide; and

(ii) any address of which the Authority is aware at which a notice or other document may be served on him;

(b) in the case of an authorised unit trust scheme, the name and address of the manager and trustee of the scheme;

(c) in the case of an authorised open-ended investment company, the name and address of—

(i) the company;

(ii) if it has only one director, the director; and

(iii) its depositary (if any);

(d) in the case of a recognised scheme, the name and address of—

(i) the operator of the scheme; and

(ii) any representative of the operator in the United Kingdom;

(e) in the case of a recognised investment exchange or recognised clearing house, the name and address of the exchange or clearing house;

(f) in the case of an individual to whom a prohibition order relates—

(i) his name; and

(ii) details of the effect of the order;

(g) in the case of a person who is an approved person—

(i) his name;

(ii) the name of the relevant authorised person;

(iii) if the approved person is performing a controlled function under an arrangement with a contractor of the relevant authorised person, the name of the contractor.

[(2A) This subsection applies to—

(a) an appointed representative to whom subsection (1A) of section 39 applies for whom the applicable register (as defined by subsection (1B) of that section) is the record maintained by virtue of subsection (1)(ha) above;

(b) a person mentioned in subsection (1)(a) of section 39A if—

(i) the contract with an authorised person to which he is party complies with the applicable requirements (as defined by subsection (7) of that section), and

(ii) the authorised person has accepted responsibility in writing for the person's activities in carrying on investment services business (as defined by subsection (8) of that section); and

(c) any person not falling within paragraph (a) or (b) in respect of whom the Authority considers that a record must be maintained for the purpose of securing compliance with Article 23.3 of the markets in financial instruments directive (registration of tied agents).]

(3) If it appears to the Authority that a person in respect of whom there is an entry in the record as a result of one of the paragraphs of subsection (1) has ceased to be a person to whom that paragraph applies, the Authority may remove the entry from the record.

(4) But if the Authority decides not to remove the entry, it must—

(a) make a note to that effect in the record; and

(b) state why it considers that the person has ceased to be a person to whom that paragraph applies.

(5) The Authority must—

(a) make the record available for inspection by members of the public in a legible form at such times and in such place or places as the Authority may determine; and

(b) provide a certified copy of the record, or any part of it, to any person who asks for it—

(i) on payment of the fee (if any) fixed by the Authority; and

(ii) in a form (either written or electronic) in which it is legible to the person asking for it.

(6) The Authority may—

(a) publish the record, or any part of it;

(b) exploit commercially the information contained in the record, or any part of that information.

(7) "Authorised unit trust scheme", "authorised open-ended investment company" and "recognised scheme" have the same meaning as in Part XVII, and associated expressions are to be read accordingly.

(8) "Approved person" means a person in relation to whom the Authority has given its approval under section 59 and "controlled function" and "arrangement" have the same meaning as in that section.

(9) "Relevant authorised person" has the meaning given in section 66.

NOTES

Sub-s (1): word omitted from para (h) repealed, and para (ha) inserted by the Financial Services and Markets Act 2000 (Markets in Financial Instruments) Regulations 2007, SI 2007/126, reg 3(5), Sch 5, paras 1, 12(a), (b), subject to transitional provisions in reg 9 thereof.

Sub-s (2A): inserted by SI 2007/126, reg 3(5), Sch 5, paras 1, 12(c), subject to transitional provisions in reg 9 thereof.

Disapplication: sub-s (1)(a), (h) above is disapplied in relation to persons with an interim permission or an interim approval, by the Financial Services and Markets Act 2000 (Transitional Provisions) (General Insurance Intermediaries) Order 2004, SI 2004/3351, arts 1(3), 2, 3, 5, Schedule, paras 4, 8, 9, and the Financial Services and Markets Act 2000 (Regulated Activities) (Amendment) Order 2006, SI 2006/1969, art 7, Schedule, paras 4, 9, 10.

Disclosure of information

[235]

348 Restrictions on disclosure of confidential information by Authority etc

(1) Confidential information must not be disclosed by a primary recipient, or by any person obtaining the information directly or indirectly from a primary recipient, without the consent of—

(a) the person from whom the primary recipient obtained the information; and

(b) if different, the person to whom it relates.

(2) In this Part "confidential information" means information which—

(a) relates to the business or other affairs of any person;

(b) was received by the primary recipient for the purposes of, or in the discharge of, any functions of the Authority, the competent authority for the purposes of Part VI or the Secretary of State under any provision made by or under this Act; and

(c) is not prevented from being confidential information by subsection (4).

(3) It is immaterial for the purposes of subsection (2) whether or not the information was received—

(a) by virtue of a requirement to provide it imposed by or under this Act;

(b) for other purposes as well as purposes mentioned in that subsection.

(4) Information is not confidential information if—

(a) it has been made available to the public by virtue of being disclosed in any circumstances in which, or for any purposes for which, disclosure is not precluded by this section; or

(b) it is in the form of a summary or collection of information so framed that it is not possible to ascertain from it information relating to any particular person.

(5) Each of the following is a primary recipient for the purposes of this Part—

(a) the Authority;

(b) any person exercising functions conferred by Part VI on the competent authority;

(c) the Secretary of State;

(d) a person appointed to make a report under section 166;

(e) any person who is or has been employed by a person mentioned in paragraphs (a) to (c);

(f) any auditor or expert instructed by a person mentioned in those paragraphs.

(6) In subsection (5)(f) "expert" includes—

(a) a competent person appointed by the competent authority under section 97;

(b) a competent person appointed by the Authority or the Secretary of State to conduct an investigation under Part XI;

(c) any body or person appointed under paragraph 6 of Schedule 1 to perform a function on behalf of the Authority.

NOTES

Application: this section and ss 349, 352 apply to confidential information disclosed under the Regulated Covered Bonds Regulations 2008, SI 2008/346, as they apply to confidential information disclosed under this Act; see SI 2008/346, reg 43(1).

Modification: this section and ss 349, 351, 352 are applied, with modifications, in relation to the Financial Services Authority's functions under the Payment Services Regulations 2009, SI 2009/209; see SI 2009/209, reg 95, Sch 5, Pt 1, para 5. This section and ss 349, 352 are applied with modifications in respect of the Financial Services Authority's functions under the Cross-Border Payments in Euro Regulations 2010, SI 2010/89; see SI 2010/89, reg 19, Schedule, Pt 1, para 4.

Disapplication: in relation to the disclosure of confidential information by certain authorities or a person obtaining that information directly or indirectly from such an authority where it has been disclosed to the authority by the FSA in reliance on sub-s (1) above, see the Takeovers Directive (Interim Implementation) Regulations 2006, SI 2006/1183, reg 18(1), (2).

[236]
349 Exceptions from section 348

(1) Section 348 does not prevent a disclosure of confidential information which is—
  (a) made for the purpose of facilitating the carrying out of a public function; and
  (b) permitted by regulations made by the Treasury under this section.

(2) The regulations may, in particular, make provision permitting the disclosure of confidential information or of confidential information of a prescribed kind—
  (a) by prescribed recipients, or recipients of a prescribed description, to any person for the purpose of enabling or assisting the recipient to discharge prescribed public functions;
  (b) by prescribed recipients, or recipients of a prescribed description, to prescribed persons, or persons of prescribed descriptions, for the purpose of enabling or assisting those persons to discharge prescribed public functions;
  (c) by the Authority to the Treasury or the Secretary of State for any purpose;
  (d) by any recipient if the disclosure is with a view to or in connection with prescribed proceedings.

(3) The regulations may also include provision—
  (a) making any permission to disclose confidential information subject to conditions (which may relate to the obtaining of consents or any other matter);
  (b) restricting the uses to which confidential information disclosed under the regulations may be put.

[(3A) Section 348 does not apply to—
  (a) the disclosure by a recipient to which subsection (3B) applies of confidential information disclosed to it by the Authority in reliance on subsection (1);
  (b) the disclosure of such information by a person obtaining it directly or indirectly from a recipient to which subsection (3B) applies.

(3B) This subsection applies to—
  (a) the Panel on Takeovers and Mergers;
  (b) an authority designated as a supervisory authority for the purposes of Article 4.1 of the Takeovers Directive;
  (c) any other person or body that exercises public functions, under legislation in an EEA State other than the United Kingdom, that are similar to the Authority's functions or those of the Panel on Takeovers and Mergers.]

(4) In relation to confidential information, each of the following is a "recipient"—
  (a) a primary recipient;
  (b) a person obtaining the information directly or indirectly from a primary recipient.

(5) "Public functions" includes—
  (a) functions conferred by or in accordance with any provision contained in any enactment or subordinate legislation;
  (b) functions conferred by or in accordance with any provision contained in the Community Treaties or any Community instrument;
  (c) similar functions conferred on persons by or under provisions having effect as part of the law of a country or territory outside the United Kingdom;
  (d) functions exercisable in relation to prescribed disciplinary proceedings.

(6) "Enactment" includes—
  (a) an Act of the Scottish Parliament;
  (b) Northern Ireland legislation.

(7) "Subordinate legislation" has the meaning given in the Interpretation Act 1978 and also includes an instrument made under an Act of the Scottish Parliament or under Northern Ireland legislation.

[(8) . . .]

NOTES

Sub-ss (3A), (3B): inserted by the Companies Act 2006, s 964(1), (4).

Sub-s (8): added by the Takeovers Directive (Interim Implementation) Regulations 2006, SI 2006/1183, reg 18(3), (5); repealed by the Companies Act 2006 (Commencement No 2, Consequential Amendments, Transitional Provisions and Savings) Order 2007, SI 2007/1093, art 7, Sch 5.

Application: see the note to s 348 at **[235]**.

Modification: see the note to s 348 at **[235]**.

Regulations: the Financial Services and Markets Act 2000 (Disclosure of Confidential Information) Regulations 2001, SI 2001/2188; the Electronic Commerce Directive (Financial Services and Markets) Regulations 2002, SI 2002/1775.

[237]

350 Disclosure of information by the Inland Revenue

(1) No obligation as to secrecy imposed by statute or otherwise prevents the disclosure of Revenue information to—

(a) the Authority, or

(b) the Secretary of State,

if the disclosure is made for the purpose of assisting in the investigation of a matter under section 168 or with a view to the appointment of an investigator under that section.

(2) A disclosure may only be made under subsection (1) by or under the authority of the Commissioners of Inland Revenue.

(3) Section 348 does not apply to Revenue information.

(4) Information obtained as a result of subsection (1) may not be used except—

(a) for the purpose of deciding whether to appoint an investigator under section 168;

(b) in the conduct of an investigation under section 168;

(c) in criminal proceedings brought against a person under this Act or the Criminal Justice Act 1993 as a result of an investigation under section 168;

(d) for the purpose of taking action under this Act against a person as a result of an investigation under section 168;

(e) in proceedings before the Tribunal as a result of action taken as mentioned in paragraph (d).

(5) Information obtained as a result of subsection (1) may not be disclosed except—

(a) by or under the authority of the Commissioners of Inland Revenue;

(b) in proceedings mentioned in subsection (4)(c) or (e) or with a view to their institution.

(6) Subsection (5) does not prevent the disclosure of information obtained as a result of subsection (1) to a person to whom it could have been disclosed under subsection (1).

(7) "Revenue information" means information held by a person which it would be an offence under section 182 of the Finance Act 1989 for him to disclose.

[238]

351 Competition information

(1)–(3) . . .

(4) Section 348 does not apply to competition information.

(5) "Competition information" means information which—

(a) relates to the affairs of a particular individual or body;

(b) is not otherwise in the public domain; and

(c) was obtained under or by virtue of a competition provision.

(6) "Competition provision" means any provision of—

(a) an order made under section 95;

(b) Chapter III of Part X; or

(c) Chapter II of Part XVIII.

(7) . . .

NOTES

Sub-ss (1)–(3), (7): repealed by the Enterprise Act 2002, ss 247(k), 278(2), Sch 26.

Modification: see the note to s 348 at **[235]**.

[239]

352 Offences

(1) A person who discloses information in contravention of section 348 or 350(5) is guilty of an offence.

(2) A person guilty of an offence under subsection (1) is liable—

(a) on summary conviction, to imprisonment for a term not exceeding three months or a fine not exceeding the statutory maximum, or both;

(b) on conviction on indictment, to imprisonment for a term not exceeding two years or a fine, or both.

(3) A person is guilty of an offence if, in contravention of any provision of regulations made under section 349, he uses information which has been disclosed to him in accordance with the regulations.

(4) A person is guilty of an offence if, in contravention of subsection (4) of section 350, he uses information which has been disclosed to him in accordance with that section.

(5) A person guilty of an offence under subsection (3) or (4) is liable on summary conviction to imprisonment for a term not exceeding *three months* or a fine not exceeding level 5 on the standard scale, or both.

(6) In proceedings for an offence under this section it is a defence for the accused to prove—
(a) that he did not know and had no reason to suspect that the information was confidential information or that it had been disclosed in accordance with section 350;
(b) that he took all reasonable precautions and exercised all due diligence to avoid committing the offence.

NOTES
Sub-s (5): for the words in italics there are substituted the words "51 weeks" by the Criminal Justice Act 2003, s 280(2), (3), Sch 26, para 54(1), (3), as from a day to be appointed.
Application: see the note to s 348 at **[235]**.
Modification: see the note to s 348 at **[235]**.

[240]
353 Removal of other restrictions on disclosure
(1) The Treasury may make regulations permitting the disclosure of any information, or of information of a prescribed kind—
(a) by prescribed persons for the purpose of assisting or enabling them to discharge prescribed functions under this Act or any rules or regulations made under it;
(b) by prescribed persons, or persons of a prescribed description, to the Authority for the purpose of assisting or enabling the Authority to discharge prescribed functions.
[(c) by the scheme operator to the Office of Fair Trading for the purpose of assisting or enabling that Office to discharge prescribed functions under the Consumer Credit Act 1974].
(2) Regulations under this section may not make any provision in relation to the disclosure of confidential information by primary recipients or by any person obtaining confidential information directly or indirectly from a primary recipient.
(3) If a person discloses any information as permitted by regulations under this section the disclosure is not to be taken as a contravention of any duty to which he is subject.

NOTES
Sub-s (1): para (c) inserted by the Consumer Credit Act 2006, s 61(9).
Regulations: the Financial Services and Markets Act 2000 (Disclosure of Information by Prescribed Persons) Regulations 2001, SI 2001/1857.

Co-operation

[241]
354 Authority's duty to co-operate with others
(1) The Authority must take such steps as it considers appropriate to co-operate with other persons (whether in the United Kingdom or elsewhere) who have functions—
(a) similar to those of the Authority; or
(b) in relation to the prevention or detection of financial crime.
[(1A) The Authority must take such steps as it considers appropriate to cooperate with—
(a) the Panel on Takeovers and Mergers;
(b) an authority designated as a supervisory authority for the purposes of Article 4.1 of the Takeovers Directive;
(c) any other person or body that exercises functions of a public nature, under legislation in any country or territory outside the United Kingdom, that appear to the Authority to be similar to those of the Panel on Takeovers and Mergers.]
(2) Co-operation may include the sharing of information which the Authority is not prevented from disclosing.
(3) "Financial crime" has the same meaning as in section 6.

NOTES
Sub-s (1A): inserted by the Companies Act 2006, s 964(1), (5).

PART XXIV
INSOLVENCY

Interpretation

[242]
355 Interpretation of this Part
(1) In this Part—
"the 1985 Act" means the Bankruptcy (Scotland) Act 1985;
"the 1986 Act" means the Insolvency Act 1986;

"the 1989 Order" means the Insolvency (Northern Ireland) Order 1989;

"body" means a body of persons—

(a) over which the court has jurisdiction under any provision of, or made under, the 1986 Act (or the 1989 Order); but

(b) which is not a building society, a friendly society or an industrial and provident society; and

"court" means—

(a) the court having jurisdiction for the purposes of the 1985 Act or the 1986 Act; or

(b) in Northern Ireland, the High Court.

(2) In this Part "insurer" has such meaning as may be specified in an order made by the Treasury.

NOTES

Modification: this section is applied, with modifications, in relation to liquidation and administration by the Banking Act 2009 (Parts 2 and 3 Consequential Amendments) Order 2009, SI 2009/317, art 5(1), (3).

Orders: the Financial Services and Markets Act 2000 (Insolvency) (Definition of "Insurer") Order 2001, SI 2001/2634 at **[668]**; the Financial Services and Markets Act 2000 (Administration Orders Relating to Insurers) Order 2002, SI 2002/1242 at **[852]**.

Voluntary arrangements

[243]

356 Authority's powers to participate in proceedings: company voluntary arrangements

[(1) Where a voluntary arrangement has effect under Part I of the 1986 Act in respect of a company or insolvent partnership which is an authorised person, the Authority may apply to the court under section 6 or 7 of that Act.]

[(2) Where a voluntary arrangement has been approved under Part II of the 1989 Order in respect of a company or insolvent partnership which is an authorised person, the Authority may apply to the court under Article 19 or 20 of that Order.]

(3) If a person other than the Authority makes an application to the court in relation to the company or insolvent partnership under [any] of those provisions, the Authority is entitled to be heard at any hearing relating to the application.

NOTES

Sub-ss (1), (2): substituted by the Insolvency Act 2000, s 15(3)(a), (b).

Sub-s (3): word in square brackets substituted by the Insolvency Act 2000, s 15(3)(c).

[244]

357 Authority's powers to participate in proceedings: individual voluntary arrangements

(1) The Authority is entitled to be heard on an application by an individual who is an authorised person under section 253 of the 1986 Act (or Article 227 of the 1989 Order).

(2) Subsections (3) to (6) apply if such an order is made on the application of such a person.

(3) A person appointed for the purpose by the Authority is entitled to attend any meeting of creditors of the debtor summoned under section 257 of the 1986 Act (or Article 231 of the 1989 Order).

(4) Notice of the result of a meeting so summoned is to be given to the Authority by the chairman of the meeting.

(5) The Authority may apply to the court—

(a) under section 262 of the 1986 Act (or Article 236 of the 1989 Order); or

(b) under section 263 of the 1986 Act (or Article 237 of the 1989 Order).

(6) If a person other than the Authority makes an application to the court under any provision mentioned in subsection (5), the Authority is entitled to be heard at any hearing relating to the application.

[245]

358 Authority's powers to participate in proceedings: trust deeds for creditors in Scotland

(1) This section applies where a trust deed has been granted by or on behalf of a debtor who is an authorised person.

(2) The trustee must, as soon as practicable after he becomes aware that the debtor is an authorised person, send to the Authority—

(a) in every case, a copy of the trust deed;

(b) where any other document or information is sent to every creditor known to the trustee in pursuance of paragraph 5(1)(c) of Schedule 5 to the 1985 Act, a copy of such document or information.

(3) Paragraph 7 of that Schedule applies to the Authority as if it were a qualified creditor who has not been sent a copy of the notice as mentioned in paragraph 5(1)(c) of the Schedule.

(4) The Authority must be given the same notice as the creditors of any meeting of creditors held in relation to the trust deed.
(5) A person appointed for the purpose by the Authority is entitled to attend and participate in (but not to vote at) any such meeting of creditors as if the Authority were a creditor under the deed.
(6) This section does not affect any right the Authority has as a creditor of a debtor who is an authorised person.
(7) Expressions used in this section and in the 1985 Act have the same meaning in this section as in that Act.

Administration orders

[246]
[359 Administration order
(1) The Authority may make an administration application under Schedule B1 to the 1986 Act [or Schedule B1 to the 1989 Order] in relation to a company or insolvent partnership which—
- (a) is or has been an authorised person,
- (b) is or has been an appointed representative, or
- (c) is carrying on or has carried on a regulated activity in contravention of the general prohibition.

(2) Subsection (3) applies in relation to an administration application made (or a petition presented) by the Authority by virtue of this section.
(3) Any of the following shall be treated for the purpose of paragraph 11(a) of Schedule B1 to the 1986 Act [or paragraph 12(a) of Schedule B1 to the 1989 Order] as unable to pay its debts—
- (a) a company or partnership in default on an obligation to pay a sum due and payable under an agreement, . . .
- (b) an authorised deposit taker in default on an obligation to pay a sum due and payable in respect of a relevant deposit[, and—
- (c) an authorised reclaim fund in default on an obligation to pay a sum payable as a result of a claim made by virtue of section 1(2)(b) or 2(2)(b) of the Dormant Bank and Building Society Accounts Act 2008.]

(4) In this section—
"agreement" means an agreement the making or performance of which constitutes or is part of a regulated activity carried on by the company or partnership,
["authorised reclaim fund" means a reclaim fund within the meaning given by section 5(1) of the Dormant Bank and Building Society Accounts Act 2008 that is authorised for the purposes of this Act;]
"authorised deposit taker" means a person with a Part IV permission to accept deposits (but not a person who has a Part IV permission to accept deposits only for the purpose of carrying on another regulated activity in accordance with that permission),
"company" means a company—
- (a) in respect of which an administrator may be appointed under Schedule B1 to the 1986 Act, or
- [(b) in respect of which an administrator may be appointed under Schedule B1 to the 1989 Order,] and

"relevant deposit" shall, ignoring any restriction on the meaning of deposit arising from the identity of the person making the deposit, be construed in accordance with—
- (a) section 22,
- (b) any relevant order under that section, and
- (c) Schedule 2.

(5) The definition of "authorised deposit taker" in subsection (4) shall be construed in accordance with—
- (a) section 22,
- (b) any relevant order under that section, and
- (c) Schedule 2.]

NOTES
Substituted by the Enterprise Act 2002, s 248(3), Sch 17, paras 53, 55.
Sub-s (1): words in square brackets substituted by the Insolvency (Northern Ireland) Order 2005, SI 2005/1455, art 3(3), Sch 2, paras 56, 58(1), (2).
Sub-s (3): words in first pair of square brackets substituted by the Insolvency (Northern Ireland) Order 2005, SI 2005/1455, art 3(3), Sch 2, paras 56, 58(1), (3); word "and" (omitted) repealed and words in second pair of square brackets inserted by the Dormant Bank and Building Society Accounts Act 2008, s 15, Sch 2, para 6(1), (2).

Sub-s (4): definition "authorised reclaim fund" inserted by the Dormant Bank and Building Society Accounts Act 2008, s 15, Sch 2, para 6(1), (3); in definition "company", para (b) substituted by SI 2005/1455, art 3(3), Sch 2, paras 56, 58(1), (4).

Modification: this section and ss 367, 368 are applied, with modifications, in respect of the Financial Services Authority's functions under the Payment Services Regulations 2009, SI 2009/209; see SI 2009/209, reg 95, Sch 5, Pt 1, para 6.

[247]

360 Insurers

(1) The Treasury may by order provide that such provisions of Part II of the 1986 Act (or Part III of the 1989 Order) as may be specified are to apply in relation to insurers with such modifications as may be specified.

(2) An order under this section—

(a) may provide that such provisions of this Part as may be specified are to apply in relation to the administration of insurers in accordance with the order with such modifications as may be specified; and

(b) requires the consent of the Secretary of State.

(3) "Specified" means specified in the order.

NOTES

Orders: the Financial Services and Markets Act 2000 (Administration Orders Relating to Insurers) Order 2002, SI 2002/1242 at **[852]**.

[248]

[361 Administrator's duty to report to Authority

(1) This section applies where a company or partnership is—

(a) in administration within the meaning of Schedule B1 to the 1986 Act, or

[(b) in administration within the meaning of Schedule B1 to the 1989 Order].

(2) If the administrator thinks that the company or partnership is carrying on or has carried on a regulated activity in contravention of the general prohibition, he must report to the Authority without delay.

(3) Subsection (2) does not apply where the administration arises out of an administration order made on an application made or petition presented by the Authority.]

NOTES

Substituted by the Enterprise Act 2002, s 248(3), Sch 17, paras 53, 56.

Sub-s (1): para (b) substituted by the Insolvency (Northern Ireland) Order 2005, SI 2005/1455, art 3(3), Sch 2, paras 56, 59.

Modification: this section is applied, with modifications, in relation to liquidation and administration by the Banking Act 2009 (Parts 2 and 3 Consequential Amendments) Order 2009, SI 2009/317, art 5(1), (4).

[249]

362 Authority's powers to participate in proceedings

(1) This section applies if a person other than the Authority [makes an administration application under Schedule B1 to the 1986 Act [or Schedule B1 to the 1989 Order]] in relation to a company or partnership which—

(a) is, or has been, an authorised person;

(b) is, or has been, an appointed representative; or

(c) is carrying on, or has carried on, a regulated activity in contravention of the general prohibition.

[(1A) This section also applies in relation to—

(a) the appointment under paragraph 14 or 22 of Schedule B1 to the 1986 Act [or paragraph 15 or 23 of Schedule B1 to the 1989 Order] of an administrator of a company of a kind described in subsection (1)(a) to (c), or

(b) the filing with the court of a copy of notice of intention to appoint an administrator under [any] of those paragraphs.]

(2) The Authority is entitled to be heard—

(a) at the hearing of the [administration application . . .]; and

(b) at any other hearing of the court in relation to the company or partnership under Part II of the 1986 Act (or Part III of the 1989 Order).

(3) Any notice or other document required to be sent to a creditor of the company or partnership must also be sent to the Authority.

[(4) The Authority may apply to the court under paragraph 74 of Schedule B1 to the 1986 Act [or paragraph 75 of Schedule B1 to the 1989 Order].

(4A) In respect of an application under subsection (4)—

(a) paragraph 74(1)(a) and (b) shall have effect as if for the words "harm the interests of the applicant (whether alone or in common with some or all other members or creditors)" there were substituted the words "harm the interests of some or all members or creditors", and

[(b) paragraph 75(1)(a) and (b) of Schedule B1 to the 1989 Order shall have effect as if for the words "harm the interests of the applicant (whether alone or in common with some or all other members or creditors)" there were substituted the words "harm the interests of some or all members or creditors"].]

(5) A person appointed for the purpose by the Authority is entitled—

(a) to attend any meeting of creditors of the company or partnership summoned under any enactment;

(b) to attend any meeting of a committee established under [paragraph 57 of Schedule B1 to the 1986 Act] [or paragraph 58 of Schedule B1 to the 1989 Order]; and

(c) to make representations as to any matter for decision at such a meeting.

(6) If, during the course of the administration of a company, a compromise or arrangement is proposed between the company and its creditors, or any class of them, the Authority may apply to the court under [section 896 or 899 of the Companies Act 2006].

NOTES

Sub-s (1): words in first (outer) pair of square brackets substituted by the Enterprise Act 2002, s 248(3), Sch 17, paras 53, 57(a); words in second (inner) pair of square brackets substituted by the Insolvency (Northern Ireland) Order 2005, SI 2005/1455, art 3(3), Sch 2, paras 56, 60(1), (2).

Sub-s (1A): inserted by the Enterprise Act 2002, s 248(3), Sch 17, paras 53, 57(b); words in square brackets in para (a) inserted and word in square brackets in para (b) substituted by SI 2005/1455, art 3(3), Sch 2, paras 56, 60(1), (3).

Sub-s (2): words in square brackets substituted by the Enterprise Act 2002, s 248(3), Sch 17, paras 53, 57(c); words omitted repealed by SI 2005/1455, arts 3(3), 31, Sch 2, paras 56, 60(1), (4), Sch 9.

Sub-s (4): substituted, together with sub-s (4A), for original sub-s (4) by the Enterprise Act 2002, s 248(3), Sch 17, paras 53, 57(d); words in square brackets substituted by SI 2005/1455, art 3(3), Sch 2, paras 56, 60(1), (5).

Sub-s (4A): substituted, together with sub-s (4), for original sub-s (4) by the Enterprise Act 2002, s 248(3), Sch 17, paras 53, 57(d); para (b) substituted by SI 2005/1455, art 3(3), Sch 2, paras 56, 60(1), (6).

Sub-s (5): in para (b), words in first pair of square brackets substituted by the Enterprise Act 2002, s 248(3), Sch 17, paras 53, 57(e); words in second pair of square brackets substituted by SI 2005/1455, art 3(3), Sch 2, paras 56, 60(1), (7).

Sub-s (6): words in square brackets substituted by the Companies Act 2006 (Consequential Amendments etc) Order 2008, SI 2008/948, art 3(1)(b), Sch 1, Pt 2, para 211(4), subject to transitional provisions and savings in arts 6, 11, 12 thereof.

Modification: this section is applied, with modifications, in relation to liquidation and administration by the Banking Act 2009 (Parts 2 and 3 Consequential Amendments) Order 2009, SI 2009/317, art 5(1), (5).

[250]

[362A Administrator appointed by company or directors

(1) This section applies in relation to a company of a kind described in section 362(1)(a) to (c).

(2) An administrator of the company may not be appointed under paragraph 22 of Schedule B1 to the 1986 Act [or paragraph 23 of Schedule B1 to the 1989 Order] without the consent of the Authority.

(3) Consent under subsection (2)—

(a) must be in writing, and

(b) must be filed with the court along with the notice of intention to appoint under paragraph 27 of [Schedule B1 to the 1986 Act or paragraph 28 of Schedule B1 to the 1989 Order].

(4) In a case where no notice of intention to appoint is required—

(a) subsection (3)(b) shall not apply, but

(b) consent under subsection (2) must accompany the notice of appointment filed under paragraph 29 of [Schedule B1 to the 1986 Act or paragraph 30 of Schedule B1 to the 1989 Order].]

NOTES

Inserted by the Enterprise Act 2002, s 248(3), Sch 17, paras 53, 58.

Sub-s (2): words in square brackets inserted by the Insolvency (Northern Ireland) Order 2005, SI 2005/1455, art 3(3), Sch 2, paras 56, 61(1), (2).

Sub-ss (3), (4): words in square brackets substituted by SI 2005/1455, art 3(3), Sch 2, paras 56, 61(1), (3), (4).

Receivership

[251]

363 Authority's powers to participate in proceedings

(1) This section applies if a receiver has been appointed in relation to a company which—

(a) is, or has been, an authorised person;

(b) is, or has been, an appointed representative; or

(c) is carrying on, or has carried on, a regulated activity in contravention of the general prohibition.

(2) The Authority is entitled to be heard on an application made under section 35 or 63 of the 1986 Act (or Article 45 of the 1989 Order).

(3) The Authority is entitled to make an application under section 41(1)(a) or 69(1)(a) of the 1986 Act (or Article 51(1)(a) of the 1989 Order).

(4) A report under section 48(1) or 67(1) of the 1986 Act (or Article 58(1) of the 1989 Order) must be sent by the person making it to the Authority.

(5) A person appointed for the purpose by the Authority is entitled—

(a) to attend any meeting of creditors of the company summoned under any enactment;

(b) to attend any meeting of a committee established under section 49 or 68 of the 1986 Act (or Article 59 of the 1989 Order); and

(c) to make representations as to any matter for decision at such a meeting.

[252]

364 Receiver's duty to report to Authority

If—

(a) a receiver has been appointed in relation to a company, and

(b) it appears to the receiver that the company is carrying on, or has carried on, a regulated activity in contravention of the general prohibition,

the receiver must report the matter to the Authority without delay.

Voluntary winding up

[253]

365 Authority's powers to participate in proceedings

(1) This section applies in relation to a company which—

(a) is being wound up voluntarily;

(b) is an authorised person; and

(c) is not an insurer effecting or carrying out contracts of long-term insurance.

(2) The Authority may apply to the court under section 112 of the 1986 Act (or Article 98 of the 1989 Order) in respect of the company.

(3) The Authority is entitled to be heard at any hearing of the court in relation to the voluntary winding up of the company.

(4) Any notice or other document required to be sent to a creditor of the company must also be sent to the Authority.

(5) A person appointed for the purpose by the Authority is entitled—

(a) to attend any meeting of creditors of the company summoned under any enactment;

(b) to attend any meeting of a committee established under section 101 of the 1986 Act (or Article 87 of the 1989 Order); and

(c) to make representations as to any matter for decision at such a meeting.

(6) The voluntary winding up of the company does not bar the right of the Authority to have it wound up by the court.

(7) If, during the course of the winding up of the company, a compromise or arrangement is proposed between the company and its creditors, or any class of them, the Authority may apply to the court under [section 896 or 899 of the Companies Act 2006].

NOTES

Sub-s (7): words in square brackets substituted by the Companies Act 2006 (Consequential Amendments etc) Order 2008, SI 2008/948, art 3(1)(b), Sch 1, Pt 2, para 211(4), subject to transitional provisions and savings in arts 6, 11, 12 thereof.

[254]

366 Insurers effecting or carrying out long-term contracts or insurance

(1) An insurer effecting or carrying out contracts of long-term insurance may not be wound up voluntarily without the consent of the Authority.

(2) If notice of a general meeting of such an insurer is given, specifying the intention to propose a resolution for voluntary winding up of the insurer, a director of the insurer must notify the Authority as soon as practicable after he becomes aware of it.
(3) A person who fails to comply with subsection (2) is guilty of an offence and liable on summary conviction to a fine not exceeding level 5 on the standard scale.
[(4) A winding up resolution may not be passed—
(a) as a written resolution (in accordance with Chapter 2 of Part 13 of the Companies Act 2006), or
(b) at a meeting called in accordance with section 307(4) to (6) or 337(2) of that Act (agreement of members to calling of meeting at short notice).]
(5) A copy of a winding-up resolution forwarded to the registrar of companies in accordance with [section 30 of the Companies Act 2006] must be accompanied by a certificate issued by the Authority stating that it consents to the voluntary winding up of the insurer.
(6) If subsection (5) is complied with, the voluntary winding up is to be treated as having commenced at the time the resolution was passed.
(7) If subsection (5) is not complied with, the resolution has no effect.
(8) "Winding-up resolution" means a resolution for voluntary winding up of an insurer effecting or carrying out contracts of long-term insurance.

NOTES

Sub-s (4): substituted by the Companies Act 2006 (Commencement No 3, Consequential Amendments, Transitional Provisions and Savings) Order 2007, SI 2007/2194, art 10(1), (2), Sch 4, Pt 3, para 93(1), (2), subject to savings in art 12 thereof.

Sub-s (5): words in square brackets substituted by SI 2007/2194, art 10(1), (2), Sch 4, Pt 3, para 93(1), (3), subject to savings in art 12 thereof.

Winding up by the court

[255]

367 Winding-up petitions

(1) The Authority may present a petition to the court for the winding up of a body which—
(a) is, or has been, an authorised person;
(b) is, or has been, an appointed representative; or
(c) is carrying on, or has carried on, a regulated activity in contravention of the general prohibition.
(2) In subsection (1) "body" includes any partnership.
(3) On such a petition, the court may wind up the body if—
(a) the body is unable to pay its debts within the meaning of section 123 or 221 of the 1986 Act (or Article 103 or 185 of the 1989 Order); or
(b) the court is of the opinion that it is just and equitable that it should be wound up.
(4) If a body is in default on an obligation to pay a sum due and payable under an agreement, it is to be treated for the purpose of subsection (3)(a) as unable to pay its debts.
(5) "Agreement" means an agreement the making or performance of which constitutes or is part of a regulated activity carried on by the body concerned.
(6) Subsection (7) applies if a petition is presented under subsection (1) for the winding up of a partnership—
(a) on the ground mentioned in subsection (3)(b); or
(b) in Scotland, on a ground mentioned in subsection (3)(a) or (b).
(7) The court has jurisdiction, and the 1986 Act (or the 1989 Order) has effect, as if the partnership were an unregistered company as defined by section 220 of that Act (or Article 184 of that Order).

NOTES

Modification: see the note to s 359 at **[246]**.

[256]

368 Winding-up petitions: EEA and Treaty firms

The Authority may not present a petition to the court under section 367 for the winding up of—
(a) an EEA firm which qualifies for authorisation under Schedule 3, or
(b) a Treaty firm which qualifies for authorisation under Schedule 4,
unless it has been asked to do so by the home state regulator of the firm concerned.

NOTES

Modification: see the note to s 359 at **[246]**.

[257]

369 Insurers: service of petition etc on Authority

(1) If a person other than the Authority presents a petition for the winding up of an authorised person with permission to effect or carry out contracts of insurance, the petitioner must serve a copy of the petition on the Authority.

(2) If a person other than the Authority applies to have a provisional liquidator appointed under section 135 of the 1986 Act (or Article 115 of the 1989 Order) in respect of an authorised person with permission to effect or carry out contracts of insurance, the applicant must serve a copy of the application on the Authority.

[257A]

[369A Reclaim funds: service of petition etc on Authority

(1) If a person other than the Authority presents a petition for the winding up of an authorised reclaim fund, the petitioner must serve a copy of the petition on the Authority.

(2) If a person other than the Authority applies to have a provisional liquidator appointed under section 135 of the 1986 Act (or Article 115 of the 1989 Order) in respect of an authorised reclaim fund, the applicant must serve a copy of the application on the Authority.

(3) In this section "authorised reclaim fund" means a reclaim fund within the meaning given by section 5(1) of the Dormant Bank and Building Society Accounts Act 2008 that is authorised for the purposes of this Act.]

NOTES

Commencement: 12 March 2009.

Inserted by the Dormant Bank and Building Society Accounts Act 2008, s 15, Sch 2, para 7.

[258]

370 Liquidator's duty to report to Authority

If—

(a) a company is being wound up voluntarily or a body is being wound up on a petition presented by a person other than the Authority, and

(b) it appears to the liquidator that the company or body is carrying on, or has carried on, a regulated activity in contravention of the general prohibition,

the liquidator must report the matter to the Authority without delay.

NOTES

Modification: this section is applied, with modifications, in relation to liquidation and administration by the Banking Act 2009 (Parts 2 and 3 Consequential Amendments) Order 2009, SI 2009/317, art 5(1), (6).

[259]

371 Authority's powers to participate in proceedings

(1) This section applies if a person other than the Authority presents a petition for the winding up of a body which—

(a) is, or has been, an authorised person;

(b) is, or has been, an appointed representative; or

(c) is carrying on, or has carried on, a regulated activity in contravention of the general prohibition.

(2) The Authority is entitled to be heard—

(a) at the hearing of the petition; and

(b) at any other hearing of the court in relation to the body under or by virtue of Part IV or V of the 1986 Act (or Part V or VI of the 1989 Order).

(3) Any notice or other document required to be sent to a creditor of the body must also be sent to the Authority.

(4) A person appointed for the purpose by the Authority is entitled—

(a) to attend any meeting of creditors of the body;

(b) to attend any meeting of a committee established for the purposes of Part IV or V of the 1986 Act under section 101 of that Act or under section 141 or 142 of that Act;

(c) to attend any meeting of a committee established for the purposes of Part V or VI of the 1989 Order under Article 87 of that Order or under Article 120 of that Order; and

(d) to make representations as to any matter for decision at such a meeting.

(5) If, during the course of the winding up of a company, a compromise or arrangement is proposed between the company and its creditors, or any class of them, the Authority may apply to the court under [section 896 or 899 of the Companies Act 2006].

NOTES

Sub-s (5): words in square brackets substituted by the Companies Act 2006 (Consequential Amendments etc) Order 2008, SI 2008/948, art 3(1)(b), Sch 1, Pt 2, para 211(4), subject to transitional provisions and savings in arts 6, 11, 12 thereof.

Bankruptcy

[260]

372 Petitions

(1) The Authority may present a petition to the court—

(a) under section 264 of the 1986 Act (or Article 238 of the 1989 Order) for a bankruptcy order to be made against an individual; or

(b) under section 5 of the 1985 Act for the sequestration of the estate of an individual.

(2) But such a petition may be presented only on the ground that—

(a) the individual appears to be unable to pay a regulated activity debt; or

(b) the individual appears to have no reasonable prospect of being able to pay a regulated activity debt.

(3) An individual appears to be unable to pay a regulated activity debt if he is in default on an obligation to pay a sum due and payable under an agreement.

(4) An individual appears to have no reasonable prospect of being able to pay a regulated activity debt if—

(a) the Authority has served on him a demand requiring him to establish to the satisfaction of the Authority that there is a reasonable prospect that he will be able to pay a sum payable under an agreement when it falls due;

(b) at least three weeks have elapsed since the demand was served; and

(c) the demand has been neither complied with nor set aside in accordance with rules.

(5) A demand made under subsection (4)(a) is to be treated for the purposes of the 1986 Act (or the 1989 Order) as if it were a statutory demand under section 268 of that Act (or Article 242 of that Order).

(6) For the purposes of a petition presented in accordance with subsection (1)(b)—

(a) the Authority is to be treated as a qualified creditor; and

(b) a ground mentioned in subsection (2) constitutes apparent insolvency.

(7) "Individual" means an individual—

(a) who is, or has been, an authorised person; or

(b) who is carrying on, or has carried on, a regulated activity in contravention of the general prohibition.

(8) "Agreement" means an agreement the making or performance of which constitutes or is part of a regulated activity carried on by the individual concerned.

(9) "Rules" means—

(a) in England and Wales, rules made under section 412 of the 1986 Act;

(b) in Scotland, rules made by order by the Treasury, after consultation with the Scottish Ministers, for the purposes of this section; and

(c) in Northern Ireland, rules made under Article 359 of the 1989 Order.

NOTES

Rules: the Bankruptcy (Financial Services and Markets Act 2000) (Scotland) Rules 2001, SI 2001/3591.

[261]

373 Insolvency practitioner's duty to report to Authority

(1) If—

(a) a bankruptcy order or sequestration award is in force in relation to an individual by virtue of a petition presented by a person other than the Authority, and

(b) it appears to the insolvency practitioner that the individual is carrying on, or has carried on, a regulated activity in contravention of the general prohibition,

the insolvency practitioner must report the matter to the Authority without delay.

(2) "Bankruptcy order" means a bankruptcy order under Part IX of the 1986 Act (or Part IX of the 1989 Order).

(3) "Sequestration award" means an award of sequestration under section 12 of the 1985 Act.

(4) "Individual" includes an entity mentioned in section 374(1)(c).

[262]

374 Authority's powers to participate in proceedings

(1) This section applies if a person other than the Authority presents a petition to the court—

(a) under section 264 of the 1986 Act (or Article 238 of the 1989 Order) for a bankruptcy order to be made against an individual;
(b) under section 5 of the 1985 Act for the sequestration of the estate of an individual; or
(c) under section 6 of the 1985 Act for the sequestration of the estate belonging to or held for or jointly by the members of an entity mentioned in subsection (1) of that section.

(2) The Authority is entitled to be heard—
(a) at the hearing of the petition; and
(b) at any other hearing in relation to the individual or entity under—
(i) Part IX of the 1986 Act;
(ii) Part IX of the 1989 Order; or
(iii) the 1985 Act.

(3) A copy of the report prepared under section 274 of the 1986 Act (or Article 248 of the 1989 Order) must also be sent to the Authority.

(4) A person appointed for the purpose by the Authority is entitled—
(a) to attend any meeting of creditors of the individual or entity;
(b) to attend any meeting of a committee established under section 301 of the 1986 Act (or Article 274 of the 1989 Order);
(c) to attend any meeting of commissioners held under paragraph 17 or 18 of Schedule 6 to the 1985 Act; and
(d) to make representations as to any matter for decision at such a meeting.

(5) "Individual" means an individual who—
(a) is, or has been, an authorised person; or
(b) is carrying on, or has carried on, a regulated activity in contravention of the general prohibition.

(6) "Entity" means an entity which—
(a) is, or has been, an authorised person; or
(b) is carrying on, or has carried on, a regulated activity in contravention of the general prohibition.

Provisions against debt avoidance

[263]

375 Authority's right to apply for an order

(1) The Authority may apply for an order under section 423 of the 1986 Act (or Article 367 of the 1989 Order) in relation to a debtor if—
(a) at the time the transaction at an undervalue was entered into, the debtor was carrying on a regulated activity (whether or not in contravention of the general prohibition); and
(b) a victim of the transaction is or was party to an agreement entered into with the debtor, the making or performance of which constituted or was part of a regulated activity carried on by the debtor.

(2) An application made under this section is to be treated as made on behalf of every victim of the transaction to whom subsection (1)(b) applies.

(3) Expressions which are given a meaning in Part XVI of the 1986 Act (or Article 367, 368 or 369 of the 1989 Order) have the same meaning when used in this section.

NOTES

Modification: this section is applied, with modifications, in relation to liquidation and administration by the Banking Act 2009 (Parts 2 and 3 Consequential Amendments) Order 2009, SI 2009/317, art 5(1), (7).

Supplemental provisions concerning insurers

[264]

376 Continuation of contracts of long-term insurance where insurer in liquidation

(1) This section applies in relation to the winding up of an insurer which effects or carries out contracts of long-term insurance.

(2) Unless the court otherwise orders, the liquidator must carry on the insurer's business so far as it consists of carrying out the insurer's contracts of long-term insurance with a view to its being transferred as a going concern to a person who may lawfully carry out those contracts.

(3) In carrying on the business, the liquidator—
(a) may agree to the variation of any contracts of insurance in existence when the winding up order is made; but
(b) must not effect any new contracts of insurance.

(4) If the liquidator is satisfied that the interests of the creditors in respect of liabilities of the insurer attributable to contracts of long-term insurance effected by it require the appointment of a special manager, he may apply to the court.

(5) On such an application, the court may appoint a special manager to act during such time as the court may direct.
(6) The special manager is to have such powers, including any of the powers of a receiver or manager, as the court may direct.
(7) Section 177(5) of the 1986 Act (or Article 151(5) of the 1989 Order) applies to a special manager appointed under subsection (5) as it applies to a special manager appointed under section 177 of the 1986 Act (or Article 151 of the 1989 Order).
(8) If the court thinks fit, it may reduce the value of one or more of the contracts of long-term insurance effected by the insurer.
(9) Any reduction is to be on such terms and subject to such conditions (if any) as the court thinks fit.
(10) The court may, on the application of an official, appoint an independent actuary to investigate the insurer's business so far as it consists of carrying out its contracts of long-term insurance and to report to the official—
(a) on the desirability or otherwise of that part of the insurer's business being continued; and
(b) on any reduction in the contracts of long-term insurance effected by the insurer that may be necessary for successful continuation of that part of the insurer's business.
(11) "Official" means—
(a) the liquidator;
(b) a special manager appointed under subsection (5); or
(c) the Authority.
(12) The liquidator may make an application in the name of the insurer and on its behalf under Part VII without obtaining the permission that would otherwise be required by section 167 of, and Schedule 4 to, the 1986 Act (or Article 142 of, and Schedule 2 to, the 1989 Order).

[265]
377 Reducing the value of contracts instead of winding up
(1) This section applies in relation to an insurer which has been proved to be unable to pay its debts.
(2) If the court thinks fit, it may reduce the value of one or more of the insurer's contracts instead of making a winding up order.
(3) Any reduction is to be on such terms and subject to such conditions (if any) as the court thinks fit.

NOTES
Disapplication: this section does not apply in relation to an EEA insurer: see the Insurers (Reorganisation and Winding Up) Regulations 2004, SI 2004/353, regs 2, 4(7) at **[4271]**, **[4273]**.

[266]
378 Treatment of assets on winding up
(1) The Treasury may by regulations provide for the treatment of the assets of an insurer on its winding up.
(2) The regulations may, in particular, provide for—
(a) assets representing a particular part of the insurer's business to be available only for meeting liabilities attributable to that part of the insurer's business;
(b) separate general meetings of the creditors to be held in respect of liabilities attributable to a particular part of the insurer's business.

[267]
379 Winding-up rules
(1) Winding-up rules may include provision—
(a) for determining the amount of the liabilities of an insurer to policyholders of any class or description for the purpose of proof in a winding up; and
(b) generally for carrying into effect the provisions of this Part with respect to the winding up of insurers.
(2) Winding-up rules may, in particular, make provision for all or any of the following matters—
(a) the identification of assets and liabilities;
(b) the apportionment, between assets of different classes or descriptions, of—
(i) the costs, charges and expenses of the winding up; and
(ii) any debts of the insurer of a specified class or description;
(c) the determination of the amount of liabilities of a specified description;
(d) the application of assets for meeting liabilities of a specified description;
(e) the application of assets representing any excess of a specified description.

(3) "Specified" means specified in winding-up rules.
(4) "Winding-up rules" means rules made under section 411 of the 1986 Act (or Article 359 of the 1989 Order).
(5) Nothing in this section affects the power to make winding-up rules under the 1986 Act or the 1989 Order.

NOTES

Rules: the Insurers (Winding Up) Rules 2001, SI 2001/3635; the Insurers (Winding Up) (Scotland) Rules 2001, SI 2001/4040.

PART XXV
INJUNCTIONS AND RESTITUTION

Injunctions

[268]

380 Injunctions

(1) If, on the application of the Authority or the Secretary of State, the court is satisfied—
- (a) that there is a reasonable likelihood that any person will contravene a relevant requirement, or
- (b) that any person has contravened a relevant requirement and that there is a reasonable likelihood that the contravention will continue or be repeated,

the court may make an order restraining (or in Scotland an interdict prohibiting) the contravention.
(2) If on the application of the Authority or the Secretary of State the court is satisfied—
- (a) that any person has contravened a relevant requirement, and
- (b) that there are steps which could be taken for remedying the contravention,

the court may make an order requiring that person, and any other person who appears to have been knowingly concerned in the contravention, to take such steps as the court may direct to remedy it.
(3) If, on the application of the Authority or the Secretary of State, the court is satisfied that any person may have—
- (a) contravened a relevant requirement, or
- (b) been knowingly concerned in the contravention of such a requirement,

it may make an order restraining (or in Scotland an interdict prohibiting) him from disposing of, or otherwise dealing with, any assets of his which it is satisfied he is reasonably likely to dispose of or otherwise deal with.
(4) The jurisdiction conferred by this section is exercisable by the High Court and the Court of Session.
(5) In subsection (2), references to remedying a contravention include references to mitigating its effect.
(6) "Relevant requirement"—
- (a) in relation to an application by the Authority, means a requirement—
  - (i) which is imposed by or under this Act [or by any directly applicable Community regulation made under the markets in financial instruments directive]; or
  - (ii) which is imposed by or under any other Act and whose contravention constitutes an offence which the Authority has power to prosecute under this Act;
- (b) in relation to an application by the Secretary of State, means a requirement which is imposed by or under this Act and whose contravention constitutes an offence which the Secretary of State has power to prosecute under this Act.

(7) In the application of subsection (6) to Scotland—
- (a) in paragraph (a)(ii) for "which the Authority has power to prosecute under this Act" substitute "mentioned in paragraph (a) or (b) of section 402(1)"; and
- (b) in paragraph (b) omit "which the Secretary of State has power to prosecute under this Act".

NOTES

Sub-s (6): words in square brackets inserted by the Financial Services and Markets Act 2000 (Markets in Financial Instruments) Regulations 2007, SI 2007/126, reg 3(5), Sch 5, paras 1, 13.

[269]

381 Injunctions in cases of market abuse

(1) If, on the application of the Authority, the court is satisfied—
- (a) that there is a reasonable likelihood that any person will engage in market abuse, or
- (b) that any person is or has engaged in market abuse and that there is a reasonable likelihood that the market abuse will continue or be repeated,

the court may make an order restraining (or in Scotland an interdict prohibiting) the market abuse.

(2) If on the application of the Authority the court is satisfied—

(a) that any person is or has engaged in market abuse, and

(b) that there are steps which could be taken for remedying the market abuse,

the court may make an order requiring him to take such steps as the court may direct to remedy it.

(3) Subsection (4) applies if, on the application of the Authority, the court is satisfied that any person—

(a) may be engaged in market abuse; or

(b) may have been engaged in market abuse.

(4) The court make an order restraining (or in Scotland an interdict prohibiting) the person concerned from disposing of, or otherwise dealing with, any assets of his which it is satisfied that he is reasonably likely to dispose of, or otherwise deal with.

(5) The jurisdiction conferred by this section is exercisable by the High Court and the Court of Session.

(6) In subsection (2), references to remedying any market abuse include references to mitigating its effect.

Restitution orders

[270]

382 Restitution orders

(1) The court may, on the application of the Authority or the Secretary of State, make an order under subsection (2) if it is satisfied that a person has contravened a relevant requirement, or been knowingly concerned in the contravention of such a requirement, and—

(a) that profits have accrued to him as a result of the contravention; or

(b) that one or more persons have suffered loss or been otherwise adversely affected as a result of the contravention.

(2) The court may order the person concerned to pay to the Authority such sum as appears to the court to be just having regard—

(a) in a case within paragraph (a) of subsection (1), to the profits appearing to the court to have accrued;

(b) in a case within paragraph (b) of that subsection, to the extent of the loss or other adverse effect;

(c) in a case within both of those paragraphs, to the profits appearing to the court to have accrued and to the extent of the loss or other adverse effect.

(3) Any amount paid to the Authority in pursuance of an order under subsection (2) must be paid by it to such qualifying person or distributed by it among such qualifying persons as the court may direct.

(4) On an application under subsection (1) the court may require the person concerned to supply it with such accounts or other information as it may require for any one or more of the following purposes—

(a) establishing whether any and, if so, what profits have accrued to him as mentioned in paragraph (a) of that subsection;

(b) establishing whether any person or persons have suffered any loss or adverse effect as mentioned in paragraph (b) of that subsection and, if so, the extent of that loss or adverse effect; and

(c) determining how any amounts are to be paid or distributed under subsection (3).

(5) The court may require any accounts or other information supplied under subsection (4) to be verified in such manner as it may direct.

(6) The jurisdiction conferred by this section is exercisable by the High Court and the Court of Session.

(7) Nothing in this section affects the right of any person other than the Authority or the Secretary of State to bring proceedings in respect of the matters to which this section applies.

(8) "Qualifying person" means a person appearing to the court to be someone—

(a) to whom the profits mentioned in subsection (1)(a) are attributable; or

(b) who has suffered the loss or adverse effect mentioned in subsection (1)(b).

(9) "Relevant requirement"—

(a) *in relation to an application* by the Authority, means a requirement—

(i) which is imposed by or under this Act [or by any directly applicable Community regulation made under the markets in financial instruments directive]; or

(ii) which is imposed by or under any other Act and whose contravention constitutes an offence which the Authority has power to prosecute under this Act;

(b) in relation to an application by the Secretary of State, means a requirement which is imposed by or under this Act and whose contravention constitutes an offence which the Secretary of State has power to prosecute under this Act.

(10) In the application of subsection (9) to Scotland—

(a) in paragraph (a)(ii) for "which the Authority has power to prosecute under this Act" substitute "mentioned in paragraph (a) or (b) of section 402(1)"; and

(b) in paragraph (b) omit "which the Secretary of State has power to prosecute under this Act".

NOTES

Sub-s (9): words in square brackets inserted by the Financial Services and Markets Act 2000 (Markets in Financial Instruments) Regulations 2007, SI 2007/126, reg 3(5), Sch 5, paras 1, 14.

[271]

383 Restitution orders in cases of market abuse

(1) The court may, on the application of the Authority, make an order under subsection (4) if it is satisfied that a person ("the person concerned")—

(a) has engaged in market abuse, or

(b) by taking or refraining from taking any action has required or encouraged another person or persons to engage in behaviour which, if engaged in by the person concerned, would amount to market abuse,

and the condition mentioned in subsection (2) is fulfilled.

(2) The condition is—

(a) that profits have accrued to the person concerned as a result; or

(b) that one or more persons have suffered loss or been otherwise adversely affected as a result.

(3) But the court may not make an order under subsection (4) if it is satisfied that—

(a) the person concerned believed, on reasonable grounds, that his behaviour did not fall within paragraph (a) or (b) of subsection (1); or

(b) he took all reasonable precautions and exercised all due diligence to avoid behaving in a way which fell within paragraph (a) or (b) of subsection (1).

(4) The court may order the person concerned to pay to the Authority such sum as appears to the court to be just having regard—

(a) in a case within paragraph (a) of subsection (2), to the profits appearing to the court to have accrued;

(b) in a case within paragraph (b) of that subsection, to the extent of the loss or other adverse effect;

(c) in a case within both of those paragraphs, to the profits appearing to the court to have accrued and to the extent of the loss or other adverse effect.

(5) Any amount paid to the Authority in pursuance of an order under subsection (4) must be paid by it to such qualifying person or distributed by it among such qualifying persons as the court may direct.

(6) On an application under subsection (1) the court may require the person concerned to supply it with such accounts or other information as it may require for any one or more of the following purposes—

(a) establishing whether any and, if so, what profits have accrued to him as mentioned in subsection (2)(a);

(b) establishing whether any person or persons have suffered any loss or adverse effect as mentioned in subsection (2)(b) and, if so, the extent of that loss or adverse effect; and

(c) determining how any amounts are to be paid or distributed under subsection (5).

(7) The court may require any accounts or other information supplied under subsection (6) to be verified in such manner as it may direct.

(8) The jurisdiction conferred by this section is exercisable by the High Court and the Court of Session.

(9) Nothing in this section affects the right of any person other than the Authority to bring proceedings in respect of the matters to which this section applies.

(10) "Qualifying person" means a person appearing to the court to be someone—

(a) to whom the profits mentioned in paragraph (a) of subsection (2) are attributable; or

(b) who has suffered the loss or adverse effect mentioned in paragraph (b) of that subsection.

Restitution required by Authority

[272]
384 Power of Authority to require restitution
(1) The Authority may exercise the power in subsection (5) if it is satisfied that an authorised person ("the person concerned") has contravened a relevant requirement, or been knowingly concerned in the contravention of such a requirement, and—
(a) that profits have accrued to him as a result of the contravention; or
(b) that one or more persons have suffered loss or been otherwise adversely affected as a result of the contravention.
(2) The Authority may exercise the power in subsection (5) if it is satisfied that a person ("the person concerned")—
(a) has engaged in market abuse, or
(b) by taking or refraining from taking any action has required or encouraged another person or persons to engage in behaviour which, if engaged in by the person concerned, would amount to market abuse,
and the condition mentioned in subsection (3) is fulfilled,
(3) The condition is—
(a) that profits have accrued to the person concerned as a result of the market abuse; or
(b) that one or more persons have suffered loss or been otherwise adversely affected as a result of the market abuse.
(4) But the Authority may not exercise that power as a result of subsection (2) if, having considered any representations made to it in response to a warning notice, there are reasonable grounds for it to be satisfied that—
(a) the person concerned believed, on reasonable grounds, that his behaviour did not fall within paragraph (a) or (b) of that subsection; or
(b) he took all reasonable precautions and exercised all due diligence to avoid behaving in a way which fell within paragraph (a) or (b) of that subsection.
(5) The power referred to in subsections (1) and (2) is a power to require the person concerned, in accordance with such arrangements as the Authority considers appropriate, to pay to the appropriate person or distribute among the appropriate persons such amount as appears to the Authority to be just having regard—
(a) in a case within paragraph (a) of subsection (1) or (3), to the profits appearing to the Authority to have accrued;
(b) in a case within paragraph (b) of subsection (1) or (3), to the extent of the loss or other adverse effect;
(c) in a case within paragraphs (a) and (b) of subsection (1) or (3), to the profits appearing to the Authority to have accrued and to the extent of the loss or other adverse effect.
(6) "Appropriate person" means a person appearing to the Authority to be someone—
(a) to whom the profits mentioned in paragraph (a) of subsection (1) or (3) are attributable; or
(b) who has suffered the loss or adverse effect mentioned in paragraph (b) of subsection (1) or (3).
(7) "Relevant requirement" means—
(a) a requirement imposed by or under this Act [or by any directly applicable Community regulation made under the markets in financial instruments directive]; and
(b) a requirement which is imposed by or under any other Act and whose contravention constitutes an offence in relation to which this Act confers power to prosecute on the Authority.
(8) In the application of subsection (7) to Scotland, in paragraph (b) for "in relation to which this Act confers power to prosecute on the Authority" substitute "mentioned in paragraph (a) or (b) of section 402(1)".

NOTES
Sub-s (7): words in square brackets inserted by the Financial Services and Markets Act 2000 (Markets in Financial Instruments) Regulations 2007, SI 2007/126, reg 3(5), Sch 5, paras 1, 15.

[273]
385 Warning notices
(1) If the Authority proposes to exercise the power under section 384(5) in relation to a person, it must give him a warning notice.
(2) A warning notice under this section must specify the amount which the Authority proposes to require the person concerned to pay or distribute as mentioned in section 384(5).

[274]
386 Decision notices

(1) If the Authority decides to exercise the power under section 384(5), it must give a decision notice to the person in relation to whom the power is exercised.
(2) The decision notice must—
  (a) state the amount that he is to pay or distribute as mentioned in section 384(5);
  (b) identify the person or persons to whom that amount is to be paid or among whom that amount is to be distributed; and
  (c) state the arrangements in accordance with which the payment or distribution is to be made.
(3) If the Authority decides to exercise the power under section 384(5), the person in relation to whom it is exercised may refer the matter to the Tribunal.

PART XXVI
NOTICES

NOTES

Modification: this Part is applied, with modifications, in respect of the Authority's functions under the Payment Services Regulations 2009, SI 2009/209; see SI 2009/209, reg 95, Sch 5, Pt 1, para 7, and in respect of the Authority's functions under the Cross-Border Payments in Euro Regulations 2010, SI 2010/89, by SI 2010/89, reg 19, Schedule, Pt 1, para 5.

Warning notices

[275]
387 Warning notices

(1) A warning notice must—
  (a) state the action which the Authority proposes to take;
  (b) be in writing;
  (c) give reasons for the proposed action;
  (d) state whether section 394 applies; and
  (e) if that section applies, describe its effect and state whether any secondary material exists to which the person concerned must be allowed access under it.
(2) The warning notice must specify a reasonable period (which may not be less than 28 days) within which the person to whom it is given may make representations to the Authority.
(3) The Authority may extend the period specified in the notice.
(4) The Authority must then decide, within a reasonable period, whether to give the person concerned a decision notice.

Decision notices

[276]
388 Decision notices

(1) A decision notice must—
  (a) be in writing;
  (b) give the Authority's reasons for the decision to take the action to which the notice relates;
  (c) state whether section 394 applies;
  (d) if that section applies, describe its effect and state whether any secondary material exists to which the person concerned must be allowed access under it; and
  (e) give an indication of—
    (i) any right to have the matter referred to the Tribunal which is given by this Act; and
    (ii) the procedure on such a reference.
(2) If the decision notice was preceded by a warning notice, the action to which the decision notice relates must be action under the same Part as the action proposed in the warning notice.
(3) The Authority may, before it takes the action to which a decision notice ("the original notice") relates, give the person concerned a further decision notice which relates to different action in respect of the same matter.
(4) The Authority may give a further decision notice as a result of subsection (3) only if the person to whom the original notice was given consents.
(5) If the person to whom a decision notice is given under subsection (3) had the right to refer the matter to which the original decision notice related to the Tribunal, he has that right as respects the decision notice under subsection (3).

Conclusion of proceedings

[277]

389 Notices of discontinuance

(1) If the Authority decides not to take—

(a) the action proposed in a warning notice, or

(b) the action to which a decision notice relates,

it must give a notice of discontinuance to the person to whom the warning notice or decision notice was given.

(2) But subsection (1) does not apply if the discontinuance of the proceedings concerned results in the granting of an application made by the person to whom the warning or decision notice was given.

(3) A notice of discontinuance must identify the proceedings which are being discontinued.

[278]

390 Final notices

(1) If the Authority has given a person a decision notice and the matter was not referred to the Tribunal within the [time required by Tribunal Procedure Rules], the Authority must, on taking the action to which the decision notice relates, give the person concerned and any person to whom the decision notice was copied a final notice.

(2) If the Authority has given a person a decision notice and the matter was referred to the Tribunal, the Authority must, on taking action in accordance with any directions given by—

(a) the Tribunal, or

[(b) a court on an appeal against the decision of the Tribunal,]

give that person and any person to whom the decision notice was copied a final notice.

(3) A final notice about a statement must—

(a) set out the terms of the statement;

(b) give details of the manner in which, and the date on which, the statement will be published.

(4) A final notice about an order must—

(a) set out the terms of the order;

(b) state the date from which the order has effect.

(5) A final notice about a penalty must—

(a) state the amount of the penalty;

(b) state the manner in which, and the period within which, the penalty is to be paid;

(c) give details of the way in which the penalty will be recovered if it is not paid by the date stated in the notice.

(6) A final notice about a requirement to make a payment or distribution in accordance with section 384(5) must state—

(a) the persons to whom,

(b) the manner in which, and

(c) the period within which,

it must be made.

(7) In any other case, the final notice must—

(a) give details of the action being taken;

(b) state the date on which the action is to be taken.

(8) The period stated under subsection (5)(b) or (6)(c) may not be less than 14 days beginning with the date on which the final notice is given.

(9) If all or any of the amount of a penalty payable under a final notice is outstanding at the end of the period stated under subsection (5)(b), the Authority may recover the outstanding amount as a debt due to it.

(10) If all or any of a required payment or distribution has not been made at the end of a period stated in a final notice under subsection (6)(c), the obligation to make the payment is enforceable, on the application of the Authority, by injunction or, in Scotland, by an order under section 45 of the Court of Session Act 1988.

NOTES

Sub-s (1): words in square brackets substituted for original words "period mentioned in section 133(1)" by the Transfer of Tribunal Functions Order 2010, SI 2010/22, art 5(1), Sch 2, paras 43, 47(a), as from 6 April 2010, subject to transitional and saving provisions in art 5(4) thereof and Sch 5 thereto.

Sub-s (2): para (b) substituted for original words "(b) the court under section 137," by SI 2010/22, art 5(1), Sch 2, paras 43, 47(b), as from 6 April 2010, subject to transitional and saving provisions in art 5(4) thereof and Sch 5 thereto.

Publication

[279]
391 Publication

(1) Neither the Authority nor a person to whom a warning notice or decision notice is given or copied may publish the notice or any details concerning it.

(2) A notice of discontinuance must state that, if the person to whom the notice is given consents, the Authority may publish such information as it considers appropriate about the matter to which the discontinued proceedings related.

(3) A copy of a notice of discontinuance must be accompanied by a statement that, if the person to whom the notice is copied consents, the Authority may publish such information as it considers appropriate about the matter to which the discontinued proceedings related, so far as relevant to that person.

(4) The Authority must publish such information about the matter to which a final notice relates as it considers appropriate.

(5) When a supervisory notice takes effect, the Authority must publish such information about the matter to which the notice relates as it considers appropriate.

(6) But the Authority may not publish information under this section if publication of it would, in its opinion, be unfair to the person with respect to whom the action was taken or prejudicial to the interests of consumers.

(7) Information is to be published under this section in such manner as the Authority considers appropriate.

(8) For the purposes of determining when a supervisory notice takes effect, a matter to which the notice relates is open to review if—

(a) the period during which any person may refer the matter to the Tribunal is still running;

(b) the matter has been referred to the Tribunal but has not been dealt with;

(c) the matter has been referred to the Tribunal and dealt with but the period during which an appeal may be brought against the Tribunal's decision is still running; or

(d) such an appeal has been brought but has not been determined.

(9) "Notice of discontinuance" means a notice given under section 389.

(10) "Supervisory notice" has the same meaning as in section 395.

(11) "Consumers" means persons who are consumers for the purposes of section 138.

Third party rights and access to evidence

[280]
392 Application of sections 393 and 394

Sections 393 and 394 apply to—

(a) a warning notice given in accordance with section 54(1), 57(1), 63(3), 67(1), 88(4)(b), 89(2), 92(1), 126(1), 207(1), 255(1), 280(1), 331(1), 345(2) (whether as a result of subsection (1) of that section or section 249(1))[, 385(1) or 412B(4) or (8)];

(b) a decision notice given in accordance with section 54(2), 57(3), 63(4), 67(4), 88(6)(b), 89(3), 92(4), 127(1), 208(1), 255(2), 280(2), 331(3), 345(3) (whether as a result of subsection (1) of that section or section 249(1))[, 386(1) or 412B(5) or (9)].

NOTES

Words in square brackets substituted by the Financial Services and Markets Act 2000 (Markets in Financial Instruments) Regulations 2007, SI 2007/126, reg 3(5), Sch 5, paras 1, 16.

[281]
393 Third party rights

(1) If any of the reasons contained in a warning notice to which this section applies relates to a matter which—

(a) identifies a person ("the third party") other than the person to whom the notice is given, and

(b) in the opinion of the Authority, is prejudicial to the third party,

a copy of the notice must be given to the third party.

(2) Subsection (1) does not require a copy to be given to the third party if the Authority—

(a) has given him a separate warning notice in relation to the same matter; or

(b) gives him such a notice at the same time as it gives the warning notice which identifies him.

(3) The notice copied to a third party under subsection (1) must specify a reasonable period (which may not be less than 28 days) within which he may make representations to the Authority.

(4) If any of the reasons contained in a decision notice to which this section applies relates to a matter which—

(a) identifies a person ("the third party") other than the person to whom the decision notice is given, and
(b) in the opinion of the Authority, is prejudicial to the third party,

a copy of the notice must be given to the third party.

(5) If the decision notice was preceded by a warning notice, a copy of the decision notice must (unless it has been given under subsection (4)) be given to each person to whom the warning notice was copied.

(6) Subsection (4) does not require a copy to be given to the third party if the Authority—
(a) has given him a separate decision notice in relation to the same matter; or
(b) gives him such a notice at the same time as it gives the decision notice which identifies him.

(7) Neither subsection (1) nor subsection (4) requires a copy of a notice to be given to a third party if the Authority considers it impracticable to do so.

(8) Subsections (9) to (11) apply if the person to whom a decision notice is given has a right to refer the matter to the Tribunal.

(9) A person to whom a copy of the notice is given under this section may refer to the Tribunal—
(a) the decision in question, so far as it is based on a reason of the kind mentioned in subsection (4); or
(b) any opinion expressed by the Authority in relation to him.

(10) The copy must be accompanied by an indication of the third party's right to make a reference under subsection (9) and of the procedure on such a reference.

(11) A person who alleges that a copy of the notice should have been given to him, but was not, may refer to the Tribunal the alleged failure and—
(a) the decision in question, so far as it is based on a reason of the kind mentioned in subsection (4); or
(b) any opinion expressed by the Authority in relation to him.

(12) Section 394 applies to a third party as it applies to the person to whom the notice to which this section applies was given, in so far as the material which the Authority must disclose under that section relates to the matter which identifies the third party.

(13) A copy of a notice given to a third party under this section must be accompanied by a description of the effect of section 394 as it applies to him.

(14) Any person to whom a warning notice or decision notice was copied under this section must be given a copy of a notice of discontinuance applicable to the proceedings to which the warning notice or decision notice related.

[282]
394 Access to Authority material

(1) If the Authority gives a person ("A") a notice to which this section applies, it must—
(a) allow him access to the material on which it relied in taking the decision which gave rise to the obligation to give the notice;
(b) allow him access to any secondary material which, in the opinion of the Authority, might undermine that decision.

(2) But the Authority does not have to allow A access to material under subsection (1) if the material is excluded material or it—
(a) relates to a case involving a person other than A; and
(b) was taken into account by the Authority in A's case only for purposes of comparison with other cases.

(3) The Authority may refuse A access to particular material which it would otherwise have to allow him access to if, in its opinion, allowing him access to the material—
(a) would not be in the public interest; or
(b) would not be fair, having regard to—
(i) the likely significance of the material to A in relation to the matter in respect of which he has been given a notice to which this section applies; and
(ii) the potential prejudice to the commercial interests of a person other than A which would be caused by the material's disclosure.

(4) If the Authority does not allow A access to material because it is excluded material consisting of a protected item, it must give A written notice of—
(a) the existence of the protected item; and
(b) the Authority's decision not to allow him access to it.

(5) If the Authority refuses under subsection (3) to allow A access to material, it must give him written notice of—
(a) the refusal; and

(b) the reasons for it.

(6) "Secondary material" means material, other than material falling within paragraph (a) of subsection (1) which—

(a) was considered by the Authority in reaching the decision mentioned in that paragraph; or

(b) was obtained by the Authority in connection with the matter to which the notice to which this section applies relates but which was not considered by it in reaching that decision.

(7) "Excluded material" means material which—

[(a) is material the disclosure of which for the purposes of or in connection with any legal proceedings is prohibited by section 17 of the Regulation of Investigatory Powers Act 2000; or]

(c) is a protected item (as defined in section 413).

NOTES

Sub-s (7): para (a) substituted for original paras (a), (b) by the Regulation of Investigatory Powers Act 2000, s 82(1), Sch 4, para 11.

The Authority's procedures

[283]

395 The Authority's procedures

(1) The Authority must determine the procedure that it proposes to follow in relation to the giving of—

(a) supervisory notices; and

(b) warning notices and decision notices.

(2) That procedure must be designed to secure, among other things, that the decision which gives rise to the obligation to give any such notice is taken by a person not directly involved in establishing the evidence on which that decision is based.

(3) But the procedure may permit a decision which gives rise to an obligation to give a supervisory notice to be taken by a person other than a person mentioned in subsection (2) if—

(a) the Authority considers that, in the particular case, it is necessary in order to protect the interests of consumers; and

(b) the person taking the decision is of a level of seniority laid down by the procedure.

(4) A level of seniority laid down by the procedure for the purposes of subsection (3)(b) must be appropriate to the importance of the decision.

(5) The Authority must issue a statement of the procedure.

(6) The statement must be published in the way appearing to the Authority to be best calculated to bring it to the attention of the public.

(7) The Authority may charge a reasonable fee for providing a person with a copy of the statement.

(8) The Authority must, without delay, give the Treasury a copy of any statement which it issues under this section.

(9) When giving a supervisory notice, or a warning notice or decision notice, the Authority must follow its stated procedure.

(10) If the Authority changes the procedure in a material way, it must publish a revised statement.

(11) The Authority's failure in a particular case to follow its procedure as set out in the latest published statement does not affect the validity of a notice given in that case.

(12) But subsection (11) does not prevent the Tribunal from taking into account any such failure in considering a matter referred to it.

(13) "Supervisory notice" means a notice given in accordance with section—

(a) 53(4), (7) or (8)(b);

(b) 78(2) or (5);

[(bza)78A(2) or (8)(b);]

[(ba) 96C;]

[(bb) 87O(2) or (5);]

[(bc) 191B(1);]

(c) 197(3), (6) or (7)(b);

(d) 259(3), (8) or (9)(b);

(e) 268(3), (7)(a) or (9)(a) (as a result of subsection (8)(b));

(f) 282(3), (6) or (7)(b);

[(fa) 301J(1);]

(g) 321(2) or (5).

NOTES

Sub-s (13): para (bza) inserted by the Regulatory Reform (Financial Services and Markets Act 2000) Order 2007, SI 2007/1973, arts 2, 8; para (ba) inserted by the Financial Services and Markets Act 2000 (Market Abuse) Regulations 2005, SI 2005/381, reg 7; para (bb) inserted by the Prospectus Regulations 2005, SI 2005/1433, reg 2(1), Sch 1, para 14; paras (bc), (fa) inserted by the Financial Services and Markets Act 2000 (Controllers) Regulations 2009, SI 2009/534, reg 6.

Open-ended investment companies: this section has effect as if sub-s (13) included a reference to a notice given in accordance with the Open-Ended Investment Companies Regulations 2001, SI 2001/1228, reg 27(3), (8) or (9)(b); see reg 27(15) of the 2001 Regulations.

[284]

396 Statements under section 395: consultation

(1) Before issuing a statement of procedure under section 395, the Authority must publish a draft of the proposed statement in the way appearing to the Authority to be best calculated to bring it to the attention of the public.

(2) The draft must be accompanied by notice that representations about the proposal may be made to the Authority within a specified time.

(3) Before issuing the proposed statement of procedure, the Authority must have regard to any representations made to it in accordance with subsection (2).

(4) If the Authority issues the proposed statement of procedure it must publish an account, in general terms, of—

(a) the representations made to it in accordance with subsection (2); and

(b) its response to them.

(5) If the statement of procedure differs from the draft published under subsection (1) in a way which is, in the opinion of the Authority, significant, the Authority must (in addition to complying with subsection (4)) publish details of the difference.

(6) The Authority may charge a reasonable fee for providing a person with a copy of a draft published under subsection (1).

(7) This section also applies to a proposal to revise a statement of policy.

PART XXVII
OFFENCES

Miscellaneous offences

[285]

397 Misleading statements and practices

(1) This subsection applies to a person who—

(a) makes a statement, promise or forecast which he knows to be misleading, false or deceptive in a material particular;

(b) dishonestly conceals any material facts whether in connection with a statement, promise or forecast made by him or otherwise; or

(c) recklessly makes (dishonestly or otherwise) a statement, promise or forecast which is misleading, false or deceptive in a material particular.

(2) A person to whom subsection (1) applies is guilty of an offence if he makes the statement, promise or forecast or conceals the facts for the purpose of inducing, or is reckless as to whether it may induce, another person (whether or not the person to whom the statement, promise or forecast is made)—

(a) to enter or offer to enter into, or to refrain from entering or offering to enter into, a relevant agreement; or

(b) to exercise, or refrain from exercising, any rights conferred by a relevant investment.

(3) Any person who does any act or engages in any course of conduct which creates a false or misleading impression as to the market in or the price or value of any relevant investments is guilty of an offence if he does so for the purpose of creating that impression and of thereby inducing another person to acquire, dispose of, subscribe for or underwrite those investments or to refrain from doing so or to exercise, or refrain from exercising, any rights conferred by those investments.

(4) In proceedings for an offence under subsection (2) brought against a person to whom subsection (1) applies as a result of paragraph (a) of that subsection, it is a defence for him to show that the statement, promise or forecast was made in conformity with[—

(a) price stabilising rules;

(b) control of information rules; or

(c) the relevant provisions of Commission Regulation (EC) No 2273/2003 of 22 December 2003 implementing Directive 2003/6/EC of the European Parliament and of the Council as regards exemptions for buy-back programmes and stabilisation of financial instruments.]

(5) In proceedings brought against any person for an offence under subsection (3) it is a defence for him to show—

(a) that he reasonably believed that his act or conduct would not create an impression that was false or misleading as to the matters mentioned in that subsection;

(b) that he acted or engaged in the conduct—

(i) for the purpose of stabilising the price of investments; and

(ii) in conformity with price stabilising rules; . . .

(c) that he acted or engaged in the conduct in conformity with control of information rules[; or

(d) that he acted or engaged in the conduct in conformity with the relevant provisions of Commission Regulation (EC) No 2273/2003 of 22 December 2003 implementing Directive 2003/6/EC of the European Parliament and of the Council as regards exemptions for buy-back programmes and stabilisation of financial instruments.]

(6) Subsections (1) and (2) do not apply unless—

(a) the statement, promise or forecast is made in or from, or the facts are concealed in or from, the United Kingdom or arrangements are made in or from the United Kingdom for the statement, promise or forecast to be made or the facts to be concealed;

(b) the person on whom the inducement is intended to or may have effect is in the United Kingdom; or

(c) the agreement is or would be entered into or the rights are or would be exercised in the United Kingdom.

(7) Subsection (3) does not apply unless—

(a) the act is done, or the course of conduct is engaged in, in the United Kingdom; or

(b) the false or misleading impression is created there.

(8) A person guilty of an offence under this section is liable—

(a) on summary conviction, to imprisonment for a term not exceeding six months or a fine not exceeding the statutory maximum, or both;

(b) on conviction on indictment, to imprisonment for a term not exceeding seven years or a fine, or both.

(9) "Relevant agreement" means an agreement—

(a) the entering into or performance of which by either party constitutes an activity of a specified kind or one which falls within a specified class of activity; and

(b) which relates to a relevant investment.

(10) "Relevant investment" means an investment of a specified kind or one which falls within a prescribed class of investment.

(11) Schedule 2 (except paragraphs 25 and 26) applies for the purposes of subsections (9) and (10) with references to section 22 being read as references to each of those subsections.

(12) Nothing in Schedule 2, as applied by subsection (11), limits the power conferred by subsection (9) or (10).

(13) "Investment" includes any asset, right or interest.

(14) "Specified" means specified in an order made by the Treasury.

NOTES

Sub-s (4): words in square brackets substituted by the Financial Services and Markets Act 2000 (Market Abuse) Regulations 2005, SI 2005/381, reg 8(1), (2).

Sub-s (5): word omitted from para (b) repealed and para (d) and word "or" immediately preceding it inserted by SI 2005/381, reg 8(1), (3) (note that SI 2005/381 purports to insert a second sub-s (5)(a); however it is thought that this provision should be numbered as para (5)(d)).

Commission Regulation (EC) No 2273/2003: OJ L336, 23.12.2003, p 33.

Directive 2003/6/EC of the European Parliament and of the Council: OJ L96, 12.4.2003, p 16.

Orders: the Financial Services and Markets Act 2000 (Misleading Statements and Practices) Order 2001, SI 2001/3645 at **[838]**.

[286]

398 Misleading the Authority: residual cases

(1) A person who, in purported compliance with any requirement imposed by or under this Act, knowingly or recklessly gives the Authority information which is false or misleading in a material particular is guilty of an offence.

(2) Subsection (1) applies only to a requirement in relation to which no other provision of this Act creates an offence in connection with the giving of information.

(3) A person guilty of an offence under this section is liable—

(a) on summary conviction, to a fine not exceeding the statutory maximum;

(b) on conviction on indictment, to a fine.

NOTES

Application: sub-ss (1), (3) are applied in respect of requirements imposed by or under the Regulated Covered Bonds Regulations 2008, SI 2008/346, by SI 2008/346, reg 38(1).

[287]

399 Misleading [the OFT]

Section 44 of the Competition Act 1998 (offences connected with the provision of false or misleading information) applies in relation to any function of [the Office of Fair Trading] under this Act as if it were a function under Part I of that Act.

NOTES

Words in square brackets substituted by the Enterprise Act 2002, s 278(1), Sch 25, para 40(1), (16).

Bodies corporate and partnerships

[288]

400 Offences by bodies corporate etc

(1) If an offence under this Act committed by a body corporate is shown—

(a) to have been committed with the consent or connivance of an officer, or

(b) to be attributable to any neglect on his part,

the officer as well as the body corporate is guilty of the offence and liable to be proceeded against and punished accordingly.

(2) If the affairs of a body corporate are managed by its members, subsection (1) applies in relation to the acts and defaults of a member in connection with his functions of management as if he were a director of the body.

(3) If an offence under this Act committed by a partnership is shown—

(a) to have been committed with the consent or connivance of a partner, or

(b) to be attributable to any neglect on his part,

the partner as well as the partnership is guilty of the offence and liable to be proceeded against and punished accordingly.

(4) In subsection (3) "partner" includes a person purporting to act as a partner.

(5) "Officer", in relation to a body corporate, means—

(a) a director, member of the committee of management, chief executive, manager, secretary or other similar officer of the body, or a person purporting to act in any such capacity; and

(b) an individual who is a controller of the body.

(6) If an offence under this Act committed by an unincorporated association (other than a partnership) is shown—

(a) to have been committed with the consent or connivance of an officer of the association or a member of its governing body, or

(b) to be attributable to any neglect on the part of such an officer or member,

that officer or member as well as the association is guilty of the offence and liable to be proceeded against and punished accordingly.

(7) Regulations may provide for the application of any provision of this section, with such modifications as the Treasury consider appropriate, to a body corporate or unincorporated association formed or recognised under the law of a territory outside the United Kingdom.

NOTES

Application: this section and s 401 are applied by the Regulated Covered Bonds Regulations 2008, SI 2008/346, reg 38(2).

Institution of proceedings

[289]

401 Proceedings for offences

(1) In this section "offence" means an offence under this Act or subordinate legislation made under this Act.

(2) Proceedings for an offence may be instituted in England and Wales only—

(a) by the Authority or the Secretary of State; or

(b) by or with the consent of the Director of Public Prosecutions.

(3) Proceedings for an offence may be instituted in Northern Ireland only—

(a) by the Authority or the Secretary of State; or

(b) by or with the consent of the Director of Public Prosecutions for Northern Ireland.

(4) Except in Scotland, proceedings for an offence under section 203 may also be instituted by [the Office of Fair Trading].

(5) In exercising its power to institute proceedings for an offence, the Authority must comply with any conditions or restrictions imposed in writing by the Treasury.

(6) Conditions or restrictions may be imposed under subsection (5) in relation to—

- (a) proceedings generally; or
- (b) such proceedings, or categories of proceedings, as the Treasury may direct.

NOTES

Sub-s (4): words in square brackets substituted by the Enterprise Act 2002, s 278(1), Sch 25, para 40(1), (17).

Application: see the note to s 400 at **[288]**.

[290]

402 Power of the Authority to institute proceedings for certain other offences

(1) Except in Scotland, the Authority may institute proceedings for an offence under—

- (a) Part V of the Criminal Justice Act 1993 (insider dealing); . . .
- (b) prescribed regulations relating to money laundering[; or
- (c) Schedule 7 to the Counter-Terrorism Act 2008 (terrorist financing or money laundering).]

(2) In exercising its power to institute proceedings for any such offence, the Authority must comply with any conditions or restrictions imposed in writing by the Treasury.

(3) Conditions or restrictions may be imposed under subsection (2) in relation to—

- (a) proceedings generally; or
- (b) such proceedings, or categories of proceedings, as the Treasury may direct.

NOTES

Sub-s (1): word omitted repealed and para (c) and word "or" immediately preceding it added by the Counter-Terrorism Act 2008, s 62, Sch 7, Pt 7, para 33(4).

Regulations: the Money Laundering Regulations 2007, SI 2007/2157; the Transfer of Funds (Information on the Payer) Regulations 2007, SI 2007/3298.

[291]

403 Jurisdiction and procedure in respect of offences

(1) A fine imposed on an unincorporated association on its conviction of an offence is to be paid out of the funds of the association.

(2) Proceedings for an offence alleged to have been committed by an unincorporated association must be brought in the name of the association (and not in that of any of its members).

(3) Rules of court relating to the service of documents are to have effect as if the association were a body corporate.

(4) In proceedings for an offence brought against an unincorporated association—

- (a) section 33 of the Criminal Justice Act 1925 and Schedule 3 to the Magistrates' Courts Act 1980 (procedure) apply as they do in relation to a body corporate;
- (b) section 70 of the Criminal Procedure (Scotland) Act 1995 (procedure) applies as if the association were a body corporate;
- (c) section 18 of the Criminal Justice (Northern Ireland) Act 1945 and Schedule 4 to the Magistrates' Courts (Northern Ireland) Order 1981 (procedure) apply as they do in relation to a body corporate.

(5) Summary proceedings for an offence may be taken—

- (a) against a body corporate or unincorporated association at any place at which it has a place of business;
- (b) against an individual at any place where he is for the time being.

(6) Subsection (5) does not affect any jurisdiction exercisable apart from this section.

(7) "Offence" means an offence under this Act.

PART XXVIII
MISCELLANEOUS

Schemes for reviewing past business

[292]

404 Schemes for reviewing past business

(1) Subsection (2) applies if the Treasury are satisfied that there is evidence suggesting—

- (a) that there has been a widespread or regular failure on the part of authorised persons to comply with rules relating to a particular kind of activity; and

(b) that, as a result, private persons have suffered (or will suffer) loss in respect of which authorised persons are (or will be) liable to make payments ("compensation payments").

(2) The Treasury may by order ("a scheme order") authorise the Authority to establish and operate a scheme for—

(a) determining the nature and extent of the failure;

(b) establishing the liability of authorised persons to make compensation payments; and

(c) determining the amounts payable by way of compensation payments.

(3) An authorised scheme must be made so as to comply with specified requirements.

(4) A scheme order may be made only if—

(a) the Authority has given the Treasury a report about the alleged failure and asked them to make a scheme order;

(b) the report contains details of the scheme which the Authority propose to make; and

(c) the Treasury are satisfied that the proposed scheme is an appropriate way of dealing with the failure.

(5) A scheme order may provide for specified provisions of or made under this Act to apply in relation to any provision of, or determination made under, the resulting authorised scheme subject to such modifications (if any) as may be specified.

(6) For the purposes of this Act, failure on the part of an authorised person to comply with any provision of an authorised scheme is to be treated (subject to any provision made by the scheme order concerned) as a failure on his part to comply with rules.

(7) The Treasury may prescribe circumstances in which loss suffered by a person ("A") acting in a fiduciary or other prescribed capacity is to be treated, for the purposes of an authorised scheme, as suffered by a private person in relation to whom A was acting in that capacity.

(8) This section applies whenever the failure in question occurred.

(9) "Authorised scheme" means a scheme authorised by a scheme order.

(10) "Private person" has such meaning as may be prescribed.

(11) "Specified" means specified in a scheme order.

Third countries

[293]

405 Directions

(1) For the purpose of implementing a third country decision, the Treasury may direct the Authority to—

(a) refuse an application for permission under Part IV made by a body incorporated in, or formed under the law of, any part of the United Kingdom;

(b) defer its decision on such an application either indefinitely or for such period as may be specified in the direction;

(c) give a notice of objection to a person who has served a notice of control to the effect that he proposes to acquire a 50% stake in a UK authorised person; or

(d) give a notice of objection to a person who has acquired a 50% stake in a UK authorised person without having served the required notice of control.

(2) A direction may also be given in relation to—

(a) any person falling within a class specified in the direction;

(b) future applications, notices of control or acquisitions.

(3) The Treasury may revoke a direction at any time.

(4) But revocation does not affect anything done in accordance with the direction before it was revoked.

(5) "Third country decision" means a decision of the Council or the Commission under—

[(a) Article 15(3) of the markets in financial instruments directive;]

(b) . . .

(c) Article 29b(4) of the first non-life insurance directive; or

[(d) Article 59(4) of the life assurance consolidation directive.]

NOTES

Sub-s (5): para (a) substituted by the Financial Services and Markets Act 2000 (Markets in Financial Instruments) Regulations 2007, SI 2007/126, reg 3(5), Sch 5, paras 1, 17; para (b) repealed by the Capital Requirements Regulations 2006, SI 2006/3221, reg 29(1), Sch 3, para 1; para (d) substituted by the Life Assurance Consolidation Directive (Consequential Amendments) Regulations 2004, SI 2004/3379, reg 6(1), (4).

[294]

406 Interpretation of section 405

(1) For the purposes of section 405, a person ("the acquirer") acquires a 50% stake in a UK authorised person ("A") on first falling within any of the cases set out in subsection (2).

(2) The cases are where the acquirer—
- (a) holds 50% or more of the shares in A;
- (b) holds 50% or more of the shares in a parent undertaking ("P") of A;
- (c) is entitled to exercise, or control the exercise of, 50% or more of the voting power in A; or
- (d) is entitled to exercise, or control the exercise of, 50% or more of the voting power in P.

(3) In subsection (2) "the acquirer" means—
- (a) the acquirer;
- (b) any of the acquirer's associates; or
- (c) the acquirer and any of his associates.

(4) "Associate", "shares" and "voting power" have the same meaning as in section 422.

[295]

407 Consequences of a direction under section 405

(1) If the Authority refuses an application for permission as a result of a direction under section 405(1)(a)—
- (a) subsections (7) to (9) of section 52 do not apply in relation to the refusal; but
- (b) the Authority must notify the applicant of the refusal and the reasons for it.

(2) If the Authority defers its decision on an application for permission as a result of a direction under section 405(1)(b)—
- (a) the time limit for determining the application mentioned in section 52(1) or (2) stops running on the day of the deferral and starts running again (if at all) on the day the period specified in the direction (if any) ends or the day the direction is revoked; and
- (b) the Authority must notify the applicant of the deferral and the reasons for it.

(3) If the Authority gives a notice of objection to a person as a result of a direction under section 405(1)(c) or (d)—
- (a) sections 189 and 191 have effect as if the notice was a notice of objection within the meaning of Part XII; and
- (b) the Authority must state in the notice the reasons for it.

[296]

408 EFTA firms

(1) If a third country decision has been taken, the Treasury may make a determination in relation to an EFTA firm which is a subsidiary undertaking of a parent undertaking which is governed by the law of the country to which the decision relates.

(2) "Determination" means a determination that the firm concerned does not qualify for authorisation under Schedule 3 even if it satisfies the conditions in paragraph 13 or 14 of that Schedule.

(3) A determination may also be made in relation to any firm falling within a class specified in the determination.

(4) The Treasury may withdraw a determination at any time.

(5) But withdrawal does not affect anything done in accordance with the determination before it was withdrawn.

(6) If the Treasury make a determination in respect of a particular firm, or withdraw such a determination, they must give written notice to that firm.

(7) The Treasury must publish notice of any determination (or the withdrawal of any determination)—
- (a) in such a way as they think most suitable for bringing the determination (or withdrawal) to the attention of those likely to be affected by it; and
- (b) on, or as soon as practicable after, the date of the determination (or withdrawal).

(8) "EFTA firm" means a firm, institution or undertaking which—
- (a) is an EEA firm as a result of paragraph 5(a), (b) or (d) of Schedule 3; and
- (b) is incorporated in, or formed under the law of, an EEA State which is not a member State.

(9) "Third country decision" has the same meaning as in section 405.

[297]

409 Gibraltar

(1) The Treasury may by order—
- (a) modify Schedule 3 so as to provide for Gibraltar firms of a specified description to qualify for authorisation under that Schedule in specified circumstances;
- (b) modify Schedule 3 so as to make provision in relation to the exercise by UK firms of rights under the law of Gibraltar which correspond to EEA rights;

(c) modify Schedule 4 so as to provide for Gibraltar firms of a specified description to qualify for authorisation under that Schedule in specified circumstances;
(d) modify section 264 so as to make provision in relation to collective investment schemes constituted under the law of Gibraltar;
(e) provide for the Authority to be able to give notice under section 264(2) on grounds relating to the law of Gibraltar;
(f) provide for this Act to apply to a Gibraltar recognised scheme as if the scheme were a scheme recognised under section 264.

(2) The fact that a firm may qualify for authorisation under Schedule 3 as a result of an order under subsection (1) does not prevent it from applying for a Part IV permission.
(3) "Gibraltar firm" means a firm which has its head office in Gibraltar or is otherwise connected with Gibraltar.
(4) "Gibraltar recognised scheme" means a collective investment scheme—
(a) constituted in an EEA State other than the United Kingdom, and
(b) recognised in Gibraltar under provisions which appear to the Treasury to give effect to the provisions of a relevant Community instrument.

(5) "Specified" means specified in the order.
(6) "UK firm" and "EEA right" have the same meaning as in Schedule 3.

NOTES

Orders: the Financial Services and Markets Act 2000 (Gibraltar) Order 2001, SI 2001/3084.

International obligations

[298]
410 International obligations

(1) If it appears to the Treasury that any action proposed to be taken by a relevant person would be incompatible with Community obligations or any other international obligations of the United Kingdom, they may direct that person not to take that action.
(2) If it appears to the Treasury that any action which a relevant person has power to take is required for the purpose of implementing any such obligations, they may direct that person to take that action.
(3) A direction under this section—
(a) may include such supplemental or incidental requirements as the Treasury consider necessary or expedient; and
(b) is enforceable, on an application made by the Treasury, by injunction or, in Scotland, by an order for specific performance under section 45 of the Court of Session Act 1988.

(4) "Relevant person" means—
(a) the Authority;
(b) any person exercising functions conferred by Part VI on the competent authority;
(c) any recognised investment exchange (other than one which is an overseas investment exchange);
(d) any recognised clearing house (other than one which is an overseas clearing house);
(e) a person included in the list maintained under section 301; or
(f) the scheme operator of the ombudsman scheme.

411 (*Outside the scope of this work.*)

Gaming contracts

[299]
412 Gaming contracts

(1) No contract to which this section applies is void or unenforceable because of—
(a) . . . Article 170 of the Betting, Gaming, Lotteries and Amusements (Northern Ireland) Order 1985; or
(b) . . .

(2) This section applies to a contract if—
(a) it is entered into by either or each party by way of business;
(b) the entering into or performance of it by either party constitutes an activity of a specified kind or one which falls within a specified class of activity; and
(c) it relates to an investment of a specified kind or one which falls within a specified class of investment.

(3) Part II of Schedule 2 applies for the purposes of subsection (2)(c), with the references to section 22 being read as references to that subsection.

(4) Nothing in Part II of Schedule 2, as applied by subsection (3), limits the power conferred by subsection (2)(c).
(5) "Investment" includes any asset, right or interest.
(6) "Specified" means specified in an order made by the Treasury.

NOTES

Sub-s (1): words omitted from para (a), and the whole of para (b), repealed by the Gambling Act 2005, ss 334(1)(e), 356, (2), Sch 17. Note that s 334(2) of the 2005 Act specifically provides that the repeal of the words in sub-s (1) above does not permit enforcement of a right which is created, or which emanates from an agreement made, before 1 September 2007.

Orders: the Financial Services and Markets Act 2000 (Gaming Contracts) Order 2001, SI 2001/2510 at **[631]**.

412A, 412B *(Outside the scope of this work.)*

Limitation on powers to require documents

[300]

413 Protected items

(1) A person may not be required under this Act to produce, disclose or permit the inspection of protected items.
(2) "Protected items" means—
- (a) communications between a professional legal adviser and his client or any person representing his client which fall within subsection (3);
- (b) communications between a professional legal adviser, his client or any person representing his client and any other person which fall within subsection (3) (as a result of paragraph (b) of that subsection);
- (c) items which—
  - (i) are enclosed with, or referred to in, such communications;
  - (ii) fall within subsection (3); and
  - (iii) are in the possession of a person entitled to possession of them.

(3) A communication or item falls within this subsection if it is made—
- (a) in connection with the giving of legal advice to the client; or
- (b) in connection with, or in contemplation of, legal proceedings and for the purposes of those proceedings.

(4) A communication or item is not a protected item if it is held with the intention of furthering a criminal purpose.

NOTES

Application: this section applies for the purposes of the Payment Services Regulations 2009, SI 2009/209 and the Cross-Border Payments in Euro Regulations 2010, SI 2010/89 as it applies for the purposes of this Act; see SI 2009/209, reg 95, Sch 5, Pt 1, para 8 and SI 2010/89, reg 19, Schedule, Pt 1, para 6.

Service of notices

[301]

414 Service of notices

(1) The Treasury may by regulations make provision with respect to the procedure to be followed, or rules to be applied, when a provision of or made under this Act requires a notice, direction or document of any kind to be given or authorises the imposition of a requirement.
(2) The regulations may, in particular, make provision—
- (a) as to the manner in which a document must be given;
- (b) as to the address to which a document must be sent;
- (c) requiring, or allowing, a document to be sent electronically;
- (d) for treating a document as having been given, or as having been received, on a date or at a time determined in accordance with the regulations;
- (e) as to what must, or may, be done if the person to whom a document is required to be given is not an individual;
- (f) as to what must, or may, be done if the intended recipient of a document is outside the United Kingdom.

(3) Subsection (1) applies however the obligation to give a document is expressed (and so, in particular, includes a provision which requires a document to be served or sent).
(4) Section 7 of the Interpretation Act 1978 (service of notice by post) has effect in relation to provisions made by or under this Act subject to any provision made by regulations under this section.

NOTES

Regulations: the Financial Services and Markets Act 2000 (Service of Notices) Regulations 2001, SI 2001/1420; the Electronic Commerce Directive (Financial Services and Markets) Regulations 2002, SI 2002/1775.

Jurisdiction

[302]

415 Jurisdiction in civil proceedings

(1) Proceedings arising out of any act or omission (or proposed act or omission) of—

(a) the Authority,

(b) the competent authority for the purposes of Part VI,

(c) the scheme manager, or

(d) the scheme operator,

in the discharge or purported discharge of any of its functions under this Act may be brought before the High Court or the Court of Session.

(2) The jurisdiction conferred by subsection (1) is in addition to any other jurisdiction exercisable by those courts.

Removal of certain unnecessary provisions

[303]

416 Provisions relating to industrial assurance and certain other enactments

(1) The following enactments are to cease to have effect—

(a) the Industrial Assurance Act 1923;

(b) the Industrial Assurance and Friendly Societies Act 1948;

(c) the Insurance Brokers (Registration) Act 1977.

(2) The Industrial Assurance (Northern Ireland) Order 1979 is revoked.

(3) The following bodies are to cease to exist—

(a) the Insurance Brokers Registration Council;

(b) the Policyholders Protection Board;

(c) the Deposit Protection Board;

(d) the Board of Banking Supervision.

(4) If the Treasury consider that, as a consequence of any provision of this section, it is appropriate to do so, they may by order make any provision of a kind that they could make under this Act (and in particular any provision of a kind mentioned in section 339) with respect to anything done by or under any provision of Part XXI.

(5) Subsection (4) is not to be read as affecting in any way any other power conferred on the Treasury by this Act.

NOTES

Orders: the Financial Services and Markets Act 2000 (Dissolution of the Insurance Brokers Registration Council) (Consequential Provisions) Order 2001, SI 2001/1283; the Financial Services and Markets Act 2000 (Transitional Provisions, Repeals and Savings) (Financial Services Compensation Scheme) Order 2001, SI 2001/2967; the Financial Services and Markets Act 2000 (Consequential Amendments and Savings) (Industrial Assurance) Order 2001, SI 2001/3647.

PART XXIX
INTERPRETATION

[304]

417 Definitions

(1) In this Act—

"appointed representative" has the meaning given in section 39(2);

"auditors and actuaries rules" means rules made under section 340;

"authorisation offence" has the meaning given in section 23(2);

"authorised open-ended investment company" has the meaning given in section 237(3);

"authorised person" has the meaning given in section 31(2);

"the Authority" means the Financial Services Authority;

"body corporate" includes a body corporate constituted under the law of a country or territory outside the United Kingdom;

"chief executive"—

(a) in relation to a body corporate whose principal place of business is within the United Kingdom, means an employee of that body who, alone or jointly with one or more others, is responsible under the immediate authority of the directors, for the conduct of the whole of the business of that body; and

(b) in relation to a body corporate whose principal place of business is outside the United Kingdom, means the person who, alone or jointly with one or more others, is responsible for the conduct of its business within the United Kingdom;

["claim", in relation to the Financial Services Compensation Scheme under Part XV, is to be construed in accordance with section 214(1B);]

"collective investment scheme" has the meaning given in section 235;

"the Commission" means the European Commission (except in provisions relating to the Competition Commission);

"the compensation scheme" has the meaning given in section 213(2);

"control of information rules" has the meaning given in section 147(1);

"director", in relation to a body corporate, includes—

(a) a person occupying in relation to it the position of a director (by whatever name called); and

(b) a person in accordance with whose directions or instructions (not being advice given in a professional capacity) the directors of that body are accustomed to act;

"documents" includes information recorded in any form and, in relation to information recorded otherwise than in legible form, references to its production include references to producing a copy of the information in legible form[, or in a form from which it can readily be produced in visible and legible form];

["electronic commerce directive" means Directive 2000/31/EC of the European Parliament and the Council of 8 June 2000 on certain legal aspects of information society services, in particular electronic commerce, in the Internal Market (Directive on electronic commerce);]

"exempt person", in relation to a regulated activity, means a person who is exempt from the general prohibition in relation to that activity as a result of an exemption order made under section 38(1) or as a result of section 39(1) or 285(2) or (3);

"financial promotion rules" means rules made under section 145;

"friendly society" means an incorporated or registered friendly society;

"general prohibition" has the meaning given in section 19(2);

"general rules" has the meaning given in section 138(2);

"incorporated friendly society" means a society incorporated under the Friendly Societies Act 1992;

"industrial and provident society" means a society registered or deemed to be registered under the Industrial and Provident Societies Act 1965 or the Industrial and Provident Societies Act (Northern Ireland) 1969;

["information society service" means an information society service within the meaning of Article 2(a) of the electronic commerce directive;]

["investment services and activities" has the meaning given in Article 4.1.2 of the markets in financial instruments directive, read with—

(a) Chapter VI of Commission Regulation 1287/2006 of 10 August 2006, and

(b) Article 52 of Commission Directive 2006/73/EC of 10 August 2006;]

"market abuse" has the meaning given in section 118;

"Minister of the Crown" has the same meaning as in the Ministers of the Crown Act 1975;

"money laundering rules" means rules made under section 146;

"notice of control" [(except in Chapter 1A of Part 18)] has the meaning given in section 178(5);

"the ombudsman scheme" has the meaning given in section 225(3);

"open-ended investment company" has the meaning given in section 236;

"Part IV permission" has the meaning given in section 40(4);

"partnership" includes a partnership constituted under the law of a country or territory outside the United Kingdom;

"prescribed" (where not otherwise defined) means prescribed in regulations made by the Treasury;

"price stabilising rules" means rules made under section 144;

"private company" has [the same meaning as in the Companies Acts (see section 4 of the Companies Act 2006)];

"prohibition order" has the meaning given in section 56(2);

"recognised clearing house" and "recognised investment exchange" have the meaning given in section 285;

"registered friendly society" means a society which is—

(a) a friendly society within the meaning of section 7(1)(a) of the Friendly Societies Act 1974; and
(b) registered within the meaning of that Act;

"regulated activity" has the meaning given in section 22;
"regulating provisions" has the meaning given in section 159(1);
"regulatory objectives" means the objectives mentioned in section 2;
"regulatory provisions" has the meaning given in section 302;
"rule" means a rule made by the Authority under this Act;
"rule-making instrument" has the meaning given in section 153;
"the scheme manager" has the meaning given in section 212(1);
"the scheme operator" has the meaning given in section 225(2);
"scheme particulars rules" has the meaning given in section 248(1);
"Seventh Company Law Directive" means the European Council Seventh Company Law Directive of 13 June 1983 on consolidated accounts (No 83/349/EEC);
["Takeovers Directive" means Directive 2004/25/EC of the European Parliament and of the Council;]
"threshold conditions", in relation to a regulated activity, has the meaning given in section 41;
"the Treaty" means the treaty establishing the European Community;
["the Tribunal" means the Upper Tribunal;]
"trust scheme rules" has the meaning given in section 247(1);
"UK authorised person" has the meaning given in section 178(4); and
"unit trust scheme" has the meaning given in section 237.

(2) In the application of this Act to Scotland, references to a matter being actionable at the suit of a person are to be read as references to the matter being actionable at the instance of that person.

(3) For the purposes of any provision of this Act [(other than a provision of Part 6)] authorising or requiring a person to do anything within a specified number of days no account is to be taken of any day which is a public holiday in any part of the United Kingdom.

[(4) For the purposes of this Act—
(a) an information society service is provided from an EEA State if it is provided from an establishment in that State;
(b) an establishment, in connection with an information society service, is the place at which the provider of the service (being a national of an EEA State or a company or firm as mentioned in Article 48 of the Treaty) effectively pursues an economic activity for an indefinite period;
(c) the presence or use in a particular place of equipment or other technical means of providing an information society service does not, of itself, constitute that place as an establishment of the kind mentioned in paragraph (b);
(d) where it cannot be determined from which of a number of establishments a given information society service is provided, that service is to be regarded as provided from the establishment where the provider has the centre of his activities relating to the service.]

NOTES

Sub-s (1): definition "claim" inserted by the Banking Act 2009, s 174(2); words in square brackets in definition "documents" inserted by the Criminal Justice and Police Act 2001, s 70, Sch 2, Pt 2, para 16(1), (2)(f); definitions "electronic commerce directive" and "information society service" inserted by the Electronic Commerce Directive (Financial Services and Markets) Regulations 2002, SI 2002/1775, reg 13(1), (2)(a), (b); definition "investment services and activities" and words in square brackets in definition "notice of control" inserted by the Financial Services and Markets Act 2000 (Markets in Financial Instruments) Regulations 2007, SI 2007/126, reg 3(5), Sch 5, paras 1, 19; words in square brackets in definition "private company" substituted by the Companies Act 2006 (Consequential Amendments, Transitional Provisions and Savings) Order 2009, SI 2009/1941, art 2(1), Sch 1, para 181(1), (4); definition "Takeovers Directive" inserted by the Companies Act 2006, s 964(1), (6); definition "the Tribunal" inserted by the Transfer of Tribunal Functions Order 2010, SI 2010/22, art 5(1), Sch 2, paras 43, 48, as from 6 April 2010, subject to transitional and saving provisions in art 5(4) thereof and Sch 5 thereto.

Sub-s (4): added by SI 2002/1775, reg 13(1), (2)(c).

Directive 2000/31/EC: OJ L178, 17.7.2000, p 1.

Commission Regulation 1287/2006: OJ L241, 2.9.2006, p 1.

Commission Directive 2006/73/EC: OJ L241, 2.9.2006, p 26.

Directive 83/349/EEC: OJ L193, 18.7.1983, p 1.

Directive 2004/25/EC: OJ L142, 30.4.2004, p 12.

[305]

418 Carrying on regulated activities in the United Kingdom

(1) In the [five] cases described in this section, a person who—

(a) is carrying on a regulated activity, but
(b) would not otherwise be regarded as carrying it on in the United Kingdom,

is, for the purposes of this Act, to be regarded as carrying it on in the United Kingdom.

(2) The first case is where—
(a) his registered office (or if he does not have a registered office his head office) is in the United Kingdom;
(b) he is entitled to exercise rights under a single market directive as a UK firm; and
(c) he is carrying on in another EEA State a regulated activity to which that directive applies.

(3) The second case is where—
(a) his registered office (or if he does not have a registered office his head office) is in the United Kingdom;
(b) he is the manager of a scheme which is entitled to enjoy the rights conferred by an instrument which is a relevant Community instrument for the purposes of section 264; and
(c) persons in another EEA State are invited to become participants in the scheme.

(4) The third case is where—
(a) his registered office (or if he does not have a registered office his head office) is in the United Kingdom;
(b) the day-to-day management of the carrying on of the regulated activity is the responsibility of—
(i) his registered office (or head office); or
(ii) another establishment maintained by him in the United Kingdom.

(5) The fourth case is where—
(a) his head office is not in the United Kingdom; but
(b) the activity is carried on from an establishment maintained by him in the United Kingdom.

[(5A) The fifth case is any other case where the activity—
(a) consists of the provision of an information society service to a person or persons in one or more EEA States; and
(b) is carried on from an establishment in the United Kingdom.]

(6) For the purposes of subsections (2) to [(5A)] it is irrelevant where the person with whom the activity is carried on is situated.

NOTES

Sub-ss (1), (6): words in square brackets substituted by the Electronic Commerce Directive (Financial Services and Markets) Regulations 2002, SI 2002/1775, reg 13(1), (3)(a), (c).

Sub-s (5A): inserted by SI 2002/1775, reg 13(1), (3)(b).

[306]

419 Carrying on regulated activities by way of business

(1) The Treasury may by order make provision—
(a) as to the circumstances in which a person who would otherwise not be regarded as carrying on a regulated activity by way of business is to be regarded as doing so;
(b) as to the circumstances in which a person who would otherwise be regarded as carrying on a regulated activity by way of business is to be regarded as not doing so.

(2) An order under subsection (1) may be made so as to apply—
(a) generally in relation to all regulated activities;
(b) in relation to a specified category of regulated activity; or
(c) in relation to a particular regulated activity.

(3) An order under subsection (1) may be made so as to apply—
(a) for the purposes of all provisions;
(b) for a specified group of provisions; or
(c) for a specified provision.

(4) "Provision" means a provision of, or made under, this Act.

(5) Nothing in this section is to be read as affecting the provisions of section 428(3).

NOTES

Orders: the Financial Services and Markets Act 2000 (Carrying on Regulated Activities by Way of Business) Order 2001, SI 2001/1177 at **[591]**.

[307]

420 Parent and subsidiary undertaking

(1) In this Act, except in relation to an incorporated friendly society, "parent undertaking" and "subsidiary undertaking" have the same meaning as in [the Companies Acts (see section 1162 of, and Schedule 7 to, the Companies Act 2006)].

(2) But—

(a) "parent undertaking" also includes an individual who would be a parent undertaking for the purposes of those provisions if he were taken to be an undertaking (and "subsidiary undertaking" is to be read accordingly);

(b) "subsidiary undertaking" also includes, in relation to a body incorporated in or formed under the law of an EEA State other than the United Kingdom, an undertaking which is a subsidiary undertaking within the meaning of any rule of law in force in that State for purposes connected with implementation of the Seventh Company Law Directive (and "parent undertaking" is to be read accordingly).

(3) In this Act "subsidiary undertaking", in relation to an incorporated friendly society, means a body corporate of which the society has control within the meaning of section 13(9)(a) or (aa) of the Friendly Societies Act 1992 (and "parent undertaking" is to be read accordingly).

NOTES

Sub-s (1): words in square brackets substituted by the Companies Act 2006 (Consequential Amendments etc) Order 2008, SI 2008/948, art 3(1)(b), Sch 1, Pt 2, para 212(1), subject to transitional provisions and savings in arts 6, 12 thereof.

[308]

421 Group

(1) In this Act "group", in relation to a person ("A"), means A and any person who is—

(a) a parent undertaking of A;

(b) a subsidiary undertaking of A;

(c) a subsidiary undertaking of a parent undertaking of A;

(d) a parent undertaking of a subsidiary undertaking of A;

(e) an undertaking in which A or an undertaking mentioned in paragraph (a), (b), (c) or (d) has a participating interest;

(f) if A or an undertaking mentioned in paragraph (a) or (d) is a building society, an associated undertaking of the society; or

(g) if A or an undertaking mentioned in paragraph (a) or (d) is an incorporated friendly society, a body corporate of which the society has joint control (within the meaning of section 13(9)(c) or (cc) of the Friendly Societies Act 1992).

(2) "Participating interest" [has the meaning given in section 421A]; but also includes an interest held by an individual which would be a participating interest for the purposes of those provisions if he were taken to be an undertaking.

(3) "Associated undertaking" has the meaning given in section 119(1) of the Building Societies Act 1986.

NOTES

Sub-s (2): words in square brackets substituted by the Companies Act 2006 (Consequential Amendments etc) Order 2008, SI 2008/948, art 3(1)(b), Sch 1, Pt 2, para 212(2), subject to transitional provisions and savings in arts 6, 12 thereof.

[308A]

[421A Meaning of "participating interest"

(1) In section 421 a "participating interest" means an interest held by an undertaking in the shares of another undertaking which it holds on a long-term basis for the purpose of securing a contribution to its activities by the exercise of control or influence arising from or related to that interest.

(2) A holding of 20% or more of the shares of an undertaking is presumed to be a participating interest unless the contrary is shown.

(3) The reference in subsection (1) to an interest in shares includes—

(a) an interest which is convertible into an interest in shares, and

(b) an option to acquire shares or any such interest;

and an interest or option falls within paragraph (a) or (b) notwithstanding that the shares to which it relates are, until the conversion or the exercise of the option, unissued.

(4) For the purposes of this section an interest held on behalf of an undertaking shall be treated as held by it.

(5) In this section "undertaking" has the same meaning as in the Companies Acts (see section 1161(1) of the Companies Act 2006).]

NOTES

Commencement: 6 April 2008.

Inserted by the Companies Act 2006 (Consequential Amendments etc) Order 2008, SI 2008/948, art 3(1)(b), Sch 1, Pt 2, para 212(3).

[309]

[422 Controller

(1) In this Act "controller", in relation to an undertaking ("B"), means a person ("A") who falls within any of the cases in subsection (2).

(2) The cases are where A holds—

- (a) 10% or more of the shares in B or in a parent undertaking of B ("P");
- (b) 10% or more of the voting power in B or P; or
- (c) shares or voting power in B or P as a result of which A is able to exercise significant influence over the management of B.

(3) For the purposes of calculations relating to this section, the holding of shares or voting power by a person ("A1") includes any shares or voting power held by another ("A2") if A1 and A2 are acting in concert.

(4) In this section "shares"—

- (a) in relation to an undertaking with a share capital, means allotted shares;
- (b) in relation to an undertaking with capital but no share capital, means rights to share in the capital of the undertaking;
- (c) in relation to an undertaking without capital, means interests—
  - (i) conferring any right to share in the profits, or liability to contribute to the losses, of the undertaking; or
  - (ii) giving rise to an obligation to contribute to the debts or expenses of the undertaking in the event of a winding up.

(5) In this section "voting power"—

- (a) includes, in relation to a person ("H")—
  - (i) voting power held by a third party with whom H has concluded an agreement, which obliges H and the third party to adopt, by concerted exercise of the voting power they hold, a lasting common policy towards the management of the undertaking in question;
  - (ii) voting power held by a third party under an agreement concluded with H providing for the temporary transfer for consideration of the voting power in question;
  - (iii) voting power attaching to shares which are lodged as collateral with H, provided that H controls the voting power and declares an intention to exercise it;
  - (iv) voting power attaching to shares in which H has a life interest;
  - (v) voting power which is held, or may be exercised within the meaning of subparagraphs (i) to (iv), by a subsidiary undertaking of H;
  - (vi) voting power attaching to shares deposited with H which H has discretion to exercise in the absence of specific instructions from the shareholders;
  - (vii) voting power held in the name of a third party on behalf of H;
  - (viii) voting power which H may exercise as a proxy where H has discretion about the exercise of the voting power in the absence of specific instructions from the shareholders; and
- (b) in relation to an undertaking which does not have general meetings at which matters are decided by the exercise of voting rights, means the right under the constitution of the undertaking to direct the overall policy of the undertaking or alter the terms of its constitution.]

NOTES

Commencement: 21 March 2009.

Substituted, together with s 422A for original s 422 by the Financial Services and Markets Act 2000 (Controllers) Regulations 2009, SI 2009/534, reg 7, Sch 3, subject to transitional provisions in reg 8 thereof which provides that this section, as it stood immediately before 21 March 2009, applies in respect of any notification submitted to the FSA before that date.

[309A]

[422A Disregarded holdings

(1) For the purposes of section 422, shares and voting power that a person holds in an undertaking ("B") or in a parent undertaking of B ("P") are disregarded in the following circumstances.

(2) Shares held only for the purposes of clearing and settling within a short settlement cycle are disregarded.

(3) Shares held by a custodian or its nominee in a custodian capacity are disregarded, provided that the custodian or nominee is only able to exercise voting power attached to the shares in accordance with instructions given in writing.

(4) Shares representing no more than 5% of the total voting power in B or P held by an investment firm are disregarded, provided that it—

- (a) holds the shares in the capacity of a market maker (as defined in article 4.1(8) of the markets in financial instruments directive);
- (b) is authorised by its home state regulator under the markets in financial instruments directive; and
- (c) neither intervenes in the management of B or P nor exerts any influence on B or P to buy the shares or back the share price.

(5) Shares held by a credit institution or investment firm in its trading book are disregarded, provided that—

- (a) the shares represent no more than 5% of the total voting power in B or P; and
- (b) the credit institution or investment firm ensures that the voting power is not used to intervene in the management of B or P.

(6) Shares held by a credit institution or an investment firm are disregarded, provided that—

- (a) the shares are held as a result of performing the investment services and activities of—
  - (i) underwriting shares; or
  - (ii) placing shares on a firm commitment basis in accordance with Annex I, section A.6 of the markets in financial instruments directive; and
- (b) the credit institution or investment firm—
  - (i) does not exercise voting power represented by the shares or otherwise intervene in the management of the issuer; and
  - (ii) retains the holding for a period of less than one year.

(7) Where a management company (as defined in Article 1a.2 of the UCITS directive) and its parent undertaking both hold shares or voting power, each may disregard holdings of the other, provided that each exercises its voting power independently of the other.

(8) But subsection (7) does not apply if the management company—

- (a) manages holdings for its parent undertaking or an undertaking in respect of which the parent undertaking is a controller;
- (b) has no discretion to exercise the voting power attached to such holdings; and
- (c) may only exercise the voting power in relation to such holdings under direct or indirect instruction from—
  - (i) its parent undertaking; or
  - (ii) an undertaking in respect of which of the parent undertaking is a controller.

(9) Where an investment firm and its parent undertaking both hold shares or voting power, the parent undertaking may disregard holdings managed by the investment firm on a client by client basis and the investment firm may disregard holdings of the parent undertaking, provided that the investment firm—

- (a) has permission to provide portfolio management;
- (b) exercises its voting power independently from the parent undertaking; and
- (c) may only exercise the voting power under instructions given in writing, or has appropriate mechanisms in place for ensuring that individual portfolio management services are conducted independently of any other services.

(10) In this section "credit institution" means—

- (a) a credit institution authorised under the banking consolidation directive; or
- (b) an institution which would satisfy the requirements for authorisation as a credit institution under that directive if it had its registered office (or if it does not have a registered office, its head office) in an EEA State.]

NOTES

Commencement: 21 March 2009.

Substituted as noted to s 422 at [**309**].

[310]
423 Manager
(1) In this Act, except in relation to a unit trust scheme or a registered friendly society, "manager" means an employee who—
- (a) under the immediate authority of his employer is responsible, either alone or jointly with one or more other persons, for the conduct of his employer's business; or
- (b) under the immediate authority of his employer or of a person who is a manager by virtue of paragraph (a) exercises managerial functions or is responsible for maintaining accounts or other records of his employer.

(2) If the employer is not an individual, references in subsection (1) to the authority of the employer are references to the authority—
- (a) in the case of a body corporate, of the directors;
- (b) in the case of a partnership, of the partners; and
- (c) in the case of an unincorporated association, of its officers or the members of its governing body.

(3) "Manager", in relation to a body corporate, means a person (other than an employee of the body) who is appointed by the body to manage any part of its business and includes an employee of the body corporate (other than the chief executive) who, under the immediate authority of a director or chief executive of the body corporate, exercises managerial functions or is responsible for maintaining accounts or other records of the body corporate.

[311]
424 Insurance
(1) In this Act, references to—
- (a) contracts of insurance,
- (b) reinsurance,
- (c) contracts of long-term insurance,
- (d) contracts of general insurance,

are to be read with section 22 and Schedule 2.

(2) In this Act "policy" and "policyholder", in relation to a contract of insurance, have such meaning as the Treasury may by order specify.

(3) The law applicable to a contract of insurance, the effecting of which constitutes the carrying on of a regulated activity, is to be determined, if it is of a prescribed description, in accordance with regulations made by the Treasury.

NOTES

Orders: the Financial Services and Markets Act 2000 (Meaning of "Policy" and "Policyholder") Order 2001, SI 2001/2361 at **[625]**.

Regulations: the Financial Services and Markets Act 2000 (Law Applicable to Contracts of Insurance) Regulations 2001, SI 2001/2635 at **[670]**; the Financial Services and Markets Act 2000 (Motor Insurance) Regulations 2007, SI 2007/2403; the Financial Services and Markets Act 2000 (Law Applicable to Contracts of Insurance) Regulations 2009, SI 2009/3075 at **[1032]**.

424A *(Outside the scope of this work.)*

[312]
425 Expressions relating to authorisation elsewhere in the single market
(1) In this Act—
- [(a) "banking consolidation directive", ["life assurance consolidation directive",] "EEA authorisation", "EEA firm", "EEA right", "EEA State", . . . "first non-life insurance directive", "insurance directives", ["reinsurance directive",] "insurance mediation directive", . . . ["markets in financial instruments directive",] "single market directives"[, "tied agent"] and "UCITS directive" have the meaning given in Schedule 3; and]
- (b) "home state regulator", in relation to an EEA firm, has the meaning given in Schedule 3.

(2) In this Act—
- (a) "home state authorisation" has the meaning given in Schedule 4;
- (b) "Treaty firm" has the meaning given in Schedule 4; and
- (c) "home state regulator", in relation to a Treaty firm, has the meaning given in Schedule 4.

NOTES

Sub-s (1): para (a) substituted by the Collective Investment Schemes (Miscellaneous Amendments) Regulations 2003, SI 2003/2066, reg 2(1); in para (a) words in first pair of square brackets inserted and first words omitted repealed by the Life Assurance Consolidation Directive (Consequential Amendments) Regulations 2004, SI 2004/3379, reg 6(1), (5), second words omitted repealed and words in fourth pair of square brackets inserted by the Financial Services and Markets Act 2000 (Markets in Financial Instruments)

Regulations 2007, SI 2007/126, reg 3(5), Sch 5, paras 1, 22, words in second pair of square brackets inserted by the Reinsurance Directive Regulations 2007, SI 2007/3253, reg 2(1), Sch 1, paras 1, 5, words in third pair of square brackets inserted by the Financial Services and Markets Act 2000 (Markets in Financial Instruments) (Modification of Powers) Regulations 2006, SI 2006/2975, regs 2, 11.

PART XXX
SUPPLEMENTAL

[313]

426 Consequential and supplementary provision

(1) A Minister of the Crown may by order make such incidental, consequential, transitional or supplemental provision as he considers necessary or expedient for the general purposes, or any particular purpose, of this Act or in consequence of any provision made by or under this Act or for giving full effect to this Act or any such provision.

(2) An order under subsection (1) may, in particular, make provision—

- (a) for enabling any person by whom any powers will become exercisable, on a date set by or under this Act, by virtue of any provision made by or under this Act to take before that date any steps which are necessary as a preliminary to the exercise of those powers;
- (b) for applying (with or without modifications) or amending, repealing or revoking any provision of or made under an Act passed before this Act or in the same Session;
- (c) dissolving any body corporate established by any Act passed, or instrument made, before the passing of this Act;
- (d) for making savings, or additional savings, from the effect of any repeal or revocation made by or under this Act.

(3) Amendments made under this section are additional, and without prejudice, to those made by or under any other provision of this Act.

(4) No other provision of this Act restricts the powers conferred by this section.

NOTES

Regulations: the Financial Services and Markets Act 2000 (Recognition Requirements for Investment Exchanges and Clearing Houses) Regulations 2001, SI 2001/995; the Financial Services and Markets Act 2000 (Disclosure of Confidential Information) Regulations 2001, SI 2001/2188; the Financial Services and Markets Act 2000 (EEA Passport Rights) Regulations 2001, SI 2001/2511 at **[633]**.

Orders: the Financial Services and Markets Act 2000 (Regulated Activities) Order 2001, SI 2001/544 at **[501]**; the Financial Services and Markets Act 2000 (Transitional Provisions and Savings) (Rules) Order 2001, SI 2001/1534; the Financial Services and Markets Act 2000 (Consequential and Transitional Provisions) (Miscellaneous) Order 2001, SI 2001/1821; the Financial Services and Markets Act 2000 (Transitional Provisions) (Ombudsman Scheme and Complaints Scheme) Order 2001, SI 2001/2326; the Financial Services and Markets Act 2000 (Transitional Provisions) (Reviews of Pensions Business) Order 2001, SI 2001/2512; the Financial Services and Markets Act 2000 (Mutual Societies) Order 2001, SI 2001/2617 at **[651]**; the Financial Services and Markets Act 2000 (Transitional Provisions) (Authorised Persons etc) Order 2001, SI 2001/2636; the Financial Services and Markets Act 2000 (Transitional Provisions) (Controllers) Order 2001, SI 2001/2637; the Financial Services and Markets Act 2000 (Consequential and Transitional Provisions) (Miscellaneous) (No 2) Order 2001, SI 2001/2659; the Financial Services and Markets Act 2000 (Official Listing of Securities) (Transitional Provisions) Order 2001, SI 2001/2957; the Financial Services and Markets Act 2000 (Consequential Amendments) (Pre-Commencement Modifications) Order 2001, SI 2001/2966; the Financial Services and Markets Act 2000 (Transitional Provisions, Repeals and Savings) (Financial Services Compensation Scheme) Order 2001, SI 2001/2967; the Financial Services and Markets Act 2000 (Transitional Provisions and Savings) (Civil Remedies, Discipline, Criminal Offences etc) (No 2) Order 2001, SI 2001/3083; the Financial Services and Markets Act 2000 (Interim Permissions) Order 2001, SI 2001/3374; the Financial Services and Markets Act 2000 (Dissolution of the Board of Banking Supervision) (Transitional Provisions) Order 2001, SI 2001/3582; the Financial Services and Markets Act 2000 (Transitional Provisions) (Partly Completed Procedures) Order 2001, SI 2001/3592; the Financial Services and Markets Act 2000 (Consequential Amendments) (Taxes) Order 2001, SI 2001/3629; the Financial Services and Markets Act 2000 (Transitional Provisions and Savings) (Business Transfers) Order 2001, SI 2001/3639; the Financial Services and Markets Act 2000 (Savings, Modifications and Consequential Provisions) (Rehabilitation of Offenders) (Scotland) Order 2001, SI 2001/3640; the Financial Services and Markets Act 2000 (Transitional Provisions and Savings) (Information Requirements and Investigations) Order 2001, SI 2001/3646; the Financial Services and Markets Act 2000 (Consequential Amendments and Savings) (Industrial Assurance) Order 2001, SI 2001/3647; the Financial Services and Markets Act 2000 (Confidential Information) (Bank of England) (Consequential Provisions) Order 2001, SI 2001/3648; the Financial Services and Markets Act 2000 (Miscellaneous Provisions) Order 2001, SI 2001/3650; the Financial Services and Markets Act 2000 (Scope of Permission Notices) Order 2001, SI 2001/3771 at **[848]**; the Financial Services and Markets Act 2000 (Consequential Amendments) (No 2) Order 2001, SI 2001/3801; the Financial Services and Markets Act 2000 (Permission and Applications) (Credit Unions etc) Order 2002, SI 2002/704; the Financial Services and Markets Act 2000 (Administration Orders Relating to Insurers) Order 2002, SI 2002/1242 at **[852]**; the Financial Services and Markets Act 2000 (Consequential Amendments and Transitional Provisions) (Credit Unions) Order 2002, SI 2002/1501; the Financial Services and Markets Act 2000 (Collective Investment Schemes) (Designated Countries and Territories) Order 2003, SI 2003/1181; the

Financial Services and Markets Act 2000 (Transitional Provisions) (Complaints Relating to General Insurance and Mortgages) Order 2004, SI 2004/454 at **[914]**; the Financial Services and Markets Act 2000 (Transitional Provisions) (Mortgages) Order 2004, SI 2004/2615; the Financial Services and Markets Act 2000 (Transitional Provisions) (General Insurance Intermediaries) Order 2004, SI 2004/3351; the Financial Services and Markets Act 2000 (Administration Orders Relating to Insurers) (Northern Ireland) Order 2007, SI 2007/846.

[314]

427 Transitional provisions

(1) Subsections (2) and (3) apply to an order under section 426 which makes transitional provisions or savings.

(2) The order may, in particular—

(a) if it makes provision about the authorisation and permission of persons who before commencement were entitled to carry on any activities, also include provision for such persons not to be treated as having any authorisation or permission (whether on an application to the Authority or otherwise);

(b) make provision enabling the Authority to require persons of such descriptions as it may direct to re-apply for permissions having effect by virtue of the order;

(c) make provision for the continuation as rules of such provisions (including primary and subordinate legislation) as may be designated in accordance with the order by the Authority, including provision for the modification by the Authority of provisions designated;

(d) make provision about the effect of requirements imposed, liabilities incurred and any other things done before commencement, including provision for and about investigations, penalties and the taking or continuing of any other action in respect of contraventions;

(e) make provision for the continuation of disciplinary and other proceedings begun before commencement, including provision about the decisions available to bodies before which such proceedings take place and the effect of their decisions;

(f) make provision as regards the Authority's obligation to maintain a record under section 347 as respects persons in relation to whom provision is made by the order.

(3) The order may—

(a) confer functions on the Treasury, the Secretary of State, the Authority, the scheme manager, the scheme operator, members of the panel established under paragraph 4 of Schedule 17, the Competition Commission or [the Office of Fair Trading];

(b) confer jurisdiction on the Tribunal;

(c) provide for fees to be charged in connection with the carrying out of functions conferred under the order;

(d) modify, exclude or apply (with or without modifications) any primary or subordinate legislation (including any provision of, or made under, this Act).

(4) In subsection (2) "commencement" means the commencement of such provisions of this Act as may be specified by the order.

NOTES

Sub-s (3): words in square brackets substituted by the Enterprise Act 2002, s 278(1), Sch 25, para 40(1), (18).

Orders: the Financial Services and Markets Act 2000 (Permission and Applications) (Credit Unions etc) Order 2002, SI 2002/704; the Financial Services and Markets Act 2000 (Consequential Amendments and Transitional Provisions) (Credit Unions) Order 2002, SI 2002/1501; the Financial Services and Markets Act 2000 (Transitional Provisions) (Complaints Relating to General Insurance and Mortgages) Order 2004, SI 2004/454 at **[914]**; the Financial Services and Markets Act 2000 (Transitional Provisions) (Mortgages) Order 2004, SI 2004/2615; the Financial Services and Markets Act 2000 (Transitional Provisions) (General Insurance Intermediaries) Order 2004, SI 2004/3351.

[315]

428 Regulations and orders

(1) Any power to make an order which is conferred on a Minister of the Crown by this Act and any power to make regulations which is conferred by this Act is exercisable by statutory instrument.

(2) The Lord Chancellor's power to make rules under section 132 is exercisable by statutory instrument.

(3) Any statutory instrument made under this Act may—

(a) contain such incidental, supplemental, consequential and transitional provision as the person making it considers appropriate; and

(b) make different provision for different cases.

[316]

429 Parliamentary control of statutory instruments

(1) No order is to be made under—

(a) section 144(4), 192(b) or (e), 236(5), 404 or 419, or

(b) paragraph 1 of Schedule 8,

unless a draft of the order has been laid before Parliament and approved by a resolution of each House.

(2) No regulations are to be made under section [90B[, 214A, 214B] or] 262 unless a draft of the regulations has been laid before Parliament and approved by a resolution of each House.

(3) An order to which, if it is made, subsection (4) or (5) will apply is not to be made unless a draft of the order has been laid before Parliament and approved by a resolution of each House.

(4) This subsection applies to an order under section 21 if—

(a) it is the first order to be made, or to contain provisions made, under section 21(4);

(b) it varies an order made under section 21(4) so as to make section 21(1) apply in circumstances in which it did not previously apply;

(c) it is the first order to be made, or to contain provision made, under section 21(5);

(d) it varies a previous order made under section 21(5) so as to make section 21(1) apply in circumstances in which it did not, as a result of that previous order, apply;

(e) it is the first order to be made, or to contain provisions made, under section 21(9) or (10);

(f) it adds one or more activities to those that are controlled activities for the purposes of section 21; or

(g) it adds one or more investments to those which are controlled investments for the purposes of section 21.

(5) This subsection applies to an order under section 38 if—

(a) it is the first order to be made, or to contain provisions made, under that section; or

(b) it contains provisions restricting or removing an exemption provided by an earlier order made under that section.

(6) An order containing a provision to which, if the order is made, subsection (7) will apply is not to be made unless a draft of the order has been laid before Parliament and approved by a resolution of each House.

(7) This subsection applies to a provision contained in an order if—

(a) it is the first to be made in the exercise of the power conferred by subsection (1) of section 326 or it removes a body from those for the time being designated under that subsection; or

(b) it is the first to be made in the exercise of the power conferred by subsection (6) of section 327 or it adds a description of regulated activity or investment to those for the time being specified for the purposes of that subsection.

(8) Any other statutory instrument made under this Act, apart from one made under section 431(2) or to which paragraph 26 of Schedule 2 applies, shall be subject to annulment in pursuance of a resolution of either House of Parliament.

NOTES

Sub-s (2): words in first (outer) pair of square brackets inserted by the Companies Act 2006, s 1272, Sch 15, Pt 1, paras 1, 12; references in second (inner) pair of square brackets inserted by the Banking Act 2009, s 178.

[317]

430 Extent

(1) This Act, except Chapter IV of Part XVII, extends to Northern Ireland.

(2) Except where Her Majesty by Order in Council provides otherwise, the extent of any amendment or repeal made by or under this Act is the same as the extent of the provision amended or repealed.

(3) Her Majesty may by Order in Council provide for any provision of or made under this Act relating to a matter which is the subject of other legislation which extends to any of the Channel Islands or the Isle of Man to extend there with such modifications (if any) as may be specified in the Order.

[318]

431 Commencement

(1) The following provisions come into force on the passing of this Act—

(a) this section;

(b) sections 428, 430 and 433;

(c) paragraphs 1 and 2 of Schedule 21.

(2) The other provisions of this Act come into force on such day as the Treasury may by order appoint; and different days may be appointed for different purposes.

NOTES

Orders: the Financial Services and Markets Act 2000 (Commencement No 1) Order 2001, SI 2001/516; the Financial Services and Markets Act 2000 (Commencement No 2) Order 2001, SI 2001/1282; the Financial Services and Markets Act 2000 (Commencement No 3) Order 2001, SI 2001/1820; the Financial Services and Markets Act 2000 (Commencement No 4 and Transitional Provision) Order 2001, SI 2001/2364; the Financial Services and Markets Act 2000 (Commencement No 5) Order 2001, SI 2001/2632; the Financial Services and Markets Act 2000 (Commencement No 6) Order 2001, SI 2001/3436; the Financial Services and Markets Act 2000 (Commencement No 7) Order 2001, SI 2001/3538.

[319]

432 Minor and consequential amendments, transitional provisions and repeals

(1) Schedule 20 makes minor and consequential amendments.
(2) Schedule 21 makes transitional provisions.
(3) The enactments set out in Schedule 22 are repealed.

[320]

433 Short title

This Act may be cited as the Financial Services and Markets Act 2000.

SCHEDULE 1

THE FINANCIAL SERVICES AUTHORITY

Section 1

PART I
GENERAL

Interpretation

[321]

1.—(1) In this Schedule—

. . .

"non-executive committee" means the committee maintained under paragraph 3;

"functions", in relation to the Authority, means functions conferred on the Authority by or under any provision of this Act.

(2) For the purposes of this Schedule, the following are the Authority's legislative functions—
- (a) making rules;
- (b) issuing codes under section 64 or 119;
- (c) issuing statements under section 64, 69, 124 or 210;
- (d) giving directions under section 316, 318 or 328;
- (e) issuing general guidance (as defined by section 158(5)) [or guidance under section 158A].

Constitution

2.—(1) The constitution of the Authority must continue to provide for the Authority to have—
- (a) a chairman; and
- (b) a governing body.

(2) The governing body must include the chairman.
(3) The chairman and other members of the governing body must be appointed, and be liable to removal from office, by the Treasury.
(4) The validity of any act of the Authority is not affected—
- (a) by a vacancy in the office of chairman; or
- (b) by a defect in the appointment of a person as a member of the governing body or as chairman.

Non-executive members of the governing body

3.—(1) The Authority must secure—
- (a) that the majority of the members of its governing body are non-executive members; and
- (b) that a committee of its governing body, consisting solely of the non-executive members, is set up and maintained for the purposes of discharging the functions conferred on the committee by this Schedule.

(2) The members of the non-executive committee are to be appointed by the Authority.

(3) The non-executive committee is to have a chairman appointed by the Treasury from among its members.

Functions of the non-executive committee

4.—(1) In this paragraph "the committee" means the non-executive committee.
(2) The non-executive functions are functions of the Authority but must be discharged by the committee.
(3) The non-executive functions are—
  (a) keeping under review the question whether the Authority is, in discharging its functions in accordance with decisions of its governing body, using its resources in the most efficient and economic way;
  (b) keeping under review the question whether the Authority's internal financial controls secure the proper conduct of its financial affairs; and
  (c) determining the remuneration of—
    (i) the chairman of the Authority's governing body; and
    (ii) the executive members of that body.
(4) The function mentioned in sub-paragraph (3)(b) and those mentioned in sub-paragraph (3)(c) may be discharged on behalf of the committee by a sub-committee.
(5) Any sub-committee of the committee—
  (a) must have as its chairman the chairman of the committee; but
  (b) may include persons other than members of the committee.
(6) The committee must prepare a report on the discharge of its functions for inclusion in the Authority's annual report to the Treasury under paragraph 10.
(7) The committee's report must relate to the same period as that covered by the Authority's report.

Arrangements for discharging functions

5.—(1) The Authority may make arrangements for any of its functions to be discharged by a committee, sub-committee, officer or member of staff of the Authority.
[(2) But—
  (a) in exercising the legislative functions mentioned in paragraph 1(2)(a) to (d), the Authority must act through its governing body; and
  (b) the legislative function mentioned in paragraph 1(2)(e) may not be discharged by an officer or member of staff of the Authority.]
(3) Sub-paragraph (1) does not apply to the non-executive functions.

Monitoring and enforcement

6.—(1) The Authority must maintain arrangements designed to enable it to determine whether persons on whom requirements are imposed by or under this Act[, or by any directly applicable Community regulation made under the markets in financial instruments directive,] are complying with them.
(2) Those arrangements may provide for functions to be performed on behalf of the Authority by any body or person who, in its opinion, is competent to perform them.
(3) The Authority must also maintain arrangements for enforcing the provisions of, or made under, this Act [or of any directly applicable Community regulation made under the markets in financial instruments directive].
(4) Sub-paragraph (2) does not affect the Authority's duty under sub-paragraph (1).

Arrangements for the investigation of complaints

7.—(1) The Authority must—
  (a) make arrangements ("the complaints scheme") for the investigation of complaints arising in connection with the exercise of, or failure to exercise, any of its functions (other than its legislative functions); and
  (b) appoint an independent person ("the investigator") to be responsible for the conduct of investigations in accordance with the complaints scheme.
(2) The complaints scheme must be designed so that, as far as reasonably practicable, complaints are investigated quickly.
(3) The Treasury's approval is required for the appointment or dismissal of the investigator.
(4) The terms and conditions on which the investigator is appointed must be such as, in the opinion of the Authority, are reasonably designed to secure—
  (a) that he will be free at all times to act independently of the Authority; and
  (b) that complaints will be investigated under the complaints scheme without favouring the Authority.

(5) Before making the complaints scheme, the Authority must publish a draft of the proposed scheme in the way appearing to the Authority best calculated to bring it to the attention of the public.
(6) The draft must be accompanied by notice that representations about it may be made to the Authority within a specified time.
(7) Before making the proposed complaints scheme, the Authority must have regard to any representations made to it in accordance with sub-paragraph (6).
(8) If the Authority makes the proposed complaints scheme, it must publish an account, in general terms, of—
  (a) the representations made to it in accordance with sub-paragraph (6); and
  (b) its response to them.
(9) If the complaints scheme differs from the draft published under sub-paragraph (5) in a way which is, in the opinion of the Authority, significant the Authority must (in addition to complying with sub-paragraph (8)) publish details of the difference.
(10) The Authority must publish up-to-date details of the complaints scheme including, in particular, details of—
  (a) the provision made under paragraph 8(5); and
  (b) the powers which the investigator has to investigate a complaint.
(11) Those details must be published in the way appearing to the Authority to be best calculated to bring them to the attention of the public.
(12) The Authority must, without delay, give the Treasury a copy of any details published by it under this paragraph.
(13) The Authority may charge a reasonable fee for providing a person with a copy of—
  (a) a draft published under sub-paragraph (5);
  (b) details published under sub-paragraph (10).
(14) Sub-paragraphs (5) to (9) and (13)(a) also apply to a proposal to alter or replace the complaints scheme.

Investigation of complaints

8.—(1) The Authority is not obliged to investigate a complaint in accordance with the complaints scheme which it reasonably considers would be more appropriately dealt with in another way (for example by referring the matter to the Tribunal or by the institution of other legal proceedings).
(2) The complaints scheme must provide—
  (a) for reference to the investigator of any complaint which the Authority is investigating; and
  (b) for him—
    (i) to have the means to conduct a full investigation of the complaint;
    (ii) to report on the result of his investigation to the Authority and the complainant; and
    (iii) to be able to publish his report (or any part of it) if he considers that it (or the part) ought to be brought to the attention of the public.
(3) If the Authority has decided not to investigate a complaint, it must notify the investigator.
(4) If the investigator considers that a complaint of which he has been notified under sub-paragraph (3) ought to be investigated, he may proceed as if the complaint had been referred to him under the complaints scheme.
(5) The complaints scheme must confer on the investigator the power to recommend, if he thinks it appropriate, that the Authority—
  (a) makes a compensatory payment to the complainant,
  (b) remedies the matter complained of,
or takes both of those steps.
(6) The complaints scheme must require the Authority, in a case where the investigator—
  (a) has reported that a complaint is well-founded, or
  (b) has criticised the Authority in his report,
to inform the investigator and the complainant of the steps which it proposes to take in response to the report.
(7) The investigator may require the Authority to publish the whole or a specified part of the response.
(8) The investigator may appoint a person to conduct the investigation on his behalf but subject to his direction.
(9) Neither an officer nor an employee of the Authority may be appointed under sub-paragraph (8).
(10) Sub-paragraph (2) is not to be taken as preventing the Authority from making arrangements for the initial investigation of a complaint to be conducted by the Authority.

Records

9. The Authority must maintain satisfactory arrangements for—
(a) recording decisions made in the exercise of its functions; and
(b) the safe-keeping of those records which it considers ought to be preserved.

Annual report

10.—(1) At least once a year the Authority must make a report to the Treasury on—
(a) the discharge of its functions;
(b) the extent to which, in its opinion, the regulatory objectives have been met;
(c) its consideration of the matters mentioned in section 2(3); and
(d) such other matters as the Treasury may from time to time direct.
(2) The report must be accompanied by—
(a) the report prepared by the non-executive committee under paragraph 4(6); and
(b) such other reports or information, prepared by such persons, as the Treasury may from time to time direct.
(3) The Treasury must lay before Parliament a copy of each report received by them under this paragraph.
(4) The Treasury may—
(a) require the Authority to comply with any provisions of [the Companies Act 2006] about accounts and their audit which would not otherwise apply to it; or
(b) direct that any such provision of that Act is to apply to the Authority with such modifications as are specified in the direction.
(5) Compliance with any requirement imposed under sub-paragraph (4)(a) or (b) is enforceable by injunction or, in Scotland, an order under section 45(b) of the Court of Session Act 1988.
(6) Proceedings under sub-paragraph (5) may be brought only by the Treasury.

Annual public meeting

11.—(1) Not later than three months after making a report under paragraph 10, the Authority must hold a public meeting ("the annual meeting") for the purposes of enabling that report to be considered.
(2) The Authority must organise the annual meeting so as to allow—
(a) a general discussion of the contents of the report which is being considered; and
(b) a reasonable opportunity for those attending the meeting to put questions to the Authority about the way in which it discharged, or failed to discharge, its functions during the period to which the report relates.
(3) But otherwise the annual meeting is to be organised and conducted in such a way as the Authority considers appropriate.
(4) The Authority must give reasonable notice of its annual meeting.
(5) That notice must—
(a) give details of the time and place at which the meeting is to be held;
(b) set out the proposed agenda for the meeting;
(c) indicate the proposed duration of the meeting;
(d) give details of the Authority's arrangements for enabling persons to attend; and
(e) be published by the Authority in the way appearing to it to be most suitable for bringing the notice to the attention of the public.
(6) If the Authority proposes to alter any of the arrangements which have been included in the notice given under sub-paragraph (4) it must—
(a) give reasonable notice of the alteration; and
(b) publish that notice in the way appearing to the Authority to be best calculated to bring it to the attention of the public.

Report of annual meeting

12. Not later than one month after its annual meeting, the Authority must publish a report of the proceedings of the meeting.

NOTES

Para 1: definition "the 1985 Act" omitted from sub-para (1) repealed by the Companies Act 2006 (Consequential Amendments, Transitional Provisions and Savings) Order 2009, SI 2009/1941, art 2(1), Sch 1, para 181(1), (5)(a); words in square brackets in sub-para (2)(e) inserted by the Financial Services and Markets Act 2000 (Markets in Financial Instruments) (Modification of Powers) Regulations 2006, SI 2006/2975, regs 2, 12, subject to transitional provisions in reg 15 thereof.

Para 5: sub-para (2) substituted by the Regulatory Reform (Financial Services and Markets Act 2000) Order 2007, SI 2007/1973, arts 2, 14.

Para 6: words in square brackets in sub-paras (1), (3) inserted by the Financial Services and Markets Act 2000 (Markets in Financial Instruments) Regulations 2007, SI 2007/126, reg 3(5), Sch 5, paras 1, 23.

Para 10: words in square brackets in sub-para (4)(a) substituted by the Companies Act 2006 (Consequential Amendments etc) Order 2008, SI 2008/948, art 3(1)(b), Sch 1, Pt 2, para 213, subject to transitional provisions and savings in arts 6, 11, 12 thereof.

Modification: the reference to the Authority's functions includes its functions as a designated agency under the Financial Services Act 1986 (repealed by the Financial Services and Markets Act 2000 (Consequential Amendments and Repeals) Order 2001, SI 2001/3649, art 3(1)(c)) and the reference to the Authority's legislative functions includes its functions of issuing statements of principle, rules, regulations and codes of practice under that Act; see the Financial Services and Markets Act 2000 (Consequential and Transitional Provisions) (Miscellaneous) Order 2001, SI 2001/1821, art 2(1)(b), (c).

PART II
STATUS

[322]

13. In relation to any of its functions—

(a) the Authority is not to be regarded as acting on behalf of the Crown; and

(b) its members, officers and staff are not to be regarded as Crown servants.

Exemption from requirement of "limited" in Authority's name

14. The Authority is to continue to be exempt from the requirements of [the Companies Act 2006] relating to the use of "limited" as part of its name.

15. If the Secretary of State is satisfied that any action taken by the Authority makes it inappropriate for the exemption given by paragraph 14 to continue he may, after consulting the Treasury, give a direction removing it.

NOTES

Para 14: words in square brackets substituted by the Companies Act 2006 (Consequential Amendments, Transitional Provisions and Savings) Order 2009, SI 2009/1941, art 2(1), Sch 1, para 181(1), (5)(b).

Modification: see the note to Pt I at **[321]**.

PART III
PENALTIES AND FEES

Penalties

[323]

16.—(1) In determining its policy with respect to the amounts of penalties to be imposed by it under this Act, the Authority must take no account of the expenses which it incurs, or expects to incur, in discharging its functions.

(2) The Authority must prepare and operate a scheme for ensuring that the amounts paid to the Authority by way of penalties imposed under this Act are applied for the benefit of authorised persons.

(3) The scheme may, in particular, make different provision with respect to different classes of authorised person.

(4) Up to date details of the scheme must be set out in a document ("the scheme details").

(5) The scheme details must be published by the Authority in the way appearing to it to be best calculated to bring them to the attention of the public.

(6) Before making the scheme, the Authority must publish a draft of the proposed scheme in the way appearing to the Authority to be best calculated to bring it to the attention of the public.

(7) The draft must be accompanied by notice that representations about the proposals may be made to the Authority within a specified time.

(8) Before making the scheme, the Authority must have regard to any representations made to it in accordance with sub-paragraph (7).

(9) If the Authority makes the proposed scheme, it must publish an account, in general terms, of—

(a) the representations made to it in accordance with sub-paragraph (7); and

(b) its response to them.

(10) If the scheme differs from the draft published under sub-paragraph (6) in a way which is, in the opinion of the Authority, significant the Authority must (in addition to complying with sub-paragraph (9)) publish details of the difference.

(11) The Authority must, without delay, give the Treasury a copy of any scheme details published by it.

(12) The Authority may charge a reasonable fee for providing a person with a copy of—

(a) a draft published under sub-paragraph (6);

(b) scheme details.

(13) Sub-paragraphs (6) to (10) and (12)(a) also apply to a proposal to alter or replace the complaints scheme.

Fees

17.—(1) The Authority may make rules providing for the payment to it of such fees, in connection with the discharge of any of its functions under or as a result of this Act, as it considers will (taking account of its expected income from fees and charges provided for by any other provision of this Act) enable it—

(a) to meet expenses incurred in carrying out its functions or for any incidental purpose;

(b) to repay the principal of, and pay any interest on, any money which it has borrowed and which has been used for the purpose of meeting expenses incurred in relation to its assumption of functions under this Act or the Bank of England Act 1998; and

(c) to maintain adequate reserves.

(2) In fixing the amount of any fee which is to be payable to the Authority, no account is to be taken of any sums which the Authority receives, or expects to receive, by way of penalties imposed by it under this Act.

(3) Sub-paragraph (1)(b) applies whether expenses were incurred before or after the coming into force of this Act or the Bank of England Act 1998.

(4) Any fee which is owed to the Authority under any provision made by or under this Act may be recovered as a debt due to the Authority.

Services for which fees may not be charged

18. The power conferred by paragraph 17 may not be used to require—

(a) a fee to be paid in respect of the discharge of any of the Authority's functions under paragraphs 13, 14, 19 or 20 of Schedule 3; or

(b) a fee to be paid by any person whose application for approval under section 59 has been granted.

NOTES

Modification: see the note to Pt I at **[321]**.

Modification: paras 16, 17 are applied, with modifications, in respect of regulated covered bonds; see the Regulated Covered Bonds Regulations 2008, SI 2008/346, regs 37, 46, Schedule, Pt 1, para 5.

Para 17 is applied, with modifications, for the purposes of the Payment Services Regulations 2009, SI 2009/209; see SI 2009/209, reg 92.

PART IV
MISCELLANEOUS

Exemption from liability in damages

[324]

19.—(1) Neither the Authority nor any person who is, or is acting as, a member, officer or member of staff of the Authority is to be liable in damages for anything done or omitted in the discharge, or purported discharge, of the Authority's functions.

(2) Neither the investigator appointed under paragraph 7 nor a person appointed to conduct an investigation on his behalf under paragraph 8(8) is to be liable in damages for anything done or omitted in the discharge, or purported discharge, of his functions in relation to the investigation of a complaint.

(3) Neither sub-paragraph (1) nor sub-paragraph (2) applies—

(a) if the act or omission is shown to have been in bad faith; or

(b) so as to prevent an award of damages made in respect of an act or omission on the ground that the act or omission was unlawful as a result of section 6(1) of the Human Rights Act 1998.

[19A. For the purposes of this Act anything done by an accredited financial investigator within the meaning of the Proceeds of Crime Act 2002 who is—

(a) a member of the staff of the Authority, or

(b) a person appointed by the Authority under section 97, 167 or 168 to conduct an investigation,

must be treated as done in the exercise or discharge of a function of the Authority.]

20, 21. . . .

NOTES

Para 19A: inserted by the Proceeds of Crime Act 2002, s 456, Sch 11, paras 1, 38.

Para 20: amends the House of Commons Disqualification Act 1975, Sch 1, Pt III.

Para 21: amends the Northern Ireland Assembly Disqualification Act 1975, Sch 1, Pt III.
Modification: see the note to Pt I at **[321]**.

SCHEDULE 2

REGULATED ACTIVITIES

Section 22(2)

[PART I
REGULATED ACTIVITIES: GENERAL]

General

[325]

1. The matters with respect to which provision may be made under section 22(1) in respect of activities include, in particular, those described in general terms in this Part of this Schedule.

Dealing in investments

2.—(1) Buying, selling, subscribing for or underwriting investments or offering or agreeing to do so, either as a principal or as an agent.
(2) In the case of an investment which is a contract of insurance, that includes carrying out the contract.

Arranging deals in investments

3. Making, or offering or agreeing to make—
- (a) arrangements with a view to another person buying, selling, subscribing for or underwriting a particular investment;
- (b) arrangements with a view to a person who participates in the arrangements buying, selling, subscribing for or underwriting investments.

Deposit taking

4. Accepting deposits.

Safekeeping and administration of assets

5.—(1) Safeguarding and administering assets belonging to another which consist of or include investments or offering or agreeing to do so.
(2) Arranging for the safeguarding and administration of assets belonging to another, or offering or agreeing to do so.

Managing investments

6. Managing, or offering or agreeing to manage, assets belonging to another person where—
- (a) the assets consist of or include investments; or
- (b) the arrangements for their management are such that the assets may consist of or include investments at the discretion of the person managing or offering or agreeing to manage them.

Investment advice

7. Giving or offering or agreeing to give advice to persons on—
- (a) buying, selling, subscribing for or underwriting an investment; or
- (b) exercising any right conferred by an investment to acquire, dispose of, underwrite or convert an investment.

Establishing collective investment schemes

8. Establishing, operating or winding up a collective investment scheme, including acting as—
- (a) trustee of a unit trust scheme;
- (b) depositary of a collective investment scheme other than a unit trust scheme; or
- (c) sole director of a body incorporated by virtue of regulations under section 262.

Using computer-based systems for giving investment instructions

9.—(1) Sending on behalf of another person instructions relating to an investment by means of a computer-based system which enables investments to be transferred without a written instrument.
(2) Offering or agreeing to send such instructions by such means on behalf of another person.
(3) Causing such instructions to be sent by such means on behalf of another person.

(4) Offering or agreeing to cause such instructions to be sent by such means on behalf of another person.

NOTES

Part heading: substituted by the Dormant Bank and Building Society Accounts Act 2008, s 15, Sch 2, para 1(1), (2).

[PART 1A
REGULATED ACTIVITIES: RECLAIM FUNDS

Activities of reclaim funds

[325A]

9A.—(1) The matters with respect to which provision may be made under section 22(1) in respect of activities include, in particular, any of the activities of a reclaim fund.
(2) "Reclaim fund" has the meaning given by section 5(1) of the Dormant Bank and Building Society Accounts Act 2008.]

NOTES

Commencement: 12 March 2009.
Inserted by the Dormant Bank and Building Society Accounts Act 2008, s 15, Sch 2, para 1(1), (3).

PART II
INVESTMENTS

General

[326]

10. The matters with respect to which provision may be made under section 22(1) in respect of investments include, in particular, those described in general terms in this Part of this Schedule.

Securities

11.—(1) Shares or stock in the share capital of a company.
(2) "Company" includes—
(a) any body corporate (wherever incorporated), and
(b) any unincorporated body constituted under the law of a country or territory outside the United Kingdom,
other than an open-ended investment company.

Instruments creating or acknowledging indebtedness

12. Any of the following—
(a) debentures;
(b) debenture stock;
(c) loan stock;
(d) bonds;
(e) certificates of deposit;
(f) any other instruments creating or acknowledging a present or future indebtedness.

Government and public securities

13.—(1) Loan stock, bonds and other instruments—
(a) creating or acknowledging indebtedness; and
(b) issued by or on behalf of a government, local authority or public authority.
(2) "Government, local authority or public authority" means—
(a) the government of the United Kingdom, of Northern Ireland, or of any country or territory outside the United Kingdom;
(b) a local authority in the United Kingdom or elsewhere;
(c) any international organisation the members of which include the United Kingdom or another member State.

Instruments giving entitlement to investments

14.—(1) Warrants or other instruments entitling the holder to subscribe for any investment.
(2) It is immaterial whether the investment is in existence or identifiable.

Certificates representing securities

15. Certificates or other instruments which confer contractual or property rights—

(a) in respect of any investment held by someone other than the person on whom the rights are conferred by the certificate or other instrument; and
(b) the transfer of which may be effected without requiring the consent of that person.

Units in collective investment schemes

16.—(1) Shares in or securities of an open-ended investment company.
(2) Any right to participate in a collective investment scheme.

Options

17. Options to acquire or dispose of property.

Futures

18. Rights under a contract for the sale of a commodity or property of any other description under which delivery is to be made at a future date.

Contracts for differences

19. Rights under—
(a) a contract for differences; or
(b) any other contract the purpose or pretended purpose of which is to secure a profit or avoid a loss by reference to fluctuations in—
(i) the value or price of property of any description; or
(ii) an index or other factor designated for that purpose in the contract.

Contracts of insurance

20. Rights under a contract of insurance, including rights under contracts falling within head C of Schedule 2 to the Friendly Societies Act 1992.

Participation in Lloyd's syndicates

21.—(1) The underwriting capacity of a Lloyd's syndicate.
(2) A person's membership (or prospective membership) of a Lloyd's syndicate.

Deposits

22. Rights under any contract under which a sum of money (whether or not denominated in a currency) is paid on terms under which it will be repaid, with or without interest or a premium, and either on demand or at a time or in circumstances agreed by or on behalf of the person making the payment and the person receiving it.

Loans secured on land

23.—(1) Rights under any contract under which—
(a) one person provides another with credit; and
(b) the obligation of the borrower to repay is secured on land.
(2) "Credit" includes any cash loan or other financial accommodation.
(3) "Cash" includes money in any form.

[Other finance arrangements involving land

23A.—(1) Rights under any arrangement for the provision of finance under which the person providing the finance either—
(a) acquires a major interest in land from the person to whom the finance is provided, or
(b) disposes of a major interest in land to that person,
as part of the arrangement.
(2) References in sub-paragraph (1) to a "major interest" in land are to—
(a) in relation to land in England or Wales—
(i) an estate *in fee simple* absolute, or
(ii) a term of years absolute,
whether subsisting at law or in equity;
(b) in relation to land in Scotland—
(i) the interest of an owner of land, or
(ii) the tenant's right over or interest in a property subject to a lease;
(c) in relation to land in Northern Ireland—
(i) any freehold estate, or
(ii) any leasehold estate,
whether subsisting at law or in equity.

(3) It is immaterial for the purposes of sub-paragraph (1) whether either party acquires or (as the case may be) disposes of the interest in land—

(a) directly, or
(b) indirectly.]

Rights in investments

24. Any right or interest in anything which is an investment as a result of any other provision made under section 22(1).

NOTES

Para 23A: inserted, together with preceding cross-heading, by the Regulation of Financial Services (Land Transactions) Act 2005, s 1.

Modification: this Part of this Schedule is applied, with modifications, to eligible debt securities by the Uncertificated Securities (Amendment) (Eligible Debt Securities) Regulations 2003, SI 2003/1633, reg 15, Sch 2, paras 6(1), (2)(b), 8(1), (2)(h).

PART III
SUPPLEMENTAL PROVISIONS

The order-making power

[327]

25.—(1) An order under section 22(1) may—

(a) provide for exemptions;
(b) confer powers on the Treasury or the Authority;
(c) authorise the making of regulations or other instruments by the Treasury for purposes of, or connected with, any relevant provision;
(d) authorise the making of rules or other instruments by the Authority for purposes of, or connected with, any relevant provision;
(e) make provision in respect of any information or document which, in the opinion of the Treasury or the Authority, is relevant for purposes of, or connected with, any relevant provision;
(f) make such consequential, transitional or supplemental provision as the Treasury consider appropriate for purposes of, or connected with, any relevant provision.

(2) Provision made as a result of sub-paragraph (1)(f) may amend any primary or subordinate legislation, including any provision of, or made under, this Act.

(3) "Relevant provision" means any provision—

(a) of section 22 or this Schedule; or
(b) made under that section or this Schedule.

Parliamentary control

26.—(1) This paragraph applies to the first order made under section 22(1).

(2) This paragraph also applies to any subsequent order made under section 22(1) which contains a statement by the Treasury that, in their opinion, the effect (or one of the effects) of the proposed order would be that an activity which is not a regulated activity would become a regulated activity.

(3) An order to which this paragraph applies—

(a) must be laid before Parliament after being made; and
(b) ceases to have effect at the end of the relevant period unless before the end of that period the order is approved by a resolution of each House of Parliament (but without that affecting anything done under the order or the power to make a new order).

(4) "Relevant period" means a period of twenty-eight days beginning with the day on which the order is made.

(5) In calculating the relevant period no account is to be taken of any time during which Parliament is dissolved or prorogued or during which both Houses are adjourned for more than four days.

Interpretation

27.—(1) In this Schedule—

"buying" includes acquiring for valuable consideration;
"offering" includes inviting to treat;
"property" includes currency of the United Kingdom or any other country or territory; and
"selling" includes disposing for valuable consideration.

(2) In sub-paragraph (1) "disposing" includes—

(a) in the case of an investment consisting of rights under a contract—

(i) surrendering, assigning or converting those rights; or
(ii) assuming the corresponding liabilities under the contract;
(b) in the case of an investment consisting of rights under other arrangements, assuming the corresponding liabilities under the contract or arrangements;
(c) in the case of any other investment, issuing or creating the investment or granting the rights or interests of which it consists.

(3) In this Schedule references to an instrument include references to any record (whether or not in the form of a document).

NOTES

Orders: the Financial Services and Markets Act 2000 (Regulated Activities) Order 2001, SI 2001/544 at **[501]**; the Financial Services and Markets Act 2000 (Financial Promotion) Order 2005, SI 2005/1529 at **[966]**.

SCHEDULE 3

EEA PASSPORT RIGHTS

Sections 31(1)(b) and 37

PART I
DEFINED TERMS

The single market directives

[328]

1. "The single market directives" means—
[(a) the banking consolidation directive;]
(c) the insurance directives; . . .
[(ca) the reinsurance directive;]
(d) the [markets in financial instruments directive][; . . .
(e) the insurance mediation directive][; and
(f) the UCITS directive.]

The banking [consolidation directive]

[**2.** "The banking consolidation directive" means Directive 2006/48/EC of the European Parliament and of the Council of 14 June 2006 relating to the taking up and pursuit of the business of credit institutions.]

The insurance directives

3.—(1) "The insurance directives" means the first, second and third non-life insurance directives and the [life assurance consolidation directive].
(2) "First non-life insurance directive" means the Council Directive of 24 July 1973 on the co-ordination of laws, regulations and administrative provisions relating to the taking up and pursuit of the business of direct insurance other than life assurance (No 73/239/EEC).
(3) "Second non-life insurance directive" means the Council Directive of 22 June 1988 on the co-ordination of laws, etc, and laying down provisions to facilitate the effective exercise of freedom to provide services and amending Directive 73/239/EEC (No 88/357/EEC).
(4) "Third non-life insurance directive" means the Council Directive of 18 June 1992 on the co-ordination of laws, etc, and amending Directives 73/239/EEC and 88/357/EEC (No 92/49/EEC).
[(8) "Life assurance consolidation directive" means Directive 2002/83/EC of the European Parliament and of the Council of 5th November 2002 concerning life assurance.]

[The reinsurance directive

3A. "The reinsurance directive" means Directive 2005/68/EC of the European Parliament and of the Council of 16 November 2005 on reinsurance and amending Council Directives 73/239/EEC, 92/49/EEC as well as Directives 98/78/EC and 2002/83/EC.]

4. . . .

[The insurance mediation directive

4A. "The insurance mediation directive" means the European Parliament and Council Directive of 9th December 2002 on insurance mediation (No 2002/92/EC).]

[The UCITS directive

4B. "The UCITS directive" means the Council Directive of 20 December 1985 on the coordination of laws, regulations and administrative provisions relating to undertakings for collective investment in transferable securities (No 85/611/EEC).]

[The markets in financial instruments directive

4C. "The markets in financial instruments directive" means Directive 2004/39/EC of the European Parliament and of the Council of 21 April 2004 on markets in financial instruments.]

EEA firm

5. "EEA firm" means any of the following if it does not have its [relevant office] in the United Kingdom—

(a) an investment firm (as defined in [Article 4.1.1 of the markets in financial instruments directive]) which is authorised (within the meaning of [Article 5]) by its home state regulator;

[(b) a credit institution (as defined in Article 4.1 of the banking consolidation directive) which is authorised (within the meaning of Article 4.2) by its home state regulator,

(c) a financial institution (as defined in Article 4.5 of the banking consolidation directive) which is a subsidiary of the kind mentioned in Article 24 and which fulfils the conditions in that Article;]

(d) an undertaking pursuing the activity of direct insurance (within the meaning of [Article 2 of the life assurance consolidation directive or Article 1 of the first non-life insurance directive]) which has received authorisation under [Article 4 of the life assurance consolidation directive or Article 6 of the first non-life insurance directive] from its home state regulator[; . . .

[(da) an undertaking pursuing the activity of reinsurance (within the meaning of Article 2.1(a) of the reinsurance directive) which has received authorisation under (or is deemed to be authorised in accordance with) Article 3 of the reinsurance directive from its home state regulator;]

(e) an insurance intermediary (as defined in Article 2.5 of the insurance mediation directive), or a reinsurance intermediary (as defined in Article 2.6) which is registered with its home state regulator under Article 3][; or

(f) a management company (as defined in Article 1a.2 of the UCITS directive) which is authorised (within the meaning of Article 5) by its home state regulator.]

[5A. In paragraph 5, "relevant office" means—

(a) in relation to a firm falling within sub-paragraph (e) of that paragraph which has a registered office, its registered office;

(b) in relation to any other firm, its head office.]

EEA authorisation

[6. "EEA authorisation" means—

(a) in relation to an EEA firm falling within paragraph 5(e), registration with its home state regulator under Article 3 of the insurance mediation directive;

(b) in relation to any other EEA firm, authorisation granted to an EEA firm by its home state regulator for the purpose of the relevant single market directive.]

EEA right

7. "EEA right" means the entitlement of a person to establish a branch, or provide services, in an EEA State other than that in which he has his [relevant office]—

(a) in accordance with the Treaty as applied in the EEA; and

(b) subject to the conditions of the relevant single market directive.

[7A. In paragraph 7, "relevant office" means—

(a) in relation to a person who has a registered office and whose entitlement is subject to the conditions of the insurance mediation directive, his registered office;

(b) in relation to any other person, his head office.]

EEA State

[8. "EEA State" has the meaning given by Schedule 1 to the Interpretation Act 1978.]

Home state regulator

9. "Home state regulator" means the competent authority (within the meaning of the relevant single market directive) of an EEA State (other than the United Kingdom) in relation to the EEA firm concerned.

UK firm

10. "UK firm" means a person whose [relevant office] is in the UK and who has an EEA right to carry on activity in an EEA State other than the United Kingdom.

[10A. In paragraph 10, "relevant office" means—

(a) in relation to a firm whose EEA right derives from the insurance mediation directive and which has a registered office, its registered office;

(b) in relation to any other firm, its head office.]

[UK investment firm

10B. "UK investment firm" means a UK firm—

(a) which is an investment firm, and

(b) whose EEA right derives from the markets in financial instruments directive.]

Host state regulator

11. "Host state regulator" means the competent authority (within the meaning of the relevant single market directive) of an EEA State (other than the United Kingdom) in relation to a UK firm's exercise of EEA rights there.

[Tied agent

11A. "Tied agent" has the meaning given in Article 4.1.25 of the markets in financial instruments directive.]

NOTES

Para 1: sub-para (a) substituted for original sub-paras (a), (b) by the Banking Consolidation Directive (Consequential Amendments) Regulations 2000, SI 2000/2952, reg 8(1), (5)(a); word omitted from sub-para (c) repealed and sub-para (e) and word immediately preceding it added by the Insurance Mediation Directive (Miscellaneous Amendments) Regulations 2003, SI 2003/1473, reg 2(2)(a); sub-para (ca) inserted by the Reinsurance Directive Regulations 2007, SI 2007/3253, reg 2(1), Sch 1, paras 1, 6(a); words in square brackets in sub-para (d) substituted by the Financial Services and Markets Act 2000 (Markets in Financial Instruments) Regulations 2007, SI 2007/126, reg 3(4), Sch 4, paras 1, 2; word omitted from sub-para (d) repealed and sub-para (f) and word immediately preceding it added by the Collective Investment Schemes (Miscellaneous Amendments) Regulations 2003, SI 2003/2066, reg 2(2)(a).

Para 2: words in square brackets in cross-heading substituted by virtue of SI 2000/2952, reg 8(1), (5)(b); para 2 substituted by the Capital Requirements Regulations 2006, SI 2006/3221, reg 29(1), Sch 3, para 2(1), (2).

Para 3: words in square brackets in sub-para (1) substituted and sub-para (8) substituted for original sub-paras (5)–(7) by the Life Assurance Consolidation Directive (Consequential Amendments) Regulations 2004, SI 2004/3379, reg 6(1), (6)(a).

Para 3A: inserted, together with preceding cross-heading, by SI 2007/3253, reg 2(1), Sch 1, paras 1, 6(b).

Para 4: repealed by SI 2007/126, reg 3(4), Sch 4, paras 1, 3.

Para 4A: inserted, together with preceding cross-heading, by SI 2003/1473, reg 2(2)(b).

Para 4B: inserted, together with preceding cross-heading, by SI 2003/2066, reg 2(2)(b).

Para 4C: inserted, together with preceding cross-heading, by the Financial Services and Markets Act 2000 (Markets in Financial Instruments) (Modification of Powers) Regulations 2006, SI 2006/2975, regs 2, 13.

Para 5: words in first pair of square brackets substituted, and sub-para (e) and word immediately preceding it added by SI 2003/1473, reg 2(2)(c); words in square brackets in sub-para (a) substituted by SI 2007/126, reg 3(4), Sch 4, paras 1, 4; sub-paras (b), (c) substituted by SI 2006/3221, reg 29(1), Sch 3, para 2(1), (3); words in square brackets in sub-para (d) substituted by SI 2004/3379, reg 6(1), (6)(b); word omitted from sub-para (d) repealed and sub-para (f) and word "or" immediately preceding it added by SI 2003/2066, reg 2(2)(c); sub-para (da) inserted by SI 2007/3253, reg 2(1), Sch 1, paras 1, 6(c).

Paras 5A, 7A, 10A: inserted by SI 2003/1473, reg 2(2)(d), (g), (i).

Para 6: substituted by SI 2003/1473, reg 2(2)(e).

Paras 7, 10: words in square brackets substituted by SI 2003/1473, reg 2(2)(f), (h).

Para 8: substituted by the Financial Services (EEA State) Regulations 2007, SI 2007/108, reg 2.

Paras 10B, 11A: inserted, together with preceding cross-headings, by SI 2007/126, reg 3(4), Sch 4, paras 1, 5, 6.

European Parliament and Council Directive 2006/48/EC: OJ L177, 30.6.2006, p 1.
Council Directive 73/239/EEC: OJ L228, 16.8.1973, p 3.
Council Directive 88/357/EEC: OJ L172, 4.7.1988, p 1.
Council Directive 92/49/EEC: OJ L228, 11.8.1992, p 1.
European Parliament and Council Directive 2002/83/EC: OJ L345, 26.5.2001, p 1.
Directive 2005/68/EC: OJ L323, 9.12.2005, p 1.
European Parliament and Council Directive 2002/92/EC: OJ L9, 15.1.2003, p 1.
Council Directive 85/611/EEC: OJ L375, 31.12.85, p 3.
European Parliament and Council Directive 2004/39/EC: OJ L145, 30.4.2004, p 1.

PART II

EXERCISE OF PASSPORT RIGHTS BY EEA FIRMS

Firms qualifying for authorisation

[329]

12.—(1) Once an EEA firm which is seeking to establish a branch in the United Kingdom in exercise of an EEA right satisfies the establishment conditions, it qualifies for authorisation.

(2) Once an EEA firm which is seeking to provide services in the United Kingdom in exercise of an EEA right satisfies the service conditions, it qualifies for authorisation.

[(3) If an EEA firm falling within paragraph 5(a) is seeking to use a tied agent established in the United Kingdom in connection with the exercise of an EEA right deriving from the markets in financial instruments directive, this Part of this Schedule applies as if the firm were seeking to establish a branch in the United Kingdom.

(4) But if—

(a) an EEA firm already qualifies for authorisation by virtue of sub-paragraph (1); and

(b) the EEA right which it is exercising derives from the markets in financial instruments directive,

sub-paragraph (3) does not require the firm to satisfy the establishment conditions in respect of its use of the tied agent in question.]

[(5) An EEA firm which falls within paragraph 5(da) which establishes a branch in the United Kingdom, or provides services in the United Kingdom, in exercise of an EEA right qualifies for authorisation.

(6) Sub-paragraphs (1) and (2) do not apply to an EEA firm falling within paragraph 5(da).]

Establishment

13.—(1) [If the firm falls within paragraph 5(a), (b), [(c), (d) or (f)],] the establishment conditions are that—

(a) the Authority has received notice ("a consent notice") from the firm's home state regulator that it has given the firm consent to establish a branch in the United Kingdom;

(b) the consent notice—

(i) is given in accordance with the relevant single market directive;

(ii) identifies the activities to which consent relates; and

(iii) includes such other information as may be prescribed;

[(ba) in the case of a firm falling within paragraph 5(a), the Authority has given the firm notice for the purposes of this paragraph or two months have elapsed beginning with the date when the home state regulator gave the consent notice; and]

(c) [in the case of a firm falling within paragraph 5(b), (c), (d) or (f),] the firm has been informed of the applicable provisions or two months have elapsed beginning with the date when the Authority received the consent notice.

[(1A) If the firm falls within paragraph 5(e), the establishment conditions are that—

(a) the firm has given its home state regulator notice of its intention to establish a branch in the United Kingdom;

(b) the Authority has received notice ("a regulator's notice") from the firm's home state regulator that the firm intends to establish a branch in the United Kingdom;

(c) the firm's home state regulator has informed the firm that the regulator's notice has been sent to the Authority; and

(d) one month has elapsed beginning with the date on which the firm's home state regulator informed the firm that the regulator's notice has been sent to the Authority.]

(2) If the Authority has received a consent notice, it must—

(a) prepare for the firm's supervision;

(b) [except if the firm falls within paragraph 5(a),] notify the firm of the applicable provisions (if any); and

(c) if the firm falls within paragraph 5(d), notify its home state regulator of the applicable provisions (if any).

(3) A notice under sub-paragraph (2)(b) or (c) must be given before the end of the period of two months beginning with the day on which the Authority received the consent notice.

(4) For the purposes of this paragraph—

"applicable provisions" means the host state rules with which the firm is required to comply when carrying on a permitted activity through a branch in the United Kingdom;

"host state rules" means rules—

(a) made in accordance with the relevant single market directive; and

(b) which are the responsibility of the United Kingdom (both as to implementation and as to supervision of compliance) in accordance with that directive; and

"permitted activity" means an activity identified in the consent notice [or regulator's notice, as the case may be].

Services

14.—(1) The service conditions are that—

(a) the firm has given its home state regulator notice of its intention to provide services in the United Kingdom ("a notice of intention");

(b) if the firm falls within [paragraph 5(a), [(d), (e) or (f)]], the Authority has received notice ("a regulator's notice") from the firm's home state regulator containing such information as may be prescribed; . . .

[(ba) if the firm falls within paragraph 5(b) and is seeking to provide services in exercise of the right under Article 31.5 of the markets in financial instruments directive, the Authority has received notice ("a regulator's notice") from the firm's home state regulator stating that the firm intends to exercise that right in the United Kingdom;]

(c) if the firm falls within [paragraph 5(d) or (e)], its home state regulator has informed it that the regulator's notice has been sent to the Authority[; and

(d) if the firm falls within paragraph 5(e), one month has elapsed beginning with the date on which the firm's home state regulator informed the firm that the regulator's notice has been sent to the Authority.]

(2) If the Authority has received a regulator's notice or, where none is required by sub-paragraph (1), has been informed of the firm's intention to provide services in the United Kingdom, it must[, unless the firm falls within paragraph 5(e),]—

(a) prepare for the firm's supervision; and

(b) notify the firm of the applicable provisions (if any).

[(2A) Sub-paragraph (2)(b) does not apply in the case of a firm falling within paragraph 5(a).]

(3) A notice under sub-paragraph (2)(b) must be given before the end of the period of two months beginning on the day on which the Authority received the regulator's notice, or was informed of the firm's intention.

(4) For the purposes of this paragraph—

"applicable provisions" means the host state rules with which the firm is required to comply when carrying on a permitted activity by providing services in the United Kingdom;

"host state rules" means rules—

(a) made in accordance with the relevant single market directive; and

(b) which are the responsibility of the United Kingdom (both as to implementation and as to supervision of compliance) in accordance with that directive; and

"permitted activity" means an activity identified in—

(a) the regulator's notice; or

(b) where none is required by sub-paragraph (1), the notice of intention.

Grant of permission

15.—(1) On qualifying for authorisation as a result of [paragraph 12(1), (2) or (3)], a firm has, in respect of each permitted activity which is a regulated activity, permission to carry it on through its United Kingdom branch (if it satisfies the establishment conditions) or by providing services in the United Kingdom (if it satisfies the service conditions).

[(1A) Sub-paragraph (1) is to be read subject to paragraph 15A(3).]

(2) The permission is to be treated as being on terms equivalent to those appearing from the consent notice, regulator's notice or notice of intention.

(3) Sections [21 and 39(1)] of the Consumer Credit Act 1974 (business requiring a licence under that Act) do not apply in relation to the carrying on of a permitted activity which is Consumer Credit Act business by a firm which qualifies for authorisation as a result of paragraph 12, unless [the Office of Fair Trading] has exercised the power conferred on [it] by section 203 in relation to the firm.

(4) "Consumer Credit Act business" has the same meaning as in section 203.

[(5) A firm which qualifies for authorisation as a result of paragraph 12(5) has, in respect of each permitted activity which is a regulated activity, permission to carry it on through its United Kingdom branch or by providing services in the United Kingdom.

(6) The permission is to be treated as being on terms equivalent to those appearing in the authorisation granted to the firm under Article 3 of the reinsurance directive by its home state regulator ("its home authorisation").

(7) For the purposes of sub-paragraph (5), "permitted activity" means an activity which the firm is permitted to carry on under its home authorisation.]

[Power to restrict permission of management companies

15A.—(1) Sub-paragraph (2) applies if—

(a) a firm falling within paragraph 5(f) qualifies for authorisation as a result of paragraph 12(1) (establishment conditions satisfied); but

(b) the Authority determines that the way in which the firm intends to invite persons in the United Kingdom to become participants in any collective investment scheme which that firm manages does not comply with the law in force in the United Kingdom.

(2) The Authority may give a notice to the firm and the firm's home state regulator of the Authority's determination under sub-paragraph (1)(b).

(3) Paragraph 15(1) does not give a firm to which the Authority has given (and not withdrawn) a notice under sub-paragraph (2) permission to carry on through the firm's United Kingdom branch the regulated activity of dealing in units in the collective investment schemes which the firm manages.

(4) Any notice given under sub-paragraph (2) must be given before the end of the period of two months beginning with the day on which the Authority received the consent notice.

(5) Sections 264(4) and 265(1), (2) and (4) apply to a notice given under sub-paragraph (2) as they apply to a notice given by the Authority under section 264(2).

(6) If a decision notice is given to the firm under section 265(4), by virtue of sub-paragraph (5), the firm may refer the matter to the Tribunal.

(7) In sub-paragraph (3)—

(a) "units" has the meaning given by section 237(2); and

(b) the reference to "dealing in" units in a collective investment scheme must be read with—

(i) section 22;

(ii) any relevant order under that section; and

(iii) Schedule 2.]

Effect of carrying on regulated activity when not qualified for authorisation

16.—(1) This paragraph applies to an EEA firm which is not qualified for authorisation under paragraph 12.

(2) Section 26 does not apply to an agreement entered into by the firm.

(3) Section 27 does not apply to an agreement in relation to which the firm is a third party for the purposes of that section.

(4) Section 29 does not apply to an agreement in relation to which the firm is the deposit-taker.

Continuing regulation of EEA firms

17. Regulations may—

(a) modify any provision of this Act which is an applicable provision (within the meaning of paragraph 13 or 14) in its application to an EEA firm qualifying for authorisation;

(b) make provision as to any change (or proposed change) of a prescribed kind relating to an EEA firm or to an activity that it carries on in the United Kingdom and as to the procedure to be followed in relation to such cases;

(c) provide that the Authority may treat an EEA firm's notification that it is to cease to carry on regulated activity in the United Kingdom as a request for cancellation of its qualification for authorisation under this Schedule.

Giving up right to authorisation

18. Regulations may provide that in prescribed circumstances an EEA firm falling within paragraph 5(c) may, on following the prescribed procedure—

(a) have its qualification for authorisation under this Schedule cancelled; and

(b) seek to become an authorised person by applying for a Part IV permission.

NOTES

Para 12: sub-paras (3), (4) inserted by the Financial Services and Markets Act 2000 (Markets in Financial Instruments) Regulations 2007, SI 2007/126, reg 3(4), Sch 4, paras 1, 7; sub-paras (5), (6) inserted by the Reinsurance Directive Regulations 2007, SI 2007/3253, reg 2(1), Sch 1, paras 1, 6(d).

Para 13: words in first (outer) pair of square brackets in sub-para (1), the whole of sub-para (1A), and words in square brackets in sub-para (4) inserted by the Insurance Mediation Directive (Miscellaneous Amendments) Regulations 2003, SI 2003/1473, reg 3; words in second (inner) pair of square brackets in sub-para (1) substituted by the Collective Investment Schemes (Miscellaneous Amendments) Regulations 2003, SI 2003/2066, reg 3(1)(a); word omitted from sub-para (1)(b)(iii) repealed, sub-para (1)(ba) and words in square brackets in sub-paras (1)(c), (2)(b) inserted by SI 2007/126, reg 3(4), Sch 4, paras 1, 8, subject to transitional provisions and savings in reg 6 thereof.

Para 14: words in first (outer) pair of square brackets in sub-para (1)(b) and words in square brackets in sub-para (1)(c) substituted, word omitted from sub-para (1)(b) repealed, para (d) and word "and" immediately preceding it added and words in square brackets in sub-para (2) inserted by SI 2003/1473, reg 4; words in second (inner) pair of square brackets in sub-para (1)(b) substituted by SI 2003/2066, reg 3(1)(b); sub-paras (1)(ba), (2A) inserted by SI 2007/126, reg 3(4), Sch 4, paras 1, 9.

Para 15: words in square brackets in sub-para (1) substituted and sub-paras (5)–(7) inserted by SI 2007/3253, reg 2(1), Sch 1, paras 1, 6(e); sub-para (1A) inserted by SI 2003/2066, reg 3(1)(c); in sub-para (3), words in first pair of square brackets substituted by the Consumer Credit Act 2006, s 33(9), words in second and third pairs of square brackets substituted by the Enterprise Act 2002, s 278(1), Sch 25, para 40(1), (19)(a).

Para 15A: inserted, together with preceding cross-heading, by SI 2003/2066, reg 3(1)(d).

Regulations: the Financial Services and Markets Act 2000 (EEA Passport Rights) Regulations 2001, SI 2001/2511 at **[633]**.

PART III
EXERCISE OF PASSPORT RIGHTS BY UK FIRMS

Establishment

[330]

19.—(1) [Subject to [sub-paragraphs (5ZA) and (5A)],] a UK firm may not exercise an EEA right to establish a branch unless three conditions are satisfied.

(2) The first is that the firm has given the Authority, in the specified way, notice of its intention to establish a branch ("a notice of intention") which—

(a) identifies the activities which it seeks to carry on through the branch; and

(b) includes such other information as may be specified.

(3) [Subject to sub-paragraph (5B), the] activities identified in a notice of intention may include activities which are not regulated activities.

(4) The second is that the Authority has given notice in specified terms ("a consent notice") to the host state regulator.

[(5) The third is—

(a) if the EEA right in question derives from the insurance mediation directive, that one month has elapsed beginning with the date on which the firm received notice, in accordance with sub-paragraph (11), that the Authority has given a consent notice;

(b) in any other case, that either—

(i) the host state regulator has notified the firm (or, where the EEA right in question derives from any of the insurance directives, the Authority) of the applicable provisions; or

(ii) two months have elapsed beginning with the date on which the Authority gave the consent notice.]

[(5ZA) This paragraph does not apply to a UK firm having an EEA right which is subject to the conditions of the reinsurance directive.]

[(5A) If—

(a) the EEA right in question derives from the insurance mediation directive, and

(b) the EEA State in which the firm intends to establish a branch has not notified the Commission, in accordance with Article 6(2) of that directive, of its wish to be informed of the intention of any UK firm to establish a branch in its territory,

the second and third conditions do not apply (and so the firm may establish the branch to which its notice of intention relates as soon as the first condition is satisfied).]

[(5B) If the firm is a UK investment firm, a notice of intention may not include ancillary services unless such services are to be provided in connection with the carrying on of one or more investment services and activities.

(5C) In sub-paragraph (5B) "ancillary services" has the meaning given in Article 4.1.3 of the markets in financial instruments directive.]

(6) If the firm's EEA right derives from [the banking consolidation directive,] [the UCITS directive or, in the case of a credit institution authorised under the banking consolidation directive, the markets in financial instruments directive] and the first condition is satisfied, the Authority must give a consent notice to the host state regulator unless it has reason to doubt the adequacy of the firm's resources or its administrative structure.

(7) If the firm's EEA right derives from any of the insurance directives and the first condition is satisfied, the Authority must give a consent notice unless it has reason—

(a) to doubt the adequacy of the firm's resources or its administrative structure, or

(b) to question the reputation, qualifications or experience of the directors or managers of the firm or the person proposed as the branch's authorised agent for the purposes of those directives,

in relation to the business to be conducted through the proposed branch.

[(7A) If—

(a) the firm's EEA right derives from the insurance mediation directive,

(b) the first condition is satisfied, and
(c) the second condition applies,

the Authority must give a consent notice, and must do so within one month beginning with the date on which it received the firm's notice of intention.]

[(7B) If the firm is a UK investment firm and the first condition is satisfied, the Authority must give a consent notice to the host state regulator within three months beginning with the date on which it received the firm's notice of intention unless the Authority has reason to doubt the adequacy of the firm's resources or its administrative structure.]

(8) If the Authority proposes to refuse to give a consent notice it must give the firm concerned a warning notice.

(9) If the firm's EEA right derives from any of the insurance directives and the host state regulator has notified it of the applicable provisions, the Authority must inform the firm of those provisions.

(10) Rules may specify the procedure to be followed by the Authority in exercising its functions under this paragraph.

(11) If the Authority gives a consent notice it must give written notice that it has done so to the firm concerned.

(12) If the Authority decides to refuse to give a consent notice—
(a) it must, [within the relevant period], give the person who gave that notice a decision notice to that effect; and
(b) that person may refer the matter to the Tribunal.

[(12A) In sub-paragraph (12), "the relevant period" means—
(a) if the firm's EEA right derives from the UCITS directive, two months beginning with the date on which the Authority received the notice of intention;
(b) in any other case, three months beginning with that date.]

(13) In this paragraph, "applicable provisions" means the host state rules with which the firm will be required to comply when conducting business through the proposed branch in the EEA State concerned.

(14) In sub-paragraph (13), "host state rules" means rules—
(a) made in accordance with the relevant single market directive; and
(b) which are the responsibility of the EEA State concerned (both as to implementation and as to supervision of compliance) in accordance with that directive.

(15) "Specified" means specified in rules.

Services

20.—(1) [Subject to sub-paragraph (4D),] a UK firm may not exercise an EEA right to provide services unless the firm has given the Authority, in the specified way, notice of its intention to provide services ("a notice of intention") which—
(a) identifies the activities which it seeks to carry out by way of provision of services; and
(b) includes such other information as may be specified.

(2) [Subject to sub-paragraph (2A), the] activities identified in a notice of intention may include activities which are not regulated activities.

[(2A) If the firm is a UK investment firm, a notice of intention may not include ancillary services unless such services are to be provided in connection with the carrying on of one or more investment services and activities.

(2B) In sub-paragraph (2A) "ancillary services" has the meaning given in Article 4.1.3 of the markets in financial instruments directive.]

(3) If the firm's EEA right derives from [the banking consolidation directive, the [markets in financial instruments directive] or the UCITS directive], the Authority must, within one month of receiving a notice of intention, send a copy of it to the host state regulator [with such other information as may be specified].

[(3A) If the firm's EEA right derives from any of the insurance directives, the Authority must, within one month of receiving the notice of intention—
(a) give notice in specified terms ("a consent notice") to the host state regulator; or
(b) give written notice to the firm of—
(i) its refusal to give a consent notice; and
(ii) its reasons for that refusal.]

[(3B) If the firm's EEA right derives from the insurance mediation directive and the EEA State in which the firm intends to provide services has notified the Commission, in accordance with Article 6(2) of that directive, of its wish to be informed of the intention of any UK firm to provide services in its territory—
(a) the Authority must, within one month of receiving the notice of intention, send a copy of it to the host state regulator;

(b) the Authority, when it sends the copy in accordance with sub-paragraph (a), must give written notice to the firm concerned that it has done so; and

(c) the firm concerned must not provide the services to which its notice of intention relates until one month, beginning with the date on which it receives the notice under sub-paragraph (b), has elapsed.]

(4) When the Authority sends the copy under sub-paragraph (3) [or gives a consent notice], it must give written notice to the firm concerned.

[(4A) If the firm is given notice under sub-paragraph (3A)(b), it may refer the matter to the Tribunal.

(4B) If the firm's EEA right derives from any of the insurance directives [or from the markets in financial instruments directive], it must not provide the services to which its notice of intention relates until it has received written notice under sub-paragraph (4).

[(4BA) If the firm's EEA right derives from the markets in financial instruments directive, the Authority must comply as soon as reasonably practicable with a request for information under the second sub-paragraph of Article 31.6 of that directive from the host state regulator.]

(4C) Rules may specify the procedure to be followed by the Authority under this paragraph.]

[(4D) This paragraph does not apply to a UK firm having an EEA right which is subject to the conditions of the reinsurance directive.]

(5) . . .

(6) "Specified" means specified in rules.

[Tied agents

20A.—(1) If a UK investment firm is seeking to use a tied agent established in an EEA State (other than the United Kingdom) in connection with the exercise of an EEA right deriving from the markets in financial instruments directive, this Part of this Schedule applies as if the firm were seeking to establish a branch in that State.

(2) But if—

(a) a UK investment firm has already established a branch in an EEA State other than the United Kingdom in accordance with paragraph 19; and

(b) the EEA right which it is exercising derives from the markets in financial instruments directive,

paragraph 19 does not apply in respect of its use of the tied agent in question.]

Offence relating to exercise of passport rights

21.—(1) If a UK firm which is not an authorised person contravenes the prohibition imposed by—

(a) sub-paragraph (1) of paragraph 19, or

(b) [sub-paragraph (1), (3B)(c) or (4B)] of paragraph 20,

it is guilty of an offence.

(2) A firm guilty of an offence under sub-paragraph (1) is liable—

(a) on summary conviction, to a fine not exceeding the statutory maximum; or

(b) on conviction on indictment, to a fine.

(3) In proceedings for an offence under sub-paragraph (1), it is a defence for the firm to show that it took all reasonable precautions and exercised all due diligence to avoid committing the offence.

Continuing regulation of UK firms

22.—(1) Regulations may make such provision as the Treasury consider appropriate in relation to a UK firm's exercise of EEA rights, and may in particular provide for the application (with or without modification) of any provision of, or made under, this Act in relation to an activity of a UK firm.

(2) Regulations may—

(a) make provision as to any change (or proposed change) of a prescribed kind relating to a UK firm or to an activity that it carries on and as to the procedure to be followed in relation to such cases;

(b) make provision with respect to the consequences of the firm's failure to comply with a provision of the regulations.

(3) Where a provision of the kind mentioned in sub-paragraph (2) requires the Authority's consent to a change (or proposed change)—

(a) consent may be refused only on prescribed grounds; and

(b) if the Authority decides to refuse consent, the firm concerned may refer the matter to the Tribunal.

23.—(1) [Sub-paragraphs (2) and (2A) apply] if a UK firm—

(a) has a Part IV permission; and
(b) is exercising an EEA right to carry on any Consumer Credit Act business in an EEA State other than the United Kingdom.

(2) The Authority may exercise its power under section 45 in respect of the firm if [the Office of Fair Trading] has informed the Authority that—
(a) the firm,
(b) any of the firm's employees, agents or associates (whether past or present), or
(c) if the firm is a body corporate, a controller of the firm or an associate of such a controller,

has done any of the things specified in paragraphs [(a) to (e) of section 25(2A)] of the Consumer Credit Act 1974.

[(2A) The Authority may also exercise its power under section 45 in respect of the firm if the Office of Fair Trading has informed the Authority that it has concerns about any of the following—
(a) the firm's skills, knowledge and experience in relation to Consumer Credit Act businesses;
(b) such skills, knowledge and experience of other persons who are participating in any Consumer Credit Act business being carried on by the firm;
(c) practices and procedures that the firm is implementing in connection with any such business.]

(3) "Associate", "Consumer Credit Act business" and "controller" have the same meaning as in section 203.

24.—(1) Sub-paragraph (2) applies if a UK firm—
(a) is not required to have a Part IV permission in relation to the business which it is carrying on; and
(b) is exercising the right conferred by [[Article 24] of the banking consolidation directive] to carry on that business in an EEA State other than the United Kingdom.

(2) If requested to do so by the host state regulator in the EEA State in which the UK firm's business is being carried on, the Authority may impose any requirement in relation to the firm which it could impose if—
(a) the firm had a Part IV permission in relation to the business which it is carrying on; and
(b) the Authority was entitled to exercise its power under that Part to vary that permission.

[Information to be included in the public record

25. The Authority must include in the record that it maintains under section 347 in relation to any UK firm whose EEA right derives from the insurance mediation directive information as to each EEA State in which the UK firm, in accordance with such a right—
(a) has established a branch; or
(b) is providing services.]

NOTES

Para 19: words in first (outer) pair of square brackets in sub-para (1) and the whole of sub-paras (5A), (7A) inserted and sub-para (5) substituted by the Insurance Mediation Directive (Miscellaneous Amendments) Regulations 2003, SI 2003/1473, reg 5; words in second (inner) pair of square brackets in sub-para (1) substituted and sub-para (5ZA) inserted by the Reinsurance Directive Regulations 2007, SI 2007/3253, reg 2(1), Sch 1, paras 1, 6(f), (g); words in square brackets in sub-para (3) substituted, words in second pair of square brackets in sub-para (6) substituted, and sub-paras (5B), (5C), (7B) inserted, by the Financial Services and Markets Act 2000 (Markets in Financial Instruments) Regulations 2007, SI 2007/126, reg 3(4), Sch 4, paras 1, 10, subject to transitional provisions in regs 7, 8 thereof; words in first pair of square brackets in sub-para (6) and words in square brackets in sub-para (12) substituted and sub-para (12A) inserted by the Collective Investment Schemes (Miscellaneous Amendments) Regulations 2003, SI 2003/2066, reg 4(1)(a).

Para 20: words in square brackets in sub-para (1) and the whole of sub-para (4D) inserted by SI 2007/3253, reg 2(1), Sch 1, paras 1, 6(h), (i); words in square brackets in sub-para (2) substituted, words in second (inner) pair of square brackets in sub-para (3) substituted, words in square brackets in sub-para (4B) and the whole of sub-paras (2A), (2B), (4BA) inserted by SI 2007/126, reg 3(4), Sch 4, paras 1, 11, subject to transitional provisions in reg 7 thereof; in sub-para (3) words in first (outer) pair of square brackets substituted and words in third pair of square brackets inserted by SI 2003/2066, reg 4(1)(b); sub-paras (3A), (4A)–(4C) inserted, words in square brackets in sub-para (4) inserted, and sub-para (5) repealed by the Financial Services (EEA Passport Rights) Regulations 2001, SI 2001/1376, reg 2(1)–(5); sub-para (3B) inserted by SI 2003/1473, reg 6(1).

Para 20A: inserted, together with preceding cross-heading, by SI 2007/126, reg 3(4), Sch 4, paras 1, 12.

Para 21: words in square brackets substituted by SI 2003/1473, reg 6(2).

Para 23: words in square brackets in sub-para (1) and words in second pair of square brackets in sub-para (2) substituted and sub-para (2A) inserted by the Consumer Credit Act 2006, s 33(10)–(12); words in first pair of square brackets in sub-para (2) substituted by the Enterprise Act 2002, s 278(1), Sch 25, para 40(1), (19)(b).

Para 24: in sub-para (1)(b), words in first (outer) pair of square brackets substituted by the Banking Consolidation Directive (Consequential Amendments) Regulations 2000, SI 2000/2952, reg 8(1), (5)(f); words in second (inner) pair of square brackets substituted by SI 2006/3221, reg 29(1), Sch 3, para 2(1), (4).

Para 25: added, together with preceding cross-heading, by SI 2003/1473, reg 7.
Regulations: the Financial Services and Markets Act 2000 (EEA Passport Rights) Regulations 2001, SI 2001/2511 at **[633]**.

(Sch 4 outside the scope of this work.)

SCHEDULE 5

PERSONS CONCERNED IN COLLECTIVE INVESTMENT SCHEMES

Section 36

Authorisation

[331]

1.—(1) A person who for the time being is an operator, trustee or depositary of a recognised collective investment scheme is an authorised person.
(2) "Recognised" means recognised by virtue of section 264.
(3) An authorised open-ended investment company is an authorised person.
[(4) A body—
(a) incorporated by virtue of regulations made under section 1 of the Open-Ended Investment Companies Act (Northern Ireland) 2002 in respect of which an authorisation order is in force, and
(b) to which the UCITS directive applies,
is an authorised person.
(5) "Authorisation order" means an order made under (or having effect as made under) any provision of those regulations which is made by virtue of section 1(2)(1) of that Act (provision corresponding to Chapter 3 of Part 17 of the Act).]

Permission

2.—(1) A person authorised as a result of paragraph 1(1) has permission to carry on, so far as it is a regulated activity—
(a) any activity, appropriate to the capacity in which he acts in relation to the scheme, of the kind described in paragraph 8 of Schedule 2;
(b) any activity in connection with, or for the purposes of, the scheme.
(2) A person authorised as a result of paragraph 1(3) [or (4)] has permission to carry on, so far as it is a regulated activity—
(a) the operation of the scheme;
(b) any activity in connection with, or for the purposes of, the operation of the scheme.

NOTES
Para 1: sub-paras (4), (5) added by the Collective Investment Schemes (Miscellaneous Amendments) Regulations 2003, SI 2003/2066, reg 10(a).
Para 2: words in square brackets inserted by SI 2003/2066, reg 10(b).

SCHEDULE 6

THRESHOLD CONDITIONS

Section 41

PART I
PART IV PERMISSION

Legal status

[332]

1.—(1) If the regulated activity concerned is the effecting or carrying out of contracts of insurance the authorised person must be a body corporate [(other than a limited liability partnership)], a registered friendly society or a member of Lloyd's.
(2) If the person concerned appears to the Authority to be seeking to carry on, or to be carrying on, a regulated activity constituting accepting deposits [or issuing electronic money], it must be—
(a) a body corporate; or
(b) a partnership.

Location of offices

2.—(1) [Subject to [sub-paragraphs (2A) and (3)],] if the person concerned is a body corporate constituted under the law of any part of the United Kingdom—

(a) its head office, and

(b) if it has a registered office, that office,

must be in the United Kingdom.

(2) If the person concerned has its head office in the United Kingdom but is not a body corporate, it must carry on business in the United Kingdom.

[(2A) If—

(a) the regulated activity concerned is any of the investment services and activities, and

(b) the person concerned is a body corporate with no registered office,

sub-paragraph (2B) applies in place of sub-paragraph (1).

(2B) If the person concerned has its head office in the United Kingdom, it must carry on business in the United Kingdom.]

[(3) If the regulated activity concerned is an insurance mediation activity, sub-paragraph (1) does not apply.

(4) If the regulated activity concerned is an insurance mediation activity, the person concerned—

(a) if he is a body corporate constituted under the law of any part of the United Kingdom, must have its registered office, or if it has no registered office, its head office, in the United Kingdom;

(b) if he is a natural person, is to be treated for the purposes of sub-paragraph (2), as having his head office in the United Kingdom if his residence is situated there.

(5) "Insurance mediation activity" means any of the following activities—

(a) dealing in rights under a contract of insurance as agent;

(b) arranging deals in rights under a contract of insurance;

(c) assisting in the administration and performance of a contract of insurance;

(d) advising on buying or selling rights under a contract of insurance;

(e) agreeing to do any of the activities specified in sub-paragraph (a) to (d).

(6) Paragraph (5) must be read with—

(a) section 22;

(b) any relevant order under that section; and

(c) Schedule 2.]

[Appointment of claims representatives

2A.—(1) If it appears to the Authority that—

(a) the regulated activity that the person concerned is carrying on, or is seeking to carry on, is the effecting or carrying out of contracts of insurance, and

(b) contracts of insurance against damage arising out of or in connection with the use of motor vehicles on land (other than carrier's liability) are being, or will be, effected or carried out by the person concerned,

that person must have a claims representative in each EEA State other than the United Kingdom.

(2) For the purposes of sub-paragraph (1)(b), contracts of reinsurance are to be disregarded.

(3) A claims representative is a person with responsibility for handling and settling claims arising from accidents of the kind mentioned in Article 1(2) of the fourth motor insurance directive.

(4) In this paragraph "fourth motor insurance directive" means Directive 2000/26/EC of the European Parliament and of the Council of 16th May 2000 on the approximation of the laws of the Member States relating to insurance against civil liability in respect of the use of motor vehicles and amending Council Directives 73/239/EEC and 88/357/EEC.]

Close links

3.—(1) If the person concerned ("A") has close links with another person ("CL") the Authority must be satisfied—

(a) that those links are not likely to prevent the Authority's effective supervision of A; and

(b) if it appears to the Authority that CL is subject to the laws, regulations or administrative provisions of a territory which is not an EEA State ("the foreign provisions"), that neither the foreign provisions, nor any deficiency in their enforcement, would prevent the Authority's effective supervision of A.

(2) A has close links with CL if—

(a) CL is a parent undertaking of A;

(b) CL is a subsidiary undertaking of A;

(c) CL is a parent undertaking of a subsidiary undertaking of A;

(d) CL is a subsidiary undertaking of a parent undertaking of A;

(e) CL owns or controls 20% or more of the voting rights or capital of A; or

(f) A owns or controls 20% or more of the voting rights or capital of CL.

(3) "Subsidiary undertaking" includes all the instances mentioned in Article 1(1) and (2) of the Seventh Company Law Directive in which an entity may be a subsidiary of an undertaking.

Adequate resources

4.—(1) The resources of the person concerned must, in the opinion of the Authority, be adequate in relation to the regulated activities that he seeks to carry on, or carries on.

(2) In reaching that opinion, the Authority may—

(a) take into account the person's membership of a group and any effect which that membership may have; and

(b) have regard to—

(i) the provision he makes and, if he is a member of a group, which other members of the group make in respect of liabilities (including contingent and future liabilities); and

(ii) the means by which he manages and, if he is a member of a group, which other members of the group manage the incidence of risk in connection with his business.

Suitability

5. The person concerned must satisfy the Authority that he is a fit and proper person having regard to all the circumstances, including—

(a) his connection with any person;

(b) the nature of any regulated activity that he carries on or seeks to carry on; and

(c) the need to ensure that his affairs are conducted soundly and prudently.

NOTES

Para 1: words in square brackets in sub-para (1) inserted by the Financial Services and Markets Act 2000 (Variation of Threshold Conditions) Order 2001, SI 2001/2507, art 2; words in square brackets in sub-para (2) inserted by the Financial Services and Markets Act 2000 (Regulated Activities) (Amendment) Order 2002, SI 2002/682, art 8.

Para 2: words in first (outer) pair of square brackets in sub-para (1) inserted, and sub-paras (3)–(6) added by the Financial Services and Markets Act 2000 (Regulated Activities) (Amendment) (No 2) Order 2003, SI 2003/1476, art 19; words in second (inner) pair of square brackets in sub-para (1) substituted and sub-paras (2A), (2B) inserted by the Financial Services and Markets Act 2000 (Markets in Financial Instruments) Regulations 2007, SI 2007/126, reg 3(5), Sch 5, paras 1, 24.

Para 2A: inserted, together with preceding cross-heading, by the Financial Services and Markets Act 2000 (Variation of Threshold Conditions) Order 2002, SI 2002/2707, art 2.

Directive 2000/26/EC of the European Parliament and of the Council: OJ L181, 20.7.2000, p 65.

Council Directive 73/239/EEC: OJ L228, 16.8.1973, p 3.

Council Directive 88/357/EEC: OJ L172, 4.7.1988, p 1.

PART II
AUTHORISATION

Authorisation under Schedule 3

[333]

6. In relation to an EEA firm qualifying for authorisation under Schedule 3, the conditions set out in paragraphs 1 and 3 to 5 apply, so far as relevant, to—

(a) an application for permission under Part IV;

(b) exercise of the Authority's own-initiative power under section 45 in relation to a Part IV permission.

Authorisation under Schedule 4

7. In relation to a person who qualifies for authorisation under Schedule 4, the conditions set out in paragraphs 1 and 3 to 5 apply, so far as relevant, to—

(a) an application for an additional permission;

(b) the exercise of the Authority's own-initiative power under section 45 in relation to additional permission.

PART III
ADDITIONAL CONDITIONS

[334]

8.—(1) If this paragraph applies to the person concerned, he must, for the purposes of such provisions of this Act as may be specified, satisfy specified additional conditions.
(2) This paragraph applies to a person who—
(a) has his head office outside the EEA; and
(b) appears to the Authority to be seeking to carry on a regulated activity relating to insurance business.
(3) "Specified" means specified in, or in accordance with, an order made by the Treasury.

9. The Treasury may by order—
(a) vary or remove any of the conditions set out in Parts I and II;
(b) add to those conditions.

NOTES
Orders: the Financial Services and Markets Act 2000 (Variation of Threshold Conditions) Order 2001, SI 2001/2507 at **[628]**; the Financial Services and Markets Act 2000 (Variation of Threshold Conditions) Order 2002, SI 2002/2707.

SCHEDULE 7

THE AUTHORITY AS COMPETENT AUTHORITY FOR PART VI

Section 72(2)

General

[335]

1. This Act applies in relation to the Authority when it is exercising functions under Part VI as the competent authority subject to the following modifications.

The Authority's general functions

2. In section 2—
(a) subsection (4)(a) does not apply to [Part 6 rules];
(b) subsection (4)(c) does not apply to general guidance given in relation to Part VI; and
(c) subsection (4)(d) does not apply to functions under Part VI.

Duty to consult

3. Section 8 does not apply.

Rules

4.—(1) Sections 149, 153, 154 and 156 do not apply.
(2) Section 155 has effect as if—
(a) the reference in subsection (2)(c) to the general duties of the Authority under section 2 were a reference to its duty under section 73; and
(b) section 99 were included in the provisions referred to in subsection (9).

Statements of policy

5.—(1) Paragraph 5 of Schedule 1 has effect as if the requirement to act through the Authority's governing body applied also to the exercise of its functions of publishing statements under section 93.
(2) Paragraph 1 of Schedule 1 has effect as if section 93 were included in the provisions referred to in sub-paragraph (2)(d).

Penalties

6. Paragraph 16 of Schedule 1 does not apply in relation to penalties under Part VI (for which separate provision is made by section 100).

Fees

7. Paragraph 17 of Schedule 1 does not apply in relation to fees payable under Part VI (for which separate provision is made by section 99).

Exemption from liability in damages

8. Schedule 1 has effect as if—

(a) sub-paragraph (1) of paragraph 19 were omitted (similar provision being made in relation to the competent authority by section 102); and
(b) for the words from the beginning to "(a)" in sub-paragraph (3) of that paragraph, there were substituted "Sub-paragraph (2) does not apply".

NOTES

Para 2: words in square brackets substituted by the Financial Services and Markets Act 2000 (Market Abuse) Regulations 2005, SI 2005/381, reg 4, Sch 1, para 12.

(*Schs 8–11B outside the scope of this work.*)

SCHEDULE 12

TRANSFER SCHEMES: CERTIFICATES

Sections 111(2) and 115

PART I
INSURANCE BUSINESS TRANSFER SCHEMES

[336]

1.—(1) For the purposes of section 111(2) the appropriate certificates, in relation to an insurance business transfer scheme, are—
(a) a certificate under paragraph 2;
(b) if sub-paragraph (2) applies, a certificate under paragraph 3;
(c) if sub-paragraph (3) applies, a certificate under paragraph 4;
(d) if sub-paragraph (4) applies, a certificate under paragraph 5[;
(e) if sub-paragraph (5) applies, the certificates under paragraph 5A.]

(2) This sub-paragraph applies if—
(a) the authorised person concerned is a UK authorised person which has received authorisation under [Article 4 of the life assurance consolidation directive or Article 6] of the first non-life insurance directive from the Authority; and
(b) the establishment from which the business is to be transferred under the proposed insurance business transfer scheme is in an EEA State other than the United Kingdom.

(3) This sub-paragraph applies if—
(a) the authorised person concerned has received authorisation under [Article 4 [or Article 51] of the life assurance consolidation directive] from the Authority;
(b) the proposed transfer relates to business which consists of the effecting or carrying out of contracts of long-term insurance; and
(c) as regards any policy which is included in the proposed transfer and which evidences a contract of insurance (other than reinsurance), an EEA State other than the United Kingdom is the State of the commitment.

(4) This sub-paragraph applies if—
(a) the authorised person concerned has received authorisation under Article 6 [or Article 23] of the first non-life insurance directive from the Authority;
(b) the business to which the proposed insurance business transfer scheme relates is business which consists of the effecting or carrying out of contracts of general insurance; and
(c) as regards any policy which is included in the proposed transfer and which evidences a contract of insurance (other than reinsurance), the risk is situated in an EEA State other than the United Kingdom.

[(5) This sub-paragraph applies if—
(a) the authorised person concerned has received authorisation under Article 23 of the first non-life insurance directive or Article 51 of the life assurance consolidation directive from the Authority; and
(b) the proposed transfer is to a branch or agency, in an EEA State other than the United Kingdom, authorised under the same Article.]

Certificates as to margin of solvency

2.—(1) A certificate under this paragraph is to be given—
(a) by the relevant authority; or
(b) in a case in which there is no relevant authority, by the Authority.

(2) A certificate given under sub-paragraph (1)(a) is one certifying that, taking the proposed transfer into account—

(a) the transferee possesses, or will possess before the scheme takes effect, the necessary margin of solvency; or
(b) there is no necessary margin of solvency applicable to the transferee.

(3) A certificate under sub-paragraph (1)(b) is one certifying that the Authority has received from the authority which it considers to be the authority responsible for supervising persons who effect or carry out contracts of insurance in the place to which the business is to be transferred that, taking the proposed transfer into account—
(a) the transferee possesses or will possess before the scheme takes effect the margin of solvency required under the law applicable in that place; or
(b) there is no such margin of solvency applicable to the transferee.

(4) "Necessary margin of solvency" means the margin of solvency required in relation to the transferee, taking the proposed transfer into account, under the law which it is the responsibility of the relevant authority to apply.

(5) "Margin of solvency" means the excess of the value of the assets of the transferee over the amount of its liabilities.

(6) "Relevant authority" means—
(a) if the transferee is an EEA firm falling within paragraph 5(d) [or (da)] of Schedule 3, its home state regulator;
[(aa) if the transferee is a non-EEA branch, the competent authorities of the EEA State in which the transferee is situated or, where appropriate, the competent authorities of an EEA State which supervises the state of solvency of the entire business of the transferee's agencies and branches within the EEA in accordance with Article 26 of the first non-life insurance directive or Article 56 of the life assurance consolidation directive;]
(b) if the transferee is a Swiss general insurer, the authority responsible in Switzerland for supervising persons who effect or carry out contracts of insurance;
(c) if the transferee is an authorised person not falling within [paragraph (a), (aa)] or (b), the Authority.

(7) In sub-paragraph (6), any reference to a transferee of a particular description includes a reference to a transferee who will be of that description if the proposed scheme takes effect.

[(7A) "Competent authorities" has the same meaning as in the insurance directives.]

(8) "Swiss general insurer" means a body—
(a) whose head office is in Switzerland;
(b) which has permission to carry on regulated activities consisting of the effecting and carrying out of contracts of general insurance; and
(c) whose permission is not restricted to the effecting or carrying out of contracts of reinsurance.

[(9) "Non-EEA branch" means a branch or agency which has received authorisation under Article 23 of the first non-life insurance directive or Article 51 of the life assurance consolidation directive.]

Certificates as to consent

3. A certificate under this paragraph is one given by the Authority and certifying that the host State regulator has been notified of the proposed scheme and that—
(a) that regulator has responded to the notification; or
(b) that it has not responded but the period of three months beginning with the notification has elapsed.

Certificates as to long-term business

4. A certificate under this paragraph is one given by the Authority and certifying that the authority responsible for supervising persons who effect or carry out contracts of insurance in the State of the commitment has been notified of the proposed scheme and that—
(a) that authority has consented to the proposed scheme; or
(b) the period of three months beginning with the notification has elapsed and that authority has not refused its consent.

Certificates as to general business

5. A certificate under this paragraph is one given by the Authority and certifying that the authority responsible for supervising persons who effect or carry out contracts of insurance in the EEA State in which the risk is situated has been notified of the proposed scheme and that—
(a) that authority has consented to the proposed scheme; or
(b) the period of three months beginning with the notification has elapsed and that authority has not refused its consent.

[Certificates as to legality and as to consent

5A.—(1) The certificates under this paragraph are to be given—

(a) in the case of the certificate under sub-paragraph (2), by the Authority;

(b) in the case of the certificate under sub-paragraph (3), by the relevant authority.

(2) A certificate given under this sub-paragraph is one certifying that the relevant authority has been notified of the proposed scheme and that—

(a) the relevant authority has consented to the proposed scheme; or

(b) the period of three months beginning with the notification has elapsed and that relevant authority has not refused its consent.

(3) A certificate given under this sub-paragraph is one certifying that the law of the EEA State in which the transferee is set up permits such a transfer.

(4) "Relevant authority" means the competent authorities (within the meaning of the insurance directives) of the EEA State in which the transferee is set up.]

Interpretation of Part I

6.—(1) "State of the commitment", in relation to a commitment entered into at any date, means—

(a) if the policyholder is an individual, the State in which he had his habitual residence at that date;

(b) if the policyholder is not an individual, the State in which the establishment of the policyholder to which the commitment relates was situated at that date.

(2) "Commitment" means a commitment represented by contracts of insurance of a prescribed class.

(3) References to the EEA State in which a risk is situated are—

(a) if the insurance relates to a building or to a building and its contents (so far as the contents are covered by the same policy), to the EEA State in which the building is situated;

(b) if the insurance relates to a vehicle of any type, to the EEA State of registration;

(c) in the case of policies of a duration of four months or less covering travel or holiday risks (whatever the class concerned), to the EEA State in which the policyholder took out the policy;

(d) in a case not covered by paragraphs (a) to (c)—

(i) if the policyholder is an individual, to the EEA State in which he has his habitual residence at the date when the contract is entered into; and

(ii) otherwise, to the EEA State in which the establishment of the policyholder to which the policy relates is situated at that date.

[(4) If the insurance relates to a vehicle dispatched from one EEA State to another, in respect of the period of 30 days beginning with the day on which the purchaser accepts delivery a reference to the EEA State in which a risk is situated is a reference to the State of destination (and not, as provided by sub-paragraph (3)(b), to the State of registration).]

NOTES

Para 1: sub-paras (1)(e), (5), words in second (inner) pair of square brackets in sub-para (3)(a) and words in square brackets in sub-para (4)(a) inserted by the Reinsurance Directive Regulations 2007, SI 2007/3253, reg 2(1), Sch 1, paras 1, 2(5)(a)–(d); words in square brackets in sub-para (2)(a) and words in first (outer) pair of square brackets in sub-para (3)(a) substituted by the Life Assurance Consolidation Directive (Consequential Amendments) Regulations 2004, SI 2004/3379, reg 6(1), (7)(a).

Para 2: words in square brackets in sub-para (6)(a), sub-paras (6)(aa), (7A), (9) inserted and words in square brackets in sub-para (6)(c) substituted by SI 2007/3253, reg 2(1), Sch 1, paras 1, 2(5)(e).

Para 5A: inserted, together with preceding cross-heading, by SI 2007/3253, reg 2(1), Sch 1, paras 1, 2(5)(f).

Para 6: sub-para (4) inserted by the Financial Services and Markets Act 2000 (Motor Insurance) Regulations 2007, SI 2007/2403, reg 2.

Regulations: the Financial Services and Markets Act 2000 (Control of Business Transfers) (Requirements on Applicants) Regulations 2001, SI 2001/3625 at **[820]**.

PART II
BANKING BUSINESS TRANSFER SCHEMES

[337]

7.—(1) For the purposes of section 111(2) the appropriate certificates, in relation to a banking business transfer scheme, are—

(a) a certificate under paragraph 8; and

(b) if sub-paragraph (2) applies, a certificate under paragraph 9.

(2) This sub-paragraph applies if the authorised person concerned or the transferee is an EEA firm falling within paragraph 5(b) of Schedule 3.

Certificates as to financial resources

8.—(1) A certificate under this paragraph is one given by the relevant authority and certifying that, taking the proposed transfer into account, the transferee possesses, or will possess before the scheme takes effect, adequate financial resources.
(2) "Relevant authority" means—
  (a) if the transferee is a person with a Part IV permission or with permission under Schedule 4, the Authority;
  (b) if the transferee is an EEA firm falling within paragraph 5(b) of Schedule 3, its home state regulator;
  (c) if the transferee does not fall within paragraph (a) or (b), the authority responsible for the supervision of the transferee's business in the place in which the transferee has its head office.
(3) In sub-paragraph (2), any reference to a transferee of a particular description of person includes a reference to a transferee who will be of that description if the proposed banking business transfer scheme takes effect.

Certificates as to consent of home state regulator

9. A certificate under this paragraph is one given by the Authority and certifying that the home State regulator of the authorised person concerned or of the transferee has been notified of the proposed scheme and that—
  (a) the home State regulator has responded to the notification; or
  (b) the period of three months beginning with the notification has elapsed.

[PART 2A
RECLAIM FUND BUSINESS TRANSFER SCHEMES

Certificate as to financial resources

[337A]

9A. For the purposes of section 111(2) the appropriate certificate, in relation to a reclaim fund business transfer scheme, is a certificate given by the Authority certifying that, taking the proposed transfer into account, the transferee possesses, or will possess before the scheme takes effect, adequate financial resources.]

NOTES
Commencement: 12 March 2009.
Inserted by the Dormant Bank and Building Society Accounts Act 2008, s 15, Sch 2, para 5.

PART III
INSURANCE BUSINESS TRANSFERS EFFECTED OUTSIDE THE UNITED KINGDOM

[338]

10.—(1) This paragraph applies to a proposal to execute under provisions corresponding to Part VII in a country or territory other than the United Kingdom an instrument transferring all the rights and obligations of the transferor under general or long-term insurance policies, or under such descriptions of such policies as may be specified in the instrument, to the transferee if any of the conditions in sub-paragraphs (2), (3) or (4) is met in relation to it.
(2) The transferor is an EEA firm falling within paragraph 5(d) [or (da)] of Schedule 3 and the transferee is an authorised person whose margin of solvency is supervised by the Authority.
(3) The transferor is a company authorised in an EEA State other than the United Kingdom under [Article 51 of the life assurance consolidation directive], or Article 23 of the first non-life insurance directive and the transferee is a UK authorised person which has received authorisation under [Article 4 of the life assurance consolidation directive or Article 6 of the first non-life insurance directive].
(4) The transferor is a Swiss general insurer and the transferee is a UK authorised person which has received authorisation under [Article 4 of the life assurance consolidation directive or Article 6 of the first non-life insurance directive].
(5) In relation to a proposed transfer to which this paragraph applies, the Authority may, if it is satisfied that the transferee possesses the necessary margin of solvency, issue a certificate to that effect.
(6) "Necessary margin of solvency" means the margin of solvency which the transferee, taking the proposed transfer into account, is required by the Authority to maintain.
(7) "Swiss general insurer" has the same meaning as in paragraph 2.

(8) "General policy" means a policy evidencing a contract which, if it had been effected by the transferee, would have constituted the carrying on of a regulated activity consisting of the effecting of contracts of general insurance.
(9) "Long-term policy" means a policy evidencing a contract which, if it had been effected by the transferee, would have constituted the carrying on of a regulated activity consisting of the effecting of contracts of long-term insurance.

NOTES

Para 10: words in square brackets in sub-para (2) inserted by the Reinsurance Directive Regulations 2007, SI 2007/3253, reg 2(1), Sch 1, paras 1, 2(5)(g); words in square brackets in sub-paras (3), (4) substituted by the Life Assurance Consolidation Directive (Consequential Amendments) Regulations 2004, SI 2004/3379, reg 6(1), (7)(b), (c).

SCHEDULE 13

THE FINANCIAL SERVICES AND MARKETS TRIBUNAL

Section 132(4)

PART I
GENERAL

Interpretation

[339]

1. In this Schedule—

"panel of chairmen" means the panel established under paragraph 3(1);

"lay panel" means the panel established under paragraph 3(4);

"rules" means rules made by the Lord Chancellor under section 132.

NOTES

Schedule repealed by the Transfer of Tribunal Functions Order 2010, SI 2010/22, art 5(1), Sch 2, paras 43, 49, as from 6 April 2010, subject to transitional and saving provisions in art 5(4) thereof and Sch 5 thereto.

Modification: this Schedule is modified in respect of appeals to the Financial Services and Markets Tribunal made under the Money Laundering Regulations 2007, SI 2007/2157, reg 44, by SI 2007/2157, reg 44(4), (8), Sch 5, Pt 1, para 2, in respect of a reference to the Tribunal under the Northern Rock plc Compensation Scheme by the Northern Rock plc Compensation Scheme Order 2008, SI 2008/718, art 2, Schedule, Pt 5, paras 15–17, in respect of a reference to the Tribunal under the Bradford & Bingley plc Compensation Scheme by the Bradford & Bingley plc Compensation Scheme Order 2008, SI 2008/3249, art 2, Schedule, Pt 5, paras 14–16, and in respect of a reference to the Tribunal made under the Dunfermline Building Society Independent Valuer Order 2009, SI 2009/1810, art 13, by SI 2009/1810, arts 14(1)(a), 15–18.

PART II
THE TRIBUNAL

President

[340]

2.—(1) The Lord Chancellor must appoint one of the members of the panel of chairmen to preside over the discharge of the Tribunal's functions.
(2) The member so appointed is to be known as the President of the Financial Services and Markets Tribunal (but is referred to in this Act as "the President").
(3) The Lord Chancellor may appoint one of the members of the panel of chairmen to be Deputy President.
(4) The Deputy President is to have such functions in relation to the Tribunal as the President may assign to him.
(5) The Lord Chancellor may not appoint a person to be the President or Deputy President unless that person—

[(a) satisfies the judicial-appointment eligibility condition on a 7-year basis;]

(b) is an advocate or solicitor in Scotland of at least [7] years' standing; or

(c) is—

(i) a member of the Bar of Northern Ireland of at least [7] years' standing; or

(ii) a [solicitor of the Court of Judicature of Northern Ireland] of at least [7] years' standing.

(6) If the President (or Deputy President) ceases to be a member of the panel of chairmen, he also ceases to be the President (or Deputy President).
(7) The functions of the President may, if he is absent or is otherwise unable to act, be discharged—

(a) by the Deputy President; or

(b) if there is no Deputy President or he too is absent or otherwise unable to act, by a person appointed for that purpose from the panel of chairmen by the Lord Chancellor.

[(8) The Lord Chancellor may appoint a person under sub-paragraph (7)(b) only after consulting the following—

(a) the Lord Chief Justice of England and Wales;

(b) the Lord President of the Court of Session;

(c) the Lord Chief Justice of Northern Ireland.

(9) The Lord Chief Justice of England and Wales may nominate a judicial office holder (as defined in section 109(4) of the Constitutional Reform Act 2005) to exercise his functions under this paragraph.

(10) The Lord President of the Court of Session may nominate a judge of the Court of Session who is a member of the First or Second Division of the Inner House of that Court to exercise his functions under this paragraph.

(11) The Lord Chief Justice of Northern Ireland may nominate any of the following to exercise his functions under this paragraph—

(a) the holder of one of the offices listed in Schedule 1 to the Justice (Northern Ireland) Act 2002;

(b) a Lord Justice of Appeal (as defined in section 88 of that Act).]

Panels

3.—(1) The Lord Chancellor must appoint a panel of persons for the purposes of serving as chairmen of the Tribunal.

(2) A person is qualified for membership of the panel of chairmen if—

[(a) he satisfies the judicial-appointment eligibility condition on a 5-year basis;]

(b) he is an advocate or solicitor in Scotland of at least [5] years' standing; or

(c) he is—

(i) a member of the Bar of Northern Ireland of at least [5] years' standing; or

(ii) a [solicitor of the Court of Judicature of Northern Ireland] of at least [5] years' standing.

(3) The panel of chairmen must include at least one member who is a person of the kind mentioned in sub-paragraph (2)(b).

(4) The Lord Chancellor must also appoint a panel of persons who appear to him to be qualified by experience or otherwise to deal with matters of the kind that may be referred to the Tribunal.

Terms of office etc

4.—(1) Subject to the provisions of this Schedule, each member of the panel of chairmen and the lay panel is to hold and vacate office in accordance with the terms of his appointment.

(2) The Lord Chancellor may remove a member of either panel (including the President) on the ground of incapacity or misbehaviour.

[(2A) The Lord Chancellor may remove a person under sub-paragraph (2) only with the concurrence of the appropriate senior judge.

(2B) The appropriate senior judge is the Lord Chief Justice of England and Wales, unless—

(a) the person to be removed exercises functions wholly or mainly in Scotland, in which case it is the Lord President of the Court of Session, or

(b) the person to be removed exercises functions wholly or mainly in Northern Ireland, in which case it is the Lord Chief Justice of Northern Ireland.]

(3) A member of either panel—

(a) may at any time resign office by notice in writing to the Lord Chancellor;

(b) is eligible for re-appointment if he ceases to hold office.

Remuneration and expenses

5. The Lord Chancellor may pay to any person, in respect of his service—

(a) as a member of the Tribunal (including service as the President or Deputy President), or

(b) as a person appointed under paragraph 7(4), such remuneration and allowances as he may determine.

Staff

6.—(1) The Lord Chancellor may appoint such staff for the Tribunal as he may determine.

(2) The remuneration of the Tribunal's staff is to be defrayed by the Lord Chancellor.

(3) Such expenses of the Tribunal as the Lord Chancellor may determine are to be defrayed by the Lord Chancellor.

NOTES

Repealed as noted to Pt I of this Schedule at **[339]**.

Para 2: sub-para (5)(a) and numbers in square brackets in sub-paras (b), (c) substituted by the Tribunals, Courts and Enforcement Act 2007, s 50, Sch 10, Pt 1, para 34(1), (2), subject to transitional provisions in the Tribunals, Courts and Enforcement Act 2007 (Commencement No 5 and Transitional Provisions) Order 2008, SI 2008/1653, arts 3, 4; words in square brackets in sub-para (5)(c)(ii) substituted and sub-paras (8)–(11) added by the Constitutional Reform Act 2005, ss 15(1), 59(5), Sch 4, Pt 1, para 286(1), (2), Sch 11, Pt 3, para 5.

Para 3: sub-para (2)(a) and numbers in square brackets in sub-paras (2)(b), (c) substituted by the Tribunals, Courts and Enforcement Act 2007, s 50, Sch 10, Pt 1, para 34(1), (3), subject to transitional provisions in the Tribunals, Courts and Enforcement Act 2007 (Commencement No 5 and Transitional Provisions) Order 2008, SI 2008/1653, arts 3, 4; words in square brackets in sub-para (2)(c)(ii) substituted by the Constitutional Reform Act 2005, s 59(5), Sch 11, Pt 3, para 5.

Para 4: sub-paras (2A), (2B) inserted by the Constitutional Reform Act 2005, s 15(1), Sch 4, Pt 1, para 286(1), (3).

Application: paras 5, 6 above are applied, in relation to England and Wales, to the Claims Management Services Tribunal, by the Compensation Act 2006, s 12(5)(a), (b).

Modification: see the note to Pt I at **[339]**.

PART III
CONSTITUTION OF TRIBUNAL

[341]

7.—(1) On a reference to the Tribunal, the persons to act as members of the Tribunal for the purposes of the reference are to be selected from the panel of chairmen or the lay panel in accordance with arrangements made by the President for the purposes of this paragraph ("the standing arrangements").

(2) The standing arrangements must provide for at least one member to be selected from the panel of chairmen.

(3) If while a reference is being dealt with, a person serving as member of the Tribunal in respect of the reference becomes unable to act, the reference may be dealt with by—

- *(a) the other members selected in respect of that reference; or*
- *(b) if it is being dealt with by a single member, such other member of the panel of chairmen as may be selected in accordance with the standing arrangements for the purposes of the reference.*

(4) If it appears to the Tribunal that a matter before it involves a question of fact of special difficulty, it may appoint one or more experts to provide assistance.

NOTES

Repealed as noted to Pt I of this Schedule at **[339]**.

Application: para 7(3), (4) above is applied, in relation to England and Wales, to the Claims Management Services Tribunal, by the Compensation Act 2006, s 12(5)(c).

Modification: see the note to Pt I at **[339]**.

PART IV
TRIBUNAL PROCEDURE

[342]

8. For the purpose of dealing with references, or any matter preliminary or incidental to a reference, the Tribunal must sit at such times and in such place or places as the Lord Chancellor may[, after consulting the President of the Financial Services and Markets Tribunal,] direct.

9. Rules made by the Lord Chancellor under section 132 may, in particular, include provision—

- *(a) as to the manner in which references are to be instituted;*
- *(b) for the holding of hearings in private in such circumstances as may be specified in the rules;*
- *(c) as to the persons who may appear on behalf of the parties;*
- *(d) for a member of the panel of chairmen to hear and determine interlocutory matters arising on a reference;*
- *(e) for the suspension of decisions of the Authority which have taken effect;*
- *(f) as to the withdrawal of references;*
- *(g) as to the registration, publication and proof of decisions and orders.*

Practice directions

10. *The President of the Tribunal may give directions as to the practice and procedure to be followed by the Tribunal in relation to references to it.*

Evidence

11.—*(1) The Tribunal may by summons require any person to attend, at such time and place as is specified in the summons, to give evidence or to produce any document in his custody or under his control which the Tribunal considers it necessary to examine.*

(2) The Tribunal may—

(a) take evidence on oath and for that purpose administer oaths; or

(b) instead of administering an oath, require the person examined to make and subscribe a declaration of the truth of the matters in respect of which he is examined.

(3) A person who without reasonable excuse—

(a) refuses or fails—

(i) to attend following the issue of a summons by the Tribunal, or

(ii) to give evidence, or

(b) alters, suppresses, conceals or destroys, or refuses to produce a document which he may be required to produce for the purposes of proceedings before the Tribunal,

is guilty of an offence.

(4) A person guilty of an offence under sub-paragraph (3)(a) is liable on summary conviction to a fine not exceeding the statutory maximum.

(5) A person guilty of an offence under sub-paragraph (3)(b) is liable—

(a) on summary conviction, to a fine not exceeding the statutory maximum;

(b) on conviction on indictment, to imprisonment for a term not exceeding two years or a fine or both.

Decisions of Tribunal

12.—*(1) A decision of the Tribunal may be taken by a majority.*

(2) The decision must—

(a) state whether it was unanimous or taken by a majority;

(b) be recorded in a document which—

(i) contains a statement of the reasons for the decision; and

(ii) is signed and dated by the member of the panel of chairmen dealing with the reference.

(3) The Tribunal must—

(a) inform each party of its decision; and

(b) as soon as reasonably practicable, send to each party and, if different, to any authorised person concerned, a copy of the document mentioned in sub-paragraph (2).

(4) The Tribunal must send the Treasury a copy of its decision.

Costs

13.—*(1) If the Tribunal considers that a party to any proceedings on a reference has acted vexatiously, frivolously or unreasonably it may order that party to pay to another party to the proceedings the whole or part of the costs or expenses incurred by the other party in connection with the proceedings.*

(2) If, in any proceedings on a reference, the Tribunal considers that a decision of the Authority which is the subject of the reference was unreasonable it may order the Authority to pay to another party to the proceedings the whole or part of the costs or expenses incurred by the other party in connection with the proceedings.

NOTES

Repealed as noted to Pt I of this Schedule at **[339]**.

Para 8: words in square brackets inserted by the Constitutional Reform Act 2005, s 15(1), Sch 4, Pt 1, para 286(1), (4).

Application: paras 8, 10, 11, 12(1)–(3) above are applied, in relation to England and Wales, to the Claims Management Services Tribunal, by the Compensation Act 2006, s 12(5)(d)–(g).

Modification: see the note to Pt I at **[339]**.

SCHEDULE 14

ROLE OF THE COMPETITION COMMISSION

Section 162

Provision of information by Treasury

[343]

1.—(1) The Treasury's powers under this paragraph are to be exercised only for the purpose of assisting the Commission in carrying out an investigation under section 162.

(2) The Treasury may give to the Commission—

(a) any information in their possession which relates to matters falling within the scope of the investigation; and

(b) other assistance in relation to any such matters.

(3) In carrying out an investigation under section 162, the Commission must have regard to any information given to it under this paragraph.

Consideration of matters arising on a report

2. In considering any matter arising from a report made by the [OFT] under section 160, the Commission must have regard to—

(a) any representations made to [the Commission] in connection with the matter by any person appearing to the Commission to have a substantial interest in the matter; and

(b) any cost benefit analysis prepared by the Authority (at any time) in connection with the regulatory provision or practice, or any of the regulatory provisions or practices, which are the subject of the report.

[Investigations under section 162: application of Enterprise Act 2002

2A.—(1) The following sections of Part 3 of the Enterprise Act 2002 shall apply, with the modifications mentioned in sub-paragraphs (2) and (3), for the purposes of any investigation by the Commission under section 162 of this Act as they apply for the purposes of references under that Part—

(a) section 109 (attendance of witnesses and production of documents etc);

(b) section 110 (enforcement of powers under section 109: general);

(c) section 111 (penalties);

(d) section 112 (penalties: main procedural requirements);

(e) section 113 (payments and interest by instalments);

(f) section 114 (appeals in relation to penalties);

(g) section 115 (recovery of penalties); and

(h) section 116 (statement of policy).

(2) Section 110 shall, in its application by virtue of sub-paragraph (1), have effect as if—

(a) subsection (2) were omitted; and

(b) in subsection (9) the words from "or section" to "section 65(3))" were omitted.

(3) Section 111(5)(b) shall, in its application by virtue of sub-paragraph (1), have effect as if for sub-paragraph (ii) there were substituted—

"(ii) if earlier, the day on which the report of the Commission on the investigation concerned is made or, if the Commission decides not to make a report, the day on which the Commission makes the statement required by section 162(3) of the Financial Services and Markets Act 2000."

(4) Section 117 of the Enterprise Act 2002 (false or misleading information) shall apply in relation to functions of the Commission in connection with an investigation under section 162 of this Act as it applies in relation to its functions under Part 3 of that Act but as if, in subsections (1)(a) and (2), the words ["the OFT, OFCOM,"] and "or the Secretary of State" were omitted.

(5) Provisions of Part 3 of the Enterprise Act 2002 which have effect for the purposes of sections 109 to 117 of that Act (including, in particular, provisions relating to offences and the making of orders) shall, for the purposes of the application of those sections by virtue of sub-paragraph (1) or (4) above, have effect in relation to those sections as applied by virtue of those sub-paragraphs.

(6) Accordingly, corresponding provisions of this Act shall not have effect in relation to those sections as applied by virtue of those sub-paragraphs.

Section 162: modification of Schedule 7 to the Competition Act 1998

2B. For the purposes of its application in relation to the function of the Commission of deciding in accordance with section 162(2) of this Act not to make a report, paragraph 15(7) of Schedule 7 to the Competition Act 1998 (power of the Chairman to act on his own while a group is being constituted) has effect as if, after paragraph (a), there were inserted—

"; or

(aa) in the case of an investigation under section 162 of the Financial Services and Markets Act 2000, decide not to make a report in accordance with subsection (2) of that section (decision not to make a report where no useful purpose would be served)."

Reports under section 162: further provision

2C.—(1) For the purposes of section 163 of this Act, a conclusion contained in a report of the Commission is to be disregarded if the conclusion is not that of at least two-thirds of the members of the group constituted in connection with the investigation concerned in pursuance of paragraph 15 of Schedule 7 to the Competition Act 1998.
(2) If a member of a group so constituted disagrees with any conclusions contained in a report made under section 162 of this Act as the conclusions of the Commission, the report shall, if the member so wishes, include a statement of his disagreement and of his reasons for disagreeing.
(3) For the purposes of the law relating to defamation, absolute privilege attaches to any report made by the Commission under section 162.]

. . .

3. . . .

Publication of reports

4.—(1) If the Commission makes a report under section 162, it must publish it in such a way as appears to it to be best calculated to bring it to the attention of the public.
(2) Before publishing the report the Commission must, so far as practicable, exclude any matter which relates to the private affairs of a particular individual the publication of which, in the opinion of the Commission, would or might seriously and prejudicially affect his interests.
(3) Before publishing the report the Commission must, so far as practicable, also exclude any matter which relates to the affairs of a particular body the publication of which, in the opinion of the Commission, would or might seriously and prejudicially affect its interests.
(4) Sub-paragraphs (2) and (3) do not apply in relation to copies of a report which the Commission is required to send under section 162(10).

NOTES

Para 2: words in square brackets substituted by the Enterprise Act 2002, s 278(1), Sch 25, para 40(1), (20)(a).

Para 2A: inserted, together with preceding cross-heading and paras 2B, 2C, by the Enterprise Act 2002, s 278(1), Sch 25, para 40(1), (20)(b); words in square brackets in sub-para (4) substituted by the Communications Act 2003, s 389(1), Sch 16, para 5.

Paras 2B, 2C: inserted, together with para 2A and preceding cross-headings, by the Enterprise Act 2002, s 278(1), Sch 25, para 40(1), (20)(b).

Para 3: repealed by the Enterprise Act 2002, s 278, Sch 25, para 40(1), (20)(c), Sch 26.

SCHEDULE 15

INFORMATION AND INVESTIGATIONS: CONNECTED PERSONS

Sections 165(11) and 171(4)

PART I
RULES FOR SPECIFIC BODIES

Corporate bodies

[344]

1. If the authorised person ("BC") is a body corporate, a person who is or has been—

(a) an officer or manager of BC or of a parent undertaking of BC;
(b) an employee of BC;
(c) an agent of BC or of a parent undertaking of BC.

Partnerships

2. If the authorised person ("PP") is a partnership, a person who is or has been a member, manager, employee or agent of PP.

Unincorporated associations

3. If the authorised person ("UA") is an unincorporated association of persons which is neither a partnership nor an unincorporated friendly society, a person who is or has been an officer, manager, employee or agent of UA.

Friendly societies

4.—(1) If the authorised person ("FS") is a friendly society, a person who is or has been an officer, manager or employee of FS.
(2) In relation to FS, "officer" and "manager" have the same meaning as in section 119(1) of the Friendly Societies Act 1992.

Building societies

5.—(1) If the authorised person ("BS") is a building society, a person who is or has been an officer or employee of BS.
(2) In relation to BS, "officer" has the same meaning as it has in section 119(1) of the Building Societies Act 1986.

Individuals

6. If the authorised person ("IP") is an individual, a person who is or has been an employee or agent of IP.

Application to sections 171 and 172

7. For the purposes of sections 171 and 172, if the person under investigation is not an authorised person the references in this Part of this Schedule to an authorised person are to be taken to be references to the person under investigation.

PART II
ADDITIONAL RULES

[345]

8. A person who is, or at the relevant time was, the partner, manager, employee, agent, appointed representative, banker, auditor, actuary or solicitor of—
(a) the person under investigation ("A");
(b) a parent undertaking of A;
(c) a subsidiary undertaking of A;
(d) a subsidiary undertaking of a parent undertaking of A; or
(e) a parent undertaking of a subsidiary undertaking of A.

(*Sch 16 outside the scope of this work.*)

SCHEDULE 17

THE OMBUDSMAN SCHEME

Section 225(4)

PART I
GENERAL

Interpretation

[346]

1. In this Schedule—
"ombudsman" means a person who is a member of the panel; and
"the panel" means the panel established under paragraph 4.

NOTES

Application: this Schedule applies as if persons who fall within the Payment Services Regulations 2009, SI 2009/209, reg 122(1) or 123(1) were payment service providers within the meaning of those Regulations; see SI 2009/209, reg 125.

PART II
THE SCHEME OPERATOR

Establishment by the Authority

[347]

2.—(1) The Authority must establish a body corporate to exercise the functions conferred on the scheme operator by or under this Act.
(2) The Authority must take such steps as are necessary to ensure that the scheme operator is, at all times, capable of exercising those functions.

Constitution

3.—(1) The constitution of the scheme operator must provide for it to have—
(a) a chairman; and
(b) a board (which must include the chairman) whose members are the scheme operator's directors.
(2) The chairman and other members of the board must be persons appointed, and liable to removal from office, by the Authority (acting, in the case of the chairman, with the approval of the Treasury).
(3) But the terms of their appointment (and in particular those governing removal from office) must be such as to secure their independence from the Authority in the operation of the scheme.
(4) The function of making voluntary jurisdiction rules under section 227[, the function of making consumer credit rules, the function of making determinations under section 234A(1)] and the functions conferred by paragraphs 4, 5, 7, 9 or 14 may be exercised only by the board.
(5) The validity of any act of the scheme operator is unaffected by—
(a) a vacancy in the office of chairman; or
(b) a defect in the appointment of a person as chairman or as a member of the board.

The panel of ombudsmen

4.—(1) The scheme operator must appoint and maintain a panel of persons, appearing to it to have appropriate qualifications and experience, to act as ombudsmen for the purposes of the scheme.
(2) A person's appointment to the panel is to be on such terms (including terms as to the duration and termination of his appointment and as to remuneration) as the scheme operator considers—
(a) consistent with the independence of the person appointed; and
(b) otherwise appropriate.

The Chief Ombudsman

5.—(1) The scheme operator must appoint one member of the panel to act as Chief Ombudsman.
(2) The Chief Ombudsman is to be appointed on such terms (including terms as to the duration and termination of his appointment) as the scheme operator considers appropriate.

Status

6.—(1) The scheme operator is not to be regarded as exercising functions on behalf of the Crown.
(2) The scheme operator's board members, officers and staff are not to be regarded as Crown servants.
(3) Appointment as Chief Ombudsman or to the panel or as a deputy ombudsman does not confer the status of Crown servant.

Annual reports

7.—(1) At least once a year—
(a) the scheme operator must make a report to the Authority on the discharge of its functions; and
(b) the Chief Ombudsman must make a report to the Authority on the discharge of his functions.
(2) Each report must distinguish between functions in relation to the scheme's compulsory jurisdiction[, functions in relation to its consumer credit jurisdiction] and functions in relation to its voluntary jurisdiction.
(3) Each report must also comply with any requirements specified in rules made by the Authority.
(4) The scheme operator must publish each report in the way it considers appropriate.

Guidance

8. The scheme operator may publish guidance consisting of such information and advice as it considers appropriate and may charge for it or distribute it free of charge.

Budget

9.—(1) The scheme operator must, before the start of each of its financial years, adopt an annual budget which has been approved by the Authority.
(2) The scheme operator may, with the approval of the Authority, vary the budget for a financial year at any time after its adoption.
(3) The annual budget must include an indication of—
(a) the distribution of resources deployed in the operation of the scheme, and
(b) the amounts of income of the scheme operator arising or expected to arise from the operation of the scheme,

distinguishing between the scheme's compulsory[, consumer credit] and voluntary jurisdiction.

Exemption from liability in damages

10.—(1) No person is to be liable in damages for anything done or omitted in the discharge, or purported discharge, of any functions under this Act in relation to the compulsory jurisdiction [or to the consumer credit jurisdiction].
(2) Sub-paragraph (1) does not apply—
(a) if the act or omission is shown to have been in bad faith; or
(b) so as to prevent an award of damages made in respect of an act or omission on the ground that the act or omission was unlawful as a result of section 6(1) of the Human Rights Act 1998.

Privilege

11. For the purposes of the law relating to defamation, proceedings in relation to a complaint which is subject to the compulsory jurisdiction [or to the consumer credit jurisdiction] are to be treated as if they were proceedings before a court.

NOTES

Paras 3, 7, 9–11: words in square brackets inserted by the Consumer Credit Act 2006, s 61(10).
Application: see the note to Pt I at **[346]**.

PART III
THE COMPULSORY JURISDICTION

Introduction

[348]

12. This Part of this Schedule applies only in relation to the compulsory jurisdiction.

Authority's procedural rules

13.—(1) The Authority must make rules providing that a complaint is not to be entertained unless the complainant has referred it under the ombudsman scheme before the applicable time limit (determined in accordance with the rules) has expired.
(2) The rules may provide that an ombudsman may extend that time limit in specified circumstances.
(3) The Authority may make rules providing that a complaint is not to be entertained (except in specified circumstances) if the complainant has not previously communicated its substance to the respondent and given him a reasonable opportunity to deal with it.
(4) The Authority may make rules requiring an authorised person[, or a payment service provider within the meaning of the Payment Services Regulations 2009,] who may become subject to the compulsory jurisdiction as a respondent to establish such procedures as the Authority considers appropriate for the resolution of complaints which—
(a) may be referred to the scheme; and
(b) arise out of activity to which the Authority's powers under Part X do not apply.

The scheme operator's rules

14.—(1) The scheme operator must make rules, to be known as "scheme rules", which are to set out the procedure for reference of complaints and for their investigation, consideration and determination by an ombudsman.
(2) Scheme rules may, among other things—
(a) specify matters which are to be taken into account in determining whether an act or omission was fair and reasonable;
(b) provide that a complaint may, in specified circumstances, be dismissed without consideration of its merits;

(c) provide for the reference of a complaint, in specified circumstances and with the consent of the complainant, to another body with a view to its being determined by that body instead of by an ombudsman;
(d) make provision as to the evidence which may be required or admitted, the extent to which it should be oral or written and the consequences of a person's failure to produce any information or document which he has been required (under section 231 or otherwise) to produce;
(e) allow an ombudsman to fix time limits for any aspect of the proceedings and to extend a time limit;
(f) provide for certain things in relation to the reference, investigation or consideration (but not determination) of a complaint to be done by a member of the scheme operator's staff instead of by an ombudsman;
(g) make different provision in relation to different kinds of complaint.

(3) The circumstances specified under sub-paragraph (2)(b) may include the following—
(a) the ombudsman considers the complaint frivolous or vexatious;
(b) legal proceedings have been brought concerning the subject-matter of the complaint and the ombudsman considers that the complaint is best dealt with in those proceedings; or
(c) the ombudsman is satisfied that there are other compelling reasons why it is inappropriate for the complaint to be dealt with under the ombudsman scheme.

(4) If the scheme operator proposes to make any scheme rules it must publish a draft of the proposed rules in the way appearing to it to be best calculated to bring them to the attention of persons appearing to it to be likely to be affected.

(5) The draft must be accompanied by a statement that representations about the proposals may be made to the scheme operator within a time specified in the statement.

(6) Before making the proposed scheme rules, the scheme operator must have regard to any representations made to it under sub-paragraph (5).

(7) The consent of the Authority is required before any scheme rules may be made.

Fees

15.—(1) Scheme rules may require a respondent to pay to the scheme operator such fees as may be specified in the rules.

(2) The rules may, among other things—
(a) provide for the scheme operator to reduce or waive a fee in a particular case;
(b) set different fees for different stages of the proceedings on a complaint;
(c) provide for fees to be refunded in specified circumstances;
(d) make different provision for different kinds of complaint.

Enforcement of money awards

16. A money award, including interest, which has been registered in accordance with scheme rules may—
(a) if a county court so orders in England and Wales, be recovered *by execution issued from the county court* (or otherwise) as if it were payable under an order of that court;
(b) be enforced in Northern Ireland as a money judgment under the Judgments Enforcement (Northern Ireland) Order 1981;
(c) be enforced in Scotland by the sheriff, as if it were a judgment or order of the sheriff and whether or not the sheriff could himself have granted such judgment or order.

NOTES

Para 13: words in square brackets in sub-para (4) inserted by the Payment Services Regulations 2009, SI 2009/209, reg 126, Sch 6, Pt 1, para 1(2).

Para 16: for the words in italics in sub-para (a) there are substituted the words "under section 85 of the County Courts Act 1984" by the Tribunals, Courts and Enforcement Act 2007, s 62(3), Sch 13, para 134, as from a day to be appointed.

Application: see the note to Pt I at **[346]**.

[PART 3A
THE CONSUMER CREDIT JURISDICTION

Introduction

[348A]

16A. This Part of this Schedule applies only in relation to the consumer credit jurisdiction.

Procedure for complaints etc

16B.—(1) Consumer credit rules—
- (a) must provide that a complaint is not to be entertained unless the complainant has referred it under the ombudsman scheme before the applicable time limit (determined in accordance with the rules) has expired;
- (b) may provide that an ombudsman may extend that time limit in specified circumstances;
- (c) may provide that a complaint is not to be entertained (except in specified circumstances) if the complainant has not previously communicated its substance to the respondent and given him a reasonable opportunity to deal with it;
- (d) may make provision about the procedure for the reference of complaints and for their investigation, consideration and determination by an ombudsman.

(2) Sub-paragraphs (2) and (3) of paragraph 14 apply in relation to consumer credit rules under sub-paragraph (1) of this paragraph as they apply in relation to scheme rules under that paragraph.
(3) Consumer credit rules may require persons falling within sub-paragraph (6) to establish such procedures as the scheme operator considers appropriate for the resolution of complaints which may be referred to the scheme.
(4) Consumer credit rules under sub-paragraph (3) may make different provision in relation to persons of different descriptions or to complaints of different descriptions.
(5) Consumer credit rules under sub-paragraph (3) may authorise the scheme operator to dispense with or modify the application of such rules in particular cases where the scheme operator—
- (a) considers it appropriate to do so; and
- (b) is satisfied that the specified conditions (if any) are met.

(6) A person falls within this sub-paragraph if he is licensed by a standard licence (within the meaning of the Consumer Credit Act 1974) to carry on to any extent a business of a type specified in an order under section 226A(2)(e) of this Act.

Fees

16C.—(1) Consumer credit rules may require a respondent to pay to the scheme operator such fees as may be specified in the rules.
(2) Sub-paragraph (2) of paragraph 15 applies in relation to consumer credit rules under this paragraph as it applies in relation to scheme rules under that paragraph.

Enforcement of money awards

16D. A money award, including interest, which has been registered in accordance with consumer credit rules may—
- (a) if a county court so orders in England and Wales, be recovered by execution issued from the county court (or otherwise) as if it were payable under an order of that court;
- (b) be enforced in Northern Ireland as a money judgment under the Judgments Enforcement (Northern Ireland) Order 1981;
- (c) be enforced in Scotland as if it were a decree of the sheriff and whether or not the sheriff could himself have granted such a decree.

Procedure for consumer credit rules

16E.—(1) If the scheme operator makes any consumer credit rules, it must give a copy of them to the Authority without delay.
(2) If the scheme operator revokes any such rules, it must give written notice to the Authority without delay.
(3) The power to make such rules is exercisable in writing.
(4) Immediately after the making of such rules, the scheme operator must arrange for them to be printed and made available to the public.
(5) The scheme operator may charge a reasonable fee for providing a person with a copy of any such rules.

Verification of consumer credit rules

16F.—(1) The production of a printed copy of consumer credit rules purporting to be made by the scheme operator—
- (a) on which there is endorsed a certificate signed by a member of the scheme operator's staff authorised by the scheme operator for that purpose, and
- (b) which contains the required statements,

is evidence (or in Scotland sufficient evidence) of the facts stated in the certificate.
(2) The required statements are—
- (a) that the rules were made by the scheme operator;
- (b) that the copy is a true copy of the rules; and

(c) that on a specified date the rules were made available to the public in accordance with paragraph 16E(4).

(3) A certificate purporting to be signed as mentioned in sub-paragraph (1) is to be taken to have been duly signed unless the contrary is shown.

Consultation

16G.—(1) If the scheme operator proposes to make consumer credit rules, it must publish a draft of the proposed rules in the way appearing to it to be best calculated to bring the draft to the attention of the public.

(2) The draft must be accompanied by—

(a) an explanation of the proposed rules; and

(b) a statement that representations about the proposals may be made to the scheme operator within a specified time.

(3) Before making any consumer credit rules, the scheme operator must have regard to any representations made to it in accordance with sub-paragraph (2)(b).

(4) If consumer credit rules made by the scheme operator differ from the draft published under sub-paragraph (1) in a way which the scheme operator considers significant, the scheme operator must publish a statement of the difference.]

NOTES

Commencement: 16 June 2006.

Inserted by the Consumer Credit Act 2006, s 59(2), Sch 2.

Application: see the note to Pt I at **[346]**.

PART IV
THE VOLUNTARY JURISDICTION

Introduction

[349]

17. This Part of this Schedule applies only in relation to the voluntary jurisdiction.

Terms of reference to the scheme

18.—(1) Complaints are to be dealt with and determined under the voluntary jurisdiction on standard terms fixed by the scheme operator with the approval of the Authority.

(2) Different standard terms may be fixed with respect to different matters or in relation to different cases.

(3) The standard terms may, in particular—

(a) require the making of payments to the scheme operator by participants in the scheme of such amounts, and at such times, as may be determined by the scheme operator;

(b) make provision as to the award of costs on the determination of a complaint.

(4) The scheme operator may not vary any of the standard terms or add or remove terms without the approval of the Authority.

(5) The standard terms may include provision to the effect that (unless acting in bad faith) none of the following is to be liable in damages for anything done or omitted in the discharge or purported discharge of functions in connection with the voluntary jurisdiction—

(a) the scheme operator;

(b) any member of its governing body;

(c) any member of its staff;

(d) any person acting as an ombudsman for the purposes of the scheme.

Delegation by and to other schemes

19.—(1) The scheme operator may make arrangements with a relevant body—

(a) for the exercise by that body of any part of the voluntary jurisdiction of the ombudsman scheme on behalf of the scheme; or

(b) for the exercise by the scheme of any function of that body as if it were part of the voluntary jurisdiction of the scheme.

(2) A "relevant body" is one which the scheme operator is satisfied—

(a) is responsible for the operation of a broadly comparable scheme (whether or not established by statute) for the resolution of disputes; and

(b) in the case of arrangements under sub-paragraph (1)(a), will exercise the jurisdiction in question in a way compatible with the requirements imposed by or under this Act in relation to complaints of the kind concerned.

(3) Such arrangements require the approval of the Authority.

Voluntary jurisdiction rules: procedure

20.—(1) If the scheme operator makes voluntary jurisdiction rules, it must give a copy to the Authority without delay.
(2) If the scheme operator revokes any such rules, it must give written notice to the Authority without delay.
(3) The power to make voluntary jurisdiction rules is exercisable in writing.
(4) Immediately after making voluntary jurisdiction rules, the scheme operator must arrange for them to be printed and made available to the public.
(5) The scheme operator may charge a reasonable fee for providing a person with a copy of any voluntary jurisdiction rules.

Verification of the rules

21.—(1) The production of a printed copy of voluntary jurisdiction rules purporting to be made by the scheme operator—
- (a) on which is endorsed a certificate signed by a member of the scheme operator's staff authorised by the scheme operator for that purpose, and
- (b) which contains the required statements,

is evidence (or in Scotland sufficient evidence) of the facts stated in the certificate.
(2) The required statements are—
- (a) that the rules were made by the scheme operator;
- (b) that the copy is a true copy of the rules; and
- (c) that on a specified date the rules were made available to the public in accordance with paragraph 20(4).

(3) A certificate purporting to be signed as mentioned in sub-paragraph (1) is to be taken to have been duly signed unless the contrary is shown.

Consultation

22.—(1) If the scheme operator proposes to make voluntary jurisdiction rules, it must publish a draft of the proposed rules in the way appearing to it to be best calculated to bring them to the attention of the public.
(2) The draft must be accompanied by—
- (a) an explanation of the proposed rules; and
- (b) a statement that representations about the proposals may be made to the scheme operator within a specified time.

(3) Before making any voluntary jurisdiction rules, the scheme operator must have regard to any representations made to it in accordance with sub-paragraph (2)(b).
(4) If voluntary jurisdiction rules made by the scheme operator differ from the draft published under sub-paragraph (1) in a way which the scheme operator considers significant, the scheme operator must publish a statement of the difference.

NOTES
Application: see the note to Pt I at **[346]**.

SCHEDULE 18

MUTUALS

(*Pt I repeals the Friendly Societies Act 1974, ss 4, 10 and amends ss 7, 11, 99 thereof, repeals the Friendly Societies Act 1992, ss 31–36A, 38–43, 44–50 and amends s 37 thereof.*)

PART II
FRIENDLY SOCIETIES: SUBSIDIARIES AND CONTROLLED BODIES

[350]

9–15. . . .

References in other enactments

16. References in any provision of, or made under, any enactment to subsidiaries of, or bodies jointly controlled by, an incorporated friendly society are to be read as including references to bodies which are such subsidiaries or bodies as a result of any provision of this Part of this Schedule.

NOTES
Paras 9–15: amend the Friendly Societies Act 1992, ss 13, 52, Sch 8 and repeal Sch 7 thereto.

(Sch 18, Pts III–V, Sch 20 contain amendments outside the scope of this work; Sch 19 repealed by the Enterprise Act 2002, ss 247(k), 278(2), Sch 26.)

SCHEDULE 21

TRANSITIONAL PROVISIONS AND SAVINGS

Section 432(2)

Self-regulating organisations

[351]–[500]

1.—(1) No new application under section 9 of the 1986 Act (application for recognition) may be entertained.
(2) No outstanding application made under that section before the passing of this Act may continue to be entertained.
(3) After the date which is the designated date for a recognised self-regulating organisation—
 (a) the recognition order for that organisation may not be revoked under section 11 of the 1986 Act (revocation of recognition);
 (b) no application may be made to the court under section 12 of the 1986 Act (compliance orders) with respect to that organisation.
(4) The powers conferred by section 13 of the 1986 Act (alteration of rules for protection of investors) may not be exercised.
(5) "Designated date" means such date as the Treasury may by order designate.
(6) Sub-paragraph (3) does not apply to a recognised self-regulating organisation in respect of which a notice of intention to revoke its recognition order was given under section 11(3) of the 1986 Act before the passing of this Act if that notice has not been withdrawn.
(7) Expenditure incurred by the Authority in connection with the winding up of any body which was, immediately before the passing of this Act, a recognised self-regulating organisation is to be treated as having been incurred in connection with the discharge by the Authority of functions under this Act.
(8) "Recognised self-regulating organisation" means an organisation which, immediately before the passing of this Act, was such an organisation for the purposes of the 1986 Act.
(9) "The 1986 Act" means the Financial Services Act 1986.

Self-regulating organisations for friendly societies

2.—(1) No new application under paragraph 2 of Schedule 11 to the 1986 Act (application for recognition) may be entertained.
(2) No outstanding application made under that paragraph before the passing of this Act may continue to be entertained.
(3) After the date which is the designated date for a recognised self-regulating organisation for friendly societies—
 (a) the recognition order for that organisation may not be revoked under paragraph 5 of Schedule 11 to the 1986 Act (revocation of recognition);
 (b) no application may be made to the court under paragraph 6 of that Schedule (compliance orders) with respect to that organisation.
(4) "Designated date" means such date as the Treasury may by order designate.
(5) Sub-paragraph (3) does not apply to a recognised self-regulating organisation for friendly societies in respect of which a notice of intention to revoke its recognition order was given under section 11(3) of the 1986 Act (as applied by paragraph 5(2) of that Schedule) before the passing of this Act if that notice has not been withdrawn.
(6) Expenditure incurred by the Authority in connection with the winding up of any body which was, immediately before the passing of this Act, a recognised self-regulating organisation for friendly societies is to be treated as having been incurred in connection with the discharge by the Authority of functions under this Act.
(7) "Recognised self-regulating organisation for friendly societies" means an organisation which, immediately before the passing of this Act, was such an organisation for the purposes of the 1986 Act.
(8) "The 1986 Act" means the Financial Services Act 1986.

NOTES

Financial Services Act 1986: repealed by the Financial Services and Markets Act 2000 (Consequential Amendments and Repeals) Order 2001, SI 2001/3649, art 3(1)(c).

(Sch 22 contains repeals which, in so far as relevant to this work, have been incorporated at the appropriate place.)

B. FSMA 2000 STATUTORY INSTRUMENTS

FINANCIAL SERVICES AND MARKETS ACT 2000 (REGULATED ACTIVITIES) ORDER 2001

(SI 2001/544)

NOTES

Made: 26 February 2001.
Authority: Financial Services and Markets Act 2000, ss 22(1), (5), 426, 428(3), Sch 2, para 25.
Commencement: see art 2.

ARRANGEMENT OF ARTICLES

PART I
GENERAL

1 Citation [501]
2 Commencement [502]
3 Interpretation [503]

PART II
SPECIFIED ACTIVITIES

CHAPTER I
GENERAL

4 Specified activities: general [504]

CHAPTER III
INSURANCE

The activities

10 Effecting and carrying out contracts of insurance [505]

Exclusions

11 Community co-insurers [506]
12 Breakdown insurance [507]
12A Information society services [508]

Supplemental

13 Application of sections 327 and 332 of the Act to insurance market activities [509]

CHAPTER IV
DEALING IN INVESTMENTS AS PRINCIPAL

The activity

14 Dealing in investments as principal [510]

Exclusions

15 Absence of holding out etc [511]
16 Dealing in contractually based investments [512]
17 Acceptance of instruments creating or acknowledging indebtedness [513]
18 Issue by a company of its own shares etc [514]
18A Dealing by a company in its own shares [515]
19 Risk management [516]
20 Other exclusions [517]

CHAPTER V
DEALING IN INVESTMENTS AS AGENT

The activity

21 Dealing in investments as agent [518]

Exclusions

22 Deals with or through authorised persons [519]
23 Risk management [520]
24 Other exclusions [521]

CHAPTER VI
ARRANGING DEALS IN INVESTMENTS

The activities

25 Arranging deals in investments [522]

25A regulated mortgage contracts . . . [523]
25D Operating a multilateral trading facility . . . [523A]

Exclusions

26 Arrangements not causing a deal . . . [524]
27 Enabling parties to communicate . . . [525]
28 Arranging transactions to which the arranger is a party . . . [526]
28A Arranging contracts or plans to which the arranger is a party . . . [527]
29 Arranging deals with or through authorised persons . . . [528]
29A Arrangements made in the course of administration by authorised person . . . [529]
30 Arranging transactions in connection with lending on the security of insurance policies . . . [530]
31 Arranging the acceptance of debentures in connection with loans . . . [531]
32 Provision of finance . . . [532]
33 Introducing . . . [533]
33A Introducing to authorised persons etc . . . [534]
34 Arrangements for the issue of shares etc . . . [535]
35 International securities self-regulating organisations . . . [536]
36 Other exclusions . . . [537]

CHAPTER VII
MANAGING INVESTMENTS

The activity

37 Managing investments . . . [538]

Exclusions

38 Attorneys . . . [539]
39 Other exclusions . . . [540]
39A Assisting in the administration and performance of a contract of insurance . . . [541]
39B Claims management on behalf of an insurer etc . . . [542]
39C Other exclusions . . . [543]

CHAPTER VIII
SAFEGUARDING AND ADMINISTERING INVESTMENTS

The activity

40 Safeguarding and administering investments . . . [544]

Exclusions

41 Acceptance of responsibility by third party . . . [545]
42 Introductions to qualifying custodians . . . [546]
43 Activities not constituting administration . . . [547]
44 Other exclusions . . . [548]

CHAPTER XI
PENSION SCHEMES

The activities

52 Establishing etc a pension scheme . . . [549]

Exclusion

52A Information society services . . . [550]

CHAPTER XIA
PROVIDING BASIC ADVICE ON STAKEHOLDER PRODUCTS

The activity

52B Providing basic advice on stakeholder products . . . [551]

CHAPTER XII
ADVISING ON INVESTMENTS

The activity

53 Advising on investments . . . [552]
53A Advising on regulated mortgage contracts . . . [553]

Exclusions

54 Advice given in newspapers etc . . . [554]
54A Advice given in the course of administration by authorised person . . . [555]
55 Other exclusions . . . [556]

CHAPTER XIII
LLOYD'S

The activities

56 Advice on syndicate participation at Lloyd's . . . [557]
57 Managing the underwriting capacity of a Lloyd's syndicate . . . [558]
58 Arranging deals in contracts of insurance written at Lloyd's . . . [559]

Exclusion

58A Information society services . . . [560]

CHAPTER XIV
FUNERAL PLAN CONTRACTS

The activity

59 Funeral plan contracts . . . [561]

Exclusions

60 Plans covered by insurance or trust arrangements . . . [562]
60A Information society services . . . [563]

CHAPTER XVI
AGREEING TO CARRY ON ACTIVITIES

The activity

64 Agreeing to carry on specified kinds of activity . . . [564]

Exclusions

65 Overseas persons etc . . . [565]

CHAPTER XVII
EXCLUSIONS APPLYING TO SEVERAL SPECIFIED KINDS OF ACTIVITY

66 Trustees, nominees and personal representatives . . . [566]
67 Activities carried on in the course of a profession or non-investment business . . . [567]
68 Activities carried on in connection with the sale of goods or supply of services . . . [568]
69 Groups and joint enterprises . . . [569]
72 Overseas persons . . . [570]
72A Information society services . . . [571]
72B Activities carried on by a provider of relevant goods or services . . . [572]
72C Provision of information on an incidental basis . . . [573]
72D Large risks contracts where risk situated outside the EEA . . . [574]
72E Business Angel-led Enterprise Capital Funds . . . [575]
72F Interpretation . . . [576]

PART III
SPECIFIED INVESTMENTS

73 Investments: general . . . [577]
75 Contracts of insurance . . . [578]
82 Rights under a pension scheme . . . [579]
86 Lloyd's syndicate capacity and syndicate membership . . . [580]

PART V
UNAUTHORISED PERSONS CARRYING ON INSURANCE MEDIATION ACTIVITIES

92 Interpretation . . . [581]
93 Duty to maintain a record of unauthorised persons carrying on insurance mediation activities . . . [582]
94 Members of designated professional bodies . . . [583]
95 Exclusion from record where not fit and proper to carry on insurance mediation activities . . . [584]
96 Exclusion from the record where Authority has exercised its powers under Part XX of the Act . . . [585]

SCHEDULES:

Schedule 1—Contracts of Insurance
Part I—Contracts of general insurance . . . [586]
Part II—Contracts of long-term insurance . . . [587]
Schedule 4—Relevant Text of the Insurance Mediation Directive
Part I—Article 1.2 . . . [588]
Part II—Article 2.3 . . . [589]
Part III—Article 2.4 . . . [590]

PART I
GENERAL

[501]
1 Citation

This Order may be cited as the Financial Services and Markets Act 2000 (Regulated Activities) Order 2001.

[502]
2 Commencement

(1) Except as provided by paragraph (2), this Order comes into force on the day on which section 19 of the Act comes into force.

(2) This Order comes into force—

(a) for the purposes of articles 59, 60 and 87 (funeral plan contracts) on 1st January 2002; and

(b) for the purposes of articles 61 to 63, 88, 90 and 91 (regulated mortgage contracts) [on such a day as the Treasury may specify].

[(3) Any day specified under paragraph (2)(b) must be caused to be notified in the London, Edinburgh and Belfast Gazettes published not later than one week before that day.]

NOTES

Para (2): words in square brackets substituted by the Financial Services and Markets Act 2000 (Commencement of Mortgage Regulation) (Amendment) Order 2002, SI 2002/1777, art 2(1), (2).

Para (3): added by SI 2002/1777, art 2(1), (3).

[503]
3 Interpretation

(1) In this Order—

"the Act" means the Financial Services and Markets Act 2000;

["agreement provider" has the meaning given by article 63J(3);

"agreement seller" has the meaning given by article 63J(3);]

"annuities on human life" does not include superannuation allowances and annuities payable out of any fund applicable solely to the relief and maintenance of persons engaged, or who have been engaged, in any particular profession, trade or employment, or of the dependants of such persons;

"buying" includes acquiring for valuable consideration;

"close relative" in relation to a person means—

(a) his spouse [or civil partner];

(b) his children and step children, his parents and step-parents, his brothers and sisters and his step-brothers and step-sisters; and

(c) the spouse [or civil partner] of any person within sub-paragraph (b);

["the Commission Regulation" means Commission Regulation 1287/2006 of 10 August 2006;]

"contract of general insurance" means any contract falling within Part I of Schedule 1;

"contract of insurance" means any contract of insurance which is a contract of long-term insurance or a contract of general insurance, and includes—

(a) fidelity bonds, performance bonds, administration bonds, bail bonds, customs bonds or similar contracts of guarantee, where these are—

(i) effected or carried out by a person not carrying on a banking business;

(ii) not effected merely incidentally to some other business carried on by the person effecting them; and

(iii) effected in return for the payment of one or more premiums;

(b) tontines;

(c) capital redemption contracts or pension fund management contracts, where these are effected or carried out by a person who—

(i) does not carry on a banking business; and

(ii) otherwise carries on a regulated activity of the kind specified by article 10(1) or (2);

(d) contracts to pay annuities on human life;

(e) contracts of a kind referred to in article 1(2)(e) of the first life insurance directive (collective insurance etc); and

(f) contracts of a kind referred to in article 1(3) of the first life insurance directive (social insurance);

but does not include a funeral plan contract (or a contract which would be a funeral plan contract but for the exclusion in article 60);

"contract of long-term insurance" means any contract falling within Part II of Schedule 1;

"contractually based investment" means—

(a) rights under a qualifying contract of insurance;

(b) any investment of the kind specified by any of articles 83, 84, 85 and 87; or

(c) any investment of the kind specified by article 89 so far as relevant to an investment falling within (a) or (b);

["credit institution" means—

(a) a credit institution authorised under the banking consolidation directive other than an institution to which Article 2.1 of the markets in financial instruments directive (the text of which is set out in Schedule 3) applies, or

(b) an institution which would satisfy the requirements for authorisation as a credit institution under that directive (other than an institution to which Article 2.1 of the markets in financial instruments directive would apply) if it had its registered office (or if it does not have a registered office, its head office) in an EEA State;]

"deposit" has the meaning given by article 5;

["electronic money" means monetary value, as represented by a claim on the issuer, which is—

(a) stored on an electronic device;

(b) issued on receipt of funds; and

(c) accepted as a means of payment by persons other than the issuer;]

["financial instrument" means any instrument listed in Section C of Annex I to the markets in financial instruments directive (the text of which is set out in Part 1 of Schedule 2) read with Chapter VI of the Commission Regulation (the text of which is set out in Part 2 of Schedule 2);]

"funeral plan contract" has the meaning given by article 59;

["home Member State", in relation to an investment firm, has the meaning given by Article 4.1.20 of the markets in financial instruments directive, and in relation to a credit institution, has the meaning given by Article 4.7 of the banking consolidation directive;]

["home purchase provider" has the meaning given by article 63F(3);

"home purchaser" has the meaning given by article 63F(3);]

"instrument" includes any record whether or not in the form of a document;

["investment firm" means a person whose regular occupation or business is the provision or performance of investment services and activities on a professional basis but does not include—

(a) a person to whom the markets in financial instruments directive does not apply by virtue of Article 2 of that directive (the text of which is set out in Schedule 3);

(b) a person whose home Member State is an EEA State other than the United Kingdom and to whom, by reason of the fact that the State has given effect to Article 3 of that directive, that directive does not apply by virtue of that Article;

(c) a person who does not have a home Member State and to whom (if he had his registered office in an EEA State, or, being a person other than a body corporate or a body corporate not having a registered office, if he had his head office in an EEA State) the markets in financial instruments directive would not apply by virtue of Article 2 of that directive;]

["investment services and activities" means—

(a) any service provided to third parties listed in Section A of Annex I to the markets in financial instruments directive (the text of which is set out in Part 3 of Schedule 2) read with Article 52 of Commission Directive 2006/73/EC of 10 August 2006 (the text of which is set out in Part 4 of Schedule 2), or

(b) any activity listed in Section A of Annex I to that directive,

relating to any financial instrument;]

"joint enterprise" means an enterprise into which two or more persons ("the participators") enter for commercial purposes related to a business or businesses (other than the business of engaging in a regulated activity) carried on by them; and, where a participator is a member of a group, each other member of the group is also to be regarded as a participator in the enterprise;

"local authority" means—

(a) in England and Wales, a local authority within the meaning of the Local Government Act 1972, the Greater London Authority, the Common Council of the City of London or the Council of the Isles of Scilly;
(b) in Scotland, a local authority within the meaning of the Local Government (Scotland) Act 1973;
(c) in Northern Ireland, a district council within the meaning of the Local Government Act (Northern Ireland) 1972;

["management company" has the meaning given by Article 1a.2 of the UCITS directive as amended by Directive 2001/107/EC;]

"managing agent" means a person who is permitted by the Council of Lloyd's in the conduct of his business as an underwriting agent to perform for a member of Lloyd's one or more of the following functions—
(a) underwriting contracts of insurance at Lloyd's;
(b) reinsuring such contracts in whole or in part;
(c) paying claims on such contracts;

["market operator" means a market operator within the meaning of Article 4.1.13 of the markets in financial instruments directive, or a person who would be a market operator if he had his registered office, or if he does not have a registered office his head office, in an EEA State, but does not include—
(a) a person to whom the markets in financial instruments directive does not apply by virtue of Article 2 of that directive (the text of which is set out in Schedule 3);
(b) a person who does not have a home Member State to whom (if he had his registered office, or if he does not have a registered office his head office, in an EEA State) the markets in financial instruments directive would not apply by virtue of Article 2 of that directive;]

["multilateral trading facility" means—
(a) a multilateral trading facility (within the meaning of Article 4.1.15 of the markets in financial instruments directive) operated by an investment firm, a credit institution or a market operator, or
(b) a facility which—
(i) is operated by an investment firm, a credit institution or market operator which does not have a home Member State, and
(ii) if its operator had a home Member State, would be a multilateral trading facility within the meaning of Article 4.1.15 of the markets in financial instruments directive;]

["occupational pension scheme" has the meaning given by section 1 of the Pension Schemes Act 1993 but with paragraph (b) of the definition omitted;]

"overseas person" means a person who—
(a) carries on activities of the kind specified by any of articles 14, 21, 25, [25A,] [25B, 25C,] [25D,] [25E,] 37[, 39A], 40, 45, 51, 52[, 53, 53A [, 53B, 53C, [53D,] 61, 63B *and 63F*]] or, so far as relevant to any of those articles, article 64 (or activities of a kind which would be so specified but for the exclusion in article 72); but
(b) does not carry on any such activities, or offer to do so, from a permanent place of business maintained by him in the United Kingdom;

"pension fund management contract" means a contract to manage the investments of pension funds (other than funds solely for the benefit of the officers or employees of the person effecting or carrying out the contract and their dependants or, in the case of a company, partly for the benefit of officers and employees and their dependants of its subsidiary or holding company or a subsidiary of its holding company); and for the purposes of this definition, "subsidiary" and "holding company" are to be construed in accordance with section 736 of the Companies Act 1985 or article 4 of the Companies (Northern Ireland) Order 1986;

["personal pension scheme" means a scheme or arrangement which is not an occupational pension scheme or a stakeholder pension scheme and which is comprised in one or more instruments or agreements, having or capable of having effect so as to provide benefits to or in respect of people—
(a) on retirement,
(b) on having reached a particular age, or
(c) on termination of service in an employment;]

["plan provider" has the meaning given by paragraph (3) of article 63B, read with paragraphs (7) and (8) of that article;]

"property" includes currency of the United Kingdom or any other country or territory;

"qualifying contract of insurance" means a contract of long-term insurance which is not—

(a) a reinsurance contract; nor

(b) a contract in respect of which the following conditions are met—

(i) the benefits under the contract are payable only on death or in respect of incapacity due to injury, sickness or infirmity;

(ii) . . .

(iii) the contract has no surrender value, or the consideration consists of a single premium and the surrender value does not exceed that premium; and

(iv) the contract makes no provision for its conversion or extension in a manner which would result in it ceasing to comply with any of the above conditions;

["regulated home purchase plan" has the meaning given by article 63F(3);

"regulated home reversion plan" has the meaning given by article 63B(3);]

"regulated mortgage contract" has the meaning given by article 61(3);

["regulated sale and rent back agreement" has the meaning given by article 63J(3);]

["relevant investment" means—

(a) rights under a qualifying contract of insurance;

(b) rights under any other contract of insurance;

(c) any investment of the kind specified by any of articles 83, 84, 85 and 87; or

(d) any investment of the kind specified by article 89 so far as relevant to an investment falling within (a) or (c);]

["reversion seller" has the meaning given by article 63B(3);]

"security" means (except where the context otherwise requires) any investment of the kind specified by any of articles 76 to 82 or, so far as relevant to any such investment, article 89;

"selling", in relation to any investment, includes disposing of the investment for valuable consideration, and for these purposes "disposing" includes—

(a) in the case of an investment consisting of rights under a contract—

(i) surrendering, assigning or converting those rights; or

(ii) assuming the corresponding liabilities under the contract;

(b) in the the corresponding liabilities under the arrangements; and

(c) in the case of any other investment, issuing or creating the investment or granting the rights or interests of which it consists;

"stakeholder pension scheme" has the meaning given by section 1 of the Welfare Reform and Pensions Act 1999 [in relation to Great Britain and has the meaning given by article 3 of the Welfare Reform and Pensions (Northern Ireland) Order 1999 in relation to Northern Ireland];

"syndicate" means one or more persons, to whom a particular syndicate number has been assigned by or under the authority of the Council of Lloyd's, carrying out or effecting contracts of insurance written at Lloyd's;

"voting shares", in relation to a body corporate, means shares carrying voting rights attributable to share capital which are exercisable in all circumstances at any general meeting of that body corporate.

(2) For the purposes of this Order, a transaction is entered into through a person if he enters into it as agent or arranges, in a manner constituting the carrying on of an activity of the kind specified by article 25(1)[, 25A(1), 25B(1) *or 25C(1)*], for it to be entered into by another person as agent or principal.

(3) For the purposes of this Order, a contract of insurance is to be treated as falling within Part II of Schedule 1, notwithstanding the fact that it contains related and subsidiary provisions such that it might also be regarded as falling within Part I of that Schedule, if its principal object is that of a contract falling within Part II and it is effected or carried out by an authorised person who has permission to effect or carry out contracts falling within paragraph I of Part II of Schedule 1.

NOTES

Para (1) is amended as follows:

Definitions "agreement provider", "agreement seller", and "regulated sale and rent back agreement" inserted by the Financial Services and Markets Act 2000 (Regulated Activities) (Amendment) Order 2009, SI 2009/1342, arts 2, 3(1)(a), (b), as from 1 July 2009 (for certain purposes) and as from 30 June 2010 (for remaining purposes) (for the full commencement details and for transitional provisions etc see arts 1, 32–34 of that Order).

Words in square brackets in the definition "close relative" inserted by the Civil Partnership Act 2004 (Amendments to Subordinate Legislation) Order 2005, SI 2005/2114, art 2(16), Sch 16, Pt 1, para 1(1), (2).

Definitions "the Commission Regulation", "credit institution", "financial instrument", "home Member State", "investment firm", "investment services and activities", "management company", "market operator", and "multilateral trading facility" inserted by the Financial Services and Markets Act 2000 (Regulated Activities) (Amendment No 3) Order 2006, SI 2006/3384, arts 2, 3(b).

Definition "electronic money" inserted by the Financial Services and Markets Act 2000 (Regulated Activities) (Amendment) Order 2002, SI 2002/682, art 2.

Definitions "home purchase provider", "home purchaser", "plan provider", "regulated home purchase plan", "regulated home reversion plan", and "reversion seller" inserted by the Financial Services and Markets Act 2000 (Regulated Activities) (Amendment) (No 2) Order 2006, SI 2006/2383, arts 2, 3(1)(a), (c)–(e).

Definition "occupational pension scheme" substituted by the Financial Services and Markets Act 2000 (Regulated Activities) (Amendment) Order 2006, SI 2006/1969, art 2(1), (2)(a).

Definition "overseas person" is amended as follows: figure "25A," in square brackets inserted by the Financial Services and Markets Act 2000 (Regulated Activities) (Amendment) (No 1) Order 2003, SI 2003/1475, art 3(a); figures "25B, 25C," in square brackets inserted by SI 2006/2383, arts 2, 3(1)(b)(i); figure "25D," in square brackets inserted by SI 2006/3384, arts 2, 3(a); figures "25E," and "53D," in square brackets inserted by SI 2009/1342, arts 2, 3(1)(c)(i), (ii), as from the same dates and for the same purposes as noted above; figure ", 39A" in square brackets inserted by SI 2003/1476, arts 2, 3(1)(a); words in square brackets beginning with the figures ", 53, 53A" substituted by SI 2003/1475, art 3(b); words in square brackets beginning with the figures ", 53B, 53C" substituted by SI 2006/2383, arts 2, 3(1)(b)(ii); for the words "and 63F" in italics there are substituted the words ", 63F and 63J" by SI 2009/1342, arts 2, 3(1)(c)(iii), as from the same dates and for the same purposes as noted above.

Definition "personal pension scheme" inserted by SI 2006/1969, art 2(1), (2)(a).

In definition "qualifying contract of insurance" sub-para (b)(ii) revoked by the Financial Services and Markets Act 2000 (Regulated Activities) (Amendment) Order 2007, SI 2007/1339, arts 2, 3.

Definition "relevant investment" inserted by SI 2003/1476, art 3(1)(b).

Words in square brackets in definition "stakeholder pension scheme" added by SI 2005/593, art 2(1), (2)(b).

Para (2): words in square brackets inserted by SI 2006/2383, arts 2, 3(2), subject to transitional provisions in arts 37–39 thereof; for the words in italics there are substituted the words ", 25C(1) or 25E(1)" by SI 2009/1342, arts 2, 3(2), as from the same dates and for the same purposes as noted above.

Commission Regulation 1287/2006: OJ L241, 2.9.2006, p 1.
Commission Directive 2006/73/EC: OJ L241, 2.9.2006, p 26.
Directive 2001/107/EC: OJ L41, 13.2.2002, p 20.

PART II
SPECIFIED ACTIVITIES

CHAPTER I
GENERAL

[504]

4 Specified activities: general

(1) The following provisions of this Part specify kinds of activity for the purposes of section 22 of the Act (and accordingly any activity of one of those kinds, which is carried on by way of business, and relates to an investment of a kind specified by any provision of Part III and applicable to that activity, is a regulated activity for the purposes of the Act).

(2) The kinds of activity specified by articles [51, 52 and 63N] are also specified for the purposes of section 22(1)(b) of the Act (and accordingly any activity of one of those kinds, when carried on by way of business, is a regulated activity when carried on in relation to property of any kind).

(3) Subject to paragraph (4), each provision specifying a kind of activity is subject to the exclusions applicable to that provision (and accordingly any reference in this Order to an activity of the kind specified by a particular provision is to be read subject to any such exclusions).

[(4) Where an investment firm or credit institution—

(a) provides or performs investment services and activities on a professional basis, and

(b) in doing so would be treated as carrying on an activity of a kind specified by a provision of this Part but for an exclusion in any of articles 15, 16, 19, 22, 23, 29, 38, 67, 68, 69, 70 and 72E,

that exclusion is to be disregarded and, accordingly, the investment firm or credit institution is to be treated as carrying on an activity of the kind specified by the provision in question.]

[(4A) Where a person, other than a person specified by Article 1.2 of the insurance mediation directive (the text of which is set out in Part 1 of Schedule 4)—

(a) for remuneration, takes up or pursues insurance mediation or reinsurance mediation in relation to a risk or commitment located in an EEA State, and

(b) in doing so would be treated as carrying on an activity of a kind specified by a provision of this Part but for an exclusion in any of articles 30, 66 and 67,

that exclusion is to be disregarded (and accordingly that person is to be treated as carrying on an activity of the kind specified by the provision in question).]

(5) In this article—

. . .

["insurance mediation" has the meaning given by Article 2.3 of the insurance mediation directive, the text of which is set out in Part II of Schedule 4;]

. . .

["reinsurance mediation" has the meaning given by Article 2.4 of the insurance mediation directive, the text of which is set out in Part III of Schedule 4.]

NOTES

Para (2): words in square brackets substituted by the Financial Services and Markets Act 2000 (Regulated Activities) (Amendment) (No 2) Order 2009, SI 2009/1389, arts 2, 3.

Para (4): substituted by the Financial Services and Markets Act 2000 (Regulated Activities) (Amendment No 3) Order 2006, SI 2006/3384, arts 2, 4(a).

Para (4A): inserted by the Financial Services and Markets Act 2000 (Regulated Activities) (Amendment) (No 2) Order 2003, SI 2003/1476, arts 2, 3(2)(a).

Para (5): definitions "core investment service" and "investment firm" (omitted) revoked by SI 2006/3384, arts 2, 4(b); definitions "insurance mediation" and "reinsurance mediation" inserted by SI 2003/1476, arts 2, 3(2)(b).

5–9L *((Chs II, IIA) outside the scope of this work.)*

CHAPTER III
INSURANCE

The activities

[505]

10 Effecting and carrying out contracts of insurance

(1) Effecting a contract of insurance as principal is a specified kind of activity.

(2) Carrying out a contract of insurance as principal is a specified kind of activity.

Exclusions

[506]

11 Community co-insurers

(1) There is excluded from article 10(1) or (2) the effecting or carrying out of a contract of insurance by an EEA firm falling within paragraph 5(d) of Schedule 3 to the Act—

(a) other than through a branch in the United Kingdom; and

(b) pursuant to a Community co-insurance operation in which the firm is participating otherwise than as the leading insurer.

(2) In paragraph (1), "Community co-insurance operation" and "leading insurer" have the same meaning as in the Council Directive of 30 May 1978 on the co-ordination of laws, regulations and administrative provisions relating to Community co-insurance (No 78/473/EEC).

NOTES

Council Directive 78/473/EEC: OJ L151, 7.6.1978, p 25.

[507]

12 Breakdown insurance

(1) There is excluded from article 10(1) or (2) the effecting or carrying out, by a person who does not otherwise carry on an activity of the kind specified by that article, of a contract of insurance which—

(a) is a contract under which the benefits provided by that person ("the provider") are exclusively or primarily benefits in kind in the event of accident to or breakdown of a vehicle; and

(b) contains the terms mentioned in paragraph (2).

(2) Those terms are that—

(a) the assistance takes either or both of the forms mentioned in paragraph (3)(a) and (b);

(b) the assistance is not available outside the United Kingdom and the Republic of Ireland except where it is provided without the payment of additional premium by a person in the country concerned with whom the provider has entered into a reciprocal agreement; and

(c) assistance provided in the case of an accident or breakdown occurring in the United Kingdom or the Republic of Ireland is, in most circumstances, provided by the provider's servants.

(3) The forms of assistance are—

(a) repairs to the relevant vehicle at the place where the accident or breakdown has occurred; this assistance may also include the delivery of parts, fuel, oil, water or keys to the relevant vehicle;

(b) removal of the relevant vehicle to the nearest or most appropriate place at which repairs may be carried out, or to—

(i) the home, point of departure or original destination within the United Kingdom of the driver and passengers, provided the accident or breakdown occurred within the United Kingdom;

(ii) the home, point of departure or original destination within the Republic of Ireland of the driver and passengers, provided the accident or breakdown occurred within the Republic of Ireland or within Northern Ireland;

(iii) the home, point of departure or original destination within Northern Ireland of the driver and passengers, provided the accident or breakdown occurred within the Republic of Ireland;

and this form of assistance may include the conveyance of the driver or passengers of the relevant vehicle, with the vehicle, or (where the vehicle is to be conveyed only to the nearest or most appropriate place at which repairs may be carried out) separately, to the nearest location from which they may continue their journey by other means.

(4) A contract does not fail to meet the condition in paragraph (1)(a) solely because the provider may reimburse the person entitled to the assistance for all or part of any sums paid by him in respect of assistance either because he failed to identify himself as a person entitled to the assistance or because he was unable to get in touch with the provider in order to claim the assistance.

(5) In this article—

"the assistance" means the benefits to be provided under a contract of the kind mentioned in paragraph (1);

"breakdown" means an event—

(a) which causes the driver of the relevant vehicle to be unable to start a journey in the vehicle or involuntarily to bring the vehicle to a halt on a journey because of some malfunction of the vehicle or failure of it to function, and

(b) after which the journey cannot reasonably be commenced or continued in the relevant vehicle;

"the relevant vehicle" means the vehicle (including a trailer or caravan) in respect of which the assistance is required.

[508]
[12A Information society services

Article 10 is subject to the exclusion in article 72A (information society services), as qualified by paragraph (2) of that article.]

NOTES

Inserted by the Financial Services and Markets Act 2000 (Regulated Activities) (Amendment) (No 2) Order 2002, SI 2002/1776, art 3(1), (3).

Supplemental

[509]
13 Application of sections 327 and 332 of the Act to insurance market activities

(1) In sections 327(5) and (7) and 332(3)(b) of the Act (exemption from the general prohibition for members of the professions, and rules in relation to such persons), the references to "a regulated activity" and "regulated activities" do not include—

(a) any activity of the kind specified by article 10(1) or (2), where—

(i) P is a member of the Society; and

(ii) by virtue of section 316 of the Act (application of the Act to Lloyd's underwriting), the general prohibition does not apply to the carrying on by P of that activity; or

(b) any activity of the kind specified by article 10(2), where—

(i) P is a former underwriting member; and

(ii) the contract of insurance in question is one underwritten by P at Lloyd's.

(2) In paragraph (1)—

"member of the Society" has the same meaning as in Lloyd's Act 1982; and

"former underwriting member" has the meaning given by section 324(1) of the Act.

CHAPTER IV
DEALING IN INVESTMENTS AS PRINCIPAL

The activity

[510]

14 Dealing in investments as principal

[(1)] Buying, selling, subscribing for or underwriting securities or contractually based investments (other than investments of the kind specified by article 87, or article 89 so far as relevant to that article) as principal is a specified kind of activity.

[(2) Paragraph (1) does not apply to a kind of activity to which article 25D applies.]

NOTES

Para (1): numbered as such by the Financial Services and Markets Act 2000 (Regulated Activities) (Amendment No 3) Order 2006, SI 2006/3384, arts 2, 5(a).

Para (2): added by SI 2006/3384, arts 2, 5(b).

Exclusions

[511]

15 Absence of holding out etc

(1) Subject to paragraph (3), a person ("A") does not carry on an activity of the kind specified by article 14 by entering into a transaction which relates to a security or is the assignment (or, in Scotland, the assignation) of a qualifying contract of insurance (or an investment of the kind specified by article 89, so far as relevant to such a contract), unless—

- (a) A holds himself out as willing, as principal, to buy, sell or subscribe for investments of the kind to which the transaction relates at prices determined by him generally and continuously rather than in respect of each particular transaction;
- (b) A holds himself out as engaging in the business of buying investments of the kind to which the transaction relates, with a view to selling them;
- (c) A holds himself out as engaging in the business of underwriting investments of the kind to which the transaction relates; or
- (d) A regularly solicits members of the public with the purpose of inducing them, as principals or agents, to enter into transactions constituting activities of the kind specified by article 14, and the transaction is entered into as a result of his having solicited members of the public in that manner.

(2) In paragraph (1)(d), "members of the public" means any persons other than—

- (a) authorised persons or persons who are exempt persons in relation to activities of the kind specified by article 14;
- (b) members of the same group as A;
- (c) persons who are or who propose to become participators with A in a joint enterprise;
- (d) any person who is solicited by A with a view to the acquisition by A of 20 per cent or more of the voting shares in a body corporate;
- (e) if A (either alone or with members of the same group as himself) holds more than 20 per cent of the voting shares in a body corporate, any person who is solicited by A with a view to—
  - (i) the acquisition by A of further shares in the body corporate; or
  - (ii) the disposal by A of shares in the body corporate to the person solicited or to a member of the same group as the person solicited;
- (f) any person who—
  - (i) is solicited by A with a view to the disposal by A of shares in a body corporate to the person solicited or to a member of the same group as that person; and
  - (ii) either alone or with members of the same group holds 20 per cent or more of the voting shares in the body corporate;
- (g) any person whose head office is outside the United Kingdom, who is solicited by an approach made or directed to him at a place outside the United Kingdom and whose ordinary business involves him in carrying on activities of the kind specified by any of articles 14, 21, 25, 37, 40, 45, 51, 52 and 53 or (so far as relevant to any of those articles) article 64, or would do so apart from any exclusion from any of those articles made by this Order.

(3) This article does not apply where A enters into the transaction as bare trustee or, in Scotland, as nominee for another person and is acting on that other person's instructions (but the exclusion in article 66(1) applies if the conditions set out there are met).

[(4) This article is subject to article 4(4).]

NOTES

Para (4): added by the Financial Services and Markets Act 2000 (Regulated Activities) (Amendment No 3) Order 2006, SI 2006/3384, arts 2, 6.

[512]

16 Dealing in contractually based investments

[(1)] A person who is not an authorised person does not carry on an activity of the kind specified by article 14 by entering into a transaction relating to a contractually based investment—

(a) with or through an authorised person, or an exempt person acting in the course of a business comprising a regulated activity in relation to which he is exempt; or

(b) through an office outside the United Kingdom maintained by a party to the transaction, and with or through a person whose head office is situated outside the United Kingdom and whose ordinary business involves him in carrying on activities of the kind specified by any of articles 14, 21, 25, 37, 40, 45, 51, 52 and 53 or, so far as relevant to any of those articles, article 64 (or would do so apart from any exclusion from any of those articles made by this Order).

[(2) This article is subject to article 4(4).]

NOTES

Para (1): numbered as such by the Financial Services and Markets Act 2000 (Regulated Activities) (Amendment No 3) Order 2006, SI 2006/3384, arts 2, 7(a).

Para (2): added by SI 2006/3384, arts 2, 7(b).

[513]

17 Acceptance of instruments creating or acknowledging indebtedness

(1) A person does not carry on an activity of the kind specified by article 14 by accepting an instrument creating or acknowledging indebtedness in respect of any loan, credit, guarantee or other similar financial accommodation or assurance which he has made, granted or provided.

(2) The reference in paragraph (1) to a person accepting an instrument includes a reference to a person becoming a party to an instrument otherwise than as a debtor or a surety.

NOTES

Modification: this article is applied, with modifications, to eligible debt securities, by the Uncertificated Securities (Amendment) (Eligible Debt Securities) Regulations 2003, SI 2003/1633, reg 15, Sch 2, paras 8(1), (2)(w), 9.

[514]

18 Issue by a company of its own shares etc

(1) There is excluded from article 14 the issue by a company of its own shares or share warrants, and the issue by any person of his own debentures or debenture warrants.

(2) In this article—

(a) "company" means any body corporate other than an open-ended investment company;

(b) "shares" and "debentures" include any investment of the kind specified by article 76[, 77 or 77A];

(c) "share warrants" and "debenture warrants" mean any investment of the kind specified by article 79 which relates to shares in the company concerned or, as the case may be, debentures issued by [the person concerned].

NOTES

Para (2): words in square brackets in sub-para (b) substituted by the Financial Services and Markets Act 2000 (Regulated Activities) (Amendment) Order 2010, SI 2010/86, art 4, Schedule, para 5(a); words in square brackets in sub-para (c) substituted by the Financial Services and Markets Act 2000 (Regulated Activities) (Amendment) Order 2001, SI 2001/3544, arts 2, 4.

[515]

[18A Dealing by a company in its own shares

(1) A company does not carry on an activity of the kind specified by article 14 by purchasing its own shares where section 162A of the Companies Act 1985 (Treasury shares) applies to the shares purchased.

(2) A company does not carry on an activity of the kind specified by article 14 by dealing in its own shares held as treasury shares, in accordance with section 162D of that Act (Treasury shares: disposal and cancellation).

(3) In this article "shares held as treasury shares" has the same meaning as in that Act.]

NOTES

Inserted by the Financial Services and Markets Act 2000 (Regulated Activities) (Amendment) (No 3) Order 2003, SI 2003/2822, arts 2, 3.

[516]

19 Risk management

(1) A person ("B") does not carry on an activity of the kind specified by article 14 by entering as principal into a transaction with another person ("C") if—

(a) the transaction relates to investments of the kind specified by any of articles 83 to 85 (or article 89 so far as relevant to any of those articles);

(b) neither B nor C is an individual;

(c) the sole or main purpose for which B enters into the transaction (either by itself or in combination with other such transactions) is that of limiting the extent to which a relevant business will be affected by any identifiable risk arising otherwise than as a result of the carrying on of a regulated activity; and

(d) the relevant business consists mainly of activities other than—

(i) regulated activities; or

(ii) activities which would be regulated activities but for any exclusion made by this Part.

(2) In paragraph (1), "relevant business" means a business carried on by—

(a) B;

(b) a member of the same group as B; or

(c) where B and another person are, or propose to become, participators in a joint enterprise, that other person.

[(3) This article is subject to article 4(4).]

NOTES

Para (3): added by the Financial Services and Markets Act 2000 (Regulated Activities) (Amendment No 3) Order 2006, SI 2006/3384, arts 2, 8.

[517]

20 Other exclusions

Article 14 is also subject to the exclusions in articles 66 (trustees etc), 68 (sale of goods and supply of services), 69 (groups and joint enterprises), 70 (sale of body corporate), 71 (employee share schemes)[, 72 (overseas persons) and 72A (information society services)].

NOTES

Words in square brackets substituted by the Financial Services and Markets Act 2000 (Regulated Activities) (Amendment) (No 2) Order 2002, SI 2002/1776, art 3(1), (4).

CHAPTER V
DEALING IN INVESTMENTS AS AGENT

The activity

[518]

21 Dealing in investments as agent

[(1)] Buying, selling, subscribing for or underwriting securities or [relevant investments] (other than investments of the kind specified by article 87, or article 89 so far as relevant to that article) as agent is a specified kind of activity.

[(2) Paragraph (1) does not apply to a kind of activity to which article 25D applies.]

NOTES

Para (1): numbered as such by the Financial Services and Markets Act 2000 (Regulated Activities) (Amendment No 3) Order 2006, SI 2006/3384, arts 2, 9(a); words in square brackets substituted by the Financial Services and Markets Act 2000 (Regulated Activities) (Amendment) (No 2) Order 2003, SI 2003/1476, arts 2, 4(1).

Para (2): added by SI 2006/3384, arts 2, 9(b).

Exclusions

[519]

22 Deals with or through authorised persons

(1) A person who is not an authorised person does not carry on an activity of the kind specified by article 21 by entering into a transaction as agent for another person ("the client") with or through an authorised person if—

(a) the transaction is entered into on advice given to the client by an authorised person; or

(b) it is clear, in all the circumstances, that the client, in his capacity as an investor, is not seeking and has not sought advice from the agent as to the merits of the client's entering into the transaction (or, if the client has sought such advice, the agent has declined to give it but has recommended that the client seek such advice from an authorised person).

[(2) But the exclusion in paragraph (1) does not apply if—

(a) the transaction relates to a contract of insurance; or

(b) the agent receives from any person other than the client any pecuniary reward or other advantage, for which he does not account to the client, arising out of his entering into the transaction.]

[(3) This article is subject to article 4(4).]

NOTES

Para (2): substituted by the Financial Services and Markets Act 2000 (Regulated Activities) (Amendment) (No 2) Order 2003, SI 2003/1476, arts 2, 4(2).

Para (3): added by the Financial Services and Markets Act 2000 (Regulated Activities) (Amendment No 3) Order 2006, SI 2006/3384, arts 2, 10.

[520]

23 Risk management

(1) A person ("B") does not carry on an activity of the kind specified by article 21 by entering as agent for a relevant person into a transaction with another person ("C") if—

(a) the transaction relates to investments of the kind specified by any of articles 83 to 85 (or article 89 so far as relevant to any of those articles);

(b) neither B nor C is an individual;

(c) the sole or main purpose for which B enters into the transaction (either by itself or in combination with other such transactions) is that of limiting the extent to which a relevant business will be affected by any identifiable risk arising otherwise than as a result of the carrying on of a regulated activity; and

(d) the relevant business consists mainly of activities other than—

(i) regulated activities; or

(ii) activities which would be regulated activities but for any exclusion made by this Part.

(2) In paragraph (1), "relevant person" means—

(a) a member of the same group as B; or

(b) where B and another person are, or propose to become, participators in a joint enterprise, that other person;

and "relevant business" means a business carried on by a relevant person.

[(3) This article is subject to article 4(4).]

NOTES

Para (3): added by the Financial Services and Markets Act 2000 (Regulated Activities) (Amendment No 3) Order 2006, SI 2006/3384, arts 2, 11.

[521]

24 Other exclusions

Article 21 is also subject to the exclusions in articles 67 (profession or non-investment business), 68 (sale of goods and supply of services), 69 (groups and joint enterprises), 70 (sale of body corporate), 71 (employee share schemes)[, 72 (overseas persons)[, 72A (information society services), 72B (activities carried on by a provider of relevant goods or services) and 72D (large risks contracts where risk situated outside the EEA)]].

NOTES

Words in first (outer) pair of square brackets substituted by the Financial Services and Markets Act 2000 (Regulated Activities) (Amendment) (No 2) Order 2002, SI 2002/1776, art 3(1), (5); words in second (inner) pair of square brackets substituted by the Financial Services and Markets Act 2000 (Regulated Activities) (Amendment) (No 2) Order 2003, SI 2003/1476, arts 2, 4(3).

CHAPTER VI
ARRANGING DEALS IN INVESTMENTS

The activities

[522]
25 Arranging deals in investments

(1) Making arrangements for another person (whether as principal or agent) to buy, sell, subscribe for or underwrite a particular investment which is—

(a) a security,
(b) a [relevant investment], or
(c) an investment of the kind specified by article 86, or article 89 so far as relevant to that article,

is a specified kind of activity.

(2) Making arrangements with a view to a person who participates in the arrangements buying, selling, subscribing for or underwriting investments falling within paragraph (1)(a), (b) or (c) (whether as principal or agent) is also a specified kind of activity.

[(3) Paragraphs (1) and (2) do not apply to a kind of activity to which article 25D applies.]

NOTES

Para (1): words in square brackets substituted by the Financial Services and Markets Act 2000 (Regulated Activities) (Amendment) (No 2) Order 2003, SI 2003/1476, arts 2, 5(1).

Para (3): added by the Financial Services and Markets Act 2000 (Regulated Activities) (Amendment No 3) Order 2006, SI 2006/3384, arts 2, 12.

[523]
[25A Regulated mortgage contracts

(1) Making arrangements—

(a) for another person to enter into a regulated mortgage contract as borrower; or
(b) for another person to vary the terms of a regulated mortgage contract entered into by him as borrower after the coming into force of article 61, in such a way as to vary his obligations under that contract,

is a specified kind of activity.

(2) Making arrangements with a view to a person who participates in the arrangements entering into a regulated mortgage contract as borrower is also a specified kind of activity.

(3) In this article "borrower" has the meaning given by article 61(3)(a)(i).]

NOTES

Inserted by the Financial Services and Markets Act 2000 (Regulated Activities) (Amendment) (No 1) Order 2003, SI 2003/1475, art 4.

25B, 25C *(Outside the scope of this work.)*

[523A]
[25D Operating a multilateral trading facility

(1) The operation of a multilateral trading facility on which MiFID instruments are traded is a specified kind of activity.

(2) In paragraph (1), "MiFID instrument" means any investment—

(a) of the kind specified by article 76, 77, [77A,] 78, 79, 80, 81, 83, 84 or 85; or
(b) of the kind specified by article 89 so far as relevant to an investment falling within sub-paragraph (a),

that is a financial instrument.]

NOTES

Commencement: 1 April 2007 (certain purposes); 1 November 2007 (remaining purposes).

Inserted by the Financial Services and Markets Act 2000 (Regulated Activities) (Amendment No 3) Order 2006, SI 2006/3384, arts 2, 13.

Para (2): reference in square brackets inserted by the Financial Services and Markets Act 2000 (Regulated Activities) (Amendment) Order 2010, SI 2010/86, art 4, Schedule, para 5(b).

25E *(Outside the scope of this work.)*

Exclusions

[524]
26 Arrangements not causing a deal

There are excluded from [articles 25(1), 25A(1), 25B(1) *and 25C(1)*] arrangements which do not or would not bring about the transaction to which the arrangements relate.

NOTES

Words in square brackets substituted by the Financial Services and Markets Act 2000 (Regulated Activities) (Amendment) (No 2) Order 2006, SI 2006/2383, arts 2, 5, subject to transitional provisions in arts 37–39 thereof; for the words in italics there are substituted the words ", 25C(1) and 25E(1)" by the Financial Services and Markets Act 2000 (Regulated Activities) (Amendment) Order 2009, SI 2009/1342, arts 2, 5, as from 1 July 2009 (for certain purposes) and as from 30 June 2010 (for remaining purposes) (for the full commencement details and for transitional provisions etc see arts 1, 32–34 of that Order).

[525]

27 Enabling parties to communicate

A person does not carry on an activity of the kind specified by [article 25(2), 25A(2), 25B(2) *or 25C(2)*] merely by providing means by which one party to a transaction (or potential transaction) is able to communicate with other such parties.

NOTES

Words in square brackets substituted by the Financial Services and Markets Act 2000 (Regulated Activities) (Amendment) (No 2) Order 2006, SI 2006/2383, arts 2, 6, subject to transitional provisions in arts 37–39 thereof; for the words in italics there are substituted the words ", 25C(2) or 25E(2)" by the Financial Services and Markets Act 2000 (Regulated Activities) (Amendment) Order 2009, SI 2009/1342, arts 2, 6, as from 1 July 2009 (for certain purposes) and as from 30 June 2010 (for remaining purposes) (for the full commencement details and for transitional provisions etc see arts 1, 32–34 of that Order).

[526]

28 Arranging transactions to which the arranger is a party

(1) There are excluded from article 25(1) any arrangements for a transaction into which the person making the arrangements enters or is to enter as principal or as agent for some other person.

(2) There are excluded from article 25(2) any arrangements which a person makes with a view to transactions into which he enters or is to enter as principal or as agent for some other person.

[(3) But the exclusions in paragraphs (1) and (2) do not apply to arrangements made for or with a view to a transaction which relates to a contract of insurance, unless the person making the arrangements either—

(a) is the only policyholder; or

(b) as a result of the transaction, would become the only policyholder.]

NOTES

Para (3): added by the Financial Services and Markets Act 2000 (Regulated Activities) (Amendment) (No 2) Order 2003, SI 2003/1476, arts 2, 5(2).

[527]

[28A Arranging contracts [*or plans*] to which the arranger is a party

(1) There are excluded from [articles 25A(1), 25B(1) *and 25C(1)*] any arrangements—

(a) for a [contract *or plan*] into which the person making the arrangements enters or is to enter; or

(b) for a variation of a [contract *or plan*] to which that person is (or is to become) a party.

(2) There are excluded [articles 25A(2), 25B(2) *and 25C(2)*] any arrangements which a person makes with a view to contracts *[or plans]* into which he enters or is to enter.]

NOTES

Inserted by the Financial Services and Markets Act 2000 (Regulated Activities) (Amendment) (No 1) Order 2003, SI 2003/1475, art 7.

Article heading: words in square brackets inserted by the Financial Services and Markets Act 2000 (Regulated Activities) (Amendment) (No 2) Order 2006, SI 2006/2383, arts 2, 7(1), subject to transitional provisions in arts 37–39 thereof; for the words in italics there are substituted the words ", plans or agreements" by the Financial Services and Markets Act 2000 (Regulated Activities) (Amendment) Order 2009, SI 2009/1342, arts 2, 7(1), as from 1 July 2009 (for certain purposes) and as from 30 June 2010 (for remaining purposes) (for the full commencement details and for transitional provisions etc see arts 1, 32–34 of that Order).

Para (1): words in square brackets substituted by SI 2006/2383, art 7(2)(a), subject to transitional provisions in arts 37–39 thereof; for the first words in italics there are substituted the words ", 25C(1) and 25E(1)", and for the second and third words in italics there are substituted the words ", plan or agreement", by SI 2009/1342, arts 2, 7(2)(a), as from the same dates and for the same purposes as noted above.

Para (2): words in first pair of square brackets substituted and words in second pair of square brackets inserted by SI 2006/2383, art 7(2)(b), subject to transitional provisions in arts 37–39 thereof; for the first words in italics there are substituted the words ", 25C(2) and 25E(2)", and for the second words in italics there are substituted the words ", plans or agreements", by SI 2009/1342, arts 2, 7(2)(b), as from the same dates and for the same purposes as noted above.

[528]

29 Arranging deals with or through authorised persons

(1) There are excluded from [articles 25(1) and (2), 25A(1) and (2), 25B(1) and (2) *and 25C(1) and (2)*] arrangements made by a person ("A") who is not an authorised person for or with a view to a transaction which is or is to be entered into by a person ("the client") with or though an authorised person if—

(a) the transaction is or is to be entered into on advice to the client by an authorised person; or

(b) it is clear, in all the circumstances, that the client, in his capacity as an [*investor, borrower, reversion seller, plan provider or (as the case may be) home purchaser*], is not seeking and has not sought advice from A as to the merits of the client's entering into the transaction (or, if the client has sought such advice, A has declined to give it but has recommended that the client seek such advice from an authorised person).

[(2) But the exclusion in paragraph (1) does not apply if—

(a) the transaction relates, or would relate, to a contract of insurance; or

(b) A receives from any person other than the client any pecuniary reward or other advantage, for which he does not account to the client, arising out of his making the arrangements.]

[(3) This article is subject to article 4(4).]

NOTES

Para (1): words in square brackets substituted by the Financial Services and Markets Act 2000 (Regulated Activities) (Amendment) (No 2) Order 2006, SI 2006/2383, arts 2, 8, subject to transitional provisions in arts 37–39 thereof; for the first words in italics there are substituted the words ", 25C(1) and (2) and 25E(1) and (2)", and for the second words in italics there are substituted the words "investor, borrower, reversion seller, plan provider, home purchaser, agreement provider or (as the case may be) agreement seller", by the Financial Services and Markets Act 2000 (Regulated Activities) (Amendment) Order 2009, SI 2009/1342, arts 2, 8, as from 1 July 2009 (for certain purposes) and as from 30 June 2010 (for remaining purposes) (for the full commencement details and for transitional provisions etc see arts 1, 32–34 of that Order).

Para (2): substituted by the Financial Services and Markets Act 2000 (Regulated Activities) (Amendment) (No 2) Order 2003, SI 2003/1476, arts 2, 5(3).

Para (3): added by the Financial Services and Markets Act 2000 (Regulated Activities) (Amendment No 3) Order 2006, SI 2006/3384, arts 2, 14.

[529]

[29A Arrangements made in the course of administration by authorised person

[(1)] A person who is not an authorised person ("A") does not carry on an activity of the kind specified by article 25A(1)(b) as a result of—

(a) anything done by an authorised person ("B") in relation to a regulated mortgage contract which B is administering pursuant to an arrangement of the kind mentioned in article 62(a); or

(b) anything A does in connection with the administration of a regulated mortgage contract in circumstances falling within article 62(b).

[(2) A person who is not an authorised person ("A") does not carry on an activity of the kind specified by article 25B(1)(b) as a result of—

(a) anything done by an authorised person ("B") in relation to a regulated home reversion plan which B is administering pursuant to an arrangement of the kind mentioned in article 63C(a); or

(b) anything A does in connection with the administration of a regulated home reversion plan in circumstances falling within article 63C(b).

(3) A person who is not an authorised person ("A") does not carry on an activity of the kind specified by article 25C(1)(b) as a result of—

(a) anything done by an authorised person ("B") in relation to a regulated home purchase plan which B is administering pursuant to an arrangement of the kind mentioned in article 63G(a); or

(b) anything A does in connection with the administration of a regulated home purchase plan in circumstances falling within article 63G(b).]]

[(4) A person who is not an authorised person ("A") does not carry on an activity of the kind specified by article 25E(1)(b) as a result of—

(a) anything done by an authorised person ("B") in relation to a regulated sale and rent back agreement which B is administering pursuant to an arrangement of the kind mentioned in article 63K(a); or

(b) anything A does in connection with the administration of a regulated sale and rent back agreement in circumstances falling within article 63K(b).]

NOTES

Inserted by the Financial Services and Markets Act 2000 (Regulated Activities) (Amendment) (No 1) Order 2003, SI 2003/1475, art 9.

Para (1): numbered as such by the Financial Services and Markets Act 2000 (Regulated Activities) (Amendment) (No 2) Order 2006, SI 2006/2383, arts 2, 9(a), subject to transitional provisions in arts 37–39 thereof.

Paras (2), (3): added by SI 2006/2383, arts 2, 9(b), subject to transitional provisions in arts 37–39 thereof.

Para (4): added by the Financial Services and Markets Act 2000 (Regulated Activities) (Amendment) Order 2009, SI 2009/1342, arts 2, 9, as from 1 July 2009 (for certain purposes) and as from 30 June 2010 (for remaining purposes) (for the full commencement details and for transitional provisions etc see arts 1, 32–34 of that Order).

[530]

30 Arranging transactions in connection with lending on the security of insurance policies

(1) There are excluded from article 25(1) and (2) arrangements made by a money-lender under which either—

[(a) a relevant authorised person or a person acting on his behalf will introduce to the money-lender persons with whom the relevant authorised person has entered, or proposes to enter, into a relevant transaction, or will advise such persons to approach the money-lender, with a view to the money-lender lending money on the security of any contract effected pursuant to a relevant transaction;]

(b) a relevant authorised person gives an assurance to the money-lender as to the amount which, on the security of any contract effected pursuant to a relevant transaction, will or may be received by the money-lender should the money-lender lend money to a person introduced to him pursuant to the arrangements.

(2) In paragraph (1)—

"money-lender" means a person who is—

(a) a money-lending company within the meaning of section 338 of the Companies Act 1985;

(b) a body corporate incorporated under the law of, or of any part of, the United Kingdom relating to building societies; or

(c) a person whose ordinary business includes the making of loans or the giving of guarantees in connection with loans;

"relevant authorised person" means an authorised person who has permission to effect [contracts of insurance] or to sell investments of the kind specified by article 89, so far as relevant to such contracts;

"relevant transaction" means the effecting of a [contract of insurance] or the sale of an investment of the kind specified by article 89, so far as relevant to such contracts.

[(3) This article is subject to article 4(4A).]

NOTES

Para (1): sub-para (a) substituted by the Financial Services and Markets Act 2000 (Regulated Activities) (Amendment) Order 2001, SI 2001/3544, arts 2, 5.

Para (2): words in square brackets substituted by the Financial Services and Markets Act 2000 (Regulated Activities) (Amendment) (No 2) Order 2003, SI 2003/1476, arts 2, 5(4).

Para (3): added by the Financial Services and Markets Act 2000 (Regulated Activities) (Amendment No 3) Order 2006, SI 2006/3384, arts 2, 15.

[531]

31 Arranging the acceptance of debentures in connection with loans

(1) There are excluded from article 25(1) and (2) arrangements under which a person accepts or is to accept, whether as principal or agent, an instrument creating or acknowledging indebtedness in respect of any loan, credit, guarantee or other similar financial accommodation or assurance which is, or is to be, made, granted or provided by that person or his principal.

(2) The reference in paragraph (1) to a person accepting an instrument includes a reference to a person becoming a party to an instrument otherwise than as a debtor or a surety.

NOTES

Modification: this article is applied, with modifications, to eligible debt securities, by the Uncertificated Securities (Amendment) (Eligible Debt Securities) Regulations 2003, SI 2003/1633, reg 15, Sch 2, paras 8(1), (2)(w), 9.

[532]
32 Provision of finance

There are excluded from article 25(2) arrangements having as their sole purpose the provision of finance to enable a person to buy, sell, subscribe for or underwrite investments.

[533]
33 Introducing

There are excluded from [articles 25(2), 25A(2), 25B(2) *and 25C(2)*] arrangements where—

(a) they are arrangements under which persons ("clients") will be introduced to another person;

(b) the person to whom introductions are to be made is—

(i) an authorised person;

(ii) an exempt person acting in the course of a business comprising a regulated activity in relation to which he is exempt; or

(iii) a person who is not unlawfully carrying on regulated activities in the United Kingdom and whose ordinary business involves him in engaging in an activity of the kind specified by any of articles 14, 21, 25, [25A,] [25B, 25C,] [25E,] 37[, 39A], 40, 45, 51, [52, 53[, 53A, 53B *and 53C*]] (or, so far as relevant to any of those articles, article 64), or would do so apart from any exclusion from any of those articles made by this Order; . . .

(c) the introduction is made with a view to the provision of independent advice or the independent exercise of discretion in relation to investments generally or in relation to any class of investments to which the arrangements relate[; and

(d) the arrangements are made with a view to a person entering into a transaction which does not relate to a contract of insurance.]

NOTES

Words in first pair of square brackets and reference in seventh (inner) pair of square brackets substituted, and reference in third pair of square brackets inserted by the Financial Services and Markets Act 2000 (Regulated Activities) (Amendment) (No 2) Order 2006, SI 2006/2383, arts 2, 10, subject to transitional provisions in arts 37–39 thereof; for the first and second words in italics there are substituted the words ", 25C(2) and 25E(2)" and ", 53C and 53D" respectively, and figure in fourth pair of square brackets inserted by the Financial Services and Markets Act 2000 (Regulated Activities) (Amendment) Order 2009, SI 2009/1342, arts 2, 10, as from 1 July 2009 (for certain purposes) and as from 30 June 2010 (for remaining purposes) (for the full commencement details and for transitional provisions etc see arts 1, 32–34 of that Order); reference in second pair of square brackets inserted and words in sixth (outer) pair of square brackets substituted by the Financial Services and Markets Act 2000 (Regulated Activities) (Amendment) (No 1) Order 2003, SI 2003/1475, art 10; reference in fifth pair of square brackets inserted, word omitted from sub-para (b)(iii) revoked and sub-para (d) and word immediately preceding it added by the Financial Services and Markets Act 2000 (Regulated Activities) (Amendment) (No 2) Order 2003, SI 2003/1476, arts 2, 5(5).

[534]
[33A Introducing to authorised persons etc

(1) There are excluded from article 25A(2) arrangements where—

(a) they are arrangements under which a client is introduced to a person ("N") who is—

(i) an authorised person who has permission to carry on a regulated activity of the kind specified by any of articles 25A, 53A, and 61(1),

(ii) an appointed representative who may carry on a regulated activity of the kind specified by either of articles 25A and 53A without contravening the general prohibition, or

(iii) an overseas person who carries on activities specified by any of articles 25A, 53A and 61(1); and

(b) the conditions mentioned in paragraph (2) are satisfied.

[(1A) There are excluded from article 25B(2) arrangements where—

(a) they are arrangements under which a client is introduced to a person ("N") who is—

(i) an authorised person who has permission to carry on a regulated activity of the kind specified by any of articles 25B, 53B and 63B(1),

(ii) an appointed representative who may carry on a regulated activity of the kind specified by either of articles 25B and 53B without contravening the general prohibition, or

(iii) an overseas person who carries on activities specified by any of articles 25B, 53B and 63B(1); and

(b) the conditions mentioned in paragraph (2) are satisfied.

(1B) There are excluded from article 25C(2) arrangements where—

(a) they are arrangements under which a client is introduced to a person ("N") who is—

(i) an authorised person who has permission to carry on a regulated activity of the kind specified by any of articles 25C, 53C and 63F(1),
(ii) an appointed representative who may carry on a regulated activity of the kind specified by either of articles 25C and 53C without contravening the general prohibition, or
(iii) an overseas person who carries on activities specified by any of articles 25C, 53C and 63F(1); and
(b) the conditions mentioned in paragraph (2) are satisfied.]

[(1C) There are excluded from article 25E(2) arrangements where—
(a) they are arrangements under which a client is introduced to a person ("N") who is—
(i) an authorised person who has permission to carry on a regulated activity of the kind specified by any of articles 25E, 53D and 63J(1),
(ii) an appointed representative who may carry on a regulated activity of the kind specified by either of articles 25E or 53D without contravening the general prohibition, or
(iii) an overseas person who carries on activities specified by any of articles 25E, 53D and 63J(1); and
(b) the conditions mentioned in paragraph (2) are satisfied.]

(2) Those conditions are—
(a) that the person making the introduction ("P") does not receive any money, other than money payable to P on his own account, paid by the client for or in connection with any transaction which the client enters into with or through N as a result of the introduction; and
(b) that before making the introduction P discloses to the client such of the information mentioned in paragraph (3) as applies to P.

(3) That information is—
(a) that P is a member of the same group as N;
(b) details of any payment which P will receive from N, by way of fee or commission, for introducing the client to N;
(c) an indication of any other reward or advantage received or to be received by P that arises out of his introducing clients to N.

[(4) In this article, "client" means—
(a) for the purposes of paragraph (1), a borrower within the meaning given by article 61(3)(a)(i), or a person who is or may be contemplating entering into a regulated mortgage contract as such a borrower;
(b) for the purposes of paragraph (1A), a reversion seller, a plan provider or a person who is or may be contemplating entering into a regulated home reversion plan as a reversion seller or as a plan provider;
(c) for the purposes of paragraph (1B), a home purchaser or a person who is or may be contemplating entering into a regulated home purchase plan as a home purchaser[;
(d) for the purposes of paragraph (1C), an agreement provider, an agreement seller or a person who is or may be contemplating entering into a regulated sale and rent back agreement as an agreement provider or agreement seller.]]

NOTES

Inserted by the Financial Services and Markets Act 2000 (Regulated Activities) (Amendment) (No 1) Order 2003, SI 2003/1475, art 11.

Paras (1A), (1B): inserted by the Financial Services and Markets Act 2000 (Regulated Activities) (Amendment) (No 2) Order 2006, SI 2006/2383, arts 2, 11(a), subject to transitional provisions in arts 37–39 thereof.

Para (1C): inserted by the Financial Services and Markets Act 2000 (Regulated Activities) (Amendment) Order 2009, SI 2009/1342, arts 2, 11(a), as from 1 July 2009 (for certain purposes) and as from 30 June 2010 (for remaining purposes) (for the full commencement details and for transitional provisions etc see arts 1, 32–34 of that Order).

Para (4): substituted by SI 2006/2383, arts 2, 11(b), subject to transitional provisions in arts 37–39 thereof; sub-para (d) inserted by SI 2009/1342, arts 2, 11(b), as from the same dates and for the same purposes as noted above.

[535]

34 Arrangements for the issue of shares etc

(1) There are excluded from article 25(1) and (2)—
(a) arrangements made by a company for the purposes of issuing its own shares or share warrants; and

(b) arrangements made by any person for the purposes of issuing his own debentures or debenture warrants;

and for the purposes of article 25(1) and (2), a company is not, by reason of issuing its own shares or share warrants, and a person is not, by reason of issuing his own debentures or debenture warrants, to be treated as selling them.

(2) In paragraph (1), "company", "shares", "debentures", "share warrants" and "debenture warrants" have the meanings given by article 18(2).

[536]

35 International securities self-regulating organisations

(1) There are excluded from article 25(1) and (2) any arrangements made for the purposes of carrying out the functions of a body or association which is approved under this article as an international securities self-regulating organisation, whether the arrangements are made by the organisation itself or by a person acting on its behalf.

(2) The Treasury may approve as an international securities self-regulating organisation any body corporate or unincorporated association with respect to which the conditions mentioned in paragraph (3) appear to them to be met if, having regard to such matters affecting international trade, overseas earnings and the balance of payments or otherwise as they consider relevant, it appears to them that to do so would be desirable and not result in any undue risk to investors.

(3) The conditions are that—

(a) the body or association does not have its head office in the United Kingdom;

(b) the body or association is not eligible for recognition under section 287 or 288 of the Act (applications by investment exchanges and clearing houses) on the ground that (whether or not it has applied, and whether or not it would be eligible on other grounds) it is unable to satisfy the requirements of one or both of paragraphs (a) and (b) of section 292(3) of the Act (requirements for overseas investment exchanges and overseas clearing houses);

(c) the body or association is able and willing to co-operate with the Authority by the sharing of information and in other ways;

(d) adequate arrangements exist for co-operation between the Authority and those responsible for the supervision of the body or association in the country or territory in which its head office is situated;

(e) the body or association has a membership composed of persons falling within any of the following categories, that is to say, authorised persons, exempt persons, and persons whose head offices are outside the United Kingdom and whose ordinary business involves them in engaging in activities which are activities of a kind specified by this Order (or would be apart from any exclusion made by this Part); and

(f) the body or association facilitates and regulates the activity of its members in the conduct of international securities business.

(4) In paragraph (3)(f), "international securities business" means the business of buying, selling, subscribing for or underwriting investments (or agreeing to do so), either as principal or agent, where—

(a) the investments are securities or [relevant investments] and are of a kind which, by their nature, and the manner in which the business is conducted, may be expected normally to be bought or dealt in by persons sufficiently expert to understand the risks involved; and

(b) either the transaction is international or each of the parties may be expected to be indifferent to the location of the other;

and, for the purposes of this definition, it is irrelevant that the investments may ultimately be bought otherwise than in the course of such business by persons not so expert.

(5) Any approval under this article is to be given by notice in writing; and the Treasury may by a further notice in writing withdraw any such approval if for any reason it appears to them that it is not appropriate to it to continue in force.

NOTES

Para (4): words in square brackets substituted by the Financial Services and Markets Act 2000 (Regulated Activities) (Amendment) (No 2) Order 2003, SI 2003/1476, arts 2, 5(6).

[537]
36 Other exclusions

[(1)] Article 25 is also subject to the exclusions in articles 66 (trustees etc), 67 (profession or non-investment business), 68 (sale of goods and supply of services), 69 (groups and joint enterprises), 70 (sale of body corporate), 71 (employee share schemes)[, 72 (overseas persons)[, 72A (information society services), 72B (activities carried on by a provider of relevant goods or services), 72C (provision of information about contracts of insurance on an incidental basis) and 72D (large risks contracts where risk situated outside the EEA)]].

[(2) [Articles 25A, 25B *and 25C* are] also subject to the exclusions in articles 66 (trustees etc), 67 (profession or non-investment business), 72 (overseas persons) and 72A (information society services).]

[(3) Article 25D is also subject to the exclusion in article 72 (overseas persons).]

NOTES

Para (1): numbered as such by the Financial Services and Markets Act 2000 (Regulated Activities) (Amendment) (No 1) Order 2003, SI 2003/1475, art 12(a); words first (outer) pair of in square brackets substituted by the Financial Services and Markets Act 2000 (Regulated Activities) (Amendment) (No 2) Order 2002, SI 2002/1776, art 3(1), (6); words in second (inner) pair of square brackets substituted by the Financial Services and Markets Act 2000 (Regulated Activities) (Amendment) (No 2) Order 2003, SI 2003/1476, arts 2, 5(7)

Para (2): added by SI 2003/1475, art 12(b); words in square brackets substituted by the Financial Services and Markets Act 2000 (Regulated Activities) (Amendment) (No 2) Order 2006, SI 2006/2383, arts 2, 12, subject to transitional provisions in arts 37–39 thereof; for the words in italics there are substituted the words ", 25C and 25E" by the Financial Services and Markets Act 2000 (Regulated Activities) (Amendment) Order 2009, SI 2009/1342, arts 2, 12, as from 1 July 2009 (for certain purposes) and as from 30 June 2010 (for remaining purposes) (for the full commencement details and for transitional provisions etc see arts 1, 32–34 of that Order).

Para (3): added by the Financial Services and Markets Act 2000 (Regulated Activities) (Amendment No 3) Order 2006, SI 2006/3384, arts 2, 16.

CHAPTER VII
MANAGING INVESTMENTS

The activity

[538]
37 Managing investments

Managing assets belonging to another person, in circumstances involving the exercise of discretion, is a specified kind of activity if—

(a) the assets consist of or include any investment which is a security or a contractually based investment; or

(b) the arrangements for their management are such that the assets may consist of or include such investments, and either the assets have at any time since 29th April 1988 done so, or the arrangements have at any time (whether before or after that date) been held out as arrangements under which the assets would do so.

Exclusions

[539]
38 Attorneys

[(1)] A person does not carry on an activity of the kind specified by article 37 if—

(a) he is a person appointed to manage the assets in question under a power of attorney; and

(b) all routine or day-to-day decisions, so far as relating to investments of a kind mentioned in article 37(a), are taken on behalf of that person by—

(i) an authorised person with permission to carry on activities of the kind specified by article 37; . . .

(ii) a person who is an exempt person in relation to activities of that kind[; or

(iii) an overseas person.]

[This article is subject to article 4(4).]

NOTES

Para (1): numbered as such and final words in square brackets added by the Financial Services and Markets Act 2000 (Regulated Activities) (Amendment No 3) Order 2006, SI 2006/3384, arts 2, 17; word omitted from sub-para (b)(i) revoked and sub-para (b)(iii) and word "or" immediately preceding it added by the Financial Services and Markets Act 2000 (Regulated Activities) (Amendment) Order 2001, SI 2001/3544, arts 2, 6.

[540]

39 Other exclusions

Article 37 is also subject to the exclusions in articles 66 (trustees etc), 68 (sale of goods and supply of services)[, 69 (groups and joint enterprises)[, 72A (information society services) and 72C (provision of information about contracts of insurance on an incidental basis)]].

NOTES

Words in first (outer) pair of square brackets substituted by the Financial Services and Markets Act 2000 (Regulated Activities) (Amendment) (No 2) Order 2002, SI 2002/1776, art 3(1), (7); words in second (inner) pair of square brackets substituted by the Financial Services and Markets Act 2000 (Regulated Activities) (Amendment) (No 2) Order 2003, SI 2003/1476, arts 2, 6.

[CHAPTER VIIA
ASSISTING IN THE ADMINISTRATION AND PERFORMANCE OF A CONTRACT OF INSURANCE

The activity

[541]

39A Assisting in the administration and performance of a contract of insurance

Assisting in the administration and performance of a contract of insurance is a specified kind of activity.]

NOTES

Ch VIIA (arts 39A–39C) inserted by the Financial Services and Markets Act 2000 (Regulated Activities) (Amendment) (No 2) Order 2003, SI 2003/1476, arts 2, 7.

[Exclusions

[542]

39B Claims management on behalf of an insurer etc

(1) A person does not carry on an activity of the kind specified by article 39A if he acts in the course of carrying on the activity of—

(a) expert appraisal;

(b) loss adjusting on behalf of a relevant insurer; or

(c) managing claims on behalf of a relevant insurer,

and that activity is carried on in the course of carrying on any profession or business.

(2) In this article—

(a) "relevant insurer" means—

(i) a person who has Part IV permission to carry on an activity of the kind specified by article 10;

(ii) a person to whom the general prohibition does not apply by virtue of section 316(1)(a) of the Act (members of the Society of Lloyd's);

(iii) an EEA firm falling within paragraph 5(d) of Schedule 3 to the Act (insurance undertaking); or

(iv) a relevant reinsurer;

(b) "relevant reinsurer" means a person whose main business consists of accepting risks ceded by—

(i) a person falling within sub-paragraph (i), (ii) or (iii) of the definition of "relevant insurer"; . . .

[(ii) an EEA firm falling within paragraph 5(da) of Schedule 3 to the Act (reinsurance undertaking); or

(iii) a person established outside the United Kingdom and not falling within paragraph (ii) who carries on an activity of the kind specified by article 10 by way of business.]]

NOTES

Inserted as noted to art 39A at **[541]**.

Para (2): word omitted from sub-para (b)(i) revoked and sub-para (b)(ii), (iii) substituted for original sub-para (b)(ii) by the Financial Services and Markets Act 2000 (Reinsurance Directive) Order 2007, SI 2007/3254, art 2.

[543]

[39C Other exclusions

Article 39A is also subject to the exclusions in articles 66 (trustees etc), 67 (profession or non-investment business), 72A (information society services), 72B (activities carried on by a provider of relevant goods or services), 72C (provision of information about contracts of insurance on an incidental basis) and 72D (large risks contracts where risk situated outside the EEA).]

NOTES

Inserted as noted to art 39A at **[541]**.

CHAPTER VIII
SAFEGUARDING AND ADMINISTERING INVESTMENTS
The activity

[544]
40 Safeguarding and administering investments

(1) The activity consisting of both—
  (a) the safeguarding of assets belonging to another, and
  (b) the administration of those assets,

or arranging for one or more other persons to carry on that activity, is a specified kind of activity if the condition in sub-paragraph (a) or (b) of paragraph (2) is met.

(2) The condition is that—
  (a) the assets consist of or include any investment which is a security or a contractually based investment; or
  (b) the arrangements for their safeguarding and administration are such that the assets may consist of or include such investments, and either the assets have at any time since 1st June 1997 done so, or the arrangements have at any time (whether before or after that date) been held out as ones under which such investments would be safeguarded and administered.

(3) For the purposes of this article—
  (a) it is immaterial that title to the assets safeguarded and administered is held in uncertificated form;
  (b) it is immaterial that the assets safeguarded and administered may be transferred to another person, subject to a commitment by the person safeguarding and administering them, or arranging for their safeguarding and administration, that they will be replaced by equivalent assets at some future date or when so requested by the person to whom they belong.

Exclusions

[545]
41 Acceptance of responsibility by third party

(1) There are excluded from article 40 any activities which a person carries on pursuant to arrangements which—
  (a) are ones under which a qualifying custodian undertakes to the person to whom the assets belong a responsibility in respect of the assets which is no less onerous than the qualifying custodian would have if the qualifying custodian were safeguarding and administering the assets; and
  (b) are operated by the qualifying custodian in the course of carrying on in the United Kingdom an activity of the kind specified by article 40.

(2) In paragraph (1), "qualifying custodian" means a person who is—
  (a) an authorised person who has permission to carry on an activity of the kind specified by article 40, or
  (b) an exempt person acting in the course of a business comprising a regulated activity in relation to which he is exempt.

[546]
42 Introduction to qualifying custodians

(1) There are excluded from article 40 any arrangements pursuant to which introductions are made by a person ("P") to a qualifying custodian with a view to the qualifying custodian providing in the United Kingdom a service comprising an activity of the kind specified by article 40, where the qualifying person (or other person who is to safeguard and administer the assets in question) is not connected with P.

(2) For the purposes of paragraph (1)—
  (a) "qualifying custodian" has the meaning given by article 41(2); and
  (b) a person is connected with P if either he is a member of the same group as P, or P is remunerated by him.

[547]
43 Activities not constituting administration

The following activities do not constitute the administration of assets for the purposes of article 40—

(a) providing information as to the number of units or the value of any assets safeguarded;
(b) converting currency;
(c) receiving documents relating to an investment solely for the purpose of onward transmission to, from or at the direction of the person to whom the investment belongs.

[548]
44 Other exclusions

Article 40 is also subject to the exclusions in articles 66 (trustees etc), 67 (profession or non-investment business), 68 (sale of goods and supply of services), 69 (groups and joint enterprises)[, 71 (employee share schemes)[, 72A (information society services) and 72C (provision of information about contracts of insurance on an incidental basis)]].

NOTES

Words in first (outer) pair of square brackets substituted by the Financial Services and Markets Act 2000 (Regulated Activities) (Amendment) (No 2) Order 2002, SI 2002/1776, art 3(1), (8); words in second (inner) pair of square brackets substituted by the Financial Services and Markets Act 2000 (Regulated Activities) (Amendment) (No 2) Order 2003, SI 2003/1476, arts 2, 8.

45–51A *((Chs IX, X) outside the scope of this work.)*

CHAPTER XI
. . . PENSION SCHEMES

NOTES

Chapter heading: word omitted revoked by the Financial Services and Markets Act 2000 (Regulated Activities) (Amendment) Order 2006, SI 2006/1969, art 2(1), (3), subject to transitional provisions in art 3(1), (2), (5) thereof.

The activities

[549]
[52 Establishing etc a pension scheme

The following are specified kinds of activity—

(a) establishing, operating or winding up a stakeholder pension scheme;
(b) establishing, operating or winding up a personal pension scheme.]

NOTES

Commencement: 1 October 2006 (certain purposes); 6 April 2007 (remaining purposes).

Substituted by the Financial Services and Markets Act 2000 (Regulated Activities) (Amendment) Order 2006, SI 2006/1969, art 2(1), (4), subject to transitional provisions in art 3(1), (2), (5) thereof.

[Exclusion

[550]
52A Information society services

Article 52 is subject to the exclusion in article 72A (information society services).]

NOTES

Inserted, together with preceding cross-heading, by the Financial Services and Markets Act 2000 (Regulated Activities) (Amendment) (No 2) Order 2002, SI 2002/1776, art 3(1), (11).

[CHAPTER XIA
PROVIDING BASIC ADVICE ON STAKEHOLDER PRODUCTS

The activity

[551]
52B Providing basic advice on stakeholder products

(1) Providing basic advice to a retail consumer on a stakeholder product is a specified kind of activity.

(2) For the purposes of paragraph (1), a person ("P") provides basic advice when—

(a) he asks a retail consumer questions to enable him to assess whether a stakeholder product is appropriate for that consumer; and
(b) relying on the information provided by the retail consumer P assesses that a stakeholder product is appropriate for the retail consumer and—

(i) describes that product to that consumer;
(ii) gives a recommendation of that product to that consumer; and
(c) the retail consumer has indicated to P that he has understood the description and the recommendation in sub-paragraph (b).

(3) In this article—

"retail consumer" means any person who is advised by P on the merits of opening or buying a stakeholder product in the course of a business carried on by P and who does not receive the advice in the course of a business carried on by him;

"stakeholder product" means—
(a) an account which qualifies as a stakeholder child trust fund within the meaning given by the Child Trust Funds Regulations 2004;
[(b) rights under a relevant stakeholder pension scheme;]
(c) an investment of a kind specified in regulations made by the Treasury.]

NOTES

Ch XIA (art 52B) inserted by the Financial Services and Markets Act 2000 (Regulated Activities) (Amendment) (No 2) Order 2004, SI 2004/2737, art 3.

Para (3): in definition "stakeholder product" para (b) substituted by the Financial Services and Markets Act 2000 (Regulated Activities) (Amendment) Order 2005, SI 2005/593, art 2(1), (3).

Regulations: the Financial Services and Markets Act 2000 (Stakeholder Products) Regulations 2004, SI 2004/2738.

CHAPTER XII
ADVISING ON INVESTMENTS

The activity

[552]

53 Advising on investments

Advising a person is a specified kind of activity if the advice is—
(a) given to the person in his capacity as an investor or potential investor, or in his capacity as agent for an investor or a potential investor; and
(b) advice on the merits of his doing any of the following (whether as principal or agent)—
(i) buying, selling, subscribing for or underwriting a particular investment which is a security or a [relevant investment], or
(ii) exercising any right conferred by such an investment to buy, sell, subscribe for or underwrite such an investment.

NOTES

Words in square brackets substituted by the Financial Services and Markets Act 2000 (Regulated Activities) (Amendment) (No 2) Order 2003, SI 2003/1476, arts 2, 9(1).

[553]

[53A Advising on regulated mortgage contracts

(1) Advising a person is a specified kind of activity if the advice—
(a) is given to the person in his capacity as a borrower or potential borrower; and
(b) is advice on the merits of his doing any of the following—
(i) entering into a particular regulated mortgage contract, or
(ii) varying the terms of a regulated mortgage contract entered into by him after the coming into force of article 61 in such a way as to vary his obligations under that contract.

(2) In this article, "borrower" has the meaning given by article 61(3)(a)(i).]

NOTES

Inserted by the Financial Services and Markets Act 2000 (Regulated Activities) (Amendment) (No 1) Order 2003, SI 2003/1475, art 13.

53B–53D *(Outside the scope of this work.)*

Exclusions

[554]

54 Advice given in newspapers etc

(1) There is excluded from [articles 53, 53A, 53B *and 53C*] the giving of advice in writing or other legible form if the advice is contained in a newspaper, journal, magazine, or other periodical publication, or is given by way of a service comprising regularly updated news or information, if the principal purpose of the publication or service, taken as a whole and including any advertisements or other promotional material contained in it, is neither—

(a) that of giving advice of a kind mentioned in article 53[, 53A, 53B *or 53C*, as the case may be]; nor

[(b) that of leading or enabling persons—

(i) to buy, sell, subscribe for or underwrite securities or [relevant investments], or (as the case may be),

(ii) to enter as borrower into regulated mortgage contracts, or vary the terms of regulated mortgage contracts entered into by them as borrower[;

(iii) to enter as reversion seller or plan provider into regulated home reversion plans, or vary the terms of regulated home reversion plans entered into by them as reversion seller or plan provider,

(iv) to enter as home purchaser into regulated home purchase plans, or vary the terms of regulated home purchase plans entered into by them as home purchaser][;

(v) to enter as agreement seller or agreement provider into regulated sale and rent back agreements, or vary the terms of regulated sale and rent back agreements entered into by them as agreement seller or agreement provider]].

(2) There is also excluded from [articles 53, 53A, 53B *and 53C*] the giving of advice in any service consisting of the broadcast or transmission of television or radio programmes, if the principal purpose of the service, taken as a whole and including any advertisements or other promotional material contained in it, is neither of those mentioned in paragraph (1)(a) and (b).

(3) The Authority may, on the application of the proprietor of any such publication or service as is mentioned in paragraph (1) or (2), certify that it is of the nature described in that paragraph, and may revoke any such certificate if it considers that it is no longer justified.

(4) A certificate given under paragraph (3) and not revoked is conclusive evidence of the matters certified.

NOTES

Para (1): words in first and second pairs of square brackets substituted and sub-para (b)(iii), (iv) inserted by the Financial Services and Markets Act 2000 (Regulated Activities) (Amendment) (No 2) Order 2006, SI 2006/2383, arts 2, 14(a), subject to transitional provisions in arts 37–39 thereof; sub-para (b) substituted by the Financial Services and Markets Act 2000 (Regulated Activities) (Amendment) (No 1) Order 2003, SI 2003/1475, art 14(1), (4); words in square brackets in sub-para (b)(i) substituted by the Financial Services and Markets Act 2000 (Regulated Activities) (Amendment) (No 2) Order 2003, SI 2003/1476, arts 2, 9(2); for the words "and 53C" in italics there are substituted the words ", 53C and 53D", for the words "or 53C," in italics there are substituted the words ", 53C or 53D,", and sub-para (b)(v) inserted by the Financial Services and Markets Act 2000 (Regulated Activities) (Amendment) Order 2009, SI 2009/1342, arts 2, 14(a)–(c), as from 1 July 2009 (for certain purposes) and as from 30 June 2010 (for remaining purposes) (for the full commencement details and for transitional provisions etc see arts 1, 32–34 of that Order).

Para (2): words in square brackets inserted by inserted by SI 2006/2383, arts 2, 14(b), subject to transitional provisions in arts 37–39 thereof; for the words in italics there are substituted the words ", 53C and 53D" by SI 2009/1342, arts 2, 14(d), as from the same dates and for the same purposes as noted above.

[555]

[54A Advice given in the course of administration by authorised person

[(1)] A person who is not an authorised person ("A") does not carry on an activity of the kind specified by article 53A by reason of—

(a) anything done by an authorised person ("B") in relation to a regulated mortgage contract which B is administering pursuant to arrangements of the kind mentioned in article 62(a); or

(b) anything A does in connection with the administration of a regulated mortgage contract in circumstances falling within article 62(b).

[(2) A person who is not an authorised person ("A") does not carry on an activity of the kind specified by article 53B by reason of—

(a) anything done by an authorised person ("B") in relation to a regulated home reversion plan which B is administering pursuant to arrangements of the kind mentioned in article 63C(a); or

(b) anything A does in connection with the administration of a regulated home reversion plan in circumstances falling within article 63C(b).

(3) A person who is not an authorised person ("A") does not carry on an activity of the kind specified by article 53C by reason of—

(a) anything done by an authorised person ("B") in relation to a regulated home purchase plan which B is administering pursuant to arrangements of the kind mentioned in article 63G(a); or

(b) anything A does in connection with the administration of a regulated home purchase plan in circumstances falling within article 63G(b).]

[(4) A person who is not an authorised person ("A") does not carry on an activity of the kind specified by article 53D by reason of

(a) anything done by an authorised person ("B") in relation to a regulated sale and rent back agreement which B is administering pursuant to arrangements of the kind mentioned in article 63K(a); or

(b) anything A does in connection with the administration of a regulated sale and rent back agreement in circumstances falling within article 63K(b).]]

NOTES

Inserted by the Financial Services and Markets Act 2000 (Regulated Activities) (Amendment) (No 1) Order 2003, SI 2003/1475, art 15.

Para (1): numbered as such by the Financial Services and Markets Act 2000 (Regulated Activities) (Amendment) (No 2) Order 2006, SI 2006/2383, arts 2, 15(a), subject to transitional provisions in arts 37–39 thereof.

Paras (2), (3): added by SI 2006/2383, arts 2, 15(b), subject to transitional provisions in arts 37–39 thereof.

Para (4): added by the Financial Services and Markets Act 2000 (Regulated Activities) (Amendment) Order 2009, SI 2009/1342, arts 2, 15, as from 1 July 2009 (for certain purposes) and as from 30 June 2010 (for remaining purposes) (for the full commencement details and for transitional provisions etc see arts 1, 32–34 of that Order).

[556]

55 Other exclusions

[(1)] Article 53 is also subject to the exclusions in articles 66 (trustees etc), 67 (profession or non-investment business), 68 (sale of goods and supply of services), 69 (groups and joint enterprises), 70 (sale of body corporate)[, 72 (overseas persons)[, 72A (information society services), 72B (activities carried on by a provider of relevant goods or services) and 72D (large risks contracts where risk situated outside the EEA)]].

[(2) [Articles 53A, 53B *and 53C* are] also subject to the exclusions in articles 66 (trustees etc), 67 (profession or non-investment business) and 72A (information society services).]

NOTES

Para (1): numbered as such by the Financial Services and Markets Act 2000 (Regulated Activities) (Amendment) (No 1) Order 2003, SI 2003/1475, art 16(a); words in first (outer) pair of square brackets substituted by the Financial Services and Markets Act 2000 (Regulated Activities) (Amendment) (No 2) Order 2002, SI 2002/1776, art 3(1), (12); words in second (inner) pair of square brackets substituted by the Financial Services and Markets Act 2000 (Regulated Activities) (Amendment) (No 2) Order 2003, SI 2003/1476, arts 2, 9(3).

Para (2): added by SI 2003/1475, art 16(b); words in square brackets substituted by the Financial Services and Markets Act 2000 (Regulated Activities) (Amendment) (No 2) Order 2006, SI 2006/2383, arts 2, 16, subject to transitional provisions in arts 37–39 thereof; for the words in italics there are substituted the words ", 53C and 53D" by the Financial Services and Markets Act 2000 (Regulated Activities) (Amendment) Order 2009, SI 2009/1342, arts 2, 16, as from 1 July 2009 (for certain purposes) and as from 30 June 2010 (for remaining purposes) (for the full commencement details and for transitional provisions etc see arts 1, 32–34 of that Order).

CHAPTER XIII
LLOYD'S

The activities

[557]

56 Advice on syndicate participation at Lloyd's

Advising a person to become, or continue or cease to be, a member of a particular Lloyd's syndicate is a specified kind of activity.

[558]

57 Managing the underwriting capacity of a Lloyd's syndicate

Managing the underwriting capacity of a Lloyd's syndicate as a managing agent at Lloyd's is a specified kind of activity.

[559]

58 Arranging deals in contracts of insurance written at Lloyd's

The arranging, by the society incorporated by Lloyd's Act 1871 by the name of Lloyd's, of deals in contracts of insurance written at Lloyd's, is a specified kind of activity.

[Exclusion

[560]

58A Information society services

Articles 56 to 58 are subject to the exclusion in article 72A (information society services).]

NOTES

Inserted, together with preceding cross-heading, by the Financial Services and Markets Act 2000 (Regulated Activities) (Amendment) (No 2) Order 2002, SI 2002/1776, art 3(1), (13).

CHAPTER XIV
FUNERAL PLAN CONTRACTS

The activity

[561]

59 Funeral plan contracts

(1) Entering as provider into a funeral plan contract is a specified kind of activity.

(2) A "funeral plan contract" is a contract (other than one excluded by article 60) under which—

- (a) a person ("the customer") makes one or more payments to another person ("the provider"); and
- (b) the provider undertakes to provide, or secure that another person provides, a funeral in the United Kingdom for the customer (or some other person who is living at the date when the contract is entered into) on his death;

unless, at the time of entering into the contract, the customer and the provider intend or expect the funeral to occur within one month.

[Exclusions]

NOTES

Cross-heading: substituted by the Financial Services and Markets Act 2000 (Regulated Activities) (Amendment) (No 2) Order 2002, SI 2002/1776, art 3(1), (14).

[562]

60 Plans covered by insurance or trust arrangements

(1) There is excluded from article 59 any contract under which—

- (a) the provider undertakes to secure that sums paid by the customer under the contract will be applied towards a contract of whole life insurance on the life of the customer (or other person for whom the funeral is to be provided), effected and carried out by an authorised person who has permission to effect and carry out such contracts of insurance, for the purpose of providing the funeral; or
- (b) the provider undertakes to secure that sums paid by the customer under the contract will be held on trust for the purpose of providing the funeral, and that the following requirements are or will be met with respect to the trust—
  - (i) the trust must be established by a written instrument;
  - (ii) more than half of the trustees must be unconnected with the provider;
  - (iii) the trustees must appoint, or have appointed, an independent fund manager who is an authorised person who has permission to carry on an activity of the kind specified by article 37, and who is a person who is unconnected with the provider, to manage the assets of the trust;
  - (iv) annual accounts must be prepared, and audited by a person who is eligible for appointment as a [statutory auditor under Part 42 of the Companies Act 2006], with respect to the assets and liabilities of the trust; and
  - (v) the assets and liabilities of the trust must, at least once every three years, be determined, calculated and verified by an actuary who is a Fellow of the Institute of Actuaries or of the Faculty of Actuaries.

(2) For the purposes of paragraph (1)(b)(ii) and (iii), a person is unconnected with the provider if he is a person other than—

- (a) the provider;
- (b) a member of the same group as the provider;

(c) a director, other officer or employee of the provider, or of any member of the same group as the provider;
(d) a partner of the provider;
(e) a close relative of a person falling within sub-paragraph (a), (c) or (d); or
(f) an agent of any person falling within sub-paragraphs (a) to (e).

NOTES

Para (1): words in square brackets in sub-para (b)(iv) substituted by the Companies Act 2006 (Consequential Amendments etc) Order 2008, SI 2008/948, art 3(1)(a), Sch 1, Pt 1, para 1(tt), subject to transitional provisions and savings in arts 6, 12 thereof.

[563]
[60A Information society services

Article 59 is subject to the exclusion in article 72A (information society services).]

NOTES

Inserted by the Financial Services and Markets Act 2000 (Regulated Activities) (Amendment) (No 2) Order 2002, SI 2002/1776, art 3(1), (15).

61–63N *((Chs XV, 15A–15D) outside the scope of this work.)*

CHAPTER XVI
AGREEING TO CARRY ON ACTIVITIES

The activity

[564]
64 Agreeing to carry on specified kinds of activity

Agreeing to carry on an activity of the kind specified by any other provision of this Part (other than article 5, [9B,] 10, [25D,] [51, 52 or 63N) is a specified kind of activity.

NOTES

Reference in first pair of square brackets inserted by the Financial Services and Markets Act 2000 (Regulated Activities) (Amendment) Order 2002, SI 2002/682, art 5; reference in second pair of square brackets inserted by the Financial Services and Markets Act 2000 (Regulated Activities) (Amendment No 3) Order 2006, SI 2006/3384, arts 2, 18; words in third pair of square brackets substituted by the Financial Services and Markets Act 2000 (Regulated Activities) (Amendment) (No 2) Order 2009, SI 2009/1389, arts 2, 5.

[Exclusions

[565]
65 Overseas persons etc

Article 64 is subject to the exclusions in articles 72 (overseas persons) and 72A (information society services).]

NOTES

Substituted, together with preceding cross-heading, by the Financial Services and Markets Act 2000 (Regulated Activities) (Amendment) (No 2) Order 2002, SI 2002/1776, art 3(1), (17).

CHAPTER XVII
EXCLUSIONS APPLYING TO SEVERAL SPECIFIED KINDS OF ACTIVITY

[566]
66 Trustees, nominees and personal representatives

(1) A person ("X") does not carry on an activity of the kind specified by article 14 where he enters into a transaction as bare trustee or, in Scotland, as nominee for another person ("Y") and—
(a) X is acting on Y's instructions; and
(b) X does not hold himself out as providing a service of buying and selling securities or contractually based investments.

(2) Subject to paragraph (7), there are excluded from [articles 25(1) and (2)[, 25A(1) and (2), 25B(1) and (2) *and 25C(1) and (2)*]] arrangements made by a person acting as trustee or personal representative for or with a view to a transaction which is or is to be entered into—
(a) by that person and a fellow trustee or personal representative (acting in their capacity as such); or
(b) by a beneficiary under the trust, will or intestacy.

(3) Subject to paragraph (7), there is excluded from article 37 any activity carried on by a person acting as trustee or personal representative, unless—

(a) he holds himself out as providing a service comprising an activity of the kind specified by article 37; or

(b) the assets in question are held for the purposes of an occupational pension scheme, and, by virtue of article 4 of the Financial Services and Markets Act 2000 (Carrying on Regulated Activities by Way of Business) Order 2001, he is to be treated as carrying on that activity by way of business.

[(3A) Subject to paragraph (7), there is excluded from article 39A any activity carried on by a person acting as trustee or personal representative, unless he holds himself out as providing a service comprising an activity of the kind specified by article 39A.]

(4) Subject to paragraph (7), there is excluded from article 40 any activity carried on by a person acting as trustee or personal representative, unless he holds himself out as providing a service comprising an activity of the kind specified by article 40.

[(4A) There is excluded from article 40 any activity carried on by a person acting as trustee which consists of arranging for one or more other persons to safeguard and administer trust assets where—

(a) that other person is a qualifying custodian; or

(b) that safeguarding and administration is also arranged by a qualifying custodian.

In this paragraph, "qualifying custodian" has the meaning given by article 41(2).]

(5) A person does not, by sending or causing to be sent a dematerialised instruction (within the meaning of article 45), carry on an activity of the kind specified by that article if the instruction relates to an investment which that person holds as trustee or personal representative.

(6) Subject to paragraph (7), there is excluded from [articles 53[, 53A, 53B *and 53C*]] the giving of advice by a person acting as trustee or personal representative where he gives the advice to—

(a) a fellow trustee or personal representative for the purposes of the trust or the estate; or

(b) a beneficiary under the trust, will or intestacy concerning his interest in the trust fund or estate.

[(6A) Subject to paragraph (7), a person acting as trustee or personal representative does not carry on an activity of the kind specified by article 61(1) or (2) where the borrower under the regulated mortgage contract in question is a beneficiary under the trust, will or intestacy.]

[(6B) Subject to paragraph (7), a person acting as trustee or personal representative does not carry on an activity of the kind specified by article 63B(1) or (2) where the reversion seller under the regulated home reversion plan in question is a beneficiary under the trust, will or intestacy.

(6C) Subject to paragraph (7), a person acting as trustee or personal representative does not carry on an activity of the kind specified by article 63F(1) or (2) where the home purchaser under the regulated home purchase plan in question is a beneficiary under the trust, will or intestacy.]

[(6D) Subject to paragraph (7), a person acting as a trustee or personal representative does not carry on an activity of the kind specified by article 63J(1) or (2) where the agreement seller under the regulated sale and rent back agreement is a beneficiary under the trust, will or intestacy.]

(7) Paragraphs (2), (3)[, (3A)], [(4), (6)[, (6A), (6B) *and (6C)*]] do not apply if the person carrying on the activity is remunerated for what he does in addition to any remuneration he receives as trustee or personal representative, and for these purposes a person is not to be regarded as receiving additional remuneration merely because his remuneration is calculated by reference to time spent.

[(8) This article is subject to article 4(4A).]

NOTES

Para (2): words in first (outer) pair of square brackets substituted by the Financial Services and Markets Act 2000 (Regulated Activities) (Amendment) (No 1) Order 2003, SI 2003/1475, art 18(a); words in second (inner) pair of square brackets substituted by the Financial Services and Markets Act 2000 (Regulated Activities) (Amendment) (No 2) Order 2006, SI 2006/2383, arts 2, 19(a), subject to transitional provisions in arts 37–39 thereof; for the words in italics there are substituted the words ", 25C(1) and (2) and 25E(1) and (2)" by the Financial Services and Markets Act 2000 (Regulated Activities) (Amendment) Order 2009, SI 2009/1342, arts 2, 18(a), as from 1 July 2009 (for certain purposes) and as from 30 June 2010 (for remaining purposes) (for the full commencement details and for transitional provisions etc see arts 1, 32–34 of that Order).

Para (3A): inserted by the Financial Services and Markets Act 2000 (Regulated Activities) (Amendment) (No 2) Order 2003, SI 2003/1476, arts 2, 10(1)(a).

Para (4A): inserted by the Financial Services and Markets Act 2000 (Regulated Activities) (Amendment) Order 2005, SI 2005/593, art 2(1), (4).

Para (6): words in first (outer) pair of square brackets substituted by SI 2003/1475, art 18(b); words in second (inner) pair of square brackets substituted by SI 2006/2383, arts 2, 19(b), subject to transitional provisions in arts 37–39 thereof; for the words in italics there are substituted the words ", 53C and 53D" by SI 2009/1342, arts 2, 18(b), as from the same dates and for the same purposes as noted above.

Para (6A): inserted by SI 2003/1475, art 18(c).

Paras (6B), (6C): inserted by SI 2006/2383, arts 2, 19(c), subject to transitional provisions in arts 37–39 thereof.

Para (6D): inserted by SI 2009/1342, arts 2, 18(c), as from the same dates and for the same purposes as noted above.

Para (7): reference in first pair of square brackets inserted by the Financial Services and Markets Act 2000 (Regulated Activities) (Amendment) (No 2) Order 2003, SI 2003/1476, arts 2, 10(1)(b); words in second (outer) pair of square brackets substituted by the Financial Services and Markets Act 2000 (Regulated Activities) (Amendment) (No 1) Order 2003, SI 2003/1475, art 18(d); words in third (inner) pair of square brackets substituted by SI 2006/2383, arts 2, 19(d), subject to transitional provisions in arts 37–39 thereof; for the words in italics there are substituted the words ", (6C) and (6D)" by SI 2009/1342, arts 2, 18(d), as from the same dates and for the same purposes as noted above.

Para (8): added by the Financial Services and Markets Act 2000 (Regulated Activities) (Amendment No 3) Order 2006, SI 2006/3384, arts 2, 19.

[567]

67 Activities carried on in the course of a profession or non-investment business

(1) There is excluded from articles 21, 25(1) and (2)[, 25A], [25B, 25C,] [25E,] [39A, 40] [53[, 53A, 53B *and 53C*]] any activity which—

(a) is carried on in the course of carrying on any profession or business which does not otherwise consist of [the carrying on of regulated activities in the United Kingdom]; and

(b) may reasonably be regarded as a necessary part of other services provided in the course of that profession or business.

(2) But the exclusion in paragraph (1) does not apply if the activity in question is remunerated separately from the other services.

[(3) This article is subject to article 4(4) and (4A).]

NOTES

Para (1): reference in first pair of square brackets inserted and words in fifth (outer) pair of square brackets substituted by the Financial Services and Markets Act 2000 (Regulated Activities) (Amendment) (No 1) Order 2003, SI 2003/1475, art 19; references in second pair of square brackets inserted and references in sixth (inner) pairs of square brackets substituted by the Financial Services and Markets Act 2000 (Regulated Activities) (Amendment) (No 2) Order 2006, SI 2006/2383, arts 2, 20, subject to transitional provisions in arts 37–39 thereof; reference in third pair of square brackets inserted and for the words in italics there are substituted the words ", 53C and 53D" by the Financial Services and Markets Act 2000 (Regulated Activities) (Amendment) Order 2009, SI 2009/1342, arts 2, 19, as from 1 July 2009 (for certain purposes) and as from 30 June 2010 (for remaining purposes) (for the full commencement details and for transitional provisions etc see arts 1, 32–34 of that Order); references in fourth pair of square brackets substituted by the Financial Services and Markets Act 2000 (Regulated Activities) (Amendment) (No 2) Order 2003, SI 2003/1476, arts 2, 10(2); words in square brackets in para (a) substituted by the Financial Services and Markets Act 2000 (Regulated Activities) (Amendment) Order 2001, SI 2001/3544, arts 2, 9.

Para (3): added by the Financial Services and Markets Act 2000 (Regulated Activities) (Amendment No 3) Order 2006, SI 2006/3384, arts 2, 20.

[568]

68 Activities carried on in connection with the sale of goods or supply of services

(1) Subject to paragraphs (9), (10) and (11), this article concerns certain activities carried on for the purposes of or in connection with the sale of goods or supply of services by a supplier to a customer, where—

"supplier" means a person whose main business is to sell goods or supply services and not to carry on any activities of the kind specified by any of articles 14, 21, 25, 37[, 39A], 40, 45, 51, 52 and 53 and, where the supplier is a member of a group, also means any other member of that group; and

"customer" means a person, other than an individual, to whom a supplier sells goods or supplies services, or agrees to do so, and, where the customer is a member of a group, also means any other member of that group;

and in this article "related sale or supply" means a sale of goods or supply of services to the customer otherwise than by the supplier, but for or in connection with the same purpose as the sale or supply mentioned above.

(2) There is excluded from article 14 any transaction entered into by a supplier with a customer, if the transaction is entered into for the purposes of or in connection with the sale of goods or supply of services, or a related sale or supply.

(3) There is excluded from article 21 any transaction entered into [by a supplier as agent for a customer], if the transaction is entered into for the purposes of or in connection with the sale of goods or supply of services, or a related sale or supply, and provided that—

(a) where the investment to which the transaction relates is a security, the supplier does not hold himself out (other than to the customer) as engaging in the business of buying securities of the kind to which the transaction relates with a view to selling them, and does not regularly solicit members of the public for the purpose of inducing them (as principals or agents) to buy, sell, subscribe for or underwrite securities;

(b) where the investment to which the transaction relates is a contractually based investment, the supplier enters into the transaction—

(i) with or through an authorised person, or an exempt person acting in the course of a business comprising a regulated activity in relation to which he is exempt; or

(ii) through an office outside the United Kingdom maintained by a party to the transaction, and with or through a person whose head office is situated outside the United Kingdom and whose ordinary business involves him in carrying on activities of the kind specified by any of articles 14, 21, 25, 37, 40, 45, 51, 52 and 53 or, so far as relevant to any of those articles, article 64, or would do so apart from any exclusion from any of those articles made by this Order.

(4) In paragraph (3)(a), "members of the public" has the meaning given by article 15(2), references to "A" being read as references to the supplier.

(5) There are excluded from article 25(1) and (2) arrangements made by a supplier for, or with a view to, a transaction which is or is to be entered into by a customer for the purposes of or in connection with the sale of goods or supply of services, or a related sale or supply.

(6) There is excluded from article 37 any activity carried on by a supplier where the assets in question—

(a) are those of a customer; and

(b) are managed for the purposes of or in connection with the sale of goods or supply of services, or a related sale or supply.

(7) There is excluded from article 40 any activity carried on by a supplier where the assets in question are or are to be safeguarded and administered for the purposes of or in connection with the sale of goods or supply of services, or a related sale or supply.

(8) There is excluded from article 53 the giving of advice by a supplier to a customer for the purposes of or in connection with the sale of goods or supply of services, or a related sale or supply, or to a person with whom the customer proposes to enter into a transaction for the purposes of or in connection with such a sale or supply or related sale or supply.

(9) Paragraphs (2), (3) and (5) do not apply in the case of a transaction for the sale or purchase of a [contract of insurance], an investment of the kind specified by article 81, or an investment of the kind specified by article 89 so far as relevant to such a contract or such an investment.

(10) Paragraph (6) does not apply where the assets managed consist of qualifying contracts of insurance, investments of the kind specified by article 81, or investments of the kind specified by article 89 so far as relevant to such contracts or such investments.

(11) Paragraph (8) does not apply in the case of advice in relation to an investment which is a [contract of insurance], is of the kind specified by article 81, or is of the kind specified by article 89 so far as relevant to such a contract or such an investment.

[(12) This article is subject to article 4(4).]

NOTES

Para (1): reference in square brackets inserted by the Financial Services and Markets Act 2000 (Regulated Activities) (Amendment) (No 2) Order 2003, SI 2003/1476, arts 2, 10(3)(a).

Para (3): words in square brackets substituted by the Financial Services and Markets Act 2000 (Regulated Activities) (Amendment) Order 2001, SI 2001/3544, arts 2, 10.

Paras (9), (11): words in square brackets substituted by SI 2003/1476, arts 2, 10(3)(b), (c).

Para (12): added by the Financial Services and Markets Act 2000 (Regulated Activities) (Amendment No 3) Order 2006, SI 2006/3384, arts 2, 21.

[569]

69 Groups and joint enterprises

(1) There is excluded from article 14 any transaction into which a person enters as principal with another person if that other person is also acting as principal and—

(a) they are members of the same group; or

(b) they are, or propose to become, participators in a joint enterprise and the transaction is entered into for the purposes of or in connection with that enterprise.

(2) There is excluded from article 21 any transaction into which a person enters as agent for another person if that other person is acting as principal, and the condition in paragraph (1)(a) or (b) is met, provided that—

(a) where the investment to which the transaction relates is a security, the agent does not hold himself out (other than to members of the same group or persons who are or propose to become participators with him in a joint enterprise) as engaging in the business of buying securities of the kind to which the transaction relates with a view to selling them, and does not regularly solicit members of the public for the purpose of inducing them (as principals or agents) to buy, sell, subscribe for or underwrite securities;

(b) where the investment to which the transaction relates is a contractually based investment, the agent enters into the transaction—

(i) with or through an authorised person, or an exempt person acting in the course of a business comprising a regulated activity in relation to which he is exempt; or

(ii) through an office outside the United Kingdom maintained by a party to the transaction, and with or through a person whose head office is situated outside the United Kingdom and whose ordinary business involves him in carrying on activities of the kind specified by any of articles 14, 21, 25, 37, 40, 45, 51, 52 and 53 or, so far as relevant to any of those articles, article 64, or would do so apart from any exclusion from any of those articles made by this Order.

(3) In paragraph (2)(a), "members of the public" has the meaning given by article 15(2), references to "A" being read as references to the agent.

(4) There are excluded from article 25(1) and (2) arrangements made by a person if—

(a) he is a member of a group and the arrangements in question are for, or with a view to, a transaction which is or is to be entered into, as principal, by another member of the same group; or

(b) he is or proposes to become a participator in a joint enterprise, and the arrangements in question are for, or with a view to, a transaction which is or is to be entered into, as principal, by another person who is or proposes to become a participator in that enterprise, for the purposes of or in connection with that enterprise.

(5) There is excluded from article 37 any activity carried on by a person if—

(a) he is a member of a group and the assets in question belong to another member of the same group; or

(b) he is or proposes to become a participator in a joint enterprise with the person to whom the assets belong, and the assets are managed for the purposes of or in connection with that enterprise.

(6) There is excluded from article 40 any activity carried on by a person if—

(a) he is a member of a group and the assets in question belong to another member of the same group; or

(b) he is or proposes to become a participator in a joint enterprise, and the assets in question—

(i) belong to another person who is or proposes to become a participator in that joint enterprise; and

(ii) are or are to be safeguarded and administered for the purposes of or in connection with that enterprise.

(7) A person who is a member of a group does not carry on an activity of the kind specified by article 45 where he sends a dematerialised instruction, or causes one to be sent, on behalf of another member of the same group, if the investment to which the instruction relates is one in respect of which a member of the same group is registered as holder in the appropriate register of securities, or will be so registered as a result of the instruction.

(8) In paragraph (7), "dematerialised instruction" and "register of securities" have the meaning given by regulation 3 of the Uncertificated Securities Regulations [2001].

(9) There is excluded from article 53 the giving of advice by a person if—

(a) he is a member of a group and gives the advice in question to another member of the same group; or

(b) he is, or proposes to become, a participator in a joint enterprise and the advice in question is given to another person who is, or proposes to become, a participator in that enterprise for the purposes of or in connection with that enterprise.

[(10) Paragraph (2) does not apply to a transaction for the sale or purchase of a contract of insurance.

(11) Paragraph (4) does not apply to arrangements for, or with a view to, a transaction for the sale or purchase of a contract of insurance.

(12) Paragraph (9) does not apply where the advice relates to a transaction for the sale or purchase of a contract of insurance.]

[(13) This article is subject to article 4(4).]

NOTES

Para (8): date in square brackets substituted by the Financial Services and Markets Act 2000 (Regulated Activities) (Amendment) Order 2002, SI 2002/682, art 13(4).

Paras (10)–(12): added by the Financial Services and Markets Act 2000 (Regulated Activities) (Amendment) (No 2) Order 2003, SI 2003/1476, arts 2, 10(4).

Para (13): added by the Financial Services and Markets Act 2000 (Regulated Activities) (Amendment No 3) Order 2006, SI 2006/3384, arts 2, 22.

70, 71 (*Outside the scope of this work.*)

[570]

72 Overseas persons

(1) An overseas person does not carry on an activity of the kind specified by article 14 [or 25D] by—

(a) entering into a transaction as principal with or though an authorised person, or an exempt person acting in the course of a business comprising a regulated activity in relation to which he is exempt; or

(b) entering into a transaction as principal with a person in the United Kingdom, if the transaction is the result of a legitimate approach.

(2) An overseas person does not carry on an activity of the kind specified by article 21 [or 25D] by—

(a) entering into a transaction as agent for any person with or through an authorised person or an exempt person acting in the course of a business comprising a regulated activity in relation to which he is exempt; or

(b) entering into a transaction with another party ("X") as agent for any person ("Y"), other than with or through an authorised person or such an exempt person, unless—

(i) either X or Y is in the United Kingdom; and

(ii) the transaction is the result of an approach (other than a legitimate approach) made by or on behalf of, or to, whichever of X or Y is in the United Kingdom.

(3) There are excluded from article 25(1) [or 25D] arrangements made by an overseas person with an authorised person, or an exempt person acting in the course of a business comprising a regulated activity in relation to which he is exempt.

(4) There are excluded from article 25(2) [or 25D] arrangements made by an overseas person with a view to transactions which are, as respects transactions in the United Kingdom, confined to—

(a) transactions entered into by authorised persons as principal or agent; and

(b) transactions entered into by exempt persons, as principal or agent, in the course of business comprising regulated activities in relation to which they are exempt.

(5) There is excluded from article 53 the giving of advice by an overseas person as a result of a legitimate approach.

[(5A) An overseas person does not carry on an activity of the kind specified by article 25A(1)(a), 25B(1)(a) *or 25C(1)(a)* if each person who may be contemplating entering into the relevant type of agreement in the relevant capacity is non-resident.

(5B) There are excluded from articles 25A(1)(b), 25B(1)(b) *and 25C(1)(b)* arrangements made by an overseas person to vary the terms of a qualifying agreement.

(5C) There are excluded from articles 25A(2), 25B(2) *and 25C(2)*, arrangements made by an overseas person which are made solely with a view to non-resident persons who participate in those arrangements entering, in the relevant capacity, into the relevant type of agreement.

(5D) An overseas person does not carry on an activity of the kind specified in article 61(1), 63B(1) *or 63F(1)* by entering into a qualifying agreement.

(5E) An overseas person does not carry on an activity of the kind specified in article 61(2), 63B(2) *or 63F(2)* where he administers a qualifying agreement.

(5F) In paragraphs (5A) to (5E)—

(a) "non-resident" means not normally resident in the United Kingdom;

(b) "qualifying agreement" means—

(i) in relation to articles 25A and 61, a regulated mortgage contract where the borrower (or each borrower) is non-resident when he enters into it;

(ii) in relation to articles 25B and 63B, a regulated home reversion plan where the reversion seller (or each reversion seller) is non-resident when he enters into it;

(iii) in relation to articles 25C and 63F, a regulated home purchase plan where the home purchaser (or each home purchaser) is non-resident when he enters into it;

[(iv) in relation to articles 25E and 63J, a regulated sale and rent back agreement where the agreement seller (or each agreement seller) is non-resident when the agreement seller enters into it;]

(c) "the relevant capacity" means—

(i) in the case of a regulated mortgage contract, as borrower;

(ii) in the case of a regulated home reversion plan, as reversion seller or plan provider;

(iii) in the case of a regulated home purchase plan, as home purchaser;

[(iv) in the case of a regulated sale and rent back agreement, as agreement seller or agreement provider;]

(d) "the relevant type of agreement" means—

(i) in relation to article 25A, a regulated mortgage contract;

(ii) in relation to article 25B, a regulated home reversion plan;

(iii) in relation to article 25C, a regulated home purchase plan.]

(iv) in relation to article 25E, a regulated sale and rent back agreement]].

(6) There is excluded from article 64 any agreement made by an overseas person to carry on an activity of the kind specified by article 25(1) or (2), 37[, 39A], 40 or 45 if the agreement is the result of a legitimate approach.

(7) In this article, "legitimate approach" means—

(a) an approach made to the overseas person which has not been solicited by him in any way, or has been solicited by him in a way which does not contravene section 21 of the Act; or

(b) an approach made by or on behalf of the overseas person in a way which does not contravene that section.

[(8) Paragraphs (1) to (5) do not apply where the overseas person is an investment firm or credit institution—

(a) who is providing or performing investment services and activities on a professional basis; and

(b) whose home Member State is the United Kingdom.]

NOTES

Paras (1)–(4): words in square brackets inserted by the Financial Services and Markets Act 2000 (Regulated Activities) (Amendment No 3) Order 2006, SI 2006/3384, arts 2, 24(a)–(d).

Paras (5A)–(5F): (originally inserted by the Financial Services and Markets Act 2000 (Regulated Activities) (Amendment) (No 1) Order 2003, SI 2003/1475, art 20) substituted by the Financial Services and Markets Act 2000 (Regulated Activities) (Amendment) (No 2) Order 2006, SI 2006/2383, arts 2, 21, subject to transitional provisions in arts 37–39 thereof; for the words in italics in para (5A) there are substituted the words ", 25C(1)(a) or 25E(1)(a)", for the words in italics in para (5B) there are substituted the words ", 25C(1)(b) and 25E(1)(b)", for the words in italics in para (5C) there are substituted the words ", 25C(2) and 25E(2)", for the words in italics in para (5D) there are substituted the words ", 63F(1) or 63J(1)", for the words in italics in para (5E) there are substituted the words ", 63F(2) or 63J(2)" and in para (5F), sub-paras (b)(iv), (c)(iv), and (d)(iv) inserted by the Financial Services and Markets Act 2000 (Regulated Activities) (Amendment) Order 2009, SI 2009/1342, arts 2, 20, as from 1 July 2009 (for certain purposes) and as from 30 June 2010 (for remaining purposes) (for the full commencement details and for transitional provisions etc see arts 1, 32–34 of that Order).

Para (6): reference in square brackets inserted by the Financial Services and Markets Act 2000 (Regulated Activities) (Amendment) (No 2) Order 2003, SI 2003/1476, arts 2, 10(6).

Para (8): added by SI 2006/3384, arts 2, 24(e).

[571]

[72A Information society services

(1) There is excluded from this Part any activity consisting of the provision of an information society service from an EEA State other than the United Kingdom.

(2) The exclusion in paragraph (1) does not apply to the activity of effecting or carrying out a contract of insurance as principal, where—

(a) the activity is carried on by an undertaking which has received official authorisation in accordance with [Article 4 of the life assurance consolidation directive] or the first non-life insurance directive, and

(b) the insurance falls within the scope of any of the insurance directives.]

NOTES

Inserted by the Financial Services and Markets Act 2000 (Regulated Activities) (Amendment) (No 2) Order 2002, SI 2002/1776, art 2.

Para (2): words in square brackets substituted by the Life Assurance Consolidation Directive (Consequential Amendments) Regulations 2004, SI 2004/3379, reg 17.

[572]

[72B Activities carried on by a provider of relevant goods or services

(1) In this article—

"connected contract of insurance" means a contract of insurance which—

(a) is not a contract of long-term insurance;

(b) has a total duration (or would have a total duration were any right to renew conferred by the contract exercised) of five years or less;

(c) has an annual premium (or, where the premium is paid otherwise than by way of annual premium, the equivalent of an annual premium) of 500 euro or less, or the equivalent amount in sterling or other currency;

(d) covers the risk of—

(i) breakdown, loss of, or damage to, non-motor goods supplied by the provider; or

[(ii) damage to, or loss of, baggage and other risks linked to the travel booked with the provider ("travel risks") in circumstances where—

(aa) the travel booked with the provider relates to attendance at an event organised or managed by that provider and the party seeking insurance is not an individual (acting in his private capacity) or a small business; or

(bb) the travel booked with the provider is only the hire of an aircraft, vehicle or vessel which does not provide sleeping accommodation;]

(e) does not cover any liability risks (except, in the case of a contract which covers travel risks, where that cover is ancillary to the main cover provided by the contract);

(f) is complementary to the non-motor goods being supplied or service being provided by the provider; and

(g) is of such a nature that the only information that a person requires in order to carry on an activity of the kind specified by article 21, 25, 39A or 53 in relation to it is the cover provided by the contract;

"non-motor goods" means goods which are not mechanically propelled road vehicles;

"provider" means a person who supplies non-motor goods or provides services related to travel in the course of carrying on a profession or business which does not otherwise consist of the carrying on of regulated activities. [For these purposes, the transfer of possession of an aircraft, vehicle or vessel under an agreement for hire which is not—

(a) a hire-purchase agreement within the meaning of section 189(1) of the Consumer Credit Act 1974, or

(b) any other agreement which contemplates that the property in those goods will also pass at some time in the future,

is the provision of a service related to travel, not a supply of goods.]

["small business" means—

(a) subject to paragraph (b) a sole trader, body corporate, partnership or an unincorporated association which had a turnover in the last financial year of less than £1,000,000;

(b) where the business concerned is a member of a group within the meaning of section 262(1) of the Companies Act 1985 (and after the repeal of that section within the meaning of section 474(1) of the Companies Act 2006), reference to its turnover means the combined turnover of the group.

"turnover" means the amounts derived from the provision of goods and services falling within the business's ordinary activities, after deduction of trade discounts, value added tax and any other taxes based on the amounts so derived.]

(2) There is excluded from article 21 any transaction for the sale or purchase of a connected contract of insurance into which a provider enters as agent.

(3) There are excluded from article 25(1) and (2) any arrangements made by a provider for, or with a view to, a transaction for the sale or purchase of a connected contract of insurance.

(4) There is excluded from article 39A any activity carried on by a provider where the contract of insurance in question is a connected contract of insurance.

(5) There is excluded from article 53 the giving of advice by a provider in relation to a transaction for the sale or purchase of a connected contract of insurance.

(6) For the purposes of this article, a contract of insurance which covers travel risks is not to be treated as a contract of long-term insurance, notwithstanding the fact that it contains related and subsidiary provisions such that it might be regarded as a contract of long-term insurance, if the cover to which those provisions relate is ancillary to the main cover provided by the contract.]

NOTES

Inserted, together with arts 72C, 72D, by the Financial Services and Markets Act 2000 (Regulated Activities) (Amendment) (No 2) Order 2003, SI 2003/1476, arts 2, 11.

Para (1): in definition "connected contract of insurance", sub-para (d)(ii) substituted and words in square brackets in definition "provider" and definitions "small business" and "turnover" inserted by the Financial Services and Markets Act 2000 (Regulated Activities) (Amendment) (No 2) Order 2007, SI 2007/3510, art 2, subject to transitional provisions in arts 3–9 thereof.

[573]

[72C Provision of information on an incidental basis

(1) There is excluded from articles 25(1) and (2) the making of arrangements for, or with a view to, a transaction for the sale or purchase of a contract of insurance or an investment of the kind specified by article 89, so far as relevant to such a contract, where that activity meets the conditions specified in paragraph (4).

(2) There is excluded from articles 37 and 40 any activity—

(a) where the assets in question are rights under a contract of insurance or an investment of the kind specified by article 89, so far as relevant to such a contract; and

(b) which meets the conditions specified in paragraph (4).

(3) There is excluded from article 39A any activity which meets the conditions specified in paragraph (4).

(4) The conditions specified in this paragraph are that the activity—

(a) consists of the provision of information to the policyholder or potential policyholder;

(b) is carried on by a person in the course of carrying on a profession or business which does not otherwise consist of the carrying on of regulated activities; and

(c) may reasonably be regarded as being incidental to that profession or business.]

NOTES

Inserted as noted to art 72B at **[572]**.

[574]

[72D Large risks contracts where risk situated outside the EEA

(1) There is excluded from articles 21, 25(1) and (2), 39A and 53 any activity which is carried on in relation to a large risks contract of insurance, to the extent that the risk or commitment covered by the contract is not situated in an EEA State.

(2) In this article, a "large risks contract of insurance" is a contract of insurance the principal object of which is to cover—

(a) risks falling within paragraph 4 (railway rolling stock), 5 (aircraft), 6 (ships), 7 (goods in transit), 11 (aircraft liability) or 12 (liability of ships) of Part 1 of Schedule 1;

(b) risks falling within paragraph 14 (credit) or 15 (suretyship) of that Part provided that the risks relate to a business carried on by the policyholder; or

(c) risks falling within paragraph 3 (land vehicles), 8 (fire and natural forces), 9 (damage to property), 10 (motor vehicle liability), 13 (general liability) or 16 (miscellaneous financial loss) of that Part provided that the risks relate to a business carried on by the policyholder and that the condition specified in paragraph (3) is met in relation to that business.

(3) The condition specified in this paragraph is that at least two of the three following criteria were met in the most recent financial year for which information is available—

(a) the balance sheet total of the business (within the meaning of section 247(5) of the Companies Act 1985 or article 255(5) of the Companies (Northern Ireland) Order 1986) exceeded 6.2 million euro,

(b) the net turnover (within the meaning given to "turnover" by section 262(1) of that Act or article 270(1) of that Order) exceeded 12.8 million euro,

(c) the number of employees (within the meaning given by section 247(6) of that Act or article 255(6) of that Order) exceeded 250,

and for a financial year which is a company's financial year but not in fact a year, the net turnover of the policyholder shall be proportionately adjusted.

(4) For the purposes of paragraph (3), where the policyholder is a member of a group for which consolidated accounts (within the meaning of the Seventh Company Law Directive) are drawn up, the question whether the condition specified by that paragraph is met is to be determined by reference to those accounts.]

NOTES

Inserted as noted to art 72B at **[572]**.

[575]

[72E Business Angel-led Enterprise Capital Funds

(1) A body corporate of a type specified in paragraph (7) does not carry on the activity of the kind specified by article 21 by entering as agent into a transaction on behalf of the participants of a Business Angel-led Enterprise Capital Fund.

(2) There are excluded from article 25(1) and (2) arrangements, made by a body corporate of a type specified in paragraph (7), for or with a view to a transaction which is or is to be entered into by or on behalf of the participants in a Business Angel-led Enterprise Capital Fund.

(3) There is excluded from article 37 any activity, carried on by a body corporate of a type specified in paragraph (7), which consists in the managing of assets belonging to the participants in a Business Angel-led Enterprise Capital Fund.

(4) There is excluded from article 40 any activity, carried on by a body corporate of a type specified in paragraph (7), in respect of assets belonging to the participants in a Business Angel-led Enterprise Capital Fund.

(5) A body corporate of a type specified in paragraph (7) does not carry on the activity of the kind specified in article 51(1)(a) where it carries on the activity of establishing, operating or winding up a Business Angel-led Enterprise Capital Fund.

(6) A body corporate of a type specified in paragraph (7) does not carry on the activity of the kind specified in article 53 where it is advising the participants in a Business Angel-led Enterprise Capital Fund on investments to be made by or on behalf of the participants of that Business Angel-led Enterprise Capital Fund.

(7) The type of body corporate specified is a limited company—

- (i) which operates a Business Angel-led Enterprise Capital Fund; and
- (ii) the members of which are participants in the Business Angel-led Enterprise Capital Fund operated by that limited company and between them have invested at least 50 per cent of the total investment in that Business Angel-led Enterprise Capital Fund excluding any investment made by the Secretary of State.

(8) For the purposes of paragraph (7), "a limited company" means a body corporate with limited liability which is a company or firm formed in accordance with the law of an EEA State and having its registered office, central administration or principal place of business within the territory of an EEA State.

(9) Nothing in this article has the effect of excluding a body corporate from the application of the Money Laundering Regulations [2007], in so far as those Regulations would have applied to it but for this article.

(10) Nothing in this article has the effect of excluding a body corporate from the application of section 397 of the Act (misleading statements and practices), in so far as that section would have applied to it but for this article.

[(11) This article is subject to article 4(4).]]

NOTES

Commencement: 1 October 2005.

Inserted, together with art 72F, by the Financial Services and Markets Act 2000 (Regulated Activities) (Amendment) (No 2) Order 2005, SI 2005/1518, art 2(1), (3).

Para (9): figure in square brackets substituted by the Money laundering Regulations 2007, SI 2007/2157, reg 51, Sch 6, Pt 2, para 10.

Para (11): added by the Financial Services and Markets Act 2000 (Regulated Activities) (Amendment No 3) Order 2006, SI 2006/3384, arts 2, 25.

[576]

[72F Interpretation

(1) For the purposes of this article and of article 72E—

"Business Angel-led Enterprise Capital Fund" means a collective investment scheme which—

- (a) is established for the purpose of enabling participants to participate in or receive profits or income arising from the acquisition, holding, management or disposal of investments falling within one or more of—

(i) article 76, being shares in an unlisted company;
(ii) article 77, being instruments creating or acknowledging indebtedness in respect of an unlisted company;
[(iia) article 77A, being rights under an alternative finance investment bond issued by an unlisted company;] and
(iii) article 79, being warrants or other instruments entitling the holder to subscribe for shares in an unlisted company;

(b) has only the following as its participants—
(i) the Secretary of State;
(ii) a body corporate of a type specified in article 72E(7); and
(iii) one or more persons each of whom at the time they became a participant was—
(aa) a sophisticated investor;
(bb) a high net worth individual;
(cc) a high net worth company;
(dd) a high net worth unincorporated association;
(ee) a trustee of a high value trust; or
(ff) a self-certified sophisticated investor;

(c) is prevented, by the arrangements by which it is established, from—
(i) acquiring investments, other than those falling within paragraphs (i) to (iii) of sub-paragraph (a); and
(ii) acquiring investments falling within paragraphs (i) to (iii) of sub-paragraph (a) in an unlisted company, where the aggregated cost of those investments exceeds £2 million, unless that acquisition is necessary to prevent or reduce the dilution of an existing share-holding in that unlisted company;

"high net worth company" means a body corporate which—
(a) falls within article 49(2)(a) of the Financial Services and Markets Act 2000 (Financial Promotion) Order 2001 (high net worth companies, unincorporated associations etc); and
(b) has executed a document [(in a manner which binds the company)] in the following terms:
"This company is a high net worth company and falls within article 49(2)(a) of the Financial Services and Markets Act 2000 (Financial Promotion) Order 2001. We understand that any Business Angel-led Enterprise Capital Fund (within the meaning of article 72F of the Financial Services and Markets Act 2000 (Regulated Activities) Order 2001), in which this company participates, or any person who operates that Business Angel-led Enterprise Capital Fund, in which this company participates, will not be authorised under the Financial Services and Markets Act 2000 (and so will not have to satisfy the threshold conditions set out in Part I of Schedule 6 to that Act and will not be subject to Financial Services Authority rules such as those on holding client money). We understand that this means that redress through the Financial Services Authority, the Financial Ombudsman Scheme or the Financial Services Compensation Scheme will not be available. We also understand the risks associated in investing in a Business Angel-led Enterprise Capital Fund and are aware that it is open to us to seek advice from someone who is authorised under the Financial Services and Markets Act 2000 and who specialises in advising on this kind of investment."

"high net worth individual" means an individual who—
(a) is a "certified high net worth individual" within the meaning of article 48(2) of the Financial Services and Markets Act 2000 (Financial Promotion) Order 2001 (certified high net worth individuals); and
(b) has signed a statement in the following terms:
"I declare that I am a certified high net worth individual within the meaning of article 48(2) of the Financial Services and Markets Act 2000 (Financial Promotion) Order 2001 and that I understand that any Business Angel-led Enterprise Capital Fund (within the meaning of article 72F of the Financial Services and Markets Act 2000 (Regulated Activities) Order 2001), in which I participate, or any person who operates that Business Angel-led Enterprise Capital Fund, in which I participate, will not be authorised under the Financial Services and Markets Act 2000 (and so will not have to satisfy the threshold conditions set out in Part I of Schedule 6 to that Act and will not be subject to Financial Services

Authority rules such as those on holding client money). I understand that this means that redress through the Financial Services Authority, the Financial Ombudsman Scheme or the Financial Services Compensation Scheme will not be available. I also understand the risks associated in investing in a Business Angel-led Enterprise Capital Fund and am aware that it is open to me to seek advice from someone who is authorised under the Financial Services and Markets Act 2000 and who specialises in advising on this kind of investment.";

"high net worth unincorporated association" means an unincorporated association—

(a) which falls within article 49(2)(b) of the Financial Services and Markets Act 2000 (Financial Promotion) Order 2001; and

(b) on behalf of which an officer of that association or a member of its governing body has signed a statement in the following terms:

"This unincorporated association is a high net worth unincorporated association and falls within article 49(2)(b) of the Financial Services and Markets Act 2000 (Financial Promotion) Order 2001. I understand that any Business Angel-led Enterprise Capital Fund (within the meaning of article 72F of the Financial Services and Markets Act 2000 (Regulated Activities) Order 2001), in which this association participates, or any person who operates that Business Angel-led Enterprise Capital Fund, in which this association participates, will not be authorised under the Financial Services and Markets Act 2000 (and so will not have to satisfy the threshold conditions set out in Part I of Schedule 6 to that Act and will not be subject to Financial Services Authority rules such as those on holding client money). I understand that this means that redress through the Financial Services Authority, the Financial Ombudsman Scheme or the Financial Services Compensation Scheme will not be available. I also understand the risks associated in investing in a Business Angel-led Enterprise Capital Fund and am aware that it is open to the association to seek advice from someone who is authorised under the Financial Services and Markets Act 2000 and who specialises in advising on this kind of investment.";

"high value trust" means a trust—

(a) where the aggregate value of the cash and investments which form a part of the trust's assets (before deducting the amount of its liabilities) is £10 million or more;

(b) on behalf of which a trustee has signed a statement in the following terms:

"This trust is a high value trust. I understand that any Business Angel-led Enterprise Capital Fund (within the meaning of article 72F of the Financial Services and Markets Act 2000 (Regulated Activities) Order 2001), in which this trust participates, or any person who operates that Business Angel-led Enterprise Capital Fund, in which this trust participates, will not be authorised under the Financial Services and Markets Act 2000 (and so will not have to satisfy the threshold conditions set out in Part I of Schedule 6 to that Act and will not be subject to Financial Services Authority rules such as those on holding client money). I understand that this means that redress through the Financial Services Authority, the Financial Ombudsman Scheme or the Financial Services Compensation Scheme will not be available. I also understand the risks associated in investing in a Business Angel-led Enterprise Capital Fund and am aware that it is open to the trust to seek advice from someone who is authorised under the Financial Services and Markets Act 2000 and who specialises in advising on this kind of investment.";

"self-certified sophisticated investor" means an individual who—

(a) is a "self-certified sophisticated investor" within the meaning of article 50A of the Financial Services and Markets Act 2000 (Financial Promotion) Order 2001;

(b) has signed a statement in the following terms:

"I declare that I am a self-certified sophisticated investor within the meaning of article 50A of the Financial Services and Markets Act 2000 (Financial Promotion) Order 2001 and that I understand that any Business Angel-led Enterprise Capital Fund (within the meaning of article 72F of the Financial Services and Markets Act 2000 (Regulated Activities) Order 2001), in which I participate, or any person who operates that Business Angel-led Enterprise Capital Fund, in which I participate, will not be authorised under the Financial Services and Markets Act 2000 (and so will not have to satisfy the threshold conditions set out in Part I of Schedule 6 to that Act and will not be subject to Financial Services Authority rules such as those on holding client money). I understand that this means that redress through the Financial Services Authority, the Financial Ombudsman Scheme or the Financial Services Compensation Scheme will not be available. I also understand the risks associated in investing in a Business Angel-led

Enterprise Capital Fund and am aware that it is open to me to seek advice from someone who is authorised under the Financial Services and Markets Act 2000 and who specialises in advising on this kind of investment.";

"sophisticated investor" means an individual who—

(a) is a "certified sophisticated investor" within the meaning of article 50(1) of the Financial Services and Markets Act 2000 (Financial Promotion) Order 2001; and

(b) has signed a statement in the following terms:

"I declare that I am a certified sophisticated investor within the meaning of article 50(1) of the Financial Services and Markets Act 2000 (Financial Promotion) Order 2001 and that I understand that any Business Angel-led Enterprise Capital Fund (within the meaning of article 72F of the Financial Services and Markets Act 2000 (Regulated Activities) Order 2001), in which I participate, or any person who operates that Business Angel-led Enterprise Capital Fund, in which I participate, will not be authorised under the Financial Services and Markets Act 2000 (and so will not have to satisfy the threshold conditions set out in Part I of Schedule 6 to that Act and will not be subject to Financial Services Authority rules such as those on holding client money). I understand that this means that redress through the Financial Services Authority, the Financial Ombudsman Scheme or the Financial Services Compensation Scheme will not be available. I also understand the risks associated in investing in a Business Angel-led Enterprise Capital Fund and am aware that it is open to me to seek advice from someone who is authorised under the Financial Services and Markets Act 2000 and who specialises in advising on this kind of investment.";

"unlisted company" has the meaning given by article 3 of the Financial Services and Markets Act 2000 (Financial Promotion) Order 2001.

(2) References in this Article and in Article 72E to a participant in a Business Angel-led Enterprise Capital Fund, doing things on behalf of such a participant and property belonging to such a participant are, respectively, references to that participant in that capacity, to doing things on behalf of that participant in that capacity or to the property of that participant held in that capacity.]

NOTES

Commencement: 1 October 2005.

Inserted as noted to art 72E at **[575]**.

Para (1): in definition "Business Angel-led Enterprise Capital Fund", para (a)(iia) inserted by the Financial Services and Markets Act 2000 (Regulated Activities) (Amendment) Order 2010, SI 2010/86, art 4, Schedule, para 5(e); words in square brackets in definition "high net worth company" substituted by the Financial Services and Markets Act 2000 (Regulated Activities) (Amendment) (No 2) Order 2006, SI 2006/2383, arts 2, 22, subject to transitional provisions in arts 37–39 thereof.

PART III
SPECIFIED INVESTMENTS

[577]

73 Investments: general

The following kinds of investment are specified for the purposes of section 22 of the Act.

74, 74A *(Outside the scope of this work.)*

[578]

75 Contracts of insurance

Rights under a contract of insurance.

76–81 *(Outside the scope of this work.)*

[579]

[82 Rights under a pension scheme

(1) Rights under a stakeholder pension scheme.

(2) Rights under a personal pension scheme.]

NOTES

Commencement: 1 October 2006 (certain purposes); 6 April 2007 (remaining purposes).

Substituted by the Financial Services and Markets Act 2000 (Regulated Activities) (Amendment) Order 2006, SI 2006/1969, art 2(1), (5).

83–85 *(Outside the scope of this work.)*

[580]

86 Lloyd's syndicate capacity and syndicate membership

(1) The underwriting capacity of a Lloyd's syndicate.

(2) A person's membership (or prospective membership) of a Lloyd's syndicate.

87–91 (*Arts 87–89 outside the scope of this work; arts 90, 91 (Pt IV) amend the Consumer Credit Act 1974, ss 16, 43, 52, 53, 137, 151, the Consumer Credit (Advertisements) Regulations 1989, SI 1989/1125, reg 9 and the Consumer Credit (Content of Quotations) and Consumer Credit (Advertisements) (Amendment) Regulations 1999, SI 1999/2725, reg 2.*)

[PART V
UNAUTHORISED PERSONS CARRYING ON INSURANCE MEDIATION ACTIVITIES

[581]

92 Interpretation

In this Part—

"designated professional body" means a body which is for the time being designated by the Treasury under section 326 of the Act (designation of professional bodies);

"insurance mediation activity" means any regulated activity of the kind specified by article 21, 25(1) or (2), 39A or 53, or, so far as relevant to any of those articles, article 64, which is carried on in relation to a contract of insurance;

"the record" means the record maintained by the Authority under section 347 of the Act (public record of authorised persons etc);

"recorded insurance intermediary" has the meaning given by article 93(4);

"a relevant member", in relation to a designated professional body, means a member (within the meaning of section 325(2) of the Act) of the profession in relation to which that designated professional body is established, or a person who is controlled or managed by one or more such members.]

NOTES

Pt V (arts 92–96) inserted by the Financial Services and Markets Act 2000 (Regulated Activities) (Amendment) (No 2) Order 2003, SI 2003/1476, arts 2, 13.

[582]

[93 Duty to maintain a record of unauthorised persons carrying on insurance mediation activities

(1) Subject to articles 95 and 96, the Authority must include in the record every person who—

(a) as a result of information obtained by virtue of its rules or by virtue of a direction given, or requirement imposed, under section 51(3) of the Act (procedure for applications under Part IV), appears to the Authority to fall within paragraph (2); or

(b) as a result of information obtained by virtue of article 94, appears to the Authority to fall within paragraph (3).

(2) A person falls within this paragraph if he is, or has entered into a contract by virtue of which he will be, an appointed representative who carries on any insurance mediation activity.

(3) A person falls within this paragraph if—

(a) he is a relevant member of a designated professional body who carries on, or is proposing to carry on, any insurance mediation activity; and

(b) the general prohibition does not (or will not) apply to the carrying on of those activities by virtue of section 327 of the Act (exemption from the general prohibition).

(4) In this Part, "recorded insurance intermediary" means a person who is included in the record by virtue of paragraph (1).

(5) The record must include—

(a) in the case of any recorded insurance intermediary, its address; and

(b) in the case of a recorded insurance intermediary which is not an individual, the name of the individuals who are responsible for the management of the business carried on by the intermediary, so far as it relates to insurance mediation activities.]

NOTES

Inserted as noted to art 92 at **[581]**.

[583]

[94 Members of designated professional bodies

(1) A designated professional body must, by notice in writing, inform the Authority of—

(a) the name,

(b) the address, and

(c) in the case of a relevant member which is not an individual, the name of the individuals who are responsible for the management of the business carried on by the member, so far as it relates to insurance mediation activities,

of any relevant member who falls within paragraph (2).

(2) A relevant member of a designated professional body falls within this paragraph if, in accordance with the rules of that body, he carries on, or proposes to carry on any insurance mediation activity but does not have, and does not propose to apply for, Part IV permission on the basis that the general prohibition does not (or will not) apply to the carrying on of that activity by virtue of section 327 of the Act.

(3) A designated professional body must also, by notice in writing, inform the Authority of any change in relation to the matters specified in sub-paragraphs (a) to (c) of paragraph (1).

(4) A designated professional body must inform the Authority when a relevant member to whom paragraph (2) applies ceases, for whatever reason, to carry on insurance mediation activities.

(5) The Authority may give directions to a designated professional body as to the manner in which the information referred to in paragraphs (1), (3) and (4) must be provided.]

NOTES

Inserted as noted to art 92 at **[581]**.

[584]

[95 Exclusion from record where not fit and proper to carry on insurance mediation activities

(1) If it appears to the Authority that a person who falls within article 93(2) (appointed representatives) ("AR") is not a fit and proper person to carry on insurance mediation activities, it may decide not to include him in the record or, if that person is already included in the record, to remove him from the record.

(2) Where the Authority proposes to make a determination under paragraph (1), it must give AR a warning notice.

(3) If the Authority makes a determination under paragraph (1), it must give AR a decision notice.

(4) If the Authority gives AR a decision notice under paragraph (3), AR may refer the matter to the Tribunal.

(5) The Authority may, on the application of AR, revoke a determination under paragraph (1).

(6) If the Authority decides to grant the application, it must give AR written notice of its decision.

(7) If the Authority proposes to refuse the application, it must give AR a warning notice.

(8) If the Authority decides to refuse the application, it must give AR a decision notice.

(9) If the Authority gives AR a decision notice under paragraph (8), AR may refer the matter to the Tribunal.

(10) Sections 393 and 394 of the Act (third party rights and access to Authority material) apply to a warning notice given in accordance with paragraph (2) or (7) and to a decision notice given in accordance with paragraph (3) or (8).]

NOTES

Inserted as noted to art 92 at **[581]**.

[585]

[96 Exclusion from the record where Authority has exercised its powers under Part XX of the Act

(1) If a person who appears to the Authority to fall within article 93(3) (member of a designated professional body) falls within paragraph (2) or (3), the Authority must not include him in the record or, if that person is already included in the record, must remove him from the record.

(2) A person falls within this paragraph if, by virtue of a direction given by the Authority under section 328(1) of the Act (directions in relation to the general prohibition), section 327(1) of the Act does not apply in relation to the carrying on by him of any insurance mediation activity.

(3) A person falls within this paragraph if the Authority has made an order under section 329(2) of the Act (orders in relation to the general prohibition) disapplying section 327(1) of the Act in relation to the carrying on by him of any insurance mediation activity.]

NOTES

Inserted as noted to art 92 at **[581]**.

97 *((Pt VI) Added by the Financial Services and Markets Act 2000 (Regulated Activities) (Amendment) Order 2004, SI 2004/1610, art 3 and inserts the Financial Services and Markets Act 2000, s 49(2A) at* **[49]**.)

SCHEDULE 1
CONTRACTS OF INSURANCE

Article 3(1)

PART I
CONTRACTS OF GENERAL INSURANCE

[586]

1 Accident

Contracts of insurance providing fixed pecuniary benefits or benefits in the nature of indemnity (or a combination of both) against risks of the person insured or, in the case of a contract made by virtue of section 140, 140A or 140B of the Local Government Act 1972 (or, in Scotland, section 86(1) of the Local Government (Scotland) Act 1973), a person for whose benefit the contract is made—

(a) sustaining injury as the result of an accident or of an accident of a specified class; or
(b) dying as a result of an accident or of an accident of a specified class; or
(c) becoming incapacitated in consequence of disease or of disease of a specified class,

including contracts relating to industrial injury and occupational disease but excluding contracts falling within paragraph 2 of Part I of, or paragraph IV of Part II of, this Schedule.

2 Sickness

Contracts of insurance providing fixed pecuniary benefits or benefits in the nature of indemnity (or a combination of both) against risks of loss to the persons insured attributable to sickness or infirmity but excluding contracts falling within paragraph IV of Part II of this Schedule.

3 Land vehicles

Contracts of insurance against loss of or damage to vehicles used on land, including motor vehicles but excluding railway rolling stock.

4 Railway rolling stock

Contract of insurance against loss of or damage to railway rolling stock.

5 Aircraft

Contracts of insurance upon aircraft or upon the machinery, tackle, furniture or equipment of aircraft.

6 Ships

Contracts of insurance upon vessels used on the sea or on inland water, or upon the machinery, tackle, furniture or equipment of such vessels.

7 Goods in transit

Contracts of insurance against loss of or damage to merchandise, baggage and all other goods in transit, irrespective of the form of transport.

8 Fire and natural forces

Contracts of insurance against loss of or damage to property (other than property to which paragraphs 3 to 7 relate) due to fire, explosion, storm, natural forces other than storm, nuclear energy or land subsidence.

9 Damage to property

Contracts of insurance against loss of or damage to property (other than property to which paragraphs 3 to 7 relate) due to hail or frost or any other event (such as theft) other than those mentioned in paragraph 8.

10 Motor vehicle liability

Contracts of insurance against damage arising out of or in connection with the use of motor vehicles on land, including third-party risks and carrier's liability.

11 Aircraft liability

Contracts of insurance against damage arising out of or in connection with the use of aircraft, including third-party risks and carrier's liability.

12 Liability of ships

Contracts of insurance against damage arising out of or in connection with the use of vessels on the sea or on inland water, including third party risks and carrier's liability.

13 General liability
Contracts of insurance against risks of the persons insured incurring liabilities to third parties, the risks in question not being risks to which paragraph 10, 11 or 12 relates.

14 Credit
Contracts of insurance against risks of loss to the persons insured arising from the insolvency of debtors of theirs or from the failure (otherwise than through insolvency) of debtors of theirs to pay their debts when due.

15 Suretyship
(1) Contracts of insurance against the risks of loss to the persons insured arising from their having to perform contracts of guarantee entered into by them.
(2) Fidelity bonds, performance bonds, administration bonds, bail bonds or customs bonds or similar contracts of guarantee, where these are—
- (a) effected or carried out by a person not carrying on a banking business;
- (b) not effected merely incidentally to some other business carried on by the person effecting them; and
- (c) effected in return for the payment of one or more premiums.

16 Miscellaneous financial loss
Contracts of insurance against any of the following risks, namely—
- (a) risks of loss to the persons insured attributable to interruptions of the carrying on of business carried on by them or to reduction of the scope of business so carried on;
- (b) risks of loss to the persons insured attributable to their incurring unforeseen expense (other than loss such as is covered by contracts falling within paragraph 18);
- (c) risks which do not fall within sub-paragraph (a) or (b) and which are not of a kind such that contracts of insurance against them fall within any other provision of this Schedule.

17 Legal expenses
Contracts of insurance against risks of loss to the persons insured attributable to their incurring legal expenses (including costs of litigation).

18 Assistance
Contracts of insurance providing either or both of the following benefits, namely—
- (a) assistance (whether in cash or in kind) for persons who get into difficulties while travelling, while away from home or while away from their permanent residence; or
- (b) assistance (whether in cash or in kind) for persons who get into difficulties otherwise than as mentioned in sub-paragraph (a).

PART II
CONTRACTS OF LONG-TERM INSURANCE

[587]

I Life and annuity
Contracts of insurance on human life or contracts to pay annuities on human life, but excluding (in each case) contracts within paragraph III.

II Marriage and birth
Contract of insurance to provide a sum on marriage [or the formation of a civil partnership] or on the birth of a child, being contracts expressed to be in effect for a period of more than one year.

III Linked long term
Contracts of insurance on human life or contracts to pay annuities on human life where the benefits are wholly or party to be determined by references to the value of, or the income from, property of any description (whether or not specified in the contracts) or by reference to fluctuations in, or in an index of, the value of property of any description (whether or not so specified).

IV Permanent health
Contracts of insurance providing specified benefits against risks of persons becoming incapacitated in consequence of sustaining injury as a result of an accident or of an accident of a specified class or of sickness or infirmity, being contracts that—
- (a) are expressed to be in effect for a period of not less than five years, or until the normal retirement age for the persons concerned, or without limit of time; and
- (b) either are not expressed to be terminable by the insurer, or are expressed to be so terminable only in special circumstances mentioned in the contract.

V Tontines
Tontines.

VI Capital redemption contracts
Capital redemption contracts, where effected or carried out by a person who does not carry on a banking business, and otherwise carries on a regulated activity of the kind specified by article 10(1) or (2).

VII Pension fund management
(a) Pension fund management contracts, and
(b) pension fund management contracts which are combined with contracts of insurance covering either conservation of capital or payment of a minimum interest,
where effected or carried out by a person who does not carry on a banking business, and otherwise carries on a regulated activity of the kind specified by article 10(1) or (2).

VIII Collective insurance etc
Contracts of a kind referred to in article 1(2)(e) of the first life insurance directive.

IX Social insurance
Contracts of a kind referred to in article 1(3) of the first life insurance directive.

NOTES
Para II: words in square brackets inserted by the Civil Partnership Act 2004 (Amendments to Subordinate Legislation) Order 2005, SI 2005/2114, art 2(16), Sch 16, Pt 1, para 1(1), (5).

(Schs 2, 3 outside the scope of this work.)

[SCHEDULE 4

RELEVANT TEXT OF THE INSURANCE MEDIATION DIRECTIVE
Article 4(4A)

PART I
ARTICLE 1.2

[588]
This Directive shall not apply to persons providing mediation services for insurance contracts if all the following conditions are met:
- (a) the insurance contract only requires knowledge of the insurance cover that is provided;
- (b) the insurance contract is not a life assurance contract;
- (c) the insurance contract does not cover any liability risks;
- (d) the principal professional activity of the person is other than insurance mediation;
- (e) the insurance is complementary to the product or service supplied by any provider, where such insurance covers:
  - (i) the risk of breakdown, loss of or damage to goods supplied by that provider; or
  - (ii) damage to or loss of baggage and other risks linked to the travel booked with that provider, even if the insurance covers life assurance or liability risks, provided that the cover is ancillary to the main cover for the risks linked to that travel;
- (f) the amount of the annual premium does not exceed EUR 500 and the total duration of the insurance contract, including any renewals, does not exceed five years.]

NOTES
Added by the Financial Services and Markets Act 2000 (Regulated Activities) (Amendment) (No 2) Order 2003, SI 2003/1476, arts 2, 12.

[PART II
ARTICLE 2.3

[589]
"Insurance mediation" means the activities of introducing, proposing or carrying out other work preparatory to the conclusion of contracts of insurance, or of concluding such contracts, or of assisting in the administration and performance of such contracts, in particular in the event of a claim.

These activities when undertaken by an insurance undertaking or an employee of an insurance undertaking who is acting under the responsibility of the insurance undertaking shall not be considered as insurance mediation.

The provision of information on an incidental basis in the context of another professional activity provided that the purpose of that activity is not to assist the customer in concluding or performing an insurance contract, the management of claims of an insurance undertaking on a professional basis, and loss adjusting and expert appraisal of claims shall also not be considered as insurance mediation.]

NOTES

Added as noted to Pt I at **[588]**.

[PART III
ARTICLE 2.4

[590]

"Reinsurance mediation" means the activities of introducing, proposing or carrying out other work preparatory to the conclusion of contracts of reinsurance, or of concluding such contracts, or of assisting in the administration and performance of such contracts, in particular in the event of a claim.

These activities when undertaken by a reinsurance undertaking or an employee of a reinsurance undertaking who is acting under the responsibility of the reinsurance undertaking are not considered as reinsurance mediation.

The provision of information on an incidental basis in the context of another professional activity provided that the purpose of that activity is not to assist the customer in concluding or performing a reinsurance contract, the management of claims of a reinsurance undertaking on a professional basis, and loss adjusting and expert appraisal of claims shall also not be considered as reinsurance mediation.]

NOTES

Added as noted to Pt I at **[588]**.

FINANCIAL SERVICES AND MARKETS ACT 2000 (CARRYING ON REGULATED ACTIVITIES BY WAY OF BUSINESS) ORDER 2001

(SI 2001/1177)

NOTES

Made: 26 March 2001.
Authority: Financial Services and Markets Act 2000, ss 419, 428(3).
Commencement: 1 December 2001 (see art 1(1)).

[591]

1 Citation, commencement and interpretation

(1) This Order may be cited as the Financial Services and Markets Act 2000 (Carrying on Regulated Activities by Way of Business) Order 2001, and comes into force on the day on which section 19 of the Financial Services and Markets Act 2000 comes into force.

(2) In this Order—

(a) the "Regulated Activities Order" means the Financial Services and Markets Act 2000 (Regulated Activities) Order 2001;

(b) ["contract of insurance",] "contractually based investment", "deposit", "overseas person" and "security" have the same meaning as in that Order;

(c) "shares" and "debentures" mean any investment of the kind specified by article 76[, 77 or 77A] of that Order;

(d) "units in a collective investment scheme" means any investment of the kind specified by article 81 of that Order;

(e) "warrants" means any investment of the kind specified by article 79 of that Order.

NOTES

Para (2): words in square brackets in sub-para (b) inserted by the Financial Services and Markets Act 2000 (Regulated Activities) (Amendment) (No 2) Order 2003, SI 2003/1476, art 18(1), (2); words in square brackets in sub-para (c) substituted by the Financial Services and Markets Act 2000 (Regulated Activities) (Amendment) Order 2010, SI 2010/86, art 4, Schedule, para 6.

[592]

2 Deposit taking business

(1) A person who carries on an activity of the kind specified by article 5 of the Regulated Activities Order (accepting deposits) is not to be regarded as doing so by way of business if—

(a) he does not hold himself out as accepting deposits on a day to day basis; and

(b) any deposits which he accepts are accepted only on particular occasions, whether or not involving the issue of any securities.

(2) In determining for the purposes of paragraph (1)(b) whether deposits are accepted only on particular occasions, regard is to be had to the frequency of those occasions and to any characteristics distinguishing them from each other.

[593]

3 Investment business

(1) A person is not to be regarded as carrying on by way of business an activity to which [paragraph (2) applies], unless he carries on the business of engaging in one or more such activities.

(2) [This paragraph] applies to an activity of the kind specified by any of the following provisions of the Regulated Activities Order, namely—

(a) article 14 (dealing in investments as principal);

(b) article 21 (dealing in investments as agent);

(c) article 25 (arranging deals in investments), except in so far as that activity relates to an investment of the kind specified by article 86 of that Order (Lloyd's syndicate capacity and syndicate membership), or article 89 of that Order (rights and interests) so far as relevant to that article;

[(ca) article 25D (operating a multilateral trading facility);]

(d) article 37 (managing investments);

(e) article 40 (safeguarding and administering investments);

(f) article 45 (sending dematerialised instructions);

(g) article 51 (establishing etc a collective investment scheme);

(h) article 52 (establishing etc a . . . pension scheme);

(i) article 53 (advising on investments); and

[(j) article 64 (agreeing) so far as relevant to any of the articles mentioned in sub-paragraphs (a) to (i),

but does not apply to any insurance mediation activity.]

(3) [Paragraph (1)] is without prejudice to article 4 of this Order.

[(4) A person is not to be regarded as carrying on by way of business any insurance mediation activity unless he takes up or pursues that activity for remuneration.

(5) In this article, "insurance mediation activity" means any activity of the kind specified by article 21, 25(1) or (2), 39A or 53 of the Regulated Activities Order, or, so far as relevant to any of those articles, article 64 of that Order, which is carried on in relation to a contract of insurance.]

NOTES

Para (1): words in square brackets substituted by the Financial Services and Markets Act 2000 (Regulated Activities) (Amendment) (No 2) Order 2003, SI 2003/1476, art 18(1), (3)(a).

Para (2): words in first pair of square brackets, and sub-para (j) together with final words substituted by SI 2003/1476, art 18(1), (3)(b); sub-para (ca) inserted by the Financial Services and Markets Act 2000 (Regulated Activities) (Amendment No 3) Order 2006, SI 2006/3384, art 37; word omitted from sub-para (h) revoked by the Financial Services and Markets Act 2000 (Regulated Activities) (Amendment) Order 2006, SI 2006/1969, art 9(1), (2).

Para (3): words in square brackets substituted by SI 2003/1476, art 18(1), (3)(c).

Paras (4), (5): added by SI 2003/1476, art 18(1), (3)(d).

[594]

[3A Arranging and advising on regulated mortgage contracts

A person is not to be regarded as carrying on by way of business an activity of the kind specified by—

(a) article 25A of the Regulated Activities Order (arranging regulated mortgage contracts);

(b) article 53A of that Order (advising on regulated mortgage contracts); or

(c) article 64 of that Order (agreeing), so far as relevant to any of the articles mentioned in sub-paragraphs (a) and (b),

unless he carries on the business of engaging in that activity.]

NOTES

Inserted by the Financial Services and Markets Act 2000 (Regulated Activities) (Amendment) (No 1) Order 2003, SI 2003/1475, art 25.

3B–3D *(Outside the scope of this work.)*

[595]

4 Managing investments: occupational pension schemes

(1) A person who carries on an activity of the kind specified by article 37 of the Regulated Activities Order (managing investments), where the assets in question are held for the purposes of an occupational pension scheme, is to be regarded as carrying on that activity by way of business, except where—

(a) he is a person to whom paragraph (2) applies; or

(b) all . . . day to day decisions in the carrying on of that activity (other than decisions falling within paragraph (6)), so far as relating to relevant assets, are taken on his behalf by—

(i) an authorised person who has permission to carry on activities of the kind specified by article 37 of the Regulated Activities Order;

(ii) a person who is an exempt person in relation to activities of that kind; or

(iii) an overseas person.

(2) This paragraph applies to—

(a) any trustee of a relevant scheme who is a beneficiary or potential beneficiary under the scheme; and

(b) any other trustee of a relevant scheme who takes no . . . day to day decisions relating to the management of any relevant assets.

(3) In this article—

["occupational pension scheme" has the meaning given by section 1 of the Pension Schemes Act 1993 but with paragraph (b) of the definition omitted;]

"relevant assets" means assets of the scheme in question which are securities or contractually based investments;

"relevant scheme" means any occupational pension scheme of a kind falling within paragraph (4) or (5).

(4) A scheme falls within this paragraph if—

(a) it is constituted under an irrevocable trust:

(b) it has no more than twelve relevant members;

(c) all relevant members, other than any relevant member who is unfit to act, or is incapable of acting, as trustee of the scheme, are trustees of it; and

(d) all . . . day to day decisions relating to the management of the assets of the scheme which are relevant assets are required to be taken by all, or a majority of, relevant members who are trustees of the scheme or by a person of a kind falling within paragraph (1)(b)(i) or (ii) acting alone or jointly with all, or a majority of, such relevant members;

and for these purposes a person is a relevant member of a scheme if he is an employee or former employee by or in respect of whom contributions to the scheme are being or have been made and to or in respect of whom benefits are or may become payable under the scheme.

(5) A scheme falls within this paragraph if—

(a) it has no more than fifty members;

(b) the contributions made by or in respect of each member of the scheme are used in the acquisition of a contract of insurance on the life of that member or in the acquisition of a contract to pay an annuity on that life;

(c) the only decision of a kind described in paragraph (1)(b) which may be taken in relation to the scheme is the selection of such contracts; and

(d) each member is given the opportunity to select the contract which the contributions made by or in respect of him will be used to acquire.

(6) A decision falls within this paragraph if—

[(a) it is a decision by the trustees of an occupational pension scheme to buy, sell or subscribe for—

(i) units in a collective investment scheme;

(ii) shares or debentures (or warrants relating to such shares or debentures) issued by a body corporate having as its purpose the investment of its funds with the aim of spreading investment risk and giving its members the benefit of the results of the management of those funds by or on behalf of that body; or

(iii) rights under (or rights to or interests in) any contract of insurance;] . . .

[(b) the decision is taken after advice has been obtained and considered from a person who falls within any of the cases in paragraph (7);]

(c), (d). . .

[(7) The cases are where the person is—

(a) an authorised person who has permission to carry on activities of the kind specified by article 53 of the Regulated Activities Order in relation to the decision in question;

(b) an exempt person in relation to such activities;

(c) exempt from the general prohibition by virtue of section 327 of the Financial Services and Markets Act 2000; or

(d) an overseas person.]

NOTES

Paras (1), (2), (4): words omitted revoked by the Financial Services and Markets Act 2000 (Carrying on Regulated Activities by Way of Business) (Amendment) Order 2005, SI 2005/922, art 2(1), (2).

Para (3): definition "occupational pension scheme" substituted by the Financial Services and Markets Act 2000 (Regulated Activities) (Amendment) Order 2006, SI 2006/1969, art 9(1), (2).

Para (6): sub-paras (a), (b) substituted, words omitted from sub-para (a) and the whole of sub-paras (c), (d) revoked by SI 2005/922, art 2(1), (4)–(7).

Para (7): substituted by SI 2005/922, art 2(1), (8).

FINANCIAL SERVICES AND MARKETS ACT 2000 (EXEMPTION) ORDER 2001

(SI 2001/1201)

NOTES

Made: 26 March 2001.

Authority: Financial Services and Markets Act 2000, ss 38, 428(3).

Commencement: 1 December 2001.

ARRANGEMENT OF ARTICLES

1 Citation and commencement . . . . . [595A]

2 Interpretation . . . . . [595B]

3 Persons exempt in respect of any regulated activity other than insurance business . . . . . [595C]

4 Persons exempt in respect of accepting deposits . . . . . [595D]

5 Persons exempt in respect of particular regulated activities . . . . . [595E]

6 Transitional exemption for credit unions . . . . . [595F]

SCHEDULE:

Part I—Persons exempt in respect of any regulated activity other than insurance business . . . . . [595G]

Part II—Persons exempt in respect of accepting deposits . . . . . [595H]

Part III—Persons exempt in respect of any regulated activity mentioned in article 5(1) . . . . . [595I]

Part IV—Persons exempt in respect of particular regulated activities . . . . . [595J]

[595A]

1 Citation and commencement

This Order may be cited as the Financial Services and Markets Act 2000 (Exemption) Order 2001 and comes into force on the day on which section 19 of the Act comes into force.

[595B]

2 Interpretation

In this Order—

"the Act" means the Financial Services and Markets Act 2000;

"charity"—

(a) in relation to Scotland, means a [body entered in the Scottish Charity Register]; and

(b) otherwise, has the meaning given by section 96(1) of the Charities Act 1993 or by section 35 of the Charities Act (Northern Ireland) 1964;

["credit institution" has the meaning given by the Regulated Activities Order;]

"deposit" has the meaning given by the Regulated Activities Order;

"industrial and provident society" has the meaning given by section 417(1) of the Act but does not include a credit union within the meaning of the Credit Unions Act 1979 or the Credit Unions (Northern Ireland) Order 1985;

["investment firm" has the meaning given by the Regulated Activities Order;]

"local authority" means—

(a) in England and Wales, a local authority within the meaning of the Local Government Act 1972, the Greater London Authority, the Common Council of the City of London or the Council of the Isles of Scilly;
(b) in Scotland, a local authority within the meaning of the Local Government (Scotland) Act 1973; and
(c) in Northern Ireland, a district council within the meaning of the Local Government Act (Northern Ireland) 1972;

["non-qualifying contract of insurance" means a contract of insurance (within the meaning of the Regulated Activities Order) which is not a qualifying contract of insurance (within the meaning of that Order);]

"the Regulated Activities Order" means the Financial Services and Markets Act 2000 (Regulated Activities) Order 2001.

NOTES

Words in square brackets in definition "charity" substituted by the Charities and Trustee Investment (Scotland) Act 2005 (Consequential Provisions and Modifications) Order 2006, SI 2006/242, art 5, Schedule, Pt 2, para 11; definitions "credit institution" and "investment firm" inserted by the Financial Services and Markets Act 2000 (Exemption) (Amendment) Order 2007, SI 2007/125, art 3; definition "non-qualifying contract of insurance" inserted by the Financial Services and Markets Act 2000 (Exemption) (Amendment) (No 2) Order 2003, SI 2003/1675, art 2(1), (2).

[595C]

3 Persons exempt in respect of any regulated activity other than insurance business

Each of the persons listed in Part I of the Schedule is exempt from the general prohibition in respect of any regulated activity other than an activity of the kind specified by article 10 of the Regulated Activities Order (effecting and carrying out contracts of insurance).

[595D]

4 Persons exempt in respect of accepting deposits

Subject to the limitations, if any, expressed in relation to him, each of the persons listed in Part II of the Schedule is exempt from the general prohibition in respect of any regulated activity of the kind specified by article 5 of the Regulated Activities Order (accepting deposits).

[595E]

5 Persons exempt in respect of particular regulated activities

(1) Subject to the limitation, if any, expressed in relation to him, each of the persons listed in Part III of the Schedule is exempt from the general prohibition in respect of any regulated activity of the kind specified by any of the following provisions of the Regulated Activities Order, or article 64 of that Order (agreeing to carry on specified kinds of activity) so far as relevant to any such activity—

(a) article 14 (dealing in investments as principal);
(b) article 21 (dealing in investments as agent);
(c) article 25 (arranging deals in investments);
[(ca) article 25D (operating a multilateral trading facility);]
(d) article 37 (managing investments);
[(da) article 39A (assisting in the administration and performance of a contract of insurance);]
(e) article 40 (safeguarding and administering investments);
(f) article 45 (sending dematerialised instructions);
(g) article 51 (establishing etc a collective investment scheme);
(h) article 52 (establishing etc a . . . pension scheme);
(i) article 53 (advising on investments).

(2) Subject to the limitation, if any, expressed in relation to him, each of the persons listed in Part IV of the Schedule is exempt from the general prohibition in respect of any regulated activity of the kind referred to in relation to him, or an activity of the kind specified by article 64 of the Regulated Activities Order so far as relevant to any such activity.

NOTES

Para (1): sub-para (ca) inserted by the Financial Services and Markets Act 2000 (Exemption) (Amendment) Order 2007, SI 2007/125, art 4; sub-para (da) inserted by the Financial Services and Markets Act 2000 (Exemption) (Amendment) (No 2) Order 2003, SI 2003/1675, art 2(1), (3); word omitted from sub-para (h) revoked by the Financial Services and Markets Act 2000 (Regulated Activities) (Amendment) Order 2006, SI 2006/1969, art 10.

[595F]

6 Transitional exemption for credit unions

A credit union, within the meaning of the Credit Unions Act 1979 . . . , is exempt from the general prohibition in respect of any regulated activity of the kind specified by article 5 of the Regulated Activities Order, but only until 1st July 2002.

NOTES

Words omitted revoked by the Financial Services and Markets Act 2000 (Exemption) (Amendment) Order 2001, SI 2001/3623, arts 2, 3.

SCHEDULE

Articles 3–5

PART I
PERSONS EXEMPT IN RESPECT OF ANY REGULATED ACTIVITY OTHER THAN INSURANCE BUSINESS

[595G]

1. The Bank of England.

2. The central bank of an EEA State other than the United Kingdom.

3. The European Central Bank.

4. The European Community.

5. The European Atomic Energy Community.

6. The European Coal and Steel Community.

7. The European Investment Bank.

8. The International Bank for Reconstruction and Development.

9. The International Finance Corporation.

10. The International Monetary Fund.

11. The African Development Bank.

12. The Asian Development Bank.

13. The Caribbean Development Bank.

14. The Inter-American Development Bank.

15. The European Bank for Reconstruction and Development.

[**15A.** Bank for International Settlements.]

[**15B.** Bank of England Asset Purchase Facility Fund Limited.]

NOTES

Para 15A: added by the Financial Services and Markets Act 2000 (Exemption) (Amendment) Order 2003, SI 2003/47, art 2.

Para 15B: added by the Financial Services and Markets Act 2000 (Exemption) (Amendment) Order 2009, SI 2009/118, art 2.

PART II
PERSONS EXEMPT IN RESPECT OF ACCEPTING DEPOSITS

[595H]

16. A municipal bank, that is to say a company which was, immediately before the coming into force of this Order, exempted from the prohibition in section 3 of the Banking Act 1987 by virtue of section 4(1) of, and paragraph 4 of Schedule 2 to, that Act.

17.—(1) Keesler Federal Credit Union, in so far as it accepts deposits from members, or dependants of members, of a visiting force of the United States of America, or from members, or dependants of members, of a civilian component of such a force.

(2) In sub-paragraph (1), "member", "dependent" and "visiting force" have the meanings given by section 12 of the Visiting Forces Act 1952 and "member of a civilian component" has the meaning given by section 10 of that Act.

18. A body of persons certified as a school bank by the National Savings Bank or by an authorised person who has permission to accept deposits.

19. A local authority.

20.—(1) Any body which by virtue of any enactment has power to issue a precept to a local authority in England or Wales or a requisition to a local authority in Scotland, or to the expenses of which, by virtue of any enactment, a local authority in the United Kingdom is or can be required to contribute.
(2) In sub-paragraph (1), "enactment" includes an enactment comprised in, or in an instrument made under, an Act of the Scottish Parliament.

[21. The Council of Europe Development Bank.]

22. A charity, in so far as it accepts deposits—
(a) from another charity; or
(b) in respect of which no interest or premium is payable.

23. The National Children's Charities Fund in so far as—
(a) it accepts deposits in respect of which no interest or premium is payable; and
(b) the total value of the deposits made by any one person does not exceed £10,000.

24. An industrial and provident society, in so far as it accepts deposits in the form of withdrawable share capital.

[24A. A credit union, within the meaning of the Credit Unions (Northern Ireland) Order 1985.]

25.—(1) The Student Loans Company Limited, in so far as it accepts deposits from the Secretary of State or the Scottish Ministers in connection with, or for the purposes of, enabling eligible students to receive loans.
(2) In sub-paragraph (1), "eligible student" means—
(a) any person who is an eligible student pursuant to regulations made under Part II of the Teaching and Higher Education Act 1998;
(b) any person to whom, or in respect of whom, loans may be paid under section 73(f) of the Education (Scotland) Act 1980;
(c) any person who is an eligible student pursuant to regulations made under article 3 of the Education (Student Support) (Northern Ireland) Order 1998; or
(d) any person who is in receipt of or who is eligible to receive a loan of the kind mentioned in article 3(1) of the Teaching and Higher Education Act 1998 (Commencement No 2 and Transitional Provisions) Order 1998 or article 3(1) of the Education (Student Support) (Northern Ireland) Order 1998 (Commencement and Transitional Provisions) Order (Northern Ireland) 1998.

NOTES

Para 21: substituted by the Financial Services and Markets Act 2000 (Financial Promotion and Miscellaneous Amendments) Order 2002, SI 2002/1310, art 4(2).

Para 24A: inserted by the Financial Services and Markets Act 2000 (Exemption) (Amendment) Order 2001, SI 2001/3623, arts 2, 4.

PART III
PERSONS EXEMPT IN RESPECT OF ANY REGULATED ACTIVITY MENTIONED IN ARTICLE 5(1)

[595I]

26. The National Debt Commissioners.

[27. Partnerships UK.]

28. The International Development Association.

29. The English Tourist Board.

30. . . .

[31. VisitScotland].

32. The Northern Ireland Tourist Board.

33. Scottish Enterprise.

[33A. Invest Northern Ireland.]

34. The Multilateral Investment Guarantee Agency.

[34A. The Board of the Pension Protection Fund.]

[34B. Capital for Enterprise Limited, in so far as in carrying on any regulated activity it provides services only to the Crown.]

35. A person acting as an official receiver within the meaning of section 399 of the Insolvency Act 1986 or article 2 of the Insolvency (Northern Ireland) Order 1989.

36. . . .

37.—[(1) An Operator, in so far as he carries on—

(a) any regulated activity for the purposes of the performance of his functions as an Operator under the Uncertificated Securities Regulations 1995; or

(b) any other regulated activity for the purposes of operating a computer-based system and procedures which—

(i) enable title to investments to be evidenced and transferred without a written instrument; or

(ii) facilitate matters supplementary or incidental to those specified in sub-paragraph (i),

other than a regulated activity in respect of which a recognised clearing house is exempt from the general prohibition by virtue of section 285(3) of the Act.]

(2) In sub-paragraph (1), "Operator" means a person approved as such by the Treasury under the Uncertificated Securities Regulations 1995.

38. A person acting as a judicial factor.

39. A person acting as an insolvency practitioner within the meaning of section 388 of the Insolvency Act 1986 [or article 3 of the Insolvency (Northern Ireland) Order 1989].

NOTES

Para 27: substituted by the Financial Services and Markets Act 2000 (Exemption) (Amendment) (No 2) Order 2003, SI 2003/1675, art 2(1), (4)(a).

Para 30: revoked by the Wales Tourist Board (Transfer of Functions to the National Assembly for Wales and Abolition) Order 2005, SI 2005/3225, art 6(2), Sch 2, Pt 2, para 4.

Para 31: substituted by the Tourist Boards (Scotland) Act 2006, s 4, Sch 2, Pt 2, para 10 (in relation to Scotland), and by the Tourist Boards (Scotland) Act 2006 (Consequential Modifications) Order 2007, SI 2007/1103, art 2, Schedule, Pt 2, para 6 (in relation to England and Wales).

Para 33A: inserted by the Financial Services and Markets Act 2000 (Exemption) (Amendment No 2) Order 2007, SI 2007/1821, art 2(1), (2).

Para 34A: inserted by the Financial Services and Markets Act 2000 (Exemption) (Amendment) Order 2005, SI 2005/592, art 2(1).

Para 34B: inserted by the Financial Services and Markets Act 2000 (Exemption) (Amendment) Order 2008, SI 2008/682, art 2.

Para 36: revoked by the Financial Services and Markets Act 2000 (Exemption) (Amendment) Order 2007, SI 2007/125, art 5.

Para 37: sub-para (1) substituted by the Financial Services and Markets Act 2000 (Exemption) (Amendment) Order 2001, SI 2001/3623, arts 2, 5.

Para 39: words in square brackets added by SI 2001/3623, arts 2, 6.

PART IV
PERSONS EXEMPT IN RESPECT OF PARTICULAR REGULATED ACTIVITIES

Enterprise schemes

[595J]

40.—(1) Any body corporate which has as its principal object (or one of its principal objects)—

(a) the promotion or encouragement of industrial or commercial activity or enterprise in the United Kingdom or in any particular area of it; or

(b) the dissemination of information concerning persons engaged in such activity or enterprise or requiring capital to become so engaged;

is exempt from the general prohibition in respect of any regulated activity of the kind specified by article 25 of the Regulated Activities Order (arranging deals in investments) so long as it does not carry on that activity for, or with the prospect of, direct or indirect pecuniary gain.

(2) For the purposes of this paragraph, such sums as may reasonably be regarded as necessary to meet the costs of carrying on the activity mentioned in sub-paragraph (1) do not constitute a pecuniary gain.

[(3) This paragraph does not apply where an investment firm or credit institution—

(a) provides or performs investment services and activities on a professional basis, and

(b) in doing so, but for the operation of [sub-paragraph (1)], it would be treated as carrying on an activity of a kind specified by Part 2 of the Regulated Activities Order [in breach of the general prohibition].]

Employee share schemes in electricity industry shares

41.—(1) Each of the persons to whom this paragraph applies is exempt from the general prohibition in respect of any regulated activity of the kind specified by article 14, 21 or 25 of the Regulated Activities Order (dealing in investments as principal or agent or arranging deals in investments) which he carries on for the purpose of—

(a) enabling or facilitating transactions in electricity industry shares or debentures between or for the benefit of any qualifying person; or

(b) the holding of electricity industry shares or debentures by or for the benefit of any qualifying person.

(2) This paragraph applies to—

(a) The National Grid Holding plc;

(b) Electricity Association Limited;

(c) any body corporate in the same group as the person mentioned in sub-paragraph (a) or (b);

(d) any company listed in Schedule 1 to the Electricity Act 1989 (Nominated Companies) (England and Wales) Order 1990; and

(e) a person holding shares in or debentures of a body corporate as trustee in pursuance of arrangements made for either of the purposes mentioned in sub-paragraph (1) by the Secretary of State, by any of the bodies mentioned in sub-paragraphs (a) to (c) or by an electricity successor company or by some or all of them.

(3) In this paragraph—

(a) "electricity industry shares or debentures" means—

(i) any investment of the kind specified by article 76[, 77 or 77A] of the Regulated Activities Order (shares or instruments creating or acknowledging indebtedness [or alternative finance investment bonds]) in or of an electricity successor company;

(ii) any investment of the kind specified by article 79 or 80 of that Order (instruments giving entitlement to investments and certificates representing certain securities), so far as relevant to the investments mentioned in sub-paragraph (i); and

(iii) any investment of the kind specified by article 89 of that Order (rights to or interests in investments) so far as relevant to the investments mentioned in sub-paragraphs (i) and (ii);

(b) "qualifying person" means—

(i) the bona fide employees or former employees of The National Grid Holding plc, Electricity Association Limited or any other body corporate in the same group as either of them; and

(ii) the wives, husbands, widows, widowers[, civil partners, surviving civil partners,] or children (including, in Northern Ireland, adopted children) or step-children under the age of eighteen of such employees or former employees;

(c) references to an electricity successor company include any body corporate that is in the same group and "electricity successor company" means a body corporate which is a successor company for the purposes of Part II of the Electricity Act 1989;

(d) "former employees" of a person ("the employer") include any person who has never been employed by the employer so long as he occupied a position in relation to some other person of such a kind that it may reasonably be assumed that he would have been a former employee of the employer had the reorganisation of the electricity industry under Part II of the Electricity Act 1989 been affected before he ceased to occupy the relevant position.

Gas industry

42.—(1) Transco plc is exempt from the general prohibition in respect of any regulated activity of the kind specified by article 14, 21[, 25 or 25D] of the Regulated Activities Order (dealing in investments as principal or agent[, arranging deals in investments or operating a multilateral trading facility]) which it carries on—

(a) in its capacity as a gas transporter under the Transco Licence; and

(b) for the purposes of enabling or facilitating gas shippers to buy or sell an investment of the kind specified by article 84 or 85 of the Regulated Activities Order (futures or contracts for differences etc).

(2) ENMO Ltd is exempt from the general prohibition in respect of any regulated activity of the kind specified by article 14, 21[, 25 or 25D] of the Regulated Activities Order (dealing in investments as principal or agent[, arranging deals in investments or operating a multilateral trading facility]) which it carries on—

(a) in its capacity as the operator of the balancing market; and

(b) for the purpose of enabling or facilitating Transco plc and relevant gas shippers, for the purpose of participating in the balancing market, to buy or sell investments of the kind specified by article 84 or 85 of that Order (futures or contracts for differences etc).

(3) Transco plc and relevant gas shippers are exempt from the general prohibition in respect of any regulated activity of the kind specified by article 14 or 21 of the Regulated Activities Order (dealing in investments as principal or agent) in so far as that activity relates to an investment of the kind specified by article 84 or 85 of that Order (futures or contracts for differences etc) and is carried on for the purpose of participating in the balancing market.

(4) In this paragraph—

(a) "the balancing market" means the market to regulate the delivery and off-take of gas in Transco plc's pipeline system for the purpose of balancing the volume of gas in that system;

(b) "gas shipper" has the same meaning as in Part I of the Gas Act 1986;

(c) "relevant gas shippers" means gas shippers who have entered into a subscription agreement with ENMO Ltd for the purpose of participating in the balancing market;

(d) "Transco Licence" means the licence treated as granted to Transco plc as a gas transporter under section 7 of the Gas Act 1986;

(e) the reference to enabling or facilitating includes acting pursuant to rules governing the operation of the balancing market which apply in the event of one of the participants appearing to be unable, or likely to become unable, to meet his obligations in respect of one or more contracts entered into through the balancing market.

Trade unions and employers' associations

43.—(1) A trade union or employers' association is exempt from the general prohibition in respect of any regulated activity of the kind specified by article 10 of the Regulated Activities Order (effecting and carrying out contracts of insurance) which it carries on in order to provide provident benefits or strike benefits for its members.

(2) In sub-paragraph (1), "trade union" and "employers' association" have the meanings given by section 1 and section 122(1) of the Trade Union and Labour Relations (Consolidation) Act 1992 or, in Northern Ireland, the meanings given by article 3(1) and article 4(1) of the Industrial Relations (Northern Ireland) Order 1992.

Charities

44.—(1) A charity is exempt from the general prohibition in respect of any regulated activity of the kind specified by article 51 of the Regulated Activities Order (establishing etc a collective investment scheme) which it carries on in relation to a fund established under—

(a) section 22A of the Charities Act 1960;

(b) section 25 of the Charities Act 1993; or

(c) section 25 of the Charities Act (Northern Ireland) 1964.

(2) A charity is exempt from the general prohibition in respect of any regulated activity of the kind specified by article 51 of the Regulated Activities Order (establishing etc a collective investment scheme) which it carries on in relation to a pooling scheme fund established under—

(a) section 22 of the Charities Act 1960; or

(b) section 24 of the Charities Act 1993.

(3) In sub-paragraph (2), "pooling scheme fund" means a fund established by a common investment scheme the trusts of which provide that property is not to be transferred to the fund except by or on behalf of a charity, the charity trustees (within the meaning of section 97(1) of the Charities Act 1993) of which are the trustees appointed to manage the fund.

Schemes established under the Trustee Investments Act 1961

45. A person acting in his capacity as manager or operator of a fund established under section 11 of the Trustee Investments Act 1961 is exempt from the general prohibition in respect of any regulated activity of the kind specified by article 51 of the Regulated Activities Order (establishing etc a collective investment scheme) which he carries on in relation to that fund.

Former members of Lloyd's

46. Any person who ceased to be an underwriting member (within the meaning of Lloyd's Act 1982) of Lloyd's before 24th December 1996 is exempt from the general prohibition in respect of any regulated activity of the kind specified by article 10(2) of the Regulated Activities Order (carrying out contracts of insurance) which relates to contracts of insurance that he has underwritten at Lloyd's.

Local authorities

[47. A local authority is exempt from the general prohibition in respect of any regulated activity of the kind specified by—

(a) article 21, 25(1) or (2), 39A or 53 of the Regulated Activities Order (dealing in investments as agent, arranging deals in investments, assisting in the administration and performance of a contract of insurance or advising on investments) which relates to a non-qualifying contract of insurance; . . .

(b) article 25A, 53A or 61 of that Order (arranging, advising on, entering into or administering a regulated mortgage contract)[;

(c) article 25B, 53B or 63B of that Order (arranging, advising on, entering into or administering a regulated home reversion plan); *or*

(d) article 25C, 53C or 63F of that Order (arranging, advising on, entering into or administering a regulated home purchase plan)][; or

(e) article 25E, 53D or 63J of that Order (arranging, advising on, entering into or administering a regulated sale and rent back agreement)]].

Social housing

[48.—(1) A relevant housing body is exempt from the general prohibition in respect of any regulated activity of the kind specified by—

(a) article 21, 25(1) or (2), 39A or 53 of the Regulated Activities Order (dealing in investments as agent, arranging deals in investments, assisting in the administration and performance of a contract of insurance or advising on investments) which relates to a non-qualifying contract of insurance; . . .

(b) article 25A, 53A or 61 of that Order (arranging, advising on, entering into or administering a regulated mortgage contract)[;

(c) article 25B, 53B or 63B of that Order (arranging, advising on, entering into or administering a regulated home reversion plan); *or*

(d) article 25C, 53C or 63F of that Order (arranging, advising on, entering into or administering a regulated home purchase plan)[;

[(e) article 25E, 53D or 63J of that Order (arranging, advising on, entering into or administering a regulated sale and rent back agreement)]].

(2) In this paragraph, "relevant housing body" means any of the following—

(a) a registered social landlord within the meaning of Part I of the Housing Act 1996;

(b) a registered social landlord within the meaning of the Housing (Scotland) Act 2001;

(c) [The Regulator of Social Housing];

[(ca) the Homes and Communities Agency;]

(d) Scottish Homes;

(e) the body established under article 9 of the Housing (Northern Ireland) Order 1981 known as the Northern Ireland Housing Executive;

[(f) Communities Scotland]].

[Electricity industry

49.—(1) NGC is exempt from the general prohibition in respect of any regulated activity of the kind specified by article 14, 21, 25[, 25D] or 53 of the Regulated Activities Order (dealing in investments as principal or agent, arranging deals in investments[, operating a multilateral trading facility] or advising on investments) which it carries on in the course of—

(a) its participation in the Balancing and Settlement Arrangements as operator of the electricity transmission system in [Great Britain] under the Transmission Licence; or

(b) the acquisition by it of Balancing Services in accordance with the Electricity Act 1989 and the Transmission Licence.

(2) ELEXON Clear Limited is exempt from the general prohibition in respect of any regulated activity of the kind specified by article 14, 21[, 25 or 25D] of that Order which it carries on in the course of its participation in the Balancing and Settlement Arrangements as clearer for the purposes of (among other things) receiving from and paying to BSC Parties trading and reconciliation charges arising under the Balancing and Settlement Arrangements.

(3) Each BSC Party is exempt from the general prohibition in respect of any regulated activity of the kind specified by article 14, 21, 25[, 25D] or 53 of that Order which it carries on in the course of—

(a) its participation in the Balancing and Settlement Arrangements; or

(b) the provision by it (or, in the case of an activity of the kind specified by article 21 of that Order, its principal) of Balancing Services to NGC.

(4) ELEXON Limited is exempt from the general prohibition in respect of any regulated activity of the kind specified by article 25 [or 25D] of that Order which it carries on in the course of its participation in the Balancing and Settlement Arrangements as administrator

(5) Each BSC Agent and each Volume Notification Agent is exempt from the general prohibition in respect of any regulated activity of the kind specified by article 25 [or 25D] of that Order which it carries on in that capacity.

(6) . . .

(7) In this paragraph—

"Ancillary Services" means services which generators and suppliers of electricity and those making transfers of electricity across an Interconnector are required (as a condition of their connection to the transmission system in [Great Britain]), or have agreed, to make available to NGC for the purpose of securing the stability of the electricity transmission or any distribution system in [Great Britain] or any system linked to it by an Interconnector;

"Balancing and Settlement Arrangements" means—

(a) the Balancing Mechanism; and

(b) arrangements—

(i) for the determination and allocation to BSC Parties of the quantities of electricity that have been delivered to and taken off the electricity transmission system and any distribution system in [Great Britain]; and

(ii) which set, and provide for the determination and financial settlement of, BSC Parties' obligations arising by reference to the quantities referred to in sub-paragraph (i), including the difference between such quantities (after taking account of accepted bids and offers in the Balancing Mechanism) and the quantities of electricity contracted for sale and purchase between BSC Parties;

"Balancing Mechanism" means the arrangements pursuant to which BSC Parties may make, and NGC may accept, offers or bids to increase or decrease the quantities of electricity to be delivered to or taken off the electricity transmission system or any distribution system in [Great Britain] at any time or during any period so as to assist NGC in operating and balancing the electricity transmission system, and arrangements for the settlement of financial obligations arising from the acceptance of such offers and bids;

"Balancing Services" means—

(a) offers and bids made in the Balancing Mechanism;

(b) Ancillary Services; and

(c) other services available to NGC which assist it in operating the electricity transmission system in accordance with the Electricity Act 1989 and the Transmission Licence;

"BSC Agents" means the persons for the time being engaged by or on behalf of ELEXON Limited for the purpose of providing services to all BSC Parties, NGC, ELEXON Limited and ELEXON Clear Limited in connection with the operation of the Balancing and Settlement Arrangements;

["BSC Framework Agreement" means the agreement of that title in the form approved by the Secretary of State for the purpose of conditions of the Transmission Licence and which is dated 14 August 2000; and "conditions" for the purposes of this definition means conditions determined by the Secretary of State under powers granted by section 137(1) of the Energy Act 2004. and incorporated into existing electricity transmission licences by a scheme made by the Secretary of State pursuant to section 138 of, and Schedule 17 to, that Act;]

"BSC Parties" means those persons (other than NGC, ELEXON Limited and ELEXON Clear Limited) who have signed or acceded to (in accordance with the terms of the BSC Framework Agreement), and not withdrawn from, the BSC Framework Agreement;

"Interconnector" means the electric lines and electrical plant [and meters] used [solely] for the transfer of electricity to or from the electricity transmission system . . . in [Great Britain] into or out of [Great Britain];

"NGC" means . . . National Grid Company plc;

. . .

"the Transmission Licence" means the licence to [participate in the transmission of] electricity in [Great Britain] granted[, or treated as granted,] to NGC under section 6(1)(b) of the Electricity Act 1989; and

"Volume Notification Agents" means the persons for the time being appointed and authorised under and in accordance with the Balancing and Settlement Arrangements on behalf of BSC Parties to notify to the BSC Agent designated for that purpose pursuant to the Balancing and Settlement Arrangements quantities of electricity contracted for the sale and purchase between those BSC Parties to be taken into account for the purposes of the Balancing and Settlement Arrangements.]

[Freight Forwarders and Storage Firms

50.—(1) A freight forwarder or storage firm is exempt from the general prohibition in respect of any regulated activity of the kind specified by article 21, 25, 39A or 53 of the Regulated Activities Order (dealing in investments as agent, arranging deals in investments, assisting in the administration and performance of a contract of insurance or advising on investments) in the circumstances referred to in paragraph 2.

(2) The circumstances are—

(a) where a freight forwarder ("F")—

(i) holds a policy of insurance which insures F in respect of loss of or damage to goods which F transports or of which F arranges the transportation, and

(ii) makes available to a customer rights under that policy to enable the customer to claim directly against the insurer in respect of loss or damage to those goods; or

(b) where a storage firm ("S")—

(i) holds a policy of insurance which insures S in respect of loss of or damage to goods which S stores or for which S arranges storage, and

(ii) makes available to a customer rights under that policy to enable the customer to claim directly against the insurer in respect of loss or damage to those goods.

(3) In this paragraph—

(a) "freight forwarder" means a person whose principal business is arranging or carrying out the transportation of goods;

(b) "storage firm" means a person whose principal business is storing goods or arranging storage for goods;

(c) "customer" means a person . . . who uses the service of a freight forwarder or storage firm.

Policyholder Advocates

51.—(1) A person acting as a policyholder advocate is exempt from the general prohibition in respect of any regulated activity of the kind specified by article 25 or 53 of the Regulated Activities Order (arranging deals in investments or advising on investments) in so far as he carries on these activities in connection with, or for the purposes of, his role as policyholder advocate.

(2) In sub-paragraph (1), "policyholder advocate" means a person who is—

(a) appointed by an insurer ("I") to represent the interests of policyholders in negotiations with I about I's proposals to redefine the rights and interests in any surplus assets arising in I's with-profits fund; and

(b) approved or nominated by the Authority to carry out that role.

(3) In sub-paragraph (2), "with-profits fund" means a long-term insurance fund in which policyholders are eligible to participate in surplus assets of the fund.]

NOTES

Para 40: sub-para (3) added by the Financial Services and Markets Act 2000 (Exemption) (Amendment) Order 2007, SI 2007/125, art 6(a); words in first pair of square brackets substituted, and words in second pair of square brackets added, by the Financial Services and Markets Act 2000 (Exemption) (Amendment No 2) Order 2007, SI 2007/1821, art 2(1), (3).

Para 41: in sub-para (3)(a)(i), words in first pair of square brackets substituted and words in second pair of square brackets inserted by the Financial Services and Markets Act 2000 (Regulated Activities) (Amendment) Order 2010, SI 2010/86, art 4, Schedule, para 7; words in square brackets in sub-para (3)(b)(ii) inserted by the Civil Partnership Act 2004 (Amendments to Subordinate Legislation) Order 2005, SI 2005/2114, art 2(16), Sch 16, Pt 1, para 4.

Para 42: words in square brackets substituted by SI 2007/125, art 6(b).

Para 47: substituted by the Financial Services and Markets Act 2000 (Exemption) (Amendment) (No 2) Order 2003, SI 2003/1675, art 2(1), (4)(b); word omitted from sub-para (a) revoked, and sub-paras (c), (d) inserted, by the Financial Services and Markets Act 2000 (Regulated Activities) (Amendment) (No 2) Order 2006, SI 2006/2383, art 30(a), subject to transitional provisions in arts 37–39 thereof; word "or" in italics in sub-para (c) revoked, and sub-para (e) inserted together with word preceding it, by the Financial Services and Markets Act 2000 (Regulated Activities) (Amendment) Order 2009, SI 2009/1342, art 28(a), as from 1 July

2009 (certain purposes), and as from 30 June 2010 (otherwise) (for the full commencement details and for transitional provisions etc see arts 1, 32–34 of that Order).

Para 48: substituted by SI 2003/1675, art 2(1), (4)(c); word omitted from sub-para (1)(a) revoked, and sub-paras (1)(c), (d) inserted, by SI 2006/2383, art 30(b), subject to transitional provisions in arts 37–39 thereof; word "or" in italics in sub-para (1)(c) revoked, and sub-para (1)(e) inserted, by the Financial Services and Markets Act 2000 (Regulated Activities) (Amendment) Order 2009, SI 2009/1342, art 28(b), as from the same dates and for the same purposes as noted above; words in square brackets in sub-para (2)(c) substituted, and sub-para (2)(ca) inserted, by the Housing and Regeneration Act 2008 (Consequential Provisions) (No 2) Order 2008, SI 2008/2831, arts 3, 4, Sch 1, para 11, Sch 2, para 4; sub-para (2)(f) added by the Financial Services and Markets Act 2000 (Exemption) (Amendment) Order 2005, SI 2005/592, art 2(2).

Para 49: added by the Financial Services and Markets Act 2000 (Exemption) (Amendment) Order 2001, SI 2001/3623, arts 2, 8; words ", operating a multilateral trading facility" in square brackets in sub-para (1) inserted, figure ", 25D" in square brackets in sub-paras (1), (3) inserted, and words in square brackets in sub-paras (4), (5) inserted, by SI 2007/125, art 6(c)(i), (iii)–(v); words in square brackets in sub-para (2) substituted by SI 2007/125, art 6(c)(ii); other words in square brackets substituted or inserted, and words omitted revoked, by the Financial Services and Markets Act 2000 (Exemption) (Amendment) Order 2005, SI 2005/592, art 3.

Para 50: added, together with para 51, by SI 2007/1821, art 2(1), (4); words omitted from definition "customer" revoked by the Financial Services and Markets Act 2000 (Exemption) (Amendment) Order 2009, SI 2009/264, art 2.

Para 51: added as noted to para 50 above.

FINANCIAL SERVICES AND MARKETS ACT 2000 (APPOINTED REPRESENTATIVES) REGULATIONS 2001

(SI 2001/1217)

NOTES

Made: 28 March 2001.

Authority: Financial Services and Markets Act 2000, ss 39(1), 417(1).

Commencement: 1 December 2001 (see reg 1(1)).

[596]

1 Citation, commencement and interpretation

(1) These Regulations may be cited as the Financial Services and Markets Act 2000 (Appointed Representatives) Regulations 2001, and come into force on the day on which section 19 of the Act comes into force.

(2) In these Regulations—

"buy", "sell", "security"[, "contract of insurance", "[qualifying contract of insurance]" and "relevant investment"] have the same meaning as in the Regulated Activities Order;

["contract of long-term care insurance" means a contract of insurance in respect of which the following conditions are met—

(a) the purpose (or one of the purposes) of the policy is to protect the policyholder against the risk of becoming unable to live independently without assistance in consequence of a deterioration of mental or physical health, injury, sickness or other infirmity;

(b) benefits under the contract are payable in respect of—

(i) services,

(ii) accommodation, or

(iii) goods,

which are (or which is) necessary or desirable due to a deterioration of mental or physical health, injury, sickness or other infirmity;

(c) the contract is expressed to be in effect until the death of the policyholder (except that the contract may give the policyholder the option to surrender the policy); and

(d) the benefits under the contract are capable of being paid throughout the life of the policyholder;]

["EEA credit institution" means a credit institution authorised under the banking consolidation directive which has its relevant office in an EEA State other than the United Kingdom;

"EEA investment firm" means an investment firm as defined in section 424A of the Act which has its relevant office in an EEA State other than the United Kingdom;]

["home purchaser" has the same meaning as in article 63F(3) of the Regulated Activities Order;]

"other counterparties" means persons other than the principal;

["plan provider" has the meaning given by paragraph (3) of article 63B of the Regulated Activities Order, read with paragraphs (7) and (8) of that article;]

"the principal", in relation to a contract, means the party who is an authorised person, and "the representative" means the other party;

"the Regulated Activities Order" means the Financial Services and Markets Act 2000 (Regulated Activities) Order 2001;

["regulated home purchase plan" has the same meaning as in article 63F(3) of the Regulated Activities Order;

"regulated home reversion plan" has the same meaning as in article 63B(3) of the Regulated Activities Order;]

["regulated mortgage contract", and "borrower" in relation to such a contract, have the same meaning as in article 61(3) of the Regulated Activities Order];

["reversion seller" has the same meaning as in article 63B(3) of the Regulated Activities Order].

NOTES

Para (2): in definition beginning "buy", words in first (outer) pair of square brackets substituted by the Financial Services and Markets Act 2000 (Regulated Activities) (Amendment) (No 2) Order 2003, SI 2003/1476, art 14(1), (2); in definition beginning "buy", words in second (inner) pair of square brackets substituted and definition "contract of long-term care insurance" inserted by the Financial Services and Markets Act 2000 (Appointed Representatives) (Amendment) Regulations 2004, SI 2004/453, reg 2; definitions "EEA credit institution" and "EEA investment firm" inserted by the Financial Services and Markets Act 2000 (Appointed Representatives) (Amendment) Regulations 2006, SI 2006/3414, regs 2, 3; definitions "home purchaser", "plan provider", "regulated home purchase plan", "regulated home reversion plan", and "reversion seller" inserted by the Financial Services and Markets Act 2000 (Regulated Activities) (Amendment) (No 2) Order 2006, SI 2006/2383, art 31(1), (2), subject to transitional provisions in arts 37–39 thereof; definition "regulated mortgage contract" inserted by the Financial Services and Markets Act 2000 (Regulated Activities) (Amendment) (No 1) Order 2003, SI 2003/1475, art 23(1), (2).

[597]

2 Descriptions of business for which appointed representatives are exempt

[(1)] [Subject to paragraph (2),] any business which comprises—

[(aa) an activity of the kind specified by article 21 of the Regulated Activities Order (dealing in investments as agent), where the transaction relates to [a contract of insurance which is not a qualifying contract of insurance or a contract of long-term care insurance];]

(a) an activity of the kind specified by article 25 of [that Order] (arranging deals in investments), where the arrangements are for or with a view to transactions relating to securities or [relevant investments];

[(ab) an activity of the kind specified by article 25A of that Order (arranging regulated mortgage contracts);]

[(aba) an activity of the kind specified by article 25B of that Order (arranging regulated home reversion plans);

(abb) an activity of the kind specified by article 25C of that Order (arranging regulated home purchase plans);]

[(ac) an activity of the kind specified by article 39A of that Order (assisting in the administration and performance of a contract of insurance), . . . ;]

(b) an activity of the kind specified by article 40 of that Order (safeguarding and administering investments), where the activity consists of arranging for one or more other persons to safeguard and administer assets;

[(ba) an activity of the kind specified by article 52B of that Order (providing basic advice on stakeholder products);]

(c) an activity of the kind specified by article 53 of that Order (advising on investments); . . .

[(ca) an activity of the kind specified by article 53A of that Order (advising on regulated mortgage contracts); . . .]

[(cb) an activity of the kind specified by article 53B of that Order (advising on regulated home reversion plans);

(cc) an activity of the kind specified by article 53C of that Order (advising on regulated home purchase plans); or]

(d) an activity of the kind specified by article 64 of that Order (agreeing to carry on activities), so far as relevant to an activity falling within [sub-paragraph (aa), (a), (ab), (ac)] [(aba), (abb), (b), (c), (ca), (cb) or (cc)];

is prescribed for the purposes of subsection (1)(a)(i) of section 39 of the Act (exemption of appointed representatives).

[(1A) In its application to a contract with a principal who is an EEA investment firm or an EEA credit institution, the list in paragraph (1) shall be treated as including in addition—

(a) the activity of placing financial instruments,

(b) the activity of providing advice to clients or potential clients in relation to the placing of financial instruments.

(1B) In paragraph (1A), "clients" and "financial instruments" have the meanings given in, respectively, paragraphs 1.10 and 1.17 of Article 4 of the markets in financial instruments directive.]

[(2), (3) . . .]

NOTES

Para (1): numbered as such and words in first pair of square brackets inserted by the Financial Services and Markets Act 2000 (Appointed Representatives) (Amendment) Regulations 2001, SI 2001/2508, reg 2(a), (b); sub-paras (aa), (ac) inserted and words in square brackets in sub-para (a) and in first pair of square brackets in sub-para (d) substituted by the Financial Services and Markets Act 2000 (Regulated Activities) (Amendment) (No 2) Order 2003, SI 2003/1476, art 14(1), (3); words in square brackets in sub-para (aa) substituted and words omitted from sub-para (ac) revoked by the Financial Services and Markets Act 2000 (Appointed Representatives) (Amendment) Regulations 2004, SI 2004/453, reg 3; sub-paras (ab), (ca) inserted, word omitted from sub-para (c) revoked by the Financial Services and Markets Act 2000 (Regulated Activities) (Amendment) (No 1) Order 2003, SI 2003/1475, art 23(1), (3)(a)–(c); sub-paras (aba), (abb), (cb), (cc) inserted, word omitted from sub-para (ca) revoked, and words in second pair of square brackets in sub-para (d) substituted by the Financial Services and Markets Act 2000 (Regulated Activities) (Amendment) (No 2) Order 2006, SI 2006/2383, art 31(1), (3), subject to transitional provisions in arts 37–39 thereof; sub-para (ba) inserted by the Financial Services and Markets Act 2000 (Regulated Activities) (Amendment) (No 2) Order 2004, SI 2004/2737, art 5(1), (2).

Paras (1A), (1B): inserted by the Financial Services and Markets Act 2000 (Appointed Representatives) (Amendment) Regulations 2006, SI 2006/3414, regs 2, 4(a).

Paras (2), (3): added by SI 2001/2508, reg 2(c); revoked by SI 2006/3414, regs 2, 4(b).

[598]

3 Requirements applying to contracts between authorised persons and appointed representatives

(1) [Except where paragraph (1A) applies to a contract between a principal and a representative, it is a prescribed requirement for the purposes of section 39(1)(a)(ii) of the Act that such a contract] must (unless it prohibits the representative from representing other counterparties) contain a provision enabling the principal to—

(a) impose such a prohibition; or

(b) impose restrictions as to the other counterparties which the representative may represent, or as to the types of investment in relation to which the representative may represent other counterparties.

[(1A) This paragraph applies to a contract where the principal is an EEA investment firm or an EEA credit institution.]

(2) For the purposes of paragraph (1) a representative is to be treated as representing other counterparties where he—

[(aa) he enters into investment transactions as agent (in circumstances constituting the carrying on of an activity of the kind specified by article 21 of the Regulated Activities Order) for other counterparties;]

(a) makes arrangements (in circumstances constituting the carrying on of an activity of the kind specified by article 25 of [that Order]) for persons to enter (or with a view to persons entering) into investment transactions with other counterparties;

[(ab) he assists in the administration and performance of a contract of insurance (in circumstances constituting the carrying on of an activity of the kind specified by article 39A of that Order) for other counterparties;]

(b) arranges (in circumstances constituting the carrying on of an activity of the kind specified by article 40 of that Order) for other counterparties to safeguard and administer assets; or

(c) gives advice (in circumstances constituting the carrying on of an activity of the kind specified by article 53 of that Order) on the merits of entering into investment transactions with other counterparties;

where an "investment transaction" means a transaction to buy, sell, subscribe for or underwrite an investment which is a security or a [relevant investment].

[(3) A representative is also to be treated as representing other counterparties for the purposes of paragraph (1) where he—

(a) makes arrangements (in circumstances constituting the carrying on of an activity of the kind specified by article 25A of that Order)—

(i) for persons to enter (or with a view to persons entering) as borrowers into regulated mortgage contracts with other counterparties, or

(ii) for a person to vary a regulated mortgage contract entered into by a person as borrower after the coming into force of article 61 of that Order with other counterparties; or

(b) gives advice (in circumstances constituting the carrying on of an activity of the kind specified by article 53A of that Order) on the merits of—

(i) persons entering as borrowers into regulated mortgage contracts with other counterparties, or

(ii) persons varying regulated mortgage contracts entered into by them as borrower after the coming into force of article 61 of that Order with other counterparties.]

[(3A) A representative is also to be treated as representing other counterparties for the purposes of paragraph (1) where he—

(a) makes arrangements (in circumstances constituting the carrying on of an activity of the kind specified by article 25B of that Order)—

(i) for a person to enter (or with a view to a person entering) as reversion seller or plan provider into a regulated home reversion plan with other counterparties, or

(ii) for a person to vary a regulated home reversion plan entered into on or after 6th April 2007 by him as reversion seller or plan provider with other counterparties; or

(b) gives advice (in circumstances constituting the carrying on of an activity of the kind specified by article 53B of that Order) on the merits of—

(i) a person entering as reversion seller or plan provider into a regulated home reversion plan with other counterparties, or

(ii) a person varying a regulated home reversion plan entered into on or after 6th April 2007 by him as reversion seller or plan provider with other counterparties.

(3B) A representative is also to be treated as representing other counterparties for the purposes of paragraph (1) where he—

(a) makes arrangements (in circumstances constituting the carrying on of an activity of the kind specified by article 25C of that Order)—

(i) for a person to enter (or with a view to a person entering) as home purchaser into a regulated home purchase plan with other counterparties, or

(ii) for a person to vary a regulated home purchase plan entered into on or after 6th April 2007 by a person as home purchaser with other counterparties; or

(b) gives advice (in circumstances constituting the carrying on of an activity of the kind specified by article 53C of that Order) on the merits of—

(i) a person entering as home purchaser into a regulated home purchase plan with other counterparties, or

(ii) a person varying a regulated home purchase plan entered into on or after 6th April 2007 by him as home purchaser with other counterparties.]

[(4) Where the contract between the principal and the representative permits or requires the representative to carry on business which includes an activity—

(a) of the kind specified by article 21, 25, 39A or 53 of the Regulated Activities Order or an activity of the kind specified by article 64 of that Order, so far as relevant to any of those articles, and

(b) which relates to a contract of insurance,

paragraph (5) applies.

(5) Where this paragraph applies, it is also a prescribed requirement for the purposes of subsection (1)(a)(ii) of section 39 of the Act that the contract between the principal and the representative contain a provision providing that the representative is not permitted or required to carry on business, so far as it comprises an activity of the kind specified by paragraph (4), unless he is included in the record maintained by the Authority under section 347 of the Act by virtue of article 93 of the Regulated Activities Order (recorded insurance intermediaries).]

[(6) In the case of a representative to whom subsection (1A) of section 39 of the Act applies, it is a prescribed requirement for the purposes of subsection (1)(a)(ii) of that section, except where paragraph (1A) applies, that the contract between the principal and the representative must contain a provision that the representative is only permitted to provide the services and carry on the activities referred to in Article 4.1.25 of the markets in financial instruments directive while he is *entered on the applicable register.]*

NOTES

Para (1): words in square brackets substituted by the Financial Services and Markets Act 2000 (Appointed Representatives) (Amendment) Regulations 2006, SI 2006/3414, regs 2, 5(a).

Para (1A): inserted by SI 2006/3414, regs 2, 5(b).

Para (2): sub-paras (aa), (ab) inserted and words in square brackets in sub-para (a) and closing words substituted by the Financial Services and Markets Act 2000 (Regulated Activities) (Amendment) (No 2) Order 2003, SI 2003/1476, art 14(1), (4)(a).
Para (3): added by the Financial Services and Markets Act 2000 (Regulated Activities) (Amendment) (No 1) Order 2003, SI 2003/1475, art 23(1), (4).
Paras (3A), (3B): inserted by the Financial Services and Markets Act 2000 (Regulated Activities) (Amendment) (No 2) Order 2006, SI 2006/2383, art 31(1), (4), subject to transitional provisions in arts 37–39 thereof.
Paras (4), (5): added by SI 2003/1476, art 14(1), (4)(b).
Para (6): added by SI 2006/3414, regs 2, 5(c).

[598A]
[4 Transitional provision in relation to contracts

Regulation 3(6) does not apply in relation to a contract made on or before 31st October 2007.]

NOTES

Commencement: 1 November 2007.
Added by the Financial Services and Markets Act 2000 (Markets in Financial Instruments) (Amendment) Regulations 2007, SI 2007/763, reg 7.

FINANCIAL SERVICES AND MARKETS ACT 2000 (PROFESSIONS) (NON-EXEMPT ACTIVITIES) ORDER 2001

(SI 2001/1227)

NOTES

Made: 27 March 2001.
Authority: Financial Services and Markets Act 2000, ss 327(6), 428(3).
Commencement: see art 1.

[599]
1 Citation and commencement

(1) This Order may be cited as the Financial Services and Markets Act 2000 (Professions) (Non-Exempt Activities) Order 2001.

(2) Subject to paragraph (3), this Order comes into force on the day on which section 19 of the Act comes into force.

(3) This Order comes into force—
- (a) for the purposes of article 4(g), on 1st January 2002; and
- (b) for the purposes of [article 6A], [on such a day as the Treasury may specify].

[(4) Any day specified under paragraph (3)(b) must be caused to be notified in the London, Edinburgh and Belfast Gazettes published not later than one week before that day.]

NOTES

Para (3): words in first pair of square brackets substituted by the Financial Services and Markets Act 2000 (Miscellaneous Provisions) Order 2001, SI 2001/3650, art 3(a); words in second pair of square brackets substituted by the Financial Services and Markets Act 2000 (Commencement of Mortgage Regulation) (Amendment) Order 2002, SI 2002/1777, art 3(1), (2).
Para (4): added by SI 2002/1777, art 3(1), (3).

[600]
2 Interpretation

(1) In this Order—

"the Act" means the Financial Services and Markets Act 2000;

["agreement provider" has the meaning given by paragraph (3) of article 63J of the Regulated Activities Order, read with paragraphs (6) and (7) of that article;

"agreement seller" has the meaning given by article 63J(3) of the Regulated Activities Order"]

["contract of insurance" has the meaning given by article 3(1) of the Regulated Activities Order;]

"contractually based investment" has the meaning given by article 3(1) of the Regulated Activities Order;

["home purchase provider" has the meaning given by article 63F(3) of the Regulated Activities Order;

"home purchaser" has the meaning given by article 63F(3) of the Regulated Activities Order;]

"occupational pension scheme" and "personal pension scheme" have the meaning given by section 1 of the Pension Schemes Act 1993;

["plan provider" has the meaning given by paragraph (3) of article 63B of the Regulated Activities Order, read with paragraphs (7) and (8) of that article;]

["record of insurance intermediaries" means the record maintained by the Authority under section 347 of the Act (the public record) by virtue of article 93 of the Regulated Activities Order (recorded insurance intermediaries);]

"the Regulated Activities Order" means the Financial Services and Markets Act 2000 (Regulated Activities) Order 2001;

["regulated home purchase plan" has the meaning given by article 63F(3) of the Regulated Activities Order;

"regulated home reversion plan" has the meaning given by article 63B(3) of the Regulated Activities Order;

"regulated mortgage contract" has the meaning given by article 61 of the Regulated Activities Order;]

["regulated sale and rent back agreement" has the meaning given by article 63J(3) of the Regulated Activities Order;]

["relevant investment" has the meaning given by article 3(1) of the Regulated Activities Order;]

["reversion seller" has the meaning given by article 63B(3) of the Regulated Activities Order;]

"security" has the meaning given by article 3(1) of the Regulated Activities Order;

"syndicate" has the meaning given by article 3(1) of the Regulated Activities Order.

(2) For the purposes of this Order, a person is a member of a personal pension scheme if he is a person to or in respect of whom benefits are or may become payable under the scheme.

NOTES

Para (1): definitions "agreement provider", "agreement seller", and "regulated sale and rent back agreement" inserted by the Financial Services and Markets Act 2000 (Regulated Activities) (Amendment) Order 2009, SI 2009/1342, art 29(1), (2), as from 1 July 2009 (certain purposes), and as from 30 June 2010 (otherwise) (for the full commencement details and for transitional provisions etc see arts 1, 32–34 of that Order); definitions "contract of insurance" and "record of insurance intermediaries" inserted and definition "relevant investment" substituted by the Financial Services and Markets Act 2000 (Regulated Activities) (Amendment) (No 2) Order 2003, SI 2003/1476, art 16(1), (2); definitions "home purchase provider", "home purchaser", "plan provider", "regulated home purchase plan", "regulated home reversion plan", "regulated mortgage contract", and "reversion seller" inserted by the Financial Services and Markets Act 2000 (Regulated Activities) (Amendment) (No 2) Order 2006, SI 2006/2383, art 32(1), (2), subject to transitional provisions in arts 37–39 thereof.

[601]

3 Activities to which exemption from the general prohibition does not apply

The activities in articles 4 to 8 are specified for the purposes of section 327(6) of the Act.

[602]

4 An activity of the kind specified by any of the following provisions of the Regulated Activities Order—

(a) article 5 (accepting deposits);
[(aa) article 9B (issuing electronic money);]
(b) article 10 (effecting and carrying out contracts of insurance);
(c) article 14 (dealing in investments as principal);
(d) article 51 (establishing etc a collective investment scheme);
(e) article 52 (establishing etc a . . . pension scheme);
[(ea) article 52B (providing basic advice on stakeholder products);]
(f) article 57 (managing the underwriting capacity of a Lloyd's syndicate);
(g) article 59 (funeral plan contracts);
(h) . . .

NOTES

Para (aa) inserted by the Financial Services and Markets Act 2000 (Regulated Activities) (Amendment) Order 2002, SI 2002/682, art 7(1); word omitted from para (e) revoked by the Financial Services and Markets Act 2000 (Regulated Activities) (Amendment) Order 2006, SI 2006/1969, art 11; para (ea) inserted by the Financial Services and Markets Act 2000 (Regulated Activities) (Amendment) (No 2) Order 2004, SI 2004/2737, art 5(3), (4); para (h) revoked by the Financial Services and Markets Act 2000 (Miscellaneous Provisions) Order 2001, SI 2001/3650, art 3(b).

[603]

[4A An activity of the kind specified by article 21 or 25 of the Regulated Activities Order (dealing in investments as agent or arranging deals in investments) in so far as it—

(a) relates to a transaction for the sale or purchase of rights under a contract of insurance; and

(b) is carried on by a person who is not included in the record of insurance intermediaries.]

NOTES

Inserted by the Financial Services and Markets Act 2000 (Regulated Activities) (Amendment) (No 2) Order 2003, SI 2003/1476, art 16(1), (3).

[604]

5— (1) An activity of the kind specified by article 37 of the Regulated Activities Order (managing investments) in so far as it consists of buying or subscribing for a [security or contractually based investment].

(2) Paragraph (1) does not apply—

(a) if all routine or day to day decisions, so far as relating to that activity, are taken by an authorised person with permission to carry on that activity or by a person who is an exempt person in relation to such an activity; or

(b) to an activity undertaken in accordance with the advice of an authorised person with permission to give advice in relation to such an activity or a person who is an exempt person in relation to the giving of such advice.

NOTES

Para (1): words in square brackets substituted by the Financial Services and Markets Act 2000 (Regulated Activities) (Amendment) (No 2) Order 2003, SI 2003/1476, art 16(1), (4).

[605]

[5A An activity of the kind specified by article 39A of the Regulated Activities Order (assisting in the administration and performance of a contract of insurance) if it is carried on by a person who is not included in the record of insurance intermediaries.]

NOTES

Inserted by the Financial Services and Markets Act 2000 (Regulated Activities) (Amendment) (No 2) Order 2003, SI 2003/1476, art 16(1), (5).

[606]

6— (1) An activity of the kind specified by article 53 of the Regulated Activities Order (advising on investments) where the advice in question falls within [paragraph (2), (3) or (5)].

(2) Subject to paragraph (4), advice falls within this paragraph in so far as—

(a) it is given to an individual (or his agent) other than where the individual acts—

(i) in connection with the carrying on of a business of any kind by himself or by an undertaking of which he is, or would become as a result of the transaction to which the advice relates, a controller; or

(ii) in his capacity as a trustee of an occupational pension scheme;

(b) it consists of a recommendation to buy or subscribe for a particular [security or contractually based investment]; and

(c) the transaction to which the advice relates would be made—

(i) with a person acting in the course of carrying on the business of buying, selling, subscribing for or underwriting the [security or contractually based investment], whether as principal or agent;

(ii) on an investment exchange or any other market to which that investment is admitted for dealing; or

(iii) in response to an invitation to subscribe for [such an investment] which is, or is to be, admitted for dealing on an investment exchange or any other market.

(3) Subject to paragraph (4), advice falls within this paragraph in so far as it consists of a recommendation to a member of a personal pension scheme (or his agent) to dispose of any rights or interests which the member has in or under the scheme.

(4) Advice does not fall within paragraph (2) or (3) if it endorses a corresponding recommendation given to the individual (or, as the case may be, the member) by an authorised person with permission to give advice in relation to the proposed transaction or a person who is an exempt person in relation to the giving of such advice.

[(5) Advice falls within this paragraph in so far as—

(a) it relates to a transaction for the sale or purchase of rights under a contract of insurance; and

(b) it is given by a person who is not included in the record of insurance intermediaries.]

NOTES

Paras (1), (2): words in square brackets substituted by the Financial Services and Markets Act 2000 (Regulated Activities) (Amendment) (No 2) Order 2003, SI 2003/1476, art 16(1), (6)(a), (b).

Para (5): added by SI 2003/1476, art 16(1), (6)(c).

[607]

[6A—(1) An activity of the kind specified by article 53A of the Regulated Activities Order (advising on regulated mortgage contracts) where the advice in question falls within paragraph (2).

(2) Subject to paragraph (3), advice falls within this paragraph in so far as—

(a) it consists of a recommendation, given to an individual, to enter as borrower into a regulated mortgage contract with a particular person; and

(b) in entering into a regulated mortgage contract that person would be carrying on an activity of the kind specified by article 61(1) of the Regulated Activities Order (regulated mortgage contracts).

(3) Advice does not fall within paragraph (2) if it endorses a corresponding recommendation given to the individual by an authorised person with permission to carry on an activity of the kind specified by article 53A of the Regulated Activities Order or a person who is an exempt person in relation to an activity of that kind.]

NOTES

Inserted by the Financial Services and Markets Act 2000 (Regulated Activities) (Amendment) (No 1) Order 2003, SI 2003/1475, art 24(1), (3).

[608]

[[6B]—(1) An activity of the kind specified by article 61(1) or (2) of the Regulated Activities Order (regulated mortgage contracts).

(2) Paragraph (1) does not apply to an activity carried on by a person in his capacity as a trustee or personal representative where the borrower under the regulated mortgage contract in question is a beneficiary under the trust, will or intestacy.]

NOTES

Inserted (originally as art 6A) by the Financial Services and Markets Act 2000 (Miscellaneous Provisions) Order 2001, SI 2001/3650, art 3(c).

Renumbered as art 6B by the Financial Services and Markets Act 2000 (Regulated Activities) (Amendment) (No 1) Order 2003, SI 2003/1475, art 24(1), (2).

6C–6H *(Outside the scope of this work.)*

[609]

7— (1) Advising a person to become a member of a particular Lloyd's syndicate.

(2) Paragraph (1) does not apply to advice which endorses that of an authorised person with permission to give such advice or a person who is an exempt person in relation to the giving of such advice.

[610]

8 Agreeing to carry on any of the activities mentioned in articles 4 to 7 other than the activities mentioned in article 4(a), [(aa),] (b), (d) and (e).

NOTES

Reference in square brackets inserted by the Financial Services and Markets Act 2000 (Regulated Activities) (Amendment) Order 2002, SI 2002/682, art 7(2).

FINANCIAL SERVICES AND MARKETS ACT 2000 (COMPENSATION SCHEME: ELECTING PARTICIPANTS) REGULATIONS 2001

(SI 2001/1783)

NOTES

Made: 9 May 2001.

Authority: Financial Services and Markets Act 2000, ss 213(10), 214(5), 224(4), 417(1), 428(3).

Commencement: 18 June 2001.

[611]

1 Citation, commencement and interpretation

(1) These Regulations may be cited as the Financial Services and Markets Act 2000 (Compensation Scheme: Electing Participants) Regulations 2001 and come into force on 18th June 2001.

(2) In these Regulations—

"branch"—

(a) in relation to an investment firm, has the meaning given by Article 1.5 of the investor-compensation schemes directive;

(b) in relation to a credit institution, has the meaning given by Article 1.5 of the deposit-guarantee schemes directive;

[(c) in relation to a relevant management company, has the meaning given by Article 1.5 of the investor-compensation schemes directive (as applied by Article 5f.2 of the UCITS directive);]

"credit institution" has the meaning given by [Article 4(1)] of the banking consolidation directive;

"deposit-guarantee schemes directive" means Council and European Parliament Directive 94/19/EC on deposit-guarantee schemes;

"depositor" has the same meaning as in the deposit-guarantee schemes directive;

"Financial Services Compensation Scheme" means the compensation scheme established pursuant to Part XV of the Act;

"home State deposit-guarantee scheme" means—

(a) in relation to a credit institution which is exempted by the EEA State in which that institution has its head office from the obligation to belong to a deposit-guarantee scheme by virtue of belonging to a system which protects the credit institution as mentioned in Article 3 of the deposit-guarantee schemes directive, that system; and

(b) in all other cases, the deposit-guarantee scheme officially recognised by that EEA State for the purposes of Article 3.1 of the deposit-guarantee schemes directive;

"home State investor-compensation scheme" means—

(a) in relation to a credit institution which is exempted by the EEA State in which that institution has its head office from the obligation to belong to an investor-compensation scheme by virtue of Article 2.1 of the investor-compensation schemes directive (participation in a system that protects the credit institution), that system; and

(b) in all other cases, the investor-compensation scheme officially recognised by that EEA State for the purposes of Article 2.1 of the investor-compensation schemes directive;

["insurance intermediary" means an insurance intermediary (within the meaning of Article 2(5) of the insurance mediation directive) or a reinsurance intermediary (within the meaning of Article 2(6) of that Directive);]

"investment firm" has the meaning given by Article 1.1 of the investor-compensation schemes directive;

"investor" has the meaning given by Article 1.4 of the investor-compensation schemes directive;

"investor-compensation schemes directive" means the Council and European Parliament Directive 97/9/EC on investor-compensation schemes;

["relevant management company" means an EEA firm falling within paragraph 5(f) of Schedule 3 to the Act which—

(a) is authorised by its home state regulator to provide services of the kind specified by Article 5.3(a) of the UCITS directive (management of portfolios of investments); and

(b) is providing those services in the United Kingdom;]

NOTES

In definition "branch" para (c) inserted and definition "relevant management company" added by the Collective Investment Schemes (Miscellaneous Amendments) Regulations 2003, SI 2003/2066, reg 7(a); words in square brackets in definition "credit institution" substituted by the Capital Requirements Regulations 2006, SI 2006/3221, reg 29(4), Sch 6, para 7; definition "insurance intermediary" inserted by the Financial Services and Markets Act 2000 (Regulated Activities) (Amendment) (No 2) Order 2003, SI 2003/1476, art 15(1), (2).

Council and European Parliament Directive 94/19/EC: OJ L135, 31.5.1994, p 5.

Council and European Parliament Directive 97/9/EC: OJ L84, 26.3.1997, p 22.

[612]
2 Persons not to be regarded as relevant persons

For the purposes of section 213(10) of the Act (certain persons not to be regarded as relevant persons unless they elect to participate), the following categories are prescribed—

(a) any investment firm; . . .
(b) any credit institution[; . . . .
(c) any insurance intermediary][; and
(d) any relevant management company.]

NOTES

Word omitted from para (a) revoked and para (c) and word immediately preceding it added by the Financial Services and Markets Act 2000 (Regulated Activities) (Amendment) (No 2) Order 2003, SI SI 2003/1476, art 15(1), (3); word omitted from para (b) revoked and para (d) and word "and" immediately preceding it added by the Collective Investment Schemes (Miscellaneous Amendments) Regulations 2003, SI 2003/2066, reg 7(b).

[613]
3 Persons who may elect to participate

(1) For the purposes of section 214(5) of the Act (persons who may elect to participate), the following categories are prescribed—

(a) any investment firm [or relevant management company] which has established a branch in the United Kingdom in exercise of an EEA right and is a member of a home State investor-compensation scheme which meets the condition in paragraph (2); . . .
(b) any credit institution which has established a branch in the United Kingdom in exercise of an EEA right and is a member of a home State deposit-guarantee scheme which meets the condition in paragraph (3)[; and
(c) any insurance intermediary which is not an investment firm or a credit institution.]

(2) The condition mentioned in paragraph (1)(a) is that the scope or level (including percentage) of the protection afforded to investors by the Financial Services Compensation Scheme exceeds that afforded by the home State investor-compensation scheme.

(3) The condition mentioned in paragraph (1)(b) is that the scope or level (including percentage) of the protection afforded to depositors by the Financial Services Compensation Scheme exceeds that afforded by the home State deposit-guarantee scheme.

NOTES

Para (1): words in square brackets in sub-para (a) inserted by the Collective Investment Schemes (Miscellaneous Amendments) Regulations 2003, SI 2003/2066, reg 7(c); word omitted from para (a) revoked and para (c) and word "and" immediately preceding it added by the Financial Services and Markets Act 2000 (Regulated Activities) (Amendment) (No 2) Order 2003, SI 2003/1476, art 15(1), (4).

[614]–[617]
4 Persons in respect of whom inspection under section 224 does not apply

For the purposes of section 224(4) of the Act (power to inspect documents held by Official Receiver), the following categories are prescribed—

(a) any investment firm; . . .
(b) any credit institution[; . . .
(c) any insurance intermediary][; and
(d) any relevant management company].

NOTES

Word omitted from para (a) revoked and para (c) and word immediately preceding it added by the Financial Services and Markets Act 2000 (Regulated Activities) (Amendment) (No 2) Order 2003, SI 2003/1476, art 15(1), (5); word omitted from para (b) revoked and para (d) and word "and" immediately preceding it added by the Collective Investment Schemes (Miscellaneous Amendments) Regulations 2003, SI 2003/2066, reg 7(d).

FINANCIAL SERVICES AND MARKETS ACT 2000 (RIGHTS OF ACTION) REGULATIONS 2001

(SI 2001/2256)

NOTES

Made: 20 June 2001.
Authority: Financial Services and Markets Act 2000, ss 20(3), 71(2), (3), 150(3), (5), 202(2), 417(1), 428(3).
Commencement: 1 December 2001 (see reg 1).

ARRANGEMENT OF REGULATIONS

1 Citation and commencement . . . . [618]
2 Interpretation . . . . [619]
3 Private person . . . . [620]
4 Authorised person acting otherwise than in accordance with permission . . . . [621]
5 Prohibition orders and performance of a controlled function . . . . [622]
6 Authority rules . . . . [623]
7 Incoming firms . . . . [624]

[618]

1 Citation and commencement

These Regulations may be cited as the Financial Services and Markets Act 2000 (Rights of Action) Regulations 2001 and come into force on the day on which section 19 of the Act comes into force.

[619]

2 Interpretation

In these Regulations—

"the Act" means the Financial Services and Markets Act 2000;

"government" means—

(a) the government of the United Kingdom;

(b) the Scottish Administration;

(c) the Executive Committee of the Northern Ireland Assembly;

(d) the National Assembly for Wales; or

(e) the government of any country or territory outside the United Kingdom;

"international organisation" means any international organisation the members of which include the United Kingdom or any other state;

"local authority", in relation to the United Kingdom, means—

(a) in England and Wales, a local authority within the meaning of the Local Government Act 1972, the Greater London Authority, the Common Council of the City of London or the Council of the Isles of Scilly;

(b) in Scotland, a local authority within the meaning of the Local Government (Scotland) Act 1973; and

(c) in Northern Ireland, a district council within the meaning of the Local Government Act (Northern Ireland) 1972;

"Part IV financial resources requirement" means a requirement imposed on an authorised person by the Authority under Part IV of the Act to have or maintain financial resources;

"Part XIII financial resources requirement" means a requirement imposed on an incoming firm (within the meaning of section 193(1) of the Act) by the Authority under Part XIII of the Act to have or maintain financial resources;

"the Regulated Activities Order" means the Financial Services and Markets Act 2000 (Regulated Activities) Order 2001.

[620]

3 Private person

(1) In these Regulations, "private person" means—

(a) any individual, unless he suffers the loss in question in the course of carrying on—

(i) any regulated activity; or

(ii) any activity which would be a regulated activity apart from any exclusion made by [article 72 (overseas persons) or 72A (information society services) of the Regulated Activities Order]; and

(b) any person who is not an individual, unless he suffers the loss in question in the course of carrying on business of any kind;

but does not include a government, a local authority (in the United Kingdom or elsewhere) or an international organisation.

(2) For the purposes of paragraph (1)(a), an individual who suffers loss in the course of effecting or carrying out contracts of insurance (within the meaning of article 10 of the Regulated Activities Order) written at Lloyd's is not to be taken to suffer loss in the course of carrying on a regulated activity.

NOTES

Para (1): words in square brackets substituted by the Electronic Commerce Directive (Financial Services and Markets) Regulations 2002, SI 2002/1775, reg 18.

[621]

4 Authorised person acting otherwise than in accordance with permission

(1) A case where the conditions specified by paragraph (2) are satisfied is prescribed for the purposes of section 20(3) of the Act (and so in such a case the contravention of a requirement imposed by the Authority under the Act is actionable at the suit of a person who suffers loss as a result of that contravention).

(2) The conditions specified by this paragraph are that—

(a) the action would be brought at the suit of—

(i) a private person; or

(ii) a person acting in a fiduciary or representative capacity on behalf of a private person and any remedy would be exclusively for the benefit of that private person and could not be effected through an action brought otherwise than at the suit of the fiduciary or representative; and

(b) the contravention is not of a Part IV financial resources requirement.

[622]

5 Prohibition orders and performance of a controlled function

(1) The definition of "private person" in regulation 3 is prescribed for the purposes of section 71(3) of the Act (and so the contravention of section 56(6) or 59(1) or (2) of the Act is actionable at the suit of a person who falls within that definition and who suffers loss as a result of that contravention).

(2) A case where the condition specified by paragraph (3) is satisfied is prescribed for the purposes of section 71(2) of the Act (and so in such a case the contravention of section 56(6) or 59(1) or (2) of the Act is actionable at the suit of a person who is not a private person).

(3) The condition specified by this paragraph is that the action would be brought at the suit of a person (who is not a private person) acting in a fiduciary or representative capacity on behalf of a private person and any remedy would be exclusively for the benefit of that private person and could not be effected through an action brought otherwise than at the suit of the fiduciary or representative.

[623]

6 Authority rules

(1) The definition of "private person" in regulation 3 is prescribed for the purposes of section 150(5) of the Act (and so the contravention by an authorised person of a rule is actionable at the suit of a person who falls within that definition and who suffers loss as a result of that contravention).

(2) A case where any of the conditions specified by paragraph (3) is satisfied is prescribed for the purposes of section 150(3) of the Act (and so in such a case the contravention of a rule is actionable at the suit of a person who is not a private person).

(3) The conditions specified by this paragraph are that—

(a) the rule that has been contravened prohibits an authorised person from seeking to make provision excluding or restricting any duty or liability;

(b) the rule that has been contravened is directed at ensuring that transactions in any security or contractually based investment (within the meaning of the Regulated Activities Order) are not effected with the benefit of unpublished information that, if made public, would be likely to affect the price of that security or investment;

(c) the action would be brought at the suit of a person (who is not a private person) acting in a fiduciary or representative capacity on behalf of a private person and any remedy would be exclusively for the benefit of that private person and could not be effected through an action brought otherwise than at the suit of the fiduciary or representative;

[(d) the rule that has been contravened requires a relevant authorised person to respond to a claim for compensation within a specified time limit, or to pay interest in specified circumstances in respect of any such claim.]

[(4) In this regulation—

(a) "relevant authorised person" means an authorised person with a Part IV permission—

(i) to effect or to carry out relevant contracts of insurance; or

(ii) to manage the underwriting capacity of a Lloyd's syndicate as a managing agent, *the members of which* effect or carry out relevant contracts of insurance underwritten at Lloyd's;

where a "relevant contract of insurance" means a contract of insurance against damage arising out of or in connection with the use of motor vehicles on land (other than carrier's liability);

(b) "rule" has the meaning given by section 150(4) of the Act; and
(c) "specified" means specified in rules.]

NOTES

Para (3): sub-para (d) added by the Financial Services and Markets Act 2000 (Fourth Motor Insurance Directive) Regulations 2002, SI 2002/2706, reg 3(a).

Para (4): substituted by SI 2002/2706, reg 3(b).

[624]

7 Incoming firms

(1) A case where the conditions specified by paragraph (2) are satisfied is prescribed for the purposes of section 202(2) of the Act (and so in such a case the contravention of a requirement imposed by the Authority under Part XIII of the Act is actionable at the suit of a person who suffers loss as a result of that contravention).

(2) The conditions specified by this paragraph are that—
- (a) the action would be brought at the suit of—
  - (i) a private person; or
  - (ii) a person acting in a fiduciary or representative capacity on behalf of a private person and any remedy would be exclusively for the benefit

  of that private person and could not be effected through an action brought otherwise than at the suit of the fiduciary or representative; and
- (b) the contravention is not of a Part XIII financial resources requirement.

FINANCIAL SERVICES AND MARKETS ACT 2000 (MEANING OF "POLICY" AND "POLICYHOLDER") ORDER 2001

(SI 2001/2361)

NOTES

Made: 2 July 2001.

Authority: Financial Services and Markets Act 2000, ss 424(2), 428(3).

Commencement: 1 December 2001 (see art 1).

[625]

1 Citation, commencement and interpretation

(1) This Order may be cited as the Financial Services and Markets Act 2000 (Meaning of "Policy" and "Policyholder") Order 2001 and comes into force on the day on which section 19 of the Act comes into force.

(2) In this Order, "contract of insurance" has the meaning given by article 3 of the Financial Services and Markets Act 2000 (Regulated Activities) Order 2001.

[626]

2 Meaning of "policy"

For the purposes of section 424(2) of the Act, "policy" means, as the context requires,
- (a) a contract of insurance, including one under which an existing liability has already accrued, or
- (b) any instrument evidencing such a contract.

[627]

3 Meaning of "policyholder"

For the purposes of section 424(2) of the Act, "policyholder" means the person who for the time being is the legal holder of the policy, and includes any person to whom, under the policy, a sum is due, a periodic payment is payable or any other benefit is to be provided or to whom such a sum, payment or benefit is contingently due, payable or to be provided.

FINANCIAL SERVICES AND MARKETS ACT 2000 (VARIATION OF THRESHOLD CONDITIONS) ORDER 2001

(SI 2001/2507)

NOTES

Made: 12 July 2001.

Authority: Financial Services and Markets Act 2000, s 428(3), Sch 6, paras 8, 9.

Commencement: 3 September 2001 (see art 1(1)).

[628]

1 Citation, commencement and interpretation

(1) This Order may be cited as the Financial Services and Markets Act 2000 (Variation of Threshold Conditions) Order 2001 and comes into force on the day on which paragraphs 1 to 7 of Schedule 6 come into force.

(2) In this Order—

"section 41" and "Schedule 6" mean (respectively) section 41 of, and Schedule 6 to, the Financial Services and Markets Act 2000;

"supervisory authority" means an authority responsible for supervising persons carrying on insurance business;

"Swiss general insurance company" means a person—

(a) whose head office is in Switzerland;

(b) who is authorised by the supervisory authority in Switzerland as mentioned in Article 7.1 of the Agreement between the European Economic Community and the Swiss Confederation on direct insurance other than life insurance, signed at Luxembourg on 10 October 1989;

(c) who is seeking to carry on, or is carrying on, from a branch in the United Kingdom, a regulated activity consisting of the effecting or carrying out of contracts of insurance of a kind which is subject to that Agreement.

2 (*Amends the Financial Services and Markets Act 2000, Sch 6, para 1(1).*)

[629]

3 Non-EEA insurers

(1) If paragraph 8 of Schedule 6 (additional conditions applying to non-EEA insurers) applies to the person concerned, it must, for the purposes of section 41 and Schedule 6, satisfy the following additional conditions—

(a) it must have a representative who is resident in the United Kingdom and who has authority to bind it in its relations with third parties and to represent it in its relations with the Authority and the courts in the United Kingdom;

(b) subject to paragraph (2), if the person concerned is not a Swiss general insurance company—

(i) it must be a body corporate entitled under the law of the place where its head office is situated to effect and carry out contracts of insurance;

(ii) it must have in the United Kingdom assets of such value as may be specified;

(iii) unless the regulated activity in question relates solely to reinsurance, it must have made a deposit (of money or securities, as may be specified) of such an amount and with such a person as may be specified, and on such terms and subject to such other provisions as may be specified.

(2) Where the person concerned is seeking to carry on an activity relating to insurance business in one or more other EEA States (as well as in the United Kingdom), and the Authority and the supervisory authority in the other EEA State or States concerned so agree—

(a) the reference in paragraph (1)(b)(ii) to the United Kingdom is to be read as a reference to the United Kingdom and the other EEA State or States concerned; and

(b) the reference in paragraph (1)(b)(iii) to such a person as may be specified is to be read as a reference to such a person as may be agreed between the Authority and the other supervisory authority or authorities concerned.

[(3) The conditions set out in paragraphs 4 and 5 of Schedule 6 (adequate resources and suitability) are removed in relation to a Swiss general insurance company.]

(4) In this article, "specified" means specified in rules.

NOTES

Para (3): substituted by the Financial Services and Markets Act 2000 (Variation of Threshold Conditions) (Amendment) Order 2005, SI 2005/680, art 2(1), (2).

[630]

[4 Swiss general insurance companies

(1) A Swiss general insurance company must, for the purposes of section 41 and Schedule 6, satisfy the following additional conditions—

(a) the value of the assets of the business carried on by it in the United Kingdom must not fall below the amount of the liabilities of that business, that value and amount being determined in such manner as may be specified;

(b) such assets must be maintained in such places as may be specified and must be of such a nature as may be specified as being appropriate in relation to the currency in which the liabilities of the company are or may be required to be met; and

(c) when applying to the Authority for permission to carry on a regulated activity it must submit to the Authority a statement from the supervisory authorities in Switzerland—

(i) stating the classes of insurance business which the company is authorised to carry on in Switzerland,

(ii) specifying the risks covered there,

(iii) declaring that the company is constituted in Switzerland in a form permitted by Annex 3 of the Agreement signed on 10th October 1989 between the European Economic Community and the Swiss Confederation on direct insurance other than life assurance,

(iv) confirming that the company limits its business activities to insurance and to operations directly arising therefrom to the exclusion of all other commercial business, and

(v) declaring that the company has the required solvency margin or minimum guarantee fund.

(2) In this article, "specified" means specified in rules.]

NOTES

Added by the Financial Services and Markets Act 2000 (Variation of Threshold Conditions) (Amendment) Order 2005, SI 2005/680, art 2(1), (3).

FINANCIAL SERVICES AND MARKETS ACT 2000 (GAMING CONTRACTS) ORDER 2001

(SI 2001/2510)

NOTES

Made: 12 July 2001.
Authority: Financial Services and Markets Act 2000, s 412(2), (6).
Commencement: 1 December 2001 (see art 1).

[631]

1 This Order may be cited as the Financial Services and Markets Act 2000 (Gaming Contracts) Order 2001 and comes into force on the day on which section 19 of the Act comes into force.

[632]

2— (1) Any activity of the kind—

(a) specified by article 14 or 21 of the Financial Services and Markets Act 2000 (Regulated Activities) Order 2001 ("the Regulated Activities Order") (dealing in investments as principal or agent);

(b) specified by article 64 of that Order (agreeing to carry on specified kinds of activity), so far as relevant to either of those articles; or

(c) which would be so specified apart from any exclusion from any of those articles made by that Order;

is specified for the purposes of paragraph (b) of subsection (2) of section 412 of the Act (contracts not to be void or unenforceable because of the law relating to gaming).

(2) The class of investment consisting of securities and contractually based investments (within the meaning of the Regulated Activities Order) is specified for the purposes of paragraph (c) of subsection (2) of that section.

FINANCIAL SERVICES AND MARKETS ACT 2000 (EEA PASSPORT RIGHTS) REGULATIONS 2001

(SI 2001/2511)

NOTES

Made: 12 July 2001.

Authority: Financial Services and Markets Act 2000, ss 417(1), 426–428, Sch 3, paras 13(1)(b)(iii), 14(1)(b), 17(a), (b), (c), 18, 22.
Commencement: 1 December 2001 (see reg 1(1)).

ARRANGEMENT OF REGULATIONS

PART I
GENERAL

1 Citation, commencement and interpretation . . . [633]

PART II
EXERCISE OF PASSPORT RIGHTS BY EEA FIRMS

Contents of consent notice and regulator's notice

2 Establishment of a branch: contents of consent notice . . . [634]
3 Provision of services: contents of regulator's notice . . . [635]

Changes relating to EEA firms

6 Insurance firms: changes to branch details . . . [636]
7 Insurance firms: changes to services . . . [637]

Cancellation of qualification for authorisation

8 EEA firms ceasing to carry on regulated activities in the United Kingdom . . . [638]

Applications for approval under section 60 by EEA firms

10 Applications for approval under section 60 by EEA firms . . . [639]

PART III
EXERCISE OF PASSPORT RIGHTS BY UK FIRMS

Changes relating to UK firms

13 UK insurance firms: changes to relevant EEA details of branches . . . [640]
14 Relevant EEA details for the purposes of regulation 13 . . . [641]
15 UK insurance firms: changes to relevant UK details of branches . . . [642]
16 UK insurance firms: changes to services . . . [643]
17 Relevant details for the purposes of regulation 16 . . . [644]
18 Offences relating to failure to notify changes . . . [645]

UK firms: scope of outward passport

19 UK firms: scope of outward passport . . . [646]

PART IV
TRANSITIONAL PROVISIONS

20 Changes relating to EEA firms: procedures partly completed at commencement . . . [647]
21 Changes relating to UK firms: procedures partly completed at commencement . . . [648]

PART I
GENERAL

[633]

1 Citation, commencement and interpretation

(1) These Regulations may be cited as the Financial Services and Markets Act 2000 (EEA Passport Rights) Regulations 2001, and come into force on the day on which section 19 of the Act comes into force.

(2) In these Regulations—

"the 2BCD Regulations" means the Banking Coordination (Second Council Directive) Regulations 1992;

"the Act" means the Financial Services and Markets Act 2000;

"authorised agent" means, in relation to an EEA firm or UK firm, an agent or employee of the firm who has authority to bind the firm in its relations with third parties, and to represent the firm in its relations with the Authority or the host state regulator (as the case may be) and with the courts in the United Kingdom or the EEA State concerned (as the case may be);

"claims representative", in relation to a UK firm and an EEA State, means a person who has been designated as the firm's representative in that EEA State, and has authority—

(a) to act on behalf of the firm and to represent, or to instruct others to represent, the firm in relation to any matters giving rise to claims made against policies issued by the firm, to the extent that they cover motor vehicles risks situated in the EEA State;

(b) to pay sums in settlement of such claims (but not to settle such claims); and

(c) to accept service on behalf of the firm of proceedings in respect of such claims;

"commencement" means the beginning of the day on which section 19 of the Act comes into force;

"contract of insurance", "contract of general insurance" and "contract of long-term insurance" have the same meaning as in the Regulated Activities Order;

"credit institution" means an EEA firm falling within paragraph 5(b) of Schedule 3;

["electronic money institution" means an electronic money institution as defined in Article 1 of directive 2000/46/EC of the European Parliament and of the Council of 18th September 2000 on the taking up, pursuit of and prudential supervision of the business of electronic money institutions;]

"EEA activities" means—

(a) in relation to an EEA firm, activities which the firm is seeking to carry on in the United Kingdom in exercise of an EEA right;

(b) in relation to a UK firm, activities which the firm is seeking to carry on in another EEA State in exercise of an EEA right;

"financial institution" means an EEA firm falling within paragraph 5(c) of Schedule 3;

"the Friendly Societies Act" means the Friendly Societies Act 1992;

"health insurance risks", in relation to an EEA State, means risks of a kind mentioned in paragraph 2 of Schedule 1 to the Regulated Activities Order (sickness), where—

(a) contracts of insurance covering those risks serve as a partial or complete alternative to the health cover provided by the statutory social security system in that EEA State; and

(b) the law of that EEA State requires such contracts to be operated on a technical basis similar to life assurance in accordance with all the conditions listed in the first sub-paragraph of Article 54(2) of the third non-life insurance directive;

"the Insurance Companies Act" means the Insurance Companies Act 1982;

"insurance firm" means an EEA firm falling within paragraph 5(d) of Schedule 3;

["insurance intermediary" means an EEA firm falling within paragraph 5(e) of Schedule 3;]

"investment firm" means an EEA firm falling within paragraph 5(a) of Schedule 3;

"the ISD Regulations" means the Investment Services Regulations 1995;

["management company" means an EEA firm falling within paragraph 5(f) of Schedule 3;]

"national bureau", in relation to an EEA State, means a professional organisation—

(a) which has been constituted in that EEA State in accordance with Recommendation No 5 adopted on 25th January 1949 by the Road Transport Sub-committee of the Inland Transport Committee of the United Nations Economic Commission for Europe; and

(b) which groups together undertakings which in that EEA State are authorised to conduct the business of motor vehicle liability insurance;

"national guarantee fund", in relation to an EEA State, means a body—

(a) which has been set up or authorised in that EEA State in accordance with Article 1(4) of Council Directive 84/5/EEC on the approximation of laws of the Member States relating to insurance against civil liability in respect of the use of motor vehicles; and

(b) which provides compensation for damage to property or personal injuries caused by unidentified vehicles or vehicles for which the insurance obligation provided for in Article 1(1) of that Directive has not been satisfied;

"the Regulated Activities Order" means the Financial Services and Markets Act 2000 (Regulated Activities) Order 2001;

"relevant motor vehicle risks" means risks of damage arising out of or in connection with the use of motor vehicles on land, including third party risks (but excluding carrier's liability);

"requisite details", in relation to a branch, means—

(a) particulars of the programme of operations carried on, or to be carried on, from the branch, including a description of the particular EEA activities to be carried on, and of the structural organisation of the branch;

(b) the address in the EEA State in which the branch is, or is to be, established from which information about the business may be obtained; and

(c) the names of the managers of the business;

"Schedule 3" means Schedule 3 to the Act[;

"tied agent" has the meaning given in Article 4.1.25 of the markets in financial instruments directive;

"UK investment firm" means a UK firm—

(a) which is an investment firm [(within the meaning of section 424A of the Act)],

(b) whose EEA right derives from the markets in financial instruments directive].

NOTES

Para (2): definition "electronic money institution" inserted by the Electronic Money (Miscellaneous Amendments) Regulations 2002, SI 2002/765, reg 10(1), (2); definition "insurance intermediary" inserted by the Insurance Mediation Directive (Miscellaneous Amendments) Regulations 2003, SI 2003/1473, reg 8(1), (2); definition "management company" inserted by the Collective Investment Schemes (Miscellaneous Amendments) Regulations 2003, SI 2003/2066, reg 2(3); definitions "tied agent" and "UK investment firm" inserted by the Financial Services and Markets Act 2000 (EEA Passport Rights) (Amendment) Regulations 2006, SI 2006/3385, regs 2, 3; words in square brackets in definition "UK investment firm" inserted by the Financial Services and Markets Act 2000 (Markets in Financial Instruments) (Amendment) Regulations 2007, SI 2007/763, reg 8.

European Parliament and Council Directive 2000/46/EC: OJ L275, 27.10.2000, p 39.

Council Directive 84/5/EEC: OJ L8, 11.1.1984, p 17.

PART II
EXERCISE OF PASSPORT RIGHTS BY EEA FIRMS

Contents of consent notice and regulator's notice

[634]

2 Establishment of a branch: contents of consent notice

(1) The following information is prescribed for the purposes of paragraph 13(1)(b)(iii) of Schedule 3 (and is therefore to be included in a consent notice given to the Authority by a firm's home state regulator pursuant to paragraph 13(1)(a) of Schedule 3).

(2)–(4) . . .

(5) In the case of an insurance firm, the prescribed information is—

(a) a scheme of operations prepared in accordance with such requirements as may be imposed by the firm's home state regulator, setting out (amongst other things) the types of business to be carried on and the structural organisation of the branch;

(b) the name of the firm's authorised agent;

(c) the address in the United Kingdom from which information about the business may be obtained, and a statement that this is the address for service on the firm's authorised agent;

(d) in the case of a firm which intends to cover relevant motor vehicle risks, a declaration by the firm that it has become a member of the Motor Insurers' Bureau (being a company limited by guarantee and incorporated under the Companies Act 1929 on the 14th June 1946); and

(e) a statement by the firm's home state regulator attesting that the firm has the minimum margin of solvency calculated in accordance with such of the following as are appropriate—

(i) Articles 16 and 17 of the first non-life insurance directive [(as last amended by Directive 2002/87/EC of the European Parliament and of the Council)], and

(ii) Articles 18, 19 and 20 of the first life insurance directive.

NOTES

Paras (2)–(4): outside the scope of this work.

Para (5): words in square brackets inserted by the Financial Conglomerates and Other Financial Groups Regulations 2004, SI 2004/1862, reg 14(4).

European Parliament and Council Directive 2002/87/EC: OJ L35, 11.2.2003, p 1.

[635]

3 Provision of services: contents of regulator's notice

(1) The following information is prescribed for the purposes of paragraph 14(1)(b) of Schedule 3 (and is therefore to be included in a regulator's notice given to the Authority by a firm's home state regulator pursuant to that paragraph).

(2) . . .

[(2ZA), (2A) . . .]

(3) In the case of an insurance firm, the prescribed information is—

(a) a statement of the classes of business which the firm is authorised to carry on in accordance with Article 6 of the first non-life insurance directive or Article 6 of the first life insurance directive;

(b) the name and address of the firm;

(c) the nature of the risks or commitments which the firm proposes to cover in the United Kingdom;

(d) in the case of a firm which intends to cover relevant motor vehicle risks—

(i) the name and address of the claims representative; and

(ii) a declaration by the firm that it has become a member of the Motor Insurers' Bureau; and

(e) a statement by the firm's home state regulator attesting that the firm has the minimum margin of solvency calculated in accordance with such of the following as are appropriate—

(i) Articles 16 and 17 of the first non-life insurance directive [(as last amended by Directive 2002/87/EC of the European Parliament and of the Council)], and

(ii) Articles 18, 19 and 20 of the first life insurance directive.

[(4) In the case of an insurance intermediary, the prescribed information is that the firm intends to carry on insurance mediation or reinsurance mediation (in each case, within the meaning of the insurance mediation directive) by providing services in the United Kingdom.]

NOTES

Paras (2), (2ZA), (2A): outside the scope of this work.

Para (3): words in square brackets inserted by the Financial Conglomerates and Other Financial Groups Regulations 2004, SI 2004/1862, reg 14(4).

Para (4): added by the Insurance Mediation Directive (Miscellaneous Amendments) Regulations 2003, SI 2003/1473, reg 8(1), (3).

Directive 2002/87/EC of the European Parliament and of the Council: OJ L35, 11.2.2003, p 1.

Changes relating to EEA firms

4–5A (*Outside the scope of this work.*)

[636]

6 Insurance firms: changes to branch details

(1) An insurance firm which has established a branch in the United Kingdom in exercise of an EEA right must not make a change in any of the details referred to in regulation 2(5)(a) to (c) with respect to the branch, unless the relevant requirements have been complied with.

(2) Where the relevant requirements have been complied with, the firm's permission is to be treated as varied accordingly.

(3) For the purposes of this regulation, the relevant requirements are those of paragraph (4) or (if the change is occasioned by circumstances beyond the firm's control) paragraph (5).

(4) The requirements of this paragraph are that—

(a) the firm has given a notice to the Authority and to its home state regulator stating the details of the proposed change;

(b) the Authority has received from the home state regulator a notice stating that it has approved the proposed change;

(c) the period of one month beginning with the day on which the firm gave the Authority the notice mentioned in sub-paragraph (a) has elapsed; and

(d) either—

(i) a further period of one month has elapsed; or

(ii) the Authority has informed the home state regulator of any consequential changes in the applicable provisions (within the meaning of paragraph 13 of Schedule 3).

(5) The requirements of this paragraph are that the firm has as soon as practicable (whether before or after the change) given a notice to the Authority and to its home state regulator, stating the details of the change.

(6) The Authority must, as soon as practicable—

(a) acknowledge receipt of the documents sent under paragraph (4) or (5); and

(b) in the case of a notice under paragraph (5), inform the firm's home state regulator of any consequential changes in the applicable provisions (within the meaning of paragraph 13 of Schedule 3).

[637]

7 Insurance firms: changes to services

(1) An insurance firm which is providing services in the United Kingdom in exercise of an EEA right must not make a change in any of the matters referred to in regulation 3(3)(b), (c) or (d), unless the relevant requirements have been complied with.

(2) Where the relevant requirements have been complied with, the firm's permission is to be treated as varied accordingly.

(3) For the purposes of this regulation, the "relevant requirements" are those of paragraph (4) or (if the change is occasioned by circumstances beyond the firm's control) paragraph (5).

(4) The requirements of this paragraph are that—

(a) the firm has given a notice to its home state regulator stating the details of the proposed change; and

(b) the home state regulator has passed to the Authority the information contained in that notice.

(5) The requirements of this paragraph are that the firm has as soon as practicable (whether before or after the change) given to its home state regulator a notice stating the details of the change.

Cancellation of qualification for authorisation

[638]

8 EEA firms ceasing to carry on regulated activities in the United Kingdom

Where an EEA firm which is qualified for authorisation under Schedule 3—

(a) has ceased, or is to cease to carry on regulated activities in the United Kingdom, and

(b) gives notice of that fact to the Authority,

the notice is to be treated as a request for cancellation of the firm's qualification for authorisation under Schedule 3 (and hence as a request under section 34(2) of the Act).

9 (*Outside the scope of this work.*)

Applications for approval under section 60 by EEA firms

[639]

10 Applications for approval under section 60 by EEA firms

In section 60 of the Act (applications for approval for persons to perform controlled functions), "the authorised person concerned" includes—

[(a)] an EEA firm with respect to which the Authority has received a consent notice [or regulator's notice] under paragraph 13 of Schedule 3 or a regulator's notice under paragraph 14 of that Schedule, and which will be the authorised person concerned if it qualifies for authorisation under that Schedule[; and

(b) an EEA firm which falls within paragraph 5(da) of Schedule 3 which establishes a branch in the United Kingdom].

NOTES

Para (a) numbered as such, and para (b) and word immediately preceding it inserted by the Reinsurance Directive Regulations 2007, SI 2007/3253, reg 2(2), Sch 2, para (a); words in square brackets in para (a) inserted by the Insurance Mediation Directive (Miscellaneous Amendments) Regulations 2003, SI 2003/1473, reg 8(1), (4).

PART III

EXERCISE OF PASSPORT RIGHTS BY UK FIRMS

Changes relating to UK firms

11–12A (*Outside the scope of this work.*)

[640]

13 UK insurance firms: changes to relevant EEA details of branches

(1) A UK firm which has exercised an EEA right, deriving from any of the insurance directives, to establish a branch must not make a change in the relevant EEA details (as defined in regulation 14), unless the requirements of paragraph (2) or (if the change is occasioned by circumstances beyond the firm's control) paragraph (3) have been complied with.

(2) The requirements of this paragraph are that—

(a) the firm has given a notice to the Authority and to the host state regulator stating the details of the proposed change;

(b) the Authority has given the host state regulator a notice under paragraph (5)(a);

(c) the period of one month beginning with the day on which the firm gave the Authority the notice mentioned in sub-paragraph (a) has elapsed; and

(d) either—

(i) a further period of one month has elapsed; or

(ii) the Authority has informed the firm of any consequential changes in the applicable provisions (within the meaning of paragraph 19 of Schedule 3) of which the Authority has been notified by the host state regulator.

(3) The requirements of this paragraph are that the firm has as soon as practicable (whether before or after the change) given a notice to the Authority and to the host state regulator, stating the details of the change.

(4) The Authority must, within one month of receiving the notice referred to in paragraph (2)(a), either consent to the change or refuse to consent to the change.

(5) If the Authority consents to the change, it must—

(a) give a notice to the host state regulator informing it of the details of the proposed change; and

(b) inform the firm that it has given that notice, stating the date on which it did so.

(6) If the Authority refuses to consent to the change—

(a) the firm may refer the mater to the Tribunal; and

(b) the Authority must give notice to the firm of the refusal, stating the reasons for it, and giving an indication of the firm's right to refer the matter to the Tribunal, and the procedure on such a reference.

(7) The Authority may not refuse to consent to the change unless, having regard to the change, the Authority has reason—

(a) to doubt the adequacy of the firm's administrative structure or financial situation, or

(b) to question the reputation, qualifications or experience of the directors or managers of the firm or the authorised agent,

in relation to the business conducted, or to be conducted, through the branch.

[641]

14 Relevant EEA details for the purposes of regulation 13

(1) For the purposes of regulation 13, the relevant EEA details, with respect to a branch, are—

(a) the address of the branch;

(b) the name of the UK firm's authorised agent and, in the case of a member of Lloyd's, confirmation that the authorised agent has power to accept service of proceedings on behalf of Lloyd's;

(c) the classes or parts of classes of business carried on, or to be carried on, and the nature of the risks or commitments covered, or to be covered, in the EEA State concerned;

(d) details of the structural organisation of the branch;

(e) the guiding principles as to reinsurance of business carried on, or to be carried on, in the EEA State concerned, including the firm's maximum retention per risk or event after all reinsurance ceded;

(f) estimates of—

(i) the costs of installing administrative services and the organisation for securing business in the EEA State concerned;

(ii) the resources available to cover those costs; and

(iii) if contracts of a kind falling within paragraph 18 of Schedule 1 to the Regulated Activities Order (assistance) are, or are to be, effected or carried out, the resources available for providing assistance;

(g) for each of the first three years following the establishment of the branch—

(i) estimates of the firm's margin of solvency and the margin of solvency required, and the method of calculation;

(ii) if the firm carries on, or intends to carry on, business comprising the effecting or carrying out of contracts of long-term insurance, the details mentioned in paragraph (2) as respects the business carried on, or to be carried on, in the EEA State concerned; and

(iii) if the firm carries on, or intends to carry on, business comprising the effecting or carrying out of contracts of general insurance, the details mentioned in paragraph (3) as respects the business carried on, or to be carried on, in the EEA State concerned;

(h) if the insurer covers, or intends to cover, relevant motor vehicle risks, details of the firm's membership of the national bureau and the national guarantee fund in the EEA State concerned; and

(i) if the firm covers, or intends to cover, health insurance risks, the technical bases used, or to be used, for calculating premiums in respect of such risks.

(2) The details referred to in paragraph (l)(g)(ii) are—

(a) the following information, on both optimistic and pessimistic bases, for each type of contract or treaty—

(i) the number of contracts or treaties expected to be issued;

(ii) the total premium income, both gross and net of reinsurance ceded; and

(iii) the total sums assured or the total amounts payable each year by way of annuity;

(b) detailed estimates, on both optimistic and pessimistic bases, of income and expenditure in respect of direct business, reinsurance acceptances and reinsurance cessions; and

(c) estimates relating to the financial resources intended to cover underwriting liabilities.

(3) The details referred to in paragraph (1)(g)(iii) are—

(a) estimates relating to expenses of management (other than costs of installation), and in particular those relating to current expenses and commissions;

(b) estimates relating to premiums or contributions (both gross and net of all reinsurance ceded) and to claims (after all reinsurance recoveries); and

(c) estimates relating to the financial resources to cover underwriting liabilities.

[642]

15 UK insurance firms: changes to relevant UK details of branches

(1) A UK firm which has exercised an EEA right, deriving from any of the insurance directives, to establish a branch must not make a change falling within paragraph (2) with respect to the branch, unless—

(a) the firm has given a notice to the Authority stating the details of the proposed change at least one month before the change is effected; or

(b) if the change is occasioned by circumstances beyond the firm's control, the firm has as soon as practicable (whether before or after the change) given a notice to the Authority stating the details of the change.

(2) A change falls within this paragraph if it is a change in any of the information which the UK firm was required to provide to the Authority by or under paragraph 19(2) of Schedule 3, other than a change in the relevant EEA details referred to in regulation 13.

[643]

16 UK insurance firms: changes to services

(1) A UK firm which is providing services in exercise of an EEA right, deriving from any of the insurance directives, must not make a change in the relevant details (as defined in regulation 17), unless the relevant requirements have been complied with.

(2) For the purposes of this regulation, the "relevant requirements" are those of paragraph (3) or (if the change is occasioned by circumstances beyond the firm's control) paragraph (4).

(3) The requirements of this paragraph are that—

(a) the firm has given a notice to the Authority stating the details of the proposed change; and

(b) the Authority has given the host state regulator a notice under paragraph (6)(a).

(4) The requirements of this paragraph are that the firm has as soon as practicable (whether before or after the change) given a notice to the Authority stating the details of the change.

(5) The Authority must, within one month of receiving a notice under paragraph (3)(a), either consent to the change or refuse to consent to the change.

(6) If the Authority consents to the change, it must—

(a) give a notice to the host state regulator informing it of the details of the proposed change; and

(b) inform the firm that it has given that notice, stating the date on which it did so.

(7) If the Authority refuses to consent to the change—

(a) the firm may refer the matter to the Tribunal; and

(b) the Authority must give notice to the firm of the refusal, stating the reasons for it, and giving an indication of the firm's right to refer the matter to the Tribunal, and the procedure on such a reference.

[644]

17 Relevant details for the purposes of regulation 16

The relevant details for the purposes of regulation 16 are—

(a) the EEA State in which the EEA activities are carried on, or are to be carried on;

(b) the nature of the risks or commitments covered, or to be covered, in the EEA State concerned;

(c) if the firm covers, or intends to cover, relevant motor vehicle risks—

(i) the name and address of the claims representative; and

(ii) details of the firm's membership of the national bureau and the national guarantee fund in the EEA State concerned; and

(d) if the insurer covers, or intends to cover, health insurance risks, the technical bases used, or to be used, for calculating premiums in respect of such risks.

[645]

18 Offences relating to failure to notify changes

(1) If a UK firm which is not an authorised person contravenes the prohibition imposed by regulation 11(1), [11A(1),] 12(1), [12A(1),] 13(1), 15(1), or 16(1) it is guilty of an offence, punishable—

(a) on summary conviction, by a fine not exceeding the statutory maximum; or

(b) on conviction on indictment, by a fine.

(2) In proceedings for an offence under paragraph (1), it is a defence for the firm to show that it took all reasonable precautions and exercised all due diligence to avoid committing the offence.

NOTES

References in square brackets inserted by the Financial Services and Markets Act 2000 (EEA Passport Rights) (Amendment) Regulations 2006, SI 2006/3385, regs 2, 14.

UK firms: scope of outward passport

[646]

19 UK firms: scope of outward passport

[(1)] Where—

(a) the activities identified in a notice of intention under paragraph 19 or 20 of Schedule 3 include (in accordance with paragraph 19(3) or 20(2) of that Schedule) any activity which is not a regulated activity, and

(b) that activity is one which the UK firm in question is able to carry on in the EEA State in question without contravening any provision of the law of the United Kingdom (or any part of the United Kingdom),

the UK firm is to be treated, for the purposes of the exercise of its EEA right, as being authorised to carry on that activity.

[(2) Where—

(a) the activities of a UK firm which pursues the activity of reinsurance (within the meaning of Article 2.1(a) of the reinsurance directive) includes any activity which is not a regulated activity, and

(b) that activity is one which the UK firm in question is able to carry on in the EEA State in question without contravening any provision of the law of the United Kingdom (or any part of the United Kingdom),

the UK firm is to be treated, for the purpose of the exercise of its EEA right, as being authorised to carry on that activity.]

NOTES

Para (1): numbered as such by the Reinsurance Directive Regulations 2007, SI 2007/3253, reg 2(2), Sch 2, para (b)(i).

Para (2): added by SI 2007/3253, reg 2(2), Sch 2, para (b)(ii).

PART IV
TRANSITIONAL PROVISIONS

[647]

20 Changes relating to EEA firms: procedures partly completed at commencement

(1) If before commencement—

(a) an EEA firm which was a European institution within the meaning of the 2BCD Regulations gave a notice under paragraph 4(1)(a) of Schedule 2 to those Regulations (changes to details of branch), and

(b) not all the other requirements set out in paragraph 4(1) of that Schedule were satisfied, the notice is to be treated as given under regulation 4(4)(a), and the other requirements set out in regulation 4(4) treated as satisfied to the extent to which the corresponding requirements in paragraph 4(1) of that Schedule had been satisfied.

(2) If before commencement—

(a) an EEA firm which was a European investment firm within the meaning of the ISD Regulations gave a notice under paragraph 5(1)(a) of Schedule 3 to those Regulations (changes to details of branch), and

(b) not all the other requirements set out in paragraph 5(1) of that Schedule were satisfied,

the notice is to be treated as given under regulation 4(4)(a), and the other requirements set out in regulation 4(4) treated as satisfied to the extent to which the corresponding requirements in paragraph 5(1) of that Schedule had been satisfied.

(3) In a case falling within paragraph (1) or (2), regulation 4(6) applies unless the Authority had, before commencement, complied with the duty in regulation 8(3) of the 2BCD Regulations or regulation 8(4) of the ISD Regulations.

(4) If before commencement—

(a) an EEA firm which was an EC company within the meaning of the Insurance Companies Act gave a notice under paragraph 2(2)(a) of Schedule 2F to that Act (changes to details of branch), and

(b) not all the other requirements set out in paragraph 2(2) of that Schedule were satisfied,

the notice is to be treated as given under regulation 6(4)(a), and the other requirements set out in regulation 6(4) treated as satisfied to the extent to which the corresponding requirements in paragraph 2(2) of that Schedule had been satisfied.

(5) In a case falling within paragraph (4), regulation 6(6) applies except to the extent that the duty in paragraph 2(4) of Schedule 2F to the Insurance Companies Act had been complied with before commencement.

(6) If before commencement—

(a) an EEA firm which was an EC company within the meaning of the Insurance Companies Act gave a notice under paragraph 9(2)(a) of Schedule 2F to that Act (changes relating to the provision of services), and

(b) the requirement in paragraph 9(2)(b) of that Schedule was not satisfied,

the notice is to be treated as given under regulation 7(4)(a).

[648]

21 Changes relating to UK firms: procedures partly completed at commencement

(1) If before commencement a UK firm gave notice under paragraph 5(1)(a) of Schedule 6 to the 2BCD Regulations or paragraph 6(1)(a) of Schedule 6 to the ISD Regulations (changes to details of branch)—

(a) the notice is to be treated as given under regulation 11(2)(a), and

(b) any notice given under paragraph 5(1)(b) of Schedule 6 to the 2BCD Regulations or paragraph 6(1)(b) of Schedule 6 to the ISD Regulations is to be treated as given under regulation 11(2)(b),

unless paragraph (2) applies.

(2) This paragraph applies if, before commencement, either—

(a) all the requirements set out in paragraph 5(1) of Schedule 6 to the 2BCD Regulations or paragraph 6(1) of Schedule 6 to the ISD Regulations had been satisfied, or

(b) in response to the notice a notice of refusal was given to the firm under paragraph 6(5)(b) of Schedule 6 to the 2BCD Regulations or paragraph 7(5)(b) of Schedule 6 to the ISD Regulations, and the refusal was not at commencement capable of being reversed on an appeal, reference to a tribunal or a review as mentioned in paragraph 7(5) of Schedule 6 to the ISD Regulations.

(3) If before commencement a UK firm gave notice under paragraph 2(2)(a) of Schedule 2G to the Insurance Companies Act or Schedule 13B to the Friendly Societies Act (changes to details of branch)—

(a) the notice is to be treated as given to the Authority under regulation 13(2)(a), and

(b) the other requirements set out in regulation 13(2) are to be treated as satisfied to the extent to which the corresponding requirements in paragraph 2(2) of Schedule 2G to the Insurance Companies Act or of Schedule 13B to the Friendly Societies Act had been satisfied,

unless paragraph (4) applies.

(4) This paragraph applies if, before commencement, either—

(a) all the requirements set out in paragraph 2(2) of Schedule 2G to the Insurance Companies Act or of Schedule 13B to the Friendly Societies Act had been satisfied, or

(b) in response to the notice a notice of refusal was given to the firm under paragraph 2(5)(b) of that Schedule.

(5) If before commencement a UK firm gave notice under paragraph 6(2)(a) of Schedule 2G to the Insurance Companies Act or of Schedule 13B to the Friendly Societies Act (changes relating to the provision of services)—

(a) the notice is to be treated as given to the Authority under regulation 16(3)(a) and

(b) if a notice was sent under paragraph 6(2)(b) of Schedule 2G to the Insurance Companies Act or of Schedule 13B to the Friendly Societies Act, that notice is to be treated as given under regulation 16(3)(b),

unless, before commencement, the firm had been notified under paragraph 6(5)(a) or (b) of Schedule 2G to the Insurance Companies Act or of Schedule 13B to the Friendly Societies Act of the decision taken in response to the notice.

FINANCIAL SERVICES AND MARKETS ACT 2000 (COMMUNICATIONS BY AUDITORS) REGULATIONS 2001

(SI 2001/2587)

NOTES

Made: 17 July 2001.

Authority: Financial Services and Markets Act 2000, ss 342(5), 343(5), 428(3).

Commencement: 1 December 2001 (see reg 1(1)).

[649]

1 Citation, commencement and interpretation

(1) These Regulations may be cited as the Financial Services and Markets Act 2000 (Communications by Auditors) Regulations 2001 and come into force on the day on which section 19 of the Act (the general prohibition) comes into force.

(2) In these Regulations—

"the Act" means the Financial Services and Markets Act 2000;

"the person concerned" means—

(a) in relation to an auditor of an authorised person, that authorised person;

(b) in relation to an auditor of a person who has close links (within the meaning of section 343 of the Act) with an authorised person, that authorised person;

"relevant requirement" means—

(a) a requirement which is imposed by or under any provision of the Act other than Part VI (listing) and which relates to authorisation under the Act (whether by way of permission under Part IV of the Act or otherwise) or to the carrying on of any regulated activity; or

(b) a requirement which is imposed by or under any other Act and whose contravention constitutes an offence which the Authority has power to prosecute under the Act.

[650]

2 Circumstances in which an auditor is to communicate

(1) An auditor to whom section 342 or 343 of the Act applies must communicate to the Authority information on, or his opinion on, matters mentioned in section 342(3)(a) or 343(3)(a) of the Act (matters of which he has, or had, become aware in his capacity as auditor of an authorised person or as auditor of a person who has close links with an authorised person) in the following circumstances.

(2) The circumstances are that—

(a) the auditor reasonably believes that, as regards the person concerned—

(i) there is or has been, or may be or may have been, a contravention of any relevant requirement that applies to the person concerned; and

(ii) that contravention may be of material significance to the Authority in determining whether to exercise, in relation to the person concerned, any functions conferred on the Authority by or under any provision of the Act other than Part VI;

(b) the auditor reasonably believes that the information on, or his opinion on, those matters may be of material significance to the Authority in determining whether the person concerned satisfies and will continue to satisfy the threshold conditions;

(c) the auditor reasonably believes that the person concerned is not, may not be or may cease to be a going concern;

(d) the auditor is precluded from stating in his report that the annual accounts or, where they are required to be made by any of the following provisions, other financial reports of the person concerned—

(i) have been properly prepared in accordance with the Companies Act 1985 or, where applicable, give a true and fair view of the matters referred to in section 235(2) of that Act;

(ii) have been prepared so as to conform with the requirements of Part VIII of the Building Societies Act 1986 and the regulations made under it or, where applicable, give a true and fair view of the matters referred to in subsection (4) or (7) of section 78 of that Act;

(iii) have been prepared so as to conform with the Friendly Societies Act 1992 and the regulations made under it or, where applicable, give a true and fair view of the matters referred to in section 73(5) of that Act;

(iv) have been prepared so as to conform with the requirements of the Friendly and Industrial and Provident Societies Act 1968 or, where applicable, give a true and fair view of the matters referred to in section 9(2) and (3) of that Act; or

(v) have been prepared so as to conform with the requirements of rules made under the Act where the auditor is, by rules made under section 340 of the Act, required to make such a statement;

as the case may be; or

(e) where applicable, the auditor is required to state in his report in relation to the person concerned any of the facts referred to in subsection (2), (3) or (4A) of section 237 of the Companies Act 1985.

FINANCIAL SERVICES AND MARKETS ACT 2000 (MUTUAL SOCIETIES) ORDER 2001

(SI 2001/2617)

NOTES

Made: 18 July 2001.

Authority: Financial Services and Markets Act 2000, ss 334(1), (2), 335(1), (2), (3), (4), 336(1), (2), 337, 338(1), (2), 339(1), (2), 426, 427, 428(3).

Commencement: see art 2.

ARRANGEMENT OF ARTICLES

PART I
GENERAL

1 Citation . . . [651]
2 Commencement . . . [652]
3 Interpretation . . . [653]

PART II
TRANSFERRED FUNCTIONS

4 Transfer of functions . . . [654]
5 Consequential and transitional provisions in relation to transferred functions . . . [655]
6 Requirements to provide documents etc . . . [656]
7 Consequential modification of non-statutory provisions . . . [657]
8 Anticipatory exercise of powers . . . [658]

PART III
DISSOLUTIONS

9 The Building Societies Commission . . . [659]
10 The Friendly Societies Commission . . . [660]
11 The Building Societies Investor Protection Board . . . [661]
12 The Chief Registrar, assistant registrar for Scotland, and assistant registrars . . . [662]

PART IV
AMENDMENTS, REPEALS ETC
13 Amendments, repeals, transitional provisions and savings . . . [663]

SCHEDULES:

Schedule 1—Functions transferred to the Treasury
Part I—Functions of the Chief Registrar, assistant registrar for Scotland, assistant registrars and the central office . . . [664]
Part II—Functions of the Friendly Societies Commission . . . [665]
Part III—Functions of the Building Societies Commission . . . [666]
Schedule 2—Application of Financial Services and Markets Act 2000 to transferred functions . . . [667]

PART I
GENERAL

[651]
1 Citation

This Order may be cited as the Financial Services and Markets Act 2000 (Mutual Societies) Order 2001.

[652]
2 Commencement

This Order comes into force—

(a) for the purposes of article 8, and for the purposes of article 4(3) and Schedule 2, on 17th August 2001, and

(b) for all other purposes, on the day on which section 19 of the 2000 Act (the general prohibition) comes into force.

[653]
3 Interpretation

(1) In this Order—

"the 2000 Act" means the Financial Services and Markets Act 2000,

"assistant registrar" means an assistant registrar of friendly societies for the central registration area,

"the assistant registrar for Scotland" means the assistant registrar of friendly societies for Scotland,

"the Board" means the Building Societies Investor Protection Board,

"building society" has the same meaning as in the Building Societies Act 1986,

"the central office" means the central office of the registry of friendly societies,

"the central registration area" means the area defined by section 4(1)(a) of the Friendly Societies Act 1974 (as it had effect immediately before its repeal by the 2000 Act),

"the Chief Registrar" means the Chief Registrar of friendly societies,

"commencement" means the beginning of the day on which section 19 of the 2000 Act comes into force,

"enactment" includes an enactment contained in subordinate legislation within the meaning of the Interpretation Act 1978, and

"the last period" means the period beginning with 1st April 2001 and ending at commencement.

(2) In this Order, "transferred function" means any function transferred by article 4 and, in relation to any transferred function, "transferor" means the person from whom the function is transferred and "transferee" means the person to whom it is transferred.

(3) In this Order, unless the context otherwise requires, any reference to an article by number alone is a reference to the article so numbered in this Order.

PART II
TRANSFERRED FUNCTIONS

[654]
4 Transfer of functions

(1) The functions—

(a) of the Chief Registrar, the assistant registrar for Scotland, the assistant registrars and the central office listed in Part I of Schedule 1 to this Order,

(b) of the Friendly Societies Commission listed in Part II of Schedule 1 to this Order, and

(c) of the Building Societies Commission listed in Part III of Schedule 1 to this Order,

are transferred to the Treasury.

(2) All other functions which, immediately before commencement were functions—

(a) of the Chief Registrar, the assistant registrar for Scotland, the assistant registrars or the central office,

(b) of the Friendly Societies Commission, or

(c) of the Building Societies Commission,

are transferred to the Authority, subject to any repeal or amendment made by any provision of this Order or by any other provision of or made under the 2000 Act.

(3) Schedule 2 makes provision about the application of the 2000 Act in relation to functions transferred (or to be transferred) to the Authority by paragraph (2) above.

(4) For the purposes of the Transfer of Undertakings (Protection of Employment) Regulations 1981, paragraph (2) above is to be regarded as giving rise to the transfer of an undertaking by virtue of each of sub-paragraphs (a), (b) and (c) of that paragraph, whether or not it would otherwise be so regarded.

[655]

5 Consequential and transitional provisions in relation to transferred functions

(1) The transfer of any function by virtue of article 4 does not affect the validity of anything done before commencement—

(a) by the transferor in the exercise of the transferred function, or

(b) by any other person in relation to the exercise by the transferor of the transferred function,

and any such thing is to have effect for all purposes as if done by (or, as the case may be, in relation to the exercise of the function by) the transferee.

(2) Paragraph (1) also has effect in relation to anything which is in the process of being done at commencement, and any such thing may be carried on and completed by (or, as the case may be, in relation to the exercise of the function by) the transferee.

(3) If, at commencement, a transferor is a party to any legal proceedings in relation to its exercise of any transferred function, the transferee is substituted for the transferor in those proceedings.

(4) If, at commencement, a transferor holds any monies which have been deposited with the transferor as security for any costs in relation to its exercise of any transferred function, the monies are transferred to the transferee at commencement to be held for the same purpose and on the same terms.

(5) This article has effect subject to any transitional provision or saving contained in Schedule 5 to this Order or in any other provision made under the 2000 Act.

[656]

6 Requirements to provide documents etc

(1) Paragraph (2) applies where, by virtue of any provision of or made under any enactment, a person ("A") other than a transferor was before commencement required or entitled—

(a) to provide any account, application, list, notice, plan, report, return, or any other document or material (including a copy of any document or material),

(b) to give any explanation or provide any other information, or

(c) to notify, report on, or make representations or a statement on, any matter,

to any transferor, or to any other person ("B") on behalf of any transferor, in connection with the exercise by the transferor of any function which is transferred by article 4(2) to the Authority, but had not provided that document or material, given that explanation or information, or notified, reported on or made representations on that matter, before commencement.

(2) After commencement A is required or (as the case may be) entitled to provide that document or material, to give that explanation or information, or to notify, report on, or make representations on, that matter, to the Authority (or, as the case may be, to B on behalf of the Authority), but otherwise in the same form and containing the same particulars as would have been required before commencement.

(3) Paragraph (1) has effect no matter how the requirement or entitlement is expressed.

(4) Where the requirement or entitlement mentioned in paragraph (1) was subject to any provision requiring A to comply with the requirement or exercise the entitlement within a specified time (however expressed), that provision continues to apply in relation to the requirement imposed or entitlement given by paragraph (2), and the time period is to be treated as continuing to run without interruption.

(5) Where any person does anything after commencement in compliance with paragraph (2) in relation to which, if that thing had been done before commencement, a fee would have been payable to the transferor, he is required to pay that fee to the Authority, and the fee (insofar as it is not so paid) may be recovered by the Authority as a debt due to it.

(6) This article is without prejudice to the generality of article 5(1) and (2).

(7) This article has effect subject to any transitional provision or saving contained in Schedule 5 to this Order or in any other provision made under the 2000 Act.

[657]

7 Consequential modification of non-statutory provisions

(1) Where a relevant provision is predicated on the continuing exercise of any transferred function by the transferor, any reference in the provision to the transferor has effect, in relation to any time after commencement, as a reference to the transferee.

(2) Paragraph (3) applies where—

(a) a relevant provision contains a requirement for consent to be given by the Building Societies Commission before the repayment by a building society of any sum owed by it, and

(b) the requirement was included in the relevant provision so as to comply with the terms of—

(i) an order made under section 45(5) of the Building Societies Act 1986 as that section had effect before the coming into force of section 21 of the Building Societies Act 1997,

(ii) an order made under section 119(1) of the Building Societies Act 1986, or

(iii) guidance issued by the Building Societies Commission pursuant to section 45AA of that Act.

(3) Unless the context otherwise requires, the requirement has effect, in relation to any time after commencement, as a requirement for consent to be given by the Authority.

(4) Paragraph (5) applies where a relevant provision prohibits the payment or crediting of interest on any sum owed by a building society if the board of directors of the society is of the opinion that—

(a) there has been a failure on the part of the society to satisfy a criterion of prudent management, set out in section 45(3) of the Building Societies Act 1986 as it had effect at any time before commencement, relating to the maintenance of adequate reserves and other capital resources, or

(b) there would be such a failure if the interest was paid or credited.

(5) Unless the context otherwise requires, any reference in that provision to that criterion has effect, in relation to any time after commencement, as a reference to the condition set out in paragraph 4(1) of Schedule 6 to the 2000 Act (adequate resources).

(6) "Relevant provision" means a provision which—

(a) is contained in the rules of a building society, friendly society or industrial and provident society, or in any other contract, deed or document other than an enactment, and

(b) has effect before, as well as after, commencement,

but for the purposes only of paragraph (1) above also includes a provision in any document which is provided to the Authority after commencement pursuant to article 6(2).

[658]

8 Anticipatory exercise of powers

(1) This article applies where by virtue of any amendment made by Schedule 3 to this Order—

(a) the Authority will, with effect from commencement, have power to make rules, or have power to give directions as to the form of or particulars to be included in any document or as to the manner in which any application is to be made, or

(b) the Treasury will, with effect from commencement, have power to make any rules, order or regulations.

(2) Where this article applies, the Authority or the Treasury (as the case may be) may exercise the power referred to in paragraph (1) before commencement for the purposes of bringing the rules, directions, order or regulations into effect at commencement.

(3) In exercising any power before commencement by virtue of paragraph (2), the Authority or the Treasury (as the case may be) are to be treated as being subject to the same requirements or conditions, as to the procedure to be followed in exercising the power or otherwise, as would apply in relation to the exercise of that power if this Order were fully in force.

PART III
DISSOLUTIONS

[659]
9 The Building Societies Commission

(1) As soon as practicable after commencement, the Building Societies Commission must lay before the Treasury and before Parliament a report on the discharge of its functions during the last period.

(2) Before the end of the period of seven months beginning at commencement, the Building Societies Commission must send to the Treasury and to the Comptroller and Auditor General a statement of accounts in respect of the last period.

(3) The Comptroller and Auditor General must examine, certify and report on the statement of accounts received by him from the Building Societies Commission under paragraph (2), and lay a copy of the statement and of his report before Parliament.

(4) The Building Societies Commission is to cease to exist on the day after the first day on which paragraphs (1) and (3) have both been complied with.

(5) Immediately before the Building Societies Commission ceases to exist by virtue of paragraph (4), all assets, rights and liabilities which at that time are held or enjoyed by the Commission, or to which at that time it is subject, are transferred to the Treasury, except as provided in paragraphs (7) and (9).

(6) Paragraph (7) applies in relation to income received by the Building Societies Commission under section 2 of the Building Societies Act 1986, in respect of the last period or in relation to applications submitted to it during the last period ("relevant income").

(7) Insofar as relevant income is not applied before commencement in accordance with section 2 of the Building Societies Act 1986 towards expenses of the Commission, it is to be paid to the Authority.

(8) Paragraph (9) applies where, before commencement—
- (a) any fee or charge, or any sum in respect of costs or expenses, was payable to the Building Societies Commission, but
- (b) that fee, charge or sum, or any part of it, was not so paid ("the unpaid sum").

(9) Notwithstanding any amendment, repeal or revocation made by this Order or by any other provision of or made under the 2000 Act, the unpaid sum is payable after commencement to the Authority in substitution for the Commission and (insofar as it is not so paid) may be recovered by the Authority as a debt due to it.

(10) The Authority must, so far as practicable, ensure that—
- (a) relevant income paid to it in accordance with paragraph (7), and
- (b) any sum paid to it or recovered by it in accordance with paragraph (9),

is used only in connection with any functions of the Authority in relation to building societies or, to the extent that it is not so used, is applied for the benefit of building societies.

[660]
10 The Friendly Societies Commission

(1) As soon as practicable after commencement, the Friendly Societies Commission must lay before the Treasury and before Parliament a report on the discharge of its functions during the last period.

(2) Before the end of the period of seven months beginning at commencement, the Friendly Societies Commission must send to the Treasury and to the Comptroller and Auditor General a statement of accounts in respect of the last period.

(3) The Comptroller and Auditor General must examine, certify and report on the statement of accounts received by him from the Friendly Societies Commission under paragraph (2), and lay a copy of the statement and of his report before Parliament.

(4) The Friendly Societies Commission is to cease to exist on the day after the first day on which paragraphs (1) and (3) have both been complied with.

(5) Immediately before the Friendly Societies Commission ceases to exist by virtue of paragraph (4), all assets, rights and liabilities which at that time are held or enjoyed by the Commission, or to which at that time it is subject, are transferred to the Treasury, except as provided in paragraphs (7) and (9).

(6) Paragraph (7) applies in relation to income received by the Friendly Societies Commission under section 2 of the Friendly Societies Act 1992, in respect of the last period or in relation to applications submitted to it during the last period ("relevant income").

(7) Insofar as relevant income is not applied before commencement in accordance with section 2 of the Friendly Societies Act 1992 towards expenses of the Commission, it is to be paid to the Authority.

(8) Paragraph (9) applies where, before commencement—

(a) any fee or charge, or any sum in respect of costs or expenses, was payable to the Friendly Societies Commission, but

(b) that fee, charge or sum, or any part of it, was not so paid ("the unpaid sum").

(9) Notwithstanding any amendment, repeal or revocation made by this Order or by any other provision of or made under the 2000 Act, the unpaid sum is payable after commencement to the Authority in substitution for the Commission and (insofar as it is not so paid) may be recovered by the Authority as a debt due to it.

(10) The Authority must, so far as practicable, ensure that—

(a) relevant income paid to it in accordance with paragraph (7), and

(b) any sum paid to it or recovered by it in accordance with paragraph (9),

is used only in connection with any functions of the Authority in relation to friendly societies or, to the extent that it is not so used, is applied for the benefit of friendly societies.

[661]

11 The Building Societies Investor Protection Board

(1) As soon as practicable after commencement, the Board must prepare—

(a) a report on the discharge of its functions during the last period, and

(b) a statement of accounts showing the state of affairs and income and expenditure of the Board in respect of the last period.

(2) The statement of accounts must be audited by auditors appointed by the Board and the auditors must report to the Board stating whether in their opinion the provisions of paragraph 6(2) of Schedule 5 to the Building Societies Act 1986 (as it had effect immediately before its repeal by this Order) were complied with in respect of the last period.

(3) As soon as practicable after paragraphs (1) and (2) above have been complied with, the Board must publish, in such manner as it thinks appropriate, the report prepared in accordance with paragraph (1)(a) and the statement of accounts prepared in accordance with paragraph (1)(b).

(4) The Board is to cease to exist on the day after paragraph (3) is complied with.

[662]

12 The Chief Registrar, assistant registrar for Scotland, and assistant registrars

(1) As soon as practicable after the Building Societies Commission and the Friendly Societies Commission have ceased to exist by virtue of articles 9 and 10, the Chief Registrar must lay before Parliament a report of his proceedings and those of the assistant registrar for Scotland and the assistant registrars, of the principal matters transacted by him and them, and of the valuations returned to him or them, in relation to the period beginning with 1st October 2001 and ending at commencement.

(2) The report which the Chief Registrar is required to make by virtue of paragraph (1) may be combined with the report which he is required to make pursuant to section 6(1) of the Friendly Societies Act 1974 in respect of the year ending 30th September 2001.

(3) The office of Chief Registrar, the office of assistant registrar for Scotland, and the offices of assistant registrar are to cease to exist on the day after paragraph (1) is complied with.

(4) Immediately before the offices mentioned in paragraph (3) cease to exist by virtue of that paragraph, all assets, rights and liabilities which at that time attach to those offices (including records maintained or held by, and any other assets, rights and liabilities of, the central office) are transferred to the Treasury.

PART IV
AMENDMENTS, REPEALS ETC

[663]

13 Amendments, repeals, transitional provisions and savings

(1) The enactments specified in Schedule 3 to this Order have effect with the amendments made by that Schedule.

(2) The enactments specified in Schedule 4 to this Order are repealed to the extent specified in that Schedule.

(3) The amendments and repeals made by Schedules 3 and 4 are subject to the transitional provisions and savings contained in Schedule 5 to this Order and to any other transitional provisions or savings made under the 2000 Act.

SCHEDULE 1

FUNCTIONS TRANSFERRED TO THE TREASURY

Article 4(1)

PART I

FUNCTIONS OF THE CHIEF REGISTRAR, ASSISTANT REGISTRAR FOR SCOTLAND, ASSISTANT REGISTRARS AND THE CENTRAL OFFICE

[664]

Act	*Provision*	*Function*
The Superannuation and other Trust Funds (Validation) Act 1927 c 41.	Section 8	Making regulations prescribing the qualifications required to be held by an actuary for the purposes of the Act.
The Friendly and Industrial and Provident Societies Act 1968 c 55.	Section 4(8)	Making regulations substituting any sum or number, and prescribing receipts and payments to be taken into account, for the purposes of section 4(2) of the Act (exemption from obligation to appoint auditor).
	Section 10(1)	Making regulations prescribing maximum rates for remuneration of auditors and reporting accountants.
	Section 13(3)	Making regulations prescribing accounts to be comprised and particulars to be contained in group accounts.
The Friendly Societies Act 1974 c 46.	Section 31(5)	Making regulations substituting any sum, number or percentage, and prescribing receipts and payments to be taken into account, for the purposes of section 31(2) or (3) of the Act (exemption from obligation to appoint auditor).
	Section 40(1)	Making regulations under section 10 of the Friendly and Industrial and Provident Societies Act 1968 prescribing maximum rates for remuneration of auditors and reporting accountants.
	Section 42(1)	Making regulations specifying class of society or branch for whom application of section 41(1) of the Act is modified (valuation report required every 3 years rather than every 5 years).
	Section 42(2)	Making regulations specifying class of society or branch for whom application of section 41(1) of the Act is modified (valuation report required every 3 years rather than every 5 years in respect of specified class of business).
	Section 47(1)	Prescribing other UK Government securities for the purchase of which, on behalf of its members, a society or branch registered under the Act (and also an industrial and provident society, by virtue of section 11 of the Industrial and Provident Societies Act 1965) may set up a fund.
	Section 86(2)	Making regulations specifying requirements to be complied with in procedure for proxy voting.

Act	*Provision*	*Function*
The Industrial and Provident Societies Act 1975 c 41.	Section 2	Making an order substituting sum in section 6(1) of the Industrial and Provident Societies Act 1965 (maximum shareholding of a member of an industrial and provident society) and making related provision.
The Industrial and Provident Societies Act 1978 c 34.	Section 2	Making an order substituting sums in section 7(3) of the Industrial and Provident Societies Act 1965 (limits on taking deposits at one time or from one depositor) and making related provision.
The Credit Unions Act 1979 c 34.	Section 5(4)	Making an order substituting sum in section 5(3) of the Act (maximum shareholding of a member of a credit union).
	Section 9(4) and (5)	Making an order substituting amount in section 9(1) of the Act (limit on taking deposits from someone too young to be a member of a credit union) and making related provision.
	Section 11(7)	Making an order specifying maximum period within which loan by credit union must be repaid (section 11(4) of the Act) and maximum rate of interest charged (section 11(5) of the Act).
	Section 13(1)	Making an order authorising manner in which surplus funds of credit union may be invested.
	Section 14(4)	Making an order specifying maximum rate of dividend payable on shares of credit union.
	Section 15(3) and (4)	Making regulations prescribing matters mentioned in section 15(2)(a) and (b) of the Act (which relate to requirement to insure against fraud or dishonesty).
The Building Societies Act 1986 c 53.	Schedule 2A paragraph 3(1)	Making rules prescribing form of receipt for discharge of mortgage under paragraph 1 of the Schedule.
The Social Security Contributions and Benefits Act 1992 c 4.	Schedule 1 paragraph 11(2)	Making regulations prescribing procedure for making amendments to rules of a registered friendly society in compliance with regulations under paragraph 11(1) of the Schedule (sickness payments).

PART II
FUNCTIONS OF THE FRIENDLY SOCIETIES COMMISSION

[665]

Act	*Provision*	*Function*
The Friendly Societies Act 1974 c 46.	Section 65A(8)	Making regulations under section 11(7) of the Friendly Societies Act 1992 (manner of carrying on group insurance business etc) applying to registered friendly societies.
The Friendly Societies Act 1992 c 40.	Section 5(4)	Making an order varying Schedule 2 (activities of an incorporated friendly society).

Act	*Provision*	*Function*
	Section 11(7)	Making regulations specifying manner in which group insurance business may be carried on by incorporated friendly societies.
	Section 69(4) and (5)	Making regulations exempting incorporated friendly societies from preparing group accounts.
	Section 70(6)	Making regulations about contents and form of annual accounts.
	Section 71(1)(b)	Making regulations prescribing information to be contained in annual report.
	Section 71(2)(a)	Making regulations prescribing information to be contained in annual report of an incorporated friendly society which has subsidiaries or jointly controls other bodies.
	Section 91(8)	Making regulations providing for regulation of conversion of friendly societies into companies.
	Section 93(14)	Making an order prescribing the day on which the transitional period ends (period within which societies must comply with the Act).
	Section 99(3)	Making an order substituting sum in section 99(1) (maximum benefit payable on death under the age of 10).
	Section 112(4)	Making regulations in connection with records which are kept otherwise than in legible form.
	Schedule 3 paragraph 13(4)	Making an order prescribing maximum fee chargeable by incorporated friendly society for providing copies of its statutory documents.
	Schedule 5 paragraph 2(5)	Making an order substituting a sum in paragraph 2(3) or (4) of the Schedule (loan fund).
	Schedule 5 paragraph 3(1)	Prescribing other UK Government securities for the purchase of which, on behalf of its members, an incorporated friendly society may set up a fund.
	Schedule 11 paragraph 16(1)	Making an order prescribing series of monetary amounts ("prescribed bands") for the purposes of Part II of Schedule 11 (dealings with members of committee of management).
	Schedule 12 paragraph 5(2)	Making regulations prescribing when rules of societies may exclude or limit voting rights of members according to amount of subscriptions.
	Schedule 12 paragraph 7(6)	Making regulations prescribing requirements for procedure to be adopted for proxy voting.
	Schedule 14 paragraph 5(3)	Making regulations specifying descriptions of connections which make auditors ineligible for appointment.

Act	*Provision*	*Function*
	Schedule 14 paragraph 7(4)	Making regulations substituting sum, number or percentage, and prescribing receipts and payments which must be taken into account, for the purposes of paragraph 7(1) and (3) of the Schedule (exemption from requirement for auditor to be a member of a recognised supervisory body).
	Schedule 14 paragraph 17(1)	Making regulations to secure the disclosure of the amount of remuneration of auditors and their associates.
	Schedule 15 paragraph 3(1)(a)	Making regulations to prescribe matters to be dealt with in a statement to members (statements relating to conversion of society into a company).

PART III
FUNCTIONS OF THE BUILDING SOCIETIES COMMISSION

[666]

Act	*Provision*	*Function*
The Building Societies Act 1986 c 53.	Section 6(7) and (8)	Making an order modifying or applying section 6(2) and (3) (lending limit) in relation to assets of subsidiary or associated undertakings, and making related provision.
	Section 6A(2)(b) and (5)	Making an order prescribing description and circumstances of creation of equitable interest (for the purposes of determining when a loan is to be treated as secured on land), and making related provision.
	Section 6A(4) and (5)	Making an order providing for provisions of the Act to have effect in relation to loans secured on land outside the EEA with appropriate modifications, and making related provision.
	Section 7(7) and (8)	Making an order modifying or applying section 7(2) and (3) (funding limit) in relation to liabilities of subsidiary or associated undertakings, and making related provision.
	Section 8(12)	Making an order varying subsections (2), (9) and (10) of the section (provision about raising funds and borrowing), and making related provision.
	Section 9A(12)	Making an order substituting an amount or percentage in subsections (2), (3) or (6), or varying subsection (4)(b), of the section (restrictions on certain transactions).
	Section 42B(8)	Making regulations specifying matters of which particulars must be contained in statements under paragraphs 3 and 9 of Schedule 8A.
	Section 60(9) and (16)	Making an order substituting maximum amount which rules of a society may require as shareholding of director, and making related provision.

Act	*Provision*	*Function*
	Section 61(4) and (5)	Making an order substituting amount, number or percentage in subsections (1) to (3), or varying subsection (3A), of the section (rules as to election of directors), and making related provision.
	Section 64(3)	Making an order substituting any of the amounts in subsection (2) (requisite cash value of assets for the purposes of transactions with directors or persons connected with them).
	Section 65(8)	Making an order to substitute sums in the section (loans to directors or persons connected with them).
	Section 68(9)	Making an order substituting amounts in subsections (7) and (8) (exceptions from obligations imposed by the section in relation to transactions with directors or persons connected with them).
	Section 69(5)	Making an order designating relevant services for the purpose of the section (disclosure and record of income of related businesses), and making related provision.
	Section 69(12)	Making an order substituting a sum in the subsection in relation to volume of business.
	Section 72(7) and (8)	Making regulations as to documents to be comprised in annual accounts, and matters to be included in such documents, including modification of Part VIII of the Act, and making related provision.
	Section 73(6) to (8)	Making regulations as to contents and form of annual accounts of a building society.
	Section 74(3) and (4)	Making regulations prescribing contents and form of annual business statement.
	Section 75(1)(b)	Making regulations prescribing information to be contained in the directors' annual report.
	Section 76(3)	Making regulations with respect to the form and content of summary financial statement.
	Section 92A(10)	Making an order substituting percentages in subsections (4) and (5) of the section (acquisition or establishment of new business), and making related provision.
	Section 92A(11)	Making an order varying subsections (5) and (9) of the section, and making related provision.
	Section 96(2)	Making regulations authorising payments of compensation to directors or other officers on amalgamation or transfer of engagements.
	Section 96(5)	Making regulations authorising distribution of funds to members on amalgamation or transfer of engagements.

Act	*Provision*	*Function*
	Section 99(3)	Making regulations authorising payment of compensation to directors or other officers on transfers of business under section 97.
	Section 102(1) and (2)	Making regulations regulating transfers of business under section 97.
	Section 102D(11)	Making regulations prescribing time periods for notices under section 102B(4).
	Section 114(4)	Making regulations about records kept otherwise than in legible form.
	Section 119(1)	Making an order defining class of shares which are "deferred shares" for the purpose of the Act.
	Schedule 2 paragraphs 10A(3) and 10C(6)	Making regulations specifying words or expressions the use of which in a business name requires the Authority's approval (and specifying bodies whose comments must be sought), and making related provision.
	Schedule 2 paragraphs 10B(5) and 10C(6)	Making regulations as to form and display of notice under paragraph 10B(3) and (4) of the Schedule (notice of registered name and address of society), and making related provision.
	Schedule 2 paragraph 12(4)	Making an order prescribing amount in paragraph 12(1)(b) of the Schedule (maximum amount which may be charged by a building society for providing copies of its statutory documents).
	Schedule 2 paragraph 20A(13)	Making an order substituting number or sum in paragraph 20A(2) or (7) of the Schedule (members' requisitions of special meetings), and making related provision.
	Schedule 2 paragraph 32(4) and (6)	Making an order varying definitions of "requisite number" or "qualified member" in paragraph 31(2) or descriptions of provisions rendered void by paragraph 31(3) of the Schedule, and making related provision.
	Schedule 2 paragraph 36(1) and (3)	Making an order specifying prescribed amount for the purposes of Part III of the Schedule, and making related provision.
	Schedule 10 paragraph 9(1) and (2)	Making an order prescribing series of numbers or monetary amounts ("prescribed bands") for the purposes of Part II of the Schedule.
	Schedule 11 paragraph 5(1)(b)	Making an order designating bodies of accountants the members of whom are qualified for appointment as auditor of a building society.
	Schedule 15A paragraph 25	Making regulations prescribing the form of receivership accounts for the purposes of section 38 of the Insolvency Act 1986.

Act	Provision	Function
	Schedule 15A paragraph 47	Making regulations prescribing the form of receivership accounts for the purposes of article 48 of the Insolvency (Northern Ireland) Order 1989.
	Schedule 17 paragraph 5(1)	Specifying particulars to be given in transfer statement.
	Schedule 17 paragraph 5(2)	Specifying information to be contained in transfer summary.

SCHEDULE 2

APPLICATION OF FINANCIAL SERVICES AND MARKETS ACT 2000 TO TRANSFERRED FUNCTIONS

Article 4(3)

Interpretation

[667]

1. In this Schedule—

(a) "mutuals expenditure" means expenditure of the Authority incurred—

(i) in carrying out relevant functions, or for any purpose incidental to the carrying out of relevant functions, or

(ii) in repaying the principal of, or paying any interest on, any money which it has borrowed and which has been used for the purpose of meeting expenses incurred in relation to its assumption of relevant functions,

(b) "the mutuals legislation" means the Friendly Societies Act 1974, the Building Societies Act 1986, the Friendly Societies Act 1992, and the enactments relating to industrial and provident societies and credit unions referred to in section 338(1),

(c) "relevant functions" means functions transferred to the Authority by virtue of article 4(2) (and includes, in relation to any time before commencement, such functions as they are to be transferred with effect from commencement), and

(d) any reference to a section or Schedule is a reference to that section or Schedule in the 2000 Act.

General

2. For the purposes of section 1(3) and Schedule 1 (which make general provision in relation to the Authority and its functions), relevant functions are to be treated as functions conferred on the Authority under a provision of the 2000 Act.

3. If the Authority maintains arrangements designed to enable it to determine whether persons are complying with requirements imposed on them by or under the mutuals legislation, paragraph 6(2) of Schedule 1 (which permits functions to be performed by a body or person other than the Authority) applies to those arrangements as it applies to arrangements of the kind mentioned in paragraph 6(1) of that Schedule, but does not affect the Authority's responsibility for relevant functions or for any other matter under the mutuals legislation.

4. The Authority's determination of the general policy and principles by reference to which it performs relevant functions is not to be treated as a general function of the Authority by virtue of subsection (4)(d) of section 2 (functions of the Authority to which the Authority's general duties apply).

5. Section 8 (which requires the Authority to make arrangements for consulting consumers and practitioners on its general policies and practices) does not apply in relation to the Authority's general policies and practices with respect to the exercise of relevant functions.

6. In the application of section 12 (which makes provision for reviews of the economy, efficiency and effectiveness with which the Authority has used its resources in discharging its functions) to relevant functions, section 12(3) is to be read as if, for the words from "pursuing" to the end there were substituted "exercising its functions".

7. For the purposes of section 159(1) (interpretation of Chapter III of Part X), relevant functions are not to be treated as functions under the 2000 Act.

8. For the purposes of section 415 (jurisdiction in civil proceedings), relevant functions are to be treated as functions of the Authority under the 2000 Act.

Rules relating to fees

9. Paragraphs 10 and 11 apply where the Authority—

(a) makes (or proposes to make) rules under paragraph 17(1) of Schedule 1 which require the payment to the Authority of fees which relate in whole or in part to mutuals expenditure, or

(b) designates any provisions in accordance with article 4 of the Financial Services and Markets Act 2000 (Transitional Provisions and Savings) (Rules) Order 2001 with a view to their having effect after commencement as such rules.

10. In the application of paragraph 17(1) of Schedule 1 to the rules, the reference to fees and charges provided for by any other provision of the 2000 Act includes a reference to fees and charges provided for by any provision of the mutuals legislation.

11. To the extent that the fees relate to mutuals expenditure—

(a) the making of the rules is not to be treated as a general function of the Authority by virtue of subsection (4)(a) of section 2 (functions of the Authority to which the Authority's general duties apply),

(b) section 155(2)(c) (requirement to include in consultation a statement that rules are compatible with general duties) (or, in any case covered by paragraph 9(b) above, article 4(2)(f) of the Order referred to in that paragraph) does not apply in relation to the rules, and

(c) the rules are not to be treated as regulating provisions for the purposes of section 159(1) (interpretation of Chapter III of Part X).

Guidance

12. For the purposes of sections 157(3) and 158(5) (guidance to regulated persons generally), guidance given to building societies, friendly societies and industrial and provident societies generally or to a class of such societies is to be treated as if given to regulated persons generally or to a class of regulated persons, whether or not those societies would otherwise be "regulated persons" within the meaning of those sections.

13. Paragraph 14 applies where guidance is given by the Authority under section 157 on the operation of a rule of the kind mentioned in paragraph 9 above (whether made as mentioned in sub-paragraph (a) of that paragraph, or designated as mentioned in sub-paragraph (b) of that paragraph).

14. To the extent that the fees required to be paid by the rule relate to mutuals expenditure—

(a) the giving of the guidance is not to be treated as a general function of the Authority by virtue of subsection (4)(c) of section 2 (functions of the Authority to which the Authority's general duties apply),

(b) section 155(2)(c) (requirement to include in consultation a statement that rules are compatible with general duties) does not apply in relation to the guidance, and

(c) the guidance is not to be treated as a regulating provision for the purposes of section 159(1) (interpretation of Chapter III of Part X).

15. Paragraphs 16 and 17 apply where general guidance is given by the Authority under section 157 with respect to any matter relating to relevant functions, or with respect to any provision of or made under the mutuals legislation, unless paragraph 14 above applies.

16. The giving of the guidance is not to be treated as a general function of the Authority by virtue of subsection (4)(c) of section 2 (functions of the Authority to which the Authority's general duties apply).

17. The guidance is not to be treated as a regulating provision for the purposes of section 159(1) (interpretation of Chapter III of Part X).

(Sch 3 amends the Industrial and Provident Societies Act 1965, the Industrial and Provident Societies Act 1967, the Friendly and Industrial and Provident Societies Act 1968, the Friendly Societies Act 1974, the Industrial and Provident Societies Act 1975, the Industrial and Provident Societies Act 1978, the Credit Unions Act 1979, the Friendly Societies Act 1984, the Building Societies Act 1986, the Friendly Societies Act 1992, the Building Societies Act 1997 and repeals the Friendly Societies Act 1981; Sch 4 contains repeals; Sch 5 contains transitional provisions and savings.)

FINANCIAL SERVICES AND MARKETS ACT 2000 (INSOLVENCY) (DEFINITION OF "INSURER") ORDER 2001

(SI 2001/2634)

NOTES

Made: 20 July 2001.
Authority: Financial Services and Markets Act 2000, ss 355(2), 428(3).
Commencement: 1 December 2001 (see art 1(1)).

[668]

1— (1) This Order may be cited as the Financial Services and Markets Act 2000 (Insolvency) (Definition of "Insurer") Order 2001 and comes into force on the day on which section 19 of the Act comes into force.

(2) In this Order, the "Regulated Activities Order" means the Financial Services and Markets Act 2000 (Regulated Activities) Order 2001.

[669]

2 In Part XXIV of the Act (insolvency), . . . "insurer" means any person who is carrying on a regulated activity of the kind specified by article 10(1) or (2) of the Regulated Activities Order (effecting and carrying out contracts of insurance) but who is not—

(a) exempt from the general prohibition in respect of that regulated activity;
(b) a friendly society; or
(c) a person who effects or carries out contracts of insurance all of which fall within paragraphs 14 to 18 of Part I of Schedule 1 to the Regulated Activities Order in the course of, or for the purposes of, a banking business.

NOTES

Words omitted revoked by the Financial Services and Markets Act 2000 (Administration Orders Relating to Insurers) Order 2002, SI 2002/1242, art 2.

FINANCIAL SERVICES AND MARKETS ACT 2000 (LAW APPLICABLE TO CONTRACTS OF INSURANCE) REGULATIONS 2001

(SI 2001/2635)

NOTES

Made: 19 July 2001.
Authority: Financial Services and Markets Act 2000, ss 417(1), 424(3), 428(3).
Commencement: 1 December 2001 (see reg 1).

ARRANGEMENT OF REGULATIONS

PART I
GENERAL

1 Citation and commencement . . . [670]
2 Interpretation . . . [671]
3 Scope of these Regulations . . . [672]

PART II
CONTRACTS OF GENERAL INSURANCE

4 Applicable law . . . [673]
5 Mandatory rules . . . [674]
6 Choice of law . . . [675]
7 The 1990 Act . . . [676]

PART III
CONTRACTS OF LONG-TERM INSURANCE

8 Applicable law . . . [677]
9 Mandatory rules . . . [678]
10 The 1990 Act . . . [679]

PART I
GENERAL

[670]

1 Citation and commencement

These Regulations may be cited as the Financial Services and Markets Act 2000 (Law Applicable to Contracts of Insurance) Regulations 2001 and come into force on the day on which section 19 of the Act comes into force.

[671]

2 Interpretation

(1) In these Regulations—

"the Act" means the Financial Services and Markets Act 2000;

"the 1990 Act" means the Contracts (Applicable Law) Act 1990;

"applicable law", in relation to a contract of insurance, means the law that is applicable to that contract;

"contract of general insurance" and "contract of long-term insurance" have the meanings given by the Regulated Activities Order;

"EEA State of the commitment" means, in relation to a contract of long-term insurance entered into on a date—

(a) if the policyholder is an individual, the EEA State in which he resides on that date; or

(b) otherwise, the EEA State in which the establishment of the policyholder to which the contract relates is situated on that date;

"establishment", in relation to a person ("A"), means—

(a) A's head office;

(b) any of A's agencies;

(c) any of A's branches; or

(d) any permanent presence of A in an EEA State, which need not take the form of a branch or agency and which may consist of an office managed by A's staff or by a person who is independent of A but has permanent authority to act for A as if he were an agency;

"large risk" has the meaning given by Article 5(d) of the first non-life insurance directive and includes risks specified by paragraph (iii) of that definition insured by professional associations, joint ventures or temporary groups;

"mandatory rules" means the rules from which the law allows no derogation by way of contract;

"the Regulated Activities Order" means the Financial Services and Markets Act 2000 (Regulated Activities) Order 2001.

(2) References to the EEA State where the risk covered by a contract of insurance is situated are to—

(a) if the contract relates to buildings or to buildings and their contents (in so far as the contents are covered by the same contract of insurance), the EEA State in which the property is situated;

(b) if the contract relates to vehicles of any type, the EEA State of registration;

(c) if the contract covers travel or holidays risks and has a duration of four months or less, the EEA State in which the policyholder entered into the contract;

(d) in any other case—

(i) if the policyholder is an individual, the EEA State in which he resides on the date the contract is entered into;

(ii) otherwise, the EEA State in which the establishment of the policyholder to which the contract relates is situated on that date.

[(2A) If the contract of insurance relates to a vehicle dispatched from one EEA State to another, in respect of the period of 30 days beginning with the day on which the purchaser accepts delivery a reference to the EEA State in which a risk is situated is a reference to the State of destination (and not, as provided by paragraph (2)(b), to the State of registration).]

(3) References to the country in which a person resides are to—

(a) if he is an individual, the country in which he has his habitual residence;

(b) in any other case, the country in which he has his central administration.

(4) Where an EEA State (including the United Kingdom) includes several territorial units, each of which has its own laws concerning contractual obligations, each unit is to be considered as a separate state for the purposes of identifying the applicable law under these Regulations.

NOTES

Para (2A): inserted by the Financial Services and Markets Act 2000 (Motor Insurance) Regulations 2007, SI 2007/2403, reg 3.

[672]

3 Scope of these Regulations

(1) These Regulations do not apply to contracts of reinsurance.

[(1A) These Regulations do not apply to contracts of insurance entered into on or after 17th December 2009.]

(2) These Regulations apply to contracts of insurance which are entered into by friendly societies [before 17th December 2009] as follows—

- (a) Part II applies to a contract of insurance entered into by a friendly society to which section 37(3) of the Friendly Societies Act 1992 applies;
- (b) Part III applies to a contract of insurance entered into by a friendly society to which section 37(2) of that Act applies; and
- (c) Part II applies to any other contract of insurance entered into by a friendly society which covers a risk situated in an EEA State with the following modifications—
  - (i) paragraph (1) of regulation 4 does not apply;
  - (ii) regulation 4 applies only where the policyholder is an individual; . . .
  - [(iii) regulation 7(1) applies as if for the words "the 1990 Act is to be treated as applying", there were substituted "a court in any part of the United Kingdom must apply the general rules of private international law of that part of the United Kingdom concerning contractual obligations"; and
  - (iv) regulation 7(2) and (3) apply as if for the words "the 1990 Act is to be treated as applying" in each case, there were substituted the words "the general rules of private international law of that part of the United Kingdom concerning contractual obligations apply".]

NOTES

Para (1A): inserted by the Financial Services and Markets Act 2000 (Law Applicable to Contracts of Insurance) Regulations 2009, SI 2009/3075, reg 2(1).

Para (2): words in first pair of square brackets inserted by SI 2009/3075, reg 2(2); word omitted from sub-para (c)(ii) revoked and sub-paras (c)(iii), (iv) substituted for original sub-para (c)(iii) by the Financial Services and Markets Act 2000 (Law Applicable to Contracts of Insurance) (Amendment) Regulations 2001, SI 2001/3542, reg 2.

PART II
CONTRACTS OF GENERAL INSURANCE

[673]

4 Applicable law

(1) This Part applies to a contract of general insurance which covers risks situated in an EEA State.

(2) If the policyholder resides in the EEA State in which the risk is situated, the applicable law is the law of that EEA State unless, if such a choice is permitted under the law of that EEA State, the parties to the contract choose the law of another country.

(3) If the policyholder does not reside in the EEA State in which the risk is situated, the parties to the contract may choose as the applicable law either—

- (a) the law of the EEA State in which the risk is situated; or
- (b) the law of the country in which the policyholder resides.

(4) If the policyholder carries on a business (including a trade or profession) and the contract covers two or more risks relating to that business which are situated in different EEA States, the freedom of the parties to choose the applicable law conferred by this regulation extends to the law of any of those EEA States and of the country in which the policyholder resides.

(5) If any of the EEA States referred to in paragraph (3) or (4) grant greater freedom of choice of the applicable law, the parties to the contract may take advantage of that freedom.

(6) Notwithstanding paragraphs (2) to (4), if the risks covered by the contract are limited to events occurring in one EEA State other than the EEA State in which the risk is situated, the parties may choose the law of the former EEA State as the applicable law.

(7) Notwithstanding paragraphs (2) to (4), if the risk covered by the contract is a large risk the parties may choose any law as the applicable law.

(8) Where the foregoing provisions of this regulation allow the parties to the contract to choose the applicable law and if no choice has been made, or no choice has been made which satisfies the requirement set out in regulation 6(1), the applicable law is the law of the country, from amongst those considered in the relevant paragraph ("the relevant countries"), which is most closely connected with the contract; however, where a severable part of the contract has a closer connection with another relevant country, the law applicable to that part is, by way of exception, the law of that relevant country.

(9) For the purposes of paragraph (8), the contract is rebuttably presumed to be most closely connected with the EEA State in which the risk is situated.

[674]

5 Mandatory rules

(1) Nothing in regulation 4 restricts the application of the mandatory rules of any part of the United Kingdom, irrespective of the applicable law of the contract.

(2) If the parties to the contract choose the applicable law under regulation 4 and if all the other elements relevant to the situation at the time when the parties make their choice are connected with one EEA State only, the application of the mandatory rules of that EEA State is not prejudiced.

[675]

6 Choice of law

(1) Any choice made by the parties under regulation 4 must be expressed or demonstrated with reasonable certainty by the terms of the contract or the circumstances of the case.

(2) Where the parties to the contract may choose the applicable law under regulation 4, and where the risk to which the contract relates is covered by Community co-insurance (within the meaning of Council Directive 78/473/EEC on the coordination of laws, regulations and administrative provisions relating to Community co-insurance)), co-insurers other than the leading insurer (within the meaning of that Directive) are not to be treated as parties to the contract.

NOTES

Council Directive 78/473/EEC: OJ L151, 7.6.1978, p 25.

[676]

7 The 1990 Act

(1) Subject to the preceding provisions of this Part, the 1990 Act is to be treated as applying to the contract for the purposes of determining the applicable law.

(2) In determining whether the mandatory rules of another EEA State should be applied in accordance with regulation 5(2) where the parties have chosen the law of a part of the United Kingdom as the applicable law, the 1990 Act is to be treated as applying to the contract.

(3) In determining what freedom of choice the parties have under the law of a part of the United Kingdom, the 1990 Act is to be treated as applying to the contract.

PART III
CONTRACTS OF LONG-TERM INSURANCE

[677]

8 Applicable law

(1) This Part applies to a contract of long-term insurance if—

- (a) where the policyholder is an individual, he resides in an EEA State;
- (b) otherwise, the establishment of the policyholder to which the contract relates is situated in an EEA State.

(2) The applicable law is the law of the EEA State of the commitment unless, if such a choice is permitted under the law of that EEA State, the parties choose the law of another country.

(3) If the policyholder is an individual and resides in one EEA State but is a national or citizen of another, the parties to the contract may choose the law of the EEA State of which he is a national or citizen as the applicable law.

[678]

9 Mandatory rules

Nothing in regulation 8 affects the application of the mandatory rules of any part of the United Kingdom, irrespective of the applicable law of the contract.

[679]–[819]

10 The 1990 Act

(1) Subject to the preceding provisions of this Part, the 1990 Act is to be treated as applying to the contract for the purposes of determining the applicable law.

(2) In determining what freedom of choice the parties have under the law of a part of the United Kingdom, the 1990 Act is to be treated as applying to the contract.

FINANCIAL SERVICES AND MARKETS ACT 2000 (CONTROL OF BUSINESS TRANSFERS) (REQUIREMENTS ON APPLICANTS) REGULATIONS 2001

(SI 2001/3625)

NOTES

Made: 7 November 2001.
Authority: Financial Services and Markets Act 2000, ss 108, 417(1), 428(3), Sch 12, para 6(2).
Commencement: 1 December 2001.

[820]

1 Citation, commencement and interpretation

(1) These Regulations may be cited as the Financial Services and Markets Act 2000 (Control of Business Transfers) (Requirements on Applicants) Regulations 2001 and come into force on 1st December 2001.

(2) In these Regulations—

"the Act" means the Financial Services and Markets Act 2000;

"the parties" means the authorised person concerned and the transferee (within the meaning of section 105(2) or, as the case may be, section 106(2) of the Act);

["reclaim fund business transfer scheme" has the meaning given by section 106A(1) of the Act;]

"the report" means the scheme report mentioned in section 109(1) of the Act;

"State of the commitment" has the meaning given by paragraph 6(1) of Schedule 12 to the Act;

"State in which the risk is situated" has the meaning given by paragraph 6(3) of Schedule 12 to the Act;

"a summary of the report" means a summary of the report sufficient to indicate the opinion of the person making the report of the likely effects of the insurance business transfer scheme on the policyholders of the parties.

NOTES

Para (2): definition "reclaim fund business transfer scheme" inserted by the Financial Services and Markets Act 2000 (Control of Business Transfers) (Requirements on Applicants) (Amendment) Regulations 2009, SI 2009/1390, reg 2(a).

[821]

2 Meaning of "commitment"

There is prescribed for the purposes of paragraph 6(2) of Schedule 12 to the Act any contract of insurance of a kind referred to in [Article 2 of the life assurance consolidation directive].

NOTES

Words in square brackets substituted by the Life Assurance Consolidation Directive (Consequential Amendments) Regulations 2004, SI 2004/3379, reg 20.

[822]

3 Transfer of an insurance business

(1) An applicant under section 107 of the Act for an order sanctioning an insurance business transfer scheme ("the scheme") must comply with the following requirements.

(2) A notice stating that the application has been made must be—

(a) *published*—

(i) in the London, Edinburgh and Belfast Gazettes;

(ii) in two national newspapers in the United Kingdom; . . .

(iii) where, as regards any policy [(other than a policy which evidences a contract of reinsurance)] included in the proposed transfer, an EEA State other than the

United Kingdom is the State of the commitment or the State in which the risk is situated, in two national newspapers in that EEA State; and

[(iv) where, as regards any policy included in the proposed transfer which evidences a contract of reinsurance, an EEA State other than the United Kingdom is the State in which the establishment of the policyholder to which the policy relates is situated at the date when the contract was entered into, in one business newspaper which is published or circulated in that EEA State; . . .]

(b) sent to every policyholder of the parties[; and

(c) sent—

(i) to every reinsurer of the authorised person concerned (within the meaning of section 105(2) of the Act) any of whose contracts of reinsurance (in whole or part) are to be transferred by the scheme; or

(ii) in a case where such a contract has been placed with or through a person authorised to act on behalf of the reinsurer, then to that person; or

(iii) in a case where such a contract has been placed with more than one reinsurer, then to the person or persons authorised to act on behalf of those reinsurers or groups of reinsurers.]

(3) The notices mentioned in paragraph (2) must—

(a) be approved by the Authority prior to publication (or, as the case may be, being sent); and

(b) contain the address from which the documents mentioned in paragraph (4) may be obtained.

(4) A copy of the report and a statement setting out the terms of the scheme and containing a summary of the report must be given free of charge to any person who requests them.

(5) A copy of the application, the report and the statement mentioned in paragraph (4) must be given free of charge to the Authority.

(6) In the case of any such scheme as is mentioned in section 105(5) of the Act, copies of the documents listed in paragraph 6(1) of Schedule 15B to the Companies Act 1985 or in paragraph 6(1) of Schedule 15B to the Companies (Northern Ireland) Order 1986 (application of provisions about compromises and arrangements to mergers and divisions of public companies) must be given to the Authority by the beginning of the period referred to in paragraph 3(e) of that Schedule.

NOTES

Para (2): word omitted from sub-para (a)(ii) revoked, words in square brackets in sub-para (a)(iii), and the whole of sub-para (a)(iv) inserted by the Financial Services and Markets Act 2000 (Reinsurance Directive) Regulations 2007, SI 2007/3255, reg 2(1), (2); word omitted from sub-para (a)(iv) revoked and sub-para (c) and word "and" immediately preceding it added by the Financial Services and Markets Act 2000 (Control of Business Transfers) (Requirements on Applicants) (Amendment) Regulations 2008, SI 2008/1467, reg 2(a), (b).

[823]

4— (1) Subject to paragraph (2) [or (3)], the court may not determine an application under section 107 for an order sanctioning an insurance business transfer scheme—

(a) where the applicant has failed to comply with the requirements in regulation 3(2), (3) or (6); and

(b) until a period of not less than twenty-one days has elapsed since the Authority was given the documents mentioned in regulation 3(5).

(2) The requirements in regulation 3(2)(a)(ii)[, (iii) and (iv)][, (b) and (c)] may be waived by the court in such circumstances and subject to such conditions as the court considers appropriate.

[(3) The requirement in regulation 3(2)(a)(iv) must be waived where an applicant demonstrates that he has notified all policyholders of contracts of reinsurance.]

NOTES

Para (1): words in square brackets inserted by the Financial Services and Markets Act 2000 (Reinsurance Directive) Regulations 2007, SI 2007/3255, reg 2(1), (3).

Para (2): words in first pair of square brackets substituted by SI 2007/3255, reg 2(1), (4); words in second pair of square brackets substituted by the Financial Services and Markets Act 2000 (Control of Business Transfers) (Requirements on Applicants) (Amendment) Regulations 2008, SI 2008/1467, reg 2(c).

Para (3): added by SI 2007/3255, reg 2(1), (5).

[824]

5 [Transfer of a banking business or a reclaim fund business]

(1) An applicant under section 107 of the Act for an order sanctioning a banking business transfer scheme [or reclaim fund business transfer scheme] ("the scheme") must comply with the following

requirements.

(2) A notice stating that the application has been made must be published—

(a) in the London, Edinburgh and Belfast Gazettes; and

(b) in two national newspapers in the United Kingdom.

(3) The notice mentioned in paragraph (2) must—

(a) be approved by the Authority prior to its publication; and

(b) contain the address from which the statement mentioned in paragraph (4) may be obtained.

(4) A statement setting out the terms of the scheme must be given free of charge to any person who requests it.

(5) Copies of the application and the statement mentioned in paragraph (4) must be given free of charge to the Authority.

NOTES

Regulation heading: words in square brackets substituted by the Financial Services and Markets Act 2000 (Control of Business Transfers) (Requirements on Applicants) (Amendment) Regulations 2009, SI 2009/1390, reg 2(b).

Para (1): words in square brackets inserted by SI 2009/1390, reg 2(c).

[825]

6— (1) Subject to paragraph (2), the court may not determine an application under section 107 for an order sanctioning a banking business transfer scheme [or reclaim fund business transfer scheme]—

(a) where the applicant has failed to comply with the requirements in regulation 5(2) or (3); and

(b) until a period of not less than twenty-one days has elapsed since the Authority was given the documents mentioned in regulation 5(5).

(2) The requirement in regulation 5(2)(b) may be waived by the court in such circumstances and subject to such conditions as the court considers appropriate.

NOTES

Para (1): words in square brackets inserted by the Financial Services and Markets Act 2000 (Control of Business Transfers) (Requirements on Applicants) (Amendment) Regulations 2009, SI 2009/1390, reg 2(d).

FINANCIAL SERVICES AND MARKETS ACT 2000 (CONTROL OF TRANSFERS OF BUSINESS DONE AT LLOYD'S) ORDER 2001

(SI 2001/3626)

NOTES

Made: 7 November 2001.

Authority: Financial Services and Markets Act 2000, ss 323, 428(3).

Commencement: 1 December 2001.

[826]

1 Citation and commencement

This Order may be cited as the Financial Services and Markets Act 2000 (Control of Transfers of Business Done at Lloyd's) Order 2001 and comes into force on 1st December 2001.

[827]

2 Interpretation

In this Order—

"the Act" means the Financial Services and Markets Act 2000;

"the Council" and "the Society" have the same meaning as in Lloyd's Act 1982;

. . .

NOTES

Definition "former underwriting member" (omitted) revoked by the Financial Services and Markets Act 2000 (Control of Transfers of Business Done at Lloyd's) (Amendment) Order 2008, SI 2008/1725, art 2(1), (2).

[828]

3 The following provisions, that is to say—

(a) sections 104 and [107 to 114A] of the Act;

(b) any regulations made under section 108 of the Act; and

(c) Part I of Schedule 12 to the Act;

apply in relation to schemes for the transfer of the whole or any part of the business carried on by one or more [underwriting members of the Society or by one or more persons who have ceased to be such a member (whether before, on or after 24th December 1996)] ("the members concerned") in the same way as they apply in relation to insurance business transfer schemes, but only if the conditions specified by article 4 are satisfied.

NOTES

Words in square brackets substituted by the Financial Services and Markets Act 2000 (Control of Transfers of Business Done at Lloyd's) (Amendment) Order 2008, SI 2008/1725, art 2(1), (3).

[829]

4 The conditions referred to in article 3 are—

(a) that the scheme results in the business transferred being carried on from an establishment of the transferee in an EEA State;

[(b) that the Council of Lloyd's has—

(i) by resolution authorised one person to act, or

(ii) certified that one person has authority to act,

in connection with the transfer for the members concerned, as transferor;

(c) that a copy of the resolution or the certificate has been give to the Authority.]

NOTES

Paras (b), (c) substituted by the Financial Services and Markets Act 2000 (Control of Transfers of Business Done at Lloyd's) (Amendment) Order 2008, SI 2008/1725, art 2(1), (4).

[830]–[837]

5— (1) The provisions which apply by virtue of paragraph (a) and (b) of article 3 do so as if—

(a) any reference to the authorised person concerned were a reference to the members concerned; and

(b) anything done in connection with the transfer by the person authorised[, or the person certified to have authority,] in accordance with [paragraph (b)] of article 4 had been done by the members concerned for whom he acted.

(2) In the application of Part I of Schedule 12 to the Act to the members concerned, the conditions in sub-paragraphs (2)(a), (3)(a) and (4)(a) of paragraph 1 of that Schedule are treated as satisfied.

[(3) A transfer scheme carried out by virtue of this Order may transfer to an establishment of the transferee business written on different syndicates and in different years of account of syndicates.]

NOTES

Para (1): words in first pair of square brackets inserted and words in second pair of square brackets substituted by the Financial Services and Markets Act 2000 (Control of Transfers of Business Done at Lloyd's) (Amendment) Order 2008, SI 2008/1725, art 2(1), (5).

Para (3): added by SI 2008/1725, art 2(1), (6).

FINANCIAL SERVICES AND MARKETS ACT 2000 (MISLEADING STATEMENTS AND PRACTICES) ORDER 2001

(SI 2001/3645)

NOTES

Made: 9 November 2001.

Authority: Financial Services and Markets Act 2000, s 397(9), (10), (14).

Commencement: see art 1.

[838]

1 Citation and commencement

(1) This order may be cited as the Financial Services and Markets Act 2000 (Misleading Statements and Practices) Order 2001.

(2) This Order comes into force—

(a) for the purposes of articles 3(b) and 4(b), on 1st January 2002;

(b) for the purposes of articles 3(c) and 4(c), [on such a day as the Treasury may specify];

(c) for all other purposes, on 1st December 2001.

[(3) Any day specified under paragraph (2)(b) must be caused to be notified in the London, Edinburgh and Belfast Gazettes published not later than one week before that day.]

NOTES

Para (2): words in square brackets substituted by the Financial Services and Markets Act 2000 (Commencement of Mortgage Regulation) (Amendment) Order 2002, SI 2002/1777, art 6(1), (2).

Para (3): added by SI 2002/1777, art 6(1), (3).

[839]

2 Interpretation

In this Order—

"the Act" means the Financial Services and Markets Act 2000;

["contract of insurance" has the meaning given by article 3(1) of the Regulated Activities Order;]

"controlled activity" means an activity which falls within Part I of Schedule 1 to the Financial Promotion Order other than an activity which falls within—

(a) [paragraph 9, 10, 10A or 10B] of that Schedule, or

(b) paragraph 11 so far as relating to [paragraph 9, 10, 10A or 10B];

"controlled investment" means an investment which falls within Part II of Schedule 1 to the Financial Promotion Order other than an investment which falls within paragraph 25 or 26 of that Schedule;

"the Financial Promotion Order" means the Financial Services and Markets Act 2000 (Financial Promotion) Order 2001;

["Regulated Activities Order" means the Financial Services and Markets Act 2000 (Regulated Activities) Order 2001].

NOTES

Definitions "contract of insurance" and "Regulated Activities Order" inserted by the Financial Services and Markets Act 2000 (Regulated Activities) (Amendment) (No 2) Order 2003, SI 2003/1476, art 17(1), (2); in definition "controlled activity" words in square brackets substituted by the Financial Services and Markets Act 2000 (Misleading Statements and Practices) (Amendment) Order 2003, SI 2003/1474, art 2(1), (2).

[840]–[847]

3 Specified kinds of activity

The following kinds of activity are specified for the purposes of section 397(9)(a) of the Act—

(a) a controlled activity;

(b) an activity which falls within paragraph 9 (providing funeral plan contracts) of Schedule 1 to the Financial Promotion Order, or agreeing to carry on such an activity;

(c) an activity which falls within paragraph 10 (providing qualifying credit) of that Schedule, or agreeing to carry on such an activity;

[(ca) an activity which falls within paragraph 10A (arranging qualifying credit) or 10B (advising on qualifying credit) of that Schedule, or agreeing to carry on any such activity;]

(d) an activity of the kind specified by article 45 (sending dematerialised instructions), 51 (establishing etc a collective investment scheme), 52 (establishing etc a stakeholder pension scheme) or 57 (managing the underwriting capacity of a Lloyd's syndicate) of [the Regulated Activities Order][;

(e) (so far as not already specified by paragraph (a)), an activity of the kind specified by—

(i) article 14 of the Regulated Activities Order (dealing in investments as principal),

(ii) article 21 of that Order (dealing in investments as agent),

(iii) article 25(1) or (2) of that Order (arranging deals in investments),

(iv) article 39A of that Order (assisting in the administration and performance of a contract of insurance),

(v) article 53 of that Order (advising on investments), or

(vi) so far as relevant to any of those articles, article 64 of that Order (agreeing),

so far as it relates to a contract of insurance.]

NOTES

Para (ca) inserted by the Financial Services and Markets Act 2000 (Misleading Statements and Practices) (Amendment) Order 2003, SI 2003/1474, art 2(1), (3); words in square brackets in para (d) substituted and para (e) added by the Financial Services and Markets Act 2000 (Regulated Activities) (Amendment) (No 2) Order 2003, SI 2003/1476, art 17(1), (3).

4 (*Outside the scope of this work.*)

FINANCIAL SERVICES AND MARKETS ACT 2000 (SCOPE OF PERMISSION NOTICES) ORDER 2001

(SI 2001/3771)

NOTES

Made: 26 November 2001.
Authority: Financial Services and Markets Act 2000, ss 426–428.
Commencement: 1 December 2001.

[848]
1 Citation, commencement and interpretation

(1) This Order may be cited as the Financial Services and Markets Act 2000 (Scope of Permission Notices) Order 2001 and comes into force on 1st December 2001.

(2) In this Order—

"the Act" means the Financial Services and Markets Act 2000;

"the Authorised Persons Order" means the Financial Services and Markets Act 2000 (Transitional Provisions) (Authorised Persons etc) Order 2001;

"commencement" means the beginning of 1st December 2001;

"the Regulated Activities Order" means the Financial Services and Markets Act 2000 (Regulated Activities) Order 2001.

[849]
2 Revision of scope of permission notices

(1) This article applies where—

(a) the Authority has given, before commencement, a scope of permission notice under article 55 of the Authorised Persons Order;

(b) that notice falls within one of the cases specified in article 3;

(c) the recipient of the notice has, before commencement, notified the Authority in accordance with article 56(1)(a) of the Authorised Persons Order that he agrees with the matters stated in the notice;

(d) the Authority has, before commencement, given that recipient a notice ("the revision notice") revising the scope of permission notice in a permitted manner.

(2) If the recipient of the scope of permission notice does not, on or before 4 January 2002, notify the Authority that he objects to the revision notice, then article 57(1) of the Authorised Persons Order applies as if—

(a) the reference to the scope of permission notice in that article were to the scope of permission notice as revised by the revision notice; and

(b) the person has agreed to that notice as so revised.

(3) If the recipient of the scope of permission notice notifies the Authority on or before 4 January 2002 that he objects to the revision notice, then article 57(1) of the Authorised Persons Order applies as if the revision notice had not been sent.

[850]
3 Cases in which scope of permission notices may be revised

The cases specified in this article are as follows:

CASE 1

Where—

(a) the recipient of the scope of permission notice was, at the time the notice was sent, an authorised person within the meaning of the Financial Services Act 1986;

(b) that person is to be treated, by virtue of Part II of the Authorised Persons Order, as having a Part IV permission to carry on a regulated activity of the kind specified by article 14 of the Regulated Activities Order (dealing in investments as principal) in so far as the activity consists of his entering into a transaction relating to contractually based investments;

(c) the person is not subject, by virtue of Part III of the Authorised Persons Order, to a requirement imposed under section 43 of the Act preventing him from carrying on the regulated activity in paragraph (b); and

(d) the scope of permission notice did not specify that the person had a Part IV permission to carry on the regulated activity in paragraph (b).

CASE 2

Where—

(a) the recipient of the scope of permission notice was, at the time the notice was sent, a member of the Personal Investment Authority Limited;

(b) the scope of permission notice specified that he had a Part IV permission to carry on a regulated activity of the kind specified by article 53 of the Regulated Activities Order (advising on investments) in relation to a particular specified kind of investment ("investment A");

(c) the person is to be treated, by virtue of Part II of the Authorised Persons Order, as having a Part IV permission to carry on that regulated activity also in relation to rights to or interests in (within the meaning of activity 89 of the Regulated Activities Order) investment A;

(d) the person is not subject, by virtue of Part III of the Authorised Persons Order, to a requirement imposed under section 43 of the Act preventing him from carrying on that regulated activity in relation to rights to or interests in investment A; and

(e) the scope of permission notice did not specify that he had a Part IV permission to carry on that regulated activity in relation to rights to or interests in investment A.

CASE 3

Where—

(a) the scope of permission notice specified that the recipient of the notice has a Part IV permission to carry on a regulated activity in relation to a particular specified kind of investment ("investment B"); and

(b) the scope of permission notice purported also to specify that he had permission to carry on that regulated activity in relation to rights to and interests in investments generally rather than only in relation to rights to or interests in investment B.

CASE 4

Where—

(a) the recipient of the scope of permission notice was, at the time the notice was sent, a member of either the Investment Management Regulatory Organisation Limited or the Personal Investment Authority Limited;

(b) the scope of permission notice specified that he had a Part IV permission to carry on a regulated activity of the kind specified by article 40 of the Regulated Activities Order (safeguarding and administering investments);

(c) the scope of permission notice also specified that he was subject to a requirement under section 43 of the Act that he should not hold or control client money; and

(d) the person is not subject, by virtue of Part III of the Authorised Persons Order, to that requirement.

CASE 5

Where—

(a) the recipient of the scope of permission notice was, at the time the notice was sent, a member of either the Investment Management Regulatory Organisation Limited or the Personal Investment Authority Limited;

(b) the scope of permission notice specified that he had a Part IV permission to carry on a regulated activity of the kind specified by either article 51 of the Regulated Activities Order (establishing etc a collective investment scheme) or article 52 of that Order (establishing etc a stakeholder pension scheme);

(c) the scope of permission notice purported to limit that permission to carrying on the activity in relation to a specified kind of investment; and

(d) the Part IV permission that the person is to be treated as having by virtue of Parts II and III of the Authorised Persons Order is not subject to that limitation.

CASE 6

Where—

(a) the recipient of the scope of permission notice was, at the time the notice was sent, a member of the Investment Management Regulatory Organisation Limited;

(b) the scope of permission notice specified that he had a Part IV permission to carry on a regulated activity of the kind specified by article 21 of the Regulated Activities Order (dealing in investments as agent) for the purpose of stock lending activities;

(c) the scope of permission notice purported further to limit his permission so that he could not carry on that activity in relation to investments of the kind specified by article 78 of the Regulated Activities Order (government and public securities); and

(d) the Part IV permission that the person is to be treated as having by virtue of Parts II and III of the Authorised Persons Order is not subject to that limitation.

[851]

4 Permitted revisions

For the purposes of article 2(1)(d), a revision notice revises the scope of permission notice in a permitted manner if—

(a) in Case 1 in article 3, it results in the scope of permission notice specifying that the recipient has a Part IV permission to carry on the regulated activities described in paragraph (b) of that Case;

(b) in Case 2 in article 3, it results in the scope of permission notice specifying that the recipient has a Part IV permission to carry on the regulated activity described in paragraph (c) of that Case;

(c) in Case 3 in article 3, it results in the scope of permission notice specifying that his Part IV permission to carry on a particular regulated activity in relation to rights to or interests in investments is limited to rights to or interests in investment B (as defined in that Case);

(d) in Case 4 in article 3, it results either in the lifting of the requirement that the recipient should not control client money or in the lifting of the requirement that he should not hold or control client money;

(e) in Case 5 in article 3, it results in the removal of the limitation described in paragraph (c) of that Case;

(f) in Case 6 in article 3, it results in the removal of the limitation described in paragraph (c) of that Case;

(g) in any Case in article 3, it results in the scope of permission notice specifying that the recipient has a Part IV permission to carry on a regulated activity of the kind specified by article 64 of the Regulated Activities Order (agreeing to carry on specified kinds of activity) to the extent appropriate having regard to paragraphs (a) to (f) above.

5 *(Amends the Financial Services and Markets Act 2000 (Miscellaneous Provisions) Order 2001, SI 2001/3650, arts 29, 30.)*

FINANCIAL SERVICES AND MARKETS ACT 2000 (ADMINISTRATION ORDERS RELATING TO INSURERS) ORDER 2002

(SI 2002/1242)

NOTES

Made: 2 May 2002.
Authority: Financial Services and Markets Act 2000, ss 355(2), 360, 426, 428(3).
Commencement: 31 May 2002.

[852]

1 Citation, commencement and interpretation

(1) This Order may be cited as the Financial Services and Markets Act 2000 (Administration Orders Relating to Insurers) Order 2002 and comes into force on 31st May 2002.

(2) In this Order—

"the 1986 Act" means the Insolvency Act 1986;

["initial creditors' meeting" has the meaning given by paragraph 51(1) of Schedule B1;

"Schedule B1" means Schedule B1 to the 1986 Act].

NOTES

Para (2): definitions "initial creditors' meeting" and "Schedule B1" substituted for original definition "section 23 meeting" by the Financial Services and Markets Act 2000 (Administration Orders Relating to Insurers) (Amendment) Order 2003, SI 2003/2134, arts 2, 3, except in relation to any case where a petition for an administration order was presented to the court before 15 September 2003.

2 (*Amends the Financial Services and Markets Act 2000 (Insolvency) (Definition of "Insurer") Order 2001, SI 2001/2634, art 2 at* **[669]**.)

[853]
3 Modification of Part II of the 1986 Act in relation to insurers

Part II of the 1986 Act (administration orders)[, other than paragraph 14 of Schedule B1 (power of holder of floating charge to appoint administrator) and paragraph 22 of Schedule B1 (power of company or directors to appoint administrator),] applies in relation to insurers with the modifications specified in the Schedule to this Order, and accordingly [paragraph 9(2) of Schedule B1] does not preclude the making of an administration order in relation to an insurer.

NOTES

Words in first pair of square brackets inserted by the Insurers (Reorganisation and Winding-up) Regulations 2004, SI 2004/353, reg 52; words in second pair of square brackets substituted by the Financial Services and Markets Act 2000 (Administration Orders Relating to Insurers) (Amendment) Order 2003, SI 2003/2134, arts 2, 4, except in relation to any case where a petition for an administration order was presented to the court before 15 September 2003.

[854]
4 Modification of the Insolvency Rules 1986 in relation to insurers

The Insolvency Rules 1986, so far as they give effect to Part II of the 1986 Act, have effect in relation to insurers with the modification that in [Rule 2.12(1)] of those Rules (the hearing) there is inserted after sub-paragraph (a) the following sub-paragraph—

"(aa) the Financial Services Authority;".

NOTES

Words in square brackets substituted by the Financial Services and Markets Act 2000 (Administration Orders Relating to Insurers) (Amendment) Order 2003, SI 2003/2134, arts 2, 5, except in relation to any case where a petition for an administration order was presented to the court before 15 September 2003.

[855]
[5 Mutual credit and set-off

Where an insurer, in relation to which an administration order has been made, subsequently goes into liquidation, sums due from the insurer to another party are not to be included in the account of mutual dealings rendered under rule 4.90 of the Insolvency Rules 1986 (mutual credit and set-off) if, at the time they became due—

(a) an administration application had been made under paragraph 12 of Schedule B1 in relation to the insurer;
(b) in the case of an appointment of an administrator under paragraph 14 of Schedule B1, a notice of appointment had been filed with the court under paragraph 18 of that Schedule in relation to the insurer; or
(c) in the case of an appointment of an administrator under paragraph 22 of Schedule B1, a notice of intention to appoint had been filed with the court under paragraph 27 of that Schedule in relation to the insurer.]

NOTES

Substituted by the Financial Services and Markets Act 2000 (Administration Orders Relating to Insurers) (Amendment) Order 2003, SI 2003/2134, arts 2, 6, except in relation to any case where a petition for an administration order was presented to the court before 15 September 2003.

SCHEDULE
MODIFICATIONS OF PART II OF THE INSOLVENCY ACT 1986 IN RELATION TO INSURERS

Article 3

[856]

[**1.** In paragraph 49(4) of Schedule B1 (administrator's proposals), at the end of paragraph (c) add—

"and
(d) to the Financial Services Authority".

2. In paragraph 53(2) of Schedule B1 (business and result of initial creditors' meeting), at the end of paragraph (c), add—

"and
(d) the Financial Services Authority".

3. In paragraph 54(2)(b) of Schedule B1 (revision of administrator's proposals), after "creditor" insert "and to the Financial Services Authority".

4. In paragraph 76(1) of Schedule B1 (automatic end of administration), for "one year" substitute "30 months".

5. In paragraph 76(2)(b) of Schedule B1 (extension of administrator's term of office by consent) for "six" substitute "twelve".

6. In paragraph 79(1) of Schedule B1 (court ending administration on application of administrator), after the first reference to "company" insert "or the Financial Services Authority".

7. In paragraph 91(1) of Schedule B1 (supplying vacancy in office of administrator), at the end of paragraph (e) add—

"or

(f) the Financial Services Authority".]

[8.]—(1) The powers of the administrator referred to in Schedule 1 to the 1986 Act (powers of administrator or administrative receiver) include the power to make—
- (a) any payments due to a creditor; or
- (b) any payments on account of any sum which may become due to a creditor.

(2) Any payments to a creditor made pursuant to sub-paragraph (1) must not exceed, in aggregate, the amount which the administrator reasonably considers that the creditor would be entitled to receive on a distribution of the insurer's assets in a winding up.

(3) The powers conferred by sub-paragraph (1) may be exercised until [an initial creditors' meeting] but may only be exercised thereafter—
- (a) if the following conditions are met—
  - (i) the administrator has laid before [that meeting] or any subsequent creditors' meeting ("the relevant meeting") a statement containing the information mentioned in sub-paragraph (4); and
  - (ii) the powers are exercised with the consent of a majority in number representing three-fourths in value of the creditors present and voting either in person or by proxy at the relevant meeting; or
- (b) with the consent of the court.

(4) The information referred to in sub-paragraph (3)(a) is an estimate of the aggregate amount of—
- (a) the insurer's assets and liabilities (whether actual, contingent or prospective); and
- (b) all payments which the administrator proposes to make to creditors pursuant to sub-paragraph (1);

including any assumptions which the administrator has made in calculating that estimate.

NOTES

Paras 1–7: substituted, for original paras 1–5, by the Financial Services and Markets Act 2000 (Administration Orders Relating to Insurers) (Amendment) Order 2003, SI 2003/2134, arts 2, 7(b), except in relation to any case where a petition for an administration order was presented to the court before 15 September 2003.

Para 8: numbered as such (originally para 6) by SI 2003/2134, arts 2, 7(a); words in square brackets in sub-para (3) substituted by SI 2003/2134, arts 2, 7(c).

FINANCIAL SERVICES AND MARKETS ACT 2000 (FOURTH MOTOR INSURANCE DIRECTIVE) REGULATIONS 2002

(SI 2002/2706)

NOTES

Made: 28 October 2002.
Authority: Financial Services and Markets Act 2000, ss 150(3), 417(1).
Commencement: 20 November 2002.

[857]

1 Citation and commencement

These Regulations may be cited as the Financial Services and Markets Act 2000 (Fourth Motor Insurance Directive) Regulations 2002 and come into force on 20th November 2002.

[858]

2 Power of the Authority to make rules under section 138 of the Financial Services and Markets Act 2000

(1) Rules made by the Authority under section 138 of the Financial Services and Markets Act 2000 ("the 2000 Act") (general rule-making power) may require a relevant authorised person to pay interest in specified circumstances in respect of claims made for compensation.

(2) In paragraph (1)—

(a) "relevant authorised person" means an authorised person with a Part IV permission (within the meaning of the 2000 Act)—

(i) to effect or carry out relevant contracts of insurance; or

(ii) to manage the underwriting capacity of a Lloyd's syndicate as a managing agent, the members of which effect or carry out relevant contracts of insurance underwritten at Lloyd's;

where a "relevant contract of insurance" means a contract of insurance against damage arising out of or in connection with the use of motor vehicles on land (other than carrier's liability);

(b) "specified" means specified in the rules.

(3) Rules made pursuant to paragraph (1) may not come into force before 19th January 2003.

3 (*Amends the Financial Services and Markets Act 2000, (Rights of Action) Regulations 2001, SI 2001/2256, reg 6 at* **[623]**.)

FINANCIAL SERVICES AND MARKETS ACT 2000 (COMMUNICATIONS BY ACTUARIES) REGULATIONS 2003

(SI 2003/1294)

NOTES

Made: 12 May 2003.
Authority: Financial Services and Markets Act 2000, ss 342(5), 343(5), 428(3).
Commencement: 1 September 2003.

[859]

1 Citation, commencement and interpretation

(1) These Regulations may be cited as the Financial Services and Markets Act 2000 (Communications by Actuaries) Regulations 2003 and come into force on 1st September 2003.

(2) In these Regulations—

"the Act" means the Financial Services and Markets Act 2000;

"contract of long-term insurance" has the same meaning as in the Financial Services and Markets Act 2000 (Regulated Activities) Order 2001;

"relevant requirement" means—

(a) a requirement which is imposed by or under any provision of the Act other than Part VI (official listing); or

(b) a requirement which is imposed by or under any other Act and whose contravention constitutes an offence which the Authority has power to prosecute under the Act.

[860]–[913]

2 Circumstances in which an actuary is to communicate

(1) This regulation applies to any person who is, or has been, an actuary acting for an authorised person ("A") and who is or was—

(a) appointed under or as a result of rules made by the Authority under section 340 of the Act; or

(b) appointed under or as a result of any other statutory provision and subject to duties imposed by such rules.

(2) An actuary to whom this regulation applies must communicate to the Authority information on, or his opinion on, matters mentioned in section 342(3)(a) of the Act (matters of which he has, or had, become aware in his capacity as actuary acting for an authorised person) in the circumstances specified in paragraph (4).

(3) An actuary—

(a) to whom this regulation applies, and

(b) who is or has been an actuary acting for a person who has close links with A (within the meaning of section 343(8) of the Act),

must communicate to the Authority information on, or his opinion on, matters mentioned in section 343(3)(a) of the Act (information on a matter concerning A of which he has, or had, become aware in his capacity as actuary acting for the person who has close links with A) in the circumstances specified in paragraph (4).

(4) The circumstances are that the actuary reasonably believes that—

(a) as regards A—

(i) there is or has been, or may be or may have been, a contravention of any relevant requirement that applies to A; and

(ii) that contravention may be of material significance to the Authority in determining whether to exercise, in relation to A, any functions conferred on the Authority by or under any provision of the Act other than Part VI;

(b) the information on, or his opinion on, those matters may be of material significance to the Authority in determining whether A satisfies and will continue to satisfy the threshold conditions;

(c) where applicable, there is a significant risk that assets representing a fund or funds maintained by A in respect of contracts of long-term insurance effected or carried out by him are or may be, or may become, insufficient to meet his liabilities attributable to such contracts; or

(d) where applicable, there is a significant risk that A—

(i) did not,

(ii) does not or is unable to, or

(iii) will not, may not or may become unable to,

take into account in a reasonable and proportionate manner the interests of the policyholders of contracts of long-term insurance effected or carried out by him.

(5) In determining whether there is a significant risk of the kind specified by paragraph (4)(d), the actuary may take into account—

(a) the manner in which A exercises his discretion in relation to the operation of the fund or funds maintained by A in respect of contracts of long-term insurance effected or carried out by him, including the distribution and use of surplus assets;

(b) the methodology used to determine bonuses;

(c) the manner in which A takes into account the interests of different classes of policyholder;

(d) the application of fixed or discretionary charges or benefits payable under such contracts;

(e) representations made by A to policyholders or potential policyholders; and

(f) any obligation (however phrased) imposed on A under the Act to treat policyholders fairly.

FINANCIAL SERVICES AND MARKETS ACT 2000 (TRANSITIONAL PROVISIONS) (COMPLAINTS RELATING TO GENERAL INSURANCE AND MORTGAGES) ORDER 2004

(SI 2004/454)

NOTES

Made: 25 February 2004.
Authority: Financial Services and Markets Act 2000, ss 426–428.
Commencement: see art 1(2).

ARRANGEMENT OF ARTICLES

1 Citation, commencement and interpretation . . . . . [914]
2 Complaints made after commencement about acts or omissions before commencement . . . . [915]
3 Procedure applying to relevant transitional complaints . . . . . [916]
4 Scheme rules applying to relevant transitional complaints . . . . . [917]
5 Determination of relevant transitional complaints . . . . . [918]
6 Funding and fees . . . . . [919]
7 Exemption from liability in damages . . . . . [920]
8 Privilege . . . . . [921]
9 Record-keeping and reporting requirements relating to relevant transitional complaints . . . . . [922]

11 Information [923]
12 Application of rules etc in relation to relevant matters [924]

[914]
1 Citation, commencement and interpretation

(1) This Order may be cited as the Financial Services and Markets Act 2000 (Transitional Provisions) (Complaints Relating to General Insurance and Mortgages) Order 2004.

(2) This Order comes into force—

(a) in so far as it relates to a complaint relating to an activity to which, immediately before 31st October 2004, the MCAS Scheme applied, on 31st October 2004;

(b) for all other purposes, on 14th January 2005.

(3) In this Order—

"the Act" means the Financial Services and Markets Act 2000;

"former scheme" means the GISC Facility or, as the case may be, the MCAS Scheme;

"GISC Facility" means the Dispute Resolution Facility established by the General Insurance Standards Council;

"MCAS Scheme" means the Mortgage Code Arbitration Scheme;

"new scheme" means the ombudsman scheme provided for by Part 16 of the Act [(the ombudsman scheme)];

"relevant commencement date" means—

(a) in relation to a complaint which relates to an activity to which, immediately before 14th January 2005, the GISC Facility applied, . . . 14th January 2005;

(b) in relation to a complaint which relates to an activity to which, immediately before 31st October 2004, the MCAS Scheme applied, . . . 31st October 2004.

NOTES

Para (3): words in square brackets in definition "new scheme" substituted, and words omitted from definition "relevant commencement date" revoked, by the Financial Services and Markets Act 2000 (Transitional Provisions) (Complaints Relating to General Insurance and Mortgages) (Amendment) Order 2004, SI 2004/1609, art 2(1)–(3).

[915]
2 Complaints made after commencement about acts or omissions before commencement

(1) Subject to the provisions of this Order, the compulsory jurisdiction resulting from section 226 of the Act applies to a complaint referred to the new scheme [on or] after the relevant commencement date which relates to an act or omission occurring before that date if the conditions mentioned in paragraph (2) are satisfied (notwithstanding that the conditions in subsection (2)(b) and (c) of that section are not met).

(2) The conditions are that—

(a) the act or omission is that of a person ("R") who, at the time of that act or omission, was subject to a former scheme;

(b) R was an authorised person on or after the relevant commencement date;

(c) the act or omission occurred in the carrying on by R of an activity to which that former scheme applied; and

(d) the complainant is eligible and wishes to have the complaint dealt with under the new scheme.

(3) For the purposes of paragraph (2)(d), where the complainant is not eligible in accordance with the rules made under section 226(6) and (7) of the Act (power to specify in rules the classes of persons who are eligible complainants), an ombudsman may nonetheless, if he considers it appropriate, treat the complainant as eligible if he would have been entitled to refer an equivalent complaint to the former scheme in question immediately before the relevant commencement date.

(4) Where the former scheme in question is the GISC Facility, a complainant is not to be treated as eligible for the purposes of paragraph (2)(d) unless—

(a) he is an individual; and

(b) he is acting otherwise than solely for the purposes of his business.

(5) Where the former scheme in question is the MCAS Scheme, a complainant is not to be treated as eligible for the purposes of paragraph (2)(d) if—

(a) the complaint does not relate to a breach of the Mortgage Code;

(b) the complaint concerns physical injury, illness, nervous shock or their consequences; or

(c) the complainant is claiming a sum of money that exceeds £100,000.

(6) A complaint falling within paragraph (1) is referred to in this Order as a "relevant transitional complaint".

NOTES

Para (1): words in square brackets inserted by the Financial Services and Markets Act 2000 (Transitional Provisions) (Complaints Relating to General Insurance and Mortgages) (Amendment) Order 2004, SI 2004/1609, art 3.

[916]

3 Procedure applying to relevant transitional complaints

In paragraph 13 of Schedule 17 to the Act (Authority's procedural rules)—

(a) the references to a complaint are to be taken to include a relevant transitional complaint; and

(b) the references to the ombudsman scheme are, in relation to a relevant transitional complaint, to be taken to mean the new scheme as it applies to such complaints by virtue of this Order; and

(c) in sub-paragraph (4), the reference to complaints which may be referred to the scheme is to be taken to include any complaint which may be referred to the scheme as a relevant transitional complaint.

[917]

4 Scheme rules applying to relevant transitional complaints

(1) In paragraph 14 of Schedule 17 to the Act (the scheme operator's rules)—

(a) references to "complaints" are to be taken to include relevant transitional complaints;

(b) sub-paragraph (2)(a) (matters which are to be taken into account in making determinations) does not apply to a relevant transitional complaint.

(2) In deciding whether a relevant transitional complaint is to be dismissed without consideration of its merits as mentioned in paragraph 14(2)(b) of that Schedule, an ombudsman must take into account whether an equivalent complaint would have been so dismissed under the former scheme in question, as it had effect immediately before the relevant commencement date; and any scheme rules made under paragraph 14(2)(b) and (3) of that Schedule (rejection of a complaint without consideration of its merits) are to be construed accordingly.

[918]

5 Determination of relevant transitional complaints

(1) Sections 228 to 232 of the Act apply in relation to a relevant transitional complaint as they apply in relation to a complaint of the kind mentioned in section 226(1) of the Act (compulsory jurisdiction), subject to paragraph (2).

(2) In determining, in relation to a relevant transitional complaint—

(a) what is fair and reasonable in all the circumstances of the case, for the purposes of section 228(2) of the Act, and

(b) what amount (if any) constitutes fair compensation for the purposes of section 229(2)(a) of the Act,

an ombudsman is to take into account what determination might have been expected to be made under the former scheme in question, and what amount (if any) might have been expected to be awarded or recommended by way of compensation under that scheme, in relation to an equivalent complaint dealt with under the former scheme immediately before the relevant commencement date.

[919]

6 Funding and fees

(1) In section 234(1) of the Act (industry funding), the reference to the operation of the new scheme in relation to the compulsory jurisdiction is to be taken to include the operation of the scheme in relation to relevant transitional complaints.

(2) In paragraph 15 of Schedule 17 to the Act (fees), the references to a complaint are to be taken to include a relevant transitional complaint.

(3) Any fee which, by reason of paragraph (2), is owed to the scheme operator by a respondent who is not an authorised person, may be recovered as a debt due to the scheme operator.

[920]

7 Exemption from liability in damages

In paragraph 10(1) of Schedule 17 to the Act (exemption from liability in damages), the reference to functions under the Act in relation to the compulsory jurisdiction is to be taken to include functions exercisable by virtue of this Order.

[921]
8 Privilege

In paragraph 11 of Schedule 17 to the Act (privilege), the reference to a complaint which is subject to the compulsory jurisdiction is to be taken to include a relevant transitional complaint.

[922]
9 Record-keeping and reporting requirements relating to relevant transitional complaints

The Authority may make rules applying to authorised persons with respect to the keeping of records and the making of reports in relation to relevant transitional complaints.

10 *(Revoked by the Financial Services and Markets Act 2000 (Transitional Provisions) (Complaints Relating to General Insurance and Mortgages) (Amendment) Order 2004, SI 2004/1609, art 4.)*

[923]
11 Information

(1) Any information held by any person responsible for the operation of a former scheme ("the former holder") in connection with the operation of a former scheme may be disclosed by that person to the scheme operator or to an ombudsman ("the new holder").

(2) Any such disclosure is not to be treated as contravening any restriction on disclosure of the information (imposed by statute or otherwise) to which the former holder is subject.

(3) When information has been disclosed in accordance with this article, the new holder is to be treated as subject to any such restriction on disclosure as would have applied to the former holder (subject to any exceptions which would have so applied).

(4) But paragraph (3) does not prevent the application of section 31(4A) of the Data Protection Act 1998 to information which has been disclosed in accordance with this article.

(5) Sections 231 and 232 apply in relation to relevant transitional complaints as they apply in relation to complaints relating to acts or omissions occurring [on or after the relevant commencement date].

NOTES

Para (5): words in square brackets substituted by the Financial Services and Markets Act 2000 (Transitional Provisions) (Complaints Relating to General Insurance and Mortgages) (Amendment) Order 2004, SI 2004/1609, art 5.

[924]–[950]
[12 Application of rules etc in relation to relevant matters

(1) If the Authority proposes to make any rules or give guidance in relation to relevant matters, sections 155 and 157(3) of the Act do not apply to the proposed rules or guidance.

(2) When the scheme operator proposes to make any scheme rules in relation to relevant matters, sub-paragraphs (4) to (6) of paragraph 14 of Schedule 17 to the Act do not apply to the proposed rules.

(3) In this article, "relevant matters" means—

(a) the effect of this Order;

(b) the application of rules or guidance made or to be made before the relevant commencement date relating to relevant transitional complaints.]

NOTES

Inserted by the Financial Services and Markets Act 2000 (Transitional Provisions) (Complaints Relating to General Insurance and Mortgages) (Amendment) Order 2004, SI 2004/1609, art 6.

FINANCIAL SERVICES AND MARKETS ACT 2000 (STAKEHOLDER PRODUCTS) REGULATIONS 2004

(SI 2004/2738)

NOTES

Made: 16 November 2004.

Authority: Financial Services and Markets Act 2000, s 428; Financial Services and Markets Act 2000 (Regulated Activities) Order 2001, SI 2001/544, art 52B(3).

Commencement: 6 April 2005.

ARRANGEMENT OF REGULATIONS

1	Citation and commencement	[951]
2	Interpretation	[952]
3	Meaning of stakeholder product	[953]
5	Units in certain collective investment schemes	[954]
6	Rights under certain linked long-term contracts	[955]
7	Characteristics and conditions applicable to certain stakeholder products	[956]
8	Additional conditions applicable to smoothed linked long-term contracts	[957]
9	Permitted reductions in investor's rights and investment property	[958]

[951]

1 Citation and commencement

These Regulations may be cited as the Financial Services and Markets 2000 (Stakeholder Products) Regulations 2004 and come into force on 6th April 2005.

[952]

2 Interpretation

(1) In these Regulations—

"the 2000 Act" means the Financial Services and Markets Act 2000;

"account-holder" means the holder of a deposit account;

"Bank of England base rate" means the rate announced from time to time by the Monetary Policy Committee of the Bank of England as the official dealing rate, being the rate at which the Bank of England is willing to enter into transactions for providing short-term liquidity in the money markets;

"the Conduct of Business Rules" means the Conduct of Business Rules made by the Financial Services Authority under section 153 of the 2000 Act;

"relevant contract of insurance" means a contract of insurance—

(a) which, or any part of which, is one or more of the following kinds—

(i) life and annuity,

(ii) linked long-term, and

(b) which is carried out by an insurer who has permission, as the case may be, under—

(i) Part 4 of the 2000 Act, or

(ii) paragraph 15 of Schedule 3 to the 2000 Act,

to effect or carry out contracts of insurance of that kind, and

(c) is not a with-profits policy and does not include rights in a with-profits fund;

"deposit account" means a deposit account with a deposit-taker and includes a share account with a building society within the meaning of the Building Societies Act 1986;

"deposit-taker" means—

(a) a person who has permission under Part 4 of the 2000 Act to accept deposits, or

(b) an EEA firm of the kind mentioned in paragraph 5(b) of Schedule 3 to the 2000 Act which has permission under paragraph 15 of that Schedule (as a result of qualifying for authorisation under paragraph 12 of that Schedule) to accept deposits;

"dilution levy" has the meaning given by the handbook made by the Financial Services Authority under section 153 of the 2000 Act;

"insurer" means—

(a) a person who has permission under Part 4 of the 2000 Act to effect or carry out contracts of insurance, or

(b) an EEA firm of the kind mentioned in paragraph 5(d) of Schedule 3 to that Act, which has permission under paragraph 15 of that Schedule (as a result of qualifying for authorisation under paragraph 12 of that Schedule) to effect or carry out contracts of insurance;

"investor" means a member of a collective investment scheme which complies with regulation 5 or an underlying fund which complies with regulation 6 as the case may be;

"investment property" means the scheme property of a collective investment scheme which complies with regulation 5 or an underlying fund which complies with regulation 6 as the case may be;

"investment scheme" means a collective investment scheme which complies with regulation 5 or a linked long-term contract which complies with regulation 6 as the case may be;

"land and buildings" means interests in any land or buildings which satisfy the conditions in rule 5A.8.5R of the Collective Investment Schemes Sourcebook made by the Financial Services Authority under section 153 of the 2000 Act;

"linked long-term contract" means a contract of long-term insurance as specified in paragraph 3 of Part 2 of Schedule 1 to the principal Order;

"manager" means the manager of a relevant collective investment scheme or the insurer of a relevant linked long-term contract as the case may be;

"the principal Order" means the Financial Services and Markets Act 2000 (Regulated Activities) Order 2001;

"relevant collective investment scheme" means an authorised unit trust scheme, an authorised open-ended investment company or a recognised scheme, as the case may be, as defined in section 237(3) of the 2000 Act;

"relevant investments" means—

- (a) shares issued by a company wherever incorporated and officially listed on a recognised stock exchange;
- (b) units in a relevant collective investment scheme where a substantial proportion of the scheme property is invested, directly or indirectly, in shares, as defined in paragraph (a) or land and buildings; and
- (c) rights under a contract of insurance where a substantial proportion of the assets of the funds held in respect of that contract are invested, directly or indirectly, in shares as set out in sub-paragraph (a) or land and buildings;

"relevant linked long-term contract" means a linked long-term contract which meets the conditions and characteristics specified in regulation 6(1);

"units" means the rights or interests (however described) of the members of a relevant collective investment scheme.

(2) The definitions of "deposit-taker" and "insurer" in paragraph (1) must be read with—

- (a) section 22 of the 2000 Act,
- (b) any relevant order under that section, and
- (c) Schedule 2 to that Act.

[953]

3 Meaning of stakeholder product

These Regulations specify kinds of investment for the purposes of sub-paragraph (c) of the definition of "stakeholder product" in article 52B(3) of the principal Order and accordingly an investment of one of these kinds is a stakeholder product for the purposes of article 52B of that Order.

4 (*Outside the scope of this work.*)

[954]

5 Units in certain collective investment schemes

Units in a relevant collective investment scheme are a stakeholder product where that scheme has the characteristics, and complies with the conditions, set out in regulation 7.

[955]

6 Rights under certain linked long-term contracts

(1) Rights under a linked long-term contract are a stakeholder product where the insurer ensures that the fund held in respect of that contract ("the underlying fund")—

- (a) has the characteristics and complies with the conditions set out in regulation 7; and
- (b) where the investment returns are smoothed, complies with the conditions set out in regulation 8.

(2) For the purposes of this regulation and regulations 8 and 9, investment returns are smoothed when the insurer offers the product on the basis that the amount in respect of the investment returns earned from time to time by the underlying funds to be attributed under the contract to the policyholder will be managed and attributed with a view to reducing the volatility of such returns over given periods, and "smoothing", "smoothed" and "unsmoothed" are to be construed accordingly.

[956]

7 Characteristics and conditions applicable to certain stakeholder products

(1) The characteristics in relation to an investment scheme are—

- (a) no more than 60 per cent. in value of the investment property, calculated in accordance with paragraph (3), consists of relevant investments;

(b) the investment property should be selected and managed having regard to the need to achieve a balance between—
 (i) the opportunity for the investor to benefit from growth in the value of investments generally; and
 (ii) control of the risk of loss of value in the investment; and
(c) the manager has regard to—
 (i) the need for diversification of the investment property, in so far as appropriate to the circumstances of the investment scheme; and
 (ii) the suitability for the purposes of the scheme of any investment option proposed.

(2) The conditions with which the investment scheme must comply are—
(a) the minimum amount which an investor may contribute to the investment scheme on a single occasion is £20, except where the manager permits a smaller amount;
(b) the manager must permit [payment to the investment scheme by any of the following means, at the option of the investor]—
 (i) cheque;
 (ii) direct debit;
 (iii) standing order;
 (iv) direct credit (other than standing order),

 and excluding payments by cash, credit card or debit card or any combination including a payment by cash, credit card or debit card;
(c) the value of an investor's rights in the investment scheme and the value of the investment property may be reduced in the circumstances and to the extent set out in regulation 9; and
(d) where the stakeholder product consists of—
 (i) units in a relevant collective investment scheme, it must be a requirement of that scheme that the purchase and sale price of those units shall, at any given time, not differ from each other and that price must be made available to the public on a daily basis;
 (ii) rights under a relevant linked long-term contract which are expressed as shares in funds, it must be a requirement of that contract that the purchase and sale price of those shares shall, at any given time, not differ from each other and that price must be made available to the public on a daily basis.

(3) For the purposes of the calculation set out in paragraph (1)(a), the following provisions apply—
(a) where any of the investment property is invested in units in a relevant collective investment scheme, only such of the assets of that scheme as are invested, directly or indirectly, in relevant investments shall be taken into account; and
(b) the calculation shall be taken as an average over a period of 3 months.

(4) When calculating the average over a period of 3 months for the purposes of paragraph (3)(b) ("the average"), where the manager has specified under paragraph (5) that the calculation is to be carried out weekly or monthly—
(a) where the average is to be calculated weekly, it is to be carried out on such day of the week ("the specified day") as has been so specified by the manager (except that, where that day is not a working day, the average is to be calculated on the next working day), and the average on each subsequent day prior to the next specified day is to be taken to be the average on the previous specified day; and
(b) where the average is to be calculated monthly, it is to be so calculated on such day in each month ("the specified day") as has been so specified by the manager (except that, where that date is not a working day, the average is to be calculated on the next working day), and the average on each subsequent day prior to the next specified date is to be taken to be the average on the previous specified date.

(5) For the purposes of paragraph (3)(b)—
(a) the frequency, which must be daily, weekly or monthly, with which the average is to be calculated; and
(b) where the average is to be calculated using weekly or monthly figures, that day of the week or, as the case may be, the date in the month on which it is to take place,

must be specified in writing by the manager; and the specification may not be amended during the period of 12 months after the date on which it is made.

(6) Where, following the calculation under paragraph (4), the average value of the investment property comprises more than 60 per cent. of relevant investments, the manager must take steps to bring that average value within the limit prescribed in regulation 7(1)(a) as soon as reasonably practicable and in any event within 3 months.

NOTES

Para (2): words in square brackets substituted by the Financial Services and Markets Act 2000 (Stakeholder Products) (Amendment) Regulations 2005, SI 2005/594, reg 2(1), (3).

[957]

8 Additional conditions applicable to smoothed linked long-term contracts

The conditions under this paragraph are—

(a) the manager must make available, to each investor who is also a policyholder or to anyone else requesting it, the information necessary to enable a person making such a request properly to understand the essential elements of the insurer's commitment under the terms of the policy;

(b) the manager must make available, to each investor and anyone else requesting it, information on its policy on and charges for smoothing;

(c) no payment may be made or property attributed from the underlying fund to any person other than an investor, except for permitted reductions in the investor's rights and investment property in accordance with regulation 9;

(d) the manager must manage the underlying fund with the aim of attributing to each investor on the maturity or surrender of his rights under the linked long-term contract a value that falls within a target range which is notified to each investor before he enters into the linked long-term contract;

(e) except as provided for in paragraph (f), there is no guarantee of the value of an investor's rights under the linked long-term contract;

(f) the manager may guarantee that, on the death of an investor, the value of an investor's rights under the linked long-term contract are no more than 101 per cent of the total of the value of the units allocated to that contract.

[958]–[965]

9 Permitted reductions in investor's rights and investment property

(1) The value of an investor's rights in an investment scheme may be reduced in the circumstances, and to the extent, set out in paragraphs (3) to (5).

(2) The value of the investment property may be reduced in the circumstances, and to the extent, set out in paragraph (9).

(3) To the extent that an investor's rights in an investment scheme are represented by a fund allocated to him to the exclusion of other investors, the value of those rights may be reduced by the making of deductions from that fund no greater than, at the choice of the manager—

(a) the relevant percentage of its value for each day on which it is held; or

(b) the proportion attributable to the investor's fund of the relevant percentage of the value of the investment property for each day on which the investor's fund is held for the purposes of the scheme.

(4) To the extent that an investor's rights in an investment scheme are represented by a share of funds held for the purposes of the scheme, the amount of that share not being determined by reference to a discretion exercisable by any person, the value of those rights may be reduced by the making of deductions from that share no greater than, at the choice of the manager—

(a) the relevant percentage of its value for each day on which it is held; or

(b) the proportion attributable to the investor's share of the relevant percentage of the value of the investment property for each day on which the investor's share is held for the purposes of the scheme.

(5) To the extent that an investor's rights are represented by rights under a linked long-term contract to which regulations 6(1)(b) and 8 apply, the value of those rights may be reduced by the making of deductions from those rights no greater than, at the choice of the manager—

(a) the relevant percentage of the value of the investor's rights under the contract; or

(b) the proportion attributable to the investor's rights of the relevant percentage of the value of the underlying fund for each day on which the investor has rights under the contract.

(6) When calculating the value of the rights of an investor for the purposes of paragraphs (3) to (5) above, where the manager has specified under paragraph (7) that such rights are to be valued weekly or monthly—

(a) where such rights are to be valued weekly, they are to be valued on such day of the week ("the specified day") as has been so specified by the manager (except that, where that day is not a working day, the rights are to be valued on the next working day), and the value of the rights on each subsequent day prior to the next specified day is to be taken to be the value of the rights on the previous specified day; and

(b) where the rights are to be valued monthly, they are to be valued on such date in each month ("the specified date") as has been so specified by the manager (except that, where that date is not a working day, the rights are to be valued on the next working day), and the value of the rights on each subsequent day prior to the next specified date is to be taken to be the value of the rights on the previous specified date.

(7) For the purposes of paragraph (3) to (5)—

(a) the frequency, which must be daily, weekly or monthly, with which rights are to be valued; and

(b) where valuation is to take place weekly or monthly, the day of the week or, as the case may be, the date in the month on which it is to take place,

must be specified in writing by the manager; and the specification may not be amended during the period of 12 months after the date on which it is made.

(8) For the purposes of paragraphs (3) to (5), "the relevant percentage" means—

(a) during the period of 10 years beginning with the day on which the first contribution is made by the investor to the investment scheme or linked long-term contract (as the case may be), 3/730 per cent;

(b) otherwise 1/365 per cent.

(9) The value of the investment property may be reduced—

(a) where any stamp duty, stamp duty reserve tax, value added tax or other charge (including any dilution levy) are incurred by the manager directly or indirectly in or consequent upon the sale or purchase of investments held for the purposes of the investment scheme, by the amount of those charges;

(b) where any amount of tax is paid or anticipated to be payable in respect of income received or capital gains realised by the manager in respect of investments held for the purposes of the investment scheme, by the amount so deducted or anticipated;

(c) where any charges or expenses are incurred by the manager directly or indirectly in maintaining or repairing any land or building in which the investment property is invested or in connection with the collection of rent, service charge or other sum due under the terms of a lease from occupiers of any land or building in which the investment property is invested, by the amount of those charges or expenses;

(d) where any charges or expenses are incurred by the manager directly or indirectly in complying with an order of the court or any similar requirements imposed by law, by the amount of those charges or expenses;

(e) to the extent that the manager incurs any expenses in complying with a requirement—

(i) to arrange for the investor to receive a copy of the annual report and accounts issued to investors by any company, unit trust, open-ended investment company or other entity in which the investment scheme is invested directly or indirectly ("the relevant entities"), or

(ii) to arrange for the investor to attend, vote or receive any other information issued to investors by the relevant entities,

by the amount of such of those expenses; and

(f) in respect of a linked long-term contract referred to in regulation 6 which is subject to smoothing, by the amount of the charges or expenses incurred by the manager in providing funds to smooth investment returns but only when the provision of such funds is in accordance with the manager's stated policy on smoothing.

(10) Where the value of the investment property is reduced by reference to an amount of charges or expenses referred to in paragraph (9), then, for the purposes of calculating any reduction in the investor's rights under paragraphs (3), (4) or (5), the value of those rights is to be calculated after the deductions of any such amount.

(11) Where an investment scheme is brought to an end by a manager and the investor takes up a transfer facility to another investment scheme, the relevant percentage for the purposes of paragraphs (3) to (5) shall be the same as that which would have been applied under or in respect of the original investment scheme as if the original investment scheme were continuing, notwithstanding any rules of the new investment scheme.

FINANCIAL SERVICES AND MARKETS ACT 2000 (FINANCIAL PROMOTION) ORDER 2005

(SI 2005/1529)

NOTES

Made: 8 June 2005.
Authority: Financial Services and Markets Act 2000, ss 21(5), (6), (9), (10), 428(3), Sch 2, para 25.
Commencement: 1 July 2005.

PART I
CITATION, COMMENCEMENT AND INTERPRETATION

1 Citation and commencement [966]
2 Interpretation: general [967]

PART II
CONTROLLED ACTIVITIES AND CONTROLLED INVESTMENTS

4 Definition of controlled activities and controlled investments [968]

PART III
EXEMPTIONS: INTERPRETATION AND APPLICATION

5 Interpretation: financial promotion restriction [969]
6 Interpretation: communications [970]
7 Interpretation: real time communications [971]
8 Interpretation: solicited and unsolicited real time communications [972]
8A Interpretation: outgoing electronic commerce communications [973]
9 Degree of prominence to be given to required indications [974]
10 Application to qualifying contracts of insurance [975]
11 Combination of different exemptions [976]

PART IV
EXEMPT COMMUNICATIONS: ALL CONTROLLED ACTIVITIES

12 Communications to overseas recipients [977]
13 Communications from customers and potential customers [978]
14 Follow up non-real time communications and solicited real time communications [979]
15 Introductions [980]
16 Exempt persons [981]
17 Generic promotions [982]
17A Communications caused to be made or directed by unauthorised persons [983]
18 Mere conduits [984]
18A Electronic commerce communications: mere conduits, caching and hosting [985]
19 Investment professionals [986]
20 Communications by journalists [987]
20A Promotion broadcast by company director etc [988]
20B Incoming electronic commerce communications [989]

PART V
EXEMPT COMMUNICATIONS: DEPOSITS AND INSURANCE

21 Interpretation: relevant insurance activity [990]
24 Relevant insurance activity: non-real time communications [991]
25 Relevant insurance activity: non-real time communications: reinsurance and large risks [992]
26 Relevant insurance activity: real time communication [993]

PART VI
EXEMPT COMMUNICATIONS: CERTAIN CONTROLLED ACTIVITIES

27 Application of exemptions in this Part [994]
28 One off non-real time communications and solicited real time communications [995]
28A One off unsolicited real time communications [996]
28B Real time communications: introductions [997]
29 Communications required or authorised by enactments [998]
30 Overseas communicators: solicited real time communications [999]
31 Overseas communicators: non-real time communications to previously overseas customers [1000]
32 Overseas communicators: unsolicited real time communications to previously overseas customers [1001]
33 Overseas communicators: unsolicited real time communications to knowledgeable customers [1002]
34 Governments, central banks etc [1003]
35 Industrial and provident societies [1004]
36 Nationals of EEA States other than United Kingdom [1005]
37 Financial markets [1006]
38 Persons in the business of placing promotional material [1007]
39 Joint enterprises [1008]

45 Group companies [1009]
47 Persons in the business of disseminating information [1010]
48 Certified high net worth individuals [1011]
49 High net worth companies, unincorporated associations etc [1012]
50 Sophisticated investors [1013]
50A Self-certified sophisticated investors [1014]
51 Associations of high net worth or sophisticated investors [1015]
52 Common interest group of a company [1016]
57 Persons placing promotional material in particular publications [1017]
61 Sale of goods and supply of services [1018]
72 Pension products offered by employers [1019]
73 Advice centres [1020]

SCHEDULES:

Schedule 1
Part I—Controlled Activities [1021]
Part II—Controlled Investments [1022]
Schedule 2—Countries and Territories [1023]
Schedule 5—Statements for Certified High Net Worth Individuals and Self-Certified Sophisticated Investors
Part I—Statement for Certified High Net Worth Individuals [1024]
Part II—Statement for Self-Certified Sophisticated Investors [1025]

PART I
CITATION, COMMENCEMENT AND INTERPRETATION

[966]
1 Citation and commencement

This Order may be cited as the Financial Services and Markets Act 2000 (Financial Promotion) Order 2005 and comes into force on 1st July 2005.

NOTES
Commencement: 1 July 2005.

[967]
2 Interpretation: general

(1) In this Order, except where the context otherwise requires—

"the 1985 Act" means the Companies Act 1985;

"the 1986 Order" means the Companies (Northern Ireland) Order 1986;

"the Act" means the Financial Services and Markets Act 2000;

"close relative" in relation to a person means—

(a) his spouse [or civil partner];

(b) his children and step-children, his parents and step-parents, his brothers and sisters and his step-brothers and step-sisters; and

(c) the spouse [or civil partner] of any person within sub-paragraph (b);

"controlled activity" has the meaning given by article 4 and Schedule 1;

"controlled investment" has the meaning given by article 4 and Schedule 1;

"deposit" means a sum of money which is a deposit for the purposes of article 5 of the Regulated Activities Order;

"equity share capital" has the meaning given in the 1985 Act or in the 1986 Order;

"financial promotion restriction" has the meaning given by article 5;

"government" means the government of the United Kingdom, the Scottish Administration, the Executive Committee of the Northern Ireland Assembly, the National Assembly for Wales and any government of any country or territory outside the United Kingdom;

"instrument" includes any record whether or not in the form of a document;

"international organisation" means any body the members of which comprise—

(a) states including the United Kingdom or another EEA State; or

(b) bodies whose members comprise states including the United Kingdom or another EEA State;

"overseas communicator" has the meaning given by article 30;

"previously overseas customer" has the meaning given by article 31;

"publication" means—

(a) a newspaper, journal, magazine or other periodical publication;

(b) a web site or similar system for the electronic display of information;

(c) any programme forming part of a service consisting of the broadcast or transmission of television or radio programmes;

(d) any teletext service, that—is to say a service consisting of television transmissions consisting of a succession of visual displays (with or without accompanying sound) capable of being selected and held for separate viewing or other use;

"qualifying contract of insurance" has the meaning given in the Regulated Activities Order;

"qualifying credit" has the meaning given by paragraph 10 of Schedule 1;

"the Regulated Activities Order" means the Financial Services and Markets Act 2000 (Regulated Activities) Order 2001;

"relevant insurance activity" has the meaning given by article 21;

"relevant investment activities" has the meaning given by article 30;

"solicited real time communication" has the meaning given by article 8;

"units", in a collective investment scheme, has the meaning given by Part XVII of the Act;

"unsolicited real time communication" has the meaning given by article 8.

(2) References to a person engaging in investment activity are to be construed in accordance with subsection (8) of section 21 of the Act; and for these purposes, "controlled activity" and "controlled investment" in that subsection have the meaning given in this Order.

NOTES

Commencement: 1 July 2005.

Para (1): words in square brackets in definition "close relative" inserted by the Financial Services and Markets Act 2000 (Financial Promotion) (Amendment) Order 2005, SI 2005/3392, art 2(1), (2).

3 (*Outside the scope of this work.*)

PART II
CONTROLLED ACTIVITIES AND CONTROLLED INVESTMENTS

[968]

4 Definition of controlled activities and controlled investments

(1) For the purposes of section 21(9) of the Act, a controlled activity is an activity which falls within any of paragraphs 1 to 11 of Schedule 1.

(2) For the purposes of section 21(10) of the Act, a controlled investment is an investment which falls within any of paragraphs 12 to 27 of Schedule 1.

NOTES

Commencement: 1 July 2005.

PART III
EXEMPTIONS: INTERPRETATION AND APPLICATION

[969]

5 Interpretation: financial promotion restriction

In this Order, any reference to the financial promotion restriction is a reference to the restriction in section 21(1) of the Act.

NOTES

Commencement: 1 July 2005.

[970]

6 Interpretation: communications

In this Order—

(a) any reference to a communication is a reference to the communication, in the course of business, of an invitation or inducement to engage in investment activity;

(b) any reference to a communication being made to another person is a reference to a communication being addressed, whether orally or in legible form, to a particular person or persons (for example where it is contained in a telephone call or letter);

(c) any reference to a communication being directed at persons is a reference to a communication being addressed to persons generally (for example where it is contained in a television broadcast or web site);

(d) "communicate" includes causing a communication to be made or directed;

(e) a "recipient" of a communication is the person to whom the communication is made or, in the case of a non-real time communication which is directed at persons generally, any person who reads or hears the communication;

(f) "electronic commerce communication" means a communication, the making of which constitutes the provision of an information society service;
(g) "incoming electronic commerce communication" means an electronic commerce communication made from an establishment in an EEA State other than the United Kingdom;
(h) "outgoing electronic commerce communication" means an electronic commerce communication made from an establishment in the United Kingdom to a person in an EEA State other than the United Kingdom.

NOTES
Commencement: 1 July 2005.

[971]
7 Interpretation: real time communications
(1) In this Order, references to a real time communication are references to any communication made in the course of a personal visit, telephone conversation or other interactive dialogue.
(2) A non-real time communication is a communication not falling within paragraph (1).
(3) For the purposes of this Order, non-real time communications include communications made by letter or e-mail or contained in a publication.
(4) For the purposes of this Order, the factors in paragraph (5) are to be treated as indications that a communication is a non-real time communication.
(5) The factors are that—
(a) the communication is made to or directed at more than one recipient in identical terms (save for details of the recipient's identity);
(b) the communication is made or directed by way of a system which in the normal course constitutes or creates a record of the communication which is available to the recipient to refer to at a later time;
(c) the communication is made or directed by way of a system which in the normal course does not enable or require the recipient to respond immediately to it.

NOTES
Commencement: 1 July 2005.

[972]
8 Interpretation: solicited and unsolicited real time communications
(1) A real time communication is solicited where it is made in the course of a personal visit, telephone call or other interactive dialogue if that call, visit or dialogue—
(a) was initiated by the recipient of the communication; or
(b) takes place in response to an express request from the recipient of the communication.
(2) A real time communication is unsolicited where it is made otherwise than as described in paragraph (1).
(3) For the purposes of paragraph (1)—
(a) a person is not to be treated as expressly requesting a call, visit or dialogue—
(i) because he omits to indicate that he does not wish to receive any or any further visits or calls or to engage in any or any further dialogue;
(ii) because he agrees to standard terms that state that such visits, calls or dialogue will take place, unless he has signified clearly that, in addition to agreeing to the terms, he is willing for them to take place;
(b) a communication is solicited only if it is clear from all the circumstances when the call, visit or dialogue is initiated or requested that during the course of the visit, call or dialogue communications will be made concerning the kind of controlled activities or investments to which the communications in fact made relate;
(c) it is immaterial whether the express request was made before or after this article comes into force.
(4) Where a real time communication is solicited by a recipient ("R"), it is treated as having also been solicited by any other person to whom it is made at the same time as it is made to R if that other recipient is—
(a) a close relative of R; or
(b) expected to engage in any investment activity jointly with R.

NOTES
Commencement: 1 July 2005.

[973]

8A Interpretation: outgoing electronic commerce communications

(1) For the purposes of the application of those articles to outgoing electronic commerce communications—

(a) any reference in article 48(7)(c), 50(1)(a) or (3)(e) or 52(3)(c) to an authorised person includes a reference to a person who is entitled, under the law of an EEA State other than the United Kingdom, to carry on regulated activities in that State;

(b) any reference in article 68(1) or 71 to rules or legislation includes a reference to provisions corresponding to those rules or legislation in the law of an EEA State other than the United Kingdom;

(c) any reference in article 49 to an amount in pounds sterling includes a reference to an equivalent amount in another currency.

(2) For the purposes of the application of article 49 to outgoing electronic commerce communications, any reference in section 264(2) or 737 of the 1985 Act (or the equivalent provisions in the 1986 Order) to a body corporate or company includes a reference to a body corporate or company registered under the law of an EEA State other than the United Kingdom.

(3) For the purposes of the application of article 3 in respect of outgoing electronic commerce communications—

(a) any reference in section 163(2)(b) of the 1985 Act (or the equivalent provision in the 1986 Order) to a company includes a reference to a company registered under the law of an EEA State other than the United Kingdom;

(b) any reference in that section to an investment exchange includes a reference to an investment exchange which is recognised as an investment exchange under the law of an EEA State other than the United Kingdom.

NOTES

Commencement: 1 July 2005.

[974]

9 Degree of prominence to be given to required indications

Where a communication must, if it is to fall within any provision of this Order, be accompanied by an indication of any matter, the indication must be presented to the recipient—

(a) in a way that can be easily understood; and

(b) in such manner as, depending on the means by which the communication is made or directed, is best calculated to bring the matter in question to the attention of the recipient and to allow him to consider it.

NOTES

Commencement: 1 July 2005.

[975]

10 Application to qualifying contracts of insurance

(1) Nothing in this Order exempts from the application of the financial promotion restriction a communication which invites or induces a person to enter into a qualifying contract of insurance with a person who is not—

(a) an authorised person;

(b) an exempt person who is exempt in relation to effecting or carrying out contracts of insurance of the class to which the communication relates;

(c) a company which has its head office in an EEA State other than the United Kingdom and which is entitled under the law of that State to carry on there insurance business of the class to which the communication relates;

(d) a company which has a branch or agency in an EEA State other than the United Kingdom and is entitled under the law of that State to carry on there insurance business of the class to which the communication relates;

(e) a company authorised to carry on insurance business of the class to which the communication relates in any country or territory which is listed in Schedule 2.

(2) In this article, references to a class of insurance are references to the class of insurance contract described in Schedule 1 to the Regulated Activities Order into which the effecting or carrying out of the contract to which the communication relates would fall.

NOTES

Commencement: 1 July 2005.

[976]

11 Combination of different exemptions

(1) In respect of a communication relating to—

(a) a controlled activity falling within paragraph 2 of Schedule 1 carried on in relation to a qualifying contract of insurance; or

(b) a controlled activity falling within any of paragraphs 3 to 11 of Schedule 1,

a person may rely on the application of one or more of the exemptions in Parts IV and VI.

(2) In respect of a communication relating to—

(a) an activity falling within paragraph 1 of Schedule 1; or

(b) a relevant insurance activity,

a person may rely on one or more of the exemptions in Parts IV and V; and, where a communication relates to any such activity and also to an activity mentioned in paragraph (1)(a) or (b), a person may rely on one or more of the exemptions in Parts IV and V in respect of the former activity and on one or more of the exemptions in Parts V and VI in respect of the latter activity.

NOTES

Commencement: 1 July 2005.

PART IV
EXEMPT COMMUNICATIONS: ALL CONTROLLED ACTIVITIES

[977]

12 Communications to overseas recipients

(1) Subject to paragraphs (2) and (7), the financial promotion restriction does not apply to any communication—

(a) which is made (whether from inside or outside the United Kingdom) to a person who receives the communication outside the United Kingdom; or

(b) which is directed (whether from inside or outside the United Kingdom) only at persons outside the United Kingdom.

(2) Paragraph (1) does not apply to an unsolicited real time communication unless—

(a) it is made from a place outside the United Kingdom; and

(b) it is made for the purposes of a business which is carried on outside the United Kingdom and which is not carried on in the United Kingdom.

(3) For the purposes of paragraph (1)(b)—

(a) if the conditions set out in paragraph (4)(a), (b), (c) and (d) are met, a communication directed from a place inside the United Kingdom is to be regarded as directed only at persons outside the United Kingdom;

(b) if the conditions set out in paragraph (4)(c) and (d) are met, a communication directed from a place outside the United Kingdom is to be regarded as directed only at persons outside the United Kingdom;

(c) in any other case where one or more of the conditions in paragraph (4)(a) to (e) are met, that fact is to be taken into account in determining whether or not a communication is to be regarded as directed only at persons outside the United Kingdom (but a communication may still be regarded as directed only at persons outside the United Kingdom even if none of the conditions in paragraph (4) is met).

(4) The conditions are that—

(a) the communication is accompanied by an indication that it is directed only at persons outside the United Kingdom;

(b) the communication is accompanied by an indication that it must not be acted upon by persons in the United Kingdom;

(c) the communication is not referred to in, or directly accessible from, any other communication made to a person or directed at persons in the United Kingdom by the person directing the communication;

(d) there are in place proper systems and procedures to prevent recipients in the United Kingdom (other than those to whom the communication might otherwise lawfully have been made by the person directing it or a member of the same group) engaging in the investment activity to which the communication relates with the person directing the communication, a close relative of his or a member of the same group;

(e) the communication is included in—

(i) a web site, newspaper, journal, magazine or periodical publication which is principally accessed in or intended for a market outside the United Kingdom;

(ii) a radio or television broadcast or teletext service transmitted principally for reception outside the United Kingdom.

(5) For the purpose of paragraph (1)(b), a communication may be treated as directed only at persons outside the United Kingdom even if—

(a) it is also directed, for the purposes of article 19(1)(b), at investment professionals falling within article 19(5) (but disregarding paragraph (6) of that article for this purpose);

(b) it is also directed, for the purposes of article 49(1)(b), at high net worth persons to whom article 49 applies (but disregarding paragraph (2)(e) of that article for this purpose) and it relates to a controlled activity to which article 49 applies;

(c) it is a communication to which article 31 applies.

(6) Where a communication falls within paragraph (5)(a) or (b)—

(a) the condition in paragraph (4)(a) is to be construed as requiring an indication that the communication is directed only at persons outside the United Kingdom or persons having professional experience in matters relating to investments or high net worth persons (as the case may be);

(b) the condition in paragraph (4)(b) is to be construed as requiring an indication that the communication must not be acted upon by persons in the United Kingdom except by persons who have professional experience in matters relating to investments or who are not high net worth persons (as the case may be);

(c) the condition in paragraph (4)(c) will not apply where the other communication referred to in that paragraph is made to a person or directed at a person in the United Kingdom to whom paragraph (5) applies.

(7) Paragraph (1) does not apply to an outgoing electronic commerce communication.

[978]

13 Communications from customers and potential customers

(1) The financial promotion restriction does not apply to any communication made by or on behalf of a person ("customer") to one other person ("supplier")—

(a) in order to obtain information about a controlled investment available from or a controlled service provided by the supplier; or

(b) in order that the customer can acquire a controlled investment from that supplier or be supplied with a controlled service by that supplier.

(2) For the purposes of paragraph (1), a controlled service is a service the provision of which constitutes engaging in a controlled activity by the supplier.

NOTES

Commencement: 1 July 2005.

[979]

14 Follow up non-real time communications and solicited real time communications

(1) Where a person makes or directs a communication ("the first communication") which is exempt from the financial promotion restriction because, in compliance with the requirements of another provision of this Order, it is accompanied by certain indications or contains certain information, then the financial promotion restriction does not apply to any subsequent communication which complies with the requirements of paragraph (2).

(2) The requirements of this paragraph are that the subsequent communication—

(a) is a non-real time communication or a solicited real time communication;

(b) is made by, or on behalf of, the same person who made the first communication;

(c) is made to a recipient of the first communication;

(d) relates to the same controlled activity and the same controlled investment as the first communication; and

(e) is made within 12 months of the recipient receiving the first communication.

(3) The provisions of this article only apply in the case of a person who makes or directs a communication on behalf of another where the first communication is made by that other person.

(4) Where a person makes or directs a communication on behalf of another person in reliance on the exemption contained in this article the person on whose behalf the communication was made or directed remains responsible for the content of that communication.

(5) A communication made or directed before this article comes into force is to be treated as a first communication falling within paragraph (1) if it would have fallen within that paragraph had it been made or directed after this article comes into force.

NOTES

Commencement: 1 July 2005.

[980]

15 Introductions

(1) If the requirements of paragraph (2) are met, the financial promotion restriction does not apply to any communication which is made with a view to or for the purposes of introducing the recipient to—

(a) an authorised person who carries on the controlled activity to which the communication relates; or

(b) an exempt person where the communication relates to a controlled activity which is also a regulated activity in relation to which he is an exempt person.

(2) The requirements of this paragraph are that—

(a) the maker of the communication ("A") is not a close relative of, nor a member of the same group as, the person to whom the introduction is, or is to be, made;

(b) A does not receive from any person other than the recipient any pecuniary reward or other advantage arising out of his making the introduction; and

(c) it is clear in all the circumstances that the recipient, in his capacity as an investor, is not seeking and has not sought advice from A as to the merits of the recipient engaging in investment activity (or, if the client has sought such advice, A has declined to give it, but has recommended that the recipient seek such advice from an authorised person).

NOTES

Commencement: 1 July 2005.

[981]

16 Exempt persons

(1) The financial promotion restriction does not apply to any communication which—

(a) is a non-real time communication or a solicited real time communication;

(b) is made or directed by an exempt person; and

(c) is for the purposes of that exempt person's business of carrying on a controlled activity which is also a regulated activity in relation to which he is an exempt person.

(2) The financial promotion restriction does not apply to any unsolicited real time communication made by a person ("AR") who is an appointed representative (within the meaning of section 39(2) of the Act) where—

(a) the communication is made by AR in carrying on the business—

(i) for which his principal ("P") has accepted responsibility for the purposes of section 39 of the Act; and

(ii) in relation to which AR is exempt from the general prohibition by virtue of that section; and

(b) the communication is one which, if it were made by P, would comply with any rules made by the Authority under section 145 of the Act (financial promotion rules) which are relevant to a communication of that kind.

NOTES

Commencement: 1 July 2005.

[982]

17 Generic promotions

The financial promotion restriction does not apply to any communication which—

(a) does not identify (directly or indirectly) a person who provides the controlled investment to which the communication relates; and

(b) does not identify (directly or indirectly) any person as a person who carries on a controlled activity in relation to that investment.

NOTES

Commencement: 1 July 2005.

[983]

17A Communications caused to be made or directed by unauthorised persons

(1) If a condition in paragraph (2) is met, the financial promotion restriction does not apply to a communication caused to be made or directed by an unauthorised person which is made or directed by an authorised person.

(2) The conditions in this paragraph are that—

(a) the authorised person prepared the content of the communication; or

(b) it is a real-time communication.

NOTES

Commencement: 1 July 2005.

[984]

18 Mere conduits

(1) Subject to paragraph (4), the financial promotion restriction does not apply to any communication which is made or directed by a person who acts as a mere conduit for it.

(2) A person acts as a mere conduit for a communication if—

(a) he communicates it in the course of an activity carried on by him, the principal purpose of which is transmitting or receiving material provided to him by others;

(b) the content of the communication is wholly devised by another person; and

(c) the nature of the service provided by him in relation to the communication is such that he does not select, modify or otherwise exercise control over its content prior to its transmission or receipt.

(3) For the purposes of paragraph (2)(c) a person does not select, modify or otherwise exercise control over the content of a communication merely by removing or having the power to remove material—

(a) which is, or is alleged to be, illegal, defamatory or in breach of copyright;

(b) in response to a request to a body which is empowered by or under any enactment to make such a request; or

(c) when otherwise required to do so by law.

(4) Nothing in paragraph (1) prevents the application of the financial promotion restriction in so far as it relates to the person who has caused the communication to be made or directed.

(5) This article does not apply to an electronic commerce communication.

NOTES

Commencement: 1 July 2005.

[985]

18A Electronic commerce communications: mere conduits, caching and hosting

The financial promotion restriction does not apply to an electronic commerce communication in circumstances where—

(a) the making of the communication constitutes the provision of an information society service of a kind falling within paragraph 1 of Article 12, 13 or 14 of the electronic commerce directive ("mere conduit", "caching" and "hosting"); and

(b) the conditions mentioned in the paragraph in question, to the extent that they are applicable at the time of, or prior to, the making of the communication, are or have been met at that time.

NOTES

Commencement: 1 July 2005.

[986]

19 Investment professionals

(1) The financial promotion restriction does not apply to any communication which—

(a) is made only to recipients whom the person making the communication believes on reasonable grounds to be investment professionals; or

(b) may reasonably be regarded as directed only at such recipients.

(2) For the purposes of paragraph (1)(b), if all the conditions set out in paragraph (4)(a) to (c) are met in relation to the communication, it is to be regarded as directed only at investment professionals.

(3) In any other case in which one or more of the conditions set out in paragraph (4)(a) to (c) are met, that fact is to be taken into account in determining whether the communication is directed only at investment professionals (but a communication may still be regarded as so directed even if none of the conditions in paragraph (4) is met).

(4) The conditions are that—

(a) the communication is accompanied by an indication that it is directed at persons having professional experience in matters relating to investments and that any investment or investment activity to which it relates is available only to such persons or will be engaged in only with such persons;

(b) the communication is accompanied by an indication that persons who do not have professional experience in matters relating to investments should not rely on it;

(c) there are in place proper systems and procedures to prevent recipients other than investment professionals engaging in the investment activity to which the communication relates with the person directing the communication, a close relative of his or a member of the same group.

(5) "Investment professionals" means—

(a) an authorised person;

(b) an exempt person where the communication relates to a controlled activity which is a regulated activity in relation to which the person is exempt;

(c) any other person—

(i) whose ordinary activities involve him in carrying on the controlled activity to which the communication relates for the purpose of a business carried on by him; or

(ii) who it is reasonable to expect will carry on such activity for the purposes of a business carried on by him;

(d) a government, local authority (whether in the United Kingdom or elsewhere) or an international organisation;

(e) a person ("A") who is a director, officer or employee of a person ("B") falling within any of sub-paragraphs (a) to (d) where the communication is made to A in that capacity and where A's responsibilities when acting in that capacity involve him in the carrying on by B of controlled activities.

(6) For the purposes of paragraph (1), a communication may be treated as made only to or directed only at investment professionals even if it is also made to or directed at other persons to whom it may lawfully be communicated.

NOTES

Commencement: 1 July 2005.

[987]

20 Communications by journalists

(1) Subject to paragraph (2), the financial promotion restriction does not apply to any non-real time communication if—

(a) the content of the communication is devised by a person acting in the capacity of a journalist;

(b) the communication is contained in a qualifying publication; and

(c) in the case of a communication requiring disclosure, one of the conditions in paragraph (2) is met.

(2) The conditions in this paragraph are that—

(a) the communication is accompanied by an indication explaining the nature of the author's financial interest or that of a member of his family (as the case may be);

(b) the authors are subject to proper systems and procedures which prevent the publication of communications requiring disclosure without the explanation referred to in sub-paragraph (a); or

(c) the qualifying publication in which the communication appears falls within the remit of—

(i) the Code of Practice issued by the Press Complaints Commission;

(ii) the OFCOM Broadcasting Code; or

(iii) the Producers' Guidelines issued by the British Broadcasting Corporation.

(3) For the purposes of this article, a communication requires disclosure if—

(a) an author of the communication or a member of his family is likely to obtain a financial benefit or avoid a financial loss if people act in accordance with the invitation or inducement contained in the communication;

(b) the communication relates to a controlled investment of a kind falling within paragraph (4); and

(c) the communication identifies directly a person who issues or provides the controlled investment to which the communication relates.

(4) A controlled investment falls within this paragraph if it is—

(a) an investment falling within paragraph 14 of Schedule 1 (shares or stock in share capital);

(b) an investment falling within paragraph 21 of that Schedule (options) to acquire or dispose of an investment falling within sub-paragraph (a);

(c) an investment falling within paragraph 22 of that Schedule (futures) being rights under a contract for the sale of an investment falling within sub-paragraph (a); or

(d) an investment falling within paragraph 23 of that Schedule (contracts for differences etc) being rights under a contract relating to, or to fluctuations in, the value or price of an investment falling within sub-paragraph (a).

(5) For the purposes of this article—

(a) the authors of the communication are the person who devises the content of the communication and the person who is responsible for deciding to include the communication in the qualifying publication;

(b) a "qualifying publication" is a publication or service of the kind mentioned in paragraph (1) or (2) of article 54 of the Regulated Activities Order and which is of the nature described in that article, and for the purposes of this article, a certificate given under paragraph (3) of article 54 of that Order and not revoked is conclusive evidence of the matters certified;

(c) the members of a person's family are his spouse [or civil partner] and any children of his under the age of 18 years.

NOTES

Commencement: 1 July 2005.

Para (5): words in square brackets in sub-para (c) inserted by the Financial Services and Markets Act 2000 (Financial Promotion) (Amendment) Order 2005, SI 2005/3392, art 2(1), (3).

[988]

20A Promotion broadcast by company director etc

(1) The financial promotion restriction does not apply to a communication which is communicated as part of a qualifying service by a person ("D") who is a director or employee of an undertaking ("U") where—

(a) the communication invites or induces the recipient to acquire—

(i) a controlled investment of the kind falling within article 20(4) which is issued by U (or by an undertaking in the same group as U); or

(ii) a controlled investment issued or provided by an authorised person in the same group as U;

(b) the communication—

(i) comprises words which are spoken by D and not broadcast, transmitted or displayed in writing; or

(ii) is displayed in writing only because it forms part of an interactive dialogue to which D is a party and in the course of which D is expected to respond immediately to questions put by a recipient of the communication;

(c) the communication is not part of an organised marketing campaign; and

(d) the communication is accompanied by an indication that D is a director or employee (as the case may be) of U.

(2) For the purposes of this article, a "qualifying service" is a service—

(a) which is broadcast or transmitted in the form of television or radio programmes; or

(b) displayed on a web site (or similar system for the electronic display of information) comprising regularly updated news and information,

provided that the principal purpose of the service, taken as a whole and including any advertisements and other promotional material contained in it, is neither of the purposes described in article 54(1)(a) or (b) of the Regulated Activities Order.

(3) For the purposes of paragraph (2), a certificate given under article 54(3) of the Regulated Activities Order and not revoked is conclusive evidence of the matters certified.

NOTES

Commencement: 1 July 2005.

[989]

20B Incoming electronic commerce communications

(1) The financial promotion restriction does not apply to an incoming electronic commerce communication.

(2) Paragraph (1) does not apply to—

(a) a communication which constitutes an advertisement by the operator of a UCITS directive scheme of units in that scheme;

(b) a communication consisting of an invitation or inducement to enter into a contract of insurance, where—

(i) the communication is made by an undertaking which has received official authorisation in accordance with Article 4 of the life assurance consolidation directive or the first non-life insurance directive, and

(ii) the insurance falls within the scope of any of the insurance directives; or

(c) an unsolicited communication made by electronic mail.

(3) In this article, "UCITS directive scheme" means an undertaking for collective investment in transferable securities which is subject to Directive 85/611/EEC of the Council of the European Communities of 20 December 1985 on the co-ordination of laws, regulations and administrative provisions relating to undertakings for collective investment in transferable securities, and has been authorised in accordance with Article 4 of that Directive.

(4) For the purposes of this article, a communication by electronic mail is to be regarded as unsolicited, unless it is made in response to an express request from the recipient of the communication.

NOTES

Commencement: 1 July 2005.
Directive 85/611/EEC: OJ L375, 31.12.85, p 3.

PART V
EXEMPT COMMUNICATIONS: DEPOSITS AND INSURANCE

[990]

21 Interpretation: relevant insurance activity

In this Part, a "relevant insurance activity" means a controlled activity falling within paragraph 2 of Schedule 1 carried on in relation to an investment falling within paragraph 13 of that Schedule where that investment is not a qualifying contract of insurance.

NOTES

Commencement: 1 July 2005.

22, 23 (*Outside the scope of this work.*)

[991]

24 Relevant insurance activity: non-real time communications

(1) If the requirements of paragraph (2) are met, the financial promotion restriction does not apply to any non-real time communication which relates to a relevant insurance activity.

(2) The requirements of this paragraph are that the communication is accompanied by an indication—

(a) of the full name of the person with whom the investment which is the subject of the communication is to be made ("the insurer");

(b) of the country or territory in which the insurer is incorporated (described as such);

(c) if different, of the country or territory in which the insurer's principal place of business is situated (described as such);

(d) whether or not the insurer is regulated in respect of its insurance business;

(e) if the insurer is so regulated, of the name of the regulator of the insurer in its principal place of business or, if there is more than one such regulator, the name of the prudential regulator;

(f) whether any transaction to which the communication relates would, if entered into by the recipient and the insurer, fall within the jurisdiction of any dispute resolution scheme or compensation scheme and if so, identifying each such scheme.

(3) In this article "full name", in relation to a person, means the name under which that person carries on business and, if different, that person's corporate name.

NOTES

Commencement: 1 July 2005.

[992]

25 Relevant insurance activity: non-real time communications: reinsurance and large risks

(1) The financial promotion restriction does not apply to any non-real time communication which relates to a relevant insurance activity and concerns only—

(a) a contract of reinsurance; or

(b) a contract that covers large risks.

(2) "Large risks" means—

(a) risks falling within paragraph 4 (railway rolling stock), 5 (aircraft), 6 (ships), 7 (goods in transit), 11 (aircraft liability) or 12 (liability of ships) of Schedule 1 to the Regulated Activities Order;

(b) risks falling within paragraph 14 (credit) or 15 (suretyship) of that Schedule provided that the risks relate to a business carried on by the recipient;

(c) risks falling within paragraph 3 (land vehicles), 8 (fire and natural forces), 9 (damage to property), 10 (motor vehicle liability), 13 (general liability) or 16 (miscellaneous financial loss) of that Schedule provided that the risks relate to a business carried on by the recipient and that the condition specified in paragraph (3) is met in relation to that business.

(3) The condition specified in this paragraph is that at least two of the three following criteria were exceeded in the most recent financial year for which information is available prior to the making of the communication—

(a) the balance sheet total of the business (within the meaning of section 247(5) of the 1985 Act or article 255(5) of the 1986 Order) was 6.2 million euros;

(b) the net turnover (within the meaning given to "turnover" by section 262(1) of the 1985 Act or article 270(1) of the 1986 Order) was 12.8 million euros;

(c) the number of employees (within the meaning given by section 247(6) of the 1985 Act or article 255(6) of the 1986 Order) was 250;

and for a financial year which is a company's financial year but not in fact a year, the net turnover of the recipient shall be proportionately adjusted.

(4) For the purposes of paragraph (3), where the recipient is a member of a group for which consolidated accounts (within the meaning of the Seventh Company Law Directive) are drawn up, the question whether the condition met in that paragraph is met is to be determined by reference to those accounts.

NOTES

Commencement: 1 July 2005.

[993]

26 Relevant insurance activity: real time communication

The financial promotion restriction does not apply to any real time communication (whether solicited or unsolicited) which relates to a relevant insurance activity.

NOTES

Commencement: 1 July 2005.

PART VI
EXEMPT COMMUNICATIONS: CERTAIN CONTROLLED ACTIVITIES

[994]

27 Application of exemptions in this Part

Except where otherwise stated, the exemptions in this Part apply to communications which relate to—

(a) a controlled activity falling within paragraph 2 of Schedule 1 carried on in relation to a qualifying contract of insurance;

(b) controlled activities falling within any of paragraphs 3 to 11 of Schedule 1.

NOTES

Commencement: 1 July 2005.

[995]

28 One off non-real time communications and solicited real time communications

(1) The financial promotion restriction does not apply to a one off communication which is either a non-real time communication or a solicited real time communication.

(2) If all the conditions set out in paragraph (3) are met in relation to a communication it is to be regarded as a one off communication. In any other case in which one or more of those conditions are met, that fact is to be taken into account in determining whether the communication is a one off communication (but a communication may still be regarded as a one off communication even if none of the conditions in paragraph (3) is met).

(3) The conditions are that—

(a) the communication is made only to one recipient or only to one group of recipients in the expectation that they would engage in any investment activity jointly;

(b) the identity of the product or service to which the communication relates has been determined having regard to the particular circumstances of the recipient;

(c) the communication is not part of an organised marketing campaign.

NOTES

Commencement: 1 July 2005.

[996]

28A One off unsolicited real time communications

(1) The financial promotion restriction does not apply to an unsolicited real time communication if the conditions in paragraph (2) are met.

(2) The conditions in this paragraph are that—

(a) the communication is a one off communication;

(b) the communicator believes on reasonable grounds that the recipient understands the risks associated with engaging in the investment activity to which the communication relates;

(c) at the time that the communication is made, the communicator believes on reasonable grounds that the recipient would expect to be contacted by him in relation to the investment activity to which the communication relates.

(3) Paragraphs (2) and (3) of article 28 apply in determining whether a communication is a one off communication for the purposes of this article as they apply for the purposes of article 28.

NOTES

Commencement: 1 July 2005.

[997]

28B Real time communications: introductions . . .

(1) If the requirements of paragraph (2) are met, the financial promotion restriction does not apply to any real time communication which—

(a) relates to a controlled activity falling within [paragraph 10, 10A, 10B, 10C, 10D, 10E, 10F, *10G or 10H*] of Schedule 1; and

(b) is made for the purpose of, or with a view to, introducing the recipient to a person ("N") who is—

(i) an authorised person who carries on the controlled activity to which the communication relates,

(ii) an appointed representative, where the controlled activity to which the communication relates is also a regulated activity in respect of which he is exempt from the general prohibition, or

(iii) an overseas person who carries on the controlled activity to which the communication relates.

(2) The requirements of this paragraph are that the maker of the communication ("M")—

(a) does not receive any money, other than money payable to M on his own account, paid by the recipient for or in connection with any transaction which the recipient enters into with or through N as a result of the introduction; and

(b) before making the introduction, discloses to the recipient such of the information mentioned in paragraph (3) as applies to M.

(3) That information is—

(a) that M is a member of the same group as N;

(b) details of any payment which M will receive from N, by way of fee or commission, for introducing the recipient to N;

(c) an indication of any other reward or advantage received or to be received by M that arises out of his making introductions to N.

(4) In this article, "overseas person" means a person who carries on controlled activities which fall within paragraph 10, 10A or 10B of Schedule 1, but who does not carry on any such activity, or offer to do so, from a permanent place of business maintained by him in the United Kingdom.

NOTES

Commencement: 1 July 2005.

Heading: words omitted revoked by the Financial Services and Markets Act 2000 (Regulated Activities) (Amendment) (No 2) Order 2006, SI 2006/2383, art 35(1), (2), subject to transitional provisions in arts 37–39 thereof.

Para (1): words in square brackets substituted by SI 2006/2383, art 35(1), (3), subject to transitional provisions in arts 37–39 thereof; for the words in italics there are substituted the words "10G, 10H, 10I, 10J or 10K" by the Financial Services and Markets Act 2000 (Regulated Activities) (Amendment) Order 2009,

SI 2009/1342, art 30(1), (2), as from 1 July 2009 (certain purposes) and 30 June 2010 (remaining purposes) (for the full commencement details and for transitional provisions etc see arts 1, 32–34 of that Order).

[998]

29 Communications required or authorised by enactments

(1) Subject to paragraph (2), the financial promotion restriction does not apply to any communication which is required or authorised by or under any enactment other than the Act.

(2) This article does not apply to a communication which relates to a controlled activity falling within paragraph 10, 10A or 10B of Schedule 1 or within paragraph 11 in so far as it relates to that activity.

NOTES

Commencement: 1 July 2005.

[999]

30 Overseas communicators: solicited real time communications

(1) The financial promotion restriction does not apply to any solicited real time communication which is made by an overseas communicator from outside the United Kingdom in the course of or for the purposes of his carrying on the business of engaging in relevant investment activities outside the United Kingdom.

(2) In this article—

"overseas communicator" means a person who carries on relevant investment activities outside the United Kingdom but who does not carry on any such activity from a permanent place of business maintained by him in the United Kingdom;

"relevant investment activities" means controlled activities which fall within paragraphs 3 to 7 or 10 to 10B of Schedule 1 or, so far as relevant to any of those paragraphs, paragraph 11 of that Schedule.

NOTES

Commencement: 1 July 2005.

[1000]

31 Overseas communicators: non-real time communications to previously overseas customers

(1) The financial promotion restriction does not apply to any non-real time communication which is communicated by an overseas communicator from outside the United Kingdom to a previously overseas customer of his.

(2) In this article a "previously overseas customer" means a person with whom the overseas communicator has done business within the period of twelve months ending with the day on which the communication was received ("the earlier business") and where—

(a) at the time that the earlier business was done, the customer was neither resident in the United Kingdom nor had a place of business there; or

(b) at the time the earlier business was done, the overseas communicator had on a former occasion done business with the customer, being business of the same description as the business to which the communication relates, and on that former occasion the customer was neither resident in the United Kingdom nor had a place of business there.

(3) For the purposes of this article, an overseas communicator has done business with a customer if, in the course of carrying on his relevant investment activities outside the United Kingdom, he has—

(a) effected a transaction, or arranged for a transaction to be effected, with the customer;

(b) provided, outside the United Kingdom; a service to the customer as described in paragraph 6 of Schedule 1 (whether or not that paragraph was in force at the time the business was done); or

(c) given, outside the United Kingdom, any advice to the customer as described in paragraph 7 of that Schedule (whether or not that paragraph was in force at the time the business was done).

NOTES

Commencement: 1 July 2005.

[1001]

32 Overseas communicators: unsolicited real time communications to previously overseas customers

(1) If the requirements of paragraphs (2) and (3) are met, the financial promotion restriction does not apply to an unsolicited real time communication which is made by an overseas communicator from outside the United Kingdom to a previously overseas customer of his.

(2) The requirements of this paragraph are that the terms on which previous transactions and services had been effected or provided by the overseas communicator to the previously overseas customer were such that the customer would reasonably expect, at the time that the unsolicited real time communication is made, to be contacted by the overseas communicator in relation to the investment activity to which the communication relates.

(3) The requirements of this paragraph are that the previously overseas customer has been informed by the overseas communicator on an earlier occasion—

- (a) that the protections conferred by or under the Act will not apply to any unsolicited real time communication which is made by the overseas communicator and which relates to that investment activity;
- (b) that the protections conferred by or under the Act may not apply to any investment activity that may be engaged in as a result of the communication; and
- (c) whether any transaction between them resulting from the communication would fall within the jurisdiction of any dispute resolution scheme or compensation scheme or, if there is no such scheme, of that fact.

NOTES

Commencement: 1 July 2005.

[1002]

33 Overseas communicators: unsolicited real time communications to knowledgeable customers

(1) If the requirements of paragraphs (2), (3) and (4) are met, the financial promotion restriction does not apply to an unsolicited real time communication which is made by an overseas communicator from outside the United Kingdom in the course of his carrying on relevant investment activities outside the United Kingdom.

(2) The requirements of this paragraph are that the overseas communicator believes on reasonable grounds that the recipient is sufficiently knowledgeable to understand the risks associated with engaging in the investment activity to which the communication relates.

(3) The requirements of this paragraph are that, in relation to any particular investment activity, the recipient has been informed by the overseas communicator on an earlier occasion—

- (a) that the protections conferred by or under the Act will not apply to any unsolicited real time communication which is made by him and which relates to that activity;
- (b) that the protections conferred by or under the Act may not apply to any investment activity that may be engaged in as a result of the communication; and
- (c) whether any transaction between them resulting from the communication would fall within the jurisdiction of any dispute resolution scheme or compensation scheme or, if there is no such scheme, of that fact.

(4) The requirements of this paragraph are that the recipient, after being given a proper opportunity to consider the information given to him in accordance with paragraph (3), has clearly signified that he understands the warnings referred to in paragraph (3)(a) and (b) and that he accepts that he will not benefit from the protections referred to.

NOTES

Commencement: 1 July 2005.

[1003]

34 Governments, central banks etc

The financial promotion restriction does not apply to any communication which—

- (a) is a non-real time communication or a solicited real time communication;
- (b) is communicated by and relates only to controlled investments issued, or to be issued, by—
  - (i) any government;
  - (ii) any local authority (in the United Kingdom or elsewhere);
  - (iii) any international organisation;
  - (iv) the Bank of England;

(v) the European Central Bank;
(vi) the central bank of any country or territory outside the United Kingdom.

NOTES
Commencement: 1 July 2005.

[1004]
35 Industrial and provident societies

The financial promotion restriction does not apply to any communication which—
(a) is a non-real time communication or a solicited real time communication;
(b) is communicated by an industrial and provident society; and
(c) relates only to an investment falling within paragraph 15 [or 15A] of Schedule 1 issued, or to be issued, by the society in question.

NOTES
Commencement: 1 July 2005.
Words in square brackets inserted by the Financial Services and Markets Act 2000 (Regulated Activities) (Amendment) Order 2010, SI 2010/86, art 4, Schedule, para 9(b).

[1005]
36 Nationals of EEA States other than United Kingdom

The financial promotion restriction does not apply to any communication which—
(a) is a non-real time communication or a solicited real time communication;
(b) is communicated by a national of an EEA State other than the United Kingdom in the course of any controlled activity lawfully carried on by him in that State; and
(c) conforms with any rules made by the Authority under section 145 of the Act (financial promotion rules) which are relevant to a communication of that kind.

NOTES
Commencement: 1 July 2005.

[1006]
37 Financial markets

(1) The financial promotion restriction does not apply to any communication—
(a) which is a non-real time communication or a solicited real time communication;
(b) which is communicated by a relevant market; and
(c) to which paragraph (2) or (3) applies.
(2) This paragraph applies to a communication if—
(a) it relates only to facilities provided by the market; and
(b) it does not identify (directly or indirectly)—
(i) any particular investment issued, or to be issued, by or available from an identified person as one that may be traded or dealt in on the market; or
(ii) any particular person as a person through whom transactions on the market may be effected.
(3) This paragraph applies to a communication if—
(a) it relates only to a particular investment falling within paragraph 21, 22 or 23 of Schedule 1; and
(b) it identifies the investment as one that may be traded or dealt in on the market.
(4) "Relevant market" means a market which—
(a) meets the criteria specified in Part I of Schedule 3; or
(b) is specified in, or is established under the rules of an exchange specified in, Part II, III or IV of that Schedule.

NOTES
Commencement: 1 July 2005.

[1007]
38 Persons in the business of placing promotional material

The financial promotion restriction does not apply to any communication which is made to a person whose business it is to place, or arrange for the placing of, promotional material provided that it is communicated so that he can place or arrange for placing it.

NOTES
Commencement: 1 July 2005.

[1008]

39 Joint enterprises

(1) The financial promotion restriction does not apply to any communication which is made or directed by a participator in a joint enterprise to or at another participator in the same joint enterprise in connection with, or for the purposes of, that enterprise.

(2) "Joint enterprise" means an enterprise into which two or more persons ("the participators") enter for commercial purposes related to a business or businesses (other than the business of engaging in a controlled activity) carried on by them; and, where a participator is a member of a group, each other member of the group is also to be regarded as a participator in the enterprise.

(3) "Participator" includes potential participator.

NOTES

Commencement: 1 July 2005.

40–44 (*Outside the scope of this work.*)

[1009]

45 Group companies

The financial promotion restriction does not apply to any communication made by one body corporate in a group to another body corporate in the same group.

NOTES

Commencement: 1 July 2005.

46 (*Outside the scope of this work.*)

[1010]

47 Persons in the business of disseminating information

(1) The financial promotion restriction does not apply to any communication which is made only to recipients whom the person making the communication believes on reasonable grounds to be persons to whom paragraph (2) applies.

(2) This paragraph applies to—

(a) a person who receives the communication in the course of a business which involves the dissemination through a publication of information concerning controlled activities;

(b) a person whilst acting in the capacity of director, officer or employee of a person falling within sub-paragraph (a) being a person whose responsibilities when acting in that capacity involve him in the business referred to in that sub-paragraph;

(c) any person to whom the communication may otherwise lawfully be made.

NOTES

Commencement: 1 July 2005.

[1011]

48 Certified high net worth individuals

(1) If the requirements of paragraphs (4) and (7) are met, the financial promotion restriction does not apply to any communication which—

(a) is a non-real time communication or a solicited real time communication;

(b) is made to an individual whom the person making the communication believes on reasonable grounds to be a certified high net worth individual, and

(c) relates only to one or more investments falling within paragraph (8).

(2) "Certified high net worth individual" means an individual who has signed, within the period of twelve months ending with the day on which the communication is made, a statement complying with Part I of Schedule 5.

(3) The validity of a statement signed for the purposes of paragraph (2) is not affected by a defect in the form or wording of the statement, provided that the defect does not alter the statement's meaning and that the words shown in bold type in Part I of Schedule 5 are so shown in the statement.

(4) The requirements of this paragraph are that either the communication is accompanied by the giving of a warning in accordance with paragraphs (5) and (6) or where, because of the nature of the communication, this is not reasonably practicable,—

(a) a warning in accordance with paragraph (5) is given to the recipient orally at the beginning of the communication together with an indication that he will receive the warning in legible form and that, before receipt of that warning, he should consider carefully any decision to engage in investment activity to which the communication relates; and

(b) a warning in accordance with paragraphs (5) and (6) (d) to (h) is sent to the recipient of the communication within two business days of the day on which the communication is made.

(5) The warning must be in the following terms—

"The content of this promotion has not been approved by an authorised person within the meaning of the Financial Services and Markets Act 2000. Reliance on this promotion for the purpose of engaging in any investment activity may expose an individual to a significant risk of losing all of the property or other assets invested.".

But where a warning is sent pursuant to paragraph (4)(b), for the words "this promotion" in both places where they occur there must be substituted wording which clearly identifies the promotion which is the subject of the warning.

(6) The warning must—

(a) be given at the beginning of the communication;
(b) precede any other written or pictorial matter;
(c) be in a font size consistent with the text forming the remainder of the communication;
(d) be indelible;
(e) be legible;
(f) be printed in black, bold type;
(g) be surrounded by a black border which does not interfere with the text of the warning; and
(h) not be hidden, obscured or interrupted by any other written or pictorial matter.

(7) The requirements of this paragraph are that the communication is accompanied by an indication—

(a) that it is exempt from the general restriction (in section 21 of the Act) on the communication of invitations or inducements to engage in investment activity on the ground that it is made to a certified high net worth individual;
(b) of the requirements that must be met for an individual to qualify as a certified high net worth individual; and
(c) that any individual who is in any doubt about the investment to which the communication relates should consult an authorised person specialising in advising on investments of the kind in question.

(8) An investment falls within this paragraph if—

(a) it is an investment falling within paragraph 14 of Schedule 1 being stock or shares in an unlisted company;
(b) it is an investment falling within paragraph 15 of Schedule 1 being an investment acknowledging the indebtedness of an unlisted company;
[(ba) it is an investment falling within paragraph 15A of Schedule 1 being an investment constituting an alternative finance investment bond issued by an unlisted company;]
(c) it is an investment falling within paragraph 17 or 18 of Schedule 1 conferring entitlement or rights with respect to investments falling within sub-paragraph (a) or (b);
(d) it comprises units in a collective investment scheme being a scheme which invests wholly or predominantly in investments falling within sub-paragraph (a) or (b);
(e) it is an investment falling within paragraph 21 of Schedule 1 being an option to acquire or dispose of an investment falling within sub-paragraph (a), (b) or (c);
(f) it is an investment falling within paragraph 22 of Schedule 1 being rights under a contract for the sale of an investment falling within sub-paragraph (a), (b) or (c);
(g) it is an investment falling within paragraph 23 of Schedule 1 being a contract relating to, or to fluctuations in value or price of, an investment falling within sub-paragraph (a), (b) or (c),

provided in each case that it is an investment under the terms of which the investor cannot incur a liability or obligation to pay or contribute more than he commits by way of investment.

(9) "Business day" means any day except a Saturday, a Sunday, Christmas Day, Good Friday or a day which is a bank holiday under the Banking and Financial Dealings Act 1971 in any part of the United Kingdom.

NOTES

Commencement: 1 July 2005.

Para (8): sub-para (ba) inserted by the Financial Services and Markets Act 2000 (Regulated Activities) (Amendment) Order 2010, SI 2010/86, art 4, Schedule, para 9(d).

[1012]

49 High net worth companies, unincorporated associations etc

(1) The financial promotion restriction does not apply to any communication which—

(a) is made only to recipients whom the person making the communication believes on reasonable grounds to be persons to whom paragraph (2) applies; or

(b) may reasonably be regarded as directed only at persons to whom paragraph (2) applies.

(2) This paragraph applies to—

(a) any body corporate which has, or which is a member of the same group as an undertaking which has, a called-up share capital or net assets of not less than—

(i) if the body corporate has more than 20 members or is a subsidiary undertaking of an undertaking which has more than 20 members, £500,000;

(ii) otherwise, £5 million;

(b) any unincorporated association or partnership which has net assets of not less than £5 million;

(c) the trustee of a high value trust;

(d) any person ("A") whilst acting in the capacity of director, officer or employee of a person ("B") falling within any of sub-paragraphs (a) to (c) where A's responsibilities, when acting in that capacity, involve him in B's engaging in investment activity;

(e) any person to whom the communication may otherwise lawfully be made.

(3) For the purposes of paragraph (1)(b)—

(a) if all the conditions set out in paragraph (4)(a) to (c) are met, the communication is to be regarded as directed at persons to whom paragraph (2) applies;

(b) in any other case in which one or more of those conditions are met, that fact is to be taken into account in determining whether the communication is directed at persons to whom paragraph (2) applies (but a communication may still be regarded as so directed even if none of the conditions in paragraph (4) is met).

(4) The conditions are that—

(a) the communication includes an indication of the description of persons to whom it is directed and an indication of the fact that the controlled investment or controlled activity to which it relates is available only to such persons;

(b) the communication includes an indication that persons of any other description should not act upon it;

(c) there are in place proper systems and procedures to prevent recipients other than persons to whom paragraph (2) applies engaging in the investment activity to which the communication relates with the person directing the communication, a close relative of his or a member of the same group.

(5) "Called-up share capital" has the meaning given in the 1985 Act or in the 1986 Order.

(6) "High value trust" means a trust where the aggregate value of the cash and investments which form part of the trust's assets (before deducting the amount of its liabilities)—

(a) is £10 million or more; or

(b) has been £10 million or more at anytime during the year immediately preceding the date on which the communication in question was first made or directed.

(7) "Net assets" has the meaning given by section 264 of the 1985 Act or the equivalent provision of the 1986 Order.

NOTES

Commencement: 1 July 2005.

[1013]

50 Sophisticated investors

(1) "Certified sophisticated investor", in relation to any description of investment, means a person—

(a) who has a current certificate in writing or other legible form signed by an authorised person to the effect that he is sufficiently knowledgeable to understand the risks associated with that description of investment; and

(b) who has signed, within the period of twelve months ending with the day on which the communication is made, a statement in the following terms:

"I make this statement so that I am able to receive promotions which are exempt from the restrictions on financial promotion in the Financial Services and Markets Act 2000. The exemption relates to certified sophisticated investors and I declare that I qualify as such in relation to investments of the following kind [list them]. I accept that the contents of promotions and other material that I receive may not have been approved by an authorised person and that their content may not therefore be subject to controls which would apply if the promotion were made or approved by an authorised person. I am aware that it is open to me to seek advice from someone who specialises in advising on this kind of investment.".

(1A) The validity of a statement signed in accordance with paragraph (1)(b) is not affected by a defect in the wording of the statement, provided that the defect does not alter the statement's meaning.

(2) If the requirements of paragraph (3) are met, the financial promotion restriction does not apply to any communication which—

(a) is made to a certified sophisticated investor;

(b) does not invite or induce the recipient to engage in investment activity with the person who has signed the certificate referred to in paragraph (1)(a); and

(c) relates only to a description of investment in respect of which that investor is certified.

(3) The requirements of this paragraph are that the communication is accompanied by an indication—

(a) that it is exempt from the general restriction (in section 21 of the Act) on the communication of invitations or inducements to engage in investment activity on the ground that it is made to a certified sophisticated investor;

(b) of the requirements that must be met for a person to qualify as a certified sophisticated investor;

(c) that the content of the communication has not been approved by an authorised person and that such approval is, unless this exemption or any other exemption applies, required by section 21 of the Act;

(d) that reliance on the communication for the purpose of engaging in any investment activity may expose the individual to a significant risk of losing all of the property invested or of incurring additional liability;

(e) that any person who is in any doubt about the investment to which the communication relates should consult an authorised person specialising in advising on investments of the kind in question.

(4) For the purposes of paragraph (1)(a), a certificate is current if it is signed and dated not more than three years before the date on which the communication is made.

NOTES

Commencement: 1 July 2005.

[1014]

50A Self-certified sophisticated investors

(1) "Self-certified sophisticated investor" means an individual who has signed within the period of twelve months ending with the day on which the communication is made, a statement complying with Part II of Schedule 5.

(2) The validity of a statement signed for the purposes of paragraph (1) is not affected by a defect in the form or wording of the statement, provided that the defect does not alter the statement's meaning and that the words shown in bold type in Part II of Schedule 5 are so shown in the statement.

(3) If the requirements of paragraphs (4) and (7) are met, the financial promotion restriction does not apply to any communication which—

(a) is made to an individual whom the person making the communication believes on reasonable grounds to be a self-certified sophisticated investor; and

(b) relates only to one or more investments falling within paragraph (8).

(4) The requirements of this paragraph are that either the communication is accompanied by the giving of a warning in accordance with paragraphs (5) and (6) or where, because of the nature of the communication this is not reasonably practicable—

(a) a warning in accordance with paragraph (5) is given to the recipient orally at the beginning of the communication together with an indication that he will receive the warning in legible form and that, before receipt of that warning, he should consider carefully any decision to engage in investment activity to which the communication relates; and

(b) a warning in accordance with paragraphs (5) and (6) (d) to (h) is sent to the recipient of the communication within two business days of the day on which the communication is made.

(5) The warning must be in the following terms—

"The content of this promotion has not been approved by an authorised person within the meaning of the Financial Services and Markets Act 2000. Reliance on this promotion for the purpose of engaging in any investment activity may expose an individual to a significant risk of losing all of the property or other assets invested.".

But where a warning is sent pursuant to paragraph (4)(b), for the words "this promotion" in both places where they occur there must be substituted wording which clearly identifies the promotion which is the subject of the warning.

(6) The warning must—

(a) be given at the beginning of the communication;

(b) precede any other written or pictorial matter;

(c) be in a font size consistent with the text forming the remainder of the communication;

(d) be indelible;

(e) be legible;

(f) be printed in black, bold type;

(g) be surrounded by a black border which does not interfere with the text of the warning; and

(h) not be hidden, obscured or interrupted by any other written or pictorial matter.

(7) The requirements of this paragraph are that the communication is accompanied by an indication—

(a) that it is exempt from the general restriction (in section 21 of the Act) on the communication of invitations or inducements to engage in investment activity on the ground that it is made to a self-certified sophisticated investor;

(b) of the requirements that must be met for an individual to qualify as a self-certified sophisticated investor;

(c) that any individual who is in any doubt about the investment to which the communication relates should consult an authorised person specialising in advising on investments of the kind in question.

(8) An investment falls within this paragraph if—

(a) it is an investment falling within paragraph 14 of Schedule 1 being stock or shares in an unlisted company;

(b) it is an investment falling within paragraph 15 of Schedule 1 being an investment acknowledging the indebtedness of an unlisted company;

[(ba) it is an investment falling within paragraph 15A of Schedule 1 being an investment constituting an alternative finance investment bond issued by an unlisted company;]

(c) it is an investment falling within paragraph 17 or 18 of Schedule 1 conferring entitlement or rights with respect to investments falling within sub-paragraph (a) or (b);

(d) it comprises units in a collective investment scheme being a scheme which invests wholly or predominantly in investments falling within sub-paragraph (a) or (b);

(e) it is an investment falling within paragraph 21 of Schedule 1 being an option to acquire or dispose of an investment falling within sub-paragraph (a), (b) or (c);

(f) it is an investment falling within paragraph 22 of Schedule 1 being rights under a contract for the sale of an investment falling within sub-paragraph (a), (b) or (c);

(g) it is an investment falling within paragraph 23 of Schedule 1 being a contract relating to, or to fluctuations in value or price of, an investment falling within sub-paragraph (a), (b) or (c),

provided in each case that it is an investment under the terms of which the investor cannot incur a liability or obligation to pay or contribute more than he commits by way of investment.

(9) "Business day" means any day except a Saturday, a Sunday, Christmas Day, Good Friday or a day which is a bank holiday under the Banking and Financial Dealings Act 1971 in any part of the United Kingdom.

NOTES

Commencement: 1 July 2005.

Para (8): sub-para (ba) inserted by the Financial Services and Markets Act 2000 (Regulated Activities) (Amendment) Order 2010, SI 2010/86, art 4, Schedule, para 9(e).

[1015]

51 Associations of high net worth or sophisticated investors

The financial promotion restriction does not apply to any non-real time communication or solicited real time communication which—

(a) is made to an association, or to a member of an association, the membership of which the person making the communication believes on reasonable grounds comprises wholly or predominantly persons who are—

(i) certified or self-certified high net worth individuals within the meaning of article 48;
(ii) high net worth persons falling within article 49(2)(a) to (d);
(iii) certified or self-certified sophisticated investors within the meaning of article 50 or 50A; and

(b) relates only to an investment under the terms of which a person cannot incur a liability or obligation to pay or contribute more than he commits by way of investment.

NOTES

Commencement: 1 July 2005.

[1016]

52 Common interest group of a company

(1) "Common interest group", in relation to a company, means an identified group of persons who at the time the communication is made might reasonably be regarded as having an existing and common interest with each other and that company in—

(a) the affairs of the company; and
(b) what is done with the proceeds arising from any investment to which the communication relates.

(2) If the requirements of paragraphs (3) and either (4) or (5) are met, the financial promotion restriction does not apply to any communication which—

(a) is a non-real time communication or a solicited real time communication;
(b) is made only to persons who are members of a common interest group of a company, or may reasonably be regarded as directed only at such persons; and
(c) relates to investments falling within paragraph 14[, 15 or 15A] of Schedule 1 which are issued, or to be issued, by that company.

(3) The requirements of this paragraph are that the communication is accompanied by an indication—

(a) that the directors of the company (or its promoters named in the communication) have taken all reasonable care to ensure that every statement of fact or opinion included in the communication is true and not misleading given the form and context in which it appears;
(b) that the directors of the company (or its promoters named in the communication) have not limited their liability with respect to the communication; and
(c) that any person who is in any doubt about the investment to which the communication relates should consult an authorised person specialising in advising on investments of the kind in question.

(4) The requirements of this paragraph are that the communication is accompanied by an indication—

(a) that the directors of the company (or its promoters named in the communication) have taken all reasonable care to ensure that any person belonging to the common interest group (and his professional advisers) can have access, at all reasonable times, to all the information that he or they would reasonably require, and reasonably expect to find, for the purpose of making an informed assessment of the assets and liabilities, financial position, profits and losses and prospects of the company and of the rights attaching to the investments in question; and
(b) describing the means by which such information can be accessed.

(5) The requirements of this paragraph are that the communication is accompanied by an indication that any person considering subscribing for the investments in question should regard any subscription as made primarily to assist the furtherance of the company's objectives (other than any purely financial objectives) and only secondarily, if at all, as an investment.

(6) For the purposes of paragraph (2)(b)—

(a) if all the conditions set out in paragraph (7) are met, the communication is to be regarded as directed at persons who are members of the common interest group;
(b) in any other case in which one or more of those conditions are met, that fact shall be taken into account in determining whether the communication is directed at persons who are members of the common interest group (but a communication may still be regarded as directed only at such persons even if none of the conditions in paragraph (7) is met).

(7) The conditions are that—

(a) the communication is accompanied by an indication that it is directed at persons who are members of the common interest group and that any investment or activity to which it relates is available only to such persons;

(b) the communication is accompanied by an indication that it must not be acted upon by persons who are not members of the common interest group;

(c) there are in place proper systems and procedures to prevent recipients other than members of the common interest group engaging in the investment activity to which the communication relates with the person directing the communication, a close relative of his or a member of the same group.

(8) Persons are not to be regarded as having an interest of the kind described in paragraph (1) if the only reason why they would be so regarded is that—

(a) they will have such an interest if they become members or creditors of the company;

(b) they all carry on a particular trade or profession; or

(c) they are persons with whom the company has an existing business relationship, whether by being its clients, customers, contractors, suppliers or otherwise.

NOTES

Commencement: 1 July 2005.

Para (2): words in square brackets substituted by the Financial Services and Markets Act 2000 (Regulated Activities) (Amendment) Order 2010, SI 2010/86, art 4, Schedule, para 9(a)(iv).

53–56 (*Outside the scope of this work.*)

[1017]

57 Persons placing promotional material in particular publications

The financial promotion restriction does not apply to any communication received by a person who receives the publication in which the communication is contained because he has himself placed an advertisement in that publication.

NOTES

Commencement: 1 July 2005.

58–60 (*Outside the scope of this work.*)

[1018]

61 Sale of goods and supply of services

(1) In this article—

"supplier" means a person whose main business is to sell goods or supply services and not to carry on controlled activities falling within any of paragraphs 3 to 7 of Schedule 1 and, where the supplier is a member of a group, also means any other member of that group;

"customer" means a person, other than an individual, to whom a supplier sells goods or supplies services, or agrees to do so, and, where the customer is a member of a group, also means any other member of that group;

"a related sale or supply" means a sale of goods or supply of services to the customer otherwise than by the supplier, but for or in connection with the same purpose as the sale or supply mentioned above.

(2) The financial promotion restriction does not apply to any non-real time communication or any solicited real time communication made by a supplier to a customer of his for the purposes of, or in connection with, the sale of goods or supply of services or a related sale or supply.

(3) But the exemption in paragraph (2) does not apply if the communication relates to—

(a) a qualifying contract of insurance or units in a collective investment scheme; or

(b) investments falling within paragraph 27 of Schedule 1 so far as relating to investments within paragraph (a).

NOTES

Commencement: 1 July 2005.

62–71 (*Outside the scope of this work.*)

[1019]

72 Pension products offered by employers

(1) If the requirements of paragraph (2) are met, the financial promotion restriction does not apply to any communication which is made by an employer to an employee in relation to a group personal pension scheme or a stakeholder pension scheme.

(2) The requirements of this paragraph are that—

(a) the employer will make a contribution to the group personal pension scheme or stakeholder pension scheme to which the communication relates in the event of the

employee becoming a member of the scheme and the communication contains a statement informing the employee of this;
(b) the employer has not received, and will not receive, any direct financial benefit from the scheme;
(c) the employer notifies the employee in writing prior to the employee becoming a member of the scheme of the amount of the contribution that the employer will make to the scheme in respect of that employee; and
(d) in the case of a non-real time communication, the communication contains, or is accompanied by, a statement informing the employee of his right to seek advice from an authorised person or an appointed representative.

(3) For the purposes of paragraph (2)(b) "direct financial benefit" includes—
(a) any commission paid to the employer by the provider of the scheme; and
(b) any reduction in the amount of the premium payable by the employer in respect of any insurance policy issued to the employer by the provider of the scheme.

(4) In this article—

"group personal pension scheme" means arrangements administered on a group basis under a personal pension scheme and which are available to employees of the same employer or of employers within a group;

["personal pension scheme" means a scheme or arrangement which is not an occupational pension scheme or a stakeholder pension scheme and which is comprised in one or more instruments or agreements, having or capable of having effect so as to provide benefits to or in respect of people—
(a) on retirement,
(b) on having reached a particular age, or
(c) on termination of service in an employment;]

"stakeholder pension scheme" has the meaning given by section 1 of the Welfare Reform and Pensions Act 1999.

NOTES

Commencement: 1 July 2005.

Para (4): definition "personal pension scheme" substituted by the Financial Services and Markets Act 2000 (Regulated Activities) (Amendment) Order 2006, SI 2006/1969, art 12(1), (2).

[1020]

73 Advice centres

(1) If the requirements of paragraph (2) are met, the financial promotion restriction does not apply to any communication which is made by a person in the course of carrying out his duties as an adviser for, or employee of, an advice centre.

(2) The requirements of this paragraph are that the communication relates to—
(a) qualifying credit;
(b) rights under, or rights to or interests in rights under, qualifying contracts of insurance;

. . .

(c) a child trust fund[;
(d) a regulated home reversion plan; *or*
(e) a regulated home purchase plan][; or
(f) a regulated sale and rent back agreement].

(3) In this article—

"adequate professional indemnity insurance", in relation to an advice centre, means insurance providing cover that is adequate having regard to—
(a) the claims record of the centre;
(b) the financial resources of the centre; and
(c) the right of clients of the centre to be compensated for loss arising from the negligent provision of financial advice;

"advice centre" means a body which—
(a) gives advice which is free and in respect of which the centre does not receive any fee, commission or other reward;
(b) provides debt advice as its principal financial services activity; and
(c) *in the* case of a body which is not part of a local authority, holds adequate professional indemnity insurance or a guarantee providing comparable cover;

"child trust fund" has the meaning given by section 1(2) of the Child Trust Funds Act 2004;

"local authority" has the meaning given in article 2 of the Financial Services and Markets Act 2000 (Exemption) Order 2001.

NOTES

Commencement: 1 July 2005.

Para (2): word omitted from sub-para (b) revoked and sub-paras (d), (e) inserted by the Financial Services and Markets Act 2000 (Regulated Activities) (Amendment) (No 2) Order 2006, SI 2006/2383, art 35(1), (4), subject to transitional provisions in arts 37–39 thereof; word in italics in sub-para (d) revoked and sub-para (f) inserted together with word preceding it, by the Financial Services and Markets Act 2000 (Regulated Activities) (Amendment) Order 2009, SI 2009/1342, art 30(1), (3), as from 1 July 2009 (certain purposes) and 30 June 2010 (remaining purposes) (for the full commencement details and for transitional provisions etc see arts 1, 32–34 of that Order).

74 (*Outside the scope of this work.*)

SCHEDULE 1

Article 4

PART I
CONTROLLED ACTIVITIES

[1021]

1. . . .

Effecting or carrying out contracts of insurance

2.—(1) Effecting a contract of insurance as principal is a controlled activity.

(2) Carrying out a contract of insurance as principal is a controlled activity.

(3) There is excluded from sub-paragraph (1) or (2) the effecting or carrying out of a contract of insurance of the kind described in article 12 of the Regulated Activities Order by a person who does not otherwise carry on an activity falling within those sub-paragraphs.

Dealing in securities and contractually based investments

3.—(1) Buying, selling, subscribing for or underwriting securities or contractually based investments (other than investments of the kind specified by paragraph 25, or paragraph 27 so far as relevant to that paragraph) as principal or agent is a controlled activity.

(2) A person does not carry on the activity in sub-paragraph (1) by accepting an instrument creating or acknowledging indebtedness in respect of any loan, credit, guarantee or other similar financial accommodation or assurance which he has made, granted or provided.

(3) The reference in sub-paragraph (2) to a person accepting an instrument includes a reference to a person becoming a party to an instrument otherwise than as a debtor or a surety.

Arranging deals in investments

4.—(1) Making arrangements for another person (whether as principal or agent) to buy, sell, subscribe for or underwrite a particular investment which is—

(a) a security;

(b) a contractually based investment; or

(c) an investment of the kind specified by paragraph 24, or paragraph 27 so far as relevant to that paragraph,

is a controlled activity.

(2) Making arrangements with a view to a person who participates in the arrangements buying, selling, subscribing for or underwriting investments falling within sub-paragraph (1)(a), (b) or (c) (whether as principal or agent) is a controlled activity.

(3) A person does not carry on an activity falling within paragraph (2) merely by providing means by which one party to a transaction (or potential transaction) is able to communicate with other such parties.

[Operating a multilateral trading facility

4A. Operating a multilateral trading facility on which MiFID instruments are traded is a controlled activity.]

Managing investments

5. Managing assets belonging to another person, in circumstances involving the exercise of discretion, is a controlled activity if—

(a) the assets consist of or include any investment which is a security or a contractually based investment; or

(b) the arrangements for their management are such that the assets may consist of or include such investments, and either the assets have at any time since 29th April 1988 done so, or the arrangements have at any time (whether before or after that date) been held out as arrangements under which the assets would do so.

Safeguarding and administering investments

6.—(1) The activity consisting of both—

(a) the safeguarding of assets belonging to another; and

(b) the administration of those assets,

or arranging for one or more other persons to carry on that activity, is a controlled activity if either the condition in paragraph (a) or (b) of sub-paragraph (2) is met.

(2) The condition is that—

(a) the assets consist of or include any investment which is a security or a contractually based investment; or

(b) the arrangements for their safeguarding and administration are such that the assets may consist of or include investments of the kind mentioned in sub-paragraph (a) and either the assets have at any time since 1st June 1997 done so, or the arrangements have at any time (whether before or after that date) been held out as ones under which such investments would be safeguarded and administered.

(3) For the purposes of this article—

(a) it is immaterial that title to the assets safeguarded and administered is held in uncertificated form;

(b) it is immaterial that the assets safeguarded and administered may be transferred to another person, subject to a commitment by the person safeguarding and administering them, or arranging for their safeguarding and administration, that they will be replaced by equivalent assets at some future date or when so requested by the person to whom they belong.

(4) For the purposes of this article, the following activities do not constitute the administration of assets—

(a) providing information as to the number of units or the value of any assets safeguarded;

(b) converting currency;

(c) receiving documents relating to an investment solely for the purpose of onward transmission to, from or at the direction of the person to whom the investment belongs.

Advising on investments

7. Advising a person is a controlled activity if the advice is—

(a) given to the person in his capacity as an investor or potential investor, or in his capacity as agent for an investor or a potential investor; and

(b) advice on the merits of his doing any of the following (whether as principal or agent)—

(i) buying, selling, subscribing for or underwriting a particular investment which is a security or a contractually based investment; or

(ii) exercising any right conferred by such an investment to buy, sell, subscribe for or underwrite such an investment.

Advising on syndicate participation at Lloyd's

8. Advising a person to become, or continue or cease to be, a member of a particular Lloyd's syndicate is a controlled activity.

9–10K. . . .

Agreeing to carry on specified kinds of activity

11. Agreeing to carry on any controlled activity falling within any of paragraphs 3 to 10B [(other than paragraph 4A)] above is a controlled activity.

NOTES

Commencement: 1 July 2005.

Paras 1, 9–10K: outside the scope of this work.

Para 4A: inserted, together with preceding cross-heading, by the Financial Services and Markets Act 2000 (Regulated Activities) (Amendment No 3) Order 2006, SI 2006/3384, art 40(1), (2)(a).

Para 11: words in square brackets inserted by SI 2006/3384, art 40(1), (2)(b).

PART II
CONTROLLED INVESTMENTS

[1022]

12. . . .

13. Rights under a contract of insurance.

14–23. . . .

Lloyd's syndicate capacity and syndicate membership

24.—(1) The underwriting capacity of a Lloyd's syndicate.
(2) A person's membership (or prospective membership) of a Lloyd's syndicate.

25–26C. . . .

Rights to or interests in investments

27.—(1) Subject to sub-paragraphs (2) and (3), any right to or interest in anything which is specified by any other provision of this Part of this (other than [paragraph 26, *26A or 26B*]).
(2) Sub-paragraph (1) does not apply to interests under the trusts of an occupational pension scheme.
(2A) Sub-paragraph (1) does not apply to any right or interest acquired as a result of entering into a funeral plan contract (and for this purpose a "funeral plan contract" is a contract of a kind described in paragraph 9(2)(a) and (b)).
(3) Sub-paragraph (1) does not apply to anything which falls within any other provision of this Part of this Schedule.

Interpretation

28. In this Schedule—
["agreement provider" has the meaning given in paragraph (3) of article 63J of the Regulated Activities Order, read with paragraphs (6) and (7) of that article;
"agreement seller" has the meaning given in article 63J(3) of the Regulated Activities Order;]
"buying" includes acquiring for valuable consideration;
["Commission Regulation" means Commission Regulation 1287/2006 of 10 August 2006;]
"contract of insurance" has the meaning given in the Regulated Activities Order;
"contractually based investment" means—
(a) rights under a qualifying contract of insurance;
(b) any investment of the kind specified by any of paragraphs 21, 22, 23 and 25;
(c) any investment of the kind specified by paragraph 27 so far as relevant to an investment falling within (a) or (b);
["credit institution" has the meaning given in the Regulated Activities Order;]
["home purchase provider" and "home purchaser" have the meanings given in article 63F(3) of the Regulated Activities Order;]
["investment firm" has the meaning given in the Regulated Activities Order;
"investment services and activities" has the meaning given in the Regulated Activities Order;
"management company" has the meaning given in the Regulated Activities Order;
"market operator" has the meaning given in the Regulated Activities Order;
"MiFID instrument" has the meaning given in article 25D(2) of the Regulated Activities Order;
"multilateral trading facility" has the meaning given in the Regulated Activities Order;]
["occupational pension scheme" has the meaning given by section 1 of the Pension Schemes Act 1993 but with paragraph (b) of the definition omitted;]
["plan provider" has the meaning given by paragraph (3) of article 63B of the Regulated Activities Order, read with paragraphs (7) and (8) of that article;]
"property" includes currency of the United Kingdom or any other country or territory;
"qualifying funeral plan contract" has the meaning given by paragraph 9;
["regulated home purchase plan" has the meaning given in article 63F(3) of the Regulated Activities Order;
"regulated home reversion plan" and "reversion seller" have the meanings given in article 63B(3) of the Regulated Activities Order;]
["regulated sale and rent back agreement" has the meaning given in article 63J(3) of the Regulated Activities Order;]
"security" means a controlled investment falling within any of paragraphs 14 to 20 or, so far as relevant to any such investment, paragraph 27;

"selling", in relation to any investment, includes disposing of the investment for valuable consideration, and for these purposes "disposing" includes—

(a) in the case of an investment consisting of rights under a contract—

(i) surrendering, assigning or converting those rights; or

(ii) assuming the corresponding liabilities under the contract;

(b) in the case of an investment consisting of rights under other arrangements, assuming the corresponding liabilities under the arrangements; and

(c) in the case of any other investment, issuing or creating the investment or granting the rights or interests of which it consists;

"syndicate" has the meaning given in the Regulated Activities Order.

NOTES

Commencement: 1 July 2005.

Paras 12, 14–23, 25–26C: outside the scope of this work.

Para 27: words in square brackets substituted by the Financial Services and Markets Act 2000 (Regulated Activities) (Amendment) (No 2) Order 2006, SI 2006/2383, art 35(1), (6)(b), subject to transitional provisions in arts 37–39 thereof; for the words in italics there are substituted the words "26A, 26B or 26C" by the Financial Services and Markets Act 2000 (Regulated Activities) (Amendment) Order 2009, SI 2009/1342, art 30(1), (5)(b), as from 1 July 2009 (certain purposes) and 30 June 2010 (remaining purposes) (for the full commencement details and for transitional provisions etc see arts 1, 32–34 of that Order).

Para 28: definitions "agreement provider", "agreement seller" and "regulated sale and rent back agreement" inserted by SI 2009/1342, art 30(1), (5)(c), as from 1 July 2009 (certain purposes) and 30 June 2010 (remaining purposes) (for the full commencement details and for transitional provisions etc see arts 1, 32–34 of that Order); definitions "Commission Regulation", "credit institution", "investment firm", "investment services and activities", "management company", "market operator", "MiFID instrument" and "multilateral trading facility" inserted by the Financial Services and Markets Act 2000 (Regulated Activities) (Amendment No 3) Order 2006, SI 2006/3384, art 40(1), (6); definitions "home purchase provider" and "home purchaser", "plan provider", "regulated home purchase plan", "regulated home reversion plan" and "reversion seller" inserted by SI 2006/2383, art 35(1), (6)(c), subject to transitional provisions in arts 37–39 thereof; definition "occupational pension scheme" substituted by the Financial Services and Markets Act 2000 (Regulated Activities) (Amendment) Order 2006, SI 2006/1969, art 12(1), (4).

Commission Regulation 1287/2006: OJ L241, 2.9.2006, p 1.

SCHEDULE 2

COUNTRIES AND TERRITORIES

Article 10

[1023]

1. The Bailiwick of Guernsey.

2. The Isle of Man.

3. The Commonwealth of Pennsylvania.

4. The State of Iowa.

5. The Bailiwick of Jersey.

NOTES

Commencement: 1 July 2005.

(Schs 3, 4 outside the scope of this work.)

SCHEDULE 5

STATEMENTS FOR CERTIFIED HIGH NET WORTH INDIVIDUALS AND SELF-CERTIFIED SOPHISTICATED INVESTORS

Articles 48 and 50A

PART I
STATEMENT FOR CERTIFIED HIGH NET WORTH INDIVIDUALS

[1024]

1. The statement to be signed for the purposes of article 48(2) (definition of high net worth individual) must be in the following form and contain the following content—

"**Statement for Certified High Net Worth Individual**

I declare that I am a certified high net worth individual for the purposes of the Financial Services and Markets Act 2000 (Financial Promotion) Order 2005.

I understand that this means:

(a) I can receive financial promotions that may not have been approved by a person authorised by the Financial Services Authority;

(b) the content of such financial promotions may not conform to rules issued by the Financial Services Authority;

(c) by signing this statement I may lose significant rights;

(d) I may have no right to complain to either of the following—

(i) the Financial Services Authority; or

(ii) the Financial Ombudsman Scheme;

(e) I may have no right to seek compensation from the Financial Services Compensation Scheme.

I am a certified high net worth individual because at least one of the following applies—

(a) I had, during the financial year immediately preceding the date below, an annual income to the value of £100,000 or more;

(b) I held, throughout the financial year immediately preceding the date below, net assets to the value of £250,000 or more. Net assets for these purposes do not include—

(i) the property which is my primary residence or any loan secured on that residence;

(ii) any rights of mine under a qualifying contract of insurance within the meaning of the Financial Services and Markets Act 2000 (Regulated Activities) Order 2001; or

(iii) any benefits (in the form of pensions or otherwise) which are payable on the termination of my service or on my death or retirement and to which I am (or my dependants are), or may be, entitled.

I accept that I can lose my property and other assets from making investment decisions based on financial promotions.

I am aware that it is open to me to seek advice from someone who specialises in advising on investments.

Signature

Date ".

NOTES

Commencement: 1 July 2005.

PART II
STATEMENT FOR SELF-CERTIFIED SOPHISTICATED INVESTORS

[1025]

2. The statement to be signed for the purposes of article 50A(1) (definition of self-certified sophisticated investor) must be in the following form and contain the following content—

"Statement for Self-certified Sophisticated Investor

I declare that I am a self-certified sophisticated investor for the purposes of the Financial Services and Markets Act (Financial Promotion) Order 2005.

I understand that this means:

(a) I can receive financial promotions that may not have been approved by a person authorised by the Financial Services Authority;

(b) the content of such financial promotions may not conform to rules issued by the Financial Services Authority;

(c) by signing this statement I may lose significant rights;

(d) I may have no right to complain to either of the following—

(i) the Financial Services Authority; or

(ii) the Financial Ombudsman Scheme;

(e) I may have no right to seek compensation from the Financial Services Compensation Scheme.

I am a self-certified sophisticated investor because at least one of the following applies—

(a) I am a member of a network or syndicate of business angels and have been so for at least the last six months prior to the date below;

(b) I have made more than one investment in an unlisted company in the two years prior to the date below;

(c) I am working, or have worked in the two years prior to the date below, in a professional capacity in the private equity sector, or in the provision of finance for small and medium enterprises;

(d) I am currently, or have been in the two years prior to the date below, a director of a company with an annual turnover of at least £1 million.

I accept that I can lose my property and other assets from making investment decisions based on financial promotions.

I am aware that it is open to me to seek advice from someone who specialises in advising on investments.

Signature

Date ".

NOTES

Commencement: 1 July 2005.

(*Sch 6 outside the scope of this work.*)

FINANCIAL SERVICES AND MARKETS ACT 2000 (CONTROLLERS) (EXEMPTION) ORDER 2009

(SI 2009/774)

NOTES

Made: 24 March 2009.
Authority: Financial Services and Markets Act 2000, ss 192(a), 428(3).
Commencement: 15 April 2009.

ARRANGEMENT OF ARTICLES

1 Citation and commencement . . . [1026]
2 Interpretation . . . [1027]
3 Matters affecting calculations under this Order . . . [1028]
4 General exemption in respect of certain non-directive firms . . . [1029]
5 Specific exemptions in respect of authorised building societies . . . [1030]
6 Specific exemptions in respect of friendly societies . . . [1031]

[1026]

1 Citation and commencement

This Order may be cited as the Financial Services and Markets Act 2000 (Controllers) (Exemption) Order 2009 and comes into force on 15th April 2009.

NOTES

Commencement: 15 April 2009.

[1027]

2 Interpretation

In this Order—

"the Act" means the Financial Services and Markets Act 2000;

"authorised building society" means any UK authorised person which is a building society within the meaning of section 119 of the Building Societies Act 1986 (interpretation);

"relevant friendly society" means any UK authorised person which is a friendly society to which neither subsection (2) nor subsection (3) of section 37 of the Friendly Societies Act 1992 (restriction on combinations of business) applies; and

"relevant UK authorised person" means a UK authorised person other than—

(a) a credit institution authorised under the banking consolidation directive;

(b) an investment firm authorised under the markets in financial instruments directive;

(c) a management company as defined in Article 1a.2 of the UCITS directive, authorised under that directive;

(d) an undertaking pursuing the activity of direct insurance within the meaning of—

(i) Article 2 of the life assurance consolidation directive, authorised under that directive; or

(ii) Article 1 of the first non-life insurance directive, authorised under that directive; or

(e) an undertaking pursuing the activity of reinsurance within the meaning of Article 2.1(a) of the reinsurance directive, authorised under that directive.

NOTES

Commencement: 15 April 2009.

[1028]

3 Matters affecting calculations under this Order

For the purposes of calculations under this Order—

(a) the holding of shares or voting power by a person ("A1") includes any shares or voting power held by another ("A2") if A1 and A2 are acting in concert; and
(b) the provisions of section 184 of the Act (disregarded holdings) apply.

NOTES

Commencement: 15 April 2009.

[1029]

4 General exemption in respect of certain non-directive firms

(1) This article provides exemptions from the obligations in sections 178 and 191D of the Act (notifying the Authority) in relation to a person ("A") who decides to acquire, increase, reduce or cease to have control over a relevant UK authorised person ("B").

(2) This article does not apply where B is an authorised building society or a relevant friendly society.

(3) Where A decides to acquire or increase control over B, A is exempt from the obligation imposed by section 178 unless giving effect to the decision would result in A beginning to be in the position of holding—

(a) 20% or more of the shares in B or in a parent undertaking of B ("P");
(b) 20% or more of the voting power in B or P; or
(c) shares or voting power in B or P as a result of which A is able to exercise significant influence over the management of B.

(4) Where A decides to reduce or cease to have control over B, A is exempt from the obligation imposed by section 191D unless giving effect to the decision would result in A ceasing to be in the position of holding—

(a) 20% or more of the shares in B or in a parent undertaking of B ("P");
(b) 20% or more of the voting power in B or P; or
(c) shares or voting power in B or P as a result of which A is able to exercise significant influence over the management of B.

NOTES

Commencement: 15 April 2009.

[1030]

5 Specific exemptions in respect of authorised building societies

(1) This article provides exemptions from the obligations in sections 178 and 191D of the Act in relation to a person ("A") who decides to acquire, increase, reduce or cease to have control over an authorised building society ("B").

(2) Where A decides to acquire or increase control over B, A is exempt from the obligation imposed by section 178 unless giving effect to the decision would result in A beginning to be in the position of holding 20% or more of the capital of B.

(3) Where A decides to reduce or cease to have control over B, A is exempt from the obligation imposed by section 191D unless giving effect to the decision would result in A ceasing to be in the position of holding 20% or more of the capital of B.

(4) For the purposes of this article "capital", in relation to an authorised building society, consists of the following—

(a) any shares of a class defined as deferred shares for the purposes of section 119 of the Building Societies Act 1986 which have been issued by that society; and
(b) the general reserves of that society.

NOTES

Commencement: 15 April 2009.

[1031]

6 Specific exemptions in respect of friendly societies

(1) This article provides exemptions from the obligations in sections 178 and 191D of the Act in relation to a person ("A") who decides to acquire, increase, reduce or cease to have control over a

relevant friendly society ("B").

(2) Where A decides to acquire or increase control over B, A is exempt from the obligation imposed by section 178.

(3) Where A decides to reduce or cease to have control over B, A is exempt from the obligation imposed by section 191D.

NOTES

Commencement: 15 April 2009.

7 (*Revokes the Financial Services and Markets Act 2000 (Controllers) (Exemption) Order 2001, SI 2001/2638, the Financial Services and Markets Act 2000 (Controllers) (Exemption) (No 2) Order 2001, SI 2001/3338 and the Financial Services and Markets Act 2000 (Regulated Activities) (Amendment) (No 2) Order 2003, SI 2003/1476, reg 21.*)

FINANCIAL SERVICES AND MARKETS ACT 2000 (LAW APPLICABLE TO CONTRACTS OF INSURANCE) REGULATIONS 2009

(SI 2009/3075)

NOTES

Made: 23 November 2009.
Authority: Financial Services and Markets Act 2000, ss 424(3), 417(1), 428(3).
Commencement: 17 December 2009.

[1032]

1 Citation, commencement and interpretation

(1) These Regulations may be cited as the Financial Services and Markets Act 2000 (Law Applicable to Contracts of Insurance) Regulations 2009 and come into force on 17th December 2009.

(2) In these Regulations—

"the 2001 Regulations" means the Financial Services and Markets Act 2000 (Law Applicable to Contracts of Insurance) Regulations 2001;

"the Rome I Regulation" means Regulation (EC) No 593/2008 of the European Parliament and of the Council of 17th June 2008 on the law applicable to contractual obligations (Rome I).

(3) Expressions used in regulations 4 and 5 and in the Rome I Regulation have the same meaning as in the Rome I Regulation unless the context requires otherwise.

NOTES

Commencement: 17 December 2009.

2 (*Amends the Financial Services and Markets Act 2000 (Law Applicable to Contracts of Insurance) Regulations 2001, SI 2001/2635, reg 3 at* **[672]**.)

[1033]

3 Application of the Rome I Regulation: conflicts falling within Article 22(2)

Notwithstanding Article 22(2) of the Rome I Regulation, Article 7 of that Regulation applies in the case of conflicts between—

(a) the laws of different parts of the United Kingdom, or

(b) the laws of one or more parts of the United Kingdom and Gibraltar,

in relation to contracts of insurance described in Article 7 of the Rome I Regulation as it applies in the case of conflicts between the laws of different countries.

NOTES

Commencement: 17 December 2009.

[1034]

4 Contracts of insurance of risks other than large risks: greater freedom of choice of law

Where, in the case of a contract of insurance to which Article 7(3) of the Rome I Regulation applies, the law referred to in sub-paragraph (a) or (b) of that Article, or one of the laws referred to in sub-paragraph (e) of that Article, is a law of any part of the United Kingdom, the parties to that contract may also choose as the law applicable to the contract—

(a) the law of another country; or

(b) the law of another part of the United Kingdom,

if that choice complies with Article 3, Article 6 and Articles 9 to 22 of that Regulation.

NOTES

Commencement: 17 December 2009.

[1035]–[2000]

5 Community co-insurers

Where the parties to the contract may choose the applicable law under the Rome I Regulation or under regulation 4, and where the risk to which the contract relates is covered by Community co-insurance (within the meaning of Council Directive 78/473/EEC on the coordination of laws, regulations and administrative provisions relating to Community insurance), co-insurers other than the leading insurer (within the meaning of that Directive) are not to be treated as parties to the contract.

NOTES

Commencement: 17 December 2009.

PART II
FINANCIAL SERVICES AUTHORITY HANDBOOK MATERIALS

GLOSSARY

NOTES

Up to date as at 22 February 2010. For later amendments please see www.fsa.gov.uk.

G: GUIDANCE ON THE GLOSSARY

[2001]

(1) The *rules* and *guidance* for interpreting the *Handbook* are to be found in *GEN* 2 (Interpreting the Handbook).

(2) The *guidance* in the following paragraphs reminds the reader of some practical points for interpreting *Handbook* text.

(3) Each sourcebook or manual has a reference code of two or more letters, usually a contraction or abbreviation of its title (for example, *GEN* stands for the General provisions and *COB* for the Conduct of Business sourcebook). The meaning of each of these codes is given in the *Glossary*.

(4) Expressions used in the *Handbook* which are defined in the *Glossary* appear in the text in italic type (*GEN* 2.2.7R(1) (Use of defined expressions)). An expression which is not shown in the text in italics has its natural meaning unless the context otherwise requires (*GEN* 2.2.9G).

(5) An expression which appears in the text in italics, but is not itself defined in the *Glossary*, should be read in the same sense as the expression to which it relates (for example, "*advice on investments*" and "*advise on investments*" are related to "*advising on investments*", so the reader should refer to the definition of "*advising on investments*" for their meaning). (*GEN* 2.2.7R(2) and *GEN* 2.2.8G).

(6) The words "in writing", unless the contrary intention appears, mean in legible form and capable of reproduction on paper; they include electronic communication (*GEN* 2.2.14R (References to writing)).

(7) The Interpretation Act 1978 applies to the *Handbook*, so (unless the contrary intention appears):

   (1) the singular includes the plural, and the plural the singular (*GEN* 2.2.12G(3));

   (2) the masculine includes the feminine (*GEN* 2.2.12G(3));

   (3) a reference to a statutory provision is a reference to it as amended from time to time (*GEN* 2.2.12G(2)); under *GEN* 2.2.13R (Cross-references in the Handbook) the same applies to a provision in the *Handbook*.

(8) Many of the defined expressions in the *Glossary* are used or defined in the Act or in a statutory instrument made under it. In these cases, the *Glossary* refers to the statutory provision which is the source of the *Handbook* definition. Where there is a short statutory definition, the *Glossary* sets out the definition in full. Where the statutory definition is long, the *Glossary* gives a summary of it, and states that it is a summary.

50/50 joint venture

[deleted]

50/50 joint venture partner

[deleted]

ABCP internal assessment approach

the method for calculating the *risk weighted exposure amount* for a *securitisation position* in relation to an *asset backed commercial paper programme* as set out in BIPRU 9.12.20R.

ABCP programme

(for the purposes of BIPRU 9 (Securitisation)) an *asset backed commercial paper programme*.

absolute FX exposure limit

(in *ELM*) the amount by which an *ELMI's own funds* exceed 2.5% of its *e-money outstandings*, calculated in accordance with *ELM* 3.4.6R (FX exposure limits).

accepted channel for dissemination of information

(in relation to any *prescribed market*) an approved channel of communication by which information concerning *investments* traded on the market is formally disseminated to other market users on a structured and equitable basis.

accepted market practice

(as defined in section 130A(3) of the *Act*) practices that are reasonably expected in the financial market or markets in question and are accepted by the *FSA* or, in the case of a market situated in another *EEA State*, the competent authority of that *EEA State* within the meaning of the *Market Abuse Directive*.

accepting deposits

the *regulated activity*, specified in article 5 of the *Regulated Activities Order* (Accepting deposits), which is in summary: accepting *deposits* if:
(a) money received by way of *deposit* is lent to others; or
(b) any other activity of the *person* accepting the *deposit* is financed, wholly or to a material extent, out of the capital of or interest on money received by way of *deposit*.

accident

(in relation to a *class* of *contract of insurance*) the *class* of *contract of insurance*, specified in paragraph 1 of Part I of Schedule 1 to the *Regulated Activities Order* (Contracts of general insurance), providing fixed pecuniary benefits or benefits in the nature of indemnity (or a combination of both) against risks of the *person* insured or, in the case of a contract made under section 140, 140A or 140B of the Local Government Act 1972 (or, in Scotland, section 86(1) of the Local Government (Scotland) Act 1973), a *person* for whose benefit the contract is made:
(a) sustaining injury as the result of an accident or of an accident of a specified class; or
(b) dying as a result of an accident or an accident of a specified class; or
(c) becoming incapacitated in consequence of disease or of disease of a specified class;

including contracts relating to industrial injury and occupational disease but excluding contracts within paragraph 2 of Part I of Schedule 1 to the *Regulated Activities Order* (Sickness) and contracts within paragraph IV of Part II of that Schedule (Permanent health).

account

(in relation to a *dormant account*) has the meaning given in section 9 of the Dormant Bank and Building Society Accounts Act 2008, which is in summary:
(a) an account which has at all times consisted only of *money* and is provided by a *bank* or *building society* as part of its activity of *accepting deposits*; and
(b) in relation to a *building society*, it includes an *account* representing *shares* in the *society*, other than:
  (i) preferential *shares*; or
  (ii) deferred *shares* within the meaning given in section 119(1) of the Building Societies Act 1986.

accounting reference date

(1) (except in *COLL*):
  (a) (in relation to a *company* incorporated in the *United Kingdom* under the Companies Acts) the accounting reference date of that *company* determined in accordance with section 391 of the Companies Act 2006;
  (b) (in relation to any other body) the last *day* of its financial year.
(2) (in *COLL*): the date stipulated in the *prospectus* on which the *annual accounting period* of an *authorised fund* ends.

accumulating with-profits policy

a *with-profits insurance contract* which has a readily identifiable current benefit, whether or not this benefit is currently realisable, which is adjusted by an amount explicitly related to the amount of any *premium* payment and to which additional benefits are added in respect of participation in profits by additions directly related to the current benefit or a *policy* with similar characteristics.

accumulation unit

a *unit* in respect of which income is credited periodically to *capital property* under COLL 6.8.3R (Income allocation and distribution).

ACD

authorised corporate director.

Act

the Financial Services and Markets Act 2000.

acting as the depositary or sole director of an openended investment company

the *regulated activity*, specified in article 51(1)(c) of the *Regulated Activities Order* (Establishing etc a collective investment scheme), of acting as the depositary or sole director of an *open-ended investment company*.

acting as trustee of an authorised unit trust scheme

the *regulated activity*, specified in article 51(1)(b) of the *Regulated Activities Order* (Establishing etc a collective investment scheme), of acting as a *trustee* of an *authorised unit trust scheme*.

actuarial body

the Institute of Actuaries or the Faculty of Actuaries.

actuarial function

controlled function CF12 in the *table of controlled functions*, described more fully in *SUP* 4.3.13R and *SUP* 10.7.17R.

actuarial health insurance

(in the context of the *rules* in INSPRU 1.1 concerning the calculation of the *general insurance capital requirement*), health insurance which meets all the conditions set out in INSPRU 1.1.72R.

actuarial investigation

an investigation to which IPRU(INS) rule 9.4 applies.

actuarial valuation date

the date as at which the *mathematical reserves* are calculated.

actuary

a fellow of an *actuarial body* or (in connection with *general insurance business*) a Fellow of the Casualty Actuarial Society who is a member of an *actuarial body*.

actuating purpose

a purpose which motivates or incites a *person* to act.

additional voluntary contribution

[deleted]

adequate public disclosure

(as defined in Article 2 of the *Buy-back and Stabilisation Regulation*) disclosure made in accordance with the procedure laid down in Articles 102(1) and 103 of the *Consolidated Admissions and Reporting Directive*.

administering a home finance transaction

any of the *regulated activities* of *administering a regulated mortgage contract, administering a home purchase plan, administering a home reversion plan* or *administering a regulated sale and rent back agreement*.

administering a home purchase plan

the *regulated activity*, specified in article 63F(2) of the *Regulated Activities Order*, which is in summary: administering a *home purchase plan* where the plan was entered into by way of business on or after 6 April 2007.

administering a home reversion plan

the *regulated activity*, specified in article 63B(2) of the *Regulated Activities Order*, which is in summary: administering a *home reversion plan* where the plan was entered into on or after 6 April 2007.

administering a regulated lifetime mortgage contract

the *regulated activity*, specified in article 61(2) of the *Regulated Activities Order*, which is in summary: administering a *regulated mortgage contract* (which is a *lifetime mortgage*) where the contract was entered into on or after 31 October 2004.

administering a regulated sale and rent back agreement

the *regulated activity*, specified in article 63J(2) of the *Regulated Activities Order*, which is in summary any of the following:

(a) notifying the agreement seller of changes in payment due under a *regulated sale and rent back agreement* or of other matters of which that *agreement* requires him to be notified;

(b) taking any necessary steps for the purpose of making payments to the agreement seller under that *agreement*; and

(c) taking any necessary steps for the purposes of collecting or recovering payments due under that *agreement* from the agreement seller;

but a person is not to be treated as administering a *regulated sale and rent back agreement* because he has, or exercises, a right to take action for the purposes of enforcing that *agreement* (or to require that such action is or is not taken);

and in relation to a person who acquires obligations or rights under a *regulated sale and rent back agreement*, an activity is a specified kind of activity for the purposes of this definition only if the agreement was entered into by the agreement provider (rather than the obligations or rights acquired) on or after 1 July 2009.

administering a regulated mortgage contract

the *regulated activity*, specified in article 61(2) of the *Regulated Activities Order*, which is in summary: administering a *regulated mortgage contract* where the contract was entered into on or after 31 October 2004.

administrative expenses

has the meaning set out in the *insurance accounts rules*.

administrative functions

(a) (in relation to managing *investments*):
- (i) arranging settlement;
- (ii) monitoring and processing corporate actions;
- (iii) *client* account administration, liaison and reporting, including valuation and performance measurement;
- (iv) *ISA*, or *CTF* administration;
- (v) *investment trust savings scheme* administration;

(b) (in relation to effecting or carrying out life policies):
- (i) new business administration;
- (ii) *policy* alterations including surrenders and *policy* loans;
- (iii) preparing *projections*;
- (iv) processing claims including pension payments;
- (v) fund switching;

(c) (in relation to the operation of a *stakeholder pension scheme*):
- (a) new business administration;
- (b) receipt of or alteration to contributions;
- (c) preparing *projections* and annual statements;
- (d) administration of transfers;
- (e) handling claims, including pension payments;
- (f) fund allocation and switching.

admissible asset

(1) (for the purpose of the *rules* in GENPRU and INSPRU as they apply to *members* of the *Society* of Lloyd's, the *Society* and *managing agents*) an asset that, subject to paragraphs (2) and (3) of GENPRU 2 Ann 7R, falls into one or more categories in paragraph (1) of GENPRU 2 Ann 7R as modified by GENPRU 2.3.34R.

(2) otherwise:
- (a) (in relation to an *insurer* which is not a *pure reinsurer*) an asset that, subject to paragraphs (2) and (3) of GENPRU 2 Ann 7R, falls into one or more categories in paragraph (1) of GENPRU 2 Ann 7R; or
- (b) (in relation to a *pure reinsurer*) an asset the holding of which is consistent with compliance by the *firm* with INSPRU 3.1.61AR.

admission or admission to listing

(in LR) *admission* of *securities* to the *official list*.

admission to trading

(1) (in LR) admission of *securities* to trading on an *RIE's* market for *listed securities*.
(2) (in PR and DTR) admission to trading on a *regulated market*;
(3) (elsewhere in the *Handbook*) (in relation to an *investment* and an exchange) the process by which the exchange permits members of the exchange to enter into transactions in that *investment* under and subject to the rules of the exchange.

advanced measurement approach

one of the following:

(a) the adjusted method of calculating the *operational risk capital requirement* set out in BIPRU 6.5 (Operational risk: advanced measurement approaches);
(b) (where the approach in (a) is being applied on a consolidated basis) the method in (a) as applied on a consolidated basis in accordance with BIPRU 8 (Group risk — consolidation); or
(c) when the reference is to the rules of or administered by a *regulatory body* other than the *FSA*, whatever corresponds to the approach in (a) or (b), as the case may be, under those rules.

advanced IRB approach

one of the following:

(a) (in relation to the *sovereign, institutional and corporate IRB exposure class*) the approach under the *IRB approach* under which a *firm* supplies its own estimates of *LGD* and *conversion factors*;
(b) (where the approach in (a) is being applied on a consolidated basis) the method in (a) as applied on a consolidated basis in accordance with *BIPRU* 8 (Group risk — consolidation); or
(c) when the reference is to the rules of or administered by a *regulatory body* other than the *FSA*, whatever corresponds to the approach in (a) or (b), as the case may be, under those rules.

advanced prudential calculation approach

one of the following:
(a) the *IRB approach*; or
(b) the *advanced measurement approach*; or
(c) the *VaR model approach*; or
(d) the *CAD 1 model approach;* or
(e) the *master netting agreement internal models approach*; or
(f) the *CCR internal model method*;

including, in each case, whatever corresponds to that approach under the rules of or administered by a *regulatory body* other than the *FSA*.

advanced prudential calculation approach permission

one of the following:
(a) an *IRB permission*; or
(b) an *AMA permission*; or
(c) a *VaR model permission*; or
(d) a *CAD 1 model waiver*; or
(e) a *master netting agreement internal models approach permission*; or
(f) a *CCR internal model method permission.*

advertisement

(in PR and LR 4) (as defined in the *PD Regulation*) announcements:
(a) relating to a specific offer to the public of securities or to an admission to trading on a regulated market; and
(b) aiming to specifically promote the potential subscription or acquisition of securities.

adviser

(1) (except in IPRU(INV) 13) an individual who is a *representative*, an *appointed representative* or a *tied agent*.
(2) (in IPRU(INV) 13) a financial adviser.

advising on a home finance transaction

any of the *regulated activities* of *advising on regulated mortgage contracts, advising on a home purchase plan, advising on a home reversion plan* or *advising on a regulated sale and rent back agreement.*

advising on a home purchase plan

the *regulated activity*, specified in article 53C of the *Regulated Activities Order*, which is in summary: advising a *person* if the advice:
(a) is given to him in his capacity as a *home purchaser* or potential *home purchaser*; and
(b) is advice on the merits of his:
 (i) entering into a particular *home purchase plan*; or
 (ii) varying the terms of a *home purchase plan* entered into by him on or after 6 April 2007 in such a way as to vary his obligations under that plan.

advising on a home reversion plan

the *regulated activity*, specified in article 53B of the *Regulated Activities Order*, which is in summary: advising a *person* if the advice:
(a) is given to him in his capacity as *reversion occupier* or plan provider or potential *reversion occupier* or potential plan provider; and
(b) is advice on the merits of his:
 (i) entering into a particular *home reversion plan*; or
 (ii) varying the terms of a *home reversion plan* entered into by him on or after 6 April 2007 in such a way as to vary his obligations under that plan.

advising on investments, advising, advise

the *regulated activity*, specified in article 53 of the *Regulated Activities Order* (Advising on investments), which is in summary: advising a *person* if the advice is:
(a) given to the *person* in his capacity as an investor or potential investor, or in his capacity as agent for an investor or a potential investor; and
(b) advice on the merits of his doing any of the following (whether as principal or agent):
 (i) *buying, selling*, subscribing for or underwriting a particular *investment* which is a *security* or *relevant investment* (that is, any *designated investment, funeral plan contract, pure protection contract, general insurance contract* or *right to or interest in a funeral plan contract*); or
 (ii) exercising any right conferred by such an *investment*, to *buy, sell*, subscribe for or underwrite such an *investment*.

Part II FSA Handbook Materials

advising on investments (except pension transfers and pension optouts)

advising on investments except in respect of *pension transfers* and *pension opt-outs*.

advising on pension transfers and pension opt-outs

advising on investments in respect of *pension transfers* and *pension opt-outs*.

advising on regulated mortgage contracts

the *regulated activity*, specified in article 53A of the *Regulated Activities Order*, which is in summary: advising a *person* if the advice:
(a) is given to the *person* in his capacity as a borrower or potential borrower; and
(b) is advice on the merits of his:
  (i) entering into a particular *regulated mortgage contract*; or
  (ii) varying the terms of a *regulated mortgage contract* entered into by him on or after 31 October 2004 in such a way as to vary his obligations under that contract.

advising on a regulated sale and rent back agreement

the *regulated activity*, specified in article 53D of the *Regulated Activities Order*, which is in summary advising a *person* if the advice:
(a) is given to a *person* in his capacity as:
  (i) an agreement seller or potential agreement seller; or
  (ii) an agreement provider or potential agreement provider; and
(b) is advice on the merits of his doing either of the following:
  (i) entering into a particular regulated sale and rent back agreement; or
  (ii) varying the terms of a *regulated sale and rent back agreement* entered into on or after 1 July 2009 by him as agreement seller or agreement provider, in such a way as to vary his obligations under that *agreement* and in relation to a *person* who acquires obligations or rights under a *regulated sale and rent back agreement*, an activity is a specified kind of activity for the purposes of this part of the definition only if the *agreement* was entered into by the agreement provider (rather than the obligations or rights acquired) on or after 1 July 2009.

advising on syndicate participation at Lloyd's

the *regulated activity*, specified in article 56 of the *Regulated Activities Order* (Advice on syndicate participation at Lloyd's), of advising a *person* to become, or continue or cease to be, a member of a particular Lloyd's *syndicate*.

affected person

(in *COLL*):
(a) (in relation to an *ICVC*):
  (i) the *ICVC*;
  (ii) its *depositary*;
  (iii) a *director* of the *ICVC*;
  (iv) any *investment adviser* of the *ICVC*;
  (v) any *associate* of any *person* in (a)(i), (ii), (iii) or (iv);
  (vi) the auditor of the *scheme*;
(b) (in relation to an *AUT*):
  (i) the *manager*;
  (ii) the *trustee*;
  (iii) any *investment adviser* of the *manager*;
  (iv) any *associate* of any *person* in (b)(i), (ii) or (iii);
  (v) the auditor of the *scheme*.

affiliated company

(in relation to a *person*) an *undertaking* in the same *group* as that *person*.

agent

(in relation to *payment services*) a *person* who acts on behalf of a *payment institution* in providing *payment services*.

[**Note**: article 4(22) of the *Payment Services Directive*]

agreeing to carry on a regulated activity

the *regulated activity*, specified in article 64 of the *Regulated Activities Order* (Agreeing to carry on specified kinds of activity), of agreeing to carry on an activity specified in Part II of that Order other than:

(a) *accepting deposits;*

(aa) *issuing electronic money;*

(b) *effecting contracts of insurance;*
(c) *carrying out contracts of insurance;*
(d) *establishing, operating or winding up a collective investment scheme;*
(e) *acting as trustee of an authorised unit trust scheme;*
(f) *acting as the depositary or sole director of an open-ended investment company;*
(g) *establishing, operating or winding up a stakeholder pension scheme*
(h) *establishing, operating or winding up a personal pension scheme.*

aircraft

(in relation to a *class* of *contract of insurance*) the *class* of *contract of insurance*, specified in paragraph 5 of Part I of Schedule 1 to the *Regulated Activities Order* (Contracts of general insurance), upon aircraft or upon the machinery, tackle, furniture or equipment of aircraft.

aircraft liability

(in relation to a *class* of *contract of insurance*) the *class* of *contract of insurance*, specified in paragraph 11 of Part I of Schedule 1 to the *Regulated Activities Order* (Contracts of general insurance), against damage arising out of or in connection with the use of aircraft, including third-party risks and carrier's liability.

allocation date

the date on or before which, in respect of each *annual accounting period*, an allocation of income is to be made.

allocation period

a single 24-hour period or, with the agreement of each *intermediate customer* concerned, a period spanning five consecutive *business days*, during which an aggregated *series of transactions* may be *executed*.

allotment

(as defined in Article 2 of the *Buy-back and Stabilisation Regulation*) the process or processes by which the number of *relevant securities* to be received by investors who have previously subscribed or applied for them is determined.

alternative projection

(in *COBS*) a *projection* calculated on the basis described in paragraph 1.5R of the projection *rules* (*COBS* 13 Annex 2R), rather than in accordance with the remainder of those *rules*.

alternative standardised approach

one of the following:
(a) a version of the *standardised approach* to *operational risk* under which a *firm* uses different indicators for certain business lines as referred to in BIPRU 6.4.19 R (The alternative standardised approach);
(b) (where the approach in (a) is being applied on a consolidated basis) the method in (a) as applied on a consolidated basis in accordance with BIPRU 8 (Group risk — consolidation); or
(c) when the reference is to the rules of or administered by a *regulatory body* other than the FSA, whatever corresponds to the approach in (a) or (b), as the case may be, under those rules.

alternatively secured pension

(as defined in paragraph 5 of Schedule 28 to the Finance Act 2004) *income withdrawal.*

AMA

the *advanced measurement approach.*

AMA permission

an *Article 129 implementing measure*, a *requirement* or a *waiver* that requires a *BIPRU firm* or an *institution* to use the *advanced measurement approach* to *operational risk* on a solo basis or, if the context requires, a consolidated basis.

ancillary activity

an activity which is not a *regulated activity* but which is:
(a) carried on in connection with a *regulated activity*; or
(b) held out as being for the purposes of a *regulated activity.*

ancillary insurance services undertaking

(in relation to any *undertaking* in a *consolidation group, sub-group* or other group of *persons*) an *undertaking* complying with the following conditions:

(a) its principal activity consists of:
  (i) owning or managing property; or
  (ii) managing data-processing services; or
  (iii) any other similar activity;
(b) the activity in (a) is ancillary to the principal activity of one or more *insurance undertakings*;
(c) those *insurance undertakings* are also members of that *consolidation group*, *sub-group* or other group of *persons*.

ancillary risk

(in relation to an *insurer* with *permission* under the *Act* to insure a principal risk belonging to one *class* (as defined for the purposes of INSPRU and SUP) of *general insurance business*) a risk included in another such *class* which is:
(a) connected with the principal risk,
(b) concerned with the object which is covered against the principal risk, and
(c) the subject of the same contract insuring the principal risk.
However, the risks included in *classes* 14, 15 and 17 may not be treated as risks ancillary to other *classes*, except that the risk included in *class* 17 (legal expenses insurance) may be regarded as an ancillary risk of *class* 18 where:
(d) the conditions laid down in (a) to (c) are fulfilled, and
(e) the principal risk relates solely to assistance provided for *persons* who fall into difficulties while travelling, while away from home or while away from their permanent residence or where it concerns disputes or risks arising out of, or in connection with, the use of sea-going vessels.

ancillary service

any of the services listed in Section B of Annex I to *MiFID*, that is:
(a) safekeeping and administration of *financial instruments* for the account of *clients*, including custodianship and related services such as cash/collateral management;
(b) granting credits or loans to an investor to allow him to carry out a transaction in one or more *financial instruments*, where the firm granting the credit or loan is involved in the transaction;
(c) advice to undertakings on capital structure, industrial strategy and related matters and advice and services relating to mergers and the purchase of undertakings;
(d) foreign exchange services where these are connected to the provision of *investment services*;
(e) *investment research* and financial analysis or other forms of general recommendation relating to transactions in *financial instruments*;
(f) services related to underwriting; and
(g) *investment services and activities* as well as ancillary services within (a) to (f), above, related to the underlying of the *derivatives* included under Section C – 5, 6, 7 and 10, that is (in accordance with that Annex and Recital 21 to, and Article 39 of, the *MiFID Regulation*):
  (i) commodities;
  (ii) climatic variables;
  (iii) freight rates;
  (iv) emission allowances;
  (v) inflation rates or other official economic statistics;
  (vi) telecommunications bandwidth;
  (vii) commodity storage capacity;
  (viii) transmission or transportation capacity relating to commodities, where cable, pipeline or other means;
  (ix) an allowance, credit, permit, right or similar asset which is directly linked to the supply, distribution or consumption of energy derived from renewable resources;
  (x) a geological, environmental or other physical variable;
  (xi) any other asset or right of a fungible nature, other than a right to receive a service, that is capable of being transferred;
  (xii) an index or measure related to the price or value of, or volume of transactions in any asset, right, service or obligation;

where these are connected to the provision of *investment services* or ancillary services.

[**Note:** article 4(1)(3) of *MiFID*]

ancillary services undertaking

(1) (in accordance with Article 4(21) of the *Banking Consolidation Directive* (Definitions) and subject to (2)) and in relation to an *undertaking* in a *consolidation group*, *sub-group* or another group of *persons*) an *undertaking* complying with the following conditions:
  (a) its principal activity consists of:
    (i) owning or managing property; or
    (ii) managing data-processing services; or
    (iii) any other similar activity;
  (b) the activity in (a) is ancillary to the principal activity of one or more *credit institutions* or *investment firms*; and

(c) those *credit institutions* or *investment firms* are also members of that *consolidation group*, *subgroup* or group.

(2) (for the purpose of GENPRU 1.3 (Valuation) and INSPRU 6.1 (Group Risk: Insurance Groups) an *undertaking* in (1) and an *ancillary insurance services undertaking*.

ancillary stabilisation

(as defined in Article 2 of the *Buy-back and Stabilisation Regulation*) the exercise of an *overallotment facility* or of a *greenshoe option* by *investment firms* or *credit institutions*, in the context of a *significant distribution* of *relevant securities*, exclusively for facilitating *stabilisation* activity.

announceable information

information which is usually the subject of a public announcement, although not subject to any formal disclosure requirement.

annual accounting period

(1) [deleted]

(2) (in COLL) the period determined in accordance with COLL 6.8.2R(3) to (7) (Accounting periods).

annual accounts

(1) the Council Directive of 19 December 1991 concerning the annual accounts and consolidated accounts of insurance undertakings (No. 91/674/EEC).

(2) (in UPRU) accounts prepared to comply with:

(a) the Companies Acts 1985 to 1989 and their equivalent in Northern Ireland, where these provisions are applicable; or

(b) the Companies Act 2006; or

(c) other statutory obligations.

Annual Accounts Directive

the Council Directive of 19 December 1991 concerning the annual accounts and consolidated accounts of *insurance undertakings* (No. 91/674/EEC).

annual audited fixed expenditure

(in UPRU) has the meaning given in UPRU 2.1.3R (Annual audited fixed expenditure).

annual bonus

(in relation to a *with-profits insurance contract*) a discretionary addition to *policy* benefits under a *with-profits insurance contract* made by a *long-term insurer* as a result of the annual *actuarial investigation*.

annual budget

the annual budgeted costs of operating the *Financial Ombudsman Service*.

annual eligible income

(in FEES) the annual income (as described in Part 2 of FEES 4 Annex 1R) for the *firm's* last financial year ended in the year to 31 December preceding the date for submission of the information under FEES 6.5.13R attributable to the relevant *sub-class*; or if the *firm* prefers, that amount of that annual income attributable to business conducted with or on behalf of *eligible claimants*, but only if the *firm* notifies *FSCS* of the amount in accordance with *FSCS* reporting requirements.

annual financial statements

the financial statements in respect of the year ending on the *firm's* annual accounting reference date, which is the date to which a corporate *firm's* accounts are prepared for the purposes of the Companies Acts, or, where the *firm* is not subject to the Companies Acts, the equivalent date chosen by the *firm* and notified to the *FSA*.

annual income

(in MIPRU) the income referred to in MIPRU 4.3.

annual income allocation date

the date in any year stated in the most recently published *prospectus* as the date on or before which, in respect of each *annual accounting period*, an allocation of income is to be made.

annual information update

(in PR) the document referred to in *PR* 5.2.1R.

annual percentage rate

the annual percentage rate of charge for a contract as calculated in accordance with *MCOB* 10 (Annual percentage rate).

annual statement provisions

(in MCOB) in relation to a:
(a) *regulated mortgage contract*, MCOB 7.5;
(b) *home purchase plan*, MCOB 7.8.3R to MCOB 7.8.6R; and
(c) *instalment reversion plan*, MCOB 9.9.1R to MCOB 9.9.4R.

annualised net written premiums

(for the purposes of INSPRU 1.4) in relation to a *financial year*, the *net written premiums* received during that *financial year*, except that in relation to a *financial year* that has been validly extended beyond, or shortened from, a period of 12 months, the amount of *net written premiums* is the amount determined in accordance with the formula:

$$\frac{NWPx365}{D}$$

where:
(1) NWP is the amount of *net written premiums* received in the *financial year*; and
(2) D is the number of days in that *financial year*.

annual report and accounts

(a) (in relation to a *company* incorporated in the *United Kingdom*) an annual report and annual accounts as those terms are defined in:
  (i) section 262(1) of the Companies Act 1985, together with an auditor's report prepared in relation to those accounts under section 235 of the same Act where these provisions are applicable; or;
  (ii) section 471 of the Companies Act 2006 together with an auditor's report prepared in relation to those accounts under sections (9495 to 497 of the same Act;
(b) (in relation to any other body) any similar or analogous *documents* which it is required to prepare whether by its constitution or by the law under which it is established.

APER

the part of the *Handbook* in High Level Standards which has the title Statements of Principle and Code of Practice for Approved Persons.

APR

annual percentage rate.

applicable asset

(a) in relation to MiFID business, a financial instrument; or
(b) in relation to safeguarding and administering investments that is not MiFID business, a designated investment.

applicable provisions

the *Host State* rules with which:
(a) an *incoming EEA firm* is required to comply when carrying on a *permitted activity* through a *branch* or by providing services (as applicable) in the *United Kingdom*, as defined in paragraphs 13(4) and 14(4) of Part II of Schedule 3 to the *Act* (Exercise of passport rights by EEA firms); or
(b) a *UK firm* is required to comply when conducting business through a *branch* (in accordance with paragraph 19(13) of Part III of Schedule 3 to the *Act* (Exercise of passport rights by UK firms)) or by providing services (as applicable) in another *EEA State*.

applicable sectoral consolidation rules

(in respect of a *financial sector* and in accordance with paragraph 6.9 of GENPRU 3 Ann 1R (Applicable sectoral consolidation rules)) the *FSA's sectoral rules* about capital adequacy and solvency on a consolidated basis applicable to that *financial sector* under the table in paragraph 6.10 of GENPRU 3 Ann 1R.

applicable sectoral rules

(in respect of a *financial sector*) *applicable sectoral consolidation rules* for that *financial sector* and the *FSA's sectoral rules* about capital adequacy and solvency for:
(a) the *banking and investment services sector* as set out in paragraph 6.2 of GENPRU 3 Ann 1R; or
(b) *insurance undertakings*;
which of those sets of *rules* apply for the purpose of a particular calculation depends on the nature of that calculation.

applicant

(1) (in LR) an *issuer* which is applying for *admission* of *securities*.
(2) (in PR) an applicant for approval of a *prospectus* or *supplementary prospectus* relating to *transferable securities*.

applications day

the first *day* on which section 40 of the *Act* (Application for permission) comes into force (for any purpose).

appointed representative

(in accordance with section 39 of the *Act*) a *person* (other than an *authorised person*) who:
(a) is a party to a contract with an *authorised person* (his *principal*) which:
  (i) permits or requires him to carry on business of a description prescribed in the *Appointed Representatives Regulations*; and
  (ii) complies with such requirements as are prescribed in those Regulations; and
(b) is someone for whose activities in carrying on the whole or part of that business his *principal* has accepted responsibility in writing;

and who is therefore an *exempt person* in relation to any *regulated activity* comprised in the carrying on of that business for which his *principal* has accepted responsibility.

Appointed Representatives Regulations

the Financial Services and Markets Act 2000 (Appointed Representatives) Regulations 2001 (SI 2001/1217).

apportionment and oversight function

controlled function CF8 in the *table of controlled functions*, described more fully in *SUP* 10.7.1R.

appropriate actuary

an *actuary* appointed under *SUP* 4.4.1R (Appointment of an appropriate actuary).

appropriate charges information

(in *COBS*) information about charges which is calculated and presented in accordance with the charges *rules* in *COBS* 13.4.1R and *COBS* 13 Annex 3.

appropriate personal pension

a *personal pension scheme* or a *stakeholder pension scheme* which is an appropriate scheme under section 7(4) of the Pension Schemes Act 1993 or section 3(4) of the Pension Schemes (Northern Ireland) Act 1993.

appropriate PRA

(1) (in relation to a *position* treated under BIPRU 7.6 (Option PRR)) the percentage figure applicable to that *position* under the table in BIPRU 7.6.8R (Appropriate PRR);
(2) (for any other purpose and in relation to a *position*) the *PRA* applicable to that *position* under BIPRU 7 (Market risk).

appropriate valuer

(in *COLL*) a *person* who complies with the requirements of COLL 5.6.18R(7) (Investment in property), COLL 8.4.11R(4) (Investment in property.

approve

(in relation to a *financial promotion*) approve the content of the *financial promotion* for the purposes of section 21 of the *Act* (Restrictions on financial promotion).

approved bank

(except in *COLL*) (in relation to a bank account opened by a *firm*):
(a) if the account is opened at a branch in the *United Kingdom*:
  (i) the Bank of England; or
  (ii) the central bank of a member state of the *OECD*; or
  (iii) a *bank*; or
  (iv) a *building society*; or
  (v) a bank which is supervised by the central bank or other banking regulator of a member state of the *OECD*; or
(b) if the account is opened elsewhere:
  (i) a bank in (a); or
  (ii) a *credit institution* established in an *EEA State* other than the *United Kingdom* and duly authorised by the relevant *Home State regulator*; or
  (iii) a bank which is regulated in the Isle of Man or the Channel Islands; or
(c) a bank supervised by the South African Reserve Bank; or

(d) any other bank that:
  (i) is subject to regulation by a national banking regulator;
  (ii) is required to provide audited accounts;
  (iii) has minimum net assets of £5 million (or its equivalent in any other currency at the relevant time) and has a surplus revenue over expenditure for the last two financial years; and

has an annual audit report which is not materially qualified.

(in *COLL*) any *person* falling within (a-c).

approved collateral

any form of security for the discharge of any liability arising from a *contingent liability investment* (other than a guarantee) which:

(a) (in relation to an *on-exchange* transaction) is acceptable under the rules of the relevant exchange or *clearing house*; and
(b) (in relation to an *OTC* transaction) would be acceptable for a similar transaction to the relevant exchange or *clearing house*.

approved counterparty

any of the following:

(a) an *approved credit institution*; or
(b) a *firm* whose *permission* includes *dealing in investments as principal* with respect to *derivatives* which are not *listed*; or
(c) a *MiFID investment firm* whose authorisation (as referred to in article 5 of *MiFID*) authorises it to carry on activities of the kind referred to in (b); or
(d) in respect of a transaction involving a new issue of *securities* which are to be *listed*, the *issuer* or a *MiFID investment firm* acting on behalf of the *issuer*.

approved credit institution

a *credit institution* recognised or permitted under the law of an *EEA State* to carry on any of the activities set out in Annex 1 to the *Banking Consolidation Directive*.

approved depositary

any depositary:

(a) which is subject to regulation by a national *regulatory body* in connection with its custody services;
(b) which is required to prepare audited accounts;
(c) whose latest annual audit report is not materially qualified; and
(d) which
(e) has minimum net assets of £5 million (or its equivalent in any other currency at the relevant time) and has surplus revenue over expenditure for the last two financial years; or
(f) if not, nevertheless has adequate financial resources for its business.*approved derivative* (in *CIS*) a *derivative* which is traded or dealt in on an *eligible derivatives* market.

approved derivative

(1) (in *COLL*) a derivative which is traded or *dealt* in on an eligible derivatives *market*.
(2) (in INSPRU) a *derivative* in respect of which the conditions in INSPRU 3.2.5R are met.

approved financial institution

any of the following:

(a) the European Central Bank;
(b) the central bank of an *EEA State*;
(c) the International Bank for Reconstruction and Development;
(d) the European Bank for Reconstruction and Development;
(e) the International Finance Corporation;
(f) the International Monetary Fund;
(g) the Inter-American Development Bank;
(h) the African Development Bank;
(i) the Asian Development Bank;
(j) the Caribbean Development Bank;
(k) the European Investment Bank;
(l) the EU; and
(m) the European Atomic Energy Community.

approved index

in relation to *permitted links*:

(a) an index that is:
  (i) calculated independently;
  (ii) published at least once every week;

(iii) based on constituents that are *permitted links*; and
(iv) calculated on a basis that is made available to the public, and that includes both the rules for including and excluding constituents and the rules for valuation which must use an arithmetic average of the value of the constituents; or

(b) a national index of retail prices published by or under the authority of a government of a *Zone A country*; or

(c) an index that is:
(i) based on constituents that are *permitted links*; and
(ii) in respect of which a *derivative* contract is *listed*; or

(d) the average earnings index when used for the purposes of orders made under section 148 of the Social Security Administration Act 1992 by the Department for Work and Pensions.

approved moneymarket instrument

(in accordance with COLL 5.2.7FR) a money-market instrument which is normally dealt in on the money market, is liquid and has a value which can be accurately determined at any time.

approved person

a *person* in relation to whom the *FSA* has given its approval under section 59 of the *Act* (Approval for particular arrangements) for the performance of a *controlled function*.

approved quasi-derivative

a *quasi-derivative* in respect of which the conditions in INSPRU 3.2.5R are met.

approved reinsurance to close

(a) a *reinsurance to close* effected before 1 January 2005; or

(b) an agreement under which *members* of a *syndicate* in one *syndicate year* ("the reinsured *members*") agree with the *members* of that *syndicate* in a later *syndicate year* or the *members* of one other *syndicate* ("the reinsuring *members*") that the reinsuring *members* will discharge, or procure the discharge of, or indemnify the reinsured *members* against, all known and unknown *insurance business* liabilities of the reinsured *members* arising out of the *insurance business* carried on by the reinsured *members* in that *syndicate year* that is:
(i) effected after 1 January 2005; and
(ii) not a balance transfer between two *syndicate years* where the *syndicate* has only one *member* and the *member* is the same in each of those years; or

(c) an agreement under which *members* of a *syndicate* in one *syndicate year* ("the reinsured members") agree with a *subsidiary* of the *Society* that that *subsidiary* will discharge or procure the discharge of, or indemnify the reinsured *members* against, all known and unknown *insurance business* liabilities of the reinsured *members* arising out of the *insurance business* carried on by the reinsured *members* in that *syndicate year* ("the reinsured liabilities") and where:
(i) that *subsidiary* is wholly owned by the *Society* and if from time to time the *subsidiary* has an *asset* or cash flow deficiency such that the *subsidiary* is unable to meet any of the liabilities which it has reinsured, the Society is legally obliged to pay to the *subsidiary* a sum equal to that deficiency; and
(ii) at the effective date of the agreement, the relevant *syndicate year* has been open for at least two years after the date at which it would normally have been closed in accordance with the policies and practices in relation to the *syndicate* concerned.

approved reporting mechanism

a trade-matching or reporting system approved by the *FSA* in accordance with Section 412A of the *Act*.

approved security

(1) (in COLL) a *transferable security* that is admitted to *official listing* in an *EEA State* or is traded on or under the rules of an *eligible securities* market (otherwise than by the specific permission of the market authority).

(2) (in INSPRU) any of the following:
(a) any *security* issued or guaranteed by, or the repayment of the principal of which, or the interest on which, is guaranteed by, and any loans to or deposits with, any government, public or local authority or nationalised industry or undertaking, which belongs to a *Zone A country*;
(b) any loan to, or deposit with, an *approved financial institution*;
(c) any *debenture* issued before 31 December 1994 by the Agricultural Mortgage Corporation Limited or the Scottish Agricultural Securities Corporation Limited.

(3) (in *COBS*) any of the following:
(a) any *security* issued or guaranteed by, or the repayment of the principal of which, or the interest on which is guaranteed by, and any loan to or deposit with, any government, public or local authority or nationalised industry or undertaking that belongs to Zone A as defined in the *Banking Consolidation Directive*; or

Part II FSA Handbook Materials

(b) any loan to, or deposit with, an *approved financial institution*; or
(c) debentures issued before 31 December 1994 by the Agricultural Mortgage Corporation Ltd or the Scottish Agricultural Securities Corporation Ltd.

approved stock lending transaction

a *stock lending* transaction in respect of which the conditions in INSPRU 3.2.36R have been met.

APR rules

MCOB 10.

arrangement

(as defined in section 59(10) of the *Act* (Approval for particular arrangements)) any kind of arrangement for the performance of a function of an *authorised person* ("A") which is entered into by A or any contractor of his with another *person*, including, in particular, that other *person's* appointment to an office, his becoming a partner, or his employment (whether under a contract of service or otherwise).

arranging

(a) (except in relation to a *home finance transaction*) *arranging (bringing about) deals in investments, making arrangements with a view to transactions in investments* or *agreeing to carry on either of those regulated activities.*
(b) (in relation to a *regulated mortgage contract*) *arranging (bringing about) regulated mortgage contracts, making arrangements with a view to regulated mortgage contracts* or *agreeing to carry on either of those regulated activities.*
(c) (in relation to a *home purchase plan*) *arranging (bringing about) a home purchase plan, making arrangements with a view to a home purchase plan* or *agreeing to carry on either of those regulated activities.*
(d) (in relation to a *home reversion plan*) *arranging (bringing about) a home reversion plan, making arrangements with a view to a home reversion plan* or *agreeing to carry on either of those regulated activities.*

arranging (bringing about) a home finance transaction

any of the *regulated activities of arranging (bringing about) a regulated mortgage contract, arranging (bringing about) a home purchase plan, arranging (bringing about) a home reversion plan* or *arranging (bringing about) a regulated sale and rent back agreement.*

arranging (bringing about) a home purchase plan

the *regulated activity*, specified in article 25C(1) of the *Regulated Activities Order*, which is in summary: making arrangements for another *person* to:
(a) enter into a *home purchase plan* as *home purchaser*; or
(b) vary the terms of a *home purchase plan* entered into by him as *home purchaser* on or after 6 April 2007.

arranging (bringing about) a home reversion plan

the *regulated activity*, specified in article 25B(1) of the *Regulated Activities Order*, which is in summary: making arrangements for another *person* to:
(a) enter into a *home reversion plan* as *reversion occupier* or as plan provider; or
(b) vary the terms of a *home reversion plan* entered into by him as *reversion occupier* or as plan provider on or after 6 April 2007.

arranging (bringing about) deals in investments

the *regulated activity*, specified in article 25(1) of the *Regulated Activities Order*, which is in summary: making arrangements for another *person* (whether as *principal* or agent) to *buy*, *sell*, subscribe for or underwrite a particular *investment* which is:

(a) a *designated investment*; or
(b) a *funeral plan contract*; or
(c) the *underwriting capacity of a Lloyd's syndicate*; or
(d) *membership of a Lloyd's syndicate*; or
(da) a *pure protection contract*; or
(db) a *general insurance contract*; or
(e) *rights to or interests in investments* in (b), (c) or (d).

arranging (bringing about) regulated mortgage contracts

the *regulated activity*, specified in article 25A(1) of the *Regulated Activities Order*, which is in summary: making arrangements for another *person* to:

(a) enter into a *regulated mortgage contract* as borrower; or
(b) vary the terms of a *regulated mortgage contract* entered into by him as borrower on or after 31 October 2004.

(see also *arranging* (in relation to *regulated mortgage contracts*) and *making arrangements with a view to regulated mortgage contracts*.)

arranging (bringing about) a regulated sale and rent back agreement

the the *regulated activity*, specified in article 25E(1) of the *Regulated Activities Order*, which is in summary making arrangements:
(a) for another *person* to enter into a *regulated sale and rent back agreement* as an agreement seller or as an agreement provider; or
(b) for another *person* to vary the terms of a *regulated sale and rent back agreement*, entered into on or after 1 July 2009 by him as agreement seller or agreement provider, in such a way so as to vary his obligations under that *agreement* and in relation to a *person* who acquires obligations or rights under a *regulated sale and rent back agreement*, an activity is a specified kind of activity for the purposes of this part of the definition only if the *agreement* was entered into by the agreement provider (rather than the obligations or rights acquired) on or after 1 July 2009;

including making arrangements with a view to a *person* who participates in the arrangements *entering into a regulated sale and rent back agreement* as agreement seller or agreement provider.

arranging deals in contracts of insurance written at Lloyd's

the *regulated activity*, specified in article 58 of the *Regulated Activities Order* (Arranging deals in contracts of insurance written at Lloyd's), carried on by the *Society of Lloyd's* of arranging deals in *contracts of insurance* written at Lloyd's.

arranging qualifying credit

the *controlled activity*, specified in paragraph 10A of Schedule 1 to the *Financial Promotion Order*, of making arrangements:
(a) for another *person* to enter as borrower into an agreement for the provision of *qualifying credit*; or
(b) for a borrower under a *regulated mortgage contract*, entered into on or after 31 October 2004, to vary the terms of that contract.

arranging safeguarding and administration of assets

that part of *safeguarding and administering investments* which consists solely of arranging for one or more other *persons* to carry on both:
(a) the safeguarding of assets belonging to another; and
(b) the administration of those assets.

arrears

(in relation to a *regulated mortgage contract* or a *home purchase plan*) either:
(a) a shortfall (equivalent to two or more regular payments) in the accumulated total payments actually made by the *customer* measured against the accumulated total amount of payments due to be received from the *customer*; or
(b) remaining in breach, for more than one month, of an agreed borrowing limit or of an obligation to pay or repay where the loan or *home purchase plan* does not have a regular payment or repayment plan.

Article 129 implementing measure

any:
(a) measure taken by the *FSA* under regulations 7-9 of the *Capital Requirements Regulations 2006*; or
(b) corresponding measure taken by another *competent authority* to apply an *Article 129 permission* as referred to in the last paragraph of Article 129(2) of the *Banking Consolidation Directive*.

Article 129 permission

a permission of the type referred to in Article 129(2) of the *Banking Consolidation Directive* (permission to apply the *IRB approach*, the *AMA approach* or the *CCR internal model method* on a consolidated basis) or Article 37(2) of the *Capital Adequacy Directive* (permission to apply the *VaR model approach* on a consolidated basis) excluding an *Article 129 implementing measure*.

Article 129 procedure

the procedure described in Article 129(2) of the *Banking Consolidation Directive* (permission to apply the *IRB approach*, the *AMA approach* or the *CCR internal model method* on a consolidated basis) or that applies under Article 37(2) of the *Capital Adequacy Directive* (permission to apply the

VaR model approach on a consolidated basis) for the purpose of applying for and granting or refusing an *Article 129 permission* or the procedure for varying of revoking an *Article 129 permission* in accordance with the *Banking Consolidation Directive* or the *Capital Adequacy Directive*.

Article 134 relationship

(in accordance with Article 134 of the *Banking Consolidation Directive*) a relationship of one of the following kinds:

(a) where a *person* exercises a significant influence over one or more *persons*, but without holding a *participation* or other capital ties in these *persons* and without being a *parent undertaking* of these *persons*; or

(b) where two or more *persons* are placed under single management other than pursuant to a contract or clauses of their memoranda or articles of association.

article 9 default

(as defined in article 2(2) of the *compensation transitionals order*) any of the following:

(a) the passing of a resolution for the voluntary winding up of an authorised insurance company within the meaning of section 3 of the Policyholders Protection Act 1975 in circumstances falling within section 5(1)(a) of that Act;

(b) the making by the court of an order for the winding up of such a company in accordance with section 5(1)(b) of that Act;

(c) the appointment of a provisional liquidator in the circumstances falling within section 15 of that Act in respect of such a company;

(d) such a company becoming a company in financial difficulties within the meaning of section 16 of that Act;

(e) a *participating deposit-taker* becoming insolvent for the purposes of Part II of the Banking Act 1987;

(f) a *participating institution* becoming insolvent within the meaning of section 25A of the Building Societies Act 1986;

(g) the beginning of a dissolution or transfer of engagements of a *member society* in accordance with rule 9(2) of the Rules of the Friendly Societies Protection Scheme.

assessable mutual

(for the purposes of INSPRU 1.4) a *mutual* where the *insurance business* carried on by the *mutual* is limited to the provision of *insurance business* to its members and whose articles of association, rules or byelaws provide for the calling of additional contributions from members to meet *claims*.

asset

(in RCB) (as defined in Regulation 1(2) of the *RCB Regulations*) any property, right, entitlement or interest.

asset backed commercial paper programme

(for the purposes of BIPRU 9 (Securitisation) and in accordance with Part 1 of Annex IX of the *Banking Consolidation Directive* (Securitisation definitions)) a programme of *securitisations* (within the meaning of paragraph (2) of the definition of securitisation) the securities issued by which predominantly take the form of commercial paper with an original maturity of one year or less.

asset backed security

(as defined in the *PD Regulation*) securities which:

(a) represent an interest in assets, including any rights intended to assure servicing, or the receipt or timeliness of receipts by holders of assets of amounts payable thereunder; or

(b) are secured by assets and the terms of which provide for payments which relate to payments or reasonable projections of payments calculated by reference to identified or identifiable assets.

asset identification rules

(as defined in subsection 142(2) of the *Act* (Insurance business: regulations supplementing Authority's rules)) *rules* made by the *FSA* which require an *authorised person* who has *permission* to *effect* or *carry out contracts of insurance* to identify assets which belong to him and which are maintained in respect of a particular aspect of his business.

asset management company

a management company within the meaning of Article 1a(2) of the *UCITS Directive*, as well as an *undertaking* the registered office of which is outside the *EEA* and which would require authorisation in accordance with Article 5(1) of the *UCITS Directive* if it had its registered office within the *EEA*.

asset pool

(in RCB) (as defined in Regulation 1(2) of the *RCB Regulations*) an asset pool within the meaning of Regulation 3 of the *RCB Regulations*.

asset-related capital requirement

a component of the calculation of the *ECR* for a *firm* carrying on *general insurance business* as set out in INSPRU 2.2.

assistance

(in relation to a *class* of *contract of insurance*) the *class* of *contract of insurance*, specified in paragraph 18 of Part I of Schedule 1 to the *Regulated Activities* Order (Contracts of general insurance), providing either or both of the following benefits:

(a) assistance (whether in cash or in kind) for *persons* who get into difficulties while travelling, while away from home or while away from their permanent residence;

(b) assistance (whether in cash or in kind) for *persons* who get into difficulties otherwise than as in (a).

assisting in the administration and performance of a contract of insurance

the *regulated activity*, specified in article 39A of the *Regulated Activities Order* (Assisting in the administration and performance of a contract of insurance) of assisting in the administration and performance of a contract of insurance.

associate

(1) (in LR) (in relation to a director, substantial shareholder, or person exercising significant influence, who is an individual):
   (a) that individual's spouse, civil partner or child (together "the individual's family");
   (b) the trustees (acting as such) of any trust of which the individual or any of the individual's family is a beneficiary or discretionary object (other than a trust which is either an *occupational pension scheme* or an *employees' share scheme* which does not, in either case, have the effect of conferring benefits on persons all or most of whom are related parties;
   (c) any *company* in whose *equity securities* the individual or any member or members (taken together) of the individual's family or the individual and any such member or members (taken together) are directly or indirectly interested (or have a conditional or contingent entitlement to become interested) so that they are (or would on the fulfilment of the condition or the occurrence of the contingency be) able:
      (i) to exercise or control the exercise of 30% or more of the votes able to be cast at general meetings on all, or substantially all, matters; or
      (ii) to appoint or remove *directors* holding a majority of voting rights at board meetings on all, or substantially all, matters.

   For the purpose of paragraph (c), if more than one *director* of the *listed company*, its *parent undertaking* or any of is *subsidiary undertakings* is interested in the *equity securities* of another *company*, then the interests of those *directors* and their *associates* will be aggregated when determining whether that *company* is an associate of the *director*.

(2) (in *LR*) (in relation to a *substantial shareholder*, or *person exercising significant influence*, which is a *company*):
   (a) any other *company* which is its *subsidiary undertaking* or *parent undertaking* or fellow *subsidiary undertaking* of the *parent undertaking*;
   (b) any *company* whose *directors* are accustomed to act in accordance with the *substantial shareholder's*, or *person exercising significant influence's* directions or instructions;
   (c) any *company* in the capital of which the *substantial shareholder* or *person exercising significant influence* and any other *company* under paragraph (1) or (2) taken together, is (or would on the fulfilment of a condition or the occurrence of a contingency be) able to exercise power of the type described in paragraph (1)(c)(i) or (ii) of this definition.

(3) (except in LR) (in relation to a *person* ("A")):
   (a) an *affiliated company* of A;
   (b) an *appointed representative* of A, or a *tied agent* of A, or of any *affiliated company* of A;
   (c) any other *person* whose business or domestic relationship with A or his *associate* might reasonably be expected to give rise to a community of interest between them which may involve a conflict of interest in dealings with third parties.

associated call option

a right to acquire a particular amount of the *relevant security* or of any *associated security* at a future date at a particular *price*.

associated instrument

(as defined in Article 2 of the *Buy-back and Stabilisation Regulation*) any of the following *financial instruments* (including those which are not admitted to trading on a *regulated market*, or for which

Part II FSA Handbook Materials

a request for admission to trading on such a market has not been made, provided that the relevant competent authorities have agreed to standards of transparency for transactions in such *financial instruments*):

(a) contracts or rights to subscribe for, acquire or dispose of *relevant securities*;

(b) financial derivatives on *relevant securities*;

(c) where the *relevant securities* are convertible or exchangeable debt instruments, the securities into which such convertible or exchangeable debt instruments may be converted or exchanged;

(d) instruments which are issued or guaranteed by the *issuer* or guarantor of the *relevant securities* and whose market price is likely to materially influence the price of the *relevant securities*, or vice versa; and

(e) where the relevant securities are securities equivalent to shares, the shares represented by those securities (and any other securities equivalent to those shares).

at the money

(for the purposes of BIPRU 7 (Market risk) and in relation to an *option* or *warrant*) the strike price of that *option* or *warrant* being equal to the current market value of the underlying instrument.

Audit Directive

Directive 2006/43/EC of the European Parliament and of the Council of 17 May 2006 on statutory audits of annual accounts and consolidated accounts, amending Council Directives 78/660/EEC and 83/349/EEC and repealing Council Directive 84/253/EEC.

AUT

an *authorised unit trust scheme*.

authorisation

authorisation as an *authorised person* for the purposes of the *Act*.

authorisation order

an order made by the *FSA*:

(a) in relation to an *AUT* under section 243 of the *Act* (Authorisation orders);

(b) in relation to an *ICVC* under regulation 14 of the *OEIC Regulations* (Authorisation);

as a result of which the *AUT* becomes authorised or the body becomes incorporated as an *ICVC* under regulation 3 of the *OEIC Regulations* (Open-ended investment company).

authorised corporate director

the *director* of an *ICVC* who is the authorised corporate *director* of the *ICVC* in accordance with COLL 6.5.3R (Appointment of an ACD including, if relevant, an *EEA UCITS management company*.

authorised fund

an *ICVC* or an *AUT*.

authorised fund manager

an *ACD* or an *authorised unit trust manager*.

authorised insurance company

(In *COMP*) (in accordance with the *compensation transitionals order*) a *person* who was, at any time before *commencement*, authorised under section 3 or 4 of the Insurance Companies Act 1982 to carry on insurance business of any class in the *United Kingdom*.

authorised payment institution

(in accordance with regulation 2(1) of the *Payment Services Regualtions*) a *person* included by the FSA in the FSA Register as an authorised payment institution pursuant to regulation 4(1)(a), or a *person* deemed to have been granted authorisation by the FSA by virtue of regulation 121 of the *Payment Services Regulations*.

authorised person

(in accordance with section 31 of the *Act* (Authorised persons)) one of the following:

(a) a *person* who has a *Part IV permission* to carry on one or more regulated activities;

(b) an *incoming EEA firm;*

(c) an *incoming Treaty firm;*

(d) a *UCITS qualifier;*

(e) an *ICVC;*

(f) the *Society of Lloyd's*.

(see also *GEN* 2.2.18R for the position of an *authorised partnership* or unincorporated association which is dissolved.)

authorised professional firm

a *professional firm* which is an authorised person.

authorised UK representative

(in relation to a *firm*) a *person* resident in the *United Kingdom* who is authorised to act generally, and to accept service of any *document*, on behalf of the *firm*.

authorised unit trust manager

a *manager* of an *AUT*.

authorised unit trust scheme

(as defined in section 237(3) of the *Act* (Other definitions)) a *unit trust scheme* which is authorised for the purposes of the *Act* by an *authorisation order*.

authorised Voluntary Jurisdiction participant

a participant in the *Voluntary Jurisdiction* who is an *authorised person*.

AVC

a voluntary contribution arrangement paid by a member of an *occupational pension scheme* under the terms of the scheme or of a separate contract.

backtesting exception

(in BIPRU 7.10 (Use of a value at risk model)) an exception (excluding a *specific risk backtesting exception*) arising out of backtesting a *VaR model* as more fully defined in BIPRU 7.10.103R.

backwardation

a situation in which *futures* prices are lower than cash prices.

balance

(in relation to a *person's account*) has the meaning given in section 8 of the Dormant Bank and Building Society Accounts Act 2008, which is in summary the amount owing to the *person* in respect of the *account* at any particular time, after the appropriate adjustments have been made for such things as interest due and fees and charges payable. In relation to a time after a transfer of the *balance* to a *dormant account fund operator,* the adjustments include those that would fall to be made but for the transfer or transfers.

balancing amount

in respect of a *syndicate*, any part of the *capital resources* that:
(a) the *managing agent* of the *syndicate* has assessed to be necessary to support the *insurance business* carried on by the *members* of the *syndicate* through the *syndicate*, including those *capital resources* required to support the risks arising at *syndicate* level that affect that business; but
(b) are not managed by or at the direction of the *managing agent* of the *syndicate*.

Balancing and Settlement Code

the document designated by the Secretary of State and adopted by the National Grid Company plc as the Balancing and Settlement Code as modified from time to time in accordance with the terms of the transmission licence granted under section 6(1)(b) of the Electricity Act 1989 in respect of England and Wales, or any subsequent similar instrument or arrangements.

bank

(a) a *firm* with a *Part IV* permission which includes *accepting deposits*, and:
  (i) which is a *credit institution*; or
  (ii) whose *Part IV permission* includes a *requirement* that it comply with the *rules* in GENPRU and BIPRU relating to *banks*;
  but which is not a building society, a friendly society or a credit union;
(b) an EEA bank which is a full credit institution.

Bank Accounts Directive

Council Directive 86/635/EEC of 8 December 1986 on the annual accounts and consolidated accounts of banks and other financial institutions.

banking and investment group

a group of *persons* (at least one of which is an *EEA regulated entity* that is a *credit institution* or an *investment firm*) who:
(a) form a group in respect of which the consolidated capital adequacy requirements for the *banking sector* or the *investment services sector* under:
  (i) the *FSA's sectoral rules*; or

(ii) the *sectoral rules* of another *competent authority*; apply; or
(b) would form such a group if the scope of those *sectoral rules* were amended as described in paragraph 3.1 of GENPRU 3 Ann 2R (removing restrictions relating to place of incorporation or head office of members of those *financial sectors*).

banking and investment services conglomerate

a *financial conglomerate* that is identified in paragraph 4.3 of GENPRU 3 Ann 1R (Types of financial conglomerate) as a *banking and investment services conglomerate*

banking and investment services sector

(in relation to a *financial sector* in a *consolidation group* or a *financial conglomerate* and in accordance with GENPRU 3.1 (Cross sector groups)), the *investment services sector* and the *banking sector* taken together

Banking Consolidation Directive

the Directive of the European Parliament and the Council of 14 June 2006 relating to the taking up and pursuit of the business of credit institutions (No 2006/48/EC).

banking customer

(in BCOBS):
(a) a *consumer*;
(b) a *micro-enterprise*; or
(c) a *charity* which has an annual income of less than £1 million.

A natural person acting in a capacity as a trustee is a *banking customer* if he is acting for purposes outside his trade, business or profession.

Banking Ombudsman scheme

the *former scheme* set up, on a voluntary basis, to handle complaints against those banks which subscribed to it.

banking sector

a sector composed of one or more of the following entities:
(a) a *credit institution*;
(b) a *financial institution*; and
(c) an *ancillary ervices undertaking* that is not an *ancillary insurance services undertaking*.

base capital resources requirement

an amount of *capital resources* that an insurer must hold as set out in GENPRU 2.1.30R (Table: Base capital resources requirement for an insurer) or a *BIPRU firm* must hold under GENPRU 2.1.41R (*Base capital resources requirement* for a *BIPRU firm*) and GENPRU 2.1.48R (Table: Base capital resources requirement for a BIPRU firm) or, as the case may be, GENPRU 2.1.60R (Calculation of the base capital resources requirement for banks authorised before 1993).

base costs

management expenses, other than *establishment costs*, which are not dependent on the level of *claims* made on the *FSCS*.

base costs levy

a levy, forming part of the *management expenses levy*, to meet the *base costs* in the financial year of the *compensation scheme* to which the levy relates, each *participant firm's* share being calculated in accordance with FEES 6.4.5R.

base currency

(1) (in *COLL*) the currency specified:
    (a) in the *instrument of incorporation* of an *ICVC* as the currency in which its accounts are to be prepared; or
    (b) in the *trust deed* of an *AUT* as the base currency of the *AUT*.
(2) (in *ELM*, *GENPRU* and *BIPRU*) (in relation to a *firm*) the currency in which that *firm's* books of account are drawn up.

base prospectus

(in *Part 6 rules*) a base prospectus referred to in PR 2.2.7R.

basic advice

the *regulated activity*, specified in article 52B of the *Regulated Activities Order* (Providing basic advice on stakeholder products) which is, in summary, providing advice on *stakeholder products* using a process that involves putting pre-scripted questions to a *retail client*.

basic indicator approach

the approach to calculating the *ORCR* set out in BIPRU 6.3 (Operational risk: Basic indicator approach)

basis risk

the risk that the relationship between two financial variables will change, particularly between two sorts of interest rate or between a hedge and the position it ostensibly hedges.

BCD

Banking Consolidation Directive.

BCD credit institution

a *credit institution* that has its registered office (or, if it has no registered office, its head office) in an *EEA State*, excluding an institution to which the *BCD* does not apply under article 2 of the *BCD* (see also *full BCD credit institution.*).

BCOBS

the Banking: Conduct of Business sourcebook.

bearer certificate

(in *COLL*) a certificate or other documentary evidence of title, for which provision is made in the *instrument constituting the scheme*, which indicates that:

(a) the *holder* of the document is entitled to the *units* specified in it; and
(b) no entry will be made on the *register* identifying the *holder* of those *units*.

bearer form

(in relation to a *client's* certificate, *share* transfer or other *document*) in a form signed by the *client* so that it enables a *designated investment* or *deposit* to which it relates to be sold, transferred, surrendered or dealt with in any other way without the need to obtain further written instructions and allows the *firm* access to the sale proceeds.

behaviour

any kind of conduct, including action or inaction.

bid price

the price at which a *person* could sell a *unit* in a *dual-priced authorised fund* or a *security*.

biofuel

liquid or gaseous fuel produced from *biomass*.

biofuel collective investment scheme

a *collective investment scheme*, the property of which consists only of property which is *biofuel* or a *biofuel investment* or cash awaiting investment.

biofuel investment

any of the following:

(a) a *unit* in a *biofuel collective investment scheme*;
(b) an *option* to acquire or dispose of a *biofuel investment*;
(c) a *future* where the *commodity* in question is *biofuel*;
(d) a *contract for differences* where the property in question is *biofuel* or a *biofuel investment* or the index or other factor in question is linked to or otherwise dependent upon fluctuations in the value or price of *biofuel* or any *biofuel investments*;
(e) *rights to or interests in investments* in (a) to (d).

biomass

the biodegradable fraction of products, waste and residues from agricultural (including vegetal and animal substances), forestry and related industries, as well as the biodegradable fraction of industrial and municipal waste.

biomass investment

any of the following:

(a) a *unit* in a *biomass collective investment scheme*;
(b) an *option* to acquire or dispose of a *biomass investment*;
(c) a *future* where the *commodity* in question is *biomass*;
(d) a *contract for differences* where the property in question is *biomass* or a *biomass investment* or the index or other factor in question is linked to or otherwise dependent upon fluctuations in the value or price of *biomass* or any *biomass investments*;
(e) *rights to or interests in investments* in (a) to (d).

biomass collective investment scheme

a *collective investment scheme*, the property of which consists only of property which is *biomass* or a *biomass investment* or cash awaiting investment.

BIPRU

the Prudential sourcebook for Banks, Building Societies and Investment Firms.

BIPRU 50K firm

has the meaning in BIPRU 1.1.20R (Types of investment firm: BIPRU 50K firm) which in summary is a *BIPRU investment firm* that satisfies the following conditions:

(a) it satisfies the conditions in BIPRU 1.1.19R(1) (does not *deal on own account* or underwrite issues of *financial instruments* on a firm commitment basis) and *BIPRU* 1.1.19R(3) (offers one or more of certain specified services);

(b) it does not hold clients' money or securities in relation to *investment services* it provides and it is not authorised to do so;

(c) it is not a *UCITS investment firm*; and

(d) it does not operate a *multilateral trading facility*.

BIPRU 125K firm

has the meaning in BIPRU 1.1.19R (Types of investment firm: BIPRU 125K firm) which in summary is a *BIPRU investment firm* that satisfies the following conditions:

(1) it does not *deal on own account* or underwrite issues of *financial instruments* on a firm commitment basis;

(2) it holds clients' money or securities in relation to *investment services* it provides or is authorised to do so;

(3) it offers one or more of certain specified services;

(4) it is not a *UCITS investment firm*; and

(5) it does not operate a *multilateral trading facility*.

BIPRU 730K firm

has the meaning in BIPRU 1.1.21R (Types of investment firm: BIPRU 730K firm) which in summary is a *BIPRU investment firm* that is not a *UCITS investment firm*, a *BIPRU 50K firm* or a *BIPRU 125K firm*.

BIPRU firm

has the meaning set out BIPRU 1.1.6 (The definition of a BIPRU firm), which is in summary a *firm* that is:

(a) a *building society*; or

(b) a *bank*; or

(c) a *full scope BIPRU investment firm*; or

(d) a *BIPRU limited licence firm*; or

(e) a *BIPRU limited activity firm*;

but excluding *firms* of the type listed in *BIPRU* 1.1.7R (Exclusion of certain types of *firm* from the definition of *BIPRU firm*).

BIPRU investment firm

has the meaning set out BIPRU 1.1.8R (Definition of a *BIPRU investment firm*), which is in summary one of the following types of *BIPRU firm*:

(a) a *full scope BIPRU investment firm*; or

(b) a *BIPRU limited licence firm*; or

(c) a *BIPRU limited activity firm*;

including a *UCITS investment firm* that is not excluded under BIPRU 1.1.7R (Exclusion of certain types of *firm* from the definition of *BIPRU firm*).

BIPRU limited activity firm

has the meaning in BIPRU 1.1.17R (Types of BIPRU investment firm), which is in summary a *limited activity firm* that meets the following conditions:

(a) it is a *firm*; and

(b) its head office is in the *United Kingdom* and it is not otherwise excluded from the definition of *BIPRU firm* under BIPRU 1.1.7R (Exclusion of certain types of *firm* from the definition of *BIPRU firm*).

BIPRU limited licence firm

has the meaning in BIPRU 1.1.17R (Types of BIPRU investment firm), which is in summary a *limited licence firm* that meets the following conditions:

(a) it is a *firm*; and

(b) its head office is in the *United Kingdom* and it is not otherwise excluded from the definition of *BIPRU firm* under BIPRU 1.1.7R (Exclusion of certain types of *firm* from the definition of *BIPRU firm*).

body corporate

(in accordance with section 417(1) of the *Act* (Definitions)) any body corporate, including a body corporate constituted under the law of acountry or territory outside the *United Kingdom*.

bonded investment

a *designated investment* not held by a trustee when acting as a trustee:

(a) which, except in the case of a *unit*, is one of the following:

(i) a *readily realisable security* held for a *customer*, whether or not held under a discretionary arrangement; or

(ii) a *designated investment* in *bearer form;* or

(iii) a *designated investment* held by a *nominee company* under the control of the *firm* or a *person* whom the *firm* controls; or

(b) a *designated investment* to which the title is recorded in electronic form;

(c) which the *firm* may *sell* or procure the sale of without the signature or other action of the *customer* or an independent third party; and

(d) where the proceeds of such a sale are or could be payable to the *firm* or its *associate*.

book value of property

(in LR) (in relation to a *property company*) the value of a *property* (which is not classified as a net current asset) before the deduction of mortgages or borrowings as shown in the *company's* latest annual report and accounts.

borrow back

a feature of a *regulated mortgage contract* under which the *customer* has the ability to re-borrow monies paid by him.

branch

(a) (in relation to a *credit institution)*:

(i) a place of business which forms a legally dependent part of a *credit institution* and which carries out directly all or some of the transactions inherent in the business of *credit institutions*;

(ii) for the purposes of the *Banking Consolidation Directive*, any number of places of business set up in the same *EEA State* by a *credit institution* with headquarters in another *EEA State* are to be regarded as a single *branch*;

(b) (in relation to an *investment firm*):

(i) a place of business other than the head office which is a part of an *investment firm*, which has no legal personality and which provides *investment services and/or activities* and which may also perform *ancillary services* for which the *firm* has been authorized;

(ii) all the places of business set up in the same *EEA State* by an *investment firm* with headquarters in another *EEA State* are regarded as a single branch;

[Note: article 4(1)(26) of *MiFID*]

(c) (in relation to an *insurance undertaking*) any permanent presence of the *insurance undertaking* in an *EEA State* other than that in which it has its head office is to be regarded as a single *branch*, whether that presence consists of a single office which, or two or more offices each of which:

(i) is managed by the *insurance undertaking's* own staff; or

(ii) is an agency of the *insurance undertaking*; or

(iii) is managed by a *person* who is independent of the *insurance undertaking*, but has permanent authority to act for the *insurance undertaking* as an agency would.

(d) (in relation to an *IMD insurance intermediary*):

(i) a place of business which is a part of an *IMD insurance intermediary*, not being the principal place of business, which has no separate legal personality and which provides *insurance mediation* for which the *IMD insurance intermediary* has been registered;

(ii) for the purposes of the *Insurance Mediation Directive*, all the places of business set up in the same *EEA State* by an *IMD insurance intermediary* with headquarters in another *EEA State* are to be regarded as a single *branch*.

(e) (in relation to an *IMD reinsurance intermediary*):

(i) a place of business which is a part of an *IMD reinsurance intermediary*, not being the principal place of business, which has no separate legal personality and which provides *reinsurance mediation* for which the *IMD reinsurance intermediary* has been registered;

(ii) for the purposes of the *Insurance Mediation Directive*, all the places of business set up in the same *EEA State* by an *IMD reinsurance intermediary* with headquarters in another *EEA State* are to be regarded as a single *branch*.

(f) (in relation to an *EEA UCITS management company*):

(i) a place of business which is a part of an *EEA UCITS management company*, which has no separate legal personality and which provides the services for which the *EEA UCITS management company* has been authorised;

(ii) for the purposes of the *UCITS Directive*, all the places of business set up in the same *EEA State* by an *EEA UCITS management company* with headquarters in another *EEA State* are to be regarded as a single *branch*.

(g) (in accordance with regulation 2(1) of the *Payment Services Regulations*) (in relation to a *payment institution*, other than its head office, which forms a legally dependent part of the institution and which carries out directly all or some of the transactions inherent in its business. For the purposes of the *Payment Services Regulations*, all places of business set up in the same *EEA State* other than the *United Kingdom* by an *authorised payment institution* are to be regarded as a single branch.

[**Note**: article 4(29) of the *Payment Services Directive*]

branded fund

[deleted]

breach

in *DEPP*:

(1) misconduct in respect of which the *FSA* is empowered to take action pursuant to section 66 (Disciplinary powers) of the *Act*; or
(2) a contravention in respect of which the *FSA* is empowered to impose a penalty pursuant to section 91 (Penalties for breach of listing rules) of the *Act*; or
(3) a contravention for the purposes of Part XIV (Disciplinary Measures); or
(4) behaviour amounting to *market abuse*, or to *requiring* or *encouraging market abuse*, in respect of which the *FSA* takes action pursuant to section 123 (Power to impose penalties in cases of market abuse) of the *Act;* or
(5) a contravention of any directly applicable *EU* regulation made under MiFID.

break fee

(in LR) a fee payable by a *listed company* if certain specified events occur which have the effect of materially impeding a transaction or causing the transaction to fail.

broker

(in *MAR*, SYSC and INSPRU) any person when dealing as agent.

broker fund

(in relation to a fund for which the *firm* is or will be a *broker fund adviser*):

(a) an actual or notional fund of a *long-term insurer* or *overseas long-term insurer*, which contains or will contain contributions made or to be made by a *client* or *clients* of a *firm* in connection with a *life policy* or *policies*;
(b) a fund of a *collective investment scheme*, which contains or will contain cash contributions made or to be made by a *client* or *clients* of a *firm* in connection with the purchase of *units* in the *scheme*.

broker fund adviser

a *firm* which has, or whose *associate* being an *authorisedperson* has, an arrangement with a *long-term insurer, overseas* long-term insurer or *operator* of a *regulated collective investment scheme*, under which it is to be expected that the *long-term insurer, overseas long-term insurer* or *operator* will take into account the advice of that *firm* or its *associate:*

(a) in the case of a *long-term insurer* or *overseas long-term insurer*, on any matter likely to influence the performance of any of the *long-term insurer's* or *overseas long-term insurer's* funds or of any *investment* issued by the *long-term insurer* or *overseas long-term insurer* into which cash contributions of that *firm's customers* have been made;
(b) in the case of an *operator*, on the composition of the property of the *collective investment scheme* into which cash contributions of that *firm's customers* have been made;

in this definition, *associate* includes any *authorised person* in respect of whose services the first *firm* receives any benefit or reward, either directly or indirectly, in connection with advice of the kind described in (a) and (b) given to a *long-term insurer* or *overseas long-term insurer* or to a *collective investment scheme operator*.

brought forward amount

an amount, as defined in INSPRU 1.1.51R, used in the calculation of the *general insurance capital requirement*.

buffer securities restriction

BIPRU 12.6.16R.

building block

(in PR and LR) (as defined in the *PD Regulation*) a list of additional information requirements, not included in one of the schedules, to be added to one or more schedules, as the case may be, depending on the type of instrument and/or transaction for which a prospectus or base prospectus is drawn up.

building society

(as defined in section 119(1) of the Building Societies Act 1986) a building society incorporated (or deemed to be incorporated) under that Act.

Building Societies Ombudsman scheme

the *former scheme* set up and recognised under the Building Societies Act 1986 to handle complaints about *building societies*.

business day

(1) (in relation to anything done or to be done in (including to be submitted to a place in) any part of the *United Kingdom*):
  (a) (except in *REC*) any *day* which is not a Saturday or Sunday, Christmas Day, Good Friday or a bank holiday in that part of the *United Kingdom;*
  (b) (in *REC*) (as defined in section 167 of the Companies Act 1989) any *day* which is not a Saturday or Sunday, Christmas Day, Good Friday or a bank holiday in any part of the *United Kingdom.*

(2) (in relation to anything done or to be done by reference to a market outside the *United Kingdom*) any *day* on which that market is normally open for business.

business illustration

an *illustration* for a *regulated mortgage contract* that is for a business purpose.

business offer document

an *offer document* for a *regulated mortgage contract* that is for a business purpose.

Business Order

the Financial Services and Markets Act 2000 (Carrying on Regulated Activities by Way of Business Order) 2001 (SI 2001/1177).

Buy-back and Stabilisation Regulation

Commission Regulation (EC) of 22 December 2003 implementing the *Market Abuse Directive* as regards exemptions for buy-back programmes and stabilisation of financial instruments (No 2273/2003).

buy-back programme

(as defined in Article 2 of the *Buy-back and Stabilisation Regulation*) trading in own shares in accordance with Articles 19 to 24 of the *PLC Safeguards Directive*.

buying

(in accordance with article 3(1) of the *Regulated Activities Order* (Interpretation)) any form of buying, including acquiring for valuable consideration.

byelaw

any Byelaw, direction, regulation, or other instrument made using the powers of the *Council* under section 6 of Lloyd's Act 1982 (including any regulation ratified by the *Council* by special resolution) and any condition or requirement made under any such Byelaw, direction, regulation or other instrument.

CAD

Capital Adequacy Directive

CAD 1 model

a risk management model of the type described in BIPRU 7.9 (Use of a CAD 1 model).

CAD 1 model approach

one of the following:

(a) the approach to calculating part of the *market risk capital requirement* set out in BIPRU 7.9 (Use of a CAD 1 model);

(b) (where the approach in (a) is being applied on a consolidated basis) the method in (a) as applied on a consolidated basis in accordance with BIPRU 8 (Group risk — consolidation); or

(c) when the reference is to the rules of or administered by a *regulatory body* other than the *FSA*, whatever corresponds to the approach in (a) or (b), as the case may be, under those rules.

CAD 1 model waiver

a *waiver* that requires a *firm* to use the *CAD 1 model approach* on a solo basis or, if the context requires, a consolidated basis.

CAD Article 22 group

a *UK consolidation group* or *non-EEA sub-group* that meets the conditions in BIPRU 8.4.9R (Definition of a CAD Article 22 group).

CAD bank

a *bank* which uses the *Capital Adequacy Directive* to measure the capital requirement on its trading book.

CAD full scope firm

has the meaning set out BIPRU 1.1.13R (Types of investment firm: CAD full scope firm), which in summary is a *CAD investment firm* that is not a *limited activity firm* or a *limited licence firm.*

CAD investment firm

has the meaning set out BIPRU 1.1.14R (Types of investment firm: CAD investment firm), which in summary is an *investment firm* that is subject to the requirements imposed by the *MiFID* (or which would be subject to that Directive if its head office were in an *EEA State*) but excluding a *bank*, a *building society*, an *ELMI*, a *credit institution*, a *local* and an *exempt CAD firm*.

callable contribution

amounts that *members* are liable to pay to the *Society* (or may by resolution of the *Society* be liable to pay) as contributions to the *Central Fund.*

cancellation

(in COLL) (in relation to *units*) a cancellation of a *unit* by an *ICVC* or by the *trustee* of an *AUT.*

cancellation price

(in COLL) (in relation to the *cancellation* of *units* in a *dual-priced authorised fund*) the *price* for each *unit* payable by the *depositary* to the *authorised fund manager* on that *cancellation.*

candidate

a *person* in respect of whom an application is made for approval under section 59 of the *Act* (Approval for particular arrangements).

capacity transfer market

any method of transferring capacity in *syndicates*, including capacity auctions, bilateral arrangements, capacity offers, minority buy-outs and conversion schemes.

capital account

(in COLL) an account relating to the *capital property* of an *authorised fund.*

Capital Adequacy Directive

the Directive of the European Parliament and the Council of 14 June 2006 on capital adequacy of investment firms and credit institutions (No 2006/49/EC).

capital instrument

(in GENPRU and BIPRU and in relation to an *undertaking*) any *security* issued by or loan made to that *undertaking* or any other investment in, or external contribution to the capital of, that *undertaking*.

capital market-driven transaction

(in accordance with point 2 of Part 1 of Annex VIII of the *Banking Consolidation Directive* (Eligible forms of credit risk mitigation)) any transaction giving rise to an *exposure* secured by collateral which includes a provision conferring upon the *person* with the *exposure* the right to receive margin frequently.

capital property

(in COLL) the *scheme property*, other than *income property* and any amount for the time being standing to the credit of the *distribution account.*

capital redemption

(in relation to a *class* of *contract of insurance*) capital redemption contracts where effected or carried out by a *person* who does not carryon a banking business, and otherwise carries on the *regulated activity* of *effecting* or *carrying out contracts of insurance*, as specified in paragraph VI of Part II of Schedule 1 to the *Regulated Activities Order* (Contracts of long-term insurance).

Capital Requirements Regulations 2006

the Capital Requirements Regulations 2006 (SI 2006/3221).

capital resources

(1) in relation to a *BIPRU firm* or an *insurer*, the *firm's* capital resources as calculated in accordance with the *capital resources table* including, in relation to a *BIPRU firm*, as that calculation is adjusted under *BIPRU* 10.5 for the purposes of *BIPRU* 10 (Concentration risk requirements); or

(2) (in relation to an *institution* that is an *EEA firm* and not a *BIPRU firm* and which is required to meet the capital resources requirements of the *CRD implementation measures* for its *EEA State* on an individual basis) capital resources calculated under those *CRD implementation measures*; or

(3) (for the purposes of *GENPRU* and *BIPRU*, in relation to an *undertaking* not falling within (1) or (2) and subject to (4)), capital resources calculated in accordance with (1) on the assumption that:

  (a) it is a *BIPRU firm* with a *Part IV permission*; and

  (b) it carries on all its business in the *United Kingdom* and has obtained whatever *permissions* for doing so are required under the *Act*; or

(4) (for the purposes of *GENPRU* and *BIPRU* and in relation to any *undertaking* not falling within (1) or (2) for which the methodology in (3) does not give an answer whose *capital resources* a *BIPRU firm* (the "relevant firm") is required to calculate under a *Handbook rule*) capital resources calculated under (1) on the assumption that it is a *BIPRU firm* of the same category as the relevant firm.

capital resources gearing rules

(1) (in relation to an *insurer*) GENPRU 2.2.29R, GENPRU 2.2.30R and GENPRU 2.2.32R to GENPRU 2.2.41R.

(2) (in relation to a *bank* or *building society*) GENPRU 2.2.29R, GENPRU 2.2.30R, GENPRU 2.2.46R and GENPRU 2.2.49R.

(3) (in relation to a *BIPRU investment firm*) GENPRU 2.2.30R, GENPRU 2.2.46R and GENPRU 2.2.49R and GENPRU 2.2.50R.

capital resources requirement

an amount of *capital resources* that:

(1) a *BIPRU firm* must hold as set out in the *main BIPRU firm Pillar 1 rules*; or

(2) an *insurer* must hold as set out in GENPRU 2.1.17R to GENPRU 2.1.23R.

capital resources table

(in relation to an *insurer* or *BIPRU firm*) the table specified in GENPRU 2.2.19R (Applicable capital resources calculation) which in summary is as follows:

(1) (in the case of an *insurer*) GENPRU 2 Annex 1R;

(2) (in the case of a *bank*) GENPRU 2 Annex 2R;

(3) (in the case of a *building society*) GENPRU 2 Annex 3R; and

(4) (in relation to a *BIPRU investment firm*) whichever of the tables in GENPRU 2 Annex 4R, GENPRU 2 Annex 5R or GENPRU 2 Annex 6R applies to the *firm* under GENPRU 2.2.19R.

captive reinsurer

a *pure reinsurer* owned by:

(a) a financial *undertaking* other than an *insurance undertaking* or a *reinsurance undertaking*; or

(b) a *group* of *insurance undertakings* or *reinsurance undertakings* to which the *Insurance Groups Directive* applies; or

(c) a non-financial *undertaking*, the purpose of which is to provide *reinsurance* cover exclusively for the risks of the *undertaking* or *undertakings* to which it belongs or of an *undertaking* or *undertakings* of the *group* of which that *pure reinsurer* is a member.

CARD

Consolidated Admissions and Reporting Directive.

carrying out contracts of insurance

the *regulated activity*, specified in article 10(2) of the *Regulated Activities Order* (Effecting and carrying out contracts of insurance), of carrying out a *contract of insurance* as principal.

cash assimilated instrument

(in accordance with Article 4(35) of the *Banking Consolidation Directive* (Definitions)) a certificate of deposit or other similar instrument issued by a *lending firm.*

cash component

a *qualifying investment* prescribed in paragraph 8 of the *ISA Regulations* (Qualifying investments for a cash component).

cash deposit CTF

a *deposit* account held within a *CTF.*

cash deposit ISA

a *cash component* of an *ISA* which does not include the *qualifying investments* prescribed in paragraphs 8(2)(c), (d), (e) or (f) of the *ISA Regulations.*

cashback

(in *MCOB*) a cash amount paid by a *mortgage lender* to a *customer* (typically at the beginning of a contract) as an inducement to enter into a *regulated mortgage contract* with the *mortgage lender*.

CASS

the Client Assets sourcebook.

CAT standards

the CAT standards for *ISAs* prescribed by the Treasury on 22 December 1998.

category B firm

a personal investment firm, other than an exempt CAD firm.

category B1 firm

a *category B firm* whose *permission* includes dealing in investments as principal.

category B2 firm

a *category B firm* whose *permission* does not include *dealing* as *principal*; and is not subject to a *requirement* preventing the holding or controlling of *client money* or *custody assets*.

category B3 firm

a category B firm:

(a) whose permission includes only insurance mediation activity in relation to non-investment insurance contracts, home finance mediation activity, assisting in the administration and performance of contracts of insurances, arranging transactions in life policies and other insurance contracts, advising on investments and receiving and transmitting, on behalf of investors, orders in relation to securities and units in collective investment schemes; and

(b) which is subject to a requirement not to hold or control client money or custody assets.

causing dematerialised instructions to be sent

the *regulated activity*, specified in article 45(2) of the *Regulated Activities Order*, which is in summary: causing dematerialised instructions relating to a *security* to be sent by means of a relevant system in respect of which an operator is approved under the 1995 Regulations where the *person* causing them to be sent is a system-participant;

in this definition:

(a) "the 1995 Regulations" means the Uncertificated Securities Regulations 1995 (SI 1995/3272);

(b) "dematerialised instruction", "operator" and "system-participant" have the meaning given by regulation 3 of the 1995 Regulations.

CCR

counterparty credit risk

CCR internal model method

one of the following:

(a) the method of calculating the amount of an *exposure* set out in BIPRU 13.6 (CCR internal model method);

(b) (where the approach in (a) is being applied on a consolidated basis) the method in (a) as applied on a consolidated basis in accordance with BIPRU 8 (Group risk — consolidation); or

(c) when the reference is to the rules of or administered by a *regulatory body* other than the *FSA*, whatever corresponds to the approach in (a) or (b), as the case may be, under those rules.

CCR internal model method permission

an *Article 129 implementing measure*, *Article 129 permission*, a *requirement* or a *waiver* that requires a *BIPRU firm* or an *institution* to use the *CCR internal model method*.

CCR mark to market method

the method of calculating the amount of an *exposure* set out in BIPRU 13.4 (CCR mark to market method).

CCR standardised method

the method of calculating the amount of an *exposure* set out in BIPRU 13.5 (CCR standardised method).

ceding insurer's waiver

(in FEES) a waiver granted on the application of an insurer that waives or modifies its obligations under any one or more of GENPRU 2 Annex 7R, INSPRU 1.1.92AR and INSPRU 1.2.28R in order to enable it to:

(a) trate amounts recovereable from an ISPV as:

 (i) an admissible asset; or

 (ii) reinsurance for the purposes of calculating its mathematical reservces; or

 (iii) reinsurance reduing its MCR; or

(b) otherwise ascribe a value to such amounts.

central assets

the *Society's* own assets that are available at its discretion to meet a *member's* liabilities in respect of *insurance business*.

central bank

(in accordance with Article 4(23) of the *Banking Consolidation Directive* (Definitions) and for the purposes of GENPRU and BIPRU) includes the European Central Bank unless otherwise indicated.

central counterparty

(in accordance with Part 1 of Annex III of the *Banking Consolidation Directive* (Definitions) and for the purpose of BIPRU 13 (The calculation of counterparty risk exposure values for financial derivatives, securities financing transactions and long settlement transactions)) an entity that legally interposes itself between counterparties to contracts traded within one or more financial markets, becoming the buyer to every seller and the seller to every buyer.

Central Fund

the Central Fund established under Lloyd's Central Fund Byelaw (No 4 of 1986) and the New Central Fund established under Lloyd's New Central Fund Byelaw (No 23 of 1996).

certificate representing certain securities

the *investment* specified in article 80 of the *Regulated Activities Order* (Certificates representing certain securities), which is in summary: a certificate or other instrument which confers contractual or property rights (other than rights consisting of *options*):

(a) in respect of any *share, debenture, government and public security* or *warrant*) held by a *person* other than the *person* on whom the rights are conferred by the certificate or instrument; and

(b) the transfer of which may be effected without requiring the consent of that *person;*

but excluding any certificate or other instrument which confers rights in respect of two or more *investments* issued by different *persons* or in respect of two or more different *government and public securities* issued by the same *person*.

certificate representing debt securities

(in LR) a *certificate representing certain securities* where the certificate or other instrument confers rights in respect of *debentures* or *government and public securities*.

certificate representing equity securities

(in LR) a *certificate representing certain securities* where the certificate or other instrument confers rights in respect of *equity securities*.

certificate representing shares

(in LR) a *certificate representing certain securities* where the certificate or other instrument confers rights in respect of *equity shares*.

CESR recommendations

the recommendations for the consistent implementation of the European Commission's Regulation on Prospectuses No 809/2004 published by the Committee of European Securities Regulators.

CESR's UCITS eligible assets guidelines

The Committee of European Securities Regulators' guidelines concerning eligible assets for investment by undertakings for collective investment in transferable securities (CESR/07-044). These are available at http://www.fsa.gov.uk/pages/Library/Other_publications/EU/eu_docs/index.shtml

CFD

contract for differences.

CFPPFM

the consumer-friendly version of a *firm's PPFM*, which must be produced pursuant to *COBS* 20.4.5R.

CFTC

the Commodity Futures Trading Commission.

charge

(1) (in *LR*) (in relation to *securitised derivatives*) means any payment identified under the terms and conditions of the *securitised derivatives*.

(2) (except in LR) any *fee* or charge made to:

(a) a *client* in connection with *designated investment business*; or

(b) a *customer* in connection with any *insurance mediation activities* in respect of a *non-investment insurance contract*;

whether levied by the *firm* or any other *person*, including a *mark-up or mark-down*.

chargeable case

any *complaint* referred to the *Financial Ombudsman Service*, except where:

(a) the *Ombudsman* considers it apparent from the *complaint*, when it is received, and from any *final response* which has been issued by the *firm* or *licensee*, that the *complaint* should not proceed because:

(i) the complainant is not an *eligible complainant* in accordance with DISP 2; or

(ii) the *complaint* does not fall within the jurisdiction of the *Financial Ombudsman Service* (as described in DISP 2); or

(iii) the *Ombudsman* considers that the *complaint* should be dismissed without consideration of its merits under DISP 3.3 (Dismissal of complaints without consideration of the merits and test cases); or

(b) the *Ombudsman* considers, at any stage, that the *complaint* should be dismissed under DISP 3.3.4R(2) on the grounds that it is frivolous or vexatious.

charity

(in *BCOBS*) includes:

(a) in England and Wales, a charity as defined by section 1(1) of the Charities Act 2006;

(b) in Scotland, a charity as defined by section 106 of the Cahritees and Trustee Investment (Scoland) Act 2005; or

(c) in Northern Ireland, a charity as defined by section 1(1) of the Charities Act (Northern Ireland) 2008 or, until that section comes into force, a body which is recognised as a charity for tax purposes by Her Majesty's Revenue and Customes.

chief executive

(1) (in relation to an undertaking whose principal place of business is within the *United Kingdom*) the *person* who, alone or jointly with one or more others, is responsible under the immediate authority of the *directors* for the conduct of the whole of its business.

(2) (in relation to an undertaking whose principal place of business is outside the *United Kingdom*) the *person* who, alone or jointly with one or more others, is responsible for the conduct of its business within the *United Kingdom*.

chief executive function

controlled function CF3 in the *table of controlled functions*, described more fully in *SUP* 10.6.11R.

Chinese wall

an arrangement that requires information held by a *person* in the course of carrying on one part of its business to be withheld from, or not to be used for, *persons* with or for whom it acts in the course of carrying on another part of its business.

circular

(in LR) any document issued to holders of *listed securities* including notices of meetings but excluding *prospectuses*, *listing particulars*, annual reports and accounts, interim reports, proxy cards and dividend or interest vouchers.

CIS administrator

(in relation to *firm type* in *SUP* 16.10 (Confirmation of *standing data*)) a *person* responsible for the *administrative functions* of a *collective investment scheme*.

CIS stakeholder product

the *stakeholder product* specified by regulations 5 (units in certain collective investment schemes) and 7 of the *Stakeholder Regulations*;

CIS trustee

(in relation to *firm type* in SUP 16.10 (Confirmation of *standing data*)) a *person* holding the property of a *collective investment scheme* on trust for the participants in the *collective investment scheme*.

CIU

collective investment undertaking.

CIU look through method

one of the *standard CIU look through method* or the *modified CIU look through method*.

CIU PRR

the *collective investment undertaking PRR.*

claim

(1) (in *COMP*) a valid claim made in respect of a civil liability owed by a *relevant person* to the claimant subject to *COMP* 8.2.5R (claims extinguished by operation of law).
(2) (in *INSPRU* and *SUP*) a claim under a *contract of insurance.*

claims amount

an amount, as defined in INSPRU 1.1.47R, used in the calculation of the *general insurance capital requirement.*

claims handling

[deleted]

claims representative

[deleted]

class

(1) (in GENPRU, INSPRU and SUP) (in relation to a *contract of insurance*) any class of *contract of insurance* listed in Schedule 1 to the *Regulated Activities* Order (Contracts of insurance) and references to:
 (a) *general insurance business class* 1, 2, 3, etc. are references to *contracts of insurance* of the kind mentioned in the corresponding numbered paragraph in Part I of Schedule 1 to that Order or, as the context may require, to the *effecting* or *carrying out* of *contracts of insurance* of that kind; and
 (b) *long-term insurance business class* I, II, III, etc. are references to *contracts of insurance* of the kind mentioned in the corresponding numbered paragraph in Part II of Schedule 1 to that Order or, as the context may require, to the *effecting* or *carrying out* of *contracts of insurance* of that kind.
(2) (in COLL):
 (a) a particular class of *units* of an *authorised fund*; or
 (b) all of the *units* relating to a single *sub-fund*; or
 (c) a particular class of *units* relating to a single *sub-fund.*
(3) (in COBS) a particular category or type of *packaged product.*
(4) (in LR) *securities* the rights attaching to which are or will be identical and which form a single issue or issues.
(5) (in FEES) one of the broad classes to which *FSCS* allocates levies as described in FEES 6.5.7R.

class 1 acquisition

(in LR) a *class 1 transaction* that involves an acquisition by the relevant *listed company* or its *subsidiary undertaking.*

class 1 circular

(in *LR*) a *circular* relating to a *class 1 transaction.*

class 1 disposal

(in LR) a *class 1 transaction* that consists of a disposal by the relevant *listed company* or its *subsidiary undertaking.*

class 1 transaction

(in LR and FEES) a transaction classified as a class 1 transaction under LR 10.

class 2 transaction

(in LR) a transaction classified as a class 2 transaction under LR 10.

class 3 transaction

(in LR) a transaction classified as a class 3 transaction under LR 10.

class tests

(in LR) the tests set out in LR 10 Ann 1 (and for certain specialist companies, those tests as modified by LR 10.7), which are used to determine how a transaction is to be classified for the purposes of the *listing rules.*

class meeting

(in COLL) a separate meeting of *holders* of a *class* of *units.*

Part II FSA Handbook Materials

clean hypothetical profit and loss figure

(in BIPRU 7.10 (Use of a value at risk model) and in relation to a *business day*) the *clean profit and loss figure* that would have occurred for that *business day* if the portfolio on which the *VaR number* for that *business day* is based remained unchanged, as more fully defined in BIPRU 7.10.111R (Backtesting: Hypothetical profit and loss).

clean profit and loss figure

(in BIPRU 7.10 (Use of a value at risk model) and in relation to a *business day*) a *firm's* actual profit or loss for that day in respect of the trading activities within the scope of the *firm's VaR model permission*, adjusted by stripping out specified items, as more fully defined in BIPRU 7.10.100R (Backtesting: Calculating the clean profit and loss).

clean-up call option

(for the purposes of BIPRU 9 (Securitisation), in relation to a *securitisation* (within the meaning of paragraph (2) of the definition of securitisation) and in accordance with Part 1 of Annex IX of the *Banking Consolidation Directive* (Securitisation definitions)) a contractual option for the *originator* to repurchase or extinguish the *securitisation positions* before all of the underlying *exposures* have been repaid, when the amount of outstanding *exposures* falls below a specified level.

clearing firm

a *firm* which assumes primary responsibility (including legal liability) for the execution and settlement of transactions for *clients*.

clearing house

a clearing house through which transactions on an exchange may be cleared.

client

(1) (except in *PROF* and except in relation to a home finance transaction) has the meaning given in COBS 3.2, that is (in summary and without prejudice to the detailed effect of COBS 3.2) a *person* to whom a *firm* provides, intends to provide or has provided a service in the course of carrying on a *regulated activity*, or in the case of *MiFID or equivalent third country business*, an *ancillary service*;

(2) every client is a *customer* or an *eligible counterparty*;

(3) "client" includes:
- (i) a potential client;
- (ii) a client of an *appointed representative* of a *firm* with or for whom the *appointed representative* acts or intends to act in the course of business for which the *firm* has accepted responsibility under section 39 of the *Act* (Exemption of appointed representatives) or, where applicable, a client of a *tied agent* of a *firm*;
- (iii) a *collective investment scheme* even if it does not have separate legal personality;
- (iv) if a *person* ("C1"), with or for whom the *firm* is conducting or intends to conduct *designated investment business*, is acting as agent for another *person* ("C2"), either C1 or C2 in accordance with the *rule* on agent as client *COBS* 2.4.3R;
- (v) for a *firm* that is *establishing, operating or winding up a personal pension scheme*, a member or beneficiary of that scheme;

(4) "client" does not include:
- (i) a trust beneficiary not in (b)(v);
- (ii) a *corporate finance contact;*
- (iii) a *venture capital contact.*

(5) [deleted]

(6) (in *PROF*) (as defined in section 328(8) of the *Act* (Directions in relation to the general prohibition)) (in relation to *members* of a profession providing financial services under Part XX of the *Act*(Provision of Financial Services by Members of the Professions)):
- (a) a *person* who uses, has used or may be contemplating using, any of the services provided by the *member* of a profession in the course of carrying on *exempt regulated activities* (including, where the *member* of the profession is acting in his capacity as a trustee, a *person* who is, has been or may be a beneficiary of the trust); or
- (b) a *person* who has rights or interests which are derived from, or otherwise attributable to, the use of any such services by other *persons*; or
- (c) a *person* who has rights or interests which may be adversely affected by the use of any such services by *persons* acting on his behalf or in a fiduciary capacity in relation to him.

(7) (in relation to a *regulated mortgage contract*, except in PROF) the individual or trustee who is the borrower or potential borrower under that contract.

(8) (in relation to a *home purchase plan*, except in *PROF*) the *home purchaser* or potential *home purchaser*.

(9) (in relation to a *home reversion plan*, except in *PROF*):
- (a) the *reversion occupier* or potential *reversion occupier*; or

(b) an individual who is an *unauthorised reversion provider* and who is not, or would not, be required to have *permission* to *enter into a home reversion plan*.

(10) (in relation to a *dormant account* transferred to a *dormant account operator*) a person entitled to the *balance* in the dormant account held with a *bank* or *building society* which was transferred to a *dormant account fund operator*.

client asset rules

CASS.

client bank account

(1) (other than in CASS 7 and CASS 7A and principally in CASS 5):
   (a) an account at a bank which:
      (i) holds the *money* of one or more *clients*;
      (ii) is in the name of the *firm*;
      (iii) includes in its title an appropriate description to distinguish the *money* in the account from the *firm's money*; and
      (iv) is a current or a deposit account; or
   (b) a money market deposit of *client money* which is identified as being *client money*.

(2) (in CASS 7 and CASS 7A):
   (a) an account at a bank which:
      (i) holds the money of one or more *clients*;
      (ii) is in the name of the *firm*; and
      (iii) is a current or a deposit account; or
   (b) a money market deposit account of *client money* which is identified as being *client money*.

client's best interests rule

COBS 2.1.1R.

client equity balance

the amount which a *firm* would be liable (ignoring any non-cash *collateral* held) to pay to a *client* (or the *client* to the *firm*) in respect of his *margined transactions* if each of his open positions was liquidated at the closing or settlement prices published by the relevant exchange or other appropriate pricing source and his account closed. This refers to cash values and does not include non-cash *collateral* or other *designated investments* held in respect of a *margined transaction*.

client money

(1) [deleted]

(2) (in CASS 5) subject to the *client money rules*, *money* of any currency which, in the course of carrying on *insurance mediation activity*, a *firm* holds on behalf of a *client* or which a *firm treats as client money in accordance with the client money rules*.

(2A) (in CASS 6 and CASS 7 and CASS 7A, in so far as it relates to matters covered by CASS 6, CASS 7, or COBS) subject to the *client money rules*, *money* of any currency:
   (a) that a *firm* receives or holds for, or on behalf of, a *client* in the course of, or in connection with, its *MiFID business*; and or
   (b) which, in the course of carrying on *designated investment business* that is not *MiFID business*, a *firm* holds in respect of any *investment agreement* entered into, or to be entered into, with or for a *client*, or which a *firm* treats as *client money* in accordance with the *client money rules*.

(3) (in MIPRU):
   (a) in relation to an *insurance intermediary* when acting as such, *money* which is *client money* in (2);
   (b) in relation to a *home finance* when acting as such, *money* of any currency which in the course of carrying on *home finance mediation activity*, the *firm* holds on behalf of a *client*, either in a bank account or in the form of cash.

(4) (in UPRU) client money for the purposes of the *client money rules*.

client money chapter

CASS 7

client money (insurance) distribution rules

the *rules* in CASS 5.6 (Client money distribution).

client money (MiFID business) distribution rules

[deleted]

Part II FSA Handbook Materials

client money distribution rules

CASS 7A.

client money rules

(1) [deleted]
(2) (in CASS 5) CASS 5.1 to 5.5.
(3) (in CASS 3, CASS 6, CASS 7, CASS 7A, UPRU and COBS) CASS 7.1 to CASS 7.8.
(4) [deleted]

client money segregation requirements

CASS 7.4.1R and CASS 7.4.11R.

client transaction account

(in relation to a *firm* and an exchange, *clearing house* or *intermediate broker*) an account maintained by the exchange, *clearing house* or *intermediate broker*, as the case may be, in respect of transactions in *contingent liability investments* undertaken by the *firm* with or for its *clients*.

closed-ended

(in LR) (in relation to investment entities) an *investment company* which is not an *open-ended investment company*.

closed-ended investment fund

(in LR) an entity:
(a) which is an undertaking with limited liability, including a company, limited partnership, or *limited liability partnership*; and
(b) whose primary object is investing and managing its assets (including pooled funds contributed by holders of its *listed securities*):
 (i) in property of any description; and
 (ii) with a view to spreading investment risk.

close links

(1) (in relation to *MiFID business*) a situation in which two or more persons are linked by:
 (a) participation which means the ownership, direct or by way of control, of 20% or more of the voting rights or capital of an undertaking;
 (b) control which means the relationship between a parent undertaking and a subsidiary, in all the cases referred to in Article 1(1) and (2) of Directive 83/349/EEC, or a similar relationship between any person and an undertaking, any subsidiary undertaking of a subsidiary undertaking also being considered a subsidiary of the parent undertaking which is at the head of those undertakings.

 [Note: article 4 (1)(31) of *MiFID*]

 A situation in which two or more persons are permanently linked to one and the same person by a control relationship is also to be regarded as constituting a close link between such persons.
(2) (except where (1) applies, *SUP* 3 (Auditors) and *SUP* 4 (Actuaries)) (in accordance with paragraph 3(2) in Schedule 6 to the *Act* (Close links)) the relationship between a *person* ("A") and another *person* ("CL") which exists if:
 (a) CL is a *parent undertaking* of A; or
 (b) CL is a *subsidiary undertaking* of A; or
 (c) CL is a *parent undertaking* of a *subsidiary undertaking* of A; or
 (d) CL is a *subsidiary undertaking* of a *parent undertaking* of A; or
 (e) CL owns or controls 20% or more of the voting rights or capital of A; or
 (f) A owns or controls 20% or more of the voting rights or capital of CL.
(3) *SUP* 3 (Auditors) and *SUP* 4 (Actuaries)) (in accordance with section 343(8) of the *Act* (Information given by auditor or actuary to the Authority: persons with close links) the relationship in (2), disregarding (e) and (f).

close matching rules

for the purposes of *permitted links*, the *rules* in INSPRU 1.1.34R, INSPRU 3.1.57R, INSPRU 3.1.58R, and INSPRU 3.1.59G.

close out

(in COLL) enter into a further transaction under which the obligation to deliver or receive which arises or may, at the option of the other party to the transaction, arise under the original transaction is offset by an equivalent and opposite obligation or right to receive or deliver.

close period

(in LR) as defined in paragraph 1(a) of the *Model Code*.

close relative

(as defined in article 3(1) of the *Regulated Activities Order* and article 2(1) of the *Financial Promotion Order*) (in relation to any *person*):
(a) his spouse or civil partner;
(b) his children and step-children, his parents and step-parents, his brothers and sisters and his step-brothers and step-sisters; and
(c) the spouse or civil partner of any *person* within (b).

closed

(in relation to a *syndicate year*) closed by *reinsurance to close* in accordance with *byelaws*, either into another *syndicate year* or into an *insurer* approved by the *Council* for the purpose.

closely related

(in GENPRU and BIPRU) describes a relationship between two or more *persons* under which one or more of the following applies:
(a) the insolvency or default of one of them is likely to be associated with the insolvency or default of the others;
(b) it would be prudent when assessing the financial condition or creditworthiness of one to consider that of the others; or
(c) there is, or there is likely to be, a close relationship between the financial performance of those *persons*.

closing date

the date specified in the earliest relevant *public announcement* of the *offer* as the last date for acceptance of the *offer*, or, if no such date is specified, then the date on which the *issuer* (or seller) of the *securities* offered receives any of the proceeds of the *offer*.

CNCOM

the *concentration risk capital component*.

COAF

the part of the *Handbook* in Redress which has the title Complaints against the FSA.

COB

the Conduct of Business sourcebook up to 1 November 2007.

COBS

the Conduct of Business sourcebook from 1 November 2007.

Code of Market Conduct

the provisions in *MAR* 1 indicated by an "E" or "C" in the margin or heading, issued by the *FSA* as required by section 119 of the *Act* (The Code).

Code of Practice for Approved Persons

the provisions in *APER* 3 and *APER* 4 indicated by an "E" in the margin or heading, the purpose of which is to help determine whether or not an *approved person's* conduct complies with the *Statements of Principle* and which are issued by the *FSA* under section 64(2) of the *Act* (Conduct: statements and codes).

cold call

a *financial promotion* made in the course of a personal visit, telephone conversation or other interactive dialogue:
(a) which:
 (i) was not initiated by the recipient of the *financial promotion*; and
 (ii) does not take place in response to an express request from the recipient of the *financial promotion*; or
(b) in relation to which it was not clear from all the circumstances when the call, visit or dialogue was initiated or requested, that during the course of the call, visit or dialogue, communications would be made concerning the kind of *controlled activities* and *controlled investments* to which the communications in fact made relate.

In this definition:
(a) a *person* is not to be treated as expressly requesting a call, visit or dialogue:
 (i) because he omits to indicate that he does not wish to receive any or any further visits or calls or to engage in any or any further dialogue; or
 (ii) because he agrees to standard terms that state that such visits, calls or dialogue will take place, unless he has signified clearly that, in addition to agreeing to the terms, he is willing for them to take place;

(b) if a call, visit or dialogue is initiated or requested by a recipient (R), it is treated as also having been initiated or requested by any other *person* to whom it is made at the same time as it is made to R if that other recipient is a *close relative* of R or expected to *engage in any investment activity* jointly with R.

[**Note:** article 8 of the *Financial Promotion Order*]

COLL

the Collective Investment Schemes sourcebook

collateral

(1) (in COLL) any form of security, guarantee or indemnity provided by way of security for the discharge of any liability arising from a transaction.

(2) (in COBS and *CASS*) any of the following:

(a) an *investment* specified in articles 76 to 81 of the *Regulated Activities Order*; that is:

(i) *shares* (article 76);

(ii) *debentures* (article 77);

(iii) *government and public securities* (article 78);

(iv) *warrants* (article 79);

(v) *certificates representing certain securities* (article 80);

(vi) *units* (article 81); or

(b) *money*; or

(c) a *commodity* warrant (however title is recorded or evidenced); which belongs to a *client* and which is held or controlled by the *firm* under the terms of a deposit, pledge, charge or other security arrangement.

(3) (in INSPRU and SYSC):

(a) (in relation to any transaction) mortgage, charge, pledge or other security interest or, as the context may require, an asset that is subject to a mortgage, charge, pledge or other security interest; and

(b) (in relation to a *stock lending, repo* or *derivative* transaction only):

(i) a transfer of assets (other than by way of sale) subject to a right of the transferor to have transferred back to it the same, or equivalent, assets or, as the context may require, the assets so transferred by the original transferor; or

(ii) a letter of credit;

where the assets are transferred, or the letter of credit is issued, to secure the performance of the obligations of one of the parties to that transaction.

collateral rules

COB 9.4.

collective insurance

(in relation to a *class* of *contract of insurance*) the *class* of *contract of insurance*, specified in paragraph VIII of Part II of Schedule 1 to the *Regulated Activities Order* (Contracts of long-term insurance), of a kind referred to in article 2(2)(e) of the *Consolidated Life Directive* ("the operations carried out by insurance companies such as those referred to in Chapter 1, Title 4 of Book IV of the French "Code des assurances"").

collective investment scheme

a collective investment scheme, as defined in section 235 of the *Act* (Collective Investment Schemes), which is in summary:

(a) any arrangements with respect to property of any description, including money, the purpose or effect of which is to enable *persons* taking part in the arrangements (whether by becoming owners of the property or any part of it or otherwise) to participate in or receive profits or income arising from the acquisition, holding, management or disposal of the property or sums paid out of such profits or income; and

(b) which are not excluded by the Financial Services and Markets Act (Collective Investment Schemes) Order 2001 (SI 2001/1062).

collective investment undertaking other than the closed-end type

(in PR) (as defined in Article 2.1(o) of the *prospectus directive*) unit trusts and investment companies:

(a) the object of which is the collective investment of capital provided by the public, and which operate on the principle of risk-spreading;

(b) the units of which are, at the holder's request, repurchased or redeemed, directly or indirectly, out of the assets of these undertakings.

collective investment undertaking PRR

the part of the *market risk capital requirement* calculated in accordance with BIPRU 7.7.5R (Calculation of the collective investment undertaking PRR).

COLLG

the Collective Investment Scheme Information Guide

Combined Code

(in *LR* and DTR) in relation to an *issuer*:

(1) in respect of a reporting period commencing on or after 29 June 2008, the Combined Code on Corporate Governance published in June 2008 by the Financial Reporting Council; or

(2) in respect of a reporting period commencing before 29 June 2008, the Combined Code on Corporate Governance published in June 2008 by the Financial Reporting Council.

combined initial disclosure document

information about the *scope of advice* or *scope of basic advice* and the nature of the services offered by a *firm* in relation to two or more of the following:

(a) *packaged products* or, for *basic advice, stakeholder products*;

(b) *non-investment insurance contracts*;

(c) *regulated mortgage contracts* other than *lifetime mortgages*;

(d) *home purchase plans*;

(e) *equity release transactions*; or

which contains the keyfacts logo, headings and text in the order shown in, and in accordance with the notes in, COBS 6 Annex 2.

commencement

the beginning of the *commencement day.*

commencement day

the *day* on which section 19 of the *Act* (The general prohibition) comes into force, being 1 December 2001.

commercial customer

(in ICOBS and CASS 5) a *customer* who is not a *consumer.*

commission

any form of commission, including a benefit of any kind, offered or given in connection with:

(a) *designated investment business* (other than *commission equivalent*);

(b) insurance mediation activity in connection with a *non-investment insurance contract*; or

(c) the sale of a *packaged product*, that is offered or given by the *product provider*.

commission equivalent

the cash payments, benefits and services listed in COBS 6 Annex 6E which satisfy the criteria in COBS 6.4.3R.

commitment

a commitment represented by *insurance business* of any of the *classes* (as defined for the purposes of INSPRU and SUP) of *long-term insurance business*.

commodity

(1) (except for (2) and (3)) a physical asset (other than a financial instrument or cash) which is capable of delivery.

(2) (for the purpose of calculating *position risk requirements*) any of the following (but excluding gold):

  (a) a commodity within the meaning of paragraph (1); and

  (b) any:

    (i) physical or energy product; or

    (ii) of the items referred to in paragraph 10 of Section C of Annex I of the *MIFID* as an underlying with respect to the *derivatives* mentioned in that paragraph;

  which is, or can be, traded on a secondary market.

(3) (in relation to the *MiFID Regulation*, including the definitions of a *financial instrument* and an *ancillary service*) any goods of a fungible nature that are capable of being delivered, including metals and their ores and alloys, agricultural products, and energy such as electricity, not including services or other items that are not goods, such as currencies or rights in real estate, or that are entirely intangible.

[Note: article 2(1) of the *MiFID Regulation*]

commodity extended maturity ladder approach

the method of calculating the *commodity PRR* in BIPRU 7.4.32R (Extended maturity ladder approach).

commodity future

a *future* relating to a *commodity.*

Part II FSA Handbook Materials

commodity maturity ladder approach

the method of calculating the *commodity PRR* in BIPRU 7.4.25R (Maturity ladder approach).

commodity option

an *option* relating to a *commodity*.

commodity PRR

the part of the *market risk capital requirement* calculated in accordance with BIPRU 7.4 (Commodity PRR) or, in relation to a particular *position*, the portion of the overall *commodity PRR* attributable to that *position*.

commodity simplified approach

the method of calculating the *commodity PRR* in BIPRU 7.4.24R (Simplified approach).

common platform firm

a *firm* that is:
(a) a *BIPRU firm*; or
(b) an *exempt CAD firm*; or
(c) a UK *MiFID investment firm* which falls within the definition of 'local firm' in article 3.1P of the *Capital Adequacy Directive*; or
(d) a *dormant account fund operator*.

common platform organisational requirements

SYSC 4 to SYSC 9.

common platform outsourcing rules

SYSC 8.1.1R to SYSC 8.1.12R.

common platform record-keeping requirements

the record-keeping requirements applicable to *common platform firms* set out in SYSC 9.

common platform requirements

SYSC 4 to SYSC 10.

common platform requirements on financial crime

the requirements *on financial crime* applicable to *common platform firms* set out in SYSC 6.3.

communicate

(in relation to a *financial promotion*) to communicate in any way, including causing a communication to be made or directed.

[Note: section 21(13) of the *Act* (Restrictions on financial promotion) and article 6(d) of the *Financial Promotion Order* (Interpretation: communications)]

communicated to a person inside the United Kingdom

communicated other than *communicated to a person outside the United Kingdom.*

communicated to a person outside the United Kingdom

(a) *made to* a *person* who receives it outside the *United Kingdom*; or
(b) *directed only at persons* outside the *United Kingdom.*

In this definition:
(c) If the conditions set out in (f)(i), (ii), (iii) and (iv) are met, a *financial promotion* directed from a place inside the *United Kingdom* will be regarded as *directed only at persons* outside the *United Kingdom.*
(d) If the conditions set out in (f)(iii) and (iv) are met, a *financial promotion* directed from a place outside the *United Kingdom* will be regarded as *directed only at persons* outside the *United Kingdom.*
(e) In any other case in which one or more of the conditions in (f)(i) to (v) is met, that fact will be taken into account in determining whether a *financial promotion* is directed only at *persons* outside the *United Kingdom* (but a *financial promotion* may still be regarded as directed only at *persons* outside the *United Kingdom* even if none of these conditions is met).
(f) The conditions are that:
  (i) the *financial promotion* is accompanied by an indication that it is *directed only at persons* outside the *United Kingdom*;
  (ii) the *financial promotion* is accompanied by an indication that it must not be acted upon by *persons* in the *United Kingdom*;
  (iii) the *financial promotion* is not referred to in, or directly accessible from, any other *financial promotion* which is *made to* a *person* or *directed at persons* in the *United Kingdom* by the same communicator;

(iv) there are in place proper systems and procedures to prevent recipients in the *United Kingdom* (other than those to whom the *financial promotion* might otherwise lawfully have been made) engaging in the investment activity to which the *financial promotion* relates with the *person* directing the *financial promotion*, a *close relative* of his or a member of the same *group*;

(v) the *financial promotion* is included in:

(A) a website, newspaper, journal, magazine or periodical publication which is principally accessed in or intended for a market outside the *United Kingdom*;

(B) a radio or television broadcast or teletext service transmitted principally for reception outside the *United Kingdom*.

Community Co-Insurance Directive

the Council Directive of 30 May 1978 on the coordination of laws, regulations and administrative provisions relating to Community coinsurance (No 78/473/EEC).

community co-insurance operation

an operation to which the *Community Co-Insurance Directive* applies, as modified by article 26 of the *Second Non-Life Directive*.

COMP

the Compensation sourcebook.

company

any body corporate.

Company Announcements Office

the Company Announcements Office of the London Stock Exchange, the information dissemination provider approved by the *UKLA*.

compensation costs

the costs incurred:

(a) in paying compensation; or

(b) as a result of making the arrangements contemplated in *COMP* 3.3.2R or taking the measures contemplated in *COMP* 3.3.3R; or

(c) in making payments or giving indemnities under *COMP* 11.2.3R.

compensation costs levy

a levy imposed by the *FSCS* on *participant firms* to meet *compensation costs*, each *participant firm's* share being calculated in accordance with FEES 6.5.

compensation fund

any *policyholder* compensation scheme in any *EEA State*.

compensation scheme

the Financial Services Compensation Scheme established under section 213 of the *Act* (The compensation scheme) for compensating *persons* in cases where *authorised persons* and *appointed representatives*, or, where applicable, a *tied agent* of a firm, are unable, or are likely to be unable, to satisfy *claims* against them.

compensation transitionals order

the Financial Services and Markets Act 2000 (Transitional Provisions, Repeals and Savings) (Financial Services Compensation Scheme) Order 2001 (SI 2001/2967)

competent authority

(1) (in relation to admission to an *official listing*):

(a) the authority designated under Schedule 8 to the *Act* (Transfer of functions under Part VI (Official listing)) as responsible for admitting securities to, and for removing securities from, the *official list*; for the time being, the *FSA* in its capacity as such; or

(b) an authority exercising functions corresponding to those in (a) in another *EEA State*.

(2) (in relation to the exercise of an *EEA right*) a competent authority for the purposes of the relevant *Single Market Directive*.

(3) (in relation to a group, and for the purposes of SYSC 12 (Group risk systems and controls requirement), GENPRU, BIPRU and INSPRU, any national authority of an *EEA State* which is empowered by law or regulation to supervise *regulated entities*, whether on an individual or group-wide basis.

(4) the authority, designated by each *EEA State* in accordance with Article 48 of *MiFID*, unless otherwise specified in *MiFID*.

[Note: article 4(1)(22) of *MiFID*]

(5) (in *REC*) in relation to an *investment firm* or *credit institution*, means the competent authority in relation to that firm or institution for the purposes of *MiFID*.
(6) (in *COBS* 13.4) the authority designated by each *EEA State* in accordance with Article 11 of the *Market Abuse Directive*.
[Note: article 1(7) of the *Market Abuse Directive*]

competent employees rule

(a) for a *firm* which is not a *common platform firm*, *SYSC* 3.1.6R.
(b) for a *common platform firm*, *SYSC* 5.1.1R.

complaint

(1) (in *COAF*) any expression of dissatisfaction about the manner in which the *FSA* has carried out its statutory functions other than its legislative functions.
(2) (in *DISP*, except *DISP* 1.1 and the *complaints handling rules* and the *complaints record rule* in relation to *MiFID business*) any oral or written expression of dissatisfaction, whether justified or not, from, or on behalf of, a *person* about the provision of, or failure to provide, a financial service, which:
 (a) alleges that the complainant has suffered (or may suffer) financial loss, material distress or material inconvenience; and
 (b) relates to an activity of that *respondent*, or of any other *respondent* with whom that *respondent* has some connection in marketing or providing financial services or products, which comes under the jurisdiction of the *Financial Ombudsman Service*.
(3) (in *DISP* 1.1 and the *complaints handling rules* and the *complaints record rule* only in relation to *MiFID business*) any oral or written expression of dissatisfaction, whether justified or not, from, or on behalf of, a *person* about the provision of, or failure to provide, a financial service, which alleges that the complainant has suffered (or may suffer) financial loss, material distress or material inconvenience.
(4) (in *DISP*) reference to a *complaint* includes:
 (a) under all jurisdictions, part of a *complaint*; and
 (b) under the *Compulsory Jurisdiction*, all or part of a *relevant complaint*.

Complaints Commissioner

the *person* appointed by the *FSA* under *COAF* 1.3.1G (The Complaints Commissioner) to carry out the functions conferred on him under the *complaints scheme*.

complaints handling rules

DISP 1.3.

complaints investigator

(1) (in relation to a *UK RIE*) the independent *person* appointed under arrangements referred to in paragraph 9(3) of the Schedule to the *Recognition Requirements Regulations* to investigate a complaint and to report on the result of his investigation to that *RIE* and to the complainant.
(2) (in relation to a *UK RCH*) the independent *person* appointed under arrangements referred to in paragraph 23(3) of the Schedule to the *Recognition Requirements Regulations* to investigate a complaint and to report on the result of his investigation to that *RCH* and to the complainant.

complaints record rule

DISP 1.9.

complaints reporting rules

DISP 1.10.

complaints resolution rules

DISP 1.4.

complaints scheme

the arrangements made by the *FSA* under paragraphs 7 and 8 of Schedule 1 to the *Act* (The Financial Services Authority) for the investigation of *complaints* against the *FSA* arising in connection with the exercise of, or failure to exercise, any of its functions (other than its legislative functions) under the *Act*.

complaints time barring rule

DISP 1.8.

complaints time limits rules

DISP 1.6.

compliance oversight function

controlled function CF10 in the *table of controlled functions*, described more fully in *SUP* 10.7.8R.

composite firm

a *firm* that carries on both *long-term insurance business* and *general insurance business*.

composite insurer

(in relation to *firm type* in *SUP* 16.10 (Confirmation of *standing data*)) an *insurer* with *permission to effect* or *carry out* both *long-term insurance contracts* and *general insurance*.

Compulsory Jurisdiction

the jurisdiction of the *Financial Ombudsman Service* to which *firms* and payment service providers (and certain other *persons* as a result of the *Ombudsman Transitional Order* or section 226(2)(b) and (c) of the *Act*) are compulsorily subject.

concentration risk group counterparty

(in accordance with Article 113(2) of the *Banking Consolidation Directive* (Limits on *large exposures*) and in relation to a *person*) a *parent undertaking* of the *person*, a *subsidiary undertaking* of the *person* or a *subsidiary undertaking* of the *person's parent undertaking*, provided that (in each case) both the counterparty and the *person* satisfy the condition in BIPRU 3.2.27R (Requirement to be subject to the same consolidation for the purposes of applying a zero *risk weight* to intra-group *exposures*).

concentration risk capital component

the part of the *credit risk capital requirement* calculated in accordance with BIPRU 10.5.20R (How to calculate the concentration risk capital component).

COND

the part of the *Handbook* in High Level Standards which has the title Threshold Conditions.

conflicts of interest policy

the policy established and maintained in accordance with SYSC 10.1.10R.

conglomerate capital resources

(in relation to a *financial conglomerate* with respect to which GENPRU 3.1.29R (Application of methods 1, 2 or 3 from Annex I of the *Financial Groups Directive*) applies) capital resources as defined in whichever of paragraphs 1.1, 2.1 or 3.1 of GENPRU 3 Ann 1R (Capital adequacy calculations for financial conglomerates) applies with respect to that *financial conglomerate*.

conglomerate capital resources requirement

(in relation to a *financial conglomerate* with respect to which GENPRU 3.1.29R (Application of methods 1, 2 or 3 from Annex I of the *Financial Groups Directive*) applies) the capital resources requirement defined in whichever of paragraphs 1.3, 2.4 or 3.3 of GENPRU 3 Ann 1R (Capital adequacy calculations for financial conglomerates) applies with respect to that *financial conglomerate*.

connected client

(in LR) in relation to a *sponsor* or securities house, any client of the *sponsor* or securities house who is:

(a) a partner, *director*, employee or controller (as defined in section 422 of the Act) of the *sponsor* or securities house or of an undertaking described in paragraph (d); or
(b) the spouse, civil partner or child of any individual described in paragraph (a); or
(c) a *person* in his capacity as a trustee of a private trust (other than a pension scheme or an *employee's share scheme*) the beneficiaries of which include any *person* described in paragraph (a) or (b); or
(d) an undertaking which in relation to the *sponsor* or securities house is a group undertaking.

connected contract

a *non-investment insurance contract* which:

(a) is not a contract of long-term insurance (as defined by article 3 of the *Regulated Activities Order*);
(b) has a total duration (including *renewals*) of five years or less;
(c) has an annual *premium* (or the equivalent of annual *premium*) of €500 or less;
(d) covers the risk of:
    (i) breakdown, loss of, or damage to, nonmotor goods supplied by the provider; or
    (ii) damage to, or loss of, baggage and other risks linked to travel booked with the provider ("travel risks");
        (A) the travel booked with the provider relates to attendance at an event organised or managed by that provider and the party seeking insurance is not an individual (acting in his private capacity) or a small business; or
        (B) the travel booked with the provider is only the hire of an aircraft, vehicle or vessel which does not provide sleeping accommodation;

Part II FSA Handbook Materials

(e) does not cover any liability risks (except, in the case of a contract which covers travel risks, where the cover is ancillary to the main cover provided by the contract);
(f) is complementary to the non-motor goods being supplied or service being provided by the provider; and
(g) is of such a nature that the only information that a *person* requires in order to carry on one of the *insurance mediation activities* is the cover provided by the contract.
(h) the transfer of possession of an aircraft, vehicle or vessel under an agreement for hire which is not:
    (i) a hire-purchase agreement within the meaning of section 189(1) of the Consumer Credit Act 1974; or
    (ii) any other agreement which contemplates that the property in those goods will also pass at some time in the future; is the provision of a service related to travel, not a supply of goods;
(i) "small business" means a sole trader, *body corporate*, *partnership* or an unincorporated association which had a turnover in the last financial year of less than £1,000,000 (but where the small business is a member of a group within the meaning of section 262(1) of the Companies Act 1985 (and after the repeal of that section, within the meaning of section 474(1) of the Companies Act 2006), reference to its turnover means the combined turnover of the group);
(j) "turnover" means the amounts derived from the provision of goods and services falling within the business's ordinary activities, after deduction of trade discounts, value added tax and any other taxes based on the amounts so derived.

connected counterparty

(for the purpose of BIPRU 10 (Concentration risk requirements) and in relation to a *firm*) has the meaning set out in BIPRU 10.3.8R (Connected counterparties), which is in summary a *person* to whom the *firm* has an *exposure* and who fulfils at least one of the conditions set out in BIPRU 10.3.8R.

connected lending of a capital nature

(in accordance with GENPRU 2.2.222R (Deductions from tiers one and two: Connected lending of a capital nature)) all lending within GENPRU 2.2.227R or GENPRU 2.2.229R and guarantees within GENPRU 2.2.231R or GENPRU 2.2.233R.

connected person

(1) (in relation to the *FSA's* consideration of an application for, or of whether to vary or cancel, a *Part IV permission*) (in accordance with section 49(1) of the *Act* (Persons connected with an applicant)) any *person* appearing to the *FSA* to be, or likely to be, in a relationship with the applicant or *person* given *permission*, which is relevant.
(2) (in relation to the *FSA*'s power to gather information under section 165 of the *Act* (Authority's power to requireinformation)) (in accordance with section 165(11) of the *Act*) a *person* who has, or has at any relevant time had, the following relationship with an *authorised person* ("A"):
    (a) he is a member of A's *group*;
    (b) he is a *controller* of A;
    (c) he is a member of a *partnership* of which A is a member;
    (d) he is or has been an employee of A;
    (e) if A is a *body corporate*, he is or has been an *officer*, or *manager* or agent of A or of a *parent undertaking* of A;
    (f) if A is a *partnership*, he is or has been a member, *manager* or agent of A;
    (g) if A is an unincorporated association of *persons* which is neither a *partnership* nor an unincorporated *friendly society*, he is or has been an *officer*, *manager*, or agent of A;
    (h) if A is a *friendly society*, he is or has been an officer or manager of A ("officer" and "manager" having the same meaning as in section 119(1) of the Friendly Societies Act 1992);
    (i) if A is a *building society*, he is or has been an officer of A ("officer" having the same meaning as in section 119(1) of the Building Societies Act 1986);
    (j) if A is an individual, he is or has been an agent of A.
(3) (in relation to the FSA's powers of investigation under sections (9171 and 172 of the *Act* (Powers of persons appointed under section 167; Additional power of persons appointed as a result of section 168(1) or (4))) (in accordance with section 171(4) of the *Act*) a *person* who has, or has at any relevant time had, the following relationship with a *person* under investigation ("P"):
(4) he has the relationship specified in any of paragraphs (2) (a), (b) or (d) to (j) to P (where references in those paragraphs to A are taken to be references to P);
(5) it is a *partnership* of which P is a member;
(6) he is the partner, *manager*, employee, agent, *appointed representative*, or, where applicable, *tied agent*, banker, auditor, actuary or solicitor of:

(i) P; or
(ii) a *parent undertaking* of P; or
(iii) a *subsidiary undertaking* of P; or
(iv) a *subsidiary undertaking of a parent undertaking of* P; or
(v) a *parent undertaking of a subsidiary undertaking* of P.

(7) [to follow]

(8) (in DTR and *LR*, in relation to a *person discharging managerial responsibilities* within an *issuer*)(as defined in section 96B(2) of the *Act*):

(9) a "connected person" within the meaning of section 346 of the Companies Act 1985 (reading that section as if any reference to a director of a company were a reference to a *person discharging managerial responsibilities* within an *issuer*);

(10) a relative of a *person discharging managerial responsibilities* within an *issuer*, who, on the date of the transaction in question has shared the same household as that person for at least 12 months;

(11) a *body corporate* in which–
(i) a *person discharging managerial responsibilities* within an *issuer*, or
(ii) any *person* connected with him by virtue of subsection (a) or (b),
is a director or a senior executive who has the power to make management decisions affecting the future development and business prospects of that *body corporate*.

connected travel insurance contract

a *non-investment insurance contract* which covers the risk of damage to, or loss of, baggage and other risks linked to the travel booked with the provider but does not otherwise meet the conditions in paragraph (d)(ii) of the definition of *connected contract*.

connected travel insurance intermediary

an *insurance intermediary* whose *permission* includes a *requirement* that it must not conduct any *regulated activity* other than *insurance mediation activity* in relation to a connected travel *insurance contract*.

consent notice

a notice given by the *FSA* to a *Host State regulator* under:

(a) paragraph 19(4) (Establishment) of Part III of Schedule 3 to the *Act* (Exercise of Passport Rights by UK firms); or

(b) paragraph 20(3A) (Services) of Part III of Schedule 3 to the *Act* (Exercise of Passport Rights by UK firms).

Consolidated Admissions and Reporting Directive

Directive of the European Parliament and of the Council on the admission of securities to official stock exchange listing and on information to be published on those securities (No 2001/34/EC).

consolidated capital resources

(in relation to a *UK consolidation group* or a *non-EEA sub-group* and in GENPRU and BIPRU) that group's capital resources calculated in accordance with BIPRU 8.6 (Consolidated capital resources).

consolidated capital resources requirement

(in relation to a *UK consolidation group* or a *non-EEA sub-group* and in GENPRU and BIPRU) an amount of *consolidated capital resources* that that group must hold in accordance with BIPRU 8.7 (Consolidated capital resources requirement).

consolidated credit risk requirement

(in relation to a *UK consolidation group* or a *non-EEA sub-group* and in GENPRU and BIPRU) has the meaning in BIPRU 8.7 (Consolidated capital resources requirements) which is in summary the part of that group's *consolidated capital resources requirement* relating to credit risk calculated in accordance with BIPRU 8.7.11R (Calculation of the consolidated requirement components) and as adjusted under BIPRU 8.7.

consolidated fixed overheads requirement

(in relation to a *UK consolidation group* or a *non-EEA sub-group* and in GENPRU and BIPRU) has the meaning in *BIPRU* 8.7 (Consolidated capital resources requirements) which is in summary the part of that group's *consolidated capital resources requirement* relating to the fixed overheads requirement (as referred to Article 21 of the *Capital Adequacy Directive* and the definition of *fixed overheads requirement*) calculated in accordance with BIPRU 8.7.11R (Calculation of the consolidated requirement components) and as adjusted under BIPRU 8.7.

consolidated indirectly issued capital

has the meaning in BIPRU 8.6.12R (Indirectly issued capital and group capital resources), which is in summary any *capital instrument* issued by a member of a *UK consolidation group* or *non-EEA sub-group* where the conditions in BIPRU 8.6.12R are met.

Consolidated Life Directive information

(in *COBS*) the Consolidated Life Directive information (*COBS* 13 Annex 1R).

consolidated market risk requirement

(in relation to a *UK consolidation group* or a *non-EEA sub-group* and in GENPRU and BIPRU) has the meaning in BIPRU 8.7 (Consolidated capital resources requirement) which is in summary the part of that group's *consolidated capital resources requirement* relating to *market risk* calculated in accordance with BIPRU 8.7.11R (Calculation of the consolidated requirement components) and as adjusted under BIPRU 8.7.

consolidated operational risk requirement

(in relation to a *UK consolidation group* or a *non-EEA sub-group* and in GENPRU and BIPRU) has the meaning in BIPRU 8.7 (Consolidated capital resources requirements) which is in summary the part of that group's *consolidated capital resources requirement* relating to *operational risk* calculated in accordance with BIPRU 8.7.11R (Calculation of the consolidated requirement components) and as adjusted under BIPRU 8.7.

consolidated requirement component

has the meaning in BIPRU 8.7.11R (Calculation of the consolidated requirement components), which in summary is one of the following:

(a) the *consolidated credit risk requirement*; or
(b) the *consolidated fixed overheads requirement*; or
(c) the *consolidated market risk requirement*; or
(d) the *consolidated operational risk requirement*.

consolidated subgroup

(in *ELM*) (in relation to a *person*):

(a) that *person*, and
(b) any *financial services undertaking* that is a member of its *subgroup*.

consolidation Article 12(1) relationship

a relationship between one *undertaking* (the first undertaking) and one or more other *undertakings* satisfying the conditions set out in Article 12(1) of the *Seventh Company Law Directive*, which in summary are as follows:

(a) those *undertakings* are not connected, as described in article 1(1) or (2) of that Directive; and
(b) one of the following conditions is satisfied:
 (i) they are managed on a unified basis pursuant to a contract concluded with the first undertaking or provisions in the memorandum or articles of association of those *undertakings*; or
 (ii) the administrative, management or supervisory bodies of those *undertakings* consist, for the major part, of the same *persons* in office during the financial year in respect of which it is being decided whether such a relationship exists.

consolidation concentration risk group counterparty

has the meaning in BIPRU 8.9.11R (UK integrated groups: Definition of consolidation concentration risk group counterparty).

consolidation group

the following:

(a) a *conventional group*; or
(b) *undertakings* linked by a *consolidation Article 12(1) relationship* or (for the purposes of *BIPRU*) an *Article 134 relationship*.

If a *parent undertaking* or *subsidiary undertaking* in a *conventional group* (the first person) has a *consolidation Article 12(1) relationship* or (for the purposes of *BIPRU*) an *Article 134 relationship* with another *person* (the second person), the second person (and any *subsidiary undertaking* of the second person) is also a member of the same *consolidation group*.

consolidation UK integrated group

(with respect to a *UK consolidation group* or *non-EEA sub-group*) all *undertakings* falling into BIPRU 8.9.9R (UK integrated groups:

Definition of consolidation UK integrated group) with respect to that *UK consolidation group* or *non-EEA sub-group*.

consolidation wider integrated group

(with respect to a *UK consolidation group* or *non-EEA sub-group*) all *undertakings* falling into BIPRU 8.9.19R (Wider integrated groups: Definition of wider integrated group) with respect to that *UK consolidation group* or *non-EEA sub-group*.

constable

a police officer in the *United Kingdom* or a *person* commissioned by the Commissioners for HM Revenue and Customs.

constitution

(in LR) memorandum and articles of association or equivalent constitutional document.

consumer

(1) (except as specified in this definition) any natural person acting for purposes outside his trade, business or profession.
[**Note:** article 2 of the *Distance Marketing Directive*, article 2 of the Unfair Terms in Consumer Contracts Directive (93/13/EEC) and article 2 of the *E-Commerce Directive*, and article 4(11) of the *Payment Services Directive*]

(2) (in relation to the *FSA's* power to make general *rules* (section 138 of the *Act* (General rule-making power))) the approval requirements for *controllers* (section 186 of the *Act* (Objection to acquisition of control)), the publication of notices (section 391 of the *Act* (Publication)) and the exercise of *Treaty rights* (Schedule 4 to the *Act* (Treaty rights))) (as defined in section 138(7) of the *Act* (General rule-making power)) a *person*:
  (a) who uses, has used, or is or may be contemplating using, any of the services provided by:
    (i) an authorised person in carrying on regulated activities; or
    (ii) a person acting as an appointed representative, or, where applicable, a *tied agent*; or
  (b) who has rights or interests which are derived from, or are otherwise attributable to the use of, any such services by another *person*; or
  (c) who has rights or interests which may be adversely affected by the use of any such services by a *person* acting on his behalf or in a fiduciary capacity in relation to him; or
  (d) (in relation to the *FSA's* power to make general *rules*) a *person* within the extended definition of consumer in article 3 of the Financial Services and Markets Act 2000 (Consequential and Transitional Provisions) (Miscellaneous) Order 2001 (SI 2001/1821) (Application of definition of "consumer" to users of regulated services before commencement);
  (e) (in relation to the *FSA's* power to make general *rules*) a *person* within the extended definition of consumer in article 4 of the Financial Services and Markets Act 2000 (Consequential Amendments and Transitional Provisions) (Credit Unions) Order 2002 (SI 2002/1501) (Application of definition of "consumer" to customers of credit unions before commencement);
  for the purposes of this definition:
  (A) if an *authorised person* is carrying on a *regulated activity* in his capacity as a trustee, the *persons* who are, have been or may be beneficiaries of the trust are to be treated as *persons* who use, have used or are or may be contemplating using services provided by the *authorised person* in his carrying on of that activity;
  (B) a *person* who deals with an *authorised person* in the course of the *authorised person's* carrying on of a *regulated activity* is to be treated as using services provided by the *authorised person* in carrying on those activities.

(3) (in relation to the protection of consumers objective (section 5 of the *Act* (The protection of consumers)) and independent inquiries (section 14 of the *Act* (Cases in which the Treasury may arrange independent inquiries))) (as defined in sections (95(3) and 14(5) of the *Act*) a *person*:

(4) within (2); or

(5) who, in relation to *regulated activities* carried on otherwise than by an *authorised person*, would be a consumer within (2) if the activities were carried on by an *authorised person*.

(6) (in relation to the establishment and maintenance of the *Consumer Panel* (section 10 of the *Act* (The Consumer Panel))) (as defined in section 10(7) of the *Act*) a *person* within (3) other than an *authorised person*.

consumer awareness rules

DISP 1.2.

consumer credit activity

any one of the following activities carried on by a *licensee*, *firm* or *payment service provider*:

(a) providing credit or otherwise being a creditor under a *regulated consumer credit agreement*;

(b) the bailment or (in Scotland) the hiring of goods or otherwise being an owner under a *regulated consumer hire agreement*;

(c) credit brokerage in so far as it is the effecting of introductions of:
  (i) individuals desiring to obtain credit to persons carrying on a consumer credit business; or

Part II FSA Handbook Materials

(ii) individuals desiring to obtain goods on hire to persons carrying on a consumer hire business;

(d) in so far as they relate to *regulated consumer credit agreements* or *regulated consumer hire agreements*;
(i) debt-adjusting;
(ii) debt-counselling;
(iii) debt-collecting; or
(iv) debt administration;

(e) the provision of credit information services; or

(f) the operation of a credit reference agency;
where at the time of the act or omission complained of:

(g) the *licensee*, *firm* or *payment service provider* was:
(i) covered by a standard licence under the Consumer Credit Act 1974 (as amended); or
(ii) authorised to carry on an activity by virtue of section 34(A) of that Act; or
(iii) in accordance with regulation 26(2) of the *Payment Services Regulations*, was not required to hold a licence for consumer credit business under section 21 of the Consumer Credit Act 1974; and

(h) the activity was carried on in the course of a business of a type specified in accordance with section 226A(2)(e) of the *Act*;

and expressions used in the Consumer Credit Act 1974 (as amended) have the same meaning in this definition as they have in that Act.

Consumer Credit Jurisdiction

the jurisdiction of the *Financial Ombudsman Service* resulting from section 226A of the *Act* which applies to *licensees*.

consumer credit prohibition

(as defined in section 203(3) of the *Act* (Power to prohibit the carrying on of Consumer Credit Act business)) a prohibition on carrying on, or purporting to carry on, in the *United Kingdom* any Consumer Credit Act business which consists of or includes carrying on one or more *listed activities* or *investment services*.

consumer e-money card

any *consumer e-money device* in the form of a *plastic card*, other portable device or device intended to be included in another portable device (or a function on a *plastic card* or on such a device) that is intended to be used by a *consumer e-money holder*.

consumer e-money device

any *e-money electronic device* intended to be used by and in the presence of a *consumer e-money holder*.

consumer e-money holder

(in relation to *e-money*) a *person* who holds that *e-money* otherwise than in the course of a business or profession.

Consumer Panel

the panel of *persons* which section 10 of the *Act* (The Consumer Panel) requires the *FSA* to establish and maintain, as part of its arrangements for consultation under section 8, to represent the interests of *consumers*.

contingency funding plan

(1) (in SYSC 11) a plan for taking action to ensure that a *firm* has adequately liquid financial resources to meet its liabilities as they fall due, prepared under SYSC 11.1.24E.

(2) (in BIPRU 12) a plan for dealing with liquidity crises as required by BIPRU 12.4.10 R.

contingent liability investment

a *derivative* under the terms of which the *client* will or may be liable to make further payments (other than *charges*, and whether or not secured by *margin*) when the transaction falls to be completed or upon the earlier *closing out* of his position.

contract for differences

the *investment*, specified in article 85 of the *Regulated Activities Order* (Contracts for differences etc), which is in summary rights under:

(a) a contract for differences; or

(b) any other contract the purpose or pretended purpose of which is to secure a profit or avoid a loss by reference to fluctuations in:
(i) the value or price of property of any description; or
(ii) an index or other factor designated for that purpose in the contract; or

(c) a derivative instrument for the transfer of credit risk to which article 85(3) of the *Regulated Activities Order* applies.

[Note: paragraph 8 of Section C of Annex 1 to *MiFID*]

contract of insurance

(1) (in relation to a *specified investment*) the *investment*, specified in article 75 of the *Regulated Activities Order* (Contracts of insurance), which is rights under a contract of insurance in (2).

(2) (in relation to a contract) (in accordance with article 3(1) of the *Regulated Activities Order* (Interpretation)) any contract of insurance which is a *long-term insurance contract* or a *general insurance contract*, including:

- (a) fidelity bonds, performance bonds, administration bonds, bail bonds, customs bonds or similar contracts of guarantee, where these are:
  - (i) effected or carried out by a *person* not carrying on a banking business;
  - (ii) not effected merely incidentally to some other business carried on by the *person* effecting them; and
  - (iii) effected in return for the payment of one or more premiums;
- (b) tontines;
- (c) capital redemption contracts or pension fund management contracts, where these are effected or carried out by a person who:
  - (i) does not carry on a banking business; and
  - (ii) otherwise carries on the *regulated activity* of *effecting* or *carrying out contracts of insurance*;
- (d) contracts to pay annuities on human life;
- (e) contracts of a kind referred to in article 1(2)(e) of the *Consolidated Life Directive* (Collective insurance etc); and
- (f) contracts of a kind referred to in article 1(3) of the *Consolidated Life Directive* (Social insurance);

but not including a *funeral plan contract* (or a contract which would be a *funeral plan contract* but for the exclusion in article 60 of the *Regulated Activities Order* (Plans covered by insurance or trust arrangements));

in this definition, "annuities on human life" does not include superannuation allowances and annuities payable out of any fund applicable solely to the relief and maintenance of *persons* engaged, or who have been engaged, in any particular profession, trade or employment, or of the dependants of such *persons*.

contract of significance

(in LR) a contract which represents in amount or value (or annual amount or value) a sum equal to 1% or more, calculated on a *group* basis where relevant, of:

(a) in the case of a capital transaction or a transaction of which the principal purpose or effect is the granting of credit, the aggregate of the *group's* share capital and reserves; or

(b) in other cases, the total annual purchases, sales, payments or receipts, as the case may be, of the *group*.

contracting out comparison

a description of:

(a) the benefits that minimum contributions would secure if a *retail client* did not contract out of the State Second Pension; and

(b) the material differences between the anticipated position if a *retail client* remains contracted into the State Second Pension and the anticipated position if that *client* contracts out;

which is calculated to the *client's* state retirement age using the *lower* and *higher rates of return* and aggregate contributions for the current and the next two tax years.

contracts of large risks

(in ICOB) *contracts of insurance* covering risks within the following categories, in accordance with article 5(d) of the *First Non-Life Directive*:

(a) *railway rolling stock, aircraft, ships* (sea, lake, river and canal vessels), *goods in transit, aircraft liability* and *liability of ships* (sea, lake, river and canal vessels);

(b) *credit* and *suretyship*, where the policyholder is engaged professionally in an industrial or commercial activity or in one of the liberal professions, and the risks relate to such activity;

(c) *land vehicles* (other than *railway rolling stock*), *fire and natural forces*, other *damage to property*, *motor vehicle liability*, *general liability*, and *miscellaneous financial loss*, in so far as the *policyholder* exceeds the limits of at least two of the following three criteria:
  - (i) balance sheet total: € 6.2 million;
  - (ii) net turnover: €12.8 million;
  - (iii) average number of *employees* during the financial year: 250.

contractual cross product netting agreement

(for the purpose of BIPRU 13.7 (Contractual netting)) has the meaning set out in BIPRU 13.7.2R, which is in summary a written bilateral agreement between a *firm* and a counterparty which creates a single legal obligation covering all included bilateral master agreements and transactions belonging to different product categories.

contractually based investment

(in accordance with article 3(1) of the *Regulated Activities Order* (Interpretation)):
(a) a *life policy* (except a *long-term care insurance contract* which is not a qualifying *contract of insurance*);
(b) an *option, future, contract for differences* or *funeral plan contract;*
(c) *rights to or interests in an investment* falling within (a) or (b).

control

(1) (except in (2)) (in relation to the acquisition, increase or reduction of control of a *firm*) the relationship between a *person* and the *firm* or other *undertaking* of which the *person* is a *controller*.
(2) (in SYSC 8 and SYSC 10) control as defined in article 1 of the Seventh Council Directive 83/349/EEC (The Seventh Company Law Directive).

[Note: article 4 (1)(30) of *MiFID*]
(3) (except in (2)) (in accordance with section 182 of the *Act*) a *controller* ("A") (whether acting alone or in concert) increases control over a *firm* ("B") when:
  (a) the percentage of *shares* A holds in B or a *parent undertaking* ("P") of B increases by any of the following steps:
    (i) from less than 20% to 20% or more;
    (ii) from less than 30% to 30% or more;
    (iii) from less than 50% to 50% or more;
  (b) the percentage of *voting power* A holds in B or P increases by any of the steps mentioned above; or
  (c) becomes a *parent undertaking* of B.
(4) (except in (2)) (in accordance with section 183 of the *Act*) a *controller* ("A") (whether alone or acting in concert) reduces control over a *firm* ("B") whenever:
  (a) the percentage of *shares* which A holds in B or a *parent undertaking* ("P") of B decreases by any of the following steps:
    (i) from 50% or more to less than 50%;
    (ii) from 30% or more to less than 30%;
    (iii) from 20% or more to less than 20%;
  (b) the percentage of *voting power* which A holds in B or P decreases by any of the steps mentioned above; or
  (c) A ceases to be a *parent undertaking* of B.
(5) (except in (2)) (in accordance with section 183 of the *Act*) a *controller* ("A") (whether acting alone or in concert) ceases to have control over a *firm* ("B") if A ceases to hold any of the following:
  (a) 10% or more of the *shares* in B or a *parent undertaking* ("P") of B;
  (b) 10% or more of the *voting power* in B or P;
  (c) shares or *voting power* in B or in P as a result of which A is able to exercise significant influence over the management of B.
(6) (for the purposes of the calculations in (3) to (5)) the holding of *shares* or *voting power* by a *person* ("A1") includes any *shares* or *voting power* held by another ("A2") if A1 and A2 are acting in concert.

controlled activity

(in accordance with section 21(9) of the *Act* (The classes of activity and investment)) any of the following activities specified in Part I of Schedule 1 to the *Financial Promotions Order* (Controlled Activities):

(a) *accepting deposits* (paragraph 1)
(b) *effecting contracts of insurance* (paragraph 2(1)):
(c) *carrying out contracts of insurance* (paragraph 2(2));
(d) dealing in securities and contractually based investments as principal or agent (paragraph 3(1));
(e) *arranging (bringing about) deals in investments* (paragraph 4(1));
(f) *making arrangements with a view to transactions in investments* (paragraph 4(2));
(fa) operating a *multilateral trading facility* (paragraph 4A);
(g) *managing investments* (paragraph 5);

(h) *safeguarding and administering investments* (paragraph 6);
(i) *advising on investments* (paragraph 7);
(j) *advising on syndicate participation at Lloyd's* (paragraph 8);
(k) providing funeral plan contracts (paragraph 9);
(l) providing qualifying credit (paragraph 10);
(m) arranging qualifying credit etc. (paragraph 10A coming into force 31st October 2004);
(n) advising on qualifying credit etc. (paragraph 10B coming into force 31st October 2004);
(o) *entering into a home purchase plan* (paragraph 10C);
(p) *making arrangements with a view to a home purchase plan* (paragraph 10D);
(q) *advising on a home purchase plan* (paragraph 10E);
(r) *entering into a home reversion plan* (paragraph 10F);
(s) *making arrangements with a view to a home reversion plan* (paragraph 10G);
(t) *advising on a home reversion plan* (paragraph 10H); or
(u) agreeing to carry on specified kinds of activity (paragraph 11) which are specified in paragraphs 3 to 10H (other than paragraph 4A) of Part I of Schedule 1 to the *Financial Promotion Order.*
(v) (in relation to COBS 5.2.4R and COBS 5.4.1R) also a marketing communication made by a *MiFID investment firm* or *a third country investment firm* that relates to an *ancillary service.*

controlled agreement

(as defined in section 30 of the *Act* (Enforceability of agreements resulting from unlawful communications)) an agreement the making or performance of which by either party constitutes a *controlled activity.*

controlled function

a function, relating to the carrying on of a *regulated activity* by a *firm*, which is specified, under section 59 of the *Act* (Approval for particular arrangements), in the *table of controlled functions.*

controlled investment

(in accordance with section 21(10) of the *Act* (Restrictions on financial promotion) and article 4 of the *Financial Promotion Order* (Definitions of controlled activities and controlled investments)) an *investment* specified in Part II of Schedule 1 to the *Financial Promotion Order* (Controlled investments).

controlled undertaking

any subsidiary undertaking within the meaning of *the Act* other than one falling within section 1162(4)(b) of the Companies Act 2006 or section 420(2)(b) of *the Act.*

controller

(1) (in relation to a *firm* or other *undertaking* ("B"), other than a *non-directive firm*), a *person* ("A") who (whether acting alone or in concert):
  (a) holds 10% or more of the *shares* in B or in a *parent undertaking* ("P") of B;
  (b) holds 10% or more of the *voting power* in B or in P; or
  (c) holds *shares* or *voting power* in B or P as a result of which A is able to exercise significant influence over the management of B.
(2) (in relation to a *non-directive firm* ("B")) a *person* ("A") who (whether acting alone or in concert):
  (a) holds 20% or more of the *shares* in B or in a *parent undertaking* ("P") of B;
  (b) holds 20% or more of the *voting power* in B or in P; or (c) holds *shares or voting power* in B or P as a result of which A is able to exercise significant influence over the management of B.
(3) for the purposes of calculations relating to (1) and (2), the holding of *shares* or *voting power* by a *person* ("A1") includes any *shares* or *voting power* held by another ("A2") if A1 and A2 are acting in concert.
(4) *shares* and *voting power* that a *person* holds in a *firm* ("B") or in a *parent undertaking* of B ("P") are disregarded for the purposes of determining *control* in the following circumstances:
  (a) *shares* held for the sole purposes of clearing and settling within a short settlement cycle;

(b) *shares* held by a *custodian* or its nominee in its custodian capacity are disregarded, provided that the *custodian* or nominee is only able to exercise *voting power* attached to the *shares* in accordance with instructions given in writing;
(c) shares representing no more than 5% of the total voting power in B or P held by an *investment firm*, provided that:
  (i) it holds the *shares* in the capacity of a *market maker* (as defined in article 4.1(8) of MIFID);
  (ii) it is authorised by its *Home State regulator* under MIFID; and
  (iii) it does not intervene in the management of B or P nor exerts any influence on B or P to buy the *shares* or back the share price;
(d) *shares* held by a *credit institution* or *investment firm* in its *trading book* are disregarded, provided that:
  (i) the *shares* represent no more than 5% of the total *voting power* in B or P; and
  (ii) the *credit institution* or *investment firm* ensures that the *voting power* is not used to intervene in the management of B or P;
(e) *shares* held by a *credit institution* or an *investment firm* are disregarded, provided that:
  (i) the shares are held as a result of performing the *investment services* and activities of:
    (A) underwriting share issues; or
    (B) placing shares on a firm commitment basis in accordance with Annex I, section A.6 of MIFID; and
  (ii) the credit institution or investment firm:
    (A) does not exercise *voting power* represented by the *shares* or otherwise intervene in the management of the issuer; and
    (B) retains the holding for a period of less than one year;
(f) where a *management company* and its *parent undertaking* both hold *shares* or *voting power*, each may disregard holdings of the other, provided that each exercises its *voting power* independently of the other;
(g) but (f) does not apply if the *management company*:
  (i) manages holdings for its *parent undertaking* or an *undertaking* in respect of which the *parent undertaking* is a *controller*;
  (ii) has no discretion to exercise the *voting power* attached to such holdings; and
  (iii) may only exercise the *voting power* in relation to such holdings under direct or indirect instruction from:
    (A) its parent undertaking; or
    (B) an undertaking in respect of which of the parent undertaking is a controller;
(h) where an *investment firm* and its *parent undertaking* both hold *shares* or *voting power*, the *parent undertaking* may disregard holdings managed by the *investment firm* on a client by client basis and the *investment firm* may disregard holdings of the *parent undertaking*, provided that the *investment firm*:
  (i) has permission to provide *portfolio management*;
  (ii) exercises its *voting power* independently from the *parent undertaking*; and
  (iii) may only exercise the *voting power* under instructions given in writing, or has appropriate mechanisms in place for ensuring that individual portfolio management services are conducted independently of any other services.

conversion factor

(in accordance with Article 4(28) of the *Banking Consolidation Directive* (Definitions)) the ratio of the currently undrawn amount of a commitment that will be drawn and outstanding at default to the currently undrawn amount of the commitment; the extent of the commitment is determined by the advised limit, unless the unadvised limit is higher.

convertible

(for the purposes of BIPRU) a *security* which gives the investor the right to convert the *security* into a *share* at an agreed price or on an agreed basis.

convertible securities

(in LR) a *security* which is:
(a) convertible into, or exchangeable for, other *securities*; or
(b) accompanied by a *warrant* or *option* to subscribe for or purchase other *securities*.

conventional group

a group of *undertakings* that consists of a *parent undertaking* and the rest of its *sub-group*.

coordinator

(in relation to a *financial conglomerate*) the *competent authority* which has been appointed, in accordance with Article 10 of the *Financial Groups Directive* (Competent authority responsible for exercising supplementary supervision (the coordinator)), as the *competent authority* which is responsible for the co-ordination and exercise of supplementary supervision of that *financial conglomerate*.

core market participant

an entity of a type listed in BIPRU 5.4.64R (The financial collateral comprehensive method: Conditions for applying a 0% volatility adjustment).

core provision

(as defined in section 316(3) of the *Act* (Direction by Authority)) a provision of the *Act* mentioned in section 317 of the *Act* (The core provisions) which applies to the carrying on of an insurance market activity by a *member*, or the *members* of the *Society* taken together, if the *FSA* so directs.

core tier one capital

an item of capital that is stated in stage A of the *capital resources table* (Core tier one capital) to be core tier one capital.

corporate

(in relation to the *IRB approach* or the *standardised approach* to credit risk) a *person* an *exposure* to whom is a *corporate exposure*.

corporate exposure

(1) (in relation to the *IRB approach*) an *exposure* falling into BIPRU 4.3.2R(3) (IRB exposure classes).

(2) (in relation to the *standardised approach* to credit risk) an *exposure* falling into BIPRU 3.2.9R(7) (Standardised approach to credit risk exposure classes).

corporate finance advisory firm

a *firm* whose *permission* includes a *requirement* that the *firm* must not conduct *designated investment business* other than *corporate finance business*.

corporate finance business

(a) *designated investment business* carried on by a *firm* with or for:
- (i) any *issuer*, holder or owner of *designated investments*, if that business relates to the *offer*, issue, underwriting, repurchase, exchange or redemption of, or the variation of the terms of, those *investments*, or any related matter;
- (ii) any *market counterparty* or *intermediate customer*, or other *body corporate*, *partnership* or supranational organisation, if that business relates to the manner in which, or the terms on which, or the *persons* by whom, any business, activities or undertakings relating to it, or any *associate*, are to be financed, structured, managed, controlled, regulated or reported upon;
- (iii) any *person* in connection with:
  - (A) a proposed or actual *takeover or related operation* by or on behalf of that *person*, or involving *investments* issued by that *person* (being a *body corporate*), its *holding company*, *subsidiary* or *associate*; or
  - (B) a merger, de-merger, reorganisation or reconstruction involving any *investments* issued by that *person* (being a *body corporate*), its *holding company*, *subsidiary* or *associate*;
- (iv) any shareholder or prospective shareholder of a *body corporate* established or to be established for the purpose of effecting a *takeover or related operation*, where that business is in connection with that *takeover or related operation*;
- (v) any *person* who, acting as a *principal* for his own account:
  - (A) is involved in negotiations or decisions relating to the commercial, financial or strategic intentions or requirements of a business or prospective business; or
  - (B) (provided he is acting otherwise than solely in his capacity as an investor) assists the interests of another *person* with or for whom the *firm*, or another *authorised person* or *overseas person*, is undertaking business as specified in (a)(i), (ii), (iii) or (iv), by himself undertaking all or part of any transactions involved in such business;
- (vi) any *person* undertaking business with or for a *person* as specified in (a)(i), (ii), (iii), (iv) or (v) in respect of activities described in those sub-paragraphs;

(b) *designated investment business* carried on by a *firm* as a *principal* for its own account where such business:
- (i) is in the course of, or arises out of, activities undertaken in accordance with (a); and
- (ii) does not involve transactions with or for, or *advice on investments* to, any other *person* who is a *private customer* in respect of such business;

(c) *designated investment business* carried on by a *firm* as *principal* for its own account if such business:

Part II FSA Handbook Materials

(i) is in the course of, or arises out of:
(A) the *offer*, issue, underwriting, repurchase, exchange or redemption of, or the variation of the terms of, *shares*, share warrants, *debentures* or debenture warrants issued by the *firm*, or any related matter; or
(B) a proposed or actual *takeover or related operation* by or on behalf of the *firm*, or involving *shares*, share warrants, *debentures* or debenture warrants issued by the *firm*; or
(C) a merger, de-merger, reorganisation or reconstruction involving any *shares*, share warrants, *debentures* or debenture warrants issued by the *firm*; and
(ii) does not involve *advice on investments* to any *person* who is a *private customer*;
in this definition, "share warrants" and "debenture warrants" mean any *warrants* which relate to *shares* in the *firm* concerned or, as the case may be, *debentures* issued by the *firm*.

corporate finance contact

(when a *firm* carries on *regulated activities* with or for a *person* in the course of or as a result of either carrying on *corporate finance business* with or for a *client*, or carrying on *corporate finance business* for the *firm's* own account) that *person* in onnection with that *regulated activity* if:
(a) the *firm* does not behave in a way towards that *person* which might reasonably be expected to lead that *person* to believe that he is being treated as a *client*; and
(b) the *firm* clearly indicates to that *person* that it:
(i) is not acting for him; and
(ii) will not be responsible to him for providing protections afforded to *clients* of the *firm* or be advising him on the relevant transaction.

corporate governance rules

(in accordance with section 89O(1) of the *Act*) *rules* for the purpose of implementing, enabling the implementation of or dealing with matters arising out of or related to, any *EU* Law obligation relating to the corporate governance of *issuers* who have requested or approved *admission to trading* of their securities and about corporate governance in relation to such *issuers* for the purpose of implementing, or dealing with matters arising out of or related to, any *EU* Law obligation. The *corporate governance rules* are located in chapters 1B, 4 and 7 of *DTR*.

corporate member

a *member* that is a *body corporate* or a Scottish Limited partnership.

Council

the *governing body* of the *Society*, constituted by section 3 of Lloyd's Act 1982.

counterparty

(1) (in UPRU) any *person* with or for whom a firm carries on *designated* investment business or an ancillary activity.
(2) (for the purposes of the rules relating to insurers in GENPRU and INSPRU) (in relation to an *insurer*, the *Society*, a *syndicate* or *member* ('A')):
(3) any one individual; or
(4) any one unincorporated body of *persons*; or
(5) any *company* which is not a member of a *group*; or
(6) any *group* of *companies* excluding:
(i) (for the purposes of INSPRU 2.1) any *companies* within the *group* which are *subsidiary undertakings* of A and which fall within GENPRU 1.3.43R; and
(ii) (for all other purposes) any *companies* within the *group* which are *subsidiary undertakings* of A; or
(7) any government of a State together with all the public bodies, local authorities or nationalised industries of that State,
in which A, or any of its *subsidiary undertakings*, has made *investments* or against whom, or in respect of whom, it, or any of its *subsidiary undertakings*, has rights or obligations under a contract entered into by A or any of its *subsidiary undertakings*.
(8) (for the purposes of the *rules* relating to *BIPRU firms* in GENPRU and BIPRU and in relation to an *exposure* of a *person* ('A')) the counterparty with respect to that *exposure* or, if the context requires, another *person* in respect of whom, under that *exposure*, A is exposed to credit risk or the risk of loss if that *person* fails to meet its obligations, such as the issuer of the underlying *security* in relation to a *derivative* held by A.

counterparty credit risk

(in accordance with Part 1 of Annex III of the *Banking Consolidation Directive* (Definitions)) the risk that the counterparty to a transaction could default before the final settlement of the transaction's cash flows.

counterparty exposure

(for the purposes of BIPRU 10 (Concentration risk requirements)) has the meaning in BIPRU 10.4.19R and BIPRU 10.4.20R (Definition of counterparty exposures).

counterparty risk capital component

the part of the *credit risk capital requirement* calculated in accordance with BIPRU 14.2.1R (Calculation of the counterparty risk capital component).

country of origin

in relation to an *electronic commerce activity*, the *EEA State* in which the *establishment* from which the service in question is provided is situated.

coupon

a dividend, interest payment or any similar payment.

covered bond

(1) (in accordance with Article 22(4) of the *UCITS Directive* and except for the purposes of the *IRB approach* or the *standardised approach* to credit risk) a bond that is issued by a *credit institution* which has its registered office in an *EEA State* and is subject by law to special public supervision designed to protect bondholders and in particular protection under which sums deriving from the issue of the bond must be invested in conformity with the law in assets which, during the whole period of validity of the bond, are capable of covering claims attaching to the bond and which, in the event of failure of the issuer, would be used on a priority basis for the reimbursement of the principal and payment of the accrued interest.

(2) (in accordance with point 68 of Part 1 of Annex VI of the *Banking Consolidation Directive* (Exposures in the form of covered bonds) and for the purposes of the *IRB approach* or the *standardised approach* to credit risk) a covered bond as defined in (1) collateralised in accordance with BIPRU 3.4.107R (Exposures in the form of covered bonds).

(3) (in *RCB)* (as defined in Regulation 1(2) of the *RCB Regulations*) a bond in relation to which the claims attaching to that bond are guaranteed to be paid by an *owner* from an *asset pool* it owns.

(4) (in accordance with Article 22(4) of the *Third Non-Life Directive* and Article 24(4) of the *Consolidated Life Directive* and for the purposes of *INSPRU* 2.1) a *debenture* that is issued by a *credit institution* which:

   (a) has its head office in an *EEA State*; and

   (b) is subject by law to special official supervision designed to protect the holders of the *debenture*; in particular, sums deriving from the issue of the *debenture* must be invested in accordance with the law in assets which, during the whole period of validity of the *debenture*, are capable of covering claims attaching to the *debenture* and which, in the event of failure of the *issuer*, would be used on a priority basis for the reimbursement of the principal and payment of the accrued interest.

CRD

the *Capital Adequacy Directive* and the *Banking Consolidation Directive*.

CRD financial instrument

has the meaning set out in BIPRU 1.2.7R to BIPRU 1.2.8R (CRD financial instruments), which is in summary any contract that gives rise to both a financial asset of one party and a financial liability or equity instrument of another party.

CRD implementation measure

(in relation to an *person*, a provision of the *Banking Consolidation Directive* or the *Capital Adequacy Directive* and an *EEA State* other than the *United Kingdom*) a measure implementing that provision of that Directive for that type of *person* in that *EEA State*.

CRED

the Credit unions sourcebook.

credit

(1) (except in relation to a *class* of *contract of insurance*) any kind of loan, deferment of repayment of any loan or of interest on any loan, guarantee or indemnity, and any other kind of accommodation or facility in the nature of credit.

(2) (in relation to a *class* of *contract of insurance*) the *class* of *contract of insurance*, specified in paragraph 14 of Part I of Schedule 1 to the *Regulated Activities Order* (Contracts of general insurance), against risks of loss to the *persons* insured arising from the insolvency of debtors of theirs or from the failure (otherwise than through insolvency) of debtors of theirs to pay their debts when due.

credit default swap PRR method

the *ordinary credit default swap PRR method* or the *securitisation credit default swap PRR method*.

Part II FSA Handbook Materials

credit enhancement

(in accordance with Article 4(43) of the *Banking Consolidation Directive* (Definitions)) a contractual arrangement whereby the credit quality of a *position* in a *securitisation* (within the meaning of paragraph (2) of the definition of securitisation) is improved in relation to what it would have been if the enhancement had not been provided, including the enhancement provided by more junior *tranches* in the *securitisation* and other types of credit protection.

credit equalisation provision

the provision required to be established by INSPRU 1.4.43R.

credit institution

(1) (except in REC) (in accordance with articles 4(1) and 107 of the *BCD*):

(2) an undertaking whose business is to receive deposits or other repayable funds from the public and to grant credits for its own account; or

(3) an electronic money institution within the meaning of the *E-money Directive*;
but so that:

(4) (except for the purposes of GENPRU, ELM, BIPRU and *IPRU(INV)* (in so far as it relates to *exempt CAD firms*) an institution within (1)(b) that does not have the right to benefit from the mutual recognition arrangements under *BCD* is excluded; and

(5) for the purposes of BIPRU 10 (Concentration risk requirements) it means:
- (i) a credit institution as defined by (1)(a) to (1)(b) that has been authorised in an *EEA State*; or
- (ii) any private or public *undertaking* which meets the definition in (1)(a) – (1)(b) and which has been authorised in a *non-EEA state*.
(see also BCD credit institution, full credit institution, full BCD credit institution and Zone A credit institution.)

(6) (in REC and in SUP 11 (Controllers and close links) and SUP 16 (Reporting requirement))):
- (a) a credit institution authorised under the *Banking Consolidation Directive*; or
- (b) an institution which would satisfy the requirements for authorisation as a credit institution under the *Banking Consolidation Directive* if it had its registered office (or if it does not have a registered office, its head office) in an *EEA State*.

credit quality assessment scale

the credit quality assessment scale:

(1) onto which the credit assessments of an export credit agency are mapped under the table in BIPRU 3.4.9R (Exposure for which a credit assessment by an export credit agency is recognised); or

(2) published by the *FSA* in accordance with the *Capital Requirements Regulations 2006* which determines:
- (a) (in relation to a *eligible ECAI* whose recognition is for *risk weighting* purposes other than those in (2)(b)) with which of the *credit quality steps* set out in BIPRU 3.4 (Risk weights under the standardised approach to credit risk) the relevant credit assessments of an *eligible ECAI* are to be associated; or
- (b) (in relation to a *eligible ECAI* whose recognition is for *securitisation risk-weighting* purposes) with which of the *credit quality steps* set out in BIPRU 9 (Securitisation) the relevant credit assessments of the *eligible ECAI* are to be associated.

credit quality step

a credit quality step in a *credit quality assessment scale* as set out in BIPRU 3.4 (Risk weights under the standardised approach to credit risk) and BIPRU 9 (Securitisation).

credit risk capital component

the part of the *credit risk capital requirement* calculated in accordance with *BIPRU* 3.1.5R (Calculation of the credit risk capital component).

credit risk capital requirement

the part of the *capital resources requirement* of a *BIPRU firm* in respect of credit risk, calculated in accordance with GENPRU 2.1.51R (Calculation of the credit risk capital requirement).

credit risk mitigation

(in accordance with Article 4(30) of the *Banking Consolidation Directive* (Definitions)) a technique used by an *undertaking* to reduce the credit risk associated with an *exposure* or *exposures* which the *undertaking* continues to hold.

credit union

a body corporate registered under the Industrial and Provident Societies Act 1965 as a credit union in accordance with the Credit Unions Act, which is an *authorised person*.

credit unions day

1 July 2002.

credit valuation adjustment

(in accordance with Part 1 of Annex III of the *Banking Consolidation Directive* (Definitions)) an adjustment to the midmarket valuation of the portfolio of transactions with a counterparty; and so that this adjustment:

(a) reflects the market value of the credit risk due to any failure to perform on contractual agreements with a counterparty; and

(b) may reflect the market value of the credit risk of the counterparty or the market value of the credit risk of both the *firm* and the counterparty.

CREST

the computer-based system which enables securities to be held and transferred in uncertificated form and which is operated by CRESTCo Limited.

CRM eligibility conditions

(1) (in relation to the *standardised approach* to credit risk), BIPRU 5.3.1R-BIPRU 5.3.2R, BIPRU 5.4.1R-BIPRU 5.4.8R, BIPRU 5.5.1R, BIPRU 5.5.4R, BIPRU 5.5.8R, BIPRU 5.6.1R and BIPRU 5.7.1R-BIPRU 5.7.4R; or

(2) (in relation to the *IRB approach*), the provisions in (1) and BIPRU 4.4.83R, BIPRU 4.10.R-BIPRU 4.10.7R, BIPRU 4.10.9R, BIPRU 4.10.10R-BIPRU 4.10.12R, BIPRU 4.10.14R, BIPRU 4.10.16R, BIPRU 4.10.19R, and BIPRU 4.10.38R-BIPRU 4.10.39R.

CRM minimum requirements

(1) in relation to the *standardised approach* to credit risk); BIPRU 5.2.9R-BIPRU 5.2.10R, BIPRU 5.3.3R, BIPRU 5.4.9R-BIPRU 5.4.13R, BIPRU 5.5.2R, BIPRU 5.5.5RBIPRU 5.5.6R, BIPRU 5.6.2R-BIPRU 5.6.3R, BIPRU 5.7.6R-BIPRU 5.7.14R; or

(2) (in relation to the *IRB approach*), the provisions in (1) and BIPRU 4.4.85R, BIPRU 4.10.13R, BIPRU 4.10.15R, and BIPRU 4.10.18R-BIPRU 4.10.19R.

cross border services

(1) (in relation to a *UK firm*) services provided within an *EEA State* other than the *United Kingdom* under the freedom to provide services.

(2) (in relation to an *incoming EEA firm* or an *incoming Treaty firm*) services provided within the *United Kingdom* under the freedom to provide services.

cross product netting

(in accordance with Part 1 of Annex III of the *Banking Consolidation Directive* (Definitions) and for the purpose of BIPRU 13 (The calculation of counterparty risk exposure values for financial derivatives, securities financing transactions and long settlement transactions)) the inclusion of transactions of different product categories within the same *netting set* pursuant to the *rules* about cross-product netting set out in BIPRU 13.

cross-transaction

(a) a transaction by which a *person* matches, at the same price and on the same terms, the *buy* and *sell* orders of two or more *persons* for whom he is acting as agent;

(b) a transaction to which only one *person* is a party, by which he purports to *sell* to and *buy* from himself.

CRR

capital resources requirement.

CTF

(as defined in section 1(2) of the Child Trust Funds Act 2004) a child trust fund, that is, an account which:

(1) is held by a child who is or has been an eligible child (as defined in section 2 of that Act);

(2) satisfies the requirements imposed by or under the Child Trust Funds Act 2004; and

(3) has been opened in accordance with the Child Trust Funds Act 2004.

CTF bank account

a bank account which fulfils the requirements of Regulation 11(5) of the *CTF Regulations*.

CTF provider

(in accordance with section 3(1) of the Child Trust Funds Act 2004) a *person* approved by HM Revenue and Customs in accordance with the *CTF Regulations*.

CTF Regulations

the Child Trust Funds Regulations 2004 (SI 2004/1450).

CTF transfer

a transaction resulting from a decision by a *customer*, made with or without advice from a *firm*, to transfer the *investments* (or their value) held in an existing *CTF* into another *CTF* whether or not provided by the same *CTF provider*.

currency class unit

(in COLL) a class of *unit* denominated in a currency that is not the *base currency* of the *authorised fund*, or, if permitted, by COLL 3.3.4R(1) (Currency class units: requirements).

current customer order

(a) a *customer order* to be *executed* immediately;
(b) a *customer order* which is to be *executed* only on fulfilment of a condition, after the condition has been fulfilled.

current exposure

(in accordance with Part 1 of Annex III of the *Banking Consolidation Directive* (Definitions) and for the purpose of BIPRU 13 (The calculation of counterparty risk exposure values for financial derivatives, securities financing transactions and long settlement transactions)) the larger of zero, or the market value of a transaction or portfolio of transactions within a *netting set* with a counterparty that would be lost upon the default of the counterparty, assuming no recovery on the value of those transactions in bankruptcy.

current market value

(in accordance with Part 1 of Annex III of the *Banking Consolidation Directive* (Definitions) and for the purpose of BIPRU 13.5 (CCR standardised method)) the net market value of the portfolio of transactions within the *netting set* with the counterparty; both positive and negative market values are used in computing *current market value.*

custodian

(a) an *approved* bank;
(b) an *approved depositary*;
(c) a *member* of a *recognised investment exchange* or *designated investment exchange;*
(d) a *firm* whose *permitted activities* include *safeguarding and administering investments;*
(e) a regulated *clearing firm*;
(f) where it is not feasible to use a *custodian* in (a) to (e), and there are reasonable grounds to show that a *person* outside the *United Kingdom*, whose business includes the provision of custodial services, is able to provide such services which are appropriate to the *client* and in the *client's* best interest to use, that *person.*

custody

(in relation to clients' assets) safeguarding and administering investments.

custody asset

(a) a *designated investment* held for or on behalf of a *client*;
(b) any other asset which is or may be held with a *designated investment* held for, or on behalf of, a *client*.

custody rules

CASS 6.

customer

(1) (except in relation to ICOBS, MCOB 3 and CASS 5) a *client* who is not an *eligible counterparty* for the relevant purposes.
(2) (in relation to MCOB 3) a *person* in (1) or a *person* who would be such a *person* if he were a *client.*
(3) (in relation to ICOBS) a *policyholder*, or a prospective *policyholder* but (except in ICOBS 2 (general matters), and (in respect of that chapter) ICOBS 1 (application)) excluding a *policyholder* or prospective *policyholder* who does not make the arrangements preparatory to him concluding the *contract of insurance*.
(4) (in relation to CASS 5) a *client*.

customer function

the *controlled function* 30 in the *table of controlled functions,* described more fully in *SUP* 10.10.7AR.

customer order

(a) an order to a *firm* from a *customer* to *execute* a transaction as agent;
(b) any other order to a *firm* from a *customer* to *execute* a transaction in circumstances giving rise to duties similar to those arising on an order to *execute* a transaction as agent;
(c) a decision by a *firm* in the exercise of discretion to *execute* a transaction with or for a *customer*.

daily e-money outstandings amount

(in *ELM*) (in relation to a particular *day* or time and *ELMI*) the highest amount that that *ELMI's e-money outstandings* reached on that *day* or, as the case may be, on the *day* in question prior to that time.

damage to property

(in relation to a *class* of *contract of insurance*) the *class* of *contract of insurance*, specified in paragraph 9 of Part I of Schedule 1 to the *Regulated Activities Order* (Contracts of general insurance), against loss of or damage to property (other than property to which paragraphs 3 to 7 of that Schedule (Land vehicles, Railway rolling stock, Aircraft, Ships *and* Goods in transit) relate) due to hail or frost or any other event (such as theft) other than those mentioned in paragraph 8 of that Schedule (Fire and natural forces).

data element

A discrete fact or individual piece of information relating to a particular field within a *data item* required to be submitted to the *FSA* by a *firm* or other regulated entity.

data item

One or more related *data elements* that are grouped together into a prescribed format and required to be submitted by a *firm* or other regulated entity under SUP 16 or provisions referred to in SUP 16.

data set

One or more *data items* relating to the same *regulated activity*.

date of allotment

the date on which amounts of the *relevant security* are allotted to subscribers or purchasers and, where there is an initial or preliminary allotment subject to confirmation, the date of that initial or preliminary allotment.

day

a period of 24 hours beginning at midnight.

deal

a *dealing* transaction.

deal on own account

(for the purposes of GENPRU and BIPRU) has the meaning in BIPRU 1.1.23R (Meaning of dealing on own account) which is in summary the service referred to in point 3 of Section A Annex I to *MiFID*, subject to the adjustments in BIPRU 1.1.23R(2) and (3) (Implementation of Article 5(2) of the *Capital Adequacy Directive*).

dealing

(1) (other than in MAR 1 (The Code of Market Conduct)) (in accordance with paragraph 2 of Schedule 2 to the *Act* (Regulated activities)) buying, selling, subscribing for or underwriting *investments* or offering or agreeing to do so, either as a *principal* or as an agent, including, in the case of an *investment* which is a *contract of insurance*, carrying out the contract.

(2) (in *MAR* 1) (as defined as in section 130A(3) of the *Act*), in relation to an investment, means acquiring or disposing of the investment whether as principal or agent or directly or indirectly, and includes agreeing to acquire or dispose of the investment, and entering into and bringing to an end a contract creating it.

dealing day

(in COLL) the period in a *business day* (in accordance with the provisions of the *prospectus*) during which the *ACD* or the *operator* is open for business.

dealing in investments as principal

the *regulated activity*, specified in article 14 of the *Regulated Activities Order* (Dealing in investments as principal), which is in summary:*buying*, *selling*, subscribing for or underwriting *designated investments* as principal.

dealing on own account

trading against proprietary capital resulting in the conclusion of transactions in one or more *financial instruments*.

[Note: article 4(1)(6) of *MIFID*]

dealing period

(in COLL) the period between one *valuation point* and the next.

debenture

the *investment*, specified in article 77 of the *Regulated Activities Order* (Instruments creating or acknowledging indebtedness), which is in summary: any of the following which are not *government and public securities*:
(a) debentures;
(b) debenture stock;
(c) loan stock;
(d) bonds;
(e) certificates of deposit;
(f) any other instrument creating or acknowledging indebtedness.

debt security

(1) (in DTR 2, DTR 3 and LR) debentures, debenture stock, loan stock, bonds, certificates of deposit or any other instrument creating or acknowledging indebtedness.
(2) (in DTR 4, DTR 5 and DTR 6) (in accordance with article 2.1(b) of the *Transparency Directive*) bonds or other forms of transferable securitised debts, with the exception of securities which are equivalent to *shares* in companies or which, if converted or if the rights conferred by them are exercised, give rise to a right to acquire *shares* or securities equivalent to *shares*
(3) ((except in DTR and LR) any of the following:
   (a) a debenture;
   (b) a *government and public security*;
   (c) a *warrant* which confers a right in respect of an *investment* in (a) or (b).

decision notice

a notice issued by the *FSA* in accordance with section 388 of the *Act* (Decision notices).

dedicated

(in relation to *investments* of an *authorised fund*) intended that the *holders* should participate in or receive:
(a) profits or income arising from the acquisition, holding, management or disposal of *investments* of the relevant description; or
(b) sums paid out of profits or income in (a); or
(c) other benefits where expressly permitted by a provision in *COLL*.

deductions plan

(in *COBS*) a plan that describes the deductions from asset share that a *firm* expects to make for the cost of guarantees and the use of capital (*COBS* 20.2.8R).

default

(in relation to the *IRB approach*) has the meaning in BIPRU 4.3 (The IRB approach: Provisions common to different exposure classes).

default rules

(1) (in relation to a *UK RIE*) the default rules which it is required to have under paragraph 10 of the Schedule to the *Recognition Requirements Regulations*.
(2) (in relation to a *UK RCH*) the default rules which it is required to have under paragraph 24 of the Schedule to the *Recognition Requirements Regulations*.

deferred acquisition costs

deferred acquisition costs as defined in the *insurance accounts rules*.

deferred bonus

(in *LR*) any arrangement pursuant to the terms of which an *employee* or *director* may receive a bonus (including cash or any security) in respect of service and/or performance in a period not exceeding the length of the relevant financial year notwithstanding that the bonus may, subject only to the *person* remaining a *director* or *employee* of the group, be receivable by the *person* after the end of the period to which the award relates.

deficit reduction amount

in respect of a *defined benefit occupational pension scheme*, the sum, determined by a *firm* in conjunction with the *defined benefit occupational pension scheme's* actuaries or trustees (or both), of the additional funding (net of tax) that will be required to be paid into that scheme by the *firm* over the following five year period for the purpose of reducing the *firm's defined benefit liability*.

defined benefit asset

the excess of the value of the assets in a *defined benefit occupational pension scheme* over the present value of the scheme liabilities, to the extent that a *firm*, as employer, in accordance with the accounting principles applicable to it, should recognise that excess as an asset in its balance sheet.

defined benefit liability

the shortfall of the value of the assets in a *defined benefit occupational pension scheme* below the present value of the scheme liabilities, to the extent that a *firm*, as employer, in accordance with the accounting principles applicable to it, should recognise that shortfall as a liability in its balance sheet.

defined benefit occupational pension scheme

an occupational pension scheme which is not a *defined* contribution occupational pension scheme.

defined benefit scheme

in relation to a *director*, means a pension scheme which is not a *money purchase scheme.*

defined benefits pension scheme

(1) (except in PRU) a *pension policy* or *pension contract* under which the only *money-purchase benefits* are benefits ancillary to other benefits which are not *money-purchase benefits.*
(2) (in PRU) an *occupational pension scheme* under which the only *money-purchase benefits* are benefits ancillary to other benefits which are not *money-purchase benefits.*

defined contribution occupational pension scheme

an *occupational pension scheme* into which a *firm*, as employer, pays regular fixed contributions and will have no legal or constructive obligation to pay further contributions if the scheme does not have sufficient assets to pay all employee benefits relating to employee service in the current and prior periods.

defined liquidity group

a DLG by default or DLG by modification.

delivery by value

a transaction type, described as "delivery by value", used to deliver and receive *securities* within *CREST.*

deposit

(1) (except in *COMP*) the *investment*, specified in article 74 and defined in articles 5(2) and 5(3) of the *Regulated Activities Order*, which is in summary: a sum of money (other than one excluded by any of articles 6 to 9AB of the *Regulated Activities Order*) paid on terms:
  (a) under which it will be repaid, with or without interest or a premium, and either on demand or at a time or in circumstances agreed by or on behalf of the *person* making the payment and the *person* receiving it; and
  (b) which are not referable to the provision of property (other than currency) or services or the giving of security;
  in this definition, money is paid on terms which are referable to the provision of property or services or the giving of security if, and only if:
  (a) it is paid by way of advance or part payment under a contract for the sale, hire or other provision of property or services, and is repayable only in the event that the property or services is or are not in fact sold, hired or otherwise provided; or
  (b) it is paid by way of security for the performance of a contract or by way of security in respect of loss which may result from the non-performance of a contract; or
  (c) without prejudice to (b), it is paid by way of security for the delivery up or return of any property, whether in a particular state of repair or otherwise.
(2) (in *COMP*) the *investment* within (1), but including a sum of money that would otherwise be excluded:
  (a) by article 6(1)(a)(ii) of the *Regulated Activities Order*, where the *person* making the payment is a *credit union* (unless the *person* receiving the payment is also a *credit union*); or
  (b) by article 6(1)(d) of the *Regulated Activities Order*, where the *person* receiving it is a *credit union.*

deposit back arrangement

(in relation to any contract of *reinsurance*) an arrangement whereby an amount is deposited by the *reinsurer* with the cedant.

deposit-based stakeholder product

the *stakeholder product* specified by regulation 4 (certain deposit accounts) of the *Stakeholder Regulations*;

Deposit Guarantee Directive

the Council Directive of 13 May 1994 on deposit-guarantee schemes (No 94/19/EC).

deposit-taking firm

a firm which is a *bank, building society* or *credit union.*

depositary

(1) (except in LR):

(a) (in relation to an *ICVC*) the *person* to whom is entrusted the safekeeping of all of the *scheme property* of the *ICVC* and who has been appointed for this purpose in accordance with regulation 5 (Safekeeping of scheme property by depositary) of and Schedule 1 (Depositaries) to the *OEIC Regulations*;

(b) (in relation to an *AUT*) the *trustee*;

(c) (in relation to any other *unit trust scheme*) the *person* holding the property of the *scheme* on trust for the *participants*;

(d) (in relation to any other *collective investment scheme*) any *person* to whom the property subject to the *scheme* is entrusted for safekeeping.

(2) (in LR) a *person* that issues *certificates representing certain securities* that have been *admitted to listing* or are the subject of an application for *admission to listing*.

DEPP

the Decision Procedure and Penalties manual.

derivative

a *contract for differences*, a future or an *option*. (see also *securitised derivative*.)

designated client bank account

a *client bank account* with the following characteristics:

(a) the account holds the money of one or more *clients*;

(b) the account includes in its title the word "designated";

(c) the *clients* whose *money* is in the account have each consented in writing to the use of the bank with which the *client money* is to be held; and

(d) in the event of the *failure* of that bank, the account is not pooled with any other type of account unless a *primary pooling event* occurs.

designated client fund account

a *client bank account* with the following characteristics:

(a) the account holds at least part of the *client money* of one or more *clients*, each of whom has consented to that *money* being held in the same *client bank accounts* at the same banks (the *client money* of such *clients* constituting a designated fund);

(b) the account includes in its title the words "designated fund"; and

(c) in the event of the *failure* of a bank with which part of a designated fund is held, each *designated client fund account* held with the *failed* bank will form a pool with any other *designated client fund account* containing part of that same designated fund unless a *primary pooling event* occurs.

designated clearing house

one of the following *clearing houses*:

(a) ASX Settlement and Transfer Corporation Pty Ltd (ASTC);

(b) Austrian Kontroll Bank (OKB);

(c) Board of Trade Clearing Corporation;

(d) Cassa di Compensazione e Garanzia S.p.A (CCG);

(e) Commodity Clearing Corporation;

(f) Emerging Markets Clearing Corporation;

(g) FUTOP Clearing Centre (FUTOP Clearing Centralen A/S);

(h) Hong Kong Futures Exchange Clearing Corporation Ltd;

(i) Hong Kong Securities Clearing Company Ltd;

(j) Kansas City Board of Trade Clearing Corporation;

(k) Norwegian Futures & Options Clearing House (Norsk Opsjonssentral A.S. (NOS));

(l) N.V. Nederlandse Liquidatiekas (NLKKAS);

(m) OM Stockholm Exchange;

(n) Options Clearing Corporation;

(o) Options Clearing House Pty Ltd (OCH);

(p) Sydney Futures Exchange Clearing House (SFECH Ltd); and

(q) TNS Clearing Pty Ltd (TNSC).

designated committee

(in relation to a *firm*) a management body of the *firm* with delegated authority from the *firm's governing body* for approving either:

(a) (in relation to a *firm* that uses the *IRB approach*) all material aspects of the *firm's rating systems* and material changes to the *firm's rating systems*; or

(b) (in relation to a *firm* that uses the *advanced measurement approach*) all material aspects of the *advanced measurement approach* as carried out by the *firm* and material changes to the *firm's advanced measurement approach*; and

(c) a policy statement defining the *firm's* overall approach to material aspects of rating and estimation processes for all *rating systems* including non-material *rating systems* in relation to the *IRB approach*, or its overall approach to the *advanced measurement approach*, as relevant;

at least one of whose members is a member of the *firm's governing body*.

designated investment

a *security* or a *contractually based investment* (other than a *funeral plan contract* and a *right to or interest in a funeral plan contract*), that is, any of the following *investments*, specified in Part III of the *Regulated Activities Order* (Specified Investments), and a *long-term care insurance contract* which is a *pure protection contract*:

(a) *life policy* (subset of article 75 (Contracts of insurance));

(b) *share* (article 76);

(c) *debenture* (article 77);

(d) *government and public security* (article 78);

(e) *warrant* (article 79);

(f) *certificate representing certain securities* (article 80);

(g) *unit* (article 81);

(h) *stakeholder pension scheme* (article 82(1));

(ha) *personal pension scheme* (article 82(2));

(i) *option* (article 83); for the purposes of the *permission* regime, this is sub-divided into:

  (i) *option* (excluding a *commodity option* and an *option* on a *commodity future*);

  (ii) *commodity option* and *option* on a *commodity future*;

(j) *future* (article 84); for the purposes of the *permission* regime, this is sub-divided into:

  (i) *future* (excluding a *commodity future* and a *rolling spot forex contract*);

  (ii) *commodity future*;

  (iii) *rolling spot forex contract*;

(k) *contract for differences* (article 85); for the purposes of the *permission* regime, this is sub-divided into:

  (i) *contract for differences* (excluding a *spread bet* and a *rolling spot forex contract*);

  (ii) *spread bet*;

  (iii) *rolling spot forex contract*;

(l) *rights to or interests in investments* in (a) to (k) (article 89) but not including rights to or interests in rights under a *long-term care insurance contract* which is a *pure protection contract*.

designated investment business

any of the following activities, specified in Part II of the *Regulated Activities Order* (Specified Activities), which is carried on by way of business:

(a) *dealing in investments as principal* (article 14), but disregarding the exclusion in article 15 (Absence of holding out etc);

(b) *dealing in investments as agent* (article 21), but only in relation to *designated investments*;

(c) *arranging (bringing about) deals in investments* (article 25(1)), but only in relation to *designated investments*;

(d) *making arrangements with a view to transactions in investments* (article 25(2)), but only in relation to *designated investments*;

(da) *operating a multilateral trading facility* (article 25D);

(e) *managing investments* (article 37), but only if the assets consist of or include (or may consist of or include) *designated investments*;

(ea) assisting in the administration and performance of a *contract of insurance*, but only if the *contract of insurance* is a *designated investment*.

(f) *safeguarding and administering investments* (article 40), but only if the assets consist of or include (or may consist of or include) *designated investments*; for the purposes of the *permission* regime, this is sub-divided into:

  (i) *safeguarding and administration of assets (without arranging)*;

(ii) *arranging safeguarding and administration of assets*;

(g) *sending dematerialised instructions* (article 45(1));

(h) *causing dematerialised instructions to be sent* (article 45(2));

(i) *establishing, operating or winding up a collective investment scheme* (article 51(1)(a)); for the purposes of the *permission* regime, this is sub-divided into:

(i) *establishing, operating or winding up a regulated collective investment scheme*;

(ii) *establishing, operating or winding up an unregulated collective investment scheme*;

(j) *acting as trustee of an authorised unit trust scheme* (article 51(1)(b));

(k) *acting as the depositary or sole director of an open-ended investment company* (article 51(1)(c));

(l) *establishing, operating or winding up a stakeholder pension scheme* (article 52(a));

(la) *establishing, operating or winding up a personal pension scheme* (article 52(b));

(m) *advising on investments* (article 53), but only in relation to *designated investments*; for the purposes of the *permission* regime, this is sub-divided into:

(i) *advising on investments (except pension transfers and pension opt-outs)*;

(ii) *advising on pension transfers and pension opt-outs*;

(n) *agreeing to carry on a regulated activity* in (a) to (h) and (m) (article 64);

(o) *providing basic advice on a stakeholder product* (article 52B).

designated investment exchange

any of the following investment exchanges:

American Stock Exchange

Australian Stock Exchange

Bermuda Stock Exchange

Bolsa Mexicana de Valores

Bourse de Montreal Inc

Channel Islands Stock Exchange

Chicago Board of Trade

Chicago Board Options Exchange

Chicago Stock Exchange

Coffee, Sugar and Cocoa Exchange, Inc

Euronext Amsterdam Commodities Market

Hong Kong Exchanges and Clearing Limited

International Securities Market Association

Johannesburg Stock Exchange

Kansas City Board of Trade

Korea Stock Exchange

MidAmerica Commodity Exchange

Minneapolis Grain Exchange

New York Cotton Exchange

New York Futures Exchange

New York Stock Exchange

New Zealand Stock Exchange

Osaka Securities Exchange

Pacific Exchange

Philadelphia Stock Exchange

Singapore Exchange

South African Futures Exchange

Tokyo International Financial Futures Exchange

Tokyo Stock Exchange

Toronto Stock Exchange

designated money market fund

(in BIPRU 12) a *collective investment scheme* authorised under the UCITS Directive or which is subject to supervision and, if applicable, authorised by an authority under the national law of an *EEA State*, and which satisfies the following conditions:

(a) its primary investment objective must be to maintain the net asset value of the undertaking either constant at par (net of earnings), or at the value of the investors' initial capital plus earnings;

(b) it must, with a view to achieving that primary investment objective, invest exclusively in either or both assets (i) of the kind mentioned in BIPRU 12.7.2R(1) and (2), or (ii) sight deposits with *credit institutions* that are at all times fully secured against assets of the kind mentioned in BIPRU 12.7.2R(1) and (2);

(c) it must, for the purpose of condition (b), only count assets with a maturity or residual maturity of no more than 397 days, or regular yield adjustments consistent with such a maturity, and with a weighted average maturity of no more than 60 days;

(d) it must, for the purpose of condition (b), ensure that if it invests in sight deposits with *credit institutions* of the kind mentioned in (b)(ii), no more than 20% of those deposits are held with any one body; and (e) it must provide liquidity through same day settlement in respect of any request for redemption made at or before 1500 hours GMT or, as the case may be, BST.

designated multilateral development bank

Any of the following:

(a) African Development Bank;
(b) Asian Development Bank;
(c) Council of Europe Development Bank;
(d) European Bank for Reconstruction and Development;
(e) European Investment Bank;
(f) Inter-American Development Bank;
(g) International Bank for Reconstruction and Development;
(h) International Finance Corporation;
(i) Islamic Development Bank; and
(j) Nordic Investment Bank.

designated non-member

(in *REC*) (in relation to a *UK RIE*) a *person* in respect of whom action may be taken under the *default rules* of the *RIE* but who is not a *member* of the *RIE*.

designated professional body

a professional body designated by the Treasury under section 326 of the *Act* (Designation of professional bodies) for the purposes of Part XX of the *Act* (Provision of Financial Services by Members of the Professions); the following professional bodies have been designated in the Financial Services and Markets Act 2000 (Designated Professional Bodies) Order 2001 (SI 2001/1226), the Financial Services and Markets Act 2000 (Designated Professional Bodies) (Amendment) Order 2004 (SI 2004/3352) and the Financial Services and Markets Act 2000 (Designated Professional Bodies) (Amendment) Order 2006 (SI 2006/58):

(a) The Law Society of England & Wales;
(b) The Law Society of Scotland;
(c) The Law Society of Northern Ireland;
(d) The Institute of Chartered Accountants in England and Wales;
(e) The Institute of Chartered Accountants of Scotland;
(f) The Institute of Chartered Accountants in Ireland;
(g) The Association of Chartered Certified Accountants;
(h) The Institute of Actuaries;
(i) The Council for Licensed Conveyancers; and
(j) The Royal Institution of Chartered Surveyors.

designated State or territory

any *EEA State* (other than the *United Kingdom*), Australia, Canada or a province of Canada, Hong Kong, Singapore, South Africa, Switzerland, a State in the United States of America, the District of Columbia or Puerto Rico.

DGD

[deleted]

DGD claim

a *claim*, in relation to a *protected deposit*, against a *BCD credit institution*, whether established in the *United Kingdom* or in another *EEA State*.

dilution

(in COLL) the amount of *dealing* costs incurred, or expected to be incurred, by or for the account of a *single-priced authorised fund* to the extent that these costs may reasonably be expected to result, or have resulted, from the acquisition or disposal of *investments* by or for the account of the *single-priced authorised fund* as a consequence (whether or not immediate) of the increase or decrease in the cash resources of the *single-priced authorised fund* resulting from the *issue* or *cancellation* of *units* over a period;

for the purposes of this definition, *dealing* costs include both the costs of *dealing* in an *investment*, professional fees incurred, or expected to be incurred, in relation to the acquisition or disposal of an immovables and, where there is a spread between the *buying* and *selling prices* of the *investment*, the indirect cost resulting from the differences between those prices.

dilution adjustment

an adjustment to the *price* of a *unit* determined by the *authorised fund manager* of a *single-priced authorised fund*, under COLL 6.3.8R (Dilution) or, as the case may be, *CIS* 4.6.4R (Dilution adjustment) for the purpose of reducing *dilution*.

dilution levy

a charge of such amount or at such rate as is determined by the *authorised fund manager* of a *single-priced authorised fund* to be made for the purpose of reducing the effect of *dilution*.

dilution risk

(in accordance with Article 4(24) of the *Banking Consolidation Directive* (Definitions)) the risk that an amount receivable is reduced through cash or non-cash credits to the obligor.

Diploma Directives

the First and Second Diploma Directives, that is:

(a) the Council Directive of 21 December 1988 on a general system for the recognition of higher-education diplomas, awarded on completion of professional education and training of at least three years' duration (No 89/48/EEC);

(b) the Council Directive of 18 June 1992 on a second general system for the recognition of professional education and training to supplement Directive 89/48/EEC (No 92/51/EEC).

direct offer financial promotion

a *financial promotion* that contains:

(a) an offer by the *firm* or another *person* to enter into a *controlled agreement* with any *person* who responds to the communication; or

(b) an invitation to any *person* who responds to the communication to make an offer to the *firm* or another *person* to enter into a *controlled agreement*;

and which specifies the manner of response or includes a form by which any response may be made.

In relation to *MiFID or equivalent third country business* "controlled agreement" includes an agreement to carry on an *ancillary service*.

directed at

a *financial promotion* is directed at *persons* if it is addressed to *persons* generally (for example where it is contained in a television broadcast or web site).

directed only at

(a) If all the conditions set out in (c) are met, a communication is to be regarded as "directed only at" a certain *group* of *persons*.

(b) In any other case in which one or more of those conditions are met, that fact is to be taken into account in determining whether the communication is "directed only at" a certain *group* of *persons* (but a communication may still be regarded as so directed even if none of the conditions in (c) are met).

(c) The conditions are that:

 (i) the communication includes an indication of the description of *persons* to whom it is directed and an indication of the fact that the *investment* or service to which it relates is available only to such *persons*;

 (ii) the communication includes an indication that *persons* of any other description should not rely upon it;

 (iii) there are in place proper systems and procedures to prevent recipients other than *persons* to whom it is directed engaging in the investment activity, or participating in the *collective investment scheme*, to which the communication relates with the *person* directing the communication, a *close relative* of his or a member of the same *group*.

directive friendly society

a friendly society other than a non-directive friendly society.

director

(1) (except in COLL, DTR, LR, and PR) (in relation to any of the following (whether constituted in the *United Kingdom* or under the law of a country or territory outside it)):
(a) an unincorporated association;
(b) a *body corporate*;
(c) (in *SYSC*, PRU 9.1 (Responsibility for insurance mediation activity) and *SUP* 10 (Approved persons)) a *partnership*;
(d) (in *SYSC* and *SUP* 10 (Approved persons)) a *sole trader*;
any *person* appointed to direct its affairs, including a *person* who is a member of its *governing body* and (in accordance with section 417(1) of the *Act*):
(i) a *person* occupying in relation to it the position of a director (by whatever name called); and
(ii) a *person* in accordance with whose directions or instructions (not being advice given in a professional capacity) the directors of that body are accustomed to act.

(2) (in COLL) a director of an *ICVC*, including (in accordance with regulation 2(1) of the *OEIC Regulations*) a *person* occupying in relation to the *ICVC* the position of director, by whatever name called.

(3) (in DTR, LR and PR) (in accordance with section 417(1)(a) of the Act) a *person* occupying in relation to it the position of a director (by whatever name called) and, in relation to an *issuer* which is not a *body corporate*, a *person* with corresponding powers and duties.

director function

controlled function CF1 in the *table of controlled functions*, described more fully in *SUP* 10.6.4R.

director of unincorporated association function

controlled function CF5 in the *table of controlled* functions, described more fully in *SUP* 10.6.24R.

Disciplinary Tribunal

a Tribunal appointed under Schedule 2 to Lloyd's Disciplinary Committees Byelaw (No 31 of 1996).

disclosable information

any information which has to be disclosed in the market in accordance with any legal or regulatory requirement.

disclosable short position

a net short position which represents an economic interest of one quarter of one per cent of the issued capital of a company.

In calculating whether a holder has a *disclosable short position*, the holder should take into account any form of economic interest it has in the shares of the *issuer*, excluding any interest which he holds as a market maker in that capacity.

disclosure obligations

(in *REC*) the initial, ongoing and ad hoc disclosure requirements contained in the *relevant articles* and given effect:
(1) in the *United Kingdom* by Part 6 of the *Act* and Part 6 rules (within the meaning of section 73A of the *Act*); or
(2) in another *EEA State* by legislation transposing the *relevant articles* in that State.

disclosure rules

(in accordance with section 73A(3) of the *Act*) *rules* relating to the disclosure of information in respect of *financial instruments* which have been *admitted to trading* on a *regulated market* or for which a request for *admission to trading* on such a market has been made.

discounting

discounting or deductions to take account of investment income as set out in paragraph 48 of the *insurance accounts rules*.

discretionary investment manager

(in COBS and (in relation to *firm type*) in SUP 16.10 (Confirmation of *standing data*)) a *person* who, acting only on behalf of a *client*, manages *designated investments* in an account or portfolio on a discretionary basis under the terms of a discretionary management agreement.

DISP

Dispute resolution: the Complaints sourcebook.

distance contract

any contract concerning financial services concluded between a supplier and a *consumer* under an organised distance sales or service provision scheme run by the supplier which, for the purpose of that contract, makes exclusive use (directly or through an intermediary) of one or more means of distance communication (that is, any means which, without the simultaneous physical presence of the supplier or intermediary and the *consumer*, may be used for the distance marketing of a service between those parties) up to and including the time at which the contract is concluded.

A contract is not a distance contract if:
(a) making, performing or marketing it does not constitute or form part of a *regulated activity*;
(b) it is entered into on a strictly occasional basis outside a commercial structure dedicated to the conclusion of distance contracts; or
(c) a *consumer*, and an intermediary acting for a product provider, are simultaneously physically present at some stage before the conclusion of the contract.

[Note: recitals 15 and 18 to, and articles 2(a) and (e) of the *Distance Marketing Directive*]

distance home purchase mediation contract

a *distance contract*, the making or performance of which constitutes, or is part of:
(a) *advising on a home purchase plan*;
(b) *arranging (bringing about) a home purchase plan*;
(c) *making arrangements with a view to a home purchase plan*; or
(d) *agreeing to carry on a regulated activity* in (a) to (c).

Distance Marketing Directive

The Directive of the Council and Parliament of 23 September 2002 on distance marketing of consumer financial services (No 2002/65/EC).

distance marketing information

(1) (in COBS) the information listed in COBS 6 Annex 1R.
(2) (in MCOB) the information listed in MCOB 6 Annex 1R.

Distance Marketing Regulations

The Financial Services (Distance Marketing) Regulations 2004 (SI 2004/2095).

distance mortgage mediation contract

a *distance contract*, the making or performance of which constitutes, or is part of:
(a) *advising on regulated mortgage contracts*; or
(b) *arranging (bringing about) regulated mortgage contracts*; or
(c) *making arrangements with a view to regulated mortgage contracts*; or
(d) *agreeing to carry on a regulated mortgage activity* in (a) to (c).

distance non-investment mediation contract

[deleted]

distance selling contract

(in BCOBS) has the same meaning as "distance contract" in the Consumer Protection (Distance Selling) Regulations 2000 (SI 2000/2334).

distribution account

(in COLL) the account to which the *income property* of an *authorised fund* must be transferred as at the end of each *annual accounting period* under COLL 6.8.3R (Income allocation and distribution), COLL 8.5.15R (Income.

distribution channels

a channel through which information is, or is likely to become, publicly available. Information which is "likely to become publicly available" means information to which a large number of *persons* have access.

[Note: article 2(1) of the *MiFID implementing Directive*]

distribution of exposures

(in accordance with Part 1 of Annex III of the *Banking Consolidation Directive* (Definitions) and for the purpose of BIPRU 13 (The calculation of counterparty risk exposure values for financial derivatives, securities financing transactions and long settlement transactions)) the forecast of the probability distribution of market values that is generated by setting forecast instances of negative net market values equal to zero.

distribution of market values

(in accordance with Part 1 of Annex III of the *Banking Consolidation Directive* (Definitions) and for the purpose of BIPRU 13 (The calculation of counterparty risk exposure values for financial derivatives, securities financing transactions and long settlement transactions)) the forecast of the probability distribution of net market values of transactions within a *netting set* for some future date (the forecasting horizon), given the realised market value of those transactions up to the present time.

diverse block

(for the purposes of BIPRU 8 (Group risk – consolidation) and BIPRU 10 (Concentration risk requirements)):

(a) (in relation to a *firm* with a *wider integrated group permission* that applies on a solo basis) has the meaning in BIPRU 10.9.6R (Definition of diverse block) which is in summary all *undertakings* in the *wider integrated group* designated as a single *diverse block* by the applicable *wider integrated group permission*;

(b) (in relation to a *firm* with a *wider integrated group permission* that applies on a consolidated basis) has the meaning in BIPRU 8.9.22R (Wider integrated groups: Definition of diverse block) which is in summary a group of *exposures* that satisfy specified eligibility conditions and that are to *undertakings* that are designated by the *wider integrated group permission* as being associated with the same *diverse block*.

DLG by default

(in relation to a *UK ILAS BIPRU firm* (a *group liquidity reporting firm*) and any reporting period under *SUP* 16 (Reporting requirements)) the *firm* and each *person* identified in accordance with the following:

(a) (in a case in which the *firm* is the only *UK ILAS BIPRU firm* in its *group*) that *person* meets any of the following conditions for any part of that period:
   (i) that *person* provides material support to the *firm* against *liquidity risk*; or
   (ii) that *person* is committed to provide such support or would be committed to do so if that *person* were able to provide it; or
   (iii) the *firm* has reasonable grounds to believe that that *person* would supply such support if asked or would do so if it were able to provide it; or
   (iv) the *firm* provides material support to that *person* against *liquidity risk*; or
   (v) the *firm* is committed to provide such support to that *person* or would be committed to do so if the *firm* were able to provide it; or
   (vi) the *firm* has reasonable grounds to believe that that *person* would expect the *firm* to supply such support if asked or that the *firm* would do so if it were able to provide it; or

(b) (in a case in which the *firm* is not the only *UK ILAS BIPRU firm* in its *group*):
   (i) each of those other *UK ILAS BIPRU firm*; and
   (ii) each *person* identified by applying the tests in (a) separately to the *firm* and to each of those other *UK ILAS BIPRU firms*, so that applying (b) to the *firm* and to each of those *UK ILAS BIPRU firms* results in their having the same *defined liquidity group*.

The following provisions also apply for the purpose of this definition.

(c) A *person* is not a member of a *firm's* DLG by default unless it also satisfies one of the following conditions:
   (i) it is a member of the *firm's group*; or
   (ii) it is a *securitisation special purpose entity* or a *special purpose vehicle*; or
   (iii) it is an *undertaking* whose main purpose is to raise funds for the *firm* or for a *group* to which that *firm* belongs.

(d) *Group* has the meaning in paragraph (1) of the definition in the *Glossary* (the definition in section 421 of the *Act*).

(e) The conditions in (a) are satisfied even if the *firm* or *person* in question provides or is committed or expected to provide support for only part of the period.

(f) In deciding for the purpose of (a) or (b) whether the *firm* is the only *UK ILAS BIPRU firm* in its *group* and identifying which are the other *UK ILAS BIPRU firms* in its *group*, any *group* member that is a member of the group through no more than a *participation* is ignored.

(g) A *firm* has a *DLG by default* for a period even if it only has one during part of that period.

(h) Liquidity support may be supplied by or to the *firm* directly or indirectly.

(i) Support is material if it is material either by reference to the *person* giving it or by reference to the *person* receiving it.

(*Guidance* about this definition, and its inter-relation with other related definitions, is set out in *SUP* 16 Annex 26G (Guidance on designated liquidity groups in *SUP* 16.12).)

DLG by modification

either of the following:

(a) a DLG by modification (firm level); or

(b) a non-UK DLG by modification (DLG level).

(*Guidance* about this definition, and its inter-relation with other related definitions, is set out in *SUP* 16 Annex 26G (Guidance on designated liquidity groups in *SUP* 16.12).)

DLG by modification (firm level)

(in relation to any reporting period under *SUP* 16 (Reporting requirements) and a *UK ILAS BIPRU firm* that has an *intra-group liquidity modification* during any part of that period (a *group liquidity reporting firm*)) the *firm* and each *person* on whose liquidity support the *firm* can rely, under that *intragroup liquidity modification*, for any part of that period for the purpose of the *overall liquidity adequacy rule* (as the *overall liquidity adequacy rule* applies to the *firm* on a solo basis). A *firm* has a 'DLG by modification (firm level)' for a period even if it only has one during part of that period.

(*Guidance* about this definition, and its inter-relation with other related definitions, is set out in *SUP* 16 Annex 26G (Guidance on designated liquidity groups in *SUP* 16.12).)

DMD

[deleted]

document

any piece of recorded information, including (in accordance with section 417(1) of the *Act* (Interpretation)) information recorded in any form; in relation to information recorded otherwise than in legible form, references to its production include references to producing a copy of the information in legible form.

document evidencing title

any means of evidencing title whether in documentary form or otherwise.

document viewing facility

(in LR) a location identified on the *FSA* website where the public can inspect documents referred to in the *listing rules* as being documents to be made available at the document viewing facility.

domestic ECA provider

[deleted]

dormant account

has the meaning given in section 10 of the Dormant Bank and Building Society Accounts Act 2008, which is in summary an *account* that at a particular point in time:

(a) has been open throughout the period of 15 years ending at that time; and
(b) during that period no transactions have been carried out in relation to the *account* by or on the instructions of the holder of the *account*.

dormant account funds

has the meaning given in section 5(6) of the Dormant Bank and Building Society Accounts Act 2008, which is *money* paid to a *dormant account fund operator* by a *bank* or *building society* in respect of a *dormant account*.

dormant account fund operator

a firm with permission for operating a dormant account fund.

drawdown mortgage

a *lifetime mortgage* contract where:

(a) the amount borrowed is paid by the *mortgage lender* to the *customer* in instalments during the life of the mortgage; and
(b) the size and frequency of the instalments are:
   (1) agreed between the *mortgage lender* and the *customer*; or
   (2) set by reference to an index or interest rate (such as the Bank of England repo rate).

drawn down capital

(in SUP 16, in the case of an *investment management firm* carrying out *venture capital business*) the total current value of contributions committed by investors under contractual agreement which has been invested by the *firm*.

DTR

the Disclosure Rules and *Transparency Rules* sourcebook.

dual-priced authorised fund

an *authorised fund* or, in the case of an *umbrella*, a *sub-fund* (if it were a separate *fund*), that is not a *single-priced authorised fund*.

durable medium

(a) paper; or
(b) any instrument which enables the recipient to store information addressed personally to him in a way accessible for future reference for a period of time adequate for the purposes of the information and which allows the unchanged reproduction of the information stored. In particular, *durabe medium* covers floppy disks, CD-ROMs, DVDs and hard drives of personal computers on which electronic mail is stored, but it excludes Internet sites unless such sites meet the criteria specified in the first sentence of this paragraph.

(in relation to *MiFID or equivalent third country business*, if the relevant rule implements the *MiFID implementing Directive*) the instrument used must be:
(i) appropriate to the context in which the business is to be carried on; and
(ii) specifically chosen by the recipient when offered the choice between that instrument and paper.

For the purposes of this definition, the provision of information by means of electronic communications shall be treated as appropriate to the context in which the business between the *firm* and the *client* is, or is to be, carried on if there is evidence that the *client* has regular access to the internet. The provision by the *client* of an e-mail address for the purposes of the carrying on of that business is sufficient.

[Note: article 2(f) and Recital 20 of the *Distance Marketing Directive*, article 2(12) of the *Insurance Mediation Directive* and article 2(2) of the *MiFID implementing Directive*]

early amortisation provision

(in accordance with Article 100 of the *Banking Consolidation Directive* (Securitisation of revolving exposures) and in relation to a *securitisation* within the meaning of paragraph (2) of the definition of securitisation) a contractual clause which requires, on the occurrence of defined events, investors' positions to be redeemed prior to the originally stated maturity of the securities issued.

early repayment charge

(in *MCOB*) a charge levied by the *mortgage lender* on the *customer* in the event that the amount of the loan is repaid in full or in part before a date specified in the contract.

ECA recipient

a *person* who is a user of an *electronic commerce activity.*

ECAI

an external credit assessment institution.

ECD Regulations

the Electronic Commerce Directive (Financial Services and Markets) Regulations 2002 (SI 2002/1775).

E-Commerce Directive

the Council Directive of 8 June 2002 on legal aspects of *information society services*, in particular electronic commerce, in the Internal Market (No 2000/31/EC).

ECR

enhanced capital requirement.

EE

expected exposure.

EEA

the *European Economic Area.*

(see also EEA State.)

EEA authorisation

(in accordance with paragraph 6 of Schedule 3 to the *Act* (EEA Passport Rights))
(a) in relation to an IMD insurance intermediary or an *IMD reinsurance intermediary*, registration with its *Home State regulator* under article 3 of the *Insurance Mediation Directive*;
(b) in relation to any other *EEA firm*, authorisation granted to an *EEA firm* by its *Home State regulator* for the purpose of the relevant *Single Market Directive*).

EEA authorised payment institution

(a) (in accordance with regulation 2(1) of the *Payment Services Regulations*) a *person* authorised in an *EEA State* other than the *United Kingdom* to provide *payment services* in accordance with the *Payment Services Directive*; and
(b) (in accordance with paragraph 1 of Schedule 7 to the *Payment Services Regulations*) a firm which has its head office in Gibraltar, is authorised in Gibraltar to provide *payment services*, and has an entitlement corresponding to its passport right deriving from the *Payment Services Directive*, to establish a *branch* or provide services in the *United Kingdom.*

EEA bank

an incoming EEA firm which is a BCD credit institution.

EEA banking and investment group

a *banking and investment group* that satisfies one or more of the following conditions:
(a) it is headed by:

Part II FSA Handbook Materials

(i) an *investment firm* or *credit institution* that is authorised and incorporated in an *EEA State*; or
(ii) a *financial holding company* that has its head office in an *EEA State*; or
(b) it has as a member an *investment firm* or *credit institution* that:
(i) is authorised and incorporated in an *EEA State*; and
(ii) is linked with another member that is in the *banking sector* or the *investment services sector* by a *consolidation Article 12(1) relationship*; or
(c) it is otherwise required by *EEA prudential sectoral legislation* for the *banking sector* or the *investment services sector* (except Article 143 of the *Banking Consolidation Directive* (Third-country parent undertakings)) to be subject to consolidated supervision by a *competent authority*.

EEA consolidated group

(in *ELM*) (in relation to an *ELMI*) the *consolidated sub-group* of the *ELMI's EEA financial parent undertaking*, as established in accordance with *ELM* 7 (Consolidated financial supervision).

EEA-deposit insurer

a *non-EEA insurer* that has made a deposit in an *EEA State* (other than the *United Kingdom*) under article 23 of the *First Non-Life Directive* (as amended) in accordance with article 26 of that Directive or under article 51 of the *Consolidated Life Directive* in accordance with article 56 of that Directive.

EEA ECA recipient

[deleted]

EEA financial conglomerate

a *financial conglomerate* that is of a type that falls under Article 5(2) of the *Financial Groups Directive* (Scope of supplementary supervision of *regulated entities* referred to in Article 1 of that Directive) which in summary means a *financial conglomerate*:
(a) that is headed by an *EEA regulated entity*; or
(b) in which the *parent undertaking* of an *EEA regulated entity* is a *mixed financial holding company* which has its head office in the *EEA*; or
(c) in which an *EEA regulated entity* is linked with a member of the *financial conglomerate* in the *overall financial sector* by a *consolidation Article 12(1) relationship*.

EEA financial parent undertaking

(in *ELM*) (in relation to an *ELMI*) the highest *undertaking* in the *ELMI's group* that:
(a) is a relevant financial services company or a *financial holding company*;
(b) is formed under the law of another *EEA State*; and
(c) is a *parent undertaking* of the *ELMI*;

as established in accordance with *ELM* 7 (Consolidated financial supervision).

EEA firm

(in accordance with paragraph 5 of Schedule 3 to the *Act* (EEA Passport Rights)) any of the following, if it does not have its relevant office in the *United Kingdom*:
(a) an investment firm (as defined in article 1(2) of the *Investment Services Directive*) which is authorised (within the meaning of article 3) by its *Home State regulator*;
(b) a *credit institution* (as defined in article 4(1) of the *Banking Consolidation Directive*) which is authorised (within the meaning of article 4(2)) by its *Home State regulator*;
(c) a financial institution (as defined in article 4(5) of the *Banking Consolidation Directive*) which is a subsidiary of the kind mentioned in article 24 and which fulfils the conditions in articles 23 and 24;
(d) an undertaking pursuing the activity of direct insurance (within the meaning of article 2 of the *Consolidated Life Directive* (No 2002/83/EC) or of Article 1 of the *First Non-Life Directive*) which has received authorisation under Article 4 of the *Consolidated Life Directive* or Article 6 of the *First Non-Life Directive* from its *Home State regulator*;
(e) an *IMD insurance intermediary* or an *IMD reinsurance intermediary* (as defined in article 2 of the *IMD*) which has registered under article 3 of that directive with its *Home State regulator*;
(f) (from 13 February 2004) a management company (as defined in article 1a of the *UCITS Directive*) which has been authorised under article 5 of that directive by its *Home State regulator*;
(g) an *undertaking* pursuing the activity of reinsurance (within the meaning of article 1 of the *Reinsurance Directive*) which has received authorisation under article 3 of the *Reinsurance Directive* from its *Home State Regulator*.

in this definition, relevant office means:
(i) in relation to a *firm* falling within sub-paragraph (e), which has a registered office, its registered office;

(ii) in relation to any other *firm* falling within any other paragraph, its head office.

EEA group large exposure

(in *ELM*) (in relation to an *ELMI*) *e-money financial exposures* of members of the *ELMI's consolidated group* calculated and identified in accordance with *ELM* 7.6.2R (EEA group large exposures).

EEA group risk own funds

(in *ELM*) (in relation to an *ELMI*) are identified and calculated by applying the definition of *own funds* to the *ELMI's EEA consolidated group* in accordance with *ELM* 7.5.1R (EEA group risk own funds).

EEA group risk own funds requirement

(in *ELM*) (in relation to an *ELMI*) is calculated by applying the definition of *own funds requirement* to an *ELMI's EEA consolidated group* in accordance with *ELM* 7.5.2R (EEA group risk own funds requirement).

EEA insurance parent undertaking

an *insurance parent undertaking* that has its head office in the *United Kingdom* or another *EEA State*.

EEA insurer

an *insurer*, other than a *pure reinsurer* or a *non-directive insurer*, whose head office is in any *EEA State* except the *United Kingdom* and which has received *authorisation* under article 6 of the *First Life Directive* article 4 of the *Consolidated Life Directive* or article 6 of or the *First Non-Life Directive* from its *Home State Regulator*.

EEA ISPV

an *ISPV* (including a *UK ISPV*) whose head office is in any *EEA State* and which has received authorisation pursuant to article 46 of the *Reinsurance Directive* from its *Home State Regulator*.

EEA market operator

(in *REC*) a *person* who is a *market operator* whose *home state* is an *EEA State* other than the *United Kingdom*.

EEA MCR

the *MCR* in relation to business carried on in all *EEA States*, taken together, calculated by a *UK-deposit insurer* in accordance with INSPRU 1.5.46R.

EEA MiFID investment firm

a *MiFID investment firm* whose *Home State* is not the *United Kingdom*.

EEA parent financial holding company

(in accordance with Article 4(17) of the *Banking Consolidation Directive* (Definitions) and Article 3 of the *Capital Adequacy Directive* (Definitions)) a *parent financial holding company in a Member State* which is not a *subsidiary undertaking* of an *institution* authorised in any *EEA State* or of another *financial holding company* set up in any *EEA State*.

EEA parent institution

(in accordance with Article 4(16) of the *Banking Consolidation Directive* and Article 2 of the *Capital Adequacy Directive* (Definitions)) a *parent institution in a Member State* which is not a *subsidiary undertaking* of another *institution* authorised in any *EEA State*, or of a *financial holding company* set up in any *EEA State*.

EEA Passport Rights Regulations

the Financial Services and Markets Act 2000 (EEA Passport Rights) Regulations 2001 (SI 2001/2511).

EEA prudential sectoral legislation

(in relation to a *financial sector*) requirements applicable to *persons* in that *financial sector* in accordance with *EEA* legislation about prudential supervision of *regulated entities* in that *financial sector* and so that:

(a) (in relation to the *banking sector* and the *investment services sector*) in particular this includes the requirements laid down in the *Banking Consolidation Directive* and the *Capital Adequacy Directive*; and

(b) (in relation to the *insurance sector*) in particular this includes requirements laid down in the *First Non-Life Directive*, the *Consolidated Life Directive* and the *Insurance Groups Directive*.

EEA pure reinsurer

a *reinsurance undertaking* (other than an *ISPV*) whose head office is in any *EEA State* except the *United Kingdom* and which has received (or is deemed to have received) authorisation under article 3 of the *Reinsurance Directive* from its *Home State Regulator*.

EEA registered tied agent

a *tied agent* of a *UK MiFID investment firm* that is not an *appointed representative* and would have been an *FSA registered tied agent* but for the fact that it does business in an *EEA State* that permits *investment firms* authorised by the *competent authority* of that state to appoint *tied agents*.

EEA regulated entity

a *regulated entity* that is an *EEA firm* or a *UK firm*.

EEA regulator

a competent authority for the purposes of any of the Single Market Directives.

EEA right

(in accordance with paragraph 7 of Schedule 3 to the *Act* (EEA Passport Rights)) the entitlement of a *person* to establish a *branch* or provide services in an *EEA State* other than that in which he has his relevant office:
(a) in accordance with the *Treaty* as applied in the *European Economic Area*; and
(b) subject to the conditions of the relevant *Single Market Directive*.

in this definition, relevant office means:
(i) in relation to a *person* who has a registered office and whose entitlement is subject to the conditions of the *Insurance Mediation Directive*, his registered office; and
(ii) in relation to any other *person*, his head office.

EEA simplified prospectus

a marketing *document* which contains information about an *EEA simplified prospectus scheme* and meets the requirements of Article 28 of the *UCITS directive*.

EEA simplified prospectus scheme

a *UCITS scheme* which is a *recognised scheme* under section 264 of the *Act* (Schemes constituted in other EEA States).

EEA State

(in accordance with Schedule 1 to the Interpretation Act 1978), in relation to any time –
(a) a state which at that time is a member State; or
(b) any other state which is at that time a party to the EEA agreement.

[Note: Current non-member State parties to the EEA agreement are Norway, Iceland and Lichtenstein. Where the context requires, references to an *EEA State* include references to Gibraltar as appropriate].

EEA territorial scope rule

COBS 1 Annex 1, Part 2 paragraph 1(1) (which provides that the territorial scope of *COBS* is modified to the extent necessary to be compatible with European law).

EEA tied agent a tied agent

who is an *FSA registered tied agent* or an *EEA registered tied agent*.

EEA UCITS management company

(as defined in article 1a (2) of the *UCITS Directive*) any *incoming EEA firm*, the regular business of which is the *management* of *UCITS* in the form of unit trusts or common funds or of investment companies (collective portfolio management of *UCITS*) or of both; this includes the functions mentioned in Annex II.

effecting contracts of insurance

the *regulated activity*, specified in article 10(1) of the *Regulated Activities Order* (*Effecting and* carrying out contracts of insurance), of effecting a *contract of insurance* as principal.

effective EE

effective expected exposure.

effective EPE

effective expected positive exposure.

effective expected exposure

(in accordance with Part 1 of Annex III of the *Banking Consolidation Directive* (Definitions) and for the purpose of BIPRU 13 (The calculation of counterparty risk exposure values for financial derivatives, securities financing transactions and long settlement transactions) and as at a specific date) the maximum *expected exposure* that occurs at that date or any prior date; alternatively, it may be defined for a specific date as the greater of the *expected exposure* at that date, or the effective *exposure* at the previous date.

effective expected positive exposure

(in accordance with Part 1 of Annex III of the *Banking Consolidation Directive* (Definitions)) the weighted average over time of *effective expected exposure* over the first year, or, if all the contracts within the *netting set* mature before one year, over the time period of the longest maturity contract in the *netting set*, where the weights are the proportion that an individual *expected exposure* represents of the entire time interval.

effective maturity

(in accordance with Part 1 of Annex III of the *Banking Consolidation Directive* (Definitions), for the purpose of the *CCR internal model method* and with respect to a *netting set* with maturity greater than one year) the ratio of the sum of *expected exposure* over the life of the transactions in the *netting set* discounted at the riskfree rate of return divided by the sum of *expected exposure* over one year in a *netting set* discounted at the risk-free rate; this effective maturity may be adjusted to reflect *rollover risk* by replacing *expected exposure* with *effective expected exposure* for forecasting horizons under one year.

efficient portfolio management

(in COLL and in accordance with article 11 of the *UCITS eligible assets Directive*) techniques and instruments which relate to *transferable securities* and *approved money-market instruments* and which fulfil the following criteria:

(a) they are economically appropriate in that they are realised in a cost effective way;

(b) they are entered into for one or more of the following specific aims:

- (i) reduction of risk;
- (ii) reduction of cost;
- (iii) generation of additional capital or income for the *scheme* with a risk level which is consistent with the risk profile of the *scheme* and the risk diversification rules laid down in COLL.

EG

the Enforcement Guide.

EIS

Enterprise Investment Scheme.

EIS fund

an arrangement, specified in paragraph 2 of the Schedule to the Financial Services and Markets Act 2000 (Collective Investment Schemes) Order 2001 (SI 2001/1062), which is in summary: an arrangement in relation to *EIS shares* that would have been a *collective investment scheme* if the scheme arrangements had not provided that:

(a) the *operator* will, so far as practicable, make investments which, subject to each participant's individual circumstances, qualify for relief under Chapter III of Part VII of the Income and Corporation Taxes Act 1988; and

(b) the minimum subscription to the arrangements by each participant must be not less than £2,000.

EIS managed portfolio

a managed portfolio which is, or is to be, invested wholly or mainly in *EIS shares*.

EIS manager

(a) (in relation to an *EIS managed portfolio*) the investment manager;

(b) (in relation to an *EIS fund*) the manager of the fund.

EIS particulars

a *document* containing particulars of an *Enterprise Investment Scheme*.

EIS share

a *share* in respect of which the beneficial owner may, subject to his individual circumstances, be qualified, or has been qualified, for relief under Chapter III of Part VII of the Income and Corporation Taxes Act 1988.

EIS subscription

any *money* which is subscribed:

(a) in the case of an *EIS managed portfolio*, by the *client* of the *EIS manager* whose portfolio it is;

(b) in the case of an *EIS fund*, by the participants in the *EIS*.

EL

expected loss.

Electing Participants Order

the Financial Services and Markets Act 2000 (Compensation Scheme: Electing Participants) Regulations 2001 (SI 2001/1783).

Electing Participants Regulations

the Financial Services and Markets Act 2000 (Compensation Scheme: Electing Participants) Regulations 2001 (SI 2001/1783).

elective eligible counterparty

a *client* categorised as an elective eligible counterparty in accordance with COBS 3.6 (Eligible counterparties).

elective professional client

a *client* categorised as an elective professional client in accordance with COBS 3.5 (Professional clients).

electricity

(a) electricity in any form, including electricity as deliverable through the *Balancing and Settlement Code*;
(b) any right that relates to electricity, for example the right under a contract or otherwise to require a person to take any action in relation to electricity, including:
  (i) supplying electricity to any person or accepting supply of electricity; or
  (ii) providing any information or notice in relation to electricity; or
(c) making any payment in relation to the supply or non-supply, or acceptance or non-acceptance of supply, of electricity.

electronic commerce activity

an activity which:
(a) consists of the provision of an *information society service* from an *establishment* in an *EEA State*; and
(b) is, or but for article 72A (Information society services) of the *Regulated Activities Order* (Information society services) (and irrespective of the effect of article 72 of that Order (Overseas persons)) would be, a *regulated activity*.

electronic commerce activity direction

a direction made, or proposed to be made, by the FSA under regulation 6 of the ECD Regulations.

electronic commerce activity provider

[deleted]

electronic commerce communication

(in accordance with article 6 of the Financial Promotion Order) a communication, the making of which constitutes the provision of an information society service.

electronic communication

has the meaning given in section 15(1) of the Electronic Communications Act 2000.

electronic means

are means of electronic equipment for the processing (including digital compression), storage and transmission of data, employing wires, radio optical technologies, or any other electromagnetic means;

electronic money

The investment, specified in article 74A of the Regulated Activities Order (Electronic money), which is monetary value, as represented by a claim on the issuer, which is:
(a) stored on an electronic device;
(b) issued on receipt of funds; and
(c) accepted as a means of payment by *persons* other than the issuer.

electronic SCV rules

(in COMP) COMP 17.2.1R(2), COMP 17.2.3R(3) and COMP 17.2.5R, the application of which is determined by COMP 17.1 and COMP 17.2.7R.

eligible

(in COLL) (in relation to a securities or a derivatives market) a market that satisfies the requirements in COLL 5.2.10R (Eligible markets: requirements CIS), in relation to schemes falling under COLL 5.

eligible claimant

a *person* who is eligible to bring a *claim* for compensation under *COMP* 4.2.1R.

eligible complainant

a person eligible to have a *complaint* considered under the Financial Ombudsman Service, as defined in DISP 2.7 (Is the complainant eligible?).

eligible counterparty

(1) (for the purposes other than those set out in (2)) (in accordance with COBS 3.6.1R) a *client* that is either a *per se eligible counterparty* or an *elective eligible counterparty*.
(2) (for the purposes of *PRIN*, in relation to activities other than *designated investment business*) a *client* categorised as an *eligible counterparty* in accordance with *PRIN* 1 Ann 1R.

eligible counterparty business

the following services and activities carried on by a *firm*:
(a) *dealing on own account, execution of orders on behalf of clients* or reception and transmission of orders; or
(b) any *ancillary service* directly related to a service or activity referred to in (a); or
(c) *arranging* in relation to business which is not *MiFID or equivalent third country firm business*;

but only to the extent that the service or activity is carried on with or for an *eligible counterparty*.

eligible ECAI

an *ECAI*:
(a) (for *exposure risk weighting* purposes other than those in (b)) recognised by the *FSA* under regulation 22 of the *Capital Requirements Regulations 2006* (Recognition for exposure risk-weighting purposes); or
(b) (for *securitisation risk weighting* purposes) recognised by the *FSA* under regulation 23 of the *Capital Requirements Regulations 2006* (Recognition for securitisation riskweighting purposes).

eligible institution

(in COLL)
(a) a *BCD credit institution* authorised by its *Home State regulator;*
(b) an *ISD investment firm* authorised by its *Home State regulator.*

eligible LLP members' capital

members' capital of a *limited liability partnership* that meets the conditions in *IPRU(INV)* Annex A or, for a *BIPRU firm*, the requirements of GENPRU 2.2.94R (Core tier one capital: Eligible LLP members' capital).

eligible partnership capital

(in relation to a *BIPRU firm*) has the meaning in GENPRU 2.2.93R.

ELM

the Electronic Money sourcebook.

ELM financial rules

the *rules* in *ELM* 2 (Initial and continuing own funds requirement), *ELM* 3 (Management of the e-money float) and *ELM* 7 (Consolidated financial supervision).

ELMI

an *e-money firm* which is not a *bank, building society, incoming Treaty firm* or *incoming EEA firm.*

e-money

electronic money.

E-Money Directive

the Council Directive of 18 September 2000 relating to the taking up, pursuit of and prudential supervision of the business of electronic money institutions (No 2000/46/EC).

e-money electronic device

an electronic device referred to in paragraph (a) of the definition of *electronic money* and any other device that a holder of *electronic money* uses to hold or to spend or otherwise use his *electronic money*.

e-money firm

a *firm* whose *permitted activities* include *issuing e-money*.

e-money float

(in *ELM*) (in relation to an *ELMI*) *qualifying liquid assets* owned by an *ELMI* except those that, taking into account *ELM* 3.3.13R (Establishment of the e-money float), the *ELMI* does not need in order to comply with *ELM* 3.3.1R (Asset-liability management).

e-money float exposure

(in *ELM*) the risks of loss set out in *ELM* 3.5.3 (Large exposure risk).

e-money issue price

(in respect of *e-money* issued by an *e-money firm*) the amount paid to the *e-money firm* for the issue of that *e-money* before or on the issue of that *e-money*.

e-money issuer

(in accordance with the definition of an "electronic money institution" in article 1.3 of the *E-Money Directive*) an *undertaking* or any other legal *person*, other than a *full credit institution*, which issues means of payment in the form of *e-money*.

e-money outstandings

(in *ELM*) (in relation to an *ELMI* and at any time) the total amount (actual or contingent) of the *ELMI's* financial liabilities related to outstanding *e-money* at that time, including the total amount that would be payable by the *ELMI* if all the *e-money* in respect of which *persons* have, against the *ELMI*, a *redemption right* or any other right to require *e-money* to be redeemed were then due for redemption.

e-money scheme rules

(in *ELM*) (in relation to a scheme under which a *firm* issues *e-money*) the contracts between the participants in that scheme relating to the issue, circulation and redemption of *e-money*, including the contracts referred to in ELM 6.7.2R (Terms of reference).

employee

(1) (for all purposes except those in (2)) an individual:

(a) who is employed or appointed by a *person* in connection with that *person's* business, whether under a contract of service or for services or otherwise; or

whose services, under an arrangement between that *person* and a third party, are placed at the disposal and under the control of that *person*;

but excluding an appointed representative or a *tied agent* of that person.

(2) (for the purposes of:

(a) *COBS* 11.7 (Personal account dealing);

(aa) *GEN* 4 (Statutory status disclosure);

(b) *SUP* 12 (Appointed representatives); and

(c) *TC*)

an individual:

(i) within (1); or

(ii) who is:

(A) an *appointed representative* or, where applicable, a *tied agent* of the *person* referred to in (1); or

(B) employed or appointed by an *appointed representative* or, where applicable, a *tied agent* of that *person*, whether under a contract of service or for services or otherwise, in connection with the business of the *appointed representative* or *tied agent* for which that *person* has accepted responsibility.

employees' share scheme

has the same meaning as in section 1166 of the Companies Act 2006.

employers' liability insurance

a *contract of insurance* against risks of the *persons* insured incurring liabilities to their employees.

EMPS

the Handbook Guide for energy market participants.

endowment assurance

a *life policy* which pays a sum of *money* on the survival of the life assured to a specific date or on his earlier death.

energy

coal, *electricity*, *natural gas* (or any by-product or form of any of them), *oil* or *biofuel*.

energy collective investment scheme

a *collective investment scheme*, the property of which consists only of *energy, energy investments, greenhouse gas emissions allowances, tradable renewable energy credits* or cash awaiting investment.

energy investment

any of the following:
(a) a *unit* in an *energy collective investment scheme;*
(b) an *option* to acquire or dispose of an *energy investment;*
(c) a *future or a contract for differences* where the commodity or property of any other description in question is:
  (i) *energy*; or
  (ii) an *energy investment*; or
  (iii) a *greenhouse gas emissions allowance*; or
  (iv) a *tradable renewable energy credit;*
(d) a *contract for differences* where the index or other factor in question is linked to or otherwise dependent upon fluctuations in the value or price of any of (c)(i) to (iv) (including any prices or charges in respect of imbalances under the *Network Code* or the *Balancing and Settlement Code*);
(e) a *weather derivative;*
(f) a *greenhouse gas emissions allowance*, if it is a *specified investment;*
(g) a *tradable renewable energy credit*, if it is a *specified investment;*
(h) *rights to or interests in investments* in (a)–(g).

energy market activity

(a) any regulated activity in relation to an energy investment or to energy or in relation to a *biomass investment* or *biomass* that is ancillary to activities related to *energy investments* or *energy*, which:
  (i) is the executing of own account transactions on any recognised investment exchange or designated investment exchange; or
  (ii) if it is not the executing of transactions on such exchanges, is performed in connection with or for persons who are not private customers;
(b) establishing, operating or winding up a collective investment scheme which is an energy collective investment scheme in which private customers do not participate.

energy market participant

a *firm*:
(a) whose permission:
  (i) includes a *requirement* that the firm must not carry on any *designated investment business* other than *energy market activity*;
  (ii) does not include a *requirement* that it comply with *IPRU(INV)* 5 (Investment management firms) or 13 (Personal investment firms); and
(b) which is not an *authorised professional firm, bank, BIPRU investment firm* (unless it is an *exempt BIPRU commodities firm*), *building society, credit union, friendly society, ICVC, insurer, MiFID investment firm* (unless it is an *exempt BIPRU commodities firm*), *media firm, oil market participant, service company, insurance intermediary, home finance administrator, mortgage intermediary, home finance provider, incoming EEA firm* (without a *top-up permission*), or *incoming Treaty firm* (without a *top-up permission*).

engage in investment activity

(as defined in section 21(8) of the *Act*) (Restrictions on financial promotion)):
(a) enter or offer to enter into an agreement the making or performance of which by either party constitutes a *controlled activity*; or
(b) exercise any rights conferred by a *controlled investment* to acquire, dispose of, underwrite or convert a *controlled investment*.

enhanced capital requirement

(1) (in relation to a *firm* carrying on *general insurance business*) the amount calculated in accordance with INSPRU 1.1.72CR.
(2) (in relation to a *firm* carrying on *long-term insurance business*) an amount of *capital resources* that a *firm* must hold as set out in GENPRU 2.1.38R.

entering as provider into a funeral plan contract

the *regulated activity*, specified in article 59 of the *Regulated Activities Order* (Funeral plan contracts) which comes into force on 1 January 2002, of entering as provider into a *funeral plan contract*.

entering into a home finance transaction

any of the *regulated activities* of *entering into a regulated mortgage contract*, *entering into a home purchase plan*, *entering into a home reversion plan* or *entering into a regulated sale and rent back agreement*.

entering into a home purchase plan

the *regulated activity*, specified in article 63F(1) of the *Regulated Activities Order*, which is in summary: entering into a *home purchase plan* as provider.

entering into a home reversion plan

the *regulated activity*, specified in article 63B(1) of the *Regulated Activities Order*, which is in summary: entering into a *home reversion plan* as provider, or acquiring any obligations or rights (including his interest in land) of the plan provider under a *home purchase plan* entered into by him on or after 6 April 2007.

entering into a regulated mortgage contract

the *regulated activity*, specified in article 61(1) of the *Regulated Activities Order*, which is in summary: entering into a *regulated mortgage contract* as lender.

entering into a regulated sale and rent back agreement

the *regulated activity*, specified in article 63J(1) of the *Regulated Activities Order*, which is in summary entering into a *regulated sale and rent back agreement* as an agreement provider, including acquiring any obligations or rights of the agreement provider, including the agreement provider's interest in land or interests under one or more such *agreements*.

Enterprise Investment Scheme

an arrangement which is an *EIS managed portfolio* or an *EIS fund*.

Enterprise Zone Property Unit Trust

an *unregulated collective investment scheme* of which the underlying assets are industrial and commercial buildings in an Enterprise Zone in accordance with section 749(2) of the Finance Act 1980.

EPE

expected positive exposure.

equalisation provision

a provision required to be established under the *rules* in INSPRU 1.4.

equity

(for the purposes of BIPRU 7) a *share*.

equity exposure

(in relation to the *IRB approach*) an *exposure* falling into the *IRB exposure class* referred to in BIPRU 4.3.2R(5) (equity exposures).

equity market adjustment ratio

(1) (in relation to the *resilience capital requirement*) has the meaning set out in INSPRU 3.1.19R.

(2) (in relation to the *market risk* scenario for the *risk capital margin* of a *with-profits fund*) has the meaning set out in INSPRU 1.3.71R.

equity PRR

the part of the *market risk capital requirement* calculated in accordance with BIPRU 7.3 (Equity PRR and basic interest rate PRR for equity derivatives) but so that:

(a) the *equity PRR* excludes the part of the *market risk capital requirement* calculated under BIPRU 7.3.45R (Basic interest rate PRR for equity derivatives); and

(b) in relation to a particular *position*, it means the portion of the overall *equity PRR* attributable to that *position*.

equity release activity

any *regulated mortgage activity* carried on in relation to a *lifetime mortgage*, or a *reversion activity*.

equity release adviser

a *firm* with *permission* (or which ought to have *permission*) for:

(a) *advising on regulated mortgage contracts* (when carried on in relation to a *lifetime mortgage*); or

(b) *advising on a home reversion plan*.

equity release arranger

a *firm* with *permission* (or which ought to have *permission*) for *arranging* a:

(a) *regulated mortgage contract* (when carried on in relation to a *lifetime mortgage*); or

(b) *home reversion plan.*

equity release intermediary

a *firm* with *permission* (or which ought to have *permission*) to carry on *equity release mediation activity.*

equity release mediation activity

any of the *regulated activities* of:

(a) *arranging* a *regulated mortgage contract* (when carried on in relation to a *lifetime mortgage*) or a *home reversion plan*;

(b) *advising on a regulated mortgage contract* (when carried on in relation to a *lifetime mortgage*) or a *home reversion plan*; or

(c) *agreeing to carry on a regulated activity* in (a) or (b).

equity release provider

a *firm* with *permission* (or which ought to have *permission*) for:

(a) *entering into a regulated mortgage contract* (when carried on in relation to a *lifetime mortgage*); or

(b) *entering into a home reversion plan.*

equity release transaction

a *lifetime mortgage* or a *home reversion plan.*

equity security

(1) (in LR) *equity shares* and *securities* convertible into *equity shares*; and

(2) (in PR) (as defined in Article 2.1(b) of the *prospectus directive*) shares and other transferable securities equivalent to shares in companies, as well as any other type of transferable securities giving the right to acquire any of the aforementioned securities as a consequence of their being converted or the rights conferred by them being exercised, provided that securities of the latter type are issued by the issuer of the underlying shares or by an entity belonging to the group of the said issuer.

equity share

shares comprised in a *company's equity share capital.*

equity share capital

(for a *company*), its issued share capital excluding any part of that capital which, neither as respects dividends nor as respects capital, carries any right to participate beyond a specified amount in a distribution.

equity stake

(in relation to a *company*) any kind of equity stake in that *company*, including *shares* in it (including non-voting and non-equity *shares, debt securities* that are convertible or exchangeable into such *shares*, a call *option* on such *shares* or an in-the-money put *option* on such *shares*, but excluding a *contract for differences* or other *investment* that provides merely an economic exposure to movement in the price of the *company's shares*).

equivalent

see *commission equivalent.*

equivalent business of a third country investment firm

the business of a *third country investment firm* carried on from an establishment in the *United Kingdom* that would be *MiFID business* if that firm were a *MiFID investment firm.*

equivalent document

(in *LR*) a document containing information equivalent to a *prospectus* for the purposes of PR 1.2.2R(2) or (3) or PR 1.2.3R(3) or (4).

essential information

[deleted]

established surplus

has the meaning in IPRU(INS) 3.3(4).

establishing, operating or winding up a collective investment scheme

the *regulated activity*, specified in article 51(1)(a) of the *Regulated Activities Order* (Establishing etc a collective investment scheme), of establishing, operating or winding up a *collective investment scheme.*

establishing, operating or winding up a personal pension scheme

the *regulated activity*, specified in article 52(b) of the *Regulated Activities Order* (Establishing etc. a pension scheme), of establishing, operating or winding up a *personal pension scheme*.

establishing, operating or winding up a regulated collective investment scheme

establishing, operating or winding up a collective investment scheme if the *scheme* is a *regulated collective investment scheme*.

establishing, operating or winding up a stakeholder pension scheme

the *regulated activity*, specified in article 52(a) of the *Regulated Activities Order* (Establishing etc a pension scheme), of establishing, operating or winding up a *stakeholder pension scheme*.

establishing, operating or winding up an unregulated collective investment scheme

establishing, operating or winding up a collective investment scheme if the *scheme* is an *unregulated collective investment scheme*.

establishment

(in relation to an *information society service*) the place at which the provider of the service effectively pursues an economic activity for an indefinite period;
in this definition:
(a) the presence or use in a particular place of equipment or other technical means of providing an *information society service* does not, of itself, constitute that place as an establishment; and
(b) where it is unclear from which of a number of establishments a particular *information society service* is provided, that service is to be regarded as provided from the establishment where the provider has the centre of his activities relating to the service.

establishment conditions

(in relation to the establishment of a *branch* in the *United Kingdom*) the conditions specified in paragraph 13 of Schedule 3 to the *Act* (EEA Passport Rights), which are that:
(a) if the *firm* falls within paragraph (a), (b), (c) or (d) in the definition of "*EEA firm*":
  (i) the *FSA* has received notice ("a consent notice") from the *EEA firm's Home State regulator* that it has given the *EEA firm* consent to establish a *branch* in the *United Kingdom*;
  (ii) the consent notice:
    (A) is given in accordance with the relevant *Single Market Directive*;
    (B) identifies the activities to which consent relates; and
    (C) includes the other information prescribed in the Financial Services and Markets Act 2000 (EEA Passport Rights) Regulations 2001 (SI 2001/1376); and
  (iii) the *EEA firm* has been informed of the *applicable provisions* or two *months* have elapsed beginning with the date when the *FSA* received the consent notice.
(b) if the *firm* falls within paragraph (e) in the definition of "*EEA firm*":
  (i) the *EEA firm* has given its *Home State regulator* notice of its intention to establish a *branch* in the *United Kingdom*;
  (ii) the *FSA* has received notice ("a regulator's notice") from the *firm's Home State regulator* that the *firm* intends to establish a *branch* in the *United Kingdom*;
  (iii) the *EEA firm's Home State regulator* has informed it that the regulator's notice has been sent to the *FSA*; and
  (iv) one *month* has elapsed beginning with the date on which the *EEA firm's Home State regulator* informed the *firm* that it had sent the regulator's notice to the *FSA*.

establishment costs

(1) (in FEES 6) the costs of establishing the *compensation scheme*.
(2) (in FEES 5) the costs of establishing the *Financial Ombudsman Service*.

EU

the European Union, being the Union established by the Treaty on European Union signed at Maastricht on 7 February 1992 (as amended).

European Economic Area

the area established by the agreement on the European Economic Area signed at Oporto on 2 May 1992, as it has effect for the time being, and which consists of the *EEA States*.

evidential provision

a *rule*, contravention of which does not give rise to any of the consequences provided for by other provisions of the *Act*; and which provides, in accordance with section 149(2) of the *Act*, that:

(a) contravention may be relied on as tending to establish contravention of such other *rule* as may be specified; or
(b) compliance may be relied on as tending to establish compliance with such other *rule* as may be specified; or
(c) both (a) and (b).

ex-section 43 firm

a *firm* that was a listed institution, as defined in section 43 of the Financial Services Act 1986, immediately before *commencement*.

ex-section 43 lead regulated firm

an *ex-section 43 firm* for which the *FSA* (in its capacity as the regulatory body under section 43 of the Financial Services Act 1986) was lead regulator for financial supervision purposes, and that was subject to the *section 43 capital requirements*, immediately before *commencement*.

excepted contract

(in BCOBS) has the same meaning as in the Consumer Protection (Distance Selling) Regulations 2000 (SI 2000/2334).

excess LLP members' drawings

the amount by which the aggregate of the amounts withdrawn by a *limited liability partnership's* members exceeds the profits of that *firm*, as calculated in accordance with IPRU(INV) Annex A 2.5R (Limited liability partnership excess drawings).

excess spread

(for the purposes of BIPRU 9 (Securitisation), in relation to a *securitisation* (within the meaning of paragraph (2) of the definition of securitisation) and in accordance with Part 1 of Annex IX of the *Banking Consolidation Directive* (Securitisation definitions)) finance charge collections and other fee income received in respect of the *securitised exposures* net of costs and expenses.

excess surplus

a *firm* will have an excess surplus in a *with-profits fund* if, and to the extent that:
(a) the *regulatory surplus* (or, in the case of a *realistic basis life firm*, the excess of *realistic value of assets* over *realistic value of liabilities*) in that *with-profits fund*; and
(b) any other financial resources applied to, or expected to be applied to, that *with-profits fund*;

exceed:
(c) the amount required to meet the higher of any regulatory capital requirement or the *firm's individual capital assessment* (at the *firm's* own risk appetite) for existing business; and
(d) any further amount necessary to support the new business plans of that *with-profits fund*.

excess trading book position

has the meaning in GENPRU 2.2.264R (Deductions from total capital: Excess trading book position).

exchange traded fund

a fund:
(a) which is an *open-ended investment company*; and
(b) the *units* of which are traded on a *regulated market or designated investment exchange*.

excluded communication

the following types of *financial promotion* (a *firm* may rely on more than one of the paragraphs in relation to the same *financial promotion*):
(a) a *financial promotion* that would benefit from an exemption in the *Financial Promotion Order* if it were *communicated* by an *unauthorised person*, or which originates outside the *United Kingdom* and is not capable of having an effect in the *United Kingdom* (within the meaning of s.21(3) of the *Act*);
(b) a *financial promotion* from outside the *United Kingdom* that would be exempt under articles 30, 31, 32 or 33 of the *Financial Promotion Order* (Overseas communicators) if the office from which the *financial promotion* is *communicated* were a separate *unauthorised person*;
(c) a *financial promotion* that is subject to, or exempted from, the *Takeover Code* or to the requirements relating to takeovers or related operations in another *EEA State*;
(d) a personal quotation or illustration form;
(e) a "one-off"*financial promotion* that is not a *cold call*. If the conditions set out in (i) to (iii), below, are satisfied, a *financial promotion* is "one-off". If not, the fact that any one or more of these conditions is met is to be taken into account in determining if a *financial promotion* is "one-off". However, a *financial promotion* may be regarded as "one-off" even if none of the conditions are met. The conditions are that:

(i) the *financial promotion* is *communicated* only to one recipient or only to one group of recipients in the expectation that they would engage in any investment activity jointly;
(ii) the identity of the product or service to which the *financial promotion* relates has been determined having regard to the particular circumstances of the recipient;
(iii) the *financial promotion* is not part of an organised marketing campaign; or

(f) a communication that is exempted by the Financial Services and Markets Act 2000 (Promotion of Collective Investment Schemes) (Exemptions) Order 2001.

excluded material

(in relation to access to *FSA* material) (as defined in section 394(7) of the *Act* (Access to Authority material)) material which:

(a) has been intercepted in obedience to a warrant issued under any enactment relating to the interception of communications; or
(b) indicates that such a warrant has been issued or that material has been intercepted in obedience to such a warrant; or
(c) is a *protected item.*

execute

(in relation to a transaction) carry into effect or perform the transaction, whether as *principal* or as agent, including instructing another *person* to execute the transaction.

execution criteria

the criteria set out in COBS 11.2.6R, that is:

(a) the characteristics of the *client* including the categorisation of the *client* as retail or professional;
(b) the characteristics of the *client* order;
(c) the characteristics of *financial instruments* that are the subject of that order;
(d) the characteristics of the *execution venues* to which that order can be directed.

execution factors

price, costs, speed, likelihood of execution and settlement, size, nature or any other consideration relevant to the execution of an order.

execution of orders on behalf of clients

acting to conclude agreements to buy or sell one or more *financial instruments* on behalf of *clients.*

[Note: article 4 (1)(5) of *MiFID*]

execution-only transaction

a transaction *executed* by a *firm* upon the specific instructions of a *client* where the *firm* does not give *advice on investments* relating to the merits of the transaction and in relation to which the rules on assessment of appropriateness (COBS 10) do not apply.

execution venue

for the purposes of the provisions relating to best execution in COBS 11.2, execution venue means a *regulated market*, an *MTF*, a *systematic internaliser*, or a *market maker* or other liquidity provider or an entity that performs a similar function in a third country to the functions performed by any of the foregoing.

[Note: article 44(1) of the *MiFID implementing Directive*]

executive procedures

the procedures relating to the giving of *warning notices, decision notices* and *supervisory notices* that are described in DEPP 4 (Decisions by FSA staff under executive procedures).

exempt activity

(in relation to a *recognised body*) any *regulated activity* in respect of which the body is exempt from the *general prohibition* as a result of section 285(2) or (3) of the *Act* (Exemption for recognised investment exchanges and clearing houses).

exempt BIPRU commodities firm

a *BIPRU firm* to which the exemption in BIPRU TP 15.6R (Exemption for a *BIPRU firm* whose main business relates to *commodities*) applies.

exempt CAD firm

(1) (except in SYSC and IPRU(INV)) has the meaning set out BIPRU 1.1.16R (Types of investment firm: exempt CAD firm) which is in summary an *investment firm* that satisfies certain specified conditions.

(2) (in SYSC) a *firm* in (1) whose head office (or, if it has a registered office, that office) is in the *United Kingdom*.

exempt full scope BIPRU investment firm

a *full scope BIPRU investment firm* falling into BIPRU 12.1.4R.

exempt insurance intermediary

an *insurance intermediary*:

(a) whose *Part IV permission* is limited to or includes *insurance mediation activity*;

(b) *which, in relation to insurance mediation activity (but disregarding money or other assets held in relation to other activities)* either:

  (i) does not hold any *client money* or other *client* assets in any form; or

  (ii) holds *client money* as trustee under a statutory trust imposed by CASS 5.3 (statutory trust) but does not otherwise hold *client money*; and

(c) which (when aggregating the amount calculated in accordance with CASS 5.5.65R) does not in relation to *insurance mediation activity* hold *client money* in excess of £30,000 at any time during a *financial year*.

exempt person

(1) (as defined in section 417(1) of the *Act* (Definitions)) (in relation to a *regulated activity*) a *person* who is exempt from the *general prohibition* in respect of that activity as a result of:

  (a) the *Exemption Order;* or

  (b) being an *appointed representative;* or

  (c) section 285(2) or (3) of the *Act* (Exemption for recognised investment exchanges and clearing houses); and

(2) a *person* who is exempt from the general prohibition as a result of section 312A(2) of the *Act*.

exempt professional firm

a *person* to whom, under section 327 of the *Act*, the *general prohibition* does not apply; guidance is given in *PROF* 2.2 (Exempt regulated activities).

exempt regulated activity

(as defined in section 325(2) of the *Act* (Authority's general duty)) a *regulated activity* which may, as a result of Part XX of the *Act* (Provision of Financial Services by Members of the Professions), be carried on by *members* of a profession which is supervised and regulated by a *designated professional body* without breaching the *general prohibition.*

Exemption Order

the Financial Services and Markets Act 2000 (Exemption) Order 2001 (SI 2001/1201)

exercise notice

(in LR) (in relation to *securitised derivatives*), a document that notifies the *issuer* of a holder's intention to exercise its rights under the *securitised derivative*.

exercise price

(in LR) (in relation to *securitised derivatives*), the price stipulated by the *issuer* at which the holder can buy or sell the *underlying instrument* from or to the *issuer*.

exercise time

(in LR) (in relation to *securitised derivatives*), the time stipulated by the *issuer* by which the holder must exercise their rights.

expected exposure

(in accordance with Part 1 of Annex III of the *Banking Consolidation Directive* (Definitions) and for the purpose of BIPRU 13 (The calculation of counterparty risk exposure values for financial derivatives, securities financing transactions and long settlement transactions)) the average of the distribution of *exposures* at any particular future date before the longest maturity transaction in the *netting set* matures.

expected loss

(in accordance with Article 4(29) of the *Banking Consolidation Directive* (Definitions) and for the purposes of the *IRB approach* and the *standardised approach* to credit risk) the ratio of the amount expected to be lost on an *exposure* from a potential *default* of a counterparty or dilution over a one year period to the amount outstanding at *default*.

expected positive exposure

(in accordance with Part 1 of Annex III of the *Banking Consolidation Directive* (Definitions) and for the purpose of BIPRU 13 (The calculation of counterparty risk exposure values for financial derivatives, securities financing transactions and long settlement transactions)) the weighted average over time of *expected exposures* where the weights are the proportion that an individual *expected exposure* represents of the entire time interval; when calculating the minimum capital requirement, the average is taken over the first year or, if all the contracts within the *netting set* mature before one year, over the time period of the longest-maturity contract in the *netting set*.

expiration date

(in LR) (in relation to *securitised derivatives*), the date stipulated by the *issuer* on which the holder's rights in respect of the *securitised derivative* ends.

exposure

(1) (in relation to a *firm* but subject to (2) and (3)) the maximum loss which the *firm* might suffer if:
  (a) a counterparty or a group of connected counterparties fail to meet their obligations; or
  (b) it realises assets or off-balance sheet positions.

(2) (in accordance with Article 77 of the *Banking Consolidation Directive* and for the purposes of the calculation of the *credit risk capital component* and the *counterparty risk capital component* (including BIPRU 3 (Standardised credit risk), BIPRU 4 (The IRB approach), BIPRU 5 (Credit risk mitigation) and BIPRU 9 (Securitisation)) an asset or off-balance sheet item.

(3) (for the purposes of BIPRU 10 (Concentration risk requirements)) has the meaning in BIPRU 10.2 (Identification of exposures).

extraction

(in relation to *mineral companies*), includes mining, production, quarrying or similar activities and the reworking of mine tailings or waste dumps.

extraordinary resolution

(in COLL) a resolution passed by a majority of not less than three-quarters of the votes validly cast (whether on a show of hands or on a poll) for and against the resolution at a general meeting or (as the case may be) *class meeting* of *holders*, of which notice specifying the intention to propose the resolution as an extraordinary resolution has been duly given.

EZPUT

Enterprise Zone Property Unit Trust.

facilities

(in relation to a *recognised body*) the facilities and services which it provides in the course of carrying on *exempt activities*, and references to the use of the facilities of an *RIE* are to be construed as follows:

references to

(1) dealings on an RIE; or
(2) transactions on an RIE are
(3) references to dealings or transactions which are effected by means of the RIE's facilities; or
(4) which are governed by the rules of the RIE; and
(5) references to the use of the facilities of an RIE include use which consists of any such dealings or entering into any such transactions.

facility grade

(in relation to the *advanced IRB approach* and the *sovereign, institutional and corporate IRB exposure class* and in accordance with BIPRU 4.4.49R) a risk category within a *rating system's* facility scale to which *exposures* are assigned on the basis of a specified and distinct set of rating criteria from which own estimates of *LGDs* are derived.

failure

the appointment of a liquidator, receiver or administrator, or trustee in bankruptcy, or any equivalent procedure in any relevant jurisdiction.

fair, clear and not misleading rule

COBS 4.2.1R.

fee

any payment or remuneration offered or made by a *client* to a *firm* in connection with *designated investment business* or with any other business of the *firm*, including (where applicable) any *mark-up or mark-down*.

feeder fund

an *AUT* that is a *relevant pension scheme* and *dedicated* to *units* in a single *regulated collective investment*.

fee-paying payment service provider

any of the following when they provide *payment services*:

(a) a *payment institution*;
(b) a *full credit institution*;
(c) an *e-money issuer*;
(d) the Post Office Limited;
(e) the Bank of England, other than when acting in its capacity as a monetary authority or carrying out functions of a public nature; and
(f) government departments and local authorities, other than when carrying out functions of a public nature.

A *full credit institution* or an *e-money issuer* that is an *EEA firm* is only a *fee-paying payment service provider* if it is exercising an *EEA right* in accordance with Part 2 of Schedule 3 to the *Act* (exercise of passport rights) to provide *payment services* in the *United Kingdom*. An *EEA authorised payment institution* is only a *fee-paying payment service provider* if it is exercising a right under Article 25 of the *Payment Services Directive* to provide *payment services* in the *United Kingdom*.

FEES

the Fees manual.

field representative

an *appointed representative* or, where applicable, a *tied agent*, or an *employee* of the *firm* (or of its *appointed representative* or, where applicable, its *tied agent*,), whose normal fixed place of business is not a business address of the *firm* which appears on the *firm's* stationery.

Fifth Motor Insurance Directive

the European Parliament and Council Directive of 11 May 2005 amending Council Directives 72/166/EEC, 84/5/EEC, 88/357/ EEC and 90/232/EEC and European Parliament and Council Directive 2006/26/EC relating to insurance against civil liability in respect of the use of *vehicles* (No 2005/14/EC).

final bonus

(in relation to a *with-profits insurance contract*) a discretionary payment which might be made by a *long-term insurer*, in addition to the guaranteed benefits, when the benefits under the *with-profits insurance contract* become payable.

final notice

a notice given by the *FSA* under section 390 of the *Act* (Final notices).

final response

(1) (in CRED) a written response from the *firm* which:
  (a) accepts the complaint, and, where appropriate, offers redress; or
  (b) offers redress without accepting the complaint; or
  (c) rejects the complaint and gives reasons for doing so; and which informs the complainant that, if he remains dissatisfied with the *firm's* response, he may now refer his complaint to the *Financial Ombudsman Service* and must do so within six months.

(2) (in *DISP*) a written response from a *respondent* which:
  (a) accepts the *complaint* and, where appropriate, offers redress or remedial action; or
  (b) offers redress or remedial action without accepting the *complaint*; or
  (c) rejects the *complaint* and gives reasons for doing so; and which:
  (d) encloses a copy of the *Financial Ombudsman Service's* standard explanatory leaflet; and
  (e) informs the complainant that if he remains dissatisfied with the *respondent's* response, he may now refer his *complaint* to the *Financial Ombudsman Service* and must do so within six months.

final terms

(in LR) the document containing the final terms of each issue which is intended to be listed.

finance function

controlled function CF13 in the *table of controlled functions*, described more fully in *SUP* 10.8.1R.

Financial Action Task Force

the inter-governmental body responsible for developing and promoting policies, both nationally and internationally, to combat money laundering.

financial adviser

(a) an individual appointed by an independent intermediary or by its *appointed representative* or where applicable, *tied agent*, to provide any or all of the following services:

Part II FSA Handbook Materials

(i) giving advice on *investments* to *clients*;
(ii) *arranging (bringing about) deals in investments* or *executing* transactions involving, in each case, *designated investments* with or for *clients*;
(iii) *managing investments*;
(iv) receiving or holding *client money* or other *client assets*;
(v) *safeguarding and administering investments*.

(b) For the purposes of this definition, an independent intermediary is a *firm* acting as an intermediary but excluding:
(i) a *firm* which is a member of a *marketing group*;
(ii) a *product provider* which *sells* its own *packaged products*.

financial analyst

a *relevant person* who produces the substance of *investment research*.

[Note: article 2(4) of the *MiFID implementing Directive*]

financial collateral comprehensive method

the method for calculating the effects of *credit risk mitigation* described in those parts of BIPRU 5.4 (Financial collateral) that are expressed to apply to that method.

Financial Collateral Directive

the Council Directive of 6 June 2002 relating to financial collateral arrangements (No 2002/47/EC).

financial collateral simple method

the method for calculating the effects of *credit risk mitigation* described in those parts of BIPRU 5.4 (Financial collateral) that are expressed to apply to that method.

financial conglomerate

(in accordance with Article 2(14) of the *Financial Groups Directive* (Definitions)) a *consolidation group* that is identified as a *financial conglomerate* by the *financial conglomerate definition decision tree*.

financial conglomerate definition decision tree

the decision tree in GENPRU 3 Ann 4R.

financial crime

(in accordance with section 6(3) of the *Act*) any kind of criminal conduct relating to money or to financial services or markets, including any offence involving:

(a) fraud or dishonesty; or
(b) misconduct in, or misuse of information relating to, a financial market; or
(c) handling the proceeds of crime; in this definition, "offence" includes an act or omission which would be an offence if it had taken place in the *United Kingdom*.

financial derivative instrument

has the meaning in BIPRU 13.3.3R (Definition of a financial derivative instrument); the definition is adjusted for the purposes of the definition of *counterparty risk capital component* in accordance with BIPRU 14.2.3R (Credit derivatives).

Financial Groups Directive

Directive 2002/87/EC of the European Parliament and of the Council of 16 December 2002 on the supplementary supervision of credit institutions, insurance undertakings and investment firms in a financial conglomerate.

Financial Groups Directive Regulations

the Financial Conglomerates and Other Financial Groups Regulations 2004 (SI 2004/1862).

financial holding company

a *financial institution* that fulfils the following conditions:

(a) its *subsidiary undertakings* are either exclusively or mainly *credit institutions*, *investment firms* or *financial institutions*;
(b) at least one of those *subsidiary undertakings* is a *credit institution* or an *investment firm*; and
(c) it is not a *mixed financial holding company*.

financial information table

(in LR) financial information presented in tabular form that covers the reporting period set out in LR 13.5.13R in relation to the entities set out in LR 13.5.14R, and to the extent relevant LR 13.5.15R and LR 13.5.16R.

financial institution

(1) (in accordance with paragraph 5(c) of Schedule 3 to the *Act* (EEA Passport Rights: EEA firm) and article 4(5) of the *Banking Consolidation Directive* (Definitions), but not for the purposes of ELM, GENPRU, BIPRU and INSPRU) an undertaking, other than a *credit institution*, the

principal activity of which is to acquire holdings or to carry on one or more of the *listed activities* listed in points 2 to 12 of Annex I to the *BCD*, which is a subsidiary of the kind mentioned in article 24 of the *BCD* and which fulfils the conditions in that article of the *BCD*.

(2) (for the purposes of ELM, GENPRU, BIPRU and INSPRU and in accordance with Articles 1(3) (Scope) and 4(5) (Definitions) of the *Banking Consolidation Directive*) the following:
(a) an *undertaking*, other than a *credit institution*, the principal activity of which is to acquire holdings or to carry on one or more of the *listed activities* listed in points 2 to 12 of Annex I to the *Banking Consolidation Directive* including the services and activities provided for in Sections A and B of Annex I of the *MIFID* when referring to the financial instruments provided for in Section C of Annex I of that Directive;
(b) (for the purposes of consolidated requirements) those institutions permanently excluded by Article 2 of the *Banking Consolidation Directive* (Scope), with the exception of the *central banks* of *EEA States*; and
(c) (for the purposes of *ELM*) an *asset management company*.

financial instrument

(1) (other than in (2)) instruments specified in Section C of Annex I of *MiFID*, that is:
(a) *transferable securities*;
(b) *money-market instruments*;
(c) units in collective investment undertakings;
(d) options, futures, swaps, forward rate agreements and any other derivative contracts relating to securities, currencies, interest rates or yields, or other derivative instruments, financial indices or financial measures which may be settled physically or in cash;
(e) options, futures, swaps, forward rate agreements and any other derivative contracts relating to commodities that must be settled in cash or may be settled in cash at the option of one of the parties (otherwise than by reason of a default or other termination event);
(f) options, futures, swaps, and any other derivative contract relating to commodities that can be physically settled provided that they are traded on a *regulated market* and/or an *MTF*;
(g) options, futures, swaps, forwards and any other derivative contracts relating to commodities, that can be physically settled not otherwise mentioned in (f) and not being for commercial purposes, which have the characteristics of other derivative financial instruments, having regard to whether, inter alia, they are cleared and settled through recognised clearing houses or are subject to regular margin calls (see articles 38(1), (2) and (4) of the *MiFID Regulation*);
(h) derivative instruments for the transfer of credit risk;
(i) financial contracts for differences; and
(j) options, futures, swaps, forward rate agreements and any other derivative contracts relating to
(i) climatic variables;
(ii) freight rates;
(iii) emission allowances;
(iv) inflation rates or other official economic statistics;
(v) telecommunications bandwidth;
(vi) commodity storage capacity;
(vii) transmission or transportation capacity relating to commodities, whether cable, pipeline or other means;
(viii) an allowance, credit, permit, right or similar asset which is directly linked to the supply, distribution or consumption of energy derived from renewable resources;
(ix) a geological, environmental or other physical variable;
(x) any other asset or right of a fungible nature, other than a right to receive a service, that is capable of being transferred;
(xi) an index or measure related to the price or value of, or volume of transactions in any asset, right, service or obligation;

where the conditions in Articles 38(3) and (4) of the *MiFID Regulation* are met.
[**Note:** article 4(1)(17) and section C of Annex I to *MiFID* and articles 38 and 39 of the *MiFID Regulation*]

(2) (in *MAR* 1 and *MAR* 2, *DTR* 1, 2 and 3 and otherwise where used in relation to the *Market Abuse Directive*) (as defined in Article 5 of the *Prescribed Markets and Qualifying Investments Order* and Article 1(3) of the *Market Abuse Directive*, and which consequently carries the same meaning in the *Buy-back and Stabilisation Regulation*):
(a) transferable securities as defined in the *ISD*;
(b) units in collective investment undertakings;

Part II FSA Handbook Materials

(c) money-market instruments;
(d) financial-futures contracts, including equivalent cash-settled instruments;
(e) forward interest-rate agreements;
(f) interest-rate, currency and equity swaps;
(g) options to acquire or dispose of any instrument falling into these categories, including equivalent cash-settled instruments. This category includes in particular options on currency and on interest rates;
(h) derivatives on commodities; and
(i) any other instrument admitted to trading on a *regulated market* in an *EEA State* or for which a request for admission to trading on such a market has been made.

Financial Ombudsman Service

the scheme provided under Part XVI of the *Act* (The Ombudsman Scheme) under which certain disputes may be resolved quickly and with minimum formality by an independent *person*.

Financial Ombudsman Service Limited

the *body corporate* established by the *FSA* under paragraph 2(1) of Schedule 17 to the *Act* (The Scheme Operator) to administer the *Financial Ombudsman Service*.

financial promotion

(1) an invitation or inducement to *engage in investment activity* that is communicated in the course of business;
[Note: section 21 of the Act (Restrictions on financial promotion]
(2) (in relation to *COBS* 3.2.1R, *COBS* 4.3.1R, *COBS* 4.5.8R and *COBS* 4.7.1R) (in addition to (1)) a marketing communication within the meaning of *MiFID* made by a *firm* in connection with its *MiFID or equivalent third country investment business*.

Financial Promotion Order

the Financial Services and Markets Act 2000 (Financial Promotion) Order 2005 (SI 2005/1529).

financial promotion rules

(1) (in relation to *COBS*) any or all of the *rules* in *COBS* 4 that impose requirements in relation to a *financial promotion* but only to the extent that they apply to a *financial promotion*.
(2) (in relation to *ICOBS*) *ICOBS* 2.2.
(3) (in relation to *MCOB*) *MCOB* 3.

financial resources

(in UPRU) the financial resources calculated in accordance with UPRU 2.2.1R (Financial resources) that a *UCITS firm* needs to meet its *financial resources requirement*.

financial resources requirement

(in UPRU) has the meaning given in UPRU 2.1.2R.

financial return

(in UPRU) means *annual financial return*, *quarterly financial return* or *monthly financial return* as the case may be.

financial sector

(1) (subject to (2)) one of the *banking sector*, the *insurance sector* or the *investment services sector*.
(2) (for the purposes of the definition of *financial conglomerate* and for any other provision of GENPRU 3 that treats the *banking sector* and the *investment services sector* as one) one of the *banking and investment services sector* or the *insurance sector*.

Financial Services and Markets Tribunal

the Tribunal established under section 132 of the *Act* (The Financial Services and Markets Tribunal) and run by the Lord Chancellor's Department.

Financial Services Compensation Scheme Limited

the *body corporate* established by the *FSA* under section 212 of the *Act* (The scheme manager) to administer the *compensation scheme*.

financial services undertaking

(in *ELM*) a *financial institution*, *ancillary banking services undertaking*, *financial holding company* or *relevant financial services company*.

financial system

(as defined in section 3 of the *Act* (Market confidence)) the financial system operating in the *United Kingdom* including:

(a) financial markets and exchanges;
(b) *regulated activities;* and
(c) other activities connected with financial markets and exchanges.

financial year

(1) (in *DISP*) the 12 *months* ending with 31 March.
(2) [deleted]
(3) (in GENPRU and INSPRU) the period at the end of which the balance of the accounts of the *insurer* is struck, or, if no balance is struck, the calendar year.

financial year in question

(for the purposes of INSPRU 1.1 and of the definition of *non-directive insurer*) the last *financial year* to end before the date on which the latest accounts of the *insurer* are required to be deposited with the *FSA*; the preceding *financial year* and previous *financial years* are construed accordingly.

financing cost amount

(in relation to a *share*, *debenture* or other investment in, or external contribution to the capital of, a *firm*) an amount that represents a reasonable estimate of the part of the *coupon* on that instrument that reflects the cost of financing generally but excludes costs reflecting factors relating to the issuer, guarantor or other person to whom the instrument creates an exposure.

fire and natural forces

(in relation to a *class* of *contract of insurance*) the *class* of *contract of insurance*, specified in paragraph 8 of Part I of Schedule 1 to the *Regulated Activities Order* (Contracts of general insurance), against loss of or damage to property (other than property to which paragraphs 3 to 7 of Part I of Schedule 1 to the *Regulated Activities Order* (Land vehicles; railway rolling stock; aircraft; ships; goods in transit) relate) due to fire, explosion, storm, natural forces other than storm, nuclear energy or land subsidence.

firm

(1) an *authorised person*, but not a *professional firm* unless it is an *authorised professional firm* (see also *GEN* 2.2.18R for the position of an *authorised partnership* or unincorporated association which is dissolved).
(2) (in *DISP* 2 and 3) includes, in accordance with the *Ombudsman Transitional Order*, *unauthorised persons* subject to the *Compulsory Jurisdiction* in relation to *relevant existing complaints* and *relevant new complaints*.
(3) (in *DISP* 2 and 3) includes, in accordance with the *Mortgage and General Insurance Complaints Transitional Order*, former *firms* subject to the *Compulsory Jurisdiction* in relation to *relevant transitional complaints*.
(4) (in *DISP* 2 and 3) includes, as a result of the *insurance market direction* given in *DISP* 2.1.7D under section 316 of the *Act* (Direction by Authority), *members* of the *Society* of Lloyd's.
(5) (in *FEES* 3 to 5) includes a *fee-paying payment service provider* in accordance with *FEES* 3.1.1A R, *FEES* 4.1.1A R and *FEES* 5.1.1A R.

firm in run-off

a *firm* whose *Part IV permission* has been varied so as to remove the *regulated activity* of *effecting contracts of insurance*.

firm-specific liquidity stress

(in relation to a *firm* and any reporting obligations under *SUP* 16 (Reporting requirements)):
(a) (in the case of reporting obligations on a solo basis (including on the basis of the *firm's UK branch*) the *firm* failing to meet, not complying with or being in breach of:
 (i) the liquidity resources requirement calculated by that *firm* as adequate in its current *Individual Liquidity Adequacy Assessment* or *Individual Liquidity Systems Assessment*; or
 (ii) the level of its liquid assets buffer advised in any current *individual liquidity guidance* that the *firm* has accepted; or
 (iii) its funding profile advised in any current *individual liquidity guidance* that the *firm* has accepted; or
 (iv) the *overall liquidity adequacy rule*; or
 (v) *BIPRU* 12.2.8R (*ILAS BIPRU firm* adequate buffer of high quality, unencumbered assets) or *BIPRU* 12.2.11R (liquid assets buffer is at least equal to the *simplified buffer requirement*); or
 (vi) the *simplified buffer requirement* (taking into account *BIPRU* TP 29 (Liquid assets buffer scalar: simplified ILAS BIPRU firms) unless this has been superseded by *individual liquidity guidance* that it has accepted; or

Part II FSA Handbook Materials

(vii) any requirement imposed by or under the *regulatory system* under which the *firm* must hold a specified level of liquidity resources; or it being likely that the *firm* will do so;

(b) (in the case of reporting obligations with respect to the *firm* and a group of other *persons*) has the same meaning as in (a) except that references to any *rule* or other requirement, *Individual Liquidity Adequacy Assessment, Individual Liquidity Systems Assessment* or *individual liquidity guidance* are to any such thing so far as it applies to the *firm* and that group considered together.

firm type

one of a list of *firm types* set out in SUP 16 Annex 17R used for the purposes of checking and correcting *standing data* under SUP 16.10.4 R.

First Life Directive

the Council Directive of 5 March 1979 on the coordination of laws, regulations and administrative provisions relating to the taking up and pursuit of the business of direct life assurance (No 79/267/EEC).

First Non-Life Directive

the Council Directive of 24 July 1973 on the coordination of laws, regulations and administrative provisions relating to the taking up and pursuit of the business of direct insurance other than life insurance (No 73/239/EEC).

FIT

the part of the *Handbook* in High Level Standards which has the title the Fit and Proper test for Approved Persons.

fixed overheads requirement

the part of the *capital resources requirement* calculated in accordance with GENPRU 2.1.53R (Calculation of the fixed overheads requirement).

fixed-sum credit

(in accordance with section 10(1)(b) of the Consumer Credit Act 1974) any facility under a contract, other than *running account credit*, by which the *customer* is enabled to receive credit (whether in one amount or by instalments).

flat rate benefits business friendly society

a *friendly society* whose *insurance business* is restricted to the provision of benefits which vary according to the resources available and in which the contributions of members are determined on a flat rate basis.

foreign currency

(in ELM, GENPRU and BIPRU) (in relation to a *firm*) any currency other than the *base currency*.

foreign currency PRR

the part of the *market risk capital requirement* calculated in accordance with BIPRU 7.5 (Foreign currency PRR) or, in relation to a particular *position*, the portion of the overall *foreign currency PRR* attributable to that *position*.

former member

a *person* who has ceased to be a *member*, whether by resignation or otherwise, in accordance with Lloyd's Act 1982 and any *byelaw* made under it.

former Ombudsman

an ombudsman, arbitrator or independent investigator appointed under a *former scheme*.

former scheme

(1) (except in relation to any *relevant transitional complaint*) any of the following:
- (a) the *Banking Ombudsman scheme;*
- (b) the *Building Societies Ombudsman scheme;*
- (c) the *FSA scheme;*
- (d) the *IMRO scheme;*
- (e) the *Insurance Ombudsman scheme;*
- (f) the *Personal Insurance Arbitration Service;*
- (g) the *PIA Ombudsman scheme;*
- (h) the *SFA scheme*:

(2) (in relation to a *relevant transitional complaint*)
- (a) the *GISC facility*; or
- (b) the *MCAS scheme*.

former underwriting member

(as defined in section 324(1) of the *Act* (Interpretation of Part XIX: Lloyd's)) a *person* ceasing to be an *underwriting member* on, or at any time after, 24 December 1996.

forward

a contract to buy or sell where the date for settlement has been agreed as a particular date in the future but excluding a *future*.**forward price**

(in relation to *units*) a *price* calculated by reference to the *valuation point* next following the *authorised fund manager's* agreement to *sell* or, as the case may be, to *redeem* the *units* in question.

forward rate agreement

an agreement under which one party agrees to pay another an amount of interest based on an agreed interest rate for a specified period from a specified settlement date applied to an agreed principal amount but under which no commitment is made by either party to lend or borrow the principal amount.

FOS Ltd

Financial Ombudsman Service Limited.

foundation IRB approach

one of the following:

(a) (in relation to the *sovereign, institutional and corporate IRB exposure class*) the approach under the *IRB approach*, described in BIPRU 4.4 (The IRB approach: Exposures to corporates, institutions and sovereigns) under which a *firm* uses the values for *LGD* and *conversion factors* set out in BIPRU 4.4 rather than supplying its own estimates;

(b) (where the approach in (a) is being applied on a consolidated basis) the method in (a) as applied on a consolidated basis in accordance with BIPRU 8 (Group risk — consolidation); or

(c) when the reference is to the rules of or administered by a *regulatory body* other than the *FSA*, whatever corresponds to the approach in (a) or (b), as the case may be, under those rules.

Fourth Company Law Directive

Council Directive 78/660/EEC on the annual accounts of certain types of companies as amended by, amongst other instruments, Directive 2006/46/EC of the European Parliament and of the Council of 14 June 2006.

Fourth Motor Insurance Directive

the Directive of the European Parliament and the Council of 16 May 2000 on the approximation of the laws of the Member States relating to insurance against civil liability in respect of the use of motor vehicles and amending Council Directives 73/239/EEC and 88/357/EEC (No 2000/26/EC).

FRA

forward rate agreement.

framework contract

(in accordance with regulations 2(1) of the *Payment Services Regulations*) a contract for *payment services* which governs the future execution of individual and successive payment transactions and which may contain the obligation and conditions for setting up a payment account.

[**Note**: article 4(12) of the *Payment Services Directive*]

free delivery

a transaction of the type set out in BIPRU 14.4.2R (Requirement to hold capital resources with respect to free deliveries) which, in summary, is a transaction under which a *person*:

(a) has paid for *securities*, *foreign currencies* or *commodities* before receiving them or it has delivered *securities*, *foreign currencies* or *commodities* before receiving payment for them; and

(b) in the case of cross-border transactions, one day or more has elapsed since it made that payment or delivery.

free-standing additional voluntary contribution

[deleted]

FREN

the Handbook Guide for small Friendly societies.

friendly society

an *incorporated friendly society* or a *registered friendly society.*

front end loaded

(in relation to an *investment*) one where deductions for *charges* and expenses are loaded disproportionately on the early years.

FSA

the Financial Services Authority.

FSA Register

the public record, as required by section 347 of the *Act* (The public record) and regulation 4 of the Payment Services Regulations (The register of certain payment service providers), of every:

(a) *authorised person*;

(aa) *authorised payment institution* and its *EEA branches*;

(ab) *small payment institution*;

(ac) *agent* of an *authorised payment institution* or *small payment institution*;

(ad) credit union, municipal bank and the National Savings Bank where such *persons* provide a *payment service*;

(b) *AUT*;

(c) *ICVC;*

(d) *recognised scheme;*

(e) *recognised investment exchange;*

(f) *recognised clearing house;*

(g) individual to whom a *prohibition order* relates;

(h) *approved person*; and

(i) *person* within such other class (if any) as the *FSA* may determine; except as provided by any transitional provisions.

FSA registered tied agent

a *tied agent* who is an *agent* for the purposes of section 39A of the *Act*.

FSA regulated EEA financial conglomerate

a *financial conglomerate* (other than a *third-country financial conglomerate*) that satisfies one of the following conditions:

(a) GENPRU 3.1.26R or GENPRU 3.1.29R (Capital adequacy calculations for *financial conglomerates*) applies with respect to it; or

(b) a *firm* that is a member of that *financial conglomerate* is subject to obligations imposed through its *Part IV permission* to ensure that that *financial conglomerate* meets levels of capital adequacy based or stated to be based on Annex I of the *Financial Groups Directive*.

FSA scheme

the former scheme operated by the FSA under paragraph 4 of Schedule 7 to the Financial Services Act 1986 for the investigation of complaints arising out of the conduct of investment business.

FSA's SCV requirements

(in COMP) the *FSA's* requirements with respect to *single customer view*.

FSAVC

an arrangement which allows a member of an *occupational pension scheme* to make *AVCs* to a private *pension policy* or *pension contract*, where the policy or contract is separate from, but associated with, an *occupational pension scheme* which is a registered pension scheme under Chapter 2 of Part 4 of the Finance Act 2004.

FSCS

Financial Services Compensation Scheme Limited.

full BCD credit institution

a *BCD credit institution* that falls within paragraph (1)(a) of the definition of *credit institution* full credit institution

full credit institution

a *credit institution* that falls within paragraph (1)(a) of the definition of *credit institution*

full RSRB permission

(in FEES) an *authorisation* which is not an *interim RSRB permission* to carry on one or more *regulated sale and rent back activities*.

full scope BIPRU investment firm

has the meaning in BIPRU 1.1.17R (Types of BIPRU investment firm) which is in summary a *CAD full scope firm* that satisfies the following conditions:
(a) it is a *firm*; and
(b) its head office is in the *United Kingdom* and it is not otherwise excluded from the definition of *BIPRU firm* under BIPRU 1.1.7R (Exclusion of certain types of *firm* from the definition of *BIPRU firm*).

funded credit protection

(in accordance with Article 4(31) of the *Banking Consolidation Directive* (Definitions)) a technique of *credit risk mitigation* where the reduction of the credit risk on the *exposure* of an *undertaking* derives from the right of the *undertaking*, in the event of the default of the counterparty or on the occurrence of other specified credit events relating to the counterparty, to liquidate, or to obtain transfer or appropriation of, or to retain certain assets or amounts, or to reduce the amount of the *exposure* to, or to replace it with, the amount of the difference between the amount of the *exposure* and the amount of a claim on the *undertaking*.

funds at Lloyd's

assets (not being *syndicate assets*) provided by or on behalf of a *members* to meet the liabilities arising from the *member's insurance business* at Lloyd's which are held in a *Lloyd's trust fund* and managed by the *Society* as trustee.

funds supermarket service

a service consisting of the provision by a *firm* of *regulated activities* for a *customer* which consists of *arranging (bringing about) deals in investments* and *safeguarding and administering investments* with particular reference to *regulated collective investment schemes* where:
(a) the *schemes* are managed by other *firms*;
(b) the *customer's units* are held under arrangements in which their legal title is held by a *nominee company*; and
(c) the service relates to *schemes* offered by several *product providers*, at least one of whom is not an *affiliated company* of another *provider*.

funds under management

(in UPRU and GENPRU)
(1) *collective investment schemes* other than *OEICs managed* by the *firm* including *schemes* where it has delegated the management function but excluding *schemes* that it is *managing* as delegate; and
(2) *OEICs* for which the *firm* is the designated management company.

funeral plan contract

the *investment*, specified in articles 59(2), 60 and 87 of the *Regulated Activities Order* which come into force on 1 January 2002, which is in summary: rights under a contract under which:
(a) a *person* ("the customer") makes one or more payments to another *person* ("the provider"); and
(b) the provider undertakes to provide, or secure that another *person* provides, a funeral in the *United Kingdom* for the customer (or some other *person* who is living at the date when the contract is entered into) on his death;

unless, at the time of entering into the contract, the customer and the provider intend or expect the funeral to occur within one month; but excluding certain contracts under which sums paid will be applied towards a *contract of insurance* or will be held on trust.

future

the *investment*, specified in article 84 of the *Regulated Activities Order* (Futures), which is in summary: rights under a contract for the sale of a commodity or property of any other description under which delivery is to be made at a future date and at a price agreed on when the contract is made.

future policy-related liabilities

(in relation to a *with-profits fund*) the future *policy*-related liabilities of the *with-profits fund* calculated in accordance with the *rules* in PRU 7.4.137R to PRU 7.4.189G.

FX exposure

(in *ELM*) (in relation to an *ELMI*) its *net FX open position* multiplied by 8%, calculated in accordance with *ELM* 3.4 (Foreign exchange risk).

FX exposure limit

(in *ELM*) (in relation to an *ELMI*) the amount by which the *ELMI's own funds* exceed 3% of its *e-money outstandings*, calculated in accordance with *ELM* 3.4 (Foreign exchange risk).

GCR

group capital resources.

GCRR

group capital resources requirement.

gearing

[deleted]

GEN

the part of the *Handbook* in High Level Standards which has the title General provisions.

general application rule

COBS 1.1.1R (which in summary provides that *COBS* applies to a *firm* with respect to certain activities carried on from an establishment maintained by it in the *United Kingdom*).

general client bank account

a *client bank account* that holds *client money* of one or more *clients* and which is not:
(a) a *designated client bank account*; or
(b) a *designated client fund account.*

general insurance business

the business of *effecting* or *carrying out general insurance contracts.*

general insurance capital requirement

the highest of the *premiums amount*, *claims amount* and *brought forward amount* as set out in INSPRU 1.1.

general insurance contract

(in accordance with article 3(1) of the *Regulated Activities Order* (Interpretation: general)) any *contract of insurance* within Part I of Schedule 1 to the *Regulated Activities Order* (Contracts of general insurance), namely:
(a) *accident* (paragraph 1);
(b) *sickness* (paragraph 2);
(c) *land vehicles* (paragraph 3);
(d) *railway rolling stock* (paragraph 4);
(e) *aircraft* (paragraph 5);
(f) *ships* (paragraph 6);
(g) *goods in transit* (paragraph 7);
(h) *fire and natural forces* (paragraph 8);
(i) *damage to property* (paragraph 9);
(j) *motor vehicle liability* (paragraph 10);
(k) *aircraft liability* (paragraph 11);
(l) *liability of ships* (paragraph 12);
(m) *general liability* (paragraph 13);
(n) *credit* (paragraph 14);
(o) *suretyship* (paragraph 15);
(p) *miscellaneous financial loss* (paragraph 16);
(q) *legal expenses* (paragraph 17);
(r) *assistance* (paragraph 18).

general insurance liabilities

liabilities arising from *general insurance business.*

general levy

(in FEES) the annual fee raised from a *firm* under the *rules* to fund a part agreed between the *Financial Ombudsman Service* and the *FSA* of the *Financial Ombudsman Service's* annual budget.

general liability

(in relation to a *class of contract of insurance*) the *class* of *contract of insurance*, specified in paragraph 13 of Part I of Schedule 1 to the *Regulated Activities Order* (Contracts of general insurance), against risks of the *persons* insured incurring liabilities to third parties, the risks in question not being risks to which paragraph 10 (Motor vehicle liability), 11 (Aircraft liability) or 12 (Liability of ships) of that Schedule relates.

general market risk

(in accordance with paragraph 12 of Annex I of the *Capital Adequacy Directive*) the risk of a price change in an *investment*:

(a) (in relation to items that may or must be treated under BIPRU 7.2 (Interest Rate PRR)) owing to a change in the level of interest rates; or

(b) (in relation to items that may or must be treated under *BIPRU* 7.3 (Equity PRR and basic interest rate PRR for equity derivatives) except insofar as BIPRU 7.3 relates to the calculation of the *interest rate PRR*) owing to a broad equitymarket movement unrelated to any specific attributes of individual *securities.*

general market risk PRA

a *PRA* with respect to *general market risk.*

general prohibition

the prohibition imposed by section 19 of the *Act* (The general prohibition) which states that no *person may* carry on a *regulated activity* in the *United Kingdom*, or purport to do so, unless he is:

(a) an *authorised person;* or

(b) an *exempt person.*

General Protocol

the "General Protocol relating to the collaboration of the insurance supervisory authorities of the Member States of the European Union" issued by the Committee of European Insurance and Occupational Pensions Supervisors.

general representative

a *person* resident in the *United Kingdom* who is authorised to act generally, and to accept service of any *document*, on behalf of the *firm*.

general stress and scenario testing rule

GENPRU 1.2.42R (Stress and scenario tests).

general wrong-way risk

(in accordance with Part 1 of Annex III of the *Banking Consolidation Directive* (Definitions) and for the purpose of BIPRU 13 (The calculation of counterparty risk exposure values for financial derivatives, securities financing transactions and long settlement transactions)) the risk that arises when the probability of default of counterparties is positively correlated with general market risk factors.

generic projection

(in *COBS*) a projection which reflects the terms of a contract which is representative of the type of business normally undertaken by the *firm*, or the type of business it is promoting, rather than the terms of a particular contract with, or that will be offered to, a particular *client.*

GENPRU

the General Prudential sourcebook

Gibraltar Order

the Financial Services and Markets Act 2000 (Gibraltar) Order 2001 (SI 2001/3084)

GICR

general insurance capital requirement.

GISC facility

the Dispute Resolution Facility established by the General Insurance Standards Council

global account

the aggregate accounts produced by the *Council* in accordance with Regulation 8(1) of the Insurance Accounts Directive (Lloyd's Syndicate and Aggregate Accounts) Regulations 2004.

Glossary

the Glossary giving the meanings of the defined expressions used in the *Handbook.*

goods in transit

(in relation to a *class* of *contract of insurance*) the *class* of *contract of insurance*, specified in paragraph 7 of Part I of Schedule 1 to the *Regulated Activities Order* (Contracts of general insurance), against loss of or damage to merchandise, baggage and all other goods in transit, irrespective of the form of transport.

governing body

the board of *directors*, committee of management or other governing body of a *firm* or *recognised body*, including, in relation to a *sole trader*, the *sole trader.*

governing function

any of the *controlled functions* 1 to 7 in the *table of controlled functions*.

government and public security

the *investment*, specified in article 78 of the *Regulated Activities Order* (Government and public securities), which is in summary: a loan stock, bond or other instrument creating or acknowledging indebtedness, issued by or on behalf of:

(a) the government of the *United Kingdom;* or
(b) the Scottish Administration; or
(c) the Executive Committee of the Northern Ireland Assembly; or
(d) the National Assembly of Wales; or
(e) the government of any country or territory outside the *United Kingdom;* or
(f) a local authority in the *United Kingdom* or elsewhere; or
(g) a body the members of which comprise:
 (i) States including the *United Kingdom* or another *EEA State*; or
 (ii) bodies whose members comprise States including the *United Kingdom* or another *EEA State*; but excluding:
  (A) the instruments specified in article 77(2)(a) to (d) of the *Regulated Activities Order*;
  (B) any instrument creating or acknowledging indebtedness in respect of:
   (I) money received by the Director of Savings as *deposits* or otherwise in connection with the business of the National Savings Bank; or
   (II) money raised under the National Loans Act 1968 under the auspices of the Director of Savings or treated as so raised under section 11(3) of the National Debt Act 1972.

granting an e-money permission

(a) (in the case of a *firm* that previously had not had a *Part IV permission*) giving the *firm* a *Part IV permission* that includes *issuing e-money*;
(b) (in the case of a *firm* that does have a *Part IV permission*) a variation of a *Part IV permission* so that it includes *issuing e-money*.

greenhouse gas emissions allowance

an allowance, licence, permit, right, note, unit, credit, asset, certificate or instrument (the "allowance") where:

(a) the allowance confers or may result in a benefit or advantage to its holder or another *person*; and
(b) the allowance, or the benefit or advantage in (a), is linked to the emission or non-emission of quantities of carbon dioxide or other greenhouse gases into the environment by the holder of the allowance or someone else.

greenshoe option

(as defined in Article 2 of the *Buy-back and Stabilisation Regulation*) an option granted by the *offeror* in favour of the *investment firm*(s) or *credit institution*(s) involved in the *offer* for the purpose of covering *overallotments*, under the terms of which such firm(s) or institution(s) may purchase up to a certain amount of *relevant securities* at the offer price for a certain period of time after the offer of the relevant securities.

gross adjusted claims amount

(for the purposes of INSPRU 1.1) an amount, as defined in INSPRU 1.1.60R to INSPRU 1.1.65G, used in calculating the *claims amount*.

gross adjusted premiums amount

(for the purposes of INSPRU 1.1) an amount as defined in INSPRU 1.1.56R to INSPRU 1.1.59G, used in calculating the *premiums amount*.

gross earned premiums

(in relation to a *financial year*) such proportion of *gross written premiums* as is attributable to risk borne by the *insurer* during that *financial year*.

gross leverage

the ratio of total assets to total equity.

gross written premiums

the amounts required by the *insurance accounts rules* to be shown in the profit and loss account of an *insurer:*

(a) (for *general insurance business*) at general business technical account item I.1.(a); and
(b) (for *long-term insurance business*) at long term business technical account item II.1.(a).

group

(1) (except in relation to an *ICVC* and except for the purposes of SYSC 12 (Group risk systems and controls requirement) and LR) (as defined in section 421 of the *Act* (Group)) (in relation to a *person* ("A")) A and any *person* who is:
(2) a parent undertaking of A;
(3) a subsidiary undertaking of A;
(4) a subsidiary undertaking of a parent undertaking of A;
(5) a parent undertaking of a subsidiary undertaking of A;
(6) an undertaking in which A or an undertaking in (a) to (d) has a participating interest;
(7) if A or an undertaking in (a) or (d) is a building society, an associated undertaking of that building society;
(8) if A or an undertaking in (a) or (d) is an incorporated friendly society, a body corporate of which that friendly society has joint control (as defined in section 13(9)(c) or (cc) of the Friendly Societies Act 1992); in this definition:
  (i) "participating interest" has the same meaning as in
    (A) Part VII of the Companies Act 1985 or Part VIII of the Companies (Northern Ireland) Order 1986, where these provisions are applicable; or
    (B) paragraph 11(1) of Schedule 10 to the Large and Medium-sized Companies and Groups (Accounts and Reports) Regulations 2008 (SI 2008/410)) where applicable; or
    (C) paragraph 8 of Schedule 7 to the Small Companies and Groups (Accounts and Directors' Report) Regulations 2008 (SI 2008/409) where applicable; or
    (D) paragraph 8 of Schedule 4 to the Large and Medium-sized Limited Liability Partnerships (Accounts) Regulations 2008 (SI 2008/1913) where applicable; or
    (E) paragraph 8 of Schedule 5 to the Small Limited Liability Partnerships (Accounts) Regulations 2008 (SI 2008/1912) where applicable;

    In (A) to (E), the meaning also includes an interest held by an individual which would be a participating interest for the purposes of those provisions if he were an *undertaking*.
  (ii) "associated undertaking" has the meaning given in section 119(1) of the Building Societies Act 1986.
(9) in relation to an ICVC) a group as in (1) but (in SYSC) including also the ICVC's authorised corporate director (if any). (see also immediate group.)
(10) (for the purposes of SYSC 12 (Group risk systems and controls requirement) and GENPRU 1.2 (Adequacy of financial resources) and in relation to a *person* "A")) A and any *person*:
  (a) who falls into (1);
  (b) who is a member of the same *financial conglomerate* as A;
  (c) who has a *consolidation Article 12(1) relationship* with A;
  (d) who has a *consolidation Article 12(1) relationship* with any *person* in (3)(a);
  (e) who is a *subsidiary undertaking* of a person in (3)(c) or (3)(d); or
  (f) whose omission from an assessment of the risks to A of A's connection to any *person* coming within (3)(a)-(3)(e) or an assessment of the financial resources available to such *persons* would be misleading.
(11) (in *LR*):
  (a) (except in *LR* 6.1.19R and *LR* 8.7.8R(10)) an *issuer* and its *subsidiary undertakings* (if any); and
  (b) in *LR* 6.1.19R and *LR* 8.7.8R(10), as defined in section 421 of the *Act*.
(12) (in relation to a *common platform firm*) means the group of which that *firm* forms a part, consisting of a parent undertaking, its subsidiaries and the entities in which the parent undertaking or its subsidiaries hold a participation, as well as undertakings linked to each other by a relationship within the meaning of article 12(1) of Directive 83/349/EEC on consolidated accounts.

[Note: article 2(5) of the *MiFID implementing Directive*]

group capital resources

in relation to an *undertaking* in INSPRU 6.1.17R, that *undertaking's* group capital resources as calculated in accordance with INSPRU 6.1.36R.

group capital resources requirement

in relation to an *undertaking* in INSPRU 6.1.17R, that *undertaking's* group capital resources requirement as calculated in accordance with INSPRU 6.1.33R.

group ISA

an individual savings account of which the *plan manager* is the *authorised fund manager*, or in the same *group* as the *authorised fund manager*, of the *authorised fund* by reference to *units* in which the *plan register* is being, or is proposed to be, maintained.

group liquidity low frequency reporting conditions

(in relation to a *group liquidity reporting firm* and its *defined liquidity group*) the *defined liquidity group* meets the group liquidity low frequency reporting conditions if the *defined liquidity group* meets the following conditions:

(a) the *firm* or any other member is a *low frequency liquidity reporting firm*; and

(b) no member of that group is a *standard frequency liquidity reporting firm*.

For the purpose of deciding whether these conditions are met in relation to a *DLG by default*, any group member (other than the *group liquidity reporting firm* itself) that is a member of the group through no more than a *participation* is ignored.

group liquidity reporting firm

see the definitions of DLG by default, DLG by modification (firm level), and non-UK DLG by modification (DLG level).

(Guidance about this definition, and its inter-relation with other related definitions, is set out in SUP 16 Annex 26G (Guidance on designated liquidity groups in SUP 16.12).)

group liquidity standard frequency reporting conditions

(in relation to a *group liquidity reporting firm* and its *defined liquidity group*) the *defined liquidity group* meets the group liquidity standard frequency reporting conditions if the group does not meet the *group liquidity low frequency reporting conditions*.

group of closely related counterparties

(in *ELM*) a group of *persons* who fall within *ELM* 3.5.8R (Calculation of large exposure).

group of connected clients

(in accordance with Article 4(45) of the *Banking Consolidation Directive* (Definitions)) one of the following:

(a) two or more *persons* who, unless it is shown otherwise, constitute a single risk because one of them is the *parent undertaking*, direct or indirect, of the other or others; or

(b) two or more *persons* between whom there is no relationship as set out in (a) but who are to be regarded as constituting a single risk because they are so interconnected that, if one of them were to experience financial problems, the other or all of the others would be likely to encounter repayment difficulties.

group personal equity plan

[deleted]

group personal pension scheme

a *personal pension scheme* which is available to employees of the same employer or of employers within a *group*.

group plan

a *group ISA* or a *group savings plan*.

group policy

a *non-investment insurance contract* which a *person* enters into as legal holder of the *policy* on his own behalf and for other *persons* who are or will become *policyholders* and:

(a) those other *persons* are or become *policyholders* by virtue of a common employment, occupation or activity which has arisen independently of the *contract of insurance*;

(b) the common employment, occupation or activity is not brought about, in relation to the *contract of insurance*, by

   (i) the *insurance undertaking* which *effects* it or carries it out; or

   (ii) any activity which if carried on by a *firm* would be an *insurance mediation activity*; and

(c) the risks insured under the *policy* are related to the common employment, occupation or activity of the *policyholders*.

group savings plan

a savings plan:

(a) of which the *plan manager* is the *authorised fund manager*, or in the same *group* as the *authorised fund manager*, of the *authorised fund* by reference to *units* in which the *plan register* is being, or is proposed to be, maintained;

(b) under which *investments* are periodically acquired and held by a nominee for the absolute benefit of the respective subscribers to the savings plan; and

(c) under which all the *investments* are *units* in one or more *authorised funds* managed by (or, in the case of an *ICVC*, whose *ACD* is) the *plan manager*, or a *body corporate* in the same *group* as the *plan manager*.

guarantee

(1) (in LR) (in relation to *securitised derivatives*), either:
  (a) a guarantee given in accordance with LR 19.2.2R(3) (if any); or
  (b) any other guarantee of the issue of *securitised derivatives*.
(2) (in PR) (as defined in the *PD Regulation*) any arrangement intended to ensure that any obligation material to the issue will be duly serviced, whether in the form of guarantee, surety, keep well agreement, mono-line insurance policy or other equivalent commitment.

guarantee fund

  (a) subject to (1)(b), in relation to a *firm* carrying on *general insurance business*, the higher of one third of the *general insurance capital requirement* and the *base capital resources requirement* applicable to that *firm*;
  (b) where the *firm* is required to calculate a *UK MCR* or an *EEA MCR* under INSPRU 1.5, for the purposes of that section in (1)(a) the reference to the *general insurance capital requirement* is replaced by *UK MCR* or *EEA MCR*, as appropriate, and the reference to the *base capital resources requirement* is replaced by the amount which is one half of the *base capital resources requirement* applicable to the *firm* set out in GENPRU 2.1.30R.
(a) and the reference to the *base capital resources requirement* is replaced by the amount which is one half of the *base capital resources requirement* applicable to the *firm* set out in GENPRU 2.1.29R.
  (a) subject to (2)(b), in relation to a *firm* carrying on *long-term insurance business*, the higher of one third of the *long-term insurance capital requirement* and the *base capital resources requirement* applicable to that *firm*;
  (b) where the *firm* is required to calculate a *UK MCR* or an *EEA MCR* under PRU 7.6, for the purposes of that section in (2)(a) the reference to the *long-term insurance capital requirement* is replaced by *UK MCR* or *EEA MCR*, as appropriate, and the reference to the *base capital resources requirement* is replaced by the amount which is one half of the *base capital resources requirement* applicable to the *firm* set out in PRU 2.1.30R.

guarantor

(in PR) a *person* that provides a *guarantee*.

guidance

guidance given by the *FSA* under the *Act*.

habitual residence

(a) if the *policyholder* is an individual, the address given by the *policyholder* as his residence if it reasonably appears to be a residential address and there is no evidence to the contrary;
(b) if the *policyholder* is not an individual or a *group* of individuals, the State in which the *policyholder* has its place of establishment, or, if it has more than one, its relevant place of establishment;
(c) in respect of the variation of a *life policy*, or the purchase of a *pension annuity* related to a *life policy*, unless there is evidence to the contrary, the habitual residence of the *policyholder* at the date on which the *policyholder* signed the proposal for the *life policy*.

half-yearly accounting period

(in COLL) a period determined in accordance with COLL 6.8.2R(2) (Accounting periods).

Handbook

the *FSA's* Handbook of rules and guidance (for a table of contents, see the Reader's Guide).

hedging set

(in accordance with Part 1 of Annex III of the *Banking Consolidation Directive* (Definitions) and for the purpose of BIPRU 13 (The calculation of counterparty risk exposure values for financial derivatives, securities financing transactions and long settlement transactions)) a group of *risk positions* from the transactions within a single *netting set* for which only their balance is relevant for determining the *exposure* value under the *CCR standardised method*.

higher lending charge

a fee charged by a *mortgage lender* (under a *regulated mortgage contract*) where the amount borrowed exceeds a given percentage of the value of the property.

higher rate of return

(in *COBS*) the higher rate of return described in paragraph 2.3 of the projection *rules* (*COBS* 13 Annex 2).

higher stage of capital

(with respect to a particular item of capital in the *capital resources table*) a stage in the *capital resources table* above that in which that item of capital appears.

higher volatility fund

(a) a *regulated collective investment scheme* which is:
   (i) a *scheme* where the investment policies which the *operator* adopts, or proposes to adopt, mean that, as a result of making investments in *warrants* or *derivatives*, or through borrowing that is not temporary in nature, movements in the *price* of *units* are likely to be significantly amplified; or
   (ii) an *umbrella* with a *sub-fund* that would fall within (i) if that subfund were a separate *scheme*; or
(b) an *authorised fund dedicated* to *units* in:
   (i) a number of *regulated collective investment schemes*; or
   (ii) *sub-funds* of one or more *umbrellas* that are *regulated collective investment schemes*;
   any one of which falls within (a).

historic price

a *price* calculated by reference to the *valuation point* immediately preceding the *authorised fund manager's* agreement to *sell* or, as the case may be, to *redeem* the *units* in question.

HMRC allocated CTF

a *CTF* opened in accordance with regulation 6 of the *CTF Regulations*.

holder

(a) (in relation to a *unit* in an *authorised fund*):
   (i) the *shareholder*; or
   (ii) the *unitholder*;
(b) (in relation to a *unit* in any other *collective investment scheme*):
   (i) the *person* who is entered in the *register* of the *scheme* as the *holder* of that *unit*; or
   (ii) the bearer of a *bearer certificate* representing that *unit*.

holding company

(as defined in section 1159(1) of the Companies Act 2006 (Meaning of "subsidiary" etc)) (in relation to another *body corporate* ("S")) a *body corporate* which:
(a) holds a majority of the voting rights in S; or
(b) is a member of S and has the right to appoint or remove a majority of its board of directors; or
(c) is a member of S and controls alone, under an agreement with other shareholders and members, a majority of the voting rights in S.

Holloway sickness

a *policy* offered or effected by a *friendly society* under the Holloway *policy* system.

home finance activity

any *home finance mediation activity, home finance providing activity* or *administering a home finance transaction*.

home finance administration

any of the regulated activities of:
(a) *administering a regulated mortgage contract*;
(b) *administering a home purchase plan*;
(c) *administering a home reversion plan*;
(d) *agreeing to carry on a regulated activity* in (a) to (cc).

home finance administrator

a *firm* with *permission* (or which ought to have *permission*) for *administering a home finance transaction*.

home finance adviser

a *firm* with *permission* (or which ought to have *permission*) for *advising on a home finance transaction*.

home finance arranger

a *firm* with *permission* (or which ought to have *permission*) for *arranging a home finance transaction*.

home finance intermediary

a *firm* with *permission* (or which ought to have *permission*) to carry on a *home finance mediation activity*.

home finance mediation activity

any *mortgage mediation activity, home purchase mediation activity, reversion mediation activity* or *regulated sale and rent back mediation activity.*

home finance provider

a *firm* with *permission* (or which ought to have *permission*) for *entering into a home finance transaction.*

home finance providing activity

any of the *regulated activities* of:

(a) *entering into a regulated mortgage contract*;

(aa) *entering into a regulated sale and rent back agreement*;

(b) *entering into a home purchase plan*;

(c) *entering into a home reversion plan*; or

(d) *agreeing to carry on a regulated activity* in (a) to (c).

home finance transaction

a *regulated mortgage contract, home purchase plan, home reversion plan* or *regulated sale and rent back agreement.*

home financing

any *home finance providing activity.*

Home Member State

(in DTR; PR and LR) *Home State.*

home purchase activity

any of the *regulated activities* of:

(a) *arranging (bringing about) a home purchase plan* (article 25C(1));

(b) *making arrangements with a view to a home purchase plan* (article 25C(2));

(c) *advising on a home purchase plan* (article 53C);

(d) *entering into a home purchase plan* (article 63F(1));

(e) *administering a home purchase plan* (article 63F(2)); or

(f) *agreeing to carry on a regulated activity* in (a) to (e) (article 64).

home purchase administrator

a *firm* with *permission* (or which ought to have *permission*) for *administering a home purchase plan.*

home purchase adviser

a *firm* with *permission* (or which ought to have *permission*) for *advising on a home purchase plan.*

home purchase arranger

a *firm* with *permission* (or which ought to have *permission*) for *arranging* a *home purchase plan.*

home purchase intermediary

a *firm* with *permission* (or which ought to have *permission*) to carry on a *home purchase mediation activity.*

home purchase mediation activity

any of the following *regulated activities*:

(a) *arranging (bringing about) a home purchase plan* (article 25C(1));

(b) *making arrangements with a view to a home purchase plan* (article 25C(2));

(c) *advising on a home purchase plan* (article 53C); or

(d) *agreeing to carry on a regulated activity* in (a) to (c) (article 64).

home purchase plan

(in accordance with article 63F(3) of the *Regulated Activities Order*) an arrangement comprised in one or more instruments or agreements which meets the following conditions at the time it is entered into:

(a) the arrangement is one under which a *person* (the 'home purchase provider') buys a *qualifying interest in land* or an undivided share of a *qualifying interest in land*;

(b) where an undivided share of a *qualifying interest in land* is bought, the interest is held on trust for the home purchase provider and the individual or trustees in (c) as beneficial tenants in common;

(c) the arrangement provides for the obligation of an individual or trustees (the *home purchaser*) to buy the interest bought by the home purchase provider during the course of or at the end of a specified period; and

(d) the *home purchaser* (if he is an individual) or an individual who is a beneficiary of the trust (if the *home purchaser* is a trustee), or a related person, is entitled under the arrangement to occupy at least 40% of the land in question as or in connection with a dwelling during that period and intends to do so;

in this definition "related person" means:
(A) that *person's* spouse or civil partner;
(B) a *person* (whether or not of the opposite sex) whose relationship with that *person* has the characteristics of the relationship between husband and wife; or
(C) that *person's* parent, brother, sister, child, grandparent or grandchild.

home purchase provider

a *firm* with *permission* (or which ought to have *permission*) for *entering into a home purchase plan*.

home purchaser

the individual (or trustees), specified in article 63F(3) of the *Regulated Activities Order*, who in summary:
(a) is (or are) obliged under a *home purchase plan* to buy the interest in land bought by the home purchase provider (as defined in article 63F(3) of the *Regulated Activities Order*) over the course of or at the end of a specified period; and
  (i) in the case of an individual, is entitled under the arrangement to occupy at least 40% of the land in question as or in connection with a dwelling and intends to do so; or
  (ii) in the case of trustees, are trustees of a trust a beneficiary of which is an individual described in (i).

home reversion plan

(in accordance with article 63B(3) of the *Regulated Activities Order*) an arrangement comprised in one or more instruments or agreements which meets the following conditions at the time it is entered into:
(a) the arrangement is one under which a *person* (the *reversion provider*) buys all or part of a *qualifying interest in land* from an individual or trustees (the *reversion occupier*);
(b) the *reversion occupier* (if he is an individual) or an individual who is a beneficiary of the trust (if the *reversion occupier* is a trustee), or a related person, is entitled under the arrangement to occupy at least 40% of the land in question as or in connection with a dwelling and intends to do so; and
(c) the arrangement specifies that the entitlement to occupy will end on the occurrence of one or more of:
  (i) a *person* in (b) becoming a resident of a care home;
  (ii) a *person* in (b) dying; or
  (iii) the end of a specified period of at least twenty years from the date the *reversion occupier* entered into the arrangement;

in this definition "related person" means:
(A) that *person's* spouse or civil partner;
(B) a *person* (whether or not of the opposite sex) whose relationship with that *person* has the characteristics of the relationship between husband and wife; or
(C) that *person's* parent, brother, sister, child, grandparent or grandchild.

Home State

(1) (in relation to a *credit institution*) the *EEA State* in which the *credit institution* has been authorised in accordance with the *Banking Consolidation Directive*.
(2) (in relation to an *investment firm*):
  (a) if the *investment firm* is a natural *person*, the *EEA State* in which his head office is situated;
  (b) if the *investment firm* is a legal *person*, the *EEA State* in which its registered office is situated; or
  (c) if the *investment firm* has, under its national law, no registered office, the *EEA State* in which its head office is situated.
  [Note: article 4(1)(20) of *MiFID*]
(3) (in relation to a *UCITS management company*) the *EEA State* in which the *management company's* registered office is situated;
(4) (in relation to an *insurance undertaking* with an *EEA right*) the *EEA State* in which the registered office of the *insurance undertaking* is situated.
(5) (in relation to an *IMD insurance intermediary* or an *IMD reinsurance intermediary*):
  (a) where the *insurance intermediary* is a natural person, the *EEA State* in which his residence is situated and in which he carries on business;
  (b) where the *insurance intermediary* is a legal person, the *EEA State* in which its registered office is situated or, if under its national law it has no registered office, the *EEA State* in which its head office is situated.

(6) (except in *REC*) (in relation to a market) the *EEA State* in which the registered office of the body which provides trading facilities is situated or, if under its national law it has no registered office, the *EEA State* in which that body's head office is situated.

(7) (in relation to a *Treaty firm*) the *EEA State* in which its head office is situated, in accordance with paragraph 1 of Schedule 4 to the *Act* (Treaty Rights).

(8) (in LR and PR) (as defined in section 102C of the Act) in relation to an issuer of *transferable securities*, the *EEA State* which is the "home Member State" for the purposes of the *prospectus directive* (which is to be determined in accordance with Article 2.1(m) of that directive).

(9) (in *DTR*)

(a) in the case of an *issuer* of debt securities the denomination per unit of which is less than EUR 1 000 or an issuer of *shares*:

(i) where the *issuer* is incorporated in the *EEA*, the *EEA State* in which it has its registered office;

(ii) where the *issuer* is incorporated in a third country, the *EEA State* in which it is required to file the annual information with the competent authority in accordance with Article 10 of Directive 2003/71/EC.

The definition of *Home State* shall be applicable to debt securities in a currency other than Euro, provided that the value of such denomination per unit is, at the date of the issue, less than EUR 1 000, unless it is nearly equivalent to EUR 1 000;

(b) for an *issuer* not covered by (a), the *EEA State* chosen by the *issuer* from among the *EEA State* in which the *issuer* has its registered office and those *EEA States* which have admitted its securities to trading on a *regulated market* on their territory. The issuer may choose only one *EEA State* as its *Home Member State*. Its choice shall remain valid for at least three years unless its securities are no longer admitted to trading on any *regulated market* in the *EEA*;

Home State authorisation

(as defined in paragraph 3(1)(a) of Schedule 4 to the *Act* (Treaty Rights)) authorisation of a *firm* under the law of its *Home State* to carry on a *regulated activity*.

Home State regulator

(1) (in relation to an *EEA firm*) (as defined in paragraph 9 of Schedule 3 to the *Act* (EEA Passport Rights)) the *competent authority* (under the relevant *Single Market Directive*) of an *EEA State* (other than the *United Kingdom*) in relation to the *EEA firm* concerned.

(2) (in relation to a *UK firm*) the *FSA*.

(3) (in relation to a *Treaty firm*) (as defined in paragraph 1 of Schedule 4 to the *Act* (Treaty Rights)) the competent authority of the *firm's Home State* for the purpose of its *Home State authorisation.*

(4) (in *REC*) the competent authority (within the meaning of Article (4)(1)(22) of *MiFID*) of the *EEA State* which is the *Home State* in relation to the *EEA market operator* concerned.

home territory

(in relation to an *overseas investment exchange* or an *overseas clearing house*) the country or territory in which its head office is situated.

Host Member State

(in PR and LR) *Host State*.

Host State

(1) (in LR and PR) as defined in Article 2.1(n) of the *Prospectus Directive*) the *EEA State* where an *offer to the public* is made or *admission to trading* is sought, when different from the *Home State*.

(2) (except in LR and PR and except in relation to *MiFID*) the *EEA State* in which an *EEA firm*, a *UK firm*, or a *Treaty firm* is exercising an EEA right or *Treaty right* to establish a *branch* or provide *cross border services.*

Host State regulator

(1) (in relation to an EEA firm or a Treaty firm exercising an EEA right or Treaty right in the United Kingdom) the FSA.

(2) (in relation to a UK firm) (as defined in paragraph 11 of Schedule 3 to the Act (EEA Passport Rights)) the competent authority (under the relevant Single Market Directive) of an EEA State (other than the United Kingdom) in relation to a UK firm's exercise of EEA rights there.

(3) (in relation to *MiFID*) the *EEA State*, other than the *Home State*, in which an *investment firm* has a *branch* or performs *investment services and/or activities* or the *EEA State* in which a *regulated market* provides appropriate arrangements so as to facilitate access to trading on its system by remote members or participants established in that same *EEA State*.

[Note: article 4(1)(21) of *MiFID*]

IAS

(in LR) *International Accounting Standards*.

IBNR

(in relation to *claims* (as defined for the purposes of INSPRU, SUP and TC)) *claims* that have been incurred but not reported arising out of events that have occurred by the balance sheet date but have not been reported to the *insurance undertaking* at that date.

ICA

individual capital assessment.

ICAAP

the *internal capital adequacy assessment process*.

ICAAP rules

the *rules* in GENPRU 1.2.30R to GENPRU 1.2.39R (Systems, strategies, processes and reviews), GENPRU 1.2.42R (Main Requirements: Stress and scenario tests) and GENPRU 1.2.60R to GENPRU 1.2.61R (Documentation of risk assessments) as they apply on a solo level and on a consolidated level.

ICD

[deleted]

ICD claim

a *claim*:

(a) against a *MiFID investment firm* (including a *credit institution* which is a *MiFID investment firm*), whether established in the *United Kingdom* or in another *EEA State*; and

(b) in relation to:

   (i) any *investment services and activities* other than the making of a *personal recommendation*;

   (ii) the *ancillary service* of safekeeping and administration of *financial instruments* for the account of *clients*, including custodianship and related services such as cash/collateral management;

   (iii) the firm's inability to repay money owed to or belonging to investors and held on their behalf or the firm's inability to return to investors any instruments belonging to them and held, administered or managed on their behalf, in each case, in connection with the *investment service* of the making of a *personal recommendation* relating to a *financial instrument* in accordance with the legal and contractual conditions applicable.

[Note: Article 2(2) of the *Investor Compensation Directive*]

ICG

individual capital guidance.

ICOBS

the Insurance: New Conduct of Business sourcebook.

ICVC

investment company with variable capital.

IFA pensions review claim

a claim arising from the sale of a personal pension scheme by a former member of *PIA* which was an independent financial adviser;

in this definition:

(a) a "personal pension scheme" includes:

(b) a personal pension scheme that was approved under Chapter IV Part XIV of ICTA 88 (when that Chapter was in force);

(c) a 'section 32' buy-out policy that was approved under Section 32 of the Finance Act 1981 (when that was in force); and

(d) in relation to opt-outs and non-joiners, a retirement annuity contract that was approved under Chapter III Part XIV of ICTA 88 (when sections (9618 to 628 of that Chapter were in force); and

(e) "ICTA 88" means the Income and Corporation Taxes Act 1988.

IFRS

International Financial Reporting Standards

ILAA

Individual Liquidity Adequacy Assessment.

ILAS

Individual Liquidity Adequacy Standards.

ILAS BIPRU firm

a firm falling into BIPRU 12.1.1R, but excluding a firm that is:
(a) an *exempt full scope BIPRU investment firm*; or
(b) a *BIPRU limited licence firm*; or
(c) a *BIPRU limited activity firm*; or
(d) an *exempt BIPRU commodities firm*.

illiquid asset

has the meaning in GENPRU 2.2.260R (Deductions from total capital: Illiquid assets).

illustration

(in *MCOB*) the illustration of the costs and features of a *regulated mortgage contract* or *home reversion plan* which is required to be provided by *MCOB* 5 (Pre-application disclosure), *MCOB* 6 (Disclosure at the offer stage), *MCOB* 7 (Disclosure at start of contract and after sale) and *MCOB* 9 (Equity release: product disclosure) and the template for which is set out:
(a) for a *regulated mortgage contract* other than a *lifetime mortgage*, at *MCOB* 5 Annex 1;
(b) for a *lifetime mortgage*, at *MCOB* 9 Annex 1; and
(c) for a *home reversion plan*, at *MCOB* 9 Annex 2.

ILSA

Individual Liquidity Systems Assessment.

IMA SORP

the Statement of Recommended Practice for financial statements of *authorised funds* issued by the Investment Management Association and effective as at 1 January 2006.

image advertising

a communication that consists only of one or more of the following:
(a) the name of the *firm*;
(b) a logo or other image associated with the *firm*;
(c) a contact point; and
(d) a reference to the types of *regulated activities* provided by the *firm*, or to its fees or commissions.

IMD

[deleted]

IMD insurance intermediary

(as defined in article 2(5) of the *IMD*) any natural or legal person who, for remuneration, takes up or pursues *insurance mediation.*

IMD insurance undertaking

(as defined in article 2(1) of the *IMD*) an undertaking which has received official authorisation in accordance with article 6of the *Consolidated Life Directive* or article 6 of the *First Non-Life Directive*.

IMD minimum implementation provisions

[deleted]

IMD reinsurance intermediary

(as defined in article 2(6) of the *IMD*) any natural or legal person who, for remuneration, takes up or pursues *reinsurance mediation.*

IMD reinsurance undertaking

(as defined in article 2(2) of the *IMD*) an undertaking, other than an *IMD insurance undertaking* or a non-member-country *insurance undertaking*, the main business of which consists in accepting risks ceded by an *IMD insurance undertaking*, a non-member country *insurance undertaking* or other *IMD reinsurance undertaking.*

immediate group

(1) (in relation to an *authorised person*) (as defined in section 148(11) of the *Act* (Modification or waiver of rules)):
 (a) the authorised person;

Part II FSA Handbook Materials

(b) a parent undertaking of the authorised person;
(c) a subsidiary undertaking of the authorised person;
(d) a subsidiary undertaking of a parent undertaking of the authorised person;
(e) a parent undertaking of a subsidiary undertaking of the authorised person.
(2) (in *ELM7* and BIPRU and in relation to any *person*) has the same meaning as in paragraph (1), with the omission of (1)(e).

implicit items

(in relation to *long-term insurance business*) economic reserves arising in respect of future profits, *zillmerising* or hidden reserves as more fully described in GENPRU 2 Ann 8G.

IMRO

the Investment Management Regulatory Organisation Limited.

IMRO scheme

the *former scheme* set up by *IMRO* under the Financial Services Act 1986 and the *Investment Ombudsman* Memorandum to handle complaints against members of *IMRO*.

in default

the status of being in default following a determination made under *COMP* 6.3.1R.

in the money

(1) (in LR) (in relation to *securitised derivatives*):
(a) where the holder has the right to buy the *underlying instrument* or *instruments* from the *issuer*, when the *settlement price* is greater than the *exercise price*; or
(b) where the holder has the right to sell the *underlying instrument* or *instruments* to the *issuer*, when the *exercise price* is greater than the *settlement price*.
(2) (for the purposes of BIPRU 7 (Market risk) and in relation to an *option* or *warrant*) the strike price of that *option* or *warrant* being less than the current market value of the underlying instrument (in the case of a call *option* or *warrant*) or vice versa (for a put *option*).

in the money percentage

(for the purposes of BIPRU 7 (Market risk) and in relation to an *option* or *warrant*) the percentage calculated under BIPRU 7.6.6R (The in the money percentage).

inception

in relation to *permitted links*, refers to the time when the liability of the *insurer* under a *linked long-term* contract of insurance commenced.

income account

(in COLL) an account relating to the *income property* of an *authorised fund*.

income equalisation

(in relation to a *scheme*) a capital sum which, in accordance with a power contained in the *instrument constituting the scheme*, is included in an allocation of income for a *unit* issued or sold during the accounting period in respect of which that income allocation is made.

income property

all sums considered by an *ICVC* or by a *manager*, after consultation with the auditor, to be in the nature of income received or receivable for the account of an *authorised fund*. Income property includes income from *debt securities* calculated on a *coupon* basis or an effective yield basis if, in either case, the *coupon* figure is at least equal to the effective yield figure, but it does not include any amount for the time being standing to the credit of the *distribution account*.

income unit

a *unit* in an *AUT* which is not an *accumulation unit*.

income withdrawals

(a) (as defined in paragraph 7 of Schedule 28 to the Finance Act 2004) in relation to a member of a pension scheme:
(i) if the member has not reached the age of 75, amounts (other than the payment of annuity) which the member is entitled to be paid from the member's unsecured pension fund (as defined in paragraph 8 of that Schedule) in respect of an arrangement;
(ii) if the member has reached the age of 75, amounts which the member is entitled to be paid from the member's alternatively secured pension fund (as defined in paragraph 11 of that Schedule) in respect of an arrangement; o
(b) payments made under interim arrangements in accordance with section 28A of the Pension Schemes Act 1993;

in respect of an election to make income withdrawals, a reference to a *private customer*, an investor or a *policyholder* includes, after that *person's* death, his surviving spouse, his surviving civil partner or anyone who is, at that time, his dependant, or both.

incoming EEA firm

(in accordance with section 193(1)(a) of the *Act* (Interpretation of this Part)) an *EEA firm* which is exercising, or has exercised, its right to carry on a *regulated activity* in the *United Kingdom* in accordance with Schedule 3 to the *Act* (EEA Passport Rights).

incoming ECA provider

a *person*, other than an *exempt person* or a *person* who has been given a waiver in accordance with article 8(1) of the *E-Money Directive*, who:

(a) provides an *electronic commerce activity*, from an *establishment* in an *EEA State* other than the *United Kingdom*, with or for an *ECA recipient* present in the *United Kingdom;* and
(b) is a national of an *EEA State* or a company or firm mentioned in article 54 of the *Treaty.*

incoming electronic commerce activity

(in accordance with regulation 2(1) of the *ECD Regulations*) an activity:

(a) which consists of the provision of an *information society service* from an *establishment* in an *EEA State* other than the *United Kingdom* to a *person* or *persons* in the *United Kingdom*; and
(b) which would, but for article 72A of the *Regulated Activities Order* (Information society services) (and irrespective of the effect of article 72 of that Order (Overseas Persons)), be a *regulated activity.*

incoming electronic commerce communication

[deleted]

incoming firm

(in accordance with section 193(1) of the *Act* (Interpretation of this Part)) an *incoming EEA firm* or an *incoming Treaty firm.*

incoming Treaty firm

(in accordance with section 193(1)(b) of the *Act* (Interpretation of this Part)) a *Treaty firm* which is exercising, or has exercised, its right to carry on a *regulated activity* in the *United Kingdom* in accordance with Schedule 4 to the *Act* (Treaty rights).

incorporated friendly society

a society incorporated under the Friendly Societies Act 1992.

incremental default risk charge

(in BIPRU 7.10 (Use of a value at risk model)) has the meaning in BIPRU 7.10.116R (Capital calculations for *VaR models*), which is in summary, in relation to a *business day*, the incremental default risk charge required under the provisions in BIPRU 7.10 about *specific risk*, in respect of the previous *business day's* close-of-business *positions* with respect to which those provisions apply.

independent expert

(in *SUP* 18) the person approved or nominated by the *FSA* to make the *scheme report* for an *insurance business transfer scheme*.

Independent Investigator

the *former Ombudsman* under the *FSA scheme.*

index-linked assets

in relation to *permitted links*, the assets held by an *insurer* for the purposes of matching *index-linked liabilities.*

index-linked benefits

benefits:

(a) provided for under a *linked long-term contract of insurance*; and
(b) determined by reference to an index of the value of property of any description (whether specified in the contract or not).

index-linked contract

a *linked long-term* contract conferring *index-linked benefits.*

index-linked liabilities

insurance liabilities in respect of *index-linked benefits.*

individual capital assessment

(in INSPRU and COBS 20.2) an assessment by a *firm* of the adequacy of its capital resources undertaken as part of an assessment of the adequacy of the *firm's* overall financial resources carried out in accordance with GENPRU 1.2.

individual capital guidance

guidance given to a *firm* about the amount and quality of capital resources that the *FSA* thinks the *firm* should hold under the *overall financial adequacy rule* as it applies on a solo level or a consolidated level.

individual capital resources requirement

has the meaning in INSPRU 6.1.34R.

individual counterparty CNCOM

has the meaning in BIPRU 10.5.20R (How to calculate the concentration risk capital component), which is in summary the sum of a *firm's individual CNCOMs* with respect to a *counterparty* or *group of connected clients* or to its *connected counterparties*.

individual CNCOM

the amount calculated with respect to an individual *exposure* under BIPRU 10.5.20R (How to calculated the concentration risk capital component).

Individual Liquidity Adequacy Assessment

a *standard ILAS BIPRU firm's* assessment of the adequacy of its liquidity resources and systems and controls as required by the *rules* in BIPRU 12.5.

Individual Liquidity Adequacy Standards

the regime of liquidity assessment set out in the *rules* and *guidance* in BIPRU 12.5.

individual liquidity guidance

guidance given to a *firm* about the amount, quality and funding profile of liquidity resources that the FSA has asked the firm to maintain.

Individual Liquidity Systems Assessment

a *simplified ILAS BIPRU firm's* assessment of the adequacy of its systems and controls as required by the rules in BIPRU 12.6.

***individual* member**

a *member*, or *former member*, who is a natural *person*.

individual pension account

an account for the holding of *IPA eligible investments*, which satisfies the conditions described in regulation 2(2) of the Stamp Duty and Stamp Duty Reserve Tax (Definition of Unit Trust Scheme and Open-ended Investment Company) Regulations 2001 (SI 2001/964).

individual pension contract

a *pension policy* or *pension contract* under which contributions are paid to:
(a) a *personal pension scheme*; or
(b) a retirement benefits scheme for the provision of relevant benefits by means of an annuity contract made with an insurance company of the employee's choice where that contract:
   (i) was approved under section 591(2)(g) of the Income and Corporation Taxes Act 1988 (when that section was in force); or
   (ii) is a registered pension scheme under Chapter 2 of Part 4 of the Finance Act 2004.

individual savings account

an account which is a scheme of investment satisfying the conditions prescribed in the *ISA Regulations.*

industrial and provident society

a society registered or deemed to be registered under the Industrial and. Provident Societies Act 1965 or the Industrial and Provident Societies Act (Northern Ireland) 1969.

industrial assurance policy

a *contract of insurance* on human life, premiums in respect of which are received by means of collectors, but excluding:
(a) a *contract of insurance*, the premiums in respect of which are payable at intervals of two *months* or more;
(b) a *contract of insurance*, effected whether before or after the passing of the Industrial Assurance Act 1923 by a society or company established before the date of the passing of that Act which at that date had no *contracts of insurance* outstanding the premiums on which were payable at intervals of less than one *month* so long as the society or company continues not to effect any such contracts;
(c) a *contract of insurance* effected before the passing of the Industrial Assurance Act 1923, premiums in respect of which are payable at intervals of one *month* or more, and which have up to the passing of that Act been treated as part of the business transacted by a branch other than the industrial branch of the society or company; and

(d) a *contract of insurance* for £25 or more effected after the passing of the Industrial Assurance Act 1923, premiums in respect of which are payable at intervals of one *month* or more, and which are treated as part of the business transacted by a branch other than the industrial branch of the society or company, in cases where the relevant authority certified prior to 1 December 2001 under section 1(2)(d) of that Act that the terms and conditions of the contract is on the whole not less favourable to the assured than those imposed by that Act;

in this definition:
(i) "collector" includes every *person*, however remunerated, who, by himself or by any deputy or substitute, makes house to house visits for the purpose of receiving premiums payable on policies of insurance on human life, or holds any interest in a collecting book, and includes such a deputy or substitute;
(ii) "collecting book" includes any book or document held by a collector in which payments of premiums are recorded.

industry block

(in *DISP*) a grouping of *firms* by common business activity for the purposes of calculating the *general levy*.

information centre

a centre established by an *EEA State* to meet its obligations under article 5 of the *Fourth Motor Insurance Directive* (Information Centres).

information society service

an information society service, as defined by article 2(a) of the *ECommerce Directive* and article 1(2) of the Technical Standards and Regulations Directive (98/34/EC), which is in summary any service normally provided for remuneration, at a distance, by means of electronic equipment for the processing (including the digital compression) and storage of data at the individual request of a service recipient.

inherited estate

an amount representing the fair market value of the *with-profits assets* less the *realistic value of liabilities* of a *with-profits fund*.

initial capital

(1) (in *ELM*) items coming into stage A of the calculation in ELM 2.4.2R (Calculation of initial capital and own funds).
(2) [Deleted]
(3) (in UPRU) capital calculated in accordance with UPRU Table 2.2.1R (Method of calculation of financial resources) composed of the specified items set out in that Table.
(4) (in the case of a *BIPRU firm*) *capital resources* included in stage A (Core tier one capital) of the *capital resources table* plus *capital resources* included in stage B of the *capital resources table* (Perpetual noncumulative preference shares);
(5) (in the case of an *institution* that is an *EEA firm*) capital resources calculated in accordance with the *CRD implementation measures* of its *Home State* for Article 4 of the *Capital Adequacy Directive* (Definition of initial capital) or Article 9 of the *Banking Consolidation Directive* (Initial capital requirements);
(6) (for the purposes of the definition of *dealing on own account* and in the case of an *undertaking* not falling within (3) or (4)) *capital resources* calculated in accordance with (3) and paragraphs (3) and (4) of the definition of *capital resources*; and
(7) (in IPRU(INV) 13) the initial capital of a firm calculated in accordance with IPRU(INV) 13.1A.6 R.

initial commitment

(for the purposes of *BIPRU* and in relation to *underwriting*) the date specified in BIPRU 7.8.13R (Time of initial commitment).

initial coupon rate

(in relation to a *tier one instrument*) the *coupon* rate of the instrument at the time it is issued.

initial disclosure document

information about the *scope of advice* and nature of the services offered by a *firm* in relation to:
(a) a *regulated mortgage contract* other than a *lifetime mortgage* as required by MCOB 4.4.1R(1) and set out in MCOB 4 Annex 1;
(b) an *equity release transaction* as required by MCOB 4.4.1R(1) and set out in MCOB 8 Annex 1;
(c) a *home purchase plan* as required by MCOB 4.10.2R and set out in MCOB 4 Annex 1; or
(d) a *non-investment insurance contract* in accordance with ICOBS 4.5.1G and set out in ICOBS 4 Annex 1G.

initial fund

the items of capital which are available to a *mutual* at *authorisation*.

initial margin

[deleted]

initial offer

(in COLL) an *offer* for *sale* of *units* in an *authorised fund* or in a *sub-fund* (otherwise than in accordance with arrangements of the type described in COLL 5.5.9R(3)(b)(iii) (Guarantees and indemnities), where all or part of the consideration paid for the account of the *authorised fund* for the *units* is to be used to acquire the initial *scheme property* of the *authorised fund* or the initial *scheme property* attributable to the *sub-fund*.

initial outlay

(in relation to an *authorised fund*) the amount which the *authorised fund* is required to provide in order to obtain rights under a transaction in *derivatives*, excluding any payment or transfer on exercise of rights.

initial price

(in COLL):

in relation to a *unit* of any *class*:

(a) in a *single-priced authorised fund*, the *price* to be paid; or

(b) in a *dual-priced authorised fund*, the amount agreed by the *depositary* and *authroised fund manager* as being the maximum *price*, inclusive of any *preliminary charge* that may be paid to the *authorised fund manager*;

during the period of the *initial offer* under COLL 6.2.3R (Initial offer).

injunction

a court order made by the High Court that prohibits a *person* from doing or continuing to do a certain act or requires a *person* to carry out a certain act.

injured party

(in ICOBS)

a resident of the *EEA* entitled to compensation in respect of any loss or injury caused by *vehicles*.

[**Note:** article 1(2) of Directive 72/166/EC (First Motor Insurance Directive)]

innovative tier one capital

an item of capital that is stated in GENPRU 2.2 (Capital resources) to be innovative tier one capital.

innovative tier one capital resources

the amount of *capital resources* at stage C of the *capital resources table* (Innovative tier one capital).

innovative tier one instrument

a *potential tier one instrument* that is stated in GENPRU 2.2 (Capital resources) to be an innovative instrument.

inside information

(1) (except in DR) (as defined in section 118C of the *Act*):

(2) (in DR) *inside information* in (1) but replacing references to *qualifying investments* with references to *financial instruments*.

(1) in relation to *qualifying investments*, or *related investments*, which are not commodity derivatives, *inside information* is information of a precise nature which:

(2) is not generally available,

(3) relates, directly or indirectly, to one or more issuers of the *qualifying investments* or to one or more of the *qualifying investments*, and

(4) would, if generally available, be likely to have a significant effect on the price of the *qualifying investments* or on the price of *related investments*.

(5) in relation to *qualifying investments*, or *related investments*, which are commodity derivatives, *inside information* is information of a precise nature which:

(6) is not generally available,

(7) relates, directly or indirectly, to one or more such derivatives, and

(8) users of markets in which the derivatives are traded would expect to receive in accordance with *accepted market practices* on those markets.

(9) in relation to a person charged with the execution of orders concerning any *qualifying investments* or *related investments*, *inside information* includes information conveyed by a client and related to the client's pending orders which:

(10) is of a precise nature;
(11) is not generally available;
(12) relates, directly or indirectly, to one or more issuers of *qualifying investments* or to one or more *qualifying investments*; and
(13) would, if generally available, be likely to have a significant effect on the price of those *qualifying investments* or the price of *related investments*;
(14) information is precise if it:
(15) indicates circumstances that exist or may reasonably be expected to come into existence or an event that has occurred or may reasonably be expected to occur; and
(16) is specific enough to enable a conclusion to be drawn as to the possible effect of those circumstances or that event on the price of *qualifying investments or related investments*;
(17) information would be likely to have a significant effect on price if and only if it is infomration of that kind which a reasonable investor would be likely to use as part of the basis of his investment decisions;
(18) for the purposes of (2)(c), users of markets on which investments in commodity derivatives are traded are to be treated as expecting to receive information relating directly or indirectly to one or more such derivatives in accordances with any *accepted market practices*, which is:
(19) routinely made available to the users of those markets; or
(20) required to be disclosed in accordance with any statutory provision, market rules, or contracts or customs on the relevant underlying commodity market or commodity derivatives market;
(21) information which can be obtained by research or analysis conducted by, or on behalf of, users of a market is to be regarded, for the purposes of *market abuse*, as being generally available to them.

insider

(as defined in section 118B of the *Act*) a *person* who has *inside information*:
(a) as a result of his membership of the administrative, management or supervisory bodies of an *issuer* of *qualifying investments*;
(b) as a result of his holding in the capital of an *issuer* of *qualifying investments*;
(c) as a result of having access to the information through the exercise of his employment, profession or duties;
(d) as a result of his criminal activities; or
(e) which he has obtained by other means and which he knows, or could reasonably be expected to know, is *inside information*.

insider dealing

the activity described in section 52 of the Criminal Justice Act 1993, which is in summary:
(a) the offence of which an individual is guilty if he has information as an insider and:
  (i) in the circumstances described in (b), he deals in securities that are price-affected securities in relation to the information;
    (A) he encourages another *person* to deal in securities that are (whether or not that other knows it) price-affected securities in relation to the information, knowing or having reasonable cause to believe that the dealing would take place in the circumstances mentioned in (b); or
    (B) he discloses the information, otherwise than in the proper performance of the functions of his employment, office or profession, to another *person;*
(b) the circumstances referred to in (a) are that the acquisition or disposal in question occurs on a regulated market (identified in an Order made by the Treasury), or that the *person* dealing relies on a professional intermediary or is himself acting as a professional intermediary.

insider list

a list, as required by DR 2.8.1R, of *persons* with access to *inside information*.

insolvency order

an administration order, compulsory winding up order, bankruptcy order, or sequestration order.

INSPRU

the Prudential sourcebook for Insurers

instalment reversion plan

a *home reversion plan* under which more than one payment is made to the *customer* during the life of the plan.

institution

(in accordance with Article 3(1)(c) of the *Capital Adequacy Directive* and Article 4(6) of the *Banking Consolidation Directive* (Definitions) and for the purposes of GENPRU and BIPRU) a *credit institution* or a *CAD investment firm*, whether or not it is incorporated in, or has its head office in, an *EEA State*.

institutional linked policyholders

in relation to *permitted links*, *linked policyholders* who are trustees of a *defined benefit occupational pension scheme*.

Instrument constituting the scheme

(a) (in relation to an ICVC) the instrument of incorporation;
(b) (in relation to an AUT) the trust deed;
(c) (in relation to a collective investment scheme other than an authorised fund) any instrument to which the operator is a party setting out any arrangements with any other person relating to any aspect of the operation or management of the scheme.

instrument of incorporation

the instrument of incorporation of an *ICVC* (as from time to time amended) initially provided to the *FSA* in accordance with regulation 14(1)(c) of the *OEIC regulations*.

insurance accounts rules

Schedule 9A to the Companies Act 1985 (Form and content of accounts of insurance companies) and Schedule 9A to the Companies Act (Northern Ireland) Order 1986 where these provisions are applicable, otherwise Schedule 3 to the Large and Medium-sized Companies and Groups (Accounts and Reports) Regulations 2008 (SI 2008/410).

insurance business

the business of *effecting* or *carrying out contracts of insurance*.

insurance business grouping

a grouping comprising descriptions of *general insurance business* determined in accordance with INSPRU 1.4.12R.

insurance business transfer

a transfer in accordance with an *insurance business transfer scheme*.

insurance business transfer scheme

(a) a scheme, defined in section 105 of the *Act*, which is in summary: a scheme to transfer the whole or part of the business of an *insurer* (other than a *friendly society*) to another body;
(b) a similar scheme to transfer the whole or part of the business carried on by one or more *members* of the *Society* or *former underwriting members* that meets the conditions of article 4 of the Financial Services and Markets Act 2000 (Control of Transfers of Business Done at Lloyd's) Order 2001 (SI 2001/3626).

insurance client money chapter

CASS 5.

insurance component

a *qualifying investment* prescribed in regulation 9 of the *ISA Regulations*.

insurance conglomerate

a *financial conglomerate* that is identified in paragraph 4.3 of GENPRU 3 Ann 1R (Types of financial conglomerate) as an insurance conglomerate.

insurance death risk capital component

one of the components of the *long-term insurance capital requirement* as set out in INSPRU 1.1.81R to INSPRU 1.1.83R.

Insurance Directives

the *Consolidated Life Directive* and the *First Non-Life Directive, Second Non-Life Directive* and *Third Non-Life Directive*.

insurance expense risk capital component

one of the components of the *long-term insurance capital requirement* as set out in INSPRU 1.1.88R.

insurance group

(1) an *insurance parent undertaking* and its *related undertakings*; or
(2) a *participating insurance undertaking* (not within (1)) and its *related undertakings*.

Insurance Groups Directive

Directive of the European Parliament and of the Council of 27 October 1998 on the supplementary supervision of insurance undertakings in an insurance group (1998/78/EC).

insurance health risk and life protection reinsurance capital component

one of the components of the *long-term insurance capital requirement* as set out in INSPRU 1.1.85R and INSPRU 1.1.86R.

insurance holding company

(1) a *parent undertaking*, other than an *insurance undertaking*, the main business of which is to acquire and hold participations in *subsidiary undertakings* and which fulfils the following conditions:
   (a) its *subsidiary undertakings* are either exclusively or mainly *insurance undertakings*; and
   (b) at least one of those *subsidiary undertakings* is an *insurer* or an *EEA firm* that is a *regulated insurance entity* or a *reinsurance undertaking*;
   a *parent undertaking*, other than an *insurance undertaking*, that fulfils the conditions in paragraphs (1)(a) and (b) of this definition is not an *insurance holding company* if:
   (c) it is a *mixed financial holding company*; and
   (d) notice has been given in accordance with Article 4(2) of the *Financial Groups Directive* that the *financial conglomerate* of which it is a *mixed financial holding company* is a *financial conglomerate*.

(2) For the purposes of:
   (a) the definition of the *insurance sector*;
   (b) *ELM*; and
   (c) the definition of *material insurance holding*;
   paragraph (1)(b) of this definition does not apply.

insurance intermediary

a *firm* carrying on *insurance mediation activity other than an insurer.*

Insurance Intermediaries Order

the Financial Services and Markets Act 2000 (Regulated Activities) (Amendment) (No 2) (Insurance Intermediaries) Order 2003 (SI 2003/1476).

insurance market activity

means a *regulated activity* relating to *contracts of insurance* written at Lloyd's.

insurance market direction

a direction made by the FSA under section 316(1) of the Act (Direction by Authority).

insurance market risk capital component

one of the components of the *long-term insurance capital requirement* as set out in INSPRU 1.1.89R.

insurance mediation

(as defined in article 2(3) of the *IMD*) the activities of introducing, proposing or carrying out other work preparatory to the conclusion of contracts of insurance, or of concluding such contracts, or of assisting in the administration and performance of such contracts, in particular in the event of a claim. These activities when undertaken by an *IMD insurance undertaking* or an employee of an *IMD insurance undertaking* who is acting under the responsibility of the *IMD insurance undertaking* shall not be considered as *insurance mediation*. The provision of information on an incidental basis in the context of another professional activity provided that the purpose of that activity is not to assist the customer in concluding or performing an insurance contract, the management of claims of an *IMD insurance undertaking* on a professional basis, and loss adjusting and expert appraisal of claims shall also not be considered as *insurance mediation*.

insurance mediation activity

any of the following *regulated activities* carried on in relation to a *contract of insurance* or *rights to or interests in a life policy*:

(a) *dealing in investments as agent* (article 21);
(b) *arranging (bringing about) deals in investments* (article 25(1));
(c) *making arrangements with a view to transactions in investments* (article 25(2));
(d) *assisting in the administration and performance of a contract of insurance* (article 39A);
(e) *advising on investments* (article 53);
(f) *agreeing to carry on a regulated activity* in (a) to (e) (article 64).

Insurance Mediation Directive

the European Parliament and Council Directive of 9 December 2002 on insurance mediation (No 2002/92/EC).

Insurance Ombudsman scheme

the former scheme set up, on a voluntary basis, to handle complaints against those insurance companies which subscribed to it.

insurance parent undertaking

a *parent undertaking* which is:
(a) a *participating insurance undertaking* which has a *subsidiary undertaking* that is an *insurance undertaking*; or
(b) an *insurance holding company* which has a *subsidiary undertaking* which is an *insurer*; or
(c) an *insurance undertaking* (not within (a)) which has a *subsidiary undertaking* which is an *insurer*.

insurance-related capital requirement

a component of the calculation of the *ECR* for a *firm* carrying on *general insurance business* as set out in INSPRU 1.1.76R to INSPRU 1.1.79R.

insurance sector

a sector composed of one or more of the following entities:
(a) an *insurance undertaking*;
(b) an *insurance holding company*; and
(c) (in the circumstances described in GENPRU 3.1.39R (The financial sectors: Asset management companies)) an *asset management company*.

insurance special purpose vehicle

an *undertaking*, other than an *insurance undertaking* or *reinsurance undertaking* which has received an official authorisation in accordance with article 6 of the *First Non-Life Directive*, article 4 of the *Consolidated Life Directive* or article 3 of the *Reinsurance Directive*:
(a) which assumes risks from such *insurance undertakings* or *reinsurance undertakings*; and
(b) which fully funds its exposures to such risks through the proceeds of a debt issuance or some other financing mechanism where the repayment rights of the providers of such debt or other financing mechanism are subordinated to the *undertaking's reinsurance* obligations.

insurance undertaking

(1) (except in *COBS*) an undertaking, or (in CASS 5 and *COMP*) a *member*, whether or not an *insurer*, which carries on *insurance business*.
(2) (in *COBS*) an undertaking or a *member* which carries on *insurance business*.

insurer

a *firm* with *permission* to *effect* or *carry out contracts of insurance* (other than a *UK ISPV*).

intended retirement date

[deleted]

inter-professional business

the business of a *firm*:
(a) when it carries on:
  (i) *regulated activities*; or
  (ii) related *ancillary activities*;
  to the extent that the *regulated activity* that the *firm* is carrying on is:
    (A) dealing in investments as principal; or
    (B) dealing in investments as agent; or
    (C) acting as an arranger; or
    (D) giving transaction-specific advice or agreeing to do so;
  but only if that activity is:
    (I) in or in respect of an *inter-professional investment;*
    (II) undertaken with or for a *market counterparty*; and
    (III) carried on from an establishment maintained by the *firm* in the *United Kingdom;*
(b) but excluding the carrying on of the following activities:
  (i) the *approval* by a *firm* of a *financial promotion*;
  (ii) activities carried on between *operators*, or between *operators* and *depositaries*, of the same *collective investment scheme* (when acting in that capacity);
  (iii) *corporate finance business*;
  (iv) *safeguarding and administering investments* and *agreeing to carry on that regulated activity*;
  (v) concluding a *distance contract* with a *retail customer*;
  (vi) activities relating to *life policies*;

in this definition, the exclusion in article 15 of the *Regulated Activities Order* (Absence of holding out etc) is to be disregarded in determining whether *dealing in investments as principal* or *agreeing* to do so) is a *regulated activity*.

inter-professional investment

any of the following *investments* specified in Part III of the *Regulated Activities Order* (Specified investments) or, in the case of *units* in an *exchange traded fund*, defined in the *Glossary*:
(a) *share* (article 76);
(b) *debenture* (article 77);
(c) *government and public security* (article 78);
(d) *warrant* (article 79);
(e) *certificate representing certain securities* (article 80);
(f) *option* (article 83); for the purposes of the *permission* regime, this is sub-divided into:
 (i) *option* (excluding a *commodity option* and an *option* on a *commodity future*);
 (ii) *commodity option* and option on a commodity future;
(g) *future* (article 84); for the purposes of the *permission* regime, this is sub-divided into:
 (i) *future* (excluding a *commodity future* and a *rolling spot forex contract*);
 (ii) *commodity future;*
 (iii) *rolling spot forex contract;*
(h) *contract for differences* (article 85); for the purposes of the *permission regime*, this is sub-divided into:
 (i) *contract for differences* (excluding a *spread bet* and a *rolling spot forex contract*);
 (ii) *spread bet;*
 (iii) *rolling spot forex contract;*
(i) *rights to or interests in investments* in (a) to (h) (article 89).
(j) *units* in an *exchange traded fund.*

inter-syndicate reinsurance

reinsurance between one *syndicate year* and another, not being *reinsurance to close.*

interdict

a Scottish court order made by the Court of Session that prohibits a *person* from doing or continuing to do a certain act or requires a *person* to carry out a certain act.

interest-only mortgage

a *regulated mortgage contract* other than a *repayment mortgage.*

interest rate duration method

the method of calculating the part of the *interest rate PRR* that relates to *general market risk* set out in BIPRU 7.2.63R (General market risk calculation: Duration method).

interest rate maturity method

the method of calculating the part of the *interest rate PRR* that relates to *general market risk* set out in BIPRU 7.2.59R (General market risk calculation: The maturity method).

interest rate PRR

the part of the *market risk capital requirement* calculated in accordance with BIPRU 7.2 (Interest rate PRR) or BIPRU 7.3.45R (Basic interest rate PRR for equity derivatives) or, in relation to a particular *position*, the portion of the overall *interest rate PRR* attributable to that *position.*

interest rate simplified maturity method

the method of calculating the part of the *interest rate PRR* that relates to *general market risk* set out in BIPRU 7.2.56R (General market risk calculation: Simplified maturity method).

interested party

(in relation to an application made under section 60 of the *Act* (Applications for approval)):
(a) the *firm* making the application;
(b) the *person* in respect of whom the application is being made ("A"); and
(c) the *person* by whom A's services are to be retained, if not the *firm* making the application.

interim accounting period

(in COLL) a period within an *annual accounting period* in respect of which an allocation of income is to be made.

interim income allocation date

any date specified in the *prospectus* of an *authorised fund* as the date on or before which an allocation of income will be made.

interim RSRB permission

(in *SYSC* and *FEES*) a *Part IV permission* to carry on one or more *regulated sale and rent back activities* deemed to have been granted by article 32 (Interim permission and interim variation of permission) of the Financial Services and Markets Act 2000 (Regulated Activities) (Amendment)

Order 2009 (SI 2009/1342) to a *person* because he has submitted an application for interim permission or an interim variation of permission in accordance with article 32(1) of the Order and such permission has been given by the *FSA*.

intermediaries offer

(1) (in LR) a marketing of *securities* already or not yet in issue, by means of an offer by, or on behalf of, the *issuer* to intermediaries for them to allocate to their own clients.

(2) (for the purposes of the *Code of Market Conduct (MAR* 1)) a marketing of *securities* not yet in issue, by means of an *offer* by, or on behalf of, the *issuer* to intermediaries for them to allocate to their own clients.

intermediate broker

(in relation to a transaction in a *contingent liability investment*) any *person* acting in the capacity of an intermediary through whom the *firm* undertakes that transaction.

Intermediate customer

(for the purposes only of COBS TP 1 (Transitional Provisions in relation to Client Categorisation)):

(1) (except in *COB* 3) a *client* who is not a *market counterparty* and who is:
- (a) a local authority or public authority;
- (b) a *body corporate* whose *shares* have been *listed* or *admitted to trading* on any *EEA* exchange;
- (c) a *body corporate* whose *shares* have been *listed* or *admitted to trading* on the primary board of any *IOSCO* member country official exchange;
- (d) a *body corporate* (including a *limited liability partnership*) which has (or any of whose *holding companies* or *subsidiaries* has) (or has had at any time during the previous two years) called up share capital or net assets of at least £5 million (or its equivalent in any other currency at the relevant time);
- (e) a *special purpose vehicle;*
- (f) a *partnership* or unincorporated association which has (or has had at any time during the previous two years) net assets of at least £5 million (or its equivalent in any other currency at the relevant time) and calculated in the case of a limited *partnership* without deducting loans owing to any of the *partners;*
- (g) a trustee of a trust (other than an *occupational pension scheme*, *SSAS*, *personal pension scheme* or *stakeholder pension scheme*) which has (or has had at any time during the previous two years) assets of at least £10 million (or its equivalent in any other currency at the relevant time) calculated by aggregating the value of the cash and *designated investments* forming part of the trust's assets, but before deducting its liabilities;
- (h) a trustee of an *occupational pension scheme* or *SSAS*, or a trustee or *operator* of a *personal pension scheme* or *stakeholder pension scheme* where the scheme has (or has had at any time during the previous two years):
  - (i) at least 50 members; and
  - (ii) assets under management of at least £10 million (or its equivalent in any other currency at the relevant time);
- (i) another *firm*, or an *overseas financial services institution*, when, in relation to *designated investment business*, or related *ancillary activities*, conducted with or for that *firm* or institution, that *firm* or institution is an *intermediate customer* in accordance with COB 4.1.7R (Classification of another firm or an overseas financial services institution);
- (j) collective investment scheme;
- (k) a client when he is classified as an intermediate customer in accordance with COB 4.1.9R (Expert private customer classified as intermediate customer);
- (l) a recognised investment exchange, designated investment exchange, regulated market or clearing house, except when it is classified as a market counterparty in accordance with COB 4.1.8A R (Classification of an exchange or clearing house);

but excluding:
- (i) [deleted]
- (ii) a client who would otherwise be an intermediate customer, when he is classified in accordance with:
  - (A) *COB* 4.1.12R (Large intermediate customer classified as market counterparty); or
  - (B) (except for the purposes of *DISP*) *COB* 4.1.14R (Client classified as private customer).

(2) (in *COB* 3) a *person* in (1) or a *person* who would be such a *person* if he were a *client*.

intermediate holding vehicle

a *company*, trust or partnership but not a *collective investment scheme*, whose purpose is to enable the holding of overseas immovables on behalf of a *non-UCITS retail scheme* or a *qualified investor scheme*.

intermediate rate of return

(in *COBS*) the intermediate rate of return described in paragraph 2.3 of the *projection rules* (*COBS* 13 Annex 2).

internal audit function

controlled function CF15 in the *table of controlled functions*, described more fully in SUP 10.8.6R.

internal capital adequacy assessment process

a *firm's* assessment of the adequacy of its capital and financial resources, as required by the *ICAAP rules*.

internal controls

the whole system of controls, financial or otherwise, established by the management of a *firm* in order to:
(a) carry on the business of the *firm* in an orderly and efficient manner;
(b) ensure adherence to management policies;
(c) safeguard the assets of the *firm* and other assets for which the *firm* is responsible; and
(d) secure as far as possible the completeness and accuracy of the *firm's* records (including those necessary to ensure continuous compliance with the requirements or standards under the *regulatory system* relating to the adequacy of the *firm's* financial resources).

international accounting standards

means the international accounting standards, within the meaning of EC Regulation No 1606/2002 of the European Parliament and of the Council of 19 July 2002 on the application of international accounting standards, adopted from time to time by the European Commission in accordance with that Regulation.

International Financial Reporting Standards

international financial accounting standards within the meaning of EC Regulation No 1606/2002 of the European Parliament and of the Council of 19 July 2002 as adopted from time to time by the European Commission in accordance with that Regulation.

international organisation

(for the purposes of GENPRU and BIPRU) an organisation referred to in BIPRU 3.4.30R (Exposures to international organisations).

intra-group liquidity modification

a modification to the *overall liquidity adequacy rule* of the kind described in BIPRU 12.8.7G.

intra-group transactions

(in accordance with Article 2(18) of the *Financial Groups Directive* (Definitions)) all transactions by which *regulated entities* within a *financial conglomerate* rely either directly or indirectly upon other *undertakings* within the same *financial conglomerate* or upon any *person* linked to the *undertakings* within that *financial conglomerate* by *close links*, for the fulfilment of an obligation whether or not contractual, and whether or not for payment.

introducer

an individual appointed by a *firm*, an *appointed representative* or, where applicable, a *tied agent*, to carry out in the course of *designated investment business* either or both of the following activities:
(a) effecting introductions;
(b) distributing *non-real time financial promotions.*

introducer appointed representative

an *appointed representative* appointed by a *firm* whose scope of appointment is limited to:
(a) effecting introductions; and
(b) distributing *non-real time financial promotions.*

introducing

[deleted]

introducing broker

a *firm* which introduces transactions relating to designated investments *arranged (brought about*) for its *clients* to a *clearing firm.*

Part II FSA Handbook Materials

investment

(in accordance with sections (922(4) (The classes of activity and categories of investments) and 397(13) (Miscellaneous offences) of the *Act*) any investment, including any asset, right or interest.

investment adviser

(in relation to an *authorised fund*) a *person* who is retained by an *ICVC*, its *directors* or its *ACD* or by a *manager* of an *AUT* under a commercial arrangement which is not a contract of service:

(a) to supply any of them with advice in relation to the *authorised fund* as to the merits of investment opportunities or information relevant to the making of judgements about the merits of investment opportunities; or

(b) to exercise for any of them any function concerning the management of the *scheme property*.

investment agreement

any agreement the making or performance of which by either party constitutes a *regulated activity*, but disregarding the exclusions in Part II of the *Regulated Activities Order*.

investment analyst

[deleted]

investment business compensation scheme

(as defined in article 2(2) of the *compensation transitionals order*) any of the following:

(a) the scheme established under section 54 of the Financial Services Act 1986 and known as the Investors Compensation Scheme;

(b) the scheme established under section 22j of the Grey Paper published by the *FSA* on 26 September 1998 and known as the Section 43 Compensation Scheme;

(c) the scheme established by chapter II of part L:VIII of the *PIA* rule book and known as the PIA Indemnity Scheme;

(d) the scheme resulting from an agreement dated 1 February 1999 between the Association of British Insurers and the Investors Compensation Scheme Limited for the making of payments by way of compensation to widows, widowers and dependants of persons (since deceased), in connection with advice given to such persons in relation to pensions, or the arranging of pensions for such persons, and known as the ABI/ICS scheme.

investment company with variable capital

a body incorporated under the *OEIC Regulations*.

investment entity

(in LR) an entity whose primary object is investing and managing its assets with a view to spreading or otherwise managing investment risk.

investment firm

(1) any person whose regular occupation or business is the provision of one or more *investment services* to third parties and/or the performance of one or more investment activities on a professional basis.
[Note: article 4(1)(1) of *MiFID*]

(2) (in *REC*) a *MiFID investment firm*, or a person who would be a *MiFID investment firm* if it had its head office in the *EEA*.

investment firm consolidation waiver

a *waiver* (described in BIPRU 8.4 (CAD Article 22 groups and investment firm consolidation waiver)) that disapplies certain requirements so far as they apply on a consolidated basis with respect to a *CAD Article 22 group*.

investment management firm

subject to BIPRU TP 1.3R (Revised definition of investment management firm for certain transitional purposes)), a firm whose permitted activities include designated investment business, which is not an authorised professional firm, bank, BIPRU investment firm, ELMI, building society, credit union, energy market participant, friendly society, ICVC, insurer, media firm, oil market participant, service company, incoming EEA firm (without a top-up permission), incoming Treaty firm (without a top-up permission), UCITS management company or UCITS qualifier (without a top-up permission), whose permission does not include a requirement that it comply with IPRU(INV) 3 or 13 (Personal investment firms) and which is within (a), (b) or (c):

(a) a firm

(i) which was a member of IMRO immediately before commencement; and

(ii) which was not, immediately before commencement, subject to the financial supervision requirements of the FSA (under section 43 of the Financial Services Act 1986), or PIA or SFA (under lead regulation arrangements);

(b) a firm whose permission includes a requirement that it comply with IPRU(INV) 5 (Investment management firms);

(c) a firm:

(i) which was given a Part IV permission on or after commencement, or which was authorised under section 25 of the Financial Services Act 1986 immediately before commencement and was not a member of IMRO, PIA or the SFA; and

(ii) for which the most substantial part of its gross income (including commissions) from the designated investment business included in its Part IV permission is derived from one or more of the following activities (based, for a firm given a Part IV permission after commencement, on the business plan submitted as part of the firm's application for permission or, for a firm authorised under section 25 of the Financial Services Act 1986, on the firm's financial year preceding its authorisation under the Act):

(A) managing investments other than for private customers or where the assets managed are primarily derivatives;

(B) OPS activity;

(C) acting as the manager or trustee of an AUT;

(D) acting as the ACD or depositary of an ICVC;

(E) establishing, operating or winding up a collective investment scheme (other than an AUT or ICVC);

(Ea) establishing, operating or winding up a personal pension scheme; and

(F) safeguarding and administering investments.

investment manager

(1) (except in LR) a *person* who, acting only on behalf of a *client:*

(a) manages *designated investments* in an account or portfolio on a discretionary basis under the terms of a discretionary management agreement; or

(b) manages designated investments in an account or portfolio on a non-discretionary basis under the terms of a non-discretionary management agreement.

(2) (in LR) a *person* who, on behalf of a *client*, manages *investments* and is not a wholly-owned *subsidiary* of the *client.*

Investment Ombudsman

the former Ombudsman under the IMRO scheme.

investment professional

(in accordance with article 19(5) of the Financial Promotion Order) (in relation to a financial promotion):

(a) an *authorised person;*

(b) an *exempt person* when the *financial promotion* relates to a *controlled activity* which is a *regulated activity* in relation to which the *person* is exempt;

(c) any other *person:*

(i) whose ordinary activities involve him in carrying on the *controlled activity* to which the *financial promotion* relates for the purposes of a business carried on by him; or

(ii) who it is reasonable to expect will carry on that activity for the purposes of a business carried on by him;

(d) a government, a local authority (whether in the *United Kingdom* or elsewhere) or an international organisation;

(e) a *person* ("A") who is a *director*, *officer* or employee of a *person* ("B") falling within any of (a) to (d) where the *financial promotion* is made to A in that capacity and where A's responsibilities when acting in that capacity involve him in the carrying on by B of *controlled activities.*

investment research

research or other information recommending or suggesting an investment strategy, explicitly or implicitly, concerning one or several *financial instruments* or the issuers of *financial instruments*, including any opinion as to the present or future value or price of such instruments, intended for *distribution channels* or for the public, and in relation to which the following conditions are met:

(a) it is labelled or described as investment research or in similar terms, or is otherwise presented as an objective or independent explanation of the matters contained in the recommendation;
(b) if the recommendation in question were to be made by an *investment firm* to a *client*, it would not constitute the provision of a *personal recommendation*.
[Note: article 24(1) of the *MiFID implementing Directive*]

investment service

any of the following involving the provision of a service in relation to a *financial instrument*:
(a) reception and transmission of orders in relation to one or more *financial instruments*;
(b) execution of orders on behalf of *clients*;
(c) *dealing on own account*;
(d) *portfolio management*;
(e) the making of a *personal recommendation*;
(f) underwriting of *financial instruments* and/or placing of *financial instruments* on a firm commitment basis;
(g) placing of *financial instruments* without a firm commitment basis;
(h) operation of *multilateral trading facilities*.
[Note: article 4(1)(2) of, and section A of Annex 1 to, *MiFID*]

investment services and activities

any of the services and activities listed in Section A of Annex I to *MiFID* relating to any *financial instrument*, that is:
(a) reception and transmission of orders in relation to one or more *financial instruments*;
(b) execution of orders on behalf of *clients*;
(c) *dealing on own account*;
(d) *portfolio management*;
(e) the making of a *personal recommendation*;
(f) underwriting of *financial instruments* and/or placing of *financial instruments* on a firm commitment basis;
(g) placing of *financial instruments* without a firm commitment basis;
(h) operation of *multilateral trading facilities*.

[Note: article 4(1)(2) of, and section A of Annex 1 to, *MiFID*]

investment services and/or activities

any of the services and activities listed in Section A of Annex I to *MiFID* relating to any *financial instrument*, that is:
(a) reception and transmission of orders in relation to one or more *financial instruments*;
(b) execution of orders on behalf of *clients*;
(c) *dealing on own account*;
(d) *portfolio management*;
(e) the making of a *personal recommendation*;
(f) underwriting of *financial instruments* and/or placing of *financial instruments* on a firm commitment basis;
(g) placing of *financial instruments* without a firm commitment basis;
(h) operation of *multilateral trading facilities*.

[Note: article 4(1)(2) of, and section A of Annex 1 to, *MiFID*]

Investment Services Directive

the Council Directive of 10 May 1993 on investment services in the securities field (No 93/22/EEC).

investment services or activities

any of the services and activities listed in Section A of Annex I to *MiFID* relating to any *financial instrument*.

investment services sector

a sector composed of one or more of the following entities:
(a) an *investment firm*;
(b) a *financial institution*; and
(c) (in the circumstances described in GENPRU 3.1.39R (The financial sectors: Asset management companies)) an *asset management company*.

investment transaction

a transaction to *buy*, *sell*, subscribe for or underwrite a *security* or *contractually based investment*.

investment trust

a *company listed* in the *United Kingdom* or another *EEA State* which:
(a) is approved by the Commissioners for HM Revenue and Customs under section 842 of the Income and Corporation Taxes Act 1988 (or, in the case of a newly formed *company*, has declared its intention to conduct its affairs so as to obtain such approval); or

(b) is resident in an *EEA State* other than the *United Kingdom* and would qualify for such approval if resident and *listed* in the *United Kingdom.*

investment trust savings scheme

(a) a *dealing* service (whether or not held within a *pension contract*) dedicated to the *securities* of one or more *investment trusts*;

(b) *securities* to be acquired through an investment trust savings scheme in (a).

Investor Compensation Directive

the Council Directive of 3 March 1997 on investor compensation schemes (No 97/9/EC).

IOSCO

the International Organisation of Securities Commissions.

IPA

individual pension account.

IPA eligible investment

a type of investment specified in regulation 2(2) (condition 5) of the Stamp Duty and Stamp Duty Reserve Tax (Definition of Unit Trust Scheme and Open-ended Investment Company) Regulations 2001 (SI 2001/964).

IPRU

the Interim Prudential sourcebook, comprising *IPRU(BANK), IPRU(BSOC), IPRU(FSOC), IPRU(INS)* and *IPRU(INV)*, or according to the context one of these Interim Prudential sourcebooks.

IPRU(BANK)

the Interim Prudential sourcebook for banks.

IPRU(BSOC)

the Interim Prudential sourcebook for building societies.

IPRU(FSOC)

the Interim Prudential sourcebook for friendly societies.

IPRU(INS)

the Interim Prudential sourcebook for insurers.

IPRU(INV)

the Interim Prudential sourcebook for investment businesses.

IRB approach

one of the following:

(a) the adjusted method of calculating the *credit risk capital component* set out in BIPRU 4 (IRB approach) and BIPRU 9.12 (Calculation of risk weighted exposure amounts under the internal ratings based approach), including that approach as applied under BIPRU 14 (Capital requirements for settlement and counterparty risk);

(b) (where the approach in (a) is being applied on a consolidated basis) the method in (a) as applied on a consolidated basis in accordance with BIPRU 8 (Group risk — consolidation); or

(c) when the reference is to the rules of or administered by a *regulatory body* other than the *FSA*, whatever corresponds to the approach in (a) or (b), as the case may be, under those rules.

IRB exposure class

(in relation to the *IRB approach*) one of the classes of *exposure* set out in BIPRU 4.3.2R (exposure classes).

IRB permission

an *Article 129 implementing measure*, a *requirement* or a *waiver* that requires a *BIPRU firm* or an *institution* to use the *IRB approach.*

ISA

an *individual savings account.*

ISA manager

a *person* who is approved by HM Revenue and Customs for the purposes of the *ISA Regulations* as an account manager.

ISA Regulations

the Individual Savings Account Regulations 1998 (SI 1998/1870).

ISA transfer

a transaction resulting from a decision, made with or without advice from a *firm*, by a *customer* who is an individual, to transfer the *investments* (or their value) held in his existing *ISA* in favour of another *ISA* which may or may not be managed by the same *ISA manager*.

ISD

Investment Services Directive.

ISD instrument

[deleted]

ISD investment firm

[deleted]

ISPV

an *insurance special purpose vehicle.*

issue

(in relation to *units*)
(1) (except in EG 14) the issue of new *units* by the *trustee* of an *AUT* or by an *ICVC*;
(2) (in EG 14)
(a) an issue in accordance with (1); and
(b) the sale of *units*.

issue price

(in relation to the *issue* of *units* of a *dual-priced authorised fund*) the *price* for each *unit* payable by the *authorised fund manager* to the *trustee* on that *issue*.

issuer

(1) (except in LR and PR)
(a) (in relation to any *security*) (other than a *unit* in a *collective investment scheme*) the *person* by whom it is or is to be issued;
(b) (in relation to a *unit* in a *collective investment scheme*) the *operator* of the *scheme*;
(c) (in relation to an interest in a limited *partnership*) the *partnership*;
(d) (in relation to *certificates representing certain securities*) the *person* who issued or is to issue the *security* to which the certificate or other instrument relates;
(e) an entity which issues *transferable securities* and, where appropriate, other *financial instruments*.

[Note: article 2(2) of the *MiFID Regulation*]

(2) (in chapters 1, 2 and 3 of DR and FEES in relation to DR) (5) any *company* or other legal person or undertaking (including a *public sector issuer*), any class of whose *financial instruments*:
(a) have been *admitted to trading* on a *regulated market*; or
(b) are the subject of an application for *admission to trading* on a *regulated market*;

other than *issuers* who have not requested or approved admission of their *financial instruments* to trading on a *regulated market*.

(2A) (in chapters 1A, 1B, 4, 6 and 7 of *DTR*) a legal entity governed by private or public law, including a State, whose securities are admitted to trading on a *regulated market*, the issuer being, in the case of depository receipts representing securities, the issuer of the securities represented;

(2B) (in chapter 5 of *DTR*)
(a) a legal entity governed by private or public law, including a State whose *shares* are admitted to trading on a *regulated market*, the issuer being in the case of depositary receipts representing securities, the issuer of the *shares* represented; or
(b) a public company within the meaning of section 4(2) of the Companies Act 2006 and any other body corporate incorporated in and having a principal *place of business* in *United Kingdom*, whose shares are admitted to trading on a market which (not being a *regulated market*) is a *prescribed market*.

(3) (in LR and FEES in relation to LR) any *company* or other legal person or undertaking (including a *public sector issuer*), any *class* of whose *securities* has been *admitted* to *listing* or is the subject of an application for *admission* to *listing*.

(4) (in PR and FEES in relation to PR) (as defined in section 102A of the *Act*) a legal person who issues or proposes to issue the *transferable securities* in question.

(5) (in *RCB*) (as defined in Regulation 1(2) of the *RCB Regulations*) a person which issues a *covered bond.*

issuer exposure

(for the purposes of BIPRU 10 (Concentration risk requirements)) has the meaning in BIPRU 10.4.5R (Definition of issuer exposures).

issuing e-money

the activity specified in article 9B of the *Regulated Activities Order* (Issuing electronic money), which is issuing *e-money.*

joint enterprise

(as defined in article 3(1) of the *Regulated Activities Order* (Interpretation)) an enterprise into which two or more *persons* ("the participators") enter for commercial purposes related to a business or businesses (other than the business of engaging in a *regulated activity*) carried on by them; where a participator is a member of a *group*, each other member of the *group* is also to be regarded as a participator in the enterprise.

key features document

a *document* prepared in accordance with the *rules* on preparing product information (*COBS* 13).

key features illustration

information describing projected performance and the effect of charges prepared in accordance with the *rules* on preparing product information (*COBS* 13).

key features scheme

a *scheme* that is not:

(a) a *simplified prospectus scheme*;

(b) a *qualified investor scheme*; or

(c) a recognised scheme under section 264 of the *Act* (Schemes constituted in other EEA States).

key individual

(in relation to a *UK recognised body*):

(a) its chairman or president;

(b) its *chief executive;*

(c) a member of its *governing body*;

(d) a *person* who, alone or jointly with one or more others, is responsible under the immediate authority of a *person* in (a), (b) or (c) or a committee of the *governing body* for the conduct of any *relevant function.*

keyfacts logo provisions

GEN 5.1 and GEN 5 Annex 1G.

kind of control

(in relation to a *firm*) (in accordance with section 179(4) of the *Act* (Acquiring control)):

(a) *control* arising as a result of holding shares in the *firm;*

(b) *control* arising as a result of holding shares in a *parent undertaking* of the *firm;*

(c) *control* arising as a result of the entitlement to exercise or control the exercise of *voting power* in the *firm;*

(d) *control* arising as a result of the entitlement to exercise or *control* the exercise of *voting power* in a *parent undertaking* of the *firm;*

in this definition, "shares" has the meaning given in the definition of "*controller*".

K_{IRB}

(for the purposes of BIPRU 9 (Securitisation), in relation to a *securitisation* (within the meaning of paragraph (2) of the definition of securitisation) and in accordance with Part 1 of Annex IX of the *Banking Consolidation Directive* (Securitisation definitions)) 8% of the *risk weighted exposure amounts* that would be calculated under the *IRB approach* in respect of the *securitised exposures*, had they not been *securitised*, plus the amount of *expected losses* associated with those *exposures* calculated under the *IRB approach.*

land vehicles

(in relation to a *class* of *contract of insurance*) the *class* of *contract of insurance*, specified in paragraph 3 of Part I of Schedule 1 to the *Regulated Activities Order* (Contracts of general insurance), against loss of or damage to vehicles used on land, including motor vehicles but excluding railway rolling stock.

large business customer

(in relation to a *regulated mortgage contract* or *qualifying credit*, and in relation to an activity to be carried on by a *firm*) a *client*, if the credit is for the purposes of a business which has a group annual turnover of £1 million or more.

large company

a *body corporate* which does not qualify as a small company under section 247 of the Companies Act 1985, or section 382 of the Companies Act 2006 as applicable.

large deal

(in COLL) a transaction (or *series of transactions*) in one *dealing period*) by any *person* to *buy*, *sell* or exchange *units* in an *authorised fund*, of any value as set out in the *prospectus*, for the purposes of:

(a) an *SDRT provision*;
(b) a *dilution levy*;
(c) a *dilution adjustment*; or
(d) calculating the *prices*, for a *dual-priced authorised fund*, at which *units* may be *sold* or *redeemed*.

large e-money float exposure

(in ELM) an *e-money float exposure* or *e-money float exposures* that exceeds or together exceed 10% of an *ELMI's own funds* as specified in more detail in *ELM* 3.5.7R (Calculation of large exposure).

large exposure

has the meaning set out in BIPRU 10.5.1R, which in summary is the *total exposure* of a *firm* to a *counterparty*, *connected counterparties* or a *group of connected clients*, whether in the *firm*'s *non-trading book* or *trading book* or both, which in aggregate equals or exceeds 10% of the *firm*'s *capital resources*.

large mutual association

a mutual association or unincorporated association with net assets of more than £1.4 million (or its equivalent in any other currency at the relevant time).

large partnership

a *partnership* or unincorporated association with net assets of more than £1.4 million (or its equivalent in any other currency at the relevant time).

larger denomination share

any *share* that is not a *smaller denomination share*.

lead regulated firm

a *firm* which is the subject of the financial supervision requirements of an *overseas regulator* in accordance with an agreement between the *FSA* and that regulator relating to the financial supervision of *firms* whose head office is within the country of that regulator.

This definition is not related to the defined terms *UK lead regulated firm* or *non UK lead regulated firm*.

leading insurer

(in relation to a *community co-insurance operation*) has the same meaning as in the *Community Co-Insurance Directive*.

legal expenses

(in relation to a *class* of *contract of insurance*) the *class* of *contract of insurance*, specified in paragraph 17 of Part I of Schedule 1 to the *Regulated Activities Order* (Contracts of general insurance), against risks of loss to the *persons* insured attributable to their incurring legal expenses (including costs of litigation).

lending firm

(in accordance with Article 90 of the *Banking Consolidation Directive* (Credit risk mitigation) and for the purposes of *rules* about *credit risk mitigation*) a *firm* that has an *exposure*, whether or not deriving from a loan.

levy limit

(in *FEES*) the maximum amount of *compensation costs* that may be allocated to a particular *sub-class* or *class* in one financial year as set out in FEES 6 Annex 2R.

LGD

loss given default.

liability of ships

(in relation to a *class* of *contract of insurance*) the *class* of *contract of insurance*, specified in paragraph 12 of Part I of Schedule 1 to the *Regulated Activities Order* (Contracts of general insurance), against damage arising out of or in connection with the use of vessels on the sea or on inland water, including third party risks and carrier's liability.

liability subject to compulsory insurance

any liability required under any of the following enactments to be covered by insurance or (as the case may be) by insurance or by some. other provisions for securing its discharge:

(a) section 1(4A)(d) of the Riding Establishments Act 1964 (or any corresponding enactment for the time being in force in Northern Ireland);
(b) section 1 of the Employers' Liability (Compulsory Insurance) Act 1969 or Article 5 of the Employers' Liability Order (Defective Equipment and Compulsory Insurance) (Northern Ireland) Order 1972;
(c) Part VI of the Road Traffic Act 1988 or Part VIII of the Road Traffic (Northern Ireland) Order 1981;
(d) section 19 of the Nuclear Installations Act 1965.

liability to a policyholder

(in relation to a *firm carrying out contracts of insurance*) any liability or obligation of that *firm* to, or in respect of, a *policyholder*, including any liability or obligation arising:

(a) from the requirement to treat *customers* fairly under *Principle* 6, including with respect to *policyholders*' reasonable expectations; or
(b) from a determination of liability by an *Ombudsman*; or
(c) from any requirement to pay compensation under the *regulatory system*.

licensee

(1) (in DISP 2–4 and FEES 5) a *person* who is not a *firm* and is:
 (a) covered by a standard licence under the Consumer Credit Act 1974 (as amended); or
 (b) authorised to carry on an activity by virtue of section 34(A) of that Act.
(2) (in DISP 1) a person within (1)(a) above.

Expressions used in that Act have the same meaning in this definition.

life and annuity

(in relation to a *class* of *contract of insurance*) the *class* of *contract of insurance*, specified in paragraph I of Part II of Schedule 1 to the *Regulated Activities Order* (Contracts of long-term insurance), on human life or a contract to pay annuities on human life, but excluding (in each case) contracts within paragraph III of Part II of that Schedule (Linked long-term).

life policy

(1) (in accordance with the definition of 'qualifying contract of insurance' in article 3(1) of the *Regulated Activities Order*) a *long-term insurance contract* (other than a reinsurance contract and a *pure protection contract*); and
 (a) a *long-term care insurance contract*; and
 (b) (in *COBS*) a *pension policy*;
 unless (2) or (3) apply.
(2) In *PERG* (other than in relation to a *firm's permission* – see Note 5B to Table 1 in Annex 2, *PERG* 2) and for the purposes of the *financial promotion rules* in *COBS* 4, life policy does not include a *long-term care insurance contract*.
(3) In relation to a *firm's permission*:
 (a) (in accordance with the definition of 'qualifying contract of insurance' in article 3(1) of the *Regulated Activities Order*) a *long-term insurance contract* (other than a reinsurance contract and a *pure protection contract*);
 (b) a *long-term care insurance contract* which is a *pure protection contract*; and
 (c) a *pension term assurance policy*.

life protection reinsurance business

reinsurance acceptances which are *contracts of insurance*:

(a) falling within *long-term insurance business class* I; or
(b) falling within *long-term insurance business class* III and providing *index-linked benefits*; that are not:
(c) *with-profits insurance contracts*; or
(d) *whole life assurances*; or
(e) contracts to pay annuities on human life; or
(f) contracts which pay a sum of money on the survival of the life assured to a specific date or on his earlier death.

Part II FSA Handbook Materials

lifetime mortgage

a *regulated mortgage contract* under which:

(a) entry into the mortgage is restricted to older *customers* above a specified age; and

(b) the *mortgage lender* may or may not specify a mortgage term, but will not seek full repayment of the loan (including interest, if any, outstanding) until the occurrence of one or more of the following:

  (i) the death of the *customer*; or

  (ii) the *customer* leaves the mortgaged land to live elsewhere and has no reasonable prospect of returning (for example by moving into residential care); or

  (iii) the *customer* acquires another dwelling for use as his main residence; or

  (iv) the *customer* sells the mortgaged land; or

  (v) the *mortgage lender* exercises its legal right to take possession of the mortgaged land under the terms of the contract.

  and

(c) while the *customer* continues to occupy the mortgaged land as his main residence:

  (i) no instalment repayments of the capital and no payment of interest on the capital (other than interest charged when all or part of the capital is repaid voluntarily by the *customer*), are due or capable of becoming due; or

  (ii) although interest payments may become due, no full or partial repayment of the capital is due or capable of becoming due; or

  (iii) although interest payments and partial repayment of the capital may become due, no full repayment of the capital is due or capable of becoming due.

LIFFE

the London International Financial Futures and Options Exchange.

limit of indemnity

(in *PRU* 9.1 (Professional indemnity insurance requirements for insurance and mortgage mediation activity and mortgage lending and administering)) the sum available to indemnify a *firm* in respect of each claim made under its *professional indemnity insurance*.

limit order

an order to buy or sell a *financial instrument* at its specified price limit or better and for a specified size.

[Note: article 4(1)(16) of *MiFID*]

limitation

a limitation incorporated in a *Part IV permission* under section 42(7)(a) of the *Act* (Giving permission) or section 45(4) of the *Act* (Variation etc on the Authority's own initiative).

limited activity firm

has the meaning set out BIPRU 1.1.11R (Types of investment firm: Limited activity firms).

limited liability partnership

(a) a *body corporate* incorporated under the Limited Liability Partnerships Act 2000;

(b) a *body corporate* incorporated under legislation having the equivalent effect to the Limited Liability Partnerships Act 2000.

limited licence firm

has the meaning set out BIPRU 1.1.12R (Types of investment firm: Limited licence firms).

limited redemption arrangements

the arrangements operated by an *authorised fund manager* for the *redemption* of *units* in an *authorised fund* where the *authorised fund manager* holds himself out to *redeem units* in that *scheme* less frequently than twice in a calendar *month* in accordance with COLL 6.2.19R (Limited redemption).

linked assets

index-linked assets or *property-linked assets*.

linked benefit

(1) (in *COBS* 21 (Permitted Links)) *property-linked benefits* or *indexlinked benefits*.

(2) (other than in *COBS* 21) a benefit payable under a *life policy* or a *regulated* collective *investment scheme* the amount of which is determined by reference to:

  (a) the value of the property of any description (whether specified or not); or

  (b) fluctuations in the value of any such property; or

  (c) income from such property; or

  (d) fluctuations in an index of the value of such property.

linked borrowing

additional credit facilities (which may be secured, unsecured, or both) that are integral to a *regulated mortgage contract* but which may be the subject of a separate contract.

linked deposits

additional facilities (which may be a current account, a savings account, or both) that are linked to a *regulated mortgage contract* but which may be the subject of a separate contract.

linked fund

a real or notional account to which an *insurer* appropriates *linked assets* for the purposes of their being *permitted links*, and which may be subdivided into units, the value of each of which is determined by the *insurer* by reference to the value of those *linked assets*.

linked liabilities

property-linked liabilities or *index-linked liabilities*.

linked life stakeholder product

the *stakeholder product* specified by regulations 6 and 7 (rights under certain linked long-term contracts) of the *Stakeholder Regulations*;

linked long-term

(in relation to a *contract of insurance*) a *long-term insurance contract* where the benefits are wholly or partly to be determined by reference to the value of, or the income from, property of any description (whether or not specified in the contracts) or by reference to fluctuations in, or in an index of, the value of property of any description (whether or not so specified).

linked policyholders

policyholders under a *linked long-term* contract.

liquidity facility

(for the purposes of BIPRU 9 (Securitisation), in relation to a *securitisation* (within the meaning of paragraph (2) of the definition of securitisation) and in accordance with Part 1 of Annex IX of the *Banking Consolidation Directive* (Securitisation definitions)) the *securitisation position* arising from a contractual agreement to provide funding to ensure timeliness of cash-flows to investors.

liquidity risk

the risk that a *firm*, although solvent, either does not have available sufficient financial resources to enable it to meet its obligations as they fall due, or can secure such resources only at excessive cost.

list of sponsors

(in LR) the list of *sponsors* maintained by the *FSA* in accordance with section 88(3)(a) of the *Act*.

listed

(1) (except in LR, INSPRU and IPRU(INS)) included in an *official list*.
(2) (in INSPRU and IPRU(INS)):
  (a) included in an official list; or
  (b) in respect of which facilities for dealing on a regulated market have been granted.
(3) (in LR) admitted to the *official list* maintained by the *FSA* in accordance with section 74 of the *Act*.

listed activity

an activity listed in Annex 1 to the *Banking Consolidation Directive*.

listed company

(in LR and DEPP) a *company* that has any *class* of its *securities listed*.

listed security

any *security* that is admitted to an *official list*.

listing particulars

(in LR) (in accordance with section 79(2) of the *Act*), a document in such form and containing such information as may be specified in *listing rules*.

listing rules

(in accordance with section 73A(2) of the *Act*) *rules* relating to admission to the *official list*.

LLD

the Lloyd's sourcebook.

Lloyd's actuary

the *actuary* appointed by the *Society* under SUP 4.6.1R.

Lloyd's Arbitration Scheme

the Lloyd's Arbitration Scheme (Members and Underwriting Agents Arbitration Scheme) established under Lloyd's Arbitration Scheme (Members and Underwriting Agents Scheme) Byelaw (No 15 of 1992).

Lloyd's complaint procedures

the procedures established and maintained by the *Society* under *DISP* 1.11.1R.

Lloyd's complaint rules

DISP 1.11

Lloyd's market activities

(a) *advising on syndicate participation at Lloyd's*, including *advising* on a transaction in the *capacity transfer market*;
(b) *managing the underwriting capacity of a Lloyd's syndicate as a managing agent at Lloyd's*;
(c) agreeing to carry on the *regulated activities* in (a) and (b);
(d) carrying on *designated investment business* which is not *MiFID business* in relation to *funds at Lloyd's*; or
(e) *communicating* or *approving* a *financial promotion* in relation to:
  (i) the *underwriting capacity of a Lloyd's syndicate*; or
  (ii) *membership of a Lloyd's syndicate*; or
  (iii) *life policies* written at Lloyd's; or
  (iv) any of the activities specified in (a) or (d).

Lloyd's member's contribution

assets:
(a) provided to a *managing agent* in response to a cash call; or
(b) held by the *Society* as *funds at Lloyd's*.

Lloyd's Members' Ombudsman

the office of Ombudsman established under Lloyd's Members' Ombudsman Scheme Byelaw (No 13 of 1987).

Lloyd's Return

the financial report that the *Society* is required to submit to the *FSA* under IPRU(INS) 9.48(1).

Lloyd's trust deed

a trust deed in the form prescribed by the *Society* and notified to the *FSA*, for execution by a *member* in respect of his *insurance business*.

Lloyd's trust fund

a fund held on the terms of a *Lloyd's trust deed*.

local

(1) (except in BIPRU 1.1 (Application and purpose)) a *firm* which is a member of a *futures* and *options* exchange and whose *permission* includes a *requirement* that:
  (a) the *firm* will not conduct *designated investment business* other than:
    (i) *dealing* for its own account on that *futures* or *options* exchange; or
    (ii) *dealing* for the accounts of other members of the same *futures* and *options* exchange; or
    (iii) making a price to other members of the same *futures* and *options* exchange; or
    (iv) *dealing* for its own account in financial *futures* and *options* or other *derivatives* in the capacity of a customer; and
  (b) the performance of the *firm's* contracts must be guaranteed by and must be the responsibility of one or more of the clearing members of the same *futures* and *options* exchange.

(2) (in BIPRU 1.1 (Application and purpose) and in accordance with article 3(1)(p) of the *Capital Adequacy Directive* (Definitions)) an *undertaking* dealing for its own account on markets in financial-futures or options or other derivatives and on cash markets for the sole purpose of hedging *positions* on derivatives markets or which deals for the accounts of other members of those markets and which are guaranteed by clearing members of the same markets, where responsibility for ensuring the performance of contracts entered into by such an *undertaking* is assumed by clearing members of the same markets; for these purposes a clearing member means a member of the exchange or the clearing house which has a direct contractual relationship with the central counterparty (market guarantor).

local firm

a *firm* which falls within the definition of "local firm" in Article 3.1P of *CAD*, that is a firm dealing for its own account on markets in financial futures or options or other derivatives and on cash markets for the sole purpose of hedging positions on derivatives markets, or dealing for the accounts of other members of those markets and being guaranteed by clearing members of the same markets, where responsibility for ensuring the performance of contracts entered into by such a firm is assumed by clearing members of the same markets.

London Stock Exchange

(in LR) London Stock Exchange Plc.

long settlement transaction

(in accordance with Part 1 of Annex III of the *Banking Consolidation Directive* (Definitions)) a transaction where a counterparty undertakes to deliver a security, a *commodity*, or a *foreign currency* amount against cash, other *CRD financial instruments*, or *commodities*, or vice versa, at a settlement or delivery date that is contractually specified as more than the lower of the market standard for this particular transaction and five *business days* after the date on which the *person* enters into the transaction.

long-term admissible asset

a *long-term insurance asset* which is an *admissible asset*.

long-term care insurance contract

a *long-term insurance contract*:

(a) which provides, would provide at the *policyholder's* option, or is sold or held out as providing, benefits that are payable or provided if the *policyholder's* health deteriorates to the extent that he cannot live independently without assistance and that is not expected to change; and

(b) under which the benefits are capable of being paid for periodically for all or part of the period that the *policyholder* cannot live without assistance;

where 'benefits' are services, accommodation or goods necessary or desirable for the continuing care of the *policyholder* because he cannot live independently without assistance.

long term incentive scheme

(in LR) any arrangement (other than a retirement benefit plan, a deferred bonus or any other arrangement that is an element of an executive *director's* remuneration package) which may involve the receipt of any asset (including cash or any security) by a *director* or *employee* of the *group*:

(a) which includes one or more conditions in respect of service and/or performance to be satisfied over more than one financial year; and

(b) pursuant to which the *group* may incur (other than in relation to the establishment and administration of the arrangement) either cost or a liability, whether actual or contingent.

long-term insurance asset

has the meaning set out in INSPRU 1.5.21R.

long-term insurance business

the business of *effecting* or *carrying out long-term insurance contracts*.

long-term insurance business syndicate

a *syndicate* in which *members* carry on *long-term insurance business*.

long-term insurance capital requirement

(in relation to a *firm* carrying on *long-term insurance business*) an amount of *capital resources* that the *firm* must hold calculated in accordance with GENPRU 2.1.36R.

long-term insurance contract

(in accordance with article 3(1) of the *Regulated Activities Order* (Interpretation: general)) any *contract of insurance* within Part II of Schedule 1 to the *Regulated Activities Order* (Contracts of long-term insurance), namely:

(a) *life and annuity* (paragraph I);

(b) *marriage or the formation of a civil partnership and birth* (paragraph II);

(c) *linked long-term* (paragraph III);

(d) *permanent health* (paragraph IV);

(e) *tontines* (paragraph V);

(f) *capital redemption* (paragraph VI);

(g) *pension fund management* (paragraph VII);

(h) *collective insurance* etc (paragraph VIII);

Part II FSA Handbook Materials

(i) *social insurance* (paragraph IX).

long-term insurance fund

has the meaning set out in INSPRU 1.5.22R.

long-term insurance liabilities

liabilities arising from *long-term insurance business.*

long-term insurer

an *insurer* with *permission* to *effect* or *carry out long-term insurance contracts.*

loss

(in accordance with Article 4(26) of the *Banking Consolidation Directive* (Definitions) and for the purposes of the *IRB approach*, the *standardised approach* to credit risk and *BIPRU* 5 (Credit risk mitigation)) economic loss, including material discount effects, and material direct and indirect costs associated with collecting on the instrument.

loss given default

(in accordance with Article 4(27) of the *Banking Consolidation Directive* (Definitions) and in relation to the *IRB approach*) the ratio of the *loss* on an *exposure* due to the *default* of a counterparty to the amount outstanding at *default.*

lower rate of return

(in *COBS*) the lower rate of return described in paragraph 2.3 of the projection *rules* (*COBS* 13 Annex 2).

low frequency liquidity reporting firm

any of the following:

(a) a simplified ILAS BIPRU firm; or

(b) a standard ILAS BIPRU firm whose most recent annual report and accounts show balance sheet assets of less than £1 billion (or its equivalent in foreign currency translated into sterling at the balance sheet date); or

(c) a standard ILAS BIPRU firm that meets the following conditions:

- (i) it does not have any *annual report and accounts* and it has been too recently established to be required to have produced any;
- (ii) it has submitted a projected balance sheet to the *FSA* as part of an application for a *Part IV permission* or a variation of one; and
- (iii) the most recent such balance sheet shows that the *firm* will meet the size condition set out in (b) in all periods covered by those projections.

Paragraphs (b) and (c) apply at the level of the *firm* rather than of the *branch* in the case of any *firm* reporting on the basis of the activities of its branch operation in the *United Kingdom.*

lower stage of capital

(with respect to a particular item of capital in the *capital resources table*) a stage in the *capital resources table* below that in which that item of capital appears.

lower tier three capital

an item of capital that is specified in stage P of the *capital resources table* (Lower tier three).

lower tier three capital resources

the sum calculated at stage P of the *capital resources table* (Lower tier three).

lower tier two capital

(1) (in *ELM*) the lower tier two capital of an *ELMI* calculated in accordance with *ELM* 2.4 (Calculation of initial capital and own funds).

(2) (in BIPRU, GENPRU and INSPRU) an item of capital that is specified in stage H of the *capital resources table* (Lower tier two capital).

lower tier two capital resources

the sum calculated at stage H of the calculation in the *capital resources table* (Lower tier two capital).

lower tier two instrument

an item of capital that meets the conditions in GENPRU 2.2.194R (Lower tier two capital) and is eligible to form part of a *firm's lower tier two capital resources.*

LR

the Listing Rules sourcebook.

LTICR

long-term insurance capital requirement.

MAD

(in *LR*) the *Market Abuse Directive*.

MAD Investment Recommendations Directive

The Commission Directive of 22 December 2003 implementing the *Market Abuse Directive* as regards the fair presentation of investment recommendations and the disclosure of conflicts of interest (No 2003/125/EC).

made to; made only to; to whom it is made

a *financial promotion* is made to a *person* if it is addressed, whether orally or in legible form, to a particular *person* or *persons* (for example where it is contained in a telephone call or letter).

main BIPRU firm Pillar 1 rules

GENPRU 2.1.40R (Variable capital requirement for *BIPRU firms*), GENPRU 2.1.41R (*Base capital resources requirement* for *BIPRU firms*), GENPRU 2.1.48R (Table: Base capital resources requirement for a BIPRU firm) and, where applicable, GENPRU 2.1.60R (Calculation of base capital resources requirement for banks authorised before 1993).

major subsidiary undertaking

(in LR) a *subsidiary undertaking* that represents 25% or more of the aggregate of the gross assets or profits (after deducting all charges except taxation) of the *group*.

making arrangements with a view to a home finance transaction

any of the *regulated activities* of *making arrangements with a view to a regulated mortgage contract*, *making arrangements with a view to a home reversion plan*, *making arrangements with a view to a home purchase plan* or *making arrangements with a view to a regulated sale and rent back agreement*.

making arrangements with a view to a home purchase plan

the *regulated activity*, specified in article 25C(2) of the *Regulated Activities Order*, which is in summary: making arrangements with a view to a *person* who participates in the arrangements entering into a *home purchase plan* as *home purchaser*.

making arrangements with a view to a home reversion plan

the *regulated activity*, specified in article 25B(2) of the *Regulated Activities Order*, which is in summary: making arrangements with a view to a *person* who participates in the arrangements entering into a *home reversion plan* as *reversion occupier* or as plan provider.

making arrangements with a view to regulated mortgage contracts

the *regulated activity*, specified in article 25A(2) of the *Regulated Activities Order*, which is in summary: making arrangements with a view to a *person* who participates in the arrangements entering into a *regulated mortgage contract* as borrower.

(see also arranging (in relation to regulated mortgage contracts) and arranging (bringing about) regulated mortgage contracts.)

making arrangements with a view to a regulated sale and rent back agreement

the *regulated activity*, specified in article 25E(2) of the *Regulated Activities Order*, which is in summary making arrangements with a view to a *person* who participates in the arrangements entering into a *regulated sale and rent back agreement* as agreement seller or agreement provider.

making arrangements with a view to transactions in investments

the *regulated activity*, specified in article 25(2) of the *Regulated Activities Order* (Arranging deals in Investments), which is in summary: making arrangements with a view to a *person* who participates in the arrangements *buying*, *selling*, subscribing for or underwriting any of the following *investments* (whether as *principal* or agent):

(a) *a designated investment*; or
(b) *a funeral plan contract*; or
(c) *the underwriting capacity of a Lloyd's syndicate*; or
(d) *membership of a Lloyd's syndicate*; or
(e) *rights to or interests in investments in* (b), (c) or (d); or
(f) a *pure protection contract*; or
(g) a *general insurance contract*

management accounts

(in relation to a *UK recognised body*) accounts showing the actual and budgeted income and expenditure of that body over any period.

management company

means a company as defined in article 1a(2) of Council Directive 85/611/EEC of 20 December 1985 on the co-ordination of laws, regulations and administrative provisions relating to undertakings for collective investment in transferable securities (UCITS).

management expenses

(1) (except in INSPRU) (in accordance with section 223 of the *Act* (Management expenses))expenses incurred or expected to be incurred by the *FSCS* in connection with its function under COMP, other than *compensation costs*; for the purposes of *COMP* these are subdivided into *base costs*, *specific costs* and *establishment costs*.

(2) (in INSPRU) in relation to *long-term insurance business*, means all expenses, other than *commission*, incurred in the administration of an *insurer* or its business.

management expenses levy

a levy imposed by the *FSCS* on *participant firms* to meet the *management expenses* and which is made up of one or more of a *base cost levy* and a *specific costs levy*, each *participant firm's* share being calculated in accordance with FEES 6.4.

manager

(1) (in relation to an *AUT*) the *firm* which is the manager of the *AUT* in accordance with the *trust deed*.

(1A) (in relation to an *OEIC* which is an undertaking for collective investment in transferable securities within the meaning of the *UCITS Directive* and which has appointed a *person* to manage the scheme) the *person* appointed to manage the scheme.

(2) (as defined in section 423(1) and (2) of the *Act* (Manager)) (except in relation to a *unit trust scheme* or an undertaking for collective investment in transferable securities within the meaning of the *UCITS Directive* (other than a *unit trust scheme*) or an *undertaking* or a *registered friendly society*):

(a) an employee who:

(i) under the immediate authority of his employer, is responsible, either alone or jointly with one or more other individuals, for the conduct of his employer's business; or

(ii) under the immediate authority of his employer or of a *person* who is a manager in accordance with (i) exercises managerial functions or is responsible for maintaining accounts or other records of his employer;

(b) if the employer is not an individual, references in (a) to the authority of the employer are references to the authority:

(i) in the case of a *body corporate*, of the directors;

(ii) in the case of a *partnership*, of the partners; and

(iii) in the case of an unincorporated association, of its officers or the members of its governing body.

(3) (as defined in section 423(3) of the *Act* (Manager)) (in relation to a *body corporate* other than one covered at (1A) above):

(a) a *person* (other than an employee of the body) who is appointed by the body to manage any part of its business, including an employee of the *body corporate* (other than the *chief executive*) who under the immediate authority of a director or *chief executive* of the *body corporate* exercises managerial functions or is responsible for maintaining accounts or other records of the *body corporate*;

(b) for the purposes of (a) and in relation to a *body corporate* whose principal place of business is within the *United Kingdom*, the *chief executive* includes only a *person* who is an employee of the *body corporate* in accordance with section 417(1) of the *Act* (Definitions).

managing agent

(as defined in article 3(1) of the *Regulated Activities Order*) a *person* who is permitted by the *Council* in the conduct of his business as an *underwriting agent* to perform for a *member* one or more of the following functions:

(a) underwriting *contracts of insurance* at Lloyd's;

(b) reinsuring such contracts in whole or in part;

(c) paying claims on such contracts.

managing agent's agreement

an agreement in the form prescribed by the *Society*, between a *managing agent* and a *member*, under which the *managing agent* manages the *insurance business* of that *member*.

managing dormant account funds (including the investment of such funds)

the *regulated activity*, specified in article 63N(1)(b) of the *Regulated Activities Order*, which is the acceptance of a transfer by a *bank* or *building society* of the *balance* of a *dormant account*, or a proportion of such a balance, and the management of those funds (including the investment of such funds) in such a way as to enable the *dormant account fund operator* to meet whatever *repayment claims* it is prudent to anticipate.

managing investments

the *regulated activity*, specified in article 37 of the *Regulated Activities Order* (Managing investments), which is in summary: managing assets belonging to another *person* in circumstances which involve the exercise of discretion, if:

(a) the assets consist of or include any *security or contractually* based investment (that is, any *designated investment, funeral plan contract or right to or interest in a funeral plan contract); or*

(b) the arrangements for their management are such that the assets may consist of or include such investments, and either the assets have at any time since 29 April 1988 done so, or the arrangements have at any time (whether before or after that date) been held out as arrangements under which the assets would do so.

managing the underwriting capacity of a Lloyd's syndicate as a managing agent at Lloyd's

the *regulated activity*, specified in article 57 of the *Regulated Activities Order* (Managing the underwriting capacity of a Lloyd's syndicate), of managing the *underwriting capacity of a Lloyd's syndicate* as a *managing agent* at Lloyd's.

mandate rules

COB 9.2.

MAR

the Market conduct sourcebook.

margin

(in *COLL*) cash or other property paid, transferred or deposited under the terms of a *derivative*; for these purposes cash or property will be treated as having been paid, transferred or deposited if it must be paid, transferred or deposited in order to comply with a requirement imposed by the market on which the contract is made or traded.

margin agreement

(in accordance with Part 1 of Annex III of the *Banking Consolidation Directive* (Definitions) and for the purpose of BIPRU 13 (The calculation of counterparty risk exposure values for financial derivatives, securities financing transactions and long settlement transactions)) a contractual agreement or provisions to an agreement under which one counterparty must supply collateral to a second counterparty when an *exposure* of that second counterparty to the first counterparty exceeds a specified level.

margin lending transaction

(in accordance with Part 1 of Annex III of the *Banking Consolidation Directive* (Definitions) and for the purpose of BIPRU 13 (The calculation of counterparty risk exposure values for financial derivatives, securities financing transactions and long settlement transactions)) transactions in which a *person* extends credit in connection with the purchase, sale, carrying or trading of securities; the definition does not include other loans that happen to be secured by securities collateral.

margin period of risk

(in accordance with Part 1 of Annex III of the *Banking Consolidation Directive* (Definitions) and for the purpose of BIPRU 13 (The calculation of counterparty risk exposure values for financial derivatives, securities financing transactions and long settlement transactions)) the time period from the last exchange of collateral covering a *netting set* of transactions with a defaulting counterpart until that counterpart is closed out and the resulting market risk is re-hedged.

margin threshold

(in accordance with Part 1 of Annex III of the *Banking Consolidation Directive* (Definitions) and for the purpose of BIPRU 13 (The calculation of counterparty risk exposure values for financial derivatives, securities financing transactions and long settlement transactions)) the largest amount of an *exposure* that remains outstanding until one party has the right to call for collateral.

margined contract

(in COLL and *CIS*) any contract in *derivatives*.

margined transaction

(1) (except in *COB* 9.3) a transaction *executed* by a *firm* with or for a *client* relating to a *future*, *option* or *contract for differences* (or any right to or any interest in such an *investment*) under the terms of which the *client* will or may be liable to provide cash or *collateral* to secure performance of obligations which he may have to perform when the transaction falls to be completed or upon the earlier *closing out* of his position.

(2) (in *COB* 9.3):

(a) a transaction within (1); or

(b) an *option* purchased by a *client*, the terms of which provide that the maximum liability of the *client* in respect of the transaction will be limited to the amount payable as premium.

mark-up or mark-down

(a) (when a *firm* receives a *customer order* and takes a *principal* position in the relevant *investment* in order to fulfil that *customer order* (that is, when the *firm* takes a *principal* position in the relevant *investment* which it would not otherwise take, except to fulfil that *customer order*)) the difference, if any, between:

(i) the price at which the *firm* takes a *principal* position in the relevant *investment* in order to fulfil that *customer order;* and

(ii) the *price* at which the *firm executes* the transaction with its *customer*;

(b) (when a *firm executes* a *customer order* against its own book and owes a duty of best execution) the difference between:

(i) the *price* at which best execution would be achieved; and

(ii) the *price* at which the *firm executes* the transaction with its *customer.*

market abuse

(in accordance with section 118 of the *Act* (Market abuse)) *behaviour* (whether by one *person* alone or by two or more *persons* jointly or in concert) which:

(a) occurs in relation to *qualifying investments* traded or admitted to trading on a *prescribed market* or in respect of which a request for admission to trading on such a market has been made; and

(b) falls within any one or more of the types of *behaviour* set out in sections (9118(2) to (8) of the *Act*.

market abuse (dissemination)

the *behaviour* described in section 118(7) of the *Act*, which is the dissemination of information by any means which gives, or is likely to give, a false or misleading impression as to a *qualifying investment* by a *person* who knew or could reasonably be expected to have known that the information was false or misleading.

market abuse (distortion)

the *behaviour* described in section 118(8) of the *Act* which satisfies the condition in section 118(8)(b) and is *behaviour* (not falling within sections (9118(5), (6) or (7)) which:

(a) would be, or would be likely to be, regarded by a *regular user* of the market as behaviour that would distort, or would be likely to distort, the market in a *qualifying investment*; and

(b) is likely to be regarded by a *regular user* of the market as a failure on the part of the *person* concerned to observe the standard of *behaviour* reasonably expected of a *person* in his position in relation to the market.

market abuse (improper disclosure)

the *behaviour* described in section 118(3) of the *Act*, which is an *insider* disclosing *inside information* to another *person* otherwise than in the proper course of the exercise of employment, profession or duties.

market abuse (insider dealing)

the *behaviour* described in section 118(2) of the *Act*, which is an *insider dealing*, or attempting to *deal*, in a *qualifying investment* or *related investment* on the basis of *inside information* relating to the *investment* in question.

market abuse (manipulating devices)

the *behaviour* described in section 118(6) of the *Act*, which is effecting transactions or orders to trade which employ fictitious devices or any other form of deception or contrivance.

market abuse (manipulating transactions)

the *behaviour* described in section 118(5) of the *Act*, which is *behaviour* effecting transactions or orders to trade (otherwise than for legitimate reasons and in conformity with *accepted market practices* on the relevant market) which:

(a) give, or are likely to give a false or misleading impression as to the supply of, or demand for, or as to the price, one or more *qualifying investments*; or

(b) secure the price of one or more such investments at an abnormal or artificial level.

market abuse (misleading behaviour)

the *behaviour* described in section 118(8) of the *Act* which satisfies the condition in section 118(8)(a) and is *behaviour* (not falling within sections (9118(5), (6) or (7)) which:

(a) is likely to give a *regular user* of the market a false or misleading impression as to the supply of, demand for or price or value of, *qualifying investments*, and

(b) is likely to be regarded by a *regular user* of the market as a failure on the part of the *person* concerned to observe the standard of *behaviour* reasonably expected of a *person* in his position in relation to the market.

market abuse (misuse of information)

the *behaviour* described in section 118(4) of the *Act*, which is *behaviour* (not falling within sections (9118 (2) or (3) of the *Act*):

(a) based on information which is not generally available to those using the market but which, if available to a *regular user* of the market, would be, or would be likely to be, regarded by him as relevant when deciding the terms on which transactions in *qualifying investments* should be effected; and

(b) likely to be regarded by a *regular user* of the market as a failure on the part of the *person* concerned to observe the standard of *behaviour* reasonably expected of a *person* in his position in relation to the market.

Market Abuse Directive

Directive of the European Parliament and of the Council of 28 January 2003 on insider dealing and market manipulation (market abuse) (No 2003/6/EC).

market abuse regime

the regime established under the provisions of Part VIII of the *Act* (Penalties for market abuse).

market contract

a market contract as described in section 155 of the Companies Act 1989 or article 80 of the Companies (No 2) (Northern Ireland) Order 1990 which is in summary:

(a) a contract entered into by a *member* or *designated non-member* of an *RIE* which is either:
  (i) a contract made on the exchange or an exchange to whose undertaking the exchange has succeeded; or
  (ii) a contract in the making of which the *member* or *designated on-member* was subject to the rules of the exchange or of an exchange to whose undertaking the exchange has succeeded;

(b) a contract entered into by an *RIE* or *RCH*, in its capacity as such, with one of its *members* for the purpose of *investments*, or with an *RCH* or with an *RIE*, for the purpose of:
  (i) enabling the rights and liabilities of that *member*, or clearing house or other investment exchange, under a transaction to be settled; or
  (ii) providing central counterparty clearing services (as described in section 155(3A) of the Companies Act 1989) to that *member* or clearing house or other investment exchange.

market counterparty]

(for the purposes only of COBS TP 1 (Transitional Provisions in relation to Client Categorisation));

(1) (except in *COB* 3) a *client* who is:
  (a) a properly constituted government (including a quasi-governmental body or a government agency) of any country or territory;
  (b) a central bank or other national monetary authority of any country or territory;
  (c) a supranational whose members are either countries or central banks or national monetary authorities;
  (d) a State investment body, or a body charged with, or intervening in, the management of the public debt;
  (e) another *firm*, or an *overseas financial services institution*, except in relation to *designated investment business*, and related *ancillary activities*, conducted with or for that *firm* or institution, when that *firm* or institution is an *intermediate customer* in accordance with COB 4.1.7R (Classification of another firm or an overseas financial.M5 services institution);
  (f) any *associate* of a *firm* (except an *OPS firm*), or of an *overseas financial services institution*, if the *firm* or institution consents;
  (g) a *client* when he is classified as a *market counterparty* in accordance with COB 4.1.12R (Large intermediate customer classified as a market counterparty);
  (h) a *recognised investment exchange*, *designated investment exchange*, *regulated market* or *clearing house* when it is classified as a *market counterparty* in accordance with COB 4.1.8A R (Classification of an exchange or clearing house);

but excluding:
(A) a *regulated collective investment scheme*; and
(B) (except for the purposes of DISP) a client, who would otherwise be a market counterparty, when he is classified as a private customer in accordance with COB 4.1.14R (Client classified as private customer).
(C) (in COB 3) a *person* in (1) and a *person* who would be such a person if he were a *client*.

market liquidity stress

(in relation to a *firm* and any reporting obligations under *SUP* 16 (Reporting requirements)):
(a) (in the case of reporting obligations on a solo basis) any market that is of material significance to the *firm* being materially adversely affected by crystallised *liquidity risk* or a substantial number of participants in any such market being materially adversely affected by crystallised *liquidity risk*, whether or not the *firm* itself is so affected;
(b) (in the case of reporting obligations with respect to the *firm* and a group of other persons) has the same meaning as in (a) except that references to the *firm* are to the *firm* and that group considered together;
(c) (in the case of reporting obligations with respect to a *firm's UK branch*) has the same meaning as in (a) except that references to the *firm* are to that *branch*.

market maker

(1) (except in *COBS*) (in relation to an *investment*) a *person* who (otherwise than in his capacity as the *operator* of a *regulated collective investment scheme*) holds himself out as able and willing to enter into transactions of sale and purchase in *investments* of that description at prices determined by him generally and continuously rather than in respect of each particular transaction.
(2) (in *COBS*) a *person* who holds himself out on the financial markets on a continuous basis as being willing to deal on own account by buying and selling *financial instruments* against his proprietary capital at prices defined by him.

[**Note:** article 4 (1)(8) of *MiFID*]

market operator

a *person* who manages and/or operates the business of a *regulated market*. The *market operator* may be the *regulated market* itself.

[**Note:** article 4(1)(13) of *MiFID*]

market risk

(in relation to a *firm*) the risks that arise from fluctuations in values of, or income from, assets or in interest or exchange rates.

market risk capital requirement

the part of the *capital resources requirement* of a *BIPRU firm* in respect of *market risk*, calculated in accordance with GENPRU 2.1.52R (Calculation of the market risk capital requirement).

market value

the market value as determined in accordance with generally accepted accounting practice.

marketable investment

(a) an *investment* which is traded on or under the rules of an exchange;
(b) a debt instrument which may be transferred without the consent of the *issuer* or any other *person* (including a collateralised mortgage obligation);
(c) a *commodity*;
(d) a *warrant*, *option*, *future* or other instrument which entitles the holder to subscribe for or acquire:
  (i) an *investment* or *commodity* in (a) to (c); or
  (ii) any currency; or
  (iii) any combination of (i) and (ii);
(e) a *contract for differences* (including interest rate and currency swaps) relating to fluctuations in:
  (i) the value or price of an *investment* or *commodity* in (a) to.(d); or
  (ii) any currency; or
  (iii) the rate of interest in any currency or any index of such rates; or
  (iv) the level of any index which is derived from the prices of an *investment* or *commodity* in (a) to (c); or
  (v) any combination of (i) to (iv);
(f) *warrants*, *options*, *futures* or other instruments entitling the holder to obtain the rights of those contracts in (d) or (e);

(g) a unit in a regulated collective investment scheme.

marketing

(in COLL) (in relation to marketing *units* in a *regulated collective investment scheme* in a particular country or territory):

(a) *communicating* to a *person* in that country or territory an invitation or inducement to become, or offer to become, a *holder* in that *regulated collective investment scheme*;

(b) giving *advice on investments* to, or *arranging (bringing about) a deal in an investment* for a *person* in that country or territory to become a *holder* in that *regulated collective investment scheme*.

marketing group

a group of *persons* who:

(a) are allied together (either formally or informally) for the purposes of marketing *packaged products* of the *marketing group*; and

(b) each of whom, if it holds itself out in the *United Kingdom* as marketing *packaged products* to *private customers*, does so only as an *investment manager* or in relation to *packaged products* of the *marketing group*.

marketing group associate

a *firm* other than a *product provider* which is a member of a *marketing group*.

marriage or the formation of a civil partnership and birth

(in relation to a *class* of *contract of insurance*) the *class* of *contract of insurance*, specified in paragraph II of Part II of Schedule 1 to the *Regulated Activities Order* (Contracts of long-term insurance), to provide a sum on marriage or the formation of a civil partnership or on the birth of a child, being contracts expressed to be in effect for a period of more than one year.

master netting agreement internal models approach

one of the following:

(a) the method of calculating the effect of *credit risk mitigation* described in BIPRU 5.6.16R to BIPRU 5.6.28G;

(b) (where the approach in (a) is being applied on a consolidated basis) the method in (a) as applied on a consolidated basis in accordance with BIPRU 8 (Group risk — consolidation); or

(c) when the reference is to the rules of or administered by a *regulatory body* other than the *FSA*, whatever corresponds to the approach in (a) or (b), as the case may be, under those rules.

master netting agreement internal models approach permission

a *requirement* or a *waiver* that requires a *firm* to use the *master netting agreement internal models approach* on a solo basis or, if the context requires, a consolidated basis.

matched principal exemption conditions

the conditions set out in BIPRU 1.1.23R(2) (Meaning of dealing on own account).

material currency

(a) *Material currencies*, in respect of a *firm* at any time, are currencies determined in accordance with the following.

(b) First, the amount of its assets and the amount of its liabilities in each currency (ignoring the sign) are separately calculated. The figures are as shown in the most recent *data item* FSA054 submitted to the *FSA*.

(c) Then, each such amount is converted into the reporting currency for the *data item* referred to in (b).

(d) Each currency (which may include the reporting currency) that represents 20% or more of the total asset figure or 20% or more of the total liabilities figure is a *material currency*.

(e) A currency is also a *material currency* if it is identified by the *firm's* current:
  (i) Individual Liquidity Adequacy Assessment; or
  (ii) Individual Liquidity Systems Assessment; or
  (iii) ILG that has been accepted by the firm; as being significant in the context of cross-currency liquidity risk (as referred to in BIPRU 12.5 (Individual Liquidity Adequacy Standards)).

(f) The conversion rate for a currency into the reporting currency is the exchange rate on the date as of which the calculation is being made.

(g) The reporting currency means the currency in which the most recent *data item* FSA054 (as referred to in (b)) is reported.

(h) A currency is a *material currency* in relation to a *firm's branch* or a *defined liquidity group* of which it is *a group liquidity reporting firm* if it is identified as such in accordance with the procedures in the previous paragraphs of this definition except that the identification is carried out by reference to that *branch* or *defined liquidity group*.

For these purposes, *data item* FSA054 for the *reporting level* concerned is used.

(i) If the *firm* has not delivered *data item* FSA054 to the *FSA* at the *reporting level* concerned or is currently not required to do so at the *reporting level* concerned, the calculation is carried out using the methods for drawing up *data item* FSA054.

material holding

(1) (for the purposes of *ELM*) a holding or position set out in *ELM* 2.4.17R (Material holdings).

(2) (for the purposes of GENPRU and BIPRU) has the meaning in GENPRU 2.2.209R (Deductions from tiers one and two: Material holdings).

material insurance holding

has the meaning in GENPRU 2.2.212R (Material holdings) or, for an *exempt CAD firm* which is an *investment management firm*, in *IPRU(INV)* Table 5.2.2(1).

material interest

(in *COBS*) (in relation to a transaction) any interest of a material nature, other than:

(a) disclosable *commission* on the transaction;

(b) goods or services which can reasonably be expected to assist in carrying on *designated investment business* with or for *clients* and which are provided or to be provided in compliance with COBS 11.6.3R.

material outsourcing

outsourcing services of such importance that weakness, or failure, of the services would cast serious doubt upon the *firm's* continuing satisfaction of the *threshold conditions* or compliance with the *Principles*.

mathematical reserves

the provision made by an *insurer* to cover liabilities (excluding liabilities which have fallen due and liabilities arising from *deposit back arrangements*) arising under or in connection with *long-term insurance contracts*.

maxi-ISA

an ISA which includes a *stocks and shares component* and may also include other *qualifying investments* such as:

(a) a *cash component;*

(b) an *insurance component*;

as prescribed in paragraphs 7, 8 and 9 respectively of the ISA *Regulations*.

MCAS scheme

Mortgage Code Arbitration Scheme.

MCOB

the Mortgages: Conduct of Business sourcebook.

MCR

minimum capital requirement.

media firm

a firm whose only *permitted activities* are *advising on investments* and *agreeing to carry on that regulated activity*, and whose *Part IV permission* includes *requirements* to the effect that the *firm* must advise:

(a) only through the media; and

(b) without conveying the impression that the advice is particularly suitable for any *person*, except when it is given in response to a specific request for advice from that *person*;

in this definition, "media" means:

(i) newspapers, journals, magazines or other periodical publications;

(ii) services comprising regularly updated news or information;

(iii) services consisting of the broadcast or transmission of television or radio programmes.

meeting of repayment claims

the *regulated activity*, specified in article 63N(1)(a) of the *Regulated Activities Order*, which is the meeting of *repayment claims* by a *dormant account fund operator*.

member

(1) (except in *PROF*, *LR*, EG 16 and *REC*) a *person* admitted to membership of the *Society* or any *person* by law entitled or bound to administer his affairs.

(2) (in *PROF*, *LR* and EG 16) (as defined in section 325(2) of the *Act* (Authority's general duty)) (in relation to a profession) a *person* who is entitled to practise that profession and, in practising it, is subject to the rules of the relevant *designated professional body*, whether or not he is a member of that body.

(3) (in *REC*) (in relation to a *recognised body*) a *person* who is entitled, under an arrangement or agreement between him and that body, to use that body's *facilities*.

member contribution

any paid up contribution by a member of a *mutual* where the members' accounts meet the following criteria:

(a) the memorandum and articles of association or other constitutional documents must stipulate that payments may be made from these accounts to members only in so far as this does not cause the *firm's capital resources* to fall below the required level, or, if after dissolution of the *firm*, all the *firm's* other debts have been settled;

(b) the memorandum and articles of association or other constitutional documents must stipulate, with respect to the payments referred to in (a) made for reasons other than the individual termination of membership, that the *FSA* must be notified at least one month in advance of the intended date of such payments; and

(c) the *FSA* must be notified of any amendment to the relevant provisions of the memorandum and articles of association or other constitutional documents.

member society

(as defined in article 2(2) of the *compensation transitionals order*) a person who at any time before *commencement* was a member society within the rules of the Friendly Societies Protection Scheme established in accordance with section 141 of the Financial Services.M8 Act 1986.

members' adviser

a firm whose permission includes *advising on syndicate participation at Lloyd's*, but which is not an *underwriting agent.*

members' agent

an *underwriting agent* who carries on the *regulated activity of advising on syndicate participation at Lloyd's.*

membership of a Lloyd's syndicate

the *investment*, specified in article 86(2) of the *Regulated Activities Order*, which is a *person's* membership (or prospective membership) of a Lloyd's *syndicate*.

mesothelioma regulations

The Compensation Act 2006 (Contribution for Mesothelioma Claims) Regulations 2006 (SI 2006/3259).

mesothelioma victim

(in accordance with section 3 (1) of the Compensation Act 2006) a *person* who has contracted mesothelioma as a result of exposure to asbestos by a *responsible person*.

micro-enterprise

an enterprise which:

(a) employs fewer than 10 *persons*; and

(b) has a turnover or annual balance sheet that does not exceed €2 million.

In this definition, "enterprise" means any *person* engaged in an economic activity, irrespective of legal form an includes, in particular, self-employed *persons* and family businesses engaged in craft or other activities, and *partnerships* or associations regularly engaged in an economic activity.

[**Note:** article 4(26) of the *Payment Services Directive* and the Annex to the *Micro-enterprise Recommendation*]

Micro-enterprise Recommendation

Recommendation 2003/362/EC of the Commission of 6th May 2003 concerning the definition of micro, small and medium-sized enterprises.

MIIC

the *Motor Insurers' Information Centre.*

MiFID

The European Parliament and Council Directive on markets in financial instruments (No 2004/39/EC). See also *MiFID Regulation* and *MiFID implementing Directive*.

MiFID business

investment services and activities and, where relevant, *ancillary services* carried on by a *MiFID investment firm.*

MiFID client money chapter

[deleted]

MiFID client money (minimum implementing) rules

CASS 7.3.1R, *CASS* 7.3.2R, *CASS* 7.4.1R, *CASS* 7.4.5R, *CASS* 7.4.7R, *CASS* 7.4.8R, *CASS* 7.4.11R, *CASS* 7.6.1R, *CASS* 7.6.2R and *CASS* 7.6.9R.

MiFID client money segregation requirements

[deleted]

MiFID custody chapter

[deleted]

MiFID implementing Directive

Commission Directive No 2006/73/EC implementing Directive 2004/39/EC of the European Parliament and of the Council as regards organisational requirements and operating conditions for investment firms and defined terms for the purposes of that Directive.

MiFID implementing requirement

(1) (in relation to a *UK RIE*) any of the requirements applicable to that body under the *MiFID Regulation*.
(2) (in relation to a body applying for recognition as a *UK RIE*) any of the requirements under the *MiFID Regulation* which, if its application were successful, would apply to it.

MiFID investment firm

(in summary) a *firm* to which *MiFID* applies including, for some purposes only, a *credit institution* and *UCITS investment firm*.

(in full) a *firm* which is:
(1) an *investment firm* with its head office in the *EEA* (or, if it has a registered office, that office);
(2) a *BCD credit institution* (only when providing an *investment service or activity* in relation to the *rules* implementing the articles referred to in article 1(2) of *MiFID*);
(3) a *UCITS investment firm* (only when providing the services referred to in article 5(3) of the *UCITS Directive* in relation to the *rules* implementing the articles of *MiFID* referred to in article 5(4) of that Directive);

unless, and to the extent that, *MiFID* does not apply to it as a result of article 2 (Exemptions) or article 3 (Optional exemptions) of *MiFID*.

MiFID or equivalent third country business

MiFID business or the *equivalent business of a third country investment firm*.

MiFID outsourcing rules

SYSC 8.1.1R to *SYSC* 8.1.11R.

MiFID Regulation

Commission Regulation (EC) 1287/2006 implementing Directive 2004/39/EC of the European Parliament and of the Council as regards organisational requirements and operating conditions for investment firms and defined terms for the purposes of that Directive

mineral company

(in LR) a *company* or *group*, whose principal activity is, or is planned to be, the *extraction* of *mineral resources* (which may or may not include exploration for *mineral resources*).

mineral expert's report

(in LR) a report prepared in accordance with the *CESR recommendations*.

mineral resources

(in LR) include metallic and non-metallic ores, mineral concentrates, industrial minerals, construction aggregates, mineral oils, natural gases, hydrocarbons and solid fuels including coal.

mini-ISA

an *ISA* which contains only one of the following *qualifying investments*:
(a) a *stocks and shares component*;
(b) a *cash component*;
(c) an *insurance component*;

as prescribed in paragraph 7, 8 or 9 respectively of the *ISA Regulations*.

minimum capital requirement

an amount of *capital resources* that a *firm* must hold as set out in GENPRU 2.1.24R and GENPRU 2.1.25R.

minimum guarantee fund

a minimum guarantee fund as defined in *IPRU(INS)* 2.9 as that *rule* was in force on 30 December 2004.

minimum IRB standards

(in relation to the *IRB approach*) BIPRU 4.3.9R, BIPRU 4.3.11RBIPRU 4.3.29R, BIPRU 4.3.33R-BIPRU 4.3.40R, BIPRU 4.3.43R, BIPRU 4.3.44R, BIPRU 4.3.46R-BIPRU 4.3.48R, BIPRU 4.3.50R, BIPRU 4.3.51R, BIPRU 4.3.54R, BIPRU 4.3.56R-BIPRU 4.3.57R, BIPRU 4.3.63R, BIPRU 4.3.70R-BIPRU 4.3.71R, BIPRU 4.3.73RBIPRU 4.3.74R, BIPRU 4.3.83R-BIPRU 4.3.85R, BIPRU 4.3.88R, BIPRU 4.3.90R-BIPRU 4.3.92R, BIPRU 4.3.94R, BIPRU 4.3.99R, BIPRU 4.3.103R, BIPRU 4.3.116R-BIPRU 4.3.123R, BIPRU 4.3.125R-BIPRU 4.3.131R, BIPRU 4.4.6R-BIPRU 4.4.9R, BIPRU 4.4.11R-BIPRU 4.4.13R, BIPRU 4.4.15R-BIPRU 4.4.18R, BIPRU 4.4.21R-BIPRU 4.4.22R, BIPRU 4.4.24R-BIPRU 4.4.25R, BIPRU 4.4.27R-BIPRU 4.4.28R, BIPRU 4.4.30R-BIPRU 4.4.31R, BIPRU 4.4.48R-BIPRU 4.4.51R, BIPRU 4.4.53R, BIPRU 4.4.54R, BIPRU 4.5.5R, BIPRU 4.6.6R-BIPRU 4.6.9R, BIPRU 4.6.11R-BIPRU 4.6.12R, BIPRU 4.6.14R, BIPRU 4.6.18R, BIPRU 4.6.20R-BIPRU 4.6.21R, BIPRU 4.6.24R-BIPRU 4.6.34R, BIPRU 4.6.37R-BIPRU 4.6.39R, BIPRU 4.7.19R, BIPRU 4.7.27R-BIPRU 4.7.35R, BIPRU 4.8.5R-BIPRU 4.8.9R, BIPRU 4.8.11R-BIPRU 4.8.15R, BIPRU 4.10.40R-BIPRU 4.10.48R.

minimum levy

(in FEES) the fixed minimum *general levy* payable by a *firm*.

minimum multiplication factor

(in BIPRU 7.10 (Use of a value at risk model)) has the meaning in BIPRU 7.10.119R (Capital calculations: Multiplication factors), which is in summary the number three or any higher amount the *VaR model permission* defines it as.

MIPRU

the Prudential sourcebook for Mortgage and Home Finance Firms, and Insurance Intermediaries

miscellaneous financial loss

(in relation to a *class* of *contract of insurance*) the *class* of *contract of insurance*, specified in paragraph 16 of Part I of Schedule 1 to the *Regulated Activities Order* (General contracts of insurance), against any of the following risks:

(a) risks of loss to the *persons* insured attributable to interruptions of the carrying on of business carried on by them or to reduction of the scope of business so carried on;

(b) risks of loss to the *persons* insured attributable to their incurring unforeseen expense (other than loss such as is covered by contracts within paragraph 18 of Part I of Schedule 1 to the *Regulated Activities Order* (Assistance));

(c) risks which do not fall within paragraphs (a) or (b) and which are not of such a kind that *contracts of insurance* against them fall within any other provision of Schedule 1 to the *Regulated Activities Order*.

misleading statements and practices offence

any of the offences described in section 397 of the *Act* (Misleading statements and practices), which are in summary:

(a) the offence of:

  (i) making a statement, promise or forecast, which the *person* making the statement, promise or forecast knows.to be misleading, false or deceptive in a material particular; or

  (ii) dishonestly concealing any material facts whether in connection with a statement, promise or forecast made by the *person* concealing the facts or otherwise; or

  (iii) recklessly making (dishonestly or otherwise) a statement, promise or forecast which is misleading, false or deceptive in a material particular;

  where the *person* makes the statement, promise or forecast or conceals the facts for the purpose of inducing, or is reckless as to whether it may induce, another *person* (whether or not that *person* is the same *person* to whom the statement, promise or forecast is made):

(b) to enter or offer to enter into, or to refrain from entering or offering to enter into, a relevant agreement; or

(c) to exercise, or refrain from exercising, any rights conferred by a relevant investment;

(d) the offence of doing any act or engaging in any course of conduct which creates a false or misleading impression as to the market in or the price or value of any relevant investments where the act was done or the course of conduct engaged in for the purpose of creating that impression and of thereby inducing another *person* to acquire, dispose of, subscribe for or underwrite those investments or to refrain from doing so, or to exercise, or refrain from exercising, any rights conferred by those investments;

in this definition:

"relevant agreement" means an agreement:
(I) the entering into or performance of which by either party constitutes an activity of a kind specified in an order made by the Treasury or one which falls within a specified class of activity; and
(II) which relates to a relevant investment;

"relevant investment" means an investment of a kind specified in an order made by the Treasury or one which falls within a class of investment prescribed in regulations made by the Treasury.

mixed-activity holding company

one of the following:
(a) (in accordance with Article 4(20) of the *Banking Consolidation Directive* (Definitions)) a *parent undertaking*, other than a *financial holding company*, a *credit institution* or a *mixed financial holding company*, the *subsidiary undertakings* of which include at least one *credit institution*; or
(b) (in accordance with Articles 2(2) and 37(1) of the *Capital Adequacy Directive* (Supervision on a consolidated basis) and in relation to a *banking and investment group* without *any credit institutions* in it) a *parent undertaking*, other than a *financial holding company*, an *investment firm* or a *mixed financial holding company*, the *subsidiary undertakings* of which include at least one *investment firm*.

mixed-activity insurance holding company

(in accordance with Article 1(j) of the *Insurance Groups Directive* (Definitions)) a *parent undertaking*, other than an *insurance undertaking*, an *insurance holding company* or a *mixed financial holding company*, the *subsidiary undertakings* of which include at least one *insurance undertaking*.

mixed financial holding company

(in accordance with Article 2(15) of the *Financial Groups Directive* (Definitions)) a *parent undertaking*, other than a *regulated entity*, which meets the following conditions:
(a) it, together with its *subsidiary undertakings*, at least one of which is an *EEA regulated entity*, and other entities, constitutes a *financial conglomerate*;
(b) it has been notified by its *coordinator* that its group is a *financial conglomerate* in accordance with Article 4(2) of the *Financial Groups Directive*; and
(c) it has not been notified that its *coordinator* and other *relevant competent authorities* have agreed not to treat the group as a *financial conglomerate* in accordance with Article 3(3) of the *Financial Groups Directive*.

mixed insurer

an *insurer* (other than a *pure reinsurer*) which carries on *reinsurance* business and where one or more of the following conditions is met in respect of its *reinsurance* acceptances:
(a) the *premiums* collected in respect of those acceptances during the previous *financial year* exceeded 10% of its total *premiums* collected during that year;
(b) the *premiums* collected in respect of those acceptances during the previous *financial year* exceeded €50 million; and
(c) the *technical provisions* in respect of those acceptances at the end of the previous *financial year* exceeded 10% of its total *technical provisions* at the end of that year.

mixed remittance

a remittance that is part *client money* and part other *money*.

MLAR

(in SUP) a Mortgage Lending and Administration Return containing data specified in SUP 16 Ann 19AR and relevant to the *firm's* type and *regulated activities*

MLRO

money laundering reporting officer.

Model Code

the Model Code on directors' dealings in securities set out in LR 9 Ann 1.

model PRR

the part of the *market risk capital requirement* calculated under a *VaR model permission* as more fully defined in BIPRU 7.10 (Use of a Value at Risk Model).

modified auditor's report

(in LR) an auditor's report:
(a) in which the auditor's opinion is qualified; or
(b) which sets out:

(i) a problem relating to the business as a going concern; or
(ii) a significant uncertainty, the resolution of which is dependent upon future events.

modified CIU look through method

the method for calculating *PRR* for a *CIU* set out in BIPRU 7.7.4R, BIPRU 7.7.7R to BIPRU 7.7.8R and BIPRU 7.7.11R to BIPRU 7.7.12R

money

any form of money, including cheques and other payable orders.

money laundering

any act which:
(a) constitutes an offence under section 18 (Money laundering) of the Terrorism Act 2000; or
(b) constitutes an offence under section 327 (Concealing etc), section 328 (Arrangements) or section 329 (Acquisition, use and possession) of the Proceeds of Crime Act 2002; or
(c) constitutes an attempt, conspiracy or incitement to commit an offence specified in paragraph (b); or
(d) constitutes aiding, abetting, counselling or procuring the commission of an offence specified in paragraph (b); or
(e) would constitute an offence specified in paragraph (b), (c) or (d) if done in the *United Kingdom*.

Money Laundering Directive

the Council Directive of 10 June 1991 on the prevention of the use of the financial system for the purpose of money laundering (91/308/EEC) as amended by the Council Directive of 4 December 2001 (2001/97/EEC).

Money Laundering Regulations

the Money Laundering Regulations 2007 (SI 2007/2157).

Money Laundering Regulations 2001

[deleted]

money laundering reporting function

controlled function CF11 *in the table of controlled functions*, described more fully in SUP 10.7.13R.

money laundering reporting officer

the individual appointed by a *firm* in accordance with SYSC 3.2.6IR or SYSC 6.3.9R.

money-market instrument

any of the following *investments*:
(a) a *debenture* which is issued on terms requiring repayment not later than five years from the date of issue;
(b) any *government and public security* which is issued on terms requiring repayment not later than one year or, if issued by a local authority in the *United Kingdom*, five years from the date of issue;
(c) a *warrant* which entitles the holder to subscribe for an *investment* within (a) or (b);
(d) a *certificate representing certain securities* or *rights to or interests in investments* relating, in either case, to an *investment* within (a) or (b);
(e) an *option* relating to:
 (i) an instrument in (a) or (b); or
 (ii) currency of the *United Kingdom* or of any other country or territory; or
 (iii) gold or silver;
(f) a *future* for the sale of:
 (i) an instrument in (a) or (b); or
 (ii) currency of the *United Kingdom* or of any other country or territory; or
 (iii) gold or silver;
(g) a *contract for differences* by reference to fluctuations in:
 (i) the value or price of any instrument within any of (a) to (f); or
 (ii) currency of the *United Kingdom* or of any other country or territory; or
 (iii) the rate of interest on loans in any such currency or any index of such rates;
(h) an *option* to acquire or dispose of an instrument within (e), (f) or (g).

money market instrument activity

an activity in respect of a transaction:
(a) which involves any of the following *investments* and is not regulated by the rules of a *recognised investment exchange*:
(b) a *debenture* which is issued on terms requiring repayment not later than five years from the date of issue;

Part II FSA Handbook Materials

(c) any *government and public security* which is issued on terms requiring repayment not later than one year or, if issued by a local authority in the *United Kingdom*, five years from the date of issue; or
(d) a *warrant* which entitles the holder to subscribe for an *investment* within (a)(i) or (a)(ii);
(e) which involves any of the following *investments* and is not made on a *recognised investment exchange* or expressed to be so made:
(f) a certificate representing certain securities or rights to or interests in investments relating, in either case, to an investment within (a)(i) or (a)(ii);
(g) an option relating to:
(h) an instrument in (a)(i) or (a)(ii); or
(i) currency of the *United Kingdom* or of any other country or territory; or
(j) gold or silver;
(k) a *future* for the sale of:
(l) an instrument in (a)(i) or (a)(ii); or
(m) currency of the *United Kingdom* or of any other country or territory; or
(n) gold or silver;
(o) a contract for differences by reference to fluctuations in:
(p) the value or price of any instrument within any of (a)(i) to (a)(iii) or (b)(i) to (b)(iii); or
(q) currency of the United Kingdom or of any other country or territory; or
(r) the rate of interest on loans in any such currency or any index of such rates; or
(s) an option to acquire or dispose of an instrument within (b)(ii), (b)(iii) or (b)(iv); or
(t) where one of the parties agrees to sell or transfer a debenture or government and public security and by the same or a collateral agreement that party agrees, or acquires an option, to buy back or re-acquire that investment or an equivalent amount of a similar investment within twelve months of the sale or transfer.
For the purposes of (c) investments are regarded as similar if they entitle their holders to the same rights against the same persons as to capital and interest and the same remedies for the enforcement of those rights.

money-market instruments

those classes of *financial instruments* which are normally dealt in on the money market, such as treasury bills, certificates of deposit and commercial papers and excluding instruments of payment.

[**Note:** article 4(1)(19) of *MiFID*]

money-purchase benefits

(1) (except in COMP) (in relation to an *occupational pension scheme*) benefits the rate or amount of which are calculated by reference to a payment or payments made by a member of the scheme.
(2) (in COMP) in relation to a member of a *personal pension scheme* or an *occupational pension scheme* or the widow or widower or surviving civil partner of a member of such a scheme, means benefits the rate or amount of which is calculated by reference to a payment or payments made by the member or by any other *person* in respect of the member and which are not average salary benefits.

money-purchase occupational scheme

an *occupational pension scheme* which provides *money-purchase benefits*.

money purchase scheme

in relation to a *director*, means a pension scheme under which all of the benefits that may become payable to or in respect of the *director* are money purchase benefits.

money remittance

(in accordance with regulation 2(1) of the Payment Service Regulations) a service for the transmission of money (or any representation of monetary value), without any payment accounts being created in the name of the payer or the payee, where:

- funds are received from a payer for the sole purpose of transferring a corresponding amount to a payee or to another payment service provider acting on behalf of the apyee; or
- funds are received on behalf of, and made available to, the payee.

[**Note**: article 4(13) of the Payment Services Directive]

money service business

carrying on by way of business the activity of:
(a) operating a bureau de change; or
(b) transmitting money, or any representation of monetary value, by any means; or
(c) cashing cheques which are made payable to customers.

money service operator

a person who carries on money service business other than a *firm*, a *BCD credit institution or a financial institution.*

month

(in accordance with the Interpretation Act 1978) a calendar month.

monthly financial return

(in UPRU) means the return referred to in SUP.

Mortgage and General Insurance Complaints Transitional Order

The Financial Services and Markets Act 2000 (Transitional Provisions) (Complaints Relating to General Insurance and Mortgages) Order 2004 (SI 2004/454)

mortgage administrator

a *firm* with *permission* (or which ought to have *permission*) for *administering a regulated mortgage contract.*

mortgage adviser

a *firm* with *permission* (or which ought to have *permission*) for *advising on regulated mortgage contracts.*

mortgage arranger

a *firm* with *permission* (or which ought to have *permission*) for *arranging* (see also *arranging (bringing about) regulated mortgage contracts* and *making arrangements with a view to regulated mortgage contracts*).

mortgage credit card

a *plastic card* which is a credit card issued under a *regulated mortgage contract* and not regulated by the Consumer Credit Act 1974.

mortgage intermediary

a *firm* with *permission* (or which ought to have *permission*) to carry on *mortgage mediation activity.*

mortgage lender

a *firm* with *permission* (or which ought to have *permission*) for *entering into a regulated mortgage contract.*

mortgage mediation activity

(as defined in article 26 of the Financial Services and Markets Act 2000 (Regulated Activities) (Amendment) (No 1) Order 2003 (SI 2003/1475)) any of the following *regulated activities*:
(a) *arranging (bringing about) regulated mortgage contracts* (article 25A(1));
(b) *making arrangements with a view to regulated mortgage contracts* (article 25A(2));
(c) *advising on regulated mortgage contracts* (article 53A);
(d) *agreeing to carry on a regulated activity* in (a) to (c) (article 64).

mortgage mediation activity

any of the following *regulated activities*:
(a) *arranging (bringing about) regulated mortgage contracts* (article 25A(1));
(b) *making arrangements with a view to regulated mortgage contracts* (article 25A(2));
(c) *advising on regulated mortgage contracts* (article 53A);
(d) *agreeing to carry on a regulated activity* in (a) to (c) (article 64).

most important financial sector

(in relation to a *financial sector* in a *consolidation group* or a *financial conglomerate* and in accordance with GENPRU 3.1 (Cross sector groups)) the *financial sector* with the largest average referred to in the box titled Threshold Test 2 in the *financial conglomerate definition decision tree* (10% ratio of balance sheet size and solvency requirements); and so that the *investment services sector* and the *banking sector* are treated as one for the purpose of the definition of *financial conglomerate* and for any other purpose that *GENPRU* 3.1 (Cross sector groups) says they are.

Motor Insurers' Information Centre

the information centre appointed to meet the *United Kingdom's* obligations under article 5 of the *Fourth Motor Insurance Directive* (Information Centres).

motor vehicle liability

(in relation to a *class* of *contract of insurance*) the *class* of *contract of insurance*, specified in paragraph 10 of Part I of Schedule 1 to the *Regulated Activities Order* (Contracts of general insurance), against damage arising out of or in connection with the use of motor vehicles on land, including third-party risks and carrier's liability.

motor vehicle liability claims handling rules

[deleted]

motor vehicle liability insurance business

general insurance business of class 10, other than:
(a) carrier's liability;
(b) pure reinsurance of that class.

motor vehicle liability insurer

(a) a firm with permission to carry on motor vehicle liability insurance business;
(b) any person carrying on the regulated activity of managing the underwriting capacity of a Lloyd's syndicate in respect of members whose insurance business at Lloyd's includes motor vehicle liability insurance business.

MTF

a *multilateral trading facility*.

MTF transaction

a transaction concluded by a *firm* under the rules governing an *MTF* with another member or participant of that *MTF*.

multilateral development bank

(a) any of the following:
- (i) African Development Bank;
- (ii) Asian Development Bank;
- (iii) Caribbean Development Bank;
- (iv) Council of Europe Development Bank;
- (v) European Bank for Reconstruction & Development;
- (vi) European Investment Bank;
- (vii) European Investment Fund;
- (viii) Inter-American Development Bank;
- (ix) International Bank for Reconstruction and Development;
- (x) International Finance Corporation;
- (xa) International Finance Facility for Immunisation;
- (xb) Islamic Development Bank;
- (xi) Multilateral Investment Guarantee Agency; and
- (xi) Multilateral Investment Guarantee Agency; and
- (xii) Nordic Investment Bank;

(b) for the purposes of the standardised approach to credit risk the following are considered to be a multilateral development bank:
- (i) the Inter-American Investment Corporation;
- (ii) the Black Sea Trade and Development Bank; and
- (iii) the Central American Bank for Economic Integration

multilateral trading facility

a multilateral system, operated by an *investment firm* or a *market operator*, which brings together multiple third-party buying and selling interests in *financial instruments* – in the system and in accordance with non-discretionary rules – in a way that results in a contract in accordance with the provisions of Title II of *MiFID*.

[**Note**: article 4(1)(15) of *MiFID*]

multiplication factor

(in BIPRU 7.10 (Use of a value at risk model)) a multiplication factor applied to a *VaR measure* for the purpose of calculating the *model PRR* made up of the *minimum multiplication factor* as increased by the *plus factor*, all as more fully defined in BIPRU 7.10.118R (Capital calculations: Multiplication factors).

mutual

an *insurer* which:
(a) if it is a *body corporate* has no *share* capital (except a wholly owned *subsidiary* with no *share* capital but limited by guarantee); or
(b) is a *registered friendly society* or *incorporated friendly society*; or
(c) is a society registered or deemed to be registered under the Industrial and Provident Societies Act 1965 or the Industrial and Provident Societies (Northern Ireland) Act 1969.

name-passing broker

a *person* who *arranges (brings about) deals* between counter parties at mutually acceptable terms and passes their names to each of them to facilitate the conclusion of a transaction.

national bureau

(in relation to an *EEA State*) a professional organisation which:
(a) has been constituted in that State in accordance with Recommendation No 5 adopted on 25 January 1949 by the Road Transport Sub-committee of the Inland Transport Committee of the United Nations Economic Commission for Europe; and
(b) groups together *insurance undertakings* which in that State are authorised to conduct the business of motor vehicle liability insurance.

national guarantee fund

(in relation to an *EEA State*) a body which:
(a) has been set up or authorised in that State in accordance with article 1(4) of Council Directive (84/5/EEC); and
(b) provides compensation for damages to property or personal injuries caused by unidentified vehicles for which the insurance obligation provided for in article 1(1) of that Directive has not been satisfied.

natural gas

(a) natural gas in any form, including natural gas as deliverable through the *Network Code*; and
(b) any right that relates to natural gas, for example the right under a contract or otherwise to require a person to take any action in relation to natural gas, including:
    (i) delivering natural gas to any person or taking delivery of natural gas; or
    (ii) providing any information or notice in relation to natural gas; or
    (iii) making any payment in relation to the delivery or non-delivery, or the taking or non-taking of delivery, of natural gas.

NCIS

National Criminal Intelligence Service.

near cash

money, *deposits* or *investments* which, in each case, fall within any of the following:
(a) *money* which is deposited with an *eligible institution* or an *approved bank* in:
    (i) a current account; or
    (ii) a deposit account, if the *money* can be withdrawn immediately and without payment of a penalty exceeding seven *days'* interest calculated at ordinary commercial rates;
(b) certificates of deposit issued by an *eligible institution* or an *approved bank* if immediately redeemable at the option of the holder;
(c) *government and public securities*, if redeemable at the option of.N2 the holder or bound to be redeemed within two years;
(d) bills of exchange which are *government and public securities*;
(e) *deposits* with a *local* authority of a kind which fall within paragraph 9 of Part II of the First Schedule to the Trustee Investments Act 1961, and equivalent *deposits* with any *local* authority in another *EEA Stat*e, if the *money* can be withdrawn immediately and without payment of a penalty as described in (a).

net annual rent

(in LR) (in relation to a *property*) the current income or income estimated by the valuer:
(a) ignoring any special receipts or deductions arising from the *property*;
(b) excluding Value Added Tax and before taxation (including tax on profits and any allowances for interest on capital or loans); and
(c) after making deductions for superior rents (but not for amortisation) and any disbursements including, if appropriate, expenses of managing the *property* and allowances to maintain it in a condition to command its rent.

net earned premiums

gross earned premiums, less *reinsurance premiums* earned.

net FX open currency position

(in *ELM*) (in relation to an *ELMI*) the *ELMI's* net open foreign currency position as calculated in accordance with *ELM* (Calculation of FX exposure).

net leverage

the ratio of total assets, less those bought under reverse *repo* arrangements, to total equity.

net long position

the situation in which a *firm* holds or will hold more *units* in an *investment* than it has contracted to *sell* or, in respect of *options*, where it has bought rights which exceed rights sold.

net open foreign currency position

(in *IPRU(INV)* 13) a *firm's net long position* or *net short position*, whichever is the higher, in a currency other than that in which the *firm's* books of account are maintained.

net premium

the *premium* that is calculated to provide the basic sum assured under a *with-profits insurance contract* taking into consideration only the mortality and interest rate risks and using the same assumptions as used in the calculation of the *mathematical reserves*.

net short position

(1) (except in *IPRU(INV)* 13) a net short position which gives rise to an economic exposure to the issued *share* capital of a company.
Any calculation of whether a *person* has a short position must take account of any form of economic interest in the *shares* of the company.

(2) (in *IPRU(INV)* 13) the situation in which a *firm* has contracted to *sell* more of an *investment* than it holds or will hold or, in respect of *options*, where it has sold rights which exceed the rights bought.

net underwriting exposure

has the meaning in BIPRU 7.8.34R (Large exposure risk from underwriting securities: Calculating the net underwriting exposure) which is in summary the amount calculated by applying the reduction factors in the table in BIPRU 7.8.35R to the *net underwriting position*.

net underwriting position

the net underwriting position calculated under BIPRU 7.8.17R (Calculating the net underwriting position).

net written premiums

gross written premiums, less *reinsurance premiums* payable under *reinsurance* ceded.

netting

a process by which the claims and obligations between two counterparties are offset against each other to leave a single net sum.

netting set

(in accordance with Part 1 of Annex III of the *Banking Consolidation Directive* (Definitions) and for the purpose of BIPRU 13 (The calculation of counterparty risk exposure values for financial derivatives, securities financing transactions and long settlement transactions)) a group of transactions with a single counterparty that are subject to a legally enforceable bilateral netting arrangement and for which netting is recognised under BIPRU 13.7 (Contractual netting), BIPRU 5 (Credit risk mitigation) and, if applicable, BIPRU 4.10 (The IRB approach: Credit risk mitigation); each transaction that is not subject to a legally enforceable bilateral netting arrangement, which is recognised under BIPRU 13.7 must be interpreted as its own *netting set* for the purpose of BIPRU 13.

network

a *firm*:

(a) which has five or more *appointed representatives* (not counting *introducer appointed representatives*); or

(b) whose *appointed representatives*, not counting *introducer appointed representatives* (and being fewer than five) have, between them, 26 or more *representatives*;

but not:

- (i) a *product provider*; or
- (ii) a *firm* which markets the *packaged products* of a *product provider* which is in the same *group* as the *firm* and which does so other than by selecting *products* from the whole market; or
- (iii) an *insurer* in relation to a *non-investment insurance contract*; or
- (iv) a *mortgage lender*.

Network Code

the network code prepared by Transco plc in accordance with condition 7 of the public gas transporter licence granted or treated as granted to Transco plc under section 7(2) of the Gas Act 1986, as in force from time to time, or any subsequent similar instrument or arrangement.

new applicant

(in *LR*) an *applicant* that does not have any *class* of its *securities* already *listed*.

nominated ECAI

(a) (in the case of an eligible ECAI within paragraph (a) of the definition of that term (Recognition for exposure riskweighting purposes)) an *eligible ECAI* nominated by a *firm* in accordance with BIPRU 3.6 (Use of rating agencies' credit assessments for the determination of risk weights under the standardised approach to credit risk) for the purpose of calculating its *risk-weighted exposure amounts* under the *standardised approach* to credit risk except under (b);

(b) (in the case of an eligible ECAI within paragraph (b) of the definition of that term (Recognition *securitisation riskweighting* purposes)) an *eligible ECAI* nominated by a *firm* in accordance with BIPRU 9.8 (Use of ECAI credit assessments for the determination of applicable risk weights) for the purpose of calculating its *securitisation risk-weighted exposure amounts*.

nominee company

a *body corporate* whose business consists solely of acting as a nominee holder of *investments* or other property.

non-authorised Voluntary Jurisdiction participant

a participant in the *Voluntary Jurisdiction* who is not a *firm*.

non-core investment service

[deleted]

non-credit equalisation provision

the provision required to be established under INSPRU 1.4.17R.

non credit-obligation asset

(in relation to the *IRB approach*) an *exposure* in the form of a non credit-obligation asset or falling under BIPRU 4.9.5R (Non creditobligation assets).

non-directive client money chapter

[deleted]

non-directive custody chapter

[deleted]

non-directive firm

non-directive firm (in SUP 11 (Controllers and close links) and SUP 16 (Reporting requirements)) (in accordance with the Financial Services and Markets Act 2000 (Controllers) (Exemption) Order 2009 (SI 2009/774)) a *UK domestic firm* other than:

(a) a credit institution authorised under the Banking Consolidation Directive;

(b) an investment firm authorised under *MIFID*;

(c) a management company as defined in article 1a.2 of the UCITS Directive, authorised under that directive;

(d) an undertaking pursuing the activity of direct insurance within the meaning of:
   (i) article 2 of the *Consolidated Life Directive*, authorised under that directive; or
   (ii) article 1 of the *First Non-Life Directive*, authorised under that directive;

(e) an *undertaking* pursuing the activity of *reinsurance* within the meaning of article 2.1 (a) of the *Reinsurance Directive*, authorised under that directive.

non-directive friendly society

(a) a *friendly society* whose *insurance business* is restricted to the provision of benefits which vary according to the resources available and in which the contributions of the members are determined on a flat-rate basis;

(b) a *friendly society* whose *long-term insurance business* is restricted to the provision of benefits for employed and self-employed *persons* belonging to an undertaking or group of undertakings, or a trade or group of trades, in the event of death or survival or of discontinuance or curtailment of activity (whether or not the commitments arising from such operations are fully covered at all times by mathematical reserves);

(c) a *friendly society* which undertakes to provide benefits solely in the event of death where the amount of such benefits does not exceed the average funeral costs for a single death or where the benefits are provided in kind;

(d) a *friendly society* (carrying on *long-term insurance business*):
   (i) whose registered rules contain provisions for calling up additional contributions from members or reducing their benefits or claiming assistance from other *persons* who have undertaken to provide it; and
   (ii) whose annual gross premium income (other than from contracts of reinsurance) has not exceeded 5 million Euro for each of the three preceding financial years;

(e) a friendly society (carrying on general insurance business):
  (i) whose registered rules contain provisions for calling up additional contributions from members or reducing their benefits;
  (ii) whose gross premium income (other than from contracts of reinsurance) for the preceding financial year did not exceed 5 million Euro; and
  (iii) whose members provided at least half of that *gross premium* income;
  (i) a *friendly society* whose liabilities in respect of *general insurance contracts* are fully reinsured with or guaranteed by other *mutuals* (including *friendly societies*); and
  (ii) the *mutuals* providing the *reinsurance* or the guarantee are subject to the rules of the *First Non-Life Directive*;

and in each case whose *insurance business* is limited to that described in any of (a) to (f).

non-directive insurer

(a) an *insurer which is a provident or mutual benefit institution* whose *insurance business* is restricted to the provision of benefits which vary according to the resources available and in which the contributions are determined on a flat-rate basis; or
(b) an *insurer* whose *long-term insurance business* is restricted to the provision of benefits for employed and self-employed persons belonging to an *undertaking* or group of *undertakings*, or a trade or group of trades, in the event of death or survival or of discontinuance or curtailment of activity (whether or not the *commitments* arising from such operations are fully covered at all times by *mathematical reserves*); or
(c) an *insurer* which undertakes to provide benefits solely in the event of death where the amount of such benefits does not exceed the average funeral costs for a single death or where the benefits are provided in kind; or
(d) a *mutual* (carrying on *long-term insurance business*) whose:
  (i) articles of association contain provisions for calling up additional contributions from members or reducing their benefits or claiming assistance from other persons who have undertaken to provide it; and
  (ii) annual gross *premium* income (other than from contracts of *reinsurance*) has not exceeded 5 million Euro for each of the *financial year in question* and the two *previous financial years*; or
(e) a *mutual* (carrying on *general insurance business*) whose:
  (i) articles of association contain provisions for calling up additional contributions from members or reducing their benefits;
  (ii) business does not cover liability risks, other than *ancillary risks*, or credit or suretyship risks;
  (iii) gross *premium* income (other than from contracts of *reinsurance*) for the *financial year in question* did not exceed 5 million Euro; and
  (iv) members provided at least half of that gross *premium* income; or
(f) an *insurer* whose *insurance business* (other than *reinsurance*) is:
  (i) restricted to the provision of assistance for persons who get into difficulties while travelling, while away from home or while away from their permanent residence;
  (ii) carried out exclusively on a local basis and consists only of benefits in kind; and
  (iii) such that the gross *premium* income from the provision of assistance in the *financial year in question* did not exceed 200,000 Euro; or
  (i) a *mutual* whose liabilities in respect of *general insurance contracts* are fully reinsured with or guaranteed by other *mutuals* (including *friendly societies*); and
  (ii) the *mutuals* providing the *reinsurance* or the guarantee are subject to the rules of the *First Non-Life Directive*.

non-directive mutual

a *mutual* that falls into (d), (e) or (g) of the definition of a *non-directive insurer*.

non-discretionary investment manager

(in relation to *firm type* in SUP 16.10 (Confirmation of *standing data*)) a *person* who, acting only on behalf of a *client*, manages *designated investments* in an account or portfolio on a non-discretionary basis under the terms of a non-discretionary management agreement.

non-discretionary management agreement

an agreement for the non-discretionary management of *investments*:
(a) under which the *firm* agrees to conduct a regular review of the suitability of the *client's* account or portfolio, based on an assessment of the *client's* requirements; and
(b) that sets out the *client's* investment objectives, investment strategy, and attitude to risk, the intervals at which the portfolio will be reviewed, and the arrangements for consulting the *client* about proposed investment decisions.

non-EEA bank

a *bank* which is a *body corporate* or *partnership* formed under the law of any country or territory outside the *EEA*.

non-EEA direct insurer

an *insurer*, other than a *pure reinsurer*, whose head office is not in an *EEA State*.

non-EEA firm

a firm that has its registered office (or, if it has no registered office, its head office) in a non-EEA state.

non-EEA insurer

an *insurer* whose head office is not in an *EEA State*.

non-EEA State

a country or state that is not an *EEA State*.

non-EEA sub-group

a group of *undertakings* identified as a *non-EEA sub-group* in BIPRU 8.3.1R (Main consolidation rule for non-EEA sub-groups); however where the provision in question refers to a *non-EAA subgroup* in another *EEA State* it means a group of *undertakings* identified in Article 73(2) of the *Banking Consolidation Directive* (Non-EEA sub-groups) required to be supervised on a consolidated basis under Article 73(2) of the *Banking Consolidation Directive* by a *competent authority* in that *EEA State*.

non-equity transferable securities

(in *PR*) (as defined in section 102A of the *Act*) all *transferable securities* that are not equity securities.

non-executive director

a *director* who has no responsibility for implementing the decisions or the policies of the *governing body* of a *firm*.

non-executive director function

controlled function CF2 in the *table of controlled functions*, described. more fully in *SUP* 10.6.8R.

Non-Exempt Activities Order

the Financial Services and Markets Act 2000 (Professions) (Non-Exempt Activities) Order 2001 (SI 2001/1227).

non-ILAS BIPRU firm

a *firm* falling into BIPRU 12.1.1R which is not an *ILAS BIPRU firm*.

non-independent research

a *research recommendation* which:

(a) relates to *financial instruments* (as specified in Section C of Annex 1 of *MiFID*, whether or not they are admitted to trading on a *regulated market*); and

(b) does not constitute *investment research*.

[Note: article 24(2) of the *MiFID implementing Directive*]

non-investment financial promotion

[deleted]

non-investment insurance contract

a *contract of insurance* which is a *general insurance contract* or a *pure protection contract* but which is not a *long-term care insurance contract*.

Non-Life Directives

the *First Non-Life Directive*, the *Second Non-Life Directive* and the *Third Non-Life Directive*.

non-mainstream regulated activity

a *regulated activity* of an *authorised professional firm* in relation to which the conditions in *PROF* 5.2.1R are satisfied.

non-market-price transaction

a transaction where:

(a) the *dealing* rate or price paid by the *firm* or its *client* differs from the prevailing market rate or price to a material extent; or

(b) the *firm* or its *client* otherwise gives materially more or less in value than it receives in return.

non-profit fund

a *long-term insurance fund* which is not a *with-profits fund*.

non-profit insurance business

the business of *effecting* or *carrying out non-profit insurance contracts*.

non-profit insurance contract

a *long-term insurance contract* which is not a *with-profits insurance contract*.

non-proportional reinsurance treaty

see *proportional reinsurance treaty*.

non-real time financial promotion

(in accordance with article 7(2) of the *Financial Promotion Order*) a *financial promotion* that is not a *real time financial promotion*.

non-real time qualifying credit promotion

[deleted]

non-retail communication

a *financial promotion* and:

(a) is *made only to recipients* who the *firm* reasonably believes are *professional clients* or *eligible counterparties*; or

(b) may reasonably be regarded as *directed only at recipients* who are *professional clients* or *eligible counterparties*.

non-stakeholder CTF

a *CTF* that is not a *stakeholder CTF*.

non-trading book

positions, *exposures*, assets and liabilities that are not in the *trading book*.

non-UCITS retail scheme

an *authorised fund* which is neither a *UCITS scheme* or a *qualified investor scheme*.

non-UCITS scheme

an authorised fund that is not a *UCITS scheme*.

non-UK DLG by modification

either of the following:

(a) a non-UK DLG by modification (firm level); or

(b) a non-UK DLG by modification (DLG level).

non-UK DLG by modification (firm level)

(in relation to a group liquidity reporting firm) a DLG by modification (firm level) that is not a UK DLG by modification. A firm with a non-UK DLG by modification (firm level) cannot also have a UK DLG by modification.

(Guidance about this definition, and its inter-relation with other related definitions, is set out in SUP 16 Annex 26G (Guidance on designated liquidity groups in SUP 16.12).)

non-UK DLG by modification (DLG level)

(in relation to any reporting period under SUP 16 (Reporting requirements) and in relation to a firm that meets the following conditions (a group liquidity reporting firm):

(a) it is a UK ILAS BIPRU firm with an intra-group liquidity modification;

(b) it is a group liquidity reporting firm in a UK DLG by modification created by that intra-group liquidity modification;

(c) the overall liquidity adequacy rule applies under that intra-group liquidity modification to that UK DLG by modification; and

(d) that UK DLG by modification can rely, under that intra-group liquidity modification, for any part of that period, on a group of other persons for the purpose of the overall liquidity adequacy rule as applied to that UK DLG by modification); means the group made up of the following:

(e) *that ILAS BIPRU* firm;

(f) the other members of that UK DLG by modification; and

(g) the group of other persons mentioned in (d).

A *firm* has a 'non-UK DLG by modification (DLG level)' for a period even if it only has one during part of that period.

(*Guidance* about this definition, and its inter-relation with other new definitions, is set out in *SUP* 16 Annex 26G (Guidance on designated liquidity groups in *SUP* 16.12).)

non UK lead regulated firm

a *firm* that is not a *UK lead regulated firm*. This definition is not related to the defined term *lead regulated firm*.

normal trading hours

(in relation to a *trading venue* or an *investment firm*) those hours which the *trading venue* or *investment firm* establishes in advance and makes public as its trading hours.

[Note: article 2(5) of the *MiFID Regulation*]

normally based

(in ICOBS) (in relation to a *vehicle*):

(a) the territory of the *EEA State* of which the *vehicle* bears a registration plate; or

(b) in cases where no registration is required for the type of *vehicle*, but the *vehicle* bears an insurance plate or a distinguishing sign analogous to a registration plate, the territory of the *EEA State* in which the insurance plate or the sign is issued; or

(c) in cases where neither registration plate nor insurance plate nor distinguishing sign is required for the type of *vehicle*, the territory of the *EEA State* in which the keeper of the *vehicle* is permanently resident.

[**Note:** article 1(4) of Directive 72/166/EC (First Motor Insurance Directive)]

normally resident

(in *MCOB*) normally resident; for the purposes of this definition:

(a) an individual (whether or not acting as trustee) is to be treated as normally resident in the country which he indicates is his country of residence, unless the *firm* has reason to doubt this; and

(b) a *body corporate* acting as trustee is to be treated as resident in the country in which its registered office (or, if it has no registered office, its head office) is located.

notice of discontinuance

a notice given by the *FSA* in accordance with section 389 of the *Act* (Notices of discontinuance) which states that the *FSA* has decided not to take the action proposed in a *warning notice* or the action to which a *decision notice* relates.

notice of intention

a notice of intention (as described in SUP 13.5) given by a *UK firm* to:

(a) establish a *branch* in an *EEA State* under paragraph 19(2) of Part III of Schedule 3 to the *Act* (Exercise of passport rights by UK firms);

(b) provide services in an *EEA State* under paragraph 20(1) of Part III of Schedule 3 to the *Act* (Exercise of passport rights by UK firms).

notification rule

(1) (in relation to a *firm*) a *rule* requiring a *firm* to give the *FSA* notice of, or information regarding, an event, but excluding:
    (a) a *rule* requiring periodic submission of a report; and
    (b) a *rule* in the *listing rules*.

(2) (in relation to a *recognised body*) a *rule* made by the *FSA* under section 293 of the *Act* (Notification requirements) or section 295 of the *Act* (Notification: overseas investment exchanges and overseas clearing houses):
    (a) requiring a *recognised body* to give the *FSA*:
        (i) notice of, and specified information regarding, specified events relating to the body;
        (ii) specified information relating to the body at specified times or in respect of specified periods; and
        (iii) any other information required to be given by such a *rule*; or
    (b) specifying descriptions of *regulatory provision* in relation to which, or circumstances in which, the duty to notify the *FSA* of such *regulatory provision* in section 300B(1) of the *Act* does not apply or providing that the duty to notify applies only to specified descriptions of *regulatory provision* or in specified circumstances; or
    (c) making provision as to the form and contents of the notice required under (b), and requiring *recognised bodies* to provide specified information in connection with that notification.

notional principal

(a) (in relation to a *contract for differences* which is an index *derivative*):

Part II FSA Handbook Materials

(i) the current mark to market valuation of a *contract for differences* which resembles a *futures* contract; or
(ii) the exercise value of a *contract for differences* which resembles an *option* contract;
(b) (in relation to any other *contract for differences*) the notional lot size of the contract..N6

nuclear risks

risks falling within any *class* of *general insurance business* and arising in connection with the construction and use of any nuclear reactor or nuclear installation or the carriage of any nuclear matter.

obligor grade

(in relation to the *IRB approach* and the *sovereign, institutional and corporate IRB exposure class* and in accordance with BIPRU 4.4.8R) a risk category within a *rating system's* obligor rating scale, to which obligors are assigned on the basis of a specified and distinct set of rating criteria, from which estimates of *PD* are derived.

occupational pension fund management business

(in COMP) the business of carrying on:
(1) *pension fund management*; or
(2) (other than in connection with a *personal pension scheme*) pension fund management, written as *linked long term business*, for an *occupational pension scheme* or for an institution falling within article 2 of the Council Directive of 3 June 2003 on the activities and supervision of institutions for occupational retirement provision (No 2003/41/EC) but only to the extent that:
(a) there is no transfer to the *participant firm* of:
(i) investment, market, or credit risk;
(ii) mortality or expense risk prior to any annuity being effected; and
(b) any annuity options provide for the *participant firm* to change the annuity rates without prior notice.

occupational pension scheme

(a) (a scheme specified in article 3(1) of the *Regulated Activities Order* (Interpretation)) which is, in summary, a pension scheme established for the purpose of providing benefits to people with service in employments of a prescribed description.

OECD

Organisation for Economic Co-operation and Development.

OECD state guaranteed issuer

an *issuer* of *debt securities* whose obligations in relation to those *securities* have been guaranteed by a member state of the *OECD*.

OEIC

open-ended investment company. (see also *ICVC*.)

OEIC Regulations

the Open-Ended Investment Companies Regulations 2001 (SI 2001/1228).

off-exchange

(in relation to a transaction in an *investment*) a transaction which is not *on-exchange*.

offer

(1) (in MAR 1 (Code of market conduct)) an offer as defined in the *Takeover Code*.
(2) (in MAR 2 (Buy-backs and Stabilisation) an offer or invitation to make an offer.
(3) (in LR and PR) an *offer of transferable securities to the public*.

offer document

(in *MCOB*) a document in which the *home finance provider* offers to enter into a *home finance transaction* with a *customer*.

offer of transferable securities to the public

(in PR and LR) (as defined in section 102B of the *Act*), in summary:
(a) a communication to any person which presents sufficient information on:
(i) the transferable securities to be offered, and
(ii) the terms on which they are offered;
to enable an investor to decide to buy or subscribe for the securities in question;
(b) which is made in any form or by any means;
(c) including the placing of securities through a financial intermediary;
(d) but not including a communication in connection with trading on:

(i) a regulated market;
(ii) a multilateral trading facility; or
(iii) any market prescribed by an order under section 130A of the *Act*.

Note: This is only a summary; to see the full text of the definition, readers should consult section 102B of the Act.

offer for sale

(in LR) an invitation to the public by, or on behalf of, a third party to purchase *securities* of the *issuer* already in issue or allotted (and may be in the form of an invitation to tender at or above a stated minimum price).

offer for subscription

(in LR) an invitation to the public by, or on behalf of, an *issuer* to subscribe for *securities* of the *issuer* not yet in issue or allotted (and may be in the form of an invitation to tender at or above a stated minimum price).

offeree

(in MAR 1) an offeree as defined in the *Takeover Code*.

offering programme

(in PR) (as defined in Article 2.1(k) of the *prospectus directive*) a plan which would permit the issuance of non-equity securities, including warrants in any form, having a similar type and/or class, in a continuous or repeated manner during a specified issuing period.

offeror

(1) (in MAR 1 (The Code of Market Conduct) and LR 5.2.10R) an offeror as defined in the *Takeover Code*.
(2) (in MAR 2 (Buy-backs and Stabilisation)) (as defined in Article 2 of the *Buy-back and Stabilisation Regulation*) the prior holders of, or the entity issuing, the *relevant securities*).
(3) (in LR, PR and FEES provisions in relation to PR) a *person* who makes an *offer of transferable securities to the public*.

offer price

the price at which a *person* could purchase a *unit* in a *dual-priced authorised fund* or a *security*.

officer

(1) (in connection with the exercise of the *FSA's* power to require information) an officer of the *FSA*, a member of the *FSA's* staff or an agent of the *FSA*.
(2) (otherwise) (in relation to a *body corporate*) (as defined in section 400(5) of the *Act* (Offences by bodies corporate etc)) a director, member of the committee of management, *chief executive*, *manager*, secretary, or other similar officer of the body, or a *person* purporting to act in that capacity or a *controller* of the body.

official list

(1) (in LR) the list maintained by the *FSA* in accordance with section 74(1) of the *Act* for the purposes of Part VI of the *Act*.
(2) (except in LR):
  (a) the list maintained by the *FSA* in accordance with section 74(1) of the *Act* (The official list) for the purposes of Part VI of the *Act*.O2 (Official Listing);
  (b) any corresponding list maintained by a *competent authority* for listing in another *EEA State*.

oil

mineral oil of any description and petroleum gases, whether in liquid or vapour form, including products and derivatives of oil.

oil collective investment scheme

a *collective investment scheme*, the property of which consists only of property which is *oil* or an *oil investment* or cash awaiting investment.

oil investment

any of the following:
(a) a *unit* in an *oil collective investment scheme*;
(b) an *option* to acquire or dispose of an *oil investment*;
(c) a *future* where the *commodity* in question is *oil*;
(d) a *contract for differences* where the property in question is *oil* or an oil investment or the index or other factor in question is linked to or otherwise dependent upon fluctuations in the value or price of oil or any *oil investments*;

Part II FSA Handbook Materials

(e) *rights to or interests in investments in* (a)–(d).

oil market activity

(a) any *regulated activity* in relation to an *oil investment* or to *oil* which, or in relation to a *biofuel investment, biofuel*, a *biomass investment* or *biomass* that is ancillary to activities related to *oil investments* or *oil*,:
 (i) is the *executing* of own account transactions on any *recognised investment exchange* or *designated investment exchange*; or
 (ii) if it is not the *executing* of transactions on such exchanges, is performed in connection with or for persons who are not individuals; and

(b) *establishing, operating or winding up a collective investment scheme* which is an *oil collective investment scheme* in which individuals do not participate.

oil market participant

a *firm*:

(a) whose permission:
 (i) includes a *requirement* that the firm must not carry on any *designated investment business* other than *oil market activity*; and
 (ii) does not include a *requirement* that it comply with *IPRU(INV)* 5 (Investment management firms) or 13 (Personal investment firms); and

(b) which is not an *authorised professional firm, BIPRU investment firm* (unless it is an *exempt BIPRU commodities firm*), *bank, building society, credit union, friendly society, ICVC, insurer, MiFID investment firm* (unless it is an *exempt BIPRU commodities firm*), *media firm, service company, insurance intermediary, home finance administrator, mortgage intermediary, home finance provider*, incoming *EEA firm* (without *a top-up permission*), or *incoming Treaty firm* (without *a top-up permission*).

Ombudsman

a *person* appointed to the panel of *persons* maintained by the *FOS Ltd* to determine complaints, including the Chief Ombudsman.

Ombudsman Transitional Order

the Financial Services and Markets Act 2000 (Transitional Provisions) (Ombudsman Scheme and Complaints Scheme) Order 2001 (SI 2001/2326).

OMPS

the Handbook Guide for oil market participants.

on-exchange

(a) (in relation to a transaction in the *United Kingdom*) effected by means of the *facilities* of, or governed by the *rules* of, an *RIE* or a *regulated market*;

(b) (in relation to any other transaction) effected by means of the *facilities* of, or governed by the rules of, an exchange.

one-day VaR measure

(in BIPRU 7.10 (Use of a value at risk model)) has the meaning in BIPRU 7.10.98R (Backtesting: One day VaR measure), which is in summary and in relation to a particular *business day*, the *VaR number* for that *business day* calibrated to a one *business day* holding period and a 99% one-tailed confidence level.

one-off transaction

any transaction other than a transaction carried out in the course of an established business relationship formed by a *person* acting in the course of relevant financial business.

one-sided credit valuation adjustment

(in accordance with Part 1 of Annex III of the *Banking Consolidation Directive* (Definitions)) a *credit valuation adjustment* that reflects the market value of the credit risk of the counterparty to a *firm*, but does not reflect the market value of the credit risk of the *firm* to the counterparty.

open

in relation to a *syndicate year*, one which has not been *closed*.

open currency position

the amount calculated under BIPRU 7.5.19R (Open currency position) as part of the calculation of the *foreign currency PRR*.

open offer

(in LR) an invitation to existing *securities* holders to subscribe or purchase *securities* in proportion to their holdings, which is not made by means of a renounceable letter (or other negotiable document).

open-ended investment company

(as defined in section 236 of the *Act* (Open-ended investment companies)) a *collective investment scheme* which satisfies both the property condition and the investment condition:

(a) the property condition is that the property belongs beneficially to, and is managed by or on behalf of, a *body corporate* ("BC") having as its purpose the investment of its funds with the aim of:
   (i) spreading investment risk; and
   (ii) giving its members the benefit of the results of the management of those funds by or on behalf of that body;

(b) the investment condition is that, in relation to BC, a reasonable investor would, if he were to participate in the *scheme*:
   (i) expect that he would be able to realise, within a period appearing to him to be reasonable, his investment in the *scheme* (represented, at any given time, by the value of shares in, or securities of, BC held by him as a *participant* in the *scheme*); and be satisfied that his investment would be realised on a basis calculated wholly or mainly by reference to the value of property in respect of which the *scheme* makes arrangements.

(see also *investment company with variable capital.*)

operating a dormant account fund

any of the regulated activities of:

(a) *meeting of repayment claims; or*

(b) *managing dormant account funds (including the investment of such funds).*

operating a multilateral trading facility

the *regulated activity* in article 25D of the *Regulated Activities Order*, which is, in summary, the operation of a multilateral trading facility on which MiFID instruments are traded.

In this definition "MiFID instrument" means any investment:

(a) of the kind specified by articles 76, 77, 78, 79, 80, 81, 83, 84 or 85 of the *Regulated Activities Order*; or

(b) of the kind specified by article 89 of the *Regulated Activities Order*, so far as relevant to an investment falling within (a),

that is a *financial instrument.*

operational risk

(in accordance with Article 4(22) of the *Banking Consolidation Directive*) the risk of loss resulting from inadequate or failed internal processes, people and systems or from external events, including legal risk.

operational risk capital requirement

the part of the *capital resources requirement* of a *BIPRU firm* falling within BIPRU 6.1.1R in respect of *operational risk*, calculated in accordance with BIPRU 6.2.

operator

(1) (except in EG):
   (a) (in relation to an *AUT*) the *manager*;
   (b) (in relation to an *ICVC*) that *company* or, if applicable, the *authorised corporate director*;
   (ba) (in relation to any other *OEIC* which is an undertaking for collective investment in transferable securities within the meaning of the *UCITS Directive* and which has appointed a *person* to manage the *scheme*) the manager;
   (c) (in relation to any other *collective investment scheme* that is a *unit trust scheme* with a separate *trustee*) any *person* who, under the *trust deed* establishing the *scheme*, is responsible for the management of the property held for or within the *scheme*;
   (d) (in relation to any other *collective investment scheme* that is an *open-ended investment company*) that *company* or, if applicable, any *person* who, under the constitution or founding arrangements of the *scheme*, is responsible for the management of the property held for or within the *scheme*;
   (e) (in relation to any other *collective investment scheme*) any *person* who, under the constitution or founding arrangements of the *scheme*, is responsible for the management of the property held for or within the *scheme*;

(f) in relation to an *investment trust savings scheme*) any *person* appointed, by those responsible for managing the property of the *investment trust*, to manage the *investment trust savings scheme*.

(g) (in relation to a *personal pension scheme* or *stakeholder pension scheme*) the *person* who carries on the *regulated activity* specified in article 52 of the *Regulated Activities Order* (Establishing etc. a pension scheme).

(2) (in EG) (in accordance with section 237(2) of the *Act* (Other definitions)):

(a) (in relation to a *unit trust scheme* with a separate *trustee*) the *manager*;

(b) (in relation to an *OEIC* which is an undertaking for collective investment in transferable securities within the meaning of the *UCITS Directive* and which has appointed a *person* to manage the *scheme*) the *manager*;

(c) (in relation to any other *OEIC*) the *company*.

OPS activity

(a) *managing investments* in a case where the assets managed are:
- (i) held for the purposes of an occupational pension scheme; or
- (ii) held for the purposes of a welfare trust established by a person who is, or has been at any time during the last 12 months, an associate of the OPS firm; or
- (iii) assets of an OPS collective investment scheme;

(b) any one or more of the following activities undertaken in the course of, or incidental to, the operation of an *occupational pension scheme*, *welfare trust* or *OPS collective investment scheme*:
- (i) dealing in investments as principal;
- (ii) dealing in investments as agent;
- (iii) arranging (bringing about) deals in investments;
- (iv) making arrangements with a view to transactions in investments;
- (v) safeguarding and administering investments;
- (vi) advising on investments;
- (vii) receiving or holding client money.

OPS collective investment scheme

a *collective investment scheme* the contributions to which consist entirely of assets held for an *occupational pension scheme*.

OPS firm

(a) (except in *IPRU(INV)*) a *firm* which:
- (i) carries on *OPS activity*; and
- (ii) is one or more of the following:
  - (A) a trustee of the *occupational pension scheme* in question;
  - (B) a *company* owned by the trustees of the *occupational pension scheme* in question;
  - (C) a *company* which is:
    - (I) an employer in relation to the *occupational pension scheme* in question in respect of its employees or former employees or their dependants; or
    - (II) a *company* within the *group* which includes an employer within (I); or
    - (III) an administering authority subject to the Local Government Pension Scheme (Administration) Regulations 2008; or

(b) a *firm* which:
- (i) has satisfied the requirements set out in (a) at any time during the past 12 *months*; but
- (ii) is no longer able to comply with those requirements because of a change in the control or ownership of the employer referred to in (a)(ii) during that period.

opted-in exempt CAD firm

an *exempt CAD firm* which complies with the requirements in regulation 4C (or any successor provision) of the Financial Services and Markets Act 2000 (Markets in Financial Instruments) Regulations 2007 (SI 2007/126).

option

the *investment*, specified in article 83 of the *Regulated Activities Order* (Options), which is an option to acquire or dispose of:

(a) a *designated investment* (other than an option or one to which (d) or (e) applies); or
(b) currency of the *United Kingdom* or of any other country or territory; or
(c) palladium, platinum, gold or silver; or
(d) a commodity to which article 83(2) of the *Regulated Activities Order* applies; or

(e) a *financial instrument* in paragraph 10 of Section C of Annex 1 to *MiFID* to which article 83(3) of the *Regulated Activities Order* applies; or
(f) an option to acquire or dispose of an option specified in (a), (b) or, (c), (d) or (e)

but so that for the purposes of calculating capital requirements for *BIPRU firms* and BIPRU 10 (Concentration risk requirements) it also includes any of the items listed in the table in BIPRU 7.6.18R (Option PRR: methods for different types of option) and any cash settled option.

option hedging method

the method of calculating the *option PRR* in BIPRU 7.6.24R (The hedging method).

option PRR

the part of the *market risk capital requirement* calculated in accordance with BIPRU 7.6 (Option PRR) or, in relation to a particular *position*, the portion of the overall *option PRR* attributable to that *position*.

option standard method

the method of calculating the *option PRR* in BIPRU 7.6.20R to BIPRU 7.6.22R (The standard method).

ORCR

the *operational risk capital requirement*.

ordinary credit default swap PRR method

the method for calculating the *specific risk* portion of the *interest rate PRR* for credit default swaps that are not *securitisation positions* set out in BIPRU 7.11.24R to BIPRU 7.11.37R.

organisation

a *body corporate*, a *partnership*, a trust or an unincorporated association.

original financing cost amount

(in relation to a *share*, *debenture* or other investment in, or external contribution to the capital of, a *firm* that is subject to a *step-up*) the *financing cost amount* for the instrument for a period beginning on or near the date of issue of the instrument and ending on or near the date of the first *step-up*.

originator

(in accordance with Article 4(41) of the *Banking Consolidation Directive* (Definitions) and in relation to a *securitisation* within the meaning of paragraph (2) of the definition of securitisation) either of the following:
(a) an entity which, either itself or through related entities, directly or indirectly, was involved in the original agreement which created the obligations or potential obligations of the debtor or potential debtor giving rise to the *exposures* being *securitised*; or
(b) an entity which purchases a third party's *exposures* onto its balance sheet and then *securitises* them.

OTC

over the counter.

OTC derivative

a derivative traded solely *over the counter*.

out of the money

(for the purposes of BIPRU 7 (Market risk) and in relation to an *option* or *warrant*) that *option* or *warrant* being neither *at the money* nor *in the money*.

outgoing ECA provider

a *firm* which:
(a) provides an *electronic commerce activity*, from an *establishment in the United Kingdom*, with or for an *ECA recipient* present in an *EEA State* other than the *United Kingdom*; and
(b) is a national of an *EEA State* or a firm or company mentioned in article 48 of the *Treaty*.

outgoing electronic commerce communication

[deleted]

outsourcing

(1) (except in SYSC 8, *COBS* 11.7 and the definition of *relevant person*) the use of a *person* to provide customised services to a *firm* other than:
  (a) a member of the *firm's governing body* acting in his capacity as such; or
  (b) an individual employed by a *firm* under a contract of service.

(2) (in *SYSC* 8, *COBS* 11.7 and the definition of *relevant person*) an arrangement of any form between a *firm* and a service provider by which that service provider performs a process, a service or an activity which would otherwise be undertaken by the *firm* itself.

[Note: article 2(6) of the *MiFID implementing Directive*]

over collateralisation

(in RCB) (as defined in Regulation 3(3) of the *RCB Regulations*) the provision of additional *assets* that assist the payment from the *relevant asset pool* of claims attaching to a *regulated covered bond* in the event of the failure of the *issuer*.

over the counter

(in relation to a transaction in an *investment*) not *on-exchange*.

overall financial adequacy rule

GENPRU 1.2.26R (Requirement for certain *firms* to have adequate financial resources).

overall financial sector

sector composed of one or more the following types of entities:

(a) members of each of the *financial sectors*; and

(b) (except where GENPRU 3.1 (Cross sector groups) or GENPRU 3 Ann 1R (Capital adequacy calculations for financial conglomerates) provide otherwise) a *mixed financial holding company*.

overall liquidity adequacy rule

BIPRU 12.2.1R.

overall Pillar 2 rule

GENPRU 1.2.30R (Systems, strategies, processes and reviews for certain *firms*).

overallotment facility

(as defined in Article 2 of the *Buy-back and Stabilisation Regulation*) a clause in the underwriting agreement or lead management agreement which permits acceptance of subscriptions or offers to purchase a greater number of *relevant securities* than originally offered.

overseas

outside the *United Kingdom*

overseas clearing house

a *clearing house* which has neither its head office nor its registered office in the *United Kingdom*.

overseas company

(in LR and PR) a *company* incorporated outside the *United Kingdom*.

overseas financial services institution

an institution authorised to carry on any *regulated activity* or other financial service by an *overseas regulator*.

overseas firm

(1) (in relation to *MAR* 5) a *firm* which has its registered office (or, if it has no registered office, its head office) outside the *United Kingdom* excluding an *incoming EEA firm*.

(2) (in any other case) a *firm* which has its registered office (or, if it has no registered office, its head office) outside the *United Kingdom*.

overseas introducing broker

a *person*, who is not an *authorised person*:

(a) who is resident outside the *United Kingdom*; and

(b) who introduces transactions relating to *designated investments. arranged (brought about*) for its *clients* to a *clearing firm* in the *United Kingdom*.

overseas investment exchange

an investment exchange which has neither its head office nor its registered office in the *United Kingdom*.

overseas long-term insurer

an *insurance undertaking* which is not an *authorised person* and which:

(a) has its head office in an *EEA State* other than the *United Kingdom*, and is entitled to carry on *long-term insurance business* in that *EEA State*; or

(b) has a *branch* or agency in an *EEA State* other than the *United Kingdom* and is entitled to carry on *long-term insurance business* in that *EEA State*; or

(b) is authorised to effect or carry on *long-term insurance business* in the Bailiwick of Jersey, the Bailiwick of Guernsey, the Isle of Man, the Commonwealth of Pennsylvania or the State of Iowa;

for the purposes of (a) and (b), Gibraltar is to be regarded as if it were an *EEA State*.

overseas person

(in accordance with article 3(1) of the *Regulated Activities Order* (Interpretation)) a *person* who:

(a) carries on any of the following *regulated activities*:

(i) *dealing in investments as principal*;
(ii) *dealing in investments as agent*;
(iii) *arranging (bringing about) deals in investments*;
(iv) *arranging (bringing about) regulated mortgage contracts*;
(v) *making arrangements with a view to regulated mortgage contracts*;
(vi) *making arrangements with a view to transactions in investments*;
(vii) *managing investments*;
(viii) *safe custody and administering investments*;
(ix) *sending dematerialised instructions*;
(x) *causing dematerialised instructions to be sent*;
(xi) *establishing, operating or winding up a collective investment scheme*;
(xii) *acting as trustee of an authorised unit trust scheme*;
(xiii) *acting as the depositary or sole director of an open-ended investment company*;
(xiv) *establishing, operating or winding up a stakeholder pension scheme*;
(xiva) *establishing, operating or winding up a personal pension scheme*;
(xv) *advising on investments*;
(xvi) *advising on regulated mortgage contracts*;
(xvii) *entering into a regulated mortgage contract*;
(xviii) *administering a regulated mortgage contract*;
(xix) *arranging (bringing about) a home reversion plan*;
(xx) *making arrangements with a view to a home reversion plan*;
(xxi) *advising on a home reversion plan*;
(xxii) *entering into a home reversion plan*;
(xxiii) *administering a home reversion plan*;
(xxiv) *arranging (bringing about) a home purchase plan*;
(xxv) *making arrangements with a view to a home purchase plan*;
(xxvi) *advising on a home purchase plan*;
(xxvii) *entering into a home purchase plan*;
(xxviii) *administering a home purchase plan*;
(xxix) *agreeing to carry on those regulated activities*, disregarding the exclusion in article 72 of the *Regulated Activities Order* (Overseas persons); but

(b) does not carry on any such activities, or offer to do so, from a permanent place of business maintained by him in the *United Kingdom*.

overseas recognised body

an *ROIE* or *ROCH*.

overseas regulator

(as defined in section 195(3) of the *Act* (Exercise of power in support of overseas regulator)) an authority in a country or territory outside the *United Kingdom*:

(a) which is a *Home State regulator*; or

(b) which exercises any of the following functions:

(i) a function corresponding to any function of the *FSA* under the *Act*;
(ii) a function corresponding to any function exercised by the *FSA* in its capacity as *competent authority* in relation to the listing of securities;

(iii) a function corresponding to any function exercised by the Secretary of State under the Companies Acts (as defined in section 2 of the Companies Act 2006);
(iv) a function in connection with the investigation of conduct of the kind prohibited by Part V of the Criminal Justice Act 1993 (Insider Dealing), or with the enforcement of rules (whether or not having the force of law) relating to such conduct;
(v) a function prescribed by regulations made for the purposes of section 195(4) of the *Act* (Exercise of powers) which, in the opinion of the Treasury, relates to companies or financial services.

own account order

an order which relates to an *own account transaction.*

own account trading firm

(in relation to *firm type* in SUP 16.10 (Confirmation of *standing data*)) a *firm* that only *deals* or *arranges deals* in *securities* or *contractually based investments* for its own benefit, or for the benefit of an *associate.*

own account transaction

a transaction *executed* by the *firm* for its own benefit or for the benefit of its *associate.*

own estimates of volatility adjustments approach

the approach to calculating volatility adjustments under the *financial collateral comprehensive method* under which the *firm* uses its own estimates of such adjustments, as more fully described in BIPRU 5.4 (Financial collateral) and including that approach as applied to master netting agreements as described in BIPRU 5.6 (Master netting agreements).

own funds

(1) own funds as described in articles 56 to 67 of the *Banking Consolidation Directive.*
(2) (in *ELM*) the own funds of an *ELMI* calculated in accordance with *ELM* 2.4 (Calculation of initial capital and own funds).
(3) (in IPRU(INV) Chapter 8) capital, as defined in CRED 8.2.1R.
(4) (in *UPRU*) funds calculated in accordance with UPRU Table 2.2.1R (Method of calculation of financial resources) composed of the specified items set out in that Table.

own funds requirement

(in *ELM*) (in relation to an *ELMI*) 2% of the higher of the following amounts:
(a) the ELMI's *e-money outstandings* at that time; and
(b) the average of the ELMI's *daily e-money outstandings amount* for *the six month period* ending at that time; calculated in accordance with ELM 2.5 (Continuing capital requirement).

owner

(in *RCB*) (as defined in Regulation 4 of the *RCB Regulations*) an owner which owns an *asset pool* and issues a guarantee to pay from that *asset pool* claims attaching to a *regulated covered bond* in the event of a failure of the *issuer* of that bond.

ownership share

in accordance with the definition of a "share" in section.O9422(6) of the *Act* (Controller):
(a) (in relation to an *undertaking* with a share capital) an allotted share;
(b) (in relation to an *undertaking* with capital but no share capital) a right to share in the capital of the *undertaking*;
(c) (in relation to an *undertaking* without capital) an interest:
  (i) conferring any right to share in the profits, or liability to contribute to the losses, of the *undertaking*; or
  (ii) giving rise to an obligation to contribute to the debts or expenses of the *undertaking* in the event of a winding up.

own-initiative power

the *FSA's* power under section 45 of the *Act* (Variation etc on the Authority's own initiative) to vary or cancel a *Part IV permission* otherwise than on the application of a *firm.*

packaged product

(a) a *life policy*;
(b) a *unit* in a *regulated collective investment scheme*;
(c) *an interest in an investment trust savings scheme*;
(d) a *stakeholder pension scheme*;
(e) *a personal pension scheme*;

whether or not (in the case of (a), (b) or (c)) held within, *ISA* or a *CTF* and whether or not the *packaged product* is also a *stakeholder product.*

parent financial holding company in a Member State

(in accordance with Article 4(15) of the *Banking Consolidation Directive* (Definitions) and Article 3 of the *Capital Adequacy Directive* (Definitions)) a *financial holding company* which is not itself a *subsidiary undertaking* of an *institution* authorised in the same *EEA State*, or of a *financial holding company* set up in the same *EEA State*.

parent institution in a Member State

(in accordance with Article 4(14) of the *Banking Consolidation Directive* and Article 3 of the *Capital Adequacy Directive* (Definitions)) an *institution* which has an *institution* or a *financial institution* as a *subsidiary undertaking* or which holds a *participation* in such an institution, and which is not itself a *subsidiary undertaking* of another *institution* authorised in the same *EEA State*, or of a *financial holding company* set up in the same *EEA State*.

parent undertaking

(1) (in accordance with section 420 of the *Act* (Parent and subsidiary undertaking) and section 1162 of the Companies Act 2006 (Parent and subsidiary undertakings)):

(a) (in relation to whether an *undertaking*, other than an *incorporated friendly society*, is a parent undertaking and except for the purposes described in (c)) an *undertaking* which has the following relationship to another *undertaking* ("S"):

(i) it holds a majority of the voting rights in S; or

(ii) it is a member of S and has the right to appoint or remove a majority of its board of directors; or

(iii) it has the right to exercise a dominant influence over S through:

(A) provisions contained in S's memorandum or articles; or

(B) a control contract; or

(iv) it is a member of S and controls alone, under an agreement with other shareholders or members, a majority of the voting rights in S; or

(A) it has the power to exercise, or actually exercises, dominant influence or control over S; or

(B) it and S are managed on a unified basis; or

(vi) it is a *parent undertaking* of a *parent undertaking* of S; or

(vii) (except in *REC* or for the purposes of the *rules* in GENPRU and INSPRU as they apply to *members* of the *Society* of Lloyd's or to the *Society* or *managing agents* in respect of *members*) he is an individual and would be a *parent undertaking* if he were an *undertaking*; or

(viii) (except in *REC* or for the purposes of *rules* in GENPRU and INSPRU as they apply to *members* of the *Society* of Lloyd's or to the *Society* or *managing agents* in respect of *members*) it is incorporated in or formed under the law of another *EEA State* and is a parent undertaking within the meaning of any rule of law in that State for purposes connected with implementation of the *Seventh Company Law Directive;*

in relation to (ii) and (iv), the *undertaking* will be treated as a member of S if any of its *subsidiary undertakings* is a member of S, or if any shares in S are held by a *person* acting on behalf of the *undertaking* or any of its *subsidiary undertakings*; the provisions of Schedule 7 to the Companies Act 2006 (Parent and subsidiary undertakings: supplementary provisions) explain the expressions used in and supplement paragraphs (i) to (vi);

(b) (in relation to whether an *incorporated friendly society is a* parent undertaking and except for the purposes described in (c)) an *incorporated friendly society* which has the following relationship to a *body corporate* ("S"):

(i) it holds a majority of the voting rights in S; or

(ii) it is a member of S and has the right to appoint or remove a majority of S's board of directors; or

(iii) it is a member of S and controls alone, under an agreement with other shareholders or members, a majority of the voting rights in S; or

(iv) it is the *parent undertaking* of a *body corporate* which has the relationship in (i), (ii) or (iii) to S.

(c) (for the purposes BIPRU, GENPRU and INSPRU as they apply on a consolidated basis, for the purposes of BIPRU 10 (Concentration risk requirements) and for the purposes of SYSC 12 (Group risk systems and controls requirement)and in relation to whether an *undertaking* is a parent undertaking) an *undertaking* which has the following relationship to another *undertaking* ("S"):

(i) a relationship described in (a) other than (a)(vii); or

(ii) it effectively exercises a dominant influence over S;

and so that (a)(v) does not apply for the purpose of BIPRU as it applies on a consolidated basis (including BIPRU 8 (Group risk — consolidation)) or BIPRU 10.

(2) a *parent undertaking* within the meaning of (1) of a *controlled undertaking*.

parental responsibility

(as defined in section 3(9) of the Child Trust Fund Act 2004):

(a) parental responsibility within the meaning of the Children Act 1989 or the Children (Northern Ireland) Order 1995 (SI 1995/755 (N.I. 2)); or

(b) parental responsibilities within the meaning of the Children (Scotland) Act 1995.

Part 6 rules

(as defined in section 73A of the *Act*) *rules* made for the purposes of Part VI of the *Act*.

Part XX exemption

the exemption from the *general prohibition* conferred on an *exempt professional firm* by section 327 of the *Act* (Exemption from the general prohibition).

Part 30 exemption order

an order under regulation 30.10 of the General Regulations under the US Commodity Exchange Act, issued by the Commodity Futures Trading Commission on 15 May 1989, granting a *person* exemption from the registration requirement contained in Part 30 of those General Regulations.

Part IV permission

(as defined in section 40(4) of the *Act* (Application for permission)) a *permission* given by the *FSA* under Part IV of the *Act* (Permission to carry on regulated activities), or having effect as if so given.

participant

(in accordance with section 235(2) of the *Act* (Collective investment schemes)) a *person* who participates in a *collective investment scheme*.

participant firm

(1) (except in FEES1 and FEES 6) a *firm* or a *member* other than:

(a) (in accordance with section 210 of the *Act* (The compensation scheme) and regulation 2 of the *Electing Participants Regulations* (Persons not to be regarded as relevant persons) an incoming *EEA firm* which is:

(i) a *credit institution;*

(ii) a *MiFID investment firm*; or

(iii) a *UCITS management company*; or

(iv) both (i) and (ii); or

(v) an *IMD insurance intermediary* or an *IMD reinsurance intermediary* which is neither (i) or (ii);

in relation to its passported activities, unless it has top-up cover (and in the case of a *UCITS management company*, only in relation to the services referred to in Article 5(3) of the *UCITS Directive*, that is *managing investments* (other than of a *collective investment scheme*), *advising on investments* or *safeguarding and administering investments*);

(b) a *service company;*

(c) [deleted]

(d) [deleted]

(e) *an underwriting agent, or members' adviser*, in respect of *advising on syndicate participation at Lloyd's or managing the underwriting capacity of a Lloyd's syndicate as a managing agent at Lloyd's;*

(f) an *authorised professional firm* that is subject to the rules of the Law Society (England and Wales) or the Law Society of Scotland;

(g) an *ICVC;*

(h) a *UCITS qualifier;*

(i) an *ELMI* in relation to *issuing e-money.*

(2) (in FEES 1 and FEES 6) a *firm* specified in paragraph (1) above that is not a *member.*

participating deposit-taker

(as defined in article 2(2) of the *compensation transitionals order*) a *person* who was at any time before *commencement*:

(a) a UK institution, participating institution, former UK institution or former participating institution as defined in section 52(6) of the Banking Act 1987; or

(b) a former authorised institution (as defined in section 106(1) of the Banking Act 1987 (other than a former UK institution or former participating institution as defined in section 52(6) of that Act), which was not a recognised bank or licensed institution excluded by an order under section 23(2) of the Banking Act 1979.

participating institution

(as defined in article 2(2) of the *compensation transitionals order*) a *person* who was at any time before *commencement* a participating institution within the meaning of section 24(4) of the Building Societies Act 1986.

participating insurance undertaking

an *insurer* which:
(a) has a *subsidiary undertaking* that is an *insurance undertaking*; or
(b) holds a *participation* in an *insurance undertaking*; or
(c) is linked to an *insurance undertaking* by a *consolidation Article 12(1) relationship*.

participating security

a participating security as defined in regulation 3 of the Uncertificated Securities Regulations 1995 (SI 1995/3272), which enable title to participating securities to be evidenced otherwise than by a certificate and transferred otherwise than by a written instrument.

participation

(for the purposes of *ELM*, *UPRU* and *GENPRU* and for the purposes of *BIPRU* and *INSPRU* as they apply on a consolidated basis)):
(a) a participating interest may be defined according to:
  (i) section 421A of the Act where applicable; or
  (ii) paragraph 11(1) of Schedule 10 to the Large and Medium-sized Companies and Groups (Accounts and Reports) Regulations 2008 (SI 2008/410) where applicable; or
  (iii) paragraph 8 of Schedule 7 to the Small Companies and Groups (Accounts and Directors' Report) Regulations 2008 (SI 2008/409) where applicable; or
  (iv) paragraph 8 of Schedule 4 to the Large and Mediumsized Limited Liability Partnerships (Accounts) Regulations 2008 (SI 2008/1913) where applicable; or
  (v) paragraph 8 of Schedule 5 to the Small Limited Liability Partnerships (Accounts) Regulations 2008 (SI 2008/1912) where applicable; or
(b) otherwise the direct or indirect ownership of 20% or more of the voting rights or capital of an *undertaking*;

but excluding the interest of a *parent undertaking* in its *subsidiary undertaking*.

partner

(in relation to a *firm* which is a *partnership*) any *person* appointed to direct its affairs, including:
(a) a *person* occupying the position of a partner (by whatever name called); and
(b) a *person* in accordance with whose directions or instructions (not being advice given in a professional capacity) the partners are accustomed to act.

partner function

controlled function CF4 in the *table of controlled functions*, described more fully in *SUP* 10.6.17R.

partnership

(in accordance with section 417(1) of the *Act* (Definitions)) any partnership, including a partnership constituted under the law of a country or territory outside the *United Kingdom*, but not including a *limited liability partnership*.

passported activity

an activity carried on by an *EEA firm*, or by a *UK firm*, under an *EEA right*.

payment holiday

a feature of a *regulated mortgage contract* under which the *mortgage lender* permits the *customer* to make no payments for a specified period without being in *arrears*.

payment information

the information described in *COBS* 7.3.4R, that is, the amount and nature of any payments that the *client* will have to make, directly or indirectly, for the *personal recommendation*.

payment institution

an *authorised payment institution*, an *EEA authorised payment institution* or a *small payment institution*.

[**Note**: articles 4(4) and 26(3) of the *Payment Services Directive*]

payment instrument

(in BCOBS) any personalised device or personalised set of procedures agrees between the *banking customer* and the *firm* used by the *banking customer* to initiate an instruction or request by the *banking customer* to the *firm* to make a payment.

payment leg

(for the purposes of the *CCR standardised method* and as more fully defined in BIPRU 13.5.2R (Derivation of risk position: payment legs) the contractually agreed gross payments under a *financial derivative instrument*, including the notional amount of the transaction.

payment protection contract

A *non-investment insurance contract* which has elements of a *general insurance contract* and the benefits of which are described as enabling a *policyholder* to protect his ability to continue to make payments due to third parties, or can reasonably be expected to be used in this way.

payment routing information

a combination of letters, numbers or symbols specified by a *firm* to be provided when instructing or requesting the *firm* to make a payment from an account of a *banking customer* for the purposes of routing the payment to the correct destination and intended recipient.

payment service

(in accordance with regulation 2(1) of, and Schedule 1 to, the *Payment Services Regulations*):

(a) Any of the following activities when carried out as a regular occupation or business activity:
- (i) services enabling cash to be placed on a payment account and all of the operations required for operating a payment account;
- (ii) services enabling cash withdrawals from a payment account and all of the operations required for operating a payment account;
- (iii) execution of the following types of payment transaction:
  - (A) direct debits, including one-off direct debits;
  - (B) payment transactions executed through a payment card or a similar device;
  - (C) credit transfers, including standing orders;
- (iv) execution of the following types of payment transaction where the funds are covered by a credit line for the *payment service user*:
  - (A) direct debits, including one-off direct debits;
  - (B) payment transactions executed through a payment card or a similar device;
  - (C) credit transfers, including standing orders;
- (v) issuing payment instruments or acquiring payment transactions;
- (vi) *money remittance*;
- (vii) execution of payment transactions where the consent of the payer to execute the payment transaction is given by means of any telecommunication, digital or IT device and the payment is made to the telecommunication, IT system or network operator, acting only as an intermediary between the *payment service user* and the supplier of the goods or services.

(b) The following activities do not constitute payment services:
- (i) payment transactions executed wholly in cash and directly between the payer and the payee, without any intermediary intervention;
- (ii) payment transactions between the payer and the payee through a commercial agent authorised to negotiate or conclude the sale or purchase of goods or services on behalf of the payer or the payee;
- (iii) the professional physical transport of banknotes and coins, including their collection, processing and delivery;
- (iv) payment transactions consisting of non-professional cash collection and delivery as part of a not-for-profit or charitable activity;
- (v) services where cash is provided by the payee to the payer as part of a payment transaction for the purchase of goods or services following an explicit request by the payer immediately before the execution of the payment transaction;
- (vi) money exchange business consisting of cash-to-cash operations where the funds are not held on a payment account;
- (vii) payment transactions based on any of the following documents drawn on the *payment service provider* with a view to placing funds at the disposal of the payee:
  - (A) paper cheques of any kind, including traveller's cheques;
  - (B) bankers' drafts;
  - (C) paper-based vouchers;
  - (D) paper postal orders;
- (viii) payment transactions carried out within a payment or securities settlement system between *payment service providers* and settlement agents, central counterparties, clearing houses, central banks or other participants in the system;
- (ix) payment transactions related to securities asset servicing, including dividends, income or other distributions, or redemption or sale, carried out by *persons* referred to in (h) or by investment firms, *full credit institutions*, collective investment undertakings, asset management companies providing investment services or by any other entities allowed to have the custody of financial instruments;

(x) services provided by technical service providers, which support the provision of *payment services*, without the provider entering at any time into possession of the funds to be transferred, including:
  (A) the processing and storage of data;
  (B) trust and privacy protection services;
  (C) data and entity authentication;
  (D) information technology;
  (E) communication network provision; and
  (F) the provision and maintenance of terminals and devices used for *payment services*;
(xi) services based on instruments that can be used to acquire goods or services only:
  (A) in or on the issuer's premises; or
  (B) under a commercial agreement with the issuer, either within a limited network of service providers or for a limited range of goods or services, and for these purposes the "issuer" is the person who issues the instrument in question;
(xii) payment transactions executed by means of any telecommunication, digital or IT device, where the goods or services purchased are delivered to and are to be used through a telecommunication, digital or IT device, provided that the telecommunication, digital or IT operator does not act only as an intermediary between the *payment service user* and the supplier of the goods and services;
  (A) payment transactions carried out between *payment service providers*, or their agents or *branches*, for their own account;
  (B) payment transactions between a parent undertaking and its subsidiary or between subsidiaries of the same parent undertaking, without any intermediary intervention by a *payment service provider* other than an undertaking belonging to the same group;
  (C) services by providers to withdraw cash by means of automated teller machines acting on behalf of one or more card issuers, which are not party to the *framework contract* with the customer withdrawing money from a payment account, where no other *payment service* is conducted by the provider.

[Note: articles 3 and 4(3) of, and the Annex to, the *Payment Services Directive*]

Payment Services Directive

Directive 2007/64/EC of the European Parliament and of the Council of 13th November 2007 on payment services in the internal market.

payment service provider

(1) (except in DISP) (in accordance with regulation 2(1) of the *Payment Service Regulations*) any of the following *persons* when they carry out a *payment service*:
  (a) an *authorised payment institution*;
  (b) a *small payment institution*;
  (c) an *EEA authorised payment institution*;
  (d) a *full credit institution*;
  (e) an *e-money issuer*;
  (f) the Post Office Limited;
  (g) the Bank of England, the European Central Bank and the national central banks of *EEA States* other than the *United Kingdom*, other than when acting in their capacity as a monetary authority or carrying out other functions of a public nature; and
  (h) government departments and local authorities, other than when carrying out functions of a public nature.
(2) (in DISP and FEES 5.5) as in (1) but excluding a *full credit institution* and an *e-money firm*.

[**Note:** article 1(1) of the *Payment Services Directive*]

(2) (in DISP) as in (1) but excluding a *full credit institution* and an *e-money firm*.

payment service user

(in accordance with regulation 2(1) of the *Payment Services Regulations*) a *person* when making use of a *payment service* in the capacity of either payer or payee, or both.

[**Note:** article 4(10) of the *Payment Services Directive*]

Payment Services Regulations

the Payment Services Regulations 2009 (SI 2009/209).

PD

(1) (except in GENPRU and BIPRU) *Prospectus Directive*.
(2) (in GENPRU and BIPRU) *probability of default*.

Part II FSA Handbook Materials

PD Regulation

the Prospectus Directive Regulation (No 2004/809/EC).

PD/LGD approach

the method for treating *equity exposures* under the *IRB approach* set out in BIPRU 4.7.14R-BIPRU 4.7.22R.

peak exposure

(in accordance with Part 1 of Annex III of the *Banking Consolidation Directive* (Definitions) and for the purpose of BIPRU 13 (The calculation of counterparty risk exposure values for financial derivatives, securities financing transactions and long settlement transactions)) a high percentile of the distribution of *exposures* at any particular future date before the maturity date of the longest transaction in the *netting set*.

pending application

(as defined in article 3(1) of the *compensation transitionals order*):
(a) an application for compensation made under an *investment business compensation scheme* before *commencement* in relation to which a *terminating event* did not occur before *commencement*; and
(b) an application made to the *FSCS* after *commencement* under an *investment business compensation scheme*, even if at the time of application that scheme had otherwise ceased to exist.

penny share

a *readily realisable security* in relation to which the bid-offer spread is 10 per cent or more of the offer price, but not:
(a) a *government and public security; or*
(b) a *share* in a *company quoted* on The Financial Times Stock Exchange 100 Index; or
(c) a *security* issued by a *company* which, at the time that the *firm deals* or recommends to the *client* to *deal* in the *investment*, has a market capitalisation of £100 million or more (or its equivalent in any other currency at the relevant time).

pension annuity

an *investment* purchased with the sums derived from the vesting (partial or full) of a *pension policy* or *pension contract*, for the purposes of securing the beneficiary's entitlement to immediate or *future benefits*.

pension buy-out contract

a *pension policy* bought from an *insurer* using funds from:
(a) a scheme that was approved under Chapter 1 of Part 14 of the Income and Corporation Taxes Act 1988 when that chapter was in force; or
(b) a scheme that is a registered pension scheme under Chapter 2 of Part 4 of the Finance Act 2004.

pension contract

a contract under which rights to benefits are obtained by the making of contributions to an occupational pension scheme or to a personal pension scheme, where the contributions are paid to a regulated collective investment scheme.

pension fund management

(in relation to a *class of contract of insurance*) the *class of contract of insurance* specified in paragraph VII of Part II of Schedule 1 to the *Regulated Activities Order* (Contracts of long-term insurance) namely:
(a) *pension fund management contracts*; and
(b) *pension fund management contracts* which are combined with *contracts of insurance* covering either conservation of capital or payment of a minimum interest;

where effected or carried out by a *person* who does not carry on a banking business, and otherwise carries on *insurance business*.

pension fund management contract

(as defined in article 3(1) of the *Regulated Activities Order* (Interpretation)) a contract to manage the *investments* of pension funds (other than funds solely for the benefit of the officers or employees of the *person* effecting or carrying out the contract and their dependants or, in the case of a *company*, partly for the benefit of officers and employees of its subsidiary or holding company or a subsidiary of its holding company and their dependants;

in this definition "subsidiary" and "holding company" mean either *subsidiary* and *holding company*, or subsidiary and holding company defined in accordance with article 4 of the Companies (Northern

Ireland) Order 1986 (SI 1986) No 1032 (NI 6)) as amended by article 62 of the Companies (No 2) (Northern Ireland) Order 1990 (SI 1990 No 1504 (NI 10)).

pension opt-out

a transaction resulting from the decision of a *retail client* who is an individual, to:
(a) opt out of an *occupational pension scheme* of which he is a member; or
(b) decline to become a member of an *occupational pension scheme* which he is eligible to join, or will be eligible to join at the end of a waiting period

in favour of a *stakeholder pension scheme* or *personal pension scheme*.

pension policy

a contract under which a right to benefits results from contributions made to an *occupational pension scheme* or to a *personal pension scheme*, where the contributions are paid to a *long-term insurer*.

pension scheme

a scheme under which a right to benefits results from contributions made under a *pension contract* or *pension policy*.

pension term assurance policy

a *personal pension policy* which is a *pure protection contract* and in connection with which tax relief is available under Chapter 4 of Part 4 of the Finance Act 2004.

pension transfer

a transaction resulting from the decision of a *retail client* who is an individual, to transfer deferred benefits from:
(a) an *occupational pension scheme*;
(b) an individual pension contract providing fixed or guaranteed benefits that replaced similar benefits under a *defined benefits pension scheme; or*
(c) (in the cancellation *rules* (COBS 15)) a *stakeholder pension scheme* or *personal pension scheme*.

to:
(d) a *stakeholder pension scheme;*
(e) a *personal pension scheme;* or
(f) a *deferred annuity policy*, where the eventual benefits depend on investment performance in the period up to the date when those benefits will come into payment.

pension transfer specialist

an individual appointed by a *firm* to check the suitability of a *pension transfer* or *pension opt-out* who has passed the required examinations as specified in *TC*.

pension wrapper

(in the cancellation rules (*COBS* 15)) a *SIPP*, *pension contract* or *personal pension product*.

PEP

[deleted]

PEP manager

[deleted]

PEP transfer

[deleted]

per se eligible counterparty

a *client* categorised as a per se eligible counterparty in accordance with *COBS* 3.6.

per se professional client

a *client* categorised as a per se professional *client* in accordance with COBS 3.5.

percentage ratio

(in LR) (in relation to a transaction) the figure, expressed as a percentage, that results from applying a calculation under a *class test* to the transaction.

PERG

the Perimeter Guidance manual.

periodic information

the information identified in the table in *COBS* 16 Ann 2 R, and if the *client* has not elected to receive *trade confirmation information* on a transaction by transaction basis under *COBS* 16.3.3R, the information identified in column 2 of *COBS* 16 Ann 1R.

periodic statement

a report which a *firm* is required to provide to a *client* under *COBS* 16.3 (Periodic reporting).

permanent health

(in relation to a *class* of *contract of insurance*) the *class* of *contract of insurance*, specified in paragraph IV of Part II of Schedule 1 to the *Regulated Activities Order* (Contracts of long-term insurance), providing specified benefits against risks of persons becoming incapacitated in consequence of sustaining injury as a result of an accident or of an accident of a specified class or of sickness or infirmity, being contracts that:

(a) are expressed to be in effect for a period of not less than five years, or until the normal retirement age of the persons concerned, or without limit of time; and

(b) either are not expressed to be terminable by the insurer, or are expressed to be so terminable only in special circumstances mentioned in the contract.

permanent health reinsurance business

reinsurance acceptances which are *contracts of insurance* falling within *long-term insurance business class* IV.

permanent interest bearing shares

any shares of a class defined as deferred shares for the purposes of section 119 of the Building Societies Act 1986 which are issued as permanent interest-bearing shares and on terms which qualify them as own funds for the purposes of the *Banking Consolidation Directive*.

permanent share capital

an item of capital that is stated in GENPRU 2.2.83R (Core tier one capital: permanent share capital) to be permanent share capital.

permission

permission to carry on *regulated activities*; that is, any of the following:

(a) *a Part IV permission;*

(b) the permission that an *incoming EEA firm* has, under paragraph 15(1) of Schedule 3 to the Act (EEA Passport Rights), on qualifying for *authorisation* under paragraph 12 of that Schedule;

(c) the permission that an *incoming Treaty firm* has, under paragraph 4(1) of Schedule 4 to the Act (Treaty Rights), on qualifying for *authorisation* under paragraph 2 of that Schedule;

(d) the permission that a *UCITS qualifier* has, under paragraph 2(1) of Schedule 5 to the Act (Persons concerned in Collective Investment Schemes);

(e) the permission that an *ICVC* has, under paragraph 2(2) of Schedule 5 to the Act (Persons concerned in Collective Investment Schemes);

(f) the permission that the *Society of Lloyd's* has, under section 315(2) of the Act (The Society: authorisation and permission), which is to be treated as a *Part IV permission* for the purposes of Part IV of the *Act* (Permission to carry on regulated activities) in accordance with section 315(3) of the *Act*.

permitted activity

(1) (except in SUP 13A and *SUP* 14) a *regulated activity* which a *firm* has *permission* to carry on.

(2) (in SUP 13A and *SUP* 14) an activity identified in a consent notice, a regulator's notice or, where none is required, a notice of intention.

permitted business

(in *UPRU*) means *permitted activity*.

permitted deposits

in relation to *permitted links*, *deposits* with any of the following:

(a) an *approved credit institution*; or

(b) an *approved financial institution*; or

(c) an *approved investment firm*.

permitted derivatives contract

in relation to *permitted links*, a contract involving a *derivative* or *quasiderivative* that satisfies INSPRU 3.2.5R to INSPRU 3.2.35AG with the exception of INSPRU 3*.2.18R*, as applied in relation to assets covering liabilities in respect of *linked long-term* contracts of insurance.

permitted immovable

any interest in land or buildings which falls within COLL 5.6.18R(2) and (6) (Investment in property) and which, being a leasehold interest or its equivalent, has an unexpired term of at least 20 years, but excluding, in relation to an *ICVC*, immovable property that is necessary for the direct pursuit of its business.

permitted land and property

in relation to *permitted links*, any interest in land (and any buildings situated on it) provided that:

(a) it is considered by the *firm* to be located in a territory with a properly functioning market, indicated by the following criteria:
 (i) a lack of artificial barriers, including barriers to foreign ownership and repatriation of capital;
 (ii) fair and accurate valuation;
 (iii) suitably qualified and independent surveyors;
 (iv) accurate financial information;
 (v) enforceable contractual and other property rights;
 (vi) clarity of taxation;
 (vii) availability of reliable economic and property market data;
(b) ethical transaction standards; and
(c) it is:
 (i) owned directly by the *firm*; or
 (ii) held in a structure, or a series of structures, that do not pose a materially greater risk to *linked policyholders* than a direct holding; and
(d) it is not geared in excess of 10% of the gross asset value of the *linked fund* excluding any amounts represented by holdings in property detailed in *permitted scheme interests* (b) (i) to (iv). But this percentage restriction does not apply if the relevant *policyholder* or trustee or operator acting on behalf of an individual beneficiary requests, directly or indirectly, the *firm* to hold those investments based on the risk profile and objectives, stipulated by and specific for that individual under an investment management agreement with that individual.

permitted links

the property in *COBS* 21.3.1R that an insurer may use for the purposes of determining *property-linked benefits* or *index-linked benefits* under *linked long-term* contracts of insurance.

permitted loans

in relation to *permitted links*, a loan with any of the following:

(a) an *approved credit institution*; or
(b) an *approved financial institution*; or
(c) an *approved investment firm*; or
(d) any person, provided that the loan:
 (i) is documented in a written agreement setting out the rate of interest and the amount of, and due dates for, repayments; and
 (ii) is fully secured by a mortgage or charge on *permitted land and property* that, if made to someone other than a body corporate, is not used wholly or mainly for domestic purposes.

permitted scheme interests

(a) in respect of a firm's business with *institutional linked policyholders* only, any of the following:
 (i) a *qualified investor scheme* or its *EEA* equivalent;
 (ii) any *unregulated collective investment scheme* that invests only in *permitted links* and publishes its prices regularly;
 (iii) any of the interests set out in (b)(i) to (b)(iv);
(b) in respect of a firm's business with *linked policyholders* other than those described in (a), any of the following:
 (i) an *authorised fund*;
 (ii) a *recognised scheme*;
 (iii) a scheme falling within the *UCITS Directive*;
 (iv) a *non-UCITS retail scheme*;
 (v) a *qualified investor scheme* or its *EEA* equivalent or any *unregulated collective investment scheme* that invests only in *permitted links* and publishes its prices regularly, provided that no more than 20% of the gross assets of the *linked fund* are so invested.

permitted stock lending

in relation to *permitted links*, a *stock lending* transaction (including a *repo* transaction) that satisfies INSPRU 3.2.36AR to INSPRU 3.2.42G (inclusive).

permitted third party

a third party who is:

(a) an *authorised person*; or
(b) an *exempt person* for whom an *authorised person* is accepting responsibility; or
(c) a *person* lawfully carrying on a *regulated activity* in another *EEA State*.

permitted units

in relation to *permitted links*, units or beneficial interests in any real or notional fund that invests only in *permitted links* and is managed either:

(a) wholly by the *insurer*; or

(b) wholly or partly by:

(i) an agent on behalf of the *insurer*; or

(ii) a *reinsurer* in relation to a *reinsurance contract* with the *insurer*;

for whom the *insurer* retains all responsibility towards its *linked policyholders*.

permitted unlisted securities

in relation to *permitted links*, means any investment (including a *share, debt security, Treasury Bill*, Tax Reserve Certificate or Certificate of Tax Deposit) that is not a *listed security*, but provided always that it is realisable in the short term.

Person

(in accordance with the Interpretation Act 1978) any person, including a body of persons corporate or unincorporate (that is, a natural person, a legal person and, for example, a *partnership*).

person discharging managerial responsibilities

(in accordance with section 96B(1) of the *Act*):

(a) a director of an issuer:

(i) registered in the *United Kingdom* that has requested or approved admission of its *shares* to trading on a *regulated market*; or

(ii) not registered in the *United Kingdom* or any other *EEA State* but has requested or approved admission of its shares to trading on a *regulated market* and who is required to file annual information in relation to shares in the *United Kingdom* in accordance with Article 10 of the *Prospectus Directive*; or

(b) a senior executive of such an *issuer* who:

(i) has regular access to *inside information* relating, directly or indirectly, to the *issuer*; and

(ii) has power to make managerial decisions affecting the future development and business prospects of the *issuer*.

person exercising significant influence

(in LR) in relation to a *listed company*, a *person* or entity which exercises significant influence over that *listed company*.

person with whom a relevant person has a family relationship

any of the following:

(a) the spouse of the *relevant person* or any partner of that person considered by national law as equivalent to a spouse;

(b) a child or stepchild of the *relevant person*;

(c) any other relative of the *relevant person* who has shared the same household as that person for at least one year on the date of the personal transaction concerned.

[**Note:** article 2(7) of the *MiFID implementing Directive*]

personal account transaction

[deleted]

personal equity plan

[deleted]

Personal Insurance Arbitration Service

the *former scheme* set up on a voluntary basis and run by the Chartered Institute of Arbitrators to handle complaints against those insurance companies which subscribed to it.

personal investment firm

(subject to BIPRU TP 1.3R (Revised definition of personal investment firm for certain transitional purposes)) a *firm* whose *permitted activities* include *designated investment business*, which is not an *authorised professional firm, bank, BIPRU investment firm, ELMI, building society, credit union, energy market participant, friendly society, ICVC, insurer, media firm, oil market participant, service company, incoming EEA firm* (without a *top-up permission*), *incoming Treaty firm* (without a *top-up permission*), *UCITS management company* or *UCITS qualifier* (without a *top-up permission*), whose *permission* does not include a *requirement* that it comply with *IPRU(INV)* 3 (Securities and futures firms) or 5 (Investment management firms), and which is within (a), (b) or (c):

(a) a *firm*:

(i) which was a member of *PIA* immediately before *commencement*; and

(ii) which was not, immediately before *commencement*, subject to the financial supervision requirements of the *FSA* (under section 43 of the Financial Services Act 1986), or *IMRO* or *SFA* (under lead regulation arrangements);

(b) a *firm* whose *permission* includes a *requirement* that it comply with *IPRU(INV)* 13 (Personal investment firms);

(c) a *firm*:

(i) which was given a *Part IV permission* after *commencement*, or which was authorised under section 25 of the Financial Services Act 1986 immediately before *commencement* and not a member of *IMRO*, *PIA* or *SFA*; and

(ii) for which the most substantial part of its gross income (including *commissions*) from the *designated investment business* included in its *Part IV permission* is derived from one or more of the following activities (based, for a *firm* given a *Part IV permission* after *commencement*, on the business plan submitted as part of the *firm's* application for *permission* or, for a *firm* authorised under section 25 of the Financial Services Act 1986, on the *firm's* financial year preceding its *authorisation* under the *Act*):

(A) *advising on investments, arranging (bringing about) deals in investments* or *making arrangements with a view to transactions in investments*, in relation to *packaged products;*

(B) *managing investments* for *private customers*.

personal pension contract

a *pension contract* under which contributions (single or regular) are paid to a *personal pension scheme*.

personal pension deposit

a contract under which rights to benefits are obtained by making contributions to a *personal pension scheme* operated by a *deposit-taking firm*.

personal pension policy

a *pension policy* under which contributions (single or regular) are paid to a *personal pension scheme*.

personal pension product

a contract under which rights to benefits are obtained by making contributions to a *personal pension scheme* other than a *personal pension policy*, a *personal pension contract*, a *personal pension deposit* or a *SIPP*.

personal pension scheme

a scheme or arrangement which is not an *occupational pension scheme* or *stakeholder pension scheme* and which is comprised in one or more instruments or agreements having or capable of having effect so as to provide benefits to or in respect of people:

(a) on retirement; or

(b) on having reached a particular age; or

(c) on termination of service in an employment.

personal projection

a *projection* that reflects the terms of a particular contract with, or to be offered to, a particular *client*.

personal recommendation

a recommendation that is *advice on investments*, or *advice on a home finance transaction*, and is presented as suitable for the person to whom it is made, or is based on a consideration of the circumstances of that person.

A recommendation is not a personal recommendation if it is issued exclusively through distribution channels or to the public.

[Note: article 52 of the *MiFID implementing Directive*]

personal transaction

a trade in a *designated investment* effected by or on behalf of a *relevant person*, where at least one of the following criteria are met:

(1) that *relevant person* is acting outside the scope of the activities he carried out in that capacity;

(2) the trade is carried out for the account of any of the following *persons*:

(a) the *relevant person*;

(b) the spouse or civil partner of the *relevant person* or any partner of that *person* considered by national law as equivalent to a spouse;

(c) a dependent child or stepchild of the *relevant person*;

(d) any other relative of the *relevant person* who has shared the same household as that *person* for at least one year on the date of the *personal transaction* concerned;

(e) any *person* with whom he has *close links*;

(f) a *person* whose relationship with the *relevant person* is such that the *relevant person* has a direct or indirect material interest in the outcome of the trade, other than a fee or commission for the execution of the trade.

[Note: article 2(7) and article 11 of the *MiFID implementing Directive*]

physical commodities

a physical holding of a *commodity*, or documents evidencing title to a *commodity*.

PIA

the Personal Investment Authority Limited.

PIA Ombudsman scheme

the *former scheme* set up by *PIA* under the Financial Services Act 1986 and operated by the PIA Ombudsman Bureau Ltd to handle complaints against members of *PIA*.

PIBS

permanent interest-bearing shares.

placing

(in LR) a marketing of *securities* already in issue but not *listed* or not yet in issue, to specified *persons* or clients of the *sponsor* or any securities house assisting in the placing, which does not involve an offer to the public or to existing holders of the *issuer's securities* generally.

plan investor

a *person* entered in the *plan register* under COLL 6.4.9R (Plan registers).

plan manager

in relation to:

(a) [deleted]
(b) a *group ISA*, the *ISA manager;*
(c) a *group savings plan*, the *person* primarily responsible for that *group savings plan*.

plan register

(1) (in relation to an *ICVC*) a record of *persons* who subscribe to a *group plan* and for whom *shares* in the *ICVC* are held for the purposes of the *group plan* by the *plan manager* or a nominee (other than a record for the establishment or maintenance of which no payments are to be made out of the *scheme property*).

(2) (in relation to an *AUT*) a sub-register to the *register*, which sub-register records *persons* who subscribe to a *group plan* and for whom *units* in the *AUT* are held for the purposes of the plan by the *plan manager* or a nominee (other than any sub-register that has not been established and maintained in accordance with COLL 6.4.4R (Register: general requirements and contents or for the establishment of which no payments are to be made out of the *scheme property*).

plastic card

a card, or a token with an equivalent function, which a *customer* can use to pay for goods and services, or to obtain cash or both, such as a credit card, charge card, debit card, cash card or electronic purse.

PLC Safeguards Directive

the Second Council Directive of 13 December 1976 on coordination of safeguards for the protection of the interests of members and others in respect of the formation of public limited liability companies and the maintenance and alteration of their capital, with a view to making such safeguards equivalent (No 77/91/EEC).

plus factor

(in BIPRU 7.10 (Use of a value at risk model)) an increase to the *minimum multiplication factor* based on *backtesting exceptions* as more fully defined in BIPRU 7.10.124R (Capital calculations: Multiplication factors).

policy

(as defined in article 2 of the Financial Services and Markets Act 2000 (Meaning of "Policy" and "Policyholder") Order 2001 (SI 2001/2361)) as the context requires:

(a) a *contract of insurance*, including one under which an existing liability has already accrued; or
(b) any instrument evidencing such a contract.

policy document

[deleted]

policy summary

a summary of a *non-investment insurance contract* in the format and containing the information specified in ICOBS 6 Annex 2.

policyholder

(as defined in article 3 of the Financial Services and Markets Act 2000 (Meaning of "Policy and "Policyholder") Order 2001 (SI 2001/2361)) the *person* who for the time being is the legal holder of the *policy*, including any *person* to whom, under the *policy*, a sum is due, a periodic payment is payable or any other benefit is to be provided or to whom such a sum, payment or benefit is contingently due, payable or to be provided.

policyholder advocate

the *person* appointed under *COBS* 20.2.42R to negotiate with a *firm* on its proposals for making a *reattribution* of its *inherited estate.*

portfolio management

managing portfolios in accordance with mandates given by *clients* on a discretionary *client*-by-*client* basis where such portfolios include one or more *financial instruments*.

[Note: article 4(1)(9) of *MiFID*]

portfolio trade

a transaction in more than one security where those securities are grouped and traded as a single lot against a specific reference price.

[Note: article 2(6) of the *MiFID Regulation*]

POS Regulations

the Public Offers of Securities Regulations 1995 (SI 1995/1537).

position

(in accordance BIPRU 1.2.4 (Definition of the trading book: Positions)) includes proprietary positions and positions arising from client servicing and market making.

position risk requirement

a capital requirement applied to a *position* treated under BIPRU 7 (Market risk) as part of the calculation of the *market risk capital requirement* or, if the relevant provision of the *Handbook* distinguishes between *general market risk* and *specific risk*, the portion of that capital requirement with respect to whichever of *general market risk* or *specific risk* is specified by that provision.

post

(in relation to sending a *document* by post) sending pre-paid by a postal service which seeks to deliver documents by post within the *United Kingdom* no later than the next working day in all or the majority of cases, and to deliver by post outside the *United Kingdom* within such a period as is reasonable in all the circumstances.

Post-BCCI Directive

the European Parliament and Council Directive of 29 June 1995 amending certain directives with a view to reinforcing prudential supervision (No 95/26/EC).

post-sale notice

[deleted]

potential tier one instrument

an item of capital that falls into GENPRU 2.2.62R (Tier one capital: General).

power of intervention

the power conferred on the *FSA* under section 196 of the *Act* (The Power of Intervention) to impose a requirement on an *incoming firm.*

PPFM

Principles and Practices of Financial Management.

PPFM guidance table

the table in *COBS* 20.3.8G (Guidance on with-profits principles and practices).

PPFM issues table

The table in *COBS* 20.3.6R (Issues to be covered in PPFM).

PR

the Prospectus Rules sourcebook.

PRA

Position Risk Adjustment; a percentage applied to a *position* as part of the process of calculating the *PRR* in relation to that *position* as set out in the tables in BIPRU 7.2.44R (Specific risk PRAs), BIPRU 7.2.57R (General market risk PRAs), BIPRU 7.3.30R (Simplified equity method PRAs), BIPRU 7.3.34R (PRAs for specific risk under the standard equity method) and BIPRU 7.6.8R (The appropriate PRA) and also as set out in BIPRU 7.2.46R to BIPRU 7.2.47R.

pre-sale notice

[deleted]

precious metals

(in COLL) gold, silver or platinum.

predecessor scheme

any of the following:
(a) The Office of the Banking Ombudsman;
(b) The Office of the Building Societies Ombudsman;
(c) The Insurance Ombudsman Bureau;
(d) The Office of the Investment Ombudsman;
(e) The Personal Investment Authority Ombudsman Bureau;
(f) The Personal Insurance Arbitration Service;
(g) The Securities and Futures Authority Complaints Bureau and Arbitration Service;
(h) The FSA Complaints Unit and Independent Investigator.

preference share

(1) (except in GENPRU) a *share* conferring preference as to income or return of capital which is not convertible into an *equity share* and does not form part of the *equity share capital* of a *company*.
(2) (in GENPRU) a *share* conferring preference as to income or return of capital which does not form part of the *equity share capital* of a *company*.

preliminary charge

a *charge* upon a *sale of units* by an *authorised fund manager* whether or not acting as *principal*.

premium

(1) (except in ICOBS and CASS 5) (in relation to a *general insurance contract*) the consideration payable under the contract by the *policyholder* to the *insurer*.

(2) (except in ICOBS and CASS 5) (in relation to a *long-term insurance contract*) the consideration payable under the contract by the *policyholder* to the *insurer*; (except in *SUP* 16.8 (Persistency reports from insurers)) a premium is a regular premium if it is one of a series of payments under the contract:

(a)

(i) which are payable on dates that are certain or ascertainable at the time the contract is made;

(ii) which are payable over a period that exceeds one year in length; and

(iii) assuming the *policy* evidencing the contract is not surrendered or otherwise terminated before the *premiums* fall due, will fall due on those dates without either party to the contract exercising any option under the contract; or

(b) of which the first payment is an obligation under the contract, and subsequent payments, calculated according to an agreed formula, are payable over a period which exceeds one year in length under a collateral written arrangement with the *insurer* or *friendly society*.

(2A) (in ICOBS and CASS 5) as in (1) and (2) except that '*insurance undertaking*' is substituted for '*insurer*' (except where 'insurer' is used in the heading to SUP 16.8).

(3) (in relation to an *option*) the total amount which the purchaser of the *option* is, or may be, required to pay in consideration for the right to exercise the *option*.

premiums amount

(for the purposes of INSPRU 1.1), an amount, as defined in INSPRU 1.1.45R, used in the calculation of the *general insurance capital requirement*.

prescribed asset share methodology

the methodology described in *COBS* 20.2.5R for assessing maturity payments by reference to unsmoothed asset shares.

prescribed market

a market which has been prescribed by the Treasury in the *Prescribed Markets and Qualifying Investments Order*.

Prescribed Markets and Qualifying Investments Order

the Financial Services and Markets Act 2000 (Prescribed Markets and Qualifying Investments) Order 2001 (SI 2001/996).

prescribed pricing basis

(in relation to a *derivative* contract, or *quasi-derivative contract*), the pricing basis set out in *IPRU(INS)* 4.12R(8) (Derivative contracts) as that rule was in force on 30 December 2004.

previous regulator

(1) (in relation to a *firm* which was authorised under the Banking Act 1987 immediately before *commencement* or which was a European institution (as defined in the Banking Coordination (Second Council Directive) Regulations 1992) immediately before *commencement*) the *FSA*.
(2) (in relation to a *firm* which was a *building society* immediately before *commencement*) the Building Societies Commission.
(3) (in relation to a *firm* which was a *friendly society* immediately before *commencement*) the Friendly Societies Commission.
(4) (in relation to a *firm* authorised under the Insurance Companies Act 1982 immediately before *commencement*) the Treasury.
(5) (in relation to an *underwriting agent* which obtained the *permission* relevant to that category under the Financial Services and Markets Act 2000 (Repeals, Transitional Provisions and Savings) Order 2001 (SI 2001/2636)) the *Society of Lloyd's*.
(6) (in relation to a *firm* which was authorised, or which was an *appointed representative*, under the Financial Services Act 1986 immediately before *commencement* or which was a European investment firm (as defined in the Investment Services Regulations 1995 (SI 1995/3275)) immediately before *commencement*) any of:
 (a) IMRO;
 (b) PIA;
 (c) SFA;
 (d) a recognised professional body; and
 (e) the FSA;
 if the *firm* (or, if relevant, its principal for the purposes of section 44 of the Financial Services Act 1986) was subject in carrying on business to the rules, requirements, regulations or guidance of that body.
(7) (in relation to an *ex-section 43 firm*) the *FSA*.

price

(in COLL)

(in relation to a *unit* in an *authorised fund*) the price of the *unit* calculated in accordance with COLL 6.3 (Valuation and pricing).

price information

(in *MCOB*) information, in a *financial promotion*, that relates to:
 (a) any rate of charge; or
 (b) the presence or absence of any payments, fees or charges (other than the fees for *advising on* or *arranging a regulated mortgage contract* as required by *MCOB* 3.6.27R); or
 (c) the amount, frequency or number of any payments, repayments, fees or charges; or
 (c) any monetary amounts.

price stabilising rules

the *rules* made under section 144 of the *Act*, and appearing in MAR 2.1 to MAR 2.4, together with any other provisions available for their interpretation.

primary listed issuer

(in LR) an *issuer* with a *primary listing* of its *securities*.

primary listing

(in LR) a *listing* by the *FSA* by virtue of which the *issuer* is subject to the full requirements of the *listing rules*.

primary pooling event

[deleted]

PRIN

the part of the *Handbook* in High Level Standards that has the title Principles for Businesses.

principal

(1) in relation to a *person*:
  (a) a *person* acting on his own account;
  (b) (if the *person* is an *appointed representative* or, where applicable, a *tied agent*) the *authorised person* who is party to a contract with the *appointed representative*, or who is responsible for the acts of the *tied agent*, resulting in him being exempt under section 39 of the *Act* (Exemption of appointed representatives).
(2) in relation to an *option*, *future* or forward contract:
  (a) (except in the case of an *option* on a *future*) the amount of property or the value of the property which must be delivered in order to satisfy settlement of the *option*, *future* or forward contract;
  (b) (in relation to an *option* on a *future*) the amount of property or the value of the property which must be delivered in order to satisfy settlement of the *future*.

Principle

one of the Principles set out in *PRIN* 2.1.1R (Principles for Businesses).

Principles and Practices of Financial Management

the Principles and Practices of Financial Management, containing *with-profits principles* and *with-profits practices*, which a *firm* carrying on *with-profits business* must establish, maintain and record under *COBS* 20.3 (Principles and Practices of Financial Management).

private customer

(for the purposes only of COBS TP 1 (Transitional Provisions in relation to Client Categorisation)):
(1) (except in *COB* 3, 4.2 and 6.4) subject to (h), a *client* who is not a *market counterparty* or an *intermediate customer*, including:
  (a) an individual who is not a *firm*;
  (b) an overseas individual who is not an *overseas financial services institution*;
  (c) [deleted]
  (d) (except for the purposes of *DISP*) a *client* when he is classified as a *private customer* in accordance with *COB* 4.1.14R (Client classified as a private customer);
  (e) a *person* to whom a *firm* gives *basic advice*;
  (f) (in *COB* 6.1 to 6.5) where the *regulated activity* (except for a *personal recommendation* relating to a contribution to a *CTF*) relates to a *CTF* and there is no *registered contact*, the *person* to whom the annual statement must be sent in accordance with Regulation 10 of the *CTF Regulations*;
  (g) (in *COB* 6.7) where the *regulated activity* (except for a *personal recommendation* relating to a contribution to a *CTF*) relates to a *CTF* and there is no *registered contact*, the child, via the person to whom the annual statement must be sent in accordance with Regulation 10 of the *CTF Regulations*;
  (h) a *client* who would otherwise be excluded as a *market counterparty* or *intermediate customer* if the *client* is within (e), (f) or (g);
  but excluding a *client*, who would otherwise be a *private customer*:
    (i) when he is classified as an *intermediate customer* in accordance with *COB* 4.1.9R (Expert private customer classified as an intermediate customer); or
    (ii) when the *regulated activity* relates to a *CTF*, any *person* other than (e), (f), (g) or (h).
(2) in *COB* 3) a *person* in (1) or a *person* excluded under (1)(h)(ii) or a *person* who would be such a *person* if he were a *client*
(3) (in *COB* 4.2 and 6.1 to 6.5) a *person* in (1) and, in relation to the conclusion of a *distance contract*, a *retail customer*.

private person

(as defined in article 3 of the Financial Services and Markets Act 2000 (Rights of Action) Regulations 2000 (SI 2001/2256)):
(a) any individual, unless he suffers the loss in question in the course of carrying on:
  (i) any *regulated activity*; or
  (ii) any activity which would be a *regulated activity* apart from any exclusion made by article 72 of the Regulated Activities Order (Overseas persons); and
(b) any *person* who is not an individual, unless he suffers the loss in question in the course of carrying on business of any kind;

but not including a government, a local authority (in the *United Kingdom* or elsewhere) or an international organisation;

for the purposes of (a), an individual who suffers loss in the course of *effecting* or *carrying out contracts of insurance written at Lloyd's* is not to be taken to suffer loss in the course of carrying on a *regulated activity*;

in this definition:

(A) "government" means:
   (I) the government of the *United Kingdom*; or
   (II) the Scottish Administration; or
   (III) the Executive Committee of the Northern Ireland Assembly; or
   (IV) the National Assembly for Wales; or
   (V) the government of any country or territory outside the *United Kingdom*;

(B) "international organisation" means any international organisation the members of which include the *United Kingdom* or any other State;

(C) "local authority", in relation to the *United Kingdom*, means:
   (I) in England and Wales, a local authority as defined in the Local Government Act 1972, the Greater London Authority, the Common Council of the City of London or the Council of the Isles of Scilly;
   (II) in Scotland, a local authority as defined in the Local Government (Scotland) Act 1973; and
   (III) in Northern Ireland, a district council as defined in the Local Government Act (Northern Ireland) 1972.

probability of default

(in accordance with Article 4(25) of the *Banking Consolidation Directive* (Definitions)) the probability of default of a counterparty over a one year period; for the purposes of the *IRB approach*, default has the meaning in the definition of *default*.

probable reserves

(in LR):

(a) in respect of *mineral companies* primarily involved in the *extraction* of oil and gas resources, those reserves which are not yet *proven* but which, on the available evidence and taking into account technical and economic factors, have a better than 50% chance of being produced; and

(b) in respect of *mineral companies* other than those primarily involved in the *extraction* of oil and gas resources, those *measured* and/or *indicated mineral resources*, which are not yet *proven* but of which detailed technical and economic studies have demonstrated that *extraction* can be justified at the time of the determination and under specified economic conditions.

procuration fee

the total amount paid by a *home finance provider* to a *home finance intermediary*, whether directly or indirectly, in connection with providing applications from *customers* to enter into *home finance transactions* with that *home finance provider*.

product provider

A *firm* which is:

(i) a *long-term insurer*;

(ii) a *friendly society*;

(iii) *the operator of a regulated collective investment scheme* or an *investment trust savings scheme*; or

(iv) the *operator* of a *personal pension scheme* or *stakeholder pension scheme*.

PROF

the Professional firms sourcebook.

professional client

a *client* that is either a *per se professional client* or an *elective professional client* (see *COBS* 3.5.1R). [Note: article 4(1)(12) of *MiFID*].

professional firm

a *person* which is:

(a) an individual who is entitled to practise a profession regulated by a *designated professional body* and, in practising it, is subject to its rules, whether or not he is a member of that body; or

(b) a *person* (not being an individual) which is controlled and managed by one or more such individuals.

profit estimate

(in PR and LR) (as defined in the *PD Regulation*) a profit forecast for a financial period which has expired and for which results have not yet been published.

profit forecast

(in PR and LR) (as defined in the *PD Regulation*) a form of words which expressly states or by implication indicates a figure or a minimum or maximum figure for the likely level of profits or losses for the current financial period and/or financial periods subsequent to that period, or contains data from which a calculation of such a figure for future profits or losses may be made, even if no particular figure is mentioned and the word "profit" is not used.

programme

(in RCB) (as defined in Regulation 1(2) of the *RCB Regulations*) issues, or series of issues, of *covered bonds* which have substantially similar terms and are subject to a framework contract or contracts.

prohibited period

(in LR) as defined by paragraph 1(e) of the *Model Code*.

prohibition order

an order made by the *FSA* under section 56 of the *Act* (Prohibition orders) which prohibits an individual from performing a specified function, any function falling within a specified description or any function.

projection

a projection of the amount of any future benefit payable under a contract or *policy*, being a benefit the amount of which is not ascertainable under the terms of the contract or *policy* when the calculation is made.

projection date

the date to which the *projection* is made.

projection period

(in *COBS*) the period covered by a *standardised deterministic projection*, which begins on the date the investment is reasonably expected to be made and ends on the *projection date* described in paragraph 2.1 of *COBS* 13 Annex 2.

property

(in LR) freehold, heritable or leasehold property.

property authorised investment fund

an *open-ended investment company* to which Part 4A of the Authorised Investment Funds (Tax) Regulations 2006 (SI 2006/964) applies.

property collective investment undertaking

(in PR) (as defined in the *PD Regulation*) a collective investment undertaking whose investment objective is the participation in the holding of property in the long term.

property company

(in LR) a *company* primarily engaged in *property* activities including:
(a) the holding of *properties* (directly or indirectly) for letting and retention as investments;
(b) the development of *properties* for letting and retention as investments;
(c) the purchase and development of *properties* for subsequent sale;
(d) the purchase of land for development *properties* for retention as investments.

property enterprise trust

an *unregulated collective investment scheme* of which the underlying assets are land and buildings.

property fund

(a) a *regulated collective investment scheme* dedicated to land and interests in land;
(b) a fund of funds of which one or more of the funds to which it is dedicated falls within (a);
(c) a constituent part of an umbrella fund which, if it were a separate fund, would fall within (a).

property-linked assets

in relation to an *insurer*, *long-term insurance assets* that are, for the time being, identified in the records of the *insurer* as being assets by reference to the value of which *property-linked benefits* are to be determined.

property-linked benefits

benefits other than *index-linked benefits* provided for under a *linked long-term contract of insurance*.

property-linked liabilities

insurance liabilities in respect of *property-linked benefits*.

property valuation report

(in LR) a *property* valuation report prepared by an independent expert in accordance with:
(1) for an *issuer* incorporated in the *United Kingdom*, the Channel Islands or the Isle of Man, the Appraisal and Valuation Standards (5th edition) issued by the Royal Institution of Chartered Surveyors; or
(2) for an *issuer* incorporated in any other place, either the standards referred to in paragraph (1) or the International Valuation Standards (7th edition) issued by the International Valuation Standards Committee.

proportional reinsurance treaty

a *reinsurance* treaty under which a pre-determined proportion of each *claim* payment by the cedant under *policies* subject to the treaty is recoverable from the *reinsurer*;

non-proportional reinsurance treaty is construed accordingly.

proprietary trader

(in SUP 10 (Approved Persons) and APER) a person (A) whose responsibilites include committing another person (B) as part of B's *proprietary trading*.

proprietary trading

(in SUP 10 (Approved Persons) and APER) *dealing in investments as principal* as part of a business of trading in *specified investments*. For these purposes *dealing in investments as principal* includes any activities that would be included but for the exclusion in Article 15 (Absence of holding out) or Article 16 (Dealing in contractually based investments) of the *Regulated Activities Order*.

prospectus

(1) (in LR and PR and FEES) a prospectus required under the *prospectus directive*.
(2) (except in LR and PR) (in relation to a *collective investment scheme*) a *document* containing information about the *scheme* and complying with the requirements in COLL 4.2.5R (Table: contents of the prospectus), COLL 8.3.4R (Table: contents of qualified investor scheme prospectus) or COLL 9.3.2R (Additional information required in the prospectus for an application under section 272) applicable to a prospectus of a *scheme* of the type.P15 concerned.

Prospectus Directive

the Directive of the European Parliament and of the Council of 4 November 2003 on the prospectus to be published when securities are offered to the public or admitted to trading (No 2003/71/EC).

Prospectus Rules

(as defined in section 73A(4) of the *Act*) *rules* expressed to relate to *transferable securities*.

protected claim

a *claim* which is covered by the *compensation scheme*, as defined in COMP 5.2.1R.

protected contract of insurance

a *contract of insurance* which is covered by the *compensation scheme*, as defined in COMP 5.4.1R.

protected deposit

a *deposit* which is covered by the *compensation scheme*, as defined in COMP 5.3.1R.

protected dormant account

a *dormant account* which is covered by the *compensation scheme*, as defined in COMP 5.3.2R.

protected home finance mediation

activities in relation to *home finance transactions* which are covered by the *compensation scheme*, as defined in COMP 5.6.1R.

protected investment business

designated investment business which is covered by the *compensation scheme*, as defined in *COMP* 5.5.1R.

protected items

(as defined in section 413 of the *Act* (Protected items)) communications (and items which they enclose or refer to and which are in the possession of a *person* entitled to possession of them) between:
(a) a professional legal adviser and his client or any *person* representing his client; or
(b) a professional legal adviser, his client or any *person* representing his client and any other *person*;

where the communication or the item is made:

(i) in connection with the giving of legal advice to the client; or
(ii) in connection with, or in contemplation of, legal proceedings and for the purposes of those proceedings; and

is not held with the intention of furthering a criminal purpose.

protected non-investment insurance mediation

insurance mediation activities which are covered by the *compensation scheme*, as defined in COMP 5.7.1R.

protection buyer

(in relation to a credit derivative and in accordance with paragraph 8 of Annex I of the *Capital Adequacy Directive* (Calculating capital requirements for position risk)) the *person* who transfers credit risk.

protection seller

(in relation to a credit derivative and in accordance with paragraph 8 of Annex I of the *Capital Adequacy Directive* (Calculating capital requirements for position risk)) the *person* who assumes the credit risk.

proven reserves

(in LR):
(a) in respect of *mineral companies* primarily involved in the *extraction* of oil and gas resources, those reserves which, on the available evidence and taking into account technical and economic factors, have a better than 90% chance of being produced; and
(b) in respect of *mineral companies* other than those primarily involved in the *extraction* of oil and gas resources, those *measured mineral resources* of which detailed technical and economic studies have demonstrated that *extraction* can be justified at the time of the determination, and under specified economic conditions.

providing qualifying credit

the *controlled activity*, specified in paragraph 10 of Schedule 1 to the *Financial Promotion Order*, of providing *qualifying credit*.

proxy capital resources requirement

the *minimum capital requirement* to which an *undertaking* would have been subject if it had *permission* for each activity it carries on anywhere in the world, so far as that activity is a *regulated activity*.

PRR

position risk requirement.

PRR charge

one of the following:
(a) the *interest rate PRR*;
(b) the *equity PRR*;
(c) the *commodity PRR*;
(d) the *foreign currency PRR*;
(e) the *option PRR*;
(f) the *collective investment undertaking PRR*; and
(g) (if the context requires) the *model PRR*.

PRR item

a *commodity* or a *CRD financial instrument*.

PRR identical product netting rules

the following:
(a) BIPRU 7.2.37R (Deriving the net position in each debt security: Netting positions in the same debt security);
(b) BIPRU 7.2.40R (Deriving the net position in each debt security: Netting zero-specific-risk securities with different maturities);
(c) BIPRU 7.3.23R (Deriving the net position in each equity);
(d) BIPRU 7.4.20R and BIPRU 7.4.22R (Calculating the PRR for each commodity: General);
(e) BIPRU 7.5.19R(1) (Open currency position); and
(f) the obligation under BIPRU 7.5.20R (Net gold position) to calculate a separate *foreign exchange PRR* charge for gold).

PSE

a *public sector entity*.

PRU

the Integrated Prudential Sourcebook.

prudential context

in relation to activities carried on by a *firm*, the context in which the activities have, or might reasonably be regarded as likely to have, a negative effect on:
(a) confidence in the *financial system*; or
(b) the ability of the *firm* to meet either:
 (i) the "fit and proper" test in *threshold condition* 5 (Suitability); or
 (ii) the applicable requirements and standards under the *regulatory system* relating to the *firm's* financial resources.

public announcement

any communication made by or on behalf of the *issuer* or the *stabilising manager* being a communication made in circumstances in which it is likely that members of the public will become aware of the communication.

public censure

(1) a statement published under section 205 (Public censure) of the *Act*;
(2) a statement of misconduct published under section 66 (Disciplinary powers) of the *Act*;
(3) a statement published under section 123 (Power to impose penalties in cases of market abuse) of the *Act*;
(4) a statement published under section 87M (Public censure of issuer) of the *Act*, under section 89 (Public censure of sponsor) of the *Act* or under section 91 (Penalties for breach of listing rules) of the *Act*.

public international body

(1) (in PR) (as defined in the *PD Regulation*) a legal entity of public nature established by an international treaty between sovereign States and of which one or more Member States are members.
(2) (in LR and DR) the African Development Bank, the Asian Development Bank, the Caribbean Development Bank, the Council of Europe Development Bank, the European Atomic Energy Community, the European Bank for Reconstruction and Development, the European Company for the Financing of Railroad Stock, the EU, the European Investment Bank, the Inter-American Development Bank, the International Bank for Reconstruction and Development, the International Finance Corporation, the International Monetary Fund and the Nordic Investment Bank.

public offer

an offer of *securities* to the public and described in the *POS Regulations*.

public sector entity

(in accordance with Article 4(18) of the *Banking Consolidation Directive* (Definitions)) any of the following:
(a) non-commercial administrative bodies responsible to central governments, regional governments or local authorities; or
(b) authorities that exercise the same responsibilities as regional and local authorities; or
(c) non commercial *undertakings* owned by central governments that have explicit guarantee arrangements; or
(d) self administered bodies governed by law that are under public supervision.

public sector issuer

states and their regional and local authorities, *state monopolies*, *state finance organisations*, *public international bodies*, statutory bodies and *OECD state guaranteed issuers*.

published recommendation

any publication by or on behalf of a *firm* (including publication by sound broadcasting or television or other electronic means) which contains:
(a) the results of research into *investments*; or
(b) analysis of factors likely to influence the future performance of *investments*; or
(c) advice or recommendations based on those results or analysis, including any communication of which the content is common to a number of communications although worded as if it were a *personal recommendation*.

pure protection contract

(1) a *long-term insurance contract* in respect of which the following conditions are met:
 (a) the benefits under the contract are payable only on death or in respect of incapacity due to injury, sickness or infirmity;

Part II FSA Handbook Materials

(b) [deleted]
(c) the contract has no surrender value, or the consideration consists of a single premium and the surrender value does not exceed that premium;
(d) the contract makes no provision for its conversion or extension in a manner which would result in it ceasing to comply with (a) or (c); or
(e) [deleted]

(2) a *reinsurance contract* covering all or part of a risk to which a *person* is exposed under a *long-term insurance contract*.

pure reinsurer

an *insurer* whose *insurance business* is restricted to reinsurance.

qualified investor

(in PR) (as defined in section 86(7) of the *Act*):
(a) any entity within the meaning of Article 2(1)(e)(i), (ii) or (iii) of the *prospectus directive*; or
(b) an investor registered on the register maintained by the competent authority under section 87R of the *Act*; or
(c) an investor authorised by an *EEA State* other than the *United Kingdom* to be considered as a qualified investor for the purposes of the *prospectus directive*.

qualified investor scheme

an *authorised fund* whose *instrument constituting the scheme* contains the statement in COLL 8.2.6R1(2) (Table: contents of the instrument constituting the scheme) that it is a *qualified* investor scheme.

qualified valuer

(in relation to any particular type of land in any particular area) a fellow or professional associate of the Royal Institution of Chartered Surveyors, a fellow or associate of the Incorporated Society of Valuers and Auctioneers, or a fellow or associate of the Rating and Valuation Association, who:
(a) has knowledge of and experience in the valuation of that particular type of land in that particular area; or
(b) has knowledge of and experience in the valuation of land and has taken advice from a valuer who he is satisfied has knowledge of and experience in the valuation of that particular type of land in that particular area; or
(c) immediately before 15 June 1981 was recognised as a qualified valuer by approval by the Secretary of State under the Insurance Companies (Valuation of Assets) Regulations 1976.

qualifying capital instrument

(in UPRU) means that part of a *firm's* capital which is a security of indeterminate duration, or other instrument, that fulfils the following conditions:
(a) it may not be reimbursed on the bearer's initiative or without the prior agreement of *FSA*;
(b) the debt agreement must provide for the *firm* to have the option of deferring the payment of interest on the debt;
(c) the lender's claims on the *firm* must be wholly subordinated to those of all non-subordinated creditors;
(d) the documents governing the issue of the securities must provide for debt and unpaid interest to be such as to absorb losses, whilst leaving the *firm* in a position to continue trading; and
(e) only fully paid-up amounts shall be taken into account.

qualifying capital item

(in UPRU) means that part of a *firm's* capital which has the following characteristics:
(a) it is freely available to the *firm* to cover normal banking or other risks where revenue or capital losses have not yet been identified;
(b) its existence is disclosed in internal accounting records; and
(c) its amount is determined by the management of the *firm* and verified by independent auditors, and is made known to, and is monitored by, *FSA*.

Note: verification by internal auditors will suffice until such time as EU provisions making external auditing mandatory have been implemented.

qualifying credit

(as defined in Schedule 1 paragraph 10 (Providing qualifying credit) of the *Financial Promotion Order*) credit (including a cash loan and any other form of financial accommodation) provided in accordance with an agreement under which:
(a) the lender is a *person* who enters into or administers *regulated mortgage contracts*; and
(b) the obligation of the borrower to repay is secured (in whole or in part) on land.

qualifying credit promotion

[deleted]

qualifying credit promotion rules

[deleted]

qualifying debt security

(1) (for the purposes of ELM) a *security* falling into ELM 3.3.9R (Liquid assets).

(2) (for the purposes of BIPRU) a debt *security* that satisfies the conditions in BIPRU 7.2.49R (Definition of a qualifying debt security).

qualifying equity

a *share* that satisfies the conditions in BIPRU 7.3.35R (Definition of a qualifying equity).

qualifying equity index

an *equity* index falling into in BIPRU 7.3.38R (Definition of a qualifying equity index).

qualifying holding

(1) (in *GENPRU* and *BIPRU*) has the meaning in GENPRU 2.2.203R (Qualifying holdings), which is in summary a direct or indirect holding of a *bank* or *building society* in a non-financial *undertaking* which represents 10% or more of the capital or of the voting rights or which makes it possible to exercise a significant influence over the management of that *undertaking*.

(2) (otherwise) any direct or indirect holding in an *investment firm* which represents 10% or more of the capital or of the voting rights, as set out in Article 92 of the European Parliament and Council Directive on the admission of securities to official stock exchange listing and on information to be published on those securities (No. 2001/34/EC) or which makes it possible to exercise a significant influence over the management of the *investment firm* in which that holding subsists.

[Note: article 4(1)(27) of *MiFID*]

qualifying interest in land

(in accordance with article 63B(4)(a) of the *Regulated Activities Order*) land (other than timeshare accommodation) in the *UK* which is:

(a) in relation to land in England and Wales, an estate in fee simple absolute or a term of years absolute whether subsisting at law or in equity; or

(b) in relation to land in Scotland, the interest of an owner in land or the tenant's right over or interest in a property subject to a lease; or

(c) in relation to land in Northern Ireland, any freehold estate or any leasehold estate whether subsisting at law or in equity.

qualifying investment

an *investment* which has been prescribed by the Treasury in the *Prescribed Markets and Qualifying Investments Order.*

qualifying liquid asset

(in ELM) an *investment* falling into ELM 3.3.5R (Liquid assets).

qualifying money market fund

(1) (in *COLL* and *CASS* 7) a *collective investment scheme* authorised under the *UCITS Directive* or which is subject to supervision and, if applicable, authorised by an authority under the national law of an *EEA State*, and which satisfies the following conditions:

   (a) its primary investment objective must be to maintain the net asset value of the undertaking either constant at par (net of earnings), or at the value of the investors' initial capital plus earnings;

   (b) it must, with a view to achieving that primary investment objective, invest exclusively in high quality money market instruments with a maturity or residual maturity of no more than 397 days, or regular yield adjustments consistent with such a maturity, and with a weighted average maturity of no more than 60 days. It may also achieve this objective by investing on an ancillary basis in deposits with credit institutions;

   (c) it must provide liquidity through same day or next day settlement.

(2) For the purposes of (1)(b), a money market instrument is to be considered to be of high quality if it has been awarded the highest available credit rating by each competent rating agency which has rated that instrument. An instrument that is not rated by any competent rating agency is not to be considered to be of high quality.

(3) For the purposes of (2), a rating agency is to be considered to be competent if it issues credit ratings in respect of money market funds regularly and on a professional basis and is an eligible ECAI within the meaning of Article 81(1) of the *BCD*.

[Note: article 18(2) of the *MiFID implementing Directive*]

qualifying revolving retail exposure

(in relation to the *IRB approach*) *retail exposures* falling into BIPRU 4.6.44R(2) (Qualifying revolving retail exposures).

qualifying subordinated loan

(in UPRU) has the meaning given in IPRU(INV) 5.2.5(1) to (7)R (Qualifying subordinated loans).

qualifying undertaking

(in UPRU) has the meaning given in IPRU(INV) 5.2.6(3)R (Qualifying undertakings).

quantification date

the date as at which the liability of the *relevant person in default* is to be determined under *COMP* 12.3.

quarterly financial return

(in UPRU) means the return referred to in SUP.

quasi-derivative contract or quasi-derivative

a contract or asset having the effect of a *derivative* contract.

RAG

regulated activity group

railway rolling stock

(in relation to a *class* of *contract of insurance*) the *class* of *contract of insurance*, specified in paragraph 5 of Part I of Schedule 1 to the *Regulated Activities Order* (Contracts of general insurance), against loss of or damage to railway rolling stock.

range

see range of packaged products and range of stakeholder products

range of packaged products, range

(in relation to a *firm*) the range of *packaged products* on which the *firm* gives *advice on investments* to *retail clients* (see COBS 6.3) or if appropriate the list of *packaged products* in which the *firm* deals.

range of stakeholder products, range

(in relation to a *firm*) the range of *stakeholder products* on which the *firm* gives *advice* (see COBS 9.6);

References to a *firm's* range (or ranges) of *stakeholder products* include, where the context requires, a reference to the range (or ranges) of the *firm's appointed representatives*.

rated position

(for the purposes of BIPRU 9 (Securitisation), in accordance with Part 1 of Annex IX of the *Banking Consolidation Directive* (Securitisation definitions) and in relation to a *securitisation position*) describes a *securitisation position* which has an eligible credit assessment by an *eligible ECAI*.

ratings based method

(for the purposes of BIPRU 9 (Securitisation) and in accordance with Part 1 of Annex IX of the *Banking Consolidation Directive* (Securitisation definitions)) the method of calculating *risk weighted exposure amounts* for *securitisation positions* set out in BIPRU 9.12.10R-BIPRU 9.12.19R and BIPRU 9.14.2R.

rating system

(in relation to the *IRB approach* and in accordance with BIPRU 4.3.25R) comprises all of the methods, processes, controls, data collection and IT systems that support the assessment of credit risk, the assignment of *exposures* to grades or pools (rating), and the quantification of *default* and *loss* estimates for a certain type of *exposure*.

RCB

the Regulated Covered Bond sourcebook.

RCB Regulations

the Regulated Covered Bonds Regulations 2008 (SI 2008/346).

RCH

a *recognised clearing house.*

RDC

Regulatory Decisions Committee.

readily realisable investment

(except in UPRU)
(a) a *packaged product*;
(b) a readily realisable security.

(in *UPRU*) means a *unit* in a *regulated collective investment scheme*, a *life policy* or any *marketable investment* other than one which is traded on or under the rules of a *recognised* or *designated investment exchange* so irregularly or infrequently:
(a) that it cannot be certain that a price for that *investment* will be quoted at all times; or
(b) that it may be difficult to effect transactions at any price which may be quoted.

readily realisable security

(a) a *government or public security* denominated in the currency of the country of its *issuer*;
(b) any other *security* which is:
  (i) admitted to *official listing* on an exchange in an *EEA State*; or
  (ii) regularly traded on or under the rules of such an exchange; or
  (iii) regularly traded on or under the rules of a *recognised investment exchange* or (except in relation to *unsolicited real time financial promotions) designated investment exchange;*
(c) a newly issued *security* which can reasonably be expected to fall within (b) when it begins to be traded.

real estate market adjustment ratio

has the meaning set out, in relation to the *resilience capital requirement*, in INSPRU 3.1.21R.

real time financial promotion

(in accordance with article 7(1) of the *Financial Promotion Order*) a *financial promotion* made in the course of a personal visit, telephone conversation or other interactive dialogue.

real time qualifying credit promotion

[deleted]

realistic basis life firm

a *firm* to which GENPRU 2.1.18R applies (and which is therefore required to calculate a *with-profits insurance capital component* in accordance with INSPRU 1.3).

realistic current liabilities

(in relation to a *with-profits fund)* the realistic current liabilities of the *with-profits fund* calculated in accordance with INSPRU 1.3.190R.

realistic excess capital

(in relation to a *with-profits fund*) has the meaning set out in INSPRU 1.3.32R.

realistic value of assets

(in relation to a *with-profits fund*) has the meaning set out in INSPRU 1.3.33R.

realistic value of liabilities

(in relation to a *with-profits fund*) the sum of the *with-profits benefit reserve*, the *future policy related liabilities* and the *realistic current liabilities* for the *with-profits fund.*

reattribution

the process under which a *firm* which carries on *with-profits business* seeks to redefine the rights and interests that the *with-profits policyholders* have over the *inherited estate.*

reattribution expert

the expert appointed by a *firm* to satisfy its obligations under *COBS* 20.2.47R (Reattribution expert).

REC

the Recognised Investment Exchange and Recognised Clearing House sourcebook.

receivable

(in relation to a *member*, a period and a *premium*) a *premium* due to the *member* in respect of *contracts of insurance* effected during the period, whether or not the *premium* is received during that period.

recipient

the *person* to whom a communication is made or, in the case of a *nonreal time financial promotion* which is *directed at persons* generally, any *person* who reads or hears the communication.

reciprocal cross-holding

has the meaning in GENPRU 2.2.219R (Deductions from tiers one and two: Reciprocal cross holdings) which is in summary a holding of a *firm* of *shares*, any other interest in the capital, and subordinated debt, whether in the *trading book* or *non-trading book*, in:
(a) a *credit institution*; or
(b) a *financial institution*;

that satisfies the conditions in GENPRU 2.2.219R.

recognised body

an *RIE* or an *RCH*.

recognised clearing house

a *clearing house* which is declared by a *recognition order* for the time being in force to be a recognised clearing house.

recognised investment exchange

an investment exchange which is declared by a *recognition order* for the time being in force to be a recognised investment exchange.

recognised overseas clearing house

an *overseas clearing house* which is declared by a *recognition order* for the time being in force to be a *recognised clearing house*.

recognised overseas investment exchange

an *overseas investment exchange* which is declared by a *recognition order* for the time being in force to be a *recognised investment exchange*.

recognised professional body

any of the following professional bodies (which were the recognised professional bodies for the purposes of the Financial Services Act 1986):
(a) The Law Society (England and Wales);
(b) The Law Society of Scotland;
(c) The Law Society of Northern Ireland;
(d) The Institute of Chartered Accountants in England and Wales;
(e) The Institute of Chartered Accountants of Scotland;
(f) The Institute of Chartered Accountants in Ireland;
(g) The Association of Chartered Certified Accountants;
(h) The Institute of Actuaries.
(see also *designated professional body*.)

recognised scheme

a *scheme* recognised under:
(a) section 264 of the *Act* (Schemes constituted in other EEA States);or
(b) section 270 of the *Act* (Schemes authorised in designated countries or territories); or
(c) section 272 of the *Act* (Individually recognised overseas schemes).

recognised third country credit institution

a *full BCD credit institution* that satisfies the following conditions:
(a) its head office is outside the *EEA*;
(b) it is authorised by a *third country competent authority* in the state or territory in which the *credit institution's* head office is located;
(c) that *third country competent authority* is named in Part 1 of *BIPRU* 8 Annex 6R (Non –EEA banking regulators' requirements deemed CRD -equivalent for individual risks); and
(d) there is a tick against that *third country competent authority* in each of the columns headed "Market risk", "Credit risk" and "Operational Risk" in the table referred to in (c).

recognised third country investment firm

a *CAD investment firm* that satisfies the following conditions:
(a) its head office is outside the EEA;
(b) it is authorised by a *third country competent authority* in the state or territory in which the *CAD investment firm's* head office is located;
(c) that *third country competent authority* is named in Part 2 of BIPRU 8 Annex 6R (Non–EEA investment firm regulators' requirements deemed CRD- equivalent for individual risks); and
(d) that *investment firm* is subject to and complies with prudential rules of or administered by that *third country competent authority* that are at least as stringent as those laid down in the *EEA prudential sectoral legislation* for the *investment services sector*.

recognition order

(in accordance with section 313 of the *Act* (Interpretation of Part XVIII)) an order made under section 290 or 292 of the *Act* which declares an investment exchange or *clearing house* to be a *recognised body*.

recognition requirement

(1) (in relation to a *UK RIE* or *UK RCH*) any of the requirements applicable to that body under the *Recognition Requirements Regulations*.
(2) (in relation to a body applying for recognition as a *UK RIE* or *UK RC*H) any of the requirements under the *Recognition Requirements Regulations* which, if its application were successful, would apply to it.
(3) (in relation to an *ROIE* or *ROCH*, or to an applicant for recognition as an *ROIE* or *ROCH*) any of the requirements in section 292(3) of the *Act* (Overseas investment exchanges and overseas clearing houses).

Recognition Requirements

the Financial Services and Markets Act 2000 (Recognition Requirements for Investment Exchanges and Clearing Houses).

redemption

(1) (except in EG 14 (Collective investment schemes)) (in relation to *units* in an *authorised fund*) the purchase of them from their *holder* by the *authorised fund manager* acting as a *principal*.
(2) (in EG 14 (Collective investment schemes)) redemption as in (1) but including their cancellation by the *trustee* of an *AUT* or by an *ICVC*.

redemption charge

an amount levied by the *operator* of a *scheme* upon the *redemption* of *units*, in the case of an *authorised fund* unde COLL 6.7.7R (Charges on buying and selling units).

redemption price

(in COLL)

the *price* payable by the *authorised fund manager* for each *unit* it *redeems* from a *unitholder*, calculated in accordance with COLL 6.3 (Valuation and pricing).

redemption right

(in relation to an *e-money firm*) the right of a holder of *e-money* to require the *e-money firm* to redeem that *e-money* that corresponds to the duty of the *e-money firm* in *ELM* 6.3.1R (Duty to redeem) to redeem *e-money* issued by it.

reduced net underwriting position

the *net underwriting position* as adjusted under BIPRU 7.8.27R (Calculating the reduced net underwriting position).

register

(1) (in PR) the register of *qualified investors* maintained by the *FSA* under section 87R of the *Act*.
(2) [deleted]
(3) (in COLL) the register of *unitholders* kept under Schedule 3 to the *OEIC Regulations* or COLL 6.4.4R (Register: general requirements and contents), or COLL 8.5.8R (The register of unitholders: AUTs) as appropriate or, in relation to a *collective investment scheme* that is not an *authorised fund*, a record of the holders (other than of *bearer certificates*) of *units* in it.

registered branch

a branch of a *friendly society* which is separately registered under the Friendly Societies Act 1974.

registered contact

(as defined in regulation 8(1)(d) of the *CTF Regulations*) the *person* who is capable of giving instructions to the *CTF provider* with respect to the management of the *CTF*.

registered friendly society

a *friendly society* registered under section 7(1)(a) of the Friendly Societies Act 1974 or any enactment which it replaced, including any *registered branches*.

registrar

the *person* who maintains a *register*.

registration date

(in *RCB*) the date of the *FSA's* decision to register a *regulated covered bond*.

registration document

(in *Part 6 rules*) a registration document referred to in PR 2.2.2R.

regular user

(as defined in section 130A(3) of the *Act* (Market abuse)) a *person* who is, in relation to a particular market, a reasonable *person* who regularly deals on that market in *investments* of the kind in question.

Regulated Activities Order

the Financial Services and Markets Act 2000 (Regulated Activities) Order 2001 (SI 2001/544).

regulated activity

(in accordance with section 22 of the *Act* (The classes of activity and categories of investment)) any of the following activities specified in Part II of the *Regulated Activities Order* (Specified Activities):

(a) *accepting deposits* (article 5);

(aa) *issuing electronic money* (article 9B);

(b) *effecting contracts of insurance* (article 10(1));

(c) *carrying out contracts of insurance* (article 10(2));.

(d) *dealing in investments as principal* (article 14);

(e) *dealing in investments as agent* (article 21);

(f) arranging (bringing about) deals in investments (article 25(1));

(g) *making arrangements with a view to transactions in investments* (article 25(2));

(ga) *arranging (bringing about) regulated mortgage contracts* (article 25A(1));

(gb) *making arrangements with a view to regulated mortgage contracts* (article 25A(2));

(gc) *arranging (bringing about) a home reversion plan* (article 25B(1));

(gd) *making arrangements with a view to a home reversion plan* (article 25B(2));

(ge) *arranging (bringing about) a home purchase plan* (article 25C(1));

(gf) *making arrangements with a view to a home purchase plan* (article 25C(2));

(gg) *operating a multilateral trading facility* (article 25D);

(gh) *arranging (bringing about) a regulated sale and rent back agreement* (article 25E(1));

(gi) *making arrangements with a view to a regulated sale and rent back agreement* (article 25E(2));

(h) *managing investments* (article 37);

(ha) *assisting in the administration and performance of a contract of insurance* (article 39A);

(i) *safeguarding and administering investments* (article 40); for the purposes of the *permission* regime, this is sub-divided into:

  (i) *safeguarding and administration of assets (without arranging);*

  (ii) *arranging safeguarding and administration of assets;*

(j) *sending dematerialised instructions* (article 45(1));

(k) *causing dematerialised instructions to be sent* (article 45(2));

(l) *establishing, operating or winding up a collective investment scheme* (article 51(1)(a)); for the purposes of the permission regime, this is sub-divided into:

  (i) *establishing, operating or winding up a regulated collective investment scheme;*

  (ii) *establishing, operating or winding up an unregulated collective investment scheme;*

(m) *acting as trustee of an authorised unit trust scheme* (article 51(1)(b));

(n) *acting as the depositary or sole director of an open-ended investment company* (article 51(1)(c));

(o) *establishing, operating or winding up a stakeholder pension scheme* (article 52(a));

(oa) providing *basic advice* on *stakeholder products* (article 52B);

(ob) *establishing, operating or winding up a personal pension scheme* (article 52(b));

(p) *advising on investments* (article 53); for the purposes of the *permission regime*, this is sub-divided into:

  (i) *advising on investments (except pension transfers and pension opt-outs)*;

  (ii) *advising on pension transfers and pension opt-outs*;

(pa) *advising on regulated mortgage contracts* (article 53A);
(pb) *advising on a home reversion plan* (article 53B);
(pc) *advising on a home purchase plan* (article 53C);
(pd) *advising on a regulated sale and rent back agreement* (article 53D);
(q) *advising on syndicate participation at Lloyd's* (article 56);
(r) *managing the underwriting capacity of a Lloyd's syndicate as a managing agent at Lloyd's* (article 57);
(s) *arranging deals in contracts of insurance written at Lloyd's* (article 58);
(sa) *entering into a regulated mortgage contract* (article 61(1));
(sb) *administering a regulated mortgage contract* (article 61(2));
(sc) *entering into a home reversion plan* (article 63B(1));
(sd) *administering a home reversion plan* (article 63B(2));
(se) *entering into a home purchase plan* (article 63F(1));
(sf) *administering a home purchase plan* (article 63F(2));
(sg) *entering into a regulated sale and rent back agreement* (article 63J(1));
(sh) *administering a regulated sale and rent back agreement* (article 63J(2));
(si) *meeting of repayment claims* (article 63N(1)(a));
(sj) *managing dormant account funds (including the investment of such funds)* (article 63N(1)(b);
(t) *entering as provider into a funeral plan contract* (article 59);
(u) *agreeing to carry on a regulated activity* (article 64);

which is carried on by way of business and relates to a *specified investment* applicable to that activity or, in the case of (l), (m), (n) and (o) is carried on in relation to property of any kind.

regulated activity debt

an obligation to pay a sum due and payable under an agreement, the making or performance of which constitutes or is part of a *regulated activity* carried on by an individual who:
(a) is, or has been, an *authorised person;* or
(b) is carrying on, or has carried on, a *regulated activity* in contravention of the *general prohibition.*

regulated activity group

A set of one or more *regulated activities* (with associated *investment* types and *customer* types) referred to in SUP 16 to determine a *firm's* or other regulated person's *data item submission* requirements.

regulated collective investment scheme

(a) an ICVC; or
(b) an *AUT*; or
(c) a *recognised scheme*;
whether or not the *units* are held within an, *ISA*, or *personal pension scheme.*

regulated consumer credit agreement

in accordance with section 8 of the Consumer Credit Act 1974 (as amended) an agreement between an individual "the debtor" and any other person "the creditor" by which the creditor provides the debtor with credit of any amount and which is not an exempt agreement for the purposes of that Act;

and expressions used in that Act have the same meaning in this definition.

regulated consumer hire agreement

in accordance with section 15 of the Consumer Credit Act 1974 (as amended) an agreement made by a person with an individual "the hirer" for the bailment or (in Scotland) the hiring of goods to the hirer, being an agreement which
(a) is not a hire-purchase agreement, and
(b) is capable of subsisting for more than three months, and
(c) is not an exempt agreement;

and expressions used in that Act have the same meaning in this definition.

regulated covered bond

(in *RCB*) (as defined in Regulation 1(2) of the *RCB Regulations*) a *covered bond* or *programme* of *covered bonds*, as the case may be, which is admitted to the register of *regulated covered bonds* maintained under Regulation 7(1)(b) of the *RCB Regulations*.

regulated entity

one of the following:
(a) a *credit institution*; or
(b) a *regulated insurance entity*; or
(c) an *investment firm*;

whether or not it is incorporated in, or has its head office in, an *EEA State*.

An *asset management company* is treated as a regulated entity for the purposes described in GENPRU 3.1.39R (The financial sectors: asset management companies).

regulated information

(in PR) (as defined in the *PD Regulation*) all information which the issuer, or any person who has applied for the admission of securities to trading on a regulated market without the issuer's consent, is required to disclose under Directive 2001/34/EC or under Article 6 of Directive 2003/6/EC.

regulated information

all information which an *issuer*, or any other *person* who has applied for the admission of *financial instruments* to trading on a *regulated market* without the *issuer's* consent, is required to disclose under:
(a) the *Transparency Directive*;
(b) article 6 of the *Market Abuse Directive*; or
(c) LR, and DTR.

Regulated Information Service

a Regulated Information Service that is approved by the *FSA* as meeting the Criteria for Regulated Information Services and that is on the list of Regulated Information Services maintained by the *FSA*.

regulated institution

any of the following:
(a) an *EEA insurer* or *UK insurer*; or
(b) an *approved credit institution*; or
(c) a *friendly society* (not within (a)) which is authorised to carry on *insurance business*; or
(d) a *firm* whose *permission* includes *dealing in investments as principal* with respect to *derivatives* which are not *listed*; or
(e) a *MiFID investment firm* whose authorisation (as referred to in article 5 of *MiFID*) authorises it to carry on activities of the kind referred to in (d).

regulated insurance entity

an insurance undertaking within the meaning of Article 4 of the *Consolidated Life Directive*, Article 6 of the *First Non-Life Directive* or Article 1(b) of the *Insurance Groups Directive*.

regulated lifetime mortgage contract

a *regulated mortgage contract* which is a *lifetime mortgage*.

regulated market

(1) a multilateral system operated and/or managed by a *market operator*, which brings together or facilitates the bringing together of multiple third-party buying and selling interests in *financial instruments* – in the system and in accordance with its non-discretionary rules – in a way that results in a contract, in respect of the *financial instruments* admitted to trading under its rules and/or systems, and which is authorised and functions regularly and in accordance with the provisions of Title III of *MiFID*.

[Note: article 4(1)(14) of *MiFID*]

(2) (in addition, in INSPRU and IPRU(INS) only) a market situated outside the *EEA States* which is characterised by the fact that:
 (a) it meets comparable requirements to those set out in (1); and
 (b) the *financial instruments* dealt in are of a quality comparable to those in a regulated market in the *United Kingdom*.

regulated market transaction

a transaction concluded by a *firm* on a *regulated market* with another member or participant of that *regulated market*.

regulated mortgage activity

any of the following activities specified in Part II of the *Regulated Activities Order* (Specified Activities):
(a) *arranging (bringing about) regulated mortgage contracts* (article 25A(1));
(b) *making arrangements with a view to regulated mortgage contracts* (article 25A(2));

(c) *advising on regulated mortgage contracts* (article 53A);
(d) *entering into a regulated mortgage contract* (article 61(1));
(e) *administering a regulated mortgage contract* (article 61(2));
(f) *agreeing to carry on a regulated activity* in (a) to (e) (article 64).

regulated mortgage contract

(a) (in relation to a contract) a contract which:
  (i) (in accordance with article 61(3) of the *Regulated Activities Order*) at the time it is entered into, meets the following conditions:
    (A) a lender provides credit to an individual or to trustees (the 'borrower'); and
    (B) the obligation of the borrower to repay is secured by a first legal mortgage on land (other than timeshare accommodation) in the *United Kingdom*, at least 40% of which is used, or is intended to be used, as or in connection with a dwelling by the borrower or (in the case of credit provided to trustees) by an individual who is a beneficiary of the trust, or by a person who is in relation to the borrower or (in the case of credit provided to trustees) a beneficiary of the trust:
      (I) that person's spouse or civil partner; or
      (II) a person (whether or not of the opposite sex) whose relationship with that person has the characteristics of the relationship between husband and wife; or
      (III) that person's parent, brother, sister, child, grandparent or grandchild; and
  (ii) is not a *home purchase plan*.
(b) (in relation to a *specified investment*) the *investment*, specified in article 88 of the *Regulated Activities Order*, which is rights under a *regulated mortgage contract* within (a).

regulated related undertaking

a *related undertaking* that is any of the following:
(a) a *regulated entity*; or
(b) an *insurance undertaking* which is not a *regulated insurance entity*; or
(c) an *asset management company*; or
(d) a *financial institution* which is neither a *credit institution* nor an *investment firm*; or
(e) a *financial holding company*; or
(f) an *insurance holding company*.

regulated sale and rent back activity

any of the following regulated activities:
(a) *arranging (bringing about) a regulated sale and rent back agreement* (article 25E(1));
(b) *making arrangements with a view to a regulated sale and rent back agreement* (article 25E(2));
(c) *advising on a regulated sale and rent back agreement* (article 53D);
(d) *entering into a regulated sale and rent back agreement* (article 63J(1));
(e) *administering a regulated sale and rent back agreement* (article 63J(2)); or
(f) *agreeing to carry on a regulated activity in (a) to (e)* (article 64).

regulated sale and rent back agreement

(in accordance with article 63J(3)(a) of the *Regulated Activities Order*) an arrangement comprised in one or more instruments or agreements, in relation to which the following conditions are met at the time it is entered into:
(a) the arrangement is one under which a *person* (an agreement provider), buys all or part of *the qualifying interest in land* in the *United Kingdom* from an individual or trustees (the "agreement seller"); and
(b) the agreement seller (if he is an individual) or an individual who is the beneficiary of the trust (if the agreement seller is a trustee), or a related person, is entitled under the arrangement to occupy at least 40% of the land in question as or in connection with a dwelling, and intends to do so;

but excluding any arrangement that is a regulated *home reversion plan*.

regulated sale and rent back firm

a *firm* that carries on any *regulated sale and rent back activity*.

regulated sale and rent back mediation activity

any of the following *regulated activities*:
(a) *arranging (bringing about) regulated sale and rent back agreements* (article 25E(1));
(b) *making arrangements with a view to regulated sale and rent back agreements* (article 25E(2));
(c) *advising on regulated sale and rent back agreements* (article 53D);

(d) *agreeing to carry on a regulated activity* in (a) to (c) (article 64).

regulated sale and rent back transaction

a transaction involving a *regulated sale and rent back agreement* under which a *SRB agreement seller*, in return for the sale of a *qualifying interest in land* in whole or in part to a *SRB agreement provider*, is granted, or any member of his family is granted, a right to occupy the land in question as, or in connection with, a dwelling, and intends so to occupy it.

Recognition Requirements Regulations

the Financial Services and Markets Act 2000 (Recognition Requirements for Investment Exchanges and Clearing Houses) Regulations 2001 (SI 2001/995).

regulatory basis only life firm

a *firm* carrying on *long-term insurance business* which is not a *realistic basis life firm.*

regulatory body

any authority, body or *person* having, or who has had, responsibility for the supervision or regulation of any *regulated activities* or other financial services, whether in the *United Kingdom* or overseas.

regulatory capital resources

(in *ELM*) (in relation to a *full credit institution*) those parts of its capital that:
(a) are treated as capital for the purpose of the laws and regulations about the maintenance of adequate capital that apply to it (including those imposed by or under the *regulatory system* or by a *regulatory body*); and
(b) fall within the definition of own funds in the *Banking Consolidation Directive* or that the *Banking Consolidation Directive* allows *EEA States* to treat as own funds.

regulatory costs

the periodic fees payable to the *FSA* by a *participant firm* in accordance with FEES 4 (Periodic fees).

regulatory current liabilities

(in relation to a *with-profits fund*) the regulatory current liabilities of the *with-profits fund* calculated in accordance with INSPRU 1.3.30R.

Regulatory Decisions Committee

a committee of the Board of the *FSA*, described in DEPP 3.1 (The nature and procedure of the RDC).

regulatory excess capital

(in relation to a *with-profits fund*) has the meaning set out in INSPRU 1.3.23R.

regulatory function

as defined in section 291 of the *Act* (Liability in relation to recognised body's regulatory functions)) any function of a *recognised body* so far as relating to, or to matters arising out of, the obligations to which the body is subject under or by virtue of the *Act*.

regulatory high risk category

(for the purposes of the *standardised approach* to credit risk) an item that falls into BIPRU 3.4.104R (Items belonging to regulatory high risk categories under the standardised approach to credit risk).

regulatory information service

either:
(a) a *Regulated Information Service*; or
(b) an incoming *information society service* that is *established* in an *EEA State* other than the *United Kingdom* and that disseminates *regulated information* in accordance with the minimum standards set out in [article 12 of the *TD implementing Directive*].

regulatory objectives

(as described in sections (92(2) and 3 to 6 of the Act):
(a) market confidence;
(b) public awareness;
(c) the protection of *consumers*; and
(d) the reduction of *financial crime*.

regulatory provisions

(a) (in accordance with section 302 of the *Act* (Interpretation)) (in relation to an investment exchange or *clearing house*) the rules of or any guidance issued by the investment exchange or *clearing house*;
(b) (in relation to an investment exchange):

(i) any arrangements which it has made, or proposes to make, for the provision of clearing services in respect of transactions effected on the exchange; and

(ii) if it provides, or proposes to provide, clearing services in respect of transactions other than those effected on the exchange, the criteria which it applies, or proposes to apply, when determining to whom it will provide those services;

(c) (in relation to a *clearing house*):

(i) if it makes, or proposes to make, clearing arrangements with an *RIE*, those arrangements; and

(ii) if it provides, or proposes to provide, clearing services for persons other than *RIEs*, the criteria which it will apply when determining to whom it will provide those services;

(d) (in REC 3.26) (in accordance with section 300E of the *Act*) *regulatory provision* means any rule, guidance, arrangements, policy or practice.

regulatory surplus

(in relation to a *long-term business fund*, or sub-fund) the excess, if any, of the *regulatory value of assets* for the *withprofits fund* over the *regulatory value of liabilities* for that fund.

regulatory surplus value

has the meaning set out in GENPRU 1.3.48R.

regulatory system

the arrangements for regulating a *firm* or other *person* in or under the *Act*, including the *threshold conditions*, the *Principles* and other *rules*, *the Statements of Principle*, codes and *guidance* and including any relevant directly applicable provisions of a European Regulation such as those contained in the *MiFID Regulation* and including any relevant directly applicable provisions of a Directive or Regulation such as those contained in the *MiFID implementing Directive* and the *MiFID Regulation*.

regulatory value of assets

(in relation to a *with-profits fund*) has the meaning set out in INSPRU 1.3.24R.

regulatory value of liabilities

(in relation to a *with-profits fund*) has the meaning set out in INSPRU 1.3.29R.

reinsurance

includes retrocession.

reinsurance contract

(in COBS 21, ICOB, CASS 5 and COMP) a *contract of insurance* covering all or part of a risk to which a *person* is exposed under *a contract of insurance*.

Reinsurance Directive

the Directive of 16 November 2005 of the European Parliament and of the Council (No 2005/68/EC) on reinsurance and amending the *First Non-Life Directive* and the *Third Non-Life Directive* as well as the *Insurance Groups Directive* and the *Consolidated Life Directive*.

reinsurance mediation

(as defined in article 2.4 of the *IMD*) the activities of introducing, proposing or carrying out other work preparatory to the conclusion of contracts of reinsurance, or of concluding such contracts, or of assisting in the administration and performance of such contracts, in particular in the event of a claim. These activities when undertaken by a *IMD reinsurance undertaking* or an employee of a *IMD reinsurance undertaking* who is acting under the responsibility of the *IMD reinsurance undertaking* shall not be considered as *reinsurance mediation*. The provision of information on an incidental basis in the context of another professional activity provided that the purpose of that activity is not to assist the customer in concluding or performing a reinsurance contract, the management of claims of a *IMD reinsurance undertaking* on a professional basis, and loss adjusting and expert appraisal of claims shall also not be considered as *reinsurance mediation*.

reinsurance to close

(a) an agreement under which members of a *syndicate* in one *syndicate year* ("the reinsured members") agree with the members of that *syndicate* in a later *syndicate year* or the members of another *syndicate* ("the reinsuring members") that the reinsuring members will discharge, or procure the discharge of, or indemnify the reinsured members against, all known and unknown *insurance business* liabilities of the reinsured members arising out of the *insurance business* carried on by the reinsured members in that *syndicate year*; or

(b) a similar reinsurance agreement or arrangement that has been approved by the *Council* as a reinsurance to close.

reinsurance undertaking

an *insurance undertaking* whose *insurance business* is restricted to *reinsurance*.

reinsurer

an *insurer* whose business includes effecting or carrying out contracts of *reinsurance*; includes a retrocessionnaire.

related designated investment

(in relation to a *designated investment* (the "first investment")) a *designated investment* whose value might reasonably be expected to be directly affected by:
(a) any fluctuation in the value of the first investment; or
(b) any *published recommendation* that concerns the first investment.

related financial instrument

means a *financial instrument*, the price of which is closely affected by price movements in another *financial instrument* which is the subject of *investment research*, and includes a derivative on that other *financial instrument*.

[Note: article 25(2) of the *MiFID implementing Directive*]

related investment

(as defined in section 130A(3) of the *Act*) in relation to a *qualifying investment*, means an investment whose price or value depends on the price or value of the *qualifying investment*.

related party

(1) (in LR) as defined in LR 11.1.4R:
(2) (in relation to an agreement seller under a regulated sale and rent back agreement or, where the agreement seller is a trustee, a beneficiary of the trust):
    (a) that *person's* spouse or civil partner; or
    (b) a *person* (whether or not of the opposite sex) whose relationship with that *person* has the characteristic of the relationship between husband and wife; or
    (c) that *person's* parent, brother, sister, child, grandparent or grandchild.

related party circular

(in LR) a *circular* relating to a *related party transaction*.

related party transaction

(in LR) as defined in LR 11.1.5R.

related undertaking

in relation to an *undertaking* ("U"):
(a) any *subsidiary undertaking* of U; or
(b) any *undertaking* in which U or any of U's *subsidiary undertakings* holds a *participation*; or
(c) any *undertaking* linked to U by a *consolidation Article 12(1) relationship*; or
(d) any *undertaking* linked by a *consolidation Article 12(1) relationship* to an *undertaking* in (a), (b) or (c).

relevant articles

(in *REC*):
(1) Article 6.1 to 6.4 of the *Market Abuse Directive*;
(2) Articles 3, 5, 7, 8, 10, 14 and 16 of the *Prospectus Directive*;
(3) Articles 4 to 6, 14, 16 to 19 and 30 of the *Transparency Directive*; and
(4) *EU* legislation made under the provisions mentioned in (1) to (3).

relevant asset pool

(in *RCB*) (as defined in Regulation 1(2) of the *RCB Regulations*) in relation to a *regulated covered bond* the *asset pool* from which the claims attaching to that bond are guaranteed to be paid by the *owner* of that pool in the event of the failure of the *issuer*.

relevant business

(1) (in *DISP* and FEES) that part of a *firm's* business which it conducts with consumers and which is subject to the jurisdiction of the *Financial Ombudsman Service* as provided for in *DISP* 2.3 (To which activities does the Compulsory Jurisdiction apply?), DISP 2.4 (To which activities does the Consumer Credit Jurisdiction apply?) and DISP 2.5 (To which activities does the Voluntary Jurisdiction apply?), measured by reference to the appropriate tariff-base for each *industry block*.
(2) (in relation to information communicated to a *client* other than a *financial promotion*) *designated investment business*.
(3) (in relation to a *financial promotion*) a *controlled activity*.

relevant capital sum

for the purposes of INSPRU 1.3.43R, the sum under a *contract of insurance* which is:

(a) unless (b) applies:
  (i) for whole life assurances, the sum assured;
  (ii) for *contracts of insurance* where a sum is payable on maturity (including contracts where a sum is also payable on earlier death), the sum payable on maturity;
  (iii) for deferred annuities, the capitalised value of the annuity at the vesting date (or the cash option if it is greater);
  (iv) for *capital redemption* contracts, the sum payable at the end of the contract period; and
  (v) for *linked long-term contracts of insurance*, notwithstanding (i) to (iv), the lesser of:
    (A) the amount for the time being payable on death; and
    (B) the aggregate of the value for the time being of the units allocated to the contract (or, where entitlement is not denoted by means of units, the value for the time being of any other measure of entitlement under the contract equivalent to units) and the total amount of the *premiums* remaining to be paid during such of the term of the contract as is appropriate for *zillmerising* or, if such *premiums* are payable beyond the age of seventy-five, until that age;

  but excluding in all cases any vested reversionary bonus; and

(b) for temporary assurances, the sum assured on the *actuarial valuation date*.

relevant charitable scheme

an *authorised fund* which is:

(a) a registered charity; or
(b) a charitable unit trust scheme under regulation 7(2)(d) of the Income Tax (Definition of Unit Trust Scheme) Regulations 1988.

relevant collateral

in relation to a transaction:

(a) cash;
(b) letters of credit and guarantees to the extent of their face value, issued by an *approved bank* which is neither a counterparty nor an *associate* of a counterparty;
(c) gold and silver bullion and coinage;
(d) *marketable investments*;
(e) the performance guarantees issued in support of the securities lending and borrowing programmes of Euroclear and Cedel, in respect only of *exposure* arising from participation in such programmes;

subject in each case to:

(i) the *firm* having an unconditional right to apply or realise the relevant collateral for the purpose of repaying a counterparty's obligations;
(ii) *marketable investments*:
  (A) being marked to market daily using the valuation principles in *IPRU(INV) 3.41(9)R*;
  (B) not being issued by a counterparty nor by an *associate* of a counterparty.

relevant commencement date

(as defined in article 1 of the *Mortgage and General Insurance Complaints Transitional Order*):

(a) in relation to a complaint which relates to an activity to which, immediately before 14 January 2005, the *GISC Facility* applied, the beginning of 14 January 2005;
(b) in relation to a complaint which relates to an activity to which, immediately before 31 October 2004, the *MCAS scheme* applied, the beginning of 31 October 2004.

relevant competent authorities

(in relation to a *financial conglomerate*) those *competent authorities* which are, or which have been appointed as, relevant competent authorities in relation to that *financial conglomerate* under Article 2(17) of the *Financial Groups Directive* (Definitions).

relevant competent authority

(in relation to a *financial instrument*) means the *competent authority* of the most relevant market in terms of liquidity for that *financial instrument*.

[**Note:** article 2(7) of *MiFID Regulation*]

relevant complaint

(1) (in DISP) a *relevant existing complaint*, a *relevant new complaint* or a *relevant transitional complaint*.
(2) (in REC) (as defined in section 299(2) of the Act (Complaints about recognised bodies)) a complaint which the FSA considers is relevant to the question of whether a recognised body should remain a recognised body.

relevant date

(in MCOB 10 (Annual percentage rate)):
(a) (where a date is specified in or determinable under an agreement at the date of its making as the date on which the debtor is entitled to require provision of anything which is the subject of the agreement) the earliest such date;
(b) (in any other case) the date of making the agreement.

relevant EEA details

the details listed in regulation 14 of the *EEA Passport Rights Regulations* and set out in SUP 13 Ann 1R (Requisite details or relevant details: branches).

relevant existing complaint

(in accordance with *the Ombudsman Transitional Order*) a complaint which:
(a) was referred to a *former scheme* at any time before *commencement*, by a person who was at that time entitled, under the terms of the *former scheme*, to refer such a complaint (whether described in that scheme as the making of a complaint, the referral of a dispute, the submission of a claim, or otherwise); and
(b) has not, before *commencement*, been rejected, withdrawn, settled or determined by *the former Ombudsman* (whether by a substantive decision, or by closure of the case without a substantive decision).

relevant financial services company

(in *ELM*) an *investment firm* or *credit institution.*

relevant former scheme

(as defined in article 2(2) of the *compensation transitionals order*):
(a) in relation to a *pending application*, the *investment business compensation scheme* under which the application was made;
(b) in relation to an *article 9 default*, one of the following that applied to the default before *commencement*:
  (i) the Policyholders Protection Scheme established by the Policyholders Protection Act 1975;
  (ii) the Deposit Protection Scheme established by Part II of the Banking Act 1987;
  (iii) the Building Societies Investor Protection Scheme established by Part IV of the Building Societies Act 1986;
  (iv) the Friendly Societies Protection Scheme established in accordance with section 141 of the Financial Services Act 1986..

relevant function

(in relation to a *UK recognised body*) an *exempt activity* or a *regulatory function.*

relevant general insurance contract

(in *COMP*) any general *insurance contract* other than:
(a) [deleted]
(b) [deleted]
(c) a contract falling within any of the following classes:
  (i) *aircraft*;
  (ii) *ships*;
  (iii) *goods in transit*;
  (iv) *aircraft liability*;
  (v) *liability of ships*;
  (vi) *credit.*

relevant information

(1) (except in *REC*) (in relation to an *investment*) information which would be likely to be regarded by a *regular user* of the market in question as relevant when deciding the terms on which transactions in that *investment* should be effected.
(2) (in *REC*) (in relation to an *investment*) information which is relevant to determining the current value of that *investment.*

relevant insurer

in relation to a *community co-insurance operation*, an *insurer* which is concerned in the operation but is not the *leading insurer.*

relevant investment

(1) (in *COBS* 12.4 in relation to a research recommendation or a public appearance), a designated investment that is the subject of that research recommendation or public appearance,

(2) (other than in *COBS* 4 or *COBS* 12.4) (in accordance with article 3(1) of the *Regulated Activities Order* (Interpretation)):
   (a) a *contractually based investment*;
   (b) a *pure protection contract*;
   (c) a *general insurance contract*;
   (d) rights to or interests in an *investment* falling within (a).
(3) (in *COBS* 4) a *specified investment* or a *controlled investment*.

relevant issuer

(1) (in relation to a *designated investment* that is the subject of a *research recommendation* or a *public appearance*) the *issuer* of that *designated investment*; or
(2) (in relation to a *related designated investment* that is the subject of a public appearance) either the *issuer* of the *related designated investment* or the *issuer* of a *designated investment* that might reasonably be expected directly to affect the value of the *related designated investment*.

relevant liquid market

a market for a share determined in accordance with paragraph 2 and 8 of Article 9 of the *MiFID Regulation*, in many cases this will be the Member State where the share or the unit was first admitted to trading on a regulated market.

[Note: article 9 of the *MiFID Regulation*]

relevant net premium income

(1) (in relation to business which is not *occupational pension fund management business*) the premium income in respect of *protected contracts of insurance* of a *firm*; or
(2) (in relation to *occupational pension fund management business*) the *remuneration* retained by a *firm* in relation to its carrying on *occupational pension fund management business*;

in the year preceding that in which the date for submission of the information under FEES 6.5.13R falls, net of any relevant rebates or refunds.

relevant new complaint

(in accordance with the *Ombudsman Transitional Order*) a complaint referred to the *Financial Ombudsman Service* after *commencement* which relates to an act or omission occurring before *commencement* if:

(a) the act or omission is that of a person who was, immediately before *commencemen*t, subject to a *former scheme*;
(b) the act or omission occurred in the carrying on by that person of an activity to which that *former scheme* applied; and
(c) the complainant is eligible and wishes to have the complaint dealt with under the new scheme;

for the purposes of (c), where the complainant is not eligible in accordance with *DISP 2* (Jurisdiction of the Financial Ombudsman Service), an *Ombudsman* may, nonetheless, if he considers it appropriate, treat the complainant as eligible if he would have been entitled to refer an equivalent complaint to the *former scheme* in question immediately before *commencement*.

relevant office-holder

a relevant office-holder as defined in section 189 of the Companies Act 1989, which is in summary:

(a) the official receiver;
(b) (in relation to a company) any *person* acting as its liquidator, provisional liquidator, administrator or administrative receiver;
(c) (in relation to an individual or a debtor within the Bankruptcy (Scotland) Act 1985) a trustee in bankruptcy, interim receiver of property, or permanent or interim trustee in the sequestration of an estate;
(d) any *person* acting as administrator of an insolvent estate of a deceased *person*.

relevant pension scheme

a *pension scheme* or an *additional voluntary contribution*.

relevant person

(1) (in *COMP*) a *person* (other than a *person* with an *interim RSRB permission* because he has submitted an application for interim permission in accordance with article 32(1) of the Financial Services and Markets Act 2000 (Regulated Activities) (Amendment) Order 2009 (SI 2009/1342) which has been approved by the *FSA*) for *claims* against whom the *compensation scheme* provides cover, as defined in *COMP* 6.2.1R.
(2) any of the following:
   (a) a *director*, *partner* or equivalent, manager or *appointed representative* (or where applicable, *tied agent*) of the *firm*;

(b) a *director*, *partner* or equivalent, or manager of any *appointed representative* (or where applicable, *tied agent*) of the *firm*;
(c) an *employee* of the *firm* or of an *appointed representative* (or where applicable, *tied agent*) of the *firm*; as well as any other natural person whose services are placed at the disposal and under the control of the *firm* or an *appointed representative* or a *tied agent* of the *firm* and who is involved in the provision by the *firm* of *regulated activities*;
(d) a natural person who is directly involved in the provision of services to the *firm* or its *appointed representative* (or where applicable, *tied agent*) under an *outsourcing* arrangement for the purpose of the provision by the *firm* of *regulated activities*.

[Note: article 2(3) of the *MiFID implementing Directive*]

Relevant scheme

a *collective investment scheme* managed by an *EEA UCITS management company*.

relevant security

(1) (in MAR 2, when used with reference to the Buy-back and Stabilisation Regulation) (in accordance with Article 2(6) of the *Buy-back and Stabilisation Regulation*) *transferable securities* which are admitted to trading on a *regulated market* or for which a request for admission to trading on a *regulated market* has been made, and which are the subject of a *significant distribution*.
(2) (otherwise in MAR 2) *transferable securities*.
(3) [deleted]

relevant transitional complaint

(in accordance with the *Mortgage and General Insurance Complaints Transitional Order*) a complaint referred to the *Financial Ombudsman Service* after the *relevant commencement date* which relates to an act or omission occurring before that date if:
(a) the act or omission is that of a *person* ("R") who, at the time of that act or omission, was subject to a *former scheme*;
(b) R was an *authorised person* on or after the *relevant commencement date*;
(c) the act or omission occurred in the carrying on by R of an activity to which that *former scheme* applied; and
(d) the complainant is eligible and wishes to have the complaint dealt with under the new scheme.

relevant UK details

the details required in regulation 15 of the *EEA Passport Rights Regulations* and set out in SUP 13 Ann 2R (Relevant UK details: branches of insurance undertakings).

remedial direction

(in accordance with section 308(8) of the *Act* (Directions by the Treasury)) a direction requiring the *FSA*:
(a) to exercise its powers under section 297(2) of the Act to revoke. the *recognition order* for a *recognised body*; or
(b) to exercise its powers under section 296 of the *Act* by giving such directions to the *recognised body* concerned as may be specified in the direction.

remuneration

any form of remuneration, including benefits of any kind.

Remuneration Code

SYS 19 (Remuneration Code).

Remuneration Code general requirement

SYSC 19.2.1R.

remuneration committee

a committee or other body responsible for a *firm's remuneration policy*.

remuneration policy

the policy, procedures and practices established, implemented and maintained in accordance with the *Remuneration Code general requirement*.

renewal

carrying forward a contract, at the point of expiry and as a successive or separate operation of the same nature as the preceding contract, between the same contractual parties.

repayment claim

(in relation to a *dormant account*) a claim for repayment made by virtue of sections 1(2)(b) or 2(2)(b) of the Dormant Bank and Building Society Accounts Act 2008, that is, in summary, that the customer has against the *dormant account fund operator* whatever right to payment of the *balance* the customer would have against the *bank* or *building society* if the transfer (or in the case of section 2(2)(b), transfers) had not happened. In this definition, 'customer' is the *person* who held with a *bank* or *building society* the *balance* of a *dormant account* transferred to a *dormant account fund operator*.

repayment mortgage

a *regulated mortgage contract* under which the *customer* is obliged to make payments of interest and capital which are designed to repay the mortgage over the stated term.

repayment vehicle

the means by which the *customer* will repay the capital due under the *regulated mortgage contract*, where all or part of that contract is an *interest-only* mortgage.

repo

(a) an agreement between a seller and buyer for the sale of *securities*, under which the seller agrees to repurchase the *securities*, or equivalent securities, at an agreed date and, usually, at a stated price;
(b) an agreement between a buyer and seller for the purchase of *securities*, under which the buyer agrees to resell the *securities*, or equivalent securities, at an agreed date and, usually, at a stated price.

reportable large exposure

the same thing as *large e-money float exposure* with the following adjustments:
(a) the figure of 10% in *ELM* 3.5.7R is replaced by 25%; and
(b) *ELM* 3.5.6R does not apply.

reportable transaction

[deleted]

reporting accountant

an accountant appointed:
(a) by the *FSA*; or
(b) by a *firm*, having been nominated or approved by the *FSA* under section 166 of the *Act* Reports by skilled persons); or
(c) by an applicant for *Part IV permission*;

to report on one or more aspects of the business of a *firm* or applicant, such as its financial position, including *internal controls* and reporting returns.

reporting level

(in *SUP* 16 (Reporting requirements) and in relation to a *data item*) refers to whether that *data item* is prepared on a solo basis or on the basis of a group such as a *UK DLG by modification* and, if it is prepared on the basis of a group, refers to the type of group (such as a *UK DLG by modification* or a *non-UK DLG by modification (firm level)*).

repossess

(in MCOB) take possession of the property that is the subject of a *regulated mortgage contract* or *home purchase plan*.

representative

(1) an individual who:
    (a) is appointed by a *firm*, or by an *appointed representative* of a *firm*, to carry on any of the following activities:
        (i) *advising on investments*;
        (ii) providing *basic advice* on *stakeholder products;*
        (iii) *arranging (bringing about) deals in investments*;
        (iv) *dealing in investments*; or
    (b) although not appointed to do so, carries on any of the activities in (i) to (iii) on behalf of a *firm* or its *appointed representative*.
(2) (in PRU(INV) 13 in relation to *designated investment business*) an individual appointed by a provider firm or by an *appointed representative* or *tied agent* of that *firm* to carry out either or both of the following activities:
    (a) giving *advice on investments* to *customers* on the merits of *packaged products* offered by that *firm* (or any other provider firm within the same *marketing group*); or
    (b) *arranging (bringing about) deals in investments* in relation to those products.
(3) In (2), a provider firm is a *firm* that is:
    (1) a *product provider*; or
    (2) a *marketing group associate*.

Part II FSA Handbook Materials

repurchase agreement

see *repurchase transaction*.

repurchase transaction

(in accordance with Article 3(1)(m) of the *Capital Adequacy Directive* and Article 4(33) of the *Banking Consolidation Directive* (Definitions)) any agreement in which an *undertaking* or its counterparty transfers securities or *commodities* or guaranteed rights relating to title to securities or *commodities* where that guarantee is issued by a *designated investment exchange* or *recognised investment exchange* which holds the rights to the securities or *commodities* and the agreement does not allow an *undertaking* to transfer or pledge a particular security or *commodity* to more than one counterparty at one time, subject to a commitment to repurchase them or substituted securities or *commodities* of the same description at a specified price on a future date specified, or to be specified, by the transferor, being a *repurchase agreement* for the *undertaking* selling the securities or *commodities* and a *reverse repurchase agreement* for the *undertaking* buying them.

required function

any of *controlled functions* 8 to 12B in the *table of controlled functions* (SUP 10.4.5R).

required percentage

the *required percentage* referred to in *COBS* 20.2.17R is, for each *with-profits fund*:

(a) the percentage (if any) required in respect of that fund by:
  (i) the *firm's* articles of association, registered rules or other equivalent instrument; or
  (ii) a relevant order made by a court of competent jurisdiction;
(b) if (a) does not apply, the percentage specified in the *firm's PPFM*, if that percentage reflects the *firm's* established practice;
(c) if (a) and (b) do not apply, not less than 90 per cent.

requirement

a requirement included in a *firm's Part IV permission* under section 43 of the *Act* (Imposition of requirements), section 45(4) of the *Act* (Variation etc on the Authority's own initiative) or section 46 of the *Act* (Variation of permission on acquisition of control).

requiring or encouraging

taking or refraining from taking any action which requires or encourages another *person* to engage in *behaviour* which, if engaged in by the *person* requiring or encouraging, would amount to *market abuse*.

requisite details

the details required in regulation 1 of the *EEA Passport Rights Regulations* and set out in *SUP* 13 Ann 1R (Requisite details: branches).

research recommendation

research or other information:

(a) concerning one or several *financial instruments* admitted to trading on *regulated markets*, or in relation to which an application for admission to trading has been made, or *issuers* of such *financial instruments*;
(b) intended for distribution so that it is, or is likely to become, accessible by a large number of *persons*, or for the public, but not including:
  (i) an informal short-term investment personal recommendation expressed to *clients*, which originates from inside the sales or trading department, and which is not likely to become publicly available or available to a large number of persons; or
  (ii) advice given by a *firm* to a *body corporate* in the context of a *takeover bid* and disclosed only as a result of compliance with a legal or regulatory obligation, including rule 3 of the *Takeover Code* or its equivalents outside the *UK*; and
(c) which:
  (i) explicitly or implicitly, recommends or suggests an investment strategy; or
  (ii) directly or indirectly, expresses a particular investment recommendation; or
  (iii) expresses an opinion as to the present or future value or price of such instruments.

In this definition, "financial instruments" means the following (as defined in Article 5 of the *Prescribed Markets and Qualifying Investments Order* and Article 1(3) of the *Market Abuse Directive*, and which consequently carries the same meaning in the *Buy-back and Stabilisation Regulation*):

(a) *transferable securities*;
(b) units in collective investment undertakings;
(c) *money-market instruments*;
(d) financial futures contracts, including equivalent cash-settled instruments;
(e) forward interest-rate agreements;

(f) interest-rate, currency and equity swaps;
(g) options to acquire or dispose of any instrument falling into these categories, including equivalent cash-settled instruments. This category includes in particular options on currency and on interest rates;
(h) derivatives on commodities; and
(i) any other instrument admitted to trading on a regulated market in an *EEA State* or for which a request for admission to trading on such a market has been made.

resecuritisation

(in accordance with point 49 of Part 4 of Annex IX of the *Banking Consolidation Directive* (Ratings based method)) *securitisation* of *securitisation exposures* (securitisation having the meaning in paragraph (2) of the definition of securitisation for these purposes).

residual block

(1) (for the purposes of BIPRU 10 (Concentration risk requirements)):
  (a) (subject to (b)) has the meaning in BIPRU 10.8.12R (Definition of residual block) which is in summary, in relation to a *firm* and its *UK integrated group*, a *concentration risk group counterparty* of the *firm* which is not a member of the *firm*'s *UK integrated group*;
  (b) (if a *firm* has a *wider integrated group permission*) has the meaning in BIPRU 10.9.7R (Definition of residual block) which is in summary, in relation to a *firm* and its *wider integrated group*, a *concentration risk group counterparty* of the *firm* which is not a member of the *firm*'s *UK integrated group* or *wider integrated group*.
(2) (for the purposes of BIPRU 8 (Group risk – consolidation)) has the meaning in BIPRU 8.9.24R (Wider integrated groups: Definition of residual block) which is in summary all *exposures* to *group concentration risk group counterparties* falling into BIPRU 8.9.20R(2) not included in a *diverse block*.

resilience capital requirement

the capital component for *long-term insurance business* calculated in accordance with the *rules* in INSPRU 3.1.9G to INSPRU 3.1.26R.

respondent

(1) (in *DISP*) a *firm (except a UCITS qualifier)*, *payment service provider*, *licensee* or *VJ participant* covered by the *Compulsory Jurisdiction*, *Consumer Credit Jurisdiction* or *Voluntary Jurisdiction* of the *Financial Ombudsman Service*.
(2) (in *DISP* 2 and 3) includes, as a result of sections (9226 and 226A of the *Act*:
  (a) an *unauthorised person* who was formerly a *firm* in respect of a *complaint* about an act or omission which occurred at the time when the *firm* was *authorised*, provided that the compulsory jurisdiction rules were in force in relation to the activity in question; and
  (b) a *person* who was formerly a *licensee* in respect of a *complaint* about an act or omission which occurred at the time when it was a *licensee*, provided the *complaint* falls within a description specified in the consumer credit rules in force at the time of the act or omission.
(3) (in *DISP* 2 and 3) includes, in accordance with the *Ombudsman Transitional Order*, an *unauthorised person* subject to the *Compulsory Jurisdiction* in relation to *relevant existing complaints* and *relevant new complaints*.
(4) (in *DISP* 2 and 3) includes, in accordance with the *Mortgage and General Insurance Complaints Transitional Order*, a former *firm* subject to the *Compulsory Jurisdiction* in relation to *relevant transitional complaints*.

responsible person

(1) (except in COMP) (as defined in section 3(8) of the Child Trust Funds Act 2004) a *person* with *parental responsibility* in relation to a child under 16 who is not:
  (a) a local authority or, in Northern Ireland, an authority within the meaning of the Children (Northern Ireland) Order 1995 (SI 1995/755 (NI 2)); or
  (b) a *person* under 16.
(2) (in COMP) (in accordance with section 3 (1) of the Compensation Act 2006) a *person* who has negligently or in breach of statutory duty caused or permitted another *person* to be exposed to asbestos (including an *insurer* of such a *person*).

restricted credit

a loan for which, as a result of an existing arrangement between a supplier and a *firm*, the *customer's* application to the *firm* is submitted through the supplier and the terms of the loan require that it be paid to the supplier for goods or services supplied to the *customer*, not including loans secured by a charge over land or loans or payments by *plastic card* (other than a *store card*).

restricted-use credit agreement

(in accordance with section 11 of the Consumer Credit Act 1974) an agreement:
(a) to finance a transaction between the *customer* and the *firm*, whether forming part of that agreement or not;
(b) to finance a transaction between the *customer* and a person (the 'supplier') other than the *firm*;
(c) to refinance any existing indebtedness of the *customer's*, whether to the *firm* or another *person*.

restriction notice

a notice served under section 191B of the *Act*.

retail banking service

an agreement with a *banking customer*, under which a *firm* agrees to accept a *deposit* from a *banking customer* on terms to be held in an account for that customer, and to provide srvices in relation to that *deposit* including but not limited to repayment to the customer.

retail client

(1) (other than in relation to the *provision of basic advice on stakeholder products*) in accordance with COBS 3.4.1R, a *client* who is neither a *professional client* or an *eligible counterparty*; or
[Note: article 4(1)(12) of *MiFID*]
(2) (in relation to the provision of *basic advice* on a *stakeholder product* and in accordance with article 52B of the *RAO*) any *person* who is advised by a *firm* on the merits of opening or buying a *stakeholder product* where the advice is given in the course of a business carried on by that *firm* and it is received by a *person* not acting in the course of a business carried on by him.

retail (investment)customer

(in relation to a *firm's permission* and the *FSA Register*) a *retail client*.

retail customer

(in accordance with the meaning of 'consumer' in article 2(d) of the *Distance Marketing Directive*) an individual who is acting for purposes which are outside his trade, business or profession.

retail exposure

(1) (in relation to the *IRB approach* and with respect to an *exposure*) an *exposure* falling into the *IRB exposure class* listed in BIPRU 4.3.2R(4) (Retail exposures).
(2) (in relation to the *standardised approach* to credit risk and with respect to an *exposure*) an *exposure* falling into the *standardised credit risk exposure class* listed in BIPRU 3.2.9R(8) (Retail exposures).

retail (non-investment insurance) customer

(in relation to a *firm's permission* and the *FSA Register*) a *consumer* or a *customer* acting in the capacity of both a *consumer* and a *commercial customer* (see *ICOBS* 2.1.3G).

retail investment

(a) a *life policy*; or
(b) a *unit*; or
(c) a *stakeholder pension scheme*; or
(ca) *a personal pension scheme*; or
(d) an interest in an *investment trust savings scheme*; or
(e) *a structured capital-at-risk product.*

retail investment firm

a firm that has *permission* to carry on an activity which is a *retail investment activity*.

retail investment activity

(a) *advising on investments*;
(b) *arranging (bringing about) deals in investments;* or
(c) *making arrangements with a view to transactions in investments*,

in relation to *retail investments*, except when carried on by a *firm* exclusively with or for *intermediate customers* or *market counterparties.*

retail securitised derivative

a *securitised derivative* which is not a specialist securitised derivative; in this definition, a "specialist *securitised derivative*" is a *securitised derivative* which, in accordance with the *listing rules*, is required to be admitted to listing with a clear statement on any disclosure document that the issue is intended for a purchase by only investors who are particularly knowledgeable in investment matters.

retail SME

(1) (in relation to the *IRB approach*) a small or medium sized entity, an *exposure* to which may be treated as a *retail exposure* under BIPRU 4.6.2R (Definition of retail exposures).
(2) (in relation to the *standardised approach* to credit risk) a small or medium sized entity, an *exposure* to which may be treated as a *retail exposure* under BIPRU 3.2.10R (Definition of retail exposures).

retail SME exposure

(in relation to the *IRB approach* or the *standardised approach* to credit risk) an *exposure* to a *retail SME*.

retirement annuity

an individual *pension policy* effected before 1 July 1988 by a self-employed *person* or a *person* in non-pensionable employment and which was approved under Chapter III, Part XIV of the Income and Corporation Taxes Act 1988 (when sections (9618 to 628 of that Chapter were in force).

retirement fund

the amount which will be available, at the date on which the investor retires, for the provision of benefits.

return

the documents required (taken together) to be deposited under IPRU(INS) *rule* 9.6(1).

reverse repurchase agreement

see *repurchase transaction.*

reverse takeover

(in LR) a transaction classified as a *reverse takeover* under LR 10.

reversion activity

any of the *regulated activities* of:
(a) *arranging (bringing about) a home reversion plan* (article 25B(1));
(b) *making arrangements with a view to a home reversion plan* (article 25B(2));
(c) *advising on a home reversion plan* (article 53B);
(d) *entering into a home reversion plan* (article 63B(1));
(e) *administering a home reversion plan* (article 63B(2)); or
(f) *agreeing to carry on a regulated activity* in (a) to (e) (article 64).

reversion administrator

a *firm* with *permission* (or which ought to have *permission*) for *administering a home reversion plan*.

reversion adviser

a *firm* with *permission* (or which ought to have *permission*) for *advising on a home reversion plan*.

reversion arranger

a *firm* with *permission* (or which ought to have *permission*) for *arranging a home reversion plan*.

reversion intermediary

a *firm* with *permission* (or which ought to have *permission*) to carry on a *reversion mediation activity*.

reversion mediation activity

any of the following *regulated activities*:
(a) *arranging (bringing about) a home reversion plan* (article 25B(1));
(b) *making arrangements with a view to a home reversion plan* (article 25B(2));
(c) *advising on a home reversion plan* (article 53B); or
(d) *agreeing to carry on a regulated activity* in (a) to (c) (article 64).

reversion occupier

the individual (or trustees), specified in article 63B(3) of the *Regulated Activities Order*, who in summary:
(a) is (or are) the *person* (or *persons*) from whom all or part of an interest in land is bought as part of an arrangement comprising a *home reversion plan*; and
(i) in the case of an individual, is entitled under the arrangement to occupy at least 40% of the land in question as or in connection with a dwelling and intends to do so; or

Part II FSA Handbook Materials

(ii) in the case of trustees, are trustees of a trust a beneficiary of which is an individual described in (i).

reversion provider

a *firm* with *permission* (or which ought to have *permission*) for *entering into a home reversion plan.*

revolving exposure

(for the purpose of BIPRU 9.13 (Securitisations of revolving exposures with early amortisation provisions) and in accordance with Article 100 of the Banking Consolidation Directive (Securitisations of revolving exposures)) an *exposure* whereby customers' outstanding balances are permitted to fluctuate based on their decisions to borrow and repay, up to an agreed limit.

RIE

recognised investment exchange.

rights issue

(in LR) an offer to existing *security* holders to subscribe or purchase further *securities* in proportion to their holdings made by means of the issue of a renounceable letter (or other negotiable document) which may be traded (as "nil paid" rights) for a period before payment for the *securities* is due.

rights issue period

the period that commences on the date a *company* announces a rights issue and which ends on the date that the *shares* issued under the rights issue are admitted to trading on a *prescribed market.*

rights to or interests in investments

the *investment*, specified in article 89 of the *Regulated Activities Order* (Rights to or interests in investments), which is in summary: any right to or interest in any other *specified investment*, but excluding:

(a) interests under the trusts of an *occupational pension scheme*;
(b) rights to or interests in a *contract of insurance* of the kind referred to in paragraph (1)(a) of article 60 of the *Regulated Activities Order* (Plans covered by insurance or trust arrangements), or interests under a trust of the kind referred to in paragraph 1(b) of article 60 of the *Regulated Activities Order* (Plans covered by insurance or trust arrangements);
(c) any other *specified investment.*

risk assessment function

controlled function CF14 in the *table of controlled functions*, described more fully in *SUP* 10.8.3R.

risk capital margin

the risk capital margin for a *with-profits fund* calculated in accordance with the *rules* in INSPRU 1.3.43R to INSPRU 1.3.103G.

risk capital requirement

(1) (in relation to the *FSA's rules*) one of the following:
  (a) the *credit risk capital requirement*;
  (b) the *fixed overheads requirement*;
  (c) the *market risk capital requirement*; or
  (d) the *operational risk capital requirement*; or
(2) (in relation to the rules of another *regulatory body*) whatever corresponds to the items in (1) under the rules of that *regulatory body.*

risk concentration

(in accordance with Article 2(19) of the *Financial Groups Directive* (Definitions)) all exposures with a loss potential borne by entities within a *financial conglomerate*, which are large enough to threaten the solvency or the financial position in general of the *regulated entities* in the *financial conglomerate*; such exposures may be caused by counterparty risk, credit risk, investment risk, insurance risk, market risk, other risks, or a combination or interaction of these risks.

risk factors

(in PR) (as defined in the *PD Regulation*) a list of risks which are specific to the situation of the issuer and/or the securities and which are material for taking investment decisions.

risk position

(in accordance with Part 1 of Annex III of the *Banking Consolidation Directive* (Definitions) and for the purpose of BIPRU 13 (The calculation of counterparty risk exposure values for financial derivatives, securities financing transactions and long settlement transactions)) a risk number that is assigned to a transaction under the *CCR standardised method* following a predetermined algorithm.

risk weight

(in relation to an *exposure*) a degree of risk expressed as a percentage assigned to that *exposure* in accordance with whichever is applicable of the *standardised approach* to credit risk and the *IRB approach*, including (in relation to a *securitisation position*) under BIPRU 9 (Securitisation).

risk weighted exposure amount

(in relation to an *exposure*) the value of an *exposure* for the purposes of the calculation of the *credit risk capital component* after application of a *risk weight*.

RMAR

(in SUP) a Retail Mediation Activities Return, containing data specified in SUP 16 Ann 18A R and relevant to the *firm's* type and *regulated activities*

ROCH

recognised overseas clearing house.

ROIE

recognised overseas investment exchange.

roll-up of interest mortgage

a *regulated mortgage contract* where no payment of interest on the amount borrowed (other than interest charged when all or part of the amount borrowed is repaid voluntarily by the *customer*), is due or capable of becoming due while the *customer* continues to occupy the mortgaged property as his main residence and fulfil his obligations under the *regulated mortgage contract.*

rolling spot forex contract

either of the following:
(a) a *future*, other than a *future* traded or expressed to be as traded on a *recognised investment exchange*, where the property which is to be sold under the contract is foreign exchange or sterling; or
(b) a *contract for differences* where the profit is to be secured or loss avoided by reference to fluctuations in foreign exchange; and

in either case where the contract is entered into for the purpose of speculation.

rollover risk

(in accordance with Part 1 of Annex III of the *Banking Consolidation Directive* (Definitions) and for the purpose of BIPRU 13 (The calculation of counterparty risk exposure values for financial derivatives, securities financing transactions and long settlement transactions)) the amount by which *expected positive exposure* is understated when future transactions with a counterpart are expected to be conducted on an ongoing basis; the additional *exposure* generated by those future transactions is not included in calculation of *expected positive exposure.*

RPPD

the Regulatory Guide which contains a statement of the responsibilities of providers and distributors for the fair treatment of *customers*.

rule

(in accordance with section 417(1) of the *Act* (Definitions)) a rule made by the *FSA* under the *Act*, including:
(a) a *Principle*; and
(b) an *evidential provision*.

rule on use of dealing commission

COBS 11.6.3R.

rules on the disclosure of commission and commission equivalent

[deleted]

running-account credit

(in accordance with section 10(1)(a) of the Consumer Credit Act 1974) a facility under a contract by which the *customer* is enabled to receive from time to time (whether in his own person, or by another person) from the *firm* or a third party cash, goods and services (or any of them) to an amount or value such that, taking into account payments made by or to the credit of the *customer*, the credit limit (if any) is not at any time exceeded.

safe custody asset

(a) in relation to *MiFID business*, a *financial instrument*; or

(b) in relation to *safeguarding* and *administering investments* that is not *MiFID business*, a *safe custody investment*.

safe custody investment

a *designated investment*, which is not the property of the *firm*, but for which the *firm*, or any *nominee company* controlled by the *firm* or by its *associate*, is accountable; which has been paid for in full by the *client*; and which ceases to be a *safe custody investment* when the *firm* has disposed of it in accordance with a valid instruction.

safeguarding and administering investments

the *regulated activity*, specified in article 40 of the *Regulated Activities Order* (Safeguarding and administering investments), which is in summary: the safeguarding of assets belonging to another and the administration of those assets, or arranging for one or more other *persons* to carry on that activity, where:

(a) the assets consist of or include any *security* or *contractually based investment* (that is, any *designated investment*, *funeral plan contract* or *right to or interest in* a *funeral plan contract*); or

(b) the arrangements for their safeguarding and administration are such that the assets may consist of or include *designated investments*, and either the assets have at any time since 1 June 1997 done so, or the arrangements have at any time (whether before or after that date) been held out as ones under which *designated investments* would be safeguarded and administered.

safeguarding and administration of assets (without arranging)

that part of *safeguarding* and *administering investments* which consists of both:

(a) the safeguarding of assets belonging to another; and

(b) the administration of those assets.

sale

(in COLL) (in relation to *units* in an *authorised fund)* the sale of *units* by the *authorised fund manager* as *principal*.

sale price

(in COLL)

the *price* payable to the *authorised fund manager* for each *unit* it *sells* to a *unitholder*, calculated in accordance with COLL 6.3 (Valuation and pricing).

sale shortfall

the outstanding amount due to the *home finance provider*, under a *home finance transaction*, following the sale of the property that is its subject.

same stage of capital

(with respect to a particular item of capital in the *capital resources table*) the stage in the *capital resources table* in which that item of capital appears.

schedule

(in *Part 6 rules*) (as defined in the *PD Regulation*) a list of minimum information requirements adapted to the particular nature of the different types of *issuers* and/or the different *securities* involved.

scheme

(1) (except in *COBS*, *CASS* and *SUP*) a collective investment scheme.

(2) (in *COBS*, *CASS* and *SUP*)
  (a) a regulated collective investment scheme;
  (b) an investment trust where the relevant *shares* have been, or will be, acquired through an *investment trust savings scheme*;
  (c) an investment trust, if:
    (i) the relevant *shares* will be held in a *wrapper* or *personal pension scheme*; and
    (ii) the trust and the *wrapper* or *personal pension scheme* will be promoted together;
  (d) (in COBS 18.5) in addition to (a), (b) and (c), an *unregulated collective investment scheme*.

scheme holding

a holding of:

(a) *units* in a *collective investment scheme*; or

(b) *shares* in an *investment trust savings scheme*.

scheme management activity

the management by an *operator* of the property held for or within the *scheme* of which it is the *operator*, excluding the receiving and holding of *client money* and *safeguarding* and *administering investments*.

scheme of arrangement

(in COLL) an arrangement relating to an *authorised fund* ("transferor fund") or to a *sub-fund* of a *scheme* that is an *umbrella* ("transferor sub-fund") under which:

(a) either:
    (i) all or part of the property of the transferor fund, or all or part of the property attributed to the transferor sub-fund, is to become the property of one or more *regulated collective investment schemes* ("transferee schemes"); or
    (ii) all or part of the property attributed to the transferor sub-fund is to become part of the property attributed to one or more other *sub-funds* of the same *umbrella scheme* ("transferee sub-funds"); and

(b) *holders of units* in the transferor fund or transferor sub-fund, the property of which is being transferred or reattributed under (a), are to receive, in exchange for their respective interests in that property, either:
    (i) *units* in the transferee scheme or one or more of the transferee schemes, to which the property is transferred; or
    (ii) *units* in the transferee sub-fund or one or more of the transferee sub-funds, to which the property is reattributed.

scheme of operations a scheme which:

(a) describes the nature of the risks which the *insurer* is underwriting, or intends to underwrite, and the guiding principles which it intends to follow in reinsuring or covering those risks; and

(b) contains the information required under SUP App 2.12.1R (Content of a scheme of operations).

scheme particulars

a *document* containing information about a *regulated collective investment scheme*.

scheme pension

a scheme pension, as defined in paragraph 2 of Schedule 28 to the Finance Act 2004, which is in summary a pension payable until a pension scheme member's death, or until the later of the member's death and the end of a term not exceeding 10 years.

scheme property

(a) (in relation to an *ICVC*) the property subject to the *collective investment scheme* constituted by it;

(b) (in relation to an *AUT*) the *capital property* and the *income property*.

scheme report

(in *SUP 18*) the report on the terms of an *insurance business transfer*.

scheme required by section 109 of the Act (Scheme reports).

scientific research based company

(in LR) a *company* primarily involved in the laboratory research and development of chemical or biological products or processes or any other similar innovative science based company.

scope of advice, scope

the basis on which *personal recommendations* on *packaged products* is given by a *firm*, that is, one of the following:

(1) the whole market (or the whole of a named sector of the market); or

(2) a limited number of *product providers*; or

(3) a single *company* or single group of *companies*.

References to a *firm's* scope of *personal recommendations* of *packaged products* include, where the context requires, a reference to the scope of *personal recommendations* of the *firm's appointed representatives* or, where applicable, *tied agent*.

scope of basic advice

the basis on which a *firm* gives *basic advice* on *stakeholder products*, that is, with reference to the *stakeholder products* of one, or more than one, *stakeholder product* provider.

SDRT provision

a *charge* of such amount or at such rate as is determined by the *authorised fund manager* to be made as a provision for stamp duty reserve tax for which the *ICVC* may become liable under the Stamp

Duty and Stamp Duty Reserve Tax (Open-Ended Investment Companies) (Amendment No. 2) Regulations 2000 or the *trustee* may become liable under Schedule 19 to the Finance Act 1999 in respect of a surrender of *units* to the *authorised fund manager*.

Second Life Directive

the Council Directive of 8 November 1990 on the coordination of laws, etc and laying down provisions relating to facilitate the effective exercise of freedom to provide services and amending Directive 79/267/EEC (No 90/619/EEC).

Second Non-Life Directive

the Council Directive of 22 June 1988 on the coordination of laws, etc and laying down provisions to facilitate the effective exercise of freedom to provide services and amending Directive 73/239/EEC (No 88/357/EEC).

secondary listed issuer

(in LR) an *issuer* with a *secondary listing* of its *equity securities*.

secondary listing

(in LR) a *listing* by the *FSA* of *equity securities* which is not a *primary listing*.

secondary material

(as more fully described in section 394 of the *Act* (Access to Authority material)) material, other than that which the *FSA* relied on in reaching its decision, which:
(a) the *FSA* considered in reaching its decision; or
(b) the *FSA* obtained in connection with, that is, in the investigation of, the matter in question.

secondary pooling event

(1) [deleted]
(2) (in CASS 5) an event that occurs in the circumstances described in CASS 5.6.14R (Failure of a bank, other broker or settlement agent: secondary pooling events).
(3) (in *CASS* 7 and CASS 7A) an event that occurs in the circumstances described in *CASS* 7A.3.1R (Failure of a bank, intermediate broker, settlement agent or OTC counterparty: secondary pooling events).

section 43 capital requirements

the financial supervision requirements of the *FSA* for the purposes of the listing arrangements made under section 43 of the Financial Services Act 1986.

section 178 notice

(in accordance with section 178(3) of the *Act*) a notice given to the *FSA* under section 178 of the *Act*.

sectoral rules

(in relation to a *financial sector*) rules and requirements relating to the prudential supervision of *regulated entities* applicable to *regulated entities* in that *financial sector* as follows:
(a) (for the purposes of GENPRU 3.1.12R (Definition of financial conglomerate: Solvency requirement)) *EEA prudential sectoral legislation* for that *financial sector* together with as appropriate the rules and requirements in (c); or
(b) (for the purpose of calculating *solo capital resources*, a *solo capital resources requirement and regulatory surplus value*):
    (i) (to the extent provided for in paragraph 6.4 to 6.6 of GENPRU 3 Ann 1R) rules and requirements that are referred to in those paragraphs; and
    (ii) the rules and requirements in (c); or
(c) (for all other purposes) rules and requirements of the *FSA*;

and so that:
(d) (in relation to prudential rules about consolidated supervision for any *financial sector*) those requirements include ones relating to the form and extent of consolidation;
(e) (in relation to any *financial sector*) those requirements include ones relating to the eligibility of different types of capital;
(f) (in relation to any *financial sector*) those requirements include both ones applying on a solo basis and ones applying on a consolidated basis;
(g) (in relation to the *insurance sector*) references in this definition to consolidated supervision are to supplementary supervision, similar expressions being interpreted accordingly; and
(h) references to the *FSA's sectoral rules* are to *sectoral rules* in the form of *rules*.

secured debt

a debt fully secured on:
(a) assets whose value at least equals the amount of debt; or
(b) a letter of credit or guarantee from an *approved counterparty*.

secured lending

lending where the *mortgage lender* takes security on land for the loan provided to the *customer*.

secured lending transaction

(in accordance with point 2 of Part 1 of Annex VIII of the *Banking Consolidation Directive* (Eligibility of credit risk mitigation)) any transaction giving rise to an *exposure* secured by collateral which does not include a provision conferring upon the *person* with the *exposure* the right to receive margin frequently.

securities and futures firm

(subject to BIPRU TP 1.3R (Revised definition of securities and futures firm for certain transitional purposes))a *firm* whose *permitted activities* include *designated investment business*, which is not an *authorised professional firm, bank, BIPRU investment firm* (unless it is an *exempt BIPRU commodities firm*), *ELMI, building society, credit union, friendly society, ICVC, insurer, media firm, service company, incoming EEA firm* (without a *top-up permission*), *incoming Treaty firm* (without a *top-up permission*), *UCITS management company* or *UCITS qualifier* (without a *top-up permission*), whose permission does not include a requirement that it comply with *IPRU(INV) 5 (*Investment management firms) or 13 (Personal investment firms), and which is within (a), (b), (c), (d), (e), (f) or (g):

(a) a *firm* (other than one falling within (d)):
- (i) which was a member of *SFA* immediately before *commencement*; and
- (ii) which was not, immediately before *commencement*, subject to the financial supervision requirements of the.*FSA* (under section 43 of the Financial Services Act 1986), or *PIA* or *IMRO* (under lead regulation arrangements);

(b) a *firm* whose *permission* includes a *requirement* that it comply with *IPRU(INV) 3* (Securities and futures firms);

(c) *a firm:*
- (i) which was given a *Part IV permission* after *commencement*, or which was authorised under section 25 of the Financial Services Act 1986 immediately before *commencement* and not a member of *IMRO, PIA or SFA*; and
- (ii) for which the most substantial part of its gross income (including *commissions*) from the *designated investment business* included in its *Part IV permission* is derived from one or more of the following activities (based, for a firm given a *Part IV permission* after *commencement*, on the business plan submitted as part of the *firm's* application for *permission* or, for a *firm* authorised under section 25 of the Financial Services Act 1986, on the *firm's financial year* preceding its *authorisation* under the *Act*):
  - (A) an activity carried on as a member of an exchange;
  - (B) making a market in *securities* or *derivatives*;
  - (C) *corporate finance business*;
  - (D) *dealing* (excluding, in the case of a *home finance proviser, dealing as principal* in *contractually based investments* where this *activity* is carried out for risk management purposes and would have been excluded under article 16 of the *Regulated Activities Order* if the *firm* were an *unauthorised person* or under article 19 of the *Regulated Activities Order) arranging (bringing about) deals in investments*, in *securities* or *derivatives*;
  - (E) the provision of clearing services as a *clearing firm*;
  - (F) *managing investments*, where those *investments* are primarily *derivatives*;
  - (G) activities relating to *spread.bets*

(d) a *firm* that is:
- (i) an *ex-section 43 firm* which was not authorised under the Financial Services Act 1986 immediately before *commencement*; or
- (ii) an *ex-section 43 lead regulated firm*;

(e) an *energy market participant*;

(f) an *oil market participant*;

(g) an *exempt BIPRU commodities firm*.

securities financing transaction

(1) (in *COBS*, in *CASS*) an instance of stock lending or stock borrowing or the lending or borrowing of other *financial instruments*, a repurchase or reverse repurchase transaction, or a buy-sell back or sell-buy back transaction.
[Note: article 2(10) of the *MiFID Regulation*]

(2) (in any other case) any of the following:
- (a) a *repurchase transaction*; or
- (b) a *securities or commodities lending or borrowing transaction*; or
- (c) a *margin lending transaction*.

securities issued in a continuous and repeated manner

(in PR) (as defined in Article 2.1(l) of the *prospectus directive*) issues on tap or at least two separate issues of securities of a similar type and/or class over a period of 12 months.

securities note

(in *Part 6 rules*) a securities note referred to in PR 2.2.2R.

securities or commodities borrowing

see *securities or commodities lending or borrowing transaction.*

securities or commodities lending

see *securities or commodities lending or borrowing transaction.*

securities or commodities lending or borrowing transaction

(in accordance with Article 4(34) of the *Banking Consolidation Directive* and Article 3(1)(n) of the *Capital Adequacy Directive* (Definitions)) any transaction in which an *undertaking* or its counterparty transfers securities or *commodities* against appropriate collateral subject to a commitment that the borrower will return equivalent securities or *commodities* at some future date or when requested to do so by the transferor, that transaction being *securities or commodities lending* for the *undertaking* transferring the securities or *commodities* and being *securities or commodities borrowing* for the *undertaking* to which they are transferred.

securities PRR

the *interest rate PRR*, the *equity PRR*, the *option PRR* (but only in relation to *positions* which under BIPRU 7.6.5R (Table: Appropriate calculation for an option or warrant) may be subject to one of the other *PRR* charges listed in this definition or which would be subject to such a *PRR* charge if BIPRU 7.6.5R did not require an *option PRR* to be calculated), the *CIU PRR* and the *PRR* calculated under BIPRU 7.11 (Credit derivatives in the trading book) and so that:

(a) the *securities PRR* includes any *PRR charge* calculated under a *CAD 1 permission*; and

(b) the *securities PRR* does not include any *PRR charge* calculated under a *VaR model permission* unless the provision in question provides otherwise.

securitisation

(1) (subject to (2)) a process by which assets are sold to a bankruptcy-remote *special purpose vehicle* in return for immediate cash payment and that vehicle raises the immediate cash payment through the issue of debt securities in the form of tradable notes or commercial paper.

(2) (in accordance with Article 4(36) of the *Banking Consolidation Directive* (Definitions) and in BIPRU) a transaction or scheme whereby the credit risk associated with an *exposure* or pool of *exposures* is *tranched* having the following characteristics:

  (a) payments in the transaction or scheme are dependent upon the performance of the *exposure* or pool of *exposures*; and

  (b) the subordination of *tranches* determines the distribution of *losses* during the ongoing life of the transaction or scheme.

securitisation credit default swap PRR method

the method for calculating the *specific risk* portion of the *interest rate PRR* for credit default swaps that are *securitisation positions* set out in BIPRU 7.11.39R to BIPRU 7.11.53R.

securitisation position

(in accordance with Article 4(40) (Definitions) and Article 96 (Securitisation) of the *Banking Consolidation Directive*) an *exposure* to a *securitisation* within the meaning of paragraph (2) of the definition of securitisation; and so that:

(a) where there is an *exposure* to different *tranches* in a *securitisation*, the *exposure* to each *tranche* must be considered as a separate *securitisation position*;

(b) the providers of credit protection to *securitisation positions* must be considered to hold positions in the *securitisation*; and

(c) *securitisation positions* include *exposures* to a *securitisation* arising from interest rate or currency derivative contracts.

securitisation special purpose entity

(in accordance with Article 4(44) of the *Banking Consolidation Directive* (Definitions)) a corporation, trust or other entity, other than a *credit institution*, organised for carrying on a *securitisation* or *securitisations* (within the meaning of paragraph (2) of the definition of securitisation), the activities of which are limited to those appropriate to accomplishing that objective, the structure of which is intended to isolate the obligations of the *SSPE* from those of the *originator*, and the holders of the beneficial interests in which have the right to pledge or exchange those interests without restriction.

securitised derivative

an *option* or *contract for differences* which, in either case, is *listed* under LR 19 of the listing *rules* (including such an *option* or.*contract for differences* which is also a *debenture*).

securitised exposure

an *exposure* in the pool of *exposures* that has been securitised, either via a *traditional securitisation* or a *synthetic securitisation*. The cash-flows generated by the securitised exposures are used to make payments to the *securitisation positions*.

security

(1) (except in LR) (in accordance with article 3(1) of the *Regulated Activities Order* (Interpretation)) any of the following investments specified in that Order:
- (a) *share* (article 76);
- (b) *debenture* (article 77);
- (c) *government and public security* (article 78);
- (d) *warrant* (article 79);
- (e) *certificate representing certain securities* (article 80);
- (f) *unit* (article 81);
- (g) *stakeholder pension scheme* (article 82(1));
- (ga) *personal pension scheme* (article 82(2));
- (h) *rights to or interests in investments in (a) to (g)* (article 89).

(2) (in LR) (in accordance with section 102A of the *Act*) anything which has been, or may be admitted to the *official list*.

security-based CTF

a *CTF*, other than a *stakeholder CTF*, which is not limited to *deposit* based investment.

segregated client

a *client* whose *money* must be segregated by the *firm* under *COB* 9.3.37R (Segregation).

self-invested personal pension scheme

an arrangement which forms all or part of a *personal pension scheme*, which gives the member the power to direct how some or all of the member's contributions are invested.

sell

(in accordance with article 3(1) of the *Regulated Activities Order* (Interpretation)) (in relation to any *investment*) sell in any way, including disposing of the *investment* for valuable consideration; in this definition, "disposing" includes:
- (a) (in relation to an *investment* consisting of rights under a contract):
  - (i) surrendering, assigning or converting those rights; or
  - (ii) assuming the corresponding liabilities under the contract;
- (b) (in relation to an *investment* consisting of rights under other arrangements) assuming the corresponding liabilities under the arrangements; and
- (c) (except in COLL) (in relation to any other *investment*) issuing or creating the *investment* or granting the rights or interests of which it consists.

Sending dematerialised instructions

the *regulated activity*, specified in article 45(1) of the *Regulated Activities Order*, of sending, on behalf of another *person*, dematerialised instructions relating to a *security*, where those instructions are sent by means of a relevant system in respect of which an operator is approved under the 2001 Regulations;

in this definition:
- (a) "the 2001 Regulations" means the Uncertificated Securities Regulations 2001 (SI 2001/3755);
- (b) "dematerialised instruction" and "operator" have the meaning given by regulation 3 of the 2001 Regulations.

senior management

(in BIPRU 7.10 (Use of a value at risk model) and in relation to a *firm*) the *firm's governing body* and those of the firm's *senior managers* and other senior management who have responsibilities relating to the measurement and control of the risks which the *firm's VaR model* is designed to measure or whose responsibilities require them to take into account those risks.

senior manager

an individual other than a *director*:
- (a) who is employed by:

(i) a *firm*; or
(ii) a *body corporate* within a *group* of which the *firm* is a member;

(b) to whom the *governing body* of the *firm*, or a member of the *governing body* of the *firm*, has given responsibility, either alone or jointly with others, for management and supervision;

(c) who, if the individual is employed by the *firm*, reports directly to:
(i) the *governing body*; or
(ii) a member of the *governing body*; or
(iii) the *chief executive*; or
(iv) the head of a significant business unit; and

(d) who, if the individual is employed by a *body corporate* within the *group*, reports directly to a *person* who is the equivalent of a body or *person* referred to in (c).

senior personnel

those *persons* who effectively direct the business of the *firm*, which could include a *firm's governing body* and other *persons* who effectively direct the business of the *firm*.

senior staff committee

(in DEPP and EG) a committee consisting of senior *FSA* staff members that is empowered to make *statutory notice decisions* and *statutory notice associated decisions* by *executive procedures*.

series of transactions

a series of transactions.*executed*.with a view to achieving one investment decision or objective.

SERV

the Handbook Guide for service companies.

service company

a *firm* whose only *permitted activities* are *making arrangements with a view to transactions in investments*, and *agreeing to carry on that regulated activity*, and *whose Part IV permission*:

(a) incorporates a *limitation* substantially to the effect that the *firm* carry on *regulated activities* only with *market counterparties* or *intermediate customers*; and

(b) includes *requirements* substantially to the effect that the *firm* must not:
(i) guarantee, or otherwise accept responsibility for, the performance, by a participant in arrangements made by the *firm* in carrying on *regulated activities*, of obligations undertaken by that participant in connection with those arrangements; or
(ii) *approve* any *financial promotion* on behalf of any other *person* or any specified class of *persons*; or
(ii) in carrying on its *regulated activities*, provide services otherwise than in accordance with *documents* (of a kind specified in the *requirement*) provided by the *firm* to the. *FSA*.

service conditions

(in accordance with paragraph 14 of Schedule 3 to the *Act* (EEA Passport Rights)) the conditions that:

(a) the *firm* has given its *Home State regulator* notice of its intention to provide services in the *United Kingdom*;

(b) if the *firm* falls within paragraph (a), (d), (e) or (f) in the definition of "*EEA firm*", the *FSA* has received notice from the *firm's Home State regulator* containing such information as may be prescribed;

(c) if the *firm* falls within paragraph (d) or (e) of that definition, its *Home State regulator* has informed it that the regulator's notice has been sent to the *FSA*; and

(d) if the *firm* falls within paragraph (e) of that definition, one *month* has elapsed beginning with the date on which the *firm's Home State regulator* informed the *firm* that it had sent the regulator's notice to the *FSA*.

services and costs disclosure document

information about the *scope of advice* or *scope of basic advice* and the nature and costs of the services offered by a *firm* as described in COBS 6.3.7G, which contains the keyfacts logo, headings and text described in COBS 6 Annex 1G.

SETS

the Stock Exchange Electronic Trading Service.

settlement agent

a *person* with or through whom the *firm* effects settlement of *UK*-settled or foreign-settled transactions.

settlement decision makers

(in DEPP and EG) two members of the *FSA's* executive of at least director of division level with responsibility for deciding whether to give *statutory notices* in the circumstances described in DEPP 5.

settlement decision procedure

(in DEPP) the procedure for the making of *statutory notice decisions* in the circumstances described in DEPP 5.

settlement discount scheme

(in DEPP and EG) the scheme described in DEPP 6.7 by which the financial penalty that might otherwise be payable in respect of a *person's* misconduct or contravention may be reduced to reflect the timing of any settlement agreement.

settlement price

(in LR) (in relation to *securitised derivatives*), the reference price or prices of the *underlying instrument* or *instruments* stipulated by the *issuer* for the purposes of calculating its obligations to the holder.

Seventh Company Law Directive

the Council Directive of 13 June 1983 on consolidated accounts (No 83/349/EEC).

SFA

the Securities and Futures Authority Limited.

SFA Complaints Bureau

the first stage of the *SFA scheme*. which aimed to resolve complaints by conciliation.

SFA Consumer Arbitration Scheme

the second stage of the *SFA scheme*, which determined complaints by means of arbitration.

SFA scheme

the *former scheme* (including the *SFA Complaints Bureau* and the *SFA Consumer Arbitration Scheme*) set up by the *SFA* to handle complaints against members of the *SFA* under the Financial Services Act 1986.

SFT

securities financing transaction.

shadow director

(in LR) as in sub-paragraph (b) of the definition of director in section 417(1) of the *Act*.

share

(1) (except in COLL, LR, DR, REC, SUP 11 (Controllers and close links) and SUP 16 (Reporting requirements)) the *investment*, specified in article 76 of the *Regulated Activities Order* (Shares etc), which is in summary: a share or stock in the share capital of:
  (a) any *body corporate* (wherever incorporated);
  (b) any unincorporated body constituted under the law of a country or territory outside the *United Kingdom*.

(2) (in COLL):
  (a) (in relation to an *ICVC*) a share in the *ICVC* (including both *smaller denomination shares* and *larger denomination shares);*
  (b) (otherwise) an *investment* within (1).

(3) (in DTR and LR, and in FEES where relevant to DTR or LR) (in accordance with section 540(1) of the Companies Act 2006) a share in the share capital of a *company*, and includes:
  (a) stock (except where a distinction between shares and stock is express or implied);
  (b) *preference shares*; and
  (c) in chapters 4, 5, 6 and 7 of *DTR* a convertible share.

(4) (in *REC*) shares admitted to trading on a *regulated market*.

(5) (in SUP 11 (Controllers and close links) and SUP 16 (Reporting requirements)) (in accordance with section 422 of the *Act*):
  (a) in relation to an *undertaking* with share capital, allotted shares;
  (b) in relation to an *undertaking* with capital but no share capital, rights to share in the capital of the *undertaking*;
  (c) in relation to an *undertaking* without capital, interests@
    (i) conferring any right to share in the profits, or liability to contribute to the losses, of the *undertaking*; or

(ii) giving rise to an obligation to contribute to the debts or expenses of the undertaking in the event of a winding up.

shared appreciation mortgage

a *regulated mortgage contract*, a condition of which is that the *mortgage lender* will receive a share in any increase in value in the mortgaged property when the *customer* either sells the property or terminates the contract including a contract where, if there is a reduction in value, the *customer* is required to pay the *mortgage lender* all or part of the shortfall.

Shareholder

(1) (in relation to an *ICVC*):
(a) (in relation to a *share* that is represented by a *bearer certificate*) the *person* who holds the certificate;
(b) (in relation to a *share* that is not represented by a *bearer.certificate*) the *person* whose name is entered on the *register* in relation to that *share*.
(2) (in relation to chapters 5 [] of *DTR*) any natural person or legal entity governed by private or public law, who holds directly or indirectly:
(a) *shares* of the *issuer* in its own name and on its own account;
(b) *shares* of the *issuer* in its own name, but on behalf of another natural person or legal entity;
(c) depository receipts, in which case the holder of the depository receipt shall be considered as the shareholder of the underlying *shares* represented by the depository receipts.

ships

(in relation to a *class* of *contract of insurance*) the *class* of *contract of insurance*, specified in paragraph 6 of Part I of Schedule 1 to the *Regulated Activities Order (*Contracts of general insurance), upon vessels used on the sea or on inland water, or upon the machinery, tackle, furniture or equipment of such vessels.

short-term annuity

(as defined in paragraph 6 of Schedule 28 to the Finance Act 2004) in relation to a member of a pension scheme, an annuity payable to the member if:
(a) it is purchased by the application of sums or assets representing the whole or any part of the member's unsecured pension fund (as defined in paragraph 8 of that Schedule) in respect of an arrangement;
(b) it is payable by an insurance company;
(c) the member had an opportunity to select an insurance company;
(d) it is payable for a term which does not exceed five years and ends before the member reaches age 75; and
(e) it is either a level annuity, an increasing annuity or a relevant linked annuity.

shortfall

(1) (in relation to cancellation of an *investment agreement*) the amount a *firm* is entitled to charge a *customer* for the market loss in accordance with *COBS* 15.4.3R.
(2) (in relation to *client money*) the amount by which the *client money* in a *client bank account* is insufficient to satisfy the claims of *clients* in respect of that *money*, or not immediately available to satisfy such claims.

sickness

(in relation to a *class of contract of insurance*) the *class of contract of insurance*, specified in paragraph 2 of Part I of Schedule 1 to the *Regulated Activities Order* (Contracts of general insurance), providing fixed pecuniary benefits or benefits in the nature of indemnity (or a combination of both) against risks of loss to the *persons* insured attributable to sickness or infirmity, but excluding contracts within paragraph IV of Part II of Schedule 1 to the *Regulated Activities Order* (Permanent health).

sickness or distressed circumstances contract

any contract in accordance with which benefits are provided for the relief or maintenance of any *person* during sickness or when in distressed circumstances.

SIFA

the Handbook Guide: "Using the FSA Handbook: an Overview for small IFA firms"

significant distribution

(as defined in Article 2 of the *Buy-back and Stabilisation Regulation*) an initial or secondary *offer* of *relevant securities*, publicly announced and distinct from ordinary trading both in terms of the amount in value of the *securities* offered and the selling methods employed.

significant influence function

any of the *controlled functions* 1 to 20 in the *a*.

significant management (designated investment business) function

controlled function CF16 in the *table of controlled functions*, described more fully in *SUP* 10.9.10R.

significant management (financial resources) function

controlled function CF19 in the *table of controlled functions*, described more fully in *SUP* 10.9.16R.

significant management (insurance underwriting) function

controlled function CF18 in the *table of controlled functions*, described more fully in *SUP* 10.9.14R.

significant management (other business operations) function

controlled function CF17 in *the table of controlled functions*, described more fully in *SUP* 10.9.12R.

significant management (settlements) function

controlled function CF20 in the *table of controlled functions*, described more fully in *SUP* 10.9.18R.

significant management function

any of the *controlled functions* 16 to 20 in the *table of controlled functions.*

simple capital issuer

a *BIPRU firm* that meets the following conditions:

(a) it does not raise capital through a special purpose vehicle;

(b) it only includes non-convertible and non-exchangeable *capital instruments* in its *capital resources*;

(c) (if it includes *capital instruments* in its *capital resources* on which *coupons* are payable) such *coupons* are not subject to a *step-up*;

(d) it only includes *capital instruments* in its *tier one capital resources* consisting of ordinary *shares*, *PIBS*, perpetual noncumulative preference *shares* or partnership or *limited liability partnership* capital accounts;

(e) it only includes non-redeemable *capital instruments* in its *tier one capital resources*; and

(f) (if it includes *capital instruments* in its *tier one capital resources* on which *coupons* are payable) such *coupons* are non-cumulative, non-mandatory and in cash.

simplified buffer requirement

BIPRU 12.6.9R.

simplified equity method

the method of calculating the *equity PRR* set out in BIPRU 7.3.29R (Simplified equity method).

simplified ILAS

the approach to the calculation of the liquid assets buffer of a *simplified ILAS BIPRU firm* described in BIPRU 12.6.

Simplified ILAS BIPRU firm

an *ILAS BIPRU firm* that, in accordance with the procedures in *BIPRU* 12 (Liquidity), is using the *simplified ILAS*.

simplified ILAS waiver

a *waiver* permitting an *ILAS BIPRU firm* to operate simplified ILAS.

simplified prospectus

a marketing *document* containing information about a *simplified prospectus scheme*, which complies with *COLL 4.6.2R* (Production and publication of simplified prospectus) and COLL 4.6.8R (Table: Contents of the simplified prospectus).

simplified prospectus scheme

(a) a *UCITS scheme* that is not a recognised scheme under section 264 of the *Act* (Schemes constituted in other EEA States); or

(b) a *key features scheme* in respect of which a *simplified prospectus* has been, or will be, produced instead of a *key features document* (see *COBS* 13.1.3R (2));

single customer view

(in COMP) a single, consistent view of an *eligible claimant's* aggregate *protected deposits* with the relevant *firm* which contains the information required by COMP 17.2.4R, but excluding from that view those accounts where the *eligible claimant* is a beneficiary rather than the account holder or if the account is not active as defined in COMP 17.2.3R(2).

Single Market Directives

(a) the *Banking Consolidation Directive*;

(b) the *Insurance Directives* (within the meaning of paragraph 1 of Schedule 3 to the *Act*);

(ba) the *Reinsurance Directive*;

(c) *MiFID*;

(d) the *Insurance Mediation Directive*; and

(e) the *UCITS Directive*.

single-priced authorised fund

an *authorised fund* or, in the case of an *umbrella*, a *sub-fund* (if it were a separate *fund*), for the *units* of which there is only one *price* applicable by reference to a *valuation point*.

SIPP

a *self-invested personal pension scheme*.

skilled person

a *person* appointed to make a report required by section 166 of the *Act* (Reports by skilled persons) for provision to the *FSA* and who must be a *person*:

(a) nominated or approved by the *FSA*; and

(b) appearing to the *FSA* to have the skills necessary to make a report on the matter concerned.

SLRP

the Supervisory Liquidity Review Process.

small and medium-sized enterprise

(in PR) (as defined in Article 2.1(f) of the *prospectus directive*) companies, which, according to their last annual or consolidated accounts, meet at least two of the following three criteria: an average number of employees during the financial year of less than 250, a total balance sheet not exceeding €43,000,000 and an annual net turnover not exceeding €50,000,000.

small business

(in *COMP*) a *partnership, body corporate*, unincorporated association or mutual association with an annual turnover of less than £1 million (or its equivalent in any other currency at the relevant time).

small e-money issuer

(as defined by article 9C(10 of the *Regulated Activities Order* (Persons certified as small issuers etc)) a *person* to whom a certificate has been given by the *FSA* under that article (and whose certificate has not been revoked).

small e-money issuer certificate

a certificate given by the *FSA* under article 9C of the *Regulated Activities Order* (Persons certified as small issuers etc).

small friendly society function

controlled function CF6 in the *table of controlled functions*, described more fully in *SUP* 10.6.26R.

small payment institution

(in accordance with regulation 2(1) of the *Payment Services Regulations*) a *person* included by the *FSA* in the *FSA Register* pursuant to regulation 4(1)(b) of the *Payment Services Regulations*.

small personal investment firm

a *personal investment firm*:

(a) which is not a *MiFID investment firm*;

(b) whose *permission* does not include *establishing, operating or winding up a personal pension scheme*;

(c) which is not a *network*; and

(d) which has fewer than 26 *epresentatives*.

small self-administered scheme

an *occupational pension scheme* of a kind described in article 4(4) and 4(5) of the Financial Services and Markets Act 2000 (Carrying on Regulated Activities by Way of Business) Order 2001 (SI 2001/1177).

smaller denomination share

a *share* to which are attached rights in a smaller denomination as provided by regulation 45 of the *OEIC regulations*.

smallest financial sector

(in relation to a *financial sector* in a *consolidation group* or a *financial conglomerate* and in accordance with GENPRU 3.1 (Cross sector groups)) the *financial sector* with the smallest average referred to in the box titled Threshold Test 2 in the *financial conglomerate definition decision tree* (10% ratio of balance sheet size and solvency requirements), the *banking sector* and *investment services sector* being treated as one *financial sector* in the circumstances set out in GENPRU 3.1.

smoothed linked long term stakeholder product

the *stakeholder product* specified by regulations 6, 7 and 8 (smoothed linked long term contracts) of the *Stakeholder Regulations*;

social housing firm

(in PRU 9.3 (Capital resources for insurance and mortgage mediation activity and mortgage lending and administration)) a wholly-owned *subsidiary* of:
(a) a local authority; or
(b) a registered social landlord;
which carries on non-profit *regulated activities* in connection with housing.

social insurance

(in relation to a *class of contract of insurance*) the *class of contract of insurance*, specified in paragraph IX of Part II of Schedule 1 to the *Regulated Activities Order* (Contracts of long-term insurance), of a kind referred to in article 2(3) of the *Consolidated Life Directive* ("operations relating to the length of human life which are prescribed by or provided for in *social insurance* legislation, when they are effected or managed at their own risk by assurance undertakings in accordance with the laws of an *EEA State*").

Society

the society incorporated by Lloyd's Act 1871 by the name of Lloyd's.

Society GICR

the *general insurance capital requirement* calculated by the *Society* as if it were an *insurer* under GENPRU 2.3.13R.

Society's basic market activity

(in accordance with section 315(2)(a) of the *Act* (The Society: authorisation and permission)) *arranging deals in contracts of insurance written at Lloyd's.*

Society's regulatory functions

the Society's powers, duties or functions in relation to *members* or *underwriting agents* which are or may be exercised for the purposes of supervising or regulating the market at Lloyd's.

Society's secondary market activity

(in accordance with section 315(2)(b) of the *Act* (The Society: authorisation and permission)) arranging deals in participation in Lloyd's syndicates.

sole trader

an individual who is a *firm*.

solicited real time financial promotion

(in accordance with article 8 of the *Financial Promotion Order*) a *real time financial promotion* which is solicited, that is, it is made in the course of a personal visit, telephone call or other interactive dialogue if that call, visit or dialogue:
(a) was initiated by the recipient of the *financial promotion*; or
(b) takes place in response to an express request from the recipient of the *financial promotion.*

solicited real time qualifying credit promotion

[deleted]

solo capital resources

(1) (for the purposes of GENPRU 3 and INSPRU 6) capital resources that are or would be eligible as capital under the *sectoral rules* that apply for the purpose of calculating its *solo capital resources requirement*. Paragraph 6.8 of GENPRU 3 Ann 1R (Solo capital resources requirement: the insurance sector) applies for the purpose of this definition in the same way as it does for the definition of *solo capital resources requirement.*
(2) for the purpose of BIPRU 10 (Concentration risk requirements) the definition in (1) is adjusted in accordance with BIPRU 10.8.13R (Calculation of capital resources for a UK integrated group) so that it means *capital resources* calculated in accordance with the *rules* applicable to the category of *BIPRU firm* identified by applying the procedure in BIPRU 8.6.6R to BIPRU 8.6.9R (Consolidated capital resources).

solo capital resources requirement

(1) (for the purpose of GENPRU 3) a capital resources requirement calculated on a solo basis as defined in paragraph 6.2 to 6.7 of GENPRU 3 Ann 1R.

(2) (for the purposes of INSPRU 6) a capital resources requirement calculated on a solo basis as defined in paragraph 6.2 to 6.7 of GENPRU 3 Ann 1R as it would apply if references to *financial conglomerate* in those paragraphs were replaced with references to *insurance group*.

(3) (for the purposes of GENPRU 2.2.214R (Deductions from tiers one and two: Material holdings)) a capital resources requirement calculated on a solo basis as defined in paragraph 6.2 to 6.7 of GENPRU 3 Ann 1R as those paragraphs apply to the *insurance sector*.

solo consolidation waiver

a *waiver* of the type described in BIPRU 2.1 (Solo consolidation).

Solvency 1 Directive

the Directive of the European Parliament and of the Council of 5 March 2002 amending Council Directive 79/267/EEC as regards the solvency margin requirements for life assurance undertakings (No 2002/12/EC).

solvency deficit

(in GENPRU 3 Ann 1R (Capital adequacy calculations with respect to financial conglomerates) and in respect of a member of the *overall financial sector*) the amount (if any) by which its *solo capital resources* fall short of its *solo capital resources requirement*.

sovereign, institution and corporate IRB exposure class

(in relation to the *IRB approach*) an *exposure* falling into the *IRB exposure classes* referred to in BIPRU 4.3.2R(1)-(3) (Sovereigns, institutions and corporates).

special adjustment

(in *IPRU(INV)* 13) a *position* risk adjustment, counterparty risk adjustment and foreign exchange adjustment.

special purpose vehicle

(1) (in PR) (as defined in the *PD Regulation*) an *issuer* whose objects and purposes are primarily the issue of *securities*.

(2) (except in PR) a *body corporate*, explicitly established for the purpose of securitising assets, whose sole purpose (either generally or when acting in a particular capacity) is to carry out one or more of the following functions:
 (a) issuing *designated investments*, other than *life policies*;
 (b) redeeming or terminating or repurchasing (whether with a view o re-issue or to cancellation) an issue (in whole or part) of *designated investments*, other than *life policies*;
 (c) entering into transactions or terminating transactions involving *designated investments* in connection with the *issue*, redemption, termination or re-purchase of designated investments, other than *life policies*;

specialised lending exposure

(in relation to the *IRB approach*) an *exposure* falling into BIPRU 4.5.3R (Definition of specialised lending).

specialist investor

(in LR) an investor who is particularly knowledgeable in investment matters.

specialist securities

(in LR and FEES) *securities* which, because of their nature, are normally bought and traded by a limited number of investors who are particularly knowledgeable in investment matters.

specialist securitised derivative

(in LR) a *securitised derivative* which because of its nature is normally bought and traded by a limited number of investors who are particularly knowledgeable in investment matters.

specific costs

management expenses other than *base costs* and *establishment costs*.

specific costs levy

a levy, forming part of the *management expenses levy*, to meet the *specific costs* in the financial year of the *compensation scheme* to which the levy relates, each *participant firm's* share being calculated in accordance with FEES 6.4.7R.

specific non-real time financial promotion

a *non-real time financial promotion* which identifies and promotes a particular *investment* or service.

specific risk

(1) (in SYSC) unique risk that is due to the individual nature of an asset and can potentially be diversified.

(2) (in GENPRU and BIPRU and in accordance with paragraph 12 of Annex I of the *Capital Adequacy Directive*) the risk of a price change in an *investment* due to factors related to its issuer or, in the case of a *derivative*, the issuer of the underlying *investment*.

specific risk backtesting exception

(in BIPRU 7.10 (Use of a value at risk model) and in relation to a *firm*) an exception arising out of backtesting a *VaR model* with respect to *specific risk* as more fully defined in that *firm's VaR model permission*.

specific risk PRA

a *PRA* for *specific risk* including any such *PRA* as applied under BIPRU 7.6.8R (Table: Appropriate PRA).

specific wrong-way risk

(in accordance with Part 1 of Annex III of the *Banking Consolidation Directive* (Definitions) and for the purpose of BIPRU 13 (The calculation of counterparty risk exposure values for financial derivatives, securities financing transactions and long settlement transactions)) the risk that arises when the exposure to a particular counterparty is positively correlated with the *probability of default* of the counterparty due to the nature of the transactions with the counterparty; a *firm* is exposed to *specific wrong-way risk* if the future exposure to a specific counterparty is expected to be high when the counterparty's *probability of default* is also high.

specified investment

any of the following *investments* specified in Part III of the *Regulated Activities Order* (Specified Investments):

(a) *deposit* (article 74);

(aa) *electronic money* (article 74A);

(b) *contract of insurance* (article 75); for the purposes of the *permission* regime, this is sub-divided into:

 (i) *general insurance contract*;

 (ii) *long-term insurance contract*

 and then further sub-divided into *classes of contract of insurance*;

(c) *share* (article 76);

(d) *debenture* (article 77);

(e) *government and public security* (article 78);

(f) *warrant* (article 79);

(g) *certificate representing certain securities* (article 80);

(h) *unit* (article 81);

(i) *stakeholder pension scheme* (article 82(1));

(ia) *personal pension scheme* (article 82(2));

(j) *option* (article 83); for the purposes of the *permission* regime, this is sub-divided into:

 (i) *option* (excluding a *commodity option* and an *option* on a *commodity future*);

 (ii) *commodity option* and an *option* on a *commodity future*;

(k) *future* (article 84); for the purposes of the *permission* regime, this is sub-divided into:

 (i) *future* (excluding a *commodity future* and a *rolling spot forex contract*);

 (ii) *commodity future*;

 (iii) *rolling spot forex contract*;

(l) *contract for differences* (article 85); for the purposes of the *permission* regime, this is sub-divided into:

 (i) *contract for differences* (excluding a *spread bet* and a *rolling spot forex contract*);

 (ii) *spread bet*;

 (iii) *rolling spot forex contract*;

(m) *underwriting capacity of a Lloyd's syndicate* (article 86(1));
(n) *membership of a Lloyd's syndicate* (article 86(2));
(o) *funeral plan contract* (article 87);
(oa) *regulated mortgage contract* (article 61(3);
(ob) *home reversion plan* (article 63B(3));
(oc) *home purchase plan* (article 63F(3));
(p) *rights to or interests in investments* (article 89).

sponsor

(1) (in LR) a *person* approved, under section 88 of the *Act* by the *FSA*, as a sponsor.
(2) (in BIPRU), in accordance with Article 4(42) of the *Banking Consolidation Directive* (Definitions) and in relation to a *securitisation* within the meaning of paragraph (2) of the definition of securitisation) an *undertaking* other than an *originator* that establishes and manages an *asset backed commercial paper programme* or other *securitisation* scheme that purchases *exposures* from third party entities.

sponsor service

a service relating to a matter referred to in *LR* 8.2 that a *sponsor* provides or is requested or appointed to provide and that is for the purpose of the *sponsor* complying with *LR* 8.3.1R or *LR* 8.4. This definition includes preparatory work that a *sponsor* may undertake before a decision is taken as to whether or not it will act as *sponsor* for a *company* or in relation to a transaction. But nothing in this definition is to be taken as requiring a *sponsor* to agree to act as a *sponsor* for a *company* or in relation to a transaction

spread bet

a *contract for differences* that is a gaming contract, whether or not section 412 of the *Act* (Gaming contracts) applies to the contract; in this definition, "gaming" has the meaning given in the Gaming Act 1968, which is in summary: the playing of a game of chance for winnings in money or money's worth, whether any *person* playing the game is at risk of losing any money or money's worth or not.

spread risk

the risk that a spread (that is, the difference in price or yield) between two variables will change.

SPV

(1) (in GENPRU 2.2 (Capital resources)) has the meaning in GENPRU 2.2.126R (Other tier one capital: innovative tier one capital: indirectly issued tier one capital).
(2) (in BIPRU 8 (Group risk — consolidation)) has the meaning in BIPRU 8.6.15R (Indirectly issued capital and group capital resources).

SRB administrator

a *firm* which carries on the *regulated activity* of *administering a regulated sale and rent back agreement.*

SRB adviser

a *firm* which carries on the regulated activity of *advising on a regulated sale and rent back agreement.*

SRB agreement provider

(in accordance with article 63J(3)(a) of the *Regulated Activities Order*) a *firm* which buys all or part of the *qualifying interest in land* in the United Kingdom from a *SRB agreement seller* under a *regulated sale and rent back agreement*, including a firm which acquires obligations or rights under a *regulated sale and rent back agreement.*

SRB agreement seller

(in accordance with article 63J(3)(a) of the *Regulated Activities Order*) an individual or trustees, or a *related party* of his, who sells all or part of the *qualifying interest in land* in the *United Kingdom* to an agreement provider under a *regulated sale and rent back agreement* and who is entitled under the arrangement to occupy at least 40% of the land in question as or in connection with a dwelling, and intends to do so.

SRB arranger

a *firm* which carries on the *regulated activity* of *arranging (bringing about) a regulated sale and rent back agreement* or *making arrangements with a view to a regulated sale and rent back agreement.*

SREP

the *supervisory review and evaluation process.*

SSAS

small self-administered scheme.

SSPE

a *securitisation special purpose entity.*

stabilisation

(in *MAR* 2) (as defined in Article 2 of the *Buy-back and Stabilisation Regulation*) any purchase or offer to purchase *relevant securities*, or any transaction in *associated instruments* equivalent thereto, by *investment firms* or *credit institutions*, which is undertaken in the context of a *significant distribution* of such *relevant securities* exclusively for supporting the market price of these *relevant securities* for a predetermined period of time, due to a selling pressure in such securities.

stakeholder CTF

a *CTF* that has the characteristics, and complies with the conditions, set out in paragraph 2 of the Schedule to the *CTF Regulations*.

stakeholder pension scheme

a scheme that meets the conditions in section 1 of the Welfare Reform and Pensions Act 1999 or article 3 of the Welfare Reform and Pensions (Northern Ireland) Order 1999.

stakeholder product

(as defined in article 52B(3) of the *Regulated Activities Order*):
(a) a *stakeholder CTF*; or
(b) a *stakeholder pension scheme*; or
(c) an investment of a kind specified in the *Stakeholder Regulations*.

Stakeholder Regulations

the Financial Services and Markets Act 2000 (Stakeholder Products) Regulations 2004 (SI 2004/2738).

standard CIU look through method

the method for calculating the *PRR* for a *position* in a *CIU* set out in BIPRU 7.7.4R and BIPRU 7.7.7R to BIPRU 7.7.10R.

standard equity method

the method of calculating the *equity PRR* set out in BIPRU 7.3.32R (Standard equity method).

standard frequency liquidity reporting firm

a standard ILAS BIPRU firm that is not a low frequency liquidity reporting firm. standard ILAS BIPRU firm an ILAS BIPRU firm that is not a simplified ILAS BIPRU firm.

standard market risk PRR rules

the *rules* relating to the calculation of the *market risk capital requirement* excluding the *VaR model approach* and any *rules* modified so as to provide for the *CAD 1 model approach.*

standard method of internal client money reconciliation

CASS 7 Annex 1.

standard terms

(in *DISP*) the contractual terms made under paragraph 18 of Schedule 17 to the *Act* (The Ombudsman Scheme), under which *VJ participants* participate in the *Voluntary Jurisdiction*.

standardised approach

one of the following:
(a) (where expressed to relate to credit risk) the method for calculating capital requirements for credit risk in BIPRU 3 (Credit risk) and BIPRU 9.2.1R(1) and BIPRU 9.11 (Standardised approach);
(b) (where expressed to relate to *operational risk*) the method for calculating capital requirements for *operational risk* in BIPRU 6.3 (Standardised approach);
(c) (where not expressed to relate to any risk and used in BIPRU 3, BIPRU 4 (IRB approach), BIPRU 5 (Credit risk mitigation), BIPRU 9 (Securitisation) or BIPRU 10 (Concentration risk requirements)) it has the meaning in (a);
(d) (where not expressed to relate to any risk and used in BIPRU 6 (Operational risk)) it has the meaning in (b);
(e) (where the one of the approaches in (a) to (d) is being applied on a consolidated basis) that approach as applied on a consolidated basis in accordance with BIPRU 8 (Group risk — consolidation); or

(f) when the reference is to the rules of or administered by a *regulatory body* other than the *FSA*, whatever corresponds to the approach in (a) to (e), as the case may be, under those rules.

standardised credit risk exposure class

(in relation to the *standardised approach* to credit risk) one of the classes of *exposure* set out in BIPRU 3.2.9R (Exposure classes).

standardised deterministic projection

a *projection* which is either a *generic projection* or a *personal projection* produced in accordance with the assumptions contained in *COBS* 13 Annex 2.

standing data

the information relating to a *firm* held by the *FSA* on the matters set out in SUP 16 Annex 16R.

standing independent valuer

the *person* appointed as such under COLL 5.6.20R (Standing independent valuer and valuation) and COLL 8.4.13R(1) (Standing independent valuer and valuation.

state finance organisation

a legal person other than a *company:* (a) which is a national of an *EEA state*; (b) which is set up by or pursuant to a special law; (c) whose activities are governed by that law and consist solely of raising funds under state control through the issue of *debt securities*; (d) which is financed by means of the resources they have raised and resources provided by the *EEA state*; and (e) the *debt securities* issued by it are considered by the law of the relevant *EEA state* as securities issued or guaranteed by that state.

state monopoly

a *company* or other legal person which is a national of an *EEA state* and which:
(a) in carrying on its business benefits from a monopoly right granted by an *EEA state*; and
(b) is set up by or pursuant to a special law or whose borrowings are unconditionally and irrevocably guaranteed by an *EEA state* or one of the federated states of an *EEA state*.

State of the commitment

(in accordance with paragraph 6(1) of Schedule 12 to the *Act* (Transfer schemes: certificates)) (in relation to a commitment entered into at any date):
(a) if the *policyholder* is an individual, the State in which he had his habitual residence at that date;
(b) if the *policyholder* is not an individual, the State in which the establishment of the *policyholder* to which the commitment relates was established at that date;

in this definition, "commitment" means (in accordance with article 2 of the Financial Services and Markets Act 2000 (Control of Business Transfers) (Requirements on Applicants) Regulations 2001 001/3625 any contract of insurance of a kind referred to in article 2 of the *Consolidated Life Directive*.

State of the risk

(in accordance with paragraph 6(3) of Schedule 12 to the *Act* (Transfer schemes: certificates)) (in relation to the *EEA State* in which a risk is situated):
(a) if the insurance relates to a building or to a building and its contents (so far as the contents are covered by the same policy), the *EEA State* in which the building is situated;
(b) if the insurance relates to a vehicle of any type, the *EEA State* of registration;
(c) in the case of *policies* of a duration of four months or less covering travel or holiday risks (whatever the class concerned), the *EEA State* in which the *policyholder* took out the *policy*;
(d) in a case not covered by (a) to (c):
    (i) if the *policyholder* is an individual, the *EEA State* in which he has his habitual residence at the date when the contract is entered into; and
    (ii) otherwise, the *EEA State* in which the establishment of the *policyholder* to which the *policy* relates is situated at that date.

statement of demands and needs

[deleted]

Statement of Principle

one of the Statements of Principle issued by the *FSA* under section 64(1) of the *Act* (Conduct: Statements and codes) with respect to the conduct of *approved persons* and set out in *APER*.

statutory auditor

a statutory auditor as that term is defined in section 1210 of the Companies Act 2006.

statutory money purchase illustration

an annual illustration of the contributions made for the benefit of, and the potential benefits due to, a member of a *personal pension scheme*, which is prepared in accordance with the Personal Pension Schemes (Disclosure of Information) Regulations 1987 (SI 1987/1110).

statutory notice

a *warning notice, decision notice* or *supervisory notice.*

statutory notice decision

a decision by the *FSA* on whether or not to give a *statutory notice.*

statutory notice associated decision

a decision which is made by the *FSA* and which is associated with a decision to give a statutory notice, including a decision:

(a) to determine or extend the period for making representations;
(b) to determine whether a copy of the *statutory notice* needs to be given to any third party and the period for him to make representations;
(c) to refuse access to *FSA* material;
(d) [deleted]

step-up

(in relation to any item of capital) any change in the *coupon* rate on that item that results in an increase in the amount payable at any time, including a change already provided in the original terms governing those payments. A step-up:

(a) includes (in the case of a fixed rate) an increase in that *coupon* rate;
(b) includes (in the case of a floating rate calculated by adding a fixed amount to a fluctuating amount) an increase in that fixed amount;
(c) includes (in the case of a floating rate) a change in the benchmark by reference to which the fluctuating element of the *coupon* is calculated that results in an increase in the absolute amount of the *coupon*; and
(d) does not include (in the case of a floating rate) an increase in the absolute amount of the *coupon* caused by fluctuations in the fluctuating figure by reference to which the absolute amount of the *coupon* floats.

stochastic projection

a *projection* showing a summary of results from repeated simulations using an investment model, where the model uses key financial parameters which are subject to random variations and are projected into the future.

stock financing

a transaction where a *physical commodity* is sold forward and the cost of funding is locked in until the date of the forward sale.

stock lending

the disposal of a *designated investment* subject to an obligation or right to reacquire the same or a similar *designated investment* from the same counterparty.

stock lending activity

the activity of undertaking a *stock lending* transaction.

stocks and shares component

a *qualifying investment* as prescribed in paragraph 7 of the *ISA Regulations.*

store card

a card restricted to paying for goods or services from a particular supplier or group of suppliers and where the price of the goods or services is paid directly to the supplier or group of suppliers by the customer or the *firm*, but excluding a *plastic card* used to pay for goods or services through a network such as Visa or MasterCard.

structured capital-at-risk product

a product, other than a *derivative*, which provides an agreed level of income or growth over a specified investment period and displays the following characteristics:

(a) the *customer* is exposed to a range of outcomes in respect of the return of initial capital invested;
(b) the return of initial capital invested at the end of the investment period is linked by a pre-set formula to the performance of an index, a combination of indices, a 'basket' of selected stocks (typically from an index or indices), or other factor or combination of factors; and
(c) if the performance in (b) is within specified limits, repayment of initial capital invested occurs but if not, the *customer* could lose some or all of the initial capital invested.

structured deposit

a *deposit* paid on terms under which any interest or premium will be paid, or is at risk, according to a formula which involves the performance of:
(a) an index (or combination of indices) (other than money market indices);
(b) a stock (or combination of stocks); or
(c) a commodity (or combination of commodities).

sub-class

one of the classes of *participant firms* within a *class* set out in FEES 6 Annex 3R being sub-classes that carry on business of a similar nature or have other common characteristics, to which *compensation costs* and *specific* costs are allocated in accordance with FEES 6.4 and FEES 6.5. Class A (Deposits) is to be treated as being made up of a single *sub-class*.

sub-fund

(a) (in relation to an *authorised fund* that is an *umbrella*) a separate part of the *scheme property* of that *scheme* that is pooled separately;
(b) (in relation to a *collective investment scheme* that is not an *authorised fund*) any part of that scheme that is equivalent to (a).

sub-group

(in relation to a *person*):
(a) that *person*; and
(b) any *person* that is either:
  (i) a *subsidiary undertaking* of that *person*; or
  (ii) an *undertaking* in which that *person* or a *subsidiary undertaking* of that *person* holds a *participation*.

subsidiary

(1) (except in relation to *MiFID business*) (as defined in section 1159(1) of the Companies Act 2006 (Meaning of "subsidiary", etc)) (in relation to another *body corporate* ("H")) a *body corporate* of which H is a *holding company*.
(2) (in relation to *MiFID business*) a subsidiary undertaking as defined in Articles 1 and 2 of Seventh Council Directive on consolidated accounts (No 83/349/EEC), including any subsidiary of a subsidiary undertaking of an ultimate *parent undertaking*.

[Note: article 4 (1)(29) of *MiFID*]

subsidiary undertaking

(1) (except for the purposes of determining whether a person has *close links* with another *person*) an *undertaking* of which another *undertaking* is its *parent undertaking*.
(2) (for the purposes of determining whether a *person* has *close links* with another *person*) (in accordance with section 343(8) of the *Act* (Information given by auditor or actuary to the FSA) and paragraph 3(3) of Schedule 6 to the *Act* (Threshold conditions)):
  (a) an *undertaking* in (1);
  (b) an *undertaking* ("S") if:
    (i) another *undertaking* (its parent) is a member of S;
    (ii) a majority of S's board of directors who have held office during the financial year and during the preceding financial year have been appointed solely as a result of the exercise of the parent's voting rights; and
    (iii) no one else is the parent undertaking of S under any of (a) (i) to (iii) or b(i) or (ii) in the definition of *parent undertaking*.
(3) (in LR) as defined in section 1162 of the Companies Act 2006.

substantial shareholder

(in *LR*) any *person* who is entitled to exercise or to control the exercise of 10% or more of the votes able to be cast on all or substantially all matters at general meetings of the *company* (or of any *company* which is its *subsidiary undertaking* or *parent undertaking* or of a fellow *subsidiary undertaking* of its *parent undertaking*). Disregard for this purpose any voting rights which such a *person* exercises (or controls the exercise of) independently in its capacity as bare trustee, investment manager, collective investment undertaking or a *long term insurer* in respect of its linked long term business if no *associate* of that *person* interferes by giving direct or indirect instructions, or in any other way, in the exercise of such voting rights (except to the extent any such *person* confers or collaborates with such an *associate* which also acts in its capacity as investment manager, collective investment undertaking or long term insurer).

sufficiency liquid

(in *ELM*) (in relation to an *investment*) complying with the requirements about liquidity in *ELM* 3.3.11R (Test for liquidity).

suitability report

a report which a *firm* must provide to its *client* under COBS 9.4 (Suitability reports) which, among other things, explains why the *firm* has concluded that a recommended transaction is suitable for the *client*.

summary

(in relation to a *prospectus*) the summary included in the *prospectus*.

SUP

the Supervision manual.

supervisory formula method

(for the purposes of BIPRU 9 (Securitisation), in relation to a *securitisation* within the meaning of paragraph (2) of the definition of securitisation and in accordance with Part 1 of Annex IX of the *Banking Consolidation Directive* (Securitisation definitions)) the method of calculating *risk weighted exposure amounts* for *securitisation positions* set out in BIPRU 9.12.21R-BIPRU 9.12.23R and BIPRU 9.14.3R.

supervisory function

any function within a *common platform firm* that is responsible for the supervision of its *senior personnel*.

Supervisory Liquidity Review Process

the *FSA's* assessment of the adequacy of certain *firms'* liquidity resources as described in BIPRU 12.2 and BIPRU 12.5.

supervisory notice

(as defined in section 395(13) of the *Act* (The Authority's procedures)) a notice given by the *FSA* in accordance with section 53(4), (7) or (8)(b); 78(2) or (5); 197(3), (6) or (7)(b); 259(3), (8) or (9)(b); 268(3), (7)(a) or (9)(a) (as a result of subsection (8)(b)); 282(3), (6) or (7)(b); or 321(2) or (5).

supervisory review and evaluation process

the *FSA's* assessment of the adequacy of certain *firms'* capital, as more fully described in BIPRU 2.2.9G and INSPRU 7.1.91G to INSPRU 7.1.99G.

supervisory volatility adjustments approach

the approach to calculating volatility adjustments under the *financial collateral comprehensive method* under which the *firm* uses the adjustments specified in BIPRU 5.4 (Financial collateral) rather than in its own estimates, as more fully described in BIPRU 5.4 and including that approach as applied to master netting agreements as described in BIPRU 5.6 (Master netting agreements).

supplementary listing particulars

(in LR) (in accordance with section 81(1) of the *Act*), supplementary listing particulars containing details of the change or new matter.

supplementary prospectus

(in *Part 6 rules*) a supplementary prospectus containing details of a new factor, mistake or inaccuracy.

suretyship

(in relation to a *class of contract of insurance*) the *class of contract of insurance*, specified in paragraph 15 of Part I of Schedule 1 to the *Regulated Activities Order* (Contracts of general insurance), namely:

(a) a *contract of insurance* against the risks of loss to the *person* insured arising from their having to perform contracts of guarantee entered into by them;

(b) fidelity bonds, performance bonds, administration bonds, bail bonds or customs bonds or similar contracts of guarantee where these are:

  (i) effected or carried out by a *person* not carrying on a banking business;

  (ii) not effected merely incidentally to some other business. carried on by the *person* effecting them; and

  (iii) effected in return for the payment of one or more premiums.

surrender value

(a) where the contract is a contract of life assurance or a contract for an annuity, the amount (including a nil amount) payable by the *firm* or other body issuing the contract on surrender of the *policy*;

(b) where the contract is a *personal pension scheme* or *stakeholder pension scheme*, the amount payable on the transfer of the investor's accrued rights under that contract to another *personal pension scheme* or *stakeholder pension scheme*;

(c) where the contract is a *Holloway sickness policy*, the amount payable by the firm on surrender on or before the *projection date* for the *policy*;
(d) where the contract is for any other matter, the amount payable by the *firm* on the surrender of the *policy*.

swap

a transaction in which two counterparties agree to exchange streams of payments over time according to a predetermined basis or a *contract for differences*.

Swiss general insurance company

(in accordance with article 1(2) of the Financial Services and Markets Act 2000 (Variation of Threshold Conditions) Order 2001 (SI 201/2507)) a *person*:
(a) whose head office is in Switzerland;
(b) who is authorised by the supervisory authority in Switzerland as mentioned in article 7.1 of the *Swiss Treaty Agreement*; and
(c) who is seeking to carry on, or is carrying on, from a branch in the *United Kingdom*, a *regulated activity* consisting of the *effecting* or *carrying out* of *contracts of insurance* of a kind which is subject to that agreement.

Swiss general insurer

a *Swiss general insurance company* which has *permission* to *effect* or *carry out contracts of insurance* of a kind which is subject to the *Swiss Treaty Agreement*.

Swiss Treaty Agreement

the agreement of 10 October 1989 between the European Economic Community and the Swiss Confederation on direct insurance other than life insurance, approved on behalf of the European Economic Community by the Council Decision of 20 June 1999 (No 91/390/EEC).

syndicate

one or more *persons*, to whom a particular syndicate number has been assigned by or under the authority of the *Council*, *carrying out* or *effecting contracts of insurance* written at Lloyd's.

syndicate actuary

an *actuary* appointed to a *syndicate* as required by SUP 4.6.9R(1).

syndicate assets

assets managed by or at the direction of a *managing agent* in respect of *insurance business* carried on through a *syndicate* and overseas business regulatory deposits funded from those assets.

syndicate ICA

the capital assessment performed by a *managing agent* under *the overall Pillar 2 rule*, GENPRU 1.5.1R(1), INSPRU 7.1 and INSPRU 1.1.57R(1) in respect of each *syndicate* managed by it.

syndicate year

a year of account of a *syndicate*.

synthetic cash

a position in a *derivative* that offsets an exposure in property to the point where that exposure has effectively been neutralised, and the effect of the combined holding of both property and the position in the *derivative* is the same as if the *authorised fund* had received or stood to receive the value of the property in cash.

synthetic future

(a) a synthetic bought future, that is, a bought call *option* coupled with a written put *option*; or
(b) a synthetic sold future, that is, a bought put *option* coupled with a written call *option*;

provided that in either case the two *options*:
(i) are bought and written, whether simultaneously or not, on a single *eligible derivatives* market;
(ii) relate to the same underlying *security* or other asset;
(iii) give the purchasers of the *options* the same rights of exercise (whether at the same price or not); and
(iv) will expire together, if not exercised.

synthetic securitisation

(in accordance with Article 4(38) of the *Banking Consolidation Directive* (Definitions)) a *securitisation* (within the meaning of paragraph (2) of the definition of securitisation) where the *tranching* is achieved by the use of credit derivatives or guarantees, and the pool of *exposures* is not removed from the balance sheet of the *originator*.

SYSC

the part of the *Handbook* in High Level Standards which has the title Senior Management Arrangements, Systems and Controls.

systematic internaliser investment firm

which, on an organised, frequent and systematic basis, *deals on own account* by executing *client* orders outside a *regulated market* or an *MTF*.

[Note: article 4(1)(7) of *MiFID*]

systems and controls function

any of *controlled functions* 13 to 15 in the *table of controlled functions*.

table of controlled functions

the table of controlled functions in *SUP* 10.4.5R.

takeover bid

an offer, as the term is used in the *Takeover Code*, or any other similar conduct governed by that code.

Takeover Code

the City Code on Takeovers and Mergers issued by the *Takeover Panel*.

takeover or related operation

(a) any transaction falling within paragraph 3(b) (Companies, Transactions and Persons subject to the Code) of the introduction to the *Takeover Code* and, for this purpose, an offer for non-voting, non-equity share capital is to be regarded as falling within the *Takeover Code* even if not required by rule 15 of that Code;

(b) any transaction which would have fallen within (a) were it not for the fact that the company which is the subject of the transaction does not satisfy the tests set out in paragraph 3(a) (Companies, Transactions and Persons subject to the Code) of the introduction to the *Takeover Code*;

(c) any offer, transaction or arrangement relating to the purchase of *securities* with a view to establishing or increasing a strategic holding of a *person*, or of a *person* together with his *associates*, in the *securities* concerned;

(d) any transaction or arrangement entered into in contemplation or furtherance of any offer, transaction or arrangement falling within (a) to (c); and

(e) any transaction or arrangement entered into by way of defence or protection against any offer, transaction or arrangement falling within (a) to (d) which has taken place or which is contemplated.

Takeover Panel

the Panel on Takeovers and Mergers.

target

(in LR) the subject of a *class 1 transaction*.

tariff of charges

a list of all the charges (including amounts) that are payable on a *home finance transaction*, including the reason for, and amount of, each charge.

tax exempt policy

any contract of assurance, offered or issued by a *friendly society*, which is tax exempt life or endowment business as defined in section 466 (2) of the Income and Corporation Taxes Act 1988.

TC

the Training and Competence sourcebook.

TD implementing Directive

Commission Directive implementing Directive 2004/109/EC of the European Parliament and of the Council laying down rules for the harmonisation of transparency requirements in relation to information about issuers whose securities are admitted to trading on a regulated market (No. 2006/xx/EC);

technical provision

a technical provision established:

(a) for *general insurance business*, in accordance with INSPRU 1.1.12R; and

(b) for *long-term insurance business*, in accordance with INSPRU 1.1.16R.

tender offer

(in LR) an offer by a *company* to purchase all or some of a *class* of its *listed equity securities* or *preference shares* at a maximum or fixed price (that may be established by means of a formula) that is:

(a) communicated to all holders of that *class* by means of a *circular* or advertisement in two national newspapers;
(b) open to all holders of that *class* on the same terms for at least seven days; and
(c) open for acceptance by all holders of that *class* pro rata to their existing holdings.

terminating event

(as defined in article 2(1) of the *compensation transitionals order*) in relation to applications made under an *investment business compensation scheme*, the withdrawal, discontinuance or rejection of the application, or its determination by a final payment of. compensation to the applicant.

terms of business

a statement, in a *durable medium*, of the terms and conditions on which a *firm* will carry on a *regulated activity* with or for a *client* or *retail customer*.

third-country banking and investment group

a *banking and investment group* that meets the following conditions:

(a) it is headed by:
    (i) a *credit institution*; or
    (ii) an *asset management company*; or
    (iii) an *investment firm*; or
    (iv) a *financial holding company*;
    that has its head office outside the *EEA*; and
(b) it is not part of a wider *EEA banking and investment group*.

third country banking or investment services undertaking

(in *BIPRU*) an *institution*, a *financial institution* or an *asset management company* in a *non-EEA state*.

third country BIPRU firm

an *overseas firm* that:

(a) is not an *EEA firm*;
(b) has its head office outside the *EEA*; and
(c) would be a *BIPRU firm* if it had been a *UK domestic firm*, it had carried on all its business in the *United Kingdom* and had obtained whatever authorisations for doing so are required under the *Act*.

third country BIPRU 730k firm

an *overseas firm* that:

(a) is not an *EEA firm*;
(b) has its head office outside the *EEA*; and
(c) would be a *BIPRU 730k firm* if it had been a *UK domestic firm*, it had carried on all its business in the *United Kingdom* and had obtained whatever authorisations for doing so are required under the *Act*.

third country competent authority

a *regulatory body* of a state or territory that is not an *EEA State*.

third-country competent authority

the authority of a country or territory which is not an *EEA State* that is empowered by law or regulation to supervise (whether on an individual or group-wide basis) *regulated entities*.

third-country financial conglomerate

a *financial conglomerate* that is of a type that falls under Article 5(3) of the *Financial Groups Directive*, which in summary is a *financial conglomerate* headed by a *regulated entity* or a *mixed financial holding company* that has its head office outside the *EEA*.

third-country group

a *third-country financial conglomerate* or a *third-country banking and investment group*.

third country investment firm

a *firm* which would be a *MiFID investment firm* if it had its head office in the *EEA*;

third country issuer

an issuer which does not have its registered office in the *EEA*.

[Note: article 2(4) of the *MiFID Regulation*]

Third Life Directive

the Council Directive of 10 November 1992 on the coordination of laws, etc, and amending Directives 79/267/EEC and 90/619/EEC (No 92/96/EEC).

Third Non-Life Directive

the Council Directive of 18 June 1992 on the coordination of laws, etc, and amending Directives 73/239/EEC and 88/357/EEC (No 92/49/EEC).

third party processor

(1) A firm ("Firm A") which carries on *home finance activities* or insurance mediation activities other than *advising* on *life policies*, or both, for another firm (or an appointed representative) ("Firm B") under a properly documented outsourcing agreement, the terms of which provide that when Firm A carries on any of these activities ("the outsourced activities") for Firm B:
   (a) Firm A acts only on the instructions of Firm B;
   (b) in any communication with a *customer*, Firm A represents itself as Firm B;
   (c) Firm A undertakes to co-operate fully with Firm B in relation to any complaints arising from Firm A's performance of the outsourced activities, even if the complaint is made after Firm A has ceased to carry on the outsourced activities for Firm B; and
   (d) Firm B accepts full responsibility for the acts and omissions of Firm A when carrying on the outsourced activities and must pay any redress due to the *customer*;

   or an *appointed representative* ("Firm A") which carries on such activities for its *principal* ("Firm B") under such an agreement.

(2) A firm ("Firm C") which carries on *home finance activities* or insurance mediation activities other than *advising* on *life policies*, or both, for a third party processor within (1) ("Firm A"), where:
   (a) the *outsourcing* agreement between Firm A and the *firm* for which Firm A is carrying on outsourced activities ("Firm B") authorises Firm A to outsource some or all of those activities to third parties which are *firms*, and identifies Firm C by name as one of those third parties;
   (b) under the *outsourcing* agreement between Firm A and Firm B, Firm B accepts full responsibility for the acts and omissions of Firm C when carrying on the activities which are outsourced to it by Firm A; and
   (c) there is a properly documented *outsourcing* agreement between Firm C and Firm A the terms of which provide that when Firm C carries on any of the outsourced activities:
      (i) Firm C acts only on the instructions of Firm A;
      (ii) in any communication with a customer, Firm C represents itself as Firm B; and
      (iii) Firm C undertakes to co-operate fully with Firm A and Firm B in relation to any complaints arising from Firm C's performance of the outsourced activities, even if the complaint is made after Firm C has ceased to carry on the outsourced activities for Firm A.

third party prospectus

a communication made by a *firm* if the communication is a prospectus that has been drawn up and published in accordance with the *Prospectus Directive* and the *firm* is not responsible under that directive for the information given in the prospectus.

[**Note:** recital 52 to the *MiFID implementing Directive*]

threshold condition

(in relation to a *regulated activity*) any of the conditions set out in or under Schedule 6 to the *Act* (Threshold conditions), including the additional conditions in the Financial Services and Markets Act 2000(Variation of Threshold Conditions) Order 2001 (SI 2001/2507) (see *COND*).

tied agent

a *person* who, under the full and unconditional responsibility of only one *MiFID investment firm* or *third country investment firm* on whose behalf it acts, promotes *investment services* and/or *ancillary services* to *clients* or prospective *clients*, receives and transmits instructions or orders from the *client* in respect of *investment services* or *financial instruments*, places *financial instruments* and/or provides *advice* to *clients* or prospective *clients* in respect of those *financial instruments* or *investment services*.

[Note: article 4(1)(25) of *MiFID*]

tied product

a product, other than *linked borrowing* or a *linked deposit*, that a *customer* is obliged to purchase through a *mortgage lender* or *reversion provider* as a condition of taking out a *regulated mortgage contract* or *home reversion plan* with that *firm*.

tier one capital

(1) (in *ELM*) the tier one capital of an *ELMI* calculated in accordance with *ELM* 2.4 (Calculation of initial capital and own funds).

(2) (in BIPRU, GENPRU and INSPRU) an item of capital that is specified in stages A (Core tier one capital), B (Perpetual non-cumulative preference shares) or C (Innovative tier one capital) of the *capital resources table*.

tier one capital resources

the sum calculated at stage F of the calculation in the *capital resources table* (Total tier one capital after deductions).

tier one instrument

an item of capital that falls into GENPRU 2.2.62R (Tier one capital: General) and is eligible to form part of a *firm's tier one capital resources.*

tier three capital

an item of capital that is *upper tier three capital* or *lower tier three capital.*

tier three capital resources

the sum calculated at stage Q of the *capital resources table* (Total tier three capital).

tier three instrument

an item of capital that falls into GENPRU 2.2.242R (Tier three capital: upper tier three capital resources) and is eligible to form part of a *firm's upper tier three capital resources.*

tier two capital

(1) (in *ELM*) the tier two capital of an *ELMI* calculated in accordance with *ELM* 2.4 (Calculation of initial capital and own funds).

(2) (in BIPRU, GENPRU and INSPRU) an item of capital that is specified in stages G (Upper tier two capital) or H (Lower tier two capital) of the *capital resources table.*

tier two capital resources

the sum calculated at stage I (Total tier two capital) of the calculation in the *capital resources table.*

tier two instrument

capital instrument that meets the conditions in GENPRU 2.2.159R (General conditions for eligibility as tier two capital instruments) or GENPRU 2.2.177R (Upper tier two capital: General) and is eligible to form part of a *firm's tier two capital resources.*

time-scheduled buy-back programme

(as defined in Article 2 of the *Buy-back and Stabilisation Regulation*) a *buy-back programme* where the dates and quantities of *securities* to be traded during the time period of the programme are set out at the time of the public disclosure of the *buy-back programme.*

tontines

(in relation to a *class of contract of insurance*) tontines as specified in paragraph V of Part II of Schedule 1 to the *Regulated Activities Order* (Contracts of long-term insurance).

top-up cover

cover provided by the *compensation scheme* for *claims* against an *incoming EEA firm* (which is a *credit institution*, an *IMD insurance intermediary*, an *IMD reinsurance intermediary* or a *MiFID investment firm* or a *UCITS management company*) in relation to the *firm's passported activities* and in addition to, or due to the absence of, any cover provided by the *firm's Home State* compensation scheme (see *COMP* 14 (Participation by EEA firms)).

top-up permission

a *Part IV permission* given to an *incoming EEA firm*, an *incoming Treaty firm* or a *UCITS qualifier.*

total amount payable

the *total charge for credit* plus the total amount of credit advanced.

total charge for credit

the total of the charges (determined as at the date of making the contract) specified in MCOB 10.4.2R as applying in relation to the *secured lending* but excluding the charges specified in MCOB 10.4.4R.

total exposure

(in relation to a *counterparty* or *group of connected clients* and a *person* or in relation to a *person* and its *connected counterparties*) all that *person's exposures* to that *counterparty* or *group of connected clients* or to that *person's connected counterparties* or the total amount of those *exposures.*

total group tier one capital

the sum calculated at stage A of the calculation in INSPRU6.1.43R.

total group tier two capital

the sum calculated at stage B of the calculation in INSPRU 6.1.43R.

TPF rules

the rules and guidance in *COBS* 20.2.1R to *COBS* 20.2.39G and *COBS* 20.2.51R to *COBS* 20.2.57G.

tradable renewable energy credit

an allowance, licence, permit, right, note, unit, credit, asset, certificate or instrument (the "credit") where:

(a) the credit confers or may result in a benefit or advantage to its holder or someone else; and

(b) the credit, or the benefit or advantage in (a), is linked to the supply, distribution or consumption of energy derived from renewable sources by the holder of the credit or someone else.

trade confirmation information

the information identified in column 1 of the table in *COBS* 16 Ann 1R.

traded life policy

a *life policy* which is to be or has been assigned for value by the *policyholder* to another *person*.

trading book

(1) (in UPRU) in relation to a *firm's* business or *exposures*, means:

(a) its proprietary positions in financial instruments:

(i) which are held for resale and/or are taken on by the *firm* with the intention of benefiting in the short term from actual and/or expected differences between their buying and selling prices or from other price or interest-rate variations;

(ii) arising from matched principal broking;

(iii) taken in order to hedge other elements of the trading book;

(b) *exposures* due to unsettled securities transactions, free deliveries, *OTC derivative* instruments, repurchase agreements and securities lending transactions based on securities included in (a)(i) to (iii) above, reverse repurchase agreements and securities borrowing transactions based on securities included in (a)(i) to (iii) above; and

(c) fees, commission, interest and dividends, and margin on exchange-traded derivatives which are directly related to the items included in (a) and (b) above.

(2) (in BIPRU and GENPRU and in relation to a *BIPRU firm*) has the meaning in BIPRU 1.2 (Definition of the trading book) which is in summary, all that *firm's positions* in *CRD financial instruments* and *commodities* held either with trading intent or in order to hedge other elements of the *trading book*, and which are either free of any restrictive covenants on their tradability or able to be hedged.

(3) (in BIPRU and GENPRU and in relation to a *person* other than a *BIPRU firm*) has the meaning in (2) with references to a *firm* replaced by ones to a *person*.

trading book concentration risk excess

has the meaning in BIPRU 10.5.20R (How to calculate the concentration risk capital component).

trading book policy statement

has the meaning in BIPRU 1.2.29R (Trading book policy statements) which is in summary a single document of a *person* recording the policies and procedures referred to in BIPRU 1.2.26R and BIPRU 1.2.27R.

trading book systems and controls rules

GENPRU 1.3.13R(2) to (3) (General requirements: Methods of valuation and systems and controls), GENPRU 1.3.14R to GENPRU 1.3.16R (Marking to market), GENPRU 1.3.17R to GENPRU 1.3.25R (Marking to model), GENPRU 1.3.26R to GENPRU 1.3.28R (Independent price verification), GENPRU 1.3.30R to GENPRU 1.3.33R (Valuation adjustments or reserves), GENPRU 2.2.86R (Core tier one capital: profit and loss account and other reserves: Losses arising from valuation adjustments) and GENPRU 2.2.248R to GENPRU 2.2.249R (Tier three capital: lower tier three capital resources).

trading day

(1) (in *MAR* 7 (Disclosure of information on certain trades undertaken outside a regulated market or MTF) and *SUP* 17 (Transaction reporting)) in relation to post-trade information to be made public about a share under *MAR* 7.2.10EU, any day of normal trading in a share on a *trading venue* in the *relevant liquid market* for this share.

[**Note:** article 4(2) of the *MiFID Regulation*]

(2) other than in (1), a day included in the calendar of trading days published by *FSA* at www.fsa.gov.uk.

trading information

information of the following kinds:

(1) that *investments* of a particular kind have been or are to be acquired or disposed of, or that their acquisition or disposal is under consideration or the subject of negotiation; or

(2) that *investments* of a particular kind have not been or are not to be acquired or disposed of; or

(3) the quantity of *investments* acquired or disposed of or to be acquired or disposed of or whose acquisition or disposal is under consideration or the subject of negotiation; or

(4) the price (or range of prices) at which *investments* have been or are to be acquired or disposed of or the price (or range of prices) at which *investments* whose acquisition or disposal is under consideration or the subject of negotiation may be acquired or disposed of; or

(5) the identity of the *persons* involved or likely to be involved in any capacity in an acquisition or disposal.

trading plan

(in LR) a written pln between a restricted person and an independent third party which sets out a strategy for the acquisition and/or disposal of *securities* by a specified person and:

(a) specifies the amount of *securities* to be dealt in and the price at which the date on which the *securities* are to be dealt in; or

(b) gives discretion to that independent third party to make trading decisions about the amount of *securities* to be dealt in and the price at which and the date on which the securities are to be dealt in; or

(c) includes a written formula or algorithm, or computer program, for determining the amount of *securities* to be dealt in and the price at which and the date on which the securities are to be dealt in.

trading venue

a *regulated market*, *MTF* or *systematic internaliser* acting in its capacity as such, and, where appropriate, a system outside the *EU* with similar functions to a *regulated market* or *MTF*.

[Note: article 2(8) of the *MiFID Regulation*]

traditional securitisation

(in accordance with Article 4(37) of the *Banking Consolidation Directive* (Definitions)) a *securitisation* (within the meaning of paragraph (2) of the definition of securitisation) involving the economic transfer of the *exposures* being *securitised* to a *securitisation special purpose entity* which issues securities; and so that:

(a) this must be accomplished by the transfer of ownership of the *securitised exposures* from the *originator* or through subparticipation; and

(b) the securities issued do not represent payment obligations of the *originator*.

tranche

(in accordance with Article 4(39) of the *Banking Consolidation Directive* (Definitions) and in relation to a *securitisation* within the meaning of paragraph (2) of the definition of securitisation) a contractually established segment of the credit risk associated with an *exposure* or number of *exposures*, where a position in the segment entails a risk of credit loss greater than or less than a position of the same amount in each other such segment, without taking account of credit protection provided by third parties directly to the holders of positions in the segment or in other segments.

transaction

only the purchase and sale of a *financial instrument*. For the purposes of the *MiFID Regulation*, excluding Chapter II, this does not include:

(a) *securities financing transactions*; or

(b) the exercise of options or covered warrants; or

(c) primary market transactions (such as issuance allotment or subscription) in *financial instruments* falling within Article 4(1)(18)(a) and (b) of *MiFID*.

[Note: article 5 of the *MiFID Regulation*]

transaction report

a report of a transaction which meets the requirements of *SUP* 17.4.1R and *SUP* 17.4.2R (Information to appear in transaction reports).

transaction-specific advice

advice on investments:

(a) given in connection with:

(i) *dealing in investments as principal*; or
(ii) *dealing in investments as agent*; or
(iii) acting as an *arranger*; or
(b) with a view to carrying on any such activities;

with or for the *market counterparty* to whom the advice is given.

transfer value analysis

[deleted]

transferable securities

(as defined in section 102A of the *Act*) anything which is a transferable security for the purposes of *MiFID*, other than money-market instruments for the purposes of that directive which have a maturity of less than 12 months.

transferable security

(1) (in PR and LR) (as defined in section 102A of the *Act*) anything which is a transferable security for the purposes of *MiFID*, other than money-market instruments for the purposes of that directive which have a maturity of less than 12 months.
(2) (in COLL) an *investment* within COLL 5.2.7R (Transferable securities) in relation to schemes falling under COLL 5.
(3) those classes of securities which are negotiable on the capital market, with the exception of instruments of payment, such as:
  (a) shares in companies and other securities equivalent to shares in companies, partnerships or other entities, and depositary receipts in respect of shares;
  (b) bonds or other forms of securitised debt, including depositary receipts in respect of such securities; and
  (c) any other securities giving the right to acquire or sell any such transferable securities or giving rise to a cash settlement determined by reference to transferable securities, currencies, interest rates or yields, *commodities* or other indices or measures.

[Note: article 4(1)(18) of *MiFID*]

transitional complaints scheme

the arrangements made by the *FSA* for the investigation of complaints against the *FSA* and each of *PIA, IMRO* and *SFA* arising in connection with the carrying out of their functions under the Financial Services Act 1986 and the Banking Act 1987.

Transparency Directive/TD

the European Parliament and Council Directive on the harmonisation of transparency requirements in relation to information about issuers whose securities are admitted to trading on a regulated market or through a comparable mechanism for the disclosure of information under national requirements of a Member State concerning the dissemination of information (No 2004/109/EC).

Transparency rules

(in accordance with section 73A(6) of *the Act*) *rules* relating to the notification and dissemination of information in respect *of issuers* of *transferable securities* and relating to major shareholdings.

treasury shares

share which meet the conditions set out in paragraphs (1) and (b) of subsection 724(5) of the Companies Act 2006.

Treaty

the Treaty on the Functioning of the European Union.

Treaty activity

(as defined in section 417(1) of the *Act* (Definitions)) an activity carried on under a *permission* obtained in accordance with Schedule 4 to the *Act* (Treaty Rights).

Treaty firm

(as defined in paragraph 1 of Schedule 4 to the *Act* (Treaty Rights)) a *person*:
(a) whose head office is situated in an *EEA State* (its "*Home State*") other than the *United Kingdom*; and
(b) which is recognised under the law of that State as its national.

Treaty right

the entitlement of a *Treaty firm* to qualify for *authorisation* under Schedule 4 to the Act (Treaty Rights).

Tribunal

the *Financial Services and Markets Tribunal*.

Part II FSA Handbook Materials

trust deed

(1) (in LR) a trust deed or equivalent document securing or constituting *debt securities*.
(2) (in COLL) the deed referred to in COLL 3.2.3R (The trust deed for AUTs) together with any deed expressed to be supplemental to it, made between the *manager* and the trustee (or, in the case of a *recognised scheme* that is a *unit trust scheme*, the *instrument constituting the scheme* as amended from time to time).

trust scheme rules

rules in COLL made by the *FSA* under section 247(1) of the *Act* (Trust scheme rules) in relation to:
(a) the constitution, management and operation of AUTs;
(b) the powers, duties, rights and liabilities of the *manager* and *trustee* of any such *scheme*;
(c) the rights and duties of the *participants* in any such *scheme*; and
(d) the winding up of any such *scheme*.

trustee

(in accordance with section 237(2) of the *Act* (Other definitions)) (in relation to a *unit trust scheme*) the *person* holding the property in question on trust for the *participants*.

trustee firm

a *firm* which is not an *OPS firm* and which is acting as a:
(a) trustee; or
(b) personal representative.

turnover

(in relation to a *financial instrument*) means the sum of the results of multiplying the number of units of that instrument exchanged between buyers and sellers in a defined period of time, pursuant to *transactions* taking place on a *trading venue* or otherwise, by the unit price applicable to each such *transaction*.

[Note: article 2(9) of the *MiFID Regulation*]

Type P projection

(in relation to a *pension scheme* or a *stakeholder pension scheme*) a *projection* in real value terms based on prices where the period to the *projection date* is one year or more.

Type Q projection

(in relation to *pension scheme* or a *stakeholder pension scheme*) a *projection* in real value terms based on earnings where the period to the *projection date* is one year or more.

UCITS Directive

the Council Directive of 20 December 1985 on the coordination of laws, regulations and administrative provisions relating to undertakings for collective investment in transferable securities (UCITS) (No 85/611/EEC), as amended.

UCITS eligible assets Directive

Commission Directive 2007/16/EC implementing Council Directive 85/611/EEC on the coordination of laws, regulations and administrative provisions relating to undertakings for collective investment in transferable securities (UCITS) as regards the clarification of certain definitions.

UCITS firm

a *firm* which:
(a) is the *operator* of a *UCITS scheme* including where in addition the *firm* is also the *operator* of a *collective investment scheme* which is not a *UCITS scheme*; and
(b) does not have a Part IV *permission* to carry on any *regulated activities* other than those which are in connection with, or for the purposes of, such schemes.

UCITS investment firm

a *firm* which:
(1) is the *operator* of a *UCITS scheme* (whether or not it is also the operator of other schemes); and
(2) has a *Part IV permission* to *manage investments* where:
 (a) the *investments managed* include one or more of the instruments listed in Section C of Annex 1 to *MiFID*; and
 (b) the *permission* extends to activities permitted by article 5(3) of the *UCITS Directive* as well as those permitted by article 5(2).

UCITS management company

(1) (except in relation to *MiFID business*) a *firm* which is either:
 (a) a *UCITS firm*; or

(b) a *UCITS investment firm*.

(2) (in relation to *MiFID business*) a management company as defined in the *UCITS Directive*.

[Note: article 4 (1)(24) of *MiFID*]

UCITS qualifier

a *firm* (other than an *EEA UCITS management company*) which:

(a) for the time being is an *operator*, *trustee* or *depositary* of a *scheme* which is a *recognised scheme* under section 264 of the *ACT*; and

(b) is an *authorised person* as a result of paragraph 1(1) of Schedule 5 to the *Act* (Persons Concerned in Collective Investment Schemes);

a reference to a firm as a *UCITS qualifier* applies in relation to the carrying on by the *firm* of activities for which it has *permission* in that capacity.

UCITS scheme

(a) an *authorised fund* whose *instrument constituting the scheme* contains a statement that it is a *UCITS scheme*; or

(b) an *umbrella* that is a *UCITS scheme* each of whose *sub-funds* would be a *UCITS scheme* if it had a separate *authorisation order*;

unless:

(c) the *scheme* raises capital without promoting the *sale* of its *units* to the public within the *EEA* or any part of it; or 42

(d) the *scheme's units*, under its *trust deed* or its *instrument constituting the scheme*, may be sold only to the public in non-EEA States.

UK

United Kingdom.

UK bank

a *bank* which is a *body corporate* or *partnership* formed under the law of any part of the *United Kingdom*.

UK consolidated group

(in *ELM*) (in relation to an *ELMI*) the *consolidated sub-group* of:

(a) the *ELMI's UK financial parent undertaking*; or

(b) (if the *ELMI* has no *UK financial parent undertaking* and the *ELMI* is a *UK domestic firm*) the *ELMI*;

as established in accordance with *ELM 7* (Consolidated financial supervision).

UK consolidation group

has the meaning in BIPRU 8.2.4R (Definition of UK consolidation group), which is in summary the group that is identified as a *UK consolidation group* in accordance with the decision tree in BIPRU 8 Annex 1R (Decision tree identifying a UK consolidation group); in each case only *persons* included under BIPRU 8.5 (Basis of consolidation) are included in the *UK consolidation group*.

UK-deposit insurer

a *non-EEA insurer* that has made a deposit in the *United Kingdom* under article 23 of the *First Non-Life Directive* in accordance with article 26 of that Directive or under article 51 of the *Consolidated Life Directive* in accordance with article 56 of that Directive.

UK DLG by modification

a DLG by modification (firm level) in which each member is a UK ILAS BIPRU firm. A firm with a UK DLG by modification cannot also have a non-UK DLG by modification (firm level).

UK domestic firm

a *firm* that has its registered office (or, if it has no registered office, its head office) in the *United Kingdom*.

UK ECA recipient

[deleted]

UK financial parent undertaking

(in *ELM*) (in relation to an *ELMI*) the same thing as *EEA financial parent undertaking* except that references to another *EEA State* are replaced with ones to the *United Kingdom*.

UK financial sector company

a company that is a:

(a) *UK bank*; or

Part II FSA Handbook Materials

(b) *UK insurer*; or
(c) *UK* incorporated *parent undertaking* of a company referred to in (a) or (b) where the main business of the *group* to which the *parent undertaking* and the company belong is financial services.

UK firm

(1) (except in *REC*) (as defined in paragraph 10 of Schedule 3 to the *Act* (EEA Passport Rights)) a *person* whose head office is in the *United Kingdom* and who has an *EEA right* to carry on activity in an *EEA State* other than the *United Kingdom*.
(2) (in *REC*) means an *investment firm* or *credit institution* which has a *Part IV permission* to carry on one or more *regulated activities*.

UK group large exposure

(in *ELM*) (in relation to an *ELMI*) the same thing as the *ELMI's EEA group large exposure* except that references to its *EEA consolidated group* are replaced with references to its *UK consolidated group*, as established in accordance with *ELM* 7 (Consolidated financial. supervision).

UK group risk own funds

(in *ELM*) the same thing as *EEA group risk own funds*, subject to the adjustments required by *ELM* 7.5.5R (UK group risk own funds and UK group risk own funds requirement).

UK group risk own funds requirement

(in *ELM*) the same thing as *EEA group risk own funds requirement*, subject to the adjustments required by *ELM* 7.5.5R (UK group risk own funds and UK group risk own funds requirement).

UK ILAS BIPRU firm

an *ILAS BIPRU firm* which has its registered office (or, if it does not have a registered office, its head office) in the *United Kingdom*.

UK insurance intermediary

a *UK domestic firm* which has *Part IV permission* to carry on *insurance mediation activity* but no other *regulated activity*.

UK insurer

an *insurer*, other than a *pure reinsurer* or a *non-directive insurer*, whose head office is in the *United Kingdom*.

UK integrated group

(in relation to a *firm*) all *undertakings* which, in relation to the *firm*, satisfy the conditions set out in BIPRU 10.8.4R (Definition of UK integrated group).

UK ISPV

an *ISPV* with a *Part IV permission* to *effect* or *carry out contracts of insurance*.

UK lead regulated firm

a UK firm that:
(a) is not part of a group that is subject to consolidated supervision by the *FSA* or any other *regulatory body*; or
(b) is part of a group that is subject to consolidated supervision by the *FSA* and that group is not part of a wider group that is subject to consolidated supervision by a *regulatory body* other than the *FSA*.

For the purposes of this definition:
(c) Consolidated supervision of a group of *persons* means supervision of the adequacy of financial and other resources of that group on a consolidated basis. For example, this includes supervision under *BIPRU* 8 (Group risk consolidation).
(d) It is not relevant whether or not any supervision by another *regulatory body* has been assessed as equivalent under the *CRD* or the *Financial Groups Directive*.
(e) If the group is a *UK consolidation group* or *financial conglomerate* of which the *FSA* is lead regulator that is headed by an *undertaking* that is not itself the *subsidiary undertaking* of another *undertaking* the *firm* is a 'UK lead regulated firm'.

This definition is not related to the defined term *lead regulated firm*.

UK MCR

the *MCR* calculated in accordance with INSPRU 1.5.44R by a *non-EEA direct insurer* (except a *UK-deposit insurer*, an *EEA-deposit insurer* or a *Swiss general insurer*) in relation to business carried on by the *firm* in the *United Kingdom*.

UK MiFID investment firm

A *MiFID investment firm* whose *Home State* is the *United Kingdom* (this may include a natural *person* provided the conditions set out in *Article* 4(1)(1) of *MiFID* are satisfied).

UK parent financial holding company in a Member State

a *parent financial holding company in a Member State* where the *EEA State* in question is the *United Kingdom*.

UK pure reinsurer

a *pure reinsurer* whose head office is in the *United Kingdom*.

UK RCH

an *RCH* that is not an *ROCH*.

UK recognised body

a *UK RIE* or *UK RCH*.

UK RIE

an *RIE* that is not an *ROIE*.

UKLA

(1) (except in relation to a part of the *Handbook*) the *FSA* acting in its capacity as the *competent authority* for the purposes of Part VI of the *Act* (Official Listing).
(2) (in relation to a part of the *Handbook*) the United Kingdom Listing Authority sourcebook.

ultimate EEA insurance parent undertaking

an *EEA insurance parent undertaking* that is not itself the *subsidiary undertaking* of another *EEA insurance parent undertaking*.

ultimate insurance parent undertaking

an *insurance parent undertaking* that is not itself the *subsidiary undertaking* of another *insurance parent undertaking*.

ultimate parent undertaking

(in relation to an *insurer*) a *parent undertaking* of the *insurer* that is not itself the *subsidiary undertaking* of another *undertaking*.

umbrella

(in FFES, COLL and COBS), a *collective investment scheme* whose *instrument constituting the scheme* provides for such pooling as is mentioned in section 235(3)(a) of the Act (Collective investment schemes) in relation to separate parts of the *scheme property* and whose *unitholders* are entitled to exchange rights in one part for rights in another.

umbrella collective investment scheme

(in PR) (as defined in the *PD Regulation*) a collective investment undertaking invested in one or more collective investment undertakings, the asset of which is composed of separate class(es) or designation(s) of securities.*underlying instrument* (in LR) (in relation to *securitised derivatives*) means either:

(a) if the *securitised derivative* is an *option* or *debt security* with the characteristics of an *option*, any of the underlying investments listed in article 83 of the *Regulated Activities Order*; or
(b) if the *securitised derivative* is a *contract for differences* or *debt security* with the characteristics of a *contract for differences*, any factor by reference to which a profit or loss under article 85 of the *Regulated Activities Order* can be calculated.

unauthorised person

a *person* who is not an *authorised person*.

unauthorised reversion provider

a *person* who carries on, or proposes to carry on, the activity specified in article 63B(1) of the *Regulated Activities Order* which is entering into a *home reversion plan* as plan provider, and who does not have *permission* for, and is not an *exempt person* in relation to, *entering into a home reversion plan*.

unauthorised SRB agreement provider

a *person* who carries on, or proposes to carry on, the activity specified in article 63J(1) of the *Regulated Activities Order* which is entering into a *regulated sale and rent back agreement* as agreement provider, and who does not have *permission* for, and is not an *exempt person* in relation to, *entering into a regulated sale and rent back agreement*; and in this definition references to an agreement provider include a *person* who acquires obligations or rights under a *regulated sale and rent back agreement*.

undertaking

(as defined in section 1161(1) of the Companies Act 2006 (Meaning of "undertaking" and related expressions)):

(a) a *body corporate or partnership*; or
(b) an unincorporated association carrying on a trade or business, with or without a view to profit.

underwrite

(for the purposes of BIPRU 7 (Market risk)) to undertake a firm commitment to buy a specified quantity of new *securities* on a given date and at a given price if no other has purchased or acquired them; and so that:
(a) new is defined in BIPRU 7.8.12R (New securities);
(b) a *firm* still underwrites *securities* at a time before the exact quantity of *securities* being underwritten or their price has been determined if it is committed at that time to underwrite them when the quantity and price is fixed;
(c) (in the case of provisions of the *Handbook* that distinguish between *underwriting* and sub-*underwriting*) *underwriting* does not include sub-*underwriting*; and
(d) (in any other case) *underwriting* includes sub-*underwriting*.

underwriting agent

a *firm* permitted by the *Council* to act as an underwriting agent at Lloyd's.

underwriting capacity of a Lloyd's syndicate

the *investment*, specified in article 86(1) of the *Regulated Activities Order*, which is the underwriting capacity of a *syndicate*.

underwriting member

a *person* admitted to the *Society* as an underwriting member.

unearned premium

the amount set aside by a *firm* at the end of its *financial year* out of *premiums* in respect of risks to be borne by the *firm* after the end of the *financial year* under *contracts of insurance* entered into before the end of that year.

Unfair Terms Regulations Unit

the Unfair Terms in Consumer Contracts Regulations 1999 (SI 1999/2083), as amended by SI 2001/1186 and SI 2001/3649.the investment, specified in article 81 of the *Regulated Activities Order* (Units in a collective investment scheme) and defined in section 237(2) of the *Act* (Other definitions)), which is the right or interest (however described) of the *participants* in a *collective investment scheme*; this includes:
(a) (in relation to an *AUT*) a unit representing the rights or interests of the *unit holders* in the *AUT*;
(b) (in relation to an *ICVC*) a *share* in the *ICVC*.

UNFCOG

the Unfair Contract Terms Regulatory Guide.

unfunded credit protection

(in accordance with Article 4(32) of the *Banking Consolidation Directive* (Definitions)) a technique of *credit risk mitigation* where the reduction of the credit risk on the *exposure* of an *undertaking* derives from the undertaking of a third party to pay an amount in the event of the default of the borrower or on the occurrence of other specified events.

unit trust scheme

(as defined in section 237(1) of the Act (Other definitions)) a *collective investment scheme* under which the property in question is held on trust for the *participants*.

units of a collective investment scheme

(in PR) (as defined in Article 2.1(p) of the *prospectus directive*) securities issued by a collective investment undertaking as representing the rights of the participants in such an undertaking over its assets.

United Kingdom

England and Wales, Scotland and Northern Ireland (but not the Channel Islands or the Isle of Man).

unitholder

(in CIS) (in relation to an *AUT*, and subject to *CIS* 11.3.2R (Special meaning of unitholder)):
(a) (in relation to a *unit* represented by a *bearer certificate*) the *person* who holds the *bearer certificate*;
(b) (in relation to a *unit* that is not represented by a *bearer certificate*) the *person* whose name is entered on the *register* in relation to that *unit*.

(in COLL)
(a) (in relation to an *ICVC* or an *AUT* as appropriate, and subject to COLL 4.4.4R (Special meaning of unitholder in COLL 4.4)):
  (i) (in relation to a *unit* which is represented by a *bearer certificate*) the *person* who holds that certificate; or
  (ii) (in a relation a *unit* that is not represented by a *bearer certificate*) the *person* whose name is entered on the *register* in relation to that *unit*; or
(b) (in relation to a *unit* in a *collective investment scheme* not within (a)):
  (i) the holder of a *bearer certificate* representing that *unit; or*
  (ii) the *person* who is entered on the *register* of the *scheme* as the holder of that *unit*.

unitisation

arrangements for a newly formed *AUT* under which:
(a) the whole or part of the property of a *body corporate* (or a *collective investment scheme*) becomes the first property to be held on the trusts of the *AUT*; and
(b) the *holders* of:
  (i) *shares* in the *body corporate* being wound up; or
  (ii) *units* in the *collective investment scheme*, theproperty of which is being transferred; become the first *participants* in the *AUT*.

unpaid initial fund

part of the *initial fund* of a *mutual* which the *mutual* is prevented from including in its *tier one capital resources* as *permanent share capital* by reason of GENPRU 2.2.64R because it is not fully paid.

unrated position

(for the purposes of BIPRU 9 (Securitisation), in accordance with Part 1 of Annex IX of the *Banking Consolidation Directive* (Securitisation definitions) and in relation to a *securitisation position*) describes a *securitisation position* which does not have an eligible credit assessment by an *eligible ECAI*.

unrecognised scheme

(in *LR*) a *collective investment scheme* which is neither a *recognised scheme* nor a scheme that is constituted as an *authorised unit trust scheme*.

unregulated activity

an activity which is not a *regulated activity*.

unregulated collective investment scheme

a *collective investment scheme* which is not a *regulated collective investment scheme*.

unsecured debt

debt that does not fall within the definition of *secured debt*.

unsecured lending

lending where the *mortgage lender* does not take a mortgage or other form of security in respect of the credit provided to the *customer*.

unsecured pension

(as defined in paragraph 4 of Schedule 28 to the Finance Act 2004):
(a) a *short-term annuity*; or
(b) an *income withdrawal*.

unsolicited real time financial promotion

(in accordance with article 8 of the *Financial Promotion Order*) a *real time financial promotion* which is not a *solicited real time financial promotion*.

unsolicited real time qualifying credit promotion

[deleted]

upper tier three capital

an item of capital that is specified in stage O of the *capital resources table* (Upper tier three).

upper tier three capital resources

the sum calculated at stage O of the *capital resources table* (Upper tier three).

upper tier three instrument

an item of capital that meets the conditions in GENPRU 2.2.242R (Tier three capital: upper tier three capital resources) and is eligible to form part of a *firm's upper tier three capital resources*.

upper tier two capital

(1) (in ELM) the upper tier two capital of an ELMI calculated in. accordance with *ELM* 2.4 (Calculation of initial capital and own funds).

(2) (in BIPRU, GENPRU and INSPRU) an item of capital that is specified in stage G of the *capital resources table* (Upper tier two capital).

upper tier two capital resources

the sum calculated at stage G of the calculation in the *capital resources table* (Upper tier two capital).

upper tier two instrument

a *capital instrument* that meets the conditions in GENPRU 2.2.177R (Upper tier two capital: General) and is eligible to form part of a *firm's upper tier two capital resources.*

UPRU

the Prudential sourcebook for UCITS Firms.

valuation point

(in COLL) a valuation point fixed by the *authorised fund manager* for the purpose of COLL 6.3.4R (Valuation points), COLL 8.5.9R (Valuation, pricing and dealing).

value at risk

(in relation to risk modelling or estimation) the measure of risk described in BIPRU 7.10.146R (Requirement to use value at risk methodology).

VaR

value at risk.

VaR measure

an estimate by a *VaR model* of the worst expected loss on a portfolio resulting from market movements over a period of time with a given confidence level.

VaR model

a value at risk model as described in BIPRU 7.10 (Use of a Value at Risk Model).

VaR model approach

one of the following:

(a) the approach to calculating part of the *market risk capital requirement* set out in BIPRU 7.10 (Use of a value at risk model);

(b) (where the approach in (a) is being applied on a consolidated basis) the method in (a) as applied on a consolidated basis in accordance with BIPRU 8 (Group risk — consolidation); or

(c) when the reference is to the rules of or administered by a *regulatory body* other than the *FSA*, whatever corresponds to the approach in (a) or (b), as the case may be, under those rules.

VaR model permission

an *Article 129 implementing measure*, a *requirement* or a *waiver* that requires a *BIPRU firm* or an *institution* to use the *VaR model approach* on a solo basis or, if the context requires, a consolidated basis.

VaR number

has the meaning in BIPRU 7.10.115R (Capital calculations: General) which in summary is (in relation to a *business day* and a *VaR model*) the *VaR measure*, in respect of the previous *business day's* close-ofbusiness *positions* in products coming within the scope of the *VaR model permission*, calculated by the *VaR model* and in accordance with BIPRU 7.10 (Use of a Value at Risk Model) and any methodology set out in the *VaR model permission.*

VaR specific risk minimum requirements

BIPRU 7.10.46R to BIPRU 7.10.52R (Model standards: Risk factors: Specific risk) and BIPRU 7.10.107R (Backtesting: Specific risk backtesting).

vehicle

any motor vehicle intended for travel on land and propelled by mechanical power, but not running on rails, and any trailer whether or not coupled.

[**Note:** article 1(1) of Council Directive 72/166/EEC (First Motor Insurance Directive)]

vendor consideration placing

(in LR) a marketing, by or on behalf of vendors, of *securities* that have been allotted as consideration for an acquisition.

venture capital business

the business of carrying on any of:

(a) investing in, *advising on investments* which are, *managing investments* which are, *arranging (bringing about) transactions* in, or *making arrangements with a view to transactions in, venture capital investments;*

(b) *advising on investments or managing investments* in relation to portfolios, or *establishing, operating or winding up collective investment schemes,* where the portfolios or *collective investment schemes* (apart from funds awaiting investment) invest only in *venture capital investments*;

(c) any *custody* activities provided in connection with the activities in (a) and (b);

(d) any related *ancillary activities.*

venture capital contact

(when a *firm* carries on *regulated activities* with or for a *person* in the course of or as a result of carrying on *venture capital business*) that *person* in connection with that *regulated activity* if:

(a) the *firm* does not behave in a way towards that *person* which might reasonably be *expected* to lead that *person* to believe that he is being treated as a *client*; and

(b) the *firm* clearly indicates to that *person* that the *firm*:
   (i) is not acting for him; and
   (ii) will not be responsible to him for providing protections afforded to *clients* of the *firm* or be advising him on the relevant transaction.

venture capital firm

a *firm* whose *permission* includes a *requirement* that it must not conduct *designated investment business* other than *venture capital business.*

venture capital investment

a *designated investment* which, at the time the investment is made, is:

(a) in a new or developing *company* or venture; or

(b) in a management buy-out or buy-in; or

(c) made as a means of financing the investee *company* or venture and accompanied by a right of consultation, or rights to information, or board representation, or management rights; or

(d) acquired with a view to, or in order to, facilitate a transaction falling within (a) to (c).

venture capital trust

(in LR) a *company* which is, or which is seeking to become, approved as a venture capital trust under section 842AA of the Income and Corporation Taxes Act 1988.

verified

(in *IPRU(INV)* 13) where interim net profits are to be included in a *firm's* capital resources, checked by an external auditor who has undertaken at least to:

(a) satisfy himself that the figures forming the basis of the interim profits have been properly extracted from the underlying accounting records;

(b) review the accounting policies used in calculating the interim profits so as to obtain comfort that they are consistent with those normally adopted by the *firm* in drawing up its *annual financial statements* and are in accordance with the accounting principles set out in *IPRU(INV)* 13;

(c) perform analytical procedures on the result to date, including comparisons of actual performance to date with budget and with the results of prior period(s);

(d) discuss with management the overall performance and financial *position* of the *firm*;

(e) obtain adequate comfort that the implications of current and prospective litigation, all known claims and commitments, changes in business activities and provisioning for bad and doubtful debts have been properly taken into account in arriving at the interim profits; and

(f) follow up problem areas of which he is already aware in the course of auditing the *firm's* financial statements, a copy of whose report asserting that the interim net profits are reasonably stated has been submitted to the *FSA* (although this does not apply to *exempt CAD firms*).

version 1 credit union

a *credit union* whose *Part IV permission* includes a *requirement* (whether for all or for particular purposes) that it must not lend more. than £15,000, or such lesser amount as may be specified, in excess of a member's shareholding;

in this definition a "member's shareholding" means any shares held by a member of the *credit union* in accordance with sections (95 and 7 of the Credit Unions Act 1979.

version 2 credit union

a *credit union* which is not a *version 1 credit union.*

VJ participant

a *person* subject to the *Voluntary Jurisdiction* by contract.

volatility risk

the potential loss due to fluctuations in implied *option* volatilities.

Voluntary Jurisdiction

the jurisdiction of the *Financial Ombudsman Service* in which *persons* (whether *authorised* or *unauthorised*) participate by contract.

voting power

(in SUP 11 (Controllers and close links) and SUP 16 (Reporting requirements) (in accordance with section 422 of the *Act*):

(a) includes, in relation to a *person* ("H"):
  (i) voting power held by a third party with whom H has concluded an agreement, which obliges H and the third party to adopt, by concerted exercise of the voting power they hold, a lasting common policy towards the management of the *undertaking* in question;
  (ii) voting power held by a third party under an agreement concluded with H providing for the temporary transfer for consideration of the voting power in question;
  (iii) voting power attaching to *shares* which are lodged as collateral with H, provided that H controls the voting power and declares an intention to exercise it;
  (iv) voting power attaching to *shares* in which H has a life interest;
  (v) voting power which is held, or may be exercised within the meaning of subparagraphs (i) to (iv), by a subsidiary *undertaking* of H;
  (vi) voting power attaching to *shares* deposited with H which H has discretion to exercise in the absence of specific instructions from the shareholders;
  (vii) voting power held in the name of a third party on behalf of H;
  (viii) voting power which H may exercise as a proxy where H has discretion about the exercise of the voting power in the absence of specific instructions from the shareholders; and

(b) in relation to an *undertaking* which does not have general meetings at which matters are decided by the exercise of voting rights, the right under the constitution of the *undertaking* to direct the overall policy of the *undertaking* or alter the terms of its constitution.

waiver

a direction waiving or modifying a *rule*, given by the *FSA* under sections (9148, 250 or 294 of the *Act* (Waiver or modification of rules) or regulation 7 of the *OEIC Regulations* (Modification or waiver of FSA rules) (see *SUP* 8 and *REC* 3.3).

warning notice

a notice issued by the *FSA* in accordance with section 387 of the *Act* (Warning notices).

warrant

(1) (except in COLL) the *investment*, specified in article 79 of the *Regulated Activities Order* (Instruments giving entitlements to investments), which is in summary: a warrant or other instrument entitling the holder to subscribe for a *share, debenture* or *government and public security.*

(2) (in COLL) an *investment* in (1) and any other *transferable security* (not being a nil paid or partly paid *security*) which is:
  (i) listed on an eligible securities market; and
  (ii) akin to an investment within (1) in that it involves a down payment by the then holder and a right later to surrender the instrument and to pay more money in return for a further transferable security.

weather derivative

a *contract for differences* where the index or other factor in question is a climatic variable.

website conditions

the following conditions:

(1) the provision of information by means of a website must be appropriate to the context in which the business between the *firm* and the *client* is, or is to be, carried on (that is, there is evidence that the *client* has regular access to the internet, such as the provision by the *client* of an e-mail address for the purposes of the carrying on of that business);

(2) the *client* must specifically consent to the provision of that information in that form;

(3) the *client* must be notified electronically of the address of the website, and the place on the website where the information may be accessed;

(4) the information must be up to date; and

(5) the information must be accessible continuously by means of that website for such period of time as the *client* may reasonably need to inspect it.

[Note: article 3 of the *MiFID implementing Directive*]

welfare trust

any scheme or arrangement, not being an *occupational pension scheme*, that is comprised in one or more instruments or agreements and operates as a benevolent fund so as to provide benefits, at the discretion of the trustees and to which the beneficiaries have no contractual rights.

whole-firm liquidity modification

a modification to the *overall liquidity adequacy rule* of the kind described in BIPRU 12.8.22 G.

whole life assurance

a *contract of insurance* which, disregarding any benefit payable on surrender, secures a capital sum only on death or either on death or on disability, but does not include a term assurance.

wholesale depositor

a *person* who is:

(a) a *credit institution*; or

(b) a *large company*; or

(c) a *large mutual association* which is:

 (i) a *firm*; or

 (ii) *an overseas financial services institution*; or

 (iii) a *collective investment scheme* or an operator or trustee of a *collective investment scheme;* or

 (iv) a pension or retirement fund, or a trustee of such a fund (except a trustee of a small self-administered scheme or an occupational scheme of an employer which is not a *large company* or a *large partnership*); or

(d) a supranational institution, government or central administrative authority; or

(e) a provincial, regional, local or municipal authority; or

(f) a *body corporate* in the same *group* as the *person* with whom the *deposit* is made.

wholesale market broker

a *firm* when carrying out the activities of *name-passing broker*, or acting on a matched principal basis, with or for *market counterparties*.

wholesale only bank

(in relation to *firm type* in SUP 16.10 (Confirmation of *standing data*)) a *bank* with *permission* to accept *deposits* from *wholesale depositors* only.

wider integrated group

(in relation to a *firm*) has the meaning in BIPRU 10.9.5R (Definition of wider integrated group), which is in summary each *concentration risk group counterparty* of the *firm* that is not a member of the *firm's UK integrated group* but satisfies all the conditions for membership of the *firm's UK integrated group* except for BIPRU 10.8.4R(4) (Establishment in the *United Kingdom*).

wider integrated group waiver

a *waiver* that has the result of requiring a *firm* to apply BIPRU 10.9 (Wider Integrated Group) or, if the context requires, BIPRU 8.9.16R to BIPRU 8.9.24R (Wider integrated groups for consolidation purposes) and the other *rules* in BIPRU 8.9 (Consolidated concentration risk requirements) that relate to those *rules*.

with-profits actuary function

controlled function CF12A in the *table of controlled functions*, described more fully in *SUP* 4.3.16AR and *SUP* 10.7.17AR.

with-profits actuary

an *actuary* appointed to perform the *with-profits actuary function*.

with-profits assets

assets that match liabilities in respect of *with-profits insurance business* or represent a *with-profits surplus*.

with-profits benefits reserve

(in relation to a *with-profits fund*) the with-profits benefits reserve for the *with-profits fund* calculated in accordance with the *rules* in INSPRU 1.3.116R to INSPRU 1.3.135G.

with-profits business

any business of an *insurer* that may affect the amount or value of the assets comprising a *with-profits fund*.

with-profits committee

a committee of the *governing body*, including non-executive members of the *governing body* and possibly some external non-directors with appropriate skills and experience.

with-profits fund

(1) (except in *INSPRU*):
  (a) a *long-term insurance fund* (or that part of such a fund) in which *policyholders* are eligible to participate in any *established surplus*; and
  (b) where it is an *insurer's* usual practice to restrict *policyholders'* participation in any *established surplus* to that arising from only a part of the fund (or part fund) falling within (a), that part (or that part of the part fund).

(2) for the purposes of INSPRU, a *long-term insurance fund* in which *policyholders* are eligible to participate in any *established surplus*.

with-profits insurance business

the business of *effecting* or *carrying out with-profits insurance contracts*.

with-profits insurance capital component

the capital component for *with-profits insurance business* of a *realistic basis life firm* calculated in accordance with INSPRU 1.3.

with-profits insurance contract

a *long-term insurance contract* which provides for the *policyholder* to be eligible to participate in any surplus arising on the whole of, or any part of, the *insurer's long-term insurance business*.

with-profits insurance liabilities

insurance liabilities arising from *with-profits insurance business*.

with-profits policy

a contract falling within a *class* of *long-term insurance business* which is eligible to participate in any part of any *established surplus*.

with-profits policyholder

a *policyholder* under a *with-profits policy*.

with-profits practices

the with-profits practices that a *firm* must establish, maintain and record under *COBS* 20.3 (Principles and Practices of Financial Management).

with-profits principles

the with-profits principles that a *firm* must establish, maintain and record under *COBS* 20.3 (Principles and Practices of Financial Management).

working day

(1) (in PR and COMP) (as defined in section 103 of the *Act*) any day other than a Saturday, a Sunday, Christmas Day, Good Friday or a day which is a bank holiday under the Banking and Financial Dealings Act 1971 in any part of the *United Kingdom*.

(2) (in relation to an *underwriter* and for the purpose of BIPRU but not for the purpose of the definition of *working day 0*) the number of *business days* after *working day 0* specified by the provision in question so that, for example, *working day* one means the *business day* following *working day 0*.

working day 0

has the meaning in BIPRU 7.8.23R (Working day 0), which is in summary (in relation to an *underwriter*) the *business day* on which a *firm* that is *underwriting* or sub-*underwriting* becomes unconditionally committed to accepting a known quantity of *securities* at a specified price.

WPICC

with-profits insurance capital component.

wrapper

a *PEP*, *ISA* or *CTF*.

zero-specific-risk security

a notional debt *security* used, for the purpose of calculating *PRR*, to represent the interest rate *general market risk* arising from certain *derivative* and forward transactions as specified in BIPRU 7.2 (Interest rate PRR).

zero weighted asset

(in *ELM*) an *investment* falling into *ELM* 3.3.8R (Liquid assets).

zillmerising

the method known by that name for modifying the *net premium* reserve method of valuing a *long-term insurance contract* by increasing the part of the future *premiums* for which credit is taken so as to allow for initial expenses.

Zone A credit institution

(in *ELM*) a *full BCD credit institution* or *a full credit institution* that has its registered office (or, if it has no registered office, its head office) in a *Zone A country* that is not an *EEA State*.

Zone A country

(a) any *EEA State*;
(b) all other countries which are full members of the *OECD;* and
(c) those countries which have concluded special lending arrangements with the International Monetary Fund (IMF) associated with the Fund's general arrangements to borrow (GAB),

save that any country falling with (a), (b) or (c) which reschedules its external sovereign debt is precluded from Zone A for a period of five years

PRINCIPLES FOR BUSINESSES (PRIN)

NOTES

Up to date as at 22 February 2010. For later amendments please see www.fsa.gov.uk.

CONTENTS

PRIN 1—Introduction . . . [2002]
PRIN 2—The Principles . . . [2003]
PRIN 3—Rules about application . . . [2004]
PRIN 4—Principles: MiFID business . . . [2004A]
PRIN TP 1—Transitional provisions . . . [2005]
PRIN Sch 1—Record Keeping Requirements . . . [2006]
PRIN Sch 2—Notification requirements . . . [2007]
PRIN Sch 3—Fees and other required payments . . . [2008]
PRIN Sch 4—Powers Exercised . . . [2009]
PRIN Sch 5—Rights of action for damages . . . [2010]
PRIN Sch 6—Rules that can be waived . . . [2011]

CHAPTER 1
INTRODUCTION

1.1 Application and purpose

Application

[2002]
1.1.1 **[G]** The *Principles* (see PRIN 2) apply in whole or in part to every *firm*. The application of the *Principles* is modified for *firms* conducting *MiFID business incoming EEA firms, incoming Treaty firms* and *UCITS qualifiers*. PRIN 3 (Rules about application) specifies to whom, to what and where the *Principles* apply.

Purpose

1.1.2 **[G]** The *Principles* are a general statement of the fundamental obligations of *firms* under the *regulatory system*. This includes provisions which implement the *Single Market Directives*. They derive their authority from the *FSA's* rule-making powers as set out in the *Act* and reflect the *regulatory objectives*.

1.1.3 **[G]** [deleted].

Link to fit and proper standard in the threshold conditions

1.1.4 **[G]** In substance, the *Principles* express the main dimensions of the "fit and proper" standard set for *firms* in *threshold condition* 5 (Suitability), although they do not derive their authority from that standard or exhaust its implications. Being ready, willing and organised to abide by the *Principles* is therefore a critical factor in applications for *Part IV permission*, and breaching the *Principles* may call into question whether a *firm* with *Part IV permission* is still fit and proper.

Taking group activities into account

1.1.5 **[G]** *Principles* 3 (Management and control), 4 (Financial prudence) and (in so far as it relates to disclosing to the *FSA*) 11 (Relations with regulators) take into account the activities of members of a *firm's group*. This does not mean that, for example, inadequacy of a *group* member's risk management systems or resources will automatically lead to a *firm* contravening *Principle* 3 or 4. Rather, the potential impact of a *group* member's activities (and, for example, risk management systems operating on a *group* basis) will be relevant in determining the adequacy of the *firm's* risk management systems or resources respectively.

Standards in markets outside the United Kingdom

1.1.6 **[G]** As set out in PRIN 3.3, *Principles* 1 (Integrity), 2 (Skill, care and diligence) and 3 (Management and control) apply to world-wide activities in a *prudential context*. *Principle* 5 (Market conduct) applies to world-wide activities which might have a negative effect on confidence in the *financial system* operating in the *United Kingdom*. In considering whether to take regulatory action under these *Principles* in relation to activities carried on outside the *United Kingdom*, the *FSA* will take into account the standards expected in the market in which the *firm* is operating. Principle 11 (Relations with regulators) applies to world-wide activities; in considering whether to take regulatory action under *Principle* 11 in relation to cooperation with an overseas regulator, the *FSA* will have regard to the extent of, and limits to, the duties owed by the *firm* to that regulator. (*Principle* 4 (Financial prudence) also applies to world-wide activities.)

1.1.6A **[G]** PRIN 4 (Principles: MiFID Business) provides *guidance* on the application of the *Principles* to *MiFID business*.

Consequences of breaching the Principles

1.1.7 **[G]** Breaching a *Principle* makes a *firm* liable to disciplinary sanctions. In determining whether a *Principle* has been breached it is necessary to look to the standard of conduct required by the *Principle* in question. Under each of the *Principles* the onus will be on the *FSA* to show that a *firm* has been at fault in some way. What constitutes "fault" varies between different *Principles*. Under *Principle* 1 (Integrity), for example, the *FSA* would need to demonstrate a lack of integrity in the conduct of a *firm's* business. Under *Principle* 2 (Skill, care and diligence) a *firm* would be in breach if it was shown to have failed to act with due skill, care and diligence in the conduct of its business. Similarly, under *Principle* 3 (Management and control) a *firm* would not be in breach simply because it failed to control or prevent unforeseeable risks; but a breach would occur if the *firm* had failed to take reasonable care to organise and control its affairs responsibly or effectively.

1.1.8 **[G]** The *Principles* are also relevant to the *FSA's* powers of information-gathering, to vary a *firm's Part IV permission*, and of investigation and intervention, and provide a basis on which the *FSA* may apply to a court for an *injunction* or restitution order or require a *firm* to make restitution. However, the *Principles* do not give rise to actions for damages by a *private person* (see PRIN 3.4.4R).

1.1.9 **[G]** Some of the other *rules* and *guidance* in the *Handbook* deal with the bearing of the *Principles* upon particular circumstances. However, since the *Principles* are also designed as a general statement of regulatory requirements applicable in new or unforeseen situations, and in situations in which there is no need for *guidance*, the *FSA's* other *rules* and *guidance* should not be viewed as exhausting the implications of the *Principles* themselves.

1.1.10 **[G]** Responsibilities of product providers and distributors under the Principles *RPPD* contains *guidance* on the responsibilities of providers and distributors for the fair treatment of *customers* under the *Principles*.

1.2 Clients and the Principles

Characteristics of the client

1.2.1 **[G]** *Principles* 6 (Customers' interests), 7 (Communications with clients), 8 (Conflicts of interest), 9 (Customers: relationships of trust) and 10 (Clients' assets) impose requirements on *firms* expressly in relation to their *clients* or *customers*. These requirements depend, in part, on the characteristics of the *client* or *customer* concerned. This is because what is "due regard" (in *Principles* 6 and 7), "fairly" (in *Principles* 6 and 8), "clear, fair and not misleading" (in *Principle* 7), "reasonable care" (in *Principle* 9) or "adequate" (in *Principle* 10) will, of course, depend on those characteristics. For example, the information needs of a general insurance broker will be different from those of a retail general insurance *policyholder*.

Approach to client categorisation

1.2.2 **[G]** *Principles* 6, 8 and 9 and parts of *Principle* 7, as qualified by PRIN 3.4.1R, apply only in relation to *customers* (that is, *clients* which are not *eligible counterparties*). The approach that a *firm* needs to take regarding categorisation of *clients* into *customers* and *eligible counterparties* will depend on whether the *firm* is carrying on *designated investment business* or other activities, as described in PRIN 1.2.3G and PRIN 1.2.4G.

1.2.3 **[G]**

(1) In relation to the carrying on of *designated investment business*, a *firm's* categorisation of a *client* under the *COBS client* categorisation chapter (COBS 3) will be applicable for the purposes of *Principles* 6, 7, 8 and 9.

(2) The *person* to whom a *firm* gives *basic advice* will be a *retail client* for all purposes, including the purposes of *Principles* 6, 7, 8 and 9.

(3) In relation to carrying on activities other than *designated investment business* (for example, *general insurance business* or *accepting deposits*) the *firm* may choose to comply with *Principles* 6, 7, 8 and 9 as if all its *clients* were *customers*. Alternatively, it may choose to distinguish between *eligible counterparties* and *customers* in complying with those *Principles*. If it chooses to make such a distinction, it must comply with PRIN 1 Ann 1R in determining whether that *client* is an *eligible counterparty* (see PRIN 3.4.2R). In doing so, the requirements in SYSC will apply, including the requirement to make and retain adequate records.

(4) In relation to carrying on activities that fall within both (1) and (3) (for example, mixed *designated investment business* and *accepting deposits*), a *firm's* categorisation of a *client* under the *COBS client* categorisation chapter (COBS 3) will be applicable for the purposes of *Principles* 6, 7, 8 and 9.

Classification: other activities

1.2.4 **[G]** [deleted]

1.2.5 **[G]** [deleted]

1.2.6 **[G]** If the *person* with or for whom the *firm* is carrying on an activity is acting through an agent, the ability of the *firm* to treat the agent as its *client* under COBS 2.4.3R (Agent as client) will not be available. For example, if a general *insurer* is effecting a *general insurance contract* through a general insurance broker who is acting as agent for a disclosed *policyholder*, the *policyholder* will be a *client* of the *firm* and the *firm* must comply with the *Principles* accordingly.

PRIN 1 Annex 1 [R]
Non-designated investment business – clients that a firm may treat as an eligible counterparty for the purposes of PRIN

1 Ann 1R

1.1 A *firm* may categorise the following types of *client* as an *eligible counterparty* for the purposes of *PRIN*:

(1) a properly constituted government (including a quasi-governmental body or a government agency) of any country or territory;

(2) a central bank or other national monetary authority of any country or territory;

(3) a supranational whose members are either countries or central banks or national monetary authorities;

(4) a State investment body, or a body charged with, or intervening in, the management of the public debt;

(5) another *firm*, or an *overseas financial services institution*;

(6) any *associate* of a *firm* (except an *OPS firm*), or of an *overseas financial services institution*, if the *firm* or institution consents;

(7) a *client* when he is classified as an *eligible counterparty* in accordance with 1.2; or

(8) a *recognised investment exchange, designated investment exchange, regulated market* or *clearing house*.

1.2 A *firm* may classify a *client* (other than another *firm*, *regulated collective investment scheme*, or an *overseas financial services institution*) as an *eligible counterparty* for the purposes of *PRIN* under 1.1(7) if:

(1) the *client* at the time he is classified is one of the following:

(a) a *body corporate* (including a *limited liability partnership*) which has (or any of whose *holding companies* or *subsidiaries* has) called up share capital of at least £10 million (or its equivalent in any other currency at the relevant time);

(b) a *body corporate* that meets (or any of whose holding companies or subsidiaries meets) two of the following tests:

(i) a balance sheet total of 12.5 million euros (or its equivalent in any other currency at the relevant time);

(ii) a net turnover of 25 million euros (or its equivalent in any other currency at the relevant time);

(iii) an average number of employees during the year of 250;

(c) a local authority or public authority;

(d) a *partnership* or unincorporated association which has net assets of at least £10 million (or its equivalent in any other currency at the relevant time) (and calculated, in the case of a limited *partnership*, without deducting loans owing to any of the *partners*);

(e) a trustee of a trust (other than an *occupational pension scheme*, *SSAS*, *personal pension scheme* or *stakeholder pension scheme*) with assets of at least £10 million (or its equivalent in any other currency), calculated by aggregating the value of the cash and *designated investments* forming part of the trust's assets, but before deducting its liabilities;

(f) a trustee of an *occupational pension scheme* or *SSAS*, or a trustee or operator of a *personal pension scheme* or *stakeholder pension scheme* where the *scheme* has (or has had at any time during the previous two years):
    (i) at least 50 members; and
    (ii) assets under management of not less than £10 million (or its equivalent in any other currency at the relevant time); and

(2) the *firm* has, before commencing business with the *client* on an *eligible counterparty* basis:
  (a) advised the *client* in writing that he is being categorised as an *eligible counterparty* for the purposes of *PRIN*;
  (b) given a written warning to the *client* that he will lose protections under the *regulatory system*;
  (c) for a *client* falling under (1)(a) or (b):
    (i) taken reasonable steps to ensure that the written notices required by (a) and (b) have been delivered to a *person* authorised to take such a decision for the *client*; and
    (ii) not been notified by the *client* that the *client* objects to being classified as an *eligible counterparty*;
  (d) for a *client* falling under (1)(c), (d), (e) or (f):
    (i) taken reasonable steps to ensure that the written notices required by (a) and (b) have been delivered to a *person* authorised to take such a decision for the *client*; and
    (ii) obtained the *client*'s written consent or is otherwise able to demonstrate that consent has been given.

CHAPTER 2
THE PRINCIPLES

2.1 The Principles

[2003]
2.1.1 **[R]**

The Principles

1 Integrity	A *firm* must conduct its business with integrity.
2 Skill, care and diligence	A *firm* must conduct its business with due skill, care and diligence.
3 Management and control	A *firm* must take reasonable care to organise and control its affairs responsibly and effectively, with adequate risk management systems.
4 Financial prudence	A *firm* must maintain adequate financial resources.
5 Market conduct	A *firm* must observe proper standards of market conduct.
6 Customers' interests	A *firm* must pay due regard to the interests of its *customers* and treat them fairly.
7 Communications with clients	A *firm* must pay due regard to the information needs of its *clients*, and communicate information to them in a way which is clear, fair and not misleading.
8 Conflicts of interest	A *firm* must manage conflicts of interest fairly, both between itself and its *customers* and between a *customer* and another *client*.
9 Customers: relationships of trust	A *firm* must take reasonable care to ensure the suitability of its advice and discretionary decisions for any *customer* who is entitled to rely upon its judgment.
10 Clients' assets	A *firm* must arrange adequate protection for *clients'* assets when it is responsible for them.
11 Relations with regulators	A *firm* must deal with its regulators in an open and cooperative way, and must disclose to the *FSA* appropriately anything relating to the *firm* of which the *FSA* would reasonably expect notice.

CHAPTER 3
RULES ABOUT APPLICATION

3.1 Who?

[2004]
3.1.1 **[R]** *PRIN* applies to every *firm*, except that:
(1) for an *incoming EEA firm* or an *incoming Treaty firm*, the *Principles* apply only in so far as responsibility for the matter in question is not reserved by an *EU* instrument to the *firm's Home State regulator*;
(2) for an *incoming EEA firm* which is a *BCD credit institution* without a *top-up permission*, *Principle* 4 applies only in relation to the liquidity of a *branch* established in the *United Kingdom*;
(3) for an *incoming EEA firm* which has *permission* only for *cross border services* and which does not carry on *regulated activities* in the *United Kingdom*, the *Principles* do not apply;
(4) for a *UCITS qualifier*, only *Principles* 1, 2, 3, 7 and 9 apply, and only with respect to the activities in PRIN 3.2.2R (Communication and approval of financial promotions);
(5) *PRIN* does not apply to an *incoming ECA provider* acting as such.

3.1.2 **[G]** SYSC App 1, COBS 1 Ann 1 and the territorial *guidance* in PERG 13.6 all contain *guidance* that is relevant to the reservation of responsibility to a *Home State regulator* referred to in PRIN 3.1.1R (1).

3.1.3 **[G]** PRIN 3.1.1R (2) reflects article 41 of the *Banking Consolidation Directive* which provides that the *Host State regulator* retains responsibility in cooperation with the *Home State regulator* for the supervision of the liquidity of a *branch* of a *BCD credit institution*.

3.1.4 **[G]** PRIN 3.1.1R (3) puts *incoming EEA firms* on an equal footing with *unauthorised overseas persons* who utilise the overseas persons exclusions in article 72 of the *Regulated Activities Order*.

3.1.5 **[G]** PRIN 3.1.1R (4) reflects section 266 of the *Act* (Disapplication of rules).

3.1.6 **[R]** A *firm* will not be subject to a *Principle* to the extent that it would be contrary to the *UK's* obligations under an *EU* Instrument.

3.1.7 **[G]** PRIN 4 provides specific *guidance* on the application of the *Principles* for *MiFID business*.

3.1.8 **[G]** The Principles will not apply to the extent that they purport to impose an obligation which is inconsistent with the *Payment Services Directive*. For example, there may be circumstances in which *Principle* 6 may be limited by the harmonised conduct of business obligations applied by the *Payment Services Directive* to *credit institutions* and *e-money issuers* (see Parts 5 and 6 of the *Payment Services Regulations*).

3.2 What?

3.2.1 **[R]** *PRIN* applies with respect to the carrying on of:
(1) *regulated activities*;
(2) activities that constitute *dealing in investments as principal*, disregarding the exclusion in article 15 of the *Regulated Activities Order* (Absence of holding out etc); and
(3) *ancillary activities* in relation to *designated investment business*, *regulated home finance activity*, *insurance mediation activity* and *accepting deposits*.

3.2.2 **[R]** *PRIN* also applies with respect to the *communication* and *approval* of *financial promotions* which:
(1) if *communicated* by an *unauthorised person* without *approval* would contravene section 21(1) of the *Act* (Restrictions on financial promotion); and
(2) may be *communicated* by a *firm* without contravening section 238(1) of the *Act* (Restrictions on promotion of collective investment schemes).

3.2.3 **[R]** *Principles* 3, 4 and (in so far as it relates to disclosing to the *FSA*) 11 (and this chapter) also:
(1) apply with respect to the carrying on of *unregulated activities* (for *Principle* 3 this is only in a *prudential context*); and
(2) take into account any activity of other members of a *group* of which the *firm* is a member.

3.3 Where?

3.3.1 **[R]** Territorial application of the Principles

Principle	Territorial application
Principles 1, 2 and 3	in a *prudential context*, apply with respect to activities wherever they are carried on; otherwise, apply with respect to activities carried on from an establishment maintained by the *firm* (or its *appointed representative*) in the *United Kingdom* unless another applicable *rule* which is relevant to the activity has a wider territorial scope, in which case the *Principle* applies with that wider scope in relation to the activity described in that *rule*.
Principle 4	applies with respect to activities wherever they are carried on.
Principle 5	if the activities have, or might reasonably be regarded as likely to have, a negative effect on confidence in the *financial system* operating in the *United Kingdom*, applies with respect to activities wherever they are carried on; otherwise, applies with respect to activities carried on from an establishment maintained by the *firm* (or its *appointed representative*) in the *United Kingdom*.
Principles 6, 7, 8, 9 and 10	Principle 8, in a prudential context, applies with respect to activities wherever they are carried on; otherwise apply with respect to activities carried on from an establishment maintained by the *firm* (or its *appointed representative*) in the *United Kingdom* unless another applicable *rule* which is relevant to the activity has a wider territorial scope, in which case the *Principle* applies with that wider scope in relation to the activity described in that *rule*.
Principle 11	applies with respect to activities wherever they are carried on.

3.3.2 **[G]** [deleted]

3.4 General

Clients and the Principles

3.4.1 **[R]** Although *Principle* 7 refers to *clients*, the only requirement of *Principle* 7 relating to *eligible counterparties* is that a *firm* must communicate information to *eligible counterparties* in a way that is not misleading.

3.4.2 **[R]** For the purposes of *PRIN*, a *firm* intending to carry on, or carrying on, activities that do not involve *designated investment business*, may treat a *client* as an *eligible counterparty* in accordance with PRIN 1 Ann 1R.

3.4.3 **[G]**

(1) COBS 3 (Client categorisation) applies to a *firm* intending to conduct, or conducting, *designated investment business* (other than giving *basic advice*) and *ancillary activities* relating to *designated investment business*. Any *client* categorisation established in relation to such business will be applicable for the purposes of *Principles* 6, 7, 8 and 9.

(2) The *person* to whom a *firm* gives *basic advice* will be a *retail client* for all purposes including the purposes of *Principles* 6, 7, 8 and 9.

Actions for damages

3.4.4 **[R]** A contravention of the *rules* in *PRIN* does not give rise to a right of action by a *private person* under section 150 of the *Act* (and each of those *rules* is specified under section 150(2) of the *Act* as a provision giving rise to no such right of action).

Reference to "regulators" in Principle 11

3.4.5 **[R]** Where *Principle* 11 refers to regulators, this means, in addition to the *FSA*, other regulators with recognised jurisdiction in relation to *regulated activities*, whether in the *United Kingdom* or abroad.

CHAPTER 4
PRINCIPLES: MIFID BUSINESS

4.1 Principles: MiFID business

[2004A]
4.1.1 **[G]** PRIN 3.1.6R ensures that the *Principles* do not impose obligations upon *firms* which are inconsistent with an *EU* Instrument. If a *Principle* does purport to impose such an obligation PRIN 3.1.6R disapplies that *Principle* but only to the extent necessary to ensure compliance with European law. This disapplication has practical effect only for certain matters covered by *MiFID*, which are explained in this section.

Where?

4.1.2 **[G]** Under PRIN 3.3.1R, the territorial application of a number of *Principles* to a *UK MiFID investment firm* is extended to the extent that another applicable *rule* which is relevant to an activity has a wider territorial scope. Under PRIN 3.1.1R, the territorial application of a number of *Principles* to an *EEA MiFID investment firm* is narrowed to the extent that responsibility for the matter in question is reserved to the *firm's Home State regulator*. These modifications are relevant to *Principles* 1, 2, 3, 6, 7, 8, 9 and 10. We have added further *guidance* in *PERG* on the ability of a *Host State* to impose conduct of business requirements (see Q67).

4.1.3 **[G]** *Principles* 4, 5 and 11 will have the same scope of territorial application for *MiFID business* as for other business.

What?

4.1.4 **[G]**
(1) Certain requirements under *MiFID* are disapplied for;
  (a) *eligible counterparty business*;
  (b) transactions concluded under the rules governing a *multilateral trading facility* between its members or participants or between the *multilateral trading facility* and its members or participants in relation to the use of the *multilateral trading facility*;
  (c) transactions concluded on a *regulated market* between its members or participants.
(2) Under PRIN 3.1.6R, these disapplications may affect *Principles* 1, 2, 6 and 9. PRIN 3.1.6R applies only to the extent that the application of a *Principle* would be contrary to the *UK's* obligations under a *Single Market Directive* in respect of a particular transaction or matter. In line with *MiFID*, these limitations relating to *eligible counterparty business* and transactions under the rules of a *multilateral trading facility* or on a *regulated market* only apply in relation to a *firm's* conduct of business obligations to its *clients* under *MIFID*. They do not limit the application of those *Principles* in relation to other matters, such as *client* asset protections, systems and controls, prudential requirements and market integrity. Further information about these limitations is contained in COBS 1 Ann 1.
(3) *Principles* 3, 4, 5, 7, 8, 10 and 11 are not limited in this way.

4.1.5 **[G]** Although *Principle* 8 does not apply to *eligible counterparty business*, a *firm* will owe obligations in respect of conflicts of interest set out in SYSC 10 which are wider than those contained in *Principle* 8 in that they apply to *eligible counterparty business*.

TRANSITIONAL PROVISIONS

[2005]
(1) [deleted]

(2) [deleted]

	Material to which the transitional provision applies		Transitional Provision	Transitional Provision: dates in force	Handbook provision: coming into force
1.	PRIN 1 Ann 1R 1.2(2)	R	A *firm* need not comply with PRIN 1 Ann 1R 1.2(2) in relation to an *eligible counterparty* if the *client* was correctly categorised as a *market counterparty* on 31 October 2007 and the *firm* complied with COB 4.1.12R(2) (Large intermediate customer classified as market counterparty).	From 1 November 2007 indefinitely	1 November 2007

Part II FSA Handbook Materials

SCHEDULE 1
RECORD KEEPING REQUIREMENTS

[2006]
1.1 **[G]** There are no record keeping requirements in *PRIN*.

SCHEDULE 2
NOTIFICATION REQUIREMENTS

[2007]
2.1 **[G]** The aim of the guidance in the following table is to give the reader a quick over-all view of the relevant requirements for notification and reporting.

It is not a complete statement of those requirements and should not be relied on as if it were.

2.2 **[G]**

Handbook reference	**Matter to be notified**	**Contents of notification**	**Trigger event**	**Time allowed**
Principle 11 (PRIN 2.1.1R)	Anything relating to the firm of which the FSA would reasonably expect notice	Appropriate disclosure	Anything relating to the firm of which the FSA would reasonably expect notice	Appropriate

SCHEDULE 3
FEES AND OTHER REQUIRED PAYMENTS

[2008]
3.1 **[G]** There are no requirements for fees or other payments in *PRIN*.

SCHEDULE 4
POWERS EXERCISED

[2009]
4.1 **[G]** The following powers and related provision in the Act have been exercised by the FSA to make the rules in *PRIN*:
(1) Section 138 (General rule -making power)
(2) Section 145 (Financial promotion rules)
(3) Section 146 (Money laundering rules)
(4) section 150(2) (Actions for damages)
(5) section 156 (General supplementary powers).

The following powers in the Act have been exercised by the FSA to give the guidance in *PRIN*:

section 157(1) (Guidance).

Section 158A (Guidance on outsourcing by investment firms and credit institutions).

SCHEDULE 5
RIGHTS OF ACTION FOR DAMAGES

[2010]
5.1 **[G]** The table below sets out the *rules* in *PRIN* contravention of which by an *authorised person* may be actionable under section 150 of the *Act* (Actions for damages) by a person who suffers loss as a result of the contravention.

5.2 **[G]** If a 'Yes' appears in the column headed 'For private person?', the rule may be actionable by a '*private person*' under section 150 (or, in certain circumstances, his fiduciary or representative; see article 6(2) and (3)(c) of the Financial Services and Markets Act 2000 (Rights of Action) Regulations 2001 (SI 2001 No 2256)). A 'Yes' in the column headed 'Removed' indicates that the *FSA* has removed the right of action under section 150(2) of the Act. If so, a reference to the *rule* in which it is removed is also given.

5.3 **[G]** The column headed 'For other person?' indicates whether the *rule* may be actionable by a person other than a *private person* (or his fiduciary or representative) under article 6(2) and (3) of those Regulations. If so, an indication of the type of *person* by whom the *rule* may be actionable is given.

5.4 **[G]**

Chapter/ Appendix	**Section/ Annex**	**Paragraph**	**Right of Action**		
			For private person	**Removed?**	**For other person?**
All *rules* in *PRIN*			No	Yes PRIN 3.4.4R	No

SCHEDULE 6
RULES THAT CAN BE WAIVED

[2011]
6.1 **[G]**

The rules in *PRIN* can be waived by the FSA under section 148 of the Act (Modification or waiver of rules).

SENIOR MANAGEMENT ARRANGEMENTS, SYSTEMS AND CONTROLS (SYSC)

NOTES

Up to date as at 22 February 2010. For later amendments please see www.fsa.gov.uk.

CONTENTS

SYSC 1—Application and purpose . . . . . [2012]
SYSC 2—Senior management arrangements . . . . . [2013]
SYSC 3—Systems and Controls . . . . . [2014]
SYSC 4—General organisational requirements . . . . . [2015]
SYSC 5—Employees, agents and other relevant persons . . . . . [2016]
SYSC 6—Compliance, internal audit and financial crime . . . . . [2016A]
SYSC 7—Risk control . . . . . [2016B]
SYSC 8—Outsourcing . . . . . [2016C]
SYSC 9—Record-keeping . . . . . [2016D]
SYSC 10 . . . . . [2016E]
SYSC 11—Liquidity risk systems and controls . . . . . [2016F]
SYSC 12—Group risk systems and controls requirement . . . . . [2016G]
SYSC 13—Operational risk: systems and controls for insurers . . . . . [2016H]
SYSC 14—Prudential risk management and associated systems and controls for insurers [2016I]
SYSC 15—Credit risk management systems and controls . . . . . [2016J]
SYSC 16—Market risk management systems and controls . . . . . [2016K]
SYSC 17—Insurance risk systems and controls . . . . . [2016L]
SYSC 18—Guidance on Public Interest Disclosure Act: whistleblowing . . . . . [2016M]
SYSC 19—Remuneration code . . . . . [2016N]
SYSC TP—Transitional provisions . . . . . [2018]
SYSC Sch 1—Record keeping requirements . . . . . [2019]
SYSC Sch 2—Notification requirements . . . . . [2020]
SYSC Sch 3—Fees and other required payments . . . . . [2021]
SYSC Sch 4—Powers exercised . . . . . [2022]
SYSC Sch 5—Rights of action for damages . . . . . [2023]
SYSC Sch 6—Rules that can be waived . . . . . [2024]

CHAPTER 1
APPLICATION AND PURPOSE

1.1

[deleted]

1.1A Application

[2012]
1.1A.1**[G]** The application of this sourcebook is summarised at a high level in the following table. The detailed application is cut back in SYSC 1 Annex 1 and in the text of each chapter.

Type of firm	**Applicable chapters**
Insurer	Chapters 2, 3, 11 to 18
Managing agent	Chapters 2, 3, 11, 12, 18
Society	Chapters 2, 3, 12, 18
Every other *firm*	Chapters 4 to 12, 18, 19

1.2 Purpose

1.2.1 **[G]** The purposes of *SYSC* are:

(1) to encourage *firms' directors* and *senior managers* to take appropriate practical responsibility for their *firms'* arrangements on matters likely to be of interest to the *FSA* because they impinge on the *FSA's* functions under the *Act*;

(2) to increase certainty by amplifying *Principle* 3, under which a *firm* must "take reasonable care to organise and control its affairs responsibly and effectively, with adequate risk management systems";
(3) to encourage *firms* to vest responsibility for effective and responsible organisation in specific *directors* and *senior managers*; and
(4) to create a common platform of organisational and systems and controls requirements for all *firms*.

1.3

[deleted]

1.4 Application of SYSC 11 to SYSC 19

What?

1.4.1 **[G]** The application of each of chapters SYSC 11 to SYSC 19 is set out in those chapters.

Actions for damages

1.4.2 **[R]** A contravention of a *rule* in SYSC 11 to SYSC 19 does not give rise to a right of action by a *private person* under section 150 of the *Act* (and each of those *rules* is specified under section 150(2) of the *Act* as a provision giving rise to no such right of action).

1 Annex 1
Detailed application of SYSC

Part 1: Application of SYSC 2 and SYSC 3 to an insurer, a managing agent and the Society

Who?

1.1 **[R]** SYSC 2 and SYSC 3 only apply to an insurer, a managing agent and the Society except that:
(1) for an *incoming EEA firm* or an *incoming Treaty firm*:
  (a) SYSC 2.1.1 R and SYSC 2.1.2 G do not apply;
  (b) SYSC 2.1.3 R to SYSC 2.2.3 G apply, but only in relation to allocation of the function in SYSC 2.1.3 R (2) and only in so far as responsibility for the matter in question is not reserved by an *EU* instrument to the *firm's Home State regulator*; and
  (c) SYSC 3 applies, but only in so far as responsibility for the matter in question is not reserved by an *EU* instrument to the *firm's Home State regulator*;
(2) for an *incoming EEA firm* which has *permission* only *for cross border services* and which does not carry on *regulated activities* in the *United Kingdom*, SYSC 2 and SYSC 3 do not apply;
(3) for an *incoming Treaty firm* which has *permission* only for *cross border services* and which does not carry on *regulated activities* in the *United Kingdom*, SYSC 3.2.6AR to SYSC 3.2.6JG do not apply;
(4) for a *sole trader*:
  (a) SYSC 2 applies but only if he employs any *person* who is required to be approved under section 59 of the *Act* (Approval for particular arrangements);
  (b) SYSC 3.2.6IR does not apply if he has no *employees*; and
(5) SYSC 2 and SYSC 3 do not apply to an *incoming ECA provider* acting as such.

1.2 **[G]**
(1) Question 12 in SYSC 2.1.6 G contains guidance on SYSC 1 Annex 1.1.1R (1)(b) and (c).
(2) SYSC 1 Annex 1.1.8 R further restrict the territorial application of SYSC 2 and SYSC 3 for an *incoming EEA firm* or an *incoming Treaty firm*.
(3) SYSC 1 Annex 1.1.1R (3) puts an *incoming EEA firm* on an equal footing with *unauthorised overseas persons* who utilise the overseas persons exclusions in article 72 of the *Regulated Activities Order*.
(4) Further *guidance* on which matters are reserved to a *firm's Home State regulator* can be found at SUP 13A Annex 2G.

What?

1.3 **[R]** SYSC 2 and SYSC 3 apply with respect to the carrying on of:
(1) *Regulated activities*;
(2) Activities that constitute *dealing in investments as principal*, disregarding the exclusion in article 15 of the *Regulated Activities Order* (Absence of holding out etc); and
(3) *Ancillary activities* in relation to *designated investment business*, *home finance activity* and *insurance mediation activity*;

except that SYSC 3.2.6AR to SYSC 3.2.6JG do not apply as described in SYSC 1.Annex 1.1.4 R.

1.4 **[R]** SYSC 3.2.6AR to SYSC 3.2.6JG do not apply:

(1) with respect to the activities described in *SYSC* 1.Annex 1.1.3R(2) and (3); or
(2) in relation to the following *regulated activities*:
(a) *general insurance business*;
(b) *insurance mediation activity* in relation to a *general insurance contract* or *pure protection contract*;
(c) *long-term insurance business* which is outside the *Consolidated Life Directive* (unless it is otherwise one of the *regulated activities* specified in this *rule*);
(d) business relating to contracts which are within the *Regulated Activities Order* only because they fall within paragraph (e) of the definition of "contract of insurance" in article 3 of that Order;
(e)
(i) arranging, by *the Society of Lloyd's*, of deals in *general insurance contracts* written at Lloyd's; and
(ii) *managing the underwriting capacity of a Lloyd's syndicate as a managing agent at Lloyd's*;
(f) *home finance mediation activity* and *administering a home finance transaction*; and
(g) *reversion activity*.

1.5 **[R]** SYSC 2 and SYSC 3, except SYSC 3.2.6AR to SYSC 3.2.6JG, also apply with respect to the *communication* and *approval* of *financial promotions* which:
(1) if *communicated* by an *unauthorised person* without *approval* would contravene section 21(1) of the *Act* (Restrictions on financial promotion); and
(2) may be *communicated* by a *firm* without contravening section 238(1) of the *Act* (Restrictions on promotion of collective investment schemes).

1.6 **[R]** SYSC 2 and 3, except SYSC 3.2.6AR to SYSC 3.2.6JG, also:
(1) apply with respect to the carrying on of *unregulated activities* in a *prudential context*; and
(2) take into account any activity of other members of a *group* of which the *firm* is a member.

1.7 **[G]** SYSC 1.Annex 1.1.6R(2) does not mean that inadequacy of a *group* member's systems and controls will automatically lead to a *firm* contravening, for example, SYSC 3.1.1 R. Rather, the potential impact of a *group* member's activities, including its systems and controls, and any systems and controls that operate on a *group* basis, will be relevant in determining the appropriateness of the *firm's* own systems and controls.

Where?

1.8 **[R]** SYSC 2 and SYSC 3 apply with respect to activities carried on from an establishment maintained by the *firm* (or its *appointed representative* or, where applicable, its *tied agent*) in the *United Kingdom* unless another applicable *rule* which is relevant to the activity has a wider territorial scope, in which case SYSC 2 and SYSC 3 apply with that wider scope in relation to the activity described in that *rule*.

1.9 **[R]** SYSC 2 and SYSC 3, except SYSC 3.2.6AR to SYSC 3.2.6JG, also apply in a *prudential context* to a *UK domestic firm* with respect to activities wherever they are carried on.

1.10 **[R]** SYSC 3, except SYSC 3.2.6AR to SYSC 3.2.6JG, also applies in a *prudential context* to an *overseas firm* (other than an *incoming EEA firm* or an *incoming Treaty firm*) with respect to activities wherever they are carried on.

1.11 **[G]**
(1) In considering whether to take regulatory action under SYSC 2 or SYSC 3 in relation to activities carried on outside the *United Kingdom*, the *FSA* will take into account the standards expected in the market in which the *firm* is operating.
(2) Most of the *rules* in SYSC 3 are linked to other requirements and standards under the *regulatory system* which have their own territorial limitations so that those *SYSC rules* are similarly limited in scope.

Actions for damages

1.12 **[R]** A contravention of the *rules* in SYSC 2 and SYSC 3 does not give rise to a right of action by a *private person* under section 150 of the *Act* (and each of those *rules* is specified under section 150(2) of the *Act* as a provision giving rise to no such right of action).

Part 2: Application of the common platform requirements (SYSC 4 to 10)

Who?

2.1 **[R]** The *common platform requirements* apply to every *firm* apart from an *insurer*, a *managing agent* and the *Society* unless provided otherwise in a specific *rule*.

2.2 **[R]** For an *incoming EEA firm* or an *incoming Treaty firm*:
(1) the *rule* on responsibility of senior personnel (SYSC 4.3) does not apply;
(2) the *common platform requirements* apply only in so far as responsibility for the matter in question is not reserved by an *EU* instrument to the *firm's Home State regulator*;

(3) for an *incoming EEA firm* which has *permission* only for *crossborder services* and which does not carry on *regulated activities* in the *United Kingdom*, the *common platform requirements* do not apply;

(4) for an *incoming Treaty firm* which has *permission* only for *crossborder services* and which does not carry on *regulated activities* in the *United Kingdom*, the *common platform requirements on financial crime* do not apply.

2.3 **[R]** For a *sole trader*:

(1) SYSC 4.3 and 4.4 do not apply as long as he does not employ any *person* who is required to be approved under section 59 of the Act (Approval for particular arrangements);

(2) SYSC 4.1.4R and SYSC 6.3.9R do not apply if he has no *employees*.

2.4 **[R]** For a *UCITS qualifier*:

(1) the *rule* on responsibility of senior personnel (SYSC 4.3) does not apply; and

(2) the *common platform requirements* apply in relation to the *communication* and *approval* of *financial promotions* only as set out in SYSC 1 Annex 1.2.12R.

[**Note:** section 266 of the *Act*.]

2.5 **[R]** For an *authorised professional firm* when carrying on *non-mainstream regulated activities*, the *common platform requirements on financial crime*, conflicts of interest and *Chinese walls* do not apply.

2.6 **[R]** The *common platform requirements* do not apply to an *incoming ECA provider* acting as such.

2.7 **[G]** *EEA MiFID investment firms* are reminded in particular that they must comply with the *common platform record-keeping requirements* in relation to a *branch* in the *United Kingdom*.

What?

2.8 **[R]** The *common platform organisational requirements* apply with respect to the carrying on of the following (unless provided otherwise within a specific *rule*):

(1) *regulated activities*;

(2) activities that constitute *dealing in investments as principal*, disregarding the exclusion in article 15 of the *Regulated Activities Order* (Absence of holding out etc);

(3) *ancillary activities*; and

(4) in relation to *MiFID business*, *ancillary services*.

2.9 **[G]** The application of the provisions on the conflicts of interest in SYSC 10 is set out in SYSC 10.1.1R and SYSC 10.2.1R.

2.10 **[R]** The provisions on record-keeping in SYSC 9 apply as set out in SYSC 1 Annex 1.2.8R, except that they only apply to the carrying on of *ancillary activities* that are performed in relation to:

(1) *designated investment business*;

(2) *home finance activity*; and

(3) *insurance mediation activity*.

2.11 **[R]** The *common platform requirements on financial crime* apply as set out in SYSC 1 Annex 1.2.8R, except that they do not apply:

(1) with respect to:

  (a) activities that constitute *dealing in investments as principal*, disregarding the exclusion in article 15 of the *Regulated Activities Order* (Absence of holding out etc); and

  (b) *ancillary activities*; or

(2) in relation to the following *regulated activities*:

  (a) general insurance business;

  (b) insurance mediation activity in relation to a general insurance contract or pure protection contract;

  (c) long-term insurance business which is outside the Consolidated Life Directive (unless it is otherwise one of the regulated activities specified in this rule);

  (d) business relating to contracts which are within the Regulated Activities Order only because they fall within paragraph (e) of the definition of "contract of insurance" in article 3 of that Order;

  (e)

    (i) arranging by the *Society* of deals in *general insurance contracts* written at Lloyd's; and

    (ii) *managing the underwriting capacity of a Lloyd's syndicate as a managing agent at Lloyd's*;

  (f) *home finance mediation activity* and *administering a home finance transaction*; and

  (g) *reversion activity*; and

  (h) *meeting of repayment claims* and *managing dormant account funds (including the investment of such funds)*.

2.12 **[R]** The *common platform organisational requirements*, except the *common platform requirements on financial crime*, also apply with respect to the *communication* and *approval* of *financial promotions* which:

(1) if *communicated* by an *unauthorised person* without *approval* would contravene section 21(1) of the *Act* (Restrictions on financial promotion); and

(2) may be *communicated* by a *firm* without contravening section 238(1) of the *Act* (Restrictions on promotion of collective investment schemes).

2.13 **[R]** The *common platform organisational requirements*, except the *common platform requirements on financial crime*, also:

(1) apply with respect to the carrying on of *unregulated activities* in a *prudential context*; and

(2) take into account any activity of other members of a *group* of which the *firm* is a member.

2.14 **[G]** SYSC 1 Annex 1.2.13R(2) does not mean that inadequacy of a *group* member's systems and controls will automatically lead to a *firm* contravening any of the *common platform organisational requirements*. Rather, the potential impact of a *group* member's activities, including its systems and controls, and any systems and controls that operate on a *group* basis, will be relevant in determining the appropriateness of the *firm's* own systems and controls.

Where?

2.15 **[R]** The *common platform requirements*, except the *common platform recordkeeping requirements*, apply to a *firm* in relation to activities carried on by it from an establishment in the *United Kingdom*.

2.16 **[R]** The *common platform requirements*, except the *common platform requirements on financial crime* and the *common platform record-keeping requirements*, apply to a *firm* in relation to *passported activities* carried on by it from a *branch* in another *EEA State*.

2.17 **[R]** The *common platform record-keeping requirements* apply to activities carried on by a *firm* from an establishment maintained in the *United Kingdom*, unless another applicable *rule* which is relevant to the activity has a wider territorial scope, in which case the *common platform record-keeping requirements* apply with that wider scope in relation to the activity described in that *rule*.

[**Note**: article 13(9) of *MiFID*]

2.18 **[R]** The *common platform organisational requirements*, except the *common platform requirements on financial crime*, also apply in a *prudential context* to a *UK domestic firm* with respect to activities wherever they are carried on.

Actions for damages

2.19 **[R]** A contravention of a *rule* in the *common platform requirements* does not give rise to a right of action by a *private person* under section 150 of the *Act* (and each of those *rules* is specified under section 150(2) of the *Act* as a provision giving rise to no such right of action).

Part 3: Tables summarising the application of the common platform requirements to different types of firm.

3.1 **[G]** The *common platform requirements* apply in the following two ways (subject to the provisions in Part 2 of this Annex).

3.2 **[G]** For a *common platform firm*, they apply in accordance with Column A in the table below.

3.3 **[G]** For all other *firms* apart from *insurers, managing agents* and the *Society*, they apply in accordance with Column B in the table below. For these *firms*, where a *rule* is shown modified in Column B as 'Guidance', it should be read as *guidance* (as if "should" appeared in that rule instead of "must") and should be applied in a proportionate manner, taking into account the nature, scale and complexity of the firm's business.

Provision	**COLUMN A**	**COLUMN B**
SYSC 4	Application to a *common platform firm*	Application to all other *firms* apart from *insurers, managing agents* and the *Society*
SYSC 4.1.1R	Rule	Rule
SYSC 4.1.2R	Rule	Guidance
SYSC 4.1.2AG	Not applicable	Guidance
SYSC 4.1.3R	Rule applies only to a *BIPRU firm*	Not applicable
SYSC 4.1.4R	Rule	(1) and (3) Guidance (2) Rule

Part II FSA Handbook Materials

Provision	COLUMN A	COLUMN B
SYSC 4.1.4AG	Not applicable	Guidance
SYSC 4.1.5R	Rule applies only to a *MiFID investment firm*	Not applicable
SYSC 4.1.6R	Rule	Guidance
SYSC 4.1.7R	Rule	Guidance
SYSC 4.1.7AG	Not applicable	Guidance
SYSC 4.1.8G	Guidance	Guidance
SYSC 4.1.9R	Rule	Not applicable
SYSC 4.1.10R	Rule	Guidance – except reference to SYSC 4.1.9R which does not apply to these *firms*
SYSC 4.1.10AG	Not applicable	Guidance
SYSC 4.1.11G	Guidance	Guidance
SYSC 4.2.1R	Rule	• UK branch of *non-EEA bank*– rule applies.
		• Other *firms* – Guidance
SYSC 4.2.1AG	Not applicable	Guidance
SYSC 4.2.2R	Rule	• UK branch of a *non-EEA bank* – Rule applies
		• Other *firms* – this provision does not apply
SYSC 4.2.3G – 4.2.5G	Guidance	• UK branch of a *non-EEA bank* – Guidance
		• Other *firms* – these provisions do not apply
SYSC 4.2.6R	Rule	• UK branch of a *non-EEA bank* – Rule applies
		• Other *firms* – this provision does not apply
SYSC 4.3.1R	Rule	Rule (but not applicable to *incoming EEA firms, incoming Treaty firms* or *UCITS qualifiers*)
SYSC 4.3.2R	Rule	Guidance (but not applicable to *incoming EEA firms, incoming Treaty firms* or *UCITS qualifiers*)
SYSC 4.3.2AG	Not applicable	Guidance (but not applicable to *incoming EEA firms, incoming Treaty firms* or *UCITS qualifiers*)
SYSC 4.3.3G	Guidance	Guidance (but not applicable to *incoming EEA firms, incoming Treaty firms* or *UCITS qualifiers*)
SYSC 4.4.1R	Not applicable	Rule applies this section only to:
		(1) an *authorised professional firm* in respect of its *non-mainstream regulated activities* unless the *firm* is also conducting other *regulated activities* and has appointed *approved persons* to perform the *governing functions* with equivalent responsibilities for the *firm's non-mainstream regulated activities* and other *regulated activities*;

Provision	COLUMN A	COLUMN B
		(2) activities carried on by a *firm* whose principal purpose is to carry on activities other than *regulated activities* and which is:
		(a) an *oil market participant*;
		(b) a *service company*;
		(c) an *energy market participant*;
		(d) a wholly-owned subsidiary of:
		(i) a local authority
		(ii) a registered social landlord;
		(e) a *firm* with *permission* to carry on *insurance mediation activity* in relation to *non-investment insurance contracts* but no other *regulated activity*;
		(3) an *incoming Treaty firm*, an *incoming EEA firm* and a *UCITS qualifier*, (but only SYSC 4.4.5 R(2) applies for these *firms*); and
		(4) a *sole trader*, but only if he employs any person who is required to be approved under section 59 of the Act (Approval for particular arrangements).
SYSC 4.4.2G	Not applicable	Guidance only applying to the *firms* specified in SYSC 4.4.1R
SYSC 4.4.3R	Not applicable	Rule only applying to the *firms* specified in SYSC 4.4.1R
SYSC 4.4.4G	Not applicable	Guidance only applying to the *firms* specified in SYSC 4.4.1R
SYSC 4.4.5R	Not applicable	Rule only applying to the *firms* specified in SYSC 4.4.1R

Provision	COLUMN A	COLUMN B
SYSC 5	Application to a *common platform firm*	Application to all other *firms* apart from *insurers, managing agents* and the *Society*
SYSC 5.1.1R	Rule	Rule
SYSC 5.1.2G	Guidance	Guidance
SYSC 5.1.3G	Guidance	Guidance
SYSC 5.1.4G	Guidance	Guidance
SYSC 5.1.4AG	Guidance	Guidance
SYSC 5.1.5G	Guidance	Guidance
SYSC 5.1.5AG	Guidance	Guidance
SYSC 5.1.6R	Rule	Guidance
SYSC 5.1.7R	Rule	Guidance
SYSC 5.1.7AG	Not applicable	Guidance

Provision	COLUMN A	COLUMN B
SYSC 5.1.8G	Guidance	Guidance
SYSC 5.1.9G	Guidance	Guidance
SYSC 5.1.10G	Guidance	Guidance
SYSC 5.1.11G	Guidance	Guidance
SYSC 5.1.12R	Rule	Guidance
SYSC 5.1.12AG	Not applicable	Guidance
SYSC 5.1.13R	Rule	Rule
SYSC 5.1.14R	Rule	Guidance
SYSC 5.1.15G	Not applicable	Guidance

Provision	COLUMN A	COLUMN B
SYSC 6	Application to a common platform firm	Application to all other firms apart from insurers, managing agents and the Society
SYSC 6.1.1R	Rule	Rule
SYSC 6.1.2R	Rule	Guidance
SYSC 6.1.2AG	Not applicable	Guidance
SYSC 6.1.3R	Rule	• Guidance
		• This provision shall be read with the following additional sentence at the start.
		"Depending on the nature, scale and complexity of its business, it may be appropriate for a *firm* to have a separate compliance function. Where a *firm* has a separate compliance function, the *firm* should also take into account 6.1.3R and 6.1.4R as guidance."
SYSC 6.1.3AG	Not applicable	Guidance
SYSC 6.1.4R	Rule	(1) (3) and (4) Guidance (2)
		• Rule for *firms* which carry on *designated investment business* with or for retail clients or professional clients.
		• Guidance for all other *firms*.
SYSC 6.1.5R	Rule	• Guidance
		• "*investment services and activities*" shall be read as "*financial services and activities*"
SYSC 6.1.6G	Not applicable	Guidance
SYSC 6.2.1R	Rule	Guidance
SYSC 6.2.1AG	Not applicable	Guidance
SYSC 6.2.2G	Guidance	Guidance
SYSC 6.3.1R	Rule	Rule
SYSC 6.3.2G	Guidance	Guidance
SYSC 6.3.3R	Rule	Rule
SYSC 6.3.4G	Guidance	Guidance
SYSC 6.3.5G	Guidance	Guidance
SYSC 6.3.6G	Guidance	Guidance
SYSC 6.3.7G	Guidance	Guidance
SYSC 6.3.8R	Rule	Rule

Provision	**COLUMN A**	**COLUMN B**
SYSC 6.3.9R	Rule	Rule
SYSC 6.3.10G	Guidance	Guidance

Provision	**COLUMN A**	**COLUMN B**
SYSC 7	Application to a *common platform firm*	Application to all other *firms* apart from *insurers, managing agents* and the *Society*
SYSC 7.1.1G	Guidance	Guidance
SYSC 7.1.2 R	Rule	Guidance
SYSC 7.1.2AG	Not applicable	Guidance
SYSC 7.1.3R	Rule	Guidance
SYSC 7.1.4R	Rule	Guidance
SYSC 7.1.4AG	Not applicable	Guidance
SYSC 7.1.5R	Rule	Guidance
SYSC 7.1.6R	Rule	Guidance
SYSC 7.1.7R	Rule	Guidance
SYSC 7.1.7AG	Not applicable	Guidance
SYSC 7.1.8G(1), (2)	(1) Guidance applies only to a *BIPRU firm*	(1) Not applicable
	(2) Guidance	(2) Guidance
SYSC 7.1.9R	Rule applies only to a *BIPRU firm*	Not applicable
SYSC 7.1.10R	Rule applies only to a *BIPRU firm*	Not applicable
SYSC 7.1.11R	Rule applies only to a *BIPRU firm*	Not applicable
SYSC 7.1.12G	Guidance applies only to a *BIPRU firm*	Not applicable
SYSC 7.1.13R – 7.1.16R	Rule applies only to a *BIPRU firm*	Not applicable

Provision	**COLUMN A**	**COLUMN B**
SYSC 8	Application to a *common platform firm*	Application to all other *firms* apart from *insurers, managing agents* and the *Society*
SYSC 8.1.1R	Rule	Guidance
SYSC 8.1.1AG	Not applicable	Guidance
SYSC 8.1.2G	Guidance	Guidance
SYSC 8.1.3G	Guidance	Guidance
SYSC 8.1.4R	Rule	Guidance
SYSC 8.1.5R	Rule	Guidance
SYSC 8.1.5AG	Not applicable	Guidance
SYSC 8.1.6R	Rule	Rule
SYSC 8.1.7R	Rule	Guidance
SYSC 8.1.8R	Rule	Guidance
SYSC 8.1.9R	Rule	Guidance
SYSC 8.1.10R	Rule	Guidance
SYSC 8.1.11R	Rule	Guidance
SYSC 8.1.11AG	Not applicable	Guidance
SYSC 8.1.12G	Guidance	Guidance
SYSC 8.2	*MiFID investment firms* only	Not applicable
SYSC 8.3	*MiFID investment firms* only	Not applicable

Provision	COLUMN A	COLUMN B
SYSC 9	Application to a *common platform firm*	Application to all other *firms* apart from *insurers, managing agents* and the *Society*
SYSC 9.1.1R	Rule	Rule
SYSC 9.1.2R	Rule applies only in relation to *MiFID business*	Not applicable
SYSC 9.1.3R	Rule applies only in relation to *MiFID business*	Not applicable
SYSC 9.1.4G	Guidance	Guidance
SYSC 9.1.5G	Guidance	Guidance
SYSC 9.1.6G	Guidance	Guidance
SYSC 9.1.7G	Guidance applies only in relation to *MiFID business*	Not applicable

Provision	Column A	Column B
SYSC 10	Application to a *common platform firm*	Application to all other *firms* apart from *insurers, managing agents* and the *Society*
SYSC 10.1.1R	Rule	Rule
SYSC 10.1.2G	Guidance	Guidance
SYSC 10.1.3R	Rule	Rule
SYSC 10.1.4R	Rule	Guidance – but applies as a *rule* in relation to the production or arrangement of production of *investment research* in accordance with COBS 12.2, or the production or dissemination of *non-independent research* in accordance with COBS 12.3
SYSC 10.1.4AG	Not applicable	Guidance
SYSC 10.1.5G	Guidance	Guidance
SYSC 10.1.6R	Rule	Guidance – but applies as a *rule* in relation to the production or arrangement of production of *investment research* in accordance with COBS 12.2, or the production or dissemination of *non-independent research* in accordance with COBS 12.3
SYSC 10.1.6AG	Not applicable	Guidance
SYSC 10.1.7R	Rule	Rule
SYSC 10.1.8R	Rule	Rule
SYSC 10.1.8AR	Rule	Rule
SYSC 10.1.9G	Guidance	Guidance
SYSC 10.1.10R	Rule Guidance – but applies as a *rule* in relation to the production or arrangement of production of *investment research* in accordance with *COBS* 12.2, or the production or dissemination of *non-independent research* in accordance with *COBS* 12.3	

Provision	Column A	Column B
SYSC 10.1.11R	Rule Guidance – but applies as a *rule* in relation to the production or arrangement of production of *investment research* in accordance with *COBS* 12.2, or the production or dissemination of *non-independent research* in accordance with *COBS* 12.3	
SYSC 10.1.11AG	Not applicable	Guidance
SYSC 10.1.12G – SYSC 10.1.15G		
	Guidance	Guidance
SYSC 10.1.16R	Not applicable	Rule
SYSC 10.2.1R	Rule	Rule
SYSC 10.2.2R	Rule	Rule
SYSC 10.2.3G	Guidance	Guidance
SYSC 10.2.4R	Rule	Rule
SYSC 10.2.5G	Guidance	Guidance

CHAPTER 2
SENIOR MANAGEMENT ARRANGEMENTS

2.1 Apportionment of Responsibilities

[2013]

2.1.1 **[R]** A *firm* must take reasonable care to maintain a clear and appropriate apportionment of significant responsibilities among its *directors* and *senior managers* in such a way that:

(1) it is clear who has which of those responsibilities; and

(2) the business and affairs of the *firm* can be adequately monitored and controlled by the *directors*, relevant *senior managers* and *governing body* of the *firm*.

2.1.2 **[G]** The role undertaken by a *non-executive director* will vary from one *firm* to another. For example, the role of a *non-executive director* in a *friendly society* may be more extensive than in other *firms*. Where a *non-executive director* is an *approved person*, for example where the *firm* is a *body corporate*, his responsibility and therefore liability will be limited by the role that he undertakes. Provided that he has personally taken due care in his role, a *non-executive director* would not be held disciplinarily liable either for the failings of the *firm* or for those of individuals within the *firm*. The *non-executive director function*, for the purposes of the *approved persons* regime, is described in SUP 10.

2.1.3 **[R]** A *firm* must appropriately allocate to one or more individuals, in accordance with SYSC 2.1.4R, the functions of:

(1) dealing with the apportionment of responsibilities under SYSC 2.1.1 R; and

(2) overseeing the establishment and maintenance of systems and controls under SYSC 3.1.1 R

2.1.4 **[R]** Allocation of functions

This table belongs to SYSC 2.1.3 R

1:	2:	3:
Firm type	**Allocation of both functions must be to the following individual, if any (see Note)**	**Allocation to one or more individuals selected from this column is compulsory if there is no allocation to an individual in column 2, but is otherwise optional and additional:**
(1) A *firm* which is a *body corporate* and is a member of a *group*, other than a *firm* in row (2)	(1) the *firm's chief executive* (and all of them jointly, if more than one); or	the *firm's* and its *group's*: (1) *directors*; and

1:	2:	3:
Firm type	**Allocation of both functions must be to the following individual, if any (see Note)**	**Allocation to one or more individuals selected from this column is compulsory if there is no allocation to an individual in column 2, but is otherwise optional and additional:**
	(2) a *director* or *senior manager* responsible for the overall management of: (a) the *group*; or (b) a *group* division within which some or all of the *firm's regulated activities* fall	(2) *senior managers*
(2) An *incoming EEA firm* or *incoming Treaty firm* (note: only the function in SYSC 2.1.3R(2) must be allocated)	(not applicable)	the *firm's* and its *group's*: (1) *directors*; and (2) *senior managers*
(3) Any other *firm*	the *firm's chief executive* (and all of them jointly, if more than one)	the *firm's* and its *group's*: (1) *directors*; and (2) *senior managers*
Note: Column 2 does not require the involvement of the *chief executive* or other executive *director* or *senior manager* in an aspect of corporate governance if that would be contrary to generally accepted principles of good corporate governance.		

2.1.5 **[G]** SYSC 2.1.3R and 2.1.4R give a *firm* some flexibility in the individuals to whom the functions may be allocated. It will be common for both the functions to be allocated solely to the *firm's chief executive*. SYSC 2.1.6G contains further *guidance* on the requirements of SYSC 2.1.3R and 2.1.4R in a question and answer form.

2.1.6 **[G]** Frequently asked questions about allocation of functions in SYSC 2.1.3 R

This table belongs to SYSC 2.1.5 G

	Question	**Answer**
1	Does an individual to whom a function is allocated under SYSC 2.1.3R need to be an *approved person*?	An individual to whom a function is allocated under SYSC 2.1.3R will be performing the *apportionment and oversight function* (CF 8, see SUP 10.7.1R) and an application must be made to the FSA for approval of the individual before the function is performed under section 59 of the Act (Approval for particular arrangements). There are exceptions from this in SUP 10.1 (Approved persons – Application). In particular, an *incoming EEA firm* is referred to the *EEA investment business oversight function* (CF 9, see SUP 10.7.6R).
2	If the allocation is to more than one individual, can they perform the functions, or aspects of the functions, separately?	If the functions are allocated to joint *chief executives* under SYSC 2.1.4R, column 2, they are expected to act jointly. If the functions are allocated to an individual under SYSC 2.1.4R, column 2, in addition to individuals under SYSC 2.1.4R, column 3, the former may normally be expected to perform a leading role in relation to the functions that reflects his position. Otherwise, yes.

	Question	Answer
3	What is meant by "appropriately allocate" in this context?	The allocation of functions should be compatible with delivering compliance with *Principle* 3, SYSC 2.1.1R and SYSC 3.1.1R. The *FSA* considers that allocation to one or two individuals is likely to be appropriate for most *firms*.
4	If a committee of management governs a *firm* or *group*, can the functions be allocated to every member of that committee?	Yes, as long as the allocation re-mains appropriate (see Question 3). If the *firm* also has an individual as *chief executive*, then the functions must be allocated to that individual as well under SYSC 2.1.4R, column 2 (see Question 7).
5	Does the definition of *chief executive* include the possessor of equivalent responsibilities with another title, such as a managing *director* or managing *partner*?	Yes.
6	Is it possible for a *firm* to have more than one individual as its *chief executive*?	Although unusual, some *firms* may wish the responsibility of a *chief executive* to be held jointly by more than one individual. In that case, each of them will be a *chief executive* and the functions must be allocated to all of them under SYSC 2.1.4R, column 2 (see also Questions 2 and 7).
7	If a *firm* has an individual as *chief executive*, must the functions be allocated to that individual?	Normally, yes, under SYSC 2.1.4R, column 2. But if the *firm* is a *body corporate* and a member of a *group*, the functions may, instead of to the *firm's chief executive*, be allocated to a *director* or *senior manager* from the *group* responsible for the overall management of the *group* or of a relevant *group* division, so long as this is appropriate (see Question 3). Such individuals will nevertheless require approval by the *FSA* (see Question 1). If the *firm* chooses to allocate the functions to a *director* or *senior manager* responsible for the overall management of a relevant *group* division, the *FSA* would expect that individual to be of a seniority equivalent to or greater than a *chief executive* of the *firm* for the allocation to be appropriate. See also Question 14.
8	If a *firm* has a *chief executive*, can the functions be allocated to other individuals in addition to the *chief executive*?	Yes. SYSC 2.1.4R, column 3, permits a *firm* to allocate the functions, additionally, to the *firm's* (or where applicable the *group's*) *directors* and *senior managers* as long as this is appropriate (see Question 3).
9	What if a *firm* does not have a *chief executive*?	Normally, the functions must be allocated to one or more individuals selected from the *firm's* (or where applicable the *group's*) *directors* and *senior managers* under SYSC 2.1.4R, column 3. But if the *firm*: (1) is a *body corporate* and a member of a *group*; and (2) the *group* has a *director* or *senior manager* responsible for the overall management of the *group* or of a relevant *group* division; then the functions must be allocated to that individual (together, optionally, with individuals from column 3 if appropriate) under SYSC 2.1.4R, column 2.

	Question	Answer
10	What do you mean by "*group* division within which some or all of the *firm's regulated activities* fall"?	A "division" in this context should be interpreted by reference to geo-graphical operations, product lines or any other method by which the *group's* business is divided. If the *firm's regulated activities* fall within more than one division and the *firm* does not wish to allocate the functions to its *chief executive*, the allocation must, under SYSC 2.1.4R, be to: (1) a *director* or *senior manager* responsible for the overall management of the *group*; or (2) a *director* or *senior manager* responsible for the overall management of one of those divisions; together, optionally, with individuals from column 3 if appropriate. (See also Questions 7 and 9.)
11	How does the requirement to allocate the functions in SYSC 2.1.3R apply to an *overseas firm* which is not an *incoming EEA firm*, *incoming Treaty firm* or *UCITS qualifier*? 2	The *firm* must appropriately allocate those functions to one or more individuals, in accordance with SYSC 2.1.4R, but: (1) The responsibilities that must be apportioned and the systems and controls that must be overseen are those relating to activities carried on from a *UK* establishment with certain exceptions (see SYSC 1 Annex 1.1.7R). Note that SYSC 1 Annex 1.1.10R does not extend the territorial scope of SYSC 2 for an *overseas firm*. (2) The *chief executive* of an *over-seas firm* is the *person* responsible for the conduct of the *firm's* business within the *United Kingdom* (see the definition of "*chief executive*"). This might, for example, be the manager of the *firm's UK* establishment, or it might be the *chief executive* of the *firm* as a whole, if he has that responsibility. The *apportionment and oversight function* applies to such a *firm*, unless it falls within a particular exception from the *approved persons* regime (see Question 1).
12	How does the requirement to allocate the functions in SYSC 2.1.3R apply to an *in-coming EEA firm* or *incoming Treaty firm*?	SYSC 1 Annex 1.1.1R and SYSC 1 Annex 1.1.8R restrict the application of SYSC 2.1.3R for such a *firm*. Accordingly: (1) Such a *firm* is not required to allocate the function of dealing with apportionment in SYSC 2.1.3R(1). (2) Such a *firm* is required to allocate the function of oversight in SYSC 2.1.3R(2). However, the systems and controls that must be overseen are those relating to matters which the *FSA*, as *Host State regulator*, is entitled to regulate (there is *guidance* on this in SUP 13A Annex 2G). Those are primarily, but not exclusively, the systems and controls relating to the conduct of the *firm's* activities carried on from its *UK branch*. (3) Such a *firm* need not allocate the function of oversight to its *chief executive*; it must allocate it to one or more *directors* and *senior managers* of the *firm* or the *firm's group* under SYSC 2.1.4R, row (2).

	Question	Answer
		(4) An *incoming EEA firm* which has *provision* only for *cross border services* is not required to allocate either function if it does not carry on *regulated activities* in the *United Kingdom*; for example if they fall within the overseas persons exclusions in article 72 of the *Regulated Activities Order*. See also Questions 1 and 15.
13	What about a *firm* that is a *partnership* or a *limited liability partnership*?	The *FSA* envisages that most if not all *partners* or members will be either *directors* or *senior managers*, but this will depend on the constitution of the *partnership* (particularly in the case of a limited *partnership*) or *limited liability partnership*. A *partnership* or *limited liability partnership* may also have a *chief executive* (see Question 5). A *limited liability partnership* is a *body corporate* and, if a member of a *group*, will fall within SYSC 2.1.4R, row (1) or (2).
14	What if generally accepted principles of good corporate governance recommend that the *chief executive* should not be involved in an aspect of corporate governance?	The Note to SYSC 2.1.4R provides that the *chief executive* or other *executive director* or *senior manager* need not be involved in such circumstances. For example, the Combined Code developed by the Committee on Corporate Governance recommends that the board of a listed company should establish an audit committee of non–executive directors to be responsible for oversight of the audit. That aspect of the oversight function may therefore be allocated to the members of such a committee without involving the *chief executive*. Such individuals may require approval by the *FSA* in relation to that function (see Question 1).
15	What about *electronic commerce activities* carried on from an *establishment* in another *EEA State* with or for a *person* in the *United Kingdom*?	*SYSC* does not apply to an *incoming ECA provider* acting as such.

2.2 Recording the apportionment

2.2.1 **[R]**

(1) A *firm* must make a record of the arrangements it has made to satisfy SYSC 2.1.1R (apportionment) and SYSC 2.1.3R (allocation) and take reasonable care to keep this up to date.

(2) This record must be retained for six years from the date on which it was superseded by a more up-to-date record.

2.2.2 **[G]**

(1) A *firm* will be able to comply with SYSC 2.2.1R by means of records which it keeps for its own purposes provided these records satisfy the requirements of SYSC 2.2.1R and provided the *firm* takes reasonable care to keep them up to date. Appropriate records might, for this purpose, include organisational charts and diagrams, project management *documents*, job descriptions, committee constitutions and terms of reference provided they show a clear description of the *firm's* major functions.

(2) *Firms* should record any material change to the arrangements described in SYSC 2.2.1R as soon as reasonably practicable after that change has been made.

2.2.3 **[G]** Where responsibilities have been allocated to more than one individual, the *firm's* record should show clearly how those responsibilities are shared or divided between the individuals concerned.

CHAPTER 3
SYSTEMS AND CONTROLS

3.1 Systems and Controls

[2014]
3.1.1 **[R]** A *firm* must take reasonable care to establish and maintain such systems and controls as are appropriate to its business.

3.1.1A **[R]** [deleted]

3.1.2 **[G]**
(1) The nature and extent of the systems and controls which a *firm* will need to maintain under SYSC 3.1.1R will depend upon a variety of factors including:
   (a) the nature, scale and complexity of its business;
   (b) the diversity of its operations, including geographical diversity;
   (c) the volume and size of its transactions; and
   (d) the degree of risk associated with each area of its operation.
(2) To enable it to comply with its obligation to maintain appropriate systems and controls, a *firm* should carry out a regular review of them.
(3) The areas typically covered by the systems and controls referred to in SYSC 3.1.1R are those identified in SYSC 3.2. Detailed requirements regarding systems and controls relevant to particular business areas or particular types of *firm* are covered elsewhere in the *Handbook*.

3.1.3 **[G]** Where the Combined Code developed by the Committee on Corporate Governance is relevant to a *firm*, the *FSA*, in considering whether the *firm's* obligations under SYSC 3.1.1R have been met, will give it due credit for following corresponding provisions in the Code and related guidance.

3.1.4 **[G]** A *firm* has specific responsibilities regarding its *appointed representatives* or, where applicable, its *tied agents* (see SUP 12).

3.1.5 **[G]** SYSC 2.1.3R (2) prescribes how a *firm* must allocate the function of overseeing the establishment and maintenance of systems and controls described in SYSC 3.1.1R.

3.1.6 **[R]** A *firm* which is not a *common platform firm* must employ personnel with the skills, knowledge and expertise necessary for the discharge of the responsibilities allocated to them.

3.1.7 **[R]** When complying with the *competent employees rule*, a *firm* must take into account the nature, scale and complexity of its business and the nature and range of financial services and activities undertaken in the course of that business.

3.1.8 **[G]** The Training and Competence sourcebook (*TC*) contains additional *rules* and *guidance* relating to specified retail activities undertaken by a *firm*.

3.1.9 **[G]** *Firms* which are carrying on activities that are not subject to *TC* may nevertheless wish to take *TC* into account in complying with the training and competence requirements in SYSC.

3.1.10 **[G]** If a *firm* requires *employees* who are not subject to an examination requirement to pass a relevant examination from the list of recommended examinations maintained by the Financial Services Skills Council, the *FSA* will take that into account when assessing whether the *firm* has ensured that the *employee* satisfies the knowledge component of the *competent employees rule*.

3.2 Areas covered by systems and controls

Introduction

3.2.1 **[G]** This section covers some of the main issues which a *firm* is expected to consider in establishing and maintaining the systems and controls appropriate to its business, as required by SYSC 3.1.1R.

Organisation

3.2.2 **[G]** A *firm's* reporting lines should be clear and appropriate having regard to the nature, scale and complexity of its business. These reporting lines, together with clear management responsibilities, should be communicated as appropriate within the *firm*.

3.2.3 **[G]**
(1) A *firm's governing body* is likely to delegate many functions and tasks for the purpose of carrying out its business. When functions or tasks are delegated, either to *employees* or to *appointed representatives* or, where applicable, its *tied agents*, appropriate safeguards should be put in place.
(2) When there is delegation, a *firm* should assess whether the recipient is suitable to carry out the delegated function or task, taking into account the degree of responsibility involved.
(3) The extent and limits of any delegation should be made clear to those concerned.

(4) There should be arrangements to supervise delegation, and to monitor the discharge of delegates functions or tasks.
(5) If cause for concern arises through supervision and monitoring or otherwise, there should be appropriate follow-up action at an appropriate level of seniority within the *firm*.

3.2.4 **[G]**
(1) The *guidance* relevant to delegation within the *firm* is also relevant to external delegation ('outsourcing'). A *firm* cannot contract out its regulatory obligations. So, for example, under *Principle* 3 a *firm* should take reasonable care to supervise the discharge of outsourced functions by its contractor.
(2) A *firm* should take steps to obtain sufficient information from its contractor to enable it to assess the impact of outsourcing on its systems and controls.

3.2.5 **[G]** Where it is made possible and appropriate by the nature, scale and complexity of its business, a *firm* should segregate the duties of individuals and departments in such a way as to reduce opportunities for *financial crime* or contravention of requirements and standards under the *regulatory system*. For example, the duties of front-office and back-office staff should be segregated so as to prevent a single individual initiating, processing and controlling transactions.

3.2.5A **[R]** An *overseas bank* must ensure that at least two individuals effectively direct its business.

3.2.5B **[G]** In the case of an *overseas bank*, the *FSA* assesses whether at least two individuals effectively direct the business of the *bank* (and not just the business of its branch in the *United Kingdom*). The *FSA* also takes into account the manner in which management decisions are taken in the *United Kingdom* branch in assessing the adequacy of the *overseas bank's* systems and controls.

Systems and controls in relation to compliance, financial crime and money laundering

3.2.6 **[R]** A *firm* must take reasonable care to establish and maintain effective systems and controls for compliance with applicable requirements and standards under the *regulatory system* and for countering the risk that the *firm* might be used to further *financial crime*.

3.2.6A **[R]** A *firm* must ensure that these systems and controls:
(1) enable it to identify, assess, monitor and manage *money laundering* risk; and
(2) are comprehensive and proportionate to the nature, scale and complexity of its activities.

3.2.6B **[G]** "*Money laundering* risk" is the risk that a *firm* may be used to further *money laundering*. Failure by a *firm* to manage this risk effectively will increase the risk to society of crime and terrorism.

3.2.6C **[R]** A *firm* must carry out regular assessments of the adequacy of these systems and controls to ensure that it continues to comply with SYSC 3.2.6AR.

3.2.6D **[G]** A *firm* may also have separate obligations to comply with relevant legal requirements, including the Terrorism Act 2000, the Proceeds of Crime Act 2002 and the *Money Laundering Regulations*. SYSC 3.2.6R to SYSC 3.2.6JG are not relevant for the purposes of regulation 3(3) of the *Money Laundering Regulations*, section 330(8) of the Proceeds of Crime Act 2002 or section 21A(6) of the Terrorism Act 2000.

3.2.6E **[G]** The *FSA*, when considering whether a breach of its *rules* on systems and controls against *money laundering* has occurred, will have regard to whether a *firm* has followed relevant provisions in the guidance for the *UK* financial sector issued by the Joint Money Laundering Steering Group.

3.2.6F **[G]** In identifying its *money laundering* risk and in establishing the nature of these systems and controls, a *firm* should consider a range of factors, including:
(1) its customer, product and activity profiles;
(2) its distribution channels;
(3) the complexity and volume of its transactions;
(4) its processes and systems; and
(5) its operating environment.

3.2.6G **[G]** A *firm* should ensure that the systems and controls include:
(1) appropriate training for its employees in relation to *money laundering*;
(2) appropriate provision of information to its *governing body* and senior management, including a report at least annually by that *firm's money laundering reporting officer* (*MLRO*) on the operation and effectiveness of those systems and controls;
(3) appropriate documentation of its risk management policies and risk profile in relation to *money laundering*, including documentation of its application of those policies (see SYSC 3.2.20R to SYSC 3.2.22G);
(4) appropriate measures to ensure that *money laundering* risk is taken into account in its day-to-day operation, including in relation to:
 (a) the development of new products;
 (b) the taking-on of new customers; and
 (c) changes in its business profile; and

(5) appropriate measures to ensure that procedures for identification of new customers do not unreasonably deny access to its services to potential customers who cannot reasonably be expected to produce detailed evidence of identity.

3.2.6H **[R]** A *firm* must allocate to a *director* or *senior manager* (who may also be the *money laundering reporting officer*) overall responsibility within the *firm* for the establishment and maintenance of effective anti-*money laundering* systems and controls.

The money laundering reporting officer

3.2.6I **[R]** A *firm* must:
(1) appoint an individual as *MLRO*, with responsibility for oversight of its compliance with the *FSA's rules* on systems and controls against *money laundering*; and
(2) ensure that its *MLRO* has a level of authority and independence within the *firm* and access to resources and information sufficient to enable him to carry out that responsibility.

3.2.6J **[G]** The job of the *MLRO* within a *firm* is to act as the focal point for all activity within the *firm* relating to anti-*money laundering*. The *FSA* expects that a *firm's MLRO* will be based in the *United Kingdom*.

The compliance function

3.2.7 **[G]**
(1) Depending on the nature, scale and complexity of its business, it may be appropriate for a *firm* to have a separate compliance function. The organisation and responsibilities of a compliance function should be documented. A compliance function should be staffed by an appropriate number of competent staff who are sufficiently independent to perform their duties objectively. It should be adequately resourced and should have unrestricted access to the *firm's* relevant records as well as ultimate recourse to its *governing body*.
(2) [deleted]
(3) [deleted]

3.2.8 **[R]**
(1) A *firm* which carries on *designated investment business* with or for *retail clients* or *professional clients* must allocate to a *director* or *senior manager* the function of:
 (a) having responsibility for oversight of the *firm's* compliance; and
 (b) reporting to the *governing body* in respect of that responsibility.
(2) In (1) "compliance" means compliance with the *rules* in:
 (a) *COBS* (Conduct of Business);
 (b) *COLL* (Collective Investment Schemes sourcebook); and
 (c) *CASS* (Client Assets).

3.2.9 **[G]**
(1) SUP 10.7.8R uses SYSC 3.2.8R to describe the *controlled function*, known as the *compliance oversight function*, of acting in the capacity of a *director* or *senior manager* to whom this function is allocated.
(2) The *rules* referred to in SYSC 3.2.8R (2) are the minimum area of focus for the *firm's compliance oversight function*. A *firm* is free to give additional responsibilities to a person performing this function if it wishes.

Risk assessment

3.2.10 **[G]**
(1) Depending on the nature, scale and complexity of its business, it may be appropriate for a *firm* to have a separate risk assessment function responsible for assessing the risks that the *firm* faces and advising the *governing body* and *senior managers* on them.
(2) The organisation and responsibilities of a risk assessment function should be documented. The function should be adequately resourced and staffed by an appropriate number of competent staff who are sufficiently independent to perform their duties objectively.
(3) The term 'risk assessment function' refers to the generally understood concept of risk assessment within a *firm*, that is, the function of setting and controlling risk exposure. The risk assessment function is not a *controlled function* itself, but is part of the *systems and controls function* (CF28).

Management information

3.2.11 **[G]**
(1) A *firm's* arrangements should be such as to furnish its *governing body* with the information it needs to play its part in identifying, measuring, managing and controlling risks of regulatory concern. Three factors will be the relevance, reliability and timeliness of that information.

(2) Risks of regulatory concern are those risks which relate to the fair treatment of the *firm's customers*, to the protection of *consumers*, to confidence in the *financial system*, and to the use of that system in connection with *financial crime*.

3.2.12 **[G]** It is the responsibility of the *firm* to decide what information is required, when, and for whom, so that it can organise and control its activities and can comply with its regulatory obligations. The detail and extent of information required will depend on the nature, scale and complexity of the business.

Employees and agents

3.2.13 **[G]** A *firm's* systems and controls should enable it to satisfy itself of the suitability of anyone who acts for it.

3.2.14 **[G]**

(1) SYSC 3.2.13G includes assessing an individual's honesty, and competence. This assessment should normally be made at the point of recruitment. An individual's honesty need not normally be revisited unless something happens to make a fresh look appropriate.

(2) Any assessment of an individual's suitability should take into account the level of responsibility that the individual will assume within the *firm*. The nature of this assessment will generally differ depending upon whether it takes place at the start of the individual's recruitment, at the end of the probationary period (if there is one) or subsequently.

(3) [deleted]

(4) The requirements on *firms* with respect to *approved persons* are in Part V of the *Act* (Performance of regulated activities) and SUP 10.

Audit committee

3.2.15 **[G]** Depending on the nature, scale and complexity of its business, it may be appropriate for a *firm* to form an audit committee. An audit committee could typically examine management's process for ensuring the appropriateness and effectiveness of systems and controls, examine the arrangements made by management to ensure compliance with requirements and standards under the *regulatory system*, oversee the functioning of the internal audit function (if applicable – see SYSC 3.2.16G) and provide an interface between management and the external auditors. It should have an appropriate number of *non-executive directors* and it should have formal terms of reference.

Internal audit

3.2.16 **[G]**

(1) Depending on the nature, scale and complexity of its business, it may be appropriate for a *firm* to delegate much of the task of monitoring the appropriateness and effectiveness of its systems and controls to an internal audit function. An internal audit function should have clear responsibilities and reporting lines to an audit committee or appropriate *senior manager*, be adequately resourced and staffed by competent individuals, be independent of the day-to-day activities of the *firm* and have appropriate access to a *firm's* records.

(2) The term 'internal audit function' refers to the generally understood concept of internal audit within a *firm*, that is, the function of assessing adherence to and the effectiveness of internal systems and controls, procedures and policies. The internal audit function is not a *controlled function* itself, but is part of the *systems and controls function* (CF28).

Business strategy

3.2.17 **[G]** A *firm* should plan its business appropriately so that it is able to identify, measure, manage and control risks of regulatory concern (see SYSC 3.2.11G (2)). In some *firms*, depending on the nature, scale and complexity of their business, it may be appropriate to have business plans or strategy plans documented and updated on a regular basis to take account of changes in the business environment.

Remuneration policies

3.2.18 **[G]** It is possible that *firms'* remuneration policies will from time to time lead to tensions between the ability of the *firm* to meet the requirements and standards under the *regulatory system* and the personal advantage of those who act for it. Where tensions exist, these should be appropriately managed.

Business continuity

3.2.19 **[G]** A *firm* should have in place appropriate arrangements, having regard to the nature, scale and complexity of its business, to ensure that it can continue to function and meet its regulatory obligations in the event of an unforeseen interruption. These arrangements should be regularly updated and tested to ensure their effectiveness.

Records

3.2.20 **[R]**

(1) A *firm* must take reasonable care to make and retain adequate records of matters and dealings (including accounting records) which are the subject of requirements and standards under the *regulatory system*.

(2) Subject to (3) and to any other record-keeping *rule* in the *Handbook*, the records required by (1) or by such other *rule* must be capable of being reproduced in the English language on paper.

(3) If a *firm's* records relate to business carried on from an establishment in a country or territory outside the *United Kingdom*, an official language of that country or territory may be used instead of the English language as required by (2).

3.2.21 **[G]** A *firm* should have appropriate systems and controls in place to fulfil the *firm's* regulatory and statutory obligations with respect to adequacy, access, periods of retention and security of records. The general principle is that records should be retained for as long as is relevant for the purposes for which they are made.

3.2.22 **[G]** Detailed record-keeping requirements for different types of *firm* are to be found elsewhere in the *Handbook*. Schedule 1 to the Handbook is a consolidated schedule of these requirements.

CRD requirements

(1) General organisation requirements

3.2.23 **[R]** [deleted]

3.2.24 **[R]** [deleted]

3.2.25 **[R]** [deleted]

3.2.26 **[R]** [deleted]

3.2.27 **[R]** [deleted]

(2) Employees, agents and other relevant persons

3.2.28 **[R]** [deleted]

(3) Risk control

3.2.29 **[R]** [deleted]

3.2.30 **[R]** [deleted]

3.2.31 **[R]** [deleted]

3.2.32 **[R]** [deleted]

3.2.33 **[R]** [deleted]

3.2.34 **[R]** [deleted]

3.2.35 **[R]** [deleted]

3.2.36 **[R]** [deleted]

CHAPTER 4
GENERAL ORGANISATIONAL REQUIREMENTS

4.1 General requirements

[2015]

4.1.1 **[R]** A *firm* must have robust governance arrangements, which include a clear organisational structure with well defined, transparent and consistent lines of responsibility, effective processes to identify, manage, monitor and report the risks it is or might be exposed to, and internal control mechanisms, including sound administrative and accounting procedures and effective control and safeguard arrangements for information processing systems.

[Note: article 22(1) of the *Banking Consolidation Directive*, article 13(5) second paragraph of *MiFID*]

4.1.2 **[R]** For a *common platform firm* the arrangements, processes and mechanisms referred to in SYSC 4.1.1R must be comprehensive and proportionate to the nature, scale and complexity of the *common platform firm's* activities and must take into account the specific technical criteria described in SYSC 4.1.7R, SYSC 5.1.7R and SYSC 7.

[Note: article 22(2) of the *Banking Consolidation Directive*]

4.1.2A **[G]** Other *firms* should take account of the comprehensiveness and proportionality *rule* (SYSC 4.1.2R) as if it were *guidance* (and as if "should" appeared in that rule instead of "must") as explained in SYSC 1 Annex 1.3.3G but a *firm* with an *interim RSRB permission* to the extent that it carries on *regulated sale and rent back activity*, need not take into account the specific technical criteria described in SYSC 4.1.7R, SYSC 5.1.7R and SYSC 7.

4.1.3 **[R]** A *BIPRU firm* must ensure that its internal control mechanisms and administrative and accounting procedures permit the verification of its compliance with *rules* adopted in accordance with the *Capital Adequacy Directive* at all times.

[Note: article 35(1) final sentence of the *Capital Adequacy Directive*]

4.1.4 **[R]** A *firm* (with the exception of a *sole trader* who does not employ any *person* who is required to be approved under section 59 of the *Act* (Approval for particular arrangements)) must, taking into account the nature, scale and complexity of the business of the *firm*, and the nature and range of the (for a *common platform firm*) *investment services and activities* or (for every other *firm*) financial services and activities undertaken in the course of that business:

(1) (if it is a *common platform firm*) establish, implement and maintain decision-making procedures and an organisational structure which clearly and in a documented manner specifies reporting lines and allocates functions and responsibilities;

(2) establish, implement and maintain adequate internal control mechanisms designed to secure compliance with decisions and procedures at all levels of the *firm*; and

(3) (if it is a *common platform firm*) establish, implement and maintain effective internal reporting and communication of information at all relevant levels of the *firm*.

[Note: articles 5(1) final paragraph, 5(1)(a), 5(1)(c) and 5(1)(e) of the *MiFID implementing Directive*]

4.1.4A **[G]** A *firm* that is not a *common platform firm* should take into account the decision-making procedures and effective internal reporting *rules* (SYSC 4.1.4R(1) and (3)) as if they were *guidance* (and as if "should" appeared in those rules instead of "must") as explained in SYSC 1 Annex 1.3.3G.

4.1.5 **[R]** A *MiFID investment firm* must establish, implement and maintain systems and procedures that are adequate to safeguard the security, integrity and confidentiality of information, taking into account the nature of the information in question.

[Note: article 5(2) of the *MiFID implementing Directive*]

Business continuity

4.1.6 **[R]** A *common platform firm* must take reasonable steps to ensure continuity and regularity in the performance of its *regulated activities*. To this end the *common platform firm* must employ appropriate and proportionate systems, resources and procedures.

[Note: article 13(4) of *MiFID*]

4.1.7 **[R]** A *common platform firm* must establish, implement and maintain an adequate business continuity policy aimed at ensuring, in the case of an interruption to its systems and procedures, that any losses are limited, the preservation of essential data and functions, and the maintenance of its *regulated activities*, or, where that is not possible, the timely recovery of such data and functions and the timely resumption of its *regulated activities*.

[Note: article 5(3) of the *MiFID implementing Directive* and annex V paragraph 13 of the *Banking Consolidation Directive*]

4.1.7A **[G]** Other *firms* should take account of the business continuity rules (SYSC 4.1.6R and 4.1.7R) as if they were *guidance* (and as if "should" appeared in those rules instead of "must") as explained in SYSC 1 Annex 1.3.3G.

4.1.8 **[G]** The matters dealt with in a business continuity policy should include:

(1) resource requirements such as people, systems and other assets, and arrangements for obtaining these resources;

(2) the recovery priorities for the *firm's* operations;

(3) communication arrangements for internal and external concerned parties (including the *FSA*, *clients* and the press);

(4) escalation and invocation plans that outline the processes for implementing the business continuity plans, together with relevant contact information;

(5) processes to validate the integrity of information affected by the disruption; and

(6) regular testing of the business continuity policy in an appropriate and proportionate manner in accordance with SYSC 4.1.10R.

Accounting policies

4.1.9 **[R]** A *common platform firm* must establish, implement and maintain accounting policies and procedures that enable it, at the request of the *FSA*, to deliver in a timely manner to the *FSA* financial reports which reflect a true and fair view of its financial position and which comply with all applicable accounting standards and rules.

[Note: article 5(4) of the *MiFID implementing Directive*]

Regular monitoring

4.1.10 **[R]** A *common platform firm* must monitor and, on a regular basis, evaluate the adequacy and effectiveness of its systems, internal control mechanisms and arrangements established in accordance with SYSC 4.1.4R to SYSC 4.1.9R and take appropriate measures to address any deficiencies.

[Note: article 5(5) of the *MiFID implementing Directive*]

4.1.10A **[G]** Other *firms* should take account of the regular monitoring rule (SYSC 4.1.10r) as if it were *guidance* (and as if "should" appeared in that rule instead of "must") as explained in SYSC 1 Annex 1.3.3G but ignoring the cross-reference to SYSC 4.1.5R and 4.1.9R.

Audit committee

4.1.11 **[G]** Depending on the nature, scale and complexity of its business, it may be appropriate for a *firm* to form an audit committee. An audit committee could typically examine management's process for ensuring the appropriateness and effectiveness of systems and controls, examine the arrangements made by management to ensure compliance with requirements and standards under the *regulatory system*, oversee the functioning of the internal audit function (if applicable) and provide an interface between management and external auditors. It should have an appropriate number of *non-executive directors* and it should have formal terms of reference.

Remuneration policies

4.1.12 **[G]** Certain *banks*, *building societies* and *BIPRU 730k firms* will need to comply with the *Remuneration Code* requirement to establish, implement and maintain an effective *remuneration policy* that is consistent with effective risk management. See SYSC 19.1 for details of the application of the *Remuneration Code*.

4.2 Persons who effectively direct the business

4.2.1 **[R]** The *senior personnel* of a *common platform firm* or of the *UK* branch of a *non-EEA bank* must be of sufficiently good repute and sufficiently experienced as to ensure the sound and prudent management of the *firm*.

[Note: article 9(1) of *MiFID* and article 11(1) second paragraph of the *Banking Consolidation Directive*]

4.2.1 A **[G]** Other *firms* should take account of the senior personnel *rule* (SYSC 4.2.1R) as if it were *guidance* (and as if "should" appeared in that rule instead of "must") as explained in SYSC Annex 1.3.3G.

4.2.2 **[R]** A *common platform firm* and the *UK* branch of a *non-EEA bank* must ensure that its management is undertaken by at least two persons meeting the requirements laid down in SYSC 4.2.1R.

[Note: article 9(4) first paragraph of *MiFID* and article 11(1) first paragraph of the *Banking Consolidation Directive*]

4.2.3 **[G]** In the case of a *body corporate*, the persons referred to in SYSC 4.2.2R should either be executive *directors* or persons granted executive powers by, and reporting immediately to, the *governing body*. In the case of a *partnership*, they should be active *partners*.

4.2.4 **[G]** At least two independent minds should be applied to both the formulation and implementation of the policies of a *common platform firm* and the *UK* branch of a *non-EEA bank*. Where such a *firm* nominates just two individuals to direct its business, the *FSA* will not regard them as both effectively directing the business where one of them makes some, albeit significant, decisions relating to only a few aspects of the business. Each should play a part in the decision making process on all significant decisions. Both should demonstrate the qualities and application to influence strategy, day-to-day policy and its implementation. This does not require their day-to-day involvement in the execution and implementation of policy. It does, however, require involvement in strategy and general direction, as well as knowledge of, and influence on, the way in which strategy is being implemented through day-to-day policy.

4.2.5 **[G]** Where there are more than two individuals directing the business of a *common platform firm* or the *UK* branch of a *non-EEA bank*, the *FSA* does not regard it as necessary for all of these individuals to be involved in all decisions relating to the determination of strategy and general direction. However, at least two individuals should be involved in all such decisions. Both individuals' judgement should be engaged so that major errors leading to difficulties for the *firm* are less likely to occur. Similarly, each individual should have sufficient experience and knowledge of the business and the necessary personal qualities and skills to detect and resist any imprudence, dishonesty or other irregularities by the other individual. Where a single individual, whether a chief executive, managing *director* or otherwise, is particularly dominant in such a *firm* this will raise doubts about whether SYSC 4.2.2R is met.

4.2.6 **[R]** If a *common platform firm* (other than a *credit institution*) or the *UK* branch of a *non-EEA bank* is:

(1) a natural person; or

(2) a legal person managed by a single natural person;

it must have alternative arrangements in place which ensure sound and prudent management of the *firm*.

[Note: article 9(4) second paragraph of *MiFID*]

4.3 Responsibility of senior personnel

4.3.1 **[R]** A *firm*, (with the exception of a *sole trader* who does not employ any *person* who is required to be approved under section 59 of the *Act* (Approval for particular arrangements)), when allocating functions internally, must ensure that *senior personnel* and, where appropriate, the *supervisory function*, are responsible for ensuring that the *firm* complies with its obligations under the *regulatory system*. In particular, *senior personnel* and, where appropriate, the *supervisory function* must assess and periodically review the effectiveness of the policies, arrangements and procedures put in place to comply with the *firm's* obligations under the *regulatory system* and take appropriate measures to address any deficiencies.

[Note: article 9(1) of the *MiFID implementing Directive*]

4.3.2 **[R]** A *common platform firm* (with the exception of a *sole trader* who does not employ any *person* who is required to be approved under section 59 of the *Act* (Approval for particular arrangements)), must ensure that:

(1) that its *senior personnel* receive on a frequent basis, and at least annually, written reports on the matters covered by SYSC 6.1.2R to 6.1.5R, SYSC 6.2.1R and SYSC 7.1.2R, SYSC 7.1.3R and SYSC 7.1.5R to SYSC 7.1.7R, indicating in particular whether the appropriate remedial measures have been taken in the event of any deficiencies; and

(2) the *supervisory function*, if any, receives on a regular basis written reports on the same matters.

[Note: article 9(2) and article 9(3) of the *MiFID implementing Directive*]

4.3.2A **[G]** Other *firms* should take account of the written reports *rule* (SYSC 4.3.2R) as if it were *guidance* (and as if "should" appeared in that rule instead of "must") as explained in SYSC 1 Annex 1.3.3G.

4.3.3 **[G]** The *supervisory function* does not include a general meeting of the shareholders of a *firm*, or equivalent bodies, but could involve, for example, a separate supervisory board within a two-tier board structure or the establishment of a non-executive committee of a single-tier board structure.

4.3.4 **[G]** [deleted]

4.4 Apportionment of responsibilities

Application

4.4.1 **[R]** This section applies to:

(1) an *authorised professional firm* in respect of its *non-mainstream regulated activities* unless the *firm* is also conducting other *regulated activities* and has appointed *approved persons* to perform the *governing functions* with equivalent responsibilities for the *firm's non-mainstream regulated activities* and other *regulated activities*;

(2) activities carried on by a *firm* whose principal purpose is to carry on activities other than *regulated activities* and which is:

  (a) an *oil market participant*;

  (b) a *service company*;

  (c) an *energy market participant*;

  (d) a wholly-owned subsidiary of:

    (i) a local authority; or

    (ii) a registered social landlord;

  (e) a *firm* with *permission* to carry on *insurance mediation activity* in relation to *non-investment insurance contracts* but no other *regulated activity*;

(3) [deleted]

(4) [deleted]

(5) [deleted]

(6) [deleted]

(7) an *incoming Treaty firm*, an *incoming EEA firm* or a *UCITS qualifier* (but only SYSC 4.4.5R(2) applies for these *firms*); and

(8) a sole trader, but only if he employs any person who is required to be approved under section 59 of the Act (Approval for particular arrangements).

4.4.1A **[R]** SYSC 4.4.3R (Maintaining a clear and appropriate apportionment) also applies to a *firm* with an *interim RSRB permission* to the extent that it carries on *regulated sale and rent back activity*.

Part II FSA Handbook Materials

4.4.2 **[G]** This section does not apply to a *common platform firm*.

Maintaining a clear and appropriate apportionment

4.4.3 **[R]** A *firm* must take reasonable care to maintain a clear and appropriate apportionment of significant responsibilities among its *directors* and *senior managers* in such a way that:
(1) it is clear who has which of those responsibilities; and
(2) the business and affairs of the *firm* can be adequately monitored and controlled by the *directors*, relevant *senior managers* and *governing body* of the *firm*.

4.4.4 **[G]** The role undertaken by a *non-executive director* will vary from one *firm* to another. Where a *non-executive director* is an *approved person*, for example where the *firm* is a *body corporate*, his responsibility and therefore liability will be limited by the role that he undertakes. Provided that he has personally taken due care in his role, a *non-executive director* would not be held disciplinarily liable either for the failings of the *firm* or for those of individuals within the *firm*. The *non-executive director* function, for the purposes of the *approved persons* regime is described in *SUP* 10.

Allocating functions of apportionment and oversight

4.4.5 **[R]** A *firm* must appropriately allocate to one or more individuals, in accordance with the following table, the functions of:
(1) dealing with the apportionment of responsibilities under *SYSC* 4.4.3R; and
(2) overseeing the establishment and maintenance of systems and controls under *SYSC* 4.1.1R.

1: Firm type	**2: Allocation of both functions must be to the following individual, if any (see Note):**	**3: Allocation to one or more individuals selected from this column is compulsory if there is no allocation to an individual in column 2, but is otherwise optional and additional:**
(1) A *firm* which is a *body corporate* and is a member of a *group*, other than a *firm* in row (2)	(1) the *firm's chief executive* (and all of them jointly, if more than one); or	the *firm's* and its *group's*:
		(1) *directors*; and
		(2) *senior managers*
	(2) a *director* or *senior manager* responsible for the overall management of:	
	(a) the *group*; or	
	(b) a group division within which some or all of the *firm's regulated activities* fall	
(2) An *incoming EEA firm* or *incoming Treaty* (note: only the functions in SYSC 4.4.5R(2) must be allocated)	(not applicable)	the *firm's* and its *group's*:
		(1) *directors*; and *firm*
		(2) *senior managers*
(3) Any other *firm*	the *firm's chief executive* (and all of them jointly, if more than one)	the *firm's* and its *group's*:
		(1) *directors*; and
		(2) *senior managers*
Note: Column 2 does not require the involvement of the *chief executive* or other executive *director* or *senior manager* in an aspect of corporate governance if that would be contrary to generally accepted principles of good corporate governance.		

Frequently asked questions about allocation of functions in SYSC 4.4.5R

4.4.6 **[G]**

Question	**Answer**
1 Does an individual to whom a function is allocated under SYSC 4.4.5R need to be an *approved person*?	An individual to whom a function is allocated under SYSC 4.4.5R will be performing the *apportionment and oversight function* (CF 8, see SUP 10.7.1R) and an application must be made to the *FSA* for approval of the individual before the function is performed under section 59 of the *Act* (Approval for particular arrangements). There are exceptions from this in SUP 10.1 (Approved persons — Application).
2 If the allocation is to more than one individual, can they perform the functions, or aspects of the functions, separately?	If the functions are allocated to joint *chief executives* under SYSC 4.4.5R, column 2, they are expected to act jointly. If the functions are allocated to an individual under SYSC 4.4.5R, column 2, in addition to individuals under SYSC 4.4.5R, column 3, the former may normally be expected to perform a leading role in relation to the functions that reflects his position. Otherwise, yes.
3 What is meant by "appropriately allocate" in this context?	The allocation of functions should be compatible with delivering compliance with *Principle* 3, SYSC 4.4.3R and SYSC 4.1.1R. The *FSA* considers that allocation to one or two individuals is likely to be appropriate for most *firms*.
4 If a committee of management governs a *firm* or *group*, can the functions be allocated to every member of that committee?	Yes, as long as the allocation remains appropriate (see Question 3). If the *firm* also has an individual as *chief executive*, then the functions must be allocated to that individual as well under SYSC 4.4.5R, column 2 (see Question 7).
5 Does the definition of *chief executive* include the possessor of equivalent responsibilities with another title, such as a managing *director* or managing *partner*?	Yes.
6 Is it possible for a *firm* to have more than one individual as its *chief executive*?	Although unusual, some *firms* may wish the responsibility of a *chief executive* to be held jointly by more than one individual. In that case, each of them will be a *chief executive* and the functions must be allocated to all of them under SYSC 4.4.5R, column 2 (see also Questions 2 and 7).
7 If a *firm* has an individual as *chief executive*, must the functions be allocated to that individual?	Normally, yes, under SYSC 4.4.5R, column 2.
	But if the *firm* is a *body corporate* and a member of a *group*, the functions may, instead of being allocated to the *firm's chief executive*, be allocated to a *director* or senior manager from the *group* responsible for the overall management of the *group* or of a relevant *group* division, so long as this is appropriate (see Question 3). Such individuals will nevertheless require approval by the *FSA* (see Question 1).

Question	Answer
	If the *firm* chooses to allocate the functions to a *director* or *senior manager* responsible for the overall management of a relevant *group* division, the *FSA* would expect that individual to be of a seniority equivalent to or greater than a *chief executive* of the *firm* for the allocation to be appropriate.
	See also Question 14.
8 If a *firm* has a *chief executive*, can the functions be allocated to other individuals in addition to the *chief executive*?	Yes. SYSC 4.4.5R, column 3, permits a *firm* to allocate the functions, additionally, to the *firm's* (or where applicable the *group's*) *directors* and *senior managers* as long as this is appropriate (see Question 3).
9 What if a *firm* does not have a *chief executive*?	Normally, the functions must be allocated to one or more individuals selected from the *firm's* (or where applicable the *group's*) *directors* and *senior managers* under SYSC 4.4.5R, column 3.
	But if the *firm*:
	(1) is a *body corporate* and a member of a *group*; and
	(2) the *group* has a *director* or *senior manager* responsible for the overall management of the *group* or of a relevant *group* division; then the functions must be allocated to that individual (together, optionally, with individuals from column 3 if appropriate) under SYSC 4.4.5R, column 2.
10 What do you mean by "*group* division within which some or all of the *firm's regulated activities* fall"?	A "division" in this context should be interpreted by reference to geographical operations, product lines or any other method by which the *group's* business is divided.
	If the *firm's regulated activities* fall within more than one division and the *firm* does not wish to allocate the functions to its *chief executive*, the allocation must, under SYSC 4.4.5R, be to:
	(1) a *director* or *senior manager* responsible for the overall management of the *group*; or
	(2) a *director* or *senior manager* responsible for the overall management of one of those divisions;
	together, optionally, with individuals from column 3 if appropriate. (See also Questions 7 and 9.)
11 How does the requirement to allocate the functions in SYSC 4.4.5R apply to an *overseas firm* which is not an *incoming EEA firm*, *incoming Treaty firm* or *UCITS qualifier*?	The *firm* must appropriately allocate those functions to one or more individuals, in accordance with SYSC 4.4.5R, but:
	(1) The responsibilities that must be apportioned and the systems and controls that must be overseen are those relating to activities carried on from a *UK* establishment with certain exceptions (see SYSC 1 Annex 1.1.8R). Note that SYSC 1 Annex 1.1.10R does not extend the territorial scope of SYSC 4.4 for an *overseas firm*.

Question	Answer
	(2) The chief executive of an overseas firm is the person responsible for the conduct of the firm's business within the United Kingdom (see the definition of "chief executive"). This might, for example, be the manager of the *firm's UK* establishment, or it might be the *chief executive* of the *firm* as a whole, if he has that responsibility.
	The *apportionment and oversight function* applies to such a *firm*, unless it falls within a particular exception from the *approved persons* regime (see Question 1).
12 How does the requirement to allocate the functions in SYSC 4.4.5R apply to an *incoming EEA firm* or incoming *Treaty firm*?	SYSC 1 Annex 1.1.1R(2) and SYSC 1 Annex 1.1.8R restrict the application of SYSC 4.4.5R for such a *firm*. Accordingly:
	(1) Such a *firm* is not required to allocate the function of dealing with apportionment in SYSC 4.4.5R(1).
	(2) Such a *firm* is required to allocate the function of oversight in SYSC 4.4.5R(2). However, the systems and controls that must be overseen are those relating to matters which the *FSA*, as *Host State regulator*, is entitled to regulate (there is *guidance* on this in SUP 13A Annex 2G). Those are primarily, but not exclusively, the systems and controls relating to the conduct of the *firm's* activities carried on from its *UK branch*.
	(3) Such a *firm* need not allocate the function of oversight to its *chief executive*; it must allocate it to one or more *directors* and *senior managers* of the *firm* or the *firm's group* under SYSC 4.4.5R, row (2).
	(4) An *incoming EEA firm* which has provision only for *cross border services* is not required to allocate either function if it does not carry on *regulated activities* in the *United Kingdom*; for example if they fall within the overseas persons exclusions in article 72 of the *Regulated Activities Order*. See also Questions 1 and 15.
13 What about a *firm* that is a *partnership* or a *limited liability partnership*?	The *FSA* envisages that most if not all *partners* or members will be either *directors* or *senior managers*, but this will depend on the constitution of the *partnership* (particularly in the case of a limited *partnership*) or *limited liability partnership*. A *partnership* or *limited liability partnership* may also have a *chief executive* (see Question 5). A *limited liability partnership* is a *body corporate* and, if a member of a *group*, will fall within SYSC 4.4.5R, row (1) or (2).

Question	Answer
14 What if generally accepted principles of good corporate governance recommend that the *chief executive* should not be involved in an aspect of corporate governance?	The Note to SYSC 4.4.5R provides that the *chief executive* or other executive director or *senior manager* need not be involved in such circumstances. For example, the Combined Code developed by the Committee on Corporate Governance recommends that the board of a listed company should establish an audit committee of non-executive directors to be responsible for oversight of the audit. That aspect of the oversight function may therefore be allocated to the members of such a committee without involving the *chief executive*. Such individuals may require approval by the FSA in relation to that function (see Question 1).
15 What about *incoming electronic commerce activities* carried on from an *establishment* in another *EEA State* with or for a *person* in the *United Kingdom*?	SYSC does not apply to an *incoming ECA provider* acting as such.

CHAPTER 5
EMPLOYEES, AGENTS AND OTHER RELEVANT PERSONS

5.1 Skills, knowledge and expertise

[2016]

5.1.1 **[R]** A *firm* must employ personnel with the skills, knowledge and expertise necessary for the discharge of the responsibilities allocated to them.

[Note: article 5(1)(b) of the *MiFID implementing Directive*]

5.1.2 **[G]** A *firm's* systems and controls should enable it to satisfy itself of the suitability of anyone who acts for it. This includes assessing an individual's honesty and competence. This assessment should normally be made at the point of recruitment. An individual's honesty need not normally be revisited unless something happens to make a fresh look appropriate.

5.1.3 **[G]** Any assessment of an individual's suitability should take into account the level of responsibility that the individual will assume within the *firm*. The nature of this assessment will generally differ depending upon whether it takes place at the start of the individual's recruitment, at the end of the probationary period (if there is one) or subsequently.

5.1.4 **[G]** The Training and Competence sourcebook (*TC*) contains additional *rules* and *guidance* relating to specified retail activities undertaken by a *firm*.

5.1.4A **[G]** *Firms* which are carrying on activities that are not subject to *TC* may nevertheless wish to take *TC* into account in complying with the training and competence requirements in *SYSC*.

5.1.5 **[G]** The requirements on *firms* with respect to *approved persons* are in Part V of the *Act* (Performance of regulated activities) and SUP 10.

5.1.5A **[G]** If a *firm* requires *employees* who are not subject to an examination requirement in *TC* to pass a relevant examination from the list of recommended examinations maintained by the Financial Services Skills Council, the *FSA* will take that into account when assessing whether the *firm* has ensured that the *employee* satisfies the knowledge component of the *competent employees rule*.

Segregation of functions

5.1.6 **[R]** A *common platform firm* must ensure that the performance of multiple functions by its *relevant persons* does not and is not likely to prevent those persons from discharging any particular functions soundly, honestly and professionally.

[Note: article 5(1)(g) of the *MiFID implementing Directive*]

5.1.7 **[R]** The *senior personnel* of a *common platform firm* must define arrangements concerning the segregation of duties within the *firm* and the prevention of conflicts of interest.

[Note: annex V paragraph 1 of the *Banking Consolidation Directive*]

5.1.7A **[G]** Other *firms* should take account of the segregation of functions rules (SYSC 5.6.6R and 5.1.7R) as if they were *guidance* (and as if "should" appeared in those rules instead of "must") as explained in SYSC 1 Annex 1.3.3G.

5.1.8 **[G]** The effective segregation of duties is an important element in the *internal controls* of a *firm* in the *prudential context*. In particular, it helps to ensure that no one individual is completely free to commit a *firm's* assets or incur liabilities on its behalf. Segregation can also help to ensure that a *firm's governing body* receives objective and accurate information on financial performance, the risks faced by the *firm* and the adequacy of its systems.

5.1.9 **[G]** A *firm* should normally ensure that no single individual has unrestricted authority to do all of the following:

(1) initiate a transaction;

(2) bind the *firm*;

(3) make payments; and

(4) account for it.

5.1.10 **[G]** Where a *firm* is unable to ensure the complete segregation of duties (for example, because it has a limited number of staff), it should ensure that there are adequate compensating controls in place (for example, frequent review of an area by relevant *senior managers*).

5.1.11 **[G]** Where a *common platform firm* outsources its internal audit function, it should take reasonable steps to ensure that every individual involved in the performance of this service is independent from the individuals who perform its external audit. This should not prevent services from being undertaken by a *firm's* external auditors provided that:

(1) the work is carried out under the supervision and management of the *firm's* own internal staff; and

(2) potential conflicts of interest between the provision of external audit services and the provision of internal audit are properly managed.

Awareness of procedures

5.1.12 **[R]** A *common platform firm* must ensure that its *relevant persons* are aware of the procedures which must be followed for the proper discharge of their responsibilities.

[Note: article 5(1)(b) of the *MiFID implementing Directive*]

5.1.12A **[G]** Other *firms* should take account of the rule concerning awareness of procedures (SYSC 5.1.12R) as if it were *guidance* (and as if "should" appeared in that *rule* instead of "must") as explained in SYSC 1 Annex 1.3.3G.

General

5.1.13 **[R]** The systems, internal control mechanisms and arrangements established by a *firm* in accordance with this chapter must take into account the nature, scale and complexity of its business and the nature and range of (for a *common platform firm*) *investment services and activities* or (for every other *firm*) financial services and activities undertaken in the course of that business.

[Note: article 5(1) final paragraph of the *MiFID implementing Directive*]

5.1.14 **[R]** A *common platform firm* must monitor and, on a regular basis, evaluate the adequacy and effectiveness of its systems, internal control mechanisms and arrangements established in accordance with this chapter, and take appropriate measures to address any deficiencies.

[Note: article 5(5) of the *MiFID implementing Directive*]

5.1.15 **[G]** Other *firms* should take account of the *rule* requiring monitoring and evaluation of the adequacy and effectiveness of systems (SYSC 5.1.14R) as if it were *guidance* (and as if "should" appeared in that rule instead of "must" as explained in SYSC 1 Annex 1.3.3G.

CHAPTER 6
COMPLIANCE, INTERNAL AUDIT AND FINANCIAL CRIME

6.1 Compliance

[2016A]

6.1.1 **[R]** A *firm must establish*, implement and maintain adequate policies and procedures sufficient to ensure compliance of the *firm* including its managers, employees and *appointed representatives* (or where applicable, *tied agents*) with its obligations under the *regulatory system* and for countering the risk that the *firm* might be used to further *financial crime*.

[Note: article 13(2) of *MiFID*]

6.1.2 **[R]** A *common platform firm* must, taking in to account the nature, scale and complexity of its business, and the nature and range of *investment services and activities* undertaken in the course of that business, establish, implement and maintain adequate policies and procedures designed to detect any risk of failure by the *firm* to comply with its obligations under the *regulatory system*, as well as associated risks, and put in place adequate measures and procedures designed to minimise such risks and to enable the *FSA* to exercise its powers effectively under the *regulatory system* and to enable any other *competent authority* to exercise its powers effectively under *MiFID*.

[Note: article 6(1) of the *MiFID implementing Directive*]

6.1.2A **[G]** Other *firms* should take account of the adequate policies and procedures *rule* (SYSC 6.1.2R) as if it were *guidance* (and as if "should" appeared in that rule instead of "must") as explained in SYSC 1 Annex 1.3.3G.

6.1.3 **[R]** A *common platform firm* must maintain a permanent and effective compliance function which operates independently and which has the following responsibilities:
(1) to monitor and, on a regular basis, to assess the adequacy and effectiveness of the measures and procedures put in place in accordance with SYSC 6.1.2R, and the actions taken to address any deficiencies in the *firm*'s compliance with its obligations;
(2) to advise and assist the *relevant persons* responsible for carrying out *regulated activities* to comply with the *firm's* obligations under the *regulatory system*.

[Note: article 6(2) of the *MiFID implementing Directive*]

6.1.3A **[G]**
(1) Other *firms* should take account of the compliance function *rule* (SYSC 6.1.3R) as if it were *guidance* (and as if "should" appeared in that rule instead of "must") as explained in SYSC 1 Annex 1.3.3G.
(2) Notwithstanding SYSC 6.1.3R, as it applies under (1), depending on the nature, scale and complexity of its business, it way be appropriate for a *firm* to have a separate compliance function. Where a *firm* has a separate compliance function the *firm* should also take into account SYSC 6.1.3R and 6.1.4R as *guidance*.

6.1.4 **[R]** In order to enable the compliance function to discharge its responsibilities properly and independently, a *common platform firm* must ensure that the following conditions are satisfied:
(1) the compliance function must have the necessary authority, resources, expertise and access to all relevant information;
(2) a compliance officer must be appointed and must be responsible for the compliance function and for any reporting as to compliance required by SYSC 4.3.2R;
(3) the *relevant persons* involved in the compliance functions must not be involved in the performance of services or activities they monitor;
(4) the method of determining the remuneration of the *relevant persons* involved in the compliance function must not compromise their objectivity and must not be likely to do so.

[Note: article 6(3) first paragraph of the *MiFID implementing Directive*]

6.1.4-A **[G]** In setting the method of determining the *remuneration* of *relevant persons* involved in the compliance function, certain *banks, building societies* and *BIPRU 730k firms* will also need to comply with the *Remuneration Code*. See SYSC 19.1 for details of the application of the *Remuneration Code*.

6.1.4A **[R]**
(1) A *firm* which is not a *common platform firm* and which carries on *designated investment business* with or for retail clients or professional clients must allocate to a *director* or *senior manager* the function of:
  (a) having responsibility for oversight of the firm's compliance; and
  (b) reporting to the *governing* body in respect of that responsibility.
(2) In SYSC 6.1.4AR(1) "compliance" means compliance with the rules in:
  (a) COBS (Conduct of Business sourcebook);
  (b) COLL (Collective Investment Schemes sourcebook) and CIS (Collective Investment Schemes sourcebook) (where appropriate);
  (c) CEAA (Client Assets sourcebook); and
  (d) ICOBS (insurance: Conduct of Business sourcebook).

6.1.5 **[R]** A *common platform firm* need not comply with SYSC 6.1.4R(3) or SYSC 6.1.4R(4) if it is able to demonstrate that in view of the nature, scale and complexity of its business, and the nature and range of (for a *common platform firm*) *investment services and activities or* (for every other *firm*) financial services and activities, the requirements under those *rules* are not proportionate and that its compliance function continues to be effective.

[Note: article 6(3) second paragraph of the *MiFID implementing Directive*]

6.1.6 **[G]** Other *firms* should take account of the proportionality *rule* (SYSC 6.1.5R) as if it were *guidance* (and as if "should" appeared in that rule instead of "must") as explained in SYSC 1 Annex 1.3.3G.

6.2 Internal audit

6.2.1 **[R]** A *common platform firm* must, where appropriate and proportionate in view of the nature, scale and complexity of its business and the nature and range of *investment services and activities* undertaken in the course of that business, establish and maintain an internal audit function which is separate and independent from the other functions and activities of the *firm* and which has the following responsibilities:

(1) to establish, implement and maintain an audit plan to examine and evaluate the adequacy and effectiveness of the *firm's* systems, internal control mechanisms and arrangements;

(2) to issue recommendations based on the result of work carried out in accordance with (1);

(3) to verify compliance with those recommendations;

(4) to report in relation to internal audit matters in accordance with SYSC 4.3.2R.

[Note: article 8 of the *MiFID implementing Directive*]

6.2.1A **[G]** Other *firms* should take account of the internal audit *rule* (SYSC 6.3.1R) as if it were *guidance* (and as if "should" appeared in that rule instead of "must") as explained in SYSC 1 Annex 1.3.3G.

6.2.2 **[G]** The term 'internal audit function' in SYSC 6.2.1R (and SYSC 4.1.11G) refers to the generally understood concept of internal audit within a *firm*, that is, the function of assessing adherence to and the effectiveness of internal systems and controls, procedures and policies. The internal audit function is not a *controlled function* itself, but is part of the *systems and controls function* (CF28).

6.3 Financial crime

6.3.1 **[R]** A *firm* must ensure the policies and procedures established under SYSC 6.1.1R include systems and controls that:

(1) enable it to identify, assess, monitor and manage *money laundering* risk; and

(2) are comprehensive and proportionate to the nature, scale and complexity of its activities.

6.3.2 **[G]** "*Money laundering* risk" is the risk that a *firm* may be used to further *money laundering*. Failure by a *firm* to manage this risk effectively will increase the risk to society of crime and terrorism.

6.3.3 **[R]** A *firm* must carry out regular assessment of the adequacy of these systems and controls to ensure that they continue to comply with SYSC 6.3.1R.

6.3.4 **[G]** A *firm* may also have separate obligations to comply with relevant legal requirements, including the Terrorism Act 2000, the Proceeds of Crime Act 2002 and the *Money Laundering Regulations*. SYSC 6.1.1R and SYSC 6.3.1R to SYSC 6.3.10G are not relevant for the purposes of regulation 3(3) of the *Money Laundering Regulations*, section 330(8) of the Proceeds of Crime Act 2002 or section 21A(6) of the Terrorism Act 2000.

6.3.5 **[G]** The *FSA*, when considering whether a breach of its *rules* on systems and controls against *money laundering* has occurred, will have regard to whether a *firm* has followed relevant provisions in the guidance for the *United Kingdom* financial sector issued by the Joint Money Laundering Steering Group.

6.3.6 **[G]** In identifying its *money laundering* risk and in establishing the nature of these systems and controls, a *firm* should consider a range of factors, including:

(1) its customer, product and activity profiles;

(2) its distribution channels;

(3) the complexity and volume of its transactions;

(4) its processes and systems; and

(5) its operating environment.

6.3.7 **[G]** A *firm* should ensure that the systems and controls include:

(1) appropriate training for its employees in relation to *money laundering*;

(2) appropriate provision of information to its *governing body* and senior management, including a report at least annually by that *firm's money laundering reporting officer* (*MLRO*) on the operation and effectiveness of those systems and controls;

(3) appropriate documentation of its risk management policies and risk profile in relation to *money laundering*, including documentation of its application of those policies (see SYSC 9);

(4) appropriate measures to ensure that *money laundering* risk is taken into account in its day-to-day operation, including in relation to:

  (a) the development of new products;

  (b) the taking-on of new customers; and

  (c) changes in its business profile; and

(5) appropriate measures to ensure that procedures for identification of new customers do not unreasonably deny access to its services to potential customers who cannot reasonably be expected to produce detailed evidence of identity.

6.3.8 **[R]** A *firm* must allocate to a *director* or *senior manager* (who may also be the *money laundering reporting officer*) overall responsibility within the *firm* for the establishment and maintenance of effective anti*money laundering* systems and controls.

The money laundering reporting officer

6.3.9 **[R]** A *firm* (with the exception of a *sole trader* who does not employ any *person* who is required to be approved under section 59 of the Act (Approval for particular purposes)) must:

(1) appoint an individual as *MLRO*, with responsibility for oversight of its compliance with the *FSA's rules* on systems and controls against *money laundering*; and

(2) ensure that its *MLRO* has a level of authority and independence within the *firm* and access to resources and information sufficient to enable him to carry out that responsibility.

6.3.10 **[G]** The job of the *MLRO* within a *firm* is to act as the focal point for all activity within the *firm* relating to anti-*money laundering*. The *FSA* expects that a *firm's MLRO* will be based in the *United Kingdom*.

CHAPTER 7
RISK CONTROL

7.1 Risk control

[2016B]

7.1.1 **[G]** SYSC 4.1.1R requires a *firm* to have effective processes to identify, manage, monitor and report the risks it is or might be exposed to.

7.1.2 **[R]** A *common platform firm* must establish, implement and maintain adequate risk management policies and procedures, including effective procedures for risk assessment, which identify the risks relating to the *firm's* activities, processes and systems, and where appropriate, set the level of risk tolerated by the *firm*.

[Note: article 7(1)(a) of the *MiFID implementing Directive*, article 13(5) second paragraph of *MiFID*]

7.1.2A **[G]** Other *firms* should take account of the risk management policies and procedures *rule* (SYSC 7.1.2R) as if it were *guidance* (and as if "should" appeared in that rule instead of "must") as explained in SYSC 1 Annex 1.3.3G.

7.1.3 **[R]** A *common platform firm* must adopt effective arrangements, processes and mechanisms to manage the risk relating to the *firm's* activities, processes and systems, in light of that level of risk tolerance.

[Note: article 7(1)(b) of the *MiFID implementing Directive*]

7.1.4 **[R]** The *senior personnel* of a *common platform firm* must approve and periodically review the strategies and policies for taking up, managing, monitoring and mitigating the risks the *firm* is or might be exposed to, including those posed by the macroeconomic environment in which it operates in relation to the status of the business cycle.

[Note: annex V paragraph 2 of the *Banking Consolidation Directive*]

7.1.4A **[G]** Other *firms* should take account of the risk management *rules* (SYSC 7.1.3R and SYSC 7.1.4R) as if they were *guidance* (and as if "should" appeared in those rules instead of "must") as explained in SYSC 1 Annex 1.3.3G.

7.1.5 **[R]** A *common platform firm* must monitor the following:

(1) the adequacy and effectiveness of the *firm's* risk management policies and procedures;

(2) the level of compliance by the *firm* and its *relevant persons* with the arrangements, processes and mechanisms adopted in accordance with SYSC 7.1.3R;

(3) the adequacy and effectiveness of measures taken to address any deficiencies in those policies, procedures, arrangements, processes and mechanisms, including failures by the *relevant persons* to comply with such arrangements or processes and mechanisms or follow such policies and procedures.

[Note: article 7(1)(c) of the *MiFID implementing Directive*]

7.1.6 **[R]** A *common platform firm* must, where appropriate and proportionate in view of the nature, scale and complexity of its business and the nature and range of the *investment services and activities* undertaken in the course of that business, establish and maintain a risk management function that operates independently and carries out the following tasks:

(1) implementation of the policies and procedures referred to in SYSC 7.1.2R to SYSC 7.1.5R; and

(2) provision of reports and advice to *senior personnel* in accordance with SYSC 4.3.2R.

[Note: *MiFID implementing Directive* article 7(2) first paragraph]

7.1.7 **[R]** Where a *common platform firm* is not required under SYSC 7.1.6R to maintain a risk management function that functions independently, it must nevertheless be able to demonstrate that the policies and procedures which it has adopted in accordance with SYSC 7.1.2R to SYSC 7.1.5R satisfy the requirements of those *rules* and are consistently effective.

[Note: article 7(2) second paragraph of the *MiFID implementing Directive*]

7.1.7A **[G]** Other *firms* should take account of the risk management *rules* (SYSC 7.1.5R to 7.1.7R) as if they were *guidance* (and as if "should" appeared in those rules instead of "must") as explained in SYSC 1 Annex 1.3.3G.

7.1.7B **[G]** In setting the method of determining the *remuneration* of *employees* involved in the risk management function, certain *banks*, *building societies* and *BIPRU 730k firms* will also need to comply with the *Remuneration Code*. See SYSC 19.1 for details of the application of the *Remuneration Code*.

7.1.8 **[G]**

(1) SYSC 4.1.3R requires a *BIPRU firm* to ensure that its internal control mechanisms and administrative and accounting procedures permit the verification of its compliance with *rules* adopted in accordance with the *Capital Adequacy Directive* at all times. In complying with this obligation, a *BIPRU firm* should document the organisation and responsibilities of its risk management function and it should document its risk management framework setting out how the risks in the business are identified, measured, monitored and controlled.

(2) The term 'risk management function' in SYSC 7.1.6R and SYSC 7.1.7R refers to the generally understood concept of risk assessment within a *firm*, that is, the function of setting and controlling risk exposure. The risk management function is not a *controlled function* itself, but is part of the *systems and controls function* (CF28).

Credit and counterparty risk

7.1.9 **[R]** A *BIPRU firm* must base credit-granting on sound and well-defined criteria and clearly establish the process for approving, amending, renewing, and refinancing credits.

[Note: annex V paragraph 3 of the *Banking Consolidation Directive*]

7.1.10 **[R]** A *BIPRU firm* must operate through effective systems the ongoing administration and monitoring of its various credit risk-bearing portfolios and exposures, including for identifying and managing problem credits and for making adequate value adjustments and provisions.

[Note: annex V paragraph 4 of the *Banking Consolidation Directive*]

7.1.11 **[R]** A *BIPRU firm* must adequately diversify credit portfolios given its target market and overall credit strategy.

[Note: annex V paragraph 5 of the *Banking Consolidation Directive*]

7.1.12 **[G]** The documentation maintained by a *BIPRU firm* under SYSC 4.1.3R should include its policy for credit risk, including its risk appetite and provisioning policy and should describe how it measures, monitors and controls that risk. This should include descriptions of the systems used to ensure that the policy is correctly implemented.

Residual risk

7.1.13 **[R]** A *BIPRU firm* must address and control by means of written policies and procedures the risk that recognised credit risk mitigation techniques used by it prove less effective than expected.

[Note: annex V paragraph 6 of the *Banking Consolidation Directive*]

Market risk

7.1.14 **[R]** A *BIPRU firm* must implement policies and processes for the measurement and management of all material sources and effects of market risks.

[Note: annex V paragraph 10 of the *Banking Consolidation Directive*]

Interest rate risk

7.1.15 **[R]** A *BIPRU firm* must implement systems to evaluate and manage the risk arsing from potential changes in interest rates as they affect a *BIPRU firm's* non-trading activities.

[Note: annex V paragraph 11 of the *Banking Consolidation Directive*]

Operational risk

7.1.16 **[R]** A *BIPRU firm* must implement policies and processes to evaluate and manage the exposure to operational risk, including to low-frequency high severity events. Without prejudice to the definition of *operational risk*, *BIPRU firms* must articulate what constitutes operational risk for the purposes of those policies and procedures.

[Note: annex V paragraph 12 of the *Banking Consolidation Directive*]

CHAPTER 8
OUTSOURCING

8.1 General outsourcing requirements

[2016C]

8.1.1 **[R]** A *common platform firm* must:

(1) when relying on a third party for the performance of operational functions which are critical for the performance of *regulated activities, listed activities* or *ancillary services* (in this chapter "relevant services and activities") on a continuous and satisfactory basis, ensure that it takes reasonable steps to avoid undue additional operational risk;

(2) not undertake the *outsourcing* of important operational functions in such a way as to impair materially:

  (a) the quality of its internal control; and

  (b) the ability of the *FSA* to monitor the *firm's* compliance with all obligations under the *regulatory system* and, if different, of a *competent authority* to monitor the *firm's* compliance with all obligations under *MiFID*.

[Note: article 13(5) first paragraph of *MiFID*]

8.1.1A **[G]** Other *firms* should take account of the outsourcing *rule* (SYSC 8.1.1R) as if it were *guidance* (and as if "should" appeared in that rule instead of "must") as explained in SYSC 1 Annex 1.3.3G.

8.1.2 **[G]** The application of SYSC 8.1 to relevant services and activities (see SYSC 8.1.1R(1)) is limited by SYSC 1 Annex 1 (Part 2) (Application of the common platform requirements).

8.1.3 **[G]** SYSC 4.1.1R requires a *firm* to have effective processes to identify, manage, monitor and report risks and internal control mechanisms. Except in relation to those functions described in SYSC 8.1.5R, where a *firm* relies on a third party for the performance of operational functions which are not critical or important for the performance of relevant services and activities (see SYSC 8.1.1R(1)) on a continuous and satisfactory basis, it should take into account, in a manner that is proportionate given the nature, scale and complexity of the *outsourcing*, the *rules* in this section in complying with that requirement.

8.1.4 **[R]** For the purposes of this chapter an operational function is regarded as critical or important if a defect or failure in its performance would materially impair the continuing compliance of a *common platform firm* with the conditions and obligations of its *authorisation* or its other obligations under the *regulatory system*, or its financial performance, or the soundness or the continuity of its relevant services and activities.

[Note: article 13(1) of the *MiFID implementing Directive*]

8.1.5 **[R]** Without prejudice to the status of any other function, the following functions will not be considered as critical or important for the purposes of this chapter:

(1) the provision to the *firm* of advisory services, and other services which do not form part of the relevant services and activities of the *firm*, including the provision of legal advice to the *firm*, the training of personnel of the *firm*, billing services and the security of the *firm's* premises and personnel;

(2) the purchase of standardised services, including market information services and the provision of price feeds.

[Note: article 13(2) of the *MiFID implementing Directive*]

(3) the recording and retention of relevant telephone conversations or electronic communications subject to COBS 11.8.

8.1.5A **[G]** Other *firms* should take account of the critical functions *rules* (SYSC 8.1.4R and SYSC 8.1.5R) as if they were *guidance* (and as if "should" appeared in that rule instead of "must") as explained in SYSC 1 Annex 1.3.3G.

8.1.6 **[R]** If a *firm outsources* critical or important operational functions or any relevant services and activities, it remains fully responsible for discharging all of its obligations under the *regulatory system* and must comply, in particular, with the following conditions:

(1) the *outsourcing* must not result in the delegation by *senior personnel* of their responsibility;

(2) the relationship and obligations of the *firm* towards its *clients* under the *regulatory system* must not be altered;

(3) the conditions with which the *firm* must comply in order to be *authorised*, and to remain so, must not be undermined;

(4) none of the other conditions subject to which the *firm's authorisation* was granted must be removed or modified.

[Note: article 14(1) of the *MiFID implementing Directive*]

8.1.7 **[R]** A *common platform firm* must exercise due skill and care and diligence when entering into, managing or terminating any arrangement for the *outsourcing* to a service provider of critical or important operational functions or of any relevant services and activities.

[Note: article 14(2) first paragraph of the *MiFID implementing Directive*]

8.1.8 **[R]** A *common platform firm* must in particular take the necessary steps to ensure that the following conditions are satisfied:

(1) the service provider must have the ability, capacity, and any *authorisation* required by law to perform the *outsourced* functions, services or activities reliably and professionally;

(2) the service provider must carry out the *outsourced* services effectively, and to this end the *firm* must establish methods for assessing the standard of performance of the service provider;

(3) the service provider must properly supervise the carrying out of the *outsourced* functions, and adequately manage the risks associated with the *outsourcing*;

(4) appropriate action must be taken if it appears that the service provider may not be carrying out the functions effectively and in compliance with applicable laws and regulatory requirements;

(5) the *firm* must retain the necessary expertise to supervise the *outsourced* functions effectively and to manage the risks associated with the *outsourcing*, and must supervise those functions and manage those risks;

(6) the service provider must disclose to the *firm* any development that may have a material impact on its ability to carry out the *outsourced* functions effectively and in compliance with applicable laws and regulatory requirements;

(7) the *firm* must be able to terminate the arrangement for the *outsourcing* where necessary without detriment to the continuity and quality of its provision of services to *clients*;

(8) the service provider must co-operate with the *FSA* and any other relevant *competent authority* in connection with the *outsourced* activities;

(9) the *firm*, it auditors, the *FSA* and any other relevant *competent authority* must have effective access to data related to the *outsourced* activities, as well as to the business premises of the service provider; and the *FSA* and any other relevant *competent authority* must be able to exercise those rights of access;

(10) the service provider must protect any confidential information relating to the *firm* and its *clients*;

(11) the *firm* and the service provider must establish, implement and maintain a contingency plan for disaster recovery and periodic testing of backup facilities where that is necessary having regard to the function, service or activity that has been *outsourced*.

[Note: article 14(2) second paragraph of the *MiFID implementing Directive*]

8.1.9 **[R]** A *common platform firm* must ensure that the respective rights and obligations of the *firm* and of the service provider are clearly allocated and set out in a written agreement.

[Note: article 14(3) of the *MiFID implementing Directive*]

8.1.10 **[R]** If a *common platform firm* and the service provider are members of the same *group*, the *firm* may, for the purpose of complying with SYSC 8.1.7R to SYSC 8.1.11R and SYSC 8.2 and SYSC 8.3, take into account the extent to which the *common platform firm controls* the service provider or has the ability to influence its actions.

[Note: article 14(4) of the *MiFID implementing Directive*]

8.1.11 **[R]** A *common platform firm* must make available on request to the *FSA* and any other relevant *competent authority* all information necessary to enable the *FSA* and any other relevant *competent authority* to supervise the compliance of the performance of the *outsourced* activities with the requirements of the *regulatory system*.

[Note: article 14(5) of the *MiFID implementing Directive*]

8.1.11A **[G]** Other *firms* should take account of the outsourcing of important operational functions *rules* (SYSC 8.1.7R to SYSC 8.1.11R) as if they were *guidance* (and as if "should" appeared in that rule instead of "must") as explained in SYSC 1 Annex 1.3.3G.

8.1.12 **[G]** As SUP 15.3.8G explains, a *firm* should notify the *FSA* when it intends to rely on a third party for the performance of operational functions which are critical or important for the performance of relevant services and activities on a continuous and satisfactory basis.

[Note: recital 20 of the *MiFID implementing Directive*]

8.2 Outsourcing of portfolio management for retail clients to a non-EEA State

8.2.1 **[R]**

(1) In addition to the requirements set out in the *MiFID outsourcing rules*, when a *MiFID investment firm outsources* the *investment service* of *portfolio management* to *retail clients* to a service provider located in a *non-EEA state*, it must ensure that the following conditions are satisfied:

(a) the service provider must be authorised or registered in its home country to provide that service and must be subject to prudential supervision;

(b) there must be an appropriate cooperation agreement between the *FSA* and the supervisor in the non-*EEA State*. (in this chapter the "conditions").

[Note: article 15(1) of the *MiFID implementing Directive*]

(2) In addition to complying with the *common platform outsourcing rules*, if one or both of the conditions are not satisfied, a *MiFID investment firm* may enter into such an *outsourcing* only if it gives prior notification in writing to the *FSA* containing adequate details of the proposed *outsourcing* and the *FSA* does not object to that arrangement within a reasonable time following receipt of that notification.

[Note: article 15(2) and (4) of the *MiFID implementing Directive*]

(3) For the purposes of this *rule* a "reasonable time" is within one month of receipt of a notification. However, the *FSA* may seek further information from the *MiFID investment firm* in relation to the *outsourcing* proposal if this is necessary to enable the *FSA* to make a decision. Any effect this may have on the *FSA's* response time will be notified to the *MiFID investment firm* and that revised response time will constitute a reasonable time for the purposes of this *rule*.

8.2.2 [intentionally blank]

8.2.3 **[G]** The conditions do not apply if the *outsourcing* only concerns ancillary activities connected with *portfolio management*, for example IT processes or execution only activities.

8.2.4 **[G]** If a *firm* has received no notice of objection or no request for further information from the *FSA* within one month of the *FSA* receiving the notification, it may *outsource* the *portfolio management* on the basis set out in the notification.

8.2.5 **[G]** The *FSA* would use its powers under section 45 of the *Act* to vary a *firm's permission* if it objected to such a notification.

Notification requirements: timing of notification

8.2.6 **[G]** A *firm* should only make an *outsourcing* proposal notification to the *FSA* after it has carried out due diligence on the service provider and has had regard to the *guidance* set out in SYSC 8.3. The *FSA* will expect a *firm* to only submit an *outsourcing* proposal notification in respect of a service provider that the *firm* has determined is suitable to carry on the *outsourcing* activity.

Notification requirements: content

8.2.7 **[G]** The *guidance* set out in SYSC 8.3 includes information on what the *FSA* will expect a *firm* to check before the submission of a notification.

8.2.8 **[G]** A notification under this section should include:

(1) details on which of the conditions is not met;

(2) if applicable, details and evidence of the service provider's authorisation or regulation including the regulator's contact details;

(3) the *firm's* proposals for meeting its obligations under this chapter on an ongoing basis;

(4) why the *firm* wishes to *outsource* to the service provider;

(5) a draft of the *outsourcing* agreement between the service provider and the *firm*;

(6) the proposed start date of the *outsourcing*; and

(7) confirmation that the *firm* has had regard to the *guidance* in SYSC 8.3, or if it has not, why not.

Notification requirements – additional guidance

8.2.9 **[G]** Where the *FSA* has not objected to the *outsourcing* agreement, the *firm* should have regard to its obligations under SUP 15 which include making the *FSA* aware of any matters which could affect the *firm's* ability to provide adequate services to its *customers* or could result in serious detriment to its *customers* or where there has been material change in the information previously provided to the *FSA* in relation to the *outsourcing*.

8.3 Guidance on outsourcing portfolio management for retail clients to a non-EEA State

8.3.1 **[G]** This *guidance* is relevant regardless of whether a *firm outsources portfolio management* directly or indirectly via a third party. However, *firms* should note that they may notify a secondary or indirect outsourcing in the same notification as the direct outsourcing.

8.3.2 **[G]** This *guidance* sets out examples of the type of actions that a *firm* proposing to *outsource* should have undertaken when assessing the suitability of the service provider and its ability to carry on the *outsourced* activity.

[Note: article 15(3) of the *MiFID implementing Directive*]

8.3.3 **[G]** If a *firm* can demonstrate that it has taken the following *guidance* into account and has satisfactorily concluded that it would be able to continue to satisfy the *common platform outsourcing* *rules* and provide adequate protection for consumers despite not satisfying the conditions, the *FSA* would not be likely to object to that *outsourcing*.

8.3.4 **[G]** If the *outsourcing* allows the service provider to sub-contract any of the services to be provided under the *outsourcing*, any such sub-contracting shall not affect the service provider's responsibilities under the *outsourcing* agreement.

8.3.5 **[G]** The *outsourcing* agreement should entitle the *firm* to terminate the *outsourcing* if the service provider undergoes a change of control or becomes insolvent, goes into liquidation or receivership (or equivalent in its home state) or is in persistent material default under the agreement.

8.3.6 **[G]** The following should be taken into account where the service provider is not authorised or registered in its home country and/or not subject to prudential supervision.

(1) The *firm* should examine, and be able to demonstrate, to what extent the service provider may be subject to any form of voluntary regulation, including self-regulation in its home state.

(2) The *firm* should be able to satisfy the *FSA* that the service provider is committed for the term of the *outsourcing* agreement to devoting sufficient, competent resources to providing the service.

(3) In addition to the requirement to ensure that a service provider discloses any developments that may have a material impact on its ability carry out the *outsourcing* (SYSC 8.1.8(6)), where the conditions are not met the developments to be disclosed should include, but are not limited to:

   (a) any adverse effect that any laws or regulations introduced in the service provider's home country may have on its carrying on the *outsourced* activity; and

   (b) any changes to its capital reserve levels or its prudential risks.

(4) The *firm* should satisfy itself that the service provider is able to meet its liabilities as they fall due and that it has positive net assets.

(5) The *firm* should require that the service provider prepares annual reports and accounts which:

   (a) are in accordance with the service provider's national law which, in all material respects, is the same as or equivalent to the *international accounting standards*;

   (b) have been independently audited and reported on in accordance with the service provider's national law which is the same as or equivalent to international auditing standards.

(6) The *firm* should receive copies of each set of the audited annual report and accounts of the service provider. If the service provider expects or knows its auditor will qualify his report on the audited report and accounts, or add an explanatory paragraph, the service provider should be required to notify the *firm* without delay.

(7) The *firm* should satisfy itself, and be able to demonstrate, that it has in place appropriate procedures to ensure that it is fully aware of the service provider's controls for protecting confidential information.

(8) In addition to the requirement at SYSC 8.1.8R (10) that the service provider must protect any confidential information relating to the *firm* or its *clients*, the *outsourcing* agreement should require the service provider to notify the *firm* immediately if there is a breach of confidentiality.

(9) The *outsourcing* agreement should be governed by the law and subject to the jurisdiction of an *EEA state*.

8.3.7 **[G]** The following should be taken into account by a *firm* where there is no cooperation agreement between the FSA and the supervisory authority of the service provider or there is no supervisory authority of the service provider.

(1) The *outsourcing* agreement should ensure the *firm* can provide the *FSA* with any information relating to the *outsourced* activity the *FSA* may require in order to carry out effective supervision. The *firm* should therefore assess the extent to which the service provider's regulator and/or local laws and regulations may restrict access to information about the *outsourced* activity. Any such restriction should be described in the notification to be sent to the *FSA*.

(2) The *outsourcing* agreement should require the service provider to provide the *firm*'s offices in the *United Kingdom* with all requested information required to meet the *firm's* regulatory obligations. The *FSA* should be given an enforceable right under the agreement to obtain such information from the *firm* and to require the service provider to provide the information directly.

CHAPTER 9
RECORD-KEEPING

9.1 General rules on record-keeping

[2016D]

9.1.-1 **[R]** [deleted]

9.1.-2 **[R]** [deleted]

9.1.1 **[R]** A *firm* must arrange for orderly records to be kept of its business and internal organisation, including all services and transactions undertaken by it, which must be sufficient to enable the *FSA* or any other relevant *competent authority* under *MiFID* to monitor the *firm's* compliance with the requirements under the *regulatory system*, and in particular to ascertain that the *firm* has complied with all obligations with respect to *clients*.

[Note: article 13(6) of *MiFID* and article 5(1)(f) of the *MiFID implementing Directive*]

9.1.2 **[R]** A *common platform firm* must retain all records kept by it under this chapter in relation to its *MiFID business* for a period of at least five years.

[Note: article 51 (1) of the *MiFID implementing Directive*]

9.1.3 **[R]** In relation to its *MiFID business*, a *common platform firm* must retain records in a medium that allows the storage of information in a way accessible for future reference by the *FSA* or any other relevant *competent authority* under *MiFID*, and so that the following conditions are met:

(1) the *FSA* or any other relevant *competent authority* under *MiFID* must be able to access them readily and to reconstitute each key stage of the processing of each transaction;

(2) it must be possible for any corrections or other amendments, and the contents of the records prior to such corrections and amendments, to be easily ascertained;

(3) it must not be possible for the records otherwise to be manipulated or altered.

[Note: article 51(2) of the *MiFID implementing Directive*]

Guidance on record-keeping

9.1.4 **[G]** Subject to any other record-keeping *rule* in the *Handbook*, the records required under the *Handbook* should be capable of being reproduced in the English language on paper. Where a *firm* is required to retain a record of a communication that was not made in the English language, it may retain it in that language. However, it should be able to provide a translation on request. If a *firm's* records relate to business carried on from an establishment in a country or territory outside the *United Kingdom*, an official language of that country or territory may be used instead of the English language.

9.1.5 **[G]** In relation to the retention of records for non-*MiFID business*, a *firm* should have appropriate systems and controls in place with respect to the adequacy of, access to, and the security of its records so that the *firm* may fulfil its regulatory and statutory obligations. With respect to retention periods, the general principle is that records should be retained for as long as is relevant for the purposes for which they are made.

9.1.6 **[G]** Schedule 1 to each module of the *Handbook* sets out a list summarising the record-keeping requirements of that module.

[Note: article 51(3) of *MiFID implementing Directive*]

9.1.7 **[G]** The Committee of European Securities Regulators (CESR) has issued recommendations on the list of minimum records under article 51(3) of the *MiFID implementing Directive*. This can be found at: http://www.fsa.gov.uk/pubs/other/CESR_Minimum_List_Recommendations.pdf.

CHAPTER 10

10.1 Conflicts of interest

Application

[2016E]

10.1.1 **[R]** This section applies to a *firm* which provides services to its *clients* in the course of carrying on *regulated activities* or *ancillary activities* or providing *ancillary services* (but only where the *ancillary services* constitute *MiFID business*).

Requirements only apply if a service is provided

10.1.2 **[G]** The requirements in this section only apply where a service is provided by a *firm*. The status of the *client* to whom the service is provided (as a *retail client*, *professional client* or *eligible counterparty*) is irrelevant for this purpose.

[Note: recital 25 of *MiFID implementing Directive*]

Identifying conflicts

10.1.3 **[R]** A *firm* must take all reasonable steps to identify conflicts of interest between:

(1) the *firm*, including its managers, employees, *appointed representatives* (or where applicable *tied agents*), or any *person* directly or indirectly linked to them by *control*, and a *client* of the *firm*; or

(2) one *client* of the *firm* and another *client*;

that arise, or may arise, in the course of the *firm* providing any service referred to in SYSC 10.1.1R.
[Note: article 18(1) of *MiFID*]

Types of conflicts

10.1.4 **[R]** For the purposes of identifying the types of conflict of interest that arise, or may arise, in the course of providing a service and whose existence may entail a material risk of damage to the interests of a *client*, a *common platform firm* must take into account, as a minimum, whether the *firm* or a *relevant person*, or a *person* directly or indirectly linked by *control* to the *firm*:
(1) is likely to make a financial gain, or avoid a financial loss, at the expense of the *client*;
(2) has an interest in the outcome of a service provided to the *client* or of a transaction carried out on behalf of the *client*, which is distinct from the *client's* interest in that outcome;
(3) has a financial or other incentive to favour the interest of another *client* or group of *clients* over the interests of the *client*;
(4) carries on the same business as the *client*; or
(5) receives or will receive from a *person* other than the *client* an inducement in relation to a service provided to the *client*, in the form of monies, goods or services, other than the standard commission or fee for that service.

The conflict of interest may result from the *firm* or *person* providing a service referred to in SYSC 10.1.1R or engaging in any other activity.

[Note: article 21 of *MiFID implementing Directive*]

10.1.4A **[G]** Other *firms* should take account of the *rule* on the types of conflicts (see SYSC 10.1.4R) as if it were *guidance* (and as if "should" appeared in that rule instead of "must") as explained in SYSC 1 Annex 1.3.3G), except when they produce or arrange the production of *investment research* in accordance with COBS 12.2, or produce or disseminate *non-independent research* in accordance with COBS 12.3 (see SYSC 10.1.16R).

10.1.5 **[G]** The circumstances which should be treated as giving rise to a conflict of interest should cover cases where there is a conflict between the interests of the *firm* or certain *persons* connected to the *firm* or the *firm's group* and the duty the *firm* owes to a *client*; or between the differing interests of two or more of its *clients*, to whom the *firm* owes in each case a duty. It is not enough that the *firm* may gain a benefit if there is not also a possible disadvantage to a *client*, or that one *client* to whom the *firm* owes a duty may make a gain or avoid a loss without there being a concomitant possible loss to another such *client*.

[Note: Recital 24 of *MiFID implementing Directive*]

Record of conflicts

10.1.6 **[R]** A *common platform firm* must keep and regularly update a record of the kinds of service or activity carried out by or on behalf of the *firm* in which a conflict of interest entailing a material risk of damage to the interests of one or more *clients* has arisen or, in the case of an ongoing service or activity, may arise.

[Note: article 23 of *MiFID implementing Directive*]

10.1.6A **[G]** Other *firms* should take account of the *rule* on records of conflicts (see SYSC 10.1.6R) as if it were *guidance* (and as if "should" appeared in that rule instead of "must") as explained in SYSC 1 Annex 1.3.3G), except when they produce or arrange the production of *investment research* in accordance with COBS 12.2, or produce or disseminate *non-independent research* in accordance with COBS 12.3 (see SYSC 10.1.16R).

Managing conflicts

10.1.7 **[R]** A *firm* must maintain and operate effective organisational and administrative arrangements with a view to taking all reasonable steps to prevent conflicts of interest as defined in SYSC 10.1.3R from constituting or giving rise to a material risk of damage to the interests of its *clients*.
[Note: article 13(3) of *MiFID*]

Disclosure of conflicts

10.1.8 **[R]**
(1) If arrangements made by a *firm* under SYSC 10.1.7R to manage conflicts of interest are not sufficient to ensure, with reasonable confidence, that risks of damage to the interests of a *client* will be prevented, the *firm* must clearly disclose the general nature and/or sources of conflicts of interest to the *client* before undertaking business for the *client*.
(2) The disclosure must:
   (a) be made in a *durable medium*; and
   (b) include sufficient detail, taking into account the nature of the *client*, to enable that *client* to take an informed decision with respect to the service in the context of which the conflict of interest arises.

[Note: article 18(2) of *MiFID* and article 22(4) of *MiFID implementing Directive*]

10.1.8A **[R]** The obligation in SYSC 10.1.8R(2)(a) does not apply to a *firm* when carrying on *insurance mediation activity*.

10.1.9 **[G]** *Firms* should aim to identify and manage the conflicts of interest arising in relation to their various business lines and their *group's* activities under a comprehensive *conflicts of interest policy*. In particular, the disclosure of conflicts of interest by a *firm* should not exempt it from the obligation to maintain and operate the effective organisational and administrative arrangements under SYSC 10.1.7R. While disclosure of specific conflicts of interest is required by SYSC 10.1.8R, an over-reliance on disclosure without adequate consideration as to how conflicts may appropriately be managed is not permitted.

[Note: Recital 27 of *MiFID implementing Directive*]

Conflicts policy

10.1.10 **[R]**

(1) A *common platform firm* must establish, implement and maintain an effective conflicts of interest policy that is set out in writing and is appropriate to the size and organisation of the *firm* and the nature, scale and complexity of its business.

(2) Where the *common platform firm* is a member of a *group*, the policy must also take into account any circumstances, of which the *firm* is or should be aware, which may give rise to a conflict of interest arising as a result of the structure and business activities of other members of the *group*.

[Note: article 22(1) of *MiFID implementing Directive]*

Contents of policy

10.1.11 **[R]**

(1) The *conflicts of interest policy* must include the following content:
  - (a) it must identify in accordance with SYSC 10.1.3R and SYSC 10.1.4R, by reference to the specific services and activities carried out by or on behalf of the *common platform firm*, the circumstances which constitute or may give rise to a conflict of interest entailing a material risk of damage to the interests of one or more *clients*; and
  - (b) it must specify procedures to be followed and measures to be adopted in order to manage such conflicts.

(2) The procedures and measures provided for in paragraph (1)(b) must:
  - (a) be designed to ensure that *relevant persons* engaged in different business activities involving a conflict of interest of the kind specified in paragraph (1)(a) carry on those activities at a level of independence appropriate to the size and activities of the *common platform firm* and of the *group* to which it belongs, and to the materiality of the risk of damage to the interests of *clients*; and
  - (b) include such of the following as are necessary and appropriate for the *common platform firm* to ensure the requisite degree of independence:
    - (i) effective procedures to prevent or control the exchange of information between *relevant persons* engaged in activities involving a risk of a conflict of interest where the exchange of that information may harm the interests of one or more *clients*;
    - (ii) the separate supervision of *relevant persons* whose principal functions involve carrying out activities on behalf of, or providing services to, *clients* whose interests may conflict, or who otherwise represent different interests that may conflict, including those of the *firm*;
    - (iii) the removal of any direct link between the remuneration of *relevant persons* principally engaged in one activity and the remuneration of, or revenues generated by, different *relevant persons* principally engaged in another activity, where a conflict of interest may arise in relation to those activities;
    - (iv) measures to prevent or limit any *person* from exercising inappropriate influence over the way in which a *relevant person* carries out services or activities; and
    - (v) measures to prevent or control the simultaneous or sequential involvement of a *relevant person* in separate services or activities where such involvement may impair the proper management of conflicts of interest.

(3) If the adoption or the practice of one or more of those measures and procedures does not ensure the requisite level of independence, a *common platform firm* must adopt such alternative or additional measures and procedures as are necessary and appropriate for those purposes.

[Note: article 22(2) and (3) of *MiFID implementing Directive*]

10.1.11A **[G]** Other *firms* should take account of the *rules* relating to conflicts of interest policies (see SYSC 10.1.10R and SYSC 10.1.11R) as if they were guidance (and as if "should" appeared in those rules instead of "must", as explained in SYSC 1 Annex 1.3.3G), except when they produce or arrange the production of *investment research* in accordance with COBS 12.2, or produce or disseminate *non-independent research* in accordance with COBS 12.3 (see SYSC 10.1.16R).

10.1.12 **[G]** In drawing up a *conflicts of interest policy* which identifies circumstances which constitute or may give rise to a conflict of interest, a *firm* should pay special attention to the activities of investment research and advice, proprietary trading, portfolio management and corporate finance business, including underwriting or selling in an offering of securities and advising on mergers and acquisitions. In particular, such special attention is appropriate where the *firm* or a *person* directly or indirectly linked by *control* to the *firm* performs a combination of two or more of those activities.

[Note: Recital 26 of *MiFID implementing Directive]*

Corporate finance

10.1.13 **[G]** This section is relevant to the management of a *securities* offering by any *firm.*

10.1.14 **[G]** A *firm* will wish to note that when carrying on a mandate to manage an offering of *securities*, the *firm's* duty for that business is to its corporate finance *client* (in many cases, the corporate issuer or seller of the relevant *securities*), but that its responsibilities to provide services to its investment *clients* are unchanged.

10.1.15 **[G]** Measures that a *firm* might wish to consider in drawing up its *conflicts of interest policy* in relation to the management of an offering of *securities* include:

(1) at an early stage agreeing with its corporate finance *client* relevant aspects of the offering process such as the process the *firm* proposes to follow in order to determine what recommendations it will make about allocations for the offering; how the target investor group will be identified; how recommendations on allocation and pricing will be prepared; and whether the *firm* might place *securities* with its investment *clients* or with its own proprietary book, or with an associate, and how conflicts arising might be managed; and

(2) agreeing allocation and pricing objectives with the corporate finance *client*; inviting the corporate finance *client* to participate actively in the allocation process; making the initial recommendation for allocation to *retail clients* of the *firm* as a single block and not on a named basis; having internal arrangements under which senior personnel responsible for providing services to *retail clients* make the initial allocation recommendations for allocation to *retail clients* of the *firm*; and disclosing to the *issuer* details of the allocations actually made.

[Note: The provisions in SYSC 10.1 also implement *BCD* article 22 and *BCD* Annex V paragraph 1]

Application of conflicts of interest rules to non-common platform firms when producing investment research or non-independent research

10.1.16 **[R]** The *rules* relating to:

(1) types of conflict (see SYSC 10.1.5R);

(2) records of conflicts (see SYSC 10.1.6R); and

(3) *conflicts of interest policies* (see SYSC 10.1.10R and SYSC 10.1.11R);

also apply to a *firm* which is not a *common platform firm* when it produces, or arranges for the production of, *investment research* that is intended or likely to be subsequently disseminated to clients of the *firm* or to the public in accordance with COBS 12.2, and when it produces or disseminates *non-independent research* in accordance with COBS 12.3.

10.2 Chinese walls

Application

10.2.1 **[R]** This section applies to any *firm.*

Control of information

10.2.2 **[R]**

(1) When a *firm* establishes and maintains a *Chinese wall* (that is, an arrangement that requires information held by a *person* in the course of carrying on one part of the business to be withheld from, or not to be used for, *persons* with or for whom it acts in the course of carrying on another part of its business) it may:

   (a) withhold or not use the information held; and

   (b) for that purpose, permit *persons* employed in the first part of its business to withhold the information held from those employed in that other part of the business;

   but only to the extent that the business of one of those parts involves the carrying on of *regulated activities*, *ancillary activities* or, in the case of *MiFID business*, the provision of *ancillary services*.

Part II FSA Handbook Materials

(2) Information may also be withheld or not used by a *firm* when this is required by an established arrangement maintained between different parts of the business (of any kind) in the same *group*. This provision does not affect any requirement to transmit or use information that may arise apart from the *rules* in COBS.
(3) For the purpose of this *rule*, "maintains" includes taking reasonable steps to ensure that the arrangements remain effective and are adequately monitored, and must be interpreted accordingly.
(4) For the purposes of section 118A(5)(a) of the *Act*, behaviour conforming with paragraph (1) does not amount to market abuse.

Effect of rules

10.2.3 **[G]** SYSC 10.2.2R is made under section 147 of the *Act* (Control of information rules). It has the following effect:
(1) acting in conformity with SYSC 10.2.2R(1) provides a defence against proceedings brought under section 397(2) or (3) of the *Act* (Misleading statements and practices) – see sections 397(4) and (5)(c);
(2) behaviour in conformity with SYSC 10.2.2R(1) does not amount to *market abuse* (see SYSC 10.2.2R(4)); and
(3) acting in conformity with SYSC 10.2.2R(1) provides a defence for a firm against *FSA* enforcement action, or an action for damages under section 150 of the *Act*, based on a breach of a relevant requirement to disclose or use this information.

Attribution of knowledge

10.2.4 **[R]** When any of the *rules* of COBS or CASS apply to a *firm* that acts with knowledge, the *firm* will not be taken to act with knowledge for the purposes of that *rule* if none of the relevant individuals involved on behalf of the *firm* acts with that knowledge as a result of arrangements established under SYSC 10.2.2R.

10.2.5 **[G]** When a *firm* manages a conflict of interest using the arrangements in SYSC 10.2.2R which take the form of a *Chinese wall*, individuals on the other side of the wall will not be regarded as being in possession of knowledge denied to them as a result of the *Chinese wall*.

CHAPTER 11
LIQUIDITY RISK SYSTEMS AND CONTROLS

11.1 Application

[2016F]
11.1.1 **[R]** SYSC 11 applies to an *insurer*, unless it is:
(1) a *non-directive friendly society*; or
(2) a *Swiss general insurer*; or
(3) an *EEA deposit insurer*; or
(4) an *incoming EEA firm*; or
(5) an *incoming Treaty firm*.

11.1.2 **[R]** [deleted]

11.1.3 **[R]** [deleted]

11.1.4 **[R]** [deleted]

11.1.5 **[R]**
(1) [deleted]
(2) [deleted]

11.1.6 **[R]** If a *firm* carries on:
(1) *long-term insurance business*; and
(2) *general insurance business*;

SYSC 11 applies separately to each type of business.

Purpose

11.1.7 **[G]** The purpose of SYSC 11 is to amplify *GENPRU* and *SYSC* in their specific application to *liquidity risk* and, in so doing, to indicate minimum standards for systems and controls in respect of that risk.

11.1.8 **[G]** Appropriate systems and controls for the management of *liquidity risk* will vary with the scale, nature and complexity of the *firm's* activities. Most of the material in SYSC 11 is, therefore, *guidance*. SYSC 11 lays out some of the main issues that the *FSA* expects a *firm* to consider in relation to *liquidity risk*. A *firm* should assess the appropriateness of any particular item of *guidance* in the light of the scale, nature and complexity of its activities as well as its obligations as set out in *Principle* 3 to organise and control its affairs responsibly and effectively.

11.1.9 **[G]** SYSC 11 addresses the need to have appropriate systems and controls to deal both with liquidity management issues under normal market conditions, and with stressed or extreme situations resulting from either general market turbulence or *firm*-specific difficulties.

11.1.10 **[G]** [deleted]

11.1.11 **[R]** [deleted]

11.1.12 **[R]** [deleted]

11.1.13 **[G]** An *insurer* is also required to comply with the requirements in relation to *liquidity risk* set out in INSPRU 4.1.

11.1.14 **[G]** [deleted]

11.1.15 **[G]** [deleted]

11.1.16 **[G]** [deleted]

11.1.17 **[G]** High level requirements in relation to carrying out stress testing and scenario analysis are set out in GENPRU 1.2. In particular, GENPRU 1.2.42R requires a *firm* to carry out appropriate stress testing and scenario analysis. SYSC 11 gives *guidance* in relation to these tests in the case of *liquidity risk*.

Stress testing and scenario analysis

11.1.18 **[G]** The effect of GENPRU 1.2.30R, GENPRU 1.2.34R, GENPRU 1.2.37R(1) and GENPRU 1.2.42R is that, for the purposes of determining the adequacy of its overall financial resources, a *firm* must carry out appropriate stress testing and scenario analysis, including taking reasonable steps to identify an appropriate range of realistic adverse circumstances and events in which *liquidity risk* might occur or crystallise.

11.1.19 **[G]** GENPRU 1.2.40G and GENPRU 1.2.62G to GENPRU 1.2.78G give *guidance* on stress testing and scenario analysis, including on how to choose appropriate scenarios, but the precise scenarios that a *firm* chooses to use will depend on the nature of its activities. For the purposes of testing *liquidity risk*, however, a *firm* should normally consider scenarios based on varying degrees of stress and both *firm*-specific and market-wide difficulties. In developing any scenario of extreme market-wide stress that may pose systemic risk, it may be appropriate for a *firm* to make assumptions about the likelihood and nature of central bank intervention.

11.1.20 **[G]** A *firm* should review frequently the assumptions used in stress testing scenarios to gain assurance that they continue to be appropriate.

11.1.21 **[E]**

(1) A scenario analysis in relation to *liquidity risk* required under GENPRU 1.2.42R should include a cash-flow projection for each scenario tested, based on reasonable estimates of the impact (both on and off balance sheet) of that scenario on the *firm's* funding needs and sources.

(2) Contravention of (1) may be relied on as tending to establish contravention of GENPRU 1.2.42R.

11.1.22 **[G]** In identifying the possible on and off balance sheet impact referred to in SYSC 11.1.21E(1), a *firm* may take into account:

(1) possible changes in the market's perception of the *firm* and the effects that this might have on the *firm's* access to the markets, including:
  (a) (where the *firm* funds its holdings of assets in one currency with liabilities in another) access to foreign exchange markets, particularly in less frequently traded currencies;
  (b) access to secured funding, including by way of repo transactions; and
  (c) the extent to which the *firm* may rely on committed facilities made available to it;

(2) (if applicable) the possible effect of each scenario analysed on currencies whose exchange rates are currently pegged or fixed; and

(3) that:
  (a) general market turbulence may trigger a substantial increase in the extent to which *persons* exercise rights against the *firm* under off balance sheet instruments to which the *firm* is party;
  (b) access to *OTC derivative* and foreign exchange markets are sensitive to credit-ratings;
  (c) the scenario may involve the triggering of early amortisation in asset securitisation transactions with which the *firm* has a connection; and
  (d) its ability to securitise assets may be reduced.

Contingency funding plans

11.1.23 **[G]** GENPRU 1.2.26R states that a *firm* must at all times maintain overall financial resources adequate to ensure that there is no significant risk that its liabilities cannot be met as they fall due.

GENPRU 1.2.42R(1)(b) provides that for the purposes of determining the adequacy of its overall financial resources, a *firm* must estimate the financial resources it would need in each of the circumstances and events considered in carrying out its stress testing and scenario analysis in order to, inter alia, meet its liabilities as they fall due.

11.1.24 **[E]**

(1) A *firm* should have an adequately documented *contingency funding plan* for taking action to ensure, so far as it can, that, in each of the scenarios analysed under GENPRU 1.2.42R(1)(b), it would still have sufficient liquid financial resources to meet liabilities as they fall due.

(2) The *contingency funding plan* should cover what events or circumstances will lead the *firm* to put into action any part of the plan.

(3) [deleted]

(4) A *firm's contingency funding plan* should, where relevant, take account of the impact of stressed market conditions on:
   (a) the behaviour of any credit-sensitive liabilities it has; and
   (b) its ability to securitise assets.

(5) A *firm's contingency funding plan* should contain administrative policies and procedures that will enable the *firm* to manage the plan's implementation effectively, including:
   (a) the responsibilities of senior management;
   (b) names and contact details of members of the team responsible for implementing the *contingency funding plan*;
   (c) where, geographically, team members will be assigned;
   (d) who within the team is responsible for contact with head office (if appropriate), analysts, investors, external auditors, press, significant *client's*, regulators, lawyers and others; and
   (e) mechanisms that enable senior management and the *governing body* to receive management information that is both relevant and timely.

(6) Contravention of any of (1) to (5) may be relied upon as tending to establish contravention of GENPRU 1.2.30R(2)(c).

Documentation

11.1.25 **[G]** GENPRU 1.2.60R requires a *firm* to document its assessment of the adequacy of its liquidity financial resources, how it intends to deal with those risks, and details of the stress tests and scenario analyses carried out and the resulting financial resources estimated to be required. Accordingly, a *firm* should document both its stress testing and scenario analysis (see SYSC 11.1.18G) and its *contingency funding plan* (see SYSC 11.1.23G).

11.1.26 **[G]** [deleted]

11.1.27 **[G]** [deleted]

11.1.28 **[G]** [deleted]

11.1.29 **[G]** [deleted]

11.1.30 **[G]** [deleted]

11.1.31 **[G]** [deleted]

11.1.32 **[G]** [deleted]

CHAPTER 12
GROUP RISK SYSTEMS AND CONTROLS REQUIREMENT

12.1 Application

[2016G]

12.1.1 **[R]** Subject to SYSC 12.1.2R to SYSC 12.1.4R, this section applies to each of the following which is a member of a *group*:

(1) a *firm* that falls into any one or more of the following categories:
   (a) a *regulated entity*;
   (b) an *ELMI*;
   (c) an *insurer*;
   (d) a *BIPRU firm*;
   (e) a non-*BIPRU firm* that is a *parent financial holding company* in a *Member State* and is a member of a *UK consolidation group*; and
   (f) a *firm* subject to the *rules* in *IPRU(INV)* Chapter 14.

(2) a *UCITS firm*, but only if its *group* contains a *firm* falling into (1); and

(3) the *Society*.

12.1.2 **[R]** Except as set out in SYSC 12.1.4R, this section applies with respect to different types of *group* as follows:

(1) SYSC 12.1.8R and SYSC 12.1.10R apply with respect to all *groups*, including *FSA regulated EEA financial conglomerates*, other *financial conglomerates* and *groups* dealt with in SYSC 12.1.13R to SYSC 12.1.16R;
(2) the additional requirements set out in SYSC 12.1.11R and SYSC 12.1.12R only apply with respect to *FSA regulated EEA financial conglomerates*; and
(3) the additional requirements set out in SYSC 12.1.13R to SYSC 12.1.16R only apply with respect to *groups* of the kind dealt with by whichever of those *rules* apply.

12.1.3 **[R]** This section does not apply to:
(1) an *incoming EEA firm*; or
(2) an *incoming Treaty firm*; or
(3) a *UCITS qualifier*; or
(4) an *ICVC*; or
(5) an *incoming ECA provider* acting as such.

12.1.4 **[R]**
(1) This *rule* applies in respect of the following *rules*:
 (a) SYSC 12.1.8R(2);
 (b) SYSC 12.1.10R(1), so far as it relates to SYSC 12.1.8R(2);
 (c) SYSC 12.1.10R(2); and
 (d) SYSC 12.1.11R to SYSC 12.1.15R.
(2) The *rules* referred to in (1):
 (a) only apply with respect to a financial conglomerate if it an FSA regulated EEA financial conglomerate;
 (b) (so far as they apply with respect to a group that is not a financial conglomerate) do not apply with respect to a group for which a competent authority in another EEA state is lead regulator;
 (c) (so far as they apply with respect to a financial conglomerate) do not apply to a firm with respect to a financial conglomerate of which it is a member if the interest of the financial conglomerate in that firm is no more than a participation;
 (d) (so far as they apply with respect to other groups) do not apply to a firm with respect to a group of which it is a member if the only relationship of the kind set out in paragraph (3) of the definition of group between it and the other members of the group is nothing more than a participation; and
 (e) do not apply with respect to a third-country group.

12.1.5 **[G]** For the purpose of this section, a *group* is defined in the *Glossary*, and includes the whole of a *firm's* group, including financial and non-financial undertakings. It also covers undertakings with other links to *group* members if their omission from the scope of *group* risk systems and controls would be misleading. The scope of the *group* systems and controls requirements may therefore differ from the scope of the quantitative requirements for *groups*.

Purpose

12.1.6 **[G]** The purpose of this chapter is to set out how the systems and control requirements imposed by SYSC (Senior Management Arrangements, Systems and Controls) apply where a *firm* is part of a *group*. If a *firm* is a member of a *group*, it should be able to assess the potential impact of risks arising from other parts of its *group* as well as from its own activities.

12.1.7 **[G]** This section implements articles 73(3) (Supervision on a consolidated basis of credit institutions) and 138 (Intra-group transactions with mixed activity holding companies) of the *Banking Consolidation Directive*, article 9 of the *Financial Groups Directive* (Internal control mechanisms and risk management processes) and article 8 of the *Insurance Groups Directive* (Intra-group transactions).

General rules

12.1.8 **[R]** A *firm* must:
(1) have adequate, sound and appropriate risk management processes and internal control mechanisms for the purpose of assessing and managing its own exposure to *group* risk, including sound administrative and accounting procedures; and
(2) ensure that its *group* has adequate, sound and appropriate risk management processes and internal control mechanisms at the level of the *group*, including sound administrative and accounting procedures.

12.1.9 **[G]** For the purposes of SYSC 12.1.8R, the question of whether the risk management processes and internal control mechanisms are adequate, sound and appropriate should be judged in the light of the nature, scale and complexity of the *group's* business and of the risks that the *group* bears. Risk management processes must include the stress testing and scenario analysis required by GENPRU 1.2.42 R and GENPRU 1.2.49R(1)(b).

12.1.10 **[R]** The internal control mechanisms referred to in SYSC 12.1.8R must include:

(1) mechanisms that are adequate for the purpose of producing any data and information which would be relevant for the purpose of monitoring compliance with any prudential requirements (including any reporting requirements and any requirements relating to capital adequacy, solvency, systems and controls and large exposures):
   (a) to which the *firm* is subject with respect to its membership of a *group*; or
   (b) that apply to or with respect to that *group* or part of it; and
(2) mechanisms that are adequate to monitor funding within the *group*.

Financial conglomerates

12.1.11 **[R]** Where this section applies with respect to a *financial conglomerate*, the risk management processes referred to in SYSC 12.1.8R(2) must include:
(1) sound governance and management processes, which must include the approval and periodic review by the appropriate managing bodies within the *financial conglomerate* of the strategies and policies of the *financial conglomerate* in respect of all the risks assumed by the *financial conglomerate*, such review and approval being carried out at the level of the *financial conglomerate*;
(2) adequate capital adequacy policies at the level of the *financial conglomerate*, one of the purposes of which must be to anticipate the impact of the business strategy of the *financial conglomerate* on its risk profile and on the capital adequacy requirements to which it and its members are subject;
(3) adequate procedures for the purpose of ensuring that the risk monitoring systems of the *financial conglomerate* and its members are well integrated into their organisation; and
(4) adequate procedures for the purpose of ensuring that the systems and controls of the members of the *financial conglomerate* are consistent and that the risks can be measured, monitored and controlled at the level of the *financial conglomerate*.

12.1.12 **[R]** Where this section applies with respect to a *financial conglomerate*, the internal control mechanisms referred to in SYSC 12.1.8R(2) must include:
(1) mechanisms that are adequate to identify and measure all material risks incurred by members of the *financial conglomerate* and appropriately relate capital in the *financial conglomerate* to risks; and
(2) sound reporting and accounting procedures for the purpose of identifying, measuring, monitoring and controlling *intra-group transactions and risk concentrations*.

BIPRU firms and other firms to which BIPRU 8 applies

12.1.13 **[R]** If this *rule* applies under SYSC 12.1.14R to a *firm*, the *firm* must:
(1) comply with SYSC 12.1.8R(2) in relation to any *UK consolidation group* or *non-EEA sub-group* of which it is a member, as well as in relation to its *group*; and
(2) ensure that the risk management processes and internal control mechanisms at the level of any *UK consolidation group* or *non-EEA sub-group* of which it is a member comply with the obligations set out in the following provisions on a consolidated (or sub-consolidated) basis:
   (a) SYSC 4.1.1R and SYSC 4.1.2R;
   (b) SYSC 4.1.7R;
   (c) SYSC 5.1.7R;
   (d) SYSC 7;
   (e) BIPRU 12.3.27R and SYSC 12.4.10R;
   (f) BIPRU 2.3.7R(1);
   (g) BIPRU 9.1.6R and BIPRU 9.13.21R (Liquidity plans);
   (h) BIPRU 10.12.3R (Concentration risk policies).

[Note: article 73(3) of the Banking Consolidation Directive]

12.1.14 **[R]** SYSC 12.1.13R applies to a *firm* that is:
(1) an *ELMI*;
(2) a *BIPRU firm*; or
(3) a non-*BIPRU firm* that is a *parent financial holding company* in a *Member State* and is a member of a *UK consolidation group*.

12.1.15 **[R]** In the case of a *firm* that:
(1) is an *ELMI* or a *BIPRU firm*; and
(2) has a *mixed-activity holding company* as a *parent undertaking*;

the risk management processes and internal control mechanisms referred to in SYSC 12.1.8R must include sound reporting and accounting procedures and other mechanisms that are adequate to identify, measure, monitor and control transactions between the *firm's parent undertaking mixed-activity holding company* and any of the *mixed-activity holding company's subsidiary undertakings*.

Insurance undertakings

12.1.16 **[R]** In the case of an *insurer* that has a *mixed-activity insurance holding company* as a *parent undertaking*, the risk management processes and internal control mechanisms referred to in

SYSC 12.1.8R must include sound reporting and accounting procedures and other mechanisms that are adequate to identify, measure, monitor and control transactions between the *firm's parent undertaking mixed-activity insurance holding company* and any of the *mixed activity insurance holding company's subsidiary undertakings*.

12.1.17 **[G]** SYSC 12.1.16R cannot apply to a building society as it cannot have a mixed activity holding company as a parent undertaking. SYSC 12.1.16R cannot apply to a friendly society as it cannot have a mixed-activity insurance holding company as a parent undertaking.

Nature and extent of requirements and allocation of responsibilities within the group

12.1.18 **[G]** Assessment of the adequacy of a *group's* systems and controls required by this section will form part of the *FSA's* risk management process.

12.1.19 **[G]** The nature and extent of the systems and controls necessary under SYSC 12.1.8R(1) to address *group* risk will vary according to the materiality of those risks to the *firm* and the position of the *firm* within the *group*.

12.1.20 **[G]** In some cases the management of the systems and controls used to address the risks described in SYSC 12.1.8R(1) may be organised on a *group*-wide basis. If the *firm* is not carrying out those functions itself, it should delegate them to the *group* members that are carrying them out. However, this does not relieve the *firm* of responsibility for complying with its obligations under SYSC 12.1.8R(1). A *firm* cannot absolve itself of such a responsibility by claiming that any breach of that *rule* is caused by the actions of another member of the *group* to whom the *firm* has delegated tasks. The risk management arrangements are still those of the *firm*, even though personnel elsewhere in the *firm's group* are carrying out these functions on its behalf.

12.1.21 **[G]** SYSC 12.1.8R(1) deals with the systems and controls that a *firm* should have in respect of the exposure it has to the rest of the *group*. On the other hand, the purpose of SYSC 12.1.8R(2) and the *rules* in this section that amplify it is to require *groups* to have adequate systems and controls. However a *group* is not a single legal entity on which obligations can be imposed. Therefore the obligations have to be placed on individual *firms*. The purpose of imposing the obligations on each *firm* in the *group* is to make sure that the *FSA* can take supervisory action against any *firm* in a *group* whose systems and controls do not meet the standards in this section. Thus responsibility for compliance with the *rules* for *group* systems and controls is a joint one.

12.1.22 **[G]** If both a *firm* and its *parent undertaking* are subject to SYSC 12.1.8R(2), the *FSA* would not expect systems and controls to be duplicated. In this case, the *firm* should assess whether and to what extent it can rely on its parent's *group* risk systems and controls.

CHAPTER 13
OPERATIONAL RISK: SYSTEMS AND CONTROLS FOR INSURERS

13.1 Application

[2016H]
13.1.1 **[G]** SYSC 13 applies to an *insurer* unless it is:
(1) a *non-directive friendly society*; or
(2) an *incoming EEA firm*; or
(3) an *incoming Treaty firm*.

13.1.2 **[G]** SYSC 13 applies to:
(1) an *EEA-deposit insurer*; and
(2) a *Swiss general insurer*;

only in respect of the activities of the *firm* carried on from a *branch* in the *United Kingdom*.

13.1.3 **[G]** SYSC 13 applies to a *UK ISPV*.

13.1.4 **[G]** SYSC 13 does not apply to an *incoming ECA provider* acting as such.

13.2 Purpose

13.2.1 **[G]** SYSC 13 provides *guidance* on how to interpret SYSC 3.1.1R and SYSC 3.2.6R, which deal with the establishment and maintenance of systems and controls, in relation to the management of operational risk. Operational risk has been described by the Basel Committee on Banking Supervision as "the risk of loss, resulting from inadequate or failed internal processes, people and systems, or from external events". This chapter covers systems and controls for managing risks concerning any of a *firm's* operations, such as its IT systems and *outsourcing* arrangements. It does not cover systems and controls for managing credit, market, liquidity and insurance risk.

13.2.2 **[G]** Operational risk is a concept that can have a different application for different *firms*. A *firm* should assess the appropriateness of the *guidance* in this chapter in the light of the scale, nature and complexity of its activities as well as its obligations as set out in *Principle* 3, to organise and control its affairs responsibly and effectively.

13.2.3 **[G]** A *firm* should take steps to understand the types of operational risk that are relevant to its particular circumstances, and the operational losses to which they expose the *firm*. This should include considering the potential sources of operational risk addressed in this chapter: people; processes and systems; external events.

13.2.4 **[G]** Operational risk can affect, amongst other things, a *firm's* solvency, or lead to unfair treatment of consumers or lead to financial crime. A *firm* should consider all operational risk events that may affect these matters in establishing and maintaining its systems and controls.

13.3 Other related Handbook sections

13.3.1 **[G]** The following is a non-exhaustive list of *rules* and *guidance* in the *Handbook* that are relevant to a *firm's* management of operational risk:

(1) SYSC 14 and INSPRU 5.1 contain specific *rules* and *guidance* for the establishment and maintenance of operational risk systems and controls in a *prudential context*.

(2) COBS contains *rules* and *guidance* that can relate to the management of operational risk; for example, COBS 2 (Conduct of business obligations), COBS 4 (Communicating with clients, including financial promotions), COBS 6 (Information about the firm, its services and remuneration), COBS 7 (Insurance mediation), COBS 9 (Suitability (including basic advice)), COBS 11 (Dealing and managing), COBS 12 (Investment research), COBS 14 (Providing product information to clients) and COBS 19 (Pensions: supplementary provisions).

13.4 Requirements to notify the FSA

13.4.1 **[G]** Under *Principle* 11 and SUP 15.3.1R, a *firm* must notify the *FSA* immediately of any operational risk matter of which the *FSA* would reasonably expect notice. SUP 15.3.8G provides *guidance* on the occurrences that this requirement covers, which include a significant failure in systems and controls and a significant operational loss.

13.4.2 **[G]** Regarding operational risk, matters of which the *FSA* would expect notice under *Principle* 11 include:

(1) any significant operational exposures that a *firm* has identified;

(2) the *firm's* invocation of a business continuity plan; and

(3) any other significant change to a *firm's* organisation, infrastructure or business operating environment.

13.5 Risk management terms

13.5.1 **[G]** In this chapter, the following interpretations of risk management terms apply:

(1) a *firm's* risk culture encompasses the general awareness, attitude and behaviour of its *employees* and *appointed representatives* or, where applicable, its *tied agents*, to risk and the management of risk within the organisation;

(2) operational exposure means the degree of operational risk faced by a *firm* and is usually expressed in terms of the likelihood and impact of a particular type of operational loss occurring (for example, fraud, damage to physical assets);

(3) a *firm's* operational risk profile describes the types of operational risks that it faces, including those operational risks within a *firm* that may have an adverse impact upon the quality of service afforded to its *clients*, and its exposure to these risks.

13.6 People

13.6.1 **[G]** A *firm* should consult SYSC 3.2.2G to SYSC 3.2.5G for *guidance* on reporting lines and delegation of functions within a *firm* and SYSC 3.2.13G to SYSC 3.2.14G for *guidance* on the suitability of *employees* and *appointed representatives* or, where applicable, its *tied agents*. This section provides additional *guidance* on management of *employees* and other human resources in the context of operational risk.

13.6.2 **[G]** A *firm* should establish and maintain appropriate systems and controls for the management of operational risks that can arise from *employees*. In doing so, a *firm* should have regard to:

(1) its operational risk culture, and any variations in this or its human resource management practices, across its operations (including, for example, the extent to which the compliance culture is extended to in-house IT staff);

(2) whether the way *employees* are remunerated exposes the *firm* to the risk that it will not be able to meet its regulatory obligations (see SYSC 3.2.18G). For example, a *firm* should consider how well remuneration and performance indicators reflect the *firm's* tolerance for operational risk, and the adequacy of these indicators for measuring performance;

(3) whether inadequate or inappropriate training of *client*-facing services exposes *clients* to risk of loss or unfair treatment including by not enabling effective communication with the *firm*;

(4) the extent of its compliance with applicable regulatory and other requirements that relate to the welfare and conduct of *employees*;

(5) its arrangements for the continuity of operations in the event of *employee* unavailability or loss;
(6) the relationship between indicators of 'people risk' (such as overtime, sickness, and *employee* turnover levels) and exposure to operational losses; and
(7) the relevance of all the above to *employees* of a third party supplier who are involved in performing an *outsourcing* arrangement. As necessary, a *firm* should review and consider the adequacy of the staffing arrangements and policies of a service provider.

Employee responsibilities

13.6.3 **[G]** A *firm* should ensure that all *employees* are capable of performing, and aware of, their operational risk management responsibilities, including by establishing and maintaining:
(1) appropriate segregation of *employees*' duties and appropriate supervision of *employees* in the performance of their responsibilities (see SYSC 3.2.5G);
(2) appropriate recruitment and subsequent processes to review the fitness and propriety of *employees* (see SYSC 3.2.13G and SYSC 3.2.14G);
(3) clear policy statements and appropriate systems and procedures manuals that are effectively communicated to *employees* and available for *employees* to refer to as required. These should cover, for example, compliance, IT security and health and safety issues;
(4) training processes that enable *employees* to attain and maintain appropriate competence; and
(5) appropriate and properly enforced disciplinary and employment termination policies and procedures.

13.6.4 **[G]** A *firm* should have regard to SYSC 13.6.3G in relation to *approved persons*, people occupying positions of high personal trust (for example, security administration, payment and settlement functions); and people occupying positions requiring significant technical competence (for example, *derivatives* trading and technical security administration). A *firm* should also consider the *rules* and *guidance* for *approved persons* in other parts of the *Handbook* (including *APER* and *SUP*) and the *rules* and *guidance* on *senior manager* responsibilities in SYSC 2.1 (Apportionment of Responsibilities).

13.7 Processes and systems

13.7.1 **[G]** A *firm* should establish and maintain appropriate systems and controls for managing operational risks that can arise from inadequacies or failures in its processes and systems (and, as appropriate, the systems and processes of third party suppliers, agents and others). In doing so a *firm* should have regard to:
(1) the importance and complexity of processes and systems used in the end-to-end operating cycle for products and activities (for example, the level of integration of systems);
(2) controls that will help it to prevent system and process failures or identify them to permit prompt rectification (including pre-approval or reconciliation processes);
(3) whether the design and use of its processes and systems allow it to comply adequately with regulatory and other requirements;
(4) its arrangements for the continuity of operations in the event that a significant process or system becomes unavailable or is destroyed; and
(5) the importance of monitoring indicators of process or system risk (including reconciliation exceptions, compensation payments for *client* losses and documentation errors) and experience of operational losses and exposures.

Internal documentation

13.7.2 **[G]** Internal documentation may enhance understanding and aid continuity of operations, so a *firm* should ensure the adequacy of its internal documentation of processes and systems (including how documentation is developed, maintained and distributed) in managing operational risk.

External documentation

13.7.3 **[G]** A *firm* may use external documentation (including contracts, transaction statements or advertising brochures) to define or clarify terms and conditions for its products or activities, its business strategy (for example, including through press statements), or its brand. Inappropriate or inaccurate information in external documents can lead to significant operational exposure.

13.7.4 **[G]** A *firm* should ensure the adequacy of its processes and systems to review external documentation prior to issue (including review by its compliance, legal and marketing departments or by appropriately qualified external advisers). In doing so, a *firm* should have regard to:
(1) compliance with applicable regulatory and other requirements;
(2) the extent to which its documentation uses standard terms (that are widely recognised, and have been tested in the courts) or nonstandard terms (whose meaning may not yet be settled or whose effectiveness may be uncertain);
(3) the manner in which its documentation is issued; and
(4) the extent to which confirmation of acceptance is required (including by *customer* signature or counterparty confirmation).

IT systems

13.7.5 **[G]** IT systems include the computer systems and infrastructure required for the automation of processes, such as application and operating system software; network infrastructure; and desktop, server, and mainframe hardware. Automation may reduce a *firm's* exposure to some 'people risks' (including by reducing human errors or controlling access rights to enable segregation of duties), but will increase its dependency on the reliability of its IT systems.

13.7.6 **[G]** A *firm* should establish and maintain appropriate systems and controls for the management of its IT system risks, having regard to:

(1) its organisation and reporting structure for technology operations (including the adequacy of senior management oversight);

(2) the extent to which technology requirements are addressed in its business strategy;

(3) the appropriateness of its systems acquisition, development and maintenance activities (including the allocation of responsibilities between IT development and operational areas, processes for embedding security requirements into systems); and

(4) the appropriateness of its activities supporting the operation of IT systems (including the allocation of responsibilities between business and technology areas).

Information security

13.7.7 **[G]** Failures in processing information (whether physical, electronic or known by *employees* but not recorded) or of the security of the systems that maintain it can lead to significant operational losses. A *firm* should establish and maintain appropriate systems and controls to manage its information security risks. In doing so, a *firm* should have regard to:

(1) confidentiality: information should be accessible only to *persons* or systems with appropriate authority, which may require firewalls within a system, as well as entry restrictions;

(2) integrity: safeguarding the accuracy and completeness of information and its processing;

(3) availability and authentication: ensuring that appropriately authorised *persons* or systems have access to the information when required and that their identity is verified;

(4) non-repudiation and accountability: ensuring that the *person* or system that processed the information cannot deny their actions.

13.7.8 **[G]** A *firm* should ensure the adequacy of the systems and controls used to protect the processing and security of its information, and should have regard to established security standards such as ISO17799 (Information Security Management).

Geographic location

13.7.9 **[G]** Operating processes and systems at separate geographic locations may alter a *firm's* operational risk profile (including by allowing alternative sites for the continuity of operations). A *firm* should understand the effect of any differences in processes and systems at each of its locations, particularly if they are in different countries, having regard to:

(1) the business operating environment of each country (for example, the likelihood and impact of political disruptions or cultural differences on the provision of services);

(2) relevant local regulatory and other requirements regarding data protection and transfer;

(3) the extent to which local regulatory and other requirements may restrict its ability to meet regulatory obligations in the *United Kingdom* (for example, access to information by the *FSA* and local restrictions on internal or external audit); and

(4) the timeliness of information flows to and from its headquarters and whether the level of delegated authority and the risk management structures of the overseas operation are compatible with the *firm's* head office arrangements.

13.8 External events and other changes

13.8.1 **[G]** The exposure of a *firm* to operational risk may increase during times of significant change to its organisation, infrastructure and business operating environment (for example, following a corporate restructure or changes in regulatory requirements). Before, during, and after expected changes, a *firm* should assess and monitor their effect on its risk profile, including with regard to:

(1) untrained or de-motivated *employees* or a significant loss of *employees* during the period of change, or subsequently;

(2) inadequate human resources or inexperienced *employees* carrying out routine business activities owing to the prioritisation of resources to the programme or project;

(3) process or system instability and poor management information due to failures in integration or increased demand; and

(4) inadequate or inappropriate processes following business reengineering.

13.8.2 **[G]** A *firm* should establish and maintain appropriate systems and controls for the management of the risks involved in expected changes, such as by ensuring:

(1) the adequacy of its organisation and reporting structure for managing the change (including the adequacy of senior management oversight);

(2) the adequacy of the management processes and systems for managing the change (including planning, approval, implementation and review processes); and
(3) the adequacy of its strategy for communicating changes in systems and controls to its *employees*.

Unexpected changes and business continuity management

13.8.3 **[G]** SYSC 3.2.19G provides high level *guidance* on business continuity. This section provides additional *guidance* on managing business continuity in the context of operational risk.

13.8.4 **[G]** The high level requirement for appropriate systems and controls at SYSC 3.1.1R applies at all times, including when a business continuity plan is invoked. However, the *FSA* recognises that, in an emergency, a *firm* may be unable to comply with a particular *rule* and the conditions for relief are outlined in GEN 1.3 (Emergency).

13.8.5 **[G]** A *firm* should consider the likelihood and impact of a disruption to the continuity of its operations from unexpected events. This should include assessing the disruptions to which it is particularly susceptible (and the likely timescale of those disruptions) including through:
(1) loss or failure of internal and external resources (such as people, systems and other assets);
(2) the loss or corruption of its information; and
(3) external events (such as vandalism, war and "acts of God").

13.8.6 **[G]** A *firm* should implement appropriate arrangements to maintain the continuity of its operations. A *firm* should act to reduce both the likelihood of a disruption (including by succession planning, systems resilience and dual processing); and the impact of a disruption (including by contingency arrangements and insurance).

13.8.7 **[G]** A *firm* should document its strategy for maintaining continuity of its operations, and its plans for communicating and regularly testing the adequacy and effectiveness of this strategy. A *firm* should establish:
(1) formal business continuity plans that outline arrangements to reduce the impact of a short, medium or long-term disruption, including:
 (a) resource requirements such as people, systems and other assets, and arrangements for obtaining these resources;
 (b) the recovery priorities for the *firm's* operations; and
 (c) communication arrangements for internal and external concerned parties (including the *FSA*, *clients* and the press);
(2) escalation and invocation plans that outline the processes for implementing the business continuity plans, together with relevant contact information;
(3) processes to validate the integrity of information affected by the disruption;
(4) processes to review and update (1) to (3) following changes to the *firm's* operations or risk profile (including changes identified through testing).

13.8.8 **[G]** The use of an alternative site for recovery of operations is common practice in business continuity management. A *firm* that uses an alternative site should assess the appropriateness of the site, particularly for location, speed of recovery and adequacy of resources. Where a site is shared, a *firm* should evaluate the risk of multiple calls on shared resources and adjust its plans accordingly.

13.9 Outsourcing

13.9.1 **[G]** As SYSC 3.2.4G explains, a *firm* cannot contract out its regulatory obligations and should take reasonable care to supervise the discharge of outsourced functions. This section provides additional *guidance* on managing *outsourcing* arrangements (and will be relevant, to some extent, to other forms of third party dependency) in relation to operational risk. *Outsourcing* may affect a *firm's* exposure to operational risk through significant changes to, and reduced control over, people, processes and systems used in outsourced activities.

13.9.2 **[G]** *Firms* should take particular care to manage *material outsourcing* arrangements and, as SUP 15.3.8G(1)(e) explains, a *firm* should notify the *FSA* when it intends to enter into a *material outsourcing* arrangement.

13.9.3 **[G]** A *firm* should not assume that because a service provider is either a regulated *firm* or an intra-group entity an *outsourcing* arrangement with that provider will, in itself, necessarily imply a reduction in operational risk.

13.9.4 **[G]** Before entering into, or significantly changing, an *outsourcing* arrangement, a *firm* should:
(1) analyse how the arrangement will fit with its organisation and reporting structure; business strategy; overall risk profile; and ability to meet its regulatory obligations;
(2) consider whether the agreements establishing the arrangement will allow it to monitor and control its operational risk exposure relating to the *outsourcing*;
(3) conduct appropriate due diligence of the service provider's financial stability and expertise;

(4) consider how it will ensure a smooth transition of its operations from its current arrangements to a new or changed *outsourcing* arrangement (including what will happen on the termination of the contract); and
(5) consider any concentration risk implications such as the business continuity implications that may arise if a single service provider is used by several *firms*.

13.9.5 **[G]** In negotiating its contract with a service provider, a *firm* should have regard to:
(1) reporting or notification requirements it may wish to impose on the service provider;
(2) whether sufficient access will be available to its internal auditors, external auditors or *actuaries* (see section 341 of the *Act*) and to the *FSA* (see SUP 2.3.5R (Access to premises) and SUP 2.3.7R (Suppliers under material outsourcing arrangements);
(3) information ownership rights, confidentiality agreements and *Chinese walls* to protect *client* and other information (including arrangements at the termination of the contract);
(4) the adequacy of any guarantees and indemnities;
(5) the extent to which the service provider must comply with the *firm's* policies and procedures (covering, for example, information security);
(6) the extent to which a service provider will provide business continuity for outsourced operations, and whether exclusive access to its resources is agreed;
(7) the need for continued availability of software following difficulty at a third party supplier;
(8) the processes for making changes to the *outsourcing* arrangement (for example, changes in processing volumes, activities and other contractual terms) and the conditions under which the *firm* or service provider can choose to change or terminate the *outsourcing* arrangement, such as where there is:
 (a) a change of ownership or *control* (including insolvency or receivership) of the service provider or *firm*; or
 (b) significant change in the business operations (including subcontracting) of the service provider or *firm*; or
 (c) inadequate provision of services that may lead to the *firm* being unable to meet its regulatory obligations.

13.9.6 **[G]** In implementing a relationship management framework, and drafting the service level agreement with the service provider, a *firm* should have regard to:
(1) the identification of qualitative and quantitative performance targets to assess the adequacy of service provision, to both the *firm* and its *clients*, where appropriate;
(2) the evaluation of performance through service delivery reports and periodic self certification or independent review by internal or external auditors; and
(3) remedial action and escalation processes for dealing with inadequate performance.

13.9.7 **[G]** In some circumstances, a *firm* may find it beneficial to use externally validated reports commissioned by the service provider, to seek comfort as to the adequacy and effectiveness of its systems and controls. The use of such reports does not absolve the *firm* of responsibility to maintain other oversight. In addition, the *firm* should not normally have to forfeit its right to access, for itself or its agents, to the service provider's premises.

13.9.8 **[G]** A *firm* should ensure that it has appropriate contingency arrangements to allow business continuity in the event of a significant loss of services from the service provider. Particular issues to consider include a significant loss of resources at, or financial failure of, the service provider, and unexpected termination of the *outsourcing* arrangement.

13.10 Insurance

13.10.1 **[G]** Whilst a *firm* may take out insurance with the aim of reducing the monetary impact of operational risk events, non-monetary impacts may remain (including impact on the *firm's* reputation). A *firm* should not assume that insurance alone can replace robust systems and controls.

13.10.2 **[G]** When considering utilising insurance, a *firm* should consider:
(1) the time taken for the *insurer* to pay claims (including the potential time taken in disputing cover) and the *firm's* funding of operations whilst awaiting payment of claims;
(2) the financial strength of the *insurer*, which may determine its ability to pay claims, particularly where large or numerous small claims are made at the same time; and
(3) the effect of any limiting conditions and exclusion clauses that may restrict cover to a small number of specific operational losses and may exclude larger or hard to quantify indirect losses (such as lost business or reputational costs).

CHAPTER 14
PRUDENTIAL RISK MANAGEMENT AND ASSOCIATED SYSTEMS AND CONTROLS FOR INSURERS

14.1 Application

[2016I]
14.1.1 **[R]** This section applies to an *insurer* unless it is:

(1) a *non-directive friendly society*; or
(2) an *incoming EEA firm*; or
(3) an *incoming Treaty firm*.

14.1.2 **[R]** This section applies to:
(1) an *EEA-deposit insurer*; and
(2) a *Swiss general insurer*;

only in respect of the activities of the *firm* carried on from a *branch* in the *United Kingdom*.

14.1.2A **[R]** This section does not apply to an *incoming ECA provider* acting as such.

Purpose

14.1.3 **[G]** This section sets out some *rules* and *guidance* on the establishment and maintenance of systems and controls for the management of a *firm's* prudential risks. A *firm's* prudential risks are those that can reduce the adequacy of its financial resources, and as a result may adversely affect confidence in the financial system or prejudice *consumers*. Some key prudential risks are credit, market, liquidity, operational, insurance and group risk.

14.1.4 **[G]** The purpose of this section is to serve the *FSA's regulatory objectives* of consumer protection and market confidence. In particular, this section aims to reduce the risk that a *firm* may pose a threat to these *regulatory objectives*, either because it is not prudently managed, or because it has inadequate systems to permit appropriate senior management oversight and control of its business.

14.1.5 **[G]** Both adequate financial resources and adequate systems and controls are necessary for the effective management of prudential risks. A *firm* may hold financial resources to help alleviate the financial consequences of minor weaknesses in its systems and controls (to reflect possible impairments in the accuracy or timing of its identification, measurement, monitoring and control of certain risks, for example). However, financial resources cannot adequately compensate for significant weaknesses in a *firm's* systems and controls that could fundamentally undermine its ability to control its affairs effectively.

How to interpret this section

14.1.6 **[G]** This section is designed to amplify *Principle* 3 (Management and control) which requires that a *firm* take reasonable care to organise and control its affairs responsibly and effectively, with adequate risk management systems. This section is also designed to be complementary to SYSC 2, SYSC 3 and SYSC 13 in that it contains some additional *rules* and *guidance* on senior management arrangements and associated systems and controls for *firms* that could have a significant impact on the *FSA's* objectives in a *prudential context*.

14.1.7 **[G]** In addition to supporting *PRIN* and SYSC 2, SYSC 3 and SYSC 13, this section lays the foundations for the more specific *rules* and *guidance* on the management of credit, market, liquidity, operational, insurance and group risks that are in SYSC 11, SYSC 12, SYSC 15, SYSC 16 and INSPRU 5.1. Many of the elements raised here in general terms are expanded upon in these sections.

14.1.8 **[G]** Appropriate systems and controls for the management of prudential risk will vary from *firm* to *firm*. Therefore, most of the material in this section is *guidance*. In interpreting this *guidance*, a *firm* should have regard to its own particular circumstances. Following from SYSC 3.1.2G, this should include considering the nature, scale and complexity of its business, which may be influenced by factors such as:
(1) the diversity of its operations, including geographical diversity;
(2) the volume and size of its transactions; and
(3) the degree of risk associated with each area of its operation.

14.1.9 **[G]** The *guidance* contained within this section is not designed to be exhaustive. When establishing and maintaining its systems and controls a *firm* should have regard not only to other parts of the *Handbook*, but also to material that is issued by other industry or regulatory bodies.

The role of systems and controls in a prudential context

14.1.10 **[G]** In a *prudential context*, a *firm's* systems and controls should provide its senior management with an adequate means of managing the *firm*. As such, they should be designed and maintained to ensure that senior management is able to make and implement integrated business planning and risk management decisions on the basis of accurate information about the risks that the *firm* faces and the financial resources that it has.

The prudential responsibilities of senior management and the apportionment of those responsibilities

14.1.11 **[G]** Ultimate responsibility for the management of prudential risks rests with a *firm's governing body* and relevant *senior managers*, and in particular with those individuals that undertake the *firm's governing functions* and the *apportionment and oversight function*. In particular, these responsibilities should include:

(1) overseeing the establishment of an appropriate business plan and risk management strategy;
(2) overseeing the development of appropriate systems for the management of prudential risks;
(3) establishing adequate *internal controls*; and
(4) ensuring that the *firm* maintains adequate financial resources.

The delegation of responsibilities within the firm

14.1.12 **[G]** Although authority for the management of a *firm's* prudential risks is likely to be delegated, to some degree, to individuals at all levels of the organisation, overall responsibility for this activity should not be delegated from its *governing body* and relevant *senior managers*.

14.1.13 **[G]** Where delegation does occur, a *firm* should ensure that appropriate systems and controls are in place to allow its *governing body* and relevant *senior managers* to participate in and control its prudential risk management activities. The *governing body* and relevant *senior managers* should approve and periodically review these systems and controls to ensure that delegated duties are being performed correctly.

Firms subject to risk management on a group basis

14.1.14 **[G]** Some *firms* organise the management of their prudential risks on a standalone basis. In some cases, however, the management of a *firm's* prudential risks may be entirely or largely subsumed within a whole *group* or *subgroup* basis.

(1) The latter arrangement may still comply with the *FSA's* prudential policy on systems and controls if the *firm's governing body* formally delegates the functions that are to be carried out in this way to the *persons* or bodies that are to carry them out. Before doing so, however, the *firm's governing body* should have explicitly considered the arrangement and decided that it is appropriate and that it enables the *firm* to meet the *FSA's* prudential policy on systems and controls. The *firm* should notify the *FSA* if the management of its prudential risks is to be carried out in this way.
(2) Where the management of a *firm's* prudential risks is largely, but not entirely, subsumed within a whole *group* or *sub-group* basis, the *firm* should ensure that any prudential issues that are specific to the *firm* are:
 (a) identified and adequately covered by those to whom it has delegated certain prudential risk management tasks; or
 (b) dealt with by the *firm* itself.

14.1.15 **[G]** Any delegation of the management of prudential risks to another part of a *firm's group* does not relieve it of responsibility for complying with the *FSA's* prudential policy on systems and controls. A *firm* cannot absolve itself of such a responsibility by claiming that any breach of the *FSA's* prudential policy on systems and controls is effected by the actions of a third party *firm* to whom the *firm* has delegated tasks. The risk management arrangements are still those of the *firm*, even though personnel elsewhere in the *firm's group* are carrying out these functions on its behalf. Thus any references in *GENPRU*, *INSPRU* or *SYSC* to what a *firm*, its personnel and its management should and should not do still apply, and do not need any adjustment to cover the situation in which risk management functions are carried out on a *group*-wide basis.

14.1.16 **[G]** Where it is stated in *GENPRU*, *INSPRU* or *SYSC* that a particular task in relation to a *firm*'s systems and controls should be carried out by a *firm's governing body* this task should not be delegated to another part of its *group*. Furthermore, even where the management of a *firm*'s prudential risks is delegated as described in SYSC 14.1.14G, responsibility for its effectiveness and for ensuring that it remains appropriate remains with the *firm's governing body*. The *firm's governing body* should therefore keep any delegation under review to ensure that delegated duties are being performed correctly.

Business planning and risk management

14.1.17 **[G]** Business planning and risk management are closely related activities. In particular, the forward-looking assessment of a *firm's* financial resources needs, and of how business plans may affect the risks that it faces, are important elements of prudential risk management. A *firm's* business planning should also involve the creation of specific risk policies which will normally outline a *firm's* strategy and objectives for, as appropriate, the management of its market, credit, liquidity, operational, insurance and group risks and the processes that it intends to adopt to achieve these objectives. SYSC 14.1.18R to SYSC 14.1.25G set out some *rules* and *guidance* relating to business planning and risk management in a *prudential context* (see also SYSC 3.2.17G, which states that a *firm* should plan its business appropriately).

14.1.18 **[R]** A *firm* must take reasonable steps to ensure the establishment and maintenance of a business plan and appropriate systems for the management of prudential risk.

14.1.19 **[R]** When establishing and maintaining its business plan and prudential risk management systems, a *firm* must document:

(1) an explanation of its overall business strategy, including its business objectives;
(2) a description of, as applicable, its policies towards market, credit (including provisioning), liquidity, operational, insurance and group risk (that is, its risk policies), including its appetite or tolerance for these risks and how it identifies, measures or assesses, monitors and controls these risks;
(3) the systems and controls that it intends to use in order to ensure that its business plan and risk policies are implemented correctly;
(4) a description of how the *firm* accounts for assets and liabilities, including the circumstances under which items are netted, included or excluded from the *firm's* balance sheet and the methods and assumptions for valuation;
(5) appropriate financial *projections* and the results of its stress testing and scenario analysis (see GENPRU 1.2 (Adequacy of financial resources); and
(6) details of, and the justification for, the methods and assumptions used in financial *projections* and stress testing and scenario analysis.

14.1.20 **[G]** The prudential risk management systems referred to in SYSC 14.1.18R and SYSC 14.1.19R are the means by which a *firm* is able to:
(1) identify the prudential risks that are inherent in its business plan, operating environment and objectives, and determine its appetite or tolerance for these risks;
(2) measure or assess its prudential risks;
(3) monitor its prudential risks; and
(4) control or mitigate its prudential risks.

INSPRU 4.1.63E is an *evidential provision* relating to SYSC 14.1.18R concerning risk management systems in respect of *liquidity risk* arising from substantial exposures in foreign currencies.

14.1.21 **[G]** A *firm* should consider the relationship between its business plan, risk policies and the financial resources that it has available (or can readily access), recognising that decisions made in respect of one element may have consequences for the other two.

14.1.22 **[G]** A *firm's* business plan and risk management systems should be:
(1) effectively communicated so that all *employees* and contractors understand and adhere to the procedures related to their own responsibilities;
(2) regularly updated and revised, in particular when there is significant new information or when actual practice or performance differs materially from the documented strategy, policy or systems.

14.1.23 **[G]** The level of detail in a *firm's* business plan and its approach to the design of its risk management systems should be appropriate to the scale and complexity of its operations, and the nature and degree of risk that it faces.

14.1.24 **[G]** A *firm's* business plan and systems documentation should be accessible to the *firm's* management in line with their respective responsibilities and, upon request, to the *FSA*.

14.1.25 **[G]** SYSC 14.1.19R(5) requires a *firm* to *document* its financial projections and the results of its stress testing and scenario analysis. Such financial projections, stress tests and scenario analysis should be used by a *firm's governing body* and relevant *senior managers* when deciding upon how much risk the *firm* is willing to accept in pursuit of its business objectives and how risk limits should be set. Further *rules* and *guidance* on stress testing and scenario analysis are outlined in GENPRU 1.2 (Adequacy of financial resources) and SYSC 11 (Liquidity risk systems and controls).

Internal controls: introduction

14.1.26 **[G]** *Internal controls* should provide a *firm* with reasonable assurance that it will not be hindered in achieving its objectives, or in the orderly and legitimate conduct of its business, by events that may reasonably be foreseen. More specifically in a *prudential context, internal controls* should be concerned with ensuring that a *firm's* business plan and risk management systems are operating as expected and are being implemented as intended. The following *rule* (SYSC 14.1.27R) reflects the importance of *internal controls* in a *prudential context.*

14.1.27 **[R]** A *firm* must take reasonable steps to establish and maintain adequate *internal controls*.

14.1.28 **[G]** The precise role and organisation of *internal controls* can vary from *firm* to *firm*. However, a *firm's internal controls* should normally be concerned with assisting its *governing body* and relevant *senior managers* to participate in ensuring that it meets the following objectives:
(1) safeguarding both the assets of the *firm* and its *customers*, as well as identifying and managing liabilities;
(2) maintaining the efficiency and effectiveness of its operations;
(3) ensuring the reliability and completeness of all accounting, financial and management information; and
(4) ensuring compliance with its internal policies and procedures as well as all applicable laws and regulations.

Part II FSA Handbook Materials

14.1.29 **[G]** When determining the adequacy of its *internal controls*, a *firm* should consider both the potential risks that might hinder the achievement of the objectives listed in SYSC 14.1.28G, and the extent to which it needs to control these risks. More specifically, this should normally include consideration of:

(1) the appropriateness of its reporting and communication lines (see SYSC 3.2.2G);
(2) how the delegation or contracting of functions or activities to *employees*, *appointed representatives* or, where applicable, its *tied agents* or other third parties (for example *outsourcing*) is to be monitored and controlled (see SYSC 3.2.3G to SYSC 3.2.4G, SYSC 14.1.12G to SYSC 14.1.16G and SYSC 14.1.33G; additional guidance on the management of *outsourcing* arrangements is also provided in SYSC 13.9);
(3) the risk that a *firm's employees* or contractors might accidentally or deliberately breach a *firm's* policies and procedures (see SYSC 13.6.3G);
(4) the need for adequate segregation of duties (see SYSC 3.2.5G and SYSC 14.1.30G to SYSC 14.1.33G;
(5) the establishment and control of risk management committees (see SYSC 14.1.34G to SYSC 14.1.37G);
(6) the need for risk assessment and the establishment of a risk assessment function (see SYSC 3.2.10G and SYSC 14.1.38G to SYSC 14.1.41G;
(7) the need for internal audit and the establishment of an internal audit function and audit committee (see SYSC 3.2.15G to SYSC 3.2.16G and SYSC 14.1.42G to SYSC 14.1.45G).

Internal controls: segregation of duties

14.1.30 **[G]** The effective segregation of duties is an important internal control in the *prudential context*. In particular, it helps to ensure that no one individual is completely free to commit a *firm's* assets or incur liabilities on its behalf. Segregation can also help to ensure that a *firm's governing body* receives objective and accurate information on financial performance, the risks faced by the *firm* and the adequacy of its systems. In this regard, a *firm* should ensure that there is adequate segregation of duties between *employees* involved in:

(1) taking on or controlling risk (which could involve risk mitigation);
(2) risk assessment (which includes the identification and analysis of risk); and
(3) internal audit.

14.1.31 **[G]** In addition, a *firm* should normally ensure that no single individual has unrestricted authority to do all of the following:

(1) initiate a transaction;
(2) bind the *firm*;
(3) make payments; and
(4) account for it.

14.1.32 **[G]** Where a *firm* is unable to ensure the complete segregation of duties (for example, because it has a limited number of staff), it should ensure that there are adequate compensating controls in place (for example, frequent review of an area by relevant *senior managers*).

14.1.33 **[G]** Where a *firm* outsources a *controlled function*, such as internal audit, it should take reasonable steps to ensure that every individual involved in the performance of this service is independent from the individuals who perform its external audit. This should not prevent services from being undertaken by a *firm's* external auditors provided that:

(1) the work is carried out under the supervision and management of the *firm's* own internal staff; and
(2) potential conflicts of interest between the provision of external audit services and the provision of *controlled functions* are properly managed.

Internal controls: risk management committees

14.1.34 **[G]** In many *firms*, especially if there are multiple business lines, it is common for the *governing body* to delegate some tasks related to risk control and management to committees such as asset and liability committees (ALCO), credit risk committees and market risk committees.

14.1.35 **[G]** Where a *firm* decides to create one or more risk management committee(s), adequate *internal controls* should be put in place to ensure that these committees are effective and that their actions are consistent with the objectives outlined in SYSC 14.1.28G. This should normally include consideration of the following:

(1) setting clear terms of reference, including membership, reporting lines and responsibilities of each committee;
(2) setting limits on their authority;
(3) agreeing routine reporting and non-routine reporting escalation procedures;
(4) agreeing the minimum frequency of committee meetings; and
(5) reviewing the performance of these risk management committees.

14.1.36 **[G]** The decision to delegate risk management tasks, along with the terms of reference of the committees and their performance, should be reviewed periodically by the *firm's governing body* and revised as appropriate.

14.1.37 **[G]** The effective use of risk management committees can help to enhance a *firm's internal controls*. In establishing and maintaining its risk management committees, a *firm* should consider:

(1) their membership, which should normally include relevant *senior managers* (such as the head of group risk, head of legal, and the heads of market, credit, liquidity and operational risk, etc.), business line managers, risk management personnel and other appropriately skilled people, for example, actuaries, lawyers, accountants, IT specialists, etc.;

(2) using these committees to:

  (i) inform the decisions made by a *firm's governing body* regarding its appetite or tolerance for risk taking;

  (ii) highlight risk management issues that may require attention by the *governing body*;

  (iii) consider risk at the firm-wide level and, within delegated limits, to determine the allocation of risk limits and financial resources across business lines; and

  (iv) consider how exposures may be unwound, hedged, or otherwise mitigated, as appropriate.

Internal controls: risk assessment

14.1.38 **[G]** Risk assessment is the process through which a *firm* identifies and analyses (using both qualitative and quantitative methodologies) the risks that it faces. A *firm's* risk assessment activities should normally include consideration of:

(1) its total exposure to risk at the *firm*-wide level (that is, its exposure across business lines and risk categories);

(2) capital allocation and the need to calculate risk weighted returns for different business lines;

(3) the potential correlations that can exist between the risks in different business lines; this should also include looking for risks to which a *firm's* business plan is particularly sensitive, such as interest rate risk, or multiple dealings with the same *counterparty*;

(4) the use of stress tests and scenario analysis;

(5) whether there are risks inherent in the *firm's* business that are not being addressed adequately;

(6) the risk adjusted return that the *firm* is achieving; and

(7) the adequacy and timeliness of management information on market, credit, insurance, liquidity, operational and group risks from the business lines, including risk limit utilisation.

14.1.39 **[G]**

(1) In accordance with SYSC 3.2.10G a *firm* should consider whether it needs to set up a separate risk assessment function (or functions) that is responsible for assessing the risks that the *firm* faces and advising its *governing body* and *senior managers* on them.

(2) The term 'risk assessment function' refers to the generally understood concept of risk assessment within a *firm*, that is, the function of setting and controlling risk exposure. The risk assessment function is not a *controlled function* itself, but is part of the *systems and controls function* (CF28).

14.1.40 **[G]** Where a *firm* does decide that it needs a separate risk assessment function, the *employees* or contractors that carry out this function should not normally be involved in risk taking activities such as business line management (see SYSC 14.1.30G to SYSC 14.1.33G on the segregation of duties).

14.1.41 **[G]** A summary of the results of the analysis undertaken by a *firm's* risk assessment function in accordance with SYSC 14.4.39G (including, where necessary, an explanation of any assumptions that were adopted) should normally be reported to relevant *senior managers* as well as to the *firm's governing body*.

Internal audit

14.1.42 **[G]** A *firm* should ensure that it has appropriate mechanisms in place to assess and monitor the appropriateness and effectiveness of its systems and controls. This should normally include consideration of:

(1) adherence to and effectiveness of, as appropriate, its market, credit, liquidity, operational, insurance, and group risk policies;

(2) whether departures and variances from its documented systems and controls and risk policies have been adequately documented and appropriately reported, including whether appropriate pre-clearance authorisation has been sought for material departures and variances;

(3) adherence to and effectiveness of its accounting policies, and whether accounting records are complete and accurate;

(4) adherence to and effectiveness of its management reporting arrangements, including the timeliness of reporting, and whether information is comprehensive and accurate; and

(5) adherence to *FSA rules* and regulatory prudential standards.

14.1.43 **[G]**

(1) In accordance with SYSC 3.2.15G and SYSC 3.2.16G, a *firm* should consider whether it needs to set up a dedicated internal audit function.
(2) The term 'internal audit function' refers to the generally understood concept of internal audit within a *firm*, that is, the function of assessing adherence to and the effectiveness of internal systems and controls, procedures and policies. The internal audit function is not a *controlled function* itself, but is part of the *systems and controls function* (CF28).

14.1.44 **[G]** Where a *firm* decides to set up an internal audit function, this function should provide independent assurance to its *governing body*, audit committee or an appropriate *senior manager* of the integrity and effectiveness of its systems and controls.

14.1.45 **[G]** In forming its judgements, the *person* performing the internal audit function should test the practical operation of a *firm's* systems and controls as well as its accounting and risk policies. This should include examining the adequacy of supporting records.

Management information

14.1.46 **[G]** Many individuals, at various levels of a *firm*, need management information relating to their activities. However, SYSC 14.1.47G to SYSC 14.1.50G concentrates on the management information that should be available to those at the highest level of a *firm*, that is, the *firm's governing body* and relevant *senior managers*. In so doing SYSC 14.1.47G to SYSC 14.1.50G amplify SYSC 3.2.11G and SYSC 3.2.12G (which outline the *FSA's* high level policy on senior management information) by providing some additional *guidance* on the management information that should be available in a *prudential context*.

14.1.47 **[G]** The role of management information should be to help a *firm's governing body* and *senior managers* to understand risk at a firm-wide level. In so doing, it should help them to:
(1) determine whether a *firm* is prudently managed with adequate financial resources;
(2) make the decisions that fall within their ambit (for example, the high level business plans, strategy and risk tolerances of the *firm*); and
(3) oversee the execution of tasks for which they are responsible.

14.1.48 **[G]** A *firm* should consider what information needs to be made available to its *governing body* and *senior managers*. Some possible examples include:
(1) firm-wide information such as the overall profitability and value of a *firm* and its total exposure to risk;
(2) reports from committees to which the *governing body* has delegated risk management tasks, if applicable;
(3) reports from a *firm's* internal audit and risk assessment functions (see SYSC 14.1.43G and SYSC 14.1.39G), if applicable, including exception reports, where risk limits and policies have been breached or systems circumvented;
(4) financial projections under expected and abnormal (that is, stressed) conditions;
(5) reconciliation of actual profit and loss to previous financial projections and an analysis of any significant variances;
(6) matters which require a decision from the *governing body* or *senior managers*, for example a significant variation to a business plan, amendments to risk limits, the creation of a new business line, etc;
(7) compliance with *FSA rules* and regulatory prudential standards;
(8) risk weighted returns; and
(9) liquidity and funding requirements.

14.1.49 **[G]** The management information that is provided to a *firm's governing body* and *senior managers* should have the following characteristics:
(1) it should be timely, its frequency being determined by factors such as:
  (a) the volatility of the business in which the *firm* is engaged (that is, the speed at which its risks can change);
  (b) any time constraints on when action needs to be taken; and
  (c) the level of risk that the *firm* is exposed to, compared to its available financial resources and tolerance for risk;
(2) it should be reliable, having regard to the fact that it may be necessary to sacrifice a degree of accuracy for timeliness; and
(3) it should be presented in a manner that highlights any relevant issues on which those *undertaking governing functions* should focus particular attention.

14.1.50 **[G]** The production of management and other information may require the collation of data from a variety of separate manual and automated systems. In such cases, responsibility for the integrity of the information may be spread amongst a number of operational areas. A *firm* should ensure that it has appropriate processes to validate the integrity of its information.

Record keeping

14.1.51 **[G]** SYSC 3.2.20R requires a *firm* to take reasonable care to make and retain adequate records. The following policy on record keeping supplements SYSC 3.2.20R by providing some additional *rules* and *guidance* on record keeping in a *prudential context*. The purpose of this policy is to:

(1) facilitate the prudential supervision of a *firm* by ensuring that adequate information is available regarding its past/current financial situation and business activities (which includes the design and implementation of systems and controls); and

(2) help the *FSA* to satisfy itself that a *firm* is operating in a prudent manner and is not prejudicing the interests of its *customers* or market confidence.

14.1.52 **[G]** In addition to the record keeping requirements in *GENPRU*, *INSPRU* and *SYSC*, a *firm* should remember that it may be obliged, under other applicable laws or regulations, to keep similar or additional records.

14.1.53 **[R]**

(1) A *firm* must make and regularly update accounting and other records that are sufficient to enable the *firm* to demonstrate to the *FSA*:
  (a) that the *firm* is financially sound and has appropriate systems and controls;
  (b) the *firm's* financial position and exposure to risk (to a reasonable degree of accuracy); and
  (c) the *firm's* compliance with the *rules* in *GENPRU*, *INSPRU* and *SYSC*.

(2) The records in (1) must be retained for a minimum of three years, or longer as appropriate.

14.1.54 **[G]** A *firm* should be able to make available the records described in SYSC 14.1.53R within a reasonable timeframe when requested to do so by the *FSA*.

14.1.55 **[G]** The *FSA* recognises that not all records are specific to a particular point in time. As such, while it may be appropriate to update some records on a daily or continuous basis, for example expenditure and details of certain transactions, it may not be appropriate to update other records as regularly as this, for example those relating to its business plan and risk policies. A *firm* should decide how regularly it should update particular records.

14.1.56 **[G]** A *firm* should decide which records it needs to hold, noting that compliance with SYSC 14.1.53R does not require it to hold records on every single aspect of its activities. Some specific *guidance* on the types of records that a *firm* should hold is set out in each of the risk specific sections on systems and controls (see SYSC 11, SYSC 12, SYSC 14.1.65G, SYSC 15 to SYSC 17 and INSPRU 5.1).

14.1.57 **[G]** In deciding which records to hold, a *firm* should also take into account that failure to keep adequate records could make it harder for it to satisfy the *FSA* that it is compliant with the *rules* in *GENPRU*, *INSPRU* or *SYSC*, and to defend any enforcement action taken against it.

14.1.58 **[G]** A *firm* should keep the records required in *GENPRU*, *INSPRU* and *SYSC* in an appropriate format and language (in terms of format this could include holding them on paper or in electronic or some other form). However, whatever format or language a *firm* chooses, SYSC 3.2.20R requires that records be capable of being reproduced on paper and in English (except where they relate to business carried on from an establishment situated in a country where English is not an official language).

14.1.59 **[G]** In accordance with SYSC 3.2.20R, a *firm* should retain the records that it needs to comply with SYSC 14.1.53R for as long as they are relevant for the purposes for which they were made.

14.1.60 **[R]** A *firm* must keep the *records* required in SYSC 14.1.53R in the *United Kingdom*, except where:

(1) they relate to business carried on from an establishment in a country or territory that is outside the *United Kingdom*; and

(2) they are kept in that country or territory.

14.1.61 **[R]** When a *firm* keeps the records required in SYSC 14.1.53R outside the *United Kingdom*, it must periodically send an adequate summary of those records to the *United Kingdom*.

14.1.62 **[G]** Where a *firm* outsources the storage of some or all of its records to a third party service provider, it should ensure that these records are readily accessible and can be reproduced within a reasonable time period. The *firm* should also ensure that these records are stored in compliance with the *rules* and *guidance* on record keeping in *GENPRU*, *INSPRU* or *SYSC*. Additional *guidance* on the management of *outsourcing* agreements is provided in SYSC 13.

14.1.63 **[G]** A *firm* may rely on records that have been produced by a third party (for example, another *group* company or an external agent, such as an outsource service provider). However where the *firm* does so it should ensure that these records are readily accessible and can be reproduced within a reasonable time period. The *firm* should also ensure that these records comply with the *rules* and *guidance* on record keeping in *GENPRU*, *INSPRU* or *SYSC*.

14.1.64 **[G]** In accordance with SYSC 3.2.21G, a *firm* should have adequate systems and controls for maintaining the security of its records so that they are reasonably safeguarded against loss, unauthorised access, alteration or destruction.

Operational risk

14.1.65 **[G]** As well as covering other types of risk, the *rules* and *guidance* set out in this chapter deal with a *firm's* approach to operational risk. In particular:

(1) SYSC 14.1.18R requires a *firm* to take reasonable steps to ensure that the risk management systems put in place to identify, assess, monitor and control operational risk are adequate for that purpose;

(2) SYSC 14.1.19R(2) requires a *firm* to document its policy for operational risk, including its risk appetite and how it identifies, assesses, monitors and controls that risk; and

(3) SYSC 14.1.27R requires a *firm* to take reasonable steps to establish and maintain adequate *internal controls* to enable it to assess and monitor the effectiveness and implementation of its business plan and prudential risk management systems.

CHAPTER 15
CREDIT RISK MANAGEMENT SYSTEMS AND CONTROLS FOR INSURERS

15.1 Application

[2016J]

15.1.1 **[G]** SYSC 15.1 applies to an *insurer* unless it is:

(1) a *non-directive friendly society*; or

(2) an *incoming EEA firm*; or

(3) an *incoming Treaty firm*.

15.1.2 **[G]** SYSC 15.1 applies to:

(1) an *EEA-deposit insurer*; and

(2) a *Swiss general insurer*;

only in respect of the activities of the *firm* carried on from a *branch* in the *United Kingdom*.

15.1.2A **[G]** This section does not apply to an *incoming ECA provider* acting as such.

Purpose

15.1.3 **[G]** This section provides *guidance* on how to interpret SYSC 14 insofar as it relates to the management of credit risk.

15.1.4 **[G]** Credit risk is incurred whenever a *firm* is exposed to loss if another party fails to perform its financial obligations to the *firm*, including failing to perform them in a timely manner. It arises from both on and off balance sheet items. For contracts for traded *financial instruments*, for example the purchase and sale of *securities* or *over the counter derivatives*, risks may arise if the *firm's counterparty* does not honour its side of the contract. This constitutes counterparty risk, which can be considered a subset of credit risk. Another risk is issuer risk, which could potentially result in a *firm* losing the full price of a market instrument since default by the issuer could result in the value of its bonds or stocks falling to nil. In insurance *firms*, credit risk can arise from *premium* debtors, where cover under *contracts of insurance* may either commence before premiums become due or continue after their non-payment. Credit risk can also arise if a *reinsurer* fails to fulfil its financial obligation to repay a *firm* upon submission of a *claim*.

15.1.5 **[G]** Credit risk concerns the *FSA* in a *prudential context* because inadequate systems and controls for credit risk management can create a threat to the *regulatory objectives* of market confidence and consumer protection by:

(1) the erosion of a *firm's* capital due to excessive credit losses thereby threatening its viability as a going concern;

(2) an inability of a *firm* to meet its own obligations to depositors, *policyholders* or other market *counterparties* due to its capital erosion.

15.1.6 **[G]** Appropriate systems and controls for the management of credit risk will vary with the scale, nature and complexity of the *firm's* activities. Therefore the material in this section is *guidance*. A *firm* should assess the appropriateness of any particular item of *guidance* in the light of the scale, nature and complexity of its activities as well as its obligations as set out in *Principle* 3 to organise and control its affairs responsibly and effectively.

Requirements

15.1.7 **[G]** High level requirements for prudential systems and controls, including those for credit risk, are set out in SYSC 14. In particular:

(1) SYSC 14.1.19R(2) requires a *firm* to document its policy for credit risk, including its risk appetite and how it identifies, measures, monitors and controls that risk;

(2) SYSC 14.1.19R(2) requires a *firm* to document its provisioning policy. Documentation should describe the systems and controls that it intends to use to ensure that the policy is correctly implemented;

(3) SYSC 14.1.18R requires it to establish and maintain risk management systems to identify, measure, monitor and control credit risk (in accordance with its credit risk policy), and to take reasonable steps to ensure that its systems are adequate for that purpose; or (4) in line with SYSC 14.1.11G, the ultimate responsibility for the management of credit risk should rest with a *firm's governing body*. Where delegation of authority occurs the *governing body* and relevant *senior managers* should approve and periodically review systems and controls to ensure that delegated duties are being performed correctly.

Credit risk policy

15.1.8 **[G]** SYSC 14.1.18R requires a *firm* to establish, maintain and document a business plan and risk policies. They should provide a clear indication of the amount and nature of credit risk that the *firm* wishes to incur. In particular, they should cover for credit risk:

(1) how, with particular reference to its activities, the *firm* defines and measures credit risk;

(2) the *firm's* business aims in incurring credit risk including:

- (a) identifying the types and sources of credit risk to which the *firm* wishes to be exposed (and the limits on that exposure) and those to which the *firm* wishes not to be exposed (and how that is to be achieved, for example how exposure is to be avoided or mitigated);
- (b) specifying the level of diversification required by the *firm* and the *firm's* tolerance for risk concentrations (and the limits on those exposures and concentrations); and
- (c) drawing the distinction between activities where credit risk is taken in order to achieve a return (for example, lending) and activities where credit exposure arises as a consequence of pursuing some other objective (for example, the purchase of a *derivative* in order to mitigate *market risk*);

(3) how credit risk is assessed both when credit is granted or incurred and subsequently, including how the adequacy of any security and other risk mitigation techniques is assessed;

(4) the detailed limit structure for credit risk which should:

- (a) address all key risk factors, including intra-*group* exposures and indirect exposures (for example, exposures held by *related* and *subsidiary undertakings*);
- (b) be commensurate with the volume and complexity of activity; and
- (c) be consistent with the *firm's* business aims, historical performance, and its risk appetite;

(5) procedures for:

- (a) approving new or additional exposures to *counterparties*;
- (b) approving new products and activities that give rise to credit risk;
- (c) regular risk position and performance reporting;
- (d) limit exception reporting and approval; and
- (e) identifying and dealing with the problem exposures caused by the failure or downgrading of a *counterparty*;

(6) the methods and assumptions used for the stress testing and scenario analysis required by GENPRU 1.2 (Adequacy of financial resources), including how these methods and assumptions are selected and tested; and

(7) the allocation of responsibilities for implementing the credit risk policy and for monitoring adherence to, and the effectiveness of, the policy.

Counterparty assessment

15.1.9 **[G]** The *firm* should make a suitable assessment of the risk profile of the *counterparty*. The factors to be considered will vary according to both the type of credit and the *counterparty* being considered. This may include:

(1) the purpose of the credit, the duration of the agreement and the source of repayment;

(2) an assessment and continuous monitoring of the credit quality of the *counterparty*;

(3) an assessment of the *claims* payment record where the *counterparty* is a *reinsurer*;

(4) an assessment of the nature and amount of risk attached to the *counterparty* in the context of the industrial sector or geographical region or country in which it operates, as well as the potential impact on the *counterparty* of political, economic and market changes; and

(5) the proposed terms and conditions attached to the granting of credit, including ongoing provision of information by the *counterparty*, covenants attached to the facility as well as the adequacy and enforceability of *collateral*, security and guarantees.

15.1.10 **[G]** It is important that sound and legally enforceable documentation is in place for each agreement that gives rise to credit risk as this may be called upon in the event of a default or dispute. A *firm* should therefore consider whether it is appropriate for an independent legal opinion to be sought on documentation used by the *firm*. Documentation should normally be in place before the *firm* enters into a contractual obligation or releases funds.

15.1.11 **[G]** Where *premium* payments are made via *brokers* or *intermediaries*, the *firm* should describe how it monitors and controls its exposure to those *brokers* and *intermediaries*. In particular, the policy should identify whether the risk of default by the *broker* or *intermediary* is borne by the *firm* or the *policyholder*.

15.1.12 **[G]** Any variation from the usual credit policy should be documented.

15.1.13 **[G]** A *firm* involved in loan syndications or consortia should not rely on other parties' assessment of the credit risks involved. It will remain responsible for forming its own judgement on the appropriateness of the credit risk thereby incurred with reference to its stated credit risk policy. Similarly a *firm* remains responsible for assessing the credit risk associated with any insurance or *reinsurance* placed on its behalf by other parties.

15.1.14 **[G]** Where a credit scoring approach or other *counterparty* assessment process is used, the *firm* should periodically assess the particular approach taken in the light of past and expected future *counterparty* performance and ensure that any statistical process is adjusted accordingly to ensure that the business written complies with the *firm's* risk appetite.

15.1.15 **[G]** In assessing its contingent exposure to a *counterparty*, the *firm* should identify the amount which would be due from the *counterparty* if the value, index or other factor upon which that amount depends were to change.

Credit risk measurement

15.1.16 **[G]** A *firm* should measure its credit risk using a robust and consistent methodology which should be described in its credit risk policy; the appropriate method of measurement will depend upon the nature of the credit product provided. The *firm* should consider whether the measurement methodologies should be backtested and the frequency of such backtesting.

15.1.17 **[G]** A *firm* should also be able to measure its credit exposure across its entire portfolio or within particular categories such as exposures to particular industries, economic sectors or geographical areas.

15.1.18 **[G]** Where a *firm* is a member of a *group* that is subject to consolidated reporting, the *group* should be able to monitor credit exposures on a consolidated basis. See SYSC 12, INSPRU 6.1 and GENPRU 3.

15.1.19 **[G]** A *firm* should have the capability to measure its credit exposure to individual *counterparties* on at least a daily basis.

Risk monitoring

15.1.20 **[G]** A *firm* should implement an effective system for monitoring its credit risk which should be described in its credit risk policy.

15.1.21 **[G]** A *firm* should have a system of management reporting which provides clear, concise, timely and accurate credit risk reports to relevant functions within the *firm*. The reports could cover exceptions to the *firm's* credit risk policy, non-performing exposures and changes to the level of credit risk within the *firm's* credit portfolio. A *firm* should have procedures for taking appropriate action according to the information within the management reports, such as a review of *counterparty* limits, or of the overall credit policy.

15.1.22 **[G]** Individual credit facilities and overall limits should be periodically reviewed in order to check their appropriateness for both the current circumstances of the *counterparty* and the *firm's* current internal and external economic environment. The frequency of review should be appropriate to the nature of the facility.

15.1.23 **[G]** A *firm* should utilise appropriate stress testing and scenario analysis of credit exposures to examine the potential effects of economic or industry downturns, market events, changes in interest rates, changes in foreign exchange rates, changes in liquidity conditions and changes in levels of insurance losses where relevant.

Problem exposures

15.1.24 **[G]** A *firm* should have systematic processes for the timely identification, management and monitoring of problem exposures. These processes should be described in the credit risk policy.

15.1.25 **[G]** A *firm* should have adequate procedures for recovering exposures in arrears or that have had provisions made against them. A *firm* should allocate responsibility, either internally or externally, for its arrears management and recovery.

Provisioning

15.1.26 **[G]** SYSC 14.1.19R(2) requires a *firm* to document its provisioning policy. A *firm's* provisioning policy can be maintained either as a separate document or as part of its credit risk policy.

15.1.27 **[G]** At intervals that are appropriate to the nature, scale and complexity of its activities a *firm* should review and update its provisioning policy and associated systems.

15.1.28 **[G]** In line with SYSC 15.1.6G, the *FSA* recognises that the frequency with which a *firm* reviews its provisioning policy once it has been established will vary from *firm* to *firm*. However, the *FSA* expects a *firm* to review at least annually whether its policy remains appropriate for the business it undertakes and the economic environment in which it operates.

15.1.29 **[G]** In line with SYSC 14.1.12G, the provisioning policy referred to in SYSC 15.1.26G must be approved by the *firm's governing body* or another appropriate body to which the *firm's governing body* has delegated this responsibility.

15.1.30 **[G]** In line with SYSC 14.1.24G, the *FSA* may request a *firm* to provide it with a copy of its current provisioning policy.

15.1.31 **[G]** Provisions may be general (against the whole of a given portfolio), specific (against particular exposures identified as bad or doubtful) or both. The *FSA* expects contingent liabilities (for example guarantees) and anticipated losses to be recognised in accordance with accepted accounting standards at the relevant time, such as those embodied in the Financial Reporting Standards issued by the Accounting Standards Board.

Risk mitigation

15.1.32 **[G]** A *firm* may choose to use various credit risk mitigation techniques including the taking of *collateral*, the use of letters of credit or guarantees, or *counterparty netting* agreements to manage and control their *counterparty* exposures. The use of such techniques does not obviate the need for thorough credit analysis and procedures. The reliance placed by a *firm* on *risk* mitigation should be described in the credit risk policy.

15.1.33 **[G]** A *firm* should consider the legal and financial ability of a guarantor to fulfil the guarantee if called upon to do so.

15.1.34 **[G]** A *firm* should monitor the validity and enforceability of its *collateral* arrangements.

15.1.35 **[G]** The *firm* should analyse carefully the protection afforded by risk mitigants such as netting agreements or credit *derivatives*, to ensure that any residual risk is identified, measured, monitored and controlled.

Record keeping

15.1.36 **[G]** Prudential records made under SYSC 14.1.53R should include appropriate records of:

(1) credit exposures, including aggregations of credit exposures, as appropriate, by:
   (a) groups of connected *counterparties*; or
   (b) types of *counterparty* as defined, for example, by the nature or geographical location of the *counterparty*;

(2) credit decisions, including details of the decision and the facts or circumstances upon which it was made; and

(3) information relevant to assessing current *counterparty* and risk quality.

15.1.37 **[G]** Credit records should be retained as long as they are needed for the purpose described in SYSC 15.1.36G (subject to the minimum three year retention period). In particular, a *firm* should consider whether it is appropriate to retain information regarding *counterparty* history such as a record of credit events as well as a record indicating how credit decisions were taken.

CHAPTER 16
MARKET RISK MANAGEMENT SYSTEMS AND CONTROLS FOR INSURERS

16.1 Application

[2016K]

16.1.1 **[G]** SYSC 16.1 applies to an *insurer* unless it is:

(1) a *non-directive friendly society*; or
(2) an *incoming EEA firm*; or
(3) an *incoming Treaty firm*.

16.1.2 **[G]** SYSC 16.1 applies to:

(1) an *EEA-deposit insurer*; and
(2) a *Swiss general insurer*;

only in respect of the activities of the *firm* carried on from a *branch* in the *United Kingdom*.

16.1.2A **[G]** This section does not apply to an *incoming ECA provider* acting as such.

16.1.3 **[G]** *Firms* should also see GENPRU 1.2 (GENPRU 1.2.64G to GENPRU 1.2.78G) and INSPRU 3.1.

Purpose

16.1.4 **[G]**

(1) The purpose of this section is to amplify SYSC 14 insofar as it relates to *market risk*.

(2) *Market risk* includes equity, interest rate, foreign exchange (FX), commodity risk and interest rate risk on *long-term insurance contracts*. The price of *financial instruments* may also be influenced by other risks such as *spread risk*, *basis risk*, correlation, *specific risk* and *volatility risk*.

(3) This section does not deal with the risk management of *market risk* in a *group* context. A *firm* that is a member of a *group* should also read SYSC 12 (Group risk systems and controls) which outlines the *FSA's* requirements for the risk management of *market risk* within a *group*.

(4) Appropriate systems and controls for the management of *market risk* will vary with the scale, nature and complexity of the *firm's* activities. Therefore the material in this section is *guidance*. A *firm* should assess the appropriateness of any particular item of *guidance* in the light of the scale, nature and complexity of its activities as well as its obligations as set out in *Principle* 3 to organise and control its affairs responsibly and effectively.

Requirements

16.1.5 **[G]** High level requirements for prudential systems and controls, including those for *market risk*, are set out in SYSC 14. In particular:

(1) SYSC 14.1.19R(2) requires a *firm* to document its policy for *market risk*, including its risk appetite and how it identifies, measures, monitors and controls that risk;

(2) SYSC 14.1.19R(4) requires a *firm* to document its asset and liability recognition policy. Documentation should describe the systems and controls that it intends to use to comply with the policy;

(3) SYSC 14.1.19R requires a *firm* to establish and maintain risk management systems to identify, measure, monitor and control *market risk* (in accordance with its *market risk* policy), and to take reasonable steps to establish systems adequate for that purpose; and

(4) In line with SYSC 14.1.11G, the ultimate responsibility for the management of *market risk* should rest with a *firm's governing body*.

Where delegation of authority occurs the *governing body* and relevant *senior managers* should approve and adequately review systems and controls to check that delegated duties are being performed correctly.

Market risk policy

16.1.6 **[G]** SYSC 14 requires a *firm* to establish, maintain and document a business plan and risk policies. They should provide a clear indication of the amount and nature of *market risk* that the *firm* wishes to incur. In particular, they should cover for *market risk*:

(1) how, with particular reference to its activities, the *firm* defines and measures *market risk*;

(2) the *firm's* business aims in incurring *market risk* including:

  (a) identifying the types and sources of *market risk* to which the *firm* wishes to be exposed (and the limits on that exposure) and those to which the *firm* wishes not to be exposed (and how that is to be achieved, for example how exposure is to be avoided or mitigated); and

  (b) specifying the level of diversification required by the *firm* and the *firm's* tolerance for risk concentrations (and the limits on those exposures and concentrations).

16.1.7 **[G]** The *market risk* policy of a *firm* should be endorsed by the *firm's governing body* and implemented by its senior management, who should take adequate steps to disseminate the policy and train the relevant staff such that they can effectively implement the policy.

16.1.8 **[G]** The *market risk* policy of a *firm* should enforce the risk management and control principles and include detailed information on:

(1) the *financial instruments*, commodities, assets and liabilities (and mismatches between assets and liabilities) that a *firm* is exposed to and the limits on those exposures;

(2) the *firm's* investment strategy as applicable between each insurance fund;

(3) activities that are intended to hedge or mitigate *market risk* including mismatches caused by for example differences in the assets and liabilities and maturity mismatches; and

(4) the methods and assumptions used for measuring linear, non-linear and geared *market risk* including the rationale for selection, ongoing validation and testing. Methods might include stress testing and scenario analysis, asset/liability analysis, correlation analysis, Value-at-Risk (VaR) and *options* such as delta, gamma, vega, rho and theta. Exposure to non-linear or geared *market risk* is typically through the use of *derivatives*.

Risk identification

16.1.9 **[G]** A *firm* should have in place appropriate risk reporting systems that enable it to identify the types and amount of *market risk* to which it is, and potentially could be, exposed. The information that systems should capture may include but is not limited to:

(1) position information which may include a description of individual *financial instruments* and their cash flows; and

(2) market data which may consist of raw time series of market rates, index levels and prices and derived time series of benchmark yield curves, spreads, implied volatilities, historical volatilities and correlations.

Risk measurement

16.1.10 **[G]** Having identified the *market risk* that the *firm* is exposed to on at least a daily basis, a *firm* should be able to measure and manage that *market risk* on a consistent basis. This may be achieved by:

(1) regularly stress testing all or parts of the *firm's* portfolio to estimate potential economic losses in a range of market conditions including abnormal markets. Corporate level stress test results should be discussed regularly by risk monitors, senior management and risk takers, and should guide the *firm's market risk* appetite (for example, stress tests may lead to discussions on how best to unwind or hedge a position), and influence the internal capital allocation process;

(2) measuring the *firm's* exposure to particular categories of *market risk* (for example, equity, interest rate, foreign exchange and commodities) as well as across its entire portfolio of *market risks*;

(3) analysing the impact that new transactions or businesses may have on its *market risk* position on an on-going basis; and

(4) regularly backtesting realised results against internal model generated *market risk* measures in order to evaluate and assess its accuracy. For example, a *firm* should keep a database of daily risk measures such as VaR and *options* such as delta, gamma, vega, rho and theta, and use these to back test predicted profit and loss against actual profit and loss for all trading desks and business units, and monitor the number of exceptions from agreed confidence bands.

Valuation

16.1.11 **[G]** A *firm* should take reasonable steps to establish systems and control procedures such that the *firm* complies with the requirements of GENPRU 1.3 (Valuation).

16.1.12 **[G]** The systems and controls referred to in SYSC 16.1.11G should include the following:

(1) the department responsible for the validation of the value of assets and liabilities should be independent of the business trading area, and should be adequately resourced by suitably qualified staff. The department should report to a suitably qualified individual, independent from the business trading area, who has sufficient authority to enforce the systems and controls policies and any alterations to valuation treatments where necessary;

(2) all valuations should be checked and validated at appropriate intervals. Where a *firm* has chosen not to validate all valuations on a daily basis this should be agreed by senior management;

(3) a *firm* should establish a review procedure to check that the valuation procedures are followed and are producing valuations in compliance with the requirements in this section. The review should be undertaken by suitably qualified staff independent of the business trading area, on a regular and ad hoc basis. In particular, this review procedure should include:
   (a) the quality and appropriateness of the price sources used;
   (b) valuation reserves held; and
   (c) the valuation methodology employed for each product and consistent adherence to that methodology;

(4) where a valuation is disputed and the dispute cannot be resolved in a timely manner it should be reported to senior management. It should continue to be reported to senior management until agreement is reached;

(5) where a *firm* is marking positions to market it should take reasonable steps to establish a price source that is reliable and appropriate to enable compliance with the provisions in this section on an ongoing basis;

(6) a *firm* should document its policies and procedures relating to the entire valuation process. In particular, the following should be documented:
   (a) the valuation methodologies employed for all product categories;
   (b) details of the price sources used for each product;
   (c) the procedures to be followed where a valuation is disputed;
   (d) the valuation adjustment and reserving policies;

(e) the level at which a difference between a valuation assigned to an asset or liability and the valuation used for validation purposes will be reported on an exceptions basis and investigated;
(f) where a *firm* is using its own internal estimate to produce a valuation, it should document in detail the process followed in order to produce the valuation; and
(g) the review procedures established by a *firm* in relation to the requirements of this section should be adequately documented and include the rationale for the policy;

(7) a *firm* should maintain records which demonstrate:
(a) senior management's approval of the policies and procedures established; and
(b) management sign-off of the reviews undertaken in accordance with SYSC 16.1.11G.

Risk monitoring

16.1.13 **[G]** Risk monitoring is the operational process by which a *firm* monitors compliance with defined policies and procedures of the *market risk* policy. The *firm's* risk monitoring system should be independent of the *employees* who are responsible for exposing the *firm* to *market risk*.

16.1.14 **[G]** The *market risk* policy of a *firm* may require the production of *market risk* reports at various levels within the *firm*. These reports should provide sufficiently accurate *market risk* data to relevant functions within the *firm*, and should be timely enough to allow any appropriate remedial action to be proposed and taken, for example:
(1) at a *firm* wide level, a *market risk* report may include information:
(a) summarising and commenting on the total *market risk* that a *firm* is exposed to and *market risk* concentrations by business unit, asset class and country;
(b) on VaR reports against risk limits by business unit, asset class and country;
(c) commenting on significant risk concentrations and market developments; and
(d) on *market risk* in particular legal entities and geographical regions;
(2) at the business unit level, a *market risk* report may include information summarising *market risk* by currency, trading desk, maturity or duration band, or by instrument type;
(3) at the trading desk level, a *market risk* report may include detailed information summarising *market risk* by individual trader, instrument, position, currency, or maturity or duration band; and
(4) all risk data should be readily reconcilable back to the prime books of entry with a fully documented audit trail.

16.1.15 **[G]** Risk monitoring may also include information on:
(1) the procedures for taking appropriate action in response to the information within the *market risk* reports;
(2) ensuring that there are controls and procedures for identifying and reporting trades and positions booked at off-market rates;
(3) the process for new product approvals;
(4) the process for dealing with situations (authorised and unauthorised) where particular *market risk* exposures exceed predetermined risk limits and criteria; and
(5) the periodic review of the risk monitoring process in order to check its suitability for both current market conditions and the *firm's* overall risk appetite.

16.1.16 **[G]** Risk monitoring should be subject to periodic independent review by suitably qualified staff.

Risk control

16.1.17 **[G]** Risk control is the independent monitoring, assessment and supervision of business units within the defined policies and procedures of the *market risk* policy. This may be achieved by:
(1) setting an appropriate *market risk* limit structure to control the *firm's* exposure to *market risk*; for example, by setting out a detailed *market risk* limit structure at the corporate level, the business unit level and the trading desk level which addresses all the key *market risk* factors and is commensurate with the volume and complexity of activity that the *firm* undertakes;
(2) setting limits on risks such as price or rate risk, as well as those factors arising from *options* such as delta, gamma, vega, rho and theta;
(3) setting limits on net and gross positions, *market risk* concentrations, the maximum allowable loss (also called "stop-loss"), VaR, potential risks arising from stress testing and scenario analysis, gap analysis, correlation, liquidity and volatility; and
(4) considering whether it is appropriate to set intermediate (early warning) thresholds that alert management when limits are being approached, triggering review and action where appropriate.

Record keeping

16.1.18 **[G]** High level requirements for record keeping are set out in SYSC 14.

16.1.19 **[G]** In relation to *market risk*, a *firm* should retain appropriate prudential records of:

(1) off and on market trades in *financial instruments*;
(2) the nature and amounts of off and on balance sheet exposures, including the aggregation of exposures;
(3) trades in *financial instruments* and other assets and liabilities; and
(4) methods and assumptions used in stress testing and scenario analysis and in VaR models.

16.1.20 **[G]** A *firm* should keep a data history to enable it to perform back testing of methods and assumptions used for stress testing and scenario analysis and for VaR models.

CHAPTER 17
INSURANCE RISK SYSTEMS AND CONTROLS

17.1 Application

[2016L]

17.1.1 **[G]** SYSC 17.1 applies to an *insurer* unless it is:
(1) a *non-directive friendly society*; or
(2) an *incoming EEA firm*; or
(3) an *incoming Treaty firm*.

17.1.2 **[G]** SYSC 17.1 applies to:
(1) an *EEA-deposit insurer*; and
(2) a *Swiss general insurer*;

only in respect of the activities of the *firm* carried on from a *branch* in the *United Kingdom*.

17.1.2A **[G]** This section does not apply to an *incoming ECA provider* acting as such.

Purpose

17.1.3 **[G]** This section provides *guidance* on how to interpret SYSC 14 (Prudential risk management and associated systems and controls) in so far as it relates to the management of insurance risk. Insurance risk refers to fluctuations in the timing, frequency and severity of insured events, relative to the expectations of the *firm* at the time of underwriting. Insurance risk can also refer to fluctuations in the timing and amount of *claim* settlements. For *general insurance business* some specific examples of insurance risk include variations in the amount or frequency of *claims* or the unexpected occurrence of multiple *claims* arising from a single cause. For *long-term insurance business* examples include variations in the mortality and persistency rates of *policyholders*, or the possibility that guarantees could acquire a value that adversely affects the finances of a *firm* and its ability to treat its *policyholders* fairly consistent with the *firm's* obligations under *Principle* 6. More generally, insurance risk includes the potential for expense overruns relative to pricing or provisioning assumptions.

17.1.4 **[G]** Insurance risk concerns the *FSA* in a *prudential context* because inadequate systems and controls for its management can create a threat to the *regulatory objectives* of market confidence and consumer protection. Inadequately managed insurance risk may result in:
(1) the inability of a *firm* to meet its contractual insurance liabilities as they fall due; and
(2) the inability of a *firm* to treat its *policyholders* fairly consistent with the *firm's* obligations under *Principle* 6 (for example, in relation to bonus payments).

17.1.5 **[G]** *Guidance* on the application of this section to a *firm* that is a member of a *group* is provided in SYSC 12 (Group risk systems and controls).

17.1.6 **[G]** The *guidance* contained within this section should be read in conjunction with the rest of SYSC.

17.1.7 **[G]** Appropriate systems and controls for the management of insurance risk will vary with the scale, nature and complexity of a *firm's* activities. Therefore, the material in this section is *guidance*. A *firm* should assess the appropriateness of any particular item of *guidance* in the light of the scale, nature and complexity of its activities as well as its obligations, as set out in *Principle* 3, to organise and control its affairs responsibly and effectively.

General requirements

17.1.8 **[G]** High level *rules* and *guidance* for prudential systems and controls for insurance risk are set out in SYSC 14. In particular:
(1) SYSC 14.1.18R requires a *firm* to take reasonable steps to establish and maintain a business plan and appropriate risk management systems;
(2) SYSC 14.1.19R(2) requires a *firm* to document its policy for insurance risk, including its risk appetite and how it identifies, measures, monitors and controls that risk; and
(3) SYSC 14.1.27R requires a *firm* to take reasonable steps to establish and maintain adequate *internal controls* to enable it to assess and monitor the effectiveness and implementation of its business plan and prudential risk management systems.

Part II FSA Handbook Materials

Insurance risk policy

17.1.9 **[G]** A *firm's* insurance risk policy should outline its objectives in carrying out *insurance business*, its appetite for insurance risk and its policies for identifying, measuring, monitoring and controlling insurance risk. The insurance risk policy should cover any activities that are associated with the creation or management of insurance risk. For example, underwriting, *claims* management and settlement, assessing *technical provisions* in the balance sheet, risk mitigation and risk transfer, record keeping and management reporting. Specific matters that should normally be in a *firm's* insurance risk policy include:

(1) a statement of the *firm's* willingness and capacity to accept insurance risk;
(2) the classes and characteristics of *insurance business* that the *firm* is prepared to accept;
(3) the underwriting criteria that the *firm* intends to adopt, including how these can influence its rating and pricing decisions;
(4) its approach to limiting significant aggregations of insurance risk, for example, by setting limits on the amount of business that can be underwritten in one region or with one *policyholder*;
(5) where relevant, the *firm's* approach to pricing *long-term insurance contracts*, including the determination of the appropriate level of any reviewable *premiums*;
(6) the *firm's* policy for identifying, monitoring and managing risk when it has delegated underwriting authority to another party (additional *guidance* on the management of *outsourcing* arrangements is provided in SYSC 13.9);
(7) the *firm's* approach to managing its expense levels, including acquisition costs, recurring costs, and one-off costs, taking account of the margins available in both the prices for products and in the *technical provisions* in the balance sheet;
(8) the *firm's* approach to the exercise of any discretion (e.g. on charges or the level of benefits payable) that is available in its *long-term insurance contracts*, in the context also of the legal and regulatory constraints existing on the application of this discretion;
(9) the *firm's* approach to the inclusion of options within new *long-term insurance contracts* and to the possible exercise by *policyholders* of options on existing contracts;
(10) the *firm's* approach to managing persistency risk;
(11) the *firm's* approach to managing risks arising from timing differences in taxation or from changes in tax laws;
(12) the *firm's* approach to the use of *reinsurance* or the use of some other means of risk transfer;
(13) how the *firm* intends to assess the effectiveness of its risk transfer arrangements and manage the residual or transformed risks (for example, how it intends to handle disputes over contract wordings, potential payout delays and *counterparty* performance risks);
(14) a summary of the data and information to be collected and reported on underwriting, *claims* and risk control (including internal accounting records), management reporting requirements and external data for risk assessment purposes;
(15) the risk measurement and analysis techniques to be used for setting underwriting *premiums, technical* provisions in the balance sheet, and assessing capital requirements; and
(16) the *firm's* approach to stress testing and scenario analysis, as required by GENPRU 1.2 (Adequacy of financial resources), including the methods adopted, any assumptions made and the use that is to be made of the results.

17.1.10 **[G]** Further, more detailed, *guidance* is given in SYSC 17.1.11G to SYSC 17.1.37G on the identification, measurement, monitoring and control (including the use of *reinsurance* and other forms of risk transfer) of insurance risk. A *firm* should consider what additional material to that set out above should be included in its insurance risk policy on each of these for its various activities.

Risk identification

17.1.11 **[G]** A *firm* should seek to identify the causes of fluctuations in the occurrence, amount and timing of its insurance liabilities. A *firm* should also seek to identify aggregations of risk that may give rise to large single or multiple *claims*.

17.1.12 **[G]** The identification of insurance risk should normally include:

(1) in connection with the *firm's* business plan:
  (a) processes for identifying the types of insurance risks that may be associated with a new product and for comparing the risk types that are present in different classes of business (in order to identify possible aggregations in particular insurance risks); and
  (b) processes for identifying business environment changes (for example landmark legal rulings) and for collecting internal and external data to test and modify business plans;
(2) at the point of sale, processes for identifying the underwriting risks associated with a particular *policyholder* or a group of *policyholders* (for example, processes for identifying potential *claims* for misselling and for collecting information on the *claims* histories of *policyholders*, including whether they have made any potentially false or inaccurate claims, to identify possible adverse selection or moral hazard problems);

(3) after the point of sale, processes for identifying potential and emerging *claims* for the purposes of *claims* management and *claims* provisioning; this could include:
   (a) identifying possible judicial rulings;
   (b) keeping up to date with developments in market practice; and
   (c) collecting information on industry wide initiatives and settlements.

17.1.13 **[G]** A *firm* should also identify potential pricing risks, where the liabilities or costs arising from the sale of a product may not be as expected.

Risk measurement

17.1.14 **[G]** A *firm* should have in place appropriate systems for collecting the data it needs to measure insurance risk. At a minimum this data should be capable of allowing a *firm* to evaluate the types of *claims* experienced, *claims* frequency and severity, expense levels, persistency levels and, where relevant, potential changes in the value of guarantees and options in *long term insurance contracts*.

17.1.15 **[G]** A *firm* should ensure that the data it collects and the measurement methodologies that it uses are sufficient to enable it to evaluate, as appropriate:
(1) its exposure to insurance risk at all relevant levels, for example, by contract, *policyholder*, product line or insurance class;
(2) its exposure to insurance risk across different geographical areas and time horizons;
(3) its total, *firm*-wide, exposure to insurance risk and any other risks that may arise out of the *contracts of insurance* that it issues;
(4) how changes in the volume of business (for example via changes in *premium* levels or the number of new contracts that are underwritten) may influence its exposure to insurance risk;
(5) how changes in *policy* terms may influence its exposure to insurance risk; and
(6) the effects of specific loss scenarios on the insurance liabilities of the *firm*.

17.1.16 **[G]** A *firm* should hold data in a manner that allows for it to be used in a flexible way. For example, data should be sufficiently detailed and disaggregated so that contract details may be aggregated in different combinations to assess different risks.

17.1.17 **[G]** A *firm* should be able to justify its choice of measurement methodologies. This justification should normally be documented.

17.1.18 **[G]** A *firm* should periodically review the appropriateness of the measurement methodologies that it uses. This could, for example, include back testing (that is, by comparing actual versus expected results) and updating for changes in market practice.

17.1.19 **[G]** A *firm* should ensure that it has access to the necessary skills and resources that it needs to measure insurance risk using its chosen methodology.

17.1.20 **[G]** When measuring its insurance risks, a *firm* should consider how emerging experience could be used to update its underwriting process, in particular in relation to contract terms and pricing and also its assessment of the *technical provisions* in the balance sheet.

17.1.21 **[G]** A *firm* should have the capability to measure its exposure to insurance risk on a regular basis. In deciding on the frequency of measurement, a *firm* should consider:
(1) the time it takes to acquire and process all necessary data;
(2) the speed at which exposures could change; and
(3) that it may need to measure its exposure to certain types of insurance risk on a daily basis (for example, weather catastrophes).

Risk monitoring

17.1.22 **[G]** A *firm* should provide regular and timely information on its insurance risks to the appropriate level of management. This could include providing reports on the following:
(1) a statement of the *firm's* profits or losses for each class of business that it underwrites (with an associated analysis of how these have arisen for any *long-term insurance contracts*), including a variance analysis detailing any deviations from budget or changes in the key performance indicators that are used to assess the success of its business plan for insurance;
(2) the *firm's* exposure to insurance risk at all relevant levels (see SYSC 17.1.15G(1)), as well as across different geographical areas and time zones (see SYSC 17.1.15G(2)), also senior management should be kept informed of the *firm's* total exposure to insurance risk (see SYSC 17.1.15G(3));
(3) an analysis of any internal or external trends that could influence the *firm's* exposure to insurance risk in the future (e.g. new weather patterns, socio-demographic changes, expense overruns etc);
(4) any new or emerging developments in *claims* experience (e.g. changes in the type of *claims*, average *claim* amounts or the number of similar *claims*);
(5) the results of any stress testing or scenario analyses;

(6) the amount and details of new business written and the amount of business that has lapsed or been cancelled;
(7) identified fraudulent *claims*;
(8) a watch list, detailing, for example, material/catastrophic events that could give rise to significant numbers of new *claims* or very large *claims*, contested *claims*, client complaints, legal and other developments;
(9) the performance of any *reinsurance*/risk transfer arrangements; and
(10) progress reports on matters that have previously been referred under escalation procedures (see SYSC 17.1.23G).

17.1.23 **[G]** A *firm* should establish and maintain procedures for the escalation of appropriate matters to the relevant level of management. Such matters may include:
(1) any significant new exposures to insurance risk, including for example any landmark rulings in the courts;
(2) a significant increase in the size or number of *claims*;
(3) any breaches of the limits set out in SYSC 17.1.27G and SYSC 17.1.28G, in particular senior management should be informed where any maximum limits have been breached (see SYSC 17.1.29G); and
(4) any unauthorised deviations from its insurance risk policy (including those by a *broker*, *appointed representative* or other delegated authority).

17.1.24 **[G]** A *firm* should regularly monitor the effectiveness of its analysis techniques for setting provisions for *claims* on *general insurance contracts*.

17.1.25 **[G]** A *firm* should have appropriate procedures in place to allow managers to monitor the application (and hence the effect) of its *reinsurance* programme. This would include, for a general *insurer*, procedures for monitoring how its *reinsurance* programme affects the gross provisions that it makes for outstanding *claims* (including *claims* that are incurred but not reported).

Risk control

17.1.26 **[G]** A *firm* should take appropriate action to ensure that it is not exposed to insurance risk in excess of its risk appetite. In so doing, the *firm* should be both reactive, responding to actual increases in exposure, and proactive, responding to potential future increases. Being proactive should involve close co-ordination between the processes of risk control, risk identification and risk measurement, as potential future exposures need to be identified and understood before effective action can be taken to control them.

17.1.27 **[G]** A *firm* should consider setting limits for its exposure to insurance risk, which trigger action to be taken to control exposure. Periodically these limits should be amended in the light of new information (e.g. on the expected number or size of *claims*). For example, limits could be set for:
(1) the *firm's* aggregate exposure to a single source of insurance risk or for events that may be the result of a number of different sources;
(2) the *firm's* exposure to specific geographic areas or any other groupings of risks whose outcomes may be positively correlated;
(3) the number of fraudulent *claims*;
(4) the number of very large *claims* that could arise;
(5) the number of unauthorised deviations from its insurance risk policy;
(6) the amount of insurance risk than can be transferred to a particular *reinsurer*;
(7) the level of expenses incurred in respect of each relevant business area; and
(8) the level of persistency by product line or distribution channel.

17.1.28 **[G]** A *firm* should also consider setting individual underwriting limits for all *employees* and agents that have the authority to underwrite insurance risk. This could include both monetary limits and limits on the types of risk that they can underwrite. Where individual underwriting limits are set, the *firm* should ensure that they are adhered to.

17.1.29 **[G]** In addition to setting some 'normal' limits for insurance risk, a *firm* should consider setting some maximum limits, beyond which immediate, emergency action should be taken. These maximum limits could be determined through stress testing and scenario analysis.

17.1.30 **[G]** A *firm* should pay close attention to the wording of its *policy* documentation to ensure that these wordings do not expose it to more, or higher, *claims* than it is expecting. In so doing, the *firm* should consider:
(1) whether it has adequate in-house legal resources;
(2) the need for periodic independent legal review of *policy* documentation;
(3) the use of standardised documentation and referral procedures for variation of terms;
(4) reviewing the documentation used by other insurance companies;
(5) revising documentation for new *policies* in the light of past experience; and
(6) the operation of law in the jurisdiction of the *policyholder*.

17.1.31 **[G]** A *firm* should ensure that it has appropriate systems and controls for assessing the validity of *claims*. This could involve consideration of the evidence that will be required from *policyholders* and how this evidence is to be tested as well as procedures to determine when experts such as loss adjusters, lawyers or accountants should be used.

17.1.32 **[G]** Particular care should be taken to ensure that a *firm* has appropriate systems and controls to deal with large *claims* or large groups of *claims* that could significantly deplete its financial resources. This should include systems to ensure that senior management (that is, the *governing body* and relevant *senior managers*) is involved in the processing of such *claims* from the outset.

17.1.33 **[G]** A *firm* should consider how it intends to use *reinsurance* or some other form of insurance risk transfer agreement to help to control its exposure to insurance risk. Additional *guidance* on the use of *reinsurance*/risk transfer is provided below.

Reinsurance and other forms of risk transfer

17.1.34 **[G]** Before entering into or significantly changing a *reinsurance* agreement, or any other form of insurance risk transfer agreement, a *firm* should:

(1) analyse how the proposed *reinsurance*/risk transfer agreement will affect its exposure to insurance risk, its underwriting strategy and its ability to meet its regulatory obligations;
(2) ensure there are adequate legal checking procedures in respect of the draft agreement;
(3) conduct an appropriate due diligence of the *reinsurer's* financial stability (that is, solvency) and expertise; and
(4) understand the nature and limits of the agreement (particular attention should be given to the wording of contracts to ensure that all of the required risks are covered, that the level of available cover is appropriate, and that all the terms, conditions and warranties are unambiguous and understood).

17.1.34A **[G]** A *firm* should analyse regularly the full effect of all its *reinsurance* agreements and other risk transfer agreements (both current and proposed), including any related agreements or side-letters, on both its current and potential future financial position, and ensure that:

(1) all significant risks related to these agreements, and the residual risks borne by the *firm*, have been identified; and
(2) appropriate risk mitigation techniques have been applied to manage and control the risks.

17.1.35 **[G]** In managing its *reinsurance* agreements, or any other form of insurance risk transfer agreement, a *firm* should have in place appropriate systems that allow it to maintain its desired level of cover. This could involve systems for:

(1) monitoring the risks that are covered (that is, the scope of cover) by these agreements and the level of available cover;
(2) keeping underwriting staff informed of any changes in the scope or level of cover;
(3) properly co-ordinating all *reinsurance*/risk transfer activities so that, in aggregate, the desired level and scope of cover is maintained;
(4) ensuring that the *firm* does not become overly reliant on any one *reinsurer* or other risk transfer provider; or
(5) conducting regular stress testing and scenario analysis to assess the resilience of its *reinsurance* and risk transfer programmes to catastrophic events that may give rise to large and or numerous *claims*.

17.1.36 **[G]** In making a claim on a *reinsurance* contract (that is, its *reinsurance* recoveries) or some other risk transfer contract a *firm* should ensure:

(1) that it is able to identify and recover any money that it is due in a timely manner; and
(2) that it makes adequate financial provision for the risk that it is unable to recover any money that it expected to be due, as a result of either a dispute with or a default by the *reinsurer*/risk transfer provider.

Additional *guidance* on credit risk in *reinsurance*/risk transfer contracts is provided in INSPRU 2.1 (Credit risk in insurance)].

17.1.37 **[G]** Where the planned level or scope of cover from a *reinsurance*/risk transfer contract is not obtained, a *firm* should consider revising its underwriting strategy.

Record keeping

17.1.38 **[G]** The *FSA's* high level *rules* and *guidance* for record keeping are outlined in SYSC 3.2.20R (Records). Additional *rules* and *guidance* in relation to the *prudential context* are set out in SYSC 14.1.51G to SYSC 14.1.64G. In complying with these *rules* and *guidance*, a *firm* should retain an appropriate record of its insurance risk management activities. This may, for example, include records of:

(1) each new risk that is underwritten (noting that these records may be held by agents or cedants, rather than directly by the *firm* provided that the *firm* has adequate access to those records);
(2) any material aggregation of exposure to risk from a single source, or of the same kind or to the same potential catastrophe or event;

(3) each notified *claim* including the amounts notified and paid, precautionary notices and any re-opened *claims*;
(4) *policy* and contractual documents and any relevant representations made to *policyholders*;
(5) other events or circumstances relevant to determining the risks and commitments that arise out of *contracts of insurance* (including discretionary benefits and charges under any *long-term insurance contracts*);
(6) the formal wordings of *reinsurance* contracts; and
(7) any other relevant information on the *firm's reinsurance* or other risk-transfer arrangements, including the extent to which they:
 (a) have been exhausted by recoveries on paid *claims*; and
 (b) will be exhausted by recoveries on reported *claims* and, to the extent known, on incurred but not reported *claims*.

17.1.39 **[G]** A *firm* should retain its underwriting and *claims* histories for as long as they may be needed to inform pricing or provisioning decisions.

CHAPTER 18
GUIDANCE ON PUBLIC INTEREST DISCLOSURE ACT: WHISTLEBLOWING

18.1 Application

[2016M]
18.1.1 **[G]** This chapter is relevant to every *firm* to the extent that the Public Interest Disclosure Act 1998 ("PIDA") applies to it.

Purpose

18.1.2 **[G]**
(1) The purposes of this chapter are:
 (a) to remind *firms* of the provisions of PIDA; and
 (b) to encourage *firms* to consider adopting and communicating to workers appropriate internal procedures for handling workers' concerns as part of an effective risk management system.
(2) In this chapter "worker" includes, but is not limited to, an individual who has entered into a contract of employment.

18.1.3 **[G]** The *guidance* in this chapter concerns the effect of PIDA in the context of the relationship between *firms* and the *FSA*. It is not comprehensive guidance on PIDA itself.

18.2 Practical measures

Effect of Public Interest Disclosure Act 1998

18.2.1 **[G]**
(1) Under PIDA, any clause or term in an agreement between a worker and his employer is void in so far as it purports to preclude the worker from making a protected disclosure (that is, "blow the whistle").
(2) In accordance with section 1 of PIDA:
 (a) a protected disclosure is a qualifying disclosure which meets the relevant requirements set out in that section;
 (b) a qualifying disclosure is a disclosure, made in good faith, of information which, in the reasonable belief of the worker making the disclosure, tends to show that one or more of the following (a "failure") has been, is being, or is likely to be, committed:
  (i) a criminal offence; or
  (ii) a failure to comply with any legal obligation; or
  (iii) a miscarriage of justice; or
  (iv) the putting of the health and safety of an individual in danger; or
  (v) damage to the environment; or
  (vi) deliberate concealment relating to any of (i) to (v);

it is immaterial whether the relevant failure occurred, occurs or would occur in the *United Kingdom* or elsewhere, and whether the law applying to it is that of the *United Kingdom* or of any other country or territory.

Internal procedures

18.2.2 **[G]**
(1) *Firms* are encouraged to consider adopting (and encouraged to invite their *appointed representatives* or, where applicable, their *tied agents* to consider adopting) appropriate internal procedures which will encourage workers with concerns to blow the whistle internally about matters which are relevant to the functions of the *FSA*.

(2) Smaller *firms* may choose not to have as extensive procedures in place as larger *firms*. For example, smaller *firms* may not need written procedures. The following is a list of things that larger and smaller *firms* may want to do.

(a) For larger *firms*, appropriate internal procedures may include:

(i) a clear statement that the *firm* takes failures seriously (see SYSC 18.2.1G(2)(b));

(ii) an indication of what is regarded as a failure;

(iii) respect for the confidentiality of workers who raise concerns, if they wish this;

(iv) an assurance that, where a protected disclosure has been made, the *firm* will take all reasonable steps to ensure that no *person* under its control engages in victimisation;

(v) the opportunity to raise concerns outside the line management structure, such as with the Compliance Director, Internal Auditor or Company Secretary;

(vi) penalties for making false and malicious allegations;

(vii) an indication of the proper way in which concerns may be raised outside the *firm* if necessary (see (3));

(viii) providing access to an external body such as an independent charity for advice;

(ix) making whistleblowing procedures accessible to staff of key contractors; and

(x) written procedures.

(b) For smaller *firms*, appropriate internal procedures may include:

(i) telling workers that the *firm* takes failures seriously (see SYSC 18.2.1G(2)(b)) and explaining how wrongdoing affects the organisation;

(ii) telling workers what conduct is regarded as failure;

(iii) telling workers who raise concerns that their confidentiality will be respected, if they wish this;

(iv) making it clear that concerned workers will be supported and protected from reprisals;

(v) nominating a senior officer as an alternative route to line management and telling workers how they can contact that individual in confidence;

(vi) making it clear that false and malicious allegations will be penalised by the *firm*;

(vii) telling workers how they can properly blow the whistle outside the *firm* if necessary (see (3));

(viii) providing access to an external body for advice such as an independent charity for advice; and

(ix) encouraging managers to be open to concerns.

(3)

(a) *Firms* should also consider telling workers (through the *firm's* internal procedures, or by means of an information sheet available from the *FSA's* website, or by some other means) that they can blow the whistle to the *FSA*, as the regulator prescribed in respect of financial services and markets matters under PIDA.

(b) The *FSA* will give priority to live concerns or matters of recent history, and will emphasise that the worker's first port of call should ordinarily be the *firm* (see Frequently Asked Questions on http://www.fsa.gov.uk/Pages/Doing/Contact/Whistle/FAQ/index.shtml).

(c) For the *FSA's* treatment of confidential information, see SUP 2.2.4G.

Link to fitness and propriety

18.2.3 **[G]** The *FSA* would regard as a serious matter any evidence that a *firm* had acted to the detriment of a worker because he had made a protected disclosure (see SYSC 18.2.1G(2)) about matters which are relevant to the functions of the *FSA*. Such evidence could call into question the fitness and propriety of the *firm* or relevant members of its staff, and could therefore, if relevant, affect the *firm's* continuing satisfaction of *threshold condition* 5 (Suitability) or, for an *approved person*, his status as such.

CHAPTER 19
REMUNERATION CODE

19.1 Application

Who?

[2016N]–[2017]
19.1.1 **[R]**
(1) The *Remuneration Code* applies to a *firm* that meets at least one of the conditions in this *rule*.

Part II FSA Handbook Materials

(2) The first condition is that the *firm* is a *UK bank* or *building society* that had *capital resources* exceeding £1 billion on its last *accounting reference date*.
(3) The second condition is that the *firm* is a *BIPRU 730k firm* that had *capital resources* exceeding £750 million on its last *accounting reference date*.
(4) The third condition is that:
(a) the *firm* is a full credit institution, a *BIPRU 730k firm* or a third country *BIPRU 730k firm*;
(b) the *firm* is part of a group; and
(c) on the *firm's* last *accounting reference date* total capital resources held within the group:
(i) by *UK banks* or *building societies* exceeded £1 billion; or
(ii) by *BIPRU 730k firms* exceeded £750 million.

19.1.2 **[R]** The *Remuneration Code* does not apply to a *firm* to the extent that it is acting as an *incoming EEA firm*.

What? Where?

19.1.3 **[R]**
(1) If the *Remuneration Code* applies to a *firm*, it applies in the same way as SYSC 4.1.1R (General Requirements).
(2) In relation to an *overseas firm* the *Remuneration Code* applies only in relation to activities carried on from an establishment in the *United Kingdom*.

19.1.4 **[G]** Part 2 of SYSC 1 Annex 1 provides for the application of SYSC 4.1.1R (General Requirements).

19.2 Remuneration Code: General requirement

Remuneration policies must be consistent with effective risk management

19.2.1 **[R]** A *firm* must establish, implement and maintain *remuneration* policies, procedures and practices that are consistent with and promote effective risk management.

19.2.2 **[G]**
(1) If a *firm's remuneration policy* is not aligned with effective risk management it is likely that *employees* will have incentives to act in ways that might undermine effective risk management.
(2) The aim of the *Remuneration Code* is to ensure that *firms* have risk-focused *remuneration policies*, which are consistent with and promote effective risk management and do not expose them to excessive risk. It expands upon the general organisational requirements in SYSC 4.
(3) The *Remuneration Code* covers all aspects of *remuneration* that could have a bearing on effective risk management including wages, bonus, long term-incentive plans, options, hiring bonuses, severance packages and pension arrangements. In applying the *Remuneration Code*, a *firm* should have regard to applicable good practice on *remuneration* and corporate governance, such as guidelines on executive contracts and severance produced by the Association of British Insurers (ABI) and the National Association of Pension Funds (NAPF). In considering the risks arising from its *remuneration* policies, a *firm* will also need to take into account its statutory duties in relation to equal pay and non-discrimination.
(4) As with other aspects of a *firm's* systems and controls, what a *firm* must do in order to comply with the *Remuneration Code* will vary according to the nature, scale and complexity of the *firm* and its activities. For example, while the *Remuneration Code* refers to a *firm's remuneration committee* and risk management function, it may be appropriate for the *governing body* of a small *firm* to act as the *remuneration committee*, and for the *firm* not to have a separate risk management function.
(5) The principles in the *Remuneration Code* will be used by the *FSA* to assess the quality of a *firm's remuneration policies* and whether they encourage excessive risk-taking by a *firm's employees*.
(6) The *FSA* may also ask *remuneration committees* to provide the *FSA* with evidence of how well the *firm's remuneration policies* meet the *Remuneration Code's* principles, together with plans for improvement where there is a shortfall. The *FSA* will also expect relevant *firms* to use the principles in assessing their exposure to risks arising from their *remuneration policies as part of the internal capital adequacy assessment process (ICAAP)*.
(7) The *Remuneration Code* is concerned with the risks created by the way *remuneration* arrangements are structured, not with the absolute amount of *remuneration*, which is a matter for *firms' remuneration committees*.

19.3 Remuneration Code: Remuneration principles

Remuneration Principle 1: Role of bodies responsible for remuneration policies and their members

19.3.1 [E]

(1) A *remuneration* committee should:

(a) exercise, and be constituted in a way that enables it to exercise, independent judgment;

(b) be able to demonstrate that its decisions are consistent with a reasonable assessment of the *firm's* financial situation and future prospects;

(c) have the skills and experience to reach an independent judgment on the suitability of the policy, including its implications for risk and risk management; and

(d) be responsible for approving and periodically reviewing the *remuneration policy* and its adequacy and effectiveness.

(2) The effect of this *evidential provision* is set out in the evidential status *rule* (SYSC 19.3.18 R).

19.3.2 [G]

(1) *Remuneration* is usually the largest cost incurred by *firms* after funding costs. The risks arising from the way *employees* are recruited and managed, including the risks posed by *remuneration policies*, constitute some of the most important risks faced by *firms*. *Remuneration committees* should pay specific attention to these risks.

(2) While industry comparators may be relevant in setting *remuneration* they should not override the need for independent decisions that are consistent with the *firm's* financial situation and prospects.

(3) *Remuneration committees* should have a majority of *non-executive directors*, one or more of whom should have practical skills and experience of risk management, for example through being a member of a *firm's* risk committee or audit committee. *Remuneration committees* should receive regular reports directly from the *firm's* risk management function on the implications of the *remuneration policy* for risk and risk management.

(4) The *FSA* may ask a *remuneration committee* to prepare a statement on the *firm's remuneration policy*, including the implications of the policy for the *firm*. The *FSA* will expect the statement to include an assessment of the impact of the *firm's* policies on its risk profile and *employee* behaviour. In drawing up this assessment, the *remuneration committee* should exercise its own judgment and should not rely solely on the judgment or opinions of others. The *FSA* may seek a meeting with members of the *remuneration committee* to discuss the statement.

(5) It is good practice for a *firm's governing body* or the *remuneration committee* to issue a separate public document to inform its shareholders and other stakeholders about its *remuneration policy* and its implications for the *firm's* risk profile and for *employee* behaviour.

Remuneration Principle 2: Procedures and risk and compliance function input

19.3.3 [E]

(1) Procedures for setting *remuneration* within a *firm* should be clear and documented, and should include appropriate measures to manage conflicts of interest.

(2) A *firm's* risk management and compliance functions should have appropriate input into setting the *remuneration policy* for other business areas. The procedures for setting *remuneration* should allow risk and compliance functions to have significant input into the setting of individual *remuneration* awards where those functions have concerns about the behaviour of the individuals concerned or the riskiness of the business undertaken.

(3) The effect of this *evidential provision* is set out in the evidential status *rule* (SYSC 19.3.18 R).

19.3.4 [G]

(1) Conflicts of interest can easily arise when *employees* are involved in the determination of *remuneration* for their own business area. Where these could arise they need to be managed by having in place independent roles for control functions (including, notably, risk management and compliance) and human resources. It is good practice to seek input from a *firm's* human resources function when setting *remuneration* for other business areas.

(2) Remuneration Principle 4 stresses the importance of risk-adjustment in measuring performance, and the importance within that process of applying judgment and common sense. It is good practice for a *remuneration committee* to ask the risk management function to validate and assess risk adjustment data, and to attend a meeting of the *remuneration committee* for this purpose.

(3) Documenting procedures for setting *remuneration* includes documenting all performance appraisal processes and decisions.

Remuneration Principle 3: Remuneration of employees in risk and compliance functions

19.3.5 **[E]**

(1) *Remuneration* for *employees* in risk management and compliance functions should be determined independently of other business areas.

(2) Risk and compliance functions should have performance metrics based principally on the achievement of the objectives of those functions.

(3) The effect of this *evidential provision* is set out in the evidential status *rule* (SYSC 19.3.18 R).

19.3.6 **[G]**

(1) *Remuneration* Principle 3 is designed to manage the conflicts of interest which might arise if other business areas had undue influence over the *remuneration* of *employees* within control functions.

(2) The need to avoid undue influence is particularly important where *employees* from the control functions are embedded in other business areas. Remuneration Principle 3 does not prevent the views of other business areas being sought as an appropriate part of the assessment process.

(3) The *FSA* would generally expect the ratio of the potential variable component of *remuneration* to the fixed component of *remuneration* to be significantly lower for *employees* in risk management and compliance functions than for *employees* in other business areas whose potential bonus is a significant proportion of their *remuneration*. *Firms* should nevertheless ensure that the total *remuneration* package offered to those *employees* is sufficient to attract and retain staff with the skills, knowledge and expertise to discharge those functions. The requirement that the method of determining the *remuneration* of *relevant persons* involved in the compliance function must not comprise their objectivity or be likely to do so (see *SYSC* 6.1.4 R(4)) also applies.

Remuneration Principle 4: Profit-based measurement and risk-adjustment

19.3.7 **[E]**

(1) Assessments of financial performance used to calculate bonus pools should be based principally on profits.

(2) A bonus pool calculation should include an adjustment for current and future risk, and take into account the cost of capital employed and liquidity required.

(3) The effect of this *evidential provision* is set out in the evidential status *rule* (SYSC 19.3.18R).

19.3.8 **[G]**

(1) Measuring performance based wholly or mainly on revenues or turnover can provide an incentive for *employees* to pay insufficient regard to the quality of business undertaken or services provided, or their appropriateness for the client.

(2) Profits are a better measure, but they should be adjusted for risk, including future risks not adequately captured by accounting profits.

(3) One of the important responsibilities of the *remuneration committee* is to determine the proportion of risk-adjusted profits that should be accrued, and paid out, in the form of variable *remuneration*.

(4) Management accounts should provide profit data at such levels within the *firm's* structure as enables a *firm* to see as accurate a picture of an *employee's* contribution to a *firm's* performance as is reasonably practicable. If revenue or turnover is used as a component in performance assessment, processes should be in place to ensure that the quality of business undertaken or services provided and their appropriateness for clients are taken into account.

(5) A number of techniques are available to adjust profits and capital for risk, and a *firm* should choose those most appropriate to its circumstances. Common techniques include those based upon a calculation of economic profit or economic capital. Whichever technique is chosen, the full range of potential risks should be covered. The *FSA* expects a *firm* to be able to provide it with information relating to the workings of the calculations. The results of risk-adjustment are not foolproof, and accordingly a *firm* should apply judgment and common sense in the final decision about the performance-related component of *remuneration*.

Remuneration Principle 5: Long-term performance measurement

19.3.9 **[E]**

(1) Where the performance-related component of an *employee's remuneration* is a significant *part of his total remuneration*, the assessment process should be designed to ensure assessment is based on longer-term performance.

(2) The effect of this *evidential provision* is set out in the evidential status *rule* (SYSC 19.3.18 R).

19.3.10 **[G]**

(1) Profits from a *firm's* activities can be volatile and subject to cycles. The financial performance of *firms* and individual *employees* can be exaggerated as a result and so the performance-related component of *remuneration* should not be assessed solely on the results of the current financial year. Effective adjustment for current and future risks in line with Remuneration Principle 4 may also be relevant to compliance with Remuneration Principle 5.

(2) Performance assessment on a moving average of results can be a good way of meeting Remuneration Principle 5. However, other techniques such as good quality risk adjustment and deferment of a sufficiently large proportion of *remuneration* may also be useful (see Remuneration Principles 4 and 8).

(3) In considering whether the performance-related component of an *employee's remuneration* is a significant part of his total *remuneration*, relevant factors include:
 (a) the proportion of total *remuneration* which is performance-related; and
 (b) the absolute amount of *remuneration* which is performance-related.

So, for example, it may be consistent with effective risk management to pay a proportionately higher performance-related bonus to a relatively low-paid *employee* without basing the bonus on longer-term performance.

Remuneration Principle 6: Non-financial performance metrics

19.3.11 **[E]**

(1) Non-financial performance metrics should form a significant part of the performance assessment process.

(2) Non-financial performance metrics should include adherence to effective risk management and compliance with the *regulatory system* and with relevant overseas regulatory requirements.

(3) The effect of this *evidential provision* is set out in the evidential status *rule* (SYSC 19.3.18R).

19.3.12 **[G]**

(1) Poor performance in non-financial metrics such as poor risk management or other behaviours contrary to *firm* values can pose significant risks for a *firm* and should, as appropriate, override metrics of financial performance.

(2) The performance assessment process and the importance of non-financial assessment factors in the process should be clearly explained to relevant *employees* and implemented. A "balanced scorecard" can be a good way to do this.

Remuneration Principle 7: Measurement of performance for long-term incentive plans

19.3.13 **[E]**

(1) The measurement of performance for long-term incentive plans, including those based on the performance of *shares*, should take account of future risks.

(2) The effect of this *evidential provision* is set out in the evidential status *rule* (SYSC 19.3.18R).

19.3.14 **[G]** Many common measures of performance for long-term incentive plans, such as earnings per *share* (EPS), are not adjusted for longer-term risk factors. Total shareholder return (TSR), another common measure, includes in its measurement dividend distributions, which can also be based on unadjusted earnings data. If incentive plans mature within a two to four year period and are based on EPS or TSR, strategies can be devised to boost EPS or TSR during the life of the plan, to the detriment of the true longer-term health of a *firm*. For example, increasing leverage is a technique which can be used to boost EPS and TSR. *Firms* should take account of these factors when developing risk-adjustment methods.

Remuneration Principle 8: Remuneration structures

19.3.15 **[R]** The *evidential provision* and *guidance* on *remuneration* structures (SYSC 19.3.16E and SYSC 19.3.17G) apply in relation to:

(1) a person who performs a significant influence function for a *firm*; and

(2) an employee whose activities have, or could have, a material impact on the *firm's* risk profile.

19.3.16 **[E]**

(1) A *firm* should ensure that the structure of *remuneration* for a *person* to whom this *evidential provision* applies is consistent with and promotes effective risk management.

(2) The effect of this *evidential provision* is set out in the evidential status *rule* (SYSC 19.3.18R).

19.3.17 **[G]**

(1) It is good practice for the fixed component of an *employee's remuneration* to be a sufficient proportion of their total *remuneration* to allow a *firm* to operate a fully flexible bonus policy. This means that a *firm* (or a part of it) would have the ability not to pay a bonus in a year in which the *firm* (or part of it) makes a loss. Such a practice need not prevent a *firm* from paying a bonus despite making a loss if the bonus is justified on other grounds, for example incentivising *employees* involved in new business ventures which could be loss-making in their early stages.

(2) It is good practice for a significant proportion of any bonus to be deferred with a minimum vesting period. Both the proportion of the bonus to be deferred and the vesting period should be appropriate to the nature of the business and its risks. The vesting period of the deferred element should be at least three years. In relation to the proportion to be deferred, if the bonus is significant when compared with the fixed component of an *employee's remuneration*, a reasonable starting point would be to defer at least two-thirds of the bonus.

(3) It is good practice for a significant proportion of the variable component of *remuneration* to be linked to the future performance of:
   (a) the *firm* and, where practicable, the *employee's* division or business unit; or
   (b) the business undertaken by the *employee*.

(4) Deferred compensation paid in *shares* can meet Remuneration Principle 8 provided that the scheme satisfies appropriate criteria, including risk-adjustment of the performance measure used to determine the initial allocation of shares.

(5) Deferred *remuneration* paid in cash should also be subject to performance criteria.

(6) Bonus pools and individual bonuses should be based on *employee*, division, business unit, or *firm* performance during the period under review. Both linkage to the future performance of the *firm* and linkage to the future performance of a division or business unit can deliver important benefits. The former promotes teamwork, while the latter assures that the risks which the *employee* had a role in assuming continue to have a bearing on his *remuneration*. It is good practice for *remuneration* awards to be based on an appropriate combination of all of these factors.

(7) "Guaranteed minimum bonuses" which run for a period of more than one year and similar payments in addition to an *employee's* salary that are not based on performance during the performance period under review are likely to be inconsistent with Remuneration Principle 8.

Status of evidential provisions

19.3.18 **[R]**

(1) Compliance with the *evidential provisions* in this section tends to show compliance with the *Remuneration Code general requirement*.

(2) Non-compliance with an *evidential provision* in this section tends to show non-compliance with the *Remuneration Code general requirement*.

APPENDIX 1
MATTERS RESERVED TO A HOME STATE REGULATOR (SEE SYSC 1.1.1R (1)(B) AND SYSC 1.1.1R (1)(C))

1.1 Matters reserved to a Home State regulator (see SYSC 1.1.1R (1)(b) and SYSC 1.1.1R (1)(c))

[deleted]

TRANSITIONAL PROVISIONS

[2018]
[G]

1 *GEN* contains some technical transitional provisions that apply throughout the Handbook and which are designed to ensure a smooth transition at commencement.

Money Laundering Transitional Provisions

Extra time provisions

Compliance with ML and SYSC 3.2.6AR to SYSC 3.2.6JG

(1)	**(2) Material to which the transitional provision applies**	**(3)**	**(4) Transitional provision**	**(5) Transitional provision: dates in force**	**(6) Handbook provision: coming into force**
(1)	SYSC 3.2.6AR to SYSC *3.2.6JG*	R	Compliance with *ML* also counts as compliance with SYSC 3.2.6AR to SYSC 3.2.6JG and vice versa.	From 1 March 2006 to 31 August 2006	(1) 1 March 2006
(2)	*ML*				(2) In force until 31 August 2006

TP 1 Common platform firms

Application

1.1 **[R]** SYSC TP 1 applies to a *common platform firm*.

Commencement and expiry of SYSC TP 1

1.2 **[R]** SYSC TP 1 comes into force on 1 January 2007 and applies until 1 November 2007.

Purpose

1.3 **[G]** From 1 November 2007, a *firm* must comply with the *common platform requirements* and SYSC 3 will cease to apply to it. However, until 1 November 2007, a *firm* may choose to comply with the specific parts of the *common platform requirements* instead of SYSC 3. The purpose of SYSC TP 1 is to give a *firm* the option of complying with the *common platform requirements* sooner than 1 November 2007.

1.4 **[G]** The ability to comply with the *common platform requirements* before 1 November 2007 does not apply to SYSC 9 (Record-keeping), SYSC 8.2 (Outsourcing of portfolio management for retail clients to a non-EEA State) or SYSC 8.3 (Guidance on outsourcing portfolio management for retail clients to a non-EEA State). All *firms* must continue to comply with the record-keeping requirements in SYSC 3.2.20R until 1 November 2007, when SYSC 9 will enter into force.

The decision to comply with the common platform requirements

1.5 **[R]** SYSC 4 to 7, SYSC 8.1 and SYSC 10 do not apply to a *firm* unless it decides to comply with them sooner than 1 November 2007.

1.6 **[R]** If a *firm* decides to comply with the *common platform requirements* in accordance with SYSC TP 1.5R:

(1) it must make a record of the date of the decision and the date from which it is to be effective; and

(2) subject to SYSC TP 1.7R below, from the effective date, it must comply with SYSC 4 to 7, SYSC 8.1 and SYSC 10, and SYSC 3 will not apply to it.

1.7 **[R]** The following provisions in SYSC 3 will continue to apply to a *firm* that decides to comply with the *common platform requirements* before the 1 November 2007:

(1) SYSC 3.2.23R, SYSC 3.2.24R, SYSC 3.2.26R and SYSC 3.2.28R to SYSC 3.2.35R in so far as SYSC 12.1.13R applies to it; and

(2) SYSC 3.2.20R to SYSC 3.2.22G.

1.8 **[G]** The purpose of SYSC TP 1.7R is to ensure the effective operation of the provisions on consolidated risk management processes and internal control mechanisms in relation to a *firm* that decides to comply with the *common platform requirements* before 1 November 2007.

1.9 **[G]** A decision by a *firm* to comply with the *common platform requirements* must be made in relation to all of the *common platform requirements*. The firm may not 'cherry-pick'.

Definitions in SYSC TP1 and the common platform requirements

1.10 **[R]** The terms *common platform firm* and *MiFID investment firm* have effect in SYSC TP1 and the *common platform requirements* as if *MiFID* applied generally from 1 January 2007.

TP 2 Firms other than common platform firms, insurer, managing agents and the Society

(1)	(2) Material to which the transitional provision applies	(3)	(4) Transitional provisions	(5) Transitional provision: dates in force	(6) Handbook provisions: Coming into force
2.1	SYSC 8.1	R	If a *firm* other than a *common platform firm*, *insurer*, *managing agent* or the *Society* has in force on 1 April 2009 *outsourcing* arrangements which would be covered by SYSC 8.1 it need not amend those contracts to comply with these provisions but should comply with the new rules and guidance in respect of any *outsourcing* contracts which are entered into, or materially amended, on or after 1 April 2009.		1 April 2009

TP 3 Remuneration code

1 **[R]** TP 3 applies to a *firm* that is unable to comply with the *Remuneration Code general requirement* because of an obligation it owes to an *employee* (the "obligation") under an agreement entered into on or before 18 March 2009 (the "agreement").

2 **[R]** A *firm's* compliance with the obligation shall not cause it to be in breach of the *Remuneration Code general requirement* provided that the *firm* complies with 3R.

3 **[R]**
(1) Where a *firm* is entitled to amend the agreement in a way that enables it to comply with the *Remuneration Code general requirement* it must do so at the earliest opportunity and no later than 31 March 2010.
(2) Otherwise, a *firm* must:
  (a) take reasonable steps to amend the obligation or terminate the agreement at the earliest opportunity;
  (b) amend the obligation or terminate the agreement no later than 31 December 2010; and
  (c) adopt specific and effective arrangements, processes and mechanisms to manage the risks raised by the obligation.

4 **[G]** By 1 January 2010, a *firm* should have at least initiated a review of the extent to which the measurement of performance for any existing long term incentive plans takes account of future risks. The *FSA* may discuss the timing of that review and any remedial action with the *firm*.

SCHEDULE 1
RECORD KEEPING REQUIREMENTS

[2019]
1.1 **[G]** The aim of the guidance in the following table is to give the reader a quick over-all view of the relevant record keeping requirements.

It is not a complete statement of those requirements and should not be relied on as if it were.

1.2 **[G]**

Handbook reference	Subject of record	Contents of record	When record must be made	Retention period
SYSC 2.2.1R	Arrangements made to satisfy SYSC 2.1.1R (apportionment) and SYSC 2.1.3R (allocation)	Those arrangements	On making the arrangements and when they are updated	Six years from the date on which the record is superseded by a more up-to-date record
SYSC 3.2.20R	Matters and dealings (including accounting records) which are the subject of requirements and standards under the *regulatory system*	Adequate	Adequate time	Adequate

SCHEDULE 2
NOTIFICATION REQUIREMENTS

[2020]
2.1 **[G]** There are no notification or reporting requirements in *SYSC*.

SCHEDULE 3
FEES AND OTHER REQUIRED PAYMENTS

[2021]
3.1 **[G]** There are no requirement for fees or other payments in *SYSC*.

SCHEDULE 4
POWERS EXERCISED

[2022]
4.1 **[G]** The following powers and related provisions in the Act have been exercised by the FSA to make rules in *SYSC*:

(1) Section 138 (General rule-making power)
(2) Section 145 (Financial promotion rules)
(3) Section 146 (Money laundering rules)
(3A) Section 149 (Evidential provisions)
(4) Section 150(2) (Actions for damages)
(5) Section 156 (General supplementary powers).

The following powers in the Act have been exercised by the FSA to give the guidance in *SYSC*.
(1) Section 157(1) (Guidance).
(2) Section 158A (Guidance on outsourcing by investment firms and credit institutions).

SCHEDULE 5
RIGHTS OF ACTION FOR DAMAGES

[2023]
5.1 **[G]** The table below sets out the rules in *SYSC* contravention of which by an authorised person may be actionable under section 150 of the Act (Actions for damages) by a person who suffers loss as a result of the contravention.

5.2 **[G]** If a 'Yes' appears in the column headed 'For private person?', the rule may be actionable by a 'private person' under section 150 (or, in certain circumstances, his fiduciary or representative; see article 6(2) and (3)(c) of the Financial Services and Markets Act 2000 (Rights of Action) Regulations 2001 (SI 2001 No 2256)). A 'Yes' in the column headed 'Removed' indicates that the FSA has removed the right of action under section 150(2) of the Act. If so, a reference to the rule in which it is removed is also given.

5.3 **[G]** The column headed 'For other person?' indicates whether the rule may be actionable by a person other than a private person (or his fiduciary or representative) under article 6(2) and (3) of those Regulations. If so, an indication of the type of person by whom the rule may be actionable is given.

5.4 [G]

Chapter/ Appendix	Section/ Annex	Paragraph	Right of action under section 150		
			For private person?	Removed?	For other person?
SYSC 2 and SYSC 3			No	Yes SYSC 1 Annex 1.1.12R	No
SYSC 4 to SYSC 10			No	Yes SYSC 1 Annex 1.2.19R	No
SYSC 11 to SYSC 19			No	Yes SYSC 1.4.2R	No

SCHEDULE 6
RULES THAT CAN BE WAIVED

[2024]
6.1 **[G]** The rules in *SYSC* can be waived by the FSA under section 148 of the Act (Modification or waiver of rules) in so far as this is compatible with the *United Kingdom's* responsibilities to implement the requirements of any European Directive.

THRESHOLD CONDITIONS (COND)

NOTES

Up to date as at 22 February 2010. For later amendments please see www.fsa.gov.uk.

CONTENTS

COND 1—Introduction [2025]
COND 2—The threshold conditions [2026]
COND 3—Banking Act 2009 [2026A]
COND TP 1—Transitional Provisions [2027]
COND Sch 1—Record keeping requirements [2028]
COND Sch 2—Notification requirements [2029]
COND Sch 3—Fees and other required payments [2030]
COND Sch 4—Powers exercised [2031]
COND Sch 5—Rights of action for damages [2032]
COND Sch 6—Rules that can be waived [2033]

Part II FSA Handbook Materials

CHAPTER 1
INTRODUCTION

1.1 Application

Who?

[2025]

1.1.1 **[G]** *COND* applies to every *firm*, except that:

(1) for an *incoming EEA firm* or an *incoming Treaty firm* only *threshold conditions* 1, 3, 4 and 5 apply and only in so far as relevant to:

(a) an application for a *top-up permission* under Part IV of the *Act* (that is, *permission* to carry on *regulated activities* in addition to those permitted through the *incoming firm's authorisation* under Schedule 3 (EEA Passport Rights) or 4 (Treaty Rights) to the *Act*); and

(b) the exercise of the *FSA's own-initiative power* under section 45 of the *Act* (Variation etc on the FSA's own initiative) in relation to the *top-up permission;*

(2) *COND* also applies to an applicant for *Part IV permission*;

(3) *threshold conditions* 3,4 and 5 do not apply to a *Swiss General Insurance Company*;

(4) *COND* 2.6 (Additional conditions) is only relevant to *non-EEA insurers*; and

(5) *COND* 3.1 is only relevant to *firms* falling within the scope of the Banking Act 2009 (see *COND* 3.1.1G).

1.1.2 **[G]** In *COND*, '*firm*' includes an applicant for *Part IV permission* unless the context otherwise requires.

What?

1.1.3 **[G]** *COND* applies in relation to all of the *regulated activities* for which a *firm* has, or will have, *permission*, except as stated in *COND* 1.1.1G(1).

Where?

1.1.4 **[G]** *COND* applies in relation to all of the *regulated activities* wherever they are carried on, except as stated in *COND* 1.1.1G(1).

1.2 Purpose

1.2.1 **[G]** *COND* gives *guidance* on the *threshold conditions* set out in or under Schedule 6 to the *Act (*Threshold conditions). The *threshold conditions* represent the minimum conditions which a *firm* is required to satisfy, and continue to satisfy, in order to be given and to retain *Part IV permission.*

Applications for Part IV permission or variation of Part IV permission

1.2.2 **[G]**

(1) Under section 41(2) of the *Act (*The threshold conditions), in giving or varying a *Part IV permission* or imposing or varying any *requirement*, the *FSA* must ensure that the *firm* concerned will satisfy, and continue to satisfy, the *threshold conditions* in relation to all of the *regulated activities* for which it has or will have *permission.*

(2) If, however, the applicant for *permission* is an *incoming firm* seeking *top-up permission*, or variation of *top-up permission*, under Part IV of the *Act* (Permission to carry on regulated activities), then under paragraphs 6 and 7 of Schedule 6 to the *Act*, the *FSA* will have regard only to satisfaction of *threshold conditions* 1, 3, 4 and 5, as relevant to the *regulated activities* for which the applicant has, or will have, *Part IV permission*.

Exercise of the FSA's own-initiative power

1.2.3 **[G]**

(1) If, among other things, a *firm* is failing to satisfy any of the *threshold conditions*, or is likely to fail to do so, section 45 of the *Act* (Variation etc. on the FSA's own initiative) states that the *FSA* may exercise its *own-initiative power*. Use of the *FSA's own-initiative power* is explained in SUP 7 (Individual requirements), and EG 8 (Variation and cancellation of permission on the FSA's own initiative and intervention against incoming firms).

(2) If, when exercising its *own-initiative power* under section 45(1) of the *Act*, the *FSA* varies a *firm's permission*, or imposes or varies a *requirement*, then, under section 41(1) of the *Act*, the *FSA* must ensure that the *firm* concerned will satisfy, and continue to satisfy, the *threshold conditions* in relation to all of the *regulated activities* for which it has or will have *permission*. However, section 41(2) of the *Act* states that the duty imposed by section 41(1) of the *Act* does not prevent the *FSA* taking such steps as it considers necessary in relation to a particular *firm* in order to secure its *regulatory objective* of *consumer* protection.

(3) The *FSA* can also exercise its *own-initiative power* under section 45 of the *Act* in relation to the *top-up permission* of an *incoming firm*. But this is only on the grounds that the *incoming firm* is failing, or likely to fail, to satisfy *threshold conditions* 1, 3, 4 or 5 in relation to that *permission*.

Approval of acquisitions or increases of control

1.2.4 **[G]**

(1) Under section 186(3) of the *Act* (Objection to acquisition of control), in deciding whether the approval requirements for a proposed acquisition or increase of *control* are satisfied, the *FSA* must have regard, in relation to the *control* that the acquirer:
 (a) has over the *firm*; or
 (b) will have over the *firm* if the proposal which has been notified to the *FSA* is carried out;

 to its general duty to ensure that the *firm* will continue to satisfy the *threshold conditions*.

(2) The *FSA* must also have regard to the *threshold conditions* in imposing any conditions on its approval of an acquisition or increase of *control* (section 185(2) of the *Act* (Conditions attached to approval)). See SUP 11.7.3G (Acquisition or increase of control: procedures).

1.3 General

An overview of the threshold conditions is given in COND 1 Ann 1G

1.3.1 **[G]** The *guidance* in *COND* 2 explains each *threshold condition* in Part I of Schedule 6 (threshold conditions) to the *Act* and how the *FSA* will interpret it in practice. An overview of the *threshold conditions* is given in *COND* 1 Ann 1G. This *guidance* is not, however, exhaustive and is written in very general terms. A *firm* will need to have regard to the obligation placed upon the *FSA* under section 41 (the *threshold conditions*) of the *Act*; that is, the *FSA* must ensure that the *firm* will satisfy, and continue to satisfy, the *threshold conditions* in relation to each *regulated activity* for which it has, or will have, *permission*.

1.3.2 **[G]**

(1) The *FSA* will consider whether a *firm* satisfies, and will continue to satisfy, the *threshold conditions* in the context of the size, nature, scale and complexity of the business which the *firm* carries on or will carry on if the relevant application is granted.

(2) In relation to *threshold conditions* 4 and 5, the *FSA* will consider whether a *firm* is ready, willing and organised to comply, on a continuing basis, with the requirements and standards under the *regulatory system* which apply to the *firm*, or will apply to the *firm*, if it is granted *Part IV permission*, or a variation of its *permission*. These matters will also be considered if the *FSA* is exercising its *own-initiative power* (see *COND* 1.2.3G). Guidance to *firms* on the implications of this is given under each of those *threshold conditions*.

1.3.3 **[G]** Although the *FSA* may consider that a matter is relevant to its assessment of a *firm*, the fact that a matter is disclosed to the *FSA*, for example in an application, does not necessarily mean that the *firm* will fail to satisfy the *threshold conditions*. The *FSA* will consider each matter in relation to the *regulated activities* for which the *firm* has, or will have, *permission*, having regard to the *regulatory objectives* set out in section 2 of the *Act* (The FSA's general duties). A *firm* should disclose each relevant matter but, if it is appropriate to do so, it is encouraged to discuss it with the *FSA*. This will enable the *FSA* to consider fully how material or significant the matter is and how it affects the ability of the *firm* to satisfy, and continue to satisfy, the *threshold conditions* (see also *COND* 2.3.5G, *COND* 2.4.4G(3) and *COND* 2.5.4G(3)).

Statutory quotations

1.3.4 **[G]**

(1) For ease of reference, the *threshold conditions* in or under Schedule 6 to the *Act* have been quoted in full in *COND* 2.

(2) As these provisions impose obligations, they are printed in bold type. The use of bold type is not intended to indicate that these quotations are *rules* made by the *FSA*.

(3) Where words have been substituted for the text of these provisions the substitutions are enclosed in square brackets ([]). However, none of the changes made by the *FSA* in these quotations for the purpose of the text in *COND* can supersede or alter the meaning of the statutory provision concerned.

Annex 1
Introduction

[G]

NOTES

The flow chart in this Annex is not reproduced here. Please see FSA website at: www.fsa.gov.uk.

Annex 2
Overview of the threshold conditions (COND 1.3.1G) applicable to Non-EEA Insurers
[G]

NOTES

The flow chart in this Annex is not reproduced here. Please see FSA website at: www.fsa.gov.uk.

CHAPTER 2
THE THRESHOLD CONDITIONS

2.1 Threshold condition 1: Legal status

[2026]

2.1.1 **[UK]** Paragraph 1, Schedule 6 to the Act

(1) Subject to sub-paragraph (3), if the regulated activity concerned is the effecting or carrying out of contracts of insurance the authorised person must be a body corporate (other than a limited liability partnership), a registered friendly society or a member of Lloyd's.

(2) If the person concerned appears to the [FSA] to be seeking to carry on, or to be carrying on, a regulated activity constituting accepting deposits, it must be-
  (a) a body corporate; or
  (b) a partnership.

(3) If the regulated activity concerned is an insurance mediation activity, sub-paragraph (1) does not apply.

(4) If the regulated activity concerned is an insurance mediation activity, the person concerned—
  (a) if he is a body corporate constituted under the law of any part of the United Kingdom, must have its registered office, or if it has no registered office, its head office, in the United Kingdom;
  (b) if he is a natural person, is to be treated for the purposes of sub-paragraph (2), as having his head office in the United Kingdom if his residence is situated there.

(5) "Insurance mediation activity" means any of the following activities—
  (a) dealing in rights under a contract of insurance as agent;
  (b) arranging deals in rights under a contract of insurance;
  (c) assisting in the administration and performance of a contract of insurance;
  (d) advising on buying or selling rights under a contract of insurance;
  (e) agreeing to do any of the activities specified in sub-paragraph (a) to (d).

(6) Paragraph (5) must be read with—
  (a) section 22;
  (b) any relevant order under that section; and
  (c) Schedule 2.

2.1.2 **[G]** Section 40(1) of the *Act* (Application for permission) allows an application to be made to the *FSA* for *Part IV permission* by an individual, a *body corporate*, a *partnership* or an unincorporated association. However, in the case of the *regulated activities* of *accepting deposits* and *effecting* or *carrying out contracts of* insurance, article 1 of the *Banking Consolidation Directive* and article 8(1) of the *First Non-Life* Directive and of the *First Life Directive* place further limits on the legal forms a *firm* may take. The *Act* implements the provisions of the directives and extends some of these limits to *firms* that are outside the scope of the directives.

2.1.3 **[G]** The words "or *issuing electronic money*" in paragraph 1(2) of Schedule 6 to the *Act* were added by the Financial Services and Markets Act 2000 (Regulated Activities) (Amendment) Order 2002 with effect from 27 April 2002.

2.2 Threshold condition 2: Location of offices

2.2.1 **[UK]** Paragraph 2, Schedule 6 to the *Act*.

(1) If the person concerned is a body corporate constituted under the law of any part of the United Kingdom—

(a) its head office, and

(b) if it has a registered office, that office, must be in the United Kingdom.

(1A) If—

(a) the regulated activity concerned is any of the investment services and activities, and

(b) the person concerned is a body corporate with no registered office, sub-paragraph (1B) applies in place of sub-paragraph (1).

(1B) If the person concerned has its head office in the United Kingdom, it must carry on business in the United Kingdom.

(2) If the person concerned has its head office in the United Kingdom but is not a body corporate, it must carry on business in the United Kingdom.

2.2.2 **[G]** *Threshold condition* 2 (1) and (2) (Location of offices), implements the requirements of article 6 of the *Post BCCI Directive* and article 5(4) of *MiFID* and *threshold condition* 2(3) and (4) implements article 2.9 of the *Insurance Mediation Directive*, although the *Act* extends *threshold condition* 2 to *firms* which are outside the scope of the *Single Market Directives* and the *UCITS Directive*.

2.2.3 **[G]** Neither the *Post BCCI Directive*, *MiFID*, the *Insurance Mediation Directive* nor the *Act* define what is meant by a *firm's* 'head office'. This is not necessarily the *firm's* place of incorporation or the place where its business is wholly or mainly carried on. Although the *FSA* will judge each application on a case-by-case basis, the key issue in identifying the head office of a *firm* is the location of its central management and control, that is, the location of:

(1) the *directors* and other senior management, who make decisions relating to the *firm's* central direction, and the material management decisions of the *firm* on a day-to-day basis; and

(2) the central administrative functions of the *firm* (for example, central compliance, internal audit).

2.2A Threshold condition 2A: Appointment of claims representatives

2.2A.1 **[UK]** Paragraph 2A, Schedule 6 to the Act

Appointment of claims representatives			
2A	(1)	If it appears to the Authority that—	
		(a)	the regulated activity that the person concerned is carrying on, or is seeking to carry on, is the effecting or carrying out of contracts of insurance, and
		(b)	contracts of insurance against damage arising out of or in connection with the use of motor vehicles on land (other than carrier's liability) are being, or will be, effected or carried out by the person concerned,
		that person must have a claims representative in each EEA State other than the United Kingdom.	
	(2)	For the purposes of sub-paragraph (1)(b), contracts of reinsurance are to be disregarded.	
	(3)	A claims representative is a person with responsibility for handling and settling claims arising from accidents of the kind mentioned in Article 1(2) of the fourth motor insurance directive.	
	(4)	In this paragraph "fourth motor insurance directive" means Directive 2000/26/EC of the European Parliament and of the Council of 16 May 2000 on the approximation of the laws of the Member States relating to insurance against civil liability in respect of the use of motor vehicles and amending Council Directives 73/239/EEC and 88/357/EEC.	

2.2A.2 **[G]** *Threshold condition* 2A (Appointment of claims representatives), provides that if it appears to the *FSA* that any *person* is seeking to carry on, or carrying on, *motor vehicle liability insurance* business, that *person* must have a claims representative in each *EEA State* other than the *United Kingdom*.

2.2A.3 **[G]** *Rules* and *guidance* concerning a *motor vehicle liability insurer's* obligations in relation to the appointment of its claims representatives, and the responsibilities and duties that the *motor vehicle liability insurer* must give to, or impose on, its claims representatives are set out in ICOBS 8.2.

2.3 Threshold condition 3: Close links

2.3.1 **[UK]** paragraph 3, Schedule 6 to the *Act*.

(1) If the person concerned ("A") has close links with another person ("CL"), the *FSA* must be satisfied—
  (a) that those links are not likely to prevent the *FSA's* effective supervision of A; and
  (b) if it appears to the *FSA* that CL is subject to the laws, regulations or administrative provisions of a territory which is not an EEA State ("the foreign provisions"), that neither the foreign provisions, nor any deficiency in their enforcement, would prevent the *FSA's* effective supervision of A.

(2) A has close links with CL if:
  (a) CL is a parent undertaking of A;
  (b) CL is a subsidiary undertaking of A;
  (c) CL is a parent undertaking of a subsidiary undertaking of A;
  (d) CL is a subsidiary undertaking of a parent undertaking of A;
  (e) CL owns or controls 20% or more of the voting rights or capital of A; or
  (f) A owns or controls 20% or more of the voting rights or capital of CL.

(3) "Subsidiary undertaking" includes all the instances mentioned in Article 1(1) and (2) of the Seventh Company Law Directive in which an entity may be a subsidiary of an undertaking.

2.3.2 **[G]** *Threshold condition* 3 (Close links) implements requirements of the *Post BCCI Directive*, but the *Act* extends this condition to *firms* from outside the *EEA* and other *firms* which are outside the scope of the *Single Market Directives* and the *UCITS Directive*.

2.3.3 **[G]** In assessing this *threshold condition*, factors which the *FSA* will take into consideration include, among other things, whether:

(1) it is likely that the *FSA* will receive adequate information from the *firm*, and those *persons* with whom the *firm* has *close links*, to enable it to determine whether the *firm* is complying with the requirements and standards under the *regulatory system* and to identify and assess the impact on the *regulatory objectives* in section 2 of the *Act* (The FSA's general duties); this will include consideration of whether the *firm* is ready, willing and organised to comply with *Principle* 11 (Relations with regulators and the *rules* in *SUP* on the provision of information to the *FSA*;

(2) The structure and geographical spread of the *firm*, the *group* to which it belongs and other *persons* with whom the *firm* has *close links*, might hinder the provision of adequate and reliable flows of information to the *FSA*; factors which may hinder these flows include the fact there may be branches or connected *companies* in territories which supervise *companies* to a different standard or territories with laws which restrict the free flow of information, although the *FSA* will consider the totality of information available from all sources;

(3) the *firm* and the *group* to which it belongs are, or will be, subject to supervision on a consolidated basis (consolidated supervision) (for example, if a financial resources requirement is determined for the *group* as a whole); and

(4) it is possible to assess with confidence the overall financial position of the *group* at any particular time; factors which may make this difficult include lack of audited consolidated accounts for a *group*, if companies in the same *group* as the *firm* have different financial years and accounting dates and if they do not share common auditors.

2.3.4 **[G]** When assessing whether the *firm* will satisfy and continue to satisfy this *threshold condition*, the *FSA* will have regard to all relevant matters, whether arising in the *United Kingdom* or elsewhere.

2.3.5 **[G]** The *FSA* will take into account relevant matters only in so far as they are significant (see COND 1.3.3G). In determining the weight to be given to any relevant matter, the *FSA* will consider its significance in the context of its ability to supervise the *firm* adequately, having regard to the *regulatory objectives* in section 2 of the *Act*. In this context, a series of matters may be significant when taken together, even though each of them in isolation might not give serious cause for concern

Meaning of "parent undertaking" and "subsidiary undertaking"

2.3.6 **[G]**

Part II FSA Handbook Materials

(1) Section 420(1) of the *Act* (Parent and subsidiary undertaking) states that, except in relation to an *incorporated friendly society*, *'parent undertaking'* and *'subsidiary undertaking'* have the same meaning as in the Companies Acts (see section 1162 of, and Schedule 7 to, the Companies Act 2006). These are the cases referred to in COND 2.3.7G(1)(a) to (f).
(2) Section 420(2) of the Act supplements these definitions in two ways; these are the cases referred to in COND 2.3.7G(1)(g) and (h).
(3) Paragraph 3(3) of Schedule 6 to the *Act* extends the meaning of *'subsidiary* undertaking' for the purposes of *threshold condition* 3 (Close links) to all the cases in articles 1(1) and (2) of the *Seventh Company Law* Directive in which one *undertaking* may be a *subsidiary* of another *undertaking* (see COND 2.3.11G).

2.3.7 **[G]**
(1) For the purposes of *threshold condition* 3 (Close links) and except in relation to an *incorporated friendly society*, an undertaking is a *parent undertaking* of another *undertaking* (a *subsidiary undertaking)* if any of the following apply to it:
 (a) it holds a majority of the voting rights in the *subsidiary undertaking*; or
 (b) it is a member of the *subsidiary undertaking* and has the right to appoint or remove a majority of its board of *directors*; or
 (c) it has the right to exercise a dominant influence over the *subsidiary undertaking* through:
  (i) provisions contained in the *subsidiary undertaking's* memorandum or articles; or
  (ii) a control contract; or
 (d) it is a member of the *subsidiary undertaking* and controls alone, under an agreement with other shareholders or members, a majority of the voting rights in the *subsidiary undertaking*; or
 (e) it has a participating interest (as defined in section 421A of the *Act* (meaning of "participating interest")) in the *subsidiary undertaking* and:
  (i) actually exercises a dominant influence over it; or
  (ii) it and the *subsidiary undertaking* are managed on a unified basis; or
 (f) it is a *parent undertaking* of a *parent undertaking* of the *subsidiary undertaking*; or
 (g) it is an individual and would be a *parent undertaking* if it were an *undertaking*; or
 (h) it is incorporated in or formed under the law of another *EEA State* and is a *parent undertaking* within the meaning of any rule of law in that State for purposes connected with implementation of the *Seventh Company Law Directive*.
(2) A flowchart of COND 2.3.7G(1) is set out in COND 2 Ann 1G.

2.3.8 **[G]**
(1) In relation to COND 2.3.7G(1)(b) and (d), an *undertaking* is treated as a member of another *undertaking* if any of its *subsidiary undertakings* is a member of that *undertaking*, or if any shares in that other *undertaking* are held by a *person* acting on behalf of the *undertaking* or any of its *subsidiary undertakings.*
(2) In relation to COND 2.3.7G(1)(e), a 'participating interest' means an interest held by an *undertaking* in the shares of another *undertaking* which it holds on a long term basis, for the purpose of securing a contribution to its activities by the exercise of control or influence arising from or related to that interest. A holding of 20% or more of the shares of an *undertaking* is presumed to be a participating interest unless the contrary is shown. Examples of interests of a temporary nature which do not constitute participating interests for the purpose of this control relationship include market-makers' holdings in a trading book.
(3) Section 421A of the *Act* states that an interest held on behalf of an *undertaking* is treated as held by it. Thus, if the chain of ownership includes a trust, the *FSA* will treat the trustees as legal owners when determining whether it considers there to be a *close link*. The beneficiaries or settlors of a trust (or both) may also come within the scope of these provisions, depending on the terms of the trust. However, the *FSA* will consider each case on its merits.

2.3.9 **[G]** The provisions of Schedule 7 to the Companies Act 2006 (Parent and subsidiary undertakings supplementary provisions) explain and supplement the provisions of section 1162 of the Companies Act 2006 (outlined in COND 2.3.7G(1)(a) to (f)).

2.3.10 **[G]** Section 420(3) of the *Act* (Parent and subsidiary undertaking) (supplemented by paragraph 3(3) of Schedule 6 to the *Act)* states that an *incorporated friendly society* is a *parent undertaking* of another *body corporate* (a *subsidiary undertaking*) if it has the following relationship to it:
(1) it holds a majority of the voting rights in the *subsidiary undertaking*; or
(2) it is a member of the *subsidiary undertaking* and has the right to appoint or remove a majority of the *subsidiary undertaking's* board of *directors*; or
(3) it is a member of the *subsidiary undertaking* and controls alone, under an agreement with other shareholders or members, a majority of the voting rights in it.

2.3.11 **[G]** For the purposes of this *threshold condition* 3 (Close links), an *undertaking* is a *subsidiary undertaking* of another *undertaking* if:

(1) the other undertaking (its parent) is a member of the *undertaking;*
(2) a majority of the *undertaking's* board of *directors* who have held office during the financial year and during the preceding financial year have been appointed solely as a result of the exercise of the parent's voting rights; and
(3) no one else is the *parent undertaking* of the *undertaking* under COND 2.3.7G(1)(a) to (c) or COND 2.3.10G(1) or (2)

2.3.12 **[G]** The *guidance* in COND 2.3 is not comprehensive and is not a substitute for consulting the relevant legislation, for example the Companies Act 2006, the Friendly Societies Act 1992 and the *Seventh Company Law Directive*, or obtaining appropriate professional advice.

2.4 Threshold condition 4: Adequate resources

2.4.1 **[UK]** Paragraph 4, Schedule 6 to the *Act*

(1) The resources of the person concerned must, in the opinion of the [FSA], be adequate in relation to the regulated activities that he seeks to carry on, or carries on.
(2) In reaching that opinion, the [FSA] may-
 (a) take into account the person's membership of a group and any effect which that membership may have; and
 (b) have regard to-
  (i) the provision he makes and, if he is a member of a group, which other members of the group make in respect of liabilities (including contingent and future liabilities); and
  (ii) the means by which he manages and, if he is a member of a group, which other members of the group manage the incidence of risk in connection with his business.

Part II FSA Handbook Materials

2.4.2 **[G]**

(1) *Threshold condition* 4 (Adequate resources), requires the *FSA* to ensure that a *firm* has adequate resources in relation to the specific *regulated activity* or *regulated activities* which it seeks to carry on, or carries on.
(2) In this context, the *FSA* will interpret the term 'adequate' as meaning sufficient in terms of quantity, quality and availability, and 'resources' as including all financial resources, non-financial resources and means of managing its resources; for example, capital, provisions against liabilities, holdings of or access to cash and other liquid assets, human resources and effective means by which to manage risks.
(3) High level systems and control requirements are in *SYSC*. Detailed financial resources and systems requirements are in the relevant section of the Prudential Standards part of the *Handbook*, including specific provisions for particular types of *regulated activity*. The *FSA* will consider whether the *firm* is ready, willing and organised to comply with these requirements when assessing if it has adequate resources for the purposes of this *threshold condition.*

2.4.3 **[G]**

(1) When assessing this *threshold condition*, the *FSA* may have regard to any *person* appearing to it to be, or likely to be, in a relevant relationship with the *firm*, in accordance with section 49 of the *Act* (Persons connected with an applicant); for example, a *firm's controllers*, its *directors* or *partners*, other *persons* with *close links* to the *firm* (see COND 2.3), and other *persons* that exert influence on the *firm* which might pose a risk to the *firm's* satisfaction of the *threshold conditions* and would, therefore, be in a relevant relationship with the *firm.*
(2) In particular, although it is the *firm* that is being assessed, the *FSA* may take into consideration the impact of other members of the *firm*'s *group* on the adequacy of its resources. For example, the *FSA* may assess the consolidated solvency of the *group*. The *FSA's* approach to the consolidated supervision of a *firm* and its *group* is in the relevant part of the Prudential Standards part of the *Handbook.*

2.4.4 **[G]**

(1) When assessing whether a *firm* will satisfy and continue to satisfy *threshold condition* 4, the *FSA* will have regard to all relevant matters, whether arising in the *United Kingdom* or elsewhere.
(2) Relevant matters may include but are not limited to:
 (a) whether there are any indications that the *firm* may have difficulties if the application is granted (see COND 2.4.6G), at the time of the grant or in the future, in complying with any of the *FSA's* prudential *rules* (see the relevant part of the Prudential Standards part of the *Handbook*);
 (b) whether there are any indications that the *firm* will not be able to meet its debts as they fall due;
 (c) whether there are any implications for the adequacy of the *firm's* resources arising from the history of the *firm*; for example, whether the *firm* has:
  (i) has been adjudged bankrupt; or

(ii) entered into liquidation; or
(iii) been the subject of a receiving or been in administration; or
(iv) had a bankruptcy or winding-up petition served on it, been the subject of a bankruptcy restrictions order (including an interim bankruptcy restrictions order) or offered a bankruptcy restrictions undertaking; or
(v) had its estate sequestrated; or
(vi) entered into a deed of arrangement or an individual voluntary agreement (or in Scotland, a trust deed) or other composition in favour of its creditors, or is doing so; or
(vii) within the last ten years, failed to satisfy a judgment debt under a court order, whether in the *United Kingdom* or elsewhere;

(d) whether the *firm* has taken reasonable steps to identify and measure any risks of regulatory concern that it may encounter in conducting its business (see COND 2.4.6G) and has installed appropriate systems and controls and appointed appropriate human resources to measure them prudently at all times; see SYSC 3.1 (Systems and Controls), SYSC 3.2 (Areas covered by systems and controls) and SYSC 4.1.1R (Organisational requirements); and
(e) whether the *firm* has conducted enquiries into the financial services sector in which it intends to conduct business (see COND 2.4.6G) that are sufficient to satisfy itself that:
(i) it has access to adequate capital, by reference to the *FSA's* prudential requirements, to support the business including any losses which may be expected during its start-up period; and
(ii) *Client money, deposits, custody assets* and *policyholders'* rights will not be placed at risk if the business fails.

(3) In the context of *threshold condition* 4 (Adequate resources), the *FSA* will only take into account relevant matters which are material (see COND 1.3.3G). The *FSA* will consider the materiality of each relevant matter in relation to the *regulated activities* for which the *firm* has, or will have, *permission*, having regard to the *regulatory objectives* in section 2 of the *Act* (The FSA's general duties). It should be noted that a series of matters may be significant when taken together, even if each of them in isolation might not be significant.
(4) In making its assessment, the *FSA* will consider the individual circumstances of each *firm* on a case-by-case basis.

2.4.5 **[G]** In complying with SYSC 3.1.1R (Systems and controls), a firm should plan its business appropriately so that it is able to identify, measure and manage the likely risks of regulatory concern it will face (SYSC 3.2.17G (Business strategy) and SYSC 7 (Risk control)).

2.4.6 **[G]**
(1) Any newly-formed *firm* can be susceptible to early difficulties. These difficulties could arise from a lack of relevant expertise and judgment, or from ill-constructed and insufficiently tested business strategies. A *firm* may also be susceptible to difficulties where it substantially changes its business activities.
(2) As a result, the *FSA* would expect a *firm* which is applying for *Part IV permission*, or a substantial variation of that *permission*, to take adequate steps to satisfy itself and, if relevant, the *FSA* that:
(a) it has a well constructed business plan or strategy plan for its product or service which demonstrates that it is ready, willing and organised to comply with the relevant requirements in the Prudential Standards part of the *Handbook* and *SYSC* that apply to the *regulated activity* it is seeking to carry on;
(b) its business plan or strategy plan has been sufficiently tested; and
(c) the financial and other resources of the *firm* are commensurate with the likely risks it will face.
(3) The *FSA* would expect the level of detail in a *firm's* business plan or strategy plan in (2) to be appropriate to the complexity of the *firm's* proposed *regulated activities* and *unregulated activities* and the risks of regulatory concern it is likely to face (see SYSC 3.2.11G (Management information) and SYSC 7 (Risk control). Notes on the contents of a business plan are given in the business plan section of the application pack for *Part IV permission*. A *firm* requiring specific *guidance* on the contents and level of detail of its business plan should contact the Firm Contact Centre (020 7066 3954), or, if relevant, its usual supervisory contact at the *FSA*, or seek professional assistance.

2.5 Threshold condition 5: Suitability

2.5.1 **[UK]** Paragraph 5, *Schedule 6 to the Act*

The person concerned must satisfy the *FSA* that he is a fit and proper person having regard to all the circumstances, including-
(a) his connection with any person;
(b) the nature of any regulated activity that he carries on or seeks to carry on; and

(c) the need to ensure that his affairs are conducted soundly and prudently.

2.5.2 **[G]**

(1) *Threshold condition* 5 (Suitability), requires the *firm* to satisfy the *FSA* that it is 'fit and proper' to have *Part IV permission* having regard to all the circumstances, including its connections with other *persons*, the range and nature of its proposed (or current) *regulated activities* and the overall need to be satisfied that its affairs are and will be conducted soundly and prudently (see also *PRIN* and *SYSC)*.

(2) The *FSA* will also take into consideration anything that could influence a *firm's* continuing ability to satisfy this *threshold condition*. Examples include the *firm's* position within a *UK* or international *group*, information provided by *overseas regulators* about the *firm*, and the *firm's* plans to seek to vary its *Part IV permission* to carry on additional *regulated activities* once it has been granted that *permission* by the *FSA*.

2.5.3 **[G]**

(1) The emphasis of this *threshold condition* is on the suitability of the *firm* itself. The suitability of each *person* who performs a *controlled function* will be assessed by the *FSA* under the *approved persons* regime (see SUP 10 (Approved persons) and *FIT)*. In certain circumstances, however, the *FSA* may consider that the *firm* is not suitable because of doubts over the individual or collective suitability of *persons* connected with the *firm*.

(2) When assessing this *threshold condition* in relation to a *firm*, the *FSA* may have regard to any *person* appearing to it to be, or likely to be, in a relevant relationship with the *firm*, as permitted by section 49 of the *Act* (Persons connected with an applicant) (see COND 2.4.3G).

(3) In relation to a *firm* which is an *EEA regulated entity*, the *Financial Groups Directive* provides that the *FSA* should consult other competent authorities when assessing the suitability of the shareholders and the reputation and experience of directors involved in the management of another entity in the same group.

2.5.4 **[G]**

(1) When determining whether the *firm* will satisfy and continue to satisfy *threshold condition* 5, the *FSA* will have regard to all relevant matters, whether arising in the *United Kingdom* or elsewhere.

(2) Relevant matters include, but are not limited to, whether a *firm:*
   (a) conducts, or will conduct, its business with integrity and in compliance with proper standards;
   (b) has, or will have, a competent and prudent management; and
   (c) can demonstrate that it conducts, or will conduct, its affairs with the exercise of due skill, care and diligence.

(3) The *FSA* will take into account relevant matters only to the extent that they are significant (see COND 1.3.3G). In determining whether relevant matters are significant to the *firm*, the *FSA* will consider significance in the context of the suitability of the *firm*, having regard to the *regulatory objectives* in section 2 of the *Act* (The FSA's general duties); a series of matters may be significant when taken together, even if each of them in isolation may not be significant.

(4) In making its assessment, the *FSA* will, therefore, consider the individual circumstances of each *firm* on a case-by-case basis.

2.5.5 **[G]** Where a *firm* is applying for *Part IV permission* or a substantial variation of that *permission*, the guidance in COND 2.4.6G is relevant. For the purpose of *threshold condition* 5, however, the *FSA* would expect the *firm's* business plan or strategy plan to take into account the interests of *consumers* and demonstrate that it is ready, willing and organised to comply with the relevant requirements in the *Handbook* that apply to the *regulated activity* it is seeking to carry on.

Conducting business with integrity and in compliance with proper standards

2.5.6 **[G]** In determining whether a *firm* will satisfy, and continue to satisfy, *threshold condition* 5 in respect of conducting its business with integrity and in compliance with proper standards, the relevant matters, as referred to in COND 2.5.4G(2), may include but are not limited to whether:

(1) the *firm* has been open and co-operative in all its dealings with the *FSA* and any other regulatory body (see *Principle* 11 (Relations with regulators)) and is ready, willing and organised to comply with the requirements and standards under the *regulatory system* and other legal, regulatory and professional obligations; the relevant requirements and standards will depend on the circumstances of each case, including the *regulated activities* which the *firm* has *permission*, or is seeking *permission*, to carry on;

(2) the *firm* has been convicted, or is connected with a *person* who has been convicted, of any criminal offence; this must include, where provided for by the Exceptions Order to the Rehabilitation of Offenders Act 1974, any spent convictions; particular consideration will be given to offences of dishonesty, fraud, financial crime or an offence whether or not in the *United Kingdom* or other offences under legislation relating to companies, building societies,

industrial and provident societies, credit unions, friendly societies, banking and or other financial services, insolvency, consumer credit companies, insurance, and consumer protection, *money laundering*, market manipulation or *insider dealing*;

(3) the *firm* has been the subject of, or connected to the subject of, any existing or previous investigation or enforcement proceedings by the *FSA*, the *Society of Lloyd's* or by other regulatory authorities (including the *FSA's* predecessors), *clearing houses* or *exchanges, professional bodies* or government bodies or agencies; the *FSA* will, however, take both the nature of the *firm*'s involvement in, and the outcome of, any investigation or enforcement proceedings into account in determining whether it is a relevant matter;

(4) the *firm* has contravened, or is connected with a *person* who has contravened, any provisions of the *Act* or any preceding financial services legislation, the *regulatory system* or the rules, regulations, statements of principles or codes of practice (for example the *Society of Lloyd's* Codes) of other regulatory authorities (including the *FSA's* predecessors), *clearing houses* or *exchanges, professional bodies*, or government bodies or agencies or relevant industry standards (such as the Non-Investment Products Code); the *FSA* will, however, take into account both the status of codes of practice or relevant industry standards and the nature of the contravention (for example, whether a *firm* has flouted or ignored a particular code);

(5) the *firm*, or a *person* connected with the *firm*, has been refused registration, authorisation, membership or licence to carry out a trade, business or profession or has had that registration, authorisation, membership or licence revoked, withdrawn or terminated, or has been expelled by a regulatory or government body; whether the *FSA* considers such a refusal relevant will depend on the circumstances;

(6) the *firm* has taken reasonable care to establish and maintain effective systems and controls for compliance with applicable requirements and standards under the regulatory system that apply to the *firm* and the *regulated activities* for which it has, or will have, *permission* (see SYSC 3.2.6R to SYSC 3.2.8R (Compliance) and SYSC 6.1.1 to SYSC 6.1.5));

(7) the *firm* has put in place procedures which are reasonably designed to:

(a) ensure that it has made its *employees* aware of, and compliant with, those requirements and standards under the *regulatory system* that apply to the *firm* and the *regulated activities* for which it has, or will have *permission;*

(b) ensure that its *approved persons* (whether or not employed by the *firm)* are aware of those requirements and standards under the *regulatory system* applicable to them;

(c) determine that its *employees* are acting in a way compatible with the *firm* adhering to those requirements and standards; and

(d) determine that its *approved persons* are adhering to those requirements and standards;

(8) the *firm* or a *person* connected with the *firm* has been dismissed from employment or a position of trust, fiduciary relationship or similar or has ever been asked to resign from employment in such a position; whether the *FSA* considers a resignation to be relevant will depend on the circumstances, for example if a *firm* is asked to resign in circumstance that cast doubt over its honesty or integrity; and

(9) the *firm* or a *person* connected with the *firm* has ever been disqualified from acting as a *director*.

Competent and prudent management and exercise of due skill, care and diligence

2.5.7 **[G]** In determining whether a *firm* will satisfy and continue to satisfy *threshold condition* 5 in respect of having competent and prudent management and exercising due skill, care and diligence, relevant matters, as referred to in COND 2.5.4G(2), may include, but are not limited to whether:

(1) the *governing body* of the *firm* is made up of individuals with an appropriate range of skills and experience to understand, operate and manage the *firm*'s regulated activities;

(2) if appropriate, the *governing body* of the *firm* includes non-executive representation, at a level which is appropriate for the control of the *regulated activities* proposed, for example, as members of an audit committee (see COND 3.2.15G (Audit Committee));

(3) the *governing body* of the *firm* is organised in a way that enables it to address and control the *regulated activities* of the *firm*, including those carried on by *managers* to whom particular functions have been delegated (see SYSC 2.1 (Apportionment of responsibilities) and SYSC 3.2 (Areas covered by systems and controls) and SYSC 4.1.1 (General organisational requirements));

(4) those *persons* who perform *controlled functions* under certain *arrangements* entered into by the *firm* or its contractors (including *appointed representatives* or, where applicable, *tied agents*) act with due skill, care and diligence in carrying our their *controlled function* (see APER 4.2 (Statement of Principle 2) or managing the business for which they are responsible (see APER 4.7 (Statement of Principle 7));

(5) the *firm* has made arrangements to put in place an adequate system of internal control to comply with the requirements and standards under the *regulatory system* (see SYSC 3.1 (Systems and Controls) and SYSC 4.1 (General organisational requirements));

(6) the *firm* has approached the control of financial and other risk in a prudent manner (for example, by not assuming risks without taking due account of the possible consequences) and has taken reasonable care to ensure that robust information and reporting systems have been developed, tested and properly installed (see SYSC 3.2.10 (Risk assessment) and SYSC 7.1 (Risk control));

(7) the *firm*, or a *person* connected with the *firm*, has been a *director, partner* or otherwise concerned in the management of a *company, partnership* or other organisation or business that has gone into insolvency, liquidation or administration while having been connected with that organisation or within one year of such a connection;

(8) the *firm* has developed human resources policies and procedures that are reasonably designed to ensure that it employs only individuals who are honest and committed to high standards of integrity in the conduct of their activities (see, for example, SYSC 3.2.13G (Employees and agents) and SYSC 5.1 (Employees, agents and other relevant persons));

(9) the *firm* has conducted enquiries (for example, through market research or the previous activities of the *firm)* that are sufficient to give it reasonable assurance that it will not be posing unacceptable risks to *consumers* or the *financial system*;

(10) the *firm* has in place systems and controls against *money laundering* of the sort described in SYSC 3.2.6R to SYSC 3.2.6JG and SYSC 6.3 (Financial crime);

(11) where appropriate, the *firm* has appointed auditors and actuaries, who have sufficient experience in the areas of business to be conducted (see SUP 3.4 (Auditors' qualifications) and SUP 4.3.8G to SUP 4.3.10G (Actuary's qualifications)); and

(12) in the case of a *firm* that carries on *insurance mediation activity*:

(a) a reasonable proportion of the *persons* within its management structure who are responsible for the *insurance mediation activity*; and

(b) all other *persons* directly involved in its *insurance mediation activity*; demonstrate the knowledge and ability necessary for the performance of their duties; and

(c) all the *persons* in its management structure and any staff directly involved in *insurance mediation activity* are of good repute (see MIPRU 2.3.1R (Knowledge, ability and good repute)).

2.6 Additional conditions

2.6.1 **[UK]**

Paragraph 8 of Schedule 6 to the Act			
(1)	If this paragraph applies to the person concerned, he must, for the purposes of such provisions of this Act as may be specified, satisfy specified additional conditions.		
(2)	This paragraph applies to a person who:		
(a)	has his head office outside the EEA; and		
(b)	appears to the [FSA] to be seeking to carry on a regulated activity relating to insurance business.		
Article 3 of the financial services and Markets Act 2000 (Variation of Threshold Conditions) Order 2001 (SI 2001/2507)			
3(1)	If paragraph 8 of Schedule 6 (additional conditions applying to non-EEA insurers) applies to the person concerned, it must, for the purposes of section 41 and Schedule 6, satisfy the following additional conditions -		
	(a)	it must have a representative who is resident in the United Kingdom and who has authority to bind it in its relations with third parties and to represent it in its relations with the [FSA] and the courts in the United Kingdom;	
	(b)	subject to paragraph (2), if the person concerned is not a Swiss general insurance company -	
		(i)	it must be a body corporate entitled under the law of the place where its head office is situated to effect and carry out contracts of insurance;
		(ii)	it must have in the United Kingdom assets of such value as may be specified;
		(iii)	unless the regulated activity in question relates solely to reinsurance, it must have made a deposit (of money or securities, as may be specified) of such an amount and with such a person as may be specified, and on such terms and subject to such other provisions as may be specified.
(2)	Where the person concerned is seeking to carry on an activity relating to insurance business in one or more other EEA States (as well as in the United Kingdom), and the [FSA] and the supervisory authority in the other EEA State or States concerned so agree -		

Paragraph 8 of Schedule 6 to the Act		
	(a)	the reference in paragraph (1)(b)(ii) to the United Kingdom is to be read as a reference to the United Kingdom and the other EEA State or States concerned; and
	(b)	the reference in paragraph (1)(b)(iii) to such a person as may be specified is to be read as a reference to such a person as may be agreed between the [FSA] and the other supervisory authority or authorities concerned.

2.6.2 **[G]** The Financial Services and Markets Act 2000 (Variation of Threshold Conditions) Order 2001 (SI 2001/2507) imposes certain additional conditions on non-*EEA insurers*, as set out above.

2.6.3 **[G]** This order implements requirements under *the Insurance Directives*, and the *Act* extends these requirements to *firms* outside of the *EEA*.

2.6.4 **[G]** The effect of article 3(a) of the order is that a non-*EEA insurer* (including a *Swiss General insurance company*) must appoint an *authorised UK representative*.

2.6.5 **[G]**

(1) A non-*EEA insurer* must be a *body corporate* formed under the law of the country where its head office is situated.

(2) *A person* seeking to carry on *insurance business* in the *United Kingdom* must have assets in the *United Kingdom* to a value specified in *GENPRU*. Where the applicant wants to carry on *insurance business* in other *EEA States*, the applicant must have assets in those other *EEA States* as are agreed between the *FSA* and the supervisory authorities in the other states.

(3) Unless the *regulated activity* to be carried on by the applicant relates solely to reinsurance business, the applicant must make a deposit of an amount, and type and on terms with a *person* and agreed between the *FSA* and the supervisory authorities in other *EEA States* where the applicant wishes to carry on *insurance business*. This deposit will be subject to provisions in INSPRU 1.5.

2.6.6 **[G]**

(1) The additional conditions set out in AUTH 2.5.6G(1), (2) and (3) do not apply to *Swiss general insurance companies*.

Annex 1
The threshold conditions

Ann 1 **[G]**

NOTES
The flow chart in this Annex is not reproduced here. Please see FSA website at: www.fsa.gov.uk.

CHAPTER 3
BANKING ACT 2009

3.1 Assessing Condition 2 under section 7(3) of the Banking Act 2009

Introduction

[2026A]

3.1.1 **[G]** The Banking Act 2009 (the Banking Act) introduces new powers for HM Treasury, the Bank of England and the *FSA* to deal with failing banks. The powers, which are set out in Parts 1 to 3 of that Act, can be used to deal with UK incorporated *firms* with a *Part IV permission* to carry on the *regulated activity* of *accepting deposits*, other than *credit unions* and any other class of institution specified in secondary legislation. In relation to *building societies*, the main tools in the Act are applied with modifications. In this section the term "bank" is used to refer to those *firms* that are potentially subject to the powers in Parts 1 to 3 of the Banking Act. The powers are defined in the Banking Act, and referred to in this section as the "stabilisation powers". The Banking Act contains powers to enable HM Treasury to extend the application of the stabilisation powers to *credit unions* by secondary legislation.

3.1.2 **[G]** Section 7 of the Banking Act sets out the two conditions that must be met before a stabilisation power can be exercised in respect of a bank:

(1) Condition 1 is that the bank is failing, or is likely to fail, to satisfy the *threshold conditions*.

(2) Condition 2 is that, having regard to timing and other relevant circumstances, it is not reasonably likely that (ignoring the stabilisation powers) action will be taken by or in respect of the bank that will enable it to satisfy the *threshold conditions*.

3.1.3 **[G]** The Banking Act provides that the *FSA* is to treat Conditions 1 and 2 as met if satisfied that they would be met but for financial assistance provided by either HM Treasury or the Bank of England (disregarding ordinary market assistance offered by the Bank on its usual terms).

Assessing Condition 1

3.1.4 **[G]** The matters the *FSA* will take into account in assessing whether a bank is failing or is likely to fail to satisfy the *threshold conditions* are described in COND 2.1 to COND 2.5. The options available to the *FSA* in the case of a breach of the *threshold conditions* are outlined in Chapter 8 of the *Enforcement Guide* and SUP 7.2. These tools are available to the *FSA* at any time, and so may be used before or in conjunction with the stabilisation tools provided by the Banking Act.

Assessing Condition 2

3.1.5 **[G]** The Banking Act provides that in considering the test in Condition 2, the *FSA* should ignore the stabilisation powers. The purpose of this limitation is to make clear that in making its assessment, the *FSA* is not considering whether the stabilisation powers could successfully resolve the situation, but is considering whether alternative measures might provide for this instead.

Timing

3.1.6 **[G]** In assessing Condition 2, the *FSA* will consider the timeframe during which any actions taken by or in relation to the bank are likely to be available and to have effect. In the view of the *FSA*, the purpose of the reference to timing in Condition 2 is to require the *FSA* to consider whether a return to full compliance is likely to occur within a reasonable period of time. The following is a non-exhaustive list of factors the *FSA* may consider:

(1) the extent of any loss, or risk of loss, or other adverse effect on *consumers*. The more serious the loss or potential loss or other adverse effect, the more likely it is that the *FSA* will consider that remedial action will be needed urgently;

(2) the seriousness of any suspected breach of the requirements of the *Act* or the *rules* and the steps that need to be taken to correct that breach;

(3) the risk that the bank's conduct or business presents to the *financial system* and to confidence in that system;

(4) the likelihood that remedial action that could be taken by or in relation to the bank will take effect before *consumers* or market confidence suffers significant detriment.

3.1.7 **[G]** If the *FSA* is satisfied that the breach of *threshold conditions* is likely to be temporary and to be rectified within a reasonable time, the *FSA* is unlikely to conclude that Condition 2 has been met.

Other relevant circumstances

3.1.8 **[G]** In general the *FSA* will be concerned to determine whether any remedial action that could be taken by or in relation to the bank will be effective. This will include an assessment of both how likely it is that the action will be taken, and if it is, the impact it will have on the bank's compliance with the *threshold conditions*. Circumstances that the *FSA* may take into account include but are not limited to:

(1) where the *FSA's* concerns relate to adequacy of liquidity:
   (a) the availability of market funding to banks generally and any specific circumstances of the bank that may impact on its ability to access the market on terms which are generally available;
   (b) whether the bank's current funding structure is adequate and viable; whether the primary sources of funding continue to be available, given current market sentiment, and whether they would still be viable if market sentiment was to change;
   (c) the maturity profile of the bank's existing funding and the availability of funding from the market to replace maturing funding as the need arises;
   (d) whether liquidity problems call into question adequacy of capital;
   (e) the bank's credit rating and the likelihood and impact of any potential downgrade;
   (f) the availability and terms of liquidity support from group companies, existing funders and central banks;

(2) where the *FSA's* concerns relate to capital:
   (a) the availability of capital from the market for banks in general and any specific circumstances of the bank that may impact on its ability to access the market on terms which are generally available;
   (b) potential sources of capital and the nature of and terms on which capital may be obtained;
   (c) the success of any recent attempts by the bank to raise capital on the open market;
   (d) the willingness of existing significant institutional investors to provide or assist in a strategic solution to the bank;

(3) where the *FSA's* concerns relate to the adequacy of non-financial resources or suitability, the *FSA* will take into account the factors identified in COND 2.4 and 2.5, and other *Handbook* provisions referred to in those chapters. In assessing Condition 2, the circumstances of each case are likely to be different, but the *FSA* will be concerned to establish the likelihood of achieving a return to full compliance with the *threshold conditions*, and the timescale in which a return to compliance will be effected;

(4) the prospects of the bank securing a material and relevant transaction with a third party, for example a sale of the bank itself or of all or part of its business. In relation to any transaction, the *FSA* will have regard to factors including but not limited to:
  (a) the status of any ongoing negotiations;
  (b) the level of interest expressed and the credibility of potential counterparties;
  (c) practical constraints related to the bank itself, for example, management engagement, availability of relevant information and severability of infrastructure;
  (d) the sources, availability and firmness of financing for any transaction;
  (e) the need for shareholder approval, merger clearances or other consents;
  (f) the suitability of the counterparty and the stability of the relevant parties following completion of any transaction.

3.1.9 **[G]** When assessing whether the bank will return to compliance with *threshold condition* 4 (adequate resources) the *FSA* will also assess the reasons behind the likely or actual failure of compliance. Serious failures of management, systems or internal controls may in themselves call into question the adequacy of the bank's non-financial resources (*threshold condition* 4) or suitability (*threshold condition* 5). Therefore, in assessing whether a bank is reasonably likely to satisfy the *threshold conditions* in the future, the *FSA* will be concerned to ensure that any such failures have been adequately addressed.

TRANSITIONAL PROVISIONS

[2027]
TP 1.1 There are no transitional provisions in *COND*.

GEN contains transitional provisions that apply throughout the *Handbook*.

SCHEDULE 1
RECORD KEEPING REQUIREMENTS

[2028]
1.1 **[G]** There are no record keeping requirements in *COND*.

SCHEDULE 2
NOTIFICATION REQUIREMENTS

[2029]
2.1 **[G]** There are no notification *rules* in *COND* but *guidance* is given in COND 1.3.3G on disclosure to the *FSA* in connection with applications.

SCHEDULE 3
FEES AND OTHER REQUIRED PAYMENTS

[2030]
3.1 **[G]** There are no requirements for fees or other payments in *COND*.

SCHEDULE 4
POWERS EXERCISED

[2031]
4.1 **[G]** The following power in the *Act* has been exercised by the *FSA* to give the *guidance* in *COND:*

Section 157(1) (Guidance).

SCHEDULE 5
RIGHTS OF ACTION FOR DAMAGES

[2032]
5.1 **[G]** There are no *rules* in *COND*.

SCHEDULE 6
RULES THAT CAN BE WAIVED

[2033]
6.1 **[G]** There are no *rules* in *COND*.

STATEMENTS OF PRINCIPLE AND CODE OF PRACTICE FOR APPROVED PERSONS (APER)

NOTES

Up to date as at 22 February 2010. For later amendments please see www.fsa.gov.uk.

CONTENTS

APER 1—Application and purpose . . . . . [2034]
APER 2—The Statements of Principle for Approved Persons . . . . . [2035]
APER 3—Code of Practice for Approved Persons: general . . . . . [2036]
APER 4—Code of Practice for Approved Persons: specific . . . . . [2037]
APER TP 1—Transitional Provisions . . . . . [2038]
APER Sch 1—Record keeping requirements . . . . . [2039]
APER Sch 2—Notification requirements . . . . . [2040]
APER Sch 3—Fees and required payments . . . . . [2041]
APER Sch 4—Powers exercised . . . . . [2042]
APER Sch 5—Rights of action for damages . . . . . [2043]
APER Sch 6—Rules that can be waived . . . . . [2044]

Part II FSA Handbook Materials

CHAPTER 1
APPLICATION AND PURPOSE

1.1 Application

Who?

[2034]

1.1.1 **[G]** *APER* applies to *approved persons*.

1.1.2 **[G]** The *Statements of Principle* apply only to the extent that a *person* is performing a *controlled function* for which approval has been sought and granted.

1.1.3 **[G]** Section 64(11) of the *Act* states that the power to issue *Statements of Principle* and codes of practice includes power to make different provisions in relation to *persons*, cases or circumstances of different descriptions. *Statements of Principle* 1, 2, 3 and 4 apply to all *approved persons*, and *Statements of Principle* 5, 6 and 7 apply to those approved to perform *significant influence functions*.

1.1.4 **[G]** The relevance of *MiFID* to the *Statements of Principle* will depend on the extent to which the corresponding requirement imposed on *firms* under *MiFID* is reserved to a *Home State regulator* or has been disapplied under *MiFID* (see APER 2.1.1AP and FIT 1.2.4AG. See also COBS 1 Ann 1, Part 2, 1.1R (EEA territorial scope rule: compatibility with European law)).

Where?

1.1.5 **[G]** The territorial scope of the *approved persons* regime and its application to *incoming EEA firms* is set out in SUP 10.1 (see SUP 10.1.13R and 10.1.14R.).

1.2 Purpose

1.2.1 **[G]** The *Statements of Principle* contained in APER 2 are issued under section 64(1) of the *Act* (Conduct: statements and codes).

1.2.2 **[G]** Section 64(2) of the *Act* states that if the *FSA* issues *Statements of Principle* it must also issue a code of practice for the purpose of helping to determine whether or not a *person's* conduct complies with the *Statements of Principle*. The *Code of Practice for Approved Persons* in APER 3 and APER 4 fulfils this requirement.

1.2.3 **[G]** The *Code of Practice for Approved Persons* sets out descriptions of conduct which, in the opinion of the *FSA*, do not comply with a *Statement of Principle* and, in the case of *Statement of Principle* 3, conduct which tends to show compliance within that statement. The *Code of Practice for Approved Persons* also sets out, in certain cases, factors which, in the opinion of the *FSA*, are to be taken into account in determining whether or not an *approved person's* conduct complies with a *Statement of Principle*. The *guidance* set out in APER 3 and APER 4 does not form part of the *Code of Practice for Approved Persons*.

1.2.4 **[G]** [deleted]

1.2.5 **[G]** As set out in SUP 10.3.1R (Arrangements and regulated activities), a function is a *controlled function* only to the extent that it is performed under an *arrangement* entered into by:

(1) a *firm*; or
(2) a contractor of the *firm*;

in relation to the carrying on by the *firm* of a *regulated activity*.

1.2.6 **[G]** The *Statements of Principle* apply only to the performance of a *controlled function* (that is, to the activities carried on under the *arrangement* described in the *firm's* application for approval).

1.2.7 **[G]** The *FSA* recognises that an *approved person* may be performing functions which are unrelated to *regulated activities* or are otherwise outside the description of a *controlled function*. The fact that a *person* may be approved for one purpose does not have the effect of bringing all his functions within the *controlled function*, nor of making those functions subject to the *Statements of Principle*.

1.2.8 **[G]** The territorial scope of the *approved persons* regime is set out in SUP 10.1 (Application).

1.2.9 **[G]** The *Statements of Principle* apply only to the extent that a *person* is performing a *controlled function* for which approval has been sought and granted.

CHAPTER 2
THE STATEMENTS OF PRINCIPLE FOR APPROVED PERSONS

2.1 The Statement of Principle

[2035]
2.1.1 **[G]** APER 2.1.2P sets out the *Statements of Principle* issued by the *FSA* to which *APER* 1.2.1G refers and to which the provisions of the *Code of Practice for Approved Persons* and *guidance* in APER 3 and APER 4 apply.

2.1.1A **[P]** An approved person will not be subject to a *Statement of Principle* to the extent that it would be contrary to the *UK's* obligations under a *Single Market Directive*.

2.1.2 **[P]** Statements of Principle issued under section 64 of the Act

Statement of Principle 1

An *approved person* must act with integrity in carrying out his *controlled function*.

Statement of Principle 2

An *approved person* must act with due skill, care and diligence in carrying out his *controlled function*.

Statement of Principle 3

An *approved person* must observe proper standards of market conduct in carrying out his *controlled function*.

Statement of Principle 4

An *approved person* must deal with the *FSA* and with other regulators in an open and cooperative way and must disclose appropriately any information of which the *FSA* would reasonably expect notice.

Statement of Principle 5

An *approved person* performing a *significant influence function* must take reasonable steps to ensure that the business of the *firm* for which he is responsible in his *controlled function* is organised so that it can be controlled effectively.

Statement of Principle 6

An *approved person* performing a *significant influence function* must exercise due skill, care and diligence in managing the business of the *firm* for which he is responsible in his *controlled function*.

Statement of Principle 7

An *approved person* performing a *significant influence function* must take reasonable steps to ensure that the business of the *firm* for which he is responsible in his *controlled function* complies with the relevant requirements and standards of the *regulatory system*.

CHAPTER 3
CODE OF PRACTICE FOR APPROVED PERSONS: GENERAL

3.1 Introduction

[2036]
3.1.1 **[G]** This *Code of Practice for Approved Persons* is issued under section 64 of the *Act* (Conduct: statements and codes) for the purpose of helping to determine whether or not an *approved person's* conduct complies with a *Statement of Principle*. The code sets out descriptions of conduct which, in

the *FSA's* opinion, do not comply with the relevant *Statements of Principle*. The code also sets out certain factors which, in the opinion of the *FSA*, are to be taken into account in determining whether an *approved person's* conduct complies with a particular *Statement of Principle*. The description of conduct, the factors and related provisions are identified in the text by the letter 'E' as explained in chapter 6 of the Reader's Guide.

3.1.2 **[G]** The *Code of Practice for Approved Persons* in issue at the time when any particular conduct takes place may be relied on so far as it tends to establish whether or not that conduct complies with a *Statement of Principle*.

3.1.3 **[G]** The significance of conduct identified in the *Code of Practice for Approved Persons* as tending to establish compliance with or a breach of a *Statement of Principle* will be assessed only after all the circumstances of a particular case have been considered. Account will be taken of the context in which a course of conduct was undertaken, including the precise circumstances of the individual case, the characteristics of the particular *controlled function* and the behaviour to be expected in that function.

3.1.4 **[G]**
(1) An *approved person* will only be in breach of a *Statement of Principle* where he is personally culpable. Personal culpability arises where an *approved person's* conduct was deliberate or where the *approved person's* standard of conduct was below that which would be reasonable in all the circumstances (see DEPP 6.2.4G (Action against approved persons under section 66 of the Act)).
(2) For the avoidance of doubt, the *Statements of Principle* do not extend the duties of *approved persons* beyond those which the *firm* owes in its dealings with *customers* or others.

3.1.5 **[G]** In particular, in determining whether or not an *approved person's* conduct complies with a *Statement of Principle*, the *FSA* will take into account the extent to which an *approved person* has acted in a way that is stated to be in breach of a *Statement of Principle*.

3.1.6 **[G]** The *Code of Practice for Approved Persons* (and in particular the specific examples of behaviour which may be in breach of a generic description of conduct in the code) is not exhaustive of the kind of conduct that may contravene the *Statements of Principle*. The purpose of the code is to help determine whether or not a *person's* conduct complies with a *Statement of Principle*. The code may be supplemented from time to time. The *FSA* will amend the code if there is a risk that unacceptable practice may become prevalent, so as to make clear what conduct falls below the standards expected of *approved persons* by the *Statements of Principle*.

3.1.7 **[G]** *Statements of Principle* 1 to 4 apply to all *approved persons*. In the *Statements of Principle* and in the *Code of Practice for Approved Persons*, a reference to "his *controlled function*" is a reference to the *controlled function* to which the approval relates. A *person* performing a *significant influence function* is also subject to the additional requirements set out in *Statements of Principle* 5 to 7 in performing that *controlled function*. Those responsible under SYSC 2.1.3R or SYSC 4.4.5R (Apportionment of responsibilities) for the *firm's* apportionment obligation will be specifically subject to *Statement of Principle* 5 (and see in particular APER 4.5.6E). In addition, it will be the responsibility of any such *approved person* to oversee that the *firm* has appropriate systems and controls under *Statement of Principle* 7 (and see in particular APER 4.7.3E).

3.1.8 **[G]** In applying *Statements of Principle* 5 to 7, the nature, scale and complexity of the business under management and the role and responsibility of the individual performing a *significant influence function* within the *firm* will be relevant in assessing whether an *approved person's* conduct was reasonable. For example, the smaller and less complex the business, the less detailed and extensive the systems of control need to be. The *FSA* will be of the opinion that an individual performing a *significant influence function* may have breached *Statements of Principle* 5 to 7 only if his conduct was below the standard which would be reasonable in all the circumstances. (See also APER 3.3.1E (3) to (5))

3.1.9 **[G]** *UK domestic firms listed* on the London Stock Exchange are subject to the Combined Code developed by the Committee on Corporate Governance, whose *internal control* provisions are amplified in the Guidance for Directors issued by the Institute of Chartered Accountants in England and Wales. *FSA*-regulated *firms* in this category will thus be subject to that code as well as to the requirements and standards of the *regulatory system*. In forming an opinion whether *approved persons* have complied with its requirements, the *FSA* will give due credit for their following corresponding provisions in the Combined Code and related *guidance*.

3.2 Factors relating to all Statements of Principle

3.2.1 **[E]** In determining whether or not the particular conduct of an *approved person* within his *controlled function* complies with the *Statements of Principle*, the following are factors which, in the opinion of the *FSA*, are to be taken into account:
(1) whether that conduct relates to activities that are subject to other provisions of the *Handbook*;
(2) whether that conduct is consistent with the requirements and standards of the *regulatory system* relevant to his *firm*.

Part II FSA Handbook Materials

3.3 Factors relating to Statements of Principle 5 to 7

3.3.1 **[E]** In determining whether or not the conduct of an *approved person* performing a *significant influence function* complies with *Statements of Principle* 5 to 7, the following are factors which, in the opinion of the *FSA*, are to be taken into account:
(1) whether he exercised reasonable care when considering the information available to him;
(2) whether he reached a reasonable conclusion which he acted on;
(3) the nature, scale and complexity of the *firm's* business;
(4) his role and responsibility as an *approved person* performing a *significant influence function*;
(5) the knowledge he had, or should have had, of regulatory concerns, if any, arising in the business under his control.

CHAPTER 4
CODE OF PRACTICE FOR APPROVED PERSONS: SPECIFIC

4.1 Statement of Principle 1

[2037]
4.1.1 **[G]** The *Statement of Principle* 1 (see APER 2.1.2P) is in the following terms: "An *approved person* must act with integrity in carrying out his *controlled function*."

4.1.2 **[E]** In the opinion of the *FSA*, conduct of the type described in APER 4.1.3E, APER 4.1.5E, APER 4.1.6E, APER 4.1.8E, APER 4.1.10E, APER 4.1.12E or APER 4.1.13E does not comply with *Statement of Principle* 1 APER 2.1.2P).

4.1.3 **[E]** Deliberately misleading (or attempting to mislead) by act or omission:
(1) a *client*; or
(2) his *firm* (or its auditors or an *actuary* appointed by his *firm* under SUP 4 (Actuaries)); or
(3) the *FSA*;

falls within APER 4.1.2E.

4.1.4 **[E]** Behaviour of the type referred to in APER 4.1.3E includes, but is not limited to, deliberately:
(1) falsifying *documents*;
(2) misleading a *client* about the risks of an *investment*;
(3) misleading a *client* about the charges or surrender penalties of *investment* products;
(4) misleading a *client* about the likely performance of *investment* products by providing inappropriate *projections* of future *investment* returns;
(5) misleading a *client* by informing him that products require only a single payment when that is not the case;
(6) mismarking the value of *investments* or trading positions;
(7) procuring the unjustified alteration of prices on illiquid or *off-exchange* contracts, or both;
(8) misleading others within the *firm* about the credit-worthiness of a borrower;
(9) providing false or inaccurate documentation or information, including details of training, qualifications, past employment record or experience;
(10) providing false or inaccurate information to the *firm* (or to the *firm's* auditors or an *actuary* appointed by the *firm* under SUP 4 (Actuaries));
(11) providing false or inaccurate information to the *FSA*;
(12) destroying, or causing the destruction of, *documents* (including false documentation), or tapes or their contents, relevant to misleading (or attempting to mislead) a *client*, his *firm*, or the *FSA*;
(13) failing to disclose dealings where disclosure is required by the *firm's* personal account *dealing rules*;
(14) misleading others in the *firm* about the nature of risks being accepted.

4.1.5 **[E]** Deliberately recommending an *investment* to a *customer*, or carrying out a discretionary *transaction* for a *customer* where the *approved person* knows that he is unable to justify its suitability for that *customer*, falls within APER 4.1.2E.

4.1.6 **[E]** Deliberately failing to inform, without reasonable cause:
(1) a *customer*; or
(2) his *firm* (or its auditors or an *actuary* appointed by his *firm* under SUP 4 (Actuaries)); or
(3) the *FSA*;

of the fact that their understanding of a material issue is incorrect, despite being aware of their misunderstanding, falls within APER 4.1.2E.

4.1.7 **[E]** Behaviour of the type referred to in APER 4.1.6E includes, but is not limited to, deliberately:
(1) failing to disclose the existence of falsified *documents*;
(2) failing to rectify mismarked positions immediately.

4.1.8 **[E]** Deliberately preparing inaccurate or inappropriate records or returns in connection with a *controlled function*, falls within APER 4.1.2E.

4.1.9 **[E]** Behaviour of the type referred to in APER 4.1.8E includes, but is not limited to, deliberately:

(1) preparing performance reports for transmission to *customers* which are inaccurate or inappropriate (for example, by relying on past performance without appropriate warnings);
(2) preparing inaccurate training records or inaccurate details of qualifications, past employment record or experience;
(3) preparing inaccurate trading confirmations, contract notes or other records of *transactions* or holdings of *securities* for a *customer*, whether or not the *customer* is aware of these inaccuracies or has requested such records.

4.1.10 **[E]** Deliberately misusing the assets or confidential information of a *client* or of his *firm* falls within APER 4.1.2E.

4.1.11 **[E]** Behaviour of the type referred to in APER 4.1.10E includes, but is not limited to, deliberately:

(1) front running *client* orders;
(2) carrying out unjustified trading on *client* accounts to generate a benefit (whether direct or indirect) to the *approved person* (that is, churning);
(3) misappropriating a *client's* assets, including wrongly transferring to personal accounts cash or *securities* belonging to *clients*;
(4) wrongly using one *client's* funds to settle margin calls or to cover trading losses on another *client's* account or on *firm* accounts;
(5) using a *client's* funds for purposes other than those for which they were provided;
(6) retaining a *client's* funds wrongly;
(7) pledging the assets of a *client* as security or margin in circumstances where the *firm* is not permitted to do so.

4.1.12 **[E]** Deliberately designing *transactions* so as to disguise breaches of requirements and standards of the *regulatory system* falls within APER 4.1.2E.

4.1.13 **[E]** Deliberately failing to disclose the existence of a conflict of interest in connection with dealings with a *client* falls within APER 4.1.2E.

4.2 Statement of Principle 2

4.2.1 **[G]** The *Statement of Principle* 2 (see APER 2.1.2P) is in the following terms: "An *approved person* must act with due skill, care and diligence in carrying out his *controlled function*."

4.2.2 **[E]** In the opinion of the *FSA*, conduct of the type described in APER 4.2.3E, APER 4.2.5E, APER 4.2.6E, APER 4.2.8E, APER 4.2.10E, APER 4.2.11E or APER 4.2.13E does not comply with *Statement of Principle* 2 APER 2.1.2P).

4.2.3 **[E]** Failing to inform:

(1) a *customer*; or
(2) his *firm* (or its auditors or an *actuary* appointed by his *firm* under SUP 4 (Actuaries));

of material information in circumstances where he was aware, or ought to have been aware, of such information, and of the fact that he should provide it, falls within APER 4.2.2E.

4.2.4 **[E]** Behaviour of the type referred to in APER 4.2.3E includes, but is not limited to:

(1) failing to explain the risks of an *investment* to a *customer*;
(2) failing to disclose to a *customer* details of the charges or surrender penalties of *investment* products;
(3) mismarking trading positions;
(4) providing inaccurate or inadequate information to a *firm*, its auditors or an *actuary* appointed by his *firm* under SUP 4 (Actuaries);
(5) failing to disclose dealings where disclosure is required by the *firm's* personal account *dealing rules*.

4.2.5 **[E]** Recommending an *investment* to a *customer*, or carrying out a discretionary *transaction* for a *customer*, where he does not have reasonable grounds to believe that it is suitable for that *customer*, falls within APER 4.2.2 E

4.2.6 **[E]** Undertaking, recommending or providing advice on *transactions* without a reasonable understanding of the risk exposure of the *transaction* to a *customer* falls within APER 4.2.2E.

4.2.7 **[E]** *Behaviour* of the type referred to in APER 4.2.6E includes, but is not limited to, recommending *transactions* in *investments* to a *customer* without a reasonable understanding of the liability (either potential or actual) of that *transaction*.

4.2.8 **[E]** Undertaking *transactions* without a reasonable understanding of the risk exposure of the *transaction* to the *firm* falls within APER 4.2.2E.

4.2.9 **[E]** *Behaviour* of the type referred to in APER 4.2.8E includes, but is not limited to, trading on the *firm's* own account without a reasonable understanding of the liability (either potential or actual) of the *transaction*.

4.2.10 **[E]** Failing without good reason to disclose the existence of a conflict of interest in connection with dealings with a *client* falls within APER 4.2.2E.

4.2.11 **[E]** Failing to provide adequate control over a *client's* assets falls within APER 4.2.2E.

4.2.12 **[E]** *Behaviour* of the type referred to in APER 4.2.11E includes, but is not limited to:
(1) failing to segregate a *client's* assets;
(2) failing to process a *client's* payments in a timely manner.

4.2.13 **[E]** Continuing to perform a *controlled function* despite having failed to meet the standards of knowledge and skill set out in the Training and Competence sourcebook (*TC*) for that *controlled function* falls within APER 4.2.2E.

4.3 Statement of Principle 3

4.3.1 **[G]** The *Statement of Principle* 3 (see APER 2.1.2P) is in the following terms: "An *approved person* must observe proper standards of market conduct in carrying out his *controlled function*."

4.3.2 **[G]** [deleted]

4.3.3 **[E]** A factor to be taken into account in determining whether or not an *approved person's* conduct complies with this *Statement of Principle* (APER 2.1.2P) is whether he, or his *firm*, has complied with the *Code of Market Conduct* (MAR 1) or relevant market codes and exchange rules.

4.3.4 **[E]** Compliance with the code or *rules* described in APER 4.3.3E will tend to show compliance with this *Statement of Principle* APER 2.1.2P).

4.4 Statement of Principle 4

4.4.1 **[G]** The *Statement of Principle* 4 (see APER 2.1.2P) is in the following terms: "An *approved person* must deal with the *FSA* and with other regulators in an open and cooperative way and must disclose appropriately any information of which the *FSA* would reasonably expect notice."

4.4.2 **[G]** For the purpose of this *Statement of Principle* APER 2.1.2P), regulators in addition to the *FSA* are those which have recognised jurisdiction in relation to *regulated activities* and a power to call for information from the *approved person* in connection with his *controlled function* or (in the case of an individual performing a *significant influence function*) in connection with the business for which he is responsible. This may include an exchange or an *overseas regulator*.

4.4.3 **[E]** In the opinion of the *FSA*, conduct of the type described in APER 4.4.4E, APER 4.4.7E, or APER 4.4.9E does not comply with *Statement of Principle* 4 APER 2.1.2P).

4.4.4 **[E]** Failing to report promptly in accordance with his *firm's* internal procedures (or if none exist direct to the *FSA*), information which it would be reasonable to assume would be of material significance to the *FSA*, whether in response to questions or otherwise, falls within APER 4.4.3E.

4.4.5 **[G]** There is no duty on an *approved person* to report such information directly to the *FSA* unless he is one of the *approved persons* responsible within the *firm* for reporting matters to the *FSA*. However, if an *approved person* takes steps to influence the decision so as not to report to the *FSA* or acts in a way that is intended to obstruct the reporting of the information to the *FSA*, then the *FSA* will, in respect of that information, view him as being one of those within the *firm* who has taken on responsibility for deciding whether to report that matter to the *FSA*.

4.4.6 **[E]** In determining whether or not an *approved person's* conduct under APER 4.4.4E complies with *Statement of Principle* 4, the following are factors which, in the opinion of the *FSA*, are to be taken into account:
(1) the likely significance to the *FSA* of the information which it was reasonable for the individual to assume;
(2) whether the information related to the individual himself or to his *firm*;
(3) whether any decision not to report the matter internally was taken after reasonable enquiry and analysis of the situation.

4.4.7 **[E]** Where the *approved person* is, or is one of the *approved persons* who is, responsible within the *firm* for reporting matters to the *FSA*, failing promptly to inform the *FSA* of information of which he is aware and which it would be reasonable to assume would be of material significance to the *FSA*, whether in response to questions or otherwise, falls within APER 4.4.3E.

4.4.8 **[E]** In determining whether or not an *approved person's* conduct under APER 4.4.7E complies with *Statement of Principle* 4 APER 2.1.2P), the following are factors which, in the opinion of the *FSA*, are to be taken into account:
(1) *the likely significance of the* information to the *FSA* which it was reasonable for the *approved person* to assume;
(2) whether any decision not to inform the *FSA* was taken after reasonable enquiry and analysis of the situation.

4.4.9 **[E]** Failing without good reason to:

(1) inform a regulator of information of which the *approved person* was aware in response to questions from that regulator;
(2) attend an interview or answer questions put by a regulator, despite a request or demand having been made;
(3) supply a regulator with appropriate *documents* or information when requested or required to do so and within the time limits attaching to that request or requirement;

falls within APER 4.4.3E.

4.5 Statement of Principle 5

4.5.1 **[G]** The *Statement of Principle* 5 (see APER 2.1.2P) is in the following terms: "An *approved person* performing a *significant influence function* must take reasonable steps to ensure that the business of the *firm* for which he is responsible in his *controlled function* is organised so that it can be controlled effectively."

4.5.2 **[E]** In the opinion of the *FSA*, conduct of the type described in APER 4.5.3E, APER 4.5.4E, APER 4.5.6E or APER 4.5.8E does not comply with *Statement of Principle* 5 APER 2.1.2P).

4.5.3 **[E]** Failing to take reasonable steps to apportion responsibilities for all areas of the business under the *approved person's* control falls within APER 4.5.2E (see APER 4.5.11G).

4.5.4 **[E]** Failing to take reasonable steps to apportion responsibilities clearly amongst those to whom responsibilities have been delegated falls within APER 4.5.2E (see APER 4.5.11G).

4.5.5 **[E]** Behaviour of the type referred to in APER 4.5.4E includes, but is not limited to:
(1) implementing confusing or uncertain reporting lines (see APER 4.5.12G);
(2) implementing confusing or uncertain authorisation levels (see APER 4.5.13G);
(3) implementing confusing or uncertain job descriptions and responsibilities (see APER 4.5.13G).

4.5.6 **[E]** In the case of an *approved person* who is responsible under SYSC 2.1.3R(1) or SYSC 4.4.5R(1) for dealing with the apportionment of responsibilities under SYSC 2.1.1R or SYSC 4.4.3R, failing to take reasonable care to maintain a clear and appropriate apportionment of significant responsibilities among the *firm's directors* and *senior managers* falls within APER 4.5.2E.

4.5.7 **[E]** Behaviour of the type referred to in APER 4.5.6E includes, but is not limited to:
(1) failing to review regularly the significant responsibilities which the *firm* is required to apportion under APER 2.1.1 R;
(2) failing to act where that review shows that those significant responsibilities have not been clearly apportioned.

4.5.8 **[E]** Failing to take reasonable steps to ensure that suitable individuals are responsible for those aspects of the business under the control of the individual performing a *significant influence function* falls within APER 4.5.2E (see APER 4.5.14G).

4.5.9 **[E]** Behaviour of the type referred to in APER 4.5.8E includes, but is not limited to:
(1) failing to review the competence, knowledge, skills and performance of staff to assess their suitability to fulfil their duties, despite evidence that their performance is unacceptable (see APER 4.5.14G);
(2) giving undue weight to financial performance when considering the suitability or continuing suitability of an individual for a particular role (see APER 4.5.14G);
(3) allowing managerial vacancies which put at risk compliance with the requirements and standards of the *regulatory system* to remain, without arranging suitable cover for the responsibilities (see APER 4.5.15G).

4.5.10 **[G]** Strategy and plans will often dictate the risk which the business is prepared to take on and high level controls will dictate how the business is to be run. If the strategy of the business is to enter high-risk areas, then the degree of control and strength of monitoring reasonably required within the business will be high. In organising the business for which he is responsible, the *approved person* performing a *significant influence function* should bear this in mind.

Apportionment of responsibilities

4.5.11 **[G]** In order to comply with the obligations of *Statement of Principle* 5 (having regard to APER 4.5.3E and APER 4.5.4E), the *approved person* performing a *significant influence function* may find it helpful to review whether each area of the business for which he is responsible has been clearly assigned to a particular individual or individuals.

Reporting lines

4.5.12 **[G]** The organisation of the business and the responsibilities of those within it should be clearly defined (see APER 4.5.5E (1)). Reporting lines should be clear to staff. Where staff have dual reporting lines there is a greater need to ensure that the responsibility and accountability of each individual line manager is clearly set out and understood.

Authorisation levels and job descriptions

4.5.13 **[G]** Where members of staff have particular levels of authorisation (see APER 4.5.5E (2) and APER 4.5.5E (3)), these should be clearly set out and communicated to staff. It may be appropriate for each member of staff to have a job description of which he is aware.

Suitability of individuals

4.5.14 **[G]** If an individual's performance is unsatisfactory, then the appropriate *approved person* (if any) performing a *significant influence function* should review carefully whether to allow that individual to continue in position. In particular, if he is aware of concerns relating to the compliance with requirements and standards of the *regulatory system* (or internal controls) of the individual concerned, or of staff reporting to that individual, the *approved person* performing a *significant influence function* should take care not to give undue weight to the financial performance of the individual or group concerned when considering whether any action should be taken. An adequate investigation of the concerns should be undertaken (including, where appropriate, adherence to internal controls). The *approved person* performing a *significant influence function* should satisfy himself, on reasonable grounds, that the investigation is appropriate, the results are accurate and that the concerns do not pose an unacceptable risk to compliance with the requirements and standards of the *regulatory system* (see in particular *Statement of Principle* 6 and APER 4.5.8E and APER 4.5.9E (1) and APER 4.5.9E (2)).

Temporary vacancies

4.5.15 **[G]** In organising the business, the *approved person* performing a *significant influence function* should pay attention to any temporary vacancies which exist (see APER 4.5.9E (3)). He should take reasonable steps to ensure that suitable cover for responsibilities is arranged. This could include taking on temporary staff or external consultants. The *approved person* performing a *significant influence function* should assess the risk that is posed to compliance with the requirements and standards of the *regulatory system* as a result of the vacancy, and the higher the risk the greater the steps he should take to fill the vacancy. It may be appropriate to limit or suspend the activity if appropriate cover for responsibilities cannot be arranged. To the extent that those vacancies are in respect of one of the *customer functions*, they may only be filled by *persons* approved for that function.

4.6 Statement of Principle 6

4.6.1 **[G]** The *Statement of Principle* 6 (see APER 2.1.2P) is in the following terms: "An *approved person* performing a *significant influence function* must exercise due skill, care and diligence in managing the business of the *firm* for which he is responsible in his *controlled function*."

4.6.2 **[E]** In the opinion of the *FSA*, conduct of the type described in APER 4.6.3E, APER 4.6.5E, APER 4.6.6E or APER 4.6.8E does not comply with *Statement of Principle* 6 APER 2.1.2P).

4.6.3 **[E]** Failing to take reasonable steps adequately to inform himself about the affairs of the business for which he is responsible falls within APER 4.6.2E.

4.6.4 **[E]** Behaviour of the type referred to in APER 4.6.3E includes, but is not limited to:
(1) permitting *transactions* without a sufficient understanding of the risks involved;
(2) permitting expansion of the business without reasonably assessing the potential risks of that expansion;
(3) inadequately monitoring highly profitable *transactions* or business practices or unusual *transactions* or business practices;
(4) accepting implausible or unsatisfactory explanations from subordinates without testing the veracity of those explanations;
(5) failing to obtain independent, expert opinion where appropriate; (see APER 4.6.12G).

4.6.5 **[E]** Delegating the authority for dealing with an issue or a part of the business to an individual or individuals (whether in-house or outside contractors) without reasonable grounds for believing that the delegate had the necessary capacity, competence, knowledge, seniority or skill to deal with the issue or to take authority for dealing with part of the business, falls within APER 4.6.2E (see APER 4.6.13G).

4.6.6 **[E]** Failing to take reasonable steps to maintain an appropriate level of understanding about an issue or part of the business that he has delegated to an individual or individuals (whether in-house or outside contractors) falls within APER 4.6.2E (see APER 4.6.14G).

4.6.7 **[E]** Behaviour of the type referred to in APER 4.6.6E includes but is not limited to:
(1) disregarding an issue or part of the business once it has been delegated;

(2) failing to require adequate reports once the resolution of an issue or management of part of the business has been delegated;
(3) accepting implausible or unsatisfactory explanations from delegates without testing their veracity.

4.6.8 **[E]** Failing to supervise and monitor adequately the individual or individuals (whether in-house or outside contractors) to whom responsibility for dealing with an issue or authority for dealing with a part of the business has been delegated falls within APER 4.6.2E.

4.6.9 **[E]** Behaviour of the type referred to in APER 4.6.8E includes, but is not limited to:
(1) failing to take personal action where progress is unreasonably slow, or where implausible or unsatisfactory explanations are provided;
(2) failing to review the performance of an outside contractor in connection with the delegated issue or business.

4.6.10 **[E]** In determining whether or not the conduct of an *approved person* performing a *significant influence function* under APER 4.6.5E, APER 4.6.6E and APER 4.6.8E complies with *Statement of Principle* 6 (see APER 2.1.2P), the following are factors which, in the opinion of the *FSA*, are to be taken into account:
(1) the competence, knowledge or seniority of the delegate; and
(2) the past performance and record of the delegate.

4.6.11 **[G]** An *approved person* performing a *significant influence function* will not always manage the business on a day-to-day basis himself. The extent to which he does so will depend on a number of factors, including the nature, scale and complexity of the business and his position within it. The larger and more complex the business, the greater the need for clear and effective delegation and reporting lines. The *FSA* will look to the *approved person* performing a *significant influence function* to take reasonable steps to ensure that systems are in place which result in issues being addressed at the appropriate level. When issues come to his attention, he should deal with them in an appropriate way.

Knowledge about the business

4.6.12 **[G]**
(1) It is important for the *approved person* performing a *significant influence function* to understand the business for which he is responsible (APER 4.6.4E). An *approved person* performing a *significant influence function* is unlikely to be an expert in all aspects of a complex financial services business. However, he should understand and inform himself about the business sufficiently to understand the risks of its trading, credit or other business activities.
(2) It is important for an *approved person* performing a *significant influence function* to understand the risks of expanding the business into new areas and, before approving the expansion, he should investigate and satisfy himself, on reasonable grounds, about the risks, if any, to the business.
(3) Where unusually profitable business is undertaken, or where the profits are particularly volatile or the business involves funding requirements on the *firm* beyond those reasonably anticipated, he should require explanations from those who report to him. Where those explanations are implausible or unsatisfactory, he should take steps to test the veracity of those explanations.
(4) Where the *approved person* performing a *significant influence function* is not an expert in a business area, he should consider whether he or those with whom he works have the necessary expertise to provide him with an adequate explanation of issues within that business area. If not he should seek an independent opinion from elsewhere within or outside the *firm*.

Delegation

4.6.13 **[G]**
(1) An *approved person* performing a *significant influence function* may delegate the investigation, resolution or management of an issue or authority for dealing with a part of the business to individuals who report to him or to others.
(2) The *approved person* performing a *significant influence function* should have reasonable grounds for believing that the delegate has the competence, knowledge, skill and time to deal with the issue. For instance, if the compliance department only has sufficient resources to deal with day-to-day issues, it would be unreasonable to delegate to it the resolution of a complex or unusual issue without ensuring it had sufficient capacity to deal with the matter adequately.
(3) If an issue raises questions of law or interpretation, the *approved person* performing a *significant influence function* may need to take legal advice. If appropriate legal expertise is not available in-house, he may need to consider appointing an appropriate external adviser.

(4) The *FSA* recognises that the *approved person* performing a *significant influence function* will have to exercise his own judgment in deciding how issues are dealt with, and that in some cases that judgment will, with the benefit of hindsight, be shown to have been wrong. He will not be in breach of *Statement of Principle* 6 unless he fails to exercise due and reasonable consideration before he delegates the resolution of an issue or authority for dealing with a part of the business and fails to reach a reasonable conclusion. If he is in doubt about how to deal with an issue or the seriousness of a particular compliance problem, then, although he cannot delegate to the *FSA* the responsibility for dealing with the problem or issue, he can speak to the *FSA* to discuss his approach (see APER 4.6.5E).

Continuing responsibilities where an issue has been delegated

4.6.14 **[G]** Although an *approved person* performing a *significant influence function* may delegate the resolution of an issue, or authority for dealing with a part of the business, he cannot delegate responsibility for it. It is his responsibility to ensure that he receives reports on progress and questions those reports where appropriate. For instance, if progress appears to be slow or if the issue is not being resolved satisfactorily, then the *approved person* performing a *significant influence function* may need to challenge the explanations he receives and take action himself to resolve the problem. This may include increasing the resource applied to it, reassigning the resolution internally or obtaining external advice or assistance. Where an issue raises significant concerns, an *approved person* performing a *significant influence function* should act clearly and decisively. If appropriate, this may be by suspending members of staff or relieving them of all or part of their responsibilities (see APER 4.6.6E).

4.7 Statement of Principle 7

4.7.1 **[G]** The *Statement of Principle* 7 (see APER 2.1.2P) is in the following terms: "An *approved person* performing a *significant influence function* must take reasonable steps to ensure that the business of the *firm* for which he is responsible in his *controlled function* complies with the relevant requirements and standards of the *regulatory system*."

4.7.2 **[E]** In the opinion of the *FSA*, conduct of the type described in APER 4.7.3E, APER 4.7.4E, APER 4.7.5E, APER 4.7.7E, APER 4.7.9E, APER 4.7.10E or APER 4.7.11AE does not comply with *Statement of Principle* 7 APER 2.1.2P).

4.7.3 **[E]** Failing to take reasonable steps to implement (either personally or through a compliance department or other departments) adequate and appropriate systems of control to comply with the relevant requirements and standards of the *regulatory system* in respect of its *regulated activities* falls within APER 4.7.2E. In the case of an *approved person* who is responsible, under SYSC 2.1.3R(2) or SYSC 4.4.5R(2), with overseeing the *firm's* obligation under SYSC 3.1.1R or SYSC 4.4.1R or SYSC 4.4.1R, failing to take reasonable care to oversee the establishment and maintenance of appropriate systems and controls falls within APER 4.7.2E.

4.7.4 **[E]** Failing to take reasonable steps to monitor (either personally or through a compliance department or other departments) compliance with the relevant requirements and standards of the *regulatory system* in respect of its *regulated activities* falls within APER 4.7.2E (see APER 4.7.12G).

4.7.5 **[E]** Failing to take reasonable steps adequately to inform himself about the reason why significant breaches (whether suspected or actual) of the relevant requirements and standards of the *regulatory system* in respect of its *regulated activities* may have arisen (taking account of the systems and procedures in place) falls within APER 4.7.2E.

4.7.6 **[E]** Behaviour of the type referred to in APER 4.7.5E includes, but is not limited to, failing to investigate what systems or procedures may have failed including, where appropriate, failing to obtain expert opinion on the adequacy of the systems and procedures.

4.7.7 **[E]** Failing to take reasonable steps to ensure that procedures and systems of control are reviewed and, if appropriate, improved, following the identification of significant breaches (whether suspected or actual) of the relevant requirements and standards of the *regulatory system* relating to its *regulated activities*, falls within APER 4.7.2E (see APER 4.7.13G).

4.7.8 **[E]** Behaviour of the type referred to in APER 4.7.7E includes, but is not limited to:

(1) unreasonably failing to implement recommendations for improvements in systems and procedures;

(2) unreasonably failing to implement recommendations for improvements to systems and procedures in a timely manner.

4.7.9 **[E]** In the case of the *Money Laundering Reporting Officer*, failing to discharge the responsibilities imposed on him by the *firm* in accordance with SYSC 3.2.6IR or SYSC 6.3.9R falls within APER 4.7.2E.

4.7.10 **[E]** In the case of an *approved person* performing a *significant influence function* responsible for compliance under SYSC 3.2.8R, SYSC 6.1.4R or SYSC 6.1.4AR failing to take reasonable steps to ensure that appropriate compliance systems and procedures are in place falls within APER 4.7.2E (see APER 4.7.14G).

4.7.11 **[G]** The *FSA* expects an *approved person* performing a *significant influence function* to take reasonable steps both to ensure his *firm's* compliance with the relevant requirements and standards of the *regulatory system* and to ensure that all staff are aware of the need for compliance.

4.7.11A **[E]** Where the *approved person* is a *proprietary trader* under SUP 10.9.10R(1A), failing to maintain and comply with appropriate systems and controls in relation to that activity falls within APER 4.7.2E.

Systems of control

4.7.12 **[G]** An *approved person* performing a *significant influence function* need not himself put in place the systems of control in his business APER 4.7.4E). Whether he does this depends on his role and responsibilities. He should, however, take reasonable steps to ensure that the business for which he is responsible has operating procedures and systems which include well-defined steps for complying with the detail of relevant requirements and standards of the *regulatory system* and for ensuring that the business is run prudently. The nature and extent of the systems of control that are required will depend upon the relevant requirements and standards of the *regulatory system*, and the nature, scale and complexity of the business (see APER 3.3.2E).

Possible breaches of regulatory requirements

4.7.13 **[G]** Where the *approved person* performing a *significant influence function* becomes aware of actual or suspected problems that involve possible breaches of relevant requirements and standards of the *regulatory system* falling within his area of responsibility, then he should take reasonable steps to ensure that they are dealt with in a timely and appropriate manner APER 4.7.7E). This may involve an adequate investigation to find out what systems or procedures may have failed and why. He may need to obtain expert opinion on the adequacy and efficacy of the systems and procedures.

Review and improvement of systems and procedures

4.7.14 **[G]** Where independent reviews of systems and procedures have been undertaken and result in recommendations for improvement, the *approved person* performing a *significant influence function* should ensure that, unless there are good reasons not to, any reasonable recommendations are implemented in a timely manner APER 4.7.10E). What is reasonable will depend on the nature of the inadequacy and the cost of the improvement. It will be reasonable for the *approved person* performing a *significant influence function* to carry out a cost benefit analysis when assessing whether the recommendations are reasonable.

TRANSITIONAL PROVISIONS

[2038]

TP 1.1 There are no transitional provisions in *APER*. However, *GEN* contains some technical transitional provisions that apply throughout the Handbook and which are designed to ensure a smooth transition at commencement.

SCHEDULE 1
RECORD KEEPING REQUIREMENTS

[2039]

1.1 **[G]** There are no record keeping requirements in *APER*.

SCHEDULE 2
NOTIFICATION REQUIREMENTS

[2040]

2.1 **[G]** The aim of the guidance in the following table is to give the reader a quick over-all view of the relevant requirements for notification and reporting.

2.2 **[G]** It is not a complete statement of those requirements and should not be relied on as if it were.

2.3 **[G]**

Handbook reference	Matter to be notified	Contents of notification	Trigger event	Time allowed
Statement of Principle 4 (APER 2.1.2P)	Any information of which the *FSA* would reasonably expect notice	Appropriate disclosure	Any information of which the *FSA* would reasonably expect notice	Appropriate

SCHEDULE 3
FEES AND OTHER REQUIRED PAYMENTS

[2041]

3.1 **[G]** There are no requirements for fees or other payments in *APER*.

Part II FSA Handbook Materials

SCHEDULE 4
POWERS EXERCISED

[2042]
4.1 **[G]** The following powers in the *Act* have been exercised by the *FSA* to issue the Statements of Principle and Code of Practice for Approved Persons:

Section 64(1) and (2) (Conduct: statements and codes).

4.2 **[G]** The following power in the *Act* has been exercised by the *FSA* to give the guidance in APER:

Section 157(1) (Guidance).

SCHEDULE 5
RIGHTS OF ACTION FOR DAMAGES

[2043]
5.1 **[G]** There are no rules in *APER*.

SCHEDULE 6
RULES THAT CAN BE WAIVED

[2044]
6.1 **[G]** There are no rules in *APER*.

THE FIT AND PROPER TEST FOR APPROVED PERSONS (FIT)

NOTES

Up to date as at 22 February 2010. For later amendments please see www.fsa.gov.uk.

CONTENTS

FIT 1—General . . . . [2045]
FIT 2—Main assessment criteria . . . . [2046]
FIT TP 1—Transitional provisions . . . . [2047]
FIT Sch 1—Record keeping requirements . . . . [2048]
FIT Sch 2—Notification requirements . . . . [2049]
FIT Sch 3—Fees and other required payments . . . . [2050]
FIT Sch 4—Powers exercised . . . . [2051]
FIT Sch 5—Rights of action for damages . . . . [2052]
FIT Sch 6—Rules that can be waived . . . . [2053]

CHAPTER 1
GENERAL

1.1 Application and purpose

[2045]

1.1.1 **[G]** *FIT* applies to:

(1) a *firm*;

(2) an applicant for *Part IV permission*;

(3) and *EEA firm*, a *Treaty firm* or a *UCITS qualifier* that wishes to establish a *branch* into the *United Kingdom* using *EEA rights*, *Treaty rights* or *UCITS directive* rights (see SUP 10.1.12G and SUP 10.1.13R), or apply for a *top-up permission* (see SUP 10.1.14R);

(4) an *approved person*; and

(5) a *candidate*.

1.1.2 **[G]** The purpose of *FIT* is to set out and describe the criteria that the *FSA* will consider when assessing the fitness and propriety of a *candidate* for a *controlled function* (see generally SUP 10 on *approved persons*). The criteria are also relevant in assessing the continuing fitness and propriety of *approved persons*. The criteria that the *FSA* will consider in relation to an *authorised person* are described in *COND*.

1.2 Introduction

1.2.1 **[G]** Under section 61(1) of the *Act* (Determination of applications), the *FSA* may grant an application for approval made under section 60 (Applications for approval) only if it is satisfied that the *candidate* is fit and proper to perform the *controlled function* to which the application relates.

1.2.2 **[G]** The method of applying for *approved person* status is set out in SUP 10.

1.2.3 **[G]** Under section 63(1) of the *Act* (Withdrawal of approval), the *FSA* may withdraw its approval if it considers that the *person* in respect of whom the approval was given is not fit and proper to perform the *controlled function* to which the approval relates.

1.2.4 **[G]** The *Act* does not prescribe the matters which the *FSA* should take into account when determining fitness and propriety. However, section 61(2) states that the *FSA* may have regard (among other things) to whether the *candidate* or *approved person* is competent to carry out a *controlled function*.

1.2.4A **[G]** Under Article 5(1)(d) of the *MiFID Implementing Directive* and Article 31 and 32 of *MiFID*, the requirement to employ personnel with the knowledge, skills and expertise necessary for the discharge of the responsibilities allocated to them is reserved to the *firm's Home State*. Therefore, in assessing the fitness and propriety of a *person* to perform a *controlled function* solely in relation to the *MiFID business* of an *incoming EEA firm*, the *FSA* will not have regard to that *person's* competence and capability. Where the *controlled function* relates to matters outside the scope of *MiFID*, for example money laundering responsibilities (see CF11), or to business outside the scope of the *MiFID* business of an *incoming EEA firm*, for example *insurance mediation activities* in relation to *life policies*, the *FSA* will have regard to a *candidate's* competence and capability as well as his honesty, integrity, reputation and financial soundness.

1.3 Assessing fitness and propriety

1.3.1 **[G]** The *FSA* will have regard to a number of factors when assessing the fitness and propriety of a *person* to perform a particular *controlled function*. The most important considerations will be the *person's*:

(1) honesty, integrity and reputation;
(2) competence and capability; and
(3) financial soundness.

1.3.2 **[G]** In assessing fitness and propriety, the *FSA* will also take account of the activities of the *firm* for which the *controlled function* is or is to be performed, the *permission* held by that *firm* and the markets within which it operates.

1.3.3 **[G]** The criteria listed in FIT 2.1 to FIT 2.3 are *guidance* and will be applied in general terms when the *FSA* is determining a *person's* fitness and propriety. It would be impossible to produce a definitive list of all the matters which would be relevant to a particular determination.

1.3.4 **[G]** If a matter comes to the *FSA's* attention which suggests that the *person* might not be fit and proper, the *FSA* will take into account how relevant and how important it is.

1.3.5 **[G]** During the application process, the *FSA* may discuss the assessment of the *candidate's* fitness and propriety informally with the *firm* making the application and may retain any notes of those discussions.

CHAPTER 2
MAIN ASSESSMENT CRITERIA

2.1 Honesty, integrity and reputation

[2046]
2.1.1 **[G]** In determining a *person's* honesty, integrity and reputation, the *FSA* will have regard to all relevant matters including, but not limited to, those set out in FIT 2.1.3G which may have arisen either in the *United Kingdom* or elsewhere. The *FSA* should be informed of these matters (see SUP 10.13.16R), but will consider the circumstances only where relevant to the requirements and standards of the *regulatory system*. For example, under FIT 2.1.3G (1), conviction for a criminal offence will not automatically mean an application will be rejected. The *FSA* treats each candidate's application on a case-by-case basis, taking into account the seriousness of, and circumstances surrounding, the offence, the explanation offered by the convicted *person*, the relevance of the offence to the proposed role, the passage of time since the offence was committed and evidence of the individual's rehabilitation.

2.1.2 **[G]** In considering the matters in FIT 2.1.1G, the *FSA* will look at whether the *person's* reputation might have an adverse impact upon the *firm* for which the *controlled function* is or is to be performed and at the *person's* responsibilities.

2.1.3 **[G]** The matters referred to in FIT 2.1.1G to which the *FSA* will have regard include, but are not limited to:

(1) whether the *person* has been convicted of any criminal offence; this must include, where provided for by the Exceptions Order to the Rehabilitation of Offenders Act 1974, any spent convictions; particular consideration will be given to offences of dishonesty, fraud, financial crime or an offence whether or not in the *United Kingdom* relating to companies, building societies, industrial and provident societies, credit unions, friendly societies, banking or other financial services, insolvency, consumer credit, insurance, consumer protection, money laundering, market manipulation or *insider dealing*;
(2) whether the *person* has been the subject of any adverse finding or any settlement in civil proceedings, particularly in connection with investment or other financial business, misconduct, fraud or the formation or management of a *body corporate*;
(3) whether the *person* has been the subject of, or interviewed in the course of, any existing or previous investigation or disciplinary proceedings, by the *FSA*, by other regulatory authorities (including a *previous regulator*), *clearing houses* and exchanges, professional bodies, or government bodies or agencies;
(4) whether the *person* is or has been the subject of any proceedings of a disciplinary or criminal nature, or has been notified of any potential proceedings or of any investigation which might lead to those proceedings;
(5) whether the *person* has contravened any of the requirements and standards of the *regulatory system* or the equivalent standards or requirements of other regulatory authorities (including a *previous regulator*), *clearing houses* and exchanges, professional bodies, or government bodies or agencies;
(6) whether the *person* has been the subject of any justified complaint relating to *regulated activities*;
(7) whether the *person* has been involved with a *company*, *partnership* or other organisation that has been refused registration, authorisation, membership or a licence to carry out a trade, business or profession, or has had that registration, authorisation, membership or licence revoked, withdrawn or terminated, or has been expelled by a regulatory or government body;
(8) whether, as a result of the removal of the relevant licence, registration or other authority, the *person* has been refused the right to carry on a trade, business or profession requiring a licence, registration or other authority;

(9) whether the *person* has been a *director, partner*, or concerned in the management, of a business that has gone into insolvency, liquidation or administration while the *person* has been connected with that organisation or within one year of that connection;
(10) whether the *person*, or any business with which the *person* has been involved, has been investigated, disciplined, censured or suspended or criticised by a regulatory or professional body, a court or Tribunal, whether publicly or privately;
(11) whether the *person* has been dismissed, or asked to resign and resigned, from employment or from a position of trust, fiduciary appointment or similar;
(12) whether the *person* has ever been disqualified from acting as a *director* or disqualified from acting in any managerial capacity;
(13) whether, in the past, the *person* has been candid and truthful in all his dealings with any *regulatory body* and whether the *person* demonstrates a readiness and willingness to comply with the requirements and standards of the *regulatory system* and with other legal, regulatory and professional requirements and standards.

2.2 Competence and capability

2.2.1 **[G]** In determining a *person's* competence and capability, the *FSA* will have regard to all relevant matters including but not limited to:
(1) whether the *person* satisfies the relevant *FSA* training and competence requirements in relation to the *controlled function* the *person* performs or is intended to perform;
(2) whether the *person* has demonstrated by experience and training that the *person* is suitable, or will be suitable if approved, to perform the *controlled function*.

2.2.2 **[G]** A *person* may have been convicted of, or dismissed or suspended from employment for, drug or alcohol abuses or other abusive acts. This will be considered only in relation to a *person's* continuing ability to perform the particular *controlled function* for which the *person* is or is to be employed.

2.3 Financial soundness

2.3.1 **[G]** In determining a *person's* financial soundness, the *FSA* will have regard to any factors including, but not limited to:
(1) whether the *person* has been the subject of any judgment debt or award, in the *United Kingdom* or elsewhere, that remains outstanding or was not satisfied within a reasonable period;
(2) whether, in the *United Kingdom* or elsewhere, the *person* has made any arrangements with his creditors, filed for bankruptcy, had a bankruptcy petition served on him, been adjudged bankrupt, been the subject of a bankruptcy restrictions order (including an interim bankruptcy restrictions order), offered a bankruptcy restrictions undertaking, had assets sequestrated, or been involved in proceedings relating to any of these.

2.3.2 **[G]** The *FSA* will not normally require the *candidate* to supply a statement of assets or liabilities. The fact that a *person* may be of limited financial means will not, in itself, affect his suitability to perform a *controlled function*.

TRANSITIONAL PROVISIONS

[2047]
[G] There are no transitional provisions in *FIT*. However, *GEN* contains some technical transitional provisions that apply throughout the Handbook and which are designed to ensure a smooth transition at commencement.

SCHEDULE 1
RECORD KEEPING REQUIREMENTS

[2048]
1.1 **[G]** There are no record keeping requirements in *FIT*.

SCHEDULE 2
NOTIFICATION REQUIREMENTS

[2049]
2.1 **[G]** There are no notification requirements in *FIT*.

SCHEDULE 3
FEES AND OTHER REQUIRED PAYMENTS

[2050]
3.1 **[G]** There are no requirements for fees or other payments in *FIT*.

SCHEDULE 4
POWERS EXERCISED

[2051]
4.1 **[G]** The following power in the Act has been exercised by the FSA to give guidance in *FIT*: section 157(1) (Guidance).

SCHEDULE 5
RIGHTS OF ACTION FOR DAMAGES

[2052]
5.1 **[G]** There are no rules in *FIT*.

SCHEDULE 6
RULES THAT CAN BE WAIVED

[2053]
6.1 **[G]** There are no rules in *FIT*.

GENERAL PROVISIONS (GEN)

NOTES

Up to date as at 22 February 2010. For later amendments please see www.fsa.gov.uk.
Chapters 1–5, Schedules 1–6 outside the scope of this work.

CHAPTER 6
INSURANCE AGAINST FINANCIAL PENALTIES

Application

[2054]

6.1.1 **[R]** This chapter applies to every *firm*, but only with respect to business that can be regulated under section 138 of the *Act* (General rule-making power).

6.1.2 **[G]** For the purposes of GEN 2.2.17R (Activities covered by general rules), the chapter applies to *regulated* and *unregulated activities* carried on in the *United Kingdom* or overseas.

Purpose

6.1.3 **[G]** The purpose of this section is to ensure that financial penalties are paid by the *person* on whom they are imposed.

Interpretation

6.1.4 **[R]** In this chapter 'financial penalty' means a financial penalty that the *FSA* has imposed, or may impose, under the *Act*. It does not include a financial penalty imposed by any other body.

Insurance against financial penalties

6.1.5 **[R]** No *firm* may enter into, arrange, claim on or make a payment under a *contract of insurance* that is intended to have, or has or would have, the effect of indemnifying any *person* against all or part of a financial penalty.

6.1.6 **[R]** The *Society*, *managing agents* and *members' agents* must not cause or permit any *member*, in the conduct of his *insurance business* at Lloyd's, to enter into, arrange, claim on or make a payment under a *contract of insurance* that is intended to have, or has or would have, the effect of indemnifying any *person* against all or part of a financial penalty.

6.1.7 **[G]** GEN 6.1.5R and GEN 6.1.6R do not prevent a *firm* or *member* from entering into, arranging, claiming on or making any payment under a *contract of insurance* which indemnifies any *person* against all or part of the costs of defending *FSA* enforcement action or any costs they may be ordered to pay to the *FSA*.

GENERAL PRUDENTIAL SOURCEBOOK (GENPRU)

NOTES

Up to date as at 22 February 2010. For later amendments please see www.fsa.gov.uk.

CONTENTS

GENPRU 1—Application . . . [2055]
GENPRU 2—Capital . . . [2056]
GENPRU 3—Cross sector groups . . . [2057]
GENPRU—Transitional Provisions . . . [2058]
GENPRU Schedules
Schedule 1—Record keeping requirements . . . [2059]
Schedule 2—Notification and reporting requirements . . . [2060]
Schedule 3—Fees and other requirement payments . . . [2061]
Schedule 4—Powers exercised . . . [2062]
Schedule 5—Rights of action for damages . . . [2063]
Schedule 6—Rules than can be waived . . . [2064]

CHAPTER 1
APPLICATION AND SCOPE

1.1 Application

Application

[2055]

1.1.1 **[G]** There is no overall application statement for GENPRU. Each chapter or section has its own application statement.

1.1.2 **[G]** Broadly speaking however, GENPRU applies to:
(1) an *insurer*;
(2) a *bank*;
(3) a *building society*;
(4) a *BIPRU investment firm*; and
(5) groups containing such *firms*.

Scope

1.1.3 **[R]** GENPRU applies to a *firm* in relation to the whole of its business, except where a particular provision provides for a narrower scope.

1.2 Adequacy of financial resources

Application

1.2.1 **[R]** This section applies to:
(1) a *BIPRU firm*;and
(2) an *insurer*, unless it is:
  (a) a *non-directive friendly society*; or
  (b) a *Swiss general insurer*; or
  (c) an *EEA-deposit insurer*; or
  (d) an *incoming EEA firm*; or
  (e) an *incoming Treaty firm*
(3) [deleted]

1.2.2 **[R]** [deleted]

1.2.2A **[R]** In relation to any provision in this section which applies to a *BIPRU firm*, a reference in that provision to "financial resources" does not constitute a reference to "liquidity resources".

1.2.3 **[R]** [deleted]

1.2.3A **[G]** In relation to:
(1) a *BIPRU firm*;
(2) an *incoming EEA firm* which:

(a) is a *full BCD credit institution*; and
(b) has a *branch* in the *United Kingdom*; and
(3) a *third country BIPRU firm* which:
(a) is a *bank*; and
(b) has a *branch* in the *United Kingdom*.

BIPRU 12 contains *rules* and *guidance* in relation to the adequacy of that *firm's* liquidity resources.

1.2.4 **[R]** [deleted]

1.2.5 **[R]** [deleted]

1.2.6 **[R]** If an *insurer* carries on:
(1) *long-term insurance business*; and
(2) *general insurance business*;

This section applies separately to each type of business.

1.2.7 **[G]** The *guidance* in this section is drafted with respect to a *firm* to which this section and the other provisions of GENPRU and BIPRU (except BIPRU 12) referred to in this section apply in full.

1.2.8 **[G]** [deleted]

1.2.9 **[G]** [deleted]

1.2.10 **[G]** The scope of application of this section is not restricted to *insurers* that are subject to the relevant *EU* Directives.

1.2.11 **[G]** The adequacy of a *firm's* financial resources needs to be assessed in relation to all the activities of the *firm* and the risks to which they give rise and so this section applies to a *firm* in relation to the whole of its business. In the case of a *UCITS investment firm* this means that this section is not limited to *designated investment business* excluding *scheme management activity*. It also applies to *scheme management activity* and to activities that are not *designated investment business*.

Purpose

1.2.12 **[G]** Adequate financial resources and adequate systems and controls are necessary for the effective management of prudential risks. This section therefore has requirements relating to both of these topics.

1.2.13 **[G]** This section amplifies *Principle* 4, under which a *firm* must maintain adequate financial resources. It is concerned with the adequacy of the financial resources that a *firm* needs to hold in order to be able to meet its liabilities as they fall due. These resources include both capital and liquidity resources. As noted in GENRPU 1.2.3AG, however, the *FSA's rules* and *guidance* in relation to the adequacy of the liquidity resources of a *BIPRU firm* are set out in BIPRU 12.

1.2.14 **[G]** In the case of a *bank* or *building society* this section implements Article 123 and (in part) Annex XI of the *Banking Consolidation Directive*. In the case of a *BIPRU investment firm* this section implements Article 34 of the *Capital Adequacy Directive* so far as that Article applies Article 123 of the *Banking Consolidation Directive*.

1.2.15 **[G]** This section also has *rules* requiring a *firm* to identify and assess risks to its being able to meet its liabilities as they fall due, how it intends to deal with those risks, and the amount and nature of financial resources that the *firm* considers necessary. GENPRU 1.2.60R provides that a *firm* should document that assessment. The *FSA* will review that assessment as part of its own assessment of the adequacy of a *firm's* capital under its *supervisory review and evaluation process* (*SREP*). When forming a view of any *individual capital guidance* to be given to the *firm*, the *FSA* will also review the ARROW risk assessment and any other issues arising from day-to-day supervision.

1.2.16 **[G]** This section also has *rules* requiring a *firm* to carry out appropriate stress tests and scenario analyses for the risks it has previously identified and to establish the amount of financial resources needed in each of the circumstances and events considered in carrying out the stress tests and scenario analyses.

1.2.17 **[G]** The basic requirements in this section are drafted to apply to a *firm* on a solo basis. This section then goes on to describe when its requirements do and do not apply on a solo basis and on a consolidated basis (see GENPRU 1.2.45R to GENPRU 1.2.47R and GENPRU 1.2.57R to GENPRU 1.2.58R). It also sets out some details about how the solo requirements are adjusted when they are applied on a consolidated basis (see GENPRU 1.2.48R to GENPRU 1.2.56G and GENPRU 1.2.59R).

Outline of other related provisions

1.2.18 **[G]** GENPRU 2.1 sets out the minimum *capital resources requirements* for a *firm*. GENPRU 2.2 sets out how *capital resources* are defined and measured for the purpose of meeting the requirements of GENPRU 2.1.

1.2.19 **[G]**

(1) BIPRU 2.2 (Internal capital adequacy standards) and INSPRU 7.1 (Individual capital assessment) set out detailed *guidance* on how a *firm* should carry out the assessment referred to in GENPRU 1.2.15G. The more thorough, objective, and prudent a *firm's* assessment is, and can be demonstrated as being, the more reliance the *FSA* will be able to place on the results of that assessment.

(2) BIPRU 2.2 and INSPRU 7.1 also have information on how the *FSA* will review and respond to the assessments referred to in GENPRU 1.2.15G. In particular they deal with the giving of individual capital *guidance* to a *firm*, which is *guidance* about the amount and quality of capital resources that the *FSA* thinks a *firm* should hold under the *overall financial adequacy rule* as it applies on a solo level and a consolidated level.

1.2.20 **[G]** *SYSC* sets out general *rules* and *guidance* on the establishment and maintenance of systems and controls.

1.2.21 **[G]**

(1) SYSC 11 sets out material on systems and controls that apply specifically to *liquidity risk* as that concept relates to an *insurer*.

(2) [deleted]

(3) BIPRU 12 sets out material on systems and controls that apply specifically to *liquidity risk* in relation to a *BIPRU firm*, a *branch* of an *incoming EEA firm* that is a *full BCD credit institution* and a *branch* of a *third country BIPRU firm* that is a *bank*.

(4) [deleted]

(5) SYSC 11.1.21E is an *evidential provision* relating to the *general stress and scenario testing rule* concerning stress testing and scenario analyses. SYSC 11.1.24E is an *evidential provision* relating to the *overall Pillar 2 rule* about *contingency funding plans*. Both of these *evidential provisions* apply only to an *insurer* to which that section of SYSC applies.

(6) GENPRU 2.2 (Adequacy of financial resources) requires certain *BIPRU investment firms* to deduct *illiquid assets* when calculating their *capital resources*.

1.2.22 **[G]** *BIPRU* 2.3 contains *rules* and *guidance* on interest rate risk in the *non-trading book*. That material elaborates on the general obligation in the *overall Pillar 2 rule*.

1.2.23 **[G]** For a *BIPRU firm* using a *VaR model* BIPRU 7.10.72R (Risk management standards: Stress testing) sets out certain stress tests that the *firm* should carry out.

1.2.24 **[G]** *BIPRU* 10.6.22R (Stress testing of credit risk concentrations) sets out further stress tests that a *firm* should carry out if it uses certain approaches to collateral for the purposes of the *rules* about concentration risk.

1.2.25 **[G]** For a *BIPRU firm* using the *IRB approach* BIPRU 4.3.39R to BIPRU 4.3.40R set out a recession credit rating migration stress test that the *firm* should carry out. Further *rules* and *guidance* on such stress tests are set out in BIPRU 2.2 (Internal capital adequacy standards).

Requirement to have adequate financial resources

1.2.26 **[R]** A *firm* must at all times maintain overall financial resources, including *capital resources* and liquidity resources, which are adequate, both as to amount and quality, to ensure that there is no significant risk that its liabilities cannot be met as they fall due.

1.2.26A **[G]** BIPRU 12 contains *rules* and *guidance* in relation to the adequacy of a *BIPRU firm's* liquidity resources. Consistent with GENPRU 1.2.2AR, in assessing the adequacy of its liquidity resources, a *BIPRU firm* should do so by reference to the *overall liquidity adequacy rule*, rather than the *overall financial adequacy rule*.

1.2.27 **[G]** The liabilities referred to in the *overall financial adequacy rule* include a *firm's* contingent and prospective liabilities. They exclude liabilities that might arise from transactions that a *firm* has not entered into and which it could avoid, for example, by taking realistic management actions such as ceasing to transact new business after a suitable period of time has elapsed. They include liabilities or costs that arise both in scenarios where the *firm* is a going concern and those where the *firm* ceases to be a going concern. They also include claims that could be made against a *firm*, which ought to be paid in accordance with fair treatment of *customers*, even if such claims could not be legally enforced.

1.2.28 **[G]** A *firm* should therefore make its assessment of adequate financial resources on realistic valuation bases for assets and liabilities taking into account the actual amounts and timing of cash flows under realistic adverse projections.

1.2.29 **[G]** Risks may be addressed through holding capital to absorb losses that unexpectedly materialise. The ability to pay liabilities as they fall due also requires liquidity. Therefore, in assessing the adequacy of a *firm's* financial resources, both capital and liquidity needs should be considered. A *firm* should also consider the quality of its financial resources such as the loss-absorbency of different types of capital and the time required to liquidate different types of asset. *SYSC* 11.1.24E is an *evidential provision* relating to the *overall financial adequacy rule* concerning *contingency funding plans*.

Systems, strategies, processes and reviews

1.2.30 **[R]** A *firm* must have in place sound, effective and complete processes, strategies and systems:

(1) to assess and maintain on an ongoing basis the amounts, types and distribution of financial resources, *capital resources* and internal capital that it considers adequate to cover:
   (a) the nature and level of the risks to which it is or might be exposed;
   (b) the risk in the *overall financial adequacy rule*; and
   (c) the risk that the *firm* might not be able to meet its *CRR* in the future; and

(2) that enable it to identify and manage the major sources of risks referred to in (1), including the major sources of risk in each of the following categories where they are relevant to the *firm* given the nature and scale of its business:
   (a) credit risk;
   (b) *market risk*;
   (c) *liquidity risk*;
   (d) *operational risk*;
   (e) insurance risk;
   (f) concentration risk;
   (g) residual risk;
   (h) *securitisation* risk;
   (i) business risk;
   (j) interest rate risk (including, in the case of a *BIPRU firm*, interest rate risk in the *non-trading book*);
   (k) pension obligation risk; and
   (l) group risk.

1.2.31 **[R]**

(1) This *rule* defines some of the terms used in the *overall Pillar 2 rule*.

(2) Residual risk means the risk that *credit risk mitigation* techniques used by the *firm* prove less effective than expected.

(3) *Securitisation* risk includes the risk that the *capital resources* held by a *firm* in respect of assets which it has *securitised* are inadequate having regard to the economic substance of the transaction, including the degree of risk transfer achieved.

(4) Business risk means any risk to a *firm* arising from changes in its business, including the risk that the *firm* may not be able to carry out its business plan and its desired strategy. It also includes risks arising from a *firm's remuneration policy* (see also the *Remuneration Code* which applies to certain *banks*, *building societies* and *BIPRU 730k firms* and the detailed application of which is set out in SYSC 19.1).

(5) Pension obligation risk is the risk to a *firm* caused by its contractual or other liabilities to or with respect to a pension scheme (whether established for its employees or those of a related *company* or otherwise). It also means the risk that the *firm* will make payments or other contribution to or with respect to a pension scheme because of a moral obligation or because the *firm* considers that it needs to do so for some other reason.

1.2.32 **[G]**

(1) This paragraph gives *guidance* on some of the terms used in the *overall Pillar 2 rule*.

(2) Insurance risk refers to the inherent uncertainties as to the occurrence, amount and timing of insurance liabilities.

(3) Interest rate risk in the *non-trading book* is explained in BIPRU 2.3 (Interest rate risk in the non-trading book).

(4) In a narrow sense, business risk is the risk to a *firm* that it suffers losses because its income falls or is volatile relative to its fixed cost base. However, in a broader sense, it is exposure to a wide range of macroeconomic, geopolitical, industry, regulatory and other external risks that might deflect a *firm* from its desired strategy and business plan. GENPRU 1.2.73G provides further *guidance* on business risk.

(5) Further material on pension obligation risk can be found in GENPRU 1.2.79G–GENPRU 1.2.86G.

(6) Group risk is the risk that the financial position of a *firm* may be adversely affected by its relationships (financial or non-financial) with other entities in the same *group* or by risks which may affect the financial position of the whole *group*, for example reputational contagion. Further *guidance* on group risk can be found in GENPRU 1.2.87G to GENPRU 1.2.91G.

1.2.33 **[R]**

(1) This *rule* amplifies some of the obligations in the *overall Pillar 2 rule*.

(2) In the case of a *BIPRU firm* the processes, strategies and systems relating to concentration risk must include those necessary to ensure compliance with BIPRU 10 (Concentration risk requirements).

(3) As part of its obligations in respect of *market risk*, a *BIPRU firm* must consider whether the value adjustments and provisions taken for *positions* and portfolios in the *trading book* enable the *firm* to sell or hedge out its *positions* within a short period without incurring material losses under normal market conditions.

(4) The processes, strategies and systems required by the *overall Pillar 2 rule* must take into account stress tests and scenario analyses that the *firm* is required to carry out under any other provision of the *Handbook*.

1.2.34 **[G]** In the *overall Pillar 2 rule*, internal capital refers to the financial resources of a *firm* which it treats as being held against the risks listed in the *overall Pillar 2 rule*. The obligation in that *rule* to assess the distribution of such capital refers, in relation to a *firm* making an assessment on a solo basis, for example, to the need to take account of circumstances where part of a *firm's* financial resources are held by a *branch* of that *firm* which are subject to restrictions on its ability to transfer that capital. An assessment of internal capital distribution might also take account of such of a *firm's* financial resources as may be ring-fenced in the event of its insolvency.

1.2.35 **[R]** The processes, strategies and systems required by the *overall Pillar 2 rule* must be comprehensive and proportionate to the nature, scale and complexity of the *firm's* activities.

1.2.36 **[R]** As part of its obligations under GENPRU 1.2.30R(1) (Main requirement relating to risk processes, strategies and systems), a *firm* must identify separately the amount of *tier one capital*, *tier two capital*, *tier three capital*, other capital eligible to form part of its *capital resources* and each category of capital (if any) that is not eligible to form part of its *capital resources* which it considers adequate for the purposes described in GENPRU 1.2.30R(1).

1.2.37 **[R]** The processes and systems required by the *overall Pillar 2 rule* must:

(1) include an assessment of how the *firm* intends to deal with each of the major sources of risk identified in accordance with GENPRU 1.2.30R(2);

(2) take into account the impact of diversification effects and how such effects are factored into the *firm's* systems for measuring and managing risks; and

(3) include an assessment of the *firm*-wide impact of the risks identified in accordance with GENPRU 1.2.30R(2), to which end a *firm* must aggregate the risks across its various business lines and units, making appropriate allowance for the correlation between risks.

1.2.38 **[G]** Certain risks such as systems and controls weaknesses may not be adequately addressed by, for example, holding additional capital and a more appropriate response would be to rectify the weakness. In such circumstances, the amount of financial resources required to address these risks might be zero. However, a *firm* should consider whether holding additional capital might be an appropriate response until the identified weaknesses are rectified. A *firm*, should, in accordance with GENPRU 1.2.60R (Documentation of risk assessments), document the approaches taken to manage these risks.

1.2.39 **[R]** A *firm* must:

(1) carry out regularly the assessments required by the *overall Pillar 2 rule*; and

(2) carry out regularly assessments of the processes, strategies and systems required by the *overall Pillar 2 rule* to ensure that they remain compliant with GENPRU 1.2.35R.

1.2.40 **[G]** A *firm* should carry out assessments of the sort described in the *overall Pillar 2 rule* and GENPRU 1.2.39R at least annually, or more frequently if changes in the business, strategy, nature or scale of its activities or operational environment suggest that the current level of financial resources is no longer adequate. The appropriateness of the internal process, and the degree of involvement of senior management in the process, will be taken into account by the *FSA* when reviewing a *firm's* assessment as part of the *FSA*'s own assessment of the adequacy of a *firm*'s financial resources. The processes and systems should ensure that the assessment of the adequacy of a *firm's* financial resources is reported to its senior management as often as is necessary.

1.2.41 **[G]** The assessments undertaken by *firms in run-off* may not need to be as comprehensive or frequent compared to a *firm* not in run off since this may better reflect the reduced nature and complexity of its business and reduced access to new capital. Whilst a *firm in run-off* will still need to carefully monitor the progress of the run off, a more comprehensive assessment may only be appropriate on commencement of the run off or when considering a reduction in capital through the payment of a dividend or other capital distribution or if the *firm's* circumstances change materially.

Stress and scenario tests

1.2.42 **[R]**

(1) As part of its obligation under the *overall Pillar 2 rule*, a *firm* must, for the major sources of risk identified in accordance with GENPRU 1.2.30R(2), carry out stress tests and scenario analyses that are appropriate to the nature, scale and complexity of those major sources of risk and to the nature, scale and complexity of the firm's business.

(2) In carrying out the stress tests and scenario analyses in (1), a *firm* must identify an appropriate range of adverse circumstances of varying nature, severity and duration relevant to its business and risk profile and consider the exposure of the *firm* to those circumstances, including:

(a) circumstances and events occurring over a protracted period of time;
(b) sudden and severe events, such as market shocks or other similar events; and
(c) some combination of the circumstances and events described in (a) and (b), which may include a sudden and severe market event followed by an economic recession.

(3) In carrying out the stress tests and scenario analyses in (1), the *firm* must estimate the financial resources that it would need in order to continue to meet the *overall financial adequacy rule* and the *CRR* in the adverse circumstances being considered.

(4) In carrying out the stress tests and scenario analyses in (1), the *firm* must assess how risks aggregate across business lines or units, any material non-linear or contingent risks and how risk correlations may increase in stressed conditions.

(5) As part of its obligation under the *overall Pillar 2 rule*, a *BIPRU firm* must also incorporate and take into account any stress tests and scenario analyses that it is required to carry out under BIPRU. In particular, a *BIPRU firm* with an *IRB permission* must incorporate and take into account the stress test required to be carried out under BIPRU 4.3.40R(2).

1.2.42A **[G]** In order to comply with the *general stress and scenario testing rule*, a *firm* should undertake a broad range of stress tests which reflect a variety of perspectives, including sensitivity analysis, scenario analysis and stress testing on an individual portfolio as well as a *firm*-wide level.

1.2.42B **[G]** A *BIPRU firm* with an *IRB permission* which has any material credit *exposures* excluded from its *IRB* models should also include these *exposures* in its stress and scenario testing to meet its obligations under the *general stress and scenario testing rule*. A *BIPRU firm* without an *IRB permission*, or an *insurer* that has any material credit and counterparty credit risk exposures, should conduct analyses to assess risks to the credit quality of its counterparties, including any protection sellers, considering both on and off-balance sheet exposures.

1.2.42C **[G]** An *insurer* may choose to carry out its *ICA* through the use of stress testing and scenario analyses (see INSPRU 7.1.10G and INSPRU 7.1.68G). If it does so, in carrying out the stress tests and scenario analyses referred to in GENPRU 1.2.42 R, an *insurer* should take into account the stress tests it uses for its *ICA*.

1.2.42D **[G]** In carrying out the stress tests and scenario analyses required by GENPRU 1.2.42 R(1), a *firm* should also consider any impact of the adverse circumstances on its *capital resources*. In particular, a *firm* should consider the *capital resources gearing rules* where its *tier one capital* is eroded by the event.

1.2.42E **[G]** A *firm* should assign adequate resources, including IT systems, to stress testing and scenario analysis, taking into account the stress testing techniques employed, so as to be able to accommodate different and changing stress tests at an appropriate level of granularity.

1.2.42F **[G]** GENPRU 1.2.63 G to GENPRU 1.2.78 G provide additional *guidance* on stress testing and scenario analyses. In particular, GENPRU 1.2.73 AG provides specific *guidance* on capital planning.

1.2.43 **[G]** Stress tests and scenario analyses should be carried out at least annually. A *firm* should, however, consider whether the nature of the major sources of risks identified by it in accordance with GENPRU 1.2.30R(2) (Main requirement relating to risk processes, strategies and systems) and their possible impact on its financial resources suggest that such tests and analyses should be carried out more frequently. For instance, a sudden change in the economic outlook may prompt a *firm* to revise the parameters of some of its stress tests and scenario analyses. Similarly, if a *firm* has recently become exposed to a particular sectoral concentration, it may wish to add some stress tests and scenario analyses in order to reflect that concentration. *SYSC* 11.1.21E is an *evidential provision* relating to the *general stress and scenario testing rule* concerning scenario analysis in relation to *liquidity risk*.

Application of this section on a solo and consolidated basis: General

1.2.44 **[G]**

(1) GENPRU 1.2.45R–GENPRU 1.2.56G explain when the *ICAAP rules* apply on a solo basis and when they apply on a consolidated basis. This material also explains how the *ICAAP rules* are adjusted to apply on a consolidated basis.

(2) GENPRU 1.2.57R–GENPRU 1.2.59R provide that the *overall financial adequacy rule* always applies on a solo basis. They also explain when and how it applies on a consolidated basis.

Application of this section on a solo and consolidated basis: Processes and tests

1.2.45 **[R]** If an *insurer* is a member of an *insurance group* and INSPRU 6.1.9R, INSPRU 6.1.10R or INSPRU 6.1.15R (Requirement to maintain group capital) apply to it with respect to that *insurance group* the *ICAAP rules*:

(1) apply to that *insurer* on a consolidated basis; and
(2) do not apply to it on a solo basis.

1.2.46 **[R]** The *ICAAP rules* do not apply on a solo basis to a *BIPRU firm* to which the *ICAAP rules*:
(1) apply on a consolidated basis under BIPRU 8.2.1R (Basic consolidation *rule* for a *UK consolidation group*); or
(2) apply on a sub-consolidated basis under BIPRU 8.3.1R (Basic consolidation *rule* for a *non-EEA sub-group*).

1.2.47 **[R]** The *ICAAP rules* apply on a solo basis:
(1) to an *insurer* to which those *rules* do not apply on a consolidated basis under GENPRU 1.2.45R;
(2) to a *BIPRU firm* to which those *rules* do not apply on a consolidated or sub-consolidated basis as referred to in GENPRU 1.2.46R (including a *BIPRU investment firm* with an *investment firm consolidation waiver*); and
(3) a *firm* referred to in GENPRU 1.2.2R (Application of this section to certain non-*EEA firms*).

1.2.48 **[R]** The requirements of the *ICAAP rules* as they apply on a consolidated basis must be carried out on the basis of the consolidated position of:
(1) (if GENPRU 1.2.45R applies) that *insurance group*;
(2) (if BIPRU 8.2.1R (Basic consolidation *rule* for a *UK consolidation group*) applies) the *UK consolidation group* of which the *firm* is a member; and
(3) (if BIPRU 8.3.1R (Basic consolidation *rule* for a *non-EEA sub-group*) applies) the *non-EEA sub-group* of which the *firm* is a member.

1.2.49 **[R]**
(1) In accordance with the general principles in GENPRU 1.2.48R and BIPRU 8 (Group risk – consolidation), for the purpose of the *ICAAP rules* as they apply on a consolidated basis:
  (a) the *firm* must ensure that the relevant group as defined in (2) have the processes, strategies and systems required by the *overall Pillar 2 rule*;
  (b) the risks to which the *overall Pillar 2 rule* and the *general stress and scenario testing rule* refer are those risks as they apply to each member of the relevant group;
  (c) the reference in the *overall Pillar 2 rule* to amounts and types of financial resources, *capital resources* and internal capital (referred to in this *rule* as resources) must be read as being to the amounts and types that the *firm* considers should be held by the members of the relevant group as defined in (2);
  (d) other references to resources must be read as being to resources of the members of the relevant group as defined in (2);
  (e) references to the *CRR* are to the consolidated capital requirements applicable to the relevant group under BIPRU 8 (Group risk – consolidation) or, as the case may be, INSPRU 6 (Group risk: Insurance groups);
  (f) the reference in the *overall Pillar 2 rule* to the distribution of resources must be read as including a reference to the distribution between members of the relevant group as defined in (2); and
  (g) the reference in the *overall Pillar 2 rule* to the *overall finanaical adequacy rule* must be read as being to that *rule* as adjusted under GENPRU 1.2.59R (Application of the *overall financial adequacy rule* on a consolidated basis).
(2) For the purpose of this *rule* the relevant group is the group referred to in GENPRU 1.2.48R and the members of that group are those *undertakings* that are included in the scope of consolidation with respect to the *insurance group*, *UK consolidation group* or, as the case may be, *non-EEA sub-group* in question.

1.2.50 **[G]** GENPRU 1.2.49R means that non-financial members of the *firm's* group are excluded from the *group* assessment. Notwithstanding the scope of GENPRU 1.2.49R, a *firm* should nevertheless take account of risks arising from the activities of those excluded members in its overall assessment of risk.

1.2.51 **[R]**
(1) This *rule* relates to the assessment of the amounts, types and distribution of financial resources, *capital resources* and internal capital (referred to in this *rule* as "resources") under the *overall Pillar 2 rule* as applied on a consolidated basis and to the assessment of diversification effects as referred to in GENPRU 1.2.37R(2) as applied on a consolidated basis.
(2) A *firm* must be able to explain how it has aggregated the risks referred to in the *overall Pillar 2 rule* and the resources required by each member of the relevant group as referred to in GENPRU 1.2.49R(2) and how it has taken into account any diversification benefits with respect to the group in question.
(3) In particular, to the extent that the transferability of resources affects the assessment in (2), a *firm* must be able to explain how it has satisfied itself that resources are transferable between members of the group in question in the stressed cases and the scenarios referred to in the *general stress and scenario testing rule*.

1.2.52 **[R]**

Part II FSA Handbook Materials

(1) A *firm* must allocate the total amount of financial resources, *capital resources* and internal capital identified as necessary under the overall *Pillar 2 rule* (as applied on a consolidated basis) between different parts of the relevant group (as defined in GENPRU 1.2.49R). GENPRU 1.2.36R (Identifying different tiers of capital) does not apply to this allocation.
(2) The *firm* must carry out the allocation in (1) in a way that adequately reflects the nature, level and distribution of the risks to which the group is subject and the effect of any diversification benefits.

1.2.53 **[R]** A *firm* must also allocate the total amount of financial resources, *capital resources* and internal capital (referred to in this *rule* as "resources") identified as necessary under the *overall Pillar 2 rule* as applied on a consolidated basis between each *firm* which is a member of the relevant group (as defined in GENPRU 1.2.49R) on the following basis:
(1) the amount allocated to each *firm* must be decided on the basis of the principles in GENPRU 1.2.52R(2); and
(2) if the process in (1) were carried out for each group member, the total so allocated would equal the total amount of resources identified as necessary under the *overall Pillar 2 rule* as applied on a consolidated basis.

1.2.54 **[G]** A *firm* to which the *ICAAP rules* apply on a consolidated basis need not prepare a consolidated basis assessment if such an assessment has been prepared by another member of its *group*. Where that is the case, a *firm* may adopt such an assessment as its own. A *firm* nevertheless remains responsible for the assessment.

1.2.55 **[G]** The purpose of GENPRU 1.2.51R–GENPRU 1.2.53R is to enable the *FSA* to assess the extent, if any, to which a *firm's* assessment, calculated on a consolidated basis, is lower than it would be if each separate legal entity were to assess the amount of capital it would require to mitigate its risks (to the same level of confidence) were it not part of a group subject to consolidated supervision under BIPRU 8 (Group risk – consolidation) or INSPRU 6.1 (Group risk: Insurance groups). The reason the *FSA* wishes to make this assessment is so that individual capital *guidance* which it gives is fair and comparable as between different *firms* and groups. Group diversification benefits which a *firm* might assert exist can be a material consideration in a capital adequacy assessment. Understanding the methods used to aggregate the different risks (for example, the correlation assumptions) is crucial to a proper evaluation of such benefits.

1.2.56 **[G]** Whereas a single legal entity can generally use its capital to absorb losses wherever they arise, there are often practical and legal restrictions on the ability of a group to do so. For instance:
(1) capital which is held by overseas regulated *firms* may not be capable of being remitted to a *firm* in the *UK* which has suffered a loss;
(2) a *firm* which is insolvent or likely to become so may be obliged to look to the interests of its creditors first before transferring capital to other group *companies*; and
(3) a parent *company* may have to balance the interests of its shareholders against the protection of the creditors of a *subsidiary undertaking* which is or might become insolvent and may, rationally, conclude that a *subsidiary undertaking* should be allowed to fail rather than provide capital to support it.

Application of this section on a solo and consolidated basis: Adequacy of resources

1.2.57 **[R]** The *overall financial adequacy rule* applies to a *firm* on a solo basis whether or not it also applies to the *firm* on a consolidated basis.

1.2.58 **[R]** The *overall financial adequacy rule* applies to a *firm* on a consolidated basis if the *ICAAP rules* apply to it on a consolidated basis.

1.2.59 **[R]**
(1) When the *overall financial adequacy rule* applies on a consolidated basis, the *firm* must ensure that at all times its group maintains overall financial resources, including capital resources and liquidity resources, which are adequate, both as to amount and quality, to ensure that there is no significant risk that the liabilities of any members of its group cannot be met as they fall due.
(2) The group referred to in (1) is the relevant group as defined in GENPRU 1.2.49R.
(3) The members of the group referred to in (1) must be identified in accordance with GENPRU 1.2.49R.

Documentation of risk assessments

1.2.60 **[R]** A *firm* must make a written record of the assessments required under this section. These assessments include assessments carried out on a consolidated basis and on a solo basis. In particular it must make a written record of:
(1) the major sources of risk identified in accordance with GENPRU 1.2.30R(2) (Main requirement relating to risk processes, strategies and systems);
(2) how it intends to deal with those risks; and

(3) details of the stress tests and scenario analyses carried out, including any assumptions made in relation to scenario design, and the resulting financial resources estimated to be required in accordance with the *general stress and scenario testing rule*.

1.2.61 **[R]** A *firm* must retain the records of its assessments referred to in GENPRU 1.2.60R for at least three years.

1.2.62 **[G]** Where a *firm* assesses the adequacy of its *CRR* in its particular circumstances in accordance with BIPRU 2.2 (Internal capital adequacy standards) and INSPRU 7.1 (Individual capital assessment) as a basis for deciding what financial resources are adequate, it should include this in the documentation produced in accordance with GENPRU 1.2.60R.

Additional guidance on stress tests and scenario analyses

1.2.63 **[G]** The *general stress and scenario testing rule* requires a *firm* to carry out stress tests and scenario analyses as part of its obligations under the *overall Pillar 2 rule*. Both stress tests and scenario analyses are undertaken by a *firm* to further a better understanding of the vulnerabilities that it faces under adverse conditions. They are based on the analysis of the impact of a range of events of varying nature, severity and duration. These events can be financial, operational or legal or relate to any other risk that might have an economic impact on the *firm*.

1.2.64 **[G]** Stress testing typically refers to shifting the values of individual parameters that affect the financial position of a *firm* and determining the effect on the *firm's* financial position.

1.2.65 **[G]** Scenario analysis typically refers to a wider range of parameters being varied at the same time. Scenario analyses often examine the impact of adverse events on the *firm's* financial position, for example, simultaneous movements in a number of risk categories affecting all of a *firm's* business operations, such as business volumes, investment values and interest rate movements.

1.2.66 **[G]** There are three broad purposes of stress testing and scenario analysis. Firstly, it can be used as a means of quantifying how much capital might be absorbed if an adverse event or events occurred. As such it represents a simple 'what if' approach to estimating exposure to risks. This might be a proportionate approach to risk management for an unsophisticated business. Secondly, it can be used to provide a check on the outputs and accuracy of risk models; particularly, in identifying nonlinear effects when aggregating risks. Thirdly, it can be used to explore the sensitivities in longer term business plans and how capital needs might change over time.

1.2.67 **[G]** [deleted]

1.2.68 **[G]** Subject to GENPRU 1.2.76G, the purpose of stress tests and scenario analyses under the *general stress and scenario testing rule* is to test the adequacy of overall financial resources. Scenarios need only be identified, and their impact assessed, in so far as this facilitates that purpose. In particular, the nature, depth and detail of the analysis depend, in part, upon the *firm's* capital strength and the robustness of its risk prevention and risk mitigation measures.

1.2.69 **[G]** Both stress testing and scenario analyses are forward-looking analysis techniques, which seek to anticipate possible losses that might occur if an identified risk crystallises. In applying them, a *firm* should decide how far forward to look. This should depend upon:

(1) how quickly it would be able to identify events or changes in circumstances that might lead to a risk crystallising resulting in a loss; and

(2) after it has identified the event or circumstance, how quickly and effectively it could act to prevent or mitigate any loss resulting from the risk crystallising and to reduce exposure to any further adverse event or change in circumstance.

1.2.70 **[G]** Where a *firm* is exposed to *market risk*, the time horizon over which stress tests and scenario analyses should be carried out will depend on, among other things, the maturity and liquidity of the *positions* stressed. For example, for the *market risk* arising from the holding of investments this will depend upon:

(1) the extent to which there is a regular, open and transparent market in those assets, which would allow fluctuations in the value of the investment to be more readily and quickly identified; and

(2) the extent to which the market in those assets is sufficiently liquid (and would remain liquid in the changed circumstances contemplated in the stress test or scenario analysis) to allow the *firm*, if needed, to sell, hedge or otherwise mitigate the risks relating to its holding so as to prevent or reduce exposure to future price fluctuations. In devising stress tests and scenario analyses for *market risk*, a *BIPRU firm* should also take into account BIPRU 7.1.17 R to BIPRU 7.1.20 G.

1.2.71 **[G]** In identifying scenarios, and assessing their impact, a *firm* should take into account, where material, how changes in circumstances might impact upon:

(1) the nature, scale and mix of its future activities; and

(2) the behaviour of *counterparties*, and of the *firm* itself, including the exercise of choices (for example, options embedded in financial instruments or *contracts of insurance*).

Part II FSA Handbook Materials

1.2.72 **[G]** In determining whether it would have adequate financial resources in the event of each identified realistic adverse scenario, a *firm* should:

(1) only include financial resources that could reasonably be relied upon as being available in the circumstances of the identified scenario; and

(2) take account of any legal or other restriction on the use of financial resources.

1.2.73 **[G]** [deleted]

Capital planning

1.2.73A **[G]**

(1) In identifying an appropriate range of adverse circumstances and events in accordance with GENPRU 1.2.42 R(2):
   (a) a *firm* will need to consider the cycles it is most exposed to and whether these are general economic cycles or specific to particular markets, sectors or industries;
   (b) for the purposes of GENPRU 1.2.42 R(2)(a), the amplitude and duration of the relevant cycle should include a severe downturn scenario based on forward looking hypothetical events, calibrated against the most adverse movements in individual risk drivers experienced over a long historical period;
   (c) the adverse scenarios considered should in general be acyclical and, accordingly, the scenario should not become more severe during a downturn and less severe during an upturn. However, the *FSA* does expect scenarios to be updated with relevant new economic data on a pragmatic basis to ensure that the scenario continues to be relevant; and
   (d) the adverse scenarios considered should reflect a *firm's* risk tolerance of the adverse conditions through which it expects to remain a going concern.

(2) In making the estimate required by GENPRU 1.2.42 R(3), a *firm* should project both its *capital resources* and its required *capital resources* over a time horizon of 3 to 5 years, taking account of its business plan and the impact of relevant adverse scenarios. In making the estimate, the *firm* should consider both the *capital resources* required to meet its *CRR* and the *capital resources* needed to meet the *overall financial adequacy rule*. The *firm* should make these projections in a manner consistent with its risk management processes and systems as set out in GENPRU 1.2.37 R.

(3) In projecting its financial position over the relevant time horizon, the *firm* should:
   (a) reflect how its business plan would "flex" in response to the adverse events being considered, taking into account factors such as changing consumer demand and changes to new business assumptions;
   (b) consider the potential impact on its stress testing of dynamic feedback effects and second order effects of the major sources of risk identified in accordance with GENPRU 1.2.30 R(2);
   (c) estimate the effects on the *firm's* financial position of the adverse event without adjusting for management actions;
   (d) separately, identify any realistic management actions that the *firm* could and would take to mitigate the adverse effects of the stress scenario; and
   (e) estimate the effects of the stress scenario on the *firm's* financial position after taking account of realistic management actions.

(4) A *firm* should identify any realistic management actions intended to maintain or restore its capital adequacy. These could include ceasing to transact new business after a suitable period has elapsed, balance sheet shrinkage, restricting distribution of profits or raising additional capital. A *firm* should reflect management actions in its projections only where it could and would take such actions, taking account of factors such as market conditions in the stress scenario and any effects upon the *firm's* reputation with its counterparties and investors. The combined effect on capital and retained earnings should be estimated. In order to assess whether prospective management actions in a stress scenario would be realistic and to determine which actions the *firm* would and could take, the *firm* should take into account any preconditions that might affect the value of management actions as risk mitigants and analyse the difference between the estimates in (3)(c) and (3)(e) in sufficient detail to understand the implications of taking different management actions at different times, particularly where they represent a significant divergence from the *firm's* business plan.

(5) The *firm* should document its stress testing and scenario analysis policies and procedures, as well as the results of its tests in accordance with GENPRU 1.2.60 R. These records should be included within the *firm's ICAAP* or *ICA* submission document.

(6) The *FSA* will review the *firm's* records referred to in (5) as part of its *SREP*. The purpose of examining these is to enable the *FSA* to judge whether a *firm* will be able to continue to meet its *CRR* and the *overall financial adequacy rule* throughout the projection period.

(7) If, after taking account of realistic management actions, a *firm's* stress testing management plan shows that the *firm's* projected *capital resources* are less than those required to continue to meet its *CRR* or less than those needed to continue to meet the *overall financial adequacy rule* over the projection period, the *FSA* may require the *firm* to set out additional countervailing measures and off-setting actions to reduce such difference or to restore the *firm's* capital adequacy after the stress event.

(8) The *firm's* senior management or *governing body* should be actively involved and engaged in all relevant stages of the *firm's* stress testing and scenario analysis programme. This would include establishing an appropriate stress testing programme, reviewing the programme's implementation (including the design of scenarios) and challenging, approving and actioning the results of the stress tests.

(9) For an *insurer*:

(a) the treatment of new business when making capital projections is likely to be different from its *ICA*. In projecting its financial position, an *insurer* should take account of new business based on the *firm's* business plan, but flexed to take account of potential changes in trading conditions and strategy. When assessing its current capital adequacy under its *ICA*, an *insurer* should take account of the effects of closure to new business (see GENPRU 1.2.27 G, GENPRU 1.2.73A G(3) and (4) and INSPRU 7.1.16 G to INSPRU 7.1.19 G). Also, an *insurer* may use methods that are more approximate than used for its *ICA* (for example, in projecting the *with-profits insurance capital component* for *realistic basis life firms* and the *capital resources* needed to meet the *overall financial adequacy rule*); and

(b) where management discretion is exercised as a normal part of an *insurer's* business (for example, in changing bonus rates or *surrender values* in accordance with the *PPFM* for *with-profits business*), under (3)(c) the *insurer* does not need to estimate the effect of an adverse event on its financial position without adjusting for such changes. However, the effect on the financial position of varying such actions should be estimated and understood.

1.2.73B **[G]** The *FSA* may formulate macroeconomic and financial market scenarios which a *firm* may use as an additional input to its *ICAAP* or *ICA* submission. In addition, the *FSA* may also ask a *firm* to apply specific scenarios directly in its *ICAAP* or *ICA* submission.

1.2.74 **[G]** A *firm* may consider scenarios in which expected future profits will provide capital reserves against future risks. However, it would only be appropriate to take into account profits that can be foreseen with a reasonable degree of certainty as arising before the risk against which they are being held could possibly arise. In estimating future reserves, a *firm* should deduct future dividend payment estimates from projections of future profits.

1.2.75 **[G]**

(1) [deleted]

(2) Stress and scenario analyses should, in the first instance, be aligned with the risk appetite of the *firm*, as well as the nature, scale and complexity of its business and of the risks that it bears. The calibration of the stress and scenario analyses should be reconciled to a clear statement setting out the premise upon which the *firm's* internal capital assessment under the *overall Pillar 2 rule* is based.

(3) [deleted]

(4) A *firm* may also consider scenarios in which the amount of capital it currently holds would be exhausted. This would provide useful information about the reasonableness or remoteness of such scenarios arising. Where a *firm* uses capital models as part of its risk management processes, considering the sensitivity of model results to variations around the most likely ruin scenario focuses testing on the most relevant scenarios.

1.2.76 **[G]** A *firm* should use the results of its stress testing and scenario analysis not only to assess capital needs, but also to decide if measures should be put in place to minimise the adverse effect on the *firm* if the risk covered by the stress or scenario test actually materialises. Such measures might be a contingency plan or might be more concrete risk mitigation steps.

1.2.77 **[G]** Additional *guidance* on stress tests and scenario analyses for the assessment of *capital resources* is available in BIPRU 2.2 (Internal capital adequacy standards) and INSPRU 7.1 (Individual capital assessment).

1.2.78 **[G]** Additional *guidance* in relation to stress tests and scenario analysis for *liquidity risk* as that concept relates to an *insurer* is available in SYSC 11 (Liquidity risk systems and controls). BIPRU 12 sets out the main *Handbook* provisions in relation to *liquidity risk* for a *BIPRU firm*.

Pension obligation risk

1.2.79 **[G]** GENPRU 1.2.80G to GENPRU 1.2.86G contain *guidance* on the assessment required by GENPRU 1.2.30R(2)(k) for a *firm* exposed to pension obligation risk as defined in GENPRU 1.2.31 R(5).

1.2.80 **[G]** The pension scheme itself (i.e. the scheme's assets and liabilities) is not the focus of the risk assessment but rather it is the *firm's* obligations towards the pension scheme. A *firm* should include in its estimate of financial resources both its expected obligations to the pension scheme and any increase in obligations that may arise in a stress scenario.

1.2.81 **[G]** If a *firm* has a current funding obligation in excess of normal contributions or there is a risk that such a funding obligation will arise then, when calculating available capital resources, it should reverse out any accounting deficit and replace this in its capital adequacy assessment with its best estimate, calculated in discussion with the scheme's actuaries or trustees, of the cash that will need to be paid into the scheme in addition to normal contributions over the foreseeable future. This may differ from the approach taken in assessing pension scheme risks for the purposes of calculating resources to meet the *CRR*, where a *firm* may not need to consider funding obligations beyond the next five years.

1.2.82 **[G]** A *firm* should also assess the risks that may increase its current funding obligations towards the pension scheme and that might lead to the *firm* not being able to pay its other liabilities as they fall due.

1.2.83 **[G]** A *firm* may wish to consider the following scenarios:

(1) one in which the *firm* gets into difficulties with an effect on its ability to fund the pension scheme; and

(2) one in which the pension scheme position deteriorates (for example, because investment returns fall below expected returns or because of increases in life expectancy) with an effect on the *firm's* funding obligations; taking into account the management actions the *firm* could and would take.

1.2.83A **[G]** A firm is expected to determine where the scope of any stress impacts upon its pension obligation risk and estimate how the relevant measure of pension obligation risk will change in the scenario in question. For example, in carrying out stress tests under GENPRU 1.2.42R a *firm* must consider how a stress scenario, such as an economic recession, would impact on the *firm's* current obligations towards its pension scheme and any potential increase in those obligations. Risks such as interest rate risk or reduced investment returns may have a direct impact on a *firm's* financial position as well as an indirect impact resulting from an increase in the *firm's* pension scheme obligations. Both effects should be taken into account in a *firm's* estimate of financial resources under GENPRU 1.2.30R.

1.2.84 **[G]** Scenarios in which a *firm's* employees suffer a loss or members of a pension scheme suffer a loss do not necessarily affect the *firm's* ability to pay its liabilities as they fall due.

1.2.85 **[G]** A *firm* should consider issues such as:

(1) the extent to which trustees of the pension scheme or a pension regulator (such as the one created under the Pensions Act 2004) can compel a certain level of contributions or a one-off payment in adverse financial situations or in order to meet the minimum legal requirements under the scheme's trust deed and rules or under the applicable laws relating to the pension scheme;

(2) whether the valuation bases used to set pension scheme contribution rates are consistent with the *firm's* current business plans and anticipated changes in the workforce; and

(3) which valuation basis is appropriate given the expected investment return on scheme assets and actions the *firm* can take if those returns do not materialise.

1.2.86 **[G]** A *firm* should carry out analyses only to a degree of sophistication and complexity which is commensurate with the materiality of its pension risks.

Group risk

1.2.87 **[G]** GENPRU 1.2.88 G to GENPRU 1.2.91G contain additional *guidance* on the assessment required by GENPRU 1.2.30 R(2)(l) (Group risk).

1.2.88 **[G]** A *firm* should include in the written record referred to in GENPRU 1.2.60R a description of the broad business strategy of the *insurance group*, the *UK consolidation group* or the *non-EEA sub-group* of which it is a member, the group's view of its principal risks and its approach to measuring, managing and controlling the risks. This description should include the role of stress testing, scenario analysis and contingency planning in managing risk at the solo and consolidated level.

1.2.89 **[G]** A *firm* should satisfy itself that the systems (including IT) of the *insurance group*, the *UK consolidation group* or the *non-EEA sub-group* of which it is a member are sufficiently sound to support the effective management and, where applicable, the quantification of the risks that could affect the *insurance group*, the *UK consolidation group* or the *non-EEA sub-group*, as the case may be.

1.2.90 **[G]** In performing stress tests and scenario analyses, a *firm* should take into account the risk that its *group* may have to bring back on to its consolidated balance sheet the assets and liabilities of off-balance sheet entities as a result of reputational contagion, notwithstanding the appearance of legal risk transfer.

1.2.91 **[G]** A *firm* should carry out stress tests and scenario analyses to a degree of sophistication which is commensurate with the complexity of its *group* and the nature of its group risk.

1.3 Valuation

Application

1.3.1 **[R]**

(1) This section of the *Handbook* applies to an *insurer*, unless it is:
  (a) a *non-directive friendly society;*
  (b) an *incoming EEA firm*; or
  (c) an *incoming Treaty firm.*

(2) This section of the *Handbook* applies to a *BIPRU firm.*

(3) This section of the *Handbook* applies to a *UK ISPV.*

Purpose

1.3.2 **[G]** This section sets out, for the purposes of GENPRU, BIPRU and INSPRU, *rules* and *guidance* as to how a *firm* should recognise and value assets, liabilities, *exposures*, equity and income statement items.

1.3.3 **[G]**

(1) In the case of a *BIPRU firm*, this section implements Article 74 of the *Banking Consolidation Directive*, Article 64(4) of the *Banking Consolidation Directive* (Own funds) and Article 33 and Part B of Annex VII of the *Capital Adequacy Directive.*

(2) In the case of an *insurer*, GENPRU 1.3.4R implements the requirements of Articles 23.3(viii) and 24.2(iv) of the *Consolidated Life Directive.*

General requirements: Accounting principles to be applied

1.3.4 **[R]** Subject to GENPRU 1.3.9R to GENPRU 1.3.10R and GENPRU 1.3.36R, except where a *rule* in GENPRU, BIPRU or INSPRU provides for a different method of recognition or valuation, whenever a *rule* in GENPRU, BIPRU or INSPRU refers to an asset, liability, *exposure*, equity or income statement item, a *firm* must, for the purpose of that *rule*, recognise the asset, liability, *exposure*, equity or income statement item and measure its value in accordance with whichever of the following are applicable:

(1) the *insurance accounts rules*, or the Friendly Societies (Accounts and Related Provisions) Regulations 1994;

(2) Financial Reporting Standards and Statements of Standard Accounting Practice issued or adopted by the Accounting Standards Board;

(3) Statements of Recommended Practice, issued by industry or sectoral bodies recognised for this purpose by the Accounting Standards Board;

(4) the Building Societies (Accounts and Related Provisions) Regulation 1998;

(5) *international accounting standards*;

(6) the Companies Act 1985; and

(7) the Companies Act 2006;

as applicable to the *firm* for the purpose of its external financial reporting (or as would be applicable if the *firm* was a company with its head office in the *United Kingdom*).

1.3.5 **[G]** Except where a *rule* in GENPRU, BIPRU or INSPRU makes different provision, GENPRU 1.3.4R applies whenever a *rule* in GENPRU, BIPRU or INSPRU refers to the value or amount of an asset, liability, *exposure*, equity or income statement item, including:

(1) whether, and when, to recognise or de-recognise an asset or liability;

(2) the amount at which to value an asset, liability, *exposure*, equity or income statement item; and

(3) which description to place on an asset, liability, *exposure*, equity or income statement item.

1.3.6 **[G]** In particular, unless an exception applies, GENPRU 1.3.4R should be applied for the purposes of GENPRU, BIPRU and INSPRU to determine how to account for:

(1) netting of amounts due to or from the *firm*;

(2) the securitisation of assets and liabilities (see also GENPRU 1.3.7G);

(3) leased tangible assets;

(4) assets transferred or received under a sale and repurchase or *stock lending* transaction; and

(5) assets transferred or received by way of initial or variation margin under a *derivative* or similar transaction.

1.3.7 **[G]** In the case of an *insurer* or a *UK ISPV*, where assets or liabilities are securitised, GENPRU 1.3.4R only permits de-recognition where Financial Reporting Standards (or, where applicable, International Accounting Standards) permit either de-recognition or the linked presentation. However, the *FSA* will consider granting a *waiver* to permit de-recognition in other circumstances provided that the *firm* can demonstrate that securitisation has effectively transferred risk

1.3.8 **[G]** Articles 23.3(viii) and 24.2(iv) of the *Consolidated Life Directive* require assets of an *insurer* that are managed on its behalf by a *subsidiary undertaking* to be taken into account for the purposes of determining the *insurer's admissible assets* and its assets in excess of concentration limits. The application of GENPRU 1.3.4R will result in such assets remaining on the balance sheet of the *insurer*.

General requirements: Adjustments to accounting values

1.3.9 **[R]** For the purposes of GENPRU, BIPRU and INSPRU, except where a *rule* in GENPRU, BIPRU or INSPRU provides for a different method of recognition or valuation:

(1) when a *firm*, upon initial recognition, designates its liabilities as at fair value through profit or loss, it must always adjust any value calculated in accordance with GENPRU 1.3.4R by subtracting any unrealised gains or adding back in any unrealised losses which are not attributable to changes in a benchmark interest rate;

(2) in respect of a *defined benefit occupational pension scheme*:
  (a) a *firm* must derecognise any *defined benefit asset*;
  (b) a *firm* may substitute for a *defined benefit liability* the *firm's deficit reduction amount*.

1.3.10 **[R]** An election made under GENPRU 1.3.9R(2) must be applied consistently for the purposes of GENPRU, BIPRU and INSPRU in respect of any one financial year.

1.3.11 **[G]** A *firm* should keep a record of and be ready to explain to its supervisory contacts in the *FSA* the reasons for any difference between the *deficit reduction amount* and any commitment the *firm* has made in any public document to provide funding in respect of a *defined benefit occupational pension scheme*.

1.3.12 **[G]** The provisions of GENPRU 1.3.9R to GENPRU 1.3.10R and GENPRU 1.3.36R apply only to the extent that the items referred to in those paragraphs would otherwise be recognised under the accounting requirements applicable to the *firm*. Some of those requirements may only be relevant to a *firm* subject to *international accounting standards*.

General requirements: Methods of valuation and systems and controls

1.3.13 **[R]**

(1) Except to the extent that GENPRU, BIPRU or INSPRU provide for another method of valuation, GENPRU 1.3.14R to GENPRU 1.3.34R (Marking to market, Marking to model, Independent price verification, Adjustments or reserves) apply:
  (a) for the purposes set out in GENPRU 1.3.41R;
  (b) for the purposes set out in GENPRU 1.3.39R; and
  (c) to any balance sheet position measured at market value or fair value.

(2) A *firm* must establish and maintain systems and controls sufficient to provide prudent and reliable valuation estimates.

(3) Systems and controls under (2) must include at least the following elements:
  (a) documented policies and procedures for the process of valuation, including clearly defined responsibilities of the various areas involved in the determination of the valuation, sources of market information and review of their appropriateness, frequency of independent valuation, timing of closing prices, procedures for adjusting valuations, month-end and ad-hoc verification procedures; and
  (b) reporting lines for the department accountable for the valuation process that are:
    (i) clear and independent of the front office; and
    (ii) ultimately to a main board executive director.

General requirements: Marking to market

1.3.14 **[R]** Wherever possible, a *firm* must use mark to market in order to measure the value of the investments and positions to which this *rule* applies under GENPRU 1.3.13R and GENPRU 1.3.38R to GENPRU 1.3.41R. Marking to market is valuation (on at least a daily basis in the case of the *trading book* positions of a *BIPRU firm*) at readily available close out prices from independent sources.

1.3.15 **[R]** For the purposes of GENPRU 1.3.14R, examples of readily available close out prices include exchange prices, screen prices, or quotes from several independent reputable brokers.

1.3.16 **[R]**

(1) When marking to market, a *firm* must use the more prudent side of bid/offer unless the *firm* is a significant market maker in a particular position type and it can close out at the mid-market price.

(2) When calculating the current *exposure* value of a credit risk *exposure* for *counterparty credit risk* purposes:
  (a) a *firm* must use the more prudent side of bid/offer or the mid-market price and the *firm* must be consistent in the basis it chooses; and

(b) where the difference between the more prudent side of bid/offer and the mid-market price is material, the *firm* must consider making adjustments or establishing reserves.

General requirements: Marking to model

1.3.17 **[R]** Where marking to market is not possible, a *firm* must use mark to model in order to measure the value of the investments and positions to which this *rule* applies under GENPRU 1.3.13R and GENPRU 1.3.38R to GENPRU 1.3.41R. Marking to model is any valuation which has to be benchmarked, extrapolated or otherwise calculated from a market input. GENPRU 1.3.18R to GENPRU 1.3.25R apply when marking to model.

1.3.18 **[R]** When the model used is developed by the *firm*, that model must be:
(1) based on appropriate assumptions which have been assessed and challenged by suitably qualified parties independent of the development process;
(2) independently tested, including validation of the mathematics, assumptions, and software implementation; and
(3) (in the case of a *BIPRU firm*) developed or approved independently of the front office.

1.3.19 **[R]** A *firm* must ensure that its senior management are aware of the positions which are subject to mark to model and understand the materiality of the uncertainty this creates in the reporting of the performance of the business of the *firm* and the risks to which it is subject.

1.3.20 **[R]** A *firm* must source market inputs in line with market prices so far as possible and assess the appropriateness of the market inputs for the position being valued and the parameters of the model on a frequent basis.

1.3.21 **[R]** A *firm* must use generally accepted valuation methodologies for particular products where these are available.

1.3.22 **[R]** A *firm* must establish formal change control procedures, hold a secure copy of the model, and periodically use that model to check valuations.

1.3.23 **[R]** A *firm* must ensure that its risk management functions are aware of the weaknesses of the models used and how best to reflect those in the valuation output.

1.3.24 **[R]** A *firm* must periodically review the model to determine the accuracy of its performance.

1.3.25 **[R]** Examples of periodical review are assessing the continued appropriateness of the assumptions, analysis of profit and loss versus risk factors and comparison of actual close out values to model outputs.

General requirements: Independent price verification

1.3.26 **[R]** In addition to marking to market or marking to model, a *firm* must perform independent price verification. This is the process by which market prices or model inputs are regularly verified for accuracy and independence.

1.3.27 **[G]** For independent price verification, where independent pricing sources are not available or pricing sources are more subjective (for example, only one available broker quote), prudent measures such as valuation adjustments may be appropriate.

1.3.28 **[R]** In the case of the *trading book* positions of a *BIPRU firm*, while daily marking to market may be performed by dealers, verification of market prices and model inputs must be performed by a unit independent of the dealing room, at least monthly (or, depending on the nature of the market/trading activity, more frequently).

General requirements: Valuation adjustments or reserves

1.3.29 **[R]** The recognition of any gains or losses arising from valuations subject to GENPRU 1.3.13R and GENPRU 1.3.38R to GENPRU 1.3.41R must be recognised for the purpose of calculating *capital resources* in accordance with GENPRU 1.3.14R to GENPRU 1.3.34R (Marking to market, Marking to model, Independent price verification, Adjustments or reserves). However if GENPRU, BIPRU or INSPRU provide for another treatment of such gains or losses, that other treatment must be applied.

1.3.30 **[R]** A *firm* must establish and maintain procedures for considering valuation adjustments or reserves. These procedures must be compliant with the requirements set out in GENPRU 1.3.33R.

1.3.31 **[R]** A *firm* using third-party valuations, or marking to model, must consider whether valuation adjustments are necessary.

1.3.32 **[R]** A *firm* must consider the need for establishing reserves for less liquid positions and, on an ongoing basis, review their continued appropriateness in accordance with the requirements set out in GENPRU 1.3.33R. Less liquid positions could arise from both market events and institution-related situations e.g. concentration positions and/or stale positions.

1.3.33 **[R]**

(1) This paragraph sets out the requirements referred to in GENPRU 1.3.30R and GENPRU 1.3.32R.

(2) A *firm* must consider the following adjustments or reserves: unearned credit spreads, close-out costs, operational risks, early termination, investing and funding costs, future administrative costs and, where appropriate, model risk.

(3) A *firm* must consider several factors when determining whether a valuation reserve is necessary for less liquid positions. These factors include the amount of time it would take to hedge out the position/risks within the position; the average and volatility of bid/offer spreads; the availability of market quotes (number and identity of market makers); the average and volatility of trading volumes; market concentrations; the ageing of positions; the extent to which valuation relies on marking to model and the impact of other model risks.

1.3.34 **[R]** If the result of establishing adjustments or reserves under GENPRU 1.3.29R to GENPRU 1.3.33R is a valuation which differs from the fair value determined in accordance with GENPRU 1.3.4R, a *firm* must reconcile the two valuations.

1.3.35 **[G]** Reconciliation differences under GENPRU 1.3.34R should not be reflected in the valuations under GENPRU 1.3 but should be disclosed to the *FSA* in prudential returns.

Specific requirements: BIPRU firms
Adjustments to accounting values

1.3.36 **[R]**

(1) For the purposes of GENPRU and BIPRU, the adjustments in (2) and (3) apply to values calculated pursuant to GENPRU 1.3.4R in addition to those required by GENPRU 1.3.9R to GENPRU 1.3.10R.

(2) A *BIPRU firm* must not recognise either:

  (a) the fair value reserves related to gains or losses on cash flow hedges of financial instruments measured at amortised cost; or

  (b) any unrealised gains or losses on debt instruments held, or formerly held, in the available-for-sale category.

(3) A *BIPRU investment firm* must deduct any asset in respect of deferred acquisition costs and add back in any liability in respect of deferred income (but exclude from the deduction or addition any asset or liability which will give rise to future cash flows), together with any associated deferred tax.

(4) The items referred to in (2) and (3) must be excluded from *capital resources*.

1.3.37 **[G]** Provisions for equity instruments held in the available-for-sale category can be found in GENPRU 2.2.185R.

Trading book and revaluations

1.3.38 **[R]** GENPRU 1.3.39R to GENPRU 1.3.40R apply only to a *BIPRU firm*.

1.3.39 **[R]** *Trading book* positions are subject to prudent valuation rules as specified in GENPRU 1.3.14R to GENPRU 1.3.34R (Marking to market, Marking to model, Independent price verification, Adjustments or reserves). In accordance with those *rules*, a *firm* must ensure that the value applied to each of its *trading book* positions appropriately reflects the current market value. This value must contain an appropriate degree of certainty having regard to the dynamic nature of *trading book* positions, the demands of prudential soundness and the mode of operation and purpose of capital requirements in respect of *trading book* positions.

1.3.40 **[R]** *Trading book* positions must be re-valued at least daily.

Specific requirements: firms carrying on insurance business
Investments, derivatives and quasi-derivatives

1.3.41 **[R]**

(1) For the purposes of GENPRU and INSPRU, an *insurer* or a *UK ISPV* must apply GENPRU 1.3.14R to GENPRU 1.3.34R (Marking to market, Marking to model, Independent price verification, Adjustments or reserves) to account for:

  (a) investments that are, or amounts owed arising from the disposal of:

    (i) *debt securities*, bonds and other money- and capital-market instruments;

    (ii) loans;

    (iii) *shares* and other variable yield participations;

    (iv) *units* in *UCITS schemes, non-UCITS retail schemes, recognised schemes* and any other *collective investment scheme* falling within paragraph(1)(A)(d)(iv) of GENPRU 2 Annex 7R; and

  (b) *derivatives* and *quasi-derivatives*

(2) In the case of an *insurer*, (1) is subject to GENPRU 1.3.43R.

Shares in and debts due from related undertakings

1.3.42 **[R]** GENPRU 1.3.43R to GENPRU 1.3.57R apply only to *insurers*.

1.3.43 **[R]** GENPRU 1.3.13R and GENPRU 1.3.41R do not apply to *shares* in, and debts due from a *related undertaking* that is:

(1) a *regulated related undertaking;*

(2) an *ancillary services undertaking*; or

(3) any other *subsidiary undertaking*, the *shares* of which a *firm* elects to value in accordance with GENPRU 1.3.47R.

1.3.44 **[G]** The effect of GENPRU 1.3.43R is that *shares* in, and debts due from, *related undertakings* of the types referred to are not valued on a mark to market basis by *insurers*. As a result, debts due from these *undertakings*, and *shares* in *related undertakings* which are *ancillary services undertakings*, are valued at their accounting book value in accordance with GENPRU 1.3.4R. *Shares* in *related undertakings* referred to in GENPRU 1.3.43R(1) or (3) are valued by *insurers* in accordance with GENPRU 1.3.45R to GENPRU 1.3.50R.

1.3.45 **[R]** Except where the contrary is expressly stated in GENPRU, whenever a *rule* in GENPRU or *INSPRU* refers to *shares* held in, and debts due from, an *undertaking* referred to in GENPRU 1.3.43R(1) or GENPRU 1.3.43R(3), a *firm* must value the *shares* held in accordance with GENPRU 1.3.47R.

1.3.46 **[R]** In relation to *shares* in, and debts due from, an *undertaking* referred to in GENPRU 1.3.43R(1), GENPRU 1.3.45R does not apply for the purposes of GENPRU 2.2.256R (Adjustments for regulated related undertakings other than insurance undertakings) and *INSPRU* 6.1 (Group risk: Insurance groups).

1.3.47 **[R]** For the purposes of GENPRU 1.3.45R, the value of the *shares* held in an *undertaking* referred to in GENPRU 1.3.43R(1) or GENPRU 1.3.43R(3) is the sum of:

(1) the *regulatory surplus value* of that *undertaking*; less

(2) for the purposes of GENPRU 2.2.256R (Adjustments for regulated related undertakings other than insurance undertakings), the book value of the total investments in the *tier one capital resources* and *tier two capital resources* of that *undertaking* by the *firm* and its *related undertakings*; or

(3) for other purposes in GENPRU and INSPRU, the sum of:
  (a) the book value of the investments by the *firm* and its *related undertakings* in the *tier two capital resources* of the *undertaking*; and
  (b) if the *undertaking* is an *insurance undertaking*, its ineligible surplus capital and any restricted assets of the *undertaking* which have been excluded under *INSPRU* 6.1.41R(1).

1.3.48 **[R]** For the purposes of GENPRU 1.3.47R(1), the regulatory surplus value of an *undertaking* referred to in GENPRU 1.3.43R(1) or GENPRU 1.3.43R(3) is, subject to GENPRU 1.3.49R, the sum of:

(1) the total capital after deductions of the *undertaking*; less

(2) the *individual capital resources requirement* of the *undertaking*.

1.3.49 **[R]**

(1) Subject to GENPRU 1.3.50R, for the purposes of GENPRU 1.3.48R, only the relevant proportion of the:
  (a) total capital after deductions of the *undertaking*; and
  (b) *individual capital resources requirement* of the *undertaking*;
  is to be taken into account.

(2) In (1), the relevant proportion is the proportion of the total number of *shares* issued by the *undertaking* held, directly or indirectly, by the *firm*.

1.3.50 **[R]** If the *individual capital resources requirement* of an *undertaking* in GENPRU 1.3.43R(1) that is a *subsidiary undertaking* exceeds total capital after deductions, then the full amount of the items referred to in GENPRU 1.3.49R(1) must be taken into account for the purposes of GENPRU 1.3.48R.

1.3.51 **[R]** For the purposes of GENPRU 1.3.47R to GENPRU 1.3.50R:

(1) in relation to an *undertaking* referred to in GENPRU 1.3.43R(1):
  (a) subject to (2), *individual capital resources requirement* has the meaning given by *INSPRU* 6.1.34R;
  (b) total capital after deductions means:
    (i) when used in relation to a *regulated related undertaking* that is subject to the *capital resources table*, the total capital after deductions (as calculated at stage M of the *capital resources table)* of the *undertaking*; and
    (ii) when used in relation to a *regulated related undertaking* that is not subject to the *capital resources table*, the total capital after deductions calculated as if that *undertaking* were required to calculate its total capital after deductions in

Part II FSA Handbook Materials

accordance with stage M of the calculation in the *capital resources table*, but with such adjustments being made to secure that the *undertaking's* calculation of its total capital after deductions complies with the relevant *sectoral rules* applicable to it; and

(c) ineligible surplus capital has the meaning given by *INSPRU* 6.1.67R;

(2) in relation to an *undertaking* referred to in GENPRU 1.3.43R(3),

(a) the *individual capital resources requirement* is zero; and

(b) the total capital after deductions means the total capital after deductions of the *undertaking* calculated as if the *undertaking* were an *insurance holding company* required to calculate its total capital resources in accordance with the *capital resources table* but with such adjustments being made to secure that the *undertaking's* calculation of its total capital after deductions complies with the *sectoral rules* for the *insurance sector.*

1.3.52 **[G]** GENPRU 1.3.47R to GENPRU 1.3.51R set out several different valuation bases for an *insurer's shares* in *related undertakings*. The *regulatory surplus value* (defined in GENPRU 1.3.48R) measures the *related undertaking's* own capital surplus or deficit. This is used: (i) in GENPRU 1.3.47R as a basis for calculating the impact on the firm's position of its investments in *related undertakings*; and (ii) in INSPRU 6.1 as a starting point for the calculation of ineligible surplus capital.

1.3.53 **[G]** GENPRU 1.3.47R determines how, for the purposes of the solo capital adequacy calculation of an *insurer*, that *insurer's capital resources* should be adjusted to take into account its investments in *related undertakings*.

1.3.54 **[G]** The *rules* that specify how, for the purposes of the adjusted solo capital calculation, an *insurer* should incorporate its *related undertakings* into its *capital resources* and *capital resources requirement* are set out in *INSPRU* 6.1.

Insurance Special Purpose Vehicles

1.3.55 **[R]** Except where a *rule* in GENPRU or INSPRU makes a different provision, an *insurer* must not place any value on amounts recoverable from an *ISPV* for the purposes of any *rule* in GENPRU or INSPRU.

1.3.56 **[G]** An *insurer* may value amounts recoverable from an *ISPV* if it obtains a *waiver* of GENPRU 1.3.55R under section 148 of the *Act*. The conditions that will need to be met, in addition to the statutory tests under section 148(4) of the *Act*, before the *FSA* will consider granting such a *waiver* are set out in INSPRU 1.6.13G to INSPRU 1.6.18G.

General insurance business: Community co-insurance operations

1.3.57 **[R]** Where a *relevant insurer* determines the amount of a liability in order to make provision for outstanding *claims* under a *Community co-insurance operation*, then, if the *leading insurer* has informed the *relevant insurer* of the amount of the provision made by the *leading insurer* for such *claims*, the amount determined by the *relevant insurer*:

(1) must be at least as great as the amount of the provision made by the *leading insurer*; or

(2) in a case where it is not the practice in the *United Kingdom* to make such provision separately, must be sufficient, when all liabilities are taken into account, to include provision at least as great as that made by the *leading insurer* for such *claims*,

due regard being had in either case to the proportion of the risk covered by the *relevant insurer* and by the *leading insurer* respectively.

1.4 Actions for damages

1.4.1 **[R]** A contravention of the *rules* in GENPRU does not give rise to a right of action by a *private person* under section 150 of the *Act* (and each of those *rules* is specified under section 150(2) of the *Act* as a provision giving rise to no such right of action).

1.5 Application of GENPRU 1 to Lloyd's

Application of GENPRU 1.2

1.5.1 **[R]** GENPRU 1.2 applies to *managing agents* and to the *Society* in accordance with:

(1) for *managing agents*, INSPRU 8.1.4R; and

(2) for the *Society*, INSPRU 8.1.2R.

1.5.2 **[R]** GENPRU 1.5.7R applies to *members*, pursuant to the *insurance market direction* in GENPRU 1.5.5D.

Insurance market direction

1.5.3 **[G]** The *insurance market direction* in GENPRU 1.5.5D is given under section 316(1) of the *Act* (Direction by Authority) and applies to *members*.

1.5.4 **[G]** The purpose of the *insurance market direction* in GENPRU 1.5.5D is to enable the *FSA* to make the rule in GENPRU 1.5.7R applying to *members*, in order to:

(1) protect *policyholders* against the risk that *members* may not have adequate financial resources to meet liabilities under or in respect of *contracts of insurance* as they fall due;

(2) promote confidence in the market at Lloyd's by requiring *members* to maintain financial resources which are adequate to meet their liabilities.

1.5.5 **[D]** With effect from 1 January 2005, Part X of the *Act* (Rules and Guidance) applies to the *members* of the *Society* taken together in relation to the *insurance market activities* of *effecting* and *carrying out contracts* of insurance written at Lloyd's, for the purpose of applying the *rules* and *guidance* in GENPRU 1.5.7R to GENPRU 1.5.9G.

1.5.6 **[G]** Part X of the *Act* is a *core provision* specified in section 317(1) of the *Act* (The core provisions). Section 317(2) provides that references in an applied *core provision* to an *authorised person* are to be read as references to a *person* in the class to which the *insurance market direction* applies. From 1 January 2005, references in Part X of the *Act* are to be read as references to *members* for the purposes of GENPRU 1.5.7R to GENPRU 1.5.9G.

Members' obligation to maintain adequate financial resources

1.5.7 **[R]** The *members* taken together must at all times maintain overall financial resources, including capital and liquidity resources, that are adequate, both as to amount and quality, to ensure that there is no significant risk that liabilities under or in respect of *contracts of insurance* written at Lloyd's will not be met as they fall due.

1.5.8 **[G]** Under GENPRU:

(1) *managing agents* must ensure that adequate financial resources are available to support the *insurance business* carried on through each *syndicate* that they manage; and

(2) the *Society* must, having regard to the availability and value of the *central assets*, ensure that the financial resources supporting the *insurance business* of each *member* are adequate at all times.

1.5.9 **[G]** In practice, compliance with the requirements described in GENPRU 1.5.8G is likely to have the effect that *members* comply with GENPRU 1.5.7R.

Application of GENPRU 1.3

1.5.10 **[R]** GENPRU 1.3 applies to *managing agents* and to the *Society* in accordance with:

(1) for *managing agents*, INSPRU 8.1.4R; and

(2) for the *Society*, INSPRU 8.1.2R.

Amounts receivable but not yet received

1.5.11 **[R]** When recognising and valuing assets that are available to meet liabilities arising from a *member's insurance business*, neither the *Society* nor *managing agents* may attribute any value to any amounts receivable but not yet received from that *member* or another *member*, except for:

(1) timing differences provided that a corresponding amount has been deducted from *syndicate assets* or *funds at Lloyd's*;

(2) the *Society's callable contributions*, which are valued according to GENPRU 1.5.17R to GENPRU 1.5.18R; and

(3) debts owed by a *member* to another *member* of the *Society* where the debt is a liability arising out of the *insurance business* he carries on at Lloyd's.

Letters of credit, guarantees and life assurance policies

1.5.12 **[R]** When recognising and valuing assets held as *members' funds at Lloyd's* the *Society* may, if the conditions in GENPRU 1.5.13R are satisfied, attribute a value to letters of credit and guarantees that it holds in respect of a *member*'s *insurance business*.

1.5.13 **[R]** The conditions referred to in GENPRU 1.5.12R are that letters of credit and guarantees must be:

(1) in the form prescribed by the *Society* from time to time and notified to the *FSA*; and

(2) issued by a *credit institution* or an *insurance undertaking*.

1.5.14 **[R]** When recognising and valuing assets held as *members' funds at Lloyd's* the *Society* may attribute a value to verifiable sums arising out of life assurance policies.

1.5.15 **[R]** The *Society* must value any letter of credit, guarantee or life assurance policy at its net realisable value. The *Society* must make all appropriate deductions, including those in respect of:

(1) the expenses of realisation; and

(2) any reduction in value that would be likely to occur if the asset needed to be realised at short notice to meet liabilities falling due earlier than expected.

1.5.16 **[R]** If a *member* relies on a value attributed to a letter of credit or guarantee to meet any applicable *capital resources requirement* and that letter of credit or guarantee will expire in less than one month, the *Society* must take appropriate steps to ensure that the applicable *capital resources requirement* will continue to be met, including taking steps to ensure that sums due under the letter of credit or guarantee are drawn down when due and carried to the appropriate *Lloyd's trust fund*.

The Society's callable contributions

1.5.17 **[R]** For the purposes of GENPRU 1.5.15R(2), the amount assumed to be callable from a *member* must not exceed the lower of:

(1) the maximum *callable contribution* that *member* is or may be liable to make in that *financial year*; and

(2) the amount by which the *member*'s own *capital resources* exceed the *member*'s own *capital resources requirement*.

1.5.18 **[R]** The *Society* must value *callable contributions* taking appropriate account of any legal, constructive or other limits on its ability to call for contributions from *members* or to realise the amount called.

1.5.19 **[R]** The *Society* must give the *FSA* adequate advance notice if it proposes to change the maximum amount of the *callable contribution* that *members* may be liable to make in any *financial year*.

1.5.20 **[G]** The *FSA* would normally expect not less than six months' notice under GENPRU 1.5.19R.

Liabilities

1.5.21 **[R]** Subject to GENPRU 1.5.22R, the *Society* must recognise and value all of a *member*'s liabilities in respect of its *insurance business*.

1.5.22 **[R]** The *Society* need not recognise or value a *member*'s liabilities that are recognised and valued at *syndicate* level by *managing agents* in accordance with GENPRU 1.3.

1.5.23 **[R]** For the purposes of calculating a *member*'s *capital resources*, when valuing a *member*'s *funds at Lloyd's* the *Society* must deduct the value of a *member*'s liabilities determined under GENPRU 1.5.21R.

1.5.24 **[G]** The liabilities to be valued under GENPRU 1.5.21R and deducted under GENPRU 1.5.23R include:

(1) amounts owing to *members' agents*;

(2) amounts owing to the *Society*;

(3) an appropriate accrual for tax payable on any profits;

(4) (where required under any applicable accounting principle in accordance with GENPRU 1.3.4R), any contingent liability relating to liabilities reinsured into Equitas Reinsurance Ltd; and

(5) amounts apportioned to *members* in respect of the *credit equalisation provision* under INSPRU 1.4.

1.5.25 **[R]** In recognising and valuing a *member*'s liabilities, the *Society* and *managing agents* may, to the extent permitted by applicable accounting principles, leave out of account the liabilities in respect of 1992 and prior *general insurance business* reinsured by Equitas Reinsurance Limited.

1.5.26 **[G]** There may be contingent liabilities associated with the reinsurance into Equitas. GENPRU 1.3 requires *managing agents* and the *Society* to treat those contingent liabilities in accordance with applicable accounting principles: see GENPRU 1.3.4R. Depending on the circumstances, *managing agents* or the *Society* may need to disclose or account for such a liability.

CHAPTER 2

2.1 Calculation of capital resources requirements

Application

[2056]

2.1.1 **[R]** This section applies to:

(1) a *BIPRU firm*; and

(2) an *insurer*, unless it is:

  (a) a *non-directive friendly society*; or

  (b) a *Swiss general insurer*; or

  (c) an *EEA-deposit insurer*; or

  (d) an *incoming EEA firm*; or

  (e) an *incoming Treaty firm*.

2.1.2 **[G]** The scope of application of this section is not restricted to *firms* that are subject to the relevant *EU* Directives.

2.1.3 **[R]**

(1) This section applies to a *firm* in relation to the whole of its business, except where a particular provision provides for a narrower scope.

(2) Where an *insurer* carries on both *long-term insurance business* and *general insurance business*, except where a particular provision provides otherwise, this section applies separately to each type of business.

2.1.4 **[G]** The adequacy of a *firm's capital resources* needs to be assessed in relation to all the activities of the *firm* and the risks to which they give rise.

2.1.5 **[G]** The requirements in this section apply to a *firm* on a solo basis.

Purpose

2.1.6 **[G]** *Principle* 4 requires a *firm* to maintain adequate financial resources. GENPRU 2 sets out provisions that deal specifically with the adequacy of that part of a *firm's* financial resources that consists of *capital resources*. The adequacy of a *firm's capital resources* needs to be assessed both by that *firm* and the *FSA*. Through its *rules*, the *FSA* sets minimum *capital resources requirements* for *firms*. It also reviews a *firm's* own assessment of its capital needs, and the processes and systems by which that assessment is made, in order to see if the minimum *capital resources requirements* are appropriate (see GENPRU 1.2 (Adequacy of financial resources), BIPRU 2.2 (Internal capital adequacy standards) and INSPRU 7.1 (Individual capital assessment)).

2.1.7 **[G]** This section sets *capital resources requirements* for a *firm*. GENPRU 2.2 (Capital resources) sets out how, for the purpose of meeting *capital resources requirements*, the amounts or values of capital, assets and liabilities are to be determined. More detailed *rules* relating to capital, assets and liabilities are set out in GENPRU 1.3 (Valuation) and, for an *insurer*, *INSPRU* and, for a *BIPRU firm*, BIPRU.

2.1.8 **[G]**

(1) This section implements minimum EC standards for the *capital resources* required to be held by an *insurer* undertaking business that falls within the scope of the *Consolidated Life Directive* (2002/83/EC), the *Reinsurance Directive* (2005/68/EC) or the *First Non-Life Directive* (1973/239/EEC) as amended.

(2) This section also implements provisions of the *Capital Adequacy Directive* and *Banking Consolidation Directive* concerning the level of *capital resources* which a *BIPRU firm* is required to hold. In particular it implements (in part) Articles 9, 10 and 75 of the *Banking Consolidation Directive* and Articles 5, 9, 10 and 18 of the *Capital Adequacy Directive*.

(3) In the case of a *UCITS investment firm* this section implements (in part) Article 5a of the *UCITS Directive*.

Monitoring requirements

2.1.9 **[R]** A *firm* must at all times monitor whether it is complying with GENPRU 2.1.13R (the main capital adequacy *rule* for *insurers*) or the *main BIPRU firm Pillar 1 rules* and be able to demonstrate that it knows at all times whether it is complying with those *rules*.

2.1.10 **[G]** For the purposes of GENPRU 2.1.9R, a *firm* should have systems in place to enable it to be certain whether it has adequate *capital resources* to comply with GENPRU 2.1.13R and the *main BIPRU firm Pillar 1 rules* (as applicable) at all times. This does not necessarily mean that a *firm* needs to measure the precise amount of its *capital resources* and its *CRR* on a daily basis. A *firm* should, however, be able to demonstrate the adequacy of its *capital resources* at any particular time if asked to do so by the *FSA*.

2.1.11 **[R]** A *firm* must notify the *FSA* immediately of any breach, or expected breach, of GENPRU 2.1.13R (in the case of an *insurer*) or the *main BIPRU firm Pillar 1 rules* (in the case of a *BIPRU firm*).

Additional capital requirements

2.1.12 **[G]** The *FSA* may impose a higher capital requirement than the minimum requirement set out in this section as part of the *firm's Part IV permission* (see GENPRU 1.2 (Adequacy of financial resources), BIPRU 2.2 (Internal capital adequacy standards) and INSPRU 7.1 (Individual capital assessment)).

Main requirement: Insurers

2.1.13 **[R]**

(1) Subject to (2), an *insurer* must maintain at all times *capital resources* equal to or in excess of its *capital resources requirement* (*CRR*).

(2) An *insurer* which is a *participating insurance undertaking* and, in relation to its own *group capital resources*, is in compliance with *INSPRU* 6.1.9R (Requirement to maintain group capital), is deemed to comply with this *rule*.

Part II FSA Handbook Materials

2.1.14 **[R]** An *insurer* must comply with GENPRU 2.1.13R separately in respect of both its *long-term insurance business* and its *general insurance business* unless it is a *pure reinsurer* or a *captive reinsurer* which has a single *MCR* in respect of its entire business in accordance with GENPRU 2.1.26R.

2.1.15 **[G]** In order to comply with GENPRU 2.1.14R, an *insurer* carrying on both *general insurance business* and *long-term insurance business* will need to allocate its *capital resources* between its *general insurance business* and *long-term insurance business* so that the *capital resources* allocated to its *general insurance business* are equal to or in excess of its *CRR* for its *general insurance business* and the *capital resources* allocated to its *long-term insurance business* are equal to or in excess of its *CRR* for its *long-term insurance business*. Whereas *long-term insurance assets* cannot be used towards meeting a *firm's CRR* for its *general insurance business*, surplus general insurance assets may be used towards meeting the *CRR* for its *long-term insurance business* (see INSPRU 1.5.30R to INSPRU 1.5.32G). INSPRU 1.5 (Internal-contagion risk) sets out the detailed requirements for the separation of *long-term* and *general insurance business*.

2.1.16 **[G]** *Insurers* commonly use different terminology for the various GENPRU requirements. For example, the *MCR* is traditionally known as the required minimum margin.

Calculation of the CRR for an insurer

2.1.17 **[R]** The *CRR* for any *insurer* carrying on *general insurance business* is equal to the *MCR* in GENPRU 2.1.24R or, for a *pure reinsurer* or a *captive reinsurer* carrying on both *general insurance business* and *long-term insurance business*, in GENPRU 2.1.26R.

2.1.18 **[R]** The *CRR* for any *insurer* to which this *rule* applies (see GENPRU 2.1.19R and GENPRU 2.1.20R) is the higher of:
(1) the *MCR* in GENPRU 2.1.24AR; and
(2) the *ECR* in GENPRU 2.1.38R.

2.1.19 **[R]** Subject to GENPRU 2.1.20R, GENPRU 2.1.18R applies to an *insurer* carrying on *long-term insurance business*, other than:
(1) a *non-directive mutual*;
(2) an *insurer* which has no *with-profits insurance liabilities*; and
(3) an *insurer* which has *with-profits insurance liabilities* that are, and at all times since 31 December 2004 (the coming into force of GENPRU 2.1.18R) have remained, less than £500 million.

2.1.20 **[R]** GENPRU 2.1.18R also applies to an *insurer* of a type listed in GENPRU 2.1.19R(3) if:
(1) the *insurer* makes an election that GENPRU 2.1.18R is to apply to it; and
(2) that election is made by written notice given to the *FSA* in a way that complies with the requirements for written notice in SUP 15.7 (Form and method of notification).

2.1.21 **[G]** The effect of GENPRU 2.1.19R(3) is that an *insurer* to which GENPRU 2.1.18R applies because it has *with-profits insurance liabilities* of £500 million or more, will continue to be subject to GENPRU 2.1.18R even if its *with-profits insurance liabilities* fall below £500 million. However, if that happens, it may apply for a *waiver* from GENPRU 2.1.18R under section 148 of the *Act*. In exercising its discretion under section 148 of the *Act*, the *FSA* will have regard (among other factors) to whether there has been a material and permanent change to the *insurer's* business and to the prospects of it continuing to have *with-profits insurance liabilities* of less than £500 million.

2.1.22 **[G]** An *insurer* that has always had *with-profits insurance liabilities* of less than £500 million since GENPRU 2.1.18R came into force may wish to "opt in" to GENPRU 2.1.18R and therefore become a *realistic basis life firm*. By doing so, it becomes obliged to calculate a *with-profits insurance capital component* (see GENPRU 2.1.38R and INSPRU 1.3 (With-profits insurance capital component)), but it also becomes entitled to certain modifications to the way that a *firm* is required to calculate its *mathematical reserves* (see INSPRU 1.2.46R (Future net premiums: adjustment for deferred acquisition costs) and INSPRU 1.2.76R (Persistency assumptions)). The *firm* is also then required to report its liabilities on a realistic basis (see IPRU(INS) rule 9.31R(b)). In order to "opt in", the *insurer* must make an election under GENPRU 2.1.20R that GENPRU 2.1.18R is to apply to it. If an *insurer* that has elected to calculate and report its *with-profits insurance liabilities* on a realistic basis subsequently decides that it no longer wishes to do so, it may seek to "opt out" by applying for a *waiver* from GENPRU 2.1.18R under section 148 of the *Act*. In exercising its discretion under section 148 of the *Act*, the *FSA* will have regard (among other factors) to whether there has been a material and permanent change to the *firm's* business and to whether it continues to have *with-profits insurance liabilities* of less than £500 million.

2.1.23 **[R]** The *CRR* for an *insurer* carrying on *long-term insurance business*, but to which GENPRU 2.1.18R does not apply, is equal to the *MCR* in GENPRU 2.1.25R or, for a *pure reinsurer* or a *captive reinsurer* carrying on both *general insurance business* and *long-term insurance business*, in GENPRU 2.1.26R.

Calculation of the MCR (Insurer only)

2.1.24 **[R]** Subject to GENPRU 2.1.26R, for an *insurer* carrying on *general insurance business* the *MCR* in respect of that business is the higher of:

(1) the *base capital resources requirement* for *general insurance business* applicable to that *firm*; and

(2) the *general insurance capital requirement.*

2.1.24A **[R]** Subject to GENPRU 2.1.26R, for an *insurer* carrying on *long-term insurance business* to which GENPRU 2.1.18R applies the *MCR* in respect of that business is the higher of:

(1) the *base capital resources requirement* for *long-term insurance business* applicable to that *firm*; and

(2) the *long-term insurance capital requirement.*

2.1.25 **[R]** Subject to GENPRU 2.1.26R, for an *insurer* carrying on *long-term insurance business*, but to which GENPRU 2.1.18R does not apply, the *MCR* in respect of that business is the higher of:

(1) the *base capital resources requirement* for *long-term insurance business* applicable to that *firm*; and

(2) the sum of:

(a) the *long-term insurance capital requirement*; and

(b) the *resilience capital requirement.*

2.1.26 **[R]** For a *pure reinsurer* or a *captive reinsurer* carrying on both *general insurance business* and *long-term insurance business*:

(1) the *MCR* in respect of its *general insurance business* is the *general insurance capital requirement*; and

(2) the *MCR* in respect of its *long-term insurance business* is the sum of:

(a) the *long-term insurance capital requirement*; and

(b) the *resilience capital requirement*;

unless the sum of:

(3) the *general insurance capital requirement*; and

(4) the sum of:

(a) the *long-term insurance capital requirement*; and

(b) the *resilience capital requirement*;

is lower than the *base capital resources requirement*, in which case the *firm* has a single *MCR* in respect of its entire business equal to the *base capital resources requirement.*

2.1.27 **[G]** The *MCR* gives effect to the *EU* Directive minimum requirements. For *general insurance business*, the *EU* Directive minimum is the higher of the *general insurance capital requirement* and the relevant *base capital resources requirement*. For *long-term insurance business*, the *EU* Directive minimum is the higher of the *long-term insurance capital requirement* and the *base capital resources requirement*. For *pure reinsurers* and *captive reinsurers* carrying on both *general insurance business* and *long-term insurance business*, however, the *base capital resources requirement* is the *EU* Directive required minimum only when it is higher than the sum of the *general insurance capital requirement* and the *long-term insurance capital requirement*. The *base capital resources requirement* is the minimum guarantee fund for the purposes of article 29(2) of the *Consolidated Life Directive* (2002/83/EC), article 17(2) of the *First Non-Life Directive* (1973/239/EEC) as amended and article 40(2) of the *Reinsurance Directive* (2005/68/EC). The *resilience capital requirement* is an *FSA* minimum requirement for *long-term insurance business* for *regulatory basis only life firms* that is additional to the *EU* minimum requirement for *long-term insurance business.*

2.1.28 **[G]** The calculation of the *resilience capital requirement* is set out in INSPRU 3.1 (Market Risk in insurance).

Calculation of the base capital resources requirement for an insurer

2.1.29 **[R]** The amount of an *insurer's base capital resources requirement* is set out in the table in GENPRU 2.1.30R. If an *insurer* falls within one or more of the descriptions of type of *firm* set out in GENPRU 2.1.30R, its *base capital resources requirement* is the highest amount set out against the different types of *firm* within whose description it falls.

2.1.30 **[R]** Table: Base capital resources requirement for an insurer

This table belongs to GENPRU 2.1.29R

***Firm* category**		**Amount: Currency equivalent of**
General insurance business		
Liability *insurer* (*classes* 10–15)	Directive *mutual*	€2.625 million
	Non-directive insurer	€350,000

Firm category		Amount: Currency equivalent of
	Other (including *mixed insurer* but excluding *pure reinsurer*)	€3.5 million
Other *insurer*	Directive *mutual*	€1.725 million
	Non-directive insurer (*classes* 1 to 8, 16 or 18)	€260,000
	Non-directive insurer (*classes* 9 or 17)	€175,000
	Mixed insurer	€3.5 million
	Other (excluding *pure reinsurer* and)	€2.3 million
Long-term insurance business		
Mutual	Directive	€2.625 million
	Non-directive mutual	€700,000
Any other *insurer* (including *mixed insurer* but excluding *pure reinsurer*)		€3.5 million
All business (*general insurance business* and *long-term insurance business*)		
Pure reinsurer excluding *captive reinsurer*		€3.5 million
Captive reinsurer		€1.1 million

2.1.31 **[G]**
(1) Under the *Insurance Directives* the amount of the *base capital resources requirement* specified in the last column of the table in GENPRU 2.1.30R for an *insurer* which is not a *non-directive insurer* is subject to annual review. The relevant amounts will be increased by the percentage change in the European index of consumer prices (comprising all EU member states, as published by Eurostat) from 20 March 2002, to the relevant review date, rounded up to a multiple of €100,000, provided that where the percentage change since the last increase is less than 5%, no increase will take place.
(2) Similar provisions for the index-linking of the *base capital resources requirement* are included in the *Reinsurance Directive*, although in that case the index-linking starts from 10 December 2005. However, to ensure consistency as between all *firms* affected by the index-linking of the *base capital resources requirement* under the *Insurance Directives* and the *Reinsurance Directive*, the *FSA* intends, so far as possible, to amend the amounts in GENPRU 2.1.30R for all such *firms* (and GENPRU 2.3.9R for the *base capital resources requirements* applying to Lloyd's) when an index-linked increase is required by the *Insurance Directives*. The *FSA* may, however, have to depart from this approach where the result would be that the *base capital resources requirement* required for any type of *firm* under GENPRU 2.1.30R is less than the increased amount resulting from the operation of an index-linking provision to which it is subject.

2.1.32 **[G]** Any increases in the *base capital resources requirement* referred to in GENPRU 2.1.31G will be published on the *FSA* website.

2.1.33 **[R]** In the case of an *insurer* and for the purposes of the *base capital resources requirement*, the exchange rate from the Euro to the pound sterling for each year beginning on 31 December is the rate applicable on the last day of the preceding October for which the exchange rates for the currencies of all the European Union member states were published in the Official Journal of the European Union.

Calculation of the general insurance capital requirement (Insurer only)

2.1.34 **[R]** An *insurer* must calculate its *general insurance capital requirement* as the highest of:
(1) the *premiums amount*;
(2) the *claims amount*; and
(3) the *brought forward amount*.

2.1.35 **[G]** The calculation of each of the *premiums amount*, *claims amount* and *brought forward amount* is set out in INSPRU 1.1 (Capital resources requirement and technical provisions for insurance business).

Calculation of the long-term insurance capital requirement (Insurer only)

2.1.36 **[R]** An *insurer* must calculate its *long-term insurance capital requirement* as the sum of:
(1) the *insurance death risk capital component*;

(2) the *insurance health risk and life protection reinsurance capital component;*
(3) the *insurance expense risk capital component*; and
(4) the *insurance market risk capital component.*

2.1.37 **[G]** The calculation of each of the capital components is set out in INSPRU 1.1 (Capital resources requirement and technical provisions for insurance business).

Calculation of the ECR (Insurer only)

2.1.38 **[R]** For an *insurer* carrying on *long-term insurance business* the *ECR* in respect of that business is the sum of:
(1) the *long-term insurance capital requirement*; and
(2) the *with-profits insurance capital component.*

2.1.39 **[G]** Details of the *resilience capital requirement* and the *with-profits insurance capital component* are set out in INSPRU 3.1 (Market Risk in insurance) and INSPRU 1.3 (With-profits insurance capital component) respectively.

Main requirement: BIPRU firms

2.1.40 **[R]** A *BIPRU firm* must maintain at all times *capital resources* equal to or in excess of the amount specified in the table in GENPRU 2.1.45R (Calculation of the variable capital requirement for a BIPRU firm).

2.1.41 **[R]** A *BIPRU firm* must maintain at all times *capital resources* equal to or in excess of the *base capital resources requirement* (see the table in GENPRU 2.1.48R).

2.1.42 **[R]** At the time that it first becomes a *bank, building society* or *BIPRU investment firm*, a *firm* must hold *initial capital* of not less than the *base capital resources requirement* applicable to that *firm.*

2.1.43 **[G]** The purpose of the *base capital resources requirement* for a *BIPRU firm* is to act as a minimum capital requirement or floor. It has been written as a separate requirement as there are restrictions in GENPRU 2.2 (Capital resources) on the types of capital that a *BIPRU firm* may use to meet the *base capital resources requirement* which do not apply to some other parts of the capital requirement calculation. In order to preserve the *base capital resources requirement's* role as a floor rather than an additional requirement, GENPRU 2.2.60R allows a *BIPRU firm* to meet the *base capital resources requirement* with capital that is also used to meet the variable capital requirements in GENPRU 2.1.40R.

2.1.44 **[G]** The *base capital resources requirement* and the variable capital requirement in GENPRU 2.1.40R are together called the *capital resources requirement* (*CRR*) in the case of a *BIPRU firm.*

Calculation of the variable capital requirement for a BIPRU firm

2.1.45 **[R]** Table: Calculation of the variable capital requirement for a BIPRU firm This table belongs to GENPRU 2.1.40R

Firm category	Capital requirement		
Bank, building society or *full scope BIPRU investment firm*	the sum of the following:		
	(1)	the *credit risk capital requirement*;	
	(2)	the *market risk capital requirement*; and	
	(3)	the *operational risk capital requirement.*	
BIPRU limited activity firm	the sum of the following:		
	(1)	the *credit risk capital requirement*;	
	(2)	the *market risk capital requirement*; and	
	(3)	the *fixed overheads requirement.*	
BIPRU limited licence firm (including *UCITS investment firm*)	the higher of (1) and (2):		
	(1)	the sum of:	
		(a)	the *credit risk capital requirement*; and
		(b)	the *market risk capital requirement*; and
	(2)	the *fixed overheads requirement.*	

Adjustment of the variable capital requirement calculation for UCITS investment firms

2.1.46 **[R]** When a *UCITS investment firm* calculates the *credit risk capital requirement* and the *market risk capital requirement* for the purpose of calculating the variable capital requirement under

GENPRU 2.1.40R, it must do so only in respect of *designated investment business*. For this purpose *scheme management activity* is excluded from *designated investment business*.

Calculation of the base capital resources requirement for a BIPRU firm

2.1.47 **[R]** The amount of a *BIPRU firm's base capital resources requirement* is set out in the table in GENPRU 2.1.48R.

2.1.48 **[R]** Table: Base capital resources requirement for a BIPRU firm This table belongs to GENPRU 2.1.47R

Firm category	Amount: Currency equivalent of
Bank	€5 million
Building society	The higher of €1 million and £1 million
BIPRU 730K firm	€730,000
BIPRU 125K firm	€125,000
BIPRU 50K firm	€50,000
UCITS investment firm	€125,000 plus, if the *funds under management* exceed €250,000,000, 0.02% of the excess, subject to a maximum of €10,000,000.

Definition of BIPRU 730K firm, BIPRU 125K firm and BIPRU 50K firm

2.1.49 **[G]** The terms *BIPRU 730K firm*, *BIPRU 125K firm* and *BIPRU 50K firm* are defined in BIPRU 1.1 (Application and purpose). However for convenience the table in GENPRU 2.1.50G briefly summarises them.

2.1.50 **[G]** Table: Definition of BIPRU 730K firm, BIPRU 125K firm and BIPRU 50K firm This table belongs to GENPRU 2.1.49G

Category of BIPRU investment firm	Definition		
BIPRU 50K firm	(1)	it does not deal in any *financial instruments* for its own account or underwrite issues of *financial instruments* on a firm commitment basis;	
	(2)	it offers one or more of the following services:	
		(a)	reception and transmission of investors' orders for *financial instruments*; or
		(b)	the execution of investors' orders for *financial instruments*; or
		(c)	the management of individual portfolios of investments in *financial instruments*; and
	(3)	it does not hold clients' money and/or securities and it is not authorised to do so (it should have a *limitation* or *requirement* prohibiting the holding of client money and its *permission* should not include *safeguarding and administering investments*).	
BIPRU 125K firm	(1)	it does not deal in any *financial instruments* for its own account or underwrite issues of *financial instruments* on a firm commitment basis;	
	(2)	it offers one or more of the following services:	
		(a)	reception and transmission of investors' orders for *financial instruments*; or
		(b)	the execution of investors' orders for *financial instruments*; or
		(c)	the management of individual portfolios of investments in *financial instruments*; and
	(3)	it holds clients' money and/or securities or it is authorised to do so.	
BIPRU 730K firm	is subject to the *Capital Adequacy Directive* and is neither a *BIPRU 50K firm* nor a *BIPRU 125K firm*.		

Calculation of the credit risk capital requirement (BIPRU firm only)

2.1.51 **[R]** A *BIPRU firm* must calculate its *credit risk capital requirement* as the sum of:
(1) the *credit risk capital component*;
(2) the *counterparty risk capital component*; and
(3) the *concentration risk capital component.*

Calculation of the market risk capital requirement (BIPRU firm only)

2.1.52 **[R]**
(1) A *BIPRU firm* must calculate its *market risk capital requirement* as the sum of:
 (a) the *interest rate PRR* (including the basic *interest rate PRR* for equity derivatives set out in *BIPRU* 7.3 (Equity PRR and basic interest rate PRR for equity derivatives));
 (b) the *equity PRR*;
 (c) the *commodity PRR*;
 (d) the *foreign currency PRR*;
 (e) the *option PRR*; and
 (f) the *collective investment undertaking PRR.*
(2) Any amount calculated under BIPRU 7.1.9R–BIPRU 7.1.13R (Instruments for which no PRR treatment has been specified) must be allocated between the *PRR* charges in (1) in the most appropriate manner.

Calculation of the fixed overheads requirement (BIPRU investment firm only)

2.1.53 **[R]** In relation to a *BIPRU investment firm* which is required to calculate a *fixed overheads requirement*, the amount of that requirement is equal to one quarter of the *firm's* relevant fixed expenditure calculated in accordance with GENPRU 2.1.54R.

2.1.54 **[R]** For the purpose of GENPRU 2.1.53R, and subject to GENPRU 2.1.55R to GENPRU 2.1.57R, a *BIPRU investment firm's* relevant fixed expenditure is the amount described as total expenditure in its most recent audited *annual report and accounts*, less the following items (if they are included within such expenditure):
(1) staff bonuses, except to the extent that they are guaranteed;
(2) employees' and directors' shares in profits, except to the extent that they are guaranteed;
(3) other appropriations of profits;
(4) shared commission and fees payable which are directly related to commission and fees receivable, which are included within total revenue;
(5) interest charges in respect of borrowings made to finance the acquisition of the *firm's readily realisable investments*;
(6) interest paid to customers on *client money*;
(7) interest paid to counterparties;
(8) fees, brokerage and other charges paid to *clearing houses*, exchanges and *intermediate brokers* for the purposes of *executing*, registering or clearing transactions;
(9) foreign exchange losses; and
(10) other variable expenditure.

2.1.55 **[R]** The relevant fixed expenditure of a *firm* in the following circumstances is:
(1) where its most recent audited *annual report and accounts* do not represent a twelve month period, an amount calculated in accordance with GENPRU 2.1.54R, pro-rated so as to produce an equivalent annual amount; and
(2) where it has not completed twelve months' trading, an amount based on forecast expenditure included in the budget for the first twelve months' trading, as submitted with its application for *authorisation*.

2.1.56 **[R]** A *firm* must adjust its relevant fixed expenditure calculation so far as necessary if and to the extent that since the date covered by the most recent audited *annual report and accounts* or (if GENPRU 2.1.55R(2) applies) since the budget was prepared:
(1) its level of fixed expenditure changes materially; or
(2) its *regulated activities* comprised within its *permission* change.

2.1.57 **[R]** If a *firm* has a material proportion of its expenditure incurred on its behalf by third parties and such expenditure is not fully recharged to that *firm* then the *firm* must adjust its relevant fixed expenditure calculation by adding back in the whole of the difference between the amount of the expenditure and the amount recharged.

2.1.58 **[G]** For the purpose of GENPRU 2.1.57R, the *FSA* would consider as material 10% of a *firm's* expenditure incurred on its behalf by third parties.

2.1.59 **[G]** For the purpose of GENPRU 2.1.54R to 2.1.57R, fixed expenditure is expenditure which is inelastic relative to fluctuations in a *firm's* levels of business. Fixed expenditure is likely to include most salaries and staff costs, office rent, payment for the rent or lease of office equipment, and insurance *premiums*. It may be viewed as the amount of funds which a *firm* would require to enable it to cease business in an orderly manner, should the need arise. This is not an exhaustive list of such expenditure and a *firm* will itself need to identify (taking appropriate advice where necessary) which costs amount to fixed expenditure.

Calculation of base capital resources requirement for banks authorised before 1993

2.1.60 **[R]**
(1) This *rule* applies to a *bank* that meets the following conditions:
    (a) on 31 December 2006 it had the benefit of IPRU(BANK) *rule* 3.3.12 (Reduced minimum capital requirement for a *bank* that is a *credit institution* which immediately before 1 January 1993 was authorised under the Banking Act 1987);
    (b) the relevant amount (as referred to in IPRU(BANK) *rule* 3.3.12) applicable to it was below €5 million as at 31 December 2006; and
    (c) on 1 January 2007 it did not comply with the *base capital resources requirement* as set out in the table in GENPRU 2.1.48R (€5 million requirement).
(2) Subject to (3), the applicable *base capital resources requirement* as at any time (the "relevant time") is the higher of:
    (a) the relevant amount applicable to it under IPRU(BANK) *rule* 3.3.12 as at 31 December 2006 as adjusted under GENPRU 2.1.62R(2); and
    (b) the highest amount of eligible *capital resources* which that *bank* has held between 1 January 2007 and the relevant time.
(3) This *rule* ceases to apply when:
    (a) that *bank's* eligible *capital resources* at any time since 1 January 2007 equal or exceed €5 million; or
    (b) a *person* (other than an existing controller) becomes the *parent undertaking* of that *bank*.
(4) If this *rule* ceases to apply under (3)(a) it continues not to apply if the *bank's* eligible *capital resources* later fall below €5 million.

2.1.61 **[G]** Where two or more *banks* merge, all of which individually have the benefit of GENPRU 2.1.60R, the *FSA* may agree in certain circumstances that the *base capital resources requirement* for the *bank* resulting from the merger may be the sum of the aggregate *capital resources* of the merged *banks*, calculated at the time of the merger, provided this figure is less than €5 million.

2.1.62 **[R]** For the purpose of GENPRU 2.1.60R:
(1) an existing controller of a *bank* means:
    (a) a *person* who has been a *parent undertaking* of that *bank* since 31 December 2006 or earlier; or
    (b) a *person* who became a *parent undertaking* of that *bank* after 31 December 2006 but who, when he became a *parent undertaking* of that *bank*, was a *subsidiary undertaking* of an existing controller of that *bank*;
(2) the relevant amount of capital as referred to in GENPRU 2.1.60R(2)(a) is adjusted by identifying the time as of which the amount of capital it was obliged to hold under *IPRU(BANK) rule* 3.3.12 as referred to in GENPRU 2.1.60R(2)(a) was fixed and then recalculating the capital resources it held at that time in accordance with the definition of eligible *capital resources* (as defined in (3)); and
(3) eligible *capital resources* mean *capital resources* eligible under GENPRU 2.2 (Capital resources) to be used to meet the *base capital resources requirement*.

2.2 Capital resources

Application

2.2.1 **[R]** This section applies to:
(1) a *BIPRU firm*; and
(2) an *insurer* unless it is:
    (a) a *non-directive friendly society*; or
    (b) a *Swiss general insurer*; or
    (c) an *EEA-deposit insurer*; or
    (d) an *incoming EEA firm*; or
    (e) an *incoming Treaty firm*.

Purpose

2.2.2 **[G]** GENPRU 2.1 (Calculation of capital resources requirement) sets out minimum *capital resources requirements* for a *firm*. This section (GENPRU 2.2) sets out how, for the purpose of these requirements, *capital resources* are defined and measured.

2.2.3 **[G]** This section implements minimum EC standards for the composition of *capital resources* required to be held by an *insurer* undertaking business that falls within the scope of the *Consolidated Life Directive* (2002/83/EC), the *First Non-Life Directive* (1973/239/EEC) as amended or the *Reinsurance Directive* (2005/68/EC).

2.2.4 **[G]** This section also implements minimum EC standards for the composition of *capital resources* required to be held by a *BIPRU firm*. In particular it implements Articles 56–61, Articles 63–64, Article 66 and Articles 120–122 of the *Banking Consolidation Directive* (2006/48/EC) and Articles 12–16, Article 17 (in part), Article 22(1)(c) (in part) and paragraphs 13–15 of Part B of Annex VII of the *Capital Adequacy Directive* (2006/49/EC).

Contents guide

2.2.5 **[G]** The table in GENPRU 2.2.6G sets out where the main topics in this section can be found.

2.2.6 **[G]** Table: Arrangement of GENPRU 2.2

This table belongs to GENPRU 2.2.5G

Topic	Location of text
Application and purpose of the *rules* in this section	GENPRU 2.2.1R to GENPRU 2.2.4G
BIPRU firms that only have simple types of *capital resources* (*simple capital issuers*)	GENPRU 2.2.7G
Principles underlying the definition of *capital resources*	GENPRU 2.2.8G
Which method of calculating *capital resources* applies to which type of *firm*	GENPRU 2.2.17R to GENPRU 2.2.19R
Purpose of the limits on the use of different forms of capital	GENPRU 2.2.24G
Use of higher tier capital in lower tiers	GENPRU 2.2.25R to GENPRU 2.2.28R
Calculation of *capital resources* for *insurers*	GENPRU 2.2.22G to GENPRU 2.2.23G; GENPRU 2 Annex 1R
Limits on the use of different forms of capital for *insurers* (*capital resources gearing rules* for *insurers*)	GENPRU 2.2.29R to GENPRU 2.2.41R
Calculation of *capital resources* for *banks*	GENPRU 2 Annex 2R
Calculation of *capital resources* for *building societies*	GENPRU 2 Annex 3R
Limits on the use of different forms of capital for *banks* and *building societies* (certain types of *capital resources* cannot be used for certain purposes)	GENPRU 2.2.42R to GENPRU 2.2.45R; GENPRU 2.2.47R to GENPRU 2.2.48R
Limits on the use of different forms of capital for *banks* and *building societies* (*capital resources gearing rules*)	GENPRU 2.2.29R to GENPRU 2.2.31G; GENPRU 2.2.46R; GENPRU 2.2.49R
Calculation of *capital resources* for *BIPRU investment firms*	GENPRU 2.2.20G to GENPRU 2.2.21G; GENPRU 2 Annex 4R to GENPRU 2 Annex 6R
Limits on the use of different forms of capital for *BIPRU investment firms* (certain types of *capital resources* cannot be used for certain purposes)	GENPRU 2.2.42R to GENPRU 2.2.45R; GENPRU 2.2.47R to GENPRU 2.2.48R
Limits on the use of different forms of capital for *BIPRU investment firms* (*capital resources gearing rules*)	GENPRU 2.2.29R to GENPRU 2.2.31G; GENPRU 2.2.46R; GENPRU 2.2.50R
Example of how the *capital resources* calculation for *BIPRU firms* works	GENPRU 2.2.51G to GENPRU 2.2.59G
Capital used to meet the *base capital resources requirement* for *BIPRU firms*	GENPRU 2.2.60R to GENPRU 2.2.61G
Tier one capital instruments: general	GENPRU 2.2.9G to 2.2.10G; GENPRU 2.2.62R to 2.2.69G; GENPRU 2.2.80R to GENPRU 2.2.82G
Core tier one capital: *permanent share capital*	GENPRU 2.2.83R to GENPRU 2.2.84G

Part II FSA Handbook Materials

Topic	Location of text
Core tier one capital: profit and loss account and other reserves: material applicable to all *firms*	GENPRU 2.2.85R; GENPRU 2.2.87R to GENPRU 2.2.89G; GENPRU 2.2.91G
Core tier one capital: profit and loss account and other reserves: material specific to *BIPRU firms*	GENPRU 2.2.86R; GENPRU 2.2.90R; GENPRU 2.2.92G
Core tier one capital: provisions relating to partnerships and *limited liability partnerships*	GENPRU 2.2.93R to GENPRU 2.2.100R
Core tier one capital: *share* premium account	GENPRU 2.2.101R
Core tier one capital: externally verified interim net profits	GENPRU 2.2.102R to GENPRU 2.2.103G
Core tier one capital: valuation differences and fund for future appropriations for *insurers*	GENPRU 2.2.104R to GENPRU 2.2.108R
Tier one capital: perpetual non-cumulative *preference shares*	GENPRU 2.2.109R to GENPRU 2.2.110G
Tier one capital: *PIBS*	GENPRU 2.2.76R; GENPRU 2.2.111R to GENPRU 2.2.112G
Innovative tier one capital (excluding issues through *SPVs*)	GENPRU 2.2.76R; GENPRU 2.2.113R to GENPRU 2.2.122G
Innovative tier one capital (issues through *SPVs*)	GENPRU 2.2.123R to GENPRU 2.2.137R
Tier one capital: conversion ratio	GENPRU 2.2.138R to GENPRU 2.2.144G
Tier one capital: requirement to have sufficient unissued stock	GENPRU 2.2.145R
Deductions from *tier one capital resources*	GENPRU 2.2.155R to GENPRU 2.2.156G
Tier two capital	GENPRU 2.2.11G; GENPRU 2.2.157G to GENPRU 2.2.197G
Deductions from *tier one capital resources* and *tier two capital resources*	GENPRU 2.2.202R to GENPRU 2.2.240G
Tier three capital	GENPRU 2.2.12G; GENPRU 2.2.241R to GENPRU 2.2.249R
Deductions from total *capital resources*	GENPRU 2.2.14G to GENPRU 2.2.16G; GENPRU 2.2.250R to GENPRU 2.2.265R
The effect of swaps	GENPRU 2.2.198R to GENPRU 2.2.201R
Step-ups (*tier one capital* and *tier two capital*)	GENPRU 2.2.76R; GENPRU 2.2.146R to GENPRU 2.2.154G
Redemption of *tier one instruments*	GENPRU 2.2.64(3); GENPRU 2.2.70R to GENPRU 2.2.79G;
Redemption of *tier two instruments*	GENPRU 2.2.172R to GENPRU 2.2.174R; GENPRU 2.2.177R to GENPRU 2.2.178R (*upper tier two instruments*); GENPRU 2.2.194R to GENPRU 2.2.197G (*lower tier two instruments*)
Non-standard capital instruments	GENPRU 2.2.13G
Standard form documentation for subordinated debt	GENPRU 2.2.164G
Public sector guarantees	GENPRU 2.2.276G
Other capital resources for insurers: unpaid *share* capital or *unpaid initial funds* and calls for supplementary contributions	GENPRU 2.2.266R to GENPRU 2.2.269G
Additional requirements for *insurers* carrying on *with-profits insurance business*	GENPRU 2.2.270R to GENPRU 2.2.275G

Simple capital issuers

2.2.7 **[G]** Parts of this section are irrelevant to a *BIPRU firm* whose *capital resources* consist of straightforward *capital instruments*. Therefore the *FSA's* Personal handbooks facility available on its website allows a *BIPRU firm* to screen out those parts of this section that are not relevant to a *simple capital issuer*.

Principles underlying the definition of capital resources

2.2.8 **[G]** The *FSA* has divided its definition of capital into categories, or tiers, reflecting differences in the extent to which the *capital instruments* concerned meet the purpose and conform to the characteristics of capital listed in GENPRU 2.2.9G. The *FSA* generally prefers a *firm* to hold higher quality capital that meets the characteristics of permanency and loss absorbency that are features of *tier one capital*. *Capital instruments* falling into *core tier one capital* can be included in a *firm's* regulatory capital without limit. Typically, other forms of capital are either subject to limits (see the *capital resources gearing rules*) or, in the case of some specialist types of capital, may only be included with the express consent of the *FSA* (which takes the form of a *waiver* under section 148 of the *Act*). Details of the individual components of capital are set out in the *capital resources table*.

Tier one capital

2.2.9 **[G]** *Tier one capital* typically has the following characteristics:

(1) it is able to absorb losses;

(2) it is permanent;

(3) it ranks for repayment upon winding up, administration or similar procedure after all other debts and liabilities; and

(4) it has no fixed costs, that is, there is no inescapable obligation to pay dividends or interest.

2.2.10 **[G]** The forms of capital that qualify for *tier one capital* are set out in the *capital resources table* and include, for example, *share* capital, reserves, partnership and *sole trader* capital, verified interim net profits and, for a *mutual*, the *initial fund* plus permanent members' accounts. *Tier one capital* is divided into *core tier one capital*, perpetual non-cumulative *preference shares*, *permanent interest-bearing shares* (*PIBS*) and *innovative tier one capital*.

Upper and lower tier two capital

2.2.11 **[G]** *Tier two capital* includes forms of capital that do not meet the requirements for permanency and absence of fixed servicing costs that apply to *tier one capital*. *Tier two capital* includes, for example:

(1) capital which is perpetual (that is, has no fixed term) but cumulative (that is, servicing costs cannot be waived at the issuer's option, although they may be deferred – for example, cumulative *preference shares*); only perpetual *capital instruments* may be included in *upper tier two capital*;

(2) capital which is not perpetual (that is, it has a fixed term) or which may have fixed servicing costs that cannot generally be either waived or deferred (for example, most subordinated debt); such capital should normally be of a medium to long-term maturity (that is, an original maturity of at least five years); dated *capital instruments* are included in *lower tier two capital*;

(3) (for *BIPRU firms*) certain revaluation reserves such as reserves arising from the revaluation of land and buildings, including any net unrealised gains for the fair valuation of equities held in the available-for-sale financial assets category; and

(4) (for *BIPRU firms*) general/collective provisions.

Tier three capital

2.2.12 **[G]** *Tier three capital* consists of forms of capital conforming least well to the characteristics of capital listed in GENPRU 2.2.9G: either subordinated debt of short maturity (*upper tier three capital*) or net *trading book* profits that have not been externally verified (*lower tier three capital*).

Non-standard capital instruments

2.2.13 **[G]** There may be examples of *capital instruments* that, although based on a standard form, contain structural features that make the *rules* in this section difficult to apply. In such circumstances, a *firm* may seek individual *guidance* on the application of those *rules* to the *capital instrument* in question. See SUP 9 (Individual guidance) for the process to be followed when seeking individual *guidance*.

Deductions from capital

2.2.14 **[G]** Deductions should be made at the relevant stage of the calculation of *capital resources* to reflect capital that may not be available to the *firm* or assets of uncertain value (for example, holdings of intangible assets and assets that are inadmissible for an *insurer*, or, in the case of a *bank* or *building society*, where that *firm* has made investments in a *subsidiary undertaking* or in another *financial institution* or in respect of *participations* that it holds).

2.2.15 **[G]** Deductions should also be made, in the case of certain *BIPRU investment firms* for *illiquid assets* (see GENPRU 2.2.19R).

2.2.16 **[G]** A full list of deductions from *capital resources* is shown in the *capital resources table* applicable to the *firm*.

Which method of calculating capital resources applies to which type of firm

2.2.17 **[R]** A *firm* must calculate its *capital resources* in accordance with the version of the *capital resources table* applicable to the *firm*, subject to the *capital resources gearing rules*. The version of the *capital resources table* that applies to a *firm* is specified in the table in GENPRU 2.2.19R.

2.2.18 **[R]** In the case of a *BIPRU firm* the *capital resources table* also sets out how the *capital resources requirement* is deducted from *capital resources* in order to decide whether its *capital resources* equal or exceed its *capital resources requirement*.

2.2.19 **[R]** Table: Applicable capital resources calculation

This table belongs to GENPRU 2.2.17R

Type of *firm*	**Location of *rules***	**Remarks**
Insurer	GENPRU 2 Annex 1R	
Bank	GENPRU 2 Annex 2R	
Building society	GENPRU 2 Annex 3R	
BIPRU investment firm without an *investment firm consolidation waiver*	GENPRU 2 Annex 4R (Deducts *material holdings*)	Applies to a *BIPRU investment firm* not using GENPRU 2 Annex 5R or GENPRU 2 Annex 6R
BIPRU investment firm without an *investment firm consolidation waiver*	GENPRU 2 Annex 5R (Deducts *illiquid assets*)	A *BIPRU investment firm* must give one *Month's* prior notice to the *FSA* before starting to use or stopping using this method
BIPRU investment firm with an *investment firm consolidation waiver*	GENPRU 2 Annex 6R (Deducts *illiquid assets* and *material holdings*)	A *firm* with an *investment firm consolidation waiver* must use this method. No other *BIPRU investment firm* may use it.

Calculation of capital resources: Which rules apply to BIPRU investment firms

2.2.20 **[G]** GENPRU 2.2.19R sets out three different methods of calculating *capital resources* for *BIPRU investment firms*. The differences between the three methods relate to whether and how *material holdings* and *illiquid assets* are deducted when calculating *capital resources*. The method depends on whether a *firm* has an *investment firm consolidation waiver*. If a *firm* does have such a *waiver*, it should deduct *illiquid assets*, own *group material holdings* and certain contingent liabilities. If a *firm* does not have such a *waiver*, it should choose to deduct either *material holdings* or, subject to notifying the *FSA*, *illiquid assets*.

2.2.21 **[G]** A consequence of a *firm* deducting all of its *illiquid assets* under GENPRU 2 Annex 5R is that it is allowed a higher limit on short term subordinated debt under GENPRU 2.2.49R.

Calculation of capital resources: Insurers

2.2.22 **[G]** *Capital resources* for an *insurer* can be calculated either as the total of eligible assets less foreseeable liabilities (which is the approach taken in the *Insurance Directives*) or by identifying the components of capital. Both calculations give the same result for the total amount of *capital resources*. The approach taken in this section has been to specify the components of capital and the relevant deductions. This is set out in the *capital resources table*. This approach is the same as that used for the calculation of *capital resources* for *banks*, *building societies* and *BIPRU investment firms*. A simple example, showing the reconciliation of the two methods, is given in the table in GENPRU 2.2.23G.

2.2.23 **[G]** Table: Approaches to calculating capital resources

This table belongs to GENPRU 2.2.22G

Liabilities		**Assets**	
Borrowings	100	Admissible assets	350
Ordinary *shares*	200	Intangible assets	100
Profit and loss account and other reserves	100	Other inadmissible assets	100
Perpetual subordinated debt	150		

Liabilities		Assets	
Total	550	Total	550
Calculation of *capital resources*: eligible assets less foreseeable liabilities			
Total assets			550
less intangible assets			(100)
less inadmissible assets			(100)
less liabilities (borrowings)			(100)
Capital resources			250
Calculation of *capital resources*: components of capital			
Ordinary *shares*			200
Profit and loss account and other reserves			100
Perpetual subordinated debt			150
Less intangible assets			(100)
Less inadmissible assets			(100)
Capital resources			250

Limits on the use of different forms of capital: General

2.2.24 **[G]** As the various components of capital differ in the degree of protection that they offer the *firm* and its *customers* and *consumers*, restrictions are placed on the extent to which certain types of capital are eligible for inclusion in a *firm's capital resources*. These *rules* are called the *capital resources gearing rules*.

Limits on the use of different forms of capital: Use of higher tier capital in lower tiers

2.2.25 **[R]** A *firm* may include in a *lower stage of capital*, *capital resources* which are eligible for inclusion in a *higher stage of capital* if the *capital resources gearing rules* would prevent the use of that capital in that *higher stage of capital*. However:

(1) the *capital resources gearing rules* applicable to that *lower stage of capital* apply to *higher stage of capital* included in that *lower stage of capital*; and

(2) (subject to GENPRU 2.2.26R) the *rules* in GENPRU governing the eligibility of capital in that *lower stage of capital* continue to apply.

2.2.26 **[R]** An item of *tier one capital* which is included in a *firm's tier two capital resources* under GENPRU 2.2.25R is not subject to the requirement to obtain a legal opinion in GENPRU 2.2.159R(12).

2.2.27 **[R]** A *BIPRU firm* may include in a *lower stage of capital*, *innovative tier one capital* that it is prohibited from using under GENPRU 2.2.42R (*BIPRU firms* may not use *innovative tier one capital* to meet the *CRR*). However:

(1) the *capital resources gearing rules* applicable to that *lower stage of capital* apply to that *innovative tier one capital*; and

(2) (subject to GENPRU 2.2.28R) the *rules* in GENPRU governing the eligibility of capital in that *lower stage of capital* continue to apply.

2.2.28 **[R]** The requirement to obtain a legal opinion in GENPRU 2.2.159R(12) does not apply to *innovative tier one capital* treated under GENPRU 2.2.27R but the requirements to obtain a legal opinion in GENPRU 2.2.118R continue to apply.

Limits on the use of different forms of capital: Limits relating to tier one capital applicable to all firms except BIPRU investment firms

2.2.29 **[R]** In relation to the *tier one capital resources* of an *insurer*, *bank* or *building society*, calculated at stage F of the calculation in the *capital resources table* (Total tier one capital after deductions), at least 50% must be accounted for by *core tier one capital*.

Limits on the use of different forms of capital: Limits relating to tier one capital applicable to all firms

2.2.30 **[R]** In relation to the *capital resources* of an *insurer*, and subject to GENPRU 2.2.42R (Restriction on the use of *innovative tier one capital*), those of a *BIPRU firm*, calculated at stage F of the calculation in the *capital resources table* (Total tier one capital after deductions), no more than 15% may be accounted for by *innovative tier one capital*.

Limits on the use of different forms of capital: Limits relating to tier one capital: Purpose of the requirements

2.2.31 **[G]** The purpose of the requirement in GENPRU 2.2.29R is to ensure that at least 50% of the *firm's tier one capital resources* (net of *tier one capital* deductions) is met by *core tier one capital* which provides maximum loss absorbency on a going concern basis to protect the *firm* from insolvency. Although a perpetual non-cumulative *preference share* or a *PIBS* is in legal form a *share*, it behaves in many ways like a perpetual fixed interest debt instrument. Within the 50% limit on non-*core tier one capital*, GENPRU 2.2.30R places a further sub-limit on the amount of *innovative tier one capital* that a *firm* may include in its *tier one capital resources*. This limit is necessary to ensure that most of a *firm's tier one capital* comprises items of capital of the highest quality.

Limits on the use of different forms of capital: Insurers

2.2.32 **[R]** At least 50% of an *insurer's MCR* must be accounted for by the sum of:
(1) the amount calculated at stage A of the calculation in the *capital resources table* (Core tier one capital); and
(2) notwithstanding GENPRU 2.2.29R, the amount calculated at stage B of the calculation in the *capital resources table* (Perpetual non-cumulative preference shares);

less the amount calculated at stage E of the calculation in the *capital resources table* (Deductions from tier one capital).

2.2.33 **[R]** Subject to GENPRU 2.2.34AR, an *insurer* carrying on *long-term insurance business* must meet the higher of:
(1) ⅓ of the *long-term insurance capital requirement*; and
(2) the *base capital resources requirement*;

with the sum of the items listed at stages A (Core tier one capital), B (Perpetual non-cumulative preference shares), G (Upper tier two capital) and H (Lower tier two capital) in the *capital resources table* less the sum of the items listed at stage E in the *capital resources table* (Deductions from tier one capital).

2.2.34 **[R]** Subject to GENPRU 2.2.34AR, an *insurer* carrying on *general insurance business* must meet the higher of:
(1) ⅓ of the *general insurance capital requirement*; and
(2) the *base capital resources requirement*;

with the sum of the items listed at stages A (Core tier one capital), B (Perpetual non-cumulative preference shares), G (Upper tier two capital) and H (Lower tier two capital) in the *capital resources table* less the sum of the items listed at stage E (Deductions from tier one capital) in the *capital resources table*.

2.2.34A **[R]** A *pure reinsurer* carrying on both *long-term insurance business* and *general insurance business* must meet the higher of:
(1) ⅓ of the sum of the *long-term insurance capital requirement* and the *general insurance capital requirement*; and
(2) the *base capital resources requirement*;

with the sum of the items listed at stages A (Core tier one capital), B (Perpetual non-cumulative preference shares), G (Upper tier two capital) and H (Lower tier two capital) in the *capital resources table* less the sum of the items listed at stage E (Deductions from tier one capital) in the *capital resources table*.

2.2.35 **[R]** In GENPRU 2.2.33R, GENPRU 2.2.34R and GENPRU 2.2.34AR:
(1) items listed at stage B (Perpetual non-cumulative preference shares) in the *capital resources table* may be included notwithstanding GENPRU 2.2.29R;
(2) *innovative tier one capital* that meets the conditions (other than GENPRU 2.2.159R(12) (Requirement for a legal opinion)) for it to be included as *upper tier two capital* at stage G (Upper tier two capital) in the *capital resources table* may be treated as an item listed at stage G; and
(3) an *insurer* must exclude from the calculation the higher of the following:
   (a) the amount (if any) by which the sum of the items listed at stages G (Upper tier two capital) and H (Lower tier two capital) in the *capital resources table* exceeds the total (net of deductions) of the remaining constituents of adjusted stage M; and
   (b) the amount (if any) by which the sum of the items listed at stage H in the *capital resources table* exceeds one-third of the total (net of deductions) of the remaining constituents of adjusted stage M;

where adjusted stage M means the amount calculated at stage M of the calculation in the *capital resources table* (Total capital after deductions) less the amount of any *innovative tier one capital* that is not treated as *upper tier two capital* for the purpose of GENPRU 2.2.33R, GENPRU 2.2.34R or GENPRU 2.2.34AR, as the case may be.

2.2.36 **[G]** The purpose of the requirements in GENPRU 2.2.33R to GENPRU 2.2.34AR is to comply with the requirements of the *Insurance Directives* and the *Reinsurance Directive* that an insurer must maintain a *guarantee fund* of higher quality *capital resources* items.

2.2.37 **[R]** Subject to GENPRU 2.2.38R, an *insurer* must exclude from the calculation of its *capital resources* the following:

(1) the amount (if any) by which *tier two capital resources* exceed the amount calculated at stage F (Total tier one capital after deductions) of the calculation in the *capital resources table*; and

(2) the amount (if any) by which *lower tier two capital resources* exceed 50% of the amount calculated at stage F of the calculation in the *capital resources table*.

2.2.38 **[R]** At least 75% of an *insurer's MCR* must be accounted for by the sum of:

(1) the amount calculated at stage A (Core tier one capital) plus, notwithstanding GENPRU 2.2.29R, the amount calculated at stage B (Perpetual non-cumulative preference shares) less the amount calculated at stage E (Deductions from tier one capital) of the calculation in the *capital resources table*; and

(2) the amount calculated at stage G (Upper tier two capital) of the calculation in the *capital resources table*.

2.2.39 **[G]** In GENPRU 2.2.38R the amount of any *innovative tier one capital* that meets the conditions for it to be included as *upper tier two capital* at stage G (Upper tier two capital) in the *capital resources table* may be included in the amount calculated at stage G.

2.2.40 **[G]** GENPRU 2.2.32R, GENPRU 2.2.37R and GENPRU 2.2.38R give effect to the requirements of the *Insurance Directives* and the *Reinsurance Directive* that no more than 50% of the amount which is the lesser of the available solvency margin and the required solvency margin should consist of *tier two capital resources* and that no more than 25% of that amount should consist of *lower tier two capital resources*.

2.2.41 **[R]** An *insurer* (other than a *pure reinsurer*) that carries on both *long-term insurance business* and *general insurance business* must apply the relevant limits in GENPRU 2.2.32R to GENPRU 2.2.38R separately for each type of business.

Limits on the use of innovative tier one capital: BIPRU firm

2.2.42 **[R]** For the purpose of meeting the *main BIPRU firm Pillar 1 rules*, a *BIPRU firm* may not include *innovative tier one capital* in its *tier one capital resources*.

2.2.43 **[G]** A *BIPRU firm* may include *innovative tier one capital* in its *tier one capital resources* for the purpose of GENPRU 1.2 (Adequacy of financial resources) and BIPRU 10 (Concentration risk). A *firm* may also include it in its *upper tier two capital resources* under GENPRU 2.2.25R (Limits on the use of different forms of capital: Use of higher tier capital in lower tiers) for all purposes as long as it meets the conditions for treatment as *upper tier two capital*.

Limits on the use of different kinds of capital: Purposes for which tier three capital may not be used (BIPRU firm only)

2.2.44 **[R]** *Tier one capital* and *tier two capital* are the only type of *capital resources* that a *BIPRU firm* may use for the purpose of meeting:

(1) the *credit risk capital component*;

(2) the *operational risk capital requirement*;

(3) the *counterparty risk capital component*; and

(4) the *base capital resources requirement*.

2.2.45 **[R]** GENPRU 2.2.44R (and the *capital resources gearing rules* that relate to it) also applies for the purposes of any other requirement in the *Handbook* for which it is necessary to calculate the *capital resources* of a *BIPRU firm*, except for the purposes described in GENPRU 2.2.47R and except as may otherwise be stated in the relevant part of the *Handbook*.

Limits on the use of different kinds of capital: Tier two limits (BIPRU firm only)

2.2.46 **[R]** For the purpose of GENPRU 2.2.44R:

(1) the amount of the items which may be included in a *BIPRU firm's tier two capital resources* must not exceed the amount calculated at stage F of the calculation in the *capital resources table* (Total tier one capital after deductions); and

(2) the amount of the items which may be included in a *BIPRU firm's lower tier two capital resources* must not exceed 50% of the amount calculated at stage F of the calculation in the *capital resources table*.

Limits on the use of different kinds of capital: Purposes for which tier three capital may be used (BIPRU firm only)

2.2.47 **[R]** For the purposes of meeting:

(1) the *market risk capital requirement*;

(2) the *concentration risk capital component*; and
(3) the *fixed overheads requirement* (where applicable);
a *BIPRU firm* may only use the following parts of its *capital resources*:
(4) *tier one capital* to the extent that it is not required to meet the requirements in GENPRU 2.2.44R (GENPRU 2.2.48R explains how to calculate how much *tier one capital* is required to meet the requirements in GENPRU 2.2.44R);
(5) *tier two capital* to the extent that it:
  (a) comes within the limits in GENPRU 2.2.46R (100% limit for *tier two capital resources* and 50% limit for *lower tier two capital resources*); and
  (b) it is not required to meet the requirements in GENPRU 2.2.44R; (GENPRU 2.2.48R explains how to calculate how much *tier two capital* is required to meet the requirements in GENPRU 2.2.44R);
(6) *tier two capital* that cannot be used for the purposes in GENPRU 2.2.44R because it falls outside the limits in GENPRU 2.2.46R; and
(7) *tier three capital*.

2.2.48 **[R]** The amount of *tier one capital* and *tier two capital* that is not used to meet the requirements in GENPRU 2.2.44R as referred to in GENPRU 2.2.47R(4) and (5) is equal to the amount calculated at stage N of the calculation in the *capital resources table* (Total tier one capital plus tier two capital after deductions) less the parts of the *capital resources requirement* deducted immediately after stage N of the *capital resources table* (the parts of the *capital resources requirements* listed in GENPRU 2.2.44R).

Limits on the use of different kinds of capital: Combined tier two and tier three limits (BIPRU firm only)

2.2.49 **[R]** For the purpose of meeting the requirements in GENPRU 2.2.47R(1) to (3) and subject to GENPRU 2.2.50R, a *BIPRU firm* must not include any item in either:
(1) its *tier two capital resources* falling within GENPRU 2.2.47R(6) (excess *tier two capital*); or
(2) its *upper tier three capital resources*;
to the extent that the sum of (1) and (2) would exceed 250% of the amount resulting from the following calculation:
(3) calculate the amount at stage F of the calculation in the *capital resources table* (Total tier one capital after deductions); and
(4) deduct from (3) those parts of the *firm's tier one capital* used to meet the requirements in GENPRU 2.2.44R (1) and (2) as established by GENPRU 2.2.48R.

2.2.50 **[R]** In relation to a *BIPRU investment firm* which calculates its *capital resources* under GENPRU 2 Annex 4R (Capital resources table for a BIPRU investment firm deducting material holdings), the figure of 200% replaces that of 250% in GENPRU 2.2.49R.

Example of how the capital resources calculation for BIPRU firms works

2.2.51 **[G]** GENPRU 2.2.52G to GENPRU 2.2.59G illustrate how to calculate a *BIPRU firm's capital resources* and how the *capital resources gearing rules* work. In this example the *BIPRU firm* has a combined credit, operational and counterparty risk requirement of £100 (of which £10 is due to counterparty risk) and a market risk requirement of £90, making a total capital requirement of £190. Its *capital resources* are as set out in the table in GENPRU 2.2.52G.

2.2.52 **[G]** Table: Example of the calculation of the capital resources of a BIPRU firm

This table belongs to GENPRU 2.2.51G

Description of the stage of the capital resources calculation	Stage in the *capital resources table*	Amount (£)
Total *tier one capital* after deductions (excluding *innovative tier one instruments* – see GENPRU 2.2.53G)	Stage F	80
Total *tier two capital* (including *innovative tier one instruments* – see GENPRU 2.2.53G)	Stage K	80
Deductions	Stage M	(20)
Total *tier one capital* and *tier two capital* after deductions	Stage N	140
Upper tier three capital (this example assumes the *firm* has no *lower tier three capital* (*trading book* profits))	Stage Q	50
Total *capital resources*	Stage T	190

2.2.53 **[G]** GENPRU 2.2.42R (Limits on the use of innovative tier one capital) prohibits the inclusion of *innovative tier one instruments* in the *tier one capital* of a *BIPRU firm* for the purpose of meeting the *capital resources requirement*. Thus they are not included in the calculation of stage F of the *capital resources table*. Instead all *innovative tier one instruments* have been included in *tier two capital* in accordance with GENPRU 2.2.25R (Use of higher tiers of capital in lower tiers).

2.2.54 **[G]** In the example in the table in GENPRU 2.2.52G the *firm* has total *tier one capital* after deductions of £80. Its *tier two capital* of £80 is therefore the maximum permitted under GENPRU 2.2.46R (Tier two limits), that is 100% of *tier one capital*.

2.2.55 **[G]** The combined credit, operational and counterparty risk capital requirement is deducted after stage N of the *capital resources table* and the market risk requirement following stage T of the *capital resources table*. These calculations are shown in the table in GENPRU 2.2.56G.

2.2.56 **[G]** Table: Example of how capital resources of a BIPRU firm are measured against its capital resources requirement

This table belongs to GENPRU 2.2.55G

Description of the stage of the capital resources calculation	Stage in the *capital resources table*	Amount (£)
Total *tier one capital* and *tier two capital* after deductions	Stage N	140
Credit, operational and counterparty risk requirement		(100)
Tier one capital and *tier two capital* available to meet market risk requirement		40
Tier three capital	Stage Q	50
Total capital available to meet market risk requirement		90
Market risk requirement		(90)
Market risk requirement met subject to meeting gearing limit set out in GENPRU 2.2.49R – see GENPRU 2.2.57G		

2.2.57 **[G]** The gearing limit in GENPRU 2.2.49 (Combined tier two and tier three limits) requires that the *upper tier three capital* used to meet the market risk requirement does not exceed 250% of the relevant *tier one capital.*

2.2.58 **[G]** In this example it is assumed that the maximum possible amount of *tier one capital* is carried forward to meet the market risk requirement. There are other options as to the allocation of *tier one capital* and *tier two capital* to the credit, operational and counterparty risk requirement.

In order to calculate the relevant *tier one capital* for the *upper tier three* gearing limit in accordance with GENPRU 2.2.49R it is first necessary to allocate *tier one capital* and *tier two capital* to the individual credit, operational and counterparty risk requirements. This allocation process underlies the calculation of the overall amount referred to in GENPRU 2.2.48R. The calculation in GENPRU 2.2.49R (3) and (4) then focuses on the *tier one* element of this earlier calculation.

In this worked example, if it is assumed that the counterparty risk requirement has been met by *tier one capital*, the relevant *tier one capital* for gearing is £50. This is because the deductions of £20 and the credit and operational risk requirements of £90 have been met by *tier two capital* in the first instance. However, the total sum of deductions and credit and operational risk requirements exceed the *tier two capital* amount of £80 by £30. Hence the £80 of *tier one* capital has been reduced by £30 to leave £50.

In practical terms, the same result is achieved for the relevant *tier one capital* for gearing by taking the amount carried forward to meet market risk of £40 and adding back the £10 in respect of the counterparty risk requirement. Again, there are other options as to the allocation to credit, operational and counterparty risk of the constituent elements of Stage N of the *capital resources table*.

The outcome of these calculations can be summarised as follows:

(1) the relevant *tier one capital* for the gearing calculation is £50;

(2) 250% of the relevant *tier one capital* is £125; and

(3) the *upper tier three capital* used to meet market risk is £50.

2.2.59 **[G]** The 250% gearing limit is met as the limit of £125 is greater than the *upper tier three capital* of £50 used in this example.

Capital used to meet the base capital resources requirement (BIPRU firm only)

2.2.60 **[R]** A *BIPRU firm* may use the *capital resources* used to meet the *base capital resources requirement* to meet any other part of the *capital resources requirement*.

2.2.61 **[G]** The explanation for GENPRU 2.2.60R can be found in GENPRU 2.1.43G (Base capital resources requirement). In brief the reason is that the *base capital resources requirement* is not in practice meant to act as an additional capital resources requirement. It is meant to act as a floor to the *capital resources requirement*.

Tier one capital: General

2.2.62 **[R]** A *firm* may not include a *capital instrument* in its *tier one capital resources* unless it complies with the following conditions:

(1) it is included in one of the categories in GENPRU 2.2.63R;
(2) it complies with the conditions set out in GENPRU 2.2.64R;
(3) it is not excluded under GENPRU 2.2.65R (Connected transactions); and
(4) it is not excluded by any of the *rules* in GENPRU 2.2.

2.2.63 **[R]** The categories referred to in GENPRU 2.2.62R(1) are:

(1) *permanent share capital*;
(2) *eligible partnership capital*;
(3) *eligible LLP members' capital*;
(4) *sole trader* capital;
(5) a perpetual non-cumulative *preference share*;
(6) (in the case of a *building society*) *PIBS*; and
(7) an *innovative tier one instrument*.

General conditions for eligibility as tier one capital

2.2.64 **[R]** The conditions that an item of capital of a *firm* must comply with under GENPRU 2.2.62R(2) are as follows:

(1) it is issued by the *firm*;
(2) it is fully paid and the proceeds of issue are immediately and fully available to the *firm*;
(3) it:
 (a) cannot be redeemed at all or can only be redeemed on a winding up of the *firm*; or
 (b) complies with the conditions in GENPRU 2.2.70R (Basic requirements for redeemability) and GENPRU 2.2.76R (Redeemable instrument subject to a *step-up*);
(4) the item of capital meets the following conditions in relation to any *coupon*:
 (a) the *firm* is under no obligation to pay a *coupon*; or
 (b) (if the *firm* is obliged to pay the *coupon*) the *coupon* is payable in the form of an item of capital that is included in a *higher stage of capital* or the *same stage of capital* as that first item of capital;
(5) any *coupon* is either:
 (a) non-cumulative; or
 (b) (if it is cumulative) it must, if deferred, be paid by the *firm* in the form of *tier one capital* complying with (4)(b);
(6) it is able to absorb losses to allow the *firm* to continue trading and in particular it complies with GENPRU 2.2.80R to 2.2.81R (Loss absorption) and, in the case of an *innovative tier one instrument*, GENPRU 2.2.116R to 2.2.118R (*Innovative tier one instrument* should not constitute a liability);
(7) the amount of the item included must be net of any foreseeable tax charge at the moment of its calculation or must be suitably adjusted in so far as such tax charges reduce the amount up to which that item may be applied to cover risks or losses;
(8) it is available to the *firm* for unrestricted and immediate use to cover risks and losses as soon as these occur;
(9) it ranks for repayment upon winding up, administration or any other similar process no higher than a *share* of a company incorporated under the Companies Act 2006 (whether or not it is such a *share*); and
(10) the description of its characteristics used in its marketing is consistent with the characteristics required to satisfy (1) to (9) and, where it applies, GENPRU 2.2.271R (Other requirements: insurers carrying on with-profits business (Insurer only)).

2.2.65 **[R]** An item of capital does not qualify for inclusion as *tier one capital* if the issue of that item of capital by the *firm* is connected with one or more other transactions which, when taken together with the issue of that item, could result in that item of capital no longer displaying all of the characteristics set out in GENPRU 2.2.64R(1) to (9).

Guidance on certain of the general conditions for eligibility as tier one capital

2.2.66 **[G]** GENPRU 2.2.65R is an example of the general principle in *GEN* 2.2.1 (Purposive interpretation). Its purpose is to emphasise that an item of capital does not meet the conditions for inclusion in *tier one capital* if in isolation it does meet those requirements but it fails to meet those requirements when other transactions are taken into account. Examples of such connected transactions might include guarantees or any other side agreement provided to the holders of the *capital instrument* by the *firm* or a connected party or a related transaction designed, for example, to enhance their security or to achieve a tax benefit, but which may compromise the loss absorption capacity or permanence of the original capital item.

2.2.67 **[G]** GENPRU 2.2.64R(2) is stricter than the Companies Act definition of fully paid, which only requires an undertaking to pay.

2.2.67A **[G]** The purpose of GENPRU 2.2.64R(4) is to ensure that a *firm* retains flexibility over the payment of *coupons* and can preserve cash in times of financial stress. However, a *firm* may include, as part of the capital instrument terms, a right to make payments of a *coupon* mandatory if an item of capital becomes ineligible to form part of its *capital resources* (e.g. through a change in the relevant *rules*) and the *firm* has notified the *FSA* that the instrument is ineligible.

2.2.68 **[G]** The *FSA* considers that dividend pushers diminish the quality of capital by breaching the principle of complete discretion over *coupons* set out in GENPRU 2.2.64R(4). A dividend pusher operates so that, in a given period of time, payments must be made on senior securities if payments have previously been made on junior securities or securities ranking pari passu. As such, dividend pushers may not be included in the terms of *tier one capital*, unless the *firm* has the option to fund the "pushed payment" in stock.

2.2.69 **[G]** An item of capital does not comply with GENPRU 2.2.64R(10) if it is marketed as a *capital instrument* that would only qualify for a lower level of capital or on the basis that investing in it is like investing in an instrument in a lower tier of capital. For example, an undated *capital instrument* should not be marketed as a dated *capital instrument* if the terms of the *capital instrument* include an option by the issuer to redeem the *capital instrument* at a specified date in the future.

Redemption of tier one instruments

2.2.70 **[R]** A *firm* may not include a *capital instrument* in its *tier one capital resources*, unless its contractual terms are such that:

(1) (if it is redeemable other than in circumstances set out in GENPRU 2.2.64R(3)(a) (redemption on a winding up)) it is redeemable only at the option of the *firm*; and

(2) the *firm* cannot exercise that redemption right:
  (a) before the fifth anniversary of its date of issue;
  (b) unless it has given notice to the *FSA* in accordance with GENPRU 2.2.74R; and
  (c) unless at the time of exercise of that right it complies with GENPRU 2.1.13R (the main capital adequacy *rule* for *insurers*) or the *main BIPRU firm Pillar 1 rules* and will continue to do so after redemption.

2.2.71 **[R]** A *firm* may include a term in a *tier one instrument* allowing the *firm* to redeem it before the date in GENPRU 2.2.70R(2)(a) if the following conditions are satisfied:

(1) the other conditions in GENPRU 2.2.70R are met;

(2) the circumstance that entitles the *firm* to exercise that right is a change in law or regulation in any relevant jurisdiction or in the interpretation of such law or regulation by any court or authority entitled to do so;

(3) it would be reasonable for the *firm* to conclude that it is unlikely that that circumstance will occur, judged at the time of issue or, if later, at the time that the term is first included in the terms of the *tier one instrument*; and

(4) the *firm's* right is conditional on it obtaining the *FSA's* consent in the form of a *waiver* of GENPRU 2.2.72R.

2.2.72 **[R]** A *firm* must not redeem a *tier one instrument* in accordance with a term included under GENPRU 2.2.71R.

2.2.73 **[G]** The purpose of GENPRU 2.2.71R to GENPRU 2.2.72R is this. In general a *tier one instrument* should not be redeemable by the *firm* before its fifth anniversary. However there may be circumstances in which it would be reasonable for the *firm* to redeem it before then. GENPRU 2.2.71R allows the *firm* to include a right to redeem the instrument before the fifth anniversary in certain circumstances. A tax call is an example of a term that may be allowed. GENPRU 2.2.71R says that the terms of the *tier one instrument* should provide that the *firm* should not be able to exercise that right without the *FSA's* consent. Any such consent will be given in the form of a *waiver* allowing early repayment. Thus although a *firm* may include a right to redeem early in the terms of a *tier one instrument* without the need to apply for a *waiver* the actual exercise of that right will require a *waiver*.

2.2.74 **[R]** A *firm* must not redeem any *tier one instrument* that it has included in its *tier one capital resources* unless it has notified the *FSA* of its intention at least one month before it becomes committed to do so. When giving notice, the *firm* must provide details of its position after such redemption in order to show how it will:

(1) meet its *capital resources requirement*; and

(2) have sufficient financial resources to meet the *overall financial adequacy rule*.

2.2.75 **[R]** If a *firm* gives notice of the redemption or repayment of any *tier one instrument*, the *firm* must no longer include that instrument in its *tier one capital resources*.

Step-ups and redeemable tier one instruments

2.2.76 **[R]** In relation to an *innovative tier one instrument* or a *PIBS* which is redeemable and which satisfies the following conditions:

(1) it is or may become subject to a *step-up*; and
(2) a reasonable *person* would think that:
 (a) the *firm* is likely to redeem it before the tenth anniversary of its date of issue; or
 (b) the *firm* is likely to have an economic incentive to redeem it before the tenth anniversary of its date of issue;

the redemption date in GENPRU 2.2.70R(2)(a) is amended by replacing "fifth anniversary" with "tenth anniversary".

Meaning of redemption

2.2.77 **[R]**

(1) This *rule* applies to a *tier one instrument, tier two instrument* or *tier three instrument* (instrument A) that under its terms is exchanged for or converted into another instrument or is subject to a similar process.
(2) This *rule* also applies to instrument A if under its terms it is redeemed out of the proceeds of the issue of new securities.
(3) If the instrument with which instrument A is replaced is included in the *same stage of capital* or a *higher stage of capital* as instrument A, instrument A is treated as not having been redeemed or repaid for the purposes of GENPRU 2.2.
(4) (3) does not apply to GENPRU 2.2.114R (Redeemable instrument likely to be repaid etc), GENPRU 2.2.74R (Notice of redemption of *tier one instruments*), GENPRU 2.2.174R (Notice of redemption of *tier two instruments*) or GENPRU 2.2.245R (so far as it relates to notice of redemption of *tier three instruments*).
(5) (3) only applies if it would be reasonable (taking into account the economic substance) to treat the original instruments as continuing in issue on the same or a more favourable basis. The question of whether that basis is more or less favourable must be judged from the point of view of the adequacy of the *firm's capital resources*.

2.2.78 **[R]**

(1) A *share* is not redeemable for the purposes of this section merely because the Companies Act 1985, the Companies (Northern Ireland) Order 1986 or the Companies Act 2006 allows the *firm* that issued it to purchase it.
(2) A *capital instrument* is not redeemable for the purposes of this section merely because the *firm* that issued it has a right to purchase it similar to the right in (1).

2.2.79 **[G]** This section generally uses the term repay and redeem interchangeably.

Loss absorption

2.2.80 **[R]** A *firm* may not include a *share* in its *tier one capital resources* unless (in addition to complying with the other relevant *rules* in GENPRU 2.2):

(1) (in the case of a *firm* that is a company as defined in the Companies Act 2006) it is "called-up *share* capital" within the meaning given to that term in that Act; or
(2) (in the case of a *building society*) it is a "deferred share" as defined in the Building Societies (Deferred Shares) Order 1991; or
(3) (in the case of any other *firm*) it is:
 (a) in economic terms; and
 (b) in its characteristics as capital (including loss absorbency, permanency, ranking for repayment and fixed costs);

substantially the same as called-up *share* capital falling into (1).

2.2.81 **[R]** A *firm* may not include a *capital instrument* other than a *share* in its *tier one capital resources* unless it complies with GENPRU 2.2.80R(3).

2.2.82 **[G]** There are additional loss absorption requirements for *innovative tier one capital* in GENPRU 2.2.116R to 2.2.118R (*Innovative tier one instrument* should not constitute a liability).

Core tier one capital: permanent share capital

2.2.83 **[R]** *Permanent share capital* means an item of capital which (in addition to satisfying GENPRU 2.2.64R) meets the following conditions:

(1) it is:
 (a) an ordinary *share*; or
 (b) a *members' contribution*; or
 (c) part of the *initial fund* of a *mutual*;
(2) any *coupon* on it is not cumulative, the *firm* is under no obligation to pay a *coupon* in any circumstances and the *firm* has the right to choose the amount of any *coupon* that it pays; and

(3) the terms upon which it is issued do not permit redemption and it is otherwise incapable of being redeemed to at least the same degree as an ordinary *share* issued by a company incorporated under the Companies Act 2006 (whether or not it is such a *share*).

2.2.84 **[G]** GENPRU 2.2.83R has the effect that the *firm* should be under no obligation to make any payment in respect of a *tier one instrument* if it is to form part of its *permanent share capital* unless and until the *firm* is wound up. A *tier one instrument* that forms part of *permanent share capital* should not therefore count as a liability before the *firm* is wound up. The fact that relevant company law permits the *firm* to make earlier repayment does not mean that the *tier one instruments* are not eligible. However, the *firm* should not be required by any contractual or other obligation arising out of the terms of that capital to repay *permanent share capital*. Similarly a *tier one instrument* may still qualify if company law allows dividends to be paid on this capital, provided the *firm* is not contractually or otherwise obliged to pay them. There should therefore be no fixed costs.

Core tier one capital: profit and loss account and other reserves: Losses

2.2.85 **[R]**
(1) Negative amounts, including any interim net losses (but in the case of a *BIPRU investment firm*, only material interim net losses), must be deducted from profit and loss account and other reserves.
(2) For these purposes material interim net losses mean unaudited interim losses arising from a *firm's trading book* and *non-trading book* business which exceed 10% of the sum of its *capital resources* calculated at stages A (Core tier one capital) and B (Perpetual non-cumulative preference shares) in the *capital resources table*.
(3) If interim losses as referred to in (2) exceed the 10% figure in (2) then a *BIPRU investment firm* must deduct the whole amount of those losses and not just the excess.

Core tier one capital: profit and loss account and other reserves: Losses arising from valuation adjustments (BIPRU firm only)

2.2.86 **[R]**
(1) This *rule* applies to *trading book* valuation adjustments or reserves referred to in GENPRU 1.3.29R to GENPRU 1.3.35G (Valuation adjustments and reserves). It applies to a *BIPRU firm*.
(2) When valuation adjustments or reserves give rise to losses of the current financial year, a *firm* must treat them in accordance with GENPRU 2.2.85R.
(3) Valuation adjustments or reserves which exceed those made under the accounting framework to which a *firm* is subject must be treated in accordance with (2) if they give rise to losses and under GENPRU 2.2.248R (Net interim *trading book* profits) otherwise.

Core tier one capital: profit and loss account and other reserves: Dividends

2.2.87 **[R]** Dividends must be deducted from reserves as soon as they are foreseeable.

2.2.87A **[G]** Each *firm* must assess for itself when, in its particular circumstances, dividends are foreseeable. A dividend is foreseeable at the latest:
(1) in the case of an interim dividend, when it is declared by the *directors*; or
(2) in the case of a final dividend, when the *directors* approve the dividend to be proposed at the annual general meeting.

Core tier one capital: profit and loss account and other reserves: Capital contributions

2.2.88 **[R]** A *firm* must account for a capital contribution as an increase in reserves and may, notwithstanding GENPRU 2.2.63R, count that increase in reserves as *core tier one capital*.

2.2.89 **[G]** An item of capital qualifies as a capital contribution if it is a gift of capital (and, as such, is not repayable) and a *coupon* is not payable on it.

Core tier one capital: profit and loss account and other reserves: Securitisation (BIPRU firm only)

2.2.90 **[R]** In the case of a *BIPRU firm* which is the *originator* of a *securitisation*, net gains arising from the capitalisation of future income from the *securitised* assets and providing *credit enhancement* to *positions* in the *securitisation* must be excluded from profit and loss account and other reserves.

Core tier one capital: profit and loss account and other reserves: Valuation

2.2.91 **[G]** Profit and loss account and other reserves should be valued in accordance with the *rules* in GENPRU 1.3 (Valuation).

Core tier one capital: profit and loss account and other reserves: Revaluation reserves (BIPRU firm only)

2.2.92 **[G]** A revaluation reserve is not included as part of a *BIPRU firm's* profit and loss account and other reserves. It is dealt with separately and forms part of a *BIPRU firm's upper tier two capital*.

Core tier one capital: partnership capital account (BIPRU firm only)

2.2.93 **[R]** *Eligible partnership capital* means a partners' account:
(1) into which capital contributed by the partners is paid; and
(2) from which under the terms of the partnership agreement an amount representing capital may be withdrawn by a partner only if:
  (a) he ceases to be a partner and an equal amount is transferred to another such account by his former partners or any *person* replacing him as their partner; or
  (b) the partnership is wound up or otherwise dissolved; or
  (c) the *BIPRU firm* has ceased to be *authorised* or no longer has a *Part IV permission*.

Core tier one capital: Eligible LLP members' capital (BIPRU firm only)

2.2.94 **[R]** *Eligible LLP members' capital* means a members' account:
(1) into which capital contributed by the members is paid; and
(2) from which under the terms of the *limited liability partnership* agreement an amount representing capital may be withdrawn by a member only if:
  (a) he ceases to be a member and an equal amount is transferred to another such account by his former fellow members or any *person* replacing him as a member; or
  (b) the *limited liability partnership* is wound up or otherwise dissolved; or
  (c) the *BIPRU firm* has ceased to be *authorised* or no longer has a *Part IV permission*.

Core tier one capital: Eligible LLP members' and partnership capital accounts (BIPRU firm only)

2.2.95 **[R]** A *BIPRU firm* that is a partnership or a *limited liability partnership* may not include *eligible partnership capital* or *eligible LLP members' capital* in its *tier one capital resources* unless (in addition to GENPRU 2.2.62R (General conditions relating to *tier one capital*)) it complies with GENPRU 2.2.83R(2) (*Coupons* should not be cumulative or mandatory). However GENPRU 2.2.64R(3) (Redemption) is replaced by GENPRU 2.2.93R or GENPRU 2.2.94R.

2.2.96 **[G]** If a *firm* has surplus *eligible partnership capital* or *eligible LLP members' capital* that it wishes to repay in circumstances other than those set out in GENPRU 2.2.93R or GENPRU 2.2.94R it may apply to the *FSA* for a *waiver* to allow it to do so. If a *firm* applies for such a *waiver* the information that the *firm* supplies with the application might include:
(1) a demonstration that the *firm* would have sufficient *capital resources* to meet its *capital resources requirement* immediately after the repayment;
(2) a demonstration that the *firm* would have sufficient financial resources to meet any *individual capital guidance* and the *firm's* latest assessment under the *overall Pillar 2 rule* immediately after the repayment; and
(3) a two to three year capital plan demonstrating that the *firm* would be able to meet the requirements in (1) and (2) at all times without needing further capital injections.

Core tier one capital: Other capital items for limited liability partnerships and partnerships (BIPRU firm only)

2.2.97 **[R]** The items *permanent share capital* and *share* premium account (which form part of *core tier one capital*) and perpetual non-cumulative *preference shares* (which forms stage B of the *capital resources table*) do not apply to a *BIPRU firm* that is a partnership or a *limited liability partnership*.

2.2.98 **[R]** Without prejudice to GENPRU 2.2.62R (Tier one capital: General), the item other reserves (which forms part of the item profit and loss and other reserves) applies to a *BIPRU firm* that is a partnership or a *limited liability partnership* to the extent the reserves correspond to reserves that are eligible for inclusion as other reserves in the case of a *BIPRU firm* that is incorporated under the Companies Act 2006.

2.2.99 **[G]** A *BIPRU firm* that is a partnership or a *limited liability partnership* should include profit and loss (taking into account interim losses or material interim net losses) in its *core tier one capital*.

***Core tier one capital:* partnership and limited liability partnership excess drawings (BIPRU firm only)**

2.2.100 **[R]** A *BIPRU firm* which is a partnership or *limited liability partnership* must deduct at stage E of the calculation in the *capital resources table* (Deductions from tier one capital) the amount by which the aggregate of the amounts withdrawn by its partners or members exceeds the profits of that *firm*. Amounts of *eligible partnership capital* or *eligible LLP members' capital* repaid in accordance with GENPRU 2.2.93R or GENPRU 2.2.94R are not included in this calculation.

Core tier one capital: Share premium account

2.2.101 **[R]**

(1) A *firm* must include *share* premium account relating to the issue of a *share* forming part of its *core tier one capital* in its *core tier one capital*.

(2) A *firm* must include *share* premium account relating to the issue of a *share* forming part of another tier of capital in that other tier.

(3) (3) A *firm* that is incorporated under the Companies Act 2006 may include its *share* premium account as *core tier one capital* notwithstanding (2) to the extent that the terms of issue of the *share* concerned provide that any premium is not repayable on redemption.

(4) Paragraph (3) applies to a *firm* that is not incorporated under the Companies Act 2006 if its *share* premium account is subject to substantially the same or greater restraints on use than a *share* premium account falling into (3).

Core tier one capital: externally verified interim net profits

2.2.102 **[R]** Externally verified interim net profits are interim profits which have been verified by a *firm's* external auditors after deduction of tax, foreseeable dividends and other appropriations.

2.2.103 **[G]** A *firm* may include interim profits before a formal decision has been taken only if these profits have been verified, in accordance with the relevant Auditing Practices Board's Practice Note, by *persons* responsible for the auditing of the accounts.

Core tier one capital: valuation differences (insurer only)

2.2.104 **[R]** GENPRU 2.2.104R to GENPRU 2.2.107R only apply to an *insurer*.

2.2.105 **[R]** Valuation differences are all differences between the valuation of assets and liabilities as valued in GENPRU and the valuation that the *insurer* uses for its external financial reporting purposes, except valuation differences which are dealt with elsewhere in the *capital resources table*. The sum of these valuation differences must either be added to (if positive) or deducted from (if negative) an *insurer's capital resources* in accordance with the *capital resources table*.

2.2.106 **[G]** Additions to and deductions from *capital resources* will arise from the application of asset and liability valuation and admissibility *rules* (see GENPRU 1.3 (Valuation), GENPRU 2.2.251R (Deductions from total capital: Inadmissible assets) and GENPRU 2 Annex 7R (Admissible assets in insurance)). Downward adjustments include *discounting* of *technical provisions* for *general insurance business* (which is optional for financial reporting but not permitted for regulatory valuation – see GENPRU 2.2.107R) and derecognition of any *defined benefit asset* in respect of a *defined benefit occupational pension scheme* (see GENPRU 1.3.9R(2) (General requirements: Adjustments to accounting values)). Details of valuation differences relating to *technical provisions* and liability adjustments for *long-term insurance business* are set out in INSPRU 1.2 (Mathematical reserves). In particular, contingent loans or other arrangements which are not valued as a liability under INSPRU 1.2.79R(2) (Reinsurance) result in a positive valuation difference.

2.2.107 **[R]**

(1) Subject to (3), this *rule* applies to an *insurer* that carries on *general insurance business* and which *discounts* or reduces its *technical provisions* for *claims* outstanding.

(2) An *insurer* of a kind referred to in (1) must deduct from its *capital resources* the difference between the undiscounted *technical provisions* or *technical provisions* before deductions, and the discounted *technical provisions* or *technical provisions* after deductions. This adjustment must be made for all *general insurance business classes*, except for risks listed under *classes* 1 and 2. For *classes* other than 1 and 2, no adjustment needs to be made in respect of the discounting of annuities included in *technical provisions*. For *classes* 1 and 2 (other than annuities), if the expected average interval between the settlement date of the *claims* being discounted and the accounting date is not at least four years, the *insurer* must deduct:
   (a) the difference between the undiscounted *technical provisions* and the discounted *technical provisions*; or
   (b) where it can identify a subset of *claims* such that the expected average interval between the settlement date of the *claims* and the accounting date is at least four years, the difference between the undiscounted *technical provisions* and the discounted *technical provisions* for the other claims.

(3) This *rule* does not apply to a *pure reinsurer* which became a *firm in run-off* before 31 December 2006 and whose *Part IV permission* has not subsequently been varied to add back the *regulated activity* of *effecting contracts of insurance*.

Core tier one capital: fund for future appropriations (insurer only)

2.2.108 **[R]** In relation to an *insurer* the fund for future appropriations means the fund of the same name required by the *insurance accounts rules*, comprising all funds the allocation of which either to *policyholders* or to shareholders has not been determined by the end of the *financial year*, or the balance sheet items under *international accounting standards* which in aggregate represent as nearly as possible that fund.

Other tier one capital: perpetual non-cumulative preference shares

2.2.109 **[R]** A perpetual non-cumulative *preference share* may be included at stage B of the calculation in the *capital resources table* if (in addition to satisfying all the other requirements in relation to *tier one capital*) it satisfies the following conditions:

(1) any *coupon* on it is not cumulative, and the *firm* is under no obligation to pay a *coupon* in any circumstances; and

(2) it is not an *innovative tier one instrument*.

2.2.110 **[G]** The other main provisions relevant to the eligibility of a perpetual non-cumulative *preference share* for inclusion in *tier one capital* are GENPRU 2.2.62R (Tier one capital: General), GENPRU 2.2.64R (General conditions for eligibility as tier one capital), GENPRU 2.2.65R (Connected transactions), GENPRU 2.2.70R to GENPRU 2.2.75R (Redemption of *tier one instruments*) and GENPRU 2.2.80R (Loss absorption). The *rules* about *innovative tier one capital* are also relevant as they may result in perpetual non-cumulative *preference shares* being treated as *innovative tier one capital*. Perpetual non-cumulative *preference shares* should be perpetual and redeemable only at the *firm's* option. Perpetual *preference shares* should be non-cumulative if they are to be included at stage B of the calculation in the *capital resources table*. Any feature that, in conjunction with a call, would make a *firm* more likely to redeem perpetual non-cumulative *preference shares* would normally result in classification as an *innovative tier one instrument*. Such features would include, but not be limited to, a *step-up*, bonus *coupon* on redemption or redemption at a premium to the original issue price of the *share*.

Other tier one capital: permanent interest bearing shares (building societies only)

2.2.111 **[R]** A *building society* may include a *PIBS* at stage B of the calculation in the *capital resources table* if (in addition to satisfying all the other requirements in relation to *tier one capital*) it is a "deferred share" as defined in the Building Societies (Deferred Shares) Order 1991.

2.2.112 **[G]** The other main provisions relevant to inclusion of a *PIBS* in *tier one capital* are GENPRU 2.2.62R (Tier one capital: General), GENPRU 2.2.64R (General conditions for eligibility as tier one capital), GENPRU 2.2.65R (Connected transactions), GENPRU 2.2.70R to GENPRU 2.2.75R (Redemption of *tier one instruments*), GENPRU 2.2.76R (Step-ups and redeemable tier one instruments) and GENPRU 2.2.80R (Loss absorption). However many of the *rules* in this section about features of *capital instruments* that result in treatment as *innovative tier one capital* do not apply.

Other tier one capital: innovative tier one capital: general

2.2.113 **[R]** If an item of capital is stated to be an *innovative tier one instrument* by the *rules* in GENPRU 2.2, it cannot be included in stages A (Core tier one capital) or B (Perpetual non-cumulative preference shares) of the calculation in the *capital resources table*.

Other tier one capital: innovative tier one capital: redemption

2.2.114 **[R]** If a *tier one instrument*, other than a *PIBS*:

(1) is redeemable; and

(2) a reasonable *person* would think that:

 (a) the *firm* is likely to redeem it; or

 (b) the *firm* is likely to have an economic incentive to redeem it;

that *tier one instrument* is an *innovative tier one instrument*.

2.2.115 **[G]** Any feature that in conjunction with a call would make a *firm* more likely to redeem a *tier one instrument*, other than a *PIBS*, would normally result in classification as *innovative tier one capital resources*. *Innovative tier one instruments* include but are not limited to those incorporating a *step-up* or principal stock settlement.

Other tier one capital: innovative tier one capital: loss absorption

2.2.116 **[R]** A *firm* may include a *capital instrument* that is not a *share* in its *innovative tier one capital resources* if (in addition to satisfying all the other requirements in relation to *tier one capital* and *innovative tier one capital*) it satisfies the condition in this *rule*. In addition a *firm* may not include any other capital in its *innovative tier one capital resources* unless it satisfies the condition in this *rule*. The condition in this *rule* is that the *firm's* obligations under the instrument either:

(1) do not constitute a liability (actual, contingent or prospective) under section 123(2) of the Insolvency Act 1986; or
(2) do constitute such a liability but the terms of the instrument are such that:
   (a) any such liability is not relevant for the purposes of deciding whether:
      (i) the *firm* is, or is likely to become, unable to pay its debts; or
      (ii) its liabilities exceed its assets;
   (b) a *person* (including, but not limited to, a holder of the instrument) is not able to petition for the winding up or administration of the *firm* or for any similar procedure in relation to the *firm* on the grounds that the *firm* is or may become unable to pay any such liability; and
   (c) the *firm* is not obliged to take into account such a liability for the purposes of deciding whether or not the *firm* is, or may become, insolvent for the purposes of section 214 of the Insolvency Act 1986 (wrongful trading).

2.2.117 **[G]** The effect of GENPRU 2.2.116R is that if a *potential tier one instrument* does constitute a liability, this should only be the case when the *firm* is able to pay that liability but chooses not to do so. As *tier one capital resources* should be undated, this will generally only be relevant on a solvent winding up of the *firm*. The holder should agree that the *firm* has no liability (including any contingent or prospective liability) to pay any amount to the extent to which that liability would cause the *firm* to become insolvent if it made the payment or to the extent that its liabilities exceed its assets or would do if the payment were made. The terms of the *capital instrument* should be such that the *directors* can continue to trade in the best interests of the senior creditors even if this prejudices the interests of the holders of the instrument.

2.2.118 **[R]** A *firm* may not include an *innovative tier one instrument*, unless it is a *preference share*, in its *tier one capital resources* unless it has obtained a properly reasoned independent legal opinion from an appropriately qualified individual confirming that the criteria in GENPRU 2.2.64R(6) (Loss absorption) and GENPRU 2.2.80R to GENPRU 2.2.81R (Loss absorption) are met.

2.2.119 **[G]** For the purpose of GENPRU 2.2.118R, an independent legal opinion may be given by an *employee* of that *firm*, but if an *employee* does so he should not be part of the business unit responsible for the transaction (including the drafting of the issue documentation).

Other tier one capital: innovative tier one capital: coupons

2.2.120 **[R]** A *tier one instrument*, other than a *PIBS*, with a cumulative or mandatory *coupon* is an *innovative tier one instrument*.

Other tier one capital: innovative tier one capital: step-ups

2.2.121 **[R]** If:
(1) a *potential tier one instrument*, other than a *PIBS*, is or may become subject to a *step-up*; and
(2) that *potential tier one instrument* is redeemable at any time (whether before, at or after the time of the *step-up*);

that *potential tier one instrument* is an *innovative tier one instrument*.

2.2.122 **[G]** See GENPRU 2.2.146R to GENPRU 2.2.154G for further *rules* and *guidance* on *step-ups*.

Other tier one capital: innovative tier one capital: indirectly issued tier one capital (BIPRU firm only)

2.2.123 **[R]** GENPRU 2.2.123R to GENPRU 2.2.137R apply to a *BIPRU firm*.

2.2.124 **[R]**
(1) GENPRU 2.2.123R–GENPRU 2.2.137R apply to capital of a *firm* if:
   (a) either or both of the conditions in (2) are satisfied; and
   (b) any of the *SPVs* referred to in (2) is a *subsidiary undertaking* of the *firm*.
(2) The conditions referred to in (1) are:
   (a) that capital is issued to an *SPV*; or
   (b) the subscription for the capital issued by the *firm* is funded directly or indirectly by an *SPV*.
(3) A *BIPRU firm* may not include capital coming within this *rule* in its *capital resources* unless the requirements in the following *rules* are satisfied:
   (a) (if (2)(a) applies and (2)(b) does not) GENPRU 2.2.127R, GENPRU 2.2.129R and GENPRU 2.2.132R; or
   (a) (in any other case) GENPRU 2.2.133R.

2.2.125 **[R]** A *BIPRU firm* may only count capital to which GENPRU 2.2.124R applies as *innovative tier one capital*.

2.2.126 **[R]** For the purpose of GENPRU 2.2, an *SPV* is, in relation to a *BIPRU firm*, any *undertaking* whose main activity is to raise funds for that *firm* or for a *group* to which that *BIPRU firm* belongs.

2.2.127 **[R]** The *SPV* referred to in GENPRU 2.2.124R(2)(a) must satisfy the following conditions:
(1) it is controlled by the *firm* and may not operate independently of the *firm*;
(2) the rights of investors in the *SPV* who do not belong to the *group* of the *BIPRU firm* in question are not such as to affect the ability of the *firm* to control the *SPV*; and
(3) all or virtually all of its *exposures* (calculated by reference to the amount) consist of *exposures* to the *firm* or to that *firm's group*.

2.2.128 **[G]** An *SPV* could take the form of a limited partnership. In such an arrangement, holders of a *capital instrument* issued by the *SPV* which do not belong to the *group* of the *BIPRU firm* in question should have no right to participate in the management of the partnership, whether under the partnership's constitutional documents or the transaction documents. In general, this means that they should be treated as limited partners. It is expected that the general partner, having control of the *SPV*, would be the *firm*.

2.2.129 **[R]** The *SPV* referred to in GENPRU 2.2.124R(2)(a) must fund its subscription for the capital issued by the *firm* by the issue of capital that satisfies the following conditions:
(1) it must comply with the conditions for qualification as *tier one capital*, as amended by GENPRU 2.2.130R, as if the *SPV* was itself a *firm* seeking to include that capital in its *tier one capital resources*;
(2) its terms must include an obligation on the *firm*, when the *capital resources* of the *firm* fall below, or are likely to fall below, its *capital resources requirement*, to substitute for the instrument issued by the *SPV* a *tier one instrument* issued by that *firm* that:
   (a) is not an *innovative tier one instrument*; or
   (b) is an *innovative tier one instrument* provided that:
      (i) it is only being classified as such because it is or may become subject to a *step-up*, and
      (ii) the terms of the original instrument issued by the *SPV* included a *step-up*;
(3) the conversion ratio in respect of the substitution described in (2) must be fixed when the *SPV* issues the *capital instrument*; and
(4) to the extent that investors have the benefit of an obligation by a *person* other than the *SPV*:
   (a) that obligation must be one owed by a member of the *firm's group*; and
   (b) the extent of that obligation must be no greater than would be permitted by GENPRU if that obligation formed part of the terms of a *capital instrument* issued by that member which complied with the *rules* in GENPRU relating to *innovative tier one capital*.

2.2.130 **[R]** For the purpose of GENPRU 2.2.129R and GENPRU 2.2.132R, GENPRU 2.2.118R (Requirement to obtain a legal opinion) does not apply.

2.2.131 **[R]** In relation to the obligation to substitute described in GENPRU 2.2.129R(2), a *firm* must take all reasonable steps to ensure that it has at all times authorised and unissued *tier one instruments* that are not *innovative tier one instruments* or that are *innovative tier one instruments* only because they are or may become subject to a *step-up* (and the authority to issue them) sufficient to discharge its obligation to substitute.

2.2.131A **[G]** GENPRU 2.2.129R(2) and GENPRU 2.2.131R allow a *firm* to replace the capital issued by the *SPV* with a *tier one instrument* that is not an *innovative tier one instrument* or that is an *innovative tier one instrument* provided that:
(1) it is only being classified as such because it is or may become subject to a *step-up*, and
(2) the terms of the original instrument issued by the *SPV* included a *step-up*.

In all other respects, the *innovative tier one instrument* issued by the *firm* must meet the conditions to be an item of *tier one capital* capable of inclusion in Stage B or higher in the *capital resources table*.

2.2.132 **[R]** The capital which the *firm* seeks to include in its *capital resources* under GENPRU 2.2.124R(3)(a) must satisfy the following conditions:
(1) it meets the conditions for inclusion in *tier one capital* (subject to GENPRU 2.2.130R);
(2) its first call date (if any) must not arise before that on the instrument issued by the *SPV*; and
(3) its terms relating to repayment must be the same as those of the instrument issued by the *SPV*.

2.2.133 **[R]**
(1) This rule deals with any transaction:
   (a) under which an *SPV* directly or indirectly funds the subscription for capital issued by the *firm* as described in GENPRU 2.2.124R; or
   (b) that is directly or indirectly funded by a transaction in (1)(a).
(2) Each *undertaking* that is a party to a transaction to which this *rule* applies (other than the *firm*) must be a *subsidiary undertaking* of the *firm*.
(3) Each *SPV* that is a party to a transaction to which this *rule* applies must comply with GENPRU 2.2.127R.
(4) Any capital to which (1) applies (other than the capital that is to be included in the *firm's capital resources*) must be in the form of capital that complies with GENPRU 2.2.129R(1) and (4), whether or not issued by an *SPV*.

(5) The obligations in GENPRU 2.2.129R(2) and (3) only apply to capital issued by an *SPV* at the end of the chain of transactions beginning with the issue of capital by the *firm* referred to in GENPRU 2.2.124R.
(6) GENPRU 2.2.132R applies to the capital issued by the *firm* as referred to in GENPRU 2.2.124R. For these purposes references in GENPRU 2.2.132R to the instrument issued by the *SPV* are to the instrument referred to in (5).

2.2.134 **[G]** The purpose of GENPRU 2.2.133R is to deal with a capital-raising under which the capital raised by a special purpose vehicle is passed through a number of *undertakings* before it is invested in the *firm*. If the *capital resources* of the *firm* fall below, or are likely to fall below, its *capital resources requirement* the *firm* should replace the capital issued by that first special purpose vehicle with a *tier one instrument* directly issued by the *firm* which complies with GENPRU 2.2.129R(2).

2.2.135 **[R]** A *firm* which satisfies the conditions for the inclusion of capital set out in GENPRU 2.2.124R, must, in addition, if that transaction is in any respect unusual, notify the *FSA* at least one *Month* in advance of the date on which the *firm* intends to include that capital in its *capital resources*.

2.2.136 **[G]** The *FSA* is likely to consider as unusual a transaction which involves the raising by the *firm* of *tier one capital* through a *subsidiary undertaking* of that *firm* that is not an *SPV*. The *FSA* would expect a *firm* to request individual *guidance* in such circumstances.

2.2.137 **[R]** A *firm* must ensure that, in relation to a transaction falling within GENPRU 2.2.124R:
(1) the marketing document for the transaction contains all the information which a reasonable third party would require to understand the transaction fully and its effect on the financial position of the *firm* and its *group*; and
(2) the information in (1) and the transaction are easily comprehensible without the need for additional information about the *firm* and its *group*.

Tier one capital: Conversion ratio

2.2.138 **[R]**
(1) This *rule* applies to a *potential tier one instrument* if:
 (a) it is redeemable by the *firm* (ignoring GENPRU 2.2.77R (Meaning of redemption));
 (b) it provides that if the issuer does not exercise that right or does not do so in specified circumstances the issuer must or may have to redeem it in whole or in part through the issue of *shares* eligible for inclusion in the *firm's tier one capital resources* or the instrument converts or may convert into such *shares*; and
 (c) GENPRU 2.2.77R means that the obligation in (1)(b) is treated as not being inconsistent with GENPRU 2.2.70R(1) (*Tier one capital* should not be redeemable at the option of the holder).
(2) A *firm* must not include a *potential tier one instrument* to which this *rule* applies in its *tier one capital resources* if:
 (a) the conversion ratio as at the date of redemption may be greater than the conversion ratio as at the time of issue by more than 200%; or
 (b) the market price of the conversion instruments issued in relation to one unit of the original capital item (plus any cash element of the redemption) may be greater than the issue price of that original capital item.
(3) All determinations under this *rule* are made as at the date of issue of the original capital item.

2.2.139 **[R]** In GENPRU 2.2.138R to GENPRU 2.2.142R:
(1) the original capital item means the capital item that is being redeemed; and
(2) the conversion instrument means the *tier one capital* to be issued on its redemption.

2.2.140 **[R]** In GENPRU 2.2.138R to GENPRU 2.2.142R, the conversion ratio means the ratio of:
(1) the number of units of the conversion instrument that the *firm* must issue to satisfy its redemption obligation (so far as it is to be satisfied by the issue of conversion instruments) in respect of one unit of the original capital item; to
(2) one unit of the original capital item.

2.2.141 **[R]** In GENPRU 2.2.138R to GENPRU 2.2.142R, the conversion ratio as at the date of issue of the original capital item is calculated as if the original capital item were redeemable at that time.

2.2.142 **[R]** If the conversion instruments or the original capital item are subdivided or consolidated or subject to any other occurrence that would otherwise result in like not being compared with like, the conversion ratio calculation in GENPRU 2.2.138R must be adjusted accordingly.

2.2.143 **[G]**
(1) The significance of the limitations on conversion in GENPRU 2.2.138R(2) can be seen in the example in this paragraph.
(2) A *firm* issues innovative notes with a par value of £100 each. The terms of the instrument provide that if the instrument is not called at par at the first call date the notes convert into a variable number of ordinary *shares*.

(3) If the market price of the ordinary *shares* is 400 pence per share on the day of issue of the innovative notes then the maximum number of ordinary *shares* (M) that a single £100 par value innovative note can be converted into is calculated as follows:
(a) M = Par value of innovative instrument × 200% / market value of ordinary *share*;
(b) M = £100 × 2/£4 = 50 *shares*.

(4) The practical effect is that conversion will result in the holder of an innovative capital note receiving ordinary *shares* equal to the par value of that note only when the market price of the ordinary *shares* remains above half the market price of the *shares* at the date of issue of the notes.

(5) If the market price of the ordinary *shares* fell by half to 200 pence, the maximum permitted number of *shares* (50) would have to be issued in order to give an investor in the innovative note ordinary *shares* with a market value equal to £100. If the market price of the ordinary *shares* fell below 200 pence, the issue of the maximum permitted number of ordinary *shares* would have a market value below £100.

2.2.144 **[G]**
(1) In addition to the maximum conversion ratio of 200%, GENPRU 2.2.138R(2)(b) does not permit a *firm* to issue *shares* that would have a market value that exceeds the issue price of the instrument being redeemed.
(2) In the example in GENPRU 2.2.143G, if the market value of the ordinary *shares* was 250 pence at the conversion date, the maximum number of ordinary *shares* that may be issued to satisfy the redemption of one of the £100 par value innovative notes would be 40 (= £100/£2.5).

Tier one capital: Requirement to have sufficient unissued stock

2.2.145 **[R]**
(1) This *rule* applies to a *potential tier one instrument* of a *firm* where either:
(a) the redemption proceeds; or
(b) any *coupon* on that capital item;
can be satisfied by the issue of another *capital instrument*.
(2) A *firm* may only include an item of capital to which this *rule* applies in its *tier one capital resources* if the *firm* has authorised and unissued *capital instruments* of the kind in question (and the authority to issue them):
(a) that are sufficient to satisfy all such payments then due; and
(b) are of such amount as is prudent in respect of such payments that could become due in the future.

Step-ups: calculating the size of a step-up

2.2.146 **[R]**
(1) Where a *rule* in this section says that a particular treatment applies to an item of capital that is subject to a *step-up* of a specified amount, the question of whether that *rule* is satisfied must be judged by reference to the cumulative amount of all *step-ups* since the issue of that item of capital rather than just by reference to a particular *step-up*.
(2) Where a *step-up* arises through a change from paying a *coupon* on a debt instrument to paying a dividend on a *share* issued in settlement of the *coupon*, any net cost to the *firm* arising from the different tax treatment of the dividend compared to the tax treatment of interest may be ignored for the purpose of assessing the effect of that *step-up*.

Step-ups: Limits on the amount of step-ups on tier one and two capital

2.2.147 **[R]**
(1) A *firm* may not include in its *tier one capital resources* a *tier one instrument* that is or may be subject to a *step-up* that does not meet the definition of moderate in the press release of the Basle Committee on Banking Supervision of 27th October 1998 called "Instruments eligible for inclusion in Tier 1 capital".
(2) For the purpose of (1) the words in that press release "than, at national supervisory discretion, either" are replaced by "than the higher of the following two amounts".
(3) The calculations required by this *rule* and GENPRU 2.2.151R must be carried out as at the date of issue of the relevant instrument.

2.2.148 **[G]** The effect of GENPRU 2.2.147R is that for inclusion in *tier one capital resources*, *step-ups* in instruments should be moderate. A moderate *step-up* for these purposes is one which results in an increase over the initial rate that is no greater than the higher of the following two amounts:
(1) 100 basis points, less the swap spread between the initial index basis and the stepped-up index basis; or
(2) 50% of the initial credit spread, less the swap spread between the initial index basis and the stepped-up index basis.

2.2.149 **[G]** If a *coupon* paid on an item of capital is initially set at a specified spread above an index (the initial index basis), and the *coupon* moves to being set relative to another index (the stepped up index basis), there will be an implied *step-up* (positive or negative) even if the specified spread does not change. This is because each index may itself include a spread relative to the risk free rate and this spread may differ between the two indexes. The deduction of the swap spread in GENPRU 2.2.148G(1) and (2) above adjusts for this difference.

2.2.150 **[G]** Where the *step-up* involves a conversion from fixed to floating (or vice versa), or a switch in basis index, the swap spread should be fixed at pricing date, reflecting the differential in pricing between indices at the time. The significance of deducting the swap spread can be seen by the following example:

(1) the pricing date:
  (a) 10 year gilts (G) = 5.5% (the initial index basis);
  (b) 3 month LIBOR is the stepped up index basis and the 10 year mid swap rate (L) = 5.9%;
  (c) initial fixed *coupon* rate = G + 200bp;
  (d) swap spread = 0.4% (= 5.9% – 5.5%);
  (e) initial fixed coupon rate = 7.5%;
  (f) the swap spread shows that there is 40bps of spread in the stepped up index basis relative to the initial index basis; and
  (g) the initial fixed coupon rate of 7.5% is equivalent to the mid swap rate + 160bp, or L + 200bp – the swap spread;
(2) pricing of *stepped-up* rate at year 10 with *step-up* of 100bp without deducting swap spread:
  (a) *stepped-up* floating rate = L + 200 + 100bp step-up = 8.9%; and
  (b) effective *step-up* from initial fixed rate of 140bp (= 8.9% – 7.5%); and
(3) pricing of *stepped-up* rate at year 10 with step-up of 100bp with deduction of the swap spread:
  (a) *stepped-up* floating *coupon* rate = L + 200 less 40bp swap spread (difference between 5.5% and 5.9%) + 100bp step-up = 8.5%
  (b) effective *step-up* from initial rate of 100bp (= 8.5% – 7.5%).

2.2.151 **[R]**
(1) Subject to (2), if a *tier two instrument* is or may be subject to a *step-up* that does not meet the definition of moderate in the press release of the Basle Committee on Banking Supervision referred to in GENPRU 2.2.147R(1) as adjusted under GENPRU 2.2.147R(2), the first date that a *step-up* can take effect is deemed to be its final maturity date if that date is before its actual maturity date.
(2) If a *tier two instrument*:
  (a) is or may be subject to a *step-up* during the period beginning on the fifth anniversary of the date of issue of that item and ending immediately before the tenth anniversary of the date of issue; and
  (b) the *step-up* or possible *step-up* is one which may result in an increase over the initial rate that is greater than 50 basis points, less the swap spread between the initial index basis and the stepped-up index basis (all these terms must be interpreted in accordance with GENPRU 2.2.147R);

the first date that a *step-up* can take effect is deemed to be its final maturity date if that date is before its actual maturity date.

2.2.152 **[R]** An instrument does not breach GENPRU 2.2.147R or as the case may be, is not subject to a deemed maturity date under GENPRU 2.2.151R, even though it is or may be subject to a *step-up* that exceeds the amount specified in those *rules* if:
(1) the instrument is fungible with other instruments (the "existing stock") that are included in the *firm's tier one capital resources* (in the case of GENPRU 2.2.147R) or *tier two capital resources* (in the case of GENPRU 2.2.151R);
(2) (if there has been no more than one previous issue of the existing stock) the existing stock complied with those limits on its date of issue;
(3) (if there has been more than one previous issue of the existing stock) the first such issue of the existing stock complied with those limits on its date of issue; and
(4) the result of the *step-up* on the instrument to which this *rule* applies is that the *coupon* on that instrument and the *coupon* on the existing stock is the same.

2.2.153 **[R]**
(1) A *firm* must not include in its *tier one capital resources* a *potential tier one instrument* that is or may become subject to a *step-up* if that *step-up* can arise earlier than the tenth anniversary of the date of issue of that item of capital.
(2) A *firm* must not include in its *tier two capital resources* a *capital instrument* that is or may become subject to a *step-up* if that *step-up* can arise earlier than the fifth anniversary of the date of issue of that item of capital.

2.2.154 **[G]** Debt instruments containing embedded options, e.g. issues containing options for the interest rate after the *step-up* to be at a margin over the higher of two (or more) reference rates, or

Part II FSA Handbook Materials

for the interest rate in the previous period to act as a floor, may affect the funding costs of the borrower and imply a *step-up*. In such circumstances, a *firm* may wish to seek individual *guidance* on the application of the *rules* relating to *step-ups* to the *capital instrument* in question. See SUP 9 (Individual guidance) for the process to be followed when seeking individual *guidance*.

Deductions from tier one: Intangible assets

2.2.155 **[R]** A *firm* must deduct from its *tier one capital resources* the value of intangible assets.

2.2.156 **[G]** Intangible assets include goodwill as defined in accordance with the requirements referred to in GENPRU 1.3.4R (General requirements: accounting principles to be applied) applicable to the *firm*. The treatment of deferred acquisition cost assets for *BIPRU investment firms* is dealt with in GENPRU 1.3 (Valuation); they should not be deducted as an intangible asset.

Tier two capital: General

2.2.157 **[G]** *Tier two capital resources* are split into upper and lower tiers. A major distinction between *upper* and *lower tier two capital* is that only perpetual instruments may be included in *upper tier two capital* whereas dated instruments, such as fixed term *preference shares* and dated subordinated debt, may be included in *lower tier two capital*.

2.2.158 **[G]** *Tier two instruments* are *capital instruments* that combine the features of debt and equity in that they are structured like debt, but exhibit some of the loss absorption and funding flexibility features of equity.

General conditions for eligibility as tier two capital instruments

2.2.159 **[R]** A *capital instrument* must not form part of the *tier two capital resources* of a *firm* unless it meets the following conditions:

(1) the claims of the creditors must rank behind those of all unsubordinated creditors;

(2) the only events of default must be non-payment of any amount falling due under the terms of the *capital instrument* or the winding-up of the *firm* and any such event of default must not prejudice the subordination in (1);

(3) to the fullest extent permitted under the laws of the relevant jurisdictions, the remedies available to the subordinated creditor in the event of non-payment or other breach of the terms of the *capital instrument* must (subject to GENPRU 2.2.161R) be limited to petitioning for the winding-up of the *firm* or proving for the debt in the liquidation or administration;

(4) any:
   (a) remedy permitted by (3);
   (b) remedy that cannot be excluded under the laws of the relevant jurisdictions as referred to in (3);
   (c) remedy permitted by GENPRU 2.2.161R; and
   (d) terms about repayment as referred to in (5);

   must not prejudice the matters in (1) and (2) and in particular any damages permitted by (b) or (c) and repayment obligation must be subordinated in accordance with (1);

(5) without prejudice to (1), the debt must not become due and payable before its stated final maturity date (if any) except on an event of default complying with (2) or as permitted by GENPRU 2.2.172R (Repayment at the option of the issuer) or GENPRU 2.2.194R(2) (Repayment of *lower tier two capital* at the option of the holder) and any remedy described in (4)(a) to (c) must not prejudice this requirement;

(6) the debt agreement or terms of the *capital instrument* are governed by the law of England and Wales, or of Scotland or of Northern Ireland;

(7) to the fullest extent permitted under the laws of the relevant jurisdictions, creditors must waive their right to set off amounts they owe the *firm* against subordinated amounts included in the *firm's capital resources* owed to them by the *firm*;

(8) the terms of the *capital instrument* must be set out in a written agreement that contains terms that provide for the conditions set out in (1) to (7);

(9) the debt must be unsecured and fully paid up;

(10) the description of its characteristics used in its marketing is consistent with the characteristics required to satisfy (1) to (9) and, where it applies, GENPRU 2.2.271R (Other requirements: insurers carrying on with-profits business (Insurer only));

(11) the amount of the item included must be net of any foreseeable tax charge at the moment of its calculation or must be suitably adjusted in so far as such tax charges reduce the amount up to which that item may be applied to cover risks or losses; and

(12) the *firm* has obtained a properly reasoned independent legal opinion from an appropriately qualified individual stating that the requirements in (1) to (7) and (insofar as it relates to whether the *capital instrument* is unsecured) (9) have been met.

2.2.160 **[R]** A holder of a non-deferred share of a *building society* must be treated as a senior unsecured creditor of that *building society* for the purpose of GENPRU 2.2.159R.

General conditions for eligibility as tier two capital instruments: Additional remedies

2.2.161 **[R]** A *capital instrument* may be included in a *firm's tier two capital resources* even though the remedies available to the subordinated creditor go beyond those referred to in GENPRU 2.2.159R(3), if the following conditions are satisfied:

(1) those remedies are not available for failure to pay any amount of principal, interest or expenses or in respect of any other payment obligation; and

(2) those remedies do not in substance amount to remedies to recover payment of the amounts in (1).

2.2.162 **[G]** If damages are a remedy that cannot be excluded as referred to in GENPRU 2.2.159R(3) those damages should be subordinated in accordance with GENPRU 2.2.159R(1). Damages permitted by GENPRU 2.2.161R should also be subordinated in accordance with GENPRU 2.2.159R(1).

General conditions for eligibility as tier two capital instruments: Alternative governing laws

2.2.163 **[R]** GENPRU 2.2.159R(6) does not apply if the *firm* has obtained a properly reasoned independent legal opinion from an appropriately qualified individual confirming that the same degree of subordination has been achieved under the law that governs the debt and the agreement as that which would have been achieved under the laws of England and Wales, Scotland, or Northern Ireland.

General conditions for eligibility as tier two capital instruments: Standard form documentation

2.2.164 **[G]** The *FSA* is more concerned that the subordination provisions listed in GENPRU 2.2.159R should be effective than that they should follow a particular form. The *FSA* does not, therefore, prescribe that the loan agreement or *capital instrument* should be drawn up in a standard form.

Guidance on the general conditions for eligibility as tier two capital instruments

2.2.165 **[G]** For the purposes of GENPRU 2.2.159R(5) the debt agreement or terms of the instrument should not contain any clause which might require early repayment of the debt (e.g. cross default clauses, negative pledges and restrictive covenants). A cross default clause is a clause which says that the loan goes into default if any of the borrower's other loans go into default. It is intended to prevent one creditor being repaid before other creditors, e.g. obtaining full repayment through the courts. A negative pledge is a clause which puts the loan into default if the borrower gives any further charge over its assets. A restrictive covenant is a term of contract that directly, or indirectly, could lead to early repayment of the debt. Some covenants, e.g. relating to the provision of management information or ownership restrictions, are likely to comply with GENPRU 2.2.159R(3) as long as monetary redress is ruled out, or any payments are covered by the subordination clauses.

2.2.166 **[G]** GENPRU 2.2.159R(3) allows a *capital instrument* to form part of the *tier two capital resources* even though the laws of the relevant jurisdiction do not allow remedies to be limited in the way described there. For example it is not possible to limit certain remedies in the case of an issue in the United States that is SEC-registered and subject to the provisions of the Trust Indenture Act.

2.2.167 **[G]** The purpose of GENPRU 2.2.159R(7) is to ensure that all of the *firm's* assets are available to *consumers* ahead of subordinated creditors. The waiver should apply both before and during liquidation or administration.

2.2.168 **[G]** The *guidance* in GENPRU 2.2.119G (Employee may give legal opinion) also applies for the purpose of GENPRU 2.2.159R(12) and GENPRU 2.2.163R.

Tier two capital instruments: Connected transactions

2.2.169 **[R]** An item of capital does not comply with GENPRU 2.2.159R (General conditions for eligibility as tier two *capital instruments*) or GENPRU 2.2.177R (Upper tier two capital: General) if the issue of that item of capital by the *firm* is connected with one or more other transactions which, when taken together with the issue of that item, could result in that item of capital no longer displaying all of the characteristics set out in whichever of those *rules* apply.

2.2.170 **[G]** GENPRU 2.2.66G (*Guidance* on GENPRU 2.2.65R) applies to GENPRU 2.2.169R in the same way as it does to GENPRU 2.2.65R (The equivalent of GENPRU 2.2.169R in relation to *tier one capital*).

Amendment of tier two instruments

2.2.171 **[R]** A *firm* must not amend the terms of the capital or the documents referred to in GENPRU 2.2.159R(8) unless:

(1) at least one *Month* before the amendment is due to take effect, the *firm* has given the *FSA* notice in writing of the proposed amendment and the *FSA* has not objected; and
(2) that notice includes confirmation that the legal opinions referred to in GENPRU 2.2.159R(12) and, if applicable, GENPRU 2.2.163R (General conditions for eligibility as tier two *capital instruments*: Alternative governing laws) and GENPRU 2.2.181R (Legal opinions for *upper tier two instruments*), continue in full force and effect in relation to the terms of the debt and documents after any proposed amendment.

Redemption of tier two instruments

2.2.172 **[R]** A *tier two instrument* may be redeemable at the option of the *firm*, but any term of the instrument providing for the *firm* to have the right to exercise such an option must not provide for that right to be exercisable earlier than the fifth anniversary of the date of issue of the instrument.

2.2.173 **[R]** GENPRU 2.2.71R to GENPRU 2.2.73G (*Tier one instruments* may be redeemed by the issuer before the fifth anniversary in limited circumstances) apply to GENPRU 2.2.172R in the same way as they do to GENPRU 2.2.70R (The issuer should not redeem *tier one capital* before the fifth anniversary).

2.2.174 **[R]** In relation to a *tier two instrument*, a *firm* must notify the *FSA*:
(1) in the case of an *insurer*, six *Months*; and
(2) in the case of a *BIPRU firm*, one *Month*;

before it becomes committed to the proposed repayment (unless that *firm* intends to repay an instrument on its final maturity date). When giving notice, the firm must provide details of its position after such repayment in order to show how it will:
(3) meet its *capital resources requirement*; and
(4) have sufficient financial resources to meet the *overall financial adequacy rule*.

Tier two capital: step-ups

2.2.175 **[G]** The *rules* and *guidance* in GENPRU 2.2.146R to GENPRU 2.2.154G on *step-ups* cover *tier two capital* as well as *tier one capital*.

Upper tier two capital: General

2.2.176 **[G]** Examples of *capital instruments* which may be eligible to count in *upper tier two capital resources* include the following:
(1) perpetual cumulative *preference shares*;
(2) perpetual subordinated debt; and
(3) other instruments that have the same economic characteristics as (1) or (2).

2.2.177 **[R]** A *capital instrument* must (in addition to meeting the requirements of the *rules* about eligibility for inclusion in *tier two capital*) meet the following conditions before it can be included in a *firm's upper tier two capital resources*:
(1) it must have no fixed maturity date;
(2) the terms of the instrument must provide for the *firm* to have the option to defer any *coupon* on the debt, except that the *firm* need not have that right in the case of a *coupon* payable in the form of an item of capital that is included in the *same stage of capital* or a *higher stage of capital* as that first item of capital;
(3) the terms of the instrument must provide for the loss-absorption capacity of the *capital instrument* and unpaid *coupons*, whilst enabling the *firm* to continue its business;
(4) it meets the conditions in GENPRU 2.2.169R (Connected transactions) and GENPRU 2.2.180R (Loss absorption); and
(5) the terms of the instrument are such that either the instrument or debt is not redeemable or repayable or it is repayable or redeemable only at the option of the *firm*.

2.2.178 **[R]** If a *firm* gives notice of the redemption or repayment of an *upper tier two instrument*, the *firm* must no longer include it in its *upper tier two capital resources*.

2.2.179 **[G]**
(1) The purpose of GENPRU 2.2.177R(2) is to ensure that a *firm* which issues an item of capital with a *coupon* retains flexibility over the payments of such *coupon* and can preserve cash in times of financial stress. However, a *firm* may include, as part of the capital instrument terms, a right to make payments of a *coupon* mandatory if an item of capital becomes ineligible to form part of its *capital resources* (for example, through a change in the relevant *rules*) and the *firm* has notified the *FSA* that the instrument is ineligible.
(2) For the purpose of GENPRU 2.2.177R(2), GENPRU 2.2.68G (Dividend pushers) applies *equally in relation to the inclusion of an instrument in upper tier two capital resources*.

Upper tier two capital: Loss absorption

2.2.180 **[R]** A *capital instrument* may only be included in *upper tier two capital resources* if a *firm's* obligations under the instrument either:

(1) do not constitute a liability (actual, contingent or prospective) under section 123(2) of the Insolvency Act 1986; or
(2) do constitute such a liability but the terms of the instrument are such that:
 (a) any such liability is not relevant for the purposes of deciding whether:
  (i) the *firm* is, or is likely to become, unable to pay its debts; or
  (ii) its liabilities exceed its assets;
 (b) a *person* (including but not limited to a holder of the instrument) is not able to petition for the winding up or administration of the *firm* or for any similar procedure in relation to the *firm* on the grounds that the *firm* is or may become unable to pay any such liability; and
 (c) the *firm* is not obliged to take into account such a liability for the purposes of deciding whether or not the *firm* is, or may become, insolvent for the purposes of section 214 of the Insolvency Act 1986 (wrongful trading).

Upper tier two capital: Legal opinions

2.2.181 **[R]** A *firm* may not include an *upper tier two instrument* in its *upper tier two capital resources* unless it has obtained a properly reasoned independent legal opinion from an appropriately qualified individual confirming that the criteria in GENPRU 2.2.177R(3) and GENPRU 2.2.180R (Loss absorption) are met. This *rule* does not apply to a perpetual cumulative *preference share*.

Upper tier two capital: Guidance

2.2.182 **[G]** GENPRU 2.2.180R is an example of the general principle in GENPRU 2.2.177R(3).

2.2.183 **[G]** The *guidance* in GENPRU 2.2.117G (There should be no liability to the extent that the *firm* would become insolvent, etc) also applies for the purpose of GENPRU 2.2.180R.

2.2.184 **[G]** The *guidance* in GENPRU 2.2.119G (Employee may give legal opinion) also applies for the purpose of GENPRU 2.2.181R.

Upper tier two capital: Revaluation reserves (BIPRU firm only)

2.2.185 **[R]**
(1) This *rule* applies to a *BIPRU firm*.
(2) A *BIPRU firm* must, in relation to equities held in the available-for-sale financial assets category:
 (a) deduct any net losses at stage E of the calculation in the *capital resources table* (Deductions from tier one capital); and
 (b) include any net gains (after deduction of deferred tax) in revaluation reserves at stage G of the calculation in the *capital resources table* (Upper tier two capital).
(3) A *BIPRU firm* must include any net gains, after deduction of deferred tax, on revaluation reserves of investment properties at stage G of the calculation in the *capital resources table*. A *firm* must include any losses on such revaluation reserves in profit and loss account and other reserves.
(4) A *BIPRU firm* must include any net gains, after deduction of deferred tax, on revaluation reserves of land and buildings at stage G of the calculation in the *capital resources table*. A *firm* must include any losses on such revaluation reserves in profit and loss account and other reserves.
(5) (2) only applies to a *firm* to the extent that the category of asset referred to in that paragraph exists under the accounting framework that applies to the *firm* as referred to in GENPRU 1.3.4R (General requirements: accounting principles to be applied).
(6) (3) and (4) apply to a *firm* whatever the accounting treatment of those items is under the accounting framework that applies to the *firm* as referred to in GENPRU 1.3.4R.

2.2.186 **[G]** Subject to GENPRU 2.2.185R, a *BIPRU firm* should value its revaluation reserves in accordance with the *rules* in GENPRU 1.3 (Valuation).

Upper tier two capital: General/collective provisions (BIPRU firm only)

2.2.187 **[R]** A *BIPRU firm* which adopts the *standardised approach* to credit risk may include general/collective provisions in its *tier two capital resources* only if:
(1) they are freely available to the *firm*;
(2) their existence is disclosed in internal accounting records; and
(3) their amount is determined by the management of the *firm*, verified by independent auditors and notified to the *FSA*.

2.2.188 **[R]** The value of general/collective provisions which a *firm* may include in its *tier two capital resources* as referred to in GENPRU 2.2.187R may not exceed 1.25% of the sum of the following:
(1) the sum of the *market risk capital requirement* and the *operational risk capital requirement* (if applicable), multiplied by a factor of 12.5; and

(2) the sum of *risk-weighted* assets under the *standardised approach* for credit risk.

2.2.189 **[R]** Where a *firm* is unable to determine whether collective/general provisions relate only to *exposures* on either the *standardised approach* or the *IRB approach*, that *firm* must allocate them on a basis which is reasonable and consistent.

Upper tier two capital: Surplus provisions (BIPRU firm only)

2.2.190 **[R]** A *BIPRU firm* calculating *risk weighted exposure amounts* under the *IRB approach* may include in its *upper tier two capital resources* positive amounts resulting from the calculation in *BIPRU* 4.3.8R (Treatment of expected loss amounts), up to 0.6% of the *risk weighted exposure amounts* calculated under that approach.

2.2.191 **[R]** A *BIPRU firm* calculating *risk weighted exposure amounts* under the *IRB approach* may not include in its *capital resources* value adjustments and provisions included in the calculation in *BIPRU* 4.3.8R (Treatment of *expected loss* amounts under the *IRB approach* for *trading book exposures*) or value adjustments and provisions for *exposures* that would otherwise have been eligible for inclusion in general/collective provisions other than in accordance with GENPRU 2.2.190R.

2.2.192 **[R]** For the purpose of GENPRU 2.2.190R and GENPRU 2.2.191R, *risk weighted exposure amounts* must not include those calculated in respect of *securitisation positions* which have a *risk weight* of 1250%.

2.2.193 **[R]** If a *BIPRU firm* calculates *risk weighted exposure amounts* under the *IRB approach* for the purposes of BIPRU 14 (Capital requirements for settlement and counterparty risk) it must not include valuation adjustments referred to in BIPRU 14.2.18R(1) (Treatment of expected loss amounts) in its *capital resources* except in accordance with that *rule*.

Lower tier two capital

2.2.194 **[R]** A *firm* may include a *capital instrument* in its *lower tier two capital resources* if (in addition to meeting the requirements of the *rules* about eligibility for inclusion in *tier two capital*) either the holder has no right to repayment or it satisfies either of the following conditions:
(1) it has an original maturity of at least five years; or
(2) it is redeemable on notice from the holder, but the period of notice of repayment required to be given by the holder is five years or more.

2.2.195 **[G]** A *firm* may include perpetual *capital instruments* that do not meet the conditions in GENPRU 2.2.177R (Eligibility conditions for *upper tier two capital*) in *lower tier two capital resources* if they meet the general conditions described in GENPRU 2.2.159R (General conditions for eligibility as tier two *capital instruments*).

2.2.196 **[R]**
(1) For the purposes of calculating the amount of a *lower tier two instrument* which may be included in a *firm's capital resources*:
    (a) in the case of an instrument with a fixed maturity date, in the final five years to maturity; and
    (b) in the case of an instrument with or without a fixed maturity date but where five years' or more notice of redemption or repayment has been given, in the final five years to the date of redemption or repayment;

    the principal amount must be amortised on a straight line basis.
(2) If a *firm* gives notice of the redemption or repayment of a *lower tier two instrument* and (1) does not apply, the *firm* must no longer include it in its *lower tier two capital resources*.

2.2.197 **[G]** If a *firm* wishes to include in *lower tier two capital resources* an instrument with or without a fixed maturity date but where less than five years' notice of redemption or repayment has been given, it should seek individual *guidance* from the *FSA*.

The effect of swaps on debt capital

2.2.198 **[R]** GENPRU 2.2.198R to GENPRU 2.2.201R apply to a *tier one instrument*, *tier two instrument* or *tier three instrument* of a *firm* that is treated as a liability under the accounting framework to which it is subject as referred to in GENPRU 1.3.4R (General requirements: accounting principles to be applied) (a "debt instrument").

2.2.199 **[R]** A *firm* must recognise for the purpose of this section any effect that changes in exchange rates or interest rates have on a debt instrument (as defined in GENPRU 2.2.198R) under the *accounting framework to which the firm* is subject as referred to in GENPRU 1.3.4R (General requirements: accounting principles to be applied).

2.2.200 **[R]** A *firm* must recognise, in accordance with GENPRU 2.2.201R, the effect of a *foreign currency* hedge on a debt instrument (as defined in GENPRU 2.2.198R) denominated in a *foreign currency* or of an interest rate hedge on a fixed rate *coupon* debt instrument if:

(1) the accounting framework to which the *firm* is subject as referred to in GENPRU 1.3.4R (General requirements: accounting principles to be applied) provides for a fair value hedge accounting relationship between a liability and its related hedge;
(2) such a relationship exists under that accounting framework between that debt instrument and that hedge;
(3) (if the debt instrument is a *tier one instrument*) the *firm's* obligations under that hedge comply with the conditions in GENPRU 2.2.64R to GENPRU 2.2.65R (General conditions for eligibility as tier one capital);
(4) (if the debt instrument is a *tier two instrument* or an *upper tier three instrument*) the *firm's* obligations under that hedge comply with the conditions in GENPRU 2.2.159R to GENPRU 2.2.169R (General conditions for eligibility as tier two capital instruments) as modified, in the case of an *upper tier three instrument*, by GENPRU 2.2.244R (Application of *tier two capital rules* to *tier three capital* debt) except as follows:
    (a) GENPRU 2.2.159R(9) only applies to the extent that it requires that hedge to be unsecured; and
    (b) GENPRU 2.2.159R(12) (legal opinion) does not apply.

2.2.201 **[R]** A *firm* must recognise the effect of a hedge as referred to in GENPRU 2.2.200R by including the net accounting fair value of the hedging instrument in the valuation of the debt instrument (as defined in GENPRU 2.2.198R).

Deductions from tiers one and two: Qualifying holdings (bank or building society only)

2.2.202 **[R]** GENPRU 2.2.202R to GENPRU 2.2.207R only apply to a *bank* or *building society*.

2.2.203 **[R]** A *qualifying holding* is a direct or indirect holding of a *bank* or *building society* in a non-financial *undertaking* which represents 10% or more of the capital or of the voting rights or which makes it possible to exercise a significant influence over the management of that *undertaking*.

2.2.204 **[R]** For the purpose of GENPRU 2.2.203R, a non-financial *undertaking* is an *undertaking* other than:
(1) a *credit institution* or *financial institution*;
(2) an *undertaking* whose exclusive or main activities are a direct extension of banking or concern services ancillary to banking, such as leasing, factoring, the management of unit trusts, the management of data processing services or any other similar activity; or
(3) an *insurer*.

2.2.205 **[R]** The amount of *qualifying holdings* that a *bank* or *building society* must deduct in the calculation in the *capital resources table* is:
(1) (if the *firm* has one or more *qualifying holdings* that exceeds 15% of its relevant *capital resources*) the sum of such excesses; and
(2) to the extent not already deducted in (1), the amount by which the sum of each of that *firm's qualifying holdings* exceeds 60% of its relevant *capital resources*.

2.2.206 **[R]** The relevant *capital resources* of a *firm* mean for the purposes of this *rule* the sum of the amount of *capital resources* calculated at stages L (Total tier one capital plus tier two capital) and Q (Total tier three capital) of the calculation in the *capital resources table* as adjusted in accordance with the following:
(1) the *firm* must not take into account the items referred to in any of the following:
    (a) GENPRU 2.2.190R to GENPRU 2.2.193R (surplus provisions); or
    (b) GENPRU 2.2.236R (*expected loss* amounts and other negative amounts); or
    (c) GENPRU 2.2.237R (*securitisation positions*);
(2) the *firm* must make the deductions to be made at stage S of the calculation in the *capital resources table* (Deductions from total capital); and
(3) the *firm* need not deduct any *excess trading book position* under (2).

2.2.207 **[R]** The following are not included as *qualifying holdings*:
(1) *shares* that are not held as investments; or
(2) *shares* that are held temporarily during the normal course of underwriting; or
(3) *shares* held in a *firm's* name on behalf of others.

Deductions from tiers one and two: Material holdings (BIPRU firm only)

2.2.208 **[R]** GENPRU 2.2.208R to GENPRU 2.2.216G only apply to a *BIPRU firm*.

2.2.209 **[R]** A *material holding* is:
(1) a *BIPRU firm's* holdings of *shares* and any other interest in the capital of an individual *credit institution* or *financial institution* (held in the *non-trading book* or the *trading book* or both) exceeding 10% of the *share* capital of the issuer, and, where this is the case, any holdings of subordinated debt of the same issuer are also included as a *material holding*; the full amount of the holding is a *material holding*; or
(2) a *BIPRU firm's* holdings of *shares*, any other interest in the capital and subordinated debt in an individual *credit institution* or *financial institution* (held in the *non-trading book* or the *trading book* or both) not deducted under (1) if the total amount of such holdings exceeds

10% of that *firm's capital resources* at stage N (Total tier one capital plus tier two capital after deductions) of the calculation in the *capital resources table* (calculated before deduction of its *material holdings*); only the excess amount is a *material holding*; or
(3) a *bank* or *building society's* aggregate holdings in the *non-trading book* of *shares*, any other interest in the capital, and subordinated debt in all *credit institutions* or *financial institutions* not deducted under (1) or (2) if the total amount of such *holdings* exceeds 10% of that *firm's capital resources* at stage N of the calculation in the *capital resources table* (calculated before deduction of its *material holdings*); only the excess amount is a *material holding*; or
(4) a *material insurance holding*.

2.2.210 **[G]** For the purpose of the definition of a *material holding*, *share* capital includes *preference shares*. *Share* premium should be taken into account when determining the amount of *share* capital.

2.2.211 **[R]** When calculating the size of its *material holdings* a *firm* must only include an actual holding (that is, a long cash position). A *firm* must not net such holdings with a short position.

2.2.212 **[R]** A *material insurance holding* means the holdings of a *BIPRU firm* of items of the type set out in GENPRU 2.2.213R in any:
(1) *insurance undertaking*; or
(2) *insurance holding company*;

that fulfils one of the following conditions:
(3) it is a *subsidiary undertaking* of that *firm*; or
(4) that *firm* holds a *participation* in it.

2.2.213 **[R]** An item falls into this provision for the purpose of GENPRU 2.2.212R if it is:
(1) an *ownership share*; or
(2) subordinated debt or another item of capital that falls into Article 16(3) of the *First Non-Life Directive* or, as applicable, Article 27(3) of the *Consolidated Life Directive*.

2.2.214 **[R]** The amount to be deducted with respect to each *material insurance holding* is the higher of:
(1) the book value of the *material insurance holding*; and
(2) the *solo capital resources requirement* for the *insurance undertaking* or *insurance holding company* in question calculated in accordance with Part 3 of GENPRU 3 Annex 1R (Method 3 of the capital adequacy calculations for financial conglomerates).

2.2.215 **[R]** For the purpose of the definition of a *material holding*, holdings must be valued using the valuation method which the holder uses for its external financial reporting purposes.

2.2.216 **[G]**
(1) This paragraph gives *guidance* on how the calculation under GENPRU 2.2.214R(1) should be carried out where an *insurance undertaking* is accounted for using the embedded value method.
(2) On acquisition, any "goodwill" element (that is, the difference between the acquisition value according to the embedded value method and the actual investment) should be deducted from *tier one capital resources*.
(3) The embedded value should be deducted from the total of *tier one capital resources* and *tier two capital resources*.
(4) Post-acquisition, where the embedded value of the *undertaking* increases, the increase should be added to reserves, while the new embedded value is deducted from total *capital resources*.
(5) This means that the net impact on the level of total *capital resources* is zero, although *tier two capital resources* headroom will increase with any increase in *tier one capital resources* reserves.
(6) Embedded value is the value of the *undertaking* taking into account the present value of the expected future inflows from existing life assurance business.

2.2.216A **[G]**
(1) This paragraph gives *guidance* as to the amount to be deducted at Part 2 of stage M (Deductions from the totals of tier one and two) of GENPRU 2 Annex 2R (Capital resources table for a bank) and Annex 3R (Capital resources table for a building society) in respect of investments in *subsidiary undertakings* and *participations* (excluding any amount which is already deducted as *material holdings* or *qualifying holdings*).
(2) The effect of those *rules* is to achieve the deduction of all investments in *subsidiary undertakings* and *participations* for *banks* and *building societies* by ensuring that amounts not already deducted under other *rules* are accounted for at this stage of the calculation of *capital resources*.
(3) The following investments in *subsidiary undertakings* and *participations* should be deducted at this stage:
  (1) those not deducted in Part 1 of stage M because of the operation of the thresholds in GENPRU 2.2.205R (on qualifying holdings) and GENPRU 2.2.209R (on material holding); and

(2) those which do not meet the definition of *qualifying holding* or *material holding*.
(4) For example, an investment in an *undertaking* which is not a *qualifying holding* under GENPRU 2.2.204R(2) (on the definition of a non-financial undertaking), that is whose exclusive or main activities are a direct extension of banking or concern services ancillary to banking, such as leasing, factoring, the management of unit trusts, the management of data processing services or any other similar activity, should be deducted at this stage.

Deductions from tiers one and two: Reciprocal cross holdings (BIPRU firm only)

2.2.217 **[R]** GENPRU 2.2.217R to GENPRU 2.2.220R apply to a *BIPRU firm*.

2.2.218 **[R]** A *BIPRU firm* must deduct at stage M of the calculation in the *capital resources table* (Deductions from the totals of tier one and two) any *reciprocal cross-holdings*. However a *BIPRU firm* must not deduct such holdings to the extent that they fall to be deducted at Part 1 of stage M of the calculation in the *capital resources table* (Deductions for *material holdings*, *qualifying holdings* and certain other items).

2.2.219 **[R]** A *reciprocal cross-holding* means a holding of the *BIPRU firm* of *shares*, any other interest in the capital, and subordinated debt, whether in the *trading* or *non-trading* book, in:
(1) a *credit institution*; or
(2) a *financial institution*;
(3) that satisfies the following conditions:
(4) the holding is the subject of an agreement or arrangement between the *BIPRU firm* and either the issuer of the instrument in question or a member of a *group* to which the issuer belongs;
(5) under the terms of the agreement or arrangement described in (3) the issuer invests in the *BIPRU firm* or in a member of the *group* to which that *BIPRU firm* belongs; and
(6) the effect of that agreement or arrangement on the capital position of the *BIPRU firm*, the issuer, or any member of a *group* to which either belongs, under any relevant rules is significantly more beneficial than it is in economic terms, taking into account the agreement or arrangement as a whole.

2.2.220 **[R]** For the purpose of GENPRU 2.2.219R, a relevant rule means a *rule* in GENPRU, *BIPRU* or *INSPRU* or any other capital adequacy or solvency requirements of the *FSA* or any other regulator, territory or country.

Deductions from tiers one and two: Connected lending of a capital nature (bank only)

2.2.221 **[R]** GENPRU 2.2.221R to GENPRU 2.2.235G only apply to a *bank*.

2.2.222 **[R]** *Connected lending of a capital nature* means all lending within GENPRU 2.2.227R or GENPRU 2.2.229R and guarantees within GENPRU 2.2.231R or GENPRU 2.2.233R.

2.2.223 **[R]** A *bank* must not deduct any item as *connected lending of a capital nature* to the extent that it falls to be deducted at Part 1 of stage M of the calculation in the *capital resources table* (Deductions for *material holdings*, *qualifying holdings* and certain other items) or as a *reciprocal cross-holding*.

2.2.224 **[R]** For the purpose of the *rules* in this section about *connected lending of a capital nature* and in relation to a *bank*, a connected party means another *person* ("P") who fulfils at least one of the following conditions and is not solo-consolidated with the *bank* under BIPRU 2.1 (Solo consolidation):
(1) P is *closely related* to the *bank*; or
(2) P is an *associate* of the *bank*; or
(3) the same *persons* significantly influence the *governing body* of P and the *bank*.

2.2.225 **[R]** For the purpose of GENPRU 2.2.224R, in relation to a *person* ("P") to which a *bank* has an *exposure* when P is acting on his own behalf and also an *exposure* to P when P acts in his capacity as a trustee, custodian or general partner of an investment trust, unit trust, venture capital or other investment fund, pension fund or similar fund (a "fund") the *bank* may choose to treat this latter *exposure* as an *exposure* to the fund, unless such treatment would be misleading.

2.2.226 **[G]** BIPRU 10.3.13G (*Guidance* on BIPRU 10.3.12R) applies to GENPRU 2.2.225R as it applies to BIPRU 10.3.12R (Exposures to trustees for concentration risk purposes).

2.2.227 **[R]** A loan is *connected lending of a capital nature* if:
(1) it is made by the *bank* to a connected party; and
(2) it falls into GENPRU 2.2.228R.

2.2.228 **[R]** A loan falls into this *rule* for the purposes of GENPRU 2.2.227R(2) if, whether through contractual, structural, reputational or other factors:
(1) based on the terms of the loan and the other knowledge available to the *bank*, the borrower would be able to consider it from the point of view of its characteristics as capital as being similar to *share* capital or subordinated debt; or

Part II FSA Handbook Materials

(2) the position of the lender from the point of view of maturity and repayment is inferior to that of the senior unsecured and unsubordinated creditors of the borrower.

2.2.229 **[R]** A loan is also *connected lending of a capital nature* if:
(1) it funds directly or indirectly a loan to a connected party of the *bank* falling into GENPRU 2.2.228R or an investment in the capital of a connected party of the *bank*; and
(2) it falls into GENPRU 2.2.228R.

2.2.230 **[G]** It is likely that a loan is not *connected lending of a capital nature* if:
(1) it is secured by collateral that is eligible for the purposes of *credit risk mitigation* under the *standardised approach* to credit risk as set out in *BIPRU* 5.4 (Financial collateral) and *BIPRU* 5.5 (Other funded credit risk mitigation); or
(2) it is repayable on demand (and should be treated as such for accounting purposes by the borrower and lender) and the *bank* can demonstrate that there are no potential obstacles to exercising the right to repay, whether contractual or otherwise.

2.2.231 **[R]** A guarantee is *connected lending of a capital nature* if it is a guarantee by the *bank* of a loan from a third party to a connected party of the *bank* and:
(1) the loan meets the requirements of GENPRU 2.2.228R; or
(2) the rights that the *bank* would have against the borrower with respect to the guarantee meet the requirements of GENPRU 2.2.228R(2).

2.2.232 **[R]** A guarantee is also *connected lending of a capital nature* if it is a guarantee by the *bank* of a loan falling into GENPRU 2.2.229R(1); and
(1) the loan meets the conditions in GENPRU 2.2.228R; or
(2) the guarantee meets the conditions in GENPRU 2.2.231R(2).

2.2.233 **[R]** The amount of a guarantee that constitutes *connected lending of a capital nature* that a *firm* must deduct is the amount guaranteed.

2.2.234 **[G]** A loan may initially fall outside the definition of *connected lending of a capital nature* but later fall into it. For example, if the initial lending to a connected party is subsequently downstreamed to another connected party the relationship between the *bank* and the ultimate borrower may be such that, looking at the arrangements as a whole, the *undertaking* to which the *bank* lends is able to regard the loan to it as being capable of absorbing losses.

2.2.235 **[G]** Lending to a connected party will not normally be *connected lending of a capital nature* where that party:
(1) is acting as a vehicle to pass funding to an unconnected party; and
(2) has no other creditors whose claims could be senior to those of the lender.

Deductions from tiers one and two: Expected losses and other negative amounts (BIPRU firm only)

2.2.236 **[R]** A *BIPRU firm* calculating *risk weighted exposure amounts* under the *IRB approach* must deduct:
(1) any negative amounts arising from the calculation in BIPRU 4.3.8R (Treatment of expected loss amounts); and
(2) any *expected loss* amounts calculated in accordance with BIPRU 4.7.12R (*Expected loss* amounts under the simple risk weight approach to calculating *risk-weighted exposure amounts* for *exposures* belonging to the *equity exposure IRB exposure class*) or BIPRU 4.7.17R (*Expected loss* amounts under the *PD/LGD approach*).

Deductions from tiers one and two: Securitisation positions (BIPRU firm only)

2.2.237 **[R]** A *BIPRU firm* calculating *risk weighted exposure amounts* under the *IRB approach* or the *standardised approach* to credit risk must deduct from its *capital resources* the exposure amount of *securitisation positions* which receive a *risk weight* of 1250% under *BIPRU* 9 (Securitisation), unless the *firm* includes the *securitisation positions* in its calculation of *risk weighted exposure amounts* (see *BIPRU* 9.10 (Reduction in risk-weighted exposure amounts)).

Deductions from tiers one and two: Special treatment of material holdings and other items (BIPRU firm only)

2.2.238 **[R]** GENPRU 2.2.238R to GENPRU 2.2.241G apply to a *BIPRU firm* and relate to the deductions in respect of:
(1) *material holdings*;
(2) *expected loss* amounts and other negative amounts referred to in GENPRU 2.2.236R; and
(3) *securitisation positions* referred to in GENPRU 2.2.237R.

2.2.239 **[R]**
(1) The treatment in the *capital resources table* of the deductions in GENPRU 2.2.238R only has effect for the purpose of the *capital resources gearing rules*.

(2) In other cases (3) and (4) apply.
(3) A *BIPRU firm* making the deductions described in GENPRU 2.2.238R must deduct 50% of the total amount of those deductions at stage E (Deductions from tier one capital) and 50% at stage J (Deductions from tier two capital) of the calculation in the *capital resources table* after the application of the *capital resources gearing rules*.
(4) To the extent that half of the total of:
(a) *material holdings*;
(b) *expected loss* amounts and other negative amounts; and
(c) *securitisation positions*;
exceeds the amount calculated at stage I (Total tier two capital) of that calculation, a *firm* must deduct that excess from the amount calculated at stage F (Total tier one capital after deductions) of the *capital resources table*.

2.2.240 **[G]** The alternative calculation in GENPRU 2.2.239R(3) to (4) is only relevant to BIPRU 11 (Pillar 3 disclosures) and certain reporting requirements under *SUP*. However the deduction of *material holdings* at Part 2 of stage E of the *capital resources table* in the case of a *BIPRU investment firm* with an *investment firm consolidation waiver* has effect for all purposes.

Tier three capital: upper tier three capital resources (BIPRU firm only)

2.2.241 **[R]** GENPRU 2.2.241R to GENPRU 2.2.245R only apply to a *BIPRU firm*.

2.2.242 **[R]** A *BIPRU firm* may include subordinated debt in its *upper tier three capital resources* only if:
(1) it has an original maturity of at least two years or is subject to at least two years' notice of repayment; and
(2) payment of interest or principal is permitted only if, after that payment, the *firm's capital resources* would be not less than its *capital resources requirement*.

2.2.243 **[R]** A *BIPRU firm* which includes subordinated debt in its *tier three capital resources* must notify the *FSA* one month in advance of all payments of either interest or principal made when the *firm's capital resources* are less than 120% of its *capital resources requirement*.

2.2.244 **[R]** The *rules* in the table in GENPRU 2.2.245R apply to short term subordinated debt that a *BIPRU firm* includes in its *tier three capital resources* in the same way that they apply to a *firm's tier two capital resources* with the adjustments in that table.

2.2.245 **[R]** Table: Application of tier two capital rules to tier three debt

This table belongs to GENPRU 2.2.244R

Tier two capital rule	Adjustment
GENPRU 2.2.159R (General conditions for eligibility as tier two capital)	The references in GENPRU 2.2.159R(5) (Capital must not become repayable prior to stated maturity date except in specified circumstances) to repayment at the option of the holder are replaced by a reference to GENPRU 2.2.242R(1) (*Upper tier three capital* should have maturity or notice period of at least two years) The reference in GENPRU 2.2.159R(10) (Description of *tier two capital* in marketing documents) to GENPRU 2.2.271R (Other requirements: insurers carrying on with-profits business (Insurer only)) does not apply
GENPRU 2.2.160R (Holder of a non-deferred share of a *building society* to be treated as a senior creditor)	
GENPRU 2.2.161R (Additional remedies)	
GENPRU 2.2.163R (Legal opinion where debt subject to a law of a country outside the *United Kingdom*)	
GENPRU 2.2.169R (Ineligibility as *tier two capital* owing to connected transactions)	The reference to GENPRU 2.2.177R (General eligibility conditions for *upper tier two capital*) does not apply
GENPRU 2.2.171R (Amendments to terms of the *capital instrument*)	
GENPRU 2.2.172R to GENPRU 2.2.173R (Redeemability at the option of the issuer)	

Part II FSA Handbook Materials

GENPRU 2.2.174R (Notification of redemption)	
References in the *rules* in the first column to the fifth anniversary are amended so as to refer to the second anniversary.	

Tier three capital: lower tier three capital resources (BIPRU firm only)

2.2.246 **[R]** GENPRU 2.2.246R to GENPRU 2.2.249R only apply to a *BIPRU firm*.

2.2.247 **[R]** A *BIPRU firm's* net interim *trading book* profits mean its net *trading book* profits adjusted as follows:

(1) they are net of any foreseeable charges or dividends and less net losses on its other business; and

(2) a *firm* must not take into account items that have already been included in the calculation of *capital resources* as part of the calculation of the following items:

(a) interim net profits (see stage (A) of the *capital resources table*); or

(b) interim net losses or material interim net losses (see stage (A) of the *capital resources table*); or

(c) profit and loss and other reserves (see stage (A) of the *capital resources table*).

2.2.248 **[R]** *Trading book* profits and losses, other than those losses to which GENPRU 2.2.86R(2) (Valuation adjustment and reserves) refers, originating from valuation adjustments or reserves as referred to in GENPRU 1.3.29R to GENPRU 1.3.35G (Valuation adjustments or reserves) must be included in the calculation of net interim *trading book* profits and be added to or deducted from *tier three capital resources*.

2.2.249 **[R]** *Trading book* valuation adjustments or reserves as referred to in GENPRU 1.3.29R to GENPRU 1.3.35G which exceed those made under the accounting framework to which a *firm* is subject must be treated in accordance with GENPRU 2.2.248R if not required to be treated under GENPRU 2.2.86R(2).

Deductions from total capital: Inadmissible assets (insurers only)

2.2.250 **[R]** GENPRU 2.2.250R to GENPRU 2.2.253G only apply to an *insurer*.

2.2.251 **[R]** For the purposes of the *capital resources table*, an *insurer* which is not a *pure reinsurer* must deduct from total *capital resources* the value of any asset which is not an *admissible asset* as listed in GENPRU 2 Annex 7R (Admissible assets in insurance), unless the asset is held to cover *property-linked liabilities* or *index-linked liabilities* under INSPRU 3.1.57R or INSPRU 3.1.58R (Covering linked liabilities).

2.2.252 **[G]** GENPRU 2.2.251R does not apply to intangible assets which should be deducted from *tier one capital resources* under GENPRU 2.2.155R (Deductions from tier one: Intangible assets).

2.2.253 **[G]** The list of *admissible assets* has been drawn with the aim of excluding assets:

(1) for which a sufficiently objective and verifiable basis of valuation does not exist; or

(2) whose realisability cannot be relied upon with sufficient confidence; or

(3) whose nature presents an unacceptable custody risk; or

(4) the holding of which may give rise to significant liabilities or onerous duties.

Deductions from total capital: Adjustments for related undertakings

2.2.254 **[R]** GENPRU 2.2.254R to GENPRU 2.2.258G only apply to an *insurer*.

2.2.255 **[R]** An *insurer* must deduct from its *capital resources* the value of its investments in each of its *related undertakings* that is an *ancillary services undertaking*.

2.2.256 **[R]** In relation to each of its *related undertakings* that is a *regulated related undertaking* (other than an *insurance undertaking*) an *insurer* must add to (if positive), at stage J in the *capital resources table* (Positive adjustments for related undertakings), or deduct from (if negative), at stage L in the *capital resources table* (Deductions from total capital), its *capital resources* the value of its *shares* in that *undertaking* calculated in accordance with GENPRU 1.3.47R (Shares in and debts due from related undertakings).

2.2.257 **[G]** For the purposes of GENPRU 2.2.255R, investments must be valued at their accounting book value in accordance with GENPRU 1.3.4R (General requirements: accounting principles to be applied).

2.2.258 **[G]** *Related undertakings* which are also *insurance undertakings* are not included in GENPRU 2.2.256R because an *insurer* that is a *participating insurance undertaking* is subject to the *requirements of INSPRU 6.1 (Group Risk:* Insurance Groups).

Deductions from total capital: Illiquid assets (BIPRU investment firm only)

2.2.259 **[R]** GENPRU 2.2.259R to GENPRU 2.2.262G only apply to a *BIPRU investment firm*.

2.2.260 **[R]** *Illiquid assets* means illiquid assets including

(1) tangible fixed assets (except land and buildings if they are used by a *firm* as security for loans, but this exclusion is only up to the value of the principal outstanding on the loans); or

(2) any holdings in the *capital resources* of *credit institutions* or *financial institutions*, except to the extent that:

(a) they have already been deducted as a *material holding*; or

(b) they are *shares* which are included in a *firm's trading book* and included in the calculation of the *firm's market risk capital requirement*; or

(3) holdings of other *securities* which are not *readily realisable securities*; or

(4) deficiencies of net assets in *subsidiary undertakings*; or

(5) deposits which are not repayable within 90 days (except for payments in connection with margined *futures* or *options* contracts); or

(6) loans and other amounts owed to a *firm* except where they are due to be repaid within 90 days; or

(7) physical stocks except for *positions* in *physical commodities* which are included in the calculation of a *firm's commodity PRR*.

2.2.261 **[G]** If a loan or other amount owing to a *firm* was originally due to be paid more than 90 days from the date of the making of the loan or the incurring of the payment obligation, as the case may be, it may be treated as liquid for the purposes of GENPRU 2.2.260R(6) where through the passage of time the remaining time to the contractual repayment date falls below 90 days.

2.2.262 **[G]** If a loan or other amount is due to be paid within 90 days (whether measured by reference to original or remaining maturity), a *firm* should consider whether it can reasonably expect the amount owing to be paid within that period. If the *firm* cannot reasonably expect it to be paid within that period the *firm* should treat it as illiquid.

Deductions from total capital: Excess trading book position (bank or building society only)

2.2.263 **[R]** GENPRU 2.2.263R to GENPRU 2.2.265R only apply to a *bank* or *building society*.

2.2.264 **[R]**

(1) The *excess trading book position* is the excess of:

(a) a *bank* or *building society's* aggregate net long (including notional) *trading book positions* in *shares*, subordinated debt or any other interest in the capital of *credit institutions* or *financial institutions*;

over;

(b) 25% of that *firm's capital resources* calculated at stage T (Total capital after deductions) of the *capital resources table* (calculated before deduction of the *excess trading book position*).

(2) Only the excess amount calculated under (1) must be deducted.

2.2.265 **[R]** The *standard market risk PRR rules* apply for establishing what is a net *position* and the amount and value of that *position* for the purposes of GENPRU 2.2.264R, ignoring *rules* which would otherwise exclude such *positions* from BIPRU 7.2 (Interest rate PRR) or BIPRU 7.3 (Equity PRR and basic interest rate PRR for equity derivatives) on the basis that they are to be deducted from a *bank* or *building society's capital resources*, or for any other reason.

Other capital resources: Unpaid share capital or initial funds and calls for supplementary contributions (Insurer only)

2.2.266 **[G]** GENPRU 2.2.266G to GENPRU 2.2.269G only apply to an *insurer*.

2.2.267 **[G]** Unpaid *share* capital or, in the case of a *mutual*, *unpaid initial funds* and calls for supplementary contributions are excluded from the *capital resources* of a *firm* except to the extent allowed in a *waiver* under section 148 of the *Act* (Modification or waiver of rules).

2.2.268 **[G]** Subject to a *waiver*, under the *Insurance Directives* a maximum of one half of unpaid *share* capital or, in the case of a *mutual*, one half of the *unpaid initial fund* may be included in an *insurer's capital resources*, once the paid-up part amounts to 25% of that *share* capital or fund, up to 50% of total *capital resources*.

2.2.269 **[G]** In the case of a *mutual* carrying on *general insurance business* and subject to a *waiver*, calls for supplementary contributions within the *financial year* may only be included in a *firm's capital resources* up to a maximum of 50% of the difference between the maximum contributions and the contributions actually called in, subject to a limit of 50% of total *capital resources*. In the case of a *mutual* carrying on *long-term insurance business*, the *Consolidated Life Directive* does not permit calls for supplementary contributions to be included in a *firm's capital resources*.

Other requirements: insurers carrying on with-profits business (Insurer only)

2.2.270 **[R]** GENPRU 2.2.270R to GENPRU 2.2.275G only apply to an *insurer*.

Part II FSA Handbook Materials

2.2.271 **[R]** An *insurer* carrying on *with-profits insurance business* must, in addition to the other requirements in respect of *capital resources* elsewhere in GENPRU 2.2, meet the following conditions before a *capital instrument* can be included in that *insurer's capital resources*:

(1) the *insurer* must manage the *with-profits fund* so that discretionary benefits under a *with-profits insurance contract* are calculated and paid disregarding, insofar as is necessary for its *customers* to be treated fairly, any liability the *firm* may have to make payments under the *capital instrument*;

(2) the intention to manage the *with-profits fund* on the basis set out in (1) must be disclosed in the *firm's Principles and Practices of Financial Management*; and

(3) no amounts, whether interest, principal, or other amounts, must be payable by the *firm* under the *capital instrument* if the *firm's* assets would then be insufficient to enable it to declare and pay under a *with-profits insurance contract* discretionary benefits that are consistent with the *firm's* obligations under *Principle* 6 (Customers' interests).

2.2.272 **[G]** The purpose of GENPRU 2.2.271R is to achieve practical subordination of *capital instruments* if they are to qualify as *capital resources* to the liabilities an *insurer* has to *with-profits policyholders*, including liabilities which arise from the regulatory duty to treat *customers* fairly in setting discretionary benefits. (*Principle* 6 (Customers' interests) requires a *firm* to pay due regard to the interests of its customers and treat them fairly.) It is not sufficient for a *capital instrument* to be subordinated to such liabilities only on winding up of the *firm* because such liabilities to *policyholders* may have been reduced by the inappropriate use of management discretion to enable funds to be applied in repaying subordinated *capital instruments* before winding up proceedings commence.

2.2.273 **[G]** GENPRU 2.2.271R is an additional requirement to all other *rules* in this section concerning the eligibility of a *capital instrument* to count as a component of an *insurer's capital resources*. Subordinated debt instruments will be the main type of *capital instrument* to which this *rule* is relevant, including both *upper tier two* (undated) and *lower tier two* (dated) subordinated debt instruments. Subordinated debt instruments which are issued by a *related undertaking* are not intended to be covered by this *rule* and may be included in *group capital resources* as appropriate if the other eligibility criteria are met.

2.2.274 **[G]** GENPRU 2.2.64R(10) and GENPRU 2.2.159R(10) contain provisions concerning the marketing of a *capital instrument*. In relation to a *firm* to which GENPRU 2.2.271R applies, in order to comply with GENPRU 2.2.64R(10) and GENPRU 2.2.159R(10), it should draw to the attention of subscribers the risk that payments may be deferred or cancelled in order to operate the *with-profits fund* so as to give priority to the payment of discretionary benefits to *with-profits policyholders*.

2.2.275 **[G]**

(1) *Upper tier two instruments* should meet the requirements of GENPRU 2.2.177R(3) which goes beyond the requirement in GENPRU 2.2.271R(3) since it requires a *firm* to have the option to defer payments in all circumstances, not just if necessary to treat *customers* fairly. However, for *lower tier two instruments*, GENPRU 2.2.271R(3) represents an additional requirement since a failure to pay amounts of interest or principal on a due date must not constitute an event of default under GENPRU 2.2.159R(2) for *firms* carrying on *with-profits insurance business*.

(2) For *firms* which are *realistic basis life firms* compliance with GENPRU 2.2.271R(3) would usually be achieved if the *capital instrument* provides that no amounts will be payable under it unless the *firm's capital resources* exceed its *capital resources requirement*. However, such *firms* should ensure that the terms of the *capital instrument* refer to *FSA capital resources requirements* in force from time to time, including the current realistic reserving requirements and are not restricted to former minimum capital requirements based only on the *Insurance Directives'* required minimum margin of solvency. For *firms* which are not *realistic basis life firms*, compliance with GENPRU 2.2.271R(3) will probably require specific reference to be made to treating *customers* fairly in the terms of the *capital instrument*.

Public sector guarantees

2.2.276 **[R]** A *BIPRU firm* may not include a guarantee from a state or public authority in its *capital resources*.

2.3 Application of GENPRU 2 to Lloyd's

Application of GENPRU 2.1

2.3.1 **[R]** GENPRU 2.1 applies to the *Society* in accordance with INSPRU 8.1.2R.

2.3.2 **[R]** GENPRU 2.1.38R to GENPRU 2.1.39G apply to *managing agents* in accordance with INSPRU 8.1.4R.

2.3.3 **[G]** GENPRU 2.1.13R requires the *Society* to ensure, in relation to each *member*'s *insurance business*, that *capital resources* equal to or in excess of the *member*'s *capital resources* requirement (*CRR*) are maintained. GENPRU 2.1 sets out the overall framework of the *CRR*. INSPRU 1.1 sets out the calculation of the components of the *general insurance capital requirement* and the *long-term insurance capital requirement*.

2.3.4 **[G]** *Managing agents* are required to calculate the *ECR* for the purposes of carrying out *syndicate ICA*s under INSPRU 7.1. As *with-profits insurance business* is not carried on through any *syndicate*, the calculation of the *with-profits insurance capital component* will not be applicable. INSPRU 1.3 is not applied to Lloyd's.

Calculation of the MCR

2.3.5 **[R]** For the purposes of GENPRU 2.1.24R, the *Society* must calculate the *MCR* in respect of the *general insurance business* of each *member* as the higher of:
(1) the *member*'s share of the *base capital resources requirement* in respect of *general insurance business* for the *member*s in aggregate; and
(2) the *general insurance capital requirement* for the *member*, calculated according to GENPRU 2.3.11R.

2.3.6 **[R]** For the purposes of GENPRU 2.3.5R(1), the *Society* must determine the *member*'s share by apportioning the *base capital resources requirement* in respect of *general insurance business* for the *member*s in aggregate between *member*s in proportion to the result for each *member* of GENPRU 2.3.11R.

2.3.7 **[R]** For the purposes of GENPRU 2.1.25R, the *Society* must calculate the *MCR* in respect of the *long-term insurance business* of each *member* as the higher of:
(1) the *member*'s share of the *base capital resources requirement* in respect of *long-term insurance business* for the *member*s in aggregate; and
(2) the sum of, for each *member*:
  (a) the *long-term insurance capital requirement*; and
  (b) the *resilience capital requirement*.

2.3.8 **[R]** For the purposes of GENPRU 2.3.7R(1), the *Society* must determine the *member*'s share by applying to the aggregate long-term business *base capital resources requirement* the ratio of the result for the *member* of GENPRU 2.3.7R(2) to the aggregate of the results of GENPRU 2.3.7R(2) for all *member*s.

Calculation of the base capital resources requirement

2.3.9 **[R]** The amount of the *base capital resources requirement* for the *member*s in aggregate is:
(1) for *general insurance business*, €3.2 million; and
(2) for *long-term insurance business*, €3.2 million.

Calculation of the general insurance capital requirement

2.3.10 **[R]** For the purposes of GENPRU 2.1.34R, the *Society* must calculate the *general insurance capital requirement* for the *member*s in aggregate as the higher of:
(1) the aggregate for all *member*s of the higher of, for each *member*, the result of the *premiums amount* and the *claims amount*; and
(2) the *brought forward amount*.

2.3.11 **[R]** The *Society* must determine the *general insurance capital requirement* for each *member* by apportioning the result of GENPRU 2.3.10R between *member*s on a fair and reasonable basis, provided that the *general insurance capital requirement* for a *member* must not be less than the higher of the result of the *premiums amount* and the *claims amount* for that *member*.

2.3.12 **[G]** The *Society* should calculate the *premiums amount* and the *claims amount* for each *member* on the basis of the *member's* own *general insurance business*, including *insurance business* that attaches to the reinsuring *member* for the purposes of GENPRU following an *approved reinsurance to close* (see INSPRU 8.2.16R).

2.3.13 **[R]** The *Society* must calculate the *general insurance capital requirement* it would have to determine under GENPRU 2.1.34R if it were an *insurer* carrying on all the *general insurance business* carried on by its *member*s, but eliminating *inter-syndicate reinsurance* (the *Society GICR*).

2.3.14 **[G]** For the purpose of GENPRU 2.3.13R the *Society* may make appropriate approximations, taking reasonable care to avoid underestimating the *Society GICR*.

2.3.15 **[R]** The *Society* must determine each *member*'s share of the *Society GICR* by allocating the *Society GICR* between the *member*s in proportion to the result for each *member* of GENPRU 2.3.11R.

Application of GENPRU 2.2

2.3.16 **[R]** Subject to GENPRU 2.3.18R, GENPRU 2.3.19R and GENPRU 2.3.21R, GENPRU 2.2 applies to *managing agents* and to the *Society* in accordance with:

(1) for *managing agents*, INSPRU 8.1.4R; and
(2) for the *Society*, INSPRU 8.1.2R.

2.3.17 **[G]** GENPRU 2.1 sets out minimum *capital resources requirements* for a *firm* and for Lloyd's *members*. GENPRU 2.2 sets out how, for the purpose of these requirements, *capital resources* are defined and measured. GENPRU 2.2 applies:
(1) to *managing agents* for their calculation of the *capital resources* managed by them in respect of each *syndicate* they manage (by reference, where there is a change in the underlying capital provision, to each open *syndicate* year); and
(2) to the *Society* for its calculation of:
  (a) each *member's capital resources*; and
  (b) its own *capital resources*.

2.3.18 **[R]** GENPRU 2.2.32R to GENPRU 2.2.41R (Limits on the use of different forms of capital) do not apply to *managing agents*.

2.3.19 **[R]** GENPRU 2.2.32R to GENPRU 2.2.41R (Limits on the use of different forms of capital) do apply to the *Society* with respect to:
(1) the *capital resources* requirements for the *members* in aggregate; and
(2) the aggregate *capital resources* supporting the *insurance business* of all the *members*.

2.3.20 **[R]** GENPRU 2.2.74R does not apply to the *Society* or to *managing agents*.

2.3.21 **[R]** In this section (GENPRU 2.3), "the aggregate *capital resources* supporting the *insurance business* of all the *members*" are:
(1) the aggregate of all the *members*' *capital resources* calculated under GENPRU 2.3.25R; and
(2) the *Society*'s *capital resources* excluding callable contributions.

Calculation of capital resources

2.3.22 **[R]** *The capital resources table* applies with the modifications that:
(1) *core tier one capital* includes *Lloyd's members' contributions* in accordance with GENPRU 2.3.34R, subject, in the case of letters of credit, guarantees and verifiable sums arising out of life assurance policies, to compliance with GENPRU 1.5.8R to GENPRU 1.5.12R; and
(2) the *Society* may also recognise and value *callable contributions*, pursuant to GENPRU 2.3.24R.

2.3.23 **[G]** *Lloyd's member's contributions* are *admissible assets* under GENPRU 2.3.34R and include letters of credit, guarantees and verifiable sums arising out of life assurance policies held as *funds at Lloyd's*. Assets that may be valued as part of *capital resources* under *PRU* are not necessarily, however, permitted investments for *members* under the terms of any *Lloyd's trust deed*.

2.3.24 **[R]** In calculating its *capital resources*, the *Society* may, subject to GENPRU 1.5.13R to GENPRU 1.5.14R, recognise and value *callable contributions*.

2.3.25 **[R]** The *Society* must calculate each *member*'s *capital resources* as the sum of:
(1) a *member*'s proportionate share of the *capital resources* held at *syndicate* level for each *syndicate* in which the *member* participates; and
(2) the value of a *member's funds at Lloyd's* after deducting liabilities in compliance with GENPRU 1.5.18R.

2.3.26 **[R]** In order to comply with GENPRU 2.1.13R the *Society* must ensure at all times that:
(1) each *member*'s *capital resources requirement* is covered by:
  (a) that *member*'s *capital resources*, calculated according to GENPRU 2.3.25R; and
  (b) to the extent that (a) is insufficient, by the *Society*'s own *capital resources*; and
(2) the *Society GICR* is covered by the aggregate *capital resources* supporting the *insurance business* of all the *members*.

2.3.27 **[R]** For the purposes of GENPRU 2.3.26R(1)(b), the *Society* must maintain at all times *capital resources* sufficient to meet the aggregate of, for each *member*, the amount, if any, by which the *member's capital resources* fall short of the *member's capital resources requirement*.

2.3.28 **[R]** The *Society* must calculate each *member's* share of the amount of *capital resources* required to comply with GENPRU 2.2.33R as the higher of:
(1) 1/3 of the *long-term insurance capital requirement* for the *members* in aggregate; and
(2) the *base capital resources requirement*;

allocated between the *members* in proportion to the result for each *member* of GENPRU 2.3.7R(2).

2.3.29 ***[R]*** For the purposes of GENPRU 2.2.34R, the *Society* must ensure that the aggregate *capital resources* supporting the *insurance business* of all the *members* meet the higher of:
(1) 1/3 of the *general insurance capital requirement* for the *members* in aggregate;
(2) 1/3 of the *Society GICR*; and
(3) the *base capital resources requirement*;

with the sum of the items listed in GENPRU 2.2.34R.

2.3.30 **[R]** The *Society* must calculate each *member's* share of the amount of *capital resources* required to comply with GENPRU 2.2.34R as the higher of:

(1) 1/3 of the *general insurance capital requirement* for the *members* in aggregate;
(2) 1/3 of the *Society GICR*; and
(3) the *base capital resources requirement*;

allocated between the *members* in proportion to the result for each *member* of GENPRU 2.3.11R.

Characteristics of tier one capital

2.3.31 **[R]** A *Lloyd's member's contribution* may be included in *tier one capital resources* to the extent that:

(1) the proceeds are immediately and fully available in respect of the *member's insurance business* at Lloyd's;
(2) (except in relation to letters of credit), it complies with GENPRU 2.2.64R(3) or cannot be repaid to a *member* until all of the *member's* liabilities in respect of its *insurance business* at Lloyd's have been extinguished, covered or reinsured by an *approved reinsurance to close*;
(3) it otherwise complies with GENPRU 2.2.64R(5) to GENPRU 2.2.64R(10).

Adjustments for related undertakings

2.3.32 **[R]** GENPRU 2.2.256R (Adjustment for regulated related undertakings other than insurance undertakings) applies to the *Society* with the modification that the *Society* must also value its *insurance undertakings* in accordance with GENPRU 2.2.256R.

2.3.33 **[R]** If a *related undertaking* is an *insurance undertaking* which has a deficit in the *capital resources* available to cover its *capital resources requirement*, the *Society* must make provision for:

(1) its proportionate share of that deficit; or
(2) in the case of a *subsidiary undertaking*, the whole of that deficit.

Modification of GENPRU 2 Annex 7R for Lloyd's

2.3.34 **[R]** In the case of *members*, *Lloyd's members' contributions* are included in GENPRU 2 Annex 7R and include:

(1) letters of credit;
(2) guarantees; and
(3) verifiable sums arising out of life assurance policies;

held as *funds at Lloyd's*.

2.3.35 **[G]** The effect of GENPRU 2.3.34R is that *Lloyd's members' contributions*, including letters of credit, guarantees and life assurance policies, are *admissible assets*.

GENPRU 2 Annex 1
Capital resources table for an insurer

GENPRU 2 Ann 1 **[R]**

Capital resources calculation for an insurer		
Type of capital	**Related text**	**Stage**
Core tier one capital		**(A)**
Permanent share capital	GENPRU 2.2.83R	
Profit and loss account and other reserves (taking into account interim net losses)	GENPRU 2.2.85R; GENPRU 2.2.87R to GENPRU 2.2.88R	
Share premium account	GENPRU 2.2.101R	
Externally verified interim net profits	GENPRU 2.2.102R	
Positive valuation differences	GENPRU 2.2.105R	
Fund for future appropriations	GENPRU 2.2.108R	
Perpetual non-cumulative preference shares		**(B)**
Perpetual non-cumulative *preference shares*	GENPRU 2.2.109R	
Innovative tier one capital		**(C)**
Innovative tier one instruments	GENPRU 2.2.113R to GENPRU 2.2.121R	
Total tier one capital before deductions = A + B + C		**(D)**

Deductions from tier one capital		**(E)**
Investments in own *shares*	None	
Intangible assets	GENPRU 2.2.155R	
Amounts deducted from *technical provisions* for discounting and other negative valuation differences	GENPRU 2.2.105R to GENPRU 2.2.107R	
Total tier one capital after deductions = D – E		**(F)**
Upper tier two capital		**(G)**
Perpetual cumulative *preference shares*	GENPRU 2.2.159R to GENPRU 2.2.181R	
Perpetual subordinated debt	See previous entry	
Perpetual subordinated securities	See previous entry	
Lower tier two capital		**(H)**
Fixed term *preference shares*	GENPRU 2.2.159R to GENPRU 2.2.175G; GENPRU 2.2.194R to GENPRU 2.2.196R	
Long term subordinated debt	See previous entry	
Fixed term subordinated securities	See previous entry	
Total tier two capital = G + H		**(I)**
Positive adjustments for related undertakings		**(J)**
Related undertakings that are *regulated related undertakings* (other than *insurance undertakings*)	GENPRU 2.2.256R	
Total capital after positive adjustments for insurance undertakings but before deductions = F + I + J		**(K)**
Deductions from total capital		**(L)**
Inadmissible assets	GENPRU 2.2.250R to GENPRU 2.2.251R; GENPRU 2 Annex 7R	
Assets in excess of *market risk* and *counterparty* limits	INSPRU 2.1.22R	
Related undertakings that are *ancillary services undertakings*	GENPRU 2.2.255R	
Negative adjustments for *related undertakings* that are *regulated related undertakings* (other than *insurance undertakings*)	GENPRU 2.2.256R	
Total capital after deductions = K – L		**(M)**
Other capital resources*		**(N)**
Unpaid *share* capital or, in the case of a *mutual*, *unpaid initial funds* and calls for supplementary contributions	GENPRU 2.2.266G to GENPRU 2.2.269G	
Implicit items	GENPRU 2 Annex 8G	
Total capital resources after deductions = M + N		**(O)**
* Items in section (N) of the table can be included in *capital resources* if subject to a *waiver* under section 148 of the *Act*.		
Note: Where the table refers to related text, it is necessary to refer to that text in order to understand fully what is included in the descriptions of capital items and deductions set out in the table.		

GENPRU 2 Annex 2R
Capital resources table for a bank

GENPRU 2 Ann 2 **[R]**

The capital resources calculation for a bank		
Type of capital	**Related text**	**Stage**
Core tier one capital		**(A)**

Permanent share capital	GENPRU 2.2.83R	
Profit and loss account and other reserves (taking into account interim net losses)	GENPRU 2.2.85R to 2.2.90R	
Eligible partnership capital	GENPRU 2.2.93R; GENPRU 2.2.95R	
Eligible LLP members' capital	GENPRU 2.2.94R; GENPRU 2.2.95R	
Share premium account	GENPRU 2.2.101R	
Externally verified interim net profits	GENPRU 2.2.102R	
Perpetual non-cumulative preference shares		**(B)**
Perpetual non-cumulative *preference shares*	GENPRU 2.2.109R	
Innovative tier one capital		**(C)**
Innovative tier one instruments	GENPRU 2.2.113R to GENPRU 2.2.137R	
Total tier one capital before deductions = A + B + C		**(D)**
Deductions from tier one capital		**(E)**
Investments in own *shares*	None	
Intangible assets	GENPRU 2.2.155R	
Excess of drawings over profits for partnerships and *limited liability partnerships*	GENPRU 2.2.100R	
Net losses on equities held in the available-for-sale financial asset category	GENPRU 2.2.185R	
(For certain limited purposes only certain additional deductions are made here)	GENPRU 2.2.239R(2) to (4)	
Total tier one capital after deductions ¼ D – E		**(F)**
Upper tier two capital		**(G)**
Perpetual cumulative *preference shares*	GENPRU 2.2.159R to GENPRU 2.2.181R	
Perpetual subordinated debt	See previous entry	
Perpetual subordinated securities	See previous entry	
Revaluation reserves	GENPRU 2.2.185R	
General/collective provisions	GENPRU 2.2.187R to GENPRU 2.2.189R	
Surplus provisions	GENPRU 2.2.190R to GENPRU 2.2.193R	
Lower tier two capital		**(H)**
Fixed term *preference shares*	GENPRU 2.2.159R to GENPRU 2.2.174R; GENPRU 2.2.194R to GENPRU 2.2.196R	
Long term subordinated debt	See previous entry	
Fixed term subordinated securities	See previous entry	
Total tier two capital = G + H		**(I)**
Deductions from tier two capital		**(J)**
(For certain limited purposes only certain additional deductions are made here)	GENPRU 2.2.239R(2) to (4)	
Total tier two capital after deductions = I – J		**(K)**
Total tier one capital plus tier two capital = F + K		**(L)**
Deductions from the totals of tier one and two		**(M)**
Qualifying holdings	GENPRU 2.2.202R to GENPRU 2.2.207R	(Part 1 of stage M)
Material holdings	GENPRU 2.2.208R to GENPRU 2.2.215R	

Part II FSA Handbook Materials

Expected loss amounts and other negative amounts *Securitisation positions*	GENPRU 2.2.236R GENPRU 2.2.237R	
Reciprocal cross-holdings	GENPRU 2.2.217R to GENPRU 2.2.220R	
Investments in *subsidiary undertakings* and *participations* excluding any amount which is already deducted as *material holdings* or *qualifying holdings* *Connected lending of a capital nature*	GENPRU 2.2.216AG GENPRU 2.2.221R to GENPRU 2.2.233R	(Part 2 of stage M)
Total tier one capital plus tier two capital after deductions = L – M		**(N)**
In calculating whether a *bank's capital resources* **exceed its** *capital resources requirement*: **(1) the** *credit risk capital component*, **the** *operational risk capital requirement* **and the** *counterparty risk capital component*; **or** **(2) the** *base capital resources requirement*; **as the case may be, must be deducted here.**		
Upper tier three		**(O)**
Short term subordinated debt	GENPRU 2.2.241R to GENPRU 2.2.245R	
Lower tier three		**(P)**
Net interim *trading book* profit and loss	GENPRU 2.2.246R to GENPRU 2.2.249R	
Total tier three capital = O + P		**(Q)**
Total capital before deductions = N + Q		**(R)**
Deductions from total capital		**(S)**
Excess trading book position *Free deliveries*	GENPRU 2.2.263R to GENPRU 2.2.265R BIPRU 14.4	
Total capital after deductions (R – S)		**(T)**
In calculating whether a *bank's capital resources* **exceed its** *capital resources requirement*, **the** *market risk capital requirement* **and the** *concentration risk capital component* **must be deducted here.**		

Note (1): Where the table refers to related text, it is necessary to refer to that text in order to understand fully what is included in the descriptions of capital items and deductions set out in the table.

Note (2): If the amount calculated at:

(a) stage N less the deductions in respect of the *capital resources requirement* made immediately following stage N; or

(b) stage T less the deductions in respect of the *capital resources requirement* made immediately following stages N and T;

is a negative number the *bank's capital resources* are less than its *capital resources requirement*.

Note (3): Stage C must be omitted except where *capital resources* are being used for a purpose for which *innovative tier one capital* may be used (see GENPRU 2.2.27R).

GENPRU 2 Annex 3R
Capital resources table for a building society

GENPRU 2 Ann 3 **[R]**

The capital resources calculation for a building society		
Type of capital	**Related text**	**Stage**
Core tier one capital		**(A)**
Profit and loss account and other reserves (taking into account interim net losses)	GENPRU 2.2.85R to 2.2.90R	
Externally verified interim net profits	GENPRU 2.2.102R	

Perpetual non-cumulative preference shares		**(B)**
PIBS	GENPRU 2.2.111R	
Innovative tier one capital		**(C)**
Innovative tier one instruments	GENPRU 2.2.113R to GENPRU 2.2.137R	
Total tier one capital before deductions = A + B + C		**(D)**
Deductions from tier one capital		**(E)**
Investments in own *shares* Intangible assets Net losses on equities held in the available-for-sale financial asset category (For certain limited purposes only certain additional deductions are made here)	None GENPRU 2.2.155R GENPRU 2.2.185R GENPRU 2.2.239R(2) to (4)	
Total tier one capital after deductions = D – E		**(F)**
Upper tier two capital		**(G)**
Perpetual subordinated debt Perpetual subordinated securities	GENPRU 2.2.159R to GENPRU 2.2.181R See previous entry	
Revaluation reserves General/collective provisions Surplus provisions	GENPRU 2.2.185R GENPRU 2.2.187R to GENPRU 2.2.189R GENPRU 2.2.190R to GENPRU 2.2.193R	
Lower tier two capital		**(H)**
Long term subordinated debt Fixed term subordinated securities	GENPRU 2.2.159R to GENPRU 2.2.174R; GENPRU 2.2.194R to GENPRU 2.2.196R See previous entry	
Total tier two capital = G + H		**(I)**
Deductions from tier two capital		**(J)**
(For certain limited purposes only certain additional deductions are made here)	GENPRU 2.2.239R(2) to (4)	
Total tier two capital after deductions = I – J		**(K)**
Total tier one capital plus tier two capital = F + K		**(L)**
Deductions from the totals of tier one and two		**(M)**
Qualifying holdings *Material holdings*	GENPRU 2.2.202R to GENPRU 2.2.207R GENPRU 2.2.208R to GENPRU 2.2.215R	 (Part 1 of stage M)
Expected loss amounts and other negative amounts *Securitisation positions*	GENPRU 2.2.236R GENPRU 2.2.237R	
Reciprocal cross-holdings Investments in *subsidiary undertakings* and *participations* excluding any amount which is already deducted as *material holdings* or *qualifying holdings*	GENPRU 2.2.217R to GENPRU 2.2.220R GENPRU 2.2.216AG	(Part 2 of stage M)
Total tier one capital plus tier two capital after deductions = L – M		**(N)**
In calculating whether a *building society's capital resources* **exceed its** *capital resources requirement*:		

(1) the *credit risk capital component*, **the** *operational risk capital requirement* **and the** *counterparty risk capital component*; **or** **(2) the** *base capital resources requirement*; **as the case may be, must be deducted here.**		
Upper tier three		**(O)**
Short term subordinated debt	GENPRU 2.2.241R to GENPRU 2.2.245R	
Lower tier three		**(P)**
Net interim *trading book* profit and loss	GENPRU 2.2.246R to GENPRU 2.2.249R	
Total tier three capital = O + P		**(Q)**
Total capital before deductions = N + Q		**(R)**
Deductions from total capital		**(S)**
Excess trading book position	GENPRU 2.2.263R to GENPRU 2.2.265R	
Free deliveries	BIPRU 14.4	
Total capital after deductions (R – S)		**(T)**
In calculating whether a *building society's capital resources* **exceed its** *capital resources requirement*, **the** *market risk capital requirement* **and the** *concentration risk capital component* **must be deducted here.**		

Note (1): Where the table refers to related text, it is necessary to refer to that text in order to understand fully what is included in the descriptions of capital items and deductions set out in the table.

Note (2): If the amount calculated at:

(a) stage N less the deductions in respect of the *capital resources requirement* made immediately following stage N; or

(b) stage T less the deductions in respect of the *capital resources requirement* made immediately following stages N and T;

is a negative number the *building society's capital resources* are less than its *capital resources requirement*.

Note (3): Stage C must be omitted except where *capital resources* are being used for a purpose for which *innovative tier one capital* may be used (see GENPRU 2.2.27R).

GENPRU 2 Annex 4R
Capital resources table for a BIPRU investment firm deducting material holdings

GENPRU 2 Ann 4 **[R]**

The capital resources calculation for an investment firm deducting material holdings		
Type of capital	**Related text**	**Stage**
Core tier one capital		**(A)**
Permanent share capital	GENPRU 2.2.83R	
Profit and loss account and other reserves (taking into account material interim net losses)	GENPRU 2.2.85R to 2.2.90R	
Eligible partnership capital	GENPRU 2.2.93R; GENPRU 2.2.95R	
Eligible LLP members' capital	GENPRU 2.2.94R; GENPRU 2.2.95R	
Sole trader capital	None	
Share premium account	GENPRU 2.2.101R	
Externally verified interim net profits	GENPRU 2.2.102R	
Perpetual non-cumulative preference shares		**(B)**
Perpetual non-cumulative *preference shares*	GENPRU 2.2.109R	
Innovative tier one capital		**(C)**

Innovative tier one instruments	GENPRU 2.2.113R to GENPRU 2.2.137R	
Total tier one capital before deductions = A + B + C		**(D)**
Deductions from tier one capital		**(E)**
Investments in own *shares*	None	
Intangible assets	GENPRU 2.2.155R	
Excess of drawings over profits for partnerships, *limited liability partnerships* and *sole traders*	GENPRU 2.2.100R; there is no related text for *sole traders*	
Net losses on equities held in the available-for-sale financial asset category	GENPRU 2.2.185R	
(For certain limited purposes only certain additional deductions are made here)	GENPRU 2.2.239R(2) to (4)	
Total tier one capital after deductions = D – E		**(F)**
Upper tier two capital		**(G)**
Perpetual cumulative *preference shares*	GENPRU 2.2.159R to GENPRU 2.2.181R	
Perpetual subordinated debt	See previous entry	
Perpetual subordinated securities	See previous entry	
Revaluation reserves	GENPRU 2.2.185R	
General/collective provisions	GENPRU 2.2.187R to GENPRU 2.2.189R	
Surplus provisions	GENPRU 2.2.190R to GENPRU 2.2.193R	
Lower tier two capital		**(H)**
Fixed term *preference shares*	GENPRU 2.2.159R to GENPRU 2.2.174R; GENPRU 2.2.194R to GENPRU 2.2.196R	
Long term subordinated debt	See previous entry	
Fixed term subordinated securities	See previous entry	
Total tier two capital = G + H		**(I)**
Deductions from tier two capital		**(J)**
(For certain limited purposes only certain additional deductions are made here)	GENPRU 2.2.239R(2) to (4)	
Total tier two capital after deductions = I – J		**(K)**
Total tier one capital plus tier two capital = F + K		**(L)**
Deductions from the totals of tier one and two		**(M)**
Material holdings	GENPRU 2.2.208R to GENPRU 2.2.215R	
Expected loss amounts and other negative amounts	GENPRU 2.2.236R	(Part 1 of stage M)
Securitisation positions	GENPRU 2.2.237R	
Reciprocal cross-holdings	GENPRU 2.2.217R to GENPRU 2.2.220R	(Part 2 of stage M)
Total tier one capital plus tier two capital after deductions = L – M		**(N)**
In calculating whether a *firm's capital resources* **exceed its** *capital resources requirement*: **(1) the** *credit risk capital component*, **the** *operational risk capital requirement* **(if applicable) and the** *counterparty risk capital component*; **or**		

Part II FSA Handbook Materials

(2) the *base capital resources requirement*; as the case may be, must be deducted here.		
Upper tier three		**(O)**
Short term subordinated debt	GENPRU 2.2.241R to GENPRU 2.2.245R	
Lower tier three		**(P)**
Net interim *trading book* profit and loss	GENPRU 2.2.246R to GENPRU 2.2.249R	
Total tier three capital = O + P		**(Q)**
Total capital before deductions = N + Q		**(R)**
Deductions from total capital		**(S)**
Free deliveries	BIPRU 14.4	
Total capital after deductions (R − S)		**(T)**
In calculating whether a *firm's capital resources* exceed its *capital resources requirement*, the *market risk capital requirement*, the *concentration risk capital component* and (if applicable) the *fixed overheads requirement* must be deducted here.		

Note (1): Where the table refers to related text, it is necessary to refer to that text in order to understand fully what is included in the descriptions of capital items and deductions set out in the table.

Note (2): If the amount calculated at:

(a) stage N less the deductions in respect of the *capital resources requirement* made immediately following stage N; or

(b) stage T less the deductions in respect of the *capital resources requirement* made immediately following stages N and T;

is a negative number the *firm's capital resources* are less than its *capital resources requirement*.

Note (3): Stage C must be omitted except where *capital resources* are being used for a purpose for which *innovative tier one capital* may be used (see GENPRU 2.2.27R).

GENPRU 2 Annex 5R
Capital resources table for a BIPRU investment firm deducting illiquid assets

GENPRU 2 Ann 5 **[R]**

The capital resources calculation for an investment firm that deducts illiquid assets		
Type of capital	**Related text**	**Stage**
Core tier one capital		**(A)**
Permanent share capital	GENPRU 2.2.83R	
Profit and loss account and other reserves (taking into account material interim net losses)	GENPRU 2.2.85R to 2.2.90R	
Eligible partnership capital	GENPRU 2.2.93R; GENPRU 2.2.95R	
Eligible LLP members' capital	GENPRU 2.2.94R; GENPRU 2.2.95R	
Sole trader capital	None	
Share premium account	GENPRU 2.2.101R	
Externally verified interim net profits	GENPRU 2.2.102R	
Perpetual non-cumulative preference shares		**(B)**
Perpetual non-cumulative *preference shares*	GENPRU 2.2.109R	
Innovative tier one capital		**(C)**
Innovative tier one instruments	GENPRU 2.2.113R to GENPRU 2.2.137R	
***Total tier one capital* before deductions = A + B + C**		**(D)**
Deductions from tier one capital		**(E)**
Investments in own *shares*	None	

Intangible assets Excess of drawings over profits for partnerships, *limited liability partnerships* and *sole traders*	GENPRU 2.2.155R GENPRU 2.2.100R; there is no related text for *sole traders*	
Net losses on equities held in the available-for-sale financial asset category (For certain limited purposes only certain additional deductions are made here)	GENPRU 2.2.185R GENPRU 2.2.239R(2) to (4)	
Total tier one capital after deductions **= D – E**		**(F)**
Upper tier two capital		**(G)**
Perpetual cumulative *preference shares* Perpetual subordinated debt Perpetual subordinated securities Revaluation reserves General/collective provisions Surplus provisions	GENPRU 2.2.159R to GENPRU 2.2.181R See previous entry See previous entry GENPRU 2.2.185R GENPRU 2.2.187R to GENPRU 2.2.189R GENPRU 2.2.190R to GENPRU 2.2.193R	
Lower tier two capital		**(H)**
Fixed term *preference shares* **Long term subordinated debt** **Fixed term subordinated securities**	GENPRU 2.2.159R to GENPRU 2.2.174R; GENPRU 2.2.194R to GENPRU 2.2.196R **See previous entry** **See previous entry**	
Total tier two capital = G + H		**(I)**
Deductions from tier two capital		**(J)**
(For certain limited purposes only certain additional deductions are made here)	GENPRU 2.2.239R(2) to (4)	
Total tier two capital after deductions **= I – J**		**(K)**
Total tier one capital plus tier two capital **= F + K**		**(L)**
Deductions from the totals of tier one and two		**(M)**
Expected loss amounts and other negative amounts *Securitisation positions* *Reciprocal cross-holdings*	GENPRU 2.2.236R GENPRU 2.2.237R GENPRU 2.2.217R to GENPRU 2.2.220R	(Part 1 of stage M) (Part 2 of stage M)
Total tier one capital plus tier two capital after deductions = L – M		**(N)**
In calculating whether a *firm's capital resources* **exceed its** *capital resources requirement*: **(1) the** *credit risk capital component*, **the** *operational risk capital requirement* **(if applicable) and the** *counterparty risk capital component*; **or** **(2) the** *base capital resources requirement*; **as the case may be, must be deducted here.**		
Upper tier three		**(O)**
Short term subordinated debt	GENPRU 2.2.241R to GENPRU 2.2.245R	
Lower tier three		**(P)**
Net interim *trading book* profit and loss	GENPRU 2.2.246R to GENPRU 2.2.249R	

Total tier three capital = O + P		**(Q)**
Total capital before deductions = N + Q		**(R)**
Deductions from total capital		**(S)**
Illiquid assets	GENPRU 2.2.259R to GENPRU 2.2.260R	
Free deliveries	BIPRU 14.4	
Total capital after deductions = R – S		**(T)**
In calculating whether a *firm's capital resources* **exceed its** *capital resources requirement*, **the** *market risk capital requirement*, **the** *concentration risk capital component* **and (if applicable) the** *fixed overheads requirement* **must be deducted here.**		

Note (1): Where the table refers to related text, it is necessary to refer to that text in order to understand fully what is included in the descriptions of capital items and deductions set out in the table.

Note (2): If the amount calculated at:
(a) stage N less the deductions in respect of the *capital resources requirement* made immediately following stage N; or
(b) stage T less the deductions in respect of the *capital resources requirement* made immediately following stages N and T;

is a negative number the *firm's capital resources* are less than its *capital resources requirement*.

Note (3): Stage C must be omitted except where *capital resources* are being used for a purpose for which *innovative tier one capital* may be used (see GENPRU 2.2.27R).

GENPRU 2 Annex 6R
Capital resources table for a BIPRU investment firm with a waiver from consolidated supervision

GENPRU 2 Ann 6 **[R]**

Part 1 of the capital resources calculation for an investment firm with a waiver from consolidated supervision		
Type of capital	**Related text**	**Stage**
Core tier one capital		**(A)**
Permanent share capital	GENPRU 2.2.83R	
Profit and loss account and other reserves (taking into account material interim net losses)	GENPRU 2.2.85R to 2.2.90R	
Eligible partnership capital	GENPRU 2.2.93R; GENPRU 2.2.95R	
Eligible LLP members' capital	GENPRU 2.2.94R; GENPRU 2.2.95R	
Sole trader capital	None	
Share premium account	GENPRU 2.2.101R	
Externally verified interim net profits	GENPRU 2.2.102R	
Perpetual non-cumulative preference shares		**(B)**
Perpetual non-cumulative *preference shares*	GENPRU 2.2.109R	
Innovative tier one capital		**(C)**
Innovative tier one instruments	GENPRU 2.2.113R to GENPRU 2.2.137R	
Total tier one capital before deductions = A + B + C		**(D)**
Deductions from tier one capital		**(E)**
Investments in own *shares*	None	(Part 1 of stage E)
Intangible assets	GENPRU 2.2.155R	

Excess of drawings over profits for partnerships, *limited liability partnerships* and *sole traders*	GENPRU 2.2.100R; there is no related text for *sole traders*	
Net losses on equities held in the available-for-sale financial asset category	GENPRU 2.2.185R	(Part 1 of stage E)
(For certain limited purposes only certain additional deductions are made here. This line does not include *material holdings*.)	GENPRU 2.2.239R(2) to (4)	
Material holdings falling into Note (4)	Note (4) of Part 2 of this table; GENPRU 2.2.208R to GENPRU 2.2.215R	(Part 2 of stage E)
(For certain limited purposes only certain additional deductions of *material holdings* are made here)	Note (5) of Part 2 of this table; GENPRU 2.2.239R(2) to (4)	(Part 3 of stage E)
Total tier one capital after deductions = D – E		**(F)**
Upper tier two capital		**(G)**
Perpetual cumulative *preference shares*	GENPRU 2.2.159R to GENPRU 2.2.181R	
Perpetual subordinated debt	See previous entry	
Perpetual subordinated securities	See previous entry	
Revaluation reserves	GENPRU 2.2.185R	
General/collective provisions	GENPRU 2.2.187R to GENPRU 2.2.189R	
Surplus provisions	GENPRU 2.2.190R to GENPRU 2.2.193R	
Lower tier two capital		**(H)**
Fixed term *preference shares*	GENPRU 2.2.159R to GENPRU 2.2.174R; GENPRU 2.2.194R to GENPRU 2.2.196R	
Long term subordinated debt	See previous entry	
Fixed term subordinated securities	See previous entry	
Total tier two capital = G + H		**(I)**
Deductions from tier two capital		**(J)**
(For certain limited purposes only certain additional deductions are made here)	Note (5) of Part 2 of this table; GENPRU 2.2.239R(2) to (4)	
Total tier two capital after deductions = I – J		**(K)**
Total tier one capital plus tier two capital = F + K		**(L)**
Deductions from the totals of tier one and two		**(M)**
Material holdings falling into Note (5)	Note (5) of Part 2 of this table; GENPRU 2.2.208R to GENPRU 2.2.215R	(Part 1 of stage M)
Contingent liabilities	Note (6) of Part 2 of this table	
Expected loss amounts and other negative amounts	GENPRU 2.2.236R	
Securitisation positions	GENPRU 2.2.237R	
Reciprocal cross-holdings	GENPRU 2.2.217R to GENPRU 2.2.220R	(Part 2 of stage M)
Total tier one capital plus tier two capital after deductions = L – M		**(N)**

In calculating whether a *firm's capital resources* **exceed its** *capital resources requirement*: **(1) the** *credit risk capital component*, **the** *operational risk capital requirement* **(if applicable) and the** *counterparty risk capital component*; **or** **(2) the** *base capital resources requirement*; **as the case may be, must be deducted here.**		
Upper tier three		**(O)**
Short term subordinated debt	GENPRU 2.2.241R to GENPRU 2.2.245R	
Lower tier three		**(P)**
Net interim *trading book* profit and loss	GENPRU 2.2.246R to GENPRU 2.2.249R	
Total tier three capital = O + P		**(Q)**
Total capital before deductions = N + Q		**(R)**
Deductions from total capital		**(S)**
Illiquid assets	GENPRU 2.2.259R to GENPRU 2.2.260R	
Free deliveries	BIPRU 14.4	
Total capital after deductions = R – S		**(T)**
In calculating whether a *firm's capital resources* **exceed its** *capital resources requirement*, **the** *market risk capital requirement*, **the** *concentration risk capital component* **and (if applicable) the** *fixed overheads requirement* **must be deducted here.**		

<table>
<tr><td colspan="3">Part 2 of the capital resources calculation for an investment firm with a waiver from consolidated supervision</td></tr>
<tr><td colspan="3">Note (1): Where the table refers to related text, it is necessary to refer to that text in order to understand fully what is included in the descriptions of capital items and deductions set out in the table.</td></tr>
<tr><td colspan="3">Note (2): If the amount calculated at:
(a) stage N less the deductions in respect of the capital resources requirement made immediately following stage N; or
(b) stage T less the deductions in respect of the capital resources requirement made immediately following stages N and T;is a negative number the firm's capital resources are less than its capital resources requirement.</td></tr>
<tr><td colspan="3">Note (3): Stage C must be omitted except where capital resources are being used for a purpose for which innovative tier one capital may be used (see GENPRU 2.2.27R).</td></tr>
<tr><td colspan="3">Note (4): The material holdings that must be deducted at part 2 of stage E are material holdings issued by undertakings which would have been members of the firm's UK consolidation group or non-EEA sub-group if the firm did not have an investment firm consolidation waiver if:</td></tr>
<tr><td>(1)</td><td colspan="2">in relation to a BIPRU investment firm, the holding forms part of the undertaking's tier one capital resources; or</td></tr>
<tr><td rowspan="3">(2)</td><td colspan="2">(subject to (3)) in relation to any other undertaking, the holding would form part of the undertaking's tier one capital resources if:</td></tr>
<tr><td>(a)</td><td>that undertaking were a BIPRU firm with a Part IV permission; and</td></tr>
<tr><td>(b)</td><td>it had carried on all its business in the United Kingdom and had obtained whatever permissions for doing so are required under the Act; or</td></tr>
<tr><td>(3)</td><td colspan="2">in relation to any undertaking not falling within (1) and for which the methodology in (2) does not give an answer, the holding would form part of its tier one capital resources if the undertaking were a BIPRU firm of the same category as the firm carrying out the calculation under this Annex.</td></tr>
<tr><td colspan="3">Note (5): The material holdings that must be deducted by a firm at part 3 of stage E and at stage J or at Part 1 of stage M are material holdings issued by undertakings which would have been members of that firm's UK consolidation group or non-EEA sub-group if the firm did not have an investment firm consolidation waiver and which do not fall into Note (4).</td></tr>
</table>

Note (6): The contingent liabilities that must be deducted by a *firm* at Part 1 of stage M are any contingent liabilities which the *firm* has in favour of *investment firms*, *financial institutions*, *asset management companies* and *ancillary services undertakings* which would have been members of the *firm's UK consolidation group* or *non-EEA sub-group* if the *firm* did not have an *investment firm consolidation waiver*.

GENPRU 2 Annex 7R
Admissible assets in insurance

GENPRU 2 Ann 7 **[R]**

(1)

(A) Investments that are, or amounts owed arising from the disposal of:
- (a) *debt securities*, bonds and other money and capital market instruments;
- (b) loans;
- (c) *shares* and other variable yield participations;
- (d) *units* in:
  - (i) *collective investment schemes* falling within the *UCITS Directive*;;
  - (ii) *non-UCITS retail schemes*;
  - (iii) *recognised schemes*; and
  - (iv) any other *collective investment scheme* where the *insurer's* investment in the scheme is sufficiently small to be consistent with a prudent overall investment strategy, having regard to the investment policy of the scheme and the information available to the *insurer* to enable it to monitor the investment risk being taken by the scheme;
- (e) land, buildings and immovable property rights;
- (f) an *approved derivative* or *quasi-derivative* transaction that satisfies the conditions in INSPRU 3.2.5R or an *approved stock lending transaction* that satisfies the conditions in INSPRU 3.2.36R.

(B) Debts and claims
- (a) debts owed by *reinsurers*, including *reinsurers'* shares of *technical provisions* (but excluding amounts recoverable from an *ISPV**);
- (b) deposits with and debts owed by ceding *undertakings*;
- (c) debts owed by *policyholders* and intermediaries arising out of direct and *reinsurance* operations (except where overdue for more than 3 months and other than *commission* prepaid to agents or intermediaries);
- (d) for *general insurance business* only, claims arising out of salvage and subrogation;
- (e) for *long-term insurance business* only, advances secured on, and not exceeding the *surrender value* of, *long-term insurance contracts* issued by the *insurer*;
- (f) tax recoveries;
- (g) claims against *compensation funds*.

(C) Other assets
- (a) tangible fixed assets, other than land and buildings;
- (b) cash at *bank* and in hand, *deposits* with *credit institutions* and any other bodies authorised to receive *deposits*;
- (c) for *general insurance business* only, *deferred acquisition costs*;
- (d) accrued interest and rent, other accrued income and prepayments;
- (e) for *long-term insurance business* only, reversionary interests.

* An *insurer* may treat amounts recoverable from an *ISPV* as an *admissible asset* if it obtains a *waiver* under section 148 of the *Act*. The conditions that will need to be met, in addition to the statutory tests under section 148(4) of the *Act*, before the *FSA* will consider granting such a *waiver* are set out in INSPRU 1.6.13G to INSPRU 1.6.18G.

(2) Subject to paragraph (3) below, a *unit* in a *collective investment scheme* is only admissible for the purposes of paragraph (1) above if it falls within paragraph (1)(A)(d), notwithstanding that it may also fall into one or more other categories in paragraph (1).

(3) A *derivative*, *quasi-derivative* or *stock lending* transaction is only admissible for the purposes of paragraph (1) above if it falls within paragraph (1)(A)(f), notwithstanding that it may also fall into one or more other categories in paragraph (1).

GENPRU 2 Annex 8G
Guidance on applications for waivers relating to implicit items

GENPRU 2 Ann 8 **[G]**

Implicit items under the Act

1	The *capital resources table* does not permit *implicit items* to be included in the calculation of a *firm's capital resources*, except subject to a *waiver* under section 148 of the *Act*. Article 27(4) of the *Consolidated Life Directive* states that *implicit items* can be included in the calculation of a *firm's capital resources*, within limits, provided that the supervisory authority agrees. Certain *implicit items*, however, are not eligible for inclusion beyond 31 December 2009 (see paragraph 5). The *FSA* may be prepared to grant a *waiver* from the *capital resources table* to allow *implicit items*, in line with the purpose of the *Consolidated Life Directive*, and provided the conditions as set out in article 27(4) of the *Consolidated Life Directive* are met. Such a *waiver* would allow an *implicit item* to count towards the *firm's capital resources* available to count against its *capital resources requirement* (*CRR*) set out for *realistic basis life firms* in GENPRU 2.1.18R and for *regulatory basis only life firms* in GENPRU 2.1.23R. An *implicit item* may potentially count as *tier one capital* (but not *core tier one capital*) or *tier two capital*. Where a *waiver* is granted allowing an *implicit item* as *tier one capital*, the value of the *implicit item* so allowed must be included at stage B of the *capital resources table*. If the application of the value of the *implicit item* is restricted by GENPRU 2.2.29R, which requires that at least 50% of a *firm's tier one capital resources* must be accounted for by *core tier one capital*, the remainder may be included at stage G of the calculation in the *capital resources table*, subject to GENPRU 2.2.31R. An *implicit item* treated as *tier two capital* will also be included at stage G of the calculation, again subject to GENPRU 2.2.81R. Article 29(1) of the *Consolidated Life Directive* requires that *implicit items* be excluded from the capital eligible to cover the *guarantee fund*. Under GENPRU 2.2.33R a *firm* must meet the *guarantee fund* from the sum of the items listed at stages A, B, G and H of the *capital resources table* less the sum of the items listed at stage E of the *capital resources table*. The *FSA* will only grant an *implicit items waiver* if the *waiver* includes a modification to GENPRU 2.2.33R to ensure that the *implicit item* does not count towards meeting the *guarantee fund*.
2	Under section 148 of the *Act*, the *FSA* may, on the application of a *firm*, grant a *waiver* from *PRU*. There are general requirements that must be met before any *waiver* can be granted. As explained in SUP 8, the *FSA* may not give a *waiver* unless the *FSA* is satisfied that:
	(1) compliance by the *firm* with the *rules* will be unduly burdensome, or would not achieve the purpose for which the *rules* were made; and
	(2) the *waiver* would not result in undue risk to *persons* whose interests the *rules* are intended to protect.
3	The *FSA* will assess compliance with the requirements in the light of all the relevant circumstances. This will include consideration of the costs incurred by compliance with a particular *rule* or whether a *rule* is framed in a way that would make compliance difficult in view of the *firm's* circumstances. For example, the *firm* may demonstrate that if an *implicit item* were not allowed, the *firm* would either have to suffer increased (and unwarranted) costs in injecting further *capital resources* or operate with a lower equity backing ratio (see case studies in paragraph 43). Even if a *firm* can demonstrate a case for an *implicit item waiver*, it should not assume that the *FSA* will grant the *waiver* requested, or that any *waiver* will be granted for the full amount of the *implicit item* which could be granted, as set out in this annex. The *FSA* will consider each application on its own merits, and taking into account all relevant circumstances, including the financial situation and business prospects of the *firm*.
4	*Implicit items* are economic reserves which are contained within the long-term insurance business provisions. Article 27(4) of the *Consolidated Life Directive* identifies three types of *implicit item*, in respect of: future profits, *zillmerisation* and hidden reserves. This annex is intended to amplify the *guidance* in SUP 8 relating to the granting of *waivers* for *implicit items* and to provide *guidance* on other aspects. Whilst this *guidance* applies to applications for *waivers* for *implicit items* generally, for a *realistic basis life firm*, to the extent that an *implicit item* is allocated to a *with-profits fund*, this *guidance* relates to *implicit items* for the purposes of determining the *regulatory value of assets* (see INSPRU 1.4.24R).

5	The *Consolidated Life Directive* (reflecting the changes introduced by the Solvency 1 Directive) requires member states to end a *firm's* ability to take into account future profits *implicit items* by (at the latest) 31 December 2009. Until then, the maximum amount of the *implicit item* relating to future profits permitted under the *Consolidated Life Directive* is limited to 50% of the product of the estimated annual profits and the average period to run (not exceeding six years) on the *policies* in the portfolio. The *Consolidated Life Directive* further limits the maximum amount of these economic reserves that can be counted to 25% of the lesser of the available solvency margin and the required solvency margin. The changes introduced by the *Solvency 1 Directive* take effect for financial years beginning on or after 1 January 2004. However, the *Consolidated Life Directive* allows for a transitional period of five years, which runs from 20 March 2002 (the publication date of the *Solvency 1 Directive*), for *firms* to become fully compliant with these new requirements. *Firms* will need to consider the potential impact of these changes when engaging in future capital planning. When applying for an *implicit item waiver* a *firm* should provide the *FSA* with a plan showing how the *firm* intends to maintain its capital adequacy over the period to 31 December 2009. *Firms* should also be aware that the *FSA* will typically only grant *waivers* for a maximum of 12 months.
Future Profits	
6	The future profits *implicit item* allows *firms* to take credit for margins in the *mathematical reserves* to the extent that these are expected to emerge from in force business. The future profit from in force business should be assessed, in the first instance, on prudent assumptions, to demonstrate that there is an 'economic reserve'. Having demonstrated that it exists, the amount should be limited to an amount calculated using a formula that takes into account the actual profit which has emerged over the last five years (see paragraph 28).
Zillmerisation	
7	*Zillmerisation* is an allowance for acquisition costs that are expected, under prudent assumptions, to be recoverable from future *premiums*. *Firms* can make a direct adjustment to their reserves for *zillmerisation*, subject to the *rules* on *mathematical reserves*. However, where no such adjustment has been made, the *FSA* will consider an application for a *waiver* to take into account an *implicit item*.
Hidden reserves	
8	Hidden reserves are reserves resulting from the underestimation of assets (other than *mathematical reserves*).
Process for applying for a waiver, including limits applicable when a waiver is granted	
9	This annex sets out the procedures to be followed and the form of calculations and data which should be submitted by *firms* to the *FSA*. This *guidance* should also be read in conjunction with the general requirements relating to the *waiver* process described in SUP 8. The *FSA* expects that applications for *waivers* in respect of future profits and *zillmerising* will not normally be considered to pass the "not result in undue risk to persons whose interests the *rules* are intended to protect" test unless the relevant criteria set out in this *guidance* have been satisfied and an application for such a *waiver* may require further criteria to be satisfied for this test to be passed. As set out below, *waivers* in respect of either *zillmerising* or hidden reserves will not normally be given except in very exceptional circumstances.
Timing	
10	A *long-term insurer* may apply to the *FSA* for a *waiver* in respect of *implicit items*. A *waiver* will not apply retrospectively (see SUP 8.3.6G). Consequently, applications intended for a particular accounting reference date will normally need to be made well before that reference date. Applications by *firms* must be made to the *FSA* in writing and include the relevant details specified under SUP 8.3.3D. Given the uncertainty in predicting the future, *waivers* will normally be granted for a maximum of 12 months at a time and any further applications will need to be made accordingly.
11	The information that will be required to enable an application to be considered as set out below, should normally include a demonstration of how the *capital resources requirement* is to be met, with and without the *waiver*. Clearly, up-to-date information may not be available before the *financial year*-end. In some cases information from the previous year-end's *return* may be used, as long as any known significant changes in the structure of the *firm*, or the assumptions used, have been taken into account.

12	If the application for a *waiver* is granted, when a *firm* submits its next *return* the amount of the *implicit item* shown should not exceed that supported by the *firm's* calculations as at the valuation date. In the event that the amount of the future profits item calculated by the *firm* based on these updated assumptions is less than the amount calculated at the time of the *firm's waiver* application, the lower figure should be used in the *return*.
13	An *implicit item* in respect of *zillmerising* or hidden reserves is related to the basis on which liabilities or assets have been valued. In the case of hidden reserves, as explained below, the granting of a *waiver* will be dependent on the overall *capital resources* of the *firm*. *Waivers* in respect of these *implicit items* will, therefore, only be made in relation to the position shown in a particular set of *returns* and it will be essential for *firms* to submit applications to the *FSA* well in advance of the latest date for the submission of the relevant *return*.
14	*Waivers* may be withdrawn by the *FSA* at any time (e.g. where the *FSA* considers the amount in respect of which a *waiver* has been given can no longer be justified). This may be as a result of changes in the *firm's* position or as a result of queries arising on scrutiny of the *returns*.
Information to be submitted	
15	An application for a *waiver* (which includes an application for an extension to or other variation of a *waiver*) should be prepared using the standard application form for a *waiver* (see SUP 8 Annex 2D). In addition, the application should be accompanied by full supporting information to enable the *FSA* to arrive at a decision on the merits of the case. In particular, the application should state clearly the nature and the amounts of the *implicit items* that a *firm* wishes to count against its *capital resources requirement* and whether it proposes to treat the *implicit item* as *tier one capital* or *tier two capital*. In order to assess an application, the *FSA* needs information as to the make-up of the *firm's capital resources*, the quality of the capital items which have been categorised into each tier of capital and a breakdown of capital both within and outside the *firm's long-term insurance fund* or *funds* and between the *firm's with-profits funds* and *non-profit funds*. An explanation as to the appropriateness of the proposed treatment of the *implicit item* under the *capital resources table* should also be provided, including a demonstration that, in allowing for *implicit items*, there has been no double counting of future margins and that the basis for valuing such margins is prudent.
16	The *FSA* recognises that the assessment of the insurance *technical provisions* reflects the contractual obligations of the *firm*. *Implicit items* are therefore margins over and above an economic assessment in these *technical provisions* only. Non-contractual "constructive" obligations arising from a *firm's* regulatory duty to treat *customers* fairly e.g. regarding future terminal bonuses, are not fully captured by the *technical provisions*. A *firm* must instead be satisfied that it has sufficient *capital resources* at all times to meet its obligations under *Principle* 6. The granting of a *waiver* for an *implicit item* does not in any way detract from this requirement and a *firm* will need to be satisfied that this condition is still met.
17	As a minimum, applications for a future profits *implicit item* should be supported by the information contained in Forms 13, 14, 18, 19, 40, 41, 42, 48, 49, the answers to questions 1 to 12 of the abstract of the valuation report, Appendix 9.4 of IPRU(INS), the abstract of the valuation report for the realistic valuation, Appendix 9.4A of IPRU(INS) and Forms 51, 52, 53, 54 and 58. For a *zillmerisation* implicit item, only those items noted above forming part of the abstract valuation report will normally be needed. Applications for a *waiver* in respect of a hidden reserves *implicit item* will normally be considered only if accompanied by the information which is contained in the annual regulatory *returns*. In particular, the balance sheet forms, *long-term insurance business* revenue accounts, and abstract of the valuation report as set out in Appendices 9.1, 9.3 and 9.4 of IPRU(INS) should be provided. This is not to say that a full regulatory *return* must be provided in the specified format, simply that the information contained in these forms should be provided. Where appropriate, the information may be summarised.

18	The following supporting information relating to the calculation of the amounts claimed should be supplied for each type of *implicit item* in respect of which a *waiver* is sought: Future profits: in addition to information related to the prospective calculation and retrospective calculation described below, the profits reported in each of the last five *financial years* up to the date of the most recent available valuation under *rule* 9.4 of IPRU(INS) which has been submitted to the *FSA* prior to, or together with, the application, and the amounts and nature of any exceptional items left out of account; the method used for calculating the average period to run and the results for each of the main categories of business, both before and after allowing for premature termination (where the calculation has been made in two stages); and the basis on which this allowance has been made. *Zillmerising*: the categories of contracts for which an item has been calculated and the percentages of the *relevant capital sum* in respect of which an adjustment has been made. Hidden reserves: particulars, with supporting evidence, of the undervaluation of assets for which recognition is sought.
Continuous monitoring by firms	
19	*Firms* should take into account any material changes in financial conditions or other relevant circumstances that may have an impact on the level of future profits that can prudently be taken into account. *Firms* should also re-evaluate whether an application to vary an *implicit item waiver* should be made whenever circumstances have changed. In the event that circumstances have changed such that an amendment is appropriate, the *firm* must contact the *FSA* as quickly as possible in accordance with *Principle* 11. (See SUP 8.5.1R). In this context, the *FSA* would expect notice of any matter that materially impacts on the *firm's* financial condition, or any *waivers* granted.
Future profits – factors to take into account when submitting calculations to support waiver applications	
20	Where an application is made in respect of a *firm* which has separate *with-profits funds* and *non-profit funds*, the *firm* should ensure that the *capital resources requirement* in respect of the *non-profit fund* is not covered by future profits attributable to *policyholders* arising in the *with-profits fund*. Furthermore, for a *realistic basis life firm* the amount of the *implicit item* allocated to each *with-profits fund* should be calculated separately, as the amount allocated to each *with-profits fund* will be taken into consideration in the calculation of the *with-profits insurance capital component* (see INSPRU 1.4.24R).
21	*Firms* need to assess prospective future profit (i.e. how much can reasonably be expected to arise) and compare this to maximum limits (in article 27(4) of the *Consolidated Life Directive*), which relate to past profits.
Future profits – prospective calculation	
22	The application for a *waiver* should be supported by details of a prospective calculation of future profits arising from in-force business. The information supplied to the *FSA* should include a description of the method used in the calculation and of the assumptions made, together with the results arising. From 31 December 2009 at the latest, future profits *implicit items* will no longer be permitted under the *Consolidated Life Directive*. Where a *firm* first applies for an *implicit items waiver* after GENPRU 2.2 comes into effect, under the prospective calculation a *firm* should only take into consideration future profits that are expected to emerge in the period up to 31 December 2009. *Implicit item waivers* granted before GENPRU 2.2 comes into effect will continue to operate under the terms of those *waivers*, but an application to vary the terms of such a *waiver*, for example to extend the effective period, is an application for a new *waiver* for which a *firm* should usually only take into consideration future profits that are expected to emerge in the period up to 31 December 2009.
Assumptions	

Part II FSA Handbook Materials

23	The assumptions made should be prudent, rather than best estimate, assumptions of future experience (that is, the prudent assumptions should allow for the fair market price for assuming that risk including associated expenses). In particular, it would not normally be considered appropriate for the projected return on any asset to be taken to be higher than the risk-free yield (that is, assessed by reference to the yield arrived at using a model of future risk free yields properly calibrated from the forward gilts market). It may also be appropriate to bring future withdrawals into account on a suitably prudent basis. For *with-profits business*, the assumptions for future investment returns should not capitalise future bonus loadings except where the with-profits *policyholders* share in risks other than the investment performance of the fund. Furthermore, the rate at which future profits are discounted should include an appropriate margin over a risk free rate of return. Calculations should also be carried out to demonstrate that the prospective calculation of the future profits arising from the in-force business supporting the application for the *implicit item* would be sufficient to support the amount of the *implicit item* under each scenario described for use in determining the *resilience capital requirement* – where the *waiver* relates to an *implicit item* allocated to more than one fund, this should be demonstrated separately for that element of the *implicit item* allocated to each fund. For an *implicit item* allocated to a *with-profits fund*, proper allowance should be made for any shareholder transfers to ensure that the *implicit item* is not supported by future profits which will be required to support those transfers. To the extent, if any, that future profits are dependent on the levying of explicit expense related charges (for example as in the case of unit-linked business) the documentation submitted should include a demonstration of the prudence of the assumptions made as to the level at which future charges will be levied and expenses incurred.	
Other limitations on the extent to which waivers for implicit items will be granted to a realistic basis life firm		
24	Where a *waiver* in respect of an *implicit item* is granted to a *realistic basis life firm* additional limits may apply by reference to a comparison of *realistic excess capital* and *regulatory excess capital* including allowance for the effect of the *waiver*. Where the *waiver* relates to an *implicit item* allocated partly or entirely to a *with-profits fund*, the *waiver* will contain a limitation to the effect that the *regulatory excess capital* for that *with-profits fund*, allowing for the effect of the *waiver*, may not exceed that fund's *realistic excess capital*. This limitation will apply on an ongoing basis so that, for example, in the case of an *implicit item* allocated to a *with-profits fund*, the amount of the *implicit item* would be limited to zero whenever the *regulatory excess capital* exceeded the *realistic excess capital* of that fund.	
Other charges to future profits		
25	To avoid double counting, no account should be taken of any future surplus arising from assets corresponding to explicit items which have been counted towards the *capital resources requirement* such as shareholders funds, surplus carried forward or investment reserves. Deductions should be made in the calculation of future surpluses for the impact of any other arrangements which give rise to a charge over future surplus emerging (e.g. financial *reinsurance* arrangements, subordinated loan capital or contingent loan agreements). Deductions should also be made to the extent that any credit has been taken for the purposes of INSPRU 1.4.45R(2)(c) for the present value of future profits relating to non-profit business written in a *non-profit fund*. The information supplied to the *FSA* should identify the amount and reason for any adjustments made to the calculation of the prospective amount of future profits.	
26	The *firm* should confirm to the *FSA* that the calculations have been properly carried out and that there are no other factors that should be taken into account.	
Future profits – retrospective calculation		
Overriding limit		
27	The maximum amount of the *implicit item* relating to future profits permitted under the *Consolidated Life Directive* is 50% of the product of the estimated annual profit and the average period to run (not exceeding six years (ten years during the transitional period referred to in paragraph 5)) on the *policies* in the portfolio. Article 27(4) of the *Consolidated Life Directive* also imposes a further limit on the amount of the *implicit item* equal to 25% of the lower of:	
	(1)	the *firm's capital resources*; and
	(2)	the higher of its *base capital resources requirement* for *long-term insurance business* and its *long-term insurance capital requirement*.

	Once the transitional period set out in article 71(1) of the *Consolidated Life Directive* has expired in 2007 (see paragraph 5), the *FSA* will not allow a *waiver* for more than the amount permitted by article 27(4) of the Directive.
Definition of profits	
28	The estimated annual profit should be taken as the average annual surplus arising in the *long-term insurance fund* over the last five *financial years* up to the date of the most recent available valuation which has been submitted to the *FSA* prior to, or together with, the application. For this purpose, deficiencies arising should be treated as negative surpluses. Where a *firm's financial year* has altered, the surplus arising in a period falling partly outside the relevant five year period should be assumed to accrue uniformly over the period in question for the purpose of estimating the profits arising within the five year period. When there has been a transfer of a block of business into the *firm* (or out of the *firm*) during the period, surplus arising from the transferred block should be included (or excluded) for the full five year period. Where a portion of a block of business is transferred, the surplus included (or excluded) should be a reasonable estimate of the surplus arising from the portion transferred.
29	Where a *firm* has been carrying on *long-term insurance business* for less than 5 years, the total profits made during the past five years should be taken to be the aggregate of any surpluses that have arisen during the period in which *long-term insurance business* has been carried on less any deficiencies that may have arisen during that period. The resulting total should still be divided by five to obtain the estimated annual profit.
Exceptional items	
30	Substantial items of an exceptional nature should be excluded from the calculation of the estimated annual profit. Such items include profits arising from an exceptional change in the value at which assets are brought into account, where this is not reflected in a similar change in the amount of the liabilities, and profits arising from a change in the overall valuation approach between one year and another. An exceptional loss (i.e. a reduction of an exceptional nature in the surplus arising) may be excluded from the calculation only to the extent that it can be set against a profit or profits up to the amount of the loss and arising from a similar cause. It is not intended, however, that any adjustment should be made for the effect on surplus of a net strengthening of reserves for costs associated with an expansion of the business or for special capital expenditure, such as the purchase of computer systems.
Double counting	
31	The inclusion of investment income arising from the assets representing the explicit components of *capital resources* (as part of the estimated annual profit for the purpose of determining the future profits *implicit item*) would result in double-counting. If those assets were required to meet the effects of adverse developments, this would automatically result in the cessation of the contribution to profits from the associated investment income. It would clearly not be appropriate for the *FSA* to grant a *waiver* which would enable a *firm* to meet the *capital resources requirement* on the basis of counting both the capital values of the assets and the value of the income flow which they can be expected to generate.
32	The definition of the estimated annual profit as the surplus arising in the *long-term insurance fund* ensures that any contribution to surplus arising from transfers from the profit and loss account, including investment income on shareholders' assets, is not included in the estimated annual profit. Thus double-counting should not arise in respect of shareholders' assets. Double-counting may arise, however, in respect of the investment income from the assets representing the explicit components of *capital resources* carried within the *long-term insurance fund* (e.g. surplus carried forward or investment reserves), but the amount of such investment income is not separately identified in the *return*.
33	Where there is reason to suspect that the elimination of any such double-counting would reduce a *firm's capital resources* to close to or below the required level, or would otherwise be significant, the *FSA* will request this information with a view to taking account of this factor in determining the amount of the *implicit item*. Additional information concerning investment income should be furnished with an application for a *waiver*, if a *firm* believes that any double-counting would fall into one of the categories mentioned above.
Average period to run	

34	The average number of years remaining to run on *policies* should be calculated on the basis of the weighted average of the periods for individual *contracts of insurance*, using as weights the actuarial present value of the benefits payable under the contracts. A separate weighted average should be calculated for each of the various categories of contract and the results combined to obtain the weighted average for the portfolio as a whole. Approximate methods of calculation, which the *firm* considers will give results similar to the full calculation, will be accepted. In particular, the *FSA* will normally accept the calculation of an average period to run for a specific category of contract on the basis of the average valuation factor for future benefits derived from data contained in the abstract of the valuation report in the regulatory *returns*. A *firm* will be asked to demonstrate the validity of the method adopted only where an abnormal distribution of the business in force gives grounds for doubt about its accuracy.
35	Calculations will normally be requested only for the main categories of *insurance business*, accounting for not less than 90% of the *mathematical reserves*, except where there are grounds for expecting that the exclusion of certain categories of *policies* under this provision might have a significant effect on the resulting average period to run. Detailed calculations will not be required where a *waiver* is sought in respect of a low multiple of the annual profits, well within the average period to run for the *firm*.
36	Where, for a particular category of business, a method of valuation is used which does not involve the calculation of the value of future benefits and which is significant for the *firm* in question, the calculation of the average period to run should be based on estimates of the value of future benefits.
Premature termination of contracts	
37	Allowance should be made for the premature termination of *contracts of insurance*, based on the actual experience of the *firm* over the last five years, or other appropriate period, and taking into account specific features of contracts such as options which can be expected to lead to premature termination (e.g. guaranteed surrender values on income bonds written as *long-term insurance contracts* and option dates on flexible whole-life contracts). The adjustment should be made separately for each of the main categories of business. The use of industry-wide rates of termination will be acceptable where a *firm* is satisfied that this will result in sufficient allowance being made having regard to the *firm's* own experience. Methods of calculation that involve a degree of approximation will be permitted.
38	For certain types of contract, where the period left to run is most naturally defined as the term to a fixed maturity or expiry date, the allowance for premature termination should also take into account terminations resulting from death.
Overall limit	
39	The overall average period left to run calculated as described above should be limited to a maximum of six years under article 27(4) of the *Consolidated Life Directive* (or a maximum of ten years during the transitional period referred to in paragraph 5) before applying it to the estimated annual profit in order to determine the maximum value of the future profits *implicit item*.
Definition of period to run	
40	The definition of the period to run and the basis of the allowance for early termination should clearly be considered together. For certain types of contracts (e.g. pension contracts with a range of retirement ages or other options), there is inherent uncertainty about the likely term to run. In such circumstances any estimate for determining the amount of the future profits *implicit item* for which a *waiver* is sought should be based on prudent assumptions tending, if anything, to underestimate the average period to run.
Zillmerising	
41	The *FSA* does not normally expect to grant *waivers* permitting *implicit items* due to *zillmerisation* except in very exceptional circumstances. *Zillmerisation* is an allowance for acquisition costs that are expected, under prudent assumptions, to be recoverable from future *premiums*. *Firms* can make a direct adjustment to their reserves for *zillmerisation*, subject to the requirements on *mathematical reserves* set out in INSPRU 1.3.43R, and this is the usual approach. However, where no such adjustment has been made, or where the maximum adjustment has not been made in the *mathematical reserves*, the *FSA* will consider an application for an *implicit item*, if the amount is consistent with the amount that would have been allowed as an adjustment to *mathematical reserves* under INSPRU 1.3.43R.
Hidden reserves	

42	The *FSA* will grant *waivers* permitting *implicit items* due to hidden reserves only in very exceptional circumstances. These items relate to hidden reserves resulting from the underestimation of assets. The *rules* for the valuation of assets and liabilities (see GENPRU 1.3) which apply to assets and liabilities other than *mathematical reserves* are based on the valuation used by the *firm* for the purposes of its external accounts, with adjustments for regulatory prudence such as concentration limits for large holdings, and would not normally be expected to contain hidden reserves.
Case studies on "unduly burdensome"	
43	Some examples of situations where the existing *rules* might be considered to be unduly burdensome are given below:
•	A *firm* writes *with-profits business*. The *firm's* investment policy is affected by its published financial position. Application of the *rules* without an *implicit item* would result in the *firm* adopting a lower equity backing ratio. It may be possible to demonstrate that, in the circumstances, it would be unduly burdensome to require the *firm* to incur costs (which might prejudice *policyholders*) resulting from the lower equity backing ratio, rather than take allowance for an *implicit item*.
•	A *firm* has purchased a block of in-force business, on which the future profits may be reasonably estimated. However, this asset is given no value under the *rules*. It may be possible to demonstrate that it is unduly burdensome for the *firm* to recognise the cost of acquiring the assets whilst giving no value to the asset acquired.
•	A *firm* has a block of in-force business, on which the future profits may be reasonably estimated. Application of the *rules* without an *implicit item* would result in a need to obtain additional capital. It may be possible to demonstrate that it is unduly burdensome, having regard to the particular circumstances of the *firm*, to require it to incur the costs involved in the injection of further capital rather than take allowance for an *implicit item*.
•	A *firm* has purchased matching assets for guaranteed annuity liabilities. The operation of the asset and liability valuation *rules* leads to statutory losses in certain circumstances in spite of good matching of assets and liabilities on a realistic basis of assessment. It may be possible to demonstrate that it is unduly burdensome to require the *firm* to incur the costs involved in the injection of further capital rather than take allowance for an *implicit item*.
Conditions which will typically be applied to implicit items waivers	
Limits	
44	Where *implicit items waivers* are granted, the value cannot exceed (and will normally be less than) the monetary limits described in paragraph 27, except that during the transitional period the pre-Solvency I limits will apply. In addition, time limits will apply and *waivers* will normally only last for 12 months.
Publicity	
45	The *FSA* will publish the *waiver* (see SUP 8.6 and SUP 8.7). Public disclosure is standard practice unless the *FSA* is satisfied that publication is inappropriate or unnecessary (see section 148 of the *Act*). Any request that a direction not be published should be made to the *FSA* in writing with grounds in support, as set out in SUP 8.6. Disclosure of a *waiver* will normally be required in the *firm's* annual *returns*.

Part II FSA Handbook Materials

CHAPTER 3

3.1 Cross sector groups

Application

[2057]
3.1.1 **[R]**
(1) GENPRU 3.1 applies to every *firm* that is a member of a *financial conglomerate* other than:
  (a) an *incoming EEA firm*;
  (b) an *incoming Treaty firm*;
  (c) a *UCITS qualifier*; and
  (d) an *ICVC*.
(2) GENPRU 3.1 does not apply to a *firm* with respect to a *financial conglomerate* of which it is a member if the interest of the *financial conglomerate* in that *firm* is no more than a *participation*.
(3) GENPRU 3.1.25 (Capital adequacy requirements: high level requirement), GENPRU 3.1.26R (Capital adequacy requirements: application of Method 4 from Annex I of the Financial Groups Directive), GENPRU 3.1.29R (Capital adequacy requirements: application

of Methods 1, 2 or 3 from Annex I of the Financial Groups Directive) and GENPRU 3.1.35R (Risk concentration and intra group transactions: the main rule) do not apply with respect to a *third-country financial conglomerate*.

Purpose

3.1.2 **[G]** GENPRU 3.1 implements the *Financial Groups Directive*. However, material on the following topics is to be found elsewhere in the *Handbook* as follows:
(1) further material on *third-country financial conglomerates* can be found in GENPRU 3.2;
(2) SUP 15.9 contains notification *rules* for members of *financial conglomerates*;
(3) material on reporting obligations can be found in SUP 16.7.82R and SUP 16.7.83R; and
(4) material on systems and controls in *financial conglomerates* can be found in SYSC 12.

Introduction: identifying a financial conglomerate

3.1.3 **[G]**
(1) In general the process in (2) to (8) applies for identifying *financial conglomerates*.
(2) *Competent authorities* that have authorised *regulated entities* should try to identify any *consolidation group* that is a *financial conglomerate*. If a *competent authority* is of the opinion that a *regulated entity* authorised by that *competent authority* is a member of a *consolidation group* which may be a *financial conglomerate* it should communicate its view to the other *competent authorities* concerned.
(3) A *competent authority* may start (as described in (2)) the process of deciding whether a group is a *financial conglomerate* even if it would not be the *coordinator*.
(4) A member of a group may also start that process by notifying one of the *competent authorities* that have authorised group members that its group may be a *financial conglomerate*, for example by notification under SUP 15.9.
(5) If a group member gives a notification in accordance with (4), that does not automatically mean that the group should be treated as a *financial conglomerate*. The process described in (6) to (9) still applies.
(6) The *competent authority* that would be *coordinator* will take the lead in establishing whether a group is a *financial conglomerate* once the process has been started as described in (2) and (3).
(7) The process of establishing whether a group is a *financial conglomerate* will normally involve discussions between the *financial conglomerate* and the *competent authorities* concerned.
(8) A *financial conglomerate* should be notified by its *coordinator* that it has been identified as a *financial conglomerate* and of the appointment of the *coordinator*. The notification should be given to the *parent undertaking* at the head of the group or, in the absence of a *parent undertaking*, the *regulated entity* with the largest balance sheet total in the *most important financial sector*. That notification does not of itself make a group into a *financial conglomerate*; whether or not a group is a *financial conglomerate* is governed by the definition of *financial conglomerate* as set out in GENPRU 3.1.
(9) GENPRU 3 Annex 3G is a questionnaire (together with its explanatory notes) that the *FSA* asks groups that may be *financial conglomerates* to fill out in order to decide whether or not they are.

Introduction: The role of other competent authorities

3.1.4 **[G]** A lead supervisor (called the *coordinator*) is appointed for each *financial conglomerate*. Article 10 of the *Financial Groups Directive* describes the criteria for deciding which *competent authority* is appointed as *coordinator*. Article 11 of the *Financial Groups Directive* sets out the tasks of the *coordinator*.

Definition of financial conglomerate: basic definition

3.1.5 **[R]** A *financial conglomerate* means a *consolidation group* that is identified as a *financial conglomerate* in accordance with the decision tree in GENPRU 3 Annex 4R.

Definition of financial conglomerate: sub-groups

3.1.6 **[R]** A *consolidation group* is not prevented from being a *financial conglomerate* because it is part of a wider:
(1) *consolidation group*; or
(2) *financial conglomerate*; or
(3) group of persons linked in some other way.

Definition of financial conglomerate: the financial sectors: general

3.1.7 **[R]** For the purpose of the definition of *financial conglomerate*, there are two *financial sectors* as follows:

(1) the *banking sector* and the *investment services sector*, taken together; and
(2) the *insurance sector*.

3.1.8 **[R]**
(1) This *rule* applies for the purpose of the definition of *financial conglomerate* and the *financial conglomerate definition decision tree*.
(2) Any *mixed financial holding company* is considered to be outside the *overall financial sector* for the purpose of the tests set out in the boxes titled Threshold Test 1, Threshold Test 2 and Threshold Test 3 in the *financial conglomerate definition decision tree*.
(3) Determining whether the tests set out in the boxes titled Threshold Test 2 and Threshold Test 3 in the *financial conglomerate definition decision tree* are passed is based on considering the consolidated and/or aggregated activities of the members of the *consolidation group* within the *insurance sector* and the consolidated and/or aggregated activities of the members of the *consolidation group* within the *banking sector* and the *investment services sector*.

Definition of financial conglomerate: adjustment of the percentages

3.1.9 **[R]** Once a *financial conglomerate* has become a *financial conglomerate* and subject to supervision in accordance with the *Financial Groups Directive*, the figures in the *financial conglomerate definition decision tree* are altered as follows:
(1) the figure of 40% in the box titled Threshold Test 1 is replaced by 35%;
(2) the figure of 10% in the box titled Threshold Test 2 is replaced by 8%; and
(3) the figure of six billion Euro in the box titled Threshold Test 3 is replaced by five billion Euro.

3.1.10 **[R]** The alteration in GENPRU 3.1.9R only applies to a *financial conglomerate* during the period that:
(1) begins when the *financial conglomerate* would otherwise have stopped being a *financial conglomerate* because it does not meet one of the unaltered thresholds referred to in GENPRU 3.1.9R; and
(2) covers the three years following that date.

Definition of financial conglomerate: balance sheet totals

3.1.11 **[R]** The calculations referred to in the *financial conglomerate definition decision tree* regarding the balance sheet must be made on the basis of the aggregated balance sheet total of the members of the *consolidation group*, according to their annual accounts. For the purposes of this calculation, *undertakings* in which a *participation* is held must be taken into account as regards the amount of their balance sheet total corresponding to the aggregated proportional share held by the *consolidation group*. However, where consolidated accounts are available, they must be used instead of aggregated accounts.

Definition of financial conglomerate: solvency requirement

3.1.12 **[R]** The solvency and capital adequacy requirements referred to in the *financial conglomerate definition decision tree* must be calculated in accordance with the provisions of the relevant *sectoral rules*.

Definition of financial conglomerate: discretionary changes to the definition

3.1.13 **[G]** Articles 3(3) to 3(6), Article 5(4) and Article 6(5) of the *Financial Groups Directive* allow *competent authorities*, on a case by case basis, to:
(1) change the definition of *financial conglomerate* and the obligations applying with respect to a *financial conglomerate*;
(2) apply the scheme in the *Financial Groups Directive* to *EEA regulated entities* in specified kinds of group structures that do not come within the definition of *financial conglomerate*; and
(3) exclude a particular entity in the scope of capital adequacy requirements that apply with respect to a *financial conglomerate*.

Capital adequacy requirements: introduction

3.1.14 **[G]** The capital adequacy provisions of GENPRU 3.1 are designed to be applied to *EEA*-based *financial conglomerates*.

3.1.15 **[G]** GENPRU 3.1.25R is a high level capital adequacy *rule*. It applies whether or not the *FSA* is the *coordinator* of the *financial conglomerate* concerned.

3.1.16 **[G]** GENPRU 3.1.26R to GENPRU 3.1.31R and GENPRU 3 Annex 1R implement the detailed capital adequacy requirements of the *Financial Groups Directive*. They only deal with a *financial conglomerate* for which the *FSA* is the *coordinator*. If another *competent authority* is *coordinator* of a *financial conglomerate*, those *rules* do not apply with respect to that *financial conglomerate* and instead that *coordinator* will be responsible for implementing those detailed requirements.

3.1.17 **[G]** Annex I of the *Financial Groups Directive* lays down four methods for calculating capital adequacy at the level of a *financial conglomerate*. Those four methods are implemented as follows:
(1) Method 1 calculates capital adequacy using accounting consolidation. It is implemented by GENPRU 3.1.29R to GENPRU 3.1.31R and Part 1 of GENPRU 3 Annex 1R.
(2) Method 2 calculates capital adequacy using a deduction and aggregation approach. It is implemented by GENPRU 3.1.29R to GENPRU 3.1.31R and Part 2 of GENPRU 3 Annex 1R.
(3) Method 3 calculates capital adequacy using book values and the deduction of capital requirements. It is implemented by GENPRU 3.1.29R to GENPRU 3.1.31R and Part 3 of GENPRU 3 Annex 1R.
(4) Method 4 consists of a combination of Methods 1, 2 and 3 from Annex I of the *Financial Groups Directive*, or a combination of two of those Methods. It is implemented by GENPRU 3.1.26R to GENPRU 3.1.28R, GENPRU 3.1.30R and Part 4 of GENPRU 3 Annex 1R.

3.1.18 **[G]** Part 4 of GENPRU 3 Annex 1R (Use of Method 4 from Annex I of the *Financial Conglomerates Directive*) applies the *FSA's sectoral rules* with respect to the *financial conglomerate* as a whole, with some adjustments. Where Part 4 of GENPRU 3 Annex 1R applies the *FSA's sectoral rules* for:
(1) the *insurance sector*, that involves a combination of Methods 2 and 3; and
(2) the *banking sector* and the *investment services sector*, that involves a combination of Methods 1 and 3.

3.1.19 **[G]** Paragraph 5.7 of GENPRU 3 Annex 1R (Capital adequacy calculations for financial conglomerates) deals with a case in which there are no capital ties between entities in a *financial conglomerate*. In particular, the *FSA*, after consultation with the other *relevant competent authorities* and in accordance with Annex I of the *Financial Groups Directive*, will determine which proportional share of a solvency deficit in such an entity will have to be taken into account, bearing in mind the liability to which the existing relationship gives rise.

3.1.20 **[G]**
(1) In the following cases, the *FSA* (acting as *coordinator*) may choose which of the four methods for calculating capital adequacy laid down in Annex I of the *Financial Groups Directive* should apply:
   (a) where a *financial conglomerate* is headed by a *regulated entity* that has been authorised by the *FSA*; or
   (b) the only *relevant competent authority* for the *financial conglomerate* is the *FSA*.
(2) GENPRU 3.1.28R automatically applies Method 4 from Annex I of the *Financial Groups Directive* in these circumstances except in the cases set out in GENPRU 3.1.28R(1)(e) and GENPRU 3.1.28R(1)(f). The process in GENPRU 3.1.22G does not apply.

3.1.21 **[G]** Where GENPRU 3.1.20G does not apply, the Annex I method to be applied is decided by the *coordinator* after consultation with the *relevant competent authorities* and the *financial conglomerate* itself.

3.1.22 **[G]** The method of calculating capital adequacy chosen in respect of a *financial conglomerate* as described in GENPRU 3.1.21G will be applied with respect to that *financial conglomerate* by varying the *Part IV permission* of a *firm* in that *financial conglomerate* to include a *requirement*. That *requirement* will have the effect of obliging the *firm* to ensure that the *financial conglomerate* has capital resources of the type and amount needed to comply with whichever of the methods in GENPRU 3 Annex 1R is to be applied with respect to that *financial conglomerate*. The powers in the *Act* relating to *waivers* and varying a *firm's Part IV permission* can be used to implement one of the methods from Annex I of the *Financial Groups Directive* in a way that is different from that set out in GENPRU 3.1 and GENPRU 3 Annex 1R if that is necessary to reflect the consultations referred to in GENPRU 3.1.21G.

3.1.23 **[G]** If there is more than one *firm* in a *financial conglomerate* with a *Part IV permission*, the *FSA* would not normally expect to apply the *requirement* described in GENPRU 3.1.22G to all of them. Normally it will only be necessary to apply it to one.

3.1.24 **[G]** The *FSA* expects that in all or most cases falling into GENPRU 3.1.21G, the *rules* in Part 4 of GENPRU 3 Annex 1R will be applied.

Capital adequacy requirements: high level requirement

3.1.25 **[R]**
(1) A *firm* that is a member of a *financial conglomerate* must at all times have capital resources of such an amount and type that results in the capital resources of the *financial conglomerate* taken as a whole being adequate.
(2) This *rule* does not apply with respect to any *financial conglomerate* until notification has been made that it has been identified as a *financial conglomerate* as contemplated by Article 4(2) of the *Financial Groups Directive*.

Capital adequacy requirements: application of Method 4 from Annex I of the Financial Groups Directive

3.1.26 **[R]** If this *rule* applies under GENPRU 3.1.27R to a *firm* with respect to a *financial conglomerate* of which it is a member, the *firm* must at all times have capital resources of an amount and type:
(1) that ensure that the *financial conglomerate* has capital resources of an amount and type that comply with the *rules* applicable with respect to that *financial conglomerate* under Part 4 of GENPRU 3 Annex 1R (as modified by that annex); and
(2) that as a result ensure that the *firm* complies with those *rules* (as so modified) with respect to that *financial conglomerate*.

3.1.27 **[R]** GENPRU 3.1.26R applies to a *firm* with respect to a *financial conglomerate* of which it is a member if one of the following conditions is satisfied:
(1) the condition in GENPRU 3.1.28R is satisfied; or
(2) this *rule* is applied to the *firm* with respect to that *financial conglomerate* as described in GENPRU 3.1.30R.

Capital adequacy requirements: compulsory application of Method 4 from Annex I of the Financial Groups Directive

3.1.28 **[R]**
(1) The condition in this *rule* is satisfied for the purpose of GENPRU 3.1.27R(1) with respect to a *firm* and a *financial conglomerate* of which it is a member (with the result that GENPRU 3.1.26R automatically applies to that *firm*) if:
  (a) notification has been made in accordance with regulation 2 of the *Financial Groups Directive Regulations* that the *financial conglomerate* is a *financial conglomerate* and that the *FSA* is *coordinator* of that *financial conglomerate*;
  (b) the *financial conglomerate* is not part of a wider *FSA regulated EEA financial conglomerate*;
  (c) the *financial conglomerate* is not an *FSA regulated EEA financial conglomerate* under another *rule* or under paragraph (b) of the definition of *FSA regulated EEA financial conglomerate* (application of supplementary supervision through a *firm's Part IV permission*);
  (d) one of the following conditions is satisfied:
    (i) the *financial conglomerate* is headed by a *regulated entity* that is a *UK domestic firm*; or
    (ii) the only *relevant competent authority* for that *financial conglomerate* is the *FSA*;
  (e) this *rule* is not disapplied under paragraph 5.7 of GENPRU 3 Annex 1R (No capital ties); and
  (f) the *financial conglomerate* meets the condition set out in the box titled Threshold Test 2 (10% average of balance sheet and solvency requirements) in the *financial conglomerate definition decision tree*.
(2) Once GENPRU 3.1.26R applies to a *firm* with respect to a *financial conglomerate* of which it is a member under GENPRU 3.1.27R(1), (1)(f) ceases to apply with respect to that *financial conglomerate*. Therefore the fact that the *financial conglomerate* subsequently ceases to meet the condition in (1)(f) does not mean that the condition in this *rule* is not satisfied.

Capital adequacy requirements: application of Methods 1, 2 or 3 from Annex I of the Financial Groups Directive

3.1.29 **[R]** If with respect to a *firm* and a *financial conglomerate* of which it is a member, this *rule* is applied to the *firm* with respect to that *financial conglomerate* as described in GENPRU 3.1.30R, the *firm* must at all times have capital resources of an amount and type that ensures that the *conglomerate capital resources* of that *financial conglomerate* at all times equal or exceed its *conglomerate capital resources requirement*.

Capital adequacy requirements: use of Part IV permission to apply Annex I of the Financial Groups Directive

3.1.30 **[R]** With respect to a *firm* and a *financial conglomerate* of which it is a member:
(1) GENPRU 3.1.26R (Method 4 from Annex I of the *Financial Groups Directive*) is applied to the *firm* with respect to that *financial conglomerate* for the purposes of GENPRU 3.1.27R(2); or
(2) GENPRU 3.1.29R (Methods 1 to 3 from Annex I of the *Financial Groups Directive*) is applied to the *firm* with respect to that *financial conglomerate*;

if the *firm's Part IV permission* contains a *requirement* obliging the *firm* to comply with GENPRU 3.1.26R or, as the case may be, GENPRU 3.1.29R.

3.1.31 **[R]** If GENPRU 3.1.29R (Methods 1–3 from Annex I of the *Financial Groups Directive*) applies to a *firm* with respect to a *financial conglomerate* of which it is a member, the definitions of *conglomerate capital resources* and *conglomerate capital resources requirement* that apply for the purposes of that *rule* are the ones from whichever of Part 1, Part 2 or Part 3 of GENPRU 3 Annex 1R is specified in the *requirement* referred to in GENPRU 3.1.30R.

Risk concentration and intra-group transactions: introduction

3.1.32 **[G]** GENPRU 3.1.35R implements Article 7(4) and Article 8(4) of the *Financial Groups Directive*, which provide that where a *financial conglomerate* is headed by a *mixed financial holding company*, the *sectoral rules* regarding *risk concentration* and *intra-group transactions* of the *most important financial sector* in the *financial conglomerate*, if any, shall apply to that sector as a whole, including the *mixed financial holding company*.

3.1.33 **[G]** Articles 7(3) (Risk concentration) and 8(3) (Intra-group transactions) and Annex II (Technical application of the provisions on intra-group transactions and risk concentration) of the *Financial Groups Directive* say that Member States may apply at the level of the *financial conglomerate* the provisions of the *sectoral rules* on *risk concentrations* and *intra-group transactions*. GENPRU 3.1 does not take up that option, although the *FSA* may impose such obligations on a case by case basis.

Risk concentration and intra-group transactions: application

3.1.34 **[R]** GENPRU 3.1.35R applies to a *firm* with respect to a *financial conglomerate* of which it is a member if:

(1) the condition in Articles 7(4) and 8(4) of *the Financial Groups Directive* is satisfied (the *financial conglomerate* is headed by a *mixed financial holding company*); and

(2) that *financial conglomerate* is an *FSA regulated EEA financial conglomerate*.

Risk concentration and intra group transactions: the main rule

3.1.35 **[R]** A *firm* must ensure that the *sectoral rules* regarding *risk concentration* and *intra-group transactions* of the *most important financial sector* in the *financial conglomerate* referred to in GENPRU 3.1.34R are complied with with respect to that *financial sector* as a whole, including the *mixed financial holding company*. The *FSA's sectoral rules* for these purposes are those identified in the table in GENPRU 3.1.36R.

Risk concentration and intra-group transactions: Table of applicable sectoral rules

3.1.36 **[R]** Table: application of sectoral rules

This table belongs to GENPRU 3.1.35R

The most important financial sector	Applicable sectoral rules	
	Risk concentration	Intra-group transactions
Banking and investment services sector	BIPRU 8.9 (Consolidated concentration risk requirements) including BIPRU TP as it applies to a *UK consolidation group*.	BIPRU 10 (Concentration Risk) including BIPRU TP as it applies on a solo basis and relates to BIPRU 10.
Insurance sector	None	*Rule* 9.39 of IPRU(INS)
Note	Any *waiver* granted to a member of the *financial conglomerate*, on a solo or consolidated basis, shall not apply in respect of the *financial conglomerate* for the purposes of GENPRU 3.1.36R.	

3.1.37 **[R]**

(1) Where the *rules* for the *banking and investment services sector* are being applied, a *mixed financial holding company* must be treated as being a *financial holding company*.

(2) Where the *rules* for the *insurance sector* are being applied, a *mixed financial holding company* must be treated as being an *insurance holding company*.

3.1.38 **[R]**

(1) This *rule* applies for the purposes of the definitions of:

  (a) a *concentration risk group counterparty*; and

  (b) a *consolidation concentration risk group counterparty*;

  as they apply for the purposes of the *rules* for the *banking and investment services sector* as applied by GENPRU 3.1.36R.

(2) For the purposes of BIPRU 3.2.27R(1)(a) and (b) (as they apply to the definition in GENPRU 3.1.38R(1)(a)), the conditions are also satisfied if the *counterparty* and the *firm* are included within the scope of consolidated supervision on a full basis with respect to the same *financial conglomerate* under GENPRU 3.1 or the relevant implementation measures in another *EEA State* for the *Financial Groups Directive*.

(3) Subject to (4), for the purposes of BIPRU 8.9.11R(3) (as it applies to the definition in GENPRU 3.1.38R(1)(b)), the conditions are also satisfied if the *counterparty* and the *firm* are included within the scope of consolidated supervision on a full basis with respect to the same *financial conglomerate* under GENPRU 3.1 or the relevant implementation measures in another *EEA State* for the *Financial Groups Directive*.

(4) BIPRU 8.9.11R(3)(a) does not apply.

The financial sectors: asset management companies

3.1.39 **[R]**

(1) In accordance with Article 30 of the *Financial Groups Directive* (Asset management companies), this *rule* deals with the inclusion of an *asset management company* that is a member of a *financial conglomerate* in the scope of regulation of *financial conglomerates*. This *rule* does not apply to the definition of *financial conglomerate*.

(2) An *asset management company* is in the *overall financial sector* and is a *regulated entity* for the purpose of:
 (a) GENPRU 3.1.26R to GENPRU 3.1.36R;
 (b) GENPRU 3 Annex 1R (Capital adequacy calculations for financial conglomerates) and GENPRU 3 Annex 2R (Prudential rules for third country groups); and
 (c) any other provision of the *Handbook* relating to the supervision of *financial conglomerates*.

(3) In the case of a *financial conglomerate* for which the *FSA* is the *coordinator*, all *asset management companies* must be allocated to one *financial sector* for the purposes in (2), being either the *investment services sector* or the *insurance sector*. But if that choice has not been made in accordance with (4) and notified to the *FSA* in accordance with (4)(d), an *asset management company* must be allocated to the *investment services sector*.

(4) The choice in (3):
 (a) must be made by the *undertaking* in the *financial conglomerate* holding the position referred to in Article 4(2) of the *Financial Groups Directive* (group member to whom notice must be given that the group has been found to be a *financial conglomerate*);
 (b) applies to all *asset management companies* that are members of the *financial conglomerate* from time to time;
 (c) cannot be changed; and
 (d) must be notified to the *FSA* as soon as reasonably practicable after the notification in (4)(a).

(5) This *rule* applies even if:
 (a) a *UCITS management company* is a *BIPRU investment firm*; or
 (b) an *asset management company* is an *investment firm*.

3.2 Third-country groups

Application

3.2.1 **[R]** GENPRU 3.2 applies to every *firm* that is a member of a *third-country group*. But it does not apply to:

(1) an *incoming EEA firm*; or
(2) an *incoming Treaty firm*; or
(3) a *UCITS qualifier*; or
(4) an *ICVC*.

Purpose

3.2.2 **[G]** GENPRU 3.2 implements in part Article 18 of the *Financial Groups Directive* and Article 143 of the *Banking Consolidation Directive*.

Equivalence

3.2.3 **[G]** The first question that must be asked about a *third-country financial group* is whether the *EEA regulated entities* in that *third-country group* are subject to supervision by a *third-country competent authority*, which is equivalent to that provided for by the *Financial Groups Directive* (in the case of a *financial conglomerate*) or the *EEA prudential sectoral legislation* for the *banking sector* or *the investment services sector* (in the case of a *banking and investment group*). Article 18(1) of the *Financial Groups Directive* sets out the process for establishing equivalence with respect to *third-country financial conglomerates* and Article 143 (1) and (2) of the *Banking Consolidation Directive* does so with respect to *third-country banking and investment groups*.

Other methods: General

3.2.4 **[G]** If the supervision of a *third-country group* by a *third-country competent authority* does not meet the equivalence test referred to in GENPRU 3.2.3G, *competent authorities* may apply other

Part II FSA Handbook Materials

methods that ensure appropriate supervision of the *EEA regulated entities* in that *third-country group* in accordance with the aims of supplementary supervision under the *Financial Groups Directive* or consolidated supervision under the applicable *EEA prudential sectoral legislation.*

Supervision by analogy: introduction

3.2.5 **[G]** If the supervision of a *third-country group* by a *third-country competent authority* does not meet the equivalence test referred to in GENPRU 3.2.3G, a *competent authority* may, rather than take the measures described in GENPRU 3.2.4G, apply, by analogy, the provisions concerning supplementary supervision under the *Financial Groups Directive* or, as applicable, consolidated supervision under the applicable *EEA prudential sectoral legislation*, to the *EEA regulated entities* in the *banking sector, investment services sector* and (in the case of a *financial conglomerate*) *insurance sector.*

3.2.6 **[G]** The *FSA* believes that it will only be right to adopt the option in GENPRU 3.2.5G in response to very unusual group structures.

3.2.7 **[G]** GENPRU 3.2.8R and GENPRU 3.2.9R and GENPRU 3 Annex 2 set out *rules* to deal with the situation covered in GENPRU 3.2.5G. Those *rules* do not apply automatically. Instead, they can only be applied with respect to a particular *third-country group* through the *Part IV permission* of a *firm* in that *third-country group.* Broadly speaking the procedure described in GENPRU 3.1.22G also applies to this process.

Supervision by analogy: rules for third-country conglomerates

3.2.8 **[R]** If the *Part IV permission* of a *firm* contains a *requirement* obliging it to comply with this *rule* with respect to a *third-country financial conglomerate* of which it is a member, it must comply, with respect to that *third-country financial conglomerate*, with the *rules* in Part 1 of GENPRU 3 Annex 2R, as adjusted by Part 3 of that annex.

Supervision by analogy: rules for third-country banking and investment groups

3.2.9 **[R]** If the *Part IV permission* of a *firm* contains a *requirement* obliging it to comply with this *rule* with respect to a *third-country banking and investment group* of which it is a member, it must comply, with respect to that *third-country banking and investment group*, with the *rules* in Part 2 of GENPRU 3 Annex 2R, as adjusted by Part 3 of that annex.

GENPRU 3 Annex 1R
Capital adequacy calculations for financial conglomerates (GENPRU 3.1.26R and GENPRU 3.1.29R)

GENPRU 3 Ann 1 **[R]**

1 Table: PART 1: Method of Annex I of the Financial Groups Directive (Accounting Consolidation Method)

Capital resources	1.1	The *conglomerate capital resources* of a *financial conglomerate* calculated in accordance with this Part are the capital of that *financial conglomerate*, calculated on an accounting consolidation basis, that qualifies under paragraph 1.2.	
	1.2	The elements of capital that qualify for the purposes of paragraph 1.1 are those that qualify in accordance with the *applicable sectoral rules*, in accordance with the following:	
		(1)	the *conglomerate capital resources requirement* is divided up in accordance with the contribution of each *financial sector* to it; and
		(2)	the portion of the *conglomerate capital resources requirement* attributable to a particular *financial sector* must be met by capital resources that are eligible in accordance with the *applicable sectoral rules* for that *financial sector*.
Capital resources requirement	1.3	The *conglomerate capital resources requirement* of a *financial conglomerate* calculated in accordance with this Part is equal to the sum of the capital adequacy and solvency requirements for each *financial sector* calculated in accordance with the *applicable sectoral rules* for that *financial sector*.	

Consolidation	1.4	The information required for the purpose of establishing whether or not a *firm* is complying with GENPRU 3.1.29R (insofar as the definitions in this Part are applied for the purpose of that *rule*) must be based on the consolidated accounts of the *financial conglomerate*, together with such other sources of information as appropriate.
	1.5	The *applicable sectoral rules* that are applied under this Part are the *applicable sectoral consolidation rules*. Other *applicable sectoral rules* must be applied if required.

2 Table: PART 2: Method 2 of Annex I of the Financial Groups Directive (Deduction and aggregation Method)

Capital resources	2.1	The *conglomerate capital resources* of a *financial conglomerate* calculated in accordance with this Part are equal to the sum of the following amounts (so far as they qualify under paragraph 2.3) for each member of the *overall financial sector*:			
		(1)	(for the *person* at the head of the *financial conglomerate*) its *solo capital resources*;		
		(2)	(for any other member):		
			(a)	its *solo capital resources*; less	
			(b)	the book value of the *financial conglomerate's* investment in that member, to the extent not already deducted in the calculation of the *solo capital resources* for:	
				(i)	the *person* at the head of the *financial conglomerate*; or
				(ii)	any other member.
	2.2	The deduction in paragraph 2.1(2) must be carried out separately for each type of capital represented by the *financial conglomerate's* investment in the member concerned.			
	2.3	The elements of capital that qualify for the purposes of paragraph 2.1 are those that qualify in accordance with the *applicable sectoral rules*. In particular, the portion of the *conglomerate capital resources requirement* attributable to a particular member of a *financial sector* must be met by capital resources that would be eligible under the *sectoral rules* that apply to the calculation of its *solo capital resources*.			
Capital resources requirement	2.4	The *conglomerate capital resources requirement* of a *financial conglomerate* calculated in accordance with this Part is equal to the sum of the *solo capital resources requirement* for each member of the *financial conglomerate* that is in the *overall financial sector*.			
Partial inclusion	2.5	The capital resources and capital resources requirements of a member of the *financial conglomerate* in the *overall financial sector* must be included proportionally. If however the member is a *subsidiary undertaking* and it has a *solvency deficit*, they must be included in full.			
Accounts	2.6	The information required for the purpose of establishing whether or not a *firm* is complying with GENPRU 3.1.29R (insofar as the definitions in this Part are applied for the purpose of that *rule*) must be based on the individual accounts of members of the *financial conglomerate*, together with such other sources of information as appropriate.			

3 Table: PART 3: Method 3 of Annex I of the Financial Groups Directive (Book value/Requirement Method)

Capital resources	3.1	The *conglomerate capital resources* of a *financial conglomerate* calculated in accordance with this Part are equal to the capital resources of the *person* at the head of the *financial conglomerate* that qualify under paragraph 3.2.
	3.2	The elements of capital that qualify for the purposes of paragraph 3.1 are those that qualify in accordance with the *applicable sectoral rules*. In particular, the portion of the *conglomerate capital resources requirement* attributable to a particular member of a *financial sector* must be met by capital resources that would be eligible under the *sectoral rules* that apply to the calculation of its *solo capital resources*.

Capital resources requirement	3.3	The *conglomerate capital resources requirement* of a *financial conglomerate* calculated in accordance with this Part is equal to the sum of the following amounts for each member of the *overall financial sector*:			
		(1)	(in the case of the *person* at the head of the *financial conglomerate*) its *solo capital resources requirement*;		
		(2)	(in the case of any other member) the higher of the following two amounts:		
			(a)	its *solo capital resources requirement*; and	
			(b)	the book value of the interest of the *person* at the head of the *financial conglomerate* in that member.	
	3.4	A *participation* may be valued using the equity method of accounting.			
Partial inclusion	3.5	The capital resources requirement of a member of the *financial conglomerate* in the *overall financial sector* must be included proportionally. If however the member has a *solvency deficit* and is a *subsidiary undertaking*, it must be included in full.			
Accounts	3.6	The information required for the purpose of establishing whether or not a *firm* is complying with GENPRU 3.1.29R (insofar as the definitions in this Part are applied for the purpose of that *rule*) must be based on the individual accounts of members of the *financial conglomerate*, together with such other sources of information as appropriate.			

4 Table: PART 4: Method 4 of Annex I of the Financial Groups Directive (Combination of Methods 1, 2 and 3)

Applicable sectoral rules	4.1	The *rules* that apply with respect to a particular *financial conglomerate* under GENPRU 3.1.26R are those relating to capital adequacy and solvency set out in the table in paragraph 4.2.

5 Table: Paragraph 4.2: Application of sectoral consolidation rules

Type of financial conglomerate	Applicable sectoral consolidation rules
Banking and investment services conglomerate	BIPRU 8 and BIPRU TP, subject to paragraph 4.5.
Insurance conglomerate	INSPRU 6.1 amended in accordance with Part 5.

6 Table

Types of financial conglomerate	4.3	(1)	This paragraph sets out how to determine the category of *financial conglomerate* for the purposes of paragraphs 4.1 and 4.2.	
		(2)	If there is an *EEA regulated entity* at the head of the *financial conglomerate*, then:	
			(a)	if that entity is in the *banking sector* or the *investment services sector*, the *financial conglomerate* is a *banking and investment services conglomerate*; or
			(b)	if that entity is in the *insurance sector*, the *financial conglomerate* is an *insurance conglomerate*.
		(3)	If (2) does not apply and the *most important financial sector* is the *banking and investment services sector*, it is a *banking and investment services conglomerate*.	
		(4)	If (2) and (3) does not apply, it is an *insurance conglomerate*.	

8 Table

A mixed financial holding company	4.4	A *mixed financial holding company* must be treated in the same way as:	
		(1)	a *financial holding company* (if the *rules* in BIPRU 8) are applied; or
		(2)	an *insurance holding company* (if the *rules* in INSPRU 6.1 are applied).
E-money	4.5	If there are no *full credit institutions* or *investment firms* in a *banking and investment services conglomerate* but there are one or more *e-money issuers*, the *sectoral rules* in BIPRU 8 are amended as follows:	
		(1)	the *rules* in ELM that apply on a solo basis must be used to establish the capital requirement for the *e- money issuers*; and
		(2)	for the purpose of (1), those *rules* in ELM shall be amended by calculating the amount of the deductions in respect of *ownership shares* and capital falling into ELM 2.4.17R(6) in accordance with paragraph 3.3(2).

9 Table: PART 5: Principles applicable to all methods

Transferability of capital	5.1	Capital may not be included in:	
		(1)	a *firm's conglomerate capital resources* under GENPRU 3.1.29R; or
		(2)	in the capital resources of the *financial conglomerate* for the purposes of GENPRU 3.1.26R;
		if the effectiveness of the transferability and availability of the capital across the different members of the *financial conglomerate* is insufficient, given the objectives (as referred to in the third unnumbered sub-paragraph of paragraph 2(ii) of Annex I of the *Financial Groups Directive* (Technical principles)) of the capital adequacy rules for *financial conglomerates*.	
Double counting	5.2	Capital must not be included in:	
		(1)	a *firm's conglomerate capital resources* under GENPRU 3.1.29R; or
		(2)	the capital resources of the *financial conglomerate* for the purposes of GENPRU 3.1.26R;
		if:	
		(3)	it would involve double counting or multiple use of the same capital; or
		(4)	it results from any inappropriate intra-group creation of capital.
Cross sectoral capital	5.3	In accordance with the second sub-paragraph of paragraph 2(ii) of Section I of Annex I of the *Financial Groups Directive* (Other technical principles and insofar as not already required in Parts 1–3):	
		(1)	the solvency requirements for each different *financial sector* represented in a *financial conglomerate* required by GENPRU 3.1.26R or, as the case may be, GENPRU 3.1.29R must be covered by own funds elements in accordance with the corresponding *applicable sectoral rules*; and
		(2)	if there is a deficit of own funds at the *financial conglomerate* level, only cross sectoral capital (as referred to in that sub-paragraph) shall qualify for verification of compliance with the additional solvency requirement required by GENPRU 3.1.26R or, as the case may be, GENPRU 3.1.29R.

Application of sectoral rules: General	5.4		The following adjustments apply to the *applicable sectoral rules* as they are applied by the *rules* in this annex.
		(1)	The scope of those *rules* will be extended to cover any *mixed financial holding company* and each other member of the *overall financial sector*.
		(2)	If any of those *rules* would otherwise not apply to a situation in which they are applied by GENPRU 3 Annex 1R, those *rules* nevertheless still apply (and in particular, any of those *rules* that would otherwise have the effect of disapplying consolidated supervision (or, in the case of the *insurance sector*, supplementary supervision) do not apply).
		(3)	(If it would not otherwise have been included) an *ancillary insurance services undertaking* is included in the *insurance sector*.
		(4)	The scope of those *rules* is amended so as to remove restrictions relating to where members of the *financial conglomerate* are incorporated or have their head office, so that the scope covers every member of the *financial conglomerate* that would have been included in the scope of those *rules* if those members had their head offices in an *EEA State*.
		(5)	(For the purposes of Parts 1 to 3) those *rules* must be adjusted, if necessary, when calculating the capital resources, capital resources requirements or solvency requirements for a particular *financial sector* to exclude those for a member of another *financial sector*.
		(6)	Any *waiver* granted to a member of the *financial conglomerate* under those *rules* does not apply for the purposes of this annex.
Application of sectoral rules: Insurance sector	5.5	(1)	This *rule* applies an adjustment to the *applicable sectoral rules* for the *insurance sector* as they are applied by the *rules* in this annex.
		(2)	To the extent that:
			(a) those *rules* merely require a report on whether or not a specified level of solvency is met (a soft limit); or
			(b) the requirements in those *rules* concern having certain net assets of an amount at or above certain levels;
			those requirements are restated so as to include an obligation at all times actually to have capital at or above that level (a hard limit), thereby turning a soft limit into a hard limit and turning a limit drafted by reference to assets and liabilities into a requirement that the level of capital be maintained at or above a specified level. If those *rules* apply both a hard and a soft limit, and the level of the soft limit is higher, that soft limit is applied under this annex, but translated into a hard limit in accordance with the earlier provisions of this *rule*.

Application of sectoral rules: Banking sector and investment services sector	5.6	The following adjustments apply to the *applicable sectoral rules* for the *banking sector* and the *investment services sector* as they are applied by the *rules* in this annex.		
		(1)	References in those *rules* to *non-EEA sub-groups* do not apply.	
		(2)	(For the purposes of Parts 1 to 3), where those *rules* require a group to be treated as if it were a single *undertaking*, those *rules* apply to the *banking sector* and *investment services sector* taken together.	
		(3)	Any *investment firm consolidation waivers* granted to members of the *financial conglomerate* do not apply.	
		(4)	(For the purposes of Parts 1 to 4), without prejudice to the application of requirements in BIPRU 8 preventing the use of an *advanced prudential calculation approach* on a consolidated basis, any *advanced prudential calculation approach permission* that applies for the purpose of BIPRU 8 does not apply.	
		(5)	(For the purposes of Parts 1 to 4), BIPRU 8.5.9R and BIPRU 8.5.10R do not apply.	
		(6)	(For the purposes of Parts 1 to 4), where the *financial conglomerate* does not include a *credit institution*, the method in GENPRU 2 Annex 4R must be used for calculating the capital resources and BIPRU 8.6.8R does not apply.	
No capital ties	5.7	(1)	This *rule* deals with a *financial conglomerate* in which some of the members are not linked by capital ties at the time of the notification referred to in GENPRU 3.1.28R(1) (Capital adequacy requirements: Compulsory application of Method 4	
		(2)	from Annex I of the Financial Groups Directive). If:	
			(a)	GENPRU 3.1.26R (Capital adequacy requirements: Application of Method 4 from Annex I of the Financial Groups Directive) would otherwise apply with respect to a *financial conglomerate* under GENPRU 3.1.28R; and
			(b)	all members of that *financial conglomerate* are linked directly or indirectly with each other by capital ties except for members that collectively are of negligible interest with respect to the objectives of supplementary supervision of *regulated entities* in a *financial conglomerate* (the "peripheral members");
			GENPRU 3.1.28R continues to apply. Otherwise GENPRU 3.1.28R does not apply with respect to a *financial conglomerate* falling into (1).	
		(3)	If GENPRU 3.1.28R applies with respect to a *financial conglomerate* in accordance with (2) the peripheral members must be excluded from the calculations under GENPRU 3.1.26R.	
		(4)	If:	
			(a)	GENPRU 3.1.26R applies with respect to a *financial conglomerate* falling into (1) under GENPRU 3.1.27R(2) (Use of *Part IV permission* to apply Annex I of the *Financial Groups Directive*); or
			(b)	GENPRU 3.1.29R (Capital adequacy requirements: Application of Methods 1, 2 or 3 from Annex I of the Financial Groups Directive) applies with respect to a *financial conglomerate* falling into (1);
			then:	
			(c)	the treatment of the links in (1) (including the treatment of any *solvency deficit*) is as provided for in the *requirement* referred to in GENPRU 3.1.30R; and

			(d)	GENPRU 3.1.26R or GENPRU 3.1.29R, as the case may be, apply even if the *applicable sectoral rules* do not deal with how *undertakings* not linked by capital ties are to be dealt with for the purposes of consolidated supervision (or, in the case of the *insurance sector*, supplementary supervision).
		(5)	Once GENPRU 3.1.26R applies to a *firm* with respect to a *financial conglomerate* of which it is a member under GENPRU 3.1.27R(1) (automatic application of Method 4 from Annex I of the *Financial Groups Directive* on satisfaction of the condition in GENPRU 3.1.28R), the disapplication of GENPRU 3.1.28R under (2) ceases to apply with respect to that *financial conglomerate*.	

10 Table: PART 6: Definitions used in this Annex

Defining the financial sectors	6.1	For the purposes of Parts 1 to 3 of this annex (but, not for the purposes of the definition of *most important financial sector*):		
		(1)	an *asset management company* is allocated in accordance with GENPRU 3.1.39R; and	
		(2)	a *mixed financial holding company* must be treated as being a member of the *most important financial sector*.	
Solo capital resources requirement: Banking sector and investment service sector	6.2	(1)	The *solo capital resources requirement* of an *undertaking* in the *banking sector* or the *investment services sector* must be calculated in accordance with this *rule*, subject to paragraphs 6.5 and 6.6.	
		(2)	The *solo capital resources requirement* of a *building society* is its *CRR*.	
		(3)	The *solo capital resources requirement* of an *e-money issuer* is:	
			(a)	(in the case of *ELMI*) the capital resources requirement that applies to it under *ELM*; or
			(b)	(in any other case) the capital resources requirement that would apply to it under *ELM* if it were an *ELMI* incorporated in the *United Kingdom*.
		(4)	If there is a *credit institution* in the *financial conglomerate*, the *solo capital resources requirement* for any *undertaking* in the *banking sector* or the *investment services sector* is, subject to (2) and (3), calculated in accordance with the *rules* for calculating the *CRR* of a *bank* that is a *BIPRU firm*.	

		(5)	If:	
			(a)	the *financial conglomerate* does not include a *credit institution*;
			(b)	there is at least one *CAD investment firm* in the *financial conglomerate*; and
			(c)	all the *CAD investment firms* in the *financial conglomerate* are *limited licence firms* or *limited activity firms*;
				the *solo capital resources requirement* for any *undertaking* in the *banking sector* or the *investment services sector* is calculated in accordance with the *rules* for calculating the *CRR* of:
			(d)	(if there is a *limited activity firm* in the *financial conglomerate*), a *BIPRU limited activity firm*; or
			(e)	(in any other case), a *BIPRU limited licence firm*.
		(6)	If:	
			(a)	the *financial conglomerate* does not include a *credit institution*; and
			(b)	(5) does not apply;
				the *solo capital resources requirement* for any *undertaking* in the *banking sector* or the *investment services sector* is calculated in accordance with the *rules* for calculating the *CRR* of a *full scope BIPRU investment firm*.
		(7)	Any *CRR* calculated under a *BIPRU* TP may be used for the purposes of the *solo capital resources requirement* in this *rule* in the same way that the *CRR* can be used under BIPRU 8.	
Solo capital resources requirement: application of rules	6.3	Any exemption that would otherwise apply under any *rules* applied by paragraph 6.2 do not apply for the purposes of this Annex.		
Solo capital resources requirement: Insurance sector	6.4	(1)	The *solo capital resources requirement* of an *undertaking* in the *insurance sector* must be calculated in accordance with this *rule*.	
		(2)	Subject to (3), the *solo capital resources requirement* of an *undertaking* in the *insurance sector* is the capital resources requirement identified in INSPRU 6.1.34R (1) to (8) as applying to that *undertaking*.	
		(3)	INSPRU 6.1.34R (1)(b) does not apply for the purposes of this annex.	
Solo capital resources requirement: EEA firms in the banking sector or investment services sector	6.5	The *solo capital resources requirement* for an *EEA regulated entity* (other than a *BIPRU firm*, an *insurer* or an *EEA insurer*) that is subject to the solo capital adequacy *sectoral rules* for its *financial sector* of the *competent authority* that authorised it is equal to the amount of capital it is obliged to hold under those *sectoral rules* provided that the following conditions are satisfied:		
		(1)	(for the purposes of the *banking sector* and the *investment services sector*) those *sectoral rules* must correspond to the *FSA's sectoral rules* identified in paragraph 6.2 as applying to that *financial sector*;	
		(2)	the entity must be subject to those *sectoral rules* in (1); and	
		(3)	paragraph 6.3 applies to the entity and those *sectoral rules*.	
Solo capital resources requirement: non-EEAfirms subject to equivalent regimes in the banking sector or investment services sector	6.6	The *solo capital resources requirement* for a *recognised third country credit institution* or a *recognised third country investment firm* is the amount of capital resources that it is obliged to hold under the *sectoral rules* for its *financial sector* that apply to it in the state or territory in which it has its head office provided that:		
		(1)	there is no reason for the *firm* applying the *rules* in this annex to believe that the use of those *sectoral rules* would produce a lower figure than would be produced under paragraph 6.2; and	
		(2)	paragraph 6.3 applies to the entity and those *sectoral rules*.	

Solo capital resources requirement: mixed financial holding company	6.7	The *solo capital resources requirement* of a *mixed financial holding company* is a notional capital requirement. It is the capital adequacy requirement that applies to *regulated entities* in the *most important financial sector* under the table in paragraph 6.10.

12 Table

Solo capital resources requirement: the insurance sector	6.8	References to capital requirements in the provisions of GENPRU 3 Annex 1R defining *solo capital resources requirement* must be interpreted in accordance with paragraph 5.5.
Applicable sectoral consolidation rules	6.9	The *applicable sectoral consolidation rules* for a *financial sector* are the *FSA's sectoral rules* about capital adequacy and solvency on a consolidated basis that are applied in the table in paragraph 6.10.

13 Table: Paragraph 6.10: Application of sectoral consolidation rules

Financial sector	FSA's sectoral rules
Banking sector	BIPRU 8 and BIPRU TP, as adjusted under paragraph 4.5
Insurance sector	INSPRU 6.1.
Investment services sector	BIPRU 8 and BIPRU TP

14 Table:

Part 5	1	This Part 6 is subject to Part 5 of this Annex.

GENPRU 3 Annex 2R
Prudential rules for third country groups (GENPRU 3.2.8R to GENPRU 3.2.9R)

GENPRU 3 Ann 2 **[R]**

1 Table: PART 1: Third-country financial conglomerates

1.1	This Part of this annex sets out the *rules* with which a *firm* must comply under GENPRU 3.2.8R with respect to a *financial conglomerate* of which it is a member.	
1.2	A *firm* must comply, with respect to the *financial conglomerate* referred to in paragraph 1.1, with whichever of GENPRU 3.1.26R and GENPRU 3.1.29R is applied under paragraph 1.3.	
1.3	For the purposes of paragraph 1.2:	
	(1)	the *rule* in GENPRU 3.1 that applies as referred to in paragraph 1.2 is the one that is specified by the *requirement* referred to in GENPRU 3.2.8R;
	(2)	(where GENPRU 3.1.29R is applied) the definitions of *conglomerate capital resources* and *conglomerate capital resources requirement* that apply for the purposes of that *rule* are the ones from whichever of Part 1, Part 2 or Part 3 of GENPRU 3 Annex 1R is specified in that *requirement*; and
	(3)	the *rules* so applied (including those in GENPRU 3 Annex 1R) are adjusted in accordance with paragraph 3.1.
1.4	If the condition in Articles 7(4) and 8(4) of *the Financial Groups Directive* is satisfied (the *financial conglomerate* is headed by a *mixed financial holding company*) with respect to the *financial conglomerate* referred to in paragraph 1.1 the *firm* must also comply with GENPRU 3.1.35R (as adjusted in accordance with paragraph 3.1) with respect to that *financial conglomerate*.	
1.5	A *firm* must comply with the following with respect to the *financial conglomerate* referred to in paragraph 1.1:	
	(1)	SYSC 12 (as it applies to *financial conglomerates* and as adjusted under paragraph 3.1); and
	(2)	GENPRU 3.1.25R.

2 Table: PART 2: Third-country banking and investment groups

2.1	This Part of this annex sets out the *rules* with which a *firm* must comply under GENPRU 3.2.9R with respect to a *third-country banking and investment group* of which it is a member.	
2.2	A *firm* must comply with one of the sets of *rules* specified in paragraph 2.3 as adjusted under paragraph 3.1 with respect to the *third-country banking and investment group* referred to in paragraph 2.1.	
2.3	The *rules* referred to in paragraph 2.2 are as follows:	
	(1)	the *applicable sectoral consolidation rules* in BIPRU 8; or
	(2)	the *rules* in ELM 7.
2.4	The set of *rules* from paragraph 2.3 that apply with respect to a particular *third-country banking and investment group* (as referred to in paragraph 2.1) are those that would apply if they were adjusted in accordance with paragraph 3.1.	
2.5	The *sectoral rules* applied by Part 2 of this annex cover all prudential *rules* applying on a consolidated basis including those relating to large exposures.	
2.6	A *firm* must comply with SYSC 12 (as it applies to *banking and investment groups* and as adjusted under paragraph 3.1) with respect to the *third-country banking and investment group* referred to in paragraph 2.1.	

3 Table: PART 3: Adjustment of scope

3.1	The adjustments that must be carried out under this paragraph are that the scope of the *rules* referred in Part 1 or Part 2 of this annex, as the case may be, are amended:	
	(1)	so as to remove any provisions disapplying those *rules* for *third-country groups*;
	(2)	so as to remove all limitations relating to where a member of the *third-country group* is incorporated or has its head office; and
	(3)	so that the scope covers every member of the *third-country group* that would have been included in the scope of those *rules* if those members had their head offices in, and were incorporated in, an *EEA State*.

GENPRU 3 Annex 3G
Classification of Groups (GENPRU 3.1.3G)

GENPRU 3 Ann 3 **[G]**

[*The following form has not been reproduced for technical reasons. Please refer to the FSA website.*]

Guidance Notes for Classification of Groups

Purpose and scope

The form is designed to identify groups and sub-groups that are likely to be financial conglomerates under the Financial Groups Directive. A group may be a financial conglomerate if it contains both insurance and banking/investment businesses and meets certain threshold tests. The FSA needs to identify conglomerates with their head offices in the EEA and those with their head offices outside the EEA, although this does not necessarily mean that the latter will be subject to EEA conglomerate supervision.

This form's purpose is to enable the FSA to obtain sufficient information so as to be able to determine how likely a group/sub-group is to be a financial conglomerate. In certain cases this can only be determined after consultation with the other EU relevant competent authorities. A second purpose of the form is therefore to identify any groups and sub-groups that may need such consultation so that this can be made as soon as possible. This should allow firms time to prepare to comply.

The third purpose of the form is to gain information from firms on the most efficient way to implement the threshold calculations in detail (consistently with the directive). We have, therefore, asked for some additional information in part 4 of the form.

A copy of this form will can be found on the FSA's Financial Groups Website with current contact details.

Please include workings showing the method employed to determine the percentages in part 2 (for the threshold conditions) and giving details of all important assumptions/approximations made in doing the calculations.

The definition of financial conglomerate includes not only conventional groups made up of parent-subsidiary relationships but groups linked by control and "consolidation Article 12(1)

Part II FSA Handbook Materials

relationships". If this is the case for your group, please submit along with this form a statement that this is the case. Please include in that statement an explanation of how you have included group members not linked by capital ties in the questionnaire calculations.

A consolidation Article 12(1) relationship arises between undertakings in the circumstances set out in Article 12(1) of the Seventh Company Law Directive. These are set out in the Handbook Glossary (in the definition of consolidation Article 12(1) relationship). Broadly speaking, undertakings come within this definition if they do not form a conventional group but:

(a) are managed on a unified basis; or
(b) have common management.

General guidance

We would like this to be completed based on the most senior parent in the group, and, if applicable, for the company heading the most senior conglomerate group in the EEA. If appropriate, please also attach a list of all other likely conglomerate sub-groups.

Please use the most recent accounts for the top level company in the group together with the corresponding accounts for all subsidiaries and participations that are included in the consolidated accounts. Please indicate the names of any significant subsidiaries with a different year-end from the group's year-end.

Please note the following:

(a) Branches should be included as part of the parent entity.
(b) Include in the calculations overseas entities owned by the relevant group or sub-group.
(c) There are only two sectors for this purpose: banking/investment and insurance.
(d) You will need to assign non-regulated financial entities to one of these sectors:
   - **banking/investment** activities are listed in – Annex 1 to the Banking Consolidation Directive
   - **insurance** activities are listed in – IPRU Insurers Annex 11.1 and 11.2 p 163–168.
   - Any **operator of a UCITS scheme, insurance intermediary, mortgage broker and mixed financial holding company** does not fall into the directive definitions of either financial sector or insurance sector and should be treated for these purposes as being outside the financial sector. They should therefore be ignored for the purposes of these calculations.

Threshold tests

For the purpose of completing section 2 of the form relating to the threshold tests, the following guidance should be used. However, if you consider that for your group there is a more appropriate calculation then you may use this calculation so long as the method of computation is submitted with the form.

Calculating balance sheet totals

Generally, use total (gross) assets for the balance sheet total of a group/entity. However, investments in other entities that are part of the group will need to be deducted from the sector that has made the investment and the balance sheet total of the entity is added to the sector in which it operates.

Our expectation of how this may be achieved efficiently is as follows:

(i) Off-balance-sheet items should be excluded.
(ii) Where off-balance sheet treatment of **funds under management** and on-balance sheet treatment of **policy holders' funds** may distort the threshold calculation, groups should consult the FSA on the appropriateness of using other measures under article 3.5 of the Financial Groups Directive.
(iii) If consolidated accounts exist for a sub-group consisting of financial entities from only one of the two sectors, these consolidated accounts should be used to measure the balance-sheet total of the sub-group (i.e. total assets less investments in entities in the other sector). If consolidated accounts do not exist, intra-group balances should be netted out when calculating the balance sheet total of a single sector (but cross-sector intra-group balances should not be netted out).
(iv) Where consolidated accounts are used, minority interests should be excluded and goodwill should be included.
(v) Where accounting standards differ between entities, groups should consult the FSA if they believe this is likely materially to affect the threshold calculation.
(vi) Where there is a subsidiary or participation in the opposite sector from its parent (i.e. insurance sector for a banking/investment firm parent and vice versa), the balance sheet amount of the subsidiary or participation should be allocated to its sector using its individual accounts.
(vii) The balance-sheet total of the parent entity/sub-group is measured as total assets of the parent/sub-group less the book value of its subsidiaries or participations in the other sector (i.e. the value of the subsidiary or participation in the parent's consolidated accounts is deducted from the parent's consolidated assets).

(viii) The cross-sector subsidiaries or participations referred to above, valued according to their own accounts, are allocated pro-rata, according to the aggregated share owned by the parent/sub-group, to their own sector.

(ix) If the cross-sector entities above themselves own group entities in the first sector (i.e. that of the top parent/sub-group) these should (in accordance with the methods above) be excluded from the second sector and added to the first sector using individual accounts.

Solvency (capital adequacy) requirements

Generally, the solvency requirements should be according to sectoral rules of the FSA that would apply to the type of entity. However, you can use EEA rules or local rules in the circumstances set out in Part 6 of GENPRU 3 Annex 1R. But if this choice makes a significant difference, either with respect to whether the group is a financial conglomerate or with respect to which sector is the biggest, you should consult with the FSA. Non-regulated financial entities should have proxy requirements calculated on the basis of the most appropriate sector. If sub-groups submit single sector consolidated returns then the solvency requirement may be taken from those returns.

Our expectation of how this may be achieved efficiently is as follows:

(i) If you complete a solvency return for a sub-group consisting of financial entities from only one of the two sectors, the total solvency requirement for the sub-group should be used.

(ii) Solvency requirements taken must include any deductions from available capital so as to allow the appropriate aggregation of requirements.

(iii) Where there is a regulated subsidiary or participation in the opposite sector from its parent/sub-group, the solvency requirement of the subsidiary or participation should be from its individual regulatory return. If there is an identifiable contribution to the parent's solvency requirement in respect of the cross-sector subsidiary or participation, the parent's solvency requirement may be adjusted to exclude this.

(iv) Where there is an unregulated financial undertaking in the opposite sector from its parent/sub-group, the solvency requirement of the subsidiary or participation should be one of the following:
   (a) as if the entity were regulated by the FSA under the appropriate sectoral rules;
   (b) using EU minimum requirements for the appropriate sector; or
   (c) using non-EU local requirements* for the appropriate sector.

   Please note on the form which of these options you have used, according to the country and sector, and whether this is the same treatment as in your latest overall group solvency calculation.

(v) For banking/investment requirements, use the total amount of capital required.

(vi) For insurance requirements, use the total amount of capital required.

Market share measures

These are not defined by the directive. The aim is to identify any standard industry approaches to measuring market share in individual EU countries by sector, or any data sources which are commonly used as a proxy.

Article I.

Article II. Threshold tests

Test F2

B/S of banking/investment + insurance sector = result %

B/S total

Test F3/F4/F5

B/S of insurance sector

B/S of banking/investment sector + insurance sector = A%

B/S of banking/investment sector

B/S of banking/investment sector + insurance sector = B%

Solvency requirement of insurance sector

Solvency requirement of banking/investment sector + insurance sector = C%

Solvency requirement of banking/investment sector

Solvency requirement of banking/investment sector + insurance sector = D%

The relevant percentage for the insurance sector is:

(A% + C%)/2 = I%

The relevant percentage for the banking/investment sector is:

(B% + D%)/2 = BI %

The smallest sector is the sector with the smallest relevant percentage.

Article III. If I% < BI% then F3 is insurance, F4 = A%, and F5 = C%

Article IV. If BI% < I% then F3 is banking/investment, F4 = B% and F5 = D%

GENPRU 3 Annex 4R
(see GENPRU 3.18.4.5R)

GENPRU 3 Ann 4 **[R]**

[*The following form has not been reproduced for technical reasons. Please refer to the FSA website.*]

TP TRANSITIONAL PROVISIONS

1 Application of GENPRU TP 1 to GENPRU TP 6 and other general provisions for insurers

Application of GENPRU TP 1 to GENPRU TP 6
[2058]

1.1 **[R]** GENPRU TP 1 – GENPRU TP 6 apply to an *insurer*.

1.2 **[G]** GENPRU TP 1 – GENPRU TP 6 apply to an *insurer* to whom the relevant *GENPRU rule* listed in GENPRU TP Table 3R, GENPRU TP 4.3R, GENPRU TP 5.2R or GENPRU TP 6.2R applies. An *insurer* to whom GENPRU does not apply is not subject to GENPRU TP.

Version of IPRU to be used

1.3 **[R]** Any reference in GENPRU TP 1 – GENPRU TP 6 to IPRU(INS) or to IPRU (FSOC) is to the version in force on 30 December 2004.

2 IPRU(INS) waivers

Duration of transitional

2.1 **[R]** GENPRU TP 2 applies until the relevant *GENPRU rule* is revoked.

Continuing effect of waivers

2.2 **[R]** A *rule* in GENPRU listed in the Table at GENPRU TP 3 is disapplied, or is modified in its application, to a *firm*:
(1) in order to produce the same effect, including any conditions, as a *waiver* had on the corresponding *rule* in IPRU(INS);
(2) for the same period as the *waiver* would have lasted, if shorter than the period in GENPRU TP 2.1R;

provided the conditions set out in GENPRU TP 2.3R are satisfied.

2.3 **[R]** The conditions referred to in GENPRU TP 2.2R are:
(1) the *rule* is shown in the Table at GENPRU TP 3 as corresponding with the *rule* in IPRU(INS) in relation to which the *waiver* was granted to the *firm*;
(2) the *waiver* was current as respects the *firm* immediately before 31 December 2004; and
(3) there is no specific transitional *rule* relating to the *waiver*.

2.4 **[R]** GENPRU TP 2.2R does not have effect if, and to the extent that, it would be inconsistent with any *EU law* obligation of the *United Kingdom*.

2.5 **[R]** A *firm* which has the benefit of a *waiver* to which GENPRU TP 2.2R applies must:
(1) notify the *FSA* immediately if it becomes aware of any matter which is material to the relevance or appropriateness of the *waiver*;
(2) maintain a written record of the *rule* in GENPRU to which it considers the *waiver* applies; and
(3) make the record available to the *FSA* on request.

3 Table: IPRU(INS) waivers

3.1 **[R]** This table belongs to GENPRU TP 2.

Rules in GENPRU	Corresponding rules in IPRU(INS)
1.3.47R	4.2 (3)
2.1.13R	2.9 (3)
2.1.24R	2.9

Rules in GENPRU	Corresponding rules in IPRU(INS)
2.1.25R	2.9
2.1.34R	2.4 (6)
2.2.107R	2.10 (7)
2.2.251R	4.14
	4.5 (7)

4 Capital instruments

Duration

4.1 **[R]** GENPRU TP 4 applies until the relevant *rule* is revoked

Application

4.2 **[R]** Subject to GENPRU TP 4.4R, GENPRU TP 4 applies to a *firm* which immediately before 31 December 2004 had the benefit of a *waiver* in relation to IPRU(INS) rule 2.10 or 5.2, or a written concession in relation to a pre-*commencement* provision listed in GENPRU TP 4.7R, in either case allowing the *firm* to exclude from the calculation of its liabilities obligations under a particular capital instrument issued by the *firm*.

Waivers

4.3 **[R]** Subject to GENPRU TP 4.4R and to compliance with the conditions set out in GENPRU TP 4.6R, a *firm* will be treated as complying with GENPRU 2.2.271R(3), GENPRU 2.2.177R(2), GENPRU 2.2.177R(3), GENPRU 2.2.180R and GENPRU 2.2.181R, in relation to the capital instrument to which the *waiver* or written concession referred to in GENPRU TP 4.2R related, so long as the *firm* is not obliged to pay any interest under the terms of the capital instrument in circumstances where the *firm* does not have *capital resources* equal to or in excess of its required margin of solvency under the *Insurance Directives*.

4.4 **[R]** GENPRU TP 4.3R ceases to apply to a *firm*:

(1) once the *firm* has redeemed the capital instrument; or

(2) on or after any date upon which the *firm* has the option to redeem the capital instrument and may prudently do so.

4.5 **[R]** Subject to compliance with the conditions set out in GENPRU TP 4.6R, a *firm* will be treated as complying with GENPRU 2.2.159R(6), GENPRU 2.2.159R(10), GENPRU 2.2.159R(12), and GENPRU 2.2.163R in relation to the capital instrument to which the *waiver* or written concession referred to in GENPRU TP 4.2R related.

4.6 **[R]** The conditions referred to in GENPRU TP 4.3R and GENPRU TP 4.5R are:

(1) the *firm* must notify the *FSA* immediately if it becomes aware of any matter which is material to the relevance or appropriateness of the *waiver* or written concession;

(2) the *firm* must maintain a written record of the *rule* in GENPRU to which it considers the *waiver* or written concession applies; and

(3) the *firm* must make the record available to the *FSA* on request.

4.7 **[R]** The pre-*commencement* provisions referred to in GENPRU TP 4.2R are those contained in:

(1) the Insurance Companies Act 1982 and relevant secondary legislation; and

(2) the Friendly Societies Act 1992 and relevant secondary legislation.

5 Calls for supplementary contributions

Duration

5.1 **[R]** GENPRU TP 5 applies until the relevant *rule* is revoked

Application

5.2 **[R]** GENPRU TP 5 applies to a *firm* which immediately before 31 December 2004 had the benefit of a *waiver* in relation to IPRU(INS) rule 2.10 (4).

Waivers

5.3 **[R]** For the period specified in GENPRU TP 5.1R or the same period as the *waiver* would have lasted if shorter, subject to GENPRU TP 5.4R and to compliance with the conditions set out in GENPRU TP 5.5R, for the purposes of calculating its *capital resources* a *firm* may include the value of claims against its members by way of calls for supplementary contributions as *core tier one capital* to the same extent as it was permitted by the *waiver* to include the value of those claims in the calculation of its margin of solvency.

Part II FSA Handbook Materials

5.4 **[R]** GENPRU TP 5.3R does not apply for the purposes of GENPRU 2.2.34R (Guarantee fund) or SUP Appendix 2.4 (Capital resources below guarantee fund).

5.5 **[R]** The conditions referred to in GENPRU TP 5.3R are:

(1) the limits specified in the *waiver* on the extent to which the *firm*'s claim against its members by way of call for supplementary contributions may be brought into account apply as if the reference (if any) in the *waiver* to the *firm*'s required margin of solvency referred to its *general insurance capital requirement* and the reference (if any) in the *waiver* to the *firm*'s margin of solvency referred to its *capital resources*; and

(2) the *firm* must comply with any further conditions imposed by the *waiver.*

6 Implicit items waivers

Duration

6.1 **[R]** GENPRU TP 6 applies until the relevant *rule* is revoked

Application

6.2 **[R]** GENPRU TP 6 applies to a *firm* which immediately before 31 December 2004 had the benefit of a *waiver* in relation to IPRU(INS) rule 2.10 (5) or IPRU (FSOC) rule 4.7 (3).

Waivers

6.3 **[R]** For the period specified in GENPRU TP 6.1R or the same period as the *waiver* would have lasted if shorter, subject to GENPRU TP 6.4R and to compliance with the conditions set out in GENPRU TP 6.5R, for the purpose of calculating its *capital resources* a *firm* may include the value of *implicit items* at Stage B of the *capital resources table* applicable to the *firm* to the same extent to which it was permitted by the *waiver* to include the value of those *implicit items* in the calculation of its margin of solvency.

6.4 **[R]** GENPRU TP 6.3R does not apply for the purposes of GENPRU 2.2.41R (Limits on forms of capital apply separately to long-term insurance business and general insurance business).

6.5 **[R]** The conditions referred to in GENPRU TP 6.3R are:

(1) the limits specified in the *waiver* on the extent to which the value of *implicit items* may be brought into account apply as if the reference (if any) in the *waiver* to the *firm*'s required margin of solvency referred to its *minimum capital requirement* and the reference (if any) in the *waiver* to the *firm*'s margin of solvency referred to its *capital resources*; and

(2) the *firm* must comply with any further conditions imposed by the *waiver.*

7 Pillar 3 capital resources

Application

7.1 **[R]** This section applies to a *BIPRU firm.*

Purpose

7.2 **[G]** This section implements Article 154(4) of the *Banking Consolidation Directive.*

Duration

7.3 **[R]** This section applies until 31 December 2012.

Transitional provision

7.4 **[R]** A *firm* may elect not to apply GENPRU 2.2.239R(2) to (4) (50:50 split between deductions from *tier one capital* and *tier two capital*) to *material insurance holdings* acquired before 20 July 2006. If a *firm* elects not to apply GENPRU 2.2.239R(2) to (4), the *firm* must deduct such *material insurance holdings* from the total of *tier one capital* and *tier two capital.*

8 Miscellaneous capital resources definitions for BIPRU firms

Application

8.1 **[R]** This section applies to a *BIPRU firm.*

8.2 **[R]** Any provision of this section that applies on a consolidated basis under GENPRU TP 8.3R applies to any *firm* to which BIPRU 8 (Group risk – consolidation) applies.

Consolidation

8.3 **[R]** A provision of this section applies on a consolidated basis for the purpose of BIPRU 8 (Group risk –consolidation) to the extent that, and in the same way that, the provision in BIPRU to which it relates applies on a consolidated basis.

Specific issues of TONS and other securities

8.4 **[R]** A *bank* may treat a *security* forming part of an issue of *securities* listed in GENPRU TP 8.5R as eligible for inclusion within stage B of the *capital resources table* (Perpetual non-cumulative preference shares) if it would not otherwise be eligible if:
(1) on 31 December 2006 the *bank* was subject to IPRU(BANK);
(2) the *bank* issued it on or before 31 December 2006; and
(3) as at 31 December 2006 the *bank* included it, and was entitled to include it, in the calculation of its capital resources under IPRU(BANK) as permanent share capital and tier one capital as referred to in chapter CA of IPRU(BANK).

8.5 **[R]** The issues of *securities* referred to in GENPRU TP 8.4R are as follows:
(1) Barclays £400mn 6% perpetual TONs;
(2) Abbey National £175m 6.984% perpetual TOPIC;
(3) Northern Rock £200m 7.053% perpetual TONs;
(4) Barclays $1bn 6.86% perpetual TONs;
(5) Lloyds TSB $850m 6.90% perpetual capital securities; and
(6) Abbey National $500m 7.375% T1MBS.

PIBS

8.6 **[R]** A *building society* may treat a *PIBS* as eligible for inclusion within stage B of the *capital resources table* (Perpetual non-cumulative preference shares) if it would not otherwise be eligible if:
(1) on 31 December 2006 the *firm* was subject to IPRU(BSOC);
(2) the *building society* issued it before 18 November 2004; and
(3) as at 31 December 2006 the *building society* included it, and was entitled to include it, in the calculation of its capital resources under IPRU(BSOC) as tier one capital as referred to in Annex 1A of chapter 1 of volume 1 of IPRU(BSOC).

Preference shares

8.7 **[R]** A *bank* or *BIPRU investment firm* may treat a *preference share* as eligible for inclusion within stage B of the *capital resources table* (Perpetual non-cumulative preference shares) if it would not otherwise be eligible if:
(1) on 31 December 2006 the *firm* was subject to IPRU(BANK) or IPRU(INV);
(2) the *firm* issued it on or before 31 December 2006;
(3) as at 31 December 2006 the *firm* included it, and was entitled to include it, in the calculation of its capital resources under IPRU(BANK) or IPRU(INV) as capital of a type that corresponded to *tier one capital resources*;
(4) it would have been eligible for inclusion within stage B of the *capital resources table* except for the fact that it does not meet GENPRU 2.2.64R(4)(b) (Restrictions on mandatory *coupons* for *tier one capital*) or GENPRU 2.2.109R(1) (Restrictions on mandatory *coupons* for perpetual non-cumulative *preference shares*) or both of those *rules*;
(5) the only reason that it does not meet GENPRU 2.2.64R(4)(b) or GENPRU 2.2.109R(1) is because a mandatory cash *coupon* is payable;
(6) the *firm* has the right not to pay the cash *coupon* if it is in breach of any of the *main BIPRU firm Pillar 1 rules* or to the extent that paying such *coupon* would result in a breach of any of those *rules*; and
(7) any amount not paid under (6) does not accumulate.

Innovative tier one capital

8.8 **[R]** A *bank* may treat an item of a *capital instrument* as eligible for inclusion within stage C of the *capital resources table* (Innovative tier one capital) if it would not otherwise be eligible if:
(1) on 31 December 2006 the *firm* was subject to IPRU(BANK);
(2) the *bank* issued it on or before 31 December 2006;
(3) as at 31 December 2006 the *bank* included it, and was entitled to include it, in the calculation of its capital resources under IPRU(BANK) as innovative tier one capital as referred to in chapter CA of IPRU(BANK);
(4) it would have been eligible for inclusion within stage C of the *capital resources table* except for the fact that it does not meet GENPRU 2.2.64R(4)(b) (Restrictions on mandatory *coupons* for *tier one capital*);
(5) the only reason that it does not meet GENPRU 2.2.64R(4)(b) is because a mandatory cash *coupon* is payable;
(6) the *bank* has the right not to pay the cash *coupon* if it is in breach of any of the *main BIPRU firm Pillar 1 rules* or to the extent that paying such *coupon* would result in a breach of any of those *rules*; and
(7) any amount not paid under (6) does not accumulate.

Upper tier 2 instruments: Deferral of interest

8.9 **[R]** A *bank* or *BIPRU investment firm* may treat a *capital instrument* as eligible for inclusion within stage G of the *capital resources table* (Upper tier two capital) if it would not otherwise be eligible if:
(1) on 31 December 2006 the *firm* was subject to IPRU(BANK) or IPRU(INV);
(2) the *firm* issued it on or before 31 December 2006;
(3) as at 31 December 2006 the *firm* included it, and was entitled to include it, in the calculation of its capital resources under *IPRU(BANK)* or *IPRU(INV)* as capital of a type that corresponded to *upper tier two capital resources*;
(4) it would have been eligible for inclusion within stage G of the *capital resources table* except for the fact that it does not meet GENPRU 2.2.177R(2);
(5) the only reason that it does not meet GENPRU 2.2.177R(2) is because a mandatory cash *coupon* is payable; and
(6) the *firm* has the right not to pay the cash *coupon* if it is in breach of any of the *main BIPRU firm Pillar 1 rules* or to the extent that paying such *coupon* would result in a breach of any of those *rules*.

Lower tier 2 instruments: Additional events of default for building societies

8.10 **[R]** A *building society* may treat a *capital instrument* as eligible for inclusion within stage H of the *capital resources table* (Lower tier two capital) if it would not otherwise be eligible if:
(1) on 31 December 2006 the *building society* was subject to IPRU(BSOC);
(2) the *building society* issued it on or before 31 December 2006;
(3) as at 31 December 2006 the *building society* included it, and was entitled to include it, in the calculation of its capital resources under IPRU(BSOC) as Term Subordinated Debt falling within its Tier Two Capital (as referred to in Annex 1A of Chapter 1 and Chapter 2 of IPRU(BSOC));
(4) it would have been eligible for inclusion within stage H of the *capital resources table* except for the fact that it does not meet GENPRU 2.2.159R(2) (Events of default); and
(5) the only reason that it does not meet GENPRU 2.2.159R(2) is because it contains an event of default permitted by paragraph 2.8.10G(3) of Volume 1 of IPRU(BSOC) (cancellation of a society's registration under the Building Societies Act 1986 otherwise than under section 103(1)(a) of that Act).

Conversion ratio

8.11 **[R]** GENPRU 2.2.138R(2) (Tier one capital: Conversion ratio) does not apply to a *capital instrument* issued by a *firm* if:
(1) on 31 December 2006 the *firm* was subject to IPRU(BANK), IPRU(BSOC) or IPRU(INV);
(2) the *firm* issued it on or before 31 December 2006; and
(3) as at 31 December 2006 the *firm* included it, and was entitled to include it, in the calculation of its capital resources under:
  (a) (in the case of a *bank*) IPRU(BANK) as innovative tier one capital as referred to in chapter CA of IPRU(BANK); or
  (b) (in the case of any other type of *firm*) IPRU(BSOC) or IPRU(INV) as capital of a type that corresponded to *tier one capital*.

Legal opinions

8.12 **[R]** GENPRU 2.2.118R (Legal opinions for *innovative tier one capital*) does not apply to a *capital instrument* issued by a *firm* if:
(1) on 31 December 2006 the *firm* was subject to IPRU(BANK), IPRU(BSOC) or IPRU(INV);
(2) the *firm* issued the *capital instrument* on or before 31 December 2006;
(3) (in the case of a *bank*) as at 31 December 2006 the *bank* included the *capital instrument*, and was entitled to include it, in the calculation of its capital resources under IPRU(BANK) as innovative tier one capital as referred to in chapter CA of IPRU(BANK); and
(4) (in any other case) the *firm* included the *capital instrument*, and was entitled to include it, in the calculation of its capital resources under IPRU(BSOC) or IPRU(INV) as capital of a type that corresponded to *tier one capital*.

8.13 **[R]** The following *rules*:
(1) GENPRU 2.2.159R(12) (Legal opinions for *tier two capital*);
(2) GENPRU 2.2.163R (Legal opinions for *tier two capital* governed by a foreign law);
(3) *GENPRU* 2.2.181R (Legal opinions for *upper tier two capital*); and
(4) GENPRU 2.2.244R (Application of certain *rules* about *tier two capital* to *tier three capital*) so far as it applies the *rules* in (1) to (3);

do not apply to a *capital instrument* issued by a *firm* if:
(5) on 31 December 2006 the *firm* was subject to IPRU(BANK), IPRU(BSOC) or IPRU(INV);

(6) the *firm* issued the *capital instrument* on or before 31 December 2006; and
(7) as at 31 December 2006 the *firm* included the *capital instrument*, and was entitled to include it, in the calculation of its capital resources under IPRU(BANK), IPRU(BSOC) or IPRU(INV) as capital of the type that corresponds to:
(a) (where the *firm* disapplies the *rule* in (1) or (2)) *tier two capital*; or
(b) (where the *firm* disapplies the *rule* in (3)) *upper tier two capital*; or
(c) (where the *firm* disapplies the *rule* in (4)) *tier three capital*.

Version of IPRU

8.14 **[R]** Any reference in this section to a type of capital in *IPRU* is to a type of capital in *IPRU* in the form *IPRU* was in on 31 December 2006.

Eligibility

8.15 **[G]** If this section says that an item of capital is eligible for inclusion within a particular stage of the *capital resources table* this is still subject to the application of the *capital resources gearing rules*.

Waivers and concessions

8.16 **[G]** A reference to a *firm* being entitled to include *capital instruments* in the calculation of its capital resources under *IPRU* at a particular level includes the *firm* being able to do this under a *waiver* or, in the case of IPRU(BANK) or IPRU(BSOC), a written approval by the *FSA*.

Combinations of provisions

8.17 **[G]** A *firm* may combine the use of two or more of the provisions in this section.

9 Individual capital guidance for BIPRU firms

Application

9.1 **[G]** This section applies to a *BIPRU firm* that is a *bank* or *building society* for which the *FSA* has given:
(1) (in the case of a *building society*) a threshold ratio under IPRU(BSOC); or
(2) (in the case of a *bank*) an individual capital ratio under IPRU(BANK);

that was in effect on 31 December 2006 but to which the *FSA* has not yet given *individual capital guidance*.

Duration

9.2 **[G]** This section applies to a *firm* until it receives *individual capital guidance*.

9.3 **[G]** GENPRU TP 9.4G – GENPRU TP 9.6G only apply until 31 December 2007. Thereafter (if they do not already apply) GENPRU TP 9.7G – GENPRU TP 9.10G apply.

Pre 2007 capital requirements

9.4 **[G]** GENPRU TP 9.5G – GENPRU TP 9.6G apply if, and for as long as, a *firm* applies the treatment in BIPRU TP 3.4R (Pre CRD capital requirements applying on a solo basis during 2007) to all its *exposures*.

9.5 **[G]** If GENPRU TP 9.4G applies, any threshold ratio or individual capital ratio remains in force. However compliance with such ratios should be measured by reference to *capital resources*.

9.6 **[G]** Where necessary, a *firm* should apply the adjustment set out in section 4.1.3 of chapter CO of IPRU(BANK) (CAD banks) as it stood on 31 December 2006 to its *trading book* capital requirements.

BIPRU capital requirements

9.7 **[G]** GENPRU TP 9.8G – GENPRU TP 9.10G apply to a *firm* if GENPRU TP 9.5G – GENPRU TP 9.6G do not apply.

9.8 **[G]** Any threshold ratio or individual capital ratio remains in force adjusted as follows:
(1) the *firm* should work out the percentage of its *capital resources requirement* as at the date in GENPRU TP 9.10G represented by the absolute amount in GENPRU TP 9.9G; and
(2) the *firm* should hold *capital resources* of an amount at least equal to the percentage specified in (1) of its *capital resources requirement* from time to time.

9.9 **[G]** The absolute amount referred to in GENPRU TP 9.8G is:
(1) (if GENPRU TP 9.7G – GENPRU TP 9.10G apply to the *firm* on 1 January 2007) the amount of capital resources it had to hold under *IPRU* on 31 December 2006 in order to meet the ratio referred to in GENPRU TP 9.1G; and

(2) (in any other case) the amount of *capital resources* it had to hold immediately prior to the date in GENPRU TP 9.10G in order to meet the ratio referred to in GENPRU TP 9.1G.

9.10 **[G]** The date referred to in GENPRU TP 9.8G and GENPRU TP 9.9G is:
(1) (if GENPRU TP 9.9G(1) applies) 1 January 2007; and
(2) (if GENPRU TP 9.9G(2) applies) the date on which GENPRU TP 9.7G – GENPRU TP 9.10G first apply to the *firm*.

9.11 **[G]** The following illustrates how GENPRU TP 9.8G – GENPRU TP 9.10G work. This example relates to a *bank* to which GENPRU TP 9.7G – GENPRU TP 9.10G apply from 1 January 2007. The example is as follows (all figures in £millions):
(1) as at 31 December 2006:
 (a) the *bank* has risk-weighted assets of £1250;
 (b) its Pillar 1 capital resources requirement was £100 (8% of £1250);
 (c) its individual capital ratio was 10%; and
 (d) its capital resources requirement expressed as an absolute amount and including the individual capital ratio is £125;
(2) on 1 January 2007 its *capital resources requirement* is £80;
(3) the result is that the new individual capital ratio is 156.25% (£125m/£80m); and
(4) its capital resources requirement expressed as an absolute amount and including the individual capital ratio remains at £125 despite the fall in the Pillar 1 charge.

9.12 **[G]** Continuing the example, say that the *bank's capital resources requirement* falls to £70 on 31 July 2007. Its capital resources requirement, expressed as an amount and including the individual capital ratio, now falls to £109.375.

Adjustments

9.13 **[G]** No adjustment should be made to take into account differences between the calculation of capital resources under *IPRU* and of *capital resources*.

Consolidation

9.14 **[G]** This section also applies to threshold ratios and individual capital ratios that apply on a consolidated basis.

10 Assets of former underwriting members

Application

10.1 **[R]** GENPRU TP 10 applies to the *Society*.

Duration

10.2 **[R]** GENPRU TP 10 applies until the *Society* is no longer required to identify or value assets of *individual members* that became *former underwriting members* before 1 January 2003.

Valuation and identification of assets

10.3 **[R]** For the purposes of GENPRU 1 and 2, the *Society* must identify and value the assets of *individual members* that became *former underwriting members* before 1 January 2003 in accordance with the requirements for the identification and valuation of assets contained in the "Conditions and Requirements Relating to Solvency and Reporting" which were approved by the *FSA*, exercising the powers of HM Treasury under section 83 of the Insurance Companies Act 1982, and which were applicable immediately before *commencement*.

11 PRU waivers

Application

11.1 **[R]** GENPRU TP 11 applies to an *insurer* to whom a *GENPRU rule* listed in the Table in GENPRU TP 12 applies.

Version of PRU to be used

11.2 **[R]** A reference in GENPRU TP 11 to PRU is to the version in force on 30 December 2006.

Duration of transitional

11.3 **[R]** GENPRU TP 11 applies until the relevant *GENPRU rule* is revoked.

Continuing effect of waivers

11.4 **[R]** A *rule* in GENPRU listed in the Table at GENPRU TP 12 is disapplied, or is modified in its application, to a *firm*:

(1) in order to produce the same effect, including any conditions, as a *waiver* had on the corresponding *rule* in PRU;
(2) for the same period as the *waiver* would have lasted, if shorter than the period in GENPRU TP 11.3R;

provided the conditions set out in GENPRU TP 11.5R are satisfied.

11.5 **[R]** The conditions referred to in GENPRU TP 11.4R are:
(1) the *rule* is shown in the Table at GENPRU TP 12 as corresponding with the *rule* in *PRU* in relation to which the *waiver* was granted to the *firm*;
(2) the *waiver* was current as respects the *firm* immediately before 31 December 2006; and
(3) there is no specific transitional *rule* relating to the *waiver*.

11.6 **[R]** GENPRU TP 11.4 does not have effect if, and to the extent that, it would be inconsistent with any *EU law* obligation of the *United Kingdom*.

11.7 **[R]** A *firm* which has the benefit of a *waiver* to which GENPRU TP 11.4R applies must:
(1) notify the *FSA* immediately if it becomes aware of any matter which is material to the relevance or appropriateness of the *waiver*;
(2) maintain a written record of the *rule* in GENPRU to which it considers the *waiver* applies; and
(3) make the record available to the *FSA* on request.

12 Table: PRU waivers

12.1 **[R]** This table belongs to GENPRU TP 11.

Rules in GENPRU	Corresponding rules in PRU
1.2.1R(2)	1.2.1R
1.2.2R(1)	1.2.3R(3)
1.2.2R(2)	1.2.3R(5)
1.2.6R	1.2.6R
1.3.4R	1.3.5R
2.1	2.1
2.1.3R	2.1.3R
2.1.13R	2.1.9R
2.1.17R	2.1.14R
2.1.24R	2.1.21R
2.1.25R	2.1.22R
2.1.29R	2.1.25R
2.1.30R	2.1.26R
2.1.30R	2.1.27R
2.1.34R	2.1.30R
2.1.38R	2.1.34R
2.2	2.2
2 Annex 1R	2.2.14R
2.2.32R	2.2.16R
2.2.33R	2.2.17R
2.2.34R	2.2.18R
2.2.118R	2.2.58R
2.2.64R(2)	2.2.40R
2.2.159R(7)	2.2.108R(7)
2.2.159R(8)	2.2.108R(8)
2.2.159R(9)	2.2.108R(9)
2.2.159R(10)	2.2.108R(10)
2.2.159R(12)	2.2.108R(11)
2.2.181R	2.2.105R
2.2.255R	2.2.89R

13 EEA pure reinsurers

Application

13.1 **[R]** GENPRU TP 13 applies to a pure reinsurer:

(1) whose head office is in an *EEA State* other than the *United Kingdom*; and

(2) which is not an *incoming Treaty firm*.

Duration of transitional

13.2 **[R]** GENPRU TP 13 has effect in relation to a *firm* until 10 December 2008 or, if earlier, the date on which it becomes:

(1) an *incoming EEA firm* by reason of having exercised its right to carry on the *regulated activity* of *effecting* or *carrying out contracts of insurance* in the *United Kingdom* in accordance with Schedule 3 to the *Act* (EEA Passport Rights); or

(2) an *incoming Treaty firm* by reason of having exercised its right to carry on the *regulated activity* of *effecting* or *carrying out contracts of insurance* in the *United Kingdom* in accordance with Schedule 4 to the *Act* (Treaty Rights).

Capital resources and discounting of technical provisions

13.3 **[R]** GENPRU 2.2.107R does not apply to a *firm*.

14 Continued use of IPRU expenditure requirements by BIPRU investment firms

Application

14.1 **[R]** This section applies to a *BIPRU investment firm*.

Transitional rule

14.2 **[R]** If a *firm*:

(1) is subject to the *fixed overheads requirement*; and

(2) was on 31 December 2006 subject to one of the expenditure based requirements under *IPRU* listed in the table in GENPRU TP 14.3R;

the *firm* may treat that expenditure based requirement as being its *fixed overheads requirement*.

14.3 **[R]** Table: Continuing *IPRU* expenditure requirements

This table belongs to GENPRU TP 14.2R

IPRU expenditure requirement	Remarks
Expenditure based requirement under Chapter 5 of IPRU(INV)	If the *firm* is subject to an expenditure based requirement of 6/52 of its annual audited expenditure, the *firm* must, for the purposes of this section, use the requirement of one quarter of its annual audited expenditure under *rule* 5.2.3(4)(c)(i)
The capital requirement of 13/52 of annual audited expenditure under *rule* 7.2.3R(1) of Chapter 7 of IPRU(INV)	
The expenditure requirement under *rule* 10-73(1)(b) of Chapter 10 of IPRU(INV)	
Financial Resources Test 2 for Category A firms under section 13.5 of Chapter 13 of IPRU(INV) (Expenditure-based requirement)	A *firm* must, for the purposes of this section, calculate its requirement as 13/52 of its relevant annual expenditure even if the fraction that applies to it under Chapter 13 would otherwise be 4/52 or 8/52.
Note (1): A reference to annual expenditure covers expenditure based on a forecast, pro-rated expenditure based on a period shorter than twelve months or any other expenditure figures for which the *IPRU rules* in this table provide.	
Note (2): Any *waiver* that a *firm* has in relation to the *rules* in *IPRU* in this table has effect for the purposes of this section. Any condition, limitation or requirement to which such a *waiver* is subject also continues to apply.	

Duration

14.4 **[R]** A *firm* must stop applying this section at the date when, under the *IPRU* expenditure requirements that apply to it as described in GENPRU TP 14.3R, it would have had to start using figures for the period following the one on which the expenditure requirements to which it was subject on 31 December 2006 were based.

14.5 **[G]** Say for example that a *firm's accounting reference date* is 31 December. As at 31 December 2006 the *firm's IPRU* expenditure requirement was based on its annual accounts for the year ended 31 December 2005. Its annual accounts for the year ending 31 December 2006 are completed on 15 March 2007. From 1 January 2007 to 14 March 2007 the *firm* may treat its *IPRU* expenditure requirements as being its *fixed overheads requirement*. On 15 March 2007 the *firm* should switch to calculating its *fixed overheads requirement* under GENPRU 2.1 (Calculation of capital resources requirement).

Capital resources

14.6 **[G]** The expenditure requirement under *IPRU* is measured against the *firm's capital resources* as calculated under GENPRU 2.2 (Capital resources) and not capital resources calculated under *IPRU*.

15 Admissible assets

Application

15.1 **[R]** GENPRU TP 15 applies to an *insurer* which is not a *pure reinsurer*.

Duration of transitional

15.2 **[R]** GENPRU TP 15 applies until 30 December 2007.

GENPRU 2 Annex 7R

15.3 **[R]**
(1) In determining whether its assets are *admissible assets*, instead of applying GENPRU 2 Annex 7R, a *firm* may elect to treat as an *admissible asset* an asset that would have been an *admissible asset* for the purposes of the Integrated Prudential Sourcebook (PRU) as it was in force on 30 December 2006.
(2) (1) does not apply when determining whether a *derivative* or *quasi-derivative* is an *approved derivative* or *approved quasi-derivative*.
(3) If a *firm* applies (1) to any of its assets, it must do so for all of its assets except *derivatives* and *quasi-derivatives*.

SCHEDULE 1
RECORD KEEPING REQUIREMENTS

[2059]
Sch 1 **[G]**
(1) The aim of the *guidance* in the following table is to give the reader a quick overall view of the relevant record keeping requirements.
(2) It is not a complete statement of those requirements and should not be relied on as if it were.
(3) Table

Handbook reference	Subject of Record	Contents of record	When record must be made	Retention Period
GENPRU 1.2.60R – GENPRU 1.2.61R	*Firm's* assessment of its financial resources	(1) The major sources of risk the *firm* has identified (2) How the *firm* intends to deal with those risks (3) Details of the stress and scenario analyses carried out and the resulting financial resources estimated to be required	Not specified	At least three years
GENPRU 1.3.22R	Valuation models for marking to model	Secure copy of *firm's* own valuation model	When model is in use	Not specified

Part II FSA Handbook Materials

SCHEDULE 2
NOTIFICATION AND REPORTING REQUIREMENTS

[2060]

Sch 2 **[G]**

(1) The aim of the *guidance* in the following table is to give the reader a quick overall view of the relevant notification requirements.

(2) It is not a complete statement of those requirements and should not be relied on as if it were.

(3) Table

Handbook reference	Matter to be notified	Contents of notification	Trigger events	Time allowed
GENPRU 1.5.19R	Intention to change maximum amount of *callable contribution*	Fact of intention and details of the change	Intention to change the maximum amount	Adequate advance notice, normally not less than 6 months
GENPRU 2.1.11R	Breach or expected breach of GENPRU 2.1.13R or *main BIPRU firm Pillar 1 rules*	Fact of breach or expectation of breach	Breach or expectation of breach	Immediately
GENPRU 2.2.19R	Intention to deduct *illiquid assets* rather than *material holdings*	Fact of intention	Intention to start or stop using method in column 2	One month prior to change of method
GENPRU 2.2.74R	Intention to redeem *tier one instrument* included in *tier one capital resources*	Fact of intention and details of the *firm's* position after such redemption in order to show how it will meet the *capital resources requirement* and how it will have sufficient financial resources to meet the *overall financial adequacy rule*	Intention to redeem	At least one month prior to becoming committed to redeem
GENPRU 2.2.135R	Intention to include an unusual transaction in capital under GENPRU 2.2.124R	Fact of intention	Intention to include in capital	At least one month prior to inclusion of that capital in *capital resources*
GENPRU 2.2.171R	Proposal to amend a tier two instrument	Details of the proposed amendment	Proposal to amend	One month before amendment is due to take effect
GENPRU 2.2.174R	Intention to repay (other than on contractual repayment date) *tier two instrument*	Fact of intention and details of the *firm's* position after such repayment in order to show how it will meet the *capital resources requirement* after such repayment and how it will have sufficient financial resources to meet the *overall financial adequacy rule*	Intention to repay	Six *Months* (in the case of an *insurer*) or one *Month* (in the case of a *BIPRU firm*) prior to becoming committed to repayment

Handbook reference	Matter to be notified	Contents of notification	Trigger events	Time allowed
GENPRU 2.2.243R	Intention to pay interest or principal on subordinated debt included in *tier three capital resources* if the *firm's capital resources* are less than 120% of its *capital resources requirement*	Fact of intention	Intention to pay	One month prior to any payment of interest or principal
GENPRU 2.2.245R	Intention to repay (other than on contractual repayment date) *tier three capital resources*	Fact of intention and details of how the *firm* will meet its *capital resources requirement* after such repayment	Intention to repay	One month prior to repayment

SCHEDULE 3
FEES AND OTHER REQUIREMENT PAYMENTS

[2061]
Sch3 [G]

There are no requirements for fees or other payments in GENPRU.

SCHEDULE 4
POWERS EXERCISED

[2062]
Sch 4 **[G]**

(1) The following powers and related provisions in the *Act* have been exercised by the *FSA* to make the rules in GENPRU:
  (1) section 138 (General rule-making power);
  (2) section 149 (Evidential provisions);
  (3) section 150(2) (Actions for damages);
  (4) section 156 (General supplementary powers); and
  (5) section 316(1) (Direction by Authority).

(2) The following power in the *Act* has been exercised by the *FSA* to give *guidance* in GENPRU:
  (1) section 157(1) (Guidance).

SCHEDULE 5
RIGHTS OF ACTION FOR DAMAGES

[2063]
Sch 5 **[G]**

(1) The table below sets out the rules in GENPRU contravention of which by an *authorised person* may be actionable under section 150 of the *Act* (Actions for damages) by a person who suffers loss as a result of the contravention.

(2) If a "Yes" appears in the column headed "For private person", the rule may be actionable by a private person under section 150 (or, in certain circumstances, his fiduciary or representative; see article 6(2) and (3)(c) of the Financial Services and Markets Act 2000 (Rights of Action) Regulations 2001 (SI 2001/2256)). A "Yes" in the column headed "Removed" indicates that the *FSA* has removed the right of action under section 150(2) of the Act. If so, a reference to the rule in which it is removed is also given.

(3) The column headed "For other person" indicates whether the rule may be actionable by a person other than a private person (or his fiduciary or representative) under article 6(2) and (3) of those Regulations. If so, an indication of the type of person by whom the rule may be actionable is given.

Chapter/ Appendix	Section/ Annex	Right of action under section 150		
		For private person	Removed	For other person
All *rules* in GENPRU		No	Yes – GEN-PRU 1.4.1R	No

SCHEDULE 6
RULES THAN CAN BE WAIVED

[2064]
Sch6 **[G]**

The rules in GENPRU may be waived by the *FSA* under section 148 of the *Act* (Modification or waiver of rules). However, if the *rules* incorporate requirements laid down in European directives, it will not be possible for the *FSA* to grant a *waiver* that would be incompatible with the *United Kingdom's* responsibilities under those directives. It therefore follows that if a *rule* in GENPRU contains provisions which derive partly from a directive, and partly not, the *FSA* will be able to consider a *waiver* of the latter requirements only, unless the directive provisions are optional rather than mandatory.

PRUDENTIAL SOURCEBOOK FOR INSURERS (INSPRU)

NOTES

Up to date as at 22 February 2010. For later amendments please see www.fsa.gov.uk.

CONTENTS

INSPRU 1—Capital resources requirements and technical provisions for insurance business . . . [2065]
INSPRU 2—Credit risk in insurance . . . [2066]
INSPRU 3—Market risk . . . [2067]
INSPRU 4—Liquidity risk management . . . [2068]
INSPRU 5—Operational Risk Management . . . [2069]
INSPRU 6—Group Risk: Insurance Groups . . . [2070]
INSPRU 7—Individual Capital Assessment . . . [2071]
INSPRU 8—General provisions applying INSPRU and GENPRU to Lloyd's . . . [2072]
INSPRU 9—Actions for damages . . . [2073]
Transitional Provisions TP . . . [2074]
INSPRU Schedules
Sch 1—Record keeping requirements . . . [2075]
Sch 2—Notification and reporting requirements . . . [2076]
Sch 3—Fees and other requirement payments . . . [2077]
Sch 4—Powers exercised . . . [2078]
Sch 5—Rights of action for damages . . . [2079]
Sch 6—Rules that can be waived . . . [2080]

Part II FSA Handbook Materials

CHAPTER 1

1.1 Capital resources requirements and technical provisions for insurance business

Application

[2065]

1.1.1 **[R]** INSPRU 1.1 applies to an *insurer* unless it is:
(1) a *non-directive friendly society*; or
(2) an *incoming EEA firm*; or
(3) an *incoming Treaty firm*.

1.1.2 **[R]**
(1) This section applies to a *firm* in relation to the whole of its business, except where a particular provision provides for a narrower scope.
(2) Where a *firm* carries on both *long-term insurance business* and *general insurance business*, this section applies separately to each type of business.

1.1.3 **[R]** For a *non-EEA insurer* with a *branch* in the *United Kingdom* whose *insurance business* in the *United Kingdom* is not restricted to *reinsurance* (other than an *EEA-deposit insurer*, a *Swiss general insurer* or a *UK-deposit insurer*):
(1) the part of this section headed "Capital requirements for insurers" (INSPRU 1.1.43G to INSPRU 1.1.92BG) applies to its world-wide activities;
(2) the parts of this section headed:
 (a) "Establishing technical provisions" (INSPRU 1.1.12R to INSPRU 1.1.19G);
 (b) "Reinsurance and analogous non-reinsurance financing agreements: risk transfer principle" (INSPRU 1.1.19AR to INSPRU 1.1.19FG);
 (c) "Assets of a value sufficient to cover technical provisions and other liabilities" (INSPRU 1.1.20R to INSPRU 1.1.29G);
 (d) "Matching of assets and liabilities" (INSPRU 1.1.34R to INSPRU 1.1.40G); and
 (e) "Premiums for new business" (INSPRU 1.1.41R to INSPRU 1.1.42G);
apply separately in respect of its world-wide activities and its activities carried on from a *branch* in the *United Kingdom*; and
(3) the part of this section headed "Localisation" (INSPRU 1.1.30R to INSPRU 1.1.33R) does not apply (see INSPRU 1.5 (Internal contagion risk)).

1.1.4 **[R]** For an *EEA-deposit insurer* or a *Swiss general insurer*:
(1) the parts of this section headed:
 (a) "Establishing technical provisions" (INSPRU 1.1.12R to INSPRU 1.1.19G);

(b) "Reinsurance and analogous non-reinsurance financing agreements: risk transfer principle" (INSPRU 1.1.19AR to INSPRU 1.1.19FG);
(c) "Assets of a value sufficient to cover technical provisions and other liabilities" (INSPRU 1.1.20R to INSPRU 1.1.29G);
(d) "Matching of assets and liabilities" (INSPRU 1.1.34R to INSPRU 1.1.40G); and
(e) "Premiums for new business" (INSPRU 1.1.41R to INSPRU 1.1.42G);

apply in respect of the activities of the *firm* carried on from a *branch* in the *United Kingdom*; and

(2) the parts of this section headed "Capital requirements for insurers" (INSPRU 1.1.43G to INSPRU 1.1.92BG) and "Localisation" (INSPRU 1.1.30R to INSPRU 1.1.33R) do not apply.

1.1.5 **[R]** For a *UK-deposit insurer*:

(1) the part of this section headed "Capital requirements for insurers" (INSPRU 1.1.43G to INSPRU 1.1.92BG) applies to its world-wide activities;

(2) the parts of this section headed:
(a) "Establishing technical provisions" (INSPRU 1.1.12R to INSPRU 1.1.19G);
(b) "Reinsurance and analogous non-reinsurance financing agreements: risk transfer principle" (INSPRU 1.1.19AR to INSPRU 1.1.19FG);
(c) "Assets of a value sufficient to cover technical provisions and other liabilities" (INSPRU 1.1.20R to INSPRU 1.1.29G);
(d) "Matching of assets and liabilities" (INSPRU 1.1.34R to INSPRU 1.1.40G); and
(e) "Premiums for new business" (INSPRU 1.1.41R to INSPRU 1.1.42G);

apply separately in respect of its world-wide activities and its activities carried on from *branches* in *EEA States*; and

(3) the part of this section headed "Localisation" (INSPRU 1.1.30R to INSPRU 1.1.33R) does not apply (see INSPRU 1.5 (Internal contagion risk)).

1.1.6 **[G]** This section may apply in cases where a *firm* has its head office in another *EEA State* but is neither an *incoming EEA firm* nor an *incoming Treaty firm*; this could arise in the case of a *non-directive mutual*.

Purpose

1.1.7 **[G]** INSPRU 1.1 has the aim of reducing the risk that a *firm* may fail to meet its liabilities to its *policyholders* as a result of insurance risk, that is, the risk that arises from the inherent uncertainties as to the occurrence, amount and timing of insurance liabilities.

1.1.8 **[G]** This section requires that the *technical provisions* that *firms* establish are adequate to meet their liabilities to *policyholders* under *contracts of insurance*. It also requires that *firms* hold assets of a value sufficient to cover their liabilities, including *technical provisions*, and that there is suitable matching of assets and liabilities. *Technical provisions* are the on- balance sheet provisions made by a *firm* in respect of liabilities arising under or in connection with *contracts of insurance*. There are different *rules* and *guidance* applicable to the calculation of *technical provisions* for *general insurance business* and for *long-term insurance business*.

1.1.9 **[G]** This section implements requirements of the *Insurance Directives* for both *general insurance business* and *long-term insurance business* with regard to the *technical provisions*. The relevant articles of the Directives include:

(1) article 15 of the *First Non-Life Directive*, as substituted by article 17 of the *Third Non-Life Directive*; and

(2) article 20 of the *Consolidated Life Directive* (this Directive consolidates the provisions of the previous *First*, *Second* and *Third Life Directives*).

1.1.10 **[G]** This section also sets out detailed *rules* and *guidance* on the calculation of the following elements of a *firm's capital resources requirement* (*CRR*) (see GENPRU 2.1):

(1) the *general insurance capital requirement*; and

(2) the *long-term insurance capital requirement*.

1.1.11 **[G]** These requirements are dealt with in the part of this section headed "Capital requirements for insurers" (see INSPRU 1.1.43G to INSPRU 1.1.91R). That part of this section also contains *rules* about the calculation of the *enhanced capital requirement* for *firms* carrying on *general insurance business*, including the calculation of the *insurance-related capital requirement*. The calculation of the *asset-related capital requirement*, which also forms part of the calculation of the *ECR* for *firms* carrying on *general insurance business*, is set out in INSPRU 2.2.

Establishing technical provisions

1.1.12 **[R]** For *general insurance business*, a *firm* must establish adequate technical provisions:

(1) in accordance with the *rules* in INSPRU 1.4 for *equalisation provisions*; and

(2) otherwise, in accordance with GENPRU 1.3.4R.

1.1.13 **[G]** For *general insurance business*, the *technical provisions* include outstanding *claims* provisions, *unearned premiums* provisions, unexpired risk provisions and *equalisation provisions*.

These provisions take into account the expected ultimate cost of *claims*, including those not yet incurred, related expenses and include an allowance for smoothing *claims* (the *equalisation provision*).

1.1.14 **[G]** *Discounting* (that is discounting for the time value of money) *general insurance business technical provisions* may be carried out only in limited circumstances and on a prudent basis (see GENPRU 2.2.107R and paragraph 48 of the *insurance accounts rules*). The fact that the expected liabilities are generally not *discounted* helps to protect against risk from inherent uncertainty in the timing, but not necessarily the amount, of *claims*.

1.1.15 **[G]** For some categories of *general insurance business*, *equalisation provisions* are required. These ensure that a *firm* retains additional assets to provide some extra protection against uncertainty as to the amount of *claims*. *Equalisation provisions* are particularly suitable for volatile business, where *claims* in any future year may be subject to significant adverse deviation from recent or average expected *claims* experience, or where trends in *claims* experience may be subject to change. Such volatile *claims* experience arises in a number of types of business, for example, property, marine and aviation, nuclear, certain *non-proportional reinsurance treaty* business, and credit insurance. The *equalisation provisions* help to equalise fluctuations in loss ratios in future years (see INSPRU 1.4 (*Equalisation provisions*)).

1.1.16 **[R]** For *long-term insurance business*, a *firm* must establish adequate technical provisions in respect of its *long-term insurance contracts* as follows:
(1) *mathematical reserves* in accordance with the *rules* and *guidance* in INSPRU 1.2 relating to such reserves, and with due regard to generally accepted actuarial practice; and
(2) for liabilities in respect of such contracts that have fallen due, in accordance with GENPRU 1.3.4R.

1.1.17 **[G]** *Rules* and *guidance* for calculating *mathematical reserves* are set out in INSPRU 1.2. *Firms* are advised by the *actuarial function* (see SUP 4) on the methods and assumptions to be used in calculating the *mathematical reserves*. The standards and guidance issued by the Board for Actuarial Standards to assist actuaries appointed to the *actuarial function* are important sources of evidence as to generally accepted actuarial practice, as referred to in INSPRU 1.1.16R(1).

1.1.18 **[G]** For *long-term insurance business*, the *technical provisions* include the *mathematical reserves*. These are actuarial estimates of a *firm's* liabilities in respect of future benefits due to *policyholders*, including bonuses already declared. The *mathematical reserves* may be reduced by the actuarial value of that component of future *premiums* attributable to meeting future liabilities (see INSPRU 1.2 (*Mathematical reserves*)).

1.1.19 **[G]** For *long-term insurance business*, the *mathematical reserves* are typically valued on a discounted basis but include valuation margins intended to provide protection against adverse deviations in experience (see INSPRU 1.2).

Reinsurance and analogous non-reinsurance financing agreements: risk transfer principle

1.1.19A **[R]**
(1) A *firm* may only take credit for *reinsurance* if and to the extent that there has been an effective transfer of risk from the *firm* to a third party.
(2) In INSPRU 1.1.19AR to INSPRU 1.1.19FG, references to *reinsurance* and contracts of *reinsurance* include:
    (a) all contracts of *reinsurance* with an *ISPV*; and
    (b) analogous non-*reinsurance* financing agreements.

1.1.19B **[R]** For the purposes of INSPRU 1.1.19AR(2)(b), analogous non-*reinsurance* financing agreements include contingent loans, securitisations and any other arrangements in respect of *contracts of insurance* that are analogous to contracts of *reinsurance* in terms of the risks transferred and the finance provided.

1.1.19C **[G]** There are a number of ways in which a *firm* may be able to take credit for *reinsurance* under the *rules* in GENPRU and INSPRU. Examples include:
(1) treating the *reinsurer's* share of *technical provisions* as an *admissible asset* in accordance with GENPRU 2 Ann 7R;
(2) reducing its solvency requirements in accordance with the deduction for *reinsurance* allowed in the calculation of the *general insurance capital requirement* or the *long-term insurance capital requirement* under INSPRU 1.1; and
(3) bringing into account amounts receivable under the contract when valuing cash flows for the purpose of a prospective valuation of *mathematical reserves* under INSPRU 1.2. In particular, a contingent loan or other analogous non-*reinsurance* financing agreement may then give rise to an addition to *capital resources* as a positive valuation difference in accordance with GENPRU 2.2.105R.

1.1.19D **[G]** The amount of credit taken by a *firm* for a risk transferred should be measured by applying the standard methods for determining the regulatory balance sheet set out in INSPRU. For example, where credit is being taken so as to reduce *technical provisions*, the amount of that credit should reflect the difference in *technical provisions* that arises from changing the assumptions used to reflect the risk transferred.

1.1.19E **[G]** For the purposes of INSPRU 1.1.19AR(1), the transfer of risk from the *firm* to the third party should be effective in all circumstances in which the *firm* may wish to rely upon the transfer. Examples of factors which the *firm* should take into account in assessing whether the transaction effectively transfers risk and the extent of that transfer include:

(1) whether the documentation associated with the *reinsurance* reflects the economic substance of the transaction;
(2) whether the extent of the risk transfer is clearly defined and incontrovertible;
(3) whether the transaction contains any terms or conditions the fulfilment of which is outside the direct control of the *firm*. Such terms or conditions may include those which:
    (a) would allow the third party unilaterally to cancel the transaction, except for the non-payment of monies due from the *firm* to the third party under the contract; or
    (b) would increase the effective cost of the transaction to the *firm* in response to an increased likelihood of the third party experiencing losses under the transaction; or
    (c) would oblige the *firm* to alter the risk that had been transferred with the purpose of reducing the likelihood of the third party experiencing losses under the transaction; or
    (d) would allow for the termination of the transaction due to an increased likelihood of the third party experiencing losses under the transaction; or
    (e) could prevent the third party from being obliged to pay out in a timely manner any monies due under the transaction; or
    (f) could allow the maturity of the transaction to be reduced;
(4) whether the transaction is legally effective and enforceable in all relevant jurisdictions.

1.1.19F **[G]** A *firm* should also take into account circumstances in which the benefit to the *firm* of the transfer of risk could be undermined. For instance, where the *firm*, with a view to reducing potential or actual losses to third parties, provides support to the transaction, including support beyond its contractual obligations (implicit support). Another example of a situation where the *firm* should consider whether it should take reduced credit for a transaction is where it has invested in the bonds issued by an *ISPV* with which it has reinsured risks.

Assets of a value sufficient to cover technical provisions and other liabilities

1.1.20 **[R]** A *firm* which is not a *composite firm* must hold *admissible assets* of a value at least equal to the amount of:

(1) the *technical provisions* that it is required to establish under INSPRU 1.1.12R or INSPRU 1.1.16R; and
(2) its other *general insurance liabilities* or *long-term insurance liabilities*;

but excluding, where the *firm* is not a *pure reinsurer*, *property-linked liabilities* and *index-linked liabilities* and the assets held to cover them under INSPRU 3.1.57R and INSPRU 3.1.58R.

1.1.21 **[R]** A *composite firm* must ensure that:

(1) it holds *admissible assets* separately identified in accordance with INSPRU 1.5.18R of a value at least equal to the amount of:
    (a) the *technical provisions* that it is required to establish under INSPRU 1.1.16R; and
    (b) its other *long-term insurance liabilities*;

but excluding, where the *firm* is not a *pure reinsurer*, *property-linked liabilities* and *index-linked liabilities* and the assets held to cover them under INSPRU 3.1.57R and INSPRU 3.1.58R; and

(2) it holds other *admissible assets* (other than those excluded under (1)) of a value at least equal to the amount of:
    (a) the *technical provisions* that it is required to establish under INSPRU 1.1.12R; and
    (b) its other *general insurance liabilities*.

1.1.22 **[G]** INSPRU 1.5 (Internal-contagion risk) sets out the *rules* and *guidance* on identifying and holding in a separate fund *long-term insurance assets*.

1.1.23 **[G]** When valuing assets for the purposes of INSPRU 1.1.20R and INSPRU 1.1.21R, a *firm* should bear in mind:

(1) that the *technical provisions* and other *long-term insurance liabilities* or *general insurance liabilities* should be covered by *admissible assets* (see GENPRU 2 Annex 7R); and
(2) the market and *counterparty* limits set out in INSPRU 2.1 (Credit risk in insurance). INSPRU 2.1 requires that a *firm* restrict to prudent levels its exposure to *reinsurer* and other *counterparties*, and, in particular, that for the purpose of its balance sheet, a *firm* must not take into account any exposure which exceeds the large exposure limits.

1.1.24 **[G]** *Rules* and *guidance* on the valuation of assets are set out in GENPRU 1.3 (Valuation), including the treatment of *shares* in, and debts due from, *related undertakings* in GENPRU 1.3.43R to GENPRU 1.3.54G. INSPRU 3.1 (Market risk in insurance) addresses *market risk* and sets out the matching requirements for linked assets and liabilities. INSPRU 3.1 also sets out *rules* and *guidance* on the matching by currency of assets and liabilities, to reduce a *firm's* exposure to currency *market risk*.

1.1.25 **[R]** For the purpose of determining the value of assets available to meet *technical provisions* and other *long-term insurance liabilities* in accordance with INSPRU 1.1.20R, INSPRU 1.1.21R, INSPRU 1.1.27R and INSPRU 1.1.28R, no value is to be attributed to:
(1) debts owed by *reinsurers*; or
(2) *claims*; or
(3) tax recoveries; or
(4) claims against *compensation funds*;

to the extent already offset in the calculation of *technical provisions*.

1.1.26 **[G]** Certain debts and claims are excluded from INSPRU 1.1.20R, INSPRU 1.1.21R, INSPRU 1.1.27R and INSPRU 1.1.28R to avoid double-counting. The *rules* and *guidance* in INSPRU 1.2 (*Mathematical reserves*) set out how a *firm* may offset debts and *claims* against liabilities in calculating the *mathematical reserves* required for *long-term insurance business*.

1.1.27 **[R]** A *firm* carrying on *long-term insurance business* must ensure that it has *admissible assets* in each of its *with-profits funds* of a value sufficient to cover:
(1) the *technical provisions* in respect of all the business written in that *with- profits fund*; and
(2) its other *long-term insurance liabilities* in respect of that *with-profits fund*.

1.1.28 **[R]** In addition to complying with INSPRU 1.1.27R, a *realistic basis life firm* must also ensure that the *realistic value of assets* for each of its *with-profits funds* is at least equal to the *realistic value of liabilities* of that fund.

1.1.29 **[G]** INSPRU 1.1.27R and INSPRU 1.1.28R support the funding of *policyholder* benefits by requiring *firms* to maintain *admissible assets* in *with-profits funds* to cover the *technical provisions* and other *long-term insurance liabilities* relating to all the business in that fund and, in the case of a *realistic basis life firm*, realistic assets to cover the realistic liabilities of the *with-profits insurance contracts* written in the fund.

Localisation (UK firms only)

1.1.30 **[R]**
(1) Subject to (2), a *UK firm* must hold *admissible assets* held pursuant to INSPRU 3.1.53R:
  (a) (where the *admissible assets* cover *technical provisions* in pounds sterling), in any *EEA State*; and
  (b) (where the *admissible assets* cover *technical provisions* in any currency other than pounds sterling), in any *EEA State* or in the country of that currency.
(2) In the case of a *community co-insurance operation* and a *relevant insurer*, the *admissible assets* covering *technical provisions* must be held in any *EEA State*.

1.1.31 **[G]** INSPRU 1.5 (Internal contagion risk) sets out the *rules* and *guidance* on localisation for *firms* other than *UK firms*.

1.1.32 **[R]** INSPRU 1.1.30R does not apply to:
(1) a *pure reinsurer*; or
(2) debts owed by *reinsurers*; or
(3) *insurance business* carried on by a *UK firm* outside the *EEA States*; or
(4) *general insurance business class* groups 3 and 4 in IPRU(INS), Annex 11.2, Part II.

1.1.33 **[R]** For the purposes of INSPRU 1.1.30R:
(1) a tangible asset is to be treated as held in the country or territory where it is situated;
(2) an *admissible asset* consisting of a claim against a debtor is to be treated as held in any country or territory where it can be enforced by legal action;
(3) a *security* which is *listed* is to be treated as held in any country or territory where there is a *regulated market* on which the *security* is dealt; and
(4) a *security* which is not *listed* is to be treated as held in the country or territory in which the *issuer* has its head office.

Matching of assets and liabilities

1.1.34 **[R]**
(1) Subject to (4), the assets held by a *firm* to cover its *technical provisions* and other *long-term insurance liabilities* or *general insurance liabilities* (see INSPRU 1.1.20R and INSPRU 1.1.21R) must:
  (a) have characteristics of safety, yield and marketability which are appropriate to the type of business carried on by the *firm*;
  (b) be diversified and adequately spread; and

(c) comply with (2).

(2) The assets referred to in (1) must, in addition to meeting the criteria set out in (1)(a) and (b), be of a sufficient amount, and of an appropriate currency and term, to ensure that the cash inflows from those assets will meet the expected cash outflows from the *firm's* insurance liabilities as they become due.

(3) For the purpose of (2), a *firm* must take into consideration in determining expected cash outflows any options which exist in the *firm's contracts of insurance*.

(4) (1) does not apply to:
(a) a *pure reinsurer*; or
(b) assets held to cover *index-linked liabilities* or *property-linked liabilities*, except that where the *linked long-term contract of insurance* in question includes a guarantee of investment performance or some other guaranteed benefit, (1) will nevertheless apply to assets held to cover that guaranteed element.

1.1.34A **[G]** INSPRU 1.1.34R is not applied to *pure reinsurers* because they are subject under INSPRU 3.1.61AR to the "prudent person" investment principles from the *Reinsurance Directive*.

1.1.35 **[G]** A *firm* should take account of the amount, currency and timing of its expected cash outflows in determining whether the assets it holds to cover its *technical provisions* and other *long-term insurance liabilities* or *general insurance liabilities* meet the requirements of INSPRU 1.1.34R(2).

1.1.36 **[G]** For the purpose of INSPRU 1.1.34R(2), the relevant cash inflows are those which the *firm* reasonably expects to receive from the *admissible assets* which it holds to cover its *technical provisions* and other *long-term insurance liabilities* or *general insurance liabilities*. A *firm* may receive cash inflows as a result of:
(1) selling assets or closing out transactions;
(2) holding assets that generate dividends, interest or other income; and
(3) receiving future *premiums* for existing business.

1.1.37 **[G]** Anticipated cash inflows from future new business should not be included, for example where the *customer* has not yet contracted to pay the *premium*, and where the associated liabilities and potential cash outflows should also not be included.

1.1.38 **[G]** A *firm* should compare cash inflows and outflows based on current expectations of amounts and timings. Current market expectations of future asset values, interest rates and currency exchange rates should be used. Where inflows are received in a currency different from that in which outflows are to be paid, account should be taken of the cost of converting the currency received.

1.1.39 **[G]** In considering the value and suitability of assets required to ensure that the *firm's* liabilities are met as they become due, a *firm* should take account of the risk of default on inflows from those assets, and other risks that may mean that future inflows are reduced relative to outflows.

1.1.40 **[G]** INSPRU 1.1.20R lays down a general requirement for a *firm* that carries on *long-term insurance business* to hold *admissible assets* that are of a value sufficient to cover its *technical provisions* and other *long-term insurance liabilities*. The INSPRU 1.1.34R(2) requirement to match liabilities with assets that allow cash outflows to be met with suitable inflows as the outflows become due may mean that a *firm* has to hold assets of a value greater than would otherwise be required by the general *rule* in INSPRU 1.1.20R.

Premiums for new business

1.1.41 **[R]** A *firm* must not enter into a *long-term insurance contract* unless it is satisfied on reasonable actuarial assumptions that:
(1) the *premiums* receivable and the investment income expected to be earned from those *premiums*; and
(2) the *reinsurance* arrangements made in respect of the risk or risks covered by that new contract are sufficient to enable it, when taken together with the *firm's* other resources, to:
(a) establish adequate *technical provisions* as required by INSPRU 1.1.16R;
(b) hold *admissible assets* of a value at least equal to the amount of the *technical provisions* and other *long-term insurance liabilities* as required by INSPRU 1.1.20R to INSPRU 1.1.28R; and
(c) maintain adequate overall financial resources as required by the *overall financial adequacy rule*.

1.1.42 **[G]** For the purposes of INSPRU 1.1.41R, the adequacy of *premiums* may be assessed in the context of a *firm's* total portfolio of business and its other resources. It thus does not prevent a *firm* writing loss leaders nor writing contracts which might incur large losses, but only if the *firm* can meet the losses that might reasonably arise, including those that would arise from an event specifically insured against.

Capital requirements for insurers

1.1.43 **[G]**

(1) GENPRU 2.1.13R requires a *firm* to maintain *capital resources* equal to or in excess of its *capital resources requirement* (*CRR*). GENPRU 2.1 sets out the overall framework of the *CRR*; in particular, GENPRU 2.1.17R requires that for a *firm* carrying on *general insurance business* the *CRR* is equal to the *minimum capital requirement* (*MCR*). GENPRU 2.1.18R requires that for *realistic basis life firms* the *CRR* is the higher of the *MCR* and the *ECR*. GENPRU 2.1.23R requires that for *regulatory basis only life firms* the *CRR* is equal to the *MCR*.

(2) For non-life *firms* the *MCR* represents the *minimum capital requirement* (or margin of solvency) prescribed by the *Insurance Directives*. GENPRU 2.1.24R provides that, for a *firm* carrying on *general insurance business*, the *MCR* in respect of that business is the higher of the *base capital resources requirement* for *general insurance business* applicable to that *firm* and the *general insurance capital requirement*. GENPRU 2.1.24AR provides that, for a *firm* carrying on *long-term insurance business* which is a *realistic basis life firm*, the *MCR* in respect of that business is the higher of the *base capital resources requirement* for *long-term insurance business* applicable to that *firm* and the *long-term insurance capital requirement*. GENPRU 2.1.25R provides that, for a *firm* carrying on *long-term insurance business* which is a *regulatory basis only life firm*, the *MCR* in respect of that business is the higher of the *base capital resources requirement* for *long-term insurance business* applicable to that *firm* and the sum of the *long-term insurance capital requirement* and the *resilience capital requirement*. As specified in GENPRU 2.1.14R, a *firm* carrying on both *general insurance business* and *long-term insurance business* must apply GENPRU 2.1.13R (referred to in paragraph (1) above) separately to its *general insurance business* and its *long-term insurance business*.

(3) The calculation of the *general insurance capital requirement* is set out in INSPRU 1.1.44G to INSPRU 1.1.72R below. INSPRU 1.1.73G to INSPRU 1.1.79R set out the calculation of the *insurance-related capital requirement* for non-life *firms*. The calculation of the *long-term insurance capital requirement* is set out in INSPRU 1.1.80G to INSPRU 1.1.91R below.

General insurance capital requirement

1.1.44 **[G]** In relation to the *MCR* (see INSPRU 1.1.43G), GENPRU 2.1.34R requires a *firm* to calculate its *general insurance capital requirement* (*GICR*) as the highest of the *premiums amount*, the *claims amount*, and the *brought forward amount*. The elements for this computation are set out in INSPRU 1.1 as follows:

(1) the *premiums amount* in INSPRU 1.1.45R;

(2) the *claims amount* in INSPRU 1.1.47R; and

(3) the *brought forward amount* in INSPRU 1.1.51R.

The premiums amount

1.1.45 **[R]** The *premiums* amount is:

(1) 18% of the *gross adjusted premiums amount*; less 2% of the amount, if any, by which the *gross adjusted premiums amount* exceeds €57.5 million; multiplied by

(2) the reinsurance ratio set out in INSPRU 1.1.54R.

1.1.46 **[G]** *Rules* and *guidance* as to how the *gross adjusted premiums amount* is to be calculated are set out in INSPRU 1.1.56R to INSPRU 1.1.59G.

The claims amount

1.1.47 **[R]** The *claims amount* is:

(1) 26% of the *gross adjusted claims amount*; less 3% of the amount, if any, by which the *gross adjusted claims amount* exceeds €40.3 million; multiplied by

(2) the reinsurance ratio set out in INSPRU 1.1.54R.

1.1.48 **[G]** *Rules* and *guidance* as to how the *gross adjusted claims amount* is to be calculated are set out in INSPRU 1.1.60R to INSPRU 1.1.65G.

1.1.49 **[G]**

(1) Under the *Insurance Directives* the Euro amounts specified in INSPRU 1.1.45R(1) and INSPRU 1.1.47R(1) are subject to annual review. The relevant amounts will be increased by the percentage change in the European index of consumer prices (comprising all EU member states, as published by Eurostat) from 20 March 2002, to the relevant review date, rounded up to a multiple of €100,000, provided that where the percentage change since the last increase is less than 5%, no increase will take place.

(2) No provision for the index-linking of these amounts is made by the *Reinsurance Directive*. However, to ensure consistency as between *pure reinsurers*, *mixed insurers* and other *insurers*, the *FSA* intends to amend the Euro amounts specified in INSPRU 1.1.45R(1) and INSPRU 1.1.47R(1) for all such *firms* when an index-linked increase is required by the *Insurance Directives*.

1.1.50 **[R]** For the purposes of INSPRU 1.1.45R(1) and INSPRU 1.1.47R(1), the exchange rate from the Euro to the pound sterling for each year beginning on 31 December is the rate applicable on the last day of the preceding October for which the exchange rates for the currencies of all the European Union member states were published in the Official Journal of the European Union.

The brought forward amount

1.1.51 **[R]**
(1) Subject to (2) and (3), the *brought forward amount* is the *general insurance capital requirement (GICR)* for the prior *financial year*, multiplied, if the ratio is less than one, by the ratio (expressed as a percentage) of:
  (a) the *technical provisions* (calculated net of *reinsurance*) for *claims* outstanding at the end of the prior *financial year*, determined in accordance with INSPRU 1.1.12R; to
  (b) the *technical provisions* (calculated net of *reinsurance*) for *claims* outstanding at the beginning of the prior *financial year*, determined in accordance with INSPRU 1.1.12R.
(2) If the amount of the *technical provisions* (calculated net of *reinsurance*) in (1)(a) and (b) is in both cases zero, the *brought forward amount* is the *general insurance capital requirement (GICR)* for the prior *financial year*, multiplied, if the ratio is less than one, by the ratio (expressed as a percentage) of:
  (a) the *technical provisions* (calculated gross of *reinsurance*) for *claims* outstanding at the end of the prior *financial year*, determined in accordance with INSPRU 1.1.12R; to
  (b) the *technical provisions* (calculated gross of *reinsurance*) for *claims* outstanding at the beginning of the prior *financial year*, determined in accordance with INSPRU 1.1.12R.
(3) If the amount of the *technical provisions* (calculated gross of *reinsurance*) in (2)(a) and (b) is in both cases zero, the *brought forward amount* is the *general insurance capital requirement (GICR)* for the prior *financial year*.

1.1.52 **[G]** The *brought forward amount* is the same as the *GICR* for the prior *financial year*, except where *claims* outstanding have fallen during that *financial year*. If the *technical provisions* (calculated net of *reinsurance*) have fallen, the *brought forward amount* is itself reduced by the same percentage fall. If the *technical provisions* (calculated net of *reinsurance*) are zero at the beginning and end of that *financial year* and the *technical provisions* gross of *reinsurance* have fallen, the *brought forward amount* is reduced by the percentage fall in *technical provisions* gross of *reinsurance*.

1.1.53 **[G]** [deleted]

Reinsurance ratio used in calculating the premiums amount and the claims amount

1.1.54 **[R]** The reinsurance ratio referred to in INSPRU 1.1.45R(2) and INSPRU 1.1.47R(2) is:
(1) if the ratio lies between 50% and 100%, the ratio (expressed as a percentage) of:
  (a) the *claims* incurred (net of *reinsurance*) in the *financial year in question* and the two previous *financial years*; to
  (b) the gross *claims* incurred in that three-year period;
(2) 50%, if the ratio calculated in (a) and (b) of (1) is 50% or less; and
(3) 100%, if the ratio calculated in (a) and (b) of (1) is 100% or more.

1.1.54A **[G]** For the treatment of amounts recoverable from *ISPVs* when calculating the reinsurance ratio, see INSPRU 1.1.92AR and INSPRU 1.1.92BG.

1.1.55 **[G]** *Rules* and *guidance* as to how the net and gross *claims* are to be calculated are set out in INSPRU 1.1.66R to INSPRU 1.1.71R.

Gross adjusted premiums amount used in calculating the premiums amount

1.1.56 **[R]** For the purpose of INSPRU 1.1.45R, the *gross adjusted premiums amount* is the higher of the *gross written premiums* and *gross earned premiums* (as adjusted in accordance with INSPRU 1.1.66R) for the *financial year in question*, adjusted by:
(1) except for a *pure reinsurer* which became a *firm in run-off* before 31 December 2006 and whose *Part IV permission* has not subsequently been varied to add back the *regulated activity* of *effecting contracts of insurance*, increasing by 50% the amount included in respect of the *premiums* for *general insurance business classes* 11, 12 and 13;

(2) deducting 66.7% of the *premiums* for *actuarial health insurance* that meets the conditions set out in INSPRU 1.1.72R; and

(3) multiplying the resulting figure by 12 and dividing by the number of months in the *financial year*. For the purposes of this calculation, the number of months in the *financial year* is the number of complete calendar months in the *financial year* plus any fractions of a month at the beginning and the end of the *financial year*.

1.1.57 **[G]** A *firm* may use statistical methods in order to allocate *premiums* in respect of the *classes* 11, 12 and 13 for the purposes of INSPRU 1.1.56R.

1.1.58 **[G]** *General insurance business classes* 11, 12 and 13 are, respectively, the marine liability, aviation liability and general liability insurance classes.

1.1.59 **[G]** Where the *firm* did not carry on *insurance business* in the *financial year in question*, the *gross adjusted premiums amount*, and therefore the *premiums amount*, is nil.

Gross adjusted claims amount used in calculating the claims amount

1.1.60 **[R]** For the purpose of INSPRU 1.1.47R and subject to INSPRU 1.1.62R, the *gross adjusted claims amount* is the amount of gross *claims* incurred (as determined in accordance with INSPRU 1.1.66R) over the reference period (as specified in INSPRU 1.1.63R) and adjusted by:

(1) except for a *pure reinsurer* which became a *firm in run-off* before 31 December 2006 and whose *Part IV permission* has not subsequently been varied to add back the *regulated activity* of *effecting contracts of insurance*, increasing by 50% the amount included in respect of the *claims* incurred for *general insurance business classes* 11, 12 and 13;

(2) deducting 66.7% of the *claims* for *actuarial health insurance* that meets the conditions set out in INSPRU 1.1.72R; and

(3) multiplying the resulting figure by 12 and dividing by the number of months in the reference period. For the purposes of this calculation, the number of months in the reference period is the number of complete calendar months in the reference period plus any fractions of a month at the beginning and the end of the reference period.

1.1.61 **[G]** A *firm* may use statistical methods in order to allocate *claims* in respect of *classes* 11, 12 and 13 for the purposes of INSPRU 1.1.60R.

1.1.62 **[R]** For the purposes of INSPRU 1.1.47R, in relation to *general insurance business class* 18, the amount of *claims* incurred used to calculate the *gross adjusted claims amount* must be the amount of costs recorded in the *firm's* books in the reference period as borne by the *firm* (whether or not borne in the reference period) in respect of the assistance given.

1.1.63 **[R]**

(1) Except in those cases where paragraph (2) applies, the reference period to be used in INSPRU 1.1.60R and INSPRU 1.1.62R must be:

  (a) the *financial year in question* and the two previous *financial years*; or

  (b) the period the *firm* had been in existence at the end of the *financial year in question*, if shorter.

(2) In the case of a *firm* which underwrites only one or more of the *general insurance business* risks of credit, storm, hail or frost (including other business written in connection with such risks), the reference period to be used must be:

  (a) the *financial year in question* and the six previous *financial years*; or

  (b) the period the *firm* had been in existence at the end of the *financial year in question*, if shorter.

1.1.64 **[G]** The classification of the risks referred to in INSPRU 1.1.63R(2) is as follows: credit-as included in *general insurance business class* 14; storm – as included in *general insurance business class* 8; hail-as included in *general insurance business class* 9; and frost – as included in *general insurance business class* 9.

1.1.65 **[G]** Where the *firm* did not carry on *insurance business* in the reference period, the *gross adjusted claims amount*, and therefore the *claims amount*, is nil.

Accounting for premiums and claims

1.1.66 **[R]** For the purposes of INSPRU 1.1.54R, INSPRU 1.1.56R, INSPRU 1.1.60R and INSPRU 1.1.62R, amounts of *premiums* and *claims* must be:

(1) determined in accordance with the *insurance accounts rules* or the Friendly Societies (Accounts and Related Provisions) Regulations 1994, as appropriate; and

(2) adjusted for transfers that were approved by the relevant authority (or became effective where approval by an authority was not required) before the end of the *financial year in question*:

  (a) to exclude any amount included in, or adjustment made to, *premiums* and *claims* to reflect the consideration for a transfer of *contracts of insurance* to or from the *firm*;

Part II FSA Handbook Materials

(b) to exclude *premiums* and *claims* which arose from *contracts of insurance* that have been transferred by the *firm* to another body; and

(c) to account for *premiums* and *claims* which arose from *contracts of insurance* that have been transferred to the *firm* from another body as if they were receivable by or payable by the *firm*.

1.1.67 **[G]** To ensure that all rights and obligations under a *contract of insurance* are transferred, a number of alternative mechanisms could be used. These are: an *insurance business transfer* under Part VII of the *Act*; under earlier *United Kingdom* insurance legislation; under equivalent foreign legislation; or by novation of contracts. The term "relevant authority" in paragraph (2) of INSPRU 1.1.66R may refer to whatever body has responsibility in a country, whether within or outside the *EEA*, for the approval of transfers of portfolios of *contracts of insurance*; the body may be a supervisory authority for financial services as such or it may be a judicial authority which has the necessary responsibility.

1.1.68 **[G]** INSPRU 1.1.66R(2)(b) requires a *firm*, for the purpose of calculating its *GICR*, to account for *contracts of insurance* transferred by it to another body as if it had never written those contracts. All amounts of *premiums* and *claims* arising in respect of those contracts are excluded, including amounts that arose in the *financial year in question* or previous *financial years*.

1.1.69 **[G]** Conversely, INSPRU 1.1.66R(2)(c) requires a *firm*, for the purpose of calculating its *GICR*, to account for *contracts of insurance* transferred to it by another body as if it had been responsible for those contracts from inception and not merely from the date of transfer. All amounts of *premiums* and *claims* that arose from those contracts are included even where they arose prior to the date of transfer and were, in fact, receivable by or payable by the other body.

1.1.70 **[G]** For both transfers to and from the *firm*, the consideration receivable or payable in respect of the transfer is excluded from *premiums* and *claims* in order to avoid double counting.

1.1.71 **[R]** Where there has been a significant change in the business portfolio of the *firm* since the end of the *financial year in question*, for example, a line of business has been transferred to another *firm*, or the *firm* no longer carries on a particular *class* of *insurance business*, the *gross adjusted premiums amount* and the *gross adjusted claims amount* must both be recalculated to take into account the impact of this change. The recalculation must take into account the requirements of the *insurance accounts rules* or the Friendly Societies (Accounts and Related Provisions) Regulations 1994, as appropriate.

Actuarial health insurance

1.1.72 **[R]** The conditions referred to in INSPRU 1.1.56R(2) and INSPRU 1.1.60R(2) are that:

(1) the health insurance is underwritten on a similar technical basis to that of life insurance;

(2) the *premiums* paid are calculated on the basis of sickness tables according to the mathematical method applied in insurance;

(3) a provision is set up for increasing age;

(4) an additional *premium* is collected in order to set up a safety margin of an appropriate amount;

(5) it is not possible for the *firm* to cancel the contract after the end of the third year of insurance; and

(6) the contract provides for the possibility of increasing *premiums* or reducing payments even for current contracts.

Enhanced capital requirement for general insurance business

1.1.72A **[G]** This section sets out the requirement for *firms* carrying on *general insurance business*, other than *non-directive insurers*, to calculate their *ECR*. The *ECR* for *firms* carrying on *general insurance business* is an indicative measure of the *capital resources* that a *firm* may need to hold based on risk sensitive calculations applied to its business profile. For *firms* carrying on *general insurance business*, the *FSA* will use the *ECR* as a benchmark for its consideration of the appropriateness of the *firm's* own capital assessment. For *firms* where an *ECR* is not calculated, the *MCR* will provide a benchmark for the *firm's* own capital assessment.

1.1.72B **[R]** A *firm* carrying on *general insurance business*, other than a *non-directive insurer*, must calculate the amount of its *ECR*.

1.1.72C **[R]** A *firm* to which INSPRU 1.1.72BR applies must calculate its *ECR* in respect of its *general insurance business* as the sum of:

(1) the *asset-related capital requirement*; and

(2) the *insurance-related capital requirement*; less

(3) the *firm's equalisation provisions*.

1.1.72D **[G]** Details of the calculation of the *asset-related capital requirement* are set out in INSPRU 2.2.10R to INSPRU 2.2.16R. Details of the calculation of the *insurance-related capital requirement* are set out in INSPRU 1.1.76R to INSPRU 1.1.79R.

Insurance-related capital requirement

1.1.73 [Intentionally blank]

1.1.74 **[G]** The *insurance-related capital requirement* is a measure of the capital that a *firm* should hold against the risk of:
(1) an adverse movement in the value of a *firm's* liabilities, to recognise that there may be substantial volatility in *claims* and other *technical provisions* made by the *firm*. Such variations may be due to inflationary increases, interest rate changes, movements in the underlying provisions themselves, changes in expense costs, inadequate rate pricing or *premium* collections (or both) from intermediaries differing from projected assumptions; and
(2) the *premiums* a *firm* charges in respect of particular business not being adequate to fund future liabilities arising from that business.

1.1.75 **[G]** The *insurance-related capital requirement* is calculated by applying capital charge factors, expressed as a percentage, to the value of the *net written premiums* and the *technical provisions* in respect of different classes of business. *Firms* should refer to GENPRU 1.3.4R which sets out how a *firm* must recognise and value assets and liabilities.

Calculation of the insurance-related capital requirement

1.1.76 **[R]** A *firm* must calculate its *insurance-related capital requirement* in accordance with INSPRU 1.1.77R.

1.1.77 **[R]**
(1) The value of:
(a) the *net written premiums*; and
(b) the *technical provisions*;
in respect of each class of business listed in the table in INSPRU 1.1.79R must be multiplied by the corresponding capital charge factor.
(2) If any amount which is to be multiplied by a capital charge factor is a negative amount, that amount shall be treated as zero.
(3) The amounts resulting from multiplying the *net written premiums* in respect of each such class of business by the corresponding capital charge factor must be aggregated.
(4) The amounts resulting from multiplying the *technical provisions* in respect of each such class of business by the corresponding capital charge factor must be aggregated.
(5) The *insurance-related capital requirement* is the sum of the amounts calculated in accordance with (3) and (4).

1.1.78 **[R]** In INSPRU 1.1.77R references to *technical provisions* comprise:
(1) outstanding *claims*;
(2) provisions for incurred but not reported (*IBNR*) *claims*;
(3) provisions for incurred but not enough reported (IBNER) *claims*;
(4) *unearned premium* reserves less *deferred acquisition costs*; and
(5) unexpired risk reserves;

in each case net of *reinsurance* receivables.

1.1.79 **[R]** Table: Insurance-related Capital Charge Factors

Class of Business	**Net Written Premium capital charge factor**	**Technical provision capital charge factor**
Reporting Group: Direct and facultative business		
Direct and facultative accident and health	5.0%	7.5%
Direct and facultative personal lines motor business	10.0%	9.0%
Direct and facultative household and domestic all risks	10.0%	10.0%
Direct and facultative personal lines financial loss	25.0%	14.0%
Direct and facultative commercial motor business	10.0%	9.0%
Direct and facultative commercial lines property	10.0%	10.0%
Direct and facultative commercial lines liability	14.0%	14.0%
Direct and facultative commercial lines financial loss	25.0%	14.0%

Part II FSA Handbook Materials

Class of Business	Net Written Premium capital charge factor	Technical provision capital charge factor
Direct and facultative aviation	32.0%	14.0%
Direct and facultative marine	22.0%	17.0%
Direct and facultative goods in transit	12.0%	14.0%
Direct and facultative miscellaneous	25.0%	14.0%
Reporting Group: Non-Proportional Treaty		
Non-proportional accident & health	35.0%	16.0%
Non-proportional motor	10.0%	14.0%
Non-proportional transport	16.0%	15.0%
Non-proportional aviation	61.0%	16.0%
Non-proportional marine	38.0%	17.0%
Non-proportional property	53.0%	12.0%
Non-proportional liability (non-motor)	14.0%	14.0%
Non-proportional financial lines	39.0%	14.0%
Non-proportional aggregate cover	53.0%	12.0%
Reporting Group: Proportional Treaty		
Proportional accident & health	12.0%	16.0%
Proportional motor	10.0%	12.0%
Proportional transport	12.0%	15.0%
Proportional aviation	33.0%	16.0%
Proportional marine	22.0%	17.0%
Proportional property	23.0%	12.0%
Proportional liability (non-motor)	14.0%	14.0%
Proportional financial lines	25.0%	14.0%
Proportional aggregate cover	23.0%	12.0%
Reporting Group: Miscellaneous Reinsurance		
Miscellaneous reinsurance accepted business	39.0%	14.0%

Long-term insurance capital requirement

1.1.80 **[G]** GENPRU 2.1.13R requires an *insurer* to maintain *capital resources* equal to or in excess of its *capital resources requirement*. GENPRU 2.1.18R defines the *capital resources requirement* for a *firm* to which that *rule* applies (a *realistic basis life firm*) as the higher of the *MCR* and the *ECR*. For other *firms* carrying on *long-term insurance business* (*regulatory basis only life firms*), the *capital resources requirement* is equal to the *MCR*. Except where the *base capital resources requirement* is the higher requirement, the *MCR* in respect of *long-term insurance business* is the sum of the *long-term insurance capital requirement* (*LTICR*) and the *resilience capital requirement* or, in the case of a *realistic basis life firm*, the *LTICR* (see GENPRU 2.1.24AR, (see GENPRU 2.1.25R and GENPRU 2.1.26R). GENPRU 2.1.36R defines the *LTICR* as the sum of the *insurance death risk, health risk and life protection reinsurance*, *expense risk*, and *market risk capital components* (see INSPRU 1.1.81R to INSPRU 1.1.91R). *Rules* and *guidance* about the *resilience capital requirement* are set out in INSPRU 3.1.9G to INSPRU 3.1.26R.

Insurance death risk capital component

1.1.81 **[R]** The *insurance death risk capital component* is the aggregate of the amounts which represent the fractions specified by INSPRU 1.1.82R of the capital at risk, defined in INSPRU 1.1.83R, for each category of *contracts of insurance* (as specified in INSPRU 1.1.81AR), in respect of those contracts where the capital at risk is not a negative figure, multiplied by the higher of:

(1) 50%; and

(2) the ratio as at the end of the *financial year in question* of:

  (a) the aggregate capital at risk in respect of that category of contracts net of *reinsurance* cessions; to

  (b) the aggregate capital at risk in respect of that category of contracts gross of *reinsurance* cessions.

1.1.81A **[R]** For the purpose of INSPRU 1.1.81R, the categories of *contracts of insurance* are as follows:
(1) contracts which fall in *long-term insurance business classes* I, II or IX; and
(2) contracts which fall in *long-term insurance business classes* III, VII or VIII.

1.1.82 **[R]** For the purpose of INSPRU 1.1.81R, the fraction is:
(1) for *long-term insurance business classes* I, II and IX, except for a *pure reinsurer*:
  (a) 0.1% for temporary insurance on death where the original term of the contract is three years or less;
  (b) 0.15% for temporary insurance on death where the original term of the contract is five years or less but more than three years; and
  (c) 0.3% in any other case;
(2) 0.3% for *long-term insurance business classes* III, VII and VIII, except for a *pure reinsurer*; and
(3) 0.1% for a *pure reinsurer*.

1.1.83 **[R]** For the purpose of INSPRU 1.1.81R, the capital at risk is:
(1) where the benefit under a *contract of insurance* payable as a result of death includes periodic or deferred payments, the present value of the benefits payable; and
(2) in any other case, the amount payable as a result of death;

less, in either case, the *mathematical reserves* for the contract.

1.1.83A **[R]** INSPRU 1.1.81R does not apply to:
(1) a *pure reinsurer*; or
(2) a *mixed insurer*;

in respect of *life protection reinsurance business*.

1.1.84 **[G]** The *insurance death risk capital component* only relates to the risk of death. There is a separate risk component for insured health risks (*class* IV) which also applies to the risk of death covered in the *life protection reinsurance business* of *pure reinsurers* and *mixed insurers*. *Tontines* (*class* V) and *capital redemption* operations (*class* VI) also have separate risk components. There is no specified risk margin for other insured risks.

1.1.84A **[G]** For the treatment of amounts recoverable from *ISPVs* when calculating the *insurance death risk capital component* in accordance with INSPRU 1.1.81R, see INSPRU 1.1.92AR and INSPRU 1.1.92BG.

Insurance health risk and life protection reinsurance capital component

1.1.85 **[R]** The *insurance health risk and life protection reinsurance capital component* is the highest of:
(1) the *premiums amount* (determined in accordance with INSPRU 1.1.45R);
(2) the *claims amount* (determined in accordance with INSPRU 1.1.47R); and
(3) the *brought forward amount* (determined in accordance with INSPRU 1.1.51R); in respect of:
  (a) *contracts of insurance* falling in *long-term insurance business class* IV (see INSPRU 1.1.86R);
  (b) risks falling in *general insurance business classes* 1 or 2 that are written as part of a *long-term insurance contract*; and
  (c) in the case of a *pure reinsurer* or a *mixed insurer*, *life protection reinsurance business*.

1.1.86 **[R]** For the purposes of INSPRU 1.1.85R, in the case of *contracts of insurance* falling in *long-term insurance business class* IV, condition (3) as set out in INSPRU 1.1.72R (*Actuarial health insurance*) is modified to: "either the reserves include a provision for increasing age, or the business is conducted on a group basis.".

1.1.87 **[G]** The *insurance health risk and life protection reinsurance capital component* only applies to *permanent health* insurance (*long-term insurance business class* IV), *accident* and *sickness* insurance (*general insurance business classes* 1 and 2) and the *life protection reinsurance business* of *pure reinsurers* and *mixed insurers*.

Insurance expense risk capital component

1.1.88 **[R]** The *insurance expense risk capital component* is:
(1) in respect of *long-term insurance business classes* III, VII and VIII, an amount equivalent to 25% of the net *administrative expenses* in the *financial year in question* relevant to the business of each of those *classes*, in so far as the *firm* bears no investment risk and the allocation to cover *management expenses* in the *contract of insurance* does not have a fixed upper limit which is effective as a limit for a period exceeding 5 years from the commencement of the contract;
(2) in respect of any *tontine* (*long-term insurance business class* V), 1% of the assets of the *tontine*;

Part II FSA Handbook Materials

(3) in the case of any other *long-term insurance business*, 1% of the "adjusted *mathematical reserves*" (as defined in INSPRU 1.1.89AR).

1.1.88A **[R]** INSPRU 1.1.88R does not apply to:
(1) a *pure reinsurer*; or
(2) a *mixed insurer*;

in respect of:
(a) *life protection reinsurance business*; or
(b) *permanent health reinsurance business*.

Insurance market risk capital component

1.1.89 **[R]** The *insurance market risk capital component* is 3% of the "adjusted *mathematical reserves*" (as defined in INSPRU 1.1.89AR) for all insurance liabilities except those of a kind which:
(1) arise from *contracts of insurance* falling in *long-term insurance business classes* III, VII or VIII to the extent that the *firm* does not bear any investment risk; or
(2) arise from *contracts of insurance* falling in *long-term insurance business class* V; or
(3) for a *pure reinsurer* or a *mixed insurer*, arise from *contracts of insurance* falling within:
  (a) its *life protection reinsurance business*; or
  (b) its *permanent health reinsurance business*.

Adjusted mathematical reserves

1.1.89A **[R]**
(1) For the purpose of INSPRU 1.1.88R and INSPRU 1.1.89R, the "adjusted *mathematical reserves*" is the aggregate of the amounts which result from the performance of the calculation in INSPRU 1.1.90R for each category of insurance liability specified in (2).
(2) The categories of insurance liability referred to in (1) are:
  (a) for the purpose of INSPRU 1.1.88R, those categories described in INSPRU 1.1.91R (1), (2), (3), (4) and (5); and
  (b) for the purpose of INSPRU 1.1.89R, those categories described in INSPRU 1.191R (1), (2), (4) and (5).

1.1.90 **[R]** The calculation referred to in INSPRU 1.1.89AR (1) is the multiplication of the amount of the *mathematical reserves* (gross of *reinsurance* cessions) in respect of a category of insurance liability by the higher of:
(1) 85% or, in the case of a *pure reinsurer*, 50%; and
(2) the ratio as at the end of the *financial year in question* of:
  (a) the *mathematical reserves* in respect of that category of insurance liability net of *reinsurance* cessions; to
  (b) the *mathematical reserves* in respect of that category of insurance liability gross of *reinsurance* cessions.

1.1.91 **[R]** For the purpose of INSPRU 1.1.89AR and INSPRU 1.1.90R, the categories of insurance liability are as follows:
(1) liabilities of a kind which arise from *contracts of insurance* falling in *long-term insurance business classes* I, II or IX;
(2) liabilities of a kind which arise from *contracts of insurance* falling in *long-term insurance business classes* III, VII or VIII to the extent that the *firm* bears an investment risk;
(3) liabilities of a kind which arise from *contracts of insurance* falling in *long-term insurance business classes* III, VII or VIII to the extent that the *firm* bears no investment risk and where the allocation to cover *management expenses* in the *contract of insurance* has a fixed upper limit which is effective as a limit for a period exceeding 5 years from the commencement of the contract;
(4) liabilities of a kind which arise from *contracts of insurance* falling in *long-term insurance business class* IV; and
(5) liabilities of a kind which arise from *contracts of insurance* falling in *long-term insurance business class* VI.

1.1.92 **[G]** Where a *firm* has written a unit-linked contract, the *firm's* liability under the contract may consist of a unit liability, where the *firm* bears no investment risk, and other liabilities for which the firm bears an investment risk, and for which a separate reserve is held. INSPRU 1.1.91R(2) and (3) require a *firm* to analyse its liabilities under unit-linked contracts between those for which it bears an investment risk and those for which it does not. INSPRU 1.1.88R and INSPRU 1.1.89R taken together result in a capital requirement for any liabilities for which the *firm* bears an investment risk of 4% of "adjusted *mathematical reserves*" (1% for expense risk and 3% for market risk).

Insurance special purpose vehicles

1.1.92A **[R]** A *firm* must not treat any amounts recoverable from an *ISPV* as *reinsurance* for the purposes of the calculation of:

(1) the reinsurance ratio in accordance with INSPRU 1.1.54R; or
(2) the *insurance death risk capital component* in accordance with INSPRU 1.1.81R; or
(3) the "adjusted *mathematical reserves*" in accordance with INSPRU 1.1.90R.

1.1.92B **[G]** A *firm* may treat amounts recoverable from an *ISPV* as *reinsurance* for these purposes if it obtains a *waiver* of INSPRU 1.1.92AR under section 148 of the *Act*. The conditions that will need to be met, in addition to the statutory tests under section 148(4) of the *Act*, before the *FSA* will consider granting such a *waiver* are set out in INSPRU 1.6.13G to INSPRU 1.6.18G.

Application of INSPRU 1.1 to Lloyd's

1.1.93 **[R]** INSPRU 1.1 applies to the *Society* in accordance with INSPRU 8.1.2R.

1.1.94 **[R]** The following *rules* and *guidance* apply to *managing agents* in accordance with INSPRU 8.1.4R:
(1) INSPRU 1.1.12R to INSPRU 1.1.20R (except INSPRU 1.1.12R(1));
(2) INSPRU 1.1.42G to INSPRU 1.1.43G; and
(3) INSPRU 1.1.74G to INSPRU 1.1.80G.

1.1.95 **[R]** The *Society* must calculate the *brought forward amount* for the *members* in aggregate in accordance with INSPRU 1.1.51R, using the result of GENPRU 2.3.6R for the prior *financial year* and the aggregate of all *members' technical provisions* for the relevant periods.

1.1.96 **[R]** For the purposes of INSPRU 1.1.66R and further to that *rule*, in the case of Lloyd's *members*, amounts of *premiums* and *claims* must be adjusted for *approved reinsurance to close* to exclude any amount included in, or adjustment made to, *premiums* and *claims* to reflect the consideration for an *approved reinsurance to close*.

1.2 Mathematical reserves

Application

1.2.1 **[R]** INSPRU 1.2 applies to a *long-term insurer* unless it is:
(1) a *non-directive friendly society*; or
(2) an *incoming EEA firm*; or
(3) an *incoming Treaty firm*.

Purpose

1.2.2 **[G]** This section follows on from the overall requirement on *firms* to establish adequate *technical provisions* (see INSPRU 1.1.16R). The *mathematical reserves* form the main component of *technical provisions* for *long-term insurance business*. INSPRU 1.2 sets out *rules* and *guidance* as to the methods and assumptions to be used in calculating the *mathematical reserves*. The *rules* and *guidance* set out the minimum basis for *mathematical reserves*. Methods and assumptions that produce reserves that are demonstrably equal to or greater than the minimum basis may also be used, though they must meet the basic requirements for methods and assumptions set out in INSPRU 1.2.7R to INSPRU 1.2.27G.

1.2.3 **[G]** This section applies to all *firms* carrying on *long-term insurance business* and implements some of the requirements contained in article 20 of the *Consolidated Life Directive*. The implementation is designed to ensure that a *firm's mathematical reserves* in respect of *long-term insurance contracts* meet the minimum requirements set by the *Consolidated Life Directive*. A *firm* may use a prospective or a retrospective method to value its *mathematical reserves* (see INSPRU 1.2.7R).

1.2.4 **[G]** The required procedures are summarised in the flowchart in INSPRU 1 Annex 1G.

1.2.5 **[G]** *Firms* to which GENPRU 2.1.18R applies are required to calculate a *with- profits insurance capital component* (see GENPRU 2.1.38R). In order to calculate its *with-profits insurance capital component*, such a *firm* is required to carry out additional calculations of its liabilities on a realistic basis (see INSPRU 1.3), which it is required to report to the *FSA* (see Forms 18,19). A *firm* that reports its liabilities on a realistic basis is referred to in GENPRU and INSPRU as a *realistic basis life firm*. Such *firms* are subject to different *rules* relating to the calculation of *mathematical reserves* (see INSPRU 1.2.46R and INSPRU 1.2.76R) compared with those that apply to *firms* that report on a regulatory basis only (*regulatory basis only life firms*).

1.2.6 **[G]** A number of the *rules* in this section require a *firm* to take into account its regulatory duty to treat *customers* fairly. In this section, references to such a duty are to a *firm's* duty to pay due regard to the interests of its *customers* and to treat them fairly (see *Principle* 6 in *PRIN*). This duty is owed to both *policyholders* and potential *policyholders*.

Basic valuation method

1.2.7 **[R]**
(1) Subject to (2), a *firm* must establish its *mathematical reserves* using a prospective actuarial valuation on prudent assumptions of all future cash flows expected to arise under, or in respect of, each of its *long-term insurance contracts*.
(2) But a *firm* may use a retrospective actuarial valuation where:
(a) a prospective method cannot be applied to a particular type of contract; or
(b) the *firm* can demonstrate that the resulting amount of the *mathematical reserves* would be no lower than would be required by a prudent prospective actuarial valuation.

1.2.8 **[G]** A prospective valuation sets the *mathematical reserves* at the present value of future net cash flows. A retrospective method typically sets the *mathematical reserves* at the level of *premiums* received (and accumulated with investment return), less *claims* and expenses paid. A prospective valuation is preferred because it takes account of circumstances that might have arisen since the *premium* rate was set and of changes in the perception of future experience. Circumstances in which a retrospective valuation might be appropriate include:
(1) where the assumptions initially made in determining the *premium* rate were sufficiently prudent at inception and have not been overtaken by subsequent events; and
(2) where the liability depends on the emerging experience.

1.2.9 **[R]** Except in INSPRU 1.2.71R(1), INSPRU 1.2 does not apply to *final bonuses*. In addition, for *realistic basis life firms* only, INSPRU 1.2 does not apply to other discretionary benefits, including future *annual bonuses*.

Methods and assumptions

1.2.10 **[R]** In the actuarial valuation under INSPRU 1.2.7R, a *firm* must use methods and prudent assumptions which:
(1) are appropriate to the business of the *firm*;
(2) are consistent from year to year without arbitrary changes (see INSPRU 1.2.11G);
(3) are consistent with the method of valuing assets (see GENPRU 1.3);
(4) include appropriate margins for adverse deviation of relevant factors (see INSPRU 1.2.12G);
(5) recognise the distribution of profits (that is, emerging surplus) in an appropriate way over the duration of each *contract of insurance*;
(6) take into account its regulatory duty to treat its *customers* fairly (see *Principle* 6); and
(7) are in accordance with generally accepted actuarial practice.

1.2.11 **[G]** INSPRU 1.2.10R(2) prohibits only arbitrary changes in methods and assumptions, that is, changes made without adequate reasons. Any such changes would hinder comparisons over time as to the amount of the *mathematical reserves* and so obscure trends in solvency and the emergence of surplus.

1.2.12 **[G]** The relevant factors referred to in INSPRU 1.2.10R(4) may include, but are not limited to, factors such as future investment returns, expenses, mortality, morbidity, options, persistency and *reinsurance* (see also INSPRU 1.2.13R to INSPRU 1.2.19G).

Margins for adverse deviation

1.2.13 **[R]** The appropriate margins for adverse deviation required by INSPRU 1.2.10R(4) must be sufficiently prudent to ensure that there is no significant foreseeable risk that liabilities to *policyholders* in respect of *long-term insurance contracts* will not be met as they fall due.

1.2.14 **[G]** The margins for adverse deviation are a prudential margin in respect of the risks that arise under a *long-term insurance contract*.

1.2.15 **[G]** INSPRU 1.2.13R sets the normal standard of prudence required for margins. INSPRU 1.2.16G suggests benchmarks against which a *firm* should compare the margins it has set in accordance with INSPRU 1.2.10R(4) and INSPRU 1.2.13R. INSPRU 1.2.17G gives *guidance* where a market risk premium is not readily obtainable.

1.2.16 **[G]** When setting the margins for adverse deviation required by INSPRU 1.2.10R(4) in relation to a particular contract, a *firm* should consider, where appropriate:
(1) the margin for adverse deviation included in the *premium* for similar *long-term insurance contracts*, if any, newly issued by the *firm*; and
(2) where a sufficiently developed and diversified market for transferring a risk exists, the risk premium that would be required by an unconnected party to assume the risk in respect of the contract.

The margin for adverse deviation of a risk should generally be greater than or equal to the relevant market price for that risk.

1.2.17 **[G]** Where a risk premium is not readily available, or cannot be determined, an external proxy for the risk should be used, such as adjusted industry mortality tables. Where there is a considerable range of possible outcomes, the *FSA* expects *firms* to use stochastic techniques to evaluate these risks. In time, for example, longevity risk, where this constitutes a significant risk for the *firm*, may fall into this category.

1.2.18 **[G]** The margins for adverse deviation should be recognised as profit only as the *firm* itself is released from risk over the duration of the contract.

1.2.19 **[G]** Further detailed *rules* and *guidance* on margins for adverse deviation are included in INSPRU 1.2.32G to INSPRU 1.2.89G. In particular, the cross- references for the different assumptions used in calculating the *mathematical reserves* are as follows:
(1) expenses (INSPRU 1.2.50R to INSPRU 1.2.58G);
(2) mortality and morbidity (INSPRU 1.2.59R to INSPRU 1.2.61G);
(3) options (INSPRU 1.2.62R to INSPRU 1.2.72G);
(4) persistency (INSPRU **1.2.76R** and INSPRU 1.2.77G); and
(5) *reinsurance* (INSPRU 1.2.77AR to INSPRU 1.2.89G).

The *rules* and *guidance* on margins for adverse deviation in respect of future investment returns, which are also required in the calculation of *mathematical reserves*, are set out in INSPRU 3.1.28R to INSPRU 3.1.48G.

Record keeping

1.2.20 **[R]** A *firm* must make, and retain for an appropriate period, a record of:
(1) the methods and assumptions used in establishing its *mathematical reserves*, including the margins for adverse deviation, and the reasons for their use; and
(2) the nature of, reasons for, and effect of, any change in approach, including the amount by which the change in approach increases or decreases its *mathematical reserves*.

1.2.21 **[G]** SYSC 14.1.53R requires *firms* to maintain accounting and other records for a minimum of three years, or longer as appropriate. For the purposes of INSPRU 1.2.20R, a period of longer than three years will be appropriate for a *firm's long-term insurance business*. In determining an appropriate period, a *firm* should have regard to:
(1) the detailed *rules* and *guidance* on record keeping in SYSC 14.1.51G-SYSC 14.1.64G;
(2) the nature and term of the *firm's long-term insurance business*; and
(3) any additional provisions or statutory requirements applicable to the *firm* or its records.

Valuation of individual contracts

1.2.22 **[R]**
(1) Subject to (2) and (3), a *firm* must determine the amount of the *mathematical reserves* separately for each *long-term insurance contract*.
(2) Approximations or generalisations may be made:
  (a) in the case of non-attributable expenses, in relation to a group of contracts with the same or similar expense risk characteristics, provided that the *mathematical reserves* in respect of such expenses established by the *firm* in relation to that group of contracts have a minimum value of at least zero; and
  (b) in any other case, where they are likely to provide the same, or a higher, result than a determination made in accordance with (1).
(3) A *firm* must set up additional *mathematical reserves* on an aggregated basis for general risks that are not specific to individual contracts.
(4) For the purpose of (2), non-attributable expenses are expenses which are not directly attributable to a particular *long-term insurance contract*.

1.2.23 **[G]** INSPRU 1.2.22R to INSPRU 1.2.89G set out *rules* and *guidance* for the separate prospective valuation of each contract. These may be applied instead to groups of contracts where the conditions set out in INSPRU 1.2.22R(2)(a) or (b) are satisfied. Guidance on non-attributable expenses and the application of INSPRU 1.2.22R(2)(a) is provided in INSPRU 1.2.54AG.

Negative mathematical reserves

1.2.24 **[R]** A *firm* may calculate a negative value for the *mathematical reserves* in respect of a *long-term insurance contract* provided that:
(1) this is based on assumptions which meet the general requirements for prudent assumptions as set out in INSPRU 1.2.10R and INSPRU 1.2.13R;
(2) the contract does not have a *surrender value* which at the *actuarial valuation date* is guaranteed; and
(3) the total *mathematical reserves* established by the *firm* have a minimum value of at least:
  (i) where the *firm's long-term insurance contracts* include *linked long-term* contracts, the sum of the *surrender values* of all its *linked long-term* contracts at the *actuarial valuation date*; and
  (ii) in any other case, zero.

1.2.25 **[G]**
(1) A separate prospective valuation for each contract may identify contracts for which the value of future cash inflows under and in respect of the contract exceeds that of outflows. In these circumstances, the *firm* may calculate the *mathematical reserves* for that contract as having a negative value and treat that value as available to off-set *mathematical reserves* for other contracts which have a positive value when establishing the overall *mathematical reserves*.
(2) In complying with INSPRU 1.1.34R or INSPRU 3.1.61AR, as applicable, with respect to the matching of assets and liabilities, *insurers* should consider the suitability for offset of contracts whose *mathematical reserves* are negative against liabilities on other contracts and only offset them if it is prudent to do so. While INSPRU 1.2.24R applies at a *firm* level, it may be relevant when assessing the prudence of the offset of contracts whose mathematical reserves are negative to consider the fact that contracts with negative *mathematical reserves* written outside a *with-profits fund* are not, for the purpose of INSPRU 1.1.27R, permitted to be offset against contracts with positive *mathematical reserves* written within that *with-profits fund*.

1.2.25A **[G]** In addition, the *Consolidated Life Directive* requires that no contract should be valued at less than its guaranteed *surrender value* (see INSPRU 1.2.62AG). As a result, no contract with a guaranteed *surrender value* to which the *Consolidated Life Directive* applies should be valued as if it were an asset. Although the *Reinsurance Directive* does not require this treatment of contracts with guaranteed *surrender values* to be applied to *pure reinsurers*, the *FSA's* policy is that there should be equal treatment in this respect. INSPRU 1.2.62R makes further provision relating to the *mathematical reserves* to be established in respect of such contracts. When considering the impact that the amount payable on surrender may have on the valuation of a contract, a *firm* should have regard to INSPRU 1.2.71R.

Avoidance of future valuation strain

1.2.26 **[R]**
(1) A *firm* must establish *mathematical reserves* for a *contract of insurance* which are sufficient to ensure that, at any subsequent date, the *mathematical reserves* then required are covered solely by:
  (a) the assets covering the current *mathematical reserves*; and
  (b) the resources arising from those assets and from the contract itself.
(2) For the purposes of (1), the *firm* must assume that:
  (a) the assumptions adopted for the current valuation of liabilities remain unaltered and are met; and
  (b) discretionary benefits and charges will be set so as to fulfil its regulatory duty to treat its *customers* fairly.
(3) Subject to (4), (1) may be applied to a group of similar contracts instead of to the individual contracts within that group.
(4) (1) must be applied to a group of contracts in relation to which *mathematical reserves* in respect of non-attributable expenses are established for that group of contracts in accordance with INSPRU 1.2.22R(2)(a), instead of to the individual contracts within that group.

1.2.27 **[G]** The valuation of each contract, or group of similar contracts, should allow for the possibility, where it exists, that contracts may be surrendered (wholly or in part), lapsed or made paid-up at any time. The valuation assumptions include margins for adverse deviation (see INSPRU 1.2.13R). INSPRU 1.2.26R requires *mathematical reserves* to be established such that, if future experience is in line with the valuation assumptions, there would be no future valuation strain.

Cash flows to be valued

1.2.28 **[R]** In a prospective valuation, a *firm* must:
(1) include in the cash flows to be valued the following:
  (a) future *premiums* (see INSPRU 1.2.35G to INSPRU 1.2.47G);
  (b) expenses, including *commissions* (see INSPRU 1.2.50R to INSPRU 1.2.58G);
  (c) benefits payable (see INSPRU 1.2.29R); and
  (d) subject to (2), amounts to be received or paid in respect of the *long-term insurance contracts* under contracts of *reinsurance* or analogous non- *reinsurance* financing agreements (see INSPRU 1.2.77AR to INSPRU 1.2.89G); but
(2) exclude from those cash flows amounts recoverable from an *ISPV*.

1.2.28A **[G]** A *firm* may include amounts recoverable from an *ISPV* in the cash flows to be valued in a prospective valuation if it obtains a *waiver* of INSPRU 1.2.28R under section 148 of the *Act*. The conditions that will need to be met, in addition to the statutory tests under section 148(4) of the *Act*, before the *FSA* will consider granting such a *waiver* are set out in INSPRU 1.6.13G to INSPRU 1.6.18G.

1.2.29 **[R]** For the purpose of INSPRU 1.2.28R(1)(c), benefits payable include:
(1) all guaranteed benefits including guaranteed *surrender values* and paid- up values;

(2) vested, declared and allotted bonuses to which the *policyholder* is entitled;
(3) all options available to the *policyholder* under the terms of the contract; and
(4) discretionary benefits payable in accordance with the *firm's* regulatory duty to treat its *customers* fairly.

1.2.30 **[G]** All cash flows are to be valued using prudent assumptions in accordance with generally accepted actuarial practice. Cash flows may be omitted from the valuation calculations provided the reserves obtained as a result of leaving those cash flows out of the calculation are not less than would have resulted had all cash flows been included (see INSPRU 1.2.22R(2)(b)). Provision for future expenses in respect of *with-profits insurance contracts* (excluding *accumulating with-profits policies*) may be made implicitly, using the *net premium* method of valuation (see INSPRU 1.2.43R below). For the purposes of INSPRU 1.2.28R(1)(b), any charges included in expenses should be determined in accordance with the *firm's* regulatory duty to treat its *customers* fairly.

1.2.31 **[G]** INSPRU 1.2.29R(4) requires *regulatory basis only life firms* to make allowance for any future *annual bonus* that a *firm* would expect to grant, assuming future experience is in line with the assumptions used in the calculation of the *mathematical reserves*. *Final bonuses* do not have to be taken into consideration in these calculations except in relation to *accumulating with-profits policies* (see INSPRU 1.2.9R). The calculations required for *accumulating with-profits policies* are set out in INSPRU 1.2.71R(1). For *realistic basis life firms*, except for *accumulating with- profits policies*, the *mathematical reserves* may be calculated without taking into account discretionary benefits, including both *annual bonuses* and *final bonuses*. For such *firms* full allowance for discretionary benefits is made in the calculation of the *realistic value of liabilities* (see INSPRU 1.3.105R(5)).

Part II FSA Handbook Materials

Valuation assumptions: detailed rules and guidance

1.2.32 **[G]** More detailed *rules* and *guidance* about the valuation of cash flows are set out in INSPRU 1.2.33R to INSPRU 1.2.89G.

Valuation rates of interest

1.2.33 **[R]** In calculating the present value of future net cash flows, a *firm* must determine the rates of interest to be used in accordance with INSPRU 3.1.28R to INSPRU 3.1.47R.

1.2.34 **[G]** The *rules* in INSPRU 3.1.28R to INSPRU 3.1.47R set out the approach *firms* must take in setting margins for adverse deviation in the interest rates assumed in calculating the *mathematical reserves*. This includes a margin to allow for adverse deviation in *market risk* and, where relevant, credit risk. The requirements set out in INSPRU 3.1.28R to INSPRU 3.1.47R protect against the *market risk* that the return actually achieved on assets may fall below the market yields on assets at the *actuarial valuation date*.

Future premiums

1.2.35 **[G]** INSPRU 1.2.46R and INSPRU 1.2.47G apply to the valuation of *with-profits insurance liabilities* for a *realistic basis life firm*. INSPRU 1.2.38R to INSPRU 1.2.45G apply to a *regulatory basis only life firm*.

1.2.36 **[G]** For *non-profit insurance contracts* no specific method of valuation for future *premiums* is required by INSPRU. However, the method of valuation used should be sufficiently prudent taking into account, in particular, the risk of voluntary discontinuance by the *policyholder*.

Future premiums: firms reporting only on a regulatory basis

1.2.37 **[R]** INSPRU 1.2.38R to INSPRU 1.2.43R apply to a *regulatory basis only life firm*.

1.2.38 **[R]**
(1) This *rule* applies to with-profits insurance contracts except accumulating with-profits policies written on a recurring single premium basis.
(2) The value attributed to a *premium* due in any future *financial year* (a future *premium*) must not exceed the lower of the value of:
  (a) the actual *premium* payable under the contract; and
  (b) the *net premium*.
(3) The *net premium* may be increased for *deferred acquisition costs* in accordance with INSPRU 1.2.43R.

1.2.39 **[G]** The valuation method for future *premiums* in INSPRU 1.2.38R retains the difference, if any, between the gross *premium* and the *net premium* as an implicit margin available to finance future bonuses, expenses and other costs. It thus helps to protect against the risk that adequate resources may not be available in the future to meet those costs. Where expenses are not directly attributable to a particular contract, a *firm* may establish *mathematical reserves* in respect of such expenses in relation to a group of contracts with the same or similar expense risk characteristics in accordance with INSPRU 1.2.22R(2)(a).

1.2.40 **[R]** Where the terms of a *contract of insurance* have changed since it was first entered into, a *firm* must apply one of the methods in INSPRU 1.2.41R in determining the *net premium* for the purpose of INSPRU 1.2.38R(2)(b).

1.2.41 **[R]** A *firm* must treat the change referred to in INSPRU 1.2.40R as if either:

(1) it had been included in the original contract but came into effect from the time the change became effective; or

(2) the original contract were cancelled and replaced by a new contract (with an initial *premium* paid on the new contract equal to the liability under the original contract immediately prior to the change); or

(3) it gave rise to two separate contracts where:

   (a) all *premiums* are payable under the first contract and that contract provides only for such benefits as those *premiums* could have purchased from the *firm* at the date the change became effective; and

   (b) no *premiums* are payable under the second contract and that contract provides for all the other benefits.

1.2.42 **[G]** INSPRU 1.2.41R permits three alternative methods. However, the third method is only possible where a meaningful comparison can be made between the terms of the contract (as changed) and the terms upon which the *firm* was *effecting* its new *contracts of insurance* at the time the contract was changed.

Future net premiums: adjustment for deferred acquisition costs

1.2.43 **[R]**

(1) The amount of any increase to the *net premium* for *deferred acquisition costs* must not exceed the equivalent of the recoverable acquisition expenses spread over the period of *premium* payments and calculated in accordance with the rates of interest, mortality and morbidity assumed in calculating the *mathematical reserves*.

(2) For the purpose of (1), recoverable acquisition expenses means the amount of expenses, after allowing for the effects of taxation, which it is reasonable to expect will be recovered from future *premiums* payable under the contract.

(3) The recoverable acquisition expenses in (1) must not exceed the lower of:

   (a) the value of the excess of actual *premiums* over *net premiums*; and

   (b) 3.5% of the *relevant capital sum*.

(4) Recoverable acquisition expenses may be calculated as the average for a group of similar contracts weighted by the *relevant capital sum* for each contract.

1.2.44 **[G]** INSPRU 1.2.43R allows a *firm* to spread acquisition costs over the lifetime of a *contract of insurance*, but only if it is reasonable to expect those costs to be recoverable from future *premium* income from that contract. Further prudence is provided by the limitation of recoverable acquisition expenses to 3.5% of the *relevant capital sum*. This adjustment for acquisition costs is sometimes termed a Zillmer adjustment.

1.2.45 **[G]** In determining the extent, if any, to which it is reasonable to expect acquisition costs to be recoverable from future *premium* income, the *firm* should make prudent assumptions as to levels of voluntary discontinuance by *policyholders*.

Future premiums: firms also reporting with-profits insurance liabilities on a realistic basis

1.2.46 **[R]**

(1) Subject to (2), for a *realistic basis life firm*, the future *premiums* to be valued in the calculation of the *mathematical reserves* for its *with-profits insurance contracts* must not be greater than the gross *premiums* payable by the *policyholder*.

(2) This *rule* does not apply to *accumulating with-profits policies* written on a recurring single *premium* basis (see INSPRU 1.2.48R).

1.2.47 **[G]** The gross *premium* is the full amount of *premium* payable by the *policyholder* to the *firm*. The gross *premium* method contrasts with the *net premium* method which is required from *regulatory basis only life firms* (see INSPRU 1.2.37R to INSPRU 1.2.45G).

Future premiums: accumulating with-profits policies

1.2.48 **[R]**

(1) This *rule* applies to *accumulating with-profits policies* written on a recurring single *premium* basis.

(2) A *firm* must not attribute any value to a future *premium* under the contract.

(3) Any liability arising only upon the payment of that *premium* may be ignored except to the extent that the value of that liability upon payment would exceed the amount of that *premium*.

1.2.49 **[G]** INSPRU 1.2.48R prohibits a *firm* from taking credit for recurring single *premiums* under *accumulating with-profits policies*. As there is no contractual commitment to pay any future *premiums* the amount and timing of which are uncertain, the recognition of any potential margins would not be prudent. Where the payment of a future *premium* would give rise to a liability in excess of the *premium* a provision should be established.

Expenses

1.2.50 **[R]**

(1) A *firm* must make provision for expenses, either implicitly or explicitly, in its *mathematical reserves* of an amount which is not less than the amount expected, on prudent assumptions, to be incurred in fulfilling its *long-term insurance contracts*.

(2) For the purpose of (1), expenses must be valued:
  (a) after taking account of the effect of taxation;
  (b) having regard to the *firm's* actual expenses in the last 12 months before the *actuarial valuation date* and any increases in expenses expected to occur in the future;
  (c) after making prudent assumptions as to the effects of inflation on future increases in prices and earnings; and
  (d) at no less than the level that would be incurred if the *firm* were to cease to transact new business 12 months after the *actuarial valuation date*.

(3) A *firm* must not rely upon an implicit provision arising from the method of valuing future *premiums* except to the extent that:
  (a) it is reasonable to assume that expenses will be recoverable from future *premiums*; and
  (b) the expenses would only arise if the future *premiums* were received.

1.2.51 **[G]** For *with-profits insurance contracts* where the *net premium* valuation method applies, an implicit provision arises because the future *premiums* valued are limited to the *net premium* adjusted as permitted by INSPRU 1.2.43R. This excludes the allowance within the gross *premium* for expenses (other than recoverable acquisition expenses). It also excludes other margins within the actual *premium* that are a prudential margin in respect of the risks that arise under the contract or that are needed to provide for future discretionary benefits. To the extent that these other margins are not needed for the purpose for which they were originally established, they may also constitute an implicit provision for expenses.

1.2.52 **[G]** An implicit provision may also arise for other types of *long-term insurance contract* where, for example, no value is attributed to future *premiums*, but the *firm* is entitled to make deductions from future regular *premiums* before allocating them to secure *policyholder* benefits.

1.2.53 **[G]** A *firm* should only reduce the provision for future expenses to take account of expected taxation recoveries related to those expenses where recovery is reasonably certain, and after taking into account the assumption that the *firm* ceases to transact new business 12 months after the *actuarial valuation date*. An appropriate adjustment for discounting should be made where receipt of the taxation recoveries is not expected until significantly after the expenses are incurred.

1.2.54 **[G]** The *firm's* actual expenses in the 12 months prior to the *actuarial valuation date* may serve as a guide to the assumptions for future expenses, taking into consideration the mix of acquisition and renewal expenses. The expense assumptions should not be reduced to account for expected future improvements in efficiency until such efficiency improvements result in a reduced level of actual expenditure. However, the assumptions should take account of all factors which might increase costs including earnings and price inflation.

1.2.54A **[G]**

(1) A *firm* should attribute to an individual contract at least those expenses which are directly attributable to that contract including expenses which vary with the volume of business for that type of contract. Commission payments, charges to a fund on a 'per policy' basis and investment management fees are generally directly attributable. For expenses of the fund which are calculated directly based on actual expenses (and not calculated in accordance with a management services agreement), the attributable expenses will also include those costs which vary with the volume of business for that product, for example, salaries and accommodation costs of staff in a processing centre, printing and postage of communications to *policyholders* and associated computer services.

(2) Non-attributable expenses may include overheads which are relatively insensitive to the volume of business for the type of contract in question and an apportionment of group overheads. Examples of expenses that *firms* may consider non-attributable include salaries of head office staff involved in monitoring products and drafting standard communications to *policyholders* and allocated overheads for centralised functions such as human resources, finance and IT. Where non-attributable expenses arise in relation to a homogeneous risk group of contracts sharing the same or similar expense risk characteristics, a *firm* may determine the reserve for those expenses at the level of that risk group, provided that the reserve so established has a minimum value of at least zero (see INSPRU 1.2.22R(2)(a)). In identifying its homogeneous risk groups, a *firm* should consider all risks that impact on the level of expenses borne by contracts including persistency risk and expense inflation risk. For

example, business that is subject to bulk lapse risk, such as any large group contract that would give rise to a reduction in surplus on lapse, should be considered as forming a homogeneous risk group of its own. A *firm* must document and justify its approach to identifying homogeneous risk groups in accordance with the record-keeping requirements of INSPRU 1.2.20R. This approach to reserving for expenses ensures that prudent reserves are established in respect of both directly attributable and non-attributable expenses arising in relation to the *firm's long-term insurance business*.

1.2.54B **[G]** In valuing cash flows in respect of *commissions*, a *firm* may wish to take into account any contractual arrangements for the "clawback" or repayment of *commissions* already paid in the event of voluntary discontinuance of a *contract of insurance*. In deciding how to treat such arrangements in determining the *mathematical reserves* for a *contract of insurance*, the *firm* must use assumptions which meet the general requirements for prudent assumptions as set out in INSPRU 1.2.10R and INSPRU 1.2.13R. For example, the *firm* should establish prudent margins for adverse deviation in respect of the credit risk of the intermediary by whom the *commission* would be repayable.

1.2.55 **[R]** The provisions for expenses (whether implicit or explicit) required by INSPRU 1.2.50R must be sufficient to cover all the expenses of running off the *firm's* existing *long-term insurance business* including:

(1) all discontinuance costs (for example, redundancy costs and closure costs) that would arise if the *firm* were to cease transacting new business 12 months after the *actuarial valuation date* in circumstances where (and to the extent that) the discontinuance costs exceed the projected surplus available to meet such costs;

(2) all costs of continuing to service the existing business taking into account the loss of economies of scale from, and any other likely consequences of, ceasing to transact new business at that time; and

(3) the lower of:

 (a) any projected valuation strain from writing new business for the 12 months following the *actuarial valuation date* to the extent the actual amount of that strain exceeds the projected surplus on prudent assumptions from existing business in the 12 months following the *actuarial valuation date*; and

 (b) any projected new business expense overrun from writing new business for the 12 months following the *actuarial valuation date* to the extent the projected expenses exceed the expenses that the new business can support on a prudent basis.

1.2.56 **[G]** The provision for future expenses, whether implicit or explicit, should include a prudent margin for adverse deviation in the level and timing of expenses (see INSPRU 1.2.13R to INSPRU 1.2.19G). The margin should cover the risk of underestimating expenses whether due to, for example, initial under-calculation or subsequent increases in the amount of expenses. In setting the amount of the margin, the *firm* should take into account the extent to which:

(1) an appropriately validated method based on reliable data is used to allocate expenses as between attributable and non-attributable expenses or between acquisition and non-acquisition expenses and by product type, by distribution channel or by homogeneous risk group, as appropriate;

(2) the volume of existing and new business and its distribution by product type or distribution channel is stable or predictable;

(3) costs vary in the short, medium or long term dependent upon the volume of existing or new business and its distribution by product type or distribution channel; and

(4) cost control is well-managed.

1.2.57 **[G]** In setting the margin, the *firm* should also take into account:

(1) the length of the period over which it is necessary to project costs;

(2) the extent to which it is reasonable to expect inflation to be stable or predictable over that period; and

(3) whether, if inflation is higher than expected, it is reasonable to expect that the excess would be offset by increases in investment returns.

1.2.58 **[G]** Where a *firm* has entered into an agreement with any other person for the sharing or reimbursement of costs, in setting the margin it should take into account the potential impact of that agreement and of its discontinuance.

Mortality and Morbidity

*1.2.59 **[R]** A firm must set the* assumptions for mortality and morbidity using prudent rates of mortality and morbidity that are appropriate to the country or territory of residence of the person whose life or health is insured.

1.2.60 **[G]** The rates of mortality or morbidity should contain prudent margins for adverse deviation (see INSPRU 1.2.13R to INSPRU 1.2.19G). In setting those rates, a *firm* should take account of:

(1) the systems and controls applied in underwriting *long-term insurance contracts* and whether they provide adequate protection against anti- selection (that is, selection against the *firm*) including:
   (a) adequately defining and identifying non-standard risks; and
   (b) where such risks are underwritten, allocating to them an appropriate weighting;
(2) the nature of the contractual exposure to mortality or morbidity risk including:
   (a) whether lower mortality increases or decreases the *firm's* liability;
   (b) the period of cover and whether risk charges can be varied during that period and, if so, how quickly; and
   (c) whether the options in the contract give rise to a significant risk of anti- selection (for example, opportunities for voluntary discontinuance, guaranteed renewal at the option of the *policyholder* and rights for conversion of benefits);
(3) the credibility of the *firm's* actual experience as a basis for projecting future experience including:
   (a) whether there is sufficient data (especially for medical or financial risks and for new types of benefit or new methods of distribution); and
   (b) whether the data is reliable and has been appropriately validated;
(4) the availability and reliability of:
   (a) any published tables of mortality or morbidity for the country or territory of residence of the person whose life or health is insured; and
   (b) any other information as to the industry-wide insurance experience for that country or territory;
(5) anticipated or possible future trends in experience including, but only where they increase the liability:
   (a) anticipated improvements in mortality;
   (b) changes arising from improved detection of morbidity (including critical illnesses);
   (c) diseases the impact of which may not yet be reflected fully in current experience; and
   (d) changes in market segmentation (such as impaired life annuities) which, in the light of developing experience, may require different assumptions for different parts of the policy class.

1.2.61 **[G]** An additional provision for diseases covered by INSPRU 1.2.60G(5)(c) may be needed, in particular for unit-linked policies. In determining whether such a provision is needed a *firm* may take into consideration any ability to increase product charges commensurately (provided that such increase does not infringe on its regulatory duty to treat its *customers* fairly), but a provision would still be required for the period until such an increase could be brought into effect.

Options

1.2.62 **[R]** When a *firm* establishes its *mathematical reserves* in respect of a *long-term insurance contract*, the *firm* must include an amount to cover any increase in liabilities which might be the direct result of its *policyholder* exercising an option under, or by virtue of, that *contract of insurance*. Where the *surrender value* of a contract is guaranteed, the amount of the *mathematical reserves* for that contract at any time must be at least as great as the value guaranteed at that time.

1.2.62A **[G]** A contract has a guaranteed *surrender value* where the *policy* wording states that a *surrender value* is payable and either provides for a minimum amount payable on surrender or sets out a method for calculating such an amount. For example, where a unit-linked contract provides for a *surrender value* equal to the value of the units allocated to the contract, the *firm* must establish *mathematical reserves* for that contract greater than or equal to the value of the units allocated at the valuation date.

1.2.63 **[G]** An option exists where a *policyholder* is given a choice between alternative forms of benefit, for example, a choice between receiving a cash benefit upon maturity or an annuity at a guaranteed rate. In some cases, the contract may designate one or other of these alternatives as the principal benefit and any other as an option. This designation, in itself, is not one of substance in the context of reserving since it does not affect the *policyholder's* choices. Other forms of option include:
(1) the right to convert to a different contract on guaranteed terms;
(2) the right to increase cover on guaranteed terms;
(3) the right to a specified amount on surrender; and
(4) the right to a paid up value.

1.2.64 **[G]** The *firm* should provide for the benefit which the *firm* anticipates the *policyholder* is most likely to choose. Past experience may be used as a guide, but only if this is likely to give a reasonable estimate of future experience. For example, past experience of the take-up of a cash payment option instead of an annuity would not be a reliable guide, if, in the past, market rates exceeded those guaranteed in the annuity but no longer do so. Similarly, past experience on the take-up of options may not be relevant in the light of the assumptions made in respect of future interest rates and mortality rates in the valuation of the benefits.

1.2.65 **[G]** Many options are long-term and need careful consideration. Improving longevity, for example, can increase the value of guaranteed annuity options vesting further in the future. *Firms* also need to have regard to the fact that *policyholder* behaviour can change in the future as *policyholders* become more aware of the value of their options. The impact on *policyholder* behaviour of possible changes in taxation should also be considered.

1.2.66 **[G]** In accordance with INSPRU 1.2.7R and INSPRU 1.2.13R, take-up rates for guaranteed annuity options should be assessed on a prudent basis with assumptions that include margins for adverse deviation (see INSPRU 1.2.13R to INSPRU 1.2.19G) that take account of current experience and the potential for future change. The *firm* should reserve for option take-up at least at a prudent margin over current experience for options shortly to vest. For longer term options where the option becomes increasingly valuable in the future due to projected mortality improvements, increased take-up rates should be assumed. In view of the growing uncertainty over take-up rates for projections further in the future, for guaranteed annuity option dates 20 years or more ahead at least a 95% take-up rate assumption should be made.

1.2.67 **[G]** Where there is considerable variation in the cost of the option depending on conditions at the time the option is exercised, and where that variation constitutes a material risk for the *firm*, it will generally be appropriate to use stochastic modelling. In this case prices from the asset model used in the stochastic approach should be benchmarked to relevant market asset prices before determining the value of the option. Where stochastic modelling is not undertaken, market option prices should be used to determine suitable assumptions for the valuation of the option. If no market exists for a particular option, a *firm* should take the value of the nearest equivalent benefit or right for which a market exists and document the way in which it has adjusted that valuation to reflect the original option.

1.2.68 **[G]** Where the option offers a choice between two non-discretionary financial benefits (such as between a guaranteed cash sum or a guaranteed annuity value, or between a unit value and a maturity guarantee) and where there is a wide range of possible outcomes, the *firm* should normally model such liabilities stochastically. In carrying out such modelling *firms* should take into account the likely choices to be made by *policyholders* in each scenario. *Firms* should make and retain a record of the development and application of the model.

1.2.69 **[G]** The value of a contract with an option is greater than the value of a similar contract without the option, that is, the option has value whether it is expected to be exercised or not. Although in theory a *firm* can rebalance its investments to match the expected cost of the option to the *firm* (including the time value of the option), this takes time to achieve and the market may move more quickly than the *firm* is able to respond. Also, there are likely to be transaction costs. *Firms* should take these aspects into consideration in setting up *mathematical reserves*.

1.2.70 **[R]**

(1) Where a *policyholder* may opt to be paid a cash amount, or a series of cash payments, the *mathematical reserves* for the *contract of insurance* established under INSPRU 1.2.7R must be sufficient to ensure that the payment or payments could be made solely from:
   (a) the assets covering those *mathematical reserves*; and
   (b) the resources arising from those assets and from the contract itself.

(2) In (1) references to a cash amount or a series of cash payments include the amount or amounts likely to be paid on a voluntary discontinuance.

(3) For the purposes of (1), the *firm* must assume that:
   (a) the assumptions adopted for the current valuation remain unaltered and are met; and
   (b) discretionary benefits and charges will be set so as to fulfil the *firm's* regulatory duty to treat its *customers* fairly.

(4) (1) may be applied to a group of similar contracts instead of to the individual contracts within that group except where the cash amount or series of cash payments is the amount or amounts likely to be paid on a voluntary discontinuance.

1.2.71 **[R]** For the purposes of INSPRU 1.2.70R, a *firm* must assume that the amount of a cash payment secured by the exercise of an option is:

(1) in the case of an *accumulating with-profits policy*, the lower of:
   (a) the amount which the *policyholder* would reasonably expect to be paid if the option were exercised, having regard to the representations made by the *firm* and including any expectations of a *final bonus*; and
   (b) that amount, disregarding all discretionary adjustments;

(2) in the case of any other *policy*, the amount which the *policyholder* would reasonably expect to be paid if the option were exercised, having regard to the representations made by the *firm*, without taking into account any expectations regarding future distributions of profits or the granting of discretionary additions in respect of an *established surplus*.

1.2.72 **[G]** INSPRU 1.2.71R(1) applies only to *accumulating with-profits policies*; INSPRU 1.2.71R(2) applies to any other type of *policy*, including *non-profit insurance contracts*. In INSPRU 1.2.71R(1)(a) a *firm* must take into consideration, for example, a market value adjustment where such an adjustment has been described in representations made to *policyholders* by the *firm*. However, any discretionary adjustment, such as a market value adjustment, must not be included in the amount calculated in INSPRU 1.2.71R(1)(b).

Persistency assumptions

1.2.73 **[G]** [intentionally blank]

1.2.74 **[R]** [intentionally blank]

1.2.75 **[G]** [intentionally blank]

1.2.76 **[R]** A *firm* may make assumptions about voluntary discontinuance rates in the calculation of the *mathematical reserves* provided that those assumptions meet the general requirements for prudent assumptions as set out in INSPRU 1.2.10R and INSPRU 1.2.13R.

1.2.77 **[G]** The prudential margin in respect of assumptions of voluntary discontinuance should be validated both in relation to recent experience and to variations in future experience that might arise as a result of reasonably foreseeable changes in conditions. In particular, where estimates of experience are being made well into the future, the assumptions should contain margins that take into account the increased risk of adverse experience arising from changed circumstances. *Firms* should also consider the possibility of anti-selection by *policyholders* and of variations in persistency experience for different classes and cohorts of business.

Reinsurance

1.2.77A **[R]** In INSPRU 1.2.78G to INSPRU 1.2.89G references to:

(1) *reinsurance* and contracts of *reinsurance* include analogous non- *reinsurance* financing agreements, including contingent loans, securitisations and any other arrangements in respect of *contracts of insurance* that are analogous to contracts of *reinsurance* in terms of the risks transferred and the finance provided;

(2) reinsured risks, in relation to a contract of *reinsurance* entered into by a *firm*, means that part of:

 (a) the risks insured by the *firm* under *long-term insurance contracts* entered into by it; and

 (b) the other risks arising directly from the *firm's long-term insurance business*;

 that have been transferred to the *reinsurer* under that contract of *reinsurance*; and

(3) *reinsurance* cash outflows include any reduction in *policy* liabilities recognised as covered under a contract of *reinsurance* or any reduction of any debt to the *firm* under or in respect of a contract of *reinsurance*.

1.2.78 **[G]** The prospective valuation of future cash flows to determine the amount of the *mathematical reserves* includes amounts to be received or paid under contracts of *reinsurance* in respect of *long-term insurance business* (see INSPRU 1.2.28R(1)(d)). This applies even where those cash flows cannot be identified as related to particular *long-term insurance contracts* (see INSPRU 1.2.22R(3)).

1.2.79 **[R]** A *firm* must value *reinsurance* cash flows using methods and assumptions which are at least as prudent as the methods and assumptions used to value the underlying *contracts of insurance* which have been reinsured. In particular:

(1) *reinsurance* recoveries must not be recognised unless the underlying liabilities to which they relate have also been recognised;

(2) *reinsurance* cash outflows that are unambiguously linked to the emergence as surplus of margins included in the valuation of existing *contracts of insurance* or to the exercise by a *reinsurer* of its rights under a termination clause need not be valued (see INSPRU 1.2.85R); and

(3) *reinsurance* cash inflows that are contingent on factors or conditions other than the reinsured risks must not be valued.

1.2.80 **[G]** In valuing *reinsurance* cash flows, a *firm* should establish prudent margins for adverse deviation (see INSPRU 1.2.13R to INSPRU 1.2.19G) including margins in respect of:

(1) any uncertainty as to the amount or timing of amounts to be paid or received; and

(2) the risk of credit default by the *reinsurer*.

1.2.81 **[G]** In assessing the risk of credit default, the *firm* should take into account the *rules* and *guidance* in INSPRU 2.1 (Credit risk in insurance).

1.2.82 **[G]** It will not necessarily be appropriate to use the same assumptions in INSPRU 1.2.79R as for the underlying contracts. For example, if only a subgroup of the original contracts is reinsured, it may be appropriate to use different mortality rates.

1.2.83 **[G]** Only *reinsurance* cash inflows that are triggered unambiguously by the reinsured risks may be valued. *Reinsurance* cash inflows that depend on other contingencies where the outcome does not form part of the valuation basis should not be given credit.

1.2.84 **[G]** *Firms* should assess the extent of margins in the valuation of the existing *contracts of insurance* where these provide implicit provision for the *reinsurance* cash outflows in INSPRU 1.2.79R. Where the *reinsurance* asset exceeds the estimated value of the future surplus under reinsured contracts *firms* should assess their credit risk exposure to the *reinsurer.*

1.2.85 **[R]** For the purposes of INSPRU 1.2.79R(2), the "link" must be such that a contingent liability to pay or repay the amount to the *reinsurer* could not arise except when, and to the extent that, the margins in the valuation of the existing *contracts of insurance* emerge as surplus, or the *reinsurer* exercises its rights under a termination clause in the contract of *reinsurance* as a result of:

(1) fraudulent conduct by the *firm* under or in relation to the contract of *reinsurance*; or

(2) a representation as to the existence, at or before the time the contract of *reinsurance* is entered into, of a state of affairs which is within the knowledge or control of the *firm* and which is material to the *reinsurer's* decision to enter into the contract being discovered to be false; or

(3) the non-payment of *reinsurance premiums* by the *firm*; or

(4) a transfer by the *firm* of the whole or a specified part of its business without the agreement of the *reinsurer*, except where that agreement has been unreasonably withheld.

1.2.86 **[R]** For the purposes of INSPRU 1.2.79R(2) and INSPRU 1.2.85R, future surplus may only be offset against future *reinsurance* cash outflow in respect of surplus on *non-profit insurance contracts* and the charges or shareholder transfers arising as surplus from *with-profits insurance contracts*. Such charges and transfers may only be allowed for to the extent consistent with the regulatory duty of the *firm* to treat its *customers* fairly.

1.2.87 **[G]** For the purposes of INSPRU 1.2.85R, a contingent liability means a liability that would only arise upon the happening of a particular contingency, even where that contingency is not expected to occur. For example, if the *firm* has a *reinsurance* arrangement in force that in the event the *firm* were wound up would give rise to repayments other than out of surplus emerging, the *reinsurance* cash outflows should be valued as a liability.

1.2.88 **[G]** INSPRU 1.2.85R allows a *firm* not to value *reinsurance* cash outflows provided the contingencies in which the *reinsurance* would require repayment other than out of future surpluses are limited to termination clauses concerning fraud, material misrepresentation, non-payment of *reinsurance premiums* by the *firm* or a transfer of business by the *firm* without the agreement of the *reinsurer*, except if unreasonably withheld.

1.2.89 **[G]** Where the *reinsurance* cash outflow is payable by a fund or sub-fund that generates such profits, charges or transfers, the *firm* need make no provision for such payments provided that repayment to the *reinsurer* is linked unambiguously (as defined in INSPRU 1.2.85R) to the emergence of future surplus. Where the profits, charges or transfers arising under a block of business are payable by a fund or sub-fund to another part of the *firm* then only where the *firm* has committed to remit such profits, charges or transfers directly to the *reinsurer* would it be acceptable for no provision for payments to the *reinsurer* to be made.

1.2.90 **[R]** [deleted]

1.2.91 **[G]** [deleted]

Application of INSPRU 1.2 to Lloyd's

1.2.92 **[R]** INSPRU 1.2 applies to *managing agents* in accordance with INSPRU 8.1.4R.

Approved reinsurance to close

1.2.93 **[R]** In respect of business that has been subject to an *approved reinsurance to close*, *managing agents* must calculate *mathematical reserves* (before and after deduction of reinsurance cessions) for the reinsuring and not for the reinsured *member*.

1.3 With-profits insurance capital component

Application

1.3.1 **[R]** INSPRU 1.3 applies to a *realistic basis life firm*.

1.3.2 **[G]** A *realistic basis life firm* means a *firm* to which GENPRU 2.1.18R applies. The application of GENPRU 2.1.18R is set out in GENPRU 2.1.19R and GENPRU 2.1.20R. GENPRU 2.1.13R requires that a *firm* must maintain at all times *capital resources* equal to or in excess of its *capital resources requirement*. The *enhanced capital requirement* forms part of the *capital resources requirement* for a *realistic basis life firm*. The *with-profits insurance capital component* forms part of the *enhanced capital requirement* which a *realistic basis life firm* is required to calculate in accordance with GENPRU 2.1.38R.

Purpose

1.3.3 **[G]** This section sets out *rules* and *guidance* as to the methods and assumptions to be used in calculating the *with-profits insurance capital component*.

1.3.4 **[G]** The purpose of the *with-profits insurance capital component* is to supplement the *mathematical reserves* so as to ensure that a *firm* holds adequate financial resources for the conduct of its *with-profits insurance business*. In particular, capital in excess of the *mathematical reserves* may be needed to ensure that adequate *final bonuses* can be awarded to *policyholders*. That is, adequate in the sense that in setting bonuses payable to *policyholders* the *firm* pays due regard to the interests of its *policyholders* and treats them fairly. The *mathematical reserves* for a *realistic basis life firm* are not required to include provision for future *annual bonuses* or *final bonuses* (INSPRU 1.2.9R).

1.3.5 **[G]** The required procedures are summarised in the flowchart in INSPRU 1 Annex 1G.

Main requirements

1.3.6 **[R]** A *firm* must calculate the *with-profits insurance capital component* in accordance with INSPRU 1.3.7R.

1.3.7 **[R]**

(1) The *with-profits insurance capital component* for a *firm* is the aggregate of any amounts that:
  (a) result from the calculations specified in (2) and (3); and
  (b) are greater than zero.

(2) Subject to (3), in relation to each *with-profits fund* within the *firm*, the *firm* must deduct B from A, where:
  (a) A is the amount of the *regulatory excess capital* for that fund (see INSPRU 1.3.23R); and
  (b) B is the sum of:
    (i) the *realistic excess capital* for that fund (see INSPRU 1.3.32R);
    (ii) the value, in the most adverse scenario required by INSPRU 1.3.43R(3), of future internal transfers from the fund to shareholders or another of the *firm's* funds in respect of the future distribution of surplus between *policyholders* and shareholders; and
    (iii) an amount not exceeding the value, in the most adverse scenario required by INSPRU 1.3.43R(3), of any other future internal transfers from the fund to a *non-profit fund* in respect of expense-related charges to the extent that the future receipt of the amount transferred is not already taken into account in the calculation of the *firm's capital resources* or in establishing its *technical provisions*.

(3) Where a capital instrument that can be included in the *firm's capital resources* in accordance with GENPRU 2.2 has been attributed wholly or partly to a *with-profits fund* and that instrument meets the requirements of GENPRU 2.2.271R, the *firm* must add to the amount calculated under (2) for that fund the result, subject to a minimum of zero, of deducting D from C where:
  (a) C is the outstanding face amount of the instrument to the extent attributed to the fund; and
  (b) D is the realistic value of the instrument to the extent attributed to the fund in the single event that determines the *risk capital margin* under INSPRU 1.3.43R.

1.3.7A **[G]** Future internal transfers from a *with-profits fund* are included in the *realistic value of liabilities* (see INSPRU 1.3.105R, INSPRU 1.3.119R, INSPRU 1.3.128R and INSPRU 1.3.165R). INSPRU 1.1.27R ensures that sufficient assets are maintained in a *with-profits fund* to meet those future internal transfers. In calculating the *WPICC*, the economic value to the *firm* of those future transfers in the most adverse scenario required in calculating the *risk capital margin* (see INSPRU 1.3.43R) should be recognised. In the case of internal transfers to a *non-profit fund* in respect of expense-related charges, those transfers may only be recognised to the extent that those cash flows have not already been taken into account in calculating the *firm's capital resources* or *technical provisions*. In effect, the future asset of the shareholders or another of the *firm's* funds is available to offset the corresponding liability of the *with-profits fund* and should, therefore, subject to the limitation in INSPRU 1.3.7R(2)(b)(iii), be treated as capital arising from that fund which is available to reduce the amount of the *WPICC*.

1.3.8 **[G]** Subordinated debt which is subordinated to *policyholder* interests (see GENPRU 2.2.271R) is an example of the sort of capital instrument that may give rise to a component of the *WPICC* under INSPRU 1.3.7R(3). Such instruments are treated as capital under GENPRU 2.2, subject to the requirements of GENPRU 2.2.271R. Under realistic reserving the capital instrument is valued as a realistic liability (INSPRU 1.3.40R) and in calculating the *risk capital margin* such an instrument would be valued at its realistic value in the single event outlined in INSPRU 1.3.43R (see also INSPRU 1.3.162R). Overall, the effect of GENPRU 2.2, INSPRU 1.3.7R(3) and INSPRU 1.3.43R is to enable a *firm* that obtains subordinated debt to benefit from additional *capital resources* equal to the face amount of that debt.

1.3.9 **[G]** SUP 4 (Actuaries) sets out the role and responsibilities of the *actuarial function* and of the *with-profits actuary*.

(1) As part of his duties under SUP 4.3.13R, the *actuary* appointed by the *firm* to perform the *actuarial function* must calculate the *firm's mathematical reserves* and, in the context of the calculation of the *with-profits insurance capital component*, must also:
   (a) advise the *firm's* governing body on the methods and assumptions to be used in the calculation of the firm's *with-profits insurance capital component*;
   (b) perform that calculation in accordance with the methods and assumptions determined by the *firm's governing body*; and
   (c) report to the *firm's governing body* on the results of that calculation.

(2) As part of his duties under SUP 4.3.16G, the *with-profits actuary* must advise the *firm's governing body* on the discretion exercised by the *firm*. In the context of the calculation of the *with-profits insurance capital component*, the *with-profits actuary* must also advise the *firm's governing body* as to whether the methods and assumptions (including the allowance for management actions) used for that calculation are consistent with the *firm's Principles and Practices of Financial Management* (*PPFM*-see COBS 20.3) and with its regulatory duty to treat its *customers* fairly.

Definitions

1.3.10 **[R]** In this section, real estate means an interest in land, buildings or other immovable property.

1.3.11 **[R]** In this section, the long-term gilt yield is the annualised equivalent of the yield on the 15-year index for United Kingdom Government fixed-interest securities jointly compiled by the Financial Times, the Institute of Actuaries and the Faculty of Actuaries.

1.3.12 **[R]** For the purposes of this section, a *firm* has an exposure to an asset or liability where the *firm's* valuation of its assets or liabilities changes when the value of the asset or liability changes.

1.3.13 **[R]** Unless the context otherwise requires, all references (however expressed) in this section to realistic liabilities, or to liabilities which are included in the calculation of realistic liabilities, include discretionary benefits payable by the *firm* in accordance with the *firm's* regulatory duty to treat its *customers* fairly.

1.3.14 **[G]** In this section, any reference to a *firm's* regulatory duty to treat its *customers* fairly is a reference to the *firm's* duty under *Principle* 6 (Customers' interests). This states that a *firm* must pay due regard to the interests of its *customers* and treat them fairly.

1.3.15 **[G]** In this section, any reference to the *Principles and Practices of Financial Management* (*PPFM*) is a reference to the requirements in COBS 20.3 (Principles and Practices of Financial Management) for *firms* to establish, maintain and record the principles and practices of financial management according to which the business of its *with-profits funds* is conducted.

1.3.16 **[G]** The extent to which a *firm* requires a separate *PPFM* for each of its *with- profits funds* will depend on the *firm's* circumstances and any relevant representations made by the *firm* to its with-profits *policyholders*. In this section, any reference to a *firm's PPFM* refers to the *PPFM* which relate to the *with-profits fund* or the *with-profits insurance contracts* in question.

Record keeping

1.3.17 **[R]** A *firm* must make, and retain for an appropriate period of time, a record of:
(1) the methods and assumptions used in making any calculation required for the purposes of this section (and any subsequent changes) and the reasons for their use; and
(2) any change in practice and the nature of, reasons for, and effect of, any change in approach with respect to those methods and assumptions.

1.3.18 **[G]** SYSC 14.1.53R requires *firms* to maintain accounting and other records for a minimum of three years, or longer as appropriate. For the purposes of INSPRU 1.3.17R, a period of longer than three years will be appropriate for a *firm's long-term insurance business*. In determining an appropriate time period, a *firm* should have regard to:
(1) the detailed *guidance* on record keeping in SYSC 14.1.51G to SYSC 14.1.64G;
(2) the nature and term of the firm's *long-term insurance contracts*; and
(3) any additional provisions or statutory requirements applicable to the *firm* or its records.

1.3.19 **[R]** A *firm* must also identify in the record required to be kept by INSPRU 1.3.17R changes in practice, in particular changes in those items which will or may be significant in relation to the eventual *claim* values.

1.3.20 **[G]** Some of the changes identified in accordance with INSPRU 1.3.19R may have to be *notified to the firm's policyholders* in accordance with the *firm's PPFM*.

General principles for allocating aggregate amounts

1.3.21 **[R]** Where any calculation is required under this section which:
(1) is to be made in respect of any *with-profits fund* of a *firm*; and

(2) covers an amount that is otherwise calculated in relation to the *firm* as a whole;

the *firm* must make an allocation of that amount as between all of its funds (including funds which are not *with-profits funds*).

1.3.22 **[R]** In any case where:
(1) *non-profit insurance contracts* are written in any *with-profits fund* of a *firm*; and
(2) any calculation is required under this section which:
 (a) is to be made in respect of the *regulatory excess capital* or *realistic excess capital* for the fund; and
 (b) covers an amount that is otherwise calculated or allocated in relation to the fund as a whole;

the *firm* must make an allocation of the amount in (2)(b) as between the *with-profits insurance contracts* and *non-profit insurance contracts* written in the fund.

Calculation of regulatory excess capital

1.3.23 **[R]** A *firm* must calculate the *regulatory excess capital* for each of its *with- profits funds* by deducting B from A, where:
(1) A is the *regulatory value of assets* of the fund (INSPRU 1.3.24R); and
(2) B is the sum of:
 (a) the *regulatory value of liabilities* of the fund (INSPRU 1.3.29R); and
 (b) the *long-term insurance capital requirement* in respect of the fund's *with-profits insurance contracts*.

Regulatory value of assets

1.3.24 **[R]**
(1) For the purposes of INSPRU 1.3.23R(1), the *regulatory value of assets* of a *with-profits fund* is equal to the sum of:
 (a) the amount of the fund's *long-term admissible assets*; and
 (b) the amount of any *implicit items* allocated to that fund;
 less an amount, representing any *non-profit insurance contracts* written in that fund, determined in accordance with (2).
(2) Where *non-profit insurance contracts* are written in a *with-profits fund*, the amount representing those contracts is the sum of:
 (a) the *mathematical reserves* in respect of the *non-profit insurance contracts* written in the fund; and
 (b) an amount in respect of the *non-profit insurance contracts* written in the fund which represents an appropriate allocation of the *firm's long-term insurance capital requirement*, to the extent that it is covered by the fund's *long-term admissible assets*.

1.3.25 **[R]** For the purpose of determining the value of a fund's *long-term admissible assets* in accordance with INSPRU 1.3.24R(1)(a), no value is to be attributed to:
(1) debts owed by *reinsurers*; or
(2) *claims*; or
(3) tax recoveries; or
(4) claims against *compensation funds*;

to the extent already offset in the calculation of *technical provisions*.

1.3.26 **[R]** In making a determination in accordance with INSPRU 1.3.24R(2), a *firm* must allocate *long-term admissible assets* of an appropriate nature and term to any *non-profit insurance contracts* written in the *with-profits fund*.

1.3.27 **[G]** [intentionally blank]

1.3.28 **[G]** A *firm* needs to obtain an *implicit item waiver* from the *FSA* in order to bring in an amount under INSPRU 1.3.24R(1)(b). For *guidance* on applying for an *implicit item waiver* in respect of future surpluses relating to *with- profits funds* see GENPRU 2 Annex 8G. The amount of any *implicit item* allocated to a *with-profits fund* may be defined in the terms of any *waiver* granted.

Regulatory value of liabilities

1.3.29 **[R]** For the purposes of INSPRU 1.3.23R(2)(a), the *regulatory value of liabilities* of a *with-profits fund* is equal to the sum of:
(1) the *mathematical reserves*, in respect of the fund's *with-profits insurance contracts*, including the value of any provisions reflecting bonuses allocated at the *actuarial valuation date*; and
(2) the *regulatory current liabilities* of the fund (see INSPRU 1.3.30R).

1.3.30 **[R]** For the purposes of INSPRU 1.3.29R(2), the *regulatory current liabilities* of a *with-profits fund* are equal to the sum of the following amounts to the extent that they relate to that fund:

(1) accounting liabilities (including *long-term insurance liabilities* which have fallen due before the end of the *financial year*);
(2) liabilities from *deposit back arrangements*; and
(3) any provision for adverse variations (determined in accordance with INPSRU 3.2.17R).

1.3.31 **[G]** The amount of *regulatory current liabilities* for a *with-profits fund* refers to the sum of the amounts in (1) and (2) in respect of the fund:
(1) the amount of 'Total other insurance and non-insurance liabilities'; and
(2) the amount of 'Cash bonuses which had not been paid to *policyholders* prior to the end of the financial year';

as disclosed at lines 49 and 12 respectively of the appropriate Form 14 ('Long-term business liabilities and margins') for that fund as part of the Annual Returns required to be deposited with the *FSA* under IPRU(INS) rule 9.6R(1).

Calculation of realistic excess capital

1.3.32 **[R]** A *firm* must calculate the *realistic excess capital* for each of its *with-profits funds* by deducting B from A, where:
(1) A is the *realistic value of assets* of the fund (see INSPRU 1.3.33R); and
(2) B is the sum of:
  (a) the *realistic value of liabilities* of the fund (see INSPRU 1.3.40R); and
  (b) the *risk capital margin* for the fund (see INSPRU 1.3.43R).

Realistic value of assets

1.3.33 **[R]**
(1) For the purposes of INSPRU 1.3.32R(1), the *realistic value of assets* of a *with-profits fund* is the sum of:
  (a) the amount of the fund's *regulatory value of assets* determined in accordance with INSPRU 1.3.24R, but with no value given to any *implicit items* and excluding the regulatory value of any *shares* in a *related undertaking* which carries on *long-term insurance business*;
  (b) the amount of the fund's excess *admissible assets* (see INSPRU 1.3.36R);
  (c) the present value of future profits (or losses) on any *non-profit insurance contracts* written in the *with-profits fund* (see INSPRU 1.3.37R);
  (d) the value of any *derivative* or *quasi-derivative* held in the fund (see GENPRU 1.3.41R) to the extent its value is not reflected in (a), (b) or (c);
  (e) any amount determined under (2); and
  (f) the amount of any prepayments made from the fund.
(2) Where any equity *shares* held (directly or indirectly) by a *firm* (A):
  (a) are *shares* in a *related undertaking* (B) which carries on *long-term insurance business*; and
  (b) have been identified by A under INSPRU 1.3.21R as *long-term insurance assets* which are held in the *with-profits fund* for which the realistic value is to be determined under (1);

  the amount required under (1)(e) is the relevant proportion of the value of all B's equity *shares* as determined in (3).
(3) For the purposes of (2):
  (a) the relevant proportion is the proportion of the total number of equity *shares* issued by B which are held (directly or indirectly) by A;
  (b) the value of all B's equity *shares* must be taken as D deducted from C, where C is equal to the sum of:
    (i) the shareholder net assets of B;
    (ii) any surplus assets in the *non-profit funds* of B;
    (iii) any additional amount arising from the present value of future profits (or losses) on any *non-profit insurance contracts* written by B (calculated on a basis consistent with INSPRU 1.3.37R), excluding any amount arising from business that is written in a *with-profits fund*; and
    (iv) where B has any *with-profits funds*, the present value of projected future transfers out of those funds to shareholder funds of B; and D is equal to the sum of:
    (v) the *long-term insurance capital requirement* in respect of any *non-profit insurance contracts* written in a *non-profit fund* of B;
    (vi) where B is a *regulatory basis only life firm*, the amount of the *resilience capital requirement* in respect of any *non- profit insurance contracts* written in a *non-profit fund* of B;

(vii) any part of the *with-profits insurance capital component* of B, or of B's *long-term insurance capital requirement* or, where B is a *regulatory basis only life firm, resilience capital requirement* in respect of B's *with-profits insurance contracts*, that is not covered from the assets of the *with-profits fund* from which it arises after deducting from those assets the amount calculated under (iv); and

(viii) any assets of B that back its regulatory capital requirements and that are valued in (iii) in the calculation of the present value of future profits of *non-profit insurance business* written by B.

(4) The methods and assumptions used in the calculations under (3)(b)(iii) and (iv) must follow a consistent approach to that set out in INSPRU 1.3.37R.

1.3.34 **[G]** In INSPRU 1.3.33R(1)(d), where a *derivative* or *quasi-derivative* has a positive asset value, credit should be given within the *realistic value of assets*. If the *derivative* or *quasi-derivative* has a negative asset value it should be valued within realistic liabilities as an element of *realistic current liabilities* (see INSPRU 1.3.40R(3)).

1.3.35 **[G]** Where a *firm* identifies *shares* in a *related undertaking* which carries on *long-term insurance business* as *shares* held in one of its *with-profits funds*, INSPRU 1.3.33R(1)(e), INSPRU 1.3.33R(2) and INSPRU 1.3.33R(3) bring in a realistic valuation of the *related undertaking* equal to its net assets plus the present value of future profits, less its regulatory capital requirements (see INSPRU 1.3.33R(3)(v), (vi) and (vii)). Where the *related undertaking* has taken the present value of future profits arising from its contracts into consideration in covering its regulatory capital requirements (for example, its *risk capital margin*, under INSPRU 1.3.45R(2)(c)), INSPRU 1.3.33R(3)(b)(iii) requires a *firm* to exclude those future profits in valuing the *related undertaking*. The subtraction of the capital requirements in the calculation provides a straightforward method of allowing for the change in the *related undertaking's* value in stress conditions, as the value of the *related undertaking* is not subject to the realistic stress tests of the *risk capital margin*. In calculating the present value of future profits on *non- profit insurance business* written in the *related undertaking* under INSPRU 1.3.33R(3)(b)(iii), a *firm* may value the release of capital requirements as the business runs off (see INSPRU 1.3.38G). INSPRU 1.3.33R(3)(b)(viii) ensures that any such capital is not double-counted.

1.3.36 **[R]** Excess *admissible assets* of a *with-profits fund* means *admissible assets* which exceed any of the percentage limits referred to in INSPRU 2.1.22R.

1.3.37 **[R]** A *firm* must calculate the present value of future profits (or losses) on *non- profit insurance contracts* written in the *with-profits fund* using methodology and assumptions which:

(1) are based on current estimates of future experience;

(2) involve reasonable (but not excessively prudent) adjustments to reflect risk and uncertainty;

(3) allow for a market-consistent valuation of any guarantees or options within the contracts valued;

(4) are derived from current market yields, having regard to International Financial Reporting Standard 4: Insurance Contracts, as if it were being applied to determine the value under that standard for the first time;

(5) have regard to generally accepted actuarial practice and generally accepted industry standards appropriate for *firms* carrying on *long-term insurance business*;

(6) are consistent with the allocation, made in accordance with INSPRU 1.3.22R, of any aggregate amounts as between the *with-profits insurance contracts* and the *non-profit insurance contracts* written in the fund;

(7) allow for any tax that would be payable out of the *with-profits fund* in respect of the contracts valued; and

(8) are consistent with the allocation, made in accordance with INSPRU 1.3.26R, of *long-term admissible assets* as between the *with-profits insurance contracts* and any *non-profit insurance contracts* written in the fund.

1.3.38 **[G]** In calculating the present value of future profits (or losses) for *non-profit insurance business* required by INSPRU 1.3.33R(1)(c), to the extent that the *long-term insurance capital requirement* is covered by the *with-profits fund's long-term admissible assets*, a *firm* may take into consideration any release of this item as the relevant *policies* go off the books.

1.3.39 **[G]** Annuities do not typically fall to be valued on a market-consistent basis under INSPRU 1.3.37R(3) as they are not "options and guarantees" as defined for accounting purposes. This is because they do not have "time value" in the option-pricing meaning of that term. However where, atypically, annuities do fall to be valued on a market-consistent basis under INSPRU 1.3.37(3), the discount rate used should be appropriate to the characteristics of the liability, including its illiquidity. The appropriate interest rate, therefore, would not typically be the risk-free rate. Where illiquid assets are used to closely match similar illiquid liabilities, as could be the case in annuities business, it would be appropriate to look at the liquidity premium that is implicit in the market value of the assets as a proxy for the liquidity premium that should be included in a market consistent valuation of the liabilities. However, care should be exercised in doing this. Assets and liabilities are rarely perfectly matched and an appropriate margin needs to be included in the valuation to cover the risk of unexpected mismatch.

1.3.39A **[G]** In view of INSPRU 1.3.39G, it is likely that the discount rate to be applied to the market-consistent valuation of those annuities that fall within the scope of INSPRU 1.3.37 R(3) would not be significantly different from that which applies to other annuities (to which a discount rate based on the return on the matching assets less an allowance for risk which is reasonable but not excessively prudent, in accordance with INSPRU 1.3.37 R(2), might be applied).

1.3.39B **[G]** In determining current market yields for the purpose of INSPRU **1.3.37R**(4), a *firm* is required to have regard to IFRS 4 as if it were being applied to determine the value under that standard for the first time, that is, without reference to existing practices. Paragraph 27 of the standard is likely to be of particular relevance. In general, a *firm* should only include an allowance for future investment margins if its assumptions are limited to no more than a risk-free rate and the discount rate is set consistently. However, this does not preclude a *firm* from using a replicating portfolio of assets to determine the discount rate for the liability with suitable adjustments for differences in their characteristics (for the example of annuity business, see INSPRU 1.3.39G). In setting assumptions for future investment returns, a *firm* should also consider sections BC134 to BC144 of the Basis for Conclusions in IFRS 4.

Realistic value of liabilities: general

1.3.40 **[R]** For the purposes of INSPRU 1.3.32R(2)(a), the *realistic value of liabilities* of a *with-profits fund* is the sum of:
(1) the *with-profits benefits reserve* of the fund;
(2) the *future policy related liabilities* of the fund; and
(3) the *realistic current liabilities* of the fund.

1.3.41 **[G]** All liabilities arising under, or in connection with, *with-profits insurance contracts* written in the fund should be included in the *realistic value of liabilities* referred to in INSPRU 1.3.40R, including those in respect of guarantees and the value of options.

1.3.42 **[G]** Detailed *rules* and *guidance* for the calculation of the three elements referred to in INSPRU 1.3.40R are contained below in this section:
(1) INSPRU 1.3.116R to INSPRU 1.3.135G refer to the *with-profits benefits reserve*;
(2) INSPRU 1.3.136G to INSPRU 1.3.189G refer to the *future policy related liabilities*; and
(3) INSPRU 1.3.190R and INSPRU 1.3.191R refer to the *realistic current liabilities*.

Risk capital margin

1.3.43 **[R]**
(1) A *firm* must calculate a *risk capital margin* for each of its *with-profits funds* in accordance with (2) to (6).
(2) The *firm* must identify relevant assets (INSPRU 1.3.45R) which, in the most adverse scenario, will have a value (INSPRU 1.3.46R) which is equal to the *realistic value of liabilities* of the fund under that scenario.
(3) The most adverse scenario means the single event comprising that combination of the scenarios in INSPRU 1.3.44R which gives rise to the largest positive value that results from deducting B from A, where:
 (a) A is the value of relevant assets which will produce the result described in (2); and
 (b) B is the *realistic value of liabilities* of the fund.
(4) The *risk capital margin* for the fund is the result of deducting C from A, where C is the sum of:
 (a) B; and
 (b) any amount included within relevant assets under INSPRU 1.3.45R(2)(c).
(5) In calculating the value of relevant assets for the purpose of determining the most adverse scenario in (3), a *firm* must not adjust the valuation of any asset taken into consideration under INSPRU 1.3.33R(1)(e) (*related undertakings* carrying on *long-term insurance business*) or INSPRU 1.3.45R(2)(c) (present value of future profits arising from *insurance contracts* written outside the *with-profits fund*).
(6) In calculating the *realistic value of liabilities* of a fund under any scenario, a *firm* is not required to adjust the best estimate provision made under INSPRU 1.3.190R(1) in respect of a *defined benefits pension scheme* in accordance with INSPRU 1.3.191R.

1.3.44 **[R]** For the purposes of INSPRU 1.3.43R(3), the scenarios are one scenario selected from each of the following:
(1) in respect of *UK* and other assets within INSPRU 1.3.62R(1)(a):
 (a) the range of *market risk* scenarios identified in accordance with INSPRU 1.3.68R(1) (equities);
 (b) the range of *market risk* scenarios identified in accordance with INSPRU 1.3.68R(2) (real estate); and

(c) the range of *market risk* scenarios identified in accordance with INSPRU 1.3.68R(3) (fixed interest securities);

(2) in respect of non-*UK* assets within INSPRU 1.3.62R(1)(b):

(a) the range of *market risk* scenarios identified in accordance with INSPRU 1.3.73R(1) (equities);

(b) the range of *market risk* scenarios identified in accordance with INSPRU 1.3.73R(2) (real estate); and

(c) the range of *market risk* scenarios identified in accordance with INSPRU 1.3.73R(3) (fixed interest securities);

(3) the range of credit risk scenarios identified in accordance with INSPRU 1.3.78R(1) (bond or debt items);

(4) the range of credit risk scenarios identified in accordance with INSPRU 1.3.78R(2) (*reinsurance* items or analogous non-*reinsurance* financing agreements);

(5) the range of credit risk scenarios identified in accordance with INSPRU 1.3.78R(3) (other items including *derivatives* and *quasi-derivatives*); and

(6) the persistency risk scenario identified in accordance with INSPRU 1.3.100R.

1.3.45 **[R]**

(1) In INSPRU 1.3.43R, in relation to a *with-profits fund*, the relevant assets means a range of assets which meets the following conditions:

(a) the range is selected on a basis which is consistent with the *firm's* regulatory duty to treat its *customers* fairly;

(b) the range must include assets from within the *with-profits fund* the value of which is greater than or equal to the *realistic value of liabilities* of the fund;

(c) the range is selected in accordance with (2); and

(d) no asset of the *firm* may be allocated to the range of assets identified in respect of more than one *with-profits fund*.

(2) The range of assets must be selected from the assets specified in (a) to (c), in the order specified:

(a) assets that have a realistic value under INSPRU 1.3.33R;

(b) where a *firm* has selected all the assets within (a), any *admissible assets* that are not identified as held within the *with-profits fund*; and

(c) where a *firm* has selected all the assets within (a) and (b), any additional assets.

(3) But a *firm* must not bring any amounts into account under (2)(b) or (2)(c) in respect of any *with-profits fund* if that would result in the *firm* exceeding its overall maximum limit (determined according to whether the *firm* has only one *with-profits fund* or more than one such fund).

(4) A *firm* exceeds its overall maximum limit for amounts brought into account under (2)(b) where:

(a) in the case of a *firm* with a single *with-profits fund*, the amount the *firm* brings into account in respect of that fund;

(b) in the case of a *firm* with two or more *with-profits funds*, the aggregate of the amounts the *firm* brings into account in respect of each of those funds; exceeds the sum of the *firm's* shareholder net assets and the surplus assets in the *firm's non-profits funds*, less any regulatory capital requirements in respect of business written outside its *with-profits funds*.

(5) A *firm* exceeds its overall maximum limit for amounts brought into account under (2)(c) where:

(a) in the case of a *firm* with a single *with-profits fund*, the amount the *firm* brings into account in respect of that fund;

(b) in the case of a *firm* with two or more *with-profits funds*, the aggregate of the amounts the *firm* brings into account in respect of each of those funds; exceeds 50% of the present value of future profits arising from *insurance contracts* written by the *firm* outside its *with-profits funds*.

1.3.46 **[R]** In valuing the relevant assets identified under INSPRU 1.3.43R(2), a *firm* must use the same methods of valuation as in INSPRU 1.3.33R, except that:

(1) the value of any *admissible assets* not identified as held within the *with-profits fund* (INSPRU 1.3.45R(2)(b)) must be as determined under GENPRU 1.3; and

(2) the value of any asset which forms part of the range of assets as a result of INSPRU 1.3.45R(2)(c) must be determined on a basis consistent with that described in INSPRU 1.3.37R.

1.3.47 **[G]** The purpose of the *risk capital margin* for a *with-profits fund* is to cover adverse deviation from:

(1) the fund's *realistic value of liabilities*;

(2) the value of assets identified, in accordance with INSPRU 1.3.43R(2), to cover the amount in (1) and the fund's *risk capital margin*;

Part II FSA Handbook Materials

arising from the effects of *market risk*, credit risk and persistency risk. Other risks are not explicitly addressed by the *risk capital margin*.

1.3.48 **[G]** The amount of the *risk capital margin* calculated by the *firm* for a *with- profits fund* will depend on the *firm's* choice of assets held to cover the fund's *realistic value of liabilities* and the margin. INSPRU 1.3.43R requires the relevant assets to be sufficient, in the most adverse scenario, to cover the *realistic value of liabilities* in the event that scenario was to arise.

1.3.49 **[G]** INSPRU 1.3.45R(2)(c) allows *firms* to bring the economic value of *non- profit insurance business* written outside a *with-profits fund* into the assets available to cover the *risk capital margin*. To place a prudent limit on the amount of future profits taken into consideration a maximum of 50% of the present value of *non-profit insurance business* can be taken into the calculation (INSPRU 1.3.45R(5)). Where a contract is written in a *non-profit fund* but the assets arising from that contract are invested in a *with-profits fund* which is subject to charges for investment management or other services which benefit the *non-profit fund*, such charges can be taken into consideration in calculating the present value of future profits of the *non- profit insurance business*. Where a proportion of the present value of future profits on *non-profit insurance business* written outside a *with-profits fund* is brought in as an asset, no stress tests apply to this asset (see INSPRU 1.3.43R(5)) as the amount taken into consideration is limited to 50% of the total present value.

1.3.50 **[G]** A *firm* using a stochastic approach in INSPRU 1.3.169R(1) should keep recalibration in the post-stress scenarios to the minimum required to reflect any change in the underlying risk-free yields. A *firm* using the market costs of hedging approach, as in INSPRU 1.3.169R(2), may assume in estimating the market cost of hedging in the post-stress scenarios that market volatilities are unchanged.

1.3.51 **[G]** In the scenario tests set out in INSPRU 1.3.62R to INSPRU 1.3.103G, *firms* are required to test for worst case scenarios across a range of assumptions. The tests are, with the exception of the credit risk test, two-sided, requiring both increases and decreases in the assumptions. The *FSA* does not expect a *firm* to investigate every possible stress, but a *firm* should be able to demonstrate that it is reasonable to assume that it has successfully identified the single event that determines the *risk capital margin* for the *firm's* business, as required by INSPRU 1.3.43R(3).

1.3.51A **[G]** In the scenario tests set out in INSPRU 1.3.62R to INSPRU 1.3.103G, a *firm* is required to assess the changed value of its assets and liabilities in the economic conditions of the most adverse scenario. A *firm* is required to assess the changed value of each relevant asset (as defined in INSPRU 1.3.45R), notwithstanding any uncertainty about the appropriate valuation basis for that asset. In valuing an asset in the most adverse scenario, a *firm* should have regard to the economic substance of the asset, rather than its legal form, and assess its value accordingly. Consider, for example, a convertible bond that is close to its conversion date and where the conversion option has value. The value of the convertible bond in the most adverse scenario is likely to be sensitive primarily to equity market scenarios and to a lesser extent to interest rate scenarios. The *firm* should value the asset according to its expected market value in the economic conditions underlying the most adverse scenario.

Management actions

1.3.52 **[R]** In calculating the *risk capital margin* for a *with-profits fund*, a *firm* may reflect, in its projections of the value of assets and liabilities under the scenarios in INSPRU 1.3.44R, the *firm's* prospective management actions (INSPRU 1.3.53R).

1.3.53 **[R]** Prospective management actions refer to the foreseeable actions that would be taken by the *firm's* management, taking into account:
(1) an appropriately realistic period of time for the management actions to take effect; and
(2) the *firm's PPFM* and its regulatory duty to treat its *customers* fairly.

1.3.54 **[G]** The management actions in INSPRU 1.3.53R may include, but are not limited to, changes in future bonus rates, reductions in *surrender values*, changes in asset dispositions (taking into account the associated selling costs) and changes in the amount of charges deducted from asset shares for *with-profits insurance contracts*.

1.3.55 **[G]** A *firm* should use reasonable assumptions in incorporating management actions into its projections of *claims* such that the mitigating effects of the management actions are not overstated. In modelling management actions, a *firm* should ensure consistency with its *PPFM* and take into account its regulatory duty to treat its *customers* fairly.

1.3.56 **[G]** In accordance with INSPRU 1.3.17R, a *firm* should make and retain a record of the approach used, in particular the nature and effect of anticipated management actions (including, where practicable, the amount by which the actions would serve to reduce the projected values of assets and liabilities).

1.3.57 **[G]** A *firm* which deducts charges in respect of any adverse experience or cost of capital to *with-profits insurance contracts* should keep a record under INSPRU 1.3.17R of the amount of any such charges to its *customers* and of how it has ensured their fair treatment.

Policyholder actions

1.3.58 **[R]** In calculating the *risk capital margin* for a *with-profits fund*, a *firm* must reflect, in its projections of the value of assets and liabilities under the scenarios in INSPRU 1.3.44R, a realistic assessment of the actions of its *policyholders* (see INSPRU 1.3.59R).

1.3.59 **[R]** *Policyholder* actions refer to the foreseeable actions that would be taken by the *firm's policyholders*, taking into account:

(1) the experience of the *firm* in the past; and

(2) the changes that may occur in the future if options and guarantees become more valuable to *policyholders* than in the past.

1.3.60 **[G]** A *firm* should use realistic assumptions in incorporating *policyholder* actions into its projections of *claims* such that any mitigating effects of *policyholder* actions are not overstated and any exacerbating effects of *policyholder* actions are not understated. In modelling *policyholder* actions, a *firm* should ensure consistency with its *PPFM* and take into account its regulatory duty to treat its *customers* fairly in determining the options and information that would be available to *policyholders*.

1.3.61 **[G]** In calculating the persistency scenario in INSPRU 1.3.100R, a *firm* needs to make assumptions regarding the future termination rates exhibited by *policies*, at points described in particular in INSPRU 1.3.101R. Such assumptions should be realistic. However, the *firm* must have regard to the economic scenarios being projected. For example, if the value of an option became significantly greater in a future scenario than in the recent past, then the behaviour of *policyholders* in taking up the option is likely to differ in this future scenario compared with the recent past.

Market risk scenario

1.3.62 **[R]**

(1) For the purposes of INSPRU 1.3.44R, the ranges of *market risk* scenarios that a *firm* must assume are:

 (a) for exposures to *UK* assets and for exposures to non-*UK* assets within (2), the ranges of scenarios set out in INSPRU 1.3.68R; and

 (b) for exposures to other non-*UK* assets, the ranges of scenarios set out in INSPRU 1.3.73R.

(2) The exposures to non-*UK* assets within this paragraph are:

 (a) exposures which do not arise from a significant territory outside the *United Kingdom* (INSPRU 1.3.63R); or

 (b) exposures which do arise from a significant territory outside the *United Kingdom* but which represent less than 0.5% of the *realistic value of assets* of the *with-profits fund*, measured by *market value*.

1.3.63 **[R]** For the purposes of this section in relation to a *with-profits fund*, a significant territory is any country or territory in which more than 2.5% of the fund's *realistic value of assets* (by *market value*) are invested.

1.3.63A **[G]** *Guidance* on how a *firm* should determine where particular assets are invested is provided in INSPRU 3.1.13BG.

1.3.64 **[G]** In determining its most adverse scenario, a *firm* applying INSPRU 1.3.68R and INSPRU 1.3.73R should consider separately possible movements in *UK* and non-*UK* markets. It should not assume that market prices in different markets move in a similar way at the same time. A *firm* should also allow for the effect of the other components of the single event comprising the combination of scenarios applicable under INSPRU 1.3.43R.

1.3.65 **[G]** In relation to the *market risk* scenarios in INSPRU 1.3.68R and INSPRU 1.3.73R, the effect of INSPRU 1.3.52R and INSPRU 1.3.58R is that a *firm* may reflect management actions and must make a realistic assessment of *policyholder* actions in projecting the assets and liabilities in its calculation of the *risk capital margin* for a *with-profits fund* within the *firm*.

1.3.66 **[G]** [deleted]

1.3.67 **[G]** The relevant assets identified under INSPRU 1.3.43R(2) to calculate the *risk capital margin* may, in certain circumstances, include up to 50% of the present value of future profits arising from *insurance contracts* written by the *firm* outside its *with-profits funds*. INSPRU 1.3.43R(5) exempts such an asset from the *market risk* stress tests.

Market risk scenario for exposures to UK assets and certain non-UK assets

1.3.68 **[R]** The range of *market risk* scenarios referred to in INSPRU 1.3.62R(1)(a) is:

(1) a rise or fall in the *market value* of equities of up to the greater of:

 (a) 10%; and

 (b) 20%, less the *equity market adjustment ratio* (see INSPRU 1.3.71R);

(2) a rise or fall in real estate values of up to 12.5%; and

Part II FSA Handbook Materials

(3) a rise or fall in yields on all fixed interest securities of up to 17.5% of the long-term gilt yield.

1.3.69 **[R]** For the purposes of INSPRU 1.3.68R, a *firm* must:
(1) assume that yields on equities and real estate remain unchanged from those applicable at market levels before applying each scenario; and
(2) model a rise or fall in equity, real estate and fixed interest markets as if the movement occurred instantaneously.

1.3.70 **[G]** For example, where the long-term gilt yield is 6%, a change of 17.5% in that yield would amount to a change of 1.05 percentage points. For the purpose of the scenarios in INSPRU 1.3.68R(3), the *firm* would assume a fall or rise of up to 1.05 percentage points in yields on all fixed interest securities.

Equity market adjustment ratio

1.3.71 **[R]** The equity market adjustment ratio referred to in INSPRU 1.3.68R(1)(b) is:
(1) if the ratio calculated in (a) and (b) lies between 80% and 100%, the result of 100% less the ratio (expressed as a percentage) of:
  (a) the current value of the FTSE Actuaries All Share Index; to
  (b) the average value of the FTSE Actuaries All Share Index over the preceding 90 calendar days;
(2) 0%, if the ratio calculated in (1)(a) and (b) is more than 100%; and
(3) 20%, if the ratio calculated in (1)(a) and (b) is less than 80%.

1.3.72 **[R]** In INSPRU 1.3.71(1)(b), the average value of the FTSE Actuaries All Share Index over any period of 90 calendar days means the arithmetic mean based on levels at the close of business on each of the days in that period on which the London Stock Exchange was open for trading.

Market risk scenario for exposures to other non-UK assets

1.3.73 **[R]** The range of *market risk* scenarios referred to in INSPRU 1.3.62R(1)(b) is:
(1) an appropriate rise or fall in the *market value* of equities listed in that territory (INSPRU 1.3.75G), which must be at least equal to the percentage determined in INSPRU 1.3.68R(1);
(2) a rise or fall in real estate values in that territory of up to 12.5%; and
(3) a rise or fall in yields on all fixed interest securities of up to 17.5% of the nearest equivalent (in respect of the method of calculation) of the long-term gilt yield.

1.3.74 **[R]** For the purposes of INSPRU 1.3.73R, a *firm* must:
(1) assume that yields on equities and real estate remain unchanged from those applicable at market levels before applying each scenario; and
(2) model a rise or fall in equity, real estate and fixed interest markets as if the movement occurred instantaneously.

1.3.75 **[G]** For the purposes of INSPRU 1.3.73R(1), an appropriate rise or fall in the *market value* of equities to which a *firm* has exposure in a significant territory must be determined having regard to:
(1) an appropriate equity market index (or indices) for that territory; and
(2) the historical volatility of the equity market index (or indices) selected in (1).

1.3.76 **[G]** For the purpose of INSPRU 1.3.75G(1), an appropriate equity market index (or indices) for a territory should be such that:
(1) the constituents of the index (or indices) are reasonably representative of the nature of the equities to which the *firm* is exposed in that territory which are included in the relevant assets identified in accordance with INSPRU 1.3.43R(2); and
(2) the frequency of, and historical data relating to, published values of the index (or indices) are sufficient to enable an average value(s) and historical volatility of the index (or indices) to be calculated over at least the three preceding *financial years*.

General

1.3.77 **[G]**
(1) The purpose of the credit risk scenarios in INSPRU 1.3.78R to INSPRU 1.3.99G is to show the financial effect of specified changes in the general credit risk environment on a *firm's* direct (*counterparty*) and indirect credit risk exposures. The scenarios apply in relation to corporate bonds, debt, *reinsurance* and other exposures, including *derivatives* and *quasi-derivatives*. This is thus quite separate from any reference to allowance for credit risk in INSPRU 3.1.
(2) In the case of bonds and debts, the scenarios are described in terms of an assumed credit rating dependent on the widening of credit spreads-changes in bond and debt credit spreads will have a direct impact on the value of bond and debt assets. Credit ratings are intended to give an indication of the security of the income and capital payments for a bond-the higher the credit rating, the more secure the payments. The reaction of credit spreads to developments in markets for credit risk varies by credit rating and so the scenarios to be

assumed for bonds and debts depend on their ratings. The credit spreads on bonds and debt represent compensation to the investor for the risk of default and downgrade, but also for illiquidity, price volatility and the uncertainty of recovery rates relative to government bonds. Credit spreads on bonds tend to widen during an economic recession to reflect the increased expectations that corporate borrowers may default on their obligations or be subject to rating downgrades.

(3) Changes in bond and debt credit spreads will also be indicative of a change in direct *counterparty* exposure in relation to *reinsurance* and other exposures including *derivatives* and *quasi-derivatives*.

(4) In addition, changes in bond and debt credit spreads may indirectly impact on credit exposures, for example by affecting the payments anticipated under credit *derivative* instruments.

(5) A *firm* will also need to allow for the effect of other components of the single event comprising the combination of scenarios applicable under INSPRU 1.3.43R in assessing exposure to credit risk. For example, in the case of an equity put *option* and a fall in equity market values, the resulting increase in the level of exposure to the *firm's counterparty* for the *option* combined with a change in the quality of the *counterparty* should be allowed for.

1.3.78 **[R]** For the purposes of INSPRU 1.3.44R, the range of credit risk scenarios that a *firm* must assume is:

(1) changes in value resulting from an increase in credit spreads by an amount of up to the spread stress determined according to INSPRU 1.3.84R in respect of any bond or debt item;

(2) changes in value determined according to INSPRU 1.3.94R in respect of any *reinsurance* item or any analogous non-*reinsurance* financing agreement item; and

(3) changes in value determined according to INSPRU 1.3.98R for any other item (including any *derivative* or *quasi-derivative*).

1.3.79 **[R]** For the purposes of INSPRU 1.3.78R, a *firm* must make appropriate allowance for any loss mitigation techniques to the extent that they are loss mitigation techniques relied on for the purpose of INSPRU 2.1.8R in accordance with INSPRU 2.1.16R and INSPRU 2.1.18R.

1.3.80 **[G]** The change in asset or liability values to be determined in relation to a credit risk scenario for the purposes of INSPRU 1.3.43R and INSPRU 1.3.44R is the change in value which would arise on the occurrence of the relevant credit risk scenario as a result of bond, debt, *reinsurance* or other exposures whether or not there is a direct *counterparty* exposure.

1.3.81 **[R]** Where a bond or a debt item or *reinsurance* asset is currently in default, it may be ignored by a *firm* for the purpose of applying INSPRU 1.3.78R.

1.3.82 **[G]** Where a bond or a debt item or a *reinsurance* asset is currently in default and has been specifically provisioned, in accordance with relevant accounting standards, a *firm* is not required to increase the existing default provisions to reflect a worsening of recovery rates.

1.3.83 **[R]** Where the credit risk scenarios in INSPRU 1.3.78R to INSPRU 1.3.99G require a *firm* to assume a change in current credit spread, or a direct change in market value, the *firm* must not change the risk-free yields used to discount future cash flows in calculating the revised *realistic value of liabilities* and *realistic value of assets* (INSPRU 1.3.43R(2)) resulting from those credit risk scenarios.

Spread stresses to be assumed for bonds and debt

1.3.84 **[R]**

(1) In INSPRU 1.3.78R(1) the spread stress which a *firm* must assume for any bond or debt item is:

   (a) for any bond or debt item issued or guaranteed by an organisation which is in accordance with INSPRU 1.3.87R a credit risk scenario exempt organisation in respect of that item, zero basis points; and

   (b) for any other bond or debt item:

      (i) Y if the credit rating description of that other bond or debt item determined by reference to INSPRU 1.3.89R is not "Highly speculative or very vulnerable"; and

      (ii) otherwise the larger of Y and Z.

(2) For the purpose of (1)(b):

   (a) Y is the product of the spread factor for that bond or debt item and the square root of S, where:

      (i) the spread factor for a bond or debt item is the spread factor shown in the final column of Table INSPRU 1.3.90R, in the row of that Table corresponding to the credit rating description of the bond or debt item determined for the purpose of this *rule* by reference to INSPRU 1.3.89R; and

(ii) subject to (3), S is the current credit spread for a bond or debt item, expressed as a number of basis points, which the *firm* must determine as the current yield on that bond or debt item in excess of the current gross redemption yield on the government bond most similar to that bond or debt item in terms of currency of denomination and equivalent term; and

(b) Z is the change in credit spread expressed as a number of basis points that would result in the current market value of the bond or debt falling by 5%.

(3) Where, for the purposes of (2)(a)(ii), there is no suitable government bond, the *firm* must use its best estimate of the gross redemption yield that would apply for a notional government bond similar to the bond or debt item in terms of currency of denomination and equivalent term.

1.3.85 **[R]** For the purpose of INSPRU 1.3.84R(1)(a), a guarantee must be direct, explicit, unconditional and irrevocable.

1.3.86 **[G]**

(1) As an example, a bond item has the credit rating description "exceptional or extremely strong" and currently yields 49 basis points in excess of the most similar government bond. The spread factor for that bond item is 3.00 by reference to Table INSPRU 1.3.90R. Since S is 49, the square root of S is 7 and the spread stress for that item is 3 times 7, that is, 21 basis points. The *firm* must consider the impact of an increase in spreads by up to 21 basis points for that item.

(2) As a further example, a bond item has the credit rating description "highly speculative or very vulnerable". For this bond, S is 400, being the current spread for that bond expressed as a number of basis points. The spread factor for the bond is 24.00. So the *firm* must consider the impact of an increase in spreads by up to 24.00 times 20 i.e. 480 basis points for that item. The bond is however of short duration and the reduction in market value resulting from an additional spread of 480 basis points is less than 5 per cent of its current market value. A 5 per cent reduction in its market value would result from a spread widening of 525 basis points. The *firm* must consider the impact of an increase in spreads by up to 525 basis points for that item by virtue of its credit rating description.

(3) The calculation of the credit spread on commercial floating rate notes warrants particular consideration. Suppose, for example, that a notional floating rate note guaranteed by the *UK* government would have a market consistent price of X. This price can be estimated based on an assumed distribution of future payments under the floating rate note, and the current forward gilt curve. Suppose further that the market price of the commercial floating rate note is Y, where Y is less than X. A *firm* could calculate what parallel upward shift in the forward gilt curve would result in the notional government-backed floating rate note having a market price of Y for an unchanged assumed distribution of future payments. The size of the resulting shift could then be taken as the credit spread on the commercial floating rate note.

(4) In arriving at the estimated gross redemption yield in INSPRU 1.3.84R(3), the *firm* may have regard to any appropriate swap rates for the currency of denomination of the bond or debt item, adjusted to take appropriate account of observed differences between swap rates and the yields on government bonds.

1.3.87 **[R]** For the purposes of this section:

(1) an organisation is a credit risk scenario exempt organisation in respect of an item if the organisation is:
- (a) the European Central Bank; or
- (b) any central government or central bank which, in relation to that item, satisfies the conditions in (2); or
- (c) a multilateral development bank which is listed in (3); or
- (d) an international organisation which is listed in (4);

(2) the conditions in (1)(b) are that, for any claim against the central government or central bank denominated in the currency in which the item is denominated:
- (a) a credit rating is available from at least one listed rating agency nominated in accordance with INSPRU 1.3.92R; and
- (b) the credit rating description in the first column of Table INSPRU 1.3.90R corresponding to the lowest such credit rating is either "exceptionally or extremely strong" or "very strong";

(3) for the purposes of (1)(c) the listed multilateral development banks are:
- (a) the International Bank for Reconstruction and Development;
- (b) the International Finance Corporation;
- (c) the Inter-American Development Bank;
- (d) the Asian Development Bank;
- (e) the African Development Bank;
- (f) the Council of Europe Development Bank;
- (g) the Nordic Investment Bank;
- (h) the Caribbean Development Bank;

(i) the European Bank for Reconstruction and Development;
(j) the European Investment Bank;
(k) the European Investment Fund; and
(l) the Multilateral Investment Guarantee Agency;
(4) for the purposes of (1)(d) the listed international organisations are:
(a) the *EU*;
(b) the International Monetary Fund; and
(c) the Bank for International Settlements.

1.3.88 **[G]** Under INSPRU 1.3.87R(2), a *firm* needs to take account of the currency in which the claim is denominated when it is considering claims on or guaranteed by a central government or central bank. It is possible, for example, that a given central bank would be a credit risk scenario exempt organisation in respect of claims on it denominated in its domestic currency, while not being a credit risk scenario exempt organisation in respect of claims on it denominated in a currency other than its domestic currency-the central government or central bank may have been assigned different credit assessments depending on the currency in which the claim on it is denominated.

1.3.89 **[R]**
(1) For the purposes of this section, the credit rating description of a bond or debt item is to be determined in accordance with (2) and (3).
(2) If the item has at least one credit rating nominated in accordance with INSPRU 1.3.92R ("a rated item"), its credit rating description is:
(a) where it has only one nominated credit rating, the general description given in the first column of Table INSPRU 1.3.90R corresponding to that rating; or
(b) where it has two or more nominated credit ratings and the two highest nominated ratings fall within the same general description given in the first column of that Table, that description; or
(c) where it has two or more nominated credit ratings and the two highest nominated ratings do not fall within the same general description given in the first column of that Table, the second highest of those two descriptions.
(3) If the item is not a rated item, its credit rating description is the general description given in the first column of Table INSPRU 1.3.90R that most closely corresponds to the *firm's* own assessment of the item's credit quality.
(4) An assessment under (3) must be made by the *firm* for the purposes of the credit risk scenario having due regard to the seniority of the bond or debt and the credit quality of the bond or debt issuer.

Table: Listed rating agencies, credit rating descriptions, spread factors

1.3.90 **[R]**

Credit Rating Description	Listed rating agencies				Spread Factor
	A.M. Best Company	Fitch Ratings	Moody's Investors Service	Standard & Poor's Corpora-tion	
Exceptional or extremely strong	aaa	AAA	Aaa	AAA	3.00
Very strong	aa	AA	Aa	AA	5.25
Strong	a	A	A	A	6.75
Adequate	bbb	BBB	Baa	BBB	9.25
Speculative or less vulner-able	bb	BB	Ba	BB	15.00
Very speculative or more vulnerable	B	B	B	B	24.00
Highly speculative or very vulnerable	Below B	Below B	Below B	Below B	24.00

1.3.91 **[G]** Where listed rating agencies provide ratings by sub-category then all ratings should be allocated to the main ratings category (e.g. ratings sub-category A+ or A- would be allocated to the assigned ratings category "Strong").

1.3.92 **[R]** For the purposes of INSPRU 1.3.87R and INSPRU 1.3.89R, a *firm* may, subject to (1) to (5), nominate for use credit ratings produced by one or more of the rating agencies listed in INSPRU 1.3.93R:
(1) if the *firm* decides to nominate for use for an item the credit rating produced by one or more rating agencies, it must do so consistently for all similar items;

(2) the *firm* must use credit ratings in a continuous and consistent way over time;
(3) the *firm* must nominate for use only credit ratings that take into account both principal and interest;
(4) if the *firm* nominates for use credit ratings produced by one of the listed rating agencies then the *firm* must use solicited credit ratings produced by that listed rating agency; and
(5) the *firm* may nominate for use unsolicited credit ratings produced by one or more of the listed rating agencies except where there are reasonable grounds for believing that any unsolicited credit ratings produced by the agency are used so as to obtain inappropriate advantages in the relationship with rated parties.

1.3.93 **[R]** In this section, a listed rating agency is:
(1) A.M. Best Company; or
(2) Fitch Ratings; or
(3) Moody's Investors Service; or
(4) Standard & Poor's Corporation.

Credit risk scenario for reinsurance

1.3.94 **[R]**
(1) The contracts of *reinsurance* or analogous non-*reinsurance* financing agreements to which INSPRU 1.3.78R(2) applies are those:
(a) into which the *firm* has entered;
(b) which represent an economic asset under the single event applicable under INSPRU 1.3.43R(3); and
(c) which are material (individually or in aggregate).
(2) For the purposes of (1), no account is to be taken of *reinsurance* or analogous non-*reinsurance* financing arrangements between *undertakings* in the same *group* where:
(a) the ceding and accepting *undertakings* are regulated by the *FSA* or a regulatory body in a *designated State or territory* for insurance (including *reinsurance*);
(b) no subsequent cessions of the ceded risk which are material (individually or in aggregate) are made to subsequent accepting *undertakings* by accepting *undertakings* (including subsequent accepting *undertakings*) other than to subsequent accepting *undertakings* which are in the same *group*; and
(c) for any subsequent cession or cessions of the ceded risk which are material (individually or in aggregate) each of the ceding and accepting *undertakings* (including subsequent accepting *undertakings*) is regulated by the *FSA* or a regulatory body in a *designated State or territory* for insurance (including *reinsurance*).
(3) The change in value which a *firm* must determine for a contract of *reinsurance* or an analogous non-*reinsurance* financing agreement is the *firm's* best estimate of the change in realistic value which would result from changes in credit risk market conditions consistent, subject to (4), with the changes in credit spreads determined in accordance with INSPRU 1.3.78R(1).
(4) For the purpose of (3), 5% should be replaced by 10% in INSPRU 1.3.84R(2)(b).

1.3.95 **[G]**
(1) *Reinsurance* and analogous non-*reinsurance* financing agreements entered into by the *firm*, either with or acting as a *reinsurer*, must be included within the scope of the scenario. The combined rights and obligations under a contract of *reinsurance* or an analogous non-*reinsurance* financing agreement may represent an economic asset or liability. The value placed by the *firm* on the *reinsurance* item or non-*reinsurance* financing item should allow for a realistic assessment of the risks transferred and the risks of *counterparty* default associated with the item. In the case of analogous non-*reinsurance* financing agreements, references to terms such as "*reinsurer*", "ceding *undertakings*" and "accepting *undertakings*" include *undertakings* which by analogy are *reinsurers*, ceding or accepting *undertakings*. Analogous non-*reinsurance* financing agreements include contingent loans, securitisations and any other arrangements in respect of *contracts of insurance* that are analogous to contracts of *reinsurance* in terms of the risks transferred and the finance provided.
(2) In assessing values in accordance with INSPRU 1.3.94R, a *firm* may consider it appropriate to determine values by drawing an analogy with the approach in respect of bond and debt items set out in INSPRU 1.3.84R. (This might be the case if, in economic terms, the item being valued sufficiently resembles a bond or debt item-an alternative approach might otherwise be preferred). If the *firm* does consider it appropriate to draw an analogy, the "credit spread" assumed should be consistent with the assumed default probabilities and the values placed on the *reinsurance* asset for the purposes of determining the *realistic values of assets* and *liabilities*. A *firm* may regard it as appropriate to have regard to any financial strength ratings applicable to the *reinsurer*, but if so should apply the same principles set out in INSPRU 1.3.92R for the nomination of financial strength ratings. Table INSPRU 1.3.97G

provides *guidance* as to the allocation of spread factors which a *firm* may, by analogy, deem appropriate to apply. Appropriate allowance should be made for any change in the extent of the *counterparty* exposure under the assumed scenario.

(3) The changes in credit risk spreads determined for bond and debt items in accordance with INSPRU 1.3.78R(1) are required to result in a reduction in market value for some items of 5% of their current value through the operation of INSPRU 1.3.84R(2)(b). For *reinsurance* contracts and analogous non-*reinsurance* financing agreements, determining the change in value by reference to INSPRU 1.3.94R(3) requires a *firm* to consider the possibility of *counterparty* default in changed credit risk market conditions. Where in the changed credit risk market conditions assumed to apply the *firm's* assessment of the *counterparty* risk would result in the asset being considered equivalent to "Highly speculative or very vulnerable", the reduction in value required is at least 10% of its current value. INSPRU 1.3.94R(4) relates to this requirement.

1.3.96 **[G]** A financial strength rating of a *reinsurer* refers to a current assessment of the financial security characteristics of the *reinsurer* with respect to its ability to pay *claims* under its *reinsurance* contracts and treaties in accordance with their terms.

1.3.97 **[G]** Table: Listed rating agencies, financial strength descriptions and spread factors

Financial Strength Description	**A.M. Best Company**	**Fitch Ratings**	**Moody's Investors Service**	**Standard & Poor's Corporation**	**Spread Factor**
Superior, extremely strong	A++	AAA	Aaa	AAA	3.00
Superior, very strong	A+	AA	Aa	AA	5.25
Excellent or strong	A, A-	A	A	A	6.75
Good	B++,B+	BBB	Baa	BBB	9.25
Fair, marginal	B, B-	BB	Ba	BB	15.00
Marginal, weak	C++,C+	B	B	B	24.00
Unrated or very weak	Unrated or below C++,C+	Unrated or below B	Unrated or below B	Unrated or below B	24.00

Credit risk scenario for other exposures (including any derivative or quasi-derivative)

1.3.98 **[R]** For the purposes of INSPRU 1.3.78R(3), the change in value which must be determined for any other item (including any *derivative* or *quasi-derivative*) which represents an economic asset under the single event applicable under INSPRU 1.3.43R(3) is the *firm's* best estimate of the change in the realistic value of that item which would result from changes in credit risk market conditions consistent with the changes in credit spreads determined in accordance with INSPRU 1.3.78R(1) and the changes in value determined in accordance with INSPRU 1.3.78R(2).

1.3.99 **[G]** In applying INSPRU 1.3.98R, a *firm* should assess the total impact on the value of the item resulting from the assumed changed credit risk market conditions. The total change in value may result from the interaction of a number of separate influences. For example, a widening of credit spreads may imply an impact on the amount exposed to *counterparty* default as well as on the likelihood of that default. Each factor influencing the change in value needs separate consideration. It should be assumed, both for determining amounts exposed to *counterparty* default and the likelihood of such default that there will be no change in the likelihood of default in relation to an item issued by or guaranteed by an organisation which is in respect of that item a credit risk scenario exempt organisation (INSPRU 1.3.87R). INSPRU 1.3.77(5) is also relevant in this context.

Persistency risk scenario

1.3.100 **[R]** For the purposes of the persistency risk scenario in INSPRU 1.3.44R(6), a *firm* must allow for the effects of an increase or a decrease in persistency experience of its *with-profits insurance contract* by adjusting the termination rates in each year of projection by 32.5% of the termination rates assumed in the calculation of the *realistic value of liabilities* in INSPRU 1.3.40R.

1.3.101 **[R]** The termination rates referred to in INSPRU 1.3.100R are the rates of termination (including the paying-up of *policies*, but excluding deaths, maturities and retirements) other than on dates specified by the *firm* where:

(1) a guaranteed amount applies as the minimum amount which will be paid on *claim*; or

(2) any payments to the *policyholder* cannot be reduced at the discretion of the *firm* by its applying a market value adjustment.

1.3.102 **[R]** For the purposes of INSPRU 1.3.100R, the increase or decrease in termination rates must be applied to the projection of terminations up to *policy* guarantee dates and between *policy* guarantee dates, but not to the assumptions as to the proportion of *policyholders* taking up the guarantees at *policy* guarantee dates.

1.3.103 **[G]** INSPRU 1.3.100R to INSPRU 1.3.102R require *firms* to apply a persistency stress test to the *realistic value of liabilities*. Where a *firm* brings the present value of *non-profit insurance business* in a *with-profits fund* into the calculation of the *realistic value of assets* (see INSPRU 1.3.33R) there is no requirement to stress this asset for changes in persistency assumptions.

Realistic value of liabilities: detailed provisions

1.3.104 **[G]** INSPRU 1.3.40R sets out the three elements comprising the *realistic value of liabilities* for a *with-profits fund*. The remainder of this section contains general *rules* and *guidance* on determining the *realistic value of liabilities* plus further detail relating to each of those elements separately, as follows:
(1) general *rules* and *guidance* in INSPRU 1.3.105R to INSPRU 1.3.115G;
(2) *with-profits benefits reserve* in INSPRU 1.3.116R to INSPRU 1.3.135G;
(3) *future policy related liabilities* in INSPRU 1.3.136G to INSPRU 1.3.189G; and
(4) *realistic current liabilities* in INSPRU 1.3.190R and INSPRU 1.3.191R.

Methods and assumptions: general

1.3.105 **[R]** In calculating the *realistic value of liabilities* for a *with-profits fund*, a *firm* must use methods and assumptions which:
(1) are appropriate to the business of the *firm*;
(2) are consistent from year to year without arbitrary changes (that is, changes without adequate reasons);
(3) are consistent with the method of valuing assets (GENPRU 1.3);
(4) make full provision for tax payable out of the *with-profits fund*, based on current legislation and practice, together with any known future changes, and on a consistent basis with the other methods and assumptions used;
(5) take into account discretionary benefits which are at least equal to, and charges which are no more than, the levels required for the *firm* to fulfil its regulatory duty to treat its *customers* fairly;
(6) take into account prospective management actions (INSPRU 1.3.53R) and *policyholder* actions (INSPRU 1.3.59R);
(7) provide for shareholder transfers out of the *with-profits fund* as a liability of the fund;
(8) have regard to generally accepted actuarial practice; and
(9) are consistent with the *firm's PPFM*.

1.3.106 **[G]** More specific *rules* and *guidance* are set out below on some aspects of the methods and assumptions to be used in calculating the *realistic value of liabilities* for a *with-profits fund*. In contrast to the *mathematical reserves* requirements in INSPRU 1.2.10R(4) and INSPRU 1.2.13R, there is no requirement to include margins for adverse deviation of relevant factors in calculating the *realistic value of liabilities*. Assumptions need be no more prudent than is necessary to achieve a best estimate, taking into account the *firm's PPFM* and its regulatory duty to treat its *customers* fairly. Where there is no requirement for a *PPFM*, for example non-*UK* business, a *firm* should use assumptions that are consistent with the *firm's* documented approach to treating its *customers* fairly. A *firm* may judge that a margin should be included in its calculations to avoid an understatement of the *realistic value of liabilities* as a result of uncertainty, for example, either in its method or in its data.

1.3.107 **[G]** The amount and timing of tax charges affect the amount of assets available to meet *policyholder* liabilities. INSPRU 1.3.105R(4) requires *firms* to provide fully for all tax payable out of the *with-profits fund* on a basis consistent with the other assumptions and methods used in deriving the realistic balance sheet. So, for example, all projections which underlie the realistic valuation of assets or liabilities must allow for taxation. The approach adopted should not give any credit for any reduction in tax deriving from future expenses or deficits which is attributable to future new business. For assets backing capital requirements it is not necessary to take into consideration future tax charges on investment income generated by those assets. However, *firms* should consider this aspect in their capital planning.

1.3.108 **[G]** [intentionally blank]

Valuation of contracts: General

1.3.109 **[R]**
(1) A *firm* must determine the amount of the *with-profits benefits reserve* or the *future policy related liabilities* for a *with-profits fund* by carrying out a separate calculation in relation to each *with-profits insurance contract* or for each group of similar contracts.

(2) Appropriate approximations or generalisations may be made where they are likely to provide the same, or a higher, result than a separate calculation for each contract.

(3) A *firm* must set up additional reserves on an aggregated basis for general risks which are not specific to individual contracts or a group of similar contacts where the *firm* considers the *realistic value of liabilities* may otherwise be understated.

1.3.110 **[R]** For the purpose of INSPRU 1.3.109R(1), a group of similar contracts is such that the conditions in INSPRU 1.3.109R(2) are satisfied.

1.3.111 **[G]** Where a *firm* has grouped individual contracts for the purpose of calculating the *mathematical reserves* for a *with-profits fund* (in accordance with INSPRU 1.2.22R), the *firm* is not required to use the same grouping of contracts in calculating the *with-profits benefits reserve* or *future policy related liabilities* for that fund.

1.3.112 **[G]** In contrast to INSPRU 1.2.24R for the *mathematical reserves*, treating individual contracts as an asset is not prohibited if, and to the extent that, this treatment does not conflict with a *firm's* regulatory duty to treat its *customers* fairly.

1.3.113 **[G]** In calculating the *with-profits benefits reserve*, an overall (grouped or pooled) approach may be appropriate under either of the two methods set out in INSPRU 1.3.116R. In particular, the calculation of aggregate retrospective reserves (see INSPRU 1.3.118R) and the projection of future cash flows (see INSPRU 1.3.128R) based on suitable specimen *policies* is permitted.

1.3.114 **[G]** In calculating the *future policy related liabilities*, the grouping of *policies* for valuing the costs of guarantees, options or smoothing, and their representation by representative *policies*, is acceptable provided the *firm* can demonstrate that the grouping of *policies* does not materially misrepresent the underlying exposure and does not significantly misstate the costs. A *firm* should exercise care in grouping *policies* in order to ensure that the risk exposure is not inappropriately distorted by, for example, forming groups containing *policies* with guarantees that are "in the money" and *policies* with guarantees well "out of the money". A *firm* should also have regard to the effects of *policyholder* behaviour over time on the spread of the outstanding guarantees or options.

1.3.115 **[G]** Where a *firm* groups similar *policies* for the purpose of calculating the *with- profits benefits reserve* or the *future policy related liabilities*, the *firm* should carry out sufficient validation to be reasonably sure that the grouping of *policies* has not resulted in the loss of any significant attributes of the portfolio being valued.

With-profits benefits reserve

1.3.116 **[R]** A *firm* must calculate a with-profits benefits reserve for a with-profits fund using either:

(1) a retrospective calculation under INSPRU 1.3.118R (the retrospective method); or

(2) a prospective calculation under INSPRU 1.3.128R of all future cash flows expected to arise under, or in respect of, each of the *with-profits insurance contracts* written in that fund (the prospective method).

1.3.117 **[R]** Subject to INSPRU 1.3.105R(2), a *firm* may use different methods under INSPRU 1.3.116R for different types or generations of *with-profits insurance contracts*.

Retrospective method

1.3.118 **[R]** In the retrospective method of calculating a *with-profits benefits reserve*, a *firm* must calculate either the aggregate of the retrospective reserves in respect of each *with-profits insurance contract* or, to the extent permitted by INSPRU 1.3.109R and INSPRU 1.3.110R, the total retrospective reserve in respect of each group of *with-profits insurance contracts*.

1.3.119 **[R]** In calculating the retrospective reserve for a *with-profits insurance contract*, or the total retrospective reserve in respect of a group of *with-profits insurance contracts*, a *firm* must take account of at least the following:

(1) *premiums* received from the *policyholder*;

(2) any expenses incurred or charges made (including *commissions*);

(3) any partial benefits paid or due;

(4) any investment income on, and any increases (or decreases) in, asset values;

(5) any tax paid or payable;

(6) any amounts received (or paid) under contracts of *reinsurance* or analogous non-*reinsurance* financing agreements, where relevant to retrospective reserves;

(7) any shareholder transfers and any associated tax paid or payable; and

(8) any permanent enhancements to (or deductions from) the retrospective reserves made by the *firm*.

1.3.120 **[G]** In taking account of amounts in INSPRU 1.3.119R(6), due regard should be had to the specific details of each relevant contract of *reinsurance* or analogous non-*reinsurance* financing agreement and the relationship between the amounts received (or paid) and the value of the benefit granted (or received) under the arrangement. This should take into consideration, for example, the risk of default and differences in the *firm's* realistic assessment of the risks transferred and the contractual terms for such transfer of risk. Analogous non-*reinsurance* financing agreements include contingent loans, securitisations and any other arrangements in respect of *contracts of insurance* that are analogous to contracts of *reinsurance* in terms of the risks transferred and the finance provided.

1.3.121 **[G]** Where allowance is made for shareholder transfers, this should be in respect of the accrued bonus entitlement reflected in the retrospective reserve. This would include both *annual bonuses* already declared and accrued *final bonus*. However, shareholder transfers in respect of surplus yet to be credited to retrospective reserves should not be charged to those reserves until the corresponding surplus is credited.

1.3.122 **[R]** In calculating retrospective reserves, a *firm* must have regard to its regulatory duty to treat its *customers* fairly and must ensure that its approach is consistent with its *Principles and Practices of Financial Management.*

1.3.123 **[R]** In calculating retrospective reserves, a *firm* must ensure its treatment of past cash flows, and of any future cash flows, is consistent with those cash flows valued in its prospective calculation of the *future policy related liabilities* for that fund in accordance with the *rules* in INSPRU 1.3.136G to INSPRU 1.3.189G.

1.3.124 **[G]** An example of INSPRU 1.3.123R concerns future shareholder transfers. A *firm* must make adequate provision for future shareholder transfers within the *future policy related liabilities* (see INSPRU 1.3.165R). The basis of provisioning needs to be consistent with the amounts accrued within retrospective reserves and the amounts already transferred out of the *with-profits fund*.

1.3.125 **[G]** Another example of the application of INSPRU 1.3.123R relates to the reference in INSPRU 1.3.119R(8) to past permanent enhancements to (or deductions from) retrospective reserves made by *firms*. This item may include past miscellaneous surplus (or losses) which have been credited to (or debited from) retrospective reserves. Any other enhancements (or deductions) made on a temporary basis and any future surplus (or losses) that *firms* intend to credit to (or debit from) retrospective reserves should be included under the *future policy related liabilities* (see INSPRU 1.3.137R).

1.3.126 **[G]** *Firms* characteristically use a range of calculation methods to determine retrospective reserves. A *firm's* definition and calculation of retrospective reserves will depend on a number of factors. These include: the *firm's* practice; its administration and accounting systems; the extent of its historical records; and the composition of its with-profits portfolio. The *rules* and *guidance* for the retrospective method are drawn up to be sufficiently flexible to accommodate the diversity of calculation methods used by *firms*, rather than to enforce any particular method of calculation of retrospective reserves. INSPRU 1.3.119R simply sets minimum standards that all retrospective methods must meet.

1.3.127 **[G]** For the purposes of INSPRU 1.3.119R(2) and INSPRU 1.3.128R(2), the phrases 'charges made' or 'charges to be made' refer to circumstances where types of risk (such as mortality risk, longevity risk and investment risk) are met by the *firm* or *with-profits fund* in return for a charge deducted by the *firm* from the *with-profits benefits reserve*.

Prospective method

1.3.128 **[R]** In the prospective method of calculating a *with-profits benefits reserve*, a *firm* must take account of at least the following cash flows:
(1) future *premiums*;
(2) expenses to be incurred or charges to be made, including *commissions*;
(3) benefits payable (INSPRU 1.3.129R);
(4) tax payable;
(5) any amounts to be received (or paid) under contracts of *reinsurance* or analogous non-*reinsurance* financing agreements, where relevant to *with- profits insurance contracts* being valued; and
(6) shareholder transfers.

1.3.129 **[R]** For the purposes of INSPRU 1.3.128R(3), benefits payable include:
(1) all guaranteed benefits, including guaranteed amounts payable on death and maturity, guaranteed *surrender values* and paid-up values;
(2) vested, declared and allotted bonuses to which *policyholders* are entitled; and
(3) future *annual* and *final bonuses* at least equal to the levels required for the *firm* to fulfil its regulatory duty to treat its *customers* fairly.

1.3.130 **[R]** A *firm* must value the cash flows listed in INSPRU 1.3.128R using best estimate assumptions of future experience, having regard to generally accepted actuarial practice and taking into account the *firm's PPFM* and its regulatory duty to treat its *customers* fairly.

1.3.131 **[G]** The prospective method sets the *with-profits benefits reserve* at the net present value of future cash flows listed in INSPRU 1.3.128R.

1.3.132 **[G]** In contrast to INSPRU 1.2.10R(4) and INSPRU 1.2.13R relating to the methods and assumptions used to value the *mathematical reserves*, there is no requirement to value future cash flows using assumptions that include margins for adverse deviation. Also there are no detailed *rules* as to the future yields on assets, discount rates, *premium* levels, expenses, tax, mortality, morbidity, persistency and *reinsurance*. A *firm* should make its own assessment as to the amount of these future cash flows including bonuses and discretionary surrender or transfer values. A *firm* should make a realistic assessment of longevity risk and asset default risk (including default risk arising under contracts of *reinsurance* or analogous non-*reinsurance* financing agreements) within the best estimate assumptions of future experience required by INSPRU 1.3.130R.

1.3.133 **[G]** In valuing the future cash flows listed in INSPRU 1.3.128R, the *firm* should use a projection term which is long enough to capture all material cash flows arising from the contract or groups of contracts being valued. If the projection term does not extend to the term of the last *policy*, the *firm* should check that the shorter projection term does not significantly affect the results.

1.3.134 **[R]** Where a *firm* expects to pay additional benefits that are not included in the cash flows listed in INSPRU 1.3.128R, it must make adequate provision for these benefits in calculating the *future policy related liabilities* in accordance with the *rules* in INSPRU 1.3.136G to INSPRU 1.3.189G.

1.3.135 **[G]** The prospective assessment of the *with-profits benefits reserve* will usually be on a deterministic basis. A *firm* will have to make further provision in the *future policy-related liabilities* for, for example, the costs of potential asset fluctuations or *policy* options.

Future policy related liabilities
Overview of liabilities

1.3.136 **[G]** INSPRU 1.3.137R lists the *future policy related liabilities* for a *with-profits fund* that form part of a *firm's realistic value of liabilities* in INSPRU 1.3.40R. Detailed *rules* and *guidance* relating to particular types of liability and asset are set out in INSPRU 1.3.139R to INSPRU 1.3.168G. These are followed by *rules* and *guidance* that deal with certain aspects of several liabilities (that is, liabilities relating to guarantees, options and smoothing):

(1) INSPRU 1.3.169R to INSPRU 1.3.186G refer to valuing the costs of guarantees, options and smoothing; and
(2) INSPRU 1.3.187R to INSPRU 1.3.189G refer to the treatment of surplus on guarantees, options and smoothing.

1.3.137 **[R]** The *future policy related liabilities* for a *with-profits fund* are equal to the sum of amounts, as they relate to that fund, in respect of (1) to (11) to the extent each is valued as a liability less the sum of amounts, as they relate to that fund, in respect of (1) to (11) to the extent each is valued as an asset:

(1) past miscellaneous surplus (or deficit) planned to be attributed to the *with-profits benefits reserve* (see INSPRU 1.3.139R);
(2) planned enhancements to the *with-profits benefits reserve* (see INSPRU 1.3.141R);
(3) planned deductions for the costs of guarantees, options and smoothing from the *with-profits benefits reserve* (see INSPRU 1.3.144R);
(4) planned deductions for other costs deemed chargeable to the *with-profits benefits reserve* (see INSPRU 1.3.146R);
(5) future costs of contractual guarantees (other than financial options) (see INSPRU 1.3.148R);
(6) future costs of non-contractual commitments (see INSPRU 1.3.154R);
(7) future costs of financial options (see INSPRU 1.3.156G);
(8) future costs of smoothing (see INSPRU 1.3.158R);
(9) financing costs (see INSPRU 1.3.162R);
(10) any other further liabilities required for the *firm* to fulfil its regulatory duty to treat its *customers* fairly; and
(11) other *long-term insurance liabilities* (see INSPRU 1.3.165R).

1.3.138 **[G]** Some of the elements of the calculation set out in INSPRU 1.3.137R may have already been taken into consideration in the calculation of the *with- profits benefits reserve*, either under the retrospective method (see INSPRU 1.3.118R onwards) or the prospective method (see INSPRU 1.3.128R onwards). Where this is the case, the adjustments made under INSPRU 1.3.137R should be such that no double-counting arises.

Past miscellaneous surplus (or deficit) planned to be attributed to the with- profits benefits reserve

1.3.139 **[R]** In calculating the *future policy related liabilities* for a *with-profits fund*, a *firm* must allow for past miscellaneous surplus (or deficit) which it intends to attribute to the *with-profits benefits reserve* for that fund but which has not yet been permanently credited to (or debited from) the *with-profits benefits reserve* for that fund.

1.3.140 **[G]** Past miscellaneous surplus (or deficit) already permanently credited to (or debited from) the *with-profits benefits reserve* will have been included in the calculation of the *with-profits benefits reserve* in accordance with INSPRU 1.3.119R(8).

Planned enhancements to the with-profits benefits reserve

1.3.141 **[R]** In calculating the *future policy related liabilities* for a *with-profits fund*, a *firm* must make provision for any future planned enhancements to the *with- profits benefits reserve* for that fund that cannot be financed out of the resources of the *with-profits benefits reserve* and future *premiums*.

1.3.142 **[G]** For the purposes of INSPRU 1.3.141R, planned enhancements to the *with- profits benefits reserve* will arise when a *firm* has a contractual obligation, or a non-contractual commitment (arising from its regulatory duty to treat *customers* fairly), to enhance *claims* on some classes of *policy* (perhaps in the form of specially enhanced future bonus rates). In such circumstances, the present value of the costs of paying out a target asset share that is more than the projected *with-profits benefits reserve* for those classes of *policy* for which this practice is applicable should be included in the amount of the *future policy related liabilities*. For example, a *firm* may have a non-contractual commitment (arising from its regulatory duty to treat *customers* fairly) to pay enhanced benefits but have discretion not to make such payments in adverse circumstances. Such planned enhancements should be provided for in the realistic balance sheet, but allowance should be made for management action in the calculation of the *risk capital margin*.

1.3.143 **[G]** The valuation of *claims* in excess of targeted asset shares in respect of guarantees, options and smoothing, including those arising under guaranteed annuity rates, should be carried out in accordance with INSPRU 1.3.169R to INSPRU 1.3.186G.

Planned deductions for the costs of guarantees, options and smoothing from the with-profits benefits reserve

1.3.144 **[R]** Where a *firm* expects to deduct future charges from the *with-profits benefits reserve* for a *with-profits fund* to cover the costs of guarantees, options or smoothing for that fund, the *firm* must take credit for these future charges in calculating the *future policy related liabilities* for that fund.

1.3.145 **[G]** In calculating *future policy related liabilities* for a *with-profits fund*, a *firm* should take credit under INSPRU 1.3.137R(3) for the present value of the future "margins" available in respect of charges deducted to cover the costs of guarantees, options and smoothing. INSPRU 1.3.188R requires *firms* that accumulate the charges made less costs incurred to provide for any surplus on the experience account as a realistic liability. Any such provision should be made under INSPRU 1.3.137R(5), INSPRU 1.3.137R(7) or INSPRU 1.3.137R(8) depending on the nature of the charges made, and has no effect on the amount calculated under INSPRU 1.3.144R.

Planned deductions for other costs deemed chargeable to the with-profits benefits reserve

1.3.146 **[R]** Where a *firm* expects to deduct future charges (other than those valued in INSPRU 1.3.144R) from the *with-profits benefits reserve* for a *with-profits fund*, the *firm* must take credit for these future charges in calculating the *future policy-related liabilities* for that fund.

1.3.147 **[G]** A *firm* should take credit for the present value of the other future "margins" available. The circumstances where such margins may arise include:

(1) where a *firm* is targeting *claims* at less than 100% of the *with-profits benefits reserve*, the amount of such shortfall; and

(2) where a *firm* expects to deduct any future charges (other than those for guarantees, options and smoothing) from the *with-profits benefits reserve*.

1.3.148 **[R]** Future costs of contractual guarantees (other than financial options)

A *firm* must make provision for the costs of paying excess *claim* amounts for a *with-profits fund* where the *firm* expects that the amount in (1) may be greater than the amount in (2), calculated as at the date of *claim*:

(1) the value of guarantees arising under a *policy* or group of *policies* in the fund; and

(2) the fund's *with-profits benefits reserve* allocated in respect of that *policy* or group of *policies*.

1.3.149 **[R]** For the purposes of INSPRU 1.3.148R, the future costs of guarantees cannot be negative.

1.3.150 **[G]** In carrying out projections to calculate the cost of guarantees under INSPRU 1.3.137R the opening liability should be set equal to the *with-profits benefit reserve* (see INSPRU 1.3.118R), adjusted for miscellaneous surplus or deficits (see INSPRU 1.3.137R(1)) and planned enhancements (see INSPRU 1.3.141R).

1.3.151 **[G]** In projecting forward the *with-profits benefits reserve*, adjusted as in INSPRU 1.3.150G, to the date of *claim* for the purposes of INSPRU 1.3.148R, the *firm* should use market consistent assumptions for the expected future *premium* and investment income (including realised and unrealised gains or losses), expenses and *claims*, any charges to be deducted, tax and any other item of income or outgo. This projection should be carried out on the same basis as is described in INSPRU 1.3.130R.

1.3.152 **[G]** INSPRU 1.3.169R to INSPRU 1.3.186G contain further *rules* and *guidance* on the valuation of guarantees, options and smoothing.

1.3.153 **[G]** Some examples of contractual guarantees are:

(1) for conventional *with-profits insurance contracts*, guaranteed sums assured and bonuses on death, maturity or retirement; and

(2) for *accumulating with-profits policies*, guarantees at a point in time or guaranteed minimum bonus rates.

Future costs of non-contractual commitments

1.3.154 **[R]** A *firm* must make provision for future costs in addition to those in INSPRU 1.3.148R where the *firm* expects to pay further amounts to meet non- contractual commitments to *customers* or pay other benefits that need to be provided to fulfil a *firm's* regulatory duty to treat its *customers* fairly.

1.3.155 **[G]** Some examples of these non-contractual commitments are:

(1) statements by the *firm* regarding the ability of *policies* to cover defined amounts, such as the repayment of a mortgage;

(2) statements by the *firm* regarding regular withdrawals from a *policy* being without penalty;

(3) guaranteed annuity and cash option rates being provided beyond the strict interpretation of the *policy*; and

(4) the costs of any promises to *customers* or other benefits that need to be provided to fulfil a *firm's* regulatory duty to treat its *customers* fairly.

Future costs of financial options

1.3.156 **[G]** Financial options include guaranteed annuity and cash option rates.

1.3.157 **[G]** INSPRU 1.3.169R to INSPRU 1.3.186G contain further *rules* and *guidance* on the valuation of options.

Future costs of smoothing

1.3.158 **[R]** A *firm* must make provision for future smoothing costs of a *with-profits fund* where the *firm* expects that the *claims* paid on a *policy* or group of *policies* in the fund will vary from the greater of:

(1) the value of guarantees determined in INSPRU 1.3.148R in respect of that *policy* or group of *policies*; and

(2) the fund's *with-profits benefits reserve* allocated in respect of that *policy* or group of *policies* which must be enhanced as described in INSPRU 1.3.141R;

calculated as at the date of *claim*.

1.3.159 **[R]** For the purposes of INSPRU 1.3.158R, smoothing costs are defined as the present value of the difference between projected *claims* and the projected *with-profits benefit reserve* after enhancements (INSPRU 1.3.141R), other than payouts on guarantees (INSPRU 1.3.148R).

1.3.160 **[R]** Subject to INSPRU 1.3.188R, the future costs of smoothing can be negative.

1.3.161 **[G]** INSPRU 1.3.169R to INSPRU 1.3.186G contain further *rules* and *guidance* on the valuation of the future costs of smoothing.

Financing costs

1.3.162 **[R]** A *firm* must provide for future liabilities to repay financing costs of a *with- profits fund* where the *firm* expects to have to meet such liabilities and to the extent that these liabilities are not already provided for by amounts included in the fund's *realistic current liabilities* (INSPRU 1.3.190R and INSPRU 1.3.191R). The amount of the liabilities to repay financing costs must be assessed on a market-consistent basis.

1.3.163 **[G]** In INSPRU 1.3.162R, financing costs refer to the future costs incurred by way of capital, interest and fees payable to the provider. A *firm* should make a realistic assessment of the requirement to repay such financing in its expected future circumstances (which may be worse than currently). Having taken account of its particular circumstances:

(1) where a *firm* has no liability to repay such financing, it should not include such repayment as a liability;

(2) where a *firm* has a reduced liability to repay such financing, it should include a reduced repayment as a liability.

1.3.164 **[G]** In INSPRU 1.3.162R, financing includes *reinsurance* financing arrangements and analogous non-*reinsurance* financing arrangements, such as contingent loans, securitisations and any other arrangements in respect of *contracts of insurance* that are analogous to contracts of *reinsurance* in terms of the risks transferred and the finance provided.

Other long-term insurance liabilities

1.3.165 **[R]** A *firm* must provide for any other *long-term insurance liabilities* arising from or in connection with *with-profits insurance contracts* in a *with-profits fund*, to the extent that adequate provision has not been made in the *with- profits benefits reserve* or in any other part of the *future policy related liabilities* for that fund.

Some examples of these other long-term insurance liabilities are:

1.3.166 **[G]**
(1) pension and other mis-selling reserves;
(2) provisions for tax; and
(3) provisions for future shareholder transfers.

1.3.167 **[G]** In determining the realistic liability for taxation *firms* should apply the general principles set out in INSPRU 1.3.105R and the *guidance* given in INSPRU 1.3.107G.

1.3.168 **[G]** INSPRU 1.3.105R requires *firms* to provide for shareholder transfers out of the *with-profits fund* as a liability of the fund. The provision should be consistent with the methods and assumptions used in valuing the other realistic liabilities. So, for example, where the *with-profits benefits reserve* includes amounts that would be paid to *policyholders* through future bonuses, provision should also be made for future shareholder transfers associated with those bonuses.

Valuing the costs of guarantees, options and smoothing

1.3.169 **[R]** For the purposes of INSPRU 1.3.137R(5), INSPRU 1.3.137R(7) and INSPRU 1.3.137R(8), a *firm* must calculate the costs of any guarantees, options and smoothing using one or more of the following three methods:
(1) a stochastic approach using a market-consistent asset model (INSPRU 1.3.170R);
(2) using the market costs of hedging the guarantee or option;
(3) a series of deterministic projections with attributed probabilities.

The market-consistent asset model in INSPRU 1.3.169(1):

1.3.170 **[R]**
(1) means a model that delivers prices for assets and liabilities that can be directly verified from the market; and
(2) must be calibrated to deliver market-consistent prices for those assets that reflect the nature and term of the *with-profits insurance liabilities* of the *with-profits fund*.

1.3.171 **[G]** Deterministic approaches will not usually capture the time value of the option generated by a guarantee. In order to calculate this value properly, *firms* are expected either to use market option values where these are readily available or to undertake a stochastic approach using a market-consistent asset model.

1.3.172 **[G]** The *FSA* considers stochastic modelling to be preferable for material groups or classes of *with-profits insurance contracts* unless it can be shown that more simplistic or alternative methods are both appropriate and sufficiently robust.

1.3.173 **[G]** Where the guarantee or option is relatively simple in nature, is capable of being hedged, and has a value unlikely to be affected by management actions (INSPRU 1.3.185R) (for example, a guaranteed annuity rate option) then the cost of the guarantee or option would be the market cost of hedging the guarantee. Where that is generally the case but, in respect of a minor part of a portfolio, no market exists for hedging the option generated by the guarantee, a *firm* should take the value of the nearest equivalent benefit or right for which a market exists and record how it has adjusted the valuation to reflect the original option. Where the market value of the hedge is used *firms* should also make provisions for the credit risk arising from the hedge, both that arising from exposure to a *counterparty* and that arising from credit risk in the underlying instrument. The extent to which the guarantee or option is capable of being hedged depends on a *firm's* assumptions regarding future investment mix, persistency, annuitant mortality and take-up rates. While the *FSA* recognises that the hedge may not be perfectly matched to the underlying guarantee or option, a *firm* should ensure that hedge is reasonably well matched having regard to the sensitivity of the guarantee or option to the *firm's* choice of key assumptions.

1.3.174 **[G]** Where a *firm* has large cohorts of guarantees and uses stochastic or deterministic approaches, a *firm* should have regard to whether the cost of the guarantees determined under those approaches bears a reasonable relationship to the market cost of hedging those guarantees (where it exists).

1.3.175 **[G]** In determining the costs of smoothing, a *firm* should consider:

(1) the consistency of its assumptions (including the exercise of management discretion over bonus rates); and

(2) where targeted payouts currently exceed retrospective reserves in respect of those *claims*, the assumptions used in reducing the excess, if applicable, having regard to the *firm's PPFM* and its regulatory duty to treat its *customers* fairly.

Stochastic approach

1.3.176 **[G]** For the purposes of INSPRU 1.3.169R(1), a stochastic approach would consist of an appropriate market-consistent asset model for projections of asset prices and yields (such as equity prices, fixed interest yields and property yields), together with a dynamic model incorporating the corresponding value of liabilities and the impact of any foreseeable actions to be taken by management. Under the stochastic approach, the cost of the guarantee, option or smoothing would be equal to the average of these stochastic projections.

1.3.177 **[G]** In performing the projections of assets and liabilities under the stochastic approach in INSPRU 1.3.169R(1), a *firm* should have regard to the aspects in (1) and (2).

(1) The projection term should be long enough to capture all material cash flows arising from the contract or groups of contracts being valued. If the projection term does not extend to the term of the last *policy*, the *firm* should check that the shorter projection term does not significantly affect the results.

(2) The number of projections should be sufficient to ensure a reasonable degree of convergence in the results, including the determination of the result of the *risk capital margin*. The *firm* should test the sensitivity of the results to the number of projections.

1.3.178 **[G]** The *FSA* considers a holistic approach to stochastic modelling to be preferable so as to value all items of costs together rather than using separate methods for different items of the *realistic value of liabilities*. This approach requires the projection of all material cash flows arising under the contract or group of contracts for each stochastic projection, rather than only those arising from the guarantee or option within the contract. The advantages of this approach are that it ensures greater consistency in the valuation of different components of the contract and explicitly takes into account the underlying hedges or risk mitigation between components of the contract or group of contracts being valued. Where a *firm* can use a stochastic approach to value simultaneously all components of the contract or group of contracts, the *firm* should adopt this approach where practical and feasible.

1.3.179 **[G]** Where a stochastic approach is used, a *firm* should make and retain a record under INSPRU 1.3.17R of the nature of the asset model and of the assumptions used (including the volatility of asset values and any assumed correlations between asset classes or between asset classes and economic indicators, such as inflation).

1.3.180 **[G]** In calibrating asset models for the purposes of INSPRU 1.3.170R, a *firm* should have regard to the aspects in (1), (2) and (3).

(1) Few (if any) asset models can replicate all the observable *market values* for a wide range of asset classes. A *firm* should calibrate its asset models to reflect the nature and term of the fund's liabilities giving rise to significant guarantee and option costs.

(2) A *firm* will need to apply judgement to determine suitable estimates of those parameters which cannot be implied from observable market prices (for example, long-term volatility). A *firm* should make and retain a record under INSPRU 1.3.17R of the choice of parameters and the reasons for their use.

(3) A *firm* should calibrate the model to the current risk-free yield curve. Risk-free yields should be determined after allowing for credit and all other risks arising. *Firms* may have regard to any standards and guidance adopted or issued by the Board of Actuarial Standards on the calculation of the risk-free yield but should not assume a higher yield than suggested by any such standards and guidance.

Deterministic approach

1.3.181 **[R]** For the purposes of the deterministic approach in INSPRU 1.3.169R(3), a *firm* must calculate a series of deterministic projections of the values of assets and corresponding liabilities, where each deterministic projection corresponds to a possible economic scenario or outcome.

1.3.182 **[G]** A *firm* should determine a range of scenarios or outcomes appropriate to both valuing the costs of the guarantee, option or smoothing and the underlying asset mix, together with the associated probability of occurrence. These probabilities of occurrence should be weighted towards adverse scenarios to reflect market pricing for risk. The costs of the guarantee, option or smoothing should be equal to the expected cost based on a series of deterministic projections of the values of assets and corresponding liabilities. In using a series of deterministic projections, a *firm* should consider whether its approach provides a suitably robust estimate of the costs of the guarantee, option or smoothing.

1.3.183 **[G]** In performing the projections of assets and liabilities under the deterministic approach in INSPRU 1.3.169R(3), a *firm* should have regard to the aspects in (1) and (2).

Part II FSA Handbook Materials

(1) The projection term should be long enough to capture all material cash flows arising from the contract or group of contracts being valued. If the projection term does not extend to the term of the last contract, the *firm* should check that the shorter projection term does not significantly affect the results.
(2) The series of deterministic projections should be numerous enough to capture a wide range of possible outcomes and take into account the probability of each outcome's likelihood. The costs will be understated if only relatively benign or limited economic scenarios are considered.

1.3.184 **[G]** Where a series of deterministic projections is used, a *firm* should make and retain a record under INSPRU 1.3.17R of the range of projections and how the probabilities attributed to each projection or outcome were determined (including the period of reference for any relevant data on past experience).

Management and policyholder actions

1.3.185 **[R]** In calculating the costs of any guarantees, options or smoothing, a *firm*:
(1) may reflect its prospective management actions (within the meaning of INSPRU 1.3.53R); and
(2) must reflect a realistic assessment of the *policyholder* actions (within the meaning of INSPRU 1.3.59R);

in its projections of the value of assets and liabilities.

1.3.186 **[G]** For the purposes of INSPRU 1.3.185R, the related *guidance* in INSPRU 1.3.54G to INSPRU 1.3.57G (management actions) and in INSPRU 1.3.60G (policyholder actions) applies.

Treatment of surplus on guarantees, options and smoothing

1.3.187 **[R]** INSPRU 1.3.188R applies to *firms* calculating the costs of guarantees, options and smoothing to be included in the *future policy-related liabilities* in accordance with INSPRU 1.3.137R(5), INSPRU 1.3.137R(7) and INSPRU 1.3.137R(8).

1.3.188 **[R]** Where a *firm* accumulates past experience and deducts or is otherwise able to take credit for charges for guarantees or options or smoothing, the future costs of guarantees or options or smoothing (as appropriate) must not be less than the greater of:
(1) the prospective calculation of the future cost of guarantees (see INSPRU 1.3.148R) or options (see INSPRU 1.3.156G) or smoothing (see INSPRU 1.3.158R) (as appropriate); and
(2) the sum of:
  (a) the accumulated charges (after deduction of past costs) for guarantees or options or smoothing (as appropriate); and
  (b) the prospective calculation of the future charges deducted for guarantees or options or smoothing (see INSPRU 1.3.144R) (as appropriate).

1.3.189 **[G]** The extent to which the amount in INSPRU 1.3.188R(2) exceeds the amount in INSPRU 1.3.188R(1) will determine the surplus available to support actions that would be taken by the *firm's* management. The purpose of INSPRU 1.3.188R is to ensure that any resulting surplus at the valuation date arising from the accumulation of charges less costs remains available to support foreseeable actions that would be taken by the *firm's* management. Any additional liability arising from INSPRU 1.3.188R is added to the liabilities under INSPRU 1.3.137R(5), INSPRU 1.3.137R(7) and INSPRU 1.3.137R(8), but has no impact on the adjustment for planned deductions for the costs of guarantees, options and smoothing (INSPRU 1.3.137R(3) and INSPRU 1.3.144R).

Realistic current liabilities

1.3.190 **[R]** For the purposes of INSPRU 1.3.40R(3), the *realistic current liabilities* of a *with-profits fund* are equal to the sum of the following amounts:
(1) the *firm's* best estimate provision for those liabilities for which prudent provision is made in *regulatory current liabilities* (see INSPRU 1.3.30R); and
(2) to the extent that amounts have not been provided in (1), any tax and any other costs arising either in respect of excess *admissible assets* (within the meaning of INSPRU 1.3.36R) or on the recognition of future shareholder transfers.

1.3.191 **[R]** For the purpose of assessing the best estimate provision to be made under INSPRU 1.3.190R(1) in respect of a *defined benefit occupational pension scheme*, a *firm* must use either its *defined benefit liability* or its *deficit reduction amount*, consistent with the *firm's* election under INSPRU 1.3.5BR(2).

1.4 Equalisation provisions

Application

1.4.1 **[R]** INSPRU 1.4 applies to an *insurer* carrying on *general insurance business* unless it is:
(1) a *non-directive friendly society*; or

(2) an *incoming EEA firm*; or
(3) an *incoming Treaty firm*.

1.4.2 **[G]** The scope of INSPRU 1.4.11R to INSPRU 1.4.37G (non-credit equalisation provisions) is not restricted to *firms* subject to the relevant *EU* directives.

1.4.3 **[G]** The requirements of this section apply to a *firm* on a solo basis.

Purpose

1.4.4 **[G]** This section sets out *rules* and *guidance* on the calculation of the amount of the *equalisation provisions* that are required to be maintained by *firms* that carry on non-credit *insurance business* or credit *insurance business*.

1.4.5 **[G]** *Credit* or *non-credit equalisation provisions* form part of the *technical provisions* that a *firm* is required to establish under INSPRU 1.1.12R(1). They help to smooth fluctuations in loss ratios in future years for business where *claims* in any future year may be subject to significant deviation from recent or average *claims* experience, or where trends in experience may be subject to change. Such volatile *claims* experience might arise in the case, for example, of insurance against losses caused by major catastrophes such as hurricanes or earthquakes.

1.4.6 **[G]** In general terms, INSPRU 1.4 sets out *rules* and *guidance* as to:
(1) the circumstances in which a *firm* is required to maintain *equalisation provisions*;
(2) the methods to be used in calculating the amount of each provision;
(3) the geographical location of the business relevant to certain calculations for different types of *firm*-this is summarised in the Table in INSPRU 1.4.7G.

1.4.7 **[G]**

Table: Scope of *insurance business* to be included in calculations

Type Of Firm		Credit Equalisation Provision		Non Credit Equalisation Provision
		Threshold in INSPRU 1.4.44R	Provision in INSPRU 1.4.43R	Threshold in INSPRU 1.4.18R(2) and provision in INSPRU 1.4.17R
UK insurer		World-wide	World-wide	World-wide
Pure reinsurer with head office outside *United Kingdom*		*UK*	World-wide	*UK*
Pure reinsurer with head office in *United Kingdom*		World-wide	World-wide	World-wide
Non-EEA direct insurers	*EEA-deposit insurer*	*UK*	*UK*	*UK*
	Swiss general insurer	*UK*	*UK*	*UK*
	UK-deposit insurer	All *EEA*	World-wide	*UK*
	All other *non-EEA direct insurers*	*UK*	World-wide	*UK*

1.4.8 **[G]** The *First Non-Life Directive* (as amended) and the *Reinsurance Directive* require the calculation of *credit equalisation provisions*. *Non-credit equalisation provisions* are a domestic *United Kingdom* requirement. For insurance regulatory purposes under *EU* Directives, *credit equalisation provisions* are classified as liabilities.

1.4.9 **[G]** However, *firms* are permitted to include *equalisation provisions* within their financial resources when demonstrating compliance with non-Directive capital requirements. Hence *equalisation provisions* are deducted from the available *capital resources* of a *firm* for the purpose of meeting its *minimum capital requirement* for *general insurance business*; but, in the calculation of a *firm's enhanced capital requirement* for *general insurance business* under INSPRU **1.1.72CR**, its *equalisation provisions* (if any) are added back to its *capital resources*.

1.4.10 **[G]** Under International Accounting Standards (IAS), which will apply to the financial statements of some *insurers* from 2005, there will be no requirement to treat *equalisation provisions* as liabilities in *insurers*' published financial statements. However, they will continue to be treated as liabilities for the purposes of demonstrating compliance with Directive capital requirements.

Non-credit equalisation provision

Firms carrying on non-credit insurance business

1.4.11 **[R]**

(1) INSPRU 1.4.11R to INSPRU 1.4.37G apply to any *firm*, other than an *assessable mutual*, which carries on the business of *effecting* or *carrying out general insurance contracts* falling within any description in column 2 in Table INSPRU 1.4.12R ("non-credit *insurance business*").

(2) A *firm* falling within (1) must classify all of its non-credit *insurance business* into separate *insurance business groupings*, as specified in Table INSPRU 1.4.12R.

1.4.12 **[R]** Table: Groupings of non-credit *insurance business*

Insurance Business Grouping		**General Insurance Contracts**
A	*Contracts of insurance* which fall within *general insurance business classes* 4, 8 or 9, other than:	
	(a)	*contracts of insurance* under non-proportional reinsurance treaties; and
	(b)	*contracts of insurance* against *nuclear risks*.
B	*Contracts of insurance* which fall within *general insurance business class* 16(a), other than:	
	(a)	*contracts of insurance* under non-proportional reinsurance treaties; and
	(b)	*contracts of insurance* against *nuclear risks*.
C	*Contracts of insurance* which fall within general insurance business classes 5, 6, 11 or 12, other than:	
	(a)	*contracts of insurance* against *nuclear risks*; and
	(b)	*reinsurance* contracts corresponding to contracts in (a).
D	*Contracts of insurance* against *nuclear risks*.	
E	*Contracts of insurance* under non-proportional reinsurance treaties and which fall within general insurance business classes 4, 8, 9 or 16(a) other than contracts of insurance against nuclear risks.	

1.4.13 **[R]** For the purposes of INSPRU 1.4.11R to INSPRU 1.4.37G, a *firm* with its head office in the *United Kingdom* must take account of non-credit *insurance business* carried on by it world-wide.

1.4.14 **[R]** For the purposes of INSPRU 1.4.11R to INSPRU 1.4.37G, a *firm* with its head office outside the *United Kingdom* need only take account of non-credit *insurance business* carried on by it from a *branch* in the *United Kingdom*.

1.4.15 **[G]** The *insurers* affected by INSPRU 1.4.11R include pure reinsurers, UK- deposit insurers, EEA-deposit insurer, and Swiss general insurers.

1.4.16 **[G]** For *insurers* (including *pure reinsurers*) with a head office in the *United Kingdom*, the calculations must be made in respect of world-wide business.

Requirement to maintain non-credit equalisation provision

1.4.17 **[R]** In respect of each *financial year*, a *firm* must, unless INSPRU 1.4.18R applies:

(1) calculate the amount of its *non-credit equalisation provision* as at the end of that year in accordance with INSPRU 1.4.20R; and

(2) maintain a *non-credit equalisation provision* calculated in accordance with INSPRU 1.4.20R for the following *financial year*.

1.4.18 ***[R]***

(1) INSPRU 1.4.17R does not apply to any *firm* in respect of any *financial year* if, as at the end of that year:

(a) no *non-credit equalisation provision* has been brought forward from the preceding *financial year*; and

(b) the amount of the *annualised net written premiums* for all the non-credit *insurance business* carried on by it in the *financial year* is less than the threshold amount.

(2) The threshold amount in respect of any *financial year* is the higher of:

(a) 1,500,000 Euro; and

(b) 4% of *net written premiums* in that *financial year* in respect of all its *general insurance business*, if this amount is less than 2,500,000 Euro.

1.4.19 **[G]** For *non-EEA insurers*, the calculation of the threshold amount in INSPRU 1.4.18R(2) is limited by INSPRU 1.4.14R to the business of the *firm* carried on in the *United Kingdom*. Such a *firm* may do little *UK* non-credit *insurance business*, and so would not be required to set up a *non-credit equalisation provision* under INSPRU 1.4, but may do significant business outside the *United Kingdom* characterised by high-impact, low-frequency *claims*. Such a *firm* is required by INSPRU 1.5.41R to hold adequate world-wide financial resources to avoid internal-contagion strain on the *branch* in the *United Kingdom*. In determining the adequacy of its financial resources, the *firm* should undertake stress and scenario testing of its underwriting and other risks as set out in GENPRU 1.2.

Calculating the amount of the provision

1.4.20 **[R]**

(1) Unless INSPRU 1.4.22R applies, the amount of a *firm's non-credit equalisation provision* as at the end of a *financial year* is the higher of:

(a) zero; and

(b) whichever is the lower of:

(i) the aggregate of the amounts of the maximum provision for each *insurance business grouping* as at the end of that *financial year*; and

(ii) the sum of A and B.

(2) For the purposes of (1)(b)(ii):

(a) A is the amount of the *non-credit equalisation provision*, if any, brought forward from the *financial year* immediately preceding that in respect of which the calculation is being performed; and

(b) B is:

(i) the aggregate of the amounts of the provisional transfers-in for each *insurance business grouping*; minus

(ii) the aggregate of the amounts of the provisional transfers-out for each *insurance business grouping*.

(3) For any *insurance business grouping*:

(a) the amount of the maximum provision in (1)(b)(i) is to be determined in accordance with INSPRU 1.4.24R;

(b) the amount of the provisional transfers-in in (2)(b)(i) is to be determined in accordance with INSPRU 1.4.26R; and

(c) the amount of the provisional transfers-out in (2)(b)(ii) is to be determined in accordance with INSPRU 1.4.29R.

1.4.21 **[G]** If provisional transfers-out are in excess of provisional transfers-in, the *non- credit equalisation provision* as calculated in accordance with INSPRU 1.4.20R in respect of a particular *financial year* may be less than that calculated for the preceding *financial year* although, by virtue of INSPRU 1.4.20R(1)(a), it cannot be negative.

1.4.22 **[R]**

(1) The amount of a *firm's non-credit equalisation provision* as at the end of a *financial year* is zero if:

(a) as at the end of that year, the *firm* meets either of the conditions specified in (2) and (3); and

(b) the *annualised net written premiums* for all the non-credit *insurance business* carried on by the *firm* in that year are less than the threshold amount.

(2) The first condition is that the *firm* carried on non-credit *insurance business* in the first *financial year* of the relevant period and, for each of any two or more *financial years* of that period, the *annualised net written premiums* for business of that description were less than the threshold amount.

(3) The second condition is that the *firm* did not carry on non-credit *insurance business* in the first *financial year* of the relevant period and the average of the *annualised net written premiums* for business of that description carried on by the *firm* in each *financial year* of the relevant period was less than the threshold amount.

(4) For the purposes of this *rule*:

(a) the threshold amount is the amount determined in accordance with INSPRU 1.4.18R(2): and

(b) the relevant period is the period of four *financial years* ending immediately before the beginning of the *financial year* in (1).

1.4.23 **[G]** If INSPRU 1.4.22R applies, a *firm* may need to make sufficient transfers from its *non-credit equalisation provision* to bring the *non-credit equalisation provision* for that *financial year* to zero.

The calculation: the maximum provision

1.4.24 **[R]**
(1) For the purposes of the calculation required by INSPRU 1.4.20R, the amount of the maximum provision for any *insurance business grouping* is to be determined in accordance with (2) to (5).
(2) Unless (4) applies, the amount of the maximum provision for the grouping, as at the end of a *financial year*, is the amount determined by multiplying X and Y.
(3) For the purposes of (2):
 (a) X is the percentage specified in Table INSPRU 1.4.25R in relation to the grouping; and
 (b) Y is the average of the amount of the *annualised net written premiums* for non-credit *insurance business* in the grouping carried on by the *firm* in each *financial year* of the relevant period.
(4) Where Y is a negative amount, the maximum provision for that *insurance business grouping* is zero.
(5) For the purposes of (3)(b), the relevant period is the five-year period comprising:
 (a) the *financial year* in (2); and
 (b) the previous four *financial years*.

1.4.25 **[R]** Table: Calculation of maximum provision for any *insurance business grouping*

Insurance Business Grouping	Percentage of average annualised net written premiums
A	20
B	20
C	40
D	600
E	75

The calculation: provisional transfers-in

1.4.26 **[R]**
(1) For the purposes of the calculation required by INSPRU 1.4.20R, the amount of the provisional transfers-in for any *insurance business grouping* is to be determined in accordance with (2).
(2) The amount of the provisional transfers-in for the grouping, as at the end of a *financial year*, is the amount determined by multiplying X and Y.
(3) For the purposes of (2):
 (a) X is the percentage specified in Table INSPRU 1.4.27R in relation to the grouping; and
 (b) Y is the amount of the *net written premiums* for non-credit *insurance business* in the grouping that was carried on by the *firm* in the *financial year* in (2), including adjustments in respect of previous *financial years*.

1.4.27 **[R]** Table: Provisional transfers-in for any *insurance business grouping*

Insurance Business Grouping	Percentage of net written premiums
A	3
B	3
C	6
D	75
E	11

1.4.28 **[G]** Since each *insurance business grouping* should be assessed individually, negative *net written premiums* in relation to any *insurance business grouping* should be transferred in to the *non-credit equalisation provision*.

The calculation: provisional transfers-out

1.4.29 **[R]**
(1) For the purposes of the calculation required by INSPRU 1.4.20R, the amount of the provisional transfers-out for any *insurance business grouping* is to be determined in accordance with (2).

(2) The amount of the provisional transfers-out for the grouping, as at the end of a *financial year*, is the lower of:
 (a) the amount of the maximum provision for the grouping under INSPRU 1.4.24R for that *financial year*; and
 (b) the abnormal loss for the grouping under INSPRU 1.4.30R for that *financial year*.

1.4.30 **[R]** For each *insurance business grouping*, the abnormal loss as at the end of a *financial year* in relation to which an *equalisation provision* is calculated is:
(1) (for business within the *insurance business grouping* accounted for on an accident year basis) the amount, if any, by which the amount of net *claims* incurred exceeds the greater of:
 (a) zero; and
 (b) the percentage of *net earned premiums* in that *financial year* specified in the Table in INSPRU 1.4.31R; or
(2) (for business within the *insurance business grouping* accounted for on an underwriting year basis) the amount, if any, by which the amount of net *claims* paid (plus adjustment for change in net *technical provisions*, other than any change in provisions for *claims* handling expenses or equalisation) exceeds the greater of:
 (a) zero; and
 (b) the percentage of *net written premiums* in that *financial year* specified in the Table in INSPRU 1.4.31R.

1.4.31 **[R]** Table: Abnormal loss for any *insurance business grouping*

Insurance business grouping	Percentage of net written premiums
A	72.5
B	72.5
C	95
D	25
E	100

Adjustments to calculations

Transfers of business from the firm

1.4.32 **[R]**
(1) This *rule* applies to modify the application of INSPRU 1.4.24R and INSPRU 1.4.26R in any case where a *firm* has transferred to another *undertaking* any rights and obligations under *general insurance contracts* falling within any *insurance business grouping*.
(2) As at the end of the *financial year* in which the transfer takes place, *net written premiums* in respect of the transferred contracts in any grouping must be deducted from total *net written premiums* for that grouping before calculating the maximum provision under INSPRU 1.4.24R or provisional transfers-in under INSPRU 1.4.26R.

1.4.33 **[R]** If all the rights and obligations of a *firm* in relation to non-credit *insurance business* in any *insurance business grouping* have been transferred, the maximum provision for the grouping under INSPRU 1.4.24R is zero.

Transfers of business to the firm

1.4.34 **[R]**
(1) This *rule* applies to modify the application of INSPRU 1.4.24R, INSPRU 1.4.26R and INSPRU 1.4.29R in any case where another *undertaking* has transferred to a *firm* any rights and obligations under *general insurance contracts* falling within any *insurance business grouping*.
(2) As at the end of the *financial year* in which the transfer takes place a sum equal to that part of the consideration for the transfer that relates to business in an *insurance business grouping* must be:
 (a) excluded from *net written premiums* before performing the calculations required by INSPRU 1.4.24R (maximum provision) and INSPRU 1.4.26R (provisional transfers in);
 (b) included in net *premiums* (written or earned) before performing the calculation required by INSPRU 1.4.30R (abnormal loss); and
 (c) excluded from net *claims* (paid or incurred) before performing the calculation required by INSPRU 1.4.30R (abnormal loss).

1.4.35 **[G]** For the purposes of INSPRU 1.4.34R, the consideration payable should be apportioned between *insurance business groupings* according to the groupings within which the *general insurance contracts* which are the subject of the acquisition fall. In appropriate cases, apportionment may reflect the split of liabilities acquired, including *unearned premium*.

1.4.36 **[G]** Where business is accounted for on an accounting year basis, in any year following the transfer, *net earned premiums* must include an appropriate amount in respect of the transfer.

1.4.37 **[G]** INSPRU 1.4.32R to INSPRU 1.4.34R apply to transfers by way of transfer under Part VII of the *Act* and by novation.

Credit equalisation provisions

Firms carrying on credit insurance business

1.4.38 **[R]** INSPRU 1.4.39R to INSPRU 1.4.47G apply to any *firm* which carries on the business of *effecting* or *carrying out general insurance contracts* falling within *general insurance business class* 14 (which business is referred to in INSPRU 1.4 as "credit *insurance business*"), unless it is:

(1) a *non-directive insurer*; or

(2) a *pure reinsurer* which became a *firm in run-off* before 31 December 2006 and whose *Part IV permission* has not subsequently been varied to add back the *regulated activity* of *effecting contracts of insurance*.

1.4.39 **[R]** For the purposes of INSPRU 1.4.43R and INSPRU 1.4.44R, a *firm* whose head office is in the *United Kingdom* must take account of the credit *insurance business* carried on by it world-wide.

1.4.40 **[R]**

(1) For the purposes of INSPRU 1.4.43R:

(a) a *Swiss general insurer* or an *EEA-deposit insurer* must take account of the credit *insurance business* carried on by it in the *United Kingdom*; and

(b) any other *firm* whose head office is outside the *United Kingdom* (including a *UK-deposit insurer*) must take account of the credit *insurance business* carried on by it world-wide.

(2) For the purposes of INSPRU 1.4.44R:

(a) a *UK-deposit insurer* need only take account of the credit *insurance business* carried on by it in all *EEA States*, taken together; and

(b) any other *firm* whose head office is outside the *United Kingdom* (including an *EEA-deposit insurer* and a *Swiss general insurer*) need only take account of the credit *insurance business* carried on by it in the *United Kingdom*.

1.4.41 **[G]** For *firms* whose head office is in the *United Kingdom* both calculations must be made in respect of world-wide business.

1.4.42 **[G]** The requirements of INSPRU 1.4.39R and INSPRU 1.4.40R are summarised in the table in INSPRU 1.4.7G.

Requirement to maintain credit equalisation provision

1.4.43 **[R]** In respect of each *financial year*, a *firm* must, unless INSPRU 1.4.44R applies:

(1) calculate the amount of its *credit equalisation provision* as at the end of that year in accordance with INSPRU 1.4.45R; and

(2) maintain a *credit equalisation provision* calculated in accordance with INSPRU 1.4.45R for the following *financial year*.

1.4.44 **[R]** INSPRU 1.4.43R does not apply to a *firm* in respect of any *financial year* if, as at the end of that year, the *annualised net written premiums* for its credit *insurance business* are less than 4% of annualised *net written premiums* in that *financial year* in respect of all its *general insurance business*, if this amount is less than 2,500,000 Euro.

Calculating the amount of the provision

1.4.45 **[R]**

(1) The amount of a *firm's credit equalisation provision* as at the end of a *financial year* ("*financial year* A") is the higher of:

(a) zero; and

(b) whichever is the lower of:

(i) 150% of the highest amount of *net written premiums* for credit *insurance business* carried on by the *firm* in *financial year* A or in any of the previous four *financial years*; and

(ii) the amount of the *credit equalisation provision* brought forward from the preceding *financial year*, after making either of the adjustments in (2).

(2) The adjustments are:

(a) the deduction of the amount of any technical deficit arising in *financial year* A; or

(b) the addition of the lower of:

(i) 75% of the amount of any technical surplus arising in *financial year* A; and

(ii) 12% of the amount of the *net written premiums* for credit *insurance business* carried on by the *firm* in *financial year* A.

(3) For the purposes of (2) the amount of technical deficit or technical surplus is to be determined in accordance with INSPRU 1.4.46R.

1.4.46 **[R]** For the purposes of the adjustments in INSPRU 1.4.45R(2), technical surplus (or technical deficit) in respect of credit *insurance business* is the amount by which the aggregate of *net earned premiums* and other technical income exceeds (or falls short of) the sum of net *claims* incurred, *claims* management costs and any technical charges.

1.4.47 **[G]** The calculation of technical surplus or technical deficit should be made before tax and before any transfer to or from the *credit equalisation provision*. Investment income should not be included in these calculations.

Euro conversion

1.4.48 **[R]** For the purposes of INSPRU 1.4, the exchange rate from the Euro to the pound sterling for each year beginning on 31 December is the rate applicable on the last day of the preceding October for which the exchange rates for the currencies of all the European Union member states were published in the Official Journal of the European Union.

Application of INSPRU 1.4 to Lloyd's

1.4.49 **[R]** INSPRU 1.4 applies to the *Society* in accordance with INSPRU 8.1.2R:
(1) with the modification set out in INSPRU 1.4.50R; and
(2) except INSPRU 1.4.11R to INSPRU 1.4.37G.

1.4.50 **[R]** The *Society* must calculate a *credit equalisation provision* for the aggregate *insurance business* of all *members*; it is not required to calculate a *credit equalisation provision* separately for the business of each *member*.

1.4.51 **[R]** The *Society* must allocate the result of INSPRU 1.4.50R between itself and each of the *members* on a fair and reasonable basis.

1.5 Internal-contagion risk

Application

1.5.1 **[R]** INSPRU 1.5 applies to an *insurer*.

1.5.2 **[R]** INSPRU 1.5 does not apply, to the extent stated, to any *insurer* in (1) to (4):
(1) none of the provisions apply to *non-directive friendly societies*;
(2) none of the provisions, apart from INSPRU 1.5.33R (payment of financial penalties) apply to *firms* which qualify for authorisation under Schedule 3 or 4 of the *Act*;
(3) INSPRU 1.5.33R (payment of financial penalties) does not apply to *mutuals*;
(4) INSPRU 1.5.41R to INSPRU 1.5.57R (*UK branches* of certain *non-EEA insurers*) do not apply to:
   (a) *UK insurers*; or
   (b) *non-EEA insurers* whose *insurance business* in the *United Kingdom* is restricted to *reinsurance*; or
   (c) *EEA-deposit insurers*; or
   (d) *Swiss general insurers*.

1.5.3 **[G]** The scope of application of INSPRU 1.5 is not restricted to *firms* that are subject to the relevant *EU* directives.

1.5.4 **[R]** In its application to a *firm* with its head office in the *United Kingdom*, this section applies to the whole of the *firm's* business carried on world-wide.

1.5.5 **[R]** In the application of this section to activities carried on by a *non-EEA insurer*:
(1) INSPRU 1.5.13R to INSPRU 1.5.15G and INSPRU 1.5.41R apply in relation to the whole of its business carried on world-wide;
(2) all other provisions of this section apply only in relation to:
   (a) in the case of any *UK-deposit insurer*, activities carried on from *branches* in any *EEA State*; and
   (b) in any other case, activities carried on from a *branch* in the *United Kingdom*.

1.5.6 **[G]** The adequacy of a *firm's* financial resources needs to be assessed in relation to all the activities of the *firm* and the risks to which they give rise.

1.5.7 **[G]** The requirements of this section apply to a *firm* on a solo basis.

Purpose

1.5.8 **[G]** This section sets out requirements for a *firm* relating to 'internal-contagion risk'. This is the risk that losses or liabilities from one activity might deplete or divert financial resources held to meet liabilities from another activity. It arises where the two activities are carried on within the same

Part II FSA Handbook Materials

firm. It may also arise from the combination of activities within the same *group*, but this aspect of internal-contagion risk falls outside the scope of this section. Requirements relevant to *group* contagion risk are set out in INSPRU 6.

1.5.9 **[G]** Internal-contagion risk includes in particular the risk that arises where a *firm* carries on:
(1) both insurance and non-insurance activities; or
(2) two or more different types of insurance activity; or
(3) insurance activities from offices or *branches* located in both the *United Kingdom* and overseas.

1.5.10 **[G]** This section requires *firms* other than *pure reinsurers* to limit non-insurance activities to those that directly arise from their *insurance business*, e.g. investing assets, employing insurance staff etc. It also requires that an adequate provision be established for non-insurance liabilities. *Pure reinsurers* must limit their activities to the business of *reinsurance* and related operations.

1.5.11 **[G]** This section also sets out requirements for the separation of different types of insurance activity. However, in most circumstances the combination of different types of insurance activity within the same *firm* is a source of strength. Adequate pooling and diversification of insurance risk is fundamental to sound business practice. The requirements, therefore, only apply in two specific cases where without adequate protection the combination might operate to the detriment of *policyholders*. They apply where a *firm* carries on both:
(1) *general insurance business* and *long-term insurance business*;
(2) linked and non-linked *insurance business*.

1.5.12 **[G]** Finally, the section sets out requirements to protect *policyholders* of *branches* of non-*EEA firms* where these are supervised by the *FSA*. These apply only to a *non-EEA firm* that has established a *branch* in the *United Kingdom*.

Requirements: Non-insurance activities

Restriction of business

1.5.13 **[R]**
(1) A *firm* other than a *pure reinsurer* must not carry on any commercial business other than *insurance business* and activities directly arising from that business.
(2) (1) does not prevent a *friendly society* which was on 15 March 1979 carrying on *long-term insurance business* from continuing to carry on savings business.

1.5.13A **[R]** A *pure reinsurer* must not carry on any business other than the business of *reinsurance* and related operations.

1.5.13B **[G]** In INSPRU 1.5.13AR related operations include, for example, activities such as provision of statistical or actuarial advice, risk analysis or research for its clients. It may also include a *holding company* function and activities with respect to financial sector activities within the meaning of Article 2, point 8, of the *Financial Groups Directive*. But it does not allow the carrying on of, for example, unrelated banking and financial activities.

Financial limitation of non-insurance activities

1.5.14 **[R]** A *firm* must limit, manage and control its non-insurance activities so that there is no significant risk arising from those activities that it may be unable to meet its liabilities as they fall due.

1.5.15 **[G]** For the purpose of INSPRU 1.5.14R a *firm* should consider how the financial impact of non-insurance activities might diverge from expectations. However, it need only take into account unexpected variations in amount and timing in so far as they are reasonably possible and may take into account effective mitigating factors.

Requirements: long-term insurance business

1.5.16 **[G]** INSPRU 1.5.18R, INSPRU 1.5.21R, INSPRU 1.5.30R and INSPRU 1.5.31R require a *firm* to identify the assets attributable to the receipts of the *long-term insurance business*, called *long-term insurance assets*, and only to apply those assets for the purpose of that business. This has the effect of prohibiting a *composite firm* from using *long-term insurance assets* to meet *general insurance liabilities*. It also keeps *long-term insurance assets* separate from shareholder funds.

Permissions not to include both types of insurance

1.5.17 **[G]**
(1) Under section 19 of the *Act*, a *firm* may not carry on a *regulated activity* unless it has *permission* to do so (or is exempt in relation to the particular activity). Both *general insurance business* and *long-term insurance business* are *regulated activities* and *permission* will extend to the *effecting* or *carrying out* of one or more particular *classes* of *contracts of insurance*.

(2) A *firm's permission* can be varied so as to add other *classes*. The *permission* of an existing *composite firm* may be varied by adding *classes* of both *general insurance business* and *long-term insurance business*.

(3) It is *FSA* policy, in compliance with *EU* directives on insurance, not to grant or vary *permission* if that would allow a newly established *firm*, or an existing *firm* engaged solely in *general insurance business* or solely in *long-term insurance business* to engage in both *general insurance business* and *long-term insurance business*. This does not apply where a *firm's permission* to carry on *long-term insurance business* is or is to be restricted to *reinsurance*. It also does not apply where a *firm's permission* to carry on *general insurance business* is or is to be restricted to *effecting* or *carrying out accident* or *sickness contracts of insurance* (see article 18(2) of the *Consolidated Life Directive*).

(4) Where a *firm's permission* extends to *effecting* or *carrying out life and annuity contracts of insurance* this will normally include *permission* to *effect* or *carry out accident contracts of insurance* or *sickness contracts of insurance* on a supplementary basis (see article 2(1)(c) of the *Consolidated Life Directive*).

Separately identify and maintain long term insurance assets

1.5.18 **[R]** A *firm* carrying on *long-term insurance business* must identify the assets relating to its *long-term insurance business* which it is required to hold by virtue of:

(1) in the case of a *pure reinsurer*:

 (a) INSPRU 1.1.20R or INSPRU 1.1.21R; and

 (b) INSPRU 3.1.61AR; and

(2) in any other case:

 (a) INSPRU 1.1.20R or INSPRU 1.1.21R; and

 (b) INSPRU 3.1.57R and INSPRU 3.1.58R.

1.5.19 **[G]**

(1) INSPRU 1.1.16R requires a *firm* to establish adequate *technical provisions* for its *long-term insurance contracts*. INSPRU 1.1.20R requires a *firm* which is not a *composite firm* to hold *admissible assets* of a value at least equal to the amount of the *technical provisions* and its other *long-term insurance liabilities*. INSPRU 1.1.21R ensures that a *composite firm* identifies separate *admissible assets* with a value at least equal to the *technical provisions* for *long-term insurance business* and its other *long-term insurance liabilities* as well as holding other *admissible assets* of a value at least equal to the amount of its *technical provisions* for *general insurance business* and its other *general insurance liabilities*.

(2) In the case of a *firm* carrying on *long-term insurance business* which is not a *pure reinsurer*, there are excluded from the scope of INSPRU 1.1.20R and INSPRU 1.1.21R *property-linked liabilities* and *index-linked liabilities* and the assets held to cover them under INSPRU 3.1.57R and INSPRU 3.1.58R. The latter two *rules* do not apply to a *pure reinsurer* (see INSPRU 3.1.58AR). However, a *pure reinsurer* is required by INSPRU 3.1.61AR to invest all its assets in accordance with the requirements of that *rule*.

(3) The overall impact of these provisions in INSPRU 1.1 and INSPRU 3.1, when read together with INSPRU 1.5.18R, is that any *firm* writing *long-term insurance business* must identify separately *assets* of a value at least equal to the amount of its *long-term insurance business technical provisions*, including those in respect of any *property-linked liabilities* or *index-linked liabilities*, and its other *long-term insurance liabilities*.

1.5.20 **[G]** INSPRU 1.5.18R does not prohibit a *firm* from identifying other assets as being available to meet the liabilities of its *long-term insurance business*. It may transfer such other assets to a *long-term insurance fund* (see INSPRU 1.5.21R and INSPRU 1.5.22R) and the transfer will take effect when it is recorded in the *firm's* accounting records (see INSPRU 1.5.23R). After the transfer takes effect, a *firm* may not transfer the assets out of a *long-term insurance fund* except where they represent an *established surplus* (see INSPRU 1.5.27R).

1.5.21 **[R]**

(1) A *firm's* long-term insurance assets are the items in (2), adjusted to take account of:

 (a) outgo in respect of the *firm's long-term insurance business*; and

 (b) any transfers made in accordance with INSPRU 1.5.27R.

(2) The items are:

 (a) the assets identified under INSPRU 1.5.18R (including assets into which those assets have been converted) but excluding any assets identified as being held to cover liabilities in respect of subordinated debt;

 (b) any other assets identified by the *firm* as being available to cover its *long-term insurance liabilities* (including assets into which those assets have been converted) including, if the *firm* so elects, assets which are excluded under (a);

 (c) *premiums* and other receivables in respect of *long-term insurance contracts*;

 (d) other receipts of the *long-term insurance business*; and

 (e) all income and capital receipts in respect of the items in (2).

1.5.22 **[R]**
(1) Unless (2) applies, all the *long-term insurance assets* of the *firm* constitute its long-term insurance fund.
(2) Where a *firm* identifies particular *long-term insurance assets* in connection with different parts of its *long-term insurance business*, the assets identified in relation to each such part constitute separate long-term insurance funds of the *firm*.

1.5.23 **[R]** A *firm* must maintain a separate accounting record in respect of each of its *long-term insurance funds* (including any *with-profits fund*).

1.5.24 **[G]** *Firms* must ensure that *long-term insurance assets* are separately identified and allocated to a *long-term insurance fund* at all times. Assets in external accounts, for example at banks, custodians, or brokers should be segregated in the *firm's* books and records into separate accounts for *long-term insurance business* and *general insurance business*. Where a *firm* has more than one *long-term insurance fund*, a separate accounting record must be maintained for each fund. Accounting records should clearly document the allocation.

1.5.25 **[G]** Where the surplus arising from business is shared between *policyholders* and shareholders in different ways for different blocks of business, it may be necessary to maintain a separate fund to ensure that *policyholders* are, and will be, treated fairly. For example, if a proprietary company writes some business on a with-profits basis, this should be written in a *with-profits fund* separate from any business where the surplus arising from that business is wholly owned by shareholders.

1.5.26 **[G]** Where a *firm* merges separate funds for different types of business, it will need to ensure that the merger will not result in *policyholders* being treated unfairly. When considering merging the funds, the *firm* should consider the impact on its *PPFM* (see COBS 20.3) and on its obligations to notify the *FSA* (see SUP 15.3). In particular, a *firm* would need to consider how any *inherited estate* would be managed and how the fund would be run in future, such that *policyholders* are treated fairly.

1.5.27 **[R]** A *firm* may not transfer assets out of a *long-term insurance fund* unless:
(1) the assets represent an *established surplus*; and
(2) no more than three months have passed since the determination of that surplus.

1.5.28 **[G]** As a result of INSPRU 1.5.27R(2), an *actuarial investigation* undertaken to determine an *established surplus* remains in-date for three months from the date as at which the determination of the surplus was made. However, even where the investigation is still in-date, the *firm* should not make the transfer unless there is sufficient surplus at the time of the transfer to allow it to be made without breach of INSPRU 1.1.20R or INSPRU 1.1.21R.

1.5.29 **[G]** INSPRU 1.1.27R and INSPRU 1.1.28R provide further constraints on the transfer of assets out of a *with-profits fund*. INSPRU 1.1.27R requires a *firm* to have *admissible assets* in each of its *with-profits funds* to cover the *technical provisions* and other *long-term insurance liabilities* relating to all the business in that fund. INSPRU 1.1.28R requires a *realistic basis life firm* to ensure that the *realistic value of assets* for each of its *with-profits funds* is at least equal to the *realistic value of liabilities* of that fund.

Exclusive use of long-term insurance assets

1.5.30 **[R]**
(1) A *firm* must apply a *long-term insurance asset* only for the purposes of its *long-term insurance business*.
(2) For the purpose of (1), applying an asset includes coming under any obligation (even if only contingently) to apply that asset.

1.5.31 **[R]** A *firm* must not agree to, or allow, any mortgage or charge on its *long-term insurance assets* other than in respect of a *long-term insurance liability*.

1.5.32 **[G]** The purposes of the *long-term insurance business* include the payment of *claims*, expenses and liabilities arising from that business, the acquisition of lawful access to fixed assets to be used in that business and the investment of assets. The payment of liabilities may include repaying a loan but only where that loan was incurred for the purpose of the *long-term insurance business*. The purchase or investment of assets may include an exchange at fair *market value* of assets (including *money*) between the *long-term insurance fund* and other assets of the *firm*. A *firm* may also lend *securities* held in a *long-term insurance fund* under a *stock lending* transaction or transfer assets as *collateral* for a *stock lending* transaction where the *firm* is the borrower, where such lending or transfer is for the *benefit of the long-term insurance business*.

Payment of financial penalties

1.5.33 **[R]** If the *FSA* imposes a financial penalty on a *long-term insurer*, the *firm* must not pay that financial penalty from a *long-term insurance fund*.

1.5.34 **[G]** INSPRU 1.5.2R states that this provision applies to all *firms*, except *mutuals*, and includes *firms* qualifying for authorisation under Schedule 3 or 4 to the *Act*.

Requirements: property-linked funds

1.5.35 **[G]** INSPRU 3.1.57R requires a *firm* to cover, as closely as possible, its *property-linked liabilities* by the property to which those liabilities are linked. In order to comply with this *rule*, a *firm* should identify the assets it holds to cover *property-linked liabilities* and should not apply those assets (as long as they are needed to cover the *property-linked liabilities*) for any purpose other than to meet those liabilities.

1.5.36 **[R]** A *firm* must select, allocate and manage the assets to which its *property-linked liabilities* are linked taking into account:
(1) the *firm's* contractual obligations to holders of property-linked *policies*; and
(2) its regulatory duty to treat *customers* fairly, including in the way it makes discretionary decisions as to how it selects, allocates and manages assets.

1.5.37 **[G]** *Property-linked liabilities* may be linked either to specified assets (with no contractual discretion given to the *firm* as to the choice of assets) or to assets of a specified kind where the selection of the actual assets is left to the *firm*.

Requirements: UK branches of certain non-EEA firms

1.5.38 **[G]** The purpose of the *rules* and *guidance* set out in INSPRU 1.5.38G to INSPRU 1.5.57R is to protect against the risk that the financial resources required in respect of the activities of the *United Kingdom* (or *EEA*) *branch*(es) might be depleted by the other activities of the *non-EEA direct insurer*.

1.5.39 **[G]** By virtue of INSPRU 1.5.2R(4), the *rules* in INSPRU 1.5.41R to INSPRU 1.5.57R apply to *non-EEA direct insurers* except for *Swiss general insurers* and *EEA-deposit insurers*. Responsibility for determining the adequacy of the world-wide financial resources of *Swiss general insurers* or *EEA-deposit insurers* rests exclusively with the Swiss authorities or the authorities in the *EEA state* (other than the *United Kingdom*) in which the deposit was made.

1.5.40 **[G]**
(1) INSPRU 1.5.41R requires a *non-EEA direct insurer* to hold adequate world-wide resources to meet the needs of the world-wide business without the need to rely on *UK* or *EEA branch* assets other than to meet *branch* liabilities.
(2) INSPRU 1.5.42R to INSPRU 1.5.47R require *non-EEA direct insurers* to calculate a local *MCR* and to hold assets representing that requirement in the *EEA* or the *United Kingdom*.
(3) INSPRU 1.5.48R to INSPRU 1.5.52R require *non-EEA direct insurers* to hold a minimum level of assets in the *United Kingdom* or *EEA*.
(4) INSPRU 1.5.54R requires the deposit of a minimum level of assets in the *United Kingdom*.
(5) INSPRU 1.5.56R and INSPRU 1.5.57R require *non-EEA direct insurers* to keep adequate accounting records in the *United Kingdom*.

Worldwide financial resources

1.5.41 **[R]**
(1) A *non-EEA direct insurer* must maintain adequate worldwide financial resources, to ensure that there is no significant risk that its liabilities cannot be met as they fall due.
(2) For the purpose of (1):
  (a) a *UK-deposit insurer* must not rely upon the assets held under INSPRU 1.1.20R as available to meet liabilities other than those arising from the activities of its *branches* in *EEA States*;
  (b) other *non-EEA direct insurers* to whom (1) applies must not rely upon the assets held under INSPRU 1.1.20R as available to meet liabilities other than those arising from the activities of any *UK branch*.

UK or EEA MCR to be covered by admissible assets

1.5.42 **[R]** A *non-EEA direct insurer* must:
(1) calculate a *UK* or *EEA MCR* in accordance with INSPRU 1.5.44R to INSPRU 1.5.47R; and
(2) hold *admissible assets* (in addition to those required under INSPRU 1.1.20R) to represent its *UK* or *EEA MCR* calculated under (1).

1.5.43 **[R]** The assets held under INSPRU 1.5.42R(2) must be identified and valued as if the *non-EEA direct insurer* was a *firm* with its head office in the *United Kingdom*.

1.5.44 **[R]** For the purposes of INSPRU 1.5.42R, a *non-EEA direct insurer* (except a *UK-deposit insurer*) must calculate a *UK MCR*:
(1) for *long-term insurance business*, in accordance with GENPRU 2.1.36R but only in relation to business carried on by the *firm* in the *United Kingdom*;

(2) for *general insurance business*, in accordance with GENPRU 2.1.34R but only in relation to business carried on by the *firm* in the *United Kingdom*.

1.5.45 **[R]** For a *composite firm*, the *UK MCR* is the sum of the amounts arrived at under INSPRU 1.5.44R(1) and INSPRU 1.5.44R(2).

1.5.46 **[R]** For the purposes of INSPRU 1.5.42R, a *UK-deposit insurer* must calculate an *EEA MCR*:
(1) for *long-term insurance business*, in accordance with GENPRU 2.1.36R but only in relation to business carried on by the *firm* in all *EEA States*, taken together;
(2) for *general insurance business*, in accordance with GENPRU 2.1.34R but only in relation to business carried on by the *firm* in all *EEA States*, taken together.

1.5.47 **[R]** For a *composite firm*, the *EEA MCR* is the sum of the amounts arrived at under INSPRU 1.5.46R(1) and INSPRU 1.5.46R(2).

Localisation of assets

1.5.48 **[R]** A *non-EEA direct insurer* (except a *UK-deposit insurer*) must hold:
(1) *admissible assets* which are required to cover its *technical provisions* in accordance with INSPRU 1.1.20R(1) or INSPRU 1.1.21R(1)(a) and *(2)(a)*; and
(2) other *admissible assets* not required to cover *property-linked liabilities* or *index-linked liabilities* in accordance with INSPRU 3.1.57R or INSPRU 3.1.58R which represent its *UK MCR* as calculated in accordance with INSPRU 1.5.44R;

as follows:
(a) (where the assets cover the *technical provisions* and the *guarantee fund*) in the *United Kingdom*;
(b) (where the assets represent the amount of the *UK MCR* in excess of the *guarantee fund*) in any *EEA State*.

1.5.49 **[R]** A *UK-deposit insurer* must hold:
(1) *admissible assets* which are required to cover its technical provisions in accordance with INSPRU 1.1.20R(1) or INSPRU 1.1.21R(1)(a) and *(2)(a)*; and
(2) other *admissible assets* not required to cover *property-linked liabilities* or *index-linked liabilities* in accordance with INSPRU 3.1.57R or INSPRU 3.1.58R which represent its *EEA MCR* as calculated in accordance with INSPRU 1.5.46R; as follows:
  (a) (where the assets cover the *technical provisions* and the *guarantee fund*) within the *EEA* states where the *firm* carries on *insurance business*;
  (b) (where the assets represent the amount of the *EEA MCR* in excess of the *guarantee fund*) in any *EEA State*.

1.5.50 **[R]** INSPRU 1.5.48R and INSPRU 1.5.49R do not apply to assets covering *technical provisions* which are debts owed by *reinsurers*.

1.5.51 **[G]** The *admissible assets* in excess of the *technical provisions* and *UK* or *EEA MCR* may be held outside the *EEA*.

1.5.52 **[R]** For the purpose of INSPRU 1.5.48R and INSPRU 1.5.49R:
(1) a tangible asset is to be treated as held in the country or territory where it is situated;
(2) an *admissible asset* consisting of a claim against a debtor is to be regarded as held in any country or territory where it can be enforced by legal action;
(3) a *security* which is *listed* is to be treated as held in any country or territory where there is a *regulated market* in which the *security* is dealt; and
(4) a *security* which is not *listed* is to be treated as held in the country or territory in which the *issuer* has its head office.

1.5.53 **[G]** INSPRU 3.1.53R to INSPRU 3.1.55R (currency matching of assets and liabilities) apply to the assets held to match insurance liabilities calculated under INSPRU 1.1.12R or INSPRU 1.1.16R.

Deposit of assets as security

1.5.54 **[R]** A *non-EEA direct insurer* must keep assets of a value at least equal to one quarter of the *base capital resources requirement* on deposit in the *United Kingdom* with a *BCD credit institution*.

1.5.55 **[G]** The assets deposited as security may count towards the assets required under INSPRU 1.5.48R and INSPRU 1.5.49R. If, after the deposit is made, the value of the deposited assets falls below one quarter of the *base capital resources requirement*, the *firm* should deposit further *admissible assets* in order to comply with INSPRU 1.5.48R and INSPRU 1.5.49R. Deposited assets may be exchanged for other *admissible assets* and excess assets may be withdrawn, provided that the exchange or deposit does not cause a breach of INSPRU 1.5.48R or INSPRU 1.5.49R.

Branch accounting records in the United Kingdom

1.5.56 **[R]** A *non-EEA direct insurer* must maintain at a place of business in the *United Kingdom* adequate records relating to:

(1) the activities carried on from its *United Kingdom branch*; and
(2) if it is an *EEA-deposit insurer*, the activities carried on from the *branches* in other *EEA States*.

1.5.57 **[R]** The records maintained as required by INSPRU 1.5.56R must include a record of:
(1) the income, expenditure and liabilities arising from activities of the *branch* or *branches*; and
(2) the assets identified under INSPRU 1.1.20R as available to meet those liabilities.

Application of INSPRU 1.5 to Lloyd's

1.5.58 **[R]** INSPRU 1.5 applies to *managing agents* and to the *Society* in accordance with:
(1) for *managing agents*, INSPRU 8.1.4R; and
(2) for the *Society*, INSPRU 8.1.2R.

1.5.59 **[R]** The *Society* and *managing agents* must take all reasonable steps to ensure that:
(1) a *corporate member* does not carry on any commercial business other than *insurance business* and activities arising directly from that business; and
(2) *individual members* do not, in their capacity as *underwriting members*, carry on any commercial business other than *insurance business* and activities arising directly from that business.

1.5.60 **[R]** A *managing agent* must not permit both *general insurance business* and *long-term insurance business* to be carried on together through any *syndicate* managed by it.

1.6 Insurance Special Purpose Vehicles

Application and Purpose

1.6.1 **[R]**
(1) INSPRU 1.6.5R to INSPRU 1.6.12R apply to a *UK ISPV*.
(2) INSPRU 1.6.13G to INSPRU 1.6.18G apply to an *insurer* which has a contract of *reinsurance* with an *ISPV*.

1.6.2 **[G]** An *ISPV* is a special purpose vehicle which assumes risks from *insurance undertakings* or *reinsurance undertakings* and which fully funds its exposure to such risks through the proceeds of a debt issuance or some other financing mechanism where the repayment rights of the providers of such debt or other financing mechanism are subordinated to the *reinsurance* obligations of that vehicle. The special feature of an *ISPV*, when compared to other *reinsurers*, is that it is fully funded to meet its *reinsurance* liabilities. It is, therefore, not subject to insurance risk to the same extent as other *reinsurers*. The *Reinsurance Directive* permits *ISPVs* to be subject to different rules to those applying to other *reinsurers*.

1.6.3 **[G]** To satisfy the definition of an *ISPV* under the *Reinsurance Directive* the *ISPV* must be fully funded. The *FSA* considers that to be fully funded an *ISPV* must have actually received the proceeds of the debt issuance or other mechanism by which it is financed. The *FSA* would not, therefore, grant a *Part IV permission* to an *ISPV* where part of the financing for its *reinsurance* liabilities was on a contingent basis, for example, a standby facility or letter of credit.

1.6.4 **[G]** The purpose of INSPRU 1.6 is:
(1) to set out the *rules* applying to *UK ISPVs* in respect of:
 (a) their assets and liabilities; and
 (b) their contractual arrangements; and
(2) to set out the conditions that must be met in order for an *insurer* to claim credit for *reinsurance* with an *ISPV*.

Assets and liabilities

1.6.5 **[R]** A *UK ISPV* must ensure that at all times its assets are equal to or greater than its liabilities.

1.6.5A **[G]** The purpose of INSPRU 1.6.5R is to ensure that a *UK ISPV* may be viewed as a going concern at all times.

1.6.6 **[G]** In addition to liability under its contracts of *reinsurance*, an *ISPV* will incur liability for other expenses, for example, staff and accommodation costs, *claims* handling arrangements and professional advisers' fees. INSPRU 1.6.5R requires a *UK ISPV* to ensure that it always has sufficient assets to meet its liabilities.

1.6.7 **[R]** A *UK ISPV* must invest its assets in accordance with the requirements set out in INSPRU 3.1.61AR.

1.6.8 **[R]** A *UK ISPV's* assets must be held by, or on behalf of:
(1) the *UK ISPV*; or
(2) the *insurance undertaking* or *reinsurance undertaking* which cedes to the *UK ISPV* the risks in respect of which the relevant assets are held.

Part II FSA Handbook Materials

Contractual arrangements

1.6.9 **[R]** A *UK ISPV* must include in each of its contracts of *reinsurance* terms which secure that its aggregate maximum liability at any time under those contracts of *reinsurance* does not exceed the amount of its assets at that time.

1.6.10 **[G]** INSPRU 1.6.9R requires that a *UK ISPV's* contracts of *reinsurance* should include terms that secure that its maximum *reinsurance* liability is capped at a level that is no greater than the *ISPV's* assets. In the *FSA's* view, this is a necessary condition of the *ISPV* being fully funded, as it means that the *ISPV* should not find that its assets are insufficient to meet its *reinsurance* liabilities.

1.6.11 **[R]** A *UK ISPV* must ensure that under the terms of any debt issuance or other financing arrangement used to fund its *reinsurance* liabilities the rights of the providers of that debt or other financing are fully subordinated to the claims of creditors under its contracts of *reinsurance*.

1.6.12 **[R]** A *UK ISPV* must only enter into contracts or otherwise assume obligations which are necessary for it to give effect to the *reinsurance* arrangements which represent the special purpose for which it has been established.

Reinsurance with an ISPV

1.6.13 **[G]** As a result of GENPRU 1.3.55R, GENPRU 2 Ann 7R, INSPRU 1.1.92AR and INSPRU 1.2.28R an *insurer* may not:

(1) treat amounts recoverable from an *ISPV* as:
   (a) an *admissible asset*, or
   (b) *reinsurance* for the purposes of calculating its *mathematical reserves*, or
   (c) *reinsurance* reducing its *MCR*, or

(2) otherwise ascribe a value to such amounts,

unless it first obtains a *waiver* from the *FSA*. INSPRU 1.6.14G to INSPRU 1.6.18G set out the information which the *FSA* will expect to receive as part of the application for the *waiver*. Those paragraphs also set out the factors, in addition to the statutory tests under section 148 of the *Act*, to which the *FSA* will have regard in deciding:

(i) whether to grant such a *waiver* (assuming the section 148 conditions are met); and
(ii) the amount recoverable from the *ISPV* which it will allow the *insurer* to bring into account for these purposes.

1.6.14 **[G]** Where the *ISPV* is a *UK ISPV*, the *FSA* will wish to be satisfied that the *UK ISPV* complies with INSPRU 1.6.5R to INSPRU 1.6.12R. The *FSA* may rely on information supplied in connection with its application for *authorisation*. However, if the application for a *waiver* is made some time after *authorisation* was granted, the *FSA* may request confirmation that there has been no material change to the information originally supplied.

1.6.15 **[G]** Where the *ISPV* is not a *UK ISPV*, the *FSA* will expect to receive confirmation that the *ISPV* has received an official authorisation in accordance with article 46 of the *Reinsurance Directive* in the *EEA State* in which it has been established. In addition, it will need details of the debt issuance or other financing mechanism by which the *ISPV's reinsurance* liabilities are funded. The *FSA* will also expect to receive information about the *ISPV's* key management and control functions, including details of the *ISPV's* auditors and arrangements for *claims* handling, and any material *outsourcing* agreements. The *FSA* will also need information about the structure of any *group* of which the *ISPV* is a member.

1.6.16 **[G]** No credit may be taken for a contract of *reinsurance* with an *ISPV* unless the contract meets the risk transfer principle set out in INSPRU 1.1.19AR. The *FSA* will require evidence that the contract of *reinsurance* and the extent of the credit that the *firm* proposes to take for it satisfy the risk transfer principle.

1.6.17 **[G]** The *FSA* will require information about the impact of the *ISPV* arrangement on the ceding *firm's* individual capital assessment carried out in accordance with INSPRU 7.1. This should include evidence that all residual risks associated with the arrangement (including credit, market, liquidity and operational risks) are reflected in that assessment.

1.6.18 **[G]** The *FSA* will also expect to receive an analysis of the potential for risk to revert to the *firm* or any of its *associates* under realistic adverse scenarios or for liabilities to arise in respect of the risks transferred for which no provision has been made.

INSPRU Annex 1G

INSPRU Ann 1 **[G]** INSPRU 1.2 (Mathematical reserves) and INSPRU 1.3 (With-profits insurance capital component)

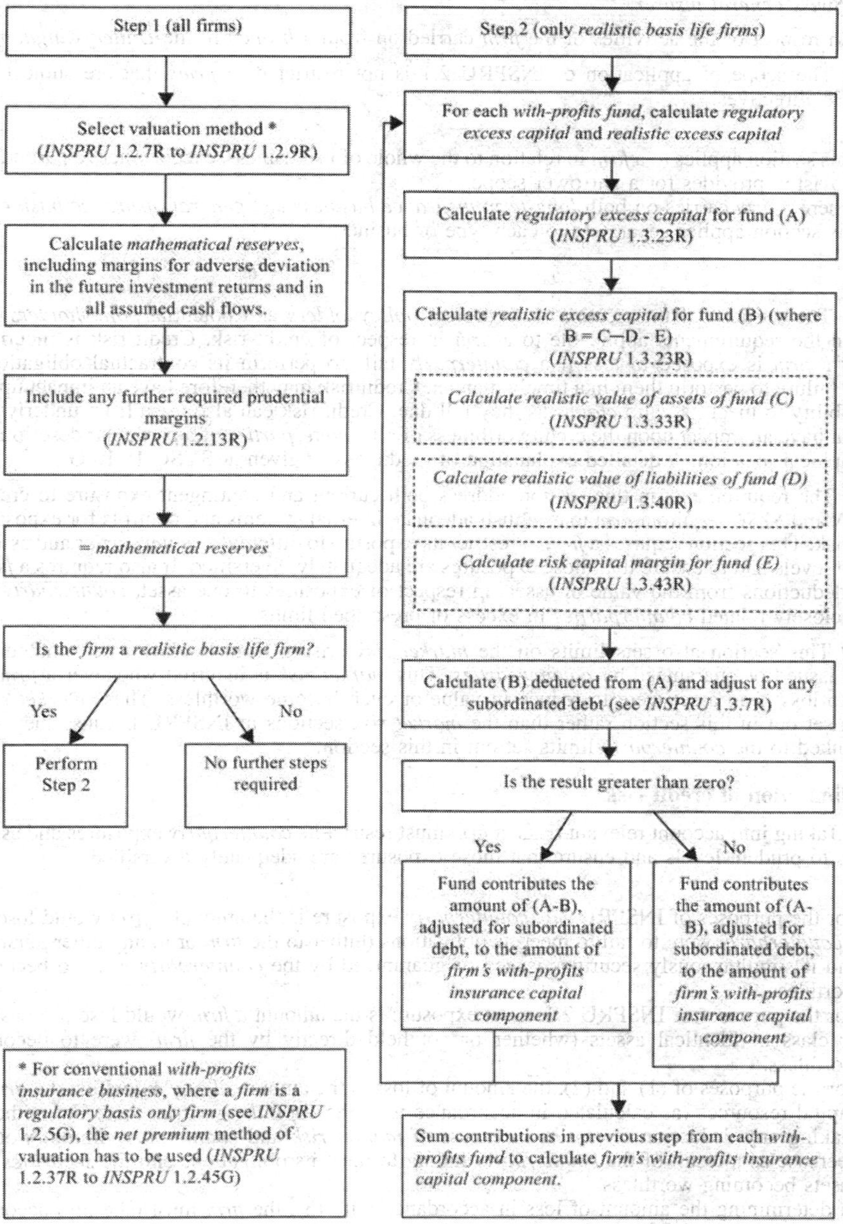
Step 1 (all firms)
Select valuation method * (INSPRU 1.2.7R to INSPRU 1.2.9R)
Calculate mathematical reserves, including margins for adverse deviation in the future investment returns and in all assumed cash flows.
Include any further required prudential margins (INSPRU 1.2.13R)
= mathematical reserves
Is the firm a realistic basis life firm?
Yes
No
Perform Step 2
No further steps required
* For conventional with-profits insurance business, where a firm is a regulatory basis only firm (see INSPRU 1.2.5G), the net premium method of valuation has to be used (INSPRU 1.2.37R to INSPRU 1.2.45G)
Step 2 (only realistic basis life firms)
For each with-profits fund, calculate regulatory excess capital and realistic excess capital
Calculate regulatory excess capital for fund (A) (INSPRU 1.3.23R)
Calculate realistic excess capital for fund (B) (where B = C–D - E) (INSPRU 1.3.23R)
Calculate realistic value of assets of fund (C) (INSPRU 1.3.33R)
Calculate realistic value of liabilities of fund (D) (INSPRU 1.3.40R)
Calculate risk capital margin for fund (E) (INSPRU 1.3.43R)
Calculate (B) deducted from (A) and adjust for any subordinated debt (see INSPRU 1.3.7R)
Is the result greater than zero?
Yes
No
Fund contributes the amount of (A-B), adjusted for subordinated debt, to the amount of firm's with-profits insurance capital component
Fund contributes the amount of (A-B), adjusted for subordinated debt, to the amount of firm's with-profits insurance capital component
Sum contributions in previous step from each with-profits fund to calculate firm's with-profits insurance capital component.

CHAPTER 2

2.1 Credit risk in insurance

Application

[2066]

2.1.1 **[R]** INSPRU 2.1 applies to an *insurer* unless it is:

(1) a *non-directive friendly society*; or

(2) an *incoming EEA firm*; or

(3) an *incoming Treaty firm*.

2.1.2 **[R]** All of INSPRU 2.1, except INSPRU 2.1.20R and INSPRU 2.1.23R to INSPRU 2.1.32G, applies to:

(1) an *EEA-deposit insurer*; and

(2) a *Swiss general insurer*;

but only in respect of the activities of the *firm* carried on from a *branch* in the *United Kingdom*.

2.1.3 **[G]** The scope of application of INSPRU 2.1 is not restricted to *firms* that are subject to relevant *EU* directives.

2.1.4 **[R]**

(1) This section applies to a *firm* in relation to the whole of its business, except where a particular provision provides for a narrower scope.

(2) Where a *firm* carries on both *long-term insurance business* and *general insurance business*, this section applies separately to each type of business.

Purpose

2.1.5 **[G]** The purpose of this section is to protect *policyholders* and potential *policyholders* by setting out the requirements applicable to a *firm* in respect of credit risk. Credit risk is incurred whenever a *firm* is exposed to loss if a *counterparty* fails to perform its contractual obligations including failure to perform them in a timely manner. Credit risk may therefore have an impact upon a firm's ability to meet its valid *claims* as they fall due. Credit risk can also arise from underlying causes that have an impact upon the creditworthiness of all *counterparties* of a particular description or geographical location. A detailed explanation of credit risk is given at SYSC 15.1.4G.

2.1.6 **[G]** The requirements in this section address both current and contingent exposure to credit risk. *PRIN* and *SYSC* require a *firm* to establish adequate internal systems and controls for exposure to credit risk. This section requires a *firm* to restrict its exposure to different *counterparties* and assets to prudent levels and to ensure that those exposures are adequately diversified. It also requires a *firm* to make deductions from the value of assets in respect of exposures to one asset, *counterparty* or group of closely related *counterparties* in excess of prescribed limits.

2.1.7 **[G]** This section also sets limits on the *market risk* arising from holding assets including securities issued or guaranteed by *counterparties*. This *market risk* is incurred whenever a *firm* is exposed to loss if an asset were to reduce in value or even become worthless. These *market risk* limits are set out in this section rather than the *market risk* sections in INSPRU because they are closely linked to the *counterparty* limits set out in this section.

Overall limitation of credit risk

2.1.8 **[R]** Taking into account relevant risks, a *firm* must restrict its *counterparty* exposures and asset exposures to prudent levels and ensure that those exposures are adequately diversified.

2.1.9 **[R]**

(1) For the purposes of INSPRU 2.1, *counterparty* exposure is the amount a *firm* would lose if a *counterparty* were to fail to meet its obligations (either to the *firm* or to any other *person*) and if simultaneously securities issued or guaranteed by the *counterparty* were to become worthless.

(2) For the purposes of INSPRU 2.1, asset exposure is the amount a *firm* would lose if an asset or class of identical assets (whether or not held directly by the *firm*) were to become worthless.

(3) For the purposes of (1) and (2), the amount of loss is the amount, if any, by which the *firm's* capital resources (as calculated in accordance with the *capital resources table* but without making any deduction for assets in excess of *market risk* and *counterparty* limits) would decrease as a result of the *counterparty* failing to meet its obligations and the *securities* or assets becoming worthless.

(4) In determining the amount of loss in accordance with (3), the *firm* must take into account decreases in its capital resources that would result not only from its own direct exposures but also from:
   (a) exposures held by any of its *subsidiary undertakings*; and
   (b) synthetic exposures arising from *derivatives* or quasi-derivatives held or entered into by the *firm* or any of its *subsidiary undertakings*.

(5) If a *firm* elects under INSPRU 2.1.35R to make a deduction in respect of *collateral*, the *firm* must deduct from the amount of loss determined in accordance with (3) so much of the value of that *collateral* as:
   (a) would be realised by the *firm* were it to exercise its rights in relation to the *collateral*; and
   (b) does not exceed any of the relevant limits in INSPRU 2.1.22R(3).

2.1.10 **[G]** Exposure is defined in terms of loss (which is decrease in capital). It does not include exposures arising from assets that are not represented in capital or exposures which if crystallised in a loss would be offset by a consequent gain, reduction in liabilities or release of provisions, but only in so far as that gain, reduction or release would itself lead to an offsetting increase in *capital resources*. Examples include:

(1) exposure from the holding of assets to which the *firm* has attributed no value;
(2) exposure from the holding of assets that the *firm* has deducted from *capital resources*; and
(3) exposure in respect of which (and to the extent that) the *firm* has established a provision.

2.1.11 **[G]** In assessing the adequacy of diversification required by INSPRU 2.1.8R, a *firm* should take into account concentrations of exposure including those arising from:

(1) different types of exposure to the same *counterparty*, such as *deposits*, loans, securities, *reinsurance* and *derivatives*;
(2) links between *counterparties* such that default by one might have an impact upon the creditworthiness of another; and
(3) possible changes in circumstance that would have an impact upon the creditworthiness of all *counterparties* of particular description or geographical location.

2.1.12 **[G]** A *firm* should consider how the spreading of credit risk will impact on overall *counterparty* quality.

2.1.13 **[G]** In assessing its exposure to a *counterparty* for the purpose of INSPRU 2.1.8R, a *firm* should take into account:

(1) the period for which the exposure to that *counterparty* might continue;
(2) the likelihood of default during that period by the *counterparty*; and
(3) the loss that might result in the event of default.

2.1.14 **[G]** In assessing the loss that might result from the default of a *counterparty* for the purposes of INSPRU 2.1.8R, a *firm* should take into account the circumstances that might lead to default and, in particular, how these might have an impact upon:

(1) the amount of exposure to the *counterparty*; and
(2) the effectiveness of any loss mitigation techniques employed by the *firm*.

2.1.15 **[G]** Often the same circumstances which lead to the crystallisation of contingent credit exposure, e.g. a significant *claims* event or a significant movement in interest, currency or asset values, also lead to an increase in the risk of default by the *counterparty*. In particular, if a *reinsurer* or *derivative counterparty* is being relied upon to provide protection against the consequences of an event or circumstance, a *firm* should take into account how that event or circumstance might have an impact upon the creditworthiness of the *reinsurer* or *derivative counterparty*.

2.1.16 **[R]** For the purposes of INSPRU 2.1.8R and of determining *counterparty* exposure and asset exposure in accordance with INSPRU 2.1.9R and *reinsurance* exposure in accordance with INSPRU 2.1.25R, a *firm* must only rely upon a loss mitigation technique where it has good reason to believe that, taking into account the possible circumstances of default, it is likely to be effective.

2.1.17 **[G]** Loss mitigation techniques include:

(1) the right, upon default, to preferential access to some or all of the *counterparty's* assets, for example by exercising rights of set off, holding *collateral* or assets deposited back, or exercising rights under fixed or floating charges;
(2) rights against third parties upon default by the *counterparty*, such as guarantees, credit insurance and credit *derivatives*; and
(3) where the *counterparty* is a *reinsurer*, having back-up or flexible *reinsurance* which covers the gap in coverage left by the *reinsurer's* default, for example 'top and drop' *reinsurance*.

2.1.18 **[R]** For the purposes of INSPRU 2.1.8R and of determining *counterparty* exposure and asset exposure in accordance with INSPRU 2.1.9R and *reinsurance* exposure in accordance with INSPRU 2.1.25R, a *firm* must not rely upon preferential access to assets unless it has taken into account appropriate professional advice as to its effectiveness.

2.1.19 **[G]** In particular, a *firm* should consider whether any preferential access to a *counterparty*'s assets would be effective even if the *counterparty* were wound up by a court or other legal process or it were to be subject to any other insolvency process. A *firm* should also consider, where it is relying upon a right against a third party, whether, in the circumstances of the *counterparty*'s default, the creditworthiness of that third party might be impaired.

Large exposure limits

2.1.20 **[R]**

(1) A *firm* must take reasonable steps to limit its *counterparty* exposure or asset exposure to:
 (a) a single *counterparty*;
 (b) each of the *counterparties* within a group of closely related counterparties; and
 (c) an asset or class of identical assets;

 to a level where, if a total default were to occur, the *firm* would not become unable to meet its liabilities as they fall due.
(2) In (1), a total default occurs where:

(a) the single *counterparty* or all of the *counterparties* within the group of closely related *counterparties* fail to meet its or their obligations and simultaneously any securities issued or guaranteed by it or any of them become worthless; or
(b) the asset becomes worthless or all of the assets within the identical class become worthless at the same time.

(3) (1) does not apply to:
(a) a *reinsurance* exposure; or
(b) a *counterparty* exposure or asset exposure to an *approved credit institution*.

2.1.21 **[G]** In assessing its exposure to a *counterparty* or group of closely related *counterparties*, a *firm* should consider exposures from different sources including *deposits*, loans, *securities* and *derivatives*.

Market risk and counterparty limits

2.1.22 **[R]**

(1) A *firm* must calculate the amount of the deduction from total capital required by stage L in the *capital resources table* in respect of assets in excess of *market risk* and *counterparty* limits as the aggregate amount by which its *counterparty* exposures and asset exposures exceed the relevant limits set out in (3).

(2) Except where the contrary is expressly stated in INSPRU, whenever:
(a) a *rule* in INSPRU refers to assets of a *firm*, or of any part of a firm, or of any fund or part of a fund within a *firm*, which are assets of a kind referred to in any of the limits in (3); and
(b) the *firm's counterparty* exposure (or aggregate exposure arising from the *counterparty* exposures to each member of a group of closely related persons) or asset exposure in respect of those assets exceeds any of the limits in (3);

the *firm* must deduct from the measure of the value of those assets (as determined in accordance with GENPRU 1.3) the amount by which that exposure exceeds the relevant limit in (3), or that portion of the deduction that relates to the part of the *firm* or fund or part of a fund in question.

(3) The limits referred to in (1) and (2) are the following, expressed as a percentage of the *firm's* business amount:
(a) for a *counterparty* exposure to an individual, unincorporated body of individuals or the aggregate exposure arising from the *counterparty* exposures to each member of a group of closely related individuals or unincorporated bodies of individuals:
(i) ¼% for that part of the exposure that arises from unsecured debt;
(ii) 1% for the whole exposure (after deduction of the excess arising from the limit in (a)(i));
(b) for a *counterparty* exposure to an *approved counterparty* or the aggregate exposure arising from the *counterparty* exposures to each member of a group of closely related *approved counterparties*:
(i) 40% for that part of the exposure arising from *covered bonds*;
(ii) 5% for that part of the exposure not arising from *covered bonds* or, if the *counterparty* is an *approved credit institution*, from short term *deposits*; this limit is increased to 10% if the total of such exposures which are greater than 5% arising from applying a 10% limit, when taken together with any exposures arising from *covered bonds* which are within the 40% limit in (i), does not exceed 40%;
(iii) 20% or £2 million, if larger, for the whole exposure (but excluding any exposure arising from *covered bonds* and after deduction of the excess arising from the limit in (b)(ii));
(c) for a *counterparty* exposure to a *person*, or the aggregate exposure arising from the *counterparty* exposures to each member of a group of closely related *persons*, who do not fall into the categories of *counterparty* to whom (a) and (b) apply:
(i) 1% for that part of the exposure arising from unsecured debt; this limit is increased to 2.5% in the case of an exposure to a *regulated institution*;

(ii) 1% for that part of the exposure arising from *shares* and other variable yield participations, bonds, *debt securities* and other *money market instruments* and capital market instruments from the same *counterparty* that are not dealt in on a *regulated market*, or a beneficial interest in a *collective investment scheme* to which INSPRU 2.1.39R applies; the limit for that part of the exposure arising from *debt securities* (other than hybrid securities) issued by the same *regulated institution* is increased to 5%;

(iii) 5% for the whole exposure (after deduction of the excesses arising from the limits in (c)(i) and (ii));

(d) 5% for the aggregate of all *counterparty* exposures that fall within (c)(i) whether or not they arise from *persons* who are closely related, but excluding amounts that are in excess of the limit in (c)(i);

(e) 10% for the aggregate of all *counterparty exposures* and asset exposures that fall within (c)(ii) above or (j) below, whether or not they arise from *persons* who are closely related, but excluding amounts that are in excess of the limit in (c)(ii) above or, in the case of an asset exposure, (j) below;

(f) 5% for the aggregate of all *counterparty* exposures arising from unsecured loans, other than those falling within (3)(b);

(g) 3% for the asset exposure arising from all cash in hand;

(h) 10% for the asset exposure (including an exposure arising from a reversionary interest) arising from any one piece of land or building, or a number of pieces of land or buildings close enough to each other to be considered effectively as one investment;

(i) 5% for the asset exposure arising from a beneficial interest in any single *non-UCITS retail scheme* or *recognised scheme* which does not fall within the *UCITS Directive*; and

(j) 1% for the asset exposure arising from a beneficial interest in any single *collective investment scheme* which does not fall within the *UCITS Directive* and is not a *non-UCITS retail scheme* or a *recognised scheme*.

(4) In (3) a *firm's* business amount means the sum of:

(a) the *firm's* total gross *technical provisions* (that is, calculated gross of *reinsurance*);

(b) the amount of its other liabilities (except those included in the calculation of capital resources in accordance with the *capital resources table*); and

(c) such amount as the *firm* may select not exceeding, in the case of a *firm* which is not a *participating insurance undertaking*, the amount of the *firm's* total capital after deductions as calculated at stage M of the *capital resources table* or, in the case of a *firm* which is a *participating insurance undertaking*, the amount calculated in accordance with (5A) or, in either case, if higher:

(i) in the case of a *firm* carrying on *general insurance business*, the amount of its *general insurance capital requirement*; and

(ii) in the case of a *firm* carrying on *long-term insurance business*, the amount of its *long-term insurance capital requirement* and, where it is a *regulatory basis only life firm*, the amount of its *resilience capital requirement*.

(5) For the purpose of (4)(a), a *firm's* total gross *technical provisions* exclude *technical provisions* in respect of *index-linked liabilities* or *property-linked liabilities*, except that where the *linked long-term contract of insurance* in question includes a guarantee of investment performance or some other guaranteed benefit, the total gross *technical provisions* include the *technical provisions* in respect of that guaranteed element.

(5A) For the purpose of (4)(c), a *firm* which is a *participating insurance undertaking* must calculate the amount of the *firm's group capital resources* less the difference between:

(a) the *firm's group capital resources requirement*; and

(b) the *firm's capital resources requirement*.

(5B) In (3)(b)(ii) short term *deposit* means a *deposit* which may be withdrawn at the discretion of the lender without penalty or loss of accrued interest by giving notice of withdrawal of one month or less.

(6) In (3)(c)(ii) hybrid security means a *debt security*, other than an *approved security*, the terms of which provide, or have the effect that, the holder does not, or would not, have an unconditional entitlement to payment of interest and repayment of capital in full within 75 years of the date on which the *security* is being valued.

(7) In (3)(a)(i) and (3)(c)(i) an unsecured debt is any debt in respect of which the conditions in INSPRU 2.1.35R or INSPRU 2.1.36R and INSPRU 2.1.37R are not satisfied or, if satisfied only in relation to part of the debt, that part of the debt which is not covered by collateral or a guarantee, letter of credit or credit derivative in accordance with those *rules*.

2.1.22A **[R]** INSPRU 2.1.22R does not apply to a *pure reinsurer*.

Large exposure calculation for reinsurance exposures

2.1.23 **[R]** A *firm* must notify the *FSA* in accordance with *SUP* 15.7 as soon as it first becomes aware that:
(1) a *reinsurance* exposure to a *reinsurer* or group of closely related *reinsurers* is reasonably likely to exceed 100% of its *capital resources*; or
(2) if (1) does not apply, that it has exceeded this limit.

2.1.24 **[R]** Upon notification under INSPRU 2.1.23R, a *firm* must:
(1) demonstrate that prudent provision has been made for the *reinsurance* exposure in excess of the 100% limit, or explain why in the opinion of the *firm* no provision is required; and
(2) explain how the *reinsurance* exposure is being safely managed.

2.1.25 **[R]**
(1) For the purposes of INSPRU 2.1, a *reinsurance* exposure is the amount of loss which a *firm* would suffer if a *reinsurer* or group of closely related *reinsurers* were to fail to meet its or their obligations under contracts of *reinsurance* reinsuring any of the firm's contracts of insurance.
(2) For the purposes of (1), the amount of loss is the amount, if any, by which the *firm's* capital resources (as calculated in accordance with the *capital resources table* but without making any deduction for assets in excess of *market risk* and *counterparty* limits) would decrease as a result of the *reinsurer* or group of closely related *reinsurers* failing to meet its or their obligations under the contracts of *reinsurance*.
(3) If a *firm* elects under INSPRU 2.1.35R to make a deduction in respect of *collateral*, the *firm* must deduct from the amount of loss determined in accordance with (2) so much of the value of that *collateral* as:
  (a) would be realised by the *firm* were it to exercise its rights in relation to the *collateral*; and
  (b) does not exceed any of the relevant limits in INSPRU 2.1.22R(3).

2.1.26 **[R]** A *firm* must, in determining its *reinsurance* exposures for the purposes of INSPRU 2.1, aggregate any *reinsurance* exposure where the identity of the *reinsurer* is not known by the *firm* with the highest *reinsurance* exposure where it does know the identity of the *reinsurer*.

2.1.27 **[G]** INSPRU 2.1.8R provides that, taking into account relevant risks, a *firm* must restrict to prudent levels, and adequately diversify, its exposure to *counterparties*.

2.1.28 **[E]**
(1) In each *financial year*, a *firm* should restrict the *gross earned premiums* which it pays to a *reinsurer* or group of closely related *reinsurers* to the higher of:
  (a) 20% of the *firm's* projected *gross earned premiums* for that *financial year*; or
  (b) £4 million.
(2) Compliance with this provision may be relied upon as tending to establish compliance with INSPRU 2.1.8R.

2.1.29 **[R]** A *firm* must notify the *FSA* immediately in accordance with SUP 15.7 if it has exceeded, or anticipates exceeding, the limit expressed in INSPRU 2.1.28E.

2.1.30 **[R]** Upon notification under INSPRU 2.1.29R, a *firm* must explain to the *FSA* how, despite the excess *reinsurance* concentration, the credit risk is being safely managed.

2.1.31 **[G]** For the purposes of INSPRU 2.1.24R and INSPRU 2.1.30R, a *firm's* explanation of how a *reinsurance* exposure is being safely managed should also describe the *reinsurance* market in which the exposure has occurred, and the nature of the *reinsurance* contract. If appropriate, the *firm* should also provide a detailed plan and timetable explaining how the excess exposure will be reduced to an acceptable level. The explanation should be approved by a person at the *firm* of appropriate seniority.

2.1.32 **[G]** Where a *firm* can demonstrate that the arrangement does not give rise to unacceptable levels of credit risk it is unlikely that further action will be required.

Exposures excluded from limits

2.1.33 **[R]** In INSPRU 2.1.20R and INSPRU 2.1.22R, references to a *counterparty* exposure or an asset exposure do not include such an exposure arising from:

(1) [deleted]

(2) *premium* debts;

(3) advances secured on, and not exceeding the *surrender value* of, *long-term insurance contracts* of the *firm*;

(4) rights of salvage or subrogation;

(5) *deferred acquisition costs*;

(6) assets held to cover *index-linked liabilities* or *property-linked liabilities*, except that where the *linked long-term contract of insurance* in question includes a guarantee of investment performance or some other guaranteed benefit, INSPRU 2.1.20R and INSPRU 2.1.22R will nevertheless apply to assets held to cover that guaranteed element;

(7) *moneys* due from, or guaranteed by, a *Zone A country*;

(8) an *approved security*;

(9) a holding in a *collective investment scheme* falling within the *UCITS Directive*.

2.1.34 **[R]** In INSPRU 2.1.22R references to a *counterparty* exposure or an asset exposure do not include such an exposure resulting from debts arising from *reinsurance* ceded and the *reinsurer's* share of *technical provisions*.

2.1.35 **[R]** If:

(1) a *firm* has a *counterparty* exposure, an asset exposure or a *reinsurance* exposure in respect of which it has rights over *collateral* (except where that *collateral* is a letter of credit – see INSPRU 2.1.36R and INSPRU 2.1.37R); and

(2) the assets constituting that *collateral* would, if owned by the *firm*, be admissible assets;

the *firm* may, in determining the amount of that exposure, deduct the value of that *collateral* in accordance with INSPRU 2.1.9R(5) or, in the case of a *reinsurance* exposure, INSPRU 2.1.25R(3).

2.1.36 **[R]** If a *firm* has a *counterparty* exposure, asset exposure or reinsurance exposure the whole or any part of which is:

(1) guaranteed by a *credit institution* or an *investment firm* subject in either case to the *Capital Adequacy Directive* or supervision by a third country (non-EEA) supervisory authority with a Capital Adequacy Directive- equivalent regime; or

(2) adequately mitigated by a credit *derivative*;

the *firm* may, for the purposes of INSPRU 2.1.20R, INSPRU 2.1.22R and INSPRU 2.1.23R, treat that exposure, or that part of the exposure which is so guaranteed or mitigated, as an exposure to the guarantor or derivative *counterparty*, rather than to the original *counterparty*, asset or *reinsurer*.

2.1.37 **[R]** For the purposes of INSPRU 2.1.36R, references to an exposure being guaranteed include an exposure secured by a letter of credit, but to fall within INSPRU 2.1.36R the guarantee or letter of credit must be direct, explicit, unconditional and irrevocable.

2.1.38 **[G]** The portion of exposure which is guaranteed or mitigated by a credit *derivative* is itself, as an exposure to the guarantor or derivative *counterparty*, subject to the limits in INSPRU 2.1.20R and INSPRU 2.1.22R.

2.1.39 **[R]** For the purposes of INSPRU 2.1.20R and INSPRU 2.1.22R, *units* in a *collective investment scheme* that does not fall within the *UCITS Directive* must be treated as a *counterparty* exposure to the *issuer* of the *units* in that scheme if the *issuer* and those *units* are to be regarded as constituting a single risk because they are so interconnected that, if the *issuer* were to experience financial problems, this would be likely to affect the value of the *units*.

2.1.39A **[G]** Where the value of *units* in a *collective investment scheme* other than one falling within the *UCITS Directive* would be likely to be adversely affected by financial problems experienced by the *issuer* of those *units*, for the purposes of INSPRU 2.1.20R and INSPRU 2.1.22R, the *units* must be treated as a *counterparty* exposure to the *issuer*, with the result that the exposure is subject to the limit in INSPRU 2.1.22R(3)(c)(ii). In all other cases, the *units* would fall to be treated as an asset exposure, with the result that they are subject to the relevant limit under INSPRU 2.1.22R(3)(i) or (j).

Meaning of closely related

2.1.40 **[R]** For the purposes of INSPRU 2.1, a group of *persons* is closely related if it consists solely of two or more *persons* who, unless it is shown otherwise, constitute a single risk because as between any two of them one or other of the following relationships apply:

(1) one of them, directly or indirectly, has control, as defined in INSPRU 2.1.41R, over the other or they are both controlled by the same third party; or

(2) there is no relationship of control as defined in INSPRU 2.1.41R but they are to be regarded as constituting a single risk because they are so interconnected that, if one of them were to experience financial problems, the other would be likely to encounter repayment difficulties.

2.1.41 **[R]** For the purposes of INSPRU 2.1.40R, control means the relationship between a *parent undertaking* and a *subsidiary undertaking*, as defined in Article 1 of the Consolidated Accounts Directive (83/349/EEC), or a similar relationship between any natural or legal person and an *undertaking*.

Meaning of reinsurance

2.1.41A **[R]** For the purposes of INSPRU 2.1, references to *reinsurance* include analogous non-*reinsurance* financing agreements, including contingent loans, securitisations and any other arrangements in respect of *contracts of insurance* that are analogous to contracts of *reinsurance* in terms of the risks transferred and the finance provided and references to *reinsurer* shall be construed accordingly.

Application of INSPRU 2.1 to Lloyd's

2.1.42 **[R]** Subject to INSPRU 2.1.43R, INSPRU 2.1 applies to *managing agents* and to the *Society* in accordance with:
(1) for *managing agents*, INSPRU 8.1.4R; and
(2) for the *Society*, INSPRU 8.1.2R.

2.1.43 **[R]** INSPRU 2.1.23R to INSPRU 2.1.32G (Large exposure calculation for reinsurance exposures) do not apply to the *Society*.

Overall limitation of credit risk

2.1.44 **[G]** For Lloyd's, *counterparty* exposure is:
(1) for *managing agents*, the amount by which the net assets managed by or under the direction of a *managing agent* in respect of a *syndicate* together with any relevant *balancing amount* would decrease if the *counterparty* were to default;
(2) for the *Society*, the amount by which its net assets (which include those of its subsidiary undertakings) would decrease if the *counterparty* were to default; and
(3) for the *Society*'s management of each *member's funds at Lloyd's*, the amount by which the *member's* net assets would decrease if the *counterparty* were to default.

Large exposures

2.1.45 **[R]** For the purposes of INSPRU 2.1.20R (Large exposure limits: counterparty exposure and asset exposure), the *Society* may determine the exposure to any letters of credit, guarantees or *members'* life assurance policies as an exposure of the *members* in aggregate.

2.1.46 **[R]** For the purposes of INSPRU 2.1.22R (Large exposure limits: market risk and counterparty limits), the *Society* must calculate the amount of and deduct from *capital resources*:
(1) an exposure (expressed as a percentage of the relevant *member's capital resources* held as *funds at Lloyd's*), other than to the assets identified in INSPRU 2.1.46R(2)(a) to INSPRU 2.1.46R(2)(c), of a *member's capital resources* held as *funds at Lloyd's* to a *counterparty*, in excess of the limits in INSPRU 2.1.22R;
(2) an exposure in excess of 20% (expressed as a percentage of the aggregate of *capital resources* held as *funds at Lloyd's*) of the aggregate of *capital resources* held as *funds at Lloyd's* to a single issuer of:
  (a) letters of credit;
  (b) guarantees; or
  (c) *members'* life assurance policies;
(3) an exposure of its own to a *counterparty*, in excess of the limits in INSPRU 2.1.22R, expressed as a percentage of the *Society*'s own assets.

2.1.47 **[R]** For the purposes of INSPRU 2.1.22R (Large exposure limits: market risk and *counterparty* limits), *managing agents* must calculate the amount of and deduct from *capital resources* an exposure (expressed as a percentage of the *admissible assets* held in respect of the relevant *syndicate*) of *admissible assets* held in respect of a *syndicate* to a *counterparty* in excess of the limits in INSPRU 2.1.22R.

2.1.48 **[R]** If the exposures of *capital resources* held as *funds at Lloyd's* for *members* in the aggregate do not exceed the limits in INSPRU 2.1.22R(3)(c), then, for each *individual member*, that limit may be replaced by 10%.

Exposures excluded from the large exposure limits

2.1.49 **[R]** For *managing agents*, in INSPRU 2.1.33R and INSPRU 2.1.35R, references to an exposure do not include exposure arising from *balancing amounts*.

2.2 Asset-related Capital Requirement

Application

2.2.1 **[R]** INSPRU 2.2 applies to an *insurer* unless it is:
(1) a *non-directive friendly society*; or
(2) a *Swiss general insurer*; or
(3) an *EEA-deposit insurer*; or
(4) an *incoming EEA firm*; or
(5) an *incoming Treaty firm*.

2.2.2 **[G]** The scope of application of INSPRU 2.2 is not restricted to *firms* that are subject to the relevant *EU* directives.

2.2.3 **[R]** INSPRU 2.2 applies to a *firm* only in relation to its *general insurance business*.

2.2.4 **[G]** The adequacy of a *firm's* financial resources needs to be assessed in relation to all the activities of the *firm* and the risks to which they give rise.

2.2.5 **[G]** The requirements in INSPRU 2.2 apply to a *firm* on a solo basis.

Purpose

2.2.6 **[G]** GENPRU 2.1.13R requires that a *firm* must maintain at all times *capital resources* equal to or in excess of its *capital resources requirement*. GENPRU 2.1.17R provides that for a *firm* carrying on *general insurance business* the *firm's capital resources requirement* is the *minimum capital requirement*.

2.2.7 **[G]** The *FSA* will use the *enhanced capital requirement* as the benchmark for *individual capital guidance* for a *firm* carrying on *general insurance business*, other than a *non-directive insurer*. The *enhanced capital requirement* is the sum of the *asset-related capital requirement* and the *insurance-related capital requirement* less the firm's equalisation provisions. This section sets out *rules* and *guidance* relating to the *asset- related capital requirement*. *Rules* and *guidance* relating to the *insurance- related capital requirement* are set out in INSPRU 1.1.

2.2.8 **[G]** The *asset-related capital requirement* is a measure of the capital that a *firm* should hold against the risk of loss if another party fails to perform its financial obligations to the *firm* or from adverse movements in the value of assets.

2.2.9 **[G]** The *asset-related capital requirement* is calculated by applying capital charge factors, expressed as a percentage, to different categories of a *firm's* assets. A *firm* should refer to GENPRU 1.3 which sets out how a *firm* must recognise and value assets and liabilities.

Calculation of asset-related capital requirement

2.2.10 **[R]** A *firm* must calculate its *asset-related capital requirement* in accordance with INSPRU 2.2.11R.

2.2.11 **[R]**
(1) The value of each of the *firm's* assets of a kind listed in the table in INSPRU 2.2.16R must be multiplied by the corresponding capital charge factor.
(2) If any amount which is to be multiplied by a capital charge factor is a negative amount, that amount shall be treated as zero.
(3) No account shall be taken of:
   (a) the value of any asset which is not an *admissible asset*;
   (b) the amount (if any) by which the value of any assets exceeds the limits on exposures to a type of asset or *counterparty* as set out in INSPRU 2.1.22R.
(4) Where a *firm* has entered into a *derivative*, then for the purposes of applying the appropriate capital charge factor as set out in INSPRU 2.2.16R, it must treat the value of the *derivative* and the value of the asset associated with the *derivative* as a single asset of a type and value which most closely reflects the economic risk to the *firm* of the combined rights and obligations associated with the *derivative* and the asset associated with the *derivative*.
(5) The amounts resulting from multiplying each of the asset items referred to in (1) by the corresponding capital charge factor must be aggregated.
(6) The *asset-related capital requirement* is the amount resulting from the aggregation in (5).

2.2.12 **[G]** *Options*: some *derivatives* may allow a *firm* an *option* whether to buy or sell a particular asset. If an *option* has a positive market value (that is, in-the- money) it is likely that the *firm* will exercise the *option* in the future and the current value of the *derivative* and associated asset will generally acquire new characteristics and volatility (a 'synthetic asset'). For instance, an *option* to acquire *shares* at a price below their current market value is likely to be exercised and the appropriate *asset-related capital requirement* calculation would be to combine the cash cost of acquiring the number of *shares* covered by the *option* with the value of the *derivative* and apply a factor of 16% to that combined value. If an *option* has no market value (that is, out- of-the-money) then it is unlikely that a *firm* would exercise the *option* in which case the appropriate *asset-related capital requirement* charge would be zero in respect of the *derivative*, and the corresponding capital charge contained in Table INSPRU 2.2.16R in relation to the asset associated with the *derivative*.

2.2.13 **[G]** *Futures* and swaps: *futures* or swaps may not allow the *firm* such an option in which case the appropriate asset-related capital charge factor to apply is the one corresponding to the asset that would be held on fulfilment of the contract and the value to which this should be applied would be the value of the asset held after the contract is fulfilled.

2.2.14 **[R]**

(1) The asset-related capital charge factor for money market funds set out in the Table INSPRU 2.2.16R must be applied to exposures to funds that meet the definition in (2).

(2) In INSPRU 2.2 an investment in a money market fund means a participation in a *collective investment scheme* which satisfies the following conditions:

- (a) the primary investment objective of the *collective investment scheme* is:
  - (i) to maintain the net asset value of the *collective investment scheme* constant at par (net of earnings); or
  - (ii) to maintain the net asset value of the *collective investment scheme* at the value of investors' initial capital plus earnings;
- (b) in order to pursue its primary investment objective the *collective investment scheme* invests exclusively in cash or in short term instruments with characteristics similar to cash or both; and
- (c) the *collective investment scheme* undertakes to abide by the following conditions:
  - (i) not to allow the assets held in the *collective investment scheme* to exceed a weighted average maturity of 60 days;
  - (ii) not to invest in equity or securities with characteristics similar to equity; and
  - (iii) on a basis of marking-to-market at least weekly, not to permit the value of each *collective investment scheme* unit at any point in time to move by more than 50 basis points (0.5% of total *collective investment scheme* value).

2.2.15 **[R]** In INSPRU 2.2.16R an insurance dependant means a *regulated related undertaking* which is an *insurance undertaking* or an *insurance holding company*.

2.2.16 **[R]** Table: Asset-related capital charge factors

Asset item				**ECR asset-related capital charge factor**
Investments	Land and Buildings			7.5%
	Investments in *group undertakings* and participating interests	*Shares* in *group undertakings* excluding participating interests	Insurance dependants	0%
			Other	7.5%
		Debt securities issued by, and loans to, *group undertakings*		3.5%
		Participating interests		7.5%
		Debt securities issued by, and loans to, *undertakings* in which the *insurer* has a participating interest		3.5%
	Other financial *investments*	*Shares* and other variable-yield *securities* and units in unit trusts		16.0%
		Money market funds		0%
		Debt securities and other fixed income securities	*Approved securities*	3.5%
			Other	3.5%
		Participation in investment pools		16.0%
		Loans secured by mortgages		2.5%
		Other loans		2.5%
		Deposits with *approved credit institutions* and *approved financial institutions*		0%
		Other		7.5%
	Deposits with ceding *undertakings*			3.5%

Asset item			ECR asset-related capital charge factor
Reinsurers' share of *technical provisions*	Provision for *unearned premium*		2.5%
	Claims outstanding		2.5%
	Other		2.5%
Debtors	Debtors arising out of direct insurance operations	*Policyholders*	4.5%
		Intermediaries	3.5%
	Debtors arising out of *reinsurance* operations		2.5%
	Other debtors		1.5%
	Called up *share* capital not paid		0%
Other Assets	Tangible assets		7.5%
	Cash at bank and in hand		0%
	Other		0%
Prepayments and accrued income	Accrued interest and rent		0%
	Deferred acquisition costs		0%
	Other prepayments and accrued income		0%

Application of INSPRU 2.2 to Lloyd's

2.2.17 **[R]** INSPRU 2.2 applies to *managing agents* and to the *Society* in accordance with:
(1) for *managing agents*, INSPRU 8.1.4R; and
(2) for the *Society*, INSPRU 8.1.2R

2.2.18 **[R]** This chapter applies to the *Society* for each *member*, including the capital charge relating to *central assets*, to the extent that those assets are held to support a particular *member*.

CHAPTER 3

3.1 Market risk in insurance

[2067]
3.1.1 **[R]** INSPRU 3.1 applies to an *insurer*, unless it is:
(1) a *non-directive friendly society*; or
(2) an *incoming EEA firm*; or
(3) an *incoming Treaty firm*.

3.1.2 **[G]** INSPRU 3.1 applies to *pure reinsurers*, with the exception of INSPRU 3.1.53R, INSPRU 3.1.57R and INSPRU 3.1.58R.

3.1.3 **[R]**
(1) INSPRU 3.1 applies to a *firm* in relation to the whole of its business, except where a particular provision provides for a narrower scope.
(2) Where a *firm* carries on both *long-term insurance business* and *general insurance business*, INSPRU 3.1 applies separately to each type of business.

Purpose

3.1.4 **[G]** This section sets out *rules* and *guidance* relating to *market risk*. Under INSPRU 1.1.20R and INSPRU 1.1.21R, a *firm* is required to hold *admissible assets* of a value sufficient to cover its *technical provisions* and its other *long-term insurance* or *general insurance liabilities*. In addition, INSPRU 1.1.34R sets the requirement that a *firm* must hold assets of appropriate amount, currency, term, safety and yield, to ensure that the cash inflows from those assets will be sufficient to meet expected cash outflows from its insurance liabilities as they are due.

3.1.5 **[G]** *Market risk is the risk that as a result of* market movements a *firm* may be exposed to fluctuations in the value of its assets, the amount of its liabilities, or the income from its assets. Sources of general *market risk* include movements in interest rates, equities, exchange rates and real estate prices. It is important to note that none of these sources of risk is independent of the others. For example, fluctuations in interest rates often have an impact upon equity and currency values and vice versa. Giving due consideration to these correlations is an important aspect of the prudent management of *market risk*.

3.1.6 **[G]** A *firm* may also be exposed to specific *market risk*, which is the risk that the *market value* of a specific asset, or income from that asset, may fluctuate for reasons that are not dependent on general market movements. The limits in INSPRU 2.1.22R cover *market risk* as well as *counterparty* risk.

3.1.7 **[G]** INSPRU 3.1 addresses the impact of *market risk* on *insurance business* in the ways set out below:

(1) Any *firm* that carries on *long-term insurance business* which is a *regulatory basis only life firm* must comply with the *resilience capital requirement*. This requires the *firm* to hold capital to cover *market risk*. The *resilience capital requirement* is dealt with in INSPRU 3.1.9G to INSPRU 3.1.26R.

(2) For a *firm* that carries on *long-term insurance business*, the assets that it must hold must be of a value sufficient to cover the *firm's technical provisions* and other *long-term insurance liabilities*. INSPRU 1.2 contains *rules* and *guidance* as to the methods and assumptions to be used in calculating the *mathematical reserves*. One of these assumptions is the assumed rate of interest to be used in calculating the present value of future payments by or to a *firm*. INSPRU 3.1.28R to INSPRU 3.1.48G set out the methodology to be used in relation to *long-term insurance liabilities*.

(3) *Firms* carrying on either *long-term insurance business* or *general insurance business* are also subject to currency risk. That is, the risk that fluctuations in exchange rates may impact adversely on a *firm*. INSPRU 3.1.49G to INSPRU 3.1.56G set out the requirements a *firm* must meet so as to cover this risk.

(4) For a *firm* carrying on general *insurance business*, the *Enhanced Capital Requirement* already captures some elements of *market risk*. In addition, the requirements as to the assumed rate of interest used in calculating the present value of *general insurance liabilities* are contained in the *insurance accounts rules*, and these requirements are outlined in INSPRU 3.1.27G.

(5) *Firms* carrying on *long-term insurance business* that have *property- linked liabilities* or *index-linked liabilities* must cover these liabilities by holding appropriate assets. INSPRU 3.1.57R and INSPRU 3.1.58R set out these cover requirements.

(6) The *Reinsurance Directive* applies to *pure reinsurers* "prudent person" investment principles in relation to the investment of their assets. INSPRU 3.1.61AR sets out these principles.

Definitions

3.1.8 **[R]** For the purposes of INSPRU 3.1:

(1) real estate means an interest in land, buildings or other immovable property;

(2) a significant territory is any country or territory in which more than 2.5% of a *firm's long-term insurance assets* (by *market value*), excluding assets held to cover *index-linked liabilities* or *property-linked liabilities* (see INSPRU 3.1.57R and INSPRU 3.1.58R), are invested;

(3) the long term gilt yield means the annualised equivalent of the fifteen year gilt yield for the *United Kingdom* Government fixed-interest *securities* index jointly compiled by the Financial Times, the Institute of Actuaries and the Faculty of Actuaries; and

(4) the member states of the European Union which have adopted the Euro as the official currency may be treated as a single territory.

Resilience capital requirement (only applicable to the long-term insurance business of regulatory basis only life firms)

3.1.9 **[G]** The *resilience capital requirement* forms part of the calculation of the *capital resources requirement* for *regulatory basis only life firms*. GENPRU 2.1.23R specifies that the *CRR* for a *regulatory basis only life firm* is equal to the *MCR* in GENPRU 2.1.25R. The *resilience capital requirement* forms part of the *MCR* for a *regulatory basis only life firm* (see GENPRU 2.1.25R(2)(b).

3.1.10 **[R]**

(1) A *regulatory basis only life firm* must calculate a *resilience capital requirement* in accordance with (2) to (5).

(2) The *firm* must identify relevant assets (see INSPRU 3.1.10AR) which, after applying the scenarios in (3), have a value that is equal to the *firm's long-term insurance liabilities* under those scenarios.

(3) For the purpose of (2), the scenarios are:
- (a) for those relevant assets invested in the *United Kingdom*, the *market risk* scenario set out in INSPRU 3.1.16R;
- (b) subject to (c) and to INSPRU 3.1.26R, for those relevant assets invested outside of the *United Kingdom*, the *market risk* scenario set out in INSPRU 3.1.23R; and
- (c) where the relevant assets in (b) are:
  - (i) held to cover *index-linked liabilities* or *property-linked liabilities*; or
  - (ii) not invested in a significant territory outside the *United Kingdom*,

the *market risk* scenario set out in INSPRU 3.1.16R.

(4) The *resilience capital requirement* is the result of deducting B from A, where:
- (a) A is the value of the relevant assets which will produce the result described in (2); and
- (b) B is the *firm's long-term insurance liabilities*.

(5) In calculating the value of the *firm's long-term insurance liabilities* under any scenario, a *firm* is not required to adjust the provision made under GENPRU 1.3.4R in respect of a *defined benefits pension scheme.*

3.1.10A **[R]** In INSPRU 3.1.10R relevant assets means a range of assets which must be selected by the *firm* from the assets specified in (1) and (2) in the order specified:

(1) its *long-term insurance assets*; and
(2) only where the *firm* has selected all the assets within (1), its shareholder assets, other than assets of an amount and kind required:
  (a) to cover its liabilities arising outside its *long-term insurance funds*; or
  (b) to meet any regulatory capital requirements in respect of business written outside its *long-term insurance funds.*

3.1.11 **[G]** The purpose of the *resilience capital requirement* is to cover adverse deviation from:

(1) the value of *long-term insurance liabilities*;
(2) the value of assets held to cover *long-term insurance liabilities*; and
(3) the value of assets held to cover the resilience capital requirement;

arising from the effects of *market risk* for equities, real estate and fixed interest securities. Other risks are not explicitly addressed by the *resilience capital requirement.*

3.1.12 **[G]** The amount of the *resilience capital requirement* calculated by the *firm* will depend on the *firm's* choice of assets held to cover the *resilience capital requirement*. The *resilience capital requirement* is held to cover not only the shortfall between the change in the value of *long-term insurance liabilities* and the change in the value of the assets identified to cover those liabilities, but also the change in the value of the assets identified to cover the *resilience capital requirement* itself.

3.1.13 **[G]** As part of the assessment of the financial resources a *firm* needs to hold to comply with the *overall financial adequacy rule*, the *general stress and scenario testing rule* requires a *firm* to carry out stress tests and scenario analyses appropriate to the major sources of risk to its ability to meet its liabilities as they fall due identified in accordance with the *overall Pillar 2 rule*. In considering the stress tests and scenario analyses relevant to the major sources of risk in the category of *market risk*, a *firm* should consider the extent to which the *market risk* scenarios set out in INSPRU 3.1.16R to INSPRU 3.1.26R are appropriate to the nature of its asset portfolio. A *firm* may judge that given the nature of its portfolio, a more severe stress should be adopted. The *firm* may also wish to bring in other asset classes, such as index-linked bonds, which should be stressed on appropriate bases, and to consider the impact of currency mismatching and any *derivative* positions held.

3.1.13A **[G]** In the *market risk* scenarios set out in INSPRU 3.1.16R to INSPRU 3.1.26R, a *firm* is required to assess the changed value of its assets and liabilities in the economic conditions of the scenarios set out in INSPRU 3.1.16R and INSPRU 3.1.23R. A *firm* is required to assess the changed value of each relevant asset (as defined in INSPRU 3.1.10AR), notwithstanding any uncertainty about the appropriate valuation basis for that asset. In valuing an asset in the specified scenarios, a *firm* should have regard to the economic substance of the asset, rather than its legal form, and assess its value accordingly. Consider, for example, a convertible bond that is close to its conversion date and where the conversion option has value. The value of the convertible bond in the specified scenarios is likely to be sensitive primarily to equity market scenarios and to a lesser extent to interest rate scenarios. The *firm* should value the asset according to its expected market value in the economic conditions underlying the specified scenarios.

3.1.13B **[G]** In determining where particular assets are invested for the purpose of determining which *market risk* scenario should be applied to those assets, or whether a country or territory in which a *firm* has invested part of its *long-term insurance assets* is a significant territory, a *firm* should generally treat:

(1) a *security* dealt in on a *regulated market* as invested in any country or territory in which a *regulated market* on which the *security* is dealt is situated;
(2) a *security* which is not dealt in on a *regulated market* as invested in the country or territory in which the *issuer* has its head office;
(3) an asset consisting of a claim against a debtor as invested in any country or territory where it can be enforced by legal action;
(4) real estate as invested in the country or territory in which the land, buildings or other immovable property is situated;
(5) a tangible asset as invested in the country or territory where it is situated; and
(6) a *derivative* or *quasi-derivative* as invested in the country or territory in which the assets to which the *firm* is exposed by reason of having entered into the *derivative* or *quasi-derivative* are situated.

Where, however, the nature of a *firm's* investment is such that the economic risks to which it is principally exposed are risks relating to assets invested in, or the currency of, a different country or territory to that in which are invested the assets directly invested in by the *firm*, then the *firm* should consider whether it would be more reasonable to treat the assets as invested in that other country or

Part II FSA Handbook Materials

territory. For example, if a *firm* has invested in the *securities* of a *collective investment scheme* which are dealt in on a *regulated market* in country A, but the scheme principally invests in real estate situated in country B, the *firm* should consider whether its principal exposure is in fact to the country in which the underlying assets are situated (that is, country B). Another example might be where a *firm* has invested in a bond or other fixed interest *security* that is denominated in the currency of a country or territory other than that in which the *security* would be treated as invested under (1) or (2) above. The *firm* may wish to consider whether that bond or fixed interest *security* should be treated as invested in the country or territory of the currency of denomination.

3.1.14 **[G]** [intentionally blank]

3.1.15 **[G]** Where the *resilience capital requirement* is affected by the presence of *derivative* or quasi-derivative instruments, the *firm* will need to consider whether the protection afforded is of suitable length or security. The *firm* should include the exposure to *counterparties* in the credit considerations of INSPRU 3.1.41R both before and after calculating the resilience capital requirement. If the *derivative* protection is very short term the *firm* should consider whether issues arise under INSPRU 1.2.26R (Avoidance of future valuation strain); when a *derivative* expires the financial position of the *firm* may deteriorate as a result of, for example, falls in asset values. Unless the *firm* holds a further reserve, the *firm* is likely to need to have either undertaken a fresh protection strategy or carried through the alternative to the *derivative* protection (such as selling equities in place of a put *option*) if the existing protection expires before the financial year end. If the existing *derivative* protection continues beyond the time of financial year end the *firm* must have sufficient confidence that it can renew its *derivative* protection or an alternative to achieve the same effect.

Market risk scenario for assets invested in the United Kingdom

3.1.16 **[R]** In INSPRU 3.1.10R(3)(a), the *market risk* scenario for assets invested in the *United Kingdom* and for assets (including assets invested outside the *United Kingdom*) held to cover *index-linked liabilities* or *property-linked liabilities* which a *firm* must assume is:

(1) a fall in the *market value* of equities of at least 10% or, if greater, the lower of:
  (a) a percentage fall in the *market value* of equities which would produce an earnings yield on the FTSE Actuaries All Share Index equal to 4/3 rds of the long-term gilt yield; and
  (b) a fall in the *market value* of equities of 25% less the *equity market adjustment ratio* (see INSPRU 3.1.19R);

(2) a fall in real estate values of 20% less the *real estate market adjustment ratio* for an appropriate real estate index (see INSPRU 3.1.21R);

(3)
  (a) the more onerous of either a fall or rise in yields on all fixed interest securities by the percentage point amount determined in (b);
  (b) for the purpose of (a), the percentage point amount is equal to 20% of the long-term gilt yield.

3.1.17 **[R]** For the purposes of INSPRU 3.1.16R(1) and INSPRU 3.1.16R(2), a *firm* must:

(1) assume that earnings for equities and rack rents for real estate fall by 10%, but dividends for equities remain unaltered (see INSPRU 3.1.36R to INSPRU 3.1.38R); and

(2) model a fall in equity and real estate markets as if the fall occurred instantaneously.

3.1.18 **[G]** An example of INSPRU 3.1.16R(3) is that, where the long-term gilt yield is currently 6%, a *firm* would assume an increase of 20% in that yield, that is, a change of 1.2 percentage points. For the purpose of the scenario in INSPRU 3.1.16R(3)(a), the *firm* would assume a fall or rise of 1.2 percentage points in yields on all fixed interest securities.

Equity market adjustment ratio

3.1.19 **[R]** The equity market adjustment ratio referred to in INSPRU 3.1.16R(1)(b) is:

(1) if the ratio calculated in (a) and (b) lies between 75% and 100%, the result of 100% less the ratio (expressed as a percentage) of:
  (a) the current value of the FTSE Actuaries All Share Index; to
  (b) the average value of the FTSE Actuaries All Share Index over the preceding 90 calendar days;

(2) 0%, if the ratio calculated in (1)(a) and (b) is more than 100%; and

(3) 25%, if the ratio calculated in (1)(a) and (b) is less than 75%.

3.1.20 **[R]** In INSPRU 3.1.19R, the average value of the FTSE Actuaries All Share Index over any period of 90 calendar days means the arithmetic mean based on levels at the close of business on each of the days in that period on which the London Stock Exchange was open for trading.

Real estate market adjustment ratio

3.1.21 **[R]** The real estate market adjustment ratio for a real estate index referred to in INSPRU 3.1.16R(2) and INSPRU 3.1.23R(2) is:

(1) if the ratio calculated in (a) and (b) lies between 90% and 100%, the result of 100% less the ratio (expressed as a percentage) of:
  (a) the current value of the real estate index; to
  (b) the average value of that real estate index over the three preceding *financial years*;
(2) 0%, if the ratio calculated in (1)(a) and (b) is more than 100%; and
(3) 10%, if the ratio calculated in (1)(a) and (b) is less than 90%.

3.1.22 **[G]** For the purpose of calculating the *real estate market adjustment ratio* in INSPRU 3.1.21R, a *firm* should select an appropriate index of real estate values such that:
(1) the constituents of the index are reasonably representative of the nature and territory of the real estate included in the range of assets identified in accordance with INSPRU 3.1.10R; and
(2) the frequency of, and historical data relating to, published values of the index are sufficient to enable an average value(s) of the index to be calculated over the three preceding *financial years*.

Market risk scenario for assets invested outside the United Kingdom

3.1.23 **[R]** In INSPRU 3.1.10R(3)(b), subject to INSPRU 3.1.26R, the *market risk* scenario for assets invested outside the *United Kingdom* (other than assets held to cover *index-linked liabilities* or *property-linked liabilities*) which a *firm* must assume is, for each significant territory in which assets are invested outside the *United Kingdom*:
(1) an appropriate fall in the *market value* of equities invested in that territory, which is at least equal to the percentage fall determined in INSPRU 3.1.16R;
(2) a fall in real estate values in that territory of 20% less the real estate market adjustment ratio for an appropriate real estate index for that territory (see INSPRU 3.1.21R); and
(3)
  (a) the more onerous of either a fall or a rise in yields on all fixed interest securities by the percentage point amount determined in (b);
  (b) for the purpose of (a), the percentage point amount is equal to 20% of the nearest equivalent (in respect of the method of calculation) to the long term gilt yield.

3.1.24 **[R]** For the purposes of INSPRU 3.1.23R(1), an appropriate fall in the *market value* of equities invested in a significant territory must be determined having regard to:
(1) an appropriate equity market index for that territory; and
(2) the historical volatility of the equity market index selected in (1).

3.1.25 **[G]** For the purpose of INSPRU 3.1.24R(1), an appropriate equity market index for a territory is such that:
(1) the constituents of the index are reasonably representative of the nature of the equities held in that territory which are included in the range of assets identified in accordance with INSPRU 3.1.10R; and
(2) the frequency of, and historical data relating to, published values of the index are sufficient to enable an average value(s) and historical volatility of the index to be calculated over at least the three preceding *financial years*.

3.1.26 **[R]** Where the assets of a *firm* invested in a significant territory of a kind referred to in INSPRU 3.1.23R(1), INSPRU 3.1.23R(2) or INSPRU 3.1.23R(3)(a) represent less than 0.5% of the *firm's long-term insurance assets* (excluding assets held to cover *index-linked liabilities* or *property-linked liabilities*), measured by *market value*, the *firm* may assume for those assets the *market risk* scenario for assets of that kind invested in the *United Kingdom* set out in INSPRU 3.1.16R instead of the *market risk* scenario set out in INSPRU 3.1.23R.

Interest rates: general insurance liabilities

3.1.27 **[G]** The rates of interest to be used for the calculation of the present values of *general insurance liabilities* are specified in the *insurance accounts rules*, except where benefits resulting from a *claim* must be paid in the form of an annuity, in which case the rules require calculation by recognised actuarial methods. In the case of *claims* not payable in the form of an annuity, the *insurance accounts rules* state that the rate of interest to be used must not exceed the lowest of:
(1) a rate prudently estimated by the *firm* to be earned by assets of the *firm* that are appropriate in magnitude and nature to cover the provisions for *claims* being discounted, during the period necessary for the payment of such *claims*;
(2) a rate justified by the performance of such assets over the preceding five years; and
(3) a rate justified by the performance of such assets during the year preceding the balance sheet date.

Interest rates: long-term insurance liabilities

3.1.28 **[R]**

(1) The rates of interest required by INSPRU 1.2.33R to be used by a *firm* for the calculation of the present value of a *long-term insurance liability* must not exceed 97.5% of the risk-adjusted yield (see INSPRU 3.1.30R to INSPRU 3.1.48G) that is expected to be achieved on:
   (a) the assets allocated to cover that liability;
   (b) the reinvestment of sums expected to be received from those assets (see INSPRU 3.1.45R to INSPRU 3.1.48G); and
   (c) the investment of future *premium* receipts (see INSPRU 3.1.45R to INSPRU 3.1.48G).

(2) (1) does not apply to a *long-term insurance contract* in respect of which the *firm* has calculated a negative value for the *mathematical reserves* in accordance with INSPRU 1.2.24R.

3.1.29 **[R]** For the purposes of INSPRU 3.1.28R, the rates of interest assumed must allow appropriately for the rates of tax that apply to the investment return on policyholder assets. The rates of tax assumed must be such that the *firm's* total implied liability for tax arising from the allocation of assets to liabilities is not less than the *firm's* actual expected liability for tax for the period in respect of which tax is to be assessed.

3.1.29A **[G]** INSPRU 3.1.28R only applies to a *long-term insurance contract* in respect of which a *firm* has calculated *mathematical reserves* with a positive value. A *firm* may, however, also have *long-term insurance contracts* where the value of future cash inflows under and in respect of the contract exceeds that of outflows, allowing the *firm* to calculate a negative value for the *mathematical reserves* for that contract (see INSPRU 1.2.24R). In calculating the present value of future net cash flows under and in respect of the contract, the *firm* must include margins for adverse variation in accordance with INSPRU 1.2.13R. These margins should include margins for *market risk* and, where relevant, credit risk. For those margins to be sufficiently prudent as required by INSPRU 1.2.13R, the rate of interest used may need to be higher than that which would apply under INSPRU 3.1.28R.

Risk-adjusted yield

3.1.30 **[R]** A risk-adjusted yield on an asset must be calculated by:

(1) taking the asset together with any covering *derivatives*, forward transactions and quasi-derivatives;
(2) assuming that the factors which affect the yield will remain unchanged after the valuation date (see INSPRU 3.1.33R);
(3) valuing the asset (together with any offsetting transaction) in accordance with GENPRU 1.3 (Valuation);
(4) making reasonable assumptions as to whether, and if so when, any options or other rights embedded in the asset (or in any offsetting transaction) will be exercised.

3.1.31 **[G]** Examples of calculating a combined yield for the purposes of INSPRU 3.1.30R(1):

(1) 1000 £1 *shares* (fully paid) of ABC plc covered by a sold *future* on the *shares*. Calculating the combined yield effectively results in a position that behaves like cash (with dividend income but no capital gain or loss on the value of the assets); and
(2) where a covering *derivative* contains an *option* exercisable by the *firm* (e.g. a bought put *option* or receiver swaption), the calculation of the risk adjusted yield should take into account the fact that on the valuation assumptions any time value will reduce over time (known as the 'wasting' nature of the time value of the *option*), for example, an at-the money *option* will expire worthless and hence the covering *derivative* will effectively be a negative yielding asset. There are various ways of allowing for this, for example a *firm* could treat the covering *derivative* and the asset as a single asset and calculate an internal rate of return on this combined asset. Alternatively, an explicit reserve could be set up equal and opposite to the time value of the covering *derivative* which would be written off in the same way as the time value on the covering *derivative*.

3.1.32 **[G]** The requirements in relation to offsetting transactions are set out in INSPRU 3.2. The options and other rights referred to in INSPRU 3.1.30R(4) include those exercisable by the *firm* as well as those exercisable by other parties.

3.1.33 **[R]** For the purpose of INSPRU 3.1.30R(2), the factors that affect yield should be ascertained as at the valuation date (that is, the date to which present values of cash flows are being calculated). All changes known to have occurred by that date must be taken into account including:

(1) changes in the rental income from real estate;
(2) changes in dividends or audited profit on equities;
(3) known or forecast changes in dividends which have been publicly announced by the issuer by the valuation date;

(4) known or forecast changes in earnings which have been publicly announced by the issuer by the valuation date;
(5) alterations in capital structure; and
(6) the value (at the most recent date at or before the valuation date for which it is known) of any determinant of the amount of any future interest or capital payment.

3.1.34 **[R]** The risk-adjusted yield is either:
(1) (for equities and real estate) a running yield (see INSPRU 3.1.36R to INSPRU 3.1.38R, INSPRU 3.1.41R and INSPRU 3.1.44R); or
(2) (for all other assets) the internal rate of return (see INSPRU 3.1.39R, INSPRU 3.1.41R and INSPRU 3.1.44R).

3.1.35 **[R]** The risk-adjusted yield on a basket of assets is the arithmetic mean of the risk-adjusted yield on each asset weighted by that asset's *market value*.

The running yield for real estate

3.1.36 **[R]** For real estate the running yield is the ratio of:
(1) the rental income arising from the real estate over the previous 12 months; to
(2) the *market value* of the real estate.

The running yield for equities

3.1.37 **[R]** For equities the running yield is:
(1) the dividend yield, if the dividend yield is more than the earnings yield;
(2) otherwise, the sum of the dividend yield and the earnings yield, divided by two.

3.1.38 **[R]** For the purposes of INSPRU 3.1.37R:
(1) the dividend yield is the ratio (expressed as a percentage) of dividend income over the previous 12 months from the equities for which the running yield is being calculated ("the relevant equities") to the *market value* of those equities;
(2) the earnings yield is the ratio (expressed as a percentage) of the audited profit (including exceptional items and extraordinary items) for the preceding *financial year* of the issuer of the relevant equities to the *market value* of those equities;
(3) the earnings yield must be calculated in accordance with whichever is most appropriate (to the issuer of the relevant equities) of *United Kingdom*, US or international generally accepted accounting practice.

The internal rate of return

3.1.39 **[R]** The internal rate of return on an asset is the annual rate of interest which, if used to calculate the present value of future income (before deduction of tax) and of repayments of capital (before deduction of tax) would result in the sum of those amounts being equal to the *market value* of the asset.

3.1.40 **[G]** The risk adjusted yield for a *collective investment scheme* may be determined as the weighted average of the yields on each of the investments held by the *collective investment scheme*.

Credit risk

3.1.41 **[R]** In both the running yield and internal rate of return the yield must be reduced to exclude that part of the yield that represents compensation for credit risk arising from the asset.

3.1.42 **[G]** An allowance for credit risk should be made for all securities except risk-free securities.

3.1.43 **[G]** Provision for credit risk for credit-rated securities may be made by reference to historic default rates of securities with a similar credit rating. However, allowance should be made both for any recent or expected changes in market conditions that may invalidate historic default rates and for the likelihood that the credit ratings on securities may deteriorate or (following such deterioration) that the issuer may default.

3.1.44 **[R]** Provision for credit risk for securities that are not credit-rated must be made on principles at least as prudent as those adopted for credit-rated securities.

Investment and reinvestment

3.1.45 **[R]** Except as provided in INSPRU 3.1.46R:
(1) the risk-adjusted yield assumed for the investment or reinvestment of sterling sums (other than sums expected to be received within the next three years) must not exceed the lowest of:
    (a) the higher of:
        (i) the long-term gilt yield; and
        (ii) the greater of:

Part II FSA Handbook Materials

(A) the forward gilts yield; and
(B) the forward rate on sterling interest rate *swaps*, reduced to exclude that part of the rate that represents compensation for credit risk;

where the forward yields and forward rates corresponding to the time when the sums are expected to be received are weighted so as to reflect the investment and reinvestment characteristics of the liabilities covered;

(b) 3% per annum, increased by two thirds of the excess, if any, of the percentage in (a) over 3% per annum; and
(c) 6.5% per annum; and

(2) the risk-adjusted yield assumed for the investment or reinvestment of those sterling sums expected to be received within the next three years must not exceed the risk-adjusted yield on the assets actually held adjusted linearly over the three-year period to the risk-adjusted yield determined under (1).

3.1.46 **[R]** For the *with-profits insurance contracts* of a *realistic basis life firm*, the risk- adjusted yield assumed for the investment or reinvestment of sums denominated in sterling must be no more than the greater of:
(1) the forward gilts yield; and
(2) the forward rate on sterling interest rate *swaps*, reduced to exclude that part of the rate that represents compensation for credit risk;

where the forward yields and forward rates corresponding to the times when the sums are expected to be received are weighted so as to reflect the investment and reinvestment characteristics of the liabilities covered.

3.1.47 **[R]** The risk-adjusted yield assumed for the investment or reinvestment of sums denominated in a currency other than sterling must be at least as prudent as in INSPRU 3.1.45R and INSPRU 3.1.46R taking into account the yields on government securities denominated in that currency.

3.1.47A **[R]** For the purpose of INSPRU 3.1.47R the yields on the government securities must be reduced to exclude that part of the yield that represents compensation for credit risk unless the following conditions are satisfied in relation to the issuer of those securities:
(1) a credit rating is available from at least one of the rating agencies listed in INSPRU 1.3.93R; and
(2) the credit rating description in the first column of Table INSPRU 1.3.90R corresponding to the lowest such credit rating is either "exceptional or extremely strong" or "very strong".

3.1.48 **[G]** The purpose of INSPRU 3.1.45R to INSPRU 3.1.47R is to help protect against 'reinvestment risk'. Reinvestment risk is the risk that, when the sums are actually received, interest rates (and so yields available on assets) might have fallen below current expectations.

Currency risk

3.1.49 **[G]** Fluctuations in foreign exchange rates may impact adversely upon a *firm*, including where it holds an open position in a foreign currency. This is where future cash outflows (that is liabilities) in one currency are matched by future cash inflows (that is assets) in a different currency. The circumstances in which this could arise include where the *firm*:
(1) has entered into contracts for the purchase or sale of foreign currency; or
(2) has entered into *contracts of insurance* under which *claims* are payable in, or determined by reference to a value or price expressed in, a foreign currency; or
(3) holds assets denominated in a foreign currency.

Cover for spot and forward currency transactions

3.1.50 **[R]** A *firm* must cover a contract providing for the purchase or sale of foreign currency by:
(1) holding the currency that must be paid by the *firm* under the contract; or
(2) being subject to an offsetting transaction.

3.1.51 **[G]** The requirements in relation to cover and offsetting transactions are set out in INSPRU 3.2.

Currency matching of assets and liabilities

3.1.52 **[G]** INSPRU 1.1.34R requires a *firm* to cover its liabilities with assets that enable it to match, in timing, amount and currency, the cash inflows and outflows from those assets and liabilities. This permits some currency mismatching of assets and liabilities, but only if sufficient excess assets are held to cover the exposure arising from such mismatching. The level of permitted currency mismatching is also limited by INSPRU 3.1.53R.

3.1.53 **[R]**
(1) Subject to INSPRU 3.1.54R, a *firm* must hold *admissible assets* in each currency of an amount equal to at least 80% of the amount of its liabilities in that currency arising under or in connection with *contracts of insurance* (but excluding, for a *firm* that carries on *general insurance business*, any *non-credit equalisation provision*), except where the amount of those assets does not exceed 7% of the assets in other currencies.

(2) In (1) references to an asset in a currency are to an asset which is expressed in or capable of being realised (without exchange risk) in that currency, and an asset is capable of being so realised if it is reasonably capable of being realised in that currency without risk that changes in exchange rates would reduce the cover for liabilities in that currency.

3.1.53A **[G]** For the purpose of INSPRU 3.1.53R, a *firm* may allocate the total *credit equalisation provisions* to different currencies in proportion to the split by currency of the *technical provisions* for credit *insurance business* established in accordance with GENPRU 1.3.4R. Alternatively, another allocation which the *firm* is able to justify as broadly appropriate may be used.

3.1.54 **[R]** INSPRU 3.1.53R does not apply to:

(1) a *pure reinsurer*; or

(2) assets held to cover *index-linked liabilities* or *property-linked liabilities*.

3.1.55 **[R]** For the purpose of INSPRU 3.1.53R, the currency of the liability under a *contract of insurance* is the currency in which the cover under the *contract of insurance* is expressed or, if the contract does not specify a currency:

(1) the currency of the country or territory in which the risk is situated; or

(2) if the *firm* on reasonable grounds so decides, the currency in which the *premium* payable under the contract is expressed; or

(3) if, taking into account the nature of the risks insured, the *firm* considers it more appropriate:

  (a) the currency (based on past experience) in which it expects the *claims* to be paid; or

  (b) if there is no past experience, the currency of the country or territory in which the *firm* or relevant branch is established:

    (i) for contracts covering risks falling within general insurance business classes 4, 5, 6, 7, 11, 12 and 13 (producer's liability only); and

    (ii) for contracts covering risks falling within any other general insurance business class where, in accordance with the nature of the risks, the *firm's* liabilities are liabilities to be provided in a currency other than that which would result from the application of (1) or (2); or

(4) (where a *claim* has been notified to the *firm* and the *firm's* liability in respect of that *claim* is payable in a currency other than that which would result from the application of (1), (2) or (3)) the currency in which the *claim* is to be paid; or

(5) (where a *claim* is assessed in a currency known to the *firm* in advance and is a currency other than that which would result from the application of (1), (2), (3) or (4)) the currency in which the *claim* is to be assessed.

3.1.56 **[G]** The reasonable grounds in INSPRU 3.1.55R(2) include if, from the time the contract is entered into, it appears likely that a *claim* will be paid in the currency of the *premium* and not in the currency of the country in which the risk is situated.

Covering linked liabilities

3.1.57 **[R]** A *firm* must cover its *property-linked liabilities* with:

(1) (as closely as possible) the assets to which those liabilities are linked; or

(2) a property-linked *reinsurance* contract; or

(3) a combination of (1) and (2).

3.1.58 **[R]** A *firm* must cover its *index-linked liabilities* with:

(1) either:

  (a) the assets which represent that index; or

  (b) assets of appropriate security and marketability which correspond, as closely as possible, to the assets which are comprised in, or which form, the index or other reference of value to which those liabilities are linked; or

(2) a portfolio of assets whose value or yield is reasonably expected to correspond closely with the *index-linked liability*; or

(3) an index-linked *reinsurance* contract; or

(4) an index-linked *approved derivative*; or

(5) an index-linked *approved quasi-derivative*; or

(6) a combination of any of (1) to (5).

3.1.58A **[R]** INSPRU 3.1.57R and INSPRU 3.1.58R do not apply to a *pure reinsurer*.

3.1.59 **[G]** For the purposes of INSPRU 3.1.57R and INSPRU 3.1.58R, a *firm* is not permitted to hold different assets and to cover the mismatch by holding excess assets.

3.1.60 **[G]** If a *firm* has incurred a *policy* liability which cannot be exactly matched by appropriate assets (for example the Limited Price Index (LPI)), the *firm* should seek to match assets that at least cover the liabilities. For example, an LPI limited to 5% per annum may be matched by an RPI bond or a fixed interest investment matching cash flows increasing at 5% per annum compound. Orders made by the Department for Work and Pensions under section 148 of the Social Security Administration Act 1992, and which are limited to 5% per annum, may also be matched by a fixed interest investment matching cash flows increasing at 5% per annum compound (see also INSPRU 3.1.61-AG).

3.1.61 **[G]** In selecting the appropriate cover, the *firm* should ensure that both credit risk, and the risk that the value or yield in the assets will not, in all circumstances, match fluctuations in the relevant index, are within acceptable limits. *Rules* and *guidance* relating to credit risk are set out in INSPRU 2.1.

3.1.61-A **[G]** Where liabilities are linked to orders made under section 148 of the Social Security Administration Act 1992, *firms* are required by COBS 21.3.5R to notify their supervisors before effecting any such business and to explain how the risks associated with this business will be safely managed. This requirement does not apply in respect of liabilities for which a limited revaluation premium has been paid to the Department for Work and Pensions so that the liability for revaluation, while still linked to section 148 orders, is limited to 5%. The risks may be mitigated by holding assets to cover an alternative index which is reasonably expected to at least cover the section 148 order (e.g. RPI plus a margin) over the duration of the link. The *firm's* exposure to an order under section 148 exceeding this index should be appropriately limited by putting a cap on the liabilities linked to the order so that risks are within acceptable limits.

Pure reinsurers

3.1.61A **[R]** A *pure reinsurer* must invest its assets in accordance with the following requirements:
(1) the assets must take account of the type of business carried out by the *firm*, in particular the nature, amount and duration of expected *claims* payments, in such a way as to secure the sufficiency, liquidity, security, quality, profitability and matching of its investments;
(2) the *firm* must ensure that the assets are diversified and adequately spread and allow the *firm* to respond adequately to changing economic circumstances, in particular developments in the financial markets and real estate markets or major catastrophic events; the *firm* must assess the impact of irregular market circumstances on its assets and must diversify the assets in such a way as to reduce such impact;
(3) investment in assets which are not admitted to trading on a *regulated market* must be kept to prudent levels;
(4) investment in *derivatives* and *quasi-derivatives* must contribute to a reduction of investment risks or facilitate efficient portfolio management and such investments must be valued on a prudent basis, taking into account the underlying assets, and included in the valuation of the *firm's* assets. The *firm* must avoid excessive risk exposure to a single *counterparty* and to other *derivative* or *quasi- derivative* operations;
(5) the assets must be properly diversified in such a way as to avoid:
  (a) excessive reliance on any one particular asset, *issuer* or *group* of *undertakings*; and
  (b) accumulations of risk in the portfolio as a whole.
  Investments in assets issued by the same *issuer* or by *issuers* belonging to the same *group* must not expose the *firm* to excessive risk concentration; and
(6) (5) does not apply to investment in government bonds.

Application of INSPRU 3.1 to Lloyd's

3.1.62 **[R]** INSPRU 3.1 applies to *managing agents* and to the *Society* in accordance with:
(1) for *managing agents* INSPRU 8.1.4R, subject to INSPRU 3.1.65R below; and
(2) for the *Society*, INSPRU 8.1.2R.

Resilience capital requirement (applicable to long-term business only)

3.1.63 **[R]** *Managing agents* must calculate the amount of the *resilience capital requirement* for the *long-term insurance business* carried on through the *syndicates* they manage.

3.1.64 **[R]** The *Society* must determine the *resilience capital requirement* for the *insurance business* of each *member* under INSPRU 3.1.10R as the *member's* proportionate share of the *resilience capital requirement* calculated by the *managing agent* for the *long-term insurance business* carried on through the syndicate.

Currency risk: matching of assets and liabilities

3.1.65 **[R]** For the purposes of INSPRU 3.1.53R, a *managing agent* must ensure that:
(1) *syndicate* liabilities are covered by matching *syndicate assets* as required by INSPRU 3.1.53R; or that
(2) it immediately notifies to the *Society* the nature and extent of any *syndicate* liabilities not covered by matching assets under (1).

3.1.66 **[R]** On receipt of a notification by a *managing agent* under INSPRU 3.1.65(2), the *Society* must ensure that the liabilities in respect of the *insurance business* of the members in aggregate are covered with matching assets complying with INSPRU 3.1.53R.

3.2 Derivatives in insurance

Application

3.2.1 **[R]** This section applies to an *insurer*, unless it is:
(1) a *non-directive friendly society*; or
(2) an *incoming EEA firm*; or
(3) an *incoming Treaty firm*; or
(4) a *pure reinsurer*.

3.2.2 **[G]** The scope of application of INSPRU 3.2 is not restricted to *firms* that are subject to the relevant *EU* directives.

3.2.3 **[R]**
(1) This section applies to a *firm* in relation to the whole of its business, except where a particular provision provides for a narrower scope.
(2) Where a *firm* carries on both *long-term insurance business* and *general insurance business*, this section applies separately to each type of business.

Purpose

3.2.4 **[G]** GENPRU 2.2.17R requires a *firm* to calculate its *capital resources* for the purpose of GENPRU in accordance with the *capital resources table*, subject to the limits in GENPRU 2.2.32R to GENPRU 2.2.41R. The *capital resources table* and GENPRU 2.2.251R require a *firm* to deduct from total *capital resources* the value of any asset included in an insurance fund which is not an *admissible asset* as listed in GENPRU 2 Annex 7R. GENPRU 2 Annex 7R provides that a *derivative*, *quasi-derivative* or *stock lending transaction* will only be an *admissible asset* if it is approved. This section sets out the criteria for determining when a *derivative*, *quasi-derivative* or *stock lending transaction* is approved for this purpose. INSPRU 3.2.5R to INSPRU 3.2.35R set out the criteria for *derivatives* and *quasi-derivatives*. INSPRU 3.2.36R to INSPRU 3.2.41R set out the criteria for *stock lending transactions*.

Derivatives and quasi-derivatives

3.2.5 **[R]** For the purpose of GENPRU 2 Annex 7R (Admissible assets in insurance), and also in relation to *permitted links*, a *derivative* or *quasi-derivative* is approved if:
(1) it is held for the purpose of efficient portfolio management (INSPRU 3.2.6R to INSPRU 3.2.7R) or reduction of investment risk (INSPRU 3.2.8R to INSPRU 3.2.13G);
(2) it is covered (INSPRU 3.2.14R to INSPRU 3.2.33G); and
(3) it is effected or issued:
  (a) on or under the rules of a *regulated market*; or
  (b) off-market with an *approved counterparty* and, except for a forward transaction, on approved terms and is capable of valuation (INSPRU 3.2.34R to INSPRU 3.2.35R).

3.2.5A **[G]**
(1) GENPRU 2 Annex 7R(3) requires *firms* to consider first whether an asset is a *derivative* or *quasi-derivative* transaction notwithstanding that it is also capable of falling within one or more other categories in GENPRU 2 Annex 7R(1). If it is a *derivative* or *quasi-derivative* transaction it is only admissible if it satisfies the conditions for it to be approved under INSPRU 3.2.5R. *Firms* should be able to justify whether or not their assets are *derivatives* or *quasi-derivatives*.
(2) A *quasi-derivative* is defined as a contract or asset that has the effect of a *derivative* contract. *Quasi-derivatives* may be regarded as those contracts or assets which are not *derivatives* but which effectively contain an embedded *derivative* component which significantly impacts the contract's or asset's cash flow and risk profile so as to mirror the economic effect of a *derivative*. A *derivative* is defined in the *Glossary* as a *contract for differences*, a *future* or an *option* and includes a *securitised derivative*, which is an *option* or *contract for differences* that is *listed*. A *securitised derivative* may also be a *debenture*.
(3) A deposit with interest or other return calculated by reference to an index or other factor is excluded from the definition of *contract for differences* by article 85(2) of the *Regulated Activities Order*. However, if the return on the deposit is in the nature of that on a *derivative* (for example, an *option* or a *future*) then the deposit is a *quasi-derivative*.
(4) A holding in a fund investing in *derivatives* may or may not be a *quasi-derivative* depending on its ongoing investment policy and governance and any investment decisions from time to time which might deviate significantly from the investment policy. It should be treated as a *quasi-derivative* if its risk profile is such that the value of *units* in the fund is expected to mirror the value of a *derivative*.
(5) The assets in the following list, which is illustrative and not exhaustive, all have features which could lead to their being assumed to be *quasi-derivatives*:
  (a) a bond whose redemption proceeds are directly linked to the performance of the FTSE 100 index but with a guaranteed minimum;

(b) an investment fund that is managed to give high leverage that mirrors a call option;
(c) an investment whose value it is reasonably foreseeable could become negative; and
(d) a credit-linked note, that is, a security with an embedded credit default swap.

Efficient portfolio management

3.2.6 **[R]** A *derivative* or *quasi-derivative* is held for the purpose of efficient portfolio management if the *firm* reasonably believes the *derivative* or *quasi-derivative* (either alone or together with any other covered transactions) enables the *firm* to achieve its investment objectives by one of the following (or, in relation to *permitted links*, in a manner which includes but is not limited to):
(1) generating additional capital or income in one of the ways described in INSPRU 3.2.7R; or
(2) reducing tax or investment cost in relation to *admissible assets* or *permitted links*; or
(3) acquiring or disposing of rights in relation to *admissible assets* or *permitted links*, or their equivalent, more efficiently or effectively.

Generation of additional capital or income

3.2.7 **[R]** The generation of additional capital or income falls within INSPRU 3.2.6R(1) where it arises from:
(1) taking advantage of pricing imperfections in relation to the acquisition and disposal (or disposal and acquisition) of rights in relation to assets the same as, or equivalent to, *admissible assets* or *permitted links*; or
(2) receiving a premium for selling a covered call *option* or its equivalent, the underlying of which is an *admissible asset* or *permitted link*, even if that additional capital or income is obtained at the expense of surrendering the chance of greater capital or income.

Reduction of investment risk

3.2.8 **[R]** A *derivative* or *quasi-derivative* is held for the purpose of reducing investment risk if the *derivative* or *quasi-derivative* (either alone or together with other fully covered transactions) reduces any aspect of investment risk without significantly increasing any other aspect of that risk.

Significant increase in risk

3.2.9 **[R]** For the purposes of INSPRU 3.2.8R, an increase in risk from a *derivative* or *quasi-derivative* is significant unless:
(1) relative to any reduction in investment risk it is both small and reasonable; or
(2) the risk is remote.

3.2.10 **[G]** INSPRU 3.2.8R does not require that a *derivative* or *quasi-derivative* has no possible adverse consequences. Often a *derivative* or *quasi-derivative* is effected to protect against a severe adverse consequence that only arises in one circumstance. In all other circumstances it may itself lead to adverse consequences, even if only because it expires worthless resulting in the loss of the purchase price. Conversely a *derivative* or *quasi-derivative* may reduce risk in a wide range of circumstances but lead to adverse consequences when a particular circumstance arises, e.g. the default of the *counterparty*. Only rarely does a *derivative* or *quasi-derivative* give rise to no adverse consequences in any circumstances. The test is merely that the increase in risk should not be significant, that is it should be both small and reasonable, or the risk should be remote.

3.2.11 **[G]** *Firms* are reminded that INSPRU 2.1 (Credit risk in insurance) sets out the different types of loss mitigation techniques.

Investment risk

3.2.12 **[R]** For the purposes of INSPRU 3.2.8R, investment risk is the risk that the assets held by a *firm*:
(1) (where they are *admissible assets* held by the *firm* to cover its *technical provisions*) might not be:
  (a) of a value at least equal to the amount of those *technical provisions* as required by INSPRU 1.1.20R; or
  (b) of appropriate safety, yield and marketability as required by INSPRU 1.1.34R(1)(a); or
  (c) of an appropriate currency match as required by INSPRU 3.1.53R;
(2) (where they are held to cover *index-linked liabilities*) might not be appropriate cover for those liabilities as required by INSPRU 3.1.58R; and
(3) (where they are held to cover *property-linked liabilities*) might not be appropriately selected in accordance with contractual and constructive liabilities as required by INSPRU 1.5.36R and appropriate cover for those liabilities as required by INSPRU 3.1.57R.

3.2.13 **[G]** In assessing whether investment risk is reduced, the impact of a transaction on both the assets and liabilities should be considered. In particular, where the amount of liabilities depends

upon the fluctuations in an index or other factor, investment risk is reduced where assets whose value fluctuates in the same way match those liabilities. In appropriate circumstances this may include:
(1) a *derivative* or *quasi-derivative* that is linked to the same index as the liabilities from the index-linked contracts; and
(2) a *derivative* or *quasi-derivative* whose value depends upon the factors which give rise to general insurance claims, e.g. a weather *quasi-derivative*.

Cover

3.2.14 **[R]** A *firm* must cover an obligation to transfer assets or pay monetary amounts that arises from:
(1) a *derivative* or *quasi-derivative*; or
(2) a contract (other than a *contract of insurance*) for the purchase, sale or exchange of assets.

3.2.15 **[R]** An obligation to transfer assets or pay monetary amounts (see INSPRU 3.2.14R) must be covered:
(1) by assets, a liability or a provision (see INSPRU 3.2.16R to INSPRU 3.2.24R); or
(2) by an offsetting transaction (see INSPRU 3.2.25R to INSPRU 3.2.27R).

3.2.16 **[R]** An obligation to transfer assets (other than *money*) or to pay monetary amounts based on the value of, or income from, assets is covered if the *firm* holds:
(1) those assets; or
(2) in the case of an index or basket of assets, a reasonable approximation to those assets.

3.2.17 **[R]** An obligation to pay a monetary amount (whether or not falling in INSPRU 3.2.16R) is covered if:
(1) the *firm* holds *admissible assets* or *permitted links* that are sufficient in value so that the *firm* reasonably believes that following reasonably foreseeable adverse variations (relying solely on cashflows from, or from realising, those assets) it could pay the monetary amount in the right currency when it falls due; or
(2) the obligation to pay the monetary amount is offset by a liability. An obligation is offset by a liability where an increase in the amount of that obligation would be offset by a decrease in the amount of that liability; or
(3) a provision at least equal to the value of the assets in (1) is implicitly or explicitly set up. A provision is implicitly set up to the extent that the obligation to pay the monetary amount is recognised under GENPRU 1.3 (Valuation) either by offset against an asset or as a separate liability. A provision is explicitly set up if it is in addition to an implicit provision.

3.2.18 **[R]** A *firm* must implicitly or explicitly set up a provision equal to the value of the assets or offsetting transactions held to cover a non-approved *derivative* or *quasi-derivative* transaction.

3.2.19 **[G]** A *firm* is required to cover a *derivative* under INSPRU 3.2.14R whether it satisfies the other conditions for approval under INSPRU 3.2.5R or not. Under INSPRU 3.2.17R a *firm* may cover an obligation to pay a monetary amount by setting up a provision. If the *derivative* is not covered at any time by other means then a provision needs to be set up to complete the cover taking into account obligations to pay monetary amounts that would arise if, for example, an obligation to transfer assets could not be met in full. By doing so, a *derivative* becomes covered. If it satisfies the other conditions under INSPRU 3.2.5R it is an *approved derivative* and may be taken into account for solvency purposes to the extent permitted by the large exposure limits and market risk and counterparty limits.

3.2.20 **[G]** Exposure to a transaction includes exposure that arises from a right at the *firm's* (or its *subsidiary undertaking's*) option to dispose of assets.

3.2.21 **[G]** Cover serves three purposes. First, it protects against exposure to loss from the transaction which is being covered. The value of the cover increases (or if the cover is a liability the amount of that liability decreases) to match any increase in obligations under the transaction.

3.2.22 **[G]** The second purpose of cover is that it prevents excessive gearing in the investment portfolio by the use of *options* and their equivalent. A *firm* is required to cover all obligations under an admissible transaction including obligations that would arise only at the option of the *firm*, e.g. the liability to pay the exercise price under a bought *option*.

3.2.23 **[G]** The third purpose of cover is that it protects against the risk that the *firm* may not be able to deliver assets (including *money* in any currency) of the right type when the obligation falls due under the transaction. An obligation to deliver assets is covered only if the *firm* holds those assets or has entered into an offsetting transaction that would deliver those assets when needed. An obligation to pay *money* is offset only if the *firm* holds cash in the right currency, its equivalent or assets that could reliably be converted into cash in the right currency.

3.2.24 **[R]** Cover used for one transaction must not be used for cover in respect of another transaction or any other agreement to acquire, or dispose of, assets or to pay or repay *money*.

Offsetting transactions

3.2.25 **[R]** An offsetting transaction means:

(1) an *approved derivative*, *approved stock lending transaction* or an *approved quasi-derivative*; or
(2) a covered transaction with an *approved counterparty* for the purchase of assets.

3.2.26 **[R]** A transaction offsets an obligation to transfer assets away from the *firm* only if it provides for the transfer to the *firm* of those assets, or their value, at the time, or before, the obligation falls due.

3.2.27 **[R]** A transaction offsets an obligation to pay a monetary amount only if it provides for that monetary amount to be paid to the *firm* at or before the earliest date on which the obligation might fall due.

Lending and borrowing assets

3.2.28 **[R]** Assets that have been lent by the *firm* are not available for cover, unless:
(1) they are non-monetary assets that have been lent under a transaction that fulfils the conditions in INSPRU 3.2.36R; and
(2) the *firm* reasonably believes the assets to be obtainable (by return or reacquisition) in time to meet the obligation for which cover is required.

3.2.29 **[R]** Assets that have been borrowed by the *firm* are not available for cover except as allowed by INSPRU 3.2.30R.

3.2.30 **[R]** Borrowed *money* may be used as cover only where:
(1) the *money* has been advanced or an *approved credit institution* has committed itself to advance the *money*; and
(2) the borrowing is or would be covered.

3.2.31 **[G]** INSPRU 3.2.30R in effect allows borrowings to be used to bridge the gap between an obligation under a transaction that might fall due at one date and cash or its equivalent that would only become due at a later date. Borrowings may not be used to gear the investment portfolio.

Examples of cover requirements

3.2.32 **[G]** Examples of cover by assets for the purposes of INSPRU 3.2.16R:
(1) a bought put *option* (or a sold call *option*) on 1000 £1 *shares* (fully paid) of ABC plc is covered by an existing holding in the fund of 1000 £1 *shares* (fully paid) of ABC plc;
(2) a bought call *option* (or sold put *option*) on 1000 ordinary £1 *shares* (fully paid) of ABC plc is covered by cash (or its equivalent) which is sufficient in amount to meet the purchase price of the *shares* on exercise of the *option*;
(3) a bought or sold *contract for differences* on short-dated sterling is covered by cash (or its equivalent), the value of which together at least match the notional principal of the contract. For example, a LIFFE short sterling contract, or a successive series of such contracts, is covered by £500,000; and
(4) a sold *future* on the FT-SE 100 index is covered by holdings of equities, which satisfy the reasonable approximation test for cover in INSPRU 3.2.16R(2) in relation to that *future*, and the values of which together at least match the current mark to market valuation of the *future*. For example, if the multiplier per full point is £10, and if the eventual obligation under the *future* is currently 2800, the valuation of the *futures* position is 2800 x £10 = £28,000.

3.2.33 **[G]** Examples of cover by offsetting transactions for the purpose of INSPRU 3.2.25R would include a bought *future* which is guaranteed to deliver to the *firm* at the relevant time sufficient assets to cover liabilities under a sold call *option*.

Off-market transactions

3.2.34 **[R]** For the purpose of INSPRU 3.2.5R(3)(b), a *derivative* or *quasi-derivative* is on approved terms only if the *firm* reasonably believes that it could, in all reasonably foreseeable circumstances and under normal market conditions, readily enter into a further transaction with the *counterparty* or a third party to close out the *derivative* or *quasi-derivative* at a price not less than the value attributed to it by the *firm*, taking into account any valuation adjustments or reserves established by the *firm* under GENPRU 1.3.29R to GENPRU 1.3.34R.

3.2.34A **[G]** In considering whether the first transaction could be readily closed out in all reasonably foreseeable circumstances under normal market conditions, the *firm* should satisfy itself that it cannot reasonably foresee any circumstances in which it would need to close out all or part of the contract at a few days' notice, and would not be able to do so.

3.2.35 **[R]** For the purpose of INSPRU 3.2.5R(3)(b), a *derivative* or *quasi-derivative* is capable of valuation only if the *firm*:
(1) is able to value it with reasonable accuracy on a reliable basis in compliance with GENPRU 1.3.41R; and
(2) reasonably believes that it will be able to do so throughout the life of the transaction.

3.2.35A **[G]** The purpose of INSPRU 3.2.34R and INSPRU 3.2.35R is to ensure the appropriate application of GENPRU 1.3 to *derivatives* and *quasi-derivatives* effected or issued off-market with an *approved counterparty*.

Stock lending

3.2.36 **[R]**
(1) For the purposes of GENPRU 2 Annex 7R (Admissible assets in insurance), a *stock lending* transaction (including a *repo* transaction) is approved if:
(a) the assets lent are *admissible assets*;
(b) the *counterparty* is an *authorised person*, an *approved counterparty*, a *person* registered as a broker-dealer with the Securities and Exchange Commission of the United States of America or a bank, or a branch of a bank, supervised, and authorised to deal in investments as principal, with respect to *OTC derivatives* by at least one of the following federal banking supervisory authorities of the United States of America:
(i) the Office of the Comptroller of the Currency;
(ii) the Federal Deposit Insurance Corporation;
(iii) the Board of Governors of the Federal Reserve System; and
(iv) the Office of Thrift Supervision; and
(c) adequate and sufficiently immediate *collateral* (INSPRU 3.2.38R to INSPRU 3.2.41R) is obtained to secure the obligation of the *counterparty*.
(2) INSPRU 3.2.36R(1)(c) does not apply to a *stock lending* transaction made through Euroclear Bank SA/NV's Securities Lending and Borrowing Programme.

3.2.36A **[R]**
(1) For the purposes of the *rules* on *permitted links*, a *stock lending* transaction (including a *repo* transaction) is approved if:
(a) the assets lent are *permitted links*;
(b) the *counterparty* is an *authorised person*, an *approved counterparty*, a *person* registered as a broker-dealer with the Securities and Exchange Commission of the United States of America or a bank, or a branch of a bank, supervised, and authorised to deal in investments as principal, with respect to *OTC derivatives* by at least one of the following federal banking supervisory authorities in the United States of America:
(i) the Office of the Comptroller of the Currency;
(ii) the Federal Deposit Insurance Corporation;
(iii) the Board of Governors of the Federal Reserve System; and
(iv) the Office of Thrift Supervision; and
(c) adequately and sufficiently immediate *collateral* (INSPRU 3.2.38R to INSPRU 3.2.41R) is obtained to secure the obligation of the *counterparty*; and
(d) provided that, for the purposes of *property-linked assets* only:
(i) where the *linked policyholder* bears the whole of the risk associated with the *stock lending* transaction, they must receive the whole of the recompense (net of fees and expenses);
(ii) the extent of any risk that the *linked policyholder* bears in relation to the *stock lending* transaction must be disclosed to them; and
(iii) where the risk associated with the *stock lending* transaction is borne outside the *linked fund*, the *linked fund* should receive a fair and reasonable recompense for the use of the *linked policyholders'* funds.
(2) INSPRU 3.2.36R(1)(c) does not apply to a *stock lending* transaction made through Euroclear Bank SA/NV's Securities Lending and Borrowing Programme.

3.2.37 **[G]** INSPRU 3.2.36R refers only to *stock lending* transactions where the *firm* is the lender. There are no special *rules* for a transaction under which the *firm* borrows securities.

Collateral

3.2.38 **[R]** For the purposes of INSPRU 3.2.36R(1)(c), *collateral* is adequate only if it:
(1) is transferred to the *firm* or its agent or, in the case of a letter of credit, meets the conditions described in INSPRU 3.2.38AR;
(2) is, at the time of the transfer or, in the case of a letter of credit, at the time of issue, at least equal in value to the value of the securities transferred, or consideration provided, by the *firm*; and
(3) is of adequate quality.

3.2.38A **[R]** The conditions referred to in INSPRU 3.2.38R(1) are that the letter of credit is:
(1) direct, explicit, unconditional and irrevocable; and
(2) issued by an *undertaking* which is:
(a) not a *related undertaking* of the *counterparty*; and

(b) either an *approved credit institution* or a bank, or a branch of a bank, whether chartered by the federal government of the United States of America or a US state, that is supervised and examined by at least one of the following US federal banking supervisory authorities:
  (i) the Office of the Comptroller of the Currency;
  (ii) the Federal Deposit Insurance Corporation;
  (iii) the Board of Governors of the Federal Reserve System; and
  (iv) the Office of Thrift Supervision.

3.2.39 **[G]** For the purposes of assessing adequate quality in INSPRU 3.2.38R(3), reference should be made to the criteria for credit risk loss mitigation set out in INSPRU 2.1.16R. The valuation rules in GENPRU 1.3 apply for the purpose of determining the value of both *collateral* received, and the *securities* transferred, by the *firm*. In addition, where *collateral* takes the form of assets transferred, under the *rules* in GENPRU any such asset that is not an *admissible asset* (see GENPRU 2 Ann 7R) does not have a value.

3.2.40 **[R]** For the purposes of INSPRU 3.2.36R(1)(c), *collateral* is sufficiently immediate only if:
(1) it is transferred or, in the case of a letter of credit, issued before, or at the same time as, the transfer of the *securities* by the *firm*; or
(2) it will be transferred or, in the case of a letter of credit, issued, at latest, by the close of business on the day of the transfer.

3.2.41 **[R]** *Collateral* continues to be adequate only if its value is at all times at least equal to the value of the *securities* transferred by the *firm*. This will be satisfied in respect of *collateral* where the validity of the *collateral* or the *firm's* interest in the *collateral* is about to expire or has expired if sufficient *collateral* will again be transferred or issued at the latest by the close of business on the day of expiry.

3.2.42 **[G]** References in INSPRU 3.2.40R(2) and INSPRU 3.2.41R to the close of business on the day of the transfer or the day of expiry are to close of business on that day in all time regions.

Application of INSPRU 3.2 to Lloyd's

3.2.43 **[R]** INSPRU 3.2 applies to *managing agents* and to the *Society* in accordance with:
(1) for *managing agents*, INSPRU 8.1.4R; and
(2) for the *Society*, INSPRU 8.1.2R.

CHAPTER 4

4.1 Liquidity risk management

Application

[2068]
4.1.1 **[R]** INSPRU 4.1 applies to an *insurer* unless INSPRU 4.1.4R applies.

4.1.2 **[R]** All of INSPRU 4.1, except INSPRU 4.1.16G, applies to:
(1) an *EEA-deposit insurer*; and
(2) a *Swiss general insurer*;

but only in respect of the activities of the *firm* carried on from a *branch* in the *United Kingdom*.

4.1.3 **[R]** If a *firm* carries on:
(1) *long-term insurance business*; and
(2) *general insurance business*;

this section applies separately to each type of business.

4.1.4 **[R]** This section does not apply to:
(1) a *non-directive friendly society*; or
(2) an *incoming EEA firm*; or
(3) an *incoming Treaty firm*.

Purpose

4.1.5 **[G]** The purpose of this section is to amplify parts of INSPRU in their application to *liquidity risk* and, in so doing, to suggest minimum standards for management of that risk. The main relevant part, SYSC 14 (Prudential risk management and associated systems and controls), itself amplifies *Principle* 3 (Management and control) and SYSC (Senior management arrangements, Systems and Controls).

4.1.6 **[G]** Appropriate management of *liquidity risk* will vary with the scale, nature and complexity of the *firm's* activities. Most of the material in this section is, therefore, *guidance*. The section lays out some of the main issues that the *FSA* expects a *firm* to consider in relation to *liquidity risk*. A *firm* should assess the appropriateness of any particular item of *guidance* in the light of the scale, nature and complexity of its activities as well as its obligations as set out in *Principle* 3 to organise and control its affairs responsibly and effectively.

4.1.7 **[G]** For *insurers*, references to *liquidity risk* in this section are intended to cover only those aspects of *liquidity risk* that do not fall under the heading of insurance risk. For such *firms*, the *FSA* sees the coverage of this section, broadly, as the management of risk arising from short-term cash-flows, rather than the risk arising from longer-term matching of assets and liabilities, which is part of insurance risk. *Guidance* on systems and controls for managing insurance risk is set out in SYSC 17 (Insurance risk systems and controls).

4.1.8 **[G]** This section addresses the need to deal both with liquidity management issues under normal market conditions, and with stressed or extreme situations resulting from either general market turbulence or firm-specific difficulties.

Requirements

4.1.9 **[G]** High level requirements for prudential systems and controls including for *liquidity risk* are set out in SYSC 14 (Prudential risk management and associated systems and controls). In particular:

(1) SYSC 14.1.18R requires a *firm*, among other things, to take reasonable steps to ensure the establishment of a business plan and appropriate systems for the management of prudential risk; and

(2) SYSC 14.1.19R(2) requires a *firm*, among other things, to document its policy for managing *liquidity risk*, including its appetite or tolerance for this risk and how it identifies, measures, monitors and controls this risk.

4.1.10 **[G]** This section sets out *guidance* on each of these areas, and notes a number of matters which the *FSA* would expect a *firm* to deal with in its *liquidity risk* policy statement as follows:

(1) its *liquidity risk* strategy (see INSPRU 4.1.12G to INSPRU 4.1.14G), including:
   (a) the role of marketable, or otherwise realisable, assets (see INSPRU 4.1.21G); and
   (b) its strategy for mitigating *liquidity risk* on the liability side (see INSPRU 4.1.26G);

(2) its method for measuring *liquidity risk* (see INSPRU 4.1.44G)

Managing liquidity risk

4.1.11 **[G]** This section amplifies the general requirements in SYSC 14 by describing the key high level arrangements that the *FSA* would normally expect to be in place to ensure that a *firm's liquidity risk* management system is adequate.

Governing body and senior management oversight

4.1.12 **[G]** SYSC 14.1.11G amplifies SYSC 2.1.1R and SYSC 2.1.3R which require the apportionment, and allocation, of significant responsibilities to be such that the business and affairs of the *firm* can be adequately monitored and controlled by the *directors*, relevant senior executives and *governing body* of the *firm*. Effective *liquidity risk* management entails an informed board, capable management and appropriate staffing. The *governing body* and senior management are responsible for understanding the nature and level of *liquidity risk* assumed by the *firm* and the tools used to manage that risk.

4.1.13 **[G]** In relation to *liquidity risk*, the *governing body's* responsibilities should normally include:

(1) approving the *firm's liquidity risk* policy, which includes taking reasonable steps to ensure that it is consistent with the *firm*'s expressed risk tolerance (see INSPRU 4.1.15G to INSPRU 4.1.17G);

(2) establishing a structure for the management of *liquidity risk* including the allocation of appropriate senior managers who have the authority and responsibility to manage *liquidity risk* effectively, including the establishment and maintenance of the *firm's liquidity risk* policy;

(3) monitoring the *firm's* overall *liquidity risk* profile on a regular basis and being made aware of any material changes in the *firm's* current or prospective *liquidity risk* profile; and

(4) taking reasonable steps to ensure that *liquidity risk* is adequately identified, measured, monitored and controlled.

4.1.14 **[G]** A *firm* should have an appropriate senior management structure in place to oversee the daily and long-term management of *liquidity risk* in line with the *governing body*- approved *liquidity risk* policy (see INSPRU 4.1.15G to INSPRU 4.1.17G). The *FSA* would normally expect the senior management to:

(1) oversee the development, establishment and maintenance of procedures and practices that translate the goals, objectives and risk tolerances approved by the *governing body* into operating standards that are consistent with the *governing body's* intent and understood by the relevant members of a *firm*'s personnel;

(2) adhere to the lines of authority and responsibility that the *governing body* has established for managing *liquidity risk*;

Part II FSA Handbook Materials

(3) oversee the establishment and maintenance of management information (see INSPRU 4.1.53G to INSPRU 4.1.55G) and other systems that identify, measure, monitor and control the *firm's liquidity risk*; and
(4) oversee the establishment of effective *internal controls* over the *liquidity risk* management process (see INSPRU 4.1.56G to INSPRU 4.1.68G (Controlling liquidity risk)).

Liquidity risk policy

4.1.15 **[G]** SYSC 3.2.17G gives *guidance*, which amplifies SYSC 3.2.6R, on the need for a *firm* to plan its business appropriately so that it is able to identify, measure, monitor and control risks of regulatory concern. A *firm* should, therefore, have an agreed policy for the day-to-day and longer term management of *liquidity risk* which is appropriate to the nature, scale and complexity of the activities carried on.

4.1.16 **[G]** The *liquidity risk* policy should cover the general approach that the *firm* will take to *liquidity risk* management, including, as appropriate, various quantitative and qualitative targets. This general approach should be communicated to all relevant functions within the organisation and be included in the *firm's liquidity risk* policy statement.

4.1.17 **[G]** The policy for managing *liquidity risk* should cover specific aspects of *liquidity risk* management. So far as appropriate to the nature, scale and complexity of the activities carried on, such aspects might include:
(1) the basis for managing liquidity (for example, regional or central);
(2) the degree of concentrations, potentially affecting *liquidity risk*, that are acceptable to the *firm*;
(3) a policy for managing the liability side of *liquidity risk* (see INSPRU 4.1.26G);
(4) the role of marketable, or otherwise realisable, assets (see INSPRU 4.1.21G);
(5) ways of managing both the *firm's* aggregate foreign currency liquidity needs and its needs in each individual currency;
(6) ways of managing market access;
(7) the use of *derivatives* to minimise *liquidity risk*; and
(8) the management of intra-day liquidity, where this is appropriate, for instance where the *firm* is a member of or participates (directly or indirectly) in a system for the intra-day settlement of payments or transactions in investments.

Identifying liquidity risk

4.1.18 **[G]** In order to manage *liquidity risk* successfully, a *firm* should be aware of the ways in which its activities can affect its *liquidity risk* profile, and how outside influences may affect its liquidity position. A *firm* should consider not only its current *liquidity risk*, but how existing activities may affect its *liquidity risk* profile in the future; it should also consider the implications of new products or business lines. This section identifies the main sources of *liquidity risk* and the key factors that a *firm* might consider when analysing its *liquidity risk* profile.

4.1.19 **[G]** The *overall financial adequacy rule* states that a *firm* must maintain overall financial resources adequate, both as to amount and quality, to ensure that there is no significant risk that its liabilities cannot be met as they fall due. The *firm* should, therefore, ensure that, overall, its financial resources are of appropriate maturity, and in a form which is sufficiently marketable or otherwise realisable, having regard to the expected timing of liabilities and the risk that liabilities may fall due earlier than expected (for which prudent allowance must be made when assessing whether assets are of appropriate maturity or sufficiently realisable).

Asset liquidity

4.1.20 **[G]** A *firm's* asset portfolio can provide liquidity in three major ways:
(a) through the maturity of an asset;
(b) the sale of an asset for cash; or
(c) the use of an asset as *collateral* to back other transactions, such as for secured borrowing (including repos), or for deposits with insureds or cedants to back insurance or *reinsurance* transactions.

4.1.21 **[G]** A *firm* may incur *liquidity risk* where inflows from the realisation of assets (at either maturity or time of sale) are less than anticipated because of the crystallisation of credit risk or *market risk*. Inflows arising from the renewal of secured funding, including repos, are similarly affected, if the haircut (the difference between the value of an asset and the amount lent to the *firm* by the counterparty using that security as *collateral*) required by a *firm's* counterparty is larger than anticipated (see INSPRU 4.1.28G).

4.1.22 **[G]** Asset concentrations often increase these sources of *liquidity risk*. A *firm* should, therefore, identify significant concentrations within its asset portfolio, including in relation to:
(1) individual counterparties or related groups of counterparties;

(2) credit ratings of the assets in its portfolio;
(3) the proportion of an issue held;
(4) instrument types;
(5) geographical regions; and
(6) economic sectors.

Marketable assets

4.1.23 **[G]** Criteria for the marketability of its assets should be decided by the *firm* and may reflect the *firm's* access to, and expertise in, individual markets. In determining the appropriateness of the marketability or realisability of assets, a *firm* may take into account:
(1) the depth and liquidity of the market, including:
  (a) the speed with which assets may be realised;
  (b) the likelihood and extent of forced-sale loss; and
  (c) the potential for using the asset as *collateral* in secured funding and the size of the haircut (see INSPRU 4.1.18G) likely to be required by the counterparty;
(2) the expected date of maturity, redemption, repayment or disposal;
(3) the proportion of an issue held;
(4) the credit ratings of the assets;
(5) the impact of exchange rate risk on the realised value of the asset, where assets are denominated in different currencies from its liabilities; and
(6) where applicable, the impact on certain assets' liquidity of their use as eligible *collateral* either in open-market operations conducted by, or in real- time or other payment systems operated by, a central bank.

4.1.24 **[G]** The role of marketable, or otherwise realisable, assets in a *firm's liquidity risk* policy, in both normal and stressed conditions, should be set out in its *liquidity risk* policy statement.

4.1.25 **[G]** In considering the marketability of an asset, a *firm* should assess how its value and liquidity would be affected in a variety of scenarios (see SYSC 11 (Liquidity risk management systems and controls) at SYSC 11.1.18G, SYSC 11.1.20G, SYSC 11.1.21E and SYSC 11.1.22G.

Adjusting for the behavioural characteristics of assets

4.1.26 **[G]** In order to manage its *liquidity risk* effectively, a *firm* should be able to adjust for the behavioural characteristics of the repayment profiles of assets, that is how their actual behaviour may vary from that suggested by their contractual terms. Such an adjustment may be necessary in order to reduce the risk of wrongly estimating the inflows in relation to, in particular:
(1) standby facilities or other commitments that have already been drawn down;
(2) retail and wholesale overdrafts;
(3) mortgages; and
(4) credit cards.

4.1.27 **[G]** The repayment profiles should be considered under both normal market conditions and stressed conditions resulting from either general market turbulence or *firm*-specific difficulties (see SYSC 11 (Liquidity risk management systems and controls) at SYSC 11.1.18G, SYSC 11.1.20G, SYSC 11.1.21E, SYSC 11.1.22G, SYSC 11.1.23G and SYSC 11.1.24E).

Inflows from off balance sheet items

4.1.28 **[G]** Where a *firm* has in place a committed facility for the provision of a portion of its funding, it should take care to monitor any covenants included in the agreement. It should also make efforts to retain a good relationship with the provider of the facility and, where possible without jeopardising that relationship, regularly test access to the funds. A *firm* should also assess the extent to which committed facilities can be relied upon under stressed conditions (see SYSC 11.1.22G and SYSC 11.1.24E).

Liability liquidity

4.1.29 **[G]** Holding marketable, or otherwise realisable, assets is not the only way for a *firm* to mitigate the *liquidity risk* it faces. There are a number of liability- side strategies that can be used to reduce a *firm's liquidity risk*, such as ensuring a spread of maturities and lengthening the term structure of its liabilities. In order to manage its *liquidity risk* effectively a *firm* should have a liability-side policy that is appropriate to the nature and scale of its activities; this policy should be described in its *liquidity risk* policy statement.

4.1.30 **[G]** When determining the appropriate mix of liabilities, a *firm's* management should consider potential concentrations. A concentration exists when a single decision or factor could cause a significant and sudden claim on liabilities. What constitutes a liability concentration depends on the nature and scale of a *firm's* activities. A *firm* should, however, normally consider:
(1) the term structure of its liabilities;

(2) the credit-sensitivity of its liabilities;
(3) the mix of secured and unsecured funding;
(4) concentrations among its liability providers, or related groups of liability providers;
(5) reliance on particular instruments or products;
(6) the geographical location of liability providers; and
(7) reliance on intra-group funding.

4.1.31 **[G]** A *firm* with credit-sensitive liabilities should be aware that, in times of market turbulence, a proportion of that funding may be withdrawn, particularly funding which is unsecured. Secured funding may also be affected, with counterparties seeking better quality *collateral* or larger haircuts (see INSPRU 4.1.18G) on *collateral*. A *firm* should recognise these characteristics of its credit-sensitive liabilities and take account of them in its stress testing and scenario analysis and *contingency funding plan* (see SYSC 11 (Liquidity risk management systems and controls) at SYSC 11.1.18G, SYSC 11.1.20G, SYSC 11.1.21E, SYSC 11.1.22G, SYSC 11.1.23G and SYSC 11.1.24E).

4.1.32 **[G]** A *firm* should consider the dynamics of its *liquidity risk* including, for example, the normal level of roll-overs, and growth, of liabilities.

Adjusting for the behavioural characteristics of liabilities

4.1.33 **[G]** In order to meet the requirement to maintain sufficient liquid financial resources (see INSPRU 4.1.16G), a *firm* should consider the behavioural characteristics of its liabilities, that is how their actual behaviour may vary from that suggested by their contractual terms.

4.1.34 **[G]** In assessing how to adjust for the behavioural characteristics of its liabilities in the context of *liquidity risk*, an *insurer* may take into account:
(1) the type of *insurance business*;
(2) the past history of volatility in the pattern of *claims* payment;
(3) options available to *policyholders* and the circumstances in which they are likely to be exercised;
(4) options available to the *insurer* and any incentive for the *insurer* to exercise them;
(5) any relevant requirements to deposit *collateral* either with the insured (or cedants) under the terms of the insurance Treaty or by requirements of overseas regulators as a condition for covering risks in a particular territory; and
(6) the other cash flow needs of the business.

Outflows from off balance sheet items

4.1.35 **[G]** The contingent or optional nature of many off balance sheet instruments adds to the complexity of managing off balance sheet cash flows. In particular, in stressed conditions off balance sheet commitments may be a significant drain on liquidity.

4.1.36 **[G]** A *firm* should consider how its wholesale off balance sheet activities affect its cash flows and *liquidity risk* profile under both normal and stressed conditions. In particular, as appropriate, it should consider the amount of funding required by:
(1) commitments given;
(2) standby facilities given;
(3) wholesale overdraft facilities given;
(4) proprietary *derivatives* positions; and
(5) liquidity facilities given for securitisation transactions.

4.1.37 **[G]** Similarly, a *firm* with retail *customers* should be able to assess the likely draw-down on retail products under a variety of circumstances and taking into account seasonal factors. In particular, as appropriate, it should consider the amount of funding required in relation to:
(1) mortgages that have been agreed but not yet drawn down;
(2) overdrafts; and
(3) credit cards.

Asset securitisations

4.1.38 **[G]** If controlled properly, asset securitisation can be a useful tool in enhancing a *firm's* liquidity. However, features of certain securitisations, such as early amortisation triggers, as well as excessive reliance on a single funding vehicle, can increase *liquidity risk*.

4.1.39 **[G]** The implications of securitisations on a *firm's* liquidity position should be considered for both day-to-day liquidity management and its contingency planning for *liquidity risk*. A contemplated securitisation should be analysed for its impact on *liquidity risk*. A *firm* using securitisation should consider:
(1) the volume of securities issued in connection with the securitisation that are scheduled to amortise during any particular period;
(2) the existence of early amortisation triggers (see also SYSC 11.1.22G);
(3) its plans for meeting its funding requirements (including their timing);

(4) strategies for obtaining substantial amounts of liquidity at short notice (see also SYSC 11.1.24E); and
(5) operational issues associated with the rollover of short-dated securities, particularly commercial paper.

4.1.40 **[G]** If a *firm* is a provider of liquidity facilities for securitisation transactions it should be able to assess the probability and scale of draw-down and make provision for it.

4.1.41 **[G]** A *firm* using securitisation should also be aware that its ability to securitise assets may diminish in stressed market conditions and take account of this in its stress testing and *contingency funding plan*. In addition, the time taken to organise a securitisation transaction may mean that it cannot be relied upon to provide liquidity at short notice.

Foreign currency liquidity

4.1.42 **[G]** Foreign currency *liquidity risk* arises where a *firm* faces actual or potential future outflows in a particular currency which it may not be able to meet from likely available inflows in that currency. A *firm's* exposure to foreign currency *liquidity risk* depends on the nature, scale and complexity of its business. Where a *firm* has significant, unhedged liquidity mismatches in particular currencies, it should consider:
(1) the volatilities of the exchange rates of the mismatched currencies;
(2) likely access to the foreign exchange markets in normal and stressed conditions; and
(3) the stickiness of deposits in those currencies with the *firm* in stressed conditions.

4.1.43 **[G]** A possible strategy for mitigating foreign currency *liquidity risk*, which is effective and simple, is for a *firm* to hold assets in a particular currency in an amount equal to, and realisable at maturities no later than, its liabilities in that currency. This strategy may be worth considering particularly where, as a result of the nature, scale and complexity of its business, a *firm's liquidity risk* is relatively small.

Intra-day liquidity

4.1.44 **[G]** SYSC 3.1.1R requires a *firm* to take reasonable care to establish and maintain systems and controls appropriate to its business. This includes appropriate systems and controls over activities that give rise to significant *market*, credit, *liquidity*, insurance, operational or group risk, including over the processes of settling and paying debts and other commitments that arise from those activities.

4.1.45 **[G]** Structural and operational changes in payment systems have increased the importance of intra-day liquidity for many *firms*. Within real time gross settlement systems, for example, a *firm* needs to take appropriate steps to ensure that it has sufficient *collateral* to cover cash positions and has systems capable of monitoring intra-day liquidity positions and cash needs.

4.1.46 **[G]** A *firm* should be aware that in stressed conditions it is likely to require more intra-day liquidity than in normal market conditions, for a variety of reasons including payments due to the *firm* being delayed and wholesale depositors withdrawing from the market. A *firm* should take account of this in its stress testing and scenario analysis.

Measuring liquidity risk

4.1.47 **[G]** A *firm* should establish and maintain a process for the measurement of *liquidity risk*, using a robust and consistent method which should be described in its *liquidity risk* policy statement.

4.1.48 **[G]** A number of techniques can be used for measuring *liquidity risk*, ranging from simple calculations to highly sophisticated modelling; a *firm* should use a measurement method which is appropriate to the nature, scale and complexity of its activities.

4.1.49 **[G]** The method that a *firm* uses for measuring *liquidity risk* should be capable of:
(1) measuring the extent of the *liquidity risk* it is incurring;
(2) dealing with the dynamic aspects of a *firm's* liquidity profile (for example, rollovers of funding and assets or new business);
(3) assessing the behavioural characteristics of its on and off balance sheet instruments; and
(4) where appropriate, measuring the *firm's* exposure to foreign currency *liquidity risk*.

Monitoring liquidity risk

4.1.50 **[G]** A *firm* should establish and maintain an appropriate system for monitoring its *liquidity risk*, which should be described in its *liquidity risk* policy statement.

4.1.51 **[G]** A *firm* should establish and maintain a system of management reporting which provides clear, concise, timely and accurate *liquidity risk* reports to relevant functions within the *firm*. These reports should alert management when the *firm* approaches, or breaches, predefined thresholds or limits, including quantitative limits imposed by the *FSA* or another regulator.

4.1.52 **[G]** Where a *firm* is a member of a *group*, it should be able to assess the potential impact on it of *liquidity risk* arising in other parts of the *group*.

Management information systems

4.1.53 **[G]** A *firm* should have adequate information systems for controlling and reporting *liquidity risk*. The management information system should be used to check for compliance with the *firm*'s established policies, procedures and limits.

4.1.54 **[G]** Reports on *liquidity risk* should be provided on a timely basis to the *firm*'s *governing body*, senior management and other appropriate personnel. The appropriate content and format of reports depends on a *firm*'s liquidity management practices and the nature, scale and complexity of the *firm*'s business. Reports to the firm's governing body may be less detailed and less frequent than reports to senior management with responsibility for managing *liquidity risk*.

4.1.55 **[G]** When considering what else might be included in *liquidity risk* management information, a *firm* should consider other types of information that may be important for understanding its *liquidity risk* profile.

Controlling liquidity risk

4.1.56 **[G]** A *firm* should establish and maintain an appropriate system for controlling its *liquidity risk*, which should be described in its *liquidity risk* policy statement. Such a system should allow the *firm's governing body* and senior management to review compliance with established limits and operating procedures.

4.1.57 **[G]** A *firm* should have in place appropriate approval processes, limits and other mechanisms designed to provide reasonable assurance that the *firm*'s *liquidity risk* management processes are adhered to.

4.1.58 **[G]** When revisions or enhancements to *internal controls* are warranted, a *firm* should implement them in a timely manner.

4.1.59 **[G]** The effectiveness of a *firm*'s *liquidity risk* management system should be regularly reviewed and evaluated by individuals unconnected with day-today *liquidity risk* management in order to check that personnel are following established policies and procedures, and that procedures accomplish the intended objectives.

4.1.60 **[G]** In addition to the regular review and evaluation described in INSPRU 4.1.59G, a *firm*'s internal audit function (see SYSC 3.2.16G or, as the case may be, SYSC 6.2.1R) should periodically review the *liquidity risk* management process in order to identify any weaknesses or problems. Any weaknesses should be addressed by management in a timely and effective manner.

Limit Setting

4.1.61 **[G]** A *firm*'s senior management should decide what limits need to be set, in accordance with the nature, scale and complexity of its activities. The structure of limits should reflect the need for a *firm* to have systems and controls in place to guard against a spectrum of possible risks, from those arising in day-to-day *liquidity risk* management to those arising in stressed conditions.

4.1.62 **[G]** SYSC 14.1.18R states that a *firm* must take reasonable steps to ensure the establishment and maintenance of a business plan and appropriate systems for the management of prudential risk.

4.1.63 **[E]**

(1) If a *firm* has *liquidity risk* that arises because it has substantial exposures in foreign currencies, the risk management systems of the *firm* referred to in SYSC 14.1.18R should include systems and procedures that are designed to ensure that the *firm* does not, except in accordance with those procedures, exceed limits that are designed to limit:
   (a) the aggregate amount of its *liquidity risk* for all exposures in foreign currencies; and
   (b) the amount of its *liquidity risk* for each individual currency in which it has a significant exposure.

(2) Contravention of (1) may be relied upon as tending to establish contravention of SYSC 14.1.18R.

4.1.64 **[G]** A *firm* should periodically review and, where appropriate, adjust its limits when conditions or risk tolerances change.

4.1.65 **[G]** Policy or limit exceptions should receive the prompt attention of the appropriate management and should be resolved according to processes described in approved policies.

Managing market access

4.1.66 **[G]** A *firm* should periodically review its efforts to establish and maintain relationships with liability providers, to maintain adequate diversification of liabilities, and to ensure adequate capacity to sell assets, or use them as *collateral* in secured funding. Where possible the *firm* should aim regularly to test its access to the individual markets in assets that it holds for liquidity purposes.

4.1.67 **[G]** Market access should be assessed under a variety of normal and stressed conditions.

4.1.68 **[G]** In some circumstances, the disclosure of information about a *firm* may be useful in managing the public perception of its organisation and soundness. A *firm* should consider the role of disclosure in managing the *liquidity risk* to which it is exposed.

Application of INSPRU 4.1 to Lloyd's

4.1.69 **[G]** INSPRU 4.1 applies to *managing agents* and to the *Society* in accordance with:
(1) for *managing agents*, INSPRU 8.1.4R; and
(2) for the *Society*, INSPRU 8.1.2R

4.1.70 **[G]** In accordance with INSPRU 8.6.2R, the *rules* and *guidance* in INSPRU 4.1 relating to the establishment and maintenance of a business plan do not apply to the *Society*.

CHAPTER 5

5.1 Operational Risk Management

Application

[2069]
5.1.1 **[G]** INSPRU 5.1 applies to an *insurer* unless it is:
(1) a *non-directive friendly society*; or
(2) an *incoming EEA firm*; or
(3) an *incoming Treaty firm*.

5.1.2 **[G]** INSPRU 5.1 applies to:
(1) an *EEA-deposit insurer*; and
(2) a *Swiss general insurer*;

only in respect of the activities of the *firm* carried on from a *branch* in the *United Kingdom*.

Purpose

5.1.3 **[G]** This section provides *guidance* on how to interpret SYSC 14.1.18R and SYSC 14.1.19R(2) (which relate to the design and documentation of risk management systems) in so far as they relate to the management of operational risk in a *prudential context*. Operational risk has been described by the Basel Committee on Banking Supervision as "the risk of loss, resulting from inadequate or failed internal processes, people and systems, or from external events". Thus this section covers management of risks concerning any of the *firm's* operations, whether caused by internal or external matters. However, it does not cover management of credit, market, liquidity and insurance risk. Examples of operational risk exposures that this section is meant to address include internal and external fraud; failure to comply with employment law or meet workplace safety standards; damage to physical assets; business disruptions and system failures; and transaction processing failures.

5.1.4 **[G]** Operational risk concerns the *FSA* in a *prudential context* because inappropriate management of operational risk can adversely affect the solvency or business continuity of a *firm*, threatening the *regulatory objectives* of market confidence and consumer protection.

5.1.5 **[G]** This section contains *guidance* on how a *firm* should determine, in a *prudential context*, its policy for operational risk management and its processes for the identification, assessment, monitoring and control of operational risk. In addition, *guidance* is provided on record keeping in relation to operational risk.

5.1.6 **[G]** The *guidance* contained within this section is not designed to be exhaustive. When establishing and maintaining its systems and controls for operational risk, a *firm* should have regard to other parts of the *Handbook* as well as the material that is issued by other industry or regulatory bodies. In particular, a *firm* should read this section in conjunction with SYSC 3A (Operational Risk Systems and Controls) which contains high level *guidance* on the management of people, processes and systems, and external events in relation to operational risk. SYSC 13 also outlines some *guidance* on the areas that are covered by operational risk systems and controls (including the *FSA's* interpretation of some frequently used risk management terms in relation to operational risk), business continuity management, outsourcing, and the role of insurance in financing operational risk. In addition, a *firm* should read SYSC 14, which contains the *FSA's* general policy on prudential systems and controls. SYSC 14 contains some *rules* and *guidance* on which this section offers additional *guidance*.

5.1.7 **[G]** *Guidance* on the application of this section to a *firm* that is a member of a *group* is provided in SYSC 12 (Group Risk Systems and Controls).

5.1.8 **[G]** Appropriate management of operational risk will vary with the scale, nature and complexity of a *firm's* activities. Therefore the material in this section is *guidance*. A *firm* should assess the appropriateness of any particular item of *guidance* in the light of the scale, nature and complexity of its activities as well as its obligations as set out in *Principle* 3 to organise and control its affairs responsibly and effectively.

Operational risk policy

5.1.9 **[G]** Much of the management of operational risk is about identifying, assessing, monitoring and controlling failures or inadequacies in a *firm's* systems and controls. As such, a *firm* may often find that there is no clear boundary between its risk management systems for operational risk and all its other systems and controls. When drafting its operational risk policy, a *firm* should try to distinguish between its systems and controls for credit, market, liquidity and insurance risk, and its systems and controls for operational risk. Where such a distinction is not possible a *firm* should still try to identify those systems and controls that are used in the management of operational risk, even when they have other purposes as well.

5.1.10 **[G]** A *firm* should document its policy for managing operational risk. This policy should outline a *firm's* strategy and objectives for operational risk management and the processes that it intends to adopt to achieve these objectives. In complying with SYSC 14.1.19R(2), the documented operational risk policy of a *firm* should include:

(1) an analysis of the *firm's* operational risk profile (see the *FSA's* interpretation of this term in SYSC 13.5.1G(3)), including where relevant some consideration of the effects that operational risk may have on the firm, including consideration of those operational risks within a *firm* that may have an adverse impact upon the quality of service afforded to its *clients*;

(2) the operational risks that the *firm* is prepared to accept and those that it is not prepared to accept, including where relevant some consideration of its appetite or tolerance (see INSPRU 5.1.12G) for specific operational risks;

(3) how the *firm* intends to identify, assess, monitor, and control its operational risks, including an overview of the people, processes and systems that are used; and

(4) where assessments of the *firm's* risk exposures are used for internal capital allocation purposes, a description of how operational risk is incorporated into this methodology.

5.1.11 **[G]** A *firm* may also wish to set threshold levels in its operational risk policy for particular types of operational risk (based on its risk appetite or tolerance for risk), which when exceeded trigger a response (such as the allocation of more resources to control the risk or a reappraisal of business plans).

5.1.12 **[G]** Given its association with a willingness to take risk, a *firm* may wish to replace the term appetite for tolerance when drafting its operational risk policy. Tolerance describes the types and degree of operational risk that a *firm* is prepared to incur (based on factors such as the adequacy of its resources and the nature of its operating environment). Tolerance may be described in terms of the maximum budgeted (that is, expected) costs of an operational risk that a *firm* is prepared to bear, or by reference to risk indicators such as the cost or number of system failures, available spare capacity and the number of failed trades.

5.1.13 **[G]** The term risk assessment can be used to represent both the qualitative and quantitative evaluation or measurement of operational exposures.

Risk identification

5.1.14 **[G]** In order to understand its operational risk profile, a *firm* should identify the types of operational risk that it is exposed to as far as reasonably possible. This might include, but is not limited to, consideration of:

(1) the nature of a *firm's customers*, products and activities, including sources of business, distribution mechanisms, and the complexity and volumes of transactions;

(2) the design, implementation, and operation of the processes and systems used in the end-to-end operating cycle for a *firm's* products and activities;

(3) the risk culture and human resource management practices at a *firm*; and

(4) the business operating environment, including political, legal, sociodemographic, technological, and economic factors as well as the competitive environment and market structure.

5.1.15 **[G]** A *firm* should recognise that it may face significant operational exposures from a product or activity that may not be material to its business strategy.

A firm should consider the appropriate level of detail at which risk identification is to take place, and may wish to manage the operational risks that it faces in risk categories that are appropriate to its organisational and legal structures.

5.1.16 **[G]** The *FSA's* interpretation of the term operational exposure is provided in SYSC 13.5.1G(2).

Risk assessment

5.1.17 **[G]** The *FSA* recognises that risk management systems for operational risk are still developing, and that it may be neither feasible nor appropriate to measure certain types of operational risk in a quantitative way. A *firm* may wish to take a qualitative approach to the assessment of its operational risks using, for example, relative estimates (such as high, medium, low) to understand its exposure to them.

5.1.18 **[G]** In order to understand the effects of its operational exposures a *firm* should continually assess its operational risks. This might include, but is not limited to, consideration of:

(1) actual operational losses that have occurred within a *firm*, or events that could have resulted in significant operational losses, but were avoided (for example, the waiving of financial penalties by a third party as a gesture of goodwill or where by chance the *firm* realised profits);

(2) internal assessment of risks inherent in its operations and the effectiveness of controls implemented to reduce these risks (through activities such as self-assessment or stress testing and scenario analysis);

(3) other risk indicators, such as *customer* complaints, processing volumes, *employee* turnover, large numbers of reconciling items, process or system failures, fragmented systems, systems subject to a high degree of manual intervention and transactions processed outside a *firm's* mainstream systems;

(4) reported external (peer) operational losses and exposures; and

(5) changes in its business operating environment.

5.1.19 **[G]** When assessing its operational risks, a *firm* may be able to differentiate between expected and unexpected operational losses. A *firm* should consider whether it is appropriate to adopt a more quantitative approach to the assessment of its expected operational losses, for example by defining tolerance, setting thresholds, and measuring and monitoring operational losses and exposures. In contrast, a *firm* may wish to take a more qualitative approach to assessing its unexpected losses.

5.1.20 **[G]** Although a *firm* may currently be unable to assess certain operational risks with a high degree of accuracy or consistency, it should, according to the nature, scale and complexity of its business, consider the use of more sophisticated qualitative and quantitative techniques as they become available.

Risk monitoring

5.1.21 **[G]** In monitoring its operational risks, a *firm* should:

(1) as appropriate, regularly report to the relevant level of management its operational exposures, loss experience (including if possible cumulative losses), and authorised deviations from the *firm's* operational risk policy;

(2) engage in exception-based escalation to management of:

  (a) unauthorised deviations from the *firm's* operational risk policy;

  (b) likely or actual breaches in predefined thresholds for operational exposures and losses, where set; and

  (c) significant increases in the *firm's* exposure to operational risk or alterations to its operational risk profile.

Risk control

5.1.22 **[G]** A *firm* should control its operational risks, as appropriate, through activities for the avoidance, transfer, prevention or reduction of the likelihood of occurrence or potential impact of an operational exposure. This might include, but is not limited to, consideration of:

(1) adjusting a *firm's* risk culture and creating appropriate incentives to facilitate the implementation of its risk control strategy (see SYSC 13.6 People);

(2) adapting internal processes and systems (see SYSC 13.7 Processes and systems);

(3) transferring or changing the operational exposure through mechanisms such as *outsourcing* (see SYSC 13.9 Outsourcing) and insurance (see SYSC 13.10 Insurance);

(4) the active acceptance of a given operational risk within the *firm's* stated risk appetite or tolerance; and

(5) providing for expected losses, and maintaining adequate financial resources against unexpected losses that may be encountered in the normal course of a *firm's* business activities.

Record keeping

5.1.23 **[G]** The *FSA's* high level *rules* and *guidance* for record keeping are outlined in SYSC 3.2.20R (Records). Additional *rules* and *guidance* in relation to the *prudential context* are set out in SYSC 14.1.51G to SYSC 14.1.64G (Record keeping). In complying with these *rules* and all associated *guidance*, a *firm* should retain an appropriate record of its operational risk management activities. This may, for example, include records of:

(1) the results of risk identification, measurement, and monitoring activities;

(2) actions taken to control identified risks;
(3) where relevant, any exposure thresholds that have been set for identified operational risks;
(4) an assessment of the effectiveness of the risk control tools that are used; and
(5) actual exposures against stated risk appetite or tolerance.

Application of INSPRU 5.1 to Lloyd's

5.1.24 **[G]** INSPRU 5.1 applies to *managing agents* and to the *Society* in accordance with:
(1) for *managing agents*, INSPRU 8.1.4R; and
(2) for the *Society*, INSPRU 8.1.2R

5.1.25 **[G]** In accordance with INSPRU 8.5.2R, the *rules* and *guidance* in INSPRU 5.1 relating to the establishment and maintenance of a business plan do not apply to the *Society*.

CHAPTER 6

6.1 Group Risk: Insurance Groups

Application

[2070]
6.1.1 **[R]** INSPRU 6.1 applies to an *insurer* that is either:
(1) a *participating insurance undertaking*; or
(2) a member of an *insurance group* which is not a *participating insurance undertaking* and which is not:
 (a) a *non-EEA insurer*; or
 (b) a *friendly society*.

6.1.2 **[R]** INSPRU 6.1 does not apply to:
(1) a *non-directive friendly society*; or
(2) a *Swiss general insurer*; or
(3) an *EEA-deposit insurer*; or
(4) an *incoming EEA firm*; or
(5) an *incoming Treaty firm*.

6.1.3 **[G]** INSPRU 6.1 applies to a *firm*:
(1) on a solo basis, as an adjusted solo calculation, where that *firm* is a *participating insurance undertaking*; and
(2) on a group basis where that *firm* is a member of an *insurance group*.

6.1.4 **[G]** For the purposes of INSPRU 6.1, an *insurer* includes a *friendly society* (other than a *non-directive friendly society*) and a *non-EEA insurer*.

Purpose

6.1.5 **[G]** The purpose of this section is to implement the *Insurance Groups Directive* on supplementary supervision of *firms* in an *insurance group*, as amended by the *Financial Groups Directive* and the *Reinsurance Directive*. The *Financial Groups Directive* (by amending the *Insurance Directives* and the *Insurance Groups Directive*) introduces specific requirements for the treatment of *related undertakings* of an *insurance parent undertaking* or a *participating insurance undertaking* that are *credit institutions, investment firms* or *financial institutions*. The *Reinsurance Directive* (by amending the *Insurance Directives* and the *Insurance Groups Directive*) introduces supplementary supervision for *firms* that are *reinsurance undertakings* in an *insurance group*.

6.1.6 **[G]** INSPRU 6.1 sets out the *sectoral rules* for *insurers* for:
(1) *firms* that are *participating insurance undertakings* carrying out an adjusted solo calculation as contemplated by GENPRU 2.1.13R(2);
(2) *insurance groups*; and
(3) *insurance conglomerates*.

6.1.6A **[G]** In accordance with the definition, an *insurance holding company* ceases to be an *insurance holding company* if:
(1) it is a *mixed financial holding company*; and
(2) notice has been given in accordance with Article 4(2) of the *Financial Groups Directive* that the *financial conglomerate* of which it is a *mixed financial holding company* is a *financial conglomerate*;

otherwise it remains an insurance holding company for the purposes of this chapter.

6.1.7 **[G]** For a *firm* that is a *participating insurance undertaking*, the *rules* in INSPRU 6.1 out the minimum capital adequacy requirements for the *firm* itself. A *firm* that satisfies the test in INSPRU 6.1.9R in relation to its *group capital resources* is deemed by GENPRU 2.1.13R(2) to be in compliance with the capital adequacy requirement set out in GENPRU 2.1.13R(1).

Requirement to calculate GCR and GCRR

6.1.8 **[R]** A *firm* must on a regular basis calculate the *group capital resources* (*GCR*) and *group capital resources requirement* (*GCRR*) of each *undertaking* referred to in INSPRU 6.1.17R.

Requirement to maintain group capital

6.1.9 **[R]** Where a *firm* is the *undertaking* referred to in INSPRU 6.1.17R(1)(c) or INSPRU 6.1.17R(2), it must maintain at all times *tier one capital resources* and *tier two capital resources* of such an amount that its *group capital resources* are equal to or exceed its *group capital resources requirement*.

6.1.10 **[R]** A *firm* that is both:
(1) a *composite firm*; and
(2) an *undertaking* referred to in INSPRU 6.1.17R(1)(c) or INSPRU 6.1.17R(2);

must comply with INSPRU 6.1.9R separately in respect of its *long-term insurance business* and its *general insurance business*.

6.1.11 **[R]** For the purposes of INSPRU 6.1.10R, a *firm* must include in the calculation of the *group capital resources* and *group capital resources requirement* of its *long-term insurance business* the *regulated related undertakings* and *ancillary services undertakings* that are *long-term insurance assets*.

6.1.12 **[G]** INSPRU 1.5 sets out the detailed requirements for the separation of *long-term* and *general insurance business*.

6.1.13 **[G]** In order to comply with INSPRU 6.1.10R, a *composite firm* will need to:
(1) establish the *group capital resources requirement* of its *general insurance business* and its *long-term insurance business* separately; and
(2) allocate its *group capital resources* between its *general insurance business* and its *long-term insurance business* so that:
  (a) the *group capital resources* allocated to its *general insurance business* are equal to or in excess of the *group capital resources requirement* of its *general insurance business*; and
  (b) the *group capital resources* allocated to its *long-term insurance business* are equal to or in excess of the *group capital resources requirement* of its *long-term insurance business*.

6.1.14 **[G]** Surplus *group capital resources* in the *long-term insurance business* cannot be used towards meeting the requirements of the *general insurance business* (see INSPRU 6.1.41R) but surplus *group capital resources* in the *general insurance business* may be used towards meeting the amount of the *group capital resources requirement* that relates to the *long-term insurance business*.

6.1.15 **[R]**
(1) Subject to INSPRU 6.1.27R, a *firm* must ensure that at all times its *capital resources* are of such an amount that the *group capital resources* of each *undertaking* referred to in INSPRU 6.1.17R (excluding those referred to in INSPRU 6.1.9R) are equal to or exceed that *undertaking's group capital resources requirement*.
(2) (1) does not apply to a *pure reinsurer* which became a *firm in run-off* before 10 December 2007 and whose *Part IV permission* has not subsequently been varied to add back the *regulated activity* of *effecting contracts of insurance*.

6.1.16 **[G]** *Principle* 4 requires a *firm* to maintain adequate financial resources, taking into account any activity of other members of the *group* of which the *firm* is a member. INSPRU 6.1 sets out provisions that deal specifically with the way the activities of other members of the *group* should be taken into account. This results in the *firm* being required to hold sufficient capital resources so that the *group capital resources* are at least equal to the *group capital resources requirement*. However, the adequacy of the *group capital resources* needs to be assessed both by the *firm* and the *FSA*. *Firms* are required to carry out an assessment of the adequacy of their financial resources under the *overall financial adequacy rule*, the *overall Pillar 2 rule* and GENPRU 1.2.39R, and the *FSA* will review this and may provide individual guidance on the amount and quality of *capital resources* the *FSA* considers adequate. As part of such reviews, the *FSA* may also form a view on the appropriateness of the *group capital resources requirement* and *group capital resources*. Where necessary, the *FSA* may also give individual *guidance* on the *capital resources* a *firm* should hold in order to comply with *Principle* 4 expressed by reference to INSPRU 6.1.9R and INSPRU 6.1.15R.

Scope – undertakings whose group capital is to be calculated and maintained

6.1.17 **[R]** The *undertakings* referred to in INSPRU 6.1.8R, INSPRU 6.1.9R, INSPRU 6.1.10R and INSPRU 6.1.15R are:
(1) for any *firm* that is not within (2), each of the following:
  (a) its *ultimate insurance parent undertaking*;

(b) its *ultimate EEA insurance parent undertaking* (if different); and
(c) the *firm* itself, if it is a *participating insurance undertaking*; and
(2) the *firm* itself, where the *firm* is a *participating insurance undertaking* and is:
(a) a *non-EEA insurer*; or
(b) a *friendly society*.

6.1.18 **[G]** Article 3(3) of the *Insurance Groups Directive* allows an *undertaking* to be excluded from supplementary supervision if:
(1) its head office is in a non-*EEA State* where there are legal impediments to the transfer of the necessary information; or
(2) in the opinion of the *competent authority* responsible for exercising supplementary supervision, having regard to the objectives of supplementary supervision:
(a) its inclusion would be inappropriate or misleading; or
(b) it is of negligible interest.

6.1.19 **[G]** If an application is made for a *waiver*, it is the policy of the *FSA* to consider the effect, in the circumstances described in INSPRU 6.1.18G, of granting a *waiver* allowing the exclusion of a *related undertaking* from the calculation of *group capital resources* and the *group capital resources requirement* required by INSPRU 6.1.8R.

6.1.20 **[G]** Examples of *related undertakings* which may be excluded from supplementary supervision by Article 3(3) of the *Insurance Groups Directive* include *insurance holding companies* in the *insurance group* that are not the *ultimate insurance parent undertaking* or, if different, the *ultimate EEA insurance parent undertaking* of a *firm*.

6.1.21 **[G]** If more than one member of the *insurance group* is to be excluded in the circumstances described in INSPRU 6.1.18G (2)(b), they may only be excluded if, considered together, they are of negligible interest in the context of the *insurance group*.

6.1.22 **[G]** When giving a *waiver* in the circumstances described in INSPRU 6.1.18G, the *FSA* may impose a condition requiring the *firm* to provide information about any member of the *insurance group* excluded pursuant to a *waiver* granted in the circumstances described in INSPRU 6.1.18G.

Optional alternative method of calculation for firms subject to supplementary supervision by another EEA competent authority

6.1.23 **[R]** If the *competent authority* in an *EEA State* other than the *United Kingdom* has agreed to be the *competent authority* responsible for exercising supplementary supervision of an *insurance group* of which a *firm* is a member under Article 4(2) of the *Insurance Groups Directive*, the *firm* may prepare the calculations required under INSPRU 6.1.8R in relation to the *ultimate EEA insurance parent undertaking* in accordance with the requirements of supplementary supervision in that *EEA State*.

6.1.24 **[G]** The *FSA* will notify the *firm* if it has reached agreement with the *competent authority* in an *EEA State* other than the *United Kingdom* in accordance with Article 4(2) of the *Insurance Groups Directive*.

Non-EEA ultimate insurance parent undertakings

6.1.25 **[R]** Where the *ultimate insurance parent undertaking* of a *firm* has its head office in a non-*EEA State*, the *firm* may:
(1) calculate the *group capital resources* and the *group capital resources requirement* of its *ultimate insurance parent undertaking* in accordance with accounting practice applicable for the purposes of the regulation of *insurance undertakings* in the state or territory of the head office of the *ultimate insurance parent undertaking* adapted as necessary to apply the general principles set out in Annex I (1) paragraphs B, C and D of the *Insurance Groups Directive*; and
(2) elect (see INSPRU 6.1.26R) to carry out the calculation referred to in (1) in accordance with the accounting consolidation method set out in Annex I
(3) of the *Insurance Groups Directive*.

6.1.26 **[R]** A *firm* may elect to use the calculation method referred to in INSPRU 6.1.25R(2) if it has made the election by written notice to the *FSA* in a way that complies with the requirements for written notice in SUP 15.7.

6.1.27 **[R]** INSPRU 6.1.15R does not apply in respect of the *group capital resources* of a firm's *ultimate insurance parent undertaking* if that *ultimate insurance parent undertaking* has its head office in a non-*EEA State*.

Proportional holdings

6.1.28 **[R]** Subject to INSPRU 6.1.30R and INSPRU 6.1.31R, when calculating *group capital resources* and the *group capital resources requirement* of an *undertaking* in INSPRU 6.1.17R, a *firm* must take only the relevant proportion of the following items ("calculation items") into account:

(1) the *solo capital resources* of a *regulated related undertaking*;
(2) the assets of a *regulated related undertaking* which are required to be deducted as part of the calculation of *group capital resources*; and
(3) the *individual capital resources requirement* of a *regulated related undertaking*.

6.1.29 **[R]** In INSPRU 6.1.28R, the relevant proportion is either:
(1) the proportion of the total number of issued *shares* in the *regulated related undertaking* held, directly or indirectly, by the *undertaking* in PRU 8.3.17R; or
(2) where a *consolidation Article 12(1) relationship* exists between *related undertakings* within the *insurance group*, such proportion as the *FSA* determines in accordance with Article 28(5) of the *Financial Groups Directive* and Regulation 15 of the *Financial Groups Directive Regulations*.

6.1.30 **[R]** Where the *undertaking* in INSPRU 6.1.17R is a *firm*, if the *individual capital resources requirement* of a *regulated related undertaking* that is a *subsidiary undertaking* and not an *insurer* exceeds the *solo capital resources* of that *undertaking* less the amount calculated in INSPRU 6.1.74R (3) (if any), the full amount of the calculation items of that *regulated related undertaking* less the amount in INSPRU 6.1.74R (3) must be taken into account in the calculation of *group capital resources* and the *group capital resources requirement*.

6.1.31 **[R]** Except where INSPRU 6.1.30R applies, if the *individual capital resources requirement* of a *regulated related undertaking* that is a *subsidiary undertaking* of the undertaking in INSPRU 6.1.17R exceeds its *solo capital resources*, the full amount of the calculation items of that *regulated related undertaking* must be taken into account in the calculation of *group capital resources* and the *group capital resources requirement*.

6.1.32 **[R]** For the purposes of INSPRU 6.1.10R, where a *composite firm* that is an *undertaking* in INSPRU 6.1.17R (1)(c) or (2):
(1) holds directly or indirectly *shares* in a *regulated related undertaking*; and
(2) the *shares* in (1) are held partly by its *long-term insurance business* and partly by its *general insurance business*;
(3) the relevant proportion of the calculation items calculated in accordance with INSPRU 6.1.29R, subject to INSPRU 6.1.30R and INSPRU 6.1.31R, must be allocated between the *long-term* and *general insurance business* in proportion to their respective holdings, directly or indirectly, in the *shares* in that *regulated related undertaking*.

Calculation of the GCRR

6.1.33 **[R]** Subject to INSPRU 6.1.23R and INSPRU 6.1.25R, a *firm* must calculate the *group capital resources requirement* of an *undertaking* in INSPRU 6.1.17R as the sum of the *individual capital resources requirement* of that *undertaking* and the *individual capital resources requirement* of each of its *regulated related undertakings*.

6.1.34 **[R]** For the purposes of INSPRU 6.1, an *individual capital resources requirement* is:
(1) in respect of any *insurer*:
  (a) its *capital resources requirement* calculated in accordance with GENPRU 2.1; less
  (b) where the *capital resources requirements* of both the *insurer* and its *insurance parent undertaking* that is an *insurer* include *with-profits insurance capital components*, any element of double-counting that may arise from the aggregation of the *individual capital resources requirements* for the purposes of INSPRU 6.1.33R;
(2) in respect of an *EEA insurer* or an *EEA pure reinsurer*, the equivalent of the *capital resources requirement* as calculated in accordance with the applicable requirements in its *Home State*;
(3) in respect of an *EEA ISPV*, the solo capital resources requirement that applies to the *ISPV* under the *sectoral rules* for the *insurance sector* of the member State of the *competent authority* that authorised the *ISPV*;
(4) in respect of an *insurance undertaking* that is not within (1), (2) or (3) and whose head office is in a *designated State or territory*, either:
  (a) its *proxy capital resources requirement*; or
  (b) the solo capital resources requirement that applies to it under the *sectoral rules* for the *insurance sector* of the *designated State or territory*;
(5) in respect of an *insurance undertaking* within (4) which is not subject to a solo capital resources requirement under the *sectoral rules* for the *insurance sector* of that *designated State or territory*, its *proxy capital resources requirement*;
(6) in respect of an *insurance undertaking* that is not within (1) to (5), its *proxy capital resources requirement*;
(7) in respect of an *insurance holding company*, zero;
(8) [intentionally blank]
(9) in respect of a *regulated entity* (excluding an *insurance undertaking*), its *solo capital resources requirement*;
(10) in respect of an *asset management company*, the *solo capital resources requirement* that would apply to it if, in connection with its activities, it were treated as being in the *investment services sector*; and

(11) in respect of a *financial institution* that is not a *regulated entity* (including a *financial holding company*), the *solo capital resources requirement* that would apply to it if, in connection with its activities, it were treated as being within the *banking sector*.

(12) [deleted]

6.1.34A **[G]** For the purposes of INSPRU 6.1.34R(4)(b), where the solo capital resources requirement under the *sectoral rules* for the *insurance sector* in a *designated State or territory* is ascertained by reference to the trigger for regulatory intervention, the *FSA* considers that the solo capital resources requirement of the *insurance undertaking* in such a *designated State or territory* will generally correspond to the highest point at which any regulatory or corrective action is triggered or which is at least comparable to the *capital resources requirement* which would apply if the *insurance undertaking* were an *insurer*.

6.1.35 **[G]** INSPRU 6.1.34R sets out the rules for calculating an *insurer's individual capital resources requirement*. Among other things, this allows the use of local rules for related entities in designated states and territories. Paragraphs 6.5 and 6.6 of GENPRU 3 Annex 1R include the equivalent provisions for *related undertakings* in the *banking sector* and *investment services sector*. The provisions of paragraphs 6.4 to 6.6 extend to the calculation of *solo capital resources*, with the references to *sectoral rules* in paragraphs 1.2, 2.3 and 3.2 of GENPRU 3 Annex 1R (that is, the capital resources requirement of a *related undertaking* must be met by capital resources that are eligible under the relevant *sectoral rules*).

Calculation of GCR

6.1.36 **[R]** For the purposes of INSPRU 6.1.8R and subject to INSPRU 6.1.23R and INSPRU 6.1.25R, a *firm* must calculate the group capital resources of an *undertaking* in INSPRU 6.1.17R in accordance with the table in INSPRU 6.1.43R, subject to the limits in INSPRU 6.1.45R.

6.1.37 **[R]** For the purposes of INSPRU 6.1, the following expressions when used in relation to either an *undertaking* in INSPRU 6.1.17R or a *regulated related undertaking* which is not subject to the *capital resources table*, are to be construed as if that *undertaking* were required to calculate its capital resources in accordance with the *capital resources table*, but with such adjustments being made to secure that the *undertaking's* calculation of its *solo capital resources* complies with the relevant *sectoral rules* applicable to it:

(1) *tier one capital resources*;
(2) *tier two capital resources*;
(3) *upper tier two capital resources*;
(4) *lower tier two capital resources*;
(5) *innovative tier one capital resources*; and
(6) *core tier one capital*.

6.1.38 **[R]** For the purposes of INSPRU 6.1.37R, the *sectoral rules* applicable to:

(1) an *insurance holding company* whose main business is to acquire and hold participations in *subsidiary undertakings* which are either exclusively or mainly *reinsurance undertakings* are the *sectoral rules* that would apply to it if, in connection with its activities, it were treated as a *pure reinsurer*;

(2) an *insurance holding company* not within (1) are the *sectoral rules* that would apply to it if, in connection with its activities, it were treated as an *insurer*;

(3) an *asset management company* are the *sectoral rules* that would apply to it if, in connection with its activities, it were treated as an *investment firm*; and

(4) subject to INSPRU 6.1.39R, a *financial institution*, that is not a *regulated entity*, are the *sectoral rules* that would apply to it if, in connection with its activities, it were treated as being within the *banking sector*.

6.1.39 **[R]** Where a *financial institution*, that is not a *regulated entity*, has invested in *tier one capital* or *tier two capital* issued by a *parent undertaking* that is:

(1) an *insurance holding company*; or
(2) an *insurer*;

the *sectoral rules* that apply to that *financial institution* are the *sectoral rules* for the *insurance sector*.

6.1.40 **[R]** For the purposes of INSPRU 6.1.36R, the capital resources of a *financial institution* within INSPRU 6.1.39R that can be included in the calculations in INSPRU 6.1.48R(2), INSPRU 6.1.50R(2), INSPRU 6.1.53R(2), INSPRU 6.1.55R(2) and INSPRU 6.1.57R(2) are:

(1) the issued *tier one capital* or *tier two capital* of that *financial institution* held, directly or indirectly, by its *parent undertaking* referred to in INSPRU 6.1.39R; and

(2) the lower of:
  (a) the *tier one capital* or *tier two capital* issued by the *parent undertaking* referred to in INSPRU 6.1.39R pursuant to the investment by the *financial institution*; and
  (b) the *tier one capital* or *tier two capital* issued by the *financial institution* to raise funds for its investment in the capital resources of the *parent undertaking* referred to in (a).

6.1.41 **[R]**

(1) In calculating *group capital resources*, a *firm* must exclude the restricted assets of a *regulated related undertaking* except insofar as those assets are available to meet the *individual capital resources requirement* of that *regulated related undertaking*.

(2) In (1), "restricted assets" means assets of a *regulated related undertaking* which are subject to a legal restriction or other requirement having the effect that those assets cannot be transferred or otherwise made available to another *regulated related undertaking* for the purposes of meeting its *individual capital resources requirement* without causing a breach of that legal restriction or requirement.

6.1.42 **[G]** For the purposes of INSPRU 6.1.41R, in respect of an *insurance undertaking* that is a member of an *insurance group*, the assets of a *long-term insurance fund* are restricted assets within the meaning of INSPRU 6.1.41R. Any excess of assets over liabilities in the *long-term insurance fund* may only be included in the calculation of the *group capital resources* up to the amount of the *undertaking's individual capital resources requirement* which relates to the *long-term insurance business* in respect of which that *long-term insurance fund* is held.

6.1.42A **[R]** For the purposes of calculating *group capital resources*, a *firm* must exclude the book value of any investment by a *related undertaking* of the *undertaking* in INSPRU 6.1.17R in shares of, or loans to, an *undertaking* that is not a *related undertaking*, where that *undertaking* has invested in the *capital resources* of a *regulated related undertaking* of the *undertaking* in INSPRU 6.1.17R.

6.1.43 **[R]** Table: Group capital resources

	Stage	**Related text**
Total group tier one capital	A	INSPRU 6.1.48R
Total group tier two capital	B	INSPRU 6.1.50R
Group capital resources before deductions	C=(A+B)	
Total deductions of inadmissible assets	D	INSPRU 6.1.59R
Total deductions under the requirement deduction method from group capital resources	E	INSPRU 6.1.62R
Total deductions of ineligible surplus capital*	F	INSPRU 6.1.65R
Deduction of assets in excess of market risk and counterparty exposure limits*	G	INSPRU 6.1.70R
Group capital resources	H=(C- (D+E+F*+ G*))	

* = section (F) of the table (the deductions for ineligible surplus capital) and section (G) of the table (assets in excess of market risk and counterparty exposure limits) only apply and are required to be calculated for the purposes of the adjusted solo calculation of an *undertaking* in INSPRU 6.1.17R that is a *participating insurance undertaking*.

Calculation of GCR – Limits on the use of different forms of capital

6.1.44 **[G]** As the various components of capital differ in the degree of protection that they offer the *insurance group*, restrictions are placed on the extent to which certain types of capital are eligible for inclusion in the *group capital resources* of the *undertaking* in INSPRU 6.1.17R. These restrictions are set out in INSPRU 6.1.45R.

6.1.45 **[R]**

(1) For the purposes of INSPRU 6.1.9R, INSPRU 6.1.10R and INSPRU 6.1.15R, a *firm* must ensure that at all times its *tier one capital resources* and *tier two capital resources* are of such an amount that the *group capital resources* of the *undertaking* in INSPRU 6.1.17R comply with the following limits:
   - (a) $(P-Q) = \frac{1}{2}(R-S)$;
   - (b) $(P-Q + T-W) = \frac{3}{4}(R-S)$;
   - (c) $V = \frac{1}{2} P$;
   - (d) $Q \leqslant 15\%$ of P;
   - (e) $T \leqslant P$; and
   - (f) $W \leqslant \frac{1}{2} P$

(2) For the purposes of INSPRU 6.1.9R and INSPRU 6.1.10R, a *firm* must ensure that at all times its *tier one capital resources* and *tier two capital resources* are of such an amount that its *group capital resources* comply with the following limit, subject to (4) $(P-Q + T) = 1/3\ X + (R-S-U-X)$.

(3) For the purposes of (1) and (2):
   - (a) P is the *total group tier one capital* of the *undertaking* in INSPRU 6.1.17R;
   - (b) Q is the sum of the *innovative tier one capital resources* calculated in accordance with INSPRU 6.1.53R;

(c) R is the *group capital resources requirement* of the *undertaking* in INSPRU 6.1.17R;
(d) S is the sum of all the *with-profits insurance capital components* of an *undertaking* in INSPRU 6.1.17R that is an *insurer* and each of its *regulated related undertakings* that is an *insurer*;
(e) T is the *total group tier two capital* of the *undertaking* in INSPRU 6.1.17R;
(f) U is the sum of all the *resilience capital requirements* of an *undertaking* in INSPRU 6.1.17R that is an *insurer* and each of its *regulated related undertakings* that is an *insurer*;
(g) V is the sum of all the *core tier one capital* calculated in accordance with INSPRU 6.1.55R;
(h) W is the sum of the *lower tier two capital resources* calculated in accordance with INSPRU 6.1.57R; and
(i) X is the *MCR* of the *firm* less its *resilience capital requirement*, if any.

(4) For the purposes of (2):
(a) INSPRU 6.1.45R (1)(a) does not apply;
(b) the *innovative tier one capital* of the *firm* or its *regulated related undertakings* that meets the conditions for it to be *upper tier two capital* may be included as *upper tier two capital* for the purpose of the calculation in INSPRU 6.1.50R; and
(c) the *firm* must exclude from the calculation of (P-Q + T) in (2) the higher of:
(i) any amount by which the *total group tier two capital* exceeds the *group capital resources* of the *firm* less any *innovative tier one capital* excluded by (b); and
(ii) any amount by which the sum of *lower tier two capital resources* calculated in accordance with INSPRU 6.1.57R exceeds one third of the *group capital resources* of the *firm* less any *innovative tier one capital* excluded by (b).

6.1.46 **[G]** The amount of any capital item excluded from *group capital resources* under INSPRU 6.1.45R (1)(d) may form part of *total group tier two capital* calculated in accordance with INSPRU 6.1.50R subject to the limits in INSPRU 6.1.45R (1)(e) and (f).

6.1.47 **[R]** For the purposes of INSPRU 6.1.10R, a *firm* must ensure that the *tier one capital resources* and *tier two capital resources* of each of its *long-term insurance business* and its *general insurance business* are of such an amount that the *group capital resources* of each its *long-term insurance business* and its *general insurance business* comply with the limits in INSPRU 6.1.45R separately for each type of business.

Calculation of GCR – Total group tier one capital

6.1.48 **[R]** For the purposes of INSPRU 6.1.43R, the *total group tier one capital* of an *undertaking* in INSPRU 6.1.17R is the sum of:
(1) the *tier one capital resources* of the *undertaking* in INSPRU 6.1.17R; and
(2) subject to INSPRU 6.1.40R, the *tier one capital resources* of each of the *related undertakings* of that *undertaking* that is a *regulated related undertaking* after the deduction in INSPRU 6.1.49R.

6.1.49 **[R]** The deduction referred to in INSPRU 6.1.48R is the sum of:
(1) the book value of the investment by the *undertaking* in INSPRU 6.1.17R in the *tier one capital resources* of each of its *related undertakings* that is a *regulated related undertaking*; and
(2) the book value of the investments by *related undertakings* of the *undertaking* in INSPRU 6.1.17R in the *tier one capital resources* of the *undertaking* in INSPRU 6.1.17R and each of its *related undertakings* that is a *regulated related undertaking*.

Calculation of GCR – Total group tier two capital

6.1.50 **[R]** For the purposes of INSPRU 6.1.43R, the *total group tier two capital* of an *undertaking* in INSPRU 6.1.17R is the sum of:
(1) the *upper tier two capital resources* and the *lower tier two capital resources* of that *undertaking*; and
(2) subject to INSPRU 6.1.40R, the *upper tier two capital resources* and the *lower tier two capital resources* of each of the *related undertakings* of that *undertaking* that is a *regulated related undertaking* after the deduction in INSPRU 6.1.51R.

6.1.51 **[R]** The deduction referred to in INSPRU 6.1.50R is the sum of:
(1) the book value of the investments by the *undertaking* in INSPRU 6.1.17R in the *upper tier two capital resources* and the *lower tier two capital resources* of each of its *related undertakings* that is a *regulated related undertaking*; and
(2) the book value of the investments by *related undertakings* of the *undertaking* in INSPRU 6.1.17R in the *upper tier two capital resources* and the *lower tier two capital resources* of the *undertaking* in INSPRU 6.1.17R and each of its *related undertakings* that is a *regulated related undertaking*.

6.1.52 **[G]** For the purposes of INSPRU 6.1.50R(2), the limits in GENPRU 2.2.37R apply to the *upper tier two capital resources* and the *lower tier two capital resources* of any *regulated related undertaking* that is an *insurer*. Similar limits may apply to other *regulated related undertakings* under the relevant *sectoral rules*.

Calculation of GCR – Innovative tier one capital resources, lower tier two capital resources and core tier one capital

6.1.53 **[R]** For the purposes of INSPRU 6.1.45R(3)(b), the *innovative tier one capital resources* is the sum of:
(1) the *innovative tier one capital resources* of the *undertaking* in INSPRU 6.1.17R; and
(2) subject to INSPRU 6.1.40R, the *innovative tier one capital resources* of each of the *related undertakings* of that *undertaking* that is a *regulated related undertaking* after the deduction in INSPRU 6.1.54R.

6.1.54 **[R]** The deduction referred to in INSPRU 6.1.53R is the sum of:
(1) the book value of the investments by the *undertaking* in INSPRU 6.1.17R in the *innovative tier one capital resources* of each of its *related undertakings* that is a *regulated related undertaking*; and
(2) the book value of the investments by *related undertakings* of the *undertaking* in INSPRU 6.1.17R in the *innovative tier one capital resources* of the *undertaking* in INSPRU 6.1.17R and each of its *related undertakings* that is a *regulated related undertaking*.

6.1.55 **[R]** For the purposes of INSPRU 6.1.45R(3)(g), the *core tier one capital* is the sum of:
(1) the *core tier one capital* of the *undertaking* of INSPRU 6.1.17R; and
(2) subject to INSPRU 6.1.40R, the *core tier one capital* of each of the *related undertakings* of that *undertaking* that is a *regulated related undertaking* after the deduction in INSPRU 6.1.56R.

6.1.56 **[R]** The deduction referred to in INSPRU 6.1.55R is the sum of:
(1) the book value of the investments by the *undertaking* in INSPRU 6.1.17R in the *core tier one capital* of each of its *related undertakings* that is a *regulated related undertaking*; and
(2) the book value of the investments by *related undertakings* of the *undertaking* in INSPRU 6.1.17R in the *core tier one capital* of the *undertaking* in INSPRU 6.1.17R and each of its *related undertakings* that is a *regulated related undertaking*.

6.1.57 **[R]** For the purposes of INSPRU 6.1.45R(3)(h), the *lower tier two capital resources* is the sum of:
(1) the *lower tier two capital resources* of the *undertaking* in INSPRU 6.1.17R; and
(2) subject to INSPRU 6.1.40R, the *lower tier two capital resources* of each of the *related undertakings* of that *undertaking* that is a *regulated related undertaking* after the deduction in INSPRU 6.1.58R.

6.1.58 **[R]** The deduction referred to in INSPRU 6.1.57R is the sum of:
(1) the book value of the investments by the *undertaking* in INSPRU 6.1.17R in the *lower tier two capital resources* of each of its *related undertakings* that is a *regulated related undertaking*; and
(2) the book value of the investments by *related undertakings* of the *undertaking* in INSPRU 6.1.17R in the *lower tier two capital resources* of the *undertaking* in INSPRU 6.1.17R and each of its *related undertakings* that is a *regulated related undertaking*.

Calculation of GCR – Inadmissible assets

6.1.59 **[R]** For the purpose of INSPRU 6.1.43R, a *firm* must deduct from the group capital resources before deduction (calculated at stage C in the table in INSPRU 6.1.43R) of the *undertaking* in INSPRU 6.1.17R, the value of all assets of the *undertaking* in INSPRU 6.1.17R and each of its *regulated related undertakings* that are not admissible assets as set out in INSPRU 6.1.60R.

6.1.60 **[R]** For the purposes of INSPRU 6.1.59R, an asset is not an admissible asset if:
(1) in respect of a *regulated related undertaking* or *undertaking* in INSPRU 6.1.17R that is an *insurer* (other than a *pure reinsurer*), it is not an *admissible asset* as listed in GENPRU 2 Annex 7R;
(2) in respect of a *regulated related undertaking* or *undertaking* in INSPRU 6.1.17R that is a *pure reinsurer*, the holding of the asset is inconsistent with compliance by that *undertaking* with INSPRU 3.1.61AR; or
(3) in respect of a *regulated related undertaking* or *undertaking* in INSPRU 6.1.17R that is not an *insurer*, it is an asset of the *undertaking* that is not admissible for the purpose of calculating that *undertaking's solo capital resources* in accordance with the *sectoral rules* applicable to it.

6.1.61 **[R]** For the purposes of INSPRU 6.1.60R(3), the *sectoral rules* applicable to:
(1) an *asset management company* are the *sectoral rules* that would apply to it if, in connection with its activities, it were treated as an *investment firm*; and

Part II FSA Handbook Materials

(2) a *financial institution* that is not a *regulated entity* are the *sectoral rules* that would apply to it if, in connection with its activities, it were treated as being within the *banking sector*.

Calculation of GCR – Deductions under requirement deduction method from group capital resources

6.1.62 **[R]** For the purposes of INSPRU 6.1.43R, a *firm* must deduct from the group capital resources before deduction (calculated at stage C in the table in INSPRU 6.1.43R) of an *undertaking* in INSPRU 6.1.17R, the sum of the value of the direct or indirect investments by the *undertaking* in INSPRU 6.1.17R in each of its *related undertakings* which is an *ancillary services undertaking*, calculated in accordance with INSPRU 6.1.63R.

6.1.63 **[R]** The value of an investment in an *undertaking* referred to in INSPRU 6.1.62R is the higher of the book value of the direct or indirect investment by the *undertaking* in INSPRU 6.1.17R and the notional capital resources requirement of that *undertaking*.

6.1.64 **[R]** For the purposes of INSPRU 6.1.63R, the notional capital resources requirement is:
(1) for an *ancillary insurance services undertaking*, zero;
(2) for any other *ancillary services undertaking*, the *capital resources requirement* that would apply to that *undertaking*, if it were a *regulated related undertaking*, in accordance with the *sectoral rules* applicable to a *regulated related undertaking* whose activities are closest in nature and scope to the activities of that *undertaking*.

Calculation of GCR – Deductions of ineligible surplus capital

6.1.65 **[R]** Where the *undertaking* in INSPRU 6.1.17R is a *participating insurance undertaking*, the *firm* must, for the purposes of INSPRU 6.1.43R, deduct from its group capital resources before deduction (calculated at stage C in the table in INSPRU 6.1.43R) the sum of the ineligible surplus capital of each of its *regulated related undertakings* that is an *insurance undertaking*, calculated in accordance with INSPRU 6.1.67R.

6.1.66 **[G]** The purpose of INSPRU 6.1.65R is to ensure that, where the *undertaking* in INSPRU 6.1.17R is a *firm*, *group capital resources* are not overstated by the inclusion of capital that, although surplus to the requirements of the relevant *regulated related undertaking* that is an *insurance undertaking*, cannot practically be transferred to support requirements arising elsewhere in the group. Therefore, ineligible surplus capital in a *regulated related undertaking* that is an *insurance undertaking* is deducted in arriving at *group capital resources*. Surplus capital in such a *regulated related undertaking* is regarded as transferable only to the extent that:
(1) it can be transferred without the *regulated related undertaking* breaching its own limits on the use of different forms of capital;
(2) it does not contain assets that are restricted within the meaning of INSPRU 6.1.41R; and
(3) in the case of a *regulated related undertaking* that has a *long-term insurance business*, it does not contain any assets allocated to the *capital resources* of that *undertaking* for the purposes of the *capital resources* of its *long-term insurance business* meeting the *capital resources requirement* of its *long-term insurance business*.

6.1.67 **[R]**
(1) For the purposes of INSPRU 6.1.65R, the ineligible surplus capital of a *regulated related undertaking* that is an *insurance undertaking* is calculated by deducting B from A where:
  (a) A is the *regulatory surplus value* of that *insurance undertaking* less any restricted assets of the *insurance undertaking* that have been excluded under INSPRU 6.1.41R; and
  (b) B is the transferable capital of that *undertaking*.
(2) If A minus B is negative, the ineligible surplus capital is zero.

6.1.68 **[R]** For the purposes of INSPRU 6.1.67R(1)(b), the transferable capital is calculated by deducting the sum of the following from the *tier one capital resources* of the *regulated related undertaking* that is an *insurance undertaking*:
(1) any restricted assets of that *insurance undertaking* that have been excluded under INSPRU 6.1.41R;
(2) any *tier one capital resources* of that *insurance undertaking* that have been allocated towards meeting the *individual capital resources requirement* of its *long-term insurance business*; and
(3) the higher of:
  (a) 50% of the *individual capital resources requirement* of the *general insurance business* of that *insurance undertaking*; and
  (b) the *individual capital resources requirement* of the *general insurance business* of that *insurance undertaking* less the difference between E and F where:
    (i) E is its *tier two capital resources*; and
    (ii) F is the amount of its *tier two capital resources* that have been allocated towards meeting the *individual capital resources requirement* of its *long-term insurance business*.

Examples of transferable and ineligible surplus capital:

6.1.69 **[G]** Example 1

Share capital	**Audited reserves**	**FFA**	**Tier two**	**Requirement**
30	20	0	40	50

(i) Under INSPRU 6.1.68R, transferable capital = *tier one capital resources* of 50, less the sum of:
 (1) restricted assets excluded under INSPRU 6.1.41R = (none);
 (2) *tier one capital resources* allocated to the *long-term insurance business* = (none); and
 (3) higher of (50% of 50 = 25 and 50-40 = 10) = (25) = (50–25) = 25
(ii) Under INSPRU 6.1.67R, ineligible surplus capital = *regulatory surplus value* (40) less restricted assets excluded under INSPRU 6.1.41R (0) less transferable capital (25) = 15.

Example 2

Share capital	**Audited reserves**	**FFA** (of which 5 is restricted)	**Tier two**	**Requirement** (of which 4 relates to the *long-term insurance business*)
30	20	10	40	50

(i) Under INSPRU 6.1.68R, transferable capital = *tier one capital resources* of 60, less the sum of:
 (1) restricted assets excluded under INSPRU 6.1.41R = (5);
 (2) *tier one capital resources* allocated to the *long-term insurance business* = (5); and
 (3) the higher of (50% of 45 = 22.5; and 45-40 = 5) = (22.5)= 60-32.5 = 27.5
(ii) Under INSPRU 6.1.67R, ineligible surplus capital = *regulatory surplus value* (50)-restricted assets excluded under INSPRU 6.1.41R of (5)-transferable capital (27.5) = 17.5.

Example 3

Share capital	**Audited reserves**	**FFA** (of which 0 is restricted)	**Tier two** (40, of which 5 is excluded at the solo level-see below)	**Requirement** (of which 25 relates to the *long-term insurance business*)
20	10	20	35	50

The requirement relating to the *long-term insurance business* is met by the FFA of 20 and *tier two capital resources* of 5. Of the remaining *tier two capital resources* of 35, 5 is excluded at the solo level because the *tier one capital resources* allocated to the *general insurance business* are 30.
(i) Under INSPRU 6.1.68R, transferable capital = *tier one capital resources* of 50, less the sum of:
 (1) restricted assets excluded under INSPRU 6.1.41R = (none);
 (2) *tier one capital resources* allocated to the *long-term insurance business* = (20); and
 (3) the higher of (50% of 25 = 12.5; and 25-(35–5) = -5) = (12.5)= 50-32.5 = 17.5.
(ii) Under INSPRU 6.1.67R, ineligible surplus capital = *regulatory surplus value* (35)-restricted assets excluded under INSPRU 6.1.41R of (0)-transferable capital (17.5) = 17.5.

Calculation of GCR – Assets in excess of market risk and counterparty exposure limits

6.1.70 **[R]** Subject to INSPRU 6.1.70AR, where the *undertaking* in INSPRU 6.1.17R is a *participating insurance undertaking*, the *firm* must deduct from its group capital resources before deduction (calculated at stage C in the table in INSPRU 6.1.43R) the assets in excess of *market risk* and *counterparty* exposure limits calculated in accordance with INSPRU 6.1.74R.

6.1.70A **[R]** Where the *undertaking* in INSPRU 6.1.17R is a *pure reinsurer* that is a *participating insurance undertaking*, the *firm* must calculate assets in accordance with INSPRU 6.1.74AR and deduct from its group capital resources before deduction (calculated at stage C in the table in INSPRU 6.1.43R) those assets the holding of which is inconsistent with compliance by that *undertaking* with INSPRU 3.1.61AR.

6.1.71 **[G]** For the purposes of INSPRU 6.1.43R, where the *undertaking* in INSPRU 6.1.17R is a *participating insurance undertaking*, the investments referred to in INSPRU 6.1.48R and INSPRU 6.1.50R are not subject to the *market risk* and *counterparty* exposure limits.

6.1.72 **[R]** The *firm* (A) must, subject to INSPRU 6.1.73R, include in the calculation in INSPRU 6.1.74R or, where A is a *pure reinsurer*, INSPRU 6.1.74AR each *related undertaking* (B) that is:
(1) a *regulated related undertaking* that is a *subsidiary undertaking*; or
(2) a *related undertaking* where the *firm* has elected to value the *shares* held in that *undertaking* by the *firm* in accordance with GENPRU 1.3.47R for the purposes of calculating the *tier one capital resources* of the *firm*.

Part II FSA Handbook Materials

6.1.73 **[R]** The *related undertakings* in INSPRU 6.1.72R need only be included in the calculation in INSPRU 6.1.74R or INSPRU 6.1.74AR if:
(1) where B is a *regulated related undertaking*, the *solo capital resources* of that *undertaking* exceed its *individual capital resources requirement*; or
(2) where B is an *undertaking* in INSPRU 6.1.72R (2), its assets that fall within one or more of the categories in GENPRU 2 Annex 7R exceed its accounting liabilities.

6.1.74 **[R]** A's assets in excess of the *market risk* and *counterparty* exposure limits are calculated as follows:
(1) Subject to (2), a *firm* must apply the *market risk* and *counterparty* exposure limits in INSPRU 2.1.22R(3) to:
 (a) where B is an *insurer* (other than a *pure reinsurer*), the *admissible assets* of B;
 (b) where B is a *pure reinsurer*, the assets of that *undertaking* less those assets identified in INSPRU 6.1.60R(2) as not being admissible; and
 (c) where B is a *regulated related undertaking* that is not an *insurer*, the assets of that *undertaking* less those assets identified in INSPRU 6.1.60R(3) as not being admissible assets.
(2) The *market risk* and *counterparty* exposure limits do not need to be applied to an *undertaking* in INSPRU 6.1.72R(2).
(3) Where the assets of B in INSPRU 6.1.74R(1) exceed the limits in INSPRU 2.1.22R(3), the assets of B in excess of the limits must be deducted by the *firm* from B's *solo capital resources* for the purposes of INSPRU 6.1.30R.
(4) After the application of (1) and (2), the surplus assets of B are aggregated with the *admissible assets* of A, where the surplus assets of B are:
 (a) where B is a *firm* (other than a *pure reinsurer*), the *admissible assets* of B that represent the amount by which the *capital resources* of B exceed its *capital resources requirement*, subject to INSPRU 6.1.77R, and limited to the amount of transferable capital calculated in accordance with INSPRU 6.1.68R;
 (b) where B is a *regulated related undertaking* that is not in (a), the assets of the *undertaking* in INSPRU 6.1.74R(1)(b) or (c) that represent the amount by which the *solo capital resources* of B exceed its *individual capital resources requirement* and, where B is an *insurance undertaking* that is not in (a), limited to the amount of transferable capital calculated in accordance with INSPRU 6.1.68R; and
 (c) where B is an *undertaking* in INSPRU 6.1.72R(2), the assets of the *undertaking* which represent those assets that fall within one or more of the categories in GENPRU 2 Annex 7R which exceed its accounting liabilities.
(5) The *market risk* and *counterparty* exposure limits are then applied to the aggregate of A's *admissible assets* and the surplus assets in INSPRU 6.1.74R(4).

6.1.74A **[R]** A must apply INSPRU 3.1.61AR to the aggregate of:
(1) the assets of A, less any assets already identified in INSPRU 6.1.60R(2) as not being admissible; and
(2) the surplus assets of B calculated in accordance with INSPRU 6.1.74R(1) to (4) as if that *rule* applied to B.

6.1.75 **[R]**
(1) Subject to (2), A must then deduct the amount by which the *admissible assets* aggregated in accordance with INSPRU 6.1.74R(5) exceed the *market risk* and *counterparty* exposure limits from A's group capital resources before deduction (calculated at stage C in the table in INSPRU 6.1.43R) in accordance with INSPRU 6.1.70R.
(2) Where A is a *pure reinsurer*, A must then deduct the amount of any assets identified by INSPRU 6.1.74AR as not complying with INSPRU 3.1.61AR in accordance with INSPRU 6.1.70AR.

6.1.76 **[R]** In relation to any of its *regulated related undertakings* that is not an *insurer*, A may modify the calculation in INSPRU 6.1.74R by:
(1) omitting the calculation in INSPRU 6.1.74R (1) and (3); and
(2) aggregating all of the assets of B identified in INSPRU 6.1.74R(1)(c) as admissible assets with the *admissible assets* of A in INSPRU 6.1.74R(4).

6.1.77 **[R]** The *admissible assets* of either A or B that are part of a *long-term insurance fund* of A or B are excluded for the purposes of the calculation in INSPRU 6.1.74R and INSPRU 6.1.74AR except insofar as those assets are available to meet the liabilities and *capital resources requirement* of that *long-term insurance fund*.

6.1.78 **[R]** If B is itself either a *participating insurance undertaking* or an *insurance parent undertaking*, the *admissible assets* of B for the purposes of INSPRU 6.1.74R (1) must be calculated as in INSPRU 6.1.75R but as if B were A.

CHAPTER 7

7.1 Individual Capital Assessment (ICA)

Application

[2071]
7.1.1 **[R]** INSPRU 7.1 applies to an *insurer* unless it is:
(1) a *non-directive friendly society*; or
(2) a *Swiss general insurer*; or
(3) an *EEA-deposit insurer*; or
(4) an *incoming EEA firm*; or
(5) an *incoming Treaty firm*.

7.1.2 **[R]** Subject to INSPRU 7.1.3R, INSPRU 7.1 applies to *managing agents* and to the *Society* in accordance with:
(1) for *managing agents*, INSPRU 8.1.4R; and
(2) for the *Society*, INSPRU 8.1.2R.

7.1.3 **[R]** *Managing agents* must carry out assessments of capital adequacy for each *syndicate* they manage by reference to all *open syndicate years* taken together.

Purpose

7.1.4 **[G]** *Principle* 4 requires a *firm* to maintain adequate financial resources. GENPRU 2 deals specifically with the adequacy of the *capital resources* element of a *firm's* financial resources.

7.1.5 **[G]** The adequacy of a *firm's capital resources* needs to be assessed both by the *firm* and the *FSA*. In GENPRU 2.1, the *FSA* sets minimum *capital resources requirements* for *firms*.

7.1.6 **[G]** The *FSA* also assesses whether the minimum *capital resources requirements* are appropriate by reviewing:
(1) a *firm's* own assessment of its capital needs; and
(2) the processes and systems by which that assessment is made.

7.1.7 **[G]** In assessing whether the minimum *capital resources requirements* are appropriate, the *FSA* is principally concerned with capital resources as calculated in accordance with GENPRU 2.2.17R. However, in carrying out its own assessment of its capital needs, a *firm* may take into account other capital available to it (see GENPRU 1.2.30R and GENPRU 1.2.36R), although it should be able to explain and justify its reliance on these other forms of capital.

7.1.8 **[G]** There are two main aims in this section:
(1) to enable *firms* to understand the issues which the *FSA* would expect to see assessed and the systems and processes which the *FSA* would expect to see in operation for *ICAs* by *firms* to be regarded as thorough, objective and prudent; and
(2) to enable *firms* to understand the *FSA's* approach to assessing whether the minimum *capital resources requirements* of GENPRU 2.1 are appropriate and what action may be taken if the *FSA* concludes that those requirements are not appropriate to a *firm's* circumstances.

General approach

7.1.9 **[G]** The *rules* in GENPRU 1.2 require a *firm* to identify and assess risks to its being able to meet its liabilities as they fall due, to assess how it intends to deal with those risks and to quantify the financial resources it considers necessary to mitigate those risks. To meet these requirements, a *firm* should consider:
(1) the extent to which capital is an appropriate mitigant for the risks identified; and
(2) assess the amount and quality of capital required.

7.1.9A **[G]** This section sets out in greater detail the approach to be taken by a *firm* when carrying out the assessment of capital described in the preceding paragraph. This is the assessment referred to as an *individual capital assessment*. GENPRU 1.2.42R is a general requirement for a *firm* to carry out stress tests and scenario analyses taking into account an appropriate range of adverse circumstances and events relevant to the *firm's* business and risk profile and to estimate the financial resources it would need to continue to meet the *overall financial adequacy rule* in the stress scenarios considered. As part of its obligations under GENPRU 1.2.42R, the *firm* must carry out stress tests and scenario analyses to estimate the financial resources it would need to support its business plans and continue adequately to cover its *CRR* and meet the *overall financial adequacy rule* over a time horizon of 3 to 5 years. This is a separate requirement from that to carry out an *ICA*, and *guidance* on this requirement is provided in GENPRU 1.2.73AG. In particular, *firms* should note that there is no requirement that the level of capital required as identified by the *ICA* should be equal to, or exceed, the *CRR*.

7.1.9B **[G]** The requirements and *guidance* in this section are drafted so as to apply to a *firm* on a solo basis. As noted in GENPRU 1.2.17G, however, in some cases the requirements in GENPRU 1.2

apply on a consolidated basis. In these cases, a *firm* should read and apply this section making appropriate adjustments to reflect the application of the GENPRU 1.2 requirements on a consolidated basis.

7.1.10 **[G]** A *firm* may choose to carry out its *ICA* in another way than through the use of stress tests and scenario analyses. The method should be proportionate to the size and nature of its business.

7.1.11 **[G]** In accordance with GENPRU 1.2.60R, these assessments must be documented so that they can be easily reviewed by the *FSA* as part of the *FSA's* assessment of the adequacy of the *firm's capital resources*.

7.1.12 **[G]** The *FSA* may ask for the results of these assessments to be provided to it together with a description of the processes by which the assessments have been made, the range of results from each stress test or scenario analysis performed and the main assumptions made. The *FSA* may also carry out a more detailed examination of the details of the *firm's* processes and calculations.

7.1.13 **[G]** Based upon this information and other information available to it, the *FSA* will consider whether the *capital resources requirement* applicable to the *firm* is appropriate. Where relevant, the *firm's ECR* will be a key input to the *FSA's* assessment of the adequacy of the *firm's capital resources*. For *firms* carrying on *general insurance business*, the *ECR* is calculated in accordance with INSPRU 1.1.72CR. For *realistic basis life firms*, the *ECR* forms part of the *CRR* and is calculated in accordance with GENPRU 2.1.38R.

7.1.14 **[G]** *Firms* that are required to calculate an *ECR* may wish to note that the *ECR* as calculated is based upon the assumptions that a *firm's* business is well diversified, well managed with assets matching its liabilities and good controls, and stable with no large, unusual, or high risk transactions. *Firms* may find it helpful to assess the extent to which their actual business differs from these assumptions and therefore what adjustments it might be reasonable to make to the *CRR* or *ECR* to arrive at an adequate level of *capital resources*.

Methodology of capital resources assessment

7.1.15 **[R]** Where a *firm* is carrying out an assessment in accordance with GENPRU 1.2 of the adequacy of its overall financial resources to cover the risk in the *overall financial adequacy rule*, that is, the risk of its being unable to meet its liabilities as they fall due, the assessment of the adequacy of the *firm's* capital resources must:
(1) reflect the *firm's* assets, liabilities, intra-group arrangements and future plans;
(2) be consistent with the *firm's* management practice, systems and controls;
(3) consider all material risks that may have an impact on the *firm's* ability to meet its liabilities to *policyholders*; and
(4) use a valuation basis that is consistent throughout the assessment.

Representative of the firm's characteristics

7.1.16 **[G]** The *ICA* should reflect both the *firm's* desire to fulfil its business objectives and its responsibility to meet liabilities to *policyholders*. This means that the *ICA* should demonstrate that the *firm* holds sufficient capital to be able to make planned investments and take on new business (within an appropriate planning horizon). It should also ensure that if the *firm* had to close to new business (if it has not already done so), it would be able to meet its existing commitments. The costs of writing new business, the expenses incurred in servicing all liabilities, including liabilities to non-*policyholders*, and the nature of intra-group arrangements and *reinsurance* arrangements should be considered as part of the assessment as well as the costs that would be incurred in the event of closure to new business.

7.1.17 **[G]** Where a *firm* has not already closed to new business, the *ICA* should be made on the basis that the *firm* closes to new business after an appropriate period. This period should allow for the time it would take for the *firm* to identify the need for closure and to implement the necessary action.

7.1.18 **[G]** Where including new business would increase the capital resources by more than any increase in the capital required, or reduce the capital required by more than any reduction in available capital, new business should be excluded. To the extent that including new business increases the required capital, a *firm* should consider whether it is appropriate to include the additional amount within the *ICA*.

7.1.19 **[G]** Any contract that the *firm* is legally obliged to renew should be considered part of the *firm's* existing liabilities and not treated as new business. Such contractual obligations include multi-year *general insurance contracts* and the exercise of options by long-term *policyholders*.

7.1.20 **[G]** For a *firm* to discharge its financial obligations to *policyholders*, it will incur certain expenses, including payments to the *firm's* own staff, contributions to any pension scheme and fees to outsourcing suppliers or service companies. All of these expenses, and risks associated with these payments, should be considered when carrying out the *ICA*. When considering the appropriate level of expenses in a projection, the *firm* should consider the acceptability of the service provided to *policyholders* and the resources required by the senior management to manage the *firm*.

7.1.21 **[G]** Where a *firm's* liabilities include payments which are subordinated to liabilities to *policyholders*, these payments do not need to be included within the *ICA*. However, the *ICA* should include all payments that must be made to avoid putting *policyholders'* interests at risk, including any payment on which a default might trigger the winding up of the *firm*. For example, if the principal of a loan could be recalled on default of a coupon payment, coupon payments over the lifetime of *policyholder* liabilities should be included in the *ICA*. As a further example, declared dividends should be treated as a liability. However, planned dividends that have not been declared need not be included in the *ICA*.

Intra-group capital considerations

7.1.22 **[G]** It is common for *firms* whose corporate *group* consists of a number of separate legal entities to have intra-group transactions in place. Capital and risk may originate within the *firm* and be passed to another company or may originate in another company and be passed to the *firm*. The *ICA* should consider the underlying effect of intra-group arrangements.

7.1.23 **[G]** Risks may exist within the individual legal entity from these intra-group transactions. Intra-group transactions should not be treated differently from external transactions just because they are intra-group. However, some intra-group transactions may carry less credit risk than the equivalent external transactions if the *firm* has access to more information regarding the financial position of an internal *reinsurer*. In assessing intra-group risks, consideration should be given, but should not be limited, to:

(1) future defaults on intra-group *reinsurance* arrangements: *Firms* should consider, for example, a test akin to the credit risk assessment undertaken on external *reinsurance* assets held or future anticipated recoveries; in other cases it may be more appropriate to perform a more explicit assessment of the *group* counterparty's own capital position, to inform the *firm's* exposure to default;

(2) non-recoverability on intra-group loans: Even though these transactions occur within the same *group*, there is a risk that an entity may default on such intra-group payments; and

(3) non-payment of future internal dividends or transfers: Many entities or funds within a *group* rely on these payments as a means to maintaining their solvency position. There is a risk that the entity paying the dividend or making the transfer may not be able to do so, and *ICAs* performed for separate regulated legal entities or funds within a *group* should consider these risks as appropriate.

7.1.24 **[G]** A *firm's* capital should normally be restricted to resources within the *firm*. Where the *firm* is relying on resources outside the direct control of the *firm*, these should only be included to the extent that the *firm* has a right to call on those resources and the provider has the ability to provide those resources without recourse to the assets of the *firm* itself, in the circumstances considered as part of the *ICA*.

Consistency with a firm's practice, systems and controls

7.1.25 **[G]** The *ICA* should reflect the *firm's* ability to react to events as they occur. When relying on prospective management actions, *firms* should understand the implications of taking such actions, including the financial effect, and taking into consideration any preconditions that might affect the value of management actions as risk mitigants.

7.1.26 **[G]** The *ICA* should assume that a *firm* will continue to manage its business having regard to the *FSA's* Principles for Businesses. In particular, a *firm* should take into account how the *FSA's* Principles for Businesses may constrain its prospective management actions, for example, *Principle* 6 (Treating Customers Fairly).

7.1.27 **[G]** *Firms* should also consider whether their systems and controls provide sufficient information to permit senior management to identify the crystallisation of risks in a timely manner so as to provide them with the opportunity to respond and allow the *firm* to obtain the full value of the modelled management action. *Firms* should also analyse the wider implications of the management actions, particularly where they represent significant divergence from the business plan and use this information to consider the appropriateness of taking this action.

7.1.28 **[G]** Where the *ICA* assumes that the *firm* may move capital from one part of its business to another across legal or geographical boundaries, the *firm* should explain the mechanisms that it would apply and satisfy itself that it could achieve the necessary capital movements in times of distress (see GENPRU 1.2.51R). The *firm* should also consider any associated costs or restrictions in the amount of capital that would be able to be relocated.

Considering all material risks

7.1.29 **[G]** The *ICA* should give the required level of confidence that the *firm's* liabilities to *policyholders* will be paid. The *ICA* should consider all material risks which may arise before the *policyholder* liabilities are paid (including those risks set out in GENPRU 1.2.30R).

7.1.30 **[G]** *Firms* should not ignore risks simply because they relate to events that occur with an expected likelihood beyond the confidence level. However, the capital required in the face of these tail events may be reduced for the purpose of carrying out the *ICA*. For example, while an A-rated bond may be assumed not to default within the required confidence level, allowance should be made for the devaluation of that bond through a more likely downgrade or change in credit spreads or other method which reflects that this investment includes a default risk to the *firm*.

7.1.31 **[G]** Notwithstanding INSPRU 7.1.30G, risks which have an immaterial effect on the *firm's* financial position or only occur with an extreme probability may be excluded from the *ICA*.

7.1.32 **[G]** The number of *claims*, the amount paid and the timing of a *firm's* liabilities may be uncertain. The *ICA* should consider risks which result in a change in the cost of those liabilities.

7.1.33 **[G]** The assets that a *firm* holds will include assets to back both the liabilities and any capital requirement. These assets carry risk, both in their own right and to the extent that they do not match the liabilities that they are backing. The risk associated with these assets should be considered over the full term for which the *firm* expects to carry the liabilities.

7.1.34 **[G]** Where the *firm* is relying on systems and controls in order to mitigate risks, the *firm* should consider the risk of those systems and controls failing at the confidence level at which the *ICA* is being carried out.

7.1.35 **[G]** If a *firm* summarises cash flows over part of the lifetime of the portfolio using a balance sheet but is exposed to risks which emerge after the balance sheet date, then these longer-dated risks may be captured by adjusting the assumptions used in the closing balance sheet.

Valuation basis

7.1.36 **[G]** The valuation of the assets and of the liabilities should reflect their economic substance. A realistic valuation basis should be used for assets and liabilities taking into account the actual amounts and timings of cash flows under any projections used in the assessment.

7.1.37 **[G]** In carrying out the *ICA*, wherever possible the value of assets should be marked to market. Where marking to market is not possible, the *ICA* should use a method suitable for assessing the underlying economic benefit of holding each asset.

7.1.38 **[G]** The methods and assumptions used in valuing the liabilities should contain no explicit margins for risk, nor should the approach be optimistic. The valuation of liabilities should be consistent with the valuation of assets. To the extent the market price includes an implicit allowance for risk, this should be included within the valuation.

7.1.39 **[G]** The methodology used to place a value on an asset or a liability following a risk event should be consistent with the methodology used prior to the risk event.

7.1.40 **[G]** Approximate valuation methods may be used by the *firm* for minor lines of business or to capture less material types of risk. However, the *firm* should avoid methods which under-estimate the risk in aggregate.

7.1.41 **[G]** The *firm* should carry out a broad reconciliation of key parts of any balance sheet used in the *ICA* with the corresponding entry from audited results.

ICA submitted to FSA: confidence level

7.1.42 **[R]** Where the *FSA* requests a *firm* to submit to it a written record of the *firm's* assessments of the adequacy of its capital resources carried out in accordance with INSPRU 7.1.15R, those assessments must include an assessment comparable to a 99.5% confidence level over a one year timeframe that the value of assets exceeds the value of liabilities, whether or not this is the confidence level otherwise used in the *firm's* own assessments.

7.1.43 **[G]** In considering the value of liabilities for the purpose of INSPRU 7.1.42R, *firms* should have regard to the guidance in INSPRU 7.1.21G, INSPRU 7.1.26G and GENPRU 1.2.27G to GENPRU 1.2.29G.

7.1.44 **[G]** The *FSA* requires *firms* to submit a capital assessment calibrated to a common confidence level, as set out in INSPRU 7.1.42R, to enable the *FSA* to assess whether the minimum *capital resources requirements* in GENPRU 2.1 are appropriate. This then allows the *FSA* to give a consistent level of *individual capital guidance* across the industry.

7.1.45 **[G]** If a *firm* selects a longer time horizon than one year it may choose to use a lower confidence level than 99.5%. In such a case, the *firm* should be prepared to justify its choice and explain why this confidence interval is appropriate and how it is comparable to a 99.5% confidence level over a one year timeframe. An assessment based on a longer timeframe should also demonstrate that there are sufficient assets to cover liabilities at all future dates. This may be illustrated by future annual balance sheets.

Measurement

7.1.46 **[G]** In determining the strength of the *ICA*, a *firm* should consider all risks in aggregate making appropriate allowance for diversification such that the assessment meets the required confidence level overall. The *firm* should be able to describe and explain each of the main diversification benefits allowed for.

7.1.47 **[G]** For risks that can be observed to crystallise over a short period of the order of a year, the confidence level may be measured with reference to the probability distribution for the impact of the risks over one year. For example, catastrophic events such as hurricanes can be measured in this way by estimating the ultimate capital cost.

7.1.48 **[G]** For risks that are not observable over a short period (such as long-tailed liability business or annuitant mortality), the confidence level may be measured with reference to the probability distribution for the emergence of that risk over the lifetime of the liabilities.

Documenting ICAs submitted to the FSA

7.1.49 **[R]** The written record of a *firm's individual capital assessments* carried out in accordance with INSPRU 7.1.15R submitted by the *firm* to the *FSA* must:

(1) in relation to the assessment comparable to a 99.5% confidence level over a one year timeframe that the value of assets exceeds the value of liabilities, document the reasoning and judgements underlying that assessment and, in particular, justify:
   (a) the assumptions used;
   (b) the appropriateness of the methodology used; and
   (c) the results of the assessment; and

(2) identify the major differences between that assessment and any other assessments carried out by the *firm* using a different confidence level.

7.1.50 **[G]** A *firm's* management should determine their own risk appetite or confidence level and a risk measure that they believe is suitable for the management of the business. The *FSA* expects that the *firm's* capital resources assessment under GENPRU 1.2 which it uses in the management of its business may well be at a different confidence level than the 99.5% one required by INSPRU 7.1.42R for a number of reasons, for example, because its view of capital adequacy is different, or to satisfy the demands of rating agencies, or to meet the proposition to *policyholders* as to the strength of the *firm*. A *firm* will maintain its own written assessment of the adequacy of its financial resources, as required by GENPRU 1.2, through the written record requirement of GENPRU 1.2.60R.

7.1.51 **[G]** INSPRU 7.1.49R(2) recognises that a *firm* may carry out a number of different assessments of the adequacy of its capital resources, using different confidence levels, in reaching its overall assessment of the adequacy of its financial resources under GENPRU 1.2. The purpose of asking the *firm* to identify the major differences between those assessments and the assessment documented under INSPRU 7.1.49R(1) is to enable the *FSA* better to understand the *firm's* approach to capital adequacy and risk management in running its business. Understanding the written record made under GENPRU 1.2.60R is therefore key to the *FSA's* understanding of the *firm's* risk and capital management processes.

7.1.52 **[G]** The written record of any other assessment by the *firm* required by GENPRU 1.2.60R is not itself part of the submission to the *FSA*, but the *FSA* is interested in the connection between that other assessment, as documented in the written record required by GENPRU 1.2.60R, and the assessment documented under INSPRU 7.1.49R(1) in terms of the *firm's* compliance with GENPRU 1.2, and the use of capital measures within the *firm*.

7.1.53 **[G]** For the purpose of the written record submitted to the *FSA*, the submitted comparison should include:

(1) A description of any direct difference in the strength of the *firm's* own assessment compared to the assessment submitted to the *FSA*. This is likely to be expressed as a different confidence level to the assessment undertaken to a 99.5% confidence level or the targeting of a defined margin about the 99.5% assessment.

(2) A description of any major differences in the definition of the assets or liabilities, the management actions used, the risks considered or the valuation methodology and assumptions included within the assessment.

7.1.54 **[G]** Some *firms* may not undertake an assessment at a separate confidence level because they consider that a 99.5% confidence level is appropriate to manage their business and meets the requirements of GENPRU 1.2. In the case of these *firms*, no analysis of the major differences is required to be submitted.

Justifying assumptions used

7.1.55 **[G]** *Firms* should provide evidence to support the choice of assumptions used within the *ICA*.

7.1.56 **[G]** Where the choice of assumptions is supported by data, the *firm* should consider the relevance of that data to the *firm's* current and future circumstances and the robustness of any estimates derived.

7.1.57 **[G]** Where the choice of assumptions is supported by expert judgement, the *firm* should consider the nature and value of the expertise being used to support this judgement and any biases that may exist. Where possible, the *firm* should use data to test and support these expert judgements.

Approach taken for significant assumptions

7.1.58 **[G]** *Firms* should be able to demonstrate how they have identified the most financially significant assumptions and calculate the sensitivity of the *ICA* to changes in these assumptions. The choice of assumption may be decided using the results of sensitivity testing.

7.1.59 **[G]** *Firms* may seek to justify their assumptions by considering the process used to determine those assumptions from relevant data. Alternatively, where historical data is either limited or not considered to be indicative of likely future experience, *firms* may justify their assumptions by reference to the suitability of the calibration for the purpose of the *ICA*. However, relatively more attention should be given to the justification where the choice of assumption has a more significant effect on the *ICA*.

7.1.60 **[G]** Where there is a concentration of business from a single source (for example, a single sales channel or cedant), consideration should be given to the greater impact of a risk crystallising, compared to that for a welldiversified portfolio.

Justification of prospective management actions

7.1.61 **[G]** Where projection of the value of assets and liabilities reflects the *firm's* prospective management actions, the *firm* should justify the choice of prospective management actions and the assumptions used.

7.1.62 **[G]** Where the prospective management action is identical to those used in another regulatory assessment of solvency (e.g. calculation of the *WPICC* for *realistic basis life firms*), no further justification is required.

7.1.63 **[G]** Where the prospective management action is not similar to those used in another regulatory assessment of solvency, or uses different assumptions, the *firm* should show the financial impact of the management action.

Regular review of assumptions

7.1.64 **[G]** *Firms* should regularly review key parameters, both to ensure their continued applicability and to reduce uncertainty over the current level of capital required. *Firms* using assumptions that are very different from past experience should present robust arguments in support of the differences.

Methodology

7.1.65 **[G]** The methodology used within the *ICA* should allow the *firm* to quantify the financial effect of material risks at the required confidence level. The methodology used should also reflect the nature of the *firm's* business and be consistent with the way in which the *firm* identifies and manages risk.

7.1.66 **[G]** *Firms* should be able to explain their rationale for choosing their approach to risk and assessment of capital required. There are no simple classifications of approach to risk and capital assessment, so the rationale should be considered in the context of a number of defining characteristics in the structure of the capital model.

7.1.67 **[G]** Generally, larger *firms* would be expected to take a more sophisticated approach to capital modelling than smaller ones.

Stress tests and scenario analyses

7.1.68 **[G]** Where a *firm* chooses to carry out its *ICA* through the use of stress testing and scenario analyses, such testing should reflect the potential range of outcomes for the risk being quantified, consistent with the prescribed confidence level for the *ICA*.

7.1.69 **[G]** The overall assessment of capital required may require the aggregation of results from the stress and scenario testing. The *firm* should explain its choice of aggregation approach and its understanding of the implications of combining the individual risks. The *firm* should be satisfied that the resultant capital provides the required degree of confidence, given the variability of the underlying risks and the uncertainty associated with modelling those risks. A useful component of this process is the characterisation and explanation of a range of possible circumstances that could give rise to a loss of this magnitude.

Documenting the results

7.1.70 **[G]** The conclusion of the *ICA* should consider whether the *firm* has adequate capital to meet its assessment of the required capital. Furthermore, the *firm* should consider any implications for its approach to risk management arising from the work carried out. The *ICA* should be supported by an explanation of the material sources of risk and financial impact of the management actions that the *firm* may take to manage those risks. Where possible, the reasonableness of the results should be supported by considering other evidence of the capital needed.

7.1.71 **[G]** The objective of capital modelling is to consider all possible outcomes, however unlikely any one outcome might be, and set capital as protection against all but the most extreme losses. It is therefore important to focus not only on the assumptions and methodology used to quantify individual risks, but also on the approach to aggregating the capital required for each risk.

7.1.72 **[G]** However the risks have been aggregated to give the *firm's* capital requirement, checks should be made as to the reasonableness of the outcome. It should be possible to characterise scenarios, or combinations of loss events, that would result in a loss of similar magnitude to that indicated by the *ICA*. *Firms* should consider a range of scenarios that could give rise to such a loss.

7.1.73 **[G]** The results of the *ICA* should be supplemented by analysis of the sources of the risks to which the *firm* is exposed, discussion of the events which are most likely to threaten the financial stability of the *firm* and the potential mitigating actions which are available to senior management.

Additional guidance for Lloyd's

7.1.74 **[G]** Responsibility for:
(1) managing the risks associated with the *insurance business*; and
(2) holding the *capital resources* that support those risks;

is divided between *managing agents* and the *Society*. To clarify the respective responsibilities of *managing agents* and the *Society* for ensuring the adequacy of financial resources, the *FSA* distinguishes between the *managing agents*' responsibility to carry out capital adequacy assessments of the *capital resources* held at *syndicate* level for each *syndicate* that they manage, and the *Society's* responsibility to carry out an assessment for each *member*.

7.1.75 **[R]** In carrying out *ICAs* in respect of the *insurance business* carried on through each *syndicate* (the *syndicate ICA*), *managing agents* must consider the risks, controls and the financial resources relevant to each *syndicate*.

7.1.76 **[R]** When carrying out the *syndicate ICA*, *managing agents* must not take into account risks to which a *member* may be exposed or controls from which a *member* may benefit:
(1) because that *member* carries on *insurance business* through another *syndicate* or more than one *syndicate year* (whether or not managed by the same *managing agent*); or
(2) because that *member's* financial resources include *funds at Lloyd's* or *central assets*.

7.1.77 **[R]** The *Society* must have regard to *syndicate ICAs* in arriving at its own capital assessment for each *member*.

7.1.78 **[G]** In assessing the adequacy of the *capital resources* supporting the *insurance business* of each *member*, the *Society* should consider the risks, controls and financial resources relevant to the totality of the *member's insurance business*, including:
(1) the adequacy of *syndicate ICAs*;
(2) the *member's* share of *syndicate ICAs*;
(3) adjustments in respect of risks and controls relating to *funds at Lloyd's*, *central assets* and the interaction of risks underwritten by the *member* through different *syndicates* and in respect of different *syndicate years*; and
(4) the ongoing validity of any relevant assumptions it makes.

7.1.79 **[G]** In taking account of a *syndicate ICA* under INSPRU 7.1.77R:
(1) if the *Society* considers a *syndicate ICA* to be adequate, it should use the *managing agent's* risk and capital assessments in carrying out its *ICA* in relation to any *member* of that *syndicate*, or it should be able to justify why it will not; and
(2) if the *Society* considers a *syndicate ICA* to be less than adequate, the *Society* should increase the *syndicate ICA* so that it is adequate for the purpose of carrying out its *ICA* in relation to the *members* of that *syndicate*.

7.1.80 **[G]** The assessment of capital adequacy for a *member* will rarely equal the proportionate share of a *syndicate ICA* (or sum of those shares, where the *member* participates on more than one *syndicate*) as attributed to that *member*, because, in determining the capital assessments for each *member*, the *Society* may make adjustments to take account of:
(1) risks and controls associated with *funds at Lloyd's* and *central assets*, which can increase the assessment for that *member*;
(2) diversification effects, including as a result of *members'* participations on more than one *syndicate year*, which can reduce the assessment for that *member*; and

Part II FSA Handbook Materials

(3) its own assessment of *syndicate* risks, which can be higher than the *managing agent's* and so increase the assessment for that *member*.

7.1.81 **[G]** *Capital resources* to meet each *syndicate ICA* could be:
(1) held within a *syndicate* and managed by the *managing agent*; or
(2) held and managed by the *Society*; or
(3) not needed in full, because of effects such as diversification that the *Society* takes into account.

7.1.82 **[G]** The *balancing amount* is a function of the relationship between the *syndicate ICA* and the amount of assets held within the *syndicate*. As illustrations:
(1) if the *syndicate* holds no *capital resources* (but its liabilities are fully covered by relevant assets), the *balancing amount* equals the *syndicate ICA* (as there are no *capital resources* at *syndicate* level, all the *capital resources* must be held as *funds at Lloyd's* or *central assets*);
(2) if *capital resources* held at *syndicate* level are negative (i.e. if relevant assets do not fully cover liabilities for the *syndicate*), the *balancing amount* should be higher than the *syndicate ICA* by an amount corresponding to the negative *capital resources* held by *managing agents* on behalf of the *syndicate*; and
(3) conversely, if a *syndicate* holds positive *capital resources* for the *syndicate*, the *balancing amount* should be lower than the *syndicate ICA* by a corresponding amount.

7.1.83 **[R]** *Managing agents* must periodically notify the *Society* of the *syndicate ICA* and the *balancing amount* in respect of each *syndicate*.

7.1.84 **[R]** For the purpose of assessing the adequacy of *capital resources* held as *funds at Lloyd's* and *central assets*, the *Society* must have regard to *balancing amounts* notified to it by *managing agents*.

7.1.85 **[R]** After notification of a *balancing amount* by a *managing agent*, the *Society* must:
(1) confirm to the *managing agent* that *capital resources* held as *funds at Lloyd's* and *central assets* are adequate to support the *balancing amount*; or
(2) notify the *managing agent* that it cannot give that confirmation.

7.1.86 **[G]** *Managing agents* should submit *syndicate ICAs* and notify *balancing amounts* to the *Society* as part of the annual capital-setting process at Lloyd's. The submission of the *syndicate ICA* and the notification of the *balancing amount* should be made in good time for the *Society* to review them and place appropriate reliance on them when it determines the capital assessments for each *member*.

7.1.87 **[G]** When communicating the *syndicate ICA* and *balancing amount* for each *syndicate* to the *Society*, *managing agents* should agree with the *Society* an allocation of the *syndicate ICA* between *syndicate years*. The purpose of the allocation is to ensure that there is an appropriate matching of assets to risk and liabilities and an equitable treatment between the *members* reflecting the provision of capital in each *syndicate year*.

7.1.88 **[G]** For the purposes of complying with their obligations under INSPRU, *managing agents* may assume that any *balancing amount* confirmed by the *Society* under INSPRU 7.1.85R is supported by *capital resources* held as *funds at Lloyd's* and *central assets*.

7.1.89 **[R]** If a *managing agent* has, at any time, a significant doubt about the adequacy of a *syndicate ICA* or *balancing amount* with respect to *syndicate* risks and controls, it must notify the *Society* immediately.

7.1.90 **[R]** If the *Society* has, at any time, a significant doubt about the adequacy of any *member's capital resources* held by it in support of any *balancing amount*, it must notify the relevant *managing agent* immediately.

FSA assessment process – all firms

7.1.91 **[G]** In assessing the adequacy of a *firm's capital resources*, the *FSA* draws on more than just a review of the submitted *ICA*. Use is made of wider supervisory knowledge of a *firm* and of wider market developments and practices. When forming a view of any *individual capital guidance* to be given to a *firm*, the review of the *firm's ICA* along with the ARROW risk assessment and any other issues arising from day-to-day supervision will be considered.

7.1.92 **[G]** The *FSA* will take a risk-based and proportionate approach to the review of a *firm's ICA*, focusing on the *firm's* approach to dealing with the key risks it faces. Any *individual capital guidance* given will reflect the judgements reached through the ARROW review process as well as the review of the *firm's ICA*.

7.1.93 **[G]** A *firm* should not expect the *FSA* to accept as adequate any particular model that the *firm* develops or that the results from the model are automatically reflected in any *individual capital guidance* given to the *firm* for the purpose of determining adequate *capital resources*. However, the *FSA* will take into account the results of any sound and prudent model when giving *individual capital guidance* or considering applications for a *waiver* under section 148 of the *Act* of the *capital resources requirement* in GENPRU 2.1.

7.1.94 **[G]** Where the *FSA* considers that a *firm* will not comply with GENPRU 1.1.26R (adequate financial resources, including *capital resources*) by holding the *capital resources* required by GENPRU 2.1, the *FSA* may give the *firm individual capital guidance* advising it of the amount and quality of *capital resources* which the *FSA* considers it needs to hold in order to meet that *rule*.

7.1.95 **[G]** In giving *individual capital guidance*, the *FSA* seeks a balance between delivering consistent outcomes across the *individual capital guidance* it gives to all *firms* and recognising that such *guidance* should reflect the individual features of the *firm*. Comparison with the assumptions used by other *firms* will be used to trigger further enquiry. Debate will be sought where good arguments are made for a particular result that differs markedly from those of a *firm's* peers. The *FSA* also takes account of the quality of the wider risk management around the development of the numbers used in the *ICA*. The aim is to deliver *individual capital guidance* that comes closest to ensuring that there is no significant risk that a *firm* is unable to pay its liabilities as they fall due.

7.1.96 **[G]** Following an internal validation process, the *FSA* will write to the Board of the *firm* being assessed providing both quantitative and qualitative feedback on the results of the *FSA's* assessment. This letter will notify the *firm* of the *individual capital guidance* considered appropriate. The letter will include reasons for any capital add-ons identified, where applicable.

7.1.97 **[G]** If a *firm* considers that the *individual capital guidance* is inappropriate to its circumstances, then the *firm* should inform the *FSA* that it does not intend to follow that *guidance*. Informing the *FSA* of such an intention would be expected if a *firm* is to comply with *Principle* 11 (Relations with regulators).

7.1.98 **[G]** The *FSA* expects most disagreements about the adequacy of capital will be resolved through further analysis and discussion. The *FSA* may consider the use of its powers under section 166 of the *Act* (Reports by skilled persons) to assist in such circumstances. If the *FSA* and the *firm* still do not agree on an adequate level of capital, then the *FSA* may consider using its powers under section 45 of the *Act* to, on its own initiative, vary a *firm's Part IV permission* so as to require it to hold capital in accordance with the *FSA's* view of the capital necessary to comply with GENPRU 1.2.26R. SUP 7 provides further information about the *FSA's* powers under section 45.

7.1.99 **[G]** Where a *firm* considers that the *capital resources requirements* of GENPRU 2.1 require the holding of more capital than is needed for the *firm* to comply with GENPRU 1.2.26R then the *firm* may apply to the *FSA* for a *waiver* of the requirements in GENPRU 2.1 under section 148 of the *Act*. In addition to the statutory tests under section 148, in deciding whether to grant a *waiver* and, if granted, its terms, the *FSA* will consider the thoroughness, objectivity and prudence of a *firm's ICA* and the extent to which the *guidance* in this section has been followed. The *FSA* will not grant a *waiver* that would cause a breach of the minimum capital requirements under the *Insurance Directives* or *Reinsurance Directive*.

Annex
INSPRU 7 Annex 1 [G]

INSPRU 7 Ann 1 **[G]**

A1	This annex provides an illustrative qualitative example of how a small *firm* could undertake its stress and scenario analysis without this being disproportionate to the size and complexity of its business so as to comply with the *general stress and scenario testing rule*. For these reasons, the example does not provide any quantitative guidance as we believe this would be impractical given the diverse nature of each *firm's* individual circumstances.
A2	This example is based on *guidance* contained in INSPRU 7.1. The areas discussed are not exhaustive and it is likely that in practice a *firm* will need to consider a range of other issues.
A3	The scenarios that the *firm* generates as part of its analysis should aim to reflect the degree of risk in a variety of areas. How extreme these scenarios are will influence the ultimate level of capital required by the *firm*. The *firm* should not necessarily develop scenarios based on the current trading or economic conditions, but on possible trading or economic conditions that could occur during the next three to five years.
A4	In addition to examining its event scenarios, a *firm* should also be able to meet any individual risk (however unlikely) that it has accepted (or proposes to accept through its business plan) from *policyholders*. It therefore should analyse its exposures and ensure that it has sufficient capital or available *reinsurance* to cover its largest individual risks and accumulations.
	Worked example

	Background	
A5	The *firm* used for this example is an *insurer* carrying on *general insurance business* within a large *group*, writing predominantly personal lines, household and motor policies of approximately £25m *gross written premium*. This business has a reasonable geographical spread, sourced significantly from within the *United Kingdom*. The *firm* has purchased appropriate *reinsurance* cover from a variety of *reinsurers* and has a demonstrated record of utilising this cover. Its settlement pattern for *claims* averages three years, however, there is a small element of the account with longer tail liability *claims*. The *firm's* investments and IT support are outsourced.	
	Insurance risk	
A6	The risk of incorrect or inaccurate pricing of business over the scenario period can be addressed by examining typical uncertainties within the pricing basis and the volatility of *claims* experience.	
A7	In examining the adequacy of its pricing, the *firm* establishes its underwriting and *claims* trend over a ten-year base period by reviewing profit and loss accounts (particularly underwriting profit). In particular it examines the following:	
	(i)	the volatility of losses in a particular line of business;
	(ii)	whether the loss ratio exceeded 100% in any line of business; and
	(iii)	whether the *deferred acquisition cost* (DAC) amount had been written down; e.g. whether an unexpired risk provision (URP) was necessary.
A8	The *firm* also examines whether its *premiums* over the last ten years have been:	
	(i)	reasonably stable;
	(ii)	responsive enough to changes in *claim* exposures (so that profitability is maintained);
	(iii)	providing adequately for contingencies (such as major losses e.g. hail, earthquake etc);
	(iv)	encouraged loss control (through the use of deductibles, no claim bonuses etc);
A9	The *firm* also reviews its method of pricing. The *firm* considers and performs the following:	
	(i)	a review of acceptable rates, e.g. *premiums* being charged by competitors for similar products;
	(ii)	an examination of whether there have been any difficulties in the past with delegated authorities in relation to pricing including the ability and experience of staff members setting or recommending *premium* prices;
	(iii)	an examination of whether the *firm* has the appropriate mechanisms in place regarding *premium* rate changes (that is, who makes these decisions, frequency, and on what basis?); and
	(iv)	a benchmark price assessment (e.g. the ability to provide adequate competitive *premium* rates). For example, indicative rates being determined through the use of industry statistics, competitor statistics and the *firm's* own analysis for all classes.
A10	Other factors the *firm* considers are:	
	(i)	changes in environment (e.g. legislation, social, economic etc);

	(ii)	changes in *policy* conditions and deductibles; and
	(iii)	impact of market segments (e.g. the effects of different *claim* frequencies and costs impacting the price charged).
A11	Having completed its analysis, the *firm* makes the following assumptions to define its underwriting risk:	
	(i)	*claims* costs. The *firm* assumes these are X% higher than in the *premium* basis;
	(ii)	*claims* inflation. The *firm* assumes a X% *claims* inflation over the scenario period, compared to Y% in the pricing basis;
	(iii)	*policy* expenses (fixed and variable) are X% higher than anticipated in the pricing basis;
	(iv)	*reinsurance* charges are X% higher than anticipated in the pricing basis; and
	(v)	investment income is X% lower than anticipated in the pricing basis.
As a result of the above analysis on a per risk basis, the *firm* considers that capital of between £X and £Y would cover the possibility of material deviations to projected results.		
	Allowing for catastrophes	
A12	The allowance for catastrophic events within the insurance risk scenario should reflect both the severity and the frequency of these events.	
A13	After considering the catastrophe *reinsurance* programme it may be clear that the upper limit is set at a level unlikely to be breached e.g. a 1 in 200 year event. Thus, for the purposes of the capital assessment, it would not be necessary to assume losses in excess of this retention.	
A14	However, it may be determined that there is possible exhaustion of free reinstatements or of horizontal cover in total. For example, if there were a significant chance of three catastrophic losses in any one period but the *reinsurance* allowed only one free reinstatement, then the assessment may be to hold two retentions and the entire gross loss for the third event.	
As a result of the above analysis, the *firm* considers it appropriate to hold capital sufficient to absorb three catastrophic losses: one European windstorm of £X, one UK flood of £Y, and one large man made explosion of £Z.		
The *reinsurance* structure in place allows for X number of reinstatements at full *premium*.		
	Deterioration of reserves	
A15	The *firm* considers the adequacy of its *claims* reserves by focussing on the liability valuation.	
A16	The liability valuation may contain a range of answers that might indicate possible reserve variability. Also, the valuation will contain areas where judgement has been applied and assumptions formulated which are subjective. These areas are considered and stressed as appropriate.	
A17	The *firm* also reviews the historic level of *claims* reserves and subsequent level of settlements to help determine the size of any historic levels of under and over reserving.	
A18	*Reinsurance* arrangements are considered and the extent to which these arrangements protect against reserve deterioration is assessed.	
A19	For *unearned premium*, where losses have yet to occur, the *firm* considers that the level of uncertainty is greater and considers similar factors to those relating to underwriting risk in addition to those discussed above.	
As a result of the above analysis, the *firm* considers it appropriate to apply a X% loading to the outstanding *claims* provision, a Y% loading to the *unearned premium* provision and Z% to all other liability values. The *firm* considers that capital of between £X and £Y would adequately cover reserve deterioration.		
	Credit risk	

A20	Credit risk relates to the risk of default by *counterparties*. The *firm* believes its exposure to credit risk results from financial transactions with *counterparties* including issuers, debtors, borrowers, brokers, *policyholders*, *reinsurers* and guarantors.
A21	When assessing credit risk the *firm* makes an assessment of the creditworthiness of *counterparties* to the assets of the *firm*.
A22	The assessment includes an evaluation of the credit risk associated with loans and investment portfolios; the quality of on and off balance sheet assets; the ongoing management of the loans and investment portfolios; as well as loss provisions and reserves.
A23	The *firm* believes its exposure to credit risk also arises due to its exposure to its *reinsurers*. In this regard, the *firm* uses the credit ratings assigned to particular *counterparties* as a measure of credit risk, most notably Standard & Poor's, Moody's Investors Service and AM Best's (particularly for *reinsurers*).
A24	When forming an opinion on credit risk the *firm* considers:
	Reinsurance
A25	The *firm's* strategy is to lessen exposure to a single lead *reinsurer* to less than 30%, with other participants holding no more than 15%. In all cases, the panel of *reinsurers* all have a specified rating. The *firm* has no prior experience of disputes, and their working relationship with the panel may be excellent, and thus the *firm* does not envisage any future difficulties arising in this regard.
A26	Bond default rates could then be used to assess a likely credit risk figure for *reinsurance* recoveries (including *IBNR* recoveries).
The *firm* considers that capital of between £X and £Y would cover *reinsurance* defaults, with no additional allowance for disputes.	
	Overseas financial institutions and banks
A27	The *firm* investigates its business relationships with overseas financial institution *counterparties* including *banks*, and decides no additional allowance is required.
	Quality of counterparties and trends in counterparty risk
A28	The *firm* assesses the level and age of debtors, focussing particularly upon unpaid *premiums*, especially those greater than three months old, and reviews the level and trend of contingent liabilities. For example, the *firm* estimates that the credit risk scenario equates to taking a 10% reduction in the asset value of debtors, based on bond default rates and age of debt.
The *firm* considers that capital of between £X and £Y would cover credit risk to counterparties.	
	Off-balance sheet transactions
A29	The *firm* investigates any unfunded commitments, credit *derivatives*, commercial or standby letters of credit. Where these exist the possibility of a loss on these instruments is considered in relation to the requirement of the credit risk scenario.
The *firm* considers that no additional capital is necessary.	
	Market risk
A30	*Market risk* encompasses an adverse movement in the value of the assets as a consequence of market movements such as interest rates, foreign exchange rates, equity prices, etc. which is not matched by a corresponding movement in the value of the liabilities.
A31	In examining possible market risks, the *firm* considers its sensitivity to *market risk* by evaluating the degree to which changes in interest rates, foreign exchange rates, equity prices, or other areas can adversely affect the *firm's* earnings or capital.
A32	The *firm* believes its assets and liabilities are approximately matched e.g. there is no existence of large unmatched or unhedged currency positions; short tail business is backed by cash/fixed interest assets of suitable term and long tail business with real assets e.g. shares/property. If mismatching does exist this should be allowed for within the estimate.

A33	In developing the scenario the *firm* estimates the effect of a X% increase in interest rates on bond values.
A34	Similarly, the *firm* estimates the effect on equity values of a major recession to estimate the possible reduction in the value of equity capital. Also, it uses a suitable equity index to determine the size of historical falls in equity values and indicate possible future falls.
A35	*Counterparty* risk might be allowed for by assuming one or several major corporate bond holding defaults.
A36	For all investments, the stability of trading revenues should be examined to determine the volatility of investment.
From the above analysis, the *firm* considers that capital of between £X and £Y would be appropriate to protect it against adverse movement in *market risk.*	
	Liquidity risk
A37	*Liquidity risk* is the potential that the *firm* may be unable to meet its obligations as they fall due as a consequence of having a timing mismatch. The *firm* considers *liquidity risk* relates to the risk associated with the processes of managing timing relationship between asset and liability cash flow patterns.
A38	When assessing *liquidity risk*, the *firm* considers the extent of mismatch between assets and liabilities and the amount of assets held in a highly liquid, marketable form should unexpected cashflows lead to a liquidity crunch.
A39	The price concession of liquidating assets is a prime concern when assessing *liquidity risk* and is built into the scenario.
A40	In examining the *liquidity risk*, the *firm* examines the following:
	Marketability, quality and liquidity of assets
A41	The *firm* considers the assets held and makes an assessment regarding the quality and liquidity of these assets. Even though the assets matched the liabilities, residual risk remains given that timings are uncertain and there is a possibility that assets will be realised at unfavourable times. This is allowed for by assuming a 2.5% reduction in the market value of assets at realisation compared to the current market value.
The *firm* considers that capital of between £X and £Y would cover timing risk to *counterparties.*	
	Reliance on new business income
A42	The *firm* relies partially upon new business cash flows to meet current liabilities as they fall due. The *firm* analyses the sensitivity of future cash flow projections and new business assumptions and considers the effect of a reduced level of new business.
A43	The *firm* finds that it did not have immediate alternatives in place in case these expected new business cash flows were reduced. In this regard, it considers that these sources should be stressed by X%.
The *firm* considers that capital of between £X and £Y would cover possible effects of adjusting the asset portfolio to switch to more liquid assets.	
A44	The *firm* also examines the volatility and cost of on- and off-balance sheet funding sources. The *firm* is satisfied that no concerns need to be raised and that there should not be any impact on its liquidity position.
A45	The *firm* believes it is well placed to manage unplanned changes in funding sources as well as react to changes in market conditions that affect its ability to quickly liquidate assets with minimal loss. The *firm* assesses that it has reasonable access to money markets and other sources of funding such as lines of credit.
A46	The *firm* has no previous problems or delays in meeting obligations (or accessing external funding).
Overall, from the above analysis, the *firm* considers that capital of between £X and £Y would be necessary to withstand the effects of deterioration in liquidity.	
	Governance Risk
A47	Governance risk relates to the risk associated with the board and/or senior management of the *firm* not effectively performing their respective roles.

A48	The existence and level of directors and officers insurance in place is investigated compared to known incidence of *claims* of this type.
A49	The *firm* assesses whether the current level of governance is appropriate for the *firm*, and the likelihood that the *firm's* practices may result in the board and/or senior management not adequately undertaking their roles. The cost of altering and strengthening the current board structure is considered.
A50	In this regard, the *firm* makes an assessment that it may be reliant on only a few senior executives, and may be exposed if they experience any misadventure.
The *firm* considers that capital of between £X and £Y would cover governance risk.	
	Strategic Risk
A51	Strategic risk arises from an inability to implement appropriate business plans and strategies, make decisions, allocate resources or adapt to changes in the business environment.
A52	The *firm* therefore assesses the prudence and appropriateness of its business strategy in the context of the *firm's* competitive and economic environment. In particular the assumptions, forecasting and projections are assessed considering the possibility of a fundamental market change due, for example, to higher numbers of competitors, changes in sales channels, new forms of insurance or changes in legislation. This review includes whether the *reinsurance* programme is appropriate for the risks selected by the *firm* and whether it adequately takes account of the underwriting and business plans of the *firm* generally.
A53	The *firm* considers the likelihood of a fundamental strategic shift too remote to include within the scenario given the maturity of the market in which they operate.
	Operational risks
A54	In reviewing the operational risk exposures, the *firm* has examined its administration, compliance, event, fraud, governance, strategic and technological risks.
	Administration
A55	The *firm* considers the risk of error or failure associated with the administrative aspects of the operation of its business. In this regard, the *firm* considers likelihood of financial loss and reputation harm due to failure or errors occurring and the likely size of these losses.
A56	None of the *firm's* administration is out-sourced to service providers.
A57	In undertaking the assessment, the *firm* considers the history of failure or error from transaction processing or control within the *firm*. Exception reports are produced on a quarterly basis. Past reports highlighted past administrative deficiencies. The biggest event in the past 10 years related to a situation where *claim*-handling staff shared access codes to the *claims* administration system. This resulted in an overpayment to some clients.
A58	The *firm* also examines the nature and extent of centralised and decentralised functions within the *firm*. Three branches report regularly to the central office and an appropriate system is in place to record financial information, handle complaints etc.
A59	The *firm* also reviews the segregation of duties between staff. It is satisfied that an adequate segregation of duties between underwriting *claims* and payments divisions exist in terms of acceptance, authorisation and payments. It is also satisfied that sufficient interaction between the front, middle and back offices exist in terms of financial control and risk management. For example, it is confident that its guidelines for accepting risks are adequate and that any breach would be picked up by exception reporting.
A60	The *firm* also investigates the level of staff expertise and training to administer its product range/services.
The *firm* considers that capital of between £X and £Y would cover the risk of future administration issues.	
	Compliance Risk

A61	The *firm* believes its main compliance risk relates to the risk of non-adherence to legislative and internal *firm* requirements.
A62	An investigation into compliance over the last 10 years finds no history of non-compliance with *firm* policy and control systems nor have there been any reported areas of non-compliance with legislation or other requirements.
A63	Regulatory reforms including corporate and consumer law are considered and it is assumed that expenses costs will rise as a result of developments in the next 5 years. As a result an additional X% of *premium* income was assumed for the expense ratio.
The *firm* considers that capital of between £X and £Y would cover the risk of future compliance issues.	
	Event risk
A64	Event risk relates to risks associated with the potential impact of significant events (e.g., financial system crisis, major change in fiscal system, natural disaster) on the operations of the *firm*.
A65	The definition of event risk is not intended to cover events that are directly associated with products and services offered, for example, events which may directly impact on the *general insurance business*.
A66	The *firm* concludes that no additional specific allocation is required.
	Fraud Risk
A67	Fraud risk relates to the risk associated with intentional misappropriation of funds, undertaken with the objective of personal benefit at the expense of the *firm*.
A68	In assessing fraud risk, the *firm* considers the possibility of fraudulent acts occurring within the *firm* and the extent of controls which management has established to mitigate such acts.
A69	The *firm* examines fraud issues over a period of 10 years and finds one major incident where it was subject to a fraudulent activity. This involved fraudulent payments being made by a member of staff which resulted in a loss for the *firm* of £Xm. Based on this previous incident and allowing for improvements in controls, the company assessed a financial figure that it believes is consistent with the probability for this scenario.
The *firm* considers that capital of between £X and £Y would cover the risk of future fraud.	
	Technology Risk
A70	The *firm* considers the risk of error or failure associated with the technological aspects (IT systems) of its operations. Specifically, technology risk refers to both the hardware systems and the software utilised to run those systems.
A71	In relation to the *firm's* information systems, the *firm* assesses the past reliability and future functionality and believes them to be adequate. It does not have any future plans to either replace its systems or make major systems modifications.
A72	Concerning business continuity management and disaster recovery planning (and testing of plans), the *firm* reviews these plans regularly and tests them quarterly. A full back-up site exists with full recovery capabilities. Costs associated with utilising the site and associated business interruption insurance was estimated.
The *firm* considers that capital of between £X and £Y would cover technology risk.	
	Group risk
A73	The size of the group risk element within operational risk will depend on the ownership structure of the *firm* and how it is funded by the parent.
A74	The *firm* considers the likelihood and financial consequences of both insolvency and credit downgrading of its parent. Given the *firm* shares the parent's name there is a large risk of association.
A75	The *firm* considers it within the scope of the scenario to allow for a single downgrade of the parent's credit rating from AA to A. It does not believe the chance of insolvency great enough to allow for directly.

Part II FSA Handbook Materials

A76	The *firm* estimates the effect on its business plan and profit margins of the downgrade. It estimates the amount of business lost and the increase in marketing costs required to maintain the client base. It also allows for a change in the pricing basis to incorporate a reduced profit margin (with knock on impacts on the business volume and loss ratios).
From the above analysis, the *firm* considers that capital of between £X and £Y would be required to cover group risks.	
	Overall assessment
A77	After individually assessing each risk area, the *firm* considers the capital that it has estimated might be absorbed under each scenario. In aggregate the range of capital absorbed is between £X and £Y. It considers how many of these scenarios might reasonably occur within a period and the extent to which it could replace capital within that period. It takes into account scenarios which might reasonably be linked, the difficulty with which capital might be replaced if the scenarios occurred, and the changes in strategy which might need to be adopted if the scenarios occurred.
A78	The *firm* decides that the worst realistic combination of circumstances that might arise would absorb capital of between £A and £B.

CHAPTER 8

8.1 General provisions applying INSPRU and GENPRU to Lloyd's

Application

[2072]
8.1.1 **[R]** INSPRU 8.1 applies to:
(1) the *Society*;
(2) *managing agents.*

8.1.2 **[R]** If a provision in INSPRU or GENPRU applies to the *Society* "in accordance with" this *rule*, the *Society* must:
(1) manage each *member's funds at Lloyd's*;
(2) manage its *central assets*; and
(3) supervise the *insurance business* carried on by each *member* at Lloyd's;

so as to achieve in relation to those assets and that *insurance business* the same effect as the relevant INSPRU or GENPRU provision would have (that is, conforming with the requirements of any *rule* and taking appropriate account of any applicable *guidance*,) when applied to a *firm* or to the *insurance business* of a *firm*.

8.1.3 **[G]** The *Society* is subject to INSPRU and GENPRU *rules* in respect of the *insurance business* of each Lloyd's *member*. These include *rules* in respect of:
(1) the calculation of the *capital resources requirements* for each *member*;
(2) the financial resources it manages on behalf of *members*; and
(3) the *Society*'s own financial resources.

8.1.4 **[R]** If a provision in INSPRU or GENPRU applies to a *managing agents* "in accordance with" this *rule*, the *managing agent* must, in relation to each *syndicate* managed by it and for each *syndicate* year, manage:
(1) the *syndicate assets*; and
(2) the *insurance business* carried on by the *members* of the *syndicate* through that *syndicate*;

so as to achieve in relation to those assets and that *insurance business* the same effect as the relevant INSPRU or GENPRU provision would have (that is, conforming with the requirements of any *rule* and taking appropriate account of any applicable *guidance*,) when applied to a *firm* or to the *insurance business* of a *firm*.

8.1.5 **[G]** *Syndicate membership* may change from year to year or it may remain constant. *Managing agents* are required to apply INSPRU and GENPRU to the *insurance business* carried on through each *syndicate* for each *syndicate year*. This should ensure that INSPRU and GENPRU are applied to Lloyd's in a way that is consistent with the provision of capital to support the *insurance business* underwritten.

8.1.6 **[G]** Where common systems and controls or processes are appropriate for all the *insurance business* carried on through more than one *syndicate* year, a single response may be adequate for all *syndicate* years. However, in some cases it will be important to consider the business of each open *syndicate* year separately, particularly for quantitative *rules*. For example, it is important that *managing agents* separately assess the financial resources (including capital) that are required and are available to support the *insurance business* carried on through each *syndicate* year, where the *syndicate membership* changes from year to year. This is because each *member*'s assets are only available to support its own business, so the assets supporting one year of account may not be available to support another. For example, if a *managing agent* were to assess the financial requirements of two or more *syndicate* years together where the capital structure had changed, there would be a risk that the *managing agent* might take account of diversification effects that were not reflected in the capital supporting the *insurance business*.

8.1.7 **[G]** There is no requirement on *managing agents* to carry out separate individual capital assessments for *syndicates* for each *syndicate* year. *Managing agents* are required to carry out individual capital assessments for each *syndicate* as if that *syndicate* were a *firm*; this would normally be on the basis of a going concern but, just as in a *firm*, account needs to be taken of any restrictions on the availability of assets (e.g. deposits with cedants), and some account needs to be taken of changes in the capital participation in the *syndicate*. The *Society* is responsible for the individual capital assessment for each *member*, which must take into account the assessments made by *managing agents* of any *syndicates* on which the *member* participates. INSPRU 7.1 contains *rules* and guidance on the assessment of capital adequacy for *firms* and INSPRU **7.1.74G** to INSPRU 7.1.90R provide for the application of INSPRU 7.1 to the *Society* and *managing agents*.

8.1.8 **[G]** The assessment which a *firm* makes should be based upon its future business plans and projections. This is the main area where the *firm's* assessment may diverge from its prescribed *capital resources requirement* which, necessarily, is based upon historic data.

8.1.9 **[G]** Key INSPRU and GENPRU requirements for Lloyd's

Key INSPRU and GENPRU requirements	**INSPRU**	**GENPRU**
Risk management, systems and controls		
The *Society* to establish and maintain systems and controls to address risks affecting the Lloyd's market	INSPRU 8.2	
The *Society* to manage prudential, credit, market, liquidity and operational risks affecting *funds at Lloyd's* and *central assets*	INSPRU 4.1, INSPRU 5.1, INSPRU 8.2 & INSPRU 8.5	
Managing agents to establish and maintain systems and controls for the management of prudential, credit, market, liquidity, operational, and insurance risks affecting each *syndicate*	INSPRU 4.1, INSPRU 5.1, INSPRU 8.2 & INSPRU 8.5	
Adequacy of financial resources		
The *Society* to ensure that *members'* financial resources are adequate		GENPRU 1.2 & GENPRU 1.5
Members taken together to maintain adequate financial resources in respect of the *insurance business* conducted at Lloyd's		GENPRU 1.5
Managing agents to ensure that financial resources are adequate for each *syndicate*		GENPRU 1.2 & GENPRU 1.5
Valuation		
The *Society* and *managing agents* to apply generally accepted accounting principles to valuing assets, liabilities, equity and income statement items for the purposes of the *rules* and *guidance* in GENPRU, INSPRU and *IPRU (INS)* unless the contrary is expressly stated	INSPRU 3.1 & INSPRU 3.2	GENPRU 1.3 & GENPRU 1.5
Capital resources requirements		
The *Society* to calculate the *MCR* in respect of the *general insurance business* of each *member*		GENPRU 2.1 & GENPRU 2.3
The *Society* to calculate the *CRR* (higher of *MCR* and *ECR*) in respect of the *long-term insurance business* of each *member*		GENPRU 2.1 & GENPRU 2.3
Capital resources		
The *Society* and *managing agents* to calculate *capital resources* in accordance with the *rules* and *guidance* in GENPRU		GENPRU 2.2 & GENPRU 2.3
Adequacy of capital resources		

Part II FSA Handbook Materials

Key INSPRU and GENPRU requirements	INSPRU	GENPRU
Managing agents to assess the adequacy of *capital resources* held at *syndicate* level in respect of *insurance business* carried on through each *syndicate* (annual ICA for each *syndicate*)	INSPRU 7.1	
The *Society* to assess the adequacy of *capital resources* available to support each *member's insurance business* (ICA for each *member*), both at *syndicate* level (taking account of *syndicate ICAs*), and as *funds at Lloyd's*	INSPRU 7.1	

8.2 Special provisions for Lloyd's

Management of insurance business

8.2.1 **[R]** Neither the *Society* nor *managing agents* may permit a *member* to carry on any *insurance business* except as a participant on one or more *syndicates*.

Obligations under INSPRU and GENPRU

8.2.2 **[R]** The *Society* must ensure that all participants in the Lloyd's market are made aware of their obligations under INSPRU and GENPRU.

Management of risk

8.2.3 **[R]** The *Society* must establish and maintain systems and controls to enable it appropriately to address the risks to which the Lloyd's market is exposed.

8.2.4 **[R]** The systems and controls in INSPRU 8.2.3 must include systems and controls to enable the *Society* to ensure that any assumptions made in calculating a *member's capital resources* or in determining the individual capital assessment for each *member* are regularly reviewed and that appropriate action is taken if any assumption is no longer valid.

8.2.5 **[R]** The *Society* must take all reasonable steps, including establishing and maintaining adequate systems and controls to enable it:

(1) to manage the risks to which *funds at Lloyd's* and *central assets* are exposed; and
(2) to ensure that *funds at Lloyd's* and *central assets* are adequate to support all *balancing amounts*.

8.2.6 **[R]** A *managing agent* must establish and maintain adequate systems and controls to manage the risks to which the *insurance business* carried on through each *syndicate* it manages is exposed.

8.2.7 **[G]** In complying with INSPRU 8.2.6R, *managing agents* should have particular regard to:

(1) transactions which may give rise to a conflict of interest, such as those to which the *counterparties* are:
    (a) other members of the *managing agent's* own *group*;
    (b) any *members* of any *syndicates* managed by the *managing agent*; or
    (c) any entity that is part of a *group* to which one or more *members* of any *syndicates* managed by the *managing agent* belong; and
(2) transactions involving:
    (a) the provision of capital;
    (b) the provision of *reinsurance*; or
    (c) the provision of other services.

8.2.8 **[R]** In complying with INSPRU 8.2.6R a *managing agent* need not take account of risks associated with assets that are not *syndicate assets*.

8.2.9 **[R]** The *Society* must take reasonable steps to ensure that systems and controls established and maintained by *managing agents* are adequate to ensure that risks to which the *insurance business* carried on through each *syndicate* is exposed do not have a detrimental effect on *funds at Lloyd's* or *central assets*.

8.2.10 **[G]** *Managing agents* and the *Society* each hold and manage some of the financial resources held to support the *insurance business* carried on through *syndicates*. In particular:

(1) the *Society* holds and manages *funds at Lloyd's* and *central assets* which must be held to support *balancing amounts*. The *Society* is required to manage the risks that affect *funds at Lloyd's* and *central assets* directly, once the effects of any aggregation and diversification have been taken into account;
(2) *managing agents* hold and manage some of the financial resources in respect of the *insurance business* carried on through each *syndicate* that they manage. *Managing agents* are required to manage all risks affecting a *syndicate* except for the risk that *funds at Lloyd's* and *central assets* are not available to support the *balancing amount*.

8.2.11 **[R]** The *Society* must establish and maintain effective arrangements to monitor and manage risk arising from:
(1) conflicts of interest (including in relation to (2) to (4));
(2) inter-*syndicate* transactions, including *reinsurance to close* and *approved reinsurance to close*;
(3) related party transactions; and
(4) transactions between *members* and itself.

8.2.12 **[R]** The arrangements in INSPRU 8.2.11R must enable the *Society* to identify any significant overstatement of financial resources resulting from any transaction falling within INSPRU 8.2.11R(2) to INSPRU 8.2.11R(4), including as a result of:
(1) any differences in the amounts recorded as due or payable by each party to any such transaction; or
(2) any actual or likely disputes between the parties to any such transaction.

8.2.13 **[R]** If the *Society* identifies a significant overstatement of the kind referred to in INSPRU 8.2.12R, it must ensure that an appropriate adjustment is made, including if appropriate by a deduction from or reduction in the value attributed to:
(1) the *capital resources* of any *member* concerned; or
(2) the *Society*'s *capital resources*.

Approved reinsurance to close

8.2.14 **[G]** As defined in the *Glossary*, "approved reinsurance to close" excludes:
(1) *reinsurance* between parties other than *members*; and
(2) balance transfers between *syndicate years* of *syndicates* having only one *member*, which have no effect on the overall liabilities of that *member*.

8.2.15 **[G]** The "approved" status of an *approved reinsurance to close* does not alter the legal status or effect of the original *contract of insurance*, or the liability of a reinsured *member* to the *policyholder* under or in respect of the original *contract of insurance*.

8.2.16 **[R]** Notwithstanding that the liability of a reinsured *member* to a *policyholder* is unaffected by an *approved reinsurance to close* as described in INSPRU 8.2.15G, for the purposes of INSPRU and GENPRU only:
(1) for an *approved reinsurance to close* which is not to a *subsidiary* of the *Society*:
 (a) a *contract of insurance* reinsured under an *approved reinsurance to close* must be treated as if the reinsuring *member* and not the reinsured *member* had effected the original *contract of insurance*; and
 (b) any payment received by a *member* as consideration for or in connection with an *approved reinsurance to close* must be treated as a *Lloyd's member's contribution* and not as *premium* or as a reinsurance recovery;
(2) for an *approved reinsurance to close* to a *subsidiary* of the *Society*, a *contract of insurance* reinsured under that *approved reinsurance to close* must be treated as if the reinsured *member* had not effected the original *contract of insurance* but:
 (a) for the purposes of the calculation of the *Society GICR*, *general insurance business* carried on by *members* and *former underwriting members* which has been reinsured to a *subsidiary* of the *Society* under an *approved reinsurance to* close must be treated as reinsured to a third party; and
 (b) for the purposes of the calculation of the *capital resources requirement* of a *subsidiary* of the *Society*, the *approved reinsurance to close* must be treated as a *reinsurance*.

Provision of information by managing agents

8.2.17 **[R]** A *managing agent* must, as soon as possible, give the *Society* any information the *managing agent* has concerning material risks to *funds at Lloyd's* or *central assets*.

8.2.18 **[R]** A *managing agent* need not comply with INSPRU 8.2.17R if the *managing agent* knows that the *Society* already has the relevant information.

Insurance receivables to be carried to trust funds

8.2.19 **[R]** The *Society* must take all reasonable steps to ensure that each *member*:
(1) executes the appropriate *Lloyd's trust deeds*; and
(2) carries to the appropriate *Lloyd's trust fund* all amounts received or receivable by the *member*, or on its behalf, in respect of any *insurance business* carried on by it.

8.2.20 **[R]** The *Society* must carry all amounts it receives on behalf of any *member* in respect of that *member*'s *insurance business* to the appropriate *Lloyd's trust fund*.

8.2.21 **[R]** A *managing agent* must carry all amounts it receives on behalf of any *member* in respect of that *member*'s *insurance business* to the appropriate *Lloyd's trust fund*.

8.2.22 **[R]** In complying with INSPRU 8.2.19R to INSPRU 8.2.21R, the *Society* and *managing agents* must take all reasonable steps to ensure that amounts received or receivable by a *member* in respect of *general insurance business* and *long-term insurance business* are carried to separate *Lloyd's trust funds*.

Amendments to byelaws, trust deeds and standard form letters of credit and guarantees

8.2.23 **[R]** The *Society* must, as soon as it is practical to do so, notify the *FSA* of its intention to approve the form of any new *Lloyd's trust deed*.

8.2.24 **[R]** The *Society* must, as soon as it is practical to do so, notify the *FSA* of its intention to make any amendment which may alter the meaning or effect of any *byelaw*, including:
(1) any *Lloyd's trust deed*;
(2) any standard form letter of credit prescribed by the *Society* from time to time; or
(3) any standard form guarantee agreement prescribed by the *Society* from time to time.

8.2.25 **[R]** The *Society* must provide the *FSA* with full details of:
(1) the form of any new *Lloyd's trust deed* it intends to approve, as described in INSPRU 8.2.23R and
(2) any amendments falling within INSPRU 8.2.24R.

8.2.26 **[R]** The *Society* must consult interested parties in relation to any new *Lloyd's trust deed* and in relation to any amendment falling within INSPRU 8.2.24R.

8.2.27 **[G]** Except in urgent cases, the *Society* should consult in relation to any new *Lloyd's trust deed* or amendments before the new deed or amendments take effect.

8.2.28 **[R]** The information provided to the *FSA* by the *Society* under INSPRU 8.2.25R must include:
(1) a statement of the purpose of any proposed amendment or new *Lloyd's trust deed* and the expected impact, if any, on *policyholders*, *managing agent*s, *members*, and potential *members*; and
(2) a description of the consultation undertaken under INSPRU 8.2.26R including a summary of any significant responses to that consultation.

8.2.29 **[G]** The *FSA* would normally expect to receive the information required under INSPRU 8.2.25R and INSPRU 8.2.28R not less than three months in advance of the proposed change.

8.3 The Central Fund

Application

8.3.1 **[R]** This section applies to the *Society*.

Purpose

8.3.2 **[G]** The *rules* and *guidance* in this section are intended to promote confidence in the market at Lloyd's, and to protect certain *consumers* of services provided by the *Society* in carrying on, or in connection with or for the purposes of, its *regulated activities*. They do this by:
(1) giving guidance to the *Society* about the protection that the *Central Fund* should provide for policyholders; and
(2) enabling the *FSA* to keep under review the protection the *Central Fund* provides for policyholders.

Enabling Provision

8.3.3 **[D]** The directions in this section are given under section 318 of the *Act* (Exercise of powers through Council) for the purpose of achieving the objective specified, as required by section 318(2) of the *Act*.

8.3.4 **[D]** The directions given in this section are given in relation to the exercise of the powers by the *Society* in respect of the *Central Fund* and are given with a view to achieving the objective of ensuring that the *Society* in making payments or in providing any other financial assistance from the *Central Fund* does so on a basis which takes no account of amounts of compensation which policyholders may receive under the provisions of the *compensation scheme* in respect of *protected claims* against *members*.

8.3.5 **[G]** The *Society* should seek to ensure that the *Central Fund* provides protection for policyholders so as to minimise the need for Lloyd's policyholders to have recourse to the *compensation scheme*.

8.3.6 **[G]** The *Society* should seek, and take appropriate account of, the *FSA's* views on all proposed changes in its arrangements relating to the *Central Fund*.

8.3.7 **[D]** The *Society* must, in the exercise of its powers to make payments from the *Central Fund* or to provide other forms of financial assistance from the *Central Fund*, ensure that in calculating and determining the amount of any such payment or the amount of any other financial assistance, it takes no account of the amounts of compensation which policyholders may receive under the provisions of the compensation scheme in respect of protected claims against *members*.

8.4 Capacity Transfer Market

Application

8.4.1 **[R]** This section applies to the *Society*.

Purpose

8.4.2 **[G]** The *rules* and *guidance* in this section are intended to promote confidence in the market at Lloyd's, and to protect certain *consumers* of services provided by the *Society* in carrying on, or in connection with or for the purposes of, its *regulated activities*. They do this by ensuring that the *Society* appropriately and effectively regulates the *capacity transfer market* so that it operates in a fair and transparent manner.

Requirement to make byelaws governing conduct in the capacity transfer market

8.4.3 **[R]** The *Society* must make appropriate *byelaws* governing conduct in the *capacity transfer market*.

8.4.4 **[G]** The *byelaws* referred to in INSPRU 8.4.3R should:
(1) ensure that adequate and effective arrangements are in place to enable *members* and *persons* applying to be admitted as *members* to enter into transactions to transfer *syndicate* capacity and settle these transactions in a timely manner;
(2) give clear and comprehensive guidance about the dissemination of information that is, or may be, relevant to the price of *syndicate* capacity and the transparency of the *capacity transfer market*; and
(3) prohibit unfair and abusive practices (including market manipulation), the misuse of information not generally available, and the dissemination of false or misleading information.

8.4.5 **[G]** The *Society* should have adequate and effective arrangements to:
(1) record and monitor transactions in the *capacity transfer market*, and maintain adequate audit trails; and
(2) suspend or annul transactions where appropriate.

8.4.6 **[G]** The *Society* should regularly review the *byelaws* referred to in INSPRU 8.4.3R, taking account of the standards of conduct required in other *UK* financial markets.

8.4.7 **[G]** The *Society* should consult *members* and *underwriting agents* before it finalises material changes in the *byelaws* referred to in INSPRU 8.4.3R, and should have timely and effective arrangements for notifying them of changes in these *byelaws*.

8.5 Former underwriting members

Application

8.5.1 **[R]** This section applies to the *Society*.

8.5.2 **[G]** The *rules* and *guidance* in this section are intended to promote confidence in the market at Lloyd's and to protect certain *consumers* of services provided by the *Society* in carrying on or in connection with or for the purposes of its *regulated activities* by:
(1) protecting policyholders against the risk that *former underwriting members* may not be able to meet any liabilities to carry out *contracts of insurance* that they underwrote at Lloyd's; and
(2) enabling the *FSA* to impose requirements under section 320(3) of the *Act* (Former underwriting members) if it considers this appropriate to protect policyholders.

Requirements relating to former underwriting members

8.5.3 **[R]** The *Society* must draw sections 320 to 322 of the *Act* (Former underwriting members, Requirements imposed under section 320, Rules applicable to former underwriting members) to the attention of any *person* ceasing to be an *underwriting member* on or after *commencement*.

8.5.4 **[R]** The *Society* must require any *person*, other than a *body corporate*, ceasing to be an *underwriting member* on or after *commencement* to:
(1) notify the *Society* of any change in his address within one month of the change;
(2) in the case of a natural person, to make arrangements for the *Society* to be notified in the event of his death.

8.6 Prudential risk management and associated systems and controls

Application of SYSC 14

8.6.1 **[R]** Subject to INSPRU 8.6.2R, SYSC 14 (Prudential risk management and associated systems and controls) applies to *managing agents* and to the *Society* in accordance with:
(1) for *managing agents*, INSPRU 8.1.4R; and
(2) for the *Society*, INSPRU 8.1.2R.

8.6.2 **[R]** The requirement in SYSC 14.1.18R to take reasonable steps to ensure the establishment and maintenance of a business plan does not apply to the *Society*.

Application of SYSC 11, 15 and 16

8.6.3 **[R]** Subject to INSPRU 8.6.5R, SYSC 11 (Liquidity risk management systems and controls), SYSC 15 (Credit risk management systems and controls) and SYSC 16 (Market risk management systems and controls) apply to *managing agents* and to the *Society* in accordance with:
(1) for *managing agents*, INSPRU 8.1.4R; and
(2) for the *Society*, INSPRU 8.1.2R

Application of SYSC 17

8.6.4 **[R]** Subject to INSPRU 8.6.5R, SYSC 17 (Insurance risk systems and controls) applies to *managing agents* in accordance with INSPRU 8.1.4R.

8.6.5 **[R]** In accordance with INSPRU 8.6.2R, the *rules* and *guidance* in SYSC 11, SYSC 15, SYSC 16 and SYSC 17 relating to the establishment and maintenance of a business plan do not apply to the *Society*.

CHAPTER 9

9.1 Actions for damages

[2073]
9.1.1 **[R]** A contravention of the *rules* in INSPRU does not give rise to a right of action by a *private person* under section 150 of the *Act* (and each of those *rules* is specified under section 150(2) of the *Act* as a provision giving rise to no such right of action).

TRANSITIONAL PROVISIONS

1 IPRU waivers

Application

[2074]
1.1 **[R]** INSPRU TP 1 applies to an *insurer* unless it is:
(1) a *non-directive friendly society*; or
(2) an *incoming EEA firm*; or
(3) an *incoming Treaty firm*.

Version of IPRU to be used

1.2 **[R]** Any reference in INSPRU TP to IPRU (INS) is to the version in force on 30 December 2004.

Duration of transitional

1.3 **[R]** INSPRU TP 1 applies until the relevant *rule* is revoked.

Continuing effect of waivers

1.4 **[R]** A *rule* in INSPRU listed in the Table at INSPRU TP Table 2 is disapplied, or is modified in its application, to a *firm*:
(1) in order to produce the same effect, including any conditions, as a *waiver* had on the corresponding *rule* in IPRU (INS);
(2) for the same period as the *waiver* would have lasted, if shorter than the period in INSPRU TP 1.3;

provided the conditions set out in INSPRU TP 1.5 are satisfied.

1.5 **[R]** The conditions referred to in INSPRU TP 1.4 are:
(1) the *rule* is shown in the Table at INSPRU TP Table 2 as corresponding with the *rule* in IPRU (INS) in relation to which the *waiver* was granted to the *firm*;
(2) the *waiver* was current as respects the *firm* immediately before 31 December 2004; and
(3) there is no specific transitional *rule* relating to the *waiver*.

1.6 **[R]** INSPRU TP 1.4 does not have effect if, and to the extent that, it would be inconsistent with any *EU* law obligation of the *United Kingdom*.

1.7 **[R]** A *firm* which has the benefit of a *waiver* to which INSPRU TP 1.4 applies must:
(1) notify the *FSA* immediately if it becomes aware of any matter which is material to the relevance or appropriateness of the *waiver*;
(2) maintain a written record of the *rule* in INSPRU to which it considers the *waiver* applies; and
(3) make the record available to the *FSA* on request.

INSPRU TP Table 2

Rules in INSPRU	Corresponding rules in IPRU (INS)
2.1.22	4.14(1)
3.1.34	5.11
3.1.39	5.11 5.11(4) 5.11(5) 5.11(9) 5.11(11)
3.1.58	2.3(2)
1.1.51	2.4(6)
1.1.56	2.4(1)
1.1.66	Appendix 2.1 2.4(1)(b) Appendix 2.2 2.4(1)(b) 5.9(1)
1.2.40	5.9(2)
1.2.41	5.9(2)
1.2.43	5.10
1.2.74	5.16
6.1.17	10.1 10.2 10.2(1) 10.2(2) 10.2(3)
6.1.23	10.2 10.2(1) 10.2(2) 10.2(3)

3 PRU waivers

Application

3.1 **[R]** INSPRU TP 3 applies to an *insurer* unless it is:
(1) a *non-directive friendly society*; or
(2) an *incoming EEA firm*; or
(3) an *incoming Treaty firm*.

Version of PRU to be used

3.2 **[R]** A reference in INSPRU TP 3 to *PRU* is to the version in force on 30 December 2006.

Duration of transitional

3.3 **[R]** INSPRU TP 3 applies until the relevant INSPRU *rule* is revoked.

Continuing effect of waivers

3.4 **[R]** A *rule* in INSPRU is disapplied, or is modified in its application, to a *firm*:
(1) in order to produce the same effect, including any conditions, as a *waiver* had on the *rule* in *PRU*;

(2) for the same period as the *waiver* would have lasted, if shorter than the period in INSPRU TP 3.3;

provided the conditions set out in INSPRU TP 3.5 are satisfied.

3.5 **[R]** The conditions referred to in INSPRU TP 3.4 are:
(1) the *rule* in *PRU* in relation to which the *waiver* was granted to the *firm* was redesignated as the relevant *rule* in INSPRU by the Prudential Sourcebook for Insurers Instrument 2006;
(2) the *waiver* was current as respects the *firm* immediately before 31 December 2006; and
(3) there is no specific transitional *rule* relating to the *waiver*.

3.6 **[R]** INSPRU TP 3.4 does not have effect if, and to the extent that, it would be inconsistent with any *EU* law obligation of the *United Kingdom*.

3.7 **[R]** A *firm* which has the benefit of a *waiver* to which INSPRU TP 3.4 applies must:
(1) notify the *FSA* immediately if it becomes aware of any matter which is material to the relevance or appropriateness of the *waiver*;
(2) maintain a written record of the *rule* in INSPRU to which it considers the *waiver* applies; and
(3) make the record available to the *FSA* on request.

4 EEA pure reinsurers

Application

4.1 **[R]** INSPRU TP 4 applies to a *pure reinsurer*:
(1) whose head office is in an *EEA State* other than the *United Kingdom*; and
(2) which is not an *incoming Treaty firm*.

Duration of transitional

4.2 **[R]** INSPRU TP 4 has effect in relation to a *firm* until 10 December 2008 or, if earlier, the date on which it becomes:
(1) an *incoming EEA firm* by reason of having exercised its right to carry on the *regulated activity* of *effecting* or *carrying out contracts of insurance* in the *United Kingdom* in accordance with Schedule 3 to the *Act* (EEA Passport Rights); or
(2) an *incoming Treaty firm* by reason of having exercised its right to carry on the *regulated activity* of *effecting* or *carrying out contracts of insurance* in the *United Kingdom* in accordance with Schedule 4 to the *Act* (Treaty Rights).

50% premiums and claims uplift for classes 11, 12 and 13; credit equalisation provision

4.3 **[R]** The following *rules* or paragraphs of a *rule* do not apply to a *firm*:
(1) INSPRU 1.1.56R(1);
(2) INSPRU 1.1.60R(1); and
(3) INSPRU 1.4.39R to INSPRU 1.4.46R.

5 Pure reinsurance groups

Application

5.1 **[R]** INSPRU TP 5 applies to a *pure reinsurer* whose *ultimate EEA insurance parent undertaking* is the *parent undertaking* of a *group* comprised solely of *reinsurance undertakings*.

Duration of transitional

5.2 **[R]** INSPRU TP 5 applies until 10 December 2007.

Group capital resources requirement

5.3 **[R]** A *firm* need not comply with INSPRU 6.1.15R.

6 Admissible assets

Application

6.1 **[R]** INSPRU TP 6 applies to an *insurer* which is not a *pure reinsurer*.

Duration of transitional

6.2 **[R]** INSPRU TP 6 applies until 30 December 2007.

GENPRU 2 Annex 7R

6.3 **[R]**

(1) In determining whether its assets are *admissible assets*, instead of applying GENPRU 2 Annex 7R, a *firm* may elect to treat as an *admissible asset* an asset that would have been an *admissible asset* for the purposes of the Integrated Prudential Sourcebook (PRU) as it was in force on 30 December 2006.

(2) (1) does not apply when determining whether a *derivative* or *quasiderivative* is an *approved derivative* or *approved quasi-derivative*.

(3) If a *firm* applies (1) to any of its assets, it must do so for all of its assets except *derivatives* and *quasi-derivatives*.

SCHEDULE 1
RECORD KEEPING REQUIREMENTS

[2075]

Sch 1 **[G]**

(1) The aim of the *guidance* in the following table is to give the reader a quick overall view of the relevant record keeping requirements.

(2) It is not a complete statement of those requirements and should not be relied on as if it were.

(3) Table

Handbook reference	Subject of Record	Contents of Record	When record must be made	Retention Period
INSPRU 1.2.20R	*Mathematical reserves*	(1) The methods and assumptions used in establishing the *firm's mathematical reserves*, including the margins for adverse deviation, and the reasons for their use (2) The nature of, reasons for, and effect of, any change in approach, including the amount by which the change in approach increases or decreases its *mathematical reserves*	Not specified	An appropriate period
INSPRU 1.3.17R, INSPRU 1.3.19R	Calculation of *with- profits insurance capital component*	(1) The methods and assumptions used in making any calculation required for the purposes of INSPRU 1.3 (and any subsequent changes) and the reasons for their use (2) Any change in practice (in particular changes in those items which will or may be significant in relation to the eventual *claim* values) and the nature of, reasons for, and effect of, any change in approach with respect to those methods and assumptions	Not specified	An appropriate period
INSPRU 1.5.23R	*Long-term insurance funds*	A separate accounting record in respect of each of a *firm's long-term insurance funds*	Not specified	Not specified

Part II FSA Handbook Materials

Handbook reference	Subject of Record	Contents of Record	When record must be made	Retention Period
INSPRU 1.5.56R, INSPRU 1.5.57R	*Branch* accounting records in the *United Kingdom*	A record of the activities carried on from a *non-EEA direct insurer's United Kingdom branch* and, if it is an *EEA-deposit insurer*, from its *branches* in other *EEA states* including a record of: (1) the income, expenditure and liabilities arising from activities of the *branch* or *branches* (2) the assets identified under INSPRU 1.1.20R as available to meet those liabilities	Not specified	Not specified

SCHEDULE 2
NOTIFICATION AND REPORTING REQUIREMENTS

[2076]
Sch 2 **[G]**
(1) The aim of the *guidance* in the following table is to give the reader a quick overall view of the relevant notification requirements.
(2) It is not a complete statement of those requirements and should not be relied on as if it were.
(3) Table

Handbook reference	Matter to be notified	Contents of notification	Trigger event	Time allowed
INSPRU 2.1.23R	That a *reinsurance* exposure to a *reinsurer* or group of closely related *reinsurers* is reasonably likely to exceed, or has exceeded, 100% of the *firm's capital resources* excluding *capital resources* held to cover *property- linked liabilities*	Fact that the limit is reasonably likely to be, or has been, exceeded Note: upon notification under INSPRU 2.1.23R the *firm* must (1) demonstrate that prudent provision has been made for the *reinsurance* exposure in excess of the 100% limit, or explain why in the opinion if the *firm* no provision is required, and (2) explain how the *reinsurance* exposure is being safely managed (see INSPRU 2.1.24R)	(1) A reasonable likelihood that the limit will be exceeded, or (2) if (1) does not apply, the limit being exceeded	As soon as the *firm* first becomes aware of the matter required to be notified

Handbook reference	**Matter to be notified**	**Contents of notification**	**Trigger event**	**Time allowed**
INSPRU 2.1.29R	That the *firm* has exceeded, or anticipates exceeding, the limit expressed in INSPRU 2.1.28E (in each *financial year* a *firm* should restrict the *gross earned premiums* which it pays to a *reinsurer* or group of closely related *reinsurers* to the higher of (a) 20% of the *firm's* projected *gross earned premiums* for that *financial year* and (b) £4 million)	Fact that the limit has been exceeded, or that the *firm* anticipates exceeding the limit Note: upon notification under INSPRU 2.1.29R the *firm* must explain to the *FSA* how, despite the excess *reinsurance* concentration, the credit risk is being safely managed (see INSPRU 2.1.30R)	The limit being exceeded, or an anticipation that the limit will be exceeded	Immediately
INSPRU 3.1.65R	*Syndicate* liabilities not covered by matching *syndicate assets* as required by INSPRU 3.1.53R	Nature and extent of *syndicate* liabilities not covered by matching *syndicate assets* as required by INSPRU 3.1.53R	*Syndicate* liabilities are no longer covered by matching *syndicate assets* as required by INSPRU 3.1.53R	Immediately
INSPRU 7.1.83R	*Syndicate ICA* and *balancing amount* in respect of each *syndicate*	*Syndicate ICA* and *balancing amount* in respect of each *syndicate*	Notification should be made periodically	As part of the annual capital-setting process, in good time for the *Society* to review and place appropriate reliance on them when determining capital assessments for each *member*

Handbook reference	Matter to be notified	Contents of notification	Trigger event	Time allowed
INSPRU 7.1.89R	Significant doubt about the adequacy of a *syndicate ICA* or *balancing amount* with respect to *syndicate* risks and controls	Revised *syndicate ICA* and *balancing amount*	The *managing agent* considers that *syndicate ICA* and *balancing amount* communicated in the capital setting process are no longer adequate in the light of the risks to which the *syndicate* business is exposed	Immediately
INSPRU 8.2.17R	Information the *managing agent* has concerning material risks to *funds at Lloyd's* or *central assets*	All information concerning relevant risk	Receipt of information	As soon as possible
INSPRU 8.2.23R	Intention to approve the form of any new *Lloyd's trust deed*	Fact of intention	Intention to approve	As soon as practical
INSPRU 8.2.24R	Intention to make any amendment which may alter the meaning or effect of any *byelaw* (including *Lloyd's trust deeds*, standard form letters of credit and guarantees)	Fact of intention	Intention to amend	As soon as practical
INSPRU 8.2.25R	Full details of form of new *Lloyd's trust deed* or amendments to *byelaw* (including *Lloyd's trust deeds*, standard form letters of credit and guarantees)	(1) Statement of purpose of amendment or new form and expected impact, if any, on *policyholders*, *managing agents*, *members* and potential *members*, and (2) Description of the consultation undertaken and summary of significant responses to consultation	Not specified	Normally not less than three months in advance of proposed change

SCHEDULE 3
FEES AND OTHER REQUIREMENT PAYMENTS

[2077]

Sch 3 **[G]** There are no requirements for fees or other payments in INSPRU.

SCHEDULE 4
POWERS EXERCISED

[2078]

Sch 4 **[G]**

(1) The following powers and related provisions in the *Act* have been exercised by the *FSA* to make the rules in INSPRU:
  (1) section 138 (General rule-making power);
  (2) section 141 (Insurance business rules);

(3) section 149 (Evidential provisions);
(4) section 150(2) (Actions for damages);
(5) section 156 (General supplementary powers;
(6) section 316(1) (Direction by Authority); and
(7) section 318(1) (Exercise of powers through Council)

(2) The following power in the *Act* has been exercised by the *FSA* to give *guidance* in INSPRU:
(1) section 157(1) (Guidance).

SCHEDULE 5
RIGHTS OF ACTION FOR DAMAGES

[2079]
Sch 5 **[G]**

(1) The table below sets out the *rules* in INSPRU contravention of which by an *authorised person* may be actionable under section 150 of the *Act* (Actions for damages) by a *person* who suffers loss as a result of the contravention.

(2) If a "Yes" appears in the column headed "For *private person*", the *rule* may be actionable by a *private person* under section 150 (or, in certain circumstances, his fiduciary or representative; see article 6(2) and (3)(c) of the Financial Services and Markets Act 2000 (Rights of Action) Regulations 2001 (SI 2001/2256)). A "Yes" in the column headed "Removed" indicates that the *FSA* has removed the right of action under section 150(2) of the *Act*. If so, a reference to the *rule* in which it is removed is also given.

(3) The column headed "For other *person*" indicates whether the *rule* may be actionable by a *person* other than a *private person* (or his fiduciary or representative) under article 6(2) and (3) of those Regulations. If so, an indication of the type of *person* by whom the *rule* may be actionable is given.

Chapter/ Appendix	**Section/ Annex**	**Right of action under section 150**		
		For *private person*	**Removed**	**For other *person***
All *rules* in INSPRU		No	Yes (INSPRU 9.1.1R)	No

Part II FSA Handbook Materials

SCHEDULE 6
RULES THAT CAN BE WAIVED

[2080]
Sch 6 **[G]** The rules in INSPRU can be waived by the *FSA* under section 148 of the *Act* (Modification or waiver of rules), except for INSPRU 9.1.1R (Actions for damages). However, if the *rules* incorporate requirements laid down in European directives, it will not be possible for the *FSA* to grant a *waiver* that would be incompatible with the *United Kingdom's* responsibilities under those directives. It therefore follows that if a *rule* in INSPRU contains provisions which derive partly from a directive, and partly not, the *FSA* will be able to consider a *waiver* of the latter requirements only, unless the directive provisions are optional rather than mandatory.

PRUDENTIAL SOURCEBOOK FOR MORTGAGE AND HOME FINANCE FIRMS, AND INSURANCE INTERMEDIARIES (MIPRU)

NOTES

Up to date as at 22 February 2010. For later amendments please see www.fsa.gov.uk.

CONTENTS

MIPRU 1—Application and general provisions . . . . [2081]
MIPRU 2—Insurance mediation activity: responsibility, knowledge, ability and good repute . . . . [2082]
MIPRU 3—Professional indemnity insurance . . . . [2083]
MIPRU 4—Capital resources . . . . [2084]
MIPRU 5—Insurance undertakings and mortgage lenders using insurance or mortgage mediation services . . . . [2085]
MIPRU TP—Transitional Provisions . . . . [2086]
MIPRU—Schedules
Schedule 1—Record keeping requirements . . . . [2087]
Schedule 2—Notification requirements . . . . [2088]
Schedule 3—Fees and other required payments . . . . [2089]
Schedule 4—Powers exercised . . . . [2090]
Schedule 5—Rights of actions for damages . . . . [2091]
Schedule 6—Rules that can be waived . . . . [2092]

Part II FSA Handbook Materials

CHAPTER 1
APPLICATION AND GENERAL PROVISIONS

1.1 Application

[2081]

1.1.1 **[G]** This sourcebook applies to a *firm* with *Part IV permission* to carry on:

(1) *insurance mediation activity*;
(2) *home finance mediation activity*;
(3) *home financing*;
(4) *home finance administration*; and
(5) *insurance business*;

as specified in the beginning of each of the remaining chapters.

1.2 Actions for damages

1.2.1 **[R]** A contravention of the *rules* in this sourcebook does not give rise to a right of action by a *private person* under section 150 of the *Act* (and each of those *rules* is specified under section 150(2) of the *Act* as a provision giving rise to no such right of action).

CHAPTER 2
INSURANCE MEDIATION ACTIVITY: RESPONSIBILITY, KNOWLEDGE, ABILITY AND GOOD REPUTE

2.1 Application and purpose

Application

[2082]

2.1.1 **[R]** This chapter applies to a *firm* with *Part IV permission* to carry on *insurance mediation activity*.

Purpose

2.1.2 **[G]** The main purpose of this chapter is to implement, in part, the provisions of the *Insurance Mediation Directive* as these apply to *firms* regulated by the *FSA*.

2.2 Allocation of the responsibility for insurance mediation activity

Responsibility for insurance mediation activity

2.2.1 **[R]** A *firm*, other than a sole trader, must allocate the responsibility for the *firm's insurance mediation activity* to a director or senior manager.

[**Note**: Article 3(1), fourth paragraph, of the *IMD*]

2.2.2 **[R]** The *firm* may allocate the responsibility for its *insurance mediation activity* to an *approved person* (or *persons*) performing:
(1) a *governing function* (other than the *non-executive director function*); or
(2) the *apportionment and oversight function*; or
(3) the *significant management function* in so far as it relates to *dealing in investments as principal*, disregarding article 15 of the *Regulated Activities Order* (Absence of holding out etc) (or *agreeing* to do so) or an activity which is not *designated investment business*.

2.2.3 **[G]**
(1) Typically a *firm* will appoint a *person* performing a *governing function* (other than the *non-executive director function*) to direct its *insurance mediation activity*. Where this responsibility is allocated to a *person* performing another function, the *person* performing the *apportionment and oversight function* with responsibility for the apportionment of responsibilities must ensure that responsibility for the *firm's insurance mediation activity* is appropriately allocated.
(2) The descriptions of *significant influence functions*, other than the *required functions*, do not extend to activities carried on by an *insurance intermediary* with *permission* only to carry on *insurance mediation activity* and whose principal purpose is to carry on activities other than *regulated activities* (see SUP 10.1.21R). In this case, the *firm* may allocate the responsibility for the *firm's insurance mediation activity* to one or more of the *persons* performing the *apportionment and oversight function* who will be required to be an *approved person*.
(3) In the case of a *sole trader*, the *sole trader* will be responsible for the *firm's insurance mediation activity*.

2.2.4 **[G]** Where a *firm* has appointed an *appointed representative* to carry on *insurance mediation activity* on its behalf, the *person* responsible for the *firm's insurance mediation activity* will also be responsible for the *insurance mediation activity* carried on by an *appointed representative*.

2.2.5 **[G]** The *FSA* will specify in the *FSA Register* the name of the *persons* to whom the responsibility for the *firm's insurance mediation activity* has been allocated by inserting after the relevant *controlled function* the words "(insurance mediation)". In the case of a *sole trader*, the *FSA* will specify in the *FSA Register* the name of the *sole trader* as the 'contact person' in the *firm*.

2.3 Knowledge, ability and good repute

2.3.1 **[R]** A *firm* (other than a *connected travel insurance intermediary*) must establish on reasonable grounds that:
(1) a reasonable proportion of the *persons* within its management structure who are responsible for *insurance mediation activity*; and
(2) all other *persons* directly involved in its *insurance mediation activity*; demonstrate the knowledge and ability necessary for the performance of their duties; and
(3) all the *persons* in its management structure and any staff directly involved in *insurance mediation activity* are of good repute.

[**Note**: Article 4(1) and (2) of the *IMD*]

2.3.2 **[G]** In determining a *person's* knowledge and ability, the *firm* should have regard to matters including, but not limited to, whether the *person*:
(1) has demonstrated by experience and training that he is able or will be able, to perform his duties related to the *firm's insurance mediation activity*; and
(2) satisfies the relevant requirements in the *FSA's* Training and Competence sourcebook and the Senior Management Arrangements, Systems and Controls sourcebook.

2.3.3 **[R]** In considering a *person's* repute, the *firm* must ensure that the *person*:
(1) has not been convicted of any serious criminal offences linked to crimes against property or other crimes related to financial activities (other than spent convictions under the Rehabilitation of Offenders Act 1974 or any other national equivalent); and
(2) has not been adjudged bankrupt (unless the bankruptcy has been discharged);

under the law of any part of the *United Kingdom* or under the law of a country or territory outside the *United Kingdom*.

[**Note**: Article 4(2) of the *IMD*]

2.3.4 **[G]** The *firm* should give particular consideration to offences of dishonesty, fraud, financial crime or other offences under legislation relating to banking and financial services, companies, insurance and consumer protection.

2.3.5 **[G]** **Firms** are reminded that *Principle* 3 requires *firms* to take reasonable care to organise and control their affairs responsibly and effectively. *Principle* 3 is amplified by the *rule* which requires *firms* to take reasonable care to establish and maintain such systems and controls as are appropriate to its business (SYSC 3.1.1R and SYSC 4.1.1R). A *firm's* systems and controls should enable it to satisfy itself of the suitability of anyone who acts for it (SYSC 3.2.13G and SYSC 5.1.2G). This includes the assessment of an individual's honesty and competence. In addition, the *competent employees rule* (SYSC 3.1.6R and SYSC 5.1.1R) sets out a high-level competence requirement which every *firm* should follow.

CHAPTER 3
PROFESSIONAL INDEMNITY INSURANCE

3.1 Application and purpose

Application

[2083]

3.1.1 **[R]** This chapter applies to a *firm* with *Part IV permission* to carry on any of the following activities:

(1) *insurance mediation activity*;

(2) *home finance mediation activity*; unless any of the following exemptions apply:

(3) in relation to *insurance mediation activity*, this chapter does not apply to a *firm* if another *authorised person* which has net tangible assets of more than £10 million provides a comparable guarantee; for this purpose:
   - (a) if the *firm* is a member of a *group* in which there is an *authorised person* with net tangible assets of more than £10 million, the comparable guarantee must be from that *person*;
   - (b) a 'comparable guarantee' means a written agreement on terms at least equal to those in a contract of professional indemnity insurance (see MIPRU 3.2.4R) to finance the claims that might arise as a result of a breach by the *firm* of its duties under the *regulatory system* or civil law;

(4) in relation to *home finance mediation activity*, this chapter does not apply to a *firm* if:
   - (a) it has net tangible assets of more than £1 million; or
   - (b) the comparable guarantee provisions of (3) apply (as if the *firm* was carrying on *insurance mediation activity*) but substituting £1 million for £10 million in (3)(a) and (b);

(5) this chapter does not apply to:
   - (a) an *insurer*; or
   - (b) a *managing agent*; or
   - (c) a *firm* to which IPRU(INV) 13.1.4(1) (Financial resource requirements for personal investment firms: requirement to hold professional indemnity insurance) applies; or
   - (d) an *exempt CAD firm* to which IPRU(INV) 9.2.5R (Initial capital and professional indemnity insurance requirements – exempt CAD firms that are also IMD insurance intermediaries) applies.

(6) in relation to *home finance mediation activity*, this chapter does not apply to an *authorised professional firm*:
   - (a) that is required by another *rule* to hold professional indemnity insurance (see IPRU(INV) 2.3.1R); and
   - (b) whose *home finance mediation activity* is incidental to its main business.

3.1.2 **[G]** The definition of *insurance mediation activity* is any of several activities 'in relation to a *contract of insurance*' which includes a contract of reinsurance. This chapter, therefore, applies to a reinsurance intermediary in the same way as it applies to any other *insurance intermediary*.

Purpose

3.1.3 **[G]** The purposes of this chapter are to:

(1) implement article 4.3 of the *Insurance Mediation Directive* in so far as it requires *insurance intermediaries* to hold professional indemnity insurance, or some other comparable guarantee, against any liability that might arise from professional negligence; and

(2) meet the *regulatory objectives* of consumer protection and maintaining market confidence by ensuring that *firms* have adequate resources to protect themselves, and their *customers*, against losses arising from breaches in its duties under the *regulatory system* or civil law.

3.1.4 **[G]** Any breach in the duty of a *firm* or of its agents under the *regulatory system* or civil law can give rise to claims being made against the *firm*. Professional indemnity insurance has an important role to play in helping to finance such claims. In so doing, this chapter amplifies *threshold condition* 4 (Adequate resources). This *threshold condition* provides that a *firm* must have, on a continuing basis, resources that are, in the opinion of the *FSA*, adequate in relation to the *regulated activities* that the *firm* carries on.

3.1.5 **[G]** Under *Principles* 3 and 4 a *firm* is required to take reasonable care to organise and control its affairs responsibly and effectively with adequate risk management systems and to maintain adequate financial resources. Under *Principle* 9 a *firm* is obliged to take reasonable care to ensure the suitability of its *advice on investments* and discretionary decisions for any *customer* who is entitled to rely upon its judgement.

3.1.6 **[G]** Although financial resources and appropriate systems and controls can generally mitigate operational risk, professional indemnity insurance has a role in mitigating the risks a *firm* faces in its day to day operations, including those arising from not meeting the legally required standard of care when *advising on investments*. The purpose of this chapter is to ensure that a *firm* has in place the type, and level, of professional indemnity insurance necessary to mitigate these risks.

3.2 Professional indemnity insurance requirements

3.2.1 **[R]** A *firm* must take out and maintain professional indemnity insurance that is at least equal to the requirements of this section from:

(1) an *insurance undertaking* authorised to transact professional indemnity insurance in the *EEA*; or

(2) a *person* of equivalent status in:

 (i) a *Zone A country*; or

 (ii) the Channel Islands, Gibraltar, Bermuda or the Isle of Man.

[**Note**: Article 4(3) of the *IMD*]

3.2.2 **[G]** The minimum *limits of indemnity* for a *firm* whose *Part IV permission* covers both *insurance mediation activity* and *home finance mediation activity* is the higher of the *limits of indemnity* for these activities. If the *firm* opts for a single comparable guarantee to finance the claims which might arise as a result of both activities, the requirements for *insurance mediation activity* apply.

3.2.3 **[G]** A non-*EEA firm* (such as a captive insurance company outside the *EEA*) will be able to provide professional indemnity insurance only if it is authorised to do so in one of the specified countries or territories. The purpose of this provision is to balance the level of protection required for the *policyholder* against a reasonable level of flexibility for the *firm*.

Terms to be incorporated in the insurance

3.2.4 **[R]** The contract of professional indemnity insurance must incorporate terms which make provision for:

(1) cover in respect of claims for which a *firm* may be liable as a result of the conduct of itself, its *employees* and its *appointed representatives* (acting within the scope of their appointment);

(2) the minimum *limits of indemnity* per year set out in this section;

(3) an excess as set out in this section;

(4) appropriate cover in respect of legal defence costs;

(5) continuous cover in respect of claims arising from work carried out from the date on which the *firm* was given *Part IV permission* for the *insurance mediation activity* or *home finance mediation activity* concerned; and

(6) cover in respect of *Ombudsman* awards made against the *firm*.

3.2.5 **[G]** A *firm* is responsible for the conduct of all of its *employees*. The *firm's employees* include, but are not limited to, its *partners*, *directors*, individuals that are self-employed or operating under a contract hire agreement and any other individual that is employed in connection with its business.

3.2.6 **[G]** A *firm* is responsible for the conduct of all of its *appointed representatives*.

Minimum limits of indemnity: insurance intermediary

3.2.7 **[R]** If the *firm* is an *insurance intermediary*, then the minimum *limits of indemnity* are:

(1) for a single claim, €1,120,200; and

(2) in aggregate, €1,680,300 or, if higher, 10% of *annual income* up to £30 million.

[**Note**: Article 4(3) of the *Insurance Mediation Directive*]

3.2.7A **[G]** Article 4(7) of the *Insurance Mediation Directive* requires the *limits of indemnity* to be reviewed every five years to take into account movements in European consumer prices. These limits will therefore be subject to further adjustments on the basis of index movements advised by the European Commission.

3.2.8 **[R]** If a *policy* is denominated in any currency other than euros, a *firm* must take reasonable steps to ensure that the *limits of indemnity* are, when the *policy* is effected and at *renewal*, at least equivalent to those required.

Minimum limits of indemnity: home finance intermediary

3.2.9 **[R]** If the *firm* is a *home finance intermediary*, then the minimum *limit of indemnity* is the higher of 10% of *annual income* up to £1 million, and:

(1) for a single claim, £100,000; or
(2) in aggregate, £500,000.

Excess

3.2.10 **[R]** In this chapter, "*client* assets" includes a *document* only if it has value, or is capable of having value, in itself (such as a bearer instrument).

3.2.11 **[R]** For a *firm* which does not hold *client money* or other *client* assets, the excess must not be more than the higher of:
(1) £2,500; and
(2) 1.5% of *annual income*.

3.2.12 **[R]** For a *firm* which holds *client money* or other *client* assets, the excess must not be more than the higher of:
(1) £5,000; and
(2) 3% of *annual income*.

Policies covering more than one firm

3.2.13 **[R]** If a *policy* provides cover to more than one *firm*, then:
(1) the *limits of indemnity* must be calculated on the combined *annual income* of all the *firms* named in the *policy*; and
(2) each *firm* named in the *policy* must have the benefit of the relevant minimum *limits of indemnity*.

Additional capital

3.2.14 **[R]** If a *firm* seeks to have an excess which is higher than the relevant limit, it must hold additional capital calculated in accordance with the appropriate table below:

Table: Calculation of additional capital for firm not holding client money or other client assets (£000's)

Income		**Excess obtained up to and including:**													
More than	**Up to**	2.5	5	10	15	20	25	30	40	50	75	100	150	200+	
0	100	0	5	9	12	14	17	19	23	26	33	39	50	59	
100	200	0	7	12	16	19	22	25	30	34	43	51	64	75	
200	300	0	7	12	16	20	24	27	32	37	47	56	71	84	
300	400	0	0	12	16	21	24	28	34	39	50	60	77	91	
400	500	0	0	11	16	21	24	28	34	40	53	63	81	96	
500	600	0	0	10	16	20	24	28	35	41	54	65	84	100	
600	700	0	0	0	15	20	24	28	35	41	55	67	87	104	
700	800	0	0	0	14	19	24	28	35	42	56	68	89	107	
800	900	0	0	0	13	18	23	27	35	42	56	69	91	109	
900	1,000	0	0	0	0	17	22	27	34	41	57	70	92	111	
1,000	1,500	0	0	0	0	0	21	26	34	41	57	71	97	118	
1,500	2,000	0	0	0	0	0	0	0	30	38	56	71	98	121	
2,000	2,500	0	0	0	0	0	0	0	24	33	53	69	99	126	
2,500	3,000	0	0	0	0	0	0	0	0	28	50	68	101	130	
3,000	3,500	0	0	0	0	0	0	0	0	0	47	67	101	132	
3,500	4,000	0	0	0	0	0	0	0	0	0	43	65	101	133	
4,000	4,500	0	0	0	0	0	0	0	0	0	39	62	101	134	
4,500	5,000	0	0	0	0	0	0	0	0	0	0	58	99	134	
5,000	6,000	0	0	0	0	0	0	0	0	0	0	54	97	133	
6,000	7,000	0	0	0	0	0	0	0	0	0	0	0	91	131	
7,000	8,000	0	0	0	0	0	0	0	0	0	0	0	84	126	
8,000	9,000	0	0	0	0	0	0	0	0	0	0	0	75	120	
9,000	10,000	0	0	0	0	0	0	0	0	0	0	0	0	113	

Income		Excess obtained up to and including:												
More than	Up to	2.5	5	10	15	20	25	30	40	50	75	100	150	200+
10,000	100,000	0	0	0	0	0	0	0	0	0	0	0	0	0
100,000	n/a	0	0	0	0	0	0	0	0	0	0	0	0	0

Table: Calculation of additional capital for firm holding client money or other client assets (£000's)

Income	Excess obtained up to and including:												
More than	Up to	5	10	15	20	25	30	40	50	75	100	150	200+
0	100	0	4	7	9	12	14	18	21	28	34	45	54
100	200	0	7	11	14	17	20	25	29	38	46	59	70
200	300	0	7	11	14	17	20	25	30	40	49	64	77
300	400	0	0	9	13	16	19	25	30	40	50	67	81
400	500	0	0	0	11	14	18	24	29	40	51	68	83
500	600	0	0	0	8	12	15	22	28	40	51	69	85
600	700	0	0	0	0	9	13	20	26	39	50	69	86
700	800	0	0	0	0	6	10	17	24	38	49	69	87
800	900	0	0	0	0	0	7	15	22	36	48	69	87
900	1,000	0	0	0	0	0	0	12	19	34	47	68	87
1,000	1,500	0	0	0	0	0	0	0	16	32	45	67	86
1,500	2,000	0	0	0	0	0	0	0	0	18	34	59	81
2,000	2,500	0	0	0	0	0	0	0	0	0	19	48	71
2,500	3,000	0	0	0	0	0	0	0	0	0	6	37	64
3,000	3,500	0	0	0	0	0	0	0	0	0	0	26	55
3,500	4,000	0	0	0	0	0	0	0	0	0	0	14	45
4,000	4,500	0	0	0	0	0	0	0	0	0	0	1	33
4,500	5,000	0	0	0	0	0	0	0	0	0	0	0	21
5,000	6,000	0	0	0	0	0	0	0	0	0	0	0	8
6,000	7,000	0	0	0	0	0	0	0	0	0	0	0	0
7,000	8,000	0	0	0	0	0	0	0	0	0	0	0	0
8,000	9,000	0	0	0	0	0	0	0	0	0	0	0	0
9,000	10,000	0	0	0	0	0	0	0	0	0	0	0	0
10,000	100,000	0	0	0	0	0	0	0	0	0	0	0	0
100,000	n/a	0	0	0	0	0	0	0	0	0	0	0	0

3.2.15 **[G]** The *rule* on the items which are eligible to contribute to the capital resources of a *firm* applies (see MIPRU 4.4.2R).

CHAPTER 4
CAPITAL RESOURCES

4.1 Application and purpose

Application

[2084]
4.1.1 **[R]** This chapter applies to a *firm* with *Part IV permission* to carry on any of the following activities, unless an exemption in this section applies:
(1) *insurance mediation activity*;
(2) *home finance mediation activity*;
(3) *home financing*;
(4) *home finance administration*.

4.1.2 **[G]** As this chapter applies only to a *firm* with *Part IV permission*, it does not apply to an *incoming EEA firm* (unless it has a *top-up permission*). An *incoming EEA firm* includes a *firm* which is passporting into the *United Kingdom* under the *IMD*.

4.1.3 **[G]** The definition of *insurance mediation activity* refers to several activities 'in relation to a *contract of insurance*' which includes a contract of reinsurance. This chapter, therefore, applies to a reinsurance intermediary in the same way as it applies to any other *insurance intermediary*.

Application: banks, building societies, insurers and friendly societies

4.1.4 **[R]** This chapter does not apply to:
(1) a *bank*; or
(2) a *building society*; or
(3) a solo consolidated *subsidiary* of a *bank* or a *building society*; or
(4) an *insurer*; or
(5) a *friendly society*.

4.1.5 **[G]** The capital resources of the *firms* above are calculated in accordance with the appropriate prudential sourcebook.

Application: firms carrying on designated investment business only

4.1.6 **[R]** This chapter does not apply to a *firm* whose *Part IV permission* is limited to *regulated activities* which are *designated investment business*.

4.1.7 **[G]** A *firm* which carries on *designated investment business*, and no other *regulated activity*, may disregard this chapter. For example, a *firm* with *permission* limited to *dealing in investments as agent* in relation to *securities* is only carrying on *designated investment business* and the Interim Prudential sourcebook for investment businesses or the Prudential sourcebook for Banks, Building Societies and Investment Firms, as appropriate, will apply. However, if its *permission* is varied to enable it to arrange motor insurance as well, this activity is not *designated investment business* so the *firm* will be subject to the higher of the requirements in this chapter and those sourcebooks (see MIPRU 4.2.5R).

Application: credit unions

4.1.8 **[R]** This chapter does not apply to:
(1) a 'small *credit union*', that is one with:
  (a) assets of £5 million or less; and
  (b) a total number of members of 5,000 or less (see CRED 8.3.14R); or
(2) a *credit union* whose *Part IV permission* includes *mortgage lending* or *mortgage administration* (or both) but not *insurance mediation activity* or *mortgage mediation activity*.

4.1.9 **[G]**
(1) For *credit unions* to which this chapter applies and which are not *CTF providers*, the capital requirements will be the higher of the requirements in this chapter and in the Credit Unions sourcebook (see MIPRU 4.2.6R).
(2) For *credit unions* to which this chapter applies and which are *CTF providers* with permission to carry on *designated investment business*, the capital requirements will be the highest of the requirements in this chapter, those in the Credit Unions sourcebook and in the Interim Prudential sourcebook for investment businesses (see MIPRU 4.2.6R).
(3) A *credit union* cannot carry on *home purchase activities* or *reversion activities* because the Credit Unions Act 1979 restricts the circumstances whereby *credit unions* can hold land.

Application: professional firms

4.1.10 **[R]**
(1) This chapter does not apply to an *authorised professional firm*:
  (a) whose main business is the practice of its profession; and
  (b) whose *regulated activities* covered by this chapter are incidental to its main business.
(2) A *firm's* main business is the practice of its profession if the proportion of income it derives from professional fees is, during its annual accounting period, at least 50% of the *firm's* total income (a temporary variation of not more than 5% may be disregarded for this purpose).
(3) Professional fees are fees, commissions and other receipts receivable in respect of legal, accountancy, actuarial, conveyancing and surveying services provided to clients but excluding any items receivable in respect of *regulated activities*.

Application: Lloyd's managing agents

4.1.11 **[R]** This chapter does not apply to a *managing agent*.

4.1.12 **[G]** The reason for excluding *managing agents* from the provisions of this chapter is twofold: first, a *member* will have accepted full responsibility for those activities under the *Soci-*

ety's managing agent agreement. Secondly, the *member* is itself subject to capital requirements which are equivalent to those applying to an *insurer* (to which this chapter is also disapplied).

Application: social housing firms

4.1.13 **[G]** There are special provisions for a *social housing firm* when it is carrying on *home financing* or *home finance administration* (see MIPRU 4.2.7R).

Purpose

4.1.14 **[G]** This chapter amplifies *threshold condition* 4 (Adequate resources) by providing that a *firm* must meet, on a continuing basis, a basic solvency requirement and a minimum capital resources requirement. This chapter also amplifies *Principle* 4 which requires a *firm* to maintain adequate financial resources by setting out capital requirements for a *firm* according to the *regulated activity* or activities it carries on.

4.1.15 **[G]** Capital has an important role to play in protecting consumers and complements the roles played by professional indemnity insurance and *client money* protection (see the *client money rules*). Capital provides a form of protection for situations not covered by a *firm's* professional indemnity insurance and it provides the funds for the *firm's* PII excess, which it has to pay out of its own finances (see MIPRU 3.2.11R and MIPRU 3.2.12R for the relationship between the *firm's* capital and its excess).

4.1.16 **[G]** More generally, having adequate capital gives the *firm* a degree of resilience and some indication to consumers of creditworthiness, substance and the commitment of its owners. It reduces the possibility of a shortfall of funds and provides a cushion against disruption if the *firm* ceases to trade.

4.1.17 **[G]** There is a greater risk to consumers, and a greater adverse impact on market confidence, if a *firm* holding *client money* or other *client* assets fails. For this reason, the capital resources *rules* in this chapter clearly distinguish between *firms* holding *client* assets and those that do not.

Purpose: social housing firms

4.1.18 **[G]** **Social housing firms** undertake small amounts of home finance business even though their main business consists of activities other than *regulated activities*. Their *home financing* is only done as an adjunct to their primary purpose (usually the provision of housing) and is substantially different in character to that done by commercial lenders. Furthermore, they are *subsidiaries* of local authorities or registered social landlords which are already subject to separate regulation. The *FSA* does not consider that it would be proportionate to the risks involved with such business to impose significant capital requirements for these *firms*. The capital resources requirement for *social housing firms* therefore simply provides that, where their *Part IV permission* is limited to *home financing* and *home finance administration*, their net tangible assets must be greater than zero.

4.1.19 **[G]** A registered social landlord is a non-profit organisation which provides and manages homes for rent and sale for people who might not otherwise be able to rent or buy on the open market. It can be a housing association, a housing society or a non-profit making housing company. The Housing Corporation, which was set up by Parliament in 1964, funds homes built by registered social landlords from money received from central government.

4.2 Capital resources requirements

General solvency requirement

4.2.1 **[R]** A *firm* must at all times ensure that it is able to meet its liabilities as they fall due.

General capital resource requirement

4.2.2 **[R]** A *firm* must at all times maintain capital resources equal to or in excess of its relevant capital resources requirement.

Capital resources: relevant accounting principles

4.2.3 **[R]** A *firm* must recognise an asset or liability, and measure its amount, in accordance with the relevant accounting principles applicable to it for the purpose of preparing its annual financial statements unless a *rule* requires otherwise.

Capital resources: client assets

4.2.4 **[R]** In this chapter, "*client* assets" includes a *document* only if it has value, or is capable of having value, in itself (such as a bearer instrument).

Capital resources requirement: firms carrying on regulated activities including designated investment business

4.2.5 **[R]** The capital resources requirement for a *firm* (other than a *credit union*) carrying on *regulated activities*, including *designated investment business*, is the higher of:
(1) the requirement which is applied by this chapter according to the activity or activities of the *firm* (treating the relevant *rules* as applying to the *firm* by disregarding its *designated investment business*); and
(2) the financial resource requirement which is applied by the Interim Prudential sourcebook for investment businesses or the Prudential sourcebook for Banks, Building Societies and Investment Firms.

Capital resources requirement: credit unions

4.2.6 **[R]** The capital resources requirement for a *credit union* to which this chapter applies is the highest of:
(1) the requirement which is applied to *firms* carrying on mediation activities only (see MIPRU 4.2.11R) treating that *rule* as applying to the *credit union* by disregarding activities which are not *insurance mediation activity* or *mortgage mediation activity*;
(2) the amount which is applied by the Credit Unions sourcebook; and
(3) if the *credit union* is a *CTF provider* that has a *permission* to carry on *designated investment business*, the amount which is applied by Chapter 8 of the Interim Prudential sourcebook for investment businesses.

Capital resources requirement: social housing firms

4.2.7 **[R]** The capital resources requirement for a *social housing firm* whose *Part IV permission* is limited to carrying on the *regulated activities* of:
(1) *home financing*; or
(2) *home finance administration* (or both);
is that the *firm's* net tangible assets must be greater than zero.

4.2.8 **[G]** If a *social housing firm* is carrying on *home financing* or *home finance administration* (and no other *regulated activity*), its net tangible assets must be greater than zero. However, if it carries on *insurance mediation activity* or *home finance mediation activity*, there is no special provision and the capital resources requirement for *firms* carrying on *designated investment business* or mediation activities only applies to it as appropriate.

Capital resources requirement: application according to regulated activities

4.2.9 **[R]** Unless any of the *rules* on capital resources for *firms* carrying on *designated investment business*, for *credit unions* or for *social housing firms* apply, the capital resources requirement for a *firm* varies according to the *regulated activity* or activities it carries on.

4.2.10 **[R]** Table: Application of capital resources requirements

	Regulated activities	Provisions
1.	(a) *insurance mediation activity*; or (b) *home finance mediation activity* (or both); and no other *regulated activity*.	MIPRU 4.2.11R
2.	(a) *home financing*; or (b) *home financing* and *home finance administration*; and no other *regulated activity*.	MIPRU 4.2.12R to MIPRU 4.2.17E
3.	*home finance administration*; and no other *regulated activity*.	MIPRU 4.2.18R to MIPRU 4.2.19R
4.	*insurance mediation activity*; and (a) *home financing*; or (b) *home finance administration* (or both).	MIPRU 4.2.20R
5.	*home finance mediation activity*; and (a) *home financing*, or (b) *home finance administration* (or both).	MIPRU 4.2.21R
6.	Any combination of *regulated activities* not within rows 1 to 5.	MIPRU 4.2.22R

Capital resources requirement: mediation activity only

4.2.11 **[R]**

Part II FSA Handbook Materials

(1) If a *firm* carrying on *insurance mediation activity* or *home finance mediation activity* (and no other *regulated activity*) does not hold *client money* or other *client* assets in relation to these activities, its capital resources requirement is the higher of:
  (a) £5,000; and
  (b) 2.5% of the *annual income* from its *insurance mediation activity* or *home finance mediation activity* (or both).
(2) If a *firm* carrying on *insurance mediation activity* or *home finance mediation activity* (and no other *regulated activity*) holds *client money* or other *client* assets in relation to these activities, its capital resources requirement is the higher of:
  (a) £10,000; and
  (b) 5% of the *annual income* from its *insurance mediation activity* or *home finance mediation activity* (or both).

Capital resources requirement: home financing and and home finance administration (but not home finance administration only)

4.2.12 **[R]**
(1) The capital resources requirement for a *firm* carrying on *home financing* or *home financing* and *home finance administration* (and no other *regulated activity*) is the higher of:
  (a) £100,000; and
  (b) 1% of:
    (i) its total assets plus total undrawn commitments and unreleased amounts under the *home reversion plan*; less:
    (ii) excluded loans or amounts plus intangible assets (see Note 1 in the table in MIPRU 4.4.4R).
(2) Undrawn commitments and unreleased amounts means the total of those amounts which a *customer* has the right to draw down or to receive from the *firm* but which have not yet been drawn down or received, excluding those under an agreement:
  (a) which has an original maturity of up to one year; or
  (b) which can be unconditionally cancelled at any time by the lender or provider.

4.2.13 **[G]** When considering what is an undrawn commitment or unreleased amount, the *FSA* takes into account an amount which a *customer* has the right to draw down or to receive under a *home finance transaction*, but which has not yet been drawn down or received, whether the commitment or obligation is revocable or irrevocable, conditional or unconditional.

4.2.14 **[R]** When calculating total assets, the *firm* may exclude a loan or plan which has been transferred to a third party only if it meets the following conditions:
(1) the first condition is that the loan or the plan has been transferred in a legally effective manner by:
  (a) novation; or
  (b) legal or equitable assignment; or
  (c) sub-participation; or
  (d) declaration of trust; and
(2) the second condition is that the *home finance provider*:
  (a) retains no material economic interest in the loan; and
  (b) has no material exposure to losses arising from it.

4.2.15 **[E]**
(1) When seeking to rely on the second condition, a *firm* should ensure that the loan or plan qualifies for the 'linked presentation' accounting treatment under Financial Reporting Standard 5 (Reporting the substance of transactions) issued in April 1994, and amended in December 1994 and September 1998 (if applicable to the *firm*).
(2) Compliance with (1) may be relied upon as tending to establish compliance with the second condition.

4.2.16 **[G]** The requirement that the loan qualifies for the 'linked presentation' accounting treatment under FRS 5 is aimed at those *firms* which report according to FRS 5. Other *firms* which report under other standards, including International Accounting Standards, need not adopt FRS 5 in order to meet the second condition.

4.2.17 **[E]**
(1) When seeking to rely on the second condition, a *firm* should not provide material credit enhancement in respect of the loan or plan unless it deducts the amount of the credit enhancement from its capital resources before meeting its capital resources requirement.
(2) Credit enhancement includes:
  (a) any holding of subordinated loans or notes in a transferee that is a special purpose vehicle; or
  (b) over collateralisation by transferring loans or plans to a larger aggregate value than the *securities* to be issued; or
  (c) any other arrangement with the transferee to cover a part of any subsequent losses arising from the transferred loan or plan.

(3) Contravention of (1) may be relied upon as tending to establish contravention the second condition.

Capital resources requirement: home finance administration only

4.2.18 **[R]** The capital resources requirement for a *firm* carrying on *home finance administration* only, which has all or part of the *home finance transactions* that it administers on its balance sheet, is the amount which is applied to a *firm* carrying on *home financing* or *home financing* and *home finance administration* (and no other *regulated activity*) (see MIPRU 4.2.12R).

4.2.19 **[R]** The capital resources requirement for a *firm* carrying on *home finance administration* only, which has all the *home finance transactions* that it administers off its balance sheet, is the higher of:
(1) £100,000; and
(2) 10% of its *annual income*.

Capital resources requirement: insurance mediation activity and home financing or home finance administration

4.2.20 **[R]** The capital resources requirement for a *firm* carrying on *insurance mediation activity* and *home financing* or *home finance administration* is the sum of the requirements which are applied to the *firm* by:
(1) the capital resources *rule* for a *firm* carrying on *insurance mediation activity* or *home finance mediation activity* (and no other *regulated activity*) (see MIPRU 4.2.11R); and
(2)
 (a) the capital resources *rule* for a *firm* carrying on *home financing* or *home financing* and *home finance administration* (and no other *regulated activity*) (see MIPRU 4.2.12R); or
 (b) if, in addition to its *insurance mediation activity*, the *firm* carries on *home finance administration* with all the assets that it administers off balance sheet, the capital resources *rule* for such a *firm* (see MIPRU 4.2.19R).

Capital resources requirement: home finance mediation activity and home financing or home finance administration

4.2.21 **[R]**
(1) If a *firm* carrying on *home finance mediation activity* and *home financing* or *home finance administration* does not hold *client money* or other *client* assets in relation to its *home finance mediation activity*, the capital requirement is the amount applied to a *firm*, according to the activities carried on by the *firm*, by:
 (a) the capital resources *rule* for a *firm* carrying on *home financing* or *home financing* and *home finance administration* (and no other *regulated activity*) (see MIPRU 4.2.12R); or
 (b) if, in addition to its *home finance mediation activity*, the *firm* carries on *home finance administration* with all the assets that it administers off balance sheet, the capital resources *rule* for such a *firm* (see MIPRU 4.2.19R).
(2) If the *firm* holds *client money* or other *client* assets in relation to its *home finance mediation activity*, the capital resources requirement is:
 (a) the amount calculated under (1); plus
 (b) the amount which is applied to a *firm* carrying on *insurance mediation activity* or *home finance mediation activity* (and no other *regulated activity*) that holds *client money* or other *client* assets in relation to these activities (see MIPRU 4.2.11R(2)).

Capital resources requirement: other combinations of activities

4.2.22 **[R]** The capital resources requirement for a *firm* carrying any other combination of *regulated activities* is the amount which is applied to a *firm* carrying on *insurance mediation activity* and *home financing* or *home finance administration* (see MIPRU 4.2.20R).

4.3 Calculation of annual income

Annual income

4.3.1 **[R]** This section contains provisions relating to the calculation of *annual income* for the purposes of:
(1) the *limits of indemnity* for professional indemnity insurance; and
(2) the capital resources requirements.

4.3.2 **[R]** 'Annual income' is the annual income given in the *firm's* most recent annual financial statement from the relevant *regulated activity* or activities.

4.3.3 **[R]** For a *firm* which carries on *insurance mediation activity* or *home finance mediation activity*, *annual income* is the amount of all brokerage, fees, *commissions* and other related income (for example, administration charges, overriders, profit shares) due to the *firm* in respect of or in relation to those activities.

4.3.4 **[G]**
(1) The purpose of the *rule* on *annual income* that applies to *insurance intermediaries* and *mortgage intermediaries* is to ensure that the capital resources requirement is calculated on the basis only of brokerage and other amounts earned by a *firm* which are its own income.
(2) *Annual income* includes *commissions* and other amounts the *firm* may have agreed to pay to other *persons* involved in a transaction, such as sub-agents or other intermediaries.
(3) A *firm's annual income* does not, however, include any amounts due to another *person* (for example, the product provider) which the *firm* has collected on behalf of that other *person*.

4.3.5 **[R]** If a *firm* is a *principal*, its *annual income* includes amounts due to its *appointed representative* in respect of activities for which the *firm* has accepted responsibility.

4.3.6 **[G]** If a *firm* is a *network*, it should include the relevant income due to all of its *appointed representatives* in its *annual income*.

Annual income for home finance administration

4.3.7 **[R]** For the purposes of the calculation of the capital resources of a *firm* carrying on *home finance administration* only with all the assets it administers off balance sheet, *annual income* is the sum of:
(1) revenue (that is, *commissions*, fees, net interest income, dividends, royalties and rent); and
(2) gains;
(3) arising in the course of the ordinary activities of the *firm*, less profit:
 (a) on the sale or termination of an operation;
 (b) arising from a fundamental reorganisation or restructuring having a material effect on the nature and focus of the *firm's* operation; and
 (c) on the disposal of fixed assets, including *investments* held in a long-term portfolio.

Annual income: periods of less than 12 months

4.3.8 **[R]** If the *firm's* most recent annual financial statement does not cover a 12 *month* period, the *annual income* is taken to be the amount in the statement converted, proportionally, to a 12 *month* period.

Annual income: no financial statements

4.3.9 **[R]** If the *firm* does not have annual financial statements, the *annual income* is to be taken from the forecast or other appropriate accounts which the *firm* has submitted to the *FSA*.

4.4 Calculation of capital resources

The calculation of a firm's capital resources

4.4.1 **[R]**
(1) A *firm* must calculate its capital resources only from the items which are eligible to contribute to a *firm's* capital resources from which it must deduct certain items (see MIPRU 4.4.4R).
(2) If the *firm* is subject to the Interim Prudential sourcebook for investment businesses, the Prudential sourcebook for Banks, Building Societies and Investment Firms or the Credit Unions sourcebook, the capital resources are the higher of:
 (a) the amount calculated under (1); and
 (b) the financial resources calculated under those sourcebooks.

4.4.2 **[R]** Table: Items which are eligible to contribute to the capital resources of a firm

	Item	Additional explanation	
1.	*Share* capital	This must be fully paid and may include:	
		(1)	ordinary *share* capital; or
		(2)	preference *share* capital (excluding preference *shares* redeemable by shareholders within two years).

	Item	Additional explanation
2.	Capital other than *share* capital (for example, the capital of a *sole trader*, *partnership* or *limited liability partnership*)	The capital of a *sole trader* is the net balance on the *firm's* capital account and current account.
		The capital of a *partnership* is the capital made up of the *partners'*:
		(1) capital account, that is the account:
		(a) into which capital contributed by the *partners* is paid; and
		(b) from which, under the terms of the *partnership* agreement, an amount representing capital may be withdrawn by a *partner* only if:
		(i) he ceases to be a *partner* and an equal amount is transferred to another such account by his former *partners* or any *person* replacing him as their *partner*; or
		(ii) the *partnership* is otherwise dissolved or wound up; and
		(2) current accounts according to the most recent financial statement.
		For the purpose of the calculation of capital resources, in respect of a *defined benefit occupational pension scheme*:
		(1) a *firm* must derecognise any *defined benefit asset*;
		(2) a *firm* may substitute for a *defined benefit liability* the *firm's deficit reduction amount*, provided that the election is applied consistently in respect of any one financial year.
3.	Reserves (Note 1)	These are, subject to Note 1, the audited accumulated profits retained by the *firm* (after deduction of tax, dividends and proprietors' or *partners'* drawings) and other reserves created by appropriations of share premiums and similar realised appropriations. Reserves also include gifts of capital, for example, from a *parent undertaking*.
		For the purposes of calculating capital resources, a *firm* must make the following adjustments to its reserves, where appropriate:
		(1) a *firm* must deduct any unrealised gains or, where applicable, add back in any unrealised losses on debt instruments held, or formerly held, in the available-for-sale financial assets category;
		(2) a *firm* must deduct any unrealised gains or, where applicable, add back in any unrealised losses on cash flow hedges of financial instruments measured at cost or amortised cost;
		(3) in respect of a *defined benefit occupational pension scheme*:
		(a) a *firm* must derecognise any *defined benefit asset*;
		(b) a *firm* may substitute for a *defined benefit liability* the *firm's deficit reduction amount*, provided that the election is applied consistently in respect of any one financial year.
4.	Interim net profits (Note 1)	If a *firm* seeks to include interim net profits in the calculation of its capital resources, the profits have, subject to Note 1, to be verified by the *firm's* external auditor, net of tax, anticipated dividends or proprietors' drawings and other appropriations.
5.	Revaluation reserves	

	Item	Additional explanation
6.	General/ collective provisions (Note 1)	These are provisions that a *firm* carrying on *home financing* or *home finance administration* holds against potential losses that have not yet been identified but which experience indicates are present in the *firm's* portfolio of assets. Such provisions must be freely available to meet these unidentified losses wherever they arise. Subject to Note 1, general/collective provisions must be verified by external auditors and disclosed in the *firm's* annual report and accounts.
7.	Subordinated loans	Subordinated loans must be included in capital on the basis of the provisions in this chapter that apply to subordinated loans.
Note:		
1	Reserves must be audited and interim net profits, general and collective provisions must be verified by the *firm's* external auditor unless the *firm* is exempt from the provisions of Part VII of the Companies Act 1985 (section 249A (Exemptions from audit)) or, where applicable, Part 16 of the Companies Act 2006 (section 477 (Small companies: Conditions for exemption from audit)) relating to the audit of accounts.	

4.4.3 **[G]** A *firm* should keep a record of and be ready to explain to its supervisory contacts in the *FSA* the reasons for any difference between the *deficit reduction amount* and any commitment the *firm* has made in any public document to provide funding in respect of a *defined benefit occupational pension scheme*.

4.4.4 **[R]** Table: Items which must be deducted from capital resources

1	*Investments* in own shares
2	Intangible assets (Note 1)
3	Interim net losses (Note 2)
4	Excess of drawings over profits for a *sole trader* or a *partnership* (Note 2)
Notes 1. Intangible assets are the full balance sheet value of goodwill (but not until 14 January 2008 – see transitional provision 1), capitalised development costs, brand names, trademarks and similar rights and licences. 2. The interim net losses in row 3, and the excess of drawings in row 4, are in relation to the period following the date as at which the capital resources are being computed.	

Personal assets

4.4.5 **[R]** In relation to a *sole trader's firm* or a *firm* which is a *partnership*, the *sole trader* or a *partner* in the *firm* may use personal assets to meet the general solvency requirement and the general capital resource requirement, to the extent necessary to make up any shortfall in meeting those requirements, unless:

(1) those assets are needed to meet other liabilities arising from:
  (a) personal activities; or
  (b) another business activity not regulated by the *FSA*; or
(2) the *firm* holds *client money* or other *client* assets.

4.4.6 **[G]** A *sole trader* or a *partner* may use any personal assets, including property, to meet the capital requirements of this chapter, but only to the extent necessary to make up a shortfall.

Subordinated loans

4.4.7 **[R]** A subordinated debt must not form part of the capital resources of the *firm* unless it meets the following conditions:

(1) (for a *firm* which carries on *insurance mediation activity* or *home finance mediation activity* (or both) but not *home financing* or *home finance administration*) it has an original maturity of:
  (a) at least two years; or
  (b) it is subject to two years' notice of repayment;
(2) (for all other *firms*) it has an original maturity of:
  (a) at least five years; or
  (b) it is subject to five years' notice of repayment;
(3) the claims of the subordinated creditors must rank behind those of all unsubordinated creditors;

(4) the only events of default must be non-payment of any interest or principal under the debt agreement or the winding up of the *firm*;
(5) the remedies available to the subordinated creditor in the event of non-payment or other default in respect of the subordinated debt must be limited to petitioning for the winding up of the *firm* or proving the debt and claiming in the liquidation of the *firm*;
(6) the subordinated debt must not become due and payable before its stated final maturity date except on an event of default complying with (4);
(7) the agreement and the debt are governed by the law of England and Wales, or of Scotland or of Northern Ireland;
(8) to the fullest extent permitted under the rules of the relevant jurisdiction, creditors must waive their right to set off amounts they owe the *firm* against subordinated amounts owed to them by the *firm*;
(9) the terms of the subordinated debt must be set out in a written agreement or instrument that contains terms that provide for the conditions set out in this *rule*; and
(10) the debt must be unsecured and fully paid up.

4.4.8 **[R]**
(1) This *rule* applies to a *firm* which:
(a) carries on:
(i) *insurance mediation activity*; or
(ii) *home finance mediation activity* (or both); and
(b) in relation to those activities, holds *client money* or other *client* assets;
but is not carrying on *home financing* or *home finance administration*.
(2) In calculating its capital resources, the *firm* must exclude any amount by which the aggregate amount of its subordinated loans and its redeemable preference *shares* exceeds the amount calculated as follows:

four times (a-b-c);		
where:		
a	=	items 1 to 5 in the Table of items which are eligible to contribute to a *firm's* capital resources (see MIPRU 4.4.2R)
b	=	the *firm's* redeemable preference *shares*; and
c	=	the amount of its intangible assets (but not goodwill until 14 January 2008 – see transitional provision 1).

4.4.9 **[G]** If a *firm* wishes to see an example of a subordinated loan agreement which would meet the required conditions, it should refer to the FSA website.

Reversion providers: additional requirement for instalment reversions

4.4.10 **[R]**
(1) If the *reversion provider* agrees under the terms of an *instalment reversion plan* to pay the *reversion occupier* for the *qualifying interest in land* over a period of time, then the *provider* must:
(a) take out and maintain adequate insurance from an *insurance undertaking* authorised in the *EEA* or a *person* of equivalent status in:
(i) a *Zone A* country; or
(ii) the Channel Islands, Gibraltar, Bermuda or the Isle of Man; or
(b) enter into a written agreement with a *credit institution*;
to meet these obligations in the event that the *reversion provider* is unable to do so.
(2) This rule does not apply if:
(a) the *instalment reversion plan* is linked to an *investment* and it is reasonably anticipated that the amounts due to the *reversion occupier* under the plan will be paid out of the proceeds of the *investment* to the *occupier* by a *product provider* other than the *reversion provider*; or
(b) the *reversion provider* acquires its interest in the property in steps proportionate to the instalments paid.

4.4.11 **[G]** The additional requirement for *reversion providers* aims to protect the *reversion occupier* against the insolvency of the *reversion provider* where the *reversion occupier* has agreed to receive the price for the part of the *qualifying interest in land* sold in instalments rather than in a lump sum. The requirement does not arise, for example, in relation to reversions linked to annuities as the *reversion occupier* has no credit risk on the *reversion provider*. Also, the requirement does not arise in relation to 'mini-reversions' (or 'staged reversions') as under these plans the *reversion occupier* continues to own the *qualifying interest in land*.

CHAPTER 5
INSURANCE UNDERTAKINGS AND HOME FINANCE PROVIDERS USING INSURANCE OR HOME FINANCE MEDIATION SERVICES

5.1 Application and purpose

Application

[2085]
5.1.1 **[R]** This chapter applies to a *firm* with a *Part IV permission* to carry on:
(1) *insurance business*; or
(2) *home financing*;
(3) and which uses, or proposes to use, the services of another person consisting of:
(a) *insurance mediation*; or
(b) *insurance mediation activity*; or
(c) *home finance mediation activity*.

Purpose

5.1.2 **[G]** The purpose of this chapter is to implement article 3.6 of the *Insurance Mediation Directive* in relation to *insurance undertakings*. The provisions of this chapter have been extended to *home finance providers* in relation to *insurance mediation activity*, and to *insurance undertakings* and *home finance providers* in relation to *home finance mediation activity*, to ensure that *firms* using these services are treated in the same way and to ensure that *clients* have the same protection. To avoid the loss of protection where an intermediary itself uses the services of an *unauthorised person*, this chapter also ensures that each person in the chain of those providing services is authorised.

5.1.3 **[G]** This chapter supports the more general duties in *Principles* 2 and 3, and the relevant *rule* in the Senior Management Arrangements, Systems and Controls sourcebook (see SYSC 3.1.1R and SYSC 4.1.1R).

5.2 Use of intermediaries

5.2.1 **[R]** A *firm* must not use, or propose to use, the services of another person consisting of:
(1) *insurance mediation*; or
(2) *insurance mediation activity*; or
(3) *home finance mediation activity*;
unless MIPRU 5.2.2R is satisfied.

[**Note**: Article 3(6) of the *IMD*]

5.2.1A **[G]** The *FSA* regards a *firm* as 'using' the services of, in particular, its immediate counterparty (typically the intermediary that passed the business to the *firm*) and of all other *persons* who have been granted the right or authority directly by the *firm* to effect a *contract of insurance* or *enter into a home finance transaction*.

5.2.2 **[R]** For the purposes of MIPRU 5.2.1R, the person, in relation to the activity must:
(1) have *permission*; or
(2) be an *exempt person*; or
(3) be an *exempt professional firm*; or
(4) be registered in another *EEA State* for the purposes of the *IMD*; or
(5) in relation to *insurance mediation activity*, not be carrying this activity on in the *EEA*; or
(6) in relation to *home finance mediation activity*, not be carrying this activity on in the *United Kingdom*.

[**Note**: Article 3(6) of the *IMD*]

5.2.3 **[E]**
(1) A *firm* should:
(a) before using the services of the intermediary, check:
(i) the *FSA Register*; or
(ii) in relation to *insurance mediation* carried on by an *EEA firm*, the register of its *Home State regulator*;
for the status of the person; and
(b) use the services of that person only if the relevant register indicates that the person is registered for that purpose.
(2)
(a) Checking the *FSA Register* before using the services of the intermediary and using the services of that person only if the *FSA Register* indicates that the person is registered for that purpose may be relied on as tending to establish that:
(i) the person, in relation to the activity, has *permission*; or
(ii) the person, in relation to *insurance mediation activity*, also is an *exempt person* or an *authorised professional firm*.

(b) In relation to *insurance mediation* carried on by an *EEA firm*, checking the register of the *firm's Home State regulator* and using the services of the *EEA firm* only if the register indicates that the *firm* is registered for that purpose may be relied on as tending to establish that the *firm* is registered for the purposes of the *IMD*.

5.2.4 **[R]** [deleted]

5.2.5 **[R]** [deleted]

5.2.6 **[G]** The *FSA Register* can be accessed through the *FSA* website under the link www.fsa.gov.uk/register.

MIPRU TP 1.1 TRANSITIONAL PROVISIONS

[2086]

(1)	(2)	(3)	(4)	(5)	(6)
	Material to which the transitional provision applies		**Transitional provision**	**Transitional provision: dates in force**	**Handbook provision: coming into force**
1	MIPRU 4.4.4R and MIPRU 4.4.8R(3)	R	expired.		
2	MIPRU 5.2.2R and MIPRU 5.2.4R	R	MIPRU 5.2.2R and MIPRU 5.2.4R have effect in respect of the use by a *firm* of the services of another *person* consisting of *insurance mediation* and provided from an establishment in an *EEA State* that has not implemented Article 3 (Registration) of the *IMD*, as if the condition in paragraph (4) of MIPRU 5.2.2R and the condition in paragraph (2) of MIPRU 5.2.4R were a condition that the *firm* has no reason to doubt the good repute, competence and financial standing of that *person*.	from 14 January 2005 until the implementation of Article 3 of the *IMD* by the relevant *EEA State*	14 January 2005
3	MIPRU 3.2.7R	R	The new *limits of indemnity* apply to a professional indemnity policy or a comparable guarantee agreement commenced, renewed or extended with effect from or after 1 March 2009. Any other existing non-annual arrangements must be aligned with the new *limits of indemnity* before 1 March 2010.	1 March 2009 to 28 February 2010	1 March 2009

SCHEDULE 1
RECORD KEEPING REQUIREMENTS

[2087]
Sch 1.1 **[G]**

There are no record keeping requirements in *MIPRU*.

SCHEDULE 2
NOTIFICATION REQUIREMENTS

[2088]
Sch 2.1 **[G]**

There are no notification requirements in *MIPRU*.

SCHEDULE 3
FEES AND OTHER REQUIRED PAYMENTS

[2089]
Sch 3.1 **[G]**

There are no requirements for fees or other payments in *MIPRU*.

SCHEDULE 4
POWERS EXERCISED

[2090]
Sch 4.1 **[G]**

The following powers and related provisions in or under the *Act* have been exercised by the *FSA* to make the *rules* in *MIPRU*:	
	Section 138 (General rule-making power);
	Section 149 (Evidential provisions);
	Section 150(2) (Actions for damages)
	Section 156 (General supplementary powers).

Sch 4.2 **[G]**

The following powers in the *Act* have been exercised by the *FSA* to give the *guidance* in *MIPRU*:	
	Section 157(1) (Guidance).

SCHEDULE 5
RIGHTS OF ACTIONS FOR DAMAGES

[2091]
Sch 5 **[G]**

(1) The table below sets out the *rules* in *MIPRU* contravention of which by an *authorised person* may be actionable under section 150 of the *Act* (Actions for damages) by a person who suffers loss as a result of the contravention.

(2) If a 'Yes' appears in the column headed 'For private person', the *rule* may be actionable by a 'private person' under section 150 of the *Act* (or, in certain circumstances, his fiduciary or representative; see article 6(2) and (3)(c) of the Financial Services and Markets Act 2000 (Rights of Action) Regulations 2001 (SI 2001 No 2256)). A 'Yes' in the column headed 'Removed' indicates that the *FSA* has removed the right of action under section 150(2) of the *Act*. If so, a reference to the *rule* in which it is removed is also given.

(3) The column headed 'For other person' indicates whether the *rule* may be actionable by a person other than a private person (or his fiduciary or representative) under article 6(2) and (3) of those Regulations. If so, an indication of the type of person by whom the *rule* may be actionable is given.

Table

Chapter/ Appendix	**Section / Annex**	**Right of action under section 150**		
		For private person	**Removed**	**For other person**
All *rules* in *MIPRU* with the status letter "E"		No	No	No
All other *rules* in *MIPRU*		No	Yes, *MIPRU* 1.2.1R	No

SCHEDULE 6
RULES THAT CAN BE WAIVED

[2092]
Sch 6 **[G]**

(1) The *rules* in *MIPRU* may be waived by the *FSA* under section 148 of the *Act* (Modification or waiver of rules). However, if the *rules* incorporate requirements laid down in European directives, it will not be possible for the *FSA* to grant a *waiver* that would be incompatible with the *United Kingdom's* responsibilities under those directives. It therefore follows that if a *rule* in *MIPRU* contains provisions which derive partly from a directive, and partly not, the *FSA* will be able to consider a *waiver* of the latter requirements only, unless the directive provisions are optional rather than mandatory.

INTERIM PRUDENTIAL SOURCEBOOK: INSURERS (IPRU(INS))

NOTES

Up to date as at 22 February 2010. For later amendments please see www.fsa.gov.uk.

Introduction

(1) The *FSA* makes the rules and guidance in this instrument on 21 June 2001.

(2) The provisions of the *Act* listed in Chapter 11 of this instrument are specified for the purpose of section 153(2).

(3) This instrument will come into force at the beginning of the day on which section 19 of the *Act* (the general prohibition) comes into force.

(4) This instrument is to be interpreted in accordance with, and applies subject to, the general provisions contained in the General Provisions Instrument 2001.

(5) This instrument may be cited as the Interim Prudential Sourcebook for Insurers Instrument 2001.

(6) This instrument, excluding the provisions in this Introduction, may be cited as the Interim Prudential Sourcebook for Insurers.

By Order of the Board

21 June 2001

CONTENTS

Volume One

Guidance: [deleted]

Chapter 1—Application rule . . . . . . [2093]

Chapter 3—Long-term insurance business

Part I—Identification and application of assets and liabilities . . . . . . [2094]

Chapter 8—Non-UK insurers

Part III—Rules applicable to branches . . . . . . [2096]

Chapter 9—Financial reporting

Part I—Accounts and statements . . . . . . [2097]

Part II—Accounts and statements for a marine mutual . . . . . . [2098]

Part III—Statistical rules . . . . . . [2099]

Part IV—Material connected-party transactions . . . . . . [2100]

Part V—Group Capital Adequacy . . . . . . [2101]

Part VI—Enhanced Capital Requirement . . . . . . [2102]

Part VII—Lloyd's of London . . . . . . [2103]

Chapter 11—Definitions

Part I—Definitions . . . . . . [2104]

Part II—General Provisions . . . . . . [2105]

Annex 11.1—Classes of long-term insurance business . . . . . . [2106]

Annex 11.2—Classes, and groups of classes, of general insurance business . . . . . . [2107]

Annex 11.3—Descriptions of FSA general insurance business reporting categories . . . [2108]

Chapter 12—Transitional arrangements . . . . . . [2109]

Volume Two

Appendices to the Rules [deleted in part, not reproduced in this work]

Volume Three

FSA Guidance Notes [deleted]

Guidance: FSA 'Dear Director' Letters [deleted]

Other Material: 'Dear Appointed Actuary' Letters [deleted]

VOLUME ONE
RULES

Interim Prudential Sourcebook for Insurers Guidance
The Purpose of the Prudential Rules for Insurers and an Overall Description

[deleted text]

CHAPTER 1
APPLICATION RULE

Application

Insurers

[2093]
1.1 An *insurer* must comply with *IPRU(INS)* unless it is—
(a) a *friendly society*[1]; or
(b) an *EEA insurer* or an *EEA pure reinsurer* qualifying for authorisation under Schedules 3 or 4 to the *Act*.

The Society of Lloyd's

1.2 No provisions of *IPRU(INS)* apply to the *Society* of Lloyd's, or *members* of the *Society* of Lloyd's except rules 9.37 and 9.38, and Part VII of Chapter 9.

1.3 [deleted]

---

1 A *non-directive friendly society* must comply with *IPRU(FSOC)*; a *directive friendly society* must comply with *GENPRU* and *INSPRU*; with Chapters 1, 2 and 3, 4 (rules 4.20 to 4.23 only), 5 (rule 5.1A only) 7, 8 and Appendix 3 of *IPRU(FSOC)*. Rule 5.1A of *IPRU(FSOC)* effectively applies most of Chapter 9 of *IPRU(INS)* to *directive friendly societies*, notwithstanding IPRU(INS) 1.1(a).

CHAPTER 2
MARGINS OF SOLVENCY

[deleted]

CHAPTER 3
LONG-TERM INSURANCE BUSINESS

Part I
Identification and Application of Assets and Liabilities

[2094]–[2095]
3.1
(1) [deleted]
(2) [deleted]

Application of assets of insurer with long-term insurance business

Limitation on use of assets in long-term insurance fund

3.2 [(1) to (5) deleted]

Restriction in relation to dividends

(6) A *long-term insurer* must not declare a dividend at any time when the value of the *long-term insurance assets*, as determined in accordance with GENPRU 1.3 and INSPRU 2.1, is less than the amount of the *long-term insurance business technical provisions* and any other liabilities connected with the *long-term insurance business*.[1]

Allocations to policy holders

Allocation of established surplus

3.3
(1) Where—
  (a) there is an 'established surplus' in which *long-term policy holders* of any category are eligible to participate; and
  (b) an amount has been allocated to *policy holders* of that category in respect of a previously 'established surplus' in which *policy holders* of that category were eligible to participate,

  an *insurer* must not by virtue of INSPRU 1.5.27R transfer or otherwise apply assets representing any part of the surplus mentioned in (a) unless the insurer has—
  (i) allocated to *policy holders* of that category in respect of that surplus an amount not less than the 'relevant minimum', or
  (ii) complied with the requirements of (3) and made to those policy holders any allocation of which notice is given under (3)(a).

(2) Subject to (6) and (7), the **relevant minimum** is the amount represented by the formula—

$$\frac{b \times c}{a} - \frac{c}{200}$$

Where—

a is the last previously 'established surplus' in respect of which an amount was allocated to *policy holders* of the category in question;

b is the amount so allocated; and

c is the surplus referred to in (1)(a).

Requirements where less than the relevant minimum is to be allocated

(3) The requirements referred to in (1)(ii) are that the *insurer*—

(a) at least 14 days before publication has given the *FSA* written notice stating that it proposes to make no allocation or an allocation of an amount (specifying it) which is smaller than the 'relevant minimum', and a copy of the statement that it proposes to publish in accordance with (b); and

(b) has published a statement in the London, Edinburgh and Belfast Gazettes and in two national newspapers explaining the allocation it proposes to make to *policy holders* and the reasons for it,

and that a period of not less than 56 days has elapsed since the date, or the last date, on which the *insurer* has published the statement mentioned in (b) as required by that paragraph.

(4) In this rule, **established surplus** means an excess of assets representing the whole or a particular part of the *long-term insurance fund* or *funds* over the liabilities, or a particular part of the liabilities, of the *insurer* attributable to that business as shown by an *actuarial investigation*.

Amounts to be treated as allocated to policy holders

(5) For the purposes of this rule, an amount is allocated to *policy holders* if, and only if—

(a) bonus payments are made to them; or

(b) reversionary bonuses are declared in their favour or a reduction is made in the premiums payable by them,

and the amount of the allocation is, in a case within (a), the amount of the payments and, in a case within (b), the amount of the liabilities assumed by the insurer in consequence of the declaration or reduction.

Bonus payments in anticipation of established surplus

(6) For the purposes of this rule, the amount of any bonus payments made in anticipation of an 'established surplus' is treated as an amount allocated in respect of the next 'established surplus' in respect of which an amount is allocated to eligible *policy holders* generally; and for the purposes of (2) the amount of any surplus in respect of which such an allocation is made is treated as increased by the amount of any such payments.

Unappropriated surplus carried forward

(7) (1) does not authorise the application for purposes other than those mentioned in INSPRU 1.5.30R of assets representing any part of the surplus mentioned in (1)(a) which the *insurer* has decided to carry forward unappropriated; and for the purposes of (2) the amount of any surplus is treated as reduced by any part of it which the *insurer* has decided to carry forward unappropriated.

Eligibility to participate in an established surplus

(8) For the purposes of (1), *policy holders* are taken to be eligible to participate in an 'established surplus' in any case where they would be eligible to participate in a later 'established surplus' representing it if it were carried forward unappropriated.

3.4 [deleted]

Arrangements to avoid unfairness between separate insurance funds

3.5

(1) An *insurer* which carries on *long-term insurance business* in the UK must have adequate arrangements for securing that transactions affecting assets of the *insurer* (other than transactions outside its control) do not operate unfairly between the *long-term insurance fund* or *funds* and the other assets of the *insurer* or, in a case where the *insurer* has more than one 'identified fund', between those funds.

(2) In this rule, **identified fund** means assets representing the *insurer's* receipts from a particular part of its *long-term insurance business* which can be identified as such by virtue of accounting or other records maintained by the *insurer*.

(3) [deleted]

3.5A [deleted]

[1] Regulations under section 142 of the *Act* may also apply to restrict a *parent undertaking* of an *insurer* from doing anything to lessen the effectiveness of the *Asset Identification Rules*.

Part II
Linked Long-Term Contracts

3.6 [deleted]

3.7 [deleted]

CHAPTER 4
VALUATION OF ASSETS

[deleted]

CHAPTER 5
DETERMINATION OF LIABILITIES

[deleted]

CHAPTER 6
GENERAL INSURANCE BUSINESS: EQUALISATION RESERVES

[deleted]

CHAPTER 7
CURRENCY MATCHING AND LOCALISATION

[deleted]

CHAPTER 8
NON-UK INSURERS

Part I
Deposits

8.1 [deleted]

Part II
Location of Accounts and Records

8.2 [deleted]

Part III
Rules Applicable to Branches

[2096]

8.3 An *insurer* which has its head office outside the United Kingdom (other than a *pure reinsurer* which has a Treaty right under Schedule 4 to the *Act*, or a *Swiss general insurer*) must appoint and maintain the appointment of a chief executive (who alone or jointly with one or more others, is responsible for the conduct of its business through an establishment in the United Kingdom).

8.4 [deleted]

8.5 [deleted]

CHAPTER 9
FINANCIAL REPORTING

Part I
Accounts and Statements

Application

[2097]

9.1 These *Accounts and Statements Rules* apply to every *insurer* other than—

(a) an *EEA-deposit insurer*, in relation to *insurance business* carried on by it outside the United Kingdom; or

(b) a *Swiss general insurer*, in relation to *general insurance business* carried on by it outside the United Kingdom.

Interpretation

9.2

(1) In rules 9.25 to 9.27, 9.29, 9.30 and 9.32, and in the Appendices relevant to the *Accounts and Statements Rules*, unless the context otherwise requires, words and expressions not defined in IPRU(INS) or the *Glossary* which are used in the *insurance accounts rules* have the same meanings as in those rules.

(2) In the *Accounts and Statements Rules*—

(a) any reference to *long-term insurance business* or *general insurance business* is, in relation to an *EEA-deposit insurer*, to *long-term insurance business* or *general insurance business* carried on by it through a branch in the United Kingdom; and

(b) any reference to *general insurance business* is, in relation to a *Swiss general insurer*, to *general insurance business* carried on by it through a branch in the United Kingdom,

and accordingly any reference to, or requirement imposed in respect of, the accounts and balance sheet (including any notes, statements, reports and certificates annexed to them) is to, or imposes a requirement in respect of, *insurance business* carried on through that branch.

(3) In the *Accounts and Statements Rules*, any reference to *long-term insurance business* or to *general insurance business* is—

(a) in relation to an *external insurer*, to its entire *long-term insurance business* or to its entire *general insurance business* and (except in the case of a *non-EEA insurer* whose *insurance business* in the United Kingdom is restricted to *reinsurance* or an *insurer* whose head office is in any *EEA State* except the United Kingdom whose *insurance business* in the *EEA* is restricted to *reinsurance*), to any *long-term insurance business* or *general insurance business* carried on by it through a branch in the United Kingdom; and

(b) in relation to a *UK-deposit insurer*, to its entire long-term insurance business or to its entire *general insurance business* and to any *long-term insurance business* or *general insurance business* carried on by it through a branch in any *EEA State*,

and accordingly any reference to, or requirement imposed in respect of, the accounts and balance sheet (including any notes, statements, reports and certificates annexed to them) relevant to *long-term insurance business* or to *general insurance business* is to, or imposes a requirement in respect of—

(i) accounts prepared in respect of its entire *long-term insurance business* or entire *general insurance business*; and

(ii) accounts prepared in respect of the *long-term insurance business* or the *general insurance business* carried on, in the case of an *external insurer* (other than a non-*EEA insurer* whose *insurance business* in the United Kingdom is restricted to *reinsurance* or an *insurer* whose head office is in any *EEA State* except the United Kingdom whose *insurance business* in the *EEA* is restricted to *reinsurance*), by the branch in the United Kingdom and, in the case of a *UK deposit insurer*, by the branches in question in the *EEA States* taken together.

(4) In the *Accounts and Statements Rules* and in Chapter 12—

(a) any reference to a numbered Form is a reference to the Form so numbered in **Appendices 9.1** to **9.3**;

(b) references to a numbered *class* of *insurance business* are references to the *class* so numbered in either **Annex 11.1** or **11.2**; and

(c) references to a numbered *FSA general insurance business reporting category* are references to the *FSA general insurance business reporting category* so numbered in **Annex 11.3**.

(5) To the extent there is a contradiction between *SUP* 16.3 and the *Accounts and Statements* Rules, the *Accounts and Statements Rules* apply.

Annual accounts and balance sheets

9.3

(1) Subject to (2) and (3), an *insurer* which does not fall within (5) must, with respect to each of its *financial years*, prepare—

(a) a revenue account for the year;

(b) a balance sheet as at the end of the year; and

(c) a *profit and loss account* for the year.

(2) An *insurer* not trading for profit must, with respect to each of its *financial years*, prepare an income and expenditure account for the year.

(3) If a form is required for—

– an account
– a balance sheet
– a note
– a statement
– a report, or
– a certificate attached to any of the above,

the account etc. must be in that form.

Part II FSA Handbook Materials

(4) An *insurer's financial year* must be a 12 month period.
(5) A *long-term insurer* which:
(a) has transferred all of its *long-term insurance business* to another *insurer*;
(b) has no intention to carry on further *long-term insurance business*; and
(c) is not carrying on *general insurance business*,
must provide to the *FSA* within three months of the date of transfer **Forms 40, 41, 42, 43, 45, 46** and **47** in respect of the period from the end of the *financial year* most recently ended to the date of transfer together with a certificate in accordance with **Appendix 9.6** paragraphs 1(1)(a) and 1(1)(b)(i) and a statement that no *long-term insurance business* has been carried on by the *insurer* since then, there is no intention to carry on further any such business and the *insurer* is not carrying on *general insurance business*.
(6) The **Forms 40, 41, 42, 43,** and **45** provided under (5) must be audited by a person qualified to do so, in accordance with the rules in SUP, who must make and annex to those documents a report in accordance with **Appendix 9.6** paragraph 4(a)(i) in respect of those documents.

Half-yearly balance sheet and report for realistic valuation

9.3A
(1) Every *long-term insurer* which is a *realistic basis life firm* must in respect of each *financial year* prepare **Forms 2, 18** and **19** of **Appendix 9.1**, as at the end of the first six months of that *financial year*.
(2) The Forms in (1) must be prepared in accordance with **Appendix 9.1**, and **Form 2** must be completed in respect of the *long-term insurance business* of the *firm* and **Forms 18 and 19** must be completed in respect of each of the *firm's with-profit funds*.
(3) The Forms in (1) must be accompanied by a report (instead of the reports required under rule 9.4(1)(b)) identifying any changes to the methods and assumptions used from those set out in the report for the realistic valuation as at the end of the *preceding financial year*.
(4) Rules 9.4, 9.6, 9.10, 9.11, 9.12, 9.33 and 9.34, **Appendices 9.1** and **9.4A** and **Part I** of **Appendix 9.6** apply to this rule and to any documents required under this rule as if—
(a) an additional balance sheet were required under rule 9.3;
(b) the documents required by (1), and only those documents, were required by rule 9.12 for the purposes of the balance sheet in (a) above;
(c) an additional investigation were required under rule 9.4(1)(a) in respect of the six-month period covered by this rule;
(d) any document required by (3) were a document required by rule 9.31(b) or the purposes of the investigation in (c) above;
(e) any reference to the *financial year in question* (however expressed) were a eference to the six-month period referred to in (1);
(f) any reference to the preceding year were a reference to the end of the *receding financial year*;
(g) the required signatory in each case were any director of the *insurer*;
(h) any reference to a particular amount shown in a document not required under (1) or (3) were a reference to the amount which would be shown in that document (subject to any modifications in (a) to (f) above) in accordance with the *Accounts and Statements Rules* if that document were required to be produced;
(i) any requirement (other than in this rule) to refer in the *return* or any certificate annexed to it by virtue of rule 9.34 to a document not required under (1) or (3) were omitted; and
(j) in 9.6(2)(a) a single printed copy is required and for both 9.6(2)(a) and 9.6(2)(b) the printed copy must be sent to the *insurer*'s normal supervisory contact.
(5) Instead of a valuation report under rule 9.31(a), the report referred to in (3) must include, in an additional numbered answer following the answers to the paragraphs in **Appendix 9.4A**—
(a) a full description of each of the changes in the methods and assumptions used in the investigation for the purposes of rule 9.4(2)(a) and (b) since the previous investigation at the end of the *preceding financial year*; or
(b) if there has been no such change, a statement to that effect.
Rules 9.3, 9.5, 9.7, 9.13 to 9.30, 9.31, 9.32 and 9.35 to 9.39 do not apply in respect of the documents required under this rule.

Periodic actuarial investigation of long-term insurer

9.4
(1) Every *long-term insurer*—
(a) must, once in every period of 12 months, cause an investigation to be made into its financial condition in respect of its *long-term insurance business*, in accordance with the methods and assumptions determined by the *insurer*, by the person or persons who for the time being are appointed to perform the *actuarial function* under the rules in *SUP*; and

(b) when such an investigation has been made, or when at any other time an investigation into the financial condition of the *insurer* in respect of its *long-term insurance business* has been made with a view to the distribution of profits, or the results of which are made public, must cause an abstract of the report or reports of the investigation to be made.

(2) An investigation to which (1)(b) relates must include—

(a) a determination of the liabilities of the *insurer* attributable to *its long-term insurance business*;

(b) a valuation of any excess over those liabilities of the assets representing the *long-term insurance fund* or *funds* and, where any rights of any long-term *policy holders* to participate in profits relate to particular parts of such a fund, a valuation of any excess of assets over liabilities in respect of each of those parts; and

(c) for the investigation in (1)(a), for every *long-term insurer* which is a *realistic basis life firm*, a calculation of the *with-profits insurance capital component*.

(3) For the purposes of any investigation to which this rule applies, the value of any assets and the amount of any liabilities must be determined in accordance with GENPRU 1.3, INSPRU 2.1 and INSPRU 1.

(4) The form and contents of any abstract under this rule must be in accordance with rule 9.31.

Audit of accounts

9.5

(1) The 'accounts and balance sheets' of every *insurer* must be audited in accordance with rule 9.35 by a person qualified in accordance with the rules in *SUP*.

(2) In (1), the reference to **accounts and balance sheets** includes a reference to any notes or statement or report annexed to them, save for—

(a) the *directors'* certificate annexed pursuant to rule 9.34, and

(b) **Forms 46** to **47A**, **50** to **55**, **57** and **59**.

Deposit of accounts etc. with the FSA

9.6

(1) Every 'account', 'balance sheet', abstract or statement required by rules 9.3, 9.3A, 9.4 and 9.36A and any report of the auditor of the *insurer* made in pursuance of rules 9.5 or 9.36E must be printed, and the 'required copies' must be deposited with the *FSA* within the periods set out in the table below.[1]

deposit period following the *financial year* end or, for documents required by rule 9.3A, the end of the first six months of the *financial year*	
where the deposit is made electronically or under rule 9.36A	**Otherwise**
3 months	2 months and 15 days

(1A) If the due date for deposit of documents required by (1) falls on a day which is not a *business day*, the documents must be submitted no later than the first *business day* after the due date.

(1B) [deleted]

(2) In (1), the reference to the **required copies** is to—

(a) five printed copies of the document; or

(b) one printed copy of the document and one copy of it in an electronic form which may be readily used or translated by the *FSA* sent by email to insurancereturns@fsa.gov.uk. The title of the email must be:

<firm name> FSA returns <dd/mm/yyyy>.

The printed copies must be sent to Insurance Returns, The Financial Services Authority, PO Box 35747, London E14 5WP (and must not be addressed to the *insurer's* normal supervisory contact).

(3) In the case of any document deposited under (1), except an auditor's report, one of the printed copies, or, as the case may be, the printed copy, of the document must be signed in accordance with rule 9.33.

(4) In the case of any auditor's report deposited under (1), one of the printed copies, or, as the case may be, the printed copy, of the document must be signed by the auditor.

(5) If within 24 months of the date of deposit, the *FSA* notifies the *insurer* that a document deposited under (1) appears to it to be inaccurate or incomplete, the *insurer* must consider the matter and within one month of the date of notification it must correct any inaccuracies and make good any omissions and deposit the relevant parts of the documents again.

(6) There must be deposited with every revenue 'account' and 'balance sheet' of an *insurer* any statement or report on the affairs of the *insurer* made or submitted:

(a) to the *insurer's* shareholders or *policyholders*; or

(b) to the *insurer's with-profits policyholders* under COBS 20.3.3G, COBS 20.4.7R or SUP 4.3.16AR (4),

in respect of the *financial year* to which the 'account' and 'balance sheet' relate.

The *insurer* may either send a printed copy or an electronic copy of these reports. The requirements in (2) above as to postal address, email address and email title apply.

(6A) Where a statement or report has not been made or submitted at the time the revenue 'account' and 'balance sheet' are deposited (see (6)), it must be deposited as soon as possible thereafter.[2]

(7) In this rule, any reference to an **account** or **balance sheet** includes a reference to any note, or statement or report annexed to it by virtue of rule 9.3 and any certificate annexed to it by virtue of rule 9.34.

Right to receive copies of deposited documents

9.7 An *insurer* must provide to any person (or the person who has already been provided with a copy under (a)) within 30 days of the date of request (or, in the case of (b), the date of deposit under rule 9.6(5)):

(a) a copy of any of the documents last deposited by the *insurer* under rule 9.6(1) in respect of the *financial year in question*, and the two *financial years* preceding the *financial year in question*;;

(b) a copy of any document deposited under rule 9.6(5) which corrects or makes good any document provided under (a); and

(c) a copy of any report deposited with any such document under rule 9.6(6),

where the deposit is made electronically, in the form (whether printed or electronic) requested or, if the deposit is not made electronically, in printed form, but (except in the case of (b)) the *insurer* may make a charge to cover its reasonable costs, including those of printing and postage.

Documents deposited with the FSA

9.8 [deleted]

Documents deposited in Northern Ireland

9.9 [deleted]

Value of assets and amount of liabilities

9.10 Unless otherwise provided in the *Accounts and Statements Rules*, in the documents which an *insurer* is required to prepare in accordance with the *Accounts and Statements Rules*—

(a) the value or amount given for an asset or a liability of the *insurer* is the value or amount of that asset or liability as determined in accordance with GENPRU 1.3 and INSPRU 1 at the end of *the financial year in question*;

(b) no value shall be given to exposures in excess of the limits set out in INSPRU 2.1.22R (3).

(c) notwithstanding (a) and (b) (but subject to the conditions set out in (d)), an *insurer* may, for the purposes of an *actuarial investigation*, elect to assign to any of its assets the value given to the asset in question in the books or other records of the *insurer*; and

(d) the conditions referred to in (c) are that—

(i) the election does not enable the *insurer* to bring into account any asset that is not an *admissible asset*; and

(ii) the value assigned to the aggregate of the *insurer's* assets is not higher than the aggregate of the value of those assets as determined in accordance with (a) and (b), without taking advantage of (c).

Content and form of accounts

9.11 Every account, balance sheet, note, statement, report and certificate required to be prepared by an *insurer* pursuant to rule 9.3(1), (2) and (3) (annual accounts and balance sheets) or 9.3(5) must be prepared in the manner set out in the *Accounts and Statements Rules* and must fairly state the information provided on the basis required by the *Accounts and Statements Rules*. Where the *rules* in IPRU(INS) require a Form to be submitted, but all entries (including comparatives) would be blank, that Form may be omitted provided that a note coded FF00 (where F is the Form number) is included stating that this why the Form has been omitted. Where a Form is omitted because of the operation of a de minimis limit, a note coded FF00 must be included stating that this is why the Form has been omitted. This note is not needed where a Form is omitted because the *rules* do not require it for a reason other than the operation of a de minimis limit.

Balance sheet

9.12

(1) The balance sheet required to be prepared by an *insurer* under rule 9.3(1) must comply with the requirements of **Appendix 9.1** and must be in **Forms 1** to **3**, **10** to **15** and **17** to **19** of that Appendix completed (as may be appropriate) as specified in (2) to (9).

(2) **Form 1** must be completed by every *insurer* that carries on *general insurance business*, other than a *Swiss general insurer* or an *EEA-deposit insurer.*

(2A) **Form 2** must be completed by every *long-term insurer* other than an *EEA-deposit insurer.*

(3) **Form 10** must be completed by every *insurer* other than a *Swiss general insurer* or an *EEA-deposit insurer.*

(3A) **Form 10** must be completed by an *external insurer* (other than a *non-EEA insurer* whose *insurance business* in the United Kingdom is restricted to *reinsurance* or an *insurer* whose head office is in any *EEA State* except the United Kingdom whose *insurance business* in the *EEA* is restricted to *reinsurance*), an *EEA-deposit insurer* or a *Swiss general insurer.*

(4) **Forms 11** and **12** must be completed by every *insurer* which carries on *general insurance business*, other than a *Swiss general insurer* or an *EEA deposit insurer* and, except when the instructions for completion of **Forms 11** and **12** specify otherwise, by every *insurer* which carries on *long-term insurance business.*

(5) **Form 13** must be completed (as appropriate)—

(a) by every *insurer* which carries on *long-term insurance business* in respect of—

(i) its total *long-term insurance assets*; and

(ii) the *long-term insurance assets* appropriated by it in respect of each *long-term insurance fund* or, where such assets have been appropriated for a group of funds, those assets;

(b) by every *insurer* in respect of its total assets other than *long-term insurance assets*;

(c) by every *external insurer* (other than a *non-EEA insurer* whose *insurance business* in the United Kingdom is restricted to *reinsurance* or an *insurer* whose head office is in any *EEA State* except the United Kingdom whose *insurance business* in the *EEA* is restricted to *reinsurance*) in respect of *long-term insurance business* or *general insurance business* carried on by it through a branch in the United Kingdom in respect of those assets which are—

(i) deposited under INSPRU 1.5.54R,

(ii) maintained in the United Kingdom, and

(iii) maintained in the United Kingdom and the other *EEA States*; and

(d) by every *UK-deposit insurer* in respect of *long-term insurance business* or *general insurance business* carried on by it through branches in the *EEA States* in respect of those assets which are—

(i) deposited under INSPRU 1.5.54R,

(ii) maintained in the United Kingdom and such other *EEA States* where *insurance business* is carried on, and

(iii) maintained in the United Kingdom and the other *EEA States.*

(6) **Form 14** must be completed by every *long-term insurer* in respect of—

(a) its total *long-term insurance liabilities* and margins;

(b) the *long-term insurance liabilities* and margins for each *long-term insurance fund* or where *long-term insurance assets* have been appropriate in respect of a group of funds, for the group; and

(c) subject to (6A), except where the information is provided by virtue of (a) or (b), each *with-profits fund*, with a supplementary note (code 1406) stating the amount, if any, of the increase or decrease, as the case may be, in the value of *non-linked assets.*

(6A) Where the amount (or part of the amount) of any increase or decrease in the value of *non-linked assets* has yet to be allocated between *with-profits funds* or between one or more *with-profits funds* and other purposes, the note required by (6) must state the total amount which has yet to be aggregated:

Part II FSA Handbook Materials

(a) identifying the *with-profits funds* to which the information relates; and

(b) describing the basis upon which increases or decreases in the value of *non-linked assets* are, or will be, allocated between the *with-profits funds* or between the *with-profits funds* and other purposes.

(7) **Form 15** must be completed by every *insurer* except an *insurer* not trading for profit which carries on only *long-term insurance business*.

(8) For each **Form 13** which an *insurer* is required to complete under (5)(a) or (b), the *insurer* must complete **Form 17** in respect of the same *insurance business*, subject to the de minimis requirement set out in instruction 1 to Form 17.

(9) **Forms 18** and **19** must be completed by every *long-term insurer* which is a *realistic basis life firm*, in respect of each of its *with profits funds*.

Profit and loss account

9.13 The *profit and loss account* required to be prepared by every *insurer* under rule 9.3 must comply with the requirements of **Appendix 9.1** and must be in **Form 16**.

Revenue account

9.14 The revenue account to be prepared by every *insurer* under rule 9.3—

(a) in the case of an *insurer* carrying on *general insurance business*, must comply with the requirements of **Appendix 9.2** and must be in **Form 20** in respect of the whole of the *general insurance business* carried on by it; and

(b) in the case of an *insurer* carrying on *long-term insurance business*, must comply with the requirements of **Appendix 9.3** and must be in **Form 40** and—

(i) separate accounts must be prepared in **Form 40** in respect of:

(A) each *long-term insurance fund* maintained by it, and

(B) except where the information is provided by virtue of (A), each *with-profits fund*, with a supplementary note [code 4010] stating the amount, if any, of investment income relating to *linked assets* included at line 12; and

(ii) where there is more than one Form 40 under (i) above, the *insurer* must also prepare a summary **Form 40** for the total long-term insurance business.

Allocation of general insurance business to risk categories

9.14A Every *insurer* preparing the Forms required under rules 9.15, 9.17, 9.19, 9.20 and 9.20A must allocate its *general insurance business* to one or more *risk categories*.

Allocation of contracts of insurance covering more than one risk category

9.14B

(1) This rule applies in any case where a *contract of insurance* falls within the description of more than one *risk category*.

(2) If the *contract of insurance* falls, to any extent, within the description of *risk category* 274, 590 or 690, an *insurer* must allocate all the *general insurance business* represented by that *contract of insurance* to that *risk category*.

(3) In any other case, an *insurer* must, unless (4) applies, allocate all the *general insurance business* represented by the *contract of insurance* to the single *risk category* that, in the reasonable opinion of the *insurer's governing body*, best describes the risk covered by the *contract of insurance*.

(4) If:

(a) the premium payable under the *contract of insurance* is separable into components relating to different *risk categories*; or

(b) in the reasonable opinion of the *insurer's governing body*, allocation under (3) would be misleading;

then the *insurer* must apply a reasonable method to allocate the *general insurance business* represented by the *contract of insurance* amongst the appropriate *risk categories* and must apportion the amounts it reports in the Forms accordingly.

General insurance business (content of revenue account and additional information as to balance sheet)

9.15

(1) Every *insurer* which carries on *general insurance business* must, in accordance with the requirements of **Appendix 9.2**, prepare—

(a) **Form 20A** in respect of the whole of the *general insurance business* carried on by it;

(b) **Form 20** in respect of each *required category*;

(c) **Forms 21, 22** and **23** for *insurance business accounted for* on an 'accident year basis' in respect of each *required category*; and

(d) **Forms 24** and **25** for *insurance business accounted for* on an 'underwriting year basis' in respect of each *required category*.

(2) For the purposes of this rule and rules 9.17(1), 9.19(1) and 9.22(2), business must be taken to be *accounted for* on an **underwriting year basis** where it relates to risks—

(a) which have been reported previously under the *Accounts and Statements Rules* on **Forms 24** and **25**;

(b) in respect of which the *claims* outstanding for such *insurance business* are calculated using the method described in paragraph 52 of *the insurance accounts rules*; or

(c) which have not previously been reported on any Form under the *Accounts and Statements Rules* and which the *insurer* accounts for on an 'underwriting year basis',

and business not *accounted for* on an 'underwriting year basis' is taken to be *accounted for* on an **accident year basis**.

(3) Every *insurer* which, in respect of any *financial year*, includes in **Form 22** or **25** amounts relating to adjustments for *discounting* must prepare **Form 30** in accordance with the requirements of **Appendix 9.2**.

9.16 [deleted]

Additional information on general insurance business (treaty reinsurance business)

9.17

(1) Every *insurer* which carries on *general insurance business* must, in accordance with the requirements of **Appendix 9.2** prepare—

(a) **Forms 26** and **27** for *treaty reinsurance business accounted for* on an 'accident year basis' in respect of each *required category*; and

(b) **Forms 28 and 29** for *treaty reinsurance business accounted for* on an 'underwriting year basis' in respect of each *required category*.

(2) [deleted]

(3) [deleted]

9.18 [deleted]

Additional information on general insurance business (direct and facultative business)

9.19

(1) Every *insurer* which carries on *general insurance business* must, in accordance with the requirements of **Appendix 9.2**, prepare—

(a) **Forms 31** or **32** for *direct and facultative insurance business*, accounted for on an 'accident year basis' in respect of each *required category*; and;

(b) **Form 34** for *direct and facultative insurance business* accounted for on an 'underwriting year basis' in respect of each *required category*.

(2) [deleted]

(3) Where any of **Forms 31, 32** or **34** has been prepared in respect of the entire *insurance business* of an *insurer*, no separate forms need be prepared—

(a) in the case of an *external insurer*, in respect of *insurance business* carried on by it through a branch in the United Kingdom; and

(b) in the case of a *UK deposit insurer*, in respect of *insurance business* carried on by it through a branch in any *EEA State*.

FSA general insurance business reporting categories falling below de minimis criteria

9.20

(1) This rule applies to any *financial year* after the first *financial year* ended on or after 31 December 2005 in any case where—

(a) for the previous *financial year*, an *insurer* was required to prepare a **Form 20 to 34** for a category of business (as set out in column 2 of paragraph 2B of **Appendix 9.2**) that was not *category number* 001 to 003, 409 or 709; and

(b) for the *financial year in question*, the 'reporting criteria' for that Form and category of business are not met.

(2) In this rule, any references to 'reporting criteria', in relation to a Form, are the reporting criteria specified for that Form in column 3 in the Table in paragraph 2B of **Appendix 9.2.**

(3) Unless paragraph (4) applies, any such business that satisfies (1) must be reported in the same category of business (as set out in column 2 of paragraph 2B of **Appendix 9.2**) in the same Form for the *financial year in question*.

(4) An *insurer* may cease to report such business on that Form in that category of business if—

(a) the *gross written premiums* in the *financial year in question* and the 'gross undiscounted provisions' at the end of that *financial year* for that category of business are each less than £0.5m; or

(b) the following conditions are met—
(i) the *financial year in question* ended on or after 31 December 2008;
(ii) the business in 1(a) has been reported on that Form for that category of business in each of the three previous *financial years*; and
(iii) the *gross written premiums* in the *financial year in question* and the 'gross undiscounted provisions' at the end of that *financial year* for that category of business are each less than 50% of the amounts respectively specified in the 'reporting criteria' for that Form in respect of that category of business.

(5) For the purpose of this rule, rule 9.20A and paragraph 2B of **Appendix 9.2**, **gross undiscounted provisions** are gross undiscounted reported claims outstanding plus gross undiscounted incurred but not reported claims plus gross provision for unearned premiums plus provision for unexpired risks.

Further information on general insurance business to ensure adequate coverage in the return

9.20A

(1) Subject to (2) and (3), if the total of all 'gross undiscounted provisions' in all the **Forms 26 to 29, 31, 32** and **34** required under rules 9.17, 9.19 and 9.20, or included despite rule 9.20(4), is less than 80% of the *insurer's* total 'gross undiscounted provisions', the *insurer* must prepare **Forms 26 to 29, 31, 32** and **34**, as appropriate, for further categories of business (as set out in column 2 of paragraph 2B of **Appendix 9.2**) in decreasing order of size (measured in 'gross undiscounted provisions'), until the 80% criterion is met.

(2) An *insurer* need not prepare a **Form 26, 27, 28, 29, 31, 32** or **34** for a category of business (as set out in column 2 of paragraph 2B of **Appendix 9.2**) if
(a) the *insurer's gross written premiums* in the *financial year in question* for that category of business are less than £1m; and
(b) the *insurer's* 'gross undiscounted provisions' at the end of the *financial year in question* for that category of business are less than £1m.

(3) An *insurer* need only prepare a **Form 26, 27, 28, 29, 31, 32** or **34** for a category of business (as set out in column 2 of paragraph 2B of **Appendix 9.2**) if it is required to prepare a **Form 20** for *category number* 110, 120, 160, 180, 220, 260, 270, 280, 330, 340, 350, 400, 500, 600 or 700 which includes that category of business.

Currencies other than sterling

9.21 Every *insurer* which, in respect of a *financial year*, prepares a Form under rules 9.17 or 9.19 containing figures in a currency other than sterling must prepare **Form 36** in accordance with the requirements of **Appendix 9.2**.

Additional information on general insurance business (claims equalisation provisions)

9.22

(1) This rule applies to non-credit *insurance business* as defined in INSPRU 1.4.11R (1) and credit *insurance business* as defined in INSPRU 1.4.38R.

(2) An *insurer* to which INSPRU 1.4.11R to INSPRU 1.4.37G apply (unless INSPRU 1.4.18R applies) and an *insurer* to which INSPRU 1.4.43R applies (unless INSPRU 1.4.44R applies) must, in accordance with the requirements of **Appendix 9.2**, prepare—
(a) **Form 37**;
(b) **Form 38** for *general insurance business* accounted for on an 'accident year basis'; and
(c) **Form 39** for *general insurance business* accounted for on an 'underwriting year basis.

Additional information on long-term insurance business

9.23 Every *insurer* which carries on *long-term insurance business* must, in respect of the *financial year in question* and in accordance with the requirements of **Appendix 9.3**, prepare—
(a) **Forms 41** to **43** in respect of each revenue account prepared separately under rule 9.14(b)(i);
(b) summary **Forms 41** to **43** if a summary **Form 40** is required under rule 9.14(b)(ii); and
(c) **Forms 44** to **59B** and, except in the case of an *EEA-deposit insurer*, **Form 60.**

as appropriate, together with the information specified in relation to those Forms.

Forms to be annexed

9.24 The forms prepared pursuant to rules 9.15, 9.17 and 9.19 to 9.23 must be annexed to the documents referred to in rules 9.12, 9.13 and 9.14.

Additional information on general insurance business: major treaty reinsurers

9.25

(1) Subject to the provisions of rule 9.28, an *insurer* which carries on *general insurance business* must annex to the documents referred to in rules 9.12, 9.13 and 9.14, and relating to the *financial year in question*, a statement of—

(a) the 'full name'[3] of each of its 'major treaty reinsurers' and the address of the registered office or of the principal office in the country where it is incorporated (or, in the case of an unincorporated body, of the principal office) of each such *reinsurer*;

(b) whether (and, if so, how) the *insurer* was at any time in the *financial year* 'connected'[4] with any such *reinsurer*;

(c) the amount of the *reinsurance* premiums payable in the *financial year* to each such *reinsurer* in respect of—

(i) *general insurance business ceded* under proportional *reinsurance* treaties; and

(ii) *general insurance business ceded* under non-proportional *reinsurance* treaties;

(d) the amount of any *debt* of each such *reinsurer* to the *insurer* in respect of *general insurance business ceded* under *reinsurance* treaties, included at line 75 of **Form 13**;

(e) the amount of any deposit received from each such *reinsurer* under *reinsurance* treaties as included at line 31 of **Form 15**; and

(f) the amount of any anticipated recoveries from each such *reinsurer* under *reinsurance* treaties to the extent that such recoveries have been taken into account by the *insurer* in determining the *reinsurers'* share of *technical provisions* in respect of *claims* outstanding as shown at line 61 of **Form 13**; except that, in respect of *claims* incurred but not reported, such recoveries need only be included to the extent that they are in respect of any specific occurrences for which provisions have been allocated by the *insurer*,

or a statement that it has no 'major treaty reinsurer'.

(2) For the purposes of this rule, a **major treaty reinsurer** of an *insurer* is a another *company*—

(a) to which (whether alone or with any *company* which is 'connected'[5] with the other *company*) the *insurer* has *ceded general insurance business* under one or more *reinsurance* treaties—

(i) in the case of proportional *reinsurance*, for which the total amount of the *reinsurance* premiums payable is equal to not less than 2% of the *gross premiums receivable* by the *insurer* in respect of *general insurance business*, or

(ii) in the case of non-proportional *reinsurance*, for which the total amount of the *reinsurance* premiums payable is equal to not less than 5% of the total premiums payable by the *insurer* in respect of all such non-proportional *reinsurance*,

in the *financial* year *in question* or in any of the five *preceding financial* years of the *insurer*; or

(b) in relation to which (whether alone or with any *company* which is 'connected' with the other *company*) the aggregate of the amounts referred to in (1)(d) and (f) exceeds the sum of 20,000 Euro and 5% of the *insurer's* liabilities arising from its *general insurance business*, net of *reinsurance ceded*.

Additional information on general insurance business: major facultative reinsurers

9.26

(1) Subject to rule 9.28, an *insurer* which carries on *general insurance business* must annex to the documents referred to in rules 9.12, 9.13 and 9.14, and relating to *the financial year in question*, for each 'major facultative reinsurance contract', a statement in respect of each 'major facultative *reinsurer*' of—

(a) its 'full name'[6] and the address of the registered office or of the principal office in the country where it is incorporated (or, in the case of an unincorporated body, of the principal office);

(b) whether (and, if so, how) the *insurer* was at any time in the *financial year* 'connected' with such *reinsurer*;

(c) the amount of the *reinsurance* premiums payable in the *financial year*;

(d) the amount of any *debt* to the *insurer* included at line 75 of **Form 13**;

(e) the amount of any deposit received as included at line 31 of **Form 15**; and

(f) the amount of any anticipated recoveries to the extent that such recoveries have been taken into account by the *insurer* in determining the *reinsurers'* share of *technical provisions* in respect of *claims* outstanding as shown at line 61 of **Form 13**; except that, in respect of *claims* incurred but not reported, such recoveries need only be included to the extent that they are in respect of any specific occurrences for which provisions have been allocated by the *insurer*,

or a statement that it has no 'major facultative reinsurer'.

(2) For the purposes of this rule, a **major facultative reinsurance contract** is a contract under which *general insurance business* has been *ceded* by the *insurer* on a facultative basis—

(a) under which the total amount of premiums payable to any *reinsurer* (a **major facultative reinsurer**) is equal to not less than 0.5% of *gross premiums receivable* by the *insurer* in respect of *general insurance business*; or
(b) in relation to which, in respect of any *reinsurer* (a **major facultative reinsurer**) the aggregate of amounts in (1)(d) and (f) exceeds the sum of 4,000 Euro and 1% of the *insurer's* liabilities arising from its *general insurance business*, net of *reinsurance ceded.*

Information on major general insurance business: reinsurance cedants

9.27
(1) Subject to rule 9.28, an *insurer* which carries on *general insurance business* must annex to the documents referred to in rules 9.12, 9.13 and 9.14, and relating to the *financial year in question*, a statement of—
(a) the 'full name' of each of its 'major cedants' and the address of the registered office or of the principal office in the country where it is incorporated (or, in the case of an unincorporated body, of the principal office) of each such cedant;
(b) whether (and, if so, how) the *insurer* was at any time in the *financial year* 'connected' with any such cedant;
(c) the amount of the total of the *gross premiums receivable* in the *financial year* from each such cedant in respect of *general insurance business* accepted under *reinsurance* treaties;
(d) the amount of any deposit made with any such cedant as included at line 57 of **Form 13**; and
(e) the amount of any *debt* of each such cedant in respect of *general insurance business* accepted under *reinsurance* treaties, included at line 74 of **Form 13**,
or a statement that it has no 'major cedant'.
(2) For the purposes of this rule, a **major cedant** of an *insurer* is another *company* from which (whether alone or with any *company* which is 'connected' with the other *company*) the *insurer* has accepted *general insurance business* under one or more *reinsurance* treaties for which the *gross premiums receivable* exceed the greater of—
(a) 5% of the *gross premiums receivable* by the *insurer* in respect of *general insurance business* accepted under *reinsurance* treaties; and
(b) 2% of the *gross premiums receivable* by the *insurer* in respect of *general insurance business*,
in the *financial year in question* or in any of the three *preceding financial years* of the *insurer*.

Provisions supplemental to rules 9.25 to 9.27

9.28
(1) For the purposes of rules 9.25(1)(b) and (2), 9.26(1)(b) and 9.27(1)(b) and (2), a *company* and another person are **connected** with each other if—
(a) the other person is—
(i) a *subsidiary undertaking* of the *company*,
(ii) a *parent undertaking* of the *company*, or
(iii) a *subsidiary undertaking* of the *parent undertaking* of the *company*; or
(b) one of them is 'controlled' by the other or both are 'controlled' by the same person,
but a *company* is not to be taken to be 'connected' with another person if the *insurer* furnishing the statement does not know and could not upon reasonable enquiry be expected to discover that it is so 'connected' with the other person.
(2) Except as provided in (3), for the purposes of (1)(b), a person is taken to **control** a *company* if he is a person—
(a) in accordance with whose directions or instructions the *directors* of the *company* or of a *company* of which it is a *subsidiary* are accustomed to act; or
(b) who, either alone or with an *associate* is entitled to exercise, or 'control' the exercise of, 15% or more of the voting power at any general meeting of the *company* or of a *company* of which it is a *subsidiary*.
(3) In relation to an *insurer*—
(a) making a statement pursuant to rules 9.25 or 9.26, a *reinsurer* is not to be taken by virtue of (2) to be 'connected' with another *reinsurer*; or
(b) making a statement pursuant to rule 9.27, a cedant is not to be taken by virtue of (2) to be 'connected' with another cedant,
for the purposes of paragraph (2) of rules 9.25, 9.26 or 9.27, as the case may be, unless it is also 'connected' by virtue of (1) with the *insurer* making the statement.
(4) In rules 9.25, 9.26 and 9.27 and in this rule, **full name** means—
(a) in the case of a company, its corporate name; and
(b) in the case of an individual or any unincorporated body, the name under which the individual or body lawfully carries on business.

(5) The following provisions of **Appendix 9.1** apply for the purposes of rules 9.25, 9.26, and 9.27—

(a) paragraphs 4 and 5 (which relate to currencies other than sterling);

(b) paragraphs 8(1) and 8(2) (which, among other things, relate to amounts due to the *insurer*); and

(c) paragraph 9 (which provides for amounts to be shown to the nearer £1,000).

(6) Rules 9.25(2), 9.26(1)(a) to (c) and 9.27 apply in relation to the members of the *Society* taken together as they apply in relation to an *insurer* and in relation to the members of the *Society* (1) to (4) of this rule do not apply.

Additional information on derivative contracts

9.29

(1) Every *insurer* must, in respect of the *financial year in question*, annex to the documents referred to in rules 9.12, 9.13 and 9.14 a statement comprising a brief description of—

(a) any investment guidelines operated by the *insurer* for the use of *derivative contracts*;

(b) any provision made by such guidelines for the use of contracts under which the *insurer* had a right or obligation to acquire or dispose of assets which was not, at the time when the contract was entered into, reasonably likely to be exercised and, if so, the circumstances in which, pursuant to that provision, such contracts would be used;

(c) the extent to which the *insurer* was during the *financial year* a party to any contracts of the kind described in (b);

(d) [deleted]

(e) [deleted]

(f) [deleted]

(g) [deleted]

(h) the circumstances surrounding the use of any *derivative* or *quasi-derivative* held at any time during the *financial year* which required a 'significant' provision to be made for it under INSPRU 3.2.17R, or (where appropriate) did not fall within the definition of a *permitted derivatives contract*; and

(i) the total value of any fixed consideration received by the *insurer* (whether in cash or otherwise) during the *financial year* in return for granting rights under *derivatives* and *quasi-derivatives* and a summary of contracts under which such rights have been granted.

(1A) For the purposes of determining in accordance with (1)(h) whether a required provision is 'significant', the *insurer* must have regard to its obligations under the contract and the volatility of the assets identified by the *insurer* as being suitable to cover such obligations; and the required provision in respect of any one *derivative contract* must be treated as **significant** if—

(a) the aggregate provision required in respect of all contracts having a similar effect is significant; or

(b) the aggregate provision required in respect of all contracts with which it is connected is significant.

(2) [deleted]

(2A) [deleted]

(2B) [deleted]

(2C) [deleted]

(2D) [deleted]

(3) [deleted]

Additional information on controllers

9.30 Every *insurer* with its head office in the United Kingdom must, in respect of the *financial year in question*, annex to the documents referred to in rules 9.12, 9.13 and 9.14—

(a) a statement naming each person who, to the knowledge of the *insurer*, has been, at any time during the *financial year*, *a controller* of that *insurer*; and

(b) in the case of each person so named, a statement of—

Part II FSA Handbook Materials

(i) the percentage of *shares* which, to the knowledge of the *insurer*, he held at the end of the *financial year in question* in the *insurer*, or in another company of which the *insurer* is a *subsidiary undertaking*; and

(ii) the percentage of the voting power which, to the knowledge of the *insurer*, he was entitled at the end of the *financial year in question* to exercise, or control the exercise of, at any general meeting of the *insurer*, or another company of which it is a *subsidiary undertaking*,

in each case, either alone or with any *associate* or *associates*.

Valuation reports on long-term insurance business

9.31 Every *insurer* which carries on *long-term insurance business* must prepare and annex to the documents referred to in rules 9.12, 9.13 and 9.14—

(a) for the purposes of rule 9.4 other than in relation to the calculation required by rule 9.4(2)(c):

(i) where an investigation into the financial condition of the *insurer* has been made in accordance with rule 9.4(1)(a), a valuation report which complies with the requirements of **Appendix 9.4** and contains the information specified in that Appendix;

(ii) where an investigation into the financial condition of the *insurer* has been made at some other time with a view to the distribution of profits or the results of which are made public, **Form 58** and a valuation report which, instead of complying with the requirements of **Appendix 9.4**, includes a full description of each of the changes in the methods and assumptions used in the investigation for the purposes of rule 9.4(2)(a) and (b) since the previous investigation at the end of the *preceding financial year* or if there has been no such change, a statement to that effect, and

(b) for the purposes of rule 9.4 in relation to the calculation required by rule 9.4(2)(c) (if applicable), a valuation report for the realistic valuation which complies with the requirements of **Appendix 9.4A** and contains the information specified in that Appendix.

Additional information on general insurance business ceded

9.32 An *insurer* which carries on *general insurance business* must annex to the documents referred to in rules 9.12, 9.13 and 9.14, and relating to the *financial year in question*, a statement of the information required by **Appendix 9.5**.

Additional information on financial reinsurance and financing arrangements: general insurers

9.32A

(1) An *insurer* which carries on *general insurance business* must annex to the documents referred to in rules 9.12, 9.13 and 9.14, and relating to the *financial year in question*, a statement of the information required by this rule.

(2) This rule applies to any *contract of insurance* under which *general insurance business* has been *ceded* by the *insurer*, where—

(a) the value placed on future payments in respect of the contract in the *return* for the *financial year in question* is not commensurate with the economic value provided by that contract, after taking account of the level of risk transferred; or

(b) there are terms or foreseeable contingencies (other than the insured event) that have the potential to affect materially the value placed on the contract in the *insurer's* balance sheet at, or any time after, the end of the *financial year in question*.

(3) In determining whether a *contract of insurance* meets one or both of the conditions in (2), the *insurer* must—

(a) treat as part of a contract any agreements, correspondence (including side-letters) or understandings that amend or modify, or purport to amend or modify, the contract or its operation; and

(b) consider whether the contract meets the condition in (2)(a) when considered together with one or more other *contracts of insurance* entered into between:

(i) the *insurer* and the *reinsurer* under the first contract; or

(ii) the *insurer* and any other *person*, where it could reasonably be predicted, at the time the most recent contract was entered into, that the contracts when considered together would meet the condition in (2)(a).

(4) Subject to (9), for each *contract of insurance* to which this rule applies the statement must contain the following information—

(a) the *financial year* of the *return* in which the contract was first reported in the *return*;

(b) the financial effect of the contract on the *insurer's capital resources* as shown in line 13 of **Form 1** of the *return* for the *financial year in question*;

(c) the amount of any undischarged obligation of the *insurer* under the contract and a brief description of the conditions for the discharge of such obligation; and

(d) how any undischarged obligations, including any contingent obligations, have been taken into account in determining the *insurer's capital resources*.

(5) The statement must include a general description of how the *insurer* makes the financial assessment that enables it to determine whether a contract satisfies the condition in (2)(a), even if there are no contracts in respect of which information is required by (4).

(6) This rule also applies to any **financing arrangement**, which for the purpose of this rule means any contract, other than a *contract of insurance*, that has been entered into by the *insurer*, in respect of *contracts of insurance* written by the *insurer*, which has the effect of increasing the *capital resources* of the *insurer* in line 13 of **Form 1**, and which includes terms for—
  (a) the transfer of assets to the *insurer*, the creation of a *debt* to the *insurer* or the transfer from the *insurer* to another party of liabilities to *policyholders* (or any combination of these); and
  (b) either an obligation for the *insurer* to return (with or without interest) some or all of such assets, a provision for the diminution of such *debt* or a provision for the recapture of such liabilities, in each case, in specified circumstances.

(7) In determining whether a contract falls within the definition of 'financing arrangement' in (6), the *insurer* must—
  (a) treat as part of a contract any agreements, correspondence (including side-letters) or understandings that amend or modify, or purport to amend or modify, the contract or its operation; and
  (b) consider whether the contract meets the conditions in (6) when considered together with one or more other contracts entered into between:
    (i) the *insurer* and the *counterparty* under the first contract; or
    (ii) the *insurer* and any other *person*, where it could reasonably be predicted, at the time the most recent contract was entered into, that the contracts when considered together would meet the conditions in (6).

(8) Subject to (9), for each 'financing arrangement' entered into by the *insurer* the statement must contain the following information—
  (a) the *financial year* of the *return* in which the 'financing arrangement' was first reported in the *return*;
  (b) the financial effect of the 'financing arrangement' on the *insurer's capital resources* as shown in line 13 of **Form 1** of the *return* for the *financial year in question*;
  (c) the amount of any undischarged obligation of the *insurer* under the 'financing arrangement' and a brief description of the conditions for the discharge of such obligation; and
  (d) how any undischarged obligations, including any contingent obligations, have been taken into account in determining the *insurer's capital resources*.

(9) No information need be supplied pursuant to (4) or (8) in respect of a *contract of insurance* or 'financing arrangement' if, when it is considered in aggregate with all such contracts with the same *reinsurer* or *counterparty* or any other *person* with whom the *insurer* has entered into a contract in the circumstances described in (3)(b)(ii) or, as the case may be, (7)(b)(ii)—
  (a) A is less than 1% of B in the *return* for the *financial year in question*; and
  (b) the *insurer* expects A to remain less than 1% of B for the foreseeable future;

  where:
  (i) A is the financial effect on the *insurer's capital resources* as a result of the existence of the contract(s); and
  (ii) B is the *insurer's* total gross amount of *technical provisions*.

(10) Where the statement required by (1) includes information about a *contract of insurance* in respect of which information has been included in the statement required by rule 9.32 relating to the *financial year in question*, the *insurer* must include in the statement under (1) a cross-reference to that other information.

Additional information on financial reinsurance and financing arrangements: guidance

9.32B

(1) In line with normal practice, an *insurer* may take account of an appropriate risk margin to reflect the nature and level of risk transferred, including any uncertainty in the amount and timing of future payments, when assessing the economic value of the transaction at the end of the *financial year in question* in order to see whether the condition in rule 9.32A(2)(a) is met. In addition, an *insurer* would be expected to take account of any credit or legal risk associated with the transaction when assessing its economic value.

(2) For most *proportional reinsurance treaties* and most standard *non-proportional reinsurance treaties*, such as contracts providing excess-of-loss cover, which include a significant transfer of risk to the *reinsurer* and do not contain any of the features described in (5) below, it is likely that the *insurer* will be able to determine that the contracts do not meet the condition in rule 9.32A(2)(a) without making a detailed calculation. The approach taken to the assessment made for the purpose of rule 9.32A(2)(a) should, however, still be described in the statement provided as required by rule 9.32A(5).

(3) When considering whether there are foreseeable contingencies, other than the insured event, that may affect the contract's given value, the *insurer* should consider the normal commercial uncertainties about the size of the *claim* that may ultimately be payable (for example, the outcome of any possible court action) to be part of the insured event. These normal commercial uncertainties would not then trigger any disclosure requirement under rule 9.32A.

(4) It is likely that one or both of the conditions in rule 9.32A(2) will be satisfied if the *contract of insurance* contains features that have the effect of materially limiting the size of the difference between—

(a) the extent of the indemnity cover provided by the contract and by any related or potentially related contracts, and

(b) the *premiums* payable under those contracts,

relative to the size of the *premiums* payable under those contracts.

(5) Some characteristic features which the *insurer* should consider carefully in relation to a *contract of insurance* before deciding whether one or both of the conditions in rule 9.32A(2) are satisfied with respect to a particular contract include (but are not limited to) the following—

(a) sliding scale fees, retrospectively rated *premiums* and profit-sharing formulae which adjust cash flows between the *insurer* and the *reinsurer* based on loss experience (for example, increasing payments from the *insurer* as losses increase and decreasing payments as losses decrease, subject to maximum and minimum limits);

(b) provision for an *experience account* or arrangements having similar effect, including arrangements which recognise an assumed rate of investment return;

(c) provision for, or a contingent obligation on, the *insurer* to make payments to the *reinsurer* or to any other *person*, where the payments—

(i) depend upon the loss experience of *general insurance business* that has been or may be carried on by the *insurer*; and

(ii) are not simply reinstatement *premiums*;

(d) provision for termination or commutation of the contract at the sole discretion of the *reinsurer*, when there is a positive balance of money due from the *reinsurer*;

(e) a provision for, or a contingent obligation on, the *insurer* to make payments to the *reinsurer* or to any other *person*, where the payments are in respect of business carried on in a period outside of the term of the contract;

(f) the contract includes a term requiring the *insurer* to enter into a further contract if the loss experience of the business subject to the contract attains a specified level;

(g) the term of the contract exceeds, or may exceed, 12 months, and the *premium* or amount of indemnity payable under the contract in subsequent years may be affected by the loss experience of earlier years;

(h) dual triggers which require the occurrence of both—

(i) an insurable event; and

(ii) a change in a separate variable specified in the contract;

in order to trigger payment of a benefit/*claim*;

(i) amounts payable under the contract could affect, or depend on, other contracts or agreements entered into by the *insurer*, or a *person connected* with the *insurer*, except where—

(i) that effect or dependence is clear from the description of that other contract or agreement given by the *insurer*; or

(ii) that effect or dependence arises solely as part of the normal market mechanism for the pricing of a risk; and

(j) terms that defer payment of *claims*—

(i) for a period of more than 12 months after the amount payable under the contract has been agreed; or

(ii) until some specified date that is more than 12 months after the end of the term of the contract.

(6) For the purpose of rule 9.32A(4), (8) and (9), the 'financial effect' of the transaction (that is, the contract or 'financing arrangement') on the *insurer's capital resources* should normally be regarded as the sum of (a) the value placed on the transaction in the *return* for the *financial year in question* plus (b) the net sum of all receipts less payments made in respect of the transaction since the transaction was first reported in the *return*.

Signature of documents

9.33

(1) In respect of any document relating to the *insurance business* of an *insurer*, wherever it may be carried on, the signatories for the purposes of rule 9.6 are—

(a) where there are more than two *directors* of the *insurer*, at least two of those *directors* and, where there are not more than two *directors*, all the *directors*, and

(b) a chief executive, if any, of the *insurer* or (if there is no chief executive) the secretary, if any.

(2) In respect of any document relating to *insurance business* carried on through a branch in the United Kingdom by a *Swiss general insurer*, an *EEA deposit insurer* or an *external insurer* or through branches in any *EEA State* (taken together) by a *UK deposit insurer*, the signatories for the purposes of rule 9.6(3) are—

(a) the authorised UK representative referred to in article 3(1)(a) of The Financial Services and Markets Act 2000 (Variation of Threshold Conditions) Order 2001 (2001/2507), and

(b) the chief executive appointed under rule 8.3 or, in the case of a *Swiss general insurer*, a person who alone or jointly with one of more others, is responsible for the conduct of its *insurance business* through the branch.

Certificates by Directors

9.34

(1) Except for reporting under rule 9.3A, there must be annexed to the documents referred to in rules 9.12, 9.13 and 9.14 a certificate in accordance with the requirements of Part I of **Appendix 9.6** which must be signed by the persons required by rule 9.33 to sign the documents to which the certificate relates.

(2) In respect of reporting under rule 9.3A, there must be annexed to the documents referred to in that rule a certificate in accordance with the requirements of Part IA of **Appendix 9.6** which must be signed by a *director* of the *insurer*.

Audit and auditor's report

9.35

(1) The documents referred to in rules 9.12, 9.13 and 9.14, together with Forms **40** to **45**, **48**, **49**, **56**, **58** (including a **Form 58** completed under rule 9.31(a)(ii)) and **60**, and every statement, analysis or report annexed pursuant to rules 9.24 to 9.27, 9.29 and 9.31 must be audited by a person, in accordance with the rules in *SUP*, who must make and annex to those documents a report in accordance with the requirements of Part II of **Appendix 9.6**.

(1A) For the purposes of rule 9.5 and (1) and **Appendix 9.6**, to the extent that any document, form, statement, analysis or report to be audited under (1) contains amounts or information abstracted from the *actuarial investigation* performed pursuant to rule 9.4, the *insurer* must ensure that the auditor obtains and pays due regard to advice from a suitably qualified *actuary* who is independent of the *insurer*.

(2) For the purposes of the Accounts and Statements Rules—

(a) section 237(1), (2) and (3) and section 389A(1) of the Companies Act 1985 and article 245(1), (2) and (3) and article 397A(1) of the *1986 Order* where applicable, otherwise sections 498(1), (2) and (3) and 499(1) of the Companies Act 2006 apply as if—

(i) the references to the *profit and loss account* in 'individual accounts' in section 226(1) of the Companies Act 1985 and article 234(1) of that Order, and section 394 of the Companies Act 2006 respectively, included references to the revenue account; and

(ii) the auditors of the insurer were not under a duty for the purposes of preparing their report to carry out any investigation into information given in **Forms 31, 32** and **34** relating wholly or partly to the number of claims notified or the amount of payments made prior to the financial year of the *insurer* in which the Insurance Companies (Accounts and Statements) Regulations 1980 first applied; and

(b) section 389A(3) and (4) of the Companies Act 1985 and article 397A(3) and (4) of the *1986 Order*, where they are applicable, otherwise section 500(1) of the Companies Act 2006 apply as if the references in them to a 'parent company' were references to the *insurer*.

Information on the actuary who has been appointed to perform the with-profits actuary function

9.36

(1) Subject to the provisions of this rule, there must be annexed to the documents referred to in rules 9.12, 9.13 and 9.14, with respect to every person who, at any time during the *financial year in question*, was the *actuary* who has been appointed to perform the *with-profits actuary function* for the insurer, a statement of the following information—

Part II FSA Handbook Materials

(a) particulars of any *shares* in, or debentures of, 'the *insurer*' in which the 'actuary' was 'interested' at any time during that year;
(b) particulars of any pecuniary interest of 'the actuary' in any transaction between 'the actuary' and 'the *insurer*' and subsisting at any time during that year or, in the case of transactions of a minor character, a general description of such interests;
(c) the aggregate amount of—
 (i) any remuneration and the value of any other benefits (other than a pension or other future or contingent benefit) under any contract of service of 'the actuary' with, or contract for services by 'the actuary' to, 'the *insurer*', and
 (ii) any emoluments, pensions or compensation as *director* of the *insurer* which are required by regulation 8 of and Schedule 5 to the Large and Medium Sized Companies and Groups (Accounts and Reports) Regulations 2008 (SI 2008/410) to be included in a note to the accounts of 'the *insurer*' receivable by 'the actuary' in respect of any period in that year; and
(d) a general description of any other pecuniary benefit (including any pension and other future or contingent benefit) received by 'the actuary' from 'the *insurer*' in that year or receivable by him from 'the *insurer*',

together with the statement specified in (2).

(2) The statement referred to in (1) is a statement that 'the *insurer*' has made a request to 'the actuary' to furnish to it the particulars specified in that paragraph and identifying any particulars furnished pursuant to that request.

(3) For the purposes of (1)(a) to (d)—
(a) references to **the actuary** include reference to—
 (i) the spouse, civil partner and any minor child (including step-child) of 'the actuary',
 (ii) any person who is a business partner of 'the actuary',
 (iii) any person (other than 'the *insurer*') of which 'the actuary' is an employee, and
 (iv) any person (other than 'the *insurer*') of which 'the actuary' is a *director* or which is 'controlled' by him;
(b) a person is deemed to be **interested** in *shares* or debentures if he is interested in them according to the rules set out in Schedule 1 to the Companies Act 2006 with the addition, in paragraph 6(4) of that Schedule, of a reference to a scheme under section 25 of the Charities Act (Northern Ireland) 1964; and
(c) a person is deemed to have an **interest** or benefit if he has a beneficial interest.

(4) For the purposes of (1)(a) to (d) and of (3)(a), references to **the** *insurer* include references to any *body corporate* which is 'the *insurer's' subsidiary undertaking* or *parent undertaking* and to any other *subsidiary undertaking* of its *parent undertaking*.

(5) For the purposes of (3), a person is taken to **control** a *body corporate* if he is a person—
(a) in accordance with whose directions or instructions the *directors* of that *body corporate* or of a *body corporate* of which it is a *subsidiary* are accustomed to act; or
(b) who, either alone or with any other person falling within (3)(a), is entitled to exercise, or control the exercise of, 15% or more of the voting power at any general meeting of the *body corporate* or of a *body corporate* of which it is a *subsidiary*.

---

1 See SUP 16.3.6 to 16.3.10R for rules on the submission of periodic reports, which take effect from 18 April 2002.

2 The amendment of rule 9.6(6) comes into force on 1 October 2002.

3 For the meaning of 'full name' in this rule, see rule 9.28(4).

4 For the meaning of 'connected', in this rule, see rule 9.28(1).

5 For the meaning of 'connected', in this rule, see rule 9.28(1).

6 For the meaning of 'full name' in this rule, see rule 9.28(4).

Part II
Accounts and Statements for a Marine Mutual

Returns

[2098]
9.36A Subject to rules 9.36B, 9.36C, 9.36D and 9.36E and **Appendix 9.8**, a *marine mutual* may complete an abbreviated *return* which comprises—
(1) **Forms 1**, **3**, **11** and **12**; and
(2) Forms M1 to M5 in Appendix 9.8,

and, if so, rules 9.3 to 9.4, 9.12 to 9.28, 9.31 and 9.32 and 9.34 to 9.36 do not apply.

Information to be annexed to the forms

9.36B A *marine mutual* must annex to the *return* provided under rule 9.36A—

(1) a description of the significant *reinsurance* arrangements which will be in operation in the *financial year* following the *financial year in question*;

(2) in respect of *insurance business* ceded by way of non-facultative reinsurance in respect of the *financial year in question* or any *previous financial year* ended on or after 20 February 1998, a statement of—

(a) in the case of contracts which are subject to no or a limited number of reinstatements, any contract not previously reported to the *FSA* under which it is anticipated that any such limit will be exhausted by such *claims* (including *claims* incurred, but not reported, in respect of any specific occurrence for which provisions have been allocated);

(b) the percentage of cover, if in excess of 10%, and if such information was not included in the *return* of the *marine mutual* for the *previous financial year*, which has been *ceded* to *reinsurers* which have ceased to pay *claims* to their reinsureds in full, whether because of insolvency or for any other reason; and

(c) if the percentage specified in (b) has increased by more than 10% since the *previous financial year* in which it was included in the *marine mutual's return*, that percentage unless, in the opinion of the *directors*, the likelihood of any *claim* being incurred under that *policy* is minimal;

(3) a statement concerning:

(a) the default rates of members (or adjusted default rates, as the case may be) on the supplementary calls collectable during the *financial year in question* and the two *previous financial years*, respectively; and

(b) the total amount of each such call, the *financial year* to which it relates, the amount paid and the amount remaining outstanding; and

(4) a copy of the rules of association of the marine mutual in force on the date of deposit of the return, unless there has been no change in a copy of the rules deposited with the return for a previous financial year.

Information to FSA

9.36C A *marine mutual* which provides a *return* under rule 9.36A must, with effect from the date of its deposit with the *FSA* until the date of deposit of the *return* for the following *financial year*, provide the *FSA* with written notice of:

(1) any change which is proposed in the rules of association of the *marine mutual*, not less than 14 days before the change is put to a meeting;

(2) any change which has been made in the rules of association, within 7 days of the change;

(3) any significant change in the *reinsurance* arrangements, a description of which has been annexed to the *return* in accordance with rule 9.36B(1), within 7 days of the change;

(4) a fall in tonnage entered by its members of 10% net or more since the end of the *financial year in question*, within 7 days of the *marine mutual* becoming aware of this; and

(5) whether tonnage entered by its members who have withdrawn from membership or who have defaulted on their obligations has increased so as to exceed 10% or more of total tonnage entered, whether before, on or after the date of deposit of the *return*, within 7 days of the date of deposit or of the *marine mutual* becoming aware of this, whichever is earlier.

Directors' certificate

9.36D A *marine mutual* must annex to the *return* provided under rule 9.36A a *directors'* certificate in accordance with Part II of **Appendix 9.8**.

Auditors' report

9.36E A *marine mutual* must annex to the *return* provided under rule 9.36A an auditors' report in accordance with Part III of **Appendix 9.8**.

Part III
Statistical Rules

Insurance statistics: EEA States

[2099]

9.37

(1) Every *UK insurer* which in any calendar year—

(a) carries on *general insurance business* in an *EEA State* other than the United Kingdom through a branch in that State; or

(b) provides general insurance in such a State through an establishment in the United Kingdom or another *EEA State*,

Part II FSA Handbook Materials

must prepare in respect of the *direct general insurance business* so carried on by it a statement in **Form 91** (analysis of financial particulars – branches), or the direct general insurance so provided by it a statement in **Form 92** (analysis of financial particulars – provision of insurance), in accordance with the requirements of **Appendix 9.7**.

(2) Every *UK insurer* which in any calendar year—

(a) carries on *long-term insurance business* in an *EEA State* other than the United Kingdom through a branch in that State; or

(b) provides long-term insurance in such a State through an establishment in the United Kingdom or another *EEA State*, must prepare in respect of the *direct long-term insurance business* so carried on by it a statement in **Form 93** (analysis of financial particulars – branches), or the direct long-term insurance so provided by it a statement in **Form 94** (analysis of financial particulars – provision of insurance), in accordance with the requirements of **Appendix 9.7**.

(3) The forms mentioned in (1) and (2) must be prepared separately in respect of each *EEA State* in which the *insurer* carries on the *insurance business* or provides the insurance.

(4) The statements required by this rule must be printed, and three copies must be deposited with the *FSA* within four months after the end of the calendar year to which they relate; but if in any case it appears to the *FSA* that the circumstances are such that a longer period than four months should be allowed, the *FSA* may extend that period by such period not exceeding three months as it thinks fit. If the due date for deposit of documents required by this rule falls on a day which is not a business day, the documents must be submitted no later than the first business day after the due date.

(5) One of the copies of the statement deposited under (4) must be signed by a *director*, a chief executive or the secretary of the *insurer*.

(6) Subject to (7), where a *UK insurer* which has notified the *FSA*—

(a) in accordance with the rules in *SUP*, of its intention to establish a branch in a *EEA State* other than the United Kingdom; or

(b) in accordance with those rules, of its intention to provide insurance in such a State,

does not in any calendar year carry on *insurance business* or, as the case may be, provide insurance in that State, it must send to the *FSA* a notification of that fact within four months after the end of the calendar year to which the notification relates, signed by a *director*, a chief executive or the secretary of the *insurer*.

(7) (6) does not apply if the *insurer* has, before the beginning of the calendar year, informed the *FSA*, in accordance with the rules in *SUP*, that it has ceased to carry on *insurance business* or, as the case may be, to provide insurance in the State in question.

(8) If within 24 months of the date of deposit under (4), the *FSA* notifies the *insurer* that a document deposited appears to it to be inaccurate or incomplete, the *insurer* must consider the matter and within one month of the date of notification it must correct any inaccuracies and make good any omissions and deposit the relevant parts of the documents again.

Application of rule 9.37 to the Society of Lloyd's

9.38

(1) Subject to (2) and (3), rule 9.37 applies in relation to the *Society* as it applies in relation to a *UK insurer*.

(2) The information required in the case of the *Society* to be included in the statements referred to in rule 9.37(4), or the notification referred to in rule 9.37(6), is that relating to the members of the *Society* taken together.

(3) Any such statements, forms or notification must be signed by the Chairman or a Deputy Chairman, for and on behalf of the Council of Lloyd's.

Part IV

Material Connected-Party Transactions

[2100]

9.39

(1) If, during the *financial year in question*, an *insurer* has agreed to, or carried out, a *material connected-party transaction*, it must provide a brief description of that transaction by way of a supplementary note to **Form 20** (note 2007) or **Form 40** (note 4009).

(2) The description to be provided in accordance with (1) must state—

(a) the names of the transacting parties;

(b) a description of the relationship between the parties;

(c) a description of the transaction;

(d) the amounts involved;

(e) any other elements of the transaction necessary for an understanding of its effect upon the financial position or performance of the *insurer*; and

(f) amounts written off in the period in respect of *debts* due to or from *connected* parties.

(3) Transactions with the same *connected* party may be disclosed on an aggregated basis unless separate disclosure is needed for a proper understanding of the effect of the transactions upon the financial position or performance of the *insurer*.

Part V
Group Capital Adequacy

[2101]
9.40

(1) Subject to (2), an *insurer* to which INSPRU 6.1 applies must, in respect of its *ultimate insurance parent undertaking* and its *ultimate EEA insurance parent undertaking* (if different), report:

(a) the name, location of the head office and principal activity of that *undertaking*;

(b) the *group capital resources* of that *undertaking* (calculated in accordance with INSPRU 6.1.36R);

(c) the *group capital resources requirement* of that *undertaking* (calculated in accordance with INSPRU 6.1.33R); and

(d) the difference between (b) and (c).

(1A) Subject to (2), an *insurer* to which INSPRU 6.1 applies must, in respect of its *ultimate EEA insurance parent undertaking*, report:

(a) where its *ultimate EEA insurance parent undertaking* has published annual consolidated accounts prepared in accordance with accounting standards, policies and legislation applicable to it, a reconciliation between:

(i) the *group capital resources* of the *ultimate EEA insurance parent undertaking*; and

(ii) the shareholders' funds, subordinated liabilities and other relevant amounts included in the published annual consolidated accounts of the *ultimate EEA insurance parent undertaking*; and

(b) where its *ultimate EEA insurance parent undertaking* includes a capital statement in the form prescribed by the Accounting Standards Board's Financial Reporting Standard 27, an explanation of any differences between:

(i) the amounts included in that capital statement; and

(ii) the amounts in (1)(b).

(2) No report is required if:

(a) The *insurer* is an *undertaking* listed in INSPRU 6.1.17R(2); or

(b) under Article 4(2) of the *Insurance Groups Directive*, a *competent authority* of an *EEA State* other than the *United Kingdom* has agreed to be the *competent authority* responsible for exercising supplementary supervision in accordance with INSPRU 6.1.23R.

(3) The report in (1) must:

(a) comply with the requirements of SUP 16.3;

(b) subject to (4), be signed by the persons described in IPRU(INS) 9.33(1); and

(c) include a statement from the auditors of the *insurer* (or of an *insurer* under (4)) that, in their opinion, the report in (1) has been properly compiled in accordance with INSPRU 6.1 from information provided by members of the *insurance group* and from the *insurer's* own records.

(4) The reports in (1) and (1A) must be provided by either the *insurer* or on behalf of the *insurer* (the first *insurer*) by any other *insurer* to which INSPRU 6.1 applies and which is a member of the *insurance group* (the second *insurer*) where:

(a) it is signed by two *directors* of the second *insurer*, and

(b) it contains a statement that it has been copied to the board of *directors* of the first *insurer*.

9.41

(1) Subject to (2), an insurer must include, in the report in rule 9.40(1), the details of any regulated related undertaking in the insurance group where the individual capital resources requirement of that undertaking exceeds its solo capital resources, stating in each case:

(a) where the *undertaking* in rule 9.41(1)(a) is a *subsidiary undertaking* of the *ultimate insurance parent undertaking* or *ultimate EEA insurance parent undertaking* (if different), the full amount of the calculation items set out in INSPRU 6.1.28R of that *undertaking* in accordance with INSPRU 6.1.30R and INSPRU 6.1.31R; or

(b) where the *undertaking* in rule 9.41(1)(a) is not a *subsidiary undertaking*, the *ultimate insurance parent undertaking's* or *ultimate EEA insurance parent undertaking's* relevant proportion, as set out in INSPRU 6.1.29R, of the calculation items set out in INSPRU 6.1.28R of that *undertaking*.

(2) Subject to paragraph (4) an insurer can exclude a regulated related undertaking where the individual capital resources requirement of that undertaking exceeds its solo capital resources if:

(a) the group capital resources of the ultimate insurance parent undertaking or the ultimate EEA insurance parent undertaking (as the case may be) exceed its group capital resources requirement;

(b) paragraph 3 applies to the regulated related undertaking.

(3) This paragraph applies to a *regulated related undertaking* if:

(a) in respect of the *insurance group*, it is not;

(i) the *insurer*; or

(ii) a *parent undertaking* of the *insurer*; or

(iii) a *participating undertaking* in the *insurer*; or

(iv) a *related undertaking* of the *insurer*; and

(b) the amount by which its *individual capital resources requirement* exceeds its *solo capital resources* does not exceed 5% of the amount that the *group capital resources* exceed the *group capital resources requirement* referred to in rule (2)(a)

(4) An *insurer* must include *regulated related undertakings* to which paragraph (2) would apply if the amount of D less E exceeds 10% of the amount that the *group capital resources* exceed the *group capital resources requirement* referred to in rule (2)(a), where:

(a) D is the sum of the *individual capital resources requirements* of the *regulated related undertakings*; and

(b) E is the sum of the *solo capital resources* of the *regulated related undertakings*.

9.42

(1) The reports in rule 9.40(1) and rule 9.40(1A) must include information and calculations required by rule 9.40 and rule 9.41:

(a) as at the end of the *financial year* of:

(i) the *insurer*; or

(ii) the *ultimate EEA insurance parent undertaking*; or

(iii) the *ultimate insurance parent undertaking*.

(b) subject to (2), as at the same date for every member of the *insurance group* to which the report relates. Where the *financial year* end of a member of the *insurance group* differs from the date chosen for the purposes of 1(a), interim calculations must be prepared for that member as at the date chosen for the purposes of 1(a); and

(c) as at a date no later than 12 months from the day after the end of the *financial year* by reference to which the information and calculations required in the report were last provided under this chapter or Chapter 10 of *I*PRU(INS).

(2) If it is not practical to prepare interim calculations for a member of the *insurance group* whose *financial year* end differs from the date chosen for the purposes of 1(a), calculations as at the member's last *financial year* end may be used, provided that:

(a) the member's *financial year* end is not more than three months before the date chosen for the purposes of 1(a); and

(b) the calculations are adjusted to take account of any changes between the *financial year* end and the date chosen for the purposes of 1(a) that materially affect the information and calculations required by rules 9.40 and 9.41.

(3) If for any reason the end of the *financial year* chosen for the purposes of (1)(a) is changed so as to end on a date later than that specified in 1(c):

(a) the report after the change takes effect must be as at the later date; but

(b) unless the report contains information and calculations that do not materially differ from what they would be as at the date specified in 1(c), the *insurer* must also provide the *FSA* with an interim statement.

(4) Subject to (4A) and (4B), an *insurer* must submit the reports in rule 9.40(1) and in *rule* 9.40(1A) to the *FSA* no later than 4 months from the end of:

(a) The *financial year in question*; or

(b) the *financial year* of the relevant parent, where the report is provided as at the end of its *financial year* under (1)(a).

The *insurer* must send one printed copy and one electronic copy to the appropriate addresses set out in rule 9.6(2) above. The electronic copy must be sent by email and the title of the email must be:

<firm name> group capital adequacy <dd/mm/yyyy>.

(4A) Where an *insurer's ultimate EEA insurance parent undertaking* publishes annual consolidated accounts in accordance with accounting standards, policies and legislation applicable to it, the report required by rule 9.40(1A) must be submitted to the *FSA* by no later than the date which is 30 days after publication of those consolidated accounts or the final date of submission required by (4), whichever is the later.

(4B) If the due date for submission of reports under (4) or (4A) falls on a day which is not a *business day*, the reports must be submitted no later than the first *business day* after that date.

(5) If within 24 months of receipt, the *FSA* notifies the *insurer* that a report appears to be inaccurate or incomplete, the *insurer* must, within one month of notification, provide a revised report correcting any inaccuracies and making good any omissions.

9.42A

(1) An *insurer* that reports under rule 9.40(1) must, subject to rule 9.42B, provide to any person, within 30 days of the date of request (or the date of submission to the *FSA* if later):

(a) the following information from the report in respect of the *financial year in question*:

(i) the name, location of the head office and principal activity of the *ultimate EEA insurance parent undertaking*;

(ii) the amount of the *group capital resources* of the *ultimate EEA insurance parent undertaking*;

(iii) the amount of the *group capital resources requirement* of the *ultimate EEA insurance parent undertaking*;

(iv) the difference between (ii) and (iii); and

(b) a copy of the report in rule 9.40(1A) in respect of the *financial year in question*; and

(c) a copy of any information provided under rule 9.42(5) that revises any information provided in (a) and (b),

where the information is available in an electronic form, in the form requested or, if the information is not available electronically, in printed form, but (except in the case of (c)) the *insurer* may make a charge to cover its reasonable costs, including those of printing and postage.

(2) (1) does not apply to a *pure reinsurer* which became a *firm in run-off* before 10 December 2007 and whose *Part IV permission* has not subsequently been varied to add back the *regulated activity* of *effecting contracts of insurance*.

9.42B

(1) An *insurer* identified at stage F of the decision tree in rule 9.42C must provide to any person within 30 days of the request the information in rule 9.42D.

(2) The information referred to in (1) must be provided, where the information is available in an electronic form, in the form requested or, if the information is not available electronically, in printed form, but the *insurer* may make a charge to cover its reasonable costs, including those of printing and postage.

9.42C

The decision tree determining application of 9.42B.

[*This decision tree has not been reproduced for technical reasons. Please refer to the FSA website.*]

9.42D

(1) An *insurer* must provide the following information from the report prepared in accordance with SUP 16.12.33R in respect of the *financial year in question* of the *financial conglomerate* identified at Stage C of the decision tree in rule 9.42C:

(a) the capital resources and capital resources requirement identified in (2) of the *financial conglomerate*;

(b) the difference between the capital resources and capital resources requirement of the *financial conglomerate* referred to in (a);

(c) where the *parent undertaking* in the *financial conglomerate* that is not a *subsidiary* of another member of the *financial conglomerate* has published annual consolidated accounts prepared in accordance with accounting standards, policies and legislation applicable to it, a reconciliation between:

(i) the amount of the capital resources of the *financial conglomerate* in (2); and

(ii) the shareholders' funds, subordinated liabilities and other relevant amounts included in the published annual consolidated accounts of that *parent undertaking*; and

(d) where the *parent undertaking* in the *financial conglomerate* that is not a *subsidiary undertaking* of another member of the *financial conglomerate* includes a capital statement in the form prescribed by the Accounting Standards Board's Financial Reporting Standard 27, an explanation of any differences between:
(i) the capital resources of the *financial conglomerate* in (2); and
(ii) the amounts included in that capital statement.

(2) The capital resources and capital resources requirement of the *financial conglomerate* identified at Stage C of the decision tree in rule 9.42C are:
(a) where GENPRU 3.1.26R applies to the *financial conglomerate*, the capital resources of the *financial conglomerate* and the minimum amount of capital resources that the *financial conglomerate* must have to meet the requirement in GENPRU 3.1.26R; or
(b) where GENPRU 3.1.29R applies to the financial conglomerate, its conglomerate capital resources and its conglomerate capital resources requirement.

Guidance

9.43
(1) An *insurer* may use Appendix 9.9 Form 95 for the purposes of the report required by rule 9.40(1).
(2) The reports required by rule 9.40 do not form part of the *insurer's return*.
(3) Where several *insurers* to which rule 9.40 applies have the same *ultimate insurance parent undertaking* or *ultimate EEA insurance parent undertaking* or both, rule 9.40 applies to all of them. In these circumstances one *insurer* may submit the reports in rule 9.40 on behalf of the other *insurers* in the *insurance group* as set out in rule 9.40(4). This should consist of one package of the relevant information with confirmation that the *insurer* submitting the information has made it available to the boards of directors of the other *insurers* in the *insurance group*. The purpose of this requirement is to ensure that all the *insurers* in the *insurance group* are aware of the relevance of the group information to themselves.
(4) Where an *insurance group* consists of an *ultimate insurance parent undertaking* or *ultimate EEA insurance parent undertaking* which is itself an *insurer* whose head office is in the *United Kingdom* and which has a *United Kingdom insurance subsidiary* or *subsidiaries* which is or are themselves *insurers*, the report in rule 9.40 will cover the same *group undertakings*. The subsidiary *insurer* need not in these circumstances deposit the report in rule 9.40. However, this does not affect the requirement to provide information under rule 9.41.

Part VI
Enhanced Capital Requirement

[2102]
9.44
(1) An *insurer* to which INSPRU 1.1.72BR applies must, in respect of each *financial year*, report its *enhanced capital requirement* (calculated in accordance with INSPRU 1.1.72CR) as at the end of that *financial year.*
(2) The report must be in the form of ECR1 set out in Appendix 9.10.
(3) An *insurer* must deposit a printed copy of the report with the *FSA* within 2 months and 15 days of the *financial year* end unless, in addition to depositing a printed copy, an *insurer* also deposits an electronic copy, then the period for deposit is within 3 months of the *financial year end*. The copies must be sent to the appropriate addresses set out in rule 9.6(2) above. If the due date for deposit of documents required by (1) falls on a day which is not a *business day*, the documents must be submitted no later than the first *business day* after the due date.
(4) The printed copy of the report must be signed by the persons described in IPRU(INS) 9.33(1).
(5) The electronic copy deposited under (3) above must be in an electronic form which may be readily used or translated by the *FSA* and must be sent by email to the appropriate address set out in rule 9.6(2) above. The title of the email must be:
<firm name> Form ECR1 <dd/mm/yyyy>

Guidance

9.45 The report required by rule 9.44(1) does not form part of the *insurer's return.*

9.46 An electronic copy that is not a completed Form ECR1 spreadsheet file template from the FSA website that can be accessed by Microsoft Excel is unlikely to be readily used or translated by the *FSA*.

Part VII
Lloyd's of London

Application

[2103]
9.47 PART VII of IPRU(INS) chapter 9 applies to the *Society* and to *managing agents.*

Requirement to report to the FSA

9.48
(1) The *Society* must report to the *FSA* within 6 months of the end of each *financial year* on its financial situation and solvency and on the whole of the *insurance business* carried on by *members*.
(2) The report in IPRU(INS) 9.48 (1) must be prepared in accordance with GENPRU 1.3.4 R and this chapter.
(3) The report in IPRU(INS) 9.48 (1) must include:
  (a) the *Lloyd's Return* which comprises a completed set of the forms set out in IPRU(INS) Appendix 9.11, together with any statements, notes, reports or certificates required by this chapter; and
  (b) a copy of the *syndicate* accounts for each *syndicate* that is required by *byelaw* to prepare accounts for the *financial year*.
(4) With the exception of the statements required to be annexed to the *Lloyd's Return* by IPRU(INS) 9.49 (6), the *Lloyd's Return* must be examined and reported on by the auditors appointed to audit the affairs of the *Society*.
(5) The *Society* must provide a printed copy of the *Lloyd's Return* to the *FSA*, with Form 9 signed by three signatories who are senior officers of the *Society* each duly authorised by the *Council* to sign the *Lloyd's Return* on behalf of the *Society*.
(6) If the *FSA* notifies the *Society* that any part of the *Lloyd's Return* is not in conformity with this chapter, the *Society* must promptly make any appropriate corrections or adjustments and if necessary re-submit the *Lloyd's Return* (or relevant part of it).

Content and form of the Lloyd's Return

9.49
(1) In preparing the *Lloyd's Return*, the *Society* must:
  (a) complete the forms in IPRU(INS) Appendix 9.11, following the requirements of and making the disclosures required under Appendices 9.1, 9.2, 9.3 and 9.4 of IPRU(INS) as if in the documents referred to in those Appendices references to an *insurer* were references to the *Society* and *members*, and adapting the requirements in those Appendices where necessary;
  (b) complete the forms in IPRU(INS) Appendix 9.11 using standard accounting *classes* as set out in IPRU(INS) Appendix 9.16 where the forms require reporting by accounting class;
  (c) report treaty reinsurance general business falling in accounting *classes* 9 to 10 as set out in IPRU(INS) Appendix 9.16 in Forms 28 and 29 in IPRU(INS) Appendix 9.11 by reference to the categories in the underlying accounting classes; and
  (d) complete forms 13, 14, 40–60 in IPRU(INS) Appendix 9.11 for each *long-term insurance business syndicate*.
(2)
  (a) Where a reinsurance contract in IPRU(INS) 9.49 (1)(c) covers more than one underlying accounting class as set out in IPRU(INS) Appendix 9.16 it must be apportioned between accounting classes in the way that best reflects its underlying composition.
  (b) However, where the apportionment in (a) cannot be made with reasonable accuracy or without disproportionate effort, then the contract must be allocated to the accounting class as set out in IPRU(INS) Appendix 9.16 that most closely reflects its underlying composition.
  (c) Whether apportioned under (a) or allocated under (b), a consistent approach must be taken to reporting:
    (i) the progress of a treaty in subsequent years; and
    (ii) substantially similar *insurance business* in subsequent years.
  (d) Where a different policy is subsequently followed a suitable explanatory note must be provided.
(3) If, during the financial year in question, the *Society* has agreed to, or carried out, a material connected party transaction, it must provide a brief description of that transaction by way of a supplementary note to the *Lloyd's Return*.
(4) The description to be provided under IPRU(INS) 9.49 (3) must state:
  (a) the names of the transacting parties;

(b) a description of the connection between the parties;
(c) a description of the transaction;
(d) the amounts involved;
(e) any other elements of the transaction needed for an understanding of its effect or potential effect upon the financial position of the *Society*; and
(f) amounts written off in the period in respect of debts due to or from transacting parties which are connected parties.

(5) Transactions with the same connected party may be disclosed on an aggregated basis unless separate disclosure is needed for a proper understanding of the effect of the transactions upon the financial position of the *Society*.

(6) The *Society* must annex to the *Lloyd's Return* a copy of each statement completed by a *managing agent* under IPRU(INS) 9.60 (7).

(7) For the purposes of the *Lloyd's Return* and IPRU(INS) 9.49 (6), the *Society* must, for each statement annexed, identify the *syndicate* to which the *contract of insurance* or 'financing arrangement' relates.

Risk groups for general insurance business

9.50

(1) The *Society* must for the purposes of reporting under this chapter:
(a) classify the direct and facultive *general insurance business* of *members* according to appropriate risk groups; and
(b) where the risks are material, complete a separate Form 34 in IPRU(INS) Appendix 9.11 for each group.

(2) The *Society* must not include:
(a) policies falling within *classes* 14, 15, 16, 17 or 18 within the same risk group as policies falling within any other *class*, except that policies falling within *class* 14 may be included in the same risk group as policies falling within *class* 15; or
(b) policies in respect of private motor car risks, within the same risk group as policies in respect of other risks falling within accounting class 2 as set out in IPRU(INS) Appendix 9.16; or
(c) policies in respect of comprehensive private motor car risks, within the same risk group as policies in respect of non-comprehensive private motor car risks; or
(d) policies transferred to *members* by way of a transfer under section 111 of the Act (Sanction of the court for business transfer schemes), within the same risk group as other policies.

(3) The *Society* must give the *FSA* notice of proposed changes to the definition or classification of the risk groups in IPRU(INS) 9.50 (1), sufficient to allow the *FSA* properly to assess the implications of the proposals.

Major treaty reinsurers

9.51

(1) The *Society* must, in connection with the *general insurance business* carried on by *members*, include in the *Lloyd's Return* a statement of major treaty reinsurers.

(2) A major treaty reinsurer is any insurance company to which in the *financial year* in question or any of the five preceding *financial years*:
(a) in the case of proportional reinsurance, 2% or more of the gross premiums receivable in respect of *general insurance business* of the *members* in aggregate has been ceded; or
(b) in the case of non-proportional reinsurance, 5% or more of the gross premiums receivable in respect of *general insurance business* has been ceded.

(3) The statement required under IPRU(INS) 9.51 (1) must include:
(a) the full name of each major treaty reinsurer;
(b) the amount of the reinsurance premiums payable in the *financial year* to each such reinsurer;
(c) whether and if so how the reinsurer was connected to any *member* or any *managing agent*;
(d) the amount of any debt of each such reinsurer included at line 75 of Form 13 in IPRU(INS) Appendix 9.11;
(e) the amount of any deposit received from each such reinsurer under reinsurance treaties included at line 31 of Form 15 in IPRU(INS) Appendix 9.11; and
(f) the reinsurers' share of *technical provisions* shown on Form 13 in IPRU(INS) Appendix 9.11 except that in respect of claims incurred but not reported, such recoveries need only be included to the extent that they are in respect of specific occurrences for which provisions have been allocated;

or, as the case may be, a statement that having aggregated the reinsurance ceded by *members* no reinsurer is a major treaty reinsurer.

(4) The requirements of IPRU(INS) 9.51 (1), IPRU(INS) 9.52 (1) and IPRU(INS) 9.53 (1) may be satisfied by giving a fair view and making use of an appropriate degree of approximation. The *Society* may employ any reasonable methods to establish the information required.

Major facultative reinsurers

9.52

(1) The *Society* must, in connection with the *general insurance business* carried on by *members*, include in the *Lloyd's Return* a statement of major facultative reinsurers.

(2) A major facultative reinsurer is an insurance company to which or with respect to which:

(a) 0.5% or more of the gross premiums *receivable* in respect of *general insurance business* of the *members* in aggregate has been ceded; or

(b) the addition of the amounts in items (d) and (e) of IPRU(INS) 9.51 (3) produces an amount exceeding 1% of the aggregate gross assets of *members*.

(3) The statement required under IPRU(INS) 9.52 (1) must include the matters listed in IPRU(INS) 9.51 (3), with appropriate amendments.

Major reinsurance cedants

9.53

(1) The *Society* must, in connection with the *general insurance business* carried on by *members*, include in the *Lloyd's Return* a statement of major reinsurance cedants.

(2) A major reinsurance cedant is an insurance company which in the *financial year* in question or any of the three preceding *financial years*:

(a) cedes an amount which exceeds 5% of the gross premiums *receivable* by *members* in respect of *general insurance business* accepted under reinsurance treaties; and

(b) cedes an amount which exceeds 2% of the gross premiums *receivable* by *members* in respect of *general insurance business*.

(3) The statement required under IPRU(INS) 9.53 (1) must include the matters listed in IPRU(INS) 9.51 (3), with appropriate amendments.

Derivative contracts

9.54

(1) The *Society* must annex a statement to the *Lloyd's Return* comprising a brief description of:

(a) any *byelaws* and guidelines issued by the *Society* governing the use of *derivative* contracts;

(b) any provision in those guidelines governing the use of contracts under which *members* have a right or obligation to acquire or dispose of assets which was not, at the time when the contract was entered into, reasonably likely to be exercised and the circumstances in which, pursuant to that provision, such contracts may be used;

(c) the extent to which *members* were during the *financial year* a party to any contracts of the kind described in (b);

(d) the extent to which any of the amounts recorded in Form 13 would be changed if assets which *members* had a right or obligation to acquire or dispose of under *derivative* contracts outstanding at the end of the *financial year* (being, in the case of *options*, only those *options* which it would have been prudent to assume would be exercised) had been acquired or disposed of;

(e) the difference between (d) and the amount which would result under (d) if such *options* had been exercised and this were reflected in Form 13 to the maximum extent;

(f) how different the information provided pursuant to (d) and (e) would have been if, instead of applying to contracts outstanding at the end of the *financial year*, (d) and (e) had applied to *derivative* contracts outstanding at such other time during the *financial year* as would have changed the amounts in Form 13 to the maximum extent;

(g) the maximum loss which would be incurred by *members* on the failure by any one other person to fulfil its obligations under *derivative* contracts outstanding at the end of the *financial year*, both under existing market conditions and in the event of other foreseeable market conditions, together with an assessment of whether such maximum loss would have been materially different at any other time during the *financial year*;

(h) the circumstances surrounding the use of any *derivative* contract held at any time during the *financial year* which did not fulfil the criteria in INSPRU 4.2.5 R; and

(i) the total value of any fixed consideration received by *members* (whether in cash or otherwise) during the *financial year* in return for granting rights under *derivative* contracts and a summary of contracts under which such rights have been granted.

(2) For the purposes of IPRU(INS) 9.54 (1), if *members* are a party to:

(a) a *contract for differences*; or

(b) any other contract which is to be, or may be, settled in cash they must be treated as having a right or obligation to acquire or dispose of the assets underlying the contract.

General insurance business ceded

9.55
(1) The *Society* must annex to the *Lloyd's Return* a statement:
(a) of each major treaty reinsurer and major facultative reinsurer; and
(b) for each of the realistic disaster scenarios set by the *Society* when fulfilling its obligations under INSPRU and GENPRU to monitor aggregation of risk within the Lloyd's market of the contribution it is assumed each such reinsurer would provide in the event of that disaster occurring.

The Society

9.56
(1) The *Society* must annex to the *Lloyd's Return* a statement naming each individual who has served:
(a) on the *Council*;
(b) as Chairman of the *Council*; and
(c) as Chief Executive Officer of the *Society*;
at any time during the *financial year*, including in each case the dates of commencement or end of service (as the case may be) of any individual who has not served for the entire year.

Capacity controlled

9.57
(1) The *Society* must annex to the *Lloyd's Return* a statement identifying any *members*, *members' agents* or *managing agents* that control a significant share of the underwriting capacity of the *Society*.
(2) To control a significant share means:
(a) in relation to a *managing agent*, managing, directing through one or more Members' Agent Pooling Arrangements or owning, whether directly or in conjunction with *connected persons*, capacity which in aggregate is greater than 5% of the total underwriting capacity of the *Society*;
(b) in relation to a *members' agent*, directing through one or more Members' Agent Pooling Arrangements or owing, whether directly or in conjunction with *connected persons*, underwriting capacity which in aggregate is greater than 2.5% of the total underwriting capacity of the *Society*; and
(c) in relation to a member, owning, whether directly or in conjunction with *connected persons*, underwriting capacity which, in aggregate, is greater than 2.5% of the total underwriting capacity of the *Society*.

Certificates and audit report

9.58
(1) Certificates
The *Society* must annex to the *Lloyd's Return*:
(a) a certificate from the *Council*, including the statements required by IPRU(INS) Appendix 9.12;
(b) a statement from the *Lloyd's actuary*, including the statements required by IPRU(INS) Appendix 9.13;
(c) a certificate from the *syndicate actuary* of each *syndicate* which carries on *long-term insurance business*, including the statements required by IPRU(INS) Appendix 9.14, and;
(d) an abstract from the *syndicate actuary* of each *syndicate* which carries on *long-term insurance business* of the *actuary's* report made under SUP 4.6.14G.
(2) Audit report
The *Society* must ensure that the *Lloyd's Return* and every document annexed to or provided with it has been examined by the *Society*'s auditors and must provide with the *Lloyd's Return* an audit certificate in respect of that examination.
(3) The certificate in IPRU(INS) 9.58 (2) must be in the form set out in IPRU(INS) Appendix 9.15.

Public disclosure

9.59
(1) The *Society* must provide within a period not exceeding 30 days:
(a) on demand to any *member* or policyholder a copy of the *Lloyd's Return* and the *global account* most recently submitted to the *FSA*; and

(b) if specifically requested by a *member* or policyholder, a copy of any *syndicate* account submitted to the *FSA*.

Syndicate-level reporting

9.60

(1) Each managing agent must:

(a) prepare a return for each *financial year* in respect of the *insurance business* carried on through each *syndicate* managed by it; and

(b) provide the return in (a) to the *Society* as soon as practicable after the end of the financial year but in any event in time to enable the *Society* to report to the *FSA* in accordance with IPRU(INS) 9.48 (1).

(2) The *Society* must:

(a) issue instructions to *managing agents* setting out the form and content of the return under IPRU(INS) 9.60 (1); and

(b) issue the instructions in (a) as soon as practicable but in any event in time to enable *managing agents* to comply with IPRU(INS) 9.60 (1).

(3) A *managing agent* must annex to each return which it prepares under IPRU(INS) 9.60 (1), a certificate signed by the persons referred to in IPRU(INS) 9.60 (4), including the statements required by IPRU(INS) Appendix 9.17.

(4) The certificate in IPRU(INS) 9.60 (3) must be signed by:

(a) where there are more than two *directors* of the *managing agent*, at least two of those *directors* and, where there are not more than two *directors*, all the *directors*; and

(b) a *chief executive*, if any, of the *managing agent* or (if there is no *chief executive*) the secretary.

(5) A *managing agent* must ensure for each *syndicate* managed by it that the return required under IPRU(INS) 9.60 (1) is examined and reported on by the *syndicate* auditor.

(6) A *managing agent* must annex to each return required under IPRU(INS) 9.60(1) an audit certificate provided by the *syndicate* auditor including the statements required by IPRU(INS) Appendix 9.18.

(7) A *managing agent* must annex to each return which it prepares under IPRU(INS) 9.60 (1) a statement of the information required by IPRU(INS) *rule* 9.32A, as if in that *rule* references to:

(a) '*insurer*' were to the *members* carrying on *insurance business* through the relevant *syndicate*;

(b) the '*return*' were to the return required to be prepared by it in respect of the business carried on through the relevant *syndicate* under IPRU(INS) 9.60 (1)

(c) the '*insurer's* balance sheet' were to the *syndicate* balance sheet;

(d) the '*insurer's capital resources*' were to the *capital resources* managed by or at the direction of the *managing agent* in respect of the *insurance business* carried on through the relevant *syndicate*; and

(e) the '*insurer's* total *technical provisions*' were to the *technical provisions* in respect of the *insurance business* carried on through the relevant *syndicate*.

The Central Fund

9.61

(1) The *Society* must give the *FSA* a report on the *Central Fund* as at the end of each calendar quarter.

(2) The report referred to in IPRU(INS) 9.61 (1) must reach the *FSA* within two weeks of the end of each calendar quarter and must include information on:

(a) the net market value of the *Central Fund*;

(b) payments made from the *Central Fund* in that quarter;

(c) the types of investment in which the *Central Fund* is held;

(d) the commencement or cessation of, or any changes in the terms of, any insurance policy taken out to protect the *Central Fund*; and

(e) any claim made, or circumstances notified that are likely to lead to a claim, under any insurance policy taken out to protect the *Central Fund*.

Information about the capacity transfer market

9.62

(1) The *Society* must give the *FSA* a report as at the end of each calendar quarter in which any capacity is transferred.

(2) The report referred to in INSPRU 8.4.3 R must reach the *FSA* within one month of the end of the relevant calendar quarter and must include information on:

(a) the total capacity in *syndicates* transferred during the quarter, analysed by *syndicate* and method of transfer;

(b) the number, and nature, of all investigations by the *Society* into conduct in the *capacity transfer market* undertaken or continued during the quarter; and
(c) the number, and nature, of all complaints received during the quarter about the operation of the *capacity transfer market*.

Guidance

9.63

(1) IPRU(INS) Chapter 9 Part VII requires the *Society* to report on the *insurance business* carried on by *members* and on the assets and liabilities of *members* and the *Society*, and requires reports from the *Society* on the *Central Fund* and the *capacity transfer market*. It also requires *managing agents* to report on the *insurance business* carried on through each *syndicate* they manage. Reporting at syndicate level is required to enable the *Society* to prepare the *Lloyd's Return*. The statements required to be annexed to the return by IPRU(INS) 9.60 (7) should not be included in the audit under IPRU(INS) 9.49 (6).

(2) The *Lloyd's Return* is made annually and contains the statement required from the *Society* that *capital resources* at least equal to the *capital resources requirements* for *general insurance business* and *long-term insurance business* under GENPRU 2 have been maintained at all times throughout the *financial year*.

(3) For *general insurance business*, the *capital resources requirement* for the *Society* is the higher of the aggregate of the *members' capital resources requirements* for *general insurance business*, calculated in accordance with GENPRU 2.3.5 R, and the *Society GICR*. For *long-term business*, the *capital resources requirement* for the *Society* is the aggregate of the *members' capital resources requirements*, calculated in accordance with GENPRU 2.3.7 R. The *Society* is required to ensure that each *member's capital resources requirement* is covered by that *member's capital resources*, or, where there is a shortfall in the *member's capital resources*, by the *Society's* own *capital resources*. For *general insurance business*, the *Society* must ensure that the *Society GICR* is covered by the aggregate *capital resources* supporting the *insurance business* of all the *members*.

(4) Where appropriate, the *Society* is also required to modify prudential reporting to make it more like that of an *insurer*. This is to aid comparisons between Lloyd's and *insurers*.

9.64 The *Society* should make the report referred to in IPRU(INS) 9.48 (1), including amendments and corrections, and amalgamated *syndicate* accounts available at its head office for inspection by policyholders and potential policyholders and *members*.

9.65

(1) In assessing what are appropriate risk groups for reporting purposes the *Society* should ensure where possible that:
   (a) each risk group should include only risks from within a single accounting class and in relation to a single country;
   (b) policies are not included in the same risk group where, having regard to the patterns of risk, *claims* incurrence and settlement patterns, it is necessary to group them separately for the purposes of applying statistical methods in calculating the provision for *claims* outstanding in accordance with generally accepted accounting practice; and
   (c) claims-made policies are not included in the same risk group as policies which are not claims-made policies, except:
      (i) where this is not possible without disproportionate expense; and
      (ii) where the policies within the risk group do not exhibit materially different characteristics.

(2) Subject to IPRU(INS) 9.50 (2)(a) and IPRU(INS) 9.50 (2)(b) and IPRU(INS) 9.65 (1)(c), the *Society* may in respect of any accounting class include all *insurance business* carried on by *members* in any country in any *financial year* as a single risk group.

(3) Notwithstanding the provisions of IPRU(INS) 9.50 (2)(a) and IPRU(INS) 9.50 (2)(b) and IPRU(INS) 9.65 (1)(c), the *Society* may classify all *insurance business* carried on by *members* in any country in respect of any accounting class in any financial year as a single risk group, as long as gross premiums written for that year in respect of that *insurance business* are less than 5% of the world-wide gross premiums written for all accounting *classes* for that year.

(4) The requirements to report a separate risk group in IPRU(INS) 9.50 (2)(a) do not apply where, in the case of any *financial year*, the gross premiums receivable for that year in respect of that risk group would be less than £1million.

9.66 The *Society* should be treated as if it were a major treaty reinsurer when *intersyndicate reinsurance* in aggregate exceeds the amounts set out in IPRU(INS) 9.51 (2)

9.67 The *Society* should be treated as if it were a major facultative reinsurer when *inter-syndicate reinsurance* in aggregate exceeds the amounts set out in IPRU(INS) 9.52 (2).

9.68 The *Society* should be treated as if it were a major reinsurance cedant when inter-syndicate cessions in aggregate exceed the amounts set out in IPRU(INS) 9.53 (2).

9.69 In relation to required disclosures of *derivative* contracts in IPRU(INS) 9.54(1), references to a *derivative* contract and related expressions should be taken to include:
(1) any *derivative* contract entered into by a *managing agent* on behalf of a *member* as part of that *member's insurance business*; and
(2) any *derivative* contract entered into by the *Society*.

9.70 Contracts that are *quasi-derivative contracts* should be treated as *derivative* contracts.

9.71 The requirements of IPRU(INS) 9.55(1) may be satisfied by giving a fair view and may make use of an appropriate degree of approximation. The *Society* may employ any reasonable methods to establish the information required. The *Society* may also include such explanation as it considers to be necessary to allow a reasonable interpretation to be put on this statement.

9.72
(1) Because of the significance of the *Central Fund* in the protection of policyholders, the *Society* should notify the *FSA* under IPRU(INS) 9.61(2)(e) of all matters relevant to any actual or potential claim. These include but are not limited to the facts on which that claim is based, the circumstances under which those facts arose and any relevant response to the claim from any *insurer* or reinsurer concerned.
(2) The report referred to in IPRU(INS) 9.61(1) must be submitted in writing in accordance with SUP 16.3.7 to SUP 16.3.10 (see SUP 16.3.6).

CHAPTER 10
PARENT UNDERTAKING SOLVENCY CALCULATION

[deleted]

CHAPTER 11
DEFINITIONS

Part I
Definitions

[2104]
11.1 For the purposes of IPRU(INS), the term or phrase in the first column has the meaning given to it in the second column unless the context otherwise requires.

Term or phrase	**Definition**
1981 Regulations	Insurance Companies Regulations 1981 (S.I. 1981 No. 1654)
1982 Act	Insurance Companies Act 1982
1983 Regulations	Insurance Companies Regulations 1983 (S.I. 1983 No. 1811)
1986 Order	Companies (Northern Ireland) Order 1986
1994 Regulations	Insurance Companies Regulations 1994 (S.I. 1994 No. 1516)
1996 Regulations	Insurance Companies (Accounts and Statements) Regulations (S.I. 1996 No. 943)
accounted for	reported pursuant to the *Accounts and Statements Rules*

Accounting class		**Corresponding groups of *classes* under paragraph 75(3) of the *insurance accounts rules***	**Corresponding general insurance business classes**
1	Accident and health	Accident and health	1 (other than 1(p)), 2
2	Motor	motor (third party liability)	1(p), 10
		motor (other classes)	3
3	Aviation	marine, aviation and transport	1(p), 5, 11
4	Marine		1(p), 6, 12
5	Transport		7
6	Property	fire and other damage to property	4, 8, 9

Part II FSA Handbook Materials

Accounting class		Corresponding groups of *classes* under paragraph 75(3) of the *insurance accounts rules*	Corresponding general insurance business classes
7	Third party liability	third party liability	13
8	Miscellaneous and pecuniary loss	credit and suretyship, legal expenses, assistance, miscellaneous	14, 15, 16, 17, 18
9	Non-proportional treaty		
10	Proportional treaty		
11	Marine, aviation and transport treaty		

Accounts and Statements Rules	rules 9.1 to 9.36E and rule 9.39 of Chapter 9
actuarial investigation	an investigation to which rule 9.4 applies
admissible asset	an asset that falls into one or more categories in GENPRU 2 Annex 7R
annuities on human life	does not include superannuation allowances and annuities payable out of any fund applicable solely to the relief and maintenance of persons engaged, or who have been engaged, in any particular profession, trade or employment, or of the dependants of such persons
approved investment firm	an investment firm as defined in the *Investment Services Directive*
associate	has the meaning given in rule 11.2
available assets	the excess of an *insurer's* assets (other than *implicit items*) over its liabilities, in each case valued in accordance with GENPRU 1.3, INSPRU 2.1 and INSPRU 1

balancing category	an *FSA general insurance business reporting category* to which any of the *category numbers* 409 or 709 has been allocated in column 1 of **Annex 11.3**

category number	the category number for the *FSA return general insurance business reporting categories* listed in column 1 of **Annex 11.3**	
cede and cession	in relation to *reinsurance*, include retrocede and retrocession	
claim	a *claim* against an *insurer* under a *contract of insurance*	
claims-made policy	a contract of liability insurance which provides that no liability is incurred by the *insurer* in respect of an incident unless—	
	(a)	the incident is notified to the *insurer* (or its agent or representative); and
	(b)	such notification is received by the *insurer* (or its agent or representative) before the end of a specified period which is no longer than three years following the final date for which cover is provided under the contract
claims management costs	refers to those claims management costs required by the *insurance accounts rules* (note (4) to the profit and loss account format) to be included in *claims* incurred other than those which, whether or not incurred through the employment of the *insurer's* own staff, are directly attributable to particular *claims*	
class	a class of *long-term insurance business*, listed in **Annex 11.1** or a class of *general insurance business* listed in **Annex 11.2**	
collecting book	includes any book or document held by a *collector* in which payments of premiums are recorded	

collector	includes every person, howsoever remunerated, who, by himself or by any deputy or substitute, makes house to house visits for the purpose of receiving premiums payable on *policies* of insurance on human life, or holds any interest in a *collecting book*, and includes such a deputy or substitute	
combined category	an *FSA general insurance business reporting category* to which any of the *category numbers* 001, 002, 003, 110, 120, 180, 220, 260, 270, 280, 330, 340, 500 or 600 has been allocated in column 1 of **Annex 11.3**	
commitment	a commitment represented by *insurance business* of any of the *classes of long-term insurance business*	
company	(a)	for the purposes of the *Accounts and Statements Rules* means an *insurance undertaking*; and
	(b)	otherwise includes any *body corporate*
Companies Act	[deleted]	
connected	a *body corporate* "A" and another *body corporate* "B" are connected with each other if:	
	(a)	B is a *related undertaking* of A;
	(b)	B is a *participating undertaking* in A; or
	(c)	B is a *related undertaking* of a *participating undertaking* in A
	a *body corporate* "C" and a natural person "D" are connected if D holds a *participation* in:	
	(d)	C or any of its *related undertakings*;
	(e)	a *participating undertaking* in C; or
	(f)	a *related undertaking* of a *participating undertaking* in A
connected company	of any *company* means—	
	(a)	that *company's holding company*;
	(b)	a *subsidiary* of that *company*; or
	(c)	a *subsidiary* of the *holding company* of that *company*
connected-party transaction	the transfer of assets or liabilities or the performance of services by, to or for a *connected* person irrespective of whether or not a price is charged	
consequential loss risk	risk falling within *general insurance business class* 16 comprising risks of the persons insured sustaining loss attributable to interruptions of the carrying on of business carried on by them or to reduction of the scope of business so carried on	
controller	has the meaning given in rule 11.2	
counterparty	in relation to an *insurer*—	
	(a)	any one individual;
	(b)	any one unincorporated body of persons;
	(c)	any one *company* not being a member of a *group*;
	(d)	any *group* of *companies* excluding any *companies* within the *group* which are *subsidiary undertakings* of the *insurer*; or
	(e)	any government of a State together with all the public bodies, local authorities or nationalised industries of that State,
	in which the *insurer* has made investments or against whom it has rights whether in pursuance of a contract entered into by the *insurer* or otherwise	

credit default swap	a *swap* contract in which a buyer makes a series of payments to a seller and, in exchange, receives the right to a payment if a credit instrument issued by a named borrower (the reference entity) goes into default or on the occurrence of a specified credit event, for example bankruptcy or restructuring of the reference entity, during the currency of the contract

debt	includes an obligation to pay a sum of money under a negotiable instrument
dependant	a dependant for a *firm* is any *subsidiary undertaking* of the *firm* that is valued in accordance with GENPRU 1.3.47R.
derivative contract	has the meaning given to *derivative* in the *Glossary*
direct and facultative	*direct insurance business* and inwards facultative *reinsurance* business
direct insurance business	*insurance business* other than *reinsurance business*
discounting	refers to discounting or deductions to take account of investment income within the meaning of paragraph 48 of the *insurance accounts rules*

equivalent securities	*securities* issued by the same *issuer* being of an identical type and having the same nominal value, description and amount
established surplus	has the same meaning as in rule 3.3(4)
exemption category	an *FSA general insurance business reporting category* to which the *category numbers* 114(p) or 710(p) have been allocated in column 1 of **Annex 11.3**
experience account	an account (whether real or notional) established under a *contract of insurance* where: (a) *premiums* payable or paid, or amounts related to *premiums* payable or paid, under the contract are credited to the account; (b) *claims* payable or paid or incurred, or amounts related to *claims* payable or paid or incurred, under the contract are deducted from the account; and (c) either: (i) some part of the amount held in the account is paid out on expiry or termination of the contract in accordance with rights specified in the contract; or (ii) the amount held in the account affects the amount payable under the contract.
external insurer	an *insurer* whose head office is outside the United Kingdom, other than an *EEA insurer*, a *Swiss general insurer* or *UK-* or *EEA-deposit insurer*

facultative business	facultative *reinsurance* business
financial year	each period at the end of which the balance of the accounts of the *insurer* is struck or, if no such balance is struck, the calendar year
financial year in question	the *financial year* which last ended before the date on which accounts and statements (as specified in the *Accounts and Statements Rules*) of the *insurer* relating to that *financial year* are required to be deposited with the *FSA* pursuant to rule 9.6, and the preceding financial year and previous financial years are construed accordingly

FSA general insurance business reporting category	a category of *general insurance business* that consists of the effecting or carrying out of *contracts of general insurance* falling within the description in column 2 of **Annex 11.3**

group	has the meaning given in section 262 of the Companies Act 1985 where applicable, otherwise section 474(1) of the Companies Act 2006

home foreign business	*general insurance business* carried on in the United Kingdom primarily relating to risks situated outside the United Kingdom, but excluding *insurance business* in *category numbers* 330, 340, 350, 500, 600 and 700 and *insurance business* where the risk commences in the United Kingdom
hybrid security	a *debt security*, other than an *approved security*, the terms of which provide or have the effect that the holder does not or would not have an unconditional entitlement to payment of interest and repayment of capital in full within 75 years of the *relevant date*

incepted	refers to the time when the liability to risk of an *insurer* under a *contract of insurance* commenced and, for this purpose, a contract providing continuous cover is deemed to commence on each anniversary date of the contract, and incepting and inception are construed accordingly	
index linked contract	a *linked long-term contract of insurance* conferring *index linked benefits*	
industrial assurance business	the business of effecting *contracts of insurance* on human life, premiums in respect of which are received by means of *collectors*;	
		But such *insurance business* does not include-
	(a)	*contracts of insurance*, the premiums in respect of which are payable at intervals of two months or more;
	(b)	*contracts of insurance*, effected whether before or after the passing of the Industrial Assurance Act 1923 by a society or company established before the date of the passing of that Act which at that date had no *contracts of insurance* outstanding the premiums on which were payable at intervals of less than one month so long as the society or company continues not to effect any such contracts;
	(c)	*contracts of insurance* effected before the passing of the Industrial Assurance Act 1923, premiums in respect of which are payable at intervals of one month or more, and which have up to the passing of that Act been treated as part of the business transacted by a branch other than the industrial branch of the society or company; or
	(d)	*contracts of insurance* for £25 or more effected after the passing of the Industrial Assurance Act 1923, premiums in respect of which are payable at intervals of one month or more, and which are treated as part of the business transacted by a branch other than the industrial branch of the society or company, in cases where the relevant authority certified prior to 1 December 2001 under section 1(2)(d) of that Act that the terms and conditions of such contracts are on the whole not less favourable to the *policy holders* than those imposed by that Act

Part II FSA Handbook Materials

initial margin	in respect of a *derivative* or *quasi-derivative*, means assets which, before or at the time the contract is entered into, are transferred by the *insurer* subject to a condition that such assets (or where the assets transferred are *securities, equivalent securities*) will be returned to the *insurer* on completion of that contract
insurance liabilities	amounts calculated in accordance with GENPRU 1.3 (Valuation) in respect of those items shown at C and D under the heading 'Liabilities' set out in paragraph 9 of the *insurance accounts rules*
international accounting standards	has the meaning given in the *Glossary* of the *FSA* Handbook.
internal linked fund	an account to which an *insurer* appropriates certain *linked assets* and which may be sub-divided into units the value of each of which is determined by the *insurer* by reference to the value of those *linked assets*

linked assets	in relation to an *insurer*, *long-term insurance business assets* of the *insurer* which are, for the time being, identified in the records of the *insurer* as being assets by reference to the value of which *property linked benefits* are to be determined, and non-linked assets is construed accordingly
long-term policy holder	a *policy holder* in respect of a *policy* the effecting of which by the *insurer* constituted the carrying on of *long-term insurance business*

management expenses	in relation to *long-term insurance business*, means all expenses, other than commission, incurred in the administration of an *insurer* or its business	
marine mutual	*an insurer*—	
	(a)	whose *insurance business* is restricted to the insurance of its members or their *associates* against loss, damage or liability arising out of marine adventures (including losses on inland waters or any risk incidental to any sea voyage); and
	(b)	whose articles of association, rules or bye laws provide for the calling of additional contributions from, or the reduction of benefits to, the majority of its members, in either case without limit, in order to ensure that the *insurer* has sufficient financial resources to meet any valid *claims* as they fall due
material connected-party transaction	*a connected-party transaction* for which (together with any similar transactions):	
	(a)	the price actually paid or received for the transfer of assets or liabilities or the performance of services; or
	(b)	the price which would have been paid or received had that transaction been negotiated at arm's length between unconnected parties,
	exceeds:	
	(c)	in the case of an *insurer* that carries on *long-term insurance business* but not *general insurance business*, 5% of the *insurer's* liabilities arising from its *long-term insurance business*, excluding *property-linked liabilities* and net of *reinsurance ceded*; or

	(d)		in the case of an *insurer* that carries on *general insurance business*, but not *long-term insurance business*, the sum of Euro 20,000 and 5% of the *insurer's* liabilities arising from its *general insurance business*, net of *reinsurance ceded*; or
	(e)		in the case of an *insurer* that carries on both types of business either—
		(i)	5% of the *insurer's* liabilities arising from its *long-term insurance business*, excluding *property-linked liabilities*, net of *reinsurance* ceded where the transaction is in connection with the *insurer's long-term insurance business*, or
		(ii)	in other cases, the sum of Euro 20,000 and 5% of the *insurer's* liabilities arising from *general insurance business* net of *reinsurance ceded*
mathematical reserves	[deleted]		
miscellaneous category	an *FSA return general insurance business reporting category* to which the *category numbers* 400 or 700 have been allocated in column 1 of **Annex 11.3**		
mortgage	in relation to Scotland, means a heritable security within the meaning of section 9(8) of the Conveyancing and Feudal Reform (Scotland) Act 1970		

non-linked assets	see *linked assets*
non-profit policy	see *with-profits policy*
non-proportional reinsurance treaty	see *proportional reinsurance treaty*

ordinary long-term insurance business	*long-term insurance business* which is not *industrial assurance business*

preceding financial year	see *financial year in question*	
previous financial years	see *financial year in question*	
Product code	has the meaning given in paragraph 3 of the Instructions for completion of **Form 47** in **Appendix 9.3**	
profit and loss account	in relation to an *insurer* not trading for profit, an income and expenditure account	
property linked benefits	*benefits* other than *index linked benefits* provided for under a *linked long-term contract of insurance*	
property linked liabilities	*insurance liabilities* in respect of *property linked benefits*	
proportional reinsurance treaty	(a)	a *reinsurance* treaty under which a pre-determined proportion of each *claim* payment by the *cedant* under *policies* subject to the treaty is recoverable from the *reinsurer*; and
	(b)	for the purposes of the *Accounts and Statements Rules*, a *reinsurance* treaty under which in return for a proportion of the premium a pre-determined proportion of each *claim* payment by the *cedant* under *policies* subject to the treaty is recoverable from the *reinsurer*, and
	non-proportional reinsurance treaty is construed accordingly	

readily realisable	in relation to an investment:

	(a)		an investment which, had negotiations for the assignment or transfer of the investment commenced not more than seven working days before the *relevant date*, it is reasonable to assume could have been assigned or transferred on the *relevant date* for an amount not less than 97.5% of the *market value* to a person other than the *issuer* or an *associate* or *associated company* of the *issuer* or of the *insurer*; or
	(b)		a *listed* investment with respect to which (a) does not apply by reason only that—
		(i)	the listing of the investment has been temporarily suspended following receipt of price sensitive information received by the stock exchange on which the investment is *listed* or the *regulated market* on which facilities for dealing have been granted, or
		(ii)	the extent of the holding would prevent an orderly disposal of the investment for an amount equal to or greater than 97.5% of *market value*
receivable	in relation to an *insurer*, a *financial year* and a premium, means due to the *insurer* whether or not the premium is received during that *financial year*		
reinsurance recoveries	amounts in respect of *claims* receivable by an *insurer* from a *reinsurer* under a contract of *reinsurance*		
related company	in relation to an *insurer*—		
	(a)		a *subsidiary undertaking* of the *insurer*;
	(b)		a company of which the *insurer* is a *subsidiary undertaking*; or
	(c)		a *subsidiary undertaking* of a company of which the *insurer* is a *subsidiary undertaking* *related undertaking* an undertaking in which a *participation* is held by another undertaking or which is a *subsidiary undertaking*
relevant company	an *insurer* whose *insurance business* is restricted to *reinsurance* of the *marine mutual* on terms that provide that the *marine mutual* can cancel the *reinsurance* arrangements at any time and can require the *insurer* immediately to transfer its assets and liabilities to the *marine mutual*		
relevant date	in relation to the valuation of any asset or liability, the date at which the value of the asset or liability falls to be determined for the purposes of reporting under the *Accounts and Statements Rules*		
required category	in relation to a Form in the *return*, a category of *general insurance business* set out in column 2 of the Table in Paragraph 2B of **Appendix 9.2** that—		
	(a)		is, or is included in, an *FSA general insurance business reporting category* for which the Table in Paragraph 2A of **Appendix 9.2** contains a tick in the row for that *FSA general insurance business reporting category* and in the column for that Form; and
	(b)		either:
		(i)	meets the reporting criteria specified in the entry in column 3 of that Table that corresponds to the entry in column 2 for that the category of *general insurance business* and the entry in column 1 for that Form, or
		(ii)	is required for that Form under rule 9.20.
return	the documents required (taken together) to be deposited under rule 9.6(1)		

risk category	any *FSA general insurance business reporting category* that is not a *combined category*, or *balancing category* or *exemption category*

secured debt	a debt fully secured on:	
	(a)	assets whose value at least equals the amount of debt; or
	(b)	a letter of credit or guarantee from an *approved counterparty*.
securities	includes *shares*, *debt securities*, *Treasury Bills*, Tax Reserve Certificates and Certificates of Tax Deposit	
share	has the meaning given in section 1161(2) of the Companies Act 2006	
Statistical Rules	rules 9.37 to 9.38	
Stock Exchange	London Stock Exchange plc	
subsidiary undertaking	has the meaning given in section 1162 of the Companies Act 2006	
Swaption	an *option* granting its owner the right but not the obligation to enter into an underlying *swap*	

technical provisions	the items required by the *insurance accounts rules* to be shown in the balance sheet of an *insurer* at liabilities items C.1 to 6
total capital resources	the sum calculated at stage O of the calculation in GENPRU 2 Annex 1R
total return swap	a financial contract which transfers both the credit risk and market risk of an underlying asset
Treasury Bills	includes bills issued by Her Majesty's Government in the United Kingdom and Northern Ireland Treasury Bills

unlisted	see *listed*

variable interest securities	*securities* which under their terms of issue provide for variable amounts of interest	
variation margin	(a)	in respect of a *derivative contract*, or a *quasi-derivative contract*, assets (other than assets transferred by way of *initial margin*) which, at the *relevant date*, have been transferred by, to, or for the benefit of the *insurer* in pursuance of a condition in that contract or a related contract; and
	(b)	in respect of an asset having the effect of a *derivative contract*, assets which, at the relevant date, have been transferred by, to, or for the benefit of, the *insurer* in pursuance of a contractual right conferred, or obligation imposed, by the holding of the asset having the effect of a *derivative contract*

with profits fund	for the purposes of the *Accounts and Statements Rules*—	
	(a)	a *long-term insurance fund* (or that part of such a fund) in which *policy holders* are eligible to participate in any *established surplus*; and
	(b)	where it is an *insurer's* usual practice to restrict *policy holders'* participation in any *established surplus* to that arising from only a part of the fund (or part fund) falling within (a), that part (or that part of the part fund)
with-profits policy	a contract falling within a *class of long-term insurance business* which is eligible to participate in any part of any *established surplus*, and non-profit policy is construed accordingly	

Part II FSA Handbook Materials

Controller

11.2
(1) For the purpose of IPRU(INS), **controller**, in relation to an undertaking ("A"), means a person who falls within any of the cases in (2).
(2) The cases are where the 'person'—
(a) holds 10% or more of the 'shares' in A;
(b) is able to exercise significant influence over the management of A by virtue of his shareholding in A;
(c) holds 10% or more of the 'shares' in a parent undertaking ("P") of A;
(d) is able to exercise significant influence over the management of P by virtue of his shareholding in P;
(e) is entitled to exercise, or control the exercise of, 10% or more of the 'voting power' in A;
(f) is able to exercise significant influence over the management of A by virtue of his 'voting power' in A;
(g) is entitled to exercise, or control the exercise of, 10% or more of the 'voting power' in P; or
(h) is able to exercise significant influence over the management of P by virtue of his 'voting power' in P.
(3) In (2) the **person** means—
(a) the person;
(b) any of the person's *associates*; or
(c) the person and any of his *associates*.
(4) **Associate**, in relation to a 'person' ("H") holding '*shares*' in an undertaking ("C") or entitled to exercise or control the exercise of 'voting power' in relation to another undertaking ("D"), means—
(a) the spouse or civil partner of H;
(b) a child or stepchild of H (if under 18);
(c) the trustee of any 'settlement' under which H has a life interest in possession (or in Scotland a life interest);
(d) an undertaking of which H is a *director*;
(e) a person who is an employee or partner of H;
(f) if H is an undertaking—
(i) a *director* of H,
(ii) a *subsidiary undertaking* of H,
(iii) a *director* or employee of such a *subsidiary undertaking*; and
(g) if H has with any other person an agreement or arrangement with respect to the acquisition, holding or disposal of '*shares*' or other interests in C or D or under which they undertake to act together in exercising their 'voting power' in relation to C or D, that other person.
(5) **Settlement**, in (4)(c), includes any disposition or arrangement under which property is held on trust (or subject to a comparable obligation).
(6) **Shares**—
(a) in relation to an undertaking with *share* capital, means allotted shares;
(b) in relation to an undertaking with capital but no *share* capital, means rights to share in the capital of the undertaking; and
(c) in relation to an undertaking without capital, means interests—
(i) conferring any right to share in the profits, or liability to contribute to the losses, of the undertaking, or
(ii) giving rise to an obligation to contribute to the debts or expenses of the undertaking in the event of a winding up.
(7) **Voting power**, in relation to an undertaking which does not have general meetings at which matters are decided by the exercise of voting rights, means the right under the constitution of the undertaking to direct the overall policy of the undertaking or alter the terms of its constitution.

Part 2
General Provisions

Powers under which the rules are made

[2105]
11.3 The rules and guidance in the IPRU(INS) are made under the following sections of the *Act*—
(a) section 138 (general rule making power);
(b) section 141 (insurance business rules);

(c) section 150(2) (actions for damages);
(d) section 156 (general supplementary powers);
(e) section 157 (guidance); and
(f) section 340 (appointment of auditors and actuaries).

Actions for damages

11.4 section 150(1) of the *Act* does not apply to a contravention of the rules in the IPRU(INS).

Use of definitions

11.5 A word or phrase which is printed in italics is used in the defined sense. Where a word or phrase is printed in italics and is not given a meaning in Part 1 of Chapter 11, that word or phrase has the meaning given to it in the Handbook *Glossary*.

11.6 Unless the context otherwise requires, a word or phrase which is defined in a related enactment bears the same meaning as in that enactment.

11.7 Unless the context otherwise requires, a word which is related to a defined word is construed by reference to the defined word.

Supplementary and ancillary provisions

11.8 For the purposes of this IPRU(INS):
(a) a *contract of insurance* is to be treated as falling within **Annex 11.1**, notwithstanding the fact that that it contains supplementary provisions falling within *class 1* or *class 2* of **Annex 11.2** if:
  (i) its principal object is that of a contract falling within **Annex 11.1**, and
  (ii) it is effected or carried out by an *insurer* who has permission to effect or carry out contracts falling within *class I* of **Annex 11.1**; and
(b) a *contract of insurance* whose principal risk falls within any of *classes* 1 to 18 of **Annex 11.2** is to be treated as falling within that *class* and no other, notwithstanding the fact that it also covers *ancillary risks*.

ANNEX 11.1
CLASSES OF LONG-TERM INSURANCE BUSINESS

[2106]

Number	**Description**	**Nature of business**	
I	Life and annuity	Effecting or carrying out *contracts of insurance* on human life or contracts to pay *annuities on human life*, but excluding (in each case) contracts within *class* III.	
II	Marriage or the formation of a civil partnership and birth	Effecting or carrying out *contracts of insurance* to provide a sum on marriage or the formation of a civil partnership or on the birth of a child, being contracts expressed to be in effect for a period of more than one year.	
III	Linked long term	Effecting or carrying out *contracts of insurance* on human life or contracts to pay *annuities on human life* where the benefits are wholly or partly to be determined by reference to the value of, or the income from, property of any description (whether or not specified in the contracts) or by reference to fluctuations in, or in an index of, the value of property of any description (whether or not so specified).	
IV	Permanent health	Effecting or carrying out *contracts of insurance* providing specified benefits against risks of persons becoming incapacitated in consequence of sustaining injury as a result of an accident or of an accident of a specified class or of sickness or infirmity, being contracts that—	
		(a)	are expressed to be in effect for a period of not less than five years, or until the normal retirement age for the persons concerned, or without limit of time; and
		(b)	either are not expressed to be terminable by the insurer, or are expressed to be so terminable only in special circumstances mentioned in the contract.
V	Tontines	Effecting or carrying out tontines.	

Number	Description	Nature of business	
VI	Capital redemption	Effecting or carrying out capital redemption contracts.	
VII	Pension fund management	Effecting or carrying out-	
		(a)	*pension fund management contracts*; or
		(b)	contracts of the kind mentioned in (a) that are combined with *contracts of insurance* covering either conservation of capital or payment of a minimum interest.
VIII	Collective insurance etc	Effecting or carrying out contracts of a kind referred to in Article 2(2)(e) of the *Consolidated Life Directive*.	
IX	Social insurance	Effecting or carrying out contracts of a kind referred to in Article 2(3) of the *Consolidated Life Directive*.	

ANNEX 11.2
CLASSES, AND GROUPS OF CLASSES, OF GENERAL INSURANCE BUSINESS

Part I
Classes of general insurance business
[2107]

Number	Description	Nature of business	
1	Accident	Effecting or carrying out *contracts of insurance* providing fixed pecuniary benefits or benefits in the nature of indemnity (or a combination of both) against risks of the person insured or, in the case of a contract made by virtue of section 140, 140A or 140B of the Local Government Act 1972, a person for whose benefit the contract is made—	
		(a)	sustaining injury as the result of an accident or of an accident of a specified class, or
		(b)	dying as the result of an accident or of an accident of a specified class, or
		(c)	becoming incapacitated in consequence of disease or of disease of a specified class,
		inclusive of contracts relating to industrial injury and occupational disease but exclusive of contracts falling within *class* 2 or within *class* IV in **Annex 11.1**.	
2	Sickness	Effecting or carrying out *contracts of insurance* providing fixed pecuniary benefits or benefits in the nature of indemnity (or a combination of the two) against risks of loss to the persons insured attributable to sickness or infirmity, but exclusive of contracts falling within *class* IV in **Annex 11.1**.	
3	Land vehicles	Effecting or carrying out *contracts of insurance* against loss of or damage to vehicles used on land, including motor vehicles but excluding railway rolling stock.	
4	Railway rolling stock	Effecting or carrying out *contracts of insurance* against loss of or damage to railway rolling stock.	
5	Aircraft Effecting	or carrying out *contracts of insurance* upon aircraft or upon the machinery, tackle, furniture or equipment of aircraft.	
6	Ships	Effecting or carrying out *contracts of insurance* upon vessels used on the sea or on inland water, or upon the machinery, tackle, furniture or equipment of such vessels.	
7	Goods in transit	Effecting or carrying out *contracts of insurance* against loss of or damage to merchandise, baggage and all other goods in transit, irrespective of the form of transport.	

Number	Description	Nature of business
8	Fire and natural forces	Effecting or carrying out *contracts of insurance* against loss of or damage to property (other than property to which *classes* 3 to 7 above relate) due to fire, explosion, storm, natural forces other than storm, nuclear energy or land subsidence.
9	Damage to property	Effecting or carrying out *contracts of insurance* against loss of or damage to property (other than property to which *classes* 3 to 7 above relate) due to hail or frost or to any event (such as theft) other than those mentioned in *class* 8 above.
10	Motor vehicle liability	Effecting or carrying out *contracts of insurance* against damage arising out of or in connection with the use of motor vehicles on land including third-party risks and carrier's liability.
11	Aircraft liability	Effecting or carrying out *contracts of insurance* against damage arising out of or in connection with the use of aircraft, including third-party risks and carrier's liability.
12	Liability for ships	Effecting or carrying out *contracts of insurance* against damage arising out of or in connection with the use of vessels on the sea or on inland water, including third-party risks and carrier's liability.
13	General liability	Effecting or carrying out *contracts of insurance* against risks of the persons insured incurring liabilities to third parties, the risks in question not being risks to which *class* 10, 11 or 12 above relates.
14	Credit Effecting	or carrying out *contracts of insurance* against risks of loss to the persons insured arising from the insolvency of debtors of theirs or from the failure (otherwise than through insolvency) of debtors of theirs to pay their debts when due.
15	Suretyship	Effecting or carrying out— (a) *contracts of insurance* against risks of loss to the persons insured arising from their having to perform contracts of guarantee entered into by them; (b) contracts for fidelity bonds, performance bonds, administration bonds, bail bonds or customs bonds or similar contracts of guarantee.
16	Miscellaneous financial loss	Effecting or carrying out *contracts of insurance* against any of the following risks, namely— (a) risks of loss to the persons insured attributable to interruptions of the carrying on of business carried on by them or to reduction of the scope of business so carried on; (b) risks of loss to the persons insured attributable to their incurring unforeseen expense (other than loss such as is covered by contracts falling within *class* 18); (c) risks neither falling within (a) or (b) nor being of a kind such that the carrying on of the business of effecting or carrying *out contracts of insurance* against them constitutes the carrying on of *insurance business* of some other class.
17	Legal expenses	Effecting or carrying out *contracts of insurance* against risks of loss to the persons insured attributable to their incurring legal expenses (including costs of litigation).
18	Assistance	Effecting or carrying out *contracts of insurance* providing either or both of the following benefits, namely – (a) assistance (whether in cash or in kind) for persons who get into difficulties while travelling, while away from home or while away from their permanent residence, or

Number	Description	Nature of business	
		(b)	assistance (whether in cash or in kind) for persons who get into difficulties otherwise than as mentioned in paragraph (a) above.

Part II
Groups of classes of general insurance business

Number	Description	Nature of business
1	Accident and health	*Classes* 1 and 2.
2	Motor	*Class* 1 (to the extent that the relevant risks are risks of the person insured sustaining injury, or dying, as the result of travelling as a passenger) and *classes* 3, 7 and 10.
3	Marine and transport	*Class* 1 (to the said extent) and *classes* 4, 6, 7 and 12.
4	Aviation	*Class* 1 (to the said extent) and *classes* 5, 7 and 11.
5	Fire and other damage to property	*Classes* 8 and 9.
6	Liability	*Classes* 10, 11, 12 and 13.
7	Credit and suretyship	*Classes* 14 and 15.
8	General	All *classes*.

ANNEX 11.3
DESCRIPTIONS OF FSA GENERAL INSURANCE BUSINESS REPORTING CATEGORIES

Part I
Categories to which contracts of general insurance business are to be allocated for the purpose of reporting in the return
[2108]

Category Number	FSA general insurance business reporting category	Map to classes of business in Annex A of 73/239/EEC
001	**Total Business** (*category numbers* 002 and 003 combined).	N/A
002	**Total Primary (Direct) and Facultative Business** (*category numbers* 110, 120, 160, 180, 220, 260, 270, 280, 330, 340, 350 and 400 combined).	N/A
003	**Total Treaty Reinsurance Accepted Business** (*category numbers* 500, 600 and 700 combined).	N/A
	PRIMARY (DIRECT) and FACULTATIVE PERSONAL LINES BUSINESS	
110	**Total primary (direct) and facultative accident & health** (*category numbers* 111 to 114 combined).	
111	**Medical expenses** *Contracts of insurance* (other than treaty reinsurance contracts) providing benefits in the nature of indemnity, with or without limit, against risks of loss to the persons insured attributable to their incurring the cost of medical treatment for sickness or infirmity or injuries sustained.	1,2
112	**HealthCare cash plan** *Contracts of insurance* (other than treaty reinsurance contracts) providing fixed pecuniary benefits against risks of the persons insured requiring health care for sickness, infirmity or injuries sustained.	2
113	**Travel**	1,2,8,9,17,18

Category Number	FSA general insurance business reporting category	Map to classes of business in Annex A of 73/239/EEC
	Contracts of insurance (other than treaty reinsurance contracts) against a combination of risks of loss to the persons insured attributable to their travelling, or to their making of travel arrangements, and which fall within *classes* 1, 2, 8, 9, 17 or 18 and do not fall within *category number* 160 (Household and domestic all risks).	
114	**Personal accident or sickness** *Contracts of insurance* (other than treaty reinsurance contracts) which fall within *classes* 1 or 2 and which do not fall within *category numbers* 111 (Medical expenses), 112 (HealthCare cash plans), 113 (Travel), 114(p), 182 (Creditor).	1,2
114(p)	**Personal accident as a result of insured travelling as a passenger** *Contracts of insurance* (other than treaty reinsurance contracts) against risks of death of, or injury to, passengers which the insurer elects to allocate to *category numbers* 121 to 123, 221 to 223, 331 to 333 or 341 to 347, notwithstanding that they would also fall within the definition of *category number* 114.	1
120	**Total primary (direct) and facultative personal motor business** (*category numbers* 121 to 123 combined).	3,10
121	**Private motor comprehensive** *Contracts of insurance* (other than treaty reinsurance contracts) against loss of, or damage to, motor vehicles used on land and against the risks of the persons insured incurring liabilities to third parties arising out of or in connection with the use of motor vehicles on land, where the motor vehicle has more than two wheels and is not a motorcycle with side-car and: (a) the primary purpose of each vehicle insured on the contract is to transport nine or fewer non-fare paying persons and each motor vehicle insured on the contract is individually rated; (b) the primary purpose of each vehicle insured on the contract is to transport nine or fewer non-fare paying persons, the persons insured are not a body corporate or partnership, and the number of vehicles insured on the contract is three or less; or (c) the primary purpose of each vehicle insured on the contract is to transport ten or more non-fare paying persons, the persons insured are not a body corporate or partnership and each motor vehicle insured on the contract is individually rated. *Contracts of insurance* (other than treaty reinsurance contracts) that fall within the definition of *category number* 114(p) which the insurer elects to allocate to this category.	3,10
122	**Private motor non-comprehensive** *Contracts of insurance* (other than treaty reinsurance contracts) against the risks of the persons insured incurring liabilities to third parties arising out of or in connection with the use of motor vehicles on land or against loss of or damage to motor vehicles used on land arising only from fire or theft, where the motor vehicle has more than two wheels and is not a motorcycle with side-car and:	3,10

Part II FSA Handbook Materials

Category Number	FSA general insurance business reporting category	Map to classes of business in Annex A of 73/239/EEC
	(a) the primary purpose of each vehicle insured on the contract is to transport nine or fewer non-fare paying persons and each motor vehicle insured in the contract is individually rated; (b) the primary purpose of each vehicle insured on the contract is to transport nine or fewer non-fare paying persons, the persons insured are not a body corporate or partnership, and the number of vehicles insured on the contract is three or less; or (c) the primary purpose of each vehicle insured on the contract is to transport ten or more non-fare paying persons and the persons insured are not a body corporate or partnership and each motor vehicle insured on the contract is individually rated. *Contracts of insurance* (other than treaty reinsurance contracts) that fall within the definition of *category numbers* 114(p) which the insurer elects to allocate to this category.	
123	**Motor cycle** *Contracts of insurance* (other than treaty reinsurance contracts) against loss of or damage to twowheeled motor vehicles or motor cycles with a side car used on land and or against the risks of the persons insured incurring liabilities to third parties arising out of or in connection with the use of such vehicles on land. *Contracts of insurance* (other than treaty reinsurance contracts) that fall within the definition of *category number* 114(p) which the insurer elects to allocate to this category.	3,10
160	**Primary (direct) and facultative household and domestic all risks.** *Contracts of insurance* (other than treaty reinsurance contracts) against loss of or damage to any of: (a) structure of domestic properties, (b) contents of domestic properties, or (c) contents of domestic properties and personal items. *Contracts of insurance* (other than treaty reinsurance contracts) against loss of or damage to structure of domestic properties and against risks to the persons insured incurring liabilities to third parties arising out of injuries sustained within the boundary of a domestic property.	8,9
180	**Total primary (direct) and facultative personal lines financial loss business** (*category numbers* 181 to 187 combined).	
181	**Assistance** *Contracts of insurance* (other than treaty reinsurance contracts) which: (a) fall within *class* 18 (such as contracts relating to vehicle assistance, household assistance and legal expense helpline); and (b) do not fall within *category number* 113 (Travel).	18
182	**Creditor**	1,2,16

Category Number	FSA general insurance business reporting category	Map to classes of business in Annex A of 73/239/EEC
	Contracts of insurance (other than treaty reinsurance contracts) against the risk that the persons insured sustain injury, suffer sickness or infirmity, suffer loss of income due to causes that may or may not be specified in the contract, where the benefits payable under the contract relate to loans, credit card balances or other debts and the contract does not fall within *category number* 185 (Mortgage indemnity).	
183	**Extended warranty** *Contracts of insurance* (other than treaty reinsurance contracts) against the risks of loss to the persons insured attributable to failure of a product, where the purpose of the contract is to put the persons insured in the position as if the manufacturer's or vendor's warranty on the product is extended for a period of time or is extended in scope.	16
184	**Legal expenses** *Contracts of insurance* (other than treaty reinsurance contracts) against risks of loss to the persons insured attributable to their incurring legal expenses including cost of litigation that do not fall within *category number* 120.	17
185	**Mortgage indemnity** *Contracts of insurance* (other than treaty reinsurance contracts) against risks of loss to the persons insured arising from the failure of debtors of theirs to pay debts relating to the purchase of a property when due and the persons insured being unable to recover the full amount of any outstanding debt by selling the property concerned.	14
186	**Pet insurance** *Contracts of insurance* (other than treaty reinsurance) against risk of loss to the person insured attributable to sickness of or accidents to domestic pets.	16
187	**Other personal financial loss** *Contracts of insurance* (other than treaty reinsurance) against risk of loss to the person insured attributable to: (a) loss, breakdown or reduction in value of a personal item that attach to the purchase of that item, or (b) to an event not taking place as intended where the persons insured are not a body corporate or partnership and the *contracts of insurance* do not fall within *category numbers* 113, 160 or 181 to 186.	16
	PRIMARY (DIRECT) and FACULTATIVE COMMERCIAL LINES BUSINESS	
220	**Total primary (direct) and facultative commercial motor business** (*category numbers* 221 to 223 combined).	3,10
221	**Fleets** *Contracts of insurance* (other than treaty reinsurance contracts) against loss of, or damage to, motor vehicles used on land and / or against the risks of the persons insured incurring liabilities to third parties arising out of or in connection with the use of motor vehicles on land, where the motor vehicle has more than two wheels and is not a motorcycle with side-car and: (a) the primary purpose of the vehicle insured on the contract is to transport non-fare paying persons;	3,10

Part II FSA Handbook Materials

Category Number	FSA general insurance business reporting category	Map to classes of business in Annex A of 73/239/EEC
	(b) the motor vehicles insured on the contract are not individually rated (that is, the premium charged is for the contract as a whole and either the firm does not disclose or record for internal management purposes a separate premium for each vehicle insured on the contract, or the premium for the contract is not necessarily the same as the sum of the premiums that would have been charged had the firm insured the vehicles under a private motor policy); and (c) the contract does not fall within *category numbers* 121 (private motor comprehensive) or 122 (private motor non-comprehensive) *Contracts of insurance* (other than treaty reinsurance contracts) that fall within the definition of *category number* 114(p) which the insurer elects to allocate to this category.	
222	**Commercial vehicles (non-fleet)** *Contracts of insurance* (other than treaty reinsurance contracts) against loss of, or damage to, motor vehicles used on land and / or against the risks of the persons insured incurring liabilities to third parties arising out of or in connection with the use of motor vehicles on land, where: (a) the persons insured are a body corporate or partnership; and (b) the primary purpose of the vehicles insured on the contract is to transport ten or more persons, to transport goods or for construction. *Contracts of insurance* (other than treaty reinsurance contracts) that fall within the definition of *category number* 114(p) which the insurer elects to allocate to this category.	3,10
223	**Motor other** *Contracts of insurance* (other than treaty reinsurance contracts) which: (a) fall within *classes* 3 or 10; and (b) do not fall within *category numbers* 120, 221 or 222. This category includes *contracts of insurance* relating to motor trade and taxis. *Contracts of insurance* (other than treaty reinsurance contracts) that fall within the definition of *category number* 114(p) which the insurer elects to allocate to this category.	3,10
260	**Total primary (direct) and facultative commercial lines property business** (*category numbers* 261 to 263 combined).	N/A
261	**Commercial property (including livestock and crops but excluding energy)** *Contracts of insurance* (other than treaty reinsurance contracts) against: (a) loss of or damage to commercial property; or (b) loss of or damage to commercial property and risks that fall within the definition of *category number* 262 (consequential loss), where the premium for the contract is rated on a single package basis and no separately identifiable premium for either the property loss or the consequential loss is charged or recorded for internal management purposes.	4,8,9

Category Number	FSA general insurance business reporting category	Map to classes of business in Annex A of 73/239/EEC
	This category does not include *contracts of insurance* that fall within *category number* 160 (Household), 263 (Contractors or engineering all risks), 274 (Mixed commercial package) or 343 (Energy).	
262	**Consequential loss (i.e. business interruption)** *Contracts of insurance* (other than treaty reinsurance contracts) against risks of loss to the persons insured attributable to interruptions of the business carried on by them, or to the reduction of the scope of the business so carried out, which result from perils insured against or other events (whether or not specified in the contract). This category does not include *contracts of insurance* that fall within *category numbers* 261 (Commercial property) or 343 (Energy).	16
263	**Contractors or engineering all risks** *Contracts of insurance* (other than treaty reinsurance contracts) against loss of or damage to property or equipment, or against the risks of the persons insured incurring liabilities to third parties, which arise from, or are attributable to: (a) materials and works in progress during construction, (b) extension or renovation work, (c) temporary sites, (d) breakdown or malfunction of or damage to plant and machinery, (e) use of equipment hired or owned by the persons insured, or (f) similar types of activities. This category excludes *contracts of insurance* that fall within *category number* 274 (Mixed commercial package).	8,9,13
270	**Total primary (direct) and facultative commercial lines liability business** (*category numbers* 271 to 274 combined).	N/A
271	**Employers liability (including the employers liability part of mixed liability packages but excluding mixed commercial packages)** *Contracts of insurance* (other than treaty reinsurance contracts) against the risks of the persons insured incurring liabilities to their employees for injury, illness or death arising out of their employment during the course of business. his category excludes *contracts of insurance* that fall within *category number* 274 (Mixed commercial package).	13
272	**Professional indemnity (including directors' and officers' liability and errors and omissions liability)** *Contracts of insurance* (other than treaty reinsurance contracts) against the risks of the persons insured incurring liabilities to third parties arising from wrongful acts (such as breach of duty, breach of trust, negligence, errors or omissions) by professionals, named individuals or businesses occurring in the course of the insured's professional activities.	13
273	**Public and products liability**	13

Category Number	FSA general insurance business reporting category	Map to classes of business in Annex A of 73/239/EEC
	Contracts of insurance (other than treaty reinsurance contracts) against the risks of the persons insured incurring liabilities to third parties for damage to property, injury, illness or death, arising in the course of the insured's business, that do not fall within *category numbers* 120 (Personal motor), 160 (Household and domestic all risks), 220 (Commercial motor), 263 (Contractors or engineering all risks), 271 (Employers liability), 272 (Professional indemnity) or 274 (Mixed commercial package).	
274	**Mixed commercial package** *Contracts of insurance* (other than treaty reinsurance contracts) against more than one of: (a) loss of or damage to property; (b) risks to the persons insured incurring liabilities to third parties; (c) risks of loss to the persons insured arising from the failure of debtors of theirs to pay their debts when due; (d) risks of loss to the persons insured attributable to interruptions of business carried on by them; (e) risks of loss to the persons insured attributable to their incurring unforeseen expenses; or (f) any other risk of loss to a commercial operation; where the risks and losses covered in the contract are rated on a single package basis and no separately identifiable premium is charged or recorded for internal management purposes for any one group of risks or losses specified in the contract. This category excludes *contracts of insurance* that fall with *category numbers* 261 (Commercial property) or 343 (Energy).	8,9,13,14,16,17
280	**Total primary (direct) and facultative commercial lines financial loss business** (*category numbers* 281 to 284 combined).	
281	**Fidelity and contract guarantee** *Contracts of insurance* (other than treaty reinsurance contracts) against risks of loss to the persons insured arising from the theft or misappropriation of money or goods by employees, or attributable to failure to complete a contract on time.	16
282	**Credit** *Contracts of insurance* (other than treaty reinsurance contracts) against risks of loss to the persons insured arising from the insolvency of debtors of theirs or from the failure (otherwise than through insolvency) of debtors of theirs to pay their debts when due, and which do not fall within *category number* 185 (Mortgage indemnity).	14
283	**Suretyship** *Contracts of insurance* (other than treaty reinsurance contracts) which fall within *class* 15.	15
284	**Commercial contingency**: *Contracts of insurance* (other than treaty reinsurance) against risk of loss to the person insured attributable to an event not taking place as intended where the persons insured are a body corporate or partnership.	16

Category Number	FSA general insurance business reporting category	Map to classes of business in Annex A of 73/239/EEC
	PRIMARY (DIRECT) and FACULTATIVE AVIATION, MARINE AND TRANSPORT	
330	**Total primary (direct) and facultative aviation business** (*category number* 331 to 333 combined).	N/A
331	**Aviation liability (including liability part of airline packages)** *Contracts of insurance* (other than treaty reinsurance contracts) against: (a) damage arising out of, or in connection with, the use of aircraft; or (b) the risks of the persons insured incurring liabilities to third parties, or carrier's liabilities, arising out of, or in connection with, the use of aircraft. This category excludes contracts that fall within *category numbers* 332 (Aviation hull) or 333 (Space and satellite) and risks relating to use of hovercraft. *Contracts of insurance* (other than treaty reinsurance contracts) that fall within the definition of *category number* 114(p) which the insurer elects to allocate to this category.	11
332	**Aviation hull (including hull part of airline packages)** *Contracts of insurance* (other than treaty reinsurance contracts) loss of or damage to aircraft, or the machinery, tackle, furniture or equipment of aircraft. This category excludes contracts that fall within *category number* 333 (Space and satellite) and risks relating to use of hovercraft. *Contracts of insurance* (other than treaty reinsurance contracts) that fall within the definition of *category number* 114(p) which the insurer elects to allocate to this category.	5
333	**Space and satellite** *Contracts of insurance* (other than treaty reinsurance contracts) upon satellites, aircraft or the machinery, tackle, furniture or equipment of satellites or aircraft-.*Contracts of insurance* (other than treaty reinsurance contracts) against: (a) damage arising out of or in connection with the use of satellites or aircraft; or (b) the risks of the persons insured incurring liabilities to third parties arising out of or in connection with the use of satellites or aircraft; where any aircraft insured in the contract is intended to transport satellites or to travel to, or be transported to, beyond the earth's atmosphere. *Contracts of insurance* (other than treaty reinsurance contracts) that fall within the definition of *category number* 114(p) which the insurer elects to allocate to this category.	5,11
340	**Total primary (direct) and facultative marine business** (*category numbers* 341 to 347 combined).	N/A
341	**Marine liability** *Contracts of insurance* (other than treaty reinsurance contracts) against damage, or against the risks of the persons insured incurring liabilities to third parties or carrier's liabilities, arising out of or in connection with the use of vessels on the sea or on inland water (including hovercraft), and which do not fall within *category numbers* 342 (Marine hull) or 347 (Yacht).	12

Category Number	FSA general insurance business reporting category	Map to classes of business in Annex A of 73/239/EEC
	Contracts of insurance (other than treaty reinsurance contracts) that fall within the definition of *category number* 114(p) which the insurer elects to allocate to this category.	
342	**Marine hull** *Contracts of insurance* (other than treaty reinsurance contracts) against loss of or damage to vessels on the sea or on inland water (including hovercraft), or upon the machinery, tackle, furniture or equipment of such vessels, which do not fall within *category numbers* 346 (War risks) or 347 (Yacht)). *Contracts of insurance* (other than treaty reinsurance contracts) that fall within the definition of *category number* 114(p) which the insurer elects to allocate to this category.	6
343	**Energy (on and off-shore)** *Contracts of insurance* (other than treaty reinsurance contracts) against loss of or damage to property, or against the risks of the persons insured incurring liabilities to third parties, or against risks of loss to the persons insured attributable to interruptions of business carried on by them, arising from the undertaking of energy operations on both land and sea. *Contracts of insurance* other than treaty reinsurance that fall within the definition of *category number* 114(p) which the insurer elects to allocate to this category.	6,8,9,12,13,16
344	**Protection and indemnity** *Contracts of insurance* (other than treaty reinsurance contracts) against the risks of the persons insured incurring liabilities to third parties for damage to property, injury, illness or death on board vessels on the sea or inland water or at locations associated with the operation of such vessels such as docks, arising from the negligence of the owner of or individuals responsible for the vessels. *Contracts of insurance* other than treaty reinsurance that fall within the definition of *category number* 114(p) which the insurer elects to allocate to this category.	12
345	**Freight demurrage and defence** *Contracts of insurance* (other than treaty reinsurance contracts) against risks of loss to the persons insured attributable to their incurring legal expenses (including costs of litigation) arising from loss of or damage to goods during a period of transit that included, or was due to include, transport of the goods via sea or inland water. *Contracts of insurance* (other than treaty reinsurance contracts) that fall within the definition of *category number* 114(p) which the insurer elects to allocate to this category.	17
346	**War risks** *Contracts of insurance* (other than treaty reinsurance contracts) against loss of or damage to property or mass transportation vehicles arising from war, civil war, revolution, rebellion, insurrection or hostile act by a belligerent power.	6

Category Number	FSA general insurance business reporting category	Map to classes of business in Annex A of 73/239/EEC
	Contracts of insurance (other than treaty reinsurance contracts) that fall within the definition of *category number* 114(p) which the insurer elects to allocate to this category.	
347	**Yacht** *Contracts of insurance* (other than treaty reinsurance contracts) upon vessels on the sea or on inland water. *Contracts of insurance* (other than treaty reinsurance contracts) against: (a) damage arising out of or in connection with the use of vessels on the sea or on inland water, or upon the machinery, tackle, furniture or equipment of such vessels; or (b) the risks of the persons insured incurring liabilities to third parties, arising out of or in connection with the use of vessels on the sea or on inland water; where the vessels insured in the contract are not used for transporting goods or fare-paying passengers. *Contracts of insurance* (other than treaty reinsurance contracts) that fall within the definition of *category number* 114(p) which the insurer elects to allocate to this category.	6,12
350	**Primary (direct) and facultative goods in transit** *Contracts of insurance* (other than treaty reinsurance contracts) against loss of, or damage to, merchandise, baggage and all other goods in transit, irrespective of the form of transport.	7
400	**Miscellaneous primary (direct) and facultative business**	N/A
	Contracts of insurance (other than treaty reinsurance) that, in the reasonable opinion of the *insurer's governing body*, do not fall within *category numbers* 110 to 350 or may mislead users of the return if allocated to one of *category numbers* 110 to 350.	
	NON-PROPORTIONAL REINSURANCE TREATY BUSINESS	
500	**Total Non-Proportional Reinsurance Treaty Business accepted** (*category numbers* 510 to 590 combined).	N/A
510	**Non-proportional accident & health** *Contracts of insurance*, effected or carried out under *non-proportional reinsurance treaties* or proportional retrocession of *non-proportional treaty reinsurance* business, which fall within *classes* 1 or 2, and do not fall within *category numbers* 590 or 710(p).	1,2
520	**Non-proportional motor** *Contracts of insurance*, effected or carried out under *non-proportional reinsurance treaties* or proportional retrocession of *non-proportional treaty reinsurance* business, which fall within *classes* 3 or 10, or *category number* 710(p), and do not fall within *category number* 590.	3,10
530	**Non-proportional aviation** *Contracts of insurance*, effected or carried out under *non-proportional reinsurance treaties* or proportional retrocession of *non-proportional treaty reinsurance* business, which fall within *classes* 5 or 11, or *category number* 710(p), and do not fall within *category number* 590.	5,11
540	**Non-proportional marine**	6,12

Category Number	FSA general insurance business reporting category	Map to classes of business in Annex A of 73/239/EEC
	Contracts of insurance, effected or carried out under *non-proportional reinsurance treaties* or proportional retrocession of *non-proportional treaty reinsurance* business, which fall within *classes* 6 or 12, or *category number* 710(p), and do not fall within *category number* 590.	
550	**Non-proportional transport** *Contracts of insurance*, effected or carried out *under non-proportional reinsurance treaties* or proportional retrocession of *non-proportional treaty reinsurance* business, which fall within *class* 7, and do not fall within *category number* 590.	7
560	**Non-proportional property** *Contracts of insurance*, effected or carried out under *non-proportional reinsurance treaties* or proportional retrocession of *non-proportional treaty reinsurance* business, which fall within *classes* 8 or 9, and do not fall within *category number* 590.	4,8,9
570	**Non-Proportional liability (non-motor)** *Contracts of insurance*, effected or carried out under *non-proportional reinsurance treaties* or proportional retrocession of *non-proportional treaty reinsurance* business, which fall within *class* 13, and do not fall within *category numbers* 520, 530, 540 or 590.	13
580	**Non-proportional financial lines** *Contracts of insurance*, effected or carried out under *non-proportional reinsurance treaties* or proportional retrocession of *non-proportional treaty reinsurance* business, which fall within *classes* 14, 15, 16, 17 or 18, and do not fall within *category number* 590.	14,15,16,17,18
590	**Non-proportional aggregate cover** *Contracts of insurance*, effected or carried out under *non-proportional reinsurance treaties* or proportional retrocession of *non-proportional treaty reinsurance* business, which fall within more than one of *category numbers* 510 to 580, where no one of these categories accounts for more than 90% of the exposure on the contract.	1 to 18
	PROPORTIONAL REINSURANCE TREATY BUSINESS	
600	**Total Proportional Reinsurance Treaty Business accepted** (*category numbers* 610 to 690 combined).	N/A
610	**Proportional accident & health** *Contracts of insurance*, effected or carried out under *proportional reinsurance treaties* other than proportional retrocession of *non-proportional treaty reinsurance* business, which fall within *classes* 1 or 2 and do not fall within *category numbers* 690 or 710(p).	1,2
620	**Proportional motor** *Contracts of insurance*, effected or carried out under *proportional reinsurance treaties* other than proportional retrocession of *non-proportional treaty reinsurance* business, which fall within *classes* 3 or 10, or *category number* 710(p) and do not fall within *category number* 690.	3,10
630	**Proportional aviation**	5,11

Category Number	FSA general insurance business reporting category	Map to classes of business in Annex A of 73/239/EEC
	Contracts of insurance, effected or carried out under *proportional reinsurance treaties* other than proportional retrocession of *non-proportional treaty reinsurance* business, which fall within *classes* 5 or 11, or *category number* 710(p) and do not fall within *category number* 690.	
640	**Proportional marine** *Contracts of insurance*, effected or carried out under *proportional reinsurance treaties* other than proportional retrocession of *non-proportional treaty reinsurance* business, which fall within *classes* 6 or 12, or *category number* 710(p) and do not fall within *category number* 690.	6,12
650	**Proportional transport**	7
	Contracts of insurance, effected or carried out under *proportional reinsurance treaties* other than proportional retrocession of *non-proportional treaty reinsurance* business, which fall within *class* 7 and do not fall within *category number* 690.	
660	**Proportional property** *Contracts of insurance*, effected or carried out under *proportional reinsurance treaties* other than proportional retrocession of *non-proportional treaty reinsurance* business, which fall within *classes* 8 or 9 and do not fall within *category number* 690.	4,8,9
670	**Proportional liability (excluding motor)** *Contracts of insurance*, effected or carried out under *proportional reinsurance treaties* other than proportional retrocession of *non-proportional treaty reinsurance* business, which fall within *class* 13 and do not fall within *category numbers* 620, 630, 640 or 690.	13
680	**Proportional financial lines** *Contracts of insurance*, effected or carried out under *proportional reinsurance treaties* other than proportional retrocession of *non-proportional treaty reinsurance* business, which fall within *classes* 14, 15, 16, 17 or 18 and do not fall within *category number* 690.	14,15,16,17,18
690	**Proportional aggregate cover (i.e. more than one of the above)** *Contracts of insurance*, effected or carried out under *proportional reinsurance treaties* other than proportional retrocession of *non-proportional treaty reinsurance* business, which fall within more than one of *category numbers* 610 to 680, where no one of these categories accounts for more than 90% of the exposure on the contract.	1 to 18
700	**Miscellaneous treaty reinsurance accepted business** *Contracts of insurance* effected or carried out under *reinsurance treaties* that, in the reasonable opinion of the *insurer's governing body*, do not fall within *category numbers* 500 or 600 or may mislead users of the *return* if allocated to one of these categories.	N/A
710(p)	**Treaty reinsurance passenger accident**	

Category Number	FSA general insurance business reporting category	Map to classes of business in Annex A of 73/239/EEC
	Contracts of insurance effected or carried out under *reinsurance treaties* against risks of death of, or injury to, passengers which the insurer elects to allocate to *category numbers* 520, 530, 540, 590, 620, 630, 640 or 690 notwithstanding that they would also fall within the definition of *category numbers* 510 or 610.	

Part II

Groups of categories of general insurance business to which categories in Part I are to be allocated for the purpose of reporting in the return

Category Number	FSA general insurance business reporting category	Map to classifications in Annex A of 73/239/EEC
409	**Balance of all primary (direct) and facultative business** All *direct and facultative insurance business* reported in a **Form 20** to **25** under *category number* 002 that is not also reported in the same Form under *category numbers* 110, 120, 160, 180, 20, 260, 270, 280, 330, 340, 350, and 400.	N/A
709	**Balance of all treaty reinsurance accepted business** All *treaty reinsurance business* reported in a **Form 20** to **25** under *category number* 003 that is not also reported in the same Form under *category numbers* 500, 600 and 700.	N/A

CHAPTER 12
TRANSITIONAL ARRANGEMENTS

Reporting of information relating to financial years prior to the financial year ending on or after 31 December 2005

[2109]

12.1

(1) An *insurer* that is required to report the information in (2) in respect of any *financial year* ending on or after 31 December 2005, may report that information as set out in (3).

(2) The information in (1) is information that is required to be inserted in—

(a) column 1 to 3 or 11 and rows relating to accident years prior to 1995 of **Forms 23**, **26** or **27**;

(b) column 1, 3 or 10 and rows relating to accident years prior to 1995 of **Forms 31** and **32**; or

(c) column 1 or 8 and rows relating to underwriting years prior to 1995 of **Form 34**.

(3) Information relating to—

(a) aggregate treaty business falling within the definition of *category number* 590 or 690, may be reported in *category numbers* 510 to 580 or 610 to 680;

(b) commercial package business falling within the definition of *category number* 274 business, may be reported in *category numbers* 261, 271 or 273;

(c) business that was reported under a single risk group or business category in the *return* for the *financial year* immediately preceding the first *financial year* that ended on or after 31 December 2005, may be reported in a single *risk category* if and 90% or more of the claim liabilities reported under the risk group or business category fall into that single *risk category*;

(d) any business covering risks relating to hovercraft which was classified under the heading 'Aviation' in the *return* for the *financial year* immediately preceding the first *financial year* that ended that ends on or after 31 December 2005, may bereported in any of *category numbers* 331 to 333 (aviation);

(e) any business covering liability for loss of, or damage to, goods in transit which was classified under the heading 'Transport' in the *return* for the *financial year* immediately preceding the first *financial year* that ended on or after 31 December 2005, may be reported in *category number* 350 (transport);

(f) any business which was classified under the heading 'Accident and Health' in the *return* for the *financial year* immediately preceding the first *financial year* that ended on or after 31 December 2005, and which would otherwise be allocated to *category number* 114(p), may be reported in *category number* 114;
(g) any business which was classified under the heading 'Marine, Aviation or Transport Treaty' in the *return* for the *financial year* immediately preceding the first *financial year* that ended on or after 31 December 2005, and which would otherwise be allocated to *category number* 550 or 650, may be reported in *category numbers* 530, 540, 630 or 640; and
(h) any business which was classified under the heading '*accounting class* 11' in the *return* for the *financial year* immediately preceding the first *financial year* that ended on or after 31 December 2005, may be reported in *category number* 510 to 590 (non-proportional treaty reinsurance).

Reporting of historical information relating to Forms 26, 27, 28, 29, 31, 32 and 34

12.2
(1) An *insurer* that is required by rule 9.17 or 9.19 to prepare any of **Forms 26, 27, 28, 29, 31, 32** or **34** in respect of the first *financial year* ending on or after 31 December 2005 must send to the *FSA* the additional information in (2).
(2) The additional information in (1)—
(a) is historical development data in respect of business reported on each relevant Form;
(b) must be prepared as set out in (3) to (8);
(c) must be submitted in the format of the **2005 Return Transitional Tables A, B, C** and **D** in the form laid out in rule 12.4;
(d) must be submitted as a computer spreadsheet file that can be accessed by Microsoft Excel; and
(e) must be submitted to *FSA* by electronic mail or a CD-ROM disk, in either case at the same time as the *return* to which it relates.
(3) An *insurer* must prepare—
(a) **2005 Return Transitional Tables A** and **B** in respect of each *required category* for which it is required to prepare **Form 26, 27, 28, 29, 31, 32** or **34** except where the *required category* is *category number* 400 or 700; and
(b) **2005 Return Transitional Table C** and **D** in respect of each *required category* for which it is required to prepare **Form 31** or **32** except where the *required category* is *category number* 400.
(4) An *insurer* must show years of origin in the first two columns of each Table where—
(a) a year of origin is a *financial year* and the columns contain the month and year, on the Gregorian calendar, in which that *financial year* ends;
(b) the month and year are to be in MM and YYYY date format, where MM is a two digit month of the year (between 01 and 12) and YYYY is a calendar year;
(c) years of origin are entered in sequence with the latest year of origin (i.e. the first *financial year* ended on or after 31 December 2005) in row 33;
(d) not report more than the 30 latest years of origin are reported;
(e) the years of origin reported on a Table are consistent with how the *insurer* has allocated claims to accident or underwriting years on the **Forms 27, 29, 31, 32** or **34**, as the case may be, on which the same business is reported.
(5) If an *insurer* is reporting business on a Table that is reported on a **Form 27, 31** or **32**, the year of origin must be an accident year and the entries along the rows of the Table must relate to claims that occurred in that origin year. If an *insurer* is reporting business on a Table that is reported on a **Form 29** or **34**, the year of origin must be an underwriting year and the entries along the rows of the Table must relate to claims arising from business written in that origin year.
(6) Historical development data must be prepared in the same currency as the Form that gave rise to the requirement to prepare the Table.
(7) In preparing any of **2005 Return Transitional Tables A, B, C** and **D**, an *insurer* must, *subject to* (9), complete—
(a) all entries relating to years of origin ending between 31/12/1996 and 30/12/2006 inclusive and all entries for the "prior years" row; and
(b) subject to the total number of years of origin reported on a Table being no more than 30, all entries relating to:
(i) years of origin ending between 23/12/1993 and 30/12/1996 inclusive for business in *category numbers* 610, 620, 650, 660 and 680,
(ii) years of origin ending between 31/12/1983 and 30/12/1996 inclusive for business in *category numbers* 510 to 580, 630, 640 and 670, and
(iii) years of origin ending prior to 31/12/1996 for business in *category numbers* 271 to 273;

(8) an *insurer* that does not maintain records of historical development data by a *required category* for which it is required to prepare any of **2005 Return Transitional Tables A, B, C** and **D**, may make a reasonable estimate of an entry required under (7) in the Table for that *required category*;

(9) an *insurer* may omit an entry required under (7) in a Table for a *required category* if—

(a) in the opinion of its *governing body*, the *insurer* does not have the information needed to complete, or make a reasonable estimate of, the entry;

(b) it does not use any data required for that entry when setting its provisions for claim liabilities for business in the *required category*; and

(c) it states in a supplementary note to the Table an explanation for the entry omitted.

(10) If for any year of origin the duration of any development year is not 12 months, an *insurer* must identify each such development year and state its duration in a supplementary note to the Tables (code TA02).

Reconciliation of information reported in the return for the first financial year ended on or after 31 December 2005 to equivalent information reported in the previous return

12.3 An *insurer* must carry out and send to the FSA, at the same time as it submits its *return* in respect of the first *financial year* ending on or after 31 December 2005, the following reconciliations—

(a) the sum of the amounts reported in column 1 plus column 3 on each **Form 27** in the *return* for the first *financial year* ended on or after 31 December 2005 to the sum of the amounts reported in the column 1 plus column 3 plus column 4 on each **Form 27** in the previous *return*;

(b) the amounts reported in the column headed 'Gross claims paid / In previous financial years' on each of **Forms 31, 32** and **34** in the *return* for the first *financial year* ended on or after 31 December 2005 to the sum of the amounts reported in the column headed 'Gross claims paid / In previous financial years' plus the amounts reported in the column headed 'Gross claims paid / In this financial year' on each **Forms 31, 32** and **34** in the previous *return*;

(c) the amounts reported in the column headed 'Gross claims outstanding brought forward / Reported' on each of **Forms 27, 31, 32** and **34** in the *return* for the first *financial year* ended on or after 31 December 2005 to the amounts reported in the column headed 'Gross claims outstanding carried forward / Reported' on each of **Forms 27, 31, 32** and **34** in the previous *return*;

(d) the amounts reported in the line titled 'Technical provisions / Brought forward / Undiscounted' (line 51) on **Form 28** in the *return* for the first *financial year* ended on or after 31 December 2005 to the amounts reported in the line titled 'Technical provisions / Carried forward / Undiscounted' (line 53) on **Form 28** in the previous *return*;

(e) the amounts in the column headed ' Total number of claims settled at non-zero cost at end of the 2004 financial year' on each **Table D** to the amounts reported in the column headed 'Number of claims / Closed at some cost during this or previous financial years' (column 1) on each **Form 31** and **32** in the previous *return*.

2005 Return Transitional Tables A, B, C and D

12.4 These Tables belong to rule 12.2.

[*The Tables have not been reproduced for technical reasons. Please refer to the FSA website.*]

Financial year ending on or after 31 December 2005

12.5 The amendments to IPRU(INS) made by the Interim Prudential Sourcebook for Insurers (Regulatory Reporting) Instrument 2005 first apply to a *firm* with respect to its *financial year* ending on or after 31 December 2005.

Pure reinsurance groups

12.5A A *pure reinsurer* whose *ultimate EEA insurance parent undertaking* is the *parent undertaking* of a *group* comprised solely of *reinsurance undertakings* need not comply with rule 9.40 (Group capital adequacy) before 10 December 2007.

Guidance

12.6

(1) Rule 12.2 requires *insurers* to prepare historical development data in triangular format for each 'required category of business' for which a **Form 26** to **29, 31, 32** or **34** is required in the *return* for the first *financial year* ended on or after 31 December 2005. The purpose of the rule is to enable users of the *return* to carry out independent analysis of the development of paid and incurred claims and claim numbers in the new categories. When preparing data required by this rule an *insurer* should consider the need of the user and provide the data as accurately as reasonably possible.

its claim development data is such that it would be highly burdensome to extract the data specified in Tables A to D in respect of business that falls into *category numbers* 590 or 690, it need not prepare the Tables for these *category numbers*. An *insurer* need not prepare Tables A to D for *category numbers* 400 and 700 (the *miscellaneous categories*).

(5) Under rule 12.2(7), an *insurer* that is required to prepare any of Tables A to D for a *required category* may omit an entry for a Table if it does not have the data needed to complete the entry and does not use that data for setting provisions for claim liabilities for business in that *required category*. An *insurer* should not omit data required to be reported on the Tables if it uses that data for its internal claim reserving. For example if an *insurer* is required to prepare Table A for *category number* 570 carried on in GBP and it does not have records of gross claims paid in development years 0 to 5 in respect of year of origin 1986 and it does not use incremental gross claims paid data to set claims provisions in respect of that business and year of origin 1986, it may omit the incremental gross claims paid in development years 0 to 5 in respect of year of origin 1986 in Table A for that *required category*.

(6) If, for example, an *insurer* has had a 30 September *financial year* end and in, say, 2002 it decided to change to a 31 March *financial year* end, the years of origin it is required to report on a Table under 12.2(4)(a) to (c) could be any of the following unless 12.2(4)(e) requires otherwise:

Actual *financial year* end	**Year of origin shown on Table**	**Actual *financial year* end**	**Year of origin shown on Table**	**Actual *financial year* end**	**Year of origin shown on Table**
	A		B		C
. . .	. . .	. . .	. . .		
30/09/2000	09-2000	30/09/2000	09-2000	. . .	. . .
30/09/2001	09-2001	30/09/2001	09-2001	30/09/2000	09-2000
31/03/2002	03-2002	30/09/2002	09-2002	30/09/2001	09-2001
31/03/2003	03-2003	31/03/2003	03-2003	31/03/2003	03-2003
31/03/2004	03-2004	31/03/2004	03-2004	31/03/2004	03-2004
31/03/2005	03-2005	31/03/2005	03-2005	30/03/2005	03-2005
31/03/2006	03-2006	31/03/2006	03-2006	31/03/2006	03-2006

Under 12.2(4)(e) if, for example the business reported on the Table is reported on a **Form 31** and claims reported on that **Form 31** relating to accident years 2002 and 2003 are claims that occurred in the periods 1 October 2001 to 31 March 2002 and 1 April 2002 to 31 March 2003 respectively, the *insurer* would be required to report the years of origin under option A. If option C applies, a calendar year (in this case 2002) would be missing from the sequence of years of origin. If the example instead had the *financial year* end changing from 31 March to 30 September in 2002, then a calendar year (in this case 2002) could appear twice in the sequence of years of origin. Thus under 12.2(4)(a) to (c) a calendar year may appear more than once or not at all in the sequence of years of origin in column 1 of a Table.

(7) If an *insurer* is unable to submit the information required in 12.2(2) to *FSA* in a computer spreadsheet file that can be accessed by Microsoft Excel, it should request guidance from *FSA* as to the format in which to submit the information. The computer spreadsheet file that an *insurer* is required to send to the *FSA*, under 12.2(2)(d), should be the computer

Annex 11.3 Part I but with the words "or against risks of loss to the persons insured attributable to interruptions of business carried on by them" omitted.

(3) If an *insurer* uses a modified definition of 343 (Energy) under (2), it must use a definition of 262 (Consequential loss) that is as stated in IPRU(INS) Annex 11.3 Part I but with the words "or 343 (energy)" omitted.

VOLUME TWO
APPENDICES TO THE RULES

NOTES

Volume Two is not reproduced in this work, but the titles of the Appendices contained in it are listed below. The full text of Volume Two can be found at www.fsa.gov.uk.

Appendix 2.1—[deleted]

Appendix 2.2—[deleted]

Appendix 2.3—[deleted]

Appendix 3.1—[deleted]

Appendix 3.2—[deleted]

Appendix 4.1—[deleted]

Appendix 4.2—[deleted]

Appendix 5.1—[deleted]

Appendix 6.1—[deleted]

Appendix 6.2—[deleted]

Appendix 9.1—Balance sheet and profit and loss account (Forms 1 to 3 and 10 to 19) (rules 9.12 and 9.13)

Appendix 9.2—General insurance business: revenue account and additional information (Forms 20 to 39) (rules 9.14 to 9.22)

Appendix 9.3—Long-term insurance business: revenue account and additional information (Forms 40 to 45) (rules 9.14 and 9.23)

Appendix 9.4—Abstract of valuation report (Forms 46 to 61) (rule 9.31)

Appendix 9.4A—Abstract of valuation report for realistic valuation (rule 9.31(b))

Appendix 9.5—General insurance business: additional information on business ceded (rule 9.32)

Appendix 9.6—Certificates by directors and report of auditors (rules 9.34 and 9.35)

Appendix 9.7—Insurance statistics: other EEA states (Forms 91 to 94) (rule 9.37)

Appendix 9.8—Marine mutuals: items to be disregarded, directors' certificates and auditors reports (rule 9.36A)

Appendix 9.9—Group Capital Adequacy (rule 9.40 to rule 9.42 and guidance 9.43)

Appendix 9.10—Enhanced Capital Requirement (Form ECR1) (rule 9.44 and guidance 9.45)

Appendix 9.11—Reporting Forms

Appendix 9.12—Certificate by the Council (rule IPRU(INS) 9.58 (1)(a))

Appendix 9.13—Statement by the Lloyd's actuary (rule IPRU(INS) 9.58 (1)(b))

Appendix 9.14—Certificate by syndicate actuary (rule IPRU(INS) 9.58 (1)

Appendix 9.15—Auditors' report (rule IPRU(INS) 9.58 (3))

Appendix 9.16—Accounting classes (rule IPRU(INS) 9.49 (1)(b))

Appendix 9.17—(rule IPRU(INS) 9.60 (3))

Appendix 9.18—(rule IPRU(INS) 9.60 (7))

VOLUME THREE
GUIDANCE

NOTES

The guidance and other material contained in Volume Three has been deleted, but the original titles are listed below.

GUIDANCE—FSA GUIDANCE NOTES

Guidance Note P.1—[deleted]

Guidance Note P.2—[deleted]

Guidance Note P.3—[deleted]

Guidance Note 2.1—[deleted]

Guidance Note 2.2—[deleted]

Guidance Note 2.3—[deleted]

Guidance Note 4.1—[deleted]

Guidance Note 4.2—[deleted]

Guidance Note 4.3—[deleted]

Guidance Note 4.4—[deleted]

Guidance Note 5.1—[deleted]

Guidance Note 9.1—[deleted]

Guidance Note 9.2—[deleted]

Guidance Note 10.1—[deleted]

GUIDANCE—FSA 'DEAR DIRECTOR' LETTERS

DD1—[deleted]

OTHER MATERIAL—'DEAR APPOINTED ACTUARY' LETTERS

DAA8—[deleted]

DAA9—[deleted]

DAA11—[deleted]

DAA13—[deleted]

DAA14—[deleted]

DAA15—[deleted]

CONDUCT OF BUSINESS SOURCEBOOK (COBS)

NOTES

Up to date as at 22 February 2010. For later amendments please see www.fsa.gov.uk.

CONTENTS

COBS 7—Insurance mediation . . . . [2110A]
COBS 20—With-profits . . . . [2110B]
COBS 21—Permitted Links . . . . [2110C]

CHAPTER 7
INSURANCE MEDIATION

7.1 Application

[2110A]

7.1.1 **[R]** This chapter applies to a *firm* carrying on *insurance mediation* in relation to a *life policy*, but only if the *State of the commitment* is an *EEA State*.

[**Note:** articles 1 and 12(4) and (5) of the *Insurance Mediation Directive*]

7.2 Information to be provided by the insurance intermediary

7.2.1 **[R]**

(1) Prior to the conclusion of any initial *life policy* and, if necessary, on amendment or renewal, a *firm* must provide a *client* with at least the following information:
   (a) its name and address;
   (b) the fact that it is registered on the *FSA register* and its *FSA register* number (or, if it is not on the *FSA register*, the register in which it has been included and the means for verifying that it has been registered);
   (c) whether it has a direct or indirect holding representing more than 10% of the voting rights or capital in a given *insurance undertaking* (that is not a *pure reinsurer*);
   (d) whether a given *insurance undertaking* (other than a *pure reinsurer*) or its *parent undertaking* has a direct or indirect holding representing more than 10% of the voting rights or capital in the *firm*; and
   (e) the procedures which allow a *client* and other interested parties to register complaints about the *firm* with the *firm* and the *Financial Ombudsman Service* or, if the *Financial Ombudsman Service* does not apply, information about the out-of-court complaint and redress procedures available for the settlement of disputes between the *firm* and its *clients*.

(2) In addition, a *firm* must inform a *client*, concerning the *life policy* that is provided, whether:
   (a) it gives advice on the basis of a fair analysis of the market; or
   (b) it is contractually obliged to conduct its *insurance mediation* business exclusively with one or more *insurance undertakings* and, if that is the case, that the *client* can request the names of those *insurance undertakings*; or
   (c) it is not contractually obliged to conduct its *insurance mediation* business exclusively with one or more *insurance undertakings* and does not give advice on the basis of a fair analysis of the market and, if that is the case, that the client can request the names of the *insurance undertakings* with which the *firm* may and does conduct business.

(3) If a *client* asks a *firm* to provide the names of the *insurance undertakings* with which the *firm* conducts, or may conduct, business (COBS 7.2.1R(2)), the *firm* must provide it.

[**Note**: article 12(1) of the *Insurance Mediation Directive*]

Interface with the services and costs disclosure document

7.2.2 **[G]** A *firm* will satisfy elements of the requirement immediately above if it provides a *services and costs disclosure document* or a *combined initial disclosure document* to a *client* (see COBS 6.3).

7.2.2A **[R]** [deleted]

7.2.2B **[G]** A *firm* may provide a *services and costs disclosure document* or a *combined disclosure document* to a *client* who buys a non-advised *life policy*.

Fair analysis for advised sales

7.2.3 **[R]** When a *firm* informs a *client* that it gives advice on the basis of a fair analysis of the market, it must give that advice on the basis of an analysis of a sufficiently large number of *life policies* available on the market to enable the *firm* to make a recommendation, in accordance with professional criteria, regarding which *life policy* would be adequate to meet the *client*'s needs.

[**Note:** article 12(2) of the *Insurance Mediation Directive*]

Specifying demands and needs

7.2.4 **[R]**
(1) Prior to the conclusion of any specific *life policy*, a *firm* must at least specify, in particular on the basis of the information provided by the *client*, the demands and needs of that *client*. Those demands and needs must be modulated according to the complexity of the relevant *policy*.
(2) This rule does not apply when a *firm* makes a personal recommendation in relation to a *life policy*.

[**Note:** article 12(3) of the *Insurance Mediation Directive*]

7.2.5 **[G]** *Firms* are reminded that they are obliged to take reasonable steps to ensure that a *personal recommendation* is suitable for the *client* and that, whenever a *personal recommendation* relates to a *life policy*, a *suitability report* is required (COBS *9*).

Means of communication to clients

7.2.6 **[R]** All information to be provided to a *client* in accordance with the *rules* in this chapter must be communicated:
(1) in a *durable medium* available and accessible to the *client*;
(2) in a clear and accurate manner, comprehensible to the *client*; and
(3) in an official language of the *State of the commitment* or in any other language agreed by the parties.

[**Note:** article 13(1) of the *Insurance Mediation Directive*]

Additional requirement: telephone selling

7.2.7 **[R]** In the case of telephone selling, the prior information given to a *client* must be in accordance with the distance marketing disclosure *rules* (COBS *5.1*). Moreover, information must be provided to the *client* in accordance with the means of communication to clients *rule* (COBS 7.2.6R) immediately after the conclusion of the *life policy*.

[**Note:** article 13(3) of the *Insurance Mediation Directive*]

Exceptions: client request or immediate cover

7.2.8 **[R]** The information referred to in the means of communication to clients *rule* (COBS 7.2.6R) may be provided orally where the *client* requests it, or where immediate cover is necessary. In those cases, the information must be provided to the *client* in accordance with that *rule* immediately after the conclusion of the *life policy*.

[**Note:** article 13(2) of the *Insurance Mediation Directive*]

CHAPTER 20
WITH-PROFITS

20.1 Application

[2110B]
20.1.1 **[R]** This chapter applies to a *firm* carrying on *with-profits business*, except to the extent modified in the following *rules*.

20.1.2 **[R]**
(1) The section on the process for *reattribution* (COBS 20.2.42R to COBS 20.2.52G):
  (a) applies to a *firm* that is proposing to make a *reattribution* of its *inherited estate*;
  (b) but not if, and to the extent that, it would require the *firm* to breach, or would prevent the *firm* from complying with, an order made by a court of competent jurisdiction.
(2) If a *firm* proposes to seek an order from a court of competent jurisdiction that would allow or require it to act in a way that is contrary to the *rules* on *reattribution* (COBS 20.2.42R to COBS 20.2.52G) (through, or because of, the exception in (1)(b)), the *firm* must:
  (a) tell the *FSA* that that is what it proposes to do;
  (b) seek the order at the earliest opportunity; and
  (c) if it wishes to take a step that would be contrary to those *rules* in anticipation of such an order, secure a *waiver* before it does so.

20.1.3 **[R]** For an *EEA insurer*:
– the *rules* and *guidance* on treating *with-profits policyholders* fairly (COBS 20.2.1G to COBS 20.2.41G and COBS 20.2.53R to COBS 20.2.60G) apply only in so far as responsibility for the matter in question has not been reserved to the *firm's Home State regulator* by an *EU* instrument;

– COBS 20.3 (Principles and Practices of Financial Management) does not apply;
– the *rule* on providing information to *with-profits policyholders* who are *habitually resident* in the United Kingdom (COBS 20.4.4R) and the *rule* on production and provision of a *CFPPFM* (COBS 20.4.5R) apply, but the rest of COBS 20.4 (Communications with *with-profits policyholders*) does not; and
– the *rule* on production and provision of a *CFPPFM* (COBS 20.4.5R) applies as if a reference to a *firm* was a reference to an *EEA insurer* in relation to any of its *with-profits policyholders* who are *habitually resident* in the *United Kingdom*.

20.1.4 **[R]** The following do not apply to a *non-directive friendly society*:
(1) COBS 20.3 (Principles and Practices of Financial Management); and
(2) COBS 20.4 (Communications with with-profits policyholders).

20.1.5 **[R]** This chapter does not apply to *with-profits business* that consists of effecting or carrying out *Holloway sickness policies*.

20.2 Treating with-profits policyholders fairly

Introduction

20.2.1 **[G]** *With-profits business*, by virtue of its nature and the extent of discretion applied by *firms* in its operation, involves numerous potential conflicts of interest that might give rise to the unfair treatment of *policyholders*. The *rules* in this section address specific situations where the risk may be particularly acute. However, a *firm* should give careful consideration to any aspect of its operating practice that has a bearing on the interests of its *with-profits policyholders* to ensure that it does not lead to an undisclosed, or unfair, benefit to *shareholders*.

20.2.2 **[R]** Neither *Principle* 6 (Customers' interests) nor the *rules* on treating *with-profits policyholders* fairly (COBS 20.2) relieve a *firm* of its obligation to deliver each *policyholder's* contractual entitlement.

Amounts payable under with-profits policies

20.2.3 **[R]** A *firm* must have good reason to believe that its pay-outs on individual *with-profits policies* are fair.

Amounts payable under with-profits policies: Maturity payments

20.2.4 **[G]** In this section, maturity payments include payments made when a *with-profits policy* provides for a minimum guaranteed amount to be paid.

20.2.5 **[R]**
(1) Unless a *firm* cannot reasonably compare a maturity payment with a calculated asset share, it must:
 (a) set a target range for the maturity payments that it will make on:
  (i) all of its *with-profits policies*; or
  (ii) each group of its *with-profits policies*;
 (b) ensure that each target range:
  (i) is expressed as a percentage of unsmoothed asset share; and
  (ii) includes 100% of unsmoothed asset share; and
 (c) manage its *with-profits business*, and the business of each *with-profit fund*, with the aim of making on each *with-profit policy* a maturity payment that falls within the relevant target range.
(2) Unsmoothed asset share means:
 (a) the unsmoothed asset share of the relevant *with-profits policy*; or
 (b) an estimate of the unsmoothed asset share of the relevant *with-profits policy* derived from the unsmoothed asset share of one or more specimen *with-profits policies*, which a *firm* has selected to represent a group, or all, of the *with-profits policies* effected in the same *with-profits fund*.
(3) A *firm* must calculate unsmoothed asset share by:
 (a) applying the methods in INSPRU 1.3.119R to INSPRU 1.3.123R;
 (b) including any amounts that have been added to the *policy* as the result of a distribution from an *inherited estate*; and
 (c) subject to (d), and where the terms of the *policy* so provide, adding or subtracting an amount that reflects the experience of the *insurance business* in the relevant *with-profits fund*; but
 (d) if a *with-profits fund* has suffered adverse experience, which results from a *firm's* failure to comply with the *rules* and *guidance* on treating *with-profits policyholders* fairly (COBS 20.2.1G to COBS 20.2.41G and COBS 20.2.53R to COBS 20.2.60G), that adverse experience may only be taken into account if, and to the extent that, in the reasonable opinion of the *firm's governing body*, the amount referred to in (c) cannot be met from:

(i) the *firm's inherited estate* (if any); or
(ii) any assets attributable to shareholders, whether or not they are held in the relevant *with-profits fund*.

20.2.6 **[R]** Notwithstanding that a *firm* must aim to make maturity payments that fall within the relevant target range, a *firm* may make a maturity payment that falls outside the target range if it has a good reason to believe that at least 90% of maturity payments on *with-profits policies* in that group have fallen, or will fall, within the relevant target range.

20.2.7 **[G]** If it is not fair or reasonable to calculate or assess a maturity payment using the *prescribed asset share methodology*, a *firm* may use another methodology to set bonus rates, if that methodology properly reflects its representations to *with-profits policyholders* and it applies that methodology consistently.

20.2.8 **[R]** A *firm* may make deductions from asset share to meet the cost of guarantees, or the cost of capital, only under a plan approved by its *governing body* and described in its *PPFM*. A *firm* must ensure that any deductions are proportionate to the costs they are intended to offset.

20.2.9 **[R]** If a *firm* has approved a plan to make deductions from asset share, it must ensure that its planned deductions do not change unless justified by changes in the business or economic environment, or changes in the nature of the *firm's* liabilities as a result of *policyholders* exercising options in their *policies*.

20.2.10 **[R]** If a *firm* calculates maturity payments using the *prescribed asset share methodology*, it must manage its *with-profits business*, and each *with-profits fund*, with the longer term aim that it will make aggregate maturity payments of 100% of unsmoothed asset share.

Amounts payable under with-profits policies: Surrender payments

20.2.11 **[G]** A *firm* may use its own methodology to calculate surrender payments, but it should have good reason to believe that its methodology produces a result which, in aggregate across all similar policies, is not less than the result of the *prescribed asset share methodology*. A *firm* might, for example, test the surrender payments on a suitable range of specimen *with-profits policies*.

20.2.12 **[R]** If a *firm* calculates surrender payments using the *prescribed asset share methodology*, it must first calculate what the surrender payment would be if it was a maturity payment calculated by that methodology.

20.2.13 **[R]** A *firm* may then make a deduction from unsmoothed asset share if necessary, in the reasonable opinion of the *firm's governing body*, to protect the interests of the *firm's* remaining *with-profits policyholders*.

20.2.14 **[G]** Amounts that might be deducted include:
(1) the *firm's* unrecovered costs, including any financing costs incurred in effecting or carrying out the surrendered *with-profits policy* to the date of surrender, including the costs that might have been recovered if the *policy* had remained in force;
(2) costs that would fall on the *with-profits fund*, if the surrender value is calculated by reference to an assumed *market value* of assets which exceeds the true *market value* of those assets;
(3) the *firm's* costs incurred in administering the surrender; and
(4) a fair contribution towards the cost of any contractual benefits due on the whole, or an appropriate part, of the continuing policies in the *with-profits fund* which would otherwise result in higher costs falling on the continuing *with-profits policies*.

20.2.15 **[G]** The provisions dealing with the calculation of surrender payments (COBS 20.2.11G to COBS 20.2.12R) do not prevent a *firm* from setting a target range for surrender payments where the top-end of the range is lower than the top-end of the relevant range for maturity payments.

20.2.16 **[R]** A *firm* must not make a market value reduction to the face value of the units of an accumulating *with-profits policy* unless:
(1) the *market value* of the *with-profits assets* in the relevant *with-profits fund* is, or is expected to be, significantly less than the assumed value of the assets on which the face value of the units of the *policy* has been based; or
(2) there has been, or there is expected to be, a high volume of surrenders, relative to the liquidity of the relevant *with-profits fund*; and

the market value reduction is no greater than is necessary to reflect the impact of (1) or (2) on the relevant surrender payment.

Conditions relevant to distributions

20.2.17 **[R]** A *firm* must:
(1) not make a distribution from a *with-profits fund*, unless the whole of the cost of that distribution can be met without eliminating the *regulatory surplus* in that *with-profits fund*;
(2) ensure that the amount distributed to *policyholders* from a *with-profits fund* is not less than the required percentage of the total amount distributed; and

(3) if it adjusts the amounts distributed to *policyholders*, apply a proportionate adjustment to amounts distributed to shareholders, so that the distribution to *policyholders* will not be less than the required percentage.

20.2.18 **[R]** A *realistic basis life firm* must not make a distribution from a *with-profits fund* to any person who is not a *with-profits policyholder*, unless the whole of the cost of that distribution (including the cost of any obligations that will or may arise from the decision to make a distribution) can be met from the excess of the *realistic value of assets* over the *realistic value of liabilities* in that *with-profits fund*.

20.2.19 **[R]** A distribution to a *person* who is not a *with-profits policyholder* includes a transfer of assets out of a *with-profits fund* that is not made to satisfy a liability of that fund.

20.2.20 **[R]** If, on a distribution, a *firm* incurs a tax liability on a transfer to shareholders, it must not attribute that tax liability to a *with-profits fund*, unless:
(1) the *firm* can show that attributing the tax liability to that *with-profits fund* is consistent with its established practice;
(2) that established practice is explained in the *firm's PPFM*; and
(3) that liability is not charged to asset shares.

Requirement relating to distribution of an excess surplus

20.2.21 **[R]** At least once a year (or, in the case of a *non-directive friendly society*, at least once in every three years), a *firm's governing body* must determine whether the *firm's with-profits fund*, or any of the *firm's with-profits funds*, has an excess surplus.

20.2.22 **[E]**
(1) If a *with-profits fund* has an *excess surplus*, and to retain that surplus would be a breach of *Principle* 6 (Customers' interests), the *firm* should:
    (a) make a distribution from that *with-profits fund*; or
    (b) carry out a *reattribution*.
(2) Compliance with (1) may be relied on as tending to establish compliance with *Principle* 6 (Customers' interests).
(3) Contravention of (1) may be relied on as tending to establish a contravention of *Principle* 6 (Customers' interests).

Charges to a with-profits fund

20.2.23 **[R]** A *firm* must only charge costs to a *with-profits fund* which have been, or will be, incurred in operating the *with-profits fund*. This may include a fair proportion of overheads.

20.2.24 **[R]** Subject to COBS 20.2.25R, COBS 20.2.25AR and COBS 20.2.25BR, a *firm* must not pay compensation or redress from a *with-profits fund*.

20.2.25 **[R]** A proprietary *firm* may pay compensation or redress due to a *policyholder*, or *former policyholder*, from assets attributable to shareholders, whether or not they are held within a *long-term insurance fund*.

20.2.25A **[R]** A *mutual* may pay compensation or redress due to a *policyholder*, or *former policyholder*, from a *with-profits fund*, but may only pay from assets that would otherwise be attributable to asset shares if, in the reasonable opinion of the *firm's governing body*, the compensation or redress cannot be paid from any other assets in the *with-profits fund*.

20.2.25B **[R]** A payment or transfer of liabilities made to correct an error and which has the effect of restoring a *policyholder*, or *former policyholder*, and the *with-profits fund* to the position they would have been in if the error had not occurred (a "rectification payment"), is not a payment of compensation or redress for the purposes of COBS 20.2.24R.

20.2.25C **[G]** Rectification payments may include, for example, a payment to a *policyholder* or *former policyholder* to correct an erroneous underpayment of policy proceeds, or a reimbursement of premiums overpaid. The effect of COBS 20.2.25BR is that a *firm* may make rectification payments using assets in a *with-profits fund*.

20.2.25D **[G]** COBS TP 2.14R has the effect that payments of compensation and redress arising out of events which took place before 31 July 2009 are subject to COBS 20.2.23R to COBS 20.2.25R as in force at 30 July 2009.

20.2.26 **[R]** A proprietary *firm* must not charge to a *with-profits fund* any amounts paid or payable to a skilled person in connection with a report under section 166 of the *Act* (Reports by skilled persons) if the report indicates that the *firm* has, or may have, materially failed to satisfy its obligations under the *regulatory system*.

Tax charge to a with-profits fund

20.2.27 **[R]** A *firm* must not charge a contribution to corporation tax to a *with-profits fund*, if that contribution exceeds the notional corporation tax liability that would be charged to that *with-profits fund* if it were assessed to tax as a separate *body corporate*.

New business

20.2.28 **[R]** If a *firm* proposes to effect new *contracts of insurance* in an existing *with-profits fund*, it must only do so on terms that are, in the reasonable opinion of the *firm's governing body*, unlikely to have a material adverse effect on the interests of its existing *with-profits policyholders*.

20.2.29 **[G]** In some circumstances, it may be difficult or impossible for a *firm* to mitigate the risk of a material adverse effect on its existing, or new, *with-profits policyholders*, unless it establishes a new bonus series or *with-profits fund*. Circumstances that might cause a *firm* to establish a new bonus series or *with-profits fund* include:
(1) where the *firm* has a high level of guarantees or options in its existing *with-profits policies*, which might place an excessive burden on new *with-profits policies*, or vice versa; and
(2) where the potential risks are likely to be so great that a single *with-profits fund* cannot provide adequately for the interests of new and existing *policyholders*, even after allowing for any beneficial effects of diversification. Such potential risks are likely to arise from significant differences in the terms and conditions of the new and existing *with-profits policies*, including the basis on which charges are levied and reviewed.

20.2.30 **[G]** When a *firm* prices the new *insurance business* that it proposes to effect in an existing *with-profits fund*, it should estimate the volume of new *insurance business* that it is likely to effect and then build in adequate margins that will allow it to recover any acquisition costs to be charged to the *with-profits fund*.

20.2.31 **[G]** When a *firm* sets a target volume for new *insurance business* in an existing *with-profits fund*, it should pay particular attention to the risk of disadvantage to existing *with-profits policyholders*. Those *policyholders* might be disadvantaged, for example, by the need to retain additional capital to support a rapid growth in new business, when that capital might have been distributed in the ordinary course of the *firm's* existing business.

Relationship of a with-profits fund with the firm and any connected persons

20.2.32 **[R]** A *firm* carrying on *with-profits business* must not:
(1) make a loan to a *connected person* using assets in a *with-profits fund*; or
(2) give a guarantee to, or for the benefit of, a *connected person*, where the guarantee will be backed using assets in a *with-profits fund*;

unless that loan or guarantee:
(3) will be on commercial terms;
(4) will, in the reasonable opinion of the *firm's* senior management, be beneficial to the *with-profits policyholders* in the relevant *with-profits fund*; and
(5) will not, in the reasonable opinion of the *firm's* senior management, expose those *policyholders* to undue *credit* or *group* risk.

Contingent loans and other forms of support for the with-profits fund

20.2.33 **[G]**
(1) If a *firm*, or a *connected person*, provides support to a *with-profits fund* (for example, by a contingent loan), no reliance should be placed on that support when the *firm* assesses the *with-profits fund's* financial position unless there are clear and unambiguous criteria governing any repayment obligations to the support provider.
(2) The degree of reliance placed on that support should depend on the subordination of the support to the fair treatment of *with-profits policyholders* and clarification of what fair treatment means in various circumstances. For a *realistic basis life firm* this would normally be evidenced by the liability for such support being capable, under stress, of a progressively lower valuation in the *future policy-related liabilities*.

20.2.34 **[G]** Where assets from outside a *with-profits fund* are made available to support that fund (and there is no ambiguity in the criteria governing any repayment obligations to the support provider), a *firm* should manage the fund disregarding the liability to repay those assets, at least in so far as that is necessary for its *policyholders* to be treated fairly.

Other guidance on the conduct of with-profit business

20.2.35 **[G]** When a *firm* determines its investment strategy, and the acceptable level of risk within that strategy, it should take into account:
(1) the extent of the guarantee in its *with-profits policies*;
(2) any representation that it has made to its *with-profits policyholders*;
(3) its established practice; and
(4) the amount of capital support available.

20.2.36 **[G]** If a proprietary *firm* is considering using *with-profits assets* to finance the purchase of another business, directly or by or through a *connected person*, or if a *firm* is considering whether it should retain such an investment, it should consider whether the purchase or retention would be, or will remain, fair to its *with-profits policyholders*. When a *firm* makes that assessment it should consider whether it would be more appropriate for the investment to be made using assets other than those in a *with-profits fund*.

20.2.37 **[G]** If a *firm* carries out *non-profit insurance business* in a *with-profits fund*, it should review the profitability of the *non-profit insurance business* regularly.

20.2.38 **[G]** If a *firm* has reinsured its *with-profits insurance business* into another *insurance undertaking*, it should take reasonable steps to discharge its responsibilities to its *with-profits policyholders*, in respect of the reinsured business. Those steps should include maintaining adequate controls.

Major changes in with-profits funds

20.2.39 **[R]** A *firm* must not enter into a material transaction relating to a *with-profits fund* unless, in the reasonable opinion of the *firm's governing body*, the transaction is unlikely to have a material adverse effect on the interests of that fund's existing *with-profits policyholders*.

20.2.40 **[R]** A material transaction includes a series of related non-material transactions which, if taken together, are material.

20.2.41 **[G]** Examples of material transactions include:
(1) a significant bulk outwards *reinsurance* contract;
(2) inwards *reinsurance* of *with-profits business* from another *insurance undertaking*;
(3) a financial engineering transaction that would materially change the profile of any surplus expected to emerge on the *with-profits fund's* existing *insurance business*; and
(4) a significant restructuring of the *with-profits fund*, especially if it involves the creation of new *sub-funds*.

Process for reattribution of inherited estates: Policyholder advocate: appointment and role

20.2.42 **[R]** A *firm* that is seeking to make a *reattribution* of its *inherited estate* must:
(1) identify at the earliest appropriate point a policyholder advocate, who is free from any conflicts of interest that may be, or may appear to be, detrimental to the interests of *policyholders*, to negotiate with the *firm* on behalf of relevant *with-profits policyholders*;
(2) seek the approval of the *FSA* for the appointment of the *policyholder advocate* as soon as he is identified, or appoint a *policyholder advocate* nominated by the *FSA* if its approval is not granted; and
(3) involve the policyholder advocate designate at the earliest possible opportunity to enable him to participate effectively in the negotiations about the proposals for the *reattribution*.

20.2.43 **[G]** The *firm* should include an independent element in the *policyholder advocate* selection process, which may include consulting representative groups of *policyholders* or using the services of a recruitment consultant. When considering an application for approval of a nominee to perform the *policyholder advocate* role, the *FSA* will have regard to the extent to which the *firm* has involved others in the selection process.

20.2.44 **[G]** The precise role of the *policyholder advocate* in any particular case will depend on the nature of the *firm* and the *reattribution* proposed. A *firm* will need to discuss with the *FSA* the precise role of the *policyholder advocate* in a particular case (COBS 20.2.45R). However, the role of the *policyholder advocate* should include:
(1) negotiating with the *firm*, on behalf of the relevant *with-profits policyholders*, the benefits to be offered to them in exchange for the rights or interests they will be asked to give up;
(2) commenting to *with-profits policyholders*, on:
  (a) the methodology used for the allocation of benefits amongst the relevant (or groups of) *with-profits policyholders* and the form of those benefits;
  (b) the criteria used for determining the eligibility of the various *with-profits policyholders*;
  (c) the terms and conditions of the proposals (to the extent that they materially affect the benefits to be offered, or the bonuses that may be added to *with-profits policies*); and
  (d) the views expressed by the *independent expert* or the *reattribution expert* (as the case may be), and the *firm's with-profits actuary* on the allocation of any benefits amongst the relevant *with-profits policyholders*; and
(3) telling *with-profits policyholders*, or each group of *with-profits policyholders*, with reasons, whether the *firm's* proposals are in their interests.

Process for reattribution of inherited estates: Policyholder advocate: terms of appointment

20.2.45 **[R]** A *firm* must:
(1) notify the *FSA* of the terms on which it proposes to appoint a *policyholder advocate* (whether or not the candidate was nominated by the *FSA*); and

(2) ensure that the terms of appointment for the *policyholder advocate*:
   (a) stress the independent nature of the *policyholder advocate's* appointment and function, and are consistent with it;
   (b) define the relationship of the *policyholder advocate* to the *firm* and its *policyholders*;
   (c) set out arrangements for communications between the *policyholder advocate* and *policyholders*;
   (d) make provision for the resolution of any disputes between the *firm* and the *policyholder advocate*;
   (e) specify when and how the *policyholder advocate's* appointment may be terminated; and
   (f) allow the *policyholder advocate* to communicate freely and in confidence with the *FSA*.

20.2.46 **[G]** A *firm* may include, within the *policyholder advocate's* terms of appointment, arrangements for the *policyholder advocate* to be indemnified in respect of certain claims that may be made against him in connection with the performance of his functions. If such indemnity is included, it should not include protection against any liability arising from acts of bad faith.

Process for reattribution of inherited estates: Reattribution expert

20.2.47 **[R]** Where a *firm* is not otherwise required to appoint an *independent expert*, it must:
(1) appoint a reattribution expert to undertake an objective assessment of its *reattribution* proposals, who must be:
   (a) nominated or approved by the *FSA* before he is appointed; and
   (b) free from any conflicts of interest that may, or may appear to, undermine his independence or the quality of his report;
(2) ensure that the *reattribution expert's* terms of appointment allow him to communicate freely and in confidence with the *FSA*; and
(3) require the *reattribution expert* to prepare a report which must be available to the *FSA*, the *policyholder advocate* and the court (if it is relevant to any court proceedings).

20.2.48 **[G]** A *reattribution expert's* report should comply with the applicable rules on expert evidence. The scope and content of the report should be substantially similar to that of the report required of an *independent expert* under SUP 18.2 (Insurance business transfers), as if (where appropriate) a reference to:
(1) the '*scheme report*' was a reference to the '*reattribution expert's* report';
(2) the '*independent expert*' was a reference to the '*reattribution expert*'; and
(3) the 'scheme' was a reference to the proposal for a '*reattribution*'.

Process for reattribution of inherited estates: Information to policyholders

20.2.49 **[R]** A *firm* must ensure that every *policyholder* that may be affected by the proposed *reattribution* is sent appropriate and timely information about:
(1) the *reattribution* process, including the role of the *policyholder advocate*, the *independent expert* or *reattribution expert*, as the case may be, and other individuals appointed to perform particular functions;
(2) the *reattribution* proposals and how they affect the relevant *policyholders*, including an explanation of any benefits they are likely to receive and the rights and interests that they are likely to be asked to give up;
(3) the *policyholder advocate's* views on the *reattribution* proposals and any benefits the relevant *policyholders* are likely to receive and the rights and interests that they are likely to be asked to give up; and
(4) the outcome of the negotiations between the *firm* and the *policyholder advocate* about the benefits that will be offered to relevant *with-profits policyholders*, in exchange for the rights and interests that they will be asked to give up.

20.2.50 **[R]** An adequate summary of the report by the *reattribution expert* must be made available to every *policyholder* that may be affected by the proposed *reattribution*.

Process for reattribution of inherited estates: Consent of policyholders

20.2.51 **[R]** A *firm* must give relevant *with-profits policyholders* the option to:
(1) individually accept or reject the final proposals for the *reattribution*; or
(2) (if the legal process to be followed allows the majority of *policyholders* to bind the minority) vote on whether the *firm* should go ahead with those proposals.

Process for reattribution of inherited estates: Costs

20.2.52 **[G]**
(1) *Reattribution* and *insurance business transfer* costs (excluding *policyholder advocate* costs) should be met from shareholder funds. A *firm* may present alternative arrangements if it can show good reasons for doing so.

(2) Shareholders should pay a reasonable proportion of the *policyholder advocate's* costs.
(3) If a *reattribution* proposal is not successful, the *FSA* would expect the costs of the *policyholder advocate* to be met by the *person* initiating the proposal. That will usually be the shareholders of the *firm*.

Ceasing to effect new contracts of insurance in a with-profits fund

20.2.53 **[R]** A *firm* must:
(1) inform the *FSA* and its *with-profits policyholders* within 28 days; and
(2) submit a run-off plan to the *FSA* as soon as reasonably practicable and, in any event, within three months;

of first ceasing to effect new *contracts of insurance* in a *with-profits fund*.

20.2.54 **[R]** A *firm* will be taken to have ceased to effect new contracts of insurance in a *with-profits fund*:
(1) when any decision by the *governing body* to cease to effect new *contracts of insurance* takes effect; or
(2) where no such decision is made, when the *firm* is no longer:
  (a) actively seeking to effect new *contracts of insurance* in that fund; or
  (b) effecting new *contracts of insurance* in that fund, except by increment.

20.2.55 **[R]** A *firm* must contact the *FSA* to discuss whether it has, or should be taken to have, ceased to effect new *contracts of insurance* if:
(1) it is no longer effecting a material volume of new *with-profits policies* in a particular *with-profits fund*, other than by *reinsurance*; or
(2) it cedes by way of *reinsurance* most of the new *with-profits policies* which it continues to effect.

20.2.56 **[R]** The run-off plan required by this section must:
(1) demonstrate how the *firm* will ensure a fair distribution of the closed *with-profits fund*, and its *inherited estate* (if any); and
(2) be approved by the *firm's governing body*.

20.2.57 **[G]** A *firm* should also include the information described in Appendix 2.15 (Run-off plans for closed *with-profits funds*) of the Supervision manual in its run-off plan.

20.2.58 **[G]** When a *firm* tells its *with-profits policyholders* that it has ceased to effect new *contracts of insurance* in a *with-profits fund*, it should also explain:
(1) why it has done so;
(2) what changes it has made, or proposes to make, to the fund's investment strategy (if any);
(3) how closure may affect *with-profits policyholders* (including any reasonably foreseeable effect on future bonus prospects);
(4) the options available to *with-profits policyholders* and an indication of the potential costs associated with the exercise of each of those options; and
(5) any other material factors that a *policyholder* may reasonably need to be aware of before deciding how to respond to this information.

20.2.59 **[G]** A *firm* may not be able to provide its *with-profits policyholders* with all of the information described above until it has prepared the run-off plan. In those circumstances, the *firm* should:
(1) tell its *with-profits policyholders* that that is the case;
(2) explain what is missing and give a time estimate for its supply; and
(3) provide the missing information as soon as possible, and within the time estimate given.

20.2.60 **[G]**
(1) If *non-profit insurance business* is written in a *with-profits fund*, a *firm* should take reasonable steps to ensure that the economic value of any future profits expected to emerge on the *non-profit insurance business* is available for distribution during the lifetime of the *with-profits business*.
(2) Where it is agreed by its *with-profits policyholders*, and subject to meeting the requirements for effecting new *contracts of insurance* in an existing *with-profits fund* (COBS 20.2.28R), a *mutual* may make alternative arrangements for continuing to carry on *non-profit insurance business*, and a *non-directive friendly society* may make alternative arrangements for continuing to carry on non-insurance related business.

20.3 Principles and Practices of Financial Management

Production of PPFM

20.3.1 **[R]**
(1) A *firm* must:

(a) establish and maintain the *PPFM* according to which its *with-profits business* is conducted (or, if appropriate, separate *PPFM* for each *with-profits fund*); and
(b) retain a record of each version of its *PPFM* for five years.

(2) A *firm's with-profits principles* must:
(a) be enduring statements of the standards it adopts in managing *with-profits funds*; and
(b) describe the business model it uses to meet its duties to *with-profits policyholders* and to respond to longer-term changes in the business and economic environment.

(3) A *firm's with-profits practices* must:
(a) describe how a *firm* manages its *with-profits funds* and how it responds to shorter-term changes in the business and economic environment; and
(b) be sufficiently detailed for a knowledgeable observer to understand the material risks and rewards from effecting or maintaining a *with-profits policy* with it.

(4) A *firm* must not change its *PPFM* unless, in the reasonable opinion of its *governing body*, that change is justified to:
(a) respond to changes in the business or economic environment; or
(b) protect the interests of *policyholders*; or
(c) change the *firm's with-profits practices* better to achieve its *with-profits principles*.

(5) A *firm* may change its *PPFM* if that change:
(a) is necessary to correct an error or omission; or
(b) would improve clarity or presentation without materially affecting the *PPFM's* substance; or
(c) is immaterial.

Governance arrangements for with-profits business

20.3.2 **[G]** In complying with the *rule* on systems and controls in relation to compliance, financial crime and money laundering (SYSC 3.2.6R or SYSC 6.1.1R), a *firm* should maintain governance arrangements designed to ensure that it complies with, maintains and records any applicable *PPFM*. These arrangements should:
(1) be appropriate to the scale and complexity of the *firm's with-profits business*;
(2) include the approval of the *firm's PPFM* by its *governing body*; and
(3) involve some independent judgment in assessing compliance with its *PPFM* and addressing conflicting rights and interests of *policyholders* and, if applicable, shareholders, which may include but is not confined to:
(a) establishing a *with-profits committee*;
(b) asking an independent person with appropriate skills and experience to report on these matters to the *governing body* or to any *with-profits committee*; or
(c) for small *firms*, asking one or more non-executive members of the *governing body* to report to the *governing body* on these matters.

20.3.3 **[G]** If a *person* or committee who provides the independent judgement wishes to make a statement or report to *with-profits policyholders*, in addition to any annual report made by a *firm* to those *policyholders*, a *firm* should facilitate this.

Scope and content of PPFM

20.3.4 **[R]** A *firm's PPFM* must cover the issues set out in the table in COBS 20.3.6R.

20.3.5 **[R]** A *firm's PPFM* must cover any matter that has, or it is reasonably foreseeable may have, a significant impact on the *firm's* management of *with-profits funds*, including but not limited to:
(1) any requirements or constraints that apply as a result of previous dealings, including previous business transfer schemes; and
(2) the nature and extent of any shareholder commitment to support the *with-profits fund*.

20.3.6 **[R]** Table: Issues to be covered in PPFM

Subject		Issues			
(1)	Amount payable under a *with-profits policy*	(a)	Methods used to guide determination of the amount that is appropriate to pay individual *with-profits policyholders*, including:		
			(i)	the aims of the methods and approximations used;	

Subject		**Issues**		
		(b)	(ii)	how the current methods, including any relevant historical assumptions used and any systems maintained to deliver results of particular methods, are documented; and
			(iii)	the procedures for changing the current method or any assumptions or parameters relevant to a particular method. Approach to setting bonus rates.
		(c)	Approach to smoothing maturity payments and surrender payments, including:	
			(i)	the smoothing policy applied to each type of *with-profits policy*;
			(ii)	the limits (if any) applied to the total cost of, or excess from, smoothing; and
			(iii)	any limits applied to any changes in the level of maturity payments between one period to another.
(2)	Investment strategy	Significant aspects of the *firm's* investment strategy for its *with-profits business* or, if different, any *with-profits fund*, including:		
		(a)	the degree of matching to be maintained between assets relevant to *with-profits business* and liabilities to *with-profits policyholders* and other creditors;	
		(b)	the *firm's* approach to assets of different credit or liquidity quality and different volatility of market values;	
		(c)	the presence among the assets relevant to *with-profits business* of any assets that would not normally be traded because of their importance to the *firm*, and the justification for holding such assets; and	
		(d)	the *firm's* controls on using new asset or liability instruments and the nature of any approval required before new instruments are used.	
(3)	Business risk	The exposure of the *with-profits business* to business risks (new and existing), including the *firm's*:		
		(a)	procedures for deciding if the *with-profits business* may undertake a particular business risk;	
		(b)	arrangements for reviewing and setting a limit on the scale of such risks; and	
		(c)	procedures for reflecting the profits or losses of such business risks in the amounts payable under *with-profits policies*.	
(4)	Charges and expenses	(a)	The way in which the *firm* applies charges and apportions expenses to its *with-profits business*, including, if material, any interaction with connected firms.	
		(b)	The cost apportionment principles that will determine which costs are, or may be, charged to a *with-profits fund* and which costs are, or may be, charged to the other parts of its business of its shareholders.	
(5)	Management of inherited estate	Management of any *inherited estate* and the uses to which the *firm* may put that *inherited estate*.		
(6)	Volumes of new business and arrangements on stopping taking new business	If a *firm's with-profits fund* is accepting new *with-profits* business, its practice for review of the limits on the quantity and type of new business and the actions that the *firm* would take if it ceased to take on new business of any significant amount.		
(7)	Equity between the with-profits fund and any shareholders	The way in which the interests of *with-profits policyholders* are, or may be, affected by the interests of any shareholders of the *firm*.		

20.3.7 **[G]** The table in COBS 20.3.8R sets out *guidance* on how various information relevant to some of the issues covered in a *firm's PPFM* (COBS 20.3.6R) might be split between *with-profits principles* and *with-profits practices.* This is an example of the matters a *firm* should address in its *with-profits principles* and *with-profits practices* and is not exhaustive. A *firm* should consider carefully the scope and content of its *PPFM* as appropriate.

20.3.8 **[G]** Table: Guidance on with-profits principles and practices

Reference to PPFM issues (COBS 20.3.6R)	**With-profits principles**		**With-profits practices**			
(1) Amount payable under a *with-profits policy*	General		General			
	(a)	Circumstances under which any historical assumptions or parameters, relevant to methods used to determine the amount payable, may be changed;	(e)	For each major class of *with-profits policy*, methods establishing the main assumptions or parameters that decide the output of methods that determine the amount payable;		
			(f)	Degree of approximation allowed when assumptions or parameters are applied across generations of *with-profits policyholders* or across different types or classes of *with-profits policies*;		
			(g)	Formality with which the methods, parameters or assumptions used are documented;		
			(h)	Target range, or target ranges, that have been set for maturity payments;		
			(i)	Factors likely to be regarded as relevant to address *policyholders'* interests or security when determining *excess surplus*; and		
			Investment return, expenses or charges and tax			
			(j)	How investment return, expenses or charges and tax are brought into account and how the impact of those items is determined on the amount payable. In particular:		
					(i)	any distinctions made in recognising the investment return from a subset of the total assets of a *with-profits fund*;
					(ii)	whether expenses are apportioned between all the policies in a *with-profits fund* or apportioned in some other way;
					(iii)	the relationship between the liability to tax attributed to a *with-profits fund* and the tax that the *firm* imputes to determine the amount payable;

Reference to PPFM issues (COBS 20.3.6R)	**With-profits principles**		**With-profits practices**		
				(iv)	impact on the amount payable of any attributed liability to tax of a *with-profits fund* as a result of the *firm* making a transfer to shareholders; and
				(v)	how any other items are brought into account.
	Bonus rates		Bonus rates		
	(b)	General aims in setting bonus rates and the constraints to which the *firm* may be subject in changing economic circumstances;	(k)	Current approach to setting bonus rates, including the weight given to recent economic experience. For final bonus rates, the description should include any distinctions made between *with-profits policies* that remain in force until contractual dates, or dates on which no market value reduction applies (for example, maturity or retirement dates) and policies that are surrendered or transferred at other dates;	
	(c)	How the range of *with-profits policies* or generations of *with-profits policies* over which the *firm* believes a single bonus rate would be appropriate is determined and the circumstances under which it believes a new bonus series would be necessary; and			
			(l)	Frequency at which bonus rates are re-set or expected to be re-set and the circumstances under which changes in the economic environment would cause the time between re-setting to change;	
			(m)	Maximum amount by which annual bonuses would alter if annual bonus rates were reset;	
			(n)	Approach to setting any interim bonus rates before the next declaration of annual bonus rates;	
			(o)	Relationship or interaction between final bonus rates and any market value reductions, if both can apply at the same time;	
			(p)	How final bonus rates influence the value of *with-profits policies* that have formulaic surrender or transfer bases (for example, older conventional policies rather than unitised policies); and	
	Smoothing		Smoothing		
	(d)	Statement as to whether smoothing is intended to be neutral over time.	(q)	Any differences in approach for:	
				(i)	the various types of *with-profits policy*;

Reference to PPFM issues (COBS 20.3.6R)	With-profits principles		With-profits practices	
				(ii) different categories of payout, such as between surrendered policies and maturing policies; and
				(iii) different generations of *with-profits policyholders*.
(2) Investment strategy	(a)	How the types, classes or mix of assets are determined; and	(c)	Whether and to what extent there is hypothecation of assets;
	(b)	Strategy in respect of derivatives and other instruments.	(d)	Period between formal reviews of investment strategy;
			(e)	Approach to investment in different asset classes, and assets of different credit or liquidity quality, including assets not normally traded; and
			(f)	Details of any external support available to the *with-profits fund* and how this affects the investment strategy.
(3) Business risk	(a)	Where a *firm* explicitly excludes business risk from a class of *with-profits policies* but there are residual risks, clarification where these risks such as guarantee and smoothing costs are borne; and	(c)	Current limits which apply to the taking on of business risk; and
			(d)	Whether and to what extent particular generations of *with-profits policyholders* or classes of *with-profits policies* bear or might bear particular business risks, including for example, crystallised or contingent guarantees to other classes of *policyholders* or whether the outturn from all business risk is pooled across all *with-profits policies*.
	(b)	Define where compensation costs from a business risk would be borne.		
(4) Charges and expenses	(a)	Factors that would drive any change to the basis on which the *firm* applies charges to or apportions its actual expenses amongst *with-profits policies*, or exercises any discretion to apply charges to particular *with-profits policies*.	(b)	Charges currently applied and the expenses currently apportioned to major classes of *with-profits policies*;
			(c)	Relationship between the *firm's* actual charges and expenses, as applied to determine the amounts payable under *with-profits policies*, and the charges and expenses borne by the *with-profits fund*;
			(d)	Circumstances under which expenses will be charged to the *with-profits fund* at an amount other than cost, and the reasons why; and

Reference to PPFM issues (COBS 20.3.6R)	With-profits principles		With-profits practices	
			(e)	Interval for reviewing any arrangements for out-sourced services, including those provided by connected parties, giving a broad indication of the terms for termination.
(5) Management of inherited estate	(a)	Preferred size or scale of *inherited estate* and implications for the values of the *with profits policies*; and	(d)	How the *inherited estate* is used, for example, in meeting costs;
	(b)	Any existing division of the *inherited estate* between *with-profits funds*; and	(e)	Whether the investment strategy for the *inherited estate* differs from the rest of the *with-profits fund*; and
	(c)	Any constraints on the freedom to deal with the *inherited estate* as a result of previous dealings.	(f)	Any current guidelines in place as to the size or scale of the *inherited estate* or as to how and over what time period the *inherited estate* would be managed, if it becomes too large or too small.
(7) Equity between the with-profits fund and any shareholders	(a)	Arrangements for, and any changes to, profit sharing between shareholders and *with-profits policyholders*.	(b)	Current basis on which profit between *with-profits policyholders* and shareholders is divided; and
			(c)	Whether the pricing of any policies being written, and particular policies open to new business, appear to be significantly and systematically reducing the *inherited estate* if the shareholder transfer is taken into account.

20.4 Communications with with-profits policyholders

Provision and publication of PPFM

20.4.1 **[R]** A *firm* must:
(1) on request, provide its *PPFM*, or the *PPFM* applicable to specified *with-profits funds*:
  (a) free of charge to its *with-profits policyholders*; or
  (b) for a reasonable charge to any person who is not its *with-profits policyholder*; and
(2) if the *firm* publishes its *PPFM* on its website, prominently signpost its location there.

Notification of changes

20.4.2 **[R]** A *firm* must send its *with-profits policyholders* who are affected by any change in its *PPFM*, written notice, setting out any:
(1) proposed changes to the *with-profits principles*, three *months* in advance of the effective date; and
(2) changes to the *with-profits practices*, within a reasonable time.

20.4.3 **[R]** A *firm* need not give the notice required if the change to its *PPFM*:
(1) is necessary to correct an error or omission; or
(2) would improve clarity or presentation without materially affecting the *PPFM's* substance; or
(3) is immaterial.

Requirements on EEA insurers

20.4.4 **[R]** In relation to any *with-profits policyholder* who is *habitually resident* in the *United Kingdom*, an *EEA insurer* must:
(1) on request, provide the information necessary to enable that *policyholder* properly to understand the *insurer's* commitment under the *policy*;

(2) ensure that the information provided is not narrower in scope or less detailed in content than the equivalent *PPFM*; and
(3) send the *policyholder* who is affected by any information being changed written notice, setting out:
  (a) any proposed changes to information that is equivalent to the *with-profits principles*, three *months* in advance of the effective date; and
  (b) any changes to information that is equivalent to the *with-profits practices*, within a reasonable time.

Consumer-friendly PPFM

20.4.5 **[R]** A *firm* must:
(1) produce a *CFPPFM* describing the most important information set out under each of the headings in its *PPFM* and keep it up to date as the *PPFM* changes over time;
(2) express its *CFPPFM* in clear and plain language that can be easily understood by a *with-profits policyholder*, or potential *with-profits policyholder* who does not possess any specialist or technical knowledge;
(3) provide its *CFPPFM* free of charge with any:
  (a) written notice sent to *with-profits policyholders* on proposed changes to its *with-profits principles* (where the firm must provide the version of the *CFPPFM* in use before the changes if this has not already been provided);
  (b) annual statements sent to its *with-profits policyholders* (unless there has been no material change in the *CFPPFM* since it was last supplied); and
  (c) *key features document* for a *with-profits policy*; and
(4) make its *CFPPFM* publicly available and prominently signpost the availability on its website.

20.4.6 **[G]** A *firm* may include the information set out in its *CFPPFM* in any other document it produces.

Annual report to with-profits policyholders

20.4.7 **[R]** A *firm* must produce an annual report to its *with-profits policyholders*, which must:
(1) state whether, throughout the *financial year* to which the report relates, the *firm* believes it has complied with its obligations relating to its *PPFM* and setting out its reasons for that belief;
(2) address all significant relevant issues, including the way in which the *firm* has:
  (a) exercised, or failed to exercise, any discretion that it has in the conduct of its *with-profits business*; and
  (b) addressed any competing or conflicting rights, interests or expectations of its *policyholders* (or groups of *policyholders*) and, if applicable, *shareholders* (or groups of *shareholders*), including the competing interests of different classes and generations.

20.4.8 **[G]** The following documents should be annexed to the annual report in this section:
(1) the report to *with-profits policyholders* made by a *with-profits actuary* in respect of each financial year (see SUP 4.3.16AR(4)); and
(2) any statement or report provided by the *person* or committee who provides the independent judgement under the *firm's* governance arrangements for its *with-profits business*.

20.4.9 **[G]** In preparing the annual report to *with-profits policyholders*, a *firm* should take advice from a *with-profits actuary*.

20.4.10 **[G]** A firm should make the annual report available to *with-profits policyholders* within six *months* of the end of the *financial year* to which it relates. A *firm* should notify its *with-profits policyholders* in any annual statements how copies of the report can be obtained.

CHAPTER 21
PERMITTED LINKS

21.1 Application

[2110C]

21.1.1 **[R]** The *rules*in this section apply on an ongoing basis to *linked long-term*contracts that are effected by:
(1) *insurers* other than *EEA insurers*; and
(2) *EEA insurers* in the United Kingdom.

21.1.2 **[R]** The *rules* in this section do not apply to:
(1) contracts that were effected before 1 July 1994, and under which *linked benefits* were permitted to be determined before that date;
(2) contracts effected by an *insurer* that are *linked long-term* contracts only because the *policyholder* is eligible to participate in any *established surplus*;

(3) contracts effected by an *EEA insurer* that are *linked long-term* contracts only because the *policyholder* is eligible to participate in an excess of assets representing the whole or a particular part of the *long-term insurance fund* over the liabilities, or a particular part of the liabilities, of the *insurer* as determined by the law of the *EEA state* in which the head office of the *insurer* is situated;
(4) [deleted]
(5) contracts effected before 30 June 1995, to the extent that they provide for benefits to be determined by reference to a *collective investment scheme* that was a *listed security* immediately before 1 July 1994; and
(6) contracts linked to *permitted units* that were effected before 1 February 1992, except to the extent that they relate to acts or omissions on or after that date.

21.2 Principles for firms engaged in linked long-term insurance business

21.2.1 **[R]** A *firm* must ensure that the values of its *permitted links* are determined fairly and accurately.

21.2.2 **[R]** A *firm* must ensure that its *linked assets*:
(1) are capable of being realised in time for it to meet its obligations to *linked policyholders*; and
(2) are matched with its *linked liabilities* as required by the *close matching rules.*

21.2.3 **[R]** A *firm* must ensure that there is no reasonably foreseeable risk that the aggregate value of any of its *linked funds* will become negative.

21.2.4 **[R]** A *firm* must notify its *linked policyholders* of the risk profile and investment strategy for the *linked fund*:
(1) at *inception*, and
(2) before making any material changes.

21.2.5 **[R]** A *firm* must ensure that its systems and controls and other resources are appropriate for the risks associated with its *linked assets* and *linked liabilities.*

21.2.6 **[R]**
(1) A *firm* must ensure when selecting *linked assets* that there is no reasonably foreseeable risk of a conflict of interest with its *linked policyholders.*
(2) If a conflict does arise, the *firm* must take reasonable steps to ensure that the interests of the *linked policyholders* are safeguarded.

21.2.7 **[R]** In applying the rules in this section, a *firm* must consider the economic effect of its *permitted links* and *linked assets* ahead of their legal form.

21.2.8 **[R]** A *firm* must notify the *FSA* in writing as soon as it becomes aware of any failure to meet the requirements of this section.

21.2.9 **[G]** In considering what action to take in response to written notification of a failure to meet the requirements of this section, the *FSA* will have regard to the extent to which the relevant circumstances are exceptional and temporary and to any other reasons for the failure.

21.3 Rules for firms engaged in linked long-term insurance business

21.3.1 **[R]** An *insurer* must not contract to provide benefits under *linked long-term* contracts of insurance that are determined:
(1) wholly or partly, or directly or indirectly, by reference to fluctuations in any index other than an *approved index*;
(2) wholly or partly by reference to the value of, or the income from, or fluctuations in the value of, property other than any of the following:
   (a) *approved securities*;
   (b) *listed securities*;
   (c) *permitted unlisted securities*;
   (d) *permitted land and property*;
   (e) *permitted loans*;
   (f) *permitted deposits*;
   (g) *permitted scheme interests*;
   (h) [deleted]
   (i) cash;
   (j) *permitted units*;
   (k) *permitted stock lending*; and
   (l) *permitted derivatives contracts.*

21.3.2 **[G]** Nothing in these rules prevents a *firm* making allowance in the value of any *permitted link* for any notional tax loss associated with the relevant *linked assets* for the purposes of fair pricing.

21.3.3 **[R]** A *firm* that has entered into a *reinsurance contract* in respect of its *linked long-term insurance business* must nevertheless discharge its responsibilities under its *linked long-term* insurance contracts as if no *reinsurance contract* had been effected.

21.3.4 **[G]** In order to comply with the requirements of COBS 21.3.3R a *firm* should:

(1) disclose to *policyholders* the implications of any credit risk exposure they may face in relation to the solvency of the reinsurer; and

(2) suitably monitor the way the reinsurer manages the business in order to discharge its continuing responsibilities to *policyholders*.

21.3.5 **[R]**

(1) Except in the case specified in (2), a *firm* which proposes to undertake *linked long-term insurance business*, which is linked to the average earnings index and used for the purposes of orders made by the Department for Work and Pensions under section 148 of the Social Security Administration Act 1992, must notify the *FSA* in writing of its intention to do so in good time before effecting any such business for the first time, or if there is a material change in the volume of such business, and explain how the risks associated with this business will be safely managed.

(2) These requirements do not apply in respect of liabilities for which a limited revaluation premium has been paid to the Department for Work and Pensions so that the liability for revaluation, while still linked to orders made under section 148 of the Social Security Administration Act 1992, is limited to 5%.

INSURANCE: NEW CONDUCT OF BUSINESS SOURCEBOOK (ICOBS)

NOTES

Up to date as at 22 February 2010. For later amendments please see www.fsa.gov.uk.

CONTENTS

ICOBS 1—Application . . . . . [2111]
ICOBS 2—General matters . . . . . [2112]
ICOBS 3—Distance communications . . . . . [2113]
ICOBS 4—Information about the firm, its services and remuneration . . . . . [2114]
ICOBS 5—Identifying client needs and advising . . . . . [2115]
ICOBS 6—Product information . . . . . [2116]
ICOBS 7—Cancellation . . . . . [2117]
ICOBS 8—Claims handling . . . . . [2118]
ICOBS TP 1—Transitional provisions . . . . . [2119]
ICOBS Sch 1—Record Keeping Requirements . . . . . [2120]
ICOBS Sch 2—Notification requirements . . . . . [2121]
ICOBS Sch 3—Fees and other required payments . . . . . [2122]
ICOBS Sch 4—Powers Exercised . . . . . [2123]
ICOBS Sch 5—Rights of action for damages . . . . . [2124]
ICOBS Sch 6—Rules that can be waived . . . . . [2125]

CHAPTER 1 APPLICATION

1.1 The general application rule

The general application rule

[2111]

1.1.1 **[R]** This sourcebook applies to a *firm* with respect to the following activities carried on in relation to a *non-investment insurance contract* from an establishment maintained by it, or its *appointed representative*, in the *United Kingdom*:

(1) an *insurance mediation activity*;
(2) *effecting* and *carrying out contracts of insurance*;
(3) *managing the underwriting capacity of a Lloyd's syndicate as a managing agent at Lloyd's*;
(4) *communicating* or *approving* a *financial promotion*;

and activities connected with them.

Modifications to the general application rule

1.1.2 **[R]** The general application *rule* is modified in ICOBS 1 Ann 1G according to the type of *firm* (Part 1), its activities (Part 2), and its location (Part 3).

1.1.3 **[R]** The general application *rule* is also modified in the chapters of this sourcebook for particular purposes, including those relating to the type of *firm*, its activities or location, and for purposes relating to connected activities.

Guidance

1.1.4 **[G]** *Guidance* on the application provisions is in ICOBS 1 Ann 1G (Part 4).

ICOBS 1 Annex 1
Application (see ICOBS 1.1.2R)

Part 1: Who?
Modifications to the general application rule according to type of firm

1 Third party processors

1 Ann 1

1.1 **[R]**

(1) This *rule* applies where a *firm* (or its *appointed representative*) ("A") has outsourced *insurance mediation activities* to a *third party processor*.

(2) Any *rule* in this sourcebook which requires the *third party processor*, when acting as such, to disclose its identity to a *customer* must be read as applying to the *third party processor* only to the extent that it applies to A and as requiring disclosure of A's identity.

2 Managing agents

2.1 **[R]**
(1) References to an *insurer* apply equally to a *managing agent* unless the context requires otherwise.
(2) A *managing agent* must give effect to the policy that a *consumer* must, where required by this sourcebook, be offered cancellation rights.
(3) References to *managing agents* in this sourcebook relate to their functions in managing the obligations of a *member* in his capacity as such.

3 Authorised professional firms

3.1 **[R]** This sourcebook does not apply to an *authorised professional firm* with respect to its *non-mainstream regulated activities* except for:
(1) the provisions on communications to *clients* and *financial promotions* (see ICOBS 2.2);
(2) the e-commerce provisions (ICOBS 3.2);
(3) status disclosure requirements in relation to complaints procedures (see ICOBS 4.1); and
(4) provisions implementing articles 12 and 13 of the *Insurance Mediation Directive* (see ICOBS 4.1, ICOBS 5.2 and ICOBS 5.3.3R), except to the extent that the *firm* is subject to equivalent rules of its *designated professional body* approved by the *FSA*.

3.2 **[G]** Compliance with provisions of the *Distance Marketing Directive* is dealt with in the Professional Firms sourcebook (see *PROF* 5.4).

4 Appointed representatives

4.1 **[R]**
(1) An *insurer* must ensure that its *appointed representative* complies with this sourcebook as it applies to an *insurance intermediary*.
(2) However, if the *appointed representative* is acting as the *insurer's third party processor* then:
   (a) this *rule* is subject to the *third party processors rule* (see paragraph 1.1R); and
   (b) the *insurer* is not required to ensure that the *appointed representative* complies with the *rules* in this sourcebook on commission disclosure (see ICOBS 4.4) or, unless they apply to an *insurer*, the *rules* on statements of demands and needs (see ICOBS 5.2).

4.2 **[G]** The cancellation requirements in chapter 7 do not apply to a *distance contract* entered into by an *appointed representative* to provide mediation services. Regulations 9 (Right to cancel) to 13 (Payment for services provided before cancellation) of the *Distance Marketing Regulations* apply instead.

5 Service companies

5.1 **[R]** This sourcebook does not apply to a *service company*, except for the provisions on communications to *clients* and *financial promotions* (see ICOBS 2.2).

6 Lloyd's

6.1 **[R]** The *Society* must ensure that no *member* carries on *motor vehicle liability insurance business* at Lloyd's unless a claims representative has been appointed to act for that *member* in each *EEA State* other than the *United Kingdom*, with responsibility for handling and settling a claim by an *injured party*. Otherwise, this sourcebook does not apply to the *Society*.

Part 2: What?
Modifications to the general application rule according to activities

1 Reinsurance

1.1 **[R]** This sourcebook does not apply to activities carried on in relation to a *reinsurance contract*.

[**Note:** article 12(4) of the *Insurance Mediation Directive*]

2 Contracts of large risks

2.1 **[R]** Subject to Part 3 of this Annex, this sourcebook does not apply to an *insurance intermediary* mediating a *contract of large risks*:
(1) where the risk is located outside the *European Economic Area*; or
(2) for a *commercial customer* where the risk is located within the *European Economic Area*.

[**Note:** article 12(4) of the *Insurance Mediation Directive*]

2.2 **[G]** *Principle* 7 continues to apply so a *firm* should provide evidence of cover promptly after inception of a *policy* to its *customer*. In respect of a *group policy*, a *firm* should provide information to its *customer* to pass on to other *policyholders* and should tell the *customer* that he should give the information to each *policyholder*.

3 Pure protection contracts: election to apply COBS rules

3.1 **[R]**

(1) This sourcebook does not apply in relation to a *pure protection contract* to the extent that a *firm* has elected to comply with the Conduct of Business sourcebook (*COBS*) in respect of such business.

(2) Within the scope of such an election, a *firm* must comply with the rest of the *Handbook*, treating the *pure protection contract* as a *life policy* and a *designated investment*, and not as a *non-investment insurance contract*.

(3) A *firm* must make, and retain indefinitely, a record in a *durable medium* of such an election (and any reversal or amendment). The record must include the effective date and a precise description of the part of the *firm's* business to which the election applies.

4 Chains of insurance intermediaries

4.1 **[R]** Where there is a chain of *insurance intermediaries* between the *insurer* and the *customer*, this sourcebook applies only to the *insurance intermediary* in contact with the *customer*.

Part 3: Where?
Modifications to the general rule of application according to location

1 EEA territorial scope rule: compatibility with European law

1.1 **[R]**

(1) The territorial scope of this sourcebook is modified to the extent necessary to be compatible with European law (see Part 4 for *guidance* on this).

(2) This *rule* overrides any other *rule* in this sourcebook.

1.2 **[R]** In addition to the *EEA* territorial scope *rule*, the effect of the *E-Commerce Directive* on territorial scope is applied in the fields covered by the 'derogations' in the Annex to that Directive other than the 'insurance derogation' in the fourth indent (see paragraph 8 of Part 4 for *guidance* on this).

[**Note:** article 3(3) of, and Annex to, the *E-Commerce Directive*]

2 Exemption for insurers: business with non-EEA customers via non-UK intermediaries

2.1 **[R]** This sourcebook does not apply to an *insurer* if:

(1) the intermediary (whether or not an *insurance intermediary*) in contact with the *customer* is not established in the *United Kingdom*; and

(2) the *customer* is not *habitually resident* in, and, if applicable, the *State of the risk* is outside, an *EEA State*.

3 Exemption for insurers: business with non-UK EEA customers

3.1 **[R]** A *rule* in this sourcebook which goes beyond the minimum required by *EU* legislation does not apply to an *insurer* if the *customer* is *habitually resident* in (and, if applicable, the *State of the risk* is) an *EEA State* other than the *United Kingdom*, to the extent that the *EEA State* in question imposes measures of like effect.

Part 4: Guidance

1 The main extensions and restrictions to the general application rule

1.1 **[G]** The general application *rule* is modified in Parts 1 to 3 of this Annex and in certain chapters of this sourcebook.

1.2 **[G]** The provisions of the *Single Market Directives* and other directives also extensively modify the general application *rule*, particularly in relation to territorial scope. However, for the majority of circumstances, the general application *rule* is likely to apply.

2 The Single Market Directives and other directives

2.1 **[G]** This *guidance* provides a general overview only and is not comprehensive.

2.2 **[G]** When considering the impact of a directive on the territorial application of a *rule*, a *firm* will first need to consider whether the relevant situation involves a non-*UK* element. The *EEA* territorial scope *rule* is unlikely to apply if a *UK firm* is doing business from a *UK establishment* for a *client* located in the *United Kingdom* in relation to a *UK* product. However, if there is a non-*UK* element, the *firm* should consider whether:

(1) it is subject to the directive;

(2) the business it is performing is subject to the directive; and

(3) the particular *rule* is within the scope of the directive.

If the answer to all three questions is 'yes', the *EEA* territorial scope *rule* may change the effect of the general application *rule*.

2.3 **[G]** When considering a particular situation, a *firm* should also consider whether two or more directives apply.

3 Insurance Mediation Directive: effect on territorial scope

3.1 **[G]** The *Insurance Mediation Directive's* scope covers most *firms* carrying on most types of *insurance mediation*. The *rules* in this sourcebook within the Directive's scope are those that require the provision of pre-contract information or the provision of advice on the basis of a fair analysis (see ICOBS 4 (Information about the firm, its services and remuneration), ICOBS 5.2 (Statement of demands and needs), ICOBS 5.3.3R (Advice on the basis of a fair analysis) and ICOBS 6 (Product information)).

3.2 **[G]** The *rules* implementing the minimum information and other requirements in articles 12 and 13 of the Directive are set out in ICOBS 4.1 (General requirements for insurance intermediaries), ICOBS 5.2 (Statement of demands and needs) and ICOBS 5.3.3R (Advice on the basis of a fair analysis).

3.3 **[G]** In the *FSA's* view, the responsibility for these minimum requirements rests with the *Home State*, but a *Host State* is entitled to impose additional requirements within the Directive's scope in the 'general good'. (See recital 19 to and article 12(5) of the *Insurance Mediation Directive*.) Accordingly, the general *rules* on territorial scope are modified so that:

(1) for a *UK firm* providing *passported activities* through a *branch* in another *EEA State* under the Directive, the *rules* implementing the Directive's minimum requirements apply, but the territorial scope of the additional *rules* within the Directive's scope is not modified;

(2) for an *EEA firm* providing *passported activities* under the Directive in the *United Kingdom*, the *rules* implementing the Directive's minimum requirements do not apply, but the additional *rules* within the Directive's scope have their unmodified territorial scope unless the *Home State* imposes measures of like effect; and

(3) an *EEA firm* acting as the principal of an *appointed representative* is required to ensure that its *appointed representative* complies with this sourcebook as it applies to a *UK firm* that is an *authorised person*.

4 Non-Life Directives: effect on territorial scope

4.1 **[G]** The *Non-Life Directives'* scope covers *insurers* authorised under those Directives conducting *general insurance business*.

4.2 **[G]** The *rules* in this sourcebook within the Directives' scope are those requiring the provision of pre-contract information or information during the term of the contract concerning the *insurer* or the *contract of insurance* (see ICOBS 2.2 (Communications to clients and financial promotions), ICOBS 4 (Information about the firm, its services and remuneration), ICOBS 6 (Product information) and ICOBS 8 (Claims handling) except ICOBS 8.2 (Motor vehicle liability insurers)).

4.3 **[G]** The Directives specify minimum information requirements and permit *EEA States* to adopt additional mandatory rules. (See article 7 of the *Second Non-Life Directive*)

4.4 **[G]** If the *State of the risk* is an *EEA State*, the Directives provide that the applicable information rules shall be determined by that state. Accordingly, if the *State of the risk* is the *United Kingdom*, the relevant *rules* in this sourcebook apply. Those *rules* do not apply if the *State of the risk* is another *EEA State*. The territorial scope of other *rules*, in particular the *financial promotion rules*, is not affected since the Directives explicitly permit *EEA States* to apply rules, including advertising rules, in the 'general good'. (See articles 28 and 41 of the *Third Non-Life Directive*)

5 Consolidated Life Directive: effect on territorial scope

5.1 **[G]** The *Consolidated Life Directive's* scope covers *long-term insurers* authorised under that Directive conducting *long-term insurance business*.

5.2 **[G]** The *rules* in this sourcebook within the Directive's scope are the cancellation *rules* (see ICOBS 7) and those *rules* requiring the provision of pre-contract information or information during the term of the contract concerning the *insurer* or the *contract of insurance* (see ICOBS 2.2 (Communications to clients and financial promotions), ICOBS 4 (Information about the firm, its services and remuneration), ICOBS 6 (Product information) and ICOBS 8 (Claims handling) except ICOBS 8.2 (Motor vehicle liability insurers)).

5.3 **[G]** The Directive specifies minimum information and cancellation requirements and permits *EEA States* to adopt additional information requirements that are necessary for a proper understanding by the *policyholder* of the essential elements of the commitment.

5.4 **[G]** If the *State of the commitment* is an *EEA State*, the Directive provides that the applicable information rules and cancellation rules shall be determined by that state. Accordingly, if the *State of the commitment* is the *United Kingdom*, the relevant *rules* in this sourcebook apply. Those *rules* do not apply if the *State of the commitment* is another *EEA State*. The territorial scope of other *rules*, in particular the *financial promotion rules*, is not affected since the Directive explicitly permits *EEA States* to apply rules, including advertising rules, in the 'general good'. (See articles 33, 35, 36 and 47 of the *Consolidated Life Directive*)

6 Motor Insurance Directives: effect on territorial scope

6.1 **[G]** The scope of the *Fourth Motor Insurance Directive* and *Fifth Motor Insurance Directive* covers *insurers* conducting *motor vehicle liability insurance business*. The *rules* in this sourcebook within the Directives' scope are those regarding the appointment of claims representatives and handling of claims by *injured parties* (see ICOBS 8.2).

6.2 **[G]** The Directives require a *motor vehicle liability insurer* to appoint a claims representative in each *EEA State* other than its *Home State*. They specify minimum requirements regarding function and powers of claims representatives in handling claims and regarding the settlement of claims by *injured parties*.

6.3 **[G]** The Directives' provisions apply to *motor vehicle liability insurers* for which the *United Kingdom* is the *Home State*. (See article 4 of the *Fourth Motor Insurance Directive*)

7 Distance Marketing Directive: effect on territorial scope

7.1 **[G]** In broad terms, a *firm* is within the *Distance Marketing Directive's* scope when conducting an activity relating to a *distance contract* with a *consumer*. The *rules* in this sourcebook within the Directive's scope are those requiring the provision of pre-contract information (see ICOBS 2.2 ((Communications to clients and financial promotions), ICOBS 4 (Information about the firm, its services and remuneration) and ICOBS 6 (Product information)), the cancellation *rules* (see ICOBS 7) and the other specific *rules* implementing the Directive (see ICOBS 3.1).

7.2 **[G]** In the *FSA's* view, the Directive places responsibility for requirements within the Directive's scope on the *Home State* except in relation to business conducted through a *branch*, in which case the responsibility rests with the *EEA State* in which the *branch* is located (this is sometimes referred to as a 'country of origin' or 'country of establishment' basis). (See article 16 of the *Distance Marketing Directive*)

7.3 **[G]** This means that relevant *rules* in this sourcebook will, in general, apply to a *firm* conducting business within the Directive's scope from an establishment in the *United Kingdom* (whether the *firm* is a national of the *United Kingdom* or of any other *EEA State* or *non-EEA state*).

7.4 **[G]** Conversely, the territorial scope of the relevant *rules* in this sourcebook is modified as necessary so that they do not apply to a *firm* conducting business within the Directive's scope from an establishment in another *EEA State* if the *firm* is a national of the *United Kingdom* or of any other *EEA State*.

7.5 **[G]** In the *FSA's* view:

(1) the 'country of origin' basis of the Directive is in line with that of the *Electronic Commerce Directive*; (see recital 6 to the *Distance Marketing Directive*)

(2) for business within the scope of both the *Distance Marketing Directive* and the *Consolidated Life Directive*, the territorial application of the *Distance Marketing Directive* takes precedence; in other words, the *rules* requiring pre-contract information and cancellation rules derived from the *Consolidated Life Directive* apply on a 'country of origin' basis rather than being based on the *State of the commitment*; (see articles 4(1) and 16 of the *Distance Marketing Directive* noting that the *Distance Marketing Directive* was adopted after the *Consolidated Life Directive*)

(3) for business within the scope of both the *Distance Marketing Directive* and the *Insurance Mediation Directive*, the minimum information and other requirements in the *Insurance Mediation Directive* continue to be those applied by the *Home State*, but the minimum requirements in the *Distance Marketing Directive* and any additional pre-contract information requirements are applied on a 'country of origin' basis. (The basis for this is that the *Insurance Mediation Directive* was adopted after the *Distance Marketing Directive* and is not expressed to be subject to it.)

8 Electronic Commerce Directive: effect on territorial scope

8.1 **[G]** The *E-Commerce Directive's* scope covers every *firm* carrying on an *electronic commerce activity*. Every *rule* in this sourcebook is within the Directive's scope.

8.2 **[G]** A key element of the Directive is the ability of a *person* from one *EEA State* to carry on an *electronic commerce activity* freely into another *EEA State*. Accordingly, the territorial application of the *rules* in this sourcebook is modified so that they apply at least to a *firm* carrying on an *electronic commerce activity* from an *establishment* in the *United Kingdom* with or for a *person* in the *United Kingdom* or another *EEA State*.

8.3 **[G]** Conversely, a *firm* that is a national of the *United Kingdom* or another *EEA State*, carrying on an *electronic commerce activity* from an *establishment* in another *EEA State* with or for a *person* in the *United Kingdom*, need not comply with the *rules* in this sourcebook. (See article 3(1) and (2) of the *E-Commerce Directive*).

8.4 **[G]** The effect of the Directive on this sourcebook is subject to the 'insurance derogation', which is the only 'derogation' in the Directive that the *FSA* has adopted for this sourcebook. The derogation applies to an *insurer* that is authorised under, and carrying on an *electronic commerce activity* within, the scope of the *Insurance Directives* and permits *EEA States* to continue to apply their advertising rules in the 'general good'.

8.5 **[G]** Where the derogation applies, the *rules* on *financial promotion* continue to apply for incoming *electronic commerce activities* (unless the *firm's* 'country of origin' applies rules of like effect), but do not apply for outgoing *electronic commerce activities*. (See article 3(3) and Annex, fourth indent of the *E-Commerce Directive*; Annex to European Commission Discussion Paper MARKT/2541/03)

8.6 **[G]** In the *FSA's* view, the Directive's effect on the territorial scope of this sourcebook (including the use of the 'insurance derogation'):
(1) is in line with the *Distance Marketing Directive*;
(2) overrides that of any other Directive discussed in this Annex to the extent that it is incompatible.

8.7 **[G]** The 'derogations' in the Directive may enable other *EEA States* to adopt a different approach to the *United Kingdom* in certain fields. (See recital 19 to the *Insurance Mediation Directive*, recital 6 to the *Distance Marketing Directive*, article 3 of, and the Annex to, the *E-Commerce Directive*)

CHAPTER 2
GENERAL MATTERS

2.1 Client categorisation

Introduction

[2112]
2.1.1 **[G]** Different provisions in this sourcebook may apply depending on the type of *person* with whom a *firm* is dealing:
(1) A *policyholder* includes anyone who, upon the occurrence of the contingency insured against, is entitled to make a claim directly to the *insurance undertaking*.
(2) Only a *policyholder* or a prospective *policyholder* who makes the arrangements preparatory to him concluding a *contract of insurance* (directly or through an agent) is a *customer*. In this sourcebook, *customers* are either *consumers* or *commercial customers*.
(3) A *consumer* is any natural person who is acting for purposes which are outside his trade or profession.
(4) A *commercial customer* is a *customer* who is not a *consumer*.

Customer to be treated as consumer when status uncertain

2.1.2 **[R]** If it is not clear in a particular case whether a *customer* is a *consumer* or a *commercial customer*, a *firm* must treat the *customer* as a *consumer*.

Customer covered in both a private and business capacity

2.1.3 **[G]** If a *customer* is acting in the capacity of both a *consumer* and a *commercial customer* in relation to a particular *contract of insurance*, the *customer* is a *commercial customer*.

Customer classification examples

2.1.4 **[G]** In practice, private individuals may act in a number of capacities. The following table sets out a number of examples of how an individual acting in certain capacities should, in the *FSA's* view, be categorised.

Customer classification examples

Capacity	Classification
Personal representatives, including executors, unless they are acting in a professional capacity, for example, a solicitor acting as executor.	*Consumer*
Private individuals acting in personal or other family circumstances, for example, as trustee of a family trust.	*Consumer*
Trustee of a trust such as a housing or NHS trust.	*Commercial customer*
Member of the governing body of a club or other unincorporated association such as a trade body and a student union.	*Commercial customer*
Pension trustee.	*Commercial customer*
Person taking out a *policy* covering property bought under a buy-to-let mortgage.	*Commercial customer*
Partner in a *partnership* when taking out insurance for purposes related to his profession.	*Commercial customer*

2.2 Communications to clients and financial promotions

Application

2.2.1 **[R]** In addition to the general application *rule* for this sourcebook, this section applies to the *communication*, or *approval* for *communication*, to a *person* in the *United Kingdom* of a *financial promotion* of a *non-investment insurance contract* unless it can lawfully be *communicated* by an *unauthorised* communicator without *approval*.

Clear, fair and not misleading rule

2.2.2 **[R]** When a *firm* communicates information, including a *financial promotion*, to a *customer* or other *policyholder*, it must take reasonable steps to communicate it in a way that is clear, fair and not misleading.

Approving financial promotions

2.2.3 **[R]**

(1) Before a *firm approves* a *financial promotion* it must take reasonable steps to ensure that the *financial promotion* is clear, fair and not misleading.

(2) If, subsequently, a *firm* becomes aware that a *financial promotion* is not clear, fair and not misleading, it must withdraw its *approval* and notify any *person* that it knows to be relying on its *approval* as soon as reasonably practicable.

Pricing claims: guidance on the clear, fair and not misleading rule

2.2.4 **[G]**

(1) This *guidance* applies in relation to a *financial promotion* that makes pricing claims, including *financial promotions* that indicate or imply that a *firm* can reduce the *premium*, provide the cheapest *premium* or reduce a *customer's* costs.

(2) Such a *financial promotion* should:

  (a) be consistent with the result reasonably expected to be achieved by the majority of *customers* who respond, unless the proportion of those *customers* who are likely to achieve the pricing claims is stated prominently;

  (b) state prominently the basis for any claimed benefits and any significant limitations; and

  (c) comply with other relevant legislative requirements, including The Control of Misleading Advertisements Regulations 1988.

2.3 Inducements

2.3.1 **[G]**

(1) *Principle* 8 requires a *firm* to manage conflicts of interest fairly, both between itself and its *customers* and between a *customer* and another *client*. This principle extends to soliciting or accepting inducements where this would conflict with a *firm's* duties to its *customers*. A *firm* that offers such inducements should consider whether doing so conflicts with its obligations under *Principles* 1 and 6 to act with integrity and treat *customers* fairly.

(2) An inducement is a benefit offered to a *firm*, or any *person* acting on its behalf, with a view to that *firm*, or that *person*, adopting a particular course of action. This can include, but is not limited to, cash, cash equivalents, *commission*, goods, hospitality or training programmes.

2.4 Record-keeping

2.4.1 **[G]**

(1) The Senior Management Arrangements, Systems and Controls sourcebook contains high-level record-keeping requirements (see *SYSC* 3.2.20R). These require *firms* to take reasonable care to make and retain adequate records of matters and dealings which are the subject of requirements and standards under the *regulatory system*, which includes this sourcebook.

(2) This sourcebook does not generally have detailed record-keeping requirements: *firms* will need to decide what records they need to keep in line with the high-level record-keeping requirements and their own business needs.

(3) *Firms* should bear in mind the need to deal with requests for information from the *FSA* as well as queries and complaints from *customers* which may require evidence of matters such as:

  (a) the reasons for *personal recommendations*;

  (b) what documentation has been provided to a *customer*; and

  (c) how claims have been settled and why.

2.5 Exclusion of liability and reliance on others

Exclusion of liability

2.5.1 **[R]** A *firm* must not seek to exclude or restrict, or rely on any exclusion or restriction of, any duty or liability it may have to a *customer* or other *policyholder* unless it is reasonable for it to do so and the duty or liability arises other than under the *regulatory system*.
2.5.2 **[G]** The general law, including the *Unfair Terms Regulations*, also limits the scope for a *firm* to exclude or restrict any duty or liability to a *consumer*.

Reliance on others

2.5.3 **[G]**
(1) Where it is compatible with the nature of the obligation imposed by a particular *rule* and with the *Principles*, in particular *Principles* 1 (Integrity), 2 (Skill, care and diligence) and 3 (Management and control), *firms* may rely on third parties in order to comply with the *rules* in this sourcebook.
(2) For example, where a *rule* requires a *firm* to take reasonable steps to achieve an outcome, it will generally be reasonable for a *firm* to rely on information provided to it in writing by an unconnected *authorised person* or a *professional firm*, unless it is aware or ought reasonably to be aware of any fact that would give reasonable grounds to question the accuracy of that information. However, a *firm* cannot delegate its responsibility under the *regulatory system*. For example, where a *rule* imposes an absolute obligation (such as the requirement for an *insurer* to handle claims promptly and fairly) although a *firm* could use outsourcing arrangements to fulfil its obligation, it retains regulatory responsibility for achieving the outcome required.

CHAPTER 3
DISTANCE COMMUNICATIONS

3.1 Distance marketing

Application

[2113]
3.1.1 **[R]** This section applies to a *firm* that carries on any distance marketing activity from an establishment in the *United Kingdom*, with or for a *consumer* in the *United Kingdom* or another *EEA* State.

Guidance on the Distance Marketing Directive

3.1.2 **[G]** *Guidance* on expressions derived from the *Distance Marketing Directive* and on the Directive's application in the context of *insurance mediation activity* can be found in ICOBS 3 Annex 1G.

The distance marketing disclosure rules

3.1.3 **[R]** A *firm* must provide a *consumer* with the distance marketing information (ICOBS 3 Annex 2R) in good time before conclusion of a *distance contract*.

[**Note:** article 3(1) of the *Distance Marketing Directive*]

3.1.4 **[G]** The *rules* setting out the responsibilities of *insurers* and *insurance intermediaries* for producing and providing information apply to requirements in this section to provide information (see ICOBS 6.1.1R).

3.1.5 **[R]** A *firm* must ensure that the distance marketing information, the commercial purpose of which must be made clear, is provided in a clear and comprehensible manner in any way appropriate to the means of distance communication used, with due regard, in particular, to the principles of good faith in commercial transactions, and the legal principles governing the protection of those who are unable to give their consent, such as minors.

[**Note:** article 3(2) of the *Distance Marketing Directive*]

3.1.6 **[R]** When a *firm* makes a voice telephony communication to a *consumer*, it must make its identity and the purpose of its call explicitly clear at the beginning of the conversation.

[**Note:** article 3(3)(a) of the *Distance Marketing Directive*]

3.1.7 **[R]** A *firm* must ensure that the information on contractual obligations to be communicated to a *consumer* during the pre-contractual phase is in conformity with the contractual obligations which would result from the law presumed to be applicable to the *distance contract* if that contract is concluded.

[**Note:** article 3(4) of the *Distance Marketing Directive*]

Terms and conditions, and form

3.1.8 **[R]** A *firm* must communicate to the *consumer* all the contractual terms and conditions and the information referred to in the distance marketing disclosure *rules* in writing or another *durable medium* available and accessible to the *consumer* in good time before conclusion of any *distance contract*.

[**Note:** article 5(1) of the *Distance Marketing Directive*]

3.1.9 **[G]** A *firm* will provide or communicate information or contractual terms and conditions to a *consumer* if another *person* provides or communicates it to the *consumer* on its behalf.

Commencing performance of the distance contract

3.1.10 **[R]** The performance of the *distance contract* may only begin after the *consumer* has given his approval.

[**Note:** article 7(1) of the *Distance Marketing Directive*]

Exception: distance contract as a stage in the provision of another service

3.1.11 **[R]** This section does not apply to a *distance contract* to act as *insurance intermediary*, if the *distance contract* is concluded merely as a stage in the provision of another service by the *firm* or another *person*.

[**Note:** recital 19 to the *Distance Marketing Directive*]

Exception: successive operations

3.1.12 **[R]** In the case of a *distance contract* comprising an initial service agreement, followed by successive operations or a series of separate operations of the same nature performed over time, the *rules* in this section only apply to the initial agreement.

[**Note:** article 1(2) of the *Distance Marketing Directive*]

3.1.13 **[R]** If there is no initial service agreement but the successive operations or separate operations of the same nature performed over time are performed between the same contractual parties, the distance marketing disclosure *rules* will only apply:

(1) when the first operation is performed; and

(2) if no operation of the same nature is performed for more than a year, when the next operation is performed (the next operation being deemed to be the first in a new series of operations).

[**Note:** recital 16 and article 1(2) of the *Distance Marketing Directive*]

Exception: voice telephony communications

3.1.14 **[R]**

(1) In the case of a voice telephony communication, and subject to the explicit consent of the *consumer*, only the abbreviated distance marketing information (ICOBS 3 Annex 3R) needs to be provided during that communication.

(2) However, unless another exemption applies (such as the exemption for means of distance communication not enabling disclosure) a *firm* must still provide the distance marketing information (ICOBS 3 Annex 2R) in writing or another *durable medium* available and accessible to the *consumer* in good time before conclusion of any *distance contract*.

[**Note:** articles 3(3)(b) and 5(1) of the *Distance Marketing Directive*]

Exception: Means of distance communication not enabling disclosure

3.1.15 **[R]** A *firm* may provide the distance marketing information (ICOBS 3 Annex 2R) and the contractual terms and conditions in writing or another *durable medium* immediately after the conclusion of a *distance contract*, if the contract has been concluded at a *consumer's* request using a means of distance communication that does not enable the provision of that information in that form in good time before conclusion of any *distance contract*.

[**Note:** article 5(2) of the *Distance Marketing Directive*]

Consumer's right to request paper copies and change the means of communication

3.1.16 **[R]** At any time during the contractual relationship the *consumer* is entitled, at his request, to receive the contractual terms and conditions on paper. The *consumer* is also entitled to change the means of distance communication used unless this is incompatible with the contract concluded or the nature of the service provided.

Part II FSA Handbook Materials

[**Note:** article 5(3) of the *Distance Marketing Directive*]

Unsolicited services

3.1.17 **[R]**
(1) A *firm* must not enforce, or seek to enforce, any obligations under a *distance contract* against a *consumer*, in the event of an unsolicited supply of services, the absence of reply not constituting consent.
(2) This *rule* does not apply to the tacit *renewal* of a *distance contract*.

[**Note:** article 9 of the *Distance Marketing Directive*]

Mandatory nature of consumer's rights

3.1.18 **[R]** If a *consumer* purports to waive any of the *consumer's* rights created or implied by the *rules* in this section, a *firm* must not accept that waiver, nor seek to rely on or enforce it against the *consumer*.

[**Note:** article 12 of the *Distance Marketing Directive*]

3.1.19 **[R]** If a *firm* proposes to enter into a *distance contract* with a *consumer* that will be governed by the law of a country outside the *EEA*, the *firm* must ensure that the *consumer* will not lose the protection created by the *rules* in this section if the *distance contract* has a close link with the territory of one or more *EEA States*.

[**Note:** articles 12 and 16 of the *Distance Marketing Directive*]

3.2 E-Commerce

Application

3.2.1 **[R]** This section applies to a *firm* carrying on an *electronic commerce activity* from an *establishment* in the *United Kingdom*, with or for a *person* in the *United Kingdom* or another *EEA* State.

Information about the firm and its products or services

3.2.2 **[R]** A *firm* must make at least the following information easily, directly and permanently accessible to the recipients of the *information society services* it provides:
(1) its name;
(2) the geographic address at which it is established;
(3) the details of the *firm*, including its e-mail address, which allow it to be contacted and communicated with in a direct and effective manner;
(4) an appropriate statutory status disclosure statement (GEN 4 Annex 1R), together with a statement which explains that it is on the *FSA register* and includes its *FSA register* number;
(5) if it is a *professional firm*, or a *person* regulated by the equivalent of a *designated professional body* in another *EEA State*:
 (a) the name of the professional body (including any *designated professional body*) or similar institution with which it is registered;
 (b) the professional title and the *EEA State* where it was granted;
 (c) a reference to the applicable professional rules in the *EEA State* of establishment and the means to access them; and
 (d) where the *firm* undertakes an activity that is subject to VAT, its VAT number.

[**Note:** article 5(1) of the *E-Commerce Directive*]

3.2.3 **[R]** If a *firm* refers to price, it must do so clearly and unambiguously, indicating whether the price is inclusive of tax and delivery costs.

[**Note:** article 5(2) of the *E-Commerce Directive*]

3.2.4 **[R]** A *firm* must ensure that commercial communications which are part of, or constitute, an *information society service*, comply with the following conditions:
(1) the commercial communication must be clearly identifiable as such;
(2) the *person* on whose behalf the commercial communication is made must be clearly identifiable;
(3) promotional offers must be clearly identifiable as such, and the conditions that must be met to qualify for them must be easily accessible and presented clearly and unambiguously; and
(4) promotional competitions or games must be clearly identifiable as such, and the conditions for participation must be easily accessible and presented clearly and unambiguously.

[**Note:** article 6 of the *E-Commerce Directive*]

3.2.5 **[R]** An unsolicited commercial communication sent by e-mail by a *firm* established in the *United Kingdom* must be identifiable clearly and unambiguously as an unsolicited commercial communication as soon as it is received by the recipient.

[**Note:** article 7(1) of the *E-Commerce Directive*]

Requirements relating to the placing and receipt of orders

3.2.6 **[R]** A *firm* must (except when otherwise agreed by parties who are not *consumers*):

(1) give an *ECA recipient* the following information, clearly, comprehensibly and unambiguously, and prior to the order being placed by the recipient of the service:
  (a) the different technical steps to follow to conclude the contract;
  (b) whether or not the concluded contract will be filed by the *firm* and whether it will be accessible;
  (c) the technical means for identifying and correcting input errors prior to the placing of the order; and
  (d) the languages offered for the conclusion of the contract;

(2) indicate any relevant codes of conduct to which it subscribes and provide information on how those codes can be consulted electronically;

(3) (when an *ECA recipient* places an order through technological means), acknowledge the receipt of the recipient's order without undue delay and by electronic means (an order and an acknowledgement of receipt are deemed to be received when the parties to whom they are addressed are able to access them); and

(4) make available to an *ECA recipient* appropriate, effective and accessible technical means allowing the recipient to identify and correct input errors prior to the placing of an order.

[**Note:** articles 10(1) and (2) and 11(1) and (2) of the *E-Commerce Directive*]

3.2.7 **[R]** Contractual terms and conditions provided by a *firm* to an *ECA recipient* must be made available in a way that allows the recipient to store and reproduce them.

[**Note:** article 10(3) of the *E-Commerce Directive*]

Exception: contract concluded by e-mail

3.2.8 **[R]** The requirements relating to the placing and receipt of orders do not apply to contracts concluded exclusively by exchange of e-mail or by equivalent individual communications.

[**Note:** article 10(4) and 11(3) of the *E-Commerce Directive*]

ICOBS 3 Annex 1G
Guidance on the Distance Marketing Directive

ICOBS 3 Ann 1 **[G]** This Annex belongs to ICOBS 3.1.2G

Q1. What is a distance contract?

To be a *distance contract*, a contract must be concluded under an 'organised distance sales or service-provision scheme' run by the contractual provider of the service who, for the purpose of the contract, makes exclusive use (directly or otherwise) of one or more means of distance communication up to and including the time at which the contract is concluded.

So:

- the *firm* must have put in place facilities designed to enable a *consumer* to deal with it exclusively at a distance; and
- there must have been no simultaneous physical presence of the *firm* and the *consumer* throughout the offer, negotiation and conclusion of the contract. So, for example, contracts offered, negotiated and concluded over the internet, through a telemarketing operation or by *post*, will normally be *distance contracts*.

Q2. What about a firm that normally operates face-to-face but occasionally uses distance means?

If a *firm* normally operates face-to-face and has no facilities in place enabling a *consumer* to deal with it customarily by distance means, there will be no *distance contract*. A one-off transaction effected exclusively by distance means to meet a particular contingency or emergency will not be a *distance contract*.

Q3. What is meant by "simultaneous physical presence"?

A *consumer* may visit the *firm's* local office in the course of the offer, negotiation or conclusion of a contract. Wherever, in the literal sense, there has been "simultaneous physical presence" of the *firm* and the *consumer* at the time of such a visit, any ensuing contract will not be a *distance contract*.

Q4. Does the mere fact that an intermediary is involved make the sale of a product or service a distance contract?

No.

Q5. When is a contract concluded?

A contract is concluded when an offer to be bound by it has been accepted. An offer in the course of negotiations (for example, an offer by an *insurer* to consider an application) is not an offer to be bound, but is part of a pre-contractual negotiation.

A *consumer* will provide all the information an *insurer* needs to decide whether to accept a risk and to calculate the *premium*. The *consumer* may do this orally, in writing or by completing a proposal form. The response by an *insurer*, giving a quotation to the *consumer* specifying the *premium* and the terms, is likely to amount to an offer of the terms on which the *insurer* will insure the risk. Agreement by the *consumer* to those terms is likely to be an acceptance which concludes the contract.

In other cases where the *insurer* requires a signed proposal form (for example, some *pure protection contracts*), the proposal form may amount to an offer by the *consumer* on which the *insurer* decides whether to insure the risk and in such cases the *insurer's* response is likely to be the acceptance.

Q6. What if the contract has not been concluded but cover has commenced?

Where the parties to a contract agree that insurance cover should commence before all the terms and conditions have been agreed, the *consumer* should be provided with information required to be provided before conclusion of the contract to the extent that agreement has been reached.

Q7. How does the Directive apply to insurance intermediaries' services?

The *FSA* expects the *Distance Marketing Directive* to apply to *insurance intermediaries'* services only in the small minority of cases where:

- the *firm* concludes a *distance contract* with a *consumer* covering its *insurance mediation activities* which is additional to any insurance contract which it is marketing; and
- that *distance contract* is concluded other than merely as a stage in the *effecting* or *carrying out* of an insurance contract by the *firm* or another *person*: in other words it has some continuity independent of an insurance contract, as opposed, for example, to being concluded as part of marketing an insurance contract.

Q8. Can you give examples of when the Directive would and would not apply to insurance intermediaries' services?

The *rules* implementing the *Distance Marketing Directive* will not apply in the typical case where an *insurance intermediary* sells an insurance contract to a *consumer* on a one-off basis, even if the *insurance intermediary* is involved in the *renewal* of that contract and handling claims under it.

Nor will the Directive apply if an *insurance intermediary*, in its terms of business, makes clear that it does not, in conducting *insurance mediation activities*, act contractually on behalf of, or for, the *consumer*.

An example of when the *Distance Marketing Directive* would apply would be a *distance contract* under which an *insurance intermediary* agrees to provide advice on a *consumer's* insurance needs as and when they arise.

Q9. When would the exception for successive operations apply?

We consider that the *renewal* of a *policy* falls within the scope of this exception. So, the distance marketing disclosure *rules* would only apply in relation to the initial sale of a *policy*, and not to subsequent *renewals* provided that the new *policy* is of the same nature as the initial *policy*. However, unless there is an initial service agreement in place, the exclusion would only apply where the *renewal* takes place no later than one year after the initial *policy* was taken out or one year after its last *renewal*. If the *policy* terms have changed, *firms* will need to consider what information should be disclosed about those changes in accordance with the requirement to disclose appropriate information about a *policy* (see ICOBS 6.1.5R), as well as ensuring their effectiveness under contract law.

ICOBS 3 Annex 2R
Distance marketing information

ICOBS Ann 2 **[R]** This Annex belongs to ICOBS 3.1.3R

Distance marketing information	
The firm	
(1)	The name and the main business of the *firm*, the geographical address at which it is established and any other geographical address relevant for the *consumer's* relations with the *firm*.
(2)	Where the *firm* has a representative established in the *consumer's EEA State* of residence, the name of that representative and the geographical address relevant for the *consumer's* relations with the representative.
(3)	When the *consumer's* dealings are with any professional other than the *firm*, the identity of that professional, the capacity in which he is acting with respect to the *consumer*, and the geographical address relevant for the *consumer's* relations with that professional.

Distance marketing information	
(4)	An appropriate statutory status disclosure statement (GEN 4), a statement that the firm is on the *FSA Register* and its *FSA* registration number.
The financial service	
(5)	A description of the main characteristics of the service the *firm* will provide.
(6)	The total price to be paid by the *consumer* to the *firm* for the financial service, including all related *fees*, charges and expenses, and all taxes paid through the *firm* or, when an exact price cannot be indicated, the basis for the calculation of the price enabling the *consumer* to verify it.
(7)	Where relevant, notice indicating that the financial service is related to instruments involving special risks related to their specific features or the operations to be executed or whose price depends on fluctuations in the financial markets outside the *firm's* control and that past performance is no indicator of future performance.
(8)	Notice of the possibility that other taxes or costs may exist that are not paid through the *firm* or imposed by it.
(9)	Any limitations on the period for which the information provided is valid, including a clear explanation as to how long a *firm's* offer applies as it stands.
(10)	The arrangements for payment and for performance.
(11)	Details of any specific additional cost for the *consumer* for using a means of distance communication.
The distance contract	
(12)	The existence or absence of a right to cancel under the cancellation *rules* (ICOBS 7) and, where there is such a right, its duration and the conditions for exercising it, including information on the amount which the *consumer* may be required to pay (or which may not be returned to the *consumer*) in accordance with those *rules*, as well as the consequences of not exercising the right to cancel.
(13)	The minimum duration of the contract, in the case of services to be performed permanently or recurrently.
(14)	Information on any rights the parties may have to terminate the contract early or unilaterally under its terms, including any penalties imposed by the contract in such cases.
(15)	Practical instructions for exercising any right to cancel, including the address to which any cancellation notice should be sent.
(16)	The *EEA State* or *States* whose laws are taken by the *firm* as a basis for the establishment of relations with the *consumer* prior to the conclusion of the contract.
(17)	Any contractual clause on law applicable to the contract or on the competent court, or both.
(18)	In which language, or languages, the contractual terms and conditions and the other information in this Annex will be supplied, and in which language, or languages, the *firm*, with the agreement of the *consumer*, undertakes to communicate during the duration of the contract.
Redress	
(19)	How to complain to the *firm*, whether complaints may subsequently be referred to the *Financial Ombudsman Service* and, if so, the methods for having access to it, together with equivalent information about any other applicable named complaints scheme.
(20)	Whether compensation may be available from the *compensation scheme*, or any other named compensation scheme, if the *firm* is unable to meet its liabilities, and information about any other applicable named compensation scheme.

[**Note:** Recitals 21 and 23 to, and article 3(1) of, the *Distance Marketing Directive*]

ICOBS 3 Annex 3R
Abbreviated distance marketing information

ICOBS Ann 3 **[R]** This Annex belongs to ICOBS 3.1.14R

Abbreviated distance marketing information	
(1)	The identity of the *person* in contact with the *consumer* and his link with the *firm*.
(2)	A description of the main characteristics of the financial service.
(3)	The total price to be paid by the *consumer* to the *firm* for the financial service including all taxes paid through the *firm* or, when an exact price cannot be indicated, the basis for the calculation of the price enabling the *consumer* to verify it.
(4)	Notice of the possibility that other taxes or costs may exist that are not paid through the *firm* or imposed by it.
(5)	The existence or absence of a right to cancel in accordance with the cancellation *rules* (ICOBS 7) and, where the right to cancel exists, its duration and the conditions for exercising it, including information on the amount the *consumer* may be required to pay (or which may not be returned to the *consumer*) on the basis of those *rules*.
(6)	That other information is available on request and what the nature of that information is. [**Note:** article 3(3)(b) of the *Distance Marketing Directive*]

CHAPTER 4
INFORMATION ABOUT THE FIRM, ITS SERVICES AND REMUNERATION

4.1 General requirements for insurance intermediaries

Application: who?

[2114]
4.1.1 **[R]** This section applies to an *insurance intermediary*.

Status disclosure: general

4.1.2 **[R]** Prior to the conclusion of an initial *contract of insurance* and, if necessary, on its amendment or *renewal*, a *firm* must provide the *customer* with at least:
(1) its name and address;
(2) the fact that it is included in the *FSA Register* and the means for verifying this;
(3) whether it has a direct or indirect holding representing more than 10% of the voting rights or capital in a given *insurance undertaking* (that is not a *pure reinsurer*);
(4) whether a given *insurance undertaking* (that is not a *pure reinsurer*) or its *parent undertaking* has a direct or indirect holding representing more than 10% of the voting rights or capital in the *firm*; and
(5) the procedures allowing *customers* and other interested parties to register complaints about the *firm* with the *firm* and the *Financial Ombudsman Service* or, if the *Financial Ombudsman Service* does not apply, information about the out-of-court complaint and redress procedures available for the settlement of disputes between the *firm* and its *customers*.

[**Note:** article 12(1) of the *Insurance Mediation Directive*]

Status disclosure exemption: introducers

4.1.3 **[R]** A *firm* whose contact with a *customer* is limited to effecting introductions (see PERG 5.6) need only provide its name and address and whether it is a member of the same *group* as the *firm* to which it makes the introduction.

4.1.4 **[G]** If a *firm* goes further than putting a *customer* in contact with another *person* (for example, by *advising* him on a particular *policy* available from the *firm*) the full status disclosure requirements will apply.

4.1.5 **[R]** In relation to a *connected travel insurance contract*, a *firm* need only provide the procedures allowing *customers* and other interested parties to register *complaints* about the *firm* with the *firm* and the *Financial Ombudsman Service* or, if the *Financial Ombudsman Service* does not apply, information about the out-of-court *complaint* and redress procedures available for the settlement of disputes between the *firm* and its *customers*.

Scope of service

4.1.6 **[R]**

(1) Prior to the conclusion of an initial *contract of insurance* (other than a *connected travel insurance contract*) and, if necessary, on its amendment or *renewal*, a *firm* must tell the *customer* whether:
 (a) it gives advice on the basis of a fair analysis of the market; or
 (b) it is under a contractual obligation to conduct *insurance mediation* business exclusively with one or more *insurance undertakings*; or
 (c) it is not under a contractual obligation to conduct *insurance mediation* business exclusively with one or more *insurance undertakings* and does not give advice on the basis of a fair analysis of the market.

(2) A *firm* that does not *advise* on the basis of a fair analysis of the market must inform its *customer* that he has the right to request the name of each *insurance undertaking* with which the *firm* may and does conduct business. A *firm* must comply with such a request.

[**Note:** article 12(1) of the *Insurance Mediation Directive*]

4.1.7 **[R]** Prior to conclusion of an initial *contract of insurance* with a *consumer* a *firm* must state whether it is giving a *personal recommendation* or information.

Guidance on using panels to advise on the basis of a fair analysis

4.1.8 **[G]**

(1) One way a *firm* may give advice on a fair analysis basis is by using 'panels' of *insurance undertakings* which are sufficient to enable the *firm* to give advice on a fair analysis basis and are reviewed regularly.

(2) A *firm* which provides a service based on a fair analysis of the market (or from a sector of the market) should ensure that its analysis of the market and the available contracts is kept adequately up-to-date. For example, a *firm* should update its selection of contracts if aware that a contract has generally become available offering an improved product feature, or a better *premium*, compared with its current selection. The update frequency will depend on the extent to which new contracts are made available on the market.

(3) The panel selection criteria will be important in determining whether the panel is sufficient to meet the 'fair analysis' criteria. Selection should be based on product features, *premiums* and services offered to *customers*, not solely on the benefit offered to the *firm*.

Means of communication to customers

4.1.9 **[R]**

(1) All information to be provided to a *customer* in accordance with this chapter must be communicated:
 (a) on paper or on any other *durable medium* available and accessible to the *customer*;
 (b) in a clear and accurate manner, comprehensible to the *customer*; and
 (c) in an official language of the *State of the commitment* or in any other language agreed by the parties.

(2) The information may be provided orally where the *customer* requests it, or where immediate cover is necessary.

(3) In the case of telephone selling, the information may be given in accordance with the distance marketing disclosure *rules* (see ICOBS 3.1.14R).

(4) If the information is provided orally, it must be provided to the *customer* in accordance with (1) immediately after the conclusion of the *contract of insurance*.

[**Note:** article 13 of the *Insurance Mediation Directive*]

4.2 Additional requirements for protection policies for insurance intermediaries and insurers

Application: what?

4.2.1 **[R]** This section applies in relation to a *pure protection contract* or a *payment protection contract* for a *consumer*.

Ensuring customers can make an informed decision

4.2.2 **[G]** In considering a *customer's* information needs for the purposes of *Principle* 7, a *firm* should have regard to the importance of information for a *customer's* purchasing decision when deciding when and how to give it.

4.2.3 **[G]** If a *firm* provides elements of status disclosure information orally as part of an interactive dialogue, it should do so for all elements of the information. In the case of telephone selling, the information may be given in accordance with the distance marketing disclosure *rules* (see ICOBS 3.1.14R).

Disclosing the limits of the service provided

4.2.4 **[R]**

Part II FSA Handbook Materials

(1) In a sale that does not involve a *personal recommendation*, a *firm* must take reasonable steps to ensure a *customer* understands he is responsible for deciding whether a *policy* meets his demands and needs.
(2) If this is done orally, the information must be provided to the *customer* in writing or any other *durable medium* no later than immediately after the conclusion of the contract.
(3) If a *firm* anticipates providing, or provides, information on any main characteristic of a *policy* orally during a non-advised sale, taking reasonable steps includes explaining the *customer's* responsibility orally.
(4) A *policy's* main characteristics include its significant benefits, its significant exclusions and limitations, its duration and price information.

Status disclosure for insurers

4.2.5 **[R]**
(1) Prior to the conclusion of an initial contract and, if necessary, on its amendment or *renewal*, an *insurer* must disclose to the *customer* at least:
 (a) the statutory status disclosure statement (see GEN 4);
 (b) whose *policies* it offers; and
 (c) whether it is providing a *personal recommendation* or information.
(2) If this is done orally, the disclosure must be provided in writing or any other *durable medium* no later than immediately after the conclusion of the contract.

4.2.6 **[G]** *Insurers* cannot carry on an *insurance mediation activity* in respect of a third party's products unless they can show a natural fit or necessary connection between their insurance business and the third party's products (see the restriction of business in *INSPRU* 1.5.13R).

4.3 Fee disclosure

4.3.1 **[R]**
(1) A *firm* must provide its *customer* with details of the amount of any *fees* other than *premium* monies for an *insurance mediation activity*.
(2) The details must be given before the *customer* incurs liability to pay the *fee*, or before conclusion of the contract, whichever is earlier.
(3) To the extent that an actual *fee* cannot be given, a *firm* must give the basis for calculation.

4.3.2 **[G]** The *fee* disclosure requirement extends to all such *fees* that may be charged during the life of a *policy*.

4.4 Commission disclosure for commercial customers

Commission disclosure rule

4.4.1 **[R]**
(1) An *insurance intermediary* must, on a *commercial customer's* request, promptly disclose the *commission* that it and any *associate* receives in connection with a *policy*.
(2) Disclosure must be in cash terms (estimated, if necessary) and in writing or another *durable medium*. To the extent this is not possible, the *firm* must give the basis for calculation.

4.4.2 **[G]** An *insurance intermediary* should include all forms of remuneration from any arrangements it may have. This includes arrangements for sharing profits, for payments relating to the volume of sales, and for payments from premium finance companies in connection with arranging finance.

4.4.3 **[G]**
(1) The commission disclosure *rule* is additional to the general law on the fiduciary obligations of an agent in that it applies whether or not the *insurance intermediary* is an agent of the *commercial customer*.
(2) In relation to *contracts of insurance*, the essence of these fiduciary obligations is generally a duty to account to the agent's principal. But where a *customer* employs an *insurance intermediary* by way of business and does not remunerate him, and where it is usual for the *firm* to be remunerated by way of *commission* paid by the *insurer* out of *premium* payable by the *customer*, then there is no duty to account but if the *customer* asks what the *firm's* remuneration is, it must tell him.

4.5 Initial disclosure document

4.5.1 **[G]** Using an *initial disclosure document* (see ICOBS 4 Annex 1G) or *combined initial disclosure document* satisfies the status disclosure, scope of service and *fee* disclosure requirements if it is used in accordance with its notes and provided to the *customer* at the correct time.

ICOBS 4 Annex 1G
Initial disclosure document

ICOBS 4 Ann 1**[G]** This annex belongs to ICOBS 4.5.1G.

A *firm* should omit the notes and square brackets in the following *initial disclosure document*, but must not include the keyfacts logo unless it uses the *initial disclosure document* in full and in accordance with its notes. Subject to this, a *firm* may use its own house style and brand.

keyfacts®

about our insurance services [Note 1]

XYZ **Financial Services**

[Note 3]
[123 Any Street
Some Town
ST21 7QB]

[Note 2]

1 The Financial Services Authority (FSA)

The FSA is the independent watchdog that regulates financial services. Use this information to decide if our services are right for you.

2 Whose products do we offer? [Note 4]

- We offer products from a range of insurers [for . . .].
- We [can] **[Note 5]** only offer products from a limited number of insurers [for . . .].
- Ask us for a list of insurers we offer insurance from. **[Note 6]**
- We [can] **[Note 5]** only offer [a] product[s] from [a single insurer] [name of single *insurance undertaking*] [for . . .]. **[Note 7]**
- [or] **[Note 8]**
- We only offer products from a single insurer.
- [or] **[Note 9]**
- We only offer our own products for [list the types of *policies*].

3 Which service will we provide you with? [Note 10] [Note 11]

- We will advise and make a recommendation for you after we have assessed your needs [for] [list the types of *policies*].
- You will not receive advice or a recommendation from us [for] [list the types of *policies*]. We may ask some questions to narrow down the selection of products that we will provide details on. You will then need to make your own choice about how to proceed.

4 What will you have to pay us for our services? [Note 12]

- A fee [of £ [ ]] [for] [list the types of insurance services provided].
- No fee [for] [list the types of insurance services provided].

You will receive a quotation which will tell you about any other fees relating to any particular insurance policy.

5 Who regulates us? [Note 13]

[Registered name and address as shown on *FSA Register* (trading name(s) may also be stated)] is authorised and regulated by the Financial Services Authority. Our FSA Register number is []. **[Note 14]**

Our permitted business is [short, plain language description of relevant *permitted* business].

[or] **[Note 15]**

[Name of *appointed representative*] **[Note 2]** is an appointed representative of [registered name and address of *principal* as shown on *FSA Register*] which is authorised and regulated by the Financial Services Authority. [Name of *principal*]'s FSA Register number is [].

[Name of *principal*]'s permitted business is [short, plain language description of relevant business].

You can check this on the FSA's Register by visiting the FSA's website www.fsa.gov.uk/register or by contacting the FSA on 0845 606 1234.

6 Ownership [Note 16]

[Short description of any direct or indirect holding representing more than 10% of the voting rights or capital in the *firm* held by an *insurance undertaking* (other than a *reinsurance undertaking*) or its *parent undertaking*, e.g. "B&C Insurer owns 20% of our share capital."]

[Short description of any direct or indirect holding by the *firm* representing more than 10% of the voting rights or capital in a given *insurance undertaking* (other than a *reinsurance undertaking*), e.g. "We have 20% of the voting rights in Royal Edinburgh."]

7 What to do if you have a complaint [Note 13]

If you wish to register a complaint, please contact us:

. . . in writing	Write to [XYZ Financial Services], [Complaints Department, 123 Any Street, Some Town, ST21 7QB].
. . . by phone	Telephone [0121 100 1234] **[Note 25]**

If you cannot settle your complaint with us, you may be entitled to refer it to the Financial Ombudsman Service. **[Note 18] [Note 19]**

8 Are we covered by the Financial Services Compensation Scheme (FSCS)? [Note 13] [Note 20]

We are covered by the FSCS. You may be entitled to compensation from the scheme if we cannot meet our obligations. This depends on the type of business and the circumstances of the claim.

Insurance advising and arranging is covered for 90% of the claim, without any upper limit.

[or] **[Note 21]**

For compulsory classes of insurance, insurance advising and arranging is covered for 100% of the claim, without any upper limit.

Further information about compensation scheme arrangements is available from the FSCS.

The following notes do not form part of the *initial disclosure document*.

Note 1 – For requirements on using the keyfacts logo, see GEN 5.1 and GEN 5 Annex 1G.

Note 2 – Insert the *firm's* or *appointed representative's* name (either the name under which it is *authorised* or the name under which it trades). If an individual who is employed or engaged by an *appointed representative* provides the information, the individual should not put his or her own name on the *initial disclosure document*. A corporate logo or logos may be included.

Note 3 – Insert the head office or if more appropriate the principal place of business from which the *firm* or *appointed representative* expects to conduct business with *customers*. An *appointed representative* should state its own name and address.

Section 2: Whose products do we offer?

Note 4 – Select, for example by ticking, the box(es) which are appropriate for the service that it expects to provide to the *customer*. More than one box can be selected if the scope of the service provided to a particular *customer* varies by type of contract, for example, if a *firm* deals with a single *insurance undertaking* for motor insurance and a range of *insurance undertakings* for household insurance. If more than one box is selected, specify which relates to which type of *policy*, by adding text to the *initial disclosure document*. This needs to be done only in relation to the service offered to a particular *customer*. Do not remove boxes that are not selected.

Note 5 – Insert "can" if the range of *policies* is determined by any contractual obligation. This does not apply to an *insurer* selling its own products.

Note 6 – This sentence is required only if this service option is selected.

Note 7 – If the *firm* deals with a different *insurance undertaking* for different types of *policy*, identify all the *insurance undertakings* and specify the types of contract to which they relate. This needs to be done only in relation to the service offered to a particular *customer*. For example, "we can only offer products from ABC Insurance for motor insurance and XYZ Insurance for household insurance".

Note 8 – If this box is not selected, use this alternative text.

Note 9 –An *insurer* offering only its own *policies*, or part of an *insurer* offering only *policies* sold under that part's trading name, should use this alternative text.

Section 3: Which service will we provide you with?

Note 10 – This section may be omitted if the *customer* receives this information as part of a demands and needs statement. Renumber remaining sections.

Note 11 – Select, for example by ticking, the box which is appropriate for the service expected to be provided to the *customer*. Both boxes can be selected if different services are offered in relation to different types of *policy*. If more than one box is selected, specify which box relates to which type of *policy*. Do not remove an unselected box.

Section 4: What will you have to pay us for our services?

Note 12 – If the *customer* will be charged a *fee* for *insurance mediation activities*, insert a plain language description of what each *fee* is for and when each *fee* is payable. This should include any *fees* over the life of the contract, for example, for mid-term adjustments. If a *firm* does not charge a *fee* the first box should be abbreviated to 'A fee'. If more than one type of service is offered, *fees* may be aggregated over all the services provided and the services for which there is no *fee* identified.

Section 5: Who regulates us?

Note 13 – This section may be omitted if the information is provided by other means. Renumber remaining sections.

Note 14 – Modify this section for *incoming EEA firms* (see GEN 4 Ann 1R(2)).

Note 15 – An *appointed representative* should use this text instead. It should give the details of its *principal* for each type of *policy* that it is offering to a particular *customer*.

Section 6: Ownership

Note 16 – Omit this section (and renumber remaining sections) if there are no relevant ownership arrangements under the following notes or the *firm* is an *insurer* selling its own *policies*. In an *initial disclosure document* provided by an *appointed representative*, cover holdings in or held by that *appointed representative*, as appropriate.

Section 7: What to do if you have a complaint

Note 17 – If different to the address in note 5, give the address and telephone number which is to be used by *customers* wishing to complain.

Note 18 – This text may be omitted for a *customer* who would not be an *eligible complainant*.

Note 19 – An *authorised professional firm* which is exclusively carrying on *non-mainstream regulated activities* should delete this sentence and refer to the alternative complaints handling arrangements.

Section 8: Are we covered by the Financial Services Compensation Scheme (FSCS)?

Note 20 – An *incoming EEA firm* should modify this section as appropriate. A *firm* which is not a *participant firm* must answer this question 'No' and should state the amount of cover provided (if any) and from whom further information about the compensation arrangements may be obtained.

Note 21 – Use this alternative text if providing a service in relation to a compulsory class of insurance, such as *employer's liability insurance*. If providing a service in relation to a contract which covers both a compulsory class of insurance and a class of insurance which is not compulsory, indicate the level of compensation that applies to each class.

Part II FSA Handbook Materials

CHAPTER 5
IDENTIFYING CLIENT NEEDS AND ADVISING

5.1 General

Eligibility to claim benefits: general insurance contracts and pure protection contracts

[2115]
5.1.1 **[G]**
(1) In line with *Principle* 6, a *firm* should take reasonable steps to ensure that a *customer* only buys a *policy* under which he is eligible to claim benefits.
(2) If, at any time while *arranging* a *policy*, a *firm* finds that parts of the cover apply, but others do not, it should inform the *customer* so he can take an informed decision on whether to buy the *policy*.

Eligibility to claim benefits: payment protection contracts

5.1.2 **[R]** A *firm arranging* a *payment protection contract* must:
(1) take reasonable steps to ensure that the *customer* only buys a *policy* under which he is eligible to claim benefits; and
(2) if, at any time while *arranging* the *policy*, it finds that parts of the cover do not apply, inform the *customer* so he can take an informed decision on whether to buy the *policy*.

5.1.3 **[G]** For a typical *payment protection contract* the reasonable steps required in the first part of the eligibility *rule* are likely to include checking that the *customer* meets any qualifying requirements for different parts of the *policy*.

Disclosure of material facts

5.1.4 **[G]** A *firm* should bear in mind the restriction on rejecting claims for non-disclosure (ICOBS 8.1.1R(3)). Ways of ensuring a *customer* knows what he must disclose include:

(1) explaining the duty to disclose all circumstances material to a *policy*, what needs to be disclosed, and the consequences of any failure to make such a disclosure; or

(2) ensuring that the *customer* is asked clear questions about any matter material to the *insurance undertaking*.

5.2 Statement of demands and needs

Application: who? what?

5.2.1 **[R]** This section applies to:

(1) an *insurance intermediary* in relation to any *policy* (other than a *connected travel insurance contract*); and

(2) an *insurer* when it has given a *personal recommendation* to a *consumer* on a *payment protection contract* or a *pure protection contract*.

Statement of demands and needs

5.2.2 **[R]**

(1) Prior to the conclusion of a contract, a *firm* must specify, in particular on the basis of information provided by the *customer*, the demands and the needs of that *customer* as well as the underlying reasons for any advice given to the *customer* on that *policy*.

(2) The details must be modulated according to the complexity of the *policy* proposed.

[**Note:** article 12(3) of the *Insurance Mediation Directive*]

Means of communication to customers

5.2.3 **[R]**

(1) A statement of demands and needs must be communicated:

  (a) on paper or on any other *durable medium* available and accessible to the *customer*;

  (b) in a clear and accurate manner, comprehensible to the *customer*; and

  (c) in an official language of the *State of the commitment* or in any other language agreed by the parties.

(2) The information may be provided orally where the *customer* requests it, or where immediate cover is necessary.

(3) In the case of telephone selling, the information may be given in accordance with the distance marketing disclosure *rules* (see ICOBS 3.1.14R).

(4) If the information is provided orally, it must be provided to the *customer* in accordance with (1) immediately after the conclusion of the *contract of insurance*.

[**Note:** article 13 of the *Insurance Mediation Directive*]

Statement of demands and needs: non-advised sales

5.2.4 **[G]** The format of a statement of demands and needs is flexible. Examples of approaches that may be appropriate where a *personal recommendation* has not been given include:

(1) providing a demands and needs statement as part of an application form, so that the demands and needs statement is made dependent upon the *customer* providing personal information on the application form. For instance, the application form might include a statement along the lines of: "If you answer 'yes' to questions a, b and c your demands and needs are those of a pet owner who wishes and needs to ensure that the veterinary needs of your pet are met now and in the future";

(2) producing a demands and needs statement in product documentation that will be appropriate for anyone wishing to buy the product. For example, "This product meets the demands and needs of those who wish to ensure that the veterinary needs of their pet are met now and in the future";

(3) giving a *customer* a record of all his demands and needs that have been discussed; and

(4) providing a *key features document*.

5.3 Advised sales

Suitability

5.3.1 **[R]** A *firm* must take reasonable care to ensure the suitability of its advice for any *customer* who is entitled to rely upon its judgment.

Suitability guidance for protection policies

5.3.2 **[G]** In taking reasonable care to ensure the suitability of advice on a *payment protection contract* or a *pure protection contract* a *firm* should:

(1) establish the *customer's* demands and needs. It should do this using information readily available and accessible to the *firm* and by obtaining further relevant information from the *customer*, including details of existing insurance cover; it need not consider alternatives to *policies* nor *customer* needs that are not relevant to the type of *policy* in which the *customer* is interested;

(2) take reasonable care to ensure that a *policy* is suitable for the *customer's* demands and needs, taking into account its level of cover and cost, and relevant exclusions, excesses, limitations and conditions; and

(3) inform the *customer* of any demands and needs that are not met.

Advice on the basis of a fair analysis

5.3.3 **[R]** If an *insurance intermediary* informs a *customer* that it gives advice on the basis of a fair analysis, it must give that advice on the basis of an analysis of a sufficiently large number of *contracts of insurance* available on the market to enable it to make a recommendation, in accordance with professional criteria, regarding which *contract of insurance* would be adequate to meet the *customer's* needs.

[**Note:** article 12(2) of the *Insurance Mediation Directive*]

CHAPTER 6
PRODUCT INFORMATION

6.1 General

Responsibilities of insurers and insurance intermediaries

[2116]

6.1.1 **[R]** An *insurer* is responsible for producing, and an *insurance intermediary* for providing to a *customer*, the information required by this chapter and by the distance communication *rules* (see ICOBS 3.1). However, an *insurer* is responsible for providing information required on mid-term changes, and an *insurance intermediary* is responsible for producing price information if it agrees this with an *insurer*.

6.1.2 **[R]** If there is no *insurance intermediary*, the *insurer* is responsible for producing and providing the information.

6.1.3 **[R]** An *insurer* must produce information in good time to enable the *insurance intermediary* to comply with the *rules* in this chapter, or promptly on an *insurance intermediary's* request.

6.1.4 **[R]** These general *rules* on the responsibilities of *insurers* and *insurance intermediaries* are modified by ICOBS 6 Annex 1R if one of the *firms* is not based in the *United Kingdom*, and in certain other situations.

Ensuring customers can make an informed decision

6.1.5 **[R]** A *firm* must take reasonable steps to ensure a *customer* is given appropriate information about a *policy* in good time and in a comprehensible form so that the *customer* can make an informed decision about the arrangements proposed.

6.1.6 **[G]** The appropriate information *rule* applies pre-conclusion and post-conclusion, and so includes matters such as mid-term changes and *renewals*. It also applies to the price of the *policy*.

6.1.7 **[G]** The level of information required will vary according to matters such as:

(1) the knowledge, experience and ability of a typical *customer* for the *policy*;

(2) the *policy* terms, including its main benefits, exclusions, limitations, conditions and its duration;

(3) the *policy's* overall complexity;

(4) whether the *policy* is bought in connection with other goods and services;

(5) distance communication information requirements (for example, under the distance communication *rules* less information can be given during certain telephone sales than in a sale made purely by written correspondence (see ICOBS 3.1.14R)); and

(6) whether the same information has been provided to the *customer* previously and, if so, when.

6.1.8 **[G]** In determining what is "in good time", a *firm* should consider the importance of the information to the *customer's* decision-making process and the point at which the information may be most useful. Distance communication timing requirements are also relevant (for example, the distance communication *rules* enable certain information to be provided post-conclusion in telephone and certain other sales (see ICOBS 3.1.14R and ICOBS 3.1.15R)).

6.1.9 **[G]** Cancellation rights do not affect what information it is appropriate to give to a *customer* in order to enable him to make an informed purchasing decision.

6.1.10 **[G]** A *firm* dealing with a *consumer* may wish to provide information in a *policy summary* or as a *key features document* (see ICOBS 6 Annex 2).

Providing evidence of cover

6.1.11 **[G]** Under *Principle* 7 a *firm* should provide evidence of cover promptly after inception of a *policy*. *Firms* will need to take into account the type of *customer* and the effect of other information requirements, for example those under the distance communication *rules* (ICOBS 3.1).

Group policies

6.1.12 **[G]** Under *Principle* 7, a *firm* that sells a *group policy* should provide appropriate information to the *customer* to pass on to other *policyholders*. It should tell the *customer* that he should give the information to each *policyholder*.

Price disclosure: connected goods or services

6.1.13 **[R]**
(1) If a *policy* is bought by a *consumer* in connection with other goods or services a *firm* must, before conclusion of the contract, disclose its *premium* separately from any other prices and whether buying the *policy* is compulsory.
(2) In the case of a *distance contract*, disclosure of whether buying the *policy* is compulsory may be made in accordance with the timing requirements under the distance communication *rules* (see ICOBS 3.1.8R, ICOBS 3.1.14R and ICOBS 3.1.15R).

Exception to the timing rules: distance contracts and voice telephony communications

6.1.14 **[R]** Where a *rule* in this chapter requires information to be provided in writing or another *durable medium* before conclusion of a contract, a *firm* may instead provide that information in accordance with the distance communication timing requirements (see ICOBS 3.1.14R and ICOBS 3.1.15R).

6.2 Pre-contract information: general insurance contracts

Application: what?

6.2.1 **[R]** This section applies in relation to a *general insurance contract*.

Non-life insurance directive disclosure requirements

6.2.2 **[R]** Before a *general insurance contract* is concluded, a *firm* must inform a *customer* who is a natural *person* of:
(1) the law applicable to the contract where the parties do not have a free choice, or the fact that the parties are free to choose the law applicable and, in the latter case, the law the *firm* proposes to choose; and
(2) the arrangements for handling *policyholders'* complaints concerning contracts including, where appropriate, the existence of a complaints body (usually the *Financial Ombudsman Service*), without prejudice to the *policyholders'* right to take legal proceedings.

[**Note:** article 31 of the *Third Non-Life Directive*]

6.2.3 **[R]**
(1) If the *insurance undertaking* is an *EEA firm*, the *firm* must inform the *customer*, before any commitment is entered into, of the *EEA State* in which the head office or, where appropriate, the *branch* with which the contract is to be concluded, is situated.
(2) Any documents issued to the *customer* must convey the information required by this *rule*.

[**Note:** article 43(2) of the *Third Non-Life Directive*]

6.2.4 **[R]** The contract or any other document granting cover, together with the insurance proposal where it is binding upon the *customer*, must state the address of the head office, or, where appropriate, of the *branch* of the *insurance undertaking* which grants the cover.

[**Note:** article 43(2) of the *Third Non-Life Directive*]

Disclosure of cancellation right

6.2.5 **[R]**
(1) A *firm* must provide a *consumer* with information on the right to cancel a *policy*.
(2) The information to be provided on the right to cancel is:
(a) its existence;

(b) its duration;
(c) the conditions for exercising it;
(d) information on the amount which the *consumer* may be required to pay if he exercises it;
(e) the consequences of not exercising it; and
(f) the practical instructions for exercising it.

(3) The information must be provided in good time before conclusion of the contract and in writing or another *durable medium*.

6.3 Pre- and post-contract information: pure protection contracts

Life insurance directive disclosure requirements

6.3.1 **[R]**
(1) Before a *pure protection contract* is concluded, a *firm* must inform a *customer* of the information in the table below.
(2) The information must be communicated in a clear and accurate manner, in writing, and in an official language of the *State of the commitment* or in another language agreed by the parties.

Information to be communicated before conclusion	
(1)	The name of the *insurance undertaking* and its legal form.
(2)	The name of the *EEA State* in which the head office and, where appropriate, the agency or *branch* concluding the contract is situated.
(3)	The address of the head office and, where appropriate, of the agency or *branch* concluding the contract.
(4)*	Definition of each benefit and each option.
(5)*	Term of the contract.
(6)*	Means of terminating the contract.
(7)*	Means of payment of *premiums* and duration of payments.
(8)*	Information on the *premiums* for each benefit, both main benefits and supplementary benefits, where appropriate.
(9)	Arrangements for application of the cancellation period.
(10)	General information on the tax arrangements applicable to the type of *policy*.
(11)	The arrangements for handling complaints concerning contracts by *policyholders*, lives assured or beneficiaries under contracts including, where appropriate, the existence of a complaints body (usually the *Financial Ombudsman Service*), without prejudice to the right to take legal proceedings.
(12)	The law applicable to the contract where the parties do not have a free choice or, where the parties are free to choose the law applicable, the law the *insurance undertaking* proposes to choose.
Note: The *rule* on mid-term changes applies to items marked with an asterisk (see ICOBS 6.3.3R).	

[**Note:** Annex III(A) to the *Consolidated Life Directive*]

6.3.2 **[G]** If the contract is concluded with a *commercial customer* by telephone, the information in this section may be provided immediately after conclusion.

Mid-term changes

6.3.3 **[R]** In addition to the *policy* conditions, both general and special, a *customer* must, throughout the term of a *pure protection contract*, receive:
(1) any change in the name of the *insurance undertaking*, its legal form or the address of its head office and, where appropriate, of the agency or *branch* which concluded the contract; and
(2) all the information marked '*' in the table of information to be communicated before conclusion, in the event of a change in the *policy* conditions or amendment of the law applicable to the contract.

[**Note:** Annex III(B) to the *Consolidated Life Directive*]

6.4 Pre- and post-contract information: protection policies

Application: what?

6.4.1 **[R]** This section applies in relation to a *payment protection contract* or a *pure protection contract* except as otherwise stated.

Oral sales: ensuring customers can make an informed decision

6.4.2 **[R]**

(1) If a *firm* provides information orally during a sales dialogue with a *customer* on a main characteristic of a *policy*, it must do so for all the *policy's* main characteristics.

(2) A *firm* must take reasonable steps to ensure that the information provided orally is sufficient to enable the *customer* to take an informed decision on the basis of that information, without overloading the *customer* or obscuring other parts of the information.

6.4.3 **[G]**

(1) A *policy's* main characteristics include its significant benefits, its significant exclusions and limitations, its duration and price information.

(2) A significant exclusion or limitation is one that would tend to affect the decision of *customers* generally to buy. In determining what exclusions or limitations are significant, a *firm* should particularly consider the exclusions or limitations that relate to the significant features and benefits of a *policy* and factors which may have an adverse effect on the benefit payable under it. Another type of significant limitation might be that the contract only operates through certain means of communication, e.g. telephone or internet.

Policy summary

6.4.4 **[R]** A *firm* must provide a *consumer* with a *policy summary* in good time before the conclusion of a contract.

Payment protection contracts: importance of reading documentation

6.4.5 **[R]**

(1) A *firm* must draw a *consumer's* attention to the importance of reading *payment protection contract* documentation before the end of the cancellation period to check that the *policy* is suitable for the *consumer*.

(2) This must be done orally if a *firm* provides information orally on any main characteristic of a *policy*.

Price information: general

6.4.6 **[R]** A *firm* must provide price information in a way calculated to enable the *customer* to relate it to a regular budget.

6.4.7 **[G]** Price information is likely also to include at least the total *premium* (or the basis for calculating it so that the *customer* can verify it) and, where relevant:

(1) for *policies* of over one year with reviewable *premiums*, the period for which the quoted *premium* is valid, and the timing of reviews;

(2) other *fees*, administrative charges and taxes payable by the *customer* through the *firm*; and

(3) a statement identifying separately the possibility of any taxes not payable through the *firm*.

6.4.8 **[G]** Price information should be given in writing or another *durable medium* in good time before conclusion of the contract. This is in addition to any requirement or decision to provide the information orally. In the case of a *distance contract* concluded over the telephone, it may be provided in writing or another *durable medium* no later than immediately after conclusion.

Price information: premiums paid using a non-revolving credit agreement

6.4.9 **[R]**

(1) This *rule* applies when a *premium* will be paid using a credit agreement other than a revolving credit agreement.

(2) A *firm* must provide price information in a way calculated to enable the *customer* to understand the additional repayments that relate to the purchase of the *policy*, and the total cost of the *policy*.

(3) Price information must reflect any difference between the duration of the *policy* and that of the credit agreement.

(4) A *firm* must explain to a *customer*, as applicable, that the *premium* will be added to the amount provided under the credit agreement and that interest will be payable on it.

Price information: policies sold in connection with revolving credit arrangements

6.4.10 **[G]**

(1) This *guidance* applies to *policies* bought as secondary products to revolving credit agreements (such as store cards or credit cards).

(2) Price information should be given in a way calculated to enable a typical *customer* to understand the typical cumulative cost of taking out the *policy*. This does not require oral disclosure where there is a sales dialogue with a *customer*. However, consistent with *Principle* 7, a *firm* should ensure that this element of price information is not undermined by any information given orally.

Mid-term changes

6.4.11 **[R]**

(1) Throughout the term of a *policy*, a *firm* must provide a *customer* with information about any change to:

(a) the *premium*, unless the change conforms to a previously disclosed formula; and

(b) any term of the *policy*, together with an explanation of any implications of the change where necessary.

(2) This information must be provided in writing or another *durable medium* in good time before the change takes effect or, if the change is at the *customer's* request, as soon as is practicable provided the *firm* explains the implications of the change before it takes effect.

6.4.12 **[G]**

(1) When explaining the implications of a change, a *firm* should explain any changes to the benefits and significant or unusual exclusions arising from the change.

(2) *Firms* will need to consider whether mid-term changes are compatible with the original *policy*, in particular whether it reserves the right to vary *premiums*, charges or other terms. *Firms* also need to ensure that any terms which reserve the right to make variations are not themselves unfair under the *Unfair Terms Regulations*.

ICOBS 6 Annex 1R
Responsibilities of insurers and insurance intermediaries in certain situations

This annex belongs to ICOBS 6.1.4R

The table in this annex modifies the general *rules* on the responsibilities of *insurers* and *insurance intermediaries* for producing and providing to a *customer* the information required by this chapter.

	Situation	***Insurance intermediary's* responsibility**	***Insurer's* responsibility**
(1)	*Insurance intermediary* operates from *UK* establishment*Insurer* does not operate from *UK* establishment	Production and providing	None
(2)	*Insurance intermediary* does not operate from *UK* establishment, is not *authorised*, is selling *connected contracts* or is an *authorised professional firm* carrying on *non-mainstream regulated activitiesInsurer* operates from *UK* establishment *Customer habitually resident* in the *EEA*	None	Production and providing (but no *policy summary* is required unless the *insurance intermediary* does not operate from a *UK* establishment)
(3)	As (2) but *customer habitually resident* outside the *EEA* and *insurer* not in contact with the *customer*	None	None
(4)	As (2) but *customer habitually resident* outside the *EEA* and *insurer* in contact with the *customer*	None	Production and providing
(5)	*Insurance intermediary* does not operate from *UK* establishment*Insurer* does not operate from *UK* establishment	None	Production and providing

ICOBS 6 Annex 2
Policy summary for consumers

This annex belongs to ICOBS 6.1.10G and ICOBS 6.4.4R

1 Format

1.1 **[R]**

(1) A *policy summary* must be in writing or another *durable medium*.

(2) A *policy summary* must be in a separate document, or within a prominent separate section of another document clearly identifiable as containing key information that the *consumer* should read.

1.2 **[G]** The quality and presentation standard of a *policy summary* should be consistent with that used for other *policy* documents.

2 Content

2.1 **[R]** A *policy summary* must contain the information in the table below and no other information.

Policy summary content	
•	Keyfacts logo in a prominent position at the top of the *policy summary*. Further requirements regarding the use of the logo and the location of specimens are set out in GEN 5.1 and GEN 5 Annex 1G.
•	Statement that the *policy summary* does not contain the full terms of the *policy*, which can be found in the policy document.
•	Name of the *insurance undertaking*.
•	Type of insurance and cover.
•	Significant features and benefits.
•	Significant or unusual exclusions or limitations, and cross-references to the relevant policy document provisions.
•	Duration of the *policy*.
•	A statement, where relevant, that the *consumer* may need to review and update the cover periodically to ensure it remains adequate.
•	Price information (optional).
•	Existence and duration of the right of cancellation (other details may be included).
•	Contact details for notifying a claim.
•	How to complain to the *insurance undertaking* and that complaints may subsequently be referred to the *Financial Ombudsman Service* (or other applicable named complaints scheme).
•	That, should the *insurance undertaking* be unable to meet its liabilities, the consumer may be entitled to compensation from the *compensation scheme* (or other applicable compensation scheme), or that there is no compensation scheme. Information on the extent and level of cover and how further information can be obtained is optional.

2.2 **[G]** A *policy summary* should properly describe the *policy* but, in line with *Principle* 7, should not overload the *consumer* with detail.

3 Significant or unusual exclusions or limitations

3.1 **[G]**

(1) A significant exclusion or limitation is one that would tend to affect the decision of *consumers* generally to buy. An unusual exclusion or limitation is one that is not normally found in comparable contracts.

(2) In determining what exclusions or limitations are significant, a *firm* should, in particular, consider the exclusions or limitations that relate to the significant features and benefits of a *policy* and factors which may have an adverse effect on the benefit payable under it.

(3) Another type of significant limitation might be that the contract only operates through certain means of communication, e.g. telephone or internet.

Examples of significant or unusual exclusions or limitations	
•	Deferred payment periods
•	Exclusion of certain conditions, diseases or pre-existing medical conditions
•	Moratorium periods
•	Limits on the amounts of cover
•	Limits on the period for which benefits will be paid
•	Restrictions on eligibility to claim such as age, residence or employment status
•	Excesses

4 Key features document as an alternative to a policy summary

4.1 *[R] A firm may provide a document that has the contents of a key features document* instead of a *policy summary*. The document must include contact details for notifying a claim but need not include the title 'key features of the [name of product]'.

CHAPTER 7
CANCELLATION

7.1 The right to cancel

The right to cancel

[2117]
7.1.1 **[R]** A *consumer* has a right to cancel, without penalty and without giving any reason, within:
(1) 30 *days* for a *contract of insurance* which is, or has elements of, a *pure protection contract* or *payment protection contract*; or
(2) 14 *days* for any other *contract of insurance* or *distance contract.*

[**Note:** article 6(1) of the *Distance Marketing Directive* in relation to a *distance contract* and article 35 of the *Consolidated Life Directive* in relation to a *pure protection contract*]

7.1.2 **[G]** A *firm* may provide longer or additional cancellation rights voluntarily, but if it does these should be on terms at least as favourable to the *consumer* as those in this chapter, unless the differences are clearly explained.

Exceptions to the right to cancel

7.1.3 **[R]** The right to cancel does not apply to:
(1) a travel and baggage *policy* or similar short-term *policy* of less than one *month's* duration;
(2) a *policy* the performance of which has been fully completed by both parties at the *consumer's* express request before the *consumer* exercises his right to cancel;
(3) a *pure protection contract* of six *months'* duration or less which is not a *distance contract*;
(4) a *pure protection contract* effected by the trustees of an *occupational pension scheme*, an employer or a *partnership* to secure benefits for the *employees* or the *partners* in the *partnership*;
(5) a *general insurance contract* which is neither a *distance contract* nor a *payment protection contract*, sold by an intermediary who is an *unauthorised person* (other than an *appointed representative*); and
(6) a *connected contract* which is not a *distance contract.*

[**Note:** articles 6(2)(b) and (c) of the *Distance Marketing Directive* and 35(1) and (2) of the *Consolidated Life Directive*]

7.1.4 **[G]** A 'similar short-term *policy*' is any *policy* where the event or activity being insured is less than one *month's* duration. 'Duration' refers to the period of cover rather than the period of the contract.

Start of the cancellation period

7.1.5 **[R]** The cancellation period begins either:
(1) from the day of the conclusion of the contract, except in respect of a *pure protection contract* where the time limit begins when the *customer* is informed that the contract has been concluded; or
(2) from the day on which the *consumer* receives the contractual terms and conditions and any other pre-contractual information required under this sourcebook, if that is later than the date referred to above.

[**Note:** article 35 of the *Consolidated Life Directive* and article 6(1) of the *Distance Marketing Directive*]

Exercising a right to cancel

7.1.6 **[R]** If a *consumer* exercises the right to cancel he must, before the expiry of the relevant deadline, notify this following the practical instructions given to him. The deadline shall be deemed to have been observed if the notification, if on paper or another *durable medium*, is dispatched before the deadline expires.

[**Note:** article 6(1) and (6) of the *Distance Marketing Directive*]

7.2 Effects of cancellation

Termination of contract

7.2.1 **[R]** By exercising the right to cancel, the *consumer* withdraws from the contract and the contract is terminated.

Payment for the service provided before cancellation

7.2.2 **[R]**

(1) When a *consumer* exercises the right to cancel he may only be required to pay, without any undue delay, for the service actually provided by the *firm* in accordance with the contract.
(2) The amount payable must not:
  (a) exceed an amount which is in proportion to the extent of the service already provided in comparison with the full coverage of the contract; and
  (b) in any case be such that it could be construed as a penalty.
(3) A *firm* must not require a *consumer* to pay any amount:
  (a) unless it can prove that the *consumer* was duly informed about the amount payable; or
  (b) if it commenced the performance of the contract before the expiry of the cancellation period without the *consumer's* prior request.
(4) A *consumer* cannot be required to pay any amount when exercising the right to cancel a *pure protection contract.*
(5) A *consumer* cannot be required to pay any amount when exercising the right to cancel a *payment protection contract* unless a claim is made during the cancellation period and settlement terms are subsequently agreed.

[**Note:** article 7(1), (2) and (3) of the *Distance Marketing Directive*]

7.2.3 **[G]** The amount payable may include:
(1) any sums that a *firm* has reasonably incurred in concluding the contract, but should not include any element of profit;
(2) an amount for cover provided (i.e. a proportion of the *policy's* exposure that relates to the time on risk);
(3) a proportion of the *commission* paid to an *insurance intermediary* sufficient to cover its costs; and
(4) a proportion of any *fees* charged by an *insurance intermediary* which, when aggregated with any *commission* to be repaid, would be sufficient to cover its costs.

7.2.4 **[G]** In most cases, the *FSA* would expect the proportion of a *policy's* exposure that relates to the time on risk to be a pro rata apportionment. However, where there is material unevenness in the incidence of risk, an *insurer* could use a more accurate method. The sum should be reasonable and should not exceed an amount commensurate to the risk incurred.

7.2.5 **[G]** An *insurer* and an *insurance intermediary* should take reasonable steps to ensure that double recovery of selling costs is avoided, particularly where the contract for the *insurance intermediary's* services is a *distance contract*, or where both *commission* and *fees* are recouped by the *insurer* and *insurance intermediary* respectively.

Firm's obligation on cancellation

7.2.6 **[R]**
(1) A *firm* must, without any undue delay and no later than within 30 *days*, return to a *consumer* any sums it has received from him in accordance with the contract, except as specified in this section.
(2) This period shall begin from the day on which the *firm* receives the notification of cancellation.

[**Note:** article 7(4) of the *Distance Marketing Directive*]

Consumer's obligation on cancellation

7.2.7 **[R]**
(1) A *firm* is entitled to receive from a *consumer* any sums and/or property he has received from the *firm* without any undue delay and no later than within 30 *days*.
(2) This period shall begin from the day on which the *consumer* dispatches the notification of cancellation.

[**Note:** article 7(5) of the *Distance Marketing Directive*]

7.2.8 **[G]** If an *insurer* has made a charge for services provided, the sums and property to be returned by a *consumer* should not include any money or property provided in settling a claim.

Set off

7.2.9 **[R]** Any sums payable under this section are owed as simple contract debts and may be set off against each other.

Automatic cancellation of an attached distance contract

7.2.10 **[G]** A *consumer's* notice to cancel a *distance contract* may also operate to cancel any attached contract which is also a distance financial services contract. This is unless the *consumer* gives notice that cancellation of the contract is not to operate to cancel the attached contract. (See the *Distance Marketing Regulations*.) Where relevant, this should be disclosed to the *consumer* along with other information on cancellation.

CHAPTER 8
CLAIMS HANDLING

8.1 Insurers: general

[2118]

8.1.1 **[R]** An *insurer* must:

(1) handle claims promptly and fairly;

(2) provide reasonable guidance to help a *policyholder* make a claim and appropriate information on its progress;

(3) not unreasonably reject a claim (including by terminating or avoiding a *policy*); and

(4) settle claims promptly once settlement terms are agreed.

8.1.2 **[R]** A rejection of a *consumer policyholder's* claim is unreasonable, except where there is evidence of fraud, if it is for:

(1) non-disclosure of a fact material to the risk which the *policyholder* could not reasonably be expected to have disclosed; or

(2) non-negligent misrepresentation of a fact material to the risk; or

(3) breach of warranty or condition unless the circumstances of the claim are connected to the breach and unless (for a *pure protection contract*):

(a) under a 'life of another' contract, the warranty relates to a statement of fact concerning the life to be assured and, if the statement had been made by the life to be assured under an 'own life' contract, the *insurer* could have rejected the claim under this *rule*; or

(b) the warranty is material to the risk and was drawn to the *customer's* attention before the conclusion of the contract.

8.2 Motor vehicle liability insurers

Application: who? what?

8.2.1 **[R]**

(1) This section applies to a *motor vehicle liability insurer*.

(2) The *rules* in this section relating to the appointment of claims representatives apply in relation to claims by *injured parties* resulting from accidents occurring in an *EEA State* other than the *injured party's EEA State* of residence which are caused by the use of *vehicles* insured through an establishment in, and *normally based* in, an *EEA State* other than the *injured party's EEA State* of residence.

(3) The *rules* in this section relating to claims handling apply in respect of claims arising from any accident caused by a *vehicle normally based* in the *United Kingdom*.

[**Note:** article 1 of the *Fourth Motor Insurance Directive* and article 4(4)(4e) of the *Fifth Motor Insurance Directive*]

Requirement to appoint claims representatives

8.2.2 **[G]** A *firm* must have a claims representative in each *EEA State* other than the *United Kingdom* (see *threshold condition* 2A).

Conditions for appointing claims representatives

8.2.3 **[R]** A *firm* must ensure that each claims representative:

(1) is responsible for handling and settling a claim by an *injured party*;

(2) is resident or established in the *EEA State* where it is appointed;

(3) collects all information necessary in connection with the settlement of a claim and takes the measures necessary to negotiate its settlement;

(4) possesses sufficient powers to represent the *firm* in relation to an *injured party* and to meet an *injured party's* claim in full; and

(5) is capable of examining cases in the official language(s) of the *EEA State* of residence of the *injured party*.

[**Note:** article 4(1), (4) and (5) of the *Fourth Motor Insurance Directive*]

8.2.4 **[G]** The requirement to possess sufficient powers does not prevent a claims representative from seeking additional authority or instructions if needed. It does prevent it from declining to deal with, or transferring responsibility for, claims properly referred to it by an *injured party*, or their representative.

Notifying the appointment of claims representatives

8.2.5 **[R]**

(1) A *firm* must notify to the *information centres* of all *EEA States*:

Part II FSA Handbook Materials

(a) the name and address of the claims representative which they have appointed in each of the *EEA States*; [**Note:** article 5(2) of the *Fourth Motor Insurance Directive*]
(b) the telephone number and effective date of appointment; and
(c) any material change to information previously notified.

(2) Notification must be made within ten *business days* of an appointment or of a material change.

Motor vehicle liability claims handling rules

8.2.6 **[R]** Within three *months* of the *injured party* presenting his *claim* for compensation:

(1) the *firm* of the *person* who caused the accident or its claims representative must make a reasoned offer of compensation in cases where liability is not contested and the damages have been quantified; or
(2) the *firm* to whom the claim for compensation has been addressed or its claims representative must provide a reasoned reply to the points made in the claim in cases where liability is denied or has not been clearly determined or the damages have not been fully quantified.

[**Note:** article 4(6) of the *Fourth Motor Insurance Directive* and article 4(4)(4e, first paragraph) of the *Fifth Motor Insurance Directive*]

8.2.7 **[R]**

(1) If liability is initially denied, or not admitted, within three *months* of any subsequent admission of liability, the *firm* must (directly, or through a claims representative) make a reasoned offer of settlement, if, by that time, the relevant claim for damages has been fully quantified.
(2) If an *injured party's* claim for damages is not fully quantified when it is first made, within three *months* of the subsequent receipt of a fully quantified claim for damages, the *firm* must (directly, or through a claims representative) make a reasoned offer of damages, if liability is admitted at that time.

8.2.8 **[R]** A claim for damages will be fully quantified for the purpose of this section when the *injured party* provides written evidence which substantiates or supports the amounts claimed.

Interest on compensation

8.2.9 **[R]**

(1) If the *firm*, or its claims representative, does not make an offer as required by this section, the *firm* must pay simple interest on the amount of compensation offered by it or awarded by the court to the *injured party*, unless interest is awarded by any tribunal.
(2) The interest calculation period begins when the offer should have been made and ends when the compensation is paid to the *injured party*, or his authorised representative.
(3) The interest rate is the Bank of England's base rate (from time to time), plus 4%.

[**Note:** article 4(6) of the *Fourth Motor Insurance Directive*. Regulation 6 of the Financial Services and Markets Act 2000 (Rights of Action) Regulations 2001 makes this *rule* actionable under section 150 of the Act (Actions for damages) by any person who suffers loss as a result of its contravention]

8.2.10 **[R]** A *firm* will be taken to have received a claim, or a fully quantified claim, for damages when the claim is delivered to it, or a claims representative, by any *person* by any method of delivery which is lawful in the *firm's*, or its claims representative's, respective State of residence or establishment.

8.2.11 **[G]** The provisions in this section are not intended to, and do not, restrict any rights which the *injured party*, or its *motor vehicle liability insurer*, or any other *insurer* acting on its behalf, may have and which would enable any of them to begin legal proceedings against the *person* causing the accident or that *person's*, or the *vehicle's*, *insurers*.

8.3 Insurance intermediaries (and insurers handling claims on another insurer's policy)

Application: who?

8.3.1 **[G]** This section applies to an *insurance intermediary*, and to an *insurer* handling a claim on another *insurance undertaking's policy*.

Interaction with the general law

8.3.2 *[G]* A *firm is* expected to comply with the general law on the duties of an insurance intermediary. This section does not seek to set out the full extent of those duties.

Conflicts of interest

8.3.3 **[G]**

(1) *Principle* 8 requires a *firm* to manage conflicts of interest fairly. SYSC 10 also requires an *insurance intermediary* to take all reasonable steps to identify conflicts of interest, and maintain and operate effective organisational and administrative arrangements to prevent conflicts of interest from constituting or giving rise to a material risk of damage to its *clients*.

(2) [deleted].

(3) If a *firm* acts for a *customer* in *arranging* a *policy*, it is likely to be the *customer*'s agent (and that of any other *policyholders*). If the *firm* intends to be the *insurance undertaking's* agent in relation to claims, it needs to consider the risk of becoming unable to act without breaching its duty to either the *insurance undertaking* or the *customer* making the *claim*. It should also inform the *customer* of its intention.

(4) A *firm* should in particular consider whether declining to act would be the most reasonable step where it is not possible to manage a conflict, for example where the *firm* knows both that its *customer* will accept a low settlement to obtain a quick payment, and that the *insurance undertaking* is willing to settle for a higher amount.

Dealing with claims notifications without claims handling authority

8.3.4 **[G]** A *firm* that does not have authority to deal with a claim should forward any claim notification to the *insurance undertaking* promptly, or inform the *policyholder* immediately that it cannot deal with the notification.

Part II FSA Handbook Materials

TP 1 Transitional Provisions

Fifth Motor Insurance Directive

[2119]
1 **[R]** In relation to a claim by an *injured party* received by a *motor vehicle liability insurer* or its claims representative on or before 10 June 2007, the motor vehicle liability claims handling *rules* (see ICOBS 8.2.6R to ICOBS 8.2.11G) only apply if the claim results from an accident occurring in an *EEA State* other than the *injured party's EEA State* of residence which was caused by the use of a *vehicle* insured through an establishment in, and *normally based* in, an *EEA State* other than the *injured party's EEA State* of residence.

Initial disclosure document

2 **[R]** A *firm* may use the keyfacts logo on a document that meets the requirements for an *initial disclosure document* except that it includes the sentence "It requires us to give you this document" in section 1 of the document. This *rule* applies until 5 January 2009.

3 [Expired]

4 [Expired]

5 [Expired]

Series of events

6 **[R]** If, for a *connected travel insurance intermediary*, the application of any provision in this sourcebook is dependent on the occurrence of a series of events, the provision applies with respect to the events that occur on or after 1 January 2009.

SCHEDULE 1
RECORD KEEPING REQUIREMENTS

[2120]
[G] Notes

(1) The aim of the *guidance* in the following table is to give the reader a quick overall view of the relevant record keeping requirements.

(2) It is not a complete statement of those requirements and should not be relied on as if it were.

Handbook reference	**Subject of record**	**Contents of record**	**When record must be made**	**Retention period**
ICOBS 1 Ann 1, Part 2 3.1R(3)	Record of election to comply with *COBS rules* for *pure protection policies* (including amendment or reversal)	Date of election and precise description of parts of the *firm's* business that will comply with *COBS* provisions	Not specified	Indefinitely

SCHEDULE 2
NOTIFICATION REQUIREMENTS

[2121]
Sch 2.1 **[G]** There are no notification requirements in ICOBS.

SCHEDULE 3
FEES AND OTHER REQUIRED PAYMENTS

[2122]
Sch 3.1 **[G]** There are no requirements for fees or other payments in ICOBS.

SCHEDULE 4
POWERS EXERCISED

[2123]
[G] The following powers and related provisions in or under the *Act* have been exercised by the *FSA* to make the *rules* in this sourcebook:

section 138 (General rule-making power)

section 139(4) (Miscellaneous ancillary matters)

section 145 (Financial promotion rules)

section 149 (Evidential provisions)

section 156 (General supplementary powers)

regulation 2 of the Financial Services and Markets Act 2000 (Fourth Motor Insurance Directive) Regulations 2002 (SI 2002/2706).

The following powers in the *Act* have been exercised by the *FSA* to give the *guidance* in this sourcebook: section 157(1) (Guidance).

SCHEDULE 5
RIGHTS OF ACTION FOR DAMAGES

[2124]
Sch 5.1 **[G]** The table below sets out the *rules* in ICOBS contravention of which by an *authorised person* may be actionable under section 150 of the *Act* (Actions for damages) by a *person* who suffers loss as a result of the contravention.

Sch 5.2 **[G]** If a "Yes" appears in the column headed "For private person?", the *rule* may be actionable by a *private person* under section 150 (or, in certain circumstances, his fiduciary or representative; see article 6(2) and (3)(c) of the Financial Services and Markets Act 2000 (Rights of Action) Regulations 2001 (SI 2001/2256)). A "Yes" in the column headed "Removed" indicates that the *FSA* has removed the right of action under section 150(2) of the *Act*. If so, a reference to the *rule* in which it is removed is also given.

Sch 5.3 **[G]** The column headed "For other person?" indicates whether the *rule* may be actionable by a *person* other than a *private person* (or his fiduciary or representative) under article 6(2) and (3) of those Regulations. If so, an indication of the type of *person* by whom the *rule* may be actionable is given.

Sch 5.4 **[G]**

Rule	**Right of action under section 150**			
	For *private person*?	**Removed?**	**For other *person*?**	
All *rules* in ICOBS with the status letter "E"	No	No	No	
Any *rule* in ICOBS which prohibits an *authorised person* from seeking to make provision excluding or restricting any duty or liability	Yes	No	Yes	Any other *person*
ICOBS 8.2.9 R	Yes	No	Yes	Any other *person*
All other *rules* in ICOBS	Yes	No	No	

SCHEDULE 6
RULES THAT CAN BE WAIVED

[2125]
Sch 6.1 **[G]** As a result of regulation 10 of the Regulatory Reform (Financial Services and Markets

Act 2000) Order 2007 (SI 2007/1973) the *FSA* has power to waive all its *rules*. However, if the *rules* incorporate requirements laid down in European directives, it will not be possible for the *FSA* to grant a waiver that would be incompatible with the *United Kingdom's* responsibilities under those directives.

CLIENT ASSETS (CASS)

NOTES
Up to date as at 22 February 2010. For later amendments please see www.fsa.gov.uk.

CONTENTS

CASS 1—Application and general provisions . . . [2126]
CASS 3—Collateral . . . [2128]
CASS 5—Client money and mandates: insurance mediation activity . . . [2130]
CASS 6—Custody: MiFID business . . . [2131]
CASS 7—Client money rules . . . [2132]
CASS 7A—Client money distribution . . . [2132A]
CASS 8—Mandates . . . [2133]
CASS TP 1—CASS Transitional provisions . . . [2134]
CASS Sch 1—Record keeping requirements . . . [2135]
CASS Sch2—Notification requirements . . . [2136]
CASS Sch 3—Fees and other required payments . . . [2137]
CASS Sch 4—Powers exercised . . . [2138]
CASS Sch 5—Rights of actions for damages . . . [2139]
CASS Sch 6—Rules that can be waived . . . [2140]

CHAPTER 1
APPLICATION AND GENERAL PROVISIONS

1.1 Application and purpose

Application

[2126]–[2127]
1.1.1 **[G]** *CASS* applies to a *firm* as specified in the remainder of this chapter.

Purpose

1.1.2 **[G]** The purpose of this chapter is to set out to whom, for what activities, and within what territorial limits the *rules*, *evidential provisions* and *guidance* in *CASS* apply.

1.2 General application: who? what?

General application: who?

1.2.1 **[G]** The *rules* in CASS 1.2 set out the maximum scope of this sourcebook. The application of *CASS* is modified for certain activities by CASS 1.4. Also particular chapters or sections of *CASS* may have provisions which limit their application.

1.2.2 **[R]** *CASS* applies to every *firm*, except as provided for in CASS 1.2.3R, with respect to the carrying on of:
(1) all *regulated activities* except to the extent that a provision of *CASS* provides for a narrower application; and
(2) *unregulated activities* to the extent specified in any provision of *CASS*.

1.2.3 **[R]** *CASS* does not apply to:
(1) an *ICVC*; or
(2) an *incoming EEA firm* other than an *insurer*, with respect to its *passported activities*; or
(3) a *UCITS qualifier*.

1.2.4 **[R]** With the exception of this chapter and the *insurance client money chapter*, *CASS* does not apply to:
(1) an *authorised professional firm* with respect to its *non-mainstream regulated activities*; or
(2) the *Society*.

1.2.5 **[R]** The *insurance client money chapter* does not apply to an *authorised professional firm* with respect to its *non-mainstream regulated activities*, which are *insurance mediation activities*, if:
(1) the *firm's designated professional body* has made rules which implement article 4 of the *IMD*;
(2) those rules have been approved by the *FSA* under section 332(5) of the *Act*; and
(3) the *firm* is subject to the rules in the form in which they were approved.

1.2.6 **[G]** [deleted]

General application: what?

1.2.7 **[G]**

(1) The approach in *CASS* is to ensure that the *rules* in a chapter are applied to *firms* in respect of particular *regulated activities* or *unregulated activities*.

(2) The scope of the *regulated activities* to which *CASS* applies is determined by the description of the activity as it is set out in the *Regulated Activities Order*. Accordingly, a *firm* will not generally be subject to *CASS* in relation to any aspect of its business activities which fall within an exclusion found in the *Regulated Activities Order*. The definition of *designated investment business* includes, however, activities within the exclusion from *dealing in investments as principal* in article 15 of the *Regulated Activities Order* (Absence of holding out etc).

(3) The *custody chapter* and the *client money chapter* apply in relation to *regulated activities*, conducted by *firms*, which fall within the definition of *MiFID business* and/or *designated investment business*.

(3A) The *collateral rules* apply in relation to *regulated activities*, conducted by *firms*, which fall within the definition of *designated investment business* (including *MiFID business*).

(4) The *insurance client money chapter* applies in relation to *regulated activities*, conducted by *firms*, which fall within the definition of *insurance mediation activities*.

(5) [deleted]

(6) The *mandate rules* apply in relation to *regulated activities*, conducted by *firms*, which fall within the definition of *designated investment business* (including *MiFID business*) and *insurance mediation activity*, except where it relates to a *reinsurance contract*.

Application for retail clients, professional clients and eligible counterparties

1.2.8 **[G]**

(1) *CASS* applies directly in respect of activities conducted with or for all categories of *clients*.

(2) [deleted]

(3) The *insurance client money chapter* does not generally distinguish between different categories of *client*. However, the term *consumer* is used for those to whom additional obligations are owed, rather than the term *retail client*. This is to be consistent with the *client* categories used in the Insurance: New Conduct of Business sourcebook.

(4) Each provision in the *custody chapter* and the *client money chapter* makes it clear whether it applies to activities carried on for *retail clients*, *professional clients* or both. There is no further modification of the *rules* in these chapters in relation to activities carried on for *eligible counterparties*. Such *clients* are treated in the same way as other *professional clients* for the purposes of these *rules*.

1.2.9 **[G]** [deleted]

Investments and money held under different regimes

1.2.10 **[R]** [deleted]

1.2.11 **[R]** Where a *firm* is subject to the *client money chapter* and the *insurance client money chapter*, it must ensure segregation between *money* held under each chapter, including that money held under different chapters is held, in different, separately designated, *client bank accounts* or *client transaction accounts*.

1.2.12 **[G]** The purpose of the *rules* regarding the segregation of investments and *money* held under different regimes is to reduce the risk of confusion between assets held under different regimes either on an on-going basis or on the *failure* of a *firm* or a third party holding those assets.

1.2.13 **[G]** A *firm* may opt to hold under a single chapter *money* that would otherwise be held under different chapters (see CASS 5.1.1R(3) and CASS 7.1.3R).

1.3 General application: where?

1.3.1 **[G]** The *rules* in CASS 1.3 set out the maximum territorial scope of this sourcebook. Particular *rules* may have express territorial limitations.

UK establishments: general

1.3.2 **[R]** Except as provided for in CASS 1.2.3R(2), *CASS* applies to every *firm*, in relation to *regulated activities* carried on by it from an *establishment* in the *United Kingdom*.

UK firms: passported activities from EEA branches

1.3.3 **[R]** *CASS* applies to every *UK firm*, other than an *insurer*, in relation to *passported activities* carried on by it from a *branch* in another *EEA State*.

1.3.4 **[R]** *CASS* does not apply to an *incoming ECA provider* acting as such.

1.4 Application: particular activities

Occupational pension scheme firms (OPS firms)

1.4.1 **[R]** In the case of *OPS activity* undertaken by an *OPS firm*, *CASS* applies with the following general modifications:

(1) references to *customer* are to the *OPS* or *welfare trust*, whichever fits the case, in respect of which the *OPS firm* is acting or intends to act, and with or for the benefit of which the relevant activity is to be carried on; and

(2) if an *OPS firm* is required by any *rule* in *CASS* to provide information to, or obtain consent from, a *customer*, that *firm* must ensure that the information is provided to, or consent obtained from, each of the trustees of the *OPS* or *welfare trust* in respect of which that *firm* is acting, unless the context requires otherwise.

Stock lending activity with or for clients

1.4.2 **[G]**

(1) The *custody chapter* and the *client money chapter* apply in respect of any *stock lending activity* that is undertaken with or for a *client* by a *firm*.

(2) The *collateral rules* apply, where relevant, in respect of *stock lending activity*.

Corporate finance business

1.4.3 **[G]**

(1) The *custody chapter* and the *client money chapter* apply in respect of *corporate finance business* that is undertaken by a *firm*.

(2) The *collateral rules* apply, where relevant, in respect of *corporate finance business*.

Oil market activity and energy market activity

1.4.4 **[G]**

(1) The *custody chapter* and the *client money chapter* apply in respect of *oil market activity* and other *energy market activity* that is undertaken by a *firm*.

(2) The *collateral rules* apply, where relevant, in respect of *energy market activity*.

Appointed representatives and tied agents

1.4.5 **[G]**

(1) Although *CASS* does not apply directly to a *firm's appointed representatives*, a *firm* will always be responsible for the acts and omissions of its *appointed representatives* in carrying on business for which the *firm* has accepted responsibility (section 39(3) of the *Act*). In determining whether a *firm* has complied with any provision of *CASS*, anything done or omitted by a *firm's appointed representative* (when acting as such) will be treated as having been done or omitted by the *firm* (section 39(4) of the *Act*). Equally, *CASS* does not apply directly to *tied agents*. A *MiFID investment firm* will be fully and unconditionally responsible for the acts and omission of the *tied agents* that it appoints.

(2) *Firms* should also refer to SUP 12 (Appointed representatives), which sets out requirements which apply to *firms* using *appointed representatives* and *tied agents*.

Depositaries

1.4.6 **[R]** The *client money chapter* does not apply to a *depositary* when acting as such.

1.4.7 **[R]** The remainder of *CASS* applies to a *depositary*, when acting as such, with the following general modifications:

(1) except in the *mandate rules*, '*client*' means '*trustee*', 'trust' or '*collective investment scheme*' as appropriate; and

(2) in the *mandate rules*, '*client*' means '*trustee*', '*collective investment scheme*' or '*collective investment scheme* instrument' as appropriate.

1.4.8 **[R]**

(1) Other than the *mandate rules*, *CASS* does not apply to a *trustee firm* which is not a *depositary*, or the trustee of a *personal pension scheme* or *stakeholder pension scheme*, unless *MiFID* applies to it, in which case the *custody chapter* and the *client money chapter* do apply.

(2) In the *custody chapter*, the *client money chapter* and the *mandate rules*, '*client*' means '*trustee*', 'trust', 'trust instrument' or 'beneficiary', as appropriate.

1.5 Application: electronic media and e-commerce

Application to electronic media

1.5.1 **[G]** GEN 2.2.14R (References to writing) has the effect that electronic media may be used to make communications that are required by the *Handbook* to be "in writing" unless a contrary intention appears.

1.5.2 **[G]** For any electronic communication with a *customer*, a *firm* should:

(1) have in place appropriate arrangements, including contingency plans, to ensure the secure transmission and receipt of the communication; it should also be able to verify the authenticity and integrity of the communication; the arrangements should be proportionate and take into account the different levels of risk in a *firm's* business;

(2) be able to demonstrate that the *customer* wishes to communicate using this form of media; and

(3) if entering into an agreement, make it clear to the *customer* that a contractual relationship is created that has legal consequences.

1.5.3 **[G]** *Firms* should note that GEN 2.2.14R does not affect any other legal requirement that may apply in relation to the form or manner of executing a *document* or agreement.

1.5.4 **[G]** [deleted]

CHAPTER 2

[deleted]

CHAPTER 3
COLLATERAL

3.1 Application and purpose

Application

[2128]–[2129]

3.1.1 **[R]** This chapter applies to a *firm* when it receives or holds assets in connection with an arrangement to secure the obligation of a *client* in the course of, or in connection with, its *designated investment business*, including *MiFID business*.

3.1.2 **[G]** *Firms* are reminded that, this chapter does not apply to an *incoming EEA firm*, other than an *insurer*, with respect to its *passported activities*. The application of this chapter is also dependent on the location from which the activity is undertaken (see CASS 1.3.2R and CASS 1.3.3R).

3.1.3 **[R]** This chapter does not apply to a *firm* that has only a bare security interest (without rights to hypothecate) in the *client's* asset. In such circumstances, the *firm* must comply with the *custody rules* or *client money rules* as appropriate.

3.1.4 **[G]** For the purpose of this chapter only, a bare security interest in the *client's* asset gives a *firm* the right to realise the assets only on a *client's* default and without the right to use other than in default.

Purpose

3.1.5 **[G]** The purpose of this chapter is to ensure that an appropriate level of protection is provided for those assets over which a *client* gives a *firm* certain rights. The arrangements covered by this chapter are those under which the *firm* is given a right to use the asset, and the *firm* treats the asset as if legal title and associated rights to that asset had been transferred to the *firm* subject only to an obligation to return equivalent assets to the *client* upon satisfaction of the *client's* obligation to the *firm*. The rights covered in this chapter do not include those arrangements by which the *firm* has only a bare security interest in the *client's* asset (in which case the *custody rules* or *client money rules* apply).

3.1.6 **[G]** Examples of the arrangements covered by this chapter include the taking of collateral by a *firm*, under the ISDA English Law (transfer of title) and the New York Law Credit Support Annexes (assuming the right to rehypothecate has not been disapplied).

3.1.7 **[G]** This chapter recognises the need to apply a differing level of regulatory protection to the assets which form the basis of the two different types of arrangement described in CASS 3.1.5G. Under the bare security interest arrangement, the asset continues to belong to the *client* until the *firm's* right to realise that asset crystallises (that is, on the *client's* default). But under a "right to use arrangement", the *client* has transferred to the *firm* the legal title and associated rights to the asset, so that when the *firm* exercises its right to treat the asset as its own, the asset ceases to belong to the *client* and in effect becomes the *firm's* asset and is no longer in need of the full range of *client* asset protection. The *firm* may exercise its right to treat the asset as its own by, for example, clearly so identifying the asset in its own books and records.

3.2 Requirements

Application

3.2.1 **[R]** [deleted]

Requirements

3.2.2 **[R]** A *firm* that receives or holds a *client's* assets under an arrangement to which this chapter applies and which exercises its right to treat the assets as its own must ensure that it maintains adequate records to enable it to meet any future obligations including the return of equivalent assets to the *client*.

3.2.3 **[G]** If the *firm* has the right to use the *client's* asset under a "right to use arrangement" but has not yet exercised its right to treat the asset as its own, the *client money rules* or the *custody rules* will continue to apply as appropriate until such time as the *firm* exercises its right, at which time CASS 3.2.2R will apply.

3.2.4 **[G]** When appropriate, *firms* that enter into the arrangements covered in this chapter with *retail clients* will be expected to identify in the statement of *custody assets* sent to the *client* in accordance with CASS 2.3.12R (Production and despatch of client statements) details of the assets which form the basis of the arrangements. Where the *firm* utilises global netting arrangements, a statement of the assets held on this basis will suffice.

CHAPTER 4

[deleted]

CHAPTER 5
CLIENT MONEY AND MANDATES: INSURANCE MEDIATION ACTIVITY

5.1 Application

[2130]
5.1.1 **[R]**

(1) CASS 5.1 to 5.6 apply, subject to (2), (3) and CASS 5.1.3R to 5.1.6R, to a *firm* that receives or holds *money* in the course of or in connection with its *insurance mediation activity*.

(2) CASS 5.1 to 5.6 do not, subject to (3), apply:
   - (a) to a *firm* to the extent that it acts in accordance with the *non-directive client money chapter* or *the MiFID client money chapter*; or
   - (b) to a *firm* in carrying on an *insurance mediation activity* which is in respect of a *reinsurance contract*; or
   - (c) to an *insurance undertaking* in respect of its *permitted activities*; or
   - (d) to a *managing agent* when acting as such; or
   - (e) with respect to *money* held by a *firm* which:
     - (i) is an *approved bank*; and
     - (ii) has requisite capital under article 4(4)(b) of the *IMD*;

     but only when held by the *firm* in an account with itself, in which case the *firm* must notify the *client* (whether through a *client* agreement, *terms of business*, or otherwise in writing) that:
     - (iii) *money* held for that *client* in an account with the *approved bank* will be held by the *firm* as banker and not as trustee (or in Scotland as agent); and
     - (iv) as a result, the *money* will not be held in accordance with CASS 5.1 to CASS 5.6.

(3) A *firm* may elect to comply with:
   - (a) CASS 5.1 to CASS 5.6 in respect of *client money* which it receives in the course of carrying on *insurance mediation activity* in respect of *reinsurance contracts*; and
   - (b) CASS 5.1, CASS 5.2 and CASS 5.4 to CASS 5.6 in respect of *money* which it receives in the course of carrying on an activity which would be *insurance mediation activity*, and which *money* would be *client money*, but for article 72D of the *Regulated Activities Order* (Large risks contracts where risk situated outside the EEA);
   - (c) but the election must be in respect of all the *firm's* business which consists of that activity.

(4) A *firm* must keep a record of any election in (3).

5.1.2 **[G]** A *firm* that is an *approved bank*, and relies on the exemption under CASS 5.1.1 R(2)(e), should be able to account to all of its *clients* for amounts held on their behalf at all times. A bank account opened with the *firm* that is in the name of the *client* would generally be sufficient. When

Part II FSA Handbook Materials

money from *clients* deposited with the *firm* is held in a pooled account, this account should be clearly identified as an account for *clients*. The *firm* should also be able to demonstrate that an amount owed to a specific *client* that is held within the pool can be reconciled with a record showing that individual's *client* balance and is, therefore, identifiable at any time.

5.1.3 **[R]** An *authorised professional firm* regulated by The Law Society (of England and Wales), The Law Society of Scotland or The Law Society of Northern Ireland must comply with the rules of its *designated professional body* as specified in CASS 5.1.4R, in force on 14 January 2005, and if it does so, it will be deemed to comply with CASS 5.2 to 5.6.

5.1.4 **[R]** For the purposes of CASS 5.1.3R the relevant rules are:

(1) If regulated by the Law Society (of England and Wales);
  (a) the Solicitors' Accounts Rules 1998; or
  (b) where applicable, the Solicitors Overseas Practice Rules 1990;

(2) if regulated by the Law Society of Scotland, the Solicitors' (Scotland) Accounts, Accounts Certificate, Professional Practice and Guarantee Fund Rules 2001;

(3) if regulated by the Law Society of Northern Ireland, the Solicitors' Accounts Regulations 1998.

5.1.4A **[R]**

(1) A *firm* will, subject to (3), be deemed to comply with CASS 5.3 to CASS 5.6 if it receives or holds *client money* and it either:
  (a) in relation to a service charge, complies with the requirement to segregate such money in accordance with section 42 of the Landlord and Tenant Act 1987 ("the 1987 Act"); or
  (b) in relation to money which is clients' money for the purpose of the Royal Institution of Chartered Surveyors' Rules of Conduct ("RICS rules") in force as at 14 January 2005, it complies with the requirement to segregate and account for such money in accordance with the RICS Members' Accounts rules.

(2) Paragraph (1)(a) also applies to a *firm* in Scotland or in Northern Ireland if in acting as a property manager the *firm* receives or holds a service charge and complies (so far is practicable) with section 42 of the 1987 Act as if the requirements of that provision applied to it.

(3) In addition to complying with (1), a *firm* must ensure that an account in which *money* held pursuant to the trust fund mentioned in section 42(3) of the 1987 Act or an account maintained in accordance with the RICS rules satisfies the requirements in CASS 5.5.49R to the extent that the *firm* will hold money as trustee or otherwise on behalf of its clients.

5.1.5 **[R]** Subject to CASS 5.1.5AR *money* is not *client money* when:

(1) it becomes properly due and payable to the *firm*:
  (a) for its own account; or
  (b) in its capacity as agent of an *insurance undertaking* where the *firm* acts in accordance with CASS 5.2; or

(2) it is otherwise received by the *firm* pursuant to an arrangement made between an *insurance undertaking* and another *person* (other than a *firm*) by which that other *person* has authority to underwrite risks, settle claims or handle refunds of *premiums* on behalf of that *insurance undertaking* outside the *United Kingdom* and where the *money* relates to that business.

5.1.5 A **[R]** CASS 5.1.5R(1)(b) and (2) do not apply, and hence *money* is *client money*, in any case where:

(1) in relation to an activity specified in CASS 5.2.3R(1)(a) to (c), the *insurance undertaking* has agreed that the *firm* may treat *money* which it receives and holds as agent of the *undertaking*, as *client money* and in accordance with the provisions of CASS 5.3 to 5.6; and

(2) the agreement in (1) is in writing and adequate to show that the *insurance undertaking* consents to its interests under the trusts (or in Scotland agency) in CASS 5.3.2R or CASS 5.4.7R being subordinated to the interests of the *firm's* other *clients*.

5.1.6 **[R]** Except where a firm and an insurance undertaking have (in accordance with CASS 5.1.5AR) agreed otherwise, for the purposes of CASS 5.1 to 5.6 an *insurance undertaking* (when acting as such) with whom a *firm* conducts *insurance mediation activity* is not to be treated as a *client* of the *firm*.

Purpose

5.1.7 **[G]**

(1) *Principle* 10 (Clients' assets) requires a *firm* to arrange adequate protection for *clients'* assets when the *firm* is responsible for them. An essential part of that protection is the proper accounting and handling of *client money*. The *rules* in CASS 5.1 to 5.6 also give effect to the requirement in article 4.4 of the *IMD* that all necessary measures should be taken to protect *clients* against the inability of an *insurance intermediary* to transfer *premiums* to an *insurance undertaking* or to transfer the proceeds of a claim or *premium* refund to the insured.

(2) There are two particular approaches which *firms* can adopt which reflect options given in article 4.4. The first is to provide by law or contract for a transfer of risk from the *insurance intermediary* to the *insurance undertaking* (CASS 5.2). The second is that *clients' money* is strictly segregated by being transferred to *client accounts* that cannot be used to reimburse other creditors in the event of the *firm's* insolvency (CASS 5.3 and 5.4 provide different means of achieving such segregation). CASS 5.1.5AR permits a *firm* subject to certain conditions to treat *money* which it collects as agent of an *insurance undertaking* as *client money*; the principle of strict segregation is, however, satisfied because such *undertakings* must agree to their interests being subordinated to the interests of the *firm's* other *clients*.

5.1.8 **[G]** *Firms* which carry on *designated investment business* which may, for example, involve them handling *client money* in respect of life assurance business should refer to the *non-directive client money chapter* which includes provisions enabling *firms* to elect to comply solely with that chapter or with the *insurance client money chapter* in respect of that business. *Firms* that also carry on *MiFID or equivalent third country business* may elect to comply solely with the *MiFID client money chapter* with respect of *client money* in respect of which the *non-directive client money chapter* or the *insurance client money chapter* apply.

5.1.9 **[G]** *Firms* are reminded that SUP 3 contains provisions which are relevant to the preparation and delivery of reports by auditors.

5.2 Holding money as agent of insurance undertaking

Introduction

5.2.1 **[G]** If a *firm* holds *money* as agent of an *insurance undertaking* then the *firm's clients* (who are not *insurance undertakings*) will be adequately protected to the extent that the *premiums* which it receives are treated as being received by the *insurance undertaking* when they are received by the agent and claims *money* and *premium* refunds will only be treated as received by the *client* when they are actually paid over. The *rules* in CASS 5.2 make provision for agency agreements between *firms* and *insurance undertakings* to contain terms which make clear when *money* should be held by a *firm* as agent of an undertaking. *Firms* should refer to CASS 5.1.5R to determine the circumstances in which they may treat *money* held on behalf of *insurance undertakings* as *client money*.

5.2.2 **[G]**

(1) Agency agreements between *insurance intermediaries* and *insurance undertakings* may be of a general kind and facilitate the introduction of business to the *insurance undertaking*. Alternatively, an agency agreement may confer on the *intermediary* contractual authority to commit the *insurance undertaking* to risk or authority to settle claims or handle *premium* refunds (often referred to as "binding authorities"). CASS 5.2.3R requires that binding authorities of this kind must provide that the *intermediary* is to act as the agent of the *insurance undertaking* for the purpose of receiving and holding *premiums* (if the *intermediary* has authority to commit the *insurance undertaking* to risk), claims *monies* (if the *intermediary* has authority to settle claims on behalf of the *insurance undertaking*) and *premium* refunds (if the *intermediary* has authority to make refunds of *premiums* on behalf of the *insurance undertaking*). Accordingly such *money* is not, except here a *firm* and an *insurance undertaking* have in compliance with CASS 5.1.5AR agreed otherwise, *client money* for the purpose of CASS 5.

(2) Other introductory agency agreements may also, depending on their precise terms, satisfy some or all of the requirements of the type of written agreement described in CASS 5.2.3R. It is desirable that an *intermediary* should, before informing its *clients* (in accordance with CASS 5.2.3R(3)) that it will receive *money* as agent of an *insurance undertaking*, agree the terms of that notification with the relevant *insurance undertakings*.

Requirement for written agreement before acting as agent of insurance undertaking

5.2.3 **[R]**

(1) A *firm* must not agree to:

(a) *deal in investments as agent* for an *insurance undertaking* in connection with *insurance mediation activity*; or

(b) act as agent for an *insurance undertaking* for the purpose of settling claims or handling *premium* refunds; or

(c) otherwise receive *money* as agent of an *insurance undertaking*;

unless:

(d) it has entered into a written agreement with the *insurance undertaking* to that effect; and

(e) it is satisfied on reasonable grounds that the terms of the policies issued by the *insurance undertaking* to the *firm's clients* are likely to be compatible with such an agreement; and

(f)

Part II FSA Handbook Materials

(i) (in the case of (a)) the agreement required by (d) expressly provides for the *firm* to act as agent of the *insurance undertaking* for the purpose of receiving *premiums* from the *firm's clients*; and

(ii) (in the case of (b)) the agreement required by (d) expressly provides for the *firm* to act as agent of the *insurance undertaking* for the purpose of receiving and holding claims *money* (or, as the case may be, *premium* refunds) prior to transmission to the client making the *claim* (or, as the case may be, entitled to the *premium refund*) in question.

(2) A *firm* must retain a copy of any agreement it enters pursuant to (1) for a period of at least six years from the date on which it is terminated.

(3) Where a *firm* holds, or is to hold, *money* as agent for an *insurance undertaking* it must ensure that it informs those of its *clients* which are not *insurance undertakings* and whose transactions may be affected by the arrangement (whether in its *terms of business, client agreements* or otherwise in writing) that it will hold their *money* as agent of the *insurance undertaking* and if necessary the extent of such agency and whether it includes all items of *client money* or is restricted, for example, to the receipt of *premiums*.

(4) A *firm* may (subject to the consent of the *insurance undertaking* concerned) include in an agreement in (1) provision for *client money* received by its *appointed representative, field representatives* and other agents to be held as agent for the *insurance undertaking* (in which event it must ensure that the *representative* or agent provides the information to *clients* required by (3)).

5.2.4 **[G]** *Firms* are reminded that CASS 5.1.5AR provides that, if the *insurance undertaking* has agreed in writing, *money* held in accordance with an agreement made under CASS 5.2.3R may be treated as *client money* and may (but not otherwise) be kept in a *client bank account.*

5.2.5 **[G]** A *firm* which provides for the protection of a *client* (which is not an *insurance undertaking*) under CASS 5.2 is relieved of the obligation to provide protection for that *client* under CASS 5.3 or CASS 5.4 to the extent of the items of *client money* protected by the agency agreement.

5.2.6 **[G]** A *firm* may, in accordance with CASS 5.2.3R (4), arrange for an *insurance undertaking* to accept responsibility for the *money* held by its *appointed representatives, field representatives,* and other agents, in which event CASS 5.5.18R to CASS 5.5.25G will not apply.

5.2.7 **[G]** A *firm* may operate on the basis of an agency agreement as provided for by CASS 5.2.3R for some of its *clients* and with protection provided by a *client money* trust in accordance with CASS 5.3 or 5.4 for other *clients.* A *firm* may also operate on either basis for the same *client* but in relation to different transactions. A *firm* which does so should be satisfied that its administrative systems and controls are adequate and, in accordance with CASS 5.2.4G, should ensure that *money* held for both types of *client* and business is kept separate.

5.3 Statutory trust

5.3.1 **[G]** Section 139(1) of the *Act* (Miscellaneous ancillary matters) provides that *rules* may make provision which result in *client money* being held by a *firm* on trust (England and Wales and Northern Ireland) or as agent (Scotland only). CASS 5.3.2R creates a fiduciary relationship between the *firm* and its *client* under which *client money* is in the legal ownership of the *firm* but remains in the beneficial ownership of the *client.* In the event of failure of the *firm*, costs relating to the distribution of *client money* may have to be borne by the trust.

5.3.2 **[R]** A *firm* (other than a *firm* acting in accordance with CASS 5.4) receives and holds *client money* as trustee (or in Scotland as agent) on the following terms:

(1) for the purposes of and on the terms of CASS 5.3, CASS 5.5 and the *client money (insurance) distribution rules*;

(2) subject to (4), for the *clients* (other than *clients* which are *insurance undertakings* when acting as such) for whom that *money* is held, according to their respective interests in it;

(3) after all valid claims in (2) have been met, for *clients* which are *insurance undertakings* according to their respective interests in it;

(4) on the *failure* of the *firm*, for the payment of the costs properly attributable to the distribution of the *client money* in accordance with (2) and (3); and

(5) after all valid claims and costs under (2) to (4) have been met, for the *firm* itself.

5.3.3 **[G]**

(1) A *firm* which holds *client money* can discharge its obligation to ensure adequate protection for its *clients* in respect of such *money* by complying with CASS 5.3 which provides for such *money* to be held by the *firm* on the terms of a trust imposed by the *rules.*

(2) The trust imposed by CASS 5.3 is limited to a trust in respect of *client money* which a *firm* receives and holds. The consequential and supplementary requirements in CASS 5.5 are designed to secure the proper segregation and maintenance of adequate *client money* balances. In particular, CASS 5.5 does not permit a *firm* to use *client money* balances to provide credit for *clients* (or potential *clients*) such that, for example, their *premium* obligations may be met in advance of the *premium* being remitted to the *firm.* A *firm* wishing to provide credit for *clients* may however do so out of its own funds.

5.4 Non-statutory client money trust

Introduction

5.4.1 **[G]**

(1) CASS 5.4 permits a *firm*, which has adequate resources, systems and controls, to declare a trust on terms which expressly authorise it, in its capacity as trustee, to make advances of credit to the *firm's clients*. The *client money* trust required by CASS 5.4 extends to such debt obligations which will arise if the *firm*, as trustee, makes credit advances, to enable a client's *premium* obligations to be met before the *premium* is remitted to the *firm* and similarly if it allows claims and *premium* refunds to be paid to the *client* before receiving remittance of those *monies* from the *insurance undertaking*.

(2) CASS 5.4 does not permit a *firm* to make advances of credit to itself out of the *client money* trust. Accordingly, CASS 5.4 does not permit a *firm* to withdraw *commission* from the *client money* trust before it has received the *premium* from the *client* in relation to the *non-investment insurance contract* which generated the *commission*.

Voluntary nature of this section

5.4.2 **[R]** A *firm* may elect to comply with the requirements in this section, and may do so for some of its business whilst complying with CASS 5.3 for other parts.

5.4.3 **[R]** A *firm* is not subject to CASS 5.3 when and to the extent that it acts in accordance with this section.

Conditions for using the non-statutory client money trust

5.4.4 **[R]** A *firm* may not handle *client money* in accordance with the *rules* in this section unless each of the following conditions is satisfied:

(1) the *firm* must have and maintain systems and controls which are adequate to ensure that the *firm* is able to monitor and manage its *client money* transactions and any credit risk arising from the operation of the trust arrangement and, if in accordance with CASS 5.4.2R a *firm* complies with both the *rules* in CASS 5.3 and CASS 5.4, such systems and controls must extend to both arrangements;

(2) the *firm* must obtain, and keep current, written confirmation from its auditor that it has in place systems and controls which are adequate to meet the requirements in (1);

(3) the *firm* must designate a *manager* with responsibility for overseeing the *firm's* day to day compliance with the systems and controls in (1) and the *rules* in this section;

(4) the *firm* (if, under the terms of the non-statutory trust, it is to handle *client money* for *retail customers*) must have and at all times maintain capital resources of not less than £50,000 calculated in accordance with MIPRU 4.4.1R; and

(5) in relation to each of the *clients* for whom the *firm* holds *money* in accordance with CASS 5.4, the *firm* must take reasonable steps to ensure that its *terms of business* or other *client agreements* adequately explain, and obtain the *client's* informed consent to, the *firm* holding the *client's money* in accordance with CASS 5.4 (and in the case of a *client* which is an *insurance undertaking* (when acting as such) there must be an agreement which satisfies CASS 5.1.5AR).

5.4.5 **[G]** The amount of a *firm's* capital resources maintained for the purposes of MIPRU 4.2.11R will also satisfy (in whole or in part) the requirement in CASS 5.4.4R (4).

Client money to be received under the non-statutory client money trust

5.4.6 **[R]** Except to the extent that a *firm* acts in accordance with CASS 5.3, a *firm* must not receive or hold any *client money* unless it does so as trustee (or, in Scotland, as agent) and has properly executed a deed (or equivalent formal document) to that effect.

Contents of trust deed

5.4.7 **[R]** The deed referred to in CASS 5.4.6R must provide that the *money* (and, if appropriate, *designated investments*) are held:

(1) for the purposes of and on the terms of:
   (a) CASS 5.4;
   (b) the applicable provisions of CASS 5.5; and
   (c) the *client money (insurance) distribution rules*.

(2) subject to (4), for the *clients* (other than *clients* which are *insurance undertakings* when acting as such) for whom that *money* is held, according to their respective interests in it;

(3) after all valid claims in (2) have been met for *clients* which are *insurance undertakings* according to their respective interests in it;

(4) on *failure* of the *firm*, for the payment of the costs properly attributable to the distribution of the *client money* in accordance with (2) and (3); and

Part II FSA Handbook Materials

(5) after all valid claims and costs under (2) to (4) have been met, for the *firm* itself.

5.4.8 **[R]** The deed (or equivalent formal document) referred to in CASS 5.4.6R may provide that:
(1) the *firm*, acting as trustee (or, in Scotland, as agent), has power to make advances or give credit to *clients* or *insurance undertakings* from *client money*, provided that it also provides that any debt or other obligation of a *client* or resulting obligation of an *insurance undertaking*, in relation to an advance or credit, is held on the same terms as CASS 5.4.7R;
(2) the benefit of a letter of credit or unconditional guarantee provided by an *approved bank* on behalf of a *firm* to satisfy any shortfall in the *firm's client money* resource (as calculated under CASS 5.5.65R) when compared with the *firm's client money* requirement (as calculated under CASS 5.6.66R or as appropriate CASS 5.5.68R), is held on the same terms as CASS 5.4.7R.

5.5 Segregation and the operation of client money accounts

Application

5.5.1 **[R]** Unless otherwise stated each of the provisions in CASS 5.5 applies to *firms* which are acting in accordance with CASS 5.3 (Statutory trust) or 5.4 (Nonstatutory trust).

5.5.2 **[G]** One purpose of CASS 5.5 is to ensure that, unless otherwise permitted, *client money* is kept separate from the *firm's* own *money*. Segregation, in the event of a *firm's* failure, is important for the effective operation of the trust that is created to protect *client money*. The aim is to clarify the difference between *client money* and general creditors' entitlements in the event of the *failure* of the *firm*.

Requirement to segregate

5.5.3 **[R]** A *firm* must, except to the extent permitted by CASS 5.5, hold *client money* separate from the *firm's money*.

Money due to a client from a firm

5.5.4 **[R]** If a *firm* is liable to pay *money* to a *client*, it must as soon as possible, and no later than one *business day* after the *money* is due and payable:
(1) pay it into a *client bank account*, in accordance with CASS 5.5.5R; or
(2) pay it to, or to the order of, the *client*.

Segregation

5.5.5 **[R]** A *firm* must segregate *client money* by either:
(1) paying it as soon as is practicable into a *client bank account*; or
(2) paying it out in accordance with CASS 5.5.80R.

5.5.6 **[G]** The *FSA* expects that in most circumstances it will be practicable for a *firm* to pay *client money* into a *client bank account* by not later than the next *business day* after receipt.

5.5.7 **[G]** Where an insurance transaction involves more than one *firm* acting in a chain such that for example *money* is transferred from a "producing" broker who has received *client money* from a *consumer* to an intermediate broker and thereafter to an *insurance undertaking*, each broker *firm* will owe obligations to its immediate *client* to segregate *client money* which it receives (in this example the producing broker in relation to the *consumer* and the intermediate broker in relation to the producing broker). A *firm* which allows a third party broker to hold or control *client money* will not thereby be relieved of its fiduciary obligations (see CASS 5.5.34R).

5.5.8 **[R]** A *firm* may segregate *client money* in a different currency from that of receipt. If it does so, the *firm* must ensure that the amount held is adjusted at intervals of not more than twenty five *business days* to an amount at least equal to the original currency amount (or the currency in which the *firm* has its liability to its *clients*, if different), translated at the previous day's closing spot exchange rate.

5.5.9 **[R]** A *firm* must not hold *money* other than *client money* in a *client bank account* unless it is:
(1) a minimum sum required to open the account, or to keep it open; or
(2) *money* temporarily in the account in accordance with CASS 5.5.16R (Withdrawal of commission and mixed remittance); or
(3) interest credited to the account which exceeds the amount due to *clients* as interest and has not yet been withdrawn by the *firm*.

5.5.10 **[R]** If it is prudent to do so to ensure that *client money* is protected (and provided that doing so would otherwise be in accordance with CASS 5.5.63R(1)(b)(ii)), a *firm* may pay into, or maintain in, a *client bank account money* of its own, and that *money* will then become *client money* for the purposes of CASS 5 and the *client money (insurance) distribution rules*.

5.5.11 **[R]** A *firm*, when acting in accordance with CASS 5.3 (statutory trust), must ensure that the total amount of *client money* held for each *client* in any of the *firm's client money bank accounts* is positive and that no payment is made from any such account for the benefit of a *client* unless the *client* has provided the *firm* with cleared funds to enable the payment to be made.

5.5.11A **[G]** When a *firm* acts in accordance with CASS 5.3 (Statutory trust) it should not make a payment from the *client bank account* unless it is satisfied on reasonable grounds that the *client* has provided it with cleared funds. Accordingly, a *firm* should normally allow a reasonable period of time for cheques to clear. If a withdrawal is made and the *client's* cheque is subsequently dishonoured it will be the *firm's* responsibility to make good the *shortfall* in the account as quickly as possible (and without delay whilst a cheque is re-presented).

5.5.12 **[R]** If *client money* is received by the *firm* in the form of an automated transfer, the *firm* must take reasonable steps to ensure that:
(1) the *money* is received directly into a *client bank account*; and
(2) if *money* is received directly into the *firm's* own account, the *money* is transferred into a *client bank account* no later than the next *business day* after receipt.

5.5.13 **[G]** A *firm* can hold *client money* in either a *general client bank account* (CASS 5.5.38R) or a *designated client bank account* (CASS 5.5.39R). A *firm* holds all *client money* in *general client bank accounts* for its *clients* as part of a common pool of *money* so those particular *clients* do not have a claim against a specific sum in a specific account; they only have a claim to the *client money* in general. A *firm* holds *client money* in *designated client bank accounts* for those *clients* who requested that their *client money* be part of a specific pool of *money*, so those particular *clients* do have a claim against a specific sum in a specific account; they do not have a claim to the *client money* in general unless a *primary pooling event* occurs. If the *firm* becomes insolvent, and there is (for whatever reason) a *shortfall* in *money* held for a *client* compared with that *client's* entitlements, the available funds will be distributed in accordance with the *client money (insurance) distribution rules*.

Part II FSA Handbook Materials

Non-statutory trust-segregation of designated investments

5.5.14 **[R]**
(1) A *firm* which handles *client money* in accordance with the *rules* for a non-statutory trust in CASS 5.4 may, to the extent it considers appropriate, but subject to (2), satisfy the requirement to segregate *client money* by segregating or arranging for the segregation of *designated investments* with a value at least equivalent to such *money* as would otherwise have been segregated into a *client bank account*.
(2) A *firm* may not segregate *designated investments* unless it:
   (a) takes reasonable steps to ensure that any *consumers* whose *client money* interests may be protected by such segregation are aware that the *firm* may operate such an arrangement and have (whether through its *terms of business, client agreements* or otherwise in writing) an adequate opportunity to give their informed consent;
   (b) ensures that the terms on which it will segregate *designated investments* include provision for it to take responsibility for meeting any *shortfall* in its *client money* resource which is attributable to falls in the market value of a segregated *investment*;
   (c) provides in the deed referred to in CASS 5.4.6R for *designated investments* which it segregates to be held by it on the terms of the non-statutory trust; and
   (d) takes reasonable steps to ensure that the segregation is at all times in conformity with the range of permitted *investments*, general principles and conditions in CASS 5, Annex 1R.

5.5.15 **[G]** A *firm* which takes advantage of CASS 5.5.14R will need to consider whether its *permission* should include the *permitted activity* of *managing investments*. If the *firm* is granted a power to manage with discretion the funds over which it is appointed as trustee under the trust deed required by CASS 5.4 then it will be likely to need a *permission* to *manage investments*. It is unlikely to need such a permission however if it is merely granted a power to invest but the deed stipulates that the funds may only be managed with discretion by another *firm* (which has the necessary *permission*). Such an arrangement would not preclude the *firm* holding *client money* as trustee from appointing another *firm* (or *firms*) as manager and setting an appropriate strategy and overall asset allocation, subject to the limits set out in CASS 5, Annex 1R. A *firm* may also need to consider whether it needs a *permission* to operate a *collective investment scheme* if any of its *clients* are to participate in the income or gains arising from the acquisition or disposal of *designated investments*.

Withdrawal of commission and mixed remittance

5.5.16 **[R]**
(1) A *firm* may draw down *commission* from the *client bank account* if:
   (a) it has received the *premium* from the *client* (or from a third party *premium* finance provider on the *client's* behalf); and
   (b) this is consistent with the *firm's terms of business* which it maintains with the relevant *client* and the *insurance undertaking* to whom the *premium* will become payable;
   (c) and the *firm* may draw down *commission* before payment of the *premium* to the *insurance undertaking*, provided that the conditions in (a) and (b) are satisfied.

(2) If a *firm* receives a *mixed remittance* (that is part *client money* and part other *money*), it must:
 (a) pay the full sum into a *client bank account* in accordance with CASS 5.5.5R; and
 (b) pay the *money* that is not *client money* out of the *client bank account* as soon as reasonably practicable and in any event by not later than twenty-five *business days* after the day on which the remittance is cleared (or, if earlier, when the *firm* performs the *client money* calculation in accordance with CASS 5.5.63R(1)).

5.5.17 **[G]**
(1) As soon as *commission* becomes due to the *firm* (in accordance with CASS 5.5.16R(1)) it must be treated as a remittance which must be withdrawn in accordance with *CASS* 5.5.16R (2). The procedure required by CASS 5.5.16R will also apply where *money* is due and payable to the *firm* in respect of *fees* due from *clients* (whether to the *firm* or other professionals).
(2) *Firms* are reminded that *money* received in accordance with CASS 5.2 must not, except where a *firm* and an *insurance undertaking* have (in accordance with CASS 5.1.5AR) agreed otherwise, be kept in a *client bank account. Client money* received from a third party *premium* finance provider should however be segregated into a *client bank account*.
(3) Where a *client* makes payments of *premium* to a *firm* in instalments, CASS 5.5.16R(1) applies in relation to each instalment.
(4) If a *firm* is unable to match a remittance with a transaction it may be unable to immediately determine whether the payment comprises a *mixed remittance* or is *client money*. In such cases the remittance should be treated as *client money* while the *firm* takes steps to match the remittance to a transaction as soon as possible.

Appointed representatives, field representatives and other agents

5.5.18 **[R]**
(1) Subject to (4), a *firm* must in relation to each of its *appointed representatives, field representatives* and other agents comply with CASS 5.5.19R to CASS 5.5.21R (Immediate segregation) or with CASS 5.5.23R (Periodic segregation and reconciliation).
(2) A *firm* must in relation to each *representative* or other agent keep a record of whether it is complying with CASS 5.5.19R to CASS 5.5.21R or with CASS 5.5.23R.
(3) A *firm* is, but without affecting the application of CASS 5.5.19R to CASS 5.5.23R, to be treated as the recipient of client money which is received by any of its appointed representatives, field representatives or other agents.
(4) (1) to (3) do not apply in relation to an *appointed representative*, *field representative* or other agent to which (if it were a *firm*) CASS 5.1.4AR(1) or (2) would apply, but subject to the *representative* or agent maintaining an account which satisfies the requirements of CASS 5.5.49R to the extent that the *representative* or agent will hold *client money* on trust or otherwise on behalf of its clients.

Immediate segregation

5.5.19 **[R]** A *firm* must establish and maintain procedures to ensure that *client money* received by its *appointed representatives*, *field representatives* or other agents of the *firm* is:
(1) paid into a *client bank account* of the *firm* in accordance with CASS 5.5.5R; or
(2) forwarded to the *firm*, or in the case of a *field representative* forwarded to a specified business address of the *firm*, so as to ensure that the *money* arrives at the specified business address by the close of the third *business day*.

5.5.20 **[G]** For the purposes of CASS 5.5.19R, the *client money* received on *business day* one should be forwarded to the *firm* or specified business address of the *firm* no later than the next *business day* after receipt (*business day* two) in order for it to reach that *firm* or specified business address by the close of the third *business day*. Procedures requiring the *client money* to be sent to the *firm* or the specified business address of the *firm* by first class post no later than the next *business day* after receipt would meet the requirements of CASS 5.5.19R.

5.5.21 **[R]** If *client money* is received in accordance with CASS 5.5.19R, the *firm* must ensure that its *appointed representatives*, *field representatives* or other agents keep *client money* (whether in the form of *premiums*, claims *money* or *premium* refunds) separately identifiable from any other *money* (including that of the *firm*) until the *client money* is paid into a *client bank account* or sent to the *firm*.

5.5.22 *[G] A firm which acts in accordance with* CASS 5.5.19R to CASS 5.5.21R need not comply with CASS 5.5.23R.

Periodic segregation and reconciliation

5.5.23 **[R]**

(1) A *firm* must, on a regular basis, and at reasonable intervals, ensure that it holds in its *client bank account* an amount which (in addition to any other amount which it is required by these *rules* to hold) is not less than the amount which it reasonably estimates to be the aggregate of the amounts held at any time by its *appointed representatives, field representatives* and other agents.
(2) A *firm* must, not later than ten *business days* following the expiry of each period in (1):
 (a) carry out, in relation to each such *representative* or agent, a reconciliation of the amount paid by the *firm* into its *client bank account* with the amount of *client money* actually received and held by the *representative* or other agent; and
 (b) make a corresponding payment into, or withdrawal from, the account.

5.5.24 **[G]**
(1) CASS 5.5.23R allows a *firm* with *appointed representatives, field representatives* and other agents to avoid the need for the *representative* to forward *client money* on a daily basis but instead requires a *firm* to segregate into its *client money bank account* amounts which it reasonably estimates to be sufficient to cover the amount of *client money* which the *firm* expects its *representatives* or agents to receive and hold over a given period. At the expiry of each such period, the *firm* must obtain information about the actual amount of *client money* received and held by its *representatives* so that it can reconcile the amount of *client money* it has segregated with the amounts actually received and held by its *representatives* and agents. The frequency at which this reconciliation is to be performed is not prescribed but it must be at regular and reasonable intervals having regard to the nature and frequency of the *insurance business* carried on by its *representatives* and agents. For example a period of six *months* might be appropriate for a *representative* which conducts business involving the receipt of *premiums* only infrequently whilst for other *representatives* a periodic reconciliation at *monthly* intervals (or less) may be appropriate.
(2) Where a *firm* operates on the basis of CASS 5.5.23R, the *money* which is segregated into its *client bank account* is *client money* and will be available to meet any obligations owed to the *clients* of its *representatives* who for this purpose are treated as the *firm's clients*.

5.5.25 **[G]** A *firm* which acts in accordance with CASS 5.5.23R need not comply with CASS 5.5.19R to CASS 5.5.21R.

Client entitlements

5.5.26 **[R]** A *firm* must take reasonable steps to ensure that it is notified promptly of any receipt of *client money* in the form of *client* entitlements.

5.5.27 **[G]** The 'entitlements' mentioned in CASS 5.5.26R refer to any kind of miscellaneous payment which the *firm* receives on behalf of a *client* and which are due to be paid to the *client*.

5.5.28 **[R]** When a *firm* receives a *client* entitlement on behalf of a *client*, it must pay any part of it which is *client money*:
(1) for *client* entitlements received in the *United Kingdom*, into a *client bank account* in accordance with CASS 5.5.5R; or
(2) for *client* entitlements received outside the *United Kingdom*, into any bank account operated by the *firm*, provided that such *client money* is:
 (a) paid to, or in accordance with, the instructions of the *client* concerned; or
 (b) paid into a *client bank account* in accordance with CASS 5.5.5R (1), as soon as possible but no later than five *business days* after the *firm* is notified of its receipt.

5.5.29 **[R]** A *firm* must take reasonable steps to ensure that a *client* entitlement which is *client money* is allocated within a reasonable period of time after notification of receipt.

Interest and investment returns

5.5.30 **[R]**
(1) In relation to *consumers*, a *firm* must, subject to (2), take reasonable steps to ensure that its *terms of business* or other *client agreements* adequately explain, and where necessary obtain a *client's* informed consent to, the treatment of interest and, if applicable, investment returns, derived from its holding of *client money* and any segregated *designated investments*.
(2) In respect of interest earned on *client bank accounts*, (1) does not apply if a *firm* has reasonable ground to be satisfied that in relation to *insurance mediation activities* carried on with or for a *consumer* the amount of interest earned will be not more than £20 per transaction.

5.5.31 **[G]** If no interest is payable to a *consumer*, that fact should be separately identified in the *firm's* client agreement or *terms of business*.

5.5.32 **[G]** If a *firm* outlines its *policy* on its payment of interest, it need not necessarily disclose the actual rates prevailing at any particular time; the *firm* should disclose the terms, for example, LIBOR plus or minus 'x' percentage points.

Transfer of client money to a third party

5.5.33 **[G]** CASS 5.5.34R sets out the requirements a *firm* must comply with when it transfers *client money* to another *person* without discharging its fiduciary duty owed to that *client*. Such circumstances arise when, for example, a *firm* passes *client money* to another broker for the purposes of the *client's* transaction being effected. A *firm* can only discharge itself from its fiduciary duty by acting in accordance with, and in the circumstances permitted by, CASS 5.5.80R.

5.5.34 **[R]** A *firm* may allow another *person*, such as another broker to hold or control *client money*, but only if:

(1) the *firm* transfers the *client money* for the purpose of a transaction for a *client* through or with that *person*; and

(2) in the case of a *consumer*, that *customer* has been notified (whether through a *client agreement*, *terms of business*, or otherwise in writing) that the *client money* may be transferred to another *person*.

5.5.35 **[G]** In relation to the notification required by CASS 5.5.34R(2), there is no need for a *firm* to make a separate disclosure in relation to each transfer made.

5.5.36 **[G]** A *firm* should not hold excess *client money* with another broker. It should be held in a *client bank account*.

Client bank accounts

5.5.37 **[G]** The *FSA* generally requires a *firm* to place *client money* in a *client bank account* with an *approved bank*. However, a *firm* which is an *approved bank* must not (subject to CASS 5.1.1R(2)(e)) hold *client money* in an account with itself.

5.5.38 **[R]**

(1) A *firm* must ensure that *client money* is held in a *client bank account* at one or more *approved banks*.

(2) If the *firm* is a bank, it must not hold *client money* in an account with itself.

5.5.39 **[R]** A *firm* may open one or more *client bank accounts* in the form of a *designated client bank account*. Characteristics of these accounts are that:

(1) the account holds *money* of one or more *clients*;

(2) the account includes in its title the word 'designated';

(3) the *clients* whose *money* is in the account have each consented in writing to the use of the bank with which the *client money* is to be held; and

(4) in the event of the *failure* of that bank, the account is not pooled with any other type of account unless a *primary pooling event* occurs.

5.5.40 **[G]**

(1) A *firm* may operate as many *client accounts* as it wishes.

(2) A *firm* is not obliged to offer its *clients* the facility of a *designated client bank account*.

(3) Where a *firm* holds *money* in a *designated client bank account*, the effect upon either:

  (a) the *failure* of a bank where any other *client bank account* is held; or

  (b) the *failure* of a third party to whom *money* has been transferred out of any other *client bank account* in accordance with CASS 5.5.34R;

  (each of which is a *secondary pooling event*) is that *money* held in the *designated client bank account* is not pooled with *money* held in any other account. Accordingly *clients* whose *money* is held in a *designated client bank account* will not share in any *shortfall* resulting from a *failure* of the type described in (a) or (b).

(4) Where a *firm* holds *client money* in a *designated client bank account*, the effect upon the failure of the *firm* (which is a *primary pooling event*) is that *money* held in the *designated client bank account* is pooled with *money* in every other *client bank account* of the *firm*. Accordingly, *clients* whose *money* is held in a *designated client bank account* will share in any *shortfall* resulting from a *failure* of the *firm*.

5.5.41 **[R]** A *firm* may hold *client money* with a bank that is not an *approved bank* if all the following conditions are met:

(1) the *client money* relates to one or more insurance transactions which are subject to the law or market practice of a jurisdiction outside the *United Kingdom;*

(2) because of the applicable law or market practice of that overseas jurisdiction, it is not possible to hold the *client money* in a *client bank account* with an *approved bank*;

(3) the *firm* holds the *money* with such a bank for no longer than is necessary to effect the transactions;

(4) the *firm* notifies each relevant *client* and has, in relation to a *consumer*, a client agreement or *terms of business* which adequately explain that:

  (a) the *client money* will not be held with an *approved bank*;

(b) in such circumstances, the legal and regulatory regime applying to the bank with which the *client money* is held will be different from that of the *United Kingdom* and, in the event of a *failure* of the bank, the *client money* may be treated differently from the treatment which would apply if the *client money* were held by an *approved bank* in the *United Kingdom*; and

(c) if it is the case, the particular bank has not accepted that it has no right of set-off or counterclaim against *money* held in a *client bank account*, in respect of any sum owed on any other account of the *firm*, notwithstanding the *firm's* request to the bank as required by CASS 5.5.49R; and

(5) the *client money* is held in a designated bank account.

A firm's selection of a bank

5.5.42 **[G]** A *firm* owes a duty of care to a *client* when it decides where to place *client money*. The review required by CASS 5.5.43R is intended to ensure that the risks inherent in placing *client money* with a bank are minimised or appropriately diversified by requiring a *firm* to consider carefully the bank or banks with which it chooses to place *client money*. For example, a *firm* which is likely only to hold relatively modest amounts of *client money* will be likely to be able to satisfy this requirement if it selects an *authorised* UK clearing bank.

5.5.43 **[R]** Before a *firm* opens a *client bank account* and as often as is appropriate on a continuing basis (and no less than once in each financial year), it must take reasonable steps to establish that the bank is appropriate for that purpose.

5.5.44 **[G]** A *firm* should consider diversifying placements of *client money* with more than one bank where the amounts are, for example, of sufficient size to warrant such diversification.

5.5.45 **[G]** When considering where to place *client money* and to determine the frequency of the appropriateness test under CASS 5.5.43R, a *firm* should consider taking into account, together with any other relevant matters:

(1) the capital of the bank;

(2) the amount of *client money* placed, as a proportion of the bank's capital and *deposits;*

(3) the credit rating of the bank (if available); and

(4) to the extent that the information is available, the level of risk in the investment and loan activities undertaken by the bank and its *affiliated companies*.

5.5.46 **[G]** A *firm* will be expected to perform due diligence when opening a *client bank account* with a bank that is authorised by an *EEA regulator*. Any continuing assessment of that bank may be restricted to verification that it remains authorised by an *EEA regulator*.

Group banks

5.5.47 **[R]** Subject to CASS 5.5.41R, a *firm* that holds or intends to hold *client money* with a bank which is in the same *group* as the *firm* must:

(1) undertake a continuous review in relation to that bank which is at least as rigorous as the review of any bank which is not in the same *group*, in order to ensure that the decision to use a *group* bank is appropriate for the *client*;

(2) disclose in writing to its *client* at the outset of the *client* relationship (whether by way of a *client agreement*, *terms of business* or otherwise in writing) or, if later, not less than 20 *business days* before it begins to hold *client money* of that *client* with that bank:

(a) that it is holding or intends to hold *client money* with a bank in the same *group*;

(b) the identity of the bank concerned; and

(c) that the *client* may choose not to have his *money* placed with such a bank.

5.5.48 **[R]** If a *client* has notified a *firm* in writing that he does not wish his *money* to be held with a bank in the same *group* as the *firm*, the *firm* must either:

(1) place that *client money* in a *client bank account* with another bank in accordance with CASS 5.5.38R; or

(2) return that *client money* to, or pay it to the order of, the *client*.

Notification and acknowledgement of trust (banks)

5.5.49 **[R]** When a *firm* opens a *client bank account*, the *firm* must give or have given written notice to the bank requesting the bank to acknowledge to it in writing:

(1) that all *money* standing to the credit of the account is held by the *firm* as trustee (or if relevant in Scotland, as agent) and that the bank is not entitled to combine the account with any other account or to exercise any right of set-off or counterclaim against *money* in that account in respect of any sum owed to it on any other account of the *firm*; and

(2) that the title of the account sufficiently distinguishes that account from any account containing *money* that belongs to the *firm*, and is in the form requested by the *firm*.

5.5.50 **[R]** In the case of a *client bank account* in the *United Kingdom*, if the bank does not provide the acknowledgement referred to in CASS 5.5.49R within 20 *business days* after the *firm* dispatched the notice, the *firm* must withdraw all *money* standing to the credit of the account and deposit it in a *client bank account* with another bank as soon as possible.

5.5.51 **[R]** In the case of a *client bank account* outside the *United Kingdom*, if the bank does not provide the acknowledgement referred to in CASS 5.5.49R within 20 *business days* after the *firm* dispatched the notice, the *firm* must notify the *client* of this fact as set out in CASS 5.5.53R.

5.5.52 **[G]** *Firms* are reminded of the provisions of CASS 5.5.41R(4), which sets out the notification and consents required when using a bank that is not an *approved bank*

Notification to clients: use of an approved bank outside the United Kingdom

5.5.53 **[R]** A *firm* must not hold, for a *consumer, client money* in a *client bank account* outside the *United Kingdom*, unless the *firm* has previously disclosed to the *consumer* (whether in its *terms of business, client agreement* or otherwise in writing):
(1) that his *money* may be deposited in a *client bank account* outside the *United Kingdom* but that the *client* may notify the *firm* that he does not wish his *money* to be held in a particular jurisdiction;
(2) that in such circumstances, the legal and regulatory regime applying to the *approved bank* will be different from that of the *United Kingdom* and, in the event of a *failure* of the bank, his *money* may be treated in a different manner from that which would apply if the *client money* were held by a bank in the *United Kingdom*; and
(3) if it is the case, that a particular bank has not accepted that it has no right of set-off or counterclaim against *money* held in a *client bank account* in respect of any sum owed on any other account of the *firm*, notwithstanding the *firm's* request to the bank as required by CASS 5.5.49R.

5.5.54 **[G]** There is no need for a *firm* to make a separate disclosure under CASS 5.5.53R (1) and (2) in relation to each jurisdiction.

5.5.55 **[G]** *Firms* are reminded of the provisions of CASS 5.5.41R (4), which sets out the notification and consents required when using a bank that is not an *approved bank*.

5.5.56 **[R]** If a *client* has notified a *firm* in writing before entering into a transaction that *client money* is not to be held in a particular jurisdiction, the *firm* must either:
(1) hold the *client money* in a *client bank account* in a jurisdiction to which the *client* has not objected; or
(2) return the *client money* to, or to the order of, the *client*.

5.5.57 **[G]** *Firms* are reminded of the provisions of CASS 5.5.41R (4), which sets out the notification and consents required when using a bank that is not an *approved bank*.

Notification to consumers: use of broker or settlement agent outside the United Kingdom

5.5.58 **[R]** A *firm* must not undertake any transaction for a *consumer* that involves *client money* being passed to another broker or *settlement agent* located in a jurisdiction outside the *United Kingdom*, unless the *firm* has previously disclosed to the *consumer* (whether in its *terms of business, client agreement* or otherwise in writing):
(1) that his *client money* may be passed to a *person* outside the *United Kingdom* but the *client* may notify the *firm* that he does not wish his *money* to be passed to a *person* in a particular jurisdiction; and
(2) that, in such circumstances, the legal and regulatory regime applying to the broker or *settlement agent* will be different from that of the *United Kingdom* and, in the event of a *failure* of the broker or *settlement agent*, this *money* may be treated in a different manner from that which would apply if the *money* were held by a broker or *settlement agent* in the *United Kingdom*.

5.5.59 **[G]** There is no need for a *firm* to make a separate disclosure under CASS 5.5.58R in relation to each jurisdiction.

5.5.60 **[R]** If a *client* has notified a *firm* before entering into a transaction that he does not wish his *money* to be passed to another broker or *settlement agent* located in a particular jurisdiction, the *firm* must either:
(1) hold the *client money* in a *client bank account* in the *United Kingdom* or a jurisdiction to which the *client* has not objected and pay its own *money* to the *firm's* own account with the broker, agent or counterparty; or
(2) return the *money* to, or to the order of, the *client*.

Notification to the FSA: failure of a bank, broker or settlement agent

5.5.61 **[R]** On the *failure* of a third party with which *client money* is held, a *firm* must notify the *FSA*:
(1) as soon as it becomes aware, of the *failure* of any bank, other broker or *settlement agent* or other entity with which it has placed, or to which it has passed, *client money*; and

(2) as soon as reasonably practical, whether it intends to make good any *shortfall* that has arisen or may arise and of the amounts involved.

Client money calculation and reconciliation

5.5.62 **[G]**

(1) In order that a *firm* may check that it has sufficient *money* segregated in its *client bank account* (and held by third parties) to meet its obligations to *clients* it is required periodically to calculate the amount which should be segregated (the *client money* requirement) and to compare this with the amount shown as its *client money* resource. This calculation is, in the first instance, based upon the *firm's* accounting records and is followed by a reconciliation with its banking records. A *firm* is required to make a payment into the *client bank account* if there is a shortfall or to remove any *money* which is not required to meet the *firm's* obligations.

(2) For the purpose of calculating its *client money* requirement two alternative calculation methods are permitted, but a *firm* must use the same method in relation to CASS 5.3 and CASS 5.4. The first refers to individual *client* cash balances; the second to aggregate amounts of *client money* recorded on a *firm's* business ledgers.

5.5.63 **[R]**

(1) A *firm* must, as often as is necessary to ensure the accuracy of its records and at least at intervals of not more than 25 *business days*:
  - (a) check whether its *client money* resource, as determined by CASS 5.5.65R on the previous *business day*, was at least equal to the *client money* requirement, as defined in CASS 5.5.66R or CASS 5.5.68R, as at the close of business on that day; and (2) ensure that:
  - (b) ensure that:
    - (i) any *shortfall* is paid into a *client bank account* by the close of business on the day the calculation is performed; or
    - (ii) any excess is withdrawn within the same time period unless CASS 5.5.9R or CASS 5.5.10R applies to the extent that the *firm* is satisfied on reasonable grounds that it is prudent to maintain a positive margin to ensure the calculation in (a) is satisfied having regard to any unreconciled items in its business ledgers as at the date on which the calculations are performed; and
  - (c) include in any calculation of its *client money* requirement (whether calculated in accordance with CASS 5.5.66R or CASS 5.5.68R) any amounts attributable to *client money* received by its *appointed representatives*, *field representatives* or other agents and which, as at the date of calculation, it is required to segregate in accordance with CASS 5.5.19R.

(2) A *firm* must within ten *business days* of the calculation in (a) reconcile the balance on each *client bank account* as recorded by the *firm* with the balance on that account as set out in the statement or other form of confirmation used by the bank with which that account is held.

(3) When any discrepancy arises as a result of the reconciliation carried out in (2), the *firm* must identify the reason for the discrepancy and correct it as soon as possible, unless the discrepancy arises solely as a result of timing differences between the accounting systems of the party providing the statement or confirmation and those of the *firm*.

(4) While a *firm* is unable to resolve a difference arising from a reconciliation, and one record or a set of records examined by the *firm* during its reconciliation indicates that there is a need to have a greater amount of *client money* than is in fact the case, the *firm* must assume, until the matter is finally resolved, that the record or set of records is accurate and either pay its own *money* into a relevant account or make a withdrawal of any excess.

5.5.64 **[R]** A *firm* must keep a record of whether it calculates its *client money* requirement in accordance with CASS 5.5.66R or CASS 5.5.68R and may only use one method during each annual accounting period (which method must be the same in relation to both CASS 5.3 and CASS 5.4).

Client money resource

5.5.65 **[R]** The *client money* resource, for the purposes of CASS 5.5.63R(1)(a), is:

(1) the aggregate of the balances on the *firm's client money bank accounts*, as at the close of business on the previous *business day* and, if held in accordance with CASS 5.4, *designated investments* (valued on a prudent and consistent basis) together with *client money* held by a third party in accordance with CASS 5.5.34R;

(2) (but only if the *firm* is comparing the *client money* resource with its *client's money* (accruals) requirement in accordance with CASS 5.5.68R) to the extent that *client money* is held in accordance with CASS 5.3 (statutory trust), insurance debtors (which in this case cannot include pre-funded items); and

(3) (but only if the firm is comparing the *client money* resource with its *client's money* (accruals) requirement in accordance with CASS 5.5.68R) to the extent that *client money* is held in accordance with CASS 5.4 (non-statutory trust):

Part II FSA Handbook Materials

(a) all insurance debtors (including pre-funded items whether in respect of advance *premiums*, claims, *premium* refunds or otherwise) shown in the *firm's* business ledgers as amounts due from *clients*, *insurance undertakings* and other *persons*, such debts valued on a prudent and consistent basis to the extent required to meet any shortfall of the *client money* resource compared with the *firm's client money* requirement; and

(b) the amount of any letter of credit or unconditional guarantee provided by an *approved bank* and held on the terms of the trust (or, in Scotland, agency), limited to:
  (i) the maximum sum payable by the *approved bank* under the letter of credit or guarantee; or
  (ii) if less, the amount which would, apart from the benefit of the letter of credit or guarantee, be the *shortfall* of the *client money* resource compared with the *client money* requirement under CASS 5.5.66R or CASS 5.5.68R.

But a *firm* may treat a transaction with an *insurance undertaking* which is not a *UK domestic firm* as complete, and accordingly may (but only for the purposes of the calculation in (1)) disregard any unreconciled items of *client money* transferred to an intermediate broker relating to such a transaction, if:
(4) it has taken reasonable steps to ascertain whether the transaction is complete; and
(5) it has no reason to consider the transaction has not been completed; and
(6) a period of at least 12 *months* has elapsed since the *money* was transferred to the intermediate broker for the purpose of the transaction.

Client money (client balance) requirement

5.5.66 **[R]** A *firm's client money* (*client* balance) requirement is the sum of, for all *clients*, the individual *client* balances calculated in accordance with CASS 5.5.67R but excluding any individual balances which are negative (that is, uncleared *client* funds).

5.5.67 **[R]** The individual *client* balance for each *client* must be calculated as follows:
(1) the amount paid by a *client* to the *firm* (to include all *premiums*); plus
(2) the amount due to the *client* (to include all claims and *premium* refunds); plus
(3) the amount of any interest or investment returns due to the *client*;
(4) less the amount paid to *insurance undertakings* for the benefit of the *client* (to include all *premiums* and *commission* due to itself) (ie *commissions* that are due but have not yet been removed from the *client account*);
(5) less the amount paid by the *firm* to the *client* (to include all claims and *premium* refunds);
and where the individual *client* balance is found by the sum ((1) + (2) + (3))-((4) + (5)).

Client money (accruals) requirement

5.5.68 **[R]** A *firm's client money* (accruals) requirement is the sum of the following:
(1) all insurance creditors shown in the *firm's* business ledgers as amounts due to *insurance undertakings, clients* and other *persons*; plus
(2) unearned *commission* being the amount of *commission* shown as accrued (but not shown as due and payable) as at the date of the calculation (a prudent estimate must be used if the *firm* is unable to produce an exact figure at the date of the calculation).

5.5.69 **[R]** A *firm* which calculates its *client money* requirement on the preceding basis must in addition and within a reasonable period be able to match its *client money* resource to its requirement by reference to individual *clients* (with such matching being achieved for the majority of its *clients* and transactions).

5.5.70 **[R]** [deleted]

5.5.71 **[G]** [deleted]

5.5.72 **[R]** [deleted]

5.5.73 **[R]** [deleted]

5.5.74 **[R]** [deleted]

5.5.75 **[R]** [deleted]

Failure to perform calculations or reconciliation

5.5.76 **[R]** A *firm* must notify the *FSA* immediately if it is unable to, or does not, perform the calculation required by CASS 5.5.63R(1).

5.5.77 **[R]** A *firm* must notify the *FSA* immediately it becomes aware that it may not be able to make good any *shortfall* identified by CASS 5.5.63R(1) by the close of business on the day the calculation is performed and if applicable when the reconciliation is completed.

5.5.78 **[R]** [deleted]

Discharge of fiduciary duty

5.5.79 **[G]** The purpose of CASS 5.5.80R to CASS 5.5.83R is to set out those situations in which a *firm* will have fulfilled its contractual and fiduciary obligations in relation to any *client money* held for or on behalf of its *client*, or in relation to the *firm's* ability to require repayment of that *money* from a third party.

5.5.80 **[R]** *Money* ceases to be *client money* if it is paid:
(1) to the *client*, or a duly authorised representative of the *client*; or
(2) to a third party on the instruction of or with the specific consent of the *client*, but not if it is transferred to a third party in the course of effecting a transaction, in accordance with CASS 5.5.34R; or
(3) into a bank account of the *client* (not being an account which is also in the name of the *firm*); or
(4) to the *firm* itself, when it is due and payable to the *firm* in accordance with CASS 5.1.5R (1); or
(5) to the *firm* itself, when it is an excess in the *client bank account* as set out in CASS 5.5.63R(1)(b)(ii).

5.5.81 **[G]**
(1) A *firm* which pays professional fees (for example to a loss adjuster or valuer) on behalf of a *client* may do so in accordance with CASS 5.5.80R (2) where this is done on the instruction of or with the consent of the *client*.
(2) When a *firm* wishes to transfer *client money* balances to a third party in the course of transferring its business to another *firm*, it should do so in compliance with CASS 5.5.80R and a transferee *firm* will come under an obligation to treat any *client money* so transferred in accordance with these *rules*.
(3) *Firms* are reminded of their obligation, when transferring *money* to third parties in accordance with CASS 5.5.34R, to use appropriate skill, care and judgment in their selection of third parties in order to ensure adequate protection of *client money*.
(4) *Firms* are reminded that, in order to calculate their *client money* resource in accordance with CASS 5.5.63R to CASS 5.5.65R, they will need to have systems in place to produce an accurate accounting record showing how much *client money* is being held by third parties at any point in time. For the purposes of CASS 5.5.63R to CASS 5.5.65R, however, a *firm* must assume that *monies* remain at an intermediate broker awaiting completion of the transaction unless it has received confirmation that the transaction has been completed.

5.5.82 **[R]** When a *firm* draws a cheque or other payable order to discharge its fiduciary duty under CASS 5.5.80R, it must continue to treat the sum concerned as *client money* until the cheque or order is presented and paid by the bank.

5.5.83 **[R]** For the purposes of CASS 5.1.5R, if a *firm* makes a payment to, or on the instructions of, a *client*, from an account other than a *client bank account*, until that payment has cleared, no equivalent sum will become due and payable to the *firm* or may be withdrawn from a *client bank account* by way of reimbursement.

Records

5.5.84 **[R]** A *firm* must ensure that proper records, sufficient to show and explain the *firm's* transactions and commitments in respect of its *client money*, are made and retained for a period of three years after they were made.

5.6 Client money distribution

Application

5.6.1 **[R]**
(1) CASS 5.6 (the *client money (insurance) distribution rules*) applies to a *firm* that in holding *client money* is subject to CASS 5.3 (statutory trust) or CASS 5.4 (Non-statutory trust) when a *primary pooling event* or a *secondary pooling event* occurs.
(2) In the event of there being any discrepancy between the terms of the trust as required by CASS 5.4.7R (1) (c) and the provisions of CASS 5.6, the latter shall apply.

5.6.2 **[G]**
(1) The *client money (insurance) distribution rules* have force and effect on any *firm* that holds *client money* in accordance with CASS 5.3 or CASS 5.4. Therefore, they may apply to a *UK branch* of a non-*EEA firm*. In this case, the *UK branch* of the *firm* may be treated as if the *branch* itself is a free-standing entity subject to the *client money (insurance) distribution rules*.
(2) *Firms* that act in accordance with CASS 5.4 (Non-statutory trust) are reminded that the *client money (insurance) distribution rules* should be given effect in the terms of trust required by CASS 5.4.

Purpose

5.6.3 **[G]** The *client money (insurance) distribution rules* seek to facilitate the timely return of *client money* to a *client* in the event of the *failure* of a *firm* or third party at which the *firm* holds *client money*.

Failure of the authorised firm: primary pooling event

5.6.4 **[G]** A *primary pooling event* triggers a notional pooling of all the *client money*, in every type of *client money* account, and the obligation to distribute it.

5.6.5 **[R]** A *primary pooling event* occurs:
(1) on the *failure* of the *firm*; or
(2) on the vesting of assets in a trustee in accordance with an 'assets *requirement*' imposed under section 48(1)(b) of the *Act*; or
(3) on the coming into force of a *requirement* for all *client money* held by the *firm*; or
(4) when the *firm* notifies, or is in breach of its duty to notify, the *FSA*, in accordance with CASS 5.5.77R, that it is unable correctly to identify and allocate in its records all valid claims arising as a result of a *secondary pooling event*.

5.6.6 **[R]** CASS 5.6.5R (4) does not apply so long as:
(1) the *firm* is taking steps, in consultation with the *FSA*, to establish those records; and
(2) there are reasonable grounds to conclude that the records will be capable of rectification within a reasonable period.

Pooling and distribution

5.6.7 **[R]** If a *primary pooling event* occurs:
(1) *client money* held in each *client money* account of the *firm* is treated as pooled;
(2) the *firm* must distribute that *client money* in accordance with CASS 5.3.2R or, as appropriate, CASS 5.4.7R, so that each *client* receives a sum which is rateable to the *client money* entitlement calculated in accordance with CASS 5.5.66R; and
(3) the *firm* must, as trustee, call in and make demand in respect of any debt due to the *firm* as trustee, and must liquidate any *designated investment*, and any letter of credit or guarantee upon which it relies for meeting any *shortfall* in its *client money* resource and the proceeds shall be pooled together with other *client money* as in (1) and distributed in accordance with (2).

5.6.8 **[G]** A *client's* main claim is for the return of *client money* held in a *client bank account*. A *client* may claim for any *shortfall* against *money* held in a *firm's* own account. For that claim, the *client* will be an unsecured creditor of the *firm*.

Client money received after the failure of the firm

5.6.9 **[R]** *Client money* received by the *firm* (including in its capacity as trustee under CASS 5.4 (Non-statutory trust)) after a *primary pooling event* must not be pooled with *client money* held in any *client money* account operated by the *firm* at the time of the *primary pooling event*. It must be placed in a *client bank account* that has been opened after that event and must be handled in accordance with the *client money rules*, and returned to the relevant *client* without delay, except to the extent that:
(1) it is *client money* relating to a transaction that has not completed at the time of the *primary pooling event*; or
(2) it is *money* relating to a *client*, for whom the *client money* requirement, calculated in accordance with CASS 5.5.66R or CASS 5.5.68R, shows that *money* is due from the *client* to the *firm* including in its capacity as trustee under CASS 5.4 (Non-statutory trust) at the time of the *primary pooling event*.

5.6.10 **[G]** *Client money* received after the *primary pooling event* relating to an incomplete transaction should be used to complete that transaction.

5.6.11 **[R]** If a *firm* receives a *mixed remittance* after a *primary pooling event*, it must:
(1) pay the full sum into the separate *client bank account* opened in accordance with CASS 5.6.9R; and
(2) pay the *money* that is not *client money* out of that *client bank account* into the *firm's* own bank account within one *business day* of the *day* on which the remittance is cleared.

5.6.12 **[G]** Whenever possible the *firm* should seek to split a *mixed remittance* before the relevant accounts are credited.

Failure of a bank, other broker or settlement agent: secondary pooling events

5.6.13 **[R]** If both a *primary pooling event* and a *secondary pooling event* occur, the provisions of this section relating to a *primary pooling event* apply.

5.6.14 **[R]** A *secondary pooling event* occurs on the *failure* of a third party to which *client money* held by the *firm* has been transferred under CASS 5.5.34R.

5.6.15 **[R]** CASS 5.6.20R to CASS 5.6.31R do not apply if, on the *failure* of the third party, the *firm* repays to its *clients* or pays into a *client bank account*, at an unaffected bank, an amount equal to the amount of *client money* which would have been held if a *shortfall* had not occurred at that third party.

5.6.16 **[G]** When *client money* is transferred to a third party, a *firm* continues to owe a fiduciary duty to the *client*. However, consistent with a fiduciary's responsibility (whether as agent or trustee) for third parties under general law, a *firm* will not be held responsible for a *shortfall* in *client money* caused by a third party *failure* if it has complied with those duties.

5.6.17 **[G]** To comply with its duties, the *firm* should show proper care:
(1) in the selection of a third party; and
(2) when monitoring the performance of the third party.

In the case of *client money* transferred to a bank, by demonstrating compliance with CASS 5.5.43R, a *firm* should be able to demonstrate that it has taken reasonable steps to comply with its duties.

Failure of a bank

5.6.18 **[G]** When a bank *fails* and the *firm* decides not to make good the *shortfall* in the amount of *client money* held at that bank, a *secondary pooling event* will occur in accordance with CASS 5.6.20R. The *firm* would be expected to reflect the *shortfall* that arises at the *firm's* bank in the periodic *client money* calculation by reducing the *client money* resource and *client money* requirement accordingly.

5.6.19 **[G]** The *client money (insurance) distribution rules* seek to ensure that *clients* who have previously specified that they are not willing to accept the risk of the bank that has *failed*, and who therefore requested that their *client money* be placed in a *designated client bank account* as a different bank, should not suffer the loss of the bank that has *failed*.

Failure of a bank: pooling

5.6.20 **[R]** If a *secondary pooling event* occurs as a result of the *failure* of a bank where one or more *general client bank accounts* are held, then:
(1) in relation to every *general client bank account* of the *firm*, the provisions of CASS 5.6.22R and CASS 5.6.26R to CASS 5.6.28G will apply;
(2) in relation to every *designated client bank account* held by the *firm* with the *failed* bank, the provisions of CASS 5.6.24R and CASS 5.6.26R to CASS 5.6.28G will apply; and
(3) any *money* held at a bank, other than the bank that has *failed*, in *designated client bank accounts* is not pooled with any other *client money*.

5.6.21 **[R]** If a *secondary pooling event* occurs as a result of the *failure* of a bank where one or more *designated client bank accounts* are held then in relation to every *designated client bank account* held by the *firm* with the *failed* bank, the provisions of CASS 5.6.24R and CASS 5.6.26R to CASS 5.6.28G will apply.

5.6.22 **[R]** *Money* held in each *general client bank account* of the *firm* must be treated as pooled and:
(1) any *shortfall* in *client money* held, or which should have been held, in *general client bank accounts*, that has arisen as a result of the *failure* of the bank, must be borne by all the *clients* whose *client money* is held in a *general client bank account* of the *firm*, rateably in accordance with their entitlements;
(2) a new *client money* entitlement must be calculated for each *client* by the *firm*, to reflect the requirements in (1), and the *firm's* records must be amended to reflect the reduced *client money* entitlement;
(3) the *firm* must make and retain a record of each *client's* share of the *client money shortfall* at the *failed* bank until the *client* is repaid; and
(4) the *firm* must use the new *client* entitlements, calculated in accordance with (2), when performing the *client money* calculation in accordance with CASS 5.5.63R to CASS 5.5.69R.

5.6.23 **[G]** The term 'which should have been held' is a reference to the *failed* bank's failure (and elsewhere, as appropriate, is a reference to the other *failed* third party's failure) to hold the *client money* at the time of the pooling event.

5.6.24 **[R]** For each *client* with a *designated client bank account* held at the *failed* bank:
(1) any *shortfall* in *client money* held, or which should have been held, in *designated client bank accounts* that has arisen as a result of the *failure*, must be borne by all the *clients* whose *client money* is held in a *designated client bank account* of the *firm* at the *failed* bank, rateably in accordance with their entitlements;
(2) a new *client money* entitlement must be calculated for each of the relevant *clients* by the *firm*, and the *firm's* records must be amended to reflect the reduced *client money* entitlement;

(3) the *firm* must make and retain a record of each *client's* share of the *client money shortfall* at the *failed* bank until the *client* is repaid; and
(4) the *firm* must use the new *client money* entitlements, calculated in accordance with (2), when performing the periodic *client money* calculation, in accordance with CASS 5.5.63R to CASS 5.5.69R.

5.6.25 **[R]** A *client* whose *money* was held, or which should have been held, in a *designated client bank account* with a bank that has *failed* is not entitled to claim in respect of that *money* against any other *client bank account* or *client transaction account* of the *firm.*

Client money received after the failure of a bank

5.6.26 **[R]** *Client money* received by the *firm* after the *failure* of a bank, that would otherwise have been paid into a *client bank account* at that bank:
(1) must not be transferred to the *failed* bank unless specifically instructed by the *client* in order to settle an obligation of that *client* to the *failed* bank; and
(2) must be, subject to (1), placed in a separate *client bank account* that has been opened after the *secondary pooling event* and either:
 (a) on the written instruction of the *client*, transferred to a bank other than the one that has *failed*; or
 (b) returned to the *client* as soon as possible.

5.6.27 **[R]** If a *firm* receives a *mixed remittance* after the *secondary pooling event* which consists of *client money* that would have been paid into a *general client bank account*, a *designated client bank account* or a *designated client fund account* maintained at the bank that has *failed*, it must:
(1) pay the full sum into a *client bank account* other than one operated at the bank that has *failed*; and
(2) pay the *money* that is not *client money* out of that *client bank account* within one *business day* of the day on which the remittance is cleared.

5.6.28 **[G]** Whenever possible the *firm* should seek to split a *mixed remittance* before the relevant accounts are credited.

Failure of an intermediate broker or settlement agent: pooling

5.6.29 **[R]** If a *secondary pooling event* occurs as a result of the *failure* of another broker or *settlement agent* to whom the *firm* has transferred *client's money* then, in relation to every *general client bank account* of the *firm*, the provisions of CASS 5.6.26R to CASS 5.6.28G and CASS 5.6.30R will apply.

5.6.30 **[R]** *Money* held in each *general client bank account* of the *firm* must be treated as pooled and:
(1) any *shortfall* in *client money* held, or which should have been held, in *general client bank accounts*, that has arisen as a result of the *failure*, must be borne by all the *clients* whose *client money* is held in a *general client bank account* of the *firm*, rateably in accordance with their entitlements;
(2) a new *client money* entitlement must be calculated for each *client* by the *firm*, to reflect the requirements of (1), and the *firm's* records must be amended to reflect the reduced *client money* entitlement;
(3) the *firm* must make and retain a record of each *client's* share of the *client money shortfall* at the *failed* intermediate broker or *settlement agent* until the *client* is repaid; and
(4) the *firm* must use the new *client money* entitlements, calculated in accordance with (2), when performing the periodic *client money* calculation, in accordance with CASS 5.5.63R to CASS 5.5.69R.

Client money received after the failure of a broker or settlement agent

5.6.31 **[R]** *Client money* received by the *firm* after the *failure* of another broker or *settlement agent*, to whom the *firm* has transferred *client money* that would otherwise have been paid into a *client bank account* at that broker or *settlement agent*:
(1) must not be transferred to the *failed* thirty party unless specifically instructed by the *client* in order to settle an obligation of that *client* to the *failed* broker or *settlement agent*; and
(2) must be, subject to (1), placed in a separate *client bank account* that has been opened after the *secondary pooling event* and either:
 (a) on the written instruction of the *client*, transferred to a third party other than the one that has *failed*; or
 (b) returned to the *client* as soon as possible.

Notification on the failure of a bank, other broker or settlement agent

5.6.32 **[R]** The provisions of CASS 5.5.61R apply.

5.7 Mandates

Application

5.7.1 **[R]** [deleted]

5.7.2 **[R]** [deleted]

5.7.3 **[G]** [deleted]

5.7.4 **[G]** [deleted]

Purpose

5.7.5 **[G]** [deleted]

General

5.7.6 **[R]** [deleted]

5.8 Safe keeping of client's documents and other assets

Application

5.8.1 **[R]**

(1) CASS 5.8 applies to a *firm* (including in its capacity as trustee under CASS 5.4) which in the course of *insurance mediation activity* takes into its possession for safekeeping any *client* title *documents* (other than *documents* of no value) or other tangible assets belonging to *clients*.

(2) CASS 5.8 does not apply to a *firm* when:

(a) carrying on an *insurance mediation activity* which is in respect of a *reinsurance contract*; or

(b) acting in accordance with CASS 2 (Custody rules).

Purpose

5.8.2 **[G]** The *rules* in this section amplify the obligation in *Principle* 10 which requires a *firm* to arrange adequate protection for *client's* assets. *Firms* carrying on *insurance mediation activities* may hold, on a temporary or longer basis, *client* title *documents* such as *policy documents* (other than *policy documents* of no value) and also items of physical property if, for example, a *firm* arranges for a valuation. The *rules* are intended to ensure that *firms* make adequate arrangements for the safe keeping of such property.

Requirement

5.8.3 **[R]**

(1) A *firm* which has in its possession or control *documents* evidencing a *client's* title to a *contract of insurance* or other similar *documents* (other than *documents* of no value) or which takes into its possession or control tangible assets belonging to a *client*, must take reasonable steps to ensure that any such *documents* or items of property:

(a) are kept safe until they are delivered to the *client*;

(b) are not delivered or given to any other *person* except in accordance with instructions given by the *client*; and that

a record is kept as to the identity of any such *documents* or items of property and the dates on which they were received by the *firm* and delivered to the *client* or other *person*.

(2) A *firm* must retain the record required in (1) for a period of three years after the document or property concerned is delivered to the *client* or other *person*.

CASS 5 Annex 1R

5 Ann 1 **[R]**

This Annex belongs to CASS 5.5.14R.

(1) The general principles which must be followed when *client money* segregation includes *designated investments*:

(a) there must be a suitable spread of *investments*;

(b) *investments* must be made in accordance with an appropriate liquidity strategy;

(c) the *investments* must be in accordance with an appropriate credit risk policy;

(d) any foreign exchange risks must be prudently managed.

(2) Table of permitted designated investments for the purpose of CASS 5.5.14R (1).

Part II FSA Handbook Materials

Investment type	Qualification
1. Negotiable debt security (including a certificate of deposit)	(a) Remaining term to maturity of 5 years or less; and (b) The issuer or investment must have a short-term credit rating of A1 by Standard and Poor's, or P1 by Moody's Investor Services, or F1 by Fitch if the instrument has a remaining term to maturity of 366 days or less; or a minimum long term credit rating of AA- by Standards and Poor's, or Aa- by Moody's Investor Services or AA- by Fitch if the instrument has a term to maturity of more than 366 days.
2. A repo in relation to negotiable debt security	As for 1 above and where the credit rating of the counterparty also meets the criteria in 1.
3. Bond funds	(a) An authorised fund or a recognised scheme or an investment company which is registered by the Securities and Exchanges Commission of the United States of America under the Investment Company Act 1940; (b) A minimum credit rating and risk rating of Aaf and S2 respectively by Standard and Poor's or Aa and MR2 respectively by Moody's Investor Services or AA and V2 respectively by Fitch.
4. Money market fund	(a) An authorised fund or a recognised scheme; (b) A minimum credit and risk rating of Aaa and MR1+ respectively by Moody's Investor Services or AAAm by Standard and Poor's or AAA and V1+ respectively by Fitch.
5. Derivatives	Only for the purpose of prudently managing foreign currency risks.

(3) The general conditions which must be satisfied in the segregation of *designated investments* are:

(a) any redemption of an *investment* must be by payment into the *firm's client money bank account*;

(b) where the credit or risk rating of a *designated investment* falls below the minimum set out in the Table, the *firm* must dispose of the *investment* as soon as possible and in any even not later than 20 *business days* following the downgrade;

(c) where any *investment* or issuer has more than one rating, the lowest shall apply.

CHAPTER 6
CUSTODY RULES

6.1 Application

[2131]

6.1.1 **[R]** This chapter (the *custody rules*) applies to a *firm*:

(1) [deleted]

(a) [deleted]

(b) [deleted]

(1A) when it holds *financial instruments* belonging to a *client* in the course of its *MiFID business*; and/or

(1B) when it is *safeguarding and administering investments*, in the course of business that is not *MiFID business*.

(2) [deleted]

6.1.1A **[G]** The *regulated activity* of *safeguarding and administering investments* covers both the *safeguarding and administration of assets (without arranging)* and arranging the *safeguarding and administration of assets*, when those assets are either *safe custody investments* or *custody assets*. A *safe custody investment* is, in summary, a *designated investment* which a *firm* receives or holds on behalf of a *client*. *Custody assets* include *designated investments*, and any other assets that the *firm* holds or may hold in the same portfolio as a *designated investment* held for or on behalf of the *client*.

6.1.1B **[R]** *Firms* to which the *custody rules* apply by virtue of CASS 6.1.1R(1B) must also apply the *custody rules* to those *custody assets* which are not *safe custody investments* in a manner appropriate to the nature and value of those *custody assets*.

6.1.1C **[G]** In accordance with article 42 of the *Regulated Activities Order*, a *firm* ("I") will not be *arranging safeguarding and administration of assets* if it introduces a *client* to another *firm* whose *permitted activities* include the *safeguarding and administration of investments*, or to an *exempt person* acting as such, with a view to that other *firm* or *exempt person*:

(1) providing a safe custody service in the *United Kingdom*; or

(2) arranging for the provision of a safe custody service in the *United Kingdom* by another *person*;

and the other *firm*, *exempt person* or other *person* who is to provide the safe custody service is not in the same *group* as I, and does not remunerate I.

6.1.2 **[G]** *Firms* are reminded that dividends (actual or payments in lieu), *stock lending* fees and other payments received for the benefit of a *client*, and which are due to the *clients* should be held in accordance with the *client money chapter* where appropriate.

6.1.3 **[G]** [deleted]

Business in the name of the firm

6.1.4 **[R]** The *custody rules* do not apply where a *firm* carries on business in its name but on behalf of the *client* where that is required by the very nature of the transaction and the *client* is in agreement.

[**Note:** recital 26 to *MiFID*]

6.1.5 **[G]** For example, this chapter does not apply where a *firm* borrows *safe custody assets* from a client as principal under a *stock lending* agreement.

Title transfer collateral arrangements

6.1.6 **[R]** The *custody rules* do not apply where a *client* transfers full ownership of a *safe custody asset* to a *firm* for the purpose of securing or otherwise covering present or future, actual, contingent or prospective obligations.

[**Note:** recital 27 to *MiFID*]

6.1.7 **[G]** A title transfer financial collateral arrangement under *the Financial Collateral Directive* is a type of transfer of instruments to cover obligations where the *financial instrument* will not be regarded as belonging to the *client*.

6.1.8 **[G]** *Firms* are reminded of the *client's best interests rule*, which requires them to act honestly, fairly and professionally in accordance with the best interests of their *clients* when structuring their business particularly in respect of the effect of that structure on *firms'* obligations under this chapter.

6.1.9 **[G]** *Firms* are reminded that, in certain cases, the *collateral rules* apply where a *firm* receives collateral from a *client* in order to secure the obligations of the *client*.

Affiliated companies – MiFID business

6.1.10 **[G]** The fact that a *client* is an *affiliated company* in respect of *MiFID business* does not affect the operation of the *custody rules* in relation to that *client*.

Affiliated companies – non-MiFID business

6.1.10A **[G]** In respect of business which is not *MiFID business*, the *custody rules* do not apply to a *firm* when it safeguards and administers a *designated investment* on behalf of an *affiliated company*, unless:

(1) the *firm* has been notified that the *designated investment* belongs to a *client* of the *affiliated company*; or

(2) the *affiliated company* is a *client* dealt with at arm's length.

6.1.11 **[G]** [deleted]

Delivery versus payment transactions

6.1.12 **[R]**

(1) A *firm* need not treat this chapter as applying in respect of a delivery versus payment transaction through a commercial settlement system if it is intended that the *safe custody asset* is either to be:

  (a) in respect of a *client's* purchase, due to the *client* within one *business day* following the *client's* fulfilment of a payment obligation; or

  (b) in respect of a *client's* sale, due to the firm within one *business day* following the fulfilment of a payment obligation;

unless the delivery or payment by the *firm* does not occur by the close of business on the third *business day* following the date of payment or delivery of the *safe custody asset* by the *client*.

(2) Until such a delivery versus payment transaction through a commercial settlement system settles, a *firm* may segregate *money* (in accordance with the *client money chapter*) instead of the *client's safe custody assets*.

6.1.13 **[G]** [deleted]

6.1.14 **[G]** [deleted]

Temporary handling of safe custody assets

6.1.15 **[G]** The *custody rules* do not apply if a *firm* temporarily handles a *safe custody asset* belonging to a *client*. A *firm* should temporarily handle a *safe custody asset* for no longer than is reasonably necessary. In most transactions this would be no longer than one *business day*, but it may be longer or shorter depending upon the transaction in question. For example, when a *firm* executes an order to sell shares which have not been registered on a dematerialised exchange, handling documents for longer periods may be reasonably necessary. However, in the case of *safe custody assets* in *bearer form*, the *firm* is expected to handle them for less than one *business day*. When a *firm* temporarily handles *safe custody assets*, it is still obliged to comply with *Principle* 10 (Clients' assets).

6.1.16 **[G]** When a *firm* temporarily handles a *safe custody asset*, in order to comply with its obligation to act in accordance with *Principle* 10 (Clients' assets), the following are guides to good practice:

(1) a *firm* should keep the *safe custody asset* secure, record it as belonging to that *client*, and forward it to the *client* or in accordance with the *client's* instructions as soon as practicable after receiving it; and

(2) a *firm* should make and retain a record of the fact that the *firm* has handled that *safe custody asset* and of the details of the *client* concerned and of any action the *firm* has taken.

Exemptions which do not apply to MiFID business

6.1.16A **[R]** The exemptions in CASS 6.1.16BR to 6.1.16DG do not apply to a *MiFID investment firm* which holds *financial instruments* belonging to a client in the course of *MiFID business*.

Operators of regulated collective investment schemes

6.1.16B **[R]** The *custody rules* do not apply to a *firm* when it acts as the *operator* of a *regulated collective investment scheme*, in relation to activities carried on for the purpose of, or in connection with, the operation of the *scheme*.

Personal investment firms

6.1.16C **[R]** The *custody rules* do not apply to a *personal investment firm* when it temporarily holds a *designated investment*, other than in *bearer form*, belonging to a *client*, if the *firm*:

(1) keeps it secure, records it as belonging to that *client*, and forwards it to the *client* or in accordance with the *client's* instructions, as soon as practicable after receiving it;

(2) retains the *designated investment* for no longer than the *firm* has taken reasonable steps to determine is necessary to check for errors and to receive the final *document* in connection with any series of transactions to which the *documents* relate; and

(3) makes a record, which must then be retained for a period of 5 years after the record is made, of all the *designated investments* handled in accordance with (1) and (2) together with the details of the *clients* concerned and of any action the *firm* has taken.

6.1.16D **[G]** Administrative convenience alone should not lead a *personal investment firm* to rely on CASS 6.1.16CR. *Personal investment firms* should consider what is in the *client's* interest and not rely on CASS 6.1.16CR as a matter of course.

Trustees and depositaries

6.1.16E **[R]** The specialist regime in CASS 6.1.16FR to 6.1.16IG does not apply to a *MiFID investment firm* which holds *financial instruments* belonging to a client in the course of *MiFID business*.

6.1.16F **[R]** When a *trustee firm* or *depositary* acts as a *custodian* for a trust or *collective investment scheme* and:

(1) the trust or *scheme* is established by written instrument; and

(2) the *trustee firm* or *depositary* has taken reasonable steps to determine that the relevant law and provisions of the trust instrument or *scheme* constitution will provide protections at least equivalent to the *custody rules* for the trust property or *scheme* property;

the *trustee firm* or *depositary* need comply only with the *custody rules* listed in the table below.

Reference	Rule
CASS 6.1.1R to CASS 6.1.9G and CASS 6.1.15G to CASS 6.1.16C R	Application
CASS 6.1.16ER to CASS 6.1.16IG	Trustees and depositaries
CASS 6.1.22G to CASS 6.1.24G	General purpose
CASS 6.2.1R and CASS 6.2.2R	Protection of clients' safe custody assets
CASS 6.2.3R and CASS 6.2.6G	Registration and recording
CASS 6.2.7R	Holding
CASS 6.4.1R and CASS 6.4.2G	Use of safe custody assets
CASS 6.5	Records, accounts and reconciliations

6.1.16G **[G]** The reasonable steps referred in CASS 6.1.16FR (2) could include obtaining an appropriate legal opinion to that effect.

6.1.16H **[R]** When a *trustee firm* or *depositary* within CASS 6.1.16FR arranges for, or delegates the provision of safe custody services by or to another *person*, the *trustee firm* or *depositary* must also comply with CASS 6.3.1R (Depositing and arranging assets to be deposited with third parties) in addition to the custody rules listed in the table in CASS 6.1.16FR.

6.1.16I **[G]** A *trustee firm* or *depositary* that just *arranges safeguarding and administration of assets* may also take advantage of the exemption in CASS 6.1.16JR (Arrangers).

Arrangers

6.1.16J **[R]** Only the *custody rules* in the table below apply to a *firm* when arranging *safeguarding and administration of assets*.

Reference	Rule
CASS 6.1.1R to CASS 6.1.9G and CASS 6.1.15G to CASS 6.1.16BR	Application
CASS 6.1.16JR	Arrangers
CASS 6.1.22G to CASS 6.1.24G	General purpose
CASS 6.3.1R(1A) and CASS 6.3.2G	Arranging for assets to be deposited with third parties
CASS 6.1.16KR	Records

6.1.16K **[R]** When a *firm arranges safeguarding and administration of assets*, it must ensure that proper records of the *custody assets* which it arranges for another to hold or receive, on behalf of the *client*, are made and retained for a period of 5 years after they are made.

6.1.17 **[R]** [deleted]

6.1.18 **[G]** [deleted]

6.1.19 **[G]** [deleted]

6.1.20 **[G]** [deleted]

6.1.20A **[G]** [deleted]

6.1.21 **[R]** [deleted]

General purpose

6.1.22 **[G]** *Principle* 10 (Clients' assets) requires a *firm* to arrange adequate protection for *clients'* assets when it is responsible for them. As part of these protections, the *custody rules* require a *firm* to take appropriate steps to protect *safe custody assets* for which it is responsible.

6.1.23 **[G]** The *rules* in this chapter are designed primarily to restrict the commingling of *client* and the *firm's* assets and minimise the risk of the *client's safe custody assets* being used by the *firm* without the *client's* agreement or contrary to the *client's* wishes, or being treated as the *firm's* assets in the event of its insolvency.

6.1.24 **[G]** The *custody rules* also, where relevant, implement the provisions of *MiFID* which regulate the obligations of a *firm* when it holds *financial instruments* belonging to a *client* in the course of its *MiFID business*.

Part II FSA Handbook Materials

6.2 Holding of client assets

Requirement to protect clients' safe custody assets

6.2.1 **[R]** A *firm* must, when holding *safe custody assets* belonging to *clients*, make adequate arrangements so as to safeguard *clients'* ownership rights, especially in the event of the *firm's* insolvency, and to prevent the use of *safe custody assets* belonging to a *client* on the *firm's* own account except with the *client's* express consent.

[**Note:** article 13(7) of *MiFID*]

Requirement to have adequate organisational arrangements

6.2.2 **[R]** A *firm* must introduce adequate organisational arrangements to minimise the risk of the loss or diminution of *clients' safe custody assets*, or the rights in connection with those *safe custody assets*, as a result of the misuse of the *safe custody assets*, fraud, poor administration, inadequate record-keeping or negligence.

[**Note:** article 16(1)(f) of the *MiFID implementing Directive*]

6.2.3 **[R]** To the extent practicable, a *firm* must effect appropriate registration or recording of legal title to a *safe custody asset* in the name of:

(1) the *client* (or, where appropriate, the *trustee firm*), unless the *client* is an *authorised person* acting on behalf of its *client*, in which case it may be registered in the name of the *client* of that *authorised person;*

(2) a *nominee company* which is controlled by:
- (a) the *firm*;
- (b) an *affiliated company;*
- (c) a *recognised investment exchange* or a *designated investment exchange*; or
- (d) a *third party* with whom *financial instruments* are deposited under CASS 6.3;

(3) any other third party if:
- (a) the *safe custody assets* is subject to the law or market practice of a jurisdiction outside the *United Kingdom* and the *firm* has taken reasonable steps to determine that it is in the *client's* best interests to register or record it in that way, or that it is not feasible to do otherwise, because of the nature of the applicable law or market practice; and
- (b) the *firm* has notified the *client* in writing;

(4) the *firm* if:
- (a) the *safe custody asset* is subject to the law or market practice of a jurisdiction outside the *United Kingdom* and the *firm* has taken reasonable steps to determine that it is in the *client's* best interests to register or record it in that way, or that it is not feasible to do otherwise, because of the nature of the applicable law or market practice; and
- (b) the *firm* has notified the *client* if a *professional client*, or obtained prior written consent if a *retail client*.

6.2.4 **[R]** A *firm* must accept the same level of responsibility to its *client* for any *nominee company* controlled by the *firm* with respect of any requirements of the *custody rules*.

6.2.5 **[R]** A *firm* may register or record legal title to its own *applicable assets* in the same name as that in which legal title to a *safe custody asset* is registered or recorded, but only if:

(1) the *firm's applicable assets* are separately identified in the *firm's* records from the *safe custody assets*; or

(2) the *firm* registers or records a *safe custody asset* in accordance with CASS 6.2.3R(4).

6.2.6 **[G]** A *firm* when complying with CASS 6.2.3R(3) or CASS 6.2.3R(4) will be expected to demonstrate that adequate investigations have been made of the market concerned by reference to local sources, which may include an appropriate legal opinion.

6.2.7 **[R]** A *firm* must ensure that any documents of title to *applicable assets* in *bearer form*, belonging to the *firm* and which it holds in its physical possession, are kept separately from any document of title to a *client's safe custody assets* in *bearer form*.

6.3 Depositing assets and arranging for assets to be deposited with third parties

6.3.1 **[R]**

(1) A firm may deposit safe custody assets held by it on behalf of its clients into an account or accounts opened with a third party, but only if it exercises all due skill, care and diligence in the selection, appointment and periodic review of the third party and of the arrangements for the holding and safekeeping of those safe custody assets.

(1A) A firm which arranges the registration of a safe custody investment through a third party must exercise all due skill, care and diligence in the selection and appointment of the third party.

(2) A firm must take the necessary steps to ensure that any client's safe custody assets deposited with a third party, in accordance with this rule are identifiable separately from the applicable assets belonging to the firm and from the applicable assets belonging to that third party, by means of differently titled accounts on the books of the third party or other equivalent measures that achieve the same level of protection.

(3) When a firm makes the selection, appointment and conducts the periodic review referred to under this rule, it must take into account:

(a) the expertise and market reputation of the third party; and

(b) any legal requirements or market practices related to the holding of those safe custody assets that could adversely affect clients' rights.

(4) A firm must make a record of the grounds upon which it satisfies itself as to the appropriateness of its selection of a third party as required in this rule. The firm must make the record on the date it makes the selection and must keep it from the date of such selection until five years after the firm ceases to use the third party to hold safe custody assets belonging to clients.

[**Note:** articles 16(1)(d) and 17(1) of the *MiFID implementing Directive*]

6.3.2 **[G]** In discharging its obligations under this section, a *firm* should also consider, together with any other relevant matters:

(1) once a *safe custody asset* has been lodged by the *firm* with the third party, the third party's performance of its services to the *firm*;

(2) the arrangements that the third party has in place for holding and safeguarding the *safe custody asset*;

(3) current industry standard reports, for example Financial Reporting and Auditing Group (FRAG) 21 report or its equivalent;

(4) the capital or financial resources of the third party;

(5) the credit rating of the third party; and

(6) any other activities undertaken by the third party and, if relevant, any *affiliated company*.

6.3.3 **[G]** A *firm* should consider carefully the terms of its agreements with third parties with which it will deposit *safe custody assets* belonging to a *client*. The following terms are examples of the issues *firms* should address in this agreement:

(1) that the title of the account indicates that any *safe custody asset* credited to it does not belong to the *firm*;

(2) that the third party will hold or record a *safe custody asset* belonging to the *firm's client* separately from any *applicable asset* belonging to the *firm* or to the third party;

(3) the arrangements for registration or recording of the *safe custody asset* if this will not be registered in the *client's* name;

(4) the restrictions over the third party's right to claim a lien, right of retention or sale over any *safe custody asset* standing to the credit of the account;

(5) the restrictions over the circumstances in which the third party may withdraw assets from the account;

(6) the procedures and authorities for the passing of instructions to or by the *firm*;

(7) the procedures regarding the claiming and receiving of dividends, interest payments and other entitlements accruing to the *client*; and

(8) the provisions detailing the extent of the third party's liability in the event of the loss of a *safe custody asset* caused by the fraud, wilful default or negligence of the third party or an agent appointed by him.

6.3.4 **[R]**

(1) A *firm* must only deposit *safe custody assets* with a third party in a jurisdiction which specifically regulates and supervises the safekeeping of *safe custody assets* for the account of another person with a third party who is subject to such regulation.

(2) A *firm* must not deposit *safe custody assets* held on behalf of a *client* with a third party in a country that is not an *EEA State* (third country) and which does not regulate the holding and safekeeping of *safe custody assets* for the account of another person unless:

(a) the nature of the *safe custody assets* or of the *investment services* connected with those *safe custody assets* requires them to be deposited with a third party in that third country; or

(b) the *safe custody assets* are held on behalf of a *professional client* and the *client* requests the *firm* in writing to deposit them with a third party in that third country.

(3) [deleted]

[**Note:** article 17(2) and (3) of the *MiFID implementing Directive*]

6.4 Use of safe custody assets

6.4.1 **[R]**

Part II FSA Handbook Materials

(1) A *firm* must not enter into arrangements for *securities financing transactions* in respect of *safe custody assets* held by it on behalf of a *client* or otherwise use such *safe custody assets* for its own account or the account of another *client* of the *firm*, unless:
 (a) the *client* has given express prior consent to the use of the *safe custody assets* on specified terms; and
 (b) the use of that *client's safe custody assets* is restricted to the specified terms to which the *client* consents.

(2) A *firm* must not enter into arrangements for *securities financing transactions* in respect of *safe custody assets* held by it on behalf of a *client* in an omnibus account held by a third party, or otherwise use *safe custody assets* held in such an account for its own account or for the account of another *client* unless, in addition to the conditions set out in (1):
 (a) each *client* whose *safe custody assets* are held together in an omnibus account has given express prior consent in accordance with (1)(a); or
 (b) the *firm* has in place systems and controls which ensure that only *safe custody assets* belonging to *clients* who have given express prior consent in accordance with the requirements of (1)(a) are used.

(3) For the purposes of obtaining the express prior consent of a *retail client* under this *rule* the signature of the *retail client* or an equivalent alternative mechanism is required.

(4) A *firm* which does not undertake *MiFID business* does not need to comply with (1), (2) and (3) until 1 May 2009.

[**Note:** article 19 of the *MiFID implementing Directive*]

6.4.2 **[G]** *Firms* are reminded of the *client's best interests rule*, which requires the *firm* to act honestly, fairly and professionally in accordance with the best interests of their *clients*. An example of what is generally considered to be such conduct, in the context of *stock lending activities* involving *retail clients* is that:
(1) the *firm* ensures that *relevant collateral* is provided by the borrower in favour of the *client*;
(2) the current realisable value of the *safe custody asset* and of the *relevant collateral* is monitored daily; and
(3) the *firm* provides *relevant collateral* to make up the difference where the current realisable value of the collateral falls below that of the *safe custody asset*, unless otherwise agreed in writing by the *client*.

6.4.3 **[R]** Where a *firm* uses *safe custody assets* as permitted in this section, the records of the *firm* must include details of the *client* on whose instructions the use of the *safe custody assets* has been effected, as well as the number of *safe custody assets* used belonging to each *client* who has given consent, so as to enable the correct allocation of any loss.

[**Note:** article 19(2) of the *MiFID implementing Directive*]

6.5 Records, accounts and reconciliations

Records and accounts

6.5.1 **[R]** A *firm* must keep such records and accounts as necessary to enable it at any time and without delay to distinguish *safe custody assets* held for one *client* from *safe custody assets* held for any other *client*, and from the *firm's* own *applicable assets*.

[**Note:** article 16(1)(a) of the *MiFID implementing Directive*]

6.5.2 **[R]** A *firm* must maintain its records and accounts in a way that ensures their accuracy, and in particular their correspondence to the *safe custody assets* held for *clients*.

[**Note:** article 16(1)(b) of the *MiFID implementing Directive*]

Record keeping

6.5.3 **[R]** A *firm* must ensure that the records made under this section are retained for a period of five years after they are made.

Internal reconciliation of safe custody assets held for clients

6.5.4 **[G]**
(1) Carrying out internal reconciliations of the *safe custody assets* held for each *client* with the *safe custody assets* held by the *firm* and third parties is an important step in the discharge of the *firm's* obligations under CASS 6.5.2R, and where relevant, SYSC 4.1.1R and SYSC 6.1.1R.
(2) A *firm* should perform such internal reconciliations:
 (a) as often as is necessary; and
 (b) as soon as reasonably practicable after the date to which the reconciliation relates;
 to ensure the accuracy of the *firm's* records and accounts.

(3) Reconciliation methods which can be adopted for these purposes include the 'total count method', which requires that all *safe custody assets* be counted and reconciled as at the same date.

(4) If a *firm* chooses to use an alternative reconciliation method (for example the 'rolling stock method') it needs to ensure that:
  (a) all of a particular *safe custody asset* are counted and reconciled as at the same date; and
  (b) all *safe custody assets* are counted and reconciled during a period of six months.

6.5.5 **[R]** A *firm* that uses an alternative reconciliation method must first send a written confirmation to the *FSA* from the *firm's* auditor that the *firm* has in place systems and controls which are adequate to enable it to use the method effectively.

Reconciliations with external records

6.5.6 **[R]** A *firm* must conduct on a regular basis, reconciliations between its internal accounts and records and those of any third parties by whom those *safe custody assets* are held.

[**Note:** article 16(1)(c) of the *MiFID implementing Directive*]

6.5.7 **[G]** Where a *firm* deposits *safe custody assets* belonging to a *client* with a third party, in complying with the requirements of CASS 6.5.6R, the *firm* should seek to ensure that the third party will deliver to the *firm* a statement as at a date or dates specified by the *firm* which details the description and amounts of all the *safe custody assets* credited to the account, and that this statement is delivered in adequate time to allow the *firm* to carry out the periodic reconciliations required in CASS 6.5.6R.

Frequency of external reconciliations

6.5.8 **[G]** A *firm* should perform the reconciliation required by CASS 6.5.6R:
(1) as regularly as is necessary; and
(2) as soon as reasonably practicable after the date to which the reconciliation relates;

to ensure the accuracy of its internal accounts and records against those of third parties by whom *safe custody assets* are held.

Independence of person conducting reconciliations

6.5.9 **[G]** Whenever possible, a *firm* should ensure that reconciliations are carried out by a *person* (for example an *employee* of the *firm*) who is independent of the production or maintenance of the records to be reconciled.

Reconciliation discrepancies

6.5.10 **[R]** A *firm* must promptly correct any discrepancies which are revealed in the reconciliations envisaged by this section, and make good, or provide the equivalent of, any unreconciled *shortfall* for which there are reasonable grounds for concluding that the *firm* is responsible.

6.5.11 **[G]** Items recorded or held within a suspense or error account fall within the scope of discrepancies.

6.5.12 **[G]** A *firm* may, where justified, conclude that another *person* is responsible for an irreconcilable *shortfall* despite the existence of a dispute with that other *person* about the unreconciled item. In those circumstances, the *firm* is not required to make good the *shortfall* but is expected to take reasonable steps to resolve the position with the other *person*.

Notification requirements

6.5.13 **[R]** A *firm* must inform the *FSA* in writing without delay:
(1) if it has not complied with, or is unable, in any material respect, to comply with the requirements in CASS 6.5.1R, CASS 6.5.2R or CASS 6.5.6R; or
(2) if, having carried out a reconciliation, it has not complied with, or is unable, in any material respect, to comply with CASS 6.5.10R.

Audit of compliance with the MiFID custody rules

6.5.14 **[G]** *Firms* are reminded that the auditor of the *firm* has to confirm in the report submitted to the *FSA* under SUP 3.10 (Duties of auditors: notification and report on client assets) that the *firm* has maintained systems adequate to enable it to comply with the *rules* in this chapter.

6.5.15 **[G]** *Firms* that use an alternative reconciliation method are reminded that the *firm's* auditor must confirm to the *FSA* in writing that the *firm* has in place systems and controls which are adequate to enable it to use another method effectively (see CASS 6.5.5R).

CHAPTER 7
CLIENT MONEY RULES

7.1 Application and Purpose

Application

[2132]
7.1.1 **[R]** This chapter (the *client money rules*) applies to a *firm* that receives *money* from or holds *money* for, or on behalf of, a *client* in the course of, or in connection with:
(1) [deleted]
(2) [deleted]
(3) its *MiFID business*; and/or
(4) its *designated investment business*, that is not *MiFID business* in respect of any *investment agreement* entered into, or to be entered into, with or for a *client*;

unless otherwise specified in this section.

7.1.2 **[G]** [deleted]

Opt-in to the client money rules

7.1.3 **[R]**

(1) A firm that receives or holds money to which this chapter applies in relation to:
 (a) its MiFID business; or
 (b) its MiFID business and its designated investment business which is not MiFID business;

 and holds money in respect of which CASS 5 applies, may elect to comply with the provisions of this chapter in respect of all such money and if it does so, this chapter applies as if all such money were money that the firm receives and holds in the course of, or in connection with, its MiFID business.

(1A) [deleted]

(1B) A firm that receives or holds money to which this chapter applies solely in relation to its designated investment business which is not MiFID business and receives or holds money in respect of which the insurance client money chapter applies, may elect to comply with the provisions of this chapter in respect of all such money and if it does so, this chapter applies as if all such money were money that the firm receives and holds in the course of or in connection with its designated investment business.

(2) A firm must make and retain a written record of any election it makes under this rule, including the date from which the election is to be effective. The firm must make the record on the date it makes the election and must keep it for a period of five years after ceasing to use it.

7.1.4 **[G]** The opt-in to the *client money rules* in this chapter does not apply in respect of *money* that a *firm* holds outside of the scope of the *insurance client money chapter*.

7.1.5 **[G]** If a *firm* has opted to comply with this chapter, the *insurance client money chapter* will have no application to the activities to which the election applies.

7.1.6 **[G]** A *firm* that is only subject to the *insurance client money chapter* may not opt to comply with this chapter.

7.1.7 **[G]** [deleted]

7.1.7A **[G]** [deleted]

Professional client opt-out

7.1.7B **[R]** CASS 7.1.7CG to CASS 7.1.7IG do not apply to a *firm* in relation to *money* held in connection with its *MiFID business* to which this chapter applies or in relation to *money* for which the *firm* has made an election under CASS 7.1.3R(1).

Money that is not client money: 'opt outs' for any business other than insurance mediation activity

7.1.7C **[G]** The 'opt out' provisions provide a *firm* with the option of allowing a *professional client* to choose whether their *money* is subject to the *client money rules* (unless the *firm* is conducting *insurance mediation activity*).

7.1.7D **[R]** Subject to CASS 7.1.7FR, *money* is not *client money* when a *firm* (other than a *sole trader*) holds that *money* on behalf of, or receives it from, a *professional client*, other than in the course of *insurance mediation activity*, and the *firm* has obtained written acknowledgement from the *professional client* that:

(1) *money* will not be subject to the protections conferred by the *client money rules*;
(2) as a consequence, this *money* will not be segregated from the *money* of the *firm* in accordance with the *client money rules* and will be used by the *firm* in the course of its own business; and
(3) the *professional client* will rank only as a general creditor of the *firm*.

'Opt-outs' for non-IMD business

7.1.7E **[G]** For a *firm* whose business is not governed by the *Insurance Mediation Directive*, it is possible to 'opt out' on a one-way basis. However, in order to maintain a comparable regime to that applying to *MiFID business*, all '*MiFID* type' business undertaken outside the scope of *MiFID*, should comply with the *client money rules* or be 'opted out' on a two-way basis.

7.1.7F **[R]** *Money* is not *client money* if a *firm*, in respect of *designated investment business* which is not an *investment service or activity*, an *ancillary service*, a *listed activity* or *insurance mediation activity*:
(1) holds it on behalf of or receives it from a *professional client* who is not an *authorised person*; and
(2) has sent a separate written notice to the *professional client* stating the matters set out in CASS 7.1.7DR(1) to 7.1.7DR(3).

7.1.7G **[G]** When a *firm* undertakes a range of business for a *professional client* and has separate agreements for each type of business undertaken, the *firm* may treat *client money* held on behalf of the *client* differently for different types of business; for example, a *firm* may, under CASS 7.1.7DR or CASS 7.1.7FR, elect to segregate *client money* in connection with *securities* transactions and not segregate (by complying with CASS 7.1.7DR or CASS 7.1.7FR) money in connection with *contingent liability investments* for the same *client*.

7.1.7H **[R]** When a *firm* transfers *client money* to another *person*, the *firm* must not enter into an agreement under CASS 7.1.7DR or CASS 7.1.7FR with that other *person* in relation to that *client money* or represent to that other *person* that the *money* is not *client money*.

7.1.7I **[G]** CASS 7.1.7HR prevents a *firm*, when passing *client money* to another *person* under CASS 7.5.2R (transfer of client money to a third party), from making use of the 'opt out' provisions under CASS 7.1.7DR or CASS 7.1.7FR.

Credit institutions and approved banks

7.1.8 **[R]** The *client money rules* do not apply to a *BCD credit institution* in relation to deposits within the meaning of the *BCD* held by that *institution*.

[**Note:** article 13(8) of *MiFID* and article 18(1) of the *MiFID implementing Directive*]

7.1.9 **[G]** If a *credit institution* that holds *money* as a deposit with itself is subject to the *requirement to disclose information before providing services*, it should, in compliance with that obligation, notify the *client* that:
(1) *money* held for that *client* in an account with the *credit institution* will be held by the *firm* as banker and not as trustee (or in Scotland as agent); and
(2) as a result, the *money* will not be held in accordance with the *client money rules*.

7.1.10 **[G]** Pursuant to *Principle* 10 (Clients' assets), a *credit institution* that holds *money* as a deposit with itself should be able to account to all of its *clients* for amounts held on their behalf at all times. A bank account opened with the *firm* that is in the name of the *client* would generally be sufficient. When *money* from *clients* deposited with the *firm* is held in a pooled account, this account should be clearly identified as an account for *clients*. The *firm* should also be able to demonstrate that an amount owed to a specific *client* that is held within the pool can be reconciled with a record showing that individual's *client* balance and is, therefore, identifiable at any time. Similarly, where that *money* is reflected only in a *firm's* bank account with other banks (nostro accounts), the *firm* should be able to reconcile amounts owed to that *client* within a reasonable period of time.

7.1.11 **[G]** A *credit institution* is reminded that the exemption for deposits is not an absolute exemption from the *client money rules*.

7.1.11A **[R]**
(1) This *rule* applies to a *firm* which is an *approved bank* but not a *BCD credit institution*.
(2) The *client money rules* do not apply to *money* held by the *approved bank* if it is undertaking business which is not *MiFID business* but only when the money is held in an account with itself, in which case the *firm* must notify the *client* in writing that:
   (a) *money* held for that *client* in an account with the *approved bank* will be held by the *firm* as banker and not as trustee (or in Scotland as agent); and
   (b) as a result, the *money* will not be held in accordance with the *client money rules*.

Affiliated companies – MiFID business

7.1.12 **[G]** A *firm* that holds *money* on behalf of, or receives *money* from, an *affiliated company* in respect of *MiFID business* must treat the *affiliated company* as any other *client* of the *firm* for the purposes of this chapter.

Affiliated companies – non-MiFID business

7.1.12A **[R]** A *firm* that holds *money* on behalf of, or receives *money* from, an *affiliated company* in respect of *designated investment business* which is not *MiFID business* must not treat the *money* as *client money* unless:

(1) the *firm* has been notified by the *affiliated company* that the *money* belongs to a *client* of the *affiliated company*; or

(2) the *affiliated company* is a *client* dealt with at arm's length; or

(3) the *affiliated company* is a manager of an *occupational pension scheme* or is an overseas company; and

  (a) the *money* is given to the *firm* in order to carry on *designated investment business* for or on behalf of the *clients* of the *affiliated company*; and

  (b) the *firm* has been notified by the *affiliated company* that the *money* is to be treated as *client money*.

7.1.13 **[G]** [deleted]

Coins

7.1.14 **[R]** The *client money rules* do not apply with respect to coins held on behalf of a *client* if the *firm* and the *client* have agreed that the *money* (or *money* of that type) is to be held by the *firm* for the intrinsic value of the metal which constitutes the coin.

Solicitors

7.1.15 **[R]**

(1) An *authorised professional firm* regulated by the Law Society (of England and Wales), the Law Society of Scotland or the Law Society of Northern Ireland must comply with the following rules of its *designated professional body* and, where relevant paragraph (3), and if it does so, it will be deemed to comply with the *client money rules*.

(2) The relevant rules are:

  (a) if the *firm* is regulated by the Law Society (of England and Wales):

    (i) the Solicitors' Accounts Rules 1998; or

    (ii) where applicable, the Solicitors Overseas Practice Rules 1990;

  (b) if the *firm* is regulated by the Law Society of Scotland, the Solicitors' (Scotland) Accounts, Accounts Certificate, Professional Practice and Guarantee Fund Rules 2001; and

  (c) if the *firm* is regulated by the Law Society of Northern Ireland, the Solicitors' Accounts Regulations 1998.

(3) If the *firm* in (1) is a *MiFID investment firm* that receives or holds *money* for, or on behalf of a *client* in the course of, or in connection with its *MiFID business*, it must also comply with the *MiFID client money (minimum implementing) rules* in relation to that business.

Long term insurers and friendly societies

7.1.15A **[R]** This chapter does not apply to the *permitted activities* of a *long-term insurer* or a *friendly society*, unless it is a *MiFID investment firm* that receives *money* from or holds *money* for or on behalf of a *client* in the course of, or in connection with, its *MiFID business*.

Contracts of insurance

7.1.15B **[R]** This chapter does not apply to *client money* held by a *firm* which:

(1) receives or holds *client money* in relation to *contracts of insurance*; but which

(2) in relation to such *client money* elects to act in accordance with the *insurance client money chapter*.

7.1.15C **[R]** A *firm* should make and retain a written record of any election which it makes under CASS 7.1.15BR.

Life assurance business

7.1.15D **[G]**

(1) A *firm* which receives and holds *client money* in respect of life assurance business in the course of its *designated investment business* that is not *MiFID business* may:

  (a) under CASS 7.1.3R(1B) elect to comply with the *client money chapter* in respect of such *client money* and in doing so avoid the need to comply with the *insurance client money chapter* which would otherwise apply to the *firm* in respect of *client money* received in the course of its *insurance mediation activity*; or

(b) under CASS 7.1.15BR, elect to comply with the *insurance client money chapter* in respect of such *client money*.

(2) These options are available to a *firm* irrespective of whether it also receives and holds *client money* in respect of other parts of its *designated investment business*. A *firm* may not however choose to comply with the *insurance client money chapter* in respect of *client money* which it receives and holds in the course of any part of its *designated investment business* which does not involve an *insurance mediation activity*.

Trustee firms (other than trustees of unit trust schemes)

7.1.15E **[R]** A *trustee firm* which holds *money* in relation to its *designated investment business* which is not *MiFID business* to which this chapter applies, must hold any such *client money* separate from its own *money* at all times.

7.1.15F **[R]** Only the *client money rules* listed in the table below apply to a *trustee firm* in connection with *money* that the firm receives, or holds for or on behalf of a client in the course of or in connection with its *designated investment business* which is not *MiFID business*.

Reference	Rule
CASS 7.1.1R to CASS 7.1.6G, and CASS 7.1.8R to CASS 7.1.14R	Application
CASS 7.1.15ER and CASS 7.1.15FR	Trustee firms (other than trustees of unit trust schemes)
CASS 7.1.16G	General principle
CASS 7.7.2R to CASS 7.7.4G	Requirement
CASS 7.4.1R to CASS 7.4.6G	Depositing client money
CASS 7.4.7R to CASS 7.4.13G	A firm's selection of credit institution, bank or money market fund
CASS 7.6.6G to CASS 7.6.16R	Reconciliation of client money balances

General purpose

7.1.16 **[G]**

(1) *Principle* 10 (Clients' assets) requires a *firm* to arrange adequate protection for *clients'* assets when the *firm* is responsible for them. An essential part of that protection is the proper accounting and treatment of *client money*. The *client money rules* provide requirements for *firms* that receive or hold *client money*, in whatever form.

(2) The *client money rules* also where relevant implement the provisions of *MiFID* which regulate the obligations of a *firm* when it holds *client money* in the course of its *MiFID business*.

7.2 Definition of client money

7.2.1 **[R]** [deleted]

7.2.2 **[R]** [deleted]

Title transfer collateral arrangements

7.2.3 **[R]** Where a *client* transfers full ownership of *money* to a *firm* for the purpose of securing or otherwise covering present or future, actual or contingent or prospective obligations, such *money* should no longer be regarded as *client money*.

[**Note:** recital 27 to *MiFID*]

7.2.4 **[G]** A title transfer financial collateral arrangement under *the Financial Collateral Directive* is an example of a type of transfer of *money* to cover obligations where that *money* will not be regarded as *client money*.

7.2.5 **[G]** Where a *firm* has received full title or full ownership to *money* under a collateral arrangement, the fact that it has also taken a security interest over its obligation to repay that *money* to the *client* would not result in the *money* being *client money*. This can be compared to a situation in which a *firm* takes a charge or other security interest over *money* held in a *client bank account*, where that *money* would still be *client money* as there would be no absolute transfer of title to the *firm*. However, if that security interest includes a "right to use arrangement", under which the *client* agrees to transfer all of its rights to *money* in that account to the *firm* upon the exercise of the right to use, the *money* may cease to be *client money*, but only once the right to use is exercised and the *money* is transferred out of the account to the *firm*.

7.2.6 **[G]** *Firms* are reminded of the *client's best interest rule*, which requires a *firm* to act honestly, fairly and professionally in accordance with the best interests of its *clients* when structuring its business particularly in respect of the effect of that structure on *firms'* obligations under the *client money rules*.

7.2.7 **[G]** Pursuant to the *client's best interests rule*, a *firm* should ensure that where a *retail client* transfers full ownership of *money* to a *firm*:

(1) the *client* is notified that full ownership of the *money* has been transferred to the *firm* and, as such, the *client* no longer has a proprietary claim over this *money* and the *firm* can deal with it on its own right;

(2) the transfer is for the purposes of securing or covering the *client's* obligations;

(3) an equivalent transfer is made back to the *client* if the provision of collateral by the *client* is no longer necessary; and

(4) there is a reasonable link between the timing and the amount of the collateral transfer and the obligation that the *client* owes, or is likely to owe, to the *firm*.

Money in connection with a "delivery versus payment" transaction

7.2.8 **[R]** *Money* need not be treated as *client money* in respect of a delivery versus payment transaction through a commercial settlement system if it is intended that either:

(1) in respect of a *client's* purchase, *money* from a *client* will be due to the *firm* within one *business day* upon the fulfilment of a delivery obligation; or

(2) in respect of a *client's* sale, *money* is due to the *client* within one *business day* following the *client's* fulfilment of a delivery obligation;

unless the delivery or payment by the *firm* does not occur by the close of business on the third *business day* following the date of payment or delivery of the *investments* by the *client*.

7.2.8A **[G]** The exclusion from the *client money rules* for delivery versus payment transactions under CASS 7.2.8R is an example of an exclusion from the *client money rules* which is permissible by virtue of recital 26 of *MiFID*.

7.2.8B **[R]** *Money* need not be treated as *client money* in respect of a delivery versus payment transaction, for the purpose of settling a transaction in relation to *units* in a *regulated collective investment scheme*, if:

(1) the *authorised fund manager* receives it from a *client* in relation to the *authorised fund manager's* obligation to issue *units*, in an *AUT* or to arrange for the issue of *units* in an *ICVC*, in accordance with COLL, unless the *price* of those *units* has not been determined by the close of business on the next *business day*:

   (a) following the date of the receipt of the *money* from the *client*; or

   (b) if the *money* was received by an *appointed representative* of the *authorised fund manager*, in accordance with CASS 7.4.24G, following the date of receipt at the specified business address of the *authorised fund manager*; or

(2) the *money* is held in the course of redeeming *units* where the proceeds of that redemption are paid to a *client* within the time specified in COLL; when an *authorised fund manager* draws a cheque or other payable order within these timeframes the provisions of CASS 7.2.17R and CASS 7.2.9R(2) will not apply.

Money due and payable to the firm

7.2.9 **[R]**

(1) *Money* is not *client money* when it becomes properly due and payable to the *firm* for its own account.

(2) For these purposes, if a *firm* makes a payment to, or on the instructions of, a *client*, from an account other than a *client bank account*, until that payment has cleared, no equivalent sum from a *client bank account* for reimbursement will become due and payable to the *firm*.

7.2.10 **[G]** *Money* held as *client money* becomes due and payable to the *firm* or for the *firm's* own account, for example, because the *firm* acted as *principal* in the contract or the *firm*, acting as agent, has itself paid for *securities* in advance of receiving the purchase *money* from its *client*. The circumstances in which it is due and payable will depend on the contractual arrangement between the *firm* and the *client*.

7.2.11 **[G]** When a *client's* obligation or liability, that is secured by that *client's* asset, crystallises, and the *firm* realises the asset in accordance with an agreement entered into between the *client* and the *firm*, the part of the proceeds of the asset to cover such liability that is due and payable to the *firm* is not *client money*. However, any proceeds of sale in excess of the amount owed by the *client* to the *firm* should be paid over to the *client* immediately or be held in accordance with the *client money rules*.

Commission rebate

7.2.12 **[G]** When a *firm* has entered into an arrangement under which *commission* is rebated to a *client*, those rebates need not be treated as *client money* until they become due and payable to the *client* in accordance with the terms of the contractual arrangements between the parties.

7.2.13 **[G]** When *commission* rebate becomes due and payable to the *client*, the *firm* should:
(1) treat it as *client money*; or
(2) pay it out in accordance with the *rule* regarding the discharge of a *firm's* fiduciary duty to the *client* (see CASS 7.2.15R);

unless the *firm* and the *client* have entered into an arrangement under which the *client* has agreed to transfer full ownership of this *money* to the *firm* as collateral against payment of future professional fees (see CASS 7.2.3R (Title transfer collateral arrangements)).

Interest

7.2.14 **[R]** Unless a *firm* notifies a *retail client* in writing whether or not interest is to be paid on *client money* and, if so, on what terms and at what frequency, it must pay that *client* all interest earned on that *client money*. Any interest due to a *client* will be *client money*.

Discharge of fiduciary duty

7.2.15 **[R]** *Money* ceases to be *client money* if it is paid:
(1) to the *client*, or a duly authorised representative of the *client*; or
(2) to a third party on the instruction of the *client*, unless it is transferred to a third party in the course of effecting a transaction, in accordance with CASS 7.5.2R (Transfer of client money to a third party); or
(3) into a bank account of the *client* (not being an account which is also in the name of the *firm*); or
(4) to the *firm* itself, when it is due and payable to the *firm* (see CASS 7.2.9R (Money due and payable to the firm)); or
(5) to the *firm* itself, when it is an excess in the *client bank account* (see CASS 7.6.13R(2) (Reconciliation discrepancies)).

7.2.16 **[G]** When a *firm* wishes to transfer *client money* balances to a third party in the course of transferring its business to another *firm*, it should do so in a way which it discharges its fiduciary duty to the *client* under this section.

7.2.17 **[R]** When a *firm* draws a cheque or other payable order to discharge its fiduciary duty to the *client*, it must continue to treat the sum concerned as *client money* until the cheque or order is presented and paid by the bank.

Allocated but unclaimed client money

7.2.18 **[G]** The purpose of the *rule* on allocated but unclaimed *client money* is to allow a *firm*, in the normal course of its business, to cease to treat as *client money* any balances, allocated to an individual *client*, when those balances remain unclaimed.

7.2.19 **[R]** A *firm* may cease to treat as *client money* any unclaimed *client money* balance if it can demonstrate that it has taken reasonable steps to trace the *client* concerned and to return the balance.

7.2.20 **[E]**
(1) Reasonable steps should include:
  (a) entering into a written agreement, in which the *client* consents to the *firm* releasing, after the period of time specified in (b), any *client money* balances, for or on behalf of that *client*, from *client bank accounts*;
  (b) determining that there has been no movement on the *client's* balance for a period of at least six years (notwithstanding any payments or receipts of charges, interest or similar items);
  (c) writing to the *client* at the last known address informing the *client* of the *firm's* intention of no longer treating that balance as *client money*, giving the *client* 28 days to make a claim;
  (d) making and retaining records of all balances released from *client bank accounts*; and
  (e) undertaking to make good any valid claim against any released balances.
(2) Compliance with (1) may be relied on as tending to establish compliance with CASS 7.2.19R.
(3) Contravention of (1) may be relied on as tending to establish contravention of CASS 7.2.19R.

7.2.21 **[G]** When a *firm* gives an undertaking to make good any valid claim against released balances, it should make arrangements authorised by the *firm's* relevant *controllers* that are legally enforceable by any *person* with a valid claim to such *money*.

7.3 Organisational requirements: client money

Requirement to protect client money

7.3.1 **[R]** A *firm* must, when holding *client money*, make adequate arrangements to safeguard the *client's* rights and prevent the use of *client money* for its own account.

[**Note:** article 13(8) of *MiFID*]

Requirement to have adequate organisational arrangements

7.3.2 **[R]** A *firm* must introduce adequate organisational arrangements to minimise the risk of the loss or diminution of *client money*, or of rights in connection with *client money*, as a result of misuse of *client money*, fraud, poor administration, inadequate record-keeping or negligence.

[**Note:** article 16(1)(f) of the *MiFID implementing Directive*]

7.4 Segregation of client money

Depositing client money

7.4.1 **[R]** A *firm*, on receiving any *client money*, must promptly place this *money* into one or more accounts opened with any of the following:
(1) a central bank;
(2) a *BCD credit institution*;
(3) a bank authorised in a third country;
(4) a *qualifying money market fund*.

[**Note:** article 18(1) of the *MiFID implementing Directive*]

7.4.2 **[G]** An account with a central bank, a *BCD credit institution* or a bank authorised in a third country in which *client money* is placed is a *client bank account*.

Qualifying money market funds

7.4.3 **[G]** Where a *firm* deposits *client money* with a *qualifying money market fund*, the units in that fund should be held in accordance with CASS 6.

[**Note:** recital 23 to the *MiFID implementing Directive*]

7.4.4 **[G]** A *firm* that places *client money* in a *qualifying money market fund* should ensure that it has the *permissions* required to invest in and hold units in that fund and must comply with the *rules* that are relevant for those activities.

7.4.5 **[R]** A *firm* must give a *client* the right to oppose the placement of his *money* in a *qualifying money market fund*.

[**Note:** article 18(3) of the *MiFID implementing Directive*]

7.4.6 **[G]** If a *firm* that intends to place *client money* in a *qualifying money market fund* is subject to the *requirement to disclose information before providing services*, it should, in compliance with that obligation, notify the *client* that:
(1) *money* held for that *client* will be held in a *qualifying money market fund*; and
(2) as a result, the *money* will not be held in accordance with the *client money rules* but in accordance with the *custody rules*.

A firm's selection of a credit institution, bank or money market fund

7.4.7 **[R]** A *firm* that does not deposit *client money* with a central bank must exercise all due skill, care and diligence in the selection, appointment and periodic review of the *credit institution*, bank or *qualifying money market fund* where the *money* is deposited and the arrangements for the holding of this *money*.

[**Note:** article 18(3) of the *MiFID implementing Directive*]

7.4.8 **[R]** When a *firm* makes the selection, appointment and conducts the periodic review of a *credit institution*, a bank or a *qualifying money market fund*, it must take into account:
(1) the expertise and market reputation of the third party; and
(2) any legal requirements or market practices related to the holding of *client money* that could adversely affect *clients'* rights.

[**Note:** article 18(3) of the *MiFID implementing Directive*]

7.4.9 **[G]** In discharging its obligations when selecting, appointing and reviewing the appointment of a *credit institution*, a bank or a *qualifying money market fund*, a *firm* should also consider, together with any other relevant matters:
(1) the need for diversification of risks;

(2) the capital of the *credit institution* or bank;
(3) the amount of *client money* placed, as a proportion of the *credit institution* or bank's capital and *deposits*, and, in the case of a *qualifying money market fund*, compared to any limit the fund may place on the volume of redemptions in any period;
(4) the credit rating of the *credit institution* or bank; and
(5) to the extent that the information is available, the level of risk in the investment and loan activities undertaken by the *credit institution* or bank and *affiliated companies*.

7.4.10 **[R]** A *firm* must make a record of the grounds upon which it satisfies itself as to the appropriateness of its selection of a *credit institution*, a bank or a *qualifying money market fund*. The *firm* must make the record on the date it makes the selection and must keep it from the date of such selection until five years after the *firm* ceases to use the third party to hold *client money*.

Client bank accounts

7.4.11 **[R]** A *firm* must take the necessary steps to ensure that *client money* deposited, in accordance with *CASS* 7.4.1R, in a central bank, a *credit institution*, a bank authorised in a third country or a *qualifying money market fund* is held in an account or accounts identified separately from any accounts used to hold *money* belonging to the *firm*.

[**Note:** article 16(1)(e) of the *MiFID implementing Directive*]

7.4.12 **[G]** A *firm* may open one or more *client bank accounts* in the form of a *general client bank account*, a *designated client bank account* or a *designated client fund account* (see CASS 7.9.3G).

7.4.13 **[G]** A *designated client fund account* may be used for a *client* only where that *client* has consented to the use of that account and all other *designated client fund accounts* which may be pooled with it. For example, a *client* who consents to the use of bank A and bank B should have his *money* held in a different *designated client fund account* at bank B from a *client* who has consented to the use of banks B and C.

Payment of client money into a client bank account

7.4.14 **[G]** Two approaches that a *firm* can adopt in discharging its obligations under the *client money segregation requirements* are:
(1) the 'normal approach'; or
(2) the 'alternative approach'.

7.4.15 **[R]** A *firm* that does not adopt the normal approach must first send a written confirmation to the *FSA* from the *firm's* auditor that the *firm* has in place systems and controls which are adequate to enable it to operate another approach effectively.

7.4.16 **[G]** The alternative approach would be appropriate for a *firm* that operates in a multi-product, multi-currency environment for which adopting the normal approach would be unduly burdensome and would not achieve the *client* protection objective. Under the alternative approach, *client money* is received into and paid out of a *firm's* own bank accounts; consequently the *firm* should have systems and controls that are capable of monitoring the *client money* flows so that the *firm* comply with its obligations to perform reconciliations of records and accounts (see CASS 7.6.2R). A *firm* that adopts the alternative approach will segregate *client money* into a *client bank account* on a daily basis, after having performed a reconciliation of records and accounts of the entitlement of each *client* for whom the *firm* holds *client money* with the records and accounts of the *client money* the *firm* holds in *client bank account* and *client transaction accounts* to determine what the *client money* requirement was at the close of the previous *business day*.

7.4.17 **[G]** Under the normal approach, a *firm* that receives *client money* should either:
(1) pay it promptly, and in any event no later than the next *business day* after receipt, into a *client bank account*; or
(2) pay it out in accordance with the *rule* regarding the discharge of a *firm's* fiduciary duty to the *client* (see CASS 7.2.15R).

7.4.18 **[G]** Under the alternative approach, a *firm* that receives *client money* should:
(1)
(a) pay any *money* to or on behalf of *clients* out of its own account; and
(b) perform a reconciliation of records and accounts required under CASS 7.6.2R (Records and accounts), and where relevant SYSC 4.1.1R and SYSC 6.1.1R, adjust the balance held in its *client bank accounts* and then segregate the *money* in the *client bank account* until the calculation is re-performed on the next *business day*; or
(2) pay it out in accordance with the *rule* regarding the discharge of a *firm's* fiduciary duty to the *client* (see CASS 7.2.15R).

7.4.19 **[G]** A *firm* that adopts the alternative approach may:
(1) receive all *client money* into its own bank account;
(2) choose to operate the alternative approach for some types of business (for example, overseas equities transactions) and operate the normal approach for other types of business (for example, *contingent liability investments*) if the *firm* can demonstrate that its systems and controls are adequate (see CASS 7.4.15R); and

(3) use an historic average to account for uncleared cheques (see paragraph 4 of CASS 7 Annex 1).

7.4.20 **[G]** Pursuant to the *client money segregation requirements*, a *firm* should ensure that any *money* other than *client money* deposited in a *client bank account* is promptly paid out of that account unless it is a minimum sum required to open the account, or to keep it open.

7.4.21 **[R]** If it is prudent to do so to ensure that *client money* is protected, a *firm* may pay into a *client bank account money* of its own, and that *money* will then become *client money* for the purposes of this chapter.

Automated transfers

7.4.22 **[G]** Pursuant to the *client money segregation requirements*, a *firm* operating the normal approach that receives *client money* in the form of an automated transfer should take reasonable steps to ensure that:
(1) the *money* is received directly into a *client bank account*; and
(2) if *money* is received directly into the *firm's* own account, the *money* is transferred into a *client bank account* promptly, and in any event, no later than the next *business day* after receipt.

Mixed remittance

7.4.23 **[G]** Pursuant to the *client money segregation requirements*, a *firm* operating the normal approach that receives a *mixed remittance* (that is part *client money* and part other *money*) should:
(1) pay the full sum into a *client bank account* promptly, and in any event, no later than the next *business day* after receipt; and
(2) pay the *money* that is not *client money* out of the *client bank account* promptly, and in any event, no later than one *business day* of the day on which the *firm* would normally expect the remittance to be cleared.

Appointed representatives, tied agents, field representatives and other agents

7.4.24 **[G]**
(1) Pursuant to the *client money segregation requirements*, a *firm* operating the normal approach should establish and maintain procedures to ensure that *client money* received by its *appointed representatives, tied agents, field representatives* or other agents is:
  (a) paid into a *client bank account* of the *firm* promptly, and in any event, no later than the next *business day* after receipt; or
  (b) forwarded to the *firm*, or in the case of a *field representative* forwarded to a specified business address of the *firm*, so as to ensure that the *money* arrives at the specified business address promptly, and in any event, no later than the close of the third *business day*.
(2) For the purposes of 1(b), *client money* received on *business day* one should be forwarded to the *firm* or specified business address of the *firm* promptly, and in any event, no later than the next *business day* after receipt (*business day* two) in order for it to reach that *firm* or specified business address by the close of the third *business day*. Procedures requiring the *client money* in the form of a cheque to be sent to the *firm* or the specified business address of the *firm* by first class post promptly, and in any event, no later than the next *business day* after receipt, would be in line with 1(b).

7.4.25 **[G]** The *firm* should ensure that its *appointed representatives, tied agents, field representatives* or other agents keep *client money* separately identifiable from any other *money* (including that of the *firm*) until the *client money* is paid into a *client bank account* or sent to the *firm*.

7.4.26 **[G]** A *firm* that operates a number of small branches, but holds or accounts for all *client money* centrally, may treat those small branches in the same way as *appointed representatives* and *tied agents*.

Client entitlements

7.4.27 **[G]** Pursuant to the *client money segregation requirements*, a *firm* operating the normal approach that receives outside the *United Kingdom* a *client* entitlement on behalf of a *client* should pay any part of it which is *client money*:
(1) to, or in accordance with, the instructions of the *client* concerned; or
(2) into a *client bank account* promptly, and in any event, no later than five *business days* after the *firm* is notified of its receipt.

7.4.28 **[G]** Pursuant to the *client money segregation requirements*, a *firm* operating the normal approach should allocate a *client* entitlement that is *client money* to the individual *client* promptly and, in any case, no later than ten *business days* after notification of receipt.

Money due to a client from a firm

7.4.29 **[G]** Pursuant to the *client money segregation requirements*, a *firm* operating the normal approach that is liable to pay *money* to a *client* should promptly, and in any event no later than one *business day* after the *money* is due and payable, pay the *money*:
(1) to, or to the order of, the *client*; or
(2) into a *client bank account*.

Segregation in different currency

7.4.30 **[R]** A *firm* may segregate *client money* in a different currency from that of receipt. If it does so, the *firm* must ensure that the amount held is adjusted each *day* to an amount at least equal to the original currency amount (or the currency in which the *firm* has its liability to its *clients*, if different), translated at the previous day's closing spot exchange rate.

7.4.31 **[G]** The *rule* on segregation of *client money* in a different currency (CASS 7.4.30R) does not apply where the *client* has instructed the *firm* to convert the *money* into and hold it in a different currency.

Commodity Futures Trading Commission Part 30 exemption order

7.4.32 **[G]** United States (US) legislation restricts the ability of non-US firms to trade on behalf of US customers on non-US futures and options exchanges. The relevant US regulator (the *CFTC*) operates an exemption system for *firms* authorised by the *FSA*. The *FSA* sponsors the application from a *firm* for exemption from Part 30 of the General Regulations under the US Commodity Exchange Act in line with this system. The application forms and associated information can be found on the *FSA* website in the "Forms" section.

7.4.33 **[G]** A *firm* with a *Part 30 exemption order* undertakes to the *CFTC* that it will refuse to allow any US customer to opt not to have his *money* treated as *client money* if it is held or received in respect of transactions on non-US exchanges, unless that US customer is an "eligible contract participant" as defined in section 1a(12) of the Commodity Exchange Act, 7 U.S.C. In doing so, the *firm* is representing that if available to it, it will not make use of the opt-out arrangements in CASS 7.1.7BR to CASS 7.1.7FR in relation to that business.

7.4.34 **[R]** A *firm* must not reduce the amount of, or cancel a letter of credit issued under, an LME bond arrangement where this will cause the *firm* to be in breach of its *Part 30 exemption order*.

7.4.35 **[R]** A *firm* must notify the *FSA* immediately it arranges the *issue* of an individual letter of *credit* under an LME bond arrangement.

7.5 Transfer of client money to a third party

7.5.1 **[G]** This section sets out the requirements a *firm* must comply with when it transfers *client money* to another *person* without discharging its fiduciary duty owed to that *client*. Such circumstances arise when, for example, a *firm* passes *client money* to a *clearing house* in the form of margin for the *firm's* obligations to the *clearing house* that are referable to transactions undertaken by the *firm* for the relevant clients. They may also arise when a *firm* passes *client money* to an *intermediate broker* for *contingent liability investments* in the form of initial or variation margin on behalf of a *client*. In these circumstances, the *firm* remains responsible for that *client's equity balance* held at the *intermediate broker* until the contract is terminated and all of that *client's* positions at that *broker* closed. If a *firm* wishes to discharge itself from its fiduciary duty, it should do so in accordance with the *rule* regarding the discharge of a *firm's* fiduciary duty to the *client* (CASS 7.2.15R).

7.5.2 **[R]** A *firm* may allow another *person*, such as an exchange, a *clearing house* or an *intermediate broker*, to hold or control *client money*, but only if:
(1) the *firm* transfers the *client money*:
  (a) for the purpose of a transaction for a *client* through or with that *person*; or
  (b) to meet a *client's* obligation to provide collateral for a transaction (for example, an *initial margin* requirement for a *contingent liability investment*); and
(2) in the case of a *retail client*, that *client* has been notified that the *client money* may be transferred to the other *person*.

7.5.3 **[G]** A *firm* should not hold excess *client money* in its *client transaction accounts* with *intermediate brokers*, *settlement agents* and *OTC* counterparties; it should be held in a *client bank account*.

7.6 Records, accounts and reconciliations

Records and accounts

7.6.1 **[R]** A *firm* must keep such records and accounts as are necessary to enable it, at any time and without delay, to distinguish *client money* held for one *client* from *client money* held for any other *client*, and from its own *money*.

[**Note:** article 16(1)(a) of the *MiFID implementing Directive*]

7.6.2 **[R]** A *firm* must maintain its records and accounts in a way that ensures their accuracy, and in particular their correspondence to the *client money* held for *clients*.

[**Note:** article 16(1)(b) of the *MiFID implementing Directive*]

Client entitlements

7.6.3 **[G]** Pursuant to CASS 7.6.2R, and where relevant SYSC 4.1.1R and SYSC 6.1.1R, a *firm* should take reasonable steps to ensure that is notified promptly of any receipt of *client money* in the form of a *client* entitlement.

Record keeping

7.6.4 **[R]** A *firm* must ensure that records made under CASS 7.6.1R and CASS 7.6.2R are retained for a period of five years after they were made.

7.6.5 **[G]** A *firm* should ensure that it makes proper records, sufficient to show and explain the *firm's* transactions and commitments in respect of its *client money*.

Internal reconciliations of client money balances

7.6.6 **[G]**

(1) Carrying out internal reconciliations of records and accounts of the entitlement of each *client* for whom the *firm* holds *client money* with the records and accounts of the *client money* the *firm* holds in *client bank accounts* and *client transaction accounts* should be one of the steps a *firm* takes to satisfy its obligations under CASS 7.6.2R, and where relevant SYSC 4.1.1R and SYSC 6.1.1R.

(2) A *firm* should perform such internal reconciliations:
   (a) as often as is necessary; and
   (b) as soon as reasonably practicable after the date to which the reconciliation relates;
   (c) to ensure the accuracy of the *firm's* records and accounts.

(3) The *standard method of internal client money reconciliation* sets out a method of reconciliation of *client money* balances that the *FSA* believes should be one of the steps that a *firm* takes when carrying out internal reconciliations of *client money*.

Records

7.6.7 **[R]**

(1) A *firm* must make records, sufficient to show and explain the method of internal reconciliation of *client money* balances under CASS 7.6.2R used, and if different from the *standard method of internal client money reconciliation*, to show and explain that:
   (a) the method of internal reconciliation of *client money* balances used affords an equivalent degree of protection to the *firm's clients* to that afforded by the *standard method of internal client money reconciliation*; and
   (b) in the event of a *primary pooling event* or *a secondary pooling event*, the method used is adequate to enable the *firm* to comply with the *client money distribution rules*.

(2) A *firm* must make these records on the date it starts using a method of internal reconciliation of *client money* balances and must keep it made for a period of five years after ceasing to use it.

7.6.8 **[R]** A *firm* that does not use the *standard method of internal client money reconciliation* must first send a written confirmation to the *FSA* from the *firm's* auditor that the *firm* has in place systems and controls which are adequate to enable it to use another method effectively.

Reconciliations with external records

7.6.9 **[R]** A *firm* must conduct, on a regular basis, reconciliations between its internal accounts and records and those of any third parties by whom *client money* is held.

[**Note:** article 16(1)(c) of the *MiFID implementing Directive*]

Frequency of external reconciliations

7.6.10 **[G]**

(1) A *firm* should perform the required reconciliation of *client money* balances with external records:
   (a) as regularly as is necessary; and
   (b) as soon as reasonably practicable after the date to which the reconciliation relates; to ensure the accuracy of its internal accounts and records against those of third parties by whom *client money* is held.

(2) In determining whether the frequency is adequate, the *firm* should consider the risks which the business is exposed, such as the nature, volume and complexity of the business, and where and with whom the *client money* is held.

Method of external reconciliations

7.6.11 **[G]** A method of reconciliation of *client money* balances with external records that the *FSA* believes is adequate is when a *firm* compares:

(1) the balance on each *client bank account* as recorded by the *firm* with the balance on that account as set out on the statement or other form of confirmation issued by the bank with which those accounts are held; and

(2) the balance, currency by currency, on each *client transaction account* as recorded by the *firm*, with the balance on that account as set out in the statement or other form of confirmation issued by the *person* with whom the account is held;

and identifies any discrepancies between them.

7.6.12 **[R]** Any *approved collateral* held in accordance with the *client money rules* must be included within this reconciliation.

Reconciliation discrepancies

7.6.13 **[R]** When any discrepancy arises as a result of a *firm's* internal reconciliations, the *firm* must identify the reason for the discrepancy and ensure that:

(1) any *shortfall* is paid into a *client bank account* by the close of business on the day that the reconciliation is performed; or

(2) any excess is withdrawn within the same time period (but see CASS 7.4.20G and CASS 7.4.21R).

7.6.14 **[R]** When any discrepancy arises as a result of the reconciliation between a *firm's* internal records and those of third parties that hold *client money*, the *firm* must identify the reason for the discrepancy and correct it as soon as possible, unless the discrepancy arises solely as a result of timing differences between the accounting systems of the party providing the statement or confirmation and that of the *firm*.

7.6.15 **[R]** While a *firm* is unable to resolve a difference arising from a reconciliation between a *firm's* internal records and those of third parties that hold *client money*, and one record or a set of records examined by the *firm* during its reconciliation indicates that there is a need to have a greater amount of *client money* or *approved collateral* than is in fact the case, the *firm* must assume, until the matter is finally resolved, that the record or set of records is accurate and pay its own *money* into a relevant account.

Notification requirements

7.6.16 **[R]** A *firm* must inform the *FSA* in writing without delay:

(1) if it has not complied with, or is unable, in any material respect, to comply with the requirements in CASS 7.6.1R, CASS 7.6.2R or CASS 7.6.9R;

(2) if having carried out a reconciliation it has not complied with, or is unable, in any material respect, to comply with CASS 7.6.13R to CASS 7.6.15R.

Audit of compliance with the MiFID client money rules

7.6.17 **[G]** *Firms* are reminded that the auditor of the *firm* has to confirm in the report submitted to the *FSA* under SUP 3.10 (Duties of auditors: notification and report on client assets) that the *firm* has maintained systems adequate to enable it to comply with the *client money rules*.

7.6.18 **[G]** *Firms* that do not adopt the normal approach are reminded that the *firm's* auditor must confirm to the *FSA* in writing that the *firm* has in place systems and controls which are adequate to enable it to operate the alternative approach effectively (see CASS 7.4.15R).

7.6.19 **[G]** *Firms* that do not use the *standard method of internal client money reconciliation* are reminded that the *firm's* auditor must confirm to the *FSA* in writing that the *firm* has in place systems and controls which are adequate to enable it to use another method effectively (see CASS 7.6.8R).

7.7 Statutory trust

7.7.1 **[G]** Section 139(1) of the *Act* (Miscellaneous ancillary matters) provides that *rules* may make provision which result in *client money* being held by a *firm* on trust (England and Wales and Northern Ireland) or as agent (Scotland only). This section creates a fiduciary relationship between the *firm* and its *client* under which *client money* is in the legal ownership of the *firm* but remains in the beneficial ownership of the *client*. In the event of *failure* of the *firm*, costs relating to the distribution of *client money* may have to be borne by the trust.

Requirement

7.7.2 **[R]** A *firm* receives and holds *client money* as trustee (or in Scotland as agent) on the following terms:

Part II FSA Handbook Materials

(1) for the purposes of and on the terms of the *client money rules* and the *client money distribution rules*;
(2) subject to (3), for the *clients* (other than *clients* which are *insurance undertakings* when acting as such with respect of *client money* received in the course of *insurance mediation activity* and that was opted in to this chapter) for whom that *money* is held, according to their respective interests in it;
(3) after all valid claims in (2) have been met, for *clients* which are *insurance undertakings* with respect of *client money* received in the course of *insurance mediation activity* according to their respective interests in it;
(4) on *failure* of the *firm*, for the payment of the costs properly attributable to the distribution of the *client money* in accordance with (2); and
(5) after all valid claims and costs under (2) to (4) have been met, for the *firm* itself.

7.7.3 **[R]** A *trustee firm* which is subject to the *client money rules* by virtue of CASS 7.1.1R(4):
(1) must receive and hold *client money* in accordance with the relevant instrument of trust;
(2) subject to that, receives and holds *client money* on trust on the terms (or in Scotland on the agency terms) specified in CASS 7.7.2R.

7.7.4 **[G]** If a *trustee firm* holds *client money* in accordance with CASS 7.7.3R(2), the *firm* should follow the provisions in CASS 7.1.15ER and CASS 7.1.15FR.

7.8 Notification and acknowledgement of trust

Banks

7.8.1 **[R]**
(1) When a *firm* opens a *client bank account*, the *firm* must give or have given written notice to the bank requesting the bank to acknowledge to it in writing that:
 (a) all *money* standing to the credit of the account is held by the *firm* as trustee (or if relevant, as agent) and that the bank is not entitled to combine the account with any other account or to exercise any right of set-off or counterclaim against *money* in that account in respect of any sum owed to it on any other account of the *firm*; and
 (b) the title of the account sufficiently distinguishes that account from any account containing *money* that belongs to the *firm*, and is in the form requested by the *firm*.
(2) In the case of a *client bank account* in the *United Kingdom*, if the bank does not provide the required acknowledgement within 20 *business days* after the *firm* dispatched the notice, the *firm* must withdraw all *money* standing to the credit of the account and *deposit* it in a *client bank account* with another bank as soon as possible.

Exchanges, clearing houses, intermediate brokers or OTC counterparties

7.8.2 **[R]**
(1) A *firm* which undertakes any *contingent liability investment* for *clients* through an exchange, *clearing house*, *intermediate broker* or *OTC* counterparty must, before the *client transaction account* is opened with the exchange, *clearing house*, *intermediate broker* or *OTC* counterparty:
 (a) notify the *person* with whom the account is to be opened that the *firm* is under an obligation to keep *client money* separate from the *firm's* own *money*, placing *client money* in a *client bank account*;
 (b) instruct the *person* with whom the account is to be opened that any *money* paid to it in respect of that transaction is to be credited to the *firm's client transaction account*; and
 (c) require the person with whom the account is to be opened to acknowledge in writing that the *firm's client transaction account* is not to be combined with any other account, nor is any right of set-off to be exercised by that *person* against *money* credited to the *client transaction account* in respect of any sum owed to that *person* on any other account.
(2) If the exchange, *clearing house*, *intermediate broker* or *OTC* counterparty does not provide the required acknowledgement within 20 *business days* of the dispatch of the notice and instruction, the *firm* must cease using the *client transaction account* with that *broker* or counterparty and arrange as soon as possible for the transfer or liquidation of any open positions and the repayment of any *money*.

7.9 Client money distribution

[deleted]

CASS 7 Annex 1G

7 Ann 1 **[G]** As explained in CASS 7.6.6G, in complying with its obligations under CASS 7.6.2R (Records and accounts), and where relevant SYSC 4.1.1R (General organisational requirements) and

SYSC 6.1.1R (Compliance), a *firm* should carry out internal reconciliations of records and accounts of *client money* the *firm* holds in *client bank accounts* and *client transaction accounts*. This Annex sets out a method of reconciliation that the *FSA* believes is appropriate for these purposes (the *standard method of internal client money reconciliation*).

1. Each *business day*, a *firm* that adopts the normal approach (see CASS 7.4.17G) should check whether its *client money* resource, being the aggregate balance on the *firm's client bank accounts*, as at the close of business on the previous *business day*, was at least equal to the *client money* requirement, as defined in paragraph 6 below, as at the close of business on that day.

2. Each *business day*, a *firm* that adopts the alternative approach (see CASS 7.4.18R) should ensure that its *client money* resource, being the aggregate balance on the *firm's client bank accounts*, as at the close of business on that *business day* is at least equal to the *client money* requirement, as defined in paragraph 6 below, as at the close of business on the previous *business day*.

3. No excess or *shortfall* should arise when adopting the alternative approach.

4. If a *firm* is operating the alternative approach and draws a cheque on its own bank account, it will be expected to account for those cheques that have not yet cleared when performing its reconciliations of records and accounts under paragraph 2. An historic average estimate of uncleared cheques may be used to satisfy this obligation (see CASS 7.4.19G(3)).

5. For the purposes of performing its reconciliations of records and accounts under paragraphs 1 or 2, a *firm* should use the values contained in its accounting records, for example its cash book, rather than values contained in statements received from its banks and other third parties.

Client money requirement

6. The *client money* requirement is either:

(1) (subject to paragraph 18) the sum of, for all *clients*:

  (a) the individual *client* balances calculated in accordance with paragraph 7, excluding:

    (i) individual *client* balances which are negative (that is, debtors); and

    (ii) *clients' equity balances*; and

  (b) the total *margined transaction* requirement calculated in accordance with paragraph 14; or

(2) the sum of:

  (a) for each client bank account:

    (i) the amount which the *firm's* records show as held on that account; and

    (ii) an amount that offsets each negative net amount which the *firm's* records show attributed to that account for an individual *client*; and

  (b) the total *margined transaction* requirement calculated in accordance with paragraph 14.

General transactions

7. The individual *client* balance for each *client* should be calculated in accordance with this table:

Individual client balance calculation			
Free *money* (no trades) and			A
sale proceeds due to the *client*:			
(a)	in respect of *principal deals* when the *client* has delivered the *designated investments*; and		B
(b)	in respect of agency *deals*, when either:		
	(i)	the sale proceeds have been received by the *firm* and the *client* has delivered the *designated investments*; or	C1
	(ii)	the *firm* holds the *designated investments* for the *client*; and	C2
the cost of purchases:			
(c)	in respect of *principal deals*, paid for by the *client* but the *firm* has not delivered the *designated investments* to the *client*; and		D
(d)	in respect of agency *deal*, paid for by the *client* when either:		
	(i)	the *firm* has not remitted the *money* to, or to the order of, the counterparty; or	E1
	(ii)	the *designated investments* have been received by the *firm* but have not been delivered to the *client*;	E2

Individual client balance calculation		
Less		
	money owed by the *client* in respect of unpaid purchases by or for the *client* if delivery of those *designated investments* has been made to the *client*; and	F
	Proceeds remitted to the *client* in respect of sales transactions by or for the *client* if the *client* has not delivered the *designated investments*.	G
Individual *Client* Balance 'X' = (A+B+C1+C2+D+E1+E2)-F-G		X

8. A *firm* should calculate the individual *client* balance using the contract value of any *client* purchases or sales.

9. A *firm* may choose to segregate *designated investments* instead of the value identified in paragraph 7 (except E1) if it ensures that the *designated investments* are held in such a manner that the *firm* cannot use them for its own purposes.

10. Segregation in the context of paragraph 9 can take many forms, including the holding of a *safe custody investment* in a nominee name and the safekeeping of certificates evidencing title in a fire resistant safe. It is not the intention that all the *custody rules* in the *custody chapter* should be applied to *designated investments* held in the course of settlement.

11. In determining the *client money* requirement under paragraph 6, a *firm* need not include *money* held in accordance with CASS 7.2.8R (Delivery versus payment transaction).

12. In determining the *client money* requirement under paragraph 6, a *firm*:
(1) should include dividends received and interest earned and allocated;
(2) may deduct outstanding *fees*, calls, rights and interest charges and other amounts owed by the *client* which are due and payable to the *firm* (see CASS 7.2.9R);
(3) need not include *client money* in the form of *client* entitlements which are not required to be segregated (see CASS 7.4.27G) nor include *client money* forwarded to the *firm* by its *appointed representatives*, *tied agents*, field representatives and other agents, but not received (see CASS 7.4.24G);
(4) should take into account any *client money* arising from CASS 7.6.13R (Reconciliation discrepancies); and
(5) should include any unallocated *client money*.

Equity balance

13. A *firm's* equity balance, whether with an exchange, *intermediate broker* or *OTC* counterparty, is the amount which the *firm* would be liable to pay to the exchange, *intermediate broker* or *OTC* counterparty (or vice-versa) in respect of the *firm's margined transactions* if each of the open positions of the *firm's clients* was liquidated at the closing or settlement prices published by the relevant exchange or other appropriate pricing source and the *firm's* account with the exchange, *intermediate broker* or *OTC* counterparty is closed.

Margined transaction requirement

14. The total *margined transaction* requirement is:
(1) the sum of each of the *client's equity balances* which are positive;
Less
(2) the proportion of any individual negative *client equity balance* which is secured by *approved collateral*; and
(3) the net aggregate of the *firm's* equity balance (negative balances being deducted from positive balances) on transaction accounts for *customers* with exchanges, *clearing houses*, *intermediate brokers* and *OTC* counterparties.

15. To meet a shortfall that has arisen in respect of the requirement in paragraph 6(1)(b) or 6(2)(b), a *firm* may utilise its own *approved collateral* provided it is held on terms specifying when it is to be realised for the benefit of *clients*, it is clearly identifiable from the *firm's* own property and the relevant terms are evidenced in writing by the *firm*. In addition, the proceeds of the sale of that *collateral* should be paid into a *client bank account*.

16. If a *firm's* total *margined transaction* requirement is negative, the *firm* should treat it as zero for the purposes of calculating its *client money* requirement.

17. The terms '*client equity balance*' and '*firm's* equity balance' in paragraph 13 refer to cash values and do not include non-cash *collateral* or other *designated investments* held in respect of a *margined transaction*.

17A. A *firm* with a *Part 30 exemption order* which also operates an LME bond arrangement for the benefit of US-resident investors, should exclude the *client equity balances* for transactions undertaken on the London Metal Exchange on behalf of those US-resident investors from the calculation of the *margined transaction* requirement.

Reduced client money requirement option

18.
(1) When, in respect of a *client*, there is a positive individual *client* balance and a negative *client equity balance*, a *firm* may offset the credit against the debit and hence have a reduced individual *client* balance in paragraph 7 for that *client*.
(2) When, in respect of a *client*, there is a negative individual *client* balance and a positive *client equity balance*, a *firm* may offset the credit against the debit and hence have a reduced *client equity balance* in paragraph 14 for that *client*.

19. The effect of paragraph 18 is to allow a *firm* to offset, on a *client* by *client* basis, a negative amount with a positive amount arising out of the calculations in paragraphs 7 and 14, and, by so doing, reduce the amount the *firm* is required to segregate.

CHAPTER 7A
CLIENT MONEY DISTRIBUTION

7A.1 Application and purpose

Application

7A.1.1 **[R]** This chapter (the *client money distribution rules*) applies to a *firm* that holds *client money* which is subject to the *client money rules* when a *primary pooling event* or a *secondary pooling event* occurs.

Purpose

7A.1.2 **[G]** The *client money distribution rules* seek to facilitate the timely return of *client money* to a *client* in the event of the *failure* of a *firm* or third party at which the *firm* holds *client money*.

7A.2 Primary pooling events

Failure of the authorised firm: primary pooling event

7A.2.1 **[G]**
(1) A *firm* can hold *client money* in a *general client bank account*, a *designated client bank account* or a *designated client fund account*.
(2) A *firm* holds all *client money* in *general client bank accounts* for its *clients* as part of a common pool of *money* so those particular *clients* do not have a claim against a specific sum in a specific account; they only have a claim to the *client money* in general.
(3) A *firm* holds *client money* in *designated client bank accounts* or *designated client fund accounts* for those *clients* that requested their *client money* be part of a specific pool of *money*, so those particular *clients* do have a claim against a specific sum in a specific account; they do not have a claim to the *client money* in general unless a *primary pooling event* occurs. A *primary pooling event* triggers a notional pooling of all the *client money*, in every type of client money account, and the obligation to distribute it.
(4) If the *firm* becomes insolvent, and there is (for whatever reason) a *shortfall* in *money* held for a *client* compared with that *client's* entitlements, the available funds will be distributed in accordance with the *client money distribution rules*.

7A.2.2 **[R]** A *primary pooling event* occurs:
(1) on the *failure* of the *firm*;
(2) on the vesting of assets in a *trustee* in accordance with an 'assets *requirement*' imposed under section 48(1)(b) of the *Act*;
(3) on the coming into force of a *requirement* for all *client money* held by the *firm*; or
(4) when the *firm* notifies, or is in breach of its duty to notify, the *FSA*, in accordance with CASS 7.6.16R (Notification requirements), that it is unable correctly to identify and allocate in its records all valid claims arising as a result of a *secondary pooling event*.

7A.2.3 **[R]** CASS 7A.2.2R(4) does not apply so long as:
(1) the *firm* is taking steps, in consultation with the *FSA*, to establish those records; and
(2) there are reasonable grounds to conclude that the records will be capable of rectification within a reasonable period.

Pooling and distribution

7A.2.4 **[R]** If a *primary pooling event* occurs:
(1) *client money* held in each *client money* account of the *firm* is treated as pooled; and

(2) the *firm* must distribute that *client money* in accordance with CASS 7.7.2R, so that each *client* receives a sum which is rateable to the *client money* entitlement calculated in accordance with CASS 7A.2.5R.

7A.2.5 **[R]**
(1) When, in respect of a *client*, there is a positive individual *client* balance and a negative *client equity balance*, the credit must be offset against the debit reducing the individual *client* balance for that *client*.
(2) When, in respect of a *client*, there is a negative individual *client* balance and a positive *client equity balance*, the credit must be offset against the debit reducing *client equity balance* for that *client*.

7A.2.6 **[G]** A *client's* main claim is for the return of *client money* held in a *client bank account*. A *client* may be able to claim for any *shortfall* against *money* held in a *firm's* own account. For that claim, the *client* will be an unsecured creditor of the *firm*.

Client money received after the failure of the firm

7A.2.7 **[R]** *Client money* received by the *firm* after a *primary pooling event* must not be pooled with *client money* held in any *client money* account operated by the *firm* at the time of the *primary pooling event*. It must be placed in a *client bank account* that has been opened after that event and must be handled in accordance with the *client money rules*, and returned to the relevant *client* without delay, except to the extent that:
(1) it is *client money* relating to a transaction that has not settled at the time of the *primary pooling event*; or
(2) it is *client money* relating to a *client*, for whom the *client money* entitlement, calculated in accordance with CASS 7A.2.5R, shows that *money* is due from the *client* to the *firm* at the time of the *primary pooling event*.

7A.2.8 **[G]** *Client money* received after the *primary pooling event* relating to an unsettled transaction should be used to settle that transaction. Examples of such transactions include:
(1) an equity transaction with a trade date before the date of the *primary pooling event* and a settlement date after the date of the *primary pooling event*; or
(2) a *contingent liability investment* that is 'open' at the time of the *primary pooling event* and is due to settle after the *primary pooling event*.

7A.2.9 **[R]** If a *firm* receives a *mixed remittance* after a *primary pooling event*, it must:
(1) pay the full sum into the separate *client bank account* opened in accordance with CASS 7A.2.7R; and
(2) pay the *money* that is not *client money* out of that *client bank account* into a *firm's* own bank account within one *business day* of the *day* on which the *firm* would normally expect the remittance to be cleared.

7A.2.10 **[G]** Whenever possible the *firm* should seek to split a *mixed remittance* before the relevant accounts are credited.

7A.2.11 **[R]** If both a *primary pooling event* and a *secondary pooling event* occur, the provisions of this section relating to a *primary pooling event* apply.

7A.3 Secondary pooling events

Failure of a bank, intermediate broker, settlement agent or OTC counterparty: secondary pooling events

7A.3.1 **[R]** A *secondary pooling event* occurs on the *failure* of a third party to which *client money* held by the *firm* has been transferred under CASS 7.4.1R(1) to CASS 7.4.1R(3) (Depositing client money) or CASS 7.5.2R (Transfer of client money to a third party).

7A.3.2 **[R]** CASS 7A.3.6R to CASS 7A.3.18R do not apply if, on the *failure* of the third party, the *firm* repays to its *clients* or pays into a *client bank account*, at an unaffected bank, an amount equal to the amount of *client money* which would have been held if a *shortfall* had not occurred at that third party.

7A.3.3 **[G]** When *client money* is transferred to a third party, a *firm* continues to owe fiduciary duties to the *client*. Whether a *firm* is liable for a *shortfall* in *client money* caused by a third party failure will depend on whether it has complied with its duty of care as agent or trustee.

Failure of a bank

7A.3.4 **[G]** When a bank *fails* and the *firm* decides not to make good the *shortfall* in the amount of *client money* held at that bank, a *secondary pooling event* will occur in accordance with CASS 7A.3.6R. The *firm* would be expected to reflect the *shortfall* that arises at the *failed* bank in its records of the entitlement of *clients* and of *money* held with third parties.

7A.3.5 **[G]** The *client money distribution rules* seek to ensure that *clients* who have previously specified that they are not willing to accept the risk of the bank that has *failed*, and who therefore requested that their *client money* be placed in a *designated client bank account* at a different bank, should not suffer the loss of the bank that has *failed*.

Failure of a bank: pooling

7A.3.6 **[R]** If a *secondary pooling event* occurs as a result of the *failure* of a bank where one or more *general client bank accounts* are held, then:

(1) in relation to every *general client bank account* of the *firm*, the provisions of CASS 7A.3.8R, CASS 7A.3.13R and CASS 7A.3.14R will apply;

(2) in relation to every *designated client bank account* held by the *firm* with the *failed* bank, the provisions of CASS 7A.3.10R, CASS 7A.3.13R and CASS 7A.3.14R will apply;

(3) in relation to each *designated client fund account* held by the *firm* with the *failed* bank, the provisions of CASS 7A.3.11R, CASS 7A.3.13R and CASS 7A.3.14R will apply;

(4) any *money* held at a bank, other than the bank that has *failed*, in *designated client bank accounts*, is not pooled with any other *client money*; and

(5) any *money* held in a *designated client fund account*, no part of which is held by the bank that has *failed*, is not pooled with any other *client money*.

7A.3.7 **[R]** If a *secondary pooling event* occurs as a result of the *failure* of a bank where one or more *designated client bank accounts* or *designated client fund accounts* are held, then:

(1) in relation to every *designated client bank account* held by the *firm* with the *failed* bank, the provisions of CASS 7A.3.10R, CASS 7A.3.13R and CASS 7A.3.14R will apply; and

(2) in relation to each *designated client fund account* held by the *firm* with the *failed* bank, the provisions of CASS 7A.3.11R, CASS 7A.3.13R and CASS 7A.3.14R will apply.

7A.3.8 **[R]** *Money* held in each general *client bank account* and *client transaction account* of the *firm* must be treated as pooled and:

(1) any *shortfall* in *client money* held, or which should have been held, in *general client bank accounts* and *client transaction accounts*, that has arisen as a result of the *failure* of the bank, must be borne by all the *clients* whose *client money* is held in either a *general client bank account* or *client transaction account* of the *firm*, rateably in accordance with their entitlements;

(2) a new *client money* entitlement must be calculated for each *client* by the *firm*, to reflect the requirements in (1), and the *firm's* records must be amended to reflect the reduced *client money* entitlement;

(3) the *firm* must make and retain a record of each *client's* share of the *client money shortfall* at the *failed* bank until the *client* is repaid; and

(4) the *firm* must use the new *client money* entitlements, calculated in accordance with (2), for the purposes of reconciliations pursuant to CASS 7.6.2R (Records and accounts), and where relevant SYSC 4.1.1R (General organisational requirements) and SYSC 6.1.1R (Compliance).

7A.3.9 **[G]** The term "which should have been held" is a reference to the *failed* bank's *failure* to hold the *client money* at the time of the pooling event.

7A.3.10 **[R]** For each *client* with a *designated client bank account* held at the *failed* bank:

(1) any *shortfall* in *client money* held, or which should have been held, in *designated client bank accounts* that has arisen as a result of the *failure*, must be borne by all the *clients* whose *client money* is held in a *designated client bank account* of the *firm* at the *failed bank*, rateably in accordance with their entitlements;

(2) a new *client money* entitlement must be calculated for each of the relevant *clients* by the *firm*, and the *firm's* records must be amended to reflect the reduced *client money* entitlement;

(3) the *firm* must make and retain a record of each *client's* share of the *client money shortfall* at the *failed* bank until the *client* is repaid; and

(4) the *firm* must use the new *client money* entitlements, calculated in accordance with (2), for the purposes of reconciliations pursuant to CASS 7.6.2R (Records and accounts), and where relevant SYSC 4.1.1R (General organisational requirements) and SYSC 6.1.1R (Compliance).

7A.3.11 **[R]** *Money* held in each *designated client fund account* with the *failed bank* must be treated as pooled with any other *designated client fund accounts* of the *firm* which contain part of the same designated fund and:

(1) any *shortfall* in *client money* held, or which should have been held, in *designated client fund accounts* that has arisen as a result of the *failure*, must be borne by each of the *clients* whose *client money* is held in that designated fund, rateably in accordance with their entitlements;

(2) a new *client money* entitlement must be calculated for each *client* by the *firm*, in accordance with (1), and the *firm's* records must be amended to reflect the reduced *client money* entitlement;

(3) the *firm* must make and retain a record of each *client's* share of the *client money shortfall* at the *failed* bank until the *client* is repaid; and

(4) the *firm* must use the new *client money* entitlements, calculated in accordance with (2), for the purposes of reconciliations pursuant to CASS 7.6.2R (Records and accounts), and where relevant SYSC 4.1.1R (General organisational requirements) and SYSC 6.1.1R (Compliance).

7A.3.12 **[R]** A *client* whose *money* was held, or which should have been held, in a *designated client bank account* with a bank that has *failed* is not entitled to claim in respect of that *money* against any other *client bank account* or *client transaction account* of the *firm*.

Client money received after the failure of a bank

7A.3.13 **[R]** *Client money* received by the *firm* after the failure of a bank, that would otherwise have been paid into a *client bank account* at that bank:

(1) must not be transferred to the *failed* bank unless specifically instructed by the *client* in order to settle an obligation of that *client* to the *failed* bank; and

(2) must be, subject to (1), placed in a separate *client bank account* that has been opened after the *secondary pooling event* and either:

   (a) on the written instruction of the *client*, transferred to a bank other than the one that has *failed*; or

   (b) returned to the *client* as soon as possible.

7A.3.14 **[R]** If a *firm* receives a *mixed remittance* after the *secondary pooling event* which consists of *client money* that would have been paid into a *general client bank account*, a *designated client bank account* or a *designated client fund account* maintained at the bank that has *failed*, it must:

(1) pay the full sum into a *client bank account* other than one operated at the bank that has *failed*; and

(2) pay the *money* that is not *client money* out of that *client bank account* within one *business day* of the day on which the *firm* would normally expect the remittance to be cleared.

7A.3.15 **[G]** Whenever possible the *firm* should seek to split a *mixed remittance* before the relevant accounts are credited.

Failure of an intermediate broker, settlement agent or OTC counterparty: Pooling

7A.3.16 **[R]** If a *secondary pooling event* occurs as a result of the *failure* of an *intermediate broker*, *settlement agent* or *OTC* counterparty, then in relation to every *general client bank account* and *client transaction account* of the *firm*, the provisions of CASS 7A.3.17R and CASS 7A.3.18R will apply.

7A.3.17 **[R]** *Money* held in each *general client bank account* and *client transaction account* of the *firm* must be treated as pooled and:

(1) any *shortfall* in *client money* held, or which should have been held, in *general client bank accounts* and *client transaction accounts*, that has arisen as a result of the *failure*, must be borne by all the *clients* whose *client money* is held in either a *general client bank account* or a *client transaction account* of the *firm*, rateably in accordance with their entitlements;

(2) a new *client money* entitlement must be calculated for each *client* by the *firm*, to reflect the requirements of (1), and the *firm's* records must be amended to reflect the reduced *client money* entitlement;

(3) the *firm* must make and retain a record of each *client's* share of the *client money shortfall* at the *failed intermediate broker*, *settlement agent* or *OTC* counterparty until the *client* is repaid; and

(4) the *firm* must use the new *client money* entitlements, calculated in accordance with (2), for the purposes of reconciliations pursuant to CASS 7.6.2R (Records and accounts), and where relevant SYSC 4.1.1R (General organisational requirements) and SYSC 6.1.1R (Compliance).

Client money received after the failure of an intermediate broker, settlement agent or OTC counterparty

7A.3.18 **[R]** *Client money* received by the *firm* after the *failure* of an *intermediate broker*, *settlement agent* or *OTC* counterparty, that would otherwise have been paid into a *client transaction account* at that *intermediate broker*, *settlement agent* or *OTC* counterparty:

(1) must not be transferred to the *failed* third party unless specifically instructed by the *client* in order to settle an obligation of that *client* to the *failed intermediate broker*, *settlement agent* or *OTC* counterparty; and

(2) must be, subject to (1), placed in a separate *client bank account* that has been opened after the *secondary pooling event* and either:

   (a) on the written instruction of the *client*, transferred to a third party other than the one that has *failed*; or

   (b) returned to the *client* as soon as possible.

Notification to the FSA: failure of a bank, intermediate broker, settlement agent or OTC counterparty

7A.3.19 **[R]** On the *failure* of a third party with which *money* is held, a *firm* must notify the *FSA*:

(1) as soon as it becomes aware of the *failure* of any bank, *intermediate broker*, *settlement agent*, *OTC* counterparty or other entity with which it has placed, or to which it has passed, *client money*; and

(2) as soon as reasonably practical, whether it intends to make good any *shortfall* that has arisen or may arise and of the amounts involved.

CHAPTER 8
MANDATES

Application

[2132A]–[2133]

8.1.1 **[R]** This chapter applies to a *firm* (including in its capacity as trustee under CASS 5.4) in respect of any written authority from a *client* under which the *firm* may control a *client's* assets or liabilities in the course of, or in connection with, the *firm's*:

(1) *designated investment business* (including *MiFID business*); and

(2) *insurance mediation activity*, except where it relates to a *reinsurance contract*.

8.1.2 **[G]** Mandates or similar authorities for the purpose of this chapter include a *firm's* authority over a *client's* safe custody account, for example for stock lending purposes, a *firm's* authority over a *client's* bank or building society account including direct debits in favour of the *firm*, and a *firm* holding a *client's* credit card details.

8.1.3 **[G]** *Firms* are reminded that the *mandate rules* do not apply to an *incoming EEA firm*, other than an *insurer*, with respect to its *passported activities*. The application of the *mandate rules* is also dependent on the location from which the activity is undertaken (see CASS 1.4.3G).

Purpose

8.1.4 **[G]** The *mandate rules* apply to those *firms* that control, rather than hold, *clients'* assets or are able to create liabilities in the name of a *client*. These *rules* seek to ensure that *firms* establish and maintain records and *internal controls* to prevent the misuse of the authority granted by the *client*.

General

8.1.5 **[R]** A *firm* that holds authorities of the sort referred to in this chapter, must establish and maintain adequate records and *internal controls* in respect of its use of the mandates, which must include:

(1) an up-to-date list of the authorities and any conditions placed by the *client* or the *firm's* management on the use of them;

(2) a record of all transactions entered into using the authority and *internal controls* to ensure that they are within the scope of authority of the *person* and the *firm* entering into the transaction;

(3) the details of the procedures and authorities for the giving and receiving of instructions under the authority; and

(4) where the *firm* holds a passbook or similar documents belonging to the *client*, *internal controls*, for the safeguarding (including against loss, unauthorised destruction, theft, fraud or misuse) of any passbook or similar document belonging to the *client* held by the *firm*.

CASS TRANSITIONAL PROVISIONS

[2134]

(1)	(2)	(3)	(4)	(5)	(6)
	Material to which the *transitional* provision applies		**Transitional provision**	**Transitional Provision: dates in force**	**Handbook provision: coming into force**
1	CASS 2 to CASS 4	R	[deleted]		
2	Every *rule* in the *Handbook*	R	Expired		
		G	Expired		

(1)	(2)	(3)	(4)	(5)	(6)
	Material to which the transitional provision applies		**Transitional provision**	**Transitional Provision: dates in force**	**Handbook provision: coming into force**
2A		G	[deleted]		
3	CASS 5.1 to 5.6	R	Apply in relation to *money* (and where appropriate *designated investments*) held by a *firm* on 14 January 2005 (being *money* or *designated investments* to which *CASS* 5.1 to 5.6 would not otherwise apply) to the extent that any such *money* (or *designated investments*) relate to business carried on before 14 January 2005 and which would, if conducted on or after 14 January 2005, be an *insurance mediation activity*.	Indefinitely	14 January 2005
4	CASS 5.1.5A	R	A *firm* will satisfy the requirements of this paragraph, and *money* is *client money*, notwithstanding that an *insurance undertaking* which is the *firm's* counterparty to an agreement required by CASS 5.1.5AR has not given written consent to its interests under the trusts (or in Scotland agency) in CASS 5.3.2R or CASS 5.4.7R being subordinated to the interests of the *firm's* other *clients*.	14 January 2005 for 6 months	14 January 2005
5	CASS 5.3.2	R	The interests of a *firm's clients* which are *insurance undertakings* will rank equally with the interests of the *firm's* other *clients*.	14 January 2005 for 6 months	14 January 2005
6	CASS 5.4.7	R	A *firm* will satisfy the requirements of this rule notwithstanding that the deed referred to in CASS 5.4.6R provides that *money* (and if appropriate *designated investments*) are held on terms which provide for the interests of the *firm's clients* which are *insurance undertakings* to rank equally with the interests of the *firm's* other *clients*.	14 January 2005 for 6 months	14 January 2005
7	CASS 5.5.65	R	A *firm* may for the purpose of calculating its *client money resource* disregard any *money* which the *firm* had before 14 January 2005 transferred to an intermediate broker in circumstances analogous to those described in CASS 5.5.34R.	14 January 2005 for 12 months	14 January 2005

SCHEDULE 1
RECORD KEEPING REQUIREMENTS

[2135]
Sch 1 **[G]**

(1) The aim of the *guidance* in the following table is to give the reader a quick overall view of the relevant record keeping requirements.
(2) It is not a complete statement of those requirements and should not be relied on as if it were.
(3) Table

Handbook reference	**Subject of record**	**Contents of record**	**When record must be made**	**Retention period**
[deleted]				
[deleted]				
[deleted]				
[deleted]				
[deleted]				
[deleted]				
[deleted]				
[deleted]				
CASS 5.1.1R(4)	Record of election of compliance with specified *CASS* rules	Record of compliance with specified *CASS* rules	Not specified	Not specified
CASS 5.2.3R(2)	Holding *client money* as agent	The terms of the agreement	Not specified	Six years
CASS 5.4.4R(2)	Adequacy of systems and controls	Written confirmation of adequate systems and controls from its auditor	Not specified	Not specified
CASS 5.5.64R	*Client money* calculation	Whether the *firm* calculates its *client money* requirements according to CASS 5.5.67R or CASS 5.5.68R	Not specified	Not specified
CASS 5.5.84R	Transactions and commitments for *client money*	Explanation of the *firm's* transactions and commitments for *client money.*	Not specified	Three years
CASS 5.8.3R(1)	Client's title to a *contract of insurance*	Identity of such *documents* and/or property and dates received and delivered to *client*	Not specified	Three years
CASS 6.1.16CR(3)	A *personal investment firm* that temporarily holds a *client's designated investments* which is not in the course of *MiFID business*	Client details and any actions taken by the firm		5 years (from the making of the record)
CASS 6.1.16KR	Client custody assets which the firm has arranged for another to hold or receive	Full details	On receipt	5 years
[deleted]				

Part II FSA Handbook Materials

Handbook reference	**Subject of record**	**Contents of record**	**When record must be made**	**Retention period**
CASS 6.3.1R(4)	Appropriateness of a *firm's* selection of a third party	Grounds upon which a *firm* satisfies itself as to the appropriateness of the *firm's* selection of a third party to hold *safe custody assets* belonging to *clients*	Date of the selection	5 years (from the date the *firm* ceases to use the third party to hold *safe custody assets* belonging to *clients*)
CASS 6.4.3R	Details of *clients* and *safe custody assets* used for the *firm's* own account or the account of another *client* of the *firm*	Details of the *client* on whose instructions the use of the *safe custody assets* has been effected and the number of *safe custody assets* used belonging to each *client*	Maintain up-to-date records	5 years (from the date the record was made)
CASS 6.5.1R	*Safe custody assets* held for each *client* and the *firm's* own *applicable assets.*	All that is necessary to enable the *firm* to distinguish *safe custody assets* held for one *client* from *safe custody assets* held for any other *client*, and from the *firm's* own *applicable assets*	Maintain up-to-date records	5 years (from the date the record was made)
CASS 6.5.2R	*Safe custody assets* held for *clients*	Accurate records which ensure their correspondence to the *safe custody assets* held for *clients*	Maintain up-to-date records	5 years (from the date the record was made)
CASS 7.1.3R(2)	Record of election to comply with the *client money chapter*	Record of election to comply with the *client money chapter*, including the date from which the election is to be effective	Date of the election	5 years (from the date the *firm* ceases to use the election)
CASS 7.1.15CR	Record of election in relation to CASS 7.1.15CR	Record of election in relation to CASS 7.1.15CR	Date of election	Not specified
CASS 7.4.10R	Appropriateness of a *firm's* selection of a third party	Grounds upon which a *firm* satisfies itself as to the appropriateness of the *firm's* selection of a third party to hold *client money*	Date of the selection	5 years (from the *firm* ceases to use the third party to hold *client money*)

Handbook reference	Subject of record	Contents of record	When record must be made	Retention period
CASS 7.6.1R	*Client money* held for each *client* and the *firm's* own *money*	All that is necessary to enable the *firm* to distinguish *client money* held for one *client* from *client money* held for any other *client*, and from the *firm's* own *money*	Maintain up-to-date records	5 years (from the date the record was made)
CASS 7.6.2R	*Client money* held for each *client*	Accurate records to ensure the correspondence between the records and accounts of the entitlement of each *client* for whom the *firm* holds *client money* with the records and accounts of the *client money* the *firm* holds in *client bank accounts* and *client transaction accounts*	Maintain up-to-date records	5 years (from the date the record was made)
CASS 7.6.7R	Internal reconciliation of *client money* balances	Explanation of method of internal reconciliation of *client money* balances used by the *firm*, and if different from the *standard method of internal client money reconciliation*, an explanation as to how the method used affords equivalent degree of protection to *clients*, and how it enables the *firm* to comply with the *client money distribution rules*	Date the *firm* starts using the method	5 years (from the date the *firm* ceases to use the method)
CASS 7A.3.8R(3)	*Client money shortfall*	Each *client's* entitlement to *client money shortfall* at the failed bank	Maintain up to date records	Until *client* is repaid
CASS 7A.3.10R(3)	*Client money shortfall*	Each *client's* entitlement to *client money shortfall* at the failed bank	Maintain up to date records	Until *client* is repaid

Handbook reference	Subject of record	Contents of record	When record must be made	Retention period
CASS 7A.3.11R(3)	*Client money shortfall*	Each *client's* entitlement to *client money shortfall* at the failed bank	Maintain up to date records	Until *client* is repaid
CASS 7A.3.17R(3)	*Client money shortfall*	Each *client's* entitlement to *client money shortfall* at the failed intermediate broker, *settlement agent* or OTC counterparty	Maintain up to date records	Until *client* is repaid
CASS 8.1.5R	Adequate records and internal controls in respect of the *firm's* use of mandates (see CASS 8.1.5R(1) to CASS 8.1.5R(4))	Up to date list of *firm's* authorities and any conditions regarding the use of authorities, all transactions entered into, details of procedures and authorities for giving and receiving of instructions under authorities, and important *client* documents held by the *firm*	Maintain current full details	Not specified

SCHEDULE 2
NOTIFICATION REQUIREMENTS

[2136]
Sch 2 **[G]**
(1) Table

Handbook reference	Matter to be notified	Contents of notification	Trigger event	Time allowed
[deleted]				
[deleted]				
[deleted]				
[deleted]				
[deleted]				
[deleted]				
[deleted]				
[deleted]				
[deleted]				
[deleted]				
CASS 5.5.61R	Failure of *bank*, *broker* or *settlement agent*	Full details including whether it intends to make good any *shortfall* that may have arisen in the amounts involved	As soon as the *firm* becomes aware	Immediately

Handbook reference	Matter to be notified	Contents of notification	Trigger event	Time allowed
CASS 5.5.76R	Inability to perform the calculation required by CASS 5.5.63R	Inability to perform the calculation	Inability to perform the calculation	Immediately
CASS 5.5.77R	Inability to make good any *shortfall* identified by CASS 5.5.63R	Inability to make good any *shortfall* in *client money*	Inability to make good any *shortfall*	Immediately
CASS 5.5.78R	Inability to comply with the requirements in CASS 5.5.70R; CASS 5.5.72R; CASS 5.5.73R; CASS 5.5.74R; CASS 5.5.75R	Inability to comply with the requirements of the *rules* listed	Inability to comply with the requirements of the *rules* listed	As soon as reasonably practical
CASS 6.5.13R(1)	Non-compliance or inability, in any material respect, to comply with the requirements in CASS 6.5.1R (Records and accounts), CASS 6.5.2R (Records and accounts, including internal reconciliations) or CASS 6.5.6R (Reconciliations with external records)	The fact that the *firm* has not complied or is unable, in any material respect, to comply with the requirements and the reasons for that	Non-compliance or inability, in any material respect, to comply with the requirements	Without delay
CASS 6.5.13R(2)	Non-compliance or inability, in any material respect, to comply with the requirements in CASS 6.5.10R (Reconciliation discrepancies)	The fact that the *firm* has not complied or is unable, in any material respect, to comply with the requirements and the reasons for that	Non-compliance or inability, in any material respect, to comply with the requirements	Without delay
CASS 7.4.35R	LME bond arrangements	Issue of an individual letter of credit issued by the *firm*	Upon issue of an individual letter of credit under an LME bond arrangement	Immediately

Handbook reference	**Matter to be notified**	**Contents of notification**	**Trigger event**	**Time allowed**
CASS 7.6.16R(1)	Non-compliance or inability, in any material respect, to comply with the requirements in CASS 7.6.1R (Records and accounts), CASS 7.6.2R (Records and accounts, including internal reconciliations) or CASS 7.6.9R (Reconciliations with external records)	The fact that the *firm* has not complied or is unable, in any material respect, to comply with the requirements and the reasons for that	Non-compliance or inability, in any material respect, to comply with the requirements	Without delay
CASS 7.6.16R(2)	Non-compliance or inability, in any material respect, to comply with the requirements in CASS 7.6.13R to CASS 7.6.15R (Reconciliation discrepancies)	The fact that the *firm* has not complied or is unable, in any material respect, to comply with the requirements and the reasons for that	Non-compliance or inability, in any material respect, to comply with the requirements	Without delay
CASS 7A.3.19R(1)	*Failure* of a third party with which *money* is held – ie: bank, *intermediate broker*, *settlement agent* or OTC counterparty or other entity with which it has placed or to which it has passed *client money*	Full details	*Firm* becomes aware of the *failure* of the entity	As soon as the *firm* becomes aware
CASS 7A.3.19R(2)	*Failure* of a third party with which money is held – ie: bank, *intermediate broker*, *settlement agent* or OTC counterparty or other entity with which it has placed or to which it has passed *client money*	Intentions regarding making good any *shortfall* that has arisen or may arise, and of the amounts involved	*Failure* of third party with which *client money* is held	As soon as reasonably practical

SCHEDULE 3
FEES AND OTHER REQUIRED PAYMENTS

[2137]
Sch 3 **[G]**

(1) There are no requirements for fees or other payments in CASS.

SCHEDULE 4
POWERS EXERCISED

[2138]
Sch 4 **[G]**

The following powers and related provisions in or under the *Act* have been exercised by the *FSA* to make the *rules* in CASS:

(1) Section 138 (General rule-making power)
(2) Section 139(1) (Miscellaneous ancillary matters)
(3) Section 149 (Evidential provisions)
(4) Section 156 (General supplementary powers)

The following powers in the *Act* have been exercised by the *FSA* to give the *guidance* in *CASS*:

(5) 5 Section 157(1) (Guidance)

SCHEDULE 5
RIGHTS OF ACTIONS FOR DAMAGES

[2139]
Sch 5 **[G]**

(1) The table below sets out the *rules* in *CASS* contravention of which by an *authorised person* may be actionable under section 150 of the *Act* (Actions for damages) by a *person* who suffers loss as a result of the contravention.

(2) If a 'Yes' appears in the column headed 'For private person?', the *rule* may be actionable by a 'private person' under section 150 (or, in certain circumstances, his fiduciary or representative; see article 6(2) and (3)(c) of the Financial Services and Markets Act 2000 (Rights of Action) Regulations 2001 (SI 2001 No 2256)). A 'Yes' in the column headed 'Removed' indicates that the *FSA* has removed the right of action under section 150(2) of the *Act*. If so, a reference to the *rule* in which it is removed is also given.

(3) The column headed 'For other person?' indicates whether the *rule* may be actionable by a *person* other than a *private person* (or his fiduciary or representative) under article 6(2) and (3) of those Regulations. If so, an indication of the type of *person* by whom the *rule* may be actionable is given.

Chapter/ Appendix	**Section/ Annex**	**Paragraph**	**Right of action under section 150**			
			For private person?	**Removed?**	**For other person?**	
All rules in CASS with the status letter "E"			No	No	No	
All other rules in *CASS*.			Yes	No	No	

SCHEDULE 6
RULES THAT CAN BE WAIVED

[2140]
Sch 6 **[G]**

(1) The rules in CASS can be waived by the FSA under section 148 of the *Act* (Modification or waiver of rules).

TRAINING AND COMPETENCE (TC)

NOTES

Up to date as at 22 February 2010. For later amendments please see www.fsa.gov.uk.

CONTENTS

TC 1—Application and Purpose . . . . . [2141]
TC 2—Competence . . . . . [2142]
TC 3—Record Keeping . . . . . [2143]
TC App 1R—Activities and Products/Sectors to which TC applies subject to TC Appendices 2 and 3 . . . . . [2144]
TC App 2R—TC's Territorial Scope subject to the limitation in TC Appendix 3 . . . . . [2145]
TC App 3R—Circumstances in which TC does not apply . . . . . [2146]
TC—Transitional Provisions . . . . . [2147]
TC Sch 1—Record keeping requirements . . . . . [2148]
TC Sch 2—Notification requirements . . . . . [2149]
TC Sch 3—Fees and other required payments . . . . . [2150]
TC Sch 4—Powers exercised . . . . . [2151]
TC Sch 5—Rights of action for damages . . . . . [2152]
TC Sch 6—Rules that can be waived . . . . . [2153]

CHAPTER 1
APPLICATION AND PURPOSE

1.1 Who, what and where?

Who and what?

[2141]
1.1.1 **[R]** This sourcebook applies to a *firm* where its *employee* carries on an activity in TC Appendix 1 for *retail clients, customers* or *consumers* (subject to the limitations set out in TC Appendix 3).

Where?

1.1.2 **[R]** The territorial scope of this sourcebook is set out in TC Appendix 2.

Purpose

1.1.3 **[G]** The *competent employees rule* is the main *Handbook* requirement relating to the competence of *employees*. The purpose of this sourcebook is to support the FSA's supervisory function by supplementing the *competent employees rule* for retail activities.

Meaning of competence

1.1.4 **[G]** In this sourcebook, competence means having the skills, knowledge and expertise needed to discharge the responsibilities of an *employee's* role. This includes achieving a good standard of ethical behaviour.

1.2 Actions for damages

1.2.1 **[R]** A contravention of the *rules* in TC does not give rise to a right of action by a *private person* under section 150 of the *Act* (and each of those *rules* is specified under section 150(2) of the *Act* as a provision giving rise to no such right of action).

CHAPTER 2
COMPETENCE

2.1 Assessing and maintaining competence

Assessment of competence and supervision

[2142]
2.1.1 **[R]**

(1) A *firm* must not assess an *employee* as competent to carry on an activity in TC Appendix 1 until the *employee* has demonstrated the necessary competence to do so and has (if required by TC Appendix 1) passed each module of an appropriate examination. This assessment need not take place before the *employee* starts to carry on the activity.

(2) A *firm* may assess an *employee* who is subject to, but has not satisfied, an appropriate examination requirement as competent to the extent that:
  (a) that *employee* works in a *branch* in an *EEA State* other than the *United Kingdom*;
  (b) the *employee* is engaging in *MiFID business*; and
  (c) there is no appropriate examination or equivalent in that *EEA State*.

2.1.2 **[R]** A *firm* must not allow an *employee* to carry on an activity in TC Appendix 1 without appropriate supervision.

2.1.3 **[G]** *Firms* should ensure that *employees* are appropriately supervised at all times. It is expected that the level and intensity of that supervision will be significantly greater in the period before the *firm* has assessed the *employee* as competent, than after. A *firm* should therefore have clear criteria and procedures relating to the specific point at which the *employee* is assessed as competent in order to be able to demonstrate when and why a reduced level of supervision may be considered appropriate. At all stages *firms* should consider the level of relevant experience of an *employee* when determining the level of supervision required.

Supervisors

2.1.4 **[G]** *Firms* should ensure that those supervising *employees* carrying on an activity in TC Appendix 1 have the necessary coaching and assessment skills as well as technical knowledge to act as a competent supervisor and assessor. In particular *firms* should consider whether it is appropriate to require those supervising *employees* not assessed as competent to pass an appropriate examination as well except where the *employee* is giving advice on *packaged products*, see TC 2.1.5R.

2.1.5 **[R]** Where an *employee* is giving advice on packaged products to *retail clients* and has not been assessed as competent to do so, the *firm* must ensure that the individual supervising and assessing that *employee* has passed an appropriate examination.

Examination requirements before starting activities

2.1.6 **[R]** A *firm* must ensure that an *employee* does not carry on an activity in TC Appendix 1 (other than an overseeing activity) for which there is an examination requirement without first passing the relevant regulatory module of an appropriate examination.

2.1.7 **[R]** A *firm* must ensure that an *employee* does not carry on any of the following activities without first passing each module of an appropriate examination:
(1) "advising and dealing" activities in TC Appendix 1;
(2) the activity of a *broker fund adviser*;
(3) *advising on syndicate participation at Lloyd's*; or
(4) the activity of a *pension transfer specialist*.

2.1.8 **[G]** Where there is an examination requirement, *firms* may wish to impose limits on the time they allow their *employees* to pass an appropriate examination or place limits on the number of times the examination can be taken.

Exemption from appropriate examination requirements

2.1.9 **[R]**
(1) If a *firm* is satisfied that an *employee* meets the conditions in this *rule* then the requirements to have passed each module of an appropriate examination will only apply if that employee is carrying on one of the activities specified in this *rule*.

(2) The conditions are that a *firm* should be satisfied that an *employee:*
  (a) has at least three years' up-to-date relevant experience in the activity in question obtained while employed outside the *United Kingdom*;
  (b) has not previously been required to comply fully with the relevant examination requirements in TC 2.1.1R; and
  (c) has passed the relevant regulatory module of an appropriate examination;

  but (b) and (c) do not apply to an *employee* who is benefiting from the "30-day rule" exemption in SUP 10.10.7BR, unless the *employee* benefits from that rule because he is advising *retail clients* on *packaged products* or is a *broker fund adviser*.

(3) The relevant activities are:
  (a) *advising on investments* which are *packaged products*, if that advice is given to *retail clients*;
  (b) the activity of a *broker fund adviser*;
  (c) *advising on syndicate participation at Lloyd's*; or
  (d) the activity of a *pension transfer specialist*.

Selecting an appropriate examination

2.1.10 **[E]**
(1) This *rule* applies for the purposes of TC 2.1.1R, TC 2.1.5R, TC 2.1.6R, TC 2.1.7R and TC 2.1.9R.
(2) In ensuring that an examination is appropriate, a *firm* should select an appropriate examination from the list of examinations maintained by The Financial Services Skills Council.
(3) Compliance with (2) may be relied on as tending to establish compliance with the *rules* referred to in (1).

Training needs

2.1.11 **[G]** *Firms* should ensure that their *employees'* training needs are assessed at the outset and at regular intervals (including if their role changes). Appropriate training and support should be provided to ensure that any relevant training needs are satisfied. *Firms* should also review at regular intervals the quality and effectiveness of such training.

Maintaining competence

2.1.12 **[R]** A *firm* must review on a regular and frequent basis *employees'* competence and take appropriate action to ensure that they remain competent for their role.

2.1.13 **[G]** A firm should ensure that maintaining competence for an employee takes into account such matters as:
(1) technical knowledge and its application;
(2) skills and expertise; and
(3) changes in the market and to products, legislation and regulation.

CHAPTER 3
RECORD KEEPING

3.1 Record-keeping requirements

[2143]
3.1.1 **[R]** A *firm* must make appropriate records to demonstrate compliance with the *rules* in this sourcebook and keep them for the following periods after an *employee* stops carrying on the activity:
(1) at least 5 years for *MiFID business*;
(2) 3 years for non-*MiFID business*; and
(3) indefinitely for a *pension transfer specialist*.

TC APPENDIX 1R
ACTIVITIES AND PRODUCTS/SECTORS TO WHICH TC APPLIES SUBJECT TO TC APPENDICES 2 AND 3

[2144]

Activity	Products/Sectors	Is there an appropriate examination requirement?
Designated investment business carried on for a *retail client*		
Providing basic advice	1. *Stakeholder products* excluding a *deposit-based stakeholder product*	No
Advising	2. *Securities* which are not *stakeholder pension schemes* or *broker funds*	Yes
	3. *Derivatives*	Yes
	4. *Packaged products* which are not *broker funds*	Yes
	5. *Friendly Society life policies* where the *employee* is not reasonably expected to receive a remuneration of greater than £1000 a year in respect of such sales	No
	6. *Friendly Society* tax-exempt policies	Yes
	7. *Long-term care insurance contracts*	Yes
	8. *Investments* in the course of *corporate finance business*	Yes
	9. *Advising on syndicate participation at Lloyd's*	Yes
Undertaking the activity in column 2	10. *Broker fund adviser*	Yes

Activity	**Products/Sectors**	**Is there an appropriate examination requirement?**
	11. *Pension transfer specialist*	Yes
Advising and dealing	12. *Securities* which are not *stakeholder pension schemes* or *broker funds*	Yes
	13. *Derivatives*	Yes
Managing	14. *Investments*	Yes
Overseeing on a day-to-day basis	15. Operating a *collective investment scheme* or undertaking the activities of a *trustee* or *depositary* of a *collective investment scheme*	Yes
	16. *Safeguarding and administering investments* or holding *client money*	Yes
	17. *Administrative functions* in relation to *managing investments*	Yes
	18. *Administrative functions* in relation to *effecting* or *carrying out contracts of insurance*, which are *life policies*	Yes
	19. *Administrative functions* in relation to the operation of *stakeholder pension schemes*	Yes
Regulated mortgage activity and *reversion activity* carried on for a *customer*		
Advising	20. *Regulated mortgage contracts* for a non-business purpose	Yes
	21. *Equity release transactions*	Yes
Designing scripted questions for non-advised sales	22. *Equity release transactions*	Yes
Overseeing non-advised sales on a day-to-day basis	23. *Equity release transactions*	Yes
Non-investment *insurance business* carried on for a *consumer*		
Advising	24. *Non-investment insurance contracts*	No
Regulated sale and rent back activity carried on for a *customer*		
Advising	25. *Regulated sale and rent back agreements*	No
Overseeing non-advised sales on a day-to-day basis	26. *Regulated sale and rent back agreements*	No

Notes:

(1) In the Appendix the heading and types of business specified in the headings are to be read in conjunction with the paragraphs appearing beneath them.

(2) Thus, for example, paragraph 24, consistent with the heading above it, refers only to advice on *non-investment insurance contracts* given to a *consumer*.

TC APPENDIX 2R
TC'S TERRITORIAL SCOPE SUBJECT TO THE LIMITATION IN TC APPENDIX 3

[2145]

	UK domestic firm	***Incoming EEA firm***	***Overseas firm* (other than an *incoming EEA firm*)**
MiFID business and *equivalent third country business*	TC applies in respect of *employees* who carry on activities from an establishment maintained by the *firm* (or its *appointed representative*) in the *United Kingdom* and	TC does not apply	TC applies in respect of *employees* who carry on activities from an establishment maintained by the *firm* (or its *appointed representative*) in the *United Kingdom*

	UK domestic firm	***Incoming EEA firm***	***Overseas firm*** **(other than an** ***incoming EEA firm*****)**
	TC also applies insofar as an activity is carried on from an establishment maintained by the *firm* (or its *appointed representative* or, where applicable, its *tied agent)* in, and within the territory of, another *EEA State*		
Insurance mediation activities	TC applies in respect of *employees* who carry on activities from an establishment maintained by the *firm* (or its *appointed representative*) in the *United Kingdom* and TC also applies in respect of *employees* who engage in or oversee activities from a branch established in another *EEA state*	TC does not apply	TC does not apply
Regulated mortgage activity and *reversion activity*	TC applies if the *customer* is resident in the *United Kingdom* at the time the *regulated mortgage activity* or *reversion activity* is carried on and TC also applies if the *customer* is resident in another *EEA State* (at the time that the activity is carried on) but only if the activity is carried on from an establishment maintained by the *firm* or its *appointed representative* in the *United Kingdom*	Same as for *UK domestic firm*	Same as for *UK domestic firm*
Any other activity in Appendix 1	TC applies in respect of *employees* who carry on these activities from an establishment maintained by the *firm* (or its *appointed representative*) in the *United Kingdom* and TC also applies in respect of *employees* who carry on activities with or for a *client* in the *United Kingdom*	TC applies in respect of its *employees* who carry on activities from an establishment maintained by the *firm* (or its *appointed representative*) in the *United Kingdom*	TC applies in respect of its *employees* who carry on activities from an establishment maintained by the *firm* (or its *appointed representative*) in the *United Kingdom*

TC APPENDIX 3R
CIRCUMSTANCES IN WHICH TC DOES NOT APPLY

[2146]

Type of firm / activity	**Application**
Incoming EEA firm	This sourcebook does not apply where responsibility for any matter it covers is reserved by an *EU* instrument to the *firm's Home State regulator*
Incoming Treaty firm	This sourcebook does not apply where responsibility for any matter it covers is reserved by an *EU* instrument to the *firm's Home State regulator*
UCITS qualifier	This sourcebook only applies where it is relevant to the manner in which a *firm communicates* or *approves* a *financial promotion*
Authorised professional firm	*TC* does not apply with respect to its *non-mainstream regulated activities* (see PROF 5.2)
Incoming ECA provider	*TC* does not apply to an *incoming ECA provider* acting as such.

TRANSITIONAL PROVISIONS

1 Designated Investment Business: Assessments of competence before commencement

[2147]

1.1 **[R]**

(1) This *rule* applies in respect of an *employee* of a *firm* employed at *commencement* who had, before *commencement*, been assessed as competent by a *firm* in accordance with the applicable *rules* of its *previous regulator*.

(2) An *employee* described in (1) is exempt from the requirements in this sourcebook to pass an appropriate examination if the activity (or role of a supervisor) carried on by that *employee* after *commencement* is the same or substantially the same as that for which the *employee* had been assessed as competent before *commencement*.

1.2 **[R]** If an employee of a *firm* is exempted from an examination requirement under TC TP 1.1R and any other *firm* subsequently employs the individual, that exemption continues to apply in respect of that subsequent employment on the same basis provided that:

(1) the activity which the *employee* carries on (or the role of the supervisor) continues to be the same, or substantially the same, as that in respect of which the *employee* had previously enjoyed the benefit of the exemption; and

(2) the individual had not experienced any significant break in employment since the last employment in respect of which the individual had the benefit of an exemption under TC TP 1.

2 Designated Investment Business: Assessments of competence in 12 month period after commencement

2.1 **[R]**

(1) This *rule* applies in respect of an *employee* who had, on 31 October 2007, the benefit of an exemption under transitional rule 2 in TC TP 1.1 in the form it was in on 31 October 2007.

(2) An *employee* described in (1) is exempt from the requirements in this sourcebook to pass an appropriate examination but only in respect of the activities in respect of which the *employee* had the benefit of that exemption as at 31 October 2007.

2.2 **[R]** If an *employee* of a *firm* is exempted from an examination requirement under TC TP 2.1R and any other *firm* subsequently employs the individual, that exemption continues to apply in respect of that subsequent employment on the same basis provided that:

(1) the activity which the *employee* carries on continues to be the same, or substantially the same, as that in respect of which the *employee* had previously enjoyed the benefit of the exemption; and

(2) the individual had not experienced any significant break in employment since the last employment in respect of which the individual had the benefit of an exemption under TC TP 2.

2.3 **[G]** At 31 October 2007 transitional rule 2 in TC TP 1.1 applied to a *firm* whose *employees* at *commencement* had not been subject to any specific training and competence requirements of a *previous regulator*. This *rule* allowed the *firm* to assess such individuals as competent in the first twelve months after *commencement* without their having to pass an exam. The exemption applied only in respect of the activities which the individual was able to carry on before *commencement* where they were the same or substantially the same.

3 Regulated Mortgage Contracts: Assessments of competence under the Mortgage Code Compliance Board Rules

3.1 **[R]**

(1) This *rule* applies:

(a) in relation to *regulated mortgage contracts*; and

(b) in respect of an individual employed by a *firm* at 31 October 2004.

(2) If the individual described in (1) was assessed as competent by the *firm* before 31 October 2004 in accordance with the rules of the Mortgage Code Compliance Board applying immediately before 31 October 2004, the individual is exempt from the requirements in this sourcebook to pass an appropriate examination provided that:

(a) the activity which the individual carries on continues to be the same, or substantially the same, as that immediately before 31 October 2004; and

(b) the individual had not experienced any significant break in employment since the last employment in respect of which the individual had the benefit of an exemption under this *rule*.

3.2 **[R]** If an *employee* of a *firm* is exempted from an examination requirement under TC TP 3.1R and any other *firm* subsequently employs the individual, that exemption continues to apply in respect of that subsequent employment on the same basis provided that:

(1) the conditions in TC TP 3.1R(2)(a) and (b) are met; and

(2) the firm assesses the individual to be competent in accordance with TC 2.1.1R.

4 Home Reversion Plans: Assessments of competence before 6 April 2007 in relation to lifetime mortgages

4.1 **[R]**

(1) This *rule* applies in respect of an individual employed by a *firm* at 6 April 2007, if that individual had before that date been assessed as competent by the *firm* in relation to:

(a) advising on *lifetime mortgages*;

(b) designing scripted questions for use in non-advised sales to *customers* of *lifetime mortgages*; or

(c) overseeing non-advised sales of *lifetime mortgages*.

(2) An individual in (1) is exempt from the examination requirements in this sourcebook in relation to activities carried on concerning *home reversion plans* that correspond to those in (1) provided that:

(a) the individual has been assessed as competent to apply the knowledge and skills necessary to carry on the relevant home reversion activity before 6 April 2007;

(b) the home reversion activity which the individual carries on continues to be the same, or substantially the same as that which the individual carried on immediately before 6 April 2007; and

(c) the individual had not experienced any significant break in employment since the last employment in respect of which the individual had the benefit of an exemption under this *rule*.

4.2 **[R]** If an *employee* of a *firm* is exempted from an examination requirement under TC TP 4.1R and any other *firm* subsequently employs the individual, that exemption continues to apply in respect of that subsequent employment on the same basis provided that:

(1) the conditions in TC TP 4.1R(2)(b) and (c) are met; and

(2) the firm assesses the individual to be competent in accordance with TC 2.1.1R.

4.3 **[R]** TC TP 4 does not apply to an individual in TC TP 4.1R(1) after 6 April 2009 unless the individual passes an appropriate home reversions top-up examination before that date.

5 Home Reversion Plans: Assessments of competence before 6 April 2007 in relation to Home Reversion Plans only

5.1 **[R]**

(1) This *rule* applies in respect of an individual employed by a *firm* at 6 April 2007 (other than an individual described in TC TP 4.1R).

(2) The individual in (1) is exempt from the examination requirements in this sourcebook in relation to the following:

(a) advising on *home reversion plans*;

(b) designing scripted questions for use in non-advised sales to customers of *home reversion plans*; or

(c) overseeing non-advised sales of *home reversion plans*.

(3) The exemption in (2) only applies if:

(a) the individual has been assessed as competent to apply the knowledge and skills necessary to engage in or oversee the relevant home reversion activity before 6 April 2007;

(b) the home reversion activity which the individual carries on continues to be the same, or substantially the same as that immediately before 6 April 2007; and
(c) the individual had not experienced any significant break in employment since the last employment in respect of which the individual had the benefit of an exemption under this *rule*.

5.2 **[R]** If the individual has not passed an appropriate examination before 6 April 2009, the individual in TC TP 5.1R(1) will cease to be exempt from the appropriate examination requirement.

5.3 **[R]** If an employee of a *firm* is exempted from an examination requirement under TC TP 5.1R and any other *firm* subsequently employs the individual, that exemption continues to apply in respect of that subsequent employment on the same basis provided that:
(1) the conditions in TC TP 5.1R3(b) and (c) are met; and
(2) the firm assesses the individual to be competent in accordance with TC 2.1.1R.

6 Transitional provisions relating to assessments of competence generally

6.1 **[G]** If appropriate, a *firm* may treat a competence assessment carried out under TC in the form it was in before 1 November 2007 as being sufficient to satisfy TC 2.1.1R.

7 Transitional provisions relating to waivers from existing examination requirements

7.1 **[R]**
(1) This provision applies to a *firm* which benefited from a waiver from an examination requirement in TC prior to 1 November 2007 in respect of an *employee*. If such a *firm* would otherwise find itself in breach of an examination requirement in TC from that date as a result of the re-categorisation of *clients* in *COBS*, the *firm* may allow that *employee* to continue carrying on the activities in respect of which the waiver was granted until 31 October 2008 though he has yet to satisfy the relevant examination requirement in TC.
(2) If an *employee* of a *firm* is exempted from an examination requirement under TC TP 7.1(1) and any other *firm* subsequently employs the individual, that exemption continues to apply in respect of that subsequent employment on the same basis provided that:
 (a) the activity which the *employee* carries on continues to be the same, or substantially the same, as that in respect of which the *employee* had previously enjoyed the benefit of the exemption; and
 (b) the *employee* had not experienced any significant break in employment since the last employment in respect of which the relevant exemption was granted.

SCHEDULE 1
RECORD KEEPING REQUIREMENTS

[2148]
TC Sch 1.1 **[G]** TC 3.1.1R provides:

A *firm* must make appropriate records to demonstrate compliance with the *rules* in this sourcebook and keep them for the following periods after an *employee* stops carrying on the activity:
(1) at least 5 years for *MiFID business*;
(2) 3 years for non-*MiFID business*; and
(3) indefinitely for a *pension transfer specialist*.

SCHEDULE 2
NOTIFICATION REQUIREMENTS

[2149]
TC Sch 2.1 **[G]** There are no notification or reporting requirements in TC.

SCHEDULE 3
FEES AND OTHER REQUIRED PAYMENTS

[2150]
TC Sch 3.1 **[G]** There are no requirements for fees or other payments in TC.

SCHEDULE 4
POWERS EXERCISED

[2151]
TC Sch 4.1 **[G]** The following powers and related provisions in the *Act* have been exercised to make the *rules* in
(1) section 138 (General rule making power)
(2) section 149 (Evidential provisions)
(3) section 150(2) (Actions for damages)
(4) section 156 (General supplementary powers)

TC Sch 4.2 **[G]** The following power in the *Act* has been exercised by the *FSA* to give the guidance in TC:
(1) section 157(1) (Guidance)

SCHEDULE 5
RIGHTS OF ACTION FOR DAMAGES

[2152]
TC Sch 5.1 **[G]** The table below sets out the *rules* in TC contravention of which by an *authorised person* may be actionable under section 150 of the *Act* (Actions for damages) by a *person* who suffers loss as a result of the contravention.

TC Sch 5.2 **[G]** If a "Yes" appears in the column headed "For private person?", the *rule* may be actionable by a "*private person*" under section 150 (or, in certain circumstances, his fiduciary or representative). A "Yes" in the column headed "Removed" indicates that the *FSA* has removed the right of action under section 150(2) of the *Act*. If so, a reference to the *rule* in which it is removed is also given.

TC Sch 5.3 **[G]** The column headed "For other person?" indicates whether the *rule* is actionable by a *person* other than a *private person* (or his fiduciary or representative). If so, an indication of the type of *person* by whom the *rule* is actionable is given.

TC Sch 5.4 **[G]** Table: Actions for damages: Training and Competence sourcebook

			Right of action under section 150		
Chapter/Appendix	Section/Annex	Paragraph	For private person	Removed	For other person
Rules in TC			No	Yes TC 1.2.1R	No

SCHEDULE 6
RULES THAT CAN BE WAIVED

Schedule 6 Rules that can be waived

[2153]
TC Sch 6.1 **[G]** The *rules* in TC can be *waived* by the *FSA* under section 148 of the *Act* (Modification or waiver of *rules*).

SUPERVISION (SUP)

NOTES

Up to date as at 22 February 2010. For later amendments please see www.fsa.gov.uk.

CONTENTS

SUP 1—The FSA's approach to supervision . . . [2154]
SUP 2—Information gathering by the FSA on its own initiative . . . [2155]
SUP 3—Auditors . . . [2156]
SUP 4—Actuaries . . . [2157]
SUP 5—Reports by skilled persons . . . [2158]
SUP 6—Applications to vary and cancel Part IV permission . . . [2159]
SUP 7—Individual requirements . . . [2160]
SUP 8—Waiver and modification of rules . . . [2161]
SUP 9—Individual guidance . . . [2162]
SUP 10—Approved persons . . . [2163]
SUP 11—Controllers and close links . . . [2164]
SUP 12—Appointed representatives . . . [2165]
SUP 13—Exercise of passport rights by UK firms . . . [2166]
SUP 13A—Qualifying for authorisation under the Act . . . [2167]
SUP 14—Incoming EEA firms changing details, and cancelling qualification for authorisation . . . [2168]
SUP 15—Notifications to the FSA . . . [2169]
SUP 16—Reporting requirements . . . [2170]
SUP 17—Transaction reporting . . . [2171]
SUP 18—Transfers of business . . . [2172]
SUP 20—Fees Rules . . . [2173]
SUP 21—Waiver . . . [2174]
SUP App 1—Prudential categories and sub-categories . . . [2175]
SUP App 2—Insurers: Scheme of operations . . . [2176]
SUP App 3—Guidance on passporting issues . . . [2177]
SUP TP 1—Transitional provisions . . . [2178]
SUP Sch 1—Record keeping requirements . . . [2179]
SUP Sch 2—Notification requirements . . . [2180]
SUP Sch 4—Powers exercised . . . [2181]
SUP Sch 5—Rights of actions for damages . . . [2182]

CHAPTER 1
THE FSA'S APPROACH TO SUPERVISION

1.1 Application and purpose

Application

[2154]
1.1.1 **[G]** This chapter applies to every *firm*, except that its relevance for an *ICVC* is limited as the *FSA* does not intend to carry out an assessment of an *ICVC* that is specific to that *ICVC*.

Purpose

1.1.2 **[G]** The *Act* requires the *FSA* to "maintain arrangements designed to enable it to determine whether persons on whom requirements are imposed by or under this Act, or by any directly applicable Community regulation made under *MiFID*, are complying with them" (paragraph 6(1) of Schedule 1 to the *Act*).

1.1.3 **[G]** The design of these arrangements is shaped by the *regulatory objectives*. These are set out in section 2 of the *Act* (The Authority's general duties) and are:

(1) maintaining confidence in the *financial system*;
(2) promoting public understanding of the *financial system*;
(3) securing the appropriate degree of protection for *consumers*; and

(4) reducing the extent to which it is possible for a business carried on by a regulated person, or in contravention of the *general prohibition*, to be used for a purpose connected with financial crime.

1.1.4 **[G]** In designing its approach to supervision, the *FSA* has regard to the principles of good regulation set out in section 2(3) of the *Act*. In particular, the *FSA's* regulatory approach aims to focus and reinforce the responsibility of the management of each *firm* (section 2(3)(b) of the *Act)* to ensure that it takes reasonable care to organise and control the affairs of the *firm* responsibly and effectively and develops and maintains adequate risk management systems. It is the responsibility of management to ensure that the *firm* acts in compliance with its regulatory requirements. The *FSA* will have regard to the principle that a burden or restriction which is imposed on a *firm* should be proportionate to the benefits, considered in general terms, which are expected to result from the imposition of that burden or restriction (section 2(3)(c) of the *Act*).

1.2 Introduction

1.2.1 **[G]**

(1) The Supervision manual (SUP) and Decision, Procedure and Penalties manual (DEPP) form the regulatory processes part of the *Handbook*.

(2) [deleted]

(3) SUP sets out the relationship between the *FSA* and *authorised persons* (referred to in the *Handbook* as *firms*). As a general rule, material that is of continuing relevance after *authorisation* is in SUP.

(4) [deleted]

(5) *DEPP* is principally concerned with and sets out the FSA's decision making procedures that involve the giving of *statutory notices*, the *FSA's* policy in respect to the imposition and amount of penalties, and the conduct of interviews to which a direction under section 169(7) of the *Act* has been given or the *FSA* is considering giving.

1.2.2 **[G]** For a *firm* which undertakes business internationally (or is part of a *group* which does), the *FSA* will have regard to the context in which it operates, including the nature and scope of the regulation to which it is subject in jurisdictions other than the *United Kingdom*. For a *firm* with its head office outside the *United Kingdom*, the regulation in the jurisdiction where the head office is located will be particularly relevant. As part of its supervision of such a *firm*, the *FSA* will usually seek to cooperate with relevant *overseas regulators*, including exchanging information on the *firm*. Different arrangements apply for an *incoming EEA firm*, an *incoming Treaty firm* and a *UCITS qualifier*. The arrangements applying for an *incoming EEA firm* and an *incoming Treaty firm* are addressed in SYSC App1. For *UCITS qualifiers* see also COLLG.

1.2.3 **[G]** The *FSA* continues to develop the risk assessment approach set out in this chapter. The approach will not be introduced for all *firms* at *commencement*. For those *firms* where the approach is not introduced at *commencement*, the *FSA* continues to operate the risk assessment approach of the *firm's previous regulator*.

1.3 The FSA's risk based approach to supervision

Purpose

1.3.1 **[G]** The purpose of taking a risk-based approach to supervision is to focus the *FSA's* resources on the mitigation of risks to the *regulatory objectives*, and to have regard to the need to use the *FSA's* resources in the most efficient and economic way. The approach to risk assessment of *firms* is based on the extent to which they pose risks to the *FSA* meeting the *regulatory objectives*. This extent encompasses both the impact of such risks were they to crystallise and the probability of their doing so. The probability of risks crystallising depends on the inherent risks run by *firms*, the environment within which they operate and the internal systems and controls designed to mitigate such risks. This approach permits a matching of the intensity of the *FSA's* supervisory effort with the degree of risk posed by *firms* to meeting the *regulatory objectives.*

Impact and probability assessment

1.3.2 **[G]** The *FSA* uses a standard risk assessment process applied consistently across all its activities. It involves assessing the risk posed by the *firm* against a number of impact and probability factors, both initially and on a continuing basis.

1.3.3 **[G]** The impact of a *firm* is assessed by reference to a range of factors derived from the *regulatory objectives*, including:

(1) the degree to which risks related to the *firm*, were they to materialise, would damage market confidence;

(2) the extent to which the *firm* may pose risks to the achievement of the objective of promoting public understanding;

(3) the extent to which *consumers* may be adversely affected either directly or indirectly by the *firm* as a result of prudential failure, misconduct, market malfunction, market manipulation or the need to contribute to the financial reconstitution of compensation schemes;
(4) the incidence and materiality of any *financial crime* which may be perpetrated through or by the *firm*.

1.3.4 **[G]** The probability of a *firm* posing a risk to meeting the *regulatory objectives* is, where applicable, assessed in terms of "risk groups". These are discrete sources of risks to meeting the *regulatory objectives* which arise from:
(1) the *firm's* strategy;
(2) the *firm's* business risk: those risks (such as credit, market and operational risk) which are inherent in the business;
(3) the financial soundness of the *firm*;
(4) the nature of the *firm's customers* and the products and services it offers;
(5) the internal systems and controls and the compliance culture of the *firm*; and
(6) the organisation of the *firm* and the role played by its governing body, management and staff in effectively mitigating risk.

1.3.5 **[G]** The impact and probability assessments are combined to give an overall judgment as to the *firm's* priority for the *FSA* and therefore the nature of the relationship which the *FSA* will seek to have with the *firm* (see 'A new regulator for the new millennium' and 'Building the new regulator, Progress report').

1.3.6 **[G]** In addition to assessing the *firm* in terms of these impact and probability factors, the *FSA* takes into account three further factors which may affect the choice of supervisory approach and activities:
(1) the level of confidence in the information on which the risk assessment is based;
(2) the quality of the home regulatory regime (for *firms* with their head office overseas); and
(3) any anticipated material change in impact and probability factors.

The scope of the risk assessment process for firms

1.3.7 **[G]** The risk assessment process applies to all *firms*, although the detail required may vary from *firm* to *firm*. *Firms* judged as high impact are likely to require a more detailed assessment. A peer review process within the *FSA* assists consistency.

1.3.8 **[G]** The main steps in the risk assessment process are:
(1) preliminary assessment of a *firm's* potential impact on the *regulatory objectives*;
(2) probability assessment—the level of detail depends on the impact rating and the complexity of the *firm* (in the case of low impact *firms*, the firm—specific probability analysis will be minimal);
(3) for a sample of *firms*, validation panel for peer review of risk grading and resource allocation;
(4) letter to *firm* regarding risk assessment and any remedial actions (see REC 1.3.10G); and
(5) continuing review of risk assessment as necessary.

1.3.9 **[G]** In order to create incentives for *firms* to raise standards and to maximise the success of the *FSA's* supervisory arrangements, it is important that a *firm* understands the *FSA's* evaluation of its risk so that it can take appropriate action.

1.3.10 **[G]** The *FSA* intends to communicate the outcomes of its risk assessment to the *firm*. In the case of *firms* in which risks have been identified which could have a material bearing on the *FSA* meeting the *regulatory objectives*, the *FSA* will also outline a programme intended to address these. The *FSA* considers that it would generally be inappropriate for the *firm* to disclose the *FSA* risk assessment to third parties, except those who have a right to be aware of it, for example external auditors. The assessment is directed towards a very specific purpose—to illustrate the risk posed by the *firm* to the *regulatory objectives* and to enable the *FSA* to allocate its resources accordingly. Using it for any other purpose might well be misleading. The *FSA* therefore discourages *firms* from disclosing their assessments.

The nature of the FSA's relationship with firms

1.3.11 **[G]** The *FSA's* relationship with *firms* has five main elements:
(1) Determining satisfaction of the threshold conditions: in order to carry on *regulated activities*, a *firm* must demonstrate that it can satisfy, initially and on a continuing basis, the *threshold conditions* (see *COND*) (for example, the need to maintain adequate resources).
(2) Baseline monitoring which is designed to ensure that *firms* comply, on a continuing basis, with the regulatory requirements which apply to them (see SUP 1.1.2G): the *FSA* collects and analyses data supplied by *firms* (see for example SUP 16) and by third parties such as the *Financial Ombudsman Service Limited, consumers*, and by other regulators.

(3) Sectoral reviews and thematic work which will be used, for example, to validate information provided by a *firm* and to collect up to date information on a particular sector, in order to assess whether a *firm* meets required standards: thematic work is carried out to assess the risks posed by a particular issue (rather than by a sector or group of *firms*). The issues selected for such work are likely to be broader and proportionately more significant to the *FSA's regulatory objectives*.

(4) Programmes designed to mitigate specific risks in individual *firms*: these programmes depend on the *firm's* priority for the *FSA* (see SUP 1.3.5G).

(5) Work undertaken after particular risks have escalated or crystallised: once the *FSA* has identified an issue, it will need to use its regulatory judgment to determine how it should respond, if at all.

1.3.12 **[G]** The exact mixture of elements will thus vary with the *firm's* risk categorisation. Moreover, the elements being used at a particular time will depend on the *firm's* circumstances—for example, whether it is applying for *permission* to conduct other *regulated activities*, or is being investigated by the *FSA*.

1.4 Tools of supervision

1.4.1 **[G]** In order to meet the *regulatory objectives* and address identified risks to those objectives, the *FSA* has a range of supervisory tools available to it.

1.4.2 **[G]** The *FSA* classifies these tools under four headings:

(1) diagnostic: designed to identify, assess and measure risks;

(2) monitoring: to track the development of identified risks, wherever these arise;

(3) preventative: to limit or reduce identified risks and so prevent them crystallising or increasing; and

(4) remedial: to respond to risks when they have crystallised.

1.4.3 **[G]** Tools may serve more than one purpose. For example, supervisory powers can be used to address risks which have materialised or to assist in preventing risks from escalating. In the first instance they are remedial, in the second, preventative.

1.4.4 **[G]** Certain of these tools, for example the use of public statements to deliver messages to *firms* or *consumers* of financial services, do not involve the *FSA* in direct oversight of the business of *firms*. Other tools do involve a direct relationship with *firms*. The *FSA* also has powers to act on its own initiative to impose individual *requirements* on a *firm* (see SUP 7).

1.4.5 **[G]** The *FSA* uses a variety of tools to monitor whether a *firm*, once *authorised*, remains in compliance with regulatory requirements. These tools include:

(1) desk-based reviews;

(2) liaison with other agencies or regulators;

(3) meetings with management and other representatives of a *firm*;

(4) on-site inspections;

(5) reviews and analysis of periodic returns and notifications;

(6) reviews of past business;

(7) transaction monitoring;

(8) use of auditors;

(9) use of *skilled persons*.

1.4.6 **[G]** The *FSA* also uses a variety of tools to address specific risks identified in *firms*. These tools include:

(1) making recommendations for preventative or remedial action;

(2) giving other individual *guidance* to a *firm*;

(3) imposing individual *requirements*;

(4) varying a *firm's permission* in another way.

1.4.7 **[G]** For further discussion of the *FSA's* regulatory approach, see publications on the *FSA* website (www.fsa.gov.uk): in particular, 'A new regulator for the new millennium' and 'Building the new regulator, Progress report 1'.

1.5 Lead supervision

Application

1.5.1 **[G]** This section applies to a *firm* which is a member of a *group* with more than one supervisory contact at the *FSA*.

Purpose

1.5.2 **[G]** The *FSA* has developed arrangements for lead supervision in order to achieve more efficient and more effective supervision of *firms* and their *groups*. Lead supervision is designed to deliver a coordinated approach to the supervision of *groups* with more than one supervisory contact at the *FSA*, assisting the *FSA* to monitor them effectively and respond to the risks that arise.

Process

1.5.3 **[G]** The *FSA* appoints a lead supervisor for a *group* with more than one supervisory contact at the *FSA*. The choice of lead supervisor depends principally on the predominant business of the *group*.

1.5.4 **[G]** The lead supervisor has three key responsibilities:
(1) to produce an overall assessment of the *group*: this comprises an assessment of the strengths and weaknesses of the business of the *group* and each of the *firms* within a *group* and a risk assessment of the *group* as a whole;
(2) to coordinate the supervision programme: based on the overall assessment, the coordinated supervision programme is a single, risk-based supervision plan for the whole *group* for a specified period; and
(3) to act as the central point of contact for the *group* with the *FSA*, where the *group* decides to use the lead supervisor in this way; this removes the need for duplicate communication between the *FSA* and *firms* in *groups* on group-wide issues.

CHAPTER 2
INFORMATION GATHERING BY THE FSA ON ITS OWN INITIATIVE

2.1 Application and purpose

Application

[2155]
2.1.1 **[R]** The application of this chapter is the same as the application of *Principle* 11 (Relations with regulators).

2.1.2 **[G]** PRIN 3 (Rules about application) specifies to whom, to what and where *Principle* 11 applies.

Purpose

2.1.3 **[G]** Achieving the *regulatory objectives* involves the *FSA* informing itself of developments in *firms* and in markets. The *Act* requires the *FSA* to monitor a *firm's* compliance with requirements imposed by or under the *Act* (paragraph 6 (1) of Schedule 1). The *Act* also requires the *FSA* to take certain steps to cooperate with other regulators (section 354). For these purposes, the *FSA* needs to have access to a broad range of information about a *firm's* business.

2.1.4 **[G]** The *FSA* receives the information in SUP 2.1.3G through a variety of means, including notifications by *firms* (see SUP 15) and regular reporting by *firms* (see SUP 16). This chapter is concerned with the methods of information gathering that the *FSA* may use on its own initiative in the discharge of its functions under the *Act*. This chapter does not deal with the information gathering powers that the *FSA* has under the *Unfair Terms Regulations*. These are dealt with in *UNFCOG*.

2.1.5 **[G]** Part XI of the *Act* (Information Gathering and Investigations) gives the *FSA* statutory powers, including:
(1) to require the provision of information (see section 165 and *EG* 3);
(2) to require reports from *skilled persons* (see section 166 and SUP 5);
(3) to appoint investigators (see sections 167, 168 and 169 of the *Act* and *EG* 3); and
(4) to apply for a warrant to enter premises (see section 176 of the *Act* and *EG* 4).

2.1.6 **[G]** The *FSA* prefers to discharge its functions by working in an open and cooperative relationship with *firms*. The *FSA* will look to obtain information in the context of that relationship unless it appears that obtaining information in that way will not achieve the necessary results, in which case it will use its statutory powers. The *FSA* has exercised its *rule*-making powers to make *Principle* 11 which requires that a *firm* must deal with its regulators in an open and cooperative way, and must disclose to the *FSA* appropriately anything relating to the *firm* of which the *FSA* would reasonably expect notice.

2.1.7 **[G]** The *FSA* operates in the context of the *Act* and the general law. The purpose of SUP 2.2 is to explain how certain provisions of the *Act* and the general law are relevant to the *FSA's* methods of information gathering described in SUP 2.3 and SUP 2.4.

2.1.8 **[G]** The purpose of SUP 2.3 is to amplify *Principle* 11 in the context of information gathering by the *FSA* on its own initiative in the discharge of its functions under the *Act*. SUP 2.3 therefore sets out, in *guidance* on *Principle* 11 and in *rules*, how the *FSA* expects *firms* to deal with the *FSA* in that context, including the steps that a *firm* should take with a view to ensuring that certain connected persons should also cooperate with the *FSA*.

2.1.9 **[G]** The purpose of SUP 2.4 is to explain a particular method of information gathering used by the *FSA*, known as "mystery shopping". Information about how a *firm* sells financial products can be very difficult to obtain, and the purpose of this method is to obtain such information from individuals who approach a *firm* in the role of potential retail *consumers* on the *FSA's* initiative. The *FSA* may seek information about particular issues or the activities of individual *firms* by means of mystery shopping.

2.2 Information gathering by the FSA on its own initiative: background

Link to the statutory information gathering and investigation powers

2.2.1 **[G]** Breaching *Principle* 11, or the *rules* in this chapter, makes a *firm* liable to regulatory sanctions, including discipline under Part XIV of the *Act* (Disciplinary Measures), and may be relevant to the use of the *FSA's* other powers, including the statutory information gathering and investigation powers (see further PRIN 1.1.7G to PRIN 1.1.9G). But, unlike a breach of a requirement imposed under the statutory powers listed in SUP 2.1.5G, a breach of *Principle* 11 or a *rule*:

(1) is not a criminal offence; and
(2) cannot lead to a *person* being treated as if in contempt of court (see section 177 of the *Act* (Offences).

2.2.2 **[G]** Neither *Principle* 11 nor SUP 2.3.5R(1) (Access to premises) enable the *FSA* to force access to premises.

Banking confidentiality and legal privilege

2.2.3 **[G]** The *FSA* would not normally seek to gather information using the methods described in SUP 2.3 or SUP 2.4 in a situation where the *FSA* could not have obtained it under the powers in Part XI of the *Act* (Information Gathering and Investigations). In particular, the limitations in the following sections of the *Act* are relevant to this chapter:

(1) section 175(5) (Information and documents: supplementary powers) under which no *person* may be required under Part XI of the *Act* (Information Gathering and Investigations) to disclose information or produce a document subject to banking confidentiality (with exceptions); the *FSA* would not normally seek such information using the methods described in SUP 2.3 or SUP 2.4; and
(2) section 413 (Protected items), under which no *person* may be required under the *Act* to produce, disclose or permit the inspection of *protected items*; a *firm* would not breach *Principle* 11 or the *rules* in this chapter by not producing such items.

Confidentiality of information

2.2.4 **[G]** When the *FSA* obtains confidential information using the methods of information gathering described in SUP 2.3 or SUP 2.4, it is obliged under Part XXIII of the *Act* (Public Record, Disclosure of Information and Co-operation) to treat that information as confidential. The *FSA* will not disclose confidential information without lawful authority, for example if an exception applies under the Financial Services and Markets Act 2000 (Disclosure of Confidential Information) Regulations 2001(SI 2001/2188) or with the consent of the *person* from whom that information was received and (if different) to whom the information relates.

Admissibility of information in proceedings

2.2.5 **[G]** Information obtained by the *FSA* using the methods described in SUP 2.3 and SUP 2.4 is admissible in evidence in any proceedings, so long as it complies with any requirements governing the admissibility of evidence in the circumstances in question.

2.3 Information gathering by the FSA on its own initiative: cooperation by firms

Introduction: Methods of information gathering requiring cooperation

2.3.1 **[G]** The *FSA* uses various methods of information gathering on its own initiative which require the cooperation of *firms*:

(1) Visits may be made by representatives or appointees of the *FSA*. These visits may be made on a regular basis, on a sample basis, for special purposes such as theme visits (looking at a particular issue across a range of *firms*), or when the *FSA* has a particular reason for visiting a *firm*. Appointees of the *FSA* may include *persons* who are not *FSA* staff, but who have been appointed to undertake particular monitoring activities for the *FSA* (paragraph 6(2) of Schedule 1 to the *Act*). The *FSA* needs to have access to a *firm's documents*, personnel and business premises to carry out a visit.
(2) The *FSA* may seek meetings at the *FSA's* offices or elsewhere.
(3) The *FSA* may seek information or request *documents* by telephone, at meetings or in writing, including by electronic communication.

2.3.2 **[G]** The *FSA* expects to request meetings or access to business premises during reasonable business hours. The *FSA* also normally expects to be able to give reasonable notice to a *firm* or connected person when it seeks information, *documents*, meetings or access to business premises. On rare occasions, however, the *FSA* may seek access to premises without notice. The prospect of unannounced visits is intended to encourage *firms* to comply with the requirements and standards under the *regulatory system* at all times.

Access to a firm's documents and personnel

2.3.3 **[G]** In complying with *Principle* 11, the *FSA* considers that a *firm* should, in relation to the discharge by the *FSA* of its functions under the *Act*:
(1) make itself readily available for meetings with representatives or appointees of the *FSA* as reasonably requested;
(2) give representatives or appointees of the *FSA* reasonable access to any records, files, tapes or computer systems, which are within the *firm's* possession or control, and provide any facilities which the representatives or appointees may reasonably request;
(3) produce to representatives or appointees of the *FSA* specified *documents*, files, tapes, computer data or other material in the *firm's* possession or control as reasonably requested;
(4) print information in the *firm's* possession or control which is held on computer or on microfilm or otherwise convert it into a readily legible *document* or any other record which the *FSA* may reasonably request;
(5) permit representatives or appointees of the *FSA* to copy *documents* or other material on the premises of the *firm* at the *firm's* reasonable expense and to remove copies and hold them elsewhere, or provide any copies, as reasonably requested; and
(6) answer truthfully, fully and promptly all questions which are reasonably put to it by representatives or appointees of the *FSA*.

2.3.4 **[G]** In complying with *Principle* 11, the *FSA* considers that a *firm* should take reasonable steps to ensure that the following *persons* act in the manner set out in SUP 2.3.3G:
(1) its *employees*, agents and *appointed representatives*; and
(2) any other members of its *group*, and their *employees* and agents.

(See also, in respect of *appointed representatives*, SUP 12.5.3G(2)).

Access to premises

2.3.5 **[R]**
(1) A *firm* must permit representatives of the *FSA*, or *persons* appointed for the purpose by the *FSA*, to have access, with or without notice, during reasonable business hours to any of its business premises in relation to the discharge of the *FSA's* functions under the *Act*.
(2) A *firm* must take reasonable steps to ensure that its agents, suppliers under *material outsourcing* arrangements and *appointed representatives* permit such access to their business premises. (See also, in respect of *appointed representatives*, SUP 12.5.3G(2)).

2.3.6 **[G]** The *FSA* normally expects to give reasonable notice of a visit (See SUP 2.3.2G).

Suppliers under material outsourcing arrangements

2.3.7 **[R]** A *firm* must take reasonable steps to ensure that each of its suppliers under *material outsourcing* arrangements deals in an open and cooperative way with the *FSA* in the discharge of its functions under the *Act* in relation to the *firm*.

2.3.8 **[G]** The cooperation that a *firm* is expected to procure from such suppliers is similar to that expected of the *firm*, in the light of the *guidance* in SUP 2.3.3G to SUP 2.3.4G, but does not extend to matters outside the scope of the *FSA's* functions in relation to the *firm*. SUP 2.3.5R(2) also requires a *firm* to take reasonable steps regarding access to the premises of such suppliers.

2.3.9 **[G]** When a *firm* appoints or renews the appointment of a supplier under a *material outsourcing* arrangement, it should satisfy itself that the terms of its contract with the supplier require the supplier to give the *FSA* access to its premises as described in SUP 2.3.5R(2), and to cooperate with the *FSA* as described in SUP 2.3.7R. The *FSA* does not consider that the 'reasonable steps' in SUP 2.3.7R would require a *firm* to seek to change a contract, already in place when that *rule* was made by the *FSA*, until renewal of the contract.

2.3.10 **[G]** The *FSA* will normally seek information from the *firm* in the first instance, but reserves the right to seek it from a supplier under a *material outsourcing* arrangement if the *FSA* considers it appropriate.

Information requested on behalf of other regulators

2.3.11 **[G]** The *FSA* may ask a *firm* to provide it with information at the request of or on behalf of other regulators to enable them to discharge their functions properly. Those regulators may include *overseas regulators* or the *Takeover Panel*. The *FSA* may also, without notifying a *firm*, pass on to those regulators information which it already has in its possession. The *FSA's* disclosure of information to other regulators is subject to the obligation described in SUP 2.2.4G (Confidentiality of information).

2.3.12 **[G]** In complying with *Principle* 11, the *FSA* considers that a *firm* should cooperate with it in providing information for other regulators. Section 169 of the *Act* (Investigations etc. in support of overseas regulator) gives the *FSA* certain statutory powers to obtain information and appoint investigators for *overseas regulators* if required (see *DEPP* 7 and *EG* 3).

2.4 'Mystery shopping'

2.4.1 **[G]** Representatives or appointees of the *FSA* (which may include individuals engaged by a market research firm) may approach a *firm*, its agents or its *appointed representatives* in the role of potential retail *consumers* with any authorisation under the Regulation of Investigatory Powers Act 2000 that is considered appropriate. This is known as 'mystery shopping'.

2.4.2 **[G]** The *FSA* uses mystery shopping to help it protect *consumers*. This may be by seeking information about a particular practice across a range of *firms* (SUP 2.4.3G(1)) or the practices of a particular *firm* (SUP 2.4.3G(2)). One of the risks *consumers* face is that they may be sold financial products which are inappropriate to them. A problem in protecting *consumers* from this risk is that it is very difficult to establish after the event what a *firm* has said to a 'genuine' *consumer* in discussions. By recording what a *firm* says in discussions with a 'mystery shopper', the *FSA* can establish a *firm's* normal practices in a way which would not be possible by other means.

2.4.3 **[G]** The *FSA* may carry out mystery shopping:

(1) together with a programme of visits to obtain information about a particular practice, looking at a particular issue across a range of *firms*, when the *FSA* may advise the *firms* of the issues beforehand; the practice being scrutinised may be that of *firms* or a class of *firms* in carrying on *regulated activities* or *ancillary activities* or in *communicating* or *approving financial promotions*;

(2) together with focused visits (concentrating on particular aspects of a *firm's* business) to obtain information about the practices of a *firm*; these practices may be in carrying on *regulated activities* or *ancillary activities* or in *communicating* or *approving financial promotions* when the *FSA* has particular concerns about those practices;

(3) using recording devices, telephonic or other communications; the *FSA* may monitor and store the contents of the materials obtained by these devices or communications.

2.4.4 **[G]** Telephone calls and meetings held during mystery shopping will be recorded. The *FSA* expects that any mystery shopping it arranges will be conducted in accordance with the Market Research Society Code of Practice.

CHAPTER 3
AUDITORS

3.1 Application

[2156]

3.1.1 **[R]** This chapter applies to:

(1) every *firm* within a category listed in column (1) of the table in SUP 3.1.2R; and

(2) the external auditor of such a *firm* (if appointed under SUP 3.3 or appointed under or as a result of a statutory provision other than in the *Act*);

in accordance with column (2) or (3) of that table, except as described in the remainder of this section.

3.1.1A **[G]** For the avoidance of doubt, this chapter does not apply to the following *firms* if they do not hold *client money* or client assets and do not appoint an auditor under or as a result of a statutory provision other than in the *Act*:

(1) *authorised professional firms*;

(2) *energy market participants, including oil market participants*, to whom IPRU(INV) 3 does not apply;

(3) *exempt insurance intermediaries*;

(4) *insurance intermediaries* not subject to SUP 3.1.2R(10);

(5) *investment management firms*;

(6) *home finance administrators*;

(7) *home finance intermediaries*;

(8) *home finance providers*;

(9) *personal investment firms*, including *small personal investment firms*;

(10) *securities and futures firms*; and

(11) *service companies*.

3.1.2 **[R]**

Table: Applicable sections (see SUP 3.1.1R)

(1) Category of firm		(2) Sections applicable to the firm	(3) Sections applicable to its auditor
(1)	*Authorised professional firm* which is required by *IPRU(INV)* 2.1.2R to comply with chapter 3, 5, 10 or 13 of *IPRU(INV)* and which has an auditor appointed under or as a result of a statutory provision other than in the *Act* (Note 1)	SUP 3.1 – SUP 3.7	SUP 3.1, SUP 3.2, SUP 3.8, SUP 3.10
(2)	*Authorised professional firm* not within (1) to which the *non-directive custody chapter*, *non-directive client money chapter*, *MiFID custody chapter* or *MiFID client money chapter* apply, unless the *firm* is regulated by The Law Society (England and Wales), The Law Society of Scotland or The Law Society of Northern Ireland (Note 2)	SUP 3.1 – SUP 3.7	SUP 3.1, SUP 3.2, SUP 3.8, SUP 3.10
(3)	*Authorised professional firm* not within (1) or (2) which has an auditor appointed under or as a result of a statutory provision other than in the *Act*	SUP 3.1, SUP 3.2, SUP 3.7	SUP 3.1, SUP 3.2, SUP 3.8
(4)	*Bank, building society or dormant account fund operator* which in each case carries on *designated investment business* (Note 2A)	SUP 3.1 – SUP 3.7	SUP 3.1, SUP 3.2, SUP 3.8, SUP 3.10
(5)	*Bank, building society or dormant account fund operator* which in each case does not carry on *designated investment business* (Note 2A)	SUP 3.1 – SUP 3.7	SUP 3.1, SUP 3.2, SUP 3.8
(5A)	*Credit union*	SUP 3.1 – SUP 3.7	SUP 3.1, SUP 3.2, SUP 3.8
(5B)	*ELMI*	SUP 3.1 – SUP 3.7	SUP 3.1, SUP 3.2, SUP 3.8
(6)	*Insurer*, the *Society of Lloyd's*, *underwriting agent* or *members' adviser*; *UK ISPV* (Note 5)	SUP 3.1 – SUP 3.7	SUP 3.1, SUP 3.2, SUP 3.8
(7)	*Investment management firm* (other than an *exempt CAD firm*), *personal investment firm* (other than a *small personal investment firm* or *exempt CAD firm*), or *securities and futures firm* (other than an *exempt CAD firm* or an *exempt BIPRU commodities firm*) which, in each case, has an auditor appointed under or as a result of a statutory provision other than in the *Act* (Notes 3 and 3A)	SUP 3.1 – SUP 3.7	SUP 3.1, SUP 3.2, SUP 3.8, SUP 3.10
(7A)	*Investment management firm* (other than an *exempt CAD firm*), *personal investment firm* (other than a *small personal investment firm* or *exempt CAD firm*), or *securities and futures firm* (other than an *exempt CAD firm* or an *exempt BIPRU commodities firm*) not within (7) to which the *non-directive custody chapter*, *non-directive client money chapter*, *MiFID custody chapter* or *MiFID client money chapter* apply	SUP 3.1 – SUP 3.7	SUP 3.1, SUP 3.2, SUP 3.8, SUP 3.10

(1) Category of firm		**(2) Sections applicable to the firm**	**(3) Sections applicable to its auditor**
(7B)	*UCITS firm*	SUP 3.1 – SUP 3.7	SUP 3.1, SUP 3.2, SUP 3.8, SUP 3.10
(7C)	*UK MiFID investment firm*, which has an auditor appointed under or as a result of a statutory provision other than in the *Act* (Note 3B)	SUP 3.1 – 3.7	SUP 3.1, SUP 3.2, SUP 3.8, SUP 3.10
(7D)	*Sole trader* or *partnership* that is a *UK MiFID investment firm* (other than an *exempt CAD firm*) (Note 3C)	SUP 3.1 – SUP 3.7	SUP 3.1, SUP 3.2, SUP 3.8, SUP 3.10
(8)	*Small personal investment firm* or *service company* which, in either case, has an auditor appointed under or as a result of a statutory provision other than in the *Act*	SUP 3.1, SUP 3.2, SUP 3.7	SUP 3.1, SUP 3.2, SUP 3.8
(9)	*Home finance provider* which has an auditor appointed under or as a result of a statutory provision other than in the *Act*	SUP 3.1 – SUP 3.7	SUP 3.1, SUP 3.2, SUP 3.8
(10)	*Insurance intermediary* (other than an *exempt insurance intermediary*) to which the *insurance client money chapter* (except for CASS 5.2 (Holding money as agent)) applies (see Note 4)	SUP 3.1 – SUP 3.7	SUP 3.1, SUP 3.2, SUP 3.8, SUP 3.10
(11)	Exempt insurance intermediary *and* insurance intermediary *not subject to* SUP 3.1.2R (10) *which has an auditor appointed under or as a result of a statutory provision other than in the* Act	SUP 3.1, SUP 3.2, SUP 3.7	SUP 3.1, SUP 3.2, SUP 3.8
(12)	*Home finance intermediary* or *home finance administrator* which has an auditor appointed under or as a result of a statutory provision other than in the *Act*.	SUP 3.1, SUP 3.2, SUP 3.7	SUP 3.1, SUP 3.2, SUP 3.8

Note 1 = This chapter applies to an *authorised professional firm* in row (1) (and its auditor) as if the *firm* were of the relevant type in the right-hand column of *IPRU(INV)* 2.1.4R.

Note 2 = In row (2):

(a) The *non-directive custody chapter* is treated as applying only if (i) the *firm safeguards and administers investments* in connection with *managing investments* (other than when acting as trustee) or (ii) it *safeguards and administers investments* in relation to *bonded investments* (and, in either case, it has not opted to conduct all business that would fall within the *non-directive custody chapter* under the *MiFID custody chapter*);

(b) The *non-directive client money chapter* is treated as applying only if the *firm* receives or holds *client money* other than under an arrangement where commission is rebated to the *client* (and assuming that it has not opted to conduct all business that would fall within the *non-directive client money chapter* under the *MiFID client money chapter*);

but, if the *custody rules* or the *client money rules* above are treated as applying, then SUP 3.10 (Duties of auditors: notification and report on client assets) applies to the whole of the business within the scope of the *custody rules* or the *client money rules* above.

Note 2A = For this purpose, *designated investment business* does not include either or both:

(a) *dealing* which falls within the exclusion in article 15 of the *Regulated Activities Order* (Absence of holding out etc) (or agreeing to do so); and

(b) dealing in investments as principal (or agreeing to do so):

(i) by a *firm* whose *permission* to *deal in investments as principal* is subject to a *limitation* to the effect that the *firm*, in carrying on this *regulated activity*, is limited to entering into transactions in a manner which, if the *firm* was an *unauthorised person*, would come within article 16 of the *Regulated Activities Order* (Dealing in contractually based investments); and

(ii) in a manner which comes within that *limitation*;

having regard to article 4(4) of the *Regulated Activities Order* (Specified activities).

Note 3 = This note applies in relation to an *oil market participant* to which *IPRU(INV)* 3 does not apply and in relation to an *energy market participant* to which *IPRU(INV)* 3 does not apply. In SUP 3:

(a) only SUP 3.1, SUP 3.2 and SUP 3.7 are applicable to such a *firm*; and
(b) only SUP 3.1, SUP 3.2 and SUP 3.8 are applicable to its auditor;

and, in each case, only if it has an auditor appointed under or as a result of a statutory provision other than in the *Act*.

Note 3A = If the *firm* has elected to comply with the *MiFID custody chapter* or the *MiFID client money chapter* also in respect of its *non-MiFID business* then SUP 3.10 will apply to the whole of the business within the scope of the *MiFID custody chapter* or the *MiFID client money chapter*.

Note 3B = *UK MiFID investment firms* include *exempt CAD firms*. An *exempt CAD firm* that has opted into *MiFID* can benefit from the audit exemption for small companies in the Companies Act legislation if it meets the relevant criteria in that legislation and fulfils the conditions of regulation 4C(3) of the Financial Services and Markets Act 2000 (Markets in Financial Instruments) Regulations 2007. If a *firm* does so benefit then SUP 3 will not apply to it. For further details about *exempt CAD firms*, see PERG 13, Q58.

Note 3C = A *sole trader* or a *partnership* that is a *MiFID investment firm* to which the *MiFID custody chapter* or *MiFID client money chapter* apply must have its annual accounts audited.

Note 4 = The *client money* audit requirement in SUP 3.1.2R(10) therefore applies to all *insurance intermediaries* except:

- those which do not hold *client money or other client assets* in relation to *insurance mediation activities*; or
- those which only hold up to, but not exceeding, £30,000 of *client money* under a statutory trust arising under CASS 5.3.

Insurance intermediaries which, in relation to *insurance mediation activities*, hold no more than that amount of *client money* only on a statutory trust are *exempt insurance intermediaries*.

Note (5) = In row (6):

(a) SUP 3.1–SUP 3.7 applies to a *managing agent* in respect of its own business and in respect of the *insurance business* of each *syndicate* which it manages; and
(b) SUP 3.1, SUP 3.2 and SUP 3.8 apply to the auditors of a *managing agent* and the auditors of *the insurance business* of each *syndicate* which the *managing agent* manages.

3.1.2A **[G]** If a *firm* falls within more than one row in column (1) of the table in SUP 3.1.2R, SUP 3.1.1R requires the *firm* and its external auditor to comply with all the sections referred to in column (2) or (3). For example, a *bank* which carries on *designated investment business* which is also a *mortgage lender*, falls in rows (4) and (9). Therefore, the *bank* must comply with SUP 3.1 to SUP 3.7, and its external auditor must comply with SUP 3.1, SUP 3.2, SUP 3.8 and SUP 3.10.

Incoming firms

3.1.3 **[R]** This chapter does applies to an *incoming EEA firm* (and the auditor of such a *firm*) only if it has a *top-up permission.*

3.1.4 **[G]** The application of SUP 3.10 to the auditor of an *incoming EEA firm* with a *top-up permission* is qualified in SUP 3.10.3R.

3.1.5 **[R]** This chapter does not apply to an *incoming Treaty firm*, which:

(1) does not have a *top-up permission*; and
(2) is not required to comply with the *client asset rules.*

3.1.6 **[G]** The application of SUP 3.7 to an *incoming Treaty firm* or an auditor of such a *firm* is further qualified in SUP 3.7.1G.

Auditors of lead regulated firms

3.1.7 **[G]** The application of SUP 3.10 to the auditor of a *lead regulated firm* is qualified in SUP 3.10.3R.

Authorised professional firms

3.1.8 **[G]** This chapter applies to an *authorised professional firm* as set out in rows (1) to (3) of SUP 3.1.2R:

(1) a *firm* in row (1) is treated in the same way as its equivalent in row (7);
(2) large parts of this chapter apply to a *firm* in row (2) and its auditor; the report on client assets under SUP 3.10 (Duties of auditors: notification and report on client assets) must cover compliance for the whole of the business within the scope of whichever of the *custody rules* and the *client money rules* are treated as applying; but there is no requirement for the auditor to prepare a report to the *FSA* on the *firm's* financial statements;

(3) this chapter has limited application to a *firm* in row (3) and its auditor.

Material elsewhere in the Handbook

3.1.9 **[G]** A *firm* which is a *friendly society* or other *insurer, investment management firm, personal investment firm* or a *securities and futures firm* should see the Prudential Standards part of the *Handbook* for further provisions on auditors as set out in SUP 3.1.10G. For the categorisations employed in SUP 3.1.2R and SUP 3.1.10G see SUP App1.

3.1.10 **[G]** Other relevant sections of the Handbook (see SUP 3.1.9G)

Friendly society	IPRU(FSOC)
Insurer (other than a friendly society)	IPRU(INS)
Investment management firm, personal investment firm, securities and futures firm (other than *BI-PRU investment firms*)	IPRU(INV)
UCITS firm	(UPRU)
Society of Lloyd's and Lloyd's *managing agents*	IPRU(INS)

Lloyd's
Enabling provision and application

3.1.11 **[G]** The *insurance market direction* in this chapter is given under section 316(1) of the *Act* (Direction by Authority) and applies to *members*.

Purpose

3.1.12 **[G]** The *insurance market direction* in this chapter is intended to enable the *rules* in SUP 3 and SUP 4 to be applied to a *managing agent* in respect of the *insurance business* of each *syndicate* which it manages.

Insurance market direction on rules concerning auditors and actuaries

3.1.13 **[D]**

(1) With effect from 1 January 2005, Part XXII of the *Act* (Auditors and Actuaries) applies to the carrying on of *insurance business* by *members* as modified by paragraph (3).

(2) For the purposes of (1) "insurance business" means the *regulated activities* of *effecting* or *carrying out contracts of insurance* written at Lloyd's.

(3) Regulations made by the Treasury under section 342(5) and section 343(5) of Part XXII of the *Act* apply only to *actuaries* appointed by a *managing agent* in respect of the *insurance business* of a *syndicate*, in relation to the *long-term insurance business* of that *syndicate*.

(4) In Part XXII of the *Act* (Auditors and Actuaries) as applied by this *insurance market direction*:

 (a) a reference to an auditor of an *authorised person* is to be read as including an auditor appointed by a *managing agent* in respect of the *insurance business* of a *syndicate*; and

 (b) a reference to an *actuary* acting for an *authorised person* is to be read as including an *actuary* appointed by a *managing agent* in respect of the *insurance business* of a *syndicate*.

3.1.14 **[G]** Part XXII (Auditors and Actuaries) is a *core provision* mentioned in section 317(1) of the *Act* (The core provisions).

3.1.15 **[G]** Section 317(2) of the *Act* (The core provisions) provides that references in an applied *core provision* to an *authorised person* are to be read as references to a *person* in the class to which the *insurance market direction* applies. The effect of this, and of the *insurance market direction* set out at SUP 3.1.13D, is that Part XXII of the *Act* (Auditors and Actuaries), applies also to auditors and *actuaries* who are appointed to report on the underwriting business of *members*. Part XXII is modified in its application to *members* by paragraph (3) of SUP 3.1.13D with the effect that the regulations made under sections 342(5) and 343(5) of the *Act* relating to communications by *actuaries* will only apply where the *actuary* is appointed to evaluate the *long-term insurance business* of the *syndicate*. The regulations made under sections 342(5) and 343(5) in relation to communications by auditors will apply in relation to both *general insurance business* and *long-term insurance business*.

3.1.16 **[G]** SUP 3.3 sets out *rules* the effect of which is to require a *managing agent* to appoint an auditor in respect of its own business and the *insurance business* of each *syndicate* which it manages.

3.1.17 **[G]** References in SUP 3, as applied by SUP 3.1.2R, to a *firm* include, where appropriate:

(1) a *managing agent*; and

(2) one or more *members* carrying on *insurance business* at Lloyd's through a *syndicate*,

and references to an *actuary* of a *firm* should be read accordingly.

3.1.18 **[G]** SUP 4.6 sets out *rules* the effect of which is to require a *managing agent* to appoint an *actuary* in respect of the *insurance business* of each *syndicate* which it manages.

3.2 Purpose

3.2.1 **[G]** This chapter sets out *rules* and *guidance* on the role auditors play in the *FSA's* monitoring of *firms'* compliance with the requirements and standards under the *regulatory system*. In determining whether a *firm* satisfies the *threshold conditions*, the *FSA* has regard to whether the *firm* has appointed auditors with sufficient experience in the areas of business to be conducted by the *firm* (SUP 2.5.7G(11)). Auditors act as a source of information for the *FSA* in its supervision. They report, where required, on the financial resources of the *firm*, the accuracy of its reports to the *FSA* and its compliance with particular *rules*, such as the *client asset rules*.

3.2.2 **[G]** The *Act*, together with other legislation such as the Companies Acts 1985, 1989 and 2006, the Building Societies Act 1986 and the Friendly Societies Act 1992, provides the statutory framework for *firms'* and auditors' obligations.

3.2.3 **[G]** The requirements in SUP 3.9 represent an interim approach to the use of auditors, based mainly on the requirements which *previous regulators* applied to *firms*.

3.2.4 **[G]** [deleted]

3.2.5 **[G]** It is the responsibility of an *insurance intermediary's* senior management to determine, on a continuing basis, whether the *insurance intermediary* is an *exempt insurance intermediary* and to appoint an auditor if management determines the *firm* is no longer exempt. SUP 3.7 (amplified by SUP 15) sets out what a *firm* should consider when deciding whether it should notify the *FSA* of matters raised by its auditor.

Rights and duties of auditors

3.2.6 **[G]** The rights and duties of auditors are set out in SUP 3.8 (Rights and duties of all auditors) and SUP 3.10 (Duties of auditors: notification and report on client assets). SUP 3.8.10G includes the auditor's statutory duty to report certain matters to the *FSA* imposed by regulations made by the Treasury under sections 342(5) and 343(5) of the *Act* (information given by auditor or actuary to the *FSA*). An auditor should bear these rights and duties in mind when carrying out *client* asset report work, including whether anything should be notified to the *FSA* immediately.

3.3 Appointment of auditors

Purpose

3.3.1 **[G]** This section requires a *firm* to appoint an auditor and supply the *FSA* with information about its auditor. The *FSA* requires such information to ensure that the *firm* has an auditor.

Appointment by firms

3.3.2 **[R]** A *firm* to which this section applies (see SUP 3.1) must:

(1) appoint an auditor;

(2) notify the *FSA*, without delay, on the form in SUP 15 Ann 2R (Standing data form), in accordance with the instructions on the form, when it is aware that a vacancy in the office of auditor will arise or has arisen, giving the reason for the vacancy;

(3) appoint an auditor to fill any vacancy in the office of auditor which has arisen;

(4) ensure that the replacement auditor can take up office at the time the vacancy arises or as soon as reasonably practicable after that; and

(5) notify the *FSA* of the appointment of an auditor, on the form in SUP 15 Ann 2R (Standing data form), in accordance with the instructions on the form, advising the *FSA* of the name and business address of the auditor appointed and the date from which the appointment has effect.

3.3.3 **[G]**

(1) SUP 3.3.2R applies to every *firm* to which this section applies. That includes a *firm* which is under an obligation to appoint an auditor under an enactment other than the *Act*, such as the Companies Act 1985 or the Companies Act 2006, as appropriate. Such a *firm* is expected to wish to have a single auditor who is appointed to fulfil both obligations. SUP 3.3.2R is made under section 138 of the *Act* (General rule-making power), in relation to such *firms*, and under section 340(1) (Appointment) in relation to other *firms*.

(2) *Building societies* and *friendly societies* are reminded that they are subject to the provisions of Schedule 11 to the Building Societies Act 1986 and Schedule 14 to the Friendly Societies Act 1992 relating to auditors, in addition to the provisions in this chapter. In relation to SUP 3.3.2R(2), such *firms* may give the *FSA* a single notification of a vacancy in the office of auditor provided that the notification complies with the requirements of the relevant Act and SUP 3.3.2R(2).

3.3.4 **[D]** [deleted]

3.3.5 **[R]** [deleted]

3.3.6 **[G]** [deleted]

Appointment by the FSA

3.3.7 **[R]**

(1) Paragraph (2) applies to a *firm* which is not under an obligation to appoint an auditor imposed by an enactment other than the *Act*.

(2) If a *firm* fails to appoint an auditor within 28 days of a vacancy arising, the *FSA* may appoint an auditor for it on the following terms:

(a) the auditor to be remunerated by the *firm* on the basis agreed between the auditor and *firm* or, in the absence of agreement, on a reasonable basis; and

(b) the auditor to hold office until he resigns or the *firm* appoints another auditor.

3.3.8 **[G]** In addition, in the case of a *building society* or *friendly society*, Schedule 11 of the Building Societies Act 1986 and Schedule 14 of the Friendly Societies Act 1992 allow the *FSA* to appoint an auditor if this is not done at the society's annual general meeting.

3.3.9 **[G]** SUP 3.3.7R allows but does not require the *FSA* to appoint an auditor if the *firm* has failed to do so within the 28 day period. When it considers whether to use this power, the *FSA* will take into account the likely delay until the *firm* can make an appointment and the urgency of any pending duties of the appointed auditor.

3.3.10 **[R]** A *firm* must comply with and is bound by the terms on which an auditor has been appointed by the *FSA*, whether under SUP 3.3.7R, the Building Societies Act 1986 or the Friendly Societies Act 1992.

3.4 Auditors' qualifications

Purpose

3.4.1 **[G]** The *FSA* is concerned to ensure that the auditor of a *firm* has the necessary skill and experience to audit the business of the *firm* to which he has been appointed. This section sets out the *FSA's rules* and *guidance* aimed at achieving this.

Qualifications

3.4.2 **[R]** Before a *firm*, to which SUP 3.3.2R applies, appoints an auditor, it must take reasonable steps to ensure that the auditor has the required skill, resources and experience to perform his functions under the *regulatory system* and that the auditor:

(1) is eligible for appointment as an auditor under Part II of the Companies Act 1989 or Part III of the Companies (Northern Ireland) Order 1990 (Eligibility for appointment) where applicable, otherwise Chapters 1, 2 and 6 of Part 42 of the Companies Act 2006; or

(2) if appointed under an obligation in another enactment, is eligible for appointment as an auditor under that enactment; or

(3) in the case of an *overseas firm*, is eligible for appointment as an auditor under any applicable equivalent laws of that country or territory.

3.4.3 **[G]** Enactments within SUP 3.4.2R(2) include the Building Societies Act 1986 and the Friendly Societies Act 1992.

3.4.4 **[G]** An auditor which a *firm* proposes to appoint should have skills, resources and experience commensurate with the nature, scale and complexity of the *firm's* business and the requirements and standards under the *regulatory system* to which it is subject. A *firm* should have regard to whether its proposed auditor has expertise in the relevant requirements and standards (which may involve access to *UK* expertise) and possesses or has access to appropriate specialist skill, for example actuarial expertise in carrying out audits of insurance companies or *friendly societies* where appropriate. The *firm* should seek confirmation of this from the auditor concerned as appropriate.

Disqualified auditors

3.4.5 **[R]** A *firm* must not appoint as auditor a *person* who is disqualified by the *FSA* under section 345 of the *Act* (Disqualification) from acting as an auditor either for that *firm* or for a relevant class of *firm*.

3.4.6 **[G]** If it appears to the *FSA* that an auditor of a *firm* has failed to comply with a duty imposed on him under the *Act*, it may disqualify him under section 345 of the *Act*. For more detail about what happens when the disqualification of an auditor is being considered or put into effect, see *EG* 15. A list of *persons* who are disqualified by the *FSA* under section 345 of the *Act* may be found on the *FSA* website (www.fsa.gov.uk).

Requests for information on qualifications by the FSA

3.4.7 **[R]** A *firm* must take reasonable steps to ensure that an auditor, which it is planning to appoint or has appointed, provides information to the *FSA* about the auditor's qualifications, skills, experience and independence in accordance with the reasonable requests of the *FSA*.

3.4.8 **[G]** To enable it to assess the ability of an auditor to audit a *firm*, the *FSA* may seek information about the auditor's relevant experience and skill. The *FSA* will normally seek information by letter from an auditor who has not previously audited any *firm*. The *firm* should instruct the auditor to reply fully to the letter (and should not appoint an auditor who does not reply to the *FSA*). The *FSA* may also seek further information on a continuing basis from the auditor of a *firm* (see also the auditor's duty to cooperate under SUP 3.8.2R).

3.5 Auditors' independence

Purpose

3.5.1 **[G]** If an auditor is to carry out his duties properly, he needs to be independent of the *firm* he is auditing, so that he is not subject to conflicts of interest. Many *firms* are also subject to requirements under the Companies Act 1989, or the Companies Act 2006, the Building Societies Act 1986 or the Friendly Societies Act 1992 on auditor's independence.

Independence

3.5.2 **[R]** A *firm* must take reasonable steps to ensure that the auditor which it appoints is independent of the *firm*.

3.5.3 **[R]** If a *firm* becomes aware at any time that its auditor is not independent of the *firm*, it must take reasonable steps to ensure that it has an auditor independent of the *firm*. The *firm* must notify the *FSA* if independence is not achieved within a reasonable time.

3.5.4 **[G]** The *FSA* will regard an auditor as independent if his appointment or retention does not breach the ethical guidance in current issue from the auditor's recognised supervisory body on the appointment of an auditor in circumstances which could give rise to conflicts of interest.

3.5.5 **[G]** *Firms* are reminded that the Building Societies Act 1986 and Friendly Societies Act 1992 provide that an auditor who is ineligible under section 27 of the Companies Act 1989 where applicable, otherwise sections 1214 and 1215 of the Companies Act 2006 for appointment as auditor of a company (which is a subsidiary undertaking of a *building society* or a subsidiary of a *friendly society*) is ineligible for appointment as auditor to the *building society* or *friendly society* concerned.

3.6 Firms' cooperation with their auditors

3.6.1 **[R]** A *firm* must cooperate with its auditor in the discharge of his duties under this chapter.

Auditor's access to accounting records

3.6.2 **[G]** In complying with SUP 3.6.1R, a *firm* should give a right of access at all times to the *firm's* accounting and other records, in whatever form they are held, and *documents* relating to its business. A *firm* should allow its auditor to copy *documents* or other material on the premises of the *firm* and to remove copies or hold them elsewhere, or give him such copies on request.

3.6.3 **[G]** Section 341 of the *Act* (Access to books etc.) provides that an auditor of a *firm* appointed under SUP 3.3.2R:

(1) has a right of access at all times to the *firm's* books, accounts and vouchers; and

(2) is entitled to require from the *firm's* officers such information and explanations as he reasonably considers necessary for the performance of his duties as auditor.

3.6.4 **[G]** Section 389A of the Companies Act 1985 where applicable, otherwise sections 499 and 500 of the Companies Act 2006, section 79 of the Building Societies Act 1986 and section 75 of the Friendly Societies Act 1992 give similar rights to auditors of companies, *building societies* and *friendly societies* respectively.

3.6.5 **[G]** Section 413 (Protected items), under which no person may be required under the *Act* to produce, disclose or permit the inspection of *protected items*, is relevant to SUP 3.6.1R and SUP 3.6.3G.

Access and cooperation: appointed representatives, material outsourcing, employees

3.6.6 **[G]** In complying with SUP 3.6.1R, a *firm* should take reasonable steps to ensure that each of its *appointed representatives* or, where applicable, *tied agents* gives the *firm's* auditor the same rights of access to the books, accounts and vouchers of the *appointed representative* or *tied agent* and entitlement to information and explanations from the *appointed representative's* or *tied agent's* officers as are given in respect of the *firm* by section 341 of the *Act* (see also SUP 12.5.5G(3)).

3.6.7 **[G]** In complying with SUP 3.6.1R, a *firm* should take reasonable steps to ensure that each of its suppliers under a *material outsourcing* arrangement gives the *firm's* auditor the same rights of access to the books, accounts and vouchers of the *firm* held by the supplier, and entitlement to information and explanations from the supplier's officers as are given in respect of the *firm* by section 341 of the *Act*.

3.6.8 **[G]** In complying with SUP 3.6.1R, a *firm* should take reasonable steps to ensure that all its employees cooperate with its auditor in the discharge of his duties under this chapter.

Provision of false or misleading information to auditors

3.6.9 **[G]** *Firms* and their officers, *managers* and *controllers* are reminded that, under section 346 of the *Act* (Provision of false or misleading information to auditor or actuary), knowingly or recklessly giving false information to an auditor appointed under SUP 3.3.2R constitutes an *offence* in certain circumstances, which could render them liable to prosecution. This applies even when an auditor is also appointed under an obligation in another enactment.

3.7 Notification of matters raised by auditor

Application

3.7.1 **[G]** SUP 3.7 does not apply to an *incoming Treaty firm* which does not have a *top-up permission.*

Notification

3.7.2 **[G]** A *firm* should consider whether it should notify the *FSA* under *Principle* 11 if:

(1) the *firm* expects or knows its auditor will qualify his report on the audited annual financial statements or add an explanatory paragraph; or

(2) the *firm* receives a written communication from its auditor commenting on *internal controls* (see also SUP 15.3).

3.7.3 **[G]** [deleted]

3.8 Rights and duties of all auditors

Purpose

3.8.1 **[G]** The auditor of a *firm* has various rights and duties to obtain information from the *firm* and both to enable and to require him to pass information to the *FSA* in specified circumstances. This section imposes or gives *guidance* on those rights and duties.

Cooperation with the FSA

3.8.2 **[R]** An auditor of a *firm* must cooperate with the *FSA* in the discharge of its functions under the *Act*.

3.8.3 **[G]** The *FSA* may ask the auditor to attend meetings and to supply it with information about the *firm*. In complying with SUP 3.8.2R, the auditor should attend such meetings as the *FSA* requests and supply it with any information the *FSA* may reasonably request about the *firm* to enable the *FSA* to discharge its functions under the *Act*.

3.8.4 **[R]** An auditor of a *firm* must give any *skilled person* appointed by the *firm* all assistance that *person* reasonably requires (see SUP 5 and section 166(5) of the *Act* (Reports by skilled persons)).

Auditor's independence

3.8.5 **[R]** An auditor of a *firm* must be independent of the *firm* in performing his duties in respect of that *firm*.

3.8.6 **[R]** An auditor of a *firm* must take reasonable steps to satisfy himself that he is free from any conflict of interest in respect of that *firm* from which bias may reasonably be inferred. He must take appropriate action where this is not the case.

3.8.7 **[G]** SUP 3.5.4G explains that an auditor whose appointment does not breach the ethical guidance in current issue from the auditor's recognised supervisory body will be regarded as independent by the *FSA*.

Auditors' rights to information

3.8.8 **[G]** SUP 3.6.1R requires a *firm* to cooperate with its auditor. SUP 3.6.3G refers to the rights to information which an auditor is granted by the *Act*. SUP 3.6.4G refers to similar rights granted by the Companies Act 1985 or where applicable, the Companies Act 2006, the Building Societies Act 1986 and the Friendly Societies Act 1992.

Communication between the FSA, the firm and the auditor

3.8.9 **[G]** Within the legal constraints that apply, the *FSA* may pass on to an auditor any information which it considers relevant to his function. An auditor is bound by the confidentiality provisions set out in Part XXIII of the Act (Public record, disclosure of information and cooperation) in respect of confidential information he receives from the *FSA*. An auditor may not pass on such confidential information without lawful authority, for example if an exception applies under the Financial Services and Markets Act 2000 (Disclosure of Confidential Information) Regulations 2001 (SI 2001/2188) or with the consent of the *person* from whom that information was received and (if different) to whom the information relates.

Auditors' statutory duty to report

3.8.10 **[G]**
(1) Auditors are subject to regulations made by the Treasury under sections 342(5) and 343(5) of the *Act* (Information given by auditor or actuary to the *FSA*). Section 343 and the regulations also apply to an auditor of an *authorised person* in his capacity as an auditor of a *person* who has *close links* with the *authorised person*.
(2) These regulations oblige auditors to report certain matters to the *FSA*. Sections 342(3) and 343(3) of the *Act* provide that an auditor does not contravene any duty by giving information or expressing an opinion to the *FSA*, if he is acting in good faith and he reasonably believes that the information or opinion is relevant to any functions of the *FSA*. These provisions continue to have effect after the end of the auditor's term of appointment. In relation to Lloyd's, an effect of the *insurance market direction* set out at SUP 3.1.13D is that sections 342(5) and 343(5) of the *Act* (Information given by an auditor or actuary to the *Authority*) apply also to auditors appointed to report on the *insurance business* of *members*.

Part II FSA Handbook Materials

Termination of term of office, disqualification

3.8.11 **[R]** An auditor must notify the *FSA* without delay if he:
(1) is removed from office by a *firm*; or
(2) resigns before his term of office expires; or
(3) is not re-appointed by a *firm*.

3.8.12 **[R]** If an auditor ceases to be, or is formally notified that he will cease to be, the auditor of a *firm*, he must notify the *FSA* without delay:
(1) of any matter connected with his so ceasing which he thinks ought to be drawn to the *FSA's* attention; or
(2) that there is no such matter.

3.8.13 **[R]** [deleted]

3.8.14 **[G]** [deleted]

3.9

[deleted]

3.10 Duties of auditors: notification and report on client assets

Application

3.10.1 **[R]** Where this section requires an auditor of a *firm* to report on a *firm's* compliance with *rules*, this section applies to the auditor only to the extent that the *firm* is required to comply with the relevant *rules*.

3.10.2 **[R]** An auditor of an *authorised professional firm* need not report under this section in relation to that *firm's* compliance with the *client money rules* in the *non-directive client money chapter*, if that *firm* is regulated by:
(1) the Law Society (England and Wales);
(2) the Law Society of Scotland;
(3) the Law Society of Northern Ireland.

3.10.3 **[R]** SUP 3.10.5R(3) does not apply to an auditor of a *lead regulated firm* or an *incoming EEA firm*.

Client assets report: content

3.10.4 **[R]** An auditor of a *firm* must submit a report addressed to the *FSA*, signed in his capacity as auditor, which:
(1) states the matters set out in SUP 3.10.5R; or
(2) if the *firm* claims not to hold *client money* or *custody assets*, states whether anything has come to the auditor's attention that causes him to believe that the *firm* held *client money* or *custody assets* during the period covered by the report.

3.10.5 **[R]**

Table: Client assets report

Whether in the auditor's opinion		
(1)	the *firm* has maintained systems adequate to enable it to comply with the *custody rules*, the *collateral rules* and the *client money rules* (except CASS 5.2) throughout the period since the last date as at which a report was made;	
(2)	the *firm* was in compliance with the *custody rules*, the *collateral rules* and the *client money rules* (except CASS 5.2) at the date as at which the report has been made; and	
(3)	in the case of an *investment management firm*,*personal investment firm*, a *UCITS firm*, *securities and futures firm*, or *BIPRU investment firm*, when a *subsidiary* of the *firm* is a *nominee company* in whose name *custody assets* of the *firm* are registered, that *nominee company* has maintained throughout the year systems for the custody, identification and control of *custody assets* which:	
	(a)	are adequate; and
	(b)	include reconciliations at appropriate intervals between the records maintained (whether by the *firm* or the *nominee company*) and statements or confirmations from *custodians* or from the *person* who maintains the record of legal entitlement.
(4)	if there has been a *secondary pooling event* during the period) the *firm* has complied with the *rules* in CASS 4.4, CASS 5.6 and CASS 7.9 (Client money distribution) in relation to that pooling event.	

Client assets report: period covered

3.10.6 **[R]** The period covered by a report under SUP 3.10.4R must end not more than 53 weeks after the period covered by the previous report on such matters, or, if none, after the *firm* is *authorised* or becomes a *firm* to which SUP 3.10 applies.

Client assets report: timing of submission

3.10.7 **[R]** An auditor must deliver a report under SUP 3.10.4R to the *FSA* within a reasonable time from the end of each period covered, unless it is the auditor of a *firm* falling within category (10) of SUP 3.1.2R.

3.10.7A **[G]** A period of four months, in ordinary circumstances, would be considered by the *FSA* as a reasonable time for the auditor to deliver the client assets report to the *FSA*.

3.10.8 **[R]** If an auditor is unable to report to the *FSA* within a reasonable time, the auditor must notify the *FSA* and advise the *FSA* of the reasons why it has been unable to meet the requirements of SUP 3.10.7R.

3.10.8A **[R]** The auditor of a *firm* falling within category (10) of SUP 3.1.2R must deliver a report under SUP 3.10.4R:

(1) to the *firm* so as to be received within four months of the end of each period covered; and

(2) to the *FSA* upon request within six years of the end of the period covered.

3.10.8B **[G]** The rights and duties of auditors are set out in SUP 3.8 (Rights and duties of all auditors) and SUP 3.10 (Duties of auditors: notification and report on client assets). SUP 3.8.10G also refers to the auditor's statutory duty to report certain matters to the *FSA* imposed by regulations made by the Treasury under sections 342(5) and 343(5) of the *Act* (information given by auditor or actuary to the *FSA*). An auditor should bear these rights and duties in mind when carrying out *client* asset report work, including whether anything should be notified to the *FSA* immediately.

3.10.8C **[G]** It is the responsibility of an *insurance intermediary's* senior management to determine, on a continuing basis, whether the *firm* is an *exempt insurance intermediary* for the purposes of this requirement and to appoint an auditor if management determines the *firm* is no longer exempt. SUP 3.7 (amplified by SUP 15) sets out what a *firm* should consider when deciding whether it should notify the *FSA* of matters raised by its auditor.

Client assets report: requirements not met or inability to form opinion

3.10.9 **[R]** If the report under SUP 3.10.4R states that one or more of the applicable requirements described in SUP 3.10.5R have not been met, the auditor must specify in the report those requirements and the respects in which they have not been met.

3.10.10 **[R]** If an auditor is unable to form an opinion as to whether one or more of the applicable requirements described in SUP 3.10.5R have been met, the auditor must specify in the report under SUP 3.10.4R those requirements and the reasons why the auditor has been unable to form an opinion.

3.10.11 **[G]** An auditor may at the *firm's* request include the matters required under this section in a separate report to that required under section SUP 3.9.

Method of submission of reports

3.10.12 **[R]** An auditor of a *firm* must submit a report under SUP 3.4.10R in accordance with the rules in SUP 16.3.6R to SUP 16.3.13R as if those *rules* applied directly to the auditor.

Service of Notice Regulations

3.10.13 **[G]** The Financial Services and Markets Act 2000 (Service of Notices) Regulations 2001 (SI 2001/1420) contain provisions relating to the service of documents on the *FSA*. They do not apply to reports required by SUP 3.10 because of the specific provisions in SUP 3.10.12R.

CHAPTER 4
ACTUARIES

4.1 Application

[2157]
4.1.1 **[R]** This chapter applies to:
(1) every *firm* within a category listed in column (1) of the table in SUP 4.1.3R; and
(2) every *actuary* or *appropriate actuary* appointed under this chapter;

in accordance with column (2) of that table.

4.1.2 **[G]** This chapter applies to *long-term insurers* (including *friendly societies*) and other *friendly societies* and to the *Society of Lloyd's* and *managing agents* at Lloyd's. This chapter does not apply to *actuaries* advising the *auditors* of *long-term insurers* under IPRU(INS) 9.35(1A) or IPRU(FSOC) 5.11(2A), as they are not appointed to act on behalf of the *firm*.
4.1.3 **[R]**

Table: Applicable sections (see SUP 4.1.1R)

(1) Category of firm			(2) Applicable sections
(1)	A *long term insurer*, other than:		SUP 4.1, SUP 4.2, SUP 4.3 and SUP 4.5
	(a)	a *registered friendly society* which is a *non-directive friendly society*;	
	(b)	an *incorporated friendly society* that is a *flat rate benefits business friendly society*; and	
	(c)	an *incoming EEA firm*	
(2)	A *friendly society*, other than a *friendly society* within (1).		SUP 4.1, SUP 4.2, SUP 4.4 and SUP 4.5
(3)	A Lloyd's *managing agent*, in respect of each *syndicate* it manages		SUP 4.1, SUP 4.2, SUP 4.5, SUP 4.6
(4)	The *Society of Lloyd's*		SUP 4.1, SUP 4.2, SUP 4.5, SUP 4.6

4.2 Purpose

4.2.1 **[G]** Section 340 of the *Act* gives the *FSA* power to make *rules* requiring an *authorised person*, or an *authorised person* falling into a specified class, to appoint an *actuary*. Section 340 further empowers the *FSA* to make *rules* governing the manner, timing and notification to the *FSA* of such an appointment and, where an appointment is not made, for the *FSA* to make an appointment on the *firm's* behalf. The *FSA's* rule-making powers under section 340 of the *Act* also extend to an *actuary's* duties and to the cessation of an *actuary's* term of office.

4.2.2 **[G]** This chapter defines the relationship between *firms* and their *appointed actuaries* and clarifies the role which *actuaries* play in the *FSA's* monitoring of *firms'* compliance with the requirements and standards under the *regulatory system*. The chapter sets out *rules* and *guidance* on the appointment of *actuaries*, and the termination of their term of office, as well as setting out their respective rights and duties. The purpose of the chapter is to ensure that:
(1) *long-term insurers* (other than certain *friendly societies)* have access to adequate actuarial advice, both in valuing their *liabilities to policyholders* and in exercising discretion affecting the interests of their *with-profits policyholders*; and
(2) other *friendly societies* carrying on *insurance business* (and which have traditionally relied upon actuarial expertise) employ or use an *actuary* of appropriate seniority and experience to evaluate the liabilities of that business; and

(3) *managing agents* of Lloyd's *syndicates* employ or use an *actuary* of appropriate seniority and experience to evaluate the liabilities associated with *insurance business* carried on at Lloyd's.

4.2.3 **[G]** The functions described by SUP 4.2.2G(1) are performed by one or more *actuaries* who are required to hold office continuously and must be *approved persons*. The principal duty of an *actuary* appointed to perform these functions is to advise the *firm* (see SUP 4.3.13R to SUP 4.3.18G for the rights and duties of such an *actuary*).

4.2.4 **[G]** The function described by SUP 4.2.2G(2) is performed by an *appropriate actuary* who is appointed to prepare the triennial investigation and interim certificate or statement required by SUP 5.2(1) (see SUP 4.4.6R and SUP 4.5.12G to SUP 4.5.14G for the rights and duties of an *appropriate actuary*).

4.2.5 **[G]** *Actuaries* act as a valuable source of information to the *FSA* in carrying out its functions. For example, in determining whether a *firm* satisfies the *threshold conditions*, the *FSA* has regard to whether the *firm* has appointed an *actuary* with sufficient experience in the areas of business to be conducted by the *firm* (SUP 2.5.7G(11)).

4.2.6 **[G]** In making appointments under this chapter and in allocating duties to *actuaries*, *firms* are reminded of their obligation under SYSC 2.1.1R to maintain a clear and appropriate apportionment of significant responsibilities so that it is clear who has which of those responsibilities and that the business and affairs of the *firm* can be adequately monitored and controlled by the *directors*, relevant *senior managers* and *governing body* of the *firm*.

4.3 Appointment of actuaries

Appointment by firms

4.3.1 **[R]** A *firm* to which this section applies (see SUP 4.1) must:

(1) appoint one or more *actuaries* to perform:
  (a) the *actuarial function* (see SUP 4.3.13R) in respect of all classes of its *long-term insurance business*; and
  (b) the *with-profits actuary function* (see SUP 4.3.16AR) in respect of all classes of its *with-profits business* (if any);

(2) notify the *FSA*, without delay, when it is aware that a vacancy in the office of any such *actuary* will arise or has arisen, giving the reason for the vacancy;

(3) appoint an *actuary* to fill any such vacancy that has arisen; and

(4) ensure a replacement *actuary* can take up office at the time the vacancy arises or as soon as reasonably practicable after that.

4.3.2 **[G]** The provisions relating to the duties of an *actuary* appointed to perform these functions are set out in SUP 4.3.13R to SUP 4.3.18G. The functions performed by *actuaries* appointed by a *firm* under SUP 4.3.1R are specified as a *controlled functions* (CF 12, the *actuarial function*, and CF 12A, the *with-profits actuary function*) in SUP 10 (*Approved persons*). As a result, an application must be made to the *FSA* under section 60 of the *Act* (Applications for approval) for approval of the *person* proposing to take up such an appointment. Section 61(3) of the *Act* (Determination of applications) gives the *FSA* three months to grant its approval or give a *warning notice* that it proposes to refuse the application. A *firm* should not appoint an *actuary* until the *FSA* has approved the *actuary*. In order to comply with SUP 4.3.1R, a *firm* should ensure it applies to the *FSA* as soon as practicable before the date when it needs the *actuary* to take office. The *FSA* will need time to consider the application before deciding whether to grant approval. See SUP 10 (*Approved persons*).

Appointment by the FSA

4.3.3 **[R]** If a *firm*, which is required to appoint one or more *actuaries* under SUP 4.3.1R, fails to do so within 28 days of a vacancy arising, the *FSA* may appoint one or more *actuaries* to perform any function corresponding to the *actuarial function* or the *with-profits actuary function* on the following terms:

(1) the *actuary* to be remunerated by the *firm* on the basis agreed between the *actuary* and the *firm* or, in the absence of agreement, on a reasonable basis; and

(2) the *actuary* to hold office until he resigns or the *firm* appoints another *actuary*.

4.3.4 **[G]** SUP 4.3.3R allows but does not require the *FSA* to appoint an *actuary* if the *firm* has failed to do so within the 28 day period. When it considers whether to use this power, the *FSA* will take into account the likely delay until the *firm* can make an appointment and the urgency of any pending duties of the *actuary*.

4.3.5 **[G]** The *FSA* will not normally seek to appoint an *actuary* under SUP 4.3.3R if a notification under SUP 10 (*Approved persons*) has been received from the *firm* in relation to a proposed appointment of an *actuary* under SUP 4.3.1R, and that application is still being considered.

4.3.6 **[R]** A *firm* must comply with and is bound by the terms on which an *actuary* has been appointed by the *FSA* under SUP 4.3.3R.

4.3.7 **[G]** If the *FSA* appoints an *actuary* under SUP 4.3.3R, he will not be an *approved person* (not being appointed under SUP 4.3.1R). However, the *firm* is still under an obligation to appoint an *actuary* under SUP 4.3.1R and will need to seek prior approval of that person (even if the individual it proposes to appoint is the person who has been appointed by the *FSA* under SUP 4.3.3R).

Actuaries qualifications

4.3.8 **[G]** The *FSA* is concerned to ensure that every *actuary* appointed by a *firm* under this section has the necessary skill and experience to provide the *firm* with appropriate actuarial advice. SUP 4.3.9R to SUP 4.3.10G set out the *FSA's rules* and *guidance* aimed at achieving this.

4.3.9 **[R]** Before a *firm* applies for approval of the *person* it proposes to appoint as an *actuary* under SUP 4.3.1R, it must take reasonable steps to ensure that the *actuary*:

(1) has the required skill and experience to perform his functions under the *regulatory system*; and

(2) is a Fellow of the Institute of Actuaries or of the Faculty of Actuaries.

4.3.10 **[G]** To comply with SUP 4.3.9R and *Principle* 3, before an *actuary* takes up his appointment the *firm* should ensure that the *actuary*:

(1) has skills and experience appropriate to the nature, scale and complexity of the *firm's* business and the requirements and standards under the *regulatory system* to which it is subject; and

(2) has adequate qualifications and experience, which includes holding an appropriate practising certificate under the rules of the Institute of Actuaries or the Faculty of Actuaries;

and seek confirmation of these from the *actuary*, or the *actuary's* current and previous employers, as appropriate.

Disqualified actuaries

4.3.11 **[R]** A *firm* must not appoint under SUP 4.3.1R an *actuary* who is disqualified by the *FSA* under section 345 of the *Act* (Disqualification) from acting as an *actuary* either for that *firm* or for a relevant class of *firm*.

4.3.12 **[G]** If it appears to the *FSA* that an *actuary* has failed to comply with a duty imposed on him under the *Act*, it may disqualify him under section 345 of the *Act*. For more detail about what happens when the disqualification of an *actuary* is being considered or put into effect, see *EG* 15 (Disqualification of auditors and actuaries). A list of *actuaries* who are disqualified by the *FSA* may be found on the *FSA* website (www.fsa.gov.uk).

Conflicts of interest

4.3.12A **[R]** A *firm* must take reasonable steps to ensure that an *actuary* who is to be, or has been, appointed under SUP 4.3.1R:

(1) does not perform the function of chairman or *chief executive* of the *firm*, or does not, if he is to perform the *with-profits actuary function*, become a member of the *firm's governing body*; and

(2) does not perform any other function on behalf of the *firm* which could give rise to a significant conflict of interest.

4.3.12B **[G]** Both the *actuarial function* and the *with-profits actuary function* may be performed by *employees* of the *firm* or by external consultants, and performing other functions on behalf of the *firm* will not necessarily give rise to a significant conflict of interest. However, being a *director*, or a senior manager responsible, say, for sales or marketing in a *firm* (or for finance in a proprietary *firm*), is likely to give rise to a significant conflict of interest for an *actuary* performing the *with-profits actuary function*. He nevertheless retains direct access to the *firm's governing body* under SUP 4.3.17R(2).

The actuarial function

4.3.13 **[R]** An *actuary* appointed to perform the *actuarial function* must, in respect of those classes of the *firm's long-term insurance business* which are covered by his appointment:

(1) advise the *firm's* management, at the level of seniority that is reasonably appropriate, on the risks the *firm* runs in so far as they may have a material impact on the *firm's* ability to meet *liabilities to policyholders* in respect of *long-term insurance contracts* as they fall due and on the capital needed to support the business, including regulatory capital requirements;

(2) monitor those risks and inform the *firm's* management, at the level of seniority that is reasonably appropriate, if he has any material concerns or good reason to believe that the *firm*:

    (a) is not meeting *liabilities to policyholders* under *long-term insurance contracts* as they fall due, or may not be doing so, or might not have done so, or might, in reasonably foreseeable circumstances, not do so;

Part II FSA Handbook Materials

(b) is, or may be, effecting new *long-term insurance contracts* on terms under which the resulting income earned is insufficient, under reasonable actuarial methods and assumptions, and taking into account the other financial resources that are available for the purpose, to enable the *firm* to meet its *liabilities* to *policyholders* as they fall due (including reasonable bonus expectations);

(c) does not, or may not, have sufficient financial resources to meet *liabilities to policyholders* as they fall due (including reasonable bonus expectations) and the capital needed to support the business, including regulatory capital requirements or, if the *firm* currently has sufficient resources, might, in reasonably foreseeable circumstances, not continue to have them;

(3) advise the *firm's governing body* on the methods and assumptions to be used for the investigations required by IPRU(INS) 9.4R or IPRU(FSOC) 5.1R and the calculation of the *with-profits insurance capital component* under INSPRU 1.3 as applicable;

(4) perform those investigations and calculations in (3), in accordance with the methods and assumptions determined by the *firm's governing body*;

(5) report to the *firm's governing body* on the results of those investigations and calculations in (3); and

(6) in the case of a *friendly society* to which this section applies, perform the functions of the appropriate actuary under section 87 (Actuary's report as to margin of solvency) of the Friendly Societies Act 1992.

4.3.14 **[G]** IPRU(INS) 9.4R and IPRU(FSOC) 5.1R require *firms* to which this section applies to cause an investigation to be made at least yearly by the *actuary* or *actuaries* appointed to perform the *actuarial function*, and to report on the result of that investigation. INSPRU 1.3 requires *realistic basis life firms* to calculate the *with-profits insurance component* as part of their capital resources requirements. The *firm* is responsible for the methods and assumptions used to determine the *liabilities* attributable to its *long-term insurance business*. The obligation on *friendly societies* to obtain a report from the 'appropriate actuary' under section 87 of the Friendly Societies Act 1992 applies to a *friendly society* which is to receive a transfer of engagements under section 86 (transfer of engagements to or by a friendly society). The 'appropriate actuary' in this context is the *actuary* appointed to perform the *actuarial function*, rather than the *appropriate actuary* under SUP 4.4 (Appropriate actuaries).

4.3.15 **[G]** SUP 4.3.13R is not intended to be exhaustive of the professional advice that a *firm* should take whether from an *actuary* appointed under this chapter or from any other *actuary* acting for the *firm*. *Firms* should consider what systems and controls are needed to ensure that they obtain appropriate professional advice on financial and risk analysis; for example:

(1) risk identification, quantification and monitoring;
(2) stress and scenario testing;
(3) ongoing financial conditions;
(4) financial projections for business planning;
(5) investment strategy and asset-liability matching;
(6) individual capital assessment;
(7) pricing of business, including unit pricing;
(8) variation of any charges for benefits or expenses;
(9) discretionary surrender charges; and
(10) adequacy of reinsurance protection.

The with-profits actuary function

4.3.16 [deleted]

4.3.16A **[R]** An *actuary* appointed to perform the *with-profits actuary function* must:

(1) advise the *firm's management*, at the level of seniority that is reasonably appropriate, on key aspects of the discretion to be exercised affecting those classes of the *with-profits business* of the *firm* in respect of which he has been appointed;

(2) where the *firm* is a *realistic basis life firm* advise the *firm's governing body* as to whether the assumptions used to calculate the *with-profits insurance component* under INSPRU 1.3 are consistent with the *firm*'s *PPFM* in respect of those classes of the *firm's with-profits business*;

(3) at least once a year, report to the *firm*'s *governing body* on key aspects (including those aspects of the *firm*'s application of its *Principles and Practices of Financial Management* on which the advice described in (1) has been given) of the discretion exercised in respect of the period covered by his report affecting those classes of *with-profits business* of the *firm*;

(4) in respect of each financial year, make a written report addressed to the relevant classes of the *firm*'s *with-profits policyholders*, to accompany the *firm*'s annual report under COBS 20.4.7R, as to whether, in his opinion and based on the information and explanations provided to him by the *firm*, and taking into account where relevant the *rules* and *guidance* in COBS 20, the annual report and the discretion exercised by the *firm* in respect of the period covered by the report may be regarded as taking, or having taken, their interests into account in a reasonable and proportionate manner;

(5) request from the *firm* such information and explanations as he reasonably considers necessary to enable him properly to perform the duties in (1) to (4);
(6) advise the *firm* as to the data and systems that he reasonably considers necessary to be kept and maintained to provide the duties in (5); and
(7) in the case of a *friendly society* to which this section applies, perform the function of appropriate actuary under section 12 (Reinsurance) of the Friendly Societies Act 1992 or section 23A (Reinsurance) of the Friendly Societies Act 1974 as applicable, in respect of those classes of its *with-profits business* covered by his appointment.

4.3.16B **[G]** In advising or reporting on the exercise of discretion, an *actuary* performing the *with-profits actuary function* should cover the implications for the fair treatment of the *firm*'s *with-profits policyholders*. His opinion on any communication or report to them should also take into account their information needs and the extent to which the communication or report may be regarded as clear, fair and not misleading. Aspects of the business that should normally be included are:
(1) bonus rates to be applied to *policies* at maturity or on the death of a *policyholder*, or when calculating the annual bonus;
(2) investment policy in the light of product descriptions disclosed to *customers*;
(3) surrender value methodology (including market value adjusters);
(4) new business plans and premium rates;
(5) allocation of expenses to *with-profits business*;
(6) investment fees to be charged to *with-profits business*;
(7) changes to the *Principles and Practices of Financial Management*; and
(8) communications with *policyholders* or potential *policyholders* on the issues in (1) to (7).

4.3.16C **[G]** The reports in SUP 4.3.16AR(3) and (4) should be proportionate to the nature of the *with-profits business*. For smaller *firms* with fewer products, the extent of reporting would be proportionately less.

4.3.16D **[G]** *Firms* should normally obtain advice, from the *actuary* appointed to perform the *with-profits actuary function* in respect of the affected class or classes of *with-profits business*, whenever they are preparing to make key decisions based on the exercise of discretion affecting their *with-profits business*. *Firms* should also have risk management processes in place to ensure that all relevant matters are referred to the *actuary* for advice.

4.3.17 **[R]** A *firm* must require and allow any *actuary* appointed to perform the *with-profits actuary function* to perform his duties and must:
(1) keep him informed of the *firm's business* and other plans (including, where relevant, those of any related *firm*, to the extent it is aware of these);
(2) provide him with sufficient resources (including his own time and access to the time of others);
(3) hold such data and establish such systems as he reasonably requires;
(4) request his advice about the likely effect of material changes in the *firm's* business plans, practices or other circumstances on the fair treatment of *with-profits policyholders*; and
(5) pay due regard to his advice, whether provided in response to a request under (4) or on the *actuary's* own initiative; this will include, if he requests it, allowing him to present his advice directly to the *firm's governing body* (that is, the board of *directors* or, for a *friendly society*, the committee of management).

4.3.18 **[G]** A *firm's* duty to keep an *actuary* appointed to perform the *with-profits actuary function* informed includes providing relevant information, even where the *actuary* does not ask for it. The *firm* needs to appreciate that the *actuary* may be unaware of certain business developments and so unable to request relevant information.

4.3.19 **[G]** [deleted]

4.3.20 **[R]** [deleted]

4.3.21 **[G]** [deleted]

4.4 Appropriate actuaries

Appointment of an appropriate actuary

4.4.1 **[R]** A *firm* to which this section applies (see SUP 4.1) and required by *IPRU(FSOC)* 5.2(1) to ensure that an investigation is carried out must:
(1) appoint an *actuary* (the "*appropriate actuary*") to carry out the triennial investigation and prepare an abstract of the report as required by *IPRU(FSOC)* 5.2(2) and provide the interim certificate or statement as required by *IPRU(FSOC)* 5.2(3); and
(2) appoint a replacement for that *actuary* if he ceases to hold office before he has carried out the duty described in (1).

Appropriate actuaries' qualifications

4.4.2 **[R]** Before a *friendly society* appoints an *appropriate actuary*, it must take reasonable steps to ensure that the *actuary* is a Fellow of the Institute of Actuaries or of the Faculty of Actuaries.

4.4.3 **[G]** An *appropriate actuary* should have skills and experience appropriate to the nature, scale and complexity of the *firm's* business and the requirements and standards under the *regulatory system* to which it is subject. In complying with *Principle* 3, a *firm* should have regard to whether its proposed *appropriate actuary* has adequate qualifications and experience, and seek confirmation of this from the *actuary*, or the *actuary's* current and previous employers, as appropriate.

4.4.4 **[R]** A *firm* must not appoint as *appropriate actuary* an *actuary* who has been disqualified by the *FSA* under section 345 of the *Act* (Disqualification) from acting as an *actuary* either for that *firm* or for a relevant class of *firm*.

4.4.5 **[G]** If it appears to the *FSA* that an *appropriate actuary* has failed to comply with a duty imposed on him under the *Act*, it may disqualify him under section 345 of the *Act*. For more detail about what happens when the disqualification of an *actuary* is being considered or put into effect, see *EG* 15 (Disqualification of auditors and actuaries). A list of *actuaries* who have been disqualified by the *FSA* may be found on the *FSA* website (www.fsa.gov.uk).

Specific duties of the appropriate actuary

4.4.6 **[R]** An *appropriate actuary* must carry out the triennial investigation and prepare an abstract of the report as required by *IPRU(FSOC)* 5.2(2) and provide the interim certificate or statement as required by *IPRU(FSOC)* 5.2(3).

4.4.7 **[G]** [deleted]

4.4.8 **[R]** [deleted]

4.4.9 **[G]** [deleted]

4.5 Provisions applicable to all actuaries

Objectivity

4.5.1 **[R]** An *actuary* appointed under this chapter must be objective in performing his duties.

4.5.2 **[G]** Objectivity requires the *actuary* to perform his duties in such a manner that he can have an honest belief in his work and does not compromise the quality of his work or his judgment. An *actuary* should not allow himself to be placed in situations where he feels unable to make objective professional judgments.

4.5.3 **[R]** An *actuary* appointed under this chapter must take reasonable steps to satisfy himself that he is free from bias, or from any conflict of interest from which bias may reasonably be inferred. He must take appropriate action where this is not the case.

4.5.4 **[G]** The appropriate action may include asking the *firm's governing body* to re-assign temporarily some or all of his duties to another competent *actuary*. Where this is insufficient, the *actuary* should resign his office.

4.5.5 **[G]** If the *actuary* is an *employee* of the *firm*, the ordinary incentives of employment, including profit-related pay, *share options* or other financial interests in the *firm* or any *associate*, give rise to a conflict of interest only where they are disproportionate, or exceptional, relative to those of other employees of equivalent seniority.

4.5.6 **[G]** The guidance and professional conduct standards in current issue from the Institute of Actuaries and the Faculty of Actuaries are relevant to compliance with SUP 4.5.1R and SUP 4.5.3R.

Actuaries' statutory duty to report

4.5.7 **[G]**

(1) *Actuaries* appointed under this chapter are subject to regulations made by the Treasury under sections 342(5) and 343(5) of the *Act* (Information given by *auditor* or actuary to the Authority). Section 343 and the regulations also apply to an actuary of an *authorised person* in his capacity as an actuary of a *person* who has *close links* with the *authorised person*.

(2) These regulations oblige *actuaries* to report certain matters to the *FSA*. Sections 342(3) and 343(3) of the *Act* provide that an *actuary* does not contravene any duty by giving information or expressing an opinion to the *FSA*, if he is acting in good faith and he reasonably believes that the information or opinion is relevant to any functions of the *FSA*. These provisions continue to have effect after the end of the *actuary's* term of appointment. In relation to Lloyd's, an effect of the *insurance market direction* set out at SUP 3.1.13D is that sections 342(5) and 343(5) of the *Act* (Information given by auditor or actuary to the FSA) apply also to *actuaries* who are appointed to evaluate the *long-term insurance business* of a *syndicate*.

Termination of term of office

4.5.8 **[G]** SUP 4.5.9R to SUP 4.5.11G apply to a *person* who is or has been an *actuary* appointed under this chapter.

4.5.9 **[R]** An *actuary* appointed under this chapter must notify the *FSA* without delay if he:
(1) is removed from office by a *firm*; or
(2) resigns before his term of office expires; or
(3) is not reappointed by a *firm*.

4.5.10 **[R]** An *actuary* who has ceased to be appointed under this chapter, or who has been formally notified that he will cease to be so appointed, must notify the *FSA* without delay:
(1) of any matter connected with the cessation which he thinks ought to be drawn to the *FSA's* attention; or
(2) that there is no such matter.

4.5.11 **[G]** When an *actuary* appointed under SUP 4.3.1R ceases to hold office, he ceases to perform a *controlled function*. A *firm* is therefore required under SUP 10.13.6R to tell the *FSA* within seven *business days* of its *actuary* ceasing to hold office and to complete a withdrawal form (Form C, SUP 10Ann6R). Note also the requirement of SUP 10.13.7R in relation to qualified withdrawals.

Rights and duties

4.5.12 **[G]** Section 341 of the *Act* (Access to books etc.) provides that an *actuary* appointed under or as a result of the *Act*:
(1) has a right of access at all times to the *firm's* books, accounts and vouchers; and
(2) is entitled to require from the *firm's* officers such information and explanations as he reasonably considers necessary to perform his duties as *actuary*.

4.5.13 **[R]** When carrying out his duties, an *actuary* appointed under this chapter must pay due regard to generally accepted actuarial practice.

4.5.14 **[G]** The standards and guidance issued from time to time by the Institute of Actuaries and the Faculty of Actuaries are important sources of generally adopted actuarial practice.

4.6 Lloyd's

Appointment of the Lloyd's actuary and syndicate actuaries

4.6.1 **[R]** The *Society* must:
(1) appoint an *actuary* to perform the *Lloyd's actuary function*;
(2) notify the *FSA*, without delay, when it is aware that a vacancy in the office of *Lloyd's actuary* will arise or has arisen, giving the reason for the vacancy;
(3) appoint an *actuary* to fill any vacancy in the office of *Lloyd's actuary* that has arisen; and
(4) ensure that the replacement *actuary* can take up office at the time the vacancy arises or as soon as reasonably practicable after that.

4.6.2 **[G]** The functions performed by the *actuary* appointed as the *Lloyd's actuary* under SUP 4.6.1R are specified as *controlled functions* in SUP 10 (Approved persons).As a result, an application must be made to the *FSA* under section 60 of the *Act* (Applications for approval) for approval of the *person* proposing to take up such an appointment. Section 61(3) of the *Act* (Determination of applications) gives the *FSA* three months to grant its approval or give a *warning notice* that it proposes to refuse the application. An *actuary* should not be appointed until the *FSA* has approved the *actuary*. In order to comply with SUP 4.6.1R, the *Society* should ensure it applies to the *FSA* as soon as practicable before the date when it needs the *actuary* to take office. The *FSA* will need time to consider the application before deciding whether to grant approval.

Qualifications

4.6.3 **[R]** Before the *Society* applies for approval of its proposed appointment of the *Lloyd's actuary* under SUP 4.6.1R, it must take reasonable steps to ensure that the *actuary*:
(1) has the required skill and experience to perform his functions under the *regulatory system*; and
(2) is a Fellow of the Institute of Actuaries or of the Faculty of Actuaries.

4.6.4 **[G]** To comply with SUP 4.6.3R and *Principle 3*, before the *Lloyd's actuary* takes up his appointment the *Society* should ensure that the *actuary*:
(1) has skills and experience appropriate to the nature, scale and complexity of the *Society's* business and the requirements and standards under the *regulatory system* to which it is subject; and
(2) has adequate qualifications and experience, which includes holding an appropriate practising certificate under the rules of the Institute of Actuaries or the Faculty of Actuaries;

and seek confirmation of these from the *actuary*, or the *actuary*'s current and previous employers, as appropriate.

Disqualified actuaries

4.6.5 **[R]** The *Society* must not appoint under SUP 4.6.1R as *Lloyd's actuary* an *actuary* who is disqualified by the *FSA* under section 345 of the *Act* (Disqualification) from acting:
(1) as an *actuary* for the *Society*; or
(2) as a *syndicate actuary*; or
(3) as an *actuary* for any other relevant class of *firm*.

4.6.6 **[G]** If it appears to the *FSA* that an *actuary* has failed to comply with a duty imposed on him under the *Act*, it may disqualify him under section 345 of the *Act*. For more detail about what happens when the disqualification of an *actuary* is being considered or put into effect, see *EG* 15. A list of *actuaries* who are disqualified by the *FSA* may be found on the *FSA* website.

Conflicts of interest

4.6.7 **[R]** The *Society* must take reasonable steps to ensure that an *actuary* who is to be, or has been, appointed under SUP 4.6.1R:
(1) does not perform the function of chairman or *chief executive* of the *Society*; and
(2) does not perform any other function on behalf of the *Society* which could give rise to a significant conflict of interest.

The Lloyd's actuary function

4.6.8 **[R]** An *actuary* who has been appointed to perform the *Lloyd's actuary function* must:
(1) prepare the statement required under LLD 15.9.1R(2) to be annexed to the *Lloyd's Return*; and
(2) take reasonable steps to ensure that the *general insurance business technical provisions* for each *syndicate year* have been reviewed by the *syndicate actuary* and that an appropriate opinion has been obtained under SUP 4.6.15R; and
(3) where a *syndicate actuary's* opinion has not been provided, sets appropriate *technical provisions* and, within six months of the end of the *financial year*, submits a report to the *FSA* on the setting of those *technical provisions*.

Appointment of syndicate actuaries

4.6.9 **[R]** Each *managing agent* must, in respect of each *syndicate* it manages:
(1) appoint an *actuary* (the "*syndicate actuary*") to carry out the duties described in SUP 4.6.15R or SUP 4.6.16R; and
(2) appoint a replacement for that *actuary* if he ceases to hold office before he has carried out the duties described in SUP 4.6.15R or SUP 4.6.16R; and
(3) ensure that the replacement *syndicate actuary* can take up office at the time the vacancy arises or as soon as reasonably practicable after that.

4.6.10 **[G]**
(1) The *insurance market direction* and guidance set out in SUP 3.1.4G to SUP 3.1.15G is relevant to *actuaries* appointed to report on the *insurance business* of *members*.
(2) References in SUP 4, as applied by SUP 4.1.3R, to a *firm* include, where appropriate:
 (a) a *managing agent*; and
 (b) one or more *members* carrying on *insurance business* at Lloyd's through a *syndicate*;

and references to an *actuary* of a *firm* should be read accordingly.

Syndicate actuaries' qualifications

4.6.11 **[R]** Before a *managing agent* appoints a *syndicate actuary*, it must take reasonable steps to ensure that the *syndicate actuary*:
(1) has the required skill and experience to perform his duties; and
(2) is a fellow of an *actuarial body* or (except for a *syndicate actuary* of a *long-term insurance business syndicate*) is a fellow of the Casualty Actuarial Society who is a member of an *actuarial body*.

4.6.12 **[G]** To comply with SUP 4.6.11R and *Principle* 3, before a *syndicate actuary* takes up his appointment a *managing agent* should ensure that the *syndicate actuary*:
(1) has skills and experience appropriate to the nature, scale and complexity of a *syndicate's* business and the requirements and standards under the *regulatory system* applicable to the *activities* of *managing agents* in relation to each *syndicate* which they manage; and
(2) has adequate qualifications and experience, which includes holding an appropriate practising certificate under the rules of the Institute of Actuaries or the Faculty of Actuaries;

and seeks confirmation of these from the *syndicate actuary*, or the *syndicate actuary's* current and previous employers, as appropriate.

Disqualified actuaries

4.6.13 **[R]** A *managing agent* must not appoint under SUP 4.6.9R as *syndicate actuary* an *actuary* who is disqualified by the *FSA* under section 345 of the *Act* (Disqualification) from acting:
(1) as a *syndicate actuary*; or
(2) as a *Lloyd's actuary*; or
(3) as an *actuary* for a relevant class of *firm*.

4.6.14 **[G]** If it appears to the *FSA* that an *actuary* has failed to comply with a duty imposed on him under the *Act*, it may disqualify him under section 345 of the *Act*. For more detail about what happens when the disqualification of an *actuary* is being considered or put into effect, see *EG* 15. A list of *actuaries* who are disqualified by the *FSA* may be found on the *FSA* website.

Duties of syndicate actuaries

4.6.15 **[R]** The *syndicate actuary* of a *long-term insurance business syndicate* must:
(1) make an investigation at the end of each *financial year* into the financial condition of the business carried on through each *syndicate year* (other than a *closed* year);
(2) make an abstract of his report of the investigation; and
(3) prepare the certificate required under LLD 15.9.1R(3) to be annexed to the *Lloyd's Return*.

4.6.16 **[R]** The *syndicate actuary* of a *general insurance business syndicate* must:
(1) review the *technical provisions* (both gross and net of reinsurance recoveries) of each *syndicate year* (other than a *closed* year); and
(2) provide his opinion confirming that the *technical provisions* for each *syndicate year* are no less prudent than his best estimate of the amounts required.

4.6.17 **[R]** If a *managing agent* becomes aware that the *syndicate actuary* of a *general insurance business syndicate* will or may be unable to produce an unqualified opinion under SUP 4.6.16R, the *managing agent* must promptly inform the *FSA* that this is the case.

4.6.18 **[R]** In carrying out his duties a *syndicate actuary* must pay due regard to generally accepted actuarial best practice.

4.6.19 **[G]** The standards and guidance issued by the Institute of Actuaries and the Faculty of Actuaries are important sources of actuarial best practice.

CHAPTER 5
REPORTS BY SKILLED PERSONS

5.1 Application and purpose

Application

[2158]
5.1.1 **[R]**
(1) This chapter applies to every *firm*.
(2) The *rules*, and the *guidance* on *rules* in SUP 5.5 (Duties of firms), do not apply to a *UCITS qualifier*.

5.1.2 **[G]** This chapter (other than the *rules*, and *guidance* on *rules*, in SUP 5.5 (Duties of firms)) is also relevant to certain unauthorised *persons* within the scope of section 166 of the *Act* (Reports by skilled persons) (see SUP 5.2.1G).

Purpose

5.1.3 **[G]** The purpose of this chapter is to give *guidance* on the *FSA's* use of the power in section 166 of the *Act* (Reports by skilled persons). The purpose is also to make *rules* requiring a *firm* to include certain provisions in its contract with a *skilled person* and to give assistance to a *skilled person*. These *rules* are designed to ensure that the *FSA* receives certain information from a *skilled person* and that a *skilled person* receives assistance from a *firm*.

5.2 The FSA's power

Who may be required to provide a report?

5.2.1 **[G]** Under section 166 of the *Act* (Reports by skilled persons), the *FSA* may, by giving a written notice, require any of the following *persons* to provide it with a report by a *skilled person*:
(1) a *firm*;
(2) any other *member* of the *firm's group*;
(3) a *partnership* of which the *firm* is a *member*;
(4) a *person* who has at any relevant time been a *person* falling within (1), (2) or (3);

but only if the *person* is, or was at the relevant time, carrying on a business.

5.3 Policy on the use of skilled persons

5.3.1 **[G]** The appointment of a *skilled person* to produce a report under section 166 of the *Act* (Reports by skilled persons) is one of the *FSA's* regulatory tools. The tool may be used:
(1) for diagnostic purposes, to identify, assess and measure risks;
(2) for monitoring purposes, to track the development of identified risks, wherever these arise;
(3) in the context of preventative action, to limit or reduce identified risks and so prevent them from crystallising or increasing; and
(4) for remedial action, to respond to risks when they have crystallised.

SUP 5Ann1G gives examples of circumstances in which the *FSA* may use the *skilled persons* tool.

5.3.2 **[G]** The decision to require a report by a *skilled person* will normally be prompted by a specific requirement for information, analysis of information, assessment of a situation or expert advice or recommendations or by a decision to seek assurance in relation to a regulatory return. It may be part of the risk mitigation programme applicable to a *firm*, or the result of an event or development relating or relevant to a *firm*, prompted by a need for verification of information provided to the *FSA* or part of the *FSA's* regular monitoring of a *firm*.

5.3.3 **[G]** When making the decision to require a report by a *skilled person*, the *FSA* will have regard, on a case-by-case basis, to all relevant factors. Those are likely to include:
(1) circumstances relating to the *firm;*
(2) alternative tools available, including other statutory powers;
(3) legal and procedural considerations;
(4) the objectives of the *FSA's* enquiries;
(5) cost considerations; and
(6) considerations relating to *FSA* resources.

SUP 5.3.4G to SUP 5.3.10G give further guidance on these listed factors.

5.3.4 **[G]** Circumstances relating to the firm

The *FSA* will have regard to circumstances relating to the *firm*, for example:
(1) attitude of the *firm*: whether the *firm* is being cooperative;
(2) history of similar issues: whether similar issues have arisen in the past and, if so, whether timely corrective action was taken;
(3) quality of a *firm's* systems and records: whether the *FSA* has confidence that the *firm* has the ability to provide the required information;
(4) objectivity: whether the *FSA* has confidence in the *firm's* willingness and ability to deliver an objective report;
(5) conflicts of interest: whether the subject matter of the enquiries or the report involves actual or potential misconduct and it would be inappropriate for the *FSA* to rely on the *firm* itself to enquire into the matter; and
(6) knowledge or expertise available to the *firm*: whether it would be appropriate to involve a third party with the required technical expertise.

Alternative tools available, including other statutory powers

5.3.5 **[G]** The *FSA* will have regard to alternative tools that may be available, including for example:
(1) obtaining what is required without using specific statutory powers (for example, by a visit by *FSA* staff or a request for information on an informal basis);
(2) requiring information from *firms* and others, including authorising an agent to require information, under section 165 of the *Act* (Authority's power to require information);
(3) appointing investigators to carry out general investigations under section 167 of the *Act* (Appointment of persons to carry out general investigations) (see *EG* 3 for the *FSA's* policy on the use of this power); and
(4) appointing investigators to carry out investigations in particular cases under section 168 of the *Act* (Appointment of persons to carry out investigations in particular cases) (see *EG* 3 for the *FSA's* policy on the use of this power).

Legal and procedural considerations

5.3.6 **[G]** The *FSA* will have regard to legal and procedural considerations including:
(1) statutory powers: whether one of the other available statutory powers is more appropriate for the purpose than the power in section 166 of the *Act* (Reports by skilled persons);
(2) subsequent proceedings: whether it is desirable to obtain an authoritative and independent report for use in any subsequent proceedings; and
(3) application of the *Handbook rules*: whether it is important that the relevant *rules* in the *Handbook* should apply, for example SUP 5.5.1R which obliges the *firm* to require and permit the skilled person to report specified matters to the *FSA*.

The objectives of the FSA's enquiries

5.3.7 **[G]** The *FSA* will have regard to the objectives of its enquiries, and the relative effectiveness of its available powers to achieve those objectives. For example:

(1) historic information or evidence: if the objectives are limited to gathering historic information, or evidence for determining whether enforcement action may be appropriate, the *FSA's* information gathering and investigation powers under sections 165 (Authority's power to require information), 167 (Appointment of persons to carry out general investigations) and 168 (Appointment of persons to carry out investigations in particular cases) of the *Act* are likely to be more appropriate than the section 166 power (Reports by skilled persons); and

(2) expert analysis or recommendations: if the objectives include obtaining expert analysis or recommendations (or both) for diagnostic, monitoring, preventative or remedial purposes, the section 166 power (Reports by skilled persons) may be an appropriate power to use, instead of, or in conjunction with, the *FSA's* other available powers.

Cost considerations

5.3.8 **[G]** In accordance with its general policy the *FSA* will have regard to the question of cost, which is particularly pertinent in relation to *skilled persons* because:

(1) if the *FSA* uses the section 166 power (Reports by skilled persons) the *firm* will appoint, and will have to pay for the services of, the *skilled person*;

(2) if the *FSA* uses its other information gathering and investigation powers, it will either authorise or appoint its own staff to undertake the information gathering or investigation (or both), or it will pay for the services of external competent persons to do so; in either case the costs will be recovered under the FSA's general fee scheme.

5.3.9 **[G]** In having regard to the cost implications of using the section 166 power (Reports by skilled persons) alternative options (such as visits) or other powers, the *FSA* will take into account relevant factors, including:

(1) whether the *firm* may derive some benefit from the work carried out and recommendations made by the *skilled person*, for instance a better understanding of its business and its risk profile, or the operation of its information systems, or improvements to its systems and controls;

(2) whether the work to be carried out by the *skilled person* is work that should reasonably have been carried out by the *firm*, or by persons instructed by the *firm* on its own initiative; for instance a compliance review or the development of new systems;

(3) whether the *firm's* record-keeping and management information systems are poor and:

  (a) the required information and *documents* are not readily available; or

  (b) an analysis of the required information cannot readily be performed without expert assistance;

(4) whether the *firm* appears to have breached requirements or standards under the *regulatory system* or otherwise put the interests of consumers at risk, and it is unable or unwilling to review and remedy the matters of concern, or the *FSA* considers that it cannot rely on the *firm* to do so; and

(5) the perceived probability and seriousness of possible breaches of regulatory requirements and the possible need for further action.

5.3.9A **[G]** [deleted]

Considerations relating to FSA resources

5.3.10 **[G]** The *FSA* will have regard to *FSA*-related considerations including:

(1) *FSA* expertise: whether the *FSA* has the necessary expertise; and

(2) *FSA* resources: whether the resources required to produce a report or to make enquiries are available within the *FSA*, or whether the exercise will be the best use of the *FSA's* resources at the time.

5.4 Appointment and reporting process

Scope of report

5.4.1 **[G]** The *FSA* will send a notice in writing requiring the *person* in SUP 5.2.1G to provide a report by a *skilled person* on any matter if it is reasonably required in connection with the exercise of its functions conferred by or under the *Act*. The *FSA* may require the report to be in whatever form it specifies in the notice (SUP 5Ann2G summarises the appointment and reporting processes).

5.4.2 **[G]** As part of the decision making process the *FSA* will normally contact the *person* in SUP 5.2.1G to discuss its needs before finalising its decision to require a report by a *skilled person*. This will provide an opportunity for discussion about the appointment, whether an alternative means of obtaining the information would be better, what the scope of a report should be, who should be appointed, and the likely cost.

5.4.3 **[G]** The *FSA* will give written notification to the *person* in SUP 5.2.1G of the purpose of the report, its scope, the timetable for completion and any other relevant matters. The *FSA* will state the matters which the report is to contain as well as any requirements as to the report's format. For example, a report on controls may be required to address key risks, key controls and the control environment. The *FSA* attaches importance to there being a timetable for each report and to the *skilled person*, with the cooperation of the *person* in SUP 5.2.1G, keeping to that timetable.

5.4.4 **[G]** The written notification in SUP 5.4.3G may be preceded or followed by a discussion of the *FSA's* requirements and the reasons for them. This may involve the *FSA*, the *person* in SUP 5.2.1G and the person who has been, or is expected to be, appointed as the *skilled person*. The *FSA* recognises that there will normally be value in holding discussions involving the *skilled person* at this stage. These discussions may include others if appropriate.

5.4.5 **[G]** The *FSA* will wish to conduct the discussion with the *firm*, its *skilled person* and any others within a timescale appropriate to the circumstances of the case.

Appointment process

5.4.6 **[G]** The *skilled person* is appointed by the *person* in SUP 5.2.1G. The *FSA* will normally seek to agree in advance with the person in SUP 5.2.1G the *skilled person* who will make the report. The *Act* requires that the *skilled person* be nominated or approved by the *FSA*:

(1) if the *FSA* decides to nominate the *skilled person* who is to make the report, it will notify the *person* in SUP 5.2.1G accordingly; and

(2) alternatively, if the *FSA* is content to approve a *skilled person* selected by the *person* in SUP 5.2.1G, it will notify the latter *person* of that fact.

The *FSA* may give the *person* in SUP 5.2.1G a shortlist from which to choose.

5.4.7 **[G]** A *skilled person* must appear to the *FSA* to have the skills necessary to make a report on the matter concerned. A *skilled person* may be an accountant, lawyer, *actuary* or *person* with relevant business, technical or technological skills.

5.4.8 **[G]** When considering whether to nominate or approve a *skilled person* to make a report, the *FSA* will have regard to the circumstances of the case, including whether the proposed *skilled person* appears to have:

(1) the skills necessary to make a report on the matter concerned;

(2) the ability to complete the report within the time expected by the *FSA*;

(3) any relevant specialised knowledge, for instance of the *person* in SUP 5.2.1G, the type of business carried on by the *person* in SUP 5.2.1G, or the matter to be reported on;

(4) any professional difficulty or potential conflict of interest in reviewing the matters to be reported on, for instance because the matters to be reported on may involve questions reflecting on the quality or reliability of work previously carried out by the proposed *skilled person*; and

(5) enough detachment, bearing in mind the closeness of an existing professional or commercial relationship, to give an objective opinion on matters such as:

    (a) matters already reported on by the *skilled person* (for example, on the financial statements of the *person* in SUP 5.2.1G or in relation to their systems and controls);

    (b) matters that are likely to be contentious and may result in disciplinary or other enforcement action against the *person* in SUP 5.2.1G, its management, *shareholders* or *controllers*; or

    (c) matters that the *skilled person* has been involved in, in another capacity (for example, when a *skilled person* has been involved in developing an information system it may not be appropriate for him to provide a subsequent opinion on the adequacy of the system).

5.4.9 **[G]** In appropriate circumstances, it may be cost effective for the *FSA* to nominate or approve the appointment of a *skilled person* who has previously acted for, or advised, the *person* in SUP 5.2.1G. For example, the *FSA* may nominate, or approve the appointment of, the auditor of a *person* in SUP 5.2.1G to prepare a report taking into account, where relevant, the considerations set out in SUP 5.4.7G.

Reporting process

5.4.10 **[G]** The *FSA* will normally require the *person* in SUP 5.2.1G to appoint a *skilled person* to report to the *FSA* through that *person*. In the normal course of events the *FSA* expects that the *person* in SUP 5.2.1G will be given the opportunity to provide written comments on the report prior to its submission to the *FSA* (SUP 5Ann2G summarises the reporting process).

5.4.11 **[G]** The *FSA* may enter into a dialogue with the *skilled person*, and is ready to discuss matters relevant to the report with him, during the preparation of the report. Such discussions will normally involve or be through the *person* in SUP 5.2.1G.

5.4.12 **[G]** The *FSA* will normally specify a time limit within which it expects the *skilled person* to deliver the report. The *skilled person* should, in complying with its contractual duty under SUP 5.5.1R, take reasonable steps to achieve delivery by that time. If the *skilled person* becomes aware that the report may not be delivered on time, he should inform the *FSA* and the *person* in SUP 5.2.1G as soon as possible. If the *skilled person* becomes aware that there may be difficulties delivering the report within cost estimates, he will no doubt wish to advise the *firm*.

5.4.13 **[G]** The *FSA* may meet with the *person* in SUP 5.2.1G and the *skilled person* together to discuss the final report. The *FSA* may also wish to discuss the final report with the *skilled person* present but without the *person* in SUP 5.2.1G.

5.5 Duties of firms

Contract with the skilled person

5.5.1 **[R]** When a *firm* appoints a skilled person to provide a report under section 166 of the *Act* (Reports by skilled persons), the *firm* must, in a contract with the *skilled person*:

(1) require and permit the *skilled person* during and after the course of his appointment:
  (a) to cooperate with the *FSA* in the discharge of its functions under the *Act* in relation to the *firm*; and
  (b) to communicate to the *FSA* information on, or his opinion on, matters of which he has, or had, become aware in his capacity as *skilled person* reporting on the *firm* in the following circumstances:
    (i) the *skilled person* reasonably believes that, as regards the *firm* concerned
      (A) there is or has been, or may be or may have been, a contravention of any relevant *requirement* that applies to the *firm* concerned; and
      (B) that the contravention may be of material significance to the *FSA* in determining whether to exercise, in relation to the *firm* concerned, any functions conferred on the *FSA* by or under any provision of the *Act* other than Part VI. (Official Listing); or
    (ii) the *skilled person* reasonably believes that the information on, or his opinion on, those matters may be of material significance to the *FSA* in determining whether the *firm* concerned satisfies and will continue to satisfy the *threshold conditions; or*
    (iii) the *skilled person* reasonably believes that *firm* is not, may not be or may cease to be a going concern;

(2) require the *skilled person* to prepare a report, as notified to the *firm* by the *FSA, within the time specified by the FSA*; and

(3) waive any duty of confidentiality owed by the *skilled person* to the *firm* which might limit the provision of information or opinion by that *skilled person* to the *FSA* in accordance with (1) or (2). (See also SUP 5.5.13G. and SUP 5.6)

5.5.2 **[G]** In complying with the contractual duty in SUP 5.5.1R(1) the *FSA* expects that a *skilled person* appointed under section 166 of the *Act* (Reports by skilled persons) will cooperate with the *FSA* by, amongst other things, providing information or documentation about the planning and progress of the report and its findings and conclusions, if requested to do so. A *firm* should therefore ensure that the contract it makes with the *skilled person* requires and permits the *skilled person* to provide the following to the *FSA* if requested to do so:

(1) interim reports;
(2) source data, *documents* and working papers;
(3) copies of any draft reports given to the *firm*; and
(4) specific information about the planning and progress of the work to be undertaken (which may include project plans, progress reports including percentage of work completed, details of time spent, costs to date, and details of any significant findings and conclusions).

5.5.3 **[G]** If the *FSA* is considering asking for the information specified in SUP 5.5.2G it will take into consideration the cost of the *skilled person* complying with the request, and the benefit that the *FSA* may derive from the information. For example, in most cases, the *FSA* will not need to request a *skilled person* to give it source data, *documents* and working papers. However, the *FSA* may do so when it reasonably believes that this information will be relevant to any investigation it may be conducting, or any action it may need to consider taking against the *firm*.

5.5.4 **[G]** In complying with the contractual duty in SUP 5.5.1R, the *FSA* expects that, in the case of substantial or complex reports, the *skilled person* will give a periodic update on progress and issues to allow for a re-focusing of the report if necessary. The channel of communication would normally be directly between the *skilled person* and the *FSA*. However, the *FSA* would also expect *firms* normally to be informed about the passage of information, and the *skilled person* would usually be expected to keep the *firm* informed of any communication between the *skilled person* and the *FSA*.

5.5.5 **[R]** A *firm* must ensure that the contract required by SUP 5.5.1R:

(1) is governed by the laws of a part of the *United Kingdom*;
(2) expressly
  (a) provides that the *FSA* has a right to enforce the provisions included in the contract under SUP 5.5.1R and SUP 5.5.5R(2);

(b) provides that, in proceedings brought by the *FSA* for the enforcement of those provisions, the *skilled person* is not to have available by way of defence, set-off or counterclaim any matter that is not relevant to those provisions;

(c) (if the contract includes an arbitration agreement) provides that the *FSA* is not, in exercising the right in (a), to be treated as a party to, or bound by, the arbitration agreement; and

(d) provides that the provisions included in the contract under SUP 5.5.1R and SUP 5.5.5R(2) are irrevocable and may not be varied or rescinded without the *FSA's* consent; and

(3) is not varied or rescinded in such a way as to extinguish or alter the provisions referred to in (2)(d).

5.5.6 **[G]** The Contracts (Rights of Third Parties) Act 1999, or Scots common law, enables the *FSA* to enforce the rights conferred on it under the contract against the *skilled person.*

5.5.7 **[G]** If the *FSA* considers it appropriate, it may request the *firm* to give it a copy of the draft contract before it is made with the *skilled person.* The *FSA* will inform the *firm* of any matters that it considers require further clarification or discussion before the contract is finalised.

5.5.8 **[G]** The *FSA* expects the *firm*, in complying with *Principle* 11, to give the *FSA* information about the cost of the *skilled persons* report. This may include both an initial estimate of the cost as well as the cost of the completed report. This information is required to help inform the *FSA's* decision making in the choice of regulatory tools. Information about the number and cost of reports by *skilled persons* will be published by the *FSA*.

Assisting the skilled person

5.5.9 **[R]** A *firm* must provide all reasonable assistance to any *skilled person* appointed to provide a report under section 166 of the *Act* (Reports by skilled persons).

5.5.10 **[G]** In providing reasonable assistance under SUP 5.5.9R, a *firm* should take reasonable steps to ensure that, when reasonably required by the *skilled person*, each of its *appointed representatives* or, where applicable, *tied agents* waives any duty of confidentiality and provides reasonable assistance as though SUP 5.5.1R(3) and SUP 5.5.9R applied directly to the *appointed representative* or *tied agent*.

5.5.11 **[G]** Reasonable *assistance* in SUP 5.5.9R should include:

(1) access at all reasonable business hours for the *skilled person* to the *firm's* accounting and other records in whatever form;

(2) providing such information and explanations as the *skilled person* reasonably considers necessary or desirable for the performance of his duties; and

(3) permitting a *skilled person* to obtain such information directly from the *firm's* auditor as he reasonably considers necessary or desirable for the proper performance of his duties.

Responsibility for delivery

5.5.12 **[G]** In complying with *Principle* 11, a *firm* is expected to take reasonable steps to ensure that a *skilled person* delivers a report in accordance with the terms of his appointment.

Assistance to skilled persons from others

5.5.13 **[G]** Section 166(5) of the *Act* (Authority's power to require information) imposes a duty on certain *persons* to give assistance to a *skilled person*. The *persons* on whom this duty is imposed are those who are providing, or have at any time provided, services to any *person* falling within SUP 5.2.1G. They include suppliers under *material outsourcing arrangements.*

5.6 Confidential information and privilege

Confidential information

5.6.1 **[G]** Within the legal constraints that apply, the *FSA* may pass on to a *skilled person* any information which it considers relevant to the *skilled person's* function. A *skilled person*, being a primary recipient under section 348 of the *Act* (Restrictions on disclosure of confidential information by Authority etc.), is bound by the confidentiality provisions in Part XXIII of the *Act* (Public record, disclosure of information and cooperation) as regards confidential information he receives from the *FSA* or directly from a *firm* or other *person*. A *skilled person* may not pass on confidential information without lawful authority, for example, where an exception applies under the Financial Services and Markets Act 2000 (Disclosure of Confidential Information) Regulations 2001 (SI 2001/2188) or with the consent of the *person* from whom that information was received and (if different) to whom the information relates. The *FSA* will indicate to a *skilled person* if there is any matter which cannot be discussed with the *person* in SUP 5.2.1G

5.6.2 **[G]** Banking confidentiality and legal privilege

The *limitations* in the following sections of the *Act* are relevant to this chapter:

(1) section 175(5) (Information and documents: supplemental provisions) under which a person may be required under Part XI of the *Act* (Information Gathering and Investigations) to disclose information or produce a document subject to banking confidentiality (with exceptions); and

(2) section 413 (Protected items), under which no *person* may be required to produce, disclose or allow the inspection of *protected items*.

Annex 1
SUP 5 Ann 1 [G]

Ann1 **[G]**

Toolkit purpose		**Purpose for use of tool**		**Examples of reasons for use of tool**
Diagnostic	•	To find out more about a concern (e.g. the result of a visit, risk assessment, or notification) and determine whether action is needed to mitigate a risk to the *regulatory objectives* or to determine whether there may have been a breach of a *rule* or of a *threshold condition.*	•	Concern about effectiveness of the *firm's** internal audit department.
			•	Concern about reliability of submitted financial returns
			•	Inability of a *firm** to quantify its current financial position.
			•	Assessment of consequences of incomplete customer files.
			•	Concern about quality of systems and controls.
			•	Indication of financial crime or money laundering.
			•	Concern about a *firm's** *controller*.
	•	To assess the implications of, and *firm's** response to, a change of circumstances e.g.	•	Assessment of control structure when a *bank* (specialising in consumer lending) diversifies into commercial lending.
		– proposed entry into new business area;		
		– new control structure;		
		– merger or take-over;		
		– new IT system; or		
		– launch of an e-commerce venture.		
Diagnostic/ monitoring	•	To verify information provided to the *FSA*.	•	Verification of a specific return to give the *FSA* assurance of the quality of information provided.
Monitoring	•	To review systems and controls	•	Assessment of systems and controls in *firms** where identified as a risk mitigation priority.
	•	To complement baseline monitoring	•	In-depth review of part of a *firm** which is material to the *firm's* risk profile but of which the *FSA* does not consider it has an adequate, up-to-date understanding.

Toolkit purpose		Purpose for use of tool		Examples of reasons for use of tool
Preventative	*	To gather and analyse information on an identified risk and develop recommendations for resolution.	•	Review of identified control weaknesses over *client money* to obtain recommendations to ensure compliance with the relevant *rules*.
Remedial	•	To assist in the design of a customer redress programme.	•	Where possible, the *FSA* has identified possible losses from failure to reconcile assets or from misposting of transactions to the general ledger.
	•	To assist in the design of a remedial action plan.		
	•	To oversee and report on remedial action plan.	•	To report on quality of work undertaken and adherence to milestones in the action plan.

* or, where applicable, the other *persons* in SUP 5.2.1G.

Annex 2
SUP 5: Reports by skilled persons
Ann2 [G]

An overview of the appointment and report development process

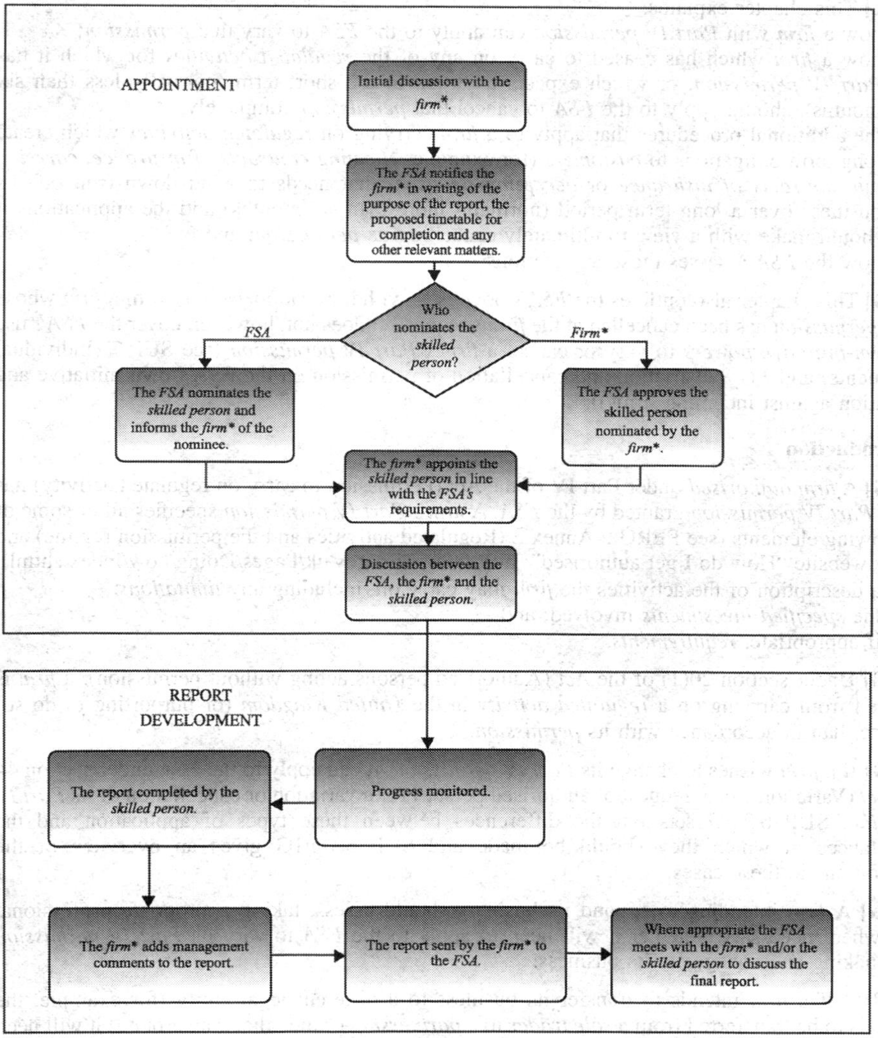

*or where applicable the other persons in *SUP* 5.2.1G

CHAPTER 6
APPLICATIONS TO VARY AND CANCEL PART IV PERMISSION

6.1 Application and purpose

Application

[2159]
6.1.1 **[G]** This chapter applies to every *firm* with a *Part IV permission* which wishes to:
(1) vary its *Part IV permission*; or
(2) cancel its *Part IV permission* and end its *authorisation*.

6.1.2 **[G]** If appropriate, a *firm* which is an *authorised fund manager* should also refer to COLL 7 for *guidance* on the termination of *ICVCs* and *AUTs* and on winding up *authorised funds* that are not commercially viable.

6.1.3 **[G]** This chapter applies to an *incoming firm* or a *UCITS qualifier* only in respect of a *top-up permission*. An *incoming firm* or a *UCITS qualifier* should refer to SUP 14 (Variation of passport rights by incoming EEA firms and ending authorisation) for the procedures for changes to *permission* granted under Schedules 3, 4 or 5 of the *Act*.

Purpose

6.1.4 **[G]** This chapter explains:
(1) how a *firm* with *Part IV permission* can apply to the *FSA* to vary that *permission*;
(2) how a *firm* which has ceased to carry on any of the *regulated activities* for which it has *Part IV permission*, or which expects to do so in the short term (normally less than six months), should apply to the *FSA* to cancel that *permission* completely;
(3) the additional procedures that apply to a *firm* carrying on *regulated activities* which create long term obligations to *customers* (for example, *effecting contracts of insurance*, *carrying out contracts of insurance* or *accepting deposits*) that needs to wind down (run off) its business over a long term period (normally more than six months) and the applications it should make with a view to ultimately cancelling its *permission*; and
(4) how the *FSA* assesses those applications.

6.1.5 **[G]** This chapter also outlines the *FSA's* powers to withdraw *authorisation* from a *firm* whose *Part IV permission* has been cancelled at the *firm's* request. It does not, however, cover the *FSA's* use of its *own-initiative powers* to vary or cancel a *firm's Part IV permission* (see SUP 7 (Individual requirements) and *EG* 8 (Variation and cancellation of permission on the FSA's own initiative and intervention against incoming firms)).

6.2 Introduction

6.2.1 **[G]** A *firm authorised* under Part IV of the *Act* (Permission to carry on regulated activity) has a single *Part IV permission* granted by the *FSA*. A *firm's Part IV permission* specifies all or some of the following elements (see PERG 2 Annex 2 (Regulated activities and the permission regime) and the FSA website "How do I get authorised": http://www.fsa.gov.uk/Pages/Doing/how/index.shtml):
(1) a description of the activities the *firm* may carry on, including any *limitations*;
(2) the *specified investments* involved; and
(3) if appropriate, *requirements*.

6.2.2 **[G]** Under section 20(1) of the *Act* (Authorised persons acting without permission), a *firm* is prohibited from carrying on a *regulated activity* in the *United Kingdom* (or purporting to do so) otherwise than in accordance with its *permission*.

6.2.3 **[G]** If a *firm* wishes to change its *Part IV permission*, it can apply to the *FSA* under section 44 of the *Act* (Variation etc. at request of authorised person) for a variation or cancellation of its *Part IV permission*. SUP 6.2.5G sets out the differences between these types of application and the circumstances in which they should be made and SUP 6Ann1G gives an overview of the considerations in these cases.

6.2.4 **[G]** A *firm* intending to expand its business should assess, taking appropriate professional advice where necessary, whether it will need to apply to the *FSA* to vary its *Part IV permission* before making any changes to its business.

6.2.4A **[G]** If a *firm* intends to transfer its business to a different legal entity (for example, the business is to be transferred from a *sole trader* to a *partnership* or the other way around) it will need to apply to the *FSA* for cancellation of its *Part IV permission* and the entity to which the business is to be transferred will need to apply for a *Part IV permission*.

6.2.5 **[G]**

Table: Variation and cancellation of Part IV permission. See SUP 6.2.3G

Question	**Variation of Part IV permission**	**Cancellation of Part IV permission**
What does the application apply to?	Individual elements of a *firm's Part IV permission*. Variations may involve adding or removing categories of *regulated activity* or *specified investments* or varying or removing any *limitations* or *requirements* in the *firm's Part IV permission*.	A *firm's* entire *Part IV permission* and not individual elements within it.

Question	Variation of Part IV permission	Cancellation of Part IV permission
In what circumstances is it usually appropriate to make an application?	If a *firm*: 1. wishes to change the *regulated activities* it carries on in the *United Kingdom* under a *Part IV permission* (SUP 6.3); or 2. has the ultimate intention of ceasing carrying on *regulated activities* but due to the nature of those *regulated activities* (for example, *accepting deposits*, or *insurance business*) it will require a long term (normally over six months) to wind down (run off) its business (see SUP 6.2.8G to SUP 6.2.11G and SUP 6 Ann 4G).	If a *firm*: 1. has ceased to carry on all of the *regulated activities* for which it has *Part IV permission* (SUP 6.4); or 2. wishes or expects to cease carrying on all of the *regulated activities* for which it has *Part IV permission* in the short term (normally not more than six months). In this case, the *firm* may apply to cancel its *Part IV permission* prior to ceasing the *regulated activities* (see SUP 6.4.3G).
Where do I find a summary of the application procedures?	See SUP 6 Ann 2G.	See SUP 6 Ann 3G.

6.2.6 **[G]** A *firm* which is seeking to:
(1) vary its *Part IV permission* substantially; or
(2) cancel its *Part IV permission*;

should discuss its plans with its usual supervisory contact at the *FSA* as early as possible before making an application, in order to comply with *Principle* 11 (see SUP 15.3.7G (Notifications to the FSA)). These discussions will help the *FSA* and the *firm* to agree the correct approach for the *firm*.

6.2.7 **[G]** If a *firm* intends to cease carrying on one or more *regulated activities* permanently, it should give prompt notice to the *FSA* to comply with *Principle* 11 (see SUP 15.3.8G(1)(d)). A *firm* should consider whether it needs to notify the *FSA* before applying to vary or cancel its *Part IV permission*.

Firms with long term liabilities to customers

6.2.8 **[G]** Discussions with the *FSA* are particularly relevant where the *firm* has to discharge obligations to its *customers* or policyholders before it can cease carrying on a *regulated activity*. This may be the case, for example, where the *firm* is an *insurer*, a *bank*, a *dormant account fund operator*, or, as is often the case, holding *client money* or *customer assets*.

6.2.9 **[G]** If an *insurer*, a *bank*, or a *dormant account fund operator* wishes to cease carrying on all *regulated activities* for which it has *Part IV permission*, it will usually be necessary to wind down the business over a long term period which is normally more than six months. This may also be the case for a *firm* holding *client money* or *customer assets*. In these circumstances, it will usually be appropriate for the *firm* to apply for variation of its *Part IV permission* before commencing the wind-down. A *firm* should only make an application for cancellation of *permission* when it expects to complete its wind-down (run-off) within six months.

6.2.10 **[G]** A *firm* which is winding down (running off) its activities should contact its usual supervisory contact at the *FSA* to discuss its circumstances. The *FSA* will discuss the *firm's* winding down plans and the need for the *firm* to vary or cancel its *Part IV permission*. Following these discussions, an application for variation or cancellation of *Part IV permission*, as appropriate, should usually be made by the *firm*, although, in certain circumstances, the *FSA* may use its *own-initiative powers* under section 45 of the *Act* (Variation etc. on the *FSA's* own initiative) (see SUP 7 and *EG* 8 (Variation and cancellation of permission on the FSA's own initiative and intervention against incoming firms)).

6.2.11 **[G]**
(1) Specific guidance on the additional procedures for a *firm* winding down (running off) its business in the circumstances discussed in SUP 6.2.8G is in SUP 6Ann4G.
(2) The guidance in SUP 6Ann4G applies to any *firm* that is applying for variation of *Part IV permission* before it applies for cancellation of *Part IV permission* to enable it to wind down (run off) its business over a long term period of six months of more. It will apply to most *insurers* and *banks* and, in some circumstances, as advised by the *FSA*, to *firms* holding *client money* or *customer assets*.
(3) If a *firm* wishes to cease carrying on some of its *regulated activities*, or the *specified investments* in respect of which the activities are carried on, the *FSA* may consider it appropriate for the *firm* to comply with the additional procedures in SUP 6Ann4G. This

would depend on the scale and nature of the *regulated activities* concerned. This might be the case, for example, if the *firm* is ceasing a significant part of its business in respect of which it has outstanding obligations to *customers* and the *FSA* believes that the additional procedures would protect *consumers*.

UK firms exercising EEA or Treaty rights

6.2.12 **[G]** A *UK firm* should assess the effect of any change to its *Part IV permission* on its ability to continue to exercise any *EEA right* or *Treaty right* and discuss any concerns with its usual supervisory contact at the *FSA*. A variation of *Part IV permission* may also change the *applicable provisions* with which it is required to comply by a *Host State*.

6.2.13 **[G]** A *UK firm* which, as well as applying to vary or cancel its *Part IV permission*, wishes to vary or terminate any business which it is carrying on in another *EEA State* under one of the *Single Market Directives*, should follow the procedures in SUP 13 (Exercise of passport rights by UK firms) on varying or terminating its *branch* or *cross border services* business.

The Lloyd's market

6.2.14 **[G]** A *firm* making an application to vary or cancel its *Part IV permission* which requires any approval from the *Society of Lloyd's* should apply to the *Society* for this at the same time as applying to the *FSA* for the variation or cancellation. See SUP 6Ann4G for additional procedures.

6.3 Applications for variation of permission

What is a variation of permission?

6.3.1 **[G]** Under section 44 of the *Act*, a *firm* may apply to the *FSA* to vary its *Part IV permission* to:

(1) allow it to carry on further *regulated activities*; or
(2) reduce the number of *regulated activities* it is permitted to carry on; or
(3) vary the *FSA's* description of its *regulated activities* (including by the removal or variation of any *limitations*); or
(4) cancel any *requirement* applied for by the *firm* or imposed by the *FSA* under section 43 of the *Act* (Imposition of requirements); or
(5) vary any such *requirement*.

6.3.2 **[G]** An application for variation of *Part IV permission* may include one or more of SUP 6.3.1G (1)–(5). For example, a *firm* may apply to vary its *Part IV permission* to add a new *regulated activity* and at the same time remove a *regulated activity* for which it currently has *permission*.

6.3.3 **[G]** In applying for a variation of *Part IV permission*, a branch of a *firm* from outside the *EEA* should be mindful of any continuing requirements referred to in the rest of the *Handbook*.

Applications to add additional regulated activities

6.3.4 **[G]** In determining the activities and *specified investments* for which a *Part IV permission* is required, and whether to apply for a variation of that *permission*, a *firm* may need to take professional advice and may also wish to discuss this with its usual supervisory contact at the *FSA*.

6.3.5 **[G]** Before applying to vary its *permission*, a *firm* should determine whether there are any statutory restrictions that do not allow combinations of certain types of *regulated activity*, particularly for *insurance business* or *UCITS* managers. For example, the *FSA* will not grant a variation of *Part IV permission* to allow a *friendly society* to carry on reinsurance business as this is not permitted under the Friendly Societies Acts 1974 and 1992. A *firm* should discuss its plans with its usual supervisory contact at the *FSA*.

6.3.6 **[G]** If a *firm* is seeking a variation of *Part IV permission* to add categories of *regulated activities*, it should be mindful of the directive requirements referred to at SUP 6.3.42G relating to the need to commence new activities within 12 months.

Applications to remove certain regulated activities

6.3.7 **[G]** If a *firm* wishes to cease carrying on an activity for which it has *Part IV permission*, it will usually apply to vary its *Part IV permission* to remove that activity. If a *firm* wishes to cease carrying on an activity in relation to any *specified investment*, it will usually apply to vary its *Part IV permission* to remove that *specified investment* from the relevant activity.

How a variation of permission may affect the firm's approved persons

6.3.8 **[G]**

(1) Where a *firm* is submitting an application for variation of *Part IV permission* which would lead to a change in the *controlled functions* of its *approved persons*, it should, at the same time and as appropriate:

(a) make an application to the *FSA* for an internal transfer of an *approved person*, Form E (Internal transfer), or make an application to the *FSA* for an individual to perform additional *controlled functions*, the relevant Form A (Application); see SUP 10.13.3G to SUP 10.13.5G;

(b) notify the *FSA* of any *approved person* who has ceased to perform a *controlled function*, Form C (Ceasing to perform controlled functions); see SUP 10.13.6G to SUP 10.13.13G.

(2) If the *firm* intends to recruit new individuals to perform *controlled functions*, it should apply to the *FSA* for approval of the individuals as *approved persons* as soon as possible using Form A (Application); see SUP 10.12.

How a variation of permission may change a firm's prudential category

6.3.9 **[G]** A variation of *Part IV permission* may, in some cases, lead to a change in a *firm's* prudential category or sub-category (see SUP App1). For example, an *investment management firm* which varies its *Part IV permission* to include *accepting deposits* and as a result meets the definition of a *bank*, would move to the prudential category for a *bank* (see SUP App1.3.1G).

6.3.10 **[G]** Even if a variation of *permission* does not itself lead to a change in a *firm's* prudential category or sub-category, the *FSA* may use its *own-initiative powers* to require a *firm* to comply with a different category or sub-category of prudential *rules* where it considers this to be appropriate. For details of when and how the *FSA* may use its *own-initiative powers* in this context, see SUP 7.

Variation of permission involving insurance business

6.3.11 **[G]** A *firm* with *Part IV permission* to carry on *insurance business*, which is applying for a variation of its *Part IV permission* to add further *insurance* activities or *specified investments*, will be required to submit particular information on its existing activities as part of its application. This includes the *scheme of operations* which is required to be submitted as part of the application pack (for further details on the *scheme of operations*, see SUP App2 (Insurers: scheme of operations)).

6.3.12 **[G]** In applying to vary its *Part IV permission* to add categories of *specified investments*, in relation to *insurance business*, a *firm* carrying *on insurance business* will need to determine the *classes* of *specified investments* relating to *effecting* and *carrying out contracts of insurance* for which variation of *Part IV permission* will be necessary, having regard to whether certain *classes* of contract may qualify to be effected or carried out on an ancillary or supplementary basis (see SUP 3.12.6G to SUP 3.12.12G).

6.3.13 **[G]** The application for variation of *Part IV permission* will need to provide information about the *classes* of *contract of insurance* for which variation of *Part IV permission* is requested and also those *classes* qualifying to be carried on on an ancillary or supplementary basis. For example, an *insurer* applying to vary its *permission* to include *class* 10 (motor vehicle liability, other than carrier's liability) must satisfy the *FSA* that it will meet, and continue to meet, *threshold condition* 2A (Appointment of claims representatives). *Firms* should note that, although the FSA is able in principle to use its power to give *Part IV permission* for an applicant to carry on a *regulated activity* for which it did not originally apply, this is not possible under the Insurance Directives, which set out minimum information requirements for an application for *authorisation* including information on the specified investments the applicant proposes to deal in.

6.3.14 **[G]**

(1) A *firm* carrying on *insurance business* which is seeking to cease such business in respect of one or more classes of *specified investment*, but which is not intending to cease all *insurance business*, should apply to vary its *Part IV permission* to remove the activity of *effecting contracts of insurance* in respect of those *specified investments* in relation to which it no longer wishes to carry on business. A *firm* intending to cease all *insurance business* should refer to SUP 6Ann4G.

(2) If the application for variation of *Part IV permission* is granted by the *FSA*, the *firm* will have *Part IV permission* only to *carry out contracts of insurance* in respect of the *specified investments* in relation to which it no longer wishes to carry on business (see SUP 6Ann4G). This will allow the *firm* to run off this aspect of its business. When the business in question has been run-off completely, the *firm* should then apply to vary its *Part IV permission* to remove the relevant *classes* of *specified investment*.

The application for variation of permission

6.3.15 **[D]**

(1) If a *firm* wishes to apply for a variation of *Part IV permission*, it must complete and submit to the *FSA* the form in SUP 6 Ann 5D (Variation of permission application form).

(2) A *firm's* application for variation of *Part IV permission* must be given or addressed, and delivered in the way set out in SUP 15.7.4R to SUP 15.7.6R (Form and method of notification).

(3) Until the application has been determined, a *firm* which submits an application for variation of *Part IV permission* must inform the *FSA* of any significant change to the information given in the application immediately it becomes aware of the change.

6.3.16 **[G]**

(1) Section 51(2) of the *Act* (Applications under this Part) requires that the application for variation of *Part IV permission* must contain a statement:
   (a) of the desired variation; and
   (b) of the *regulated activity* or *regulated activities* which the *firm* proposes to carry on if its *permission* is varied.

(2) The full form and content of the application for variation of *Part IV permission* is a matter for direction by the *FSA*, who will determine the additional information and documentation required on a case by case basis.

6.3.17 **[G]**

(1) [deleted]

(2) A *firm* is advised to discuss its application with its usual supervisory contact at the *FSA* before submission, particularly if it is seeking a variation of *permission* within a short timescale. A *firm* is also advised to include as much detail as possible (including any additional information identified by its supervisors at this stage) with its application.

6.3.18 **[G]** The *FSA*, as soon as possible after receipt of an application, will advise the *firm* of any additional information which is required as part of its application (see SUP 6.3.23G to SUP 6.3.27G). The amount of information the *FSA* will require will vary depending on the scale of the variation in the context of the *firm* as a whole, and the nature, risk profile and complexity of the variation.

Applications from firms winding down (running off) business over the long term

6.3.19 **[G]** A *firm* which is making an application for variation of *Part IV permission* to wind down (run off) its business before applying for a cancellation of that *permission* (see SUP 6.2.9G) should read SUP 6Ann4G for details of the additional procedures that apply.

Applications involving significant changes

6.3.20 **[G]** In certain cases, *FSA* may consider that granting an application for variation of *Part IV permission* which includes adding further *regulated activities* or changing a *requirement* or *limitation* would cause a significant change in the *firm's* business or risk profile. In these circumstances, the *FSA* may require the *firm* to complete appropriate parts of the full application pack (see the FSA website "How do I get authorised": http://www.fsa.gov.uk/Pages/Doing/how/index.shtml), as directed by the *FSA*. Applications for variation involving significant changes may be processed by the *firm's* usual supervisory contact at the *FSA*, in conjunction with the Permissions department. Examples of an application for variation of *Part IV permission* which may represent a significant change include, but are not limited to, an application:

(1) to carry on new *regulated activities* such as *accepting deposits*;

(2) to extend the *insurance business* of a *firm* which already has *Part IV permission* which includes *carrying out* or *effecting contracts of insurance* (or both), to new *classes* of *specified investment*; or

(3) to remove a *requirement* preventing a *firm* from holding or controlling *client money*; or

(4) which causes the *firm* to change prudential category by, for example, removing a *requirement* relating to prudential category (see SUP App1).

6.3.21 **[G]** A *firm* that wishes to make a significant change to its business, or is unsure whether the changes it is proposing would be considered to be significant, should contact its usual supervisory contact at the *FSA*. The *FSA* will discuss with the *firm* whether it will be required to submit parts of the application pack and whether any reports from third parties may be required.

6.3.22 **[R]** The fees payable for a *firm* applying for a variation of its *Part IV permission* are set out in FEES 3.

Information to be supplied to the FSA as part of the application

6.3.23 **[G]**

(1) The *FSA* may ask for any information it reasonably requires before determining the application. The information required will be determined on a case by case basis, taking into account the *FSA's* existing knowledge of the *firm* and the variation requested. The *FSA* will advise the *firm* of the information required at an early stage in the application process.

(2) *The nature of the information* and documents requested will be related to the risks posed to the *FSA's regulatory objectives* by the *regulated activities* and any *unregulated activities* that the *firm* is seeking to carry on. This information will be proportional to the nature of the business which the *firm* intends to carry on or the risks posed by the *firm*.

6.3.24 **[G]**

(1) The information the *FSA* may require includes, but is not limited to, the examples given in SUP 6.3.25G:

6.3.25 **[G]**

Table: Information which may be required. See SUP 6.3.24G

Type of business	**Information which may be required**	
All	1.	Details of how the *firm* plans to comply with the *FSA's* regulatory requirements relating to any additional *regulated activities* it is seeking to carry on.
	2.	Descriptions of the *firm's* key controls, senior management arrangements and audit and proposed compliance arrangements in respect of any new *regulated activity* (see *SYSC*).
	3.	Organisation charts and details of individuals transferring or being recruited to perform new *controlled functions* (see SUP 10 for details of the application or transfer procedures under the *approved persons* regime).
Insurance business	1.	A *scheme of operations* in accordance with SUP Appendix 2.
	2.	(If the application seeks to vary a *permission* to include *motor vehicle liability insurance business*) details of the *claims representatives* required by *threshold condition* 2A (Appointment of claims representatives), if applicable.
Accepting deposits and *designated investment business*	1.	A business plan which includes the impact of the variation on the *firm's* existing or continuing business financial projections for the *firm*, including the impact of the requested variation of *Part IV permission* on the *firm's* financial resources and capital adequacy requirements.

6.3.26 **[G]** Specific information may also be required by the *FSA* on the activities the *firm* intends to cease, or cease carrying on in relation to any *specified investments* (see SUP 6 Ann4G).

6.3.27 **[G]** When determining whether to grant an application, the *FSA* may request further information, including reports from third parties such as the *firm's* auditors, and may require meetings with, and visits to, the *firm*. The *FSA* may also require a statement from members of the *firm's governing body* confirming, to the best of their knowledge, the completeness and accuracy of the information supplied. The *FSA* may also discuss the application with other regulators, exchanges.

When will the FSA grant an application for variation of permission?

6.3.28 **[G]**

(1) The *FSA* is required by section 41(2) of the *Act* to ensure that a *firm* applying to vary its *Part IV permission* satisfies and will continue to satisfy the *threshold conditions* in relation to all the regulated activities for which the *firm* has or will have *Part IV permission* after the variation. However, the *FSA's* duty under the *Act* does not prevent it, having regard to that duty, from taking such steps as it considers necessary in relation to a particular *firm*, to secure its *consumer* protection objective. This may include granting a *firm's* application for variation of *Part IV permission* when it wishes to wind down (run off) its business activities and cease to carry on new business as a result of no longer being able to satisfy the *threshold conditions*.

(2) In addition, the *FSA* may refuse the application if it appears that the interests of *consumers*, or a group of *consumers*, would be adversely affected if the application were to be granted and it is desirable in the interests of *consumers*, or that group of *consumers*, for the application to be refused.

6.3.29 **[G]** In determining whether the *firm* satisfies and continues to satisfy the *threshold conditions*, the *FSA* will consider whether the *firm* is ready, willing and organised to comply with the regulatory requirements it will be subject to if the requested variation of *Part IV permission* is granted.

6.3.30 **[G]** The *FSA* will also consider the specific requirements that apply to certain types of activity as these may not allow certain combinations of activity.

6.3.31 **[G]** In considering whether to grant a *firm's* application to vary its *Part IV permission*, the *FSA* will also have regard, under section 49(1) of the *Act* (Persons connected with an applicant), to any person appearing to be, or likely to be, in a relationship with the *firm* which is relevant. The *Financial Groups Directive Regulations* make special consultation provisions where the *FSA* is exercising its functions under Part IV of the *Act* (Permission to carry on regulated activities) for the purposes of carrying on supplementary supervision. Broadly, where the *FSA*, in the course of carrying on supplementary supervision, is considering varying the *Part IV permission* of a *person* who is a member of a *group* which is a *financial conglomerate*, the consultation provisions in section 49(2) of the *Act* are disapplied. In their place, the regulations impose special obligations, linked to the *Financial Groups Directive*, to obtain the consent of the relevant competent authorities, to consult those authorities and to consult with the *group* itself.

The FSA's powers in respect of application for variation of Part IV permission

6.3.32 **[G]** The *FSA's* power to vary a *Part IV permission* after it receives an application from a *firm* extends to including in the *Part IV permission* as varied any provision that could be included as though a fresh *permission* was being given in response to an application under section 40 of the *Act* (Application for permission). Under sections 42 (Giving permission) and 43 of the *Act* (Imposition of requirements), the *FSA* may:

(1) incorporate in the description of a *regulated activity* a *limitation* (for example, as to the circumstance in which a *regulated activity* may or may not be carried on); or
(2) specify a narrower or wider description of *regulated activity* than the *firm* applied for in the application for variation of *Part IV permission* (see SUP 3.9.29G(3) for restrictions on *insurers*); or
(3) require the *firm* not to take a specified action (for example, not to hold *client money*); or
(4) require the *firm* to take a specified action (for example, to submit financial returns more frequently than normal).

6.3.33 **[G]** Thus, when determining an application for variation of *Part IV permission*, the *FSA* can, therefore:

(1) include new *limitations* and vary existing *limitations*, either on application from the *firm* (for example, the *customer* categories with which a *firm* may carry on a specified activity), or if considered appropriate by the *FSA* under section 42(7)(a) of the *Act*; or
(2) include any new *requirements* and vary existing *requirements*, either on application from the *firm* or where considered appropriate by the *FSA* under section 43 of the *Act* to ensure that the *firm* satisfies and continues to satisfy the *threshold conditions*.

6.3.34 **[G]** If *limitations* or *requirements* are varied or imposed by the *FSA* which were not included in the *firm's* application for variation of *Part IV permission*, the *FSA* will be required to issue the *firm* with a *warning notice* and *decision notice* (see SUP 6.3.39G).

How long will an application take?

6.3.35 **[G]** Under section 52(1) of the *Act* (Determination of applications), the *FSA* has six months to consider a completed application from the date of receipt.

6.3.36 **[G]** If the *FSA* receives an application which is incomplete (that is, if information or a document required as part of the application is not provided), section 52(2) of the *Act* requires the *FSA* to determine that incomplete application within 12 months of the initial receipt of the application.

6.3.37 **[G]** Within these time limits, however, the length of the process will relate directly to the complexity of the variation requested. The *FSA* publishes standard response times on its website at www.fsa.gov.uk setting out how long the application process is expected to take in practice. From time to time, the *FSA* also publishes its performance against these times.

6.3.38 **[G]** At any time after receiving an application and before determining it, the *FSA* may require the applicant to provide additional information or documents. The circumstances of each application will dictate what additional information or procedures are appropriate.

6.3.39 **[G]** How will the FSA make the decision?

A decision to grant an application for variation of *Part IV permission*, as applied for, will be taken by appropriately experienced *FSA* staff. However, if the *FSA* staff dealing with the application recommend that a *firm's* application for variation of *Part IV permission* be either refused or granted subject to *limitations* or *requirements* or a narrower description of *regulated activities* than applied for, the decision will be taken by either the *RDC* or *executive procedures*.

6.3.40 **[G]** *DEPP* gives guidance on the *FSA's* decision making procedures including the procedures it will follow if it proposes to refuse an application for variation of *Part IV permission* either in whole or in part (for example, an application granted by the *FSA* but subject to *limitations* or *requirements* not applied for).

Commencing new regulated activities

6.3.41 **[G]** If the variation of *Part IV permission* is given, the *FSA* will expect a *firm* to commence a new *regulated activity* in accordance with its business plan (revised as necessary to take account of changes during the application process) or scheme of operations for an *insurer*. *Firms* should take this into consideration when determining when to make an application to the *FSA*.

6.3.42 **[G]**

(1) *Firms* should be aware that the *FSA* may exercise its *own-initiative power* to vary or cancel their *Part IV permission* if they do not (see EG 8 (Variation and cancellation of permission on the FSA's own initiative and intervention against incoming firms)):

(a) commence a *regulated activity* for which they have *Part IV permission* within a period of at least 12 months from the date of being given; or

(b) carry on a *regulated activity* for which they have *Part IV permission* for a period of at least 12 months (irrespective of the date of grant).

(1A) The *FSA* may exercise its *own-initiative power* to cancel an *investment firm's Part IV permission* if the *investment firm* has provided or performed no *investment services and activities* at any time during the period of six months ending with the day on which the *warning notice* under section 54(1) of the *Act* is given (see EG 8).

(2) If the *FSA* considers that such a variation or cancellation of the *firm's Part IV permission* is appropriate, it will discuss the proposed action with the *firm* and its reasons for not commencing or carrying on the *regulated activities* concerned.

6.3.43 **[G]** When a *firm* commences new *regulated activities* following a variation of a *Part IV permission*, it should have particular regard to the requirements of *Principle* 11 (Relations with regulators) (see SUP 15.3.8G(1)(c)).

6.4 Applications for cancellation of permission

6.4.1 **[G]** Under section 44(2) of the *Act* (Variation etc. at request of authorised person), if an *authorised person* with a *Part IV permission* applies to the *FSA*, the *FSA* may cancel that *permission*. Cancellation applies to a *firm's* entire *Part IV permission*; that is to every activity and every *specified investment* and not to the individual elements such as *specified investments*. Changes to the individual elements of a *permission* would require a variation.

6.4.2 **[G]** Under section 44(3) of the *Act*, the *FSA* may refuse an application from a *firm* to cancel its *Part IV permission* if it appears that:

(1) the interests of *consumers*, or potential *consumers*, would be adversely affected if the application were to be granted; and

(2) it is desirable in the interests of *consumers*, or potential *consumers*, for the application to be refused.

6.4.3 **[G]**

(1) A *firm* may apply to the *FSA* to cancel its *Part IV permission* before it has ceased carrying on all *regulated activities*. However, where a *firm* makes a formal application for cancellation of its *permission* when it has not yet ceased carrying on *regulated activities*, the *FSA* will expect the *firm*:

(a) to cease those *regulated activities* within the short term (normally no more than six months from the date of application for cancellation); and

(b) to have formal plans to cease its *regulated activities* in an orderly manner.

(2) *Firms* should note, however, that the *FSA* will not grant an application for cancellation of *Part IV permission* until the *firm* can demonstrate that it has ceased carrying on all *regulated activities* (SUP 6.4.19G).

(3) The *FSA* may apply additional procedures or require additional information, as if the *firm* had entered into a long term wind down of business (see SUP 6 Ann4G), if it considers it appropriate to the circumstances of the *firm*.

6.4.4 **[G]** Additional guidance for a *firm* carrying on *insurance business, accepting deposits, operating a dormant account fund* or which holds *client money* or *customer's* assets is given in SUP 6Ann4G. As noted in SUP 6.2.9G, it will usually be appropriate for a *firm* to apply for variation of its *Part IV permission* while winding down (running off) its *regulated activities* and before applying to cancel its *Part IV permission*.

The application for cancellation of permission

6.4.5 **[D]**

(1) If a *firm* wishes to cancel its *Part IV permission*, it must complete and submit to the *FSA* the form in SUP 6 Ann 6D (Cancellation of permission application form).

(2) A *firm's* application for cancellation of *Part IV permission* must be:

(a) given to a member of, or addressed for the attention of, the Cancellations Team at the *FSA*; and

(b) delivered to the *FSA* by one of the methods in SUP 15.7.5R (Form and method of notification).

(3) [deleted]

(4) Until the application has been determined, a *firm* which submits an application for cancellation of *Part IV permission* must inform the *FSA* of any significant change to the information given in the application immediately it becomes aware of the change.

6.4.6 **[G]**

(1) In addition to applying for cancellation of *Part IV permission* in accordance with SUP 6.4.5D, a *firm* may discuss prospective cancellations with its usual supervisory contact at the *FSA*.

(2) To contact the Cancellations Team:
  (a) telephone on 020 7676 1102; fax on 020 7066 9701; or
  (b) write to: Cancellations Team, The Financial Services Authority, 25 The North Colonnade, Canary Wharf, London, E14 5HS; or
  (c) email cancellation.team@fsa.gov.uk

6.4.7 **[G]** When an application is received, the *FSA* will send the *firm* a written acknowledgement. The *firm* will be required to provide information which, in the opinion of the *FSA*, is necessary for it to determine whether to grant or refuse the application for cancellation of *Part IV permission*. The Cancellations Team will work with the *firm's* usual supervisory contact at the *FSA* during this process.

Information to be supplied to the FSA as part of the application for cancellation of permission

6.4.8 **[G]** The information which the *FSA* may request on the circumstances of the application for cancellation and the confirmations which the *FSA* may require a *firm* to provide will differ according to the nature of the *firm* and the activities it has *Part IV permission* to carry on.

6.4.9 **[G]** A *firm* will be expected to demonstrate to the *FSA* that it has ceased carrying on *regulated activities*. The *FSA* may require, as part of the application, a report from the *firm* that includes, but is not limited to, the confirmations referred to in SUP 6.4.12G (as appropriate to the *firm's* business). The *FSA* may also require additional information to be submitted with the report including, in some cases, confirmation or verification from a professional adviser on certain matters to supplement the report (see SUP 6.4.15G).

6.4.10 **[G]**

(1) If a *firm* is subject to the complaints rules in *DISP*, the *FSA* may request confirmation from the *firm* that there are no unresolved, unsatisfied or undischarged complaints against the *firm* from a *customer* of the *firm*.

(2) If there are unresolved or undischarged complaints against a *firm* from a *customer* of the *firm*, the *FSA* may request confirmation, as appropriate, of the steps (if any) which have been taken under the *firm's* complaints procedures and the amount of compensation claimed. The *FSA* may also request an explanation of the arrangements made for the future consideration of such complaints.

6.4.11 **[G]** If the *firm* is carrying on *designated investment business* with *private customers*, the *FSA* may request confirmation that the *firm* has written, or intends to write, to all *private customers* with, or for whom, the *firm* has conducted *regulated activities* within a certain period.

Confirmations and resolutions

6.4.12 **[G]** The *FSA* will usually require the report in SUP 6.4.9G to be signed by a *director* or other officer with authority to bind the *firm*. It may include confirmations from the *firm* that, in relation to business carried on under its *Part IV permission*, it has:

(1) ceased carrying on all *regulated activities*;
(2) properly disbursed funds in its *client bank accounts* and closed those accounts;
(3) discharged all insurance or *deposit* liabilities; and
(4) properly transferred all *investments*, title documents and other property that it held on behalf of *clients*.

6.4.13 **[G]** The *FSA* may also require a resolution from the *firm's governing body*, for example to support the application for cancellation of *permission*, expressed to be irrevocable, and to give the signatory the authority to sign the formal report to the *FSA*.

6.4.14 **[G]** Under section 397 of the *Act* (Misleading statements and practices), it is an *offence*, in purported compliance with a requirement imposed by or under the *Act* (including the directions in SUP 6.4.5D), for a *person* to knowingly or recklessly give the *FSA* information that is false or misleading. If necessary, a *firm* should take appropriate professional advice when supplying information required by the *FSA*. An *insurer*, for example, may ask an *actuary* to check assumptions in respect of future *claims* made under *contracts of insurance*.

Reports from professionals

6.4.15 **[G]** The *FSA* may require additional information, including professional advice, to supplement or support the report in SUP 6.4.9G where it considers this appropriate. Examples of reports that may be requested by the *FSA* include, but are not limited to those detailed in SUP 6.4.16G.

6.4.16 **[G]**

Table: Types of reports. See SUP 6.4.15G

Category of firm	Type of report
A *bank* or *building society*	• an audited balance sheet which confirms that, in the auditor's opinion, the *firm* has no remaining *deposit* liabilities to *customers*;
	• a report from auditors or *reporting accountants*;
A *securities and futures firm*	• a report from auditors or *reporting accountants*
an *insurer*	• an audited closing balance sheet which demonstrates that the *firm* has no insurance liabilities to *policyholders*;
	• a report from the auditors or *reporting accountants*: and
	• in some cases, an actuarial opinion as to the likelihood of any remaining liabilities to *policyholders*.

6.4.17 **[G]** If a *firm* is transferring its business, the *FSA* may require a professional opinion in respect of certain aspects of the transfer. For example, the *FSA* may require a legal opinion on the validity of arrangements to transfer *regulated activities*, *client money*, *client deposits*, *custody assets* or any other *property* belonging to *clients*, to another *authorised person*. Alternatively, an auditor or *reporting accountant* may be requested to verify that a transfer has been properly accounted for in the *firm's* books and records. Transfers of *insurance* and *banking business* are subject to statutory requirements (see SUP 18).

Approved persons

6.4.18 **[G]** A *firm* which is applying for cancellation of *Part IV permission* and which is not otherwise *authorised* by, or under, the *Act* should, at the same time, comply with SUP 10.13.6R and notify the *FSA* of persons ceasing to perform *controlled functions*. These forms should give the effective date of withdrawal, if known (see SUP 10 (Approved persons)).

When will the FSA grant an application for cancellation of permission?

6.4.19 **[G]** The *FSA* will usually not cancel a *firm's Part IV permission* until the *firm* can demonstrate that, in relation to business carried on under that permission, it has, as appropriate:

(1) ceased carrying on *regulated activities* or fully run off or transferred all insurance liabilities;
(2) repaid all *client money* and *client deposits*;
(3) discharged *custody assets* and any other *property* belonging to *clients*; and
(4) discharged, satisfied or resolved complaints against the *firm*.

6.4.20 **[G]** If it is not possible for a *firm* to demonstrate a relevant matter referred to in SUP 6.4.19G, for example, depositors are uncontactable, the *firm* will be expected to have satisfied the *FSA* that it has made adequate provisions for discharging any liabilities to *clients* which do not involve the *firm* carrying on *regulated activities*.

6.4.21 **[G]** Before the *FSA* cancels a *firm's Part IV permission*, the *firm* will be expected to be able to demonstrate that it has ceased or transferred all *regulated activities* under that *permission*. For example, the *firm* may be asked to provide evidence that a transfer of business (including, where relevant, any *client money, customer* assets or *deposits* or insurance liabilities) is complete. As noted in SUP 6.4.9G, the *FSA* may require the *firm* to confirm this by providing a report, in a form specified by the *FSA*:

(1) as part of the application for cancellation of *permission*, if the *firm* has ceased carrying on all *regulated activities* under its *Part IV permission* at the time of application (see SUP 6.4.9G); or
(2) after the application but before its determination, if the *firm* has not ceased carrying on *regulated activities* under its *Part IV permission* at the time of application.

6.4.22 **[G]** In deciding whether to cancel a *firm's Part IV permission*, the *FSA* will take into account all relevant factors in relation to business carried on under that *permission*, including whether:

(1) there are unresolved, unsatisfied or undischarged complaints against the *firm* from any of its *customers*;
(2) the *firm* has complied with CASS 4.3.99R, CASS 5.5.80R and CASS 7.2.15R (Client money: discharge of fiduciary duty) and CASS 4.3.10R and CASS 7.2.19R (Client money: allocated but unclaimed client money) if it has ceased to hold *client money*; these *rules* apply to both repayment and transfer to a third party;

(3) the *firm* has ceased to hold or control *custody assets* in accordance with instructions received from *clients* (including instructions set out in an agreement entered into in accordance with CASS 2.3.2R and COBS 6.1.7R (Information concerning safeguarding of designated investments belonging to clients and client money));
(4) the *firm* has repaid all *client deposits*, if it is ceasing to carry on *regulated activities* including *accepting deposits*;
(5) the *FSA* or another regulator has commenced an investigation against the *firm* or continuing enforcement action against the *firm*;
(6) there are any matters affecting the *firm* which should be investigated before a decision on whether the *firm* should have its *Part IV permission* cancelled by the *FSA* or be disciplined;
(7) the *firm* has unsettled or unexpired liabilities to *consumers*, for example, outstanding contracts (such as *deposits* or insurance liabilities);
(8) the *firm* has settled all its debts to the *FSA*; and
(9) the factors set out in SUP 6.4.19G apply.

The FSA's enforcement and investigation powers against a former authorised person

6.4.23 **[G]** If the *FSA* has granted an application for cancellation of *Part IV permission* and withdrawn a *firm's* status as an *authorised person* (see SUP 6.5) it will retain certain investigative and enforcement powers in relation to the *firm* as a former *authorised person*. These include:
(1) information gathering and investigation powers in Part XI of the *Act* (Investigation gathering and investigations) (see EG 3 (Use of information gathering and investigation powers));
(2) powers to apply to court for *injunctions* and restitution orders in Part XXV of the *Act* (Injunctions and restitution) (see *EG* 10 (Injunctions) and *EG* 11 (Restitution and redress));
(3) powers in Part XXIV of the *Act* (Insolvency) to petition for administration *orders* or winding up *orders* against *companies* or insolvent *partnerships*, or bankruptcy *orders* (or in Scotland sequestration awards) against individuals (see EG 13 (Insolvency));
(4) powers in Part XXVII of the *Act* (Offences) to prosecute *offences* under the *Act* and other specified provisions (see *EG* 12 (Prosecution of criminal offences)).

6.4.24 **[G]** However, the *FSA* will not be able to use the following powers against former *authorised persons*:
(1) powers to take disciplinary action against *firms* by publishing statements of misconduct under section 205 of the *Act* (Public censure) or imposing financial penalties under section 206(1) of the *Act* (Financial penalties); and
(2) the power to require *firms* to make restitution under section 384 of the *Act* (Power of the FSA to require restitution).

6.4.25 **[G]** Consequently, the *FSA* considers that it will have good reason not to grant a *firm's* application for cancellation of *permission* where:
(1) it proposes to exercise any of the powers described in SUP 6.4.24G; or
(2) it has already begun disciplinary and restitution proceedings against the *firm* by exercising either or both of these powers against the *firm*.

6.4.26 **[G]** The *FSA's* use of those powers is outlined in *DEPP* 6 (Penalties).

How long will an application take?

6.4.27 **[G]**
(1) Under section 52(1) of the *Act* (Determination of applications), the *FSA* has six months to consider a completed application.
(2) If the *FSA* receives an application which is incomplete, that is, where information or a *document* required as part of the application is not provided, section 52(2) of the *Act* requires the *FSA* to determine the incomplete application within 12 months of the initial receipt of the application.
(3) Within these time limits, however, the length of the process will relate directly to the complexity of variation requested and whether the *firm* has fully wound down (run off) its activities at the time it applies. The *FSA* publishes standard response times on its website setting out how long the application process is expected to take in practice. From time to time, the *FSA* also publishes its performance against these times.

How will FSA make the decision?

6.4.28 **[G]** A decision to grant an application for cancellation of *permission* will be taken by appropriately experienced *FSA* staff. Where, however, the *FSA* staff dealing with the application recommend that a *firm's* application for cancellation of *Part IV permission* be refused, the decision will be taken by the *RDC* if the applicant makes representations to the *FSA*. If there are no representations, the decision will be made under *executive procedures*.

6.4.29 **[G]** See *DEPP* for *guidance* on the *FSA's* decision making procedures, including the procedures it will follow if it proposes to refuse an application for cancellation of *Part IV permission*.

6.5 Ending authorisation

6.5.1 **[G]** Under section 33(2) of the *Act* (Withdrawal of authorisation by the FSA), if the *FSA* cancels a *firm's Part IV permission*, and as a result there is no *regulated activity* for which the *firm* has *permission*, the *FSA* is required to give a *direction* withdrawing the *firm's* status as an *authorised person.*

6.5.2 **[G]** If the *FSA* concludes that it should grant a *firm's* application for cancellation of *permission* and end its *authorisation*, the *FSA* will:

(1) cancel the *firm's Part IV permission* under section 44(2) of the *Act*;

(2) withdraw the *firm's authorised* status under section 33(2) of the *Act* by giving the *firm* a direction in writing; and

(3) update the *firm's* entry in the *FSA register* to show it has ceased to be *authorised.*

Annex 1

SUP 6 Ann 1 [G]: Applications for variation and cancellation of Part IV permission

Ann1 **[G]**

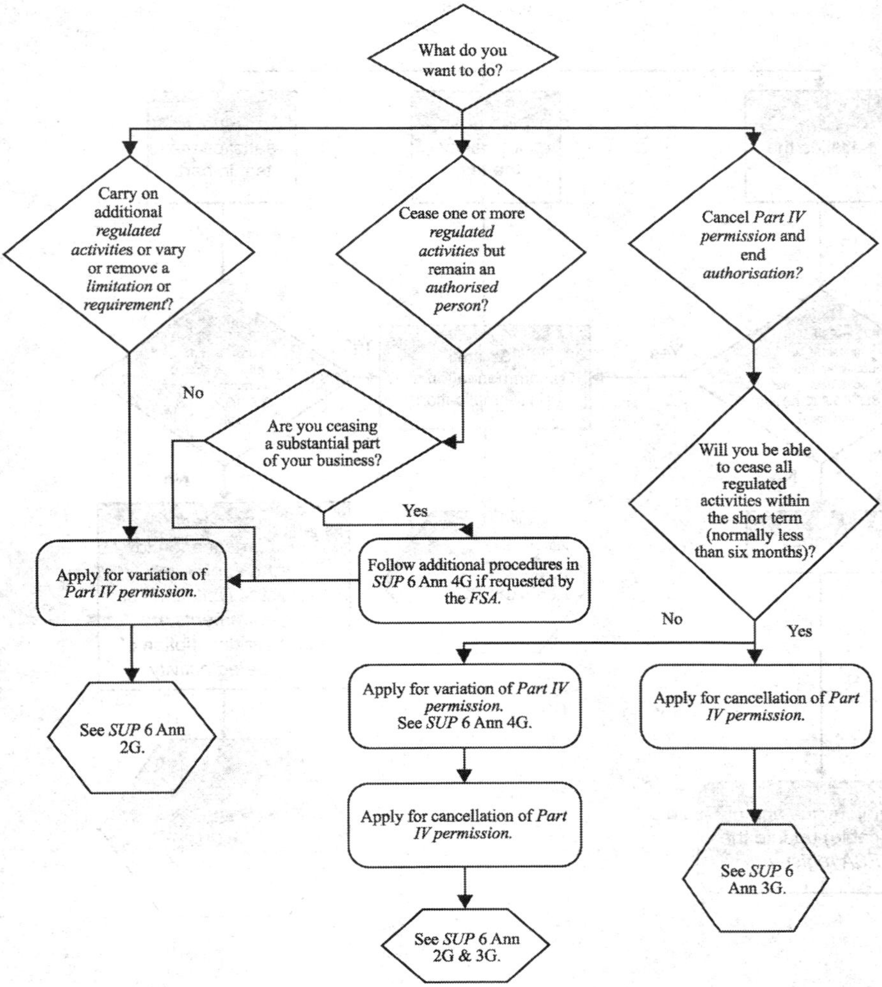

Annex 2

SUP 6 Ann 2 [G]: Summary of procedures on application for variation of Part IV permission

Ann2 **[G]**

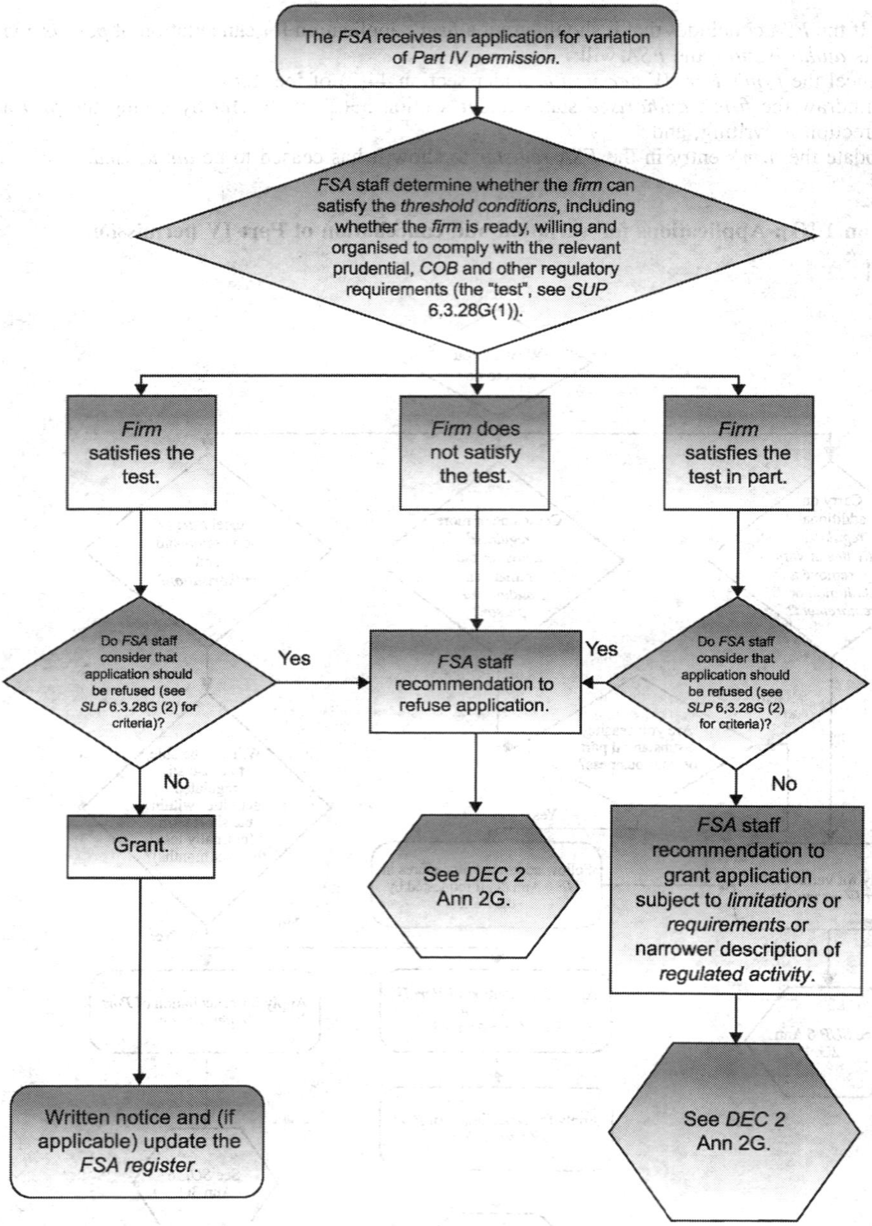

Annex 3

SUP 6 Ann 3 [G]: Summary of procedures on application for cancellation of Part IV permission

Ann3 **[G]**

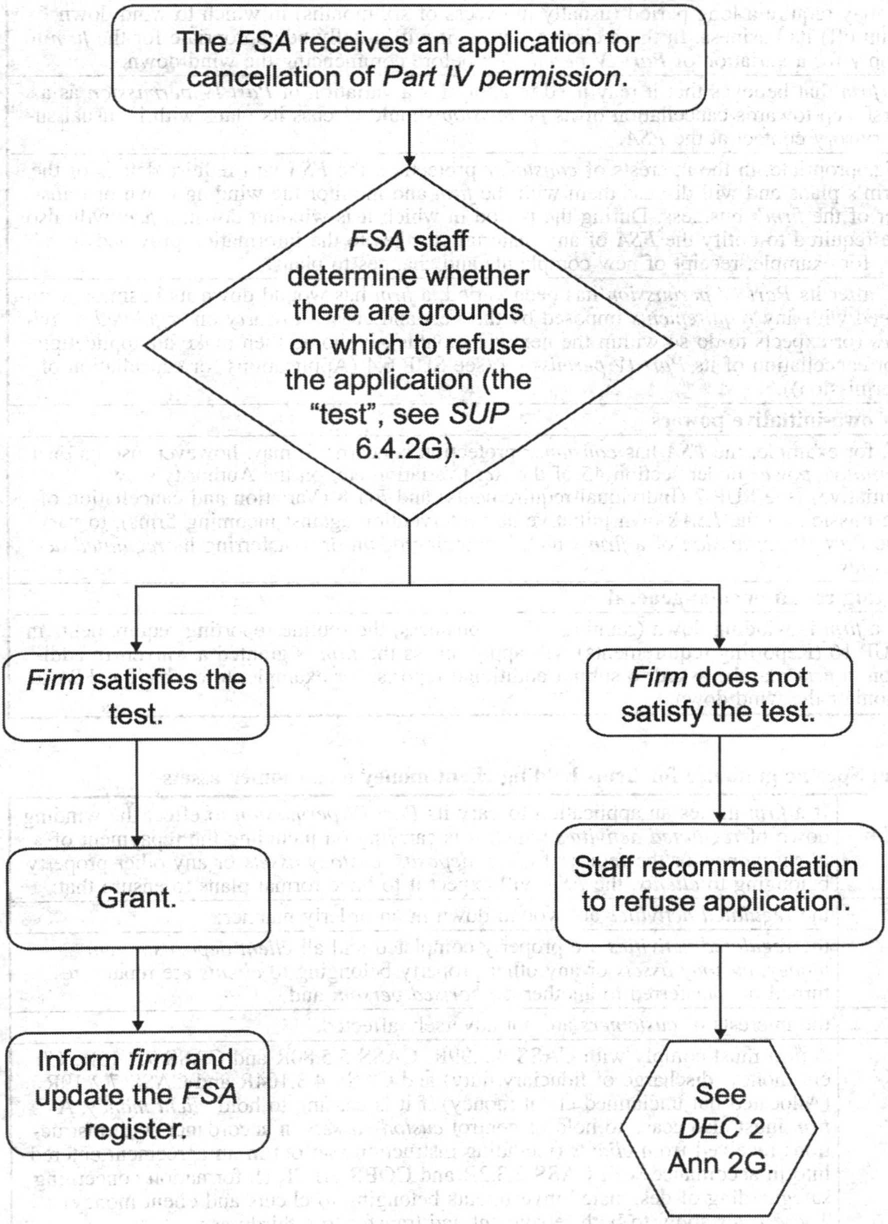
The *FSA* receives an application for cancellation of *Part IV permission*.
FSA staff determine whether there are grounds on which to refuse the application (the "test", see *SUP* 6.4.2G).
Firm satisfies the test.
Firm does not satisfy the test.
Grant.
Staff recommendation to refuse application.
Inform *firm* and update the *FSA* register.
See *DEC* 2 Ann 2G.

Annex 4

SUP 6 Ann 4 [G]: Additional guidance for a firm winding down (running off) its business

Ann4 **[G]**

1 Table: General

1.	If a *firm* has *Part IV permission* which enables it to hold *client money* or to carry on *regulated activities* including:

	(a)	*carrying out contracts of insurance* and *effecting contracts of insurance*; or
	(b)	*accepting deposits*;
	(c)	*safeguarding and administration of assets*;
	(d)	*meeting of repayment claims* or managing *dormant account funds* (including the investment of such funds;
	it may require a long period (usually in excess of six months) in which to wind down (run off) its business. In these circumstances, it will usually be appropriate for the *firm* to apply for a variation of *Part IV permission* before commencing the wind down.	
2.	A *firm* that believes that it may need to apply for a variation of *Part IV permission* as a first step towards cancellation of its *permission* should discuss its plans with its usual supervisory contact at the *FSA*.	
3.	If appropriate, in the interests of *consumer* protection, the *FSA* will require details of the firm's plans and will discuss them with the *firm* and monitor the winding down or transfer of the *firm's* business. During the period in which it is winding down, a *firm* will also be required to notify the *FSA* of any material changes to the information provided such as, for example, receipt of new complaints and changes to plans.	
4.	If, after its *Part IV permission* has been varied, a *firm* has wound down its business, complied with any *requirements* imposed by the *FSA* and ceased to carry on *regulated activities* (or expects to do so within the next six months), it should then make an application for cancellation of its *Part IV permission* (see SUP 6.4 (Applications for cancellation of permission)).	
Use of own-initiative powers		
5	If, for example, the *FSA* has *consumer* protection concerns, it may, however, use its *own-initiative power* under section 45 of the *Act* (Variation etc. on the Authority's own initiative) (see SUP 7 (Individual requirements) and *EG* 8 (Variation and cancellation of permission on the *FSA's* own initiative and intervention against incoming firms), to vary the *Part IV permission* of a *firm* which is winding down or transferring its *regulated activities*.	
Reporting requirements: general		
6	If a *firm* is winding down (running-off) its business, the routine reporting requirements in SUP 16 (Reporting requirements) will apply unless the *firm* is granted a waiver. In addition, a *firm* may be asked to submit additional reports, for example, to enable the *FSA* to monitor the wind down.	

2 Table: Specific guidance for firms holding client money or customer assets

1.	If a *firm* makes an application to vary its *Part IV permission* to effect the winding down of *regulated activities* which it is carrying on including the repayment of *client money*, or the return of *client deposits*, *custody assets* or any other property belonging to *clients*, the *FSA* will expect it to have formal plans to ensure that:
(1)	the *regulated activities* are wound down in an orderly manner;
(2)	the *regulated activities* are properly completed and all *client deposits*, *client money*, *custody assets* or any other property belonging to *clients* are repaid, returned or transferred to another *Authorised person*; and
(3)	the interests of *customers* are not adversely affected.
2.	A *firm* must comply with CASS 4.3.99R, CASS 5.5.80R and CASS 7.2.15R (Client money: discharge of fiduciary duty) and CASS 4.3.104R and CASS 7.2.19R (Allocated but unclaimed client money) if it is ceasing to hold *client money*. A *firm* must also cease to hold or control *custody assets* in accordance with instructions received from *clients* (including instructions set out in an agreement entered into in accordance with CASS 2.3.2R and COBS 7.1.7R (Information concerning safeguarding of designated investments belonging to clients and client money). These *rules* apply to both repayment and transfer to a third party.

3 Table: Specific guidance for insurers

1.		A *firm* carrying on *insurance business* which, ultimately, intends to cease *insurance business* completely, will first need to apply for a variation of its *Part IV permission* while it is running off its business. The *firm* should apply for a variation of *Part IV permission* to remove the activity of *effecting contracts of insurance* from its *permission*, thus restricting its activities to *carrying out insurance contracts* to enable it to run off its remaining insurance liabilities (see SUP 6.2.9G).
2.		Examples of variations of *Part IV permission* which may be appropriate in the context of winding down *insurance business* include:
	(1)	removing one or more *regulated activities* (for example, when a *firm* which has *Part IV permission* to carry on *insurance business* enters into run-off, its *Part IV permission* will need to be varied to remove the activity of *effecting contracts of insurance* in relation to new *contracts of insurance*); a new *contract of insurance* excludes contracts effected under a term of a subsisting *contract of insurance*. Thus the *firm's permission* will be restricted to *carrying out contracts of insurance* to enable it to run off its existing liabilities; or
	(2)	imposing a *limitation* on *regulated activities* in a firm's *Part IV permission* or imposing a *requirement* on the type of investments a *firm* holds to support its insurance liabilities.
3.		An *insurer* ceasing to *effect contracts of insurance* is required to submit a *scheme of operations* in accordance with SUP App 2 (Insurers: scheme of operations). The *FSA* may require other information depending on the circumstances, for example an actuarial assessment of the *firm's* run-off.
4.		A *firm* that is ceasing *effecting* new *contracts of insurance* in all categories of *specified investment* should refer to SUP App 2 for details of the specific reporting requirements that apply.
5.		An *insurer* should note that the *FSA* will not cancel a *firm's permission* until all the firm's insurance liabilities have been discharged, including any potential insurance liabilities. A *firm* is, therefore, advised to submit an application for cancellation of its *Part IV permission* when its run-off is completed.

4 Table: Specific guidance for firms in the Lloyd's market

1.		A *firm* making an application to vary or cancel its *Part IV permission* which requires any approval from the *Society of Lloyd's* should apply to the *Society* for this in addition to applying to the *FSA* for the variation or cancellation.
2.		Where a *firm* has *Part IV permission* to *manage the underwriting capacity of a Lloyd's syndicate as a managing agent at Lloyd's* then, if it wishes to vary its *Part IV permission* to remove this *regulated activity* or to cancel its *Part IV permission* completely, special procedures will apply.
3.	(1)	As a first step, the *firm* should apply to the *FSA* for a variation of its *Part IV permission* to limit the *regulated activity*, after the Lloyd's *syndicates* have been closed, to permit no new business. Once the *syndicates* have been closed, the *firm's* consent from the *Society* to manage *syndicates* will also lapse
	(2)	After a period of one year from the date of closure of the Lloyd's *syndicates* the *firm* may apply to the *FSA* to vary its *Part IV permission*, to remove the *regulated activity* or to cancel its *Part IV permission* entirely, as appropriate. At this time, a *firm's* approval from the *Society of Lloyd's* as a *managing agent* will cease.
4.		*Firms* which wish to discuss these procedures in more detail should contact their usual supervisory contact at the *FSA* and the *Society of Lloyd's*, as appropriate.

5 Table: Specific guidance for firms accepting deposits

1.	As stated in SUP 6.2.9G, where a *bank*, or other *firm* with permission that includes *accepting deposits*, wishes to cancel its *Part IV permission*, it will generally need to apply for a variation of that *permission* while it winds down its business.	
2.	When a firm is winding down its business activities, it may be appropriate to vary its *Part IV permission* by imposing:	
	(1)	a *limitation* that no new *deposits* will be accepted; or
	(2)	a *limitation* on the purchasing of *investments* for its own account; or
	(3)	*requirements* concerning solvency.
3.	After a *bank* has discussed with the *FSA* the type of variation of *Part IV permission* the *bank* requires to wind down its business, it should make an application for variation of *Part IV permission* as directed in SUP 6.3.15D and follow the *guidance* and procedures in SUP 6 as well as the additional procedures set out in this annex.	
4.	The *FSA* may vary the *firm's Part IV permission* to impose one or more of:	
	(1)	a *requirement* that the *firm* takes certain steps or refrains from adopting or pursuing a particular course of action or to restrict the scope of its business in a particular way;
	(2)	a *limitation* on *accepting deposits*, for example a *limitation* that no new deposits will be accepted;
	(3)	a *requirement* restricting the granting of *credit* or the making of investments;
	(4)	a *requirement* prohibiting the *firm* from soliciting *deposits* either generally or from *persons* who are not already depositors.
5.	The information concerning the circumstances of the application for variation of *Part IV permission* and the confirmations a *firm* is required to give to the *FSA* will differ according to the nature of the *bank* and its *Part IV permission*. If appropriate, it may include, but will not necessarily be limited to:	
	(1)	a plan containing the arrangements made in respect of the business of any current depositors, for example how and when the *firm* intends to repay or novate arrangements with depositors; or
	(2)	confirmation that the *bank* will not take any new *deposits*, will not roll over or renew any existing *deposits* at maturity and will repay all remaining *deposits* (including accrued interest) as they fall due for repayment
Dealing with residual deposits: general		
6.	Where a *firm* has residual *deposits* which, for whatever reason, cannot be repaid, they may be protected by a number of different methods. The precise applicability of the courses to be followed depends upon the particular circumstances of the individual *firm*. The *FSA*'s supervisory approach will be determined by the course of action taken.	
Holding funds on trust		
7.	In some circumstances, it may be appropriate for the *firm* to make an irrevocable transfer of funds, at least equal to the total of its *deposits*, to an independent *trustee* to be held on *trust* for the benefit of the depositors. Any such proposal should be discussed in advance with the *FSA*. The amount of funds held on trust should at all times exceed the total of all *deposits*, in order to provide for contingencies. Trust account arrangements are appropriate only in respect of solvent institutions. The *guidance* in paragraph 13 of this section applies in most cases.	
8.	(1)	A plan containing the arrangements should be made by the *firm* in respect of the business of any current depositors, for example how and when the *firm* intends to repay or novate arrangements with depositors.
	(2)	The *trustee* should be an independent and appropriately qualified third party, nominated by the institution and acceptable to the *FSA*.
		(a) The *trustee* should usually be a major *UK bank*. If appropriate, an additional trustee from within the institution may be appointed, preferably in an advisory role. An internal trustee may help to ensure continuity if the *firm* and the trust are likely to remain in existence for the foreseeable future.
		(b) The *FSA* should be consulted about, or pre-notified of, a potential change of trustee.

		(c) Trustees are responsible for fulfilling their obligations under the trust deed. In practice, the *FSA* may wish to point out that certain factors need to be given consideration by the trustees and the institution (for example, the procedures for paying out to depositors).
9.	The *FSA* would require to see an opinion by the *firm's* legal advisers, confirming the validity and enforceability of the *trust* and in particular specifying the extent (if any) to which the trust arrangements may be set aside in future. The *FSA* reserves the right to request sight of the proposed trust documentation itself.	
10.	The trustee has the right (and probably the obligation) to invest the funds, and in doing so should normally seek to "match" the maturity profile of the *firm's deposit* base. However, the following could result in *deposit* liabilities exceeding *trust* funds at any time:	
	(a)	maturity mismatches, that is, whether there are insufficient liquid funds across the maturity bands to repay depositors; or
	(b)	changes in interest rates; or
	(c)	the trustee's fees and disbursements.
11.	The trustee should not deposit, or otherwise invest, trust funds except in segregated accounts with third-party authorised institutions.	
	(1)	An auditor's report, similar to that used to determine whether all the *deposits* have been repaid by a *firm*, should be provided to confirm that all depositors have been repaid before the discharge of a trust is allowed.
	(2)	Auditors' reports, from the trust's auditors, should subsequently be obtained at intervals to demonstrate that funds in the trust continue to be at least equal to the remaining liabilities to depositors and that repayments have been properly made. The *firm* retains the ultimate responsibility to provide information to the *FSA*.
	(3)	The *FSA* may, however, require the inclusion of a clause in the trust deed requiring the trustee to provide such information as may be requested.
12.	Entering into a trust arrangement does not "transfer" deposits or discharge the *firm's* contractual obligations to its depositors.	
Holding the funds in segregated accounts		
13.	*The firm* may place and retain an amount at all times at least equal to its *deposit* liabilities in a segregated account with its usual bankers. The advantage of this course of action is that if all deposit liabilities are matched by funds in such an account, then the *firm* is not carrying on the *regulated activity* of *accepting deposits* in contravention of the *Act*.	
14.	Placing funds in a segregated account does not discharge a *firm's* contractual obligations to its depositors.	

Annex 5
SUP 6 Ann 5 [D]: Variation of permission application form

Ann5 **[D]**

This form has not been reproduced for technical reasons. Please refer to the FSA website.

Annex 6
SUP 6 Ann 6 [D]: Cancellation of permission application form

Ann6 **[D]**

This form has not been reproduced for technical reasons. Please refer to the FSA website.

CHAPTER 7
INDIVIDUAL REQUIREMENTS

7.1 Application and purpose

Application

[2160]
7.1.1 **[G]** This chapter applies to every *firm* which has a *Part IV permission.*

7.1.2 **[G]** The application of this chapter to an *incoming EEA firm, incoming Treaty firm* or *UCITS qualifier* with a *Part IV permission* (a "*top-up permission*") is limited as explained in SUP 7.2.4G.

Purpose

7.1.3 **[G]** The *Handbook* primarily contains provisions which apply to all *firms* or to certain categories of *firm*. However, a *firm* may apply for a waiver or modification of *rules* in certain circumstances as set out in SUP 8; or it may receive individual *guidance* on the application of the *rules*, as set out in SUP 9.

7.1.4 **[G]** The *FSA*, in the course of its supervision of a *firm*, may sometimes judge it necessary or desirable to impose additional *requirements* on a *firm* or in some way amend or restrict the activities which the firm has *permission* to undertake. The *guidance* in this chapter describes when and how the *FSA* will seek to do this.

7.1.5 **[G]** By waiving or modifying the requirements of a *rule* or imposing an additional *requirement* or *limitation*, the *FSA* can ensure that the *rules*, and any other *requirements* or *limitations* imposed on a *firm*, take full account of the *firm's* individual circumstances, and so assist the *FSA* in meeting the *regulatory objectives* (for example, to protect *consumers* and maintain market confidence).

7.2 The FSA's powers to set individual requirements on its own initiative

7.2.1 **[G]** The *FSA* has the power under section 45 of the *Act* (Variation on the Authority's own initiative) to vary a *firm's Part IV permission*. This includes imposing a statutory *requirement* or *limitation* on that *Part IV permission*.

7.2.2 **[G]** The circumstances in which the *FSA* may vary a *firm's Part IV permission* on its own initiative under section 45 of the *Act* include where it appears to the *FSA* that:
(1) one or more of the threshold conditions is or is likely to be no longer satisfied; or
(2) it is desirable to vary a *firm's permission* in order to protect the interests of consumers or potential consumers.

7.2.3 **[G]** The *FSA* may also use its powers under section 45 for enforcement purposes. EG 8 sets out in detail the *FSA's* powers under section 45 and the circumstances under which the *FSA* may vary a *firm's permission* in this way, whether for enforcement purposes or as part of its day to day supervision of *firms*. This chapter provides additional guidance on when the *FSA* will use these powers for supervision purposes.

7.2.4 **[G]** The *FSA* may use its powers under section 45 of the *Act* only in respect of a *Part IV permission*; that is, a *permission* granted to a *firm* under section 42 of the *Act* (Giving permission) or having effect as if so given. In respect of an *incoming EEA firm*, an incoming *Treaty firm*, or a *UCITS qualifier*, this power applies only in relation to any *top-up permission* that it has. There are similar but more limited powers under Part XIII of the *Act* in relation to the *permission* of an *incoming EEA firm* or incoming *Treaty firm* under Schedules 3 or 4 to the *Act* (see EG 8.26 to 8.27).

7.2.5 **[G]** If the *FSA* exercises its powers under section 45 of the *Act*, it will do so by issuing a *supervisory notice*. The procedure that will be followed is set out in DEPP 2.

7.2.6 **[G]** A *firm* has a right of referral to *the Financial Services and Markets Tribunal* in respect of the exercise by the *FSA* of its powers to vary, on its own initiative, the *firm's Part IV permission*.

7.3 Criteria for varying a firm's permission

7.3.1 **[G]** The *FSA* expects to maintain a close working relationship with certain types of *firm* and expects that routine supervisory matters arising can be resolved during the normal course of this relationship by, for example, issuing individual *guidance* where appropriate (see SUP 9.3). However, the *FSA* may seek to vary a *firm's Part IV permission*:
(1) in circumstances where it considers it appropriate for the *firm* to be subject to a formal *requirement*, breach of which could attract enforcement action; or
(2) if a variation is needed to enable the *firm* to comply with the *requirement*, due to agreements the *firm* may have with third parties. (For example a *firm* may be under a contractual obligation to do something, but only if it can do so lawfully. In this case, if the *FSA* considers the *firm* must not do it, then the *FSA* would need to prevent it doing so through a variation in its *Part IV permission* to enable the *firm* to avoid breaching the contractual obligation.)

7.3.2 **[G]** The *FSA* may seek to vary a *firm's Part IV permission* on its own initiative in certain situations, including the following:
(1) If the *FSA* determines that a *firm's* management, business or *internal controls* give rise to material risks that are not fully addressed by its *rules*, the *FSA* may seek to vary the *firm's Part IV permission* and impose an additional *requirement* or *limitation* on the *firm*.
(2) If a *firm* becomes or is to become involved with new products or selling practices which present risks not adequately addressed by existing requirements, the *FSA* may seek to vary the *firm's Part IV permission* in respect of those risks.
(3) If there has been a change in a *firm's* structure, *controllers*, activities or strategy which generate material uncertainty or create unusual or exceptional risks, then the *FSA* may seek to vary the *firm's Part IV permission*. (See also SUP 11.7.14G to SUP 11.7.18G for a description of the *FSA's* ability to vary a *firm's Part IV permission* on a change in *control* under section 46 of the *Act*.)

(4) If a *firm* is a member of a *financial conglomerate* and the *FSA* is implementing supplementary supervision under the *Financial Groups Directive* with respect to that *financial conglomerate* by imposing obligations on the *firm*. Further material on this can be found in GENPRU 3.1 (Cross sector groups) and SUP 16.7.82R to SUP 16.7.83R (reporting requirements with respect to *financial conglomerates*).

7.3.3 **[G]** The *FSA* may seek to impose *requirements* or *limitations* which include but are not restricted to:

(1) requiring a *firm* to submit regular reports covering, for example, trading results, management accounts, *customer* complaints, connected party transactions;
(2) requiring a *firm* to maintain prudential limits, for example on large *exposures*, foreign currency *exposures* or liquidity gaps;
(3) requiring a *firm* to submit a business plan (or for an *insurer*, a *scheme of operations* (see SUP App2));
(4) limiting the *firm's* activities;
(5) requiring a *firm* to maintain a particular amount or type of financial resources.

7.3.4 **[G]** The *FSA* will seek to give a *firm* reasonable notice of an intent to vary its *permission* and to agree with the *firm* an appropriate timescale. However, if the *FSA* considers that a delay may be prejudicial to the interest of *consumers*, the *FSA* may need to act immediately using its powers under section 45 of the *Act* to vary a *firm's Part IV permission* with immediate effect.

CHAPTER 8
WAIVER AND MODIFICATION OF RULES

8.1 Application and purpose

[2161]

8.1.1 **[R]** This chapter applies to every:

(1) *firm* or *person* who is subject to *FSA rules* that wishes to apply for, consent to, or has been given a modification of or waiver of the *FSA's rules*;
(2) *person*, as respects a particular *AUT* or *ICVC*, who wishes to apply for, consent to, or has been given a modification of or waiver of the *rules* in COLL.

8.1.1A **[G]** This chapter is relevant to an applicant for a *Part IV permission*, as if that applicant were a *firm*. Where the chapter refers to usual supervisory contact, the applicant should read this as being the usual contact in the Permissions Department. Further, this chapter is relevant to a *person* who is subject to rules made by the *FSA* and where the chapter refers to a *firm*, this includes that person.

8.1.2 **[G]** A *recognised body* should see REC 3.3 for information on *waivers* of *rules* in *REC* under section 294 of the *Act*.

8.1.3 **[G]** This chapter is not relevant to the functions of the *FSA* acting in its capacity as the *competent authority* for the purposes of Part VI of the *Act* (Official Listing).

Purpose

8.1.4 **[G]** This chapter explains how the regime for the *waiver* of *rules* works.

8.2 Introduction

Waivers under section 148 of the Act

8.2.1 **[G]** Under section 148 of the *Act* (Modification or waiver of rules), the *FSA* may, on the application or with the consent of a *firm*, direct that its *rules*:

(1) are not to apply to the *firm*; or
(2) are to apply to the *firm* with such modifications as may be specified.

8.2.2 **[G]** The directions referred to in SUP 8.2.1G (1) and (2) are collectively referred to in the *Handbook* as *waivers*.

Waivers of rules in COLL

8.2.3 **[G]** Section 250 of the *Act* and regulation 7 of the *OEIC Regulations* allow the *FSA* to *waive* the application of certain *rules* in COLL to:

(1) a *person*, as respects a particular *AUT* or *ICVC*, on the application or with the consent of that *person*; and
(2) an *AUT* or *ICVC* on the application or with the consent of the *manager* and *trustee* (in the case of an *AUT*) or the *ICVC* and its *depositary* (in the case of an *ICVC*).

8.2.4 **[G]** Those *persons* to whom section 250 and regulation 7 of the *OEIC Regulations* are relevant, but who are not *firms*, should follow SUP 8 as if they were *firms*.

8.2.5 **[G]** Section 250 of the *Act* and regulation 7 of the *OEIC Regulations* work by giving effect to section 148 of the *Act* in respect of *waivers* given under section 250(2) and (3) and regulation 7(1) and (2) of the *OEIC Regulations*.

Rules which can be waived

8.2.6 **[G]** [deleted]

8.2.7 **[G]** [deleted]

8.2.8 **[G]** [deleted]

8.3 Applying for a waiver

Conditions for giving a waiver

8.3.1 **[G]** Under section 148(4) of the *Act*, the *FSA* may not give a *waiver* unless it is satisfied that:

(1) compliance by the *firm* with the *rules*, or with the *rules* as unmodified, would be unduly burdensome, or would not achieve the purpose for which the *rules* were made; and

(2) the *waiver* would not result in undue risk to *persons* whose interests the *rules* are intended to protect.

8.3.1A **[G]** Even if the conditions in section 148(4) of the *Act* are satisfied, the *FSA* will consider other relevant factors before giving a *waiver*, such as whether the *waiver* would be compatible with European law, including relevant EC Directives.

Publication of waivers

8.3.2 **[G]** The *FSA* is required by section 148(6) of the *Act* to publish a *waiver* unless it is satisfied that it is inappropriate or unnecessary to do so (see SUP 8.6).

Form and method of application

8.3.3 **[D]**

If a *firm* wishes to apply for a *waiver*, it must complete and submit the form in SUP 8 Ann 2D (Application form for a waiver or modification). The application must be given or addressed, and delivered, in the way set out in SUP 15.7.4R to SUP 15.7.9R (Form and method of notification).

(1)–(7) [deleted]

8.3.3A **[G]**

(1) The *FSA's* preferred method of submission for *waiver* applications is by e-mail or by online submission at www.fsa.gov.uk.

(2) The form is available on the *FSA's* website (see http://www.fsa.gov.uk/waivers/application_form).

8.3.4 **[G]** Before sending in a *waiver* application, a *firm* may find it helpful to discuss the application with its usual supervisory contact at the *FSA*. However, the *firm* should still ensure that all relevant information is included in the application.

Procedure on receipt of an application

8.3.5 **[G]** The *FSA* will acknowledge an application promptly and if necessary will seek further information from the *firm*. The time taken to determine an application will depend on the issues it raises. However, the *FSA* will aim to give *waiver* decisions within 20 *business days* of receiving an application which includes sufficient information. If the *FSA* expects to take longer, it will tell the *firm* and give an estimated decision date. A *firm* should make it clear in the application if it needs a decision within a specific time.

8.3.5A **[G]** The *FSA* will treat a *firm's* application for a *waiver* as withdrawn if it does not hear from the *firm* within 20 *business days* of sending a communication which requests or requires a response from the *firm*. The *FSA* will not do this if the *firm* has made it clear to the *FSA* in some other way that it intends to pursue the application.

8.3.6 **[G]** In some cases, the *FSA* may give a modification of a *rule* rather than direct that the *rule* is not to apply. The *FSA* may also impose conditions on a *waiver*, for example additional reporting requirements. A *waiver* may be given for a specified period of time only, after which time it will cease to apply. A *firm* wishing to extend the duration of a *waiver* should follow the procedure in SUP 8.3.3D. A *waiver* will not apply retrospectively.

8.3.7 **[G]** If the *FSA* decides not to give a *waiver*, it will give reasons for the decision.

8.3.8 **[G]** A *firm* may withdraw its application at any time up to the giving of the *waiver*. In doing so, a *firm* should give the *FSA* its reasons for withdrawing the application.

8.3.9 **[G]** If the *FSA* believes that a particular *waiver* given to a *firm* may have relevance to other *firms*, it may publish general details about the possible availability of the *waiver*. For example, IPRU(INV) 3-80(10)G explains that a *firm* that wishes to use its own internal model to calculate its position risk requirement (PRR) will need to apply for a *waiver* of the relevant *rules*.

Giving a waiver with consent rather than on an application

8.3.10 **[G]** Under section 148(2) of the *Act* the *FSA* may give a *waiver* with the consent of a *firm*. This power may be used by the *FSA* in exceptional circumstances where the *FSA* considers that a *waiver* should apply to a number of *firms* (for example, where a *rule* unmodified may not meet the particular circumstances of a particular category of *firm*). In such cases the *FSA* will inform the *firms* concerned that the *waiver* is available, either by contacting *firms* individually or by publishing details of the availability of the *waiver* on the *FSA's* website. The *firms* concerned will not have to make a formal application but will have to give their written consent for the *waiver* to apply.

Waiver of an evidential provision

8.3.11 **[G]** An application for a *waiver* of an *evidential provision* will normally be granted only if a breach of the underlying binding *rule* is actionable under section 150 of the *Act*. Individual *guidance* would normally be a more appropriate response (see SUP 9 (Individual Guidance)) if there is no right of action.

8.3.12 **[G]** An application for a *waiver* of the presumption of compliance created by an *evidential provision* would not normally be granted.

8.3.13 **[G]** For an application for a *waiver* of the presumption of contravention of a binding *rule*, which is actionable under section 150 of the *Act*, the *FSA* would normally wish to be satisfied that the evidential *rule* is itself unduly burdensome or does not achieve the purpose of the *rule*.

Waiver of a two-way evidential provision

8.3.14 **[G]** In the case of an application for a *waiver* of a two-way *evidential provision* relating to an actionable binding *rule*, the policy in SUP 8.3.12G would apply to the presumption of compliance and the policy in SUP 8.3.13G would apply to the presumption of contravention. In other words, any modification is likely to be in relation to the second presumption only.

8.4 Reliance on waivers

Application of waived rules

8.4.1 **[G]** If the *FSA* gives a *firm* a *waiver*, then the relevant *rule* no longer applies to the *firm*. But:

(1) if a *waiver* directs that a *rule* is to apply to a *firm* with modifications, then contravention of the modified *rule* could lead to *FSA* enforcement action and (if applicable) a right of action under section 150 of the *Act* (Actions for damages); and

(2) if a *waiver* is given subject to a condition, it will not apply to activities conducted in breach of the condition, and those activities, if in breach of the original *rule*, could lead to *FSA* enforcement action or such a right of action.

The effect of rule changes on waivers

8.4.2 **[G]** Substantive changes to the *rules* (this would not include simple editorial changes) in the *Handbook* may affect existing *waivers*, changing their practical effect and creating a need for a change to the original *waiver*. The *FSA* will consult on proposed *rule* changes. A *firm* should note proposed *rule* changes and discuss the impact on a *waiver* with its usual supervisory contact at the *FSA*.

8.5 Notification of altered circumstances relating to waivers

8.5.1 **[R]** A *firm* which has applied for or has been granted a *waiver* must notify the *FSA* immediately if it becomes aware of any matter which could affect the continuing relevance or appropriateness of the application or the *waiver*.

8.5.2 **[G]** *Firms* are also referred to SUP 15.6 (Inaccurate, false or misleading information). This requires, in SUP 15.6.4R, a *firm* to notify the *FSA* if false, misleading, incomplete or inaccurate information has been provided. This would apply in relation to information provided in an application for a *waiver*.

8.6 Publication of waivers

Requirement to publish

8.6.1 **[G]** The *FSA* is required by section 148(6) of the *Act* to publish a *waiver* unless it is satisfied that it is inappropriate or unnecessary to do so. If the *FSA* publishes a *waiver*, it will not publish details of why a *waiver* was required or any of the supporting information given in a *waiver* application.

Matters for consideration

8.6.2 **[G]** When considering whether it is satisfied under section 148(6), the *FSA* is required by section 148(7) of the *Act*:

Part II FSA Handbook Materials

(1) to take into account whether the *waiver* relates to a *rule* contravention of which is actionable under section 150 of the *Act* (Actions for damages); Schedule 5 identifies such *rules*;
(2) to consider whether its publication would prejudice, to an unreasonable degree, the commercial interests of the *firm* concerned, or any other member of its *immediate group*; and
(3) to consider whether its publication would be contrary to an international obligation of the *United Kingdom* (for example, the confidentiality obligations in the *Single Market Directives*).

8.6.3 **[G]** *Waivers* can affect the legal rights of third parties, including *consumers*. In the *FSA's* view it is important that the fact and effect of such *waivers* should be transparent. So the fact that a *waiver* relates to a *rule* that is actionable under section 150 of the *Act* (see SUP 8.6.2G(1)) will tend to argue in favour of publication.

8.6.4 **[G]** In making *waiver* applications under section 250 of the *Act* or regulation 7 of the *OEIC Regulations*, SUP 8.6.2G(2) should be read in application to *rules* in COLL as if the word "commercial" were omitted.

8.6.5 **[G]** In considering whether commercial interests would be prejudiced to an unreasonable degree (see SUP 8.6.2G(2)), the *FSA* will weigh the prejudice to *firms'* commercial interests against the interests of *consumers*, markets and other third parties in disclosure. In doing so the *FSA* will consider factors such as the extent to which publication of the *waiver* would involve the premature release of proprietary information to commercial rivals, for example relating to a product innovation, or reveal information which could reasonably be regarded as the *firm's* own intellectual property. In line with section 148(8) of the *Act*, the *FSA* will also consider whether prejudice to a *firm's* commercial interests could be avoided or mitigated by publication of the *waiver* without disclosing the identity of the *firm*.

8.6.6 **[G]** The *FSA* may consider publication unnecessary where, for example, the *waiver* relates to a minor matter that does not affect any third party and is unlikely to be of relevance or interest to other *firms*.

Firm's objection to publication

8.6.7 **[G]** If, after taking into account the matters in SUP 8.6.2G to SUP 8.6.6G, a *firm* believes there are good grounds for the *FSA* either to withhold publication or to publish the *waiver* without disclosing the identity of the *firm*, it should make this clear in its application (see SUP 8.3.3D(7)). If the *FSA* proposes to publish a *waiver* against the wishes of the *firm*, the *FSA* will give the *firm* the opportunity to withdraw its application before the *waiver* is given.

Withholding publication for a limited period

8.6.8 **[G]** A decision to withhold a *waiver* or identity of a *firm* from publication may be for a limited period only, usually as long as the duration of the relevant grounds for non-publication. If the *FSA* proposes to publish information about a *waiver* that had previously been withheld, it will first give the *firm* an opportunity to make representations.

Means of publication

8.6.9 **[G]** The principal means of publication of *waiver* information will be the *FSA's* website (www.fsa.gov.uk).

8.7 Varying waivers

8.7.1 **[G]** Once the *FSA* has given a *waiver*, it may vary it with the *firm's* consent, or on the *firm's* application. If a *firm* wishes the *FSA* to vary a *waiver*, it should follow the procedures in SUP 8.3.3D, giving reasons for the application. In a case where a *waiver* has been given to a number of *firms* (see SUP 8.3.10G), if the *FSA* wishes to vary such *waivers* with the consent of those *firms*, it will follow the procedures in SUP 8.3.10G.

8.7.2 **[G]** If the *waiver* that has been varied has previously been published, the *FSA* will publish the variation unless it is satisfied that it is inappropriate or unnecessary to do so, having regard to any representation made by the *firm*.

8.8 Revoking waivers

8.8.1 **[G]** The *FSA* may revoke a *waiver* at any time. In deciding whether to revoke a *waiver*, the FSA will consider whether the conditions in section 148(4) of the *Act* are no longer satisfied (see *SUP 8.3.1G), and whether the* *waiver* is otherwise no longer appropriate. The *FSA* may revoke a *waiver* with immediate effect, if it considers that this is necessary, for example, in order to prevent undue risk to *consumers*.

8.8.2 **[G]** If the *FSA* proposes to revoke a *waiver*, or revokes a *waiver* with immediate effect, it will:
(1) give the *firm* written notice either of its proposal, or of its action, giving reasons;

(2) state in the notice a reasonable period (usually 28 *days*) within which the *firm* can make representations about the proposal or action; if a *firm* wants to make oral representations, it should inform the *FSA* as quickly as possible, specify who will make the representations and which matters will be covered; the *FSA* will inform the *firm* of the time and place for hearing the representations and may request a written summary;

(3) after considering any representations, in the case of a proposed revocation, give the *firm* written confirmation of its decision to revoke the *waiver* or not; or, in the case of a revocation that has already taken effect, either confirm the revocation or seek the *firm's* consent to a new *waiver*.

8.8.3 **[G]** If the *waiver* that has been revoked has previously been published, the *FSA* will publish the revocation unless it is satisfied that it is inappropriate or unnecessary to do so, having regard to any representations made by the *firm*.

8.9 Decision making

8.9.1 **[G]** The *waivers* regime is overseen by a staff committee. Its responsibility is to ensure that the giving of *waivers* is in accordance with the requirements of the *Act*, of the *guidance* in SUP 8 and of other relevant *guidance*. Decisions on individual applications are made under arrangements designed to result in rapid, responsive and well-informed decision making. The arrangements include arrangements for collective decision making to set general policies, and, as necessary, determine cases for applications with substantially common characteristics (for example, *waivers* in relation to the same *rule* or related *rules* or by *firms* in a similar position). It also includes arrangements for decision making by individuals within established precedents and policies.

8.9.2 **[G]** If the *FSA*, in the course of carrying on supplementary supervision of a *financial conglomerate*, is considering exercising its powers under section 148 of the *Act* (Modification or waiver of rules), regulation 4 of the *Financial Groups Directive Regulations* contains special provisions. The *FSA* must, in broad terms, do two things. Where required by those regulations, it must obtain the consent of the relevant competent authorities of the group. And, where required by those Regulations, it must consult those competent authorities.

Annex 1
SUP 8: Waiver and modification of rules

Ann1 **[G]**

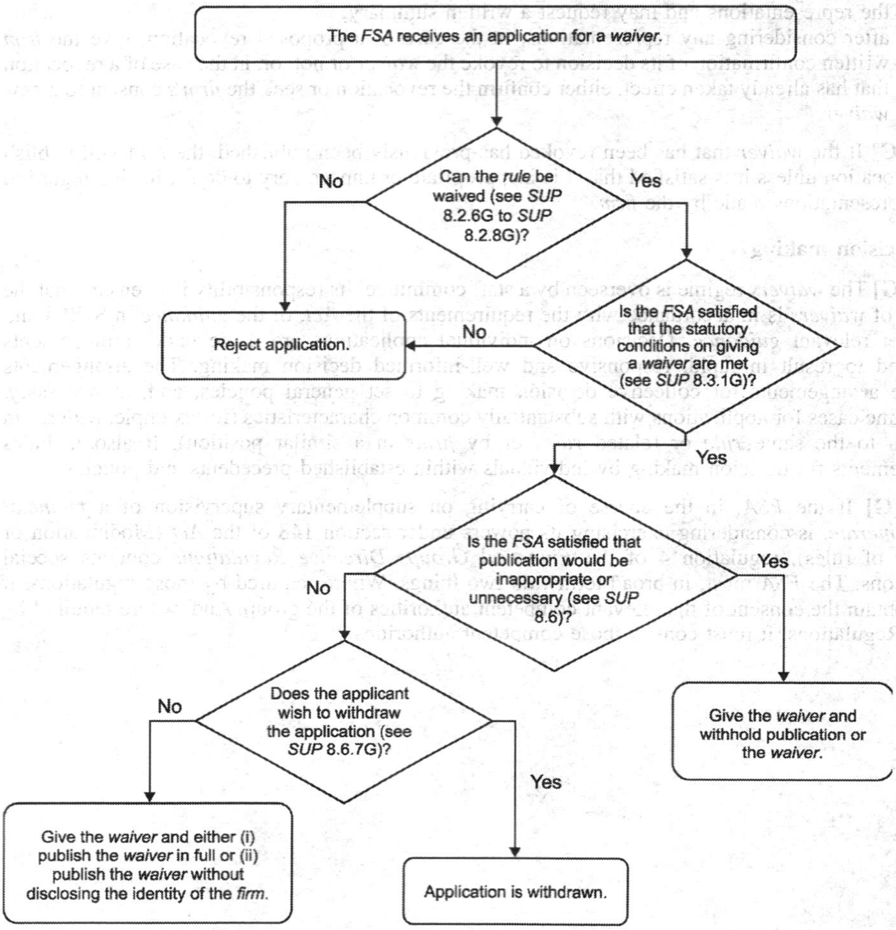

The FSA receives an application for a waiver.
Can the rule be waived (see SUP 8.2.6G to SUP 8.2.8G)?
No
Yes
Is the FSA satisfied that the statutory conditions on giving a waiver are met (see SUP 8.3.1G)?
No
Reject application.
Yes
Is the FSA satisfied that publication would be inappropriate or unnecessary (see SUP 8.6)?
No
Yes
Give the waiver and withhold publication or the waiver.
Does the applicant wish to withdraw the application (see SUP 8.6.7G)?
No
Yes
Give the waiver and either (i) publish the waiver in full or (ii) publish the waiver without disclosing the identity of the firm.
Application is withdrawn.

Annex 2
Application form for a waiver or modification of rules

This annex consists only of one or more forms. Forms are to be found through the 'Forms' link at www.fsa.gov.uk/handbook or through the Handbook section of the CD-ROM under Forms.

CHAPTER 9
INDIVIDUAL GUIDANCE

9.1 Application and purpose

Application

[2162]
9.1.1 **[G]**
(1) This chapter applies to:
 (a) every *firm*
 (b) *persons* that are subject to the requirements of the *Part 6 rules*; and
 (c) *persons* generally.
(2) SUP 9.3 (Giving individual guidance to a firm on the FSA's own initiative) is, however, only relevant to a *firm*.

Purpose

9.1.2 **[G]** Individual *guidance* is *guidance* that is not given to *persons* or regulated *persons* generally or to a class of regulated *person*. It will normally be given to one particular *person*, which relates to its own particular circumstances or plans. It may be oral or written. Individual *guidance* will not be published but may at the *FSA's* discretion be converted to general *guidance* and published in the *Handbook*. Written individual *guidance* will often be labelled as such

9.1.3 **[G]** A *person* may need to ask the *FSA* for individual *guidance* on how the *rules* and general *guidance* in the *Handbook*, the *Act* or other regulatory requirements apply in their particular circumstances. This chapter describes how a *person* may do this. Section 157 of the *Act* gives the *FSA* the power to give *guidance* consisting of such information and advice as it considers appropriate.

9.1.4 **[G]** The *FSA* may at times also consider it appropriate to give a *firm* individual *guidance* on its own initiative, for example on how it considers a *firm* should comply with a *rule*. SUP 9.3 describes when and how the *FSA* will seek to do this.

9.2 Making a request for individual guidance

How to make a request

9.2.1 **[G]** Requests for individual *guidance* may be made in writing or orally. If oral queries raise complex or significant issues, the *FSA* will normally expect the details of the request to be confirmed in writing. Simple requests for *guidance* may often be dealt with orally, although it is open to a *person* to seek a written confirmation from the *FSA* of oral *guidance* given by the *FSA*.

9.2.2 **[G]** Who to address a request to

A *firm* and its professional advisers should address requests for individual *guidance* to the *firm's* usual supervisory contact at the *FSA*, with the exception of requests for *guidance* on the *Code of Market Conduct* (MAR 1) which should be addressed to the specialist team within the Markets and Exchanges Division. A *firm* may wish to discuss a request for *guidance* with the relevant contact before making a written request.

9.2.3 **[G]** A *person* who is not a *firm* should address his request for individual *guidance* to the appropriate department within the *FSA*. A *person* who is unsure of where to address his request may address his enquiry to the *FSA*, making clear the nature of the request.

Discussions on a no-names basis

9.2.4 **[G]** The *FSA* does not expect to enter into discussions on a 'no-name' basis about the affairs of an individual *person* except in relation to SUP 9.2.4AG.

9.2.4A **[G]** The *FSA* may enter into discussions with a *person* on a 'no-names' basis about how a particular requirement in *the Part 6 rules* should be interpreted, but:

(1) the *FSA* will not be bound by any *guidance* given in response to the request; and

(2) the *person* receiving the *guidance* will not be able to rely upon it.

The FSA's response to a reasonable request

9.2.5 **[G]** The *FSA* will aim to respond quickly and fully to reasonable requests. The *FSA* will give high priority to enquiries about areas of genuine uncertainty or about difficulties in relating established requirements to innovative practices or products. What constitutes a 'reasonable request' is a matter for the *FSA*. It will depend on the nature of the request and on the resources of the *firm* or other *person* making it. The *FSA* will expect the *person* to have taken reasonable steps to research and analyse a topic before approaching the *FSA* for individual *guidance*. The *FSA* should not be viewed as a first port of call for *guidance*, except where it is only the *FSA* that can give the *guidance*, for example in confirming non-standard reports that it wishes to receive from a *firm*.

Information required by the FSA

9.2.6 **[G]** The *FSA* will always need sufficient information and time before it can properly evaluate the situation and respond to a request. If a request is time-critical, the *person* or its professional adviser should make this clear. The more notice a *person* can give the *FSA*, the more likely it is that the *FSA* will be able to meet the *person's* timetable. However, the time taken to respond will necessarily depend upon the complexity and novelty of the issues involved. In making a request, a *person* should identify the *rule*, general *guidance*, or other matter on which individual *guidance* is sought, and provide a description of the circumstances relating to the request. The *FSA* may request further information if it considers that it does not have sufficient information.

9.3 Giving individual guidance to a firm on the FSA's own initiative

9.3.1 **[G]** Business and internal control risks vary from *firm* to *firm*, according to the nature and complexity of the business. The *FSA's* assessment of these risks is reflected in how its *rules* apply to different categories of *firm* as well as in the use of its other regulatory tools. One of the tools the *FSA* has available is to give a *firm* individual *guidance* on the application of the requirements or standards under the *regulatory system* in the *firm's* particular circumstances.

9.3.2 **[G]** The *FSA* may give individual *guidance* to a *firm* on its own initiative if it considers it appropriate to do so. For example:

(1) the *FSA* may consider that general *guidance* in the *Handbook* does not appropriately fit a *firm's* particular circumstances (which may be permanent or temporary) and therefore decide to give additional individual *guidance* to the *firm*;

(2) some of the *FSA's* requirements are expressed in general terms; however, there may be times when the *FSA* will wish to respond to a *firm's* particular circumstances by giving individual *guidance* on the application of the general requirement in these circumstances;

(3) the *FSA* may consider that a *firm* should be given more detailed *guidance* than that contained in the *Handbook*; for example, where a *firm* holds positions in instruments of a non-standard form it may be appropriate to give the *firm* additional or more detailed *guidance* on how the *FSA* considers that it should calculate its financial resources requirement;

(4) in some instances a *rule* allows a *firm* to select which requirement, within a range of alternative requirements, a *firm* should comply with; in many instances, the *Handbook* gives *guidance* setting out the circumstances in which compliance with a particular requirement is appropriate; the *FSA* may sometimes consider it necessary to give additional individual *guidance* to tell a *firm* which requirement it considers appropriate;

(5) in relation to the maintenance of adequate financial resources, the *FSA* may give a *firm* individual *guidance* on the amount or type of financial resources the *FSA* considers appropriate, for example *individual capital guidance* for *BIPRU firms* and *insurers*; further *guidance* on how and when the *FSA* may give *individual capital guidance* on financial resources is contained in the Prudential Standards part of the *Handbook*:

  (a) for a *BIPRU firm*: GENPRU 1.2 and BIPRU 2.2;

  (b) for an *insurer*: GENPRU 1.2 and INSPRU 7.1;

  (c) for a *securities and futures firm* (or other *firm* required to comply with IPRU(INV) 3): IPRU(INV) 3-79R; and

  (d) for an *insurer*: INSPRU 7.

9.3.3 **[G]** If the *FSA* intends to give a *firm* individual *guidance* on its own initiative, it will normally seek to discuss the issue with the *firm* and agree suitable individual *guidance*.

9.3.4 **[G]** Individual *guidance* given to a *firm* on the *FSA's* own initiative will normally be given in writing.

9.4 Reliance on individual guidance

9.4.1 **[G]** Reliance by recipient of individual guidance

If a *person* acts in accordance with current individual written *guidance* given to him by the *FSA* in the circumstances contemplated by that *guidance*, then the *FSA* will proceed on the footing that the *person* has complied with the aspects of the *rule* or other requirement to which the *guidance* relates.

9.4.2 **[G]** The extent to which a *person* can rely on individual *guidance* given to him will depend on many factors. These could include, for example, the degree of formality of the original query and the *guidance* given, and whether all relevant information was submitted with the request. Individual *guidance* is usually given in relation to a set of particular circumstances which exist when the *guidance* is given. If the circumstances later change, for example, because of a change in the circumstances of the *person* or a change in the underlying *rule* or other requirement, and the premises upon which individual *guidance* was given no longer apply, the *guidance* will cease to be effective.

9.4.3 **[G]** If the circumstances relating to individual *guidance* change it will be open to a *person* to ask for further *guidance*.

Effect on rights of third parties

9.4.4 **[G]** Rights conferred on third parties (such as a *firm's clients*) cannot be affected by *guidance* given by the *FSA*. *Guidance* on *rules*, the *Act* or other legislation represents the *FSA's* view, and does not bind the courts, for example in relation to an action for damages brought by a *private person* for breach of a *rule* (section 150 of the *Act* (Actions for damages)) or in relation to enforceability of a contract if the *general prohibition* is breached (sections 26 and 27 of the *Act* (Enforceability of agreements)). A *person* may need to seek his own legal advice.

9.5 Disputes as to the interpretation of the Part 6 rules

9.5.1 **[G]** Where a *person* that is subject to any requirement of the *Part 6 rules* disagrees with the individual *guidance* given by the *FSA*, he can request that the *guidance* be reviewed at a meeting of senior *FSA* staff.

9.5.2 **[G]** Upon receiving a request under SUP 9.5.1G senior *FSA* staff will review:
(1) the initial request for *guidance*;
(2) the individual circumstances of the *person* seeking the review; and
(3) the reasons why the *person* does not agree with the individual *guidance*.

9.5.3 **[G]** The outcome of the senior *FSA* staff meeting will be communicated to the *person*.

9.5.4 **[G]** A *person* that does not agree with the individual *guidance* that results from a senior *FSA* staff meeting, or a third party that is directly affected by that individual *guidance* may request that the *guidance* be reviewed by the Listing Authority Review Committee.

9.5.5 **[G]** The Listing Authority Review Committee has powers, delegated by the *FSA* Board, to resolve disputes on the application and interpretation of the requirements set out in LR, DR and PR. A managing *director* of the *FSA* sits as chairman of the Listing Authority Review Committee.

9.5.6 **[G]** The *person* requesting the review can make representations to the Listing Authority Review Committee either orally or in writing.

9.5.7 **[G]** All decisions of the Listing Authority Review Committee are final and are determinative of the *FSA's* opinion as to the interpretation or application of the requirement in question.

CHAPTER 10
APPROVED PERSONS

10.1 Application

General

[2163]
10.1.1 **[R]** This chapter applies to every *firm*.

10.1.2 **[G]** This chapter is also relevant to every *approved person*.

10.1.3 **[G]** The *rules* in this chapter specify descriptions of *controlled functions* under section 59 of the *Act* (Approval for particular arrangements).

10.1.4 **[G]** The directions in this chapter relate to the manner in which a *firm* must apply for the *FSA's* approval under section 59 of the *Act* and other procedures.

10.1.5 **[G]** [deleted]

Overseas firms: UK services

10.1.6 **[R]** This chapter does not apply to an *overseas firm* in relation to *regulated activities* which are carried on in the *United Kingdom* other than from an establishment maintained by it or its *appointed representative* in the *United Kingdom*.

Overseas firms: UK establishments

10.1.7 **[R]** Only the following *controlled functions* apply to an *overseas firm* which maintains an establishment in the *United Kingdom* from which *regulated activities* are carried on:
(1) the *director function* where the person performing that function:
  (a) has responsibility for the *regulated activities* of a *UK branch* which are likely to enable him to exercise significant influence over that branch; or
  (b) is someone whose decisions or actions are regularly taken into account by the governing body of that branch.
(2) the *non-executive director function* where the person performing the function:
  (a) has responsibility for the *regulated activities* of a UK branch which is likely to enable him to exercise significant influence over that branch; or
  (b) is someone whose decisions or actions are regularly taken into account by the *governing body* of that branch.
(3) the *chief executive function*;
(4) the *required functions*;
(5) the *systems and controls function*;
(6) the *significant management function* in so far as the function relates to:
  (a) *designated investment business* other than *dealing in investments* as principal, disregarding article 15 of the *Regulated Activities Order*; or
  (b) processing confirmations, payments, settlements, insurance claims, *client money* and similar matters in so far as this relates to *designated investment* business; and
(7) the *customer function*.

10.1.8 **[G]** [deleted]

Incoming EEA firms, incoming Treaty firms and UCITS qualifiers

10.1.9 **[R]** This chapter does not apply to:
(1) an *incoming EEA firm*; or

(2) an *incoming Treaty firm*; or
(3) a *UCITS qualifier*;

if and in so far as the question of whether a *person* is fit and proper to perform a particular *function* in relation to that *firm* is reserved, under any of the *Single Market Directives*, the *Treaty* or the *UCITS Directive* to an authority in a country or territory outside the *United Kingdom*.

10.1.10 **[G]** SUP 10.1.9R reflects the provisions of section 59(8) of the *Act* and, in relation to an *incoming Treaty firm* and a *UCITS qualifier*, the *Treaty* and the *UCITS Directive*. It preserves the principle of *Home State* prudential regulation. In relation to an *incoming EEA firm* exercising an *EEA right*, or an *incoming Treaty firm* exercising a *Treaty right*, the effect is to reserve to the *Home State regulator* the assessment of the fitness and propriety of a *person* performing a function in the exercise of that right. A member of the *governing body*, or the notified *UK branch manager*, of an *incoming EEA firm*, acting in that capacity, will not therefore have to be approved by the *FSA* under the *Act*.

10.1.11 **[G]** But an *incoming EEA firm* (other than an *EEA pure reinsurer*), or *incoming Treaty firm*, will have had to consider the impact of the *Host State rules* with which it is required to comply when carrying on a *passported activity* or *Treaty activity* through a *branch* in the *United Kingdom*. An *incoming EEA firm* (other than an *EEA pure reinsurer*) will have been notified of those provisions under Part II of Schedule 3 to the *Act* in the course of satisfying the conditions for *authorisation* in the *United Kingdom*.

10.1.12 **[G]** An *incoming EEA firm* will have to consider, for example, the position of a *branch manager* based in the *United Kingdom* who may also be performing a function in relation to the carrying on of a *regulated activity* not covered by the *EEA right* of the *firm*. In so far as the function is within the description of a *controlled function*, the *firm* will need to seek approval for that *person* to perform that *controlled function*.

Incoming EEA firms: passported activities from a branch

10.1.13 **[R]** Only the following *controlled functions* apply to an *incoming EEA firm* with respect to its *passported activities* carried on from a *branch* in the *United Kingdom*:
(1) [deleted]
(2) [deleted]
(3) the *money laundering reporting function*;
(4) the *significant management function* in so far as the function relates to:
  (a) *designated investment business* other than *dealing in investments as principal*, disregarding article 15 of the *Regulated Activities Order*; or
  (b) processing confirmations, payments, settlements, insurance claims, *client money* and similar matters in so far as this relates to *designated investment business*; and
(5) [deleted]
(6) the *customer function* other than where this relates to the function in SUP 10.10.7AR (4).

10.1.13A **[R]** [deleted]

10.1.13B **[G]** [deleted]

10.1.13C **[G]** [deleted]

10.1.13D **[R]** If an *incoming EEA firm* is an *EEA pure reinsurer* then SUP 10.1.13R does not apply.
10.1.14 **[R]** Incoming EEA firms etc with top-up permission activities from a UK branch

In relation to the activities of a *firm* for which it has a *top-up permission*, only the following *controlled functions* apply:
(1) the *required functions*, other than the *apportionment and oversight function* and the *compliance oversight function*;
(2) the *significant management function* in so far as it relates to:
  (a) *designated investment business* other than *dealing in investments as principal*, disregarding article 15 of the *Regulated Activities Order*; or
  (b) processing confirmations, payments, settlements, insurance claims, *client money* and similar matters in so far as this relates to *designated investment business*; and
(3) [deleted]
(4) the *customer functions*.

10.1.15 **[G]** [deleted]

Appointed representatives

10.1.16 **[R]** The descriptions of the following *controlled functions* apply to an *appointed representative* of a *firm*, except an *introducer appointed representative*, as they apply to a *firm*:
(1) the *governing functions*, subject to SUP 10.1.16A R and except for a *tied agent* of an *EEA MiFID investment firm*;

(2) the *customer function* other than in relation to acting in the capacity of an *investment manager* (see SUP 10.10.7AR(6)).

10.1.16A **[R]**

(1) SUP 10.1.16R(1) is modified in relation to an *appointed representative* meeting the conditions in (2) so that only one of the following *governing functions*:
  (a) *director function*; or
  (b) *chief executive function*; or
  (c) *partner function*; or
  (d) *director of unincorporated association function*;

  applies, as appropriate, to an individual within that *appointed representative* who will be required to be an *approved person*.

(2) The conditions are that:
  (a) the scope of appointment of the *appointed representative* includes *insurance mediation activity* in relation to *non-investment insurance contracts* but no other *regulated activity*, and
  (b) the principal purpose of the *appointed representative* is to carry on activities other than *regulated activities*.

10.1.17 **[G]** [deleted]

Members of a profession

10.1.18 **[R]**

(1) This chapter, except in respect of the *required functions*, does not apply to an *authorised professional firm* in respect of its *non-mainstream regulated activities*, subject to (2).

(2) Where the *authorised professional firm* has appointed *approved persons* to perform the *governing functions* with equivalent responsibilities for the firm's *non-mainstream regulated activities* and other *regulated activities*, for the firm's *non-mainstream regulated activities* this chapter applies with respect to the *governing functions* and the *required functions* (other than the *apportionment and oversight function*) only.

10.1.19 **[G]** [deleted]

10.1.20 **[G]** [deleted]

Oil market participants, service companies, energy market participants, subsidiaries of local authorities or registered social landlords and insurance intermediaries

10.1.21 **[R]** The descriptions of *significant influence functions*, other than the *required functions*, and if the *firm* is a *MiFID investment firm*, the *governing functions*, do not extend to activities carried on by a *firm* whose principal purpose is to carry on activities other than *regulated activities* and which is:

(1) an *oil market participant*; or
(2) a *service company*; or
(3) an *energy market participant*; or
(4) a wholly owned *subsidiary* of:
  (a) a local authority; or
  (b) a registered social landlord; or
(5) a *firm* with *permission* to carry on *insurance mediation activity* in relation to *non-investment insurance contracts* but no other *regulated activity*.

10.1.22 **[G]** It will be a matter of fact in each case whether, having regard to all the circumstances, including in particular where the balance of the business lies, a *firm's* principal purpose is to carry on activities other than *regulated activities*. If a *firm* wishes to rely on SUP 10.1.21R, it should be in a position to demonstrate that its principal purpose is to carry on activities other than *regulated activities*.

Committees of the Society of Lloyd's

10.1.23 **[R]**

(1) For the purpose of SUP 10.6.4R (the *director function*), "director" includes an executive member of a committee to which the *Council* of the *Society of Lloyd's* directly delegates authority to carry out the *Society's* regulatory functions.

(2) For the purpose of SUP 10.6.8R (the *non-executive director function*), "*non-executive director*" includes a non-executive member of a committee to which the *Council* of the *Society of Lloyd's* directly delegates authority to carry out the *Society's* regulatory functions.

10.1.24 **[G]** [deleted]

10.1.25 **[G]** [deleted]

Insolvency practitioners

10.1.26 **[R]** This chapter does not apply to a function performed by:

(1) a *person* acting as an insolvency practitioner within the meaning of section 388 of the Insolvency Act 1986; or
(2) a *person* acting as a nominee in relation to a voluntary arrangement under Parts I (Company Voluntary Arrangements) and VIII (Individual Voluntary Arrangements) of the Insolvency Act 1986; or
(3) a *person* acting as an insolvency practitioner within the meaning of Article 3 of the Insolvency (Northern Ireland) Order 1989; or
(4) a *person* acting as a nominee in relation to a voluntary arrangement under Parts II (Company Voluntary Arrangements) and VIII (Individual Voluntary Arrangements) of the Insolvency (Northern Ireland) Order 1989.

10.2 Purpose

10.2.1 **[G]** The immediate purpose of SUP 10.3 to SUP 10.10 is to specify, under section 59 of the *Act*, descriptions of the 16 *controlled functions* which are listed in SUP 10.4.5R. The underlying purpose is to establish, and mark the boundaries of, the "approved persons regime".

10.2.2 **[G]** [deleted]

10.2.3 **[G]** [deleted]

10.2.4 **[G]** [deleted]

10.3 Provisions related to the act

Arrangements and regulated activities

10.3.1 **[R]** A function is a *controlled function* only to the extent that it is performed under an *arrangement* entered into by:
(1) a *firm*; or
(2) a contractor of the *firm*;

in relation to the carrying on by the *firm* of a *regulated activity*.

10.3.2 **[G]** Sections 59(1) and (2) of the *Act* provide that approval is necessary in respect of a *controlled function* which is performed under an *arrangement* entered into by a *firm*, or its contractor (typically an *appointed representative*), in relation to a *regulated activity*.

10.3.3 **[G]** *Arrangement* is defined in section 59(10) of the *Act* as any kind of *arrangement* for the performance of a function which is entered into by a *firm* or any of its contractors with another *person* and includes the appointment of a *person* to an office, his becoming a *partner*, or his employment (whether under a contract of service or otherwise). For the provisions in this chapter relating to outsourcing, see SUP 10.12.3G and SUP 10.12.4G.

10.3.4 **[G]** If, however, a *firm* is a member of a *group*, and the *arrangements* for the performance of a *controlled function* of the *firm* are made by, say, the *holding company*, the *person* performing the function will only require approval if there is an *arrangement* (under section 59(1)) or a contract (under section 59(2)) between the *firm* and *holding company* permitting this. This need not be a written contract but could arise, for example, by conduct, custom and practice.

10.3.5 **[G]** The *arrangement* must be "in relation to" the carrying on of a *regulated activity*. *Regulated activities* are defined in the *Glossary* by reference to the *Regulated Activities Order*. This order prescribes the activities which are *regulated activities* for the purposes of the *Act*.

10.4 Specification of functions

10.4.1 **[R]** [deleted]

10.4.2 **[G]** SUP 10.4.1R, together with the *table of controlled functions* in SUP 10.4.5R, specifies, in brief terms, the descriptions of the *controlled functions*. Other *rules* in this chapter contain the detail of the description for each function. Further *rules* in this chapter contain provisions which will apply to each description as indicated in those *rules*: see in particular SUP 10.1 for the application provisions.

10.4.3 **[G]** The fact that a *person* may be approved for one purpose does not have the effect of bringing all his activities within that *controlled function*.

10.4.4 **[G]** [deleted]

10.4.5 **[R]**

Table: Controlled functions

Type	**CF**	**Description of controlled function**
*Governing functions**	1	*Director function*
	2	*Non-executive director function*

Type	CF	Description of controlled function
	3	*Chief executive function*
	4	*Partner function*
	5	*Director of unincorporated association function*
	6	*Small friendly society function*
	7	[deleted]
*Required functions**	8	*Apportionment and oversight function*
	9	[deleted]
	10	*Compliance oversight function*
	11	*Money laundering reporting function*
	12	*Actuarial function*
	12A	*With profits actuary function*
	12B	*Lloyd's actuary* function
*Systems and controls function**	28	*Systems and controls function*
*Significant management function**	29	*Significant management function*
Customer functions	21	[deleted]
	22	[deleted]
	23	[deleted]
	24	[deleted]
	25	[deleted]
	26	[deleted]
	27	[deleted]
	30	*Customer function*

* significant influence functions

10.5 Significant influence functions

What are the significant influence functions?

10.5.1 **[G]** The *significant influence functions*, which are specified in SUP 10.4.1R, comprise the *governing functions* (see SUP 10.6), the *required functions* (see SUP 10.7), the *systems and controls function* (see SUP 10.8) and the *significant management function* (see SUP 10.9). SUP 10.5 applies to each of the *significant influence functions*.

The first condition

10.5.2 **[R]** Each *significant influence function* is one which is likely to result in the *person* responsible for its performance exercising a significant influence on the conduct of a *firm*'s affairs, so far as relating to a *regulated activity* of the *firm*.

10.5.3 **[G]** SUP 10.5.2R gives effect to section 59(5) of the *Act* (where this provision is referred to as the first condition).

10.5.4 **[G]** Whether a *controlled function* is likely to result in the *person* responsible for its performance exercising significant influence on the conduct of the *firm*'s affairs is a question of fact in each case. The *FSA* has identified the *significant influence functions* as satisfying this condition.

Periods of less than 12 weeks

10.5.5 **[R]** If:

(1) a *firm* appoints an individual to perform a function which, but for this rule, would be a *significant influence function*;

(2) the appointment is to provide cover for an *approved person* whose absence is:

  (a) temporary; or

  (b) reasonably unforeseen; and

(3) the appointment is for less than 12 weeks in a consecutive 12 month period;

the description of the relevant *significant influence function* does not relate to those activities of that individual.

Part II FSA Handbook Materials

10.5.6 **[G]** SUP 10.5.5R enables cover to be given for, say, holidays and emergencies and avoids the need for the precautionary approval of, for example, a deputy. However, as soon as it becomes apparent that a *person* will be performing a *controlled function* for more than 12 weeks, the *firm* should apply for approval.

10.6 Governing functions

Introduction

10.6.1 **[G]** Every *firm* will have one or more *persons* responsible for directing its affairs. These *persons* will be performing the *governing functions* and will be required to be *approved persons* unless the application provisions in SUP 10.1, or the particular description of a *controlled function*, provide otherwise. For example, each *director* of a *company* incorporated under the Companies Acts will perform the *governing function* in relation to that *company*.

10.6.1A **[G]** A *sole trader* does not fall within the description of the *governing functions*.

What the governing functions include

10.6.2 **[R]** Each of the *governing functions* (other than the *non-executive director function*) and the function described in SUP 10.6.4R(2)) includes where apportioned under SYSC 2.1.1R or SYSC 4.3.1R and SYSC 4.4.3R:
(1) the *systems and controls function*; and
(2) the *significant management function*.

10.6.3 **[G]** The effect of SUP 10.6.2R is that a *person* who is *approved* to perform a *governing function* (other than the *non-executive function* and the function described in SUP 10.6.4R(2)) will not have to be specifically approved to perform the *systems and controls functions* or the *significant management functions*. A *person* who is *approved* to perform a *governing function* will have to be additionally approved before he can perform any of the *required functions* or the *customer function*.

10.6.3A **[G]** A *firm* carrying on *insurance mediation activity*, other than a *sole trader*, must allocate to a *director* or *senior manager* the responsibility for the *firm's insurance mediation activity* (MIPRU 2.2.1R). MIPRU 2.2.2R(1) provides that the *firm* may allocate this responsibility to one or more of the *persons* performing a *governing function* (other than the *non-executive director function*).

10.6.3B **[G]** Where a *person* performing a *governing function* is also responsible for the *firm's insurance mediation activity*, the words "(insurance mediation)" will be inserted after the relevant *controlled function* (see MIPRU 2.2.5G).

Director function (CF1)

10.6.4 **[R]** If a *firm* is a *body corporate* (other than a *limited liability partnership*), the *director function* is the function of acting in the capacity of either a:
(1) *director* (other than *non-executive director*) of that *firm*; or
(2) a *person*:
   (a) who is a *director*, partner, officer, member (if the *parent undertaking* or *holding company* is a *limited liability partnership*), *senior manager*, or employee (other than a *non-executive director*) of a *parent undertaking* or *holding company* (except where that *parent undertaking* or *holding company* has a Part IV permission or is regulated by an EEA regulator); and
   (b) whose decisions or actions are regularly taken into account by the governing body of the *firm*.

10.6.5 **[G]** Examples of where SUP 10.6.4R(2) would apply include (but are not limited to):
(1) a chairman of an audit committee of a *parent undertaking* or *holding company* of a *UK firm* where that audit committee is working for that *UK firm* (that is, functioning as the audit committee for the *group*); or
(2) a *director* (other than *a non-executive director*) of a *parent undertaking* or *holding company* of a *UK firm* exercising significant influence by way of his involvement in taking decisions for that *UK firm*; or
(3) an individual (such as a *senior manager*) of a *parent undertaking* or *holding company* of a *UK firm* who is responsible for and/or has significant influence in setting the objectives for and the remuneration of executive *directors* of that *UK firm*; or
(4) an individual who is a *director* (other than *a non-executive director*) or a *senior manager* of a *parent undertaking* or *holding company* of a *UK firm* who is accustomed to influencing the operations of that *UK firm*, and acts in a manner in which it can reasonably be expected that an *executive director* or *senior manager* of that *UK firm* would act; or
(5) an individual of an *overseas firm* which maintains an establishment in the *United Kingdom* from which *regulated activities* are carried on where that individual has responsibilities for those *regulated activities* which are likely to enable him to exercise significant influence over the *UK branch*.

10.6.6 **[G]** [deleted]

10.6.7 **[G]** A *director* can be a *body corporate* and may accordingly require approval as an *approved person* in the same way as a natural *person* may require approval.

Non-executive director function (CF2)

10.6.8 **[R]**

(1) If a *firm* is a *body corporate*, the *non-executive director function* is the function of acting in the capacity of either a:

(a) *non-executive director* of that *firm*; or

(b) *non-executive director* of a *parent undertaking* or *holding company* (except where that *parent undertaking* or *holding company* has a *Part IV permission* or is regulated by an *EEA regulator*) whose decisions, or actions are regularly taken into account by the *governing body* of the *firm*.

(2) If a *firm* is a *long-term insurer*, the *non-executive director function* is also the function of acting in the capacity of an individual (other than an individual performing the *director function* or the *non-executive director function* under (1)) who, as a member of a committee having the purpose of a *with-profits committee*, has responsibility in relation to governance arrangements for *with-profits business* under COBS 20.3 (Principles and Practices of Financial Management).

10.6.9 **[G]** Examples of where SUP 10.6.8R(1)(b) would apply include (but are not limited to):

(1) an individual who is a *non-executive director* of a *parent undertaking* or *holding company* who takes an active role in the running of the business of a *UK firm*, for example, as a member of a board or committee (on audit or remuneration) of that *firm*; or

(2) an individual who is a *non-executive director* of a *parent undertaking* or *holding company* having significant influence in setting and monitoring the business strategy of the *UK firm*; or

(3) an individual who is a *non-executive director* of a *parent undertaking* or *holding company* of a *UK firm* involved in carrying out responsibilities such as scrutinising the approach of executive management, performance, or standards of conduct of the *UK firm*; or

(4) an individual who is a *non-executive director* of a *parent undertaking* or *holding company* of a *UK firm* who is accustomed to influence the operations of the *UK firm*, and acts in a way in which it can reasonably be expected that a *non-executive director* of the *UK firm* would act; or

(5) an individual who is a *non-executive director* of an *overseas firm* which maintains a branch in the *United Kingdom* from which *regulated activities* are carried on where that individual has responsibilities for those *regulated activities* which are likely to enable him to exercise significant influence over the *UK branch*.

Guidance on CF1 and CF2

10.6.10 **[G]**

(1) This paragraph explains the basis on which the *director function* and *non-executive director function* are applied to *persons* who have a position with the *firm's parent undertaking* or *holding company* under SUP 10.6.4R(2) or SUP 10.6.8R(1)(b).

(2) The basic position is set out in SUP 10.3.4G. As is the case with all *controlled functions*, SUP 10.6.4R(2) and SUP 10.6.8R(1)(b) are subject to the overriding provisions in SUP 10.3.1R, which sets out the requirements of sections 59(1) and (2) of the *Act*. This means that unless the *firm* has an *arrangement* or a contract permitting the performance of these roles by the *persons* concerned, these *persons* will not be performing these *controlled functions*. Therefore, the *FSA* accepts that there will be cases in which a *person* performing these roles will not require approval.

(3) However the *FSA* expects that in general a *person* who performs these roles will perform the *director function* or the *non-executive director function*. This is because the *FSA* would expect that a *firm* that allows major decisions to be taken by a group decision-making body will do so on the basis of a formal delegation from the *firm's governing body*. This delegation will amount to an *arrangement* for the purposes of section 59 of the *Act*.

Chief executive function (CF3)

10.6.11 **[R]** The *chief executive function* is the function of acting in the capacity of a *chief executive* of a *firm*.

10.6.12 **[G]** [deleted]

10.6.13 **[G]** This function is having the responsibility, alone or jointly with one or more others, under the immediate authority of the *governing body*, for the conduct of the whole of the business (or relevant activities); or, in the case of a *branch* in the *United Kingdom* of an *overseas firm*, for all of the activities subject to the *UK regulatory system*.

10.6.14 **[G]** For a *branch* in the *United Kingdom* of an *overseas firm*, the *FSA* would not normally expect the overseas *chief executive* of the *firm* as a whole to be approved for this function where there is a *senior manager* under him with specific responsibility for those activities of the *branch* which are subject to the *UK regulatory system*. In some circumstances, the *person* within the *firm* responsible for *UK* operations may, if the function is likely to enable him to exercise significant influence over the *branch*, also perform the *chief executive function* (see SUP 10.7.4G).

10.6.15 **[G]** A *person* performing the *chief executive function* may be a *member* of the *governing body* but need not be. If the chairman of the *governing body* is also the *chief executive*, he will be discharging this function. If the responsibility is divided between more than one *person* but not shared, there is no *person* exercising the *chief executive function*. But if that responsibility is discharged jointly by more than one *person*, each of those *persons* will be performing the *chief executive function*.

10.6.16 **[G]** Note that a *body corporate* may be a *chief executive*. If so, it will need to be approved to perform the *chief executive function*.

Partner function (CF4)

10.6.17 **[R]**

(1) If a *firm* is a *partnership*, the *partner function* is the function of acting in the capacity of a *partner* in that *firm*.

(2) If the principal purpose of the *firm* is to carry on one or more *regulated activities*, each *partner* performs the *partner function*.

(3) If the principal purpose of the *firm* is other than to carry on *regulated activities*:
   (a) a *partner* performs the *partner function* to the extent only that he has responsibility for a *regulated activity*; and
   (b) a *partner* in a *firm* will be taken to have responsibility for each *regulated activity* except where the *partnership* has apportioned responsibility to another *partner* or group of *partners*.

10.6.18 **[G]** [deleted]

10.6.19 **[G]** Any apportionment referred to in SUP 10.6.17R(3)(b) will have taken place under SYSC 2.1.1R or SYSC 4.3.1R and SYSC 4.4.3R. The *FSA* may ask to see details of the apportionment but will not require, as a matter of course, a copy of the material which records this (see SYSC 2.2).

10.6.20 **[G]** The effect of SUP 10.1.18R is that *regulated activity* in SUP 10.6.17R (and elsewhere) is to be taken as not including an activity that is a *non-mainstream exempt regulated activity*. Therefore, a *partner* whose only *regulated activities* are incidental to his professional services, in a *partnership* whose principal purpose is to carry on other than *regulated activities*, need not be an *approved person*. What amounts to the principal purpose of the *firm* is a matter of fact in each case having regard to all the circumstances, including the activities of the *firm* as a whole. Any *regulated activities* which such a *partner* carries on are not within the description of the *partner function*.

10.6.21 **[R]** If a *firm* is a *limited liability partnership*, the *partner function* extends to the *firm* as if the *firm* were a *partnership* and a member of the *firm* were a *partner*.

10.6.22 **[G]** [deleted]

10.6.23 **[R]** If a *partnership* is registered under the Limited Partnership Act 1907, the *partner function* does not extend to any function performed by a limited partner.

Director of unincorporated association function (CF5)

10.6.24 **[R]** If a *firm* is an unincorporated association, the *director of unincorporated association function* is the function of acting in the capacity of a *director* of the unincorporated association.

10.6.25 **[G]** [deleted]

Small friendly society function (CF6)

10.6.26 **[R]**

(1) If a *firm* is a *non-directive friendly society*, the *small friendly society function* is the function of directing its affairs, either alone or jointly with others.

(2) If the principal purpose of the *firm* is to carry on *regulated activities*, each *person* with responsibility for directing its affairs performs the *controlled function*.

(3) If the principal purpose of the *firm* is other than to carry on *regulated activities*, a *person* performs the *small friendly society function* only to the extent that he has responsibility for a *regulated activity*.

10.6.27 **[G]** [deleted]

10.6.28 **[R]**

(1) Each *person* on the *non-directive friendly society's governing body* will be taken to have responsibility for its *regulated activities*, unless the *firm* has apportioned this responsibility to one particular individual to whom it is reasonable to give this responsibility.
(2) The individual need not be a member of the *governing body*.

10.6.29 **[G]**
(1) Typically a *non-directive friendly Society* will appoint a "committee of management" to direct its affairs. However, the governing arrangements may be informal and flexible. If this is the case, the *FSA* would expect the society to resolve to give responsibility for the carrying on of *regulated activities* to one individual who is appropriate in all the circumstances. That individual may, for example, have the title of *chief executive* or similar. The individual would have to be an *approved person* under SUP 10.6.26R.
(2) Any apportionment of responsibilities will have taken place under SYSC 2.1.1R. The *FSA* may ask to see details of the apportionment but will not require, as a matter of course, a copy of the material which records this (see SYSC 2.2).

Sole trader function (CF7)

10.6.30 **[R]** [deleted]

10.6.31 **[G]** [deleted]

10.6.32 **[G]** [deleted]

10.7 Required functions

Apportionment and oversight function (CF8)

10.7.1 **[R]** The *apportionment and oversight function* is the function of acting in the capacity of a *director* or *senior manager* responsible for either or both of the apportionment function and the oversight function set out in SYSC 2.1.3R or SYSC 4.4.5R.

10.7.2 **[G]** [deleted]

10.7.2A **[G]** In requiring someone to apportion responsibility, a *common platform firm* should not apply for that *person* or *persons* to be approved to perform the *apportionment and oversight function* (see SUP 10.7.1R, SYSC 2.1.3R and SYSC 1.1.3R(5)).

10.7.3 **[G]** The fact that there is a *person* performing the *apportionment and oversight function*, and who has responsibility for activities subject to regulation by the *FSA*, may have a bearing on whether a manager who is based overseas will be performing a *controlled function*. It is a factor to take into account when assessing the likely influence of the overseas manager.

10.7.4 **[G]** Generally, in relation to a *UK* establishment of an *overseas firm* or a *firm* which is part of an overseas *group*, where an overseas manager's responsibilities in relation to the *United Kingdom* are strategic only, he will not need to be an *approved person*. However, where, in accordance with SYSC 3 or SYSC 4 to SYSC 10, he is responsible for implementing that strategy in the *United Kingdom*, and has not delegated that responsibility to a *senior manager* in the *United Kingdom*, he is likely to be performing a *controlled function*, such as, for example, the *chief executive function*. This is subject to SUP 10.1.13AR, which applies where the *firm* is a *MiFID investment firm* and the only *regulated activities* carried out by it in the *United Kingdom* are *MiFID business*.

10.7.4A **[G]** A *firm* carrying on *insurance mediation activity*, other than a *sole trader*, must allocate to a *director* or *senior manager* the responsibility for the *firm's insurance mediation activity* (MIPRU 2.2.1R). MIPRU 2.2.2R(2) provides that the *firm* may allocate this responsibility to the *person* performing the *apportionment and oversight function*.

10.7.4B **[G]** Where the *person* performing the *apportionment and oversight function* is also responsible for the *firm's insurance mediation activity*, the words "(insurance mediation)" will be inserted after this *controlled function* (see MIPRU 2.2.5G).

10.7.5 **[G]** [deleted]

EEA investment business oversight function (CF9)

10.7.6 **[R]** [deleted]

10.7.7 **[G]** [deleted]

Compliance oversight function (CF10)

10.7.8 **[R]** The *compliance oversight function* is the function of acting in the capacity of a *director* or *senior manager* who is allocated the function set out in SYSC 3.2.8R or SYSC 6.1.4R(2).

10.7.9 **[G]** [deleted]

10.7.10 **[G]** [deleted]

10.7.11 **[G]** [deleted]

10.7.12 **[G]** [deleted]

Money laundering reporting function (CF11)

10.7.13 **[R]** The *money laundering reporting function* is the function of acting in the capacity of the *money laundering reporting officer* of a *firm*.

10.7.13A **[G]** A *firm's* obligations in respect of its *money laundering reporting officer* are set out elsewhere in the *Handbook* (see SYSC 3.2.61R and SYSC 6.3.9R and for their scope, see the application provisions in SYSC 1 Annex 1).

10.7.13B **[G]** A *firm's* obligations in respect of its *money laundering reporting officer* are set out in SYSC 3.2.61R and SYSC 6.

10.7.14 **[G]** [deleted]

10.7.15 **[G]** [deleted]

10.7.16 **[G]** [deleted]

Appointed actuary function (CF12)

10.7.17 **[R]** The *actuarial function* is the function of acting in the capacity of an *actuary* appointed by a *firm* under SUP 4.3.1R to perform the duties set out in SUP 4.3.13R.

10.7.17A **[R]** The *with-profits actuary function* is the function of acting in the capacity of an *actuary* appointed by a *firm* under SUP 4.3.1R to perform the duties set out in SUP 4.3.16AR.

10.7.18 **[G]** [deleted]

10.7.19 **[G]** [deleted]

10.7.20 **[G]** [deleted]

10.7.21 **[G]** [deleted]

Lloyd's actuary function (CF12B)

10.7.22 **[R]** The *Lloyd's actuary function* is the function of acting in the capacity of the *actuary* appointed under SUP 4.6.1R to perform the duties set out in SUP 4.6.7R.

10.7.23 **[G]** [deleted]

10.8 Systems and control function

Systems and controls function (CF28)

10.8.1 **[R]** The *systems and controls function* is the function of acting in the capacity of an *employee* of the *firm* with responsibility for reporting to the *governing body* of a *firm*, or the audit committee (or its equivalent) in relation to:
(1) its financial affairs;
(2) setting and controlling its risk exposure (see SYSC 3.2.10G and SYSC 7.1.6R);
(3) adherence to internal systems and controls, procedures and policies (see SYSC 3.2.16G and SYSC 6.2).

10.8.2 **[G]** [deleted]

10.8.2A **[G]** Where an *employee* performs the *systems and controls function* the *FSA* would expect the *firm* to ensure that the *employee* had sufficient expertise and authority to perform that function effectively. A *director* or *senior manager* would meet this expectation.

10.8.3 **[R]** [deleted]

10.8.4 **[G]** [deleted]

10.8.5 **[G]** [deleted]

10.8.6 **[R]** [deleted]

10.8.7 **[G]** [deleted]

10.8.8 **[G]** [deleted]

10.9 Significant management functions

Application

10.9.1 **[R]** SUP 10.9 applies only to a *firm* which:

(1) under SYSC 2.2.1R and SYSC 4.4.3R, apportions a significant responsibility, within the description of the *significant management function*, to a *senior manager* of a significant business unit; or

(2) undertakes *proprietary trading*.

10.9.2 **[G]** The *FSA* anticipates that there will be only a few *firms* needing to seek approval for an individual to perform the *significant management function* set out in SUP 10.9.1R(1). In most *firms*, those approved for the *governing functions*, *required functions* and, where appropriate, the *systems and controls functions*, are likely to exercise all the significant influence at senior management level.

10.9.2A **[G]** A *proprietary trader* undertakes activities with the *firm's money* and has the ability to commit to the *firm*. By virtue of this role, all *proprietary traders* have potential to be able to exercise significant influence on the *firm* for the purposes of section 59(4) and (5) of the *Act*. It is therefore the *FSA's* expectation that all *firms* will assess all their *proprietary traders* to ascertain the ones for whom approval is required.

10.9.3 **[G]** The scale, nature and complexity of the *firm's* business may be such that a *firm* apportions, under SUP 10.9.1R(1), a significant responsibility to an individual who is not approved to perform the *governing functions required functions* or, where appropriate, the *systems and controls functions*. If so, the *firm* should consider whether the functions of that individual fall within the *significant management function*. For the purposes of the description of the *significant management functions*, the following additional factors about the *firm* should be considered:

(1) the size and significance of the *firm's* business in the *United Kingdom*; for example, a *firm* carrying on *designated investment business* may have a large number of *approved persons* (for example, in excess of 100 individuals); or a *firm* carrying on *general insurance business* may have gross written *premiums* in excess of £100mn;

(2) the number of *regulated activities* carried on, or proposed to be carried on, by the *firm* and (if relevant) other members of the *group*;

(3) its *group* structure (if it is a member of a *group*);

(4) its management structure (for example matrix management); and

(5) the size and significance of its international operations, if any.

10.9.4 **[G]** When considering whether a business unit is significant, the *firm* should take into account all relevant factors in the light of the *firm's* current circumstances and its plans for the *future*, including:

(1) the risk profile of the unit; or

(2) its use or commitment of a *firm's* capital; or

(3) its contribution to the profit and loss account; or

(4) the number of *employees* or *approved persons* in the unit; or

(5) the number of *customers* of the unit; or

(6) any other factor which makes the *unit* significant to the conduct of the *firm's* affairs so far as relating to the *regulated activity*.

10.9.5 **[G]** The question may arise whether a manager who is based overseas will be performing the *significant management function* under SUP 10.9.10R(1) and should therefore be an *approved person*. This is especially true where the *firm* operates matrix management. The fact there is a *person* performing the *apportionment and oversight function*, and who has responsibility for activities subject to regulation by the *FSA*, may have a bearing on this. It is a factor to take into account when assessing the likely influence of the overseas manager.

10.9.6 **[G]** Generally, in relation to a *branch* of a *firm*, or a *firm* which is part of an overseas *group*, where an overseas *manager* is responsible for strategy, he will not need to be an *approved person* under SUP 10.9.10R. However, where he is responsible for implementing that strategy in the *United Kingdom*, and has not delegated that responsibility to a *senior manager* in the *United Kingdom*, he is likely to be performing that *controlled function*.

10.9.7 **[G]** See also SUP 10.7.3G to SUP 10.7.4BG in relation to matrix management.

10.9.8 **[R]** [deleted]

10.9.9 **[G]** [deleted]

Significant management function (CF29)

10.9.10 **[R]**

(1) The *significant management function* is the function of acting as a *senior manager* with significant responsibility for a significant business unit that:

(a) carries on *designated investment business* or other activities not falling within (b) to (d);

(b) *effects contracts of insurance* (other than *contractually based investments*);

Part II FSA Handbook Materials

(c) makes material decisions on the commitment of a *firm's* financial resources, its financial commitments, its assets acquisitions, its liability management and its overall cash and capital planning;

(d) processes confirmations, payments, settlements, insurance claims, *client money* and similar matters.

(1A) The *significant management function* also includes the function of acting as a *proprietary trader.*

(2) This *controlled function* does not include any of the activities described in any other *controlled function.*

10.9.10A **[G]** A *senior manager* carrying on the *significant management function* under SUP 10.9.10R(1) with significant responsibility for a significant business unit that carries on activities other than *designated investment business* for the purposes of SUP 10.9.10R(1)(a) could, for example, be the head of a unit carrying on the activities of: retail banking, personal lending, corporate lending, salvage or loan recovery, or *proprietary trading*; or a member of a committee (that is, a *person* who, together with others, has authority to commit the *firm*) making decisions in these functions.

10.9.10B **[G]** A *proprietary trader* also undertakes activities which may have a significant influence on the *firm.* Such activities may require approval for CF29 under SUP 10.9.10R(1A).

10.9.11 **[G]** [deleted]

10.9.12 **[R]** [deleted]

10.9.13 **[G]** [deleted]

10.9.13A **[G]** A *firm* carrying on *insurance mediation activity*, other than a *sole trader*, must allocate to a *director* or *senior manager* the responsibility for the *firm's insurance mediation activity* (MIPRU 2.2.1R). MIPRU 2.2.2R(3) provides that the *firm* may allocate this responsibility to the *person* performing the *significant management function.*

10.9.13B **[G]** Where the *person* performing the *significant management function* is also responsible for the *firm's insurance mediation activity*, the words "(insurance mediation)" will be inserted after this *controlled function* (see MIPRU 2.2.5G).

10.9.14 **[R]** [deleted]

10.9.15 **[G]** [deleted]

10.9.16 **[R]** [deleted]

10.9.17 **[G]** [deleted]

10.9.18 **[R]** [deleted]

10.9.19 **[G]** [deleted]

10.9.20 **[G]** [deleted]

10.10 Customer function

10.10.1 **[R]** SUP 10.10 (*Customer functions*) applies with respect to activities carried on from an establishment maintained by the *firm* (or by its *appointed representative*) in the *United Kingdom.*

10.10.2 **[G]** Without SUP 10.10.1R the descriptions of the *customer functions* would extend to this function wherever it was performed. The effect of SUP 10.10.1R is that the descriptions is limited, in relation to *regulated activities* with an overseas element, in a manner which is broadly consistent with the scope of *conduct of business* regulation.

10.10.3 **[G]** The *customer function* has to do with giving advice on, *dealing* and arranging deals in and *managing investments*; it has no application to banking business such as deposit taking and lending, nor to *general insurance business.*

The customer conditions (the second and third conditions)

10.10.4 **[R]** The *customer function* is one which will involve the *person* performing it in dealing with *clients*, or dealing with property of *clients*, of a *firm* in a manner substantially connected with the carrying on of a *regulated activity* of the *firm.*

10.10.5 **[G]** SUP 10.10.4R gives effect to sub-sections (6) and (7) of section 59 of the *Act* (referred to in that section as the second and third conditions).

10.10.6 **[G]** The *FSA* interprets the phrase "dealing with" as including having contact with *customers* and extending beyond "dealing" as used in the phrase "dealing in investments". "Dealing in" is used in Schedule 2 to the *Act* to describe in general terms the *regulated activities* which are specified in Part II of the *Regulated Activities Order.*

10.10.7 **[R]** [deleted]

Customer function (CF 30)

10.10.7A **[R]** The *customer function* is the function of:

(1) *advising on investments* other than a *non-investment insurance contract* (but not where this is *advising on investments* in the course of carrying on the activity of *providing basic advice on a stakeholder product*) and performing other functions related to this such as *dealing* and *arranging*;

(2) giving advice to *clients* solely in connection with *corporate finance business* and performing other functions related to this;

(3) giving advice or performing related activities in connection with *pension transfers* or opt-outs for *retail clients*;

(4) giving advice to a *person* to become, or continue or cease to be, a member of a particular *Lloyd's syndicate*;

(5) *dealing*, as principal or as agent, and *arranging (bringing about) deals in investments* other than a *non-investment insurance contract* with or for, or in connection with customers where the *dealing* or *arranging deals* is governed by COBS 11 (Dealing and managing);

(6) acting in the capacity of an *investment manager* and carrying on functions connected to this.

10.10.7B **[R]** The *customer function* does not extend to an individual who is performing the functions in SUP 10.10.7AR (1) to (2) or SUP 10.10.7AR (5) to (6) and who is based overseas and who, in a 12 *month* period, spends no more than 30 *days* in the *United Kingdom* to the extent that he is appropriately supervised by a *person* approved for this function.

10.10.7C **[G]** The *FSA* would expect an individual from overseas to be accompanied on a visit to a *customer*. TC 2.1.9R (2) provides that the *firm* will have to be satisfied that the individual has at least three years' up-to-date relevant experience obtained outside the *United Kingdom*. However, the remaining provisions of TC 2.1.9R (2) are disapplied in these circumstances (except for an individual who gives advice to *retail clients* on *packaged products* or is a *broker fund adviser*). The effect of this is that such individuals need not pass the relevant regulatory module of an appropriate examination (see TC 2.1.9R (2)).

10.10.7D **[G]** The *customer function* in SUP 10.10.7AR (5) does not extend to the individual who, on the instructions of the *customer*, simply inputs the *customer's* instructions into an automatic execution system where no discretion is or may be exercised by the individual performing the activity. Nor does it extend to merely introducing a *customer* to a firm or distributing advertisements.

10.10.7E **[G]** An individual may *advise on investments* prior to being assessed as competent in accordance with the *rules* in the Senior Management Arrangements, Systems and Controls sourcebook (*SYSC*) and, where relevant, the Training and Competence sourcebook (*TC*). The *firm* shall record when that person subsequently becomes competent.

10.10.8 **[G]** [deleted]

10.10.9 **[G]** [deleted]

10.10.10 **[G]** [deleted]

10.10.11 **[R]** [deleted]

10.10.12 **[G]** [deleted]

10.10.13 **[R]** [deleted]

10.10.13A **[G]** [deleted]

10.10.14 **[R]** [deleted]

10.10.15 **[R]** [deleted]

10.10.16 **[R]** [deleted]

10.10.17 **[G]** [deleted]

10.10.18 **[G]** [deleted]

10.10.19 **[G]** [deleted]

10.10.20 **[R]** [deleted]

10.10.21 **[G]** [deleted]

10.10.22 **[G]** [deleted]

10.11 Procedures relating to approved persons

Forms

10.11.1 **[G]** The forms listed in SUP 10.11.2G are referred to in SUP 10.11 (Procedures relating to approved persons) to SUP 10.14 (Further questions).

10.11.2 **[G]**

Table: Approved persons forms

the relevant Form A	SUP 10 Ann 4D	Application to perform controlled functions under the approved persons regime
Form B	SUP 10 Ann 5R	Notice to withdraw an application to perform controlled functions under the approved persons regime
Form C	SUP 10 Ann 6R	Notice of ceasing to perform controlled functions
Form D	SUP 10 Ann 7R	Notification of changes in personal information or application details
Form E	SUP 10 Ann 8G	Internal transfer of an approved person

10.11.3 **[G]** A summary of the forms and their purposes is in SUP 10Ann2G. A summary of *FSA* procedures is in SUP 10Ann3G. For the method of notification to the *FSA*, see SUP 15.7 (Form and method of notification).

10.11.4 **[G]** Unless the context otherwise requires, in SUP 10.11 (Procedures relating to *approved persons*) to SUP 10.14 (Further questions) where reference is made to a *firm*, this also includes an applicant for *Part IV permission*, and other *persons* seeking to carry on *regulated activities* as an *authorised person*.

10.11.5 **[G]** Forms B, C, D and E can only be submitted in respect of an *approved person* by the *firm* that submitted an *approved person's* original application (that is, the relevant Form A).

10.11.6 **[G]** Copies of Forms A, B, C, D and E may be obtained from the *FSA* website or from the Individuals, Mutuals and Policy Department. To contact the Individuals, Mutuals and Policy Department for general enquiries:

(1) telephone 020 7066 0019; or
(2) fax 020 7066 0017; or
(3) write to:
Individuals, Mutuals and Policy Department,
The Financial Services Authority
25 The North Colonnade
Canary Wharf
LONDON E14 5HS; or
(4) e-mail iva@fsa.gov.uk

10.12 Application for approval and withdrawing an application for approval

When to apply for approval

10.12.1 **[G]** In accordance with section 59 of the *Act* (Approval for particular arrangements), where a *candidate* will be performing one or more *controlled functions*, a *firm* must take reasonable care to ensure that the *candidate* does not perform these functions unless he has prior approval from the *FSA*.

How to apply for approval

10.12.2 **[D]** An application by a *firm* for the *FSA's* approval under section 59 of the *Act* (Approval for particular arrangements) must be made by completing the Form A which relates to the particular type of *firm*, that is, a *UK firm*, *overseas firm* or *incoming EEA firm*.

Who should make the application?

10.12.3 **[G]**

(1) In accordance with section 60 of the *Act* (Applications for approval), applications must be submitted by, or on behalf of, the *firm* itself, not by:
  (a) the *candidate;* or
  (b) (where the candidate works for the *firm's parent undertaking* or *holding company*) by the *firm's parent undertaking* or *holding company*.
(2) Usually this will be the *firm* that is employing the *candidate* to perform the *controlled function*. Where a *firm* has outsourced the performance of a *controlled function*, the details of the outsourcing determine where responsibility lies and whom the *FSA* anticipates will submit *approved persons* application forms. SUP 10.12.4G describes some common situations. The *firm* which is outsourcing is referred to as "A" and the *person* to whom the

performance of the *controlled function* has been outsourced, or which makes the *arrangement* for the *controlled function* to be performed, is referred to as "B". In each situation, A must take reasonable care to ensure that, in accordance with section 59(2) of the *Act*, no *person* performs a *controlled function* under an *arrangement* entered into by its contractor in relation to the carrying on by A of a *regulated activity*, without approval from the *FSA*. See also SYSC 3.2.4G and SYSC 8.1.1R, and for *insurers* SYSC 13.9.

10.12.4 **[G]**

Table: *Outsourcing arrangements*

Outsourcing arrangements		**Submitting forms**
Firm A to firm B	The FSA will consider A to have taken reasonable care if it enters into a contract with B under which B is responsible for ensuring that the relevant controlled functions are performed by approved persons, and that it is reasonable for A to rely on this	Firm B submits approved persons forms on behalf of firm A
Outsourcing by A to B (both being a member of the same United Kingdom group and each having its registered office in the United Kingdom)	See SUP 10.3.4G	See SUP 15.7.8G
(i) A to B, where B is a non-authorised person not part of the same group as A (ii) A to B, where A is a branch of an overseas firm in the United Kingdom, and B is an overseas undertaking of the same group (iii) A to B, where A is a UK authorised subsidiary of an overseas firm, and B is an overseas undertaking of the same group	Responsibility for (as opposed to the performance of) any activity outsourced to B will remain with A. See SYSC 3.2.4G and SYSC 8	A ensures that an individual approved under one of the significant influence functions has responsibility for the outsourced arrangement and A submits a form in relation to that individual

10.12.4A **[G]** Where the notification of an *appointed representative* (SUP 12.7.1R) is linked to an application for approval (SUP 10.12 (Applications for approval and withdrawing an application for approval)), any delay in receiving the notification under SUP 12.7.1R may delay the *FSA's* approval of the individuals employed by that *appointed representative* who will be performing *controlled functions* for the *firm*.

10.12.5 **[G]** Processing an application

The *Act* allows the *FSA* three *months* from the time it receives a properly completed application to consider it and come to a decision. The *FSA* must either grant the application or, if it proposes not to grant an application, issue a *warning notice* (see *DEPP* 2). The *FSA* will deal with cases more quickly than this whenever circumstances allow and will try to meet the standard response times published on the website and in its Annual Report. However, if an application is incomplete when received, or the *FSA* has knowledge that, or reason to believe that, the information is incomplete, then the processing time will be longer than the published standard response times.

10.12.6 **[G]** Application forms must always be completed fully and honestly. Further notes on how to complete the form are contained in each form. If forms are not completed fully and honestly, applications will be subject to investigation and the candidate's suitability to be approved to undertake a *controlled function* will be called into question. A *person* who provides information to the *FSA* that is false or misleading may commit a criminal offence, and could face prosecution under section 398 of the *Act* regardless of the status of their application.

10.12.7 **[G]** If there is a delay in processing the application within the standard response time, the *FSA* will tell the *firm* making the application as soon as this becomes apparent.

10.12.8 **[G]** Before making a decision to grant the application or give a *warning notice*, the *FSA* may ask the *firm* for more information about the *candidate*. If it does this, the three *month* period in which the *FSA* must determine a completed application:

(1) will stop on the *day* the *FSA* requests the information; and
(2) will start running again on the *day* on which the *FSA* finally receives all the requested information.

10.12.9 **[G]** The *FSA* may grant an application only if it is satisfied that the *candidate* is a fit and proper *person* to perform the *controlled function* stated in the application form. Responsibility lies with the *firm* making the application to satisfy the *FSA* that the *candidate* is fit and proper to perform the *controlled function* applied for.

10.12.10 **[G]** For further *guidance* on criteria for assessing whether a *candidate* is fit and proper, see *FIT*.

Decisions on applications

10.12.11 **[G]** Whenever it grants an application, the *FSA* will confirm this in writing to all *interested parties*.

10.12.12 **[G]** If the *FSA* proposes to refuse an application in relation to one or more *controlled functions*, it must follow the procedures for issuing *warning* and *decision notices* to all *interested parties*. The *requirements* relating to *warning* and *decision notices* are in *DEPP* 2.

Withdrawing an application for approval

10.12.13 **[R]** A *firm* applying to withdraw an application must notify the *FSA*, using Form B.

10.12.14 **[G]** Under section 61(5) of the *Act* (Determination of applications), the *firm* may withdraw an application only if it also has the consent of the *candidate* and the *person* by whom the *candidate* is or would have been employed, if this is not the *firm* making the application.

10.13 Changes to an approved person's details

Moving within a firm

10.13.1 **[G]** An *approved person's* job may change from time to time as a result, for instance, of a change in personal job responsibilities or a *firm's regulated activities*. Where the changes will involve the *person* performing one or more different *controlled functions* from those for which approval has already been granted, then an application must be made to the *FSA* for approval for the *person* to perform those *controlled functions*. The *firm* must take reasonable care to ensure that an individual does not begin performing a *controlled function* until the *FSA* has granted *approved person* status to that individual in respect of that *controlled function*. This applies to *individuals* seeking approval in respect of a *controlled function* within the *firm* for which they already perform *controlled functions*. If the *approved person* is ceasing to perform *controlled functions*, as well as applying for *approval* in respect of additional *controlled functions*, then refer to SUP 10.13.3G.

10.13.2 **[G]** The relevant Form A must be used to apply for an individual to perform further *controlled functions* for a *firm* for which he already performs a *controlled function* as an *approved person* (see SUP 10.12.2D). It is not mandatory to complete all parts of the form. See the notes relevant to each form for full details.

10.13.3 **[D]**A *firm* must use Form E where an *approved person* is both ceasing to perform one or more *controlled functions* and needs to be approved in relation to one or more new *controlled functions* within the same *firm* or *group*.

Moving between firms

10.13.4 **[G]** If it is proposed that an *approved person* will no longer be performing a *controlled function* under an *arrangement* entered into by one *firm* or one of its contractors, but will be performing the same or a different *controlled function* under an *arrangement* entered into by a new *firm* or one of its contractors (whether or not the new *firm* is in the same *group* as the old *firm*), the new *firm* will be required to make a fresh application for the performance of the *controlled function* by that *person*.

10.13.5 **[G]** In certain circumstances, when the *FSA* already has the information it would usually require, a shortened version of the relevant Form A may be completed. See the notes relevant to each form for full details.

Ceasing to perform a controlled function

10.13.6 **[R]** A *firm* must submit to the *FSA* a completed Form C no later than seven *business days* after an *approved person* ceases to perform a *controlled function*.

10.13.7 **[R]**

(1) A *firm* must notify the *FSA* as soon as practicable after it becomes aware, or has information which reasonably suggests, that it will submit a qualified Form C in respect of an *approved person.*

(2) Form C is qualified if the information it contains:
   (a) relates to the fact that the *firm* has dismissed, or suspended, the *approved person* from its employment; or
   (b) relates to the resignation by the *approved person* while under investigation by the *firm*, the *FSA* or any other *regulatory body*; or
   (c) otherwise reasonably suggests that it may affect the *FSA's* assessment of the *approved person's* fitness and propriety.

10.13.8 **[G]** Notification under SUP 10.13.7R may be made by telephone, fax or email and should be made, where possible, within one *business day* of the *firm* becoming aware of the information. If the *firm* does not submit Form C, it should inform the *FSA* in due course of the reason. This could be done using Form D, if appropriate.

10.13.9 **[G]** A *firm* is responsible for notifying the *FSA* if any *approved person* has ceased to perform a *controlled function* under an *arrangement* entered into by its *appointed representative* or former *appointed representative.*

10.13.10 **[G]** A *firm* can submit Form C or Form E to the *FSA* in advance of the cessation date. When a *person* ceases the *arrangement* under which he performs a *controlled function*, he will automatically cease to be an *approved person* in relation to that *controlled function.* A *person* can only be an *approved person* in relation to a specific *controlled function.* Therefore, a *person* is not an *approved person* during any period between ceasing to perform one *controlled function* (when he is performing no other *controlled function*) and being *approved* in respect of another *controlled function.*

10.13.11 **[G]** Sending forms promptly will help to ensure that any fresh application can be processed within the standard response times.

10.13.12 **[R]**

(1) If a *firm* (A):
   (a) is considering appointing a *person* to perform any of the *controlled functions*;
   (b) requests another *firm* (B), as a current or former *employer* of that *person*, for a reference or other information in connection with that appointment; and
   (c) indicates to B the purpose of the request;

B must, as soon as reasonably practicable, give to A all relevant information of which it is aware.

(2) When giving the information to A under (1), B must have regard to the purpose of the request and in particular to:
   (a) any outstanding liabilities of that *person* from commission payments;
   (b) any relevant outstanding or upheld complaint from an *eligible complainant* against that *person*;
   (c) section 5 of the relevant Form A in SUP 10 Annex 4D (Application to perform controlled functions under approved persons regime);
   (d) *FIT* 2 (Main assessment criteria); and
   (e) if SUP 16.8.1R (*Persistency* reports from *insurers*) applies to B, the persistency of any *life policies* sold by that *person.*

10.13.12A **[G]**The requirement in SUP 10.13.12(1)R for *firm* (B) to give to *firm* (A) all relevant information of which it is aware concerning a *person firm* A is considering appointing to perform and of the *controlled functions*, also applies where *firm* A has outsourced the collection of that information to another (unregulated) third party, where *firm* B has been made aware that the unregulated third party is acting on behalf of *firm* A.

10.13.13 **[G]** A *firm* supplying a reference in accordance with SUP 10.13.12R owes a duty to its former *employee* and the recipient *firm* to exercise due skill and care in the preparation of the reference. The reference should be accurate and based on documented fact. The *firm* may give frank and honest views, but only after taking reasonable care both as to factual content, and as to the opinions expressed, and verifying the information upon which they are based.

Changes to an approved person's personal details

10.13.14 **[R]** If an *approved person's* title, name or national insurance number changes, the *firm* for which the *person* performs a *controlled function* must notify the *FSA* on Form D of that change within seven *business days* of the *firm* becoming aware of the matter.

10.13.15 **[G]** The duty to notify in SUP 10.13.14R does not apply to changes to an *approved person's* private address.

10.13.16 **[R]** If a *firm* becomes aware of information which would reasonably be material to the assessment of an *approved person's*, or a *candidate's*, fitness and propriety (see *FIT*), it must inform the *FSA* on Form D, or (if it is more practical to do so and with the prior agreement of the *FSA*) by fax or e-mail, as soon as practicable.

10.13.17 **[G]** The duty to notify in SUP 10.13.16R extends to any circumstances that would normally be declared when giving the information required for section 5 of Form A or matters considered in FIT 2.

10.13.18 **[R]**

(1) If, in relation to a *firm* which has completed the relevant Form A (SUP 10 Ann 4D), any of the details in section 3.01 (Arrangements and controlled functions) are to change, the *firm* must notify the *FSA* on Form D, or (if it is more practical to do so and with the prior agreement of the *FSA*) by fax or e-mail.

(2) The notification must be made as soon as reasonably practicable after the *firm* becomes aware of the proposed change.

(3) Paragraphs (1) and (2) also apply to a *firm* in respect of an *approved person*, to whom the grandfathering arrangements applied as if the *firm* had completed the relevant Form A for that *person*.

10.13.19 **[G]** An example of where a *firm* should use Form D is when an individual who is appointed by one *appointed representative* becomes employed by another *appointed representative* but continues to perform the *investment adviser function* for the *firm*. The *firm* should notify the *FSA* by completing Section 1.07 of Form D.

10.13.20 **[G]** The grandfathering arrangements applying to an *approved person* referred to in SUP 10.13.18 R are contained in Part VI (Approved persons) of the Financial Services and Markets Act (Transitional Provisions) (Authorised Persons etc.) Order 2001 (SI 2001/2636). Article 72 of that Order provides, in general terms, that, where a *person* was performing a function at the beginning of 1 December 2001 which became a *controlled function* under the *Act*, the continued performance of that function by that *person* was taken to be approved by the *FSA*. That *person* therefore became an *approved person* without the need for a Form A.

10.14 Further questions

10.14.1 **[G]** A list of frequently asked questions and answers is at SUP 10Ann1G.

10.14.2 **[G]** If the *firm* or its advisers have further questions, they should contact the *FSA's* Individuals, Mutuals and Policy Department (see SUP 10.11.6G).

Annex 1
SUP 10 Ann 1 [G]: Frequently asked questions

Ann1 **[G]**

Question		*Answer*
Requirements of the regime		
1	Does pre-approval apply to individuals taking up a new *controlled function* within the same *firm*?	Yes. Pre-approval applies in all circumstances (see section 59 of the *Act* (Approval for particular arrangements)) except under the temporary ('12 weeks') provision. See SUP 10.5.5R and question 2.
2	What are the procedures for 'emergency situations'?	Individuals may perform the *significant influence functions* for up to 12 weeks in any consecutive 12 *month* period without requiring approval. When it becomes clear that a *person* will be performing the function on a permanent basis, then an application for approval should be made. However, there is no provision for individuals to perform the *customer function* on a continuing basis without approval. See SUP 10.5.5.R.
3	Can a *person* be approved for more than one *controlled function*?	Yes. A *firm* will need to seek approval in respect of each *controlled function* a *person* is to perform.
4	Do the *controlled functions* apply to an *incoming EEA firm* that is providing *cross border services* into the *United Kingdom*?	No. The *approved persons* regime does not apply to *cross border services*. See SUP 10.1.6R
5	May any activity be outsourced by a *firm*?	Yes. But if that activity constitutes a *regulated activity*, the *person* to whom it is outsourced will itself need permission.

Question		*Answer*
6	Can a *significant influence function* be outsourced?	It is a question of fact in each case who is performing a *significant influence function.* These functions are mostly described at a high level of responsibility, that is, for example, the *director* of a *company* or a *partner* in a *partnership*. The *persons* performing these functions cannot avoid their ultimate responsibility and therefore the need for approval. However, some of the *significant influence functions* may be performed by a *person* who is specifically brought in to do the job, for example the *chief executive function* (where it is to be performed by a *body corporate*) and the *actuarial* and *with-profits actuary functions.*
7	Do Lloyd's underwriting agents still require registration with Lloyd's?	Yes. Approval for a *controlled function* is not sufficient.
8	What should a *firm* do if it is unsure whether an individual needs approval?	The *firm* should contact the Individuals, Mutuals and Policy Department. See SUP 10.11.6G.
Submitting an application		
9	Who applies for approval?	The *firm*. See section 60 of the *Act* (Applications for approval).
10	What is the role of the *candidate* in the application process?	Before the *firm* submits the relevant Form A, it must verify the information contained in it. As part of this verification, the Form provides for the *candidate* to confirm the accuracy of the information given by the *firm* so far as it relates to him.
11	What checks should a *firm* make on a *candidate* before submitting an application for approval from the *FSA*?	The *FSA* expects *firms* to perform due and diligent enquiries into their *candidates* before they submit an application to us for approval. Our approval process is not a substitute for the checks that a *firm* should be carrying out on its prospective recruits. It is for the *firm* to determine what checks are appropriate but in making its decision, a *firm* should have regard to the *controlled function* to which the application relates. *Firms'* enquiries should include checks to verify relevant qualifications and previous employment. Note also the provisions of EG 6.
11A	Should these checks include a check of criminal records?	It is for senior management to decide what checks should be made. In deciding if it is necessary to carry out a check of criminal records, the *firm* should consider that the *FSA* does not routinely carry out these checks during the approval process. By virtue of the Rehabilitation of Offenders Act 1974 (Exceptions) Order 1975 (see Articles 3 and 4 of the Order), the *FSA* and the industry also have a right to ask about spent, as well as unspent, criminal convictions for employment purposes about *candidates* for *approved person* status (see section 5 of the relevant Form A (Application to perform controlled functions under the approved persons regime)). Note also the provisions of *EG* 6 (Publicity).

Part II FSA Handbook Materials

Question		*Answer*
12	What is the "fit and proper" test for approval?	Section 61(1) of the *Act* (Determination of applications) provides that the *FSA* may grant an application only if it is satisfied that the *candidate* is a fit and proper *person* to perform the relevant function. In determining this question, the *Act* sets out the matters to which the *FSA* may have regard (section 61(2)) and the *FSA* has given guidance on this in *FIT*.
13	If a *firm* is unsure whether or not something may have an impact upon an individual's fitness and propriety, should it be disclosed?	Yes, always. The deliberate non-disclosure of material facts is taken very seriously by the *FSA* as it is seen as possible evidence of current dishonesty. Therefore, if in doubt, disclose.
14	What happens if adverse information comes to light after the application form has been submitted or after the individual has been approved?	The *firm* must inform the *FSA* at the earliest opportunity. See SUP 10.13.16R.
15	Will the *FSA* consider an application in respect of a *candidate* who has not yet signed a contract with the *firm*?	Yes, as the *FSA* will consider the *arrangement* under which the *candidate* will perform the function. However, the *FSA* will not consider speculative or provisional applications – such as for the candidates in an election to a mutual society Board.
		The *FSA* must be informed immediately of any material changes to the information provided on the application form which arises before the application has been determined. All changes must be communicated to the *FSA* by the *firm* making the application (see SUP 15.6.4R). Failure to notify the *FSA* may result in a delay in processing or rejection or both.
16	How can we get a supply of application forms (Form A)?	These can either be ordered through the Individuals, Mutuals and Policy Department or obtained from the *FSA* website at www.fsa.gov.uk. There is no charge for an application form.
17	Is there a separate fee for making an application for *approved person* status?	No.
18	Must all gaps in previous employment be explained?	Yes.
FSA procedures		
19	Does the *FSA* verify the information provided to it?	Yes, as far as possible, information is verified.
20	Will the *FSA* handle information confidentially?	Yes. The *FSA* is obliged to handle all information confidentially and is subject to the provisions of the Data Protection Act 1998.
21	How long will the *FSA* take to process an application for *approved person* status?	Generally the *FSA* will handle this within seven *business days* for *significant influence functions* and four *business days* for *customer functions*. However, if information is missing, or the information provided gives the *FSA* cause for concern, processing time will almost always be longer. In each case, the *FSA* will notify the *firm* of any extension to the processing times.

Question		*Answer*
22	Will the *firm* and individual be notified if there is a delay in processing the application form?	Yes. The *FSA* will contact the firm explaining the position and, where appropriate, giving the reasons for delay. It will then be the responsibility of the *firm* to keep the *candidate* and any other *interested party* informed.
23	How are non-routine cases handled?	Refer to *DEPP* 2.
24	Can the *FSA* apply conditions to an *approved person*?	No. The application can either be granted or refused. The *Act* provides no equivalent to the *limitations* or *requirements* which may be included in *permissions*. If the application is refused, the *firm* may re-apply in respect of the same individual but a different *controlled function*. If it is considering doing this, the *firm* is encouraged to discuss the matter with the *FSA*.
		Where there are reasonable grounds for doing so, the *FSA* may require a *firm* to provide information about an *approved person* (see section 165 of the *Act* (Power to require information)).
25	Will the *firm* be issued with confirmation of approval?	Yes. The *firm* will be sent a letter setting out the effective date of approval together with the *controlled function* for which the individual has been approved. It will then be the *firm's* responsibility to inform the individual and any other *interested party*, for example any *appointed representative*.
Withdrawing an application		
26	Can a *firm* withdraw its application?	Yes, but only with the consent of the *candidate*. See section 61(5) of the *Act* (Determination of applications).
27	What happens if the individual refuses to consent to the withdrawal of the application?	The *FSA* will consider with all *interested parties* what to do. If it proposes to refuse the application, it will give a *warning notice* to all *interested parties*. See section 62 of the *Act* (Applications for approval: procedure and right to refer to the Tribunal).
28	Can the *firm* withdraw only part of an application – say, in relation to a specific *controlled function*?	The *FSA* will allow the *firm* to amend its application at any time before determination with the consent of all other *interested parties*. Whether the amendment will have the effect of amounting to a fresh application will be considered on a case by case basis.
Conduct of approved persons		
29	How and when must the *firm* report to the *FSA* potentially adverse information about an *approved person's* fitness and propriety?	Normally, the *firm* should report such matters to the *FSA* on Form D once it is reasonably satisfied as to the information's validity. See SUP 10.13.16R. See also, Principle for Businesses 11 (*PRIN*) and Statements of Principle 4 (*APER*).
		However, if an *approved person* is dismissed, is suspended, or resigns while under investigation by the *firm*, the *FSA* or another regulatory body, or there are any other matters that might affect the individual's fitness and propriety to perform a *controlled function*, the *firm* should inform the *FSA* (SUP 10.13.7R) that it will be submitting a Form C containing adverse information. Full details must then be provided within seven *business days*, on the Form C. See SUP 10.13.6R.

Part II FSA Handbook Materials

Question		*Answer*
30	For how long are individuals accountable to the *FSA* after ceasing to be an *approved person*?	A *person* is guilty of misconduct if, while an *approved person*, he fails to comply with a *Statement of Principle* or is knowingly concerned in the contravention by a *firm* of a requirement in the *Act* or the *Handbook*. But the *FSA* may not bring proceedings after two years from when it first knew of the misconduct.

How does the customer function relate to the training and competence requirements?

Activity	Products/sectors in TC Appendix 1 R	Controlled Function	SUP
Advising only, Undertaking an activity, Advising and dealing Managing investments	2–9, 10–11, 12–13, 14	*customer function* (CF30)	10.10.4R

Annex 2

SUP 10 Ann 2 [G]: Approved person regime: summary of forms and their use

Ann2 **[G]**

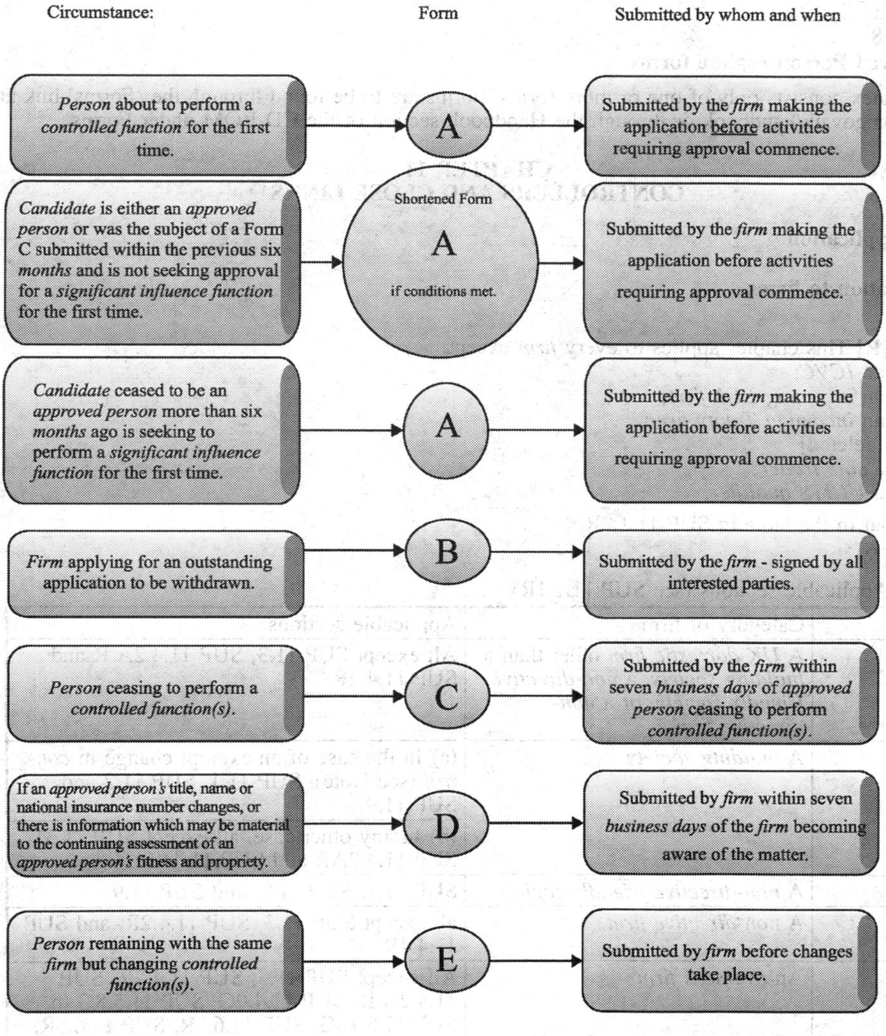

Circumstance:
Form
Submitted by whom and when
Person about to perform a controlled function for the first time.
A
Submitted by the firm making the application before activities requiring approval commence.
Candidate is either an approved person or was the subject of a Form C submitted within the previous six months and is not seeking approval for a significant influence function for the first time.
Shortened Form
A
if conditions met.
Submitted by the firm making the application before activities requiring approval commence.
Candidate ceased to be an approved person more than six months ago is seeking to perform a significant influence function for the first time.
A
Submitted by the firm making the application before activities requiring approval commence.
Firm applying for an outstanding application to be withdrawn.
B
Submitted by the firm - signed by all interested parties.
Person ceasing to perform a controlled function(s).
C
Submitted by the firm within seven business days of approved person ceasing to perform controlled function(s).
If an approved person's title, name or national insurance number changes, or there is information which may be material to the continuing assessment of an approved person's fitness and propriety.
D
Submitted by firm within seven business days of the firm becoming aware of the matter.
Person remaining with the same firm but changing controlled function(s).
E
Submitted by firm before changes take place.

Annex 3

SUP 10 Ann 3 [G]: Summary of procedures on application for approved status

[deleted]

Annex 4

Approved Person regime forms

This form has not been reproduced for technical reasons. Please refer to the FSA website.

Annex 5

Approved Person regime forms

This annex consists only of one or more forms. Forms are to be found through the 'Forms' link at www.fsa.gov.uk/handbook or through the Handbook section of the CD-ROM under Forms.

Annex 6

Approved Person regime forms

This annex consists only of one or more forms. Forms are to be found through the 'Forms' link at www.fsa.gov.uk/handbook or through the Handbook section of the CD-ROM under Forms.

Annex 7
Approved Person regime forms

This annex consists only of one or more forms. Forms are to be found through the 'Forms' link at www.fsa.gov.uk/handbook or through the Handbook section of the CD-ROM under Forms.

Annex 8
Approved Person regime forms

This annex consists only of one or more forms. Forms are to be found through the 'Forms' link at www.fsa.gov.uk/handbook or through the Handbook section of the CD-ROM under Forms.

CHAPTER 11
CONTROLLERS AND CLOSE LINKS

11.1 Application

Application to firms

[2164]
11.1.1 **[R]** This chapter applies to every *firm* except:
(1) an *ICVC*;
(2) an *incoming EEA firm*;
(3) an *incoming Treaty firm*;
(4) [deleted]
(5) a *sole trader*;
(6) a *UCITS qualifier*;

as set out in the table in SUP 11.1.2R.

11.1.2 **[R]**

Table: Applicable sections (see SUP 11.1.1R)

	Category of firm	Applicable sections
(1)	A *UK domestic firm* other than a *building society*, a *non-directive friendly society*, or a *non-directive firm*	All except SUP 11.3, SUP 11.4.2A R and SUP 11.4.4R
(1A)	A *building society*	(a) In the case of an exempt change in *control* (see Note), SUP 11.1, SUP 11.2 and SUP 11.9
		(b) In any other case, all except SUP 11.3, SUP 11.4.2AR and SUP 11.4.4R
(2)	A *non-directive friendly society*	SUP 11.1, SUP 11.2, and SUP 11.9
(2A)	A *non-directive firm*	all except SUP 11.3, SUP 11.4.2R, and SUP 11.4.4R
(3)	An *overseas firm*	All except SUP 11.3, SUP 11.4.2R, SUP 11.4.2A R, SUP 11.4.9G, SUP 11.5.8G to SUP 11.5.10G, SUP 11.6.2R, SUP 11.6.3R, SUP 11.7

Note: In row (1A), a change in *control* is exempt if the *controller* or proposed *controller* is exempt from any obligation to notify the *FSA* under Part XII of the *Act* (Notices of acquisitions of control over UK authorised persons) because of The Financial Services and Markets Act 2000 (Controllers) (Exemption) Order 2009 (SI 2009/774). (See SUP 11.3.2AG(2).)

11.1.3 **[G]** This chapter may apply to *directive friendly societies* in the circumstances described in SUP 16.4.2G (1) to (3).

Application to controllers

11.1.4 **[D]** SUP 11.1, SUP 11.2, SUP 11.3 and SUP 11.7 apply to a *controller* or a proposed *controller* of a *UK domestic firm* not listed in SUP 11.1.1R (1) to (6).

11.1.5 **[G]** This chapter may apply to *controllers* and *proposed controllers* of *directive friendly societies* in the circumstances described in SUP 16.4.2G (1) to (3).

11.2 Purpose

11.2.1 **[G]** Part XII of the *Act* (Notices of acquisitions of control over UK authorised persons) places an obligation on the *controllers* and proposed *controllers* of those *UK domestic firms* not listed in

SUP 11.1.1R (1) to (6) to notify the *FSA* of changes in *control*, including acquiring, increasing or reducing *control* or ceasing to have *control* over a *firm*. Furthermore, those *persons* are required to obtain the *FSA's approval* before becoming a *controller* or increasing their *control* over a firm. SUP 11.3 is intended to assist those *persons* in complying with their obligations under Part XII of the *Act*.

11.2.2 **[G]** The *rules* in SUP 11.4 to SUP 11.6 are aimed at ensuring that the *FSA* receives information it needs to assist the *FSA* with its responsibility to monitor and, in some cases, give prior approval to *firms' controllers*.

11.2.2A **[G]** [deleted]

11.2.3 **[G]** As the approval of the *FSA* is not required under the *Act* for a new *controller* of an *overseas firm*, the *notification rules* on such *firms* are less prescriptive than they are for *UK domestic firms*. Nevertheless, the *FSA* still needs to monitor such an *overseas firm's* continuing satisfaction of the *threshold conditions*, which normally includes consideration of a *firm's* connection with any *person*, including its *controllers* and *parent undertakings* (see *COND*). The *FSA* therefore needs to be notified of *controllers* and *parent undertakings* of *overseas firms*.

11.2.4 **[G]** As part of the *FSA's* function of monitoring a *firm's* continuing satisfaction of the *threshold conditions*, the *FSA* needs to consider the impact of any significant change in the circumstances of one or more of its *controllers*, for example, in their financial standing and, in respect of corporate *controllers*, in their *governing bodies*. Consequently, the *FSA* needs to know if there are any such changes. SUP 11.8 therefore requires a *firm* to tell the *FSA* if it becomes aware of particular matters relating to a *controller*.

11.2.5 **[G]** Similarly, the *FSA* needs to monitor a *firm's* continuing satisfaction of *threshold condition* 3 (Close links) (see COND 2.3), which requires that a *firm's close links* are not likely to prevent the *FSA's* effective supervision of that *firm*. Accordingly the *FSA* needs to be notified of any changes in a *firm's close links*. This requirement is contained in SUP 11.9.

11.2.6 **[G]** Every *firm* other than a *firm* listed in SUP 11.1.1R (1) to (6) or a firm excluded from the operation of SUP 16.4 or SUP 16.5 by SUP 16.1.3R, is required to submit an annual report on its *controllers* and *close links* as set out in SUP 16.4 and SUP 16.5.

11.2.7 **[G]** The requirements in SUP 11 implement certain provisions relating to changes in *control* and *close links* required under the *Single Market Directives*.

11.2.8 **[G]** An event described in SUP 11.4.2R, SUP 11.4.2AR and SUP11.4.4R is referred to in this chapter as a "change in *control*".

11.3 Requirements on controllers or proposed controllers under the Act

11.3.1 **[G]** The notification requirements are set out in sections 178, 179, 191D and 191E of the *Act* and holdings which may be disregarded are set out in section 184 of the *Act*. A summary of the notification requirements described in this section is given in SUP 11Ann1G.

Requirement to notify a proposed change in control

11.3.2 **[G]** Sections 178(1) and 191D(1) of the *Act* requires a *person* (whether or not he is an *authorised person*) to notify the *FSA* in writing if he decides to acquire, increase or reduce *control* or to cease to have *control* over a UK *domestic firm*. Failure to notify is an offence under section 191F of the *Act* (Offences under this Part).

11.3.2A **[G]** The Treasury have made the following exemptions from the obligations under section 178 of the Act:

(1) *controllers* and potential *controllers* of *non-directive friendly societies* are exempt from the obligation to notify a change in *control* (The Financial Services and Markets Act 2000 (Controllers) (Exemption) Order 2009 (SI 2009/774));

(2) *controllers* and potential *controllers* of *building societies* are exempt from the obligation to notify a change in *control* unless the change involves the acquisition of a holding of a specified percentage of a *building society's* capital or the increase or reduction by a specified percentage of a holding of a *building society's* capital (The Financial Services and Markets Act 2000 (Controllers) (Exemption) Order 2009 (SI 2009/774.)). The "capital" of a *building society* for these purposes consists of:
   (a) any shares of a class defined as deferred shares for the purposes of section 119 of the Building Societies Act 1986 which have been issued by the society (in practice, likely to be permanent interest bearing shares (PIBS)); and
   (b) the general reserves of that *building society*.

(3) potential *controllers* of *non-directive firms* ("A") are exempt from the obligation to notify a change in *control* unless the change results in the potential *controller* holding:
   (a) 20% or more of the *shares* in A or in a *parent undertaking* of A ("P");
   (b) 20% or more of the voting power in A or P; or
   (c) *shares* or *voting power* in A or P as a result of which the *controller* is able to exercise significant influence over the management of A;

Part II FSA Handbook Materials

or where the change in *control* over A would lead to the *controller* ceasing to fall into any of the cases (a), (b) or (c) above (The Financial Services and Markets Act 2000 (Controllers) (Exemption) Order 2009 (SI 2009/774)).

11.3.3 **[G]** [deleted]

Approval required before acquiring or increasing control

11.3.4 **[G]** If a *person* decides to acquire *control* or increase *control* over a *UK domestic firm* in a way described in SUP 11.4.2R or acquire *control* in a way described in SUP 11.4.2A R(1), he must obtain the *FSA's* approval before doing so. Making an acquisition before the *FSA* has approved of it is an offence under section 191F of the *Act* (Offences under this Part).

11.3.5 **[G]** The *FSA's* approval is not required before a *controller* reduces *control* or ceases to have *control* over a *UK domestic firm*.

Pre-notification and approval for fund managers

11.3.5A **[G]** The *FSA* recognises that *firms* acting as *investment managers* may have difficulties in complying with the prior notification requirements in sections 178 and 191D of the *Act* as a result of acquiring or disposing of listed *shares* in the course of that fund management activity. To ameliorate these difficulties, the *FSA* may accept pre-notification of proposed changes in *control*, made in accordance with SUP 11.3.5BD, and may grant approval of such changes for a period lasting up to a year.

11.3.5B **[D]** The *FSA* may treat as notice given in accordance with sections 178 and 191D of the *Act* a written notification from a *firm* which contains the following statements:

(1) that the *firm* proposes to acquire and/or dispose of *control*, on one or more occasions, of any *UK domestic firm* whose *shares* or those of its ultimate *parent undertaking* are, at the time of the acquisition or disposal of *control*, *listed* or which are admitted to listing on a *designated investment exchange*:

(2) that any such acquisitions and/or disposals of *control* will occur only in the course of the *firm's* business as an *investment manager*,

(3) that the level of *control* the *firm* so acquires in the preapproval period will at all times remain less than 20%; and.

(4) that the *firm* will not exercise any influence over the *UK domestic firm* in which the shares are held, other than by exercising its voting rights as a shareholder or by exercising influence intended to promote generally accepted principles of good corporate governance.

11.3.5C **[G]** Where the *FSA* approves changes in *control* proposed in a notice given under SUP 11.3.5BD:

(1) the *controller* remains subject to the requirement to notify the *FSA* when a change in *control* actually occurs; and

(2) the notification of change in *control* should be made no later than five *business days* after the end of each *month* and set out all changes in the *controller's control* position for each *UK domestic firm* for the *month* in question.

At that stage, the *FSA* may seek from the *controller* further information.

11.3.6 **[G]** [deleted]

11.3.6A **[G]** [deleted]

11.3.6B **[D]** [deleted]

11.3.6C **[G]** [deleted]

Forms of notifications when acquiring or increasing control

11.3.7 **[D]** A *section 178 notice* given to the *FSA* by a *person* who is acquiring *control* or increasing *control* over a *UK domestic firm*, in a way described in SUP 11.4.2R, or acquiring *control* in a way described in SUP 11.4.2A R(1), must contain the information and be accompanied by such documents as are required by the controllers form approved by the *FSA* for the relevant application.

11.3.7A **[G]** The controllers forms approved by the *FSA* may be found at the FSA's website (http://www.fsa.gov.uk/Pages/Doing/Regulated/Notify/Control/index.shtml).

11.3.8 **[D]** [deleted]

11.3.9 **[D]** [deleted]

11.3.10 **[D]**

(1) A *person* who has submitted a *section 178 notice* under SUP 11.3.7D must notify the *FSA* immediately if he becomes aware, or has information that reasonably suggests, that he has or may have provided the *FSA* with information which was or may have been false, misleading, incomplete or inaccurate, or has or may have changed, in a material particular. The notification must include:

(a) details of the information which is or may be false, misleading, incomplete or inaccurate, or has or may have changed;
(b) an explanation why such information was or may have been provided; and
(c) the correct information.

(2) If the information in (1)(c) cannot be submitted with the *section 178 notice* (because it is not immediately available), it must instead be submitted as soon as possible afterwards.
(3) The requirement in (1) ceases if the change in *control* occurs or will not take place.

11.3.11 **[G]** The *FSA* will inform a *section 178 notice* giver as soon as reasonably practicable if it considers the *section 178 notice* to be incomplete.

11.3.12 **[G]** The *FSA* has power, under section 179(3) of the *Act* (Requirements for *section 178 notices*), to vary or waive these requirements in relation to *a section 178 notice* in particular cases if it considers it appropriate to do so.

11.3.13 **[G]** A *controller* or proposed *controller* which is an *authorised person* is required to submit less information under SUP 11.3.7D than other *persons* and consequently the *FSA* may ask for confirmation of details already held or any additional information required under SUP 11.5.1R.

11.3.14 **[G]** Pursuant to section 188 of the Act (Assessment: consultation with *EU* competent authorities), the *FSA* is obliged to consult any appropriate *Home State Regulator* before making a determination under section 185 of the *Act* (Assessment: general).

Notification when reducing control

11.3.15 **[G]** [deleted]

11.3.15A **[D]** A notice given to the *FSA* by a *person* who is reducing or ceasing to have *control* over a *UK domestic firm*, as set out in SUP 11.4.2R or SUP 11.4.2AR must:
(1) be in writing; and
(2) provide details of the extent of *control* (if any) which the *controller* will have following the change in *control*.

11.3.16 **[G]** [deleted]

Joint notifications

11.3.17 **[G]** Notifications to the *FSA* by proposed *controllers* and *controllers* under Part XII of the *Act* may be made on a joint basis outlined in SUP 11.5.8G to SUP 11.5.10G.

11.4 Requirements on firms

11.4.1 **[G]** A summary of the notification requirements in this section is given in SUP 11Ann1G.

Requirement to notify a change in control

11.4.2 **[R]** A *UK domestic firm* other than a *non-directive firm*, must notify the *FSA* of any of the following events concerning the *firm*:
(1) a *person* acquiring *control*;
(2) an existing *controller* increasing *control*;
(3) an existing *controller* reducing *control*;
(4) an existing *controller* ceasing have *control*.

11.4.2A **[R]** A *non-directive firm* must notify the *FSA* of any of the following events concerning the *firm*:
(1) a *person* becoming *controller* of the firm; or
(2) an existing *controller* ceasing to be *controller* of the firm.

11.4.3 **[G]** [deleted]

11.4.4 **[R]** An *overseas firm* must notify the *FSA* if a *person* becomes a *controller* of the *firm*, increases or reduces *control* over the *firm* or ceases to have *control* over the *firm*.

11.4.5 **[G]** [deleted]

11.4.6 **[G]** If a *firm* is required to obtain approval from the *Society of Lloyd's* for any changes in its *controllers*, it should apply for this approval as well as notifying the *FSA*.

Content and timing of the notification

11.4.7 **[R]** The notification by a *firm* under SUP 11.4.2R, SUP 11.4.2A R or SUP 11.4.4R must:
(1) be in writing;
(2) contain the information set out in:
(a) in the case of acquiring or increasing *control*, SUP 11.5.1R (subject to SUP 11.5.2R); or
(b) in the case of reducing *control*, SUP 11.5.7R; and

(3) be made:
(a) as soon as the *firm* becomes aware that a *person*, whether alone or acting in concert, has decided to acquire *control* or to increase or reduce *control*; or
(b) if the change in *control* takes place without the knowledge of the *firm*, within 14 *days* of the *firm* becoming aware of the change in *control* concerned.

11.4.8 **[G]** *Principle* 11 requires *firms* to be open and cooperative with the *FSA*. A *firm* should discuss with the *FSA*, at the earliest opportunity, any prospective changes of which it is aware, in a *controller's* or proposed *controller's* shareholdings or *voting power* (if the change is material). These discussions may take place before the formal notification requirement in SUP 11.4.2R, SUP 11.4.2AR or SUP 11.4.4R arises. (See also SUP 11.3.2G.) As a minimum, the *FSA* considers that such discussions should take place before a *person*:
(1) enters into any formal agreement in respect of the purchase of shares or a proposed acquisition or merger which would result in a change in *control* (whether or not the agreement is conditional upon any matter, including the *FSA's* approval); or
(2) purchases any *share options*, *warrants* or other financial instruments, the exercise of which would result in the *person* acquiring *control* or any other change in *control*.

11.4.9 **[G]** The obligations in SUP 11.4.2R and SUP 11.4.2AR apply whether or not the *controller* himself has given or intends to give a notification, in accordance with his obligations under the *Act*.

Identity of controllers

11.4.10 **[R]** A *firm* must take reasonable steps to keep itself informed about the identity of its *controllers*.

11.4.11 **[G]** The steps that the *FSA* expects a *firm* to take to comply with SUP 11.4.10R include, if applicable:
(1) monitoring its register of shareholders (or equivalent);
(2) monitoring notifications to the *firm* in accordance with Part 22 of the Companies Act 2006;
(3) monitoring public announcements made under the relevant disclosure provisions of the *Takeover Code* or other rules made by the *Takeover Panel*;
(4) monitoring the entitlement of delegates, or *persons* with voting rights in respect of group insurance contracts, to exercise or control *voting power* at general meetings.

11.5 Notifications by firms

11.5.1

Table Information to be submitted by the *firm* (see SUP 11.4.7R(2)(a))

(1)	The name of the *firm*;
(2)	the name of the *controller* or proposed *controller* and, if it is a *body corporate* and is not an *authorised person*, the names of its *directors* and its *controllers*;
(3)	a description of the proposed event including the shareholding and *voting power* of the *person* concerned, both before and after the change in *control*; and
(4)	any other information of which the *FSA* would reasonably expect notice.

11.5.2 **[R]** The notification from a *firm* under SUP 11.4.7R(2)(a) need only contain as much of the information set out in SUP 11.5.1R as the *firm* is able to provide, having made reasonable enquiries from *persons* and other sources as appropriate.

11.5.3 **[G]** [deleted]

11.5.4 **[G]** *Firms* are reminded that a change in *control* may give rise to a change in the *group companies* to which the *FSA's* consolidated financial supervision requirements apply. Also, the *firm* may for the first time become subject to the *FSA's* requirements on consolidated financial supervision (or equivalent requirements imposed by another *EEA State*). This may apply, for example, if the *controller* is itself an authorised *undertaking*. The *FSA* may therefore request such a *firm, controller* or proposed *controller* to provide evidence that, following the change in *control*, the *firm* will meet the requirements of these *rules*, if appropriate.

11.5.4A **[G]** *Firms* are also reminded that a change in *control* may give rise to a notification as a *financial conglomerate* or a change in the supplementary supervision of a *financial conglomerate* (see GENPRU 3.1 (Cross sector groups) and GENPRU 3.2 (Third country groups)).

11.5.5 **[G]** [deleted]

11.5.6 **[G]** *[deleted]*

Form of notification when a person reduces control

11.5.7 **[R]** A notification of a proposed reduction in *control* must:
(1) give the name of the *controller*; and

(2) provide details of the extent of *control* (if any) which the *controller* will have following the change in *control*.

Joint notifications

11.5.8 **[G]** A *firm* and its *controller* or proposed *controller* may discharge an obligation to notify the *FSA* by submitting a single joint *section 178 notice* containing the information required from the *firm* and the *controller* or proposed *controller*. In this case, the *section 178 notice* may be used on behalf of both the *firm* and the *controller* or proposed *controller*.

11.5.9 **[G]** If a *person* is proposing a change in *control* over more than one *firm* within a *group*, then the *controller* or proposed *controller* may submit a single *section 178 notice* in respect of all those *firms*. The *section 178 notice* should contain all the required information as if separate notifications had been made, but information and documentation need not be duplicated.

11.5.10 **[G]** When an event occurs (for example, a *group* restructuring or a merger) as a result of which:

(1) more than one *firm* in a *group* would undergo a change in *control*; or
(2) a single *firm* would experience more than one change in *control*;

then, to avoid duplication of documentation, all the *firms* and their *controllers* or proposed *controllers* may discharge their respective obligations to notify the *FSA* by submitting a single *section 178 notice* containing one set of information.

11.6 Subsequent notification requirements by firms

Changes in the information provided to the FSA

11.6.1 **[G]** *Firms* are reminded that SUP 15.6.4R requires them to notify the *FSA* if information notified under SUP 11.4.2R, SUP **11.4.2A R** or SUP 11.4.4R was false, misleading, inaccurate, incomplete, or changes, in a material particular. This would include a *firm* becoming aware of information that it would have been required to provide under SUP 11.5.1R if it had been aware of it.

11.6.2 **[R]** After submitting a *section 178 notice* under SUP 11.4.2R or SUP 11.4.2AR and until the change in *control* occurs (or is no longer to take place), SUP 15.6.4R and SUP 15.6.5R apply to a *UK domestic firm* in relation to any information its *controller* or proposed *controller* provided to the *FSA* under SUP 11.5.1R or SUP 11.3.7D.

11.6.3 **[R]** During the period in SUP 11.6.2R, a *UK domestic firm* must take reasonable steps to keep itself informed about the circumstances of the *controller* or the proposed *controller* to which the notification related.

Notification that the change in control has taken place

11.6.4 **[R]** A *firm* must notify the *FSA*:

(1) when a change in *control* which was previously notified under SUP 11.4.2R, SUP 11.4.2AR or SUP 11.4.4R has taken place; or
(2) if the *firm* has grounds for reasonably believing that the event will not now take place.

11.6.5 **[R]** The notification under SUP 11.6.4R must be given within 14 *days* of the change in *control* or of having the grounds (as applicable).

11.6.6 **[G]** [deleted]

11.7 Acquisition or increase of control: assessment process and criteria

11.7.1 **[G]** The assessment process and the assessment criteria are set out in sections 185 to 191 of the Act.

11.7.2 **[G]** Section 191A deals with the procedure the *FSA* must follow where there has been a failure to notify or a default.

11.7.3 **[G]** The *FSA* may serve *restriction notices* in certain circumstances in accordance with section 191B of the *Act*.

11.7.4 **[G]** The *FSA* may apply to the court for an order for the sale of *shares* in accordance with section 191C of the *Act*.

11.7.5 **[G]** [deleted]

11.7.6 **[G]** [deleted]

11.7.7 **[G]** [deleted]

11.7.8 **[G]** [deleted]

11.7.9 **[G]** [deleted]

11.7.10 **[G]** [deleted]

11.7.11 **[G]** [deleted]

11.7.12 **[G]** [deleted]

11.7.13 **[G]** Before making a determination under section 185 or giving a *warning notice* under section 191A, the *FSA* must comply with the requirements as to consultation with EC competent authorities set out in section 188 of the *Act*.

11.7.14 **[G]** [deleted]

11.7.15 **[G]** [deleted]

11.7.16 **[G]** [deleted]

11.7.17 **[G]** [deleted]

11.7.18 **[G]** [deleted]

11.8 Changes in the circumstances of existing controllers

11.8.1 **[R]** A *firm* must notify the *FSA* immediately it becomes aware of any of the following matters in respect of one or more of its *controllers*:

(1) if a *controller*, or any entity subject to his *control*, is or has been the subject of any legal action or investigation which might put into question the integrity of the *controller*;

(2) if there is a significant deterioration in the financial position of a *controller*;

(3) if a corporate *controller* undergoes a substantial change or series of changes in its *governing body*;

(4) if a *controller*, who is authorised in another *EEA State* as an *ISD investment firm* or *BCD credit institution* or under the *Insurance Directives* or the *Insurance Mediation Directive*, ceases to be so authorised (registered in the case of an *IMD insurance intermediary*).

11.8.2 **[G]** In assessing whether a matter should be notified to the *FSA* under SUP 11.8.1R (1), (2) or (3), a *firm* should have regard to the *guidance* on satisfying *threshold condition* 5 (Suitability) contained in COND 2.5.

11.8.3 **[G]** In respect of SUP 11.8.1R(3), the *FSA* considers that, in particular, the removal or replacement of a majority of the members of a *governing body* (in a single event or a series of connected events) is a substantial change and should be notified.

11.8.4 **[G]** If a matter has already been notified to the *FSA* (for example, as part of the *firm's* application for a *Part IV permission*), the *firm* need only inform the *FSA* of any significant developments.

11.8.5 **[G]** The level of a *firm's* awareness of its *controller's* circumstances will depend on its relationship with that *controller*. The *FSA* does not expect *firms* to implement systems or procedures so as to be certain of any changes in its *controllers'* circumstances. However, the *FSA* does expect *firms* to notify it of such matters if the *firm* becomes aware of them, and it expects *firms* to make enquiries of its *controllers* if it becomes aware that one of the events in SUP 11.8.1R may occur or has occurred.

11.8.6 **[G]** The *FSA* may ask the *firm* for additional information following a notification under SUP 11.8.1R in order to satisfy itself that the *controller* continues to be suitable (see SUP 2: Information gathering by the FSA on its own initiative).

11.9 Changes in close links

Requirement to notify changes in close links

11.9.1 **[R]** A *firm* must notify the *FSA* that it has become or ceased to be *closely linked* with any *person*. The notification must include the information set out in SUP 16.5.4R(4).

11.9.2 **[G]** *Guidance* on what constitutes a *close link* is provided in COND 2.3.

11.9.3 **[G]** The *FSA* may ask the *firm* for additional information following a notification under SUP 11.9.1R in order to satisfy itself that the *firm* continues to satisfy the *threshold conditions* (see SUP 2: Information gathering by the FSA on its own initiative).

Timing of notification requirement

11.9.4 **[R]** The *firm* must make a notification to the *FSA* under SUP 11.9.1R:

(1) as soon as reasonably practicable and no later than one *month* after it becomes aware that it has become or ceased to be *closely linked* with any *person*; or

(2) where a *firm* has elected to report on a *monthly* basis, within fifteen *business days* of the end of each *month* and:

(a) including the information set out in SUP 16.5.4R(4) for that *month*; and

(b) if there is no *person* required to be included in the notification for a particular *month*, confirming this fact in the notification.

Electing to notify changes in close links monthly

11.9.5 **[R]**

(1) A *firm* elects to report changes in *close links* on a *monthly* basis by sending a written notice of election to the *firm's* usual supervisory contact at the *FSA*.

(2) An election to report changes in *close links* on a *monthly* basis will stand until such time as the *firm* gives its usual supervisory contact at the *FSA* at least one *month's* written notice of its intention to cease reporting changes in *close links* on a *monthly* basis.

11.9.6 **[G]** The *FSA* considers that *monthly* reporting of changes in *close links* will ordinarily only be appropriate for *firms* forming part of large *groups*.

Annex 1

SUP 11 Ann 1 [G]: Summary of notification requirements

Ann1 **[G]**

Event triggering a notification		Requirement reference	
		When	**How**
Notifications from a controller or proposed controller of a UK domestic firm other than a non-directive firm			
1	When a *person* decides to become a *controller* or an existing *controller* decides to increase *control*	SUP 11.3.2G	SUP 1.3.7D to SUP 11.3.14G
2	When an existing *controller* decides to reduce *control* or to cease to have *control*	SUP 11.3.2G	SUP 11.3.15AD
Notifications from a controller or potential controller of a non-directive firm			
1	When a potential *controller* of a *non-directive firm* ("A") decides to acquire (a) 20% or more of the *shares* in A or in a *parent undertaking* of A ("P"); (b) 20% or more of the *voting power* in A or P; or (c) shares or *voting power* in A or P as a result of which the potential *controller* will be able to exercise significant influence over the management of A	SUP 11.3.2AG(3)	SUP 11.3.7D to SUP 11.3.14G
2	When an existing *controller* decides to reduce *control* over A in a manner which will result in the *controller* failing to fall in any of the cases described in 1 above	SUP 11.3.2AG(3)	SUP 11.3.15AD
Notifications from a UK domestic firm other than a non-directive firm relating to a change in control			
1	When a *firm* becomes aware of a person proposing to become a *controller* or an existing *controller* proposing to increase his *control* over the *firm*	SUP 11.4.2R SUP 11.4.7R SUP 11.4.8G	SUP 11.5.1R SUP 11.5.1AG SUP 11.5.2R SUP 11.5.3G SUP 15.7
2	When a *firm* becomes aware that an existing *controller* is proposing to reduce his *control* over the *firm* or is proposing to cease to be a *controller* of the *firm*	SUP 11.4.2R SUP 11.4.7R SUP 11.4.8G	SUP 11.5.7R SUP 15.7
3	When a *firm* becomes aware of any material inaccuracies, omissions or changes in information previously provided to the *FSA* either by the *firm* or by the *controller*	SUP 11.6.1G SUP 11.6.2R	SUP 15.7

Part II FSA Handbook Materials

Event triggering a notification		Requirement reference	
		When	**How**
4	When a change in *control* actually takes place or, although a notification has been submitted, is not, after all, going to take place	SUP 11.6.4R SUP 11.6.5R	SUP 15.7
Notification from a non-directive firm relating to a change in control			
1	When a *firm* becomes aware that a *person* is acquiring (a) 20% or more of the *shares* in the *firm* ("B") or in a *parent undertaking* of B ("P"); (b) 20% or more of the *voting power* in B or P; or (c) *shares* or *voting power* in B or P as a result of which the *controller* is able to exercise significant influence over the management of B	SUP 11.4.2A R SUP 11.4.7R SUP 11.4.8G	SUP 11.5.1R SUP 11.5.2R SUP 11.5.3G
2	When a *firm* becomes aware that A is ceasing to fall in any of the cases described in 1 above	SUP 11.4.2R SUP 11.4.7R SUP 11.4.8G	SUP 11.5.7R SUP 15.7
3	When a *firm* becomes aware of any material inaccuracies omissions or changes in information previously provided to the *FSA* either by the *firm* or by the *controller*	SUP 11.6.1G SUP 11.6.2R	SUP 15.7
4	When a change in *control* actually takes place or, although a notification has been submitted, is not, after all, going to take place	SUP 11.6.4R SUP 11.6.5R	SUP 15.7
Notifications from an overseas firm relating to a change in control			
1	When a *firm* becomes aware that a person becomes a *controller* of the *firm*, increases or reduces his *control* over the *firm* or ceases to be have *control* over the *firm*	SUP 11.4.4R SUP 11.4.7R SUP 11.4.8G	SUP 11.5.1R SUP 11.5.2R SUP 11.5.3G SUP 15.7
2	When a *firm* becomes aware of any material inaccuracies, omissions or changes in information previously provided to the *FSA* by the *firm*	SUP 11.6.1G	SUP 15.7
3	When a change in *control* actually takes place or, although a notification has been submitted, is not, after all, going to take place	SUP 11.6.4R SUP 11 6.5R	SUP 15.7
Other ongoing notifications from a firm (UK domestic or overseas)			
1	When a *firm* becomes aware of a change in the circumstances of an existing *controller*	SUP 11.8.1R to SUP 11.8.4G	SUP 15.7
2	When a *firm* becomes aware that it has become or ceased to be *closely linked* with any person	SUP 11.9.1R	SUP 15.7

Annex 2

[deleted]

Annex 3

[deleted]

Annex 4

[deleted]

Annex 5
[deleted]

CHAPTER 12
APPOINTED REPRESENTATIVES

12.1 Application and purpose

Application

[2165]
12.1.1 **[R]**

(1) This chapter applies to a *firm* which is considering appointing, has decided to appoint or has appointed an *appointed representative*.

(1A) This chapter applies to a *UK MiFID investment firm* which is considering appointing, has decided to appoint or has appointed an *EEA tied agent*.

(2) This chapter does not apply to a *UCITS qualifier*.

(3) This chapter does not apply in relation to a *tied agent* acting on behalf of an *EEA MiFID investment firm* unless that *tied agent* is established in the *UK*.

Purpose

12.1.2 **[G]** This chapter gives *guidance* to a *firm*, which is considering appointing an *appointed representative*, on how the provisions of section 39 of the *Act* (Exemption of appointed representatives) work. For example, it gives *guidance* on the conditions that must be satisfied for a *person* to be appointed as an *appointed representative*. It also gives *guidance* to a *firm* on the implications, for the *firm* itself, of appointing an *appointed representative*.

12.1.3 **[G]** The chapter also sets out the *FSA's rules*, and guidance on these *rules*, that apply to a *firm* before it appoints, when it appoints and when it has appointed an *appointed representative*. The main purpose of these *rules* is to place responsibility on a *firm* for seeking to ensure that:

(1) its *appointed representatives* are fit and proper to deal with *clients* in its name; and

(2) *clients* dealing with its *appointed representatives* are afforded the same level of protection as if they had dealt with the *firm* itself.

12.1.4 **[G]** A separate leaflet will be produced to give guidance to *appointed representatives* themselves. For a copy of this leaflet (when available) please contact the Corporate Authorisation department (see SUP 12.7.5G).

12.1.5 **[G]** This chapter also sets out *guidance* about section 39A of the *Act*, which is relevant to a *UK MiFID investment firm* that is considering appointing an *FSA registered tied agent*. It also sets out the *FSA's rules*, and *guidance* on those *rules*, in relation to the appointment of an *EEA tied agent* by a *UK MiFID investment firm*.

12.2 Introduction

What is an appointed representative?

12.2.1 **[G]**

(1) Under section 19 of the *Act* (The general prohibition), no *person* may carry on a *regulated activity* in the *United Kingdom*, or purport to do so, unless he is an *authorised person*, or he is an *exempt person* in relation to that activity.

(2) A *person* will be an *exempt person* if he satisfies the conditions in section 39(1) of the *Act*, *guidance* on which is given in SUP 12.2.2G. A *person* who is exempt as a result of satisfying these conditions is referred to in the *Act* as an *appointed representative*.

(3) If an *appointed representative* is also a *tied agent* he must also satisfy the condition in section 39(1A) of the *Act* in order to be an *exempt person*. See SUP 12.4.12G for *guidance* on that condition and SUP 12.2.16G for more general *guidance* about *tied agents*.

12.2.2 **[G]**

(1) A *person* must satisfy the conditions in section 39(1) of the *Act* to become an *appointed representative*. These are that:

    (a) the *person* must not be an *authorised person*, that is, he must not have *permission* under the *Act* to carry on any *regulated activity* in his own right (section 39(1) of the *Act*);

    (b) the *person* must have entered into a contract with an *authorised person*, referred to in the *Act* as the '*principal*', which:

        (i) permits or requires him to carry on business of a description prescribed in the *Appointed Representatives Regulations* (section 39(1)(a)(i) of the *Act*) (see SUP 12.2.7G); and

(ii) complies with any requirements that may be prescribed in the *Appointed Representatives Regulations* (section 39(1)(a)(ii) of the *Act*) (see SUP 12.5.2G); and

(c) the *principal* must have accepted responsibility, in writing, for the activities of the *person* in carrying on the whole, or part, of the business specified in the contract.

(2) The *appointed representative* is an *exempt person* in relation to any *regulated activity* comprised in the carrying on of the business for which his *principal* has accepted responsibility.

12.2.3 **[G]** Who can be an appointed representative?

As long as the conditions in section 39 of the *Act* are satisfied, any *person*, other than an *authorised person*, may become an *appointed representative*, including a *body corporate*, a *partnership* or an individual in business on his own account. However, an *appointed representative* cannot be an *authorised person* under the *Act*; that is, it cannot be exempt for some *regulated activities* and *authorised* for others.

12.2.4 **[G]** Can an appointed representative have more than one principal?

The *Act* and the *Appointed Representative Regulations* do not prevent an *appointed representative* from acting for more than one *principal*. However, SUP 12.5.6A R (Prohibition of multiple principals for certain activities) prevents this for particular kinds of business.

12.2.5 **[G]** [deleted]

What is a "network"?

12.2.6 **[G]** A *firm* is referred to as a *'network'* if it appoints five or more *appointed representatives* (not counting *introducer appointed representatives*) or if it appoints fewer than five *appointed representatives* (again, not counting *introducer appointed representatives*) which have, between them, twenty-six or more *representatives*. However, a *network* does not include:

(a) a *product provider*;

(b) a *firm* which markets the *packaged products* of a *product provider* in the same *group* as the *firm* and which does so other than by selecting *products* from the whole market;

(c) an *insurer* in relation to a *non-investment insurance contract*; or

(d) a *home finance provider*.

Business for which an appointed representative is exempt

12.2.7 **[G]**

(1) The *Appointed Representatives Regulations* are made by the Treasury under section 39(1) of the *Act*. These regulations describe, among other things, the business for which an *appointed representative* may be exempt, which is business which comprises any of:

(a) *dealing in investments as agent* (article 21 of the *Regulated Activities Order*) where the transaction relates to a *pure protection contract* (but only where the contract is not a *long-term care insurance contract*) or *general insurance contract*;

(b) *arranging (bringing about) deals in investments* (article 25(1) of the *Regulated Activities Order*) (that is in summary, deals in a *designated investment, funeral plan contract, pure protection contract, general insurance contract* or *right to or interest in a funeral plan*);

(c) *making arrangements with a view to transactions in investments* (article 25(2) of the *Regulated Activities Order*) (that is in summary, transactions in a *designated investment, funeral plan contract, pure protection contract, general insurance contract* or *right to or interest in a funeral plan*);

(d) *arranging (bringing about) a home finance transaction* (articles 25A(1), 25B(1) and 25C(1) of the *Regulated Activities Order*);

(e) *making arrangements with a view to a home finance transaction* (articles 25A(2), 25B(2) and 25C(2) of the *Regulated Activities Order*);

(f) *assisting in the administration and performance of a contract of insurance* (article 39A of the *Regulated Activities Order*);

(g) *arranging safeguarding and administration of assets* (part of article 40 of the *Regulated Activities Order*);

(h) providing *basic advice* on *stakeholder products* (article 52B of the *Regulated Activities Order*);

(i) advising on *investments* (article 53 of the *Regulated Activities Order*) (that is in summary, on any *designated investment, funeral plan contract* or *right to or interest in a funeral plan*)

(j) *advising on a home finance transaction* (articles 53A, 53B and 53C of the *Regulated Activities Order*); and

(k) *agreeing to carry on a regulated activity* (article 64 of the *Regulated Activities Order*) where the *regulated activity* is one of those in (a) to (h).

(2) If the *appointed representative* is a *tied agent* of an *EEA firm*, the business for which the *appointed representative* may be exempt includes the following additional activities:
(a) placing *financial instruments*;
(b) providing advice to *clients* or potential *clients* in relation to the placing of *financial instruments*.
(3) [deleted]

What is an introducer appointed representative?

12.2.8 **[G]**
(1) An *introducer appointed representative* is an *appointed representative* appointed by a *firm* whose scope of appointment must, under SUP 12.5.7R, be limited to:
(a) effecting introductions to the *firm* or other members of the *firm's group*; and
(b) distributing *non-real-time financial promotions* which relate to products or services available from or through the *firm* or other members of the *firm's group*.
(2) The permitted scope of appointment of an *introducer appointed representative* does not include in particular:
(a) *dealing in investments as agent*; or
(b) *arranging (bringing about) deals in investments* or *arranging (bringing about) regulated mortgage contracts*; or
(c) *assisting in the administration and performance of a contract of insurance*; or
(d) *advising on investments*, providing *basic advice* on *stakeholder products*, *advising on a home finance transaction* or other activity that might reasonably lead a *customer* to believe that he had received *basic advice* or *advice on investments* or on *home finance transactions* or that the *introducer appointed representative* is permitted to give *basic advice* or give *personal recommendations* on investments or on *home finance transactions*.
(3) An *introducer appointed representative* may have more than one *principal*, but will need a contract with each *principal*.
(4) The *approved persons* regime does not apply to an *introducer appointed representative* (see SUP 10.1.16R).

12.2.9 **[G]** To become an *introducer appointed representative*, a *person* must meet the conditions in the *Act* to become an *appointed representative* (see SUP 12.2.2G).

12.2.10 **[G]** All *rules* in SUP 12 apply in relation to *introducer appointed representatives* except for:
(1) SUP 12.4.2R, SUP 12.4.5B R and SUP 12.4.5C R, on the appointment of *appointed representatives*, which are replaced by SUP 12.4.6R;
(2) SUP 12.5.6AR on required contract terms, which is replaced by SUP 12.5.7R; and
(3) SUP 12.9.1R(4) (Record keeping).

12.2.11 **[G]** If an *introducer appointed representative* is an individual in business on his own, then he will also be an *introducer* (see SUP 12.2.13G). This has certain implications in COBS.

Introducers and representatives: what do these terms mean and what is the relationship with an appointed representative?

12.2.12 **[G]** A *firm* or its *appointed representative* may appoint or employ individuals to act as *introducers* or *representatives* in respect of *designated investment business*.

12.2.13 **[G]**
(1) An *introducer* is an individual appointed by a *firm* or by an *appointed representative* of such a *firm* to carry out, in the course of *designated investment business*, either or both of the following activities:
(a) effecting introductions;
(b) distributing *non-real-time financial promotions*.
(2) An *introducer* is not an *exempt person* under section 39 of the *Act* (unless he is also an *introducer appointed representative*) and hence cannot benefit from the exemption to carry on *regulated activities* in his own right. As a result, an *introducer* that is not an *introducer appointed representative* works in the name of his *firm* or the *firm's appointed representative* but he does not fall within the scope of the *approved persons* regime as he does not, as such, perform a *controlled function*.

12.2.14 **[G]**
(1) A *representative* is an individual who is appointed by a *firm* or an *appointed representative*, to carry on any of the activities in (1)(a) to (c):
(a) *advising on investments*;
(b) *arranging (bringing about) deals in investments*;
(c) *dealing in investments as agent*.
(2) If a *firm* appoints an *appointed representative* who is an individual in (1), that *appointed representative* will also be a *representative*. The individual may need to be approved to perform the *customer function*, (see SUP 12.6.8G and SUP 12.6.9G). In these circumstances,

in addition to complying with the requirements of SUP 12 and other regulatory requirements, the *firm* should ensure that the *rules* for *representatives* in COBS 6 (Information about the firm, its services and remuneration) are complied with.

12.2.15 **[G]** [deleted]

What is a tied agent?

12.2.16 **[G]**

(1) A *tied agent* is a *person* who acts for and under the responsibility of a *MiFID investment firm* (or a *third country investment firm*) in respect of *MiFID business* (or the *equivalent business of the third country investment firm*). Most *tied agents* appointed by *firms* are also *appointed representatives.*

(2) Unless otherwise provided, this chapter applies to a *firm* that appoints a *tied agent* that is an *appointed representative* in the same way as it applies to the appointment of any other *appointed representative*.

(3) This chapter sets out the provisions which apply to *tied agents*:
 (a) established in the *UK*; or
 (b) established in another *EEA State* and appointed by a *UK MiFID investment firm.*

(4) A *tied agent* appointed by a *firm* to carry on *investment services and activities* or *ancillary services* on its behalf may not provide *cross border services* or establish a *branch* in another *EEA State* in its own right. This is because *tied agents* do not have passporting rights. The *tied agent* of a *MiFID investment firm* may, however, provide *cross border services* or establish a *branch* in another *EEA State* by availing itself of the appointing *firm*'s passport. *MiFID investment firms* may also appoint *tied agents* established in different *EEA States.*

(5) A *tied agent* will not be an *appointed representative* if it does not and is not likely to conduct any business as a *tied agent* in the *UK*. If such a *tied agent* is appointed by a *UK MiFID investment firm* it will be an *EEA tied agent*. *EEA tied agents* are either *FSA registered tied agents* or *EEA registered tied agents.*

(6) This chapter only applies to a *firm* that appoints a *tied agent* that is not an *appointed representative* where it expressly refers to *tied agents.*

(7) Under *MiFID*, an *EEA State* may prohibit the appointment of *tied agents* by *MiFID investment firms* for which it is the *Home State*. If a *UK MiFID investment firm* appoints a *tied agent* established in such an *EEA State*, the *tied agent* must be registered with the *FSA*. Such an *EEA tied agent* is referred to in the *Handbook* as an *FSA registered tied agent.*

(8) If a *UK MiFID investment firm* appoints a *tied agent* established in an *EEA State* that allows *MiFID investment firms* for which it is the *home State* to appoint *tied agents*, the *tied agent* must be registered with the *competent authority* of the *EEA State* in which it is established. Such an *EEA tied agent* is referred to in the *Handbook* as an *EEA registered tied agent.*

12.3 What responsibility does a firm have for its appointed representatives or EEA tied agent?

Responsibility for appointed representatives

12.3.1 **[G]** In determining whether a *firm* has complied with any provision in or under the *Act* such as any *Principle* or other *rule*, anything that an *appointed representative* has done or omitted to do as respects the business for which the *firm* has accepted responsibility will be treated as having been done or omitted to be done by the *firm* (section 39(4) of the *Act*).

12.3.2 **[G]** The *firm* is responsible, to the same extent as if it had expressly permitted it, for anything the *appointed representative* does or omits to do, in carrying on the business for which the *firm* has accepted responsibility (section 39(3) of the *Act*).

12.3.3 **[G]** In determining whether the *firm* has committed any *offence*, however, the knowledge or intentions of an *appointed representative* are not attributable to the *firm*, unless in all the circumstances it is reasonable for them to be attributed to it (section 39(6) of the *Act*).

12.3.4 **[G]** SYSC 6.1.1R requires a *MiFID investment firm* to ensure the compliance of its *appointed representative* with obligations under the *regulatory system*. The concept of a *relevant person* in *SYSC* includes an officer or employee of a *tied agent.*

Responsibility for EEA tied agents

12.3.5 **[R]** A *UK MiFID investment firm* must not appoint an *EEA registered tied agent* or allow such an agent to continue to act for it unless it accepts or has accepted responsibility in writing for the agent's activities in acting as its *EEA registered tied agent*.

[Note: paragraph 1 of article 23(2) of *MiFID*]

12.3.6 **[G]** The effect of section 39A(6)(b) of the *Act* is to prohibit a *UK MiFID investment firm* from appointing an *FSA registered tied agent* unless it has accepted responsibility in writing for the agent's activities in acting as a *tied agent*.

12.4 What must a firm do when it appoints an appointed representative or an EEA tied agent?

The permission that the firm needs

12.4.1 **[R]** [Deleted]

12.4.1A **[G]** The effect of sections 20 (Authorised persons acting without permission) and 39(4) (Exemption of appointed representatives) of the *Act* is that the *regulated activities* covered by an *appointed representative's* appointment need to:

(1) fall within the scope of the *principal's permission*; or

(2) be excluded from being *regulated activities* when carried on by the *principal*, for example because they fall within article 28 of the *Regulated Activities Order* (Arranging transactions to which the arranger is a party).

Appointment of an appointed representative (other than an introducer appointed representative)

12.4.2 **[R]** Before a *firm* appoints a *person* as an *appointed representative* (other than an *introducer appointed representative*) and on a continuing basis, it must establish on reasonable grounds that:

(1) the appointment does not prevent the *firm* from satisfying and continuing to satisfy the *threshold conditions*;

(2) the *person*:

  (a) is solvent;

  (b) is otherwise suitable to act for the *firm* in that capacity; and

  (c) has no *close links* which would be likely to prevent the effective supervision of the *person* by the *firm*;

(3) the *firm* has adequate:

  (a) controls over the *person's regulated activities* for which the *firm* has responsibility (see SYSC 3.1 or SYSC 4.1); and

  (b) resources to monitor and enforce compliance by the *person* with the relevant requirements applying to the *regulated activities* for which the *firm* is responsible and with which the *person* is required to comply under its contract with the *firm* (see SUP 12.5.3G(2)); and

(4) the *firm* is ready and organised to comply with the other applicable requirements contained or referred to in this chapter.

12.4.2A **[R]** A *firm* must ensure that a *tied agent* that is an *appointed representative* is of sufficiently good repute and that it possesses appropriate general, commercial and professional knowledge so as to be able to communicate accurately all relevant information regarding the proposed service to the *client* or potential *client*. This does not limit a *firm's* obligations under SUP 12.4.2 R.

[Note: paragraphs 3 and 4 of article 23(3) of *MiFID*]

12.4.3 **[G]** In assessing, under SUP 12.4.2R(2)(a) and (b), whether an *appointed representative* or prospective *appointed representative* is solvent and otherwise suitable, a *firm* should determine, among other matters, whether the *person* is likely to be adversely influenced by its financial position in the conduct of the business for which the *firm* is responsible. This might arise, for example, if the *person* has cashflow problems and is not able to service its debts. Guidance for *firms* on assessing the financial position of an *appointed representative* or prospective *appointed representative* is given in SUP 12Ann1G.

12.4.4 **[G]** In assessing, under SUP 12.4.2R(2)(b), whether an *appointed representative* or prospective *appointed representative* is otherwise suitable to act for the *firm* in that capacity, a *firm* should consider:

(1) whether the *person* is fit and proper; *guidance* on the information that *firms* should take reasonable steps to obtain and verify is given in SUP 12Ann2G; and

(2) the fitness and propriety (including good character and competence) and financial standing of the *controllers*, *directors*, *partners*, proprietors and *managers* of the *person*; *firms* seeking *guidance* on the information which they should take reasonable steps to obtain and verify should refer to *FIT* and the questions in the relevant Form A (Application to perform controlled functions under the approved person regime) in SUP 10Ann4D.

12.4.5 **[G]** In determining, under SUP 12.4.2R(2)(c), whether an *appointed representative* or prospective *appointed representative* has any *close links* which would be likely to prevent the *firm's* effective supervision, a *firm* should consider the *guidance* to *threshold condition* 3 (Close links) in COND 2.3.

Appointment representative who may be appointed by other principals

12.4.5A **[G]** If a *firm* proposes to appoint an *appointed representative*, but not to prohibit its appointment by any other *principals* (see SUP 12.5.2G(3)), the *firm* should, in particular:

(1) require, in the contract, that the *appointed representative* notifies the *firm* about other *principals* (see SUP 12.5.5R(3)); and

(2) unless the *appointed representative* is an *introducer appointed representative*:

(a) take reasonable steps to check whether the *appointed representative* is already appointed by one or more other *principals* and, if it is, contact those other *principals*; such steps should include asking the *appointed representative* and checking the *Register*;

(b) if there are any other *principals*, agree arrangements with the other *principals* (see SUP 12.4.5B R); and

(c) establish effective systems and controls for ensuring that the *appointed representative* complies with all contractual restrictions imposed, including those relating to multiple *principals* under the *Appointed Representatives Regulations* and under SUP 12.5.6AR (see SUP 12.6.11AR).

Multiple principals

12.4.5B **[R]**

(1) A *firm* must not appoint a *person* as its *appointed representative* until it has entered into a written agreement (a "multiple principal agreement") with every other *principal* the person may have; but this does not apply to the appointment of an *introducer appointed representative* nor does it require an agreement with another *principal* which has appointed a *person* as an *introducer appointed representative*.

(2) A *firm* must not unreasonably decline to enter into a multiple principal agreement with any *principal* of his *appointed representative* unless the *firm* is relying on a prohibition on the *appointed representative* from representing any other *firms* (or is seeking to impose such a prohibition) as permitted by article 3 of the *Appointed Representative Regulations*.

(3) A multiple principal agreement must contain all the provisions which are necessary or desirable to:

(a) set out the relationship between the *principals* of that *appointed representative*; and

(b) protect the interests of *clients*;

including the matters set out in SUP 12.4.5C R.

12.4.5C **[R]** Table: Multiple principal agreement

	Matter	Explanation
1.	Scope of appointment	The scope of appointment given by each *principal* to the *appointed representative*.
2.	Complaints handling	The identity of the *principal* which will be the point of contact for a complaint from a *client* (referred to as the "lead-principal" in SUP 12.4.5D G to SUP *12.4.5E G*).
		An agreement that each *principal* will co-operate with each other *principal* in resolving a complaint from a *client* in relation to the *appointed representative's* conduct.
		The arrangements for complaints handling, including arrangements for resolving disputes between the *principals* in relation to their liability to a *client* in respect of a complaint and arrangements for dealing with referrals to the *Financial Ombudsman Service*.
3.	*Financial promotions*	The arrangements for *approving financial promotions*.
4.	Control and monitoring	The arrangements for the control and monitoring of the activities of the *appointed representative* (see in particular SUP 12.6.6R (Regulated activities and investment services outside the scope of appointment) and SUP 12.6.7G (Senior management responsibility for appointed representatives)).
5.	*Approved person* status	The arrangements for making applications for *approved person* status (see SUP 10 (Approved persons)).
6.	Training and competence	The arrangements for training and competence (see TC).
7.	Co-operation	The arrangements for co-operation over any other issues which may arise from the multiple appointments, including issues which may damage the interests of *clients* dealing with the *appointed representative* and administrative issues.

	Matter	Explanation
		An agreement by each *principal* to take reasonable steps to ensure that it does not cause the *appointed representative* or any of its other *principals* to be in breach of their obligations to each other or under the *regulatory system*.
8.	Sharing information	The arrangements for sharing information on matters relevant to the matters covered under the multiple principal agreement and each *principal's* obligations under SUP 12.6 (Continuing obligations of firms with appointed representatives).
		An agreement that each *principal* will notify each other *principal* of any information which is materially relevant to the multiple principal agreement.

12.4.5D **[G]** One effect of the multiple principal agreement is to introduce a 'lead principal' concept in relation to complaints handling for the benefit of the *client*. For example, where the *client* has been given advice by an *appointed representative* who has two *principals*, and the advice could have led to a transaction being arranged with either *principal*, the *client* will know that he may pursue his complaint with (but not necessarily against) one of the *principals*. Whether he later decides to refer his complaint to the *Financial Ombudsman Service*, and if so, against which *principal*, will depend on the circumstances.

12.4.5E **[G]**

(1) Under the relevant provisions in *COBS*, *ICOBS* and *MCOB*, the *customer* will receive details of how to complain to the *appointed representative* and, when a product is purchased, details of the complaints procedure for the *product provider*, *insurer* or *home finance provider*.

(2) Under DISP 1.2.1R, a *firm* must among other things, supply summary details of its internal process for dealing promptly and fairly with *complaints* to the *customer* when it receives a *complaint*. In complying with DISP 1.2.1R, a *firm* should ensure that the "lead-principal" is clearly identified in the procedures.

(3) The complaints procedure should also explain that the *customer* has a choice of whether to contact the *appointed representative*, the "lead-principal" or the *product provider*, *insurer* or *home finance provider* and that the "lead-principal" will be the appropriate point of contact where the *customer* does not wish to complain about a specific product or is unsure who to contact.

(4) In other words, where the *customer* has a doubt who to complain to the "lead-principal" is to be the point of contact for all complaints arising out of the activities of the *appointed representative*.

12.4.5F **[G]** When considering the provisions for complaints handling (see SUP 12.4.5C R(2)) *firms* should consider the use of a mediation clause. If a complaint is made by a *client*, *principals* which are unable to resolve a dispute about liability to the *client* should consider all quick and effective ways of resolving the dispute, including referring the matter to the *Financial Ombudsman Service* and mediation.

12.4.5G **[G]** It is for the *principals* to consider in each case whether it would be appropriate to show the multiple principal agreement to their *appointed representative*, or in some circumstances make their *appointed representative* a party to it.

Appointment of an introducer appointed representative

12.4.6 **[R]** Before a *firm* appoints a *person* as an *introducer appointed representative*, and on a continuing basis, it must take reasonable care to ensure that:

(1) the *person* is suitable to act for the *firm* in that capacity (having regard, in particular, to other *persons* connected with the *person* who will be, or who are, directly responsible for its activities); and

(2) the *firm* is ready and organised to comply with the other applicable requirements contained or referred to in this chapter.

12.4.7 **[G]** In assessing, under SUP 12.4.6R(1), whether an *introducer appointed representative* or prospective *introducer appointed representative* is otherwise suitable to act for the *firm* in that capacity, the *firm* should determine whether the *introducer appointed representative* and those *persons* who will be, or who are, directly responsible for its activities are of sufficiently good reputation and otherwise fit and proper for that appointment. The *firm* should, as a minimum, verify the identity of a prospective *introducer appointed representative* and relevant *persons* but need not carry out the more extensive due diligence required for the appointment of an *appointed representative* under SUP 12.4.2R.

12.4.8 **[G]** If a *firm* has doubts that a prospective *introducer appointed representative* or other *person* is of sufficiently good reputation and otherwise fit and proper, the *FSA* will expect it to resolve those

Part II FSA Handbook Materials

doubts before appointing the prospective *introducer appointed representative*. For example, if a *firm* is aware that a *person's* previous appointment as an *introducer appointed representative* or *representative* was terminated, it should take reasonable steps to find out the reasons for the termination and the extent to which those reasons reflect on the *person* concerned.

Appointed representative carrying on insurance mediation

12.4.8A **[R]** Before a *firm* appoints a *person* as an *appointed representative* to carry on *insurance mediation activity*, it must in relation to *insurance mediation activity* ensure that the *person* will comply on appointment, and will continue to comply with, the provisions of PRU 9.1.8R and PRU 9.1.10R (Knowledge and ability, and good repute) as if the *appointed representative* were a *firm*.

12.4.8B **[G]** In assessing, under SUP 12.4.8A R, whether an *appointed representative*, or prospective *appointed representative*, has established the knowledge and ability requirements for *persons* within its management structure and for those directly involved in its *insurance mediation activity*, a *firm* should refer to *TC*.

12.4.9 **[G]**

(1) An *appointed representative* must not commence an *insurance mediation activity* until he is included on the *Register* as carrying on such *activities* (see SUP 12.5.2G(3)).

(2) If an *appointed representative's* scope of appointment is to include an *insurance mediation activity*, the *principal* must notify the *FSA* of the appointment before the *appointed representative* commences that *activity* (see SUP 12.7.1R(1)).

(3) As an exception, pre-notification is not required if the *appointed representative* is already included on the *Register* as carrying on *insurance mediation activities* in another capacity (for example, as the *appointed representative* of another *principal*).

12.4.10 **[G]**

(1) The *FSA* has the power to decide not to include on the *Register* (or to remove from the *Register*) an *appointed representative* whose scope of appointment includes an *insurance mediation activity*, if it appears to the *FSA* that he is not a fit and proper *person* to carry on those *activities* (article 95 of the *Regulated Activities Order*).

(2) If the *FSA* proposes to use the power in (1), it must give the *appointed representative* a *warning notice*. If the *FSA* decides to proceed with its proposal, it must give the *appointed representative* a *decision notice*. The procedures followed by the *FSA* in relation to the giving of *warning notices* and *decision notices* are set out in DEPP 2.

(3) An *appointed representative* may apply to the *FSA* for a determination of the kind referred to in (1) to be revoked. If the *FSA* proposes to refuse the application, it must give the *appointed representative* a *warning notice*, and if the *FSA* decides to proceed with the refusal, it must give the *appointed representative* a *decision notice*.

Appointment of an FSA registered tied agent

12.4.11 **[R]** If a *UK MiFID investment firm* appoints an *FSA registered tied agent*, SUP 12.4.2R and SUP 12.4.2AR apply to that *firm* as though the *FSA registered tied agent* were an appointed representative.

[Note: paragraphs 3 and 4 of article 23(3) of *MiFID*]

Tied agents

12.4.12 **[G]**

(1) A *tied agent* that is an *appointed representative* may not start to act as a *tied agent* until it is included on the applicable register (section 39(1A) of the *Act*). If the *tied agent* is established in the *UK*, the register maintained by the *FSA* is the applicable register for these purposes. If the *tied agent* is established in another *EEA State*, it should consult section 39(1B) of the *Act* to determine the applicable register.

(2) A *UK MiFID investment firm* that appoints an *FSA registered tied agent* who is not registered with the *FSA* will, subject to certain conditions, be taken to have contravened a requirement imposed on it by or under the *Act* (see section 39A(6)(c) and (d) of the *Act*).

(3) A *UK MiFID investment firm* that appoints an *EEA registered tied agent* will be required to register that agent with the *competent authority* of the *EEA State* in which it is established. This requirement will be imposed by the rules of that *EEA State*.

(4) If the *tied agent* is not established in the *UK* and is appointed by an *EEA MiFID investment firm*, it cannot commence acting as a *tied agent* until it is included on the public register of *tied agents* in the *EEA State* in which it is established (or in certain cases, of the *Home State* of the *firm*).

(5) If an *appointed representative's* scope of appointment is to include acting as a *tied agent*, the principal must notify the *FSA* of the appointment before the *appointed representative* starts acting as such (see SUP 12.7.7R (1A)).

(6) A *tied agent* can only act as such for one *MiFID investment firm* or *third country investment firm* (see SUP 12.5.6AR(1A)).

12.5 Contracts: required terms

Required contract terms for all appointed representatives

12.5.1 **[G]** The *Appointed Representative Regulations* include, among other things, the prescribed requirements applying to contracts between *firms* and *appointed representatives* for the purposes of section 39(1)(a)(ii) of the *Act*.

12.5.2 **[G]**

(1) Regulations 3(1) and (2) of the *Appointed Representatives Regulations* makes it a requirement that the contract between the *firm* and the *appointed representative* (unless it prohibits the *appointed representative* from representing other counterparties) contains a provision enabling the *firm* to:

(a) impose such a prohibition; or

(b) impose restrictions as to the other counterparties which the *appointed representative* may represent, or as to the types of *investment* in relation to which the *appointed representative* may represent other counterparties.

(1A) The requirement described in paragraph (1) does not apply if the *firm* is an *EEA MiFID investment firm.*

(2) Under the *Appointed Representative Regulations*, an *appointed representative* is treated as representing other counterparties if, broadly, it:

(a) makes arrangements (within article 25 of the *Regulated Activities Order*) for *persons* to enter into investment transactions with other counterparties; or

(b) *arranges the safeguarding and administration of assets* by other counterparties; or

(c) gives *advice* (within article 53 of the *Regulated Activities Order* (Advising on investments)) on the merits of entering into investment transactions with other counterparties;

(d) *assists in the administration and performance of a contract of insurance* (article 39A of the *Regulated Activities Order*);

where an "investment transaction" means a transaction to *buy*, *sell*, subscribe for or underwrite a *security*, a *relevant investment* (that is, a *designated investment, funeral plan contract, pure protection contract, general insurance contract* or *right to or interest in a funeral plan*); or

(e) *arranges*:

(i) for *persons* to enter (or with a view to *persons* entering) as customers into *home finance transactions* (or as plan providers in the case of a *home reversion plan*) with other counterparties; or

(ii) for a *person* to vary a *home finance transaction* entered into by a *person* as customer (or as plan provider in the case of a *home reversion plan*) on or after 31 October 2004 (in the case of a *regulated mortgage contract*) or 6 April 2007 (in all other cases) with other counterparties; or

(f) gives advice (within articles 53A, 53B or 53C of the *Regulated Activities Order*) on the merits of:

(i) *persons* entering as customers into *home finance transactions* (or as plan provider in the case of a *home reversion plan*) with other counterparties; or

(ii) *persons* varying *home finance transactions* entered into by them as customer (or as plan provider in the case of a *home reversion plan*) on or after 31 October 2004 (in the case of a *regulated mortgage contract*) or 6 April 2007 (in all other cases) with other counterparties.

(g) provides *basic advice* on *stakeholder products*.

(3) If the scope of appointment covers, in relation to a *contract of insurance*, *dealing in investments as agent*, *arranging*, *assisting in the administration and performance of a contract of insurance* or *advising on investments*, regulation 3(4) of the *Appointed Representatives Regulations* makes it a requirement that the contract between the *firm* and the *appointed representative* contains a provision providing that the *appointed representative* is not permitted or required to carry on such business unless he is included in the *Register* as carrying on *insurance mediation activities*.

12.5.2A **[G]** If a *UK MiFID investment firm* or a *third country investment firm* appoints an *appointed representative* that is a *tied agent*, regulation 3(6) of the *Appointed Representative Regulations* requires the contract between the *firm* and the *appointed representative* to contain a provision that the representative is only permitted to provide the services and carry on the activities referred to in Article 4(1)(25) of *MiFID* while he is entered on the applicable register.

12.5.3 **[G]** A *firm* should satisfy itself that the terms of the contract with its *appointed representative* (including an *introducer appointed representative*):

(1) are designed to enable the *firm* to comply properly with any *limitations* or *requirements* on its own *permission*;

(2) require the *appointed representative* to cooperate with the *FSA* as described in SUP 2.3.4G (Information gathering by the FSA on its own initiative: cooperation by firms) and give access to its premises, as described in SUP 2.3.5G(2); and

(3) require the *appointed representative* to give the *firm's* auditors the same rights as are provided by section 341 of the *Act*, as described in SUP 3.6.6G.

12.5.4 **[G]** A *firm* should have the ability to terminate the contract with its *appointed representative* in the circumstances in SUP 12.6.1R(2). However, such a termination provision should not be automatic (see SUP 12.8.3R(1)).

12.5.5 **[R]** A *firm* must ensure that its written contract with each of its *appointed representatives*:

(1) complies with the requirements prescribed in regulation 3 of the *Appointed Representatives Regulations* (see SUP 12.5.2G);

(2) requires the *appointed representative* to comply, and to ensure that any *persons* who provide services to the *appointed representative* under a contract of services or a contract for service comply, with the relevant requirements in or under the *Act* (including the *rules*) that apply to the activities which it carries on as *appointed representative* of the *firm*; and

(3) (unless the written contract prohibits appointments by other *principals*) requires the *appointed representative* to notify the *firm*:

   (a) that it is seeking appointment as an *appointed representative* of another *person*, who the *person* is and the business for which the other *person* will accept responsibility;

   (b) (as soon as possible) of any change in the business notified under (a); and

   (c) (as soon as possible) of the termination of any such appointment.

12.5.6 **[G]**

(1) If the *appointed representative* is appointed to give *advice on investments* to *private customers* concerning *packaged products*, the *firm* should also satisfy itself that the contract requires compliance with the *rules* in COBS 6 (Information about the firm, its services and remuneration).

(2) The contractual requirements in SUP 12.5.5R should extend to:

   (a) the activities of the *appointed representative*, if the *appointed representative* is and individual; and

   (b) the activities of the *employees* of, *representatives* and *introducers* appointed by, the *appointed representative*.

Prohibition of multiple principals for certain activities

12.5.6A **[R]**

(1) A *firm* must ensure that, if appointing an *appointed representative* (other than an *introducer appointed representative*), to carry on any of the following *regulated activities*, its written contract prohibits the *appointed representative* from carrying on any of the specified activities as an *appointed representative* for another *firm*:

   (a) any *designated investment* business for *private customers*: the prohibition must cover all *designated investment* business for *private customers*;

   (b) any *regulated mortgage activities* (other than in relation to *lifetime mortgages*): the prohibition must cover all *regulated mortgage activities* (other than *lifetime mortgages*);

   (c) any *regulated mortgage activities* in relation to *lifetime mortgages*: the prohibition must cover all *lifetime mortgages*;

   (d) any *reversion activities*: the prohibition must cover all *reversion activities*;

   (e) any *home purchase activities*: the prohibition must cover all *home purchase activities*.

(1A) If the *appointed representative* is a *tied agent*, the prohibition must prevent the *appointed representative* acting as a *tied agent* for any other *MiFID investment firm* or *third country investment firm*.

(2) As an exception to (1), if the *firm* is a *long-term insurer* or an *operator* of a *UCITS* scheme, it may permit an *appointed representative* to carry on *designated investment business* as the *appointed representative* of one or more other *firms* provided that:
   (a) each of those other *firms* is a *long-term insurer* or an *operator* of a *UCITS scheme*;
   (b) the first *firm* and each of those other *firms* is a member of the same group; "group" means for this purpose a group of *bodies corporate* all having the same *holding company* including the *holding company*; and
   (c) the scope of each appointment does not overlap, as to both activities and *investments*.

[Note: articles 4(1)(25) and 23(1) of *MiFID*]

12.5.6B **[G]**

(1) The effect of SUP 12.5.6A R(1)(a) is that, in relation to designated investment business with *private customers*, *appointed representatives* are restricted to one *principal*.

(1A) The effect of SUP 12.5.6AR(1A) is that *tied agents* are restricted to one *principal* when acting as such. A *tied agent who has a MiFID investment firm* or a *third country investment firm* as a *principal* may have other *principals* who are not *MiFID investment firms* or *third country investment firms*.

(2) The effect of the *rule* prohibiting multiple principals for certain activities is that, in relation to *home finance activities*, *appointed representatives* are restricted to having four *principals*: one for *regulated mortgage contracts* other than *lifetime mortgages*, one for *lifetime mortgages*, one for *home reversion plans* and one for *home purchase plans*.

12.5.6C **[G]** As SUP 12.5.6A R does not apply to *non-investment insurance contracts*, there are no restrictions on the number of *principals* an *appointed representative* may have in relation to those contracts.

Required contract terms for an introducer appointed representative

12.5.7 **[R]** A *firm* must ensure that its written contract with each of its *introducer appointed representatives* limits the scope of the appointment to:

(1) effecting introductions to the *firm* or other members of the *firm's group*; and
(2) distributing *non-real-time financial promotions* which relate to products or services available from or through the *firm* or other members of the *firm's group*.

Required contract terms for EEA tied agents

12.5.8 **[R]** If a *UK MiFID investment firm* appoints an *EEA tied agent*, SUP 12.5.6AR(1A) applies to that *firm* as though the *EEA tied agent* were an *appointed representative*.

[Note: articles 4(1)(25) and 23(1) of *MiFID*]

Required contract terms for FSA registered tied agents

12.5.9 **[G]** Under section 39A(6)(a) of the *Act* a *UK MiFID investment firm* must ensure that the contract it uses to appoint an *FSA registered tied agent* complies with the requirements that would apply under the *Appointed Representative Regulations* if it were appointing an *appointed representative*.

12.6 Continuing obligations of firms with appointed representatives or EEA tied agents

Suitability etc. of appointed representatives

12.6.1 **[R]** If at any time a *firm* has reasonable grounds to believe that the conditions in SUP 12.4.2R, SUP 12.4.6R or SUP 12.4.8A R (as applicable) are not satisfied, or are likely not to be satisfied, in relation to any of its *appointed representatives*, the *firm* must:

(1) take immediate steps to rectify the matter; or
(2) terminate its contract with the *appointed representative*.

12.6.1A **[R]** A *firm* that is a principal of a *tied agent* that is an *appointed representative* must monitor the activities of that *tied agent* so as to ensure the *firm* complies with obligations imposed under *MiFID* (or equivalent obligations relating to the *equivalent business of a third country investment firm*) when acting through that *tied agent*.

[Note: paragraph 3 of Article 23(2) of *MiFID*]

12.6.2 **[G]** The *FSA* would normally expect a *firm* to carry out a check on its *appointed representative's* financial position every year (more often, if necessary) and to review critically the information obtained. An appropriately experienced *person* (for example, a financial accountant) should carry out these checks.

12.6.3 **[G]** Consideration should be given, among other things, to the impact on the *appointed representative's* financial position of any debts owed to, or by, the *appointed representative*. Indicators that an *appointed representative* is experiencing financial problems may include failure to adhere to repayment schedules for any debts, failure to meet any other financial commitments or requests for advances of *commission*.

12.6.4 **[G]** A *firm* should look into any concerns that may arise at any time about an *appointed representative's* financial standing and take the necessary action. The necessary action may include, for example, increased monitoring or, if appropriate, suspension or termination of the appointment.

Appointed representatives not to hold client money

12.6.5 **[R]**

(1) A *firm* must not permit an *appointed representative* to hold *client money* unless the *firm* is an *insurance intermediary* acting in accordance with CASS 5.5.18R to CASS 5.5.23R (which include provision for periodic segregation and reconciliation).

(2) The *firm* must take reasonable steps to ensure that if *client money* is received by the *appointed representative*, it is paid into *a client bank account* of the *firm*, or forwarded to the *firm*, in accordance with:

- (a) CASS 4.3.15R to CASS 4.3.17R; or
- (b) CASS 5.5.18R to CASS 5.5.21R unless acting in accordance with CASS 5.5.23R (Periodic segregation and reconciliation); or
- (c) the *MiFID client money segregation requirements*.

12.6.5A **[G]** When complying with the *MiFID client money segregation requirements*, *firms'* attention is drawn to the *guidance* in *CASS* 7.4.24 G to *CASS* 7.4.27 G.

Regulated activities and investment services outside the scope of appointment

12.6.6 **[R]** A *firm* must take reasonable steps to ensure that each of its *appointed representatives*:

(1) does not carry on *regulated activities* in breach of the *general prohibition* in section 19 of the *Act*; and

(2) carries on the *regulated activities* for which the *firm* has accepted responsibility in a way which is, and is held out as being, clearly distinct from any of the *appointed representative's* other business:

- (a) which is performed as an *appointed representative* of another *firm*; or
- (b) which:
  - (i) is, or is held out as being, primarily for the purposes of investment or obtaining credit, or obtaining insurance cover; and
  - (ii) is not a *regulated activity*.

Senior management responsibility for appointed representatives

12.6.7 **[G]** The senior management of a *firm* should be aware that the activities of *appointed representatives* are an integral part of the business that they manage. The responsibility for the control and monitoring of the activities of *appointed representatives* rests with the senior management of the *firm*.

Obligations of firms under the approved persons regime

12.6.8 **[G]**

(1) Some of the *controlled functions*, as set out in SUP 10.4.1R, apply to an *appointed representative* of a *firm*, other than an *introducer appointed representative*, just as they apply to a *firm* (see SUP 10.1.16R). These are the *governing functions* and the *customer function*. As explained in SUP 10.1.17G(1) and SUP 10.3.2G respectively:

- (a) the effect of SUP 10.1.16R is that the *directors* (or their equivalent) and *senior managers* (or their equivalent) of an *appointed representative*, other than an *introducer appointed representative*, must also be approved under section 59 of the *Act* for the performance of certain *controlled functions*;
- (b) although the *customer function* applies to an *appointed representative*, the descriptions of the functions themselves do not extend to *home finance mediation activity* or *insurance mediation activity*; and
- (c) sections 59(1) and 59(2) of the *Act* (Approval for particular arrangements) provide that approval is necessary in respect of a *controlled function* which is performed under an *arrangement* entered into by a *firm*, or its contractors (typically an *appointed representative*), in relation to a *regulated activity*.

(2) The *approved persons* regime applies differently to an *appointed representative* whose scope of appointment includes *insurance mediation activity* in relation to *non-investment insurance contracts* but no other *regulated activity* and whose principal purpose is to carry on activities other than *regulated activities*. These *appointed representatives* need only one *person*

performing one of the *governing functions*. This means that only one *director* (or equivalent) of these *appointed representatives* must be approved under section 59 of the *Act* for the performance of the *director function*, the *chief executive function*, the *partner function* or the *director of unincorporated association function*, whichever is the most appropriate (see SUP 10.1.16A R).

12.6.9 **[G]** *Firms* should be aware that, under the *approved persons* regime, the *firm* is responsible for submitting applications to the *FSA* for the approval as an *approved person* of:

(1) any individual who performs a *controlled function* and who is an *appointed representative*; and

(2) any *person* who performs a *controlled function* under an *arrangement* entered into by any of the *firm's appointed representatives*.

Applications for approval should be submitted as early as possible since a *person* may not perform a *controlled function* if he has not been approved by the *FSA* (see SUP 10.12).

Obligations of firms under the training and competence rules

12.6.10 **[G]** The *rules* and *guidance* relating to training and competence in SYSC 3 and 5 and in *TC* for a *firm* carrying on retail business extend to any *employee* of the *firm* in respect of whom the relevant *rules* apply. For these purposes, an *employee* of a *firm* includes:

(1) an individual who is an *appointed representative* of a *firm*; and

(2) an individual who is employed or appointed by an *appointed representative* of a *firm* (whether under a contract of service or for services) in connection with the business of *the appointed representative* for which the *firm* has accepted responsibility.

12.6.11 **[G]** A *firm* should take reasonable care to ensure that:

(1) it has satisfied SYSC 3 or SYSC 4 to 9 and TC in respect of the relevant staff of the *appointed representative*; and

(2) its *appointed representative* has adequate arrangements in respect of training and competence, which meet the requirements in SYSC and *TC*.

Compliance by an appointed representative with the contract

12.6.11A **[R]** A *firm* must take reasonable steps to establish and maintain effective systems and controls for ensuring that each of its *appointed representatives* complies with those terms of its contract which are imposed under the requirements contained or referred to in SUP 12.5 (Contracts: required terms).

12.6.12 **[R]** [deleted]

Continuing obligations of firms with tied agents

12.6.13 **[R]** A *firm* must ensure that its *tied agent* discloses the capacity in which he is acting and the *firm* he is representing when contacting a *client* or potential *client* or before dealing with a *client* or potential *client*.

[Note: paragraph 1 of article 23(2) of *MiFID*]

12.6.14 **[R]** A *firm* must take adequate measures in order to avoid any negative impact of the activities of its *tied agent* not covered by the scope of *MiFID* (or relating to the *equivalent business of a third country investment firm*) could have on the activities carried out by the *tied agent* on behalf of the *firm*.

[Note: paragraph 1 of article 23(4) of *MiFID*]

Continuing obligations of firms with EEA tied agents

12.6.15 **[R]** If a *UK MiFID investment firm* appoints an *EEA tied agent*, SUP 12.6.1R, SUP 12.6.1AR, SUP 12.6.5R and SUP 12.6.11AR apply to that firm as though the *EEA tied agent* were an *appointed representative*.

12.7 Notification requirements

Notification of appointment of an appointed representative

12.7.1 **[R]**

(1) This *rule* applies to a *firm* which intends to appoint:
   (a) an *appointed representative* to carry on *insurance mediation activities*; or
   (b) a *tied agent*.

(2) This *rule* also applies to a *firm* which has appointed an *appointed representative*.

(3) A *firm* in (1) must complete and submit the form in SUP 12 Ann 3 before the appointment.

(4) A *firm* in (2) must complete and submit the form in SUP 12 Ann 3 within ten *business days* after the commencement of activities.

Part II FSA Handbook Materials

12.7.2 **[G]** A *firm's* notice under SUP 12.7.1R should give details of the *appointed representative* and the *regulated activities* which the *firm* is, or intends to, carry on through the *appointed representative*, including:

(1) the name of the *firm's* new *appointed representative* (if the *appointed representative* is a *body corporate*, this is its registered name);

(2) any trading name under which the *firm's* new *appointed representative* carries on a *regulated activity* in that capacity;

(3) a description of the *regulated activities* which the *appointed representative* is permitted or required to carry on and for which the *firm* has accepted responsibility;

(4) any restrictions imposed on the *regulated activities* for which the *firm* has accepted responsibility; and

(5) where the *appointed representative* is not an individual, the name of the individuals who are responsible for the management of the business carried on by the *appointed representative* so far as it relates to *insurance mediation activity*.

12.7.3 **[G]** A *firm* need not notify the *FSA* of any restrictions imposed on the *regulated activities* for which the *firm* has accepted responsibility (under SUP 12.7.2G(4)) if the *firm* accepts responsibility for the unrestricted scope of the *regulated activities*.

12.7.3A **[G]** Where a notification is linked to an application for approval under section 59 of the *Act* (Approval for particular arrangements), see SUP 10.12.4AG.

12.7.4 **[G]** [deleted]

12.7.5 **[G]** To contact the Individuals, Mutuals and Policy Department:

(1) telephone on 020 7066 0019; fax on 020 7066 1099; or

(2) write to: Individuals, Mutuals and Policy Department, The Financial Services Authority, 25 The North Colonnade, Canary Wharf, London E14 5HS; or

(3) email iva@fsa.gov.uk.

12.7.6 **[G]** [deleted]

Notification of changes in information given to the FSA

12.7.7 **[R]**

(1) If:

(a)

(i) the scope of appointment of an *appointed representative* is extended to cover *insurance mediation activities* for the first time; and

(ii) the *appointed representative* is not included on the *Register* as carrying on *insurance mediation activities* in another capacity; or

(b) the scope of appointment of an *appointed representative* ceases to include *insurance mediation activity*;

the *appointed representative's principal* must give written notice to the *FSA* of that change before the *appointed representative* begins to carry on *insurance mediation activities* under the contract (see SUP 12.4.9G) or as soon as the scope of appointment of the *appointed representative* ceases to include *insurance mediation activity*.

(1A) If:

(a)

(i) the scope of appointment changes such that the *appointed representative* acts as a *tied agent* for the first time; and

(ii) the *appointed representative* is not included on the *Register*; or

(b) the *appointed representative* ceases to act as a *tied agent*;

the *appointed representative's* principal must give written notice to the *FSA* of that change before the *appointed representative* begins to act as a *tied agent* (see SUP 12.4) or as soon as the *appointed representative* ceases to act as a *tied agent*.

(2) Where there is a change in any of the information provided to the *FSA* under SUP 12.7.1R or SUP 12.7.7R(1A), a *firm* must complete and submit to the *FSA* the form in SUP 12 Ann 4R (Appointed representative notification form) in accordance with the instructions on the form and within ten *business days* of that change being made or, if later, as soon as the *firm* becomes aware of the change. The Appointed representative *notification form must* state the information that has changed.

(3) A *firm's* notification under (1) and (2) must be given to a member of or addressed for the attention of the Monitoring and Notifications Department at the address given in SUP 12.7.5G.

Notification of changes in conditions of appointment

12.7.8 **[R]**

(1) As soon as a *firm* has reasonable grounds to believe that any of the conditions in SUP 12.4.2R, SUP 12.4.6R or SUP 12.4.8A R (as applicable) are not satisfied, or are likely not to be satisfied, in relation to any of its *appointed representatives*, it must complete and submit to the *FSA* the form in SUP 12 Ann 4R (Appointed representative notification form), in accordance with the instructions on the form.

(2) In its notification under SUP 12.7.8R(1), the *firm* must state either:

(a) the steps it proposes to take to rectify the matter; or

(b) the date of termination of its contract with the *appointed representative* (see SUP 12.8).

(c) [deleted]

Notifications relating to EEA tied agents

12.7.9 **[R]** If a *UK MiFID investment firm* appoints an *EEA tied agent* this section applies to that *firm* as though the *EEA tied agent* were an *appointed representative*.

12.8 Termination of a relationship with an appointed representative or EEA tied agent

Notification of termination or prohibited amendment of the contract

12.8.1 **[R]** If either the *firm* or the *appointed representative* notifies the other that it proposes to terminate the contract of appointment or to amend it so that it no longer meets the requirements contained or referred to in SUP 12.5 (Contracts: required terms), the *firm* must:

(1) complete and submit to the *FSA* the form in SUP 12 Ann 5R (Appointed representative termination form) in accordance with the instructions on the form and no more than ten *business days* after the date of the decision to terminate or so amend the contract or, if later, as soon as it becomes aware that the contract is to be or has been terminated or amended.

(2) [deleted]

(3) [deleted]

(4) [deleted]

12.8.2 **[G]** In assessing whether to terminate a relationship with an *appointed representative*, a *firm* should be aware that the *notification rules* in SUP 15 require notification to be made immediately to the *FSA* if certain events occur. Examples include a matter having a serious regulatory impact or involving an *offence* or a breach of any requirement imposed by the *Act* or by regulations or orders made under the *Act* by the Treasury.

Steps to be taken on termination or prohibited amendment of the contract

12.8.3 **[R]** If a contract with an *appointed representative* is terminated, or if it is amended in a way which gives rise to a requirement to notify under SUP 12.8.1R, a *firm* must take all reasonable steps to ensure that:

(1) if the termination is by the *firm*, the *appointed representative* is notified in writing before, or if not possible, immediately on, the termination of the contract and informed that it will no longer be an *exempt person* for the purpose of the *Act* because of the contract with the *firm*;

(2) outstanding *regulated activities* and obligations to *customers* are properly completed and fulfilled either by itself or another of its *appointed representatives*;

(3) where appropriate, *clients* are informed of any relevant changes; and

(4) all the other *principals* of the *appointed representative* of which the *firm* is aware are notified.

Notification of approved persons on termination

12.8.4 **[G]** The *firm* is responsible for notifying the *FSA* of any *approved person* who no longer performs a *controlled function* under an *arrangement* entered into by a *firm* or its *appointed representative* (see SUP 10.3).

Removal of an appointed representative from the Register

12.8.5 **[G]** The *FSA* has the power to remove from the *Register* an *appointed representative*, whose scope of appointment covers *insurance mediation activities* (see SUP 12.4.9G and SUP 12.4.10G).

Termination of a UK MiFID investment firm's relationship with an EEA tied agent

12.8.6 **[R]** If a *UK MiFID investment firm* has appointed an *EEA tied agent* this section applies to that *firm* as though the *EEA tied agent* were an *appointed representative*.

12.9 Record keeping

12.9.1 **[R]** A *firm* must make the following records on each of its *appointed representatives*:

(1) the *appointed representative's* name;

(2) a copy of the original contract with the *appointed representative* and any subsequent amendments to it (including details of any restrictions placed on the activities which the *appointed representative* may carry on);
(3) the date and reason for terminating or amending its contract with the *appointed representative*, whenever such termination or amendment gives rise to a requirement to notify under SUP 12.8.1R; and
(4) any arrangements agreed with other *principals* under SUP 12.4.5B R (Multiple principals).

12.9.2 **[R]** A *firm* must retain these records for at least three years from the date of termination or the amendment of the contract with the *appointed representative* other than in respect of *tied agents* when the records must be retained for a period of five years.

12.9.3 **[G]** The *firm* should also satisfy itself that:
(1) the *appointed representative* is making and retaining records in accordance with the relevant record keeping *rules* in the *Handbook*, if these records are not maintained by the *firm*;
(2) the *appointed representative* (other than an *introducer appointed representative*) is making and retaining records sufficient to disclose with reasonable accuracy the financial position of the *business* it carries on in its capacity as the *firm's appointed representative*; and
(3) the *firm* has full access to the *appointed representative's* records under (1) and (2) and any other records relevant to the *regulated activities* that the *appointed representative* carries on in that capacity.

12.9.4 **[G]** *Firms* are reminded that they should make and retain records in relation to any *person* who falls within the scope of the *rules* in *TC* or who performs a *controlled function* under an *arrangement* entered into by a *firm* or by an *appointed representative*. See SUP 10 and *TC* for the applicable record keeping *rules*.

Record keeping in relation to EEA tied agents

12.9.5 **[R]** If a *UK MiFID investment firm* appoints an *EEA tied agent* this section applies to that *firm* as though the *EEA tied agent* were an *appointed representative*.

SUP 12 Annex 1G
Guidance on steps a firm should take in assessing the financial position of an appointed representative (other than an introducer appointed representative). See SUP 12.4.3G

1.	The *guidance* in this annex applies to a *firm* which intends to appoint, or has appointed, an *appointed representative* (other than an *introducer appointed representative*).
2.	All of the items in this annex should be applied, as appropriate, to an individual who is in business on his own.
3.	*Partners* in *partnerships* (other than limited partners in *limited liability partnerships*) have joint and several unlimited liability. It follows that any assessment of the financial position of an *appointed representative* which is a *partnership* should take into account the final position of the individual *partners* as well as the *partnership* itself.

Accounts	1.	Consider whether the type of accounts obtained is appropriate to the type of *appointed representative* (for example, *companies* should supply audited accounts prepared in accordance with Companies Act provisions while individuals in business on their own may only prepare unaudited accounts, for example, for submission to HM Revenue and Customs or their bankers).
	2.	Consider whether the accounts have been prepared on a timely basis. Consider the content of the audit report, including all detail and explanations given, and any qualifications which it may contain. Investigate any concerns.
	3.	If relevant, obtain the most recent management accounts to assess whether the *appointed representative's* financial position has changed materially since the most recent audited accounts.
	4.	If audited accounts are not available, be more circumspect about the accounts as they have not been independently audited. If necessary, consider obtaining third party verification of material balances.

Unusual items/ recoverability of debts/ goodwill	1.	Investigate fully any unusual items – in particular any amounts outstanding with *directors*, *partners*, *connected persons* or *associates* and any guarantees.
	2.	Consider whether any amounts due to the *appointed representative* would be recoverable; and whether the *appointed representative* would be in a position to pay any debts if it were required to do so at short notice.
	3.	Any balance for goodwill should be ignored since this will normally represent stream of potential future income which may not be forthcoming if the equity interest in the *appointed representative* were sold.
Financial stability/ cashflows	1.	Critically review the accounts to ensure that the *appointed representative* is financially stable. The review should take into account the overall position of the *appointed representative* and its cashflow.
	2.	The review should also consider the nature of the *appointed representative's* assets and whether or not they are liquid and readily available to the *appointed representative*, if required. *Investments* in (for example) unquoted *companies* or *property* may be difficult to realise if there were a sudden need for *cash*.
Income / financial pressures	1.	Assess the overall financial pressures on the *appointed representative* and *connected persons*. Account should be taken of the full range of the *appointed representative's* activities (and not merely those activities in which the *appointed representative* will be acting for the *firm*). Careful consideration should be given to any debts arising out of previous activities within the financial services industry.
	2.	If relevant, review the accounts of any *associates* where there is a possibility that their performance – or any commitments entered into in respect of them – may affect the financial position of the *appointed representative*.
	3.	Establish whether the *appointed representative's* income is sufficient both to service any debts and to provide an acceptable level of income to the proprietors.
Credit checks /dealings *government* bodies	1.	Undertake a *credit* reference check on the *appointed representative* itself (in the case of a *company*); on the *partners* (in the case of a *partnership*); or on the individual (in the case of a *sole trader*).
	2.	Ask the *appointed representative* whether it is up to date in its dealings with HM Revenue and Customs (etc).
Forecasts	1.	If relevant, obtain a *forecast* of the next year's figures and review it to ensure that the *appointed representative* is likely to remain in a satisfactory financial position. This is particularly important where a material change is expected in the *appointed representative's* operations; or where the *appointed representative* has only recently been established so that accounts are not available for the previous three complete financial years.
	2.	If the *firm* decides to appoint the *appointed representative*, the *firm* should keep the *appointed representative's* actual performance under close review so as to assess whether the *forecasts* were realistic and to enable any problems to be addressed.

SUP 12 Annex 2G

Guidance on information firms should take reasonable steps to obtain to verify and to assess the fitness and propriety of an appointed representative (other than an introducer appointed representative). See SUP 12.4.4G(1).

(1) The *guidance* in this annex applies to a *firm* which intends to appoint or has appointed an *appointed representative* (except an *introducer appointed representative*).

(2) Items 1(c) and 1(d) in the following table will not be relevant in the case of an individual who is himself an *appointed representative*, unless, in the case of 1(d), the individual is in business on his own.

(3) If the *appointed representative* is a *partnership*, the information a *firm* should obtain, having regard to SUP 12.4.4(1)G, is that contained in this annex on the basis that the information sought applies to each *partner*. When considering the fitness and propriety of each *partner*,

having regard to SUP 12.4.4(1)G, information a firm should obtain will also include information in this annex. Therefore, a *firm* may wish to assess the fitness and propriety of *partners* as suggested in SUP 12.4.4(2)G and then consider if any additional information is recommended under this annex.

(1)	Information about the *appointed representative*	(a)		Name
		(b)		Address, and, where applicable and different, address of the registered office and the principal place of *business*
		(c)		full name of every *director*, *senior manager* and *controller*
		(d)		accounts (see SUP 12 Ann 1G) for the last three complete financial years
	The *appointed representative's* professional reputation	(a)		Disciplinary proceedings
			(i)	whether the *appointed representative* has ever been publicly censored, disciplined, suspended or expelled by the *FSA*, another regulator, a *clearing house*, an *exchange*, a *professional body*, or a *government* body or agency;
			(ii)	whether the *appointed representative* is currently the subject of any disciplinary proceedings by a body referred to in (i) above or is aware that such proceedings are pending;
			(iii)	whether the *appointed representative* has ever been the subject of a formal investigation under the powers in the Companies Acts 1985 to 2006; and
			(iv)	whether the *appointed representative* has had anything equivalent to (i) to (iii) above occur under relevant overseas provisions.
		(b)		Criminal or civil proceedings. Whether the *appointed representative* is a defendant in any current civil proceedings connected with professional activities in which an allegation of fraud or dishonesty is being made, the subject of any current criminal proceedings, or has been convicted of any criminal offence, either in the *United Kingdom* or overseas.
		(c)		Insolvency, bankruptcy and winding up. Whether the *appointed representative* has:
			(i)	been wound up or had a petition presented, or had a meeting called to consider a resolution, for winding it up; or
			(ii)	in the case of a company, been the subject of an application to dissolve it or to strike it off the Register of Companies; or
			(iii)	made, or proposed to make, a composition or voluntary arrangement with any one of more of its creditors; or
			(iv)	had an administrator or trustee in bankruptcy appointed to it or had an application made for such an appointment; or
			(v)	had a receiver appointed to it (whether an administrative receiver or a receiver appointed over particular property); or
			(vi)	had an application for an interim order made against it under section 252 of the Insolvency Act 1986 (or, in Northern Ireland, section 227 of the Insolvency (Northern Ireland) Order 1989); or
			(vii)	if it is a *sole trader*, been the subject of an application for a sequestration order or a petition for bankruptcy; or

			(viii)	ceased trading in circumstances in which any of its creditors did not receive full payment; or.
			(ix)	had anything equivalent to (i) to (viii) above occur under relevant overseas law.

SUP 12 Annex 3R
Appointed representative appointment form

SUP 12 Ann 3 **[R]**

This form has not been reproduced for technical reasons. Please refer to the FSA website.

SUP 12 Annex 4R
Appointed representative notification form

SUP 12 Ann 4 **[R]**

This form has not been reproduced for technical reasons. Please refer to the FSA website.

SUP 12 Annex 5
Appointed representative termination form

SUP 12 Ann 5 **[R]**

This form has not been reproduced for technical reasons. Please refer to the FSA website.

CHAPTER 13
EXERCISE OF PASSPORT RIGHTS BY UK FIRMS

13.1 Application and purpose

Application

[2166]
13.1.1 **[G]** This chapter applies to a *UK firm*, that is, a *person* whose head office is in the *United Kingdom* and which is entitled to carry on an activity in another *EEA State* subject to the conditions of a *Single Market Directive*. Such an entitlement is referred to in the *Act* as an *EEA right* and its exercise is referred to in the *Handbook* as passporting.

13.1.2 **[G]** This chapter also applies to a *UK firm* which wishes to establish a *branch* in, or provide *cross border services* into, Gibraltar. The Financial Services and Markets Act 2000 (Gibraltar) Order 2001 provides that a *UK firm* is to be treated as having an entitlement corresponding to its *EEA right*, to establish a *branch* in, or provide *cross border services* into, Gibraltar under any of the *Single Market Directives*. So, references in this chapter to an *EEA State* or an *EEA right* include references to Gibraltar and the entitlement under the *Gibraltar Order* respectively.

13.1.3 **[G]** This chapter does not apply to:

(1) a *firm* established in an *EEA State* other than the *United Kingdom*; passporting by such a *firm* in or into the *United Kingdom* is a matter for its *Home State regulator* although *guidance* is given in SUP 13A (Qualifying for authorisation under the Act);

(2) other *overseas firms* (that is, *overseas firms* established outside the *EEA*); such *firms* are not entitled to passport into another *EEA State* and, where relevant, may need to obtain authorisation in each *EEA State* in which they carry on business;

(3) any insurance activity by way of provision of services which is provided by an *EEA firm* participating in a *community co-insurance operation* otherwise than as *leading insurer*; article 26.2 of the *Second Non-Life Directive* provides that only the *leading insurer* in such an operation is required to complete any passporting formalities (see also article 11 of the *Regulated Activities Order)*; or

(4) the marketing of a *UCITS* scheme by its operator in another *EEA State* under the *UCITS Directive* (see COLLG 2.1.8G).

13.1.4 **[G]** SUP Appendix 3 contains *guidance* on the *Single Market Directives*.

Purpose

13.1.5 **[G]** This chapter gives *guidance* on Schedule 3 to the *Act* for a *UK firm* which wishes to exercise its *EEA right* and establish a *branch* in, or provide *cross border services* into, another *EEA State*. That is, when a *UK firm* wishes to establish its first *branch* in, or provide *cross border services* for the first time into, a particular *EEA State*.

13.1.6 **[G]** The chapter also explains how a *UK firm* which has already established a *branch* in, or is providing *cross border services* into, another *EEA State*, may change the details of its *branch* or of the *cross border services* it is providing: for example, where a *UK firm* wishes to establish additional *branches* in an *EEA State* in which it has already established a *branch* where this would result in a change to the details provided previously. Such changes are governed by the *EEA Passport Rights Regulations*.

13.2 Introduction

13.2.1 **[G]** This *chapter* gives *guidance* to *UK firms*. In most cases *UK firms* will be *authorised persons* under the *Act*. However, under the *Banking Consolidation Directive*, a subsidiary of a *firm* which is a *credit institution* which meets the criteria set out in that Directive also has an *EEA right*. Such an unauthorised subsidiary is known as a *financial institution*. References in this chapter to a *UK firm* include a *financial institution*.

13.2.2 **[G]** A *UK firm* should be aware that the *guidance* is the *FSA's* interpretation of the *Single Market Directives*, the *Act* and the legislation made under the *Act*. The *guidance* is not exhaustive and is not a substitute for *firms* consulting the legislation or taking their own legal advice in the *United Kingdom* and in the relevant *EEA States*.

13.2.3 **[G]** In some circumstances, a *UK firm* that is carrying on business which is outside the scope of the *Single Market Directives* has a right under the *Treaty* to carry on that business. For example, for an *insurer* carrying on both direct insurance and *reinsurance* business, the authorisation of *reinsurance* business is not covered by the *Insurance Directives*. The *firm* may, however, have rights under the *Treaty* in respect of its *reinsurance* business. Such *UK firms* may wish to consult with the FSA on their particular circumstances (see SUP 13.12.2G).

13.3 Establishing a branch in another EEA State

What constitutes a branch

13.3.1 **[G]** *Guidance* on what constitutes a *branch* is given in SUP Appendix 3. Note that if a *UK MiFID investment firm* is seeking to use a *tied agent* established in another *EEA State*, the *rules* in SUP 13 will apply as if that *firm* were seeking to establish a *branch* in that *EEA State* unless the *firm* has already established a *branch* in that *EEA State* (paragraph 20A of Schedule 3 to the *Act*).

The conditions for establishing a branch

13.3.2 **[G]** A *UK firm* other than a *UK pure reinsurer* cannot establish a *branch* in another *EEA State* for the first time under an *EEA right* unless the conditions in paragraphs 19(2), (4) and (5) of Part III of Schedule 3 to the *Act* are satisfied. It is an offence for a *UK firm* which is not an *authorised person* to contravene this prohibition (paragraph 21 of Part III of Schedule 3 to the *Act*). These conditions are that:

(1) the *UK firm* has given the *FSA*, in accordance with the *FSA rules* (see SUP 13.5.1R), notice of its intention to establish a *branch* (known as a *notice of intention*) which:
   (a) identifies the activities which it seeks to carry on through the *branch*; and
   (b) includes such other information as may be specified by the *FSA* (see SUP 13.5.1R);
(2) the *FSA* has given notice (known as a *consent notice*) to the *Host State regulator*; and
(3)
   (a) if the *UK firm's EEA right* derives from the *Insurance Mediation Directive* one *month* has elapsed beginning on the date on which the *UK firm* received notice that the *FSA* had given a *consent notice* as described in SUP 13.3.6 G(1) (see SUP 13.3.2AG);
   (b) in any other case:
      (i) the *Host State regulator* has notified the *UK firm* (or, where the *UK firm* is passporting under the *Insurance Directives*, the *FSA*) of the *applicable provisions* or, in the case of a *UK firm* passporting under *MiFID*, that the *branch* may be established; or
      (ii) two months have elapsed beginning with the date on which the *FSA* gave the *consent notice*.

13.3.2A **[G]** If the *UK firm* is passporting under the *Insurance Mediation Directive* and the *EEA State* in which the *UK firm* is seeking to establish a *branch* has not notified the European Commission of its wish to be informed of the intention of *persons* to establish a *branch* in its territory in accordance with article 6(2) of that directive, SUP 13.3.2G (2) and (3) do not apply. Accordingly, the *UK firm* may establish the *branch* to which its *notice of intention* relates as soon as the conditions referred to in SUP 13.3.2G(1) are satisfied. The list of *EEA States* that have notified the European Commission of their wish to be informed in accordance with article 6(2) of the *Insurance Mediation Directive* is published on the *FSA's* website at www.fsa.gov.uk.

13.3.2B **[G]** An *appointed representative* appointed by a *firm* to carry on *insurance mediation activity* on its behalf may establish a *branch* in another *EEA State* under the *Insurance Mediation Directive*. In this case, the *notice of intention* in SUP 13.3.2G(1) should be given to the *FSA* by the *firm* on behalf of the *appointed representative*.

13.3.2C **[G]** An *exempt professional firm* which is included in the record of *unauthorised persons* carrying on *insurance mediation activity* maintained by the *FSA* under article 93 of the *Regulated Activities Order* may establish a *branch* in another *EEA State* under the *Insurance Mediation Directive* (see PROF 7.2).

13.3.2D **[G]** A *tied agent* appointed by a *MiFID investment firm* to carry on *investment services and activities* (and *ancillary services* where relevant) does not have its own passporting right to establish a *branch* in another *EEA State*. However, a *MiFID investment firm* remains free to appoint a *tied agent* to do business in another *EEA State* and where it does so, the *tied agent* will benefit from its passport.

13.3.2E **[G]** Once authorised in the *United Kingdom*, a *UK pure reinsurer* has an automatic *EEA right* to carry on *reinsurance* business in another *EEA State* by establishing a *branch* in that state or providing *cross border services* into that state. There are no additional requirements to be satisfied before the *firm* can commence business in that state.

13.3.3 **[G]** Where the *UK firm* is passporting under the *Insurance Directives* and the *Host State regulator* has notified the *FSA* of the *applicable provisions*, then under paragraph 19(9) of Part III of Schedule 3 to the *Act*, the *FSA* is required to inform the *firm* of these provisions.

13.3.3A **[G]**
(1) SUP 13.3.3G does not apply to *UK pure reinsurers* as they have automatic passport rights on the basis of their *Home State authorisation* under the *Reinsurance Directive*.
(2) Under section 3 of Part III of the *General Protocol*, *Home State regulators* have agreed to inform *Host State regulators* if a *pure reinsurer* for which the *Home State* is responsible carries on business through a *branch* in the *Host State*. Therefore SUP 13.5.1AR requires a *UK firm* passporting under the *Reinsurance Directive* to notify the *FSA* of certain information relating to the *branch*.

13.3.4 **[G]** [deleted]

13.3.4A **[G]** [deleted]

Issue of a consent notice to the Host State regulator

13.3.5 **[G]**
(1) If the *UK firm's EEA right* derives from the *Banking Consolidation Directive*, the *Investment Services Directive* or the *UCITS Directive*, the *FSA* will give the *Host State regulator* a *consent notice* within three *months* unless it has reason to doubt the adequacy of a *UK firm's* resources or its administrative structure.
(2)
  (a) If the *UK firm's EEA right* derives from the *Insurance Directives*, the *FSA* will give the *Host State regulator* a *consent notice* within three *months* unless it has reason to:
    (i) doubt the adequacy of the *UK firm's* resources or its administrative structure; or
    (ii) question the reputation, qualifications or experience of the *directors* or managers of the *UK firm* or its proposed authorised agent;

  in relation to the business the *UK firm* intends to conduct through the proposed *branch*. The *Host State regulator* then has a further two *months* to notify the *applicable provisions* (if any) and prepare for the supervision, as appropriate, of the *UK firm*.
  (b) In assessing the matters in (2)(a), the *FSA* may, in particular, seek further information from the *firm* or require a report from a *skilled person* (see SUP 5 (skilled persons)).
  (c) If the *FSA* has required a financial recovery plan of a *UK firm* of the kind mentioned in paragraph 1 of article 38 of the *Consolidated Life Directive* or paragraph 1 of article 20a of the *First Non-Life Directive*, the *FSA* will not give a *consent notice* for so long as it considers that *policyholders* are threatened within the meaning of those provisions.
  (d) If the *UK firm's EEA right* derives from the *Insurance Mediation Directive* and SUP 13.3.2G (2) applies, the *FSA* will give the *Host State regulator* a *consent notice* within one *month* of the date on which it received the *UK firm's notice of intention*. In cases where SUP 13.3.2 G (2) does not apply (see SUP 13.3.2AG), the *UK firm* may establish a *branch* as soon as it satisfies the conditions referred to in SUP 13.3.2G.

13.3.6 **[G]**
(1) If the *FSA* gives a *consent notice*, it will inform the *UK firm* in writing that it has done so.
(2) The *consent notice* will contain, among other matters, the *requisite details* or, if the *firm* is passporting under the *Insurance Directives*, the *EEA relevant details* (see SUP 13 Ann 1R) provided by the *UK firm* in its *notice of intention* (see SUP 13.5 (Notices of intention)).

13.3.7 **[G]**

(1) If the *FSA* proposes to refuse to give a *consent notice*, then paragraph 19(8) of Part III of Schedule 3 to the *Act* requires the *FSA* to give the *UK firm* a *warning notice*.

(2) If the *FSA* decides to refuse to give a *consent notice*, then paragraph 19(12) of Part III of Schedule 3 to the *Act* requires the *FSA* to give the *UK firm* a *decision notice* within three *months* of the date on which it received the *UK firm's notice of intention* (two *months* in the case of a *UK firm* which is a *UCITS management company*). The *UK firm* may refer the matter to the *Tribunal*.

(3) For details of the *FSA's* procedures for the giving of *warning notices* or *decision notices* see DEPP 2 (Statutory notices and the allocation of decision making).

13.4 Providing cross border services into another EEA State

Where is the service provided?

13.4.1 **[G]** *Guidance* on where a *cross border service* is provided is given in SUP Appendix 3.

The conditions for providing cross border services into another EEA State

13.4.2 **[G]** A *UK firm*, other than a *UK pure reinsurer*, cannot start providing *cross border services* into another *EEA State* under an *EEA right* unless it satisfies the conditions in paragraphs 20(1) of Part III of Schedule 3 to the *Act* and, if it derives its *EEA right* from the *Insurance Directives*, paragraph 20(4B) of Part III of Schedule 3 to the *Act*. It is an offence for a *UK firm* which is not an *authorised person* to breach this prohibition (paragraph 21 of Part III of Schedule 3 to the *Act*). The conditions are that:

(1) the *UK firm* has given the *FSA*, in the way specified by *FSA rules* (see SUP 13.5.2R), notice of its intention to provide *cross border services* (known as a *notice of intention*) which:
   (a) identifies the activities which it seeks to carry on by way of provision of *cross border services*; and
   (b) includes such other information as may be specified by the *FSA* (see SUP 13.5.2R); and

(2) if the *UK firm* is passporting under the *Insurance Directives*, the *firm* has received written notice from the *FSA* as described in SUP 13.4.5G; or

(3) if the *UK firm* is passporting under the *Insurance Mediation Directive* and the *EEA State* in which the *UK firm* is seeking to provide services has notified *the* European Commission of its wish to be informed of the intention of *persons* to provide *cross border services* in its territory in accordance with article 6(2) of that directive, one *month* has elapsed beginning with the date on which the *UK firm* received written notice from the *FSA* as described in SUP 13.4.5 G (paragraph 20 (3B)(c) of Schedule 3 to the *Act*).

13.4.2A **[G]** An *appointed representative* appointed by a *firm* to carry on *insurance mediation activity* on its behalf may provide *cross border services* in another *EEA State* under the *Insurance Mediation Directive*. In this case, the *notice of intention* in SUP 13.4.2G(1) should be given to the *FSA* by the *firm* on behalf of the *appointed representative*.

13.4.2B **[G]** An *exempt professional firm* which is included in the record of *unauthorised persons* carrying on *insurance mediation activity* maintained by the *FSA* under article 93 of the *Regulated Activities Order* may provide *cross border services* in another *EEA State* under the *Insurance Mediation Directive* (see PROF 7.2).

13.4.2C **[G]** A *tied agent* appointed by a *MiFID investment firm* to carry on *investment services and activities* (and *ancillary services* where relevant) does not have its own passporting right to provide *cross border services* in another *EEA State*. However, a *MiFID investment firm* remains free to appoint a *tied agent* to do business in another *EEA State* and where it does so, the *tied agent* will benefit from its passport.

13.4.2D **[G]** A *MiFID investment firm* that wishes to obtain a passport for the activity of *operating an MTF* should follow the procedures described in this chapter. A *UK market operator* that operates a *recognised investment exchange* or an *MTF* and wishes to provide *cross border services* into another *EEA State* should follow the procedure described in REC 4.2BG.

13.4.2E **[G]** SUP 13.4.2G does not apply to *UK pure reinsurers* as they have automatic passport rights on the basis of their *Home State authorisation* under the *Reinsurance Directive*. No notification is required from *UK pure reinsurers* in respect of the provision of *cross border services*.

13.4.3 **[G]** [deleted]

13.4.3A **[G]** [deleted]

Issuing a consent notice or notifying the Host State regulator

13.4.4 **[G]**

(1) If the *UK firm's EEA right* derives from *MiFID*, the *Banking Consolidation Directive* or the *UCITS Directive*, paragraph 20(3) of Part III of Schedule 3 to the *Act* requires the *FSA* to send a copy of the *notice of intention* to the *Host State regulator* within one *month* of receipt. However, a *UK firm* passporting under the *Banking Consolidation Directive* or *MiFID Investment Services Directive* may start providing *cross border services* as soon as it satisfies the relevant conditions (see SUP 13.4.2G).

(2)

(a) If the *UK firm's EEA right* derives from the *Insurance Directives*, paragraph 20(3A) of Part III of Schedule 3 to the *Act* requires the *FSA*, within one *month* of receiving the *notice of intention*, to:

(i) give notice in a specified form (known as a *consent notice*) to *the Host State regulator*; or

(ii) give written notice to the *UK firm* of its refusal to give a *consent notice* and the reasons for that refusal.

(b) The issue or refusal of a *consent notice* under paragraph 20(3A) of Part III of Schedule 3 to the *Act* is the consequence of a regulatory decision, and this *consent notice* (unlike the *consent notice* for establishment of a *branch*)is not a *statutory notice* as set out in section 395 of the *Act*. A *UK firm* that receives notice that the *FSA* refuses to give a *consent notice* may refer the matter to the *Tribunal* under paragraph 20(4A) of Part III of Schedule 3 to the *Act*.

(c) If the *FSA* has required of a *UK firm* a financial recovery plan of the kind mentioned in paragraph 1 of article 38 of the *Consolidated Life Directive* or paragraph 1 of article 20a of the *First Non-Life Directive*, the *FSA* will not give a *consent notice* for so long as it considers that *policyholders'* rights are threatened within the meaning of those provisions.

(2A)

(a) If the *UK firm's EEA right* derives from the *Insurance Mediation Directive*, and the *EEA State* in which the *UK firm* is seeking to provide services has notified the European Commission of its wish to be informed of the intention of *persons* to provide *cross border services* in its territory in accordance with article 6(2) of that directive, paragraph 20(3B)(a) of Part III of Schedule 3 to the *Act* requires the *FSA* to send a copy of the *notice of intention* to the *Host State regulator* within one *month* of receipt. Otherwise, the *UK firm* may start providing *cross border services* as soon as it satisfies the relevant conditions (see SUP 13.4.2G).

(b) The list of the *EEA States* that have notified the European Commission of their wish to be informed in accordance with article 6(2) of the *Insurance Mediation Directive* is published on the *FSA's* website at www.fsa.gov.uk.

13.4.5 **[G]** When the *FSA* sends a copy of a *notice of intention*, or if it gives a *consent notice* to the *Host State regulator*, it must inform the *UK firm* in writing that it has done so (paragraphs 20 (3B)(b) and (4) of Schedule 3 to the *Act*).

Applicable provisions for cross border services

13.4.6 **[G]**

(1) If the *UK firm* is passporting under the *UCITS Directive*, then when the *Host State regulator* receives the *notice of intention*, it should inform the *UK firm* of any *applicable provisions*.

(2) If the *UK firm* is passporting under the *Insurance Directives*, then the *Host State regulator* may notify the *FSA* if there are any applicable provisions. If so, the *FSA* will inform the *UK firm* of the *applicable provisions*.

(3) If a *UK firm* is not notified of the *applicable provisions*, it should, for its own protection, take all reasonable steps to determine the *applicable provisions* for itself.

13.5 Notices of intention

Specified contents: notice of intention to establish a branch

13.5.1 **[R]** A *UK firm*, other than a *UK pure reinsurer*, wishing to establish a *branch* in a particular *EEA State* for the first time under an *EEA right* must include in its *notice of intention* given to the *FSA*:

(1)

(a) the information specified in SUP 13 Ann 1R; and

(b) if the *UK firm* is passporting under the *Insurance Directives*, the information specified in SUP 13 Ann 2R; or

(2) if the *UK firm* is passporting under the *Insurance Mediation Directive*, only a statement that it intends to carry on *insurance mediation* in that State by establishing a *branch*.

13.5.1A **[R]** A *UK pure reinsurer* establishing a *branch* in a particular *EEA state* for the first time under the *Reinsurance Directive* must notify the *FSA*. Whenever possible, this notification must be made as soon as the information specified in SUP 13 Annex 1R is known by the *firm*.

13.5.1B **[G]** SUP 13.5.1R does not apply to *UK pure reinsurers* as they have automatic passport rights on the basis of their *Home State authorisation* under the *Reinsurance Directive*.

Specified contents: notice of intention to provide cross border services

13.5.2 **[R]** A *UK firm* wishing to provide *cross border services* into a particular *EEA State* for the first time under an *EEA right* must include, in its *notice of intention* given to the *FSA*:

(1) if the *UK firm* is passporting under *MiFID* or the *Insurance Directives*, the information specified in SUP 13 Ann 3R;

(2) if the *UK firm* is passporting under the *Banking Consolidation Directive*, the activities which it intends to carry on.

(3) if the *UK firm* is passporting under the *Insurance Mediation Directive*, only a statement that it intends to carry on *insurance mediation* in that State by provision of *cross border services*.

13.5.2A **[G]** SUP 13.5.2R does not apply to *UK pure reinsurers* as they have automatic passport rights on the basis of their *Home State authorisation* under the *Reinsurance Directive*.

13.5.3 **[R]**

(1) The *notice of intention* under SUP 13.5.1R and SUP 13.5.2R, and the notice required under SUP 13.5.1AR, must be:

(a) given to a member of, or addressed for the attention of, the Corporate Authorisation department, if submitted with an application for *Part IV permission*, or the Passport Notifications Unit in any other circumstances; and

(b) delivered to the *FSA* by one of the methods in (2).

(2) The *notice of intention* or notice required under SUP 13.5.1AR may be delivered by:

(a) *post* to the address in (3); or

(b) leaving the application at the address in (3) and obtaining a time-stamped receipt; or

(c) hand delivery to a member of the Authorisation department (if submitted with an application for *Part IV permission*) or to the Passport Notification Unit; or

(d) electronic mail to the address in (4) if not submitted with an application for *Part IV permission* and obtaining an electronic confirmation of receipt; or

(e) fax to the Passport Notifications Unit on 0207 676 9798 (if not submitted with an application for *Part IV permission*) provided that the *FSA* receives a copy by one of the methods (a) to (d) above within five *business days* after the date of the faxed notification; or

(f) online submission via the *FSA's* website at www.fsa.gov.uk (when available).

(g) The address for notices referred to in (2) is: The Financial Services Authority, 25 The North Colonnade, Canary Wharf, London E14 5HS.

(h) Email: passport.notifications@fsa.gov.uk

13.5.4 **[G]** A standard form of *notice of intention* that a *UK firm* may wish to use is available from the Passport Notifications Unit (see SUP 13.12 (Sources of further information)).

13.5.4A **[G]** A *UK pure reinsurer* giving notice as required under SUP 13.5.1AR may wish to use the passporting notification form available on the *FSA* website (http://www.fsa.gov.uk/pubs/forms/passporting/branch_eea.doc), adapted as appropriate to reflect the information required by SUP 13 Annex 1R paragraph 4.

Unregulated activities

13.5.5 **[G]** A *notice of intention* may include activities within the scope of the relevant *Single Market Directive* which are not *regulated activities* (paragraphs 19(3) and 20(2) of Part III of Schedule 3 to the *Act*), although in the case of a *MiFID investment firm* a notice of intention may only include *ancillary services* which are to be carried on with one or more *investment services and activities* (paragraphs 19(5B) and 20(2A) of Part III of Schedule 3 to the *Act*). Regulation 19 of the *EEA Passport Rights Regulations* states that where a *UK firm* is able to carry on such an *unregulated activity* in the *EEA State* in question without contravening any law of the *United Kingdom* (or any *part of the United Kingdom*) the *UK firm* is treated, for the purposes of the exercise of its *EEA right*, as being *authorised* to carry on that activity.

Translations

13.5.6 **[G]**

(1) A *UK firm* passporting under the *Banking Consolidation Directive*, the *Insurance Directives* or the *Reinsurance Directive* may have to submit the *requisite details* or relevant details in the language of the *Host State* as well as in English. For a *UK firm* passporting under the *Insurance Directives* this translated document will not include the relevant UK details. Further information is available from the Passport Notifications Unit.

(2) A *UK firm* may wish to discuss with the Passport Notifications Unit the appropriate time for providing the translations in (1), given that further information or clarification of the details provided may be required by the *FSA*.

(3) A *UK firm* passporting under the *Insurance Directives* should keep the *EEA* and *UK* relevant details separate as, if the application is approved, only the former will be sent to the *Host State regulator.*

Notifications to more than one EEA State

13.5.7 **[G]** If a *UK firm* wishes to establish *branches* in, or *provide cross border services* into, more than one *EEA State*, a single notification may be provided but the relevant information for each *EEA State* should be clearly identifiable.

13.6 Changes to branches

13.6.1 **[G]** Where a *UK firm* is exercising an *EEA right*, other than under the *Insurance Mediation Directive* (see SUP 13.6.9AG) or the *Reinsurance Directive* (see SUP 13.6.9BR), and has established a *branch* in another *EEA State*, any changes to the details of the *branch* are governed by the *EEA Passport Rights Regulations.* References to regulations in this section are to the *EEA Passport Rights Regulations*. A *UK firm* which is not an *authorised person* should note that, under regulation 18, contravention of the prohibition imposed by regulation 11(1), 13(1) or 15(1) is an offence. It is a defence, however, for the *UK firm* to show that it took all reasonable precautions and exercised due diligence to avoid committing the offence.

13.6.2 **[G]** *UK firms* should note that if a *branch* in another *EEA State* ceases to provide services, this may represent a change in *requisite details* or, if the *firm* is passporting under the *Insurance Directives*, the *relevant EEA details* or *relevant UK details*.

13.6.3 **[G]** *UK firms* should also note that changes to the details of *branches* may lead to changes to the *applicable provisions* to which the *UK firm* is subject. These changes should be communicated to the *UK firm* either by the *Host State regulator*, or, if the *firm* is passporting under *Insurance Directives*, via the *FSA*.

Firms passporting under the Banking Consolidation Directive and the UCITS Directive

13.6.4 **[G]** If a *UK firm* has exercised an *EEA right*, under the *Banking Consolidation Directive* or the *UCITS Directive*, and established a *branch* in another *EEA State*, regulation 11(1) states that the *UK firm* must not make a change in the *requisite details* of the *branch* (see SUP 13 Ann 1R), unless it has satisfied the requirements of regulation 11(2), or, where the change arises from circumstances beyond the *UK firm's* control, regulation 11(3) (see SUP 13.6.10G).

13.6.5 **[G]** Where the change arises from circumstances within the control of the *UK firm*, the requirements in regulation 11(2) are that:

(1) the *UK firm* has given notice to the *FSA* and to the *Host State regulator* stating the details of the proposed change;

(2) the *FSA* has given the *Host State regulator* a notice informing it of the details of the change; and

(3) either the *Host State regulator* has informed the *UK firm* that it may make the change, or the period of one *month* beginning with the day on which the *UK firm* gave the *Host State regulator* the notice in (1) has elapsed.

Firms passporting under MiFID

13.6.5A **[G]** If a *UK firm* has exercised an *EEA right* to establish a *branch* under *MiFID*, it must not make a change in the *requisite details* of the *branch* (see SUP 13 Annex 1), use, for the first time, a *tied agent* established in the *EEA State* in which the *branch* is established, or cease to use a *tied agent* established in the *EEA State* in which the *branch* is established, unless it has satisfied the requirements of regulation 11A(2) (see SUP 13.6.5BG).

13.6.5B **[G]** The requirements of regulation 11A(2) are that:

(1) the *UK firm* has given a notice to the *FSA* stating the details of the proposed change; and

(2) the period of one *month* beginning with the day on which the *UK firm* gave the notice has elapsed.

Firms passporting under the Insurance Directives

13.6.6 **[G]** If a *UK firm* has exercised an *EEA right* under the *Insurance Directives* and established a *branch* in another *EEA State*, regulation 13(1) states that the *UK firm* must not make a change in the *relevant EEA details*, unless it has satisfied the requirements of regulation 13(2), or, where the change arises from circumstances beyond the *UK firm's* control, regulation 13(3) (see SUP 13.6.10G).

13.6.7 **[G]** Where the change arises from circumstances within the control of the *UK firm*, the requirements in regulation 13(2) are that:

(1) the *UK firm* has given notice to the *FSA* and to the *Host State regulator* stating the details of the proposed change;
(2) the *FSA* has given the *Host State regulator* a notice informing it of the details of the proposed change;
(3) the period of at least one *month* beginning on the day on which the *UK firm* gave the *FSA* the notice in (1) has elapsed; and
(4) either:
  (a) a further period of one *month* has elapsed; or
  (b) the *FSA* has informed the *UK firm* of any consequential changes in the applicable provisions of which the *FSA* has been notified by the *Host State regulator*.

13.6.8 **[G]** If a *UK firm* has exercised an *EEA right* under the *Insurance Directives* and established a *branch* in another *EEA State*, regulation 15(1) states that the *UK firm* cannot make a change in any of the *relevant UK details* unless the *UK firm* has given a notice to the *FSA* stating the details of the proposed change at least one *month* before the change is effected.

13.6.9 **[G]** Where a *UK firm* with *Part IV permission* to carry on both *long-term* and *general insurance business*, is passporting under the *Insurance Directives* and wishes to extend its *general insurance business* to include *long term insurance business* (or vice versa), it should complete a new *notice of intention* and not a change to details notice.

Firms passporting under the Insurance Mediation Directive

13.6.9A **[G]** A *UK firm* exercising its *EEA right* under the *Insurance Mediation Directive* to establish a *branch* in another *EEA State* is not required to supply a change to the details of *branches* notice.

Firms passporting under the Reinsurance Directive

13.6.9B **[R]** A *UK firm* exercising its *EEA right* under the *Reinsurance Directive* to establish a branch in another *EEA State* must notify the *FSA* of any changes in the information specified in SUP 13 Annex 1R. Whenever possible, this notification must be made as soon as the change in information is known by the *firm*.

Changes arising from circumstances beyond the control of a UK firm

13.6.10 **[G]**

(1) If the change arises from circumstances beyond the *UK firm's* control, the *UK firm*:
  (a) is required by regulation 11(3) or regulation 13(3) to give a notice to the *FSA* and to the *Host State regulator* stating the details of the change as soon as reasonably practicable;
  (b) may, if it is passporting under the *Insurance Directives*, make a change to its *relevant UK details* under regulation 15(1) if it has, as soon as practicable (whether before or after the change), given notice to the *FSA* stating the details of the change.
(2) The *FSA* believes that for a change to arise from circumstances beyond the control of a *UK firm*, the circumstances should be outside the control of the *firm* as a whole and not just the *branch* in the *EEA State*.
(3) Neither this *guidance* nor that set out at SUP 13.6.4G or SUP 13.6.5G is applicable to *MiFID investment firms*.

The process

13.6.11 **[G]** When the *FSA* receives a notice from a *UK firm* other than a *MiFID investment firm* (see SUP 13.6.5G (1) and SUP 13.6.7G (1)) or a *pure reinsurer* (see SUP 13.6.9BR) it is required by regulations 11(4) and 13(4) to either refuse, or consent to the change within a period of one *month* from the day on which it received the notice.

13.6.12 **[G]** If the *FSA* consents to the change, then under regulations 11(5) and 13(5) it will:

(1) give a notice to the *Host State regulator* informing it of the details of the change; and
(2) inform the *UK firm* that it has given the notice, stating the date on which it did so.

13.6.13 **[G]** If a *UK firm* is passporting under the *Banking Consolidation Directive*, then regulation 11(7) states that the *FSA* may not refuse to consent to a change unless, having regard to the change and to the EEA activities the *UK firm* is seeking to carry on, it doubts the adequacy of the administrative structure or the financial situation of the *UK firm*. In reaching its determination, the *FSA* may have regard to the adequacy of management, systems and the presence of relevant skills needed for the EEA activities to be carried on.

13.6.14 **[G]** If a *UK firm* is passporting under the *Insurance Directives*, then regulation 13(7) states that the *FSA* may not refuse to consent to a change unless, having regard to the change, the *FSA* has reason:

(1) to doubt the adequacy of the *UK firm's* administrative structure or financial situation; or
(2) to question the reputation, qualifications or experience of the directors or managers of the firm or the authorised agent;

in relation to the business conducted, or to be conducted, through the branch.

13.6.15 **[G]** If the *FSA* refuses to consent to a change, then under regulations 11(6) and 13(6):

(1) the *FSA* will give notice of the refusal to the *UK firm*, stating its reasons and giving an indication of the *UK firm's* right to refer the matter to the *Tribunal* and the procedures on such a reference; and
(2) the *UK firm* may refer the matter to the *Tribunal*.

13.6.16 **[G]** *UK firms* may wish to use the standard form available from the Passport Notifications Unit (see SUP 13.12 (Sources of further information)) to give the notices to the *FSA* described in SUP 13.6.5G(1), SUP 13.6.5BG, SUP 13.6.7G(1), SUP 13.6.8G and SUP 13.6.10G(1).

The process: MiFID investment firms

13.6.17 **[G]** When the *FSA* receives a notice from a *UK MiFID investment firm* (see SUP 13.6.5BG(1)), it is required by regulation 11A(3) to inform the relevant *Host State regulator* of the proposed change as soon as reasonably practicable. The *firm* in question may make the change once the period of one *month* beginning with the day on which it gave notice has elapsed.

13.7 Changes to cross border services

13.7.1 **[G]** Where a *UK firm* is exercising an *EEA right* under the *UCITS Directive*, *MiFID* or the *Insurance Directives*, and is providing *cross border services* into another *EEA State*, any changes to the details of the services are governed by the *EEA Passport Rights Regulations*. References to regulations in this section are to the *EEA Passport Rights Regulations*. A *UK firm* which is not an *authorised person* should note that contravention of the prohibition imposed by regulation 12(1), 12A(1) or 16(1) is an offence. It is a defence, however, for the *UK firm* to show that it took all reasonable precautions and exercised due diligence to avoid committing the offence.

13.7.2 **[G]** *UK firms* should also note that changes to the details of *cross border services* may lead to changes to the *applicable provisions* to which the *UK firm* is subject.

Firms passporting under the UCITS Directive

13.7.3 **[G]** If a *UK firm* is passporting under the *UCITS Directive*, regulation 12(1) states that the *UK firm* must not make a change in its programme of operations, or the activities to be carried on under its *EEA right*, unless the relevant requirements in regulation 12(2) have been complied with. These requirements are:

(1) the *UK firm* has given a notice to the *FSA* and to the *Host State regulator* stating the details of the proposed change; or
(2) if the change arises as a result of circumstances beyond the *UK firm's* control, the *UK firm* has as soon as practicable (whether before or after the change) given a notice to the *FSA* and to the *Host State regulator*, stating the details of the change.

UK firms may wish to use the standard form available from the Passport Notifications Unit (see SUP 13.12 (Sources of further information)) to give the notices to the *FSA* required by SUP 13.7.3G(1) and SUP 13.7.3AG.

Firms passporting under MiFID

13.7.3A **[G]** If a *UK firm* is providing *cross border services* in a particular *EEA State* in exercise of an *EEA right* deriving from *MiFID*, the *UK firm* must comply with the requirements of regulation 12A(2) before it makes a change to its programme of operations, including:

(1) changing the activities to be carried on in exercise that *EEA right*;
(2) using, for the first time, any *tied agent* to provide services in the territory of that *EEA State*; or
(3) ceasing to use any *tied agent* to provide services in the territory of that *EEA State*.

13.7.3B **[G]** The requirements of regulation 12A(2) are that:

(1) the *UK firm* has given notice to the *FSA* stating the details of the proposed change; and
(2) the period of one *month* beginning with the day on which the *UK firm* gave the notice mentioned in (1) has elapsed.

Firms passporting under the Insurance Directives

13.7.4 **[G]** If a *UK firm* has exercised an *EEA right* under the *Insurance Directives* and is providing *cross border services* into another *EEA State*, regulation 16(1) states that the *UK firm* must not make a change in the relevant details (as defined in regulation 17 – see also SUP 13 Ann 3R) unless the relevant requirements in regulation 16(3) or, where the change arises from circumstances beyond the *UK firm's* control, regulation 16(4), have been complied with.

13.7.5 **[G]** Regulation 16(3) provides that:

(1) the *UK firm* has given a notice to the *FSA* stating the details of the proposed change; and

(2) the *FSA* has given the *Host State regulator* a notice informing it of the details of the proposed change.

13.7.6 **[G]** If the change arises from circumstances beyond the *UK firm's* control, the *UK firm* is required by regulation 16(4) to give a notice to the *FSA* stating the details of the change as soon as reasonably practicable (whether before or after the change). See also SUP 13.6.10G (2), as relevant to *cross border services.*

13.7.6A **[G]** *UK firms* may wish to use the standard form available from the Passport Notifications Unit (see SUP 13.12 (Sources of further information)) to give the notices to the *FSA* required by SUP 13.7.3(1)G, SUP 13.7.3AG, SUP 13.7.3BG, SUP 13.7.5G(1) and SUP 13.7.6G.

13.7.7 **[G]** When the *FSA* receives a notice from a *UK firm* (see SUP 13.7.5G(**1**) and SUP **13.7.6G**), it is required by regulation 16(5) to either refuse or consent to the change within one *month* of receipt.

13.7.8 **[G]** If the *FSA* consents to the change it will:

(1) give a notice to the *Host State regulator* informing it of the details of the proposed change; and

(2) inform the *UK firm* that it has given the notice, stating the date on which it did so.

13.7.9 **[G]** If the *FSA* refuses to consent to a change it is required by regulation 16(7) to give notice of the refusal to the *UK firm*, stating its reasons and giving an indication of the *UK firm's* right to refer the matter to the *Tribunal* and the procedures that apply to such a reference.

13.7.10 **[G]** Where a *UK firm* with *Part IV permission* to carry on both *long-term* and *general insurance business* is passporting under the *Insurance Directives* and wishes to extend its *general insurance business* to include *long term insurance business* (or vice versa), it should complete a new *notice of intention* and not a change to details notice.

Firms passporting under the Banking Consolidation Directive and Insurance Mediation Directive

13.7.11 **[G]** A *UK firm* providing *cross border services* under the *Banking Consolidation Directive* or *Insurance Mediation Directive* is not required to supply a change to the details of *cross border services* notice.

Firms passporting under the Reinsurance Directive

13.7.12 **[G]** A *UK firm* providing *cross border services* under the *Reinsurance Directive* is not required to supply notification of, or a change to the details of, its *cross border services.*

13.8 Changes of details: provision of notices to the FSA

13.8.1 **[R]**

(1) A notice of a change to a *branch* referred to in SUP 13.6.5 G(1), SUP 13.6.5BG(1), SUP 13.6.7G(1), SUP 13.6.8G, SUP 13.6.9BR and SUP 13.6.10G(1) and a notice of a change to *cross border services* referred to in SUP 13.7.3G(1), SUP 13.7.3AG(1)), SUP 13.7.5G(1) and SUP 13.7.6G must be:
   (a) given to a member of, or addressed for the attention of, the Passport Notifications Unit; and
   (b) delivered to the *FSA* by one of the methods in (2).

(2) The notice may be delivered by:
   (a) *post* to the address in (3); or
   (b) leaving the application at the address in (3) and obtaining a time-stamped receipt; or
   (c) hand delivery to a member of the Passport Notifications Unit; or
   (d) electronic mail to the address in (4) and obtaining an electronic confirmation of receipt; or
   (e) fax to the Passport Notifications Unit on 0207 676 9798 provided that the FSA receives a copy by one of the methods (a) to (d) above within five *business days* after the date of the faxed notification; or
   (f) online submission via the *FSA's* website at www.fsa.gov.uk (when available).

(3) The address for notices is: The Financial Services Authority, 25 The North Colonnade, Canary Wharf, London E14 5HS.

(4) Email: passport.notifications@fsa.gov.uk

13.8.2 **[G]** *UK firms* passporting under the *Banking Consolidation Directive* or the *Insurance Directives* may be required to submit the change to details notice in the language of the *Host State* as well as in English.

13.9

[deleted]

13.9.1 **[G]** [deleted]

13.10 Applicable provisions

13.10.1 **[G]** *UK firms* are reminded that conduct of business rules, and other rules made for the general good, may apply to business carried on in the *Host State* by a *UK firm*. These are known in the *Act* as the *applicable provisions*(paragraph 19(13) of Part III of Schedule 3 to the *Act*).

13.10.2 **[G]** *UK firms* passporting under the *Banking Consolidation Directive* should note that, under the Directive, the *Host State* is responsible, together with the *FSA*, for monitoring the liquidity of a *branch* established by a *UK firm* in another *EEA State*.

13.10.3 **[G]** These *Host State* provisions often have requirements about the soliciting of business, for example, advertising and cold-calling rules. A *UK firm* should ensure it is familiar with, and acts in compliance with, the relevant requirements of its *Host State regulator*.

13.11 Record keeping

13.11.1 **[R]**

(1) A *UK firm* which is exercising an *EEA right* must make and retain a record of:
  - (a) the services or activities it carries on from a *branch* in, or provides cross-border into, another *EEA State* under that *EEA right*; and
  - (b) the details relating to those services or activities (as set out in SUP 13.6 and SUP 13.7).

(2) The record in (1) must be kept for five years (for *firms* passporting under *MiFID*) or three years (for other *firms*) from the earlier of the date on which:
  - (a) it was superseded by a more up-to-date record; or
  - (b) the *UK firm* ceased to have a *branch* in, or carry on *cross border services* into, any *EEA State* under an *EEA right*.

13.11.2 **[G]** The record in SUP 13.11.1R need not relate to the level of business carried on. A *UK firm* may comply with SUP 13.11.1R by, for example, keeping copies of all notices of intention and change to details notices.

13.11.3 **[G]** A *UK firm* should monitor the business carried on under an *EEA right* to ensure that any changes to details are notified as required by SUP 13.6 (Changes to branches) and SUP 13.7 (Changes to cross border services).

13.12 Sources of further information

13.12.1 **[G]**

(1) Given the complexity of issues raised by passporting, *UK firms* are advised to consult legislation and also to obtain legal advice at earliest opportunity. Firms are encouraged to contact their usual supervisory contact at the *FSA* to discuss their proposals. However, a *UK firm* which is seeking *guidance* on procedural or notification issues relating to passporting should contact the Passport Notifications Unit.

(2) An applicant for *Part IV permission* which is submitting a *notice of intention* with its application for such *permission* should contact the Permissions department (020 7066 3954) in the first instance.

13.12.2 **[G]** To contact the Passport Notifications Unit, from which a standard form of *notice of intention* can be obtained:

(1) telephone on 020 7676 1000; fax on 020 7676 9798; or

(2) write to: The Passport Notifications Unit, The Financial Services Authority, 25 The North Colonnade, Canary Wharf, London E14 5HS; or

(3) Email: passport.notifications@fsa.gov.uk

SUP 13 Annex 1 [R]
Requisite details: branches

	Type of firm	Requisite details (see notes 1 & 2)	
1	*Credit institution*	(a)	Particulars of the programme of operations carried on, or to be carried on, from the *branch*, including a description of the particular *EEA* activities to be carried on, and of the structural organisation of the *branch*;
		(b)	the address in the *EEA State* in which the *branch* is, or is to be, established from which information about the business may be obtained; and

	Type of firm	Requisite details (see notes 1 & 2)			
		(c)	the names of the managers of the *branch*.		
1A	*MiFID investment firm*	(a)	The *EEA States* within the territory of which the *UK firm* plans to establish a *branch*; [Note: Article 32(2)]		
		(b)	the programme of operations to be carried on from the *branch*, including a description of the *investment services and activities* and *ancillary activities* to be carried on and of the structural organisation of the *branch;*		
		(c)	the address in the *EEA State* in which the branch is to be established from which information about the business may be obtained;		
		(d)	the names of the managers of the *branch*; and		
		(e)	whether the *branch* intends to use *tied agents*.		
2	*UCITS management company*		The information required under 1 above, plus: the *EEA State* within the territory of which the *UCITS management company* plans to establish a *branch*;		
3	*Insurance undertaking*	(1)(a)	The address of the *branch*;		
		(b)	the name of the *UK firm's* authorised agent (see note 3) and, in the case of a *member* of *Lloyd's*, confirmation that the authorised agent has power to accept service of proceedings on behalf of *Lloyd's*;		
		(c)	the *classes* or parts of *classes* of business carried on, or to be carried on, and the nature of the risks or commitments covered, or to be covered, in the *EEA State* concerned;		
		(d)	details of the structural organisation of the *branch*;		
		(e)	the guiding principles as to reinsurance of business carried on, or to be carried on, in the *EEA State* concerned, including the *firm's* maximum retention per risk or event after all reinsurance ceded;		
		(f)	estimates of:		
			(i)	the costs of installing administrative services and the organisation for securing business in the *EEA State* concerned;	
			(ii)	the resources available to cover those costs; and	
			(iii)	if contracts of a kind falling within paragraph 18 of Schedule 1 to the *Regulated Activities Order* (assistance) are, or are to be, effected or carried out, the resources available for providing assistance;	
		(g)	for each of the first three years following the establishment of the *branch*:		
			(i)	estimates of the *firm's* margin of solvency and the margin of solvency required and the method of calculation;	
			(ii)	if the *firm* carries on, or intends to carry on, business comprising the effecting or carrying out of contracts of *long-term insurance*, the details mentioned in paragraph (2) as respects the business carried on, or to be carried on, in the *EEA State* concerned; and	
			(iii)	if the *firm* carries on, or intends to carry on, business comprising the effecting or carrying out of contracts of *general insurance*, the details mentioned in paragraph (3) as respects the business carried on, or to be carried on, in the *EEA State* concerned;	

	Type of firm	Requisite details (see notes 1 & 2)		
		(h)	if the *firm* covers, or intends to cover, relevant motor vehicle risks, details of the *firm's* membership of the national bureau and the national guarantee fund in the *EEA State* concerned; and	
		(i)	if the *firm* covers, or intends to cover, health insurance risks, the technical bases used, or to be used, for calculating premiums in respect of such risks.	
		(2)	The details referred to in (1)(g)(ii) are:	
		(a)	the following information, on both optimistic and pessimistic bases, for each type of contract or treaty:	
			(i)	the number of contracts or treaties expected to be issued;
			(ii)	the total premium income, both gross and net of reinsurance ceded;
			(iii)	the total sums assured or the total amounts payable each year by way of annuity;
			(b)	detailed estimates, on both optimistic and pessimistic bases, of income and expenditure in respect of direct *business*, reinsurance acceptances and reinsurance cessions; and
			(c)	estimates relating to the financial resources intended to cover underwriting liabilities.
		(3)	The details referred to in (1)(g)(iii) are:	
			(a)	estimates relating to the expenses of management (other than the costs of installation), and in particular those relating to current general expenses and *commissions*;
			(b)	estimates relating to premiums or contributions (both gross and net of all reinsurance ceded) and to claims (after all reinsurance recoveries); and
			(c)	estimates relating to the financial resources intended to cover underwriting liabilities.
4	*Pure reinsurer*	(a)	the address of the *branch*;	
		(b)	the name of the *firm's* authorised agent (see note 3);	
		(c)	whether the *firm* will be, or is, carrying on life or non-life *reinsurance* business, or both;	
		(d)	confirmation that the *firm* fulfils the solvency requirements of the *Reinsurance Directive*.	

Notes

Note 1: The *requisite details* or relevant details specified in this annex are those in the *EEA Passport Rights Regulations*; that is, those in regulation 1 for *credit institutions* and *MiFID investment firms*, and those in regulation 14 for *insurance undertakings*. The relevant details specified for *pure reinsurers* are those in the *General Protocol*, under which *Home State regulators* have agreed to inform *Host State regulators* if a *pure reinsurer* carries on business through a *branch* in the *Host State*.

Note 2: In this table, the references to classes of insurance have the meaning given to them in Schedule 1 to the *Regulated Activities Order*.

Note 3: For the purposes of this table, 'authorised agent' means an agent or employee of the *insurance undertaking* who has authority (a) to bind the *insurance undertaking* in its relations with third parties, and (b) to represent the *insurance undertaking* in its relations with *overseas regulators* and courts in the *EEA State* of the *branch*.

SUP 13 Annex 2 [R]
Relevant UK details: branches of insurance undertakings

Relevant UK details	
(1)	The names of the *UK firm's* managers and main agents in the *EEA State* concerned;
(2)	particulars of any association which exists or is proposed to exist between:

Relevant UK details		
	(a)	the directors and controllers of the *UK firm*;
	(b)	any *person* who will act as insurance broker, agent, loss adjuster or reinsurer for the *UK firm* in the *EEA State* concerned;
(3)	the names of the principal reinsurers of business to be carried on in the *EEA State* concerned;	
(4)	the sources of business in the *EEA State* concerned (for, example, insurance brokers, agents, own employees or direct selling) with the approximate percentage expected from each of these sources;	
(5)	copies or drafts of:	
	(a)	any separate reinsurance treaties covering business to be written in the *EEA State* concerned;
	(b)	any standard agreements which the *UK firm* will enter into with brokers or agents in the *EEA State* concerned;
	(c)	any agreements which the insurance undertaking will enter into with persons (other than employees of the *UK firm*) who will manage the business to be carried on in the *EEA State* concerned;
(6)	in the case of a *UK firm* which intends to carry on long-term business:	
	(a)	the technical bases which the actuary appointed in accordance with SUP 4.3.1R proposes to use for each class of business to be carried on in the *EEA State*, including the bases needed for calculating premium rates and mathematical reserves;
	(b)	a statement by the actuary so appointed whether he considers that the premium rates which will be used in the *EEA State* concerned are suitable;
	(c)	a statement by that actuary whether he agrees with the information provided under relevant EEA details (1)(e) and (2)(b) and (c);
	(d)	the technical bases used to calculate the statements and estimates referred to in relevant EEA details (2); and
(7)	in the case of a *UK firm* which intends to carry on general business, copies or drafts of any agreements which the *UK firm* will have with main agents in the *EEA State* concerned.	

SUP 13 Annex 3 [R]
Specified information: Cross Border Services

	Type of firm	Specified information		
1	*MiFID investment firm*	(a)	The *EEA State* in which the *UK firm* intends to operate.	
		(b)	Details of the programme of operations, stating in particular the *investment services and activities* and the *ancillary services* which it intends to perform.	
		(c)	Whether the *UK firm* intends to use *tied agents* in the territory of the *EEA State* in which the *UK firm* intends to operate.	
2	*UCITS management company*	(a)	The information required under 1 above; and	
		(b)	the *EEA State* within the territory of which the *UCITS management company* plans to operate.	
3	*Insurance undertaking* (note 1)	(a)	The *EEA State* in which the EEA activities are carried on, or are to be carried on;	
		(b)	the nature of the risks or commitments covered, or to be covered, in the *EEA State* concerned;	
		(c)	if the *firm* covers, or intends to cover, relevant motor vehicle risks (note 2):	
			(i)	the name and address of the claims representative (note 3); and

	Type of firm	**Specified information**		
			(ii)	details of the *firm's* membership of the national bureau and the national guarantee fund in the *EEA State* concerned (if required by the *EEA State* concerned as part of the *consent notice*); and
		(d)	if the *insurer* covers, or intends to cover, health insurance, the technical bases used, or to be used, for calculating premiums in respect of such risks.	
4.	*MiFID investment firm* wishing to *operate an MTF*	(a)	The *EEA State* in which arrangements are to be made.	
		(b)	A description of the arrangements the *firm* wishes to make.	
Note 1: See regulation 17 of the *EEA Passport Rights Regulations*.				
Note 2: In this table, the reference to 'relevant motor risks' has the meaning given to *motor vehicle liability* in Schedule 1 to the *Regulated Activities Order*.				
Note 3: In this table, the reference to 'claims representative' has the meaning given to it in the *EEA Passport Rights Regulations* .				

CHAPTER 13A
QUALIFYING FOR AUTHORISATION UNDER THE ACT

13A.1 Application and purpose

Application

[2167]
13A.1.1 **[G]**
(1) This chapter applies to an *EEA firm* that wishes to exercise an entitlement to establish a *branch* in, or provide *cross border services* into, the *United Kingdom* under a *Single Market Directive*. (The *Act* refers to such an entitlement as an *EEA right* and its exercise is referred to in the *Handbook* as "passporting".) (See SUP App 3 (Guidance on passporting issues) for further *guidance* on passporting.)
(2) This chapter also applies to:
 (a) a *Treaty firm* that wishes to exercise rights under the *Treaty* in respect of *regulated activities*, those rights not being covered by passporting rights provided by the *Single Market Directives*, and qualifies for *authorisation* under Schedule 4 to the *Act* (Treaty Rights); and
 (b) *a UCITS qualifier*, that is, an *operator*, *trustee* or *depositary* of a recognised *collective investment scheme*, constituted in another *EEA State*, and which qualifies for *authorisation* under Schedule 5 to the *Act* (Persons concerned in collective investment schemes).
(3) The provisions implementing the *Single Market Directives* are within the coordinated field (see PERG 2.9.18G(1)). So, where an *incoming ECA provider* intends to provide *electronic commerce activity* that consists of activities that fall within one of the *Single Market Directives*, the passporting requirements on exercising an *EEA right* in this chapter will apply.

13A.1.2 **[G]** This chapter does not apply to:
(1) an *EEA firm* that wishes to carry on in the *United Kingdom* activities which are outside the scope of its *EEA right* and the scope of a *permission* granted under Schedule 4 to the *Act*; in this case the *EEA firm* requires a "*top-up permission*" under Part IV of the *Act* (see the *FSA* website "How do I get authorised": http://www.fsa.gov.uk/Pages/Doing/how/index.shtml); or
(2) an *EEA firm* that carries on any insurance activity:
 (a) by the provision of services; and
 (b) pursuant to a *community co-insurance operation* in which the *firm* is participating otherwise than as *leading insurer* (see Article 11 of the *Regulated Activities Order*); or
(3) a *Treaty firm* that wishes to provide *electronic commerce activities* into the *United Kingdom*.
(4) a *market operator* that operates a *regulated market* or an *MTF* in an *EEA State* other than the *UK* and wishes to make appropriate arrangements so as to facilitate access to and use of its system by remote users or participants in the *UK*. See SUP App 3.6.25G for *guidance*.

13A.1.3 **[G]**

(1) Under the *Gibraltar Order* made under section 409 of the *Act* (*Gibraltar Order*), a Gibraltar firm is treated as an *EEA firm* under Schedule 3 to the *Act* if it is:
 (a) authorised in Gibraltar under the *Insurance Directives*; or
 (aa) authorised in Gibraltar under the *Reinsurance Directive*; or
 (b) authorised in Gibraltar under the *Banking Consolidation Directives*; or
 (c) authorised in Gibraltar under the *Insurance Mediation Directive*; or
 (d) authorised in Gibraltar under the *Investment Services Directive*.

(1A) Similarly, an *EEA firm* which:
 (a) has satisfied the Gibraltar establishment conditions and has established a *branch* in the *UK*; or
 (b) has satisfied the Gibraltar service conditions and is providing *cross border services* into the *UK*;

is treated as having satisfied the *establishment conditions* or *service conditions* (as appropriate) under Schedule 3 to the *Act*. Regulations 4 to 7 of the *EEA Passport Rights Regulations* will apply to the establishment of the *branch* or the provision of *cross border services*.

(2) Gibraltar insurance companies, *credit institutions*, *insurance intermediaries* and *investment firms* are allowed to passport their services into the *United Kingdom* if they comply with the relevant notification procedures. So, any references in this chapter to *EEA State* or *EEA right* include references to Gibraltar and the entitlement under the *Gibraltar Order* where appropriate.

(3) [deleted]

Purpose

13A.1.4 **[G]**

(1) This chapter explains how an *EEA firm* and a *Treaty firm* can qualify for *authorisation* under Schedules 3 and 4 to the *Act* and how a *UCITS qualifier* is *authorised* under Schedule 5 to the *Act*.

(2) This chapter also provides *guidance* on Schedule 3 to the *Act* for an *incoming EEA firm* that wishes to establish a *branch* in the *United Kingdom* instead of, or in addition to, providing *cross border services* into the *United Kingdom* or vice versa.

13A.1.5 **[G]**

(1) *EEA firms* should note that this chapter only addresses the procedures which the *FSA* will follow under the *Act*. So, an *EEA firm* should consider this *guidance* in conjunction with the requirements with which it will have to comply in its *Home State*.

(2) The *guidance* in this chapter represents the *FSA's* interpretation of the *Single Market Directives*, the *Act* and the secondary legislation made under the *Act*. The *guidance* is not exhaustive and should not be seen as a substitute for a *person* consulting the legislation or taking legal advice.

13A.2 EEA firms and Treaty firms

13A.2.1 **[G]** A *person* will only be an *EEA firm* or a *Treaty firm* if it has its head office in an *EEA State* other than the *United Kingdom*. *EEA firms* and *Treaty firms* are entitled to exercise both the right of establishment and the freedom to provide services under the *Treaty*. The difference, however, is that an *EEA firm* has a right to passport under a *Single Market Directive*, whereas a *Treaty firm* carries on activities for which the right to carry on those activities does not fall within the scope of a *Single Market Directive*. An *EEA firm* may also be a *Treaty firm* if it carries on such activities. A *person* may be a *Treaty firm*, where, for example, it carries on business that includes *regulated activities*, the right to carry on which does not fall within the scope of the *Single Market Directive* under which it is entitled to exercise an *EEA right*, for example, *reinsurance* in the case of a direct insurer to which the *Insurance Directives* apply.

13A.2.2 **[G]** An *EEA firm* may passport those activities which fall within the scope of the relevant *Single Market Directive* as long as they are included in its *Home State authorisation*.

13A.3 Qualification for authorisation under the Act

EEA firms

13A.3.1 **[G]** Section 31 of the *Act* (Authorised persons) states that an *EEA firm* is *authorised* for the purposes of the *Act* if it qualifies for *authorisation* under Schedule 3 to the *Act* (EEA Passport Rights). Under paragraph 12 of Part II of that Schedule, an *EEA firm* that is an *EEA pure reinsurer* qualifies for *authorisation* without condition. An *EEA firm* that is not an *EEA pure reinsurer* qualifies for *authorisation* if:

(1) it is seeking to establish a *branch* in *the United Kingdom* in exercise of an *EEA right* and satisfies the *establishment conditions* (see SUP 13A.4.1G and SUP 13A.4.2G); or
(2) it is seeking to provide *cross border services* into the *United Kingdom* in exercise of an *EEA right* and satisfies the *service conditions* (see SUP 13A.5.3G).

13A.3.1A **[G]** If an *EEA MiFID investment firm* seeks to use a *tied agent* established in the *UK*, the *EEA MiFID investment firm* will be treated as if it were seeking to establish a *branch* and must satisfy the *establishment conditions* (see SUP 13A.4.1 G).

13A.3.1B **[G]** A *pure reinsurer* with its head office in an *EEA State* that has not fully implemented the *Reinsurance Directive* may nevertheless be accepted as satisfying the conditions to be an *EEA pure reinsurer* if the *firm* provides satisfactory evidence that the prudential requirements of the *Reinsurance Directive* have been implemented by that *EEA State* and that they apply to the *firm*. The *firm* may then be deemed to be authorised under the *Reinsurance Directive* in that *EEA State*.

13A.3.2 **[G]**
(1) On qualifying for *authorisation*, subject to SUP 13A.3.2G (2), an *EEA firm* will have *permission* to carry on each *permitted activity* (see (3) below) which is a *regulated activity*.
(2)
(a) Paragraph (1) does not apply to the activity of *dealing* in *units* in a *collective investment scheme* in the *United Kingdom* where:
(i) the *firm* is an *EEA UCITS management company*;
(ii) the *firm* satisfies the *establishment conditions* in SUP 13A.4.1G; and
(iii) the *FSA* notifies the *EEA firm* and the *EEA firm's Home State regulator* that the way in which it intends to market a *relevant scheme* in the *United Kingdom* does not comply with the law in force in the *United Kingdom*.
(b) The *FSA's* notice under (2)(a)(iii) has to be given to the *EEA firm* within two *months* of receiving the consent notice (see paragraph 13(1) of Part II of Schedule 3 to the *Act*) and will be similar to a *warning notice*.
(c) For details of the *FSA's* procedures for the giving of *warning notices* see DEPP 2 (Statutory notices and allocation of decision making).
(3) The *permitted activities* of an *EEA firm* are those activities identified in the consent notice, regulator's notice or notice of intention. *Permitted activities* may include activities that are within the scope of a *Single Market Directive* but which are *unregulated activities* in the *United Kingdom*.
(4) The *permission* will be treated as being on terms equivalent to those appearing in the consent notice, regulator's notice or notice of intention. For example, it will reflect any limitations or requirements which are included in the *firm's Home State* authorisation.

13A.3.3 **[G]** An *EEA firm* which has qualified for *authorisation* is referred to in the *Handbook* as an *incoming EEA firm*.

Treaty firms

13A.3.4 **[G]** Under section 31 of the *Act*, a *Treaty firm* is *authorised* for the purposes of the *Act* if it qualifies for *authorisation* under Schedule 4 (Treaty Rights), that is:
(1) the *Treaty firm* is seeking to carry on a *regulated activity*; and
(2) the conditions set out in paragraph 3(1) of Schedule 4 to the *Act* are satisfied.

13A.3.5 **[G]** On qualifying for *authorisation* a *Treaty firm* will have *permission* to carry on each *permitted activity* which is a *regulated activity*. This *permission* will be treated on the same terms as those which apply to the *Treaty firm's Home State authorisation*. For example, it will reflect any limitations or requirements which are included in the *firm's Home State authorisation*.

13A.3.6 **[G]** The effect of paragraph 5(1) and 5(2) of Schedule 4 to the *Act* is that a *Treaty firm* which qualifies for *authorisation* under that Schedule must, at least seven *days* before it carries on any of the *regulated activities* covered by its *permission*, give the *FSA* written notice of its intention to do so. Failure to do so is a criminal offence under paragraph 6(1) of that Schedule.

13A.3.7 **[D]**
(1) A written notice from a *Treaty firm* under paragraph 5(2) of Schedule 4 to the *Act* must be:
(a) given to a member of, or addressed for the attention of, the Authorisation Department; and
(b) delivered to the *FSA* by one of the methods in (2).
(2) The written notice may be delivered by:
(a) *post* to the address in SUP 13A.3.9G below; or
(b) leaving the application at the address in SUP 13A.3.9G below and obtaining a time-stamped receipt; or
(c) hand delivery to a member of the Authorisation Department.

13A.3.8 **[G]** The written notice required by paragraph 5(2) of Schedule 4 to the *Act* should be accompanied by confirmation of the *Treaty firm's* authorisation from the *Home State regulator*, as referred to in paragraph 3(2) of Schedule 4 to the *Act*.

13A.3.9 **[G]**

(1) For further information, a *Treaty firm* may contact the Authorisation Department:
 (a) telephone on +4420 7066 3954; or
 (b) write to: Authorisation Department, The Financial Services Authority, 25 The North Colonnade, Canary Wharf, London, E14 5HS; or
 (c) email corporate.authorisation@fsa.gov.uk.

13A.3.10 **[G]**

(1) The *guidance* in PERG 2 is relevant to *Treaty firms* to help them determine if they require *authorisation* under the *Act*.

(2) A *Treaty firm* which qualifies for *authorisation* is referred to in the *Handbook* as an *incoming Treaty firm*.

13A.3.11 **[G]**

(1) An *EEA firm* that is carrying on both direct insurance and *reinsurance* business will be entitled to passport under Schedule 3 to the *Act* in relation to the direct *insurance business*. It will also have a *Treaty right* under Schedule 4 to the *Act* in relation to the *reinsurance* business if the *firm* has received *Home State authorisation* for the *regulated activity* of effecting and/or carrying out the relevant class of *insurance business* that includes *reinsurance* business for that class and the relevant provisions of the law of the *Home State* satisfy the conditions laid down by the *Insurance Directives* relating to the carrying on of that activity (see SUP App 3.10.13G).

(1A) An insurance company with its head office in an *EEA State* other than the *United Kingdom* that is carrying on pure *reinsurance* business in that State, and which has received authorisation (or is deemed to be authorised) under the *Reinsurance Directive* from its *Home State* (an *EEA pure reinsurer*), has an automatic *EEA right* to passport into the *United Kingdom* by establishing a *branch* in the *United Kingdom* or by the provision of *cross border services*. Under the *General Protocol*, *Home State regulators* have agreed to inform *Host State regulators* if a *pure reinsurer* carries on business through a *branch* in the *Host State*.

(2) An insurance company with its head office in an *EEA State* other than the *United Kingdom* that is carrying on pure *reinsurance* business in that State, and which wishes to carry on such business in the *United Kingdom* and is authorised by its *Home State* but not yet under the *Reinsurance Directive*, is advised to discuss its particular requirements with the Authorisation Department. It may be entitled to exercise a *Treaty right* provided it satisfies the conditions in paragraph 3(1) of Schedule 4 to the *Act* (see SUP 13A.3.4G). Otherwise, it will have to seek a *Part IV permission* (see the *FSA* website "How do I get authorised": http://www.fsa.gov.uk/Pages/Doing/how/index.shtml)).

UCITS qualifiers

13A.3.12 **[G]** Under Schedule 5 to the *Act* (Persons concerned in collective investment schemes), a *person* who for the time being is an *operator, trustee* or *depository* of a *scheme* which is a *recognised scheme* under section 264 of the *Act* is an *authorised person*. Such a *person* is referred to in the *Handbook* as a *UCITS qualifier*.

13A.3.13 **[G]** A *UCITS qualifier* has *permission* under paragraph 2 of Schedule 5 to the *Act*, to carry on, as far as is appropriate to the capacity in which it acts in relation to the scheme:

(1) the *regulated activity* of *establishing, operating or winding up a collective investment scheme*; and

(2) any activity in connection with, or for the purposes of, the scheme.

13A.3.14 **[G]** A *UCITS qualifier* should refer to COLLG or to the following sections of COLL for requirements for *recognised schemes*:

(1) COLL 9.2.1G for *guidance* on notifications;

(2) COLL 9.2.1G for *guidance* on information and documentation requirements; and

(3) COLL 9.4 which includes *rules* on what facilities need to be maintained.

13A.4 EEA firms establishing a branch in the United Kingdom

The conditions for establishing a branch

13A.4.1 **[G]**

(1) Before an *EEA firm* other than an *EEA pure reinsurer* exercises an *EEA right* to establish a *branch* in the *United Kingdom* other than under the *Insurance Mediation Directive*, the *Act* requires it to satisfy the *establishment conditions*, as set out in paragraph 13(1) of Part II of Schedule 3 to the *Act*.

(2) For the purposes of paragraph 13(1)(b)(iii) of Part II of Schedule 3 to the *Act*, the information to be included in the consent notice has been prescribed under regulation 2 of the *EEA Passport Rights Regulations*.

13A.4.2 **[G]** Where an *EEA firm* exercises its *EEA right* to establish a *branch* in the *United Kingdom* under the *Insurance Mediation Directive*, the *Act* requires it to satisfy the *establishment conditions*, as set out in paragraph 13(1A) of Part II of Schedule 3 to the *Act*.

13A.4.3 **[G]** For the purposes of paragraph 13(2)(b) of Part II of Schedule 3 to the *Act*, the *applicable provisions* may include *FSA rules*. The *EEA firm* is required to comply with relevant *rules* when carrying on a *passported activity* through a *branch* in the *United Kingdom* as well as with relevant *UK* legislation.

13A.4.3A **[G]** *Guidance* on the matters that are reserved to a *firm's Home State regulator* is located in SUP 13A Annex 2G.

The notification procedure

13A.4.4 **[G]**

(1) When the *FSA* receives a consent notice from the *EEA firm's Home State regulator*, it will, under paragraphs 13(2)(b), (c) and 13(3) of Part II of Schedule 3 to the *Act*, notify the *applicable provisions* (if any) to:

- (a) the *EEA firm*; and
- (b) in the case of an *EEA firm* passporting under the *Insurance Directives*, the *Home State regulator*;

within two *months* of the notice date.

(1A) The notice date is:

- (a) for a *MiFID investment firm*, the date on which the *Home State* gave the consent notice; and
- (b) in any other case, the date on which the *FSA* received the consent notice.

(2) Although the *FSA* is not required to notify the *applicable provisions* to an *EEA firm* passporting under the *Insurance Mediation Directive*, these provisions are set out in SUP 13A Annex 1G (Application of the Handbook to Incoming EEA Firms).

13A.5 EEA firms providing cross border services into the United Kingdom

Is the service provided within the United Kingdom?

13A.5.1 **[G]** There is *guidance* for *UK firms* in SUP Appendix 3.6 on when a service is provided cross border. *EEA firms* may find this of interest although they should follow the guidance of their *Home State regulators*.

13A.5.2 **[G]** An *EEA firm* other than an *EEA pure reinsurer* should note that the requirement under the *Single Market Directives* to give a notice of intention to provide *cross border services* applies whether or not:

(1) it has established a *branch* in the *United Kingdom*; or
(2) those *cross border services* are *regulated activities*.

The conditions for providing cross border services into the United Kingdom

13A.5.3 **[G]**

(1) Before an *EEA firm* other than an *EEA pure reinsurer* exercises an *EEA right* to provide *cross border services* into the *United Kingdom*, the *Act* requires it to satisfy the *service conditions*, as set out in paragraph 14 of Part II of Schedule 3 to the *Act*.

(2) For the purposes of paragraph 14(1)(b) of Part II of Schedule 3 to the *Act*, the information to be contained in the regulator's notice has been prescribed under regulation 3 of the *EEA Passport Rights Regulations*.

The notification procedure

13A.5.4 **[G]**

(1) Unless the *EEA firm* is passporting under the *Insurance Mediation Directive*, if the *FSA* receives a regulator's notice or, where no notice is required (in the case of an *EEA firm* passporting under the *Banking Consolidation Directive*), is informed of the *EEA firm's* intention to provide *cross border services* into the *United Kingdom*, the *FSA* will, under paragraphs 14(2)(b) and 14(3) of Part II of Schedule 3 to the *Act*, notify the *EEA firm* of the *applicable provisions* (if any) within two *months* of the *day* on which the *FSA* received the regulator's notice or was informed of the *EEA firm's* intention.

(2) Although the *FSA* is not required to notify the *applicable provisions* to an *EEA Firm* passporting under the *Insurance Mediation Directive*, these provisions are set out in SUP 13A Annex 1G (Application of the Handbook to Incoming EEA Firms).

13A.5.5 **[G]** An *EEA firm* that has satisfied the *service conditions* in paragraph 14 of Part II of Schedule 3 to the *Act* is entitled to start providing *cross border services* into the *United Kingdom*.

However, an *EEA firm* that wishes to start providing *cross border services* but has not yet received notification of the *applicable provisions* may wish to contact the *FSA's* Passport Notifications Unit (see SUP 13A.8.1G(2)).

13A.6 Which rules will an incoming EEA firm be subject to?

13A.6.1 **[G]**
(1) SUP 13A Annex 1G summarises how the *Handbook* applies to *incoming EEA firms*.
(2) SUP 13A Annex 2G summarises the matters that are reserved to a *firm's Home State regulator*.

13A.6.2 **[G]** An *incoming EEA firm* (other than an *EEA pure reinsurer*) or *incoming Treaty firm* carrying on business in the *United Kingdom* must comply with the *applicable provisions* (see SUP 13A.4.4G and SUP 13A.5.4G) and other relevant *UK* legislation. For example where the business includes:
(1) business covered by the Consumer Credit Act 1974, then an *incoming EEA firm* or *incoming Treaty firm* must comply with the provisions of that Act, as modified by paragraph 15(3) of Schedule 3 to the *Act*; or
(2) effecting or carrying out contracts covering motor vehicle third party liability risks as part of direct *insurance business*, then an *incoming EEA firm* or *incoming Treaty firm* is required to become a member of the Motor Insurers' Bureau.

13A.6.3 **[G]** In particular, an *EEA firm* (other than an *EEA pure reinsurer*) or *Treaty firm* must comply with the *applicable provisions* in SUP 10 (Approved persons). An *EEA firm* or *Treaty firm* should also refer to SUP 10.1 (Application) which sets out the territorial provisions of the *approved persons* regime.

13A.6.4 **[G]** Under the *EEA Passport Rights Regulations*, references in section 60 of the *Act* (applications for approval for persons to perform controlled functions) to "the authorised person concerned" include:
(1) an *EEA MiFID investment firm* whose *Home State regulator* has given a consent notice under paragraph 13 of Schedule 3 to the *Act* (see SUP 13A.4.1G (1) and SUP 13A.4.2G) or a regulator's notice under paragraph 14 of that Schedule (see SUP 13A.5.3G (1)), and which will be the *authorised person* concerned if the *EEA firm* qualifies for *authorisation* under that Schedule; and
(2) any other *EEA firm* with respect to which the *FSA* has received a consent notice or regulator's notice under paragraph 13 of Schedule 3 to the *Act* (see SUP 13A.4.1G(1)) and SUP 13A.4.2G) or a regulator's notice under paragraph 14 of that Schedule (see SUP 13A.5.3G (1)), and which will be the *authorised person* concerned if the *EEA firm* qualifies for *authorisation* under that Schedule.

13A.6.5 **[G]** SUP 13A Annex 1G does not apply to *incoming ECA providers* acting as such.

13A.7 Top-up permission

13A.7.1 **[G]** If a *person* established in the *EEA*:
(1) does not have an *EEA right*;
(2) does not have *permission* as a *UCITS qualifier*; and
(3) does not have, or does not wish to exercise, a *Treaty right* (see SUP 13A.3.4G to SUP 13A.3.11G);

to carry on a particular *regulated activity* in the *United Kingdom*, it must seek *Part IV permission* from the *FSA* to do so (see the *FSA* website "How do I get authorised": http://www.fsa.gov.uk/Pages/Doing/how/index.shtml). This might arise if the activity itself is outside the scope of the *Single Market Directives*, or where the activity is included in the scope of a *Single Market Directive* but is not covered by the *EEA firm's Home State authorisation*. If a *person* also qualifies for *authorisation* under Schedules 3, 4 or 5 of the *Act* as a result of its other activities, the *Part IV permission* is referred to in the *Handbook* as a *top-up permission*.

13A.7.2 **[G]** Where the *FSA* grants a *top-up permission* to an *incoming EEA firm* to carry on *regulated activities* for which it has neither an *EEA right* nor a *Treaty right*, the *FSA* is responsible for the prudential supervision of the *incoming EEA firm*, to the extent that the responsibility is not reserved to the *incoming EEA firm's Home State regulator*.

13A.7.3 ***[G]*** *[deleted]*

13A.7.4 **[G]** For *guidance* on how to apply for *Part IV permission* under the *Act*, see the *FSA* website "How do I get authorised": http://www.fsa.gov.uk/Pages/Doing/how/index.shtml. If an *EEA firm* or *Treaty firm* wishes to make any subsequent changes to its *top-up permission*, it can make an application for variation of that *permission* (see SUP 6 (Applications to vary and cancel Part IV permission)).

13A.8 Sources of further information

13A.8.1 **[G]** For further information on *UK* regulation, an *EEA firm*, a *Treaty firm* or a *UCITS qualifier* should contact the Perimeter Guidance team at the *FSA*. Questions about the passporting notification procedures can be addressed to the Passport Notifications Unit.

(1) To contact the Perimeter Guidance team:
  (a) telephone on +44 20 7066 0082 or fax on +44 20 7066 9719;
  (b) write to: Perimeter Guidance team, The Financial Services Authority, 25 The North Colonnade, Canary Wharf, London E14 5HS.

(2) To contact the Passport Notifications Unit:
  (a) telephone on +44 20 7066 1000 or fax on +44 20 7066 9798;
  (b) write to: Passport Notifications Unit, The Financial Services Authority, 25 The North Colonnade, Canary Wharf, London E14 5HS;
  (c) email: passport.notifications@fsa.gov.uk.

13A.9 The precautionary measure rule for incoming EEA firms

Application

13A.9.1 **[R]**

(1) The precautionary measure rule (SUP 13A.9.2R) applies to an *incoming EEA firm* which:
  (a) is authorised by a *home state regulator* with respect to its *MiFID business*; or
  (b) has a *top-up permission* which covers *MiFID business*;

  but which is not subject to provisions adopted by the *Home State* which transpose, in full, *MiFID* or the *MiFID implementing Directive*.

(2) The precautionary measure rule applies:
  (a) with respect to the *regulated activities* carried on by the *firm* in the *United Kingdom*; and
  (b) to the extent that the *firm* is not subject to provisions which are comparable to provisions transposing *MiFID* or the *MiFID implementing Directive*.

(3) This section (SUP 13A.9) is effective from 1 November 2007 until 31 October 2008.

The precautionary measure rule

13A.9.2 **[R]**

(1) A *firm* must comply with standards which are comparable to those required by the provisions of *MiFID* and the *MiFID implementing Directive* specified in rows (1) and (4) of the table in SUP 13A.9.3R.

(2) An *MTF* must also comply with standards in row (2).

(3) The following *firms* must also comply with standards in row (3):
  (a) a *systematic internaliser*;
  (b) a *firm*, which, either on its own account or on behalf of *clients*, concludes *transactions* in shares *admitted to trading* on a *regulated market* outside a *regulated market* or *MTF* (see MAR 7.1.2R).

13A.9.3 **[R]** Table: MiFID provisions for incoming EEA firms

	Articles of MiFID or the MiFID implementing directive
(1)	Articles 13(3) and (6), 18 to 22 and 24 and Annex II of MiFID
(2)	Articles 12, 14, 26, 29 and 30 of MiFID
(3)	Articles 27 and 28 of MiFID
(4)	All related Articles of MiFID and the MiFID implementing Directive

13A.9.4 **[E]**

(1) A *firm* should comply with the provisions of the *Handbook* which transpose the provisions of *MiFID* and the *MiFID implementing Directive* referred to in SUP 13A.9.3R (even if they are expressed not to apply to an *incoming EEA firm*).

(2) Compliance with (1) may be relied upon as tending to establish compliance with the precautionary measure rule.

13A.9.5 **[G]**

(1) The purpose of the precautionary measure rule is to ensure that an *incoming EEA firm* is subject to the standards of *MiFID* and the *MiFID implementing Directive* to the extent that the *Home State* has not transposed *MiFID* or the *MiFID implementing Directive* by 1 November 2007. It is to 'fill a gap'.

(2) The *rule* is made in the light of the duty of the *United Kingdom* under Article 62 of *MiFID* to adopt precautionary measures to protect investors.

(3) The *rule* will be effective for 12 months only; it reflects the scope of the *Regulated Activities Order* (including, for example, the overseas persons exclusion); and it allows for the possibility of a partial transposition by the *Home State*.

(4) An indication of the *Handbook* provisions which transpose *MiFID* and the *MiFID implementing Directive* can be found in the websites http://www.hm-treasury.gov.uk/media/C/7/transfinal1b120707.pdf and http://www.hm-treasury.gov.uk/media/C/E/transfinal2b120707.pdf. For the purposes of the precautionary measure rule, the principal provisions are the *rules* in *COBS* (including in particular those relating to inducements in *COBS* 2.3) and the conflicts and record keeping provisions in *SYSC*.

(5) The provisions applying to an *incoming EEA firm* are set out in SUP 13A Annex 1G. The effect of SUP 13A.9.4E(1) is that some of the provisions which are expressed as not applying may need to be applied by a *firm* in order to meet a *MiFID* standard.

SUP 13A Annex 1 [G]
Application of the Handbook to Incoming EEA Firms

SUP 13A Ann 1 **[G]**

(1) The table below summarises the application of the *Handbook* to an *incoming EEA firm*. Where the table indicates that a particular module of the *Handbook* may apply, its application in relation to any particular activity is dependent on the detailed application provisions in that module. The table does not apply to *incoming ECA providers*. These should refer to COBS 1 Ann 1 Part 3 section 7 for *guidance* on how COBS applies to them. The table does not apply to *EEA pure reinsurers* as these *firms* have automatic passport rights on the basis of their *Home State authorisation*.

(2) In some cases, the application of the *Handbook* depends on whether responsibility for a matter is reserved under an *EU* instrument to the *incoming EEA firm's Home State regulator*. *Guidance* on the reservation of responsibility is contained in SUP 13A Ann 2 (Matters reserved to a Home State regulator). *Guidance* on the territorial application of *MiFID* is contained in PERG 13.6 and 13.7 and SUP 13A Annex 2G.

(3) For an *incoming EEA firm* which has *permission* for *cross-border services* only, many parts of the *Handbook* apply only if the *firm* carries on *regulated activities* in the *United Kingdom*. Those parts of the *Handbook* will therefore not apply if the *firm* confines its activities to those within the *overseas persons* exclusions in article 72 of the *Regulated Activities Order*, or which would not be regarded as carried on in the *United Kingdom*. Further *guidance* may be found in PERG 2.4 (Link between activities and the *United Kingdom*) and PERG 2.9.15G to PERG 2.9.17G (Overseas persons).

2 **[G]**

(1) Module of Handbook	(2) Potential application to an incoming EEA firm with respect to activities carried on from an establishment of the firm (or its appointed representative) in the United Kingdom	(3) Potential application to an incoming EEA firm with respect to activities carried on other than from an establishment of the firm (or its appointed representative) in the United Kingdom
PRIN	The *Principles* apply only in so far as responsibility for the matter in question is not reserved by an *EU* instrument to the *firm's Home State regulator* (PRIN 3.1.1R(1)). For an *incoming EEA firm* which is a *BCD credit institution* without a *top-up permission*, *Principle* 4 applies only in relation to the liquidity of a *branch* established in the *United Kingdom* (PRIN 3.1.1R(2)).	The *Principles* do not apply if the *firm* has *permission* only for *cross-border services* and does not carry on *regulated activities* in the *United Kingdom* (PRIN 3.1.1R(2). The *Principles* have limited application for activities which are not carried on from a *UK* establishment (see PRIN 3.3.1R). Otherwise, see column (2).
SYSC	SYSC 1 and SYSC 1 Annex 1 (Application of SYSC 2 and SYSC 3) contain application provisions only. SYSC 2 and SYSC 3 apply only to an *insurer*, a *managing agent* and the *Society* as set out in SYSC 1 Annex 1.1.1 R, which include the following exceptions: (1) SYSC 2.1.1R and SYSC 2.1.2G do not apply;	SYSC 2 and SYSC 3 do not apply if the *firm* has *permission* only for *cross-border services* and does not carry on *regulated activities* in the *United Kingdom* (SYSC 1 Annex 1.1.1 R). SYSC 2 and SYSC 3 have limited application for activities which are not carried on from a *UK* establishment (see SYSC 1 Annex 1.1.1 R(2A)). Otherwise, see column (2).

(1) Module of Handbook	**(2) Potential application to an incoming EEA firm with respect to activities carried on from an establishment of the firm (or its appointed representative) in the United Kingdom**	**(3) Potential application to an incoming EEA firm with respect to activities carried on other than from an establishment of the firm (or its appointed representative) in the United Kingdom**
	(2) SYSC 2.1.3R to SYSC 2.2.3G apply, but only in relation to allocation of the function in SYSC 2.1.3R(2) and only in so far as responsibility for the matter in question is not reserved by an *EU* instrument to the *firm's Home State regulator*; and	
	(3) SYSC 3 applies, but only in so far as responsibility for the matter in question is not reserved by an *EU* instrument to the *firm's Home State regulator*.	
	SYSC 1.1.7R (Where?) further restricts the territorial application of SYSC 1 to SYSC 3 for an *incoming EEA firm*. Further *guidance* is contained in SYSC 2.1.6G, Question 12.	
	SYSC 18 applies to the extent that the Public Interest Disclosure Act 1998 applies to the *firm*.	
	The *common platform requirements* in SYSC 4–10 apply as set out in Part 2 of SYSC 1 Annex 1 (Application of the common platform requirement).	The *common platform requirements* in SYSC 4 to SYSC 10 apply as set out in SYSC 1 Annex 1.2.2R.
	SYSC 1 Annex 1.2.7G reminds *EEA MiFID investment firms* that they must comply with the *common platform record-keeping requirements* in relation to a *branch* in the *United Kingdom*.	
	SYSC 9 applies to activities carried on from an establishment in the *United Kingdom*, unless another applicable *rule* which is relevant to the activity has a wider territorial scope, in which case the *common platform record-keeping requirements* apply with that wider scope in relation to the activity described in that *rule* (SYSC 1 Annex 1.2.17R).	
	SYSC 12 does not apply (SYSC 12.1.3R).	SYSC 11–17 do not apply.
	SYSC 13 does not apply (SYSC 13.1.1G).	
	SYSC 14 does not apply (SYSC 14.1.1R).	
	SYSC 15 does not apply (SYSC 15.1.1G).	
	SYSC 16 does not apply (SYSC 16.1.1G).	
	SYSC 17 does not apply (SYSC 17.1.1G).	
	SYSC 18 applies.	SYSC 18 applies

(1) Module of Handbook	**(2) Potential application to an incoming EEA firm with respect to activities carried on from an establishment of the firm (or its appointed representative) in the United Kingdom**	**(3) Potential application to an incoming EEA firm with respect to activities carried on other than from an establishment of the firm (or its appointed representative) in the United Kingdom**
	SYSC 19 does not apply to an *incoming EEA firm* when acting as such	SYSC 19 does not apply
COND	*COND* does not apply if the *firm* does not have, or apply for, a *top-up permission*. Otherwise, only *threshold conditions* 1, 3, 4 and 5 apply and only in so far as relevant to: (1) an application for a *top-up permission* under Part IV of the *Act* (that is, a *permission* to carry on *regulated activities* in addition to those permitted through its *authorisation* under Schedule 3 to the *Act* (EEA Passport Rights)); and (2) the exercise of the *FSA's own-initiative power* in relation to the *top-up permission*. (COND 1.1.1G.)	As column (2).
APER	APER applies to *approved persons* (APER 1.1.1G). See below under SUP 10 as to whether *controlled functions* are performed, and approval therefore required.	Not relevant because SUP 10 does not apply.
FIT	*FIT* applies to a *firm* wishing to establish a *branch* in the *United Kingdom* or to apply for a *top-up permission* in respect of any application that it makes for the approval of a *person* to perform a *controlled function* (FIT 1.1). See under SUP 10 below as to whether such approval is required. *FIT* applies in a limited way in relation to an incoming *MiFID investment firm* (see FIT 1.2.4AG).	Does not apply.
GEN	GEN applies (GEN 1.1, GEN 2.1, GEN 3.1, GEN 4.1, GEN 5.1 and GEN 6.1). However, (a) GEN 4 does not apply to the extent that the *firm* is subject to equivalent *rules* imposed by its *Home State* (GEN 4.1.1R(3)), and (b) GEN 6 only applies to business that can be regulated under section 138 of the *Act* (General rule-making power). It does not therefore apply if, or to the extent that, responsibility has been reserved to an *incoming firm's Home State regulator* by an *EU* instrument. Only GEN 4.5 applies in relation to *MiFID or equivalent third country business* (see GEN 4.1.1R).	GEN 4 does not apply if the *firm* has *permission* only for *cross-border services* and does not carry on *regulated activities* in the *United Kingdom* (see GEN 4.1.1R). The general licence to use or reproduce the FSA logo in GEN 5 Annex 1G does not apply (see 3.1(1) of GEN 5 Annex 1G). Otherwise, as column (2).

(1) Module of Handbook	**(2) Potential application to an incoming EEA firm with respect to activities carried on from an establishment of the firm (or its appointed representative) in the United Kingdom**	**(3) Potential application to an incoming EEA firm with respect to activities carried on other than from an establishment of the firm (or its appointed representative) in the United Kingdom**
GENPRU	Does not apply.	Does not apply if the *firm* has *permission* only for *cross border services* and does not carry on *regulated activities* in the *United Kingdom*.
BIPRU	*EEA firms* are subject to the prudential standards of their home state regulator (BIPRU 1.1.7R and BIPRU 1.1.9G). However, BIPRU 12 applies to an *EEA firm* as respects the activities of its *UK branch*, but in relation to *liquidity risk* only.	Does not apply if the *firm* has *permission* only for *cross border services* and does not carry on *regulated activities* in the *United Kingdom*.
MIPRU	MIPRU 1 (Application and general provisions) does not apply unless the *firm* has a *top-up permission*. MIPRU 2 (Responsibility for insurance mediation activity) does not apply unless the *firm* has a *top-up permission*. MIPRU 3 (Requirement to hold professional indemnity insurance) does not apply unless the *firm* has a *top-up permission*. MIPPRU 4 (Requirement to hold capital resources) does not apply unless the *firm* has a *top-up permission*. See MIPRU 4.1.2G for more detailed *guidance*. MIPRU 5 (Insurance undertakings and mortgage lenders using insurance or mortgage mediation services) does not apply unless the *firm* has a *top-up permission*.	As column (2)
INSPRU	INSPRU does not apply unless the firm is an *insurer* to which INSPRU 1.5.33R applies.	
IPRU(BANK)	Only the following apply, and only if the *firm* is a *credit institution* other than an electronic money institution within the meaning of article 1(3)(a) of the *E-Money Directive* that has the right to benefit from the mutual recognition arrangements under the *Banking Consolidation Directive* (IPRU(BANK) 3.2.1R): (1) IPRU(BANK) 3.5.1R; and (2) IPRU(BANK) chapters LM and LS.	Does not apply. But if the *firm* is a *credit institution* whose notification to the *FSA* of its intention to provide services in the *United Kingdom* covers services provided through a *branch*, see column (2).
IPRU(BSOC)	Does not apply because an *incoming EEA firm* cannot be a *building society* (IPRU(BSOC) X.2.1R).	Does not apply because an *incoming EEA firm* cannot be a *building society* (IPRU(BSOC) X.2.1R).
IPRU(FSOC)	Does not apply because an *incoming EEA firm* cannot be a *friendly society* (IPRU(FSOC) 1.1).	Does not apply because an *incoming EEA firm* cannot be a *friendly society* (IPRU(FSOC) 1.1).
IPRU(INS)	[deleted]	[deleted]
IPRU(INV)	IPRU(INV) does not apply unless the *firm*:	As column (2).

Part II FSA Handbook Materials

(1) Module of Handbook	**(2) Potential application to an incoming EEA firm with respect to activities carried on from an establishment of the firm (or its appointed representative) in the United Kingdom**	**(3) Potential application to an incoming EEA firm with respect to activities carried on other than from an establishment of the firm (or its appointed representative) in the United Kingdom**
	(1) has a *top-up permission*; (2) is an *authorised professional firm, investment management firm, members' adviser, personal investment firm, securities and futures firm, service company* or *underwriting agent*; and (3) is not a *lead regulated firm;* a *media firm* or a *BIPRU investment firm*. (IPRU(INV) 1.1.1R and 1.2R)	
COB	[deleted]	[deleted]
COBS	*Guidance* on the territorial application of COBS is contained in COBS 1 Ann 1 Part 3.	*Guidance* on the territorial application of COBS is contained in COBS 1 Ann 1 Part 3.
ICOBS	ICOBS applies except to the extent necessary to be compatible with European law. *Guidance* on the territorial application of ICOBS is contained in ICOBS 1 Ann 1 Part 4.	ICOBS does not apply, except to the extent necessary to be compatible with European law. *Guidance* on the territorial application of ICOBS is contained in ICOBS 1 Ann 1 Part 4.
MCOB	Applies where the activity is carried on with or for a *customer* resident in the *United Kingdom* or another *EEA State* at the time that the activity is carried on, but see the territorial scope in MCOB 3.3 (Application: where?).	Applies where the activity is carried on with or for a *customer* resident in the *United Kingdom* at the time that the activity is carried on but see MCOB 1.3.4R (Distance contracts entered into from an establishment in another EEA State) and MCOB 3.3 (Application: where?).
CASS	*CASS* does not apply with respect to the *firm's passported activities* unless the *firm* is an *insurer* (CASS 1.2.3R (2)).	As column (2).
MAR	MAR 1 (Code of market conduct) Applies if the *firm* is seeking *guidance* as to whether or not *behaviour* amounts to *market abuse* (*MAR* 1.1.1G). MAR 2 (Price stabilising rules) Applies if the *firm* undertakes *stabilising action* and wishes to show that it has acted in conformity with *price stabilising rules*, or that its *behaviour* conforms with *rules* in accordance with section 118A(5)(a) of the *Act* (Market abuse) (MAR 2.1 Application). MAR 4 (Endorsement of the Take-over Code) Applies to *firms* whose *permission* includes, or ought to include, any *designated investment business*, except as set out in MAR 4.4.1R. MAR 5 (Multilateral Trading Facilities) Does not apply (MAR 5.1.1G).	MAR 1 (Code of market conduct) As column (2). MAR 2 (Price stabilising rules) Only applies in so far as the *firm* undertakes *stabilising action* and wishes to rely on a defence that it has acted in conformity with *price stabilising rules*, or that its *behaviour* conforms with *rules* in accordance with section 118A(5)(a) of the *Act* (Market abuse) (MAR 2.1 and in particular MAR 2.1.3R). MAR 4 (Endorsement of the Take-over Code) Does not apply (MAR 4.4.1R(4)(b)). MAR 5 (Multilateral Trading Facilities) Does not apply (MAR 5.1.1G).

(1) Module of Handbook	(2) Potential application to an incoming EEA firm with respect to activities carried on from an establishment of the firm (or its appointed representative) in the United Kingdom	(3) Potential application to an incoming EEA firm with respect to activities carried on other than from an establishment of the firm (or its appointed representative) in the United Kingdom
TC	*TC* applies, but only in so far as responsibility for any matter it covers is not reserved by an *EU* instrument to the *firm's Home State regulator*	TC Appendix 1 R sets out the activities to which TC applies. TC Appendix 2 R sets out the sourcebook's territorial scope. TC Appendix 3 R sets out the limitations on TC Appendix 2.
SUP	SUP 1 (The FSA's approach to supervision)	SUP 1 (The FSA's approach to supervision)
	Applies, but contains only *guidance*.	As column (2).
	SUP 2 (Information gathering by the FSA on its own initiative)	SUP 2 (Information gathering by the FSA on its own initiative)
	The application of this chapter is the same as for *Principle* 11 (see under *PRIN* above).	As column (2).
	SUP 3 (Auditors)	SUP 3 (Auditors)
	Applies to the *firm* (and its auditor) only if the *firm* has a *top-up permission*.	As column (2).
	SUP 4 (Actuaries)	SUP 4 (Actuaries)
	Does not apply.	Does not apply
	SUP 5 (Skilled persons)	SUP 5 (Skilled persons)
	Applies only if the *firm* is required by the *FSA* to provide a report under section 166 of the *Act* (Reports by skilled persons).	As column (2).
	SUP 6 (Applications to vary and cancel Part IV permission)Applies only if the *firm* has a *top-up permission*.	SUP 6 (Applications to vary and cancel Part IV permission)As column (2).
	SUP 7 (Individual requirements)	SUP 7 (Individual requirements)
	Applies only if the *firm* has a *top-up permission*. It contains only *guidance* on the exercise of the *FSA's own initiative power* to vary that *permission*. The *FSA* has similar, but more limited, powers of intervention under Part XIII of the *Act* in relation to the *permission* of the *firm* under Schedule 3 to the *Act* (see *ENF* 4).	As column (2).
	SUP 8 (Waiver and modification of rules)	SUP 8 (Waiver and modification of rules)
	Applies only if the *firm* wishes to apply for, or consent to, or has been given, a *waiver* of the *FSA's* rules (SUP 8.1.1R).	As column (2).
	SUP 9 (Individual guidance)	SUP 9 (Individual guidance)
	Applies only if the *firm* wishes to obtain individual *guidance* from the *FSA* or if the *FSA* gives the *firm* individual *guidance* on its own initiative (SUP 9.1.1G).	As column (2).
	SUP 10 (Approved persons)	SUP 10 (Approved persons)

(1) Module of Handbook	(2) Potential application to an incoming EEA firm with respect to activities carried on from an establishment of the firm (or its appointed representative) in the United Kingdom	(3) Potential application to an incoming EEA firm with respect to activities carried on other than from an establishment of the firm (or its appointed representative) in the United Kingdom
	Applies, but the applicable *controlled functions* are limited. See SUP 10.1 (Application) for more detailed *guidance*.	Does not apply (SUP 10.1.6R).
	SUP 11 (Controllers and close links)	SUP 11 (Controllers and close links)
	Does not apply (SUP 11.1.1R (2)).	Does not apply (SUP 11.1.1R (2)).
	SUP 12 (Appointed representatives)	SUP 12 (Appointed representatives)
	Applies only if the *firm* has *permission* to carry on *designated investment business*, *insurance mediation activity* or *mortgage mediation activity* and wishes to appoint, or has appointed, an *appointed representative* (SUP 12.1.1R (1)).	As column (2).
	SUP 13 (Exercise of passport rights by UK firms)	SUP 13 (Exercise of passport rights by UK firms)
	Does not apply.	Does not apply.
	SUP 13A (Qualifying for authorisation under the Act)	SUP 13A (Qualifying for authorisation under the Act)
	SUP 13A applies to the *firm* if it: (1) is considering carrying on activities in the *United Kingdom* which may fall within the scope of the *Act* and is seeking *guidance* on whether it needs a *top-up permission*; or (2) is, or is considering, applying to the *FSA* to carry on *regulated activities* in the *United Kingdom* under a *top-up permission*; or (3) is, or is considering, establishing a *branch* or providing *cross border services* into the *United Kingdom* using *EEA rights*.	As column (2).
	SUP 14 (Incoming EEA Firms: Changing detail and cancelling qualifications for authorisation)	SUP 14 (Incoming EEA Firms: Changing detail and cancelling qualifications for authorisation)
	Applies.	Applies.
	SUP 15 (Notifications to the FSA)	SUP 15 (Notifications to the FSA)
	Applies in full if the *firm* has a *top-up permission*. Otherwise, the application is modified as set out in SUP 15 Ann 1R.	Does not apply if the *firm* has *permission* only for *cross border services* and does not carry on *regulated activities* in the *United Kingdom* (SUP 15 Ann 1R).Otherwise, as column (2).
	SUP 16 (Reporting requirements)	SUP 16 (Reporting requirements)
	Parts of this chapter may apply if the *firm* has a *top-up permission* or if the *firm* is: (a) a *bank*; or (b) a *depositary* of an *ICVC*; or (c) an *OPS firm*; or (d) a *trustee* of an *AUT*; or	Parts of this chapter may apply if the *firm* has a *top-up permission* or if the *firm* is: (a) a *depositary* of an *ICVC*; or (b) an *OPS firm*; or (c) a *trustee* of an *AUT*; or (d) an *insurer* with *permission* to effect or carry out *life policies*; or

(1) Module of Handbook	(2) Potential application to an incoming EEA firm with respect to activities carried on from an establishment of the firm (or its appointed representative) in the United Kingdom	(3) Potential application to an incoming EEA firm with respect to activities carried on other than from an establishment of the firm (or its appointed representative) in the United Kingdom
	(e) an *insurer* with *permission* to effect or carry out *life policies*; or	(e) a *firm* with *permission* to *establish, operate or wind up* a *personal pension scheme* or a *stakeholder pension scheme*; or
	(f) a *firm* with *permission* to *establish, operate or wind up* a *personal pension scheme* or a *stakeholder pension scheme*; or	(f) a *firm* with *permission* to *advise on investments, arrange (bring about) deals in investments, make arrangements with a view to transactions in investments*, or *arrange safeguarding and administration of assets*
	(g) a *firm* with *permission* to *advise on investments, arrange (bring about) deals in investments, make arrangements with a view to transactions in investments*, or *arrange safeguarding and administration of assets*.	
	(SUP 16.1)	(SUP 16.1)
	SUP 17 (Transaction reporting)	SUP 17 (Transaction reporting)
	Applies to *UK* branches of *incoming EEA firms* which are *MiFID investment firms* in respect of reportable *transactions* executed in the course of services provided, whether within in the *United Kingdom* and outside. (SUP 17.1.2G and SUP 17.1.3AG)	Applies as appropriate to *incoming EEA firms* which are *MiFID investment firms* in respect of reportable *transactions*. (SUP 17.1.1R and SUP 17.1.4R).
	SUP 18 (Transfers of business)	SUP 18 (Transfers of business)
	SUP 18.4 does not apply. SUP 18.1, SUP 18.2 and SUP 18.3 may be relevant if the *firm* proposes to transfer the whole or part of its business by an *insurance business transfer scheme* or to accept such a transfer or proposes to accept certain transfers of *insurance business* taking place outside the *United Kingdom*.	As column (2).
	SUP 20 (Fees Rules)	SUP 20 (Fees Rules)
	Applies (SUP 20.1.1R) but modified (SUP 20.4.7G to SUP 20.4.10R).	As column (2).
	SUP App 1 (Prudential categories)	SUP App 1 (Prudential categories)
	Applies and provides *guidance* on the prudential categories used in the *Handbook*.	As column (2).
	SUP App 2 (Insurers: Scheme of operations)	SUP App 2 (Insurers: Scheme of operations)
	Does not apply (SUP App 2.1.1R).	Does not apply (SUP App 2.1.1R).
DEPP	*DEPP* applies and contains a description of the FSA's procedures for taking statutory notice decisions, the FSA's policy on the imposition and amount of penalties and the conduct of interviews to which a direction under section 169(7) of the Act has been given or the FSA is considering giving.	DEPP applies and contains a description of the FSA's procedures for taking statutory notice decisions, the FSA's policy on the imposition and amount of penalties and the conduct of interviews to which a direction under section 169(7) of the Act has been given or the FSA is considering giving.

Part II FSA Handbook Materials

(1) Module of Handbook	(2) Potential application to an incoming EEA firm with respect to activities carried on from an establishment of the firm (or its appointed representative) in the United Kingdom	(3) Potential application to an incoming EEA firm with respect to activities carried on other than from an establishment of the firm (or its appointed representative) in the United Kingdom
DISP	Applies (DISP 1.1.1R) and applies in a limited way in relation to *MiFID business*.	Does not apply (DISP 1.1.1R).
COMP	Applies, except in relation to the *passported activities* of an *ISD investment firm* or a *BCD credit institution* (see the definition of "*participant firm*") other than an electronic money institution within the meaning of article 1(3)(a) of the *E-Money Directive* that has the right to benefit from the mutual recognition arrangements under the *Banking Consolidation Directive*. However, an *ISD investment firm* or *BCD credit institution* may be able to apply for *top-up cover* in relation to its *passported activities* (see COMP 14 (Participation by EEA Firms)).	Does not apply in relation to the passported activities of an *ISD investment firm* or a *BCD credit institution* (see the definition of "*participant firm*"). Otherwise, COMP may apply, but the coverage of the *compensation scheme* is limited for non-*UK* activities (see COMP 5).
COAF	Applies if the *firm* wishes to bring a *complaint* under the *complaints scheme*, provided the *complaint* meets the requirements of the *complaints scheme* (COAF 1.2).	As column (2).
COLL	COLL applies if the *firm*: (a) is the *operator* or *depositary* of an *AUT* or *ICVC*; or (b) wishes to apply for an *authorisation order* to establish an *AUT* or *ICVC*; or (c) is the *operator* of a *recognised scheme*; or (d) wishes to apply for recognition of a *recognised scheme*.	As column (2).
CRED	Does not apply.	Does not apply.
ELM	ELM 6 applies.	Does not apply.
LLD	Does not apply.	Does not apply.
PROF	PROF applies only if the *firm* is an *authorised professional firm*.	As column (2).
REC	Does not apply.	Does not apply.
LR	LR (Listing Rules) May apply if the *firm* is applying for *listing* in the *United Kingdom*, is a *listed issuer* in the *United Kingdom*, is a *sponsor* or is applying for approval as a *sponsor*.	LR (Listing Rules) As column (2).
PR	PR (Prospectus Rules) May apply if the *firm* makes an *offer of transferable securities to the public* in the *United Kingdom* or is seeking the *admission to trading* of *transferable securities* on a *regulated market* situated or operating in the *United Kingdom*.	PR (Prospectus Rules) As column (2).

(1) Module of Handbook	(2) Potential application to an incoming EEA firm with respect to activities carried on from an establishment of the firm (or its appointed representative) in the United Kingdom	(3) Potential application to an incoming EEA firm with respect to activities carried on other than from an establishment of the firm (or its appointed representative) in the United Kingdom
DR	DR (Disclosure Rules) May apply if the *firm* is an *issuer*, any class of whose *financial instruments* have been *admitted to trading* on a *regulated market*, or are the subject of an application for *admission to trading* on a *regulated market*, other than *issuers* who have not requested or approved admission of their *financial instruments* to trading on a *regulated market*.	DR (Disclosure Rules) As column (2).
EG describes the FSA's approach to exercising the main enforcement powers given to it by FSMA and by regulation 12 of the Unfair Terms Regulations. EG is a Regulatory Guide and as such does not form part of the Handbook.		

SUP 13A Annex 2 [G]:
Matters reserved to a Home State regulator
SUP 13A Ann 2 **[G]**

Introduction

(1) The application of certain provisions in the *Handbook* to an *incoming EEA firm* or *incoming Treaty firm* depends on whether responsibility for the matter in question is reserved to the *firm's Home State regulator*. This annex contains *guidance* designed to assist such *firms* in understanding the application of those provisions. This annex is not concerned with the *FSA's* rights to take enforcement action against an *incoming EEA firm* or an *incoming Treaty firm*, which are covered in the Enforcement Guide (*EG*), or with the position of a *firm* with a *top-up permission*.

Requirements in the interest of the general good

(2) The *Single Market Directives*, and the *Treaty* (as interpreted by the European Court of Justice) adopt broadly similar approaches to reserving responsibility to the *Home State regulator*. To summarise, the *FSA*, as *Host State regulator*, is entitled to impose requirements with respect to activities carried on within the *United Kingdom* if these can be justified in the interests of the "general good" and are imposed in a non-discriminatory way. This general proposition is subject to the following in relation to activities passported under the *Single Market Directives*:

(1) the *Single Market Directives* expressly reserve responsibility for the prudential supervision of a *MiFID investment firm*, *BCD credit institution*, *UCITS management company* or passporting *insurance undertaking* to the *firm's Home State regulator*. The *Insurance Mediation Directive* reaches the same position without expressly referring to the concept of prudential supervision. Accordingly, the *FSA*, as *Host State regulator*, is entitled to regulate only the conduct of the *firm's* business within the *United Kingdom*;

(2) there is no "general good" provision in *MiFID*. Rather, *MiFID* states exactly what the *Host State regulator* regulates (see paragraphs 8–10);

(3) for a *BCD credit institution*, the *FSA*, as *Host State regulator*, is jointly responsible with the *Home State regulator* under article 41 of the *Banking Consolidation Directive* for supervision of the liquidity of a *branch* in the *United Kingdom*;

(4) for a *MiFID investment firm* including a *BCD credit institution* which is a *MiFID investment firm*), the protection of *clients'* money and *clients'* assets is reserved to the *Home State regulator* under *MiFID*; and

(5) responsibility for participation in compensation schemes for *BCD credit institutions* and *MiFID investment firm* is reserved in most cases to the *Home State regulator* under the *Deposit Guarantee Directive* and the *Investor Compensation Directive*.

(3) It is necessary to refer to the case law of the European Court of Justice to interpret the concept of the "general good". To summarise, to satisfy the general good test, *Host State* rules must come within a field which has not been harmonised at an *EU* level, satisfy the

Part II FSA Handbook Materials

general requirements that they pursue an objective of the general good, be non-discriminatory, be objectively necessary, be proportionate to the objective pursued and not already be safeguarded by rules to which the *firm* is subject in its *Home State*.

Application of SYSC 2 and SYSC 3

(4) SYSC 2 and SYSC 3 only apply to an *insurer*, a *managing agent* and the *Society*. See paragraph 8 below for a discussion of how the *common platform requirements* apply. SYSC 2.1.1R and SYSC 2.1.2G do not apply for a relevant *incoming Treaty firm*. The *FSA* considers that it is entitled, in the interests of the general good, to impose the requirements in SYSC 2.1.3R to SYSC 2.2.3G (in relation to the allocation of the function in SYSC 2.1.3R (2)) and SYSC 3 on an *incoming EEA firm* and an *incoming Treaty firm*; but only in so far as they relate to those categories of matter responsibility for which is not reserved to the *firm's Home State regulator*.

(5) Should the *FSA* become aware of anything relating to an *incoming EEA firm* or *incoming Treaty firm* (whether or not relevant to a matter for which responsibility is reserved to the *Home State regulator*), the *FSA* may disclose it to the *Home State regulator* in accordance with any directive and the applicable restrictions in Part XXIII of the *Act* (Public Record, Disclosure of Information and Co-operation).

(6) This Annex represents the *FSA's* views, but a *firm* is also advised to consult the relevant *EU* instrument and, where necessary, seek legal advice. The views of the European Commission in the banking and insurance sectors are contained in two Commission Interpretative Communications (Nos. 97/C209/04 and C(1999)5046).

(7) [deleted]

Application of the common platform requirements in SYSC to EEA MiFID investment firms

(8) Whilst the *common platform requirements* (located in *SYSC* 4–10) do not generally apply to *incoming EEA firms*, *EEA MiFID investment firms* must comply with the *common platform record-keeping requirements* in relation to a *branch* in the *United Kingdom*.

Requirements under MiFID

(9) Article 31(1) of *MiFID* prohibits *Member States* from imposing additional requirements on a *MiFID investment firm* in relation to matters covered by *MiFID* if the *firm* is providing services on a cross-border basis. Such firms will be supervised by their Home State regulator.

(10) Article 32 of *MiFID* requires the *FSA* as the *Host State regulator* to apply certain obligations to an *incoming EEA firm* with an establishment in the *UK*. In summary, these are Articles:

(1) 19 (conduct of business obligations);
(2) 21 (execution of orders on terms most favourable to the client);
(3) 22 (client order handling);
(4) 25 (upholding the integrity of markets, reporting transactions and maintaining records);
(5) 27 (making public firm quotes); and
(6) 28 (post-trade disclosure).

The remaining obligations under *MiFID* are reserved to the *Home State regulator*.

(11) *MiFID* is more highly harmonising than other *Single Market Directives*. Article 4 of the *MiFID implementing Directive* permits Member States to impose additional requirements only where certain tests are met. The *FSA* has made certain requirements that fall within the scope of Article 4. These requirements apply to an *EEA MiFID investment firm* with an establishment in the *United Kingdom* as they apply to a *UK MiFID investment firm*.

(12) Further *guidance* on the territorial application of the *Handbook* can be found at PERG 13.6 and 13.7.

(13) Examples of how SYSC 3 and/or the common platform provisions apply in practice.

(1) The Prudential Standards part of the *Handbook* (with the exception of INSPRU 1.5.33R on the payment of financial penalties and the Interim Prudential sourcebook (insurers) (IPRU(INS)) (rules 3.6 and 3.7) do not apply to an *insurer* which is an *incoming EEA firm*. Similarly, SYSC 3 does not require such a *firm*:

(a) to establish systems and controls in relation to financial resources (SYSC 3.1.1R); or
(b) to establish systems and controls for compliance with that Prudential Standards part of the *Handbook* (SYSC 3.2.6R); or
(c) to make and retain records in relation to financial resources (SYSC 3.2.20R and SYSC 9.1.1R to 9.1.4G).

(2) The Conduct of Business sourcebook (COBS) applies to *an incoming EEA firm*. Similarly, SYSC 3 and SYSC 4-10 do require such a *firm*:

(a) to establish systems and controls in relation to those aspects of the conduct of its business covered by applicable sections of COBS (SYSC 3.1.1R and SYSC 4.1.1R);

(b) to establish systems and controls for compliance with the applicable sections of COBS (SYSC 3.2.6R and SYSC 6.1.1R); and

(c) to make and retain records in relation to those aspects of the conduct of its business (SYSC 3.2.20R and SYSC 9.1.1R to 9.1.4G).

See also Question 12 in SYSC 2.1.6G for guidance on the application of SYSC 2.1.3R(2)

CHAPTER 14
INCOMING EEA FIRMS CHANGING DETAILS, AND CANCELLING QUALIFICATION FOR AUTHORISATION.

14.1 Application and purpose

Application

[2168]
14.1.1 **[G]** This chapter applies to an *incoming EEA firm* other than an *EEA pure reinsurer* which has established a *branch* in, or is providing *cross border services* into, the *United Kingdom* under one of the *Single Market Directives* and, therefore, qualifies for *authorisation* under Schedule 3 to the *Act*.

14.1.2 **[G]** SUP 14.6 (Cancelling qualification for authorisation), which sets out how to cancel qualification for *authorisation* under the *Act*, also applies to:

(1) an *incoming Treaty firm* that qualifies for *authorisation* under Schedule 4 to the *Act*; and

(2) a *UCITS qualifier* that is an *authorised person* under Schedule 5 to the *Act*; a *UCITS qualifier* should, however, refer to COLL 3.1.11G for full details of applicable *rules* and *guidance*.

14.1.3 **[G]**

(1) Under the *Gibraltar Order* made under section 409 of the *Act*, a Gibraltar firm is treated as an *EEA firm* under Schedule 3 to the *Act* if it is:

(a) authorised in Gibraltar under the *Insurance Directives*; or

(b) authorised in Gibraltar under the *Banking Consolidation Directive*; or

(c) authorised in Gibraltar under the *Insurance Mediation Directive*; or

(d) authorised in Gibraltar under the *Investment Services Directive*.

(1A) Similarly, an *EEA firm* which:

(a) has satisfied the Gibraltar establishment conditions and has established a *branch* in the *UK*; or

(b) has satisfied the Gibraltar service conditions and is providing *cross border services* into the *UK*;

is treated as having satisfied the *establishment conditions* or *service conditions* (as appropriate) under Schedule 3 to the *Act*.

(2) Gibraltar insurance companies, *credit institutions, insurance intermediaries* and *investment firms* are allowed to passport their services into the *United Kingdom* if they comply with the relevant notification procedures. So, any references in SUP 14 to *EEA State* or *EEA right* include references to Gibraltar and the entitlement under the *Gibraltar Order* where appropriate.

Purpose

14.1.4 **[G]** This chapter gives *guidance* on the *Act* and the *EEA Passport Rights Regulations* made under the *Act*, for an *incoming EEA firm* which has established a *branch* in, or is providing *cross border services* into, the *United Kingdom* and wishes to change the details of the *branch* or *cross border services*.

14.1.5 **[G]** This chapter also explains how an *incoming EEA firm*, an *incoming Treaty firm* or a *UCITS qualifier* may cancel its qualification for *authorisation* under the *Act*.

14.1.6 **[G]** This chapter does not, however, give *guidance* on the procedures for the establishment of a *branch* in, or the providing of *cross border services* into, the *United Kingdom* for the first time. So, an *incoming EEA firm* that wishes to change or supplement the nature of its operations in the *United Kingdom* from the providing of *cross border services* to the establishment of a *branch* (or vice versa) should refer to SUP 13A (Qualifying for authorisation under the Act).

14.1.7 **[G]** In addition, the chapter does not give *guidance* on the procedures for making an application for *top-up permission*, to carry on *regulated activities* in the *United Kingdom* which are outside the scope of the *Single Market Directives* and for which the firm cannot exercise *Treaty rights*. *Incoming EEA firms* seeking a *top-up permission* should refer to SUP 13A.

14.2 Changes to branch details

14.2.1 **[G]** Where an *incoming EEA firm* is exercising an *EEA right*, other than under the *Insurance Mediation Directive*, and has established a *branch* in the United Kingdom, the *EEA Passport Rights Regulations* govern any changes to the details of that *branch*. Where an *incoming EEA firm* has complied with the relevant requirements in the *EEA Passport Rights Regulations*, then the *firm's permission* given under Schedule 3 to the *Act* is to be treated as varied accordingly. All references to regulations in SUP 14 are to the *EEA Passport Rights Regulations*.

Firms passporting under the Banking Consolidation Directive and the UCITS Directive

14.2.2 **[G]**

(1) Where an *incoming EEA firm*, passporting under the *Banking Consolidation Directive* or the *UCITS Directive* has established a *branch* in the *United Kingdom*, regulation 4 states that it must not make a change in the *requisite details* of the *branch* unless it has complied with the relevant requirements.

(2) The relevant requirements are set out in regulation 4(4) or, where the change arises from circumstances beyond the *incoming EEA firm's* control, in regulation 4(5) (see SUP 14.2.8G).

14.2.3 **[G]** Where the change arises from circumstances within the control of the *incoming EEA firm*, the requirements in regulation 4(4) are that:

(1) the *incoming EEA firm* has given notice to the *FSA* (see SUP 14.4.1G) and to its *Home State regulator* stating the details of the proposed change;

(2) the *FSA* has received a notice stating those details; and

(3) either:

  (a) the *FSA* has informed the firm that it may make the change; or

  (b) the period of one month beginning with the date on which the *incoming EEA firm* gave the *FSA* the notice mentioned in (1) has elapsed.

14.2.4 **[G]** Changes to the *requisite details* may lead to changes to the *applicable provisions* to which the *incoming EEA firm* is subject. The *FSA* will, as soon as practicable after receiving a notice in SUP 14.2.3G or SUP 14.2.8G, inform the incoming *EEA firm* of any consequential changes in the *applicable provisions* (regulation 4(6)).

Firms passporting under the Insurance Directives

14.2.5 **[G]**

(1) Where an *incoming EEA firm*, passporting under the *Insurance Directives* has established a *branch* in the *United Kingdom*, regulation 6 states that it must not make a change to the information referred to in regulation 2(5)(a) to (c) unless it has complied with the relevant requirements.

(2) The relevant requirements are set out in regulation 6(4) or, where the change arises from circumstances beyond the *incoming EEA firm's* control, regulation 6(5) (see SUP 14.2.8G).

14.2.6 **[G]** Where the change arises from circumstances within the control of the *incoming EEA firm*, the relevant requirements in regulation 6(4) are that:

(1) the *incoming EEA firm* has given a notice to the *FSA* (see SUP 14.4.1G) and to its *Home State regulator* stating the details of the proposed change;

(2) the *FSA* has received from the *Home State regulator* a notice stating that it has approved the proposed change;

(3) the period of at least one month beginning with the day on which the *incoming EEA firm* gave the *FSA* the notice in (1) has elapsed; and

(4) either:

  (a) a further period of one month has elapsed; or

  (b) the *FSA* has informed the *Home State regulator* of any consequential changes in the *applicable provisions*.

14.2.7 **[G]** Under regulation 6(6) the *FSA* is required, as soon as practicable, to:

(1) acknowledge receipt of the documents sent under regulation 6(4) or 6(5); and

(2) in the case of a notice under regulation 6(5), inform the *incoming EEA firm's Home State regulator* of any consequential changes in the *applicable provisions*.

Changes arising from circumstances beyond the control of an incoming EEA firm passporting under the Banking Consolidation Directive, UCITS Directive or Insurance Directive

14.2.8 **[G]** If the change arises from circumstances beyond the *incoming EEA firm's* control, the *firm* is required by regulation 4(5) (see SUP 14.2.2G) or regulation 6(5) (see SUP 14.2.5G(2)) to give a notice to the *FSA* (see SUP 14.4.1G) and to its *Home State regulator* stating the details of the change as soon as reasonably practicable.

14.2.9 **[G]** The *FSA* believes that for a change to arise from circumstances beyond the control of an *incoming EEA firm*, the circumstances should be outside the control of the *firm* as a whole and not just its *UK branch*. For example, the *FSA* considers that this provision would be unlikely to apply to circumstances in which lack of planning at the *incoming EEA firm's* head office resulted in a problem arising in a *UK branch* which was outside its control. In practice, therefore, use of this provision is likely to be rare.

Firms passporting under MiFID

14.2.10 **[G]** Where an *EEA MiFID investment firm* has established a *branch* in the *UK*, regulation 4A states that it must not make a change in the requisite details of the *branch* unless it has complied with the relevant requirements.

14.2.11 **[G]** The relevant requirements in regulation 4A(3) are that:
(1) the *EEA MiFID investment firm* has given notice to its *Home State regulator* stating the details of the proposed change; and
(2) the period of one *month* beginning with the date on which the *EEA MiFID investment firm* gave the notice mentioned in (1) has elapsed.

14.2.12 **[G]** Changes to the *requisite details* may lead to changes to the applicable provisions to which the *EEA MiFID investment firm* is subject. The *FSA* will, as soon as practicable after receiving a notice in SUP 14.2.11 G inform the *EEA MiFID investment firm* of any consequential changes in the applicable provisions.

14.3 Changes to cross border services

14.3.1 **[G]** Where an *incoming EEA firm* passporting under the *MiFID, UCITS Directive or Insurance Directives* is exercising an *EEA right* and is providing *cross border services* into the *United Kingdom*, the *EEA Passport Rights Regulations* govern any changes to the details of those services. Where an *incoming EEA firm* has complied with the relevant requirements in the *EEA Passport Rights Regulations*, then the *firm's permission* given under Schedule 3 to the *Act* is to be treated as varied accordingly.

Firms passporting under the UCITS Directive

14.3.2 **[G]** Where an *incoming EEA firm*, passporting under the *UCITS Directive* is providing *cross border services* into the *United Kingdom*, it must not make a change in the details referred to in regulation 5(1) unless it has complied with the relevant requirements in regulation 5(3).

14.3.3 **[G]** The relevant requirements in regulation 5(3) are that:
(1) the *incoming EEA firm* has given a notice to the *FSA* (see SUP 14.4.1G) and to its *Home State regulator* stating the details of the proposed change;
(2) if the change arises from circumstances beyond *the incoming EEA firm's* control, that firm has, as soon as practicable, given to the *FSA* and to its *Home State regulator* the notice in (1).

Firms passporting under MiFID

14.3.3A **[G]** The requirement in regulation 5(3A) is that the *incoming EEA firm* has.

14.3.4 **[G]** Under regulation 5(4), the *FSA* is required, as soon as practicable after receiving the notice in SUP 14.3.3G, to inform the *incoming EEA firm* of any consequential changes in the *applicable provisions*.

14.3.4A **[G]** Where an *incoming EEA firm* passporting under *MiFID* is providing *cross border services* into the *United Kingdom*, it must not make a change in the details referred to in regulation 5(1) unless it has given at least one *month*'s notice to its *Home State regulator* stating the details of the proposed change.

Firms passporting under the Insurance Directives

14.3.5 **[G]** If an *incoming EEA firm* passporting under the *Insurance Directives* is providing *cross border services* into the *United Kingdom*, it must not make a change to the details referred to in regulation 7(1) unless it has complied with the relevant provisions.

14.3.6 **[G]** The relevant provisions are those set out in regulation 7(4), namely that:
(1) the *incoming EEA firm* has given a notice to its *Home State regulator* stating the details of the proposed change; and
(2) the *Home State regulator* has passed on to the *FSA* the information contained in that notice.

14.3.7 **[G]** If the change arises from circumstances beyond the *incoming EEA firm's* control, the *incoming EEA firm* is required to comply with the relevant provisions referred to in SUP 14.3.6G as soon as reasonably practicable (whether before or after the change). See also SUP 14.2.9, as relevant to *cross border services*.

14.4 Notices of proposed changes: form and delivery

14.4.1 **[G]**
(1) Regulation 7 to 9 of the Financial Services and Markets Act 2000 (Services of Notices) Regulations 2001 (SI 2001/1420) govern the manner in which notices may be submitted to the FSA under the *EEA Passport Rights Regulations*. In summary, they should be delivered or posted to the FSA's address (See (2) below) and will be treated as given when received by the FSA. They should not be sent by fax or electronic mail.
(2) The address for notices is: The Passport Notifications Unit, The Financial Services Authority, 25 The North Colonnade, Canary Wharf, London, E14 5HS

14.5 Variation of a top-up permission to carry on regulated activities outside the scope of the Single Market Directives

14.5.1 **[G]** Where an *incoming EEA firm* has been granted *top-up permission* by the *FSA* and wishes to vary that *permission*, the *Act* requires it to apply to the *FSA* for a variation of the *top-up permission*.

14.5.2 **[G]** Guidance on the procedures for applying for a variation of a *permission* granted under Part IV of the *Act*, including a *top-up permission*, is given in SUP 6 (Applications to vary and cancel Part IV Permission).

14.6 Cancelling qualification for authorisation

Incoming EEA firms

14.6.1 **[G]** Section 34 of the *Act* states that an *incoming EEA firm* no longer qualifies for *authorisation* under Schedule 3 to the *Act* if it ceases to be an *incoming EEA firm* as a result of:
(1) having its *EEA authorisation* withdrawn by its *Home State regulator*; or
(2) ceasing to have an *EEA right* in circumstances in which *EEA* authorisation is not required; this is relevant to a *financial institution* that is a subsidiary of a *credit institution* (of the kind mentioned in Article 19 of the *Banking Consolidation Directive*) which fulfils the conditions in articles 18 and 19 of that *Directive*.

14.6.2 **[G]** In addition, under section 34(2) an *incoming EEA firm* may ask the *FSA* to give a direction cancelling its *authorisation* under Schedule 3 to the *Act*.

14.6.3 **[G]** Regulation 8 states that where an *incoming EEA firm* which qualifies for *authorisation* under Schedule 3:
(1) has ceased, or is to cease, to carry on *regulated activities* in the *United Kingdom*; and
(2) gives notice of that fact to the *FSA*;

the notice is treated under regulation 8 as a request for cancellation of the *incoming EEA firm's* qualification for *authorisation* under Schedule 3 to the *Act* and so as a request under section 34(2) of the *Act*.

14.6.4 **[G]** Where a *financial institution* (that is, a subsidiary of a *credit institution*) is passporting under the *Banking Consolidation Directive* (see SUP 14.6.1G(2)), regulation 9(1) states that the *incoming EEA firm* may request the *FSA* to direct that its qualification for *authorisation* under Schedule 3 to the *Act* is cancelled from such date as may be specified in the direction.

14.6.5 **[G]** The *FSA* may not, however, give a direction referred to in SUP 14.6.4G unless:
(1) the *incoming EEA firm* has given notice to its *Home State regulator*; and
(2) the *FSA* has agreed with the *Home State regulator* that the direction should be given.

14.6.6 **[G]** Regulation 9(3) requires that the date specified by the *FSA* in a direction referred to in SUP 14.6.4G:
(1) must not be earlier than the date requested in the application; but
(2) subject to (1), is as agreed between the *FSA* and the *incoming EEA firm's Home State regulator*.

14.6.7 **[G]** The *FSA* is required to send, as soon as practicable, a copy of the direction to the *incoming EEA firm* and to its *Home State regulator* (regulation 9(4)).

14.6.8 **[G]** Where the *FSA* gives a direction referred to in SUP 14.6.4G, the *incoming EEA firm* may apply for *Part IV permission* (see the *FSA* website "How do I get authorised": http://www.fsa.gov.uk/Pages/Doing/how/index.shtml) to take effect not earlier than the date that its qualification for *authorisation* is cancelled (as specified in the direction).

Incoming Treaty firms

14.6.9 **[G]** Section 35 of the *Act* states that an *incoming Treaty firm* no longer qualifies for *authorisation* under Schedule 4 to the *Act* if its *Home State* authorisation is withdrawn.

14.6.10 **[G]** In addition, under section 35(2) an *incoming Treaty firm* may ask the *FSA* to give a direction cancelling its *authorisation* under Schedule 4 to the *Act*.

UCITS qualifiers

14.6.11 **[G]** Section 36 of the *Act* states that a *UCITS qualifier* may ask the *FSA* to give a direction cancelling its *authorisation* under paragraph 1(1) of Schedule 5 to the *Act*. *UCITS qualifiers* should also refer to COLLG 3.1.11G (Revocation of recognition of overseas schemes (section 279)).

14.7 Cancellation of a top-up permission to carry on regulated activities outside the scope of the Single Market Directives

14.7.1 **[G]** Where an *incoming EEA firm*, an *incoming Treaty firm* or a *UCITS qualifier* wishes to cancel its *top-up permission*, either with or without cancellation of its qualification for *authorisation* under Schedule 3, 4, or 5 to the *Act*, it should make an application following the procedures set out in SUP 6 (Applications to vary and cancel Part IV Permission).

14.8 Further guidance

14.8.1 **[G]** For further *guidance* on passporting procedures, an *incoming EEA firm* should contact the *FSA's* Passport Notifications Unit or their usual supervisory contact at the *FSA*. *Incoming Treaty firms* and *UCITS qualifiers* should speak to their usual supervisory contact at the *FSA* in the first instance

CHAPTER 15
NOTIFICATIONS TO THE FSA

15.1 Application

Who?

[2169]

15.1.1 **[R]** This chapter applies to every *firm* except that:

(1) only SUP 15.10 applies to an *ICVC* or a *UCITS qualifier*; and

(2) SUP 15.3.22D to SUP 15.3.25D apply only to the *Society*.

15.1.2 **[R]** The application of this chapter to an *incoming EEA firm* or an *incoming Treaty firm* is set out in SUP 15 Ann 1R.

15.1.3 **[G]** In some cases, the application of provisions set out in SUP 15 Ann 1R depends on whether responsibility is reserved to a *Home State regulator*. SYSC App 1 contains *guidance* on this.

What?

15.1.4 **[R]** This chapter:

(1) applies with respect to the carrying on of both *regulated activities* and *unregulated activities*; and

(2) takes into account any activity of other members of a *group* of which the *firm* is a member.

Where?

15.1.5 **[G] Firms** are reminded that unless expressly stated otherwise, where a *rule* or *guidance* includes a reference to a *firm* this includes all *UK* and overseas branches and representative offices of that *firm*, whether or not those branches or offices carry on any *regulated activities*.

15.1.6 **[R]** This chapter does not apply to an *incoming ECA provider* acting as such.

15.2 Purpose

15.2.1 **[G]** A *firm* is required to provide the *FSA* with a wide range of information to enable the *FSA* to meet its responsibilities for monitoring the *firm's* compliance with requirements imposed by or under the *Act*. Some of this information is provided through regular reports, including those set out in SUP 16 (Reporting requirements) and SUP 17 (Transaction reporting). In addition, other chapters in the *Handbook* set out specific notification and reporting requirements. *Principle* 11 includes a requirement for a *firm* to disclose to the *FSA* appropriately anything relating to the *firm* of which the *FSA* would reasonably expect notice.

15.2.2 **[G]** This chapter sets out:

(1) *guidance* on the type of event or change in condition which a *firm* should consider notifying in accordance with *Principle* 11; the purpose of this *guidance* is to set out examples and not to give comprehensive advice to *firms* on what they should notify in order to be in compliance with *Principle* 11;

(2) *rules* on events and changes in condition that a *firm* must notify; these are the types of event that the *FSA* must be informed about, usually as soon as possible, if it is to be able to carry out its monitoring function effectively and react in good time to developments that may require a regulatory response;

Part II FSA Handbook Materials

(3) *rules* on the core information that a *firm* must provide to the *FSA*, for example its name and address and the names of its other regulators, so that the *FSA* is able to maintain a relationship with the *firm* and with those regulators;
(4) *rules* requiring a *firm* to ensure that information provided to the *FSA* is accurate and complete; section 398 of the *Act* makes it an *offence* knowingly or recklessly to provide the *FSA* with information which is false or misleading in a material particular, in purported compliance with any requirement imposed by or under the *Act*; the purpose of the *rules* in SUP 15.6 is to ensure that *firms* take due care to ensure the accuracy of information and to require them to ensure that information is not only accurate but also complete; and
(5) material (in SUP 15.10 (Notification of suspicious transactions (market abuse))) to implement the provisions of the *Market Abuse Directive* for the reporting of transactions about which there is reasonable suspicion of *market abuse*.

15.2.3 **[G]** *Rules* and *guidance* have also been included to set out how *firms* should make a notification and to determine when it may be appropriate to discuss matters with their usual supervisory contact by telephone (SUP 15.7).

15.2.4 **[G]** Schedule 2 contains a consolidated summary of all the *notification rules* applicable to *firms* set out in the *Handbook*.

15.3 General notification requirements

Matters having a serious regulatory impact

15.3.1 **[R]** A *firm* must notify the *FSA* immediately it becomes aware, or has information which reasonably suggests, that any of the following has occurred, may have occurred or may occur in the foreseeable future:
(1) the *firm* failing to satisfy one or more of the *threshold conditions*; or
(2) any matter which could have a significant adverse impact on the *firm's* reputation; or
(3) any matter which could affect the *firm's* ability to continue to provide adequate services to its *customers* and which could result in serious detriment to a *customer* of the *firm*; or
(4) any matter in respect of the *firm* which could result in serious financial consequences to the *financial system* or to other *firms*.

15.3.2 **[G]** The circumstances which may give rise to any of the events in SUP 15.3.1R are wide-ranging and the probability of any matter resulting in such an outcome, and the severity of the outcome, may be difficult to determine. However, the *FSA* expects *firms* to consider properly all potential consequences of events.

15.3.3 **[G]** In determining whether an event that may occur in the foreseeable future should be notified to the *FSA*, a *firm* should consider both the probability of the event happening and the severity of the outcome should it happen.

15.3.4 **[G]** *Guidance* on satisfaction of the *threshold conditions* is given in *COND*.

15.3.5 **[G]** A *firm* making a notification in accordance with SUP 15.3.1R should consider the *guidance* in SUP 15.7.2G and notify the *FSA* by telephone if appropriate.

15.3.6 **[G]** An *insurer* or *friendly society* making a notification under SUP 15.3.1R(1) relating to satisfaction of *threshold condition* 4 (Adequate resources) should be aware of the requirements in SUP App 2 (Scheme of operations).

Communication with the FSA in accordance with Principle 11

15.3.7 **[G]** *Principle* 11 requires a *firm* to deal with its regulators in an open and cooperative way and to disclose to the *FSA* appropriately anything relating to the *firm* of which the *FSA* would reasonably expect notice. *Principle* 11 applies to *unregulated activities* as well as *regulated activities* and takes into account the activities of other members of a *group*.

15.3.8 **[G]** Compliance with *Principle* 11 includes, but is not limited to, giving the *FSA* notice of:
(1) any proposed restructuring, reorganisation or business expansion which could have a significant impact on the *firm's* risk profile or resources, including, but not limited to:
 (a) setting up a new *undertaking* within a *firm's group*, or a new branch (whether in the *United Kingdom* or overseas); or
 (b) commencing the provision of cross border services into a new territory; or
 (c) commencing the provision of a new type of product or service (whether in the *United Kingdom* or overseas); or
 (d) ceasing to undertake a *regulated activity* or *ancillary activity*, or significantly reducing the scope of such activities; or
 (e) entering into, or significantly changing, a *materia outsourcing* arrangement (a *bank*, a *building society* and a *dormant account fund operator* should also see SYSC 3.2.4G and SYSC 8, and an *insurer* should also see SYSC 13.9 for further details); or

(f) a substantial change or a series of changes in the *governing body* of an *overseas firm* (other than an *incoming firm*); or
(g) any change to the *firm's* prudential category or sub-category, as used in the Interim Prudential sourcebooks and SUP and on which *guidance* is given in SUP App 1; or
(h) any proposed change which limits the liability of any of the *members* or *partners* of a *firm* such as a general *partner* becoming a limited *partner* or re-registration as a limited liability *company* of a *company* incorporated with unlimited liability; or
(i) in relation to a *dormant account fund operator*, notify the *FSA* when the operator intends to rely on a third party for the performance of operational functions which are critical or important for the performance of relevant services and activities in connection with *operating a dormant account fund* on a continuous and satisfactory basis;

(2) any significant failure in the *firm's* systems or controls, including those reported to the *firm* by the *firm's* auditor;
(3) any action which a *firm* proposes to take which would result in a material change in its capital adequacy or solvency, including, but not limited to:
(a) any action which would result in a material change in the *firm's* financial resources or financial resources requirement; or
(b) a material change resulting from the payment of a special or unusual dividend or the repayment of *share* capital or a subordinated loan; or
(c) for *firms* which are subject to the *rules* on consolidated financial supervision, any proposal under which another *group company* may be considering such an action; or
(d) significant trading or non-trading losses (whether recognised or unrecognised).

15.3.9 **[G]** The period of notice given to the *FSA* will depend on the event, although the *FSA* expects a *firm* to discuss relevant matters with it at an early stage, before making any internal or external commitments.

15.3.10 **[G]** A notification under *Principle* 11 may be given orally or in writing (as set out in SUP 15.7.1R and SUP 15.7.2G), although the *FSA* may request written confirmation of a matter. However, it is the responsibility of a *firm* to ensure that matters are properly and clearly communicated to the *FSA*. A *firm* should provide a written notification if a matter either is complex or may be such as to make it necessary for the *FSA* to take action. A *firm* should also have regard to *Principle* 11 and the *guidance* in SUP 15.7.2G in respect of providing important information promptly.

Part II FSA Handbook Materials

Breaches of rules and other requirements in or under the Act

15.3.11 **[R]**

(1) A *firm* must notify the *FSA* of:
(a) a significant breach of a *rule* (which includes a *Principle*) or *Statement of Principle*; or
(b) a breach of any requirement imposed by the *Act* or by regulations or an order made under the *Act* by the Treasury (except if the breach is an *offence*, in which case (c) applies); or
(c) the bringing of a prosecution for, or a conviction of, any *offence* under the *Act*;
(d) a breach of a directly applicable provision in the *MiFID Regulation*; or
(e) a breach of any requirement in regulation 4C(3) (or any successor provision) of the Financial Services and Markets Act 2000 (Markets in Financial Instruments) Regulations 2007;

by (or as regards (c) against) the *firm* or any of its *directors*, *officers*, *employees*, *approved persons*, or *appointed representatives* or, where applicable, *tied agents*.

(2) A *firm* must make the notification in (1) immediately it becomes aware, or has information which reasonably suggests, that any of the matters in (1) has occurred, may have occurred or may occur in the foreseeable future.

15.3.11A **[G]** SUP 15.3.11R(1)(e) relates to the standard requirement in the *permission* of those *firms* which fall outside *MiFID* because of the Treasury's implementation of Article 3 of *MiFID*. *Guidance* on how the Treasury has exercised the Article 3 exemption for the *United Kingdom* is given in Q48 and the following questions and answers in PERG 13.5 (Exemptions from MiFID).

15.3.12 **[G]** In SUP 15.3.11R (1)(a), significance should be determined having regard to potential financial losses to *customers* or to the *firm*, frequency of the breach, implications for the *firm's* systems and controls and if there were delays in identifying or rectifying the breach.

15.3.13 **[G]** In assessing whether an event that may occur in the foreseeable future should be notified to the *FSA*, a *firm* should consider the *guidance* in SUP 15.3.3G.

15.3.14 **[G]** A notification under SUP 15.3.11R should include:

(1) information about any circumstances relevant to the breach or *offence*;
(2) identification of the *rule* or requirement or *offence*; and

(3) information about any steps which a *firm* or other *person* has taken or intends to take to rectify or remedy the breach or prevent any future potential occurrence.

Civil, criminal or disciplinary proceedings against a firm

15.3.15 **[R]** A *firm* must notify the *FSA* immediately if:
(1) civil proceedings are brought against the *firm* and the amount of the claim is significant in relation to the *firm's* financial resources or its reputation; or
(2) any action is brought against the *firm* under section 71 of the *Act* (Actions for damages) or section 150 (Actions for damages); or
(3) disciplinary measures or sanctions have been imposed on the *firm* by any statutory or regulatory authority, professional organisation or trade body (other than the *FSA*) or the *firm* becomes aware that one of those bodies has started an investigation into its affairs; or
(4) the *firm* is prosecuted for, or convicted of, any *offence* involving fraud or dishonesty, or any penalties are imposed on it for tax evasion; or
(5) it is an *OPS firm*, which is a trustee, and is removed as trustee by a court order.

15.3.16 **[G]** A notification under SUP 15.3.15R should include details of the matter and an estimate of the likely financial consequences, if any.

Fraud, errors and other irregularities

15.3.17 **[R]** A *firm* must notify the *FSA* immediately if one of the following events arises and the event is significant:
(1) it becomes aware that an *employee* may have committed a fraud against one of its *customers*; or
(2) it becomes aware that a *person*, whether or not *employed* by it, may have committed a fraud against it; or
(3) it considers that any *person*, whether or not *employed* by it, is acting with intent to commit a fraud against it; or
(4) it identifies irregularities in its accounting or other records, whether or not there is evidence of fraud; or
(5) it suspects that one of its *employees* may be guilty of serious misconduct concerning his honesty or integrity and which is connected with the *firm's regulated activities* or *ancillary activities*.

15.3.18 **[G]** In determining whether a matter is significant, a *firm* should have regard to:
(1) the size of any monetary loss or potential monetary loss to itself or its *customers* (either in terms of a single incident or group of similar or related incidents);
(2) the risk of reputational loss to the *firm*; and
(3) whether the incident or a pattern of incidents reflects weaknesses in the *firm's internal controls*.

15.3.19 **[G]** The notifications under SUP 15.3.17R are required as the *FSA* needs to be aware of the types of fraudulent and irregular activity which are being attempted or undertaken, and to act, if necessary, to prevent effects on *consumers* or other *firms*. A notification under SUP 15.7.3R should provide all relevant and significant details of the incident or suspected incident of which the *firm* is aware.

15.3.20 **[G]** In addition, the *firm* may have suffered significant financial losses as a result of the incident, or may suffer reputational loss, and the *FSA* will wish to consider this and whether the incident suggests weaknesses in the *firm's internal controls*.

Insolvency, bankruptcy and winding up

15.3.21 **[R]** A *firm* must notify the *FSA* immediately of any of the following events:
(1) the calling of a meeting to consider a resolution for winding up the *firm*; or
(2) an application to dissolve the *firm* or to strike it off the Register of Companies; or
(3) the presentation of a petition for the winding up of the *firm*; or
(4) the making of, or any proposals for the making of, a composition or arrangement with any one or more of its creditors; or
(5) an application for the appointment of an administrator or trustee in bankruptcy to the *firm*; or
(6) the appointment of a receiver to the *firm* (whether an administrative receiver or a receiver appointed over particular property); or
(7) an application for an interim order against the *firm* under section 252 of the Insolvency Act 1986 (or, in Northern Ireland, section 227 of the Insolvency (Northern Ireland) Order 1989); or
(8) if the *firm* is a *sole trader*:
    (a) an application for a sequestration order on the *firm*; or
    (b) the presentation of a petition for bankruptcy; or

(9) anything equivalent to (1) to (8) above occurring in respect of the *firm* in a jurisdiction outside the *United Kingdom*.

Lloyd's of London

15.3.22 **[D]** SUP 15.3.23D to SUP 15.3.25D are given in relation to the exercise of the powers of the *Society* and of the *Council* generally, with a view to achieving the objective of enabling the *FSA* to:

(1) comply with its general duty under section 314 of the *Act* (Authority's general duty);
(2) determine whether *underwriting agents*, or *approved persons* acting for them or on their behalf, are complying with the requirements imposed on them by or under the *Act*;
(3) enforce the provisions of the *Act*, or requirements made under the *Act*, by enabling the *FSA* to consider, where appropriate, whether it should use its powers, for example, to:
  (a) vary or cancel the *permission* of an *underwriting agent*, under section 45 of the *Act* (Variation etc on the Authority's own initiative);
  (b) withdraw approval from an *approved person* acting for or on behalf of an *underwriting agent*, under section 63 of the *Act* (Withdrawal of approval) (see EG 9);
  (c) prohibit an individual acting for or on behalf of an *underwriting agent* from involvement in *regulated activities*, under section 56 of the *Act* (Prohibition orders) (see EG 9);
  (d) require an *underwriting agent* to make restitution, under section 384 of the *Act* (Power of Authority to require restitution) (see EG 11);
  (e) discipline an *underwriting agent*, or an *approved person* acting for it or on its behalf, for a breach of a requirement made under the *Act*, including the *Principles*, *Statements of Principle* and *rules* (see DEPP 6 and EG 7);
  (f) apply to court for an *injunction*, restitution order or *insolvency order* (see EG 10, EG 11 and EG 13); and
  (g) prosecute any criminal offence that the *FSA* has power to prosecute under the *Act* (see EG 12).

15.3.23 **[D]** The *Society* must immediately inform the *FSA* in writing if it becomes aware that any matter likely to be of material concern to the *FSA* may have arisen in relation to:

(1) the *regulated activities* for which the *Society* has *permission*; or
(2) *underwriting agents*; or
(3) *approved persons* or individuals acting for or on behalf of *underwriting agents*.

15.3.24 **[D]** The *Society* must inform the *FSA* if it commences investigations or disciplinary proceedings relating to apparent breaches:

(1) of the *Act* or requirements made under the *Act*, including the *threshold conditions* or the *Principles* or other *rules*, by an *underwriting agent*; or
(2) of the *Statements of Principle* by an individual or other *person* who carries out *controlled functions* for or on behalf of an *underwriting agent*.

15.3.25 **[D]** The *Society* must inform the *FSA* if it commences investigations or disciplinary proceedings which do not fall within the scope of SUP 15.3.24D but which:

(1) involve an *underwriting agent*, or an *approved person* who carries out *controlled functions* for it or on its behalf; or
(2) may indicate that an individual acting for or on behalf of an *underwriting agent* may not be a fit and proper *person* to perform functions in relation to *regulated activities*.

15.4 Notified persons

15.4.1 **[R]**

(1) An *overseas firm*, which is not an *incoming firm*, must notify the *FSA* within 30 *business days* of any *person* taking up or ceasing to hold the following positions:
  (a) the *firm's* worldwide chief executive (that is, the *person* who, alone or jointly with one or more others, is responsible under the immediate authority of the *directors* for the whole of its business) if the *person* is based outside the *United Kingdom*;
  (b) the *person* within the *overseas firm* with a purely strategic responsibility for *UK* operations (see SUP 10.7.4G);
  (c) for a *bank* or an *ELMI*: the two or more *persons* who effectively direct its business in accordance with SYSC 4.2.2R and ELM 5.3.1R, respectively;
  (d) for an *insurer*: the *authorised UK representative*.
(2) The notification in (1) must be submitted using Form F (SUP 15 Ann 2R). However, if the person is an *approved person*, notification giving details of his name, the *approved person's* FSA individual reference number and the position to which the notification relates, is sufficient.

15.4.2 **[G]** SUP 15.4.1R is not made under the powers conferred on the *FSA* by Part V of the *Act* (Performance of Regulated Activities). A *person* notified to the *FSA* under SUP 15.4.1R is not subject to the *Statements of Principle* or *Code of Practice for Approved Persons*, unless he is also an *approved person*.

15.4.3 **[G]** Copies of Form F may be obtained from the *FSA* website at www.fsa.gov.uk or from the Individual Vetting and Approval department. See SUP 10.11.6G for contact details.

15.4.4 **[G]** If adverse information is revealed about a *person* notified to the *FSA* under SUP 15.4.1R, the *FSA* may exercise its *own initiative power* against the *firm* (see SUP 7 (Individual requirements)).

15.5 Core information requirements

Change in name

15.5.1 **[R]** A *firm* must give the *FSA* reasonable advance notice of a change in:
(1) the *firm's* name (which is the registered name if the *firm* is a *body corporate*);
(2) any business name under which the *firm* carries on a *regulated activity* or *ancillary activity* either from an establishment in the *United Kingdom* or with or for clients in the *United Kingdom*.

15.5.2 **[G]** A notification under SUP 15.5.1R should include the details of the proposed new name and the date on which the *firm* intends to implement the change of name.

15.5.3 **[G]** **Firms** are reminded that certain name changes (for example, to include 'Limited') may also require a notification under SUP 15.5.5R.

Change in address

15.5.4 **[R]** A *firm* must give the *FSA* reasonable advance notice of a change in any of the following addresses, and give details of the new address and the date of the change:
(1) the *firm's* principal place of business in the *United Kingdom*;
(2) in the case of an *overseas firm*, its registered office (or head office) address.

15.5.5 **[R]** [deleted]

15.5.6 **[G]** [deleted]

Other regulators

15.5.7 **[R]** A *firm* must notify the *FSA* immediately if it becomes subject to or ceases to be subject to the supervision of any *overseas regulator* (including a *Home State regulator*).

15.5.8 **[G]** The *FSA's* approach to the supervision of a *firm* is influenced by the regulatory regime and any legislative or foreign provisions to which that *firm*, including its branches, is subject.

15.6 Inaccurate, false or misleading information

15.6.1 **[R]** A *firm* must take reasonable steps to ensure that all information it gives to the *FSA* in accordance with a *rule* in any part of the *Handbook* (including *Principle* 11) is:
(1) factually accurate or, in the case of estimates and judgments, fairly and properly based after appropriate enquiries have been made by the *firm*; and
(2) complete, in that it should include anything of which the *FSA* would reasonably expect notice.

15.6.2 **[G]** SUP 15.6.1R applies also in relation to *rules* outside this chapter, and even if they are not *notification rules*. Examples of *rules* and chapters to which SUP 15.6.1R is relevant, are:
(1) *Principle* 11, and the guidance on *Principle* 11 in SUP 2 (Information gathering by the FSA on its own initiative);
(2) SUP 15 (Notifications to the FSA);
(3) SUP 16 (Reporting requirements);
(4) SUP 17 (Transaction reporting);
(5) any *notification rule* (see Schedule 2 which contains a consolidated summary of such *rules*);
(6) DISP 1.9 (Complaints record rule); and
(7) DISP 1.10 (Complaints reporting rule).

15.6.3 **[G]** If a *firm* is unable to obtain the information required in SUP 15.6.1R (2), then it should inform the *FSA* that the scope of the information provided is, or may be, limited.

15.6.4 **[R]** If a *firm* becomes aware, or has information that reasonably suggests that it has or may have provided the *FSA* with information which was or may have been false, misleading, incomplete or inaccurate, or has or may have changed in a material particular, it must notify the *FSA* immediately. Subject to SUP 15.6.5R, the notification must include:
(1) details of the information which is or may be false, misleading, incomplete or inaccurate, or *has or may have changed;*
(2) an explanation why such information was or may have been provided; and
(3) the correct information.

15.6.5 **[R]** If the information in SUP 15.6.4R(3) cannot be submitted with the notification (because it is not immediately available), it must instead be submitted as soon as possible afterwards.

15.6.6 **[G]** The *FSA* may request the *firm* to provide revised documentation containing the correct information, if appropriate.

15.6.7 **[G]** *Firms* are reminded that section 398 of the *Act* (Misleading the Authority: residual cases) makes it an *offence* for a *firm* knowingly or recklessly to provide the *FSA* with information which is false or misleading in a material particular in purported compliance with the *FSA's rules* or any other requirement imposed by or under the *Act*. An offence by a *body corporate*, *partnership* or unincorporated association may be attributed to an *officer* or certain other *persons* (section 400 of the *Act* (Offences by bodies corporate etc)).

15.7 Form and method of notification

Form of notification: oral or written

15.7.1 **[R]** A notification required from a *firm* under any *notification rule* must be given in writing, and in English, and must be submitted on the form specified for that notification rule, or if no form is specified, on the form in SUP 15 Ann 3R (Notification form), and must give the *firm's* FSA Firm Reference Number unless:
(1) the *notification rule* states otherwise; or
(2) the notification is provided solely in compliance with *Principle* 11 (see SUP 15.3.7G).

15.7.2 **[G]** A *firm* should have regard to the urgency and significance of a matter and, if appropriate, should also notify its usual supervisory contact at the *FSA* by telephone or by other prompt means of communication, before submitting a written notification. Oral notifications should be given directly to the *firm's* usual supervisory contact. An oral notification left with another person or left on a voicemail or other automatic messaging service is unlikely to have been given appropriately.

15.7.3 **[G]** The *FSA* is entitled to rely on any information it receives from a *firm* and to consider any notification received as being made by a *person* authorised by the *firm* to do so. A *firm* should therefore consider whether it needs to put procedures in place to ensure that only appropriate *employees* make notifications to the *FSA* on its behalf.

Method of notification

15.7.4 **[R]** Unless otherwise stated in the *notification rule* or on the relevant form (if specified), a written notification required from a *firm* under any *notification rule* must be:
(1) given to or addressed for the attention of the *firm's* usual supervisory contact at the *FSA*; and
(2) delivered to the *FSA* by one of the methods in SUP 15.7.5R:

15.7.5 **[R]**
(1) Table Methods of notification

Method of delivery	
1.	*Post* to the appropriate address in SUP 15.7.6R
2.	Leaving the notification at the appropriate address in SUP 15.7.6R and obtaining a time-stamped receipt
3.	Electronic mail to an address for the *firm's* usual supervisory contact at the *FSA* and obtaining an electronic confirmation of receipt
4.	Hand delivery to the *firm's* usual supervisory contact at the *FSA*
5.	Fax to a fax number for the *firm's* usual supervisory contact at the *FSA*, and receiving a successful transmission report for all pages of the notification
6.	Online submission via the *FSA's* website at www.fsa.gov.uk.

15.7.6 **[G]** The current published address of the *FSA* for postal submission or hand delivery of notifications is:
(1) The Financial Services Authority
25 The North Colonnade
Canary Wharf
London E14 5HS
if the *firm's* usual supervisory contact at the *FSA* is based in London, or
(2) The Financial Services Authority
Sutherland House
108–114 Dundas Street
Edinburgh EH3 5DQ
if the *firm's* usual supervisory contact at the *FSA* is based in Edinburgh.

15.7.7 **[G]** If the *firm* or its *group* is subject to lead supervision arrangements by the *FSA*, the *firm* or *group* may give or address a notice under SUP 15.7.4R (1) to the supervisory contact at the *FSA*, designated as lead supervisor, if the *firm* has chosen to make use of the lead supervisor as a central point of contact (see SUP 1.5).

15.7.8 **[G]** If a *firm* is a member of a *group* which includes more than one *firm*, any one *undertaking* in the *group* may notify the *FSA* on behalf of all *firms* in the *group* to which the notification applies. In this way, that *undertaking* may satisfy the obligation of all relevant *firms* in the *group* to notify the *FSA*. Nevertheless, the obligation to make the notification remains the responsibility of the individual *firm* itself. See also SUP 15.7.3G.

15.7.9 **[G]** *Firms* wishing to communicate with the *FSA* by electronic mail or fax should obtain the appropriate address or number from the *FSA*.

Timely notification

15.7.10 **[R]** If a *notification rule* requires notification within a specified period:

(1) the *firm* must give the notification so as to be received by the *FSA* no later than the end of that period; and

(2) if the end of that period falls on a *day* which is not a *business day*, the notification must be given so as to be received by the *FSA* no later than the first *business day* after the end of that period.

15.7.11 **[G]** If a *notification rule* does not require notification within a specified period, the *firm* should act reasonably in deciding when to notify.

Underwriting agents: notification to the Society of Lloyd's

15.7.12 **[R]**

(1) paragraph (2) applies in relation to notifications required under this chapter within the scope of any arrangements made by the *FSA* with the *Society of Lloyd's* under paragraph 6(2) of Schedule 1 to the *Act*.

(2) An *underwriting agent* must submit the notifications in (1) to the *Society of Lloyd's* rather than to the *FSA*.

15.7.13 **[G]** paragraph 6(2) of Schedule 1 to the *Act* enables the *FSA* to make arrangements which provide for monitoring functions to be performed by any body or *person* who, in its opinion, is competent to perform them. Arrangements made under this provision are published by the *FSA*.

15.7.14 **[G]** The *FSA* has made arrangements with the *Society of Lloyd's* with respect to the monitoring of *underwriting agents*. *Underwriting agents* should check whether these arrangements provide for any notifications required under this chapter to be sent to the *Society* instead of to the *FSA*. [For further details see the *FSA* website.]

Consequences of breach of form and method rules

15.7.15 **[G]** If a *firm* fails to comply with the *rules* in this section then the notification is invalid and there may be a breach of the *rule* that required the notification to be given.

Service of Notices Regulations

15.7.16 **[G]** The Financial Services and Markets Act 2000 (Service of Notices) Regulations 2001 (SI 2001/1420) contain provisions relating to the service of documents on the *FSA*. They do not apply to notifications required under *notification rules* because of the specific *rules* in this section.

15.8 Notification in respect of particular products and services

Management of occupational pension scheme assets

15.8.1 **[R]** A *firm* which manages the assets of an *occupational pension scheme* must notify the *FSA* as soon as reasonably practicable if it receives any request or instruction from a trustee which it:

(1) knows; or

(2) on substantial grounds:

  (a) suspects; or

  (b) has cause reasonably to suspect;

is at material variance with the trustee's duties.

Individual Pension Accounts

15.8.2 **[R]** If a *firm* begins or ceases to administer *individual pension accounts*, it must notify the *FSA* as soon as reasonably practicable that it has done so.

Insurers' commission clawback

15.8.3 **[R]**

(1) An *insurer* must notify the *FSA* in respect of any *firm* (the "intermediary") as soon as reasonably practicable if:

(a) any amount of *commission* due from the intermediary to the *insurer* in accordance with an indemnity commission clawback arrangement remains outstanding for four *months* after the date when the *insurer* gave notice to the intermediary that the relevant *premium* had not been paid; or
(b) any amount of *commission* due from the intermediary to the *insurer* as a result of either the cancellation of an investment agreement or overpayment of *commission* remains outstanding for four *months* after the date on which the *insurer* gave notice to the intermediary that cancellation or overpayment had occurred.

(2) A notification in (1):
(a) must give the identity of the intermediary and the amount of *commission* which remains outstanding;
(b) need not be given unless the total amounts outstanding under 1(a) and (b) in respect of the intermediary exceed £1000; and
(c) need not be given if the *insurer* has reported the events in SUP 15.8.3R(1)(a) and (b) on the database run for these purposes by Elixir.

(3) In (1) an "indemnity commission clawback arrangement" is an arrangement under which:
(a) an insurer pays *commission* to an intermediary before the date on which the *premium* is due under the relevant *investment agreement*; and
(b) the *insurer* requires repayment of the *commission*, if the *investment agreement* is terminated by reason of a failure to pay a premium.

Money service business and trust or company service providers

15.8.4 **[G]**
(1) In accordance with article 31 of the Money Laundering Regulations 2003, with effect from 15 December 2007, a *firm* is required to notify the *FSA*:
(a) before it begins or within 28 days of it beginning; and
(b) immediately after it ceases;
to operate a money service business or a trust or company service provider.
(2) The notification referred to in (1) should be made in accordance with the requirements in SUP 15.7 (Form and method of notification).

15.8.5 **[G]** A *firm* which is already operating a money service business or a trust or company service provider as at 15 December 2007 is required by the Money Laundering Regulations 2003 to notify the *FSA* of that fact and should do so in the manner specified in SUP 15.8.4G(2) before 15 January 2008.

Delegation by UCITS management companies

15.8.6 **[R]** A *UCITS management company* must notify the *FSA* as soon as reasonably practicable if it delegates any of its functions to a third party.

15.8.7 **[G]** A *UCITS management company* which delegates any of its functions to a third party must, as well as complying with SUP 15.8.6R, comply with the requirements in COLL 6.6.15R(2).

CTF providers

15.8.8 **[R]**
(1) If a *firm* begins or ceases to hold itself out as acting as a *CTF provider*, it must notify the *FSA* as soon as reasonably practicable that it has done so.
(2) A *firm* that acts as a *CTF provider* must provide the *FSA*, as soon as reasonably practicable, with details of:
(a) any third party administrator that it engages;
(b) details of whether it intends to offer *Revenue allocated CTFs*; and
(c) whether it intends to provide its own *stakeholder CTF* account.

15.8.9 **[R]** A *BIPRU firm* must report to the *FSA* immediately any case in which its counterparty in a *repurchase agreement* or *reverse repurchase agreement* or *securities or commodities lending or borrowing transaction* defaults on its obligations.

15.9 Notifications by members of financial conglomerates

15.9.1 **[R]** A *firm* that is a *regulated entity* must notify the *FSA* immediately it becomes aware that any *consolidation group* of which it is a member:
(1) is a *financial conglomerate*; or
(2) has ceased to be a *financial conglomerate*.

15.9.2 **[R]**
(1) A *firm* that is a *regulated entity* must establish whether or not any *consolidation group* of which it is a member:
(a) is a *financial conglomerate*; or

Part II FSA Handbook Materials

(b) has ceased to be a *financial conglomerate*;
if:
(c) the *firm* believes; or
(d) a reasonable *firm* that is complying with the requirements of the *regulatory system* would believe;
that it is likely that (a) or (b) is true.

(2) A *firm* does not need to determine whether (1)(a) is the case if the *consolidation group* is already being regulated as a *financial conglomerate*.

(3) A *firm* does not need to determine whether (1)(b) is the case if notification has already been given as contemplated by SUP 15.9.4R.

15.9.3 **[G]** A *firm* should consider the requirements in SUP 15.9.2R on a continuing basis, and in particular, when the *group* prepares its financial statements and on the occurrence of an event affecting the *consolidated group*. Such events include, but are not limited to, an acquisition, merger or sale.

15.9.4 **[R]** A *firm* does not have to give notice to the *FSA* under SUP 15.9.1R if it or another member of the *consolidation group* has already given notice of the relevant fact to:
(1) the *FSA*; or
(2) (if another *competent authority* is *co-ordinator* of the *financial conglomerate*) that *competent authority*; or
(3) (in the case of a *financial conglomerate* that does not yet have a *co-ordinator*) the *competent authority* who would be *co-ordinator* under Article 10(2) of the *Financial Groups Directive* (Competent authority responsible for exercising supplementary supervision (the co-ordinator)).

15.10 Reporting suspicious transactions (market abuse)

Application: where

15.10.1 **[R]** This section applies in relation to activities carried on from an establishment maintained by the *firm* or its *appointed representative* in the *United Kingdom*. [**Note:** Article 7 2004/72/EC]

Notification of suspicious transactions: general

15.10.2 **[R]** A *firm* which *arranges* or *executes* a transaction with or for a *client* in a *qualifying investment* admitted to trading on a *prescribed market* and which has reasonable grounds to suspect that the transaction might constitute *market abuse* must notify the *FSA* without delay. [**Note:** Article 6(9) *Market Abuse Directive*]

Notification of suspicious transactions: investment firms and credit institutions

15.10.3 **[R]** A *firm*, that is an *investment firm* or a *credit institution*, must decide on a case-by-case basis whether there are reasonable grounds for suspecting that a transaction involves *market abuse*, taking into account the elements constituting *market abuse*. [**Note:** Articles 1(3) and 7 2004/72/EC]

15.10.4 **[G]**
(1) Notification of suspicious transactions to the *FSA* requires sufficient indications (which may not be apparent until after the transaction has taken place) that the transaction might constitute *market abuse*. In particular a *firm* will need to be able to explain the basis for its suspicion when notifying the *FSA* (see SUP 15.10.6 R). Certain transactions by themselves may seem completely devoid of anything suspicious, but might deliver such indications of possible *market abuse*, when seen in perspective with other transactions, certain behaviour or other information (though *firms* are not expected to breach effective information barriers put in place to prevent and avoid conflicts of interest so as actively to seek to detect suspicious transactions). [**Note:** Recital 9 2004/72/EC]
(2) Assistance in identifying the elements constituting *market abuse* may be derived from the *Code of Market Conduct* (*MAR* 1), and some example indications of *market abuse* are set out in SUP 15 Ann 5 G. A fuller set of example indications is published by the Committee of European Securities Regulators (CESR).

Timeframe for notification: investment firms and credit institutions

15.10.5 **[R]** If an *investment firm* or a *credit institution* becomes aware of a fact or information that gives reasonable ground for suspicion concerning a transaction, it must make its notification under this section without delay. [**Note:** Article 8 2004/72/EC]

Content of notification: investment firms and credit institutions

15.10.6 **[R]**
(1) If an *investment firm* or a *credit institution* is obliged to make a notification to the *FSA* under this section, it must transmit to the *FSA* the following information:

(a) a description of the transaction, including the type of order (such as limit order, market order or other characteristics of the order) and the type of trading market (such as block trade); and
(b) the reasons for suspicion that the transaction might constitute *market abuse*.

(2) In addition the following information must be provided to the *FSA* as soon as it becomes available:
(a) the means for identification of the *persons* on behalf of whom the transaction has been carried out, and of other *persons* involved in the relevant transaction;
(b) the capacity in which the *firm* operates (such as for own account or on behalf of third parties); and
(c) any other information which may have significance in reviewing the suspicious transaction. [**Note:** Article 9 2004/72/EC]

Means of notification: investment firms and credit institutions

15.10.7 **[R]** An *investment firm* or a *credit institution* making a notification to the *FSA* under this section may do so:
(1) by mail to:
Market Conduct Team
25 The North Colonnade
Canary Wharf
London E14 5HS; or
(2) by electronic mail to market.abuse@fsa.gov.uk;
(3) by facsimile to the Market Conduct Team on 020 7066 1099; or
(4) by telephone to the market abuse helpline 020 7066 4900. [**Note:** Article 10 2004/72/EC]

15.10.8 **[G]**
(1) If a notification is made by telephone, the *FSA* may subsequently request confirmation of the notification in writing. [**Note:** Article 10 2004/72/EC]
(2) When making a notification in writing it may be convenient to use the form for suspicious transaction reports provided on the *FSA's* website. This form follows the common standard approved by CESR.

Liability and professional secrecy: investment firms and credit institutions

15.10.9 **[R]**
(1) An *investment firm* or a *credit institution* which notifies the *FSA* under this section must not inform any other *person*, in particular the *persons* on behalf of whom the transaction has been carried out or parties related to those persons, of this notification, except in accordance with an obligation imposed by or under statute.
(2) Notwithstanding any other provision of the *Handbook* a notification in good faith under this section to the *FSA* does not constitute a breach of any restriction on disclosure of information imposed by the *Handbook*. [**Note:** Article 11 2004/72/EC]

Note: Section 131A of the *Act* sets out additional protections from liability for a *person* who makes a notification to the *FSA* under this section (or who passes the relevant information to someone designated by his employer to do so).

SUP 15 Annex 1R
Application of SUP 15 to incoming EEA firms and incoming Treaty firms
(1) Table

1.	SUP 15 applies in full to an incoming EEA firm, or incoming Treaty firm, which has a top up permission.
2.	SUP 15 does not apply to an incoming EEA firm which has permission for cross border services only and which does not carry on regulated activities in the United Kingdom.
2A.	SUP 15 does not apply to an *EEA pure reinsurer* which does not have a *top-up permission*.
3.	For any other incoming EEA firm or incoming Treaty firm, SUP 15 applies as set out in the following table.

(2) Table Application of SUP 15 to an incoming EEA firm or an incoming Treaty firm which does not have a top-up permission

Applicable sections		Application
SUP 15.1 SUP 15.2	Application, Purpose	Apply in full

Part II FSA Handbook Materials

Applicable sections		Application
SUP 15.3.1R to SUP 15.3.6G	Matters having a serious regulatory impact	SUP 15.3.1R(1) does not apply, otherwise apply in full
SUP 15.3.7G to SUP 15.3.10G	Communication with the FSA in accordance with Principle 11	Apply in so far as responsibility for the matter in question is not reserved by an *EU*instrument to the *firm's Home State regulator*
SUP 15.3.11R to SUP 15.3.14G	Breaches of rules and other requirements in or under the Act	Apply in full
SUP 15.3.15R and SUP 15.3.16G	Civil, criminal or disciplinary proceedings against a firm	Apply in so far as responsibility for the matter in question is not reserved by an *EU* instrument to the *firm's Home State regulator*
SUP 15.3.17R to SUP 15.3.20G	Fraud, errors and other irregularities	Apply in so far as responsibility for the matter in question is not reserved by an *EU* instrument to the *firm's Home State regulator*
SUP 15.3.21R	Insolvency, bankruptcy and winding up	Apply in so far as responsibility for the matter in question is not reserved by an *EU* instrument to the *firm's Home State regulator*
SUP 15.4	Notified persons	Does not apply
SUP 15.5.1R to SUP 15.5.3G	Change in name	Apply in full
SUP 15.5.4R(1)	Change in address: principal place of business in the UK	Applies in full
SUP 15.5.4R(2)	Change in address: registered office	Applies to an *incoming Treaty firm*. Does not apply to an *incoming EEA firm*, but see SUP 14 (Incoming EEA firms: changing authorisation and cancelling qualification for authorisation).
SUP 15.5.5R and SUP 15.5.6G	Change in legal status	Do not apply
SUP 15.5.7R and SUP 15.5.8G	Other regulators	Apply in so far as responsibility for the matter in question is not reserved by an *EU* instrument to the *firm's Home State regulator*
SUP 15.6	Inaccurate, false or misleading information	Applies in full
SUP 15.7	Form and method of notification	Applies in full
SUP 15.8	Notifications in respect of particular products and services	Applies in full
SUP 15.10	Reporting suspicious transactions (market abuse)	Applies in relation to activities carried on from an establishment maintained by the *firm* or its *appointed representative* in the *United Kingdom*. [**Note**: Article 7 2004/72/EC]

SUP 15 Annex 2R
Form F

SUP 15 Ann 2 **[R]**

This form has not been reproduced for technical reasons. Please refer to the FSA website.

SUP 15 Annex 3R
Standing data form

SUP 15 Ann 3 **[R]**

This form has not been reproduced for technical reasons. Please refer to the FSA website.

SUP 15 Annex 4R
Notification form

SUP 15 Ann 4 **[R]** This form has not been reproduced for technical reasons. Please refer to the FSA website.

This form has not been reproduced for technical reasons. Please refer to the FSA website.

SUP 15 Annex 5G
Indications of Possible Suspicious Transactions

SUP 15 Ann 5 **[G]**
(1) The following examples of indications are intended to be a starting point for consideration of whether a transaction is suspicious. They are neither conclusive nor comprehensive.

Possible signals of Insider Dealing
(2) A client opens an account and immediately gives an order to conduct a significant transaction or, in the case of a wholesale client, an unexpectedly large or unusual order, in a particular security – especially if the client is insistent that the order is carried out very urgently or must be conducted before a particular time specified by the client.
(3) A transaction is significantly out of line with the client's previous investment behaviour (e.g. type of security; amount invested; size of order; time security held).
(4) A client specifically requests immediate execution of an order regardless of the price at which the order would be executed (assuming more than a mere placing of 'at market' order by the client).
(5) There is unusual trading in the shares of a company before the announcement of price sensitive information relating to the company.
(6) An employee's own account transaction is timed just before clients' transactions and related orders in the same financial instrument.

Possible signals of Market Manipulation
(7) An order will, because of its size in relation to the market in that security, clearly have a significant impact on the supply of or demand for or the price or value of the security, especially an order of this kind to be executed near to a reference point during the trading day – e.g. near the close.
(8) A transaction appears to be seeking to modify the valuation of a position while not decreasing/increasing the size of that position.
(9) A transaction appears to be seeking to bypass the trading safeguards of the market (e.g. as regards volume limits; bid/offer spread parameters; etc).

CHAPTER 16
REPORTING REQUIREMENTS

16.1 Application

[2170]
16.1.1 **[R]** This chapter applies to every *firm* within a category listed in column (2) of the table in SUP 16.1.3R and in accordance with column (3) of that table.

16.1.2 **[G]** The only categories of *firm* to which no section of this chapter applies are:
(1) an *ICVC*;
(2) an *incoming EEA firm* or *incoming Treaty firm*, unless it is:
  (a) a *firm* of a type listed in SUP 16.1.3R as a type of *firm* to which SUP 16.6, SUP 16.7, SUP 16.9 or SUP 16.12 applies; or
  (b) an *insurer* with *permission* to *effect* or *carry out life policies*;
  (c) a *firm* with *permission* to *establish, operate or* wind up a *personal pension scheme* or a *stakeholder pension scheme*;
(3) a *UCITS qualifier*.

16.1.3 **[R]**

Table: Application of different sections of SUP 16

(1) Section(s)	(2) Categories of firm to which section applies	(3) Applicable rules and guidance
SUP 16.1, 16.2 and SUP 16.3	All categories of *firm* except: (a) an *ICVC*; (b) an *incoming EEA firm* or *incoming Treaty firm*, which is not: (i) a *firm* of a type to which SUP 16.6 or SUP 16.12 applies; or (ii) an *insurer* with *permission* to *effect* or *carry out life policies*; or (iii) a *firm* with *permission* to *establish, operate or wind up* a *personal pension scheme* or a *stakeholder pension scheme*; (c) a *UCITS qualifier*.	Entire sections
SUP 16.4 and SUP 16.5	All categories of *firm* except: (a) a *credit union*; (a) an *ICVC*; (b) an *incoming EEA firm*; (c) an *incoming Treaty firm*; (d) a *non-directive friendly society*; (e) [deleted] (f) a *sole trader*; (g) a *service company*; (h) a *UCITS qualifier* (i) a *firm* with *permission* to carry on only *retail investment activities*; (j) a *firm* with *permission* to carry on only *insurance mediation activity*, *home finance mediation activity*, or both; (k) a *firm* falling within both (i) and (j).	Entire sections
SUP 16.6	*Bank, ELMI*	SUP 16.6.4R to SUP 16.6.5R
	Depositary of an *ICVC*	SUP 16.6.6R to SUP 16.6.9G
	OPS firm	SUP 16.6.6R to SUP 16.6.8R
	Trustee of an *AUT*	SUP 16.6.6R to SUP 16.6.9G
SUP 16.7	*Bank*, other than an *EEA bank* with *permission* for *cross border services* only.	SUP 16.7.7R to SUP 16.7.15R
	Building society	SUP 16.7.16R to SUP 16.7.19R
	Service company	SUP 16.7.20R to SUP 16.7.21R
	UK ISPV	SUP 16.7.21AR and SUP 16.7.21BR
	Securities and futures firm (other than an *oil market participant* to which *IPRU(INV)* 3 does not apply)	SUP 16.7.22R to SUP 16.7.34G
	Investment management firm	SUP 16.7.35R to SUP 16.7.41R
	Authorised professional firm (note)	SUP 16.7.54R and SUP 16.7.54AR

(1) Section(s)	(2) Categories of firm to which section applies	(3) Applicable rules and guidance
	Society of Lloyd's	SUP 16.7.55R to SUP 16.7.56R and SUP 16.7.59R(1) and (2)
	Members' adviser	SUP 16.7.57R to SUP 16.7.58R, SUP 16.7.59R(3), SUP 16.7.60G and SUP 16.7.61G
	Credit Union	SUP 16.7.62R to SUP 16.7.63R
	ELMI	SUP 16.7.64R to SUP 16.7.66R
	UCITS management company	SUP 16.7.67R to SUP 16.7.72R
	Insurer Friendly society	SUP 16.7.73R to SUP 16.7.75R
	A *firm* not subject to other reporting requirements in SUP 16.7.1–16.7.75 (nor to reporting requirements in IPRU(INS) or IPRU(FSOC)): (1) with *permission* to carry on one or more of: (a) *insurance mediation activity*; or (b) *home finance mediation activity*; or (c) *home finance providing activity*; or (d) *administering a home finance transaction*; or (2) which is a *personal investment firm*	SUP 16.7.76R to SUP 16.7.81G
SUP 16.8	*Insurer* with *permission* to *effect* or *carry out life policies*, unless it is a *non-directive friendly society*	Entire section
	Firm with *permission* to *establish, operate or wind up a personal pension scheme* or a *stakeholder pension scheme*	Entire section
SUP 16.9	*Firm* with *permission* to *advise on investments; arrange (bring about) deals in investments; make arrangements with a view to transactions in investments*; or *arrange safeguarding and administration of assets*	Entire section
SUP 16.10	All categories of *firm* except: (a) an *ICVC*; (b) a *UCITS qualifier*; (c) a *credit union*; and (d) a *dormant account fund operator*.	Entire section
SUP 16.11	A *firm*, other than a *managing agent*, which is: (1) a *home finance provider*; or (2) an *insurer*; or	Entire section

Part II FSA Handbook Materials

(1) Section(s)	(2) Categories of firm to which section applies	(3) Applicable rules and guidance
	(3) the operator of a *regulated collective investment scheme* or an *investment trust savings scheme*; or (4) a *person* who issues or manages the relevant assets of the issuer of a *structured capital-at-risk product*.	
SUP 16.12	A *firm* undertaking the *regulated activities* as listed in SUP 16.12.4R, unless exempted in SUP 16.12.1R	Sections as relevant to *regulated activities* as listed in SUP 16.12.4R

Note = Where an *authorised professional firm* is required by *IPRU(INV)* 2.1.2R(1) to comply with chapter 3, 5, 10 or 13 of *IPRU(INV)*, section 16.7 applies to such a *firm* as if it were the relevant *firm* category in the right hand column of *IPRU(INV)* 2.1R).

16.1.4 **[G]**

(1) This chapter contains requirements to report to the *FSA* on a regular basis. These requirements include reports relating to a *firm's* financial condition, and to its compliance with other *rules* and requirements which apply to the *firm*. Where the relevant requirements are set out in another section of the *Handbook*, this chapter contains cross references. An example of this is financial reporting for *insurers* and *friendly societies*.

(2) Where such requirements already apply to a *firm* under legislation other than the *Act*, they are not referred to in this chapter. An example of this is reporting to the *FSA* by *building societies* under those parts of the Building Societies Act 1986 which have not been repealed.

(3) Requirements for individual *firms* reflect:
   (a) the category of *firm*;
   (b) the nature of business carried on;
   (c) whether a *firm* has its registered office (or if it does not have a registered office, its head office) in the *United Kingdom*;
   (d) whether a *firm* is an *incoming EEA firm* or *incoming Treaty firm*; and
   (e) the regulated activities the *firm* undertakes.

16.1.5 **[G]** [deleted]

16.1.6 **[G]** [deleted]

16.2 Purpose

16.2.1 **[G]**

(1) In order to discharge its functions under the *Act*, the *FSA* needs timely and accurate information about *firms*. The provision of this information on a regular basis enables the *FSA* to build up over time a picture of *firms'* circumstances and behaviour.

(2) *Principle* 11 requires a *firm* to deal with its regulators in an open and cooperative way, and to tell the *FSA* appropriately anything of which the *FSA* would reasonably expect notice. The reporting requirements are part of the *FSA's* approach to amplifying *Principle* 11 by setting out in more detail the information that the *FSA* requires. They supplement the provisions of SUP 2 (Information gathering by the FSA on its own initiative) and SUP 15 (Notifications to the FSA). The reports required under these *rules* help the *FSA* to monitor *firms'* compliance with *Principles* governing relationships between *firms* and their *customers*, with *Principle* 4, which requires *firms* to maintain adequate financial resources, and with other requirements and standards under the *regulatory system*.

16.3 General provisions on reporting

Application

16.3.1 **[G]** The effect of SUP 16.1.1R is that this section applies to every *firm* except:

(1) an *ICVC*;

(2) an *incoming EEA firm* or *incoming Treaty firm*, which is not:
   (a) a *firm* of a type listed in SUP 16.1.3R as a *firm* to which section SUP 16.6, SUP 16.7 or SUP 16.12 applies;
   (b) an *insurer* with *permission* to *effect* or *carry out life policies*;

(3) a *UCITS qualifier*.

Structure of the chapter

16.3.2 **[G]** This chapter has been split into the following sections, covering:
(1) annual controllers reports (SUP 16.4);
(2) annual close links reports (SUP 16.5);
(3) compliance reports (SUP 16.6);
(4) financial reports (SUP 16.7);
(5) persistency reports (SUP 16.8);
(6) annual appointed representatives reports (SUP 16.9);
(7) verification of *standing data* (SUP 16.10);
(8) product sales data reporting (SUP 16.11);
(9) integrated regulatory reporting (SUP 16.12).

16.3.3 **[G]** The annual controllers, annual close links, persistency and annual appointed representatives reports sections are the same for all categories of *firm* to which they apply.

16.3.4 **[G]** The compliance sections is set out by category of *firm*, with detailed requirements set out in tables giving:
(1) a brief description of each report;
(2) the frequency with which the report is required; and
(3) the due date for submission of the report.

16.3.5 **[G]** Further requirements about the reports, such as form and content, are set out in the sections for each category of *firm*, where this is appropriate. In many cases, however, it is more appropriate to provide this information by means of a separate annex; in these cases the relevant section refers to the annex.

16.3.6 **[R]** A periodic report required to be submitted under this chapter, or under any other *rule*, must be submitted in writing in accordance with SUP 16.3.7R to SUP 16.3.10G, unless:
(1) a contrary intention appears; or
(2) the report is required under the *listing rules*.

16.3.7 **[R]** A report or *data item* must:
(1) give the *firm's FSA* firm reference number (or all the *firms'* FSA firm reference numbers in those cases where a report is submitted on behalf of a number of *firms*, as set out in SUP 16.3.25 G); and
(2) if submitted in paper form, be submitted with the cover sheet contained in SUP 16 Ann 13R fully completed.

16.3.8 **[R]** A written report must be:
(1) given to or addressed for the attention of the *firm's* usual supervisory contact at the *FSA*; and
(2) delivered to the *FSA* by one of the methods listed in SUP 16.3.9R.

16.3.9 **[R]**

Table: Method of submission of reports (see SUP 16.3.8R)

Method of delivery	
1.	*Post* to the published address of the *FSA* for postal submission of reports
2.	Leaving the report at the published address of the *FSA* for hand delivery of reports and obtaining a dated receipt
3.	Electronic mail to an address for the *firm's* usual supervisory contact at the *FSA* and obtaining an electronic confirmation of receipt
4.	Hand delivery to the *firm's* usual supervisory contact at the *FSA* and obtaining a dated receipt
5.	Fax to the number notified by the *firm's* usual supervisory contact at the *FSA* and receiving a successful transmission report for all pages of the report.
6.	Online submission via the *FSA's* website at www.fsa.gov.uk
7.	Electronic submission via the Early Reporting System available from

16.3.10 **[G]**
(1) The current published address of the *FSA* for postal submission of reports is:
The Financial Services Authority
PO BOX 35747
London E14 5WP
(2) The current published address of the *FSA* for hand delivery of reports is:
(a) The Financial Services Authority
25 The North Colonnade
Canary Wharf
London E14 5HS

Part II FSA Handbook Materials

if the *firm's* usual supervisory contact at the *FSA* is based in London, or:

(b) The Financial Services Authority
Sutherland House
108–114 Dundas Street
Edinburgh EH3 5DQ
if the *firm's* usual supervisory contact at the *FSA* is based in Edinburgh.

Complete reporting

16.3.11 **[R]** A *firm* must submit reports required under this chapter to the *FSA* containing all the information required.

16.3.12 **[G]** SUP 15.6 refers to and contains requirements regarding the steps that *firms* must take to ensure that information provided to the *FSA* is accurate and complete. Those requirements apply to reports required to be submitted under this chapter.

Timely reporting

16.3.13 **[R]**

(1) A *firm* must submit a report required by this chapter in the frequency, and so as to be received by the *FSA* no later than the due date, specified for that report.

(2) If the due date for submission of a report required by this chapter falls on a day which is not a *business day*, the report must be submitted so as to be received by the *FSA* no later than the first *business day* after the due date.

(3) If the due date for submission of a report required by this chapter is a set period of time after the quarter end, the quarter ends will be the following dates, unless another *rule* or the reporting form states otherwise:
   (a) the *firm's accounting reference date*;
   (b) 3 months after the *firm's accounting reference date*;
   (c) 6 months after the *firm's accounting reference date*; and
   (d) 9 months after the *firm's accounting reference date*.

(4) If the due date for submission of a report required by this chapter is a set period of time after the end of a half-year, a quarter, or a month, the dates will be determined by (a) or (b) below except where otherwise indicated:
   (a) the *firm's accounting reference date*;
   (b) monthly, 3 monthly or 6 months after the *firm's accounting reference date*, as the case may be.

Failure to submit reports

16.3.14 **[R]**

(1) If a *firm* does not submit a complete report by the date on which it is due in accordance with the *rules* in, or referred to in, this chapter or the provisions of relevant legislation and any prescribed submission procedures, the *firm* must pay an administrative fee of £250.

(2) The administrative fee in (1) does not apply in respect of quarterly reports required to be submitted by *credit unions* whose liability to pay a periodic fee under FEES 4.2.1 R in respect of the A.1 activity group in FEES 4 Annex 1R, for the financial year prior to the due date for submission of the report, was limited to the payment of the minimum fee.

16.3.14A **[G]** Failure to submit a report in accordance with the *rules* in, or referred to in, this chapter or the provisions of relevant legislation may also lead to the imposition of a financial penalty and other disciplinary sanctions (see DEPP 6.6.1–6.6). A *firm* may be subject to reporting requirements under relevant legislation other than the Act, not referred to in this chapter. An example of this is reporting to the *FSA* by *building societies* under those parts of the Building Societies Act 1986 which have not been repealed (see SUP 16.1.4G). If it appears to the *FSA* that, in the exceptional circumstances of a particular case, the payment of any fee would be inequitable, the *FSA* may reduce or remit all or part of the fee in question which would otherwise be payable (see FEES 2.3).

16.3.15 **[G]** The *FSA* may from time to time send reminders to *firms* when reports are overdue. *Firms* should not, however, assume that the *FSA* has received a report merely because they have not received a reminder.

16.3.16 **[G]** The *firm* is responsible for ensuring delivery of the required report at the *FSA's* offices by the due date. If a report is received by the *FSA* after the due date and the *firm* believes its delivery arrangements were adequate, it may be required to provide proof of those arrangements. Examples of such proof would be:

(1) "proof of posting" receipts from a *UK* post office or overseas equivalent which demonstrates that the report was posted early enough to allow delivery by the due date in accordance with the delivery service standards prescribed by the relevant postal authority; or

(2) recorded postal delivery receipts showing delivery on the required day; or

(3) records of a courier service provider showing delivery on the required day.

Change of accounting reference date

16.3.17 **[R]**
(1) A *firm* must notify the *FSA* if it changes its *accounting reference date.*
(2) When a *firm* extends its accounting period, it must make the notification in (1) before the date which otherwise would have been the *accounting reference date.*
(3) When a *firm* shortens its accounting period, it must make the notification in (1) before the new *accounting reference date.*

16.3.18 **[G]** SUP 16.2.1G emphasises the importance to the *FSA* of timely and accurate information. The extension of a *firm's* accounting period to more than 15 months may hinder the timely provision of relevant and important information to the *FSA*. This is because many due dates for reporting to the *FSA* are linked to *firms' accounting reference dates*. Indeed, for some categories of *firm*, the only reports required by the *FSA* have due dates for submission which are linked to the *firm's accounting reference date*. If the extension of a *firm's* accounting period appears likely to impair the effectiveness of the *FSA's* supervisory work, the *FSA* may take action to ensure that it continues to receive the information it requires on a timely basis. This may include the use of any of the tools of supervision set out in SUP 1.4.5G.

16.3.19 **[G]** If more than one *firm* in a *group* intends to change its *accounting reference date* at the same time, a single notification may be given to the *FSA*, as described in SUP 15.7.8G.

Underwriting agents: submission to the Society of Lloyd's

16.3.20 **[R]**
(1) paragraph (2) applies in relation to reports required under this chapter within the scope of any arrangements made by the *FSA* with the *Society of Lloyd's* under paragraph 6(2) of Schedule 1 to the *Act*.
(2) An *underwriting agent* must submit the reports in (1) to the *Society of Lloyd's* rather than to the *FSA*.

16.3.21 **[G]** See SUP 15.7.13G and SUP 15.7.14G for *guidance* on arrangements in SUP 16.3.20R.

Service of Notices Regulations

16.3.22 **[G]** The Financial Services and Markets Act 2000 (Service of Notices) Regulations 2001 (SI 2001/1420) contain provisions relating to the service of documents on the *FSA*. They do not apply to reports required under SUP 16, because of the specific *rules* in this section.

Confidentiality and sharing of information

16.3.23 **[G]** When the *FSA* receives a report which contains confidential information and whose submission is required under this chapter, it is obliged under Part XXIII of the Act (Public Record, Disclosure of Information and Co-operation) to treat that information as confidential. (See SUP 2.2.4G)

16.3.24 **[G]** SUP 2.3.12G states that the *FSA* may pass to other regulators information which it has in its possession. Such information includes information contained in reports submitted under this chapter. The *FSA's* disclosure of information to other regulators is subject to SUP 2.2.4G (Confidentiality of information).

Reports from groups

16.3.25 **[G]** If this chapter requires the submission of a report or *data item* covering a *group*, a single report or *data item* may be submitted, and so satisfy the requirements of all *firms* in the *group*. Such a report or *data item* should contain the information required from all of them, meet all relevant due dates and indicate all the *firms* on whose behalf it is submitted; if necessary a separate covering sheet should list the *firms* on whose behalf a report or *data item* is submitted.

Nevertheless, the requirement to provide a report or *data item*, and the responsibility for the report or *data item*, remain with each *firm* in the *group*. However, reporting requirements that apply to a *firm*, by reason of the *firm* being a member of a *financial conglomerate*, are imposed on only one member of the *financial conglomerate* (see, for example, SUP 16.12.32R).

16.3.26 **[G]** Examples of reports covering a *group* are:
(1) the compliance reports required from *banks* under SUP 16.6.4R;
(2) annual controllers reports required under SUP 16.5.4R;
(3) annual close links reports required under SUP 16.5.4R
(4) consolidated financial reports required from *banks* under SUP 16.7.7R;
(5) consolidated reporting statements required from *securities and futures firms* under SUP 16.7.24R;

(6) reporting in relation to *defined liquidity groups* under SUP 16.12.

16.4 Annual controllers report

Application

16.4.1 **[G]** This section applies to every *firm* except those *firms* excluded from its operation by SUP 16.1.1R and SUP 16.1.3R.

16.4.2 **[G]** This section may be of relevance to a *directive friendly society*:
(1) if it has 10 members or less;
(2) if it has a delegate voting system and has 10 delegates or less; or
(3) if it has 20 members or less and effects or carries out group insurance contracts where one person may exercise one vote on behalf of the members of a group and one vote in their private capacity; or

where a member or delegate, whether alone or acting in concert, is entitled to exercise, or control the exercise of, 10% or more of the total voting power.

16.4.2A **[G]** This section may be of relevance to *non-directive firms*.

16.4.3 **[G]** Requirements for notifications of a change in *control* can be found in SUP 11 (Controllers and close links).

Purpose

16.4.4 **[G]** A *firm* and its *controllers* are required to notify certain changes in *control* (see SUP 11 (Controllers and close links)). The purpose of the *rules* and *guidance* in this section is:
(1) to ensure that, in addition to such notifications, the *FSA* receives regular and comprehensive information about the identities of all of the *controllers* of a *firm*, which is relevant to a *firm's* continuing to satisfy the *threshold conditions* (see COND 2.3);
(2) to implement certain requirements relating to annual reporting of *controllers* which must be imposed on *firms* under the *Investment Services Directive*, the *Banking Consolidation Directive*, the *Consolidated Life Directive* and the *Third Non-Life Directive*; and
(3) to support the *FSA's* functions under Part XII of the *Act* (Notices of acquisitions of control over UK authorised persons) (see SUP 11 (Controllers and close links)).

Reporting requirement

16.4.5 **[R]**

(1) A *firm* must submit a report to the *FSA* annually, containing the information in (3) or (4) (as applicable).

(2) A *firm* must submit the report in (1) to the *FSA* within four months of the *firm's accounting reference date*.

(3) If a *firm* is not aware:
  (a) that it has any *controllers*; or
  (b) of any changes in the identity of its *controllers* since the submission of its previous report under (1); or
  (c) of any changes in the percentage of shares or *voting power* in the *firm* held by any *controllers* (alone or acting in concert) since the submission of its previous report;

then the report in (1) must confirm this.

(4) Unless (3) applies, the report in (1) must contain a list of all the *controllers* as at the *firm's accounting reference date* of which it is aware and, for each such *controller*, state:
  (a) its name;
  (b) the percentage of *voting power* in the *firm*, or in the *firm's parent undertaking*, which it is entitled to exercise or control the exercise of, whether alone or acting in concert;
  (c) the percentage of shares in the *firm*, or in the *firm's parent undertaking*, which it holds, whether alone or acting in concert;
  (d) if the *controller* is a *body corporate*, its country of incorporation, address and registered number; and
  (e) if the *controller* is an individual, his date and place of birth.

(4A) A *firm* that is a *regulated entity* must include in its report to the *FSA* under (1) whether any *consolidation group* of which it is a member is a *third-country banking and investment group*.

(4B) A *firm* does not have to give notice to the *FSA* under (4A) if it, or another member of the *third-country banking and investment group*, has already given notice to the *FSA* of the relevant fact.

(5) [deleted]

16.4.6 **[G]** The information required by SUP 16.4.5R (4) may be provided in the form of a group organisation chart.

16.4.7 **[G]** If a *group* includes more than one *firm*, a single annual controllers report may be submitted, and so satisfy the requirements of all *firms* in the *group*. Such a report should contain the information required from all of them, meet all relevant due dates, indicate all the *firms* on whose behalf it is submitted and give their *FSA* firm reference numbers. Nevertheless, the requirement to provide a report, and the responsibility for the report, remain with each *firm* in the *group*.

16.4.8 **[G]** A *firm* may submit a single report satisfying the requirements of its annual controllers report (SUP 16.4.5R) and its annual close links report (SUP 16.5.4R). Such a report should contain the information required on both *controllers* and *close links*.

16.4.9 **[G]** *Firms* are reminded of the requirement in SUP 11.4.10R to take reasonable steps to keep themselves informed about the identity of their *controllers*.

Exceptions: friendly societies and building societies

16.4.10 **[R]** If a *firm* is a *friendly society* or a *building society*, then it is required to submit a report under SUP 16.4.5R only if it is aware that it has a *controller*.

16.4.11 **[R]** In SUP 16.4.5R and SUP 16.4.10R, a *building society* may regard a *person* as not being a *controller* if that *person* is exempt from the obligation to notify a change in *control* under The Financial Services and Markets Act 2000 (Controllers) (Exemption) Order 2009 (SI 2009/774) (see SUP 11.3.2AG(2)).

Exception: insurers

16.4.12 **[R]** An *insurer* need not submit a report under SUP 16.4.5R to the extent that the information has already been provided to the *FSA* under *IPRU(INS)* 9.30R (Additional information on controllers).

16.5 Annual close links report

Application

16.5.1 **[G]** This section applies to every *firm* except those *firms* excluded from its operation by SUP 16.1.1R and SUP 16.1.3R.

Purpose

16.5.2 **[G]** A *firm* is required to notify the *FSA* of changes to its *close links* (see SUP 11.9). *Threshold condition* 3 (Close links) provides that, if a *firm* has *close links* with another *person*, the *FSA* must be satisfied that:

(1) those *close links* are not likely to prevent the *FSA's* effective supervision of the *firm*; and

(2) where it appears to the *FSA* that the person is subject to the laws, regulations or administrative provisions of a territory which is not an *EEA State*, neither the foreign provisions, nor any deficiency in their enforcement, would prevent the *FSA's* effective supervision of the *firm*.

16.5.3 **[G]** The purposes of the *rules* and *guidance* in this section are:

(1) to ensure that, in addition to such notifications, the *FSA* receives regular and comprehensive information about the identities of all persons with whom a *firm* has *close links*, which is relevant to a *firm's* continuing to satisfy the *threshold condition* 3 (Close links) (see SUP 2.3) and to the protection of *consumers*; and

(2) to implement certain requirements relating to the provision of information on *close links* which must be imposed on *firms* under the "*Post-BCCI Directive*".

Report

16.5.4 **[R]**

(1) A *firm* must submit a report to the *FSA* annually, containing the information in (3) or (4) (as applicable).

(2) A *firm* must submit the report in (1) to the *FSA* within four months of the firm's *accounting reference date*.

(3) If a *firm* is not aware:

(a) that it has any *close links*; or
(b) of any material changes to the details in (4) (a) to (c) in respect of its *close links* since the submission of its previous report under (1);

then the report in (1) must confirm this.

(4) Unless (3) applies, the report in (1) must contain a list of all *persons* with whom the *firm* has *close links* as at the *firm's accounting reference date* of which it is aware, and for each such *person* state:
(a) its name;
(b) the nature of the *close links*;
(c) if the *close link* is with a *body corporate*, its country of incorporation, address and registered number; and
(d) if the *close link* is with an individual, his date and place of birth.

16.5.5 **[G]** The information required by SUP 16.5.4R(4) may be provided in the form of a group organisation chart.

16.5.6 **[G]** If a *group* includes more than one *firm*, a single annual close links report may be submitted and so satisfy the requirements of all *firms* in the *group*. Such a report should contain the information required from all of them, meet all relevant due dates, indicate all the *firms* on whose behalf it is submitted and give their FSA firm reference numbers. Nevertheless, the requirement to provide a report, and the responsibility for the report, remain with each *firm* in the *group*.

16.5.7 **[G]** A *firm* may submit a single report satisfying the requirements of its annual controllers report (SUP 16.4.5R) and its annual close links report (SUP 16.5.4R). Such a report should contain the information required on both *controllers* and *close links*.

16.5.8 **[R]** If a *firm* is an unincorporated *friendly society*, then it is only required to submit a report under SUP 16.5.4R if it is aware that it has *close links*.

16.6 Compliance reports

Application

16.6.1 **[G]** The effect of SUP 16.1.1R is that this section applies to every *firm* within a category listed in the left hand column of the table in SUP 16.6.2G.

16.6.2 **[G]**

Table: Applicable provisions of this section (see SUP 16.6.1G)

Category of firm	**Applicable provisions**
Bank, ELMI	SUP 16.6.4R – SUP 16.6.5R
Trustee of an *AUT Depositary* of an *ICVC*	SUP 16.6.6R – SUP 16.6.9G
OPS firm	SUP 16.6.6R – SUP 16.6.8R

Purpose

16.6.3 **[G]** The *FSA* performs part of its supervision work by reviewing and analysing information about *firms'* records of compliance with the requirements and standards under the *regulatory system*. The type of report the *FSA* requires will vary, depending on the type of business a *firm* undertakes. The requirements in SUP 16.6 represent an interim approach to compliance reporting, based mainly on the reporting requirements, which *previous regulators* applied to *firms*. This information helps the *FSA* to determine whether a *firm* is complying with the requirements applicable to its business, and what procedures it is operating to ensure its compliance.

Banks

16.6.4 **[R]** A *bank* and an *ELMI* must submit compliance reports to the *FSA* in accordance with SUP 16.6.5R.

16.6.5 **[R]**

Table: Compliance reports from a bank and an ELMI (see SUP 16.6.4R)

Report	**Frequency**	**Due date**
List of all *overseas regulators* for each legal entity in the *firm's group*	Annually	6 months after the *firm's accounting reference date*
Organogram showing the *authorised* entities in the *firm's group*	Annually	6 months after the *firm's accounting reference date*

Trustees of authorised unit trust schemes, depositaries of ICVCs, and OPS firms

16.6.6 **[R]** A *firm* within a category listed in the left-hand column of SUP 16.6.7R must submit compliance reports in accordance with SUP 16.6.7R.

16.6.7 **[R]**

Table: Compliance reports from trustees of AUTs, depositaries of ICVCs, and OPS firms (see SUP 16.6.6R)

Report	Frequency	Due date
Report from a *trustee* of an *AUT* on *manager's* failures as set out in SUP 16.6.8R(1)	Quarterly	1 month after quarter end (Note)
Report from a *depositary* of an *ICVC* on failures by the *authorised corporate director* as set out in SUP 16.6.8R(2)	Quarterly	1 month after quarter end (Note)
OPS firms only: Annual accounts of each *occupational pension scheme* in respect of which the *firm* is acting	Annually	7 months after end of the scheme year
OPS firms only: Audited annual accounts of each *OPS collective investment scheme* in respect of which the *firm* is acting	Annually	7 months after end of the scheme year

Note = The quarter ends are 31 March, 30 June, 30 September, 31 December.

16.6.8 **[R]**

(1) The report from a *trustee* of an *AUT* to the *FSA* must state, in relation to the *manager* of each *AUT* for which it is a *trustee*, the number of times during the quarter in which facts came to the *firm's* knowledge from which it appeared, or might have appeared, that the *manager* had failed (materially or otherwise) to:
  - (a) give correct instructions to the *trustee* to create or cancel *units* in the *AUT* when the *manager* should have done so, and the error:
    - (i) resulted in the creation of too few *units* or in the cancellation of too many *units*; and
    - (ii) was not corrected in accordance with the *FSA's guidance* as set out in COLL 6.2.12G;
  - (b) price *units* in the *AUT* in accordance with COLL 6.3, where the pricing error was:
    - (i) greater than 0.5% of the price of a *unit*; or
    - (ii) less than 0.5% of the price of a *unit*, and the *trustee* did not consider the *manager's* controls to be adequate;

  unless the failure was an isolated incident.

(2) The report from a *depositary* of an *ICVC* to the *FSA* must state, in relation to the *authorised corporate director* of each *ICVC* for which the *firm* is a *depositary*, the number of times during the quarter in which facts came to the *firm's* knowledge from which it appeared or might have appeared that the *authorised corporate director* had failed (materially or otherwise) to:
  - (a) arrange for the issue or cancellation of *shares* in the *ICVC* when the *authorised corporate director* should have done so, and the error:
    - (i) resulted in the creation of too few *shares* or in the cancellation of too many *shares*; and
    - (ii) was not corrected in accordance with the *FSA's guidance* as set out in COLL 6.2.12G;
  - (b) price *shares* in the *ICVC* in accordance with the provisions of COLL 6.3 where the pricing error was:
    - (i) greater than 0.5% of the price of a *share*; or
    - (ii) less than 0.5% of the price of a *share*, and the *depositary* did not consider the *authorised corporate director's* controls to be adequate;

  unless the failure was an isolated incident.

(3) An *OPS firm* must notify the *FSA* of any change in the date of commencement of the scheme year of an *OPS* or *OPS collective investment scheme*, in respect of which the *firm* is acting, not less than 15 *business days* before the date on which such a change is to become effective.

16.6.9 **[G]** SUP 16 Ann 12G provides *guidance* on the completion of the report from a *trustee* of an *AUT* on a *manager's* failures as set out in SUP 16.6.8R (1), and the report from a *depositary* of an *ICVC* on failures by the *authorised corporate director* as set out in SUP 16.6.8R (2). This *guidance* includes suggested formats for the submission of the reports.

16.7 Financial reports

[deleted]

16.8 Persistency reports from insurers and data reports on stakeholder pensions

Application

16.8.1 **[G]** The effect of SUP 16.1.1R is that this section applies to:

(1) every *insurer* with *permission* to *effect* or *carry out life policies*, unless it is a *non-directive friendly society;* and

(2) every *firm* with *permission* to establish, operate or wind up a *stakeholder pension scheme.*

Purpose

16.8.2 **[G]** The purpose of this section is to enable information on the persistency of life policies and data on stakeholder pensions to be prepared and provided to the *FSA* in a standard format. This information is used in the monitoring of *firms* both individually and collectively.

Requirement to submit persistency and data reports

16.8.3 **[R]**

(1) An *insurer* with *permission* to *effect* or *carry out life policies* must submit to the *FSA* a persistency report in respect of *life policies* by 30 April each year in accordance with this section.

(2) A *firm* with *permission* to establish, operate or wind up a *stakeholder pension scheme* must submit to the *FSA*:

  (a) a data report on stakeholder pensions by 30 April each year prepared in accordance with this section; and

  (b) two extra data reports on stakeholder pensions prepared in accordance with this section as follows:

    (i) by 31 October 2002, of the number effected in the period to 30 June 2001 and the number of those still in force 12 months after the contract was effected;

    (ii) by 31 January 2003, of the number effected in the period 1 July 2001 to 30 September 2001 and the number of those still in force 12 months after the contract was effected.

Interpretation of this section

16.8.4 **[R]** In this section, and Forms 1R(1) to (4) in SUP 16 Annex 6R:

(1) '12 month report' means the part of a persistency report or data report reporting on *life policies* or stakeholder pensions *effected* in Y–2, '24 month report' means the part of a persistency report or data report reporting on *life policies* or stakeholder pensions effected in Y–3, and so on;

(2) 'CC' means the number of *life policies* or stakeholder pensions which:

  (a) were effected during the period to which the calculation relates; and

  (b) are reported on in the persistency report or data report (see SUP 16.8.8R to SUP 16.8.15R);

(3) 'CF' means the number of *life policies* or stakeholder pensions within 'CC' which are treated as in force at the end of Y–1 or, for a report under SUP 16.8.3R (2)(b), the relevant 12 month period (see SUP 16.8.16R to SUP 16.8.18R);

(4) 'contract anniversary' means the anniversary of the date on which the *life policy* or stakeholder pension was effected falling within Y–1;

(5) 'data report' means a report in respect of stakeholder pensions complying with SUP 16.8.19R to SUP 16.8.21R;

(6) Forms 1R(1), 1R(2), 1R(3) and 1R(4) mean the forms in SUP 16 Ann 6R;

(7) 'group personal pension policy' means a *life policy* which is not a separate *pension scheme*, effected under a collecting arrangement made for the *employees* of a particular employer to participate in a personal pension arrangement on a group basis;

(8) [deleted]

(9) 'mortgage endowment' means an *endowment assurance effected* or believed to be *effected* for the purposes of paying off a loan on land;

(10) 'new', in relation to a stakeholder pension, has the meaning given in SUP 16.8.11R (2);

(11) '*ordinary assurance policy*' means a *life policy* which is not an *industria assurance policy*;

(12) 'other life assurance' means a *life policy* other than a *pension policy*, *endowment assurance* or *whole life assurance*;

(13) 'other pension policy' means a *pension policy* other than a *persona pension policy*;

(14) 'persistency rate' means a rate calculated using this formula:

CF × 100 / CC

(see the example in SUP 16.8.5R);

(15) 'persistency report' means a report in respect of life policies complying with SUP 16.8.19R to SUP 16.8.21R;

(16) 'regular premium life policy' means a *life policy* where there is (or could be, or has been) a commitment by the policyholder to make a regular stream of contributions (for example by means of a direct debit mandate);

(17) 'regular premium stakeholder pension' means a stakeholder pension where there is (or could be, or has been) a commitment by the policyholder to make a regular stream of contributions;

(18) 'single premium life policy' means a *life policy* that is not a regular premium *life policy*, except that a recurrent single premium *life policy* must be treated as a regular premium *life policy*;

(19) 'single premium stakeholder pension' means a stakeholder pension which is not a regular premium stakeholder pension, except that a recurrent single premium stakeholder pension must be treated as a regular premium stakeholder pension;

(20) 'stakeholder pension' means an individual's rights under a *stakeholder pension scheme*;

(21) 'substitute', in relation to stakeholder pension, has the meaning given in SUP 16.8.11R (2);

(22) 'Y' means the year in which the report must be submitted, 'Y–1' means the preceding year, 'Y–2' means the next earlier year and so on;

(23) 'year' means calendar year, unless SUP 16.8.7R applies.

16.8.5 **[G]** Table Example of calculation of persistency rate for life policies that commenced during 1996 (see SUP 16.8.3R)

Y year of reporting)	**Number of *life policies* which commenced during 1996**	**Number of 1996 *policies* that cease to be in force during Y–1**	**Deaths and retirements (not included in CC and CF)**	**CF**	**CC**
1998	1000	143	2	1000 – 143 – 2 = 855	1000 – 2 = 998
1999	1000	25	1	1000 – 143 – 25 – 2 – 1 = 829	1000 – 2 – 1 = 997

Report submitted in 1998 Persistency rate for *life policies* that commenced during Y–2 (that is 1996)

$$\frac{CF \times 100}{CC} = \frac{855 \times 100}{998} = 85.7\%$$

Report submitted in 1999 Persistency rate for *life policies* that commenced during Y–3 (that is 1996)

$$\frac{CF \times 100}{CC} = \frac{829 \times 100}{997} = 83.1\%$$

16.8.6 **[G]** **Firms** are reminded that annuity contracts other than deferred annuity contracts are not within the definition of *'life policy'*.

16.8.7 **[R]** In relation to a persistency report, a *firm* may treat a 12-month period ending between 1 October and 31 March as a 'year' for the purposes of this section and Forms 1R(1) to (3):

(1) if the *firm's* financial year does not end on 31 December; or

(2) for *industria assurance policy* business;

provided that the use of an alternative period is disclosed in the persistency report.

Part II FSA Handbook Materials

Life policies and stakeholder pension to be reported on in the persistency or data reports

16.8.8 **[R]** A persistency report or data report must report on a *life policy* or stakeholder pension if:
(1) it is not of a type listed in SUP 16.8.13R or SUP 16.8.14R;
(2) it was effected by:
 (a) the *firm* submitting the report; or
 (b) an *unauthorised* member of the *group* of the *firm* submitting the report and in circumstances in which that *firm* was responsible for the promotion of that *life policy* or stakeholder pension; or
 (c) another *firm*, but is being carried out by the *firm* submitting the report; and
(3) the *person* who sold it or who was responsible for its promotion was, in so doing, subject to *rules* in *COBS*.

16.8.9 **[G] Life policies** and stakeholder pensions falling within SUP 16.8.8R (2) (c) are those which have been transferred from another *firm*, for example under an insurance business transfer scheme under Part VII of the *Act* (Control of Business Transfers).

16.8.10 **[R] Life policies** falling within SUP 16.8.8R, which were sold subject to the conduct of business rules of a *previous regulator*, need to be reported only if they were required to be reported on by the rules of the *previous regulator* of the *firm* submitting the report.

16.8.11 **[R]**
(1) A *life policy* or stakeholder pension which was issued in substitution for a similar contract may be treated as being effected on the inception date of the previous *life policy* or stakeholder pension, provided that the *firm* is satisfied that no loss to the *policyholder* is attributable to the substitution;
(2) A stakeholder pension which is treated as in (1) is a "substitute" stakeholder pension. A "new" stakeholder pension is any other stakeholder pension.

16.8.12 **[G]** Examples of loss to the *policyholder* under SUP 16.8.11R are losses resulting from higher charges and more restrictive benefits and options.

16.8.13 **[R]** A persistency or data report must not report on any of the following:
(1) a *life policy* or stakeholder pension that was cancelled from inception whether or not this was as a result of service of a notice under the *rules* on cancellation (COBS 15);
(2) an *appropriate persona pension scheme* to which contributions are made only by the Department of Social Security;
(3) a *life policy* (excluding *income withdrawal*) or stakeholder pension which has terminated as a result of death, critical illness, retirement, maturity or other completion of the contract term;
(4) *income withdrawals* that have ceased as a result of the death of the *policyholder*;
(5) in the case of a persistency report only, a *life policy* which is a stakeholder pension;
(6) a *life policy* purchased by the trustees of an *occupationa pension scheme* which is a *defined benefits pension scheme*;
(7) a *life policy* purchased by the trustees of *an executive money purchase occupationa pension scheme*.

16.8.14 **[R]** A persistency report required by SUP 16.8.3R (1) need not report on a *life policy* if the number of *life policies* on substantially the same terms effected by the relevant *firm* (or member of the *firm's group*) in the relevant year did not exceed the higher of fifty and 1% of the total reportable *life policies* effected by the *person* in that year.

16.8.15 **[R]** If the term of an *endowment assurance* is less than five years, the *life policy* must only be included in a persistency report in respect of years up to and including the anniversary prior to maturity.

Life policies and stakeholder pensions to be treated as in force

16.8.16 **[R]** Subject to SUP 16.8.17R and SUP 16.8.18R, a *life policy* or stakeholder pension must be treated as in force at the end of Y-1 (that is, included in CF) if and only if:
(1) in the case of a regular premium life policy:
 (a) in the case of an *industria assurance policy* on which the *premiums* are paid at intervals of four weeks, the *premium* has been paid in respect of the four-week period in which the policy anniversary falls; or
 (b) in any other case, the *premium* has been paid in respect of the month in which the policy anniversary falls;
(2) in the case of a single premium life policy, the policy has not been surrendered as at the policy anniversary;
(3) in the case of a regular premium stakeholder pension:
 (a) for a report required by SUP 16.8.3R (2) (a), the premium has been paid in respect of the month in which the contract anniversary falls;
 (b) for a report required by SUP 16.8.3R (2) (b), the premium has been paid in respect of the month 12 months after the contract was effected;

(4) in the case of a single premium stakeholder pension:
  (a) for a report required by SUP 16.8.3R (2) (a), the contract has not been surrendered as at the contract anniversary; or
  (b) for a report required by SUP 16.8.3R (2) (b), the contract has not been surrendered as at the end of the 12 month period.

16.8.17 **[R]** A cluster *life policy* must be reported as a single *life policy* and must be treated as in force (that is included in CF) even if some of the constituent *life policies* have been terminated.

16.8.18 **[R]** An *income withdrawal* that has terminated other than by death of the *policyholder* must be treated as not in force at the end of Y-1 (that is, not included in CF).

Contents of the persistency or data report

16.8.19 **[R]**
(1) A persistency report on life policies must be a report in the format of Forms 1R(1), (2) and (3).
(2) A data report on stakeholder pensions must be a report in the format of Form 1R(4).
(3) A persistency and a data report must include:
  (a) for a report required by SUP 16.8.3R (1) or (2) (a), a separate copy of each Form reporting on *life policies* or stakeholder pensions effected during each of Y-2, Y-3, Y-4, Y-5;
  (b) for a persistency report, a separate copy of Forms IR(1) and IR(2) reporting on:
    (i) regular premium life policies and single premium *life policies*; and
    (ii) *life policies* classified as ordinary assurance policies and *industrial* assurance policies.

16.8.20 **[R]** If, in relation to any Form, a *firm* has no *life policies* or stakeholder pensions to report on in a copy of that Form, the *firm* need not submit that copy provided that it confirms in writing to the *FSA*, as part of the persistency or data report, that it is not doing so and the reason for not doing so.

16.8.21 **[R]** The *firm* must, if a persistency report reports on;
(1) an *endowment assurance* with a term of five years or less:
  (a) report on such a *policy* in Form 1R(2); and
  (b) not report on such a policy in Form 1R(1);
(2) a group personal pension policy, include the policy as a personal pension policy in Forms 1R(1) and 1R(3);
(3) a mortgage endowment, also include the policy as an endowment assurance in Forms 1R(1) and 1R(3);
(4) an *income withdrawal*, not include the policy under any other relevant category in Forms 1R(1) and 1R(3).

16.8.22 **[G]**
(1) Under SUP 16.8.16R, a *life policy* must be treated as not in force if *premiums* have not been paid at the relevant date. Form 1R(3) seeks additional information on the number of *policies* treated as not in force which are subject to genuine contribution holidays.
(2) A *firm* should treat a *life policy* as 'subject to a contribution holiday' if:
  (a) the terms of the *policy* allow the *policyholder* to take a contribution holiday;
  (b) the *policyholder* has opted to take a contribution holiday in accordance with those terms;
  (c) the *policyholder* has clearly stated his intention to resume payments; and
  (d) at the end of Y-1, not more than 12 months have elapsed from the date that *premiums* ceased to be paid.

Records

16.8.23 **[R]** A *firm* must make and retain such records as will enable it to:
(1) monitor regularly the persistency of *life policies* and stakeholder pensions effected through each of its *representatives*; and
(2) make persistency reports or data reports to the *FSA* in accordance with SUP 16.8.3R.

16.8.24 **[G]** In order to comply with SUP 16.8.23R, a *firm* will as a minimum need to make and retain separate records for:
(1) *life policies* and stakeholder pensions originally promoted:
  (a) *by representatives*; or
  (b) *by independent intermediaries*; or
  (c) through the *firm's* own *direct offer financia promotions*; or
  (d) as *adopted packaged products*;
(2) *life policies* and stakeholder pensions not within (1), including those *effected* as execution-only transactions, for inclusion in the relevant form under 'Otherwise';

Part II FSA Handbook Materials

(3) *life policies* and stakeholder pensions written assuming the payment of:
(a) regular premiums;
(b) a single premium;
(4) *life policies* written as:
(a) ordinary assurance policies;
(b) *industria assurance policies*;
(5) the categories of *life policies* and stakeholder pensions referred to in Forms 1R(1) to (4).

16.9 Appointed representatives annual report

Application

16.9.1 **[G]** The effect *of* SUP 16.1.1R is that this section applies to every *firm* with a *Part IV permission to advise on investments, arrange (bring about) deals in investments, make arrangements with a view to transactions in investments, or arrange safeguarding and administration of assets.*

Purpose

16.9.2 **[G]** The purpose of the *rules* and *guidance* in this section is to ensure that, in addition to the notifications made under SUP 12.7 (Appointed representatives: notification requirements), the *FSA* receives regular and comprehensive information about the *appointed representatives* engaged by a *firm*, so that the *FSA* is in a better position to pursue the *regulatory objective* of the protection of *consumers.*

Report

16.9.3 **[R]**
(1) A *firm* must:
(a) submit a report to the *FSA* annually, in the form of an amended copy of the relevant extract from the *FSA* Register, containing the information in (2); and
(b) submit the report in (1) to the *FSA* within four *months* of the *firm's accounting reference date*.
(2) The report in (1) must contain a list of all the current *appointed representatives* of the *firm* as at the *firm's accounting reference date*.
(3) The report in (1) is not required if:
(a) the *firm* has no *appointed representatives* as at the *firm's accounting reference date*; and
(b) this is reflected in the relevant extract from the *FSA Register*.

16.9.4 **[G]** The *FSA Register* is maintained under section 347 of the *Act* (The record of authorised persons, etc.) and may be viewed at the *FSA's* website at www.fsa.gov.uk/register/.

16.9.5 **[G]** [deleted]

16.9.6 **[G]** If a *group* includes more than one *firm*, a single annual *appointed representatives* report may be submitted on behalf of all *firms* in the *group*. Such a report should contain the information required from all the *firms*, meet all relevant due dates, indicate all the *firms* on whose behalf it is submitted and give their *FSA* firm reference numbers. The requirement to provide a report, and the responsibility for the report, remains with each *firm* in the *group*.

16.10 Verification of standing data

Application

16.10.1 **[G]** The effect of SUP 16.1.1R is that this section applies to every *firm* except:
(1) an *ICVC*; or
(2) a *UCITS qualifier*;
(3) a *credit union*; or
(4) a *dormant account fund operator*.

Purpose

16.10.2 **[G]** **Standing data** is used by the *FSA*:
(1) to ensure that a *firm* is presented with the correct regulatory return when it seeks to report electronically;
(2) in order to communicate with a *firm*;
(3) as the basis for some sections of the *FSA Register*; and
(4) in order to carry out thematic analysis across sectors and groups of *firms*.

16.10.3 [G] In view of the importance attached to *standing data*, and the consequences which may result if it is wrong, this section provides the framework for a *firm* to check and correct it.

Requirement to check the accuracy of standing data and to report changes to the FSA

16.10.4 **[R]**

(1) Within 30 *business days* of its *accounting reference date*, a *firm* must check the accuracy of its *standing data* through the relevant section of the *FSA* website.
(2) [to follow]
(3) If any *standing data* is incorrect, the *firm* must give the corrected *standing data* to the *FSA* using the appropriate form submitted in accordance with instructions on that form.

16.10.5 **[G]** The *standing data* is made available to the *firm* when the *firm* logs into the appropriate section of the *FSA* website. The *firm* should check the *standing data* and send any corrections to the *FSA*. The *FSA's* preferred method of receiving corrections to *standing data* is by the online forms available at the *FSA's* website.

16.10.6 **[G]** A *firm* may check, and submit corrections to, its *standing data* more frequently than annually.

16.10.7 **[G]** For the purpose of SUP 16.10.4 R (3), the appropriate form will be determined by the *standing data* to be corrected. Appropriate forms will include (but are not limited to) the form in SUP 15 Ann 3R (standing data form) and the form in SUP 15 Ann 4R (notification form).

16.11 Product Sales Data Reporting

Application

16.11.1 **[R]**

This section applies to a firm which is a *home finance provider*; or in respect of sales to a *private customer* or a *retai customer*:
(1) an *insurer*; or
(2) the *operator* of a *regulated collective investment scheme*, an *investment trust savings scheme*, or a *persona pension scheme*; or
(3) a *person* who issues or manages the relevant assets of the issuer of a *structured capital-at-risk product*, unless the *firm* is a *managing agent*.

Purpose

16.11.2 **[G]**
(1) The purpose of this section is to set out the requirements for *firms* in the retail mortgage, investment, and *pure protection contract* markets specified in SUP 16.11.1R to report individual product sales data to the *FSA*. This requirement applies whether the *regulated activity* has been carried out by the *firm*, or through an intermediary which has dealt directly with the *firm*.
(2) The purpose of collecting this data is to assist the *FSA* in the ongoing supervision of *firms* engaged in retail activities and to enable the *FSA* to gain a wider understanding of market trends in the interests of protecting *consumers*.

Reporting requirement

16.11.3 **[R]**
(1) A *firm* must submit a report (the 'data report') containing the information required by SUP 16.11.5R quarterly, within 20 *business days* of the end of the quarter, unless (3) applies.
(2) The reporting periods are the four calendar quarters of each year beginning on 1 January.
(3) A *firm* need not submit a data report if no relevant sales have occurred in the quarter.

16.11.4 **[G]**
(1) A *firm* may submit a data report more frequently than quarterly if it wishes.
(2) If it is easier and more practical for a *firm* to submit additional data relating to products other than those specified in SUP 16.11.5R, it may submit that additional data to the *FSA* in a data report.

Content of the report

16.11.5 **[R]**

The data report must contain sales data in respect of the following products:
(1) *retai investments*;
(2) *pure protection contracts*;
(3) *regulated mortgage contracts* (but not further advances);
(4) *home purchase plans*; and
(5) *home reversion plans*.

16.11.6 **[G] Guidance** on the type of products covered by SUP 16.11.5R is contained in SUP 16 Ann 20G.

16.11.7 **[R]** The data report must comply with the provisions of SUP 16 Ann 21R.

16.11.8 **[R]** The data report must relate both to transactions undertaken by the *firm* and to transactions undertaken by an intermediary which has dealt directly with the *customer* on the *firm's* behalf.

16.11.8A **[G]** Where the *operator* of a *collective investment scheme* receives business from a *firm* which operates a nominee account, the data report in respect of those transactions submitted by the *operator* should treat those transactions as transactions undertaken by the *operator* with the *firm*.

16.11.9 **[R]** A *firm* must provide the data report to the *FSA* electronically in a standard format provided by the *FSA*.

16.11.10 **[G]** A data report will have been provided to the *FSA* in accordance with SUP 16.11.9R only if all mandatory data reporting fields (as set out in SUP 16 Ann 21R) have been completed correctly and the report has been accepted by the relevant *FSA* reporting system.

Use of reporting agents

16.11.11 **[R]**

(1) A *firm* may appoint another *person* to provide the data report on the *firm's* behalf if the *firm* has informed the *FSA* of that appointment in writing.

(2) Where (1) applies, the *firm* must ensure that the data report complies with the requirements of SUP 16.11 and identifies the originator of the transaction.

16.12 Integrated Regulatory Reporting

Application

16.12.1 **[G]** The effect of SUP 16.1.1R is that this section applies to every *firm* carrying on business set out in column (1) of SUP 16.12.4R except:

(1) an *incoming EEA firm* with *permission* for *cross border services* only;

(2) an *oi market participant* that is not subject to the requirements of IPRU(INV) Chapter 3;

(3) an *authorised professiona firm* (other than one that must comply with IPRU(INV) 3, 5 or 13 in accordance with IPRU(INV) 2.1.4R, where SUP 16.12.4R will apply in respect of the business the firm undertakes), which must comply with SUP 16.12.30R and SUP 16.12.31R; and

(4) a *financia conglomerate*, which must comply with SUP 16.12.32R: *firms* that are members of a *financia conglomerate* will have their own reporting requirements under SUP 16.12.32R.

Purpose

16.12.2 **[G]**

(1) *Principle* 4 requires *firms* to maintain adequate financial resources. The Interim Prudential sourcebooks, *PRU*, *BIPRU* and *GENPRU* set out the *FSA's* detailed capital adequacy requirements. By submitting regular data, *firms* enable the *FSA* to monitor their compliance with *Principle* 4 and their prudential requirements in the FSA Handbook.

(2) The *data items* submitted help the *FSA* analyse *firms'* financial and other conditions and performance and to understand their business. By means of further collation and review of the data which the *data items* provide, the *FSA* also uses the *data items* to identify developments across the financial services industry and its constituent sectors.

(3) The requirements in this section differ according to a *firm's regulated activity group (RAG)*, as different information is required to reflect different types of business. Standard formats are used for reporting, to assist compatibility between *firms* which carry on similar types of business. Timely submission is important to ensure the *FSA* has up-to-date information.

Reporting requirement

16.12.3 **[R]**

(1) Any *firm* permitted to carry on any of the activities within each of the *RAG*s set out in column (1) of the table in SUP 16.12.4 R must:

(a)

(i) unless (ii) or (iii) applies, submit to the *FSA* the duly completed *data items* or other items applicable to the *firm* as set out in the provision referred to in column (2) of that table;

(ii) unless (iii) applies, where a *firm* is required to submit completed *data items* for more than one *RAG*, that *firm* must only submit the *data item* of the same name and purpose in respect of the lowest numbered *RAG* applicable to it, *RAG* 1 being the lowest and *RAG* 10 the highest;

(iii) where a *firm* is, but for this *rule*, required to submit *data items* for more than one *RAG* and this includes the submission of *data items* in respect of *FSA* fees, the *FOS* or *FSCS* levy, or threshold conditions, that *firm* must only submit these *data items* if the belong to the lowest numbered of the *RAGs* applicable to it;

(iv) in the case of a *non-EEA bank*, or an *EEA bank* (whether or not it has *permission* for *accepting deposits*) other than one with *permission* for *cross border services* only, any *data items* submitted should, unless indicated otherwise, only cover the activities of the branch operation in the *United Kingdom*;

in the format specified as applicable to the *firm* in the provision referred to in column (2);

(b) submit this information at the frequency and in respect of the periods set out in the provision referred to in column (3); and

(c) submit this information by the due date referred to in the provision referred to in column (4).

(2) Unless (3) applies, any *data item* in (1) must be submitted by electronic means made available by the *FSA*;

(3) does not apply to:

(a) *credit unions* solely in relation to the reporting requirement for *RAG* 1 activities, where SUP 16.3.6R to SUP 16.3.10G will apply;

(b) *firms* in *RAG* 2 in relation to the reporting requirements for *RAG* 2 activities; and

(c) those data items specified as "No standard format", where SUP 16.3.6R to SUP 16.3.10G will apply.

(4) A *firm* that is a member of a *financia conglomerate* must also submit financial reports as required by SUP 16.12.32R

16.12.3A **[G]** The following is designed to assist *firms* to understand how the reporting requirements set out in this chapter operate when the circumstances set out in SUP 16.12.3R(1)(a)(ii) apply.

(1) Example 1

A *BIPRU 730k firm* that undertakes activities in both RAG 3 and RAG 7
Overlaying the requirements of RAG 3 (*data items*) with the requirements of RAG 7 shows the following:

RAG 3 (SUP 16.12.11R) data items	**RAG 7 (SUP 16.12.22AR) data items**
Annual reports and accounts	*Annual reports and accounts*
Annual report and accounts of the *mixed-activity holding company*	*Annual report and accounts* of the *mixed-activity holding company* (note 10)
Solvency statement	Solvency statement
Balance sheet	Balance Sheet
Income statement	Income Statement
Capital adequacy	Capital Adequacy
Credit risk	Credit risk
Market risk	Market risk
Market risk – supplementary	Market risk – supplementary
Operational risk	Operational risk
Large exposures	Large exposures
UK integrated group large exposures	UK integrated group large exposures
Solo consolidation data	Solo consolidation data
Pillar 2 questionnaire	Pillar 2 questionnaire
Non-EEA sub-group	Non-EEA sub-group
	Professional indemnity insurance
	Threshold Conditions
	Training and Competence
	COBS data
Client money and client assets	Client money and client assets
	Fees and levies
CFTC	
IRB portfolio risk	IRB portfolio risk
Securitisation	Securitisation
Daily Flows (if it is an *ILAS BIPRU firm*)	
Enhanced Mismatch Report (if it is an *ILAS BIPRU firm*)	

RAG 3 (SUP 16.12.11R) data items	RAG 7 (SUP 16.12.22AR) data items
Liquidity Buffer Qualifying Securities (if it is an *ILAS BIPRU firm*)	
Funding Concentration (if it is an *ILAS BIPRU firm*)	
Pricing data (if it is an *ILAS BIPRU firm*)	
Retail and corporate funding (if it is an *ILAS BIPRU firm*)	
Currency Analysis (if it is a *ILAS BIPRI firm*)	
Systems and Controls Questionnaire (if it is a *non-ILAS BIPRU firm*)	

From this, the additional reports that are required are:
(a) [deleted]
(b) Professional indemnity insurance, where RAG 7 *firms* complete Section E of the RMAR, and therefore a RAG 3 *firm* should complete that;
(c) [deleted]
(d) Training and competence data, where RAG 3 *firms* should also complete Section G of RMAR;
(e) Conduct of business data, where RAG 3 *firms* should complete Section H of RMAR;
(f) [deleted]
(g) [deleted]

The reporting frequency and submission times for items (b), (d) and (e) above are then derived from the rules applicable to *BIPRU firms* in SUP 16.12.23R and SUP 16.12.24R. Threshold conditions and fees and levies reports do not need to be submitted as they are not required under the lowest numbered of the two *RAGs* in this example, see SUP 16.12.3R(1)(a)(iii).

(2) Example 2

A *UK bank* in RAG 1 that also carries on activities in RAG 5
Again, overlaying the RAG 1 reporting requirements with the requirements for a RAG 5 *firm* gives the following:

RAG 1 requirements (SUP 16.12.5R)	RAG 5 requirements (SUP 16.12.18AR)
Annual report and accounts	*Annual report and accounts*
Annual report and accounts of the *mixed-activity holding company* (note 9)	
Solvency statement (note 10)	
Balance sheet	Balance Sheet
Income statement	Income Statement
Capital adequacy	Capital Adequacy
Credit risk	
Market risk	
Market risk -supplementary	
Operational risk	
Large exposures	
UK integrated group large exposures	
Liquidity (other than stock)	
Liquidity – stock	
Forecast data	
Solo consolidation data	
Interest rate gap report	
Non-EEA sub-group	
Sectoral information, including arrears and impairment	
Maturity *analysis of assets* and deposits	
IRB portfolio risk	
Securitisation	

RAG 1 requirements (SUP 16.12.5R)	RAG 5 requirements (SUP 16.12.18AR)
Daily Flows (if it is an *ILAS BIPRU firm*	
Enhanced Mismatch Report (if it is an *ILAS BIPRU firm*	
Liquidity Buffer Qualifying Securities (if it is an *ILAS BIPRU firm*	
Funding Concentration (if it is an *ILAS BIPRU firm*	
Pricing data (if it is an *ILAS BIPRU firm*	
Retail and corporate funding (if it is an *ILAS BIPRU firm*	
Currency Analysis (if it is a *ILAS BIPRI firm*	
	Lending – Business flow and rates
	Residential Lending to individuals – New business profile
	Lending – Arrears analysis
	Mortgage administration – Business profile
	Mortgage Administration – Arrears analysis
	Analysis of loans to customers
	Provisions analysis
	Fees and levies

In this case, it is more obvious that the firm's reporting requirement in RAG 1 is not all the data items listed above. However, for the purposes of this exercise, it is the list of potential data items that is important. Thus comparing RAG 1 with RAG 5, the additional reporting requirements are:

(a) Lending – Business flow and rates, where Section D MLAR is required;
(b) Residential Lending to individuals – New business profile, where Section E MLAR is required;
(c) Lending – Arrears analysis, where Section F MLAR is required;
(d) Mortgage administration – Business profile, where Section G MLAR is required;
(e) Mortgage Administration – Arrears analysis, where Section H MLAR is required
(f) Analysis of loans to customers, where section A3 of MLAR is required
(g) Provisions analysis, where Section B2 of MLAR is required; and
(h) [deleted]

Fees and levies are not applicable as they are not required to be submitted under the lowest numbered RAG in this example. The reporting frequency and submission times for items (a) to (g) above are then derived from the rules applicable to RAG 5 *firms* in SUP 16.12.18R.

16.12.3B **[G] Firms'** attention is drawn to SUP *16.3.25G* regarding a single submission for all *firms* in the group

16.12.4 **[R]** Table of applicable rules containing *data items*, frequency and submission periods

	(1)	(2)	(3)	(4)
RAG number	**Regulated Activities**	**Provisions containing:**		
		applicable *data items*	**reporting frequency/ period**	**Due date**
RAG 1	• accepting deposits • issuing electronic money • meeting of repayment claims • managing dormant account funds (including the investment of such funds)	SUP 16.12.5R	SUP 16.12.6R	SUP 16.12.7R
RAG 2.1	• effecting contracts of insurance • carrying out contracts of insurance	SUP 16.12.8R	SUP 16.12.8R	SUP 16.12.8R

Part II FSA Handbook Materials

	(1)	(2)	(3)	(4)
RAG number	**Regulated Activities**	**Provisions containing:**		
		applicable *data items*	**reporting frequency/ period**	**Due date**
	• entering as provider into a funeral plan contract			
RAG 2.2	• managing the underwriting capacity of a Lloyds syndicate as a managing agent at Lloyds	SUP 16.12.9R	SUP 16.12.9R	SUP 16.12.9R
	• advising on syndicate participation at Lloyds			
	• arranging deals in contracts of insurance written at Lloyds			
RAG 3	• dealing in investment as principal	SUP 16.12.10R	SUP 16.12.10R	SUP 16.12.10R
	• dealing in investments as agent	SUP 16.12.11R	SUP 16.12.12R	SUP 16.12.13R
	• advising on investments (excluding retail investment activities)			
	• arranging (bringing about) deals in investments (excluding retail investment activities)			
RAG 4	• managing investments	SUP 16.12.14R	SUP 16.12.14R	SUP 16.12.14R
	• establishing, operating or winding up a regulated collective investment scheme	SUP 16.12.15R	SUP 16.12.16R	SUP 16.12.17R
	• establishing, operating or winding up an unregulated collective investment scheme			
	• establishing, operating or winding up a stakeholder pension scheme			
	• establishing, operating or winding up a personal pension scheme			
RAG 5	• *home finance administration or home finance providing activity*	SUP 16.12.18AR	SUP 16.12.18AR	SUP 16.12.18AR
RAG 6	• acting as trustee of an authorised unit trust	SUP 16.12.19R	SUP 16.12.20R	SUP 16.12.21R
	• safeguarding and administration of assets (without arranging)			
	• arranging safeguarding and administration of assets			
	• acting as depository or sole director of an OEIC			
RAG 7	• retail investment activities	SUP 16.12.22R	SUP 16.12.23R	SUP 16.12.24R
	• advising on pensions transfers & opt-outs			
	• arranging (bringing about deals) in retail investments			

	(1)	(2)	(3)	(4)
RAG number	**Regulated Activities**	**Provisions containing:**		
		applicable *data items*	**reporting frequency/ period**	**Due date**
RAG 8	• making arrangements with a view to transactions in investments • operating a multilateral trading facility	SUP 16.12.25R	SUP 16.12.26R	SUP 16.12.27R
RAG 9	• mortgage mediation activity • insurance mediation activity (non-investment insurance contracts)	SUP 16.12.28R	SUP 16.12.28R	SUP 16.12.28R
RAG 10	• the activities of an *RIE/RCH*	SUP 16.12.29R	SUP 16.12.29R	SUP 16.12.29R

16.12.4A **[G]** **RAG** 1 includes an *incoming EEA firm* exercising a *BCD* right through a *UK* branch.

Group liquidity reporting

16.12.4B **[G]** Reporting at group level for liquidity purposes by *firms* falling within BIPRU 12 (Liquidity) is by reference to *defined liquidity groups*. Guidance about the different types of *defined liquidity groups* and related material is set out in SUP 16 Annex 26 (Guidance on designated liquidity groups in SUP 16.12).

Regulated Activity Group 1

16.12.5 **[R]** The applicable *data items* and forms or reports referred to in SUP 16.12.4R are set out according to *firm* type in the table below:

Description of *data item*	Prudential category of *firm*, applicable data items and reporting format (Note 1)							
	UK bank	*Building society*	*Non-EEA bank*	*EEA bank* that has *permission* to accept deposits, other than one with permission for cross border services only	*EEA bank* that does not have permission to accept deposits, other than one with permission for cross border services only	Electronic money institutions	*Credit union*	*Dormant account fund operator* (note 15)
Annual report and accounts	No standard format		No standard format, but in English			No standard format		No standard format
Annual report and accounts of the *mixed-activity holding company* (note 9)	No standard format							
Solvency statement (note 10)	No standard format							
Balance sheet	FSA001 (note 2)	FSA001 (note 2)				FSA020	CQ; CY	
Income statement	FSA002 (note 2)	FSA002 (note 2)	FSA002			FSA021	CQ; CY	
Capital adequacy	FSA003 (note 2)	FSA003 (note 2)				FSA022	CQ; CY	
Credit risk	FSA004 (note 2)	FSA004 (note 2)						
Market risk	FSA005 (notes 2, 4)	FSA005 (notes 2, 4)				FSA023		
Market risk – supplementary	FSA006 (note 5)							
Operational risk	FSA007 (notes 2, 6)	FSA007 (notes 2, 6)						

Description of *data item*	**Prudential category of *firm*, applicable data items and reporting format (Note 1)**							
	UK bank	***Building society***	***Non-EEA bank***	***EEA bank* that has *permission* to accept deposits, other than one with permission for cross border services only**	***EEA bank* that does not have permission to accept deposits, other than one with permission for cross border services only**	**Electronic money institutions**	***Credit union***	***Dormant account fund operator* (note 15)**
Large exposures	FSA008 (note 2)	FSA008 (note 2)				FSA024	CQ; CY	
UK integrated group large exposures	FSA018 (note 12)	FSA018 (note 12)						
Liquidity (other than stock)		FSA011				FSA025	CQ; CY	
Forecast data	FSA014 (note 11)	FSA014 (note 11)						
Solo consolidation data	FSA016 (note 7)	FSA016 (note 7)						
Interest rate gap report	FSA017	FSA017						
ELMI questions						FSA026		
Non-EEA sub-group	FSA028 (note 8)					FSA028 (note 8)		
Sectoral information, including arrears and impairment	FSA015	FSA015						
Maturity analysis of assets and deposits	FSA044 (note 11)	FSA044 (note 11)	FSA044 (note 11)	FSA044 (note 11)				

Description of *data item*	**Prudential category of *firm*, applicable data items and reporting format (Note 1)**							
	UK bank	***Building society***	***Non-EEA bank***	***EEA bank* that has *permission* to accept deposits, other than one with permission for cross border services only**	***EEA bank* that does not have permission to accept deposits, other than one with permission for cross border services only**	**Electronic money institutions**	***Credit union***	***Dormant account fund operator* (note 15)**
IRB portfolio risk	FSA045 (note 13)	FSA045 (note 13)						
Securitisation	FSA046 (note 14)	FSA046 (note 14)						
Daily flows	FSA047 (Notes 16, 20 and 22)	FSA047 (Notes 16, 20 and 22)	FSA047 (Notes 16, 18, 20 and 22)	FSA047 (Notes 16, 18, 20 and 22)	FSA047 (Notes 16, 18, 20 and 22)			
Enhanced Mismatch Report	FSA048 (Notes 16, 20 and 22)	FSA048 (Notes 16, 20 and 22)	FSA048 (Notes 16, 18, 20 and 22)	FSA048 (Notes 16, 18, 20 and 22)	FSA048 (Notes 16, 18, 20 and 22)			
Liquidity Buffer Qualifying Securities	FSA050 (Notes 17, 21 and 22)	FSA050 (Notes 17, 21 and 22)	FSA050 (Notes 17, 19, 21 and 22)	FSA050 (Notes 17, 19, 21 and 22)	FSA050 (Notes 17, 19, 21 and 22)			
Funding Concentration	FSA051 (Notes 17, 21 and 22)	FSA051 (Notes 17, 21 and 22)	FSA051 (Notes 17, 19, 21 and 22)	FSA051 (Notes 17, 19, 21 and 22)	FSA051 (Notes 17, 19, 21 and 22)			
Pricing Data	FSA052 (Notes 17, 21 and 22)	FSA052 (Notes 17, 21 and 22)	FSA052 (Notes 17, 19, 21 and 22)	FSA052 (Notes 17, 19, 21 and 22)	FSA052 (Notes 17, 19, 21 and 22)			
Retail and corporate funding	FSA052 (Notes 17, 21 and 22)	FSA052 (Notes 17, 21 and 22)	FSA052 (Notes 17, 19, 21 and 22)	FSA052 (Notes 17, 19, 21 and 22)	FSA053 (Notes 17, 19, 21 and 22)			
Currency Analysis	FSA052 (Notes 17, 21 and 22)	FSA052 (Notes 17, 21 and 22)	FSA052 (Notes 17, 19, 21 and 22)	FSA052 (Notes 17, 19, 21 and 22)	FSA054 (Notes 17, 19, 21 and 22)			

Note 1	When submitting the completed *data item* required, a *firm* must use the format of the *data item* set out in SUP 16 Ann 24R, except for credit union reports that are in SUP 16 Ann 14R. Guidance notes for completion of the data items are contained in SUP 16 Ann 25G (or Ann 15G for credit unions).
Note 2	Firms that are members of a *UK consolidation group* subject to the capital resources requirement at stage 1 of BIPRU 8 Annex 5R are also required to submit this *data item* on a *UK consolidation group* basis. *Firms'* attention is drawn to SUP 16.3.25G regarding a single submission for all *firms* in the *group*.
Note 3	[deleted]
Note 4	This applies to a *firm* that is required to submit *data item* FSA003 and, at any time within the 12 *months* up to its latest *accounting reference date* ("the relevant period"), was reporting *data item* FSA004 ("Firm A") or not reporting this item ("Firm B"). In the case of Firm A it must report this *data item* if one or both of its last two submissions in the relevant period show that the threshold was exceeded. In the case of Firm B it must report this item if both the last two submissions in the relevant period show that the threshold has been exceeded. The threshold is exceeded where *data element* 93A in *data item* FSA003 is greater than £50 million, or its currency equivalent, at the relevant reporting date for the *firm*.
Note 5	Only applicable to *firms* with a *VaR model permission*.
Note 6	This is only applicable to a *firm* that has adopted, in whole or in part, either the standardised approach, alternative standardised approach, or advanced measurement approach under BIPRU 6
Note 7	Only applicable to a *firm* that has a *solo consolidation waiver*.
Note 8	This will be applicable to *firms* (other than *building societies*) that are members of a *UK consolidation group* on a half-yearly reporting date. *Firms'* attention is drawn to SUP 16.3.25G regarding a single submission for all *firms* in the *group*.
Note 9	Only applicable to a *firm* whose ultimate *parent* is a *mixed activity holding company*.
Note 10	Only applicable to a *firm* that is a *partnership*, when the report must be submitted by each *partner*.
Note 11	Members of a *UK consolidation group* should only submit this *data item* at the *UK consolidation group* level.
Note 12	Members of a *UK integrated group* should only submit this *data item* at the *UK integrated group* level.
Note 13	Only applicable to *firms* that have an *IRB permission*.
Note 14	Only applicable to *firms* that undertake *securitisations*.
Note 15	Only applies to a *dormant account fund operator* that does not fall into any of the other prudential categories in this table.
Note 16	A *firm* must complete this item separately on each of the following bases that are applicable. (1) It must complete it on a solo basis (including on the basis of the *firm's UK branch*). Therefore even if it has a *solo consolidation waiver* it must complete the item on an unconsolidated basis by reference to the *firm* alone. (2) If it is a *group liquidity reporting firm* in a *DLG by default* and is a *UK lead regulated firm*, it must complete the item on the basis of that group. (3) If it is a *group liquidity reporting firm* in a *UK DLG by modification*, it must complete the item on the basis of that group. (4) If it is a *group liquidity reporting firm* in a *non-UK DLG by modification*, it must complete the item on the basis of that group.
Note 17	A *firm* must complete this item separately on each of the following bases that are applicable. (1) It must complete it on a solo basis (including on the basis of the *firm's UK branch*) unless it is a *group liquidity reporting firm* in a *UK DLG* by *modification*. Therefore even if it has a *solo consolidation waiver* it must complete the item on an unconsolidated basis by reference to the *firm* alone. (2) If it is a *group liquidity reporting firm* in a *UK DLG by modification*, it must complete the item on the basis of that group.

Note 18	(1) If the *firm* has a *whole-firm liquidity modification* it must complete this item on the basis of the whole *firm* (or at any other *reporting level* the *whole-firm liquidity modification* may require) and not just its *UK branch*. (2) Otherwise the *firm* must complete this item by reference to the activities of its branch operation in the *United Kingdom* in accordance with SUP 16.12.3R(1)(a)(iv).
Note 19	(1) If the *firm* has a *whole-firm liquidity modification* there is no obligation to report this item. (2) Otherwise the *firm* must complete this item by reference to the activities of its branch operation in the *United Kingdom* in accordance with SUP 16.12.3R(1)(a)(iv).
Note 20	(1) This item must be reported in the reporting currency. (2) If any *data element* is in a currency or currencies other than the reporting currency, all currencies (including the reporting currency) must be combined into a figure in the reporting currency. (3) In addition, all *material currencies* (which may include the reporting currency) must each be recorded separately (translated into the reporting currency). However if: (a) the reporting frequency is (whether under a *rule* or under a *waiver*) quarterly or less than quarterly; or (b) The only *material currency* is the reporting currency; (3) does not apply. (4) If there are more than three *material currencies* for this *data item*, (3) only applies to the three largest in amount. A *firm* must identify the largest in amount in accordance with the following procedure. (a) For each currency, take the largest of the asset or liability figure as referred to in the definition of *material currency*. (b) Take the three largest figures from the resulting list of amounts. (5) The date as at which the calculations for the purposes of the definition of *material currency* are carried out is the last day of the reporting period in question. (6) The reporting currency for this *data item* is whichever of the following currencies the *firm* chooses, namely USD (the United States Dollar), EUR (the euro), GBP (sterling), JPY (the Japanese Yen), CHF (the Swiss Franc), CAD (the Canadian Dollar) or SEK (the Swedish Krona).
Note 21	Note 20 applies, except that paragraph (3) does not apply, meaning that *material currencies* must not be recorded separately.
Note 22	Any changes to reporting requirements caused by a *firm* receiving an *intra-group liquidity modification* or a *whole-firm liquidity modification* (or a variation to one) do not take effect until the first day of the next reporting period applicable under the changed reporting requirements for the *data item* in question if the *firm* receives that *intra-group liquidity modification*, *whole-firm liquidity modification* or variation part of the way through such a period. If the change is that the *firm* does not have to report a particular *data item* or does not have to report it at a particular *reporting level*, the *firm* must nevertheless report that item or at that *reporting level* for any reporting period that has already begun. This paragraph is subject to anything that the *intra-group liquidity modification* or a *whole-firm liquidity modification* says to the contrary.

16.12.6 **[R]** The applicable reporting frequencies for submission of *data items* and periods referred to in SUP 16.12.5R are set out in the table below according to *firm* type. Reporting frequencies are calculated from a *firm's accounting reference date*, unless indicated otherwise.

Data item	Unconsolidated *UK banks* and *building societies*	Solo consolidated *UK banks* and *building societies*	Report on a *UK consolidation group* or, as applicable, *defined liquidity group* basis by *UK banks* and *building societies*	Other members of RAG 1
Annual report and accounts	Annual			Annual
Annual report and accounts of the *mixed-activity holding company*	Annual			
Solvency statement	Annual			
CQ				Quarterly
CY				Annually (note 2)
FSA001	Quarterly		Half yearly	
FSA002	Quarterly		Half yearly	Half yearly
FSA003	Quarterly or monthly (note 1)		Half yearly	
FSA004	Quarterly		Half yearly	
FSA005	Quarterly		Half yearly	
FSA006	Quarterly			
FSA007	Annually (note 3)			
FSA008	Quarterly			
FSA011	Quarterly			
FSA014	Half yearly			
FSA015	Quarterly		Half yearly	
FSA016		Half yearly		
FSA017	Quarterly		Half yearly	
FSA018	Quarterly			
FSA020				Half yearly
FSA021				Half yearly
FSA022				Half yearly
FSA023				Half yearly
FSA024				Half yearly
FSA025				Half yearly
FSA026				Half yearly
FSA028	Half yearly			
FSA044	Quarterly		Half yearly	Quarterly
FSA045	Quarterly		Half yearly	
FSA046	Half yearly		Half yearly	
FSA047	Daily, weekly, monthly or quarterly (Notes 4, 6 and 9)	Daily, weekly, monthly or quarterly (Notes 4, 5, 6 and 9)	Daily, weekly, monthly or quarterly (Notes 4, 8 and 9)	Daily, weekly, monthly or quarterly (Notes 4, 7 and 9)
FSA048	Daily, weekly, monthly or quarterly (Notes 4, 6 and 9)	Daily, weekly, monthly or quarterly (Notes 4, 5, 6 and 9)	Daily, weekly, monthly or quarterly (Notes 4, 8 and 9)	Daily, weekly, monthly or quarterly (Notes 4, 7 and 9)
FSA050	Monthly (Note 4)	Monthly (Notes 4 and 5)	Monthly (Note 4)	Monthly (Note 4)
FSA051	Monthly (Note 4)	Monthly (Notes 4 and 5)	Monthly (Note 4)	Monthly (Note 4)

Data item	**Unconsolidated** ***UK banks*** **and** ***building societies***	**Solo consolidated** ***UK banks*** **and** ***building societies***	**Report on a** ***UK consolidation group*** **or, as applicable,** ***defined liquidity group*** **basis by** ***UK banks*** **and** ***building societies***	**Other members of RAG 1**
FSA052	Weekly or Monthly (Notes 4 and 10)	Weekly or Monthly (Notes 4, 5 and 10)	Weekly or Monthly (Notes 4 and 11)	Weekly or Monthly (Notes 4 and 10)
FSA053	Quarterly (Note 4)	Quarterly (Notes 4 and 5)	Quarterly (Note 4)	Quarterly (Note 4)
FSA054	Quarterly (Note 4)	Quarterly (Notes 4 and 5)	Quarterly (Note 4)	Quarterly (Note 4)

Note 1 Monthly submission only applicable if the *firm* has been notified in writing that it is required to report (when, on an annual review, it has two consecutive quarterly submissions of FSA003 showing *data element* 93A being greater than £50 million, or its currency equivalent, and also greater than 50% of *data element* 70A or, during 2007, it has two consecutive quarterly submissions of FSA009 showing *data element* 27A and *data element* 33A combined being greater than £50 million, or its currency equivalent, and also greater than 50% of *data element* 36A.

Note 2 The annual report required from a *credit union* by SUP 16.12.5R must be made up for the same period as the audited accounts published by the *credit union* in accordance with section 3A of the Friendly and Industrial and Provident Societies Act 1968 (see CRED 14 Ann 1). CRED 14.10.10R (2)(a) states that the audited accounts referred to in SUP 16.12.5R are to be made up for the period beginning with the date of the *credit union's* registration or with the date to which the *credit union's* last annual accounts were made up, and ending on the *credit union's* most recent financial year end.

Note 3 The reporting date for this *data item* is six months after a *firm's* most recent *accounting reference date.*

Note 4 Reporting frequencies and reporting periods for this *data item* are calculated on a calendar year basis and not from a *firm's accounting reference date*. In particular:

(1) A week means the period beginning on Saturday and ending on Friday.

(2) A month begins on the first day of the calendar month and ends on the last day of that month.

(3) Quarters end on 31 March, 30 June, 30 September and 31 December.

(4) Daily means each *business day.*

All periods are calculated by reference to London time.

Any changes to reporting requirements caused by a *firm* receiving an *intra-group liquidity modification* or a *whole-firm liquidity modification* (or a variation to one) do not take effect until the first day of the next reporting period applicable under the changed reporting requirements if the *firm* receives that *intra-group liquidity modification*, *whole-firm liquidity modification* or variation part of the way through such a period, unless the *whole-firm liquidity modification* or *intra-group liquidity modification* says otherwise.

Note 5 As specified in SUP 16.12.5R, solo consolidation has no application to liquidity reporting. Therefore it does not make any difference to the reporting of this item whether or not the *firm* is solo consolidated.

Note 6 If the report is on a solo basis (and the *firm* is a *UK firm*) the reporting frequency is as follows:

(1) if the *firm* does not have an *intra-group liquidity modification* the frequency is:

(a) weekly if the *firm* is a *standard frequency liquidity reporting firm*; and

(b) monthly if the *firm* is a *low frequency liquidity reporting firm*;

(2) if the *firm* is a *group liquidity reporting firm* in a *non-UK DLG by modification (firm level)* the frequency is:

	(a) weekly if the *firm* is a *standard frequency liquidity reporting firm*; and (b) monthly if the *firm* is a *low frequency liquidity reporting firm*; (3) the frequency is quarterly if the *firm* is a *group liquidity reporting firm* in a UK DLG by modification.
Note 7	(1) If the report is on a solo basis (and the *firm* is not a *UK firm*) the reporting frequency is as follows: (a) weekly if the *firm* is a *standard frequency liquidity reporting firm*; and (b) monthly if the *firm* is a *low frequency liquidity reporting firm*. (2) If the *firm* has a *whole-firm liquidity modification* (1) does not apply and instead the frequency of solo reporting is quarterly (or whatever other frequency the *whole-firm liquidity modification* requires).
Note 8	(1) If the report is by reference to the *firm's DLG by default* the reporting frequency is: (a) weekly if the *group liquidity standard frequency reporting conditions* are met; (b) monthly if the *group liquidity low frequency reporting conditions* are met. (2) If the report is by reference to the *firm's UK DLG by modification* the reporting frequency is: (a) weekly if the *group liquidity standard frequency reporting conditions* are met; (b) monthly if the *group liquidity low frequency reporting conditions* are met. (3) If the report is by reference to the *firm's non-UK DLG by modification* the reporting frequency is quarterly.
Note 9	(1) If the reporting frequency is otherwise weekly, the item is to be reported on every *business day* if (and for as long as) there is a *firm-specific liquidity stress* or *market liquidity stress* in relation to the *firm, branch* or group in question. (2) If the reporting frequency is otherwise monthly, the item is to be reported weekly if (and for as long as) there is a *firm-specific liquidity stress* or *market liquidity stress* in relation to the *firm*, *branch* or group in question. (3) A *firm* must ensure that it would be able at all times to meet the requirements for daily or weekly reporting under paragraph (1) or (2) even if there is no *firm-specific liquidity stress* or *market liquidity stress* and none is expected.
Note 10	If the report is on a solo basis (including by reference to the *firm's UK branch*) the reporting frequency is as follows: (1) weekly if the *firm* is a *standard frequency liquidity reporting firm*; and (2) monthly if the *firm* is a low frequency liquidity reporting *firm*.
Note 11	If the report is by reference to *the firm's UK DLG by modification* the reporting frequency is: (1) weekly if the *group liquidity standard frequency reporting conditions* are met; (2) monthly if the *group liquidity low frequency reporting conditions* are met.

16.12.7 **[R]** The applicable due dates for submission referred to in SUP 16.12.4R are set out in the table below. The due dates are the last day of the periods given in the table below following the relevant reporting frequency period set out in SUP 16.12.6R, unless indicated otherwise.

Data item	**Daily**	**Weekly**	**Monthly submission**	**Quarterly submission**	**Half yearly submission**	**Annual submission**
Annual reports and accounts of the *mixed-activity holding company*						80 business days (note 1) 7 months (note 2)
Solvency statement						3 months
CQ				1 month		
CY						7 months
FSA001				20 business days	45 business days	
FSA002				20 business days	45 business days	
FSA003			15 business days	20 business days	45 business days	
FSA004				20 business days	45 business days	
FSA005				20 business days	45 business days	
FSA006				20 business days		
FSA007						2 months
FSA008				20 business days (note 3) 45 business days (note 4)		
FSA011				15 business days		
FSA014					30 business days (note 3) 45 business days (note 4)	
FSA015				30 business days	45 business days	
FSA016					30 business days	
FSA017				20 business days	45 business days	
FSA018				45 business days		
FSA020					30 business days	
FSA021					30 business days	
FSA022					30 business days	
FSA023					30 business days	
FSA024					30 business days	

Data item	Daily	Weekly	Monthly submission	Quarterly submission	Half yearly submission	Annual submission
FSA025					30 business days	
FSA026					30 business days	
FSA028					30 business days	
FSA044				25 business days	25 business days	
FSA045				20 business days	45 business days	
FSA046					30 business days (note 3), 45 business days (note 4)	
FSA047	22.00 hours (London time) on the business day immediately following the last day of the reporting period for the item in question	22.00 hours (London time) on the business day immediately following the last day of the reporting period for the item in question	15 *business days*	15 *business days* or one *Month* (Note 5)		
FSA048	22.00 hours (London time) on the business day immediately following the last day of the reporting period for the item in question	22.00 hours (London time) on the business day immediately following the last day of the reporting period for the item in question	15 *business days*	15 *business days* or one *Month* (Note 5)		
FSA050			15 *business days*			
FSA051			15 *business days*			
FSA052		22.00 hours (London time) on the business day immediately following the last day of the reporting period for the item in question	15 *business days*			
FSA053				15 *business days*		
FSA054				15 *business days*		

Note 1	Applicable to *UK banks, dormant account fund operators* and electronic money institutions.
Note 2	Applicable to *non-EEA banks*.
Note 3	Applicable to unconsolidated and solo consolidated reports
Note 4	Applicable to *UK consolidation group* reports
Note 5	It is one *Month* if the report relates to a *non-UK DLG by modifications* or the *firm* has a *whole-firm liquidity modification*.

Regulated Activity Group 2.1

16.12.8 **[R]**

(1) The financial reporting requirements for *RAG* 2.1 activities for *insurers*, excluding *friendly societies*, are set out in *IPRU(INS)*.

(2) The financial reporting requirements for *RAG* 2.1 activities for *friendly societies* are set out in *IPRU(FSOC)*.

(3) A *UK insurance specia purpose vehicle* must submit a copy of its annual audited financial statements within 3 months of its *accounting reference date*, but the report is only required if it was audited as a result of a statutory provision other than under the *Act*.

Regulated Activity Group 2.2

16.12.9 **[R]** The applicable *data items* referred to in SUP 16.12.4R are set out according to type of *firm* in the table below.

The applicable reporting frequencies for submission of *data items* and periods referred to in SUP 16.12.4R are set out in the table below and are calculated from a *firm's accounting reference date*, unless indicated otherwise.

The applicable due dates for submission referred to in SUP 16.12.4R are set out in the table below. The due dates are the last day of the periods given in the table below following the relevant reporting frequency period.

	Member's advisor **(note 3)**		**the *Society* (note 3)**		
Description of *data item* and *data item*	**Frequency**	**Submission deadline**	**Description of *data item***	**Fre-quency**	**Submission deadline**
			Annual report and accounts	Annually	6 months after the Society's *accounting reference date*
			Annual Lloyd's return	Annually	6 months after the Society's *accounting reference date*
			Syndicate accounts and reports (note 2)	Annually	6 months after the Society's *accounting reference date*
Quarterly reporting statement	Quarterly	15 *business days* after the quarter end			
Balance Sheet					
FSA001 (notes 15, 20) or	Quarterly or half yearly (note 14)	(note 14)			
FSA029	Quarterly (note 14)	(note 14)			
Income statement					

	Member's advisor (note 3)		*the Society* (note 3)		
Description of *data item* and *data item*	**Frequency**	**Submission deadline**	**Description of *data item***	**Frequency**	**Submission deadline**
FSA002 (note 20), or	Quarterly or half yearly (note 14)	(note 14)			
FSA030	Quarterly	(note 14)			
Capital Adequacy					
FSA003 (notes 4, 20) or	Monthly, Quarterly or half yearly (note 14)	(note 14)			
FSA033 (note 12) or	Quarterly	(note 14)			
FSA034 (note 13) or	Quarterly	(note 14)			
FSA035 (note 13)	Quarterly	(note 14)			
Credit Risk					
FSA004 (notes 5, 20)	Quarterly or half yearly (note 14)	(note 14)			
Market risk					
FSA005 (notes 6, 20)	Quarterly of half yearly (note 14)	(note 14)			
Large Exposures					
FSA008 (note 20)	Quarterly	20 business days (note 19)			

Note 1 The *Society* must prepare its reports in the format specified in IPRU(INS) Appendix 9.11, unless Note 2 applies

Note 2 The *Society* must ensure that the annual syndicate accounts and reports are prepared in accordance with the Insurance Accounts Directive (Lloyd's Syndicate and Aggregate Accounts) Regulations 2008 (SI 2008/1950).

Note 3 A *member's adviser* must prepare its reports in accordance with, and in the format set out in, SUP 16 Annex 10 and as required by section 6 of that annex. Guidance notes for the completion of the reports is contained in SUP 16 Annex 11.

Note 4 Only *firms* subject to IPRU(INV) 4 report *data item* FSA003.

Note 5 This applies to a *firm* that is required to submit *data item* FSA003 and, at anytime within the 12 *months* up to its latest *accounting reference date* ("the relevant period"), was reporting *data item* FSA004 ("*Firm* A") or not reporting this item ("*Firm* B"). In the case of *Firm* A it must report this *data item* if one or both of its last two submissions in the relevant period show that the threshold was exceeded. In the case of *Firm* B it must report this item if both the last two submissions in the relevant period show that the threshold has been exceeded. The threshold is exceeded where *data element* 77A in *data item* FSA003 is greater than £10 million, or its currency equivalent, at the relevant reporting date for the *firm*.

Note 6	This applies to a *firm* that is required to submit *data item* FSA003 and, at anytime within the 12 *months* up to its latest *accounting reference date* ("the relevant period"), was reporting *data item* FSA005 ("*Firm* A") or not reporting this item ("*Firm* B"). In the case of *Firm* A it must report this *data item* if one or both of its last two submissions in the relevant period show that the threshold was exceeded. In the case of *Firm* B it must report this item if both the last two submissions in the relevant period show that the threshold has been exceeded. The threshold is exceeded where *data element* 93A in *data item* FSA003 is greater than £50 million, or its currency equivalent, at the relevant reporting date for the *firm*.
Note 7	[deleted]
Note 8	[deleted]
Note 9	[deleted]
Note 10	[deleted]
Note 11	[deleted]
Note 12	FSA033 is only applicable to *firms* subject to IPRU(INV) 3.
Note 13	Only applicable to *firms* subject to IPRU(INV) 5. FSA034 must be completed by a *firm* not subject to the exemption in IPRU(INV) 5.2.3(2)R. FSA035 must be completed by a *firm* subject to the exemption in IPRU(INV) 5.2.3(2)R.
Note 14	*BIPRU 50K firms* report half yearly on 30 *business days* submission, all other *BIPRU firms* on unconsolidated basis report quarterly on 20 *business days* submission. All *UK consolidation group* reports *report* half yearly on 45 *business days* submission. All other *firms* report monthly on 20 *business days* submission.
Note 15	This *data item* only applies to *BIPRU firms*.
Note 16	[deleted]
Note 17	[deleted]
Note 18	[deleted]
Note 19	*UK consolidation group* reports have 45 *business days* submission.
Note 20	*Firms* that are members of a *UK consolidation group* are also required to submit FSA001, FSA002, FSA003, FSA004, FSA005 and FSA008 on a *UK consolidation group* basis.

16.12.9A **[G]** A *Member's adviser* that is also a *BIPRU investment firm* will also fall under one of the higher number RAGs that apply to *BIPRU investment firms*. That means that it will have to report a number of *data items* in addition to the ones that it has to supply under RAG 2.2.

Regulated Activity Group 3

16.12.10 **[R]**

(1) SUP 16.12.11R to SUP 16.12.13R do not apply to:
   - (a) a *lead regulated* firm (except in relation to *data items* 47 to 55 (inclusive));
   - (b) *an OPS firm*;
   - (c) a local authority;
   - (d) a *service company*.

(2) A *lead regulated* firm and an *OPS firm* must submit a copy of its annual report and audited accounts within 80 *business days* from its *accounting reference date*.

(3) A *service company* must submit a copy of its annual audited financial statements within 6 months from its *accounting reference date*. However, the *firm* need only submit this if the report was audited as a result of a statutory provision other than the *Act*.

16.12.11 **[R]** The applicable *data items* referred to in SUP 16.12.4R are set out according to *firm* type in the table below:

Description of *data item*	*Firms* prudential category and applicable *data items* (note 1)							
	BIPRU firms (note 17)			*Firms* other than *BIPRU firms*				
	730K	**125K and *UCITS investment firms***	**50K**	**IPRU (INV) Chapter 3**	**IPRU (INV) Chapter 5**	**IPRU (INV) Chapter 9**	**IPRU (INV) Chapter 13**	**UPRU**
Annual report and accounts	No standard format			No standard format (note 19)	No standard format		No standard format	No standard format
Annual report and accounts of the *mixed-activity holding company* (note 10)	No standard format							
Solvency statement	No standard format (note 11)			No standard format (note 20)	No standard format (note 11)			No standard format (note 11)
Balance sheet	FSA001 (note 2)	FSA001 (note 2)	FSA001 (note 2)	FSA029 (note 18)	FSA029	FSA029	FSA029 (note 15) or Section A RMAR (note 15)	FSA029
Income statement	FSA002 (note 2)	FSA002 (note 2)	FSA002 (note 2)	FSA030 (note 18)	FSA030	FSA030	FSA030 (note 15) or Section B RMAR (note 15)	FSA030
Capital adequacy	FSA003 (note 2)	FSA003 (note 2)	FSA003 (note 2)	FSA033 (note 18)	FSA034 or FSA035 (note 14)	FSA031	FSA032 (note 15) or Sections D1 and D2 RMAR (note 15)	FSA036
Credit risk	FSA004 (notes 2, 3)	FSA004 (notes 2, 3)	FSA004 (notes 2, 3)					
Market risk	FSA005 (notes 2, 4)	FSA00 5 (notes 2, 4)	FSA00 5 (notes 2, 4)					

Description of *data item*	***Firms* prudential category and applicable *data items* (note 1)**							
	***BIPRU firms* (note 17)**			***Firms* other than *BIPRU firms***				
	730K	**125K and *UCITS investment firms***	**50K**	**IPRU (INV) Chapter 3**	**IPRU (INV) Chapter 5**	**IPRU (INV) Chapter 9**	**IPRU (INV) Chapter 13**	**UPRU**
Market risk – supplementary	FSA006 (note 5)	FSA006 (note 5)	FSA006 (note 5)					
Operational risk	FSA007 (notes 2, 6, 7)	FSA007 (notes 2, 6, 7)	FSA007 (notes 2, 6, 7)					
Large exposures	FSA008 (note 2)	FSA008 (note 2)	FSA008 (note 2)					
UK integrated group large exposures	FSA018 (note 12)	FSA018 (note 12)	FSA018 (note 12)					
Solo consolidation data	FSA016 (note 25)	FSA016 (note 25)	FSA016 (note 25)					
Pillar 2 questionnaire	FSA019 (note 8)	FSA019 (note 8)	FSA019 (note 8)					
Non-EEA sub-group	FSA028 (note 9)	FSA028 (note 9)	FSA028 (note 9)					
Threshold conditions							Section F RMAR (note 21)	
Client money and client assets	FSA039	FSA039	FSA039	FSA039 (note 18)	FSA039	FSA039	Section C RMAR (note 21) or FSA039	FSA039
CFTC	FSA040 (note 24)	FSA040 (note 24)	FSA040 (note 24)	FSA040 (note 24)	FSA040 (note 24)	FSA040 (note 24)	FSA040 (note 24)	FSA040 (note 24)
IRB portfolio risk	FSA045 (note 22)	FSA045 (note 22)	FSA045 (note 22)					
Securitisation	FSA046 (note 23)	FSA046 (note 23)	FSA046 (note 23)					
Daily Flows	FSA047 (Notes 26, 29 and 31)							

Description of *data item*	***Firms* prudential category and applicable *data items* (note 1)**							
	***BIPRU firms* (note 17)**			***Firms* other than *BIPRU firms***				
	730K	**125K and *UCITS investment firms***	**50K**	**IPRU (INV) Chapter 3**	**IPRU (INV) Chapter 5**	**IPRU (INV) Chapter 9**	**IPRU (INV) Chapter 13**	**UPRU**
Enhanced Mismatch Report	FSA048 (Notes 26, 29 and 31)							
Liquidity Buffer Qualifying Securities	FSA050 (Notes 27, 30 and 31)							
Funding Concentration	FSA051 (Notes 27, 30 and 31)							
Pricing data	FSA052 (Notes 27, 30 and 31)							
Retail and corporate funding	FSA053 (Notes 27, 30 and 31)							
Currency Analysis	FSA054 (Notes 27, 30 and 31)							
Systems and Controls Questionnaire	FSA055 (Note 28)							

Note 1	When submitting the completed *data item* required, a *firm* must use the format of the *data item* set out in SUP 16 Ann 24R. Guidance notes for completion of the data items are contained in SUP 16 Ann 25G.
Note 2	*Firms* that are members of a *UK consolidation group* are also required to submit this report on a *UK consolidation group* basis.
Note 3	This applies to a *firm* that is required to submit *data item* FSA003 and, at any time within the 12 *months* up to its latest *accounting reference date* ("the relevant period"), was reporting *data item* FSA004 ("*Firm* A") or not reporting this item ("*Firm* B"). In the case of *Firm* A it must report this *data item* if one or both of its last two submissions in the relevant period show that the threshold was exceeded. In the case of *Firm* B it must report this item if both the last two submissions in the relevant period show that the threshold has been exceeded. The threshold is exceeded where *data element* 77A in *data item* FSA003 is greater than £10 million, or its currency equivalent, at the relevant reporting date for the *firm*.
Note 4	This applies to a *firm* that is required to submit *data item* FSA003 and, at anytime within the 12 *months* up to its latest *accounting reference date* ("the relevant period"), was reporting *data item* FSA005 ("*Firm* A") or not reporting this item ("*Firm* B"). In the case of *Firm* A it must report this *data item* if one or both of its last two submissions in the relevant period show that the threshold was exceeded. In the case of *Firm* B it must report this item if both the last two submissions in the relevant period show that the threshold has been exceeded. The threshold is exceeded where data element 93A in *data item* FSA003 is greater than £50 million, or its currency equivalent, at the relevant reporting date for the *firm*.
Note 5	Only applicable to *firm*s with a *VaR model permission*.
Note 6	This will not be applicable to *BIPRU* limited activity *firms* or *BIPRU* limited licence *firm*s unless they have a waiver under BIPRU 6.1.2G.
Note 7	This is only applicable to a *firm* that has adopted, in whole or in part, either the *standardised approach*, *alternative standardised approach*, or *advanced measurement approach* under BIPRU 6.
Note 8	Only applicable to *BIPRU investment firms* that: (a) are subject to consolidated supervision under BIPRU 8, except those that are either included within the consolidated supervision of a group that includes a UK *credit institution*, or that have been granted an *investment firm consolidation waiver*; (b) have been granted an *investment firm consolidation waiver*; or (c) are not subject to consolidated supervision under BIPRU 8. A *BIPRU investment firm* under (a) must complete the report on the basis of its *UK consolidation group*. A *BIPRU investment firm* under (b) or (c) must complete the report on the basis of its solo position.
Note 9	This will be applicable to *firm*s that are members of a *UK consolidation group* on the reporting date.
Note 10	Only applicable to a *firm* whose ultimate parent is a mixed activity *holding company*.
Note 11	Only applicable to a *firm* that is a *sole trader* or a *partnership*, when the report must be submitted by each *partner*.
Note 12	Members of a *UK integrated group* should only submit this *data item* at the *UK integrated group* level.
Note 13	This does not apply to a *firm* subject to *IPRU(INV)* Chapter 13 which is an *exempt CAD firm*.
Note 14	FSA034 must be completed by a *firm* not subject to the exemption in IPRU(INV) 5.2.3(2)R. FSA035 must be completed by a *firm* subject to the exemption in IPRU(INV) 5.2.3(2)R.
Note 15	FSA029, FSA030 and FSA032 must be completed by a *firm* subject to *IPRU(INV)* Chapter 13 which is an *exempt CAD firm*. Section A or Section B RMAR and Sections D1 and D2 RMAR only apply to a *firm* subject to *IPRU(INV)* Chapter 13 which is not an *exempt CAD firm*.
Note 16	[deleted]

Note 17	An exempt *BIPRU commodity firm* will, by virtue of the definition of BIPRU TP 15, be exempt from completing FSA003 (and thus FSA004, FSA005, FSA006 and FSA007) for the duration of the transitional provision. It is however required to submit all other data items applicable according to the *firm*'s *BIPRU* classification including, for the avoidance of doubt, BIPRU TP 16.
Note 18	Except if the *firm* is an *adviser, local* or traded options market maker (as referred to in *IPRU(INV)* 3-60(4)R.
Note 19	In the case of an *adviser, local* or traded options market maker (as referred to in *IPRU(INV)* 3-60(4)R), it is only required from partnerships and bodies *corporate*, and then only if the report was audited as a result of a statutory provision other than under the *Act*.
Note 20	Only required in the case of an *adviser, local* or traded options market maker (as referred to in *IPRU(INV)* 3-60(4)R) that is a *sole trader*.
Note 21	[deleted]
Note 22	Only applicable to *firms* that have an *IRB permission.*
Note 23	Only applicable to *firms* that undertake securitisations.
Note 24	Only applicable to *firms* granted a *Part 30 exemption order* and operating an arrangement to cover forward profits on the London Metals Exchange.
Note 25	Only applicable to a *firm* that has a *solo consolidation waiver.*
Note 26	A *firm* must complete this item separately on each of the following bases (if applicable). (1) It must complete it on a solo basis. Therefore even if it has a *solo consolidation waiver* it must complete the item on an unconsolidated basis by reference to the *firm* alone. (2) If it is a *group liquidity reporting firm* in a *DLG by default* and is a *UK lead regulated firm*, it must complete the item on the basis of that group. (3) If it is a *group liquidity reporting firm* in a *UK DLG by modification*, it must complete the item on the basis of that group. (4) If it is a *group liquidity reporting firm* in a *non-UK DLG by modification*, it must complete the item on the basis of that group.
Note 27	A *firm* must complete this item separately on each of the following bases that are applicable. (1) It must complete it on a solo basis unless it is a *group liquidity reporting firm* in a *UK DLG by modification*. Therefore even if it has a *solo consolidation waiver* it must complete the item on an unconsolidated basis by reference to the *firm* alone. (2) If it is a *group liquidity reporting firm* in a *UK DLG by modification*, it must complete the item on the basis of that group.
Note 28	If it is a *non-ILAS BIPRU firm*, it must complete it on a solo basis. Therefore even if it has a *solo consolidation waiver* it must complete the item on an unconsolidated basis by reference to the *firm* alone.
Note 29	(1) This item must be reported in the reporting currency. (2) If any *data element* is in a currency or currencies other than the reporting currency, all currencies (including the reporting currency) must be combined into a figure in the reporting currency. (3) In addition, all *material currencies* (which may include the reporting currency) must each be recorded separately (translated into the reporting currency). However if: (a) the reporting frequency is (whether under a *rule* or under a *waiver*) quarterly or less than quarterly; or (b) the only *material currency* is the reporting currency; (3) does not apply. (4) If there are more than three *material currencies* for this *data item*, (3) only applies to the three largest in amount. A *firm* must identify the largest in amount in accordance with the following procedure. (a) For each currency, take the largest of the asset or liability figure as referred to in the definition of *material currency.* (b) Take the three largest figures from the resulting list of amounts. (5) The date as at which the calculations for the purposes of the definition of *material currency* are carried out is the last day of the reporting period in question.

(6) The reporting currency for this *data item* is whichever of the following currencies the *firm* chooses, namely USD (the United States Dollar), EUR (the euro), GBP (sterling), JPY (the Japanese Yen), CHF (the Swiss Franc), CAD (the Canadian Dollar) or SEK (the Swedish Krona).

Note 30 Note 29 applies, except that paragraph (3) does not apply, meaning that *material currencies* must not be recorded separately.

Note 31 Any changes to reporting requirements caused by a *firm* receiving an *intragroup liquidity modification* (or a variation to one) do not take effect until the first day of the next reporting period applicable under the changed reporting requirements for the *data item* in question if the *firm* receives that *intragroup liquidity modification* or variation part of the way through such a period. If the change is that the *firm* does not have to report a particular *data item* or does not have to report it at a particular *reporting level*, the *firm* must nevertheless report that item or at that *reporting level* for any reporting period that has already begun. This paragraph is subject to anything that the intra-group liquidity modification says to the contrary.

16.12.11A **[G]** The columns in the table in SUP 16.12.11 R that deal with *BIPRU 50K firms* and *BIPRU 125K firms* cover some liquidity items that only have to be reported by an *ILAS BIPRU firm*. In fact a *BIPRU 50K firm* and a *BIPRU 125K firm* cannot be an *ILAS BIPRU firm*. One reason for drafting the table in this way is that the classification of *firms* into *ILAS BIPRU firms* and *non-ILAS BIPRU firms* is not based on the classification into *BIPRU 50K firms*, *BIPRU 125K firms* and *BIPRU 730K firms* and the drafting of the table emphasises that. Also, the table covers consolidated reports and the conditions about what sort of group has to supply what type of liquidity report do not always depend on how the individual *firm* is classified.

16.12.12 **[R]** The applicable reporting frequencies for *data items* referred to in SUP 16.12.4 R are set out in the table below according to *firm* type. Reporting frequencies are calculated from a *firm's accounting reference date*, unless indicated otherwise.

Data item	**BIPRU 730K** ***firm***	**BIPRU 125K** ***firm*** **and** ***UCITS investment firm***	**BIPRU 50K** ***firm***	***UK consolidation group*** **or** ***defined liquidity group***	***Firms*** **other than** ***BIPRU firms***
Annual reports and accounts	Annually	Annually	Annually		Annually
Annual reports and accounts of the *mixed-activity holding company*	Annually	Annually	Annually		
Solvency statement	Annually	Annually	Annually		Annually
FSA001	Quarterly	Quarterly	Half yearly	Half yearly	
FSA002	Quarterly	Quarterly	Half yearly	Half yearly	
FSA003	Monthly	Quarterly	Half yearly	Half yearly	
FSA004	Quarterly	Quarterly	Half yearly	Half yearly	
FSA005	Quarterly	Quarterly	Half yearly	Half yearly	
FSA006	Quarterly	Quarterly	Quarterly	Quarterly	
FSA007	Annually (note 4)	Annually (note 4)	Annually (note 4)	Annually (note 4)	
FSA008	Quarterly	Quarterly	Quarterly	Quarterly	
FSA016	Half yearly	Half yearly	Half yearly		
FSA018	Quarterly	Quarterly	Quarterly		
FSA019	Annually	Annually	Annually	Annually	
FSA028	Half yearly	Half yearly	Half yearly		
FSA029					Quarterly
FSA030					Quarterly
FSA031					Quarterly
FSA032					Quarterly
FSA033					Quarterly

Data item	**BIPRU 730K** ***firm***	**BIPRU 125K** ***firm*** **and** ***UCITS investment firm***	**BIPRU 50K** ***firm***	***UK consolidation group*** **or** ***defined liquidity group***	***Firms*** **other than** ***BIPRU firms***
FSA034					Quarterly
FSA035					Quarterly
FSA036					Quarterly
FSA039	Half yearly	Half yearly	Half yearly		Half yearly
FSA040	Quarterly	Quarterly	Quarterly		Quarterly
FSA045	Quarterly	Quarterly	Half yearly	Half yearly	
FSA046	Half yearly	Half yearly	Half yearly	Half yearly	
FSA047	Daily, weekly, monthly or quarterly (Notes 5, 6 and 8)			Daily, weekly, monthly or quarterly (Notes 5, 7 and 8)	
FSA048	Daily, weekly, monthly or quarterly (Notes 5, 6 and 8)			Daily, weekly, monthly or quarterly (Notes 5, 7 and 8)	
FSA050	Monthly (Note 5)			Monthly (Note 5	
FSA051	Monthly (Note 5)			Monthly (Note 5	
FSA052	Weekly or monthly (Notes 5 and 9)			Weekly or monthly (Notes 5 and 10)	
FSA053	Quarterly (Note 5)			Quarterly (Note 5)	
FSA054	Quarterly (Note 5)			Quarterly (Note 5)	
FSA055	Annually (Note 5)			Annually (Note 5)	
Section A RMAR					Half yearly (note 2) Quarterly (note 3)
Section B RMAR					Half yearly (note 2) Quarterly (note 3)
Section C RMAR					Half yearly (note 2) Quarterly (note 3)
Section D1 and D2 RMAR					Half yearly (note 2) Quarterly (note 3)
Section F RMAR					Half yearly

Note 1 [deleted]

Note 2 Annual regulated business revenue up to and including £5 million.

Note 3 Annual regulated business revenue over £5 million.

Note 4	The reporting date for this *data item* is six months after a *firm's* most recent *accounting reference date*.
Note 5	Reporting frequencies and reporting periods for this *data item* are calculated on a calendar year basis and not from a *firm's accounting reference date*. In particular: (1) A week means the period beginning on Saturday and ending on Friday. (2) A month begins on the first day of the calendar month and ends on the last day of that month. (3) Quarters end on 31 March, 30 June, 30 September and 31 December. (4) Daily means each *business day*. All periods are calculated by reference to London time. Any changes to reporting requirements caused by a *firm* receiving an *intragroup liquidity modification* (or a variation to one) do not take effect until the first day of the next reporting period applicable under the changed reporting requirements if the *firm* receives that *intra-group liquidity modification* or variation part of the way through such a period, unless the *intra-group* liquidity modification says otherwise.
Note 6	If the report is on a solo basis the reporting frequency is as follows: (1) if the *firm* does not have an *intra-group liquidity modification* the frequency is: (a) weekly if the *firm* is a *standard frequency liquidity reporting firm*; and (b) monthly if the *firm* is a *low frequency liquidity reporting firm*; (2) if the *firm* is a *group liquidity reporting firm* in a *non-UK DLG by modification (firm level)* the frequency is: (a) weekly if the *firm* is a *standard frequency liquidity reporting firm*; and (b) monthly if the *firm* is a *low frequency liquidity reporting firm*; (3) the frequency is quarterly if the *firm* is a *group liquidity reporting firm* in a UK DLG by modification.
Note 7	(1) If the report is by reference to the *firm's DLG by default* the reporting frequency is: (a) weekly if the *group liquidity standard frequency reporting conditions* are met; (b) monthly if the *group liquidity low frequency reporting conditions* are met. (2) If the report is by reference to the *firm's UK DLG by modification* the reporting frequency is: (a) weekly if the *group liquidity standard frequency reporting conditions* are met; (b) monthly if the *group liquidity low frequency reporting conditions* are met. (3) If the report is by reference to the *firm's non-UK DLG by modification* the reporting frequency is quarterly.
Note 8	(1) If the reporting frequency is otherwise weekly, the item is to be reported on every *business day* if (and for as long as) there is a *firm specific liquidity stress* or *market liquidity stress* in relation to the *firm* or group in question. (2) If the reporting frequency is otherwise monthly, the item is to be reported weekly if (and for as long as) there is a *firm-specific liquidity stress* or *market liquidity stress* in relation to the *firm* or group in question. (3) A *firm* must ensure that it would be able at all times to meet the requirements for daily or weekly reporting under paragraph (1) or (2) even if there is no *firm-specific liquidity stress* or *market liquidity stress* and none is expected.
Note 9	If the report is on a solo basis the reporting frequency is as follows: (1) weekly if the *firm* is a *standard frequency liquidity reporting firm*; and (2) monthly if the *firm* is a low frequency liquidity reporting *firm*.
Note 10	If the report is by reference to the *firm's UK DLG by modification* the reporting frequency is: (1) weekly if the *group liquidity standard frequency reporting conditions* are met; (2) monthly if the *group liquidity low frequency reporting conditions* are met.

16.12.13 **[R]** The applicable due dates for submission referred to in SUP 16.12.4R are set out in the table below. The due dates are the last day of the periods given in the table below following the relevant reporting frequency period set out in SUP 16.12.12R, unless indicated otherwise.

Data item	**Daily**	**Weekly**	**Monthly submission**	**Quarterly submission**	**Half yearly submission**	**Annual submission**
Annual reports and accounts						80 business days
Annual reports and accounts of the *mixed-activity holding company*						7 months
Solvency statement						3 months
FSA001				20 business days	30 business days (note 1) 45 business days (note 2)	
FSA002				20 business days	30 business days (note 1) 45 business days (note 2)	
FSA003			15 business days	20 business days	30 business days (note 1) 45 business days (note 2)	
FSA004				20 business days	30 business days (note 1) 45 business days (note 2)	
FSA005				20 business days	30 business days (note 1) 45 business days (note 2)	
FSA006				20 business days		
FSA007						2 months
FSA008				20 business days (note 1); 45 business days (note 2)		

Data item	**Daily**	**Weekly**	**Monthly submission**	**Quarterly submission**	**Half yearly submission**	**Annual submission**
FSA016					30 business days	
FSA018				45 business days		
FSA019						2 months
FSA028					30 business days	
FSA029				20 business days		
FSA030				20 business days		
FSA031				20 business days		
FSA032				20 business days		
FSA033				20 business days		
FSA034				20 business days		
FSA035				20 business days		
FSA036				20 business days		
FSA039					30 business days	
FSA040				15 business days		
FSA045				20 business days	30 business days (note 1), 45 business days (note 2)	
FSA046					30 business days (note 1), 45 business days (note 2)	
FSA047	22.00 hours (London time) on the *business day* immediately following the last day of the reporting period for the item in question	22.00 hours (London time) on the *business day* immediately following the last day of the reporting period for the item in question	15 *business days*	15 *business days* or one *Month* (Note 3)		

Data item	**Daily**	**Weekly**	**Monthly submission**	**Quarterly submission**	**Half yearly submission**	**Annual submission**
FSA048	22.00 hours (London time) on the *business day* immediately following the last day of the reporting period for the item in question	22.00 hours (London time) on the *business day* immediately following the last day of the reporting period for the item in question	15 *business days*	15 *business days* or one *Month* (Note 3)		
FSA050			15 *business days*			
FSA051			15 *business days*			
FSA052		22.00 hours (London time) on the *business day* immediately following the last day of the reporting period for the item in question	15 *business days*			
FSA053					15 *business days*	
FSA054					15 *business days*	
FSA055						15 *business days*
Section A RMAR				30 business days	30 business days	
Section B RMAR				30 business days	30 business days	
Section C RMAR				30 business days	30 business days	
Section D1 and D2 RMAR				30 business days	30 business days	
Section F RMAR					30 business days	

Note 1 For unconsolidated and solo-consolidated reports.
Note 2 For *UK consolidation group* reports.
Note 3 It is one *Month* if the report relates to a *non-UK DLG by modification*.

Regulated Activity Group 4

16.12.14 **[R]**

(1) SUP 16.12.15 R to SUP 16.12.17 R do not apply to:
- (a) a *lead regulated* firm (except in relation to *data items* 47 to 55 (inclusive));
- (b) an *OPS firm*;
- (c) a local authority.

(2) A *lead regulated* firm and an *OPS firm* must submit a copy of its annual report and audited accounts within 80 *business days* from its *accounting reference date*.

16.12.15 **[R]** The applicable *data items* referred to in SUP 16.12.4R according to type of *firm* are set out in the table below:

	Firms prudential category and applicable data items (note 1)							
Description of data item	***BIPRU***			**Firms other than *BIPRU firms***				
	730K	**125K and *UCITS investment firms***	**50K**	***IPRU (INV)* Chapter 3**	***IPRU (INV)* Chapter 5**	***IPRU (INV)* Chapter 9**	***IPRU (INV)* Chapter 13**	**UPRU**
Annual report and accounts	No standard format (note 13)							
Annual report and accounts of the *mixed-activity holding company* (note 10)	No standard format							
Solvency statement (note 11)	No standard format				No standard format			No standard format
Balance sheet	FSA001 (note 2)	FSA001 (note 2)	FSA001 (note 2)	FSA029	FSA029	FSA029	FSA029 (note 15) or Section A RMAR (note 15)	FSA029 (note 16)
Income statement	FSA002 (note 2)	FSA002 (note 2)	FSA002 (note 2)	FSA030	FSA030	FSA030	FSA030 (note 15) or Section B RMAR (note 15)	FSA030 (note 16)
Capital adequacy	FSA003 (note 2)	FSA003 (note 2)	FSA003 (note 2)	FSA030	FSA034 or FSA035 (note 14)	FSA031	Section D1 and D2 RMAR or FSA032 (note 15)	FSA036
Credit risk	FSA004 (notes 2, 3)	FSA004 (notes 2, 3)	FSA004 (notes 2, 3)					
Market risk	FSA005 (notes 2, 4)	FSA005 (notes 2, 4)	FSA005 (notes 2, 4)					
Market risk – supplementary	FSA006 (note 5)	FSA006 (note 5)	FSA006 (note 5)					

	Firms prudential category and applicable data items (note 1)							
Description of data item	***BIPRU***			***Firms* other than *BIPRU firms***				
	730K	**125K and *UCITS investment firms***	**50K**	***IPRU (INV)* Chapter 3**	***IPRU (INV)* Chapter 5**	***IPRU (INV)* Chapter 9**	***IPRU (INV)* Chapter 13**	**UPRU**
Operational risk	FSA007 (notes 2, 6, 7)	FSA007 (notes 2, 6, 7)	FSA007 (notes 2, 6, 7)					
Large exposures	FSA008 (note 2)	FSA008 (note 2)	FSA008 (note 2)					
UK integrated group large exposures	FSA018 (note 12)	FSA018 (note 12)	FSA018 (note 12)					
Solo consolidation data	FSA016 (note 20)	FSA016 (note 20)	FSA016 (note 20)					
Pillar 2 questionnaire	FSA019 (note 8)	FSA019 (note 8)	FSA019 (note 8)					
Non-EEA sub-group	FSA028 (note 9)	FSA028 (note 9)	FSA028 (note 9)					
Threshold conditions							Section F RMAR (note 15)	
Volumes and type of business (note 21)	FSA038	FSA038	FSA038	FSA038	FSA038	FSA038	FSA038	FSA038
Client money and client assets	FSA039	FSA039	FSA039	FSA039	FSA039	FSA039	Section C RMAR (note 15) or FSA039	FSA039
Asset managers that use hedge fund techniques (note 21)	FSA041	FSA041	FSA041	FSA041	FSA041	FSA041	FSA041	FSA041
UCITS (note 22)	FSA042	FSA042	FSA042	FSA042	FSA042	FSA042	FSA042	FSA042

	Firms prudential category and applicable data items (note 1)							
Description of data item	***BIPRU***			***Firms* other than *BIPRU firms***				
	730K	**125K and *UCITS investment firms***	**50K**	***IPRU (INV)* Chapter 3**	***IPRU (INV)* Chapter 5**	***IPRU (INV)* Chapter 9**	***IPRU (INV)* Chapter 13**	**UPRU**
IRB portfolio risk	FSA045 (note 18)	FSA045 (note 18)	FSA045 (note 18)					
Securitisation	FSA046 (note 19)	FSA046 (note 19)	FSA046 (note 19)					
Daily Flows	FSA047 (Notes 23, 26 and 28)							
Enhanced Mismatch Report	FSA048 (Notes 23, 26 and 28)							
Liquidity Buffer Qualifying Securities	FSA050 (Notes 24, 27 and 28)							
Funding Concentration	FSA051 (Notes 24, 27 and 28)							
Pricing data	FSA052 (Notes 24, 27 and 28)							
Retail and corporate funding	FSA053 (Notes 24, 27 and 28)							
Currency Analysis	FSA054 (Notes 24, 27 and 28)							
Systems and Controls Questionnaire	FSA055 (Note 25)							

Note 1:	When submitting the completed *data item* required, a *firm* must use the format of the *data item* set out in SUP 16 Ann 24R. Guidance notes for completion of the *data items* are contained in SUP 16 Ann 25G.
Note 2	*Firms* that are members of a *UK consolidation group* are also required to submit this report on a *UK consolidation group* basis.
Note 3	This applies to a *firm* that is required to submit *data item* FSA003 and at anytime within the 12 *months* up to its latest *accounting reference date* ("the relevant period"), was reporting *data item* FSA004 ("*Firm* A") or not reporting this item ("*Firm* B"). In the case of *Firm* A it must report this *data item* if one or both of its last two submissions in the relevant period show that the threshold was exceeded. In the case of *Firm* B it must report this item if both the last two submissions in the relevant period show that the threshold has been exceeded. Threshold is exceeded if *data element* 77A in *data item* FSA003 is greater than £10 million, or its currency equivalent at the relevant reporting date for the *firm*.
Note 4	This applies to a *firm* that is required to submit *data item* FSA003 and at any time within the 12 *months* up to its latest *accounting reference date* ("the relevant period"), was reporting *data item* FSA005 ("*Firm* A") or not reporting this item ("*Firm* B"). In the case of *Firm* A it must report this *data item* if one or both of its last two submissions in the relevant period show that the threshold was exceeded. In the case of *Firm* B it must report this item if both the last two submissions in the relevant period show that the threshold has been exceeded. Threshold is exceeded if *data element* 93A in *data item* FSA003 is greater than £50 million, or its currency equivalent at the relevant reporting date for the *firm*.
Note 5	Only applicable to *firms* with a *VaR model permission*.
Note 6	This will not be applicable to *BIPRU* limited activity *firms* or *BIPRU* limited licence *firms* unless they have a waiver under BIPRU 6.1.2G.
Note 7	This is only applicable to a *firm* that has adopted, in whole or in part, either the *standardised approach*, *alternative standardised approach*, or *advanced measurement approach* under BIPRU 6.
Note 8	Only applicable to *BIPRU investment firms* that: (a) are subject to consolidated supervision under BIPRU 8, except those that are either included within the consolidated supervision of a group that includes a UK *credit institution*, or that have been granted an *investment firm consolidation waiver*; or (b) been granted an *investment firm consolidation waiver*; or (c) are not subject to consolidated supervision under BIPRU 8. A *BIPRU investment firm* under (a) must complete the report on the basis of its *UK consolidation group*. A *BIPRU investment firm* under (b) or (c) must complete the report on the basis of its solo position.
Note 9	This will be applicable to *firms* that are members of a *UK consolidation group* on the reporting date.
Note 10	Only applicable to a *firm* whose ultimate parent is a mixed activity *holding company*.
Note 11	Only applicable to a *firm* that is a *sole trader* or a *partnership*, when the report must be submitted by each *partner*.
Note 12	Members of a *UK integrated group* should only submit this *data item* at the *UK integrated group* level.
Note 13	This *data item* is applicable to all *firms* in this table except a *firm* subject to *IPRU(INV)* Chapter 13 which is not an *exempt CAD firm*.
Note 14	FSA034 must be completed by a *firm* not subject to the exemption in IPRU(INV) 5.2.3(2)R. FSA035 must be completed by a *firm* subject to the exemption in IPRU(INV) 5.2.3(2)R.
Note 15	FSA029, FSA030 and FSA032 must be completed by a *firm* subject to *IPRU(INV)* Chapter 13 which is an exempt CAD *firm*. Section A, B, C or F RMAR and Sections D1 and D2 RMAR only apply to a *firm* subject to *IPRU(INV)* Chapter 13 which is not an *exempt CAD firm*.

Note 16	[deleted]
Note 17	[deleted]
Note 18	Only applicable to *firms* that have an *IRB permission*.
Note 19	Only applicable to *firms* that undertake securitisations.
Note 20	Only applicable to a *firm* that has a *solo consolidation waiver*.
Note 21	Only applicable to *firms* that have a *managing investments permission*.
Note 22	Only applicable to *firms* that have *permission* for *establishing, operating or winding up a regulated collective investment scheme*.
Note 23	A *firm* must complete this item separately on each of the following bases (if applicable). (1) It must complete it on a solo basis. Therefore even if it has a *solo consolidation waiver* it must complete the item on an unconsolidated basis by reference to the *firm* alone. (2) If it is a *group liquidity reporting firm* in a *DLG by default* and is a *UK lead regulated firm*, it must complete the item on the basis of that group. (3) If it is a *group liquidity reporting firm* in a *UK DLG by modification*, it must complete the item on the basis of that group. (4) If it is a *group liquidity reporting firm* in a *non-UK DLG by modification*, it must complete the item on the basis of that group.
Note 24	A *firm* must complete this item separately on each of the following bases that are applicable. (1) It must complete it on a solo basis unless it is a *group liquidity reporting firm* in a *UK DLG by modification*. Therefore even if it has a *solo consolidation waiver* it must complete the item on an unconsolidated basis by reference to the *firm* alone. (2) If it is a *group liquidity reporting firm* in a *UK DLG by modification*, it must complete the item on the basis of that group.
Note 25	If it is a *non-ILAS BIPRU firm*, it must complete it on a solo basis. Therefore even if it has a *solo consolidation waiver* it must complete the item on an unconsolidated basis by reference to the *firm* alone.
Note 26	(1) This item must be reported in the reporting currency. (2) If any *data element* is in a currency or currencies other than the reporting currency, all currencies (including the reporting currency) must be combined into a figure in the reporting currency. (3) In addition, all *material currencies* (which may include the reporting currency) must each be recorded separately (translated into the reporting currency). However if: (a) the reporting frequency is (whether under a *rule* or under a *waiver*) quarterly or less than quarterly; or (b) the only *material currency* is the reporting currency; (3) does not apply. (4) If there are more than three *material currencies* for this *data item*, (3) only applies to the three largest in amount. A *firm* must identify the largest in amount in accordance with the following procedure. (a) For each currency, take the largest of the asset or liability figure as referred to in the definition of *material currency*. (b) Take the three largest figures from the resulting list of amounts. (5) The date as at which the calculations for the purposes of the definition of *material currency* are carried out is the last day of the reporting period in question. (6) The reporting currency for this *data item* is whichever of the following currencies the *firm* chooses, namely USD (the United States Dollar), EUR (the euro), GBP (sterling), JPY (the Japanese Yen), CHF (the Swiss Franc), CAD (the Canadian Dollar) or SEK (the Swedish Krona).
Note 27	Note 26 applies, except that paragraph (3) does not apply, meaning that *material currencies* must not be recorded separately.

Note 28 Any changes to reporting requirements caused by a *firm* receiving an *intragroup liquidity modification* (or a variation to one) do not take effect until the first day of the next reporting period applicable under the changed reporting requirements for the *data item* in question if the *firm* receives that *intra-group liquidity modification* or variation part of the way through such a period. If the change is that the *firm* does not have to report a particular *data item* or does not have to report it at a particular *reporting level*, the *firm* must nevertheless report that item or at that *reporting level* for any reporting period that has already begun. This paragraph is subject to anything that the intra-group liquidity modification says to the contrary.

16.12.15A **[G]** The columns in the table in SUP 16.12.15 R that deal with *BIPRU 50K firms* and *BIPRU 125K firms* cover some liquidity items that only have to be reported by an *ILAS BIPRU firm*. In fact a *BIPRU 50K firm* and a *BIPRU 125K firm* cannot be an *ILAS BIPRU firm*. One reason for drafting the table in this way is that the classification of *firms* into *ILAS BIPRU firms* and *non-ILAS BIPRU firms* is not based on the classification into *BIPRU 50K firms*, *BIPRU 125K firms* and *BIPRU 730K firms* and the drafting of the table emphasises that. Also, the table covers consolidated reports and the conditions about what sort of group has to supply what type of liquidity report do not always depend on how the individual *firm* is classified.

16.12.16 **[R]** The applicable reporting frequencies for *data items* referred to in SUP 16.12.15R are set out in the table below according to *firm* type. Reporting frequencies are calculated from a *firm's accounting reference date*, unless indicated otherwise.

Data item	***Firms'* prudential category**				
	BIPRU 730K *firm*	**BIPRU 125K *firm* and *UCITS investment firm***	**BIPRU 50K *firm***	***UK consolidation group* or *defined liquidity group***	***Firms* other than *BIPRU firms***
Annual report and accounts	Annually	Annually	Annually		Annually
Annual report and accounts of the *mixed-activity holding company*	Annually	Annually	Annually		
Solvency statement	Annually	Annually	Annually		Annually
FSA001	Quarterly	Quarterly	Half yearly	Half yearly	
FSA002	Quarterly	Quarterly	Half yearly	Half yearly	
FSA003	Monthly	Quarterly	Half yearly	Half yearly	
FSA004	Quarterly	Quarterly	Half yearly	Half yearly	
FSA005	Quarterly	Quarterly	Half yearly	Half yearly	
FSA006	Quarterly	Quarterly	Half yearly	Half yearly	
FSA007	Annually (note 4)	Annually (note 4)	Annually (note 4)	Annually (note 4)	
FSA008	Quarterly	Quarterly	Quarterly	Quarterly	
FSA016	Half yearly	Half yearly	Half yearly		
FSA018	Quarterly	Quarterly	Quarterly		
FSA019	Annually	Annually	Annually	Annually	
FSA028	Half yearly	Half yearly	Half yearly		
FSA029					Quarterly
FSA030					Quarterly
FSA031					Quarterly
FSA032					Quarterly
FSA033					Quarterly
FSA034					Quarterly
FSA035					Quarterly
FSA036					Quarterly
FSA038	Half yearly	Half yearly	Half yearly		Half yearly

Data item	*Firms'* **prudential category**				
	BIPRU 730K ***firm***	**BIPRU 125K** ***firm*** **and** ***UCITS investment firm***	**BIPRU 50K** ***firm***	***UK consolidation group*** **or** ***defined liquidity group***	***Firms*** **other than** ***BIPRU firms***
FSA039	Half yearly	Half yearly	Half yearly		Half yearly
FSA041	Annually	Annually	Annually		Annually
FSA042	Quarterly	Quarterly	Quarterly		Quarterly
FSA045	Quarterly	Quarterly	Half yearly	Half yearly	
FSA046	Half yearly	Half yearly	Half yearly	Half yearly	
FSA047	Daily, weekly, monthly or quarterly (Notes 5, 6 and 8)			Daily, weekly, monthly or quarterly (Notes 5, 7 and 8)	
FSA048	Daily, weekly, monthly or quarterly (Notes 5, 6 and 8)			Daily, weekly, monthly or quarterly (Notes 5, 7 and 8)	
FSA050	Monthly (Note 5)			Monthly (Note 5	
FSA051	Monthly (Note 5)			Monthly (Note 5	
FSA052	Weekly or monthly (Notes 5 and 9)			Weekly or monthly (Notes 5 and 10)	
FSA053	Quarterly (Note 5)			Quarterly (Note 5)	
FSA054	Quarterly (Note 5)			Quarterly (Note 5)	
FSA055	Annually (Note 5)			Annually (Note 5)	
Section A RMAR					Half yearly (note 2) Quarterly (note 3)
Section B RMAR					Half yearly (note 2) Quarterly (note 3)
Section C RMAR					Half yearly (note 2) Quarterly (note 3)
Section D1 and D2 RMAR					Half yearly (note 2) Quarterly (note 3)
Section F RMAR					Half yearly

Note 1 [deleted]

Note 2 Annual regulated business revenue up to and including £5 million.

Note 3 Annual regulated business revenue over £5 million.

Note 4 The reporting date for this *data item* is six months after a *firm's* most recent *accounting reference date*.

Note 5	Reporting frequencies and reporting periods for this *data item* are calculated on a calendar year basis and not from a *firm's accounting reference date*. In particular: (1) A week means the period beginning on Saturday and ending on Friday (2) A month begins on the first day of the calendar month and ends on the last day of that month. (3) Quarters end on 31 March, 30 June, 30 September and 31 December. (4) Daily means each *business day*. All periods are calculated by reference to London time. Any changes to reporting requirements caused by a *firm* receiving an *intragroup liquidity modification* (or a variation to one) do not take effect until the first day of the next reporting period applicable under the changed reporting requirements if the *firm* receives that *intra-group liquidity modification* or variation part of the way through such a period, unless the *intra-group* liquidity modification says otherwise.
Note 6	If the report is on a solo basis the reporting frequency is as follows: (1) if the *firm* does not have an *intra-group liquidity modification* the frequency is: (a) weekly if the *firm* is a *standard frequency liquidity reporting firm*; and (b) monthly if the *firm* is a *low frequency liquidity reporting firm*; (2) if the *firm* is a *group liquidity reporting firm* in a *non-UK DLG by modification (firm level)* the frequency is: (a) weekly if the *firm* is a *standard frequency liquidity reporting firm*; and (b) monthly if the *firm* is a *low frequency liquidity reporting firm*; (3) the frequency is quarterly if the *firm* is a *group liquidity reporting firm* in a UK DLG by modification.
Note 7	(1) If the report is by reference to the *firm's DLG by default* the reporting frequency is: (a) weekly if the *group liquidity standard frequency reporting conditions* are met; (b) monthly if the *group liquidity low frequency reporting conditions* are met. (2) If the report is by reference to the *firm's UK DLG by modification* the reporting frequency is: (a) weekly if the *group liquidity standard frequency reporting conditions* are met; (b) monthly if the *group liquidity low frequency reporting conditions* are met. (3) If the report is by reference to the *firm's non-UK DLG by modification* the reporting frequency is quarterly.
Note 8	(1) If the reporting frequency is otherwise weekly, the item is to be reported on every *business day* if (and for as long as) there is a *firm specific liquidity stress* or *market liquidity stress* in relation to the *firm* or group in question. (2) If the reporting frequency is otherwise monthly, the item is to be reported weekly if (and for as long as) there is a *firm-specific liquidity stress* or *market liquidity stress* in relation to the *firm* or group in question. (3) A *firm* must ensure that it would be able at all times to meet the requirements for daily or weekly reporting under paragraph (1) or (2) even if there is no *firm-specific liquidity stress* or *market liquidity stress* and none is expected.
Note 9	If the report is on a solo basis the reporting frequency is as follows: (1) weekly if the *firm* is a *standard frequency liquidity reporting firm*; and (2) monthly if the *firm* is a low frequency liquidity reporting *firm*.
Note 10	If the report is by reference to the *firm's UK DLG by modification* the reporting frequency is: (1) weekly if the *group liquidity standard frequency reporting conditions* are met; (2) monthly if the *group liquidity low frequency reporting conditions* are met.

16.12.17 **[R]** The applicable due dates for submission referred to in SUP 16.12.4R are set out in the table below. The due dates are the last day of the periods given in the table below following the relevant reporting frequency period set out in SUP 16.12.16R, unless indicated otherwise.

Data item	**Daily**	**Weekly**	**Monthly submission**	**Quarterly submission**	**Half yearly submission**	**Annual submission**
Annual report and accounts						80 business days
Annual report and accounts of the *mixed-activity holding company*						7 months
Solvency statement						3 months
FSA001				20 business days	30 business days (note 2); 45 business days (note 3)	
FSA002				20 business days	30 business days (note 2); 45 business days (note 3)	
FSA003			15 business days	20 business days	30 business days (note 2); 45 business days (note 3)	
FSA004				20 business days	30 business days (note 2); 45 business days (note 3)	
FSA005				20 business days	30 business days (note 2); 45 business days (note 3)	
FSA006				20 business days		
FSA007						2 months
FSA008				20 business days (note 2); 45 business days (note 3)		
FSA016					30 business days	

Data item	**Daily**	**Weekly**	**Monthly submission**	**Quarterly submission**	**Half yearly submission**	**Annual submission**
FSA018				45 business days		
FSA019						2 months
FSA028					30 business days	
FSA029				20 business days		
FSA030				20 business days		
FSA031				20 business days		
FSA032				20 business days		
FSA033				20 business days		
FSA034				20 business days		
FSA035				20 business days		
FSA036				20 business days		
FSA038					30 business days	
FSA039					30 business days	
				[deleted]		
FSA041						30 business days
FSA042				20 business days		
FSA045				20 business days	30 business days (note 2) 45 business days (note 3)	
FSA046					30 business days (note 2) 45 business days (note 3)	
FSA047	22.00 hours (London time) on the *business day* immediately following the last day of the reporting period for the item in question	22.00 hours (London time) on the *business day* immediately following the last day of the reporting period for the item in question	15 *business days*	15 *business days* or one *Month* (Note 4)		

Data item	Daily	Weekly	Monthly submission	Quarterly submission	Half yearly submission	Annual submission
FSA048	22.00 hours (London time) on the *business day* immediately following the last day of the reporting period for the item in question	22.00 hours (London time) on the *business day* immediately following the last day of the reporting period for the item in question	15 *business days*	15 *business days* or one *Month* (Note 4)		
FSA050			15 *business days*			
FSA051			15 *business days*			
FSA052		22.00 hours (London time) on the *business day* immediately following the last day of the reporting period for the item in question	15 *business days*			
FSA053				15 *business days*		
FSA054				15 *business days*		
FSA055						15 *business days*
Section A RMAR				30 business days	30 business days	
Section B RMAR				30 business days	30 business days	
Section C RMAR				30 business days	30 business days	
Section D1 and D2 RMAR				30 business days	30 business days	
Section F RMAR					30 business days	

Note 1 [deleted]
Note 2 For unconsolidated and solo-consolidated reports.
Note 3 For *UK consolidation group* reports.
Note 4 In one *Month* if the report relates to a *non-UK DLG by modification.*

Regulated Activity Group 5

16.12.18 **[R]**
(1) SUP 16.12.18AR does not apply to:
 (a) a *lead regulated* firm;
 (b) an *OPS firm*;
 (c) a local authority.

(2) A *lead regulated* firm and an *OPS firm* must submit a copy of its annual report and audited accounts within 80 *business days* from its *accounting reference date*.

16.12.18A **[R]** The applicable *data items*, reporting frequencies and submission deadlines referred to in SUP 16.12.4R are set out in the table below. Reporting frequencies are calculated from a *firm's accounting reference date*, unless indicated otherwise. The due dates are the last day of the periods given in the table below following the relevant reporting frequency period.

Description of data item	**Data item (note 1)**	**Frequency**	**Submission deadline**
Annual *report and* accounts	No standard format	Annually	80 *business days*
Balance Sheet	Sections A.1 and A.2 MLAR	Quarterly	20 *business days*
Income Statement	Sections B.0 and B.1 MLAR	Quarterly	20 *business days*
Capital Adequacy	Section C MLAR	Quarterly	20 *business days*
Lending – Business flow and rates	Section D MLAR	Quarterly	20 *business days*
Residential Lending to individuals – New business profile	Section E MLAR	Quarterly	20 *business days*
Lending – Arrears analysis	Section F MLAR	Quarterly	20 *business days*
Mortgage administration –Business profile	Section G MLAR	Quarterly	20 *business days*
Mortgage Administration –Arrears analysis	Section H MLAR	Quarterly	20 *business days*
Analysis of loans to customers	Section A3 MLAR	Quarterly	20 *business days*
Provisions analysis	Section B2 MLAR	Quarterly	20 *business days*
Fees and levies	Section J MLAR	Annually	30 *business days*

Note 1 When submitting the completed *data item* required, a *firm* must use the format of the *data item* set out in SUP 16 Ann 19AR. Guidance notes for the completion of the data items is set out in SUP 16 Ann19BG.

Regulated Activity Group 6

16.12.19 **[R]**

(1) SUP 16.12.19AR to SUP 16.12.21R do not apply to:

(a) a *lead regulated* firm;

(b) an *OPS firm*;

(c) a local authority.

(2) A *lead regulated* firm and an *OPS firm* must submit a copy of its annual report and audited accounts within 80 *business days* from its *accounting reference date*.

16.12.19A **[R]** The applicable *data items* referred to in SUP 16.12.4R are set out according to type of *firm* in the table below:

Description of data item	**Firm's prudential category and applicable data item (note 1)**				
	IPRU(INV) Chapter 3	**IPRU(INV) Chapter 5**	**IPRU(INV) Chapter 9**	**IPRU(INV) Chapter 13**	**UPRU**
Annual report and accounts	No standard format				
Solvency statement (note 6)		No standard format			No standard format
Balance sheet	FSA029	FSA029	FSA029	FSA029 or Section A RMAR (note 7)	FSA029

Description of data item	Firm's prudential category and applicable data item (note 1)				
	IPRU(INV) Chapter 3	IPRU(INV) Chapter 5	IPRU(INV) Chapter 9	IPRU(INV) Chapter 13	UPRU
Income statement	FSA030	FSA030	FSA030	FSA030 or Section B RMAR (note 7)	FSA030
Capital adequacy	FSA033	FSA034 or FSA035 (note 4)	FSA031	FSA032 (note 5) or Section D1 and D2 RMAR (note 7)	FSA036
Threshold conditions				Section F RMAR	
Client money and client assets	FSA039	FSA039	FSA039	Section C RMAR (note 7) or FSA039	FSA039

Note 1 When submitting the completed *data item* required, a *firm* must use the format of the *data item* set out in SUP 16 Ann 24R. Guidance notes for completion of the data items are contained in SUP 16 Ann 25G.

Note 2 This does not apply to a *firm* subject to IPRU(INV) Chapter 13 which is an *exempt CAD firm*.

Note 3 [deleted]

Note 4 FSA034 must be completed by a *firm* not subject to the exemption in IPRU(INV) 5.2.3(2)R.

FSA035 must be completed by a *firm* subject to the exemption in IPRU(INV) 5.2.3(2)R.

Note 5 FSA032 must be completed by a *firm* subject to IPRU(INV) Chapter 13 which is an *exempt CAD firm*.

Note 6 Only applicable to a firm that is a *partnership*, when the report must be submitted by each *partner*.

Note 7 FSA029 and FSA030 only apply to a *firm* subject to *IPRU(INV)* Chapter 13 which is an *exempt CAD firm* and Sections A and B RMAR only apply to a *firm* subject to *IPRU(INV)* Chapter 13 which is an *exempt CAD firm*.

16.12.20 **[R]** The applicable reporting frequencies for submission of *data items* referred to in SUP 16.12.4R are set out in the table below. Reporting frequencies are calculated from a *firm's accounting reference date*, unless indicated otherwise.

Annual report and accounts	Annually
Annual reconciliation	Annually
Solvency statement	Annually
FSA029	Quarterly
FSA030	Quarterly
FSA031	Quarterly
FSA032	Quarterly
FSA033	Quarterly
FSA034	Quarterly
FSA035	Quarterly
FSA036	Quarterly
FSA039	Half yearly
Section A RMAR	Half yearly (note 2) Quarterly (note 3)
Section B RMAR	Half yearly (note 2) Quarterly (note 3)

Section C RMAR	Half yearly (note 2) Quarterly (note 3)
Section D1 and D2 RMAR	Half yearly (note 2) Quarterly (note 3)
Section F RMAR	Half yearly

Note 1 [deleted]

Note 2 Annual regulated business revenue up to and including £5 million.

Note 3 Annual regulated business revenue over £5 million.

16.12.21 **[R]** The applicable due dates for submission referred to in SUP 16.12.4R are set out in the table below. The due dates are the last day of the periods given in the table below following the relevant reporting frequency period set out in SUP 16.12.20R.

Data item	**Quarterly submission**	**Half yearly submission**	**Annual submission**
Annual report and accounts			80 *business days*
Solvency statement			3 months
FSA029	20 *business days*		
FSA030	20 *business days*		
FSA031	20 *business days*		
FSA032	20 *business days*		
FSA033	20 *business days*		
FSA034	20 *business days*		
FSA035	20 *business days*		
FSA036	20 *business days*		
FSA039		30 *business days*	
FSA040	15 *business days*		
Section A RMAR	30 *business days*	30 *business days*	
Section B RMAR	30 *business days*	30 *business days*	
Section C RMAR	30 *business days*	30 *business days*	
Section D1 and D2 RMAR	30 *business days*	30 *business days*	
Section F RMAR		30 *business days*	

Regulated Activity Group 7

16.12.22 **[R]**

(1) SUP 16.12.22AR to SUP 16.12.24R do not apply to:

(a) a *lead regulated* firm (except in relation to *data items* 4 to 55 (inclusive));

(b) an *OPS firm*;

(c) a local authority.

(2) A *lead regulated* firm and an *OPS firm* must submit a copy of its annual report and audited accounts within 80 *business days* from its *accounting reference date*.

16.12.22A **[R]** The applicable *data items* referred to in SUP 16.12.4R are set out according to type of *firm* in the table below:

Description of *Data item*	***Firm* prudential category and applicable *data item* (note 1)**					
	BIPRU 730K *firm*	**BIPRU 125K *firm* and *UCITS investment firm***	**BIPRU 50K *firm***	***Exempt CAD firms* subject to *IPRU(INV)* Chapter 13**	***Firms* (other than *exempt CAD firms*) subject to *IPRU(INV)* Chapter 13**	***Firms* that are also in one or more of RAGS I to 6 and not subject to *IPRU(INV)* Chapter 13**
Annual report and accounts	No standard format			No standard format		
Annual report and accounts of the *mixed-activity holding company* (note 10)	No standard format					
Solvency statement	No standard format (note 11)					
Balance Sheet	FSA001 (note 2)	FSA001 (note 2)	FSA001 (note 2)		Section A RMAR	
Income Statement	FSA002 (note 2)	FSA002 (note 2)	FSA002 (note 2)	Section B RMAR	Section B RMAR	
Capital Adequacy	FSA003 (note 2)	FSA003 (note 2)	FSA003 (note 2)	FSA032	Section D1 and D2 RMAR	
Credit risk	FSA004 (notes 2, 3)	FSA004 (notes 2, 3)	FSA004 (notes 2, 3)			
Market risk	FSA005 (notes 2, 4)	FSA005 (notes 2, 4)	FSA005 (notes 2, 4)			
Market risk – supplementary	FSA006 (note 5)	FSA006 (note 5)	FSA006 (note 5)			
Operational risk	FSA007 (notes 2, 6, 7)	FSA007 (notes 2, 6, 7)	FSA007 (notes 2, 6, 7)			
Large exposures	FSA008 (note 2)	FSA008 (note 2)	FSA008 (note 2)			
UK integrated group large exposures	FSA018 (note 12)	FSA018 (note 12)	FSA018 (note 12)			
Solo consolidation data	FSA016	FSA016	FSA016			
Pillar 2 questionnaire	FSA019 (note 8)	FSA019 (note 8)	FSA019 (note 8)			

Description of *Data item*	*Firm* **prudential category and applicable** *data item* **(note 1)**					
	BIPRU 730K *firm*	**BIPRU 125K** *firm* **and** *UCITS investment firm*	**BIPRU 50K** *firm*	*Exempt CAD firms* **subject to** *IPRU(INV)* **Chapter 13**	*Firms* **(other than** *exempt CAD firms*) **subject to** *IPRU(INV)* **Chapter 13**	*Firms* **that are also in one or more of RAGS I to 6 and not subject to** *IPRU(INV)* **Chapter 13**
Non-EEA sub-group	FSA028 (note 9)	FSA028 (note 9)	FSA028 (note 9)			
Professional indemnity insurance	Section E RMAR	Section E RMAR	Section E RMAR		Section E RMAR	Section E RMAR
Threshold Conditions				Section F RMAR	Section F RMAR	
Training and Competence	Section G RMAR	Section G RMAR	Section G RMAR	Section G RMAR	Section G RMAR	Section G RMAR
COBS data	Section H RMAR	Section H RMAR	Section H RMAR	Section H RMAR	Section H RMAR	Section H RMAR
[deleted]	[deleted]	[deleted]	[deleted]	[deleted]	[deleted]	
Client money and client assets	Section C RMAR	Section C RMAR	Section C RMAR	Section C RMAR	Section C RMAR	
Fees and levies	Section J RMAR	Section J RMAR	Section J RMAR	Section J RMAR	Section J RMAR	
IRB portfolio risk	FSA045 (note 13)	FSA045 (note 13)	FSA045 (note 13)			
Securitisation	FSA046 (note 14)	FSA046 (note 14)	FSA046 (note 14)			
Daily Flows	FSA047 (Notes 16, 19 and 21)					
Enhanced Mismatch Report	FSA048 (Notes 16, 19 and 21)					
Liquidity Buffer Qualifying Securities	FSA050 (Notes 17, 20 and 21)					
Funding Concentration	FSA051 (Notes 17, 20 and 21)					
Pricing data	FSA052 (Notes 17, 20 and 21)					
Retail and corporate funding	FSA053 (Notes 17, 20 and 21)					

Description of *Data item*	*Firm* prudential category and applicable *data item* (note 1)					
	BIPRU 730K *firm*	**BIPRU 125K *firm* and *UCITS investment firm***	**BIPRU 50K *firm***	***Exempt CAD firms* subject to *IPRU(INV)* Chapter 13**	***Firms* (other than *exempt CAD firms*) subject to *IPRU(INV)* Chapter 13**	***Firms* that are also in one or more of RAGS I to 6 and not subject to *IPRU(INV)* Chapter 13**
Currency Analysis	FSA054 (Notes 17, 20 and 21)					
Systems and Controls Questionnaire	FSA055 (Note 18)					

Note 1 When submitting the completed *data item* required, a *firm* must use the format of the *data item* set out in SUP 16 Ann 24R, or SUP 16 Ann 18AR in the case of the RMAR. Guidance notes for completion of the data items are contained in SUP 16 Ann 25G, or SUP 16 Ann 18BG in the case of the RMAR.

Note 2 *Firms* that are members of a *UK consolidation group* are also required to submit this report on a *UK consolidation group* basis.

Note 3 This applies to a *firm* that is required to submit *data item* FSA003 and, at any tine within the 12 *months* up to its latest *accounting reference date* ("the relevant period"), was reporting *data item* FSA004 ("*Firm* A") or not reporting this item ("*Firm* B"). In the case of *Firm* A it must report this *data item* if one or both of its last two submissions in the relevant period show that the threshold was exceeded. In the case of *Firm* B it must report this item if both the last two submissions in the relevant period show that the threshold has been exceeded. The threshold is exceeded where *data element* 77A in *data item* FSA003 is greater than £10 million, or its currency equivalent at the relevant reporting date for the *firm*.

Note 4 This applies to a *firm* that is required to submit *data item* FSA003 and, at any time within the 12 *months* up to its latest *accounting reference date* ("the relevant period"), was reporting *data item* FSA005 ("*Firm* A") or not reporting this item ("*Firm* B"). In the case of *Firm* A it must report this *data item* if one or both of its last two submissions in the relevant period show that the threshold was exceeded. In the case of *Firm* B it must report this item if both the last two submissions in the relevant period show that the threshold has been exceeded. The threshold is exceeded where *data element* 93A in *data item* FSA003 is greater than £50 million, or its currency equivalent at the relevant reporting date for the *firm*.

Note 5 Only applicable to *firms* with a *VaR model permission*.

Note 6 This will not be applicable to *BIPRU* limited activity *firms* or *BIPRU* limited licence *firms* unless they have a waiver under BIPRU 6.1.2G.

Note 7 This is only applicable to a *firm* that has adopted, in whole or in part, either the *standardised approach*, *alternative standardised approach*, or *advanced modelling approach* under BIPRU 6.

Note 8 Only applicable to *BIPRU investment firms* that are:

(a) subject to consolidated supervision under BIPRU 8, except those that are either included within the consolidated supervision of a group that includes a UK *credit institution*, or that have been granted an *investment firm consolidation waiver*; or

(b) have been granted an *investment firm consolidation waiver*; or

(c) not subject to consolidated supervision under BIPRU 8.

A *BIPRU investment firm* under (a) must complete the report on the basis of its *UK consolidation group*. A *BIPRU investment firm* under (b) or (c) must complete the report on the basis of its solo position.

Note 9	This will be applicable to *firms* that are members of a *UK consolidation group* on the reporting date.
Note 10	Only applicable to a *firm* whose ultimate parent is a *mixed activity holding company*.
Note 11	Only applicable to a *firm* that is a *sole trader* or a *partnership*, when the report must be submitted by each *partner*.
Note 12	Members of a *UK integrated group* should only submit this *data item* at the *UK integrated group* level.
Note 13	Only applicable to *firms* that have an IRB permission.
Note 14	Only applicable to *firms* that undertake securitisations.
Note 15	This item only applies to *firms* that are subject to an *FSA* requirement to hold professional indemnity insurance and are not *exempt CAD firms*.
Note 16	A *firm* must complete this item separately on each of the following bases (if applicable). (1) It must complete it on a solo basis. Therefore even if it has a *solo consolidation waiver* it must complete the item on an unconsolidated basis by reference to the *firm* alone. (2) If it is a *group liquidity reporting firm* in a *DLG by default* and is a *UK lead regulated firm*, it must complete the item on the basis of that group. (3) If it is a *group liquidity reporting firm* in a *UK DLG by modification*, it must complete the item on the basis of that group. (4) If it is a *group liquidity reporting firm* in a *non-UK DLG by modification*, it must complete the item on the basis of that group.
Note 17	A *firm* must complete this item separately on each of the following bases that are applicable. (1) It must complete it on a solo basis unless it is a *group liquidity reporting firm* in a *UK DLG by modification*. Therefore even if it has a *solo consolidation waiver* it must complete the item on an unconsolidated basis by reference to the *firm* alone. (2) If it is a *group liquidity reporting firm* in a *UK DLG by modification*, it must complete the item on the basis of that group.
Note 18	If it is a *non-ILAS BIPRU firm*, it must complete it on a solo basis. Therefore even if it has a *solo consolidation waiver* it must complete the item on an unconsolidated basis by reference to the *firm* alone.
Note 19	(1) This item must be reported in the reporting currency. (2) If any *data element* is in a currency or currencies other than the reporting currency, all currencies (including the reporting currency) must be combined into a figure in the reporting currency. (3) In addition, all *material currencies* (which may include the reporting currency) must each be recorded separately (translated into the reporting currency). However if: (a) the reporting frequency is (whether under a *rule* or under a *waiver*) quarterly or less than quarterly; or (b) the only *material currency* is the reporting currency; (3) does not apply. (4) If there are more than three *material currencies* for this *data item*, (3) only applies to the three largest in amount. A *firm* must identify the largest in amount in accordance with the following procedure. (a) For each currency, take the largest of the asset or liability figure as referred to in the definition of *material currency*. (b) Take the three largest figures from the resulting list of amounts. (5) The date as at which the calculations for the purposes of the definition of *material currency* are carried out is the last day of the reporting period in question. (6) The reporting currency for this *data item* is whichever of the following currencies the *firm* chooses, namely USD (the United States Dollar), EUR (the euro), GBP (sterling), JPY (the Japanese Yen), CHF (the Swiss Franc), CAD (the Canadian Dollar) or SEK (the Swedish Krona).

Note 20	Note 19 applies, except that paragraph (3) does not apply, meaning that *material currencies* must not be recorded separately.
Note 21	Any changes to reporting requirements caused by a *firm* receiving an *intragroup liquidity modification* (or a variation to one) do not take effect until the first day of the next reporting period applicable under the changed reporting requirements for the *data item* in question if the *firm* receives that *intra-group liquidity modification* or variation part of the way through such a period. If the change is that the *firm* does not have to report a particular *data item* or does not have to report it at a particular *reporting level*, the *firm* must nevertheless report that item or at that *reporting level* for any reporting period that has already begun. This paragraph is subject to anything that the intra-group liquidity modification says to the contrary.

16.12.22B **[G]** The columns in the table in SUP 16.12.22A R that deal with *BIPRU 50K firms* and *BIPRU 125K firms* cover some liquidity items that only have to be reported by an *ILAS BIPRU firm*. In fact a *BIPRU 50K firm* and a *BIPRU 125K firm* cannot be an *ILAS BIPRU firm*. One reason for drafting the table in this way is that the classification of *firms* into *ILAS BIPRU firms* and *non-ILAS BIPRU firms* is not based on the classification into *BIPRU 50K firms*, *BIPRU 125K firms* and *BIPRU 730K firms* and the drafting of the table emphasises that. Also, the table covers consolidated reports and the conditions about what sort of group has to supply what type of liquidity report do not always depend on how the individual *firm* is classified.

16.12.23 **[R]** The applicable reporting frequencies for *data items* referred to in SUP 16.12.22AR are set out in the table below. Reporting frequencies are calculated from a *firm's accounting reference date*, unless indicated otherwise.

Data item	**Frequency**				
	Unconsolidated *BIPRU investment firm*	**Solo consolidated *BIPRU investment firm***	**UK consolidation group or defined liquidity group**	**Annual regulated business revenue up to and including £5 million**	**Annual regulated business revenue over £5 million**
Annual reports and accounts	No standard format				
Annual accounts of the *mixed-activity holding company*	No standard format				
Solvency statement	No standard format				
FSA001	Quarterly or half yearly (note 1)	Quarterly or half yearly (note 1)	Half yearly		
FSA002	Quarterly or half yearly (Note 1)	Quarterly or half yearly (note 1)	Half yearly		
FSA003	Monthly, quarterly or half yearly (note 2)	Monthly, quarterly or half yearly (note 2)	Half yearly		
FSA004	Quarterly or half yearly (note 1)	Quarterly or half yearly (note 1)	Half yearly		
FSA005	Quarterly or half yearly (note 1)	Quarterly or half yearly (note 1)	Half yearly		
FSA006	Quarterly	Quarterly	Quarterly		
FSA007	Annually (note 3)	Annually (note 3)	Annually (note 3)		
FSA008	Quarterly	Quarterly	Quarterly		
FSA016		Half yearly			

Data item	Frequency				
	Unconsolidated *BIPRU investment firm*	**Solo consolidated *BIPRU investment firm***	**UK consolidation group or defined liquidity group**	**Annual regulated business revenue up to and including £5 million**	**Annual regulated business revenue over £5 million**
FSA018	Quarterly	Quarterly	Quarterly		
FSA019	Annually	Annually	Annually		
FSA028	Half yearly	Half yearly			
FSA032				Quarterly	Quarterly
FSA045	Quarterly or Half yearly (note 1)	Quarterly or Half yearly (note 1)	Half yearly		
FSA046	Half yearly	Half yearly	Half yearly		
FSA047	Daily, weekly, monthly or quarterly (Notes 4, 5 and 7)	Daily, weekly, monthly or quarterly (Notes 4, 5, 7 and 10)	Daily, weekly, monthly or quarterly (Notes 4, 6 and 7)		
FSA048	Daily, weekly, monthly or quarterly (Notes 4, 5 and 7)	Daily, weekly, monthly or quarterly (Notes 4, 5, 7 and 10)	Daily, weekly, monthly or quarterly (Notes 4, 6 and 7)		
FSA050	Monthly (Note 4)	Monthly (Notes 4 and 10)	Monthly (Note 4)		
FSA051	Monthly (Note 4)	Monthly (Notes 4 and 10)	Monthly (Note 4)		
FSA052	Weekly or monthly (Notes 4 and 8)	Weekly or monthly (Notes 4, 8 and 10)	Weekly or monthly (Notes 4 and 9)		
FSA053	Quarterly (Note 4)	Quarterly (Notes 4 and 10)	Quarterly (Note 4)		
FSA054	Quarterly (Note 4)	Quarterly (Notes 4 and 10)	Quarterly (Note 4)		
FSA055	Annually (Note 4)	Annually(Notes 4 and 10)	Annually(Note 4)		
Section A RMAR				Half yearly	Quarterly
Section B RMAR				Half yearly	Quarterly
Section C RMAR				Half yearly	Quarterly
Section D1 and D2 RMAR				Half yearly	Quarterly
Section E RMAR	Half yearly	Half yearly	Half yearly	Half yearly	Quarterly
Section F RMAR	Half yearly	Half yearly	Half yearly	Half yearly	Half yearly
Section G RMAR	Half yearly	Half yearly	Half yearly	Half yearly	Half yearly

Data item	Frequency				
	Unconsolidated *BIPRU investment firm*	**Solo consolidated *BIPRU investment firm***	**UK consolidation group or defined liquidity group**	**Annual regulated business revenue up to and including £5 million**	**Annual regulated business revenue over £5 million**
Section H RMAR	Half yearly	Half yearly	Half yearly	Half yearly	Half yearly
Section J RMAR	Annually	Annually	Annually	Annually	Annually

Note 1: *BIPRU 730K firms* and *BIPRU 125K firms* – quarterly;

BIPRU 50K firms – half yearly.

Note 2: *BIPRU 730K firms* – monthly;

BIPRU 125K firms – quarterly;

BIPRU 50K firms – half yearly.

Note 3: The reporting date for this *data item* is six months after a *firm*'s most recent *accounting reference date*.

Note 4 Reporting frequencies and reporting periods for this *data item* are calculated on a calendar year basis and not from a *firm's accounting reference date*. In particular:

(1) A week means the period beginning on Saturday and ending on Friday.

(2) A month begins on the first day of the calendar month and ends on the last day of that month.

(3) Quarters end on 31 March, 30 June, 30 September and 31 December.

(4) Daily means each *business day*.

All periods are calculated by reference to London time.

Any changes to reporting requirements caused by a *firm* receiving an *intragroup liquidity modification* (or a variation to one) do not take effect until the first day of the next reporting period applicable under the changed reporting requirements if the *firm* receives that *intra-group liquidity modification* or variation part of the way through such a period, unless the *intra-group* liquidity modification says otherwise.

Note 5 If the report is on a solo basis the reporting frequency is as follows:

(1) if the *firm* does not have an *intra-group liquidity modification* the frequency is:

(a) weekly if the *firm* is a *standard frequency liquidity reporting firm*; and

(b) monthly if the *firm* is a *low frequency liquidity reporting firm*;

(2) if the *firm* is a *group liquidity reporting firm* in a *non-UK DLG by modification (firm level)* the frequency is:

(a) weekly if the *firm* is a *standard frequency liquidity reporting firm*; and

(b) monthly if the *firm* is a *low frequency liquidity reporting firm*;

(3) the frequency is quarterly if the *firm* is a *group liquidity reporting firm* in a UK DLG by modification.

Note 6 (1) If the report is by reference to the *firm's DLG by default* the reporting frequency is:

(a) weekly if the *group liquidity standard frequency reporting conditions* are met;

(b) monthly if the *group liquidity low frequency reporting conditions* are met.

(2) If the report is by reference to the *firm's UK DLG by modification* the reporting frequency is:

(a) weekly if the *group liquidity standard frequency reporting conditions* are met;

(b) monthly if the *group liquidity low frequency reporting conditions* are met.

(3) If the report is by reference to the *firm's non-UK DLG by modification* the reporting frequency is quarterly.

Note 7	(1) If the reporting frequency is otherwise weekly, the item is to be reported on every *business day* if (and for as long as) there is a *firm specific liquidity stress* or *market liquidity stress* in relation to the *firm* or group in question. (2) If the reporting frequency is otherwise monthly, the item is to be reported weekly if (and for as long as) there is a *firm-specific liquidity stress* or *market liquidity stress* in relation to the *firm* or group in question. (3) A *firm* must ensure that it would be able at all times to meet the requirements for daily or weekly reporting under paragraph (1) or (2) even if there is no *firm-specific liquidity stress* or *market liquidity stress* and none is expected.
Note 8	If the report is on a solo basis the reporting frequency is as follows: (1) weekly if the *firm* is a *standard frequency liquidity reporting firm*; and (2) monthly if the *firm* is a low frequency liquidity reporting *firm*.
Note 9	If the report is by reference to the *firm's UK DLG by modification* the reporting frequency is: (1) weekly if the *group liquidity standard frequency reporting conditions* are met; (2) monthly if the *group liquidity low frequency reporting conditions* are met.
Note 10	As specified in SUP 16.12.22A R, solo consolidation has no application to liquidity reporting. Therefore it does not make any difference to the reporting of this item whether or not the *firm* is solo consolidated.

16.12.24 **[R]** The applicable due dates for submission referred to in SUP 16.12.4R are set out in the table below. The due dates are the last day of the periods given in the table below following the relevant reporting frequency period set out in SUP 16.12.23R, unless indicated otherwise.

Data item	**Daily**	**Weekly**	**Monthly submission**	**Quarterly submission**	**Half yearly submission**	**Annual submission**
Annual reports and accounts						80 business days
Annual report and accounts of the *mixed-activity holding company*						7 months
Solvency statement					3 months	
FSA001				20 business days	30 business days (note 1);	
					45 business days (note 2)	
FSA002				20 business days	30 business days (note 1);	
					45 business days (note 2)	
FSA003			15 business days	20 business days	30 business days (note 1);	
					45 business days (note 2)	

Data item	**Daily**	**Weekly**	**Monthly submission**	**Quarterly submission**	**Half yearly submission**	**Annual submission**
FSA004				20 business days	30 business days (note 1); 45 business days (note 2)	
FSA005				20 business days	30 business days (note 1); 45 business days (note 2)	
FSA006				20 business days		
FSA007						2 months
FSA008				20 business days (note 1); 45 business days (note 2)		
FSA016					30 business days	
FSA018				45 business days		
FSA019						2 months
FSA028					30 business days	
FSA032				20 business days		
FSA045				20 business days	30 business days (note 1), 45 business days (note 2)	
FSA046					30 business days (note 1), 45 business days (note 2)	
FSA047	22.00 hours (London time) on the *business day* immediately following the last day of the reporting period for the *item in* question	22.00 hours (London time) on the *business day* immediately following the last day of the reporting period for the item in question	15 *business days*	15 *business days* or one *Month* (Note 3)		

Data item	**Daily**	**Weekly**	**Monthly submission**	**Quarterly submission**	**Half yearly submission**	**Annual submission**
FSA048	22.00 hours (London time) on the *business day* immediately following the last day of the reporting period for the item in question	22.00 hours (London time) on the *business day* immediately following the last day of the reporting period for the item in question	15 *business days*	15 *business days* or one *Month* (Note 3)		
FSA050			15 *business days*			
FSA051			15 *business days*			
FSA052		22.00 hours (London time) on the *business day* immediately following the last day of the reporting period for the item in question	15 *business days*			
FSA053				15 *business days*		
FSA054				15 *business days*		
FSA055						15 *business days*
Section A RMAR				30 business days	30 business days	
Section B RMAR				30 business days	30 business days	
Section C RMAR				30 business days	30 business days	
Section D1 and D2 RMAR				30 business days	30 business days	
Section E RMAR				30 business days	30 business days	
Section F RMAR					30 business days	
Section G RMAR					30 business days	
Section H RMAR					30 business days	
Section J RMAR						30 business days

Note 1	For unconsolidated and solo consolidated reports
Note 2	For *UK consolidation group* reports
Note 3	It is one *Month* if the report relates to a *non-UK DLG by modification.*

Regulated Activity Group 8

16.12.25 **[R]**

(1) SUP 16.12.25AR does not apply to:
  (a) a *lead regulated firm* (except in relation to data items 47 to 55 (inclusive));
  (b) an *OPS firm*;
  (c) a local authority;
  (d) a service company.

(2) A *lead regulated* firm and an *OPS firm* must submit a copy of its annual report and audited accounts within 80 *business days* from its *accounting reference date.*

(3) A *service company* must submit a copy of its annual audited financial statements (only if the report was audited as a result of a statutory provision other than under the Act) within 6 months from its *accounting reference date.*

16.12.25A **[R]** The applicable *data items* referred to in SUP 16.12.4R are set out according to type of *firm* in the table below:

Description of *data item*	*Firms* prudential category and applicable data item (note 1)							
	BIPRU			Firms other than *BIPRU firms*				
	730K	**125K**	**50K**	**IPRU (INV) Chapter 3**	**IPRU (INV) Chapter 5**	**IPRU (INV) Chapter 9**	**IPRU (INV) Chapter 13**	**UPRU**
Annual report and accounts	No standard format							
Annual report and accounts of the *mixed-activity holding company* (note 10)	No standard format							
Solvency statement (note 11)	No standard format							No standard format
Balance sheet	FSA001 (note 2)	FSA001 (note 2)	FSA001 (note 2)	FSA029	FSA029	FSA029	Section A RMAR (note 17) or FSA029	
Income statement	FSA002 (note 2)	FSA002 (note 2)	FSA002 (note 2)	FSA030	FSA030	FSA030	Section B RMAR (note 17) or FSA030	FSA030
Capital adequacy	FSA003 (note 2)	FSA003 (note 2)	FSA003 (note 2)	FSA033	FSA034 or FSA035 (note 14)	FSA031	Section D1 and D2 RMAR (note 17) or FSA032 (note 15)	FSA036
Credit risk	FSA004 (note 2, 3)	FSA004 (note 2, 3)	FSA004 (note 2, 3)					
Market risk	FSA005 (notes 2, 4)	FSA005 (notes 2, 4)	FSA005 (notes 2, 4)					
Market risk – supplementary	FSA006 (note 5)	FSA006 (note 5)	FSA006 (note 5)					
Operational risk	FSA007 (notes 2, 6, 7)	FSA007 (notes 2, 6, 7)	FSA007 (notes 2, 6, 7)					
Large exposures	FSA008 (note 2)	FSA008 (note 2)	FSA008 (note 2)					

Description of *data item*	*Firms* prudential category and applicable data item (note 1)							
	BIPRU			Firms other than *BIPRU firms*				
	730K	**125K**	**50K**	**IPRU (INV) Chapter 3**	**IPRU (INV) Chapter 5**	**IPRU (INV) Chapter 9**	**IPRU (INV) Chapter 13**	**UPRU**
UK Integrated group large exposures	FSA018 (note 12)	FSA018 (note 12)	FSA018 (note 12)					
Solo consolidation data	FSA016 (note 20)	FSA016 (note 20)	FSA016 (note 20)					
Pillar 2 questionnaire	FSA019 (note 8)	FSA019 (note 8)	FSA019 (note 8)					
Non-EEA sub-group	FSA028 (note 9)	FSA02 8 (note 9)	FSA028 (note 9)					
Threshold conditions							Section F RMAR (note 17)	
Client money and client assets	FSA039	FSA039	FSA039	FSA039	FSA039	FSA039	FSA039 or Section C RMAR (note 17)	FSA039
IRB portfolio risk	FSA045 (note 18)	FSA045 (note 18)	FSA045 (note 18)					
Securitisation	FSA046 (note 19)	FSA046 (note 19)	FSA046 (note 19)					
Daily Flows	FSA047 (Notes 21, 24 and 26)							
Enhanced Mismatch Report	FSA048 (Notes 21, 24 and 26)							
Liquidity Buffer Qualifying Securities	FSA050 (Notes 22, 25 and 26)							
Funding Concentration	FSA051 (Notes 22, 25 and 26)							
Pricing data	FSA052 (Notes 22, 25 and 26)							

Description of *data item*	*Firms* prudential category and applicable data item (note 1)							
	BIPRU			Firms other than *BIPRU firms*				
	730K	125K	50K	IPRU (INV) Chapter 3	IPRU (INV) Chapter 5	IPRU (INV) Chapter 9	IPRU (INV) Chapter 13	UPRU
Retail and corporate funding	FSA053 (Notes 22, 25 and 26)							
Currency Analysis	FSA054 (Notes 22, 25 and 26)							
Systems and Controls Questionnaire	FSA055 (Note 23)							

Note 1:	When submitting the completed *data item* required, a *firm* must use the format of the *data item* set out in SUP 16 Ann 24R. Guidance notes for completion of the data items are contained in SUP 16 Ann 25G.
Note 2	*Firms* that are members of a *UK consolidation group* are also required to submit this report on a *UK consolidation group* basis.
Note 3	This applies to a *firm* that is required to submit *data item* FSA003 and, at any time within the 12 *months* up to its latest *accounting reference date* ("the relevant period"), was reporting *data item* FSA004 ("*Firm* A") or not reporting this item ("*Firm* B"). In the case of *Firm* A it must report this *data item* if one or both of its last two submissions in the relevant period show that the threshold was exceeded. In the case of *Firm* B it must report this item if both the last two submissions in the relevant period show that the threshold has been exceeded. The threshold is exceeded if *data element* 77A in *data item* FSA003 is greater than £10 million, or its currency equivalent at the relevant reporting date for the *firm*.
Note 4	This applies to a *firm* that is required to submit *data item* FSA003 and, at any time within the 12 *months* up to its latest *accounting reference date* ("the relevant period"), was reporting *data item* FSA005 ("*Firm* A") or not reporting this item ("*Firm* B"). In the case of *Firm* A it must report this *data item* if one or both of its last two submissions in the relevant period show that the threshold was exceeded. In the case of *Firm* B it must report this item if both the last two submissions in the relevant period show that the threshold has been exceeded. The threshold is exceeded if *data element* 93A in *data item* FSA003 greater than £50 million, or its currency equivalent at the relevant reporting date for the *firm*.
Note 5	Only applicable to *firms* with a *VaR model permission*.
Note 6	This will not be applicable to *BIPRU* limited activity *firms* or *BIPRU* limited licence *firms* unless they have a waiver under BIPRU 6.1.2G.
Note 7	This is only applicable to a *firm* that has adopted, in whole or in part, either the *standardised approach*, *alternative standardised approach*, or *advanced modelling approach* under BIPRU 6
Note 8	Only applicable to *BIPRU investment firms* that : (a) are subject to consolidated supervision under BIPRU 8, except those that are either included within the consolidated supervision of a group that includes a UK *credit institution*, or that have been granted an *investment firm consolidation waiver*; or (b) have been granted an *investment firm consolidation waiver*; or (c) not subject to consolidated supervision under BIPRU 8. A *BIPRU investment firm* under (a) must complete the report on the basis of its *UK consolidation group*. A *BIPRU investment firm* under (b) or (c) must complete the report on the basis of its solo position.
Note 9	This will be applicable to *firms* that are members of a *UK consolidation group* on the reporting date.
Note 10	Only applicable to a *firm* whose ultimate parent is a *mixed activity holding company*.
Note 11	Only applicable to a *firm* that is a *sole trader* or a *partnership*, when the report must be submitted by each *partner*.
Note 12	Members of a *UK integrated group* should only submit this *data item* at the *UK integrated group* level.
Note 13	This does not apply to *firm* subject to *IPRU(INV)* Chapter 13 which is an *exempt CAD firm*.
Note 14	FSA034 must be completed by a *firm* not subject to the exemption in IPRU(INV) 5.2.3(2)R. FSA035 must be completed by a *firm* subject to the exemption in IPRU(INV) 5.2.3(2)R.
Note 15	FSA032 must be completed by a *firm* subject to *IPRU(INV)* Chapter 13 which is an *exempt CAD firm*.

Part II FSA Handbook Materials

Note 16 [deleted]

Note 17 This is only applicable to a *firm* subject to *IPRU(INV)* Chapter 13 that is not an *exempt CAD firm*.

Note 18 Only applicable to *firms* that have an *IRB permission*.

Note 19 Only applicable to *firms* that undertake securitisations.

Note 20 Only applicable to a *firm* that has a *solo consolidation waiver*.

Note 21 A *firm* must complete this item separately on each of the following bases (if applicable).

(1) It must complete it on a solo basis. Therefore even if it has a *solo consolidation waiver* it must complete the item on an unconsolidated basis by reference to the *firm* alone.

(2) If it is a *group liquidity reporting firm* in a *DLG by default* and is a *UK lead regulated firm*, it must complete the item on the basis of that group.

(3) If it is a *group liquidity reporting firm* in a *UK DLG by modification*, it must complete the item on the basis of that group.

(4) If it is a *group liquidity reporting firm* in a *non-UK DLG by modification*, it must complete the item on the basis of that group.

Note 22 A *firm* must complete this item separately on each of the following bases that are applicable.

(1) It must complete it on a solo basis unless it is a *group liquidity reporting firm* in a *UK DLG by modification*. Therefore even if it has a *solo consolidation waiver* it must complete the item on an unconsolidated basis by reference to the *firm* alone.

(2) If it is a *group liquidity reporting firm* in a *UK DLG by modification*, it must complete the item on the basis of that group.

Note 23 If it is a *non-ILAS BIPRU firm*, it must complete it on a solo basis.

Therefore even if it has a *solo consolidation waiver* it must complete the item on an unconsolidated basis by reference to the *firm* alone.

Note 24 (1) This item must be reported in the reporting currency.

(2) If any *data element* is in a currency or currencies other than the reporting currency, all currencies (including the reporting currency) must be combined into a figure in the reporting currency.

(3) In addition, all *material currencies* (which may include the reporting currency) must each be recorded separately (translated into the reporting currency). However if:

(a) the reporting frequency is (whether under a *rule* or under a *waiver*) quarterly or less than quarterly; or

(b) the only *material currency* is the reporting currency;

(3) does not apply.

(4) If there are more than three *material currencies* for this *data item*,

(3) only applies to the three largest in amount. A *firm* must identify the largest in amount in accordance with the following procedure.

(a) For each currency, take the largest of the asset or liability figure as referred to in the definition of *material currency*.

(b) Take the three largest figures from the resulting list of amounts.

(5) The date as at which the calculations for the purposes of the definition of *material currency* are carried out is the last day of the reporting period in question.

(6) The reporting currency for this *data item* is whichever of the following currencies the *firm* chooses, namely USD (the United States Dollar), EUR (the euro), GBP (sterling), JPY (the Japanese Yen), CHF (the Swiss Franc), CAD (the Canadian Dollar) or SEK (the Swedish Krona).

Note 25 Note 24 applies, except that paragraph (3) does not apply, meaning that *material currencies* must not be recorded separately.

Note 26 Any changes to reporting requirements caused by a *firm* receiving an *intragroup liquidity modification* (or a variation to one) do not take effect until the first day of the next reporting period applicable under the changed reporting requirements for the *data item* in question if the *firm* receives that *intra-group liquidity modification* or variation part of the way through such a period. If the change is that the *firm* does not have to report a particular *data item* or does not have to report it at a particular *reporting level*, the *firm* must nevertheless report that item or at that *reporting level* for any reporting period that has already begun. This paragraph is subject to anything that the intra-group liquidity modification says to the contrary.

16.12.25B **[G]** The columns in the table in SUP 16.12.25A R that deal with *BIPRU 50K firms* and *BIPRU 125K firms* cover some liquidity items that only have to be reported by an *ILAS BIPRU firm*. In fact a *BIPRU 50K firm* and a *BIPRU 125K firm* cannot be an *ILAS BIPRU firm*. One reason for drafting the table in this way is that the classification of *firms* into *ILAS BIPRU firms* and *non-ILAS BIPRU firms* is not based on the classification into *BIPRU 50K firms*, *BIPRU 125K firms* and *BIPRU 730K firms* and the drafting of the table emphasises that. Also, the table covers consolidated reports and the conditions about what sort of group has to supply what type of liquidity report do not always depend on how the individual *firm* is classified.

16.12.26 **[R]** The applicable reporting frequencies for *data items* referred to in SUP 16.12.25R are set out according to the type of *firm* in the table below. Reporting frequencies are calculated from a *firm's accounting reference date*, unless indicated otherwise.

	BIPRU 730K firm	***BIPRU 125K firm***	***BIPRU 50K firm***	***UK consolidation group* or *defined liquidity group***	***Firms* other than *BIPRU firms***
Annual reports and accounts	Annually	Annually	Annually		Annually
Annual reports and accounts of the *mixed-activity holding company*	Annually	Annually	Annually	Annually	
Solvency statement	Annually	Annually	Annually		Annually
FSA001	Quarterly	Quarterly	Half yearly	Half yearly	
FSA002	Quarterly	Quarterly	Half yearly	Half yearly	
FSA003	Monthly	Quarterly	Half yearly	Half yearly	
FSA004	Quarterly	Quarterly	Half yearly	Half yearly	
FSA005	Quarterly	Quarterly	Half yearly	Half yearly	
FSA006	Quarterly	Quarterly	Quarterly		
FSA007	Annually (note 4)	Annually (note 4)	Annually (note 4)	Annually (note 4)	
FSA008	Quarterly	Quarterly	Quarterly	Quarterly	
FSA016	Half yearly	Half yearly	Half yearly		
FSA018	Quarterly	Quarterly	Quarterly		
FSA019	Annually	Annually	Annually	Annually	
FSA028	Half yearly	Half yearly	Half yearly		
FSA029					Quarterly
FSA030					Quarterly
FSA031					Quarterly
FSA032					Quarterly
FSA033					Quarterly
FSA034					Quarterly
FSA035					Quarterly
FSA036					Quarterly
FSA039	Half yearly	Half yearly	Half yearly		Half yearly
FSA045	Quarterly	Quarterly	Half yearly	Half yearly	

	BIPRU 730K firm	***BIPRU 125K firm***	***BIPRU 50K firm***	***UK consolidation group* or *defined liquidity group***	**Firms other than *BIPRU firms***
FSA046	Half yearly	Half yearly	Half yearly	Half yearly	
FSA047	Daily, weekly, monthly or quarterly (Notes 5, 6 and 8)			Daily, weekly, monthly or quarterly (Notes 5, 7 and 8)	
FSA048	Daily, weekly, monthly or quarterly (Notes 5, 6 and 8)			Daily, weekly, monthly or quarterly (Notes 5, 7 and 8)	
FSA050	Monthly (Note 5)			Monthly (Note 5	
FSA051	Monthly (Note 5)			Monthly (Note 5	
FSA052	Weekly or monthly (Notes 5 and 9)			Weekly or monthly (Notes 5 and 10)	
FSA053	Quarterly (Note 5)			Quarterly (Note 5)	
FSA054	Quarterly (Note 5)			Quarterly (Note 5)	
FSA055	Annually (Note 5)			Annually (Note 5)	
Section A RMAR					Half yearly (note 2) Quarterly (note 3)
Section B RMAR					Half yearly (note 2) Quarterly (note 3)
Section C RMAR					Half yearly (note 2) Quarterly (note 3)
Section D1 and D2 RMAR					Half yearly (note 2) Quarterly (note 3)
Section F RMAR					Half yearly

Note 1	[deleted]
Note 2	Annual regulated business revenue up to and including £5 million.
Note 3	Annual regulated business revenue over £5 million.
Note 4	The reporting date for this *data item* is six months after a *firm's* most recent *accounting reference date*.
Note 5	Reporting frequencies and reporting periods for this *data item* are calculated on a calendar year basis and not from a *firm's accounting reference date*. In particular: (1) A week means the period beginning on Saturday and ending on Friday.

	(2) A month begins on the first day of the calendar month and ends on the last day of that month. (3) Quarters end on 31 March, 30 June, 30 September and 31 December. (4) Daily means each *business day*. All periods are calculated by reference to London time. Any changes to reporting requirements caused by a *firm* receiving an *intragroup liquidity modification* (or a variation to one) do not take effect until the first day of the next reporting period applicable under the changed reporting requirements if the *firm* receives that *intra-group liquidity modification* or variation part of the way through such a period, unless the *intra-group* liquidity modification says otherwise.
Note 6	If the report is on a solo basis the reporting frequency is as follows: (1) if the *firm* does not have an *intra-group liquidity modification* the frequency is: (a) weekly if the *firm* is a *standard frequency liquidity reporting firm*; and (b) monthly if the *firm* is a *low frequency liquidity reporting firm*; (2) if the *firm* is a *group liquidity reporting firm* in a *non-UK DLG by modification (firm level)* the frequency is: (a) weekly if the *firm* is a *standard frequency liquidity reporting firm*; and (b) monthly if the *firm* is a *low frequency liquidity reporting firm*; (3) the frequency is quarterly if the *firm* is a *group liquidity reporting firm* in a UK DLG by modification.
Note 7	(1) If the report is by reference to the *firm's DLG by default* the reporting frequency is: (a) weekly if the *group liquidity standard frequency reporting conditions* are met; (b) monthly if the *group liquidity low frequency reporting conditions* are met. (2) If the report is by reference to the *firm's UK DLG by modification* the reporting frequency is: (a) weekly if the *group liquidity standard frequency reporting conditions* are met; (b) monthly if the *group liquidity low frequency reporting conditions* are met. (3) If the report is by reference to the *firm's non-UK DLG by modification* the reporting frequency is quarterly.
Note 8	(1) If the reporting frequency is otherwise weekly, the item is to be reported on every *business day* if (and for as long as) there is a *firm specific liquidity stress* or *market liquidity stress* in relation to the *firm* or group in question. (2) If the reporting frequency is otherwise monthly, the item is to be reported weekly if (and for as long as) there is a *firm-specific liquidity stress* or *market liquidity stress* in relation to the *firm* or group in question. (3) A *firm* must ensure that it would be able at all times to meet the requirements for daily or weekly reporting under paragraph (1) or (2) even if there is no *firm-specific liquidity stress* or *market liquidity stress* and none is expected.
Note 9	If the report is on a solo basis the reporting frequency is as follows: (1) weekly if the *firm* is a *standard frequency liquidity reporting firm*; and (2) monthly if the *firm* is a low frequency liquidity reporting *firm*.
Note 10	If the report is by reference to the *firm's UK DLG by modification* the reporting frequency is: (1) weekly if the *group liquidity standard frequency reporting conditions* are met; (2) monthly if the *group liquidity low frequency reporting conditions* are met.

16.12.27 **[R]** The applicable due dates for submission referred to in SUP 16.12.4R are set out in the table below. The due dates are the last day of the periods given in the table below following the relevant reporting frequency period set out in SUP 16.12.26R, unless indicated otherwise.

Data item	**Daily**	**Weekly**	**Monthly submission**	**Quarterly submission**	**Half yearly submission**	**Annual submission**
Annual reports and accounts						80 business days
Annual report and accounts of the *mixed-activity holding company*						
Solvency statement						3 months
FSA001				20 business days	30 business days (note 1);	
					45 business days (note 2)	
FSA002				20 business days	30 business days (note 1);	
					45 business days (note 2)	
FSA003			15 business days	20 business days	30 business days (note 1);	
					45 business days (note 2)	
FSA004				20 business days	30 business days (note 1);	
					45 business days (note 2)	
FSA005				20 business days	30 business days (note 1);	
					45 business days (note 2)	
FSA006				20 business days	30 business days (note 1);	
					45 business days (note 2)	
FSA007						2 months
FSA008				20 business days (note 1);		
				45 business days (note 2)		
FSA016					30 business days	
FSA018				45 business days		
FSA019						2 months

Data item	**Daily**	**Weekly**	**Monthly submission**	**Quarterly submission**	**Half yearly submission**	**Annual submission**
FSA028					30 business days	
FSA029				20 business days		
FSA030				20 business days		
FSA031				20 business days		
FSA032				20 business days		
FSA033				20 business days		
FSA034				20 business days		
FSA035				20 business days		
FSA036				20 business days		
FSA039					30 business days	
FSA045				20 business days	30 business days (note 1), 45 business days (note 2)	
FSA046					30 business days (note 1), 45 business days (note 2)	
FSA047	22.00 hours (London time) on the *business day* immediately following the last day of the reporting period for the item in question	22.00 hours (London time) on the *business day* immediately following the last day of the reporting period for the item in question	15 *business days*	15 *business days* or one *Month* (Note 3)		
FSA048	22.00 hours (London time) on the *business day* immediately following the last day of the reporting period for the item in question	22.00 hours (London time) on the *business day* immediately following the last day of the reporting period for the item in question	15 *business days*	15 *business days* or one *Month* (Note 3)		
FSA050			15 *business days*			

Part II FSA Handbook Materials

Data item	Daily	Weekly	Monthly submission	Quarterly submission	Half yearly submission	Annual submission
FSA051			15 *business days*			
FSA052		22.00 hours (London time) on the *business day* immediately following the last day of the reporting period for the item in question	15 *business days*			
FSA053					15 *business days*	
FSA054					15 *business days*	
FSA055						15 *business days*
Section A RMAR				30 business days	30 business days	
Section B RMAR				30 business days	30 business days	
Section C RMAR				30 business days	30 business days	
Section D1 and D2 RMAR				30 business days	30 business days	
Section F RMAR					30 business days	

Note 1 For unconsolidated and solo consolidated reports.

Note 2 For *UK consolidation group* reports

Note 3 It is one *Month* if the report to a *non-UK DL by modification.*

Regulated Activity Group 9

16.12.28 **[R]**

(1) SUP 16.12.28AR does not apply to:
 (a) a *lead regulated* firm;
 (b) an *OPS firm*;
 (c) a local authority;
 (d) a *third party processor* in respect of any *home finance activity*.

(2) A *lead regulated* firm and an *OPS firm* must submit a copy of its annual report and audited accounts within 80 *business days* from its *accounting reference date.*

16.12.28A **[R]** The applicable *data items*, reporting frequencies and submission deadlines referred to in SUP 16.12.4R are set out in the table below. Reporting frequencies are calculated from a *firm's accounting reference date*, unless indicated otherwise. The due dates are the last day of the periods given in the table below following the relevant reporting frequency period.

Description of data item	Data item (note 1)	Frequency		Submission deadline
		Annual regulated business revenue up to and including £5 million	Annual regulated business revenue over £5 million	

Description of data item	Data item (note 1)	Frequency		Submission deadline
Balance Sheet	Section A RMAR	Half yearly	Quarterly	30 *business days*
Income Statement	Section B RMAR	Half yearly	Quarterly	30 *business days*
Capital Adequacy	Section D1 RMAR	Half yearly	Quarterly	30 *business days*
Professional indemnity insurance (note 2)	Section E RMAR	Half yearly	Quarterly	30 *business days*
Threshold Conditions	Section F RMAR	Half yearly	Half yearly	30 *business days*
Training and Competence	Section G RMAR	Half yearly	Half yearly	30 *business days*
COBS data	Section H RMAR	Half yearly	Half yearly	30 *business days*
Supplementary product sales data	Section I RMAR	Half yearly	Annually	30 *business days*
Client money and client assets	Section C RMAR	Half yearly	Quarterly	30 *business days*
Fees and levies	Section J RMAR	Annually	Annually	30 *business days*

Note 1 When submitting the completed *data item* required, a *firm* must use the format of the *data item* set out in SUP 16 Ann 18AR. Guidance notes for the completion of the data items is set out in SUP 16 Ann 18BG.

Note 2 This item only applies to *firms* that may be subject to an *FSA* requirement to hold professional indemnity insurance and are not *exempt CAD firms*.

Regulated Activity Group 10

16.12.29 **[G] Recognised bodies** (RIEs and RCHs) have separate reporting requirements agreed between the *recognised body* and the *FSA*.

Authorised professional firms

16.12.30 **[R]**

(1) An *authorised professional firm*, other than one that must comply with IPRU(INV) 3, 5 or 13 in accordance with IPRU(INV) 2.1.4R, must submit an annual questionnaire, contained in SUP 16 Ann 9R, unless:
- (a) its only *regulated activities* are one or more of:
  - (i) *insurance mediation*;
  - (ii) *mortgage mediation*;
  - (iii) *retail investment*;
  - (iv) *mortgage lending*;
  - (v) *mortgage administration*; or
- (b) its "main business" as determined by IPRU(INV) 2.1.2R(3) is *advising* on, or *arranging deals* in, *packaged products*, or *managing investments* for *private customers*;

in which case the *authorised professional firm* must complete the appropriate report specified in SUP 16.12.31R.

(2) The due date for submission of the annual questionnaire is four months after the *firm's accounting reference date*.

(3) An *authorised professional firm* must also, where applicable, submit the other report to the *FSA* in accordance with SUP 16.12.31R in respect of the other *regulated activities* it undertakes under (1)(a).

16.12.30A **[R]** An *authorised professional firm* that must comply with IPRU(INV) 3, 5, 10 or 13 in accordance with IPRU(INV) 2.1.4R must submit the relevant reports in SUP 16.12.4R to SUP 16.12.29R, according to the *regulated activity groups* that its business falls into.

16.12.31 **[R]** Table of data items from an *authorised professional firm*

Report	Return (note 1)	Frequency	Due date
Adequate information relating to the following activities:	RMAR (Note 3)	Half yearly (quarterly for sections A to E for larger *firms*, subject to Note 3 exemptions) (note 2)	For half yearly report: 30 *business days* after period end. For quarterly report: 30 *business days* after quarter end
(1) *insurance mediation activity*;			
(2) *mortgage mediation activity*;			
(3) *Retail investment activity*;			
(4) advising on, or arranging deals in, *packaged products*, or *managing investments* for *private customers* where these activities are the *authorised professional firm's* "main business" as determined by IPRU(INV) 2.1.2 R(3)			
Adequate information relating to mortgage lending and mortgage administration	MLAR	Quarterly	20 *business days* after quarter end

Note 1 When giving the report required, a *firm* must use the return indicated. The RMAR and MLAR are located at SUP 16 Ann 18AR and SUP 16 Ann 19AR respectively. Guidance on the completion of the *data items* are located at SUP 16 Ann 18BG and SUP 16 Ann 19BG respectively.

Note 2 For the purposes of RMAR reporting, a larger *firm* is a *firm* whose annual regulated business revenue in its previous financial year was greater than £5m. Annual regulated business revenue for these purposes is a *firm's* total revenue relating to *insurance mediation activity, mortgage mediation activity* and *retail investment activity*.

Note 3 A *firm* which submits an MLAR is not required to submit sections A and B of the RMAR.

Note 4 Reporting dates are calculated from a firm's *accounting reference date*.

Financial conglomerates

16.12.32 **[R]**

(1) A *firm* that is a member of a *financial conglomerate* must submit financial reports to the *FSA* in accordance with the table in SUP 16.12.33R if:
  (a) it is at the head of an *FSA regulated EEA financial conglomerate*; or
  (b) its *Part IV permission* contains a relevant *requirement*.

(2) In (1)(b), a relevant *requirement* is one which:
  (a) applies SUP 16.12.33R to the *firm*; or
  (b) applies SUP 16.12.33R to the *firm* unless the *mixed financial holding company* of the *financial conglomerate* to which the *firm* belongs submits the report required under this *rule* (as if the *rule* applied to it).

16.12.33 **[R]** Financial reports from a member of a financial conglomerate (see SUP 16.12.32R)

Content of Report	Form (Note 1)	Frequency	Due Date
Calculation of supplementary capital adequacy requirements in accordance with one of the *four technical calculation methods*	Note 2	Note 5	Note 5
Identification of significant *risk concentration* levels	Note 3	Yearly	4 months after year end

Content of Report	Form (Note 1)	Frequency	Due Date
Identification of significant *intra-group transactions*	Note 4	Yearly	4 months after year end
Report on compliance with *GENPRU* 3.1.35R where it applies	Note 6	Note 5	Note 5

Note 1 When giving the report required, a *firm* must use the form indicated, if any.

Note 2 If Part 1 of *GENPRU* 3 Annex 1R (method 1), Part 2 of *GENPRU* 3 Annex 1R (method 2), or Part 3 of *GENPRU* 3 Annex 1R (method 3) applies, there is no specific form. Adequate information must be provided, and each *financial conglomerate* for which the *FSA* is the *co-ordinator* must discuss with the *FSA* how to do this.

If Part 4 of *GENPRU* 3 Annex 1R applies (method 4):

(1) a *banking and investment services conglomerate* must use FSA003; and

(2) an *insurance conglomerate* must use:

(a) (where SUP 16.12.32(1)(a) applies), Forms 1, 2 and 3 in Appendix 9.1 of *IPRU(INS)* prepared in accordance with *IPRU (INS)* 9.35(1); or

(b) (in any other case),the Insurance Group Capital Adequacy Reporting Form (Form 95) in Appendix 9.9 of *IPRU(INS)*

For the purposes of (b), *rules* 9.40(1), 9.40(1A), 9.40(3) and 9.40(4) of *IPRU(INS)* apply as they would if the *insurance conglomerate* were an *insurance group*.

Note 3 Rather than specifying a standard format for each *financial conglomerate* to use, each *financial conglomerate* for which the *FSA* is the *co-ordinator* must discuss with the *FSA* the form of the information to be reported. This should mean that usual information management systems of the *financial conglomerate* can be used to the extent possible to generate and analyse the information required. When reviewing the *risk concentration* levels, the *FSA* will in particular monitor the possible risk of contagion in the *financial conglomerate*, the risk of a conflict of interests, the risk of circumvention of sectoral *rules*, and the level or volume of risks.

Note 4 For the purposes of this reporting requirement, an *intra-group transaction* will be presumed to be significant if its amount exceeds 5% of the total amount of capital adequacy requirements at the level of the *financial conglomerate*. Rather than specifying a standard format for each *financial conglomerate* to use, each *financial conglomerate* for which the *FSA* is the *co-ordinator* must discuss with the *FSA* the form of the information to be reported. This should mean that usual information management systems of the *financial conglomerate* can be used to the extent possible to generate and analyse the information required. When reviewing the *intra-group transactions*, the *FSA* will in particular monitor the possible risk of contagion in the *financial conglomerate*, the risk of a conflict of interests, the risk of circumvention of *sectoral rules*, and the level or volume of risks.

Note 5 The frequency and due date will be as follows:

(1) *banking and investment services conglomerate*: frequency is half-yearly with due date 45 *business days* after period end

(2) *insurance conglomerate*: frequency is yearly with due date four months after period end for the capital adequacy return and three months after period end for the report on compliance with *GENPRU* 3.1.[35]R where it applies.

Note 6 Adequate information must be added as a separate item to the relevant form for sectoral reporting.

SUP 16 Annex 1R

SUP 16 Ann 1 **[R]** [deleted]

SUP 16 Annex 2G

SUP 16 Ann 2 **[G]** [deleted]

SUP 16 Annex 3R

SUP 16 Ann 3 **[R]** [deleted]

Part II FSA Handbook Materials

SUP 16 Annex 4G

SUP 16 Ann 4 **[G]** [deleted]

SUP 16 Annex 5R

SUP 16 Ann 5 **[R]** [deleted]

SUP 16 Annex 6R
Reporting requirements

SUP 16 Ann 6 **[R]**

[This annex consists of one or more forms which can be accessed through the 'Forms' link at www.fsa.gov.uk/handbook.]

SUP 16 Annex 7R
Section 5: Personal investment firms: requirements applying to the completion of reports

SUP 16 Ann 7 **[R]** [deleted]

SUP 16 Annex 8G
Reporting requirements

SUP 16 Ann 8 **[G]** [deleted]

SUP 16 Annex 9R
Reporting requirements

SUP 16 Ann 9 **[R]**

[This annex consists of one or more forms which can be accessed through the 'Forms' link at www.fsa.gov.uk/handbook.]

SUP 16 Annex 10R
Securities and Futures Firms' Reporting Forms and Requirements Applying to their Completion

16 Ann 10 **[R]**

[This annex consists of one or more forms which can be accessed through the 'Forms' link at www.fsa.gov.uk/handbook.]

SUP 16 Annex 11G
Reporting requirements

SUP 16 Ann 11 **[G]**

[This annex consists of one or more forms which can be accessed through the 'Forms' link at www.fsa.gov.uk/handbook.]

SUP 16 Annex 12G
Reports from trustees of AUTs and depositaries of ICVCs (see SUP 16.6.9G)

SUP 16 Ann 12 **[G]**

(1) Table

- (1) Trustees of AUTs
  - (1) Form 1 at the end of this annex provides a suggested format for the submission of the reports.
  - (2) The quarterly report should be completed each year as at 31 March, 30 June, 30 September, and 31 December.
  - (3) The report should be signed by an *approved person* who has responsibility for the *firm's trustee* area.
  - (4) A *firm* should refer to COLL 6, and CIS 4, 7, 15 and Appendix CIS or COLL 6.2.12G (Box management errors guidance) before completing this report.
- (2) Depositaries of ICVCs
  - (1) Form 2 at the end of this annex provides a suggested format for the submission of the reports.
  - (2) The quarterly report should be completed each year as at 31 March, 30 June, 30 September, and 31 December.
  - (3) The report should be signed by an *approved person* who has responsibility for the *firm's depositary* area.
  - (4) A *firm* should refer to COLL 6 and CIS 4, 7 and Appendix CIS or COLL 6.2.12G before completing this report.

[Forms 1, 2 can be accessed through the 'Forms' link at www.fsa.gov.uk/handbook.]

SUP 16 Annex 13R
Reporting requirements

SUP 16 Ann 13 **[R]**

[This annex consists of one or more forms which can be accessed through the 'Forms' link at www.fsa.gov.uk/handbook.]

SUP 16 Annex 14R
Reporting requirements

SUP 16 Ann 14 **[R]**

[This annex consists of one or more forms which can be accessed through the 'Forms' link at www.fsa.gov.uk/handbook.]

SUP 16 Annex 15G
Reporting requirements

SUP 16 Ann 15 **[G]**

[This annex consists of one or more forms which can be accessed through the 'Forms' link at www.fsa.gov.uk/handbook.]

SUP 16 Annex 16R

SUP 16 Ann 16 **[R]** [deleted]

SUP 16 Annex 16AR
Standing data (see SUP 16.10.4R)

SUP 16 Ann 16A **[R]**

A: Communications with a *firm*
(1) Name of the *firm*
(2) Trading name(s) of the *firm*
(3) Country of incorporation
(4) Registered office
(5) Principal place of business
(6) Website address
(7) Telephone number
(8) The name and email address of the principal compliance contact

B: Information about a firm on the *FSA Register*
(9) *Regulated activities* for which a *firm* has *permission*
(10) Whether the *firm* holds *client money*
(11) Whether the *firm* is an "*ISD investment firm*"

C: Other information about a *firm*
(12) *Firm* types
(13) *Passported activities*
(14) Name and address of *firm's* auditor
(15) Legal status
(16) *Accounting reference date*

SUP 16 Annex 17G

16 Ann17 **[G]** [deleted]

SUP 16 Annex 18AR
Retail Mediation Activities Return ('RMAR')

SUP 16 Ann 18A **[R]**

Illustration of reporting requirements for firms carrying on retail mediation activities

Retail Mediation Activities Return ('RMAR')

This form has not been reproduced for technical reasons. Please refer to the FSA website.

SUP 16 Annex 18BG
Notes for Completion of the Retail Mediation Activities Return ('RMAR')

SUP 16 Ann 18B **[G]**

These notes have not been reproduced for technical reasons. Please refer to the FSA website.

SUP 16 Annex 19

[deleted]

SUP 16 Annex 19AR
Mortgage Lending and Administration Return ('MLAR')

SUP 16 Ann 19A **[R]**

Illustration of reporting requirements for firms carrying on mortgage lending and administration activities

This form has not been reproduced for technical reasons. Please refer to the FSA website.

SUP 16 Annex 19BG
Notes For Completion of the Mortgage Lending & Administration Return ('MLAR')

SUP 16 Ann 19B **[G]**

These notes have not been reproduced for technical reasons. Please refer to the FSA website.

SUP 16 Annex 20G
Products covered by the reporting requirement in SUP 16.11

SUP 16 Ann 20 **[G]**

This is the *guidance* referred to in SUP 16.11.6G.

SUP 16.11.3R requires certain *firms* to report product sales data. A reportable sale is when a new contract has been made and the premium has been paid. A reportable sale does not include a policy renewal, a policy top-up, or any alteration to an existing policy.

In the case of mortgage transactions, the reporting requirement only applies to loans for house purchase and remortgages and not to further advances. A reportable mortgage transaction applies where the mortgage transaction has completed (i.e. funds have been transferred and have been applied for the purpose of the mortgage).

Part 1 – Products

The following tables provide *guidance* on the products for which sales data is to be reported.

These tables are not intended to be a complete list of relevant products; *firms* should report sales data on all products which would fall within the scope of *retail investments*, *pure protection contracts*, and *regulated mortgage contracts* and other *home finance transactions*.

Table 1 – RETAIL INVESTMENTS

Relevant products include:

Unit in a *regulated unit trust scheme/OEIC*
Investment trust
ISA
Structured capital-at-risk product
With profit bond
Unit linked bond
Distribution bond
Mortgage Endowment
With profit endowment
Endowment savings plan
Guaranteed income/growth/investment bond
Trustee investment bond
Life annuity
Pension annuity
Long term care insurance contract
Stakeholder pension
Self-invested personal pension
Personal pension
Group personal pension

FSAVC
Individual pension transfer
Pension opt out
Section 32 buy out
Group section 32 buy out
Income drawdown
Executive pension
SSAS
Group money purchase
AVC final salary
AVC group money purchase

Table 2 – PURE PROTECTION CONTRACTS

Relevant products include:

Income protection
Standalone critical illness
Critical illness sold as a rider benefit to mortgage protection and mortgage term assurances

Table 3 – MORTGAGES

Relevant mortgage types include:

Fixed rate mortgages
Discounted variable rate mortgages
Tracker mortgages
Capped rate mortgages
Standard variable rate mortgages

Table 4 – OTHER HOME FINANCE TRANSACTIONS

Relevant products include:
Home reversion plans
Home purchase plans

Part 2: Supporting product definitions/guidance for product sales data reporting

Part 2 contains *guidance* on the terms used in part 1 and on other relevant material.

Where products have not been defined in the *Glossary*, an explanatory description is provided.

Retail investments

PRODUCT	Guidance
With profit bond	**Includes all single premium policies where a lump sum is paid into a with profits fund made up of investments such as company shares, fixed interest securities , commercial property and money . Unitised with profit bonds should be reported under this category.**
Unit linked bond	**A contract where the premium buys, or is deemed to buy investment units in a selected fund. The value of the policyholder's fund is linked to the value of the units (see guidance relating to distribution bonds).**
Distribution bond	**A single premium investment policy. The funds are invested in equities and gilts and an income is paid each year to the policyholder, dependent on the performance of the investments**. Only report as a distribution bond where over 50% of the fund allocation relates to the distribution fund. If less than a 50% allocation is made, the product should be reported as a unit linked bond.
Guaranteed income/growth/investment bond	This includes income and growth bonds which include guaranteed income and guaranteed equity bonds that include guarantees and pay a percentage of the movement of more one or more index.

Part II FSA Handbook Materials

PRODUCT	Guidance
Structured capital-at-risk product	*Defined in the Handbook Glossary.*
Life/pension annuity	An arrangement by which a life company pays someone a regular income, usually for life, in return for a lump sum premium. This would include • deferred and immediate annuities • compulsory purchase annuities • home income plans; and • all other types of life annuities.
Unit trust scheme	*Defined in the Handbook Glossary.*
Investment trust	*Defined in the Handbook Glossary.*
ISA	*Defined in the Handbook Glossary.* Cash and insurance ISAs should not be reported.
Endowment savings plan	An endowment plan with a fixed term with benefits paid on death within the term or on maturity.
Mortgage endowment	This should include any regular premium low cost endowments plus unitised with profit endowments.
Long-term care insurance contract	[The FSA consulted in CP 200 on the definition of long-term care insurance contract that will apply from 14 January 2005. The guidance here will cross-refer to the finalised definition.]
Stakeholder Pension	*See Handbook Glossary for definition of 'stakeholder pension scheme'.*
Self-invested personal pension	*See Handbook Glossary for definition of 'self-invested personal pension scheme'.*
Personal pension	*See Handbook Glossary for definition of 'personal pension scheme'.* For reporting purposes do not include Rebate Only Pension business.
Group personal pension	*See Handbook Glossary for definition of 'group personal pension scheme'.* Phased retirement should include transfer plans that permit staggered annuities to subsequently be purchased. Deferred transfer plans should be excluded. Report each individual policy as a separate case.
FSAVC	*Defined in the Handbook Glossary.* Do not include Rebate Only Pension business.
Individual pension transfer	*See Handbook Glossary for definition of 'pension transfer'.*
Pension opt out	*Defined in the Handbook Glossary.*
Section 32 buy out/Group section 32 buy out	An arrangement where trustees accept capital from employees who have left *occupational pension scheme* service and the transfer value is reinvested in an attempt to provide better benefits when the employee retires.
Income drawdown	*See Handbook Glossary for definition of 'income withdrawal'.* This should include transfer plans that allow income from a pension plan in advance of an annuity being purchased.
Executive pension scheme	An arrangement where each premium paid is identifiable to an individual employee and where an employer has discretion as to whether a pension arrangement is made for a particular employee and to the level of contribution or target benefit under the policy. Report each individual policy as a separate case. Pension premiums should be reported gross.
SSAS	*Defined in the Handbook Glossary.* Pension premiums should be reported gross. *SSAS* business should not be reported if you only provide an administration service. Report each individual policy as a separate case.

PRODUCT	Guidance
Trustee investment bond	A lump sum *investment* vehicle designed for use by *pension scheme* trustees. Includes *SSAS* Trustee Investment Bonds and SIPP Trustee Investment Bonds.
Group money purchase	An *occupational pension scheme* which provides *money-purchase benefits* which is available to employees of the same employer or of employers within a group.
AVC Final salary	Pension premiums should be reported gross.
AVC Group money purchase	Pension premiums should be reported gross.

Mortgages

(a) Types of interest rate

Types of interest rate	Description
Fixed rate	where the interest rate is fixed for a stated period.
Discounted rate	where a discount is applied to the lender's standard variable rate usually for a limited period of time.
Tracker	where the interest rate is guaranteed to move in line with either the Bank of England Base (or repo) Rate (BBR) or another index such as LIBOR (London InterBank Offered Rate).
Capped (and collared) rate mortgage	where the interest rate is guaranteed not to exceed a stated maximum rate (the 'capped' rate) for specific period of time, but where the standard variable interest rate applies when the rate is lower than the capped rate. Also includes products where the interest rate is subject to a minimum rate (the 'collared' rate).
Cashback	a cash amount paid by a *mortgage lender* to a *customer* (typically at the beginning of a contract) as an inducement to enter into a *regulated mortgage contract* with the *mortgage lender.*
Standard variable rate	the lender's underlying interest rate.

(b) Features

Data item	Description
Flexible mortgage	A mortgage where you can change the monthly payments and pay off part or all of the loan whenever you like. It is normally linked to any interest rate type. Details vary from one mortgage to another, but for reporting purposes, to be reported as a flexible mortgage, the mortgage should have the following features: • interest must be calculated monthly or daily; and • must have an overpayment facility.
Offset mortgage – positive and/or negative offset	An offset mortgage will typically have similar facilities to a flexible mortgage, but will also allow the borrower to offset positive (savings and/or current account) and/or negative balances (credit card and/or personal loans) against their outstanding mortgage balance.
Loans where income is not evidenced	This applies to loans which are based on one or more *persons'* incomes. These loans are those where the lender has no independent documentary evidence to verify income (e.g. as provided by an employer's reference, a bank statement, a salary slip, a P60, or audited/certified accounts).

Data item	Description
Total gross income	This is the total of the gross annual incomes (before tax or other deductions) of each of the individual borrowers whose incomes were taken into account when the lender made the lending assessment/decision. For these purposes, each borrower's gross income is the sum of that person's main income and any other reckonable income (e.g., overtime, income from other sources etc to the extent that the lender takes such additional income into account in whole or in part). For example if borrower A has gross income of £25,000 and borrower B has gross income of £20,000 then total gross income for the loan would be £45,000.

Pure protection contracts

Policy type	Description
Standalone critical illness	These policies are 'pure' critical illness policies i.e. there is no life cover sold alongside them. Under these policies the *insurer* provides the sum insured to the *policyholder* in the event of diagnosis of a life threatening condition.
Critical illness sold as a rider benefit to term assurance	For reporting purposes, this applies where critical illness is offered as a rider benefit to either a mortgage protection policy (a *life policy* that provides by means of decreasing term assurance for a mortgage to be paid off in the event of the borrower's death) or a protection term assurance contract.
Income protection	Insurance contracts arranged by an individual to provide for payment of income during a period of incapacity, due to ill health or accident.

Other home finance transactions

Finance type	Description
Home reversion plan	Defined in the Handbook *Glossary*.
Home purchase plan	Defined in the Handbook *Glossary*.

SUP 16 Annex 21R
Reporting Fields

SUP 16 Ann 21 **[R]**

This is the annex referred to in SUP 16.11.7R.

1 General Reporting Fields

The following data reporting fields must be completed, where applicable, for all reportable transactions and submitted in a prescribed format. Shaded boxes represent non-compulsory data items.

Data reporting field	Code (where applicable)	Notes
FSA reference number of product provider	6 digit number	This field must contain the FSA reference number of the *firm* providing the data report.
FSA reference number of *firm* which sold the product	6 digit number	This field must contain the FSA reference number of the *firm* which sold the product. For *firm's* own direct sales, enter *firm's* own FSA reference number. For sales via an intermediary enter the intermediary's reference number.

Advice at point of sale	**Y = advised** **N = non-advised**	**This information will not have to be reported until July 2006.** ***Firms* will however be able to report his information before then if appropriate by using the appropriate code to indicate whether the sale was advised or non-advised.** **For reporting purposes non-advised includes execution only and direct offer transactions.**
FSA reference number of the intermediary's *principal* or *network*	6 digit number	This field only applies if the sale has been made by an intermediary who has a *principal* or is part of a *network*.

2 Specific Reporting Fields

(a) Retail investments

The following data reporting fields must be completed, where applicable, for all *retail investment* transactions, including *structured capital-at-risk products*:

Data reporting field	**Illustrative code (where applicable)**	**Notes**
Product type	Numeric	Enter relevant product code. If none of the existing codes apply report sale as 'O' for other.
Post code of customer	**e.g. XY45 6XX**	**Applies to first named customer only.**
Method of *premium* / contribution payment	S = single R = regular	Use code to indicate method of payment.
Total *premium*/contribution amount	Numeric £	Enter annualised amount rounded to nearest £.
Date of birth	**DD/MM/YYYY**	**Applies to first named customer at time of sale i.e. age obtained at proposal stage.**

(b) Pure protection contracts

The following data reporting fields must be completed, where applicable:

Data reporting field	**Illustrative code (where applicable)**	**Notes**
Policy type	Numeric	Enter relevant product code. If none of the existing codes apply report sale as 'O' for other.
Method of *premium* payment	S = single R = regular	Use code to indicate method of payment.
Total *premium* amount	Numeric	Enter annualised amount rounded to nearest £.

(c) Mortgages

The following data reporting fields must be completed, where applicable for all regulated mortgage transactions (with the exception of further advances):

Note: In the case of mixed interest rate options/combination mortgages, sales data should only be provided for the rate applying to the largest portion of the overall mortgage balance.

Data reporting field	**Illustrative code (where applicable)**	**Notes**
Date mortgage account opened	DD/MM/YYYY	Date of mortgage completion or drawdown of the funds.

Data reporting field	Illustrative code (where applicable)	Notes
Interest rate type	F = fixed rate C = capped rate D = discount T = tracker V = standard variable rate O = other	Enter the relevant code. If none of the existing codes apply enter sale as 'O' to denote 'other'. Only 1 code can be entered
Mortgage characteristics	**CB = cashback** **FF = flexible features (allowing overpayments and underpayments)** **OS = offset positive and or negative balances.** **L = the loan is a lifetime mortgage** **SAM = the loan is a shared appreciation** mortgage	**Use code to indicate additional mortgage characteristics if applicable.** **Cashback should only be reported where it is linked to a variable interest rate and where the cashback is not being provided as an incentive to pay legal costs and valuation fees.** **Where more than 1 code applies, report all.**
Post code of the mortgaged property	e.g. XY45 6XX	
Type of borrower	F = first time buyers M = home movers (2nd or subsequent buyers) R = remortgagors C = council/ registered social landlord tenant exercising their right to buy O = other N = not known	Use code to indicate type of borrower. Only 1 code should be entered
Method of repayment	C = capital and interest E = interest only/endowment I = interest only/ISA P = interest only/pension U = interest only/unknown M = mix of capital and interest only N = not known	Use code to indicate method of mortgage repayment Only 1 code should be entered
Term of mortgage	Numeric	Number in whole years. (Optional for *Lifetime* and *Shared appreciation mortgages*)
Size of loan	Numeric £	Report the original interest bearing balance at completion of the mortgage.
Value of the mortgaged property	Numeric £	The value reported should be based on: • the surveyors valuation (or from a valuation index) or • from the customers estimated value as captured on the application form. In the case of staged construction or self build schemes, value means 'expected final value of property at the time lending decision is made'.

Data reporting field	**Illustrative code (where applicable)**	**Notes**
Income Basis	S = single income J = joint income	Use code to indicate whether the income assessment has been made on a single or joint basis (Optional for *Lifetime* and *Shared appreciation mortgages*)
Age of main borrower	DD/MM/YYYY	Report age of main borrower only.
Remortgage transactions only	**N = no extra money raised** **H = extra money raised for home improvements** **D = extra money raised for debt consolidation** **M = extra money raised for home improvements and debt consolidation** **O = other**	**Use code to indicate the purpose of the remortgage.** **Only 1 code can be entered**
Employment status of main borrower	E = employed S = self employed R = retired O = other	Applies to main borrower only. Only 1 code can be entered
Total gross income	Numeric £	The total income of all borrowers whose income was used in the credit assessment (see guidance notes for further explanation) (Optional for *Lifetime* and *Shared appreciation mortgages*)
Income verification	Y = income evidenced N = income not evidenced	Applies to loans based on one or more persons' incomes (see guidance notes relating to 'loans where income is not evidenced') (Optional for *Lifetime* and *Shared appreciation mortgages*)
County court judgments (CCJs) Value	**Numeric £**	**Applies where borrower/s has one or more CCJs within the last 3 years – either satisfied or unsatisfied – with a total value greater than £500.**
Impaired credit history	**A = arrears** **V = IVA** **Bankruptcy**	**Use code/s to indicate applicable credit history** **A = applies to secured loans and unsecured loans where the borrower/s has arrears on a previous (or current) mortgage or other secured loan within the last 2 years where the cumulative amount overdue at any point reached three or more monthly payments or** **V = applies where the borrower/s have been subject to an individual voluntary arrangement (IVA) at any time within the last 3 years** **B = applies where the borrower/s have been subject to a bankruptcy order at any time within the last 3 years**

(d) Other home finance transactions

(i) Home Reversion Plans

The following data reporting fields must be completed, where applicable:

Data reporting field	**Illustrative code (where applicable)**	**Notes**
Date reversion plan commenced	DD/MM/YYYY	
Reversion Characteristics	F = Full reversion FI = Full reversion linked to an investment with a view to providing income P = Partial reversion PI = Partial reversion linked to an investment with a view to providing income O = Other	Only 1 code can be entered
Property postcode	e.g. XY45 6XX	
Reversion Sum	Numeric £	Amount of reversion lump sum or sum used to provide income
Full market value of property	Numeric £	The actual market value of the property or portion of property that is intended for reversion
Discounted value of reverted property	Numeric £	The actual discounted value of the property or portion of property on which the reversion plan is based
Date of birth of main XXX	DD/MM/YYYY	Report the age of the main plan holder only
Purpose of reversion	H = Extra money for home improvements D = Extra money for debt consolidation M = Extra money for home improvements and debt consolidation O = Other	Only 1 code can be entered

(ii) Home Purchase Plans

The following data reporting fields must be completed, where applicable:

Data reporting field	**Illustrative code (where applicable)**	**Notes**
Date HPP account opened	DD/MM/YYYY	
Type of rental rate	V = Variable F = Fixed O = Other	Only 1 code can be entered
HPP Characteristics	I = Ijara D = Diminishing Musharaka O = Other	
Type of home buyer	F = First time buyer H = Home mover R = Re-finance C = Council/Registered social landlord exercising their right to buy O = Other N = Not known	Only 1 code can be entered
Term of HPP	Numeric	Number in whole years
Amount granted to home buyer	Numeric £	The sum of money advanced to the consumer in respect of their house purchase

Value of property	Numeric £	The value should be based on: • The surveyors valuation (or from a valuation index) • From the customers estimated value as captured on the application form.
Income basis	S = Single income J = Joint income	Use code to indicate whether the income assessment has been made on a single or joint basis.
Date of birth of main home buyer	DD/MM/YYYY	Report the age of the main home buyer only
Main home buyer employment status	F = Full time employed S = Self employed R = Retired O = Other	Applies to main home buyer only Only 1 code can be entered.
Total gross income	Numeric £	The total gross income of all home buyers whose income was used in the credit assessment (see guidance notes for further explanation)
Income verification	Y = Income evidenced N = Income not evidenced	Applies to plans based on one or more persons' incomes (see guidance notes relating to where income is not evidenced)
County court judgements (CCJs) Value	**Numeric £**	**Applies where home buyer/s has had one or more CCJs within the last 3 years – either satisfied or unsatisfied with a total value greater than £500.**
Impaired credit history of main home buyer	**A = Arrears** **V = IVA** **B = Bankruptcy**	**Use codes to indicate applicable credit history** **A = applies to previous home finance transactions where the home buyer/s has had arrears within the last 2 years where the cumulative amount overdue at any point reached three or more monthly payments or** **V = applies where the home buyer/s have been subject to an individual voluntary arrangement at anytime within the last 3 years** **B = applies where the home buyer/s have been subject to a bankruptcy order at any time within the last 3 years.**

3 Optional Reporting Fields

1. The following data items are not currently mandatory reporting fields.

However, without this information, we will not be able to identify individual incorrect transactions. A *firm* would need to trawl through all submitted transactions until they could match the original transaction details and thus, correct and resubmit the information to us. These data items are essential for the smooth running of the regulatory reporting process both from the *FSA's* and the *firm's* perspective and because we understand that these data items are generally available to *firms* is it is our intention to make these data items mandatory in due course. In the interim, we would encourage *firms* to build these extra items into their PSD reporting systems.

Data reporting field	Code (where applicable)	Notes
Initial gross charging rate of interest	**numeric**	**The amount of interest reported should be the initial gross nominal rate charged on the loan and should take into account any discount being provided. Where the advance is split, the interest rate applying to the largest part of the advance should be entered.**

Data reporting field	Code (where applicable)	Notes
Date incentivised rate ends	**DD/MM/YYYY**	**Only applies to fixed, capped or discounted rates where the customer is paying an incentivised rate for a set period.**
Date *early repayment charge* ends	**DD/MM/YYYY**	**If applicable, report date early repayment charge ends.**
Product sale reference	free text field	This can be any unique number such as the policy/account number but must be a number that the a firm can use to trace the original transaction information.
Date sale of product concluded	DD/MM/YYYY	Enter date

2. The following data items are not required for regulatory purposes and should only be reported by *mortgage lenders* who currently support the RMS (Regulated Mortgage Survey) and other *home finance providers*.

Data reporting field	Code (where applicable)	Notes
Purchase price of property (Purchases only)	**£ numeric**	**Purchase price as stated on application form.**
Type of dwelling	**B = bungalow** **D = detached house** **S = semi-detached house** **T = terraced house** **F = flat or maisonette in converted house** **P = purpose built flat or maisonette** **O = other**	**Use code to indicate property type** **Only 1 code can apply**
Number of habitable rooms	**numeric**	**Include kitchen but not bathroom/toilet**
Number of bedrooms	**numeric**	
Does the property have a garage	**Y = Yes** **N = No**	**The garage should be a permanent structure but does not have to stand on the main site of the property.**
Is the dwelling new?	**Y = Yes** **N = No**	**New refers to the period in which the main structure of the dwelling was completed and also means where a dwelling is being occupied for the first time. Does not therefore include new conversions of older dwellings.**
Is mortgage payment protection insurance (MPPI) being taken out with the mortgage?	**Y = Yes** **N = No**	**MPPI can be any of the following:** **– full accident, sickness and unemployment insurance; or** **– accident and sickness only; or** **– unemployment only.** **Report 'Yes' even where the policy was sold or provided free and irrespective of whether the premiums are collected by the lender or the insurer.**

Is payment protection insurance (PPI) being taken out with the home purchase plan ?	**Y = Yes** **N = No**	**PPI can be any of the following:** **– full accident, sickness and unemployment insurance; or** **– accident and sickness only; or** **– unemployment only.** **Report 'Yes' even where the policy was sold or provided free and irrespective of whether the premiums are collected by the lender or the insurer.**

SUP 16 Annex 22R

SUP 16 Ann 22 **[R]** [deleted]

SUP 16 Annex 23G

SUP 16 Ann 23 **[G]** [deleted]

SUP 16 Annex 24R

SUP 16 Ann 24 **[R]**

This form has not been reproduced for technical reasons. Please refer to the FSA website.

SUP 16 Annex 25G

SUP 16 Ann 25 **[G]**

These forms have not been reproduced for technical reasons. Please refer to the FSA website.

SUP 16 Annex 26G
Guidance on designated liquidity groups in SUP 16.12

SUP 16 Ann 26 **[G]**

Purpose of this guidance

1 **[G]** The purpose of this Annex is to explain the different types of *defined liquidity group* dealt with in SUP 16.12 (Integrated Regulatory Reporting) and what a group liquidity reporting *firm* is.

2 **[G] Defined liquidity groups** are relevant to liquidity reporting by *ILAS BIPRU firms*. Liquidity reporting under SUP 16.12 relates to a *firm* on a solo or *branch* basis and in addition by reference to a *firm's designated liquidity group*.

The two main types of designated liquidity groups

3 **[G] Defined liquidity groups** are divided into two types:
(1) a DLG by default; and
(2) a DLG by modification (this type is subdivided into other types as explained in this Annex).

DLG by default

4 **[G]** Broadly speaking, a *firm's DLG by default* is made up of the members of the *firm's group* on which it relies for liquidity or that rely on the *firm*. It also includes certain funding vehicles. It covers each entity:
(1) that provides or is committed to provide material support to the *firm* against *liquidity risk*; or
(2) to which the *firm* provides or is committed to provide material support against *liquidity risk*; or
(3) that has reasonable grounds to believe that the *firm* would supply such support, and vice *versa*.

5 **[G]** Paragraph (b) of the definition of *DLG by default* deals with a case in which there are several *UK ILAS BIPRU firms* in the same *group*. The effect is this. Say that there are two *UK ILAS BIPRU firms*, A and B in the group. Say that A relies on, or is relied on by, companies M, N, O and P. B relies on, or is relied on by, companies P, Q, R and S. The result is that A and B have the same *DLG by default*, which is made up of companies A, B, M, N, O, P, Q, R and S.

6 **[G]** There is an exclusion relating to *participations*. Say that 70% of B is owned by unconnected third party shareholders and that A and B rely on each other. A will report on the basis of a group made up of A, B, M, N, O and P. B will report on the basis of a group made up of A, B, P, Q, R and S.

Part II FSA Handbook Materials

7 **[G]** The full definition is set out in the *Glossary*.

8 **[G]** The definition applies automatically. It does not depend, for example, on the *firm* getting a waiver under BIPRU 12 (Liquidity). However, in practice it is likely that the *firm* and the FSA will agree who is in the *firm*'s DLG by default.

9 **[G]** A *DLG by default* is only relevant to a *UK lead regulated firm*.

10 **[G]** A *firm* may have a *DLG by default* and a *DLG by modification* at the same time.

Types of DLG by modification

11 **[G]** A *DLG by modification* only applies to a *firm* with an *intra-group liquidity modification*. BIPRU 12.8 has more *about intra-group liquidity modifications*.

12 **[G]** Every *firm* subject to BIPRU 12 (Liquidity) is subject to the *overall liquidity adequacy rule*. The effect of that *rule* is that every *firm* is required to be self-sufficient in terms of liquidity adequacy and to be able to satisfy that *rule* relying on its own liquidity resources.

13 **[G]** The *FSA* recognises that a *firm* may be part of a wider *group* which manages its liquidity on a *group*-wide basis. This is recognised by an *intra-group liquidity modification*. A *DLG by modification* arises out of the *intra-group liquidity modification*.

14 **[G]** There are two types of DLG by modification:
(1) a DLG by modification (*firm* level); and
(2) a *non-UK DLG by modification* (DLG level).

Types of DLG by modification (*firm* level)

15 **[G]** If the *firm* obtains an *intra-group liquidity modification* it will permit the *firm* to rely on liquidity support from elsewhere in its *group* for the purposes of the *overall liquidity adequacy rule*. A *DLG by modification (firm level)* is made up of the *group* members on which the *firm* can rely for these purposes, together with the *firm* itself. It is called '*firm* level' because it relates to the way that the *overall liquidity adequacy rule* is applied to the *firm*.

16 **[G]** There are two types of DLG by modification (*firm* level):
(1) a UK DLG by modification; and
(2) a *non-UK DLG by modification* (*firm* level).

17 **[G]** It is not possible for a *firm* to have both types.

18 **[G]** A *UK DLG by modification* is made up solely of *UK ILAS BIPRU firms*. That means that the *intra-group liquidity modification* will permit the *firm* to rely on liquidity support from other specified *UK ILAS BIPRU firms* elsewhere in its *group*, but no one else.

19 **[G]** A *non-UK DLG by modification (firm level)* is defined to mean any kind of *DLG by modification (firm level)* except for a *UK DLG by modification*. In practice though an *intra-group liquidity modification* setting up a *non-UK DLG by modification (firm level)* will be expected to allow the *firm* to rely on support from a *parent undertaking* which is constituted under the law of a country or territory outside the United Kingdom or on subsidiary undertakings of that parent which are themselves constituted under the law of a country or territory outside the *United Kingdom*. These parents and their subsidiaries (together with the firm itself) will make up the *non-UK DLG by modification (firm level)*. It is not envisaged that a *non-UK DLG by modification (firm level)* will include *UK* members (other than the *firm* itself). That is why this type of defined liquidity group is called a *non-UK DLG by modification (firm level)*.

***Non-UK DLG by modification* (DLG level)**

20 **[G]** It is envisaged that if a firm has a *UK DLG by modification*, the intra-group liquidity modification will apply the overall liquidity adequacy rule to the *UK DLG by modification* as a whole. The starting position is that the *UK DLG by modification* should be self-sufficient for liquidity purposes.

21 **[G]** However, the *intra-group liquidity modification* may permit the *UK DLG by modification* to rely on liquidity support from elsewhere in the *group*. In this case this other part of the group, together with the *UK DLG by modification*, forms the *non-UK DLG by modification (DLG level)*. It is called 'DLG level' because it relates to the way that the *overall liquidity adequacy rule* is applied to the *firm's DLG*.

22 **[G]** It is not envisaged that a *firm* with a non-UK DLG by modification (firm level) will have a *non-UK DLG by modification* (DLG level).

23 **[G]** It is envisaged that the only *group* members on which the *non-UK DLG by modification (firm level)* will be able to rely for these purposes will be foreign parents and others described in paragraph 19 of SUP 16 Annex 26.

That is why it is called a *non-UK DLG by modification (DLG level).*

Combinations of DLG

24 **[G]** That means that the types of *DLG by modification* a *firm* may have are these:
(1) a *UK DLG by modification* and nothing else; or
(2) a *non-UK DLG by modification* (*firm level)* and nothing else; or
(3) a *UK DLG by modification* and *non-UK DLG by modification (DLG level).*

Group liquidity reporting *firm*

25 **[G]** The defined term *group liquidity reporting firm* is also used in connection with reporting at the level of a *defined liquidity group.* Its purpose is to identify the *firms* on which the reporting obligation falls.

26 **[G]** The general principle is that reporting is done by *UK ILAS BIPRU firms.* In the case of a *DLG by modification,* the reporting will be done by *UK ILAS BIPRU firms* that have been granted the *intra-group liquidity modification.*

27 **[G]** However there may be other types members of the *defined liquidity group.* For example, say that *UK ILAS BIPRU firm* A has a *defined liquidity group* made up of companies B, C, D and E. Say that B is an *authorised person* but is not a *UK ILAS BIPRU firm,* that C is a *UK* company that is not *authorised* and that D and E are foreign and not *authorised.* A, B, C, D and E are all members of the *defined liquidity group.* However B, C, D and E do not have to report on the *defined liquidity group* under SUP 16.12. That obligation falls on A. A is the *group liquidity reporting firm.*

CHAPTER 17
TRANSACTION REPORTING

17.1 Application

Who?

[2171]
17.1.1 **[R]** This chapter applies to:
(1) a *MiFID investment firm*;
(2) a *third country investment firm*; and to
(3) a *person* who is the operator of an *approved reporting mechanism* or of a *regulated market* or *MTF* that is used by a *firm* to report *transactions* to the *FSA*; and
(4) a firm acting in its capacity as a manager or operator of:
  (i) a collective investment undertaking; or
  (ii) a *pension scheme*; or
  (iii) an *occupational pension scheme*; or
  (iv) a *personal pension scheme*; or
  (v) a *stakeholder pension scheme*.

17.1.2 **[G]** Article 32(7) of *MiFID* requires the *FSA* to apply the *transaction* reporting requirements in Article 25 to the *UK branches* of *EEA* investment firms and branches of *credit institutions* in respect of reportable transactions arising in the course of services provided in the UK.

17.1.3 **[G]** Article 32(7) of *MiFID* provides that the branch of a *UK firm* operating from an establishment in another *EEA state* must satisfy the *transaction* reporting requirements of the *competent authority* in that other Member State in respect of reportable transactions arising in the course of services provided in that other Member State.

17.1.3 A **[G]** In line with guidance from CESR, the *FSA* acknowledges that, from a practical point of view, it would be burdensome for *branches* of *investment firms* to be obliged to report their *transactions* to two *competent authorities*. Therefore, all *transactions* executed by *branches* may be reported to the *competent authority* of the *Host State*, if the *investment firm* elects to do so. In these cases *transaction reports* should follow the rules of the *competent authority* to which the report is made. However, where an *investment firm* chooses to report to two *competent authorities*, this choice will not be challenged by the *FSA*.

What?

17.1.4 **[R]** A *firm* which executes a *transaction*:
(1) in any *financial instrument* admitted to trading on a *regulated market* or a *prescribed market* (whether or not the *transaction* was carried out on such a market); or
(2) in any *OTC derivative* the value of which is derived from, or which is otherwise dependent upon, an equity or debt-related *financial instrument* which is *admitted to trading* on a *regulated market* or on a *prescribed market*;

must report the details of the *transaction* to the *FSA*.

[Note: article 25(3) of *MiFID*].

17.1.4A **[R]** SUP 17.1.4R(2) does not apply to a transaction in any *OTC derivative* the value of which is derived from, or which is otherwise dependent upon, multiple equity or multiple debt-related *financial instruments* except where the multiple *financial instruments* are all issued by the same *issuer*.

Where?

17.1.5 **[R]** This chapter applies in respect of *transactions* which are to be reported to the *FSA*.

Status of EU provisions as rules in certain instances

17.1.6 **[R]** In this chapter, paragraphs marked "EU", including SUP 17 Ann 1EU, shall apply to a *firm* as if those provisions were *rules* to the extent that it executes a transaction in a *financial instrument* which is specified by SUP 17.1.4R but which is beyond the scope of article 25(3) of *MiFID*.

Guidance on the reporting of certain transactions

17.1.7 **[G]**

(1) The movement, reallocation or transfer of *financial instruments* within the accounts of one legal entity will be reportable where the movement, reallocation or transfer is as a result of an agreement to transfer rights in a *financial instrument* to which this chapter applies between *clients* of the *firm* or between the *firm* (or a member of its *group)* and a *client*, and where the movement, reallocation or transfer involves a transaction within the meaning of Article 5 of the *MiFID Regulation*.

(2) For a rolling *spread bet*, only the initial opening of the betting contract and the final closure of the contract need to be reported. Openings and closings for technical purposes such as daily roll-over, which are intended to maintain a particular *spread bet* position, need not be reported. Final closings of a portion of a bet should be reported as required by SUP 17.2.7R.

17.2 Making transaction reports

Transaction reports made through third party agents

17.2.1 **[R]** A *firm* may rely on a third party acting on the firm's behalf to make a *transaction* report to the *FSA*.

[Note: article 25(5) of *MiFID*]

17.2.2 **[G]** The *FSA* will treat a *firm* as acting in accordance with SUP 17.2.1R in circumstances where the *firm* enters into a *transaction* with another *person* in the course of providing a service of *portfolio management* on behalf of one or more clients, provided it:

(1) enters into the *transaction* in the exercise of a discretion conferred on it by an investment mandate or does so having specifically recommended the *transaction* to its *client*;

(2) has reasonable grounds to be satisfied that the other *person* will, in respect of the *transaction*, make a *transaction report* to the *FSA* (or to another *competent authority*) which, as to content, will include all such information as would have been contained in a *transaction report* by the *firm* (other than as to the identity of the *firm's client*).

Approved reporting mechanisms, regulated markets or MTFs

17.2.3 **[R]** A *firm* is relieved of its obligation to make a *transaction* report if the *transaction* is instead reported directly to the *FSA* by an *approved reporting mechanism*, or by a *regulated market* or *MTF* through whose systems the *transaction* was completed.

[Note: article 25(5) of *MiFID*]

17.2.3A **[G]** The *regulated markets* and *MTFs* that report *transactions* undertaken on their systems to the *FSA* are listed on the *FSA's* website at: http://www.fsa.gov.uk/Pages/Doing/Regulated/Returns/mtr/regulated_markets/index.shtml.

Verifying that transaction reports will be made

17.2.4 **[G]** The *FSA* will expect a *firm* which seeks to rely upon the waiver in SUP 17.2.3R to take reasonable steps to verify that *transaction* reports will be made in accordance with the standards laid down in this chapter and in particular should ascertain and remain satisfied that:

(1) the provider of the *transaction* reporting facility maintains an automated reporting system which the *firm* is able to access through the efficient inputting of *transactions* into the system;

(2) the terms of the agreement between itself and the relevant trade matching or reporting system, *regulated market* or *MTF*, make appropriate provision obliging the provider of the transaction reporting service to make *transaction* reports on its behalf;

(3) the arrangements provide for confirmation in each case that a *transaction* report has been made on its behalf.

Compliance by approved reporting mechanisms or MTFs with the provisions of this Chapter

17.2.5 **[R]**

(1) The operator of an *approved reporting mechanism*, or the operator of an *MTF* or a *market operator* through whose systems a reportable *transaction* is to be completed and which has, pursuant to SUP 17.2.3R, agreed to make *transaction* reports to the *FSA* on behalf of a *firm*, must:
   (a) make reports to the *FSA* in respect of each *transaction* to which the agreement relates;
   (b) ensure such reports contain the reporting fields specified in SUP 17 Ann 1, where applicable; and
   (c) ensure that, once received from the reporting *firm*, such reports are submitted to the *FSA* within the time limit for making reports.

(2) The obligations of the operator under this Rule do not affect the liability of the reporting *firm* for ensuring the accuracy of the information contained in the *transaction* report that it submits to the operator.

17.2.6 **[G]**

(1) A *transaction* report should distinguish each individual *transaction*, using the *firm's* identifying code.

(2) Reporting obligations under this chapter do not affect any obligation to report *transactions* under the rules of any market, trading system, matching or reporting system or exchange, whether or not that market, system or exchange is a *regulated market*.

Time period for making reports

17.2.7 **[R]** A *firm* must report the required details of the *transaction* to the *FSA* as quickly as possible and by not later than the close of the working day following the day upon which that *transaction* took place.

[Note: article 25(3) of *MiFID*]

17.3 Reporting channels

17.3.1 **[EU]**

The reports of *transactions* in *financial instruments* shall be made in an electronic form except under exceptional circumstances, when they may be made in a medium which allows for the storing of the information in a way accessible for future reference by the competent authorities other than an electronic form, and the methods by which those reports are made shall satisfy the following conditions:

(a) they ensure the safety and confidentiality of the data reported;
(b) they incorporate mechanisms for identifying and correcting errors in a *transaction* report;
(c) they incorporate mechanisms for authenticating the source of the *transaction* report;
(d) they include appropriate precautionary measures to enable the timely resumption of reporting in the case of system failure;
(e) they are capable of reporting the information required under Article 13 of the *MiFID Regulation* in the format specified in SUP 17 Ann 1EU required by the *FSA* and in accordance with this paragraph, within the time-limits set out in SUP 17.2.7R.

[Note: article 12(1) of the *MiFID Regulation*]

Methods of a firm reporting transactions either directly or through a third party acting on its behalf

17.3.2 **[G]** [deleted]

Approval and monitoring of trade matching and reporting systems

17.3.3 **[EU]**

A trade matching or reporting system shall be approved by the *FSA* for the purposes of Article 25(5) of *MiFID* if the arrangements for reporting *transactions* established by that system comply with SUP 17.3.1EU and are subject to monitoring by a *competent authority* in respect of their continuing compliance.

[Note: article 12(2) of the *MiFID Regulation*]

17.3.4 **[G]** The *approved reporting mechanisms* are listed on the FSA's website at: http://www.fsa.gov.uk/pages/Doing/Regulated/Returns/mtr/arms/index.shtml.

17.3.5 **[G]** Section 412A of the *Act* contains provisions which are concerned with the manner in which the *FSA* will carry out its approval and monitoring of trade matching or reporting systems.

Receipt of transaction reports by the FSA

17.3.6 **[G]** A report is made to the *FSA* when it is received by the *FSA*. The delivery of a report by a *MiFID investment firm* to a reporting *person*, channel or system by the close of the working day following the day of the *transaction* does not amount to the making of a report to the *FSA*.

17.4 Information in transaction reports

Information to appear in transaction reports

17.4.1 **[EU]**

Reports of *transactions* made in accordance with Articles 25 (3) and (5) of *MiFID* shall contain the information specified in SUP 17 Ann1EU which is relevant to the type of *financial instrument* in question and which the *FSA* declares is not already in its possession or is not available to it by other means.

[Note: article 13(1) of the *MiFID Regulation*.]

17.4.2 **[R]** The reports referred to in SUP 17.4.1EU shall, in particular include details of the names and the numbers of the instruments bought or sold, the quantity, the dates and times of execution and the *transaction* prices and means of identifying the *firms* concerned.

[Note: article 25(4) of *MiFID*]

Data retention

17.4.3 **[R]** A *firm* must keep at the disposal of the *FSA*, for at least five years, the relevant data relating to all *transactions* in *financial instruments* which it has carried out, whether on own account or on behalf of a *client*. In the case of *transactions* carried out on behalf of *clients*, the records shall contain all the information and details of the identity of the *client*, and the information required under the *money laundering directive*.

[Note: article 25(2) of *MiFID*]

Maintenance of information by firm

17.4.4 **[G]** The requirement to keep information at the disposal of the *FSA* means that a *firm* should maintain that information in such a form that it can readily be gathered and transmitted to the *FSA* upon request. Where more than one *firm* has given effect to a *transaction*, each *firm* should be considered to have carried out the *transaction* for the purposes of SUP 17.4.3R and should keep the records, even where only one *firm* makes a *transaction* report as contemplated in this Chapter.

SUP 17 Annex 1
Minimum content of a transaction report

17 Ann 1 List of fields for reporting purposes

[Note: This table includes information required under MiFID Article 25 (4) and contains additional *FSA* requirements permitted under Articles 13 (3) and (4) of the *MiFID Regulation*]

Where appropriate, *firms* should complete these fields in the formats described, or these formats must be contained in the fields that their *approved reporting mechanism* will use when sending a *transaction report* to the *FSA* on behalf of a *firm*.

	Field Identifier	**Description**
EU	1. Reporting Firm Identification	A unique code to identify the *firm* which executed the *transaction*.
G		This code should be the *FSA* reference number of the *firm* or the Swift Bank Identifier Code (BIC).
EU	2. Trading Day	The trading day on which the *transaction* was executed.
EU	3. Trading Time	The time at which the *transaction* was executed, reported in London local time.
G		The time should be specified in hours, minutes and seconds (hhmmss). Where it is not possible to input seconds, '00' may be entered in this field.
EU	4. Buy/Sell Indicator	Identifies whether the *transaction* was a buy or sell from the perspective of the reporting *MiFID investment firm*.
EU	5. Trading Capacity	Identifies whether the *firm* executed the *transaction*

			transaction in such a capacity.
G		Where a *firm* has executed a *transaction* in an agency cross capacity, it may submit two reports rather than a single report, in which case this field should indicate that the *firm* is acting on behalf of a *client*.	
G		–	Where the *firm* has executed a *transaction* in a principal cross capacity (that is where the *firm* has simultaneously executed a buy and sell *transaction* as principal in a single product at the same price and quantity) and the *firm* has chosen to submit a single report to the *FSA* representing both of these *transactions* this field should be used to indicate that the *firm* has executed the *transaction* in such a capacity.
G		Where a *firm* has executed a transaction in a principal cross capacity, and prefers to submit two reports rather than a single report, this field should indicate that the *firm* is acting on its own account.	
EU	6. Instrument Identification	This shall consist in:	
		–	a unique code, decided by the *FSA*, identifying the *financial instrument* which is the subject of the *transaction*;
G			The unique code should be an ISO 6166 ISIN. This code must always be used for, but is not limited to, reporting transactions in warrants.
EU		–	or, if the *financial instrument* in question does not have a unique identification code, the report must include the name of the instrument or, in the case of a *derivative* contract, the characteristics of the *derivative*.
G		The FSA considers that where the financial instrument in question (which includes derivatives) is admitted to trading on a market where the ISO 6166 ISIN is not the industry method of identification, it will be sufficient to insert in this field the code assigned to the instrument by that market.	
R		–	or, in the case of an *OTC derivative*, the characteristics of the *OTC derivative*.
G			Where an *OTC derivative* is the subject of the *transaction* a full description of the *OTC derivative* should be provided.
EU	7. Instrument code type	The code type used to report the instrument.	

	Field Identifier	Description
G		– on its own account (either on its own behalf or on behalf of a *client*) (that is as principal);
		– for the account and on behalf of a *client* (that is as agent);
		– Where the *firm* has executed a *transaction* in an agency cross capacity; (that is where the *firm* has acted as agent for both the selling and the buying counterparties) and the *firm* has chosen to submit a single report to the *FSA* representing both of these *transactions* this field should be used to indicate that the *firm* has executed the

		a derivative contract.
G		This field is only mandatory when the *transaction* involves an *OTC derivative* or a *financial instrument admitted to trading* on a market where the ISIN is not the industry method of identification. Where the derivative type is spreadbet on an equity option or contract for difference on an equity option, this field must be used to indicate the expiry of the option.
EU	12. Derivative Type	The harmonised description of the derivative type.
G		This field is only mandatory when the *transaction* involves an *OTC derivative* or a *financial instrument admitted to trading* on a market where the ISIN is not the industry method of identification, and must indicate the derivative type, e.g. option, future, contract for difference (other than a contract for difference on an equity option), contract for difference on an equity option, complex derivative, warrant, spreadbet (other than a spreadbet on an equity option), spreadbet on an equity option, credit default swap or other swap.
EU	13. Put/Call	Specification whether an option or any other *financial instrument* is a put or call.

	Field Identifier	Description	
G		This field is only mandatory when (i) the *transaction* involves an *OTC derivative* or a *financial instrument admitted to trading* on a market where the ISIN is not the industry method of identification; and (ii) the *derivative* type is option, warrant, spreadbet on an equity option or contract for difference on an equity option. Where the *financial instrument* is a spreadbet on an equity option or a contract for difference on an equity option this field should be used to indicate the put/call status of the equity option.	
EU	14. Strike Price	The strike price of an option or other *financial instrument*.	
G		This field is only mandatory when (i) the *transaction* involves an *OTC derivative* or a *financial instrument admitted to trading* on a market where the ISIN is not the industry method of identification; and (ii) the *derivative* type is option, warrant, spreadbet on an equity option or contract for difference on an equity option. Where the *financial instrument* is a spreadbet on an equity option or a contract for difference on an equity option this field should be used to indicate the strike price of the equity option.	
EU	15. Price Multiplier	The number of units of the *financial instrument* in question which are contained in a trading lot; for example, the number of derivatives or securities represented by one contract.	
G		This field is only mandatory where the transaction involves an *OTC derivative*.	
EU	16. Unit Price	The price per security or derivative contract excluding commission and (where relevant) accrued interest. In the case of a debt instrument, the price may be expressed either in terms of currency or as a percentage.	
EU	17. Price Notation	The currency in which the price is expressed. If, in the case of a bond or other form of securitised debt, the price is expressed as a percentage, that percentage shall be included.	
G		The ISO 4217 currency code must be used. The major currency must be used (e.g. pounds rather than pence). If the price is expressed as a percentage of nominal value then the ISO 4217 currency code of the nominal value must be used.	
EU	18. Quantity	The number of units of the *financial instruments*, the nominal value of bonds, or the number of derivative contracts included in the *transaction*.	
EU	19. Quantity notation	An indication as to whether the quantity is the number of units of *financial instruments*, the nominal value of bonds, or the number of derivative contracts.	
G		*Firms* do not need to complete this field since the *FSA* already has access to this information.	
EU	20. Counterparty	Identification of the counterparty to the *transaction*. That identification shall consist of:	
		–	where the counterparty is a *MiFID investment firm*, a unique code for that firm, to be determined by the *FSA*; or

Part II FSA Handbook Materials

	Field Identifier	Description
		– where the counterparty is a *regulated market* or *MTF* or an entity acting as its central counterparty, the unique harmonised identification code for that market, *MTF* or entity acting as central counterparty, as specified in the list published by the competent authority of the *home Member State* of that entity in accordance with Article 13(2).
G		The *FSA* has determined that where an *FSA* reference number or a Swift Bank Identification Code (BIC) exists for the counterparty, one of these codes must be used, or in the case that a counterparty has neither an *FSA* reference number or a BIC, a unique internal code allocated by the reporting *firm* must be used and that unique internal code must be used consistently across all instrument types and platforms for that counterparty.
EU	21. Venue Identification	Identification of the venue where the *transaction* was executed. That identification shall consist in:
		– where the venue is a trading venue: its unique harmonised identification code,
G		Where the venue is a *regulated market, prescribed market* or an *MTF* (or, where appropriate, an equivalent venue outside the *EEA*), the four character Swift Market Identifier Code ISO 10383 must be used. However, where the venue has been identified as a *systematic internaliser*, a Swift Bank Identification Code (BIC) should be used.
EU		– where the *transaction* is made off market or the subject of the *transaction* is an *OTC derivative* this should be made clear.
EU	22. Transaction Reference Number	A unique identification number for the *transaction* provided by the *MiFID investment firm* or a third party reporting on its behalf.
EU	23. Cancellation Flag	An indication as to whether the *transaction* was cancelled.
EU	24. Customer/*Client* Identification	This field contains the identification of the *client* or customer on whose behalf the reporting *firm* was acting.
G		For agency transactions a customer/*client* identifier is required to identify the *client* on whose behalf the *transaction* has been conducted. Where an *FSA* reference number or a Swift Bank Identification Code (BIC) exists, one of these codes must be used or, in the case that a customer/*client* has neither an *FSA* reference number or a BIC, a unique internal code allocated by the reporting *firm* must be used and that unique internal code must be used consistently across all instrument types and platforms for that counterparty.
EU	25.	Any other fields Any other mandatory fields required by the reporting system.

SUP 17 Annexes 2–5

[deleted]

CHAPTER 18
TRANSFERS OF BUSINESS

18.1 Application

[2172]

18.1.1 **[G]** This chapter provides *guidance* in relation to business transfers.

(1) SUP 18.2 applies to any *firm* or to any *member* of Lloyd's proposing to transfer the whole or part of its business by an *insurance business transfer scheme* or to accept such a transfer. SUP 18.2.31G to SUP 18.2.41G also apply to the *independent expert* making the *scheme report*.

(2) SUP 18.3 applies to any *firm* proposing to accept certain transfers of *insurance business* taking place outside the *United Kingdom*.

(3) SUP 18.4 applies to any *friendly societies* proposing to amalgamate under section 85 of the Friendly Societies Act 1992, to any *friendly society* proposing to transfer engagements under section 86 of that Act to another body and to any body (whether or not it is a *friendly society*) proposing to accept such a transfer. SUP 18.4 also provides *guidance* to those wishing to make representations to the *FSA* about an application for confirmation of an amalgamation or transfer.

18.1.2 **[G]** *Guidance* on *building society* transfers and mergers is given in the Building Societies Regulatory Guide.

Introduction

18.1.3 **[G]** *Insurance business transfers* are subject to Part VII of the *Act* and must be approved by the court under section 111. The Financial Services and Markets Act 2000 (Control of Business Transfers)(Requirements on Applicants) Regulations 2001 (SI 2001/3625) also apply. These regulations set out minimum requirements for publicising schemes, notifying certain interested parties directly (subject to the discretion of the court), and giving information to anyone who requests it.

18.1.4 **[G]** An *insurance business transfer scheme* is defined in section 105 of the *Act* and the definition has been extended to transfers from *members* of Lloyd's to reflect the effect of the Financial Services and Markets Act 2000 (Control of Transfers of Business Done at Lloyd's) Order 2001(SI 2001/3626). With certain exclusions (relating to some schemes approved under foreign legislation, some novations of reinsurance or some captive *insurers*), it includes, in broad terms, any scheme to transfer *insurance business* from one *firm* (other than a *friendly society*) or *members* of Lloyd's to another body (which may be a *friendly society*), if:

(1)
- (a) the transferor is an "UK authorised person" and the business is being carried on in one or more *EEA States*; or
- (b) the business is reinsurance carried on in the *United Kingdom*; or
- (c) the business is carried on in the *United Kingdom* and the transferor is not an *EEA firm*; and

(2) in each case, the transferred business will be carried on from an establishment in the *EEA*.

The business transferred may include liabilities and potential liabilities on expired *policies*, liabilities on current *policies* and liabilities on contracts to be written in the period until the transfer takes effect. The parties to schemes approved under foreign legislation or involving novations of reinsurance or a captive *insurer* can apply to the court for an order sanctioning the scheme.

18.1.5 **[G]** In the opinion of the *FSA*, a novation or a number of novations would constitute an *insurance business transfer* only if their number or value were such that the novation was to be regarded as a transfer of part of the business. A novation is an agreement between the *policyholder* and two *insurers* whereby a contract with one *insurer* is replaced by a contract with the other. In the opinion of the *FSA*, where an *insurer* agrees to meet the liabilities (this may include undertaking the administration of the *policies*) of another *insurer* by means of a reinsurance contract, including Lloyd's *reinsurance to close*, this would not constitute an *insurance business transfer* because the contractual liability remains with the original *insurer*; nor would an arrangement whereby an *insurer* offers to renew the *policies* of another *insurer* on their expiry date.

18.1.6 **[G]** Under section 112 of the *Act*, the court has wide discretion to transfer property and liabilities to the transferee and to make orders in relation to incidental, consequential and supplementary matters. In the opinion of the *FSA*, the court has the power in such cases and on such terms as may be appropriate, to transfer the benefit of reinsurance contracts protecting the transferred business and to make such amendments to the terms of those contracts as may be necessary to give effect to that transfer of benefit.

18.1.7 **[G]** Amalgamations of *friendly societies* and transfers of engagements from *friendly societies* to other bodies (whether or not *friendly societies*) are governed by part VIII of the Friendly Societies Act 1992 and Schedule 15 to that Act applies.

18.2 Insurance business transfers

Purpose

18.2.1 **[G]** Transfers enable *firms* to manage their affairs more effectively, both for their own benefit and for that of their *customers*. However they represent an interference in the contracts between a *firm* and its *customers*, unless the *customers* individually consent, and may also affect the rights of third parties. An important protection is the requirement for the consent of the court. Under section 110 of the *Act*, the *FSA* is entitled to be heard by the court. In deciding whether it should appear, the *FSA* will consider the potential risk to its *regulatory objectives* of the scheme compared to not implementing the scheme.

18.2.2 **[G]** The *FSA's regulatory objectives* include market confidence and the protection of *consumers*. Either or both of these might be impaired if a transfer were approved that led to loss, or perceived loss, to *consumers* or other market participants. On the other hand a transfer that led to improved security or benefits for *consumers* would promote the *FSA's regulatory objectives*. When considering a transfer, the *FSA* needs to take into account the interests of existing *consumers* of the transferee and of *consumers* remaining with the transferor as well as of those whose contracts are being transferred. The *guidance* in this section is intended to protect *consumers*. By so doing it promotes the market confidence objective.

18.2.3 **[G]** Under section 5(2) of the *Act*, in considering what degree of protection may be appropriate for *consumers*, the *FSA* must have regard to their need for accurate information. Under *Principle* 7, a *firm* must pay due regard to the information needs of *clients* (the scope of the *Principle* is not precisely *consumers*). The extent and nature of the information provided to *consumers* about a proposed scheme will therefore be a factor for the *FSA* in determining its attitude to the scheme. For the court process to be an effective protection, *consumers* and others affected need to learn of the proposed transfer and receive sufficient information on the transfer and its effects in such a form as to enable them to decide if they are likely to be adversely affected, and whether they wish to be heard by the court. The information needed depends on the circumstances and cannot be precisely specified in advance but this chapter contains *guidance* aimed at ensuring that *consumers*, the *FSA* and the court receive adequate information.

18.2.4 **[G]** Under *Principle* 11, a *firm* must deal with the *FSA* in an open and cooperative way and disclose to the *FSA* appropriately anything relating to the *firm* of which the *FSA* would reasonably expect notice. This chapter contains *guidance* on the information that the *FSA* expects to receive from *firms* and *members* of Lloyd's in the context of *insurance business transfer schemes*.

18.2.5 **[G]** Under *Principle* 6, a *firm* must treat *customers* fairly (the scope of the *Principle* is not precisely *consumers*) and, under *Principle* 8, manage conflicts of interest fairly. A criterion for the *FSA* in considering a proposed scheme would be whether it appears that either *Principle* is not being followed. Transfers may have both positive and negative effects on individual *consumers*. In such circumstances it is for *consumers* to balance these effects and assess whether the proposed scheme as a whole is in their interests and whether to make representations to the court about the scheme. The *FSA's* main concern then becomes to ensure that *consumers* have appropriate information and not to set its judgment over theirs.

18.2.6 **[G]** A scheme may have a material effect on the transferor or the transferee. The *FSA* will take any scheme into account in its future regulation of the *firms*, where it continues to regulate them. This could include, for instance, the exercise of own-initiative powers under section 45 of the *Act* to vary a *firm's Part IV permission*, for instance, by requiring a *scheme of operations* (SUP 7 contains *guidance* on criteria for varying a *firm's Part IV permission*).

18.2.7 **[G]** For many transfers it is necessary to cooperate with *overseas regulators*. This section contains *guidance* on such cooperation.

18.2.8 **[G]** Section 86(8) of the Friendly Societies Act 1992 requires, where a transferee is a *friendly society*, that consent to accept the engagements is passed by special resolution in accordance with paragraph 7 of Schedule 12 to that Act. This section includes *guidance* about the information needed in these circumstances.

18.2.9 **[G]** Under section 109 of the *Act*, an *insurance business transfer scheme* must be accompanied by a *scheme report* in a form approved by the *FSA*. This section contains *guidance* on the form of a *scheme report*.

18.2.10 **[G]** Also under section 109 of the *Act*, the *scheme report* must be made by a *person* nominated or approved by the *FSA*. This section contains *guidance* on the procedures and general criteria that the *FSA* proposes to adopt for this purpose.

18.2.11 **[G]** The *FSA* has a duty under section 2(3) of the *Act* "to have regard to the need to use its resources in the most efficient and economic way". The extent to which (if at all) it examines and considers the details of a scheme and the resources it devotes to such consideration will depend on the potential risk to its *regulatory objectives*.

Procedure: initial steps

18.2.12 **[G]** When an *insurance business transfer scheme* is being considered, the scheme promoters (including the transferor and, except possibly if it is a new *company*, the transferee) should discuss the scheme with the *FSA* as soon as reasonably practical, to enable the *FSA* to consider what issues are likely to arise, and to enable a practical timetable for the scheme to be agreed. The *FSA* will wish to consider material issues relating to *policyholder* rights (such as the reasonable expectations of with-profits *policyholders*) or *policyholder* security at the earliest opportunity. In any case the *FSA* will need time to:

(1) consider the application, if an application by the transferee for a *Part IV permission* or a variation of *permission* is necessary (SUP 6 provides *guidance* on this);
(2) seek information or approvals from other supervisors (where this applies);
(3) consider what skills are needed to make a proper report on the scheme and what criteria should therefore be applied to the choice of *independent expert*;
(4) consider whether the promoters' nominee for *independent expert* is suitable for approval or, if the *FSA* proposes to nominate someone, who the *FSA* should nominate; and
(5) consider whether to object to the scheme in the light of the report and other circumstances.

18.2.13 **[G]** The initial information on the scheme provided to the *FSA* under SUP 18.2.12G should include its broad outline and its purpose. The *FSA* will indicate to the promoters how closely it wishes to monitor the progress of the scheme, including the extent to which it wishes to see draft documentation.

Independent expert: qualifications

18.2.14 **[G]** Under section 109(2) of the *Act* a *scheme report* may only be made by a *person*:
(1) appearing to the *FSA* to have the skills necessary to enable him to make a proper report; and
(2) nominated or approved for the purpose by the *FSA*.

18.2.15 **[G]** The general principles set out in SUP 5.4.8G, for suitability of a *skilled person*, apply also to the *independent expert*. The *FSA* expects the *independent expert* making the *scheme report* to be a natural person, who:
(1) is independent, that is any direct or indirect interest or connection he has or has had in either the transferor or transferee should not be such as to prejudice his status in the eyes of the court; and
(2) has relevant knowledge, both practical and theoretical, and experience of the types of *insurance business* transacted by the transferor and transferee.

18.2.16 **[G]** For a transfer of *long-term insurance business* the *independent expert* should be an *actuary* familiar with the role and responsibilities of the *actuarial function* holder and (if the relevant *insurance business* includes *with-profits insurance business*) a *with-profits actuary*.

18.2.17 **[G]** For a transfer of *general insurance business* the *independent expert* should normally be competent at assessing technical provisions and the uncertainties of the liabilities they represent (such as an *actuary*). Exceptionally, where issues other than the ability of the transferee to meet the liabilities to be transferred are much more significant in assessing the likely effects of the scheme, this criterion might not be applied. In such a case the *independent expert* would be expected to take advice from an appropriately qualified practitioner about the adequacy of the financial resources of the transferee.

18.2.18 **[G]** The *independent expert* would not normally be expected to be knowledgeable:
(1) about *general insurance business* if the business being transferred is *long-term insurance business* only; nor
(2) about *long-term insurance business* if the business being transferred is *general insurance business* only;

but, where either the transferor or transferee is a composite, he should understand the relevance of the *general insurance business* to the security of the *long-term insurance business policyholders* and vice versa and may need to seek independent specialist advice.

Independent expert: appointment

18.2.19 **[G]** The suitability of a *person* to act as an *independent expert* depends on the nature of the scheme and the *firms* concerned. On the basis of the preliminary information supplied by the scheme promoters (and any other knowledge it has of the circumstances and the *firms*), the *FSA* will consider what skills are needed to make a proper report on the scheme and what criteria should therefore be applied to the choice of *independent expert*. The *FSA* will inform the promoters of any such criteria it is minded to apply.

18.2.20 **[G]** Under section 107(2) of the *Act*, the application to the court may be made by the transferor or the transferee or both. As soon as reasonably practical, the intended applicant should choose their nominee for *independent expert* in the light of any criteria advised by the *FSA* and advise the *FSA* of their choice, unless the *FSA* wishes them to defer nomination or to make its own nomination. The notification should be accompanied by reasons why the party considers the nominee to be a suitable *person* to act as *independent expert*, together with relevant details of his experience and qualifications.

18.2.21 **[G]** The *FSA* may wish to have preliminary discussions with the nominee about the transfer to help the *FSA* determine whether he is suitably qualified to address issues arising from the transfer. The *FSA* will consider the suitability of the nominee and inform the *firm* that nominated him whether it approves him. Since the nature of the scheme is a factor in determining the suitability of the nominee, the *FSA* cannot approve a nominee before the broad outlines of the scheme have been determined. If the *FSA* rejects a nominee, it will normally inform him and, with the agreement of the nominee, the applicant of the reasons for the rejection.

18.2.22 **[G]** The *FSA* may itself nominate the *independent expert*, either where it indicates that a nomination is not required by the parties, or where it does not approve the parties' own nomination. In either case it will inform the promoters of its nominee.

18.2.23 **[G]** *Firms* should co-operate fully with the *independent expert* and provide him with access to all relevant information and appropriate staff.

Consultation with other regulators

18.2.24 **[G]** The *guidance* set out in SUP 18.2.25G to SUP 18.2.30G derives from the requirements of the *Insurance Directives* and the associated agreements between *EEA regulators*. Schedule 12 of the *Act* implements some of these requirements.

18.2.25 **[G]**

(1) If the transferee is (or will be) an *EEA firm* (authorised in its *Home State* to carry on *insurance business* under the *Insurance Directives*) or a *Swiss general insurance company*, then the *FSA* has to consult the transferee's *Home State regulator*, who has 3 months to respond. It will be necessary for the *FSA* to obtain from the transferee's *Home State regulator* a certificate confirming that the transferee will meet the *Home State's* solvency margin requirements (if any) after the transfer.

(2) If the transferee is *authorised* in the *United Kingdom*, the *FSA* will need to certify that the transferee will meet its solvency margin requirements after the transfer. If the *FSA* has required of a *UK firm* a financial recovery plan of the kind mentioned in paragraph 1 of article 38 of the Life Directive (2002/83/EC) or paragraph 1 of article 20a of the *First Non-Life Directive*, the *FSA* will not issue a certificate for so long as it considers that *policyholders'* rights are threatened within the meaning of paragraph 1.

18.2.26 **[G]** The transferor will need to provide the *FSA* with the information that the *Home State regulator* requires from *FSA*. This information includes:

(1) the transfer agreement or a draft, with:
 (a) the names and addresses of the transferor and transferee; and
 (b) the *classes* of *insurance business* and details of the nature of the risks or commitments to be transferred;

(2) for the business to be transferred (both before and after reinsurance):
 (a) the amount of technical provisions;
 (b) the amount of *premiums* (in the most recent financial period); and
 (c) for *general insurance business*, the *claims* incurred (in the most recent financial period);

(3) details of assets to be transferred;

(4) details of any guarantees (including reinsurance), whether provided by the transferor or a third party, to protect the provisions for the business transferred against deterioration; and

(5) the *states of the risks* or the *states of the commitments* being transferred.

18.2.27 **[G]** If the transferee is not (and will not be) *authorised* and will be neither an *EEA firm* nor a *Swiss general insurance company*, then the *FSA* will need to consult its insurance supervisor in the place where the business is to be transferred. The *FSA* will need confirmation from this supervisor that the transferee will meet his solvency margin requirements there (if any) after the transfer.

18.2.28 **[G]** If the transferor is an *UK insurer* and the business to be transferred includes business carried on from a branch in another *EEA State*, then the *FSA* has to consult the *Host State regulator*, who has 3 months to respond. The *FSA* will need to be given the information that the *Host State regulator* requires from it. This information should identify the parties to the transfer and include the transfer agreement or draft transfer agreement or a summary containing relevant information, and describe arrangements for settling *claims* if the branch is to be closed.

18.2.29 **[G]** If the transferor is an *UK insurer* and the business to be transferred includes a long-term insurance contract (other than reinsurance) for which the *state of the commitment* is an *EEA state* other than the *United Kingdom*, then the *FSA* has to consult the *Host State regulator*. If the transferor is an *UK insurer* and the business to be transferred includes a general insurance contract (other than reinsurance) for which the *state of the risk* is an *EEA state* other than the *United Kingdom*, then the *FSA* must consult the *Host State regulator*. The *FSA* will need to be given the information that the *Host State regulator* requires from it. This information should identify the parties to the transfer and include the transfer agreement or draft transfer agreement or a summary containing relevant information. It would be helpful (especially for *long-term insurance business*) if a draft of the *scheme report* was also available. The consent of the *Host State regulator* to the transfer is required, unless he does not respond within 3 months.

18.2.30 **[G]** Where the transferor is an *UK-deposit insurer* and, following the transfer, it will no longer be carrying on *insurance business* in the *United Kingdom*, the *FSA* will need to collaborate with *regulatory bodies* in the other *EEA States* in which it is carrying on business to ensure that effective supervision of the business carried on in the *EEA* continues. The transferor should cooperate with the *FSA* and the other *regulatory bodies* in this process and demonstrate that it will meet the requirements of its regulators following the transfer.

Form of scheme report

18.2.31 **[G]** Under section 109 of the *Act*, a *scheme report* must accompany an application to the court to approve an *insurance business transfer scheme*. This report must be made in a form approved by the *FSA*. The *FSA* would not expect to approve the form of a *scheme report* unless it complies with SUP 18.2.33G and would expect to approve the form of a *scheme report* that complies. SUP 18.2.32G and SUP 18.2.34G to SUP 18.2.41G provide additional *guidance* for the *independent expert*.

18.2.32 **[G]** There may be matters relating to the scheme or the parties to the transfer that the *FSA* wishes to draw to the attention of the *independent expert*. The *FSA* may also wish the report to address particular issues. The *independent expert* should therefore contact the *FSA* at an early stage to establish whether there are such matters or issues. The *independent expert* should form his own opinion on such issues, which may differ from the opinion of the *FSA*.

18.2.33 **[G]** The *scheme report* should comply with the applicable rules on expert evidence and contain the following information:

(1) who appointed the *independent expert* and who is bearing the costs of that appointment;
(2) confirmation that the *independent expert* has been approved or nominated by the *FSA*;
(3) a statement of *independent expert's* professional qualifications and (where appropriate) descriptions of the experience that fits him for the role;
(4) whether the *independent expert* has, or has had, direct or indirect interest in any of the parties which might be thought to influence his independence, and details of any such interest;
(5) the scope of the report;
(6) the purpose of the scheme;
(7) a summary of the terms of the scheme in so far as they are relevant to the report;
(8) what documents, reports and other material information the *independent expert* has considered in preparing his report and whether any information that he requested has not been provided;
(9) the extent to which the *independent expert* has relied on:
    (a) information provided by others; and
    (b) the judgment of others;
(10) the people on whom the *independent expert* has relied and why, in his opinion, such reliance is reasonable;
(11) his opinion of the likely effects of the scheme on *policyholders* (this term is defined to include *persons* with certain rights and contingent rights under the *policies*), distinguishing between:
    (a) transferring *policyholders*;
    (b) *policyholders* of the transferor whose contracts will not be transferred; and
    (c) *policyholders* of the transferee;
(12) what matters (if any) that the *independent expert* has not taken into account or evaluated in the report that might, in his opinion, be relevant to *policyholders*' consideration of the scheme; and
(13) for each opinion that the *independent expert* expresses in the report, an outline of his reasons.

18.2.34 **[G]** The purpose of the *scheme report* is to inform the court and the *independent expert* therefore has a duty to the court. However reliance will also be placed on it by *policyholders*, by others affected by the scheme and by the *FSA*. The amount of detail that it is appropriate to include will depend on the complexity of the scheme, the materiality of the details themselves and the circumstances. For instance where it is clear that no-one will be adversely affected by the transfer, a simple explanation for this conclusion plus the details required by SUP 18.2.33G might be an adequate report.

18.2.35 **[G]** The summary of the terms of the scheme should include:

(1) a description of any reinsurance arrangements that it is proposed should pass to the transferee under the scheme; and

(2) a description of any guarantees or additional reinsurance that will cover the transferred business or the business of the transferor that will not be transferred.

18.2.36 **[G]** The *independent expert's* opinion of the likely effects of the scheme on *policyholders* should:

(1) include a comparison of the likely effects if it is or is not implemented;
(2) state whether he considered alternative arrangements and, if so, what;
(3) where different groups of *policyholders* are likely to be affected differently by the scheme, include comment on those differences he considers may be material to the *policyholders*; and
(4) include his views on:
 (a) the effect of the scheme on the security of *policyholders'* contractual rights, including the likelihood and potential effects of the insolvency of the *insurer*;
 (b) the likely effects of the scheme on matters such as investment management, new business strategy, administration, expense levels and valuation bases in so far as they may affect:
  (i) the security of *policyholders'* contractual rights;
  (ii) levels of service provided to *policyholders*; or
  (iii) for *long-term insurance business*, the reasonable expectations of *policyholders*; and
 (c) the cost and tax effects of the scheme, in so far as they may affect the security of *policyholders'* contractual rights, or for *long-term insurance business*, their reasonable expectations.

18.2.37 **[G]** The *independent expert* is not expected to comment on the likely effects on new *policyholders*, that is, those whose contracts are entered into after the effective date of the transfer.

18.2.38 **[G]** For any mutual *company* involved in the scheme, the report should:

(1) describe the effect of the scheme on the proprietary rights of members of the *company*, including the significance of any loss or dilution of the rights of those members to secure or prevent further changes which could affect their entitlements as *policyholders*;
(2) state whether, and to what extent, members will receive compensation under the scheme for any diminution of proprietary rights; and
(3) comment on the appropriateness of any compensation, paying particular attention to any differences in treatment between members with voting rights and those without.

18.2.39 **[G]** For a scheme involving *long-term insurance business*, the report should:

(1) describe the effect of the scheme on the nature and value of any rights of *policyholders* to participate in profits;
(2) if any such rights will be diluted by the scheme, how any compensation offered to *policyholders* as a group (such as the injection of funds, allocation of shares, or cash payments) compares with the value of that dilution, and whether the extent and method of its proposed division is equitable as between different classes and generations of *policyholders*;
(3) describe the likely effect of the scheme on the approach used to determine:
 (a) the amounts of any non-guaranteed benefits such as bonuses and *surrender values*; and
 (b) the levels of any discretionary charges;
(4) describe what safeguards are provided by the scheme against a subsequent change of approach to these matters that could act to the detriment of existing *policyholders* of either *firm*;
(5) include the *independent expert's* overall assessment of the likely effects of the scheme on the reasonable expectations of *long-term insurance business policyholders*;
(6) state whether the *independent expert* is satisfied that for each *firm* the scheme is equitable to all classes and generations of its *policyholders*; and
(7) state whether, in the *independent expert's* opinion, for each relevant *firm* the scheme has sufficient safeguards (such as principles of financial management or certification by a *with-profits actuary* or *actuarial function* holder) to ensure that the scheme operates as presented.

18.2.40 **[G]** Where the transfer forms part of a wider chain of events or corporate restructuring, it may not be appropriate to consider the transfer in isolation and the *independent expert* should seek sufficient explanations on corporate plans to enable him to understand the wider picture. Likewise he will need information on the operational plans of the transferee and, if only part of the business of the transferor is transferred, of the transferor. These will need to have sufficient detail to allow him to understand in broad terms how the business will be run. He would not normally be expected to assess the adequacy of systems and controls in detail.

18.2.41 **[G]** A transfer may provide for benefits to be reduced for some or all of the *policies* being transferred. This might happen if the transferor is in financial difficulties. If there is such a proposal, the *independent expert* should report on what reductions he considers ought to be made, unless either:

(1) the information required is not available and will not become available in time for his report, for instance it might depend on future events; or
(2) otherwise, he is unable to report on this aspect in the time available.

Under such circumstances, the transfer might be urgent and it might be appropriate for the reduction in benefits to take place after the event, by means of an order under section 112 of the *Act*. The *FSA* would wish to consider the fairness of any such reduction and section 113 allows the court to appoint an independent *actuary* to report to the *FSA* on any such post-transfer reduction in benefits.

Notice provisions

18.2.42 **[G]** Under the Financial Services and Markets Act 2000 (Control of Business Transfers) (Requirements on Applicants) Regulations 2001 (SI 2001/3625), unless the court directs otherwise, notice of the application must be sent to all *policyholders* of the parties. It may also be appropriate to give notice to others affected, in particular to:
(1) reinsurers of the transferor where it is proposed that benefits or liabilities under their contracts should pass to the transferee; and
(2) anyone with an interest in the *policies* being transferred who has notified the transferor of their interest.

18.2.43 **[G]** The regulations referred to in SUP 18.2.42G require that notice of the application must be published in:
(1) the London, Edinburgh and Belfast Gazettes; and
(2) unless the court directs otherwise, in:
  (a) two national newspapers in the *United Kingdom*; and
  (b) in two national newspapers in any other *EEA State* that is the *state of the risk* or the *state of the commitment*.

Wider publication may be appropriate in some circumstances (especially if not all *policyholders* are sent notices).

18.2.44 **[G]** The regulations referred to in SUP 18.2.44G require that the *FSA* approves in advance the notices sent to *policyholders* and published in the press.

18.2.45 **[G]** Where a transfer involves *members* of Lloyd's as transferor or transferee, any notice requirements of the *Society* will also apply.

18.2.46 **[G]** The *FSA* is entitled to be heard by the court on any application for a transfer. A consideration for the *FSA* in determining whether to oppose a transfer would be its view on whether adequate steps had been taken to tell *policyholders* about the transfer and whether they had adequate information and time to consider it. The *FSA* would not normally consider adequate a period of less than six weeks between sending notices to *policyholders* and the date of the court hearing. Therefore it would be sensible, before requesting the court for a waiver of the publication requirements or the requirement to send statements direct to *policyholders*, to consult the *FSA* on its views about what waivers might be appropriate and what substitute arrangements might be made. The *FSA* will take into account the practicality and costs of sending notices to *policyholders* (especially for *firms* in financial difficulty), the likely benefits for *policyholders* of receiving notices and the efficacy of other arrangements proposed for informing *policyholders* (including additional advertising or, where appropriate, electronic communication). For instance, the *FSA* would be unlikely to object to a transfer on the grounds that *policyholders* had not been sent notices, if cover for the *policies* concerned had expired and the probability of them making a *claim* was so small as to make the sending disproportionately expensive (particularly if there had been additional advertising). A *firm* may not be able to send notices to some or all of its *policyholders*, because it does not have their address, or may not even know their identity. This situation is not uncommon for business written through brokers or other agents. In such a case, alternative ways of informing *policyholders* need to be considered.

18.2.47 **[G]** As the consent (or presumed consent) of the *Host State* is required for a transfer covering contracts for which another *EEA State* is the *state of the risk* (for *general insurance business*) or the *state of the commitment* (for *long-term insurance business*), it is advisable to obtain the consent of *regulatory body* in the *Host State* to any waiver of publication in that state. The approval of the court will still be required.

Statement to policyholders

18.2.48 **[G]** It would normally be appropriate to include with the notice referred to in SUP 18.2.42G a statement setting out the terms of the scheme and containing a summary of the *scheme report*. Ideally every recipient should understand in broad terms from the summary how the scheme is likely to affect him. This objective will be most nearly achieved if the summary is clear and concise while containing sufficient detail for the purpose. A lengthy summary or one that was hard to understand would not be appropriate. Regulations require the *scheme report*, the notice and the statement to be made available to anyone requesting them. The internet can be used for this purpose if it is suitable for the *person* making the request.

18.2.49 **[G]** Where the transferee is a *friendly society*, the notice should include information about the meeting at which a special resolution in accordance with paragraph 7 of Schedule 12 to the Friendly Societies Act 1992 is to be voted on, including the date of the meeting, how notice of the meeting is to be given to members and the terms of the special resolution. After the meeting the *friendly society* should inform the *FSA* whether the special resolution has been passed. The court will also need to be informed, so an appropriate way of informing the *FSA* may be to include it in the affidavit to the court.

18.2.50 **[G]** The *FSA* should be given the opportunity to comment on the statement referred to in SUP 18.2.48G before it is sent, unless the *FSA* has informed the promoters in writing that it does not wish to do so.

FSA assessment of scheme

18.2.51 **[G]** The assessment is a continuing process, starting when the scheme promoters first approach the *FSA* about a proposed scheme. Among the considerations that may be relevant to both the depth of consideration given to, and the *FSA's* opinion on, a scheme are:

(1) the potential risk posed by the transfer to the *regulatory objectives*;
(2) the purpose of the scheme;
(3) how the security of *policyholders*' (who include *persons* with certain rights and contingent rights under the *policies*) contractual rights appears to be affected;
(4) how the scheme compares with possible alternatives, particularly those that do not require approval (whether by the court or the *FSA*);
(5) how *policyholders'* rights and reasonable expectations appear to be affected;
(6) the compensation offered to *policyholders* for any loss of rights or expectations;
(7) how for other *persons* (besides *policyholders*) who have an interest in *policies*, their rights and the security of those rights appear to be affected;
(8) the opportunity given to *policyholders* to consider the scheme, that is whether they have been properly notified, whether they have had adequate information and whether they have had adequate time to consider that information;
(9) the opinion of the *independent expert*;
(10) for a transfer that involves *members* of Lloyd's as transferor or transferee, the effect on the *Society*;
(11) the views of other *regulatory bodies* consulted in connection with the proposed transfer; and
(12) any views expressed by *policyholders*.

18.2.52 **[G]** The *scheme report* will be an important factor in the view the *FSA* forms on a scheme. The *FSA* will place considerable reliance on the opinions of the *independent expert* and the reasons for them. However it will form its own view taking into account other information and having regard to its *regulatory objectives*.

18.2.53 **[G]** The *FSA* is likely to object to a scheme if it concludes that it is unfair to a class of *policyholders*, unless the *policyholders* of that class have approved the scheme on the basis of information the *FSA* considers clear and accurate. *Policyholders* are not required to vote on a scheme but would, for instance, normally vote on a demutualisation or on a scheme of arrangement under the Companies Act 2006. The *FSA* is also likely to object to a scheme if it concludes that it has a material adverse effect on *policyholders'* security. The *FSA* may wish to satisfy itself that questions of systems and controls are properly addressed. There may also be conduct of business issues, particularly if the market has not fully absorbed the impact of the scheme by its effective date. The *FSA* would seek to resolve such issues through discussion with the scheme promoters in advance of the application to the court for approval, giving them the opportunity to amend the scheme or documentation, or otherwise to allay the *FSA's* concerns. Scheme promoters should keep the *FSA* informed to allow this discussion.

18.2.54 **[G]** The *FSA* may exercise its other powers under the *Act*, if it considers this a more effective method of achieving its *regulatory objectives*.

18.2.55 **[G]** The *FSA* is not required under its *regulatory objectives* to object to a scheme merely because some other scheme might have been in the better interests of *policyholders*, if the scheme itself is not adverse to their interests. However there may be circumstances where treating *customers* fairly would require a *firm* to consider or to implement an alternative scheme.

18.2.56 **[G]** Where a transfer involves *members* of Lloyd's as transferor or transferee, the *FSA* will consult the *Society*. Where the business of a *syndicate* is being transferred, the transfer involves all *members* participating in the relevant *syndicate years*.

18.2.57 **[G]** Regulations require that copies of the application to the court, the *scheme report* and the statement for *policyholders* referred to in SUP 18.2.48G are also given to the *FSA*. This enables the *FSA* to consider these and determine whether it wishes to be heard by the court. It might assist the *FSA* if these items were given to the *FSA* in draft, in the first instance. This would enable:

(1) the *FSA* to seek clarification before the documents were finalised; and
(2) if the promoters so choose, allow them to amend the scheme to meet any concerns of the *FSA*.

18.2.58 **[G]** For *long-term insurance business*, the affidavit evidence to the court would normally include copies of reports on the transfer by the *actuarial function* holder and (if the *insurance business* includes *with-profits business*) the *with-profits actuary* of both *firms*, which should be provided to the *FSA* at an early stage. SUP 4.3.17G (4) requires a *firm* to request the advice of its *with-profits actuary* about the likely effect of material changes in its business plans on the rights and reasonable expectations of *long-term insurance business policyholders*. A transfer would be material unless the liabilities transferred were not material relative to the total liabilities of the *firm*. The advice on a transfer would normally be in the form of a formal report by the *with-profits actuary*.

18.2.59 **[G]** The scheme promoters should advise the *FSA* about any material representations made to them in response to the transfer scheme. Where it is proposed that reinsurance arrangements should pass to the transferee under the scheme, the *FSA* should also be informed about the steps being taken to consult with, or seek the consent of, the reinsurers and the reactions received.

18.2.60 **[G]** The court is likely to wish to know the *FSA's* opinion on the scheme and, if the *FSA* does not intend to be heard, the affidavit may include a summary of the views expressed by the *FSA*. The applicants to the court should provide the *FSA* with a copy of all the affidavit evidence that they intend to submit to the court.

18.3 Insurance business transfers outside the United Kingdom

Purpose

18.3.1 **[G]** Under section 115 of the *Act*, the *FSA* has the power to give a certificate confirming that a *firm* possesses any *required minimum margin*, to facilitate an *insurance business* transfer to the *firm* under overseas legislation from a firm authorised in another *EEA State* or from a *Swiss general insurance company*. This section provides *guidance* on how the *FSA* would exercise this power and on related matters.

FSA response to proposal

18.3.2 **[G]** Under cooperation agreements between *EEA regulators*, if it has serious concerns about the proposed transferee, the *FSA* should inform the *regulatory body* of the transferor within 3 months of the original request from that *regulatory body*. The *FSA* is not obliged to reply, but if it does not, its opinion is taken to be favorable. Although the protocol does not apply to Switzerland, the *FSA* is required to cooperate with the Swiss *regulatory body* and would apply similar principles to a proposed transfer from a *Swiss general insurance company*.

18.3.3 **[G]** The information that the *regulatory body* of the transferor is required to supply will normally be sufficient for the *FSA* to determine whether the transfer is likely to have a material effect on the transferee.

18.3.4 **[G]** If the effect of the transfer is not likely to be material and the *FSA* does not already have serious concerns about the transferee, the *FSA* can reply favorably.

18.3.5 **[G]** If the effect of the transfer may be material, the *FSA* will need to consider whether to request a *scheme of operations* or other information from the proposed transferee to assist in determining whether the likely effect of the transfer is such that the *FSA* should have serious concerns.

18.3.6 **[G]** If the effect of the transfer may have a material adverse effect on the transferee or the security of *policyholders*, the *FSA* will consider whether it is appropriate to exercise its powers under the *Act* to achieve its *regulatory objectives*.

18.4 Friendly Society transfers and amalgamations

Purpose

18.4.1 **[G]** It is for the committee of management of a *friendly society* to decide whether to recommend an amalgamation or a transfer of engagements to the society's members. This section provides some *guidance* on the procedures to be followed and the information to be provided to a *friendly society's* members so that they are appropriately informed before they exercise their right to vote on the proposals.

General considerations

18.4.2 **[G]** *Friendly societies* are encouraged to discuss a proposed transfer or amalgamation with the *FSA*, at an early stage to help ensure that a workable timetable is developed. This is particularly important where there are notification requirements for supervisory authorities in *EEA States* other than the *United Kingdom*, or for an amalgamation where additional procedures are required.

18.4.3 **[G]** The *FSA* will want to satisfy itself that after an amalgamation or a transfer the business will be prudently managed and continue to comply with the *Principles*. It may therefore require prudential information to be provided. It may request prudential information at an early stage to provide itself with adequate time to assess the information.

18.4.4 **[G]** For a transfer to another *friendly society*, if the conditions of 87(1) and 87(2) of the Friendly Societies Act 1992 are met a report is required from the *appropriate actuary* of the transferee to confirm that it will meet the *required minimum margin*. Where the conditions of 87(1) and 87(3) are met the *FSA* may require a report from the *appropriate actuary* of the transferee to confirm that it will have an excess of assets over liabilities.

18.4.5 **[G]** For a transfer of *long-term insurance business*, the *FSA* may, under section 88 of the Friendly Societies Act 1992, require a report from an independent *actuary* on the terms of the proposed transfer and on his opinion of the likely effects of the transfer on long-term *policyholder* members of either the transferor or (if it is a *friendly society*) the transferee. A summary is included in the statement sent to members (see SUP 18.4.13G) and the full report is required to be made available to anyone on payment of a reasonable fee. The general principles in SUP 18.2.32G to SUP 18.2.40G apply to the independent *actuary's* report.

18.4.6 **[G]** Under the Friendly Societies Act 1992 the *FSA* may not confirm a transfer of engagements unless it is satisfied that the transfer is in the interests of the members of each *friendly society* participating in the transfer (see SUP 18.4.25G (2)(b)). It will therefore ask that the participating societies' *actuaries* confirm that the transfer is in the interests of the members.

18.4.7 **[G]** Under the Friendly Societies Act 1992, members will normally have the opportunity to vote on a proposed transfer or amalgamation (SUP 18.4.11G and SUP 18.4.12G describe exceptions). A *friendly society* has to ensure that, before casting their votes, its members are clearly and fully informed of the terms on which the amalgamation or transfer of engagements is to take place and that they have all the information needed to understand how their interests will be affected. If the society's rules permit, delegates can vote except on an "affected members' resolution" under section 86. The *FSA* may not confirm an amalgamation or a transfer if it considers that information material to the members' decision was not made available to all the members eligible to vote.

18.4.8 **[G]** Amendments to a *friendly society's* registered rules may be necessary to permit a transfer to it. The *FSA* will need to be consulted in the usual way about registration of the appropriate rules. Similarly for an amalgamation, each of the amalgamating societies has to approve the memorandum and rules of the new society and the requirements of schedule 3 to the Friendly Societies Act 1992 have to be met. It will be necessary to allow adequate time for these processes.

18.4.9 **[G]** For an amalgamation the successor society, and for a transfer the transferee, may need to apply for *permission*, or to vary its *permission*, under Part IV of the *Act*. The *FSA* will need time before confirming a transfer to consider whether any necessary *permission* or variation should be given. If the transferee is an *EEA firm* or a *Swiss general insurance company*, then confirmation will be needed from its *Home State regulator* that it meets the *Home State's* solvency margin requirements (see SUP 18.4.25G (3)).

18.4.10 **[G]** It is likely that the information sent to members will include a statement explaining the reasons for the amalgamation or transfer and the choice of partner. Although this is not a statutory statement and not subject to *FSA* approval, the *FSA* will take the statement into account when considering whether to confirm the amalgamation or transfer. A *friendly society* will therefore find it helpful to consult the *FSA* about the content of such a statement.

FSA discretion

18.4.11 **[G]** The *FSA* has discretion under section 86(3)(b) of the Friendly Societies Act 1992 to allow a transferee society to resolve to undertake to fulfil the engagements of a transferor society by resolution of the committee of management, rather than by special resolution. Among the issues on which the *FSA* will wish to satisfy itself before exercising this discretion, are that the transfer will be in the interests of the members of both societies and that the transfer will not mean a change of policy by the transferee society. The *FSA* is unlikely to exercise this discretion unless the transferee is significantly larger than the business to be transferred.

18.4.12 **[G]** The *FSA* has discretion under section 89 of the Friendly Societies Act 1992 to modify some of the requirements for a transfer of engagements from a *friendly society*, on the application of a specified number of its members, if it is satisfied that it is expedient to do so in the interests of its members or potential members.

Schedule 15 statement to members

18.4.13 **[G]** Schedule 15 to the Friendly Societies Act 1992 requires a statement to be sent to every member of a *friendly society* entitled to vote on a transfer or amalgamation. Among other matters this statement has to cover the financial position of the *friendly society* and every other participant in the transfer or amalgamation. The members should be provided with sufficient financial information about the respective financial positions of the participants to gain an understanding of the relative financial strengths and key features of the participants. The statement has to include a summary of any *actuary's* report under section 88, though the *FSA* may direct that the summary is to be provided separately if inclusion appears impractical.

18.4.14 **[G]** The financial information provided under SUP 18.4.13G would normally contain comparative statements of balance sheets at the same date, and include main investments, reserves and funds or technical provisions, with details of the number of members of each participant as at the balance sheet date and the *premium* income of the relevant fund of each participant during the financial year to which the balance sheet relates. SUP 18.4.15G to SUP 18.4.18G give further *guidance* on the financial information to be included.

18.4.15 **[G]** If the information relates to a position some time in the past, the information should state that there has been no significant change or include a clear description of the changes. Differences in accounting *policies* and reporting requirements could lead to the loss of some comparability between participants. Such differences and their estimated financial effects (if any) should be explained.

18.4.16 **[G]** The information should state whether any of the participants has any significant future capital commitments. The *FSA* will require it to state that the transfer of engagements or amalgamation will not conflict with any contractual commitment by a society, any *subsidiary* or any body jointly controlled by it and others.

18.4.17 **[G]** Brief details should be given of the date of the last actuarial valuation and the position revealed (surplus/deficit, *required minimum margin* and free assets) for each participant.

18.4.18 **[G]** The *FSA* may require confirmation from the auditors of either *friendly society* involved in the transfer or amalgamation about the reasonableness of any part of the information in the statement. For instance such confirmation would normally be required if the financial information relates to a date more than six months previously.

18.4.19 **[G]** The statement is required to include particulars of:

(1) any interest of the members of the committee of management in the amalgamation or transfer; and

(2) any compensation or other consideration proposed to be paid to committee members or other *officers* of the society and to the *officers* of every other society or *person* participating in the amalgamation or transfer.

Under section 92 of the Friendly Societies Act 1992, any compensation must be approved by a special resolution, separate from any resolution approving other terms of the amalgamation or transfer. This enables members to vote on this as a separate issue.

18.4.20 **[G]** Under schedule 15 to the Friendly Societies Act 1992, the *FSA* may require the statement to include any other matter. The *FSA* would normally require inclusion of the terms on which the amalgamation or the transfer of engagements is to be made.

18.4.21 **[G]** The statement should be clearly separate from other information sent to members. It has to be approved by the *FSA* and if it is not in a self-contained document, the approved element should appear in a separate section.

18.4.22 **[G]** SUP 18 Ann 1G provides an example of the information for members required by Schedule 15.

Confirmation procedures and criteria

18.4.23 **[G]** Under the Friendly Societies Act 1992:

(1) when the members of a transferor society have approved the transfer of its engagements by passing a special resolution and the transferee has approved the transfer (by passing a resolution where the transferee is a *friendly society*); or

(2) when two or more societies have approved a proposed amalgamation by passing a special resolution;

it, or they jointly, must then obtain confirmation by the *FSA* of the transfer. Notice of the application will need to be published in one or more of the London, Edinburgh or Belfast Gazettes and other newspapers as directed by the *FSA*. If the *FSA* confirms a transfer, then it will register the society's instrument of transfer after receiving an application on the appropriate form by the transferor society and the transferee. If the *FSA* confirms an amalgamation, it will register the successor society. All the property, rights and liabilities pass on the transfer date specified by the *FSA*.

18.4.24 **[G]** For a *directive friendly society*, if the transfer or amalgamation includes *policies* where the *state of the risk* or the *state of the commitment* is an *EEA State* other than the *United Kingdom*, consultation with the *Host State regulator* is required and SUP 18.2.25G to SUP 18.2.29G apply (for an amalgamation they apply as if the business of the amalgamating societies is to be transferred to the successor society). paragraph 6(1) of Schedule 15 to the Friendly Societies Act 1992 requires publication of the application to the *FSA* for confirmation of an amalgamation or transfer and the *FSA* may require the notice of the application to be published in two national newspapers in the *Host State*.

18.4.25 **[G]** The criteria that the *FSA* must use in determining whether to confirm a proposed amalgamation or transfer are set out in schedule 15 to the Friendly Societies Act 1992. These criteria include that:

(1) confirmation must not be given if the *FSA* considers that:
  (a) there is a substantial risk that the successor society or transferee will be unable lawfully to carry out the engagements to be transferred to it;
  (b) information material to the members' decision about the amalgamation or transfer was not made available to all the members eligible to vote;
  (c) the vote on any resolution approving the amalgamation or transfer does not represent the views of the members eligible to vote; or
  (d) some relevant requirement of the Friendly Societies Act 1992 or the rules of any of the participating societies was not fulfilled (but it can modify some requirements and direct that certain failures may be disregarded, see SUP 18.4.12G and SUP 18.4.27G);

(2) the *FSA* must be satisfied that:
  (a) the transferee or successor society will have any *permissions* necessary under Part IV of the *Act*;
  (b) for a transfer, it is in the interests of the members of each *friendly society* participating in it (see SUP 18.4.6G); and
  (c) for a *directive friendly society* where a transfer includes *policies* where the *state of the risk* or the *state of the commitment* is an *EEA State* other than the *United Kingdom*, the *Host State regulator* has been notified of the transfer and has consented or has not refused consent to the transfer; and

(3) for a transfer, the transferee possesses the *required minimum margin* after taking the proposed transfer into account or, where it is not required to maintain a *required minimum margin*, possesses an excess of assets over liabilities (for a transferee that is a *Swiss general insurance company* or an *EEA firm*, this is evidenced by a certificate from its *home state regulator*).

18.4.26 **[G]** If *authorisation* or a *Part IV permission* is needed, the *FSA* will need to consider the application for *authorisation* or *permission* in the usual way. If the *authorisation* or *permission* is refused, confirmation cannot be given even if all the other criteria are met. As part of the *regulatory objective* to protect *consumers*, the *FSA* may consider whether an amalgamation is in the interests of members.

18.4.27 **[G]** The *FSA* may (as an alternative to refusing confirmation) direct the society or societies to remedy certain procedural defects in a proposed transfer or amalgamation, and after they have been remedied confirm the application. If it appears to the *FSA* that failure to meet a "relevant requirement" of the Friendly Societies Act 1992 or the rules of the *friendly society* could not be material to the members' decision, then it may direct that this failure is to be disregarded.

Confirmation procedures: representations

18.4.28 **[G]** Any interested party has the right to make representations to the *FSA* about an application for confirmation of a transfer or amalgamation. This includes any *person* (whether a member of the *friendly society* or not) who claims that he would be adversely affected by the amalgamation or transfer. The *person* making the representations should state clearly why he or she claims to be an interested party and the ground or grounds to which the representations are directed.

18.4.29 **[G]** Written representations, or written notice of a *person's* intention to make oral representations, or both, are required to reach the *FSA* by the date published in the relevant Gazettes and other newspapers. Those giving notice of intent to make oral representations are advised to state the nature and general grounds of the oral representations they intend to make. *Persons* who make written representations but subsequently decide also to make oral representations are required, nevertheless, to give notice of that intention, in writing, to the *FSA* by the same date.

18.4.30 **[G]** The *FSA* will send copies of all written representations to the society(ies), and will afford them an opportunity to comment on the representations. It may consider the written representations and a society's response to them, before the date set for hearing oral representations. A synopsis of the written representations (probably in the form of a summary of each of the points made and the numbers of *persons* making each point) and a society's responses will be made available to those participating in the hearing. This is intended to inform those making oral representations of the points already being considered by the *FSA*.

18.4.31 **[G]** The *FSA* expects that any documents referred to in a society's comments will be made available by the society for inspection at its registered office and, if reasonably possible, at the venue of the hearing on the date of the hearing. However if a society applies to put documents which it considers to be sensitive to the *FSA* in confidence, the *FSA* will balance any disadvantage this might cause interested parties in making representations against the commercial damage that publication of the documents might cause, and may permit the documents or sensitive parts of them not to be available for inspection.

Confirmation hearing

18.4.32 **[G]** Interested parties may be represented and may make collective representations. Such arrangements should be notified to the *FSA* in advance to enable it to make appropriate arrangements.

18.4.33 **[G]** The hearing referred to in SUP 18.4.30G will be at a time and place that will be notified to the participants and will be conducted by *FSA* representatives. The hearing may last longer than one day and may be adjourned. The *FSA* will try to tell participants when they may expect to make their representations and when the society may be expected to respond.

18.4.34 **[G]** The *FSA* expects that oral hearings will be held in public though this is not required. At the start members of the general public and the press will be asked to wait outside while participants are asked if any of them has good reason to object to the admission of the general public or the press. Unless an objection by a participant is upheld by the *FSA* representatives, the press and the general public will then be admitted, within the limits of the space available. However, the *FSA* representatives may decide that parts of the hearing will be in private if that appears to them to be desirable.

18.4.35 **[G]** The procedure will be informal. All participants will be expected to speak concisely and avoid repetition. The *FSA* will, as far as practicable, help those who are not professionally represented. Those taking the hearing may question the participants. The sequence of events will normally be broadly:

(1) any preliminary matters (such as the admission of the public or other procedural questions) will be dealt with;
(2) the chair of the hearing will introduce the proceedings;
(3) the society representatives will be invited to speak on the application, including a description of the events at the meeting at which the resolution to amalgamate or transfer was put to the members, a statement of the voting on the resolution, and any other matters which they wish to introduce at that stage;
(4) the other participants will be invited to speak to their representations. The *FSA* expects to call them in order of a list arranged, so far as possible, by subject matter;
(5) the society representatives will be invited to reply to, or comment on, the points made by the other participants; and
(6) the other participants will be invited to comment on the society replies.

18.4.36 **[G]** The above procedure may be varied according to the circumstances at the hearing, and is intended only as a guide. The hearing may be adjourned if the *FSA* representatives consider that necessary to enable facts to be checked or additional information to be obtained.

18.4.37 **[G]** The *FSA* will not decide whether to confirm the transfer or amalgamation at the hearing. A copy of its written decision, including its findings on the points made in representations, will be sent to the society(ies) and to those making representations. It will also be available to any other *person* on request and may be published.

Annex 1

SUP 18 Annex 1 **[G]**
(1) Table Example of Schedule 15 statement G

Transfer/Amalgamation of [Society A] to/with [Society B]		
Proposed effective date:		
Comparative financial positions		
(a) Balance Sheet as at 31 December 20—		
	Society A	Society B
ASSETS		
Land and buildings (4)		
Government securities		
Equities		
Other investments (6)		
Fixed assets		
Other assets		
Cash at bank and in hand		
LIABILITIES		

Transfer/Amalgamation of [Society A] to/with [Society B]		
Benefit funds [technical provisions] (7)		
[Management fund]		
Other liabilities and provisions		
Reserve funds [Reserves] (8)		

NOTES

(1) The above figures are extracted from the audited accounts [unaudited accounts] of [Society A and Society B] for the year [period] ended:

(2) There has been no significant change in the financial position of the [participants] [except for]

(3) The future capital commitments of [the participants] are: [None of [the participants] has any significant future capital commitments.]

(4) Land and buildings have been brought into account on the following bases: (include statement of any differences in accounting policies and where material any estimated financial effects)

(5) Investments have been brought into account on the following bases: (include statement of any differences in accounting policies and where material any estimated financial effects)

(6) Other investments comprise: (include statement of any differences in accounting policies and where material any estimated financial effects)

(7) Benefit Funds [Technical Provisions] comprise: include statement of any differences in accounting policies and where material any estimated financial effects)

(8) Reserve Funds [Reserves] comprise:

(9) The membership at [ ] and premium income received during [ ] for each [participant] were:

(10) Brief summary of the financial position of each [participant] as shown in the last actuarial investigation:

(11) Summary of independent actuary's report under section 88 of the Friendly Societies Act 1992:

(12) The interests of committee members of the [participants] in the transfer [amalgamation] are:

(13) Proposed compensation to be paid to committee members and[/or] to other officers is:

(14) The terms of the transfer[amalgamation] are:

CHAPTER 19
COMMODITY FUTURES TRADING COMMISSION PART 30 EXEMPTION

[deleted]

CHAPTER 20
FEES RULES

20.1–20.7

[2173]
The periodic fees rules are set out in FEES 4 (Periodic fees).

CHAPTER 21
WAIVER

21.1 Form of waiver for energy market participants

[2174]
21.1.1 **[G]** EMPS 2Ann1G sets out a form of *waiver* that the *FSA* will be minded to give to *energy market participants* in the exercise of its statutory discretion under section 148 of the *Act* to grant a *waiver* of its *rules*.

21.1.2 **[G]** *Energy market participants* should bear in mind that section 148 of the *Act* requires that in order to give a *waiver* of particular *rules*, the *FSA* must be satisfied that:

(1) compliance with the *rules*, or with the *rules* as unmodified, would be unduly burdensome or would not achieve the purpose for which the *rules* were made; and

(2) the *waiver* would not result in undue risk to persons whose interests the *rules* are intended to protect.

21.1.3 **[G]** Accordingly, the *FSA* must be satisfied that the statutory criteria will be met in each case where an *energy market participant* applies for a *waiver* in the form in EMPS 2Ann1G.

21.1.4 **[G]** In particular, clause 4 of the form of *waiver* in EMPS 2Ann1G will not ordinarily be inserted in *waivers* for *energy market participants* that will not, at the time the *waiver* will take effect, clearly satisfy the conditions set out in that clause. For these purposes the *FSA* will take into account the relative proportions of the *energy market participant's* assets and revenues that are referable to the various parts of its business, as well as to any other factor that the *FSA* considers is relevant to an assessment of the prudential risk presented by the *energy market participant*.

Annex 1
Form of waiver: Energy market participants

21 Ann 1

This form has not been reproduced for technical reasons. Please refer to the FSA website.

APPENDIX 1
PRUDENTIAL CATEGORIES AND SUB-CATEGORIES

1.1 Application

[2175]
App 1.1.1 **[G]** This appendix applies to every *firm*.

1.2 Purpose

App 1.2.1 **[G]** The purpose of this appendix is to give *guidance* on the prudential categories and sub-categories of *firm* used in the Interim Prudential sourcebooks and the Supervision manual. The prudential categories are defined in the *Glossary*, and some of the sub-categories are defined there and some in the glossaries of the Interim Prudential sourcebooks.

App 1.2.2 **[G]** Prudential requirements for *firms* are set out in the Prudential Standards part of the *Handbook* according to their prudential category. Certain reporting requirements and other prudential material are contained in the Supervision manual, for example SUP 16 (Reporting requirements).

App 1.2.3 **[G]** If there is any doubt about prudential categorisation, a *firm* should seek individual *guidance* from its usual supervisory contact at the *FSA* and an applicant for authorisation should seek *guidance* from the Corporate Authorisation department.

1.3 Prudential categories and sub-categories

App 1.3.1 **[G]**

Table: Prudential categories and sub-categories used in the Interim Prudential sourcebooks and the Supervision manual

***Prudential categories* (Note 1)**	**Applicable prudential requirements (Note 2)**	**Prudential sub-categories**
*Authorised professional firm**	*IPRU(INV)* 1 and 2	
*Bank**	*GENPRU*, *BIPRU* and *IPRU(BANK)*	*EEA bank* Overseas bank *UK bank*
BIPRU investment firm	*GENPRU* and *BIPRU*	*Full scope BIPRU investment firm* *BIPRU limited licence firm* *BIPRU limited activity firm*
*Building society**	*GENPRU*, *BIPRU* and *IPRU(BSOC)*	
Credit union	*CRED* 7, 8, 9, and 10	*Version 1 credit union* *Version 2 credit union*
ELMI	*ELM*	
Friendly society	*IPRU(FSOC)*	*Directive friendly society* *Incorporated friendly society* *Non-directive friendly society* *Registered friendly society* *Flat rate benefits business friendly society*
Home finance administrator	*MIPRU*	
Home finance intermediary	*MIPRU*	

Part II FSA Handbook Materials

***Prudential categories* (Note 1)**	**Applicable prudential requirements (Note 2)**	**Prudential sub-categories**
Home finance provider	*MIPRU*	
*ICVC**	None, but see *COLL*	
Incoming EEA firm	None (unless another prudential category applies)	
Incoming Treaty firm	*GENPRU*, *BIPRU*, *INSPRU* and *IPRU(BANK)*	*EEA bank*
Insurance intermediary	*MIPRU*	
*Insurer**	*IPRU(INS)* or *IPRU(FSOC)*, *GENPRU*, *INSPRU* and *MIPRU*	*Long term insurer* General insurer *Friendly society* (see above)
*Investment management firm**	IPRU(INV) 1 and 5	*Exempt CAD firm* (see also IPRU(INV) 9) *OPS firm* Non-OPS life office Non-OPS local authority Individuals admitted to authorisation collectively Individual whose sole investment business is giving investment advice to institutional or corporate investors Other
Lead regulated firm	None (unless another prudential category applies)	
*Media firm**	None	
Members' adviser	IPRU(INV) 1 and 4	
*Personal investment firm**	IPRU(INV) 1 and 13	Category B firm Category B1 firm Category B2 firm Category B3 firm *Exempt CAD firm* Low resource firm *Network* *Small personal investment firm*
*Securities and futures firm**	IPRU(INV) 1 and either 3 or 9 There is a special transitional regime for *ex-section 43 lead regulated firms* – see transitional rules to *IPRU(INV)*.	IPRU(INV) 3: *Adviser* *Arranger* *Broad scope firm* *Corporate finance advisory firm* *Dematerialised instruction transmitter* *Derivative fund manager* *Energy market participant* *Local* *Oil market participant* *Venture capital firm* Other IPRU(INV) 9: *Exempt CAD firm* *Exempt BIPRU commodities firm*
*Service company**	IPRU(INV) 1 and 6	
*Society of Lloyd's**	INSPRU and IPRU(INS)	

Prudential categories (Note 1)	Applicable prudential requirements (Note 2)	Prudential sub-categories
UCITS firm	UPRU	
UCITS investment firm	GENPRU and BIPRU	
UK ISPV		
UCITS qualifier	None (unless another prudential category applies)	
Underwriting agent	IPRU(INV) 1 and 4	*Managing agent* *Members' agent*

Note 1 = It is possible for a *firm* to have more than one prudential category. But it cannot have more than one of the prudential categories marked with a '*'.

Note 2 = Only the requirements in the Prudential sourcebooks and *CRED* are listed in the column. Requirements in other parts of the *Handbook* will also apply.

1.4 Relevance of prudential categories

App 1.4.1 **[G]** Many, but not all, of the categories are used only in the Prudential Standards part of the *Handbook* and the Supervision manual. The prudential category of a *firm* will normally determine:

(1) which module of the Prudential Standards part of the *Handbook* is applicable to the *firm*;
(2) if the *firm* is subject to the *IPRU(INV)*, which chapter of that sourcebook is applicable to the *firm*;
(3) whether particular chapters of the Supervision manual are applicable to the *firm*; and
(4) if the *firm* is subject to SUP 3 (Auditors), SUP 16 (Reporting) or SUP 17 (Transaction reporting), which parts of those chapters apply to the *firm*.

App 1.4.2 **[G]** In some cases, a *firm* may also fall within a prudential sub-category. This will determine which provisions within a particular sourcebook or chapter apply to the *firm*.

App 1.4.3 **[G]** If a *firm* is part of a *group*, each *authorised* member of the *group* will have its own prudential category. *Firms* should refer to the provisions of the relevant module of the Prudential Standards part of the *Handbook* to determine whether and, if so, how consolidated supervision applies.

1.5 Determining the prudential categories of a firm

App 1.5.1 **[G]** This appendix includes flow diagrams (Figures 1 and 2) to assist in determining the prudential category of a *firm*.

App 1.5.2 **[G]** For a *firm* which became an *authorised person* after *commencement*, the *FSA* will have confirmed the applicable prudential category of the *firm* as part of the *authorisation* process.

App 1.5.3 **[G]** For a *firm* with automatic *authorisation* by passporting under the *Single Market Directives*, exercising rights under the *Treaty* or as a *UCITS qualifier*, the *FSA* will have notified the *firm* of its prudential category at the same time as the *FSA* notified it of the *applicable provisions* to which it is subject (see SUP 13A for further details on inward passporting). If it has a *top-up permission*, then SUP App1 1.5.2G may also apply.

1.6 Changing prudential category after authorisation

App 1.6.1 **[G]** A *firm's* prudential category may change in the following circumstances:

(1) A variation in the *firm's permission* may, in some cases, lead to an automatic change in the *firm's* prudential category or sub-category because of the way those categories are defined. For example, if an *investment management firm* is granted *permission* to *accept deposits*, it may become a *bank* and cease to be an *investment management firm*. Figures 1 and 2 may be used, even if a *firm's permission* is varied after *commencement*. They should enable a *firm* to determine whether any variation in its *permission* will lead to a change in prudential category.
(2) The *FSA* may vary the *firm's permission* and thereby require a *firm* to comply with the *rules* applicable to a different prudential category, either through using its *own-initiative power* or on the application of the *firm*.

App 1.6.2 **[G]** A *firm* should notify the *FSA* immediately if it believes that its prudential category or sub-category has changed (see SUP 15.3.8G (1)(g)), or if there has been an expansion or reduction in its business that could be relevant to its prudential categorisation or sub-categorisation (see SUP 15.3.8G).

1.7 Prudential categories and sub-categories

App 1.7.1 **[G]** Figure 1: Determination of a firm's prudential category - general

[This form has not been reproduced for technical reasons. Please refer to the FSA website.]

App 1.7.2 **[G]** Figure 2: Determination of a firm's prudential category (cont'd)

[This figure has not been reproduced for technical reasons. Please refer to the FSA website.]

1.8 Notes to Figures 1 and 2

App 1.8.1 **[G]**

Table: Note 1

Chapter of IPRU(INV) that requirement on permission requires the firm to comply with	Firm's prudential category
Chapter 3	*Securities and futures firm*
Chapter 5	*Investment management firm*
Chapter 13	*Personal investment firm*

App 1.8.2 **[G]**

Table: Note 2

The table below shows how a *firm's* main *regulated activities* determine its prudential category. A firm's 'main *regulated activities*' in this context are the *regulated activities* included in the *firm's Part IV permission* from which the *firm* derives or is expected to derive the most substantial part of its gross income, including *commissions*. The aggregate gross income from all of the activities listed against each prudential category should be considered to determine which source is the most substantial.

The gross income is based on the business plan submitted as part of the *firm's* application for a *Part IV permission* (for a *firm* given a *Part IV permission* after *commencement*) or on the *firm's* financial year preceding its *authorisation* under the *Act* (for a *firm authorised* under section 25 of the Financial Services Act 1986 prior to *commencement*).

If the *firm's* prudential categorisation is not clear, please consult the *FSA* for *guidance*.

Activities from which the most substantial part of the firm's gross income, including commissions, from regulated activities is derived	Firm's prudential category
(i) *Managing investments* other than for *retail clients* ***or*** if the assets managed are primarily *derivatives*; (ii) *OPS activity*; (iii) acting as the *manager* or *trustee* of an *AUT*; (iv) acting as the *ACD* or *depository* of an *ICVC*; (v) *establishing, operating or winding-up* a *collective investment scheme* other than an *AUT* or *ICVC*; (va) *establishing, operating or winding up a personal pension scheme*; and (vi) *safeguarding and administering investments*.	*Investment management firm*
(i) *Advising on investments*, or *arranging (bringing about) deals in investments*, in relation to *packaged products*; and (ii) *managing investments* for *private customers*.	*Personal investment firm*
(i) An activity carried on as a member of an *exchange*; (ii) making a market in *securities* or *derivatives*; (iii) *corporate finance business*; (iv) *dealing*, or *arranging (bringing about) deals in investments*, in *securities* or *derivatives*; (v) the provision of clearing services as a *clearing firm*; (vi) *managing investments* where the assets managed are primarily *derivatives*; and (vi) activities relating to *spread bets*.	*Securities and futures firm*

App 1.8.3 **[G]**

Table: Note 3

Single SRO membership	Firm's prudential category
IMRO	*Investment management firm*
PIA	*Personal investment firm*
SFA	*Securities and futures firm*

App 1.8.4 **[G]**

Table: Note 4

SRO to whose Financial Supervision requirements the firm was subject	Firm's prudential category
IMRO	*Investment management firm*
PIA	*Personal investment firm*
SFA	*Securities and futures firm*

App 1.8.5 **[G]** Note 5

Only a small number of *firms* are expected to be authorised under section 25 of the Financial Services Act 1986 immediately prior to *commencement* and not be a member of one of the SROs. These *firms* are directly regulated by the *FSA* under the Financial Services Act 1986.

APPENDIX 2
INSURERS: SCHEME OF OPERATIONS AND RUN-OFF PLANS

2.1 Application

[2176]

App 2.1.1 **[R]** SUP App 2.1 to 2.15 apply to an *insurer*, unless it is:

(1) a *Swiss general insurer*; or
(2) an *EEA-deposit insurer*; or
(3) an *incoming EEA firm*; or
(4) an *incoming Treaty firm*.

App 2.1.2 **[G]** SUP App 2.1 to 2.15 apply to every *friendly society* that is an *insurer*.

App 2.1.3 **[G]** SUP App 2.15 applies to an *insurer* carrying on *with-profits business*, but only if COBS 20.2.53R (Ceasing to effect new contracts of insurance in a with-profits fund) also applies.

App 2.1.3 **[R]** SUP App 2.16 applies to the *Society*.

2.2 Interpretation

App 2.2.1 **[R]** For the purpose of SUP App 2.1 to 2.14:

(1) "capital resources":
  (a) in relation to a *non-directive friendly society*, has the meaning given to "margin of solvency" in *rule* 4.1(4) of IPRU(FSOC);
  (b) in relation to a *participating insurance undertaking*, means P+T, where P and T have the meanings given by INSPRU 6.1.45R(3)(a) and (e) respectively, as calculated in accordance with INSPRU 6.1.43R; and
  (c) in relation to any other *firm*, means the *firm's capital resources* as calculated in accordance with GENPRU 2.2.12R;

(2) "guarantee fund":
  (a) in relation to a *non-directive friendly society*, has the meaning given to that term in IPRU(FSOC);
  (b) in relation to a *participating insurance undertaking*, means the amount of capital resources which that *firm* must hold to comply with INSPRU 6.1.45R(2);
  (c) in relation to a *firm* which is not covered by (a) or (b), carrying on *general insurance business*, means the amount of capital resources which that *firm* must hold to comply with GENPRU 2.2.34R; and
  (d) in relation to a *firm* which is not covered by (a) or (b), carrying on *long-term insurance business*, means the amount of capital resources which that *firm* must hold to comply with GENPRU 2.2.33R;

(3) "material transaction" means a transaction (when aggregated with any similar transactions) in which:
  (a) the price actually paid or received for the transfer of assets or liabilities or the performance of services; or
  (b) the price which would have been paid or received had that transaction been negotiated at arm's length between unconnected parties; exceeds:

(c) in the case of a *firm* which carries on *long-term insurance business*, but not *general insurance business*, the sum of €20,000 and 5% of the *firm's* liabilities arising from its *long-term insurance business*, excluding *property-linked liabilities* and net of *reinsurance* ceded; or
(d) in the case of a *firm* which carries on *general insurance business*, but not *long-term insurance business*, the sum of €20,000 and 5% of the *firm's* liabilities arising from its *general insurance business*, net of *reinsurance* ceded; or
(e) in the case of a *firm* which carries on both *long-term insurance business* and *general insurance business*:
(i) where the transaction is in connection with the *firm's long-term insurance business*, the sum of €20,000 and 5% of the *firm's* liabilities arising from its *long-term insurance business*, excluding *property-linked liabilities* and net of *reinsurance* ceded; and
(ii) in all other cases, the sum of €20,000 and 5% of the *firm's* liabilities arising from its *general insurance business*, net of *reinsurance* ceded; and

(4) "required margin of solvency":
(a) in relation to a *non-directive friendly society*, has the meaning given to that term in IPRU(FSOC);
(b) in relation to a *participating insurance undertaking*, means R-S-U, where R, S and U have the meanings given by INSPRU 6.1.45R(3)(c), (d) and (f) respectively;
(c) in relation to a *firm* which is not covered by (a) or (b), carrying on *general insurance business*, means the *general insurance capital requirement* applicable to that *firm*; and
(d) in relation to a *firm* which is not covered by (a) or (b), carrying on *long-term insurance business*, means the *long-term insurance capital requirement* applicable to that *firm*.

App 2.2.2 **[G]** The calculation of each of the *base capital resources requirement*, the *long-term insurance capital requirement* and the *general insurance capital requirement* is set out in GENPRU 2.1. The calculation of each of the "guarantee fund" and "required margin of solvency" for *nondirective friendly societies* is set out in chapter 4 of IPRU(FSOC).

2.3 Purpose

App 2.3.1 **[G]** To fulfil its obligations under the *Insurance Directives*, and as part of the *FSA's* risk-based approach to supervision, there are certain times when the *FSA* needs to monitor a *firm* more closely than it normally would. This is so the *FSA* can fulfil its function of supervising *firms* properly and meet the *regulatory objective* of securing an appropriate degree of protection for *consumers*.

App 2.3.2 **[G]** The *rules* in SUP App 2.1 to 2.14 require a *firm* to submit reports and information to the *FSA* when:
(1) a *firm* is failing to satisfy *threshold condition* 4 (Adequate resources) (see COND 2.2), and its capital resources have fallen below its required margin of solvency, or its guarantee fund; or
(2) the capital resources of a *firm* have fallen below its *capital resources requirement*; or
(3) a *firm* has decided to cease to *effect* new *contracts of insurance*; or
(4) a *firm* is going through periods of potential uncertainty, for example, when it has come under the *control* of a new *parent undertaking* or following the grant or variation of *permission*.

App 2.3.3 **[G]** The *FSA* may also ask a *firm* to submit reports and information to it when the *firm's* capital resources fall below the level advised in *individual capital guidance* given to the *firm*.

App 2.3.4 **[G]** In accordance with the *Insurance Directives*, a *firm* whose capital resources have fallen below its required margin of solvency, or its guarantee fund, is required, by the *rules* set out in this appendix, to submit a *scheme of operations*, together with an explanation of how its capital resources will be adequately restored. In order to secure an appropriate degree of protection for *consumers*, the *FSA* applies the *rules* in this appendix to *firms* to which the provisions of the *Insurance Directives* would not otherwise apply.

App 2.3.5 **[G]** A *firm* which is entering into run-off is required to submit a *scheme of operations*, including an explanation of how its *liabilities to policyholders* will be met in full. Where the capital resources of such a *firm* subsequently fall below its required margin of solvency, the *firm* is required to submit a plan for restoration.

App 2.3.6 **[G]** Following a change in *control*, or the grant or variation of *permission*, the reports submitted help the *FSA* to identify when a *firm* departs from the *scheme of operations* submitted as part of the notification of a change in *control*, or an application for the grant or variation of *permission*, and on which basis such notification or application was approved.

App 2.3.7 **[G]** *Principle* 4 of the *FSA's* Principles for Businesses provides that *firms* should hold adequate financial resources, while GENPRU 1.2.26R requires a *firm* to maintain overall financial resources which are adequate to ensure that there is no significant risk that it cannot meet its liabilities as they fall due. In considering these requirements, a *firm* may decide to maintain capital resources above the level advised in *individual capital guidance* given by the *FSA*, or, if no *individual capital guidance* has been given, above its *capital resources requirement*. The amount of any such additional capital resources held is at the discretion of the *firm*. However, the extent to which a *firm* matches these additional capital resources to the volatility of its capital base, in conjunction with the strength of its systems and controls environment, is likely to affect the frequency with which it is subject to intervention under this appendix.

App 2.3.8 **[G]** In relation to a *firm* carrying on *with-profits insurance business*, action which it takes either to restore its capital resources to the levels set by the intervention points in this appendix, or to prevent its capital resources falling below those points, should be consistent with *Principle* 6 of the *FSA's* Principles for Businesses. *Principle* 6 requires a *firm* to pay due regard to the interests of its *customers* and treat them fairly.

App 2.3.9 **[G]** These *rules* are in addition to the other *rules* and *guidance* in SUP, in particular SUP 2 (Information gathering by the *FSA* on its own initiative), SUP 15 (Notifications to the *FSA*), SUP 16 (Reporting requirements) and the Principles for Businesses (PRIN).

2.4 Capital resources below guarantee fund

App 2.4.1 **[R]** If a *firm's* capital resources fall below its guarantee fund, it must, within 14 days of the *firm* becoming aware of this event, submit to the *FSA* a short-term financial plan, including:
(1) a *scheme of operations* (see SUP App 2.12); and
(2) an explanation of how, if at all, and by when, it expects its capital resources to be adequately restored to the guarantee fund.

App 2.4.2 **[G]** See SUP App 2.11.2G for *guidance* on the period that the *scheme of operations* should cover.

2.5 Capital resources below required margin of solvency

App 2.5.1 **[R]** Unless SUP App 2.5.3R applies:
(1) if a *firm's* capital resources are such that they no longer equal or exceed its required margin of solvency; or
(2) if a *firm* no longer complies with GENPRU 2.2.32R and GENPRU 2.2.28R, or INSPRU 6.1.45R(1)(a) and INSPRU 6.1.45R(1)(b), as applicable;

it must, within 28 days of becoming aware of this event, submit to the *FSA* a plan for the restoration of a sound financial position, including:
(3) a *scheme of operations*; and
(4) an explanation of how, if at all, and by when:
  (a) it expects its capital resources to be restored to the required margin of solvency; or
  (b) as the case may be, it expects to comply with GENPRU 2.2.32R and GENPRU 2.2.28R, or INSPRU 6.1.45R(1)(a) and INSPRU 6.1.45R(1)(b), as applicable.

App 2.5.2 **[G]** See SUP App 2.11.2G for *guidance* on the period that the *scheme of operations* should cover.

App 2.5.3 **[R]** If a *firm*:
(1) falls into SUP App 2.5.1R(1) or (2); and
(2) it has previously submitted either a run-off plan in accordance with SUP App 2.8.1R or a *scheme of operations* in accordance with SUP App 2.5.1R;

it must, within 28 days of becoming aware that it falls into SUP App 2.5.1R(1) or (2):
(3) notify the *FSA*; and
(4) submit a plan for restoration which:
  (a) explains why the *firm's* capital resources have fallen below its required margin of solvency or, as the case may be, it no longer complies with GENPRU 2.2.32R or GENPRU 2.2.28R, or INSPRU 6.1.45R(1)(a) and INSPRU 6.1.45R(1)(b), as applicable; and
  (b) demonstrates how, if at all, and by when, the *firm* will restore it or, as the case may be, resume compliance with GENPRU 2.2.32R and GENPRU 2.2.28R, or INSPRU 6.1.45R(1)(a) and INSPRU 6.1.45R(1)(b), as applicable.

2.6 Capital resources below capital resources requirement

App 2.6.1 **[R]** Unless any of SUP App 2.4.1R, 2.5.1R or 2.5.3R applies, if a *firm's* capital resources fall below its *capital resources requirement*, it must, within 28 days of becoming aware of this event:
(1) notify the *FSA*; and
(2) submit a plan for restoration, which:
  (a) explains why the *firm's* capital resources have fallen below its *capital resources requirement*; and

(b) demonstrates how, if at all, and by when, the *firm* will restore it.

2.7 Capital resources below the level of individual capital guidance

App 2.7.1 **[G]** Unless any of SUP App 2.4.1R, 2.5.1R, 2.5.3R or 2.6.1R applies, if a *firm's* circumstances change, such that its capital resources have fallen, or are expected to fall, below the level advised in *individual capital guidance* given to the *firm* by the *FSA*, then, consistent with PRIN 2.1.1R *Principle* 11 (Relations with regulators), a *firm* should inform the *FSA* of this fact as soon as practicable, explaining why capital resources have fallen, or are expected to fall, below the level advised in *individual capital guidance*, and:
(1) what action the *firm* intends to take to increase its capital resources; or
(2) what modification the *firm* considers should be made to the *individual capital guidance* which it has been given.

App 2.7.2 **[G]** In the circumstance set out in SUP App 2.7.1G, the *FSA* may ask a *firm* for alternative or more detailed proposals and plans or further assessments and analyses of capital adequacy and risks faced by the *firm*. The *FSA* will seek to agree with the *firm* appropriate timescales and scope for any such additional work, in light of the circumstances which have arisen.

App 2.7.3 **[G]** In relation to a *firm* carrying on *with-profits insurance business*, if it intends either (a) to remedy a fall in the level of capital resources advised in its *individual capital guidance*, or (b) to prevent a fall in the level advised in that *guidance*, for example, in either case, by taking management action to de-risk a *with-profits fund* or by reducing non-contractual benefits for *policyholders*, it should explain to the *FSA* how such proposed actions are consistent with the *firm's* obligations under PRIN 2.1 *Principle* 6 (Customers' interests).

App 2.7.4 **[G]** If a *firm's* capital resources fall below the level advised in *individual capital guidance* given to the *firm* and, at the same time, any one or more of SUP App 2.4.1R, 2.5.1R, 2.5.3R or 2.6.1R applies, the *firm* should first comply with those *rules*. Those *rules* are concerned with circumstances where capital resources are likely to have fallen to levels much lower than the level advised in *individual capital guidance* and are, in some cases, requirements imposed by the *Insurance Directives*.

App 2.7.5 **[G]** If a *firm* has not accepted *individual capital guidance* given by the *FSA* it should, nevertheless, inform the *FSA* as soon as practicable if its capital resources have fallen below the level suggested by that *individual capital guidance*. In such circumstances, the *FSA* may ask the *firm* for further explanation as to why it does not consider the *individual capital guidance* to be appropriate. The *FSA* may also consider using its powers under section 45 of the *Act* to, on its own initiative, vary a *firm's Part IV permission*, so as to require it to hold such capital as the *FSA* considers is necessary for the *firm* to comply with GENPRU 1.2.26R.

2.8 Ceasing to effect contracts of insurance

App 2.8.1 **[R]** If a *firm* decides to cease to *effect* new *contracts of insurance*, it must, within 28 days of that decision, submit a run-off plan to the *FSA* including:
(1) a scheme of operations; and
(2) an explanation of how, or to what extent, all liabilities to policyholders (including, where relevant, liabilities which arise from the regulatory duty to treat customers fairly in setting discretionary benefits) will be met in full as they fall due.

App 2.8.2 **[G]** SUP App 2.8.1R only applies if a *firm* ceases to *effect* new *contracts of insurance* in respect of the whole of its *insurance business*.

App 2.8.3 **[G]** For the purposes of SUP App 2.8.1R, a new *contract of insurance* excludes contracts effected under a term in a subsisting *contract of insurance*.

App 2.8.4 **[G]** Under *Principle* 11, the *FSA* normally expects to be notified by a *firm* when it decides to cease *effecting* new *contracts of insurance* in respect of one or more *classes* of *contract of insurance* (see SUP 15.3.8G). At the same time, the *FSA* would normally expect the *firm* to discuss with it the need for the *firm* to apply to vary its *permission* (see SUP 6.2.6G and SUP 6.2.7G) and, if appropriate, to submit a *scheme of operations* in accordance with SUP App 2.8.1R.

App 2.8.5 **[G]** See SUP App 2.11.2G for *guidance* on the period that the *scheme of operations* should cover.

2.9 Under control of a new parent undertaking

App 2.9.1 **[G]** A *firm* that has notified the *FSA* of a new *parent undertaking* may be requested to submit a *scheme of operations* (see SUP 11.5.5G). A *scheme of operations* would be requested if the significance and circumstances of the change were considered to be sufficient to merit that level of scrutiny. This is normally only likely to be necessary when there has been an ultimate change in *control*, or when, as a result of the change in *control*, significant changes are proposed to the *firm's regulated activities*, business plan or strategy. A *firm* which has submitted a *scheme of* *operations* under SUP 11.5.5G, is not required to submit a further *scheme of operations* under this appendix unless SUP App 2.4, 2.5 or 2.8 applies. SUP App 2.13 does, however, apply to such a *firm*.

2.10 Grant or variation of permission

App 2.10.1 **[G]** The *FSA* may ask a *firm* seeking a grant or variation of *permission* to provide a *scheme of operations* as part of the application process (see SUP 6.3.25G). Such a *firm* is not required to submit a further *scheme of operations* under this appendix unless SUP App 2.4, 2.5 or 2.8 applies. SUP App 2.13 and SUP 6 Ann 4G do, however, apply to such a *firm*.

2.11 Submission of a scheme of operations or a plan for restoration

App 2.11.1 **[G]** A *firm* should discuss its plan in draft with the *FSA* before submitting it. If a plan is submitted which does not satisfy the *FSA* that the *firm* can restore its capital resources (as appropriate), or meet its liabilities as they fall due, the *FSA* may use its *own-initiative power* to vary or cancel the *firm's permission*. If a *firm* submitting a plan is part of a *group* of *companies*, the *FSA* may ask that *firm* to provide additional information in relation to other *companies* in the *group*, if this is necessary to establish how the *firm* will restore its own sound financial position. The *firm* should agree in discussion with the *FSA* the nature of such additional information.

App 2.11.2 **[G]** The *schemes of operations* required when a *firm's* capital resources have fallen below its required margin of solvency or its guarantee fund (see SUP App 2.5.1R and SUP App 2.4.1R, respectively) should cover a period which is sufficient to demonstrate that the *firm's* capital resources will be adequately restored. Typically this would be a period of at least three years. However, if a *scheme of operations* has expired, but SUP App 2.4.1R or 2.5.1R continues to apply, the *firm* should submit a new *scheme of operations*. The *scheme of operations* required by SUP App 2.8.1R, when a *firm* ceases to *effect* new *contracts of insurance*, should cover the run-off period until all *liabilities to policyholders* are met.

App 2.11.3 **[G]** The period to be covered by, and the details to be included in, the plan for restoration required by SUP App 2.5.3R will depend on the circumstances of the *firm*, why its capital resources have fallen below its required margin of solvency and the degree of risk that that fall will be repeated, even if the *firm* restores its capital resources in accordance with its plan.

App 2.11.4 **[G]** In relation to a *firm* which carries on *with-profits insurance business* and which submits a plan, the *FSA* would expect an explanation of how any actions it plans to take to restore capital resources to the level of the guarantee fund, required margin of solvency or *capital resources requirement* are consistent with the *firm's* obligations under *Principle* 6 (Customers' interests).

2.12 Content of a scheme of operations

App 2.12.1 **[R]** A scheme of operations must:

(1) describe the *firm's* business strategy;

(2) include financial projections (including appropriate scenarios and stress-tests) as follows:
  (a) a forecast summary profit and loss account in accordance with SUP App 2.12.7R;
  (b) a forecast summary balance sheet in accordance with SUP App 2.12.8R; and
  (c) a forecast statement of capital resources in accordance with SUP App 2.12.9R; and

(3) as at the end of each *financial year* which falls (in whole or part) within the period to which the *scheme of operations* relates:
  (a) describe the assumptions which underlie those forecasts and the reasons for adopting those assumptions; and
  (b) identify any material transactions proposed to be effected or carried out with, or in respect of, any *associate*.

App 2.12.2 **[G]** The business strategy referred to at SUP App 2.12.1R(1) should include a description of the nature of the risks which the *firm* is underwriting, or intends to underwrite. It should also give an explanation of the *firm's* strategy for managing the risks associated with carrying on *insurance business* (including, in particular, *reinsurance*).

App 2.12.3 **[G]** The amount of detail to be given on the *firm's* business strategy required by SUP App 2.12.1R(1) should be appropriate to the scale and complexity of the *firm's* operations and the degree of risk involved.

App 2.12.4 **[R]** The information required by SUP App 2.12.1R must reflect the nature and content of the *rules* relating to capital resources applicable to a *firm*.

App 2.12.5 **[G]** In relation to *firms* covered by SUP App 2.1 to 2.14, IPRU(FSOC) 4.1 sets out the *rules* relating to capital resources for *non-directive friendly societies* and GENPRU 2.1, 2.2 and INSPRU 6.1 set out the *rules* relating to capital resources for every other *firm*. The capital resources which a *firm* is required to maintain vary according to whether the *firm* has its head office in the *United Kingdom* or overseas, and depending on the nature of the *insurance business* it carries on. The information which a *firm* is required to submit under SUP App 2.12.1R should reflect the nature and content of the *rules* relating to capital resources identified above. For example, in order to satisfy

Part II FSA Handbook Materials

SUP App 2.12.1R, a *firm* with its head office outside the *United Kingdom* which is carrying on direct *insurance business* in the *United Kingdom* should submit separate information concerning its world-wide activities and its *UK* activities.

App 2.12.6 **[G]** To reflect its obligations under GENPRU 2.2.22R or IPRU(FSOC) 4.1(2) (as applicable), in order to comply with SUP App 2.12.1R, a *firm* which carries on both *long-term insurance business* and *general insurance business* should submit separate information for each type of *insurance business*.

App 2.12.7 **[R]** Summary profit and loss account (see SUP App 2.12.1R(2)(a))

(1)	*Premiums* and *claims* (gross and net of *reinsurance*) analysed by *accounting class* of *insurance business*
(2)	Investment return
(3)	Expenses
(4)	Other charges and income
(5)	Taxation
(6)	Dividends paid and accrued

App 2.12.8 **[R]** Summary balance sheet (see SUP App 2.12.1R (2)(b))

(1)	Investments analysed by type
(2)	Assets held to cover linked liabilities
(3)	Other assets and liabilities separately identifying cash at bank and in hand
(4)	Capital and reserves analysed into called up *share* capital or equivalent funds, *share* premium account, revaluation reserve, other reserves and profit and loss account
(5)	Subordinated liabilities
(6)	The fund for future appropriations
(7)	Technical provisions gross and net of *reinsurance* analysed by accounting *class* of *insurance business* and separately identifying the provision for linked liabilities, *unearned premiums*, unexpired risks and equalisation
(8)	Other liabilities and credits

App 2.12.9 **[R]** A forecast statement of capital resources (under SUP App 2.12.1R(2)(c)) must include the forecast capital resources and the forecast required margin of solvency at the end of each *financial year* or part *financial year*.

2.13 Obligations on firms which have previously submitted a scheme of operations

App 2.13.1 **[R]** A *firm* which has submitted a *scheme of operations* to the *FSA*, whether required by SUP App 2.4, 2.5 or 2.8, or as part of an application under SUP 6.3 (see SUP 6.3.25G), SUP 6.4 (see SUP 6 Ann 4G), or SUP 11.5 (see SUP 11.5.5G), or an amended *scheme of operations*, must during the period covered by that *scheme of operations*:

(1) notify the *FSA* at least 28 days before entering into or carrying out any material transaction with, or in respect of, an *associate*, unless that transaction is in accordance with a *scheme of operations* which has been submitted to the *FSA*;

(2) submit a quarterly financial return to the *FSA* which must include for, or as at the end of, each quarter:
   (a) a summary profit and loss account prepared in accordance with SUP App 2.12.7R;
   (b) a summary balance sheet prepared in accordance with SUP App 2.12.8R; and
   (c) a statement of capital resources prepared in accordance with SUP App 2.12.9R;

   and which must identify and explain differences between the actual results and the forecasts submitted in the *scheme of operations*; and

(3) notify the *FSA* promptly of any matter which has either happened or is likely to happen and which represents a significant departure from the *scheme of operations*; the *firm* must either:
   (a) explain the nature of the departure and the reasons for it and provide revised forecast financial information in the *scheme of operations* for its remaining term; or
   (b) include an amended *scheme of operations* and explain the amendments and the reasons for them.

App 2.13.2 **[R]** A report under SUP App 2.13.1R(2) must be submitted in accordance with the *rules* in SUP 16.3.6R to SUP 16.3.13R. 2.13.3 G For the purpose of SUP App 2.13.1R(1), the *FSA* considers that transactions with, or in respect of, *associates* include:

(1) contracting (as either party), advancing, repaying, writing off or agreeing to change the terms of any loan;

(2) entering into (in any capacity), releasing, calling upon or agreeing to change the terms of any guarantee, pledge, security, charge or any off-balance-sheet transaction;
(3) entering into agreements to acquire or dispose of property or which otherwise affect the nature or value of the *firm's* assets;
(4) making an investment (directly or indirectly) in an *associate*;
(5) entering into (as either party), commuting or agreeing to change the terms of, any contract of *reinsurance*; and
(6) entering into, or changing the terms of, any agreement to give or provide services or to share costs.

App 2.13.4 **[G]** The *FSA* considers that a significant departure referred to in SUP App 2.13.1R(3) includes:
(1) entry or withdrawal from a line of *insurance business*;
(2) significant revision of the *firm's* strategy for managing risks, in particular the basis upon which risks are reinsured;
(3) forecast *premiums* being exceeded, by more than 10%, for a single *financial year* (or part year if the period covered by the *scheme of operations* is or includes part of a *financial year*);
(4) *claims* experience being significantly worse than forecast for a single *financial year* (or part year if the period covered by the *scheme of operations* is or includes part of a *financial year*);
(5) the actual level of capital resources being significantly worse than forecast;
(6) paid or proposed dividends being greater than those forecast; and
(7) any other transaction or circumstance which is likely to have a material effect upon available assets (as defined in IPRU(INS) 11.1).

2.14 Financial Recovery Plan

App 2.14.1 **[G]** When:
(1) the *FSA* has required a financial recovery plan within the meaning of article 20a of the *First Non-Life Directive*;
(2) the *FSA* is of the view that *policyholders*' rights are threatened because the financial position of the *firm* is deteriorating; and
(3) the *FSA* decides to require the *firm* to hold more capital than would otherwise be required under the *Handbook* to ensure that the *firm* will be able to fulfil the required margin of solvency in the near future;

any such higher capital requirement will be based on the financial recovery plan.

2.15 Run-off plans for closed with-profits funds

App 2.15.1 **[G]** The run-off plan required by COBS 20.2.53R should include the information described in SUP App 2.15.2G to SUP App 2.15.13G in respect of the relevant *with-profits fund*.

Funding

App 2.15.2 **[G]** A *firm's* run-off plan should describe how the *firm* proposes to manage the run-off of the *with-profits fund*. That description should include:
(1) details of the expected duration and costs of fully running off the fund's liabilities;
(2) an explanation as to how a solvent run-off will be funded; and
(3) details of the *firm's* future strategy for managing the risks associated with the run-off of the fund.

Investment risk

App 2.15.3 **[G]** A *firm's* run-off plan should include an explanation of its future investment strategy, including:
(1) its strategy for matching the *with-profits fund's* liabilities with appropriate assets; and
(2) any changes it expects to make to the *with-profits fund's* investment strategy as a result of the closure of the *with-profits fund*, including any changes to the proportions of different types of investments.

Credit risk

App 2.15.4 **[G]** A *firm's* run-off plan should include an explanation of its strategy for managing the *with-profits fund's* counterparty and credit risk, both within and external to the *firm's* group.

Operational risk

App 2.15.5 **[G]** A *firm's* run-off plan should show how it will address any additional operational risks that may flow from the closure of the *with-profits fund*, including:
(1) any changes that it proposes to make to staffing arrangements for the run-off;
(2) an estimate of the cost of proposed operational changes, including redundancy costs; and

(3) any *material outsourcing* arrangements it proposes to enter into, explaining how the *firm* will address any specific operational risks created by those arrangements.

Reinsurance

App 2.15.6 **[G]** A *firm's* run-off plan should explain how it will use and manage *reinsurance* (if it will), including:

(1) any new inwards or outwards reinsurance it proposes to enter into as a result of the closure of the *with-profits fund* identifying, in each case, the proposed counterparty and the counterparty's relationship to the *firm's group* (if any); and

(2) how it will manage the risk that the *reinsurance* in (1) will not perform as expected.

Governance and impact on policyholders

App 2.15.7 **[G]** A *firm's* run-off plan should include:

(1) details of any changes that will be made to the *firm's* corporate governance arrangements as a consequence of closure; 4

(2) an explanation of how costs charged to the *with-profits fund* may change in the light of closure;

(3) an explanation of any changes it will make, as a consequence of closure, to any charges for guarantees, including:
 (a) the circumstances in which those charges may be varied in the future; or
 (b) the manner by which the level of any appropriate variation to those charges may be determined;

(4) an explanation of any actual or potential changes in the maturity payment or surrender payment target ranges that the *firm* will apply to determine benefits under its *with-profits policies*;

(5) an explanation of any actual or potential changes in the *firm's* smoothing policy as a consequence of closure;

(6) an explanation of any changes to the *firm's projection* rates as a consequence of closure;

(7) details of any new deductions to be made from the *firm's* surrender payments, together with an explanation as to how those deductions are consistent with:
 (a) Principle 6 (Customers' interests); and
 (b) COBS 20.2.11G to COBS 20.2.16R (Amounts payable under with-profits policies: Surrender payments);

(8) if there are groups of unitised *with-profits policies* in the *with-profits fund* with similar market value reduction free dates, an explanation as to whether:
 (a) the *firm* expects surrenders to peak around any of those dates; and
 (b) if it does, how it proposes to deal with those peaks;

(9) details of the information that the *firm* gives to its *with-profits policyholders* about their right (if any) to use the proceeds of a *personal pension scheme*, *stakeholder pension scheme*, *FSAVC*, *retirement annuity* contract or *pension buy-out contract* to purchase an annuity on the open market when the relevant contracts or schemes vest or mature and any changes that will be made to that information as a result of the closure;

(10) details of how the *firm* will deal with any potential mis-selling costs that may arise in the future in respect of *contracts of insurance* effected in the *with-profits fund*;

(11) an explanation of how the *firm*:
 (a) anticipates capital will become available for distribution to *policyholders* (and shareholders where appropriate); and
 (b) will ensure a full and fair distribution of the closed *with-profits fund*, including any *inherited estate*;

including details of:
 (c) how the *firm* plans to provide in the long term for *annuity* payments on any *with-profits* and non-profits *policies* under which benefits have vested;
 (d) how the *firm* will address future adverse circumstances in relation to these (e.g. increased annuitant longevity); and
 (e) details of the *firm's* plans for distributing the embedded value in any major *subsidiaries* held in or by the closed *with-profits fund*;

(12) an explanation of any material differences between the *firm's* run-off plan and relevant parts of its *PPFM*, together with details of any changes that will be made to the *PPFM* as a consequence of closure (The *firm* should provide the *FSA* with a copy of the revised sections of its *PPFM* when it submits its run-off plan.);

(13) an explanation of whether the *firm* will be seeking to expand any other business following closure of the *with-profits fund*. (This explanation should include whether the *firm* will effect any new *with-profits policies* in a different *with-profits fund* and whether it will seek to expand its unit-linked or *non-profit insurance business*. It should also include an explanation

of how such plans will impact on the closed *with-profits fund*. For example, will the *firm* offer *policyholders* in the closed *with-profits fund* the opportunity to switch into another *with-profits fund* or into unit-linked business?)

Financial projections

App 2.15.8 **[G]** A *firm's* run-off plan should include:
(1) a forecast summary revenue account for the *with-profits fund*, in the form of SUP App 2.15.9G Table 1;
(2) a forecast summary balance sheet and statement of solvency for the *with-profits fund*, which has been prepared in the form of SUP App 2.15.9G Table 2 and on a regulatory basis; and
(3) a forecast summary balance sheet and statement of solvency for the entire *firm*, which has been prepared in the form of SUP App 2.15.9G Table 3 and on a regulatory basis;
in each case, for at least a three year period, beginning on the date of closure; and
(4) a description of the assumptions underlying the forecasts at (1) to (3) and the reasons for adopting those assumptions.

App 2.15.9 **[G]** These tables belong to SUP App 2.15.8G

Table 1 – forecast summary revenue account for the relevant *with-profits fund*	
(1)	*Premiums* and *claims* (gross and net of *reinsurance*) analysed by major *class* of *insurance business*
(2)	Investment return
(3)	Expenses
(4)	Other charges and income
(5)	Taxation
(6)	Increase (decrease) in fund in financial year
(7)	Fund brought forward
(8)	Fund carried forward

Table 2 – forecast summary balance sheet and statement of solvency for the relevant *with-profits fund*	
	Assets analysed by type (excluding *implicit items*):
(1)	Equities
(2)	Land and buildings
(3)	Fixed interest investments
(4)	All other assets
(5)	Total assets (excluding *implicit items*)
(6)	*Policyholder* liabilities
(7)	Other liabilities
(8)	Total liabilities
(9)	Excess/(deficiency) of assets over liabilities before *implicit items*
(10)	*Implicit items* allocated to the *with-profits fund*
(11)	*Long-term insurance capital requirement* for the *with-profits fund*
(12)	*Resilience capital requirement* for the *with-profits fund*
(13)	*With-profits insurance capital component* (for *realistic basis life firms* only)
(14)	Net excess/(deficiency) of assets in the *with-profits fund*

Table 3 – forecast summary balance sheet and statement of solvency for the *firm*		
L1	Surplus *long-term insurance assets*, *with-profit fund(s)*	
L2	Surplus *long-term insurance assets*, *non-profit fund(s)*	
L3	Total *long-term insurance assets*	L1+L2
L4	Total *long-term insurance liabilities* (excluding *resilience capital requirement*)	
L5	Total *long-term insurance fund* surplus	L3–L4
L6	Shareholder fund assets	
L7	*Implicit items*	
L8	*Long-term insurance capital requirement*	

Part II FSA Handbook Materials

L9	Excess of regulatory assets over *long-term insurance capital requirement*	L5+L6+L7–L8
L10	*With-profits insurance capital component*	For realistic basis life *firms* only.
L11	*Resilience capital requirement*	
L12	Net excess assets	L9–L10–L11
L13	FTSE level at which the *long-term insurance capital requirement would be* breached	

App 2.15.10 **[G]** If a *firm* is a *realistic basis life firm,* its run-off plan should include:
(1) a realistic balance sheet and statement of solvency position in the form of SUP App 2.15.9G Table 2, if the financial position of the relevant *with-profits fund* would, when stated in that form, be materially different from the *firm's* most recent realistic solvency submission for that fund; or
(2) a statement that the *firm* is satisfied that the closure of the *with-profits fund* will not materially affect the realistic solvency position of that fund, as reflected in the *firm's* most recent realistic solvency submission for that fund.

App 2.15.11 **[G]** A *firm's* run-off plan should include:
(1) a revised individual capital assessment for the *firm* (see INSPRU 7.1), which reflects the impact of the closure of the relevant *with-profits fund*; or
(2) a statement that the *firm* is satisfied that the closure will not materially affect the *firm's* most recent assessment.

App 2.15.12 **[G]** A *firm's* run-off plan should include details of any:
(1) intra-*group* balances held by the *with-profits fund*;
(2) *group company* investments held by the *with-profits fund*; and
(3) guarantees given by the *firm*;
(4) which, in each case, have a value in excess of 5% of the *firm's* gross technical provisions.

App 2.15.13 **[G]** A *firm's* run-off plan should include any other information that the *firm* considers relevant to the run-off of the closed *with-profits fund.*

App 2.15.14 **[G]** The *FSA* may request additional information and explanations from the *firm.* (See section 165 (Authority's power to require information) of the *Act.*)

App 2.15.15 **[G]** Significant changes to, or departures from, a *firm's* run-off plan are likely to trigger one or more of the *firm's* obligations to notify the *FSA*. (See, for example, *Principle* 11 (Relations with regulators). The guidance in SUP 15.3 (General notification requirements) may also be relevant.)

2.16 Regulatory intervention points for Lloyd's

Application

App 2.16.1 **[R]** The *rules* and *guidance* in SUP App 2 apply to the *Society*:
(1) with the modifications set out in SUP App 2.16.2R to SUP App 2.16.5G; but
(2) except SUP App 2.8.1G to SUP App 2.8.5G, SUP App 2.9.1R, SUP App 2.10.1R, SUP App 2.12.1R(2)(a), SUP App 2.12.2G and SUP App 2.12.7R.

Interpretation

App 2.16.2 **[R]** For the purpose of SUP App 2.16 and the application of SUP App 2 to the *Society*:
(1) "capital resources", as the context requires:
    (a) in relation to the *Society's* own capital resources, means its own *capital resources* calculated in accordance with the *capital resources table*;
    (b) in relation to a *member's* capital resources, means the *member's capital resources* calculated in accordance with GENPRU 2.3.22R;
    (c) in relation to the aggregate *capital resources* of the *Society* and the *members* supporting the *insurance business* of the *members*, means the aggregate of the *capital resources* in (1)(a) and (b) but excluding the *Society's callable contributions*;
(2) "guarantee fund":
    (a) in relation to the *general insurance business* carried on by *members*, means the amount of capital resources required in order to comply with GENPRU 2.2.26R, GENPRU 2.3.17R and GENPRU 2.3.26R; and the "member's share of the guarantee fund" for *general insurance business* means the result of the calculation set out in GENPRU 2.3.27R;
    (b) in relation to the *long-term insurance business* carried on by *members*, means the amount of capital resources required in order to comply with GENPRU 2.2.25R and GENPRU 2.3.17R; and the "*member's* share of the guarantee fund" for *long-term insurance business* means the result of the calculation set out in GENPRU 2.3.25R;

(3) "required margin of solvency":
   (a) in relation to the *general insurance business* carried on by *members*, means the higher of the *Society GICR* and the *general insurance capital requirement* for the *members* in aggregate; and
   (b) in relation to the *long-term insurance business* carried on by *members*, means the *long-term insurance capital requirement* for the *members* in aggregate.

Capital resources below guarantee fund

App 2.16.3 **[R]** For the purposes of SUP App 2.4.1R and SUP App 2.4.2G, *capital resources* will have fallen below the guarantee fund if the *Society's* own capital resources are such that they are no longer sufficient to meet the aggregate of, for each *member*, the amount, if any, by which the *member's* capital resources fall short of the *member's* share of the guarantee fund.

Capital resources below required margin of solvency

App 2.16.4 **[R]** For the purposes of SUP App 2.5.1R to SUP App 2.5.3G, capital resources will be such that they no longer equal or exceed the required solvency margin if the *Society's* own capital resources are insufficient to meet the aggregate of, for each *member*, the amount, if any, by which the *member's* capital resources fall short of the *member's* share of the required solvency margin.

Capital resources below capital resources requirement

App 2.16.5 **[R]** For the purposes of SUP App 2.6.1G, capital resources will have fallen below the *capital resources requirement* if the *Society's* own capital resources are insufficient to meet the aggregate of, for each *member*, the amount, if any, by which the *member's* capital resources fall short of the *member's* share of the *capital resources requirement* for the *members* in aggregate.

Capital resources below the level of individual capital guidance

App 2.16.6 **[G]** For the purposes of SUP App 2.7.1G to SUP App 2.7.5G, capital resources will have fallen below the level of *individual capital guidance* if the *Society's* own capital resources have fallen below the level advised in *individual capital guidance* given to the *Society* in respect of those capital resources.

APPENDIX 3
GUIDANCE ON PASSPORTING ISSUES

3.1 Application

[2177]

App 3.1.1 **[G]** This appendix applies to all *firms* when passporting.

3.2 Purpose

App 3.2.1 **[G]** The purpose of this appendix is to give *guidance*:
(1) to *UK firms* on some of the issues that arise when carrying on *passported activities* (see SUP App 3.5 and SUP App 3.6);
(2) to all *firms* on the relationship between *regulated activities* and activities passported under the *Single Market Directives* (see SUP App 3.9 and SUP App 3.10).

3.3 Background

The Treaty on the Functioning of the European Union

App 3.3.1 **[G]**
(1) The *Treaty* establishes in *EU* law the rights of freedom of establishment and freedom to provide services in the *EU*.
(2) The *Treaty* lays down central principles governing the legal framework for freedom of establishment and the free movement of services in the *EU*. There are, however, a number of areas where the legal position is not clear. This includes, for example, identifying whether a service is provided through an establishment, where the issues involved are complex. Therefore, this Appendix is intended to provide *guidance* but cannot be regarded as comprehensive. Ultimately, the construction of the *Treaty* and relevant Directive provisions is a matter for the European Court of Justice.

App 3.3.2 **[G]** The *Treaty* provides the framework for the provision of banking, insurance business, investment business, *UCITS* management services and insurance mediation, while the *Single Market Directives* clarify the rights and freedoms within that framework.

EU and EEA

App 3.3.3 **[G]** The agreement on the *European Economic Area*, signed at Oporto on 2 May 1992, extends certain *EU* legislation to those *EEA States* that are not Member States of the *EU*.

Interpretative communications

App 3.3.4 **[G]** In 1997, the European Commission published an interpretative communication (Freedom to provide services and the interests of the general good in the Second Banking Directive (97/C 209/04)) (the text of this directive and the First Banking Directive is now consolidated in the *Banking Consolidation Directive*). The European Commission's objective in publishing this communication was to explain and clarify the EU rules. The European Commission deemed it desirable " . . . to restate in a Communication the principles laid down by the Court of Justice and to set out its position regarding the application of these Principles to the specific problems raised by the Second Banking Directive".

App 3.3.5 **[G]** In 2000, the European Commission published a further interpretative communication (Freedom to provide services and the general good in the insurance sector (2000/C43/03)). This allowed the European Commission to publicise its own interpretation of the rules on the freedom to provide services.

App 3.3.6 **[G]**

(1) The European Commission has not produced an interpretive communication on *MiFID*. It is arguable, however, that the principles in the communication on the Second Banking Directive can be applied to *investment services and activities*. This is because Chapter II of Title II of *MiFID* (containing provisions relating to operating conditions for investment firms) also applies to the *investment services and activities* of *firms* operating under the *Banking Consolidation Directive*.

(2) The European Commission has not produced an interpretative communication on either the *Insurance Mediation Directive* or on the *UCITS Directive*.

App 3.3.7 **[G]** In giving its views, communications made by the European Commission have the status of guidance and are not binding on the national courts of *EEA States*. This is because it is the European Court of Justice that has ultimate responsibility for interpreting the *Treaty* and secondary legislation. Accordingly, the communications " . . . do not prejudge the interpretation that the Court of Justice, which is responsible in the final instance for interpreting the *Treaty* and secondary legislation, might place on the matter at issue." (European Commission interpretative communication: Freedom to provide services and the general good in the insurance sector (C(99) 5046). However, the Courts may take account of European Commission communications when interpreting the *Treaty* and secondary legislation.

App 3.3.8 **[G]** *Firms* should also note that European Commission communications do not necessarily represent the views taken by all *EEA States*.

E-commerce

App 3.3.9 **[G]** The *E-Commerce Directive* covers services provided at a distance by means of electronic equipment for the processing (including digital compression) and storage of data. The services would normally be provided in return for remuneration and must be provided at the individual request of a recipient (see recital 17 of the *E-Commerce Directive*). The Directive implements the *country of origin* approach to regulation. This approach makes *firms* subject to the conduct of business requirements of the *EEA State* from which the service is provided. This is subject to certain derogations (see SUP App 3.3.11G).

App 3.3.10 **[G]** The *E-Commerce Directive* does not affect the responsibilities of *Home States* under the *Single Market Directives*. This includes the obligation of a *Home State regulator* to notify the *Host State regulator* of a *firm's* intention to establish a *branch* in, or provide *cross border services* into, the other *EEA State*.

App 3.3.11 **[G]** There are, however, general derogations from the internal market provisions under article 3(3) of the *E-Commerce Directive*. The derogations include consumer contracts, the permissibility of unsolicited e-mail and certain insurance services (both life and non-life). Where these derogations apply, the *EEA States* in which the recipients of the service are based may continue to be able to impose their own requirements.

App 3.3.12 **[G]** [deleted]

Notification of establishing a branch or of providing cross border services

App 3.3.13 **[G]** The *Single Market Directives* require *credit institutions*, *insurance undertakings* (other than *reinsurance* undertakings), *MiFID investment firms, UCITS management companies* and *insurance intermediaries* to make a notification to the *Home State* before establishing a *branch* or provide *cross border services*. SUP 13.5 (Notices of intention) sets out the notification requirements for a *firm* seeking to establish a *branch* or provide *cross border services*. As *firms* will note, the decision whether a passport notification needs to be made will be a matter of interpretation. The onus is on *firms* to comply with the requirements of the *Act* and, where relevant, the laws of other *EEA States*. So, in cases of doubt, *firms* should obtain their own legal advice on the specific issues involved.

App 3.3.14 **[G]** Blanket notification is the practice of the *Home State regulator* notifying all *Host State regulators* in respect of all activities regardless of any genuine intention to carry on the activity. This practice is discouraged by the *FSA*. However, a *firm* may be carrying on activities in the *United Kingdom* or elsewhere in a way that necessarily gives rise to a real possibility of the provision of services in other *EEA States*. In such cases, the *firm* should consider with its advisers whether it should notify the relevant authorities and include that possibility in its business plan.

3.4 Introduction

[deleted]

3.5 The right of establishment

[deleted]

3.6 Freedom to provide services

App 3.6.1 **[G]** Article 56 (Services) of the *Treaty* grants to *EEA* nationals established in one *EEA State* the freedom to provide *cross border services* to other *EEA States*.

How services may be provided

App 3.6.2 **[G]** Under the *Treaty*, the freedom to provide services within the EC may be exercised in three broad ways:

(1) where the provider of a service moves temporarily to another *EEA State* in order to provide the service;

(2) where the service is provided without either the provider or the recipient moving (in this situation the provision, and receipt, of the service may take place by post, telephone or fax, through computer terminals or by other means of remote control);

(3) where the recipient of a service moves temporarily to another *EEA State* in order to receive (or, perhaps, commission the receipt of) the service within that State.

App 3.6.3 **[G]** Under the *Single Market Directives*, however, *EEA rights* for the provision of services are concerned only with services provided in one of the ways referred to in SUP App 3.6.2G(1) and (2) (How services may be provided).

App 3.6.4 **[G]** [deleted]

Place of supply

App 3.6.5 **[G]** In the opinion of the European Commission (and in the wording of the *Single Market Directives*) "only activities carried on within the territory of another Member State should be the subject of prior notification" (Commission interpretative communication: Freedom to provide services and the interests of the general good in the Second Banking Directive (97/C 209/04)). In determining, for the purposes of notification, whether a service is to be provided 'within' another *EEA State*, it is necessary to determine the place of supply of the service.

App 3.6.6 **[G]** An *insurance undertaking* that effects *contracts of insurance* covering risks or commitments situated in another *EEA State* should comply with the notification procedures for the provision of services within that *EEA State*. The location of risks and commitments is found by reference to the rules set out in paragraph 6 of schedule 12 to the *Act*, which derive from article 1 of the *Consolidated Life Directive* and article 2 of the *Second Non-Life Directive*. It may be appropriate for insurers to take legal advice as to how these rules are interpreted and applied in other *EEA States*. The need to passport may arise because of only one of the risks covered by an insurance policy. This includes, for example, where a policy covers a number of property risks and one of those properties is in another *EEA State*.

App 3.6.7 **[G]** In respect of banking services, the European Commission believes that " . . . to determine where the activity was carried on, the place of provision of what may be termed the 'characteristic performance' of the service i.e. the essential supply for which payment is due, must be determined" (Commission interpretative communication: Freedom to provide services and the interests of the general good in the Second Banking Directive (97/C 209/04)). In the *FSA's* view, this requires consideration of where the service is carried out in practice.

App 3.6.8 **[G]** The *FSA* is of the opinion that *UK firms* that are *credit institutions* and *MiFID investment firms* should apply the 'characteristic performance' test (as referred to in SUP App 3.6.7G) when considering whether prior notification is required for services business. *Firms* should note that other *EEA States* may take a different view. Some *EEA States* may apply a solicitation test. This is a test as to whether it is the consumer or the provider that initiates the business relationship.

App 3.6.9 **[G]** In the case of a *UK firm* conducting portfolio management, for example, this would mean looking at where the investment decisions and management are actually carried on in order to determine where the service is undertaken. Similarly, a *UK* stockbroker that receives orders by telephone from a customer in France for execution on a *UK* exchange may be deemed to be dealing or receiving and transmitting orders within the territory of the *United Kingdom*. In such a case, whether the *firm* solicited the overseas investor would be irrelevant.

App 3.6.10 **[G]** Where, however, a *credit institution* or *MiFID investment firm*:

(1) intends to send a member of staff or a temporarily authorised intermediary to the territory of another *EEA State* on a temporary basis to provide financial services; or

(2) provides advice, of the type that requires notification under either *MiFID* or the *Banking Consolidation Directive*, to customers in another *EEA State;*

the *firm* should make a prior notification under the freedom to provide services.

Temporary activities

App 3.6.11 **[G]** The key distinction in relation to temporary activities is whether a *firm* should make its notification under the freedom of establishment in a *Host State*, or whether it should notify under the freedom to provide services into a *Host State*. It would be inappropriate to discuss such a complex issue in *guidance* of this nature. It is recommended that, where a *firm* is unclear on the distinction, it should seek appropriate advice. In either case, where a *firm* is carrying on activities in another *EEA State* under a *Single Market Directive*, it should make a notification.

App 3.6.12 **[G]** [deleted]

App 3.6.13 **[G]** [deleted]

App 3.6.14 **[G]** [deleted]

Monitoring procedures

App 3.6.15 **[G]** The *FSA* considers that, in order to comply with *Principle* 3:

Management and control (see *PRIN* 2.1.1R), a *firm* should have appropriate procedures to monitor the nature of the services provided to its customers. Where a *UK firm* has non-resident customers but has not notified the *EEA State* in which the customers are resident that it wishes to exercise its freedom to provide services, the *FSA* would expect the *firm's* systems to include appropriate controls. Such controls would include procedures to prevent the supply of services covered by the *Single Market Directives* in the *EEA State* in which the customers are resident if a notification has not been made and it is proposed to provide services otherwise than by remote communication. In respect of *insurance business*, the *insurer's* records should identify the location of the risk at the time the policy is taken out or last renewed. That will, in most cases, remain the location of the risk thereafter, even if, for example, the *policyholder* changes his habitual residence after that time.

App 3.6.16 **[G]** [deleted]

App 3.6.17 **[G]** [deleted]

App 3.6.18 **[G]** [deleted]

App 3.6.19 **[G]** [deleted]

App 3.6.20 **[G]** [deleted]

App 3.6.21 **[G]** [deleted]

App 3.6.22 **[G]** [deleted]

App 3.6.23 **[G]** [deleted]

App 3.6.24 **[G]** [deleted]

Membership of regulated markets

App 3.6.25 **[G]**

(1) The *FSA* is of the opinion that where a *UK firm* becomes a member of:

  (a) a *regulated market* that has its registered office or, if it has no registered office, its head office, in another *EEA State*; or

  (b) an *MTF* operated by a *MiFID investment firm* or a *market operator* in another *EEA State*,

  the same principles as in the 'characteristic performance' test should apply. Under this test, the fact that a *UK firm* has a screen displaying the *regulated market's* or the *MTF's* prices in its *UK* office does not mean that it is *dealing* within the territory of the *Home State* of the *regulated market* or of the *MTF*.

(2) In such a case, we would consider that:

  (a) the *market operator* operating the *regulated market* or the *MTF* is providing a *cross-border service* into the *UK* and so, provided it has given notice to its *Home State regulator* in accordance with articles 42(6) or 31(5) *MiFID*, it will be exempt from the *general prohibition* in respect of any *regulated activity* carried on as part of the business of the *regulated market* or of *operating an MTF* (see section 312A of the *Act*);

(b) the *MiFID investment firm* operating the *MTF* is providing a *cross-border service* into the *UK* and so needs to comply with SUP 13A.

App 3.6.26 **[G]** *Firms* are reminded of their rights, under article 33 of *MiFID*, to become members of, or have access to, the *regulated markets* in other Member States.

App 3.6.27 **[G]** *Firms* should note that, in circumstances where the *FSA* takes the view that a notification would not be required, other *EEA States* may take a different view.

App 3.6.28 **[G]** [deleted]

App 3.6.29 **[G]** [deleted]

App 3.6.30 **[G]** [deleted]

App 3.6.31 **[G]** [deleted]

3.7 Simultaneous exercise of the freedom to provide services and the right of establishment

[deleted]

3.8 Avoidance

[deleted]

3.9 Mapping of MiFID, the Banking Consolidation Directive, UCITS Directive and Insurance Mediation Directive to the Regulated Activities Order

App 3.9.1 **[G]** The following Tables 1, 2, 2A and 2B provide an outline of the *regulated activities* and *specified investments* that may be of relevance to *firms* considering undertaking *passported activities* under the *Banking Consolidation Directive*, *MiFID*, the *UCITS Directive* and the *Insurance Mediation Directive*. The tables may be of assistance to *UK firms* that are thinking of offering financial services in another *EEA State* and to *EEA firms* that may offer those services in the *United Kingdom*.

App 3.9.2 **[G]** The tables provide a general indication of the *investments* and activities specified in the *Regulated Activities Order* that may correspond to categories provided for in either the *Banking Consolidation Directive*, *MiFID*, the *UCITS Directive* or the *Insurance Mediation Directive*. The tables do not provide definitive *guidance* as to whether a *firm* is carrying on an activity that is capable of being passported, nor do the tables take account of exceptions that remove the effect of articles. Whether a *firm* is carrying on a *passported activity* will depend on the particular circumstances of the *firm*. If a *firm's* activities give rise to potential passporting issues, it should obtain specialist advice on the relevant issues.

App 3.9.3 **[G]** In considering the issues raised in the tables, *firms* should note that:

(1) article 64 of the *Regulated Activities Order* (Agreeing to carry on specific kinds of activity) applies in respect of agreeing to undertake the specified activity; and

(2) article 89 of the *Regulated Activities Order* (Rights to or interests in investments) applies in respect of rights to and interests in the types of *investments* to which the category applies.

App 3.9.4 **[G]** Table: Activities set out in Annex I of the BCD

Table 1: BCD activities		**Part II RAO Activities**	**Part III RAO Investments**
1.	Acceptance of deposits and other repayable funds from the public	Article 5	Article 74
2.	Lending	Article 61, 64	Article 88
3.	Financial leasing		
4.	Money transmission services		
5.	Issuing and administering means of payment (eg credit cards, travellers' cheques and bankers' drafts)		
6.	*Guarantees and commitments*		
7.	Trading for own account or for account of customers in:		
	(a) money market instruments	Article 14, 21, 25 (see Note 1), 64 Article 14, 21, 25, 64	Article 77, 78, 80, 83–85, 89
	(b) foreign exchange	Article 14, 21, 25, 64	Article 83–85, 89
	(c) financial futures and options	Article 14, 21, 25, 64	Article 83–85, 89
	(d) exchange and interest rate instruments	Article 14, 21, 25, 64	Article 83–85, 89

Part II FSA Handbook Materials

Table 1: BCD activities		Part II RAO Activities	Part III RAO Investments
	(e) transferable securities		Article 76–81, 89
8.	Participation in share issues and the provision of services relating to such issues	Article 14, 21, 25, 53, 64	Article 76–81, 89
9.	Advice to undertakings on capital structure, industrial strategy and related questions and advice and services relating to mergers and the purchase of undertakings	Article 14, 21, 25, 53, 64	Article 76–80, 83–85, 89
10.	Money broking	Article 25, 64	Article 77, 78, 89
11.	Portfolio management and advice	Article 14, 21, 25, 37, 53, 64	Article 76–81, 83–85, 89
12.	Safekeeping and administration of securities	Article 40, 45, 64	Article 76–81, 83–85, 89
13.	Credit reference services		
14.	Safe custody services		

Note 1: The services and activities provided for in Sections A and B of Annex I of *MiFID* when referring to the *financial instruments* provided for in Section C of Annex I of that Directive are subject to mutual recognition according to the *BCD* from 1 November 2007. See the table at SUP App 3.9.5 below for mapping of *MiFID investment services and activities*. For further details relating to this residual category, please see the "Banking Consolidation Directive" section of the passporting forms entitled "Notification of intention to establish a branch in another EEA State" and "Notification of intention to provide cross border services in another EEA State".

App 3.9.5 **[G]** Table: Services set out in Annex I to MiFID

Table 2: *MiFID investment services and activities*		**Part II RAO Activities**	**Part III RAO Investments**
	A *MiFID investment services and activities*		
1.	Reception and transmission of orders in relation to one or more financial instruments	Article 25	Article 76–81, 83–85, 89
2.	Execution of orders on behalf of clients	Article 14, 21	A Article 76–81, 83–85, 89
3.	Dealing on own account	Article 14	Article 76–81, 83–85, 89
4.	Portfolio management	Article 37 (14, 21, 25 – see Note 1)	Article 76–81, 83–85, 89
5.	Investment advice	Article 53	Article 76–81, 83–85, 89
6.	Underwriting of financial instruments and/or placing of financial instruments on a firm commitment basis	Article 14, 21	Article 76–81, 83–85, 89
7.	Placing of financial instruments without a firm commitment basis	Article 21, 25	Article 76–81, 83–85, 89
8.	Operation of Multilateral Trading Facilities	Article 25B (see Note 2)	Article 76–81, 83–85, 89
	Ancillary services	Part II RAO Activities	Part III RAO Investments
1.	Safekeeping and administration of financial instruments for the account of clients, including custodianship and related services such as cash/collateral management	Article 40, 45, 64	Article 76–81, 83–85, 89
2.	Granting credits or loans to an investor to allow him to carry out a transaction in one or more of the relevant instruments where the firm granting the credit or loan is involved		

Table 2: *MiFID investment services and activities*		Part II RAO Activities	Part III RAO Investments
3.	Advice to undertakings on capital structure, industrial strategy and related matters and advice and services relating to mergers and the purchase of undertakings	Article 14, 21, 25, 53, 64	Article 76–80, 83–85, 89
4.	Foreign exchange services where these are connected with the provision of investment services	Article 14, 21, 25, 53, 64	Article 83–85, 89
5.	Investment research and financial analysis or other forms of general recommendation relating to transactions in financial instruments	Article 53, 64	Article 76–81, 83–85, 89
6.	Services related to underwriting	Article 25, 53, 64	Article 76–81, 83–85, 89
7.	Investment services and activities as well as ancillary services of the type included under Section A or B of Annex I related to the underlying of the derivatives included under Section C 5, 6, 7 and 10 – where these are connected to the provision of investment or ancillary services.	Article 14, 21, 25, 25B, 37, 53, 64	Article 83 and 84

Note 1. A *firm* may also carry on these other activities when it is *managing investments*.

Note 2. A *firm* operating an *MTF* under article 25B does not need to have a *permission* covering other *regulated activities*, unless it performs other *regulated activities* in addition to *operating an MTF*.

App 3.9.6 **[G]** Table: Activities set out in Article 5(2) and (3) of the UCITS Directive

Table 2A: UCITS Directive activities		Part II RAO Activities	Part III RAO Investments
1.	The management of UCITS in the form of unit trusts / common funds or of investment companies; this includes the functions mentioned in Annex II of the *UCITS Directive* (see Note 2).	Article 14, 21, 25, 37, 51, 53, 64	Article 76–81, 83–85, 89
2.	Managing portfolios of investments, including those owned by pension funds, in accordance with mandates given by investors on a discretionary, client-by-client basis, where such portfolios include one or more of the instruments listed in Section C of Annex I to *MiFID*.	Article 14, 21, 25, 37, 53, 64	Article 76–81, 83–85, 89
3.	Investment advice concerning one or more of the instruments listed in Section C of Annex to *MiFID*.	Article 53, 64	Article 76–81, 83–85, 89
4.	Safekeeping and administration services in relation to units of collective investment undertakings.	Article 40, 45, 64	Article 76–81, 83–85, 89

Note 1. A *UCITS management company* can only exercise passport rights under the *UCITS Directive* (article 2(1)(h) of *MiFID*). A *UCITS management company* can only be *authorised* to carry on the non-core services set out in rows (3) and (4) of Table 2A if it is also *authorised* to carry on the activity set out in row (2) of the table.

Note 2. The functions set out in Annex 2 to the *UCITS Directive* are:

(1) Investment management.

(2) Administration:

- (a) legal and fund management accounting services;
- (b) customer inquiries;
- (c) valuation and pricing (including tax returns);
- (d) regulatory compliance monitoring;
- (e) maintenance of unit-holder register;
- (f) distribution of income;
- (g) unit issues and redemptions;

Part II FSA Handbook Materials

(h) contract settlements (including certificate dispatch);
(i) record keeping.
(3) Marketing.

App 3.9.7 **[G]** Table: Activities set out in Article 2(3) of the IMD

Table 2B: IMD activities		Part II RAO Activities	Part III RAO Investments
1.	Introducing, proposing or carrying out other work preparatory to the conclusion of contracts of insurance.	Articles 25, 53 and 64	Article 75, 89 (see Note 1)
2.	Concluding contracts of insurance	Article 21, 25, 53 and 64	Article 75, 89
3.	Assisting in the administration and performance of contracts of insurance, in particular in the event of a claim.	Article 39A, 64	Article 75, 89

Note 1. Rights to or interests in *life policies* are *specified investments* under Article 89 of the *Regulated Activities Order*, but rights to or interests in *general insurance* contracts are not.

3.10 Mapping of Insurance Directives to the Regulated Activities Order

Introduction

App 3.10.1 **[G]** The *guidance* in Table 3 describes in broad outline the relationship between:
(1) the insurance-related *regulated activities* specified in the *Regulated Activities Order*; and
(2) the activities within the scope of the *Insurance Directives.*

App 3.10.2 **[G]** This is a guide only and should not be used as a substitute for legal advice in individual cases.

Table 3: Insurance Directive activities		Part II RAO Activities	Part III RAO Investments
	1. Non-life Insurance Directive activities		
1.	Taking up and carrying on direct non-life insurance business	Article 10	Article 75
2.	Classes 1 to 18 of direct non-life insurance business in Point A of the Annex to the First Directive		Corresponding paragraphs 1 to 18 of Schedule 1, Part I
	2. Consolidated Life Directive activities		
1.	Taking up and carrying on direct life insurance business	Article 10	Article 75
2.	Classes I to IX of direct life insurance business in the Annex 1 to the Consolidated Life Directive		Corresponding paragraphs I to IX of Schedule 1, Part II
	It will normally be the case that the activities of taking up and carrying on direct non-life or life insurance business will also embrace the activity of accepting deposits	Article 5	Article 74

Meaning of contract of insurance

App 3.10.3 **[G]** The meaning of *contract of insurance* is set out in article 3(1) of the *Regulated Activities Order* (Interpretation). It does not include benefit-in-kind funeral plans, which are specified in article 60 of the *Regulated Activities Order* (plans covered by insurance or trust arrangements). Such funeral plans (to the extent that they are insurance) are also excluded from the *Insurance Directives.* It covers some contracts which might not otherwise be viewed as insurance in the *United Kingdom* (for example, contracts of guarantee). These contracts are also governed by the *Insurance Directives.* For the purpose of the *Regulated Activities Order,* a *contract of insurance* includes a contract of reinsurance as well as a contract of direct insurance.

The Insurance Directives

App 3.10.4 **[G]** Article 1 of the *First Non-Life Directive* and article 2 of the *Consolidated Life Directive* provides that the Directives "concern the taking up and pursuit of the self-employed activity of direct insurance". By contrast, article 10 of the *Regulated Activities Order* (Effecting and carrying out contracts of insurance) also covers reinsurance.

App 3.10.5 **[G]** Articles 2, 3 and 4 of the *First Non-Life Directive* and *article 3 of the Consolidated Life Directive* set out certain exclusions by reference to:
(1) types of insurance;
(2) types of insurer;
(3) particular conditions under which insurance activities are carried out;
(4) annual income; and
(5) particular identified institutions.

App 3.10.6 **[G]** Some of the exclusions referred to in SUP App 3.11.2G mirror exclusions in the *Regulated Activities Order*. So, the exclusion for breakdown insurance in article 2(3) of the *First Non-Life Directive* is matched by a slightly narrower exclusion in article 12 of the *Regulated Activities Order* (Breakdown insurance). The separate treatment of benefit-in-kind funeral plans under the *Regulated Activities Order* (see SUP App 3.10.4G) is matched by their exclusion on a slightly wider basis in article 3(5) of the *Consolidated Life Directive*. Other requirements from these Directives are also excluded from regulation by the *Exemption Order*.

App 3.10.7 **[G]** Most of the exclusions under the Directives, however, are not excluded from being *regulated activities*. For example, article 3 of the *Consolidated Life Directive* and article 3 of the *Non-Life Directive* exclude certain mutual associations whose annual contribution income falls below a defined threshold. In the *United Kingdom*, these include certain smaller *friendly societies* commonly referred to as "*non-directive friendly societies*". The activities of such societies are regulated under the *Act*, on a "lighter basis" than the activities of other insurers.

Territorial scope of the Regulated Activities Order and the Directives

App 3.10.8 **[G]** Under the *Act* and the *Regulated Activities Order*, the activities of *effecting* and *carrying out contracts of insurance* are treated as being carried on in the *United Kingdom* on the basis of legal tests under which the location of the risk is only one factor. If the risk is located in the *United Kingdom*, then (other relevant factors being taken into account) the activity will, in the vast majority of cases, also be viewed as carried on in the *United Kingdom*. There are exceptions, however, and overseas insurers may insure risks in the *United Kingdom* without carrying on business here and so without requiring to be regulated (although the *financial promotion* regime may apply). By contrast, under the Directives, the responsibility, as between *EEA States*, for regulating the conduct of passported insurance services is determined by reference to the location of the risk or commitment, as defined in article 1 of the *Consolidated Life Directive* and article 2 of the *Second Non-Life Directive*.

App 3.10.9 **[G]** So, the effect of SUP App 3.12.1G is that an *insurer* may be carrying on *insurance business* in the *United Kingdom* which is to be treated as a *regulated activity* under article 10 to the *Regulated Activities Order* (Effecting and carrying out contracts of insurance) in circumstances where the risks covered are treated as located in another *EEA State*. In that event, the *insurer* is required by Schedule 3 to the *Act* to passport into the State concerned and may be subject to conduct of business requirements in that State (see SUP 13.10 (Applicable provisions)).

App 3.10.10 **[G]** An *insurer* authorised in another *EEA State* who is insuring *UK* risks and so passports on a services basis under the *Insurance Directives* into the *United Kingdom* (see SUP App 3.12.1 G), may not be carrying on a *regulated activity* in the *United Kingdom*. But, if it passports into the *United Kingdom*, it will qualify for *authorisation* under paragraph 12 of Schedule 3 to the *Act* (Firms qualifying for authorisation). Where this is the case, the *insurer* will be subject to conduct of business requirements in the *United Kingdom* (see SUP 13A.6 (Which rules will an incoming EEA firm be subject to?)).

Activities carried on by incoming EEA firms in connection with insurance business.

App 3.10.11 **[G]** Although the *Insurance Directives* are concerned with the *regulated activities* of *effecting and carrying out contracts of insurance*, an *incoming EEA firm* passported under the *Insurance Directives* will be entitled to carry on certain other *regulated activities* without the need for *top-up permission*. This is where the *regulated activities* are carried on for the purposes of or in connection with the *incoming EEA Firm's insurance business*. These *regulated activities* may include:
(1) *dealing in investments as principal*;
(2) *dealing in investments as agent*;
(3) *arranging (bringing about) deals in investments*;
(4) *making arrangements with a view to transactions in investments*;
(5) *managing investments*;
(6) *safeguarding and administering investments*;
(7) *advising on investments*;
(8) *agreeing to carry on a regulated activity* of the above kind.

Financial promotion

App 3.10.12 **[G]** The *financial promotion* regime under section 21 of the *Act* (Restrictions on financial promotion) may also apply to *EEA insurance undertakings* regardless of whether they carry on a *regulated activity* in the *United Kingdom* or passport into the *United Kingdom*.

Position of EEA insurers carrying out both direct and reinsurance business

App 3.10.13 **[G]** The *Insurance Directives* do not apply to the authorisation to carry on *reinsurance*. But, the *Insurance Directives* do not prevent *insurance undertakings* authorised under those Directives from carrying out *reinsurance* as well as direct insurance business. Article 13(2) of the *First Non-Life Directive* and article 10(2) of the *Consolidated Life Directive* state that financial supervision of *insurance undertakings* "shall include verification, with respect to the *insurance undertaking's* entire business, of its state of solvency, of the establishment of technical provisions and of the assets covering them". On that basis, an *insurance undertaking* authorised in another *EEA State* which carries on a mixed direct insurance and *reinsurance* business, and is, therefore, subject to the requirements of the Directives, will generally be treated as satisfying the conditions laid down by an *EU* instrument relating to the carrying on of the *regulated activity* of *effecting* or *carrying out contracts of insurance*. This is for the purpose of paragraph 3 of Schedule 4 to the *Act* (Exercise of treaty rights). The *insurance undertaking* will, therefore, generally be able to qualify for *permission* as a *Treaty firm* for its *reinsurance* business if it follows the procedure provided for by Schedule 4 (see SUP 13A.3.4G to SUP 13A.3.11G (Treaty Firms)). This will be in addition to the *insurance undertaking* being an *EEA firm* under Schedule 3 of the *Act* for its direct insurance business.

TRANSITIONAL PROVISIONS

[2178]

1.1 Table: Transitional provisions applying to the Supervision manual only

Definitions for these transitional provisions, additional to those in the *Glossary*, are provided at paragraph 16 of the table.

1.2 Table

(1)	(2) Material to which the transitional provision applies	(3)	(4) Transitional provision	(5) Transitional provision: dates in force	(6) Handbook provision: coming into force
1	SUP 3.3.2R(1)	R	Auditors A *firm* will not contravene SUP 3.3.2R(1), if the office of auditor is filled at *commencement*. The auditor filling the office at that time will be deemed to be appointed under SUP 3.3.2R.	From *commencement*	*Commencement*
2	SUP 3.9 and SUP 3.10	R	Expired		
3	SUP 3.9.4R	R	Expired		
3A	SUP 3.10	R	Expired		
3B	SUP 3.10.6R, SUP 3.10.7R	G	Expired		
3C	SUP 3.10	R	Expired		
4	SUP 4.3.1R(1) and SUP 4.4.1R(1)	R	Actuaries A *firm* will not contravene SUP 4.3.1R(1) or SUP 4.4.1R(1) to the extent that the office of *actuarial function holder*, *with-profits actuary* or *appropriate actuary* is filled by an *actuary* appointed on or before 31 December 2004, provided that that *actuary* was appointed in accordance with the statutory requirements, or the requirements of the *regulatory system*, in force at that time.	From *commencement*	*Commencement*
4A	SUP 4	R	Anything done before 31 December 2004 for the purposes of an amended provision in SUP 4 has effect as if done under that provision.	From 31 December 2004	31 December 2004
4B	[deleted]				
4BA	SUP 4.3.16AR(3) and (4)	R	The *rules* apply in respect of each financial year commencing on or after 1 January 2005.	From 31 December 2004	31 December 2004
4C	[deleted]				
4D	[deleted]				
4E	[deleted]				

(1)	(2) Material to which the transitional provision applies	(3)	(4) Transitional provision	(5) Transitional provision: dates in force	(6) Handbook provision: coming into force
5	SUP 4.3.3R	R	If a *firm's actuary* has been appointed by a *previous regulator* under statutory or contractual powers and remains in office immediately before *commencement*, that appointment will be deemed to have been made under SUP 4.3.3R, but on the terms of the actual appointment.	From *commencement*	*Commencement*
6	SUP 8.6.1R	R	Expired		
6A	SUP 9.4	G	Individual guidance	From 19 July 2001	
			(1) If a *person* acts in accordance with individual written guidance:		
			(a) given to him by any *previous regulator* (or body whose functions were assumed by a *previous regulator*);		
			(b) relating to any pre-commencement provision; and		
			(c) in the circumstances contemplated by that guidance;		
			then the *FSA* will proceed on the footing that the *person* has complied with the aspects of any provision in or under the *Act* (including a *rule* or *guidance* in the *Handbook*) to which the guidance relates if:		
			(d) that provision is substantially similar to the pre-commencement provision in relation to the matter with which the guidance is concerned;		
			(e) the guidance was current immediately before *commencement*; and		
			(f) the guidance has not been superseded.		
			(2) SUP 9.4.2G – SUP 9.4.4G are relevant for individual guidance in (1) in the same way as for individual written *guidance* given by the *FSA*.		
			(3) References to "individual written guidance" in (1) and (2) include a written concession from a pre-commencement provision which is substantially similar to *guidance* in the *Handbook*.		

(1)	(2) Material to which the transitional provision applies	(3)	(4) Transitional provision	(5) Transitional provision: dates in force	(6) Handbook provision: coming into force
8	SUP 10.13.6R	R	Expired		
8A	SUP 10.4.1R	R	(1) An application made under section 60 of the *Act* received before 31 October 2007 will be taken to relate to the *controlled function* existing at the date of determination.	From 1 November 2007	From 1 November 2007
			(2) The *controlled functions* CF 13 (*finance function*), CF 14 (*risk assessment function*) and CF 15 (*internal audit function*) are subsumed in the new *controlled function* CF 28 (*systems and controls function*) to the extent that they fall within the description of the *systems and controls function*.	On 1 November 2007	On 1 November 2007
			(3) The *controlled functions* CF 16 (*significant management (designated investment business) function*), CF 17 (*significant management (other business operations) function*), CF 18 (*significant management (insurance underwriting) function*), CF 19 (*significant management (financial resources) function*) and CF 20 (*significant management (settlements) function*) are subsumed in the new *controlled function* CF 29 (*significant management function*) to the extent that they fall within the description of the *significant management function*.	On 1 November 2007	On 1 November 2007
			(4) The *controlled functions* CF 21 (*investment adviser function*), CF 22 (*investment adviser (trainee) function*), CF 23 (*corporate finance adviser function*), CF 24 (*pension transfer specialist function*), CF 25 (*adviser on syndicate participation at Lloyd's function*), CF 26 (*customer trading function*) and CF 27 (*investment management function*) are subsumed in the new *controlled function* CF 30 (*customer function*) to the extent that they fall within the description of the *customer function*.	On 1 November 2007	On 1 November 2007

(1)	(2) Material to which the transitional provision applies	(3)	(4) Transitional provision	(5) Transitional provision: dates in force	(6) Handbook provision: coming into force
8B		G	(1) The effect of TP 8AR is that if immediately prior to 1 November 2007 a *person* was an *approved person* in relation to any of the *controlled functions* to be subsumed into the *systems and controls function* the original grant of approval by the *FSA* will remain valid in relation to the *systems and controls function* and no new approval to perform that *controlled function* will be required.		
			(2) The effect of TP 8AR is that if immediately prior to 1 November 2007 a *person* was an *approved person* in relation to any of the *controlled functions* to be subsumed into the *significant management function* the original grant of approval by the *FSA* will remain valid in relation to the *significant management function* and no new approval to perform that *controlled function* will be required.		
			(3) The effect of TP 8AR is that if immediately prior to 1 November 2007 a *person* was an *approved person* in relation to any of the *controlled functions* to be subsumed into the *customer function* the original grant of approval by the FSA will remain valid in relation to the *customer function* and no new approval to perform controlled function will be required.		
8C		G	*Firms* are reminded of their obligation under SUP 10.13.16R to notify the *FSA* if the *firm* becomes aware of information which would be reasonably material to the continuing assessment of an *approved person's* fitness and propriety and in particular their competence to perform a function.		

(1)	(2) Material to which the transitional provision applies	(3)	(4) Transitional provision	(5) Transitional provision: dates in force	(6) Handbook provision: coming into force
8D	SUP 10.13.6R (Ceasing to perform a controlled function) and SUP 10.13.3D (Moving within a firm)	R	The obligation to submit Form C or Form E does not apply in relation to a person who: (a) ceases to perform a *controlled function* because that *controlled function* ceases to exist on 1 February 2007; or (b) performs a function which falls within the description of a different *controlled function* after 1 November 2007 as a result of TP 8AR.	From 1 February 2007 in relation to the *sole trader function* and 1 November 2007 in all other cases.	From 1 February 2007 in relation to the *sole trader function* and 1 November 2007 in all other cases.
8E	SUP 10.6.4R(2)	R	(1) This *rule* deals with a *person* (a "director") who would otherwise have been performing the *director function* for a *firm* under SUP 10.6.4R(2) on 6 August 2009 but who was not otherwise performing the *director function* for that *firm* at that date. This *rule* only applies if he was not approved at that date to perform the *director function* for that *firm*.	6 August 2009 to 6 February 2010	6 February 2010
			(2) Between the dates in column (5), the functions described in SUP 10.6.4R(2) are not treated as forming part of the *director function* as respects that *firm* and that director unless they also fall under SUP 10.6.4R(1).		
			(3) If this transitional rule has not already expired under column (5), this *rule* comes to an end as respects that director and that *firm* if and when an application is made for the director to perform the *director function* for that *firm* and that application is granted.		
8F	SUP 10.6.8R(1)(b)	R	(1) This *rule* deals with a *person* (a "non-executive director") who would otherwise have been performing the *non-executive director function* for a *firm* under SUP 10.6.8R(1)(b) on 6 August 2009 but who was not otherwise performing the *non-executive director function* for that *firm* at that date. This rule only applies if he was not approved at that date to perform the *non-executive director function* for that *firm*.	6 August 2009 to 6 February 2010	6 February 2010

(1)	(2) Material to which the transitional provision applies	(3)	(4) Transitional provision	(5) Transitional provision: dates in force	(6) Handbook provision: coming into force
			(2) Between the dates in column (5), the functions described in SUP 10.6.8R(1)(b) are not treated as forming part of the *non-executive director function* as respects the *firm* and that non-executive director unless they also fall under SUP 10.6.8.R(1)(a).		
			(3) If this transitional rule has not already expired under column (5), this *rule* comes to an end as respects that non-executive director and that *firm* if and when an application is made for the non-executive director to perform the *non-executive director function* for that *firm* and that application is granted.		
8G	SUP 10.9.1R(2)	R	(1) This *rule* deals with a *person* (a "proprietary trader") who would otherwise have been performing the *significant management function* for a *firm* under SUP 10.9.10R(1A) on 6 August 2009 but who was not otherwise performing the *significant management function* for that *firm* at that date. This *rule* only applies if he was not approved at that date to perform the *significant management function* for that *firm*.	6 August 2009 to 6 February 2010	6 February 2010
			(2) Between the dates in column (5), the functions described in SUP 10.9.10R(1A) are not treated as forming part of the *significant management function* as respects that *firm* and that proprietary trader unless they also fall under SUP 10.9.10R(1).		
			(3) If this transitional rule has not already expired under column (5), this *rule* comes to an end as respects that proprietary trader and that *firm* if and when an application is made for the proprietary trader to perform the *significant management function* for that *firm* and that application is granted.		

(1)	(2) Material to which the transitional provision applies	(3)	(4) Transitional provision	(5) Transitional provision: dates in force	(6) Handbook provision: coming into force
8H	SUP 10.1.7R(1)	R	(1) This *rule* deals with the application of the *director function* under SUP 10.1.7R(1) to a *person* (a "director") who would otherwise have been performing the *director function* on 6 August 2009 in an *overseas firm* which maintains an establishment in the *United Kingdom* from which *regulated activities* are carried on (or would have been doing so but for a *waiver*).	6 October 2009 to 6 February 2010	6 February 2010
			(2) Between the dates in column (5), the functions described in SUP 10.1.7R(1) are not treated as forming part of the *director function* as respects that establishment in the *United Kingdom*, and that director.		
			(3) If this transitional rule has not already expired under column (5), this *rule* comes to an end as respects that director and that establishment in the *United Kingdom*, if and when an application is made for the director to perform the *director function* for that establishment in the *United Kingdom* and that application is granted.		
8I	SUP 10.1.7R(2)	R	(1) This *rule* deals with the application of the *non-executive director function* under SUP 10.1.7R(2) to a *person* (a "non-executive director") who would otherwise have been performing the *non-executive director function* on 6 August 2009 in an *overseas* firm which maintains an establishment in the *United Kingdom* from which *regulated activities* are carried on (or would have been doing so but for a *waiver*).	6 October 2009 to 6 February 2010	6 February 2010
			(2) Between the dates in column (5), the functions described in SUP 10.1.7R(2) are not treated as forming part of the *non-executive director function* as respects that establishment in the *United Kingdom*, and that non-executive director.		

(1)	(2) Material to which the transitional provision applies	(3)	(4) Transitional provision	(5) Transitional provision: dates in force	(6) Handbook provision: coming into force
			(3) If this transitional rule has not already expired under column (5), this *rule* comes to an end as respects that non-executive director and that establishment in the *United Kingdom*, if and when an application is made for the non-executive director to perform the *non-executive director function* for that establishment in the *United Kingdom* and that application is granted.		
8J	SUP 10.1.7R(5)	R	(1) This *rule* deals with the application of the *systems and controls function* under SUP 10.1.7R(5) to *persons* who would otherwise have been performing the *systems and controls function* on 6 August 2009 in an *overseas firm* which maintains an establishment in the *United Kingdom* from which *regulated activities* are carried on (or would have been doing so but for a *waiver*).	6 October 2009 to 6 February 2010	6 February 2010
			(2) Between the dates in column (5), the functions described in SUP 10.1.7R(5) are not treated as forming part of the *systems and controls function* as respects that establishment in the *United Kingdom* and that person.		
			(3) If this transitional rule has not already expired under column (5), this *rule* comes to an end as respects that person and that establishment in the *United Kingdom*, if and when an application is made for that person to perform the *systems and controls function* for that establishment in the *United Kingdom* and that application is granted.		
9	SUP 12.5.5R SUP 12.5.7R	R	Expired		
9A	SUP 15.8.4	R	Notification of Delegation (1) Subject to (2), SUP 15.8.4 R does not apply to a *UCITS management company* which became *authorized* before 13 February 2004.	From 13 February 2004 to 13 February 2007	13 February 2004

(1)	(2) Material to which the transitional provision applies	(3)	(4) Transitional provision	(5) Transitional provision: dates in force	(6) Handbook provision: coming into force
			(2) paragraph (1) does not apply in relation to any *UK firm* which exercises an *EEA right* under the *UCITS Directive* (in which event the rule applies in relation to acts of delegation occurring on or after the date on which the firm begins to exercise such rights).		
9B	SUP 12.5	R	A *firm* conducting *designated investment business* need not amend its written contract with an *appointed representative* (appointed before 15 January 2004) to take account of amendments to SUP 12.5 coming into force between 30 June 2004 and 30 June 2005, until 30 June 2005 or the date on which the contract is next updated (whichever is earlier).	From 30 June 2004 until 30 June 2005, that is, 12 *months*.	*Commencement*, and as amended with effect from 30 June 2004
10	SUP 16.4.5R SUP 16.5.5R	R	Expired		
10A	SUP 16.4 SUP 16.5	R	SUP 16.4 (Annual controllers report) and 16.5 (Annual close links report) do not apply to a *firm* with *permission* to carry on only *insurance mediation activity*, *mortgage mediation activity*, or both.	(1) in respect of *mortgage mediation activities*, 31 October 2004 – 31 March 2005; (2) in respect of *insurance mediation activities*, 14 January 2005 – 31 March 2005.	1 April 2005
11	SUP 16.6 SUP 16.7 SUP 16.8	R	Expired		

(1)	(2) Material to which the transitional provision applies	(3)	(4) Transitional provision	(5) Transitional provision: dates in force	(6) Handbook provision: coming into force
12	SUP 16.7.7R; SUP 16.7.9R, SUP 16.7.11R, SUP 16.7.16R, SUP 16.7.24R, SUP 16.7.26R, SUP 16.7.35R, SUP 16.7.44R, SUP 16.7.46R, SUP 16.7.48R, SUP 16.7.57R	R	Expired		
12A	SUP 16.7.38	R	An *investment management firm* which, before 1 December 2003, was already submitting consolidated financial returns using the form in: (a) SUP 16 Ann 10R; or (b) SUP 16 Ann 7R (with associated guidance in SUP 16 Ann 8G); may continue to use these forms instead of the consolidated financial resources return in SUP 16 Ann 5R.	From 1 December 2003 until, but not including, the date on which the provisions of the Financial Groups Directive take effect in the *United Kingdom*.	1 December 2003
12B	SUP 16.7.54R; SUP 16.7.76R; SUP 16.7.79R; SUP 16.7.80R	R	(1) Where a *rule* in SUP 16.7 requires a *firm* to submit information using the *RMAR* on a half-yearly basis, and the *firm* has:	From 1 April 2005	1 April 2005
			(a) annual income of less than £5m but more than £60,000 in total from *insurance mediation activity, mortgage mediation activity* and its *permitted activities* as a *personal investment firm*, and		
			(b) an *accounting reference date* which		
			(i) falls between 31 December 2004 and 31 March 2005; or		

(1)	(2) Material to which the transitional provision applies	(3)	(4) Transitional provision	(5) Transitional provision: dates in force	(6) Handbook provision: coming into force
			(ii) falls between 30 June 2005 and 30 September 2005 this must be read as a reference to providing the first return in accordance with SUP TR 12CR.		
			(2) Where a *rule* in SUP 16.7 requires a *firm* to submit information using the *RMAR* on a half-yearly basis, and the *firm* has:		
			(a) annual income of less than £5m but more than £60,000 in total from *insurance mediation activity, mortgage mediation activity* and its *permitted activities* as a *personal investment firm*, and		
			(b) an *accounting reference date* which is not within (1)(b);		
			the first return must cover the *firm's* first full financial half-year which starts on or after 1 April 2005 and be submitted 30 *business days* after period end.		
			(3) Where a *firm* is carrying on *regulated activities* before 1 April 2005 and is required under a *rule* in SUP 16.7 to submit information using the *MLAR*, the first return must cover the *firm's* first full financial quarter which starts on or after this date and be submitted 20 *business days* after period end.		
			(4) Where a *rule* in SUP 16.7 requires a *firm* to submit information using the *RMAR* on a half-yearly basis, and the *firm* has:		
			(a) annual income of less than £60,000 in total from *insurance mediation activity, mortgage mediation activity* and its *permitted activities* as a *personal investment firm*, and		
			(b) an *accounting reference date* which falls between 31 December 2004 and 30 December 2005 the relevant *rule* must be read as requiring the first return to be provided in accordance with SUP TR 12DR.		

<table>
<tr><th>(1)</th><th>(2)
Material to which the transitional provision applies</th><th>(3)</th><th colspan="4">(4)
Transitional provision</th><th>(5)
Transitional provision: dates in force</th><th>(6)
Handbook provision: coming into force</th></tr>
<tr><td></td><td></td><td></td><td colspan="4">(5) Where a rule in SUP 16.7 requires a firm to submit information using the RMAR on a quarterly basis, and the firm has an accounting reference date which falls between 31 December 2004 and 30 December 2005 the relevant rule must be read as requiring the first return to be provided with SUP TR 14B.</td><td></td><td></td></tr>
<tr><td>12C</td><td></td><td>R</td><td colspan="4">If SUP TR 12B R (1)–(3) applies, the firm's first return must be provided as follows:</td><td></td><td></td></tr>
<tr><td></td><td></td><td></td><td>Accounting reference date</td><td>Reporting period starts</td><td>Reporting period ends</td><td>Return to be provided</td><td></td><td></td></tr>
<tr><td></td><td></td><td></td><td>Between 30 June 2005 and 30 September 2005</td><td>1 April 2005</td><td>Accounting reference date within 2005</td><td>30 business days after period end.</td><td></td><td></td></tr>
<tr><td></td><td></td><td></td><td>31 December 2004</td><td>1 April 2005</td><td>30 June 2005</td><td>30 business days after the period end</td><td></td><td></td></tr>
<tr><td></td><td></td><td></td><td>Between 1 January 2005 and 31 March 2005</td><td>1 April 2005</td><td>6 months after the accounting reference date within 2005</td><td>30 business days after period end</td><td></td><td></td></tr>
<tr><td>12D</td><td></td><td>R</td><td colspan="4">(1) If SUP TR 12BR (4) applies, the firm's first return must be provided as follows:</td><td></td><td></td></tr>
<tr><td></td><td></td><td></td><td>Accounting reference date</td><td>Reporting period starts</td><td>Reporting period ends</td><td>Return to be provided</td><td></td><td></td></tr>
<tr><td></td><td></td><td></td><td>31 December 2004</td><td>1 April 2005</td><td>30 June 2005</td><td>30 business days after period end (Note 1)</td><td></td><td></td></tr>
</table>

(1)	(2) Material to which the transitional provision applies	(3)	(4) Transitional provision				(5) Transitional provision: dates in force	(6) Handbook provision: coming into force
			Between 1 January 2005 and 31 March 2005	1 April 2005	6 months after the *accounting reference date* within 2005	30 *business days* after period end (Note 1)		
			Between 1 April 2005 and 29 June 2005	the day following the accounting reference date within 2005	6 months after the accounting reference date within 2005	30 business days after period end. (Note 1)		
			Between 30 June 2005 and 29 September 2005	1 April 2005	*Accounting reference date* within 2005	30 *business days* after period end		
			Between 30 September 2005 and 30 December 2005	The day after 6 months preceding the *accounting reference date* within 2005	*Accounting reference date* within 2005	30 *business days* after period end		
12E		R	(2) If SUP TR 12BR (4) applies, the *firm's* second return must be provided as follows:					
			Accounting reference date	Reporting period starts	Reporting period ends	Return to be provided		
			Between 30 June 2005 and 29 September 2005	the day following the *accounting reference date* within 2005	6 months after the *accounting reference date* within 2005	30 *business days* after period end (Note 1)		
12F	SUP 16.7.77R	R	A *mortgage administrator or mortgage lender* must submit an annual report and audited accounts annually, 3 months after the *firm's accounting reference date*				31 October 2004 – 31 March 2005	1 April 2005

(1)	(2) Material to which the transitional provision applies	(3)	(4) Transitional provision				(5) Transitional provision: dates in force	(6) Handbook provision: coming into force
12G	SUP 16.7.7R; SUP 16.7.9R; SUP 16.7.11R; SUP 16.7.16R; SUP 16.7.20R; SUP 16.7.24R;	R	(1)	Where a *rule* in SUP 16.7 requires a firm to submit information using the *RMAR* on a half yearly basis the relevant *rule* must be read as requiring the first return to be provided in accordance with SUP TR 12HR.			From 1 January 2007 – 31 December 2007	1 January 2007
			(2)	Where a *firm* is carrying on *regulated activities* on or before 1 January 2007 and is required under a *rule* in SUP 16.7 to submit information using the *MLAR*, the first return must cover the *firm's* first full financial quarter which starts on or after this date and be submitted 20 *business days* after period end.				
12H	SUP 16.7.26R; SUP 16.7.28R; SUP 16.7.35R; SUP 16.7.57R; SUP 16.7.62R; SUP 16.7.65R; SUP 16.7.73R;	R	If SUP TR 12G R (1) applies, the *firm's* first return must be provided as follows:					
			Accounting reference date (dates inclusive)	Reporting period starts	Reporting period ends	Return to be provided		
			Between 1 January and 31 March	The day after the *accounting reference date* within 2007	6 months after the *accounting reference date* within 2007	30 *business days* after period end.		
			Between 1 April and 30 June	1 January 2007	*Accounting reference date* within 2007	30 *business days* after period end		

(1)	(2) Material to which the transitional provision applies	(3)	(4) Transitional provision				(5) Transitional provision: dates in force	(6) Handbook provision: coming into force
			Between 1 July and 30 September	The day after 6 months preceding the *accounting reference date* within 2007	*Accounting reference date* within 2007	30 *business days* after period end.		
			Between 1 October and 31 December	1 January 2007	6 months before the *accounting reference date* within 2007	30 *business days* after period end		
12I	SUP 16.7.54R	R	Until 6 September 2006, an *authorised professional firm* will not contravene SUP 16.7.54R if it submits to the FSA the annual questionnaire that was contained in SUP 16 Annex 9 immediately prior to 6 July 2006.				6 July 2006 – 6 September 2006	6 July 2006
12J	(1) SUP 16.7.24, 16.7.25 and 16.7.25A, SUP 16.7.27 and 16.7.27A	R	A *securities and futures firm* that is a *BIPRU investment firm* is not required to submit the Annual Reporting Statement, the Annual Reconciliation and the Consolidated Supervision Return under SUP 16.7.25R and SUP 16.7.27R (as appropriate).				1 January 2007 to 31 December 2007	*Commencement* and 1 January 2007
	(2) SUP 16.7.35, SUP 16.7.36 and 16.7.36A	R	An *investment management firm* that is a *BIPRU investment firm* is not required to submit the Annual Financial Return, the Consolidated Supervision Return and the Consolidated Financial Resources Return under SUP 16.7.36R.				1 January 2007 to 31 December 2007	*Commencement* and 1 January 2007
	(3) SUP 16.7.67, SUP 16.7.68 and SUP 16.7.68A	R	A *UCITS investment firm* is not required to submit the Annual Financial Return and the Consolidated Supervision Return under SUP16.7.68R.				1 January 2007 to 31 December 2007	13 February 2004 and 1 January 2007
	(4) SUP 16.7.76, 16.7.77 and 16.7.77 A	R	A *personal investment firm* that is a *BIPRU investment firm* is not required to submit the Consolidated Supervision Return under SUP 16.7.77R.				1 January 2007 to 31 December 2007	1 April 2005 and 1 January 2007

(1)	(2) Material to which the transitional provision applies	(3)	(4) Transitional provision	(5) Transitional provision: dates in force	(6) Handbook provision: coming into force
	(5) SUP 16.7.16 and SUP 16.7.17	R	A *building society* will not be required to submit reports MFS1, MFS1 Supp, MFS2 and QFS2 for reporting dates after 1 January 2008	From 1 January 2008	*Commencement*
12K	SUP 16.7.7R, SUP 16.7.8R, SUP 16.7.9R, SUP 16.7.10R, SUP 16.7.11R, SUP 16.7.12R, SUP 16.7.16R, SUP 16.7.17R, SUP 16.7.24R, SUP 16.7.25R, SUP 16.7.26R, SUP 16.7.27R, SUP 16.7.28R, SUP 16.7.29R, SUP 16.7.35R, SUP 6.7.36R, SUP 16.7.54R, SUP 16.7.54AR, SUP 16.7.57R, SUP 16.7.58R, SUP 16.7.62R, SUP 16.7.63R, SUP 16.7.65R, SUP 16.7.66R. SUP 16.7.73R, SUP 16.7.74R, SUP 16.7.75R, SUP 16.7.76R and SUP 16.7.77R	R	Solely in respect of information regarding any *reversion activity* or *home purchase activity* required to be reported in the *RMAR* and *MLAR*, a *firm*: (1) is not required to include such information in respect of the applicable reporting periods (as set out in the relevant provisions in SUP 16.7) ending before 1 October 2007; (2) must include such information in respect of reporting periods ending on or after 1 October 2007; (3) must include such information under existing mortgage headings (for the *RMAR*) or loan headings (for the *MLAR*) as set out in the guidance in SUP 16 Annex 18BG and SUP 16 Annex 19BG respectively.	1 April 2007 to 31 December 2008	*Commencement*

(1)	(2) Material to which the transitional provision applies	(3)	(4) Transitional provision	(5) Transitional provision: dates in force	(6) Handbook provision: coming into force
12L	(1) SUP 16.7.7R, SUP 16.7.8R, SUP 16.7.8AR, SUP 16.7.16R, SUP 16.7.17R, SUP 16.7.17AR, SUP 16.7.24R, SUP 16.7.25R, SUP 16.7.25AR, SUP 16.7.26R, SUP 16.7.27R, SUP 16.7.27AR, SUP 16.7.30R, SUP 16.7.35R, SUP 16.7.36R, SUP 16.7.36AR, SUP 16.7.67R, SUP 16.7.68R, SUP 16.7.68AR, SUP 16.7.76R, SUP 16.7.77R SUP 16.7.77AR	R	Except to the extent required by a transitional provision in TP12M, a *BIPRU firm* will not be required to report under these rules in respect of reporting dates after 31 December 2007, but will instead report under SUP 16.12.	1 January 2008 to 1 April 2009	1 January 2008
	(2) SUP 16.7.9R, SUP 16.7.10R	R	Except to the extent required by a transitional provision in TP12M, an *EEA Bank*, other than one with *permission* for *cross border services* only, will not be required to report under these rules in respect of reporting dates after 31 December 2007 but will instead report under SUP 16.12.5R.	1 January 2008 to 1 April 2009	1 January 2008
	(3) SUP 16.7.11R, SUP 16.7.12R	R	Except to the extent required by a transitional provision in TP12M, a *bank* established outside the *EEA* will not be required to report under these rules in respect of reporting dates after 31 December 2007 but will instead report under SUP 16.12.5R.	1 January 2008 to 1 April 2009	1 January 2008

(1)	(2) Material to which the transitional provision applies	(3)	(4) Transitional provision	(5) Transitional provision: dates in force	(6) Handbook provision: coming into force
	(4) SUP 16.7.62R, SUP 16.7.63R	R	A *credit union* will not be required to report under these rules in respect of reporting dates after 31 December 2007 but will instead report under SUP 16.12.5R.	1 January 2008 to 1 April 2009	1 January 2008
	(5) SUP 16.7.66	R	An *ELMI* that is required to report a consolidated reporting statement on capital adequacy in the case of ELM 7.3.2R in respect of reporting dates after 31 December 2007 will use FSA003 in place of FSA009. FSA003 should be submitted in accordance with SUP 16.12.3R (3).	1 January 2008	1 January 2008
	(6) SUP 16.7.82R, SUP 16.7.83R	R	(1) A *firm* that is a member of a *financial conglomerate*: (a) that is at the head of an *FSA regulated EEA financial conglomerate*; or (b) whose *Part IV permission* contains a relevant *requirement*; will not be required to report under these rules in respect of reporting dates after 31 December 2007 but will instead report under SUP 16.12.32R and SUP 16.12.33R. (2) In (1)(b), a relevant *requirement* is one as set out in SUP 16.7.82R (2).	1 January 2008 to 1 April 2009	1 January 2008
	(7) SUP 16.7.65R, SUP 16.7.66R	R	An *ELMI* will not be required to report under these rules in respect of reporting dates after 31 December 2007 but will instead report under SUP 16.12.5R.	1 January 2008 to 1 April 2009	1 January 2008
12M	(1) SUP 16.12.5R	R	Firms in *Regulated Activity Group* 1 are not required to submit the following data items: (i) for reporting dates falling prior to 30 June 2008: FSA001 FSA002 FSA008 FSA010 FSA012	1 January 2008 to 29 September 2008	1 January 2008

(1)	(2) Material to which the transitional provision applies	(3)	(4) Transitional provision	(5) Transitional provision: dates in force	(6) Handbook provision: coming into force
			FSA013 FSA016 FSA018 FSA045 (ii) for reporting dates falling prior to 31 August 2008: FSA005 FSA006 FSA007 FSA014 FSA020 FSA021 FSA022 FSA023 FSA024 FSA025 FSA026 and (iii) for reporting dates falling prior to 30 September 2008: FSA015 FSA044 FSA046		
	(2) SUP 16.12.5	R	*UK banks* in *Regulated Activity Group* 1 should not submit FSA017 for reporting dates prior to 31 August 2008.	1 January 2008 to 30 August 2008	1 January 2008
	(3) SUP 16.12.5	R	A *building society* in *Regulated Activity Group* 1: (i) should not submit FSA017 for reporting dates prior to 31 August 2008;	1 January 2008 to 30 August 2008	1 January 2008

(1)	(2) Material to which the transitional provision applies	(3)	(4) Transitional provision	(5) Transitional provision: dates in force	(6) Handbook provision: coming into force
			(ii) should instead submit an 'Analysis of interest rate gap' quarterly, within 15 *business days* of the quarter end, except in the case of a building society on the "Administered" approach (see *IPRU(BSOC)* 4 Ann 4A 4A.2) which is not required to submit the 'Analysis of interest rate gap'. In the case of (ii), reports should be prepared as at the end of March, June, September and December of each year. The 'Analysis of interest rate gap' must be submitted in accordance with TP 12L (4).		
	(4) SUP 16.12.5	R	In respect of the transitional reporting requirements in this transitional provision TP12L (3), the report should be submitted in accordance with SUP 16.3.6R to SUP 16.3.10R.	1 January 2008 to 31 December 2008	1 January 2008
	(5) SUP 16.12.11R	R	*Firms* in *Regulated Activity Group* 3, other than *exempt BIPRU commodity firms*, are not required to submit the following data items: (i) for reporting dates falling prior to 30 June 2008: FSA001 FSA002 FSA008 FSA016 FSA018 FSA019 FSA045 (ii) for reporting dates falling prior to 31 August 2008: FSA005 FSA006 FSA007 FSA039 FSA040	1 January 2008 to 29 September 2008	1 January 2008

(1)	(2) Material to which the transitional provision applies	(3)	(4) Transitional provision	(5) Transitional provision: dates in force	(6) Handbook provision: coming into force
			and (iii) for reporting dates falling prior to 30 September 2008: FSA046		
	(6) SUP 16.12.15R	R	*Firms* in *Regulated Activity Group* 4 are not required to submit the following data items: (i) for reporting dates falling prior to 30 June 2008: FSA001 FSA002 FSA008 FSA016 FSA018 FSA019 FSA045 (ii) for reporting dates falling prior to 31 August 2008: FSA005 FSA006 FSA007 FSA038 FSA039 FSA040 FSA041 FSA042 and (iii) for reporting dates falling prior to 30 September 2008: FSA046	1 January 2008 to 29 September 2008	1 January 2008

(1)	(2) Material to which the transitional provision applies	(3)	(4) Transitional provision	(5) Transitional provision: dates in force	(6) Handbook provision: coming into force
	(7) SUP 16.12.22R	R	*Firms* in *Regulated Activity Group* 7 are not required to submit the following data items: (i) for reporting dates falling prior to 30 June 2008: FSA001 FSA002 FSA008 FSA016 FSA018 FSA019 FSA045 (ii) for reporting dates falling prior to 31 August 2008: FSA005 FSA006 FSA007 and (iii) for reporting dates falling prior to 30 September 2008: FSA046	1 January 2008 to 29 September 2008	1 January 2008
	(8) SUP 16.12.25R	R	*Firms* in *Regulated Activity Group* 8 are not required to submit the following data items: (i) for reporting dates falling prior to 30 June 2008: FSA001 FSA002 FSA008 FSA016 FSA018 FSA019	1 January 2008 to 29 September 2008	1 January 2008

(1)	(2) Material to which the transitional provision applies	(3)	(4) Transitional provision	(5) Transitional provision: dates in force	(6) Handbook provision: coming into force
			FSA045 (ii) for reporting dates falling prior to 31 August 2008: FSA005 FSA006 FSA007 FSA039 FSA040 and (iii) for reporting dates falling prior to 30 September 2008: FSA046		
	(9) SUP 16.12.11R	R	*Exempt BIPRU commodity firms* are not required to submit the following data items for reporting dates: (i) falling prior to 30 June 2008: FSA008 (ii) falling prior to 31 August 2008: FSA001 FSA002 FSA016 FSA018 FSA028 FSA033 FSA038 FSA039 FSA040 FSA041 FSA042	1 January 2008 to 30 August 2008	1 January 2008

(1)	(2) Material to which the transitional provision applies	(3)	(4) Transitional provision	(5) Transitional provision: dates in force	(6) Handbook provision: coming into force
	(10) SUP 16.12.11	R	*Exempt BIPRU commodity firms*, are not required to submit the following data items for reporting dates falling prior to 1 January 2011: FSA003 FSA004 FSA005 FSA006 FSA007 FSA019	1 January 2008 to 31 December 2010	1 January 2008
	(11) SUP 16.12.5R	R	(1) A *UK bank* must submit the following reports for reporting dates falling between 1 January 2008 and 29 June 2008 in accordance with the rules set out in SUP 16.7.8R: BSD3 (unconsolidated, solo consolidated); BSD3 (consolidated); LE3 (unconsolidated, solo consolidated); LE3 (consolidated); M1 (unconsolidated, solo consolidated); and M1 (consolidated). Consolidated reports are only required from *UK consolidation groups*. (2) In addition, a *UK bank* subject to IPRU(BANK) Chapter LS must submit the SLR1 for reporting dates between 1 January 2008 and 31 May 2008 in accordance with the rules set out in SUP 16.7.8R. (3) Also, a *UK bank* subject to IPRU(BANK) Chapter LM must submit the LR for reporting dates between 1 January 2008 and 31 March 2008 in accordance with the rules set out in SUP 16.7.8R.	1 January 2008 to 29 June 2008	1 January 2008

(1)	(2) Material to which the transitional provision applies	(3)	(4) Transitional provision	(5) Transitional provision: dates in force	(6) Handbook provision: coming into force
	(12) SUP 16.7.9R, SUP 16.7.10R	R	An *EEA Bank*, other than one with *permission* for *cross border services* only, must submit the LR for reporting dates between 1 January 2008 and 31 March 2008 in accordance with the rules set out in SUP 16.7.10R.	1 January 2008 to 31 March 2008	1 January 2008
	(13) SUP 16.7.11R, SUP 16.7.12R	R	A *bank* established outside the *EEA* must submit: (a) the LR for reporting dates between 1 January 2008 and 31 March 2008; and (b) the B7 for reporting dates between 1 January 2008 and 29 June 2008 in accordance with the rules set out in SUP 16.7.12R.	1 January 2008 to 29 June 2008	1 January 2008
	(14) SUP 16.7.16R, SUP 16.7.17R	R	A *building society* must submit: (a) the QFS1 and AFS1 for reporting dates between 1 January 2008 and 29 June 2008; and (b) the interest rate gap report for reporting dates between 1 January 2008 and 30 August 2008 in accordance with the rules set out in SUP 16.7.17R.	1 January 2008 to 30 August 2008	1 January 2008
	(15) SUP 16.7.24R, SUP 16.7.25R	R	A *securities and futures firm* which is a category A or B firm or a broad scope firm, and is a *BIPRU investment firm*, must submit the large exposures quarterly reporting statement (Form LEM 1 or LEM 2) (consolidated and unconsolidated) and monthly reporting statement for reporting dates between 1 January 2008 and 29 June 2008 in accordance with the rules set out in SUP 16.7.25R, except that the monthly reporting statement should be submitted quarterly.	1 January 2008 to 29 June 2008	1 January 2008

(1)	(2) Material to which the transitional provision applies	(3)	(4) Transitional provision	(5) Transitional provision: dates in force	(6) Handbook provision: coming into force
	(16) SUP 16.7.26R, SUP 16.7.27R		A *securities and futures firm* which is a category C or D firm or an arranger or venture capital firm, and is a *BIPRU investment firm*, must submit the large exposures quarterly reporting statement (Form LEM 1 or LEM 2) (consolidated and unconsolidated) and quarterly reporting statement for reporting dates between 1 January 2008 and 29 June 2008 in accordance with the rules set out in SUP 16.7.27R, except that *BIPRU 50K firms* should submit the quarterly reporting statement half yearly.	1 January 2008 to 29 June 2008	1 January 2008
	(17) SUP 16.7.35R, SUP 16.7.36R	R	An *investment management firm* which is a *BIPRU investment firm* must submit either a quarterly financial return or a monthly financial return (depending on whether the firms is subject to a Liquid Capital Requirement or is an ISD firm subject to the Own Funds Requirement of Euro 730,000) for reporting dates between 1 January 2008 and 29 June 2008 in accordance with the rules set out in SUP 16.7.36R, except that *BIPRU 50K firms* should submit the quarterly financial return half yearly, and *BIPRU 730K firms* should submit the monthly financial return on a quarterly basis.	1 January 2008 to 29 June 2008	1 January 2008
	(18) SUP 16.7.65R, SUP 16.7.66R	R	An ELMI must submit the ELM CA/LE (unconsolidated and consolidated) for reporting dates between 1 January 2008 and 30 August 2008 in accordance with the rules set out in SUP 16.7.66R.	1 January 2008 to 30 August 2008	1 January 2008
	(19) SUP 16.7.67R, SUP 16.7.68R	R	A *UCITS firm* must submit the Quarterly Financial Return for reporting dates between 1 January 2008 and 29 June 2008 in accordance with the rules set out in SUP 16.7.68R.	1 January 2008 to 29 June 2008	1 January 2008

(1)	(2) Material to which the transitional provision applies	(3)	(4) Transitional provision	(5) Transitional provision: dates in force	(6) Handbook provision: coming into force
	(20) SUP 16.7.76R, SUP 16.7.77R	R	A firm that was not subject to other reporting requirements in SUP 16.7 (other than in SUP 16.7.76R and SUP 16.7.77R) at 31 December 2007, and is a *BIPRU firm*, must submit sections A, B, C and E of the RMAR and sections A and B of the MLAR for reporting dates between 1 January 2008 and 29 June 2008 in accordance with the rules set out in SUP 16.7.77R, except that the frequency for these sections of the RMAR and MLAR is amended as follows: (a) for *BIPRU 730K firms* and *BIPRU 125K firms*, quarterly; and (b) for *BIPRU 50K firms*, half-yearly	1 January 2008 to 29 June 2008	1 January 2008
	(21) SUP 16.12.23R	R	*Firms* in RAGs 3, 4, 6, 7 and 8 that are required to complete Section J of the RMAR, with an *accounting reference date* falling between 1 July 2007 and 31 August 2007 inclusive, must additionally report on section J of the RMAR at their half year (i.e. for reporting dates falling between 1 January 2008 and 29 February 2008 inclusive), to be submitted within 30 *business days* of the half year date.	1 January 2008 to 29 February 2008	1 January 2008
12N	(1) SUP 16.7.36	R	(1) Subject to (2), SUP 16.7.36R does not apply from 6 April 2007 to 30 August 2008 to an *investment management firm* which: (a) was not a *firm* before 6 April 2007; and (b) carries on only the activity of *establishing, operating or winding up a personal pension scheme*. (2) Notwithstanding (1), a *firm* described in (1) with an *accounting reference date* of between 6 April 2007 and 30 August 2008 (inclusive) must submit a copy of its annual accounts to the *FSA* in accordance with SUP 16.7.36R, unless (3) applies. The annual accounts must give a true and fair view of the state of affairs of the *firm* and of the *firm's* profit or loss.	6 April 2007 to 30 August 2008	6 April 2007
12O	(1)		[deleted]		

(1)	(2) Material to which the transitional provision applies	(3)	(4) Transitional provision	(5) Transitional provision: dates in force	(6) Handbook provision: coming into force
	(2) SUP 16.7.24, SUP 16.7.25, SUP 16.7.27	R	A *securities and futures firm* which is either (1) an *exempt CAD firm*, or (2) an *exempt BIPRU commodity firm* to which the requirements of *IPRU(INV)* Chapter 3 apply is not required to submit the Annual Reporting Statement and the Annual Reconciliation under SUP 16.7.25R and SUP 16.7.27R (as appropriate).	1 November 2007 to 31 December 2008	*Commencement* and 1 November 2007
	(3) SUP 16.7.35, SUP 16.7.36	R	An *investment management firm* which is an *exempt CAD firm* is not required to submit the Annual Financial Return under SUP 16.7.36R.	1 November 2007 to 31 December 2008	*Commencement* and 1 November 2007
	(4) SUP 16.7.67, SUP 16.7.68	R	A *UCITS firm* which is an *exempt CAD firm* is not required to submit an Annual Financial Return under SUP 16.7.68R, Note 3.	1 November 2007 to 31 December 2008	13 February 2004 and 1 November 2007
	(5) SUP 16.12.11R, SUP 16.12.12R	R	An *exempt BIPRU commodity firm* that does not meet the conditions in BIPRU TP16 is not required to submit FSA008 for reporting dates prior to 30 June 2008.	1 January 2008 to 29 June 2008	1 January 2008

(1)	(2) Material to which the transitional provision applies	(3)	(4) Transitional provision	(5) Transitional provision: dates in force	(6) Handbook provision: coming into force
12P	(1) SUP 16.7.20R, SUP 16.7.21R, SUP 16.7.21AR, SUP 16.7.21BR, SUP 16.7.26R, SUP 16.7.27R, SUP 16.7.28R, SUP 16.7.29R, SUP 16.7.30R, SUP 16.7.35R, SUP 16.7.36R, SUP 16.7.54R, SUP 16.7.54AR, SUP 16.7.55R, SUP 16.7.56R, SUP 16.7.57R, SUP 16.7.58R, SUP 16.7.67R, SUP 16.7.68R, SUP 16.7.76R, SUP 16.7.77R	R	Except to the extent required by a transitional provision in TP12Q, a *firm*, other than a *BIPRU firm*, will not be required to report under these rules in respect of reporting dates after 31 December 2007, but will instead report under SUP 16.12.	1 January 2008 to 31 March 2009	1 January 2008
12Q	(1) SUP 16.12.11R	R	*Firms* in *Regulated Activity Group* 3:	1 January 2008 to 30 August 2008	1 January 2008
			(1) are not required to submit the following data items for reporting dates falling prior to 31 August 2008: FSA029 FSA030 FSA031 FSA032 FSA033 FSA034		

(1)	(2) Material to which the transitional provision applies	(3)	(4) Transitional provision	(5) Transitional provision: dates in force	(6) Handbook provision: coming into force
			FSA035 FSA036 FSA037 FSA039 FSA040		
			(2) are instead required to report as set out in TP12Q(5)		
	(2) SUP 16.12.14R	R	*Firms* in *Regulated Activity Group* 4:	1 January 2008 to 30 August 2008	1 January 2008
			(1) are not required to submit the following data items for reporting dates falling prior to 31 August 2008: FSA029 FSA030 FSA031 FSA032 FSA033 FSA034 FSA035 FSA036 FSA037 FSA038 FSA039 FSA040 FSA041 FSA042		
			(2) are instead required to report as set out in TP12N(1), TP12Q(5) or TP12R(1)		

(1)	(2) Material to which the transitional provision applies	(3)	(4) Transitional provision	(5) Transitional provision: dates in force	(6) Handbook provision: coming into force
	(3) SUP 16.12.19R	R	*Firms* in *Regulated Activity Group* 6:	1 January 2008 to 30 August 2008	1 January 2008
			(1) are not required to submit the following data items for reporting dates falling prior to 31 August 2008: FSA029 FSA030 FSA031 FSA032 FSA033 FSA034 FSA035 FSA036 FSA037 FSA039 FSA040		
			(2) are instead required to report as set out in TP12Q(5)		
	(4) SUP 16.12.25R	R	*Firms* in *Regulated Activity Group* 8:	1 January 2008 to 30 August 2008	1 January 2008
			(1) are not required to submit the following data items for reporting dates falling prior to 31 August 2008: FSA029 FSA030 FSA031 FSA032 FSA033 FSA034 FSA035		

(1)	(2) Material to which the transitional provision applies	(3)	(4) Transitional provision	(5) Transitional provision: dates in force	(6) Handbook provision: coming into force
			FSA036 FSA037 FSA039 FSA040		
			(2) are instead required to report as set out in TP12Q(5)		
	(5) SUP 16.12.11R, SUP 16.12.14R, SUP 16.12.19R, SUP 16.12.25R	R	(1) A *securities and futures firm* that is:	1 January 2008 to 30 August 2008	1 January 2008
			(a) not a *BIPRU firm*, an *exempt CAD firm* or an *exempt BIPRU commodity firm* must submit the quarterly reporting statement in the manner and to the timescales set out in SUP 16.7.27R, and SUP 16.7.31R to SUP 16.7.34G;		
			(b) an *exempt CAD firm* must submit the quarterly reporting statement in the manner and to the timescales set out in SUP 16.7.27R, and SUP 16.7.31R to SUP 16.7.34G;		
			(c) an *exempt BIPRU commodity firm* (to which the requirements of IPRU(INV) Chapter 3 apply) must submit the quarterly reporting statement in the manner and to the timescales set out in SUP 16.7.27R, and SUP 16.7.31R to SUP 16.7.34G;		
			(2) except in the case of an *investment management firm* that is not a *BIPRU firm*, is not an *exempt CAD firm* and is authorised by the FSA after 5 April 2007, an *investment management firm* that is:		
			(a) neither a *BIPRU firm* nor an *exempt CAD firm* must submit the quarterly financial return in the manner and to the timescales set out in SUP 16.7.36R to SUP 16.7.38R;		

(1)	(2) Material to which the transitional provision applies	(3)	(4) Transitional provision	(5) Transitional provision: dates in force	(6) Handbook provision: coming into force
			(b) an *exempt CAD firm* must submit the quarterly financial return in the manner and to the timescales set out in SUP 16.7.36R to SUP 16.7.38R, and FSA043 in the manner and to the timescale set out in SUP 16.7.36BR;		
			(3) a *UCITS firm*:		
			(a) other than an *exempt CAD firm* must submit the Quarterly Financial Return in the manner and to the timescales set out in SUP 16.7.68R and SUP 16.7.69R;		
			(b) that is an *exempt CAD firm* must submit the Quarterly Financial Return in the manner and to the timescales set out in SUP 16.7.68R and SUP 16.7.69R and FSA043 in the manner and to the timescale set out in SUP 16.7.68BR; and		
			(4) a *firm* that satisfies the criteria in SUP 16.7.76R and is:		
			(a) neither a *BIPRU investment firm* nor an *exempt CAD firm* must submit the RMAR and MLAR in the manner and to the timescales set out in SUP 16.7.77R;		
			(b) that is an *exempt CAD firm* must submit the RMAR and MLAR in the manner and to the timescales set out in SUP 16.7.77R and FSA043 in the manner and to the timescale set out in SUP 16.7.77BR.		
12R	(1) SUP 16.12.14	R	(1) An *investment management firm* that is not a *BIPRU firm* and is authorised by the *FSA* on or after 6 April 2007, and which carries on only the activity of *establishing, operating or winding up a personal pension scheme*, must submit FSA029, FSA030 and either FSA034 or FSA035 (subject to (2) below) six monthly, based on the firm's *accounting reference date*, and within 20 *business days* in the manner set out in (3) below;	1 February 2008 to 31 December 2008	1 February 2008
			(2) FSA034 must be completed by a *firm* not subject to the exemption in IPRU(INV) 5.2.3(2)R, while FSA035 must be completed by a firm subject to the exemption in IPRU(INV) 5.2.3(2)R; and		

(1)	(2) Material to which the transitional provision applies	(3)	(4) Transitional provision	(5) Transitional provision: dates in force	(6) Handbook provision: coming into force
			(3) FSA029, FSA030, FSA034 and FSA035 should be submitted to the FSA in the manner to be specified by the FSA.		
	(2) SUP 16.12.11	R	An *exempt BIPRU commodity firm* that, at the reporting date for large exposures *data item* FSA008, satisfies the conditions of BIPRU TP 16 is not required to submit FSA008 for that reporting date.	1 February 2008 to 31 December 2010	1 February 2008
12S	SUP 16.12.15, SUP 16.12.16, SUP 16.12.17	R	In the case of an *exempt BIPRU commodity firm* that is subject to the requirements of IPRU(INV) Chapter 3, it is required to submit the capital adequacy *data item* FSA033 in the manner and to the frequency and timescales set out for *firms* other than *BIPRU firms* that are subject to IPRU(INV) Chapter 3 in SUP 16.12.15R to SUP 16.12.17R.	1 January 2009 to 31 December 2010	1 January 2009
12T	SUP 16.12.5 R to SUP 16.12.7 R; SUP 16.12.10 R to SUP 16.12.17 R; SUP 16.12.22 R to SUP 16.12.27 R	R	(1) This *rule* deals with: (a) the date (the "start date") on which the (4) requirements (the "new requirements") relating to *data items* FSA047 to FSA055 (inclusive) (the "new *data items*") made by the Supervision Manual (Integrated Regulatory Reporting of Liquidity for Banks, Building Societies and Investment Firms) Instrument 2009 (the "instrument") begin; (b) the date on which the requirements relating to *data items* FSA010 and FSA013 end; and (c) the date on which the changes in the requirements relating to *data item* FSA011 made by the instrument take effect.	As set out in column (4)	As set out in column (4)

(1)	(2) Material to which the transitional provision applies	(3)	(4) Transitional provision	(5) Transitional provision: dates in force	(6) Handbook provision: coming into force
			(2) The start date for reporting on a solo basis for a *firm* that as at 30 November 2009 or, as the case may be, 1 December 2009, or as the case may be, 30 November 2009 and 1 June 2010, falls into one of the classes covered by BIPRU TP 26.2 (Transitional rules for quantitative aspects of BIPRU 12 that apply to all *firms* to which BIPRU 12 applies) is the day immediately following the last day on which that transitional provision is in force as specified in column (5) of BIPRU TP 26.2. (3) The start date for reporting on a solo basis for other *firms* (other than a *non-ILAS BIPRU firm*) is 1 December 2009. (4) The reporting period for the first report on a solo basis for *non-ILAS BIPRU firms* ends on 31 December 2010. (5) Reporting on the basis of a *defined liquidity group* applies for all reporting periods beginning on or after 1 November 2010. (6) For a *firm* falling into paragraph (2), the following start dates apply to the following *data items* (a) The date for *data items* FSA047, FSA048 and FSA052 is 1 June 2010. (b) The date for *data items* FSA050, FSA051, FSA053 and FSA054 is 1 November 2010. (7) For a *firm* falling into paragraph (3), the following start dates apply to the following data items. (a) The date for *data items* FSA047 and FSA048 is 1 December 2009. (b) The date for *data item* FSA052 is 1 June 2010. (c) The date for *data items* FSA050, FSA051, FSA053 and FSA054 is 1 November 2010.		

(1)	(2) Material to which the transitional provision applies	(3)	(4) Transitional provision	(5) Transitional provision: dates in force	(6) Handbook provision: coming into force
			(8) If the start date under paragraphs (6) or (7) (taking into account paragraph (9)) falls before the start date in paragraphs (2) or (3), the dates in paragraphs (2) or (3) apply. However if the start date in paragraphs (6) or (7) (taking into account paragraph (9)) fall after the dates in paragraphs (2) or (3), the start dates in paragraphs (6) or (7) apply. (9) If the start date for a new *data item* occurs part of the way through what would have been a reporting period for that *data item* under SUP **16.12** if the relevant part of SUP **16.12** had been in force, the first reporting period for that *data item* begins on the first day ("the first day") of what would have been that reporting period (as specified in SUP **16.12**), even though the first day falls before the start date. The time for submission of the *data item* and the length of the reporting period are calculated as if the new requirements relating to that data item had been in force from the first day. (10) (a) The requirements relating to *data items* FSA010 and FSA013 are as follows. (b) If a *firm* does not fall into RAG 1 as at 30 November 2009, it does not have to submit these *data items*. (c) Otherwise, the last reporting period for the *data item* concerned ends on the first date when the start date for that *firm* in relation to both *data item* FSA047 and FSA048 has occurred. That last reporting period for *data item* FSA010 or FSA013 is shortened accordingly if necessary. (d) Any notes in SUP **16.12** relating to those *data items* continue in force as long as required by (a) to (c).		

(1)	(2) Material to which the transitional provision applies	(3)	(4) Transitional provision	(5) Transitional provision: dates in force	(6) Handbook provision: coming into force
			(11) The changes to *data item* FSA011 only take effect with respect reporting periods beginning on or after the commencement date for those changes as specified in the instrument (1 October 2010).		
12U	SUP 16.12.5 R to SUP 16.12.7 R; SUP 16.12.10 R to SUP 16.12.17 R; SUP 16.12.22 R to SUP 16.12.27 R	G	The effect of paragraph 12T is that a *firm* which becomes an *ILAS BIPRU firm* or *non-ILAS BIPRU firm* after 1 December 2009 and before the end of the transitional period which would otherwise have applied will be expected to comply with the requirements listed in column (2) from the date on which it becomes either an *ILAS BIPRU firm* or a *non-ILAS BIPRU firm* (as the case may be). However such a *firm* does have the benefit of the delayed start dates as specified in paragraphs (4), (5) and (7) of paragraph 12T.		
12V	SUP 16.12.5 R to SUP 16.12.7 R; SUP 16.12.10 R to SUP 16.12.17 R; SUP 16.12.22 R to SUP 16.12.27 R	G	An example of how paragraph 12T(6) and (9) work is as follows. Say that the start date for a *firm* under paragraph 12T(2) is 1 June 2010. If the *firm* reports *data item* FSA047 weekly, the first reporting period for that *data item* starts on Saturday 29 May 2010 and ends on Friday 4 June 2010. It has to be submitted to the *FSA* by 2200 on Monday 7 June.		
12W	SUP 16.12.5 R to SUP 6.12.7 R	R	If BIPRU TP 30.4R (Liquidity floor for certain banks) applies to a *firm* the regulatory intervention point mentioned in that *rule* is added to the list in paragraph (a) of the definition of *firm-specific liquidity stress* in the case of that *firm* for as long as BIPRU TP 30.4R applies to it.	For as long as BIPRU TP 30.4 R applies to the firm	At the end of period set out in column (5)
13	SUP 16.8	R	In Forms 1R(1) to (3) in SUP 16 Ann 6R, for any *life policy* promoted before *commencement*, a reference to "direct offer financial promotion" must be read as a reference to "direct offer advertisement", as defined in the rulebook of the *PIA* at the time the *policy* was promoted.	From *commencement* for 6 years	*Commencement*

(1)	(2) Material to which the transitional provision applies	(3)	(4) Transitional provision				(5) Transitional provision: dates in force	(6) Handbook provision: coming into force
13A	(1) SUP 3.1.2	R	In relation to an *investment management firm* which carries on only the activity of *establishing, operating or winding up a personal pension scheme* and which is authorised by the *FSA* after 6 April 2007, SUP 3.9 will not apply to the *firm's* auditor.				6 April 2007 to 31 December 2008	6 April 2007
14	SUP 16.8	R	SUP 16.8 does not apply to an *insurer* (including a *friendly society*) which was not a member of the *PIA* immediately before *commencement*.				From *commencement* for 6 years	*Commencement*
14A	SUP 16.11.7R	R	Until 1 July 2006, a *firm* will not contravene SUP 16.11.7R if it does not complete the data reporting field 'Advice at the point of sale' (see SUP 16 Ann 21R).				1 April 2005 – 30 June 2006	1 April 2005
14B		R	If SUP TR 12B R (5) applies, the *firm's* first return must be provided as follows:					
			Accounting reference date	Reporting period starts	Reporting period ends	Return to be provided		
			31 December 2004	1 April 2005	30 June 2005	30 *business days* after period end		
			Between 1 January 2005 and 31 March 2005	1 April 2005	6 months after the *accounting reference date* within 2005	30 *business days* after period end (Note 2)		
			Between 1 April 2005 and 29 June 2005	The day following the *accounting reference date* within 2005	3 months after the *accounting reference date* within 2005	30 *business days* after period end (Note 2)		
			Between 30 June 2005 and 29 September 2005	1 April 2005	*Accounting reference date* within 2005	30 *business days* after period end (Note 2)		

(1)	(2) Material to which the transitional provision applies	(3)	(4) Transitional provision				(5) Transitional provision: dates in force	(6) Handbook provision: coming into force
			Between 30 September 2005 and 30 December 2005	The day after 6 months preceding the *accounting reference date* within 2005	3 months preceding the *accounting reference date* within 2005	30 *business days* after period end (Note 3)		
14C	16.10.4	R	A *firm* whose *accounting reference date* falls between 1 April 2005 and 30 June 2005 (inclusive) need not comply with SUP 16.10.4 R until its *accounting reference date* in 2006.				1 April 2005 – 30 June 2005	1 April 2005
14D	16.11.3	R	The report under SUP 16.11.3 R (1) for the quarter 1 April to 30 June 2005, together with the report for the quarter 1 July to 30 September 2005 must be submitted within 20 *business days* after the end of the 1 July – 30 September 2005 quarter.				1 April 2005 – 30 June 2005	1 April 2005
15			[deleted]					
15A	*Rules* in SUP 20	R	Expired					
15B	Transitional *rule* SUP 15A	G	Expired					
15C	The Supervision manual (SUP)		A *regulated sale and rent back firm* need not comply with the *rules* in this sourcebook to the extent that they carry on *regulated sale and rent back activity*, provided that within a period of 3 months after submitting an application for interim authorisation in accordance with article 32 of the Financial Services and Markets Act 2000 (Regulated Activities) (Amendment) Order (SI 2009/1342), and every 6 months after such date until 30 June 2010, they provide to the *FSA* for the relevant period the following information: (a) management accounts for the *firm*, including a balance sheet, profit/loss statement and management report; (b) details of the *firm's* funding arrangements; and				1 July 2009 to 30 June 2010	1 July 2009

(1)	(2) Material to which the transitional provision applies	(3)	(4) Transitional provision		(5) Transitional provision: dates in force	(6) Handbook provision: coming into force
			(c) where the firm is a *SRB agreement provider*, the number of *regulated sale and rent back agreements* it has entered into in that period, distinguishing between direct sales (both advised and non-advised) and indirect sales (advised and non-advised).			
16	Paragraphs 1 to 15	R	Definitions		From *commencement*	*Commencement*
			In these transitional provisions:			
			(1)	"pre-commencement provision"		
				means a provision repealed or revoked by or under the *Act* or a rule or guidance of the *firm's previous regulator*, including (where the context permits) any relevant provision which it replaced before *commencement*; and		
			(2)	"substantially similar" means substantially similar in purpose and effect.		
	SUP	G	*GEN* contains some technical transitional provisions that apply throughout the *Handbook* and which are designed to ensure a smooth transition at *commencement*. These include transitional provisions relevant to record keeping and *notification rules*.		From commencement of the relevant provision in SUP	Various dates
17	SUP 20.4.4R(4)	R	The periodic fee modification set out in SUP 20.4.4R(4) does not apply to the A.2, A.18 and A.19 activity groups until 1 April 2005.		From 31 October 2004 to 31 March 2005	1 April 2002

Note 1 = The return need not provide data for sections A, B, C, D, E of the RMAR.

Note 2 = Sections A, B, C, D, E of the *RMAR* should be reported for the 3 months to the reporting end date.

Note 3 = This should only cover sections A, B, C, D, E of the *RMAR*

1.3 Transitional provisions relating to written concessions

(1) The purpose of the transitional provisions in the following table is to carry forward existing written concessions relating to pre-commencement provisions – for example, formal waivers or modifications given by IMRO, PIA or SFA ("an SRO") and the recognised professional bodies, written concessions from the standards in the FSA's Guide to Banking Supervisory Policy, and formal written consents and determinations made by an SRO under an SRO rule.

(2) An existing written concession is only carried forward if the pre-commencement provision to which it relates is substantially similar to a *rule* in the *Handbook*. The substantially similar test should be applied to the specific element of the *rule* to which the written concession relates. An existing written concession from a pre-commencement provision which is substantially similar to written *guidance* in the *Handbook* is carried forward in the same way as pre-commencement individual guidance; see transitional provision 6A (Individual guidance) in the schedule of Transitional provisions applying to the Supervision manual only.

(3) An existing written concession is carried forward on a temporary basis only – for 12 months from *commencement* or, in the case of modifications relating to the Interim Prudential sourcebooks or SUP 16.6 (Compliance reports) or 16.7 (Financial reports), until the relevant provisions cease to apply. A *firm* wishing to retain the benefit of a concession after that time will need to apply in good time for a *waiver* (see SUP 8 (Waiver and modification of rules)).

(4) An existing written concession is carried forward as an amendment to the *rule* to which it relates. Any such amendment has effect for all purposes (including *FSA* enforcement action and actions for damages under section 150 of the *Act*).

(5) An existing written concession is not carried forward if, and to the extent that, doing so would be inconsistent with any *EU* law obligation of the *United Kingdom*, in particular with the proper implementation of a directive.

(6) These transitional provisions do not apply to *rules* which are continued by designation of pre-commencement provisions rather than made as new *rules*. Written concessions of such *rules* are carried forward, to similar effect, as *waivers* (given under section 148 of the *Act*) by article 8 of The Financial Services and Markets Act 2000 (Transitional Provision and Savings) (Rules) Order 2001 (SI 2001/1534). The relevant *rules* are in *IPRU(INV)*, those identified as designated *rules* in the schedule to *IPRU(INV)* entitled "Powers exercised".

(7) Definitions for these transitional provisions, additional to those in the *Glossary*, are provided at paragraph 4 of the table.

1.4 Table

(1)	(2) Material to which the transitional provision applies	(3)	(4) Transitional provision		(5) Transitional provision: dates in force	(6) Handbook provision: coming into force
1	*Rules* in: IPRU, SUP 16.6 and 16.7	R	(1)	A *rule* listed in column (2) (including *evidential provisions*, transitional *rules* and relevant defined expressions) is disapplied, or is modified in its application, to a *firm*:	From *commencement* until revoked.	*Commencement*
			(a)	in order to produce the same effect, including any conditions, as a written concession had on a pre-commencement provision listed in paragraph 2; and		
			(b)	for the same period as the written concession would have lasted, if shorter than the period in column (5);		
			If			
			(c)	the *rule* is substantially similar to the pre-commencement provision in relation to the matter with which the written concession is concerned;		

Part II FSA Handbook Materials

(1)	(2) Material to which the transitional provision applies	(3)	(4) Transitional provision	(5) Transitional provision: dates in force	(6) Handbook provision: coming into force
			(d) the written concession was current as respects the *firm* immediately before *commencement*;		
			(e) there is no specific transitional *rule* relating to the written concession; and		
			(f) the written concession has not been superseded by a *waiver* from the *FSA*.		
			(2) Paragraph (1) does not have effect if, and to the extent that, it would be inconsistent with any *EU* law obligation of the *United Kingdom*.		
2	*Rules* in: IPRU, SUP 16.6 and 16.7	R	The pre-commencement provisions referred to in paragraph 1(1) are those contained in any of the following (including relevant defined expressions):	From *commencement* until revoked.	*Commencement*
			(1) The legislative provisions of the *FSA* as designated agency under the Financial Services Act 1986;		
			(2) the rules of *IMRO, PIA, SFA* and the *recognised professional bodies*;		
			(3) the Insurance Companies Act 1982 and relevant secondary legislation;		
			(4) the Friendly Societies Act 1992, and relevant secondary legislation;		
			(5) the Banking Act 1987, relevant secondary legislation and the *FSA's* Guide to Banking Supervisory Policy;		
			(6) the Building Societies Act 1986, relevant secondary legislation and the Building Societies Commission's Prudential Notes, Guidance Notes and DCE (Dear Chief Executive) letters.		
3	*Rules* in: IPRU, SUP 16.6 and 16.7	R	<u>Notification of relevance etc of concession</u> A *firm* which has the benefit of a written concession to which paragraph 1 applies must notify the *FSA* immediately if it becomes aware of any matter which is material to the relevance or appropriateness of the written concession.	From *commencement* until revoked.	*Commencement*
4	*Rules* in: IPRU, SUP 16.6 and 16.7	R	<u>Definitions</u>	From *commencement* until revoked.	*Commencement*
			In these transitional provisions:		

(1)	(2) Material to which the transitional provision applies	(3)	(4) Transitional provision		(5) Transitional provision: dates in force	(6) Handbook provision: coming into force
			(1)	"substantially similar" means substantially similar in purpose and effect; and		
			(2)	"written concession" means a waiver, exemption, concession, modification, consent, approval, determination or similar exercise of discretion which:		
			(a)	disapplied, or tended to reduce the burden of complying with, a pre-commencement provision (with or without conditions); and		
			(b)	was evidenced in writing.		

1.5 **[R]**

(1) A *firm* may, in the written contract with its *introducer appointed representative*, extend the scope of appointment to include:

(a) receiving and forwarding to an *insurer* or *insurance intermediary* an application by a *customer* for a *connected travel insurance contract* together with any associated documentation; and

(b) receiving *client money* from a *customer* in respect of a *connected travel insurance contract*, and holding that *client money*.

(2) The extension of the scope of the appointment must apply only where the receipt of an application or of *client money* results from documentation given to a *customer*, where the deadline for submission of this documentation to the publishers for publishing was on or before 15 November 2008.

(3) This *rule* applies until 31 December 2009.

SCHEDULE 1
RECORD KEEPING REQUIREMENTS

[2179]

Sch1 **[G]**

Sch 1.1

The aim of the guidance in the following table is to give the reader a quick overall view of the relevant record keeping requirements.

It is not a complete statement of those requirements and should not be relied on as if it were.

Sch 1.2

Handbook reference	Subject of record	Contents of record	When record must be made	Retention period
SUP 4.3.17R(3)	Data for *actuary* (or *actuaries*) appointed under SUP 4 (Actuaries)	Such data as the *actuary* (or *actuaries*) appointed under SUP 4 (Actuaries) reasonably require	Not Specified	Not specified
SUP 12.9.1R, SUP 12.9.2R	*Appointed representatives*	(1) *Appointed representative's* name	On appointment, amendment of contract or termination of contract	3 years from termination or amendment of the contract, other than in respect of *tied agents* when period is five years.

Handbook reference	Subject of record	Contents of record	When record must be made	Retention period
		(2) Copy of the original contract with the *appointed representative* and any subsequent amendments to it (including details of any restrictions placed on the activities which the *appointed representative* may carry on)		
		(3) Date and reason for terminating or amending the contract		
		(4) Arrangements agreed with other *principals* under SUP 12.4.5BR		
SUP 12.9.5R	*EEA tied agents*	If a *UK MiFID investment firm* appoints an *EEA tied agent* the record keeping requirements in SUP 12.9 applies to that *firm* as though the *EEA tied agent* were an *appointed representative*.		
SUP 13.11	*UK firm* exercising *EEA right*	(a) the services or activities it carries on from a *branch* in, or provide *cross border services* into, another *EEA State* under that *EEA right*; and the *requisite details* or relevant details relating to those services or activities (if applicable)	Not specified	Three years from the earlier of the date on which: (a) it was superseded by a more up-to-date record; or
				(a) the *UK firm* ceased to have a *branch* in, or carry *cross border services* into, any *EEA State* under an *EEA right*
SUP 13.11.1R	Exercise of passport rights by *UK firms*	(1) Services or activities carried on from a *branch* in, or provided cross-border into, another *EEA State* under an *EEA right*	Not specified	Five years (for *firms* passporting under *MiFID*) or three years (for other *firms*) from earlier of:

Handbook reference	Subject of record	Contents of record	When record must be made	Retention period
				(1) record being superseded;
		(2) The details relating to those services or activities (as set out in SUP 13.6 and SUP 13.7).		(2) *firm* ceasing to have any *EEA branches* or *cross-border services*.
SUP 15.8.8R	*CTF provider* status	The fact of the *firm* beginning or ceasing to hold itself out as a *CTF provider*	*Firm* beginning or ceasing to hold itself out as a *CTF provider*	As soon as reasonably practicable
	CTF third party administrator	Engagement of third party administrator	Thirds party administrator engaged	As soon as reasonably practicable
	Intention to offer *Revenue allocated CTFs*	Whether it intends to offer *Revenue allocated CTFs*	Becoming a *CTF provider*	As soon as reasonably practicable
	Intention to provide *stakeholder CTF*	Whether it intends to provide its own *stakeholder CTFs*	Becoming a *CTF provider*	As soon as reasonably practicable
SUP 16.8.23R	Persistency reports and data reports	Records to enable the *firm* to monitor regularly the persistency of *life policies* and stakeholder pensions effected through each of its *representatives* and make the required reports to the *FSA*.	Not specified	Not specified

SCHEDULE 2
NOTIFICATION REQUIREMENTS

[2180]
Sch2 **[G]**

Sch 2.1

The aim of the *guidance* in the following table is to give the reader a quick overall view of the relevant requirements for notification and reporting.

It is not a complete statement of those requirements and should not be relied on as if it were.

Sch 2.2

Handbook reference	Matter to be notified	Contents of notification	Trigger event	Time allowed
SUP 3.3.2(2)R	Vacancy in the office of auditor	The fact of the vacancy and the reason for it	Vacancy in the office of auditor will arise or has arisen	Without delay
SUP 3.3.2(5)R	Appointment of auditor	The fact of the appointment, name and business address of the auditor and the date the appointment takes effect	Appointment of auditor	Not specified

Part II FSA Handbook Materials

Handbook reference	Matter to be notified	Contents of notification	Trigger event	Time allowed
SUP 3.3.5R	Vacancy in the office of auditor to a Lloyd's *underwriting agent* or the auditor of the *insurance business* of a Lloyd's *syndicate*	The fact of the vacancy and the reason for it	Vacancy in the office of auditor will arise or has arisen.	Without delay
	Appointment of auditor by Lloyd's *underwriting agent*	The fact of the appointment, name and business address of the auditor and the date the appointment takes effect.	Appointment of auditor	Not specified
SUP 3.5.3R	Auditor not independent of the *firm*	The fact of the lack of independence	*Firm* aware that its auditor not independent of the *firm*	A reasonable time
SUP 3.7.2G (1)	Expectation that auditor will qualify his report on the audited annual financial statements or add an explanatory paragraph	Fact of expectation	*Firm* decides qualification or explanatory paragraph is probable and the matter justifies notifying the *FSA*.	Not specified
SUP 3.7.2G (2)	The *firm* receives a written communication from its auditor commenting on *internal controls*	Content of written communication	*Firm* receives written communication and decides that it is appropriate that the *FSA* should be informed	Not specified
SUP 3.8.10G	Matters requiring reporting under sections 342(5) and 343(5) of the *Act*	Information on or the auditor's opinion on the matters which have caused the auditor to believe the circumstances set out in Statutory Instrument 2001 No. 2587 apply	Auditor believes that the circumstances set out in Statutory Instrument 2001 No 2587 paragraph 2 apply	Not specified
SUP 3.8.11R	Auditor: termination of office	The fact of the termination	Auditor removed from office by the *firm*, resigns before his term of office expires or is not re-appointed by the *firm*.	Without delay
SUP 3.8.12R	Auditor: termination of office	Any matter connected with ceasing which he thinks ought to be drawn to the *FSA's* attention; or the fact that there is no such matter	Auditor ceasing to be (or being formally notified that he will cease to be) auditor of the *firm*.	Without delay

Handbook reference	**Matter to be notified**	**Contents of notification**	**Trigger event**	**Time allowed**
SUP 3.10	Auditor: *client* assets	Either:	Report period must end no more than 53 weeks after previous report	A reasonable time
		(1) Whether *firm* has: maintained systems to comply with *COB* 9 (*client* assets), is in compliance with the *client asset rules* at the report date, and *nominee company* records are adequate; or		
		(2) if the *firm* claims not to hold *client money* or *custody assets* whether anything has come to the auditor's attention that causes him to believe that they were held.		
SUP 3.10.8R	Failure by auditor to report under SUP 3.10.4R	Auditor to report the failure and the reasons why it has been unable to meet the requirements of SUP 3.10.7R	Failure by the auditor to deliver a report under SUP 3.10.4R to the *FSA* so as to be received within four months of the end of each period covered	Not specified
SUP 4.3.1R (2)	Vacancy in the office of *actuary*	The fact of the vacancy and the reason for it	Vacancy in the office of *actuary* will arise or has arisen	Without delay
SUP 4.3.1R (3) and SUP 4.3.2G	Appointment of *actuary*	Matters specified in SUP 10 (because the *actuarial function* and the *with-profits actuary function* are specified as *controlled functions*)	Appointment of *actuary*	Before appointment
SUP 4.5.9R	*Actuary*: termination of office	The fact of the termination	*Actuary* removed from office by the *firm*, resigns before his term of office expires or is not re-appointed by the *firm*.	Without delay
SUP 4.5.10R	*Actuary: ceasing* to hold office	Any matter connected with ceasing which he thinks ought to be drawn to the *FSA's* attention; or the fact that there is no such matter	*Actuary* ceasing to be (or being formally notified that he will cease to be) *actuary* of the *firm*.	Without delay

Part II FSA Handbook Materials

Handbook reference	Matter to be notified	Contents of notification	Trigger event	Time allowed
SUP 4.5.11G	*Actuary*: ceasing to hold office	Matters specified in SUP 10.13.6R and SUP 10.13.7R (because the *actuarial function* and the *with-profits actuary function* are specified as *controlled functions*)	*Actuary* ceasing to hold office	Seven *business days*; or, if *approved persons* Form C is qualified, as soon as reasonably practicable
SUP 4.6.1R	Vacancy in the office of *Lloyd's actuary* will arise or has arisen	Fact of the vacancy and the reason for the vacancy	The *Society of Lloyd's* becomes aware that a vacancy will arise or has arisen	Without delay
SUP 4.6.17R	*Syndicate actuary* of a *general insurance business syndicate* will or may be unable to produce an unqualified opinion under SUP 4.6.16R	Fact that the *syndicate actuary* will or may be unable to produce an unqualified opinion (to be notified by the *managing agent* to the *FSA*)	The *managing agent* becomes aware that the *syndicate actuary* will or may be unable to produce an unqualified opinion	Notification to be made promptly
SUP 5.4.12G	Delay in producing a *skilled person* report	*Skilled person*: inform the *FSA* and the *person* in SUP 5.2.1G that the report may not be delivered on time.	The *skilled person* becomes aware that the report may not be delivered on time	As soon as possible
SUP 5.5.1R	Matters which the *skilled person* is required and permitted to report to the *FSA*	As set out in SUP 5.5.1R.	*Skilled person* becomes aware of reportable matter	Not specified
SUP 5.5.8G	Cost of *skilled person* report	As set out in SUP 5.5.8G	On request	Not specified
SUP 6.2.6G	*Firm* seeking to vary its *Part IV permission* substantially or cancel its *Part IV permission*	The fact of seeking such applications to initiate discussion.	*Firm* seeking to vary its *Part IV permission* substantially or cancel its *Part IV permission*	As early as possible before making the application
SUP 6.2.7G	*Firm* intending to cease carrying on one or more *regulated activities* permanently	The fact of intending to cease carrying on one or more *regulated activities* permanently	*Firm* intending to cease carrying on one or more *regulated activities* permanently	Prompt notice
SUP 6.2.10G	*Firm* winding down (running off) its activities.	The fact of winding down (running off) its activities.	*Firm* winding down (running off) its activities.	Before making an application for variation of *permission* or *cancellation* of *Part IV permission*.
SUP 6.3.15D	Variation of *permission*	The desired variation and the *regulated activity* or *regulated activities* which the *firm* proposes to carry on.	*Firm* wishes to vary its *Part IV permission*	Before variation is required; the *FSA* has six months to consider a completed application.

Hand-book ref-erence	Matter to be noti-fied	Contents of notifi-cation	Trigger event	Time allowed
		The *FSA* will advise the *firm* of any additional information required (see SUP 6.3.15D to SUP 6.3.27G)		
SUP 6.3.15D (3)	Variation of *permission* – any significant change in information provided	Any significant change in the information given in the application	Until the application has been determined, a change in information provided on the application for variation of *Part IV permission*	Immediately
SUP 6.4.5D	Cancellation of *Part IV permission*	Reasons for the application, the date on which the *firm* has ceased, or expects to cease, to carry on *regulated activities* and an explanation of the full circumstances of its application.	*Firm* wishes to cancel its *Part IV permission*	Before cancellation is required; the *FSA* has six months to consider a completed application. See SUP 6.4.3G
		The *FSA* will advise the *firm* of any additional information required (see SUP 6.4.8G to SUP 6.4.17G)		
SUP 6.4.5 (4)D	Cancellation of *Part IV permission* – any significant change in information provided	Any significant change in the information given in the application	Until the application has been determined, a change in information provided on the application for a cancellation of *Part IV permission*	Immediately
SUP 8.3.3D	Application for a *waiver*	The form in SUP 8 Ann 2D (Application form for a waiver or modification).	*Firm* seeks a *waiver*	Before the *waiver* is required; the *FSA* will aim to give a *waiver* decision within 20 *business days* of receiving the application.
SUP 8.5.1R	*Waiver*: altered circumstances	The matter that affects the continuing relevance or appropriateness of the application or *waiver*	*Firm* that has applied for or has been granted a *waiver* becoming aware of any matter which could affect the continuing relevance or appropriateness of the application or *waiver*	Immediately

Handbook reference	Matter to be notified	Contents of notification	Trigger event	Time allowed
SUP 9.2.6G	*Guidance* request	Sufficient information to enable the *FSA* to properly evaluate the situation and respond. In particular, identification of the *rule*, general *guidance* or other matter on which the individual *guidance* is sought and a description of the circumstances relating to the request.	A *firm* seeks individual *guidance*	Before individual *guidance* required (the *FSA* will aim to respond quickly and fully to reasonable request)
SUP 10.12.2D	*Approved persons* – application	*Approved persons* the relevant Form A Application to perform *controlled functions* under the *approved persons* regime (see SUP 10 Ann 4D)	*Firm* wishes to appoint a *person* to a *controlled function*	Before appointment takes effect (the *FSA* has three months to consider a properly completed application but will deal with cases more quickly whenever circumstances allow)
SUP 10.12.13R	*Approved persons* – withdrawal of an application	*Approved persons* Form B Notice to withdraw an application to perform *controlled functions* under the *approved persons* regime (see SUP 10 Ann 5R)	*Firm* wishes to withdraw an application for *approved person* status	Not specified
SUP 10.13.1G	*Approved persons* – moving within a *firm*	*Approved persons* Form E Internal transfer of an *approved person* (see SUP 10 Ann 8G)	An *approved person* is both ceasing to perform one or more *controlled functions* and needs to be approved in relation to one or more new *controlled functions* within the same *firm*	Before appointment takes effect (the *FSA* has three months to consider a properly completed application but will deal with cases more quickly whenever circumstances allow)
SUP 10.13.6R	*Approved persons* – ceasing to perform a *controlled function*	*Approved persons* Form C Notice of ceasing to perform *controlled functions* (see SUP 10 Ann 6R)	An *approved person* ceasing to perform a *controlled function*	Seven *business days* after an *approved person* ceases to perform a *controlled function*

Handbook reference	Matter to be notified	Contents of notification	Trigger event	Time allowed
SUP 10.13.7R	*Approved persons* – ceasing to perform a *controlled function* – qualified withdrawal	The fact of the qualified withdrawal	An *approved person* ceasing to perform a *controlled function* and the *firm* becoming aware, or has information which reasonably suggests, that it will submit a qualified Form C in respect of that *approved person* (qualified defined in SUP 10.13.7R (2): *approved person* dismissed; *approved person* under investigation; *approved person's* fitness and propriety affected)	As soon as practicable (*guidance* in SUP 10.13.8G states, where possible, within one *business day*)
SUP 10.13.14R	*Approved persons* – change to personal details – title, name or national insurance number	*Approved persons* Form D Notification of changes in personal information or application details (see SUP 10 Ann 7R)	An *approved person's* title, name or national insurance number changes	Seven *business days* of the *firm* becoming aware
SUP 10.13.16R	*Approved persons* – change to personal details – information reasonably material to fitness and propriety	*Approved persons* Form D Notification of changes in personal information or application details (see SUP 10 Ann 7R)	*Firm* becomes aware of information which would reasonably be material to the assessment of an *approved person's*, or a *candidate's*, fitness and propriety	As soon as practicable
SUP 11.3.7D	*Controllers* – *person* proposing to acquire or increase *control* – notification from *controller* or proposed *controller*	If the *controller* or proposed *controller* is an *authorised person*: those sections of Controllers Form A which deal with details of the proposed change in *control*, joint notifications and supplementary information (see SUP 11 Ann 4D). If the *controller* or proposed *controller* is an *authorised person* and a *fund manager* which satisfies SUP 11.3.5D: notification in accordance with SUP 11.3.5D	Proposing to take a step which would result in acquiring the specified *control*	Before acquiring *control* (the *FSA* has up to three *months* to consider whether to approve *control*)

Handbook reference	Matter to be notified	Contents of notification	Trigger event	Time allowed
		In other cases: all of Controllers Form A (see SUP 11 Ann 4D) and one or more of Controllers Form B (see SUP 11 Ann 5D) for relevant individuals (see SUP 11.3.8D)		
SUP 11.3.10D	*Controllers* – correction to previously submitted information by *controller*	Details of the information which may be false, misleading, incomplete or inaccurate, or has or may have changed	A *person* who submitted a notification under SUP 11.3.7D becoming aware, or has information which reasonably suggests, that he has or may have provided the *FSA* with information which was or may have been false, misleading, incomplete or inaccurate or has or may have changed, in a material particular	Immediately
SUP 11.3.15G	*Controllers* – proposing to reduce *control* – notification from *controller*	Extent of *control* (if any) which the *controller* will have following the change in *control* If the *controller* is a *fund manager* which satisfies SUP 11.3.5D: notification in accordance with SUP 11.3.5D	Reduction in *control*	Before reducing *control*
SUP 11.3.16G	*Controllers* – change in *control* occurs – notification from *controller*	Date relevant change of *control* occurred. If a *person* has reduced *control*, details of the extent of *control* retained (if any)	Change in *control* has occurred	Not specified
SUP 11.4.2R	*Controllers* – proposed change of *control* – notification from a *UK domestic firm*	When acquiring or increasing *control*:	(1) A *person* acquiring *control* or ceasing to have *control*;	As soon as the *firm* becomes aware that a *person* is proposing to take a step that would result in the event concerned; or if the event takes place without the knowledge of the *firm*, within 14 *days* of the *firm* becoming aware of the event concerned

Handbook reference	Matter to be notified	Contents of notification	Trigger event	Time allowed
		(1) the name of the *firm*;	(2) an existing *controller* acquiring an additional *kind of control* or ceasing to have a *kind of control*;	
		(2) the name of the *controller* or proposed *controller* and, if it is a *body corporate* and is not an *authorised person*, the names of its *directors* and its *controllers*; (3) a description of the proposed event including the shareholding and *voting power* of the *person* concerned, both before and after the proposed event; and	(3) an existing *controller* increasing or decreasing a *kind of control* which he already has so that the percentage of shares or *voting power* concerned becomes or ceases to be equal to or greater than 20, 33 or 50	
		(4) any other information of which the *FSA* would reasonably expect notice, including information which could have a material impact on any of the approval requirements in section 186(2) of the *Act* and any relevant supporting documentation. The notification need only contain as much of the information the *firm* is able to provide, having made reasonable enquiries from *persons* and other sources as appropriate. When reducing *control*: (1) the name of the *controller*; and (2) details of the extent of *control* (if any) which the *controller* will have following the change in *control*	(4) an existing *controller* becoming or ceasing to be a *parent undertaking*	

Part II FSA Handbook Materials

Handbook reference	**Matter to be notified**	**Contents of notification**	**Trigger event**	**Time allowed**
SUP 11.4.2AR	*Controllers* – proposed change of *control* notification from a *UK insurance intermediary*	When acquiring *control*:	(1) A *person* acquiring *control* or ceasing to have *control*;	As soon as the *firm* becomes aware that a *person* is proposing to take such a step that would result in the event concerned; or if the event takes place without the knowledge of the *firm*, 14 *days* of the *firm* becoming aware of the event concerned
		(1) the name of the *firm*;	(2) a *person* becoming or ceasing to be a *parent undertaking*	
		(2) the name of the *controller* or proposed *controller* and, if it is a *body corporate* and is not an *authorised person*, the names of its *directors* and its *controllers*;		
		(3) a description of the proposed event including the shareholding and *voting power* of the *person* concerned, both before and after the proposed event; and		
		(4) any other information of which the *FSA* would reasonably expect notice, including information which could have a material impact on any of the approval requirements in section 186(2) of the *Act* and any relevant supporting documentation.		
		The notification need only contain as much of the information the *firm* is able to provide, having made reasonable enquiries from *persons* and other sources as appropriate.		
		When reducing *control*:		

Handbook reference	Matter to be notified	Contents of notification	Trigger event	Time allowed
		(1) name of the *controller*; and (2) details of the extent of *control* (if any) which the *controller* will have following the change in *control*		
SUP 11.4.4R	*Controllers* – proposed change of *control* – notification from an *overseas firm* (1) the name of the *firm*; (2) the name of the *controller* or proposed *controller* and, if it is a *body corporate* and is not an *authorised person*, the names of its *directors* and its *controllers*; (3) a description of the proposed event including the shareholding and *voting power* of the *person* concerned, both before and after the proposed event; and	When acquiring or increasing *control*: (1) A *person* acquiring *control* or ceasing to have *control*; (2) an existing *controller* becoming or ceasing to be a *parent undertaking* (4) any other information of which the *FSA* would reasonably expect notice, including information which could have a material impact on any of the approval requirements in section 186(2) of the *Act* and any relevant supporting documentation. The notification need only contain as *much of the information* the *firm* is able to provide, having made reasonable enquiries from *persons* and other sources as appropriate. When reducing *control*:		As soon as the *firm* becomes aware that a *person* is proposing to take a step that would result in the event concerned; or if the event takes place without the knowledge of the *firm*, within 14 days of the *firm* becoming aware of the event concerned

Hand-book reference	Matter to be notified	Contents of notification	Trigger event	Time allowed
		(1) the name of the *controller*; details of the extent of *control* (if any) which the *controller* will have following the change in *control*		
SUP 11.4.8G	*Controllers* – notification under *Principle* 11 by *firms*	Proposed change of *control*	Any prospective changes of which the *firm* is aware, in *controllers'* or proposed *controllers'* shareholdings or *voting power* (if the change is material)	The earliest opportunity and before the formal notifications. As a minimum, the *FSA* considers such discussions should take place before a *person*:
				(1) enters into any formal agreement in respect of the purchase of *shares* or a proposed acquisition or merger which would result in a change in *control* (whether or not the agreement is conditional upon any matter, including the *FSA's* approval) or
				(2) purchases any *share options, warrants* or other financial instruments, the exercise of which would result in the *person* acquiring *control* or any other changes in *control*
SUP 11.6.2R to SUP 11.6.5R	*Controllers* – change in information provided by a *UK domestic firm*	(1) Details of the information which is or may be false, misleading, incomplete or inaccurate, or has or may have changed (2) An explanation why such information was or may have been provided; and (3) The correct information	After submitting a notification under SUP 11.4.2R or SUP 11.4.2AR and until the change in *control* occurs, the *firm* becomes aware, or has information that reasonably suggests, that information provided by the *controller* or proposed *controller* is false, misleading, incomplete or inaccurate, or has or may have changed in a material particular.	Immediately

Handbook reference	**Matter to be notified**	**Contents of notification**	**Trigger event**	**Time allowed**
SUP 11.6.4R	*Controllers* – change in notification has taken place – notification by *firm*	The fact that the change in *control* has taken place or that there are grounds for reasonably believing that the event will not now take place.	A change in *control* previously notified under SUP 11.4.2R, SUP 11.4.2AR or SUP 11.4.4R taking place; or the *firm* having grounds for reasonably believing that the event will not now take place	14 *days* of the change in *control* or having grounds for reasonably believing that the event will not now take place
SUP 11.8.1R	*Controllers* – changes in the circumstances of existing *controllers*	The fact of: (1) a *controller*, or any entity subject to his *control*, being the subject of any legal action or investigation which might put into question the integrity of the *controller*;	The *firm* becoming aware of: (1) a *controller*, or any entity subject to his *control*, is or has been the subject of any legal action or investigation which might put into question the integrity of the *controller*;	Immediately
		(2) a significant deterioration in the financial position of a *controller*;	(2) a significant deterioration in the financial position of a *controller*;	
		(3) a corporate *controller* undergoing a substantial change or series of changes in its *governing body*;	(3) a corporate *controller* undergoing a substantial change or series of changes in its *governing body*;	
		(4) a *controller*, who is authorised in *another EEA State* as an *ISD investment firm* or *BCD credit institution* or under the *Insurance Directives* or the *Insurance Mediation Directive*, ceasing to be so authorised (registered in the case of an *IMD insurance intermediary*)	(4) a *controller*, who is authorised in *another EEA State* as an *ISD investment firm* or *BCD credit institution* or under the *Insurance Directives* or the *Insurance Mediation Directive*, ceasing to be so authorised (registered in the case of an *IMD insurance intermediary*)	

Handbook reference	Matter to be notified	Contents of notification	Trigger event	Time allowed
SUP 11.9.1R	*Close links*	(a) the name of the *person* (b) the nature of the *close links* (c) if the *close link* is with a *body corporate*, its country of incorporation, address and registered number; and (d) if the *close link* is with an individual, his date and place of birth	The *firm* becoming aware that it has become or ceased to be *closely linked* with any *person*.	As soon as reasonably practicable and no later than one *month* after the *firm* becomes aware that it has become or ceased to be *closely linked* or if the *firm* has elected to report *monthly*, within 15 *business days* of the end of each *month* (see SUP 11.9.4R)
SUP 12.7.1R	*Appointed representatives*	The notification should give details of the *appointed representative* and the *regulated activities* which the *firm* is, or intends to, carry on through the *appointed representative*, including:	A *firm* appointing an *appointed representative*	(1) (if the appointment covers *insurance mediation activities* and the *appointed representative* is not included on the *Register* as carrying on such *activities* in another capacity) before; or
		(1) the name of the *firm's* new *appointed representative* (if the *appointed representative* is a *body corporate*, this is its registered name)		(2) if the *firm* appoints a *tied agent* and the *tied agent* is not included in the *Register* (see SUP 12.4.11G), before; or
		(2) any trading name under which the *firm's* new *appointed representative* carries on a *regulated activity* in that capacity;		(3) (otherwise) ten *business days* after the *appointed representative* begins to carry on *regulated activities* under the contract.
		(3) a description of the *regulated activities* which the *appointed representative* is permitted or required to carry on and for which the *firm* has accepted responsibility		

Handbook reference	Matter to be notified	Contents of notification	Trigger event	Time allowed
SUP 12.7.7R(1)	*Appointed representatives* – extension of scope of appointment to cover *insurance mediation activities* for the first time	That fact	Extension of scope of appointment to cover *insurance mediation activities* for the first time and the *appointed representative* is not included on the *Register* as carrying on *insurance mediation activities* in another capacity	Before the *appointed representative* begins to carry on *insurance mediation activities* under the contract
SUP 12.7.7R (1A)	*Appointed Representatives* – commencing as *tied agent.*	That fact.	Change of scope of *tied agent's* appointment	Notification must be made prior to *tied agent* acting.
SUP 12.7.7R(2)	*Appointed representatives* – change in other information	The information that has changed	A change being made to other information provided under SUP 12.7.1R or the *firm* becoming aware of the change	Ten *business days* of a change being made, or if later, as soon as it becomes aware of the change
SUP 12.7.8R	*Appointed representatives* – belief that appointment conditions not met	The fact that the *firm* has reasonable grounds for believing that the appointment conditions are not being met; and: (a) the steps the *firm* proposes to take to rectify the matter; and	The *firm* having reasonable grounds for believing that the conditions in SUP 12.4.2R, SUP 12.4.6R or SUP 12.4.8AR are not being satisfied. The SUP 12.4.2R conditions are that:	As soon as the *firm* has reasonable grounds for believing that the *approval* conditions have not been met
		(b) the date of the termination of the contract with the *appointed representative*	(1) the appointment does not prevent the *firm* from satisfying and continuing to satisfy the *threshold conditions*;	
			(2) the *appointed representative*:	
			(a) is solvent;	
			(b) is suitable to act for the *firm* in that capacity;	
			(c) has no *close links* which would be likely to prevent the effective supervision of the *appointed representative* by the *firm*; and	
			(3) the *firm* has adequate:	

Part II FSA Handbook Materials

Handbook reference	Matter to be notified	Contents of notification	Trigger event	Time allowed
			(a) *controls* over the *appointed representative's regulated activities* for which the *firm* has responsibility (see *SYSC* 3.1); and	
			(b) resources to monitor and enforce compliance by the *appointed representative* with the relevant requirements applying to the *regulated activities* for which the *firm* is responsible and with which the *appointed representative* is required to comply under its contract with the *firm* (see SUP 12.5.3R(2))	
			The SUP 12.4.6R conditions are that: On a continuing basis the *firm* must take reasonable care to ensure that the *appointed representative* is suitable to act for the *firm* in that capacity (having regard, in particular, to other *persons* connected with the *appointed representative* who will be, or who are, directly responsible for its activities).	
SUP 12.7.9R	*EEA tied agents*	If a *UK MiFID investment firm* appoints an *EEA tied agent* the notification requirements in SUP 12.7 apply to that *firm* as though the *EEA tied agent* were an *appointed representative*.		

Handbook reference	**Matter to be notified**	**Contents of notification**	**Trigger event**	**Time allowed**
SUP 12.8.1R	*Appointed representatives* – termination of appointment	(1) Written notice of the notification by the *firm* or the *appointed representative*	Either the *firm* or the *appointed representative* notifying the other that it proposes to terminate the contract of appointment or to amend it so that it no longer meets the requirements contained in or referred to in SUP 12.5.	Ten *business days* after the date of the decision to terminate or so amend the contract or, if later, as soon as the *firm* becomes aware that the contract is to be or has been terminated or amended
		(2) The reason for the termination or amendment, if the termination or amendment is due to misconduct or the *appointed representative* is resigning while under investigation by the *firm*, the *FSA*, another regulator, a *clearing house*, an exchange, a *designated professional body*, or a government body or agency		
		(3) If relevant, details of action taken by the *firm* and, if applicable, its outcome		
SUP 12.8.1R	*Appointed representatives* – termination of appointment	(1) Written notice of the notification by the *firm* or the *appointed representative*	Either the *firm* or the *appointed representative* notifying the other that it proposes to terminate a contract or to amend it so that it no longer meets the requirements in the *Appointed Representatives Regulations*.	Ten *business days* after the date of the decision to terminate or so amend the contract or, if later, as soon as the *firm* becomes aware that the contract is to be or has been terminated or amended

Handbook reference	**Matter to be notified**	**Contents of notification**	**Trigger event**	**Time allowed**
		(2) The reason for the termination or amendment, if the termination or amendment is due to misconduct or the *appointed representative* is resigning while under investigation by the *firm*, the *FSA*, another regulator, a *clearing house*, an exchange, a *designated professional body*, or a government body or agency	Also, in the case of an *introducer appointed representative*, if the contract no longer meets the requirements of SUP 12.5.7R, namely that the contract prohibits the *introducer* from: (1) in relation to a *designated investment* or *designated investment business*:	
		(3) If relevant, details of action taken by the *firm* and, if applicable, its outcome	(a) effecting an introduction between a *customer* and a *person* other than the *firm* or another member of the *firm's marketing group*; and	
			(b) distributing *non-real-time financial promotions approved* by a *person* other than the *firm* or another member of the *firm's marketing group* or the producer of an *adopted packaged product*; and	
			(2) carrying on any *regulated activity* on behalf of any *person* other than the *firm* or another member of the *firm's marketing group*.	
SUP 12.8.4G	*Appointed representatives* – termination of appointment – *approved persons*	*Approved persons* Form C Notice of ceasing to perform *controlled functions* (see SUP 10 Ann 6R)	An *approved person* ceasing to perform a *controlled function* under an *arrangement* entered into by a *firm* or its *appointed representative*	Seven *business days* after an *approved person* ceases to perform a *controlled function*

Handbook reference	Matter to be notified	Contents of notification	Trigger event	Time allowed
SUP 12.8.4G	*Appointed representatives* – termination of appointment – *approved persons* (qualified withdrawal)	The fact of the qualified withdrawal	An *approved person* ceasing to perform a *controlled function* under an *arrangement* entered into by a *firm* or its *appointed representative* and the *firm* becoming aware, or has information which reasonably suggest, that it will submit a qualified Form C in respect of that *approved person* (qualified defined in SUP 10.13.7 (2); *approved person* dismissed, *approved person* under investigation, *approved person's* fitness and propriety affected)	As soon as practicable (*guidance* in SUP 10.13.8G states, where possible, within one *business day*)
SUP 13.3.2G (1)	Intention to establish a *branch* in another *EEA State*	(a) activities which it seeks to carry on through *branch* (b) other information as specified in SUP 13.5.1R	Decision to establish a *branch* in other *EEA State*	Before establishing a *branch*
SUP 13.4.2G (1)	Intention to provide *cross border services* into another *EEA State*	(a) identifies activities which it seeks to carry on by way of provision of *cross border services* (b) other information as specified in SUP 13.5.2R	Decision to provide *cross border services* into another *EEA State*	Before providing *cross border services*
SUP 13.5.1AR	*UK pure reinsurer* establishing a *branch* in another *EEA State*	(a) the address of the *branch* (b) the name of the *firm's* authorised agent (c) whether the *firm* will be, or is, carrying on life or non-life *reinsurance* business, or both (d) confirmation that the *firm* fulfils the solvency requirements of the *Reinsurance Directive*	Decision to establish a *branch* in other *EEA State*	Whenever possible, as soon as the information specified in SUP 13 Annex 1R is known by the *firm*

Handbook reference	Matter to be notified	Contents of notification	Trigger event	Time allowed
SUP 13.6.5G (1)	Changes to *branches* (*Firms* passporting under the *UCITS Directive*, and *Banking Consolidation Directive*)	Details of proposed change	Change in circumstances within control of *UK firm*	Before making change
SUP 13.6.5BG	Changes to *branches* (*Firms* passporting under *MiFID*)	Details of proposed change	Change in circumstances, including using for the first time or ceasing to use a *tied agent* established in the *EEA State* in which the *branch* is established	Before making change
SUP 12.8.6R	*EEA tied agents*	If a *UK MiFID investment firm* appoints an *EEA tied agent* the notification requirements in SUP 12.8 apply to that *firm* as though the *EEA tied agent* were an *appointed representative*.		
SUP 13.6.7G (1)	Changes to relevant *EEA* details of *branches* (*Firms* passporting under the *Insurance Directives*)	Details of proposed change	Change in circumstances within control of *UK firm*	Before making change
SUP 13.6.8G	Changes to relevant *UK* details of *branches* (*Firms* passporting under the *Insurance Directives*)	Details of proposed change	Change arising from circumstances within control of *UK firm*	At least one month before change is effected
SUP 13.6.10G	Changes to *branches* (not *firms* passporting under *MiFID*)	Details of change	Changes to *branch* arising from circumstances beyond control of a *UK firm*	As soon as reasonably practicable
SUP 13.7.3G	*Firms* passporting under the *UCITS Directive*: Change in program of operations, or activities to be carried on under its *EEA right*	Details of proposed change	Change in programme of operations, or activities to be carried on under its *EEA right*	(a) change arises from circumstances within control of *firm*: before making change.
				(b) change arises from circumstances beyond *UK firm's* control: as soon as practicable (whether before or after change)

Handbook reference	Matter to be notified	Contents of notification	Trigger event	Time allowed
SUP 13.7.3BG	*Firms* passporting under *MiFID (cross-border services)*: Change in program of operations, or activities to be carried on under its *EEA right*	Details of proposed change	Change in activities to be carried on, using for the first time or ceasing to use a *tied agent*	Before making change.
SUP 13.7.4G	*Firms* passporting under *Insurance Directives* (providing *cross border services*) – change in relevant details	Details of proposed change	Change in relevant details	(a) change arises from circumstances within control of *firm*: at least one month before proposed change
				(b) change arises from circumstances beyond *UK firm's* control: as soon as reasonably practicable
SUP 13A.3.6G– SUP 13A.3.8G	Intention of *incoming Treaty firm* to carry on a *regulated activity* in the *United Kingdom*	Matters relevant to the notice as indicated in SUP 13A.3.6G.	Intention to carry on a *regulated activity.*	At least seven *days* in advance.
SUP 14.2.3G	Change to *branch* details in circumstances within control of the *firm* (*firms* passporting under the *UCITS Directive*, and *Banking Consolidation Directive)*	Details of proposed change	Change to *branch* details	Before making the change
SUP 14.2.6G	Change to *branch* details in circumstances within control of the *firm* (*firms* passporting under the *Insurance Directives*)	Details of proposed change	Change to *branch* details	Before making the change
SUP 14.2.8G	Changes to *branch* details arising from circumstances beyond control of incoming *EEA firm*	Change to *branch* details	Details of the change	As soon as reasonably practicable
SUP 14.2.11G	Changes to *UK branch* details for *EEA MiFID investment firms*	Details of proposed change	Changes to *branch* details	Before making the change
SUP 14.3.3G	Changes to *cross border services* (*firms* passporting under the *UCITS Directive*)	Details of proposed change	Changes to *cross border services*	(a) change arises from circumstances within control of *firm*: before making change

Handbook reference	**Matter to be notified**	**Contents of notification**	**Trigger event**	**Time allowed**
				(b) change arises from circumstances beyond *UK firm's* control: as soon as reasonably practicable
SUP 14.3.3BG	*Incoming EEA firm* passporting under *MiFID*	Details of the proposed change to *cross-border services*	Change in details	Before the change
SUP 14.6.3G	Incoming *EEA firm* – cancelling qualification for *authorisation*		Incoming *firm* ceased, or intends to cease, to carry on *regulated activities* in the *United Kingdom*	
SUP 15.3.1R	Notifications – matters having a serious regulatory impact	The fact of any of the trigger events occurring	Becoming aware or having information which reasonably suggests, that any of the following has occurred, may have occurred or may occur in the foreseeable future:	Immediately
			(1) the *firm* failing to satisfy one or more of the *threshold conditions*;	
			(2) any matter which could have a significant adverse impact on the *firm's* reputation;	
			(3) any matter which could affect the *firm's* ability to continue to provide adequate services to its *customers* and which could result in serious detriment to a *customer* of the *firm*; or	
			(4) any matter in respect of the *firm* which could result in serious financial consequences to the *financial system* or to other *firms*.	

Handbook reference	Matter to be notified	Contents of notification	Trigger event	Time allowed
SUP 15.3	Commencement, continuation and cessation of relevant investigations and disciplinary proceedings	Commencement, continuation and cessation of relevant investigations and disciplinary proceedings listed in SUP 15.3.24D and 15.3.25D	Commencement of proceedings	Not specified
SUP 15.3.7G and SUP 15.3.8G	Notifications – anything relating to the *firm* of which the *FSA* would expect notice	The matters specified in 'trigger events' which must be disclosed appropriately.	A *firm* must deal with its regulators in an open and co-operative way, and must disclose to the *FSA* appropriately anything relating to the *firm* of which the *FSA* would reasonably expect notice. (*Principle* 11 and SUP 15.3.7G)	A *firm* should have regard to the urgency and significance of a matter. (SUP 15.7.2G)
			Compliance with *Principle* 11 includes, but is not limited to, giving the *FSA* notice of:	The period of notice will depend on the event, although the *FSA* expects a *firm* to discuss relevant matters with it at an early stage, before making any internal or external commitments. (SUP 15.3.9G)
			(1) any proposed restructuring, reorganisation or business expansion which could have a significant impact on the *firm's* risk profile or resources, including, but not limited to:	
			(a) setting up a new *undertaking* within a *firm's group*, or a new *branch* (whether in the *United Kingdom* or overseas); or	
			(b) commencing the provision of *cross border services* into a new territory;	
			(c) commencing the provision of a new type of product or service (whether in the *United Kingdom* or overseas);	

Hand-book reference	Matter to be notified	Contents of notification	Trigger event	Time allowed
			(d) ceasing to undertake a *regulated activity* or *ancillary activity*, or significantly reducing the scope of such activities; or	
			(e) entering into, or significantly changing, a *material outsourcing* arrangement; or	
			(f) a substantial change or a series of changes in the *governing body* of an *overseas firm* (other than an *incoming firm*); or	
			(g) any change to the *firm's* prudential category or sub-category, as used in the Interim Prudential sourcebooks and the Supervision manual and on which *guidance* is given in SUP App 1;	
			(2) any significant *failure* in the *firm's* systems or *controls*, including those reported to the *firm* by the *firm's* auditor;	
			(3) any action which a *firm* proposes to take which would result in a material change in its capital adequacy or solvency, including, but not limited to:	
			(a) any action which would result in a material change in the *firm's* financial resources or financial resources requirement; or	

Handbook reference	Matter to be notified	Contents of notification	Trigger event	Time allowed
			(b) a material change resulting from the payment of a special or unusual dividend or the repayment of *share* capital or a subordinated loan; or	
			(c) for *firms* which are subject to the *rules* on consolidated financial supervision, any proposal under which another *group company* may be considering such an action; or	
			(d) significant trading or non-trading losses (whether recognised or unrecognised).	
SUP 15.3.11R	Notifications – breaches of *rules* and other requirements in or under the *Act*	(1) information about any circumstances relevant to the breach or offence; (2) identification of the *rule* or *requirement* or offence; and (3) information about any steps which a *firm* or other *person* has taken or intends to take to rectify or remedy the breach or prevent any future potential occurrence.	Becoming aware, or having information which reasonably suggests, that any of the following matters has occurred, may have occurred or may occur in the foreseeable future as regards the *firm*, any of its *directors*, *officers*, *employees*, *approved persons*, *appointed representatives*, or *tied agents*:	Immediately
			(a) a significant breach of a *rule* (which includes a *Principle*) or *Statement of Principle*; or	
			(b) a breach of any requirement imposed by the *Act* or by regulations or an order made under the *Act* by the Treasury (except if the breach is an offence, in which case (c) applies);	

Part II FSA Handbook Materials

Handbook reference	**Matter to be notified**	**Contents of notification**	**Trigger event**	**Time allowed**
			(c) the bringing of a prosecution for, or a conviction of, any offence under the *Act*.	
SUP 15.3.15R	Notifications – civil, criminal or disciplinary proceedings against a *firm*	Details of the matter and an estimate of the likely financial consequences, if any.	(1) Civil proceedings being brought against the *firm* and the amount of the claim being significant in relation to the *firm's* financial resources or its reputation; or	Immediately
			(2) any action being brought against the *firm* under section 71 of the *Act* (Actions for damages) or section 150 (Actions for damages); or	
			(3) disciplinary measures or sanctions being imposed on the *firm* by any statutory or regulatory authority, professional organisation or trade body (other than the *FSA*) or the *firm* becoming aware that one of those bodies has started an investigation into its affairs: or	
			(4) the *firm* being prosecuted for, or convicted of, any offence involving fraud or dishonesty, or any penalties being imposed on it for tax evasion; or	
			(5) if it is an *OPS firm*, which is a trustee, being removed as trustee by a court order.	

Handbook reference	Matter to be notified	Contents of notification	Trigger event	Time allowed
SUP 15.3.17R	Notifications – Fraud, errors and other irregularities	All relevant and significant details of the incident or suspected incident of which the *firm* is aware.	The following events arising, if significant: (1) the *firm* becoming aware that an *employee* may have committed a fraud against one of its *customers*; or	Immediately
			(2) the *firm* becoming aware that a *person*, whether or not *employed* by it, may have committed a fraud against it; or	
			(3) the *firm* considering that any *person*, whether or not *employed* by it, acting with intent to commit a fraud against it; or	
			(4) the *firm* identifying irregularities in its accounting or other records, whether or not there is evidence of fraud; or	
			(5) the *firm* suspecting that one of its *employees* may be guilty of serious misconduct concerning his honesty or integrity and which is committed with the *firm's regulated activities* or *ancillary activities*.	
SUP 15.3.21R	Notifications – insolvency, bankruptcy and winding up	The fact of the event	(1) the calling of a meeting to consider a resolution for winding up the *firm*;	Immediately
			(2) an application to dissolve the *firm* or to strike it off the Register of Companies;	
			(3) the presentation of a petition for the winding up of the *firm*;	

Handbook reference	Matter to be notified	Contents of notification	Trigger event	Time allowed
			(4) the making of, or any proposals for the making of, a composition or arrangement with any one or more of its creditors;	
			(5) an application for the appointment of an administrator or trustee in bankruptcy to the *firm*;	
			(6) the appointment of a receiver to the *firm* (whether an administrative receiver or receiver appointed over particular property): or	
			(7) an application for an interim order against the *firm* under section 252 of the Insolvency Act 1986 (or, in Northern Ireland, section 227 of the Insolvency (Northern Ireland) Order 1989); or	
			(8) if the *firm* is a *sole trader*:	
			(a) an application for a sequestration order; or	
			(b) the presentation of a petition for bankruptcy; or	
			(9) anything equivalent to (1) to (8) above in respect of the *firm* in a jurisdiction outside the *United Kingdom*	
SUP 15.3.23D	Any matter likely to be of material concern in relation to the *FSA* which may have arisen in relation to: (1) the *regulated activities* for which the *Society* has *permission*; or (2) *underwriting agents*; or	Details of the matters arisen.	The *Society* becomes aware	Immediately

Handbook reference	Matter to be notified	Contents of notification	Trigger event	Time allowed
	(3) *approved persons* or individuals acting for or on behalf of *underwriting agents*.			
SUP 15.4.1R	Notifications – notified *persons* – *overseas firm* which is not an *incoming firm*	Form F Changes in notified *persons* (see SUP 15 Ann 2R)	Any *person* taking up or ceasing to hold the following positions:	30 *business days*
		However, if the *person* is an *approved person*, notification giving details of his name, the *approved person's FSA* individual reference number and the position to which the notification relates, is sufficient.	(a) the *firm's* worldwide chief executive (that is, the *person* who, alone or jointly with one or more others, is responsible under the immediate authority of the *directors* for the whole of its business) if the *person* is based outside the *United Kingdom*;	
			(b) the *person* within the *overseas firm* with a purely strategic responsibility for *UK* operations;	
			(c) for a *bank*: the two or more *persons* who effectively direct its business in accordance with SYSC 4.2.2R;	
			(d) for an *insurer*: the *authorised UK representative*.	
SUP 15.5.1R	Notifications – change in name	Details of the proposed new name and the date on which the *firm* intends to implement the change of name	A change in:	Reasonable advance notice
			(1) the *firm's* name (which is the registered name if the *firm* is a *body corporate*);	

Handbook reference	**Matter to be notified**	**Contents of notification**	**Trigger event**	**Time allowed**
			(2) any business name under which the *firm* carries on a *regulated activity* or *ancillary activity* either from an establishment in the *United Kingdom* or with or for clients in the *United Kingdom*	
SUP 15.5.4R	Notifications – change in address	Details of the new address and the date of the change	A change in any of the following addresses: (1) the *firm's principal* place of business in the *United Kingdom*;	Reasonable advance notice
			(2) in the case of an *overseas firm*, its registered office (or head office) address	
SUP 15.5.5R	Notifications – change in legal status	The fact of the proposed change in liability	A proposed change in a *firm's* legal status which limits the liability of any of its members or *partners*. This includes:	Reasonable advance notice
			(1) re-registration as a limited liability *company* of a *company* incorporated with unlimited liability; and	
			(2) a general *partner* in a *firm* becoming a limited *partner*	
SUP 15.5.7R	Notifications – other regulators	The fact of becoming subject to or ceasing to be subject to the supervision of any *overseas regulator* (including a *Home State regulator*)	A *firm* becoming subject to or ceasing to be subject to the supervision of any *overseas regulator* (including a *Home State regulator*)	Immediately

Handbook reference	Matter to be notified	Contents of notification	Trigger event	Time allowed
SUP 15.6.4R	Notification – inaccurate, false or misleading information	(1) details of the information which is or may be false, misleading, incomplete or inaccurate, or has or may have changed; (2) an explanation why such information was or may have been provided; and (3) the correct information	A *firm* becoming aware, or having information that reasonably suggests that it has or may have provided the *FSA* with information which was or may have been false, misleading, incomplete or inaccurate, or has or may have changed in a material particular	Immediately If the information required cannot be submitted with the notification (because it is not immediately available), it must instead be submitted as soon as possible afterwards
SUP 15.8.1R	Notification – management of *occupational pension scheme* assets	The fact of receiving the request or instruction	A *firm* which manages the assets of an *occupational pension scheme* receiving a request or instruction from a trustee which it knows or on substantial grounds suspects or has cause reasonably to suspect is at material variance with the trustee's duties.	As soon as reasonably practical
SUP 15.8.2R	Administration of *individual pension accounts*	If a *firm* begins or ceases to administer *individual pension accounts*, notify the *FSA*	Event of beginning or ceasing to administer *individual pension accounts*	As soon as reasonably practicable
SUP 15.8.3R	Insurers' commission clawback	As set out in SUP 15.8.3R	Any amount of *commission* due from an intermediary remaining outstanding for four *months* after date when *insurer* gave notice to the intermediary that (a) relevant *premium* had not been paid or (b) that cancellation or overpayment has occurred.	As soon as reasonably practicable

Part II FSA Handbook Materials

Handbook reference	**Matter to be notified**	**Contents of notification**	**Trigger event**	**Time allowed**
SUP 15.8.4R	Delegation by *UCITS management company*	The fact that a function of the *UCITS management company* has been delegated together with (a) the identity of the party to whom the function has been delegated and (b) the period during which the delegation will apply.	The delegation of a function by a *UCITS management company.*	As soon as reasonably practicable.
SUP 15.8.4G	Operating a bureau de change	That the *firm* intends to operate a bureau de change	Intending to operate a bureau de change	Before the *firm* begins to operate a bureau de change
SUP 15.8.4G	Operating a bureau de change	That the *firm* has ceased to operate a bureau de change	Ceasing to operate a bureau de change	As soon as reasonably practicable
SUP 15.8.8R	*CTF provider* status	The fact of the *firm* beginning or ceasing to hold itself out as a *CTF provider*	*Firm* beginning or ceasing to hold itself out as a *CTF provider*	As soon as reasonably practicable
	CTF third party administrator	Engagement of third party administrator	Thirds party administrator engaged	As soon as reasonably practicable
	Intention to offer *Revenue allocated CTFs*	Whether it intends to offer *Revenue allocated CTFs*	Becoming a *CTF provider*	As soon as reasonably practicable
	Intention to provide *stakeholder CTF*	Becoming a *CTF provider*	Whether it intends to provide its own *stakeholder CTFs*	As soon as reasonably practicable
SUP 15.8.9R	Default by counterparty on its obligations in a transaction of a type specified in SUP 15.8.9R.	The fact of the default.	Default by counterparty on its obligations in a *repurchase agreement* or *reverse repurchase agreement* or *securities or commodities lending or borrowing transaction.*	Immediately
SUP 15.9.1R	Being or ceasing to be a *financial conglomerate*	The fact of being or ceasing to be a *financial conglomerate*	Being or ceasing to be a *financial conglomerate*	immediately
SUP 15.9.2R	Reasonable likelihood of becoming or ceasing to be a *financial conglomerate*	Reasonable likelihood of becoming or ceasing to be a *financial conglomerate*	Reasonable likelihood of becoming or ceasing to be a *financial conglomerate*	immediately
SUP 16.3.17R	Reporting – change of *accounting reference date*	The fact of a change in *accounting reference date*	A change in *accounting reference date*	If extending its accounting reference period, before the previous *accounting reference date*

Handbook reference	**Matter to be notified**	**Contents of notification**	**Trigger event**	**Time allowed**
				If shortening its accounting period, it must make the notification in (1) before the new *accounting reference date*.
SUP 16.4.5R	Reporting – annual *controllers* report – every *firm* except: (1) an *ICVC*; (2) an *incoming EEA firm*; (3) an *incoming Treaty firm*; (4) a *non-directive friendly Society*; (5) a *partnership*; (6) a *sole trader*; (7) a *service company*; (8) a *UCITS qualifier*	If the *firm* is not aware: (a) that it has any *controllers*; or (b) of any changes in the identity of its *controllers* since the submission of its previous report; or (c) of any changes in the percentage of shares *or voting power* in the *firm* held by any *controllers* (alone or with any associate) since the submission of its previous report; then confirmation of this. If the above does not apply, the report must contain a list of all the *controllers* as at the *firm's accounting reference date* of which the *firm* is aware and, for each such *controller*, state: (a) its name; (b) the percentage of *voting power* in the *firm*, or in the *firm's parent undertaking*, which it is entitled to exercise or control the exercise of, whether alone or with any associate; (c) the percentage of shares in the *firm*, or in the *firm's parent undertaking*, which it holds, whether alone or with any associate;	Annually from the *accounting reference date* If a *firm* is a *friendly society* or a *building society*, then it is required to submit a report only if it is aware that it has a *controller*.	Four months

Handbook reference	**Matter to be notified**	**Contents of notification**	**Trigger event**	**Time allowed**
		(d) if the *controller* is a *body corporate*, its country of incorporation, address and registered number; and (e) if the *controller* is an individual, his date and place of birth. This information may be provided in the form of a group organisation chart.		
SUP 16.5.4R	Reporting – annual *close links* report – every *firm* except: (1) an *ICVC*; (2) an *incoming EEA firm*; (3) an *incoming Treaty firm*; (4) a *non-directive friendly society*; (5) a *partnership*; (6) a *sole trader*; (7) a *service company*; (8) a *UCITS qualifier*	If a *firm* is not aware: (a) that it has *close links*; or (b) of any material changes to the details since the last report; then confirmation of this. If the above does not apply, the report must contain a list of all *persons* with whom the *firm* has *close links* as at the *firm's accounting reference date* of which it is aware, and for each such *person* state: (a) its name; (b) the nature of the *close links*; (c) if the *close link* is with a *body corporate*, its country of incorporation, address and registered number; and (d) if the *close link* is with an individual, his date and place of birth. The information may be provided in the form of a group organisation chart	Annually from the *accounting reference date* If a *firm* is an unincorporated *friendly society*, then it is only required to submit a report if it is aware that it has *close links*	Four months
SUP 16.6.5R	Reporting – compliance reports – *bank* – list of *overseas regulators*	List of all *overseas regulators* for each legal entity in the *firm's group*	Annually from the *accounting reference date*	Six months

Handbook reference	Matter to be notified	Contents of notification	Trigger event	Time allowed
SUP 16.6.5R	Reporting – compliance reports – *bank – authorised* entities in the *firm's group*	Organogram showing the *authorised* entities in the *firm's group*	Annually from the *accounting reference date*	Six months
SUP 16.6.6R	Reporting – compliance reports – *trustee* of an *AUT*	In relation to the *manager* of each *AUT* for which it is a *trustee*, the number of times during the quarter in which facts came to the *firm's* knowledge from which it appeared, or might have appeared, that the *manager* had failed (materially or otherwise) to:	Quarterly (the quarter ends are 31 March, 30 June, 30 September, 31 December)	One month
		(a) give correct instructions to the *trustee* to create or cancel *units* in the *AUT* when the *manager* should have done so, and the error:		
		(i) resulted in the creation of too few *units* or in the cancellation of too many *units*; and		
		(ii) was not corrected in accordance with the *FSA's guidance* as set out in COLL 6.2.12G;		
		(b) *price units* in the *AUT* in accordance with COLL 6, where the pricing error was:		
		(i) greater than 0.5% of the price of a *unit*; or		
		(ii) less than 0.5% of the price of a *unit*, and the *trustee* did not consider the *manager's* controls to be adequate; unless the failure was an isolated incident		

Handbook reference	Matter to be notified	Contents of notification	Trigger event	Time allowed
SUP 16.6.6R	Reporting – compliance reports – *depositary* of an *ICVC*	In relation to the *authorised corporate director* of each *ICVC* for which it is a *depositary*, the number of times during the quarter in which facts came to the *firm's* knowledge from which it appeared, that the *authorised corporate director* had failed (materially or otherwise) to:	Quarterly (the quarter ends are 31 March, 30 June, 30 September, 31 December)	One month
		(a) arrange for the *issue* or cancellation of *shares* in the *ICVC* when the *authorised corporate director* should have done so, and the error:		
		(i) resulted in the creation of too few *shares* or in the cancellation of too many *shares*; and		
		(ii) was not corrected in accordance with the *FSA's guidance* as set out in COLL 6.2.12G;		
		(b) price *shares* in the *ICVC* in accordance with COLL 6, where the pricing error was:		
		(i) greater than 0.5% of the price of a *share*; or		
		(ii) less than 0.5% of the price of a *share*, and the *depositary* did not consider the *authorised corporate director's* controls to be adequate;		
		unless the failure was an isolated incident		
SUP 16.6.6R	Reporting – compliance reports – *OPS firms*	Annual accounts of each *occupational pension scheme* in respect of which the *firm* is acting	Annually	Seven months after the end of the scheme year

Handbook reference	Matter to be notified	Contents of notification	Trigger event	Time allowed
SUP 16.6.6R	Reporting – compliance reports – *OPS firms*	Audited annual accounts of each *OPS collective investment scheme* in respect of which the *firm* is acting	Annually	Seven months after the end of the scheme year
SUP 16.6.8R (3)	Reporting – compliance reports – *OPS firms*	Any change in the date of commencement of the scheme year of an *OPS* or *OPS collective investment scheme*, in respect of which the *firm* is acting, not less than 15 *business days* before the date on which such a change is to become effective.		15 *business days* before the date on which such a change is to become effective
SUP 16.7.7R to SUP 16.7.15R	Reporting financial reports – *UK bank*	Annual report and audited accounts	Annually	3 months after the *firm's accounting reference date*
SUP 16.7.7R to SUP 16.7.15R	Reporting – financial reports – *UK bank*	Adequate information on capital adequacy (unconsolidated solo consolidated) BSD3	Quarterly. Reports required on a quarterly basis must be prepared as at the end of March, June, September and December of each year, except that a *bank*, which submits the BT report to the Bank of England monthly, must prepare the Form LR (Adequate information on mismatch liquidity) as at the end of February, May, August and November each year.	10 *business days* (12 *business days* if submitted electronically)
SUP 16.7.7R to SUP 16.7.15R	Reporting – financial reports – *UK bank*	Adequate information on capital adequacy (consolidated) BSD3 The requirement to submit consolidated reports applies only to a *bank* which calculates its capital requirements on a consolidated basis.	Half yearly. All consolidated reports required on a half yearly basis must be prepared as at the end of June and December of each year.	20 *business days* (22 *business days* if submitted electronically)
		See *IPRU(BANK)* GN 3.3.13R(2) and *IPRU(BANK)* CS 4.		

Handbook reference	**Matter to be notified**	**Contents of notification**	**Trigger event**	**Time allowed**
SUP 16.7.7R to SUP 16.7.15R	Reporting – financial reports – *UK bank*	Analysis of large exposures (Unconsolidated, solo consolidated) LE2 or LE3	Quarterly. Reports required on a quarterly basis must be prepared as at the end of March, June, September and December of each year, except that a *bank*, which submits the BT report to the Bank of England monthly, must prepare the Form LR (Adequate information on mismatch liquidity) as at the end of February, May, August and November each year.	10 *business days* after quarter end (14 *business days* if LE3 submitted electronically)
SUP 16.7.7R to SUP 16.7.15R	Reporting – financial reports – *UK bank*	Analysis of large exposures (Consolidated) LE2 or LE3. The requirement to submit consolidated reports applies only to a *bank* which calculates its capital requirements on a consolidated basis. See *IPRU(BANK)* GN 3.3.13R(2) and *IPRU(BANK)* CS 4.	Quarterly. Reports required on a quarterly basis must be prepared as at the end of March, June, September and December of each year, except that a *bank*, which submits the BT report to the Bank of England monthly, must prepare the Form LR (Adequate information on mismatch liquidity) as at the end of February, May, August and November each year.	20 *business days* after quarter end (24 *business days* if LE3 submitted electronically)

Handbook reference	**Matter to be notified**	**Contents of notification**	**Trigger event**	**Time allowed**
SUP 16.7.7R to SUP 16.7.15R	Reporting – financial reports – *UK bank*	Adequate information on holdings of credit and financial institutions' and non-financial companies' capital instruments (Unconsolidated, solo consolidated) M1 This report is only required from a *bank* which reports either on a solo or unconsolidated basis and (i) has been granted a trading book concession as explained in *IPRU(BANK)* CA 10.3; or (ii) has qualifying holdings in non-financial *companies* as explained in *IPRU(BANK)* CA 10.4	Quarterly. Reports required on a quarterly basis must be prepared as at the end of March, June, September and December of each year, except that a *bank*, which submits the BT report to the Bank of England monthly, must prepare the Form LR (Adequate information on mismatch liquidity) as at the end of February, May, August and November each year.	10 *business days* (12 *business days* if submitted electronically)
SUP 16.7.7R to SUP 16.7.15R	Reporting – financial reports – *UK bank*	Adequate information on holdings of credit and financial institutions' and non-financial companies' capital instruments (Consolidated) M1 This report is only required from a *bank* which reports either on a solo or unconsolidated basis and:	Half yearly. All consolidated reports required on a half yearly basis must be prepared as at the end of June and December of each year.	20 *business days* after period end (22 *business days* if submitted electronically)

Handbook reference	Matter to be notified	Contents of notification	Trigger event	Time allowed
		(i) has been granted a trading book concession as explained in *IPRU(BANK)* CA 10.3; or (ii) has qualifying holdings in non-financial companies as explained in *IPRU(BANK)* CA 10.4 The requirement to submit consolidated reports applies only to a *bank* which calculates its capital requirements on a consolidated basis. See *IPRU(BANK)* GN 3.3.13R(2) and *IPRU(BANK)* CS 4.		
SUP 16.7.7R to SUP 16.7.15R	Reporting – financial reports – *UK bank*	Adequate information on sterling stock liquidity (SLR1)	Monthly	6 *business days* after second Wednesday of the month
		A *bank* is not required to submit both the SLR1 and LR A *bank* which monitors its liquidity according to the maturity mismatch approach as set out in *IPRU(BANK)* LM must submit the LR		This report must be prepared as at the second Wednesday of each month. See *IPRU(BANK)* LS 5.2(2) regarding submission of an SLR1 on breach of various limits
		A *bank* which monitors its liquidity according to the maturity mismatch approach as set out in *IPRU(BANK)* LS must submit the SLR1		

Handbook reference	**Matter to be notified**	**Contents of notification**	**Trigger event**	**Time allowed**
SUP 16.7.7R to SUP 16.7.15R	Reporting – financial reports – *UK bank*	Adequate information on mismatch liquidity LR	Quarterly. Reports required on a quarterly basis must be prepared as at the end of March, June, September and December of each year, except that a *bank*, which submits the BT report to the Bank of England monthly, must prepare the Form LR (Adequate information on mismatch liquidity) as at the end of February, May, August and November each year.	10 *business days* after period end (12 *business days* if submitted electronically)
		A *bank* is not required to submit both the SLR1 and LR A *bank* which monitors its liquidity according to the maturity mismatch approach as set out in *IPRU(BANK)* LM must submit the LR		
		A *bank* which monitors its liquidity according to the maturity mismatch approach as set out in *IPRU(BANK)* LS must submit the SLR1		
SUP 16.7.7R to SUP 16.7.15R	Reporting – financial reports – *UK bank*	List of *companies* in the *bank's* consolidated large exposure reporting	Annually	6 months after the *firm's accounting reference date*
SUP 16.7.7R to SUP 16.7.15R	Reporting – financial reports – *UK bank*	Annual confirmation that all *companies* included in solo consolidation meet the criteria for such consolidation as set out in *IPRU(BANK)* CS 9.2	Annually	6 months after the *firm's accounting reference date*

Handbook reference	**Matter to be notified**	**Contents of notification**	**Trigger event**	**Time allowed**
SUP 16.7.7R to SUP 16.7.15R	Reporting – financial reports – *EEA bank*, other than one with *permission* only for *cross border services*	Adequate information on mismatch liquidity (excluding deposit concentration) LR (excluding Part 5)	Quarterly. Reports required on a quarterly basis must be prepared as at the end of March, June, September and December of each year, except that a *bank*, which submits the BT report to the Bank of England monthly, must prepare the Form LR (Adequate information on mismatch liquidity) as at the end of February, May, August and November each year.	10 *business days* after period end (12 *business days* if submitted electronically)
SUP 16.7.7R to SUP 16.7.15R	Reporting – financial reports – *bank* established outside the *EEA*	Analysis of profits, large exposures, balance sheet, off balance sheet items and bad and doubtful debt provisions B7	Half yearly. Period ends are end of June and December each year.	10 *business days* after period end (12 *business days* if submitted electronically)
SUP 16.7.7R to SUP 16.7.15R	Reporting – financial reports – *bank* established outside the *EEA*	Adequate information on mismatch liquidity LR	Quarterly. Reports required on a quarterly basis must be prepared as at the end of March, June, September and December of each year, except that a *bank*, which submits the BT report to the Bank of England monthly, must prepare the Form LR (Adequate information on mismatch liquidity) as at the end of February, May, August and November each year.	10 *business days* after period end (12 *business days* if submitted electronically)
SUP 16.7.16R to SUP 16.7.19R	Reporting – financial reports – *building society*	Adequate information on *group* balance sheet, analysed between society and subsidiary undertakings MFS1 – (Table A)	Monthly	9 *business days* after month end (largest societies) 12 *business days* after month end (other societies)

Handbook reference	Matter to be notified	Contents of notification	Trigger event	Time allowed
SUP 16.7.16R to SUP 16.7.19R	Reporting – financial reports – *building society*	Adequate information on society's balance sheet and primary business transactions MFS1 – (Tables B to G)	Monthly	7 *business days* after month end (largest societies) 10 *business days* after month end (other societies)
SUP 16.7.16R to SUP 16.7.19R	Reporting – financial reports – *building society*	Largest *building societies* (see SUP 16.7.17R Note 2):	Monthly	7 *business days* after month end (largest societies)
		Sectoral breakdown of the society's balance sheet MFS1 SUP		10 *business days* after month end (other societies)
SUP 16.7.16R to SUP 16.7.19R	Reporting – financial reports – *building society*	Adequate information on balance sheets and primary business transactions of society's subsidiary undertakings accepting deposits and/or lending MFS2	Monthly	7 *business days* after month end (largest societies) 10 *business days* after month end (other societies)
SUP 16.7.16R to SUP 16.7.19R	Reporting – financial reports – *building society*	Analysis of interest rate risk gap	Monthly	15 *business days* after month end
SUP 16.7.16R to SUP 16.7.19R	Reporting – financial reports – *building society*	Adequate information on balance sheet, income and expenditure, capital, lending quality, large exposures and maturities for the society and its subsidiary undertakings, together with relevant expected and likely out-turns QFS1	Quarterly	18 *business days* after society's financial quarter end
SUP 16.7.16R to SUP 16.7.19R	Reporting – financial reports – *building society*	Largest *building societies* (see SUP 16.7.17R Note 2): Sectoral and other breakdown of assets and liabilities, gilt maturities, and derivative contracts QFS2	Quarterly	11 *business days* after calendar quarter end
SUP 16.7.16R to SUP 16.7.19R	Reporting – financial reports – *building society*	Adequate information on balance sheet, income and expenditure, the range and volume of activities undertaken by the society, its subsidiary undertakings, and where relevant, its participating interests AFS1	Annually	2 months after society's accounting reference date

Handbook reference	Matter to be notified	Contents of notification	Trigger event	Time allowed
SUP 16.7.20R to SUP 16.7.21R	Reporting – financial reports – *service companies*	Annual audited financial statements	Annually	6 months after the *firm's accounting reference date*
SUP 16.7.22R to SUP 16.7.34G	Reporting – financial reports – *securities and futures firm* (only applies to *oil market participants* if *IPRU(INV)* applies to the *firm*) – *lead regulated firm*	Annual audited financial statements	Annually	6 months after the *firm's accounting reference date*
SUP 16.7.22R to SUP 16.7.34G	Reporting – financial reports – *securities and futures firm*, except a *lead regulated firm* (only applies to *oil market participants* if *IPRU(INV)* applies to the *firm*)	Audited annual financial statements	Annually	3 months after the *firm's accounting reference date*
SUP 16.7.22R to SUP 16.7.34G	Reporting – financial reports – *securities and futures firm*, except a *lead regulated firm* (only applies to *oil market participants* if *IPRU(INV)* applies to the *firm*) Category A or B firm or broad scope firm	Annual reporting statement	Annually	3 months after the *firm's accounting reference date*
SUP 16.7.22R to SUP 16.7.34G	Reporting – financial reports – *securities and futures firm*, except a *lead regulated firm* (only applies to *oil market participants* if *IPRU(INV)* applies to the *firm*) Category A or B firm or broad scope firm	Annual reconciliation Every year a *firm* must submit: (a) a reconciliation and explanation of any differences between amounts shown in the balance sheet in the audited annual financial statements and the annual reporting statement (b) a reconciliation and explanation of any differences between the annual reporting statement and the monthly reporting statement prepared as at the same date	Annually	3 months after the *firm's accounting reference date*

Handbook reference	Matter to be notified	Contents of notification	Trigger event	Time allowed
SUP 16.7.22R to SUP 16.7.34G	Reporting – financial reports – *securities and futures firm*, except a *lead regulated firm* (only applies to *oil market participants* if *IPRU(INV)* applies to the *firm*) Category A or B firm or broad scope firm	Audited accounts of any subsidiary, unless the *rules* in this chapter require that subsidiary to submit accounts to the *FSA*	Annually	3 months after the *firm's accounting reference date*
SUP 16.7.22R to SUP 16.7.34G	Reporting – financial reports – *securities and futures firm*, except a *lead regulated firm* (only applies to *oil market participants* if *IPRU(INV)* applies to the *firm*) Category A or B firm or broad scope firm	Consolidated reporting statement (Only required for category A and B firms which are subject to the consolidation *rules* set out in *IPRU(INV)* 10-200R to 10-203R, and are not exempt from the consolidation *rules* under *IPRU(INV)* 10-200R(2) or *IPRU(INV)* 10-204R.)	Half yearly	1 month after period end
SUP 16.7.22R to SUP 16.7.34G	Reporting – financial reports – *securities and futures firm*, except a *lead regulated firm* (only applies to *oil market participants* if *IPRU(INV)* applies to the *firm*) Category A or B firm or broad scope firm	Large exposures quarterly reporting statement (Form LEM 1 or LEM 2) – solo A *firm* which was required to submit Form LEM1 in the relevant period immediately prior to *commencement* must continue to do so.	Quarterly	15 *business days* after quarter end
		A *firm* which was required to submit Form LEM2 in the relevant period immediately prior to *commencement* must continue to do so.		
		A category A or B firm authorised after the *commencement* must submit Form LEM1.		

Part II FSA Handbook Materials

Hand-book reference	**Matter to be notified**	**Contents of notification**	**Trigger event**	**Time allowed**
SUP 16.7.22R to SUP 16.7.34G	Reporting – financial reports – *securities and futures firm*, except a *lead regulated firm* (only applies to *oil market participants* if *IPRU(INV)* applies to the *firm*)	Large exposures quarterly reporting statement (Form LEM 1 or LEM 2) – consolidated A *firm* which was required to submit Form LEM1 in the relevant period immediately prior to *commencement* must continue to do so.	Quarterly	1 month after quarter end
	Category A or B firm or broad scope firm	A *firm* which was required to submit Form LEM2 in the relevant period immediately prior to *commencement* must continue to do so.		
		A category A or B firm *authorised* after the *commencement* must submit Form LEM1.		
		(Only required for category A and B firms which are subject to the consolidation *rules* set out in *IPRU(INV)* 10-200R – 10-203R, and are not exempt from the consolidation *rules* under *IPRU(INV)* 10-200R(2) or *IPRU(INV)* 10-204R.)		
SUP 16.7.22R to SUP 16.7.34G	Reporting – financial reports – *securities and futures firm*, except a *lead regulated firm* (only applies to *oil market participants* if *IPRU(INV)* applies to the *firm*) Category A or B firm or broad scope firm	Monthly reporting statement	Monthly	15 *business days* after month end
SUP 16.7.22R to SUP 16.7.34G	Reporting – financial reports – *securities and futures firm*, except a *lead regulated firm* (only applies to *oil market participants* if *IPRU(INV)* applies to the *firm*)		Annually	3 months after the *firm's accounting reference date*

Handbook reference	**Matter to be notified**	**Contents of notification**	**Trigger event**	**Time allowed**
	Category C or D firm or arranger or venture capital firm	Annual reporting statement		
SUP 16.7.22R to SUP 16.7.34G	Reporting – financial reports – *securities and futures firm*, except a *lead regulated firm* (only applies to *oil market participants* if *IPRU(INV)* applies to the *firm*)	Annual reconciliation Every year a *firm* must submit:	Annually	3 months after the *firm's accounting reference date*
	Category C or D firm or arranger or venture capital firm	(a) a reconciliation and explanation of any differences between amounts shown in the balance sheet in the audited annual financial statements and the annual reporting statement		
		(b) a reconciliation and explanation of any differences between the annual reporting statement and the monthly reporting statement prepared as at the same date		
SUP 16.7.22R to SUP 16.7.34G	Reporting – financial reports – *securities and futures firm*, except a *lead regulated firm* (only applies to *oil market participants* if *IPRU(INV)* applies to the *firm*) Category C or D firm or arranger or venture capital firm	Audited accounts of any *subsidiary*, unless the *rules* in this chapter require that *subsidiary* to submit accounts to the *FSA*	Annually	3 months after the *firm's accounting reference date*
SUP 16.7.22R to SUP 16.7.34G	Reporting – financial reports – *securities and futures firm*, except a *lead regulated firm* (only applies to *oil market participants* if *IPRU(INV)* applies to the *firm*)	Consolidated reporting statement	Half yearly	1 month from period end

Part II FSA Handbook Materials

Handbook reference	**Matter to be notified**	**Contents of notification**	**Trigger event**	**Time allowed**
	Only for category C firm (as defined in the glossaries located in *IPRU(INV)* 10, which is subject to the consolidation *rules* set out *IPRU(INV)* 10-200R to 10-203R and are not exempt from the consolidation *rules* under *IPRU(INV)* 10-200R(2) or *IPRU(INV)* 10-204R			
SUP 16.7.22R to SUP 16.7.34G	Reporting – financial reports – *securities and futures firm*, except a *lead regulated firm* (only applies to *oil market participants* if *IPRU(INV)* applies to the *firm*) Category C firm	Large exposures quarterly reporting statement (Form LEM 1 or LEM 2) – solo A *firm* which was required to submit Form LEM1 in the relevant period immediately prior to *commencement* must continue to do so.	Quarterly	15 *business days* after quarter end
		A *firm* which was required to submit Form LEM2 in the relevant period immediately prior to *commencement* must continue to do so. A firm *authorised* after the *commencement* must submit Form LEM1.		

Handbook reference	Matter to be notified	Contents of notification	Trigger event	Time allowed
SUP 16.7.22R to SUP 16.7.34G	Reporting financial reports – *securities and futures firm*, except a *lead regulated firm* (only applies to *oil market participants* if *IPRU(INV)* applies to the *firm*) Category C firm (as defined in the glossaries located in *IPRU(INV)* 10, which is subject to the consolidation *rules* set out in *IPRU(INV)* 10-200R – 10-203R and are not exempt from the consolidation *rules* under *IPRU(INV)* 10-200R(2) or *IPRU(INV)* 10-204R	Large exposures quarterly reporting statement (Form LEM 1 or LEM 2) – consolidated A *firm* which was required to submit Form LEM1 in the relevant period immediately prior to *commencement* must continue to do so. A *firm* which was required to submit Form LEM2 in the relevant period immediately prior to *commencement* must continue to do so. A firm *authorised* after the *commencement* must submit Form LEM1.	Quarterly	1 month after quarter end
SUP 16.7.22R to SUP 16.7.34G	Reporting – financial reports – *securities and futures firm*, except a *lead regulated firm* (only applies to *oil market participants* if *IPRU(INV)* applies to the *firm*) Category C or D firm or arranger or venture capital firm	Quarterly reporting statement	Quarterly	15 *business days* after quarter end
SUP 16.7.22R to SUP 16.7.34G	Reporting – financial reports – *securities and futures firm*, except a *lead regulated firm* (only applies to *oil market participants* if *IPRU(INV)* applies to the *firm*) Adviser or local, or a traded options market maker (as referred to in *IPRU(INV)* 3-60R (4) *Sole traders* only	Solvency statement	Annually	2 months after the *firm's accounting reference date*

Part II FSA Handbook Materials

Handbook reference	**Matter to be notified**	**Contents of notification**	**Trigger event**	**Time allowed**
SUP 16.7.22R to SUP 16.7.34G	Reporting – financial reports – *securities and futures firm*, except a *lead regulated firm* (only applies to *oil market participants* if *IPRU(INV)* applies to the *firm*)	Audited annual financial statements	Annually	3 months after the *firm's accounting reference date*
	Adviser or local, or a traded options market maker (as referred to in *IPRU(INV)* 3-60R (4)			
	Partnerships and *bodies corporate* only			
SUP 16.7.22R to SUP 16.7.34G	Reporting – financial reports – *securities and futures firm*, except a *lead regulated firm* (only applies to *oil market participants* if *IPRU(INV)* applies to the *firm*)	Audited accounts of any *subsidiary* unless the *rules* in this chapter require that *subsidiary* to submit accounts to the *FSA*	Annually	3 months after the *firm's accounting reference date*
	Adviser or local, or a traded options market maker (as referred to in *IPRU(INV)* 3-60R (4)			
SUP 16.7.22R to SUP 16.7.34G	Reporting – financial reports – *securities and futures firm*, except a *lead regulated firm* (only applies to *oil market participants* if *IPRU(INV)* applies to the *firm*)	Solvency statement for the *sole trader* or each *partner*	Annually	3 months after the *firm's accounting reference date*
	ISD investment firm, which is a *sole trader* or a *partnership* formed under the laws of England and Wales			
SUP 16.7.35R to SUP 16.7.41R	Reporting – financial reports – *investment management firms* Except a *lead regulated firm* or an *OPS firm* or a local authority	Annual Financial Return	Annually	4 months after the *firm's accounting reference date*

Handbook reference	Matter to be notified	Contents of notification	Trigger event	Time allowed
SUP 16.7.35R to SUP 16.7.41R	Reporting – financial reports – *investment management firms*	Annual accounts	Annually	4 months after the *firm's accounting reference date*
SUP 16.7.35R to SUP 16.7.41R	Reporting – financial reports – *investment management firms* Individuals in partnership	Annual solvency statement	Annually	4 months after the *firm's accounting reference date*
	Except a *lead regulated firm* or an *OPS firm* or a local authority			
SUP 16.7.35R to SUP 16.7.41R	Reporting –financial reports – *investment management firms*	Quarterly Financial Return	Quarterly	1 month after the *firm's* quarter end
	Firms subject to a Liquid Capital *Requirement* as set out in *IPRU(INV)* 5.2.3(1)(a)			
	Except a *lead regulated firm* or an *OPS firm*			
SUP 16.7.35R to SUP 16.7.41R	Reporting – financial reports – *investment management firms*	Monthly Financial Return	Monthly	1 month after the month end
	ISD firms (defined in the *Glossary* of *IPRU(INV)* 5 subject to the Own Funds Requirement of Euro 730,000 as set out in *IPRU(INV)* 5.2.3(1)(b)	A *firm* need not prepare a Monthly Financial Return as at the same date as a Quarterly Financial Return (see Note 4 of SUP 16.7.36R)		
	Except *a lead regulated firm* or an *OPS firm* or a local authority			
SUP 16.7.35R to SUP 16.7.41R	Reporting – financial reports – *investment management firms* Except a *lead regulated firm* or an *OPS firm* or a local authority	Why the report cannot be submitted to the *FSA* on time and the date by which it will submit the report to the *FSA*	Having reason to believe that it will be unable to submit an annual. quarterly or monthly financial return by the dates specified in the Supervision manual.	As soon as it has reason to believe it will be unable to submit by the specified date

Handbook reference	Matter to be notified	Contents of notification	Trigger event	Time allowed
SUP 16.7.42G to SUP 16.7.53G	Reporting – financial reports – *personal investment firms* except a *small personal investment firm*, a Category A1 firm a Category B1 firm or a *lead regulated firm*	Annual questionnaire	Annually	2 months after the *firm's accounting reference date*
SUP 16.7.42G to SUP 16.7.53G	Reporting – financial reports – *personal investment firms* except a *small personal investment firm* or a *lead regulated firm*	Annual financial statements The annual financial statements must include all reports for which table SUP 16.7.45R specifies a monthly or quarterly frequency	Annually	4 months after the *firm's accounting reference date*
SUP 16.7.42G to SUP 16.7.53G	Reporting – financial reports – *personal investment firms* except a *small personal investment firm* or a *lead regulated firm*	Audited consolidated statutory accounts Only required from a *firm* if it is a *holding company* or if one of its *controllers* is a *company*.	Annually	4 months after the *firm's accounting reference date*
SUP 16.7.42G to SUP 16.7.53G	Reporting – financial reports – *personal investment firms* except a *small personal investment firm* or a *lead regulated firm*	Annual reconciliation Every year a *firm* must submit a reconciliation of the amounts shown in the balance sheet in the annual financial statements with the amounts shown in the balance sheet in the last monthly or quarterly financial statements. The reconciliation must be submitted with the *firm's* annual financial statements.	Annually	4 months after the *firm's accounting reference date*
SUP 16.7.42G to SUP 16.7.53G	Reporting – financial reports – *personal investment firms* except a *small personal investment firm* or a *lead regulated firm*	Form 13A (Balance sheet)	Category A1 or B1 firm: Monthly Category B2 firm, which has less than 26 *financial advisers*: Annual	Category A1 or B1 firm: 3 weeks after month end
			Category B3 firm, which has less than 26 *financial advisers* and has *permission* to *manage investments*: Annual	Category B2 firm, which has less than 26 *financial advisers*: 4 months after year end

Handbook reference	**Matter to be notified**	**Contents of notification**	**Trigger event**	**Time allowed**
			Any other *firm*: Quarterly	Category B3 firm, which has less than 26 *financial advisers* and has *permission* to *manage investments*: 4 months after year end
				Any other *firm*: 3 weeks after quarter end
SUP 16.7.42G to SUP 16.7.53G	Reporting – financial reports – *personal investment firms* except a *small personal investment firm* or a *lead regulated firm*	Form 13Bi/ii (Profit and loss)	Category A1 or B1 firm: Monthly Category B2 firm, which has less than 26 *financial advisers*: Annual	Category A1 or B1 firm: 3 weeks after month end
			Category B3 firm, which has less than 26 *financial advisers* and has *permission* to *manage investments*: Annual	Category B2 firm, which has less than 26 *financial advisers*: 4 months after year end
			Any other *firm*: Quarterly	Category B3 firm, which has less than 26 *financial advisers* and has *permission* to *manage investments*: 4 months after year end
				Any other *firm*: 3 weeks after quarter end
SUP 16.7.42G to SUP 16.7.53G	Reporting – financial reports – *personal investment firms* except a *small personal investment firm* or a *lead regulated firm*	Form 13Ci (Statement of own funds)	Category A1 or B1 firm: Monthly Category B2 firm, which has less than 26 *financial advisers*: Annual	Category A1 or B1 firm: 3 weeks after month end
			Category B3 firm, which has less than 26 *financial advisers* and has *permission* to *manage investments*: Annual	Category B2 firm, which has less than 26 *financial advisers*: 4 months after year end
			Any other *firm*: Quarterly	Category B3 firm, which has less than 26 *financial advisers* and has *permission* to *manage investments*: 4 months after year end

Handbook reference	**Matter to be notified**	**Contents of notification**	**Trigger event**	**Time allowed**
				Any other *firm*: 3 weeks after quarter end
SUP 16.7.42G to SUP 16.7.53G	Reporting – financial reports – *personal investment firms* except a *small personal investment firm* or a *lead regulated firm*	Form 13Cii (Statement of own funds) (Unincorporated *firms* only)	Category A1 or B1 firm: Monthly Category B2 firm, which has less than 26 *financial advisers*: Annual	Category A1 or B1 firm: 3 weeks after month end
			Category B3 firm, which has less than 26 *financial advisers* and has *permission* to *manage investments*: Annual Any other *firm*: Quarterly	Category B2 firm, which has less than 26 *financial advisers*: 4 months after year end
				Category B3 firm, which has less than 26 *financial advisers* and has *permission* to *manage investments*: 4 months after year end
				Any other *firm*: 3 weeks after quarter end
SUP 16.7.42G to SUP 16.7.53G	Reporting – financial reports – *personal investment firms* except a *small personal investment firm* or a *lead regulated firm*	Form 13D (Financial resources test –current assets)	Category A1 or B1 firm: Monthly	Category A1 or B1 firm: 3 weeks after month end
			Category B2 firm, which has less than 26 *financial advisers*: Annual Category B3 firm, which has less than 26 *financial advisers* and has *permission* to *manage investments*: Annual	Category B2 firm, which has less than 26 *financial advisers*: 4 months after year end
			Any other *firm*: Quarterly	Category B3 firm, which has less than 26 *financial advisers* and has *permission* to *manage investments*: 4 months after year end
				Any other *firm*:

Hand-book reference	**Matter to be notified**	**Contents of notification**	**Trigger event**	**Time allowed**
				3 weeks after quarter end
SUP 16.7.42G to SUP 16.7.53G	Reporting – financial reports – *personal investment firms* except a *small personal investment firm* or a *lead regulated firm*	Form 13E (Financial resources test –expenditure *requirement*) Category A1 firm, Category A2 firm with *permission* to *manage investments*, or a Category A network: Form 13Ei in SUP 16 Ann7 (section 3)	Category A1 or B1 firm: Monthly Category B2 firm, which has less than 26 *financial advisers*: Annual Category B3 firm, which has less than 26 *financial advisers* and has *permission* to *manage investments*: Annual	Category A1 or B1 firm: 3 weeks after month end Category B2 firm, which has less than 26 *financial advisers*: 4 months after year end
		Category A2 firm without *permission* to *manage investments*, a Category A3 firm: Form 13Eii in SUP 16 Ann 7 (section 3)	Any other *firm*: Quarterly	Category B3 firm, which has less than 26 *financial advisers* and has *permission* to *manage investments*: 4 months after year end
		Category B1, B2 or B3 firm: Form 13E in SUP 16 Ann 7 (section 4)		Any other *firm*: 3 weeks after quarter end
SUP 16.7.42G to SUP 16.7.53G	Reporting – financial reports – *personal investment firms* except a *small personal investment firm* or a *lead regulated firm*	Form 13F (Financial resources test – assets and liabilities)	Category A1 or B1 firm: Monthly Category B2 firm, which has less than 26 *financial advisers*: Annual	Category A1 or B1 firm: 3 weeks after month end
			Category B3 firm, which has less than 26 *financial advisers* and has *permission* to *manage investments*: Annual Any other *firm*: Quarterly	Category B2 firm, which has less than 26 *financial advisers*: 4 months after year end
				Category B3 firm, which has less than 26 *financial advisers* and has *permission* to *manage investments*: 4 months after year end
				Any other *firm*: 3 weeks after quarter end

Handbook reference	**Matter to be notified**	**Contents of notification**	**Trigger event**	**Time allowed**
SUP 16.7.42G to SUP 16.7.53G	Reporting – financial reports – *personal investment firms* except a *small personal investment firm* or a *lead regulated firm*	Form 13G (Financial resources test – position risk deductions)	Category A1 or B1 firm: Monthly	Category A1 or B1 firm: 3 weeks after month end
			Category B2 firm, which has less than 26 *financial advisers*: Annual Category B3 firm, which has less than 26 *financial advisers* and has *permission* to *manage investments*: Annual Any other *firm*: Quarterly	Category B2 firm, which has less than 26 *financial advisers*: 4 months after year end Category B3 firm, which has less than 26 *financial advisers* and has *permission* to *manage investments*: 4 months after year end
				Any other *firm*: 3 weeks after quarter end
SUP 16.7.42G to SUP 16.7.53G	Reporting – financial reports – *personal investment firms* except a *small personal investment firm* or a *lead regulated firm Sole traders* only	Form 13J (*Sole trader* solvency statement)	Category A1 or B1 firm: Monthly Category B2 firm, which has less than 26 *financial advisers*: Annual	Category A1 or B1 firm: 3 weeks after month end Category B2 firm, which has less than 26 *financial advisers*: 4 months after year end
			Category B3 firm, which has less than 26 *financial advisers* and has *permission* to *manage investments*: Annual Any other *firm*: Quarterly	Category B3 firm, which has less than 26 *financial advisers* and has *permission* to *manage investments*: 4 months after year end
				Any other *firm*: 3 weeks after quarter end
SUP 16.7.42G to SUP 16.7.53G	Reporting – financial reports –*personal investment firms* except a *small personal investment firm* or a *lead regulated firm*	Consolidated financial resources return	Quarterly	3 weeks after quarter end

Handbook reference	Matter to be notified	Contents of notification	Trigger event	Time allowed
	Category A1, A2 or A3 firm If the *firm* is a member of a *group* and is subject to consolidated supervision as set out in *IPRU(INV)* 13.7.1R to 13.7.2R			
SUP 16.7.42G to SUP 16.7.53G	Reporting – financial reports – *personal investment firms* except a *small personal investment firm* or a *lead regulated firm* Category A1, A2 or A3 firm	Form CAD 13	Quarterly	3 weeks after quarter end
SUP 16.7.42G to SUP 16.7.53G	Reporting –financial reports – *personal investment firms* except a *small personal investment firm* or a *lead regulated firm* Category A1, A2 or A3 firm	Form 13H (Restrictions of Financial Resources)	Category A1 firm: monthly Category A2 or A3 firm: Quarterly	Category A1 firm: 3 weeks after month end Category A2 or A3 firm: 3 weeks after quarter end
SUP 16.7.42G to SUP 16.7.53G	Reporting – financial reports – *personal investment firms* except a *small personal investment firm* or a *lead regulated firm* Category A1, A2 or A3 firm	Form 13I (Statement of large exposures)	Quarterly	3 weeks after quarter end
SUP 16.7.42G to SUP 16.7.53G	Reporting – financial reports –*personal investment firms* except a *small personal investment firm* or a *lead regulated firm*	Form 13I Consolidated statement of large exposures	Quarterly	3 weeks after quarter end
	Category A1, A2 or A3 firm If the *firm* is a member of a *group* and is subject to consolidated supervision as set out in *IPRU(INV)* 13.7.1R to 13.7.2R			

Handbook reference	Matter to be notified	Contents of notification	Trigger event	Time allowed
SUP 16.7.42G to SUP 16.7.53G	Reporting – financial reports –*personal investment firms – small personal investment firm*	Annual questionnaire	Annually	4 months after the *firm's accounting reference date*
SUP 16.7.42G to SUP 16.7.53G	Reporting – financial reports – *personal investment firms – small personal investment firm* If the *firm* is a *holding company* or one of its *controllers* is a *company*	Audited consolidated annual financial statements The *firm* must submit the statutory accounts of the *group* to which it belongs	Annually	4 months after the *firm's accounting reference date*
SUP 16.7.54R	Reporting – financial reports –*authorised professional firm*	Annual questionnaire Form in SUP 16 Ann 9R	Annually	4 months after the *firm's accounting reference date*
SUP 16.7.55R	Reporting – financial reports – The *Society of Lloyd's*	Annual audited accounts	Annually	6 months after the *Society's accounting reference date*
SUP 16.7.55R	Reporting – financial reports – The *Society of Lloyd's*	Annual Lloyd's Return	Annually	6 months after the *Society's accounting reference date*
SUP 16.7.55R to SUP 16.7.56R	Reporting – financial reports – The *Society of Lloyd's*	Syndicate returns	Annually	6 months after the *Society's accounting reference date*
SUP 16.7.57R to SUP 16.7.58R	Reporting – financial reports – *Members' adviser*	Audited annual financial statements	Annually	3 months after the *firm's accounting reference date*
SUP 16.7.57R to SUP 16.7.58R	Reporting – financial reports – *Members' adviser*	Annual reporting statement	Annually	3 months after the *firm's accounting reference date*
SUP 16.7.57R to SUP 16.7.58R	Reporting – financial reports – *Members' adviser*	Annual reconciliation	Annually	3 months after the *firm's accounting reference date*
SUP 16.7.57R to SUP 16.7.58R	Reporting – financial reports – *Members' adviser*	Audited accounts of any *subsidiary*, unless the *rules* in this chapter require those *subsidiaries* to submit accounts to the *FSA*	Annually	3 months after the *firm's accounting reference date*
SUP 16.7.57R to SUP 16.7.58R	Reporting – financial reports – *Members' adviser*	Quarterly reporting statement	Quarterly	15 *business days* after the quarter end
SUP 16.7.62R to SUP 16.7.63R	Reporting – financial reports – *Credit union*	Form CQ – Key financial data	Quarterly	One *month* after quarter end

Handbook reference	Matter to be notified	Contents of notification	Trigger event	Time allowed
SUP 16.7.62R to SUP 16.7.63R	Reporting – financial reports – *Credit union*	Form CY – Extended financial data	Annually	Seven *months* after the financial year end
SUP 16.7.64R to SUP 16.7.65R	Reporting – financial reports – *ELMI*	Annual report and audited accounts	Annually	3 *months* after the *firm's accounting reference date*
SUP 16.7.64R to SUP 16.7.65R	Reporting – financial reports – *ELMI*	Form ELM – CA/LE – Unconsolidated reporting statement on capital adequacy	Half-yearly	20 *business days* after period end (22 *business days* if submitted electronically)
SUP 16.7.64R to SUP 16.7.65R	Reporting – financial reports – *ELMI*	Form ELM – CA/LE – Consolidated reporting statement on capital adequacy	Half-yearly	20 *business days* after period end (22 *business days* if submitted electronically)
SUP 16.7.64R to SUP 16.7.65R	Reporting – financial reports – *ELMI*	Form BSD3 – Consolidated reporting statement on capital adequacy in the case of *ELM* 7.3.2R	Half-yearly	20 *business days* after period end (22 *business days* if submitted electronically)
SUP 16.7.64R to SUP 16.7.65R	Reporting – financial reports – *ELMI*	Form ELM – CA/LE – Unconsolidated large exposures reporting statement	Half-yearly	20 *business days* after period end (22 *business days* if submitted electronically)
SUP 16.7.64R to SUP 16.7.65R	Reporting – financial reports – *ELMI*	Form ELM – CA/LE – Consolidated large exposures reporting statement	Half-yearly	20 *business days* after period end (22 *business days* if submitted electronically)
SUP 16.8	Reporting – persistency reports from *insurers*	Persistency report The report must report on every *life policy* which was promoted subject to *rules* in *COB* or COBS, is not a *life policy* of a type listed in SUP 16.8.13R or SUP 16.8.14R, and which:	Annually	By 30 April each year
		(1) was effected by the *firm* submitting the report; or		
		(2) was effected by a member of the *firm's group*, which is not an *authorised person*, and in circumstances in which the *firm* submitting the report was responsible for promoting that *life policy*; or		

Part II FSA Handbook Materials

Handbook reference	Matter to be notified	Contents of notification	Trigger event	Time allowed
		(3) was effected by another *firm*, but is carried out by the *firm* submitting the report.		
		The report must be in the format of Forms 1R(1), (2) and (3) in SUP 16 Ann 6R.		
SUP 16.9.3R	Details of appointed representatives. Every firm with a *Part IV permission* to *advise on investments, arrange (bring about) deals in investments, make arrangements with a view to transactions in investments, or arrange safeguarding and administration of assets*	A list of all the current *appointed representatives* of the *firm* as at the *firm's accounting reference date*. A report is not required if a *firm* has no *appointed representatives* as at the *firm's accounting reference date* and this is reflected in the relevant extract from the *FSA Register*.	Annually	Four months
SUP 16.10.4R	Verification of *standing data* items	Correction of inaccuracies in *standing data*	*Accounting reference date*	30 *business days* after *accounting reference date*
SUP 17	Transaction reporting This applies to (a) a *MiFID investment firm*; (b) a *third country investment firm*; (c) a *person* who is the operator of an *approved reporting mechanism* or of a *regulated market* or *MTF* that is used by a *firm* to report transactions to the *FSA*; or	A *transaction report* as specified in SUP 17.1.4R, SUP 17.4.1EU and SUP 17.4.2R.	Executing a *transaction*, subject to the exceptions in SUP 17.2.1R and SUP 17.2.3R.	As quickly as possible and by not later than the close of the working day following the day upon which that *transaction* took place.
	(d) a *firm* acting in its capacity as a manager or operator of a collective investment undertaking, *pension scheme*, *occupational pension scheme*, a *personal pension scheme* or a *stakeholder pension scheme*.			
SUP 18.2.12G	Possible proposal for *insurance business transfer scheme*	The broad outline of the scheme and its purpose	When an *insurance business transfer scheme* is being considered	As soon as reasonably practical

Handbook reference	Matter to be notified	Contents of notification	Trigger event	Time allowed
SUP 18.2.26G	The *FSA* has to be informed to enable it to consult the transferee's *Home State regulator*	As set out in 18.2.26G	If the transferee is (or will be) an *EEA firm* (authorised in its *Home State* to carry on *insurance business* under the *Insurance Directives*) or a *Swiss general insurance company*.	Not specified
SUP 18.2.28G	The *FSA* has to be informed to enable it to consult the *Host State regulator*	As set out in 18.2.28G	If the transferor is an *UK insurer* and the business to be transferred includes business carried on from a branch in another *EEA State*.	Not specified
SUP 18.2.29G	The *FSA* has to be informed to enable it to consult the *Host State regulator*	Should identify the parties to the transfer and include the transfer agreement or draft transfer agreement or a summary containing relevant information. It would be helpful if a draft of the *scheme report* was also available.	If the transferor is an *UK insurer* and the business to be transferred includes a long-term insurance contract (other than reinsurance) for which the *state of the commitment* is an *EEA state* other than the *United Kingdom*.	Not specified
			If the transferor is an *UK insurer* and the business to be transferred includes a general insurance contract (other than reinsurance) for which the *state of the risk* is an *EEA state* other than the *United Kingdom*.	Not specified
SUP 18.2.31G	*Scheme report* in a form approved by the *FSA*	As set out in SUP 18.2.33G	Decision to apply to the court to approve an *insurance business transfer scheme*.	
SUP 18.2.32G	Fact of the *independent expert* producing a *scheme report*		*Independent expert* appointed to produce a *scheme report*.	At an early stage
SUP 18.2.42G	Notice of the application to be sent to all *policyholders* of the parties. It may also be appropriate to give notice to others affected, in particular to:	In addition to the notice it would normally be appropriate to include a statement setting out the terms of the scheme and containing a summary of the *scheme report*.	Decision to apply to the court for approval of an *insurance business transfer scheme* (unless the court directs otherwise)	At least six weeks before court hearing

Part II FSA Handbook Materials

Handbook reference	**Matter to be notified**	**Contents of notification**	**Trigger event**	**Time allowed**
	(1) reinsurers of the transferor where it is proposed that benefits or liabilities under their contracts should pass to the transferee			
	(2) anyone with an interest in the *policies* being transferred who has notified the transferor of their interest.			
SUP App 2.3.1R	*Insurers*: *scheme of operations* – an *insurer* which is not an *incoming EEA firm* or an *incoming Treaty firm* – *Margin of solvency* below required level	A plan for the restoration of a sound financial position including: (1) a *scheme of operations* (see SUP App 2.9); and (2) an explanation of how, if at all, and by when it expects its *margin of solvency* to be adequately restored to the *required margin of solvency*	The firm becoming aware that its *margin of solvency* has fallen below its *required margin of solvency*	28 days
SUP App 2.4.1R	*Insurers*: *scheme of operations* – an *insurer* which is not an *incoming EEA firm* or an *incoming Treaty firm* – *Margin of solvency* below *guarantee fund*	A short term financial plan including: (1) a *scheme of operations* (see SUP App 2.9); and (2) an explanation of how, if at all, and by when it expects its *margin of solvency* to be adequately restored to the *guarantee fund*	The firm becoming aware that its *margin of solvency* has fallen below its *guarantee fund*	14 days
SUP App 2.5.1R	*Insurers*: *scheme of operations* – an *insurer* which is not an *incoming EEA firm* or an *incoming Treaty firm* – ceasing to *effect contracts of insurance*	A run-off plan including: (1) a *scheme of operations* (see SUP App 2.9); and (2) an explanation of how, or to what extent, all *liabilities* to *policyholders* (including where relevant, reasonable bonus expectations) will be met in full as they fall due	The *firm* deciding to cease to *effect* new *contracts of insurance*	28 days
[deleted]	[deleted]	[deleted]	[deleted]	[deleted]

Handbook reference	Matter to be notified	Contents of notification	Trigger event	Time allowed
SUP App 2.10.1R (2) and 2.10.2R	*Insurers*: *scheme of operations* – an *insurer* which is not an *incoming EEA firm* or an *incoming Treaty firm* – obligations on *insurers* which have previously submitted a *scheme of operations*	Quarterly financial return: (a) a summary profit and loss account prepared in accordance with SUP App 2.9.7R; (b) a summary balance sheet prepared in accordance with SUP App 2.9.8R; and (c) a statement of solvency prepared in accordance with SUP App 2.9.9R;	The end of each quarter	Not specified
		and which must identify and explain differences between the actual results and the forecasts submitted in the *scheme of operations*		
SUP App 2.10.1R (3)	*Insurers*: *scheme of operations* – an *insurer* which is not an *incoming EEA firm* or an *incoming Treaty firm* – obligations on *insurers* which have previously submitted a *scheme of operations*	(a) Explanation of the nature of the departure and the reasons for it and provide revised forecast financial information in the *scheme of operations* for its remaining term; or (b) an amended *scheme of operations* and explanation of the amendments and the reasons for them	Any matter which has either happened or is likely to happen and which represents a significant departure from the *scheme of operations*	Promptly

SCHEDULE 4
POWERS EXERCISED

[2181]
Sch4 **[G]**

Sch 4.1

The following powers and related provisions in the *Act* have been exercised by the *FSA* to make the rules in SUP:

(1) Section 59 (Approval for particular arrangements)
(2) Section 118(8) (Market abuse)
(3) Section 138 (General rule-making power)
(4) Section 139(1) and (4) (Miscellaneous ancillary matters)
(5) Section 141 (Insurance business rules)
(6) Section 144 (Price stabilising rules)
(7) Section 145 (Financial promotion rules)
(8) Section 146 (Money laundering rules)
(9) Section 147 (Control of information rules)
(10) Section 149 (Evidential provisions)
(11) Section 150(2) (Actions for damages)

(12) Section 156 (General supplementary powers)
(12A) Section 178 (Obligation to notify the Authority: acquisitions of control)
(12B) Section 191D (Obligation to notify the Authority: dispositions of control)
(13) Section 238(5) (Restrictions on promotion)
(14) Section 247 (Trust scheme rules)
(14AA) Section 293 (Notification requirements)
(14A) Section 318(1) (Exercise of powers through Council)
(15) Section 340 (Appointment)
(15A) Section 341 (Access to books etc.)
(15B) Paragraph 17(1) (Fees) of Schedule 1 (The Financial Services Authority)
(16) Regulations 6(1) (FSA rules) and 12 (Applications for authorisation) of the OEIC Regulations
(17) Article 4(1) of the Financial Services and Markets Act 2000 (Transitional Provisions and Savings) (Rules) Order 2001 (SI 2001/1534)

Sch 4.2

The following power in the *Act* has been exercised by the *FSA* to give the guidance in SUP:
(1) Section 157(1) (Guidance)
(2) Article 11(1) of the Financial Services and Markets Act 2000 (Transitional Provisions and Savings)(Rules) Order 2001 (SI 2001/1534).

Sch 4.3

The following powers and related provisions in or under the *Act* have been exercised by the *FSA* in SUP to direct or require:
(1) Section 51 (Applications under this Part)
(2) Section 60 (Applications for approval)
(3) Section 148(3) (Modification or waiver of rules)
(4) Section 182 (Notification)
(5) Section 250(4) and (5) (Modification or waiver of rules)
(6) Section 316 (Direction by Authority)
(7) Regulation 7(3) and (4) of the OEIC Regulations (Modification of waiver of rules)
(8) Paragraph 5(4) of Schedule 4 (Treaty Rights: Notice to Authority).

SCHEDULE 5
RIGHTS OF ACTIONS FOR DAMAGES

[2182]–[2183]
Sch5 **[G]**

Sch 5.1

1	The table below sets out the *rules* in SUP contravention of which by an *authorised person* may be actionable under section 150 of the *Act* (Actions for damages) by a *person* who suffers loss as a result of the contravention.
2	If a "Yes" appears in the column headed "For private person?", the *rule* may be actionable by a "*private person*" under section 150 (or, in certain circumstances, his fiduciary or representative). A "Yes" in the column headed "Removed" indicates that the *FSA* has removed the right of action under section 150(2) of the *Act*. If so, a reference to the *rule* in which it is removed is also given.
3	The column headed "For other person?" indicates whether the rule is actionable by a *person* other than a *private person* (or his fiduciary or representative). If so, an indication of the type of *person* by whom the *rule* is actionable is given.

Sch 5.2

Actions for damages: Supervision manual

Chapter/ Appendix	Section/ Annex	Paragraph	Right of action under section 150		
			For private person?	Removed?	For other person?
All *rules* in SUP with the status letter "E"			No	No	No
3	8	All *rules* in the section	No	No	No

Chapter/ Appendix	Section/ Annex	Paragraph	Right of action under section 150		
			For private person?	Removed?	For other person?
3	9	All *rules* in the section	No	No	No
3	10	All *rules* in the section	No	No	No
4	3	13	No	No	No
4	3	20	No	No	No
4	4	7	No	No	No
4	4	9	No	No	No
4	5	All *rules* in the section	No	No	No
10	All *rules* in sections SUP 10.1 to SUP 10.10		No	No	No
All other *rules* in SUP			Yes	No	No

SCHEDULE 6

[deleted]

COMPENSATION (COMP)

NOTES

Up to date as at 22 February 2010. For later amendments please see www.fsa.gov.uk.

CONTENTS

COMP 1—Introduction and Overview . . . [2184]
COMP 2—The FSCS . . . [2185]
COMP 3—The qualifying conditions for compensation . . . [2186]
COMP 4—Eligible claimants . . . [2187]
COMP 5—Protected claims . . . [2188]
COMP 6—Relevant persons in default . . . [2189]
COMP 7—Assignment of rights . . . [2190]
COMP 8—Rejection of application and withdrawal of offer . . . [2191]
COMP 9—Time limits on payment and postponing payment . . . [2192]
COMP 10—Limits on the amount of compensation payable . . . [2193]
COMP 11—Payment of compensation . . . [2194]
COMP 12—Calculating compensation . . . [2195]
COMP 13—Funding . . . [2196]
COMP 14—Participation by EEA Firms . . . [2197]
COMP 15—Accelerated compensation for depositors . . . [2197A]
COMP 16—Disclosure requirements for firms that accept deposits . . . [2197B]
COMP TP 1—Transitional Provisions . . . [2198]
COMP Sch 1—Record-keeping requirements . . . [2199]
COMP Sch 2—Notification requirements . . . [2200]
COMP Sch 3—Fees and other required payments . . . [2201]
COMP Sch 4—Powers Exercised . . . [2202]
COMP Sch 5—Rights of action for damages . . . [2203]
COMP Sch 6—Rules that can be waived . . . [2204]

FOREWORD TO THE COMPENSATION SOURCEBOOK

(This Foreword to the Compensation Sourcebook does not form part of COMP.)

The Act requires the FSA to make rules establishing a scheme for compensating consumers when authorised firms are unable, or likely to be unable, to satisfy claims against them. The body established to operate and administer the compensation scheme is the Financial Services Compensation Scheme Limited (FSCS). By making rules that allow the FSCS to pay compensation to retail consumers and small businesses, focusing protection on those who need it most, the compensation scheme rules form an important part of the toolkit the FSA will use to meet its statutory objectives.

This module of the FSA Handbook contains the rules and guidance that allow the Financial Services Compensation Scheme Limited to pay claims for compensation or secure continuity of insurance when an authorised person is unable or likely to be unable to meet claims against it. The rules specify who is eligible to receive compensation and in what circumstances, how much compensation can be paid to a claimant; and how the scheme will be funded. The compensation rules, although of interest to consumers and authorised firms, do not in fact apply to either. The rules only apply to the FSCS.

The Sourcebook is divided into 16 Chapters covering all aspects of the scheme:

Chapter 1: Introduction and Overview

This chapter provides an introduction to the FSCS rules and a table of question and answers that may be of interest to consumers.

Chapter 2: The FSCS

This chapter gives the FSCS the duty to administer the compensation scheme. It also sets out the general conditions the FSCS must follow when administering the scheme such as having regard to the efficient and economic use of resources, the requirement to publish an Annual Report, and the duty to ensure consumers are informed about how they can make a claim. The rules in this chapter also require the FSCS to have in place procedures for dealing with complaints.

Chapter 3: The qualifying conditions for paying compensation

This chapter sets out the main qualifying conditions that must be satisfied before the FSCS can pay compensation to claimants or take steps to secure continuity of insurance. These are that a claimant

Part II FSA Handbook Materials

is eligible to claim; the activity that gave rise to the loss is protected by the scheme; the firm against which the claim is being made is protected by the scheme; and that the claimant has assigned his rights to the scheme. Chapters 4–7 expand on the general conditions described in Chapter 3.

Chapter 4: Eligible claimants

This chapter specifies who is eligible to receive compensation or benefit from the continuity of insurance provided by the FSCS.

Chapter 5: What is a protected claim?

This chapter specifies the activities that are protected by the FSCS.

Chapter 6: Relevant persons in default

This chapter specifies the circumstances when a firm is in default, that is, when a firm is to be taken as being unable or likely to be unable to meet claims against it. The FSCS can only pay compensation, take steps to secure continuity of insurance, or provide assistance to an insurer in financial difficulties if the circumstances specified in Chapter 6 are met.

Chapter 7: Assignment of rights

This chapter enables the FSCS to make an offer of compensation conditional on the claimant assigning to it their rights to claim against the failed firm. If the FSCS recovers from the firm a greater sum than it has paid to the claimant, it must pay the balance to the claimant.

Chapter 8: Rejection of application and withdrawal of offer

This chapter allows the FSCS to reject an application for compensation or withdraw an offer of compensation in specified circumstances.

Chapter 9: Time limits on payment and postponing payment

This chapter requires the FSCS to pay a claim for compensation within a specified time unless specified conditions apply.

Chapter 10: Limits on the amount of compensation payable

This chapter specifies the maximum amount of compensation the FSCS can pay to a claimant, and the limits on the FSCS's duty to secure continuity of insurance for policyholders. Different limits apply depending on whether the claim is for a deposit, a claim on an insurance policy, or a claim in connection with an investment.

Chapter 11: Payment of compensation

This chapter specifies to whom the FSCS may pay compensation. In certain circumstances compensation may be paid to a person other than the claimant.

Chapter 12: Calculating compensation

This chapter specifies how the FSCS will calculate the amount of compensation it can pay to a claimant.

Chapter 13: Funding

This chapter allows the FSCS to makes levies on authorised firms to fund the operation of the scheme, to pay compensation or secure continuity of insurance. It specifies how FSCS can make levies, how costs are to be allocated, the maximum the FSCS can levy in any particular period of time, and how sums recovered from failed firms are to be treated.

Chapter 14: Participation by EEA firms

This chapter sets out the way the FSCS deals with incoming EEA firms who may choose to top-up into the FSCS to supplement the compensation available from their home state scheme.

Chapter 15: Deposit payout

This chapter provides for the FSCS to have powers to accelerate the payment of compensation for protected deposits, providing that certain conditions are met. These powers include the ability to make payments without having first received an application form from claimants, the power to pay compensation directly into a claimant's account with another authorised person, and the power to pay compensation on behalf of another compensation scheme or government and to recover the sums paid.

Chapter 16: Disclosure requirements for firms that accept deposits

This chapter sets out the format, frequency and method of communication that deposit-taking firms must use in informing eligible customers that their deposits are covered by the FSCS. It also requires deposit-taking firms to inform their customers if their deposits are not covered by the FSCS.

CHAPTER 1
INTRODUCTION AND OVERVIEW

1.1 Application, Introduction, and Purpose

Application

[2184]
1.1.1 **[G]** This chapter is relevant to:
(1) the *FSCS*;
(2) *eligible claimants*; and
(3) *firms*.

1.1.2 **[G]** This sourcebook is principally relevant to the *FSCS*. It sets out the circumstances in which compensation may be paid, to whom compensation may be paid, and on whom the *FSCS* can impose levies to meet the costs of paying compensation (see in particular COMP 3, 4, and FEES 6). It also describes how the *FSCS* is to calculate compensation in particular cases (see COMP 12).

1.1.3 **[G]** Claimants and their advisers will be particularly interested in the sections of this sourcebook which deal with eligibility for claiming compensation, the way that the *FSCS* calculates compensation, and how they can make a claim. For convenience, the relevant parts of this sourcebook are highlighted in a list of questions and answers in COMP 1.3.3G.

1.1.4 **[G]** *Firms* will be particularly interested in FEES 6, which deals with levies and COMP 16 which deals with disclosure requirements for *firms* that accept deposits.

Introduction

1.1.5 **[G]** Under section 212 of the *Act* (The scheme manager), the *FSA* must establish a body corporate to exercise the functions that are conferred on that body corporate by Part XV of the *Act*, dealing with compensation. This body is the Financial Services Compensation Scheme Limited, a company limited by guarantee (*FSCS*).

1.1.6 **[G]** The *FSA* is also required, under section 213 of the *Act* (The compensation scheme), to make *rules* establishing a compensation scheme. These *rules* are set out in the remaining chapters of this sourcebook, and are directed to the *FSCS*, claimants and potential claimants, and *firms*.

Purpose

1.1.7 **[G]** The *FSCS* will only pay *claims* if a *firm* is unable or likely to be unable to meet *claims* against it because of its financial circumstances. If a *firm* is still trading and has sufficient financial resources to satisfy a *claim*, the *firm* will be expected to meet the *claim* itself. This can, for example, be an amount the *firm* agrees with the claimant, or the amount of an *Ombudsman* award from the *Financial Ombudsman Service*.

1.1.8 **[G]** COMP 1 consists of *guidance* which is aimed at giving an overview of how this sourcebook works. The provisions of COMP 2 to 16 cover who is eligible, the amount of compensation and how it might be paid, and disclosure requirements for *firms* that *accept deposits*.

1.1.9 **[G]** This sourcebook is one of the means by which the *FSA* will meet its *regulatory objectives* of securing the appropriate degree of protection for *consumers* and maintaining confidence in the *financial system*.

1.1.10 **[G]** By setting up the *FSCS* and making *rules* that allow the *FSCS* to provide compensation at a level appropriate for the protection of retail *consumers* and *small businesses*, the *FSA* enables *consumers* to participate in the financial markets with the confidence that they will be protected, at least in part, should the *relevant person* with whom they are dealing be unable to satisfy *claims* against it.

1.2 The FSCS

1.2.1 **[G]** While this sourcebook deals with the main powers and duties of the *FSCS*, it does not provide the complete picture. Other aspects of the operation of the *FSCS* are dealt with through the powers of the Financial Services Compensation Scheme Limited under company law (such as the power to borrow, to take on premises, etc.).

1.2.2 **[G]**
(1) In addition, the *Act* itself confers certain powers upon the *FSCS*, such as a power under section 219 of the *Act* (Scheme Manager's powers to require information) to require *persons* to provide information. These powers are not, therefore, covered by this sourcebook.
(2) Of specific relevance to the way in which the *FSCS* fulfils its responsibilities is the relationship between the *FSCS* and the *FSA*. This is covered in a Memorandum of Understanding which can be found on the *FSA* website www.fsa.gov.uk.

1.3 Claimants

1.3.1 **[G]** The *FSCS* also provides information to claimants and potential claimants about the way the *FSCS* works and the procedures that need to be followed when making a *claim*. The *FSCS* can be contacted at 7th Floor, Lloyds Chambers, 1 Portsoken Street, London E1 8BN, or by telephone or fax (Tel: 020 7892 7300 or Fax: 020 7892 7301), or by e-mail (enquiries@fscs.org.uk).

1.3.2 **[G]** Information about the operation of the *FSCS* and how to claim is also available from the *FSCS* website (www.fscs.org.uk).

1.3.3 **[G]** This Table belongs to COMP 1.1.3G.

Q1	**What do I need to do in order to receive compensation?**		
A1	In order to receive compensation:		
	(1)	you must be an *eligible claimant*;	COMP 4.2–3
	(2)	you must have a *protected claim*;	COMP 5.2–6
	(3)	you must be claiming against a *relevant person*;	COMP 6.2.1R
	(4)	the *relevant person* must be *in default*.	COMP 6.3
	In addition, if the *FSCS* requires you to do so, you must assign your legal rights in the claim to the *FSCS*.		COMP 7.2
	And you must bring your claim to the *FSCS* within a set time (normally within six years of the date on which your claim against the *relevant person* occurred).		COMP 8.2.3R–8.2.5R
	It is possible, in certain circumstances, for someone else to make a *claim* on your behalf.		COMP 3.2.2R
Q2	**How much compensation will I be offered?**		
A2	This depends on whether your *protected claim* is:		
	(1)	a *claim* for a *protected deposit* or a *protected dormant account*; or	COMP 5.3
	(2)	a *claim* under a *protected contract of insurance*; or	COMP 5.4
	(3)	a *claim* in connection with *protected investment business*.	COMP 5.5
	(4)	a *claim* in connection with *protected home finance mediation*.	COMP 5.6
	Different limits apply to different types of *claim*.		COMP 10.2.3R
Q3	**How will the FSCS calculate the compensation that is offered to me?**		
A3	Again, this will depend on whether your *protected claim* is a:		
	(1)	a *claim* for a *protected deposit* or a *protected dormant account*; or	COMP 12.2.1R, 12.3.1R, and 12.4.1R
	(2)	a *claim* under a *protected contract of insurance*; or	COMP 12.2.1R, 12.3.2–4R, and 12.4.9R–12.4.16R
	(3)	a *claim* in connection with *protected investment business*; or	COMP 12.2.1R, 12.3.5–6R, and 12.4.2–8R
	(4)	a *claim* in connection with *protected home finance mediation*; or	COMP 12.4.17–19R
	(5)	a *claim* in connection with *protected non-investment insurance mediation*.	COMP 12.4.17R–18R
	Certain types of *protected investment business claim* require the *FSCS* to use a particular method of calculation.		COMP 12.4.5–7R
Q4	**What happens if an insurance undertaking is insolvent?**		

A4	If you have a *long term insurance contract* which is not a *reinsurance contract* with an insolvent *insurance undertaking*, the *FSCS* will first try to secure continuity of insurance for you.	COMP 3.3, 11.2.3R, and 12.4.11R
	If the *FSCS* achieves this, you will not necessarily receive any cash, but you will continue to be insured (though possibly with lower benefits than before).	COMP 3.3R and 11.2.3R
	You will receive cash compensation only if the *FSCS* cannot secure continuity of insurance cover or the cost of doing so would be unreasonable.	COMP 3.3.1–2ER, and 11.2.1R
	If you have a *relevant general insurance contract* which is not a *reinsurance contract* with an insolvent *insurance undertaking*, the *FSCS* will pay you cash compensation if it is unable to secure continuity of insurance cover or the cost of doing so would be unreasonable.	COMP 3.2.1–2R and 11.2.3R
	If the *insurance undertaking* is in "financial difficulties", the *FSCS* may try to arrange for another *insurance undertaking* to take over the *business*, or provide the *insurance undertaking* with financial assistance to carry on business. If this occurs, you will not receive cash compensation, but your policy will continue (though possibly with lower benefits than before).	COMP 3.3.3–6R and 11.2.3R

1.4 EEA Firms

1.4.1 **[G]** *Incoming EEA firms* which are conducting *regulated activities* in the *United Kingdom* under a *BCD*, *IMD*, *ISD* or *UCITS Directive* passport are not required to participate in the *compensation scheme* in relation to those *passported activities*. They may apply to obtain the cover of, or 'top up' into, the *compensation scheme* if there is no cover provided by the *incoming EEA firm's Home State* compensation scheme or if the level or scope of the cover is less than that provided by the *compensation scheme*. This is covered by COMP 14.

1.4.2 **[G]** If an *incoming EEA firm* "tops-up", and then becomes insolvent, the *Home State* compensation scheme will pay compensation for *claims* up to the limit and scope of the *Home State* compensation scheme, with the *FSCS* paying compensation for the additional amount in accordance with the provisions in this sourcebook.

1.4.3 **[G]** The *DGD* and *ICD* require the *FSCS* to make arrangements with the relevant *Home State* compensation scheme regarding the payment of compensation (COMP 14.3.1R).

1.5 Application to Lloyd's

1.5.1 **[G]** The *FSA* has exercised its power under section 316 of the *Act* (Direction by Authority) to direct in COMP 1.5.5D that certain *core provisions* in the *Act* should apply to *members* of the *Society* of Lloyd's (an "*insurance market direction*"). The effect of the direction is that the *FSA* may, in relation to *members*, and in respect of *insurance market activities* carried on by them, exercise any of the statutory powers conferred by the provisions which are applied by the direction. Those include the powers in Part X to make general *rules* and give *guidance* and also the powers in Part XV to make *rules* for the establishment and operation of a compensation scheme. Accordingly this sourcebook makes provision for the payment of compensation by the *FSCS* in certain cases arising from *insurance business* carried on by *members*, and for raising levies on the *Society*.

1.5.2 **[R]** Notwithstanding anything to the contrary in this sourcebook, in relation to the *Society*, *members* and *Lloyd's policies FSCS* must act, so far as is reasonably practicable, to ensure that:

(1) *Eligible claimants* have protection under this sourcebook in relation to *Lloyd's policies* equivalent to that otherwise afforded to *eligible claimants* by the *FSCS*;

(2) *FSCS* does not meet *claims* in relation to *Lloyd's policies* unless the *Central Fund* is unlikely to be able to meet them;

(3) *Claims* against *members* under the *compensation scheme* which arise from the same loss under the same *Lloyd's policy* must be treated as a single *claim*;

(4) any recovery resulting from the exercise of any rights assigned to the *FSCS* in connection with the payment of compensation to an *eligible claimant*, is treated by the *FSCS* in accordance with COMP 7.2.4R, and any such recovery which is not paid to the claimant in accordance with that rule, is used for the benefit of *FSCS* in priority to any interest that the *Society* may have.

1.5.3 **[G]** The effect of COMP 1.5.2 R(4) and COMP 7.2.4AR, and subject to 7.2.4 R(2), is that any recovery obtained by *FSCS* is retained by *FSCS* up to an amount equal to the cost to *FSCS* of paying compensation. To the extent that the *Society* is entitled to any part of the recovery (for example by agreement with *FSCS*) it is only paid out of any excess up to a maximum amount equal to that paid out of the *Central Fund*. Any recovery in excess of the compensation (including payment from the *Central Fund*) received by the policyholder is paid to the claimant in accordance with COMP 7.2.4R regardless of whether the *Society* receives the full amount paid from the *Central Fund*.

Compensation arrangements for policyholders

1.5.4 **[G]** The *insurance market direction* in COMP 1.5.5D is intended to protect the interests of *policyholders* and potential *policyholders* by:

(1) providing for the application of the *compensation scheme* in respect of *contracts of insurance* issued by *members*; and

(2) providing for the application of such other provisions of the *Act* as will enable the application of the *compensation scheme* to be effective in relation to *insurance market activities* carried on by *members*.

1.5.5 **[D]** With effect from 15 October 2003 the following *core provisions* of the *Act* apply to the carrying on of *insurance market activities* by *members*:

(1) Part X (Rules and guidance) for the purpose of applying the *rules* in COMP and relevant interpretative provisions; and

(2) Part XV (Financial Services Compensation Scheme).

1.5.6 **[G]** Section 317(2) of the *Act* (The core provisions) provides that references in an applied *core provision* to an *authorised person* are to be read as references to a *person* in the class to which the *insurance market direction* applies. In particular, with effect from 15 October 2003, references to a *relevant person* in Part XV of the *Act* include a person who was a *member* at the time the act or omission giving rise to the claim against him took place.

Compensation arrangements for individual members

1.5.7 **[G]** The *compensation scheme* will not compensate *members* or *former members* if *firms* are unable to satisfy claims made in connection with *regulated activities* relating to their participation in Lloyd's *syndicates*. Separate *rules* and *guidance* are therefore needed.

1.5.8 **[R]** The *Society* must maintain *byelaws* establishing appropriate and effective arrangements to compensate *individual members* and *former members* who were *individual members* if *underwriting agents* are unable, or likely to be unable, to satisfy claims by those *members* relating to *regulated activities* carried on in connection with their participation in Lloyd's *syndicates*.

1.5.9 **[R]** For the purposes of COMP 1.5.8R "*individual member*" includes a *member* which is a *limited liability partnership* or a *body corporate* whose members consist only of, or of the nominees for, a single natural person or a group of connected persons.

1.5.10 **[G]** The arrangements referred to in COMP 1.5.8R:

(1) will not compensate losses arising only as a result of underwriting or investment risk to which *individual members* or *former members* who were *individual members* are or were exposed by their participation in Lloyd's *syndicates*;

(2) may be restricted to compensation for losses arising out of fraud, dishonesty or failure to account; and

(3) should cover all *regulated activities* carried on by *underwriting agents* relating to Lloyd's *syndicate* capacity and *syndicate* membership.

1.5.11 **[G]** The arrangements referred to in COMP 1.5.8R should have a governance structure that is operationally independent from the *Society*, but which is nevertheless accountable to the *Society* for the proper administration of the compensation arrangements.

1.5.12 **[R]** A contravention of COMP 1.5.8R does not give rise to a right of action by a *private person* under section 150 of the *Act* (Actions for damages) and that *rule* is specified under section 150(2) of the *Act* as a provision giving rise to no such right of action.

CHAPTER 2
THE FSCS

2.1 Application and Purpose

Application

[2185]

2.1.1 **[R]** This chapter applies to the *FSCS*.

Purpose

2.1.2 **[G]** In order to carry out its functions and put into effect the provisions set out in COMP 13 – COMP 14 (which deal with determining whether compensation is payable, calculating the amount of compensation that should be paid, and making levies on *firms*), the *FSCS* needs to have a variety of powers. The purpose of this chapter is to set out these powers, and the restrictions upon them.

2.2 Duties of the FSCS

Administering the compensation scheme

2.2.1 **[R]** The *FSCS* must administer the *compensation scheme* in accordance with the *rules* in this sourcebook and any other rules prescribed by law to ensure that the *compensation scheme* is administered in a manner that is procedurally fair and in accordance with the European Convention on Human Rights.

2.2.2 **[G]** The *FSCS* may:

(1) pay compensation to *eligible claimants* or secure continuity of insurance for *eligible claimants* when a *relevant person* is unable or likely to be unable to meet *claims* against it in accordance with the sourcebook; and

(2) make levies on *participant firms*, in accordance with FEES 6 (Financial Services Compensation Scheme Funding), to enable it to pay compensation, secure continuity of insurance, or meet the costs of discharging its functions under this sourcebook.

Information for claimants

2.2.3 **[R]** The *FSCS* must publish information for claimants and potential claimants on the operation of the *compensation scheme*.

Assistance to claimants

2.2.4 **[R]** The *FSCS* may agree to pay the reasonable costs of an *eligible claimant* bringing or continuing insolvency proceedings against a *relevant person* (whether those proceedings began before or after a determination of default), if the *FSCS* is satisfied that those proceedings would help it to discharge its functions under the requirements of this sourcebook.

Annual Report

2.2.5 **[G]** The *FSCS* must make and publish an annual report to the *FSA* on the discharge of its functions (section 218 of the *Act* (Annual report)).

Finance and resources

2.2.6 **[R]** The *FSCS* must have regard to the need to use its resources in the most efficient and economic way in carrying out its functions under the requirements of this sourcebook.

Publication of defaults

2.2.7 **[R]** The *FSCS* must take appropriate steps to ensure that potential claimants are informed of how they can make a *claim* for compensation as soon as possible after a determination has been made that a *relevant person* is *in default*, whether by the *FSCS* or the *FSA*.

Complaints

2.2.8 **[R]** The *FSCS* must put in place and publish procedures which satisfy the minimum requirements of procedural fairness and comply with the European Convention on Humans Rights for the handling of any complaints of maladministration relating to any aspect of the operation of the *compensation scheme*.

Informing the FSCS

2.2.9 **[G]** The *FSA* will inform the *FSCS* if it detects problems in a *firm* that is likely to give rise to the intervention of the *FSCS*.
[**Note**: article 10(1), part of last sub-paragraph of the *Deposit Guarantee Directive*]

CHAPTER 3
THE QUALIFYING CONDITIONS FOR COMPENSATION

3.1 Application and Purpose

Application

[2186]
3.1.1 **[R]** This chapter applies to the *FSCS*.

3.1.2 **[G]** It is also relevant to claimants.

Part II FSA Handbook Materials

Purpose

3.1.3 **[G]** The purpose of this chapter is to set out in general terms the conditions that must be satisfied before the *FSCS* can make an offer of compensation, or secure continuity of insurance cover, or provide assistance to an *insurance undertaking* to enable it to continue *insurance business*.

3.1.4 **[G]** The qualifying conditions for paying compensation are set out in greater detail in COMP 4–COMP 7.

3.2 The qualifying conditions for paying compensation

3.2.1 **[R]** The *FSCS* may pay compensation to an *eligible claimant*, subject to COMP 11 (Payment of compensation), if it is satisfied that:

(1) an *eligible claimant* has, for *claims* other than *claims* under a *protected contract of insurance*, made an application for compensation;

(2) the claim is in respect of a *protected claim* against a *relevant person* who is *in default*;

(3) where the *FSCS* so requires, the claimant has assigned the whole or any part of his rights against the *relevant person* or against any third party to the *FSCS*, on such terms as the *FSCS* thinks fit; and

(4) in the case of a *claim* under a *protected contract of insurance*:

 (a) it is not reasonably practicable or appropriate to make, or continue to make, arrangements to secure continuity of insurance under COMP 3.3.1R; or

 (b) it would not be appropriate to take, or continue to take, measures under COMP 3.3.3R to safeguard policyholders of an *insurance undertaking* in financial difficulties.

3.2.2 **[R]** The *FSCS* may also pay compensation (and any recovery or other amount payable by the *FSCS* to the claimant) to a *person* who makes a *claim* on behalf of another *person* if the *FSCS* is satisfied that the *person* on whose behalf the *claim* is made:

(1) is or would have been an *eligible claimant*; and

(2) would have been paid compensation by the *FSCS* had he been able to make the *claim* himself, or to pursue his application for compensation further.

3.2.3 **[G]** Examples of the circumstances covered by COMP 3.2.2R are:

(1) when personal representatives make a *claim* on behalf of the deceased;

(2) when trustees make a *claim* on behalf of beneficiaries (for further provisions relating to *claims* by trustees, see COMP 12.6.1 to COMP 12.6.7R);

(3) when the donee of an enduring power of attorney or a lasting power of attorney makes a *claim* on behalf of the donor of the power;

(4) when the Court of Protection makes a *claim* on behalf of a *person* incapable by reason of mental disorder of managing and administering his property and affairs;

(5) when an *eligible claimant* makes a *claim* for compensation but dies before his *claim* is determined.

3.2.4 **[R]** The *FSCS* may also pay compensation to a *firm*, who makes a claim in connection with *protected non-investment insurance mediation* on behalf of its *customers*, if the *FSCS* is satisfied that:

(1) each *customer* has borne a *shortfall* in *client money* held by the *firm* caused by a *secondary pooling event* arising out of the *failure* of a broker or *settlement agent* which is a *relevant person in default*;

(2) the *customers* in respect of which compensation is to be paid satisfy the conditions set out in COMP 3.2.2R(1);

(3) the *customers* do not have a *claim* against the *relevant person* directly, nor a claim against the *firm*, in respect of the same loss;

(4) the *customers* would have been paid compensation by *FSCS* if the *customers* had a *claim* for their share of the *shortfall*, and if the *firm* were the *relevant person*; and

(5) the *firm* has agreed, on such terms as the *FSCS* thinks fit, to pay, or credit the accounts of, without deduction, each relevant *customer* in (1), that part of the compensation equal to the *customer's* financial loss, subject to the limits in COMP 10.2.

3.3 Insurance

Securing continuity of long term insurance cover

3.3.1 **[R]** The *FSCS* must make arrangements to secure continuity of insurance for an *eligible claimant* under a *protected contract of insurance* which is a *long term insurance contract* with a *relevant person*, if:

(1) the *relevant person* is the subject of any of the proceedings listed in COMP 6.3.3R(1)–(5); and

(2) it is reasonably practicable to do so;

(3) in the opinion of the *FSCS* at the time it proposes to make the arrangements, it would be beneficial to the generality of *eligible claimants* covered by the proposed arrangements, and, in situations where the cost of securing continuity of insurance might exceed the cost of paying compensation under COMP 3.2, any additional cost is likely to be justified by the benefits; and

(4) where the *relevant person* is a *member*, the *FSCS* is satisfied that the amounts which the *Society* is able to provide from the *Central Fund* are or are likely to be insufficient to ensure that *claims* against the *member* under a *protected contract of insurance* will be met to the level of protection which would otherwise be available under this sourcebook.

3.3.2 **[R]** In order to secure continuity of insurance under COMP 3.3.1R the *FSCS* may take such measures as it considers appropriate to:

(1) secure or facilitate the transfer of the business of the *relevant person in default* which consists of carrying out *long-term insurance contracts* or any part of that business, to another *firm*; and

(2) secure the issue of policies by another *firm* to *eligible claimants* in substitution for their existing policies.

3.3.2A **[R]** The *FSCS's* duty under COMP 3.3.1R and COMP 3.3.3R in respect of a *long term insurance contract* is limited to ensuring that the claimant will receive at least 90% of any benefit under his *contract of insurance*, subject to and in accordance with terms corresponding (so far as it appears to the *FSCS* to be reasonable in the circumstances) to those which have applied under the *contract of insurance*.

3.3.2B **[R]** If the *FSCS* secures less than 100% of any benefit of a claimant under a contract, then FSCS must ensure that any future *premiums* that the claimant is committed to paying under the contract will be reduced by an equivalent amount.

3.32C **[R]**

(1) In any period when the *FSCS* is seeking to secure continuity of insurance under COMP 3.3.1R, it must secure that 90% of any benefit under a *long term insurance contract* which:
    (a) falls due, or would have fallen due, to be paid to any *eligible claimant*; or
    (b) had already fallen due to be paid to any *eligible claimant* before the beginning of that period and has not yet been paid; is paid to the *eligible claimant* in question as soon as reasonably practicable after the time when the benefit in question fell due, or would have fallen due under the contract.

(2) A payment under (1) is made subject to and in accordance with any other terms which apply or would have applied under the contract.

(3) A payment made under (1) is not subject to the *FSCS* deciding that the cost of making the payment would be likely to be no more than the cost of paying compensation under COMP 3.2.

(4) Where a payment is due under (1), *FSCS* may:
    (a) make payments to or on behalf of *eligible claimants* on such terms (including any terms requiring repayment in whole or in part) and on such conditions as it thinks fit (subject to (1)); or
    (b) secure that payments (subject to (1)) are made to or on behalf of any such *eligible claimants* by the liquidator, administrator or provisional liquidator by giving him an indemnity covering any such payments or any class or description of such payments.

3.3.2D For the purposes of COMP 3.3.2AR to COMP 3.3.2CR, "benefit" does not include:

(1) any bonus provided for under the contract unless it was declared and vested before the *insurance undertaking* became the subject of one or more of the proceedings listed in COMP 6.3.3R(1) to (5); or

(2) any reduction which the *FSCS* has determined, or any benefit which the *FSCS* has decided to disregard under COMP 12.4.14R, to the extent that the *FSCS* has decided so to treat it.

3.3.2E **[R]** Unless the *FSCS* has decided to treat the liability of the *relevant person* under the contract as reduced or (as the case may be) disregarded under COMP 12.4.14R, it must not treat as a reason for failing to secure, or for delaying the securing of, payments under COMP 3.3.2CR at the level prescribed in that *rule* the fact that:

(1) it considers that any benefit referred to in COMP 3.3.2CR is or may be excessive in any respect; or

(2) it has referred the contract in question to an independent actuary under COMP 12.4.13 R; or

(3) it considers that it may at some later date decide to treat the liability of the *relevant person* under a contract as reduced or disregarded under COMP 12.4.14 R;

save where the *FSCS* decides to exclude certain benefits to the extent that they arise out of the exercise of any option under the policy and for this purpose the option includes, but is not restricted to, a right to surrender the policy.

3.3.2F **[R]** In making arrangements to secure continuity of insurance the *FSCS* must use its reasonable endeavours to seek the most cost-effective arrangements available.

Insurance undertakings in financial difficulties

3.3.3 **[R]**

(1) The *FSCS* may take such measures as it considers appropriate for the purpose of safeguarding the rights of *eligible claimants* under *protected contracts of insurance* which are:

 (a) *general insurance contracts* with a *relevant person* which is an *insurance undertaking* in financial difficulties (see COMP 3.3.6R); or

 (b) *long-term insurance contracts* with a *relevant person* which is an *insurance undertaking* in financial difficulties (see COMP 3.3.6R) but in respect of which the *FSCS* is not securing continuity of insurance within COMP 3.3.1R;

 if, in the opinion of the *FSCS* at the time it proposes to make the measures, it would be beneficial to the generality of *eligible claimants* covered by the proposed measures, and, in situations where the cost of taking those measures might exceed the cost of paying compensation under COMP 3.2, any additional cost is likely to be justified by the benefits.

(2) Measures under (1) may be taken on such terms (including terms reducing or deferring payment of any liabilities or benefits provided under any *protected contract of insurance*) as the *FSCS* considers appropriate.

3.3.4 **[R]** The measures contemplated in COMP 3.3.3R include measures to:

(1) secure or facilitate the transfer of the *insurance business* of the *relevant person*, or any part of the business, to another *firm*;

(2) give assistance to the *relevant person* to enable it to continue to *effect contracts of insurance* or *carry out contracts of insurance*; and

(3) secure the issue of policies by another *firm* to *eligible claimants* in substitution for their existing policies.

3.3.4A **[R]** If it thinks appropriate, the *FSA* may in relation to any *insurance undertaking* which is in financial difficulties:

(1) give the *FSCS* assistance in determining what measures under COMP 3.3.3R are practicable or desirable;

(2) impose constraints on the measures which may be taken by the *FSCS* under COMP 3.3.3R;

(3) require the *FSCS* to provide it with information about any measures which it is proposing to take under COMP 3.3.3R.

3.3.5 **[R]** [deleted]

3.3.6 **[R]** For the purpose of COMP 3.3.3R and COMP 3.3.4AR, a *relevant person* which is an *insurance undertaking* is in financial difficulties if any of the following events occurs:

(1) a liquidator, administrator, provisional liquidator, administrative receiver or interim manager is appointed to the *relevant person*, or a receiver is appointed by the court to manage the *relevant person's* affairs; or

(2) there is a finding by a court of competent jurisdiction that the *relevant person* is unable to pay its debts; or

(3) a resolution is passed for winding up of the *relevant person*, unless a declaration of solvency has been made in accordance with section 89 of the Insolvency Act 1986; or

(4) the *FSA* determines that the *relevant person* is unable or likely to be unable to satisfy *protected claims* against it; or

(5) approval is given to any company voluntary arrangement made by the *relevant person*; or

(6) the *relevant person* makes a composition or arrangement with any one or more of its creditors providing for the reduction of, or deferral of payment of, the liabilities or benefits provided for under any of the *relevant person's* policies; or

(7) the *relevant person* is dissolved or struck off from the Register of Companies; or

(8) a receiver is appointed over particular property of the *relevant person*; or

(9) any of (1) to (8) or anything equivalent occurs in respect of the *relevant person* in a jurisdiction outside England and Wales; or

(10) in the case of an *insurance undertaking* which is a *member*, the *FSCS* is satisfied that any of sub-paragraphs (1) to (9) apply to the *member*, and the amounts which the *Society* is able to provide from the *Central Fund* are or are likely to be insufficient to ensure that *claims* against the *member* under a *protected contract of insurance* will be met to the level of protection which would otherwise be available under this sourcebook.

Assessing the costs of paying compensation

3.3.7 **[R]** For the purposes of COMP 3.3.1R(3) and COMP 3.3.3R(1), when assessing the cost of paying compensation under COMP 3.2 *FSCS* may have regard to the likely total cost of paying compensation arising out of the default, not just the compensation amounts likely to be payable to particular eligible claimants covered by the proposed arrangements for continuity.

CHAPTER 4
ELIGIBLE CLAIMANTS

4.1 Application and Purpose

Application

[2187]
4.1.1 **[R]** This chapter applies to the *FSCS*.

4.1.2 **[G]** It is also relevant to those who may wish to bring a *claim* for compensation.

Purpose

4.1.3 **[G]** The purpose of this chapter is to set out the types of *person* who are able to claim compensation or benefit from the protection the *FSCS* is able to provide. A claimant needs to be an *eligible claimant* to satisfy COMP 3.2.1G.

4.2 Who is eligible to benefit from the protection provided by the FSCS?

4.2.1 **[R]** Unless COMP 4.2.3R applies, an *eligible claimant* is any *person* who at any material time:
(1) did not come within COMP 4.2.2R; or
(2) did come within COMP 4.2.2R, but satisfied the relevant exception in COMP 4.3 or COMP 4.4.

4.2.2 **[R]** Table COMP 4.2.2R Persons not eligible to claim unless COMP 4.3 applies (see COMP 4.2.1R).

This table belongs to COMP 4.2.1R

(1)	*Firms* (other than a *sole trader firm*; a *credit union*; a trustee of a *stakeholder pension scheme* (which is not an *occupational pension scheme*) or *personal pension scheme*; a *firm* carrying on the *regulated activity* of *operating*, or *winding up*, a *stakeholder pension scheme* (which is not an *occupational pension scheme*) or *personal pension scheme*; or a *small business*; in each case, whose *claim* arises out of a *regulated activity* for which they do not have a *permission*).		
(2)	*Overseas financial services institutions.*		
(3)	*Collective investment schemes*, and anyone who is the operator or trustee of such a scheme.		
(4)	Pension and *retirement funds*, and anyone who is a trustee of such a fund. However, this exclusion does not apply to:		
	(a)	a trustee of a *personal pension scheme* or a *stakeholder pension scheme* (which is not an *occupational pension scheme*); or	
	(b)	a trustee of a *small self-administered scheme* or an *occupational pension scheme* of an employer which is not a *large company*, *large partnership*, or *large mutual association*).	
(5)	Supranational institutions, governments, and central administrative authorities.		
(6)	Provincial, regional, local and municipal authorities.		
(7)	*Directors* and *managers* of the *relevant person in default*. However, this exclusion does not apply if:		
	(a)	both of the following apply:	
		(i)	the *relevant person in default* is a mutual association which is not a *large mutual association*; and
		(ii)	the *directors* and *managers* do not receive a salary or other remuneration for services performed by them for the *relevant person in default*, or
	(b)	the *relevant person in default* is a *credit union*.	
(8)	*Close relatives* of *persons* excluded by (7) above.		
(9)	Bodies corporate in the same *group* as the *relevant person in default* unless that *body corporate* is:		
	(i)	a trustee that falls within COMP 4.2.2 R(1) or (4); or	
	(ii)	carrying on the *regulated activity* of *operating*, or *winding up*, a *stakeholder pension scheme* (which is not an *occupational pension scheme*) or *personal pension scheme*.	

(10)	*Persons* holding 5% or more of the capital of the *relevant person in default*, or of any body corporate in the same *group*.
(11)	The auditors of the *relevant person in default*, or of any *body corporate* in the same *group* as the *relevant person in default*, or any *actuary* appointed under SUP 4 (Actuaries) by a *friendly society* or *insurance undertaking in default*.
(12)	*Persons* who in the opinion of the *FSCS* are responsible for, or have contributed to, the *relevant person's* default.
(13)	*Large companies* or *large mutual associations*.
(14)	Where the *claim* is in relation to *a protected contract of insurance* or *protected non-investment insurance mediation, bodies corporate, partnerships*, mutual associations and unincorporated associations which are not *small businesses*.
(15)	*Persons* whose claim arises from transactions in connection with which they have been convicted of an *offence* of money laundering.
(16)	*Persons* whose claim arises under the Third Parties (Rights against Insurers) Act 1930.
(17)	Where the *claim* is in relation to *a protected contract of insurance* or *protected non-investment insurance mediation, bodies corporate, partnerships*, mutual associations and unincorporated associations which are not *small businesses*.

4.2.3 **[R]** A *person* who is a *small business* is an *eligible claimant* in respect of a *relevant general insurance contract* entered into before *commencement* only if the *person* is a *partnership*.

4.3 Exceptions: Circumstances where a person coming within COMP 4.2.2R may receive compensation

Deposits and balances in dormant accounts

4.3.1 **[R]** A *person* is eligible to claim compensation in respect of a *protected deposit* or a *protected dormant account* if, at the date on which the *relevant person* is determined to be *in default*:

(1) he came within category (8) or (14) of COMP 4.2.2R; or

(2) he came within any of categories (1)–(3), (7) or (10)–(12) of COMP 4.2.2R, and was not a *large company*, *large mutual association*, or a *credit institution*.

Long term insurance

4.3.2 **[R]** A *person* other than one which comes within any of categories (7)–(12) and (15) of COMP 4.2.2R is eligible to claim compensation in respect of a *long term insurance* contract.

Relevant general insurance contracts

4.3.3 **[R]**

(1) A *person* falling within categories (1)–(4) of COMP 4.2.2R is eligible to claim compensation in respect of a *relevant general insurance contract* if, at the date the contract commenced he was a *small business*.

(2) Where the contract has been renewed, the last renewal date shall be taken as the commencement date.

4.3.4 **[R]** A *partnership* which falls within category 14 or category 17 or both of COMP 4.2.2R is eligible to claim compensation in respect of a *relevant general insurance contract* entered into before *commencement*.

4.3.5 **[R]** A *person* who comes within category (16) of COMP 4.2.2R (a 'category 16 *person*') is eligible to claim compensation if:

(1) the *person* insured would have been an *eligible claimant* at the time that his rights against the insurer were transferred to and vested in the category 16 *person*; or

(2) the liability of the *person* insured in respect of the category 16 person was a liability under a contract of employer's liability insurance which would have been a *liability subject to compulsory insurance* had the contract been entered into after 1 January 1972 or (for contracts in Northern Ireland) 29 December 1975; or

(3) the extent of the liability of the *person* insured in respect of the category 16 *person* had been agreed in writing by the insurer, or determined by a court or arbitrator, before the date on which the insurer is determined to be *in default*.

Liability subject to compulsory insurance

4.3.6 **[R]** A *person* who comes within COMP 4.2.2R is eligible to claim compensation in respect of a *liability subject to compulsory insurance* if the *claim* is:
(1) a *claim* under a *protected contract of insurance*; or
(2) a *claim* in connection with *protected non-investment insurance mediation*.

Protected investment business and protected home finance mediation

4.3.7 **[G]** There are no exceptions to COMP 4.2.2R for *claims* made in connection with *protected investment business* or *protected home finance mediation*.

4.4 Exceptions: Relevant general insurance contracts: mesothelioma claims

Application

4.4.1 **[R]** This section applies in respect of any claim for a contribution by a *responsible person* made on or after 25 July 2006 in relation to a *mesothelioma victim's* claim which is determined by agreement in writing, a court or an arbitrator on or after 3 May 2006.

Claims for contribution by responsible persons

4.4.2 **[R]** The *rules* in this sourcebook shall have effect as modified to the extent necessary to enable the *FSCS* to receive, assess, determine and make payments in respect of applications for compensation from *responsible persons* in accordance with article 9A of the *compensation transitionals order* and regulation 3 of the *mesothelioma regulations*.

4.4.3 **[R]** In particular:
(1) a *responsible person* is eligible to claim in accordance with the provisions of this section;
(2) the *FSCS* may pay compensation to a *responsible person* where it is satisfied that an *eligible claimant* has a claim under a *protected contract of insurance* issued by an *insurer in default*, which, but for satisfaction of that claim by the *responsible person*, the *FSCS* would have paid;
(3) a *responsible person* in (2) may claim compensation only if, having satisfied a claim in relation to a *mesothelioma victim*, he could claim contribution from an *insurer in default*;
(4) the *FSCS* may pay compensation in respect of any contribution for which an *insurer in default* is liable by agreement in writing, or by a determination of a court or arbitrator; and
(5) in this section, references to an *insurer* include *an authorised insurance company*, and references to *in default* include an *article 9 default*.

4.4.4 **[G]** The provisions in this section establish a scheme for contribution claims by *responsible persons*. The requirement in COMP 12.2.7R to take into account payments to the claimant do not therefore require the *FSCS*, in paying compensation in respect of such a claim, to take into account any payments referred to in that *rule* made by a *responsible person* in calculating the claimant's overall net *claim*.

Limits to amounts payable for contribution claims

4.4.5 **[R]** The amount payable by the *FSCS* in respect of a claim in accordance with the provisions of this section may not exceed the amount that it would have paid if the *mesothelioma victim* (or a *responsible person* other than an *insurer* of such a *person*) to whom the contribution claim relates had made that claim directly against *FSCS*.

CHAPTER 5
PROTECTED CLAIMS

5.1 Application and Purpose

Application

[2188]
5.1.1 **[R]** This chapter applies to the *FSCS*.

5.1.2 **[G]** It is also relevant to claimants.

Purpose

5.1.3 **[G]** The purpose of this chapter is to set out the various categories of *claim* for which compensation may be payable.

5.2 What is a protected claim?

5.2.1 **[R]** A *protected claim* is:
(1) a *claim* for a *protected deposit* or a *protected dormant account* (see COMP 5.3); or

(2) a *claim* under a *protected contract of insurance* (see COMP 5.4); or
(3) a *claim* in connection with *protected investment business* (see COMP 5.5); or
(4) a *claim* in connection with *protected mortgage business* (see COMP 5.6); or
(5) a *claim* in connection with *protected non-investment insurance mediation* (see COMP 5.7).

5.2.2 **[G]** [deleted]

5.3 Protected deposits and protected dormant accounts

5.3.1 **[R]** A *deposit* is a *protected deposit* only if:
(1) the *deposit* was made with:
 (a) an establishment of a *relevant person* in the *United Kingdom*; or
 (b) a *branch* of a *UK firm* which is a *credit institution* established in another *EEA State* under an *EEA right*; and
(2) the *deposit* is not:
 (a) a bond issued by a *credit institution* which is part of the institution's capital, as set out in the Consolidated Banking Directive (Directive 2000/12/EC); or
 (b) a secured *deposit; or*
 (c) a deferred share issued by a *building society*; or
 (d) a non-nominative *deposit* (that is, a *deposit* made without disclosing the depositor's identity).

5.3.2 **[R]** If not a *protected deposit*, a *dormant account* is a protected dormant account only if, immediately prior to transfer, it consisted of a protected deposit, the liability for which has been transferred to a *dormant account fund operator.*

5.4 Protected contracts of insurance

5.4.1 **[R]** A *protected contract of insurance* is:
(1) (if issued after *commencement*) a *contract of insurance* within COMP 5.4.2R (Contracts of insurance issued after commencement)
(2) (if issued before *commencement*) a *contract of insurance* within COMP 5.4.5R (Contracts of insurance issued before commencement)

Contracts of insurance issued after commencement

5.4.2 **[R]** A *contract of insurance* issued after *commencement* which:
(1) relates to a protected risk or commitment as described in COMP 5.4.3R;
(2) is issued by the *relevant person* through an establishment in;
 (a) the *United Kingdom*; or
 (b) another *EEA State*; or
 (c) the Channel Islands or the Isle of Man;
(3) is a *long-term insurance contract* or a *relevant general insurance contract*;
(4) is not a *reinsurance contract*; and
(5) if it is a *contract of insurance* entered into by a *member*, was entered into on or after 1 January 2004;

is a *protected contract of insurance*.

5.4.3 **[R]** A risk or commitment is a protected risk or commitment for the purpose of COMP 5.4.2R(1) if:
(1) in the case of a *contract of insurance* falling within COMP 5.4.2R(2)(a), it is situated in an *EEA State*, the Channel Islands or the Isle of Man;
(2) in the case of a *contract of insurance* falling within COMP 5.4.2R(2)(a), it is situated in an *EEA State* except that where the *relevant person* is a *firm* which is not a *UK firm* issuing a *contract of insurance* through an establishment in an *EEA State* (other than the *United Kingdom*), the risk or commitment must be situated in the *United Kingdom*;
(3) in the case of a *contract of insurance* falling within COMP 5.4.2R(2)(a), it is situated in the *United Kingdom*, the Channel Islands or the Isle of Man.

5.4.4 **[R]** For the purpose of COMP 5.4.3R and COMP 5.4.5R(1)(b), the situation of a risk or commitment is determined as follows:
(1) for a *contract of insurance* relating to a building or a building and its contents (in so far as the contents are covered by the same *contract of insurance*), the risk or commitment is situated where the building is situated;
(2) for a *contract of insurance* relating to vehicles of any type, the risk or commitment is situated where the vehicle is registered;
(3) for a *contract of insurance* lasting four months or less covering travel or holiday risks (whatever the class concerned), the risk or commitment is situated where the policyholder took out the *contract of insurance*; and
(4) in cases not covered by (1) to (3):

(a) where the policyholder who first took out the *contract of insurance* is an individual, the risk or commitment is situated where he has his *habitual residence* at the date when the *contract of insurance* commenced;

(b) where the policyholder who first took out the *contract of insurance* is not an individual, the risk or commitment is situated where the establishment to which the risk or commitment relates is situated at the date when the *contract of insurance* commenced.

Contracts of insurance issued before commencement

5.4.5 **[R]**

(1) If after *commencement*, a *relevant person* is subject to one or more of the proceedings listed in COMP 6.3.3R or is declared *in default*, then a *contract of insurance* issued by that *relevant person* before *commencement* which is within COMP 5.4.5R(2) is a *protected contract of insurance*, provided that the *relevant person* was not a *member* at the time the *contract of insurance* was issued, and:
   (a) (unless it comes within (b)) at the earlier events in (1) it was a "United Kingdom policy" for the purposes of the Policyholders Protection Act 1975;
   (b) if the *contract of insurance* is a contract of employers' liability insurance entered into before 1 January 1972 or (for contracts in Northern Ireland) 29 December 1975, and the *claim* was agreed after the default of the *insurer*, the risk or commitment was situated in the *United Kingdom* (as set out in COMP 5.4.4R).

(2) The *contracts of insurance* referred to in COMP 5.4.5R(1)) are:
   (a) a *relevant general insurance contract*;
   (b) a *contract of insurance* within the *credit* class; and
   (c) a *long-term insurance contract*;

   which in each case is not a *reinsurance contract*.

Contracts not evidenced by a policy

5.4.6 **[R]** If it appears to the *FSCS* that a *person* is insured under a contract with an *insurance undertaking* which is not evidenced by a policy, and it is satisfied that if a policy evidencing the contract had been issued, the *person* in question would have had a *protected contract of insurance*, the *FSCS* must treat the contract as a *protected contract of insurance*.

Liabilities giving rise to claims under a protected contract of insurance

5.4.7 **[R]** The *FSCS* must treat liabilities of an *insurance undertaking* which is *in default*, in respect of the following items, as giving rise to *claims* under a *protected contract of insurance*:

(1) (if the contract is not a *reinsurance contract* and has not commenced) *premiums* paid to the *insurance undertaking*; or

(2) proceeds of a *long-term insurance contract* that is not a *reinsurance contract* and that has matured or been surrendered which have not yet been passed to the claimant; or

(3) the unexpired portion of any *premium* in relation to *relevant general insurance contracts* which are not *reinsurance contracts*; or

(4) *claims* by *persons* entitled to the benefit of a judgement under section 151 of the Road Traffic Act 1988 or Article 98 of the Road Traffic (Northern Ireland) Order 1981.

5.5 Protected investment business

5.5.1 **[R]** *Protected investment business* is:

(1) *designated investment business* carried on by the *relevant person* with, or for the benefit of, the claimant (so long as that claimant has a *claim*), or as *agent* on the claimant's behalf;

(2) the activities of the manager or *trustee* of an *AUT*, provided that the *claim* is made by a *holder*;

(3) the activities of the *ACD* or *depositary* of an *ICVC*, provided that the *claim* is made by a *holder*;

provided that the condition in COMP 5.5.2R is satisfied.

5.5.2 **[R]** COMP 5.5.1R only applies if the *protected investment business* was carried on from:

(1) an *establishment* of the *relevant person* in the *United Kingdom*; or

(2) a *branch* of a *UK firm* which is:
   (a) a *MiFID investment firm*, or
   (b) a *UCITS management company* established in another *EEA State* (but only in relation to *managing investments* (other than of a *collective investment scheme*), *advising on investments* or *safeguarding and administering investments*);

   and the *claim* is an *ICD claim*; or

(3) both (1) and (2).

Part II FSA Handbook Materials

5.6 Protected home finance mediation

5.6.1 **[R]** *Protected home finance mediation* is:
(1) *advising on a home finance transaction*; or
(2) *arranging (bringing about) a home finance transaction*; or
(3) *making arrangements with a view to a home finance transaction*; or
(4) *agreeing to carry on a regulated activity* in (1) to (3); or
(5) the activities of a *home finance provider* which would be *arranging* but for article 28A of the *Regulated Activities Order* (Arranging contracts or plans to which the arranger is a party);

provided that the condition in COMP 5.6.2R is satisfied.

5.6.2 **[R]** COMP 5.6.1R applies only if the *protected home finance mediation* was carried on by a *relevant person*:
(1) with a *customer* who was resident in the *United Kingdom*; or
(2) from an establishment maintained by the *relevant person* (or its *appointed representative*) in the *United Kingdom* with a *customer* who was resident elsewhere in the *EEA*;

at the time the *protected home finance mediation* was carried on.

5.7 Protected non-investment insurance mediation

5.7.1 **[R]** *Protected non-investment insurance mediation* is an *insurance mediation activity* where the *investment* concerned is a *relevant general insurance contract* or a *pure protection contract* but which is not a *long-term care insurance contract* or a *reinsurance contract*, provided that the condition in COMP 5.7.2R is satisfied.

5.7.2 **[R]** COMP 5.7.1R only applies if the conditions in (1) and (2) are satisfied:
(1) the *protected non-investment insurance mediation* was carried on from:
   (a) an establishment of the *relevant person* in the *United Kingdom;* or
   (b) a *branch* of a *UK firm* established in another *EEA State* in the exercise of an *EEA right* derived from the *IMD*; and
(2) the *customer* making the *claim* (or where COMP 3.2.4R applies, the *customer* on behalf of whom a *firm* makes a claim) was in contact with:
   (a) a *firm* carrying on an *insurance mediation activity* in the *United Kingdom*; or
   (b) a *branch* of a UK *firm* established in another *EEA State* which is carrying on an *insurance mediation activity* in the exercise of an *EEA right* derived from the *IMD*.

CHAPTER 6
RELEVANT PERSONS IN DEFAULT

6.1 Application and Purpose

Application

[2189]
6.1.1 **[R]** This chapter applies to the *FSCS*.

6.1.2 **[G]** It is also relevant to claimants.

Purpose

6.1.3 **[G]** The purpose of this chapter is to specify the types of *person* against whom a claimant must have a *claim* in order to be eligible for compensation, and when those *persons* are "*in default*". Generally, this occurs when they are insolvent or unable to meet their liabilities to claimants.

6.1.4 **[G]** To be eligible for compensation a claimant's claim must be against a *relevant person in default*: see COMP 3.2.1R(2).

6.2 Who is a relevant person?

6.2.1 **[R]** A *relevant person* is a *person* who was, at the time the act or omission giving rise to the *claim* against it took place:
(1) a *participant firm*; or
(2) an *appointed representative* of a *participant firm*.

6.2.2 **[G]** An *incoming EEA firm*, which is a *credit institution*, an *IMD insurance intermediary*, a *MiFID investment firm* or a *UCITS management company*, and its *appointed representatives* are not *relevant persons* in relation to the *firm's passported activities*, unless it has *top-up cover* (and in the case of a *UCITS management company*, only in relation to *managing investments* (other than of a *collective investment scheme*), *advising on investments* or *safeguarding and administering investments*). (See definition of "*participant firm*").

6.3 When is a relevant person in default?

6.3.1 **[R]** A *relevant person* is *in default* if:

(1) (except in relation to an *ICD claim* or *DGD claim*) the *FSCS* has determined it to be *in default* under COMP 6.3.2R COMP 6.3.3R, COMP 6.3.4R or COMP 6.3.5R; or
(2) (in relation to an *ICD claim* or *DGD claim*):
  (a) the *FSA* has determined it to be *in default* under COMP 6.3.2R; or
  (b) a judicial authority has made a ruling that had the effect of suspending the ability of *eligible claimants* to bring *claims* against the *participant firm*, if that is earlier than (a).

6.3.1A **[G]** The *FSA* will make the determination in COMP 6.3.1R(2)(a) in relation to a *DGD claim* as soon as possible and in any event no later than five *working days* after being satisfied that either of the conditions in COMP 6.3.2R has been met.

[**Note**: article 1(3)(i) of the *Deposit Guarantee Directive*]

6.3.2 **[R]** Subject to COMP 3.3.3R to COMP 3.3.6R and COMP 6.3.6R, the *FSCS* (or, where COMP 6.3.1R(2)(a) applies, the *FSA*) may determine a *relevant person* to be *in default* when it is, in the opinion of the *FSCS* or the *FSA*:
(1) unable to satisfy *protected claims* against it; or
(2) likely to be unable to satisfy *protected claims* against it.

6.3.3 **[R]** Subject to COMP 6.3.6R, the *FSCS* may determine a *relevant person* to be *in default* if it is satisfied that a *protected claim* exists (other than an *ICD claim* or *DGD claim*), and the *relevant person* is the subject of one or more of the following proceedings in the *United Kingdom* (or of equivalent or similar proceedings in another jurisdiction):
(1) the passing of a resolution for a creditors' voluntary winding up;
(2) a determination by the *relevant person's Home State regulator* that the *relevant person* appears unable to meet *claims* against it and has no early prospect of being able to do so;
(3) the appointment of a liquidator or administrator, or provisional liquidator or interim manager;
(4) the making of an order by a court of competent jurisdiction for the winding up of a company, the dissolution of a partnership, the administration of a company or partnership, or the bankruptcy of an individual;
(5) the approval of a company voluntary arrangement, a partnership voluntary arrangement, or of an individual voluntary arrangement.

6.3.4 **[R]** For *claims* arising in connection with *protected investment business*, *protected home finance mediation* or *protected non-investment insurance mediation*, the *FSCS* has the additional power to determine that a *relevant person* is *in default* if it is satisfied that a *protected claim* exists, and:
(1) the *FSCS* is satisfied that the *relevant person* cannot be contacted at its last place of business and that reasonable steps have been taken to establish a forwarding or current address, but without success; and
(2) there appears to the *FSCS* to be no evidence that the *relevant person* will be able to meet *claims* made against it.

6.3.5 **[R]** For *claims* arising in connection with *protected contracts of insurance*, the *FSCS* must treat any term in an *insurance undertaking's* constitution or in its *contracts of insurance*, limiting the undertaking's liabilities under a *long-term insurance contract* to the amount of its assets, as limiting the undertaking's liabilities to any claimant to an amount which is not less than the gross assets of the undertaking.

Members in default and the Central Fund of the Society

6.3.6 **[R]** The *FSCS* may not declare a *member* to be in default unless it is satisfied that the amounts which the *Society* may provide from the *Central Fund* are or are likely to be insufficient to ensure that *claims* against the *member* under a *protected contract of insurance* will be met to the level of protection which would otherwise be available under this sourcebook.

6.3.7 **[G]** If a *member* is unable fully to meet *protected claims* against it then in the first instance any shortfall will be avoided by payments by the *Society* from the assets of the *Central Fund*. The *FSCS* will not consider *claims* for compensation unless it is satisfied that the amounts which the *Society* will make available from the *Central Fund* are or are likely to be insufficient to ensure that *claims* against the *member* under a *protected contract of insurance* will be met to the level of protection which would otherwise be available under this sourcebook. The amount which the *FSCS* may pay in respect of any such *claim* will be limited to the difference between the amount which the claimant will receive, or is expected to receive, from the *member* and the *Society* together and the maximum amount of compensation payable in accordance with COMP 10 and COMP 12.

Claims arising under COMP 3.2.4R

6.3.8 **[R]** For the purposes of COMP 6.3 a claim made by a *firm* under COMP 3.2.4R is to be treated as if it were a *protected claim* against the *relevant person*.

Scheme manager's power to require information

6.3.9 **[R]** For the purposes of sections 219(1A)(b) and (d) of the *Act* (Scheme manager's power to require information) whether a *relevant person* is unable or likely to be unable to satisfy claims shall be determined by reference to whether it is *in default.*

CHAPTER 7
ASSIGNMENT OF RIGHTS

7.1 Application

Application and Purpose

[2190]
7.1.1 **[R]** This chapter applies to the *FSCS.*

7.1.2 **[G]** It is also relevant to claimants.

Purpose

7.1.3 **[G]** The *FSCS* may make an offer of compensation conditional on the assignment of rights to it by a claimant. The purpose of this chapter is to make provision for and set out the consequences of an assignment of the claimant's rights.

7.2 How does the assignment of rights work?

7.2.1 **[R]** The *FSCS*:
(1) must make any payment of compensation to a claimant, in respect of a *protected deposit,* conditional on the claimant, in so far as able to do so, assigning the whole of his rights; and
(2) may make any payment of compensation to a claimant in respect of any other *protected claim* conditional on the claimant assigning the whole or any part of his rights;

against the *relevant person,* or against any third party, or both, to the *FSCS* on such terms as the *FSCS* thinks fit.

7.2.2 **[R]** If a claimant assigns the whole or any part of his rights against any *person* to the *FSCS* as a condition of payment, the effect of this is that any sum payable in relation to the rights so assigned will be payable to the *FSCS* and not the claimant.

7.2.3 **[R]**
(1) Before taking assignment of rights from the claimant under COMP 7.2.1R, the *FSCS* must inform the claimant that if, after taking assignment of rights, the *FSCS* decides not to pursue recoveries using those rights it will, if the claimant so requests in writing, reassign the assigned rights to the claimant. The *FSCS* must comply with such a request in such circumstances.
(2) If the *FSCS* takes assignment of rights from the claimant under COMP 7.2.1R, it must pursue all and only such recoveries as it considers are likely to be both reasonably possible and cost effective to pursue.
(3) [deleted]

Specific provisions relating to claims for protected deposits

7.2.3A **[R]** If the *FSCS,* in relation to a *claim* for a *protected deposit,* takes an assignment of rights from the claimant under COMP 7.2.1R and subsequently makes recoveries through those rights, the *FSCS* must:
(1) retain from those recoveries a sum equal to the "FSCS retention sum"; and
(2) as soon as reasonably possible after it makes the recoveries, pay to the claimant, or as directed by the claimant, a sum equal to the "top up payment".

7.2.3B **[R]** The *FSCS* must calculate "FSCS retention sum" and the "top up payment" as follows:
(1) calculate the "recovery ratio" of;
  (a) the amount recovered by the *FSCS* through rights assigned under COMP 7.2.1R (taking into account any deduction from that amount the FSCS may make to cover part or all of its reasonable costs of recovery and of distribution, if any); to
  (b) the claimant's overall net *claim* for *protected deposits* against the *relevant person in default* less any liability of a *Home State* deposit guarantee scheme;
(2) subtract the sum paid by the *FSCS* as compensation and any amount paid or payable by a *Home State* compensation scheme to the claimant from the total value of the claimant's overall net *claim* for *protected deposits,* to give the "compensation shortfall";
(3) apply the recovery ratio to the sum paid by the *FSCS* as compensation to the claimant, to give the "FSCS retention sum"; and
(4) apply the recovery ratio to the compensation shortfall, to give the "top up payment".

7.2.3C **[G]**

(1) For example, if the claimant's overall net *claim* for *protected deposits* against a *relevant person* was for £100,000, and the *FSCS* paid compensation of £50,000 and took assignment of all the claimant's rights in relation to that claim, and made recoveries through those rights in the sum of £80,000 (after the costs of recovery and of distribution), then:
  (a) the recovery ratio would be 80% (£80,000 ÷ £100,000);
  (b) the compensation shortfall would be £50,000 (£100,000 — £50,000);
  (c) the FSCS retention sum would be £40,000 (80% x £50,000);
  (d) the top up payment would be £40,000 (80% of £50,000);
  (e) the total payment to the claimant would be £90,000 (£50,000 of compensation plus £40,000 of top up payment); and
  (f) the total outlay by the *FSCS*, net of the FSCS retention sum, would be £10,000 (20% x £50,000).

(2) In the example above, the amount recovered exceeds the amount of compensation. However, COMP 7.2.1AR also applies where the amount recovered is less than the amount of compensation. Therefore, for example, if the claimant's overall net *claim* for *protected deposits* against a *relevant person* was for £100,000, and the FSCS paid compensation of £50,000 and took assignment of all the claimant's rights in relation to that claim, and made recoveries through those rights in the sum of £20,000 (after the costs of recovery and of distribution), then:
  (a) the recovery ratio would be 20% (£20,000 ÷ £100,000);
  (b) the compensation shortfall would be £50,000 (£100,000 — £50,000);
  (c) the FSCS retention sum would be £10,000 (20% x £50,000);
  (d) the top up payment would be £10,000 (20% of £50,000);
  (e) the total payment to the claimant would be £60,000 (£50,000 of compensation plus £10,000 of top up payment); and
  (f) the total outlay by the *FSCS*, net of the FSCS retention sum, would be £40,000 (80% x £50,000).

7.2.3D **[G]** In order to prevent a claimant suffering disadvantage arising solely from his prompt acceptance of the *FSCS*'s offer of compensation compared with what might have been the position had he delayed his acceptance, the *FSCS* shall apply the rule in COMP 12.2.7R(2).

Provisions relating to other classes of protected claim

7.2.3E **[R]** If the FSCS makes recoveries through rights assigned under COMP 7.2.1R in relation to a *claim* that is not for a *protected deposit*, it may deduct from any recoveries paid over to the claimant under COMP 7.2.4R part or all of its reasonable costs of recovery and of distribution (if any).

7.2.4 **[R]** Unless compensation was paid under COMP 9.2.3R or the *claim* was for a *protected deposit*, if a claimant agrees to assign his rights to the *FSCS* and the *FSCS* subsequently makes recoveries through those rights, those recoveries must be paid to the claimant:

(1) to the extent that the amount recovered exceeds the amount of compensation (excluding interest paid under COMP 11.2.7R) received by the claimant in relation to the *protected claim*; or

(2) in circumstances where the amount recovered does not exceed the amount of compensation paid, to the extent that a failure to pay any sums recovered to the claimant would leave a claimant who had promptly accepted an offer of compensation at a disadvantage relative to a claimant who had delayed accepting an offer of compensation (see COMP 7.2.5R).

7.2.4A **[R]** For the purposes of COMP 7.2.4R compensation received by *eligible claimants* in relation to *Lloyd's policies* may include payments made from the *Central Fund*.

7.2.5 **[R]** Except for a *claim* for a *protected deposit*, the *FSCS* must endeavour to ensure that a claimant will not suffer disadvantage arising solely from his prompt acceptance of the *FSCS's* offer of compensation compared with what might have been the position had he delayed his acceptance.

7.2.6 **[G]** As an example of the circumstances which COMP 7.2.5R is designed to address, take two claimants, A and B.

(1) Both A and B have a *protected investment business claim* of £60,000 against a *relevant person in default*. The *FSCS* offers both claimants £48,000 compensation (the maximum amount payable for such claims (COMP 10.2.3R). A accepts immediately, and assigns his rights against the *relevant person* to the *FSCS*, but B delays accepting the *FSCS's* offer of compensation.

(2) In this example, the liquidator is able to recover assets from the *relevant person in default* and makes a payment of 50p in the pound to all the *relevant person's* creditors. If the liquidator made the payment before any offer of compensation from the *FSCS* had been accepted, A and B would both receive £30,000 each from the liquidator, leaving both with a loss of £30,000 to be met by the *FSCS*. Both *claims* would be met in full.

(3) However, if the payment were made by the liquidator after A had accepted the *FSCS's* offer of compensation and assigned his rights to the *FSCS*, but before B accepted the *FSCS's* offer of compensation, A would be disadvantaged relative to B even though he has received £48,000 compensation from the *FSCS*. A would be disadvantaged relative to B because he promptly accepted the *FSCS's* offer and assigned his rights to the *FSCS*. Because A has assigned his rights to the *FSCS*, any payment from the liquidator will be made to the *FSCS* rather than A. In this case the *FSCS* has paid A more than £30,000 so the £30,000 from the liquidator that would have been payable to A will be payable in full to the *FSCS* and not to A.

(4) B is able to exercise his rights against the liquidator because he delayed accepting the *FSCS's* offer and receives £30,000 from the liquidator. B can then make a *claim* for the remaining £30,000 to the *FSCS* which the *FSCS* can pay in full (see COMP 10.2.2R). B therefore suffers no loss whereas A is left with a loss of £12,000, being the difference between his *claim* of £60,000 and the compensation paid by the *FSCS* of £48,000.

7.2.7 **[R]**

(1) For the purposes of compensation paid under COMP 3.2.4R, *FSCS* may require any *firm* (including, but not limited to, the claimant *firm*) to assign to *FSCS* any rights the *firm* may have to claim against the *relevant person* in relation to the amount of the *shortfall* in *client money* arising out of the *failure* of the *relevant person*.

(2) A *firm* required by *FSCS* to assign its rights in (1), must assign those rights as requested, unless it has a reasonable excuse for not doing so.

CHAPTER 8
REJECTION OF APPLICATION AND WITHDRAWAL OF OFFER

8.1 Application and Purpose

Application

[2191]

8.1.1 **[R]** This chapter applies to the *FSCS*.

8.1.2 **[G]** It is also relevant to claimants.

Purpose

8.1.3 **[G]** In some circumstances, it may be appropriate for the *FSCS* to reject an application for compensation, or withdraw an offer of compensation. The purpose of this chapter is to set out when those circumstances arise.

8.2 Rejection of application for compensation

8.2.1 **[R]** If an application for compensation contains any material inaccuracy or omission, the *FSCS* may reject the application unless this is considered by the *FSCS* to be wholly unintentional.

8.2.2 **[G]** A rejection under COMP 8.2.1R does not mean that the claimant cannot receive compensation. A rejected application may be resubmitted, with the appropriate amendments. An application rejected under COMP 8.2.3R may be resubmitted if COMP 8.2.5R applies.

8.2.3 **[R]** The *FSCS* must reject an application for compensation if:

(1) the *FSCS* considers that a civil claim in respect of the liability would have been defeated by a defence of limitation at the earlier of:

 (a) the date on which the *relevant person* is determined to be *in default*; and

 (b) the date on which the claimant first indicates in writing that he may have a claim against the *relevant person*;

unless COMP 8.2.4R applies; or

(2) the liability of the *relevant person* to the claimant has been extinguished by the operation of law, unless COMP 8.2.5R applies.

8.2.4 **[R]** For *claims* made in connection with *protected investment business*, *protected home finance mediation* or *protected non-investment insurance mediation*, the *FSCS* may disregard a defence of limitation where the *FSCS* considers that it would be reasonable to do so.

8.2.5 **[R]** For claims made in connection with *protected investment business* or *protected non-investment insurance mediation*, if a *relevant person*, incorporated as a *company*, has been dissolved with the result that its liability to the claimant has been extinguished by operation of law, *the FSCS must treat the claim*, for the purposes of paying compensation, as if the *relevant person* had not been dissolved.

8.2.6 **[G]** COMP 8.2.5R means that the *FSCS* will be able to pay compensation in cases where:

(1) the *company* was declared in default on or after 1 December 2001; and

(2) at the time the application for compensation is made, the *company* has been dissolved.

8.2.7 **[R]** The *FSCS* may reject an application for compensation if:
(1) it relates to an event or transaction which has been reviewed under the provisions of a 'deemed scheme' as defined in the Financial Services and Markets Act 2000 (Transitional Provisions) (Reviews of Pensions Business) Order 2001 (SI 2001/2512); and
(2) as a result of the review in (1) no redress was payable, or redress was paid, in accordance with the regulatory standards for the review of such events or transactions, and the terms of any scheme order, applicable as at the date of the review.

8.2.8 **[G]** The purpose of COMP 8.2.7R is to allow the *FSCS* to reject claims relating to pensions review cases where a review was carried out in accordance with the relevant regulatory standards applicable at the time. 'Deemed schemes' are those review schemes set up before *commencement* (that is, 30 November 2001) but which are treated as schemes for the review of past business under the *Act*, namely the pensions review and *FSAVC* review.

8.3 Withdrawal of offer of compensation

8.3.1 **[R]** The *FSCS* may withdraw any offer of compensation made to a claimant if the offer is not accepted or if it is not disputed within 90 days of the date on which the offer is made.

8.3.2 **[R]** Where the amount of compensation offered is disputed, the *FSCS* may withdraw the offer but must consider exercising its powers to make a reduced or interim payment under COMP 11.2.4R or COMP 11.2.5R before doing so.

8.3.3 **[R]** The *FSCS* may repeat any offer withdrawn under COMP 8.3.1R or COMP 8.3.2R.

8.3.4 **[R]** The *FSCS* must withdraw any offer of compensation if it appears to the *FSCS* that no such offer should have been made.

8.3.5 **[R]** The *FSCS* must seek to recover any compensation paid to a claimant if it appears to the *FSCS* that no such payment should have been made, unless the *FSCS* believes on reasonable grounds that it would be unreasonable to do so, or that the costs of doing so would exceed any amount that could be recovered.

CHAPTER 9
TIME LIMITS ON PAYMENT AND POSTPONING PAYMENT

9.1 Application and Purpose

Application

[2192]
9.1.1 **[R]** This chapter applies to the *FSCS*.

9.1.2 **[G]** It is also relevant to claimants.

Purpose
9.1.3 **[G]** The purpose of this chapter is to ensure that compensation is paid to claimants as quickly as possible and that delays in paying compensation to claimants are kept to a minimum. The *FSCS* may postpone payment of compensation only in strictly limited circumstances.

9.2 When must compensation be paid?

9.2.1 **[R]** The *FSCS* must pay a *claim* as soon as reasonably possible after:
(1) it is satisfied that the conditions in COMP 3.2.1R have been met; and
(2) it has calculated the amount of compensation due to the claimant;

and in any event within three months of that date, unless the *FSA* has granted the *FSCS* an extension, in which case payment must be made no later than six months from that date.

9.2.2 **[R]** The *FSCS* may postpone paying compensation if:
(1) in the case of a *claim* against a *relevant person* who is an *appointed representative*, the *FSCS* considers that the claimant should make and pursue an application for compensation against the *appointed representative's* relevant *principal*; or
(2) in the case of a *claim* relating to *protected investment business* which is not an *ICD claim* or a *claim* relating to *protected home finance mediation*, the *FSCS* considers that the claimant should first exhaust his rights against the *relevant person* or any third party, or make and pursue an application for compensation to any other *person*; or
(3) in the case of a *claim* relating to a *protected contracts of insurance*, the *FSCS* considers that the liability to which the *claim* relates or any part of the liability is covered by another *contract of insurance* with a solvent *insurance undertaking*, or where it appears that a *person*, other than the liquidator, may make payments or take such action to secure the continuity of cover as the *FSCS* would undertake; or
(4) the *claim* is one which falls within COMP 12.4.5R or COMP 12.4.7R and it is not practicable for payment to be made within the usual time limits laid out in COMP 9.2.1R; or

(5) the claimant has been charged with an offence arising out of or in relation to money laundering, and those proceedings have not yet been concluded; or

(6) the *claim* relates solely to a bonus provided for under a *protected contract of insurance* the value of which the *FSCS* considers to be of such uncertainty that immediate payment of compensation in respect of that bonus would not be prudent and a court has yet to attribute a value to such bonus.

9.2.3 **[R]** Notwithstanding COMP 9.2.2R(2), the *FSCS* may pay compensation to a claimant in respect of assets held by a *relevant person* if an insolvency practitioner has been appointed to the *relevant person*, and:

(1) the *FSCS* considers it likely that the insolvency practitioner would, in due course, return the assets to the claimant;

(2) the claimant has agreed to be compensated for the assets on the basis of the valuation provided by the *FSCS*; and

(3) the claimant has agreed, to the satisfaction of the *FSCS*, that his rights to the assets in respect of which compensation is payable should pass to it.

CHAPTER 10
LIMITS ON THE AMOUNT OF COMPENSATION PAYABLE

10.1 Application and Purpose

Application

[2193]

10.1.1 **[R]** This chapter applies to the *FSCS*.

10.1.2 **[G]** It is also relevant to claimants.

Purpose

10.1.3 **[G]** In most cases it is appropriate for there to be a limit on the amount of compensation payable by the *FSCS* and that there should be some part of the *claim* which is not compensatable and for which the claimant must bear the loss. The purpose of this chapter is to set these limits out.

10.1.4 **[G]** The chapter also sets out the limit on the level of protection the *FSCS* must seek to secure when the *FSCS* is ensuring that there is continuity of insurance cover.

10.2 Limits on compensation payable

10.2.1 **[R]** The limits on the maximum compensation sums payable by the *FSCS* for *protected claims* are set out in COMP 10.2.3R.

10.2.2 **[G]** The limits apply to the aggregate amount of *claims* in respect of each category of *protected claim* that an *eligible claimant* has against the *relevant person*. Consequently, a claimant who has, for example, a *claim* against a *relevant person* in connection with *protected investment business* of £30,000, and a further such *claim* of £20,000, will not receive 100% compensation for both *claims*; instead he will receive £48,000 (100% of the first £30,000 and 90% of the next £20,000). Similarly, if a claimant receives more than one payment in respect of a *claim* or *claims* on one or more *protected contract of insurance*, the claimant will only receive 100% of the first £2,000 of the total paid, and not 100% of the first £2,000 of each payment.

10.2.2 **[G]** The limits apply to the aggregate amount of *claims* in respect of each category of *protected claim* that an *eligible claimant* has against the *relevant person*. Consequently, a claimant who has, for example, a *claim* against a *relevant person* in connection with *protected investment business* of £40,000, and a further such *claim* of £20,000, will only receive the £50,000 limit.

10.2.3 **[R]** Table Limits

This table belongs to COMP 10.2.1R

Type of claim	Level of cover	Maximum payment
Protected deposit or *protected dormant account*	100% of *claim*	£50,000 or €50,000 whichever is the greater on the date the *relevant person* is determined to be in *default* or the date the *protected deposit* was due and payable, if later. [**Note**: article 7(1) of the *Deposit Guarantee Directive*] (see also below for building society and other mutual society mergers and transfers (COMP 10.2.10R) and protected deposit transfers under the special resolution regime (COMP 10.2.11R))
Protected contract of insurance when the contract is a *relevant general insurance contract*	(1) Where the claim is in respect of a liability subject to compulsory insurance: 100% of claim.	Unlimited
		Unlimited
	(2) In all other cases: 90% of *claim*.	Unlimited
Protected contract of insurance when the contract is a *long-term insurance contract*	At least 90% of *claim* as determined in accordance with *COMP* 12.	Unlimited
Protected investment business	100% of *claim*	£50,000
Protected noninvestment insurance mediation	(1) where the *claim* is in respect of a *liability subject to compulsory insurance*: 100% of *claim*	Unlimited
	(2) In all other cases: 90% of *claim*	Unlimited
protected home finance mediation	100% of *claim*	£50,000

10.2.4 **[G]** COMP 12 sets out the *rules* the *FSCS* will follow when calculating the amount of compensation payable.

10.2.5 **[G]** COMP 12.4.1R and COMP 12.4.4R include further limits relating to *DGD claims* and *ICD claims* against certain *incoming EEA firms*. These reflect the *DGD* and *ICD*, under which compensation may be payable by the *incoming EEA firm's Home State* compensation scheme.

10.2.6 **[R]** [deleted]

10.2.7 **[R]** [deleted]

Claims against more than one member in respect of a single protected contract of insurance to be treated as a single claim

10.2.8 **[R]** In applying the financial limits in COMP 10.2, and in calculating the amount of a *claim* in respect of a *protected contract of insurance* arising from the default of one or more *members*, a *policyholder* is to be treated as having a single *claim* for the aggregate of all such amounts as may be payable on the *claim* in respect of the *protected contract of insurance*.

Claims arising under COMP 3.2.4R

10.2.9 **[R]** If a *firm* has a claim under COMP 3.2.4R, the *FSCS* must treat the share of the *shortfall* of each *customer* as if it were a *protected claim* for the purposes of calculating the limits of compensation payable, within COMP 10.2, in relation to that *customer*.

Building society and other mutual society mergers

10.2.10 **[R]**

(1) This *rule* applies from 1 December 2008 to 30 December 2010.

(2) In the event of a merger between two *building societies* or a transfer of the business of a *building society* to a subsidiary of another mutual society (whether or not of the same type), there is a separate and additional £50,000 maximum payment limit for a claimant with respect to *claims* for *protected deposits* held under the name of the dissolved entity (or such part of the name as is permitted by law) provided the following conditions are satisfied:
   - (a) the merger or transfer takes effect between 1 December 2008 and 30 December 2010;
   - (b) the successor entity has notified the FSA before the merger or transfer takes effect that it wishes this *rule* to apply;
   - (c) before the merger or transfer took effect, the claimant had a *protected deposit* with each of the relevant entities; and
   - (d) the successor entity continues to operate the business of the dissolved entity under the name of the latter (or such part of the name as is permitted by law).

[Note: The *FSA* will publish the names of any successor entity and the relevant name to which a separate £50,000 limit applies.]

(3) A successor entity to which this *rule* applies must make and retain a written record of potential claimants for whom the separate limit applies.

(4) In this *rule* "mutual society" and "subsidiary" have the same meanings as in the Building Societies (Funding) and Mutual Societies (Transfers) Act 2007.

Protected deposit transfers under the special resolution regime

10.2.11 **[R]**

(1) This *rule* applies from 16:00 on 29 March 2009 to 30 December 2010.

(2) In the event of a transfer of *protected deposits* from one *deposit-taking firm* to another *deposit-taking firm* pursuant to the property transfer powers under the Banking Act 2009, there is a separate and additional £50,000 maximum payment limit for a claimant with respect to *claims* for *protected deposits* held under the name of the transferor (or such part of the name as is permitted by law) provided the following conditions are satisfied:
   - (a) the transfer takes effect between 16:00 on 29 March 2009 and 30 December 2010;
   - (b) the transferee has notified the FSA before the transfer takes effect that it wishes this *rule* to apply;
   - (c) before the transfer took effect, the claimant had a *protected deposit* with each of the transferor and the transferee; and
   - (d) the transferee continues to operate the business relating to the transferred *protected deposits* under the name of the transferor (or such part of the name as is permitted by law).

[Note: The FSA will publish the names of any transferee and the relevant name to which a separate £50,000 limit applies.]

(3) A transferee to which this *rule* applies must make and retain a written record of potential claimants for whom the separate limit applies.

Claims in respect of protected dormant accounts

10.2.12 **[R]** In the event of a default of a *dormant account fund operator*, the *FSCS* will pay compensation in accordance with COMP 10.2.3R on the basis of the *authorisation* of the *relevant person* who was liable for the *protected deposit* immediately prior to the liability being transferred to the *dormant account fund operator* (and the relevant *authorisation* of the *relevant person* is the *authorisation* that was in place at the time that the liability was transferred).

10.2.13 **[G]** The purpose of COMP 10.2.12R is to ensure that *persons* whose *balances* in a *dormant account* have been transferred to a *dormant account fund operator* do not have their entitlement to compensation reduced in the event of default of the *dormant account fund operator*. So, a *person* who held *dormant accounts* with two different *relevant persons*, the liability for which were then automatically transferred to the *dormant account fund operator*, could still be compensated by the *FSCS* on the basis of accounts with two separate *relevant persons* (and so could receive up to 2 × £50,000 in compensation) rather than just one account with one *relevant person*.

CHAPTER 11
PAYMENT OF COMPENSATION

11.1 Application and Purpose

Application

[2194]
11.1.1 **[R]** This chapter applies to the *FSCS*.

11.1.2 **[G]** It is also relevant to claimants.

Purpose

11.1.3 **[G]** The *FSCS* will usually pay compensation direct to the claimant, but in certain circumstances it may be appropriate for the *FSCS* to pay compensation to someone other than the claimant, or to make reduced or interim payments. The purpose of this chapter is to set out when those circumstances arise.

11.2 Payment

To whom must payment be made?

11.2.1 **[R]** If the *FSCS* determines that compensation is payable (or any recovery or other amount is payable by the *FSCS* to the claimant), it must pay it to the claimant, or as directed by the claimant, unless:

(1) arrangements have or are being made to secure continuity of insurance under COMP 3.3.1R to COMP 3.3.2ER or the *FSCS* is taking measures it considers appropriate to safeguard *eligible claimants* under COMP 3.3.3R to COMP 3.3.6R; or
(2) COMP 11.2.2R or COMP 11.2.3R applies.

11.2.2 **[R]** Where a claimant has a *protected claim* arising out of the circumstances described in COMP 12.4.5R, the *FSCS* must pay any compensation (and any recovery or other amount payable by the *FSCS* to the claimant) to:

(1) the trustee of an *occupational pension scheme*; or
(2) a *personal pension scheme* or other *product provider*; *or*
(3) both (1) and (2);

and not to the claimant, unless exceptional circumstances apply.

11.2.3 **[R]** Where an *eligible claimant* has a *claim* under a *protected contract of insurance* against a *relevant person* that is in administration, provisional liquidation, or liquidation, the *FSCS* may:

(1) make payments to or on behalf of *eligible claimants* on such terms (including any terms requiring repayment in whole or in part) and on such conditions as it thinks fit (subject to COMP 10); or
(2) secure that payments (subject to COMP 10) are made to or on behalf of any such *eligible claimants* by the liquidator, administrator, or provisional liquidator by giving him an indemnity covering any such payments or any class or description of such payments.

Reduced or interim payments

11.2.4 **[R]** If the *FSCS* is satisfied that in principle compensation is payable in connection with any *protected claim*, but considers that immediate payment in full would not be prudent because of uncertainty as to the amount of the claimant's overall net *claim*, it may decide to pay an appropriate lesser sum in final settlement, or to make payment on account.

11.2.5 **[R]** The *FSCS* may also decide to make a payment on account or to pay a lesser sum in final settlement if the claimant has any reasonable prospect for recovery in respect of the *claim* from any third party or by applying for compensation to any other *person*.

11.2.6 **[R]** The *FSCS* may not pay a lesser sum in final settlement under COMP 11.2.4R and COMP 11.2.5R where the *claim* is a *DGD claim* or *ICD claim*.

11.2.6A **[G]** COMP 11.2.4R applies to compensation payable in connection with any *protected claim*. It would, for example, apply to the situation where the *FSCS* considers it imprudent to make a payment in full because of uncertainty as to the value a court might attribute to a bonus provided for under a *long-term insurance contract*. In such circumstances the *FSCS* may make payment of compensation on account to the policyholder in respect of benefits under the contract the value of which is not uncertain.

Paying interest on compensation

11.2.7 **[R]** The *FSCS* may pay interest on the compensation sum in such circumstances as it considers appropriate.

11.2.8 **[R]** Interest under COMP 11.2.7R is not to be taken into account when applying the limits on the compensation sum payable in respect of a *claim* under COMP 10.

CHAPTER 12
CALCULATING COMPENSATION

12.1 Application and Purpose

Application

[2195]
12.1.1 **[R]** This chapter applies to the *FSCS*.

12.1.2 **[G]** This chapter is also relevant to claimants, since it sets out how a *claim* will be quantified. (For the process of paying compensation, including the limits on the amount of compensation that can be paid, see COMP 8 – COMP 11).

Purpose

12.1.3 **[G]** The purpose of this chapter is to set out the different ways in which the *FSCS* is to calculate compensation.

12.2 Quantification: general

12.2.1 **[R]** The amount of compensation payable to the claimant in respect of any type of *protected claim* is the amount of his overall net *claim* against the *relevant person* at the *quantification date*.

12.2.2 **[R]** COMP 12.2.1R is, however, subject to the other provisions of COMP, in particular those *rules* that set limits on the amount of compensation payable for various types of *protected claim*. The limits are set out in COMP 10.

12.2.3 **[G]** Where a liability of a *relevant person* to an *eligible claimant* could fall within more than one type of *protected claim* (see COMP 5.2.1R), for example a *claim* in connection with *money* held by an *ISD investment firm* that is also a *credit institution*, the *FSCS* should seek to ensure that the claimant does not receive any further compensation payment from the *FSCS* in cases where the claimant has already received compensation from the *FSCS* in respect of that *claim*.

Overall net claim

12.2.4 **[R]** A claimant's overall net *claim* is the sum of the *protected claims* of the same category that he has against a *relevant person in default*, less the amount of any liability which the *relevant person* may set off against any of those *claims* (see COMP 10.2.2G).

12.2.5 **[G]** For the different categories of *protected claim*, see COMP 5 and COMP 10.2.3G.

12.2.6 **[G]** In calculating the claimant's overall net *claim*, the *FSCS* may rely, to the extent that it is relevant, on any determination by:
(1) a court of competent jurisdiction;
(2) a trustee in bankruptcy;
(3) a liquidator;
(4) any other recognised insolvency practitioner;

and on the certification of any net sum due which is made in default proceedings of any exchange or clearing house.

12.2.7 **[R]** The *FSCS* must take into account any payments to the claimant (including amounts recovered by the *FSCS* on behalf of the claimant) made by the *relevant person* or the *FSCS* or any other *person*, if that payment is connected with the *relevant person's* liability to the claimant:
(1) in calculating the claimant's overall net *claim*; and
(2) for a *claim* for a *protected deposit*, by reducing the amount of compensation by the FSCS retention sum that the *FSCS* would have retained if it had made those recoveries itself.

12.2.8 **[R]** The *FSCS* must calculate the amount of compensation due to the claimant as soon as reasonably possible after it is satisfied that the conditions in COMP 3.2.1 have been met.

12.2.9 **[R]** In calculating the claimant's overall net *claim* the *FSCS* must take into account the amounts paid by, or expected to be paid by, the *Society* from the *Central Fund* to meet a *member's* liabilities under the contract which gives rise to the *claim*.

12.3 Quantification date

Protected deposits

12.3.1 **[R]** For a *protected deposit claim*, the *quantification date* is the date the *relevant person* is determined to be *in default*, or the date the *protected deposit* was due and payable, if later.

Protected contracts of insurance

12.3.2 **[R]** For a *claim* under a *protected contract of insurance* that is a *long-term insurance contract*, the *FSCS* must determine as the *quantfication date* a specific date by reference to which the liability of the *relevant person* to the *eligible claimant* is to be determined.

12.3.3 **[R]** For a claim under a *protected contract of insurance* that is a *relevant general insurance contract*, the *FSCS* must determine as the *quantification date* a specific date by reference to which the liability of the *relevant person* to the *eligible claimant* is to be determined.

12.3.4 **[R]** For a *claim* in respect of the unexpired *premiums* under a *protected contract of insurance* that is a *relevant general insurance contract* (see COMP 5.4.7R(3)), the *quantification date*, being the date by which the liability of the *relevant person* to the *eligible claimant* is to be determined, is the date the policy was terminated or cancelled.

Protected investment business

12.3.5 **[R]** For a *claim* made in connection with *protected investment business* which is not an *ICD claim*, the *FSCS* must determine a specific date as the *quantification date*, and this date may be either on, before or after the date of the determination of default.

12.3.6 **[R]** For a *claim* made in connection with *protected investment business* which is an *ICD claim*, the *quantification date* is the date the *relevant person* is determined to be *in default*.

Protected mortgage business

12.3.7 **[R]** For a *claim* made in connection with *protected home finance mediation*, the *FSCS* must determine a specific date as the *quantification date*, and this date may be either on, before or after the date of determination of default.

Protected non-investment insurance mediation

12.3.8 **[R]** For a *claim* made in connection with *protected non-investment insurance mediation*, the *FSCS* must determine a specific date as the *quantification date*, and this date may be either on, before or after the date of determination of default.

12.4 The compensation calculation

Protected deposit with incoming EEA firm

12.4.1 **[R]** If the claimant has a *DGD claim* against an *incoming EEA firm* which is a *credit institution*, the *FSCS* must take account of the liability of the *Home State* deposit-guarantee scheme in calculating the compensation payable by the *FSCS*.

Protected investment business: general

12.4.2 **[R]** The *FSCS* may pay compensation for any *claim* made in connection with *protected investment business* which is not:

(1) a *claim* for property held; or
(2) a *claim* arising from transactions which remain uncompleted at the *quantification date*;

only to the extent that the *FSCS* considers that the payment of compensation is essential in order to provide the claimant with fair compensation.

12.4.3 **[R]** The *FSCS* must not pay compensation for any *claim* in connection with *protected investment business* to the extent that it relates to or depends on:

(1) a failure of investment performance to match a guarantee given or representation made; or
(2) a contractual obligation to pay or promise to pay which the *FSCS* considers to have been undertaken without full consideration passing to the *relevant person* or in anticipation of possible insolvency; or
(3) the mere fluctuation in the value of an *investment*.

12.4.4 **[R]** If the claimant has an *ICD claim* against an *incoming EEA firm* which is an *ISD investment firm* (including a *credit institution* which is an *ISD investment firm*), the *FSCS* must take account of the liability of the *Home State* compensation scheme in calculating the compensation payable by the *FSCS*.

Protected investment business: claims covered by the pensions review

12.4.5 **[R]** If the claimant has a *claim* in connection with *protected investment business* relating to the fact that the claimant has:

(1) while eligible or reasonably likely to become eligible to be a member of an *occupational pension scheme*, instead become a member of a *personal pension scheme* or entered into a *retirement annuity*; or

(2) ceased to be a member of, or to pay contributions to, an *occupational pension scheme*, and has instead become a member of a *personal pension scheme* or entered into a *retirement annuity*; or

(3) transferred to a *personal pension scheme* accrued rights under an *occupational pension scheme* which is not a defined contribution (money purchase) scheme; or

(4) ceased to be a member of an *occupational pension scheme* and has instead (by virtue of such a provision as is mentioned in section 591(2)(g) of the Income and Corporation Taxes Act 1988) entered into arrangements for securing relevant benefits by means of an annuity;

the *FSCS* must take the steps set out in COMP 12.4.6R.

12.4.6 **[R]** If COMP 12.4.5R applies, the *FSCS* must follow the Specification of Standards and Procedures issued by the *FSA* in October 1994, as supplemented and modified by subsequent guidance issued by the *FSA* (in particular, that of November 1996) (the 'Specification') in:

(1) assessing whether a *relevant person* has complied with the relevant regulatory requirements;

(2) assessing whether non-compliance has caused the claimant loss; and

(3) calculating the amount of compensation due (where the *FSCS* may rely on calculations made by the *FSA* or any previous regulator of the *relevant person*);

unless the *FSCS* considers that departure from the Specification is essential in order to provide the claimant with fair compensation.

Protected investment business: FSAVC Review

12.4.7 **[R]** Where a *claim* made in connection with *protected investment business* relates to an Additional Voluntary Contribution policy advised on or arranged by a *relevant person*, the *FSCS* must follow the FSAVC Review Model Guidance issued by the *FSA* in May 2000 (the "Guidance") in:

(1) assessing whether the *relevant person* has complied with the relevant regulatory requirements;

(2) assessing whether non-compliance has caused the claimant loss; and

(3) calculating the compensation due (where the *FSCS* may rely on calculations made by the *FSA* or any previous regulator of the *relevant person*);

unless the *FSCS* considers that departure from the Guidance is essential in order to provide the claimant with fair compensation.

Protected investment business: excessive benefits

12.4.8 **[R]** The *FSCS* may decide to reduce the compensation that would otherwise be payable for a *claim* made in connection with *protected investment business* that is not an *ICD claim*, if it is satisfied that:

(1) there is evidence of contributory negligence by the claimant; or

(2) payment of the full amount would provide a greater benefit than the claimant might reasonably have expected or than the benefit available on similar *investments* with other *relevant persons*; and

it would be inequitable for the *FSCS* not to take account of (1) or (2).

Protected contracts of insurance: liabilities subject to compulsory insurance

12.4.9 **[R]** The *FSCS* must pay a sum equal to 100% of any liability of a *relevant person* who is an *insurance undertaking* in respect of a *liability subject to compulsory insurance* to the claimant as soon as reasonably practicable after it has determined the *relevant person* to be *in default*.

Protected contracts of insurance: general insurance

12.4.10 **[R]** The *FSCS* must calculate the liability of a *relevant person* to the claimant under a *relevant general insurance contract* in accordance with the terms of the contract, and (subject to any limits in COMP 10.2.3R) pay that amount to the claimant.

Protected contracts of insurance: long-term insurance

12.4.11 **[R]** Unless the *FSCS* is making arrangements to secure continuity of insurance cover under COMP 3.3.1R to COMP 3.3.2ER, the *FSCS* must calculate the liability of a *relevant person* to the claimant under a *long-term insurance contract* in accordance with the terms of the contract as valued *in a liquidation of the relevant person*, or (in the absence of such relevant terms) in accordance with such reasonable valuation techniques as the *FSCS* considers appropriate.

12.4.11A **[R]**

(1) Unless the *FSCS* is seeking to secure continuity of cover for a *relevant person* under COMP 3.3.1 to COMP 3.3.2ER, it must:

(a) pay compensation in accordance with COMP 12.4.11R for any benefit provided for under a protected *long-term insurance contract* which has fallen due or would have fallen due under the contract to be paid to any *eligible claimant* and has not already been paid; and

(b) do so as soon as reasonably practicable after the time when the benefit in question fell due or would have fallen due under the contract (but subject to and in accordance with any other terms which apply or would have applied under the contract).

(2) If the *FSCS* decides to treat the liability of the *relevant person* under the contract as reduced or (as the case may be) disregarded under COMP 12.4.14R then, for the purposes of (1), the value of benefits falling due after the date of that decision must be treated as reduced or disregarded to that extent.

(3) Unless it has decided to treat the liability of the *relevant person* under the contract as reduced or disregarded under COMP 12.4.14R the *FSCS* must not treat as a reason for failing to pay, or for delaying the payment of compensation in accordance with (1), the fact that:

(a) it considers that any benefit referred to in (1) is or may be excessive in any respect; or

(b) it has referred the contract in question to an independent actuary under COMP 12.4.13R; or

(c) it considers that it may at some later date decide to treat the liability of the *relevant person* under a contract as reduced or (as the case may be) disregarded under COMP 12.4.14R;

save where the *FSCS* decides to exclude certain benefits to the extent that they arise out of the exercise of any option under the policy (for this purpose option includes, but is not restricted to, a right to surrender the policy).

12.4.12 **[R]** The *FSCS* must not treat any bonus provided for under a *long term insurance contract* as part of the claimant's claim except to the extent that:

(1) a value has been attributed to it by a court in accordance with the Insurers (Winding Up) Rules 2001 or any equivalent rules or legislative provision in force from time to time; or

(2) the *FSCS* considers that a court would be likely to attribute a value to the bonus if it were to apply the method set out in those rules.

12.4.13 **[R]**

(1) If the *FSCS* is:

(a) seeking to secure continuity of cover under COMP 3.3.1R to COMP 3.3.2ER or to calculate the liability owed to an *eligible claimant* under COMP 12.4.11R; and

(b) considers that the benefits provided for under a protected *long term insurance contract* are or may be excessive in any respect,

it must refer the contract to an actuary who is independent of the *eligible claimant* and of the *relevant person*.

(2) In this *rule* and in COMP 12.4.14R, a benefit is only "excessive" if, at the time when the *relevant person* decided to confer or to offer to confer that benefit, no reasonable and prudent *insurer* in the position of the *relevant person* would have so decided given the *premiums* payable and other contractual terms.

12.4.14 **[R]** If the *FSCS* is satisfied, following the actuary's written recommendation, that any of the benefits provided for under the contract are or may be excessive, it may treat the liability of the *relevant person* under the contract as reduced or (as the case may be) disregarded for the purpose of any payment made after the date of that decision.

12.4.15 **[R]** The *FSCS* may rely on the value attributed to the contract by the actuary when calculating the compensation payable to the claimant, or when securing continuity of cover.

12.4.16 **[R]** For *claims* arising in connection with *protected contracts of insurance*, the *FSCS* must treat any term in an *insurance undertaking's* constitution or in its *contracts of insurance*, limiting the undertaking's liabilities under a *long-term insurance contract* to the amount of its assets, as limiting the undertaking's liabilities to any claimant to an amount which is not less than the gross assets of the undertaking.

Protected mortgage business

12.4.17 **[R]** The *FSCS* may pay compensation for any *claim* made in connection with any *protected home finance mediation* only to the extent that the *FSCS* considers that the payment of compensation is essential in order to provide the claimant with fair compensation.

12.4.18 **[R]** The *FSCS* must not pay compensation for any *claim* in connection with *protected home finance mediation* to the extent that it relates to or depends on:

(1) a failure of investment performance to match a guarantee given or representation made; or

(2) the mere fluctuation in the value of property.

12.4.19 **[R]** The *FSCS* may decide to reduce the compensation that would otherwise be payable for a *claim* made in connection with *protected home finance mediation* if it is satisfied that there is evidence of contributory negligence by the claimant and it would be inequitable for *FSCS* not to take account of that fact.

Protected non-investment insurance mediation

12.4.20 **[R]** The *FSCS* may pay compensation for any *claim* made in connection with *protected non-investment insurance mediation* only to the extent that the *FSCS* considers that the payment of compensation is essential in order to provide the claimant with fair compensation.

12.4.21 **[R]** The *FSCS* may decide to reduce the compensation that would otherwise be payable for a *claim* made in connection with *protected non-investment insurance mediation* if it is satisfied that:

(1) there is evidence of contributory negligence by the claimant; or

(2) payment of the full amount would provide a greater benefit than the claimant might reasonably have expected or than the benefit available on similar contracts with other *relevant persons*; and

it would be inequitable for *FSCS* not to take account of (1) or (2).

12.5.1 **[R]** [deleted]

12.5.2 **[R]** [deleted]

12.6 Quantification: trustees, operators of pension schemes, persons winding up pension schemes, personal representatives, agents, and joint claims

Trustees, operators of pension schemes and persons winding up pension schemes

12.6.1 **[R]** If a claimant's *claim* includes a *claim* as:

(1) trustee; or

(2) the *operator* of, or the *person* carrying on the *regulated activity* of *winding up*, a *stakeholder pension scheme* (which is not an *occupational pension scheme*) or *personal pension scheme*,

the *FSCS* must treat him in respect of that *claim* as if his *claim* was the *claim* of a different *person*.

12.6.2 **[R]** If a claimant has a *claim* as a bare trustee or *nominee company* for one or more beneficiaries, the *FSCS* must treat the beneficiary or beneficiaries as having the *claim*, and not the claimant.

12.6.2A **[R]** If a claimant has a *claim* as:

(1) the trustee of a *small self-administered scheme* or an *occupational pension scheme* of an employer which is not a *large company*, *large partnership* or *large mutual association* or the trustee or *operator* of, or the *person* carrying on the *regulated activity* of *winding up*, a *stakeholder pension scheme* (which is not an *occupational pension scheme*) or *personal pension scheme*,

(2) for one or more members of a pension scheme (or, where relevant, the beneficiary of any member) whose benefits are *money-purchase benefits*,

the *FSCS* must treat the member or members (or, where relevant, the beneficiary of any member) as having the *claim*, and not the claimant.

12.6.3 **[R]** If any group of *persons* has a *claim* as:

(1) trustees; or

(2) *operators* of, or as *persons* carrying on the *regulated activity* of *winding up*, a *stakeholder pension scheme* (which is not an *occupational pension scheme*) or a *personal pension scheme*,

(or any combination thereof), the *FSCS* must treat them as a single and continuing *person* distinct from the *persons* who may from time to time be the trustees, *operators* or *persons* winding up the relevant pension scheme.

12.6.4 **[R]** Where the same *person* has a *claim* as:

(1) trustee for different trusts, or for different *stakeholder pension schemes* (which are not *occupational pension schemes*) or *personal pension schemes*; or

(2) the *operator* of, or the *person* carrying on the *regulated activity* of *winding up*, different *stakeholder pension schemes* (which are not *occupational pension schemes*) or *personal pension schemes*,

COMP applies as if the *claims* relating to each of these trusts or schemes were *claims* of different *persons*.

12.6.5 **[R]** Where the claimant is a trustee, and some of the beneficiaries of the trust are *persons* who would not be *eligible claimants* if they had a claim themselves, the *FSCS* must adjust the amount of the overall net *claim* to eliminate the part of the claim which, in the *FSCS's* view, is a claim for those beneficiaries.

12.6.6 **[R]** Where any of the provisions of COMP 12.6.1R to COMP 12.6.5R apply, the *FSCS* must try to ensure that any amount paid to:

(1) the trustee; or

(2) the *operator* of, or the *person* carrying on the *regulated activity of winding up*, a *stakeholder pension scheme* (which is not an *occupational pension scheme*) or *personal pension scheme*,

is, in each case:

(3) for the benefit of members or beneficiaries who would be *eligible claimants* if they had a *claim* themselves; and

(4) no more than the amount of the loss suffered by those members or beneficiaries.

12.6.7 **[R]** Where a *person* A is entitled (whether as trustee or otherwise) to a *deposit* made out of a clients' or other similar account containing money to which one or more *persons* are entitled, the *FSCS* must treat each of those other persons, and not A, as entitled to the part of the *deposit* that corresponds to the proportion of the money in the account to which the other person is entitled.

Personal representative

12.6.8 **[R]** Where a *person* numbers among his *claims* a *claim* as the personal representative of another, the *FSCS* must treat him in respect of that *claim* as if he were standing in the shoes of that other *person*.

Agents

12.6.9 **[R]** If a claimant has a *claim* as agent for one or more *principals*, the *FSCS* must treat the *principal* or *principals* as having the *claim*, not the claimant.

Joint claims

12.6.10 **[R]** If two or more *persons* have a joint beneficial *claim*, the *claim* is to be treated as a *claim* of the partnership if they are carrying on business together in partnership. Otherwise each of those *persons* is taken to have a *claim* for his share, and in the absence of satisfactory evidence as to their respective shares, the *FSCS* must regard each *person* as entitled to an equal share.

Foreign law

12.6.11 **[R]** In applying COMP to *claims* arising out of business done with a *branch* or *establishment* of the *relevant person* outside the *United Kingdom*, the *FSCS* must interpret references to:

(1) *persons* entitled as personal representatives, trustees, bare trustees or agents, *operators* of *pension schemes* or *persons* carrying on the *regulated activity* of winding up *pension schemes*; or

(2) *persons* having a joint beneficial *claim* or carrying on business in partnership,

as references to *persons* entitled, under the law of the relevant country or territory, in a capacity appearing to the *FSCS* to correspond as nearly as may be to that capacity.

Claims arising under COMP 3.2.4R

12.6.12 **[R]** If a *firm* has a claim under COMP 3.2.4R, the *FSCS* must treat each *customer* of the *firm* as having the claim for the purposes of calculating compensation within COMP 12.

CHAPTER 13
FUNDING

[2196]
[deleted: the provisions in relation to the funding of the Financial Services Compensation Scheme are set out in FEES 6 (Financial Services Compensation Scheme Funding)]

COMP 13 Annex 1R

COMP 13 Ann 1 **[R]** [deleted: the provisions in relation to the funding of the Financial Services Compensation Scheme are set out in FEES 6 (Financial Services Compensation Scheme Funding)]

CHAPTER 14
PARTICIPATION BY EEA FIRMS

14.1 Application and Purpose

Application

[2197]
14.1.1 **[R]** This chapter applies to the *FSCS*.

14.1.2 **[R]** This chapter also applies to an *incoming EEA firm* which is *a credit institution*, an *ISD investment firm* (or both), an *IMD insurance intermediary* or a *UCITS management company*.

Purpose

14.1.3 **[G]** This chapter provides supplementary *rules* and *guidance* for an *incoming EEA firm* which is a *credit institution*, an *IMD insurance intermediary*, an *ISD investment firm* or *UCITS management company*. It reflects in part the implementation of the *Deposit Guarantee Directive*, *Investors Compensation Directive*, and *UCITS Directive*. This sourcebook applies in the usual way to an *incoming EEA firm* which is exercising *EEA rights* under the *Insurance Directives*. Such a *firm* is not affected by the *Deposit Guarantee Directive*, the *Investors Compensation Directive* or the *UCITS Directive*.

14.1.4 **[G]** An *incoming EEA firm*, which is a *credit institution*, an *IMD insurance intermediary*, an *ISD investment firm* or *UCITS management company*, is not a "*participant firm*" in relation to its *passported activities* unless it obtains the cover of, or "tops-up" into, the *compensation scheme* (for a *UCITS management company*, this is only for certain *passported activities*). This reflects section 213(10) of the *Act* (The compensation scheme) and regulation 2 of the *Electing Participants Regulations* (Persons not to be regarded as relevant persons). If an *incoming EEA firm* also carries on non-*passported activities* (or, for a *UCITS management company*, certain *passported activities*) for which the *compensation scheme* provides cover, it will be a *participant firm* in relation to those activities and will be covered by the *compensation scheme* for those activities in the usual way.

14.1.5 **[G]** In relation to an *incoming EEA firm's passported activities*, its *Home State* compensation scheme must provide compensation cover in respect of business within the scope of the *Deposit Guarantee Directive*, *Investors Compensation Directive* and article 5(3) of the *UCITS Directive*, whether that business is carried on from a *UK branch* or on a *cross border services* basis. (For a *UCITS management company*, this is only for certain *passported activities*.) *Insurance mediation activity* relating to *non-investment insurance contracts* is not within the scope of the *Deposit Guarantee Directive* and *Investors Compensation Directive*.

14.1.6 **[G]** If there is no cover provided by the *incoming EEA firm's Home State* or the scope and/or level of cover is less than that provided by the *compensation scheme*, this chapter enables the *firm* to obtain cover or 'top-up cover' from the *compensation scheme* for its *passported activities* carried on from a *UK branch*, up to the *compensation scheme's* limits (set out in COMP 10). This reflects section 214(5) of the *Act* (General) and regulation 3 of the *Electing Participants Regulations* (Persons who may elect to participate). If the *firm* "tops-up" and then becomes insolvent, the *Home State* compensation scheme will pay compensation up to the limit and scope of the *Home State* compensation scheme, with the *FSCS* paying compensation for the additional amount in accordance with the provisions in this sourcebook (COMP 12.4.1R and COMP 12.4.4R).

14.2 Obtaining top-up cover

14.2.1 **[R]** An *incoming EEA firm* may, by notice in writing to the *FSCS*, elect to receive *top-up cover* from the *compensation scheme* if it falls within one of the categories prescribed in regulation 3 of the *Electing Participants Regulations* (Persons who may elect to participate).

14.2.2 **[R]** An election under COMP 14.2.1R takes effect on the date when the *FSCS* notifies the *incoming EEA firm* that its election has been accepted.

14.2.3 **[G]** A notice under COMP 14.2.1R should include details confirming that the *incoming EEA firm* falls within a prescribed category. In summary:

(1) the *firm* must be a *credit institution*, an *IMD reinsurance intermediary*, an *ISD investment firm* or a *UCITS management company*;

(2) the *firm* must have established a *branch* in the *United Kingdom* in the exercise of an *EEA right*; and

(3) the scope and/or level of cover provided by the *firm's Home State* compensation scheme must be less than that provided by the *compensation scheme*.

14.2.4 **[R]** When the *FSCS* accepts an application, it must allocate the *incoming EEA firm* to the *contribution group* (or groups) which seems to the *FSCS* to be most appropriate, taking into account the nature of the business for which the *incoming EEA firm* is seeking cover from the *compensation scheme*.

14.2.5 **[R]** The *FSCS* must put in place and publish procedures to enable an appeal by an *incoming EEA firm* against a rejection by the *FSCS* of an election to receive *top-up cover* or a decision to allocate an *incoming EEA firm*, once the *firm's* election has been accepted, to a particular *contribution group*. Such procedures must satisfy the minimum requirements of procedural fairness and comply with the European Convention on Human Rights.

14.3 Co-operation between the FSCS and Home State compensation schemes

14.3.1 **[R]** Where an *incoming EEA firm* obtains *top-up cover* under COMP 14.2, the *FSCS* must co-operate with that *firm's Home State* compensation scheme. In particular, the *FSCS* must seek to establish with that *firm's Home State* compensation scheme appropriate procedures for the payment of compensation to claimants, following the principles set out in Annex II of the *Deposit Guarantee Directive* or Annex II of the *Investor Compensation Directive*, as appropriate.

[**Note**: article 4(5) of the *Deposit Guarantee Directive*]

14.4 Ending top-up cover

FSCS terminating top-up cover

14.4.1 **[R]** The *FSCS* must terminate an *incoming EEA firm's top-up cover* where it has ascertained that the conditions in COMP 14.2.1R are no longer satisfied.

14.4.2 **[R]** If an *incoming EEA firm* which has *top-up cover* fails to observe any of the *rules* in this sourcebook which apply to *participant firms*, the *FSCS* must notify the *FSA* and the *incoming EEA firm's Home State regulator*.

14.4.3 **[R]** In cases where COMP 14.4.2R applies, the *FSCS* must co-operate with the *incoming EEA firm's Home State regulator* so that appropriate measures can be taken to ensure that the *incoming EEA firm* meets its obligations under this sourcebook.

14.4.4 **[R]** If the *incoming EEA firm* fails to meet its obligations for a period of twelve months following the notice, the *FSCS* may, subject to obtaining the consent of the *incoming EEA firm's Home State regulator*, terminate its *top-up cover*. Notwithstanding the termination of *top-up cover* under this *rule*, cover will continue for:

(1) *protected deposits* which are not repayable on demand without penalty; and

(2) *protected investment business* transacted before that termination.

Resignation of an EEA firm from the compensation scheme

14.4.5 **[R]** An *incoming EEA firm* which has *top-up cover* may terminate that *top-up cover* by giving six month's notice in writing to the *FSCS*.

Notice to customers and the FSCS

14.4.6 **[R]** When an *incoming EEA firm's top-up cover* comes to an end under COMP 14.4.1R, COMP 14.4.4R or COMP 14.4.5R, it must:

(1) inform all the clients of its *UK branch* no later than six weeks after the date that its participation ends that they are no longer protected (or, if appropriate, of the more limited protection provided) by the *compensation scheme*, and of the level of compensation which is then available to them; and

(2) within two months, notify the *FSCS* whether it has done so.

14.4.7 **[R]** If an *incoming EEA firm* fails to comply with COMP 14.4.6R(1), the *FSCS* must inform the *firm's Home State regulator* of that fact.

14.4.8 **[R]** The *FSCS* must bring the ending of an *incoming EEA firm's top-up cover* to the attention of the *incoming EEA firm's* clients by means of a public notice.

CHAPTER 15
SPECIAL SITUATIONS

15.1 Accelerated compensation for depositors

Purpose

[2197A]

15.1.1 **[G]** When a *relevant person* is *in default* with claims against it for *protected deposits*, it may be desirable for the *FSCS* to make accelerated payments of compensation, for the protection of consumers and to maintain market confidence.

15.1.2 **[G]** To facilitate an accelerated payment of compensation, this section provides additional and alternative powers for the *FSCS*. These powers include the ability for the *FSCS* to pay compensation to *eligible claimants* without an application, to provide compensation by a variety of means and subject to conditions including by making a payment directly into an account maintained by another *authorised person*, to administer the payment of compensation on behalf of, or to pay compensation and recover from, another scheme or a government and/or to be subrogated automatically to the claimant's rights against the *relevant person* and/or any third party.

Application

15.1.3 **[R]** This section applies in respect of compensation for *claims* for *protected deposits*.

15.1.4 **[R]** Before using any power in this section, the *FSCS* must determine that using that power:

(1) would be beneficial to the generality of *eligible claimants* with *protected deposits* made with a *relevant person in default* in respect of whom the power is to be used; and
(2) is unlikely to result in any additional cost to the *FSCS* which would require the imposition of increased levies on *participant firms*, over and above those required if the power was not exercised, or any additional cost is likely to be justified by the benefits.

15.1.5 **[R]** The *FSCS's* powers in this section may be used:
(1) separately or in any combination as an alternative and in substitution for the powers and processes elsewhere in this sourcebook;
(2) in respect of a *relevant person in default* irrespective of when the default occurred;
(3) in relation to all or any part of a *protected deposit* or class of *protected deposits* made with the *relevant person*; and/or
(4) (where the *FSCS* uses its powers to administer the payment of compensation on behalf of, or to pay compensation or make a payment on account or an advance and recover from, a Non-UK Scheme or Other Funder (see COMP 15.1.14R)) in respect of all or part of any *protected deposit* which is compensatable by and/or recoverable from the Non-UK Scheme or Other Funder, and the *FSCS* may make different provision for those parts of a *protected deposit* (and references to paying compensation shall be treated as referring to making a payment, making a payment on account or making an advance as appropriate).

15.1.6 **[R]** The *FSCS* may determine that the exercise of any power in this section is subject to such incidental, consequential or supplemental conditions as the *FSCS* considers appropriate.

Determinations by the FSCS

15.1.7 **[R]**
(1) Any power conferred on the *FSCS* to make determinations under this section is exercisable in writing.
(2) An instrument by which the *FSCS* makes the determination must specify the provision under which it is made, the date and time from which it takes effect and the *relevant person* and *protected deposits*, parts of *protected deposits* and/or classes of *protected deposits* in respect of which it applies.
(3) The *FSCS* must take appropriate steps to publish the determination as soon as possible after it is made.
(4) Failure to comply with any requirement in this *rule* does not affect the validity of the determination.
(5) A determination by the *FSCS* under this section may be amended, remade or revoked at any time and subject to the same conditions.

Verification of determinations

15.1.8 **[R]**
(1) The production of a copy of a determination purporting to be made by the *FSCS* under this section:
  (a) on which is endorsed a certificate, signed by a member of the *FSCS's* staff authorised by it for that purpose; and
  (b) which contains the required statements; is evidence (or in Scotland sufficient evidence) of the facts stated in the certificate.
(2) The required statements are:
  (a) that the determination was made by the *FSCS*; and
  (b) that the copy is a true copy of the determination.
(3) A certificate purporting to be signed as mentioned in (1) is to be taken to have been properly signed unless the contrary is shown.
(4) A *person* who wishes in any legal proceedings to rely on a determination may require the *FSCS* to endorse a copy of the determination with a certificate of the kind mentioned in (1).

Effect of this section on other provisions in this sourcebook etc

15.1.9 **[R]** Other provisions in this sourcebook and FEES 6 are modified to the extent necessary to give full effect to the powers provided for in this section.

15.1.10 **[R]** Other than as expressly provided for, nothing in this section is to be taken as limiting or modifying the rights or obligations of or powers conferred on the *FSCS* elsewhere in this sourcebook or in FEES 6.

Payment of compensation without an application

15.1.11 **[R]** The *FSCS* may treat an *eligible claimant* as if the *eligible claimant* had made a *claim* under the *compensation scheme* and pay compensation to an *eligible claimant* without having received an application and/or an assignment of the whole or any part of the claimant's rights against the *relevant person* and/or any third party (and COMP 3.2.1R(1) and COMP 7.2.1R are modified accordingly).

Early compensation for term or notice accounts

15.1.12 **[R]** If a *protected deposit* was not due and payable on or before the date that the *relevant person* was determined to be *in default*, the *FSCS* may nevertheless treat that date as the *quantification date* for that *deposit* and pay compensation on the basis that the principal sum (including any interest attributable up to that date) is due and payable on that date either (as determined by the *FSCS*):

(1) with the consent of the *eligible claimant* (express or implied, including by conduct); or

(2) without that consent, but in this case the amount that the *eligible claimant* is entitled to claim from the *FSCS* is the lesser of:

  (a) the amount which the *FSCS* quantifies as being the value of that *claim* as at the *quantification date*; and

  (b) the amount that would have been payable at the date the *deposit* was due and payable; and

COMP 12.3.1R is modified accordingly.

Form and method of paying compensation

15.1.13 **[R]** The *FSCS* may pay compensation in any form and by any method (or any combination of them) that it determines is appropriate including, without limitation:

(1) by paying the compensation (on such terms as the *FSCS* considers appropriate) to an *authorised person* with *permission* to *accept deposits* which agrees to become liable to the claimant in a like sum;

(2) by paying compensation directly into an existing deposit account of (or for the benefit of) the claimant, or as otherwise identified by (or on behalf of) the claimant, with an *authorised person* (but before doing so the *FSCS* must take such steps as it considers appropriate to verify the existence of such an account and to give notice to the claimant of its intention to exercise this power); and/or

(3) (where two or more *persons* have a joint beneficial *claim*) by accepting communications from and/or paying compensation to any one of those *persons* where this is in accordance with the terms and conditions for communications and withdrawals of the *protected deposit*.

Payment of compensation to which claimant is entitled from another scheme etc

15.1.14 **[R]** If the *FSCS* is satisfied that:

(1) a claimant is or is likely at some future date to become entitled to receive a payment of compensation in respect of his actual, contingent or future rights against a *relevant person in default*:

  (a) under a scheme which is maintained by an *EEA State* or any other state or *person* comparable to the *compensation scheme* (in this section, a "Non-UK Scheme"); and/or

  (b) as a result of a guarantee given or arrangements made by the Government of the *United Kingdom*, an *EEA State*, any other government or any other authority (in this section, an "Other Funder"); and

(2) the *FSCS* has received prior funding in respect of, or is satisfied that it will be able to recover, the amount of that payment from the Non-UK Scheme or Other Funder; the *FSCS* may, irrespective of whether or not the *relevant person* is in default under the laws or regulations of any other *EEA State* or any other state or law-country:

(3) make a payment in respect of all or part of that compensation (whether or not yet due or payable) from the Non-UK Scheme or Other Funder, with or without the Non-UK Scheme or Other Funder's prior agreement;

(4) make a payment on account of, or advance to the claimant, the whole or part of the amount in (3) on such terms as the *FSCS* considers appropriate;

(5) (having been satisfied as to the total amount to be paid or advanced to the claimant) ascertain the proportion of any such payment or advance attributable to the Non-UK Scheme or Other Funder at any time, whether before or after making the payment or advance;

(6) (to the extent that prior funding has not been provided by the Non-UK Scheme or Other Funder) recover from the Non-UK Scheme or Other Funder the whole or any part of the amount of compensation paid or monies paid on account or advanced in respect of potential compensation which is or is likely to be payable to a claimant by the Non-UK Scheme or Other Funder, in accordance with COMP 15.1.17R to COMP 15.1.20R; and/or

(7) take such other steps in connection with such payment or advance by the *FSCS* or to facilitate the payment of compensation that is due or may become due from the Non-UK Scheme or Other Funder as the *FSCS* considers appropriate; and references to payment of compensation, payment on account or advance to the claimant include taking such action for the claimant's benefit or on the claimant's behalf.

15.1.15 **[R]** In determining the proportion of any such payment or advance attributable to the *FSCS*, a Non UK Scheme or Other Funder, the *FSCS* may use any methodology or approach it considers appropriate if (and to the extent that) it considers that the cost of ascertaining the proportion by reference to each claimant would exceed or be disproportionate to the benefit of doing so.

15.1.16 **[R]** If the ***FSCS*** has made a payment or advance attributable to a Non-UK Scheme or Other Funder, and has acquired a right of recovery against the *relevant person* or any third party in respect of that amount, the *FSCS* may determine that the whole or any part of any recoveries which it makes shall be held by it for the benefit of and/or shared amongst the *FSCS*, that Non- UK Scheme, that Other Funder and/or any other *person* which has provided prior funding in respect of a payment or advance attributable to any such body (and COMP 7.2.3AR is modified accordingly).

Rights and obligations against the relevant person and third parties

15.1.17 **[R]** The *FSCS* may determine that:
(1) the payment of compensation by the *FSCS*; and/or
(2) the following actions by the *FSCS* (under COMP 15.1.14R):
  (a) administering the payment of compensation on behalf of; and/or
  (b) paying and/or making a payment on account of compensation from; a Non-UK Scheme or Other Funder; shall have all or any of the following effects:
(3) the *FSCS* shall immediately and automatically be subrogated, subject to such conditions as the *FSCS* determines are appropriate, to all or any part (as determined by the *FSCS*) of the rights and claims in the *United Kingdom* and elsewhere of the claimant against the *relevant person* and/or any third party (whether such rights are legal, equitable or of any other nature whatsoever and in whatever capacity the *relevant person* or third party is acting) in respect of or arising out of the *claim* in respect of which the payment of or on account of compensation was made;
(4) the *FSCS* may claim and take legal or any other proceedings or steps in the *United Kingdom* or elsewhere to enforce such rights in its own name or in the name of, and on behalf of, the claimant or in both names against the *relevant person* and/or any third party;
(5) the subrogated rights and claims conferred on the *FSCS* shall be rights of recovery and claims against the *relevant person* and/or any third party which are equivalent (including as to amount and priority and whether or not the *relevant person* is insolvent) to and not exceed the rights and claims that the claimant would have had; and/or
(6) such rights and/or obligations (as determined by the *FSCS*) as between the *relevant person* and the claimant arising out of the *protected deposit* in respect of which the payment was made shall be transferred to, and subsist between, another *authorised person* with *permission* to *accept deposits* and the claimant provided that the *authorised person* has consented (but the transferred rights and/or obligations shall be treated as existing between the *relevant person* and the *FSCS* to the extent of any subrogation, transfer or assignment for the purposes of (3) to (5) and COMP 15.1.18R).

15.1.18 **[R]** The *FSCS* may alternatively or additionally make the actions in COMP 15.1.17R(1) and (2) conditional on the claimant assigning or transferring the whole or any part of all such rights as he may have against the *relevant person* and/or any third party (including, for the avoidance of any doubt, any Non-UK Scheme or Other Funder) on such terms as the *FSCS* determines are appropriate.

15.1.19 **[R]** The *FSCS* may determine that the making of an advance by the *FSCS* to the claimant (under COMP 15.1.14R(4)) shall have the effect that the *FSCS* may claim and take legal or any other proceedings or steps in the *United Kingdom* or elsewhere to enforce the rights and claims of the claimant referred to in COMP 15.1.17R(3) in the name of, and on behalf of, the claimant against the *relevant person* and/or any third party.

15.1.20 **[R]**
(1) The *FSCS* may determine that:
  (a) if the claimant does not assign or transfer his rights under COMP 15.1.18R;
  (b) if it is impractical to obtain such an assignment or transfer; and/or
  (c) if it is otherwise necessary or desirable in conjunction with the exercise of the *FSCS's* powers under COMP 15.1.17R to COMP 15.1.19R; that claimant shall be treated as having irrevocably and unconditionally appointed the chairman of the *FSCS* for the time being to be his attorney and agent and on his behalf and in his name or otherwise to do such things and execute such deeds and documents as may be required under such laws of the *United Kingdom*, another *EEA State* or any other state or law-country to create or give effect to such assignment or transfer or otherwise give full effect to those powers.
(2) The execution of any deed or document under (1) shall be as effective as if made in writing by the claimant or by his agent lawfully authorised in writing or by will.

CHAPTER 16
DISCLOSURE REQUIREMENTS FOR FIRMS THAT ACCEPT DEPOSITS

16.1 Application and purpose

[2197B]
16.1.1 **[R]** This chapter applies to:
(1) a *UK domestic firm* that *accepts deposits*;
(2) a *non-EEA firm* that *accepts deposits* in the *United Kingdom*; and
(3) an *incoming EEA firm* that *accepts deposits* through a *UK branch*.

16.1.2 **[G]** The purpose of this chapter is to set out the information about compensation that these *firms* must disclose, how frequently that information should be disclosed and the methods of communication which should be used.

16.2 Informing depositors of limitations to coverage

16.2.1 **[R]**
(1) If a *protected deposit* is not protected by the *compensation scheme*, the *firm* must inform the depositor accordingly.
(2) A *firm* must make the information required by (1) available in a readily comprehensible manner.

[**Note**: article 9(1) of the *Deposit Guarantee Directive*]

16.2.2 **[R]** When providing the information required by COMP 16.2.1R, a *firm* must use the communication channels it normally uses when communicating with its depositors.

16.3 UK domestic firms, non-EEA firms and incoming EEA firms

UK domestic firms and non-EEA firms

16.3.1 **[R]** A *firm* that is a *UK domestic firm* or a *non-EEA firm* must disclose the following information to any *protected deposit* holder with that *firm* who is or is likely to be an *eligible claimant*.

> **"Important information about compensation arrangements**
>
> We are covered by the Financial Services Compensation Scheme (FSCS). The FSCS can pay compensation to depositors if a [bank/building society/credit union – delete as appropriate] is unable to meet its financial obligations. Most depositors – including most individuals and small businesses – are covered by the scheme.
>
> In respect of deposits, an eligible depositor is entitled to claim up to [insert FSCS maximum payment for *protected deposits*]. For joint accounts each account holder is treated as having a claim in respect of their share so, for a joint account held by two eligible depositors, the maximum amount that could be claimed would be [insert FSCS maximum payment for *protected deposits*] each (making a total of [insert FSCS maximum payment for *protected deposits* × 2]). The [insert FSCS maximum payment for *protected deposits*] limit relates to the combined amount in all the eligible depositor's accounts with the [bank/building society/credit union – delete as appropriate], including their share of any joint account, and not to each separate account.
>
> For further information about the scheme (including the amounts covered and eligibility to claim) please ask at your local branch, refer to the FSCS website www.FSCS.org.uk or call [insert FSCS phone number]."

16.3.2 **[G]** A *UK domestic firm* that discloses the information required to be disclosed by COMP 16.3.1 R to *persons* that hold *protected deposits* through an overseas *branch* may do so in the local language.

Incoming EEA firms that accept deposits through UK branches and have not obtained top-up cover

16.3.3 **[R]** An *incoming EEA firm* that *accepts deposits* through a *UK branch* and has not obtained *top-up cover* must disclose the following information to any *protected deposit* holder with that *branch* who is or is likely to be eligible to claim for compensation from the *firm's Home State* compensation scheme.

> **"Important information about compensation arrangements**
>
> We are part of [insert name of *firm*] which is based in [insert name of *Home State*]. Most depositors are covered by [insert name of *Home State* compensation scheme] which is also based in [insert name of *Home State*].

> This means that if our bank is unable to meet its financial obligations, our eligible UK depositors would be entitled to claim up to £ [insert *Home State* compensation scheme maximum payment for *protected deposits*] from the [insert name of *Home State* compensation scheme]. [State any significant conditions that compensation is subject to e.g. if paid on a per account or per depositor basis, and if set-off applies].
>
> For further information about the [insert name of *Home State* compensation scheme] (including the amounts covered and eligibility to claim) please contact your branch or refer to [insert contact details of the *Home State* compensation scheme]."

Incoming EEA firms that accept deposits through UK branches and have obtained top-up cover

16.3.4 **[R]** An *incoming EEA firm* that *accepts deposits* through a *UK branch* and has obtained *top-up cover* must disclose the following information to any *protected deposit* holder with that *firm* who is or is likely to be an *eligible claimant*.

> **"Important information about compensation arrangements**
>
> We are part of [insert name of *firm*] which is based in [insert name of *Home State*]. Most depositors are covered by [insert name of *Home State* compensation scheme] compensation scheme which is also based in [insert name of *Home State*]. In addition, for depositors with our UK branch we have joined the UK compensation scheme, the Financial Services Compensation Scheme (FSCS).
>
> This means that if our bank is unable to meet its financial obligations, eligible depositors with our UK branch could claim up to £ [insert *Home State* compensation scheme maximum payment for *protected deposits*] from the [insert name of *Home State* compensation scheme] and if they have more saved with us,. they could also claim for the remainder up to [insert *FSCS* maximum payment for *protected deposits*] from the *FSCS*. This is because the [insert name of *Home State* compensation scheme] is only responsible for paying the first part of the compensation up to £ [insert *Home State* compensation scheme maximum payment for *protected deposits*] and the *FSCS* is only responsible for paying the second part of compensation – being above £ [insert *Home State* compensation scheme maximum payment for *protected deposits*] and up to [insert *FSCS* maximum payment for *protected deposits*].
>
> The FSCS will also try to help depositors with our UK branch, for example, to get in touch with the [insert name of *Home State* compensation scheme] compensation scheme and to understand the process involved.
>
> For further information on how compensation would apply to you please contact:
>
> - [insert name of *firm*] by dropping into one of our branches, at [insert website link] or by calling [insert phone number].
>
> General information is also available from:
>
> - the FSCS by calling [insert *FSCS* phone number] or at http://www.fscs.org.uk/.
> - [insert name of *Home State* compensation scheme] compensation scheme by contacting [insert relevant phone number and website link]."

Incoming EEA firms: conversion of home state compensation scheme limit to sterling

16.3.5 **[G]** When an incoming *EEA firm* inserts the *Home State* compensation scheme maximum payment for *protected deposits* in the disclosure required by this section, that amount should be converted into pounds sterling and the exchange rate noted in a footnote. The exchange rate used should be updated regularly.

Frequency of communication

16.3.6 **[R]**

(1) A *firm* must provide the information required to be disclosed by this section on at least a 6 monthly basis.

(2) If a *firm* normally communicates with a *protected deposit* holder less frequently than every 6 months (1) does not apply and the *firm* must provide the information required to be disclosed by this section on at least an annual basis.

16.3.7 **[G]** The *FSA* considers monthly, quarterly or 6 monthly account statements to be a means of communication for these purposes.

Method of communication

16.3.8 **[R]**

(1) If the recipient receives paper statements, the information required to be disclosed by this section must be prominently displayed in the relevant paper statement.

(2) If the recipient uses internet banking, the information required to be disclosed by this section must be communicated by electronic means in a way that brings it to the attention of the recipient.

(3) If the recipient does not receive paper statements or use internet banking the information required to be disclosed by this section must be communicated in a way that brings it to the attention of the recipient.

16.3.9 **[G]** The *FSA* considers that if information required to be disclosed by this section is communicated by letter/leaflet sent through the post, email or a pop up box on the *firm's* internet website the requirement to communicate in a way that brings the information to the attention of the recipient will have been satisfied.

Trading name disclosure

16.3.10 **[R]** Where a *firm* operates under more than one trading name, the *firm* must, in any communication required by this section to a *protected deposit* holder who is or is likely to be eligible to claim for compensation from the *compensation scheme* or other *Home State* compensation scheme and generally in its *UK branches* and on its website, prominently disclose the trading names under which it operates and explain the impact this has on any *protected deposit* holder's entitlement to compensation from the *compensation scheme* and any relevant *Home State* or *Host State* compensation scheme.

Further disclosure

16.3.11 **[G]** A *firm* should ensure that all communications to consumers about compensation for *protected deposits* are clear, fair and not misleading.

16.3.12 **[G]** A *firm* should also consider its obligations under the Credit Institutions (Protection of Depositors) Regulations 1995.

Transitional Provisions Table
[2198]

(1)	(2) **Material to which the transitional provision applies**	(3)	(4) **Transitional Provision**		(5) **Transitional provision: dates in force**	(6) **Handbook Provisions coming into force**
1	COMP 5	R	Protected claims		Indefinitely	Commencement
			(1)	A *claim* for a *protected deposit* or under a *protected contract of insurance* includes a *claim* in respect of an *article 9 default*, subject to (2)		
			(2)	A *claim* must be treated as a *claim* in relation to a *protected contract of insurance* under COMP 5.4.5R if the conditions in article 9A or 10(1)(a)–(d) of the *compensation transitionals order* are satisfied.		*Commencement* but on 6 December 2006 for article 9A of the *compensation transitionals order*
			(3)	A *claim* in connection with *protected investment business* includes a claim in respect of a *pending application*.		

(1)	(2) Material to which the transitional provision applies	(3)	(4) Transitional Provision			(5) Transitional provision: dates in force	(6) Handbook Provisions coming into force
			(4)	Where the *claim* is in respect of an *article 9 default* or a *pending application*, the *FSCS* must apply the rules of the *relevant former scheme*, as they applied to the default before *commencement*, unless (2) applies.			
			(5)	The rules of each *investment business compensation scheme* are amended so that references to the person managing the scheme are replaced by references to the *FSCS*.			
			(6)	The rules of the Friendly Societies Protection Scheme are amended so that:			
				(a)	references to the person managing the scheme are replaced by references to the *FSCS*; and		
				(b)	references to functions conferred upon the Friendly Societies Protection Scheme Board are replaced by references to functions conferred upon the *FSCS*.		
			(7)	Where the default occurs after *commencement*, a *claim* for a *protected deposit* includes a *claim* that arose before *commencement* in respect of:			
				(a)	a deposit within the meaning of the Banking Act 1987; and		
				(b)	a *claim* in respect of a protected investment within the meaning of section 27 of the Building Societies Act 1986.		

(1)	(2) **Material to which the transitional provision applies**	(3)	(4) **Transitional Provision**	(5) **Transitional provision: dates in force**	(6) **Handbook Provisions coming into force**
			(8) Where the default occurs after *commencement*, a *claim* in connection with *protected investment business* includes a *claim* that could have been entertained under an *investment business compensation scheme* (provided that the person making the claim has not also made a *pending application* arising out of the same set of facts).		
2	COMP 13.5R and COMP 13.6R	R	Expired		
3	COMP 13.4.6R and COMP 13.6.7R	R	Expired		
4	COMP 13.5.8R	R	Expired		
5	COMP 6.2.1R	R	Credit unions	Indefinitely	Commencement
			In relation to a *claim* or potential *claim* referred to in (1) or (2), a *relevant person* is also any credit union which:		
			(1) becomes unable, or is likely to become unable, to satisfy *claims* against it which relate to *deposits* which were accepted before 2 July 2002; or		
			(2) (a) has ceased to have *Part IV permission* by virtue of article 3(4) of the Financial Services and Markets Act 2000 (Permission and Applications) (Credit Unions etc.) Order 2002 (SI 2002/704) (failure to comply with a direction to re-apply for *Part IV permission*); and		

(1)	(2) Material to which the transitional provision applies	(3)	(4) Transitional Provision		(5) Transitional provision: dates in force	(6) Handbook Provisions coming into force
			(b)	thereafter, becomes unable, or is likely to become unable, to satisfy *claims* against it which relate to *deposits* which were accepted on or after 2 July 2002 but before the date on which it ceased to have *Part IV permission.*		
6	COMP 6.2.1R	G	In consequence of transitional provision 5R, compensation can be provided:			
			(a)	in respect of a credit union which is unable, or likely to become unable, to satisfy *claims* for *protected deposits* accepted before 2 July 2002; and		
			(b)	where a credit union has ceased to hold a *Part IV permission* (because of failure to comply with a direction to re-apply for the *Part IV permission*), for *protected deposits* accepted on or after 2 July 2002 but before the date at which it ceased to have the *Part IV permission*.		
7	COMP 6.2.1R	G	In consequence of transitional provision 5R(1), a credit union becomes a *relevant person* in respect of *deposits* accepted before 2 July 2002.			
8	Amendments introduced by the Compensation Sourcebook (Amendment No 2) Instrument 2003	R	Provisions and definitions arising out of (2) only apply to defaults, or circumstances giving rise to arrangements made under COMP 3.3.1R or to measures taken under COMP 3.3.3R, occurring after the date in (6).		Indefinitely	1 December 2003
9	COMP 13.6.8R	R	Expired			
10	COMP 5.7.1R, 13.4.7BR and 13.6.9BR	R	Rules not in effect.		31 October 2004 to 13 January 2005	31 October 2004

(1)	(2) **Material to which the transitional provision applies**	(3)	(4) **Transitional Provision**	(5) **Transitional provision: dates in force**	(6) **Handbook Provisions coming into force**
11	FEES 6.3.1R, FEES 6.3.22R, FEES 6.4.8R, FEES 6.4.6R, FEES 6.5.1R and FEES 6.5.6R	R	With regard to *contribution group* A.18 – Mortgage lenders, advisers and arrangers, the *management expenses levy* and *compensation costs levy* for 2005/2006 may also take account of expenditure in the period 31 October 2004 to 31 March 2005.	31 October 2004 to 31 March 2006	31 October 2004
12	FEES 6.5.7R(4), FEES 6.3.22R, FEES 6.4.6R, FEES 6.4.8R, FEES 6.5.1R and FEES 6.5.6R	R	With regard to *contribution group* A.19 – General insurance mediation, the *management expenses levy* and *compensation costs levy* for 2005/2006 may also take account of expenditure in the period 14 January 2005 to 31 March 2005.	14 January 2005 to 31 March 2006	31 October 2004
13	FEES 6.5.7(4)R, FEES 6.5.10R and FEES 6.5.13R(2)	R	For the period 31 October 2004 to 31 March 2006 the tariff base will be the annual income (relating to the relevant *contribution group*) reported in accordance with note 3 to *AUTH* 4 Ann 2 or, if the *firm* prefers, that amount of its annual income which is attributable to business conducted with *eligible claimants* but only if the *firm* notifies *FSCS* of the amount by 28 February 2005.	31 October 2004 to 31 March 2006	31 October 2004
14	FEES 6.5.7R(5), FEES 6.5.11R and FEES 6.5.13R (2)		For the period 14 January 2005 to 31 March 2006 the tariff base will be the annual income (relating to the relevant *contribution group*) reported in accordance with note 3 to *AUTH* 4 Ann 2 or, if the *firm* prefers, that amount of its annual income which is attributable to business conducted with *eligible claimants* but only if the *firm* notifies *FSCS* of the amount by 28 February 2005.	14 January 2005 to 31 March 2006	31 October 2004
15	COMP 5.4.4R (4)(a) and 5.4.4R (4)(b)	R	The changes to COMP 5.4.4R (4) made in the Compensation Sourcebook (Amendment No 7) Instrument 2006 do not apply in relation to defaults declared before 6 June 2006.	Indefinitely	6 June 2006
16	COMP 10.2.3R	R	The change to the limit for *protected deposits* made by the Compensation Sourcebook (Protected Deposits Limit) Instrument 2007 does not apply in relation to a *claim* against a *relevant person* that was *in default* before 1 October 2007.	From 1 October 2007 indefinitely	Amended with effect from 1 October 2007

(1)	(2) Material to which the transitional provision applies	(3)	(4) Transitional Provision		(5) Transitional provision: dates in force	(6) Handbook Provisions coming into force
17	Amendments introduced by the Compensation Sourcebook (Amendment No 8) Instrument 2008	R	Provisions and definitions arising out of (2) only apply to defaults on or occurring after 7 October 2008		From 7 October 2008 indefinitely	7 October 2008
18	COMP 10.2.3R	R	The change to the limit for *protected deposits* made by the Compensation Sourcebook (Deposit Guarantee Schemes Directive Amendments) Instrument 2009 does not apply in relation to a *claim* against a *relevant person* that was *in default* before 30 June 2009		From 30 June 2009	30 June 2009 indefinitely
19	Amendments to COMP 10.2.3R introduced by the Financial Services Compensation Scheme (Limits Amendment) Instrument 2009	R	Provisions and definitions arising out of (2) only apply to defaults on or occurring after 1 January 2010		From 1 January 2010 indefinitely	1 January 2010
20	COMP 4.3.1R	R	The change to the eligibility requirements for claimants for *protected deposits* made by the Financial Services Compensation Scheme (Banking Compensation Reform) Instrument 2009 does not apply in relation to a *claim* against a *relevant person* that was *in default* before 1 August 2009		From 1 August 2009 indefinitely	1 August 2009
21	COMP 17.3 and COMP 17.2.7R	R	(1)	This transitional provision applies to a firm to which COMP 17 will apply	From 6 December 2009 until 30 December 2010	31 December 2010
			(2)	If a firm operates less than 5,000 accounts held by eligible claimants, it may make revoke an election (under COMP 17.2.7R) that the *electronic SCV rules* do not apply.		
			(3)	A *firm* that made a valid election under (2) must provide the *FSA* with an SCV pre-implementation report by 31 July 2010 based on the *firm's* progress as at 30 June 2010 which must:		

(1)	(2) Material to which the transitional provision applies	(3)	(4) Transitional Provision			(5) Transitional provision: dates in force	(6) Handbook Provisions coming into force
				(a)	state the number of accounts held by *eligible claimants* as at 30 June 2010;		
				(b)	confirm that the *firm* is making the election in (2); and		
				(c)	state whether the *firm's* board of directors believes the *firm* will comply with the *FSA's SCV requirements* by 31 December 2010 and if not why not.		
			(4)	A *firm* that has not made a valid election under (2) must provide the *FSA* with an SCV pre-implementation report by 30 July 2010 based on the *firm's* progress as at 30 June 2010 which must state:			
				(a)	whether the *firm* has a plan for implementing the *FSA's SCV requirements*;		
				(b)	how the *firm* proposes to transfer to the *FSCS* a *single customer view* for each *eligible claimant* including specifying the transfer method and format;		
				(c)	the dates the *firm* started implementation and plans to end implementation and whether implementation is on time;		
				(d)	whether the *firm's* board of directors believes implementation will be completed by 31 December 2010 and if not why not; and		

(1)	(2) Material to which the transitional provision applies	(3)	(4) Transitional Provision		(5) Transitional provision: dates in force	(6) Handbook Provisions coming into force
			(e)	any issues that may impact on the *firm's* ability to implement by 31 December 2010.		

SCHEDULE 1
RECORD-KEEPING REQUIREMENTS

[2199]

Sch 1.1 **[G]**

(1) The aim of the guidance in the following able is to give the reader a quick overall view of the relevant record keeping requirements. The Rules listed below apply only to FSCS (the scheme manager).

(2) It is not a complete statement of those requirements and should not be relied upon as it were.

Sch 1.2 **[G]** Table

Handbook reference	Subject of record	Contents of record	When record must be made	Retention period
FEES 6.3.14R	FSCS funding	Full details of the movement of funds within sub-schemes.	Ongoing requirement.	N/A
COMP 10.2.10R(3)	Potential claimants for whom the separate limit under COMP 10.2.10R(2) applies	Sufficient details to enable the identification of claimants for whom the separate limit under COMP 10.2.10R(2) applies	As implicit from the *rules* in COMP	As implicit from the *rules* in COMP
COMP 10.2.11R	Potential claimants for whom the separate limit under COMP 10.2.11R(2) applies	Sufficient details to enable the identification of claimants for whom the separate limit under COMP 10.2.11R(2) applies	As implicit from the *rules* in COMP	As implicit from the *rules* in COMP

SCHEDULE 2
NOTIFICATION REQUIREMENTS

[2200]

Sch 2.1 **[G]**

(1) The aim of the guidance in the following table is to give the reader a quick overall view of the relevant requirements for notification and reporting. In all cases, other than those concerning Chapter 13 and Chapter 14, the notification rules in COMP apply only to FSCS (the scheme manager).

(2) It is not a complete statement of those requirements and should not be relied on as if it were.

Sch 2.2 **[G]** Table

Handbook reference	Matter to be notified	Contents of notification	Trigger event	Time allowed
COMP 2.2.5G	Annual Report	Not specified in COMP – see Memorandum of Understanding (MoU) between FSA and FSCS	End of Financial Year	Not specified in COMP (see MoU)

Handbook reference	**Matter to be notified**	**Contents of notification**	**Trigger event**	**Time allowed**
COMP 2.2.7R	Default of relevant person	Not specified – although FSCS must take appropriate steps to ensure claimants are informed about how they can claim compensation	Default of a relevant person	Not specified – but as soon as practicable after determining default
FEES 6.2.1R	Right to exemption for specific costs and compensation costs levy	Notice that firm does not conduct business that could give rise to a claim on the FSCS and has no reasonable likelihood of doing so	If it does not, or if it ceases to, conduct business with persons eligible to claim on FSCS, unless it has already given such notice	None specified though exemption generally only takes effect from the date of receipt of notice by FSCS
FEES 6.2.4R	Loss of right to seek exemption from specific costs & compensation costs levy	Statement that firm no longer qualifies for exemption because it carries on business with persons eligible to claim on FSCS	Firm looses the right to claim the exemption	As soon as reasonably practicable
FEES 6.5.13R	Levy base for participant firm	The contribution groups to which the participant firm belongs. The total amount of business (measured in accordance with the appropriate tariff bases, which it conducted as at 31 December of the previous year	The end of the calendar year (the occasion of 31 December every year beginning with 31 December 2001)	By end February
FEES 6.7	Participant firms compensation levy for the financial year	Amount of levy payable by the participant firm	The decision by the FSCS that it must impose a levy	30 days before the levy is payable
COMP 14.2.1R	Application by eligible inward passporting EEA firm to obtain *top-up cover* into compensation scheme	That firm is qualifying incoming EEA firm. The sub-scheme(s) the firm wishes to participate in	The firm's decision that it wishes to obtain *top-up cover* into the UK scheme	N/A
		Confirmation that the level or scope of cover offered by its home state scheme(s) is less than that available in the UK		
COMP 14.4.5R	Termination of top-up cover	Statement that incoming EEA firm is terminating top-up cover	Decision by firm to resign from FSCS	6 months notice

Handbook reference	**Matter to be notified**	**Contents of notification**	**Trigger event**	**Time allowed**
COMP 14.4.6R	Termination of inward passporting EEA firm's top-up cover into compensation scheme	The firm's resignation from the compensation scheme and the level of compensation available to clients of the firm's UK branch following its decision to resign from FSCS	Termination of firm's top-up cover	No later than six weeks after the end of the firms participation in compensation scheme
COMP TP 21R(2) and COMP 17.2.7 R	Election or revocation of election that the *electronic SCV rules* do not apply.	See Matter to be notified	See Matter to be notified	Immediately

SCHEDULE 3
FEES AND OTHER REQUIRED PAYMENTS

[2201]
Sch 3.1 **[G]** The rules in FEES 6 give FSCS (the scheme manager) the power to raise levies on participant firms in order to meet its expenses. The rules in FEES 6 do not specify the amount of any levy but do specify how a participant firm's share of a levy is to be calculated and any limit on the amount leviable by the FSCS is a particular period.

SCHEDULE 4
POWERS EXERCISED

[2202]
Sch 4.1 **[G]** The following powers and related provisions in or under the *Act* and the Financial Services and Markets Act 2000 (Transitional Provisions, Repeals and Savings) (Financial Services Compensation Scheme) Order 2001 ("the *compensation transitionals order*") have been exercised by the *FSA* to make the *rules* in COMP:

(1) Section 138 (General rule making power)
(2) Section 156 (General supplementary powers)
(3) Section 213 (The compensation scheme)
(4) Section 214 (General)
(5) Section 215 (Rights of the scheme in insolvency)
(6) Section 216 (Continuity of long term insurance policies)
(7) Section 217 (Insurers in financial difficulties)
(8) Section 218 (Annual report)
(9) Section 218A (Authority's power to require information)
(10) Section 219 (Scheme manager's power to require information)
(11) Section 316(1) (Direction by Authority)
(12) Article 4 (Pending Applications) of the *compensation transitionals order*
(13) Article 6 (Post-commencement applications) of the *compensation transitionals order*
(14) Article 9 (Article 9 defaults occurring before commencement) of the *compensation transitionals order*
(15) Article 9A (Contributions in relation to mesothelioma claims) of the *compensation transitionals order*
(16) Article 10 (Applications in respect of compulsory liability insurance) of the *compensation transitionals order*
(17) Article 12 (Applications under the new scheme) of the *compensation transitionals order*

Sch 4.2 **[G]** The following additional powers have been exercised by the *FSA* to make the *rules* in COMP:

(1) Articles 3 (Further power for Authority to make rules concerning mesothelioma claims) and 4 (Modification of FSMA in relation to FSA rules for mesothelioma claims) of the *mesothelioma regulations*.
(2) Section 123 (Role of FSCS) of the Banking Act 2009

Sch 4.3 **[G]** The following powers in the *Act* have been exercised by the *FSA* to give the *guidance* in COMP:

(1) Section 157(1) (Guidance)

SCHEDULE 5
RIGHTS OF ACTION FOR DAMAGES

[2203]
Sch 5.1 **[G]**
(1) The table below sets out the *rules* in COMP contravention of which by an *authorised person* may be actionable under section 150 of the *Act* (Actions for damages) by a *person* who suffers loss as a result of the contravention.
(2) If a "yes" appears in the column headed "For private person?", the *rule* may be actionable by a "*private person*" under section 150 unless a "yes" appears in the column headed "Removed". A "yes" in the column headed "Removed" indicates that the *FSA* has removed the right of action under section 150(2) of the *Act*. If so, a reference to the *rule* in which it is removed is also given.
(3) In accordance with the Financial Services and Markets Act 2000 (Rights of Action) Regulations 2001 (SI 2001/2256) a "private person" is:
(i) any individual, except when acting in the course of carrying on a *regulated activity*; and
(ii) any *person* who is not an individual, except when acting in the course of carrying on business of any kind;
but does not include a government, local authority or an international organisation.
(4) The column headed "For other person?" indicates whether the rule is actionable by a *person* other than a *private person*, in accordance with those Regulations. If so, an indication of the type of person by whom the rule is actionable is given.
(5) The vast majority of *rules* in COMP are *rules* to which the *FSCS* is subject. No right of action arises under section 150 for breach of these *rules*, as the *FSCS* is not an *authorised person*.

Sch 5.2 **[G]** Table

				Right of action under section 150		
Chapter/Appendix		Section/ Annex	Paragraph	For private person?	Removed?	For other person?
COMP 1		5	8	**No**	**Yes** – COMP 1.5.11R	**No**
COMP 13	Funding (all rules)			**Yes**	**No**	**No**
COMP 14.4.6R				**Yes**	**No**	**No**

SCHEDULE 6
RULES THAT CAN BE WAIVED

[2204]
Sch 6.1 **[G]** The *rules* in COMP cannot be *waived* by the *FSA*, except:
(1) FEES 6.5.13R;
(2) COMP 14.4.6R.

PROFESSIONAL FIRMS (PROF)

NOTES

Up to date as at 22 February 2010. For later amendments please see www.fsa.gov.uk.

CONTENTS

PROF 1—Professional firms . . . . [2205]
PROF 2—Status of exempt professional firm . . . . [2206]
PROF 3—The FSA's duties and powers . . . . [2207]
PROF 4—Disclosure . . . . [2208]
PROF 5—Non-mainstream regulated activities . . . . [2209]
PROF 6—Fees . . . . [2210]
PROF 7—Professional firms – Insurance mediation activity . . . . [2211]
PROF TP 1—Transitional provisions . . . . [2212]
PROF Sch 1—Record keeping requirements . . . . [2213]
PROF Sch 2—Notification requirements . . . . [2214]
PROF Sch 3—Fees and other required payments . . . . [2215]
PROF Sch 4—Powers exercised . . . . [2216]
PROF Sch 5—Rights of action for damages . . . . [2217]
PROF Sch 6—Rules that can be waived . . . . [2218]

CHAPTER 1
PROFESSIONAL FIRMS

1.1 Application and Purpose

Application

[2205]
1.1.1 **[R]** This sourcebook applies as follows:
(1) PROF 1 to PROF 4 apply to *exempt professional firms*;
(2) PROF 5 applies to *authorised professional firms*; and
(3) [deleted]
(4) PROF 7 applies to every *designated professional body* and every *exempt professional firm* that is carrying on, or proposing to carry on, *insurance mediation activity*.

1.1.1A **[R]** This sourcebook does not apply to an *incoming ECA provider* acting as such.

1.1.2 **[G]** This sourcebook is also relevant to *designated professional bodies*.

Purpose

1.1.3 **[G]** Under Part XX of the *Act* (Provision of Financial Services by Members of the Professions) certain individuals, partnerships or corporate entities, known as *exempt professional firms*, can carry on particular *regulated activities* (which the *Act* terms *exempt regulated activities*) under supervision and regulation by *designated professional bodies*.

1.1.4 **[G]** This sourcebook outlines:
(1) the arrangements for designation of professional bodies;
(2) the conditions for activities to be treated as *exempt regulated activities* (see PROF 2.1.3 G);
(3) the *FSA's* duty to keep itself informed about how *designated professional bodies* supervise and regulate the *exempt regulated activities* of *exempt professional firms* and how *exempt professional firms* carry on *exempt regulated activities*;
(4) the *FSA's* power under section 328 of the *Act* (Directions in relation to the general prohibition) to make a direction to deny the exemption to different classes of *person* or to different descriptions of *regulated activity*;
(5) the implications for an *authorised professional firm* that carries on *non-mainstream regulated activities*; and
(6) the arrangements made by the *FSA* for complying with its obligations under the *IMD* in relation to:
 (a) maintaining a record of *unauthorised persons*, including *exempt professional firms*, that carry on, or are proposing to carry on, *insurance mediation activity*; and
 (b) *exempt professional firms* that wish to passport under the *IMD*.

1.1.5 **[G]** This sourcebook also contains disclosure *rules* made by the *FSA* under the power conferred by section 332(1) of the *Act* (Rules in relation to persons to whom the general prohibition does not apply). These *rules* apply to *exempt professional firms* for the purpose of ensuring that their *clients* are made aware that *exempt professional firms* are not *authorised persons*.

1.1.6 **[G]** The *rules* and *guidance* in this sourcebook are intended to:

(1) assist the protection of *clients* of *exempt professional firms* by ensuring that the *FSA* has information which allows it to keep under review the exercise of the direction power under section 328 of the *Act* (see PROF 1.1.4G (4));

(2) promote public understanding of the *financial system* by ensuring that the *clients* of an *exempt professional firm* are made aware that the firm is not an *authorised person*;

(3) enable the *FSA* to use its resources in an efficient and effective way in the collection of information relevant to its duty to keep itself informed under section 325 of the *Act* (Authority's general duty); and

(4) explain the background to and the arrangements made by the *FSA* for:

  (a) the registration of *unauthorised persons*, including *exempt professional firms*, that carry on, or are proposing to carry on, *insurance mediation activity*; and

  (b) *authorised professional firms* and *exempt professional firms* that wish to exercise their *EEA right* under the *IMD* to establish a *branch* or provide *cross border services* in another *EEA State*.

1.1.7 **[G]** *Professional firms* should refer to AUTH App1 (Financial promotion and related activities) for general *guidance* on financial promotion and to AUTH App1.15 (Financial promotions by members of the professions (articles 55 and 55A)) for *guidance* on the exemptions which are specifically intended for *professional firms*.

CHAPTER 2
STATUS OF EXEMPT PROFESSIONAL FIRM

2.1 Designated professional bodies and exempt regulated activities

Designated professional bodies

[2206]

2.1.1 **[G]** The Treasury designates professional bodies. Section 326 of the *Act* (Designation of professional bodies) sets out the conditions a body must satisfy before it can be designated.

2.1.2 **[G]** The professional bodies that have been designated by the Treasury are listed in PROF 2 Ann 1 G.

Exempt regulated activities

2.1.3 **[G]** Section 327 of the *Act* (Exemption from the general prohibition) sets out the conditions which must be met for a *person* to be treated as an *exempt professional firm*, and for the *person's regulated activities* to be treated as *exempt regulated activities*. If the exemption in section 327 does not apply to a *person* and the *person* carries on a *regulated activity*, the *person* may contravene the *general prohibition* and be committing a criminal offence. The *FSA's* approach to the use of its powers in respect of alleged contraventions of the *general prohibition* is explained in EG 12.

2.1.4 **[G]** If the *FSA* has made a direction under section 328 of the *Act* (Directions in relation to the general prohibition) (see PROF 3.2) in relation to classes of *person* (or *regulated activity*), then a *person* within the class (or carrying on the *regulated activity*) specified will not be an *exempt professional firm*. In addition, section 329 of the *Act* (Orders in relation to the general prohibition) gives the *FSA* power to make an order disapplying the Part XX exemption from a *person* named in the Order. The *FSA's* general approach to the use of this power is explained in EG 16.

2.1.5 **[G]** Section 327(2) provides that an *exempt professional firm* must be a *member* of a profession or be controlled or managed by one or more *members*.

2.1.6 **[G]** The effect of section 327(7) of the *Act* is that an *exempt professional firm* can carry on *regulated activities* in that capacity or as an *exempt person* but not otherwise. Therefore, an *exempt professional firm* cannot be an *authorised person*.

2.1.7 **[G]** The *Act* does not, however, prevent an *exempt professional firm* from carrying on, in addition to *exempt regulated activities*, any *regulated activities* in relation to which it is an *exempt person*. For example, it is possible for an *exempt professional firm* to carry on *regulated activities* as an *appointed representative*.

2.1.8 **[G]** Section 327 also sets out the conditions which determine the particular *regulated activities* an *exempt professional firm* may carry on.

2.1.9 **[G]** Section 327(6) of the *Act* gives the Treasury power to make an order specifying activities, or activities relating to specified *investments*, that a *person* cannot carry on as an *exempt professional firm*. The relevant order is listed in PROF 2 Ann 2 G.

2.1.10 **[G]** Section 332(3) of the *Act* requires a *designated professional body* to make rules that define the particular *regulated activities* which its *members* are allowed to carry on. Section 332(4) of the *Act* provides that those rules must be designed to secure that, in providing a particular professional service to a particular *client*, a *member* must carry on only *regulated activities* which arise out of, or are complementary to, the provision by the *member* of that professional service to the *client*.

2.1.11 **[G]** The *FSA* is required to approve the rules *designated professional bodies* make under section 332(3) of the *Act*. These rules must be in place in order to allow a *person* to be an *exempt professional firm*. They add to the other conditions within section 327 but do not override them, and a firm may need to refer to section 327 if it is in doubt whether an activity is an *exempt regulated activity*.

2.1.12 **[G]** Section 327(3) deals with the treatment by a firm of a pecuniary reward or other advantage received from anyone other than the firm's *client*. For a *regulated activity* to be treated as an *exempt regulated activity*, the firm must account to its *client* for any such receipt. The *FSA* considers this to mean that an *exempt professional firm* must hold to the order of its *client* any such reward or other advantage that it receives.

2.1.13 **[G]** Section 327(4) states that the manner of the provision of any service in the course of carrying on *regulated activities* must be incidental to the provision by the *exempt professional firm* of professional services. For this purpose, professional services are services which do not constitute carrying on a *regulated activity*, and the provision of which is supervised and regulated by a *designated professional body*.

2.1.14 **[G]** The *FSA* considers that to satisfy the condition in section 327(4) *regulated activities* cannot be a major part of the practice of the firm. The *FSA* also considers the following further factors to be among those that are relevant:

(1) the scale of *regulated activity* in proportion to other professional services provided;

(2) whether and to what extent activities that are *regulated activities* are held out as separate services; and

(3) the impression given of how the firm provides *regulated activities*, for example through its advertising or other promotions of its services.

2.1.15 **[G]** The *FSA's* view is that, in the context of section 327 as an exemption from the *general prohibition*, the conditions in section 327 should be interpreted as not imposing any restriction on the *regulated activities* that an *exempt professional firm* may carry on outside the *United Kingdom*. For further guidance on when a *regulated activity* is carried on '*in the United Kingdom*', *exempt professional firms* are referred to section 418 of the *Act* and the *guidance* in PERG 2.4 (Link between activities and the United Kingdom).

PROF 2 Annex 1
Status of exempt professional firm G

Annex 1 **[G]**

1 Table Designated professional bodies (see PROF 2.1.2 G)

On 28 March 2001 the following professional bodies were designated by the Treasury under section 326(1) of the *Act*:

the Law Society of England & Wales

the Law Society of Scotland

the Law Society of Northern Ireland

the Institute of Chartered Accountants in England and Wales

the Institute of Chartered Accountants of Scotland

the Institute of Chartered Accountants in Ireland

the Association of Chartered Certified Accountants

the Institute of Actuaries.

On 14 January 2005, the Council for Licensed Conveyancers was designated by the Treasury under section 326(1) of the *Act*.

On 10 February 2006, the Royal Institution of Chartered Surveyors was designated by the Treasury under section 326(1) of the *Act*.

PROF 2 Annex 2G
Status of exempt professional firm G

PROF 2 Ann 2 **[G]**

1 Table Non Exempt activities orders under section 327(6) of the Act (see PROF 2.1.9 G)

As at 31 October 2004 the Treasury had made the following orders under section 327(6):

The Financial Services and Markets Act 2000 (Professions) (Non-Exempt Activities) Order 2001 (SI 2001/1227), as amended by: article 3 of the Financial Services and Markets Act 2000 (Miscellaneous Provisions) Order 2001 (SI 2001/3650); article 7 of the Financial Services and Markets Act 2000 (Regulated Activities) (Amendment) Order 2002 (SI 2002/682)); article 3 of the Financial Services and Markets Act 2000 (Commencement of Mortgage Regulation) (Amendment) Order 2002 (SI 2002/1777); article 24 of the Financial Services and Markets Act 2000 (Regulated Activities) (Amendment) (No 1) Order 2003 (SI 2003/1475), and article 16 of the Financial Services and Markets Act 2000 (Regulated Activities) (Amendment) (No 2) Order 2003 (SI 2003/1476).

CHAPTER 3
THE FSA'S DUTIES AND POWERS

3.1 The FSA's duty to keep itself informed

[2207]
3.1.1 **[G]** Section 325 of the *Act* (Authority's general duty) imposes on the *FSA* a duty to keep itself informed about:
(1) the way in which *designated professional bodies* supervise and regulate the carrying on of *exempt regulated activities* by *exempt professional firms*; and
(2) the way in which *exempt professional firms* carry on *exempt regulated activities*.

3.1.2 **[G]** The *FSA* keeps itself informed in a number of ways. A *designated professional body* has a duty under section 325(4) of the *Act* to cooperate with the *FSA*. Article 94 of the *Regulated Activities Order* requires each *designated professional body* to provide the *FSA* with the information it needs to maintain a public record of *persons* that are registered with the *FSA* to conduct *insurance mediation activity*. The *FSA* has made arrangements with each of the *designated professional bodies* about the information they provide to it, to include information about:
(1) complaints and redress arrangements;
(2) complaints volumes and their analysis;
(3) disciplinary action;
(4) supervisory activity;
(5) the activities carried on by *exempt professional firms*, the risks arising from them and how they are mitigated, for example by monitoring activity or training and competence arrangements; and
(6) the names and addresses of each of their *exempt professional firms* that carry on, or are proposing to carry on, *insurance mediation activity*, together with the details of the individuals within the management of the *exempt professional firms* who are responsible for the *insurance mediation activity* and, where relevant, the passporting information required by the *FSA* for the purposes of paragraph 25 of Schedule 3 to the *Act* (EEA Passport Rights).

3.1.3 **[G]** Information may also be obtained from *exempt professional firms*, government departments, trade bodies, consumer organisations and *clients* of *exempt professional firms*. The *FSA* may also commission or carry out reviews of the supervisory and regulatory activities of a *designated professional body* and commission or carry out research about, or surveys of, *exempt professional firms* or their *clients*.

3.2 The FSA's power to make a direction

3.2.1 **[G]** Section 328 of the *Act* (Directions in relation to the general prohibition) gives the *FSA* power to make a direction that the exemption under section 327 of the *Act* (see PROF 2.1.3 G) does not apply to the extent specified in the direction. Section 328 allows the *FSA* to make a direction in relation to different classes of *person* or different descriptions of *regulated activity*. Section 325(3) of the *Act* requires the *FSA* to keep under review the desirability of exercising its powers under Part XX of the *Act* (Provision of Financial Services by Members of the Professions), including its direction powers under section 328 of the *Act*.

3.2.2 **[G]** If the *FSA* gives a direction in relation to specified classes of *person*, then any *person* within those classes may be in contravention of the *general prohibition* unless:
(1) it ceases to carry on *regulated activities*; or
(2) it is an *authorised person*; or
(3) it is an *exempt person*.

3.2.3 **[G]** A direction might also cover classes of *persons* who are *members* of different *designated professional bodies*.

3.2.4 ***[G]*** Were the *FSA* to give a direction in relation to a description of *regulated activity* (for example, *dealing in investments as agent*), then that activity could no longer be carried on within the terms of the exemption.

3.2.5 **[G]**
(1) The *FSA* may exercise its direction powers under section 328(6) of the *Act* in two situations, as set out in (2) and (3).
(2) First, the *FSA* may exercise its direction power under section 328(6)(a) of the *Act* if it is satisfied that it is desirable in order to protect the interests of *clients*. In considering whether it is satisfied, the *FSA* is required by section 328(7) of the *Act* to have regard, among other things, to the effectiveness of any arrangements made by a *designated professional body*:
   (a) for securing compliance with *rules* made under section 332(1) of the *Act* (see PROF 4.1.1 G);
   (b) for dealing with complaints against its *members* in relation to the carrying on by them of *exempt regulated activities* (see PROF 4.1.4G (2)(d));
   (c) in order to offer redress to *clients* who suffer, or claim to have suffered, loss as a result of misconduct by its *members* in their carrying on of *exempt regulated activities* (see PROF 4.1.4G (2)(d)); and
   (d) for cooperating with the *FSA* under section 325(4) of the *Act* (see PROF 3.1.2 G).
(3) Second, the *FSA* may exercise its direction power under section 328(6)(b) of the *Act* if it is satisfied that it is necessary to do so in order to comply with an obligation imposed by the *IMD*. For example, the *FSA* might wish to do so if it was not receiving from a *designated professional body* the information it needs to maintain the *FSA Register* (see *PROF* 7.1).

3.2.6 **[G]** Section 330 of the *Act* (Consultation) sets out procedures which the *FSA* must follow if it wishes to make a direction under section 328(6)(a) or (b). Except as specifically provided in section 330:
(1) the *FSA* must consult publicly on its proposed direction;
(2) the *FSA* must have regard to any representations made in response to the consultation; and
(3) if the *FSA* then gives the proposed direction, it must publish an account of the representations made and its response to them.

3.2.7 **[G]** The directions the *FSA* has made under section 328 are set out in PROF 3 Ann 1 G. Directions made by the *FSA* under section 328(6)(b) of the *Act* are listed in PROF 3 Ann 2G (The FSA's duties and powers).

PROF 3 Annex 1G
The FSA's duties and powers

PROF 3 Ann 1 **[G]**

1 Directions made by the FSA under section 328(6)(a) of the *Act* (see PROF 3.2.7G)

As at 31 October 2004 the *FSA* had made no directions under section 328(6)(a) of the *Act*.

PROF 3 Annex 2G
The FSA's duties and powers

1 Directions made by the *FSA* under section 328(6)(b) of the *Act* (see PROF 3.2.7G)

As at 31 October 2004, the *FSA* had made no directions under section 328(6)(b) of the *Act*.

CHAPTER 4
DISCLOSURE

4.1 Disclosure rules

[2208]
4.1.1 **[G]** The effectiveness of arrangements made by a *designated professional body* for securing compliance with the *rules* in this chapter is one of the factors that the *FSA* must take into account in considering whether to exercise its power to give a direction under section 328 of the *Act* (see PROF 3.2.5(2)G and (3)G).

4.1.2 **[R]** An *exempt professional firm* must avoid making any representation to a *client* that:
(1) it is authorised under the *Act* or regulated by the *FSA*; or
(2) the regulatory protections provided by or under the *Act* to a *person* using the services of an *authorised person* are available.

4.1.3 **[R]**
(1) An *exempt professional firm* must, before it provides a service which includes the carrying on of a *regulated activity* in the *United Kingdom*, other than an *insurance mediation activity*, with or for a *client*, disclose in writing to the *client* in a manner that is clear, fair and not misleading that it is not authorised under the *Act*.
(2) An *exempt professional firm* must, before it provides a service which includes the carrying on of an *insurance mediation activity* with or for a *client*, make the following statement in writing to the *client* in a way that is clear, fair and not misleading and no less prominent than any other information provided to the *client* at the same time:

"[This firm is]/[We are] not authorised by the Financial Services Authority. However, we are included on the register maintained by the Financial Services Authority so that we can carry on insurance mediation activity, which is broadly the advising on, selling and administration of insurance contracts. This part of our business, including arrangements for complaints or redress if something goes wrong, is regulated by [DPB]. The register can be accessed via the Financial Services Authority website at www.fsa.gov.uk/register."

4.1.4 **[G]**

(1) The *FSA* considers that material provided to satisfy PROF 4.1.3 R(1) and (2) need not be tailored to the individual *client*. The disclosures in PROF 4.1.3 R(1) and (2) may be provided alongside or integrated with other material provided to a *client*. *Exempt professional firms* may therefore include the information within engagement letters or client care letters, if they wish.

(2) The *FSA* considers that it is important that *clients* understand the implications for them of receiving services from an *exempt professional firm* that is not authorised under the *Act*. It is also important that *clients* understand the implications of the difference between authorisation under the *Act* and being on the register maintained by the *FSA*, so that the *exempt professional firm* can conduct *insurance mediation activity*, in relation to which activity the regulatory protections established by the *Act* for the benefit of *consumers* will not apply. The *FSA* therefore expects *designated professional bodies* to make rules covering the information to be provided to *clients*. These rules should require *exempt professional firms* to make a disclosure to *clients* containing the following elements:

   (a) where the *exempt professional firm* conducts a *regulated activity* other than an *insurance mediation activity*, a statement that the *exempt professional firm* is not an *authorised person*;

   (b) the nature of the *regulated activities* carried on by the *exempt professional firm*, and the fact that they are limited in scope;

   (c) a statement that the *exempt professional firm* is regulated for these *regulated activities* by the *exempt professional firm's designated professional body*, identifying the *designated professional body* concerned;

   (d) the nature of the complaints and redress mechanisms available to *clients* in respect of these *regulated activities*; and

   (e) where the *regulated activity* consists of *insurance mediation activity*, the statement contained at *PROF* 4.1.3R (2).

(3) *Exempt professional firms* should also ensure that any statement that makes reference to the *FSA* does not lead a *client* to suppose that the *FSA* has direct regulatory responsibility for the *exempt professional firm*. This could be a breach of PROF 4.1.2R. This consideration is particularly important in relation to *insurance mediation activity*, where *clients* may well fail to appreciate the difference between authorisation under the *Act* and being included on the register maintained by the *FSA* so as to permit the *exempt professional firm* to carry on *insurance mediation activity*.

4.1.5 **[G]** For further guidance on when a *regulated activity* is carried on 'in the *United Kingdom*', *exempt professional firms* are referred to section 418 of the *Act* and the *guidance* in AUTH 2.4.

CHAPTER 5
NON-MAINSTREAM REGULATED ACTIVITIES

5.1 Application and purpose

Application

[2209]
5.1.1 **[R]** This chapter applies to an *authorised professional firm* that carries on *non-mainstream regulated activities*.

Purpose

5.1.2 **[G]** This chapter:

(1) contrasts "*exempt regulated activities*" with "*non-mainstream regulated activities*";

(2) sets out the conditions which must be satisfied for a *regulated activity* of an *authorised professional firm* to constitute a *non-mainstream regulated activity*;

(3) refers to other parts of the *Handbook* in which provisions are disapplied or modified in relation to *authorised professional firms* when carrying on *non-mainstream regulated activities*;

(4) gives effect to the *Distance Marketing Regulations* with respect to the *non-mainstream regulated activities* of *authorised professional firms*.

Exempt regulated activities contrasted with non-mainstream regulated activities

5.1.3 **[G]**

(1) The *FSA's* policy is designed to provide so far as possible a level playing field for authorised and unauthorised members of the professions in relation to the carrying on of similar activities.

(2) Subject to conditions (see PROF 2), members of *designated professional bodies* that are not authorised can carry on particular *regulated activities*, known as *exempt regulated activities*, and obtain the benefit of the exemption under section 327 of the *Act* from the *general prohibition*.

(3) In contrast, *non-mainstream regulated activities* are particular *regulated activities* carried on by an *authorised professional firm*. If the *professional firm* were not authorised under the *Act*, these same activities would be *exempt regulated activities* which, if the *firm* could meet the necessary conditions in section 327, would enable it to benefit from the section 327 exemption.

(4) Therefore, a number of provisions of the *Handbook* (see PROF 5.3) have been disapplied or modified in respect of these *non-mainstream regulated activities* of *authorised professional firms*.

5.1.4 **[G]** A "*non-mainstream regulated activity*" is defined in the *Glossary* as "a *regulated activity* of an *authorised professional firm* in relation to which the conditions in PROF 5.2.1R are satisfied". Conditions (1) to (5) of PROF 5.2.1R replicate section 327(1)(b)(i), (3), (4), (5) and (6) of the *Act*, as if those conditions applied to an *authorised professional firm*.

5.2 Nature of non-mainstream regulated activities

Conditions for non-mainstream regulated activity

5.2.1 **[R]** A "*non-mainstream regulated activity*" is a *regulated activity* of an *authorised professional firm* in relation to which the following conditions are satisfied:

(1) the *firm* must not receive from a *person* other than his client any pecuniary reward or other advantage, for which he does not account to his client, arising out of the carrying on of the *regulated activity*;

(2) the manner of the provision by the *firm* of any service in the course of carrying on the *regulated activity* must be incidental to the provision by it of professional services (see PROF 5.2.2R);

(3) the *regulated activity* must not be of a description, or relate to an investment of a description, specified in The Financial Services and Markets Act 2000 (Professions) (Non-Exempt Activities) Order 2001 (SI 2001/1227) or in any other order made by the Treasury under section 327(6) of the *Act* (see PROF 2 Annex 2 G);

(4) there must not be in force any direction under section 328 of the *Act* (Directions in relation to the general prohibition) in relation to:

   (a) a class of *person* which would have included the *firm* were it not an *authorised person*; or

   (b) a description of *regulated activity* which includes the *regulated activity* the *firm* proposes to carry on; and

(5) the *regulated activity* must be an activity which *exempt professional firms* which are *members* of the same *designated professional body* as the *authorised professional firm* are permitted to carry on under rules made by that body as required by section 332(3) of the *Act*.

5.2.2 **[R]** In PROF 5.2.1R(2), "professional services" means services:

(1) which do not constitute a *regulated activity*; and

(2) the provision of which is supervised and regulated by a *designated professional body*.

5.3 Reference to other sourcebooks and manuals

Introduction

5.3.1 **[G]** The parts of the *Handbook* in which provisions are disapplied or modified in relation to *authorised professional firms* when carrying on *non-mainstream regulated activities* include those described in PROF 5.3.1AG to PROF 5.3.9G.

General provisions

5.3.1A **[G]** GEN 4.3.5R provides that GEN 4.3.1 (Disclosure in letters to private customers) does not apply to an *authorised professional firm* with respect to its *non-mainstream regulated activities*.

Conduct of business sourcebook

5.3.2 **[G]** COBS 18.11 provides that COBS does not apply to an *authorised professional firm* with respect to its *non-mainstream regulated activities*, except for:

(1) the *fair, clear and not misleading rule*; and

(1A) the *financial promotion rules*, but only in limited circumstances;

(2) (where these are *insurance mediation activities*) COBS 7 (Insurance mediation) unless:

(a) the *designated professional body* of the *firm* has made rules which implement some or all of articles 12 and 13 of the *Insurance Mediation Directive*;

(b) those rules have been approved by the *FSA* under section 332(5) of the *Act*; and

(c) the *firm* is subject to the rules in the form in which they were approved;

(3) COBS 8.1.3R (Client agreements), except for the requirement to provide information on conflicts of interest; and

(4) COBS 5.2 (E-commerce).

Training and Competence sourcebook

5.3.3 **[G]** TC Appendix 3R provides that TC, which imposes the substantive training and competence requirements for *retail clients or customers*, does not apply to an *authorised professional firm* with respect to its *non-mainstream regulated activities*.

Senior Management Arrangements, Systems and Controls

5.3.4 **[G]** SYSC 3.2.6AR to SYSC 3.2.6JG and SYSC 6.3 (Financial crime), in relation to *money laundering*, do not apply to *authorised professional firms* when carrying on *non-mainstream regulated activities*.

Supervision manual

5.3.5 **[G]** SUP 10.1.18R provides that SUP 10 (Approved persons) does not apply (except in respect of the *required functions*) to an *authorised professional firm* in respect of its *non-mainstream regulated activities*. So a person such as a *partner*, whose only *regulated activities* are incidental to his professional services, in an *authorised professional firm* whose principal purpose is to carry on activities other than *regulated activities*, need not be an *approved person*.

Dispute resolution: Complaints sourcebook

5.3.6 **[G]** DISP 1.1.5R(3) provides that DISP 1 (Treating complainants fairly) only applies to an *authorised professional firm* in so far as its mainstream regulated activities are concerned. DISP 2.3.4R further provides that a *complaint* about an *authorised professional firm* cannot be handled under the *Compulsory Jurisdiction* of the *Financial Ombudsman Service* if it relates solely to *non-mainstream regulated activity* and can be handled by a *designated professional body*. This is because such a *complaint* will be handled by the relevant professional body.

Market Conduct sourcebook

5.3.7 **[G]** MAR 4.4.1R(3) provides that MAR 4, which deals with the endorsement of the City Code on Takeovers and Mergers and the Rules Governing Substantial Acquisitions of Shares, does not have effect in relation to an *authorised professional firm* in respect of *non-mainstream regulated activity*.

Mortgages: Conduct of business sourcebook

5.3.8 **[G]** MCOB 1.2.10R provides that *MCOB* does not apply to an *authorised professional firm* with respect to its *non-mainstream regulated activities* except for *MCOB* 2.2 (Clear, fair and not misleading communication), *MCOB* 3 (Financial promotion) and to a limited extent *MCOB* 4.4 (Initial disclosure requirements).

5.3.9 **[G]** CASS 1.2.4R(1) provides that with the exception of CASS 1 and the *insurance client money chapter*, CASS does not apply to *authorised professional firms* when carrying on *non-mainstream regulated activities*. CASS 1.2.5 further provides that if the *non-mainstream regulated activities* are *insurance mediation activity*, CASS 5 (the insurance client money chapter) does not apply to an *authorised professional firm*, if the *firm's designated professional body* has rules applicable to the *firm* which implement the *Insurance Mediation Directive* and which are in the form approved by the *FSA* under section 332(5) of the *Act*.

Insurance: Conduct of Business sourcebook

5.3.10 **[G]**

(1) ICOB 1.2.10R provides that *ICOB* does not apply to an *authorised professional firm* with respect to its *non-mainstream regulated activities*, except for:

(a) ICOB 2.2 (Clear, fair and not misleading communication);

(b) ICOB 3 (Financial promotion);
(c) ICOB 4.2.2R in relation to the information for customers in table ICOB 4.2.8R items numbered (8), (9) and Note 4 covering complaints and compensation; and
(d) those sections in *ICOB* which implement articles 12 and 13 of the *IMD*, unless:
  (i) the *designated professional body* of the *firm* has made rules which implement articles 12 and 13 of the *IMD*;
  (ii) those rules have been approved by the *FSA* under section 332(5) of the *Act*; and
  (iii) the *firm* is subject to the rules in the form in which they were approved.

(2) ICOB 1.2.11G (2) provides that the effect of ICOB 1.2.10R(4) is that if the relevant *designated professional body* of an *authorised professional firm* does not make rules implementing articles 12 and 13 of the *IMD* applicable to *authorised professional firms* those *authorised professional firms* will need to comply with those sections of *ICOB* which implement articles 12 and 13 of the *IMD*, namely ICOB 4.1 to 4.4 (but not 4.2.20G to 4.2.28G), and ICOB 4.8.

5.4 Application of the Distance Marketing Regulations

5.4.1 **[R]**
(1) In addition to those provisions of the *Distance Marketing Regulations* which apply directly, an *authorised professional firm* must, with respect to its *non-mainstream regulated activities*, comply with regulations 7 to 11 and 15 of the *Distance Marketing Regulations*. Those regulations have effect to cancel *distance contracts* the making or performance of which by such *firms* constitutes a *non-mainstream regulated activity*.
(2) Paragraph (1) does not apply in relation to regulations 7 to 8 and 15 if the *designated professional body* of the *authorised professional firm* has rules equivalent to some or all of those regulations and:
  (a) those rules have been approved by the *FSA* under section 332(5) of the *Act*; and
  (b) the *authorised professional firm* is subject to those rules in the form in which they have been approved

in which case those regulations are disapplied to the extent that they are implemented by the rules of the *designated professional body*.

5.4.2 **[G]** The effect of PROF 5.4.1R is that it allows *designated professional bodies* to make rules which allow an *authorised professional firm* to comply with the *Distance Marketing Regulations* in respect of its *non-mainstream regulated activities* in the same way as an *exempt professional firm* which is a member of the same *designated professional body* in respect of its *exempt regulated activities*.

CHAPTER 6
FEES

6.1

[2210]
[deleted: the provisions in relation to *designated professional bodies* are set out in FEES 1, 2, 3 and 4]

6.2

[deleted: the provisions in relation to *designated professional bodies* are set out in FEES 1, 2, 3 and 4]

6.3

6.3.1 **[R]** [deleted: the provisions in relation to *designated professional bodies* are set out in FEES 1, 2, 3 and 4]
PROF 6: Annex 2R [deleted]

CHAPTER 7
PROFESSIONAL FIRMS
INSURANCE MEDIATION ACTIVITY

7.1 Register of persons carrying on *insurance mediation activity*

Background

[2211]
7.1.1 **[G]** The Financial Services and Markets Act 2000 (Regulated Activities) Amendment) (No. 2) Order 2003 (SI 2003/1476) implements in part the provisions of the *IMD* and amends the *Regulated Activities Order*.

Part II FSA Handbook Materials

The FSA's obligation to maintain a record

7.1.2 **[G]** Article 93 of the amended *Regulated Activities Order* requires the *FSA* to maintain an up-to-date record of every *unauthorised person*, whether an *appointed representative* or an *exempt professional firm* that carries on, or is proposing to carry on, *insurance mediation activity* and to whom the *general prohibition* does not apply in relation to the carrying on of such an activity. In relation to *exempt professional firms* the *general prohibition* does not apply by virtue of section 327 of the *Act*.

7.1.3 **[G]** The *FSA* is not to include an *exempt professional firm* in the register relating to *unauthorised persons* if:
(1) under a direction given by the *FSA* under section 328(1) of the *Act*, section 327(1) of the *Act* does not apply in relation to the carrying on by it of *insurance mediation activity*; or
(2) the *FSA* has made an order under section 329(2) of the *Act* disapplying section 327(1) of the *Act* in relation to the carrying on by the *exempt professional firm* of *insurance mediation activity*.

Provision of information to the FSA

7.1.4 **[G]** Article 94 of the *Regulated Activities Order* obliges a *designated professional body* to provide the *FSA* with the information it needs to maintain the record referred to in *PROF* 7.1.2G of every *unauthorised person* that carries on, or proposes to carry on, *insurance mediation activity* and keep it up to date. This information needs to include the details referred to in *PROF* 7.1.7 G. This is the responsibility of the *designated professional body* and not each *exempt professional firm*.

Financial Services and Markets Act 2000 (Professions) (Non-Exempt) Activities Order 2001 (S1 2001/1227)

7.1.5 **[G]**
(1) The attention of *exempt professional firms* is drawn to the significance of The Financial Services and Markets Act 2000 (Professions) (Non-Exempt) Activities Order 2001 (SI 2001/1227), as amended by The Financial Services and Markets Act 2000 (Regulated Activities) (Amendment) (No 2) Order 2003 (SI 2003/1476). The effect of these amendments is that *exempt professional firms* may not carry on certain *regulated activities* which relate to a *contract of insurance* in reliance on the *Part XX exemption* unless the *exempt professional firm* is included in the record of *unauthorised persons* carrying on *insurance mediation activity* maintained by the *FSA* under article 93 of the *Regulated Activities Order*.
(2) Each *exempt professional firm* carrying on, or proposing to carry on, *insurance mediation activity* should ensure that at all material times the name of the firm and the requisite details are included in the record maintained by the *FSA*. Any such *exempt professional firm* carrying on, or proposing to carry on, *insurance mediation activity* whose name does not appear in the record maintained by the *FSA* is likely to be breaching the *general prohibition* which is a criminal offence under section 23 of the *Act*.

FSA Register

7.1.6 **[G]** In order to comply with its obligations to maintain a record of *unauthorised persons* that carry on, or are proposing to carry on, *insurance mediation activity*, the *FSA* has established an appropriate record which forms part of the record maintained by the *FSA* under section 347 of the *Act*. The record maintained by the *FSA* under section 347 of the *Act* is known as the *FSA Register*. The *FSA Register* therefore contains a record of each *authorised* and *unauthorised person* that carries on, or proposes to carry on, *insurance mediation activity*.

7.1.7 **[G]** The information to be included on the record in relation to *exempt professional firms* will, as required by the *IMD*, include details of:
(1) the name and address of each *exempt professional firm* that carries on, or is proposing to carry on, *insurance mediation activity*;
(2) where the *exempt professional firm* is not an individual, the names of the individuals within the management of the *exempt professional firm* who are responsible for the *insurance mediation activity*; and
(3) each *EEA State* in which the *exempt professional firm* under an *EEA right* derived from the *IMD*:
    (a) has established a *branch*; or
    (b) is providing *cross border services*.

FSA Website

7.1.8 **[G]** The *FSA Register* can be accessed through the *FSA* website under the link www.fsa.gov.uk/register.

7.2 Passporting under the Insurance Mediation Directive

7.2.1 **[G]** All *persons* that are on the register maintained by the *FSA* in accordance with article 3 of the *IMD*, and so permitted to conduct *insurance mediation activity*, are entitled to exercise the *EEA right* conferred upon them by article 6 of the *IMD* to establish a *branch* or provide services relating to *insurance mediation activity* in another *EEA State*. Both *authorised professional firms* and *exempt professional firms* that are so registered by the *FSA* get the benefit of these passporting rights.

7.2.2 **[G]** Any *authorised professional firm* or *exempt professional firm* that is contemplating the exercise of rights under article 6 of the *IMD* to establish a *branch* or provide services relating to *insurance mediation activity* in another *EEA State* is referred to SUP 13 (Exercise of passport rights by UK firms) for further details as to the applicable process. Note that both *authorised professional firms* and *exempt professional firms* are *UK firms* for the purposes of the *Handbook*, including SUP 13.

7.2.3 **[G]** A *UK firm* proposing to establish a *branch* in another *EEA State* for the first time under an *EEA right* derived from the *IMD* must first satisfy the conditions in paragraphs 19(2), (4) and (5) of Part III of Schedule 3 to the *Act* (EEA Passport Rights). These include the requirement that the firm must at the outset give the *FSA* a notice in the required form of its intention to establish the *branch*. SUP 13.3.2G to SUP 13.3.5G detail the procedure to be followed once such a *notice of intention* has been received by the *FSA*. SUP 13.5.1R (Specified contents: notice of intention to establish a branch) and SUP 13.6.9AG (Firms passporting under the IMD) will also be relevant.

7.2.4 **[G]** A *UK firm* proposing to provide *cross border services* into another *EEA State* for the first time under an *EEA right* derived from the *IMD* must first satisfy the conditions in paragraph 20(1) of Part III of Schedule 3 to the *Act* (EEA Passport Rights). The *UK firm* must at the outset give the *FSA* a notice in the required form of its intention to provide the *cross border services* into another *EEA State*. In this instance, the relevant procedure to be followed is outlined in SUP 13.4.2G to SUP 13.4.5 G. SUP 13.5.2R (Specified contents: notice of intention to provide cross border services) and SUP 13.7.11G will also be relevant.

Part II FSA Handbook Materials

TP 1 TRANSITIONAL PROVISIONS

[2212]
1 Table

(1)	(2) Material to which the transitional provision applies	(3)	(4) Transitional provision	(5) Transitional provision: dates in force	(6) Handbook provision: coming into force
1	*PROF* 4.1.2R	G	The *FSA* considers that the issue by an *exempt professional firm* of a letter to a client on a letterhead that includes a statement that it is "authorised" will be in breach of *PROF* 4.1.2R. This includes a statement such as: 'This firm is authorised in the conduct of investment business by [name of recognised professional body] under the *Financial Services* Act 1986.'	From *commencement*	*Commencement*

(1)	(2) Material to which the transitional provision applies	(3)	(4) Transitional provision	(5) Transitional provision: dates in force	(6) Handbook provision: coming into force
			However, an *exempt professional firm* which has been authorised for investment business by a recognised professional body under the Financial Services Act 1986 may continue to use stocks of notepaper and other material that discloses its status under that act, provided that it strikes through the disclosure statement.		
2	*PROF*	G	**General transitional provisions** *GEN* contains some technical transitional provisions that apply throughout the *Handbook* and which are designed to ensure a smooth transition at *commencement*.	From *commencement*	*Commencement*

SCHEDULE 1
RECORD KEEPING REQUIREMENTS

[2213]
Sch 1 **[G]**

1 There are no record keeping requirements in PROF.

SCHEDULE 2
NOTIFICATION REQUIREMENTS

[2214]
Sch 2 **[G]**

1 There are no notification or reporting requirements in *PROF*.

SCHEDULE 3
FEES AND OTHER REQUIRED PAYMENTS

[2215]
Sch 3 **[G]**

1 There are no requirements for fees or other payments in *PROF*.

SCHEDULE 4
POWERS EXERCISED

[2216]
Sch 4 **[G]**

(1) The following powers and related provisions in the *Act* have been exercised by the *FSA* to make the *rules* in *PROF*:
  - (1) Section 138 (General rule-making power)
  - (2) Section 156 (General supplementary powers)
  - (3) Section 332(1) (Rules in relation to persons to whom the general prohibition does not apply)

(2) The following power in the *Act* has been exercised by the *FSA* to give the *guidance* in *PROF*:
  - (1) Section 157(1) (Guidance)

SCHEDULE 5
RIGHTS OF ACTION FOR DAMAGES

[2217]
Sch 5 **[G]**

(1) The table below sets out the *rules* in *PROF* contravention of which by an *authorised person* may be actionable under section 150 of the *Act* (Actions for damages) by a *person* who suffers loss as a result of the contravention.

(2) If a "YES" appears in the column headed "For private person?", the *rule* may be actionable by a "*private person*" under section 150 (or, in certain circumstances, his fiduciary or representative; see article 6(2) and (3)(c) of the Financial Services and Markets Act 2000 (Rights of Action) Regulations 2001 (SI 2001 No. 2256)). A "Yes" in the column headed "Removed" indicates that the *FSA* has removed the right of action under section 150(2) of the *Act*. If so, a reference to the *rule* in which it is removed is also given.

(3) The column headed "For other person?" indicates whether the *rule* may be actionable by a *person* other than a *private person* (or his fiduciary or representative) under article 6(2) and (3) of those Regulations. If so, an indication of the type of *person* by whom the *rule* may be actionable is given.

(4) Actions for damages: Professional firms sourcebook

Chapter/ Appendix	**Section/ Annex**	**Paragraph**	**Right of action under section 150**		
			For private person?	**Removed?**	**For other person?**
PROF 5.2.1R Conditions for non-mainstream regulated activity			Yes	No	No

SCHEDULE 6
RULES THAT CAN BE WAIVED

[2218]
Sch 6 **[G]**

(1) No *rules* in PROF can be *waived* by the *FSA* under section 148 of the *Act* (Modification or waiver of rules), except for PROF 5.2.1R and PROF 5.2.2R (Conditions for non-mainstream regulated activity).

SERVICE COMPANIES (SERV)

NOTES
Up to date as at 22 February 2010. For later amendments please see www.fsa.gov.uk.

CONTENTS

SERV 1—Handbook requirements for service companies . . . . [2219]

CHAPTER 1
HANDBOOK REQUIREMENTS FOR SERVICE COMPANIES

1.1 Application and Purpose

[2219]

1.1.1 **[G]** This special guide is for *service companies*. Its purpose is to help *service companies* find their way around the *Handbook* by setting out which parts of it apply to them.

1.1.2 **[G]** *Service companies* are *firms* whose *regulated activities* are restricted to *making arrangements with a view to transactions in investments* and *agreeing to carry on that regulated activity*. They are, in the main, technology companies who provide order routing, post-trade processing, or other services to market participants which assist them to *deal* in *investments* or *arrange (bring about) deals in investments* among themselves. A light-touch regulatory regime applies to *service companies* as set out in this Special guide.

1.2 Parts of the Handbook applicable to service companies

1.2.1 **[G]** The parts of the *Handbook* applicable to *service companies* are listed in SERV 1.2.2G. *Service companies* should read applicable parts of the *Handbook* to find out what the detailed regulatory requirements for *service companies* are.

1.2.2 **[G]** This table belongs to SERV 1.2.1G

	Part of Handbook	**Applicability to service companies**
High Level Standards	Principles for Businesses (PRIN)	This applies.
	Senior management arrangements, Systems and Controls (SYSC)	This applies.
	Threshold Conditions (COND)	This applies.
	Statements of Principle and Code of Practice for Approved Persons (APER)	This applies to an *approved person* who performs a *controlled function* for a *service company*.
	The Fit and Proper test for Approved Persons (FIT)	This applies.
	General provisions (GEN)	This applies.
Prudential Standards	Interim Prudential sourcebooks (IPRU)	In the Interim Prudential sourcebook for investment business (*IPRU(INV)*), only Chapters 1 (Application and General) and 6 (Service Companies) apply: see IPRU(INV) 1.2.4R. The other Interim Prudential sourcebooks do not apply.
Business Standards	Conduct of Business sourcebook (COBS)	Only some parts of COBS apply to *service companies*: see COBS 18.10. The *permission* given to *service companies* means that they must not approve *financial promotions* on behalf of another *person* or specified class of *person*, or deal with private customers. If the *firm* communicates *financial promotions* to *eligible counterparties* and *professional clients* only, the *financial promotion rules* will have only very limited application.
	Mortgages: Conduct of Business sourcebook (MCOB)	
	Client Assets sourcebook (CASS)	This applies. However, *service companies* should not, ordinarily, hold client assets.

Part II FSA Handbook Materials

	Part of Handbook	Applicability to service companies
	Market Conduct sourcebook (MAR)	MAR 1 (Code of market conduct), MAR 2 (Price stabilising rules) and MAR 4 (Endorsement of the Takeover Code) apply to *service companies* *MAR* 5 (Multilateral Trading Systems), MAR 6 (Systematic Internalisers) and MAR 7 (Disclosure of information on certain trades undertaken outside a regulated market or *MTF*) do not apply to *service companies*.
	Training and Competence sourcebook (TC)	TC does not apply to *service companies* as they do not carry on activities for *retail clients*. But they are subject to the *competent employees rule* in SYSC 3.
Regulatory processes	Supervision manual (SUP)	This applies, with the following qualifications:
		(a) in SUP 3 (Auditors), only sections 3.1, 3.2, and 3.7 apply to a *service company* (and only if it has an auditor) and only sections 3.1, 3.2 and 3.8 apply to its auditor (if it has one): see SUP 3.1.2R;
		(b) SUP 4 (Actuaries) does not apply: see SUP 4.1.1R;
		(c) in SUP 10 (Approved persons), if a *service company's* principal purpose is to carry on activities other than *regulated activities*, then the scope of the *significant influence functions* is restricted to the *required functions*: see SUP 10.1.21R – SUP 10.1.22G;
		(d) SUP 13 (Exercise of passport rights by UK firms) does not apply because *service companies* do not *conduct investment service and activities*;
		(e) SUP 14 (Incoming EEA firms changing details and cancelling qualification for authorisation) does not apply because a *service company* cannot be an *incoming EEA firm* (see explanation in (d));
		(f) in SUP 16 (Reporting requirements), sections 16.4 – 16.6 do not apply and in section 16.7, only SUP 16.7.20R – SUP 16.7.21R apply: see SUP 16.1.1R;
		(g) SUP 17 (Transaction reporting) does not apply: see SUP 17.1.1R; and
		(h) SUP App 2 (Insurers: Scheme of operations) does not apply.
	Decision Procedure and Penalties Manual (DEPP)	This applies.

	Part of Handbook	Applicability to service companies
Redress	Dispute resolution: the Complaints sourcebook (DISP)	All *firms* are subject to the *Compulsory Jurisdiction* of the *Financial Ombudsman Service*. However, a *firm* which does not, and notifies the *FSA* under *DISP* 1.1.12R that it does not, conduct business with *eligible complainants* (*persons* eligible to have a *complaint* considered under the *Financial Ombudsman Service*, as defined in *DISP* 2.4) will be *exempt* from the rules on treating complainants fairly (*DISP* 1.2 to *DISP* 1.11) and from the Financial Ombudsman Funding *rules* (*FEES* 5.1 to *DISP* 5.7). The definition of a *service company* means that a *service company* will qualify for these exemptions if it applies for them: see *DISP* 2.4.3R(2)(a).
	Compensation sourcebook (COMP)	COMP does not apply to *service companies*, which are not *participant firms* under the *compensation scheme*, and are exempt from funding it.
	Complaints against the FSA (COAF)	This applies to *service companies*, although it contains no requirements for *service companies*.
Specialist sourcebooks	Collective Investment Schemes sourcebook (CIS)	None of the other specialist sourcebooks applies.
	Professional firms sourcebook (PROF)	
	Recognised Investment Exchange and Recognised Clearing House sourcebook (REC)	
Special guides	Special guide for service companies (SERV)	This applies.
	Special guide for energy market participants (EMPS)	This does not apply because an *energy market participant* is defined to exclude a *service company*.
	Special guide for small friendly societies (FREN)	This does not apply.
	Special guide for oil market participants (OMPS)	This does not apply because an *oil market participant* is defined to exclude a *service company*.
	Summary schedules Record keeping requirements Notification requirements Fees and other required payments Powers exercised in making the Handbook Rights of action for damages Rules that can be waived Releases	These apply, but only to the extent that the sourcebook or manual to which they relate applies.
Schedules	This applies.	
Glossary of definitions		This applies.

ENFORCEMENT GUIDE (EG)

NOTES

Up to date as at 22 February 2010. For later amendments please see www.fsa.gov.uk.

CONTENTS

EG 1—Introduction . . . [2219A]

Overview

EG 2—The FSA's approach to enforcement . . . [2219B]
EG 3—Use of information gathering and investigation powers . . . [2219C]
EG 4—Conduct of investigations . . . [2219D]
EG 5—Settlement . . . [2219E]
EG 6—Publicity . . . [2219F]

Specific enforcement powers

EG 7—Penalties and censures . . . [2219G]
EG 8—Variation and cancellation of permission on the FSA's own initiative and intervention against incoming firms . . . [2219H]
EG 9—Prohibition orders and withdrawal of approval . . . [2219I]
EG 10—Injunctions . . . [2219J]
EG 11—Restitution and redress . . . [2219K]
EG 12—Prosecution of criminal offences . . . [2219L]
EG 13—Insolvency . . . [2219M]
EG 14—Collective investment schemes . . . [2219N]
EG 15—Disqualification of auditors and actuaries . . . [2219O]
EG 16—Disapplication orders against members of the professions . . . [2219P]
EG 18—Cancellation of approval as a sponsor . . . [2219Q]
EG 19—Non-FSMA powers . . . [2219R]
Annex 2—Guidelines on the investigation of cases of interest or concern to the FSA and other prosecuting and other investigating authorities . . . [2219S]
Transitional Provisions . . . [2219T]

CHAPTER 1
INTRODUCTION

[2219A]

1.1 This guide describes the FSA's approach to exercising the main enforcement powers given to it by the Financial Services and Markets Act 2000 (the *Act*) and by regulation 12 of the *Unfair Terms Regulations*. It is broken down into two parts. The first part provides an overview of enforcement policy and process, with chapters about the FSA's approach to enforcement (chapter 2), the use of its main information gathering and investigation powers under the *Act* (chapter 3), the conduct of investigations (chapter 4), settlement (chapter 5) and publicity (chapter 6). The second part contains an explanation of the FSA's policy concerning specific enforcement powers such as its powers to: vary a *firm's Part IV permission* on its own initiative (chapter 8); make *prohibition orders* (chapter 9); and prosecute criminal offences (chapter 12); and powers which the *FSA* has been given under legislation other than the *Act* (chapter 19).

1.2 In the areas set out below, the *Act* expressly requires the FSA to prepare and publish statements of policy or procedure on the exercise of its enforcement and investigation powers and in relation to the giving of *statutory notices*.

(1) sections 69 and 210 require the FSA to publish statements of policy on the imposition, and amount, of financial penalties on *firms* and *approved persons*;

(2) section 93 requires the FSA to publish a statement of its policy on the imposition, and amount, of financial penalties under section 91 of the *Act* (penalties for breach of Part 6 rules);

(3) section 124 requires the FSA to publish a statement of its policy on the imposition, and amount, of financial penalties for *market abuse*;

(4) section 169 requires the FSA to publish a statement of its policy on the conduct of certain interviews in response to requests from *overseas regulators*; and

(5) section 395 requires the FSA to issue a statement of procedures relating to the giving of *supervisory notices*, *warning notices* and *decision notices*.

These policies are set out in the Decision Procedure and Penalties manual (DEPP), a module of the FSA Handbook. References to the policies are made at appropriate places in the guide.

1.3 This guide includes material on the investigation, disciplinary and criminal prosecution powers that are available to the FSA when it is performing functions as the competent authority under Part VI of the *Act* (Official listing). The *Act* provides a separate statutory framework within which the FSA must operate when it acts in that capacity. When determining whether to exercise its powers in its capacity as competent authority under Part VI, the FSA will have regard to the matters and objectives which apply to the competent authority function.

1.4 The FSA has a range of enforcement powers, and in any particular enforcement situation, the FSA may need to consider which power to use and whether to use one or more powers. So in any particular case, it may be necessary to refer to a number of chapters of the guide.

1.5 Since most of the FSA's enforcement powers are derived from it, this guide contains a large number of references to the *Act*. Users of the guide should therefore refer to the *Act* as well as to the guide where necessary. In the event of a discrepancy between the *Act*, or other relevant legislation, and the description of an enforcement power in the guide, the provisions of the *Act* or the other relevant legislation prevail. Defined terms used in the text are shown in italic type. Where a word or phrase is in italics, its definition will be the one used for that word or phrase in the glossary to the FSA Handbook.

1.6 [deleted]

1.7 This guide will be kept under review and amended as appropriate in the light of further experience and developing law and practice.

1.8 The material in this guide does not form part of the FSA Handbook and is not guidance on rules, but it is 'general guidance' as defined in section 158 of the *Act*. If you have any doubt about a legal or other provision or your responsibilities under the *Act* or other relevant requirements, you should seek appropriate legal advice from your legal adviser.

CHAPTER 2
THE FSA'S APPROACH TO ENFORCEMENT

[2219B]

2.1 The FSA's effective and proportionate use of its enforcement powers plays an important role in the pursuit of its *regulatory objectives* of protecting *consumers*, maintaining confidence in the *financial system*, promoting public awareness and reducing *financial crime*. For example, using enforcement helps to contribute to the protection of *consumers* and to deter future contraventions of FSA and other applicable requirements and *financial crime*. It can also be a particularly effective way, through publication of enforcement outcomes, of raising awareness of regulatory standards.

2.2 There are a number of principles underlying the FSA's approach to the exercise of its enforcement powers:

(1) The effectiveness of the regulatory regime depends to a significant extent on maintaining an open and co-operative relationship between the FSA and those it regulates.

(2) The FSA will seek to exercise its enforcement powers in a manner that is transparent, proportionate, responsive to the issue, and consistent with its publicly stated policies.

(3) The FSA will seek to ensure fair treatment when exercising its enforcement powers.

(4) The FSA will aim to change the behaviour of the *person* who is the subject of its action, to deter future non-compliance by others, to eliminate any financial gain or benefit from non-compliance, and where appropriate, to remedy the harm caused by the non-compliance.

2.3 Enforcement is only one of a number of regulatory tools available to the FSA. As a risk based regulator with limited resources, throughout its work the FSA prioritises its resources in the areas which pose the biggest threat to its *regulatory objectives*. This applies as much to the enforcement tool as it does to any other tool available to it. The next section of this chapter summarises how in practice the FSA takes a risk based approach towards its use of the enforcement tool, and the subsequent sections comment on other aspects of the FSA's approach to enforcement.

2.4 Where a *firm* or other *person* has failed to comply with the requirements of the *Act*, the *rules*, or other relevant legislation, it may be appropriate to deal with this without the need for formal disciplinary or other enforcement action. The proactive supervision and monitoring of *firms*, and an open and cooperative relationship between *firms* and their supervisors, will, in some cases where a contravention has taken place, lead the FSA to decide against taking formal disciplinary action. However, in those cases, the FSA will expect the *firm* to act promptly in taking the necessary remedial action agreed with its supervisors to deal with the FSA's concerns. If the *firm* does not do this, the FSA may take disciplinary or other enforcement action in respect of the original contravention.

Case selection: Firms and approved persons, market abuse cases and listing matters

2.5 Other than in the area of a *firm's* failure to satisfy the FSA's *Threshold Conditions* for authorisation (as to which, see paragraph 2.11), the selection method for cases involving *firms* and *approved persons*, *market abuse* and listing matters (for example, breaches of the listing, prospectus or disclosure rules) occurs at two main levels:

(1) strategic planning; and
(2) decisions on individual cases.

2.6 The FSA does not have a set of enforcement priorities that are distinct from the priorities of the FSA as a whole. Rather, the FSA consciously uses the enforcement tool to deliver its overall strategic priorities. The areas and issues which the FSA as an organisation regards as priorities at any particular time are therefore key in determining at a strategic level how enforcement resource should be allocated. FSA priorities will influence the use of resources in its supervisory work and as such, make it more likely that the FSA will identify possible breaches in these priority areas. Further, should evidence emerge of potential breaches, these areas are more likely to be supported by enforcement action than non-priority areas.

2.7 One way in which the FSA focuses on priority areas is through its thematic work. This work involves the FSA looking at a particular issue or set of issues across a sample of *firms*. Themes are, in general, selected to enable the FSA to improve its understanding of particular industry areas or to assess the validity of concerns the FSA has about risks those areas may present to the *regulatory objectives*. Thematic work does not start with the presumption that it will ultimately lead to enforcement outcomes. But if the FSA finds significant issues, these may become the subject of enforcement investigations as they would if the FSA had discovered them in any other circumstance. Also, by definition, the fact they are in areas that are of importance to the FSA means, following the FSA's risk-based approach through, that they are proportionately more likely to result in the FSA determining that an enforcement investigation should be carried out than issues in lower priority areas.

2.8 This does not mean that the FSA will only take enforcement action in priority strategic areas. There will always be particularly serious cases where enforcement action is necessary, ad hoc cases of particular significance in a markets, *consumer* protection or *financial crime* context, or cases that the FSA thinks are necessary to achieve effective deterrence.

2.9 The combination of the priority given to certain types of misconduct over others and the FSA's risk-based approach to enforcement means that certain cases will be subject to enforcement action and others not, even where they may be similar in nature or impact. The FSA's choice as to the use of the enforcement tool is therefore a question of how the FSA uses its resources effectively and efficiently and how it ensures that it is an effective regulator.

2.10 Before it proceeds with an investigation, the FSA will satisfy itself that there are grounds to investigate under the statutory provisions that give the FSA powers to appoint investigators. If the statutory test is met, it will decide whether to carry out an investigation after considering all the relevant circumstances. To assist its consideration of cases, the FSA has developed a set of assessment criteria. The current criteria (which are published on the Enforcement section of the FSA web site[1]) are framed as a set of questions. They take account of the FSA's *regulatory objectives*, its strategic/supervision priorities (see above) and other issues such as the response of the *firm* or individual to the issues being referred. Not all of the criteria will be relevant to every case and there may be other considerations which are not mentioned in the list but which are relevant to a particular case. The FSA's assessment will include considering whether using alternative tools is more appropriate taking into account the overall circumstances of the *person* or *firm* concerned and the wider context. Another consideration will be whether the FSA is under a Community obligation to take action on behalf of, or otherwise to provide assistance to, an authority from another *EU* member state. Paragraph 2.15 discusses the position where other authorities may have an interest in a case.

Case selection: Threshold Conditions cases

2.11 The FSA often takes a different approach to that described above where *firms* no longer meet the *threshold conditions*. The FSA views the *threshold conditions* as being fundamental requirements for *authorisation* and it will generally take action in all such cases which come to its attention and which cannot be resolved through the use of supervisory tools. The FSA does not generally appoint investigators in such cases. Instead, *firms* are first given an opportunity to correct the failure. If the *firm* does not take the necessary remedial action, the FSA will consider whether its *permission* to carry out regulated business should be varied and/or cancelled. However, there may be cases where the FSA considers that a formal investigation into a *threshold conditions* concern is appropriate.

Case selection: Unauthorised business

2.12 Where this poses a significant risk to the *consumer* protection objective or to the FSA's other *regulatory objectives*, *unauthorised* activity will be a matter of serious concern for the FSA. The FSA deals with cases of suspected *unauthorised* activity in a number of ways and it will not use its investigation powers and/or take enforcement action in every single instance.

2.13 The FSA's primary aim in using its investigation and enforcement powers in the context of suspected *unauthorised* activities is to protect the interests of *consumers*. The FSA's priority will be to confirm whether or not a *regulated activity* has been carried on in the United Kingdom by someone without *authorisation* or exemption, and, if so, the extent of that activity and whether other related contraventions have occurred. It will seek to assess the risk to *consumers'* assets and interests arising from the activity as soon as possible.

2.14 The FSA will assess on a case-by-case basis whether to carry out a formal investigation, after considering all the available information. Factors it will take into account include:
(1) the elements of the suspected contravention or breach;
(2) whether the FSA considers that the *persons* concerned are willing to co-operate with it;
(3) whether obligations of confidentiality inhibit individuals from providing information unless the FSA compels them to do so by using its formal powers;
(4) whether the *person* concerned has offered to undertake or undertaken remedial action.

Cases where other authorities have an interest

2.15 Action before or following an investigation may include, for example, referring some issues or information to other authorities for consideration, including where another authority appears to be better placed to take action. For example, when considering whether to use its powers to conduct formal investigations into market misconduct, the FSA will take into account whether another regulatory authority is in a position to investigate and deal with the matters of concern (as far as a *recognised investment exchange* or *recognised clearing house* is concerned, the FSA will consider the extent to which the relevant exchange or clearing house has adequate and appropriate powers to investigate and deal with a matter itself). Equally, in some cases, the FSA may investigate and/or take action in parallel with another domestic or international authority. This topic is discussed further in DEPP 6.2.19G to DEPP 6.2.28 G, paragraph 3.16 of this guide and in the case of action concerning criminal offences, paragraph 12.11.

Assisting overseas regulators

2.16 The FSA views co-operation with its overseas counterparts as an essential part of its regulatory functions. Section 354 of the *Act* imposes a duty on the FSA to take such steps as it considers appropriate to co-operate with others who exercise functions similar to its own. This duty extends to authorities in the UK and overseas. In fulfilling this duty the FSA may share information which it is not prevented from disclosing, including information obtained in the course of the FSA's own investigations, or exercise certain of its powers under Part XI of the *Act*. Further details of the FSA's powers to assist overseas regulators are provided at EG 3.12–3.15 (Investigations to assist overseas authorities), EG 4.8 (Use of statutory powers to require the production of documents, the provision of information or the answering of questions), EG 4.25–4.27 (Interviews in response to a request from an overseas regulator), and EG 8.18–8.25 (Exercising the power under section 47 to vary or cancel a firm's part IV permission in support of an overseas regulator). The FSA's statement of policy in relation to interviews which representatives of overseas regulators attend and participate in is set out in DEPP 7.

Sources of cases

2.17 The FSA may be alerted to possible contraventions or breaches by complaints from the public or *firms*, by referrals from other authorities or through its own enquiries and supervisory activities. *Firms* may also bring their own contraventions to the FSA's attention, as they are obliged to do under Principle 11 of the *Principles for Businesses* and *rules* in the FSA's Supervision manual.

Enforcement and the FSA's Principles for Businesses ('the Principles')

2.18 The FSA's approach to regulation involves a combination of high-level principles and detailed rules and guidance. While this broad structure is both necessary and desirable, the FSA is moving towards a more principles-based approach. This is because the FSA believes an approach that is based less on detailed rules and that focuses more on outcomes will allow it to achieve its *regulatory objectives* in a more efficient and effective way. The FSA regards the increased emphasis on the *Principles* as a development of its current approach rather than a fundamental change of direction.

2.19 This policy approach is leading to increased focus on principles-based enforcement action. The use of the *Principles* in enforcement cases is far from new. They have been used regularly in an enforcement context over many years. However, as part of its overall strategy in this area, the FSA will be giving more prominence to the *Principles* including, in appropriate cases, taking enforcement action on the basis of the *Principles* alone (see also DEPP 6.2.14 G). This will have the benefit of providing further clear examples of how the *Principles* work in practice.

2.20 The FSA wishes to encourage firms to exercise judgement about, and take responsibility for, what the *Principles* mean for them in terms of how they conduct their business. But we also recognise the importance of an environment in which *firms* understand what is expected of them. So we have indicated that *firms* must be able reasonably to predict, at the time of the action concerned, whether the conduct would breach the *Principles*. This has sometimes been described as the "reasonable predictability test" or "condition of predictability", but it would be wrong to think of this as a legal test to be met in deciding whether there has been a breach of FSA rules. Rather, our intention has been to acknowledge that firms may comply with the *Principles* in different ways; and to indicate that the FSA will not take enforcement action unless it was possible to determine at the time that the relevant conduct fell short of our requirements.

2.21 To determine whether there has been a failure to comply with a *Principle*, the standards we will apply are those required by the *Principles* at the time the conduct took place. The FSA will not apply later, higher standards to behaviour when deciding whether to take enforcement action for a breach of the *Principles*. Importantly, however, where conduct falls below expected standards the FSA considers that it is legitimate for consequences to follow, even if the conduct is widespread within the industry or the *Principle* is expressed in general terms.

FSA guidance and supporting materials

2.22 The FSA uses *guidance* and other materials to supplement the *Principles* where it considers this would help *firms* to decide what action they need to take to meet the necessary standard.

2.23 *Guidance* is not binding on those to whom the FSA's *rules* apply. Nor are the variety of materials (such as case studies showing good or bad practice, FSA speeches, and generic letters written by the FSA to Chief Executives in particular sectors) published to support the rules and *guidance* in the Handbook. Rather, such materials are intended to illustrate ways (but not the only ways) in which a person can comply with the relevant rules.

2.24 DEPP 6.2.1(4)G explains that the FSA will not take action against someone where we consider that they have acted in accordance with what we have said. However, *guidance* does not set out the minimum standard of conduct needed to comply with a rule, nor is there any presumption that departing from *guidance* indicates a breach of a rule. If a *firm* has complied with the *Principles* and other rules, then it does not matter whether it has also complied with other material the FSA has issued.

2.25 *Guidance* and supporting materials are, however, potentially relevant to an enforcement case and a decision maker may take them into account in considering the matter. Examples of the ways in which the FSA may seek to use *guidance* and supporting materials in an enforcement context include:

(1) To help assess whether it could reasonably have been understood or predicted at the time that the conduct in question fell below the standards required by the *Principles*.

(2) To explain the regulatory context.

(3) To inform a view of the overall seriousness of the breaches eg the decision maker could decide that the breach warranted a higher penalty in circumstances where the FSA had written to chief executives in the sector in question to reiterate the importance of ensuring a particular aspect of its business complied with relevant regulatory standards.

(4) To inform the consideration of a *firm's* defence that the FSA was judging the *firm* on the basis of retrospective standards.

(5) To be considered as part of expert or supervisory statements in relation to the relevant standards at the time.

2.26 The extent to which *guidance* and supporting materials are relevant will depend on all the circumstances of the case, including the type and accessibility of the statement and the nature of the *firm's* defence. It is for the decision maker (see paragraphs 2.37 to 2.39) – whether the *RDC*, *Tribunal* or an executive decision maker – to determine this on a case-by-case basis.

2.27 The FSA may take action in areas in which it has not issued *guidance* or supporting materials.

Industry guidance

2.28 The FSA recognises that Industry Guidance has an important part to play in a principles-based regulatory environment, and that firms may choose to follow such guidance as a means of seeking to meet the FSA's requirements. This will be true especially where Industry Guidance has been 'confirmed' by the FSA. DEPP 6.2.1(4)G confirms that, as with FSA *guidance* and supporting materials, the FSA will not take action against a firm for behaviour that we consider is in line with FSA-confirmed Industry Guidance that was current when the conduct took place.

2.29 Equally, however, FSA-confirmed Industry Guidance is not mandatory. The FSA does not regard adherence to Industry Guidance as the only means of complying with FSA rules and *Principles*. Rather, it provides examples of behaviour which meets the FSA's requirements; and non-compliance with confirmed Industry Guidance creates no presumption of a breach of those requirements.

2.30 Industry Guidance may be relevant to an enforcement case in ways similar to those described at paragraph 2.25. But the FSA is aware of the concern that firms must have scope to exercise their own judgement about what FSA rules require, and that Industry Guidance should not become a new prescriptive regime in place of detailed FSA rules. This, and the specific status of FSA-confirmed Industry Guidance, will be taken into account when the FSA makes judgements about the relevance of Industry Guidance in enforcement cases.

Senior management responsibility

2.31 The FSA is committed to ensuring that senior managers of *firms* fulfil their responsibilities. The FSA expects senior management to take responsibility for ensuring *firms* identify risks, develop appropriate systems and controls to manage those risks, and ensure that the systems and controls are effective in practice. The FSA will not pursue senior managers where there is no personal culpability. However, where senior managers are themselves responsible for misconduct, the FSA will, where appropriate, bring cases against individuals as well as *firms*. The FSA believes that deterrence will most effectively be achieved by bringing home to such individuals the consequences of their actions. The FSA's policy on disciplinary action against senior management and against other *approved persons* under section 66 of the *Act* is set out in DEPP 6.2.4G to DEPP 6.2.9 G. The FSA's policy on prohibition and withdrawal of approval is set out in chapter 9 of this guide.

2.32 The FSA recognises that cases against individuals are very different in their nature from cases against corporate entities and the FSA is mindful that an individual will generally face greater risks from enforcement action, in terms of financial implications, reputation and livelihood than would a corporate entity. As such, cases against individuals tend to be more strongly contested, and at many practical levels are harder to prove. They also take longer to resolve. However, taking action against individuals sends an important message about the FSA's *regulatory objectives* and priorities and the FSA considers that such cases have important deterrent values. The FSA is therefore committed to pursuing appropriate cases robustly, and will dedicate sufficient resources to them to achieve effective outcomes.

Co-operation

2.33 An important consideration before an enforcement investigation and/or enforcement action is taken forward is the nature of a *firm's* overall relationship with the FSA and whether, against that background, the use of enforcement tools is likely to further the FSA's aims and objectives. So, for any similar set of facts, using enforcement tools will be less likely if a *firm* has built up over time a strong track record of taking its senior management responsibilities seriously and been open and communicative with the FSA. In addition, a *firm's* conduct in response to the specific issue which has given rise to the question of whether enforcement tools should be used will also be relevant. In this respect, relevant matters may include whether the *person* has self-reported, helped the FSA establish the facts and/or taken remedial action such as addressing any systems and controls issues and compensating any consumers who have lost out. Such matters will not, however, necessarily mean that enforcement tools will not be used. The FSA has to consider each case on its merits and in the wider regulatory context, and any such steps cannot automatically lead to no enforcement sanction. However, they may in any event be factors which will mitigate the penalty.

2.34 On its web site, the FSA has given anonymous examples of where it has decided not to investigate or take enforcement action in relation to a possible *rule* breach because of the way in which the *firm* has conducted itself when putting the matter right. This is part of an article entitled 'The benefits to firms and individuals of co-operating with the FSA'.[2] However, in those cases where enforcement action is not taken and/or a formal investigation is not commenced, the FSA will expect the *firm* to act promptly to take the necessary remedial action agreed with its supervisors to deal with the FSA's concerns. If the *firm* does not do this, the FSA may take disciplinary or other enforcement action in respect of the original contravention.

Late reporting or non-submission of reports to the FSA

2.35 The FSA attaches considerable importance to the timely submission by *firms* of reports required under FSA rules. This is because the information contained in such reports is essential to the FSA's assessment of whether a *firm* is complying with the requirements and standards of the regulatory system and to the FSA's understanding of that *firm's* business. So, in the majority of cases involving non-submission of reports or repeated failure to submit complete reports on time, the FSA considers that it will be appropriate to seek to cancel the *firm's permission*. Where the FSA does not cancel a *permission*, it may take action for a financial penalty against a *firm* that submits a report after the due date (see DEPP 6.6.1G to DEPP 6.6.5 G).

Legal review

2.36 Before a case is referred to the *RDC*, it will be subject to a legal review by a lawyer who has not been a part of the investigation team. This will help to ensure that there is consistency in the way in which our cases are put and that they are supported by sufficient evidence. A lawyer who has not been a part of the investigation team will also review *warning notices* before they are submitted to the *settlement decision makers*.

Decision making in the context of regulatory enforcement action

2.37 When the FSA is proposing to exercise its regulatory enforcement powers, the *Act* generally requires the FSA to give *statutory notices* (depending on the nature of the action, a *warning notice* and *decision notice* or *supervisory notice*) to the subject of the action. The person to whom a *warning notice* or *supervisory notice* is given has a right to make representations on the FSA's proposed decision.

2.38 The procedures the FSA will follow when giving *supervisory notices*, *warning notices* and *decision notices* are set out in DEPP 1 to 5. Under these procedures, the decisions to issue such notices in contested enforcement cases are generally taken by the *RDC*, an FSA Board committee that is appointed by, and accountable to, the FSA Board for its decisions generally. Further details about the *RDC* can be found in DEPP 3 and on the pages of the FSA web site relating to the *RDC*.[3] However, decisions on settlements and *statutory notices* arising from them are taken by two members of FSA senior management of at least director level, under a special settlement decision procedure (see chapter 5).

2.39 A *person* who receives a *decision notice* or *supervisory notice* has a right to refer the matter to the *Tribunal* within prescribed time limits. The *Tribunal* is independent of the FSA and members of the *Tribunal* are appointed by the Lord Chancellors Department. Where a matter has been referred to it, the *Tribunal* will determine what action, if any, it is appropriate for the FSA to take in relation to that matter. Further details about the *Tribunal* can be found in an item on the *Tribunal* on the Enforcement pages of the FSA web site[4] and on the *Tribunal's* own web site.[5]

---

1 http://www.fsa.gov.uk/pages/Doing/Regulated/Law/criteria.shtml

2 http://www.fsa.gov.uk/Pages/doing/regulated/law/focus/co-operating.shtml

3 http://www.fsa.gov.uk/Pages/About/Who/board/committees/RDC/index.shtml

4 http://www.fsa.gov.uk/pages/doing/regulated/law/focus/tribunal.shtml

5 http://www.financeandtaxtribunals.gov.uk

CHAPTER 3
USE OF INFORMATION GATHERING AND INVESTIGATION POWERS

[2219C]

3.1 The FSA has various powers under sections 97, 165 to 169 and 284 of the *Act* to gather information and appoint investigators, and to require the production of a report by a *skilled person*. In any particular case, the FSA will decide which powers, or combination of powers, are most appropriate to use having regard to all the circumstances. Further comments on the use of these powers are set out below.

3.1A Information may also be provided to the FSA voluntarily. For example, *firms* may at times commission an internal investigation or a report from an external law firm or other professional adviser and decide to pass a copy of this report to the FSA. Such reports can be very helpful for the FSA in circumstances where enforcement action is anticipated or underway. The FSA's approach to using firm-commissioned reports in an enforcement context is set out at the end of this chapter.

Information requests (section 165)

3.2 The FSA may use its section 165 power to require information and documents from *firms* to support both its supervisory and its enforcement functions.

3.3 An officer with authorisation from the FSA may exercise the section 165 power to require information and documents from *firms*. This includes an FSA employee or an agent of the FSA.

Reports by skilled persons (section 166)

3.4 Under section 166 of the *Act*, the FSA has a power to require a *firm* and certain other persons to provide a report by a *skilled person*. The FSA may use its section 166 power to require reports by *skilled persons* to support both its supervision and enforcement functions.

3.5 The factors the FSA will consider when deciding whether to use the section 166 power include:

(1) If the FSA's objectives for making further enquiries are predominantly for the purposes of fact finding ie gathering historic information or evidence for determining whether enforcement action may be appropriate, the FSA's information gathering and investigation powers under sections 167 and 168 of the *Act* are likely to be more effective and more appropriate than the power under section 166.

(2) If the FSA's objectives include obtaining expert analysis or recommendations (or both) for, say, the purposes of seeking remedial action, it may be appropriate to use the power under section 166 instead of, or in conjunction with, the FSA's other available powers.

3.6 Where it exercises this power, the FSA will make clear both to the *firm* and to the *skilled person* the nature of the concerns that led the FSA to decide to appoint a *skilled person* and the possible uses of the results of the report. But a report the FSA commissions for purely diagnostic purposes could identify issues which could lead to the appointment of an investigator and/or enforcement action.

3.7 Chapter 5 of the FSA's Supervision manual (Reports by skilled persons) contains *rules* and guidance that will apply whenever the FSA uses the section 166 power.

Investigations into general and specific concerns (sections 167 and 168)

3.8 Where the FSA has decided that an investigation is appropriate (see chapter 2) and it appears to it that there are circumstances suggesting that contraventions or offences set out in section 168 may have happened, the FSA will normally appoint investigators pursuant to section 168. Where the circumstances do not suggest any specific breach or contravention covered by section 168, but, the FSA still has concerns about a *firm*, an *appointed representative*, a *recognised investment exchange* or an *unauthorised incoming ECA provider*, such that it considers there is good reason to conduct an investigation into the nature, conduct or state of the *person's* business or a particular aspect of that business, or into the ownership or control of an *authorised person*, the FSA may appoint investigators under section 167.

3.9 In some cases involving both general and specific concerns, the FSA may consider it appropriate to appoint investigators under both section 167 and section 168 at the outset. Also, where, for example, it has appointed investigators under section 167, it may subsequently decide that it is appropriate to extend the appointment to cover matters under section 168 as well.

Official listing investigations (section 97)

3.10 If the FSA has decided to carry out an investigation where there are circumstances suggesting that contraventions set out in section 97 may have happened, it will normally appoint investigators pursuant to that section. An investigator appointed under section 97 is treated under the *Act* as if they were appointed under section 167(1).

Investigations into collective investment schemes (section 284)

3.11 The FSA may appoint investigators under section 284 to conduct an investigation into the affairs of a *collective investment scheme* if it appears to it that it is in the interests of the participants or general participants to do so or that the matter is of public concern.

Investigations to assist overseas authorities (section 169)

3.12 The FSA's power to conduct investigations to assist overseas authorities is contained in section 169 of the *Act*. The section provides that at the request of an *overseas regulator*, the FSA may use its power under section 165 to require the production of documents or the provision of information under section 165 or to appoint a person to investigate any matter.

3.13 If the *overseas regulator* is a *competent authority* and makes a request in pursuance of any Community obligation, section 169(3) states that the FSA must, in deciding whether or not to exercise its investigative power, consider whether the exercise of that power is necessary to comply with that obligation.

3.14 Section 169(4) and (5) set out factors that the FSA may take into account when deciding whether to use its investigative powers. However, these provisions do not apply if the FSA considers that the use of its investigative powers is necessary to comply with a Community obligation.

3.15 When it considers whether to use its investigative power, and whether section 169(4) applies, the FSA will first consider whether it is able to assist without using its formal powers, for example by obtaining the information voluntarily. Where that is not possible, the FSA may take into account all of the factors in section 169(4), but may give particular weight to the seriousness of the case and its importance to persons in the United Kingdom, and to the public interest.

Liaison where other authorities have an interest

3.16 The FSA has agreed guidelines that establish a framework for liaison and cooperation in cases where certain other UK authorities have an interest in investigating or prosecuting any aspect of a matter that the FSA is considering for investigation, is investigating or is considering prosecuting. These guidelines are set out in Annex 2 to this guide.

FSA approach to firms conducting their own investigations in anticipation of FSA enforcement action.

Firm-commissioned reports: the desirability of early discussion and agreement where enforcement is anticipated

3.17 The FSA recognises that there are good reasons for *firms* wishing to carry out their own *investigations. This might be for*, for example, disciplinary purposes, general good management, or operational and risk control. The *firm* needs to know the extent of any problem, and it may want advice as to what immediate or short-term measures it needs to take to mitigate or correct any problems identified. The FSA encourages this proactive approach and does not wish to interfere with a *firm's* legitimate procedures and controls.

3.18 A *firm's* report – produced internally or by an external third party – can clearly assist the *firm*, but may also be useful to the FSA where there is an issue of regulatory concern. Sharing the outcome of an investigation can potentially save time and resources for both parties, particularly where there is a possibility of the FSA taking enforcement action in relation to a *firm's* perceived misconduct or failing. This does not mean that *firms* are under any obligation to share the content of legally privileged reports they are given or advice they receive. It is for the *firm* to decide whether to provide such material to the FSA. But a *firm's* willingness to volunteer the results of its own investigation, whether protected by legal privilege or otherwise, is welcomed by the FSA and is something the FSA may take into account when deciding what action to take, if any. (The FSA's approach to deciding whether to take action is described in more detail in DEPP 6.2 and paragraph 2.4 of this Guide.)

3.19 Work done or commissioned by the *firm* does not fetter the FSA's ability to use its statutory powers, for example to require a skilled person's report under section 166 of the *Act* or to carry out a formal enforcement investigation; nor can a report commissioned by the *firm* be a substitute for formal regulatory action where this is needed or appropriate. But even if formal action is needed, it may be that a report could be used to help the FSA decide on the appropriate action to take and may narrow the issues or obviate the need for certain work.

3.20 The FSA invites *firms* to consider, in particular, whether to discuss the commissioning and scope of a report with FSA staff where:

(1) *firms* have informed the FSA of an issue of potential regulatory concern, as required by SUP 15; or

(2) the FSA has indicated that an issue or concern has or may result in a referral to Enforcement.

3.21 The FSA's approach in commenting on the proposed scope and purpose of the report will vary according to the circumstances in which the report is commissioned; it does not follow that the FSA will want to be involved in discussing the scope of a report in every situation. But if the *firm* anticipates that it will proactively disclose a report to the FSA in the context of an ongoing or prospective enforcement investigation, then the potential use and benefit to be derived from the report will be greater if the FSA has had the chance to comment on its proposed scope and purpose.

3.22 Some themes or issues are common to any discussion about the potential use or value of a report to the FSA. These include:

(1) to what extent the FSA will be able to rely on the report in any subsequent enforcement proceedings;

(2) to what extent the FSA will have access to the underlying evidence or information that was relied upon in producing the report;

(3) where legal privilege or other professional confidentiality is claimed over any material gathered or generated in the investigation process, to what extent such material may nevertheless be disclosed to the FSA, on what basis and for what purposes the FSA may use that material;

(4) what approach will be adopted to establishing the relevant facts and how evidence will be recorded and retained;

(5) whether any conflicts of interest have been identified and whether there are proposals to manage them appropriately;

(6) whether the report will describe the role and responsibilities of identified individuals;

(7) whether the investigation will be limited to ascertaining facts or will also include advice or opinions about breaches of FSA rules or requirements;

(8) how the *firm* intends to inform the FSA of progress and communicate the results of the investigation; and

(9) timing.

3.23 In certain circumstances the FSA may prefer that a *firm* does not commission its own investigation (whether an internal audit report or a report by external advisers) because action by the *firm* could itself be damaging to an FSA investigation. This is true in particular of criminal investigations, where alerting the suspects could have adverse consequences. For example, where the FSA suspects that individuals are abusing positions of trust within financial institutions and that an insider dealing ring is operating, it might notify the relevant *firm* but would not want the *firm* to embark on its own investigation: to do so would alert those under investigation and prejudice on-going monitoring of the suspects and other action. *Firms* are therefore encouraged to be alive to the possibility that their own investigations could prejudice or hinder a subsequent FSA investigation, and, if in doubt, to discuss this with the FSA. The FSA recognises that *firms* may be under time and other pressures to establish the relevant facts and implications of possible misconduct, and will have regard to this in discussions with the *firm*.

3.24 Nothing in paragraphs 3.17 to 3.23 extends or increases the scope of the existing duty to report facts or issues to the FSA in accordance with SUP 15 or *Principle* 11.

Firm-commissioned reports: material gathered

3.25 Where a *firm* does conduct or commission an investigation, it is very helpful if the *firm* maintains a proper record of the enquiries made and interviews conducted. This will inform the FSA's judgment about whether any further work is needed and, if so, where the FSA's efforts should be focused.

3.26 How the results of an investigation are presented to the FSA may differ from case to case; the FSA acknowledges that different circumstances may call for different approaches. In this sense, one size does not fit all. The FSA will take a pragmatic and flexible approach when deciding how to receive the results of an investigation. However, if the FSA is to rely on a report as the basis for taking action, or not taking action, then it is important that the *firm* should be prepared to give the FSA underlying material on which the report is based as well as the report itself. This includes, for example, notes of interviews conducted by the lawyers, accountants or other professional experts carrying out the investigation.

3.27 The FSA is not able to require the production of "protected items", as defined in the *Act*, but it is not uncommon for there to be disagreement with *firms* about the scope of this protection. Arguments about whether certain documents attract privilege tend to be time-consuming and delay the progress of an investigation. If a *firm* decides to give a report to the FSA, then the FSA considers that the greatest mutual benefit is most likely to flow from disclosure of the report itself and any supporting papers. A reluctance to disclose these source materials will, in the FSA's opinion, devalue the usefulness of the report and may require the FSA to undertake additional enquiries.

Firm-commissioned reports: FSA use of reports and the protection of privileged and confidential material

3.28 For reasons that the FSA can understand, *firms* may seek to restrict the use to which a report can be put, or assert that any legal privilege is waived only on a limited basis and that the *firm* retains its right to assert legal privilege as the basis for nondisclosure in civil proceedings against a private litigant.

3.29 The FSA understands that the concept of a limited waiver of legal privilege is not one which is recognised in all jurisdictions; the FSA considers that English law does permit such "limited waiver" and that legal privilege could still be asserted against third parties notwithstanding disclosure of a report to the FSA. However, the FSA cannot accept any condition or stipulation which would purport to restrict its ability to use the information in the exercise of the FSA's statutory functions. In this sense, the FSA cannot 'close its eyes' to information received or accept that information should, say, be used only for the purposes of supervision but not for enforcement.

3.30 This does not mean that information provided to the FSA is unprotected. The FSA is subject to strict statutory restrictions on the disclosure of confidential information (as defined in section 348 of the *Act*), breach of which is a criminal offence (under section 352 of the *Act*). Reports and underlying materials provided voluntarily to the FSA by a *firm*, whether covered by legal privilege or not, are confidential for these purposes and benefit from the statutory protections.

3.31 Even in circumstances where disclosure of information would be permitted under the "gateways" set out in the Financial Services and Markets Act 2000 (Disclosure of Confidential Information) Regulations, the FSA will consider carefully whether it would be appropriate to disclose a report provided voluntarily by a *firm*. The FSA appreciates that *firms* feel strongly about the importance of maintaining confidentiality, and that *firms* are more likely to volunteer information to the regulator when they know that the regulator is mindful of this sensitivity and the impact of potential disclosure. Accordingly, if the FSA contemplates disclosing a report voluntarily provided by a *firm*, the *firm* will normally be notified and given the opportunity to make representations about the proposed disclosure. The exceptions to this include circumstances where disclosure is urgently needed, where notification might prejudice an investigation or defeat the purpose for which the information had been requested, or where notification would be inconsistent with the FSA's international obligations.

CHAPTER 4
CONDUCT OF INVESTIGATIONS

Notifying the person under investigation where notice is a requirement under section 170

[2219D]

4.1 The FSA will always give written notice of the appointment of investigators to the *person* under *investigation if it is required to* give such notice under section 170 of the *Act*. In such cases, if there is a subsequent change in the scope or conduct of the investigation and, in the FSA's opinion, the *person* under investigation is likely to be significantly prejudiced if not made aware of this, that *person* will be given written notice of the change. It is impossible to give a definitive list of the circumstances in which a *person* is likely to be significantly prejudiced by not being made aware of a change in the scope or conduct of an investigation. However, this may include situations where there may be unnecessary costs from dealing with an aspect of an investigation which the FSA no longer intends to pursue.

Notifying the person under investigation where notice is not required under the Act

4.2 The *Act* does not always require the FSA to give written notice of the appointment of investigators, for example, where investigators are appointed as a result of section 168(1) or (4) of the *Act* and the FSA believes that the provision of notice would be likely to result in the investigation being frustrated, or where investigators are appointed as a result of section 168(2) of the *Act*.

4.3 Although the FSA is not required to give written notice of the appointment of investigators appointed as a result of section 168(2), when it becomes clear who the *person* under investigation is, the FSA will, nevertheless, normally notify them that they are under investigation when it exercises its statutory powers to require information from them, providing such notification will not, in the FSA's view, prejudice the FSA's ability to conduct the investigation effectively.

Notification where a particular person is not yet under investigation

4.4 In investigations into possible *insider dealing*, *market abuse*, *misleading statements and practices offences*, breaches of the *general prohibition*, the restriction on *financial promotion*, or the prohibition on promoting *collective investment schemes*, the investigator may not know the identity of the perpetrator or may be looking into market circumstances at the outset of the investigation rather than investigating a particular *person*. In those circumstances, the FSA will give an indication of the nature and subject matter of its investigation to those who are required to provide information to assist with the investigation. As soon as a *person* becomes the focus of the FSA's enquiries, the FSA will consider whether it is appropriate to notify that *person* that they are under investigation. The FSA will usually notify them when it exercises its statutory powers to require information from them unless doing so would prejudice the FSA's ability to conduct the investigation effectively.

Appointment of additional investigators

4.5 In some cases, the FSA will appoint an additional investigator or additional investigators during the course of an investigation. If this occurs and the FSA has previously told the subject it has appointed investigators, then the FSA will normally give the person written notice of the appointment(s).

Notice of termination of investigations

4.6 Except where the FSA has issued a *warning notice*, and the FSA has subsequently discontinued the proceedings, the *Act* does not require the FSA to provide notification of the termination of an investigation or subsequent enforcement action. However, where the FSA has given a *person* written notice that it has appointed an investigator and later decides to discontinue the investigation without any present intention to take further action, it will confirm this to the *person* concerned as soon as it considers it is appropriate to do so, bearing in mind the circumstances of the case.

What a subject of investigation can say to third parties

4.7 As is explained in the chapter of this guide on publicity (chapter 6), the FSA will not normally make public the fact that it is or is not investigating a matter and its expectation is that the *person* under investigation will also treat the matter as confidential. However, subject to the restrictions on disclosure of confidential information in section 348 of the *Act*, this does not stop the *person* under investigation from seeking professional advice or making their own enquiries into the matter, from giving their auditors appropriate details of the matter or from making notifications required by law or contract.

Use of statutory powers to require the production of documents, the provision of information or the answering of questions

4.8 The FSA's standard practice is generally to use statutory powers to require the production of documents, the provision of information or the answering of questions in interview. This is for reasons of fairness, transparency and efficiency. It will sometimes be appropriate to depart from this standard practice, for example:

(1) For suspects or possible suspects in criminal or *market abuse* investigations, the FSA may prefer to question that *person* on a voluntary basis, possibly under caution. In such a case, the interviewee does not have to answer but if they do, those answers may be used against them in subsequent proceedings, including criminal or *market abuse* proceedings.

(2) In the case of third parties with no professional connection with the financial services industry, such as the victims of an alleged fraud or misconduct, the FSA will usually seek information voluntarily.

(3) In some cases, the FSA is asked by *overseas regulators* to obtain documents or conduct interviews on their behalf. In these cases, the FSA will not necessarily adopt its standard approach as it will consider with the *overseas regulator* the most appropriate method for obtaining evidence for use in their country.

4.9 *Firms* and *approved persons* have an obligation to be open and co-operative with the FSA (as a result of Principle 11 for Businesses and Statement of Principle 4 for Approved Persons respectively). The FSA will make it clear to the *person* concerned whether it requires them to produce information or answer questions under the *Act* or whether the provision of answers is purely voluntary. The fact that the *person* concerned may be a regulated person does not affect this.

4.10 The FSA will not bring disciplinary proceedings against a *person* under the above *Principles* simply because, during an investigation, they choose not to attend or answer questions at a purely voluntary interview. However, there may be circumstances in which an adverse inference may be drawn from the reluctance of a *person* (whether or not they are a *firm* or *approved person*) to participate in a voluntary interview.

4.11 If a *person* does not comply with a requirement imposed by the exercise of statutory powers, they may be held to be in contempt of court. The FSA may also choose to bring proceedings for breach of *Principle* 11 or *Statement of Principle* 4 as this is a serious form of non-cooperation.

Scoping discussions

4.12 For cases involving *firms* or *approved persons*, the FSA will generally hold scoping discussions with the *firm* or individuals concerned close to the start of the investigation (and may do so in other cases). The purpose of these discussions is to give the *firm* or individuals concerned in the investigation an indication of: why the FSA has appointed investigators (including the nature of and reasons for the FSA's concerns); the scope of the investigation; how the process is likely to unfold; the individuals and documents the team will need access to initially and so on. There is a limit, however, as to how specific the FSA can be about the nature of its concerns in the early stages of an investigation. The FSA team for the purposes of the scoping discussions will normally include the supervisor if the subject is a *firm* which is relationship-managed.

4.13 In addition to the initial scoping discussions, there will be an ongoing dialogue with the *firm* or individuals throughout the investigative process. Where the nature of the FSA's concerns changes significantly from that notified to the person under investigation and the FSA, having reconsidered the case, is satisfied that it is appropriate in the circumstances to continue the investigation, the FSA will notify the person of the change in scope.

Involvement of FSA supervisors during the investigation phase

4.14 As a general rule, the FSA supervisors of a *firm* are not directly involved in an enforcement investigation. This approach has its advantages in that it maintains a clear division between the conduct of the investigation on the one hand and the need to maintain the supervisory relationship with the *firm* on the other. However, this division of responsibility may mean that the investigation does not benefit as much as it might otherwise do from the knowledge of the *firm* or individuals that the supervisors will have built up, or from their general understanding of the *firm's* business or sector. Accordingly, the FSA takes the following general considerations into account in relation to the potential role of a supervisor in an investigation.

(1) While it is clearly essential for the day-to-day supervisory relationship to continue during the course of any enforcement action, this need not, of itself, preclude a *firm's* supervisor from assisting in an investigation.

(2) Such assistance will include: making the case team aware of the *firm's* history and compliance track record; the current supervisory approach to the area concerned; current issues with the *firm*; and acting as a sounding board on questions that emerge from the investigation about industry practices and standards.

(3) Equally, there may be circumstances where someone in the FSA other than the *firm's* supervisor can more effectively and efficiently provide information on the current supervisory approach to the area under investigation or current market standards. In this case it makes good sense for the FSA to draw on that other source of expertise.

(4) In the event that a *firm's* supervisor becomes part of the investigation team, the FSA will notify the firm of this in the normal way.

The timeframe for responding to information and document requirements

4.15 As delays in the provision of information and/or documents can have a significant impact on the efficient progression of an investigation, the FSA expects *persons* to respond to information and document requests in a timely manner to appropriate deadlines. When an investigation is complex (and the timetable allows), the FSA may decide to issue an information or document requirement in draft, allowing a specified period (of usually no more than three working days) for the *person* to comment on the practicality of providing the information or documentation by the proposed deadline. After considering any comments, the FSA will then confirm or amend the request. The FSA will not, however, send such a draft request where the request is straightforward and the FSA considers that it is reasonable to expect the information or documents to be made available within the FSA's specified timeframe.

4.16 Once it has formally issued a requirement (whether or not this has been preceded by a draft), the FSA will not usually agree to an extension of time for complying with the requirement unless compelling reasons are provided to support an extension request.

Approach to interviews and interview procedures

4.17 Paragraph 4.8 explains the FSA's approach to the use of its statutory powers to require, amongst other matters, individuals to be interviewed. The type of interview is a decision for the FSA.

4.18 A *person* required to attend an interview by the use of statutory powers has no entitlement to insist that the interview takes place voluntarily. If someone does not attend an interview required under the *Act*, then he can be dealt with by the court as if he were in contempt (where the penalties can be a fine, imprisonment or both).

4.19 Similarly, a *person* asked to attend an interview on a purely voluntary basis is not entitled to insist that he be served with a requirement. A *person* is not obliged to attend a voluntary interview or to answer questions put to them at that time. But they should be aware that in an appropriate case, an adverse inference may be drawn from the failure to attend a voluntary interview, or a refusal to answer any questions at such an interview.

Interviews generally

4.20 Where the FSA interviews a *person*, it will allow the *person* to be accompanied by a legal adviser, if they wish. The FSA will also, where appropriate, explain what use can be made of the answers in proceedings against them. Where the interview is tape-recorded, the *person* will be given a copy of the audio tape of the interview and, where a transcript is made, a copy of the transcript.

Interviews under caution

4.21 Individuals suspected of a criminal offence may be interviewed under caution. These interviews will be subject to all the safeguards of the relevant Police and Criminal Evidence Act Codes and are voluntary on the part of the suspect. The FSA will warn the suspect at the start of the interview of their right to remain silent (and the consequences of remaining silent) and will inform the suspect that they are entitled to have a legal adviser present. The FSA will also give a cautionary warning in similar terms to interviewees who are the subject of *market abuse* investigations.

Subsequent interviews

4.22 If a suspect has been interviewed by the FSA using statutory powers, before they are re-interviewed on a voluntary basis (under caution or otherwise), the FSA will explain the difference between the two types of interview. The FSA will also tell the individual about the limited use that can be made of their previous answers in criminal proceedings or in proceedings in which the FSA seeks a penalty for *market abuse* under Part VIII of the *Act*.

4.23 Conversely, where a suspect has been interviewed under caution, and the FSA later wishes to conduct a compulsory interview with them, the FSA will explain the difference between the two types of interview, and will notify the individual of the limited use that can be made of his answers in the compulsory interview.

Interviews under arrest

4.24 On occasion, where the police have a power of arrest, the FSA may make a request to the police for assistance to arrest the individual for questioning by the FSA (FSA investigators do not have powers of arrest), for example:

(1) where it appears likely that inviting an individual to attend on a voluntary basis would prejudice an ongoing investigation or risk the destruction of evidence or the dissipation of assets; or
(2) where a suspect declines an invitation to attend a voluntary interview.

The procedure the FSA may follow on such occasions in seeking assistance from the police is set out in a Memorandum of Understanding with the Association of Chief Police Officers of England, Wales and Northern Ireland dated 3 August 2005.[6]

Interviews in response to a request from an overseas regulator

4.25 Where the FSA has appointed an investigator in response to a request from an *overseas regulator*, it may, under section 169(7) of the *Act*, direct the investigator to allow a representative of that regulator to attend, and take part in, any interview conducted for the purposes of the investigation. However, the FSA may only use this power if it is satisfied that any information obtained by an *overseas regulator* as a result of the interview will be subject to safeguards equivalent to those in Part XXIII of the *Act* (section 169(8)).

4.26 The factors that the FSA may take into account when deciding whether to make a direction under section 169(7) include the following:
(1) the complexity of the case;
(2) the nature and sensitivity of the information sought;
(3) the FSA's own interest in the case;
(4) costs, where no Community obligation is involved, and the availability of resources; and
(5) the availability of similar assistance to UK authorities in similar circumstances.

4.27 Under section 169(9), the FSA is required to prepare a statement of policy with the approval of the Treasury on the conduct of interviews attended by representatives of *overseas regulators*. The statement is set out in DEPP 7.

Search and seizure powers

4.28 Under section 176 of the *Act*, the FSA has the power to apply to a justice of the peace for a warrant to enter premises where documents or information is held. The circumstances under which the FSA may apply for a search warrant include:
(1) where a *person* on whom an information requirement has been imposed fails (wholly or in part) to comply with it; or
(2) where there are reasonable grounds for believing that if an information requirement were to be imposed, it would not be complied with, or that the documents or information to which the information requirement relates, would be removed, tampered with or destroyed.

4.29 A warrant obtained pursuant to section 176 of the *Act* authorises a police constable or an FSA investigator in the company, and under the supervision of, a police constable, to do the following, amongst other things: to enter and search the premises specified in the warrant and take possession of any documents or information appearing to be documents or information of a kind in respect of which the warrant was issued or to take, in relation to any such documents or information, any other steps which may appear to be necessary for preserving them or preventing interference with them.

Preliminary findings letters and preliminary investigation reports

4.30 In cases where the FSA proposes to submit an investigation report to the *RDC* with a recommendation for regulatory action, the FSA's usual practice is to send a preliminary findings letter to the subject of an investigation before the matter is referred to the *RDC*. The letter will normally annex the investigators' preliminary investigation report. Comment will be invited on the contents of the preliminary findings letter and the preliminary investigation report.

4.31 The FSA recognises that preliminary findings letters serve a very useful purpose in focussing decision making on the contentious issues in the case. This in turn makes for better quality and more efficient decision making. However, there are exceptional circumstances in which the FSA may decide it is not appropriate to send out a preliminary findings letter. This includes:
(1) where the subject consents to not receiving a preliminary findings letter; or
(2) where it is not practicable to send a preliminary findings letter, for example where there is a need for urgent action in the interests of consumer protection, restoring market confidence or reducing *financial crime* or if the whereabouts of the subject are unknown; or
(3) where the FSA believes that no useful purpose would be achieved in sending a preliminary findings letter, for example where it has otherwise already substantially disclosed its case to the subject and the subject has had an opportunity to respond to that case.

4.32 In cases where it is sent, the preliminary findings letter will set out the facts which the investigators consider relevant to the matters under investigation (normally, as indicated above, by means of an annexed preliminary investigation report). And it will invite the *person* concerned to confirm that those facts are complete and accurate, or to provide further comment. FSA staff will allow a reasonable period (normally 28 days) for a response to this letter, and will take into account any response received within the period stated in the letter. They are not obliged to take into account any response received outside that period.

4.33 Where the FSA has sent a preliminary findings letter and it then decides not to take any further action, the FSA will communicate this decision promptly to the person concerned.

6 http://www.fsa.gov.uk/pubs/mou/fsacolp.pdf

CHAPTER 5
SETTLEMENT

Settlement and the FSA – an overview

[2219E]

5.1 The FSA resolves many enforcement cases by settlement. Early settlement has many potential advantages as it can result, for example, in *consumers* obtaining compensation earlier than would otherwise be the case, the saving of FSA and industry resources, messages getting out to the market sooner and a public perception of timely and effective action. The FSA therefore considers it is in the public interest for matters to settle, and settle early, if possible.

5.2 The possibility of settlement does not, however, change the fact that enforcement action is one of the tools available to the FSA to secure our *regulatory objectives*. The FSA seeks to change the behaviour not only of those subject to the immediate action, but also of others who will be alerted to our concerns in a particular area. There is no distinction here between action taken following agreement with the subject of the enforcement action and action resisted by a firm before the *RDC*. In each case, the FSA must be satisfied that its decision is the right one, both in terms of the immediate impact on the subject of the enforcement action but also in respect of any broader message conveyed by the action taken.

5.3 Settlements in the FSA context are not the same as 'out of court' settlements in the commercial context. An FSA settlement is a regulatory decision, taken by the FSA, the terms of which are accepted by the *firm* or individual concerned. So, when agreeing the terms of a settlement, the FSA will carefully consider its *regulatory objectives* and other relevant matters such as the importance of sending clear, consistent messages through enforcement action, and will only settle in appropriate cases where the agreed terms of the decision result in acceptable regulatory outcomes. Redress to *consumers* who may have been disadvantaged by a *firm's* misconduct may be particularly important in this respect. Other than in exceptional circumstances, FSA settlements that give rise to the issue of a *final notice* or *supervisory notice* will result in some degree of publicity (see chapter 6), unlike commercial out of court settlements, which are often confidential.

5.4 In recognition of the value of early settlement, the FSA operates a scheme to award explicit discounts for early settlement of cases involving financial penalties. Details of the scheme, which applies only to settlement of cases where investigators were appointed on or after 20 October 2005, are set out in DEPP 6.7. This chapter provides some commentary on certain practical aspects of the operation of the scheme.

5.5 Decisions on settlements and *statutory notices* arising from them are taken by two members of FSA senior management of at least director level, rather than by the *RDC* (DEPP refers to these individuals as the '*settlement decision makers*'). Full details of the special decision making arrangements for settlements are set out in DEPP 5.

When settlement discussions may take place

5.6 Settlement discussions between FSA staff and the *person* concerned are possible at any stage of the enforcement process if both parties agree.

5.7 The FSA considers that in general, the earlier settlement discussions can take place the better this is likely to be from a public interest perspective. However, the FSA will only engage in such discussions once it has a sufficient understanding of the nature and gravity of the suspected misconduct or issue to make a reasonable assessment of the appropriate outcome. At the other end of the spectrum, the FSA expects that settlement discussions following a *decision notice* or *second supervisory notice* will be rare.

5.8 In the interests of efficiency and effectiveness, the FSA will set clear and challenging timetables for settlement discussions to ensure that they result in a prompt outcome and do not divert resources unnecessarily from progressing a case through the formal process. To this end, the FSA will aim to organise its resources so that the preparation for the formal process continues in parallel with any settlement discussions. The FSA will expect *firms* and others to give it all reasonable assistance in this regard.

The basis of settlement discussions

5.9 As described above, the FSA operates special decision-making arrangements under which members of FSA senior management take decisions on FSA settlements. This means that settlement discussions will take place without involving the *RDC*. The FSA would expect to hold any settlement discussions on the basis that neither FSA staff nor the *person* concerned would seek to rely against the other on any admissions or statements made if the matter is considered subsequently by the *RDC* or the *Tribunal*. This will not, however, prevent the FSA from following up, through other means, on any new issues of regulatory concern which come to light during settlement discussions. The *RDC* may be made aware of the fact negotiations are taking place if this is relevant, for example, to an application for an extension of the period for making representations.

5.10 If the settlement negotiations result in a proposed settlement of the dispute, FSA staff will put the terms of the proposed settlement in writing and agree them with the *person* concerned. The *settlement decision makers* will then consider the settlement under the procedures set out in DEPP 5. A settlement is also likely to result in the giving of *statutory notices* (see paragraphs 2.37 to 2.39).

Multiple parties and third party rights in enforcement action involving warning and decision notices

5.11 Enforcement cases often involve multiple parties, for example a *firm* and individuals in the *firm*. Enforcement action may be appropriate against just the *firm*, just the individuals or both. In some cases, it will not be possible to reach an acceptable settlement unless all parties are able to reach agreement.

5.12 Even where action is not taken against connected parties, these parties may have what the *Act* calls 'third party rights'. Broadly, if any of the reasons contained in a *warning notice* or *decision notice* identifies a *person* (the third party) other than the *person* to whom the notice is given, and in the opinion of the FSA is prejudicial to the third party, a copy of the notice must be given to the third party unless that *person* receives a separate *warning notice* or *decision notice* at the same time. The third party has the right to make representations and ultimately can refer the matter to the *Tribunal*. Any representations made by the third party in response to a *warning notice* or *decision notice* will be considered by the *settlement decision makers*, who will also decide whether to give the *decision notice* or *final notice*.

5.13 In practice, third party rights do not frequently cause undue difficulty for settlement, either because they do not arise at all or because the third party agrees not to exercise such rights.

The settlement discount scheme

5.14 The *settlement discount scheme* allows a reduction in a financial penalty that would otherwise be imposed on a *person* according to the stage at which the agreement is reached. Full details of the scheme are set out in DEPP 6.7.

5.15 Normally, where the outcome is potentially a financial penalty, the FSA will send a letter at an early point in the enforcement process to the subject of the investigation. This is what the FSA refers to as a stage 1 letter.

5.16 The scheme does not apply to civil or criminal proceedings brought in the courts, or to *public censure*, *prohibition orders*, withdrawal of *authorisation* or approval or the payment of compensation or redress.

5.17 There is no set form for a stage 1 letter though it will always explain the nature of the misconduct, the FSA's view on penalty, and the period within which the FSA expects any settlement discussions to be concluded. In some cases, a draft *statutory notice* setting out the alleged *rule* breaches and the proposed penalty may form part of the letter, to convey the substance of the case team's concerns and reasons for arriving at a particular penalty figure.

5.18 The timing of the stage 1 letter will vary from case to case. Sufficient investigative work must have taken place for the FSA to be able to satisfy itself that the settlement is the right regulatory outcome. In many cases, the FSA can send out the stage 1 letter substantially before the *person* concerned is provided with the FSA's preliminary investigation report (see paragraphs 4.30 to 4.33). The latest point the FSA will send a stage 1 letter is when the *person* is provided with the preliminary investigation report.

5.19 The FSA considers that 28 days following a stage 1 letter will normally be the 'reasonable opportunity to reach agreement as to the amount of penalty' before the expiry of stage 1 contemplated by DEPP 6.7.3. Extensions to this period will be granted in exceptional circumstances only.

Mediation

5.20 The FSA is committed to mediating appropriate cases; mediation and the involvement of a neutral mediator may help the FSA to reach an agreement with the *person* subject to enforcement action in circumstances where settlement might not otherwise be achieved or may not be achieved so efficiently and effectively.

5.21 Further information about the FSA's approach to mediation and the mediation process are set out on our web site.[7]

The relevance of settled cases to subsequent action

5.22 Decisions recorded in FSA *final notices* or *supervisory notices* will be taken into account in any subsequent case if the later case raises the same or similar issues to those considered by the FSA when it reached its earlier decision. Not to do so would expose the FSA to accusations of arbitrary and inconsistent decision-making. The need to look at earlier cases applies irrespective of whether the decisions were reached following settlement or consideration by the *RDC* or the *Tribunal*. This reflects the fact that a person's agreement to the action proposed by the FSA in the earlier case would not have relieved the FSA of the obligation to ensure that the final decision was the right regulatory outcome, both for the person concerned and more generally.

5.23 The FSA recognises the importance of consistency in its decision-making and that it must consider the approach previously taken to, say, the application of a particular rule or *Principle* in a given context. This applies equally to consideration by the *RDC* or by the *settlement decision makers* when they look at action taken by the FSA in earlier, similar, cases. This is not to say that the FSA cannot take a different view to that taken in the earlier case: the facts of two enforcement cases are very seldom identical, and it is also important that the FSA is able to respond to the demands of a changing and principles–based regulatory environment. But any decision to depart from the earlier approach will be made only after careful consideration of the reasons for doing so.

7 http://www.fsa.gov.uk/pages/doing/regulated/law/focus/mediation.shtml

CHAPTER 6
PUBLICITY

Publicity during FSA investigations

[2219F]

6.1 The FSA will not normally make public the fact that it is or is not investigating a particular matter, or any of the findings or conclusions of an investigation except as described in other sections of this chapter. The following paragraphs deal with the exceptional circumstances in which the FSA may make a public announcement that it is or is not investigating a particular matter.

6.2 Where the matter in question has occurred in the context of a *takeover bid*, and the following circumstances apply, the FSA may make a public announcement that it is not investigating, and does not propose to investigate, the matter. Those circumstances are where the FSA:
(1) has not appointed, and does not propose to appoint, investigators; and
(2) considers (following discussion with the *Takeover Panel*) that such an announcement is appropriate in the interests of preventing or eliminating public uncertainty, speculation or rumour.

6.3 Where it is investigating any matter, the FSA will, in exceptional circumstances, make a public announcement that it is doing so if it considers such an announcement is desirable to:
(1) maintain public confidence in the *financial system* or the market; or
(2) protect *consumers* or investors; or
(3) prevent widespread malpractice; or
(4) help the investigation itself, for example by bringing forward witnesses; or
(5) maintain the smooth operation of the market.

In deciding whether to make an announcement, the FSA will consider the potential prejudice that it believes may be caused to any *persons* who are, or who are likely to be, a subject of the investigation.

6.4 The exceptional circumstances referred to above may arise where the matters under investigation have become the subject of public concern, speculation or rumour. In this case it may be desirable for the FSA to make public the fact of its investigation in order to allay concern, or contain the speculation or rumour. Where the matter in question relates to a *takeover bid*, the FSA will discuss any announcement beforehand with the *Takeover Panel.* Any announcement will be subject to the restriction on disclosure of *confidential information* in section 348 of the *Act.*

6.5 There will also be cases where publicity is unavoidable. For example, investigations into suspected criminal offences may often lead the FSA into making enquiries amongst the general public which might attract publicity.

6.6 The FSA will not normally publish details of the information found or conclusions reached during its investigations. In many cases, statutory restrictions on the disclosure of information obtained by the FSA in the course of exercising its functions are likely to prevent publication (see section 348 of the *Act*). In exceptional circumstances, and where it is not prevented from doing so, the FSA may publish details. Circumstances in which it may do so include those where the fact that the FSA is investigating has been made public, by the FSA or otherwise, and the FSA subsequently concludes that the concerns that prompted the investigation were unwarranted. This is particularly so if the *firm* under investigation wishes the FSA to clarify the matter.

Publicity during, or upon the conclusion of regulatory action

6.7 For both *supervisory notices* (as defined in section 395(13)) which have taken effect[8] and *final notices*, section 391 of the *Act* requires the FSA to publish, in such manner as it considers appropriate, such information about the matter to which the notice relates as it considers appropriate. However, section 391 provides that the FSA cannot publish information if publication of it would, in its opinion, be unfair to the *person* with respect to whom the action was taken or prejudicial to *consumers*.

Part II FSA Handbook Materials

Final notices

6.8 The FSA will consider the circumstances of each case, but will ordinarily publicise enforcement action where this has led to the issue of a *final notice*. Publication will generally include placing the notice on the FSA web site and this will often be accompanied by a press release. The FSA will also consider what information about the matter should be included on the *FSA Register*. Additional guidance on the FSA's approach to the publication of information on the *FSA Register* in certain specific types of cases is set out at the end of this chapter.

6.9 However, as required by the *Act* (see paragraph 6.7 above), the FSA will not publish information if publication of it would, in its opinion, be unfair to the *person* in respect of whom the action is taken or prejudicial to the interests of *consumers*. It may make that decision where, for example, publication could damage market confidence or undermine market integrity in a way that could be damaging to the interests of *consumers*.

6.10 Publishing *final notices* is important to ensure the transparency of FSA decision-making; it informs the public and helps to maximise the deterrent effect of enforcement action. The FSA will review *final notices* and related press releases that are published on the FSA's web site after a period of six years. The FSA will determine at that time whether continued publication is appropriate, or whether notices and publicity should be removed or amended.

Supervisory notices varying a firm's Part IV permission on the FSA's own initiative (see chapter 8 of this guide)

6.11 [deleted]

6.12 Publishing the reasons for variations of *Part IV permission* (and interventions), and maintaining an accurate public record, are important elements of the FSA's approach to its *consumer* protection objective. The FSA will always aim to balance both the interests of *consumers* and the possibility of unfairness to the *person* subject to the FSA's action. The FSA will publish relevant details of both fundamental and non fundamental variations of *Part IV permission* and interventions which it imposes on *firms*. But it will use its discretion not to do so if it considers this would be unfair to the person on whom the variation is imposed or prejudicial to the interests of consumers. Publication will generally include placing the notice on the FSA web site and this may be accompanied by a press release. As with *final notices*, *supervisory notices* and related press releases that are published on the FSA's web site will be reviewed after a period of six years. The FSA will determine at that time whether continued publication is appropriate, or whether notices and related press releases should be removed or amended.

6.12A The FSA will amend the *FSA Register* to reflect a *firm's* actual *Part IV permission* following any variation.

Directions against ECA providers

6.13 This is discussed in paragraphs 19.37 and 19.38 of this guide.

Publicity in RDC cases

6.14 The Chairman of the *RDC*, or his relevant Deputy, will approve the contents of press releases to be published by the FSA in cases in which the decision to take action was made by the *RDC*, unless the *RDC's* decision is superseded by a decision of the *Tribunal*.

Publicity during, or upon the conclusion of civil action

6.15 Civil court proceedings nearly always take place in public from the time they begin. Therefore, civil proceedings for an *injunction* (see chapter 10) or a restitution order (see chapter 11), for example, will often be public as soon as they start.

6.16 The FSA considers it generally appropriate to publish details of its successful applications to the court for civil remedies including *injunctions* or restitution orders. For example, where the court has ordered an *injunction* to prohibit further illegal *regulated activity*, the FSA thinks it is appropriate to publicise this to tell *consumers* of the position and help them avoid dealing with the *person* who is the subject of the *injunction*. Similarly, a restitution order may be publicised to protect and inform *consumers* and maintain market confidence. However, there may be circumstances when the FSA decides not to publicise, or not to do this immediately. These circumstances might, for example, be where publication could damage confidence in the *financial system* or undermine market integrity in a way that would be prejudicial to the interests of *consumers*.

Publicity during, or upon the conclusion of criminal action (see chapter 12)

6.17 Like civil proceedings, criminal court proceedings nearly always take place in public from the time they begin. However, the FSA will always be very careful to ensure that any FSA publicity does not prejudice the fairness of any subsequent trial. The FSA will normally publicise the outcome of public hearings in criminal prosecutions.

Behaviour in the context of takeover bid

6.18 Where the behaviour to which a *final notice*, civil action, or criminal action relates has occurred in the context of a *takeover bid*, the FSA will consult the *Takeover Panel* over the timing of publication if the FSA believes that publication may affect the timetable or outcome of that bid, and will give due weight to the *Takeover Panel's* views.

The FSA register: publication of prohibitions of individuals (see chapter 9)

6.19 Once the decision to make a *prohibition order* is no longer open to review, the FSA will consider what additional information about the circumstances of the *prohibition order* to include on the *FSA Register*. The FSA will balance any possible prejudice to the individual concerned against the interests of *consumer* protection. The FSA's normal approach to maintaining information about a *prohibition order* on the *FSA Register* is as follows:

(1) The FSA will maintain an entry on the *FSA Register* while a *prohibition order* is in effect. If the FSA grants an application to vary the order, it will make a note of the variation on the *FSA Register*.

(2) Where the FSA grants an application to revoke a *prohibition order*, it will make a note on the *FSA Register* that the order has been revoked giving reasons for the revocation. The availability to *firms* and *consumers* of a full record of FSA action taken in relation to an individual's fitness and propriety will help it in furthering its *regulatory objectives*. In particular, it will help with protecting *consumers* and the maintaining of confidence in the *financial system*.

(3) The FSA will maintain an annotated record of revoked *prohibition orders* for six years from the date of the revocation after which time it will remove the record from the *FSA Register*.

The FSA register: publication of disqualifications of auditors and actuaries (see chapter 15)

6.20 To help it fulfil its *regulatory objectives* of protecting *consumers* and promoting public awareness, the FSA will keep on the *FSA Register* a record of *firms* or individual auditors or actuaries who have been the subject of disqualification orders.

The FSA register: publication of disapplication orders against members of the professions (see chapter 16)

6.21 In general, the FSA considers that publishing relevant information about orders to disapply an exemption in respect of a member of a *designated professional body* will be in the interests of clients and *consumers*. The FSA will consider what additional information about the circumstances of the order to include on the record maintained on the *FSA Register* taking into account any prejudice to the *person* concerned and the interests of *consumer* protection.

6.22 The FSA's normal approach to maintaining information about a disapplication order on the *FSA Register* is as follows.

(1) While a disapplication order is in effect, the FSA will maintain a record of the order on the *FSA Register*. If the FSA grants an application to vary the order, a note of the variation will be made against the relevant entry on the *FSA Register*.

(2) The FSA's policy in relation to section 347(4) of the *Act* is that where an application to revoke an order is granted, it will make a note on the *FSA Register* saying that the order has been revoked giving reasons for its revocation. Having a full record of action the FSA has taken against *persons* granted an exemption under section 327 of the *Act* available will help the FSA to fulfil its *regulatory objectives* of protecting *consumers* and maintaining confidence in the *financial system*.

(3) This is why the FSA will maintain the annotated record of the disapplication order for a period of six years from the date of the revocation of the order, after which period the record will be removed from the record on the *FSA Register*.

---

8 Section 53(2) and section 391(8) of the *Act* define when a variation of permission under a supervisory notice takes effect

---

CHAPTER 7
FINANCIAL PENALTIES AND PUBLIC CENSURES

The FSA's use of sanctions

[2219G]

7.1 Financial penalties and *public censures* are important regulatory tools. However, they are not the only tools available to the FSA, and there will be many instances of non-compliance which the FSA considers it appropriate to address without the use of financial penalties or *public censures*. Having said that, the effective and proportionate use of the FSA's powers to enforce the requirements of the *Act*, the *rules* and the Statements of Principle for Approved Persons will play an important role in the FSA's pursuit of its *regulatory objectives*. Imposing financial penalties and *public censures* shows that the FSA is upholding regulatory standards and helps to maintain market confidence, promote public awareness of regulatory standards and deter *financial crime*. An increased public awareness of regulatory standards also contributes to the protection of *consumers*.

7.2 The FSA has the following powers to impose a financial penalty and to publish a *public censure*.

(1) It may publish a statement:
   (a) against an *approved person* under section 66 of the *Act*;
   (b) against an *issuer* under section 87M of the *Act*;
   (c) against a *sponsor* under section 89 of the *Act*;
   (d) where there has been a contravention of the Part VI rules, under section 91 of the *Act*;
   (e) where there has been *market abuse*, against a *person* under section 123 of the *Act*; and
   (f) against a *firm* under section 205 of the *Act*.

(2) It may impose a financial penalty:
   (a) on an *approved person*, under section 66 of the *Act*;
   (b) where there has been a contravention of the Part 6 rules, under section 91 of the *Act*;
   (c) where there has been *market abuse*, on any *person*, under section 123 of the *Act*; and
   (d) on a *firm*, under section 206 of the *Act*.

Alternatives to financial penalties and public censures

7.3 The FSA also has measures available to it where it considers it is appropriate to take protective or remedial action. These include:

(1) where a *firm's* continuing ability to meet the *threshold conditions* or where an *approved person's* fitness and propriety to perform the *controlled functions* to which his approval relates are called into question:
   (a) varying and/or cancelling of *permission* and the withdrawal of a *firm's* authorisation (see chapter 8); and
   (b) the withdrawal of an individual's status as an *approved person* and/or the prohibition of an individual from performing a specified function in relation to a *regulated activity* (see chapter 9);

(2) where the smooth operation of the market is, or may be, temporarily jeopardised or where protecting investors so requires, the FSA may suspend, with effect from such time as it may determine, the *listing* of any *securities* at any time and in such circumstances as it thinks fit (whether or not at the request of the *issuer* or its *sponsor* on its behalf);

(3) when the FSA is satisfied there are special circumstances which preclude normal regular dealings in any *listed securities*, it may cancel the *listing* of any *security*;

(4) where there are reasonable grounds to suspect non compliance with the *disclosure rules*, the FSA may require the suspension of trading of a financial instrument with effect from such time as it may determine; and

(5) where there are reasonable grounds for suspecting that a provision of Part VI of the *Act*, a provision contained in the *prospectus rules*, or any other provision made in accordance with the *Prospectus Directive* has been infringed, the FSA may:
   (a) suspend or prohibit the offer to the public of transferable securities as set out in section 87K of the *Act*; or
   (b) suspend or prohibit admission of transferable securities to trading on a regulated market as set out in section 87L of the *Act*.

FSA's statements of policy

7.4 The FSA's statement of policy in relation to the imposition of financial penalties is set out in DEPP 6.2 (Deciding whether to take action), DEPP 6.3 (Penalties for market abuse) and DEPP 6.4 (Financial penalty or public censure). The FSA's statement of policy in relation to the amount of a financial penalty is set out in DEPP 6.5.

Apportionment of financial penalties

7.5 In a case where the FSA is proposing to impose a financial penalty on a *person* for two or more separate and distinct areas of misconduct, the FSA will consider whether it is appropriate to identify in the *final notice* how the penalty is apportioned between those separate and distinct areas. Apportionment will not however generally be appropriate in other cases.

Payment of financial penalties

7.6 Financial penalties must be paid within the period (usually 14 days) that is stated on the FSA's *final notice*.

7.7 A *person* may ask the FSA to allow them to pay a financial penalty by instalments. However, the FSA will consider agreeing to payment of a financial penalty by instalments only where there is verifiable evidence of serious financial hardship or financial difficulties if the *person* was required to pay the full payment in a single instalment. This reflects the fact that the purpose of a penalty is not to render a *person* insolvent or to threaten solvency. The FSA will determine the appropriate level and number of instalments having regard to the overall circumstances of the case. However, in such cases, the full payment of the penalty will generally have to be made within one year from the date of the *final notice*.

7.8 Chapter 6 of the General Provisions module of the FSA Handbook contains rules prohibiting a *firm* or *member* from entering into, arranging, claiming on or making a payment under a *contract of insurance* that is intended to have, or has, the effect of indemnifying any *person* against a financial penalty.

7.9 Rule 1.5.33 in the FSA's Prudential Sourcebook for Insurers prohibits a *long-term insurer* (including a *firm* qualifying for *authorisation* under Schedule 3 or 4 to the *Act*), which is not a mutual, from paying a financial penalty from a long-term insurance fund.

Private warnings

7.10 In certain cases, despite concerns about a *person's* behaviour or evidence of a *rule* breach, the FSA may decide that it is not appropriate, having regard to all the circumstances of the case, to bring formal action for a financial penalty or *public censure*. This is consistent with the FSA's risk-based approach to enforcement. In such cases, the FSA may give a private warning to make the *person* aware that they came close to being subject to formal action.

7.11 Private warnings are a non-statutory tool. Fundamentally they are no different to any other FSA communication which criticises or expresses concern about a *person's* conduct. But private warnings are a more serious form of reprimand than would usually be made in the course of ongoing supervisory correspondence. A private warning requires that the FSA identifies and explains its concerns about a *person's* conduct and/or procedures, and tells the subject of the warning that the FSA has seriously considered formal steps to impose a penalty or censure. They are primarily used by the FSA as an enforcement tool, but they may also be used by other parts of the FSA.

7.12 Typically, the FSA might give a private warning rather than take formal action where the matter giving cause for concern is minor in nature or degree, or where the person has taken full and immediate remedial action. But there can be no exhaustive list of the conduct or the circumstances which are likely to lead to a private warning rather than more serious action. The FSA will take into account all the circumstances of the case before deciding whether a private warning is appropriate. Many of the criteria identified in *DEPP* 6 for determining whether the FSA should take formal action for a financial penalty or *public censure* will also be relevant to a decision about whether to give a private warning.

7.13 Generally, the FSA would expect to use private warnings in the context of *firms* and *approved persons*. However, the FSA may also issue private warnings in circumstances where the *persons* involved may not necessarily be authorised or approved. For example, private warnings may be issued in potential cases of *market abuse*; cases where the FSA has considered making a *prohibition order* or a disapplication order; or cases involving breaches of provisions imposed by or under Part VI of the *Act* (Official Listing).

7.14 In each case, the FSA will consider the likely impact of a private warning on the recipient and whether any risk that *person* poses to the *regulatory objectives* requires the FSA to take more serious action. Equally, where the FSA gives a private warning to an *approved person*, the FSA will consider whether it would be desirable and appropriate to inform the *approved person's firm* (or employer, if different) of the conduct giving rise to the warning and the FSA's response.

7.15 A private warning is not intended to be a determination by the FSA as to whether the recipient has breached the FSA's rules. However, private warnings, together with any comments received in response, will form part of the *person's* compliance history. In this sense they are no different to other FSA correspondence, but the weight the FSA attaches to a private warning is likely to be greater. They may therefore influence the FSA's decision whether to commence action for a penalty or censure in relation to future breaches. Where action is commenced in those circumstances, earlier private warnings will not be relied upon in determining whether a breach has taken place. However, if a *person* has previously been told about the FSA's concerns in relation to an issue, either by means of a private warning or in supervisory correspondence, then this can be an aggravating factor for the level of a penalty imposed in respect of a similar issue that is the subject of later FSA action.

7.16 Where the FSA is assessing the relevance of private warnings in determining whether to commence action for a financial penalty or a *public censure*, the age of a private warning will be taken into consideration. However, a long-standing private warning may still be relevant.

7.17 Private warnings may be considered cumulatively, although they relate to separate areas of a *firm's* or other *person's* business, where the concerns which gave rise to those warnings are considered to be indicative of a *person's* compliance culture. Similarly, private warnings issued to different subsidiaries of the same parent company may be considered cumulatively where the concerns which gave rise to those warnings relate to a common management team.

How a person will know they are receiving a private warning

7.18 It will be obvious from the terms of any letter written by the FSA whether it is intended to constitute a private warning. In particular, a warning letter will describe itself as a private warning and will refer to this chapter to explain the consequences of receiving it for the person.

The procedure for giving a private warning

7.19 The FSA's normal practice is to follow a "minded-to" procedure before deciding whether to give a private warning. This means that it will notify in writing the intended recipient of the warning that it has concerns about their conduct and inform them that the FSA proposes to give a private warning. The recipient will then have an opportunity to comment on our understanding of the circumstances giving rise to the FSA's concerns and whether a private warning is appropriate. The FSA will carefully consider any response to its initial letter before it decides whether to give the private warning. The decision will be taken by an FSA head of department or a more senior member of FSA staff.

CHAPTER 8
VARIATION AND CANCELLATION OF PERMISSION ON THE FSA'S OWN INITIATIVE AND INTERVENTION AGAINST INCOMING FIRMS

[2219H]

8.1 The FSA has powers under section 45 of the *Act* to vary or cancel an *authorised person's Part IV permission*. The FSA may use these powers where:

(1) the person is failing or is likely to fail to satisfy the threshold conditions;
(2) the person has not carried on any *regulated activity* for a period of at least 12 months; or
(3) it is desirable to vary or cancel the person's *Part IV permission* in order to protect the interests of consumers or potential consumers.

8.1A The powers to vary and cancel a person's Part IV permission are exercisable in the same circumstances. However, the statutory procedure for the exercise of each power is different and this may determine how the FSA acts in a given case. Certain types of behaviour which may cause the FSA to cancel permission in one case, may lead it to vary, or vary and cancel, permission in another, depending on the circumstances. The non-exhaustive examples provided below are therefore illustrative but not conclusive of which action the FSA will take in a given case.

Varying a firm's Part IV permission on the FSA's own initiative

8.1B When it considers how it should deal with a concern about a *firm*, the FSA will have regard to its *regulatory objectives* and the range of regulatory tools that are available to it. It will also have regard to:

(1) the responsibilities of a *firm's* management to deal with concerns about the *firm* or about the way its business is being or has been run; and
(2) the principle that a restriction imposed on a *firm* should be proportionate to the objectives the FSA is seeking to achieve.

8.2 The FSA will proceed on the basis that a *firm* (together with its directors and senior management) is primarily responsible for ensuring the *firm* conducts its business in compliance with the *Act*, the *Principles* and other *rules*.

8.3 In the course of its supervision and monitoring of a *firm*, or as part of an enforcement action, the FSA may make it clear that it expects the *firm* to take certain steps to meet regulatory requirements. In the vast majority of cases the FSA will seek to agree with a *firm* those steps the *firm* must take to address the FSA's concerns. However, where the FSA considers it appropriate to do so, it will exercise its formal powers under section 45 of the Act to vary a *firm's* permission to ensure such requirements are met. This may include where:

(1) the FSA has serious concerns about a *firm*, or about the way its business is being or has been conducted;
(2) the FSA is concerned that the consequences of a *firm* not taking the desired steps may be serious;
(3) the imposition of a formal statutory requirement reflects the importance the FSA attaches to the need for the firm to address its concerns;
(4) the imposition of a formal statutory requirement may assist the *firm* to take steps which would otherwise be difficult because of legal obligations owed to third parties.

8.3A SUP 7 provides more information about the situations in which the FSA may decide to take formal action in the context of its supervision activities.

8.4 [deleted]

8.5 Examples of circumstances in which the FSA will consider varying a *firm's Part IV permission* because it has serious concerns about a *firm*, or about the way its business is being or has been conducted include where:

(1) in relation to the grounds for exercising the power under section 45(1)(a) of the *Act*, the firm appears to be failing, or appears likely to fail, to satisfy the *threshold conditions* relating to one or more, or all, of its *regulated activities*, because for instance:
 (a) the *firm's* material and financial resources appear inadequate for the scale or type of *regulated activity* it is carrying on, for example, where it has failed to maintain professional indemnity insurance or where it is unable to meet its liabilities as they have fallen due; or
 (b) the *firm* appears not to be a fit and proper *person* to carry on a *regulated activity* because:
  (i) it has not conducted its business in compliance with high standards which may include putting itself at risk of being used for the purposes of *financial crime* or being otherwise involved in such crime;
  (ii) it has not been managed competently and prudently and has not exercised due skill, care, and diligence in carrying on one or more, or all, of its *regulated activities*;
  (iii) it has breached requirements imposed on it by or under the *Act* (including the *Principles* and the *rules*), for example in respect of its disclosure or notification requirements, and the breaches are material in number or in individual seriousness;

(2) in relation to the grounds for exercising the power under section 45(1)(c), it appears that the interests of *consumers* are at risk because the *firm* appears to have breached any of *Principles* 6 to 10 of the FSA's *Principles* (see PRIN 2.1.1R) to such an extent that it is desirable that *limitations*, restrictions, or prohibitions are placed on the *firm's regulated activity*.

Use of the own-initiative power in urgent cases

8.6 The FSA may impose a variation of permission so that it takes effect immediately or on a specified date if it reasonably considers it necessary for the variation to take effect immediately (or on the date specified), having regard to the ground on which it is exercising its *own-initiative power*.

8.7 The FSA will consider exercising its *own-initiative power* as a matter of urgency where:

(1) the information available to it indicates serious concerns about the *firm* or its business that need to be addressed immediately; and

(2) circumstances indicate that it is appropriate to use statutory powers immediately to require and/or prohibit certain actions by the *firm* in order to ensure the *firm* addresses these concerns.

8.8 It is not possible to provide an exhaustive list of the situations that will give rise to such serious concerns, but they are likely to include one or more of the following characteristics:

(1) information indicating significant loss, risk of loss or other adverse effects for *consumers*, where action is necessary to protect their interests;

(2) information indicating that a *firm's* conduct has put it at risk of being used for the purposes of *financial crime*, or of being otherwise involved in crime;

(3) evidence that the *firm* has submitted to the FSA inaccurate or misleading information so that the FSA becomes seriously concerned about the *firm's* ability to meet its regulatory obligations;

(4) circumstances suggesting a serious problem within a *firm* or with a *firm's controllers* that calls into question the *firm's* ability to continue to meet the *threshold conditions*.

8.9 The FSA will consider the full circumstances of each case when it decides whether an urgent variation of *Part IV permission* is appropriate. The following is a non-exhaustive list of factors the FSA may consider.

(1) The extent of any loss, or risk of loss, or other adverse effect on *consumers*. The more serious the loss or potential loss or other adverse effect, the more likely it is that the FSA's urgent exercise of *own-initiative powers* will be appropriate, to protect the *consumers'* interests.

(2) The extent to which *customer* assets appear to be at risk. Urgent exercise of the FSA's *own-initiative power* may be appropriate where the information available to the FSA suggests that *customer* assets held by, or to the order of, the *firm* may be at risk.

(3) The nature and extent of any false or inaccurate information provided by the *firm*. Whether false or inaccurate information warrants the FSA's urgent exercise of its *own-initiative powers* will depend on matters such as:
 (a) the impact of the information on the FSA's view of the *firm's* compliance with the regulatory requirements to which it is subject, the *firm's* suitability to conduct *regulated activities*, or the likelihood that the *firm's* business may be being used in connection with *financial crime*;
 (b) whether the information appears to have been provided in an attempt knowingly to mislead the FSA, rather than through inadvertence;
 (c) whether the matters to which false or inaccurate information relates indicate there is a risk to *customer* assets or to the other interests of the *firm's* actual or potential *customers*.

(4) The seriousness of any suspected breach of the requirements of the legislation or the *rules* and the steps that need to be taken to correct that breach.
(5) The financial resources of the *firm*. Serious concerns may arise where it appears the *firm* may be required to pay significant amounts of compensation to *consumers*. In those cases, the extent to which the *firm* has the financial resources to do so will affect the FSA's decision about whether exercise of the FSA's *own-initiative power* is appropriate to preserve the *firm's* assets, in the interests of the *consumers*. The FSA will take account of any insurance cover held by the *firm*. It will also consider the likelihood of the *firm's* assets being dissipated without the FSA's intervention, and whether the exercise of the FSA's power to petition for the winding up of the *firm* is more appropriate than the use of its *own-initiative power* (see chapter 13 of this guide).
(6) The risk that the *firm's* business may be used or has been used to facilitate *financial crime*, including *money laundering*. The information available to the FSA, including information supplied by other law enforcement agencies, may suggest the *firm* is being used for, or is itself involved in, *financial crime*. Where this appears to be the case, and the *firm* appears to be failing to meet the *threshold conditions* or has put its *customers'* interests at risk, the FSA's urgent use of its *own-initiative powers* may well be appropriate.
(7) The risk that the *firm's* conduct or business presents to the *financial system* and to confidence in the *financial system*.
(8) The *firm's* conduct. The FSA will take into account:
 (a) whether the *firm* identified the issue (and if so whether this was by chance or as a result of the *firm's* normal *controls* and monitoring);
 (b) whether the *firm* brought the issue promptly to the FSA's attention;
 (c) the *firm's* past history, management ethos and compliance culture;
 (d) steps that the *firm* has taken or is taking to address the issue.
(9) The impact that use of the FSA's *own-initiative powers* will have on the *firm's* business and on its *customers*. The FSA will take into account the (sometimes significant) impact that a variation of *permission* may have on a *firm's* business and on its *customers'* interests, including the effect of variation on the *firm's* reputation and on market confidence. The FSA will need to be satisfied that the impact of any use of the *own-initiative power* is likely to be proportionate to the concerns being addressed, in the context of the overall aim of achieving its *regulatory objectives*.

Limitations and requirements that the FSA may impose when exercising its section 45 power

8.10 When varying *Part IV permission* at its own-initiative under its section 45 power (or section 47 power), the FSA may include in the *Part IV permission* as varied any *limitation* or restriction which it could have imposed if a fresh *permission* were being given in response to an application under section 40 of the *Act*.

8.11 Examples of the *limitations* that the FSA may impose when exercising its *own-initiative power* in support of its enforcement function include *limitations* on: the number, or category, of *customers* that a *firm* can deal with; the number of specified investments that a *firm* can deal in; and the activities of the *firm* so that they fall within specific regulatory regimes (for example, so that *oil market participants*, *locals*, *corporate finance advisory firms* and service providers are permitted only to carry on those types of activities).

8.12 Examples of *requirements* that the FSA may consider including in a *firm's Part IV permission* when exercising its *own-initiative power* in support of its enforcement function are: a *requirement* not to take on new business; a *requirement* not to hold or control *client money*; a *requirement* not to trade in certain categories of *specified investment*; a *requirement* that prohibits the disposal of, or other dealing with, any of the *firm's* assets (whether in the United Kingdom or elsewhere) or restricts those disposals or dealings; and a *requirement* that all or any of the *firm's* assets, or all or any assets belonging to investors but held by the *firm* to its order, must be transferred to a *trustee* approved by the FSA.

Cancelling a firm's Part IV permission on its own initiative

8.13 The FSA will consider cancelling a *firm's Part IV permission* using its *own-initiative powers* contained in sections 45 and 47 respectively of the *Act* in two main circumstances:
(1) where the FSA has very serious concerns about a *firm*, or the way its business is or has been conducted;
(2) where the *firm's regulated activities* have come to an end and it has not applied for *cancellation* of its *Part IV permission*.

8.14 The grounds on which the FSA may exercise its power to cancel an authorised person's permission under section 45 of the *Act* are the same as the grounds for variation. They are set out in section 45(1)and described in EG 8.1. Examples of the types of circumstances in which the FSA may cancel a *firm's Part IV permission* include:

(1) non-compliance with a *Financial Ombudsman Service* award against the *firm*;
(2) material non-disclosure in an application for authorisation or approval or material non-notification after authorisation or approval has been granted. The information which is the subject of the non-disclosure or non-notification may also be grounds for cancellation;
(3) failure to have or maintain professional indemnity insurance, or other adequate financial resources, or a failure to comply with regulatory capital requirements;
(4) non-submission of, or provision of false information in, regulatory returns, or repeated failure to submit such returns in a timely fashion;
(5) non-payment of FSA fees or repeated failure to pay FSA fees except under threat of enforcement action; and
(6) failure to provide the FSA with valid contact details or failure to maintain the details provided, such that the FSA is unable to communicate with the *firm*;
(7) repeated failures to comply with rules or requirements;
(8) a failure to co-operate with the FSA which is of sufficient seriousness that the FSA ceases to be satisfied that the *firm* is fit and proper, for example failing without reasonable excuse to:
    (a) comply with the material terms of a formal agreement made with the FSA to conclude or avoid disciplinary or other enforcement action; or
    (b) provide material information or take remedial action reasonably required by the FSA.

Section 45(2A) of the *Act* sets out further grounds on which the FSA may cancel the permission of *authorised persons* which are *investment firms*.

8.15 Depending on the circumstances, the FSA may need to consider whether it should first use its *own-initiative powers* to vary a *firm's Part IV permission* before going on to cancel it. Amongst other circumstances, the FSA may use this power where it considers it needs to take immediate action against a *firm* because of the urgency and seriousness of the situation.

8.16 Where the situation appears so urgent and serious that the *firm* should immediately cease to carry on all *regulated activities*, the FSA may first vary the *firm's Part IV permission* so that there is no longer any *regulated activity* for which the *firm* has a *Part IV permission*. If it does this, the FSA will then have a duty to cancel the *firm's Part IV permission* – once it is satisfied that it is no longer necessary to keep the *Part IV permission* in force.

8.17 However, where the FSA has cancelled a *firm's Part IV permission*, it is required by section 33 of the *Act* to go on to give a direction withdrawing the *firm's authorisation*. Accordingly, the FSA may decide to keep a *firm's Part IV permission* in force to maintain the *firm's* status as an *authorised person* and enable it (the FSA) to monitor the *firm's* activities. An example is where the FSA needs to supervise an orderly winding down of the *firm's* regulated business (see SUP 6.4.22 (When will the FSA grant an application for cancellation of *permission*)). Alternatively, the FSA may decide to keep a *firm's Part IV permission* in force to maintain the *firm's* status as an *authorised person* to use administrative enforcement powers against the *firm*. This may be, for example, where the FSA proposes to impose a financial penalty on the *firm* under section 206 of the *Act*.

Exercising the power under section 47 to vary or cancel a firm's part IV permission in support of an overseas regulator: the FSA's policy

8.18 The FSA has a power under section 47 to vary, or alternatively cancel, a *firm's Part IV permission*, in support of an *overseas regulator*. Section 47(3), (4) and (5) set out matters the FSA may, or must, take into account when it considers whether to exercise these powers. The circumstances in which the FSA may consider varying *a firm's Part IV permission* in support of an *overseas regulator* depend on whether the FSA is required to consider exercising the power in order to comply with a Community obligation. This reflects the fact that under section 47, if a relevant *overseas regulator* acting under prescribed provisions has made a request to the FSA for the exercise of its *own-initiative power* to vary or cancel a *Part IV permission*, the FSA must consider whether it must exercise the power in order to comply with a Community obligation.

8.19 Relevant Community obligations which the FSA may need to consider include those under the Banking Consolidation Directive, the Insurance Directives, the Investment Services Directive/Markets in Financial Instruments Directive; and the Insurance Mediation Directive. Each of these Directives imposes general obligations on the relevant *EEA competent authority* to cooperate and collaborate closely in discharging their functions under the Directives.

8.20 The FSA views this cooperation and collaboration as essential to effective regulation of the international market in financial services. It will therefore exercise its *own-initiative power* wherever:

(1) an *EEA Competent authority* requests it to do so; and
(2) it is satisfied that the use of the power is appropriate (having regard to the considerations set out at paragraphs 8.1B to 8.5) to enforce effectively the regulatory requirements imposed under the *Single Market Directives* or other Community obligations.

8.21 The FSA will actively consider any other requests for assistance from relevant *overseas regulators* (that is requests in relation to which it is not obliged to act under a Community obligation). Section 47(4), which sets out matters the FSA may take into account when it decides whether to vary or cancel a *firm's Part IV permission* in support of the *overseas regulator*, applies in these circumstances.

8.22 Where section 47(4) applies and the FSA is considering whether to vary a *firm's Part IV permission*, it may take account of all the factors described in paragraphs 8.18 to 8.25 but may give particular weight to:

(1) the matters set out in paragraphs (c) and (d) of section 47(4) (seriousness, importance to persons in the United Kingdom, and the public interest); and

(2) any specific request made to it by the *overseas regulator* to vary, rather than cancel, the *firm's Part IV permission*.

8.23 The FSA will give careful consideration to whether the relevant authority's concerns would provide grounds for the FSA to exercise its *own-initiative power* to vary or cancel if they related to a UK *firm*. It is not necessary for the FSA to be satisfied that the overseas provisions being enforced mirror precisely those which apply to UK *firms*. However, the FSA will not assist in the enforcement of regulatory requirements or other provisions that appear to extend significantly beyond the purposes of *UK regulatory provisions*.

8.24 Similarly, the FSA will not need to be satisfied that precisely the same assistance would be provided to the United Kingdom in precisely the same situation. However, it will wish to be confident that the relevant authorities in the jurisdiction concerned would have powers available to them to provide broadly similar assistance in aid of UK authorities, and would be willing properly to consider exercising those powers. The FSA may decide, under section 47(5), not to exercise its *own-initiative power* to vary or cancel in response to a request unless the regulator concerned undertakes to make whatever contribution towards the cost of its exercise the FSA considers appropriate.

8.25 Paragraphs 8.10 and 8.12 set out some examples of *limitations* and *requirements* the FSA may impose when exercising its section 47 power to vary *a firm's Part IV permission*.

The FSA's policy on exercising its power of intervention against incoming firms under section 196 of the Act

8.26 The FSA adopts a similar approach to the exercise of its *power of intervention* under section 196 as it does to its *own-initiative powers* to vary *Part IV permission*, but with suitable modification for the differences in the statutory grounds for exercising the powers. Consequently the factors and considerations set out in paragraphs 8.1B to 8.12 and 8.18 to 8.25 may also be relevant when the FSA is considering regulatory concerns about *incoming firms*.

8.27 When it is considering action against an *incoming firm*, the FSA will co-operate with the *firm's Home State regulator* as appropriate, including notifying and informing the *firm's Home State regulator* as required by the relevant section of the *Act*.

CHAPTER 9
PROHIBITION ORDERS AND WITHDRAWAL OF APPROVAL

Introduction

[2219I]

9.1 The FSA's power under section 56 of the *Act* to prohibit individuals who are not fit and proper from carrying out functions in relation to *regulated activities* helps the FSA to work towards achieving its *regulatory objectives*. The FSA may exercise this power to make a *prohibition order* where it considers that, to achieve any of those objectives, it is appropriate either to prevent an individual from performing any function in relation to *regulated activities*, or to restrict the functions which he may perform.

9.2 The FSA's effective use of the power under section 63 of the *Act* to withdraw approval from an *approved person* will also help ensure high standards of regulatory conduct by preventing an *approved person* from continuing to perform the *controlled function* to which the approval relates if he is not a fit and proper person to perform that function. Where it considers this is appropriate, the FSA may prohibit an *approved person*, in addition to withdrawing their approval.

The FSA's general policy in this area

9.3 In deciding whether to make a *prohibition order* and/or, in the case of an *approved person*, to withdraw its approval, the FSA will consider all the relevant circumstances including whether other enforcement action should be taken or has been taken already against that individual by the FSA. As is noted below, in some cases the FSA may take other enforcement action against the individual in addition to seeking a *prohibition order* and/or withdrawing its approval. The FSA will also consider whether enforcement action has been taken against the individual by other enforcement agencies or *designated professional bodies*.

9.4 The FSA has the power to make a range of *prohibition orders* depending on the circumstances of each case and the range of *regulated activities* to which the individual's lack of fitness and propriety is relevant. Depending on the circumstances of each case, the FSA may seek to prohibit individuals from performing any class of function in relation to any class of *regulated activity*, or it may limit the *prohibition order* to specific functions in relation to specific *regulated activities*. The *FSA* may also make an order prohibiting an individual from being employed by a particular *firm*, type of *firm* or any *firm*.

9.5 The scope of a *prohibition order* will depend on the range of functions which the individual concerned performs in relation to *regulated activities*, the reasons why he is not fit and proper and the severity of risk which he poses to *consumers* or the market generally.

9.6 Where the FSA issues a *prohibition order*, it may indicate in the *final notice* that it would be minded to revoke the order on the application of the individual in the future, in the absence of new evidence that the individual is not fit and proper. If the FSA gives such an indication, it will specify the number of years after which it would be minded to revoke or vary the prohibition on an application. However, the FSA will only adopt this approach in cases where it considers it appropriate in all the circumstances. In deciding whether to adopt this approach, the factors the FSA may take into account include, but are not limited to, where appropriate, the factors at paragraphs 9.9 and at 9.17. The FSA would not be obliged to revoke an order after the specified period even where it gave such an indication. Further, if an individual's *prohibition order* is revoked, he would still have to satisfy the FSA as to his fitness for a particular role in relation to any future application for approval to perform a *controlled function*.

9.7 Paragraphs 9.8 to 9.14 set out additional guidance on the FSA's approach to making *prohibition orders* against *approved persons* and/or withdrawing such persons' approvals. Paragraphs 9.17 to 9.18 set out additional guidance on the FSA's approach to making *prohibition orders* against other individuals.

Prohibition orders and withdrawal of approval – approved persons

9.8 When the FSA has concerns about the fitness and propriety of an *approved person*, it may consider whether it should prohibit that person from performing functions in relation to *regulated activities*, withdraw its approval, or both. In deciding whether to withdraw its approval and/or make a *prohibition order*, the FSA will consider in each case whether its *regulatory objectives* can be achieved adequately by imposing disciplinary sanctions, for example, *public censures* or financial penalties, or by issuing a private warning.

9.9 When it decides whether to make a *prohibition order* against an *approved person* and/or withdraw its approval, the FSA will consider all the relevant circumstances of the case. These may include, but are not limited to those set out below.

(1) The matters set out in section 61(2) of the *Act*.

(2) Whether the individual is fit and proper to perform functions in relation to *regulated activities*. The criteria for assessing the fitness and propriety of *approved persons* are set out in FIT 2.1 (Honesty, integrity and reputation); FIT 2.2 (Competence and capability) and FIT 2.3 (Financial soundness).

(3) Whether, and to what extent, the *approved person* has:
   (a) failed to comply with the *Statements of Principle* issued by the FSA with respect to the conduct of *approved persons*; or
   (b) been knowingly concerned in a contravention by the relevant *firm* of a requirement imposed on the *firm* by or under the *Act* (including the *Principles* and other *rules*) or failed to comply with any directly applicable Community regulation made under *MiFID*.

(4) Whether the *approved person* has engaged in *market abuse*.

(5) The relevance and materiality of any matters indicating unfitness.

(6) The length of time since the occurrence of any matters indicating unfitness.

(7) The particular *controlled function* the *approved person* is (or was) performing, the nature and activities of the *firm* concerned and the markets in which he operates.

(8) The severity of the risk which the individual poses to *consumers* and to confidence in the *financial system*.

(9) The previous disciplinary record and general compliance history of the individual including whether the FSA, any *previous regulator*, *designated professional body* or other domestic or international regulator has previously imposed a disciplinary sanction on the individual.

9.10 The FSA may have regard to the cumulative effect of a number of factors which, when considered in isolation, may not be sufficient to show that the individual is fit and proper to continue to perform a *controlled function* or other function in relation to *regulated activities*. It may also take account of the particular *controlled function* which an *approved person* is performing for a *firm*, the nature and activities of the *firm* concerned and the markets within which it operates.

Part II FSA Handbook Materials

9.11 Due to the diverse nature of the activities and functions which the FSA regulates, it is not possible to produce a definitive list of matters which the FSA might take into account when considering whether an individual is not a fit and proper person to perform a particular, or any, function in relation to a particular, or any, *firm*.

9.12 The following are examples of types of behaviour which have previously resulted in the FSA deciding to issue a *prohibition order* or withdraw the approval of an *approved person*:

(1) Providing false or misleading information to the FSA; including information relating to identity, ability to work in the United Kingdom, and business arrangements;

(2) Failure to disclose material considerations on application forms, such as details of County Court Judgments, criminal convictions and dismissal from employment for regulatory or criminal breaches. The nature of the information not disclosed can also be relevant;

(3) Severe acts of dishonesty, eg which may have resulted in financial crime;

(4) Serious lack of competence; and

(5) Serious breaches of the *Statements of Principle* for *approved persons*, such as failing to make terms of business regarding fees clear or actively misleading clients about fees; acting without regard to instructions; providing misleading information to clients, consumers or third parties; giving clients poor or inaccurate advice; using intimidating or threatening behaviour towards clients and former clients; failing to remedy breaches of the general prohibition or to ensure that a firm acted within the scope of its permissions.

9.13 Certain matters that do not fit squarely, or at all, within the matters referred to above may also fall to be considered. In these circumstances the FSA will consider whether the conduct or matter in question is relevant to the individual's fitness and propriety.

9.14 Where it considers it is appropriate to withdraw an individual's approval to perform a *controlled function* within a particular *firm*, it will also consider, at the very least, whether it should prohibit the individual from performing that function more generally. Depending on the circumstances, it may consider that the individual should also be prohibited from performing other functions.

Prohibition orders against exempt persons and members of professional firms

9.15 In cases where it is considering whether to exercise its power to make a *prohibition order* against an individual performing functions in relation to *exempt regulated activities* by virtue of an exemption from the *general prohibition* under Part XX of the *Act*, the FSA will consider whether the particular unfitness might be more appropriately dealt with by making an order disapplying the exemption using its power under section 329 of the *Act*. In most cases where the FSA is concerned about the fitness and propriety of a specific individual in relation to *exempt regulated activities* by virtue of an exemption under Part XX of the *Act*, it will be more appropriate to make an order prohibiting the individual from performing functions in relation to *exempt regulated activities* than to make a disapplication order.

9.16 When considering whether to exercise its power to make a *prohibition order* against an *exempt person*, the FSA will consider all relevant circumstances including, where appropriate, the factors set out in paragraph 9.9.

Prohibition orders against other individuals

9.17 Where the FSA is considering making a *prohibition order* against an individual other than an individual referred to in paragraphs 9.8 to 9.14, the FSA will consider the severity of the risk posed by the individual, and may prohibit the individual where it considers this is appropriate to achieve one or more of its *regulatory objectives*.

9.18 When considering whether to exercise its power to make a *prohibition order* against such an individual, the FSA will consider all the relevant circumstances of the case. These may include, but are not limited to, where appropriate, the factors set out in paragraph 9.9.

Applications for variation or revocation of prohibition orders

9.19 When considering whether to grant or refuse an application to revoke or vary a *prohibition order*, the FSA will consider all the relevant circumstances of a case. These may include, but are not limited to:

(1) the seriousness of the misconduct or other unfitness that resulted in the order;

(2) the amount of time since the original order was made;

(3) any steps taken subsequently by the individual to remedy the misconduct or other unfitness;

(4) any evidence which, had it been known to the FSA at the time, would have been relevant to the FSA's decision to make the *prohibition order*;

(5) all available information relating to the individual's honesty, integrity or competence since the order was made, including any repetition of the misconduct which resulted in the prohibition order being made;

(6) where the FSA's finding of unfitness arose from incompetence rather than from dishonesty or lack of integrity, evidence that this unfitness has been or will be remedied; for example, this may be achieved by the satisfactory completion of relevant training and obtaining relevant qualifications, or by supervision of the individual by his employer;
(7) the financial soundness of the individual concerned; and
(8) whether the individual will continue to pose the level of risk to *consumers* or confidence in the *financial system* which resulted in the original prohibition if it is lifted.

9.20 When considering whether to grant or refuse an application to revoke or vary a *prohibition order*, the FSA will take into account any indication given by the FSA in the *final notice* that it is minded to revoke or vary the *prohibition order* on application after a certain number of years (see paragraph 9.6).

9.21 If the individual applying for a revocation or variation of a *prohibition order* proposes to take up an offer of employment to perform a *controlled function*, the *approved persons* regime will also apply to him. In these cases, the *firm* concerned will be required to apply to the FSA for approval of that individual's employment in that capacity. The FSA will assess the individual's fitness and propriety to perform *controlled functions* on the basis of the criteria set out in FIT 2.1 (Honesty, integrity and reputation); FIT 2.2 (Competence and capability) and FIT 2.3 (Financial soundness).

9.22 The FSA will not generally grant an application to vary or revoke a *prohibition order* unless it is satisfied that: the proposed variation will not result in a reoccurrence of the risk to *consumers* or confidence in the *financial system* that resulted in the order being made; and the individual is fit to perform functions in relation to *regulated activities* generally, or to those specific *regulated activities* in relation to which the individual has been prohibited.

Other powers that may be relevant when the FSA is considering whether to exercise its power to make a prohibition order

9.23 In appropriate cases, the FSA may take other action against an individual in addition to making a *prohibition order* and/or withdrawing its approval, including the use of its powers to: impose a financial penalty or issue a *public censure*; apply for an *injunction* to prevent dissipation of assets; stop any continuing misconduct; order restitution; apply for an insolvency order or an order against debt avoidance; and/or prosecute certain criminal offences.

The effect of the FSA's decision to make a prohibition order

9.24 The FSA may consider taking disciplinary action against a *firm* that has not taken reasonable care, as required by section 56(6) of the *Act*, to ensure that none of that *firm's* functions in relation to carrying on of a *regulated activity* is performed by a *person* who is prohibited from performing the function by a *prohibition order*. The FSA considers that a search by a *firm* of the *FSA Register* is an essential part of the statutory duty to take reasonable care to ensure that *firms* do not employ or otherwise permit prohibited individuals to perform functions in relation to *regulated activities*. In addition, the FSA expects firms to check the *FSA Register* when making applications for approval under section 59 of the *Act*. More generally, if a *firm's* search of the *FSA Register* reveals no record of a *prohibition order*, the FSA will consider taking action for breach of section 56(6) only where the *firm* had access to other information indicating that a *prohibition order* had been made.

The effect of the FSA's decision to withdraw approval

9.25 When the FSA's decision to withdraw an approval has become effective, the position of the *firm* which applied for that approval depends on whether it directly employs the *person* concerned, or whether the *person* is employed by one of its contractors.

9.26 Section 59(1) is relevant where the *firm* directly employs the *person* concerned. Under the provision, a firm ('A') must take reasonable care to ensure that no *person* performs a *controlled function* under an *arrangement* entered into by A in relation to the carrying on by it of a *regulated activity*, unless the FSA approves the performance by that *person* of the *controlled function* to which the approval relates. Therefore, if the *firm* continues to employ the *person* concerned to carry out a *controlled function*, it will be in breach of section 59(1) and the FSA may take enforcement action against it.

9.27 Section 59(2) is relevant where the *person* is employed by a contractor of the *firm*. It requires a *firm* ('A') to take reasonable care to ensure that no *person* performs a *controlled function* under an arrangement entered into by a contractor of A in relation to the carrying on by A of a *regulated activity*, unless the FSA approves the performance by that person of the *controlled function* to which the approval relates. Therefore, if a contractor of the *firm* employs the person concerned, and the contractor continues to employ the *person* to carry out a *controlled function*, the *firm* itself will be in breach of section 59(2) unless it has taken reasonable care to ensure that this does not happen. The FSA may take enforcement action against a *firm* that breaches this requirement.

9.28 *Firms* should be aware of the potential effect that these provisions may have on their contractual relationships with *approved persons* employed by them and with contractors engaged by them, and their obligations under those contracts.

CHAPTER 10
INJUNCTIONS

[2219J]

10.1A Decisions about whether to apply to the civil courts for injunctions under the Act will be made by the *RDC* Chairman or, in an urgent case and if the Chairman is not available, by an *RDC* Deputy Chairman. In an exceptionally urgent case the matter will be decided by the director of Enforcement or, in his or her absence, another member of the FSA's executive of at least director of division level.

10.1B An exceptionally urgent case in these circumstances is one where the FSA staff believe that a decision to begin proceedings

(1) should be taken before it is possible to follow the procedure described in paragraph 10.1A; and

(2) it is necessary to protect the interests of consumers or potential consumers.

10.1 The orders the court may make following an application by the FSA under the powers referred to in this chapter are generally known in England and Wales as *injunctions*, and in Scotland as *interdicts*. In the chapter, the word *'injunction'* and the word *'order'* also mean *'interdict'*. The FSA's effective use of these powers will help it work towards its *regulatory objectives*, in particular, those of protecting *consumers*, maintaining confidence in the *financial system* and reducing *financial crime*.

Section 380 (injunctions for breaches of relevant requirements[9]) and section 381 (injunctions in cases of market abuse): the FSA's policy

10.2 The court may make three types of order under these provisions: to restrain a course of conduct, to take steps to remedy a course of conduct and to secure assets. As is explained below, the court may also make an order freezing assets under its inherent jurisdiction. In certain cases, the FSA may seek only one type of order, although in others it may seek several.

10.3 The broad test the FSA will apply when it decides whether to seek an *injunction* is whether the application would be the most effective way to deal with the FSA's concerns. In deciding whether an application for an *injunction* is appropriate in a given case, the FSA will consider all relevant circumstances and may take into account a wide range of factors. The following list of factors is not exhaustive; not all the factors will be relevant in a particular case and there may be other factors that are relevant.

(1) The nature and seriousness of a contravention or expected contravention of a relevant requirement. The extent of loss, risk of loss, or other adverse effect on *consumers*, including the extent to which *client* assets may be at risk, may be relevant. The seriousness of a contravention or prospective contravention will include considerations of:
  (a) whether the losses suffered are substantial;
  (b) whether the numbers of *consumers* who have suffered loss are significant;
  (c) whether the assets at risk are substantial; and
  (d) whether the number of *consumers* at risk is significant.

(2) In cases of *market abuse*, the nature and seriousness of the misconduct or expected misconduct in question. The following may be relevant:
  (a) the impact or potential impact on the *financial system* of the conduct in question. This would include the extent to which it has resulted in distortion or disruption of the markets, or would be likely to do so if it was allowed to take place or to continue;
  (b) the extent and nature of any losses or other costs imposed, or likely to be imposed, on other users of the *financial system*, as a result of the misconduct.

(3) Whether the conduct in question has stopped or is likely to stop and whether steps have been taken or will be taken by the *person* concerned to ensure that the interests of *consumers* are adequately protected. For example, an application for an *injunction* may be appropriate where the FSA has grounds for believing that a contravention of a relevant requirement, *market abuse* or both may continue or be repeated. It is likely to have grounds to believe this where, for example, the *Takeover Panel* has requested that a person stop a particular course of conduct and that *person* has not done so.

(4) Whether there are steps a *person* could take to remedy a contravention of a relevant requirement or *market abuse*. The steps the FSA may require a *person* to take will vary according to the circumstances but may include the withdrawal of a misleading *financial promotion* or publishing a correction, writing to clients or investors to notify them of FSA action, providing financial redress and repatriating funds from an overseas jurisdiction. An application by the FSA to the court under section 380(2) or 381(2) for an order requiring a *person* to take such steps may not be appropriate if, for example, that *person* has already taken or proposes to take appropriate remedial steps at his own initiative or under a ruling imposed by another regulatory authority (such as the *Takeover Panel* or a *recognised investment exchange*). If another authority has identified the relevant steps and the *person*

concerned has failed to take them, the FSA will take this into account and (subject to all other relevant factors and circumstances) may consider it is appropriate to apply for an *injunction*. In those cases the FSA may consult with the relevant regulatory authority before applying for an *injunction*.

(5) Whether there is a danger of assets being dissipated. The main purpose of an application under section 380(3), sections 381(3) and (4) or pursuant to the court's inherent jurisdiction, is likely to be to safeguard funds containing *client* assets (eg *client* accounts) and/or funds and other assets from which restitution may be made. The FSA may seek an *injunction* to secure assets while a suspected contravention is being investigated or where it has information suggesting that a contravention is about to take place.

(6) The costs the FSA would incur in applying for and enforcing an *injunction* and the benefits that would result. There may be other cases which require the FSA's attention and take a higher priority, due to the nature and seriousness of the breaches concerned. There may, therefore, be occasions on which the FSA considers that time and resources should not be diverted from other cases in order to make an application for an *injunction*. These factors reflect the FSA's duty under the *Act* to have regard to the need to use its resources in the most efficient and economic way.

(7) The disciplinary record and general compliance history of the *person* who is the subject of the possible application. This includes whether the FSA (or a *previous regulator*) has taken any previous disciplinary, remedial or protective action against the *person*. It may also be relevant, for example, whether the *person* has previously given any undertakings to the FSA (or any *previous regulator*) not to do a particular act or engage in particular behaviour and is in breach of those undertakings.

(8) Whether the conduct in question can be adequately addressed by other disciplinary powers, for example *public censure* or financial penalties.

(9) The extent to which another regulatory authority can adequately address the matter. Certain circumstances may give rise not only to possible enforcement action by the FSA, but also to action by other regulatory authorities. The FSA will examine the circumstances of each case, and consider whether it is appropriate for the FSA to take action to address the relevant concern. In most cases the FSA will consult with other relevant regulatory authorities before making an application for an order.

(10) Whether there is information to suggest that the *person* who is the subject of the possible application is involved in *financial crime*.

(11) In any case where the FSA is of the opinion that any potential exercise of its powers under section 381 may affect the timetable or the outcome of a *takeover bid*, the FSA will consult the *Takeover Panel* before taking any steps to exercise these powers and will give due weight to its views.

Asset-freezing injunctions

10.4 Where the FSA applies to the court under section 380(3) or sections 381(3) and (4) of the *Act*, the FSA may ask the court to exercise its inherent jurisdiction to make orders on an interim basis, restraining a *person* from disposing of, or otherwise dealing with, assets. To succeed in an application for such interim relief, the FSA will have to show a good arguable case for the granting of the *injunction*. The FSA will not have to show that a contravention has already occurred or may have already occurred.

10.5 The FSA may request the court to exercise its inherent jurisdiction in cases, for example, where it has evidence showing that there is a reasonable likelihood that a *person* will contravene a requirement of the *Act* and that the contravention will result in the dissipation of assets belonging to investors.

Other relevant powers

10.6 The FSA has a range of powers it can use to take remedial, protective and disciplinary action against a *person* who has contravened a relevant requirement or engaged in *market abuse*, as well as its powers to seek *injunctions* under sections 380 and 381 of the *Act* and under the courts' inherent jurisdiction. Where appropriate, the FSA may exercise these other powers before, at the same time as, or after it applies for an *injunction* against a *person*.

10.7 When, in relation to *firms*, the FSA applies the broad test outlined in paragraph 10.3, it will consider the relative effectiveness of the other powers available to it, compared with injunctive relief. For example, where the FSA has concerns about whether a *firm* will comply with restrictions that the FSA could impose by exercising its *own-initiative powers*, it may decide it would be more appropriate to seek an *injunction*. This is because breaching any requirement imposed by the court could be punishable for contempt. Alternatively, where, for example, the FSA has already imposed requirements on a *firm* by exercising its *own-initiative powers* and these requirements have not been met, the FSA may seek an *injunction* to enforce those requirements.

10.8 The FSA's *own-initiative powers* do not apply to *unauthorised persons*. This means that an application for an *injunction* is the only power by which the FSA may seek directly to prevent *unauthorised persons* from actual or threatened breaches or *market abuse*. The FSA will decide whether an application against an *unauthorised person* is appropriate, in accordance with the approach discussed in paragraph 10.3. The FSA may also seek an *injunction* to secure assets where it intends to use its insolvency powers against an *unauthorised person*.

10.9 In certain cases, conduct that may be the subject of an *injunction* application will also be an offence which the FSA has power to prosecute under the *Act*. In those cases, the FSA will consider whether it is appropriate to prosecute the offence in question, as well as applying for *injunctions* under section 380, section 381, or both.

10.10 Where the FSA exercises its powers under section 380, section 381 and/or invokes the court's inherent jurisdiction to obtain an order restraining the disposal of assets, it may also apply to the court for a restitution order for the distribution of those assets.

Section 198: the FSA's policy

10.11 Under section 198 of the *Act* the FSA has power to apply to court on behalf of the *Home State regulator* of certain *incoming EEA firms* for an *injunction* restraining the *incoming EEA firm* from disposing of, or otherwise dealing with, any of its assets. The FSA will consider exercising this power only where a request from a *Home State regulator* satisfies the requirements of section 198(1).

Applications for injunctions under regulation 12 of the Unfair Terms Regulations: the FSA's policy

10.12 If the FSA decides to address issues using its powers under the *Unfair Terms Regulations*, and the contract is within its scope as described in the FSA's Regulatory Guide on these powers,[10] it will, unless the case is urgent, generally first write to the *person* expressing its concerns about the potential unfairness within the meaning of the *Unfair Terms Regulations* of a term or terms in the *person's* contract and inviting the *person's* comments on those concerns. If the FSA remains of the view that the term is unfair within the meaning of the *Unfair Terms Regulations*, it will normally ask the *person* to undertake to stop including the term in new contracts and stop relying on it in contracts which have been concluded.

10.13 If the *person* either declines to give an undertaking, or gives such an undertaking and fails to follow it, the FSA will consider the need to apply to court for an *injunction* under regulation 12 of the *Unfair Terms Regulations*.

10.14 In determining whether to seek an *injunction* against a *person*, the FSA will consider the full circumstances of each case. A number of factors may be relevant for this purpose. The following list is not exhaustive; not all of the factors may be relevant in a particular case, and there may be other factors that are relevant.

(1) whether the FSA is satisfied that the contract term which is the subject of the complaint may properly be regarded as unfair within the meaning of the *Unfair Terms Regulations*;
(2) the extent and nature of the detriment to *consumers* resulting from the term or the potential detriment which could result from the term;
(3) whether the *person* has fully cooperated with the FSA in resolving the FSA's concerns about the fairness of the particular contract term;
(4) the likelihood of success of an application for an *injunction*;
(5) the costs the FSA would incur in applying for and enforcing an *injunction* and the benefits that would result from that action; the FSA is more likely to be satisfied that an application is appropriate where an *injunction* would not only prevent the continued use of the particular contract term, but would also be likely to prevent the use or continued use of similar terms, or terms having the same effect, used or recommended by other *firms* concluding contracts with *consumers*.

10.15 In an urgent case, the FSA may seek a temporary *injunction*, to prevent the continued use of the term until the fairness of the term could be fully considered by the court. An urgent case is one in which the FSA considers that the actual or potential detriment is so serious that urgent action is necessary. In deciding whether to apply for a temporary *injunction*, the FSA may take into account a number of factors, including one or more of the factors set out in paragraph 10.14. In such an urgent case, the FSA may seek a temporary injunction without first consulting with the *person*.

10.16 In deciding whether to grant an *injunction*, the court will decide whether the term in question is unfair within the meaning of the *Unfair Terms Regulations* (see UNFCOG 1.3.2G). The court may grant an *injunction* on such terms as it sees fit. For example, it may require the *person* to stop including the unfair term in contracts with *consumers* from the date of the *injunction* and to stop relying on the unfair term in contracts which have been concluded. If the *person* fails to comply with the *injunction*, it will be in contempt of court.

10.17 Regulation 8 of the *Unfair Terms Regulations* provides that an unfair term is not binding on the *consumer*. This means that if the court finds that the term in question is unfair, the *person* would be unable to rely on the unfair term in existing contracts governed by the *Unfair Terms Regulations*. To the extent that it is possible, the existing contract would continue in effect without the unfair term.

10.18 When the FSA considers that a case requires enforcement action under the *Unfair Terms Regulations*, it will take the enforcement action itself if the *person* is a *firm* or an *appointed representative*.

10.19 Where the *person* is not a *firm* or an *appointed representative*, the FSA will generally pass the case to the Office of Fair Trading, with a recommendation that it take the enforcement action. The Office of Fair Trading may then decide whether or not to take enforcement action.

FSA costs

10.20 When it seeks an *injunction* under a power discussed in this chapter, the FSA may ask the court to order that the *person* who is the subject of the application should pay the FSA's costs.

---

9 Under sections 380(6)(a) and (7)(a), a 'relevant requirement' means a requirement: which is imposed by or under the *Act* or by any directly applicable Community regulation made under *MiFID*; or which is imposed by or under any other Act and whose contravention constitutes and offence which the FSA has power to prosecute under the *Act* (or in the case of Scotland, which is imposed by or under any other Act) and whose contravention constitutes an offence under Part V of the Criminal Justice Act 1993 or under the *Money Laundering Regulations*.

10 [link to UNFCOG]

CHAPTER 11
RESTITUTION AND REDRESS

Restitution orders under sections 382, 383 and 384 of the Act: the FSA's general approach

[2219K]

11.1A Decisions about whether to apply to the civil courts for restitution orders under the Act will be made by the RDC Chairman or, in an urgent case and if the Chairman is not available, by an RDC Deputy Chairman. In an exceptionally urgent case the matter will be decided by the director of Enforcement or, in his or her absence, another member of the FSA's executive of at least director of division level.

11.1B An exceptionally urgent case in these circumstances is one where the FSA staff believe that a decision to begin proceedings

(1) should be taken before it is possible to follow the procedure described in paragraph 11.1A; and

(2) it is necessary to protect the interests of consumers or potential consumers.

11.1 The FSA has power to apply to the court for a restitution order under section 382 of the *Act* and (in the case of *market abuse*) under section 383 of the *Act*. It also has an administrative power to require restitution under section 384 of the *Act*. When deciding whether to exercise these powers, the FSA will consider whether this would be the best use of the FSA's limited resources taking into account, for example, the likely amount of any recovery and the costs of achieving and distributing any sums. It will also consider, before exercising its powers: other ways that *persons* might obtain redress, and whether it would be more efficient or cost-effective for them to use these means instead; and any proposals by the *person* concerned to offer redress to any *consumers* or other *persons* who have suffered loss, and the adequacy of those proposals. The FSA expects, therefore, to exercise its formal restitution powers on rare occasions only.

11.2 Instances in which the FSA might consider using its powers to obtain restitution for *market counterparties* are likely to be very limited.

Criteria for determining whether to exercise powers to obtain restitution

11.3 In deciding whether to exercise its powers to seek or require restitution under sections 382, 383 or 384 of the *Act*, the FSA will consider all the circumstances of the case. The factors which the FSA will consider may include, but are not limited to, those set out below.

(1) Are the profits quantifiable?

(2) The FSA will consider whether quantifiable profits have been made which are owed to identifiable *persons*. In certain circumstances it may be difficult to prove that the conduct in question has resulted in the *person* concerned making a profit. It may also be difficult to find out how much profit and to whom the profits are owed. In these cases it may not be appropriate for the FSA to use its powers to obtain restitution.

(3) Are the losses identifiable?

(4) The FSA will consider whether there are identifiable *persons* who can be shown to have suffered quantifiable losses or other adverse effects. In certain circumstances it may be difficult to establish the number and identity of those who have suffered loss as a result of the conduct in question. It may also prove difficult in those cases to establish the amount of that loss and whether the losses have arisen as a result of the conduct in question. In these cases it may not be appropriate for the FSA to use its powers to obtain restitution.

(5) The number of persons affected

(6) The FSA will consider the number of *persons* who have suffered loss or other adverse effects and the extent of those losses or adverse effects. Where the breach of a relevant requirement by a *person*, whether *authorised* or not, results in significant losses, or losses to a large number of *persons* which collectively are significant, it may be appropriate for the FSA to use its powers to obtain restitution on their behalf. The FSA anticipates that many individual losses resulting from breaches by *firms* may be more efficiently and effectively redressed by *consumers* pursuing their claims directly with the firm concerned or through the *Financial Ombudsman Service* or the *compensation scheme* where the *firm* has ceased trading. However, where a large number of *persons* have been affected or the losses are substantial it may be more appropriate for the FSA to seek or require restitution from a *firm*. In those cases the FSA may consider combining an action seeking or requiring restitution from a *firm* or *unauthorised person* with disciplinary action or a criminal prosecution.

(7) FSA costs

(8) The FSA will consider the cost of securing redress and whether these are justified by the benefit to *persons* that would result from that action. The FSA will consider the costs of exercising its powers to obtain restitution and, in particular, the costs of any application to the court for an order for restitution, together with the size of any sums that might be recovered as a result. The costs of the action will, to a certain extent, depend on the nature and location of assets from which restitution may be made. In certain circumstances it may be possible for the FSA to recover its costs of applying to the court for an order for restitution, or a proportion of those costs, from the party against whom a restitution order is obtained, though this would have the disadvantage of reducing the amount available to pay redress.

(9) Is redress available elsewhere?

(10) The FSA will consider the availability of redress through the *Financial Ombudsman Service* or the *compensation scheme*. This will be relevant where the loss has resulted from the conduct of a *firm*. It will not be relevant where losses have resulted from the conduct of *unauthorised persons* operating in breach of the *general prohibition*. The *Financial Ombudsman Service* and the *compensation scheme* (where the *firm* has ceased trading) may be a more efficient and effective method of redress in many cases. The *Financial Ombudsman Service* provides a way for some *consumers* to obtain redress. The *compensation scheme* may provide redress for some *consumers* and businesses. The FSA's power to obtain restitution is not intended to duplicate the functions of the *Ombudsman* or *compensation schemes* in those cases. However, in certain cases it will be more appropriate for the FSA to pursue restitution. Further details of these schemes are set out in COMP.

(11) Is redress available through another regulator?

(12) The FSA will consider the availability of redress through another regulatory authority. Where another regulatory authority, such as *the Takeover Panel*, is in a position to require appropriate redress, the FSA will not generally exercise its own powers to do so. If the FSA does consider that action is appropriate and the matters in question have happened in the context of a *takeover bid*, the FSA will only take action during the bid in the circumstances set out in DEPP 6.2.25G if the *person* concerned has responsibilities under the *Takeover Code*. If another *regulatory body* has required redress and a *person* has not met that requirement, the FSA will take this into account and (subject to all other relevant factors and circumstances) may consider it appropriate to take action to ensure that such redress is provided.

(13) Can persons bring their own proceedings?

(14) The FSA will consider whether *persons* who have suffered losses are able to bring their own civil proceedings. In certain circumstances it may be appropriate for *persons* to bring their own civil proceedings to recover losses. This might be the case where the *person* who has suffered loss is a *market counterparty* and so may be expected to have a high degree of financial experience and knowledge. When considering whether this might be a more appropriate method of obtaining redress, the FSA will consider the costs to the *person* of bringing that action and the likelihood of success in relation to the size of any sums that may be recovered.

(15) Is the firm solvent?

(16) The FSA will consider the solvency of the *firm* or *unauthorised person* concerned. Where the solvency of the *firm* or *unauthorised person* would be placed at risk by the payment of restitution, the FSA will consider whether it is appropriate to seek restitution. In those cases, *the FSA* may consider obtaining a compulsory *insolvency order* against the *firm* or *unauthorised person* rather than restitution. When considering these options, the FSA may also take account of the position of other creditors who may be prejudiced if the assets of the *firm* or *unauthorised person* are used to pay restitution payments prior to insolvency.

(17) What other powers are available to the FSA?

(18) The FSA will consider the availability of its power to obtain a compulsory *insolvency order* against the *firm* or *unauthorised person* concerned or to apply to the court for the appointment of a receiver. In certain circumstances it may be appropriate for the FSA to obtain an administration order, winding up order or bankruptcy order against a *firm* or *unauthorised person* carrying out *regulated activities* in breach of the *general prohibition*.

(19) The FSA may decide to exercise its power to obtain a compulsory *insolvency order* or to apply for the appointment of a receiver rather than to exercise its powers to obtain restitution. This could happen if the FSA has particular concerns about a *person's* conduct, or financial position and, in particular, whether it is solvent (though the appointment by the court of a receiver is not conditional on the insolvency of the *person* concerned). The FSA may also consider the cost of seeking compulsory *insolvency orders* which will be paid out of the assets of the *firm*, or of the *unauthorised person* concerned, compared to the cost of seeking restitution. In the case of *unauthorised persons* operating in breach of the *general prohibition*, a decision to apply for a compulsory *insolvency order* rather than restitution will depend on all the circumstances of the case. In particular, the FSA may consider the significance of the *unauthorised* activities compared to the whole of the business; the nature and conduct of the activities carried on in breach of the *general prohibition*; and the number and nature of the claims against the *person* or *firm* concerned. The FSA's powers to apply for compulsory *insolvency orders* are discussed in chapter 13 of this guide.

(20) The behaviour of the persons suffering loss

(21) The FSA will consider the conduct of the *persons* who have suffered loss. As part of its *regulatory objectives* of increasing consumer awareness of the *financial system* and protecting *consumers*, the FSA is required to publicise information about the *authorised* status of *persons* and is empowered to give information and guidance about the regulation of financial services. This information should help *consumers* avoid suffering losses. When the FSA considers whether to obtain restitution on behalf of *persons*, it will consider the extent to which those *persons* may have contributed to their own loss or failed to take reasonable steps to protect their own interests.

(22) Other factors which may be relevant

(23) The FSA will consider the context of the conduct in question. In any case where the FSA believes that the exercise of its powers under section 383 or 384 of the *Act* may affect the timetable or outcome of a *takeover bid*, it will consult the *Takeover Panel* before taking any steps to exercise such powers, and will give due weight to its views.

(24) Where the FSA is considering applying to court for a restitution order in relation to *market abuse* under section 383 of the *Act*, it will also consider whether the court would be prevented from making that order by section 383(3) of the *Act*. A similar provision to section 383(3) applies where the FSA proposes to exercise its powers to require restitution in relation to market abuse under section 384(2). The conditions set out in section 383(3)(a) and section 384(a) and (b) are the same as those that apply to penalties for *market abuse* and the FSA will take the same factors into account when considering whether the conditions have been met. DEPP 6.3 lists those factors.

The FSA's choice of powers

11.4 In cases where it is appropriate to exercise its powers to obtain restitution from *firms*, the FSA will first consider using its own administrative powers under section 384 of the *Act* before considering taking court action.

11.5 However, there may be circumstances in which the FSA will choose to use the powers under section 382 or section 383 of the *Act* to apply to the court for an order for restitution against a *firm*. Those circumstances may include, for example, where:

(1) the FSA wishes to combine an application for an order for restitution with other court action against the *firm*, for example, where it wishes to apply to the court for an *injunction* to prevent the *firm* breaching a relevant requirement of the *Act* or any directly applicable Community regulation made under *MiFID*; the FSA's powers to apply for *injunctions* restraining *firms* from breaching relevant requirements of the *Act* or any directly applicable Community regulation under *MiFID* are discussed in chapter 10 of this guide;

(2) the FSA wishes to bring related court proceedings against an *unauthorised person* where the factual basis of those proceedings is likely to be the same as the claim for restitution against the *firm*;

(3) there is a danger that the assets of the *firm* may be dissipated; in those cases, the FSA may wish to combine an application to the court for an order for restitution with an application for an asset-freezing *injunction* to prevent assets from being dissipated; or

(4) the FSA suspects that the *firm* may not comply with an administrative requirement to give restitution; in those cases the FSA may consider that the sanction for breach of a court order may be needed to ensure compliance; a *person* who fails to comply with a court order may be in contempt of court and is liable to imprisonment, to a fine and/or to have his assets seized.

Determining the amount of restitution

11.6 The FSA may obtain information relating to the amount of profits made and/or losses or other adverse effects resulting from the conduct of *firms* or *unauthorised persons* as a result of the exercise of its powers to appoint investigators under sections 167 or 168 of the *Act*.

11.7 As well as obtaining information through the appointment of investigators, the FSA may consider using its power under section 166 of the *Act* to require a *firm* to provide a report prepared by a *skilled person*. That report may be requested to help the FSA to:

(1) determine the amount of profits which have been made by the *firm*; or

(2) establish whether the conduct of the *firm* has caused any losses or other adverse effects to qualifying persons and/or the extent of such losses; or

(3) determine how any amounts to be paid by the *firm* are to be distributed between qualifying persons.

Other relevant powers

11.8 The FSA may apply to the court for an *injunction* if it appears that a *person*, whether *authorised* or not, is reasonably likely to breach a requirement of the *Act* or any directly applicable Community regulation made under *MiFID* or engage in *market abuse*. It can also apply for an *injunction* if a *person* has breached a requirement of the *Act* or any directly applicable Community regulation made under *MiFID* or has engaged in *market abuse* and is likely to continue doing so.

11.9 The FSA may consider taking action for a financial penalty or *public censure*, as well as seeking restitution, if a *person* has breached a relevant requirement of the *Act* or any directly applicable Community regulation under *MiFID* or has engaged in, or *required or encouraged* others to engage in, *market abuse*.

11.10 The FSA may consider exercising its power to prosecute offences under the *Act*, as well as applying to seek restitution if a *person* has breached certain requirements of the *Act*.

CHAPTER 12
PROSECUTION OF CRIMINAL OFFENCES

The FSA's general approach

[2219L]

12.1 The FSA has powers under sections 401 and 402 of the *Act* to prosecute a range of criminal offences in England, Wales and Northern Ireland. The FSA may also prosecute criminal offences for which it is not the statutory prosecutor, but where the offences form part of the same criminality as the offences it is prosecuting under the *Act*.

12.2 The FSA's general policy is to pursue through the criminal justice system all those cases where criminal prosecution is appropriate. When it decides whether to bring criminal proceedings in England, Wales or Northern Ireland, or to refer the matter to another prosecuting authority in England, Wales or Northern Ireland (see paragraph 12.11), it will apply the basic principles set out in the Code for Crown Prosecutors.[11] When considering whether to prosecute a breach of the *Money Laundering Regulations*, the FSA will also have regard to whether the person concerned has followed the Guidance for the UK financial sector issued by the Joint Money Laundering Steering Group.

12.3 The FSA's approach when deciding whether to commence criminal proceedings for *misleading statements and practices offences* and *insider dealing offences*, where the FSA also has power to impose a sanction for *market abuse*, is discussed further in paragraphs 12.7 to 12.10.

12.4 In cases where criminal proceedings have commenced or will be commenced, the FSA may consider whether also to take civil or regulatory action (for example where this is appropriate for the protection of *consumers*) and how such action should be pursued. That action might include: applying to court for an *injunction*; applying to court for a restitution order; variation and/or cancellation of *permission*; and prohibition of individuals. The factors the FSA may take into account when deciding whether to take such action, where criminal proceedings are in contemplation, include, but are not limited to the following:

(1) whether, in the FSA's opinion, the taking of civil or regulatory action might unfairly prejudice the prosecution, or proposed prosecution, of criminal offences;

(2) whether, in the FSA's opinion, the taking of civil or regulatory action might unfairly prejudice the defendants in the criminal proceedings in the conduct of their defence; and

(3) whether it is appropriate to take civil or regulatory action, having regard to the scope of the *criminal proceedings* and the powers available to the criminal courts.

12.4A Subject to 12.4C, a decision to commence criminal proceedings will be made by the *RDC* Chairman or, in an urgent case and if the Chairman is not available, by an *RDC* Deputy Chairman. In an exceptionally urgent case the matter will be decided by the director of Enforcement or, in his or her absence, another member of the FSA's executive of at least director of division level.

12.4B An exceptionally urgent case in these circumstances is one where the FSA staff believe that a decision to begin proceedings

(1) should be taken before it is possible to follow the procedure described in paragraph 12.4A; and

(2) it is necessary to protect the interests of consumers or potential consumers.

12.4C Decisions about whether to initiate criminal proceedings under the Building Societies Act 1986, the Friendly Societies Acts 1974 and 1992, the Credit Unions Act 1979, the Industrial and Provident Societies Act 1965 and the Friendly and Industrial and Provident Societies Act 1968 may either be taken by the procedure described in paragraph 12.4A above or under *executive procedures*. The less serious the offence or its impact and the less complex the issues raised, the more likely that the FSA will take the decision to prosecute under *executive procedures*.

FSA cautions

12.5 In some cases, the FSA may decide to issue a formal caution rather than to prosecute an offender. In these cases the FSA will follow the Home Office Guidance on the cautioning of offenders, currently contained in the Home Office Circular 18/1994.

12.6 Where the FSA decides to administer a formal caution, a record of the caution will be kept by the FSA and on the Police National Computer. The FSA will not publish the caution, but it will be available to parties with access to the Police National Computer. The issue of a caution may influence the FSA and other prosecutors in their decision whether or not to prosecute the offender if he offends again. If the offender is a *firm* or an *approved person*, a caution given by the FSA will form part of the *firm's* or *approved person's* regulatory record for the purposes of DEPP 6.2.1G (3). If relevant, the FSA will take the caution into account in deciding whether to take disciplinary action for subsequent regulatory misconduct by the *firm* or the *approved person*. The FSA may also take a caution into account when considering a *person's* honesty, integrity and reputation and his fitness or propriety to perform controlled or other functions in relation to *regulated activities* (see FIT 2.1.3G).

Criminal prosecutions in cases of market abuse

12.7 In some cases there will be instances of market misconduct that may arguably involve a breach of the criminal law as well as *market abuse* as defined in section 118 of the *Act*. When the FSA decides whether to commence criminal proceedings rather than impose a sanction for *market abuse* in relation to that misconduct, it will apply the basic principles set out in the Code for Crown Prosecutors. When deciding whether to prosecute market misconduct which also falls within the definition of *market abuse*, application of these basic principles may involve consideration of some of the factors set out in paragraph 12.8.

12.8 The factors which the FSA may consider when deciding whether to commence a criminal prosecution for market misconduct rather than impose a sanction for *market abuse* include, but are not limited to, the following:

(1) the seriousness of the misconduct: if the misconduct is serious and prosecution is likely to result in a significant sentence, criminal prosecution may be more likely to be appropriate;

(2) whether there are victims who have suffered loss as a result of the misconduct: where there are no victims a criminal prosecution is less likely to be appropriate;

(3) the extent and nature of the loss suffered: where the misconduct has resulted in substantial loss and/or loss has been suffered by a substantial number of victims, criminal prosecution may be more likely to be appropriate;

(4) the effect of the misconduct on the market: where the misconduct has resulted in significant distortion or disruption to the market and/or has significantly damaged market confidence, a criminal prosecution may be more likely to be appropriate;

(5) the extent of any profits accrued or loss avoided as a result of the misconduct: where substantial profits have accrued or loss avoided as a result of the misconduct, criminal prosecution may be more likely to be appropriate;

(6) whether there are grounds for believing that the misconduct is likely to be continued or repeated: if it appears that the misconduct may be continued or repeated and the imposition of a financial penalty is unlikely to deter further misconduct, a criminal prosecution may be more appropriate than a financial penalty;

(7) whether the person has previously been cautioned or convicted in relation to market misconduct or has been subject to civil or regulatory action in respect of market misconduct;

(8) the extent to which redress has been provided to those who have suffered loss as a result of the misconduct and/or whether steps have been taken to remedy any failures in systems or controls which gave rise to the misconduct: where such steps are taken promptly and voluntarily, criminal prosecution may not be appropriate; however, potential defendants will not avoid prosecution simply because they are able to pay compensation;

(9) the effect that a criminal prosecution may have on the prospects of securing redress for those who have suffered loss: where a criminal prosecution will have adverse effects on the solvency of a *firm* or individual in circumstances where loss has been suffered by *consumers*, the FSA may decide that criminal proceedings are not appropriate;

(10) whether the *person* is being or has been voluntarily cooperative with the FSA in taking corrective measures; however, potential defendants will not avoid prosecution merely by fulfilling a statutory duty to take those measures;

(11) whether an individual's misconduct involves dishonesty or an abuse of a position of authority or trust;

(12) where the misconduct in question was carried out by a group, and a particular individual has played a leading role in the commission of the misconduct: in these circumstances, criminal prosecution may be appropriate in relation to that individual;

(12A) where the misconduct in question was carried out by two or more individuals acting together and one of the individuals provides information and gives full assistance in the FSA's prosecution of the other(s), the FSA will take this cooperation into account when deciding whether to prosecute the individual who has assisted the FSA or bring market abuse proceedings against him;

(13) the personal circumstances of an individual may be relevant to a decision whether to commence a criminal prosecution.

12.9 The importance attached by the FSA to these factors will vary from case to case and the factors are not necessarily cumulative or exhaustive.

12.10 It is the FSA's policy not to impose a sanction for *market abuse* where a *person* is being prosecuted for market misconduct or has been finally convicted or acquitted of market misconduct (following the exhaustion of all appeal processes) in a criminal prosecution arising from substantially the same allegations. Similarly, it is the FSA's policy not to commence a prosecution for market misconduct where the FSA has brought or is seeking to bring disciplinary proceedings for *market abuse* arising from substantially the same allegations.

Liaison with other prosecuting authorities

12.11 The FSA has agreed guidelines that establish a framework for liaison and cooperation in cases where one or more other authority (such as the Crown Prosecution Service or Serious Fraud Office) has an interest in prosecuting any aspect of a matter that the FSA is considering for investigation, investigating or considering prosecuting. These guidelines are set out in annex 2 to this guide.

Prosecution of Friendly Societies

12.12 The FSA's power to prosecute friendly societies is discussed in EG 19.3 to 19.9 and in an article on the FSA web-site entitled 'Prosecuting Friendly Societies'.[12]

---

11 http://www.cps.gov.uk/publications/docs/code2004english.pdf

12 http://www.fsa.gov.uk/Pages/doing/regulated/law/focus/friendly.shtml

---

CHAPTER 13
INSOLVENCY

[2219M]

13.1 This chapter explains the FSA's policies on how it uses its powers under the *Act* to apply to the court for orders under existing insolvency legislation and exercise its rights under the *Act* to be involved in proceedings under that legislation. The FSA's effective use of its powers and rights in insolvency proceedings helps it pursue its *regulatory objectives* of maintaining market confidence, protecting *consumers* and reducing *financial crime* by, amongst other matters, enabling it to apply to court for action to:

(1) stop *firms* and *unauthorised persons* carrying on insolvent or unlawful business; and
(2) ensure the orderly realisation and distribution of their assets.

The FSA's general approach to use of its powers and rights in insolvency proceedings

13.2 In using its powers to seek *insolvency orders* the FSA takes full account of: the principle adopted by the courts that recourse to insolvency regimes is a step to be taken for the benefit of creditors as a whole; and the fact that the court will have regard to the public interest when considering whether to wind up a body on the grounds that it is just and equitable to do so.

13.3 The FSA will consider the facts of each particular case when it decides whether to use its powers and exercise its rights. The FSA will also consider the other powers available to it under the *Act* and to *consumers* under the *Act* and other legislation, and the extent to which the use of those other powers meets the needs of *consumers* as a whole and the FSA's *regulatory objectives*. The FSA may use its powers to seek *insolvency orders* in conjunction with its other powers, including its powers to seek *injunctions*.

13.3A Decisions about whether to apply to the civil courts for insolvency orders under the *Act* will be made by the *RDC* Chairman or, in an urgent case and if the Chairman is not available, by an *RDC* Deputy Chairman. In an exceptionally urgent case the matter will be decided by the director of Enforcement or, in his or her absence, another member of the FSA's executive of at least director of division level.

13.3B An exceptionally urgent case in these circumstances is one where the FSA staff believe that a decision to begin proceedings

(1) should be taken before it is possible to follow the procedure described in paragraph 13.3A; and

(2) it is necessary to protect the interests of consumers or potential consumers.

Petitions for administration orders or compulsory winding up orders: determining whether a company or partnership is unable to pay its debts

13.4 The FSA can petition for an administration order or compulsory winding up order on the grounds that the *company* or *partnership* is unable (or, in the case of administration orders, is likely to become unable) to pay its debts. The FSA does not have to be a creditor to petition on these grounds.

13.5 Under sections 359 (Petitions) and 367 (Winding up Petitions) of the *Act*, a *company* or *partnership* is deemed to be unable to pay its debts if it is in default on an obligation to pay a sum due and payable under an agreement where the making or performance of the agreement constitutes or is part of a *regulated activity* which the *company* or *partnership* is carrying on.

13.6 The FSA would not ordinarily petition for an administration order unless it believes that the *company* or *partnership* is, or is likely to become, insolvent. Similarly, the FSA would not ordinarily petition for a compulsory winding up order solely on the ground of inability to pay debts (as provided in the *Act*), unless it believes that the *company* or *partnership* is or is likely to be insolvent.

13.7 While a default on a single agreement of the type mentioned in paragraph 13.5 is, under the *Act*, a presumption of an inability to pay debts, the FSA will consider the circumstances surrounding the default. In particular, the FSA will consider whether:

(1) the default is the subject of continuing discussion between the *company* or *partnership* and the creditor, under the relevant agreement, which is likely to lead to a resolution;

(2) the default is an isolated incident;

(3) in other respects the *company* or *partnership* is meeting its obligations under agreements of this kind; and

(4) the FSA has information to indicate that the *company* or *partnership* is able to pay its debts or, alternatively, that in addition to the specific default the *company* or *partnership* is in fact unable to pay its debts.

Petitions for administration orders or compulsory winding up orders: determining whether to seek any insolvency order

13.8 Where the FSA believes that a *company* or *partnership* to which sections 359(1) and 367(1) of the *Act* applies is, or is likely to become, unable to pay its debts, the FSA will consider whether it is appropriate to seek an administration order or a compulsory winding up order from the court. The FSA's approach will be in two stages: the first is to consider whether it is appropriate to seek any *insolvency order*; the second is to consider which *insolvency order* will meet, or is likely to meet, the needs of *consumers*.

13.9 In determining whether it is appropriate to seek an *insolvency order* on this basis, the FSA will consider the facts of each case including, where relevant:

(1) whether the *company* or *partnership* has taken or is taking steps to deal with its insolvency, including petitioning for its own administration, placing itself in voluntary winding up or proposing to enter into a company voluntary arrangement, and the effectiveness of those steps;

(2) whether any consumer or other creditor of the *company* or *partnership* has taken steps to seek an *insolvency order* from the court;

(3) the effect on the *company* or partnership and on the creditors of the company or partnership if an *insolvency order* is made;

(4) whether the use of other powers, rights or remedies available to the FSA, *consumers* and creditors under the *Act* and other legislation will achieve the same or a more advantageous result in terms of the protection of *consumers*, and of market confidence and the restraint and remedy of unlawful activity, for example:
  (a) in the case of *authorised persons* and *appointed representatives*, the interests of *consumers* may, in certain circumstances, be met by the use of the FSA's intervention powers and by requiring restitution to *consumers*;
  (b) in the case of *unauthorised companies* and *partnerships*, the FSA will consider whether the interests of *consumers* can be achieved by seeking an *injunction* to restrain continuation of the carrying on of the *regulated activity* and/or an order for restitution to consumers;
(5) whether other regulatory authorities or law enforcement agencies propose to take action in respect of the same or a similar issue which would be adequate to address the FSA's concerns or whether it would be appropriate for the FSA to take its own action;
(6) the nature and extent of the *company* or *partnership* assets and liabilities, and in particular whether the *company* or *partnership* holds *client* assets and whether its secured and preferred liabilities are likely to exceed available assets;
(7) whether there is a significant cross border or international element to the business which the *company* or *partnership* is carrying on and the effect on foreign assets or on the continuation of the business abroad of making an *insolvency order*;
(8) whether an *insolvency order* is likely to achieve a fair and orderly realisation and distribution of assets; and
(9) whether there is a risk of creditors being preferred and any advantage in securing a moratorium in relation to proceedings against the *company* or *partnership*.

13.10 After the FSA has determined that it is appropriate to seek an *insolvency order*, and there is no moratorium in place under Schedule A1 to the Insolvency Act 1986 (as amended by the Insolvency Act 2000) (hereafter referred to in this chapter as 'the 1986 Act'), it will consider whether this order should be an administration order or a compulsory winding up order.

Petitions for administration orders or compulsory winding up orders: determining which insolvency order to seek

13.11 An administration order can be made only in relation to *companies* and *partnerships* and only where the court believes that making such an order will achieve one or more of the four purposes set out in section 8 of the 1986 Act. The FSA will apply for an administration order only where it considers that doing so will meet or is likely to meet one or more of these purposes.

13.12 Where it has the option of applying for either an administration order or a compulsory winding up order, the FSA will have regard to the purpose to be achieved by the insolvency procedure.

13.13 In addition, the FSA will consider, where relevant, factors including:
(1) the extent to which the financial difficulties are, or are likely to be attributable to the management of the *company* or *partnership*, or to external factors, for example, market forces;
(2) the extent to which it appears to the FSA that the *company* or *partnership* may, through an administrator, be able to trade its way out of its financial difficulties;
(3) the extent to which the *company* or *partnership* can lawfully and viably continue to carry on *regulated activities* through an administrator;
(4) the extent to which the sale of the business in whole or in part as a going concern is likely to be achievable;
(5) the complexity of the business of the *company* or *partnership*;
(6) whether recourse to one regime or another is likely to result in delays in redress to *consumers* or an additional cost;
(7) whether recourse to one regime or another is likely to result in better redress to *consumers*;
(8) the adequacy and reliability of the *company* or *partnership*'s accounting or administrative records;
(9) the extent to which the management of the *company* or *partnership* has co-operated with the FSA;
(10) in the case of an *unauthorised company* or *partnership* carrying on a *regulated activity* as part of a larger enterprise, the scale and importance of the unauthorised activity in relation to the whole of the *company's* or *partnership's* business;
(11) the extent to which the management of the *company* or *partnership* is likely to cooperate in determining whether one or more of the purposes of an administration order can be met;
(12) in the case of an *unauthorised company* or *partnership* carrying on a *regulated activity* as part of a larger enterprise, the extent to which the *company*'s or *partnership*'s survival can be anticipated without the continuance of the unauthorised regulated activity;
(13) where an administrative receiver is in place, whether the *debenture* holder is likely to agree to an application for an administration order;

(14) where an administrative receiver is in place, whether the FSA has reason to believe that the *debenture* under which the administrative receiver has been appointed is likely to be released, discharged, avoided or challenged.

Petitioning for compulsory winding up on just and equitable grounds

13.14 The FSA has power under section 367(3)(b) of the *Act* to petition the court for the compulsory winding up of a *company* or *partnership*, on the ground that it is just and equitable for the body to be wound up, regardless of whether or not the body is able to pay its debts. In some instances the FSA may need to consider whether to petition on this ground alone or in addition to the ground of insolvency.

13.15 When deciding whether to petition on this ground the FSA will consider all relevant facts including:

(1) whether the needs of *consumers* and the public interest require the *company* or *partnership* to cease to operate;

(2) the need to protect *consumers'* claims and *client* assets;

(3) whether the needs of *consumers* and the public interest can be met by using the FSA's other powers;

(4) in the case of an *authorised person*, where the FSA considers that the *authorisation* should be withdrawn or where it has been withdrawn, the extent to which there is other business that the *person* can carry on without *authorisation*;

(5) in the case of an *unauthorised company* or *partnership* carrying on a *regulated activity* as part of a larger enterprise, the scale and importance of the *unauthorised regulated activity* and the extent to which the enterprise is likely to survive the restraint and remedying of that activity by the use of other powers available to the FSA having regard to any continuing risk to *consumers*;

(6) whether there is reason to believe that an *injunction* to restrain the carrying on of an *unauthorised regulated activity* would be ineffective;

(7) whether the *company* or *partnership* appears to be or to have been involved in *financial crime* or appears to be or to have been used as a vehicle for *financial crime*.

13.16 Where appropriate the FSA will also take the following factors into account:

(1) the complexity of the *company* or *partnership* (as this may have a bearing on the effectiveness of winding up or any alternative action);

(2) whether there is a significant cross border or international element to the business being carried on by the *company* or *partnership* and the impact on the business in other jurisdictions;

(3) the adequacy and reliability of the *company* or *partnership*'s accounting or administrative records;

(4) the extent to which the *company* or *partnership*'s management has co-operated with the FSA.

Petitioning for compulsory winding up of a company already in voluntary winding up

13.17 Section 365(6) of the *Act* makes it clear that the FSA may petition for the compulsory winding up of a *company* even if it is already in voluntary winding up. This power is already available to creditors and contributories of *companies* in voluntary winding up. For example, the court can be asked to direct the liquidator to investigate a transaction which the *company* undertook before the winding up. In some circumstances, this power may be used in respect of partnerships (section 367 of the *Act*).

13.18 Given the powers available to creditors (or contributories), the FSA anticipates that there will only be a limited number of cases where it will exercise the right under section 365(6) to petition for the compulsory winding up of a company already in voluntary winding up. The FSA will only be able to exercise this right where one or both of the grounds on which it can seek compulsory winding up are met.

13.19 Factors which the FSA will consider when it decides whether to use this power (in addition to the factors identified in paragraphs 13.11 to 13.16 in relation to the FSA's decisions to seek compulsory winding up) include:

(1) whether the FSA's concerns can properly and effectively be met by seeking a specific direction under section 365(2) of the Act;

(2) whether the affairs of the *company* require independent investigation of the kind which follows a compulsory winding up order and whether there are or are likely to be funds available for that investigation;

(3) the composition of the creditors of the company including the ratio of *consumer* and non-*consumer* creditors and the nature of their claims;

(4) the extent to which there are creditors who are or are likely to be connected to the *company* or its directors and management;

(5) the extent to which the directors and management are cooperating with the liquidator in voluntary winding up;

(6) the need to protect and distribute *consumers'* claims and *assets*;
(7) whether a petition by the FSA for compulsory winding up is likely to have the support of the majority or a large proportion of the creditors; and
(8) the extent of any resulting delay and additional costs in seeking a compulsory winding up order.

13.20 Where the FSA is requested by a *Home State regulator* of an *EEA firm* or a *Treaty firm* to present a petition for the compulsory winding up of that firm, the FSA will first need to consider whether the presentation of the petition is necessary in order to comply with a Community obligation.

Power to apply to court for a provisional liquidator

13.21 Where a petition has been presented for the winding up of a body, the court may appoint a provisional liquidator in the interim period pending the hearing of the petition. An appointment may be sought and made to:
(1) permit the continuation of the business for the protection of *consumers*; or
(2) secure, protect, or realise assets or property in the possession or under the control of the *company* or *partnership* (in particular where there is a risk that the assets will be dissipated) for the benefit of creditors or *consumers*.

13.22 In cases where it decides to petition for the compulsory winding up of a body under section 367 of the *Act*, the FSA will also consider whether it should seek the appointment of a provisional liquidator. The FSA will have regard, in particular, to the extent to which there may be a need to protect *consumers'* claims and *consumers'* funds or other assets. Where the FSA decides to petition for the compulsory winding up of a *company* or *partnership* on the just and equitable ground and where the *company* or *partnership* is solvent but may become insolvent, the FSA will also consider whether the appointment of a provisional liquidator would serve to maintain the solvency of the *company* or *partnership*.

The FSA's use of its power to petition for a bankruptcy order or a sequestration award in relation to an individual (section 372 of the Act)

13.23 The FSA recognises that the bankruptcy of an individual or the sequestration of an individual's estate are significant measures which may have significant personal and professional implications for the individual involved. In considering whether to present a petition the FSA's principal considerations will be its *regulatory objectives* including the protection of *consumers*.

13.24 The FSA is also mindful that whilst the winding up of an *unauthorised company* or *partnership* should bring an end to any unlawful activity, this is not necessarily the effect of bankruptcy or sequestration. The FSA may, in certain cases, consider the use of powers to petition for bankruptcy or sequestration in conjunction with the use of other powers to seek *injunctions* and other relief from the court. In particular, where the individual controls assets belonging to consumers and holds, or appears to hold, those assets on trust for consumers, those assets will not vest in the insolvency practitioner appointed in the bankruptcy or sequestration. The FSA will in those circumstances consider whether separate action is necessary to protect the assets and interests of *consumers*.

13.25 If an individual appears to be unable to pay a *regulated activity debt*, or to have no reasonable prospect of doing so, then section 372 of the *Act* permits the FSA to petition for the individual's bankruptcy, or in Scotland, for the sequestration of the individual's estate. The FSA will petition for bankruptcy or sequestration only if it believes that the individual is, in fact, insolvent. In determining this, as a general rule, the FSA will serve a demand requiring the individual to establish, to the FSA's satisfaction, that there is a reasonable prospect that he will be able to pay the *regulated activity debt*.

13.26 The FSA will consider the response of the individual to that demand on its own facts and in the light of information, if any, available to the FSA. Exceptionally, the FSA may not first proceed to serve a demand if:
(1) the individual is already in default of a *regulated activity debt* which has fallen due and payable; and
(2) the FSA is satisfied, either because the individual has confirmed it or on the information already available to the FSA, that the individual is insolvent and has no reasonable prospect of paying another *regulated activity debt* when it falls due.

13.27 If the FSA believes that the individual is insolvent, the factors it will consider when it decides whether to seek a bankruptcy order or sequestration award include:
(1) whether others have taken steps to deal with the individual's insolvency, including a proposal by the individual of a voluntary arrangement, a petition by the individual for his own bankruptcy or sequestration, or a petition by a third party for the individual's bankruptcy or the sequestration of the individual's estate;

(2) whether the FSA can adequately deal with the individual using other powers available to it under the *Act*, without the need to seek a bankruptcy order or sequestration award;
(3) the extent of the individual's insolvency or apparent insolvency;
(4) the number of *consumers* affected and the extent of their claims against the individual;
(5) whether the individual has control over assets belonging to *consumers*;
(6) the individual's conduct in his dealings with the FSA, including the extent of his cooperation with the FSA;
(7) whether the individual appears to be, or to have been, involved in *financial crime*;
(8) the adequacy of the individual's accounts and administration records;
(9) in the case of an *unauthorised individual* who is carrying on or who has carried on a *regulated activity*, the nature, scale and importance of that activity and the individual's conduct in carrying on that activity;
(10) whether there would be an advantage in securing a moratorium in respect of proceedings against the individual; and
(11) whether there are any special personal or professional implications for that individual if a bankruptcy order or sequestration award is made.

Applications in relation to voluntary arrangements: the FSA's policy

13.28 In general terms, the approval of a voluntary arrangement (in relation to *companies*, *partnerships* and *individuals*) requires more than 75% of the creditors to whom notice of a meeting has been sent and who are present in person or by proxy. The arrangement must also not be opposed by more than 50% of creditors given notice of the meeting and who have notified their claim, but excluding secured creditors and creditors who are, in the case of companies or partnerships, connected persons and, in the case of individuals, associates. The FSA will therefore not normally challenge an arrangement approved by a majority of creditors.

13.29 Exceptionally, the FSA will consider making such a challenge using its powers in sections 356 and 357 of the *Act* after considering, in particular, the following matters:
(1) The composition of the creditors of the company including the ratio of *consumer* to non-*consumer* creditors or the nature of their claims;
(2) whether the FSA has concerns, or is aware of concerns of creditors, about the regularity of the meeting or the identification of connected or associated creditors and the extent to which creditors with those concerns could themselves make an application to court;
(3) whether the *company*, *partnership* or individual has control of consumer assets which might be affected by the voluntary arrangement;
(4) the complexity of the arrangement;
(5) the nature and complexity of the regulated activity;
(6) the *company's*, *partnership's* or individual's previous dealings with the FSA, including the extent of its cooperation with the FSA and its compliance history;
(7) whether the FSA is aware of any matters which would materially affect the rights and expectations of creditors under the voluntary arrangement as approved; and
(8) the extent to which the debtor has made full and accurate disclosure of assets and liabilities in the proposal to creditors.

13.30 Similarly, the FSA will not normally use its powers under section 358 of the *Act* to petition for sequestration of a debtor's estate following the grant of a trust deed, if the trust deed has been, or appears likely to be, acceded to by a majority of creditors.

13.31 In considering whether to exercise its powers under Schedule A1 to the 1986 Act to make a challenge in relation to acts, omissions or decisions of a nominee during a moratorium, the FSA will have regard to the following matters in particular:
(1) whether the FSA is aware of matters indicating that the proposed voluntary arrangement does not have a reasonable prospect of being approved and implemented or that the company is likely to have insufficient funds available to it to carry on its business during the moratorium;
(2) whether consumer assets held by the company are or may be placed at risk; and
(3) in the case of an *unauthorised company* whether that *company* is able to carry on its business lawfully during the moratorium without undertaking any *regulated activity* in contravention of the *general prohibition*.

Applications for orders against debt avoidance: the FSA's policy

13.32 When it decides whether to make an application for an order against debt avoidance pursuant to section 375 of the *Act*, the FSA will consider all relevant factors, including the following:
(1) the extent to which the relevant transactions involved dealings in *consumers*' funds;
(2) whether it would be appropriate to petition for a winding up order, bankruptcy order, or sequestration award, in relation to the debtor and the extent to which the transaction could properly be dealt with in that winding up, bankruptcy or sequestration;
(3) the number of *consumers* or other creditors likely to be affected and their ability to make an application of this nature; and

Part II FSA Handbook Materials

(4) the size of the transaction.

The FSA's arrangements for notification of petitions and other documents

13.33 Paragraphs 13.34 to 13.36 contain information for insolvency practitioners and others about sending copies of petitions, notices and other documents to the FSA, and about making reports to the FSA. Insolvency practitioners and others have duties to give that information and those documents to the FSA under various sections in Part XXIV of the *Act* (Insolvency). Paragraph 13.34 identifies the relevant sections of the Act that explain some of the duties.

Insolvency regime and relevant sections of the *Act*.

13.34

Insolvency regime	**Relevant sections of the Act**
Administration	Sections 361 and 362(3)
Compulsory winding up	Sections 369, 370, and 371(3)
Voluntary liquidation	Section 365(4)
Receivership	Sections 363(4) and 364
Bankruptcy and sequestration	Sections 373 and 374(3)
Company moratoria	Paragraph 44 of schedule A1 to the 1986 Act
Individual voluntary arrangements	Section 357(3) – relates to notices of the result of the creditors' meetings.
Trust deeds for creditors	Section 358(2)(a) and (b) – relates to copies of trust deeds and copies of certain other documents of information sent to creditors. Section 358(4) – relates to notices of any meeting of creditors held in relation to the trust deed.

13.35 Unless paragraph 13.36 applies, the information and documents identified in 13.34 should be sent to the Financial Services Authority, 25 The North Colonnade, Canary Wharf, London E14 5HS marked 'Insolvency Information'. If the *person* who is subject to the insolvency regime ('the insolvent person') is an *authorised person*, the information and documents should, in the first instance, be addressed to the insolvent person's supervisory contact at the FSA (if known).

13.36 If the insolvent person is an *authorised person* and the sender of the information or documents knows that the insolvent person's supervisory contact operates from Edinburgh, information or documents should, in the first instance, be sent to the Financial Services Authority, Quayside House, 127 Fountainbridge, Edinburgh EH3 8DJ.

Rights on petitions by third parties and involvement in creditors meetings: the FSA's policy

13.37 The FSA will exercise its rights under sections 362, 371 and 374 of the *Act* to be heard on a third party's petition or in subsequent hearings only where it believes it has information that it considers relevant to the court's consideration of the petition or application. These circumstances may include:

(1) where the FSA has relevant information which it believes may not otherwise be drawn to the court's attention; especially where the FSA has been asked to attend for a particular purpose (for example to explain the operation of its rules);

(2) where the FSA believes that the *insolvency order* being sought by a third party is inappropriate to meet the needs of *consumers* and the public interest; and

(3) where the FSA believes that the making of an *insolvency order* will affect the FSA's exercise of its other powers under the *Act*, and wishes to make the court aware of this.

13.38 The making of an *insolvency order* operates to stay any proceedings already in place against the company, partnership or individual, and prevents proceedings being commenced while the *insolvency order* is in place. Proceedings can continue or be commenced against those *persons* only with the court's permission. This may impact on the effectiveness of the FSA's use of its powers to seek *injunctions* and restitution orders from the court. The FSA will draw the court's attention to this potential effect where the FSA believes it is a relevant consideration, but it is a matter for the court to determine its relevance in a particular case.

13.39 The FSA is given power to receive the same information as creditors are entitled to receive in the winding up, administration, receivership or voluntary arrangement of an *authorised person*, of *appointed representatives* and of *persons* who have carried out a *regulated activity* while *unauthorised*. The FSA is also entitled to attend and make representation at any creditors' meeting or (where relevant) creditors' committee meeting taking place in those regimes. When it decides whether to exercise its power to attend and make representations at meetings the factors which the FSA will take into account include:

(1) the extent of claims by *consumers* upon the body or individual;
(2) the extent to which *consumer* assets are held by the body or individual;
(3) the extent to which the FSA is aware of concerns of *consumers* (or other creditors or contributories) about the way in which the insolvency regime is proceeding;
(4) whether the circumstances which gave rise to the insolvency regime might have general implications for others carrying on regulated business;
(5) whether the creditors include *shareholders*, directors, or other *persons* who have a connection with the management or ownership of the body or are associated with the individual;
(6) the complexity or specialisation of the business of the body or individual; and
(7) where there is a significant cross border or international element to the business which the *company*, *partnership* or individual is carrying out.

NOTES

There are two paras 13.29 in the original; the second para 13.29 has been renumbered as 13.30, and subsequent paragraphs have been numbered accordingly.

CHAPTER 14
COLLECTIVE INVESTMENT SCHEMES

Exercise of the powers in respect of Authorised Unit Trust Schemes (AUT): sections 254 (revocation of authorisation), 257 (directions) and 258 (power to apply to court) of the Act

[2219N]

14.1 The FSA will consider all the relevant circumstances of each case and may take a number of factors into account when it decides whether to use these powers. The following list is not exhaustive; not all these factors may be relevant in a particular case and there may be other factors that are relevant.

(1) The seriousness of the breach or likely breach by a *manager* or *trustee* of a requirement imposed by or under the *Act*. The following may be relevant:
  (a) the extent to which the *breach* was deliberate or reckless;
  (b) the extent of loss, or risk of loss, caused to existing, past or potential participants in the *AUT* as a result of the *breach*;
  (c) whether the *breach* highlights serious or systemic weaknesses in the management or control of either the *AUT* or *scheme property*;
  (d) whether there are grounds for believing a *breach* is likely to be continued or repeated;
  (e) the length of time over which the *breach* happened; and
  (f) whether existing and/or past participants in the *AUT* have been misled in a material way, for example about the investment objectives or policy of the *scheme* or the level of investment risk.
(2) The consequences of a failure to satisfy a requirement for the making of an order authorising an *AUT*. The FSA will expect the non-compliance to be resolved as soon as possible. Important factors are likely to be whether existing and/or past *participants* have suffered loss due to the non-compliance and whether remedial steps will be taken to satisfy all the requirements of the order.
(3) Whether it is necessary to suspend the issue and redemption of units to protect the interests of existing or potential *participants* in the *AUT*. For example, this may be necessary if:
  (a) information suggests the current price of units under the *AUT* may not accurately reflect the value *scheme property*; or
  (b) the *scheme property* cannot be valued accurately.
(4) The effect on the interests of *participants* within the scheme of the use of either or both of its powers under sections 254 and 257. However, the FSA will also consider the interests of past and potential *participants*.
(5) Whether the FSA's concerns can be resolved by taking enforcement action against the *manager* and/or *trustee* of the *AUT*. In some instances, the FSA may consider it appropriate to deal with a *breach* by a manager or *trustee* by taking direct enforcement action against the *manager* and/or *trustee* without using its powers under sections 254, 257, or 258. In other instances, the FSA may combine direct enforcement action against a *trustee* and/or *manager* with the use of one or more of the powers under sections 254, 257 and 258.
(6) Whether there is information to suggest that a *trustee* or *manager* has knowingly or recklessly given the FSA false information. Giving false information is likely to cause very serious concerns, particularly if it shows there is a risk of loss to the *scheme property* or that *participants*' interests have been or may be affected in some other way.
(7) The conduct of the *manager* or *trustee* in relation to, and following the identification of, the issue, for example:
  (a) whether the *manager* or *trustee* discovered the issue or problem affecting the *AUT* and brought it to the FSA's attention promptly;

(b) the degree to which the *manager* or *trustee* is willing to cooperate with the FSA's investigation and to take protective steps, for example by suspending the issue and redemption of units in the *AUT*;

(c) whether the *manager* or *trustee* has compensated past and existing *participants* who have suffered loss.

(8) The compliance history of the *trustee* or *manager*, including whether the FSA has previously taken disciplinary action against the *trustee* or *manager* in relation to the *AUT* or any other *collective investment scheme*.

(9) Whether there is information to suggest that the *AUT* is being used for criminal purposes and/or that the *manager* or *trustee* is itself involved in *financial crime*.

Choice of powers

14.2 The FSA may use its powers under sections 254, 257 and 258 individually, together, and as well as direct enforcement action against a *trustee* or *manager* in their capacity as *firms*.

14.3 Where the FSA has a concern about an *AUT* that must be dealt with urgently, it will generally use its power to give directions under section 257 in the first instance.

14.4 The following are examples of situations where the FSA may consider it appropriate to seek a court order under section 258 to remove the *manager* or *trustee*:

(1) Where there are grounds for concern over the behaviour of the *manager* or *trustee* in respect of the management of the *scheme* or of its assets.

(2) Where a *manager* or *trustee* has breached a requirement imposed on him under the *Act* or has knowingly or recklessly given the FSA false information.

14.5 The FSA recognises that participants in an *AUT* have a direct financial interest in the *scheme property*. It follows that in cases where it considers it appropriate to use its section 254 power to revoke an authorisation order, the FSA will generally first require the *manager* or *trustee* to wind up the *AUT* (or seek a court order for the appointment of a firm to wind up the *AUT*).

14.6 [deleted]

Exercise of the powers in respect of recognised schemes: section 267 of the Act – power to suspend promotion of a scheme recognised under section 264: the FSA's policy

14.7 When it decides whether a suspension order under section 267 is appropriate, the FSA will consider all the relevant circumstances. General factors that the FSA may consider include, but are not limited to:

(1) the seriousness of the breach of *financial promotion* rules by the *operator* (the matters listed at paragraph 14.1(1)(a) to (f) may be relevant in this context); and

(2) the conduct of the *operator* after the *breach* was discovered including whether the *operator* has compensated past and existing *participants* who have suffered loss.

14.8 In addition to or instead of suspending the promotion of a *scheme* recognised under section 264, the FSA may ask the *competent authorities* of the *EEA State* in which the *scheme* is constituted who are responsible for the authorisation of *collective investment schemes*, to take such action in respect of the *scheme* and/or its *operator* as will resolve the FSA's concerns. Also, Schedule 5 to the *Act* states that a *person* who for the time being is an *operator*, *trustee* or *depositary* of a *scheme* recognised under section 264 of the *Act* is an *authorised person*. So, it will also be open to the FSA to take direct enforcement action against those *persons*.

Exercise of the powers in respect of recognised schemes: sections 279 and 281 of the Act – powers to revoke recognition of schemes recognised under section 270 or section 272: the FSA's policy

14.9 The FSA will consider all the relevant circumstances of each case. The general factors which the FSA may consider include, but are not limited to, those set out in paragraph 14.1(1) to (9) (the conduct of the *operator* of the *scheme* and of the *trustee* or *depositary* will also, of course, be taken into account in relation to each of these factors).

14.10 As well as or instead of using these powers, the FSA may ask the relevant *regulatory body* of the country or territory in which the *scheme* is authorised to take such action in respect of the *scheme* and/or its *operator*, *trustee* or *depositary* as will resolve the FSA's concerns.

14.10A Decisions about whether to apply to the civil courts for *collective investment scheme* related orders under the *Act* will be made by the *RDC* Chairman or, in an urgent case and if the Chairman is not available, by an *RDC* Deputy Chairman. In an exceptionally urgent case the matter will be decided by the director of Enforcement or, in his or her absence, another member of the FSA's executive of at least director of division level.

14.10B An exceptionally urgent case in these circumstances is one where the FSA staff believe that a decision to begin proceedings

(1) should be taken before it is possible to follow the procedure described in paragraph 14.10A; and

(2) it is necessary to protect the interests of consumers or potential consumers.

CHAPTER 15
DISQUALIFICATION OF AUDITORS AND ACTUARIES

[2219O]

15.1 Auditors and *actuaries* fulfil a vital role in the management and conduct of *firms* and *AUTs*. Provisions of the *Act*, *rules* made under the *Act* and the *OEIC Regulations 2000* impose various duties on auditors and *actuaries*. These duties and the FSA's power to disqualify auditors and *actuaries* if they breach them assist the FSA in pursuing its *regulatory objectives*. The FSA's power to disqualify auditors in breach of duties imposed by *trust scheme rules* also assist the FSA to achieve these *regulatory objectives* by ensuring that auditors fulfil the duties imposed on them by these rules.

Disqualification of auditors and actuaries under its powers contained in section 345 and section 249 of the Act: the FSA's general approach

15.2 The FSA recognises that the use of its powers to disqualify auditors and *actuaries* will have serious consequences for the auditors or *actuaries* concerned and their clients; it will therefore exercise its power to impose a disqualification in a way that is proportionate to the particular breach of duty concerned. The FSA will consider the seriousness of the breach of duty when deciding whether to exercise its power to disqualify and the scope of any disqualification.

15.3 *Actuaries* appointed by *firms* under rule 4.3.1 of the FSA's Supervision Manual are *approved persons* and as such will be subject to the FSA's *Statements of Principle* and *Code of Practice for Approved Persons*. When deciding whether to exercise its power to disqualify an *actuary* who is an *approved person*, the FSA will consider whether the particular breach of duty can be adequately addressed by the exercise of its disciplinary powers in relation to *approved persons*.

15.4 In cases where the nature of the breach of duties imposed on the auditors and *actuaries* under the *Act* (and/or in the case of actuaries imposed by *trust scheme rules*) is such that the FSA has concerns about the fitness and propriety of an individual auditor or *actuary*, the FSA will consider whether it is appropriate to make a *prohibition order* instead of, or in addition to, disqualifying the individual.

15.5 A disqualification order will be made against the *person* appointed as auditor or *actuary* of the *firm*. In the case of *actuaries*, the disqualification order will be made against the individual appointed by the *firm*. In the case of auditors, the disqualification order will depend on the terms of the appointment. Where the *firm* has appointed a named individual as auditor the disqualification will be made against that individual and this will be the case where the individual concerned is a member of a *firm* of auditors. Where the *firm* has appointed a firm as auditor the disqualification order will be against that firm. Where the *person* appointed is a *limited liability partnership* the disqualification order will be against the *limited liability partnership* rather than its members.

Disqualification under section 345

15.6 When it decides whether to exercise its power to disqualify an auditor or *actuary* under section 345(1), and what the scope of any disqualification will be, the FSA will take into account all the circumstances of the case. These may include, but are not limited to, the following factors:

(1) the nature and seriousness of any breach of rules and the effect of that breach: the rules are set out in SUP 3 (Auditors) and SUP 4 (*Actuaries*), and in the case of *firms* which are *ICVCs*, in COLL 4 (Investor relations) and COLL 7 (Suspension of dealings and termination of authorised funds). The FSA will regard as particularly serious any breach of *rules* which has resulted in, or is likely to result in, loss to *consumers* or damage to confidence in the *financial system* or an increased risk that a *firm* may be used for the purposes of *financial crime*;

(2) the nature and seriousness of any breach of the duties imposed under the *Act*: the FSA will regard as particularly serious any failure to disclose to it information which has resulted in, or is likely to result in, loss to *consumers* or damage to confidence in the *financial system* or an increased risk that a *firm* may be used for the purposes of *financial crime*;

(3) action taken by the auditor or *actuary* to remedy the *breach*: this may include whether the auditor or *actuary* brought the *breach* to the attention of the FSA promptly, the degree of cooperation with the FSA in relation to any subsequent investigation, and whether remedial steps have been taken to rectify the breach and whether reasonable steps have been taken to prevent a similar breach from occurring;

(4) action taken by professional bodies: the FSA will consider whether any disciplinary action has been or will be taken against the auditor or *actuary* by a relevant professional body and whether that action adequately addresses the particular breach of duty;

(5) The previous compliance record of the auditor or *actuary* concerned: whether the FSA (or a *previous regulator*) or professional body has imposed any previous disciplinary sanctions on the *firm* or individual concerned.

Disqualification under section 249

15.7 When deciding whether or not to disqualify an auditor under section 249(1) of the *Act* (concerning the power to disqualify an auditor for breach of *trust scheme rules*), and in setting the disqualification, the FSA will take into account all the circumstances of the case. These may include, but are not limited to, the following circumstances:

(1) the effect of the auditor's breach of a duty imposed by *trust scheme rules*: the FSA will regard as particularly serious a breach of a duty imposed by *trust scheme rules* (set out in COLL 4 (Investor relations) and COLL 7 (Suspension of dealings and termination of authorised funds)) which has resulted in, or is likely to result in, loss to *consumers* or damage to confidence in the *financial system* or an increased risk that a *firm* may be used for the purposes of *financial crime*;

(2) action taken by the auditor to remedy its breach of a duty imposed by *trust scheme rules*: this may include any steps taken by the auditor to bring the breach to the attention of the FSA promptly, the degree of co-operation with the FSA in relation to any subsequent investigation, and whether any steps have been taken to rectify the breach or prevent a similar breach;

(3) action taken by a relevant professional body: The FSA will consider whether any disciplinary action has or will be taken against the auditor by a relevant professional body and whether such action adequately addresses the particular breach of a duty imposed by *trust scheme rules*;

(4) the previous compliance record of the auditor concerned: whether the FSA (or a *previous regulator*) or professional body has imposed any previous disciplinary sanctions on the *firm* or individual concerned.

Removal of a disqualification

15.8 An auditor or *actuary* may ask the FSA to remove the disqualification at any time after it has been imposed. The FSA will remove a disqualification if it is satisfied that the disqualified *person* will in future comply with the duty in question (and other duties under the *Act*). When it considers whether to grant or refuse a request that a disqualification be removed on these grounds, the FSA will take into account all the circumstances of a particular case. These circumstances may include, but are not limited to:

(1) the seriousness of the breach of duty that resulted in the disqualification;

(2) the amount of time since the original disqualification; and

(3) any steps taken by the auditor or *actuary* after the disqualification to remedy the factors which led to the disqualification and any steps taken to prevent a similar breach of duty from happening again.

CHAPTER 16
DISAPPLICATION ORDERS AGAINST MEMBERS OF THE PROFESSIONS

The FSA's general approach to making disapplication orders

[2219P]

16.1 The FSA's power under section 329 of the *Act* to make an order disapplying an exemption from the *general prohibition* in relation to a *person* who is a *member* of the professions on the grounds that the *member* is not a fit and proper person to conduct *exempt regulated activities*, and to maintain a public record of disapplication orders, will assist the FSA in pursuing its *regulatory objectives*.

16.2 The FSA may make a range of disapplication orders depending on the particular circumstances of each case, including the range of *exempt regulated activities* undertaken and the particular *exempt regulated activities* to which the *person's* lack of fitness and propriety in that context is relevant.

16.3 The FSA recognises that a decision to make a disapplication order may have serious consequences for a *member* in relation not only to the conduct by the member of *exempt regulated activities*, but also in relation to the other business carried on by the *member*. When it decides whether to exercise its power to make a disapplication order, the FSA will consider all relevant circumstances including whether other action, in particular the making of a *prohibition order* (see chapter 9 of this guide), would be more appropriate. In general, the FSA is likely to exercise its powers to make an order disapplying an exemption where it considers that a *member* of a profession presents such a risk to the FSA's *regulatory objectives* that it is appropriate to prevent the *member* from carrying out the *exempt regulated activities*. The FSA will also have regard to any disciplinary action taken, or to be taken, against the *person* by the relevant *designated professional body*.

Disapplication orders

16.4 When the FSA has concerns about the fitness and propriety of a *member* to carry out *exempt regulated activities*, it will consider all the relevant circumstances of the case, including whether those concerns arise from the fitness and propriety of specific individuals engaged to perform the *exempt regulated activities* carried out by the *member* or whether its concerns arise from wider concerns about the *member* itself.

16.5 In most cases, where the FSA is concerned about the fitness and propriety of a specific individual, it may be more appropriate for the FSA to consider whether to make an order prohibiting the individual from performing functions in relation to *exempt regulated activities* rather than a disapplication order in relation to the *member* concerned. The criteria which the FSA will apply when determining whether to make a prohibition order against an individual who is not regulated by the FSA are set out in paragraphs 9.17 to 9.18 of this guide (*prohibition orders* against other individuals). In addition to the factors referred to in these paragraphs, the FSA may also take into consideration any disciplinary action that has been, or will be taken against the individual concerned by the relevant *designated professional body*, where that disciplinary action reflects on the fitness and propriety of the individual concerned to perform *exempt regulated activities*.

16.6 The FSA will also take into account the potentially more serious consequences that a disapplication of an exemption will have for the *member* concerned compared with the consequences of a prohibition of a particular individual engaged in *exempt regulated activities*. However, the FSA may consider it appropriate in some cases to disapply an exemption where it decides that the *member* concerned is not fit and proper to carry out *exempt regulated activities* in accordance with section 327 of the *Act* (Exemption from the general prohibition).

16.7 As an alternative to making an order to disapply an exemption, the FSA may consider issuing a private warning. A private warning may be appropriate where the FSA has concerns in relation to a *member's* fitness and propriety but feels that its concerns in relation to the conduct of *exempt regulated activities* can be more appropriately addressed by a private warning than by a disapplication of the *member's* exemption.

16.8 When it decides whether to exercise its power to disapply an exemption from the *general prohibition* in relation to a *member*, the FSA will take into account all relevant circumstances which may include, but are not limited to, the following factors:

(1) Disciplinary or other action taken by the relevant *designated professional body*, where that action relates to the fitness and propriety of the *member* concerned: where the FSA considers that its concerns in relation to the fitness and propriety of the *member* concerned may be, or have been adequately addressed by disciplinary or other action taken by the relevant *designated professional body* it may consider not making a disapplication order in addition to such action; however, where the FSA considers that its concerns, and in particular, any risks presented to the *member's clients* in respect of its *exempt regulated activities*, are not adequately addressed by that action, the FSA will consider making a disapplication order;

(2) The significance of the risk which the *member* presents to its *clients*: if the FSA is satisfied that there is a significant risk to *clients* and *consumers* it may consider making a disapplication order;

(3) The extent of the *member's* compliance with rules made by the FSA under section 332(1) of the *Act* (Rules in relation to whom the general prohibition does not apply) or by the relevant *designated professional body* under section 332(3) of the *Act*.

16.9 Where the FSA is considering whether to exercise its power to make a disapplication order in relation to a *member*, it will liaise closely with the relevant *designated professional body*.

16.10 Where the FSA is considering making a disapplication order against a *member* as a result of a breach of *rules* made by the FSA under section 323(1) of the *Act*, it will take into account any proposed application by the *member* concerned for *authorisation* under the *Act*. The FSA may refrain from making a disapplication order pending its consideration of the application for *authorisation*.

Applications under section 329(3) for variation or revocation of disapplication orders

16.11 When considering whether to grant or refuse an application under section 329(3) of the *Act* to vary or revoke a disapplication order, the FSA will take into account all the relevant circumstances. These may include, but are not limited to:

(1) any steps taken by the *person* to rectify the circumstances which gave rise to the original order;

(2) whether the *person* has ceased to present the risk to *clients* and *consumers* or to the FSA's *regulatory objectives* which gave rise to the original order;

(3) the circumstances giving rise to the original order and any additional information which, had it been known by the FSA, would have been relevant to the decision to make the order;

(4) the amount of time which has elapsed since the order was made.

16.12 The FSA will not generally grant an application to vary a disapplication order unless it is satisfied that the proposed variation will not result in the *person* presenting the same degree of risk to *clients* or *consumers* that originally gave rise to the order to disapply the exemption. Similarly, the FSA will not revoke a disapplication order unless and until it is satisfied that the *person* concerned is fit and proper to carry out *exempt regulated activities* generally or those specific *exempt regulated activities* in relation to which the exemption has been disapplied.

The effect of a disapplication order

16.13 When the FSA has made a disapplication order, the *member* against which it has been made may not perform the *exempt regulated activities* to which the order relates. If the member contravenes the order, there will be a breach of the *general prohibition* that may be prosecuted under section 23 of the *Act* (see chapter 12).

16.14 A disapplication order in relation to *exempt regulated activities* made against a *member* will be relevant should that *member* subsequently apply for *authorisation* under the *Act*. Whether or not such an application for *authorisation* is successful will depend on many factors, including the FSA's grounds for making the disapplication order. For example, if the order for disapplication of the exemption was made on the grounds of a breach of *rules* made under 332(1) the FSA may accept an application for *authorisation* notwithstanding the disapplication order. If, however, the order was made on grounds of a breach of the rules of a *designated professional body* resulting in a significant risk to *clients* in relation to the provision of *exempt regulated activities*, it is unlikely that an application for approval made by the *member* would be accepted by the FSA before the revocation of the disapplication order.

CHAPTER 17

[deleted]

CHAPTER 18
CANCELLATION OF APPROVAL AS SPONSOR ON THE FSA'S OWN INITIATIVE

[2219Q]

18.1 The FSA may cancel a *sponsor's* approval under section 88 of the *Act* if it considers that a *sponsor* has failed to meet the criteria for approval as a *sponsor* as set out in LR 8.6.5R.

18.2 When considering whether to cancel a *sponsor's* approval on its own initiative, the FSA will take into account all relevant factors, including, but not limited to, the following:
(1) the competence of the *sponsor*;
(2) the adequacy of the *sponsor's* systems and controls;
(3) the *sponsor's* history of compliance with the *listing rules*;
(4) the nature, seriousness and duration of the suspected failure of the *sponsor* to meet (at all times) the criteria for approval as a *sponsor* set out in LR 8.6.5R;
(5) any matter which the FSA could take into account if it were considering an application for approval as a *sponsor* made under section 88(3)(d) of the *Act*.

CHAPTER 19
NON-FSMA POWERS

Introduction

[2219R]

19.1 This chapter describes many of the powers that the FSA has to enforce requirements imposed under legislation other than the *Act*. The chapter is ordered chronologically, ending with the most recent legislation. Where powers under different pieces of legislation are broadly the same, or apply to the same class of person, we have set out the relevant statements of policy in one section to avoid duplication.

19.2 Where conduct may amount to a breach of more than one enactment, the FSA may need to consider which enforcement powers to use and whether to use powers from one or more of the Acts. Which power or powers are appropriate will vary according to the circumstances of the case. However, where appropriate, we have tried to adopt procedures in respect of our use of powers under legislation other than the Act which are akin to those used under the *Act*. We expect, for example, to provide the subject of an investigation with confirmation of the reasons for the investigation and the legislative provisions under which it is conducted unless notification would be likely to prejudice the investigation or otherwise result in it being frustrated.

Industrial and Provident Societies Act 1965 (IPSA65)

Friendly and Industrial and Provident Societies Act 1968 (FIPSA68)

Friendly Societies Act 1974 (FSA74)

Friendly Societies Act 1992 (FSA92)

19.3 The FSA has certain functions in relation to what are described as "registrant-only" mutual societies. These societies are not regulated or supervised under the Act. Instead, they are subject to the provisions of IPSA65, FIPSA68, FSA74 and FSA92, which require them to register with the FSA and fulfil certain other obligations, such as the requirement to submit annual returns.

19.4 IPSA65, FIPSA68, FSA74 and FSA92 provide the FSA with certain powers to ensure that registrant-only societies meet the requirements imposed on them. These include the power to:

- cancel or suspend the society's registration (ss 16 and 17 IPSA65, s 91 FSA74);
- dissolve the society (ss 95 and 95A FSA74);
- appoint an accountant or actuary to inspect the society's books (s 47 IPSA65);
- require the production of documents and provision of information for certain purposes (s 48 IPSA65, s 90 FSA74);
- appoint inspectors and call special meetings (s 49 IPSA65, s 90 FSA74);
- present petitions for winding up (s 56 IPSA65; ss 22 and 52 FSA92); and
- prosecute failures to comply with requirements (s 61 IPSA65, s 18 FIPSA68 s 98 FSA74).

19.5 The FSA's enforcement activities in respect of registrant-only societies focus on prosecuting societies that fail to submit annual returns. As registrant-only societies are not subject to the rules imposed by the *Act* and by the FSA Handbook, the requirement that they submit annual returns provides an important check that the interests and investments of members, potential members, creditors and other interested parties are being safeguarded. The power to prosecute registrant-only societies who fail to meet this requirement is therefore an important tool and one which the FSA is committed to using in appropriate cases.

19.6 The FSA considers a variety of factors when deciding whether to prosecute a society for failing to submit its annual return. The FSA is more likely to prosecute a society which has previously failed to submit returns, or which poses a greater risk to the FSA's statutory objectives, for example, because of the size of its financial resources or its number of members.

19.7 The FSA may also use its power to petition for the society's winding up where it has prosecuted a society but the society continues to fail to submit the outstanding annual returns or defaults on submitting further returns.

19.8 The decision whether to initiate criminal and other proceedings under these Acts will be taken in accordance with the procedure described in EG 12.4C. Under section 18 IPSA65, a society may appeal certain decisions of the FSA relating to the refusal, cancellation or suspension of a society's registration to the High Court or, in Scotland, the Court of Session. Refusals to register a branch or to register the amendment of a society's rules and cancellations or suspensions of a society's listing under the Friendly Societies Act 1974 are also appealable in certain circumstance to the High Court or the Court in Sessions. Distinguishing features of the procedure for giving statutory notices under the FSA92, including available rights of reference to the *Tribunal*, are set out in DEPP 2.5.18G.

19.9 Further information about the FSA's powers under IPSA65 and FSA74 can be found on the FSA's website.[13]

Credit Unions Act 1979

19.10 The Credit Unions Act enables certain societies in Great Britain to be registered under IPSA65 and makes provisions in respect of these societies. It gives the FSA certain powers in addition to the powers that it has under the Act in respect of those credit unions which are *authorised persons*. The FSA's powers under the Credit Unions Act include the power to:

- require the production of books, accounts and other documents in the exercise of certain functions (section 17);
- appoint an investigator or to call a special meeting of the credit union (section 18);
- cancel the registration of the credit union (section 20); and
- petition the High Court to wind up the credit union in particular circumstances (section 20).

19.11 The FSA will use these powers in a manner consistent with its approach to using the same powers under the *Act*. Where the FSA decides to cancel or suspend a credit union's registration under section 20(1) of the Credit Unions Act, the credit union may appeal that decision to the High Court or, in Scotland, the Court of Session.

19.12 The Credit Unions Act also extends to credit unions some criminal offences under IPSA65. The FSA will act in accordance with EG 12 when prosecuting these offences.

Buildings Societies Act 1986

19.13 The Building Societies Act sets out provisions on matters relating, amongst other things, to the constitution and management of building societies. It extends certain of the FSA's enforcement powers under the *Act* so that the FSA may, for example:

- make a prohibition order against the society (section 36A);
- petition the High Court for a winding up order where a society breaches certain requirements, for example, if it contravenes a prohibition order or where it fails to comply with certain directions given to it by the FSA (section 37); and
- exercise the FSA's powers under section 45 of the *Act* to cancel or vary a *Part IV permission* where a society fails to comply with a direction from the FSA to transfer all its engagements or to transfer its business (section 42B).

19.14 The FSA will use these powers in a manner consistent with its approach to using them under the *Act*. Distinguishing features of the procedure for giving statutory notices under the Building Societies Act are set out in DEPP 2.5.18G. Decisions of the FSA made under the Building Societies Act may not be referred to the *Tribunal*.

Unfair Terms in Consumer Contracts Regulations 1999

19.15 The FSA has published a separate regulatory guide, UNFCOG, which describes how it will use the general powers under the *Unfair Terms Regulations*, including its powers to obtain undertakings and seek information from firms. In addition, EG 10 describes how the FSA will use its injunctive powers under these Regulations.

Regulation of Investigatory Powers Act 2000 (RIPA)

19.16 RIPA provides methods of surveillance and information gathering to help the FSA in the prevention and detection of crime. RIPA ensures that, where these methods are used, an individual's rights to privacy under Article 8 of the European Convention of Human Rights are considered and protected.

19.17 Under RIPA the FSA is able to:

- acquire data relating to communications;
- carry out covert surveillance;
- make use of covert human intelligence sources (CHIS); and
- access electronic data protected by encryption or passwords.

19.18 The FSA is not able to obtain warrants to intercept communications during the course of transmission.

19.19 The FSA is only able to exercise powers available to it under Parts I and II of RIPA where it is necessary for the purpose of preventing or detecting crime. All RIPA authorisations for the acquisition of communications data, the carrying out of directed surveillance and the use of CHIS must be approved by a Head of Department in the Enforcement Division. Authorisation will only be given where the authorising officer believes that the proposed action is necessary and proportionate in the specific circumstances set out in the application. Consideration will be given to any actual or potential infringement of the privacy of individuals who are not the subjects of the investigation or operation (collateral intrusion) and to the steps taken to avoid or minimise any such intrusion. When considering whether the proposed action is necessary and proportionate the following non-exhaustive list of factors is likely to be relevant:

- the seriousness of the offence;
- the amount of material that might be gathered;
- the nature of the material that might be gathered;
- whether there are other less intrusive ways of obtaining the same result;
- whether the proposed activity is likely to satisfy the objective; and
- where surveillance is proposed, the location of the surveillance operation.

Encryption

19.20 Under Part III RIPA the FSA is able to require a person who holds "protected" electronic information (that is, information which is encrypted) to put that information into an intelligible form and, where the person has a key to the encrypted information, to require the person to disclose the key so that the data may be put into an intelligible form. The FSA may impose such a requirement where it is necessary for the purpose of preventing or detecting crime or where it is necessary for the purpose of securing the effective exercise or proper performance by the FSA of its statutory powers or statutory duties. In order to serve a notice under Part III RIPA, the FSA must obtain written permission from an appropriate judicial authority. The FSA does not anticipate using powers under Part III very often as it expects firms and individuals to provide information in intelligible format pursuant to requirements to provide information under the *Act*.

Home Office Codes of Practice

19.21 In exercising powers under RIPA the FSA has regard to the relevant RIPA codes of practice. The Codes are available on the Home Office website: security.homeoffice.gov.uk/ripa/publication-search/ripa-cop/.

Complaints and Oversight

19.22 RIPA provides for the appointment of Commissioners to oversee the compliance of designated authorities with RIPA requirements, and the establishment of a tribunal with jurisdiction to consider and determine, amongst other things, complaints and referrals about the way in which the FSA and other public bodies use their RIPA powers.

Regulated Activities Order 2001 (RAO)

19.23 The RAO sets out those activities which are regulated for the purposes of the Act. Part V of the RAO also requires the FSA to maintain a register of all those people who are not authorised by the FSA but who carry on insurance mediation activities. Under article 95 RAO, the FSA has the power to remove from the register an appointed representative who carries on insurance mediation activities if it considers that he is not fit and proper. The FSA will give the person a *warning notice* informing him that it proposes to remove his registration and a *decision notice* if the decision to remove his registration is taken. The decisions to give a *warning notice* or a *decision notice* will be taken by the *RDC* following the procedures set out in DEPP 3.2 or, where appropriate, DEPP 3.3. A person who receives a decision notice under article 95 RAO may refer the matter to the *Tribunal*.

The Open-Ended Investment Companies Regulations 2001

19.24 The *OEIC Regulations* set out requirements relating to the way in which collective investment may be carried on by open-ended investment companies. Under the *OEIC Regulations*, the FSA has the power, amongst other things, to:

- revoke an open-ended investment company's authorisation in several situations, including where the firm breaches relevant requirements or provides us with false or misleading information (regulation 23);
- give, vary and revoke certain directions, including that the affairs of the company be wound up (regulations 25 and 28);
- apply to court for an order that a depositary or director of a company be removed and replaced (regulation 26);
- appoint one or more competent persons to investigate and report on the affairs of the company and specified others (regulation 30).

19.25 Factors that the FSA may take into account when it decides whether to use one or more of these powers include, but are not limited to, factors which are broadly similar to those in EG 14.1 in the context of *AUTs*. However, the relevant conduct will be that of the *ICVC*, the *director* or *directors* of the *ICVC* and its *depositary*. Another difference is that the FSA is also able to take disciplinary action against the *ICVC* itself since the *ICVC* will be an *authorised person*. When choosing which powers to use, the FSA will adopt an approach which is broadly similar to that described in EG 14.2 to 14.5.

19.26 The FSA will give a company a *warning notice* if it proposes to revoke the company's authorisation and a *decision notice* if the decision to revoke the company's authorisation is subsequently taken. The decisions to give a *warning notice* or a *decision notice* will be taken by the *RDC* following the procedures set out in DEPP 3.2 or, where appropriate, DEPP 3.3. A person who receives a decision notice under the *OEIC Regulations* may refer the matter to the *Tribunal*.

19.27 Under the *OEIC Regulations*, the FSA may also use its disqualification powers against auditors who fail to comply with a duty imposed on them under FSA rules. The procedure which the FSA will follow when exercising its disqualification powers is set out in EG 15.

Electronic Commerce Directive (Financial Services and Markets) Regulations 2002

19.28 The FSA has powers under regulation 6 of the *ECD Regulations*, provided certain policy and procedural conditions are met, to direct that an *incoming ECA provider* may no longer carry on a specified *incoming electronic commerce activity*, or may only carry it on subject to specified requirements.

Electronic commerce activity directions: the FSA's policy

19.29 The FSA will exercise the power to make an *electronic commerce activity direction* on a case-by-case basis. When deciding whether to make a direction, the FSA will undertake an assessment of whether the circumstances of the particular case meet the policy conditions set out in regulation 6.

19.30 On obtaining information concerning possible *financial crime* facilitated through or involving an *incoming ECA provider*, or detriment to UK markets or UK *ECA recipients* caused by the activities of an *incoming ECA provider*, the FSA will contact the relevant *EEA regulator* of the *incoming ECA provider*. The FSA would expect the relevant *EEA regulator* to consider the matter, investigate it where appropriate and keep the FSA informed about what action, if any, was being taken. The FSA may not need to be involved further if the action by the relevant *EEA regulator* addresses the FSA's concerns.

19.31 However, there are likely to be circumstances in which the FSA will need to use the *electronic commerce activity direction* power. Examples could include where it was necessary to stop the behaviour complained of, or to make the continued provision of services by the *incoming ECA provider* conditional upon compliance with specified requirements. Overall, the FSA may use the direction power:

(1) where:
   (a) the behaviour complained of was causing, or had the potential to cause, major detriment to *consumers* in the United Kingdom; or
   (b) the *incoming ECA provider's* activities have been used, or have the potential to be used, to facilitate serious *financial crime* or to launder the proceeds of a crime; or

(c) the making of the direction is considered to be necessary for other reasons of public policy relevant to the *regulatory objectives*; and

(2) either:

(a) the relevant *EEA regulator* is unable to take action, or has not within a reasonable time taken action which appears to the FSA to be adequate; or

(b) the relevant *EEA regulator* and the FSA agree that, having regard to the circumstances of the particular case, action against the wrong-doing would be taken more effectively by the FSA.

19.32 The question of whether the FSA decides to prevent or prohibit the *incoming electronic commerce activity*, or to make it subject to certain requirements (for example, compliance with specified rules), will depend on the overall circumstance of the case. A relevant consideration will be whether the FSA is satisfied that its concerns over the *incoming electronic commerce activity* can be adequately addressed through the imposition of a requirement, rather than a complete prohibition on the activity. Set out below is a list of factors the FSA may consider. The list is not exhaustive.

(1) The extent of any loss, or risk of loss, or other adverse effect on UK *ECA recipients*: The more serious the loss or potential loss or other adverse effect on them, the more likely it is to be appropriate for the FSA to use its powers to prohibit the activity altogether, to protect the interests of UK *ECA recipients*.

(2) The extent to which customer assets appear to be at risk.

(3) The risk that the *incoming ECA provider's* activities may be used or have been used to facilitate *financial crime* or to launder the proceeds of a crime: Information available to the FSA, including information supplied by other law enforcement agencies, may suggest that the *incoming ECA provider* is being used for, or is itself involved in, financial crime. Where this appears to be the case, a direction that the *incoming electronic commerce activity* should cease may be appropriate.

(4) The risk that the *incoming ECA provider's* activities present to the *financial system* and to confidence in the *financial system*.

(5) The impact that a complete prohibition on the activity would have on UK *ECA recipients*.

19.33 The FSA may consider that a case is urgent, in particular, where:

(1) the information available to it indicates serious concerns about the *incoming electronic commerce activity* that need to be addressed immediately; and

(2) circumstances indicate that it is appropriate to use the direction power immediately to prohibit the *incoming electronic commerce activity*, or to make the carrying on of the activity subject to specified requirements.

19.34 The FSA will consider the full circumstances of the case when deciding whether exercising the direction power, without first taking the procedural steps set out in regulation 6, is an appropriate response to such concerns. The factors the FSA may consider include those listed in paragraph 19.32 of this guide. There may be other relevant factors.

Decision making

19.35 The FSA's decision to make, revoke or vary an *electronic commerce activity direction* will generally be taken by the RDC Chairman. However, this is subject to two exceptions.

(1) In an urgent case and if the Chairman is not available, the decision will be taken by an *RDC* Deputy Chairman and where possible, but subject to the need to act swiftly, one other *RDC* member.

(2) If a provider who has been notified of the FSA's intention to make a direction or to vary a direction on its own initiative makes representations within the period and in the manner required by the FSA, then those representations will be considered by the *RDC*, rather than by the *RDC* Chairman alone. Having taken into account the provider's representations, the *RDC* will then decide whether to make the direction, or to vary the existing direction.

19.36 Where a provider must be given the opportunity to make representations in relation to a proposed direction or variation of a direction, the RDC Chairman will determine in each case the manner and the period within which those representations should be made. If the FSA decides to issue a direction or vary it at its own initiative, or if the FSA refuses an application to vary or revoke a direction, the person to whom the direction applies may refer the matter to the *Tribunal*.

Publicity

19.37 Regulation 10(8) of the ECD *Regulations* provides that if the FSA makes a direction, it may publish, in such manner as it considers appropriate, such information about the matter to which the direction relates as it considers appropriate in furtherance of any of the objectives referred to in *paragraph 19.31(1) of this guide*. However, under regulation 10(9), the FSA may not publish information relating to a direction if publication would, in the FSA's opinion, be unfair to the provider to whom the direction applies or prejudicial to the interests of *consumers*.

19.38 When deciding what information, if any, to publish and the appropriate manner of publication, the FSA will consider the full circumstances of each case. The FSA anticipates that it will generally be appropriate to publish relevant details of a direction, in order to protect and inform *consumers*. However, in accordance with the regulation 10(9) prohibition, it will not publish information if it considers that publication would be unfair to the provider or prejudicial to the interests of *consumers*.

Enterprise Act 2002

19.39 The FSA, together with several other UK authorities, has powers under Part 8 of the Enterprise Act to enforce breaches of consumer protection law. Where a breach has been committed, the FSA will liaise with other authorities, particularly the Office of Fair Trading (the OFT), to determine which authority is best placed to take enforcement action. The FSA would generally expect to be the most appropriate authority to deal with breaches by authorised firms in relation to regulated activities.

19.40 The Enterprise Act identifies two main types of breach which trigger the Part 8 enforcement powers. These are referred to as "domestic infringements", which are breaches of UK law, and "Community infringements" which are breaches of the EU legislation listed in Schedule 13 of the Enterprise Act. In both cases the breach must be regarded as harming the collective interests of consumers.

19.41 The Community legislation falling within the FSA's scope under the Enterprise Act is:

- the Unfair Terms in Consumer Contracts Directive;[14]
- the Comparative and Misleading Advertising Directive;[15]
- the E-Commerce Directive;[16]
- the Distance Marketing Directive;[17] and
- the Unfair Commercial Practices Directive.[18]

19.42 The FSA has powers under Part 8 of the Enterprise Act both as a "designated enforcer" in relation to domestic and Community infringements and as a "CPC enforcer" which gives the FSA and other CPC enforcers additional powers in relation to Community infringements so that they can meet their obligations as "competent authorities" under Regulation (EC) No 2006/2004 on co-operation between national authorities responsible for enforcement of consumer protection laws (the CPC Regulation).

The FSA's powers as a designated enforcer

19.43 As a designated enforcer, the FSA has the power to apply to the courts for an enforcement order or an interim enforcement order which requires a person who has committed a breach of applicable legislation not to engage in the conduct which constituted the breach. The FSA may also apply for orders where it thinks that a person is likely to commit a Community infringement.

19.44 The FSA has the power under the Enterprise Act to require any person to provide it with information which will enable it to (i) exercise or consider exercising its functions as an enforcer; or (ii) determine whether a person is complying with an enforcement order or an interim enforcement order. If the FSA requires a person to provide it with information, it must give him a notice setting out the information that it requires and confirming for which of purposes (i) and (ii) above the information is required.

19.45 Before the FSA may apply for an enforcement order, it must consult with:

- the OFT; and
- the person against whom the enforcement order would be made.

The period for consultation is 14 days before an application for an enforcement order can be made, or 7 days in the case of an application for an interim enforcement award. The aim of consultation is to ensure that any action taken is necessary and proportionate, and to ensure that businesses are given a reasonable opportunity to put things right before the courts become involved.

19.46 The Enterprise Act also makes provision for enforcers to accept undertakings from a person who has committed a breach. The undertaking confirms that the person will not, amongst other things, commence, continue or repeat the conduct which constituted or would constitute the breach. There is a general expectation that, if a breach of applicable legislation is committed, or if a Community infringement is likely to be committed, enforcers will seek an undertaking from the person in question before applying to court for an enforcement order against him.

19.47 The FSA may take steps to publish the undertakings it receives, and may apply to the court for an enforcement order if a person fails to comply with an undertaking that he has given.

The FSA's powers as a CPC enforcer

19.48 In addition to its powers as a designated enforcer under the Enterprise Act, the FSA also has powers, in its capacity as a "CPC enforcer", to enter premises with or without a warrant. The FSA must give at least two working days' notice of its intention to enter premises without a warrant unless it has not been possible to serve such notice despite all reasonably practicable steps having been taken. If the FSA cannot give a notice in advance, it must produce the notice on the day the premises are entered.

Use of enforcement powers under Enterprise Act

19.49 The FSA anticipates that its powers under the Act will be adequate to address the majority of breaches which it would also be able to enforce under the Enterprise Act and that there will therefore be limited cases in which it would seek to use its powers as an Enterprise Act enforcer. Where the FSA does use its powers under the Enterprise Act, it will have regard to the enforcement guidelines which are published on the OFT's website.[19]

19.50 Further information about the FSA's powers under the CPC Regulations is provided at paragraphs 19.66 to 19.70 below.

Proceeds of Crime Act 2002 (POCA)

19.51 POCA provides the legislative framework for the confiscation from criminals of the proceeds of their crime. Under POCA, the FSA can apply to the Crown Court for a restraint order when it is investigating or prosecuting criminal cases. A restraint order prevents the person(s) named in the order from dealing with the assets it covers for the duration of the order.

19.52 The FSA may apply for such an order where a criminal investigation has been started or where proceedings have started but not concluded; in either case there must be reasonable cause to believe that the defendant has benefited from criminal conduct. In this context, a person benefits from criminal conduct if he obtains property or a pecuniary advantage as a result of or in connection with conduct that would be an offence if it took place in England or Wales, regardless of whether he also obtains it in some other connection. The court is required to exercise its powers with a view to securing that the value of realisable assets is not diminished.

19.53 Once an order is made, the applicant or anyone affected by the order can apply to the court for it to be varied or discharged. The court must discharge the order if the condition for granting it is no longer satisfied, that is, if the criminal investigation has not led to criminal proceedings being started within a reasonable time or the criminal proceedings have concluded.

19.54 A restraint order may apply to any realisable property held by the specified person whether or not described in the order, or to any such property transferred to him after the order is made. The order may contain exceptions for reasonable living and business expenses, but not for legal expenses relating to the offences from which he is suspected to have benefited for the order to be made.

19.55 The order can apply to assets wherever they are held, and anyone breaching the order would be guilty of contempt of court in this country. The FSA may request that the court make ancillary orders requiring the person to disclose his assets and/or to repatriate assets held overseas.

19.56 POCA also contains various powers of investigation which the FSA may use in specified circumstances. However, where these powers overlap with powers under the Act, the FSA will in most cases consider it more appropriate to rely on its investigation powers under the *Act*.

Credit Institutions (Reorganisation and Winding Up) Regulations 2004

19.57 These Regulations implement Directive 2001/24/EC on the reorganisation and winding up of credit institutions. The Regulations only allow winding-up proceedings or reorganisation measures in respect of EEA credit institutions in certain circumstances.

19.58 Under these Regulations, the FSA is required to exercise its powers under section 45 of the *Act* to vary or cancel the UK credit institution's permission to accept deposits or to issue electronic money as soon as reasonably practicable after it is notified of any of the following:

- a decision which approves a voluntary arrangement where it includes a realisation of some or all of the assets of the credit institution with a view to terminating the whole or any part of the business of that credit institution;
- a winding-up order or an administration order in the prescribed circumstances; or
- the appointment of a provisional liquidator or the appointment of a liquidator.

19.59 This power is mandatory rather than discretionary. The FSA will follow its procedure for varying and cancelling *Part IV permission* under the *Act* when exercising its powers under these Regulations.

Financial Services (Distance Marketing) Regulations 2004

19.60 These Regulations give effect to the Distance Marketing Directive.[20] Under the Regulations, the FSA can enforce breaches of the Regulations concerning "specified contracts". Specified contracts are certain contracts for the provision of financial services which are made at a distance and do not require the simultaneous physical presence of the parties to the contract.

19.61 The FSA may apply to the courts for an injunction or interim injunction against a person who appears to it to be responsible for a breach of the Regulations. The FSA must consult with the OFT before exercising this power. The FSA may also accept undertakings from the person who committed the breach that he will comply with the Regulations. The FSA must publish details of any applications it makes for Directive 2002/65/EC injunctions; the terms of any orders that the court subsequently makes; and the terms of any undertakings given to it or to the court.

19.62 The FSA may also prosecute offences under the Regulations which relate to specified contracts. It will generally be appropriate for the FSA to seek to resolve the breach by obtaining an undertaking before it applies for an injunction or initiates a prosecution. Where a failure by a firm to meet the requirements of the Regulations also amounts to a breach of the FSA's rules, the FSA will consider all the circumstances of the case when deciding whether to take action for a breach of its rules or under the Regulations. This will include, amongst other things, having regard to appropriate factors set out in DEPP 6 and the considerations in EG 12.

Financial Conglomerates and Other Financial Groups Regulations 2004

19.63 These Regulations implement in part the Financial Conglomerates Directive,[21] which imposes certain procedural requirements on the FSA as a competent authority under the Directive. These Regulations also make specific provision about the exercise of certain supervisory powers in relation to financial conglomerates.

19.64 The FSA's power to vary a firm's *Part IV permission* under section 45 of the *Act* has been extended under these Regulations. The FSA is able to use this power where it is desirable to do so for the purpose of:

- supervision in accordance with the Financial Conglomerates Directive;
- acting in accordance with specified provisions of the Banking Consolidation Directive; and
- acting in accordance with specified provisions of the Insurance Groups Directive.

19.65 The duty imposed by section 41(2) (The threshold conditions) of the *Act* does not prevent the FSA from exercising its own-initiative power for these purposes. But subject to that, when exercising this power under the Regulations, the FSA will do so in a manner consistent with its approach generally to variation under the *Act*.

The Consumer Protection Co-operation Regulation[22]

19.66 The FSA is a competent authority under the CPC Regulation, which aims to encourage and facilitate co-operation between competent authorities across the EU in consumer protection matters. The FSA is a competent authority for the purposes of consumer protection laws. specified EU consumer protection laws[23] in the context of the regulated activities of authorised firms and of breaches by UK firms concerning "specified contracts" as defined in the Financial Services (Distance Marketing) Regulations 2004 (for which see paragraphs 19.60 to 19.62).

19.67 All CPC competent authorities have a minimum set of enforcement and investigatory powers available to them to ensure that across the EU there is a robust toolkit to protect consumers. These are powers to:

- access any relevant document related to the breach;
- require the supply by any person of relevant information related to the breach;
- carry out necessary on-site inspections;
- request in writing that a person cease the breach;
- obtain from the person responsible for the breach an undertaking to cease the breach; and, where appropriate, to publish the resulting undertaking;
- require the cessation or prohibition of any breach and where appropriate, to publish resulting decisions; and
- require the losing defendant to make payments in the event of failure to comply with the decision.

19.68 The powers are engaged when a person breaches one of the EU consumer protection laws which are scheduled to the CPC Regulation and the breach is one which harms, or is likely to harm, the collective interests of consumers who live in a member state other than the member state in which the breach was committed; where the person who committed the breach is established; or where evidence or assets relating to the breach are located.

19.69 Under the CPC Regulation the FSA can request information from competent authorities in other member states to help it determine whether a relevant breach has taken, or may take, place. The FSA can also request that competent authorities in the relevant member states take action without delay to stop or prohibit the breach. All competent authorities are required to notify their counterparts in relevant member states when they become aware of actual or possible breaches of European consumer protection law.

19.70 The FSA may use its powers under the Act or under Part 8 of the Enterprise Act (for which, see paragraphs 19.39 to 19.50 above) in order to fulfil its obligations under the CPC Regulation. The FSA will decide on a case-by-case basis which powers will enable it to obtain its desired outcomes in the most effective and efficient way. In the majority of cases this is more likely to be by using its powers under the *Act*.

Money Laundering Regulations 2007

19.71 The FSA has investigation and sanctioning powers in relation to both criminal and civil breaches of the *Money Laundering Regulations*. The *Money Laundering Regulations* impose requirements including, amongst other things, obligations to apply customer due diligence measures and conduct ongoing monitoring of business relationships on designated types of business.

19.72 The FSA is responsible for monitoring and enforcing compliance with the Regulations not only by authorised firms who are within the *Money Laundering Regulations'* scope, but also by what the Regulations describe as "Annex I financial institutions". These are businesses which are not otherwise authorised by us but which carry out certain of the activities listed in Annex I of the Banking Consolidation Directive.[24] The activities include lending (eg forfaiters and trade financiers), financial leasing, and safe custody services. Annex I financial institutions are required to register with the FSA.

19.73 The *Money Laundering Regulations* add to the range of options available to the FSA for dealing with anti-money laundering failures. These options are:

- to prosecute both authorised firms and Annex I financial institutions;
- to take regulatory action against authorised firms for failures which breach the FSA's rules and requirements (for example, under Principle 3 or SYSC 3.2.6R); and
- to impose civil penalties on both authorised firms and Annex I financial institutions under regulation 42 of the *Money Laundering Regulations*.

19.74 This means that there will be situations in which the FSA has powers to investigate and take action under both the *Act* and the *Money Laundering Regulations*. The FSA will consider all the circumstances of the case when deciding what action to take and, if it is appropriate to notify the subject about the investigation, will in doing so inform them about the basis upon which the investigation is being conducted and what powers it is using. The FSA will adopt the approach outlined in EG 12 when prosecuting *Money Laundering Regulations* offences. In the majority of cases where both the Regulations and the FSA rules apply and regulatory action, as opposed to criminal proceedings, is appropriate, the FSA generally expects to continue to discipline authorised firms under the *Act*.

19.75 The *Money Laundering Regulations* also provide investigation powers that the FSA can use when investigating whether breaches of the Regulations have taken place. These powers include:

- the power to require information from, and attendance of, relevant and connected persons (regulation 37); and
- powers of entry and inspection without or under warrant (regulations 38 and 39).

The use of these powers will be limited to those cases in which the FSA expects to take action under the Regulations.

19.76 The FSA will adopt a risk-based approach to its enforcement of the *Money Laundering Regulations*. Failures in anti-money laundering controls will not automatically result in disciplinary sanctions, although enforcement action is more likely where a firm has not taken adequate steps to identify its money laundering risks or put in place appropriate controls to mitigate those risks, and failed to take steps to ensure that controls are being effectively implemented.

19.77 However, the *Money Laundering Regulations* say little about the way in which investigation and sanctioning powers should be used, so the FSA has decided to adopt enforcement and decision making procedures which are broadly akin to those under the *Act*. Key features of the FSA's approach are described below.

The conduct of investigations under the Money Laundering Regulations

19.78 The FSA will notify the subject of the investigation that it has appointed officers to carry out an investigation under the *Money Laundering Regulations* and the reasons for the appointment, unless notification is likely to prejudice the investigation or otherwise result in it being frustrated. The FSA expects to carry out a scoping visit early on in the enforcement process in most cases. The FSA's policy in civil investigations is to use powers to compel information in the same way as it would in the course of an investigation under the *Act*.

19.79 When the FSA proposes or decides to impose a penalty under the *Money Laundering Regulations*, it must give the person on whom the penalty is to be imposed a notice. These notices are akin to *warning notices* and *decision notices* given under the *Act*, although Part XXVI (Notices) of the *Act* does not apply to notices given under the Regulations.

19.80 The *RDC* is the FSA's decision maker for contested cases in which the FSA decides to impose a penalty under the *Money Laundering Regulations*. This builds a layer of separation into the process to help ensure not only that decisions are fair but that they are seen to be fair. The *RDC* will make its decisions following the procedure set out in DEPP 3.2 or, where appropriate, DEPP 3.3. Where the FSA imposes a penalty on a person under the *Money Laundering Regulations*, that person may appeal the decision to the *Tribunal*.

19.81 Although the *Money Laundering Regulations* do not require it, the FSA will involve third parties and provide access to Authority material when it gives notices under the Regulations, in a manner consistent with the provisions of sections 393 and 394 of the *Act*. However, there is no formal mechanism under the *Money Laundering Regulations* for third parties to make representations in respect of proposed money laundering actions. If a third party asks to make representations, it will be a matter for the FSA's decision makers to decide whether this is appropriate and, if so, how best to ensure that these representations are taken into consideration. In general it is expected that decision makers would agree to consider any representations made. Third parties may not refer cases to the *Tribunal* as the *Money Laundering Regulations* give the *Tribunal* no power to hear such referrals.

19.82 When imposing or determining the level of a financial penalty under the Regulations, the FSA's policy includes having regard to relevant factors in DEPP 6.2.1G and DEPP 6.5. The FSA may not impose a penalty where there are reasonable grounds for it to be satisfied that the subject of the proposed action took all reasonable steps and exercised all due diligence to ensure that the relevant requirement of the *Money Laundering Regulations* would be met. In deciding whether a person has failed to comply with a requirement of the *Money Laundering Regulations*, the FSA must consider whether he followed any relevant guidance which was issued by a supervisory authority or other appropriate body; approved by the Treasury; and published in a manner approved by the Treasury. The Joint Money Laundering Steering Group Guidance satisfies this requirement.

19.83 As with cases under the *Act*, the FSA may settle or mediate appropriate cases involving civil breaches of the *Money Laundering Regulations* to assist it to exercise its functions under the Regulations in the most efficient and economic way. The settlement discount scheme set out in DEPP 6.7 applies to penalties imposed under the *Money Laundering Regulations*.

19.84 The FSA will apply the approach to publicity that it has outlined in EG 6. However, as the *Money Laundering Regulations* do not require the FSA to issue final notices, the FSA will publish such information about the matter to which the decision notice relates as it considers appropriate. This will generally involve publishing the decision notice on the FSA's website, with or without an accompanying press release, and updating the Public Register. The timing of publicity will be consistent with the FSA's approach in comparable cases under the *Act*.

Transfer of Funds (Information on the Payer) Regulations 2007 (The Transfer of Funds Regulations)

19.85 The FSA is required, under EU Regulation 1781/2006 (on information on the payer accompanying transfers of funds), to monitor the compliance of payment services providers which are *authorised firms* with the requirements imposed by the Regulation. The Transfer of Funds Regulations set out the FSA's powers to investigate and impose sanctions for breaches of Regulation 1781/2006. The powers are identical to those given under the *Money Laundering Regulations*. The FSA's policy in respect of the use of its powers under the Regulations is the same as the policy it has adopted for the use of *Money Laundering Regulations* powers; the FSA will adopt enforcement procedures broadly akin to those used under the *Act*, with the modifications described in paragraphs 19.78 to 19.84 above.

Regulated Covered Bonds Regulations 2008

19.86 The *RCB Regulations* provide a framework for issuing covered bonds in the UK. Covered bonds issued under the *RCB Regulations* are subject to strict quality controls and both bonds and issuers must be registered with the FSA. The *RCB Regulations* give the FSA powers to enforce these Regulations. Where a person has failed, or is likely to fail, to comply with any obligation under the *RCB Regulations*, the FSA may make a direction that the person take steps to ensure compliance with the Regulations or it may make a direction for the winding up of the owner of the asset pool. The FSA may also remove an *issuer* from the register if it fails to comply with the Regulations. In addition, the FSA may apply to court for an order restraining a person from committing a breach of the Regulations or requiring the person to take steps to remedy the breach. The *RCB Regulations* also give the FSA the power to impose a financial penalty on a person for a breach of the Regulations.

19.87 The FSA may use the information gathering powers set out in section 165 of the Act when monitoring and enforcing compliance with the *RCB Regulations*, and may appoint skilled persons as provided in section 166 of the *Act*.

19.88 The FSA's approach to the use of its enforcement powers, and its statement of policy in relation to imposing and determining financial penalties under the *RCB Regulations*, are set out in RCB 4.2. The FSA's penalty policy includes having regard to the relevant factors in DEPP 6.2.1G and DEPP 6.5 and such other specific matters as the likely impact of the penalty on the interests of investors in the relevant bonds. The FSA's statement of procedure in relation to giving *warning notices* or *decision notices* under the *RCB Regulations* is set out in RCB 6. It confirms that the *RDC* will be the decision maker in relation to the imposition of financial penalties under the *RCB Regulations*, following the procedure outlined in DEPP 3.2 or, where appropriate, DEPP 3.3 and that decision notices given under the Regulations may be referred to the *Tribunal*.

19.89 The FSA may agree to settle cases in which it proposes to impose a financial penalty under the *RCB Regulations* if the right regulatory outcome can be achieved. The settlement discount scheme set out in DEPP 6.7 applies to penalties imposed under the *RCB Regulations*. See DEPP 5 and EG 5 for further information about the settlement process.

Payment Services Regulations 2009

19.90 The *FSA* has investigation and sanctioning powers in relation to both criminal and civil breaches of the *Payment Services Regulations*. The *Payment Services Regulations* impose requirements including, amongst other things, obligations on *payment service providers* to provide users with a range of information and various provisions regulating the rights and obligations of payment service users and providers.

19.91 The *FSA's* approach to enforcing the *Payment Services Regulations* will mirror its general approach to enforcing the *Act*, as set out in EG 2. It will seek to exercise its enforcement powers in a manner that is transparent, proportionate, responsive to the issue, and consistent with its publicly stated policies. It will also seek to ensure fair treatment when exercising its enforcement powers. Finally, it will aim to change the behaviour of the *person* who is the subject of its action, to deter future noncompliance by others, to eliminate any financial gain or benefit from non-compliance, and where appropriate, to remedy the harm caused by the non-compliance.

19.92 The regulatory powers which the *Payment Services Regulations* provide to the *FSA* include:

- the power to require information;
- powers of entry and inspection;
- power of public censure;
- the power to impose financial penalties;
- the power to prosecute or fine unauthorised providers; and
- the power to vary an authorisation on its own initiative.

19.93 The *Payment Services Regulations*, for the most part, mirror the *FSA's* investigative, sanctioning and regulatory powers under the *Act*. The FSA has decided to adopt procedures and policies in relation to the use of those powers akin to those it has under the *Act*. Key features of the *FSA's* approach are described below.

The conduct of investigations under the Payment Services Regulations

19.94 The *Payment Services Regulations* apply much of Part 11 of the *Act*. The effect of this is to apply the same procedures under the *Act* for appointing investigators and requiring information when investigating breaches of the *Payment Services Regulations*.

19.95 The *FSA* will notify the subject of the investigation that it has appointed investigators to carry out an investigation under the *Payment Services Regulations* and the reasons for the appointment, unless notification is likely to prejudice the investigation or otherwise result in it being frustrated. The *FSA* expects to carry out a scoping visit early on in the enforcement process in most cases. The *FSA's* policy in civil investigations under the *Payment Services Regulations* is to use powers to compel information in the same way as it would in the course of an investigation under the *Act*.

Decision making under the Payment Services Regulations

19.96 The RDC is the FSA's decision maker for some of the decisions under the *Payment Services Regulations* as set out in DEPP 2 Annex 1G. This builds a layer of separation into the process to help ensure not only that decisions are fair but that they are seen to be fair. The RDC will make its decisions following the procedure set out in DEPP 3.2 or, where appropriate, DEPP 3.3 and 3.4. DEPP 3.4 applies for urgent notices under Regulations 11(6), (9), and (10)(b) (including as applied by Regulation 14).

19.97 For decisions made by *executive procedures* the procedures to be followed will be those described in DEPP 4.

19.98 The *Payment Service Regulations* do not require the *FSA* to have published procedures to launch criminal prosecutions. However, in these situations the *FSA* expects that it will normally follow its decision-making procedures for the equivalent decisions under the Act.

19.99 The *Payment Service Regulations* require the *FSA* to give third party rights as set out in section 393 of the Act and to give access to certain material as set out in section 394 of the *Act*.

19.100 Certain FSA decisions (for example the cancellation of an authorisation or the imposition of a financial penalty) may be referred to the *Tribunal* by an aggrieved party.

Imposition of penalties under the Payment Services Regulations

19.101 When imposing or determining the level of a financial penalty the *FSA's* policy includes having regard to relevant factors in DEPP 6.2.1G and DEPP 6.5.

19.102 As with cases under the *Act*, the *FSA* may settle or mediate appropriate cases involving civil breaches of the *Payment Services Regulations* to assist it to exercise its functions under the Regulations in the most efficient and economic way. See DEPP 5, DEPP 6.7 and EG 5 for further information on the settlement process and the settlement discount scheme.

Statement of policy in section 169(7) interviews (as implemented by the Payment Services Regulations)

19.103 The *Payment Services Regulations* apply section 169 of the *Act* which requires the *FSA* to publish a statement of policy on the conduct of certain interviews in response to requests from overseas regulators. For the purposes of the *Payment Services Regulations* the *FSA* will follow the procedures described in DEPP 7.

---

13 http://www.fsa.gov.uk/Pages/doing/regulated/law/focus/friendly.shtml

14 Directive 93/13/EEC

15 Directive 97/55/EC

16 Directive 2000/31/EC

17 Directive 2002/65/EC

18 Directive 2005/29/EC

19 www.oft.gov.uk/advice_and_resources/resource_base/legal/enterprise-act/part8

20 Directive 2002/65/EC

21 Diective 2002/87/EC

22 Regulation (EC) No 2006/2004 on co-operation between national authorities responsible for enforcement of consumer protection laws

23 These are the Unfair Terms in Consumer Contracts Directive; the Comparative and Misleading Advertising Directive; the E-Commerce Directive; the Distance Marketing Directive; and the Unfair Commercial Practices Directive

24 Credit financial institutions and money service businesses are also outside the definition of "Annex I financial institution", which is set out in Regulation 22(1)

ANNEX 1

[deleted]

ANNEX 2 – GUIDELINES ON INVESTIGATION OF CASES OF INTEREST OR CONCERN TO THE FINANCIAL SERVICES AUTHORITY AND OTHER PROSECUTING AND INVESTIGATING AGENCIES

Purpose, status and application of the guidelines

[2219S]

1. These guidelines have been agreed by the following bodies (the agencies):

- the Financial Services Authority (the FSA);
- the Serious Fraud Office (the SFO);
- the Department for Business, Enterprise and Regulatory Reform (BERR);
- the Crown Prosecution Service (the CPS);
- the Association of Chief Police Officers in England, Wales and Northern Ireland (ACPO);
- the Crown Office and Procurator Fiscal Service (COPFS);
- the Prosecution Service for Northern Ireland (the PPS);
- the Association of Chief Police Officers in Scotland (ACPOS).

2. The guidelines are intended to assist the agencies when considering cases concerning financial crime and/or regulatory misconduct that are, or may be, of mutual interest to the FSA and one or more of the other agencies. Their implementation and wider points arising from them will be kept under review by the agencies who will liaise regularly.

3. The purpose of the guidelines is to set out some broad principles which the agencies agree should be applied by them in order to assist them to:

(a) decide which of them should investigate such cases;

(b) co-operate with each other, particularly in cases where more than one agency is investigating;

(c) prevent undue duplication of effort by reason of the involvement of more than one agency;

(d) prevent the subjects of proceedings being treated unfairly by reason of the unwarranted involvement of more than one agency.

4. The guidelines are intended to apply to the relationships between the FSA and the other agencies. They are not intended to apply to the relationships between those other agencies themselves where there is no FSA interest. They are not legally binding.

5. The guidelines are subject to the restrictions on disclosure of information held by the agencies. They are not intended to override them.

6. The guidelines are relevant to ACPO and ACPO(S) only in so far as they relate to investigations. Similarly, they are relevant to the CPS, COPFS and the PPS only in so far as they relate to prosecutions.

Commencing Investigations

7. The agencies recognise that there are areas in which they have an overlapping remit in terms of their functions and powers (the powers and functions of the agencies are set out in the Appendix to this document). The agencies will therefore endeavour to ensure that only the agency or agencies with the most appropriate functions and powers will commence investigations.

8. The agencies further recognise that in certain cases concurrent investigations may be the most quick, effective and efficient way for some cases to be dealt with. However, if an agency is considering commencing an investigation and another agency is already carrying on a related investigation or proceedings or is otherwise likely to have an interest in that investigation, best practice is for the agencies concerned to liaise and discuss which agency or agencies should take action, ie investigate, bring proceedings or otherwise deal with the matter.

Indicators for deciding which agency should take action

9. The following are indicators of whether action by the FSA or one of the other agencies is more appropriate. They are not listed in any particular order or ranked according to priority. No single feature of the case should be considered in isolation, but rather the whole case should be considered in the round.

(a) Tending towards action by the FSA

- Where the suspected conduct in question gives rise to concerns regarding market confidence or protection of consumers of services regulated by the FSA.
- Where the suspected conduct in question would be best dealt with by:
  - criminal prosecution of offences which the FSA has powers to prosecute by virtue of the Financial Services and Markets Act 2000 ("the 2000 Act") (See Appendix paragraph 1.4) and other incidental offences;
  - civil proceedings under the 2000 Act (including applications for injunctions, restitution and to wind up firms carrying on regulated activities);
  - regulatory action which can be referred to the Financial Services and Markets Tribunal (including proceedings for market abuse); and
  - proceedings for breaches of Part VI of the *Act*, of *Part 6 rules* or the *Prospectus Rules* or a provision otherwise made in accordance with the *Prospectus Directive*.
- Where the likely defendants are FSA authorised or approved persons.
- Where the likely defendants are issuers or sponsors of a security admitted to the official list or in relation to which an application for listing has been made.
- Where there is likely to be a case for the use of FSA powers which may take immediate effect (eg powers to vary the permission of an authorised firm or to suspend listing of securities).
- Where it is likely that the investigator will be seeking assistance from overseas regulatory authorities with functions equivalent to those of the FSA.
- Where any possible criminal offences are technical or in a grey area whereas regulatory contraventions are clearly indicated.
- Where the balance of public interest is in achieving reparation for victims and prosecution is likely to damage the prospects of this.
- Where there are distinct parts of the case which are best investigated with regulatory expertise.

(b) Tending towards action by one of the other agencies

- Where serious or complex fraud is the predominant issue in the conduct in question (normally appropriate for the SFO).
- Where the suspected conduct in question would be best dealt with by:
  - criminal proceedings for which the FSA is not the statutory prosecutor;
  - proceedings for disqualification of directors under the Company Directors Disqualification Act 1986 (normally appropriate for BERR action);
  - winding up proceedings which FSA does not have statutory powers to bring (normally appropriate for BERR action); or
  - criminal proceedings in Scotland.
- Where the conduct in question concerns the abuse of limited liability status under the Companies Acts (normally appropriate for BERR action).
- Where powers of arrest are likely to be necessary.
- Where it is likely that the investigator will rely on overseas organisations (such as law enforcement agencies) with which the other agencies have liaison.
- Where action by the FSA is likely to prejudice the public interest in the prosecution of offences for which the FSA is not a statutory prosecutor.

- Where the case falls only partly within the regulated area (or criminal offences for which FSA is a statutory prosecutor) and the prospects of splitting the investigation are not good.

10. It is also best practice for the agencies involved or interested in an investigation to continue to liaise as appropriate throughout in order to keep under review the decisions as to who should investigate or bring proceedings. This is particularly so where there are material developments in the investigation that might cause the agencies to reconsider its general purpose or scope and whether additional investigation by others is called for.

Conduct of concurrent investigations

11. The agencies recognise that where concurrent investigations are taking place, action taken by one agency can prejudice the investigation or subsequent proceedings brought by another agency. Consequently, it is best practice for the agencies involved in concurrent investigations to notify each other of significant developments in their investigations and of any significant steps they propose to take in the case, such as:

- interviewing a key witness;
- requiring provision of significant volumes of documents;
- executing a search warrant; or
- instituting proceedings or otherwise disposing of a matter.

12. If the agencies identify that particular action by one party might prejudice an investigation or future proceedings by another, it is desirable for the parties concerned to discuss and decide what action should be taken and by whom. In reaching these decisions, they will bear in mind how the public interest is best served overall. The examples provided in paragraph 9 above may also be used as indicators of where the overall balance of interest lies.

Deciding to bring proceedings

13. The agencies will consider, as necessary, and keep under review whether an investigation has reached the point where it is appropriate to commence proceedings. Where agencies are deciding whether to institute criminal proceedings, they will have regard to the usual codes or guidance relevant to that decision. For example, agencies other than the PPS or the COPFS will have regard to the Code for Crown Prosecutors (Note: Different guidance applies to the PPS and the COPFS. All criminal proceedings in Scotland are the responsibility of the Lord Advocate. Separate arrangements have been agreed between the FSA and the Crown Office for the prosecution of offences in Scotland arising out of FSA investigations). Where they are considering whether to bring non-criminal proceedings, they will take into account whatever factors they consider relevant (for example, in the case of market abuse proceedings brought by the FSA, these are set out in paragraph 6.2 of the FSA Decision Procedure and Penalties manual).

14. The agencies recognise that in taking a decision whether to commence proceedings, relevant factors will include:

- whether commencement of proceedings might prejudice ongoing or potential investigations or proceedings brought by other agencies; and
- whether, in the light of any proceedings being brought by another party, it is appropriate to commence separate proceedings against the person under investigation.

15. Best practice in these circumstances, therefore, is for the parties concerned to liaise before a decision is taken.

Closing Cases

16. It is best practice for the agencies, at the conclusion of any investigation where it is decided that no further action need be taken, or at the conclusion of proceedings, to notify any other agencies concerned of the outcome of the investigation and/or proceedings and to provide any other helpful feedback.

Appendix to the Guidelines on Investigation of Cases of Interest or Concern to the Financial Services Authority and Other Prosecuting and Investigating Agencies

1. The FSA

1.1 The FSA is the single statutory regulator for all financial business in the UK. Its regulatory objectives under the Financial Services and Markets Act 2000 (the 2000 Act) are:

- market confidence;
- public awareness;
- the protection of consumers; and
- the reduction of financial crime.

(**Note**: The 2000 Act repealed and replaced various enactments which conferred powers and functions on the FSA and other regulators whose functions are now carried out by the FSA. Most notable in this context are the Financial Services Act 1986 and the Banking Act 1987. Transitional provisions under the 2000 Act permit the FSA to continue to investigate and bring proceedings for offences under the old legislation. Details of these transitional provisions are not set out in these guidelines)

1.2 The *FSA's regulatory objectives* as the competent authority under Part VI of the *Act* are:
- the protection of investors;
- access to capital; and
- investor confidence.

1.3 Under the 2000 Act the FSA has powers to investigate concerns including:
- regulatory concerns about authorised *firms* and individuals employed by them;
- suspected *market abuse* under s 118 of the 2000 Act;
- suspected misleading statements and practices under s 397 of the 2000 Act;
- suspected *insider dealing* under of Part V of the Criminal Justice Act 1993;
- suspected contraventions of the general prohibition under s 19 of the 2000 Act and related offences;
- suspected offences under various other provisions of the 2000 Act (see below);
- suspected breaches of Part VI of the *Act*, of *Part 6 rules* or the *prospectus rules* or a provision otherwise made in accordance with the *Prospectus Directive*.

The FSA's powers of information gathering and investigation are set out in Part XI of the 2000 Act and in s 97 in relation to its Part VI functions.

1.4 The FSA has power to take the following enforcement action:
- discipline authorised firms under Part XIV of the 2000 Act and approved persons under s 66 of the 2000 Act;
- impose civil penalties in cases of market abuse under s 123 of the 2000 Act;
- prohibit an individual from being employed in connection with a regulated activity, under s 56 of the 2000 Act;
- apply to Court for *injunctions* (or interdicts) and other orders against persons contravening relevant requirements (under s 380 of the 2000 Act) or engaging in *market abuse* (under s 381 of the 2000 Act);
- petition the court for the winding up or administration of companies, and the bankruptcy of individuals, carrying on *regulated activities*;
- apply to the court under ss 382 and 383 of the 2000 Act for restitution orders against persons contravening relevant requirements or persons engaged in *market abuse*;
- require restitution under s 384 of the 2000 Act of profits which have accrued to authorised persons contravening relevant requirements or persons engaged in *market abuse*, or of losses which have been suffered by others as a result of those *breaches*;
- (except in Scotland) prosecute certain offences under the Money Laundering Regulations 1993, Part V Criminal Justice Act 1993 (insider dealing) and various offences under the 2000 Act including (**Note:** The FSA may also prosecute any other offences which are incidental to those which it has express statutory power to prosecute):
  - carrying on *regulated activity* without authorisation or exemption, under s 23;
  - making false claims to be authorised or exempt, under s 24;
  - promoting investment activity without authorisation, under s 25;
  - breaching a prohibition order, under s 56;
  - failing to co-operate with or giving false information to FSA appointed investigators, under s 177;
  - failing to comply with provisions about influence over authorised persons, under s 191;
  - making misleading statements and engaging in misleading practices, under s 397;
  - misleading the FSA, under s 398;
  - various offences in relation to the FSA's Part VI function;
- Fine, issue public censures, suspend or cancel listing for breaches of the Listing Rules by an issuer; and
- Issue public censures or cancel a sponsor's approval.

2. BERR

2.1 The Secretary of State for Business, Enterprise and Regulatory Reform exercises concurrently with the FSA those powers and functions marked with an asterisk in paragraphs 1.3 above. The investigation functions are undertaken by Companies Investigation Branch (CIB) and the prosecution functions by the Legal Services Directorate.

2.2 The principal activities of CIB are, however, the investigations into the conduct of companies under the Companies Acts. These are fact-finding investigations but may lead to follow-up action by CIB such as petitioning for the winding up of a company, disqualification of directors of the company or referring the matter to the Solicitors Office for prosecution. CIB may also disclose information to other prosecution or regulatory authorities to enable them to take appropriate action under their own powers and functions. Such disclosure is, however, strictly controlled under a gateway disclosure regime.

2.3 The Solicitors Office advises on investigation work carried out by CIB and undertakes criminal investigations and prosecutions in respect of matters referred to it by CIB, the Insolvency Service or other directorates of the BERR or its agencies.

3. SFO

3.1 The aim of the SFO is to contribute to:
- reducing fraud and the cost of fraud;
- the delivery of justice and the rule of law;
- maintaining confidence in the UK's business and financial institutions.

3.2 Under the Criminal Justice Act 1987 the Director of the SFO may investigate any suspected offence which appears on reasonable grounds to involve serious or complex fraud and may also conduct, or take over the conduct of, the prosecution of any such offence. The SFO may investigate in conjunction with any other person with whom the Director thinks it is proper to do so; that includes a police force (or the FSA or any other regulator). The criteria used by the SFO for deciding whether a case is suitable for it to deal with are set out in paragraph 3.3.

3.3 The key criterion should be that the suspected fraud is such that the direction of the investigation should be in the hands of those who would be responsible for any prosecution.

The factors that are taken into account include:
- whether the amount involved is at least £1 million (this is simply an objective and recognisable signpost of seriousness and likely public concern rather than the main indicator of suitability);
- whether the case is likely to give rise to national publicity and widespread public concern. That includes those involving government bodies, public bodies, the governments of other countries and commercial cases of public interest;
- whether the case requires highly specialist knowledge of, for example, stock exchange practices or regulated markets;
- whether there is a significant international dimension;
- whether legal, accountancy and investigative skills need to be brought together; and
- whether the case appears to be complex and one in which the use of Section 2 powers might be appropriate.

4. CPS

4.1 The CPS has responsibility for taking over the conduct of all criminal proceedings instituted by the police in England and Wales. The CPS may advise the police in respect of criminal offences. The CPS prosecutes all kinds of criminal offences, including fraud. Fraud cases may be prosecuted by local CPS offices but the most serious and complex fraud cases will be prosecuted centrally.

5. ACPO and ACPO(S)

5.1 ACPO represents the police forces of England, Wales, and Northern Ireland. ACPO(S) represents the police forces of Scotland.

6. COPFS

6.1 The investigation and prosecution of crime in Scotland is the responsibility of the Lord Advocate, who is the head of the COPFS, which comprises Procurators Fiscal and their Deputes, who are answerable to the Lord Advocate. The Procurator Fiscal is the sole public prosecutor in Scotland, prosecuting cases reported not only by the police but all regulatory departments and agencies. All prosecutions before a jury, both in the High Court of Justiciary and in the Sheriff Court, run in the name of the Lord Advocate; all other prosecutions run in the name of the local Procurator Fiscal. The Head Office of the Procurator Fiscal Service is the Crown Office and the Unit within the Crown Office which deals with serious and complex fraud cases and with the investigation of cases of interest or concern to the Financial Services Authority is the National Casework Division: the remit of this Unit is directly comparable to that of the Serious Fraud Office.

7. The PPS

7.1 The PPS is responsible for the prosecution of all offences on indictment in Northern Ireland, other than offences prosecuted by the Serious Fraud Office. The PPS is also responsible for the prosecution of certain summary offences, including offences reported to it by any government department.

TRANSITIONAL PROVISIONS APPLYING TO THE ENFORCEMENT GUIDE

[2219T]

(1)	(2) Material to which the transitional provision applies	(3)	(4) Transitional provision	(5) Transitional provision dates in force:	(6) Regulatory Guide provision coming into force
1	EG		EG takes effect on 28 August 2007, save to the extent described below. The *FSA's* enforcement policy will continue to be as described in the Enforcement manual (ENF) in relation to any *statutory notice* or related notice given on or after 28 August where a *warning notice*, first *supervisory notice* or *decision notice* was given by the *FSA* before 28 August in relation to the same matter.	From 28 August 2007	28 August 2007

PERIMETER GUIDANCE MANUAL (PERG)

NOTES

Up to date as at 22 February 2010. For later amendments please see www.fsa.gov.uk.

CONTENTS

PERG 2—Authorisation and regulated activities . . . . [2220]
PERG 5—Guidance on insurance mediation activities . . . . [2221]
PERG 6—Guidance on the Identification of Contracts of Insurance . . . . [2222]
PERG 8—Financial promotion and related activities
8.17A—Financial promotions concerning insurance mediation activities . . . . [2223]

(*Chapter 1 outside the scope of this work.*)

CHAPTER 2
AUTHORISATION AND REGULATED ACTIVITIES

2.1 Application and purpose

Application

[2220]
2.1.1 **[G]** This chapter is relevant to any *person* who needs to know what activities fall within the scope of the *Act*.

Purpose

2.1.2 **[G]** The purpose of this chapter is to provide *guidance*:
(1) to *unauthorised persons* who wish to find out whether they need to be *authorised* and, if so, what *regulated activities* their *permission* needs to include; and
(2) to *authorised persons* who may have questions about the scope of their existing *permission*.

2.2 Introduction

2.2.1 **[G]** Under section 23 of the *Act* (Contravention of the general prohibition), a *person* commits a criminal offence if he carries on activities in breach of the *general prohibition* in section 19 of the *Act* (The general prohibition). Although a *person* who commits the criminal offence is subject to a maximum of two years imprisonment and an unlimited fine, it is a defence for a *person* to show that he took all reasonable precautions and exercised all due diligence to avoid committing the offence.

2.2.2 **[G]** Another consequence of a breach of the *general prohibition* is that certain agreements could be unenforceable (see sections 26 to 29 of the *Act*). This applies to agreements entered into by *persons* who are in breach of the *general prohibition*. It also applies to any agreement entered into by an *authorised person* if the agreement is made as a result of the activities of a *person* who is in breach of the *general prohibition*.

2.2.3 **[G]** Any *person* who is concerned that his proposed activities may require *authorisation* will need to consider the following questions (these questions are a summary of the issues to be considered and have been reproduced, in slightly fuller form in the decision tree in PERG 2 Annex 1G):
(1) Will I be carrying on my activities by way of business (see PERG 2.3)?
(2) Will I be managing the assets of an *occupational pension scheme* (see PERG 2.3.2G(3))?
(3) If the answer is 'Yes' to (1) or (2), will my activities involve *specified investments* in any way (see PERG 2.6)?
(4) If so, will my activities be, or include, *regulated activities* (see PERG 2.7)?
(5) If so, will I be carrying them on in the *United Kingdom* (see PERG 2.4)?
(6) If so, will my activities be excluded (see PERG 2.8 and PERG 2.9)?
(7) If not, will I be exempt (see PERG 2.10.5G to PERG 2.10.8G)?
(8) If not, am I allowed to carry on *regulated activities* without *authorisation* (see PERG 2.10.9G to PERG 2.10.16G)?
(9) If not, do I benefit from the few provisions of the *Act* that *authorise* me without a *permission* under Part IV of the *Act* (see PERG 2.10.10G (Members of Lloyd's))?
(10) If not, what is the scope of the *Part IV permission* that I need to seek from the *FSA* (see PERG 2 Annex 2G)?

2.2.4 **[G]** The rest of this chapter provides a high level guide through the questions set out in PERG 2.2.3G. It aims to give an overall picture but in doing so it necessarily relies on the reader referring to *UK* statutory provisions and European legislation to fill in the detail (which can be extensive).

2.2.5 **[G]** The process of applying for *Part IV permission* is available on the *FSA* website "How do I get authorised": http://www.fsa.gov.uk/Pages/Doing/how/index.shtml. But a list of the activities for which *permission* may be given is annexed to this chapter (see PERG 2 Annex 2G). You may find this helpful in providing an overview of the activities that are regulated. The list is included here because, with some exceptions, the *investments* and activities for which *permission* may be given are the same as the investments and activities specified in the *Regulated Activities Order*. This creates a few additional categories for which *permission* must be sought.

2.3 The business element

2.3.1 **[G]** Under section 22 of the *Act* (Regulated activities), for an activity to be a *regulated activity* it must be carried on 'by way of business'.

2.3.2 **[G]** There is power in the *Act* for the Treasury to change the meaning of the business element by including or excluding certain things. They have exercised this power (see the Financial Services and Markets Act 2000 (Carrying on Regulated Activities by Way of Business) Order 2001 (SI 2001/1177), the Financial Services and Markets Act 2000 (Regulated Activities) (Amendment) (No 2) Order 2003 (SI 2003/1476) and the Financial Services and Markets Act 2000 (Carrying on Regulated Activities by Way of Business) (Amendment) Order 2005 (SI 2005/922). The result is that the business element differs depending on the activity in question. This in part reflects certain differences in the nature of the activities:

(1) The activity of *accepting deposits* will not be regarded as carried on by way of business by a *person* if he does not hold himself out as *accepting deposits* on a day-to-day basis and if the *deposits* he accepts are accepted only on particular occasions. In determining whether *deposits* are accepted only on particular occasions, the frequency of the occasions and any distinguishing characteristics must be taken into account.

(2) Except as stated in PERG 2.3.2G(2A) and (3), the business element is not to be regarded as sat isfied for any of the *regulated activities* carried on in relation to *securities* or *contractually base investments* (or for those *regulated activities* carried on in relation to 'any property') unless a *person* carries on the business of engaging in one or more of the activities. This also applies to the *regulated activities* of *advising on a home finance transaction* and *arranging a home financ transaction*. This is a narrower test than that of carrying on *regulated activities* by way of business (as required by section 22 of the *Act*), as it requires the *regulated activities* to represent the carrying on of a business in their own right.

(2A) A *person* who carries on an *insurance mediation activity* will not be regarded as doing so by way of business unless he takes up or pursues that activity for remuneration. PERG 2.3.3G give *guidance* on the factors that are relevant to the meaning of 'by way of business' in section 22 c the *Act*. PERG 5.4 (The business test) gives further *guidance* on the business element as applie to *insurance mediation activities*.

(3) A *person* managing assets on a discretionary basis while acting as *trustee* of an *occupational pension scheme* may in certain circumstances be regarded as acting by way of business even if he would not, in the ordinary meaning of the phrase, be regarded as doing so. The Financial Se vices and Markets Act (Carrying on Regulated Activities by Way of Business) Order 2001 (as amended) contains some exceptions from this (see article 4).

(4) The business element for all other *regulated activities* is that the activities are carried on by wa of business. This applies to the activities of *effecting* or *carrying out contracts of insurance*, ce tain activities relating to the Lloyd's market, *entering as provider into a funeral plan contract*, *entering intoa home finance transaction* or *administering a home finance plan*, and operating a *dormant account fund*.

2.3.3 **[G]** Whether or not an activity is carried on by way of business is ultimately a question of judgement that takes account of several factors (none of which is likely to be conclusive). These include the degree of continuity, the existence of a commercial element, the scale of the activity and the proportion which the activity bears to other activities carried on by the same *person* but which are not regulated. The nature of the particular *regulated activity* that is carried on will also be relevant to the factual analysis.

2.4 Link between activities and the United Kingdom

2.4.1 **[G]** Section 19 of the *Act* (The general prohibition) provides that the requirement to be *authorised* under the *Act* only applies in relation to activities that are carried on 'in the *United Kingdom*'. In many cases, it will be quite straightforward to identify where an activity is carried on. But when there is a cross-border element, for example because a client is outside the *United Kingdom* or because some other element of the activity happens outside the *United Kingdom*, the question may arise as to where the activity is carried on.

2.4.2 **[G]** Even with a cross-border element a *person* may still be carrying on an activity 'in the *United Kingdom*'. For example, a *person* who is situated in the *United Kingdom* and who is *safeguarding and administering investments* will be carrying on activities in the *United Kingdom* even though his *client* may be overseas.

2.4.3 **[G]** Section 418 of the *Act* (Carrying on regulated activities in the United Kingdom) takes this one step further. It extends the meaning that 'in the *United Kingdom*' would ordinarily have by setting out five additional cases. The *Act* states that, in these five cases, a *person* who is carrying on a *regulated activity* but who would not otherwise be regarded as carrying on the activity in the *United Kingdom* is, for the purposes of the *Act*, to be regarded as carrying on the activity in the *United Kingdom.*

(1) The first case is where a *UK*-based *person* carries on a *regulated activity* in another *EEA State* in exercise of rights under a *Single Market Directive.*

(2) The second case consists of the *marketing* in another *EEA State* of a *UK*-based *collective investment scheme* by the *scheme*'s *manager* where the *scheme* in question is one to which the *UCITS Directive* applies.

(3) The third case is where a *regulated activity* is carried on by a *UK*-based *person* and the day-to-day management of the activity is the responsibility of an establishment in the *United Kingdom.*

(4) The fourth case is where a *regulated activity* is carried on by a *person* who is not based in the *United Kingdom* but is carried on from an establishment in the *United Kingdom.* This might occur when each of the stages that make up a *regulated activity* (such as *managing investments*) takes place in different countries. For example, a *person*'s management is in country A, the assets are held by a nominee in country B, all transactions take place in country B or country C but all decisions about what to do with the investments are taken from an office in the *United Kingdom.* Given that the investments are held, and all dealings in them take place, outside the *United Kingdom* there may otherwise be a question as to where the *regulated activity* of *managing investments* is taking place. For the purposes of the *Act*, it is carried on in the *United Kingdom.*

(5) The fifth case, inserted by the *ECD Regulations* is, in effect, where an *electronic commerce activity* is carried on, from an *establishment* in the *United Kingdom*, in another *EEA State.*

2.4.4 **[G]** The application of the third and fourth cases will depend on how the activities carried on from the *UK* establishment are set up and operated.

2.4.5 **[G]** A *person* who is based outside the *United Kingdom* but who sets up an establishment in the *United Kingdom* must therefore consider the following matters. First, he must not, unless he is *authorised*, carry on *regulated activities* in the *United Kingdom.* Second, unless he is *authorised*, the day-to-day management of the carrying on of the *regulated activity* must not be the responsibility of the *UK* establishment. This may, for example, affect those *UK* establishments that in the context of *deposit*-taking activities were, before the *commencement* of the *Act*, treated as representative offices of overseas institutions. Such institutions will need to seek *authorisation* if the responsibility for the day-to-day management of the accepting of *deposits* by them outside the *United Kingdom* is nevertheless effectively that of their *UK* establishment. Third, such a *person* will need to ensure that he does not contravene other provisions of the *Act* that apply to *persons* who are not *authorised.* These include the controls on *financial promotion* (section 21 of the *Act* (Financial promotion)), and on giving the impression that a *person* is *authorised* (section 24).

2.4.6 **[G]** A *person* based outside the *United Kingdom* may also be carrying on activities in the *United Kingdom* even if he does not have a place of business maintained by him in the *United Kingdom* (for example, by means of the internet or other telecommunications system or by occasional visits). In that case, it will be relevant to consider whether what he is doing satisfies the business test as it applies in relation to the activities in question. In addition, he may be able to rely on the exclusions from certain *regulated activities* that apply in relation to *overseas persons* (see PERG 2.9.15G).

2.4.7 **[G]** *Electronic commerce activities*, other than *insurance business* falling within the scope of the *Insurance Directives*, provided by an *incoming ECA provider* will not be *regulated activities* (see PERG 2.9.18G(2)).

2.5 Investments and activities: general

2.5.1 **[G]** In addition to the requirements as to the business test and the link to the *United Kingdom*, two other essential elements must be present before a *person* needs *authorisation* under the *Act*. The first is that the *investments* must come within the scope of the system of regulation under the *Act* (see PERG 2.6). The second is that the activities, carried on in relation to those *specified investments*, are regulated under the *Act* (see PERG 2.7). Both *investments* and activities are defined in the *Regulated Activities Order* made by the Treasury under section 22 of the *Act.*

2.5.2 **[G]** The *Regulated Activities Order* contains exclusions. Exclusions may exist in relation to both the element of investment and the element of activity. Each should therefore be checked carefully. The exclusions that relate to *specified investments* are considered in PERG 2.6, together with the outline of the *specified investments*. The exclusions that relate to activities are considered separately from the outline of activities (see PERG 2.8 and PERG 2.9).

Modification of certain exclusions as a result of MiFID and the Insurance Mediation Directive

2.5.3 **[G]** The application of certain of the exclusions considered in PERG 2.8 (Exclusions applicable to certain regulated activities) and PERG 2.9 (Regulated activities: exclusions applicable to certain circumstances) is modified in relation to *persons* who are subject to *MiFID* or the *Insurance Mediation Directive*. The reasons for this and the consequences of it are explained in PERG 2.5.4G as respects *MiFID*, and PERG 5 (Insurance mediation activities), as respects the *Insurance Mediation Directive*.

Investment services and activities

2.5.4 **[G]** It remains the Government's responsibility to ensure the proper implementation of *MiFID*. Certain *persons* subject to the requirements of *MiFID* must be brought within the scope of regulation under the *Act*. A core element of *MiFID* is the concept of "investment firm". An *investment firm* is any *person* whose regular occupation or business is the provision of one or more *investment services* to third parties or the performance of one or more *investment activities* on a professional basis. An *investment firm* is not subject to *MiFID* requirements if it falls within one or more of the exemptions in article 2 *MiFID*. Further information about these exemptions is contained in PERG 13.5. To the extent that an *investment firm* falls within one of these exemptions, it will not be a *MiFID investment firm*. Where a *firm* is not a *MiFID investment firm* because one or more of the exemptions in article 2 apply, it may still be carrying on *regulated activities* and therefore require *authorisation* unless it is an *exempt person*.

2.5.4A The *UK* has exercised the optional exemption in article 3 of *MiFID*. Further information about this exemption is contained in Q48 to 53 in PERG 13.5. It is a requirement of article 3 *MiFID* that the activities of firms relying on the exemption are "regulated at national level". The investment services to which article 3 apply (namely reception and transmission of orders and investment advice in relation to either *transferable securities* or units in collective investment undertakings) correspond to *regulated activities* (see PERG 13 Annex 2 Tables 1 and 2).

2.5.5 **[G]** For *persons* who are *MiFID investment firms*, the activities that must be caught by the *Regulated Activities Order* are those that are caught by *MiFID*. To achieve this result, some of the exclusions in the Order (that will apply to *persons* who are not caught by *MiFID*) have been made unavailable to *MiFID investment firms* when they provide or perform *investment services and activities*. A "MiFID investment firm", for these purposes, includes *credit institutions* to which *MiFID* applies (see PERG 13, Q5 and 9) and *UCITS investment firms* providing the services of *portfolio management* and *personal recommendations* in relation to *financial instruments* or the ancillary service of safekeeping and administration in relation to units of collective investment undertakings. The same exclusions are also unavailable to *third country investment firms* when they provide *investment services and activities*. Article 4(4) of the *Regulated Activities Order* (Specified activities: general) lists a number of exclusions that must be disregarded. These relate to the exclusions concerned with:

(1) the absence of holding out (see PERG 2.8.4G(1));

(2) transactions or arrangements with or through certain *persons* (see PERG 2.8.4G(2), PERG 2.8.5G(1) and PERG 2.8.6G(4));

(3) risk management (see PERG 2.8.4G(5) and PERG 2.8.5G(2));

(4) *persons* acting under powers of attorney (see PERG 2.8.7G);

(4A) professions or businesses not involving *regulated activities* (see PERG 2.9.5G);

(5) sale of goods (see PERG 2.9.7G);

(6) groups and joint enterprises (see PERG 2.9.9G);

(7) sale of a *body corporate* (see PERG 2.9.11G); and

(8) business angel-led enterprise capital funds (see PERG 2.9.20G to PERG 2.9.22G).

Insurance mediation or reinsurance mediation

2.5.6 **[G]** The *Insurance Mediation Directive* has in part been implemented through various amendments to the *Regulated Activities Order*. These include article 4(4A) (Specified activities: general) which precludes a *person* who, for remuneration, takes up or pursues *insurance mediation* or *reinsurance mediation* in relation to a risk or commitment situated in an *EEA State* from making use of certain exclusions. In other cases, some of the exclusions provided in relation to particular *regulated activities* are unavailable where the activity involves a *contract of insurance*. This is explained in more detail in PERG 5 (Insurance mediation activities).

2.6 Specified investments: a broad outline

2.6.1 **[G]** The following paragraphs describe the various *specified investments*, taking due account of any exclusion that applies.

Deposits

2.6.2 **[G]** A *deposit* is defined in article 5(2) of the *Regulated Activities Order*. This focuses on a sum of *money* paid by one *person* to another on terms that it will be repaid when a specified event occurs (for example, a demand is made).

2.6.3 **[G]** Certain transactions are excluded. The definition of *deposit* itself excludes money paid in connection with certain transactions such as advance payments for the provision of goods or services and sums paid to secure the performance of a contract. The circumstances in which payments are excluded from the definition itself are exhaustively stated in article 5(3) of the *Regulated Activities Order* (Accepting deposits). In addition, there is a separate exclusion in article 9 of the Order (Sums received in consideration for the issue of debt securities) and another in article 9A (Sums received in exchange for electronic money). PERG 3.2.15G to PERG 3.2.19G contain *guidance* on the exclusion relating to *electronic money*.

2.6.4 **[G]** In addition, several separate exclusions focus on the identity of the *person* paying the *money* or the *person* receiving it (or both).

(1) Payments by certain *persons* are excluded if they are made by specified *persons* (such as local authorities or national, or supranational, bodies) or by *persons* acting in the course of a business consisting wholly or partly of lending money.

(2) Exclusions apply for sums paid between certain *persons* who are linked in a specified way (such as *group companies* or *close relatives*).

(3) Exclusions apply to sums received by *persons* acting for specified purposes. This covers sums received by a practising solicitor acting in the course of his profession or by *authorised* or *exempt persons* carrying on one of a specified range of *regulated activities* and acting within the scope of their *permission* or exemption.

Electronic money

2.6.4A **[G]** *Electronic money* is specified as an *investment* in article 74A of the *Regulated Activities Order* (as amended by the Financial Services and Markets Act 2000 (Regulated Activities) (Amendment) Order 2002 (SI 2002/682)). It is defined, in article 2 of that Order, as monetary value, as represented by a claim on the issuer, which is stored on an electronic device, issued on receipt of funds and accepted as a means of payment by *persons* other than the issuer. Further *guidance* is given in PERG 3 (Guidance on the scope of the regulated activity of issuing e-money).

Rights under a contract of insurance

2.6.5 **[G]** *Contract of insurance* is defined to include certain things that might not be considered a *contract of insurance* at common law. Examples of such additions include *capital redemption* contracts or contracts to pay annuities on human life. Detailed *guidance* on identifying a *contract of insurance* is in PERG 6 (Guidance on the Identification of Contracts of Insurance).

2.6.6 **[G]** There are two main sorts of *contracts of insurance*. These are *general insurance contracts* and *long-term insurance contracts*. The *Regulated Activities Order* provides that, in certain specified circumstances, a contract is to be treated as a *long-term insurance contract* notwithstanding that it contains supplementary provisions that might also be regarded as relating to a *general insurance contract* (see article 3(3)).

2.6.7 **[G]** The *Regulated Activities Order* uses two further terms in relation to *contracts of insurance* to identify those contracts under which rights are treated as *contractually based investments*.

(1) The first term is 'qualifying contracts of insurance' (referred to as *life policies* in the *Handbook*). This identifies those *long-term insurance contracts* under which rights are treated as *contractually based investments*. This term does not cover *long-term insurance contracts* which are contracts of reinsurance or, if specified conditions are met, contracts under which benefits are payable only on death or incapacity.

(2) The second term is '*relevant investments*'. This term applies to:

  (a) *contractually based investments*, which includes rights under *life policies*, and rights to or interests in such *investments* under article 89 of the *Regulated Activities Order* (Rights to or interests in investments); and

  (b) rights under *contracts of insurance* other than *life policies* (but not rights to or interests in such rights).

  This term is used in connection with the treatment, under various parts of the *Regulated Activities Order*, of *persons* carrying on *insurance mediation activities* (see PERG 5 (Insurance mediation activities) for further *guidance* on such activities).

2.6.8 **[G]** Certain arrangements in relation to funeral plans are specifically excluded from being *contracts of insurance* if they would otherwise be so. The exclusion applies to arrangements that fall within the definition of a *funeral plan contract* (see PERG 2.6.26G) as well as arrangements that are excluded from the *regulated activity* of *entering as provider into funeral plan contracts* (see PERG 2.8.14G).

Shares etc

2.6.9 **[G]** *Shares* are defined in the *Regulated Activities Order* as shares or stock in a wide range of entities; that is, any *body corporate* wherever incorporated and unincorporated bodies formed under the law of a country other than the *United Kingdom*. They include deferred shares issued by *building societies* as well as transferable shares in *industrial and provident societies*, *credit unions* and equivalent *EEA* bodies. These shares are transferable and negotiable in a way similar to other shares or stock and are treated as such for the purposes of defining *regulated activities*. They are specifically mentioned as being within the *specified investment* category of *shares* because other types of share issued by these mutual bodies are not transferable and are expressly excluded (see PERG 2.6.10G).

2.6.10 **[G]** The following are excluded from the *specified investment* category of *shares*. Shares or stock in all *open-ended investment companies* are excluded from being treated in this particular category (but see PERG 2.6.17G). Exclusions from this category also apply to shares or stock in the share capital of certain mutuals or in equivalent *EEA* bodies. This takes out *building society* or *credit union* accounts and non-transferable shares in *industrial and provident societies*. These may nevertheless be *specified investments* in another category (such as *deposits* in the case of *building society* accounts).

Debt instruments

2.6.11 **[G]** Two categories of *specified investments* relating to debt instruments are dealt with under this heading. They broadly split into private debt and public sector debt.

(1) The first category of 'instruments creating or acknowledging indebtedness' (defined in article 77 of the *Regulated Activities Order* and referred to in the *Handbook* as *debentures*) expressly refers to a range of *instruments* such as *debentures*, bonds and loan stock and contains a catch-all reference to 'any other instrument creating or acknowledging indebtedness.'

(2) The second category (defined in article 78 of the *Regulated Activities Order* and referred to in the *Handbook* as *government and public securities*) refers to loan stock, bonds and other instruments creating or acknowledging indebtedness which are issued by or on behalf of any government, the assemblies for Scotland, Wales or Northern Ireland, a local authority or an international organisation.

An instrument cannot fall within both categories of *specified investments* relating to debt instruments. 'Instrument' is defined to include any record whether or not in the form of a document (see article 3(1) of the *Regulated Activities Order*).

2.6.12 **[G]** Certain instruments are excluded from both these categories of *specified investments*. These include trade bills, specified banking documents (such as cheques and banknotes though not bills of exchange accepted by a banker) and *contracts of insurance*. There is a further exclusion from this category of *specified investment* dealing with public debt for National Savings deposits and products.

Warrants

2.6.13 **[G]** The category of *specified investment* of instruments giving entitlements to investments (referred to in the *Handbook* as *warrants*) covers warrants and other instruments which confer an entitlement to subscribe for *shares*, *debentures* and *government and public securities*. This is one of several categories of *specified investments* that are expressed in terms of the rights they confer in relation to other categories of *specified investment*. The rights conferred must be rights to 'subscribe' for the relevant investments. This means that they are rights to acquire the investments directly from the *issuer* of the *investments* and by way of the *issue* of new investments (rather than by purchasing investments that have already been issued).

2.6.14 **[G]** To keep clear distinctions between the different *specified investment* categories, instruments giving entitlements to investments are not to be regarded as *options*, *futures* or *contracts for differences*.

Certificates representing securities

2.6.15 **[G]** The *specified investment* category of *certificates representing certain securities* covers certificates or other instruments which confer rights in relation to *shares* and *debt securities*. It includes depositary receipts.

2.6.16 **[G]** There is an exclusion for any instrument that would otherwise fall within the *specified investment* category of *units* in a *collective investment scheme*. But the exclusion does not apply where the underlying investments covered by the certificate are issued by the same (non-public sector) *issuer* or constitute a single issue of public sector debt (such as a single issue of gilts). Certificates or other instruments conferring rights in respect of investments in these two cases continue to be treated as *certificates representing certain securities*.

Units

2.6.17 **[G]** The *specified investment* category of *units* in a *collective investment scheme* includes *units* in a *unit trust scheme*, *shares* in *open-ended investment companies* and rights in respect of most limited *partnerships*. *Shares* in or *securities* of an *open-ended investment company* are treated differently from *shares* in other *companies*. They are excluded from the *specified investment* category of *shares*. This does not mean that they are not investments but simply that they are uniformly treated in the same way as *units* in other forms of *collective investment scheme*. The effect is that an *open-ended investment company* will, in issuing its *shares*, be subject to the restrictions on promotion of *collective investment schemes* in section 238 of the *Act* (rather than to restrictions that apply to other forms of body corporate). For exclusions from the restrictions on the provisions of *collective investment schemes*, see the Financial Services and Markets Act 2000 (Promotion of Collective Investment Schemes) (Exemptions) Order 2001 (SI 2001/1060). *Guidance* on the meaning of *open-ended investment company* is in PERG 9 (Meaning of open-ended investment company).

2.6.18 **[G]** There are no exclusions in the *Regulated Activities Order* for this *specified investment* category. This is because '*collective investment scheme*' is defined in section 235 of the *Act* (Collective investment schemes) for the purposes of the *Act* generally. But there is a separate power to provide for exemptions from that definition and the Treasury have exercised it (see the Financial Services and Markets Act 2000 (Collective Investment Schemes) Order 2001 (SI 2001/1062). The result is that *units* in certain arrangements are excluded from being *collective investment schemes* (for example, closed-ended *bodies corporate*, franchise arrangements, timeshare schemes).

Rights under a pension scheme

2.6.19 **[G]** Two types of *investment* are specified here:
(1) rights under a *stakeholder pension scheme*; and
(2) rights under a *personal pension scheme*.

2.6.19A **[G]** A *stakeholder pension scheme* is defined in section 1 of the Welfare Reform and Pensions Act 1999. Regulations made under that section set out detailed rules under which such schemes will operate (see the Stakeholder Pension Scheme Regulations 2000). Schemes must be registered with The Pensions Regulator.

2.6.19B **[G]** A *personal pension scheme* is, broadly speaking, a pension scheme which is not an *occupational pension scheme* or a *stakeholder pension scheme*. That is, a scheme or arrangement that is comprised in one or more instruments or agreements, having or capable of having effect so as to provide benefits to or in respect of people:
(1) on retirement; or
(2) on having reached a particular age; or
(3) on termination of service in an employment.

2.6.19C **[G]** Rights under *stakeholder pension schemes* and *personal pension schemes* are *specified investments* for the purposes of the *Regulated Activities Order*. There are no exclusions in the Order.

Options

2.6.20 **[G]** The *specified investment* category of *options* comprises:
(1) *options* to acquire or dispose of *securities* or *contractually based investments*, currency and certain precious metals and *options* to acquire or dispose of such *options*. *Options* to *buy* or *sell* other types of *commodity* will only fall within this *specified investment* category if they are *options* to *buy* or *sell futures*, or *options* to *buy* or *sell contracts for differences*, which are based on other *commodities*. But *options* to *buy* or *sell* other types of *commodity* may be *contracts for differences* (see PERG 2.6.23G);
(2) options to acquire or dispose of other property and falling within paragraphs 5, 6, 7 or 10 of Annex 1 to *MiFID* (see article 83(2) of the *Regulated Activities Order* and PERG 13, Q32 to Q34 for *guidance* about these instruments), but only where they are options in relation to which a *MiFID investment firm* or *a third country investment firm* provides or performs *investment services and activities* on a professional basis; and
(3) options to acquire or dispose of an option to which (2) applies. See article 83(1)(e) of the *Regulated Activities Order*.

2.6.20A **[G]** It follows therefore that options not falling within PERG 2.6.20G(1), for example physically settled options on non-precious metals, such as copper options, will not be *options* unless they meet the conditions in PERG 2.6.20G(2). Moreover, where the option in question is one to which PERG 2.6.20G(2) applies, it will be an *option* only in relation to the *investment services and activities*, or *ancillary services* where relevant, provided by that person. The same applies in the case of options falling within PERG 2.6.20G(3), for example an option on a physically settled copper option traded on a *regulated market*.

Futures

2.6.21 **[G]** *Futures* is the name given to rights under a contract for the *sale* of a *commodity*, or of property of any other description, under which delivery is to be made at a future date and at a price agreed on when the contract is made.

2.6.22 **[G]** The key issue in determining whether something is an investment in this category for the purposes of the *Regulated Activities Order* is whether the contract is made for investment purposes rather than commercial purposes. Contracts which are made for commercial purposes are excluded from this *specified investment* category and the *Regulated Activities Order* contains several tests as to when that is, or is not, the case (some are conclusive, others only indicative).

2.6.22A **[G]** As with *options*, there is an additional category of instruments which are *futures* only when they are the object of *investment services or activities* provided or performed by certain *persons*. These are contracts as described in PERG 2.6.21G:

(1) that would not be regarded as having been entered into for investment purposes because they fail one of the tests mentioned in PERG 2.6.22G;

(2) that fall within paragraphs 5, 6, 7 or 10 of Annex 1 to *MiFID* (see PERG 13, Q32 to Q34 for *guidance* about these derivatives); and

(3) in relation to which a *MiFID investment firm* or *a third country investment firm* provides or performs *investment services and activities* on a professional basis.

See article 84(1A)–(1D) of the Regulated Activities Order

2.6.22B **[G]** The transposition of *MiFID* does not have the effect of turning spot or forward foreign exchange contracts into *financial instruments* where such instruments satisfy the commercial purpose test in article 84(2) of the *Regulated Activities Order*. In our view, very few instruments are likely to fall within PERG 2.6.22AG in practice, given that this category only applies in the case of instruments not falling within PERG 2.6.22G. An example of an instrument falling within PERG 2.6.22AG could be rights under a contract for a derivative which provides for physical delivery of a commodity at a future date and which is entered into on a multilateral trading facility.

Contracts for differences

2.6.23 **[G]** The *specified investment* category of *contracts for differences* covers:

(1) rights under *contracts for differences*;

(2) rights under other contracts whose purpose or pretended purpose is to secure a profit or avoid a loss by reference to fluctuations in certain factors; and

(3) other derivative contracts (not within (1) or (2)) falling within paragraph 8 of Annex 1 to *MiFID*, that is derivative instruments for the transfer of credit risk (see PERG 13, Q30 to Q31 for *guidance* about these instruments), but only where a *MiFID investment firm* or *a third country investment firm* provides or performs *investment services and activities* on a professional basis.

The factors mentioned in (2) include the value or price of property of any description or an index or any 'other factor designated in the contract'. This catches a wide range of factors.

2.6.23A **[G]** All contracts in this category are cash-settled instruments (as opposed to being settled by way of delivering something other than cash). Many would be unenforceable as gaming contracts were it not for section 412 of the *Act* (Gaming contracts). Examples of instruments that count as *specified investments* under this category are *spread bets* and interest rate swaps.

2.6.24 **[G]** There are a number of exclusions. These include a case where the parties intend that the profit is to be secured or the loss to be avoided by taking delivery of property. This avoids overlap with the *specified investment* categories of *options* and *futures*. Also excluded are index-linked *deposits* and rights under certain contracts connected with the National Savings Bank or National Savings products. There is also provision to ensure that the *specified investment* category of *contracts for differences* does not include rights under *life policies*.

Lloyd's investments

2.6.25 **[G]** Two types of *specified investment* are relevant. These are the *underwriting capacity of a Lloyd's syndicate* and a *person's membership of a Lloyd's syndicate*. There are no exclusions from these *specified investment* categories.

Rights under a funeral plan

2.6.26 **[G]** Rights under a *funeral plan contract* are the rights to a funeral obtained by a *person* who pays for the funeral before the death of the *person* whose funeral it will be.

Rights under a regulated mortgage contract

2.6.27 **[G]** In accordance with article 61(3)(a) of the *Regulated Activities Order*, a *regulated mortgage contract* is a contract which, at the time it is entered into, satisfies the following conditions:

(1) the contract is one where the lender provides credit to an individual or trustees (the "borrower");
(2) the obligation of the borrower to repay is secured by a first legal charge on land (other than timeshare accommodation) in the *United Kingdom*; and
(3) at least 40% of that land is used, or is intended to be used, as or in connection with a dwelling by the borrower (or, where trustees are the borrower, by an individual who is a beneficiary of the trust) or by a related *person*.

Detailed guidance on this is set out in PERG 4.4 (Guidance on regulated activities connected with mortgages).

Rights under a home reversion plan

2.6.27A **[G]** In accordance with article 63B(3)(a) of the *Regulated Activities Order*, a *home reversion plan* is an arrangement under which, at the time it is entered into:
(1) a *person* (the "reversion purchaser") buys all or part of a qualifying interest in land (other than timeshare accommodation) in the *United Kingdom* from an individual or trustees (the "*reversion occupier*");
(2) the *reversion occupier* (or, where trustees are concerned, an individual who is a beneficiary of the trust), or a related *person* of either, is entitled, and intends, to use at least 40% of that land as or in connection with a dwelling; and
(3) the entitlement to occupy ends on the occurrence of any one or more of the following events:
(a) the end of a specified period of at least twenty years; or
(b) the death of the individual; or
(c) the individual enters a care home.

Detailed *guidance* on this is set out in PERG 14.3 (Guidance on home reversion and home purchase activities).

Rights under a home purchase plan

2.6.27B **[G]** In accordance with article 63F(3)(a) of the *Regulated Activities Order*, a *home purchase plan* is an arrangement under which, at the time it is entered into:
(1) a *person* (the "*home purchase provider*") buys a qualifying interest in land or an undivided share of a qualifying interest in land (other than timeshare accommodation) in the *United Kingdom*;
(2) where an undivided share of a qualifying interest is bought, the interest is held on trust for the home purchase provider and the individual or trustee as beneficial tenants in common;
(3) an individual or trustees (the "*home purchaser*") is obliged to buy the interest bought by the *home purchase provider* over the course of or at the end of a specified period; and
(4) the *home purchaser* (or, where trustees are concerned, by an individual who is a beneficiary of the trust), or a related *person* of either, is entitled, and intends, to use at least 40% of that land as or in connection with a dwelling.

Detailed *guidance* on this is set out in PERG 14.4 (Guidance on home reversion and home purchase activities).

Rights to or interests in investments

2.6.28 **[G]** Rights to, or interests in, all the *specified investments* in PERG 2.6 (except rights to, or interests in, rights under a *home finance transaction*) are themselves treated as *specified investments*. The effect is that, in most cases, an activity carried on in relation to rights or interests derived from any of those *investments* is also a *regulated activity* if the activity would be regulated if carried on in relation to the investment itself. The exception is where the rights or interests relate to a *pure protection contract* or a *general insurance contract*.

2.6.29 **[G]** There are several things that are not covered by this category (other than rights to, or interests in, rights under a mortgage contract). Anything that is covered by any other *specified investment* category is excluded, as are interests under the trusts of an *occupational pension scheme*. Finally, where a contract is excluded from the scope of the *regulated activity* of *entering as provider into a funeral plan contract* (see PERG 2.8.14G), then rights to, or interests in, the *contracts of insurance* or interests under the trusts, to which the *contracts* relate are also excluded from this *specified investment* category.

2.7 Activities: a broad outline

2.7.1 **[G]** The following paragraphs describe the various specified activities. The exclusions relating to activities are dealt with in PERG 2.8 and PERG 2.9.

Accepting deposits

2.7.2 **[G]** Whether or not *accepting deposits* is a *regulated activity* depends on the use to which the money is put. The activity is caught if money received by way of *deposit* is lent to others or if any other activity of the *person* accepting the *deposit* is financed wholly (or to a material extent) out of the capital of, or interest on, money received by way of *deposit*.

Issuing e-money

2.7.2A **[G]** *Guidance* on the *regulated activity* of *issuing e-money* is given in PERG 3.

Effecting or carrying out contracts of insurance as principal

2.7.3 **[G]** The activities of *effecting a contract of insurance* or *carrying out a contract of insurance* are separate *regulated activities*, each requiring *authorisation*. But this only applies where they are carried on by a *person* who is acting as principal. This means that the activities of agents, such as loss adjusters, will not constitute this *regulated activity*. The activities of some agents may, however, be regulated as *insurance mediation activities* (see PERG 5 (Guidance on insurance mediation activities)).

2.7.4 **[G]** In addition, certain other activities carried on in relation to rights under *contracts of insurance* are *regulated activities*. These are where the activity is carried on in relation to:

(1) *life policies*, where the *regulated activities* concerned are:
- (a) *dealing in investments as principal* (see PERG 2.7.5G);
- (b) *managing investments* (see PERG 2.7.8G);
- (c) *safeguarding and administering investments* (see PERG 2.7.9G); and
- (d) agreeing to carry on any of those activities (see PERG 2.7.21G); and

(2) rights under any *contract of insurance*, where the *regulated activities* concerned are:
- (a) *dealing in investments as agent* (see PERG 2.7.5G);
- (b) *arranging (bringing about) deals* in *investments* and *making arrangements with a view to transactions in investments* (see PERG 2.7.7AG);
- (c) *assisting in the administration and performance of a contract of insurance* (see PERG 2.7.8AG);
- (d) *advising on investments* (see PERG 2.7.15G); and
- (e) agreeing to carry on any of those activities (see PERG 2.7.21G).

PERG 5 (Insurance mediation activities) has more *guidance* on these *regulated activities* where they are *insurance mediation activities*.

Dealing in investments (as principal or agent)

2.7.5 **[G]** In relation to *securities* or *life policies* (or rights or interests in either), *dealing* as *principal* is only a *regulated activity* if certain conditions are satisfied (see PERG 2.8.4G(1)).

2.7.6 **[G]** Both the activities of *dealing in investments as principal* and *dealing in investments as agent* are defined in terms of '*buying*, *selling*, subscribing for or underwriting' certain *investments*. These *investments* are:

(1) for *dealing in investments as principal*, *securities* or *contractually based investments* (except rights under a *funeral plan contract*); and

(2) for *dealing in investments as agent*, *securities* and *relevant investments* (except rights under a *funeral plan contract*).

2.7.6A **[G]** Because of the different nature of the *specified investments* in relation to which these activities are carried on, '*buying*' and '*selling*' are defined terms that have an extended meaning. For example, some of the *specified investments* listed in PERG 2.6 are particular things that can be bought and sold in the ordinary meaning of the words. Others fall outside the ordinary meaning of 'buy' and 'sell' because their transfer involves an assumption of a potential liability under a bilateral contract (*contracts for differences* are an example of this). To deal with the possible range of circumstances, '*buying*' is defined in the *Regulated Activities Order* to include acquiring for valuable consideration. '*Selling*' is defined to include disposing for valuable consideration and 'disposing' is itself given a specified meaning that covers a range of possible transactions according to the nature of the investment being transferred (including, for example, surrendering a life insurance contract).

Arranging deals in investments and arranging a home finance transaction

2.7.7 **[G]** [not used]

2.7.7A **[G]** There are eight arranging activities that are *regulated activities* under the *Regulated Activities Order*. These are:

(1) *arranging (bringing about) deals in investments* which are *securities*, *relevant investments* or the *underwriting capacity of a Lloyd's syndicate* or *membership of a Lloyd's syndicate* (article 25(1));

(2) *making arrangements with a view to transactions in investments* which are *securities*, *relevant investments* or the *underwriting capacity of a Lloyd's syndicate* or *membership of a Lloyd's syndicate* (article 25(2));

(3) *arranging (bringing about) regulated mortgage contracts*, which includes arranging for another *person* to vary the terms of a *regulated mortgage contract* entered into by him as borrower after 31 October 2004 (article 25A(1));

(4) *making arrangements with a view to regulated mortgage contracts* (article 25A(2));
(5) *arranging (bringing about) a home reversion plan*, which includes arranging for another *person* to vary the terms of a *home reversion plan* entered into by him as the original reversion provider (and not merely as a *person* to whom the rights or obligations or the interest in land may be transferred) or as *reversion occupier* on or after 6 April 2007 (article 25B(1));
(6) *making arrangements with a view to a home reversion plan* (article 25B(2));
(7) *arranging (bringing about) a home purchase plan*, which includes arranging for another *person* to vary the terms of a *home purchase plan* entered into by him as *home purchaser* on or after 6 April 2007 (article 25C(1)); and
(8) *making arrangements with a view to a home purchase plan* (article 25C(2)).

2.7.7B **[G]** The activity of *arranging (bringing about) deals in investments* is aimed at arrangements that would have the direct effect that a particular transaction is concluded (that is, *arrangements* that bring it about). The activity of *making arrangements with a view to transactions in investments* is concerned with arrangements of an ongoing nature whose purpose is to facilitate the entering into of transactions by other parties. This activity has a potentially broad scope and typically applies in one of two scenarios. These are where a person provides facilities of some kind:
(1) to enable or assist investors to deal with or through a particular firm (such as the arrangements made by introducers); or
(2) to facilitate the entering into of transactions directly by the parties (such as multilateral trading facilities of any kind other than those excluded under article 25(3) of the *Regulated Activities Order*, exchanges, *clearing houses* and *service companies* (for example, *persons* who provide communication facilities for the routing of orders or the negotiation of transactions)).

2.7.7BA **[G]** It is of note, however, that the *regulated activity* of *making arrangements with a view to transactions in investments* is not limited to arrangements that are participated in by investors. It is also not necessary that both the buyer and the seller under the transaction that is being arranged should participate in the arrangements. So, arrangements may come within the activity if they are participated in only by product companies with a view to their issuing investments. A *person* may be carrying on this *regulated activity* even if he is only providing part of the facilities for bringing about a transaction.

2.7.7BB **[G]** It is also the *FSA's* view that certain arrangements may come within the activity even though the parties may have already committed to the transaction using other arrangements. This would typically apply to a *clearing house* whose clearing and settlement facilities may be seen to be made with a view to the members of the *clearing house*, as participants in its arrangements, entering into transactions (usually through an investment exchange) which must be cleared through the *clearing house* to be completed. The *clearing house* is providing an essential part of the market infrastructure that is necessary to support trading activities. The same principle applies outside the markets context. So for example if a company that wishes to raise capital from private investors tells the potential investors, in order to increase their confidence, that all aspects of paying for and issuing shares will be handled by a particular firm, that firm may come within article 25(2) when it provides those services.

2.7.7BC **[G]** In the *FSA's* view, it is generally the case that providers of back office administration services do not carry out the *regulated activity* of *making arrangements with a view to transactions in investments*. This is based essentially on the fact that providers of back office administration services aim to assist a broker *firm* to deal with the aftermath of transactions it has entered into on behalf of its clients. The broker *firm* has assumed full responsibility to its clients for completing their transactions, thus enabling the view to be taken that the *firm* to whom it outsources functions is making arrangements to assist the broker to complete transactions rather than with a view to the broker entering into trades as agent for its clients. The provider of back office services does not carry out the *regulated activity* of *making arrangements with a view to transactions in investments* because the transaction has already been entered into by the time of its involvement.

2.7.7BD **[G]**
(1) The scope of article 25(2) of the *Regulated Activities Order* (the subject of PERG 2.7.7BG) was considered by the High Court in the case of Watersheds Limited v. David Da Costa and Paul Gentlemen. The judgement suggests that the activity of 'introducing' does not itself constitute a *regulated activity* for the purposes of article 25(2) of the *Regulated Activities Order*. The *FSA* has considered whether the judgement necessitates any change to the views expressed in PERG 2.7.7BG and elsewhere in PERG. It appears to the *FSA* that the judgement should be considered in the light of the case to which it relates.
(2) Also, the court does not seem to have had the benefit of a relevant argument. The *Regulated Activities Order* provides an exclusion which has the effect of removing certain arrangements for making introductions from the scope of article 25(2) of the *Regulated Activities Order*. This exclusions can be found in article 33 of the *Regulated Activities Order* (*guidance* on this can be found in PERG 8.33 and PERG 5.6.17G to PERG 5.6.21G). This exclusions would

not be necessary if all 'introductions' were outside the scope of article 25(2) of the *Regulated Activities Order*. Support for this can also be found in the fact that article 25A(2) is very similar to article 25(2) and there is an exclusion from it for certain introductions. The exclusion is in article 33A of the *Regulated Activities Order* and *guidance* on it can be found in PERG 4.5.10G and the following paragraphs. For these reasons, the *FSA* remains of the view that article 25(2) of the *Regulated Activities Order* includes certain types of arrangements for making introductions whilst recognising that the judgement in the Watersheds case introduces an element of doubt.

2.7.7BE **[G]** In determining whether particular arrangements fall within the scope of Article 25(2) of the *Regulated Activities Order*, it may be necessary to consider the purpose of the arrangements. Further guidance on this can be found in PERG 8.32.3G. Although this *guidance* is in relation to the activities of publishers, broadcasters, website operators and telephone marketing services, the principle is not limited to those activities.

2.7.7BF **[G]** In the *FSA's* view, a mere passive display of literature advertising investments would not amount to the article 25(2) activity. Further *guidance* on this point can be found in PERG 5.6.4G. Although this *guidance* is in relation to *contracts of insurance*, the principle is not limited to them.

2.7.7C **[G]** Further *guidance* on the arranging activities as they relate to *home finance transactions* and *contracts of insurance* is in PERG 4.5 (Arranging regulated mortgage contracts), PERG 14.3 and PERG 14.4 (Guidance on home reversion and home purchase activities) and PERG 5.6 (The regulated activities: arranging deals in, and making arrangements with a view to transactions in, contracts of insurance) respectively.

Operating a multilateral trading facility

2.7.7D **[G]** *Guidance* on the *MiFID investment service* of *operating a multilateral trading facility* is given in PERG 13, Q24. So far as the *regulated activity* of *operating a multilateral trading facility* is concerned, this does not comprise the activities of *dealing in investments as agent*, *dealing in investments as principal*, or *arranging deals in investments*. Where a *firm* carries on one or more of these activities in addition to *operating a multilateral trading facility*, these are separate *regulated activities* for which it requires *permission*.

Managing investments

2.7.8 **[G]** The *regulated activity* of *managing investments* includes several elements.

(1) First, a *person* must exercise discretion. Non-discretionary portfolio management (where the manager *buys* and *sells*, as principal or agent, on the instructions of some other *person*) is not caught by this activity, although it may be caught by a different *regulated activity* such as the activity of *dealing in investments as principal* or *dealing in investments as agent*. The discretion must be exercised in relation to the composition of the portfolio under management and not in relation to some other function (such as proxy voting) carried on by the manager.

(2) Second, the property that is managed must belong beneficially to another *person*. This excludes from the *regulated activity* the management by a *person* of his own property. But discretionary management of assets by a *person* acting in his capacity as trustee will be caught even though he is the legal owner of the assets.

(3) Third, the property that is managed must consist of (or include) *securities* or *contractually based investments*. Alternatively, discretionary management will generally be caught if it is possible that the property could consist of or include such *securities* or investments. This is the case even if there never has been any investment in *securities* or *contractually based investments*, as long as there have been representations that there would be.

Assisting in the administration and performance of a contract of insurance

2.7.8A **[G]** The activity of *assisting in the administration and performance of a contract of insurance* is a *regulated activity* that is identified in the *Insurance Mediation Directive*. Further *guidance* on this activity is in PERG 5.7 (The regulated activities: assisting in the administration and performance of a contract of insurance).

Safeguarding and administering investments

2.7.9 **[G]** The activity of *safeguarding and administering investments* belonging to another is regulated, as is providing a service under which a *person* undertakes to arrange on a continuing basis for others actually to carry out the safeguarding and administering. In each case, both the elements of safeguarding and administering must be present before a *person* will be said to carry on the activity.

(1) Safeguarding is acting as custodian of the property, for example, holding any documents evidencing the investments such as the share certificate (although it is worth noting that there is express provision that an uncertificated investment may be safeguarded and administered).

(2) Administration covers services provided to the owner or manager of the property, such as settlement of sale transactions relating to an investment, dealing with income arising from the investment and carrying out corporate actions such as voting. The nature of administration services must be such that the custodian has no discretion (otherwise he is likely to be caught by the *regulated activity* of *managing investments* (see PERG 2.7.8G)).

2.7.10 **[G]** The property that is safeguarded and administered must belong beneficially to another *person*. It must consist of (or include) *securities* or *contractually based investments*. Alternatively, safeguarding and administration will generally be caught if it is possible that the property could consist of (or include) such *securities* or investments. This is the case even if the property in question has never consisted of (or included) such *securities* or investments, as long as there have been representations that it would do.

Sending dematerialised instructions

2.7.11 **[G]** The *regulated activities* relating to *sending dematerialised instructions* relate to the operation of the system for electronic transfer of title to *securities* or *contractually based investments*. This is the system maintained under the Uncertificated Securities Regulations 2001 (SI 2001/3755) (and currently operated by CREST). Sending instructions on behalf of another is a *regulated activity*, as is causing such instructions to be sent if the *person* causing the sending is a system-participant, as defined in those Regulations. A system-participant is the *person* who has the computer and network connection to CREST.

Establishing etc collective investment schemes

2.7.12 **[G]** The *regulated activities* carried on in relation to a *collective investment scheme* generally are the *establishing, operating or winding up a collective investment scheme*. Acting as the *depositary* and acting as sole director of an *open-ended investment company* are also separate *regulated activities*. In all these cases, the activities are regulated where the schemes themselves are authorised schemes for the purposes of the *UK* product regulation regime under Part XVII of the *Act* (Collective investment schemes) as well as where the schemes are unregulated schemes. The process for applying for authorisation of a *collective investment scheme* is described in COLLG 2 (Authorised fund applications). *Guidance* on whether certain types of scheme (property and land investment schemes) may amount to *collective investment schemes* is set out in PERG 11 (Property investment clubs and land investment schemes).

2.7.13 **[G]** In addition, express provision is included in the *Regulated Activities Order* to make *acting as trustee of an authorised unit trust scheme* a *regulated activity*. The full picture for authorised schemes (that is, schemes that can be promoted to the public) is as follows:

(1) *Acting as trustee of an authorised unit trust scheme* is expressly included as a *regulated activity*.

(2) *Acting as depositary of an open-ended investment company* that is authorised under regulations made under section 262 of the *Act* (Open-ended investment companies), is a *regulated activity*.

(3) Acting as a sole director of such a *company* is a *regulated activity*.

(4) Managing an *authorised unit trust scheme* will amount to operating the scheme and so will be a *regulated activity*. A *person* acting as *manager* is also likely to be carrying on other *regulated activities* (such as *dealing* (see PERG 2.7.5G) or *managing investments* (see PERG 2.7.8G)).

(5) An *open-ended investment company* will, once it is authorised under regulations made under section 262 of the *Act*, become an *authorised person* in its own right under Schedule 5 to the *Act* (Persons concerned in Collective Investment Schemes). Under ordinary principles, a company operates itself and an *authorised open-ended investment company* will be operating the *collective investment scheme* constituted by the *company*. It is not required to go through a separate process of *authorisation* as a *person* because it has already undergone the process of product authorisation.

(6) *Operators*, *trustees* or *depositaries* of *UCITS schemes* constituted in other *EEA States* are also *authorised persons* under Schedule 5 of the *Act* if those *schemes* qualify as recognised *collective investment schemes* for the purposes of section 264 of the *Act*.

Establishing etc pension schemes

2.7.14 **[G]** The *regulated activities* carried on in relation to pension schemes are the *establishing, operating or winding up of stakeholder pension scheme* and *establishing, operating or winding up a personal pension scheme*. The identity of the *operator* of such a pension scheme depends on the facts. However, the scheme administrator will usually be the *operator* of the scheme either on its own or jointly with the scheme trustees. More detailed *guidance* on the scope of this activity is in PERG 12 (Q4).

Providing basic advice on stakeholder products

2.7.14A **[G]** This activity covers advice in the form of a recommendation given to a retail *consumer*. The recommendation must relate to a *stakeholder product* and certain conditions must be met. These conditions are based on the need for the adviser to make an assessment of the *consumer's* needs based on the answers that the *consumer* provides to a series of pre-scripted questions. A fuller description of the activity is given in PERG 2.7.14BG and explains what is meant by "retail customer". This activity is separate to the *regulated activity* of *advising on investments* (see PERG 2.7.15G (Advising on investments)). The existence of this separate advising activity does not prevent a *person* from giving advice on *stakeholder products* in circumstances that do not satisfy the conditions set out in PERG 2.7.14BG. But such advice is likely to amount to *advising on investments* unless the *stakeholder product* is a *deposit*. Neither does the existence of the activity prevent a *person* from selling *stakeholder products* in any other manner provided the *person* has the appropriate *permission*.

2.7.14B **[G]** A *person* ('P') carries on the *regulated activity* of *providing basic advice on a stakeholder product* when:

(1) P gives the advice:
  (a) to a *person* ('C') who does not receive the advice in the course of a business that he carries on; and
  (b) in the course of a business that P carries on;

(2) the advice is on the merits of C opening or *buying* a *stakeholder product*;

(3) the following conditions are met:
  (a) P asks C questions to enable P to assess whether a *stakeholder product* is appropriate for C;
  (b) if P, relying solely on the information provided by C in response to the questions referred to in (a), assesses that a *stakeholder product* is appropriate for C, P:
    (i) describes that product to C; and
    (ii) gives a recommendation of that product to C; and

(4) C has indicated to P that he has understood the description and recommendation referred to in (3)(b).

Advising on investments

2.7.15 **[G]** The *regulated activity* of *advising on investments* under article 53 of the *Regulated Activities Order* applies to advice on *securities* or *relevant investments*. It does not, for example, include giving advice about *deposits*, or about things that are not *specified investments* for the purposes of the *Regulated Activities Order* (such as interests under the trusts of an *occupational pension scheme*). Giving advice on certain other *specified investments* is, however, regulated under other parts of the *Regulated Activities Order* (see PERG 2.7.16AG and PERG 2.7.17G(2). Giving a *person* generic advice about *specified investments* (for example, invest in Japan rather than Europe) is not a *regulated activity* nor is giving information as opposed to advice (for example, listings or company news). However, the context in which something is communicated may affect its character; for example, if a *person* gives information on share price against the background that, when he does so, that will be a good time to sell, then this will constitute *advising on investments*.

2.7.16 **[G]** The advice must also be given to someone who holds *specified investments* or is a prospective investor (including trustees, nominees or discretionary fund managers). This requirement excludes advice given to a *person* who receives it in another capacity. An example of this might be a tax professional to whom advice is given to inform the practice of his profession or advice given to an employer for the purposes of setting up a *group personal pension scheme*. Further *guidance* on the meaning of *advising on investments* is in PERG 8.24 (Advising on investments).

2.7.16A **[G]** In certain circumstances, the activity of *advising on investments* can also amount to *providing basic advice on a stakeholder product* (see PERG 2.7.14A (Providing basic advice on stakeholder products)).

Advising on regulated mortgage contracts

2.7.16B **[G]** Under article 53A of the *Regulated Activities Order*, giving advice to a *person* in his capacity as borrower or potential borrower is a *regulated activity* if it is advice on the merits of the *person*:

(1) entering into a particular *regulated mortgage contract*; or

(2) *varying the terms of a regulated mortgage contract.*

Advice on varying terms as referred to in (2) comes within article 53A only where the borrower entered into the *regulated mortgage contract* on or after 31 October 2004 and the variation varies the borrower's obligations under the contract. Further *guidance* on the scope of the *regulated activity* under article 53A is in PERG 4.6 (Advising on regulated mortgage contracts).

Advising on home reversion plans

2.7.16C **[G]** Under article 53B of the *Regulated Activities Order*, giving advice to a *person* in his capacity as *reversion occupier* or reversion provider is a *regulated activity* if it is advice on the merits of the *person*:
(1) entering into a particular *home reversion plan*; or
(2) varying the terms of a *home reversion plan*.

Advice on varying terms as referred to in (2) only comes within article 53B where the plan was entered into by the *person* on or after 6 April 2007 and the variation varies his obligations under the plan. Where a *person* is entering into the plan as reversion provider purely as a result of rights or obligations, or the interest in land, being transferred to him, advice given to him on the merits of the transaction is only regulated where the plan was originally entered into on or after 6 April 2007. Further *guidance* on the scope of the *regulated activity* under article 53B is in PERG 14.3 (Guidance on home reversion and home purchase activities).

Advising on a home purchase plan

2.7.16D **[G]** Under article 53C of the *Regulated Activities Order*, giving advice to a *person* in his capacity as *home purchaser* is a *regulated activity* if it is advice on the merits of the *person*:
(1) entering into a particular *home purchase plan*; or
(2) varying the terms of a *home purchase plan*.

Advice on varying terms as referred to in (2) only comes within article 53C where the plan is entered into by the *person* on or after 6 April 2007 and the variation varies the *person*'s obligations under the plan. Further *guidance* on the scope of the *regulated activity* under article 53C is in PERG 14.4 (Guidance on home reversion and home purchase activities).

Lloyd's activities

2.7.17 **[G]** Certain activities carried on in connection with business at Lloyd's will be regulated. In addition to those already mentioned (*arranging deals* in the *underwriting capacity of a Lloyd's syndicate* or *membership of a Lloyd's syndicate*), there are three other *regulated activities* as follows.
(1) *Managing the underwriting capacity of a Lloyd's syndicate as a managing agent at Lloyd's* is a *regulated activity*. '*Managing agent*' is defined in article 3(1) of the *Regulated Activities Order*.
(2) *Advising on syndicate participation at Lloyd's*, that is advising a *person* to become, or continue or cease to be, a member of a particular *syndicate* is also caught. Giving advice about *syndicate* participation (such as how members should use their capital within the market and arrange their *syndicate* participation) is a separate *regulated activity* to that of providing advice in relation to *securities* and *contractually based investments* (see PERG 2.7.15G). Appropriate *permission* will be needed.
(3) *Arranging deals in contracts of insurance written at Lloyd's* is also a *regulated activity* for the *Society* of Lloyd's itself.

Entering funeral plan contracts

2.7.18 **[G]** *Entering as provider into a funeral plan contract* is a *regulated activity*. The 'provider' is the *person* to whom the pre-payments are made and who undertakes to provide, or secure the provision of, the funeral at some future point. He may be the funeral director or a third party who arranges for another *person* to provide the funeral. Certain types of *funeral plan contract* are excluded (see PERG 2.8.14G).

2.7.19 **[G]** In addition, other activities carried on in relation to rights under certain *funeral plan contracts* are regulated (see PERG 2.7.5G to PERG 2.7.11G and PERG 2.7.15G and PERG 2.7.16G). This is because such rights are classified as *contractually based investments*.

Entering into and administering a regulated mortgage contract

2.7.20 **[G]** *Entering into* as lender, and *administering*, *a regulated mortgage contract* are *regulated activities* under article 61 of the *Regulated Activities Order* (Regulated mortgage contracts). *Guidance* on these *regulated activities* is in PERG 4.7 (Entering into a regulated mortgage contract) and PERG 4.8 (Administering a regulated mortgage contract).

Entering into and administering a home reversion plan

2.7.20A **[G]** *Entering into a home reversion plan* and *administering a home reversion plan* are *regulated activities* under article 63B of the *Regulated Activities Order* (Regulated home reversion plans). *Guidance* on these *regulated activities* is in *PERG* 14.3 (Guidance on home reversion and home purchase activities).

Entering into and administering a home purchase plan

2.7.20B **[G]** *Entering into a home purchase plan* and *administering a home purchase plan* are *regulated activities* under article 63F of the *Regulated Activities Order* (Regulated home purchase plans). *Guidance* on these *regulated activities* is in *PERG* 14.4 (Guidance on home reversion and home purchase activities).

Dormant account funds

2.7.20C **[G]** There are two *regulated activities* associated with the activities of a *dormant account fund operator* under the Dormant Bank and Building Society Accounts Act 2008:

(1) the *meeting of repayment claims*; and

(2) *managing dormant account funds (including the investment of such funds).*

Agreeing

2.7.21 **[G]** Agreeing to carry on most *regulated activities* is itself a *regulated activity*. But this is not the case if the underlying activities to which the agreement relates are those of *accepting deposits, issuing e-money, effecting* or *carrying out contracts of insurance, operating a multilateral trading facility, managing dormant account funds,* the *meeting of repayment claims* or carrying on any of the activities that are regulated in relation to *collective investment schemes, stakeholder pension schemes* or *personal pension schemes*. A *person* will need to make sure that he has appropriate *authorisation* at the stage of agreement and before he actually carries on the underlying activity (such as the *dealing* or *arranging*).

2.8 Exclusions applicable to particular regulated activities

2.8.1 **[G]** Most *regulated activities* are subject to exclusions that are set out in the *Regulated Activities Order* directly following each activity.

Accepting deposits

2.8.2 **[G]** Only one exclusion applies to the *regulated activity* of *accepting deposits*. A deposit taker providing its services as an *electronic commerce activity* from another *EEA State* into the *United Kingdom* (see PERG 2.9.18G) does not carry on a *regulated activity*. In addition to the situations that are excluded from being '*deposits*' (see PERG 2.6.2G to PERG 2.6.4G), several *persons* are *exempt persons* in relation to the *regulated activity* of *accepting deposits* (see PERG 2.10.8G(2)).

Issuing e-money

2.8.2A **[G]** Certain 'small issuers' of *e-money* may apply to the *FSA* for a certificate to be excluded from the *regulated activity* of *issuing e-money*. To be eligible, the issuer must be a *body corporate* or a *partnership* (other than a *full credit institution*) with its head office in the *United Kingdom* and it must meet certain conditions. The *FSA* must give that issuer a certificate if it appears to the *FSA* that the issuer meets those conditions. Further *guidance* on those conditions and how the application is made is given in ELM 8.4 (The conditions for giving a small e-money issuer certificate).

Effecting and carrying out contracts of insurance

2.8.3 **[G]** The following activities are excluded from both the *regulated activities* of *effecting* and *carrying out contracts of insurance*.

(1) In specified circumstances, the activities of an *EEA firm* when participating in a Community co-insurance operation are excluded. A Community co-insurance operation is defined in the *Community Co-insurance Directive*.

(2) Activities that are carried out in connection with the provision of on-the-spot accident or breakdown assistance for cars and other vehicles (such as repairs, vehicle retrieval, delivery of parts or fuel) are excluded.

(3) *Electronic commerce activities* provided by an *incoming ECA provider* where those activities are outside the scope of the *Insurance Directives* (see PERG 2.9.18G).

Dealing in investments as principal

2.8.4 **[G]** The *regulated activity* of *dealing in investments as principal* applies to specified transactions relating to any security or to any *contractually based investment* (apart from rights under *funeral plan contracts* or rights to or interests in such contracts). The activity is cut back by exclusions as follows.

(1) Of particular significance is the exclusion in article 15 of the *Regulated Activities Order* (Absence of holding out etc). This applies where *dealing in investments as principal* involves entering into transactions relating to any security or assigning rights under a *life policy* (or rights or interests in such a contract). In effect, it superimposes an additional condition that must be met before a *person*'s activities become *regulated activities*. The additional condition is that a *person* must hold himself out as making a market in the relevant *specified investments* or as being in the business of dealing in them, or he must regularly solicit members of the public with the purpose of inducing them to deal. This exclusion does not apply to dealing activities that relate to any *contractually based investment* except the assigning of rights under a *life policy*.

(2) Entering into a transaction relating to a *contractually based investment* is not regulated if the transaction is entered into by an *unauthorised person* and it takes place in either of the following circumstances (a transaction entered into by an *authorised person* would be caught). The first set of circumstances is where the *person* with whom the *unauthorised person* deals is either an *authorised person* or an *exempt person* who is acting in the course of a business comprising a *regulated activity* in relation to which he is exempt. The second set of circumstances is where the *unauthorised person* enters into a transaction through a non-*UK* office (which could be his own) and he deals with or through a *person* who is based outside the *United Kingdom*. This non-*UK person* must be someone who, as his ordinary business, carries on any of the activities relating to *securities* or *contractually based investments* that are generally treated as *regulated activities*.

(3) A *person* (for example, a bank) who provides another *person* with finance for any purpose can accept an instrument acknowledging the debt (and as security for it) without risk of *dealing* as *principal* as a result.

(4) A *company* does not *deal* as principal by issuing its own *shares* or *share warrants* and a *person* does not *deal* as principal by issuing his own *debentures* or *debenture warrants*.

(4A) A *company* does not carry on the activity of *dealing in investments as principal* by purchasing its own *shares* where section 162A of the Companies Act 1985 (Treasury shares) applies to the *shares* purchased or by dealing in its own *shares* held as Treasury shares, in accordance with section 162D of that Act (Treasury shares: disposal and cancellation).

(5) Risk-management activities involving *options*, *futures* and *contracts for differences* will not require *authorisation* if specified conditions are met. The conditions include the *company's* business consisting mainly of *unregulated activities* and the sole or main purpose of the risk management activities being to limit the impact on that business of certain kinds of identifiable risk.

(6) A *person* will not be treated as carrying on the activity of *dealing in investments as principal* if, in specified circumstances (outlined in PERG 2.9), he enters as principal into a transaction:

(a) while acting as bare trustee (or, in Scotland, as nominee);

(b) in connection with the sale of goods or supply of services;

(c) that takes place between members of a *group* or *joint enterprise*;

(d) in connection with the sale of a *body corporate*;

(e) in connection with an employee share scheme;

(g) as an *overseas person*;

(f) as an *incoming ECA provider* (see PERG 2.9.18G).

2.8.4A **[G]** *Persons* who enter as principal into transactions involving rights under a *contract of insurance* of any kind will need to consider whether they may, as a result, be carrying on the *regulated activity* of:

(1) *arranging (bringing about) deals in investments*; or

(2) *making arrangements with a view to transactions in investments*; or

(3) agreeing to do (1) or (2).

2.8.4B **[G]** The possibility referred to in PERG 2.8.4AG will only arise where it is not the case that the *person* who enters into the transaction as principal either:

(1) is the only *policyholder*; or

(2) as a result of the transaction, would become the only *policyholder*.

2.8.4C **[G]** The exclusions referred to in PERG 2.8.4G(1), (2), (5) and (6)(b), (c) and (d) will not be available to *persons* who, when carrying on the activity of *dealing in investments as principal*, are *MiFID investment firms or third country investment firms* (see PERG 2.5.4G to PERG 2.5.5G (Investment services and activities)).

Dealing in investments as agent

2.8.5 **[G]** The *regulated activity* of *dealing in investments as agent* applies to specified transactions relating to any *security* or to any *relevant investment* (apart from rights under *funeral plan contracts* or rights to or interests in such rights). In addition, the activity is cut back by exclusions as follows.

(1) An exclusion applies to certain transactions entered into by an agent who is not an *authorised person* which depend on him dealing with (or through) an *authorised person*. It does not apply if the transaction relates to a *contract of insurance*. There are certain conditions which must be satisfied for the exclusion to apply. These are that the agent must not give any relevant advice on the transaction and that he must not receive any remuneration from the transaction unless account is made to his client.

(2) There is an exclusion for risk-management transactions where the agent is dealing on behalf of a *group* company or a co-participant in a *joint enterprise*.

(3) In addition, exclusions apply in specified circumstances (outlined in PERG 2.9 (Regulated activities: exclusions available in certain circumstances)) where a *person* enters as agent into a transaction:
  (a) in connection with the carrying on of a profession or of a business not otherwise consisting of *regulated activities* (see PERG 2.9.5G);
  (b) in connection with the sale of goods or supply of services (see PERG 2.9.7G);
  (c) that takes place between members of a *group* or *joint enterprise* (see PERG 2.9.9G);
  (d) in connection with the sale of a *body corporate* (see PERG 2.9.11G);
  (e) in connection with an employee share scheme (see PERG 2.9.13G);
  (f) as an *overseas person* (see PERG 2.9.15G);
  (g) as an *incoming ECA provider* (see PERG 2.9.18G);
  (h) as a provider of non-motor goods or travel services where the transaction involves a *general insurance contract* that satisfies certain conditions (see PERG 2.9.19G);
  (i) that involves a *contract of insurance* covering large risks situated outside the *EEA* (see PERG 2.9.19G);
  (j) on behalf of the participants of a business angel-led enterprise capital fund and that person is a *body corporate* as specified in article 72E(7) of the *Regulated Activities Order*.

  More detailed *guidance* on the exclusions that relate to *contracts of insurance* is in PERG 5 (Insurance mediation activities).

2.8.5A **[G]** The exclusions referred to in PERG 2.8.5G (1), (2) and (3)(a), (b), (c), (d) and (j) will not be available to *persons* who, when carrying on the activity of *dealing in investments as agent*, are *MiFID investment firms* or *third country investment firms* (see PERG 2.5.4G to PERG 2.5.5G (Investment services and activities)).

Arranging deals in investments and arranging a home finance transaction

2.8.6 **[G]** The various activities that involve *arranging* fall into two general types. These are:

(1) those relating to arranging a particular transaction or a contract or plan variation (articles 25(1), 25A(1), 25B(1) and 25C(1) of the *Regulated Activities Order*); and

(2) those relating to making arrangements with a view to persons entering into certain transactions (articles 25(2), 25A(2), 25B(2) and 25C(2) of the *Regulated Activities Order*).

The exclusions in relation to the *regulated activities* of *arranging* under articles 25(1) and (2) are of particular relevance in the context of raising corporate finance. Some of the exclusions outlined in PERG 2.8.6A relate to all of the arranging activities but most relate only to certain of those activities as indicated.

[1–13 deleted and moved to 2.8.6A]

2.8.6A **[G]** The exclusions in the *Regulated Activities Order* that relate to the various *arranging* activities are as follows.

(1) Under article 26, arrangements that do not or would not bring about the transaction to which they relate are excluded from the *arranging* activities that relate to a particular transaction (see PERG 2.8.6G(1)) only. A *person* will bring about a transaction or a contract or plan variation only if his involvement in the chain of events leading to a transaction or contract or plan variation is of sufficient importance that, without that involvement, it would not take place. This will require something more than the mere giving of advice (although giving such advice may be the *regulated activity* of *advising on investments* or *advising on home finance transactions*).

(2) Under article 27, simply providing the means by which parties to a transaction (or possible transaction) are able to communicate with each other is excluded from arrangements made with a view to persons entering into certain transactions (see PERG 2.8.6G(2)) only. This will ensure that *persons* such as Internet service providers or telecommunications networks are excluded if all they do is provide communication facilities (and these would otherwise be considered to be arrangements made with a view to the participants entering into transactions). If a *person* makes arrangements that go beyond providing the means of communication, and add value to what is provided, he will lose the benefit of this exclusion.

(3) Under article 28, arranging investment transactions to which the arranger is to be a party is excluded from both article 25(1) and (2). The main purpose is to ensure that a person is not regarded as arranging deals for another when the transaction in question is one to which he intends to be a party. As a result, a person cannot both be engaging in a dealing activity (as principal or agent) and arranging deals for another as regards any particular transaction. But where the transaction involves a contract of insurance, article 28 will not apply if the person making the arrangements:
(a) is the only policyholder; or
(b) as a result of the transaction, would become the only policyholder.
Under article 28A, a *person* is excluded from any of the *arranging* activities that relate to *home finance transactions* (2) if he is to enter into the contract or plan to which the *arrangements* relate or if he is or is to become a party to a contract or plan that is varied or to be varied.

(4) Under article 29, an *unauthorised person* who, on behalf of a client, arranges transactions or contract or plan variations, with or through an *authorised person*, is excluded from each of the *arranging* activities if specified conditions as to advice and remuneration are satisfied. For example, the exclusion is dependent on the client not receiving any advice on the transactions or variations from the *unauthorised person* making the arrangements. The exclusion does not apply where the *investment* is a *contract of insurance*.

(5) Under article 29A, an *unauthorised person* is excluded from the *regulated activity* of *arranging* for another *person* to vary the terms of a *regulated mortgage contract* entered into on or after 31 October 2004 (article 25A(1)(b)) or a *home reversion plan* or *home purchase plan* entered into on or after 6 April 2007 (articles 25B(1)(b) and 25C(1)(b)). This is if the *arranging* is the result of:
(a) anything done in the course of the administration, by an *authorised person*:
(i) of a *regulated mortgage contract* in the way set out in article 62(a);
(ii) of a *home reversion plan* in the way set out in article 63C(a);
(iii) of a *home purchase plan* in the way set out in article 63G(a); or
(b) anything done by the *unauthorised person* in connection with the administration:
(i) of a *regulated mortgage contract* in the way set out in article 62(b);
(ii) of a *home reversion plan* in the way set out in article 63C(b);
(iii) of a *home purchase plan* in the way set out in article 63G(b).

(6) Under article 30, arranging investment transactions in connection with lending on the security of contracts of insurance is excluded, from article 25(1) and (2) but only where a person is not carrying on insurance mediation or reinsurance mediation.

(7) Under article 31, making arrangements for finance (in whatever form) to be supplied to a person by a third party is excluded from article 25(1) and (2) if the finance is given in exchange for an instrument acknowledging the debt. This mirrors the exclusion from dealing in investments as principal in similar circumstances (see PERG 2.8.4G (3)).

(8) Under article 32, arrangements the only purpose of which is to provide finance to enable persons to enter into investment transactions are excluded from article 25(2) only. There is no equivalent exemption from article 25(1). But arrangements for the provision of finance will only be caught by that provision if the arrangements actually bring about the transaction.

(9) Under article 33, making arrangements under which *persons* will be introduced to third parties who will provide independent services (consisting of advice or the exercise of discretion in relation to certain investments) is excluded from articles 25(2), 25A(2), 25B(2) and 25C(2) only. The party to whom the introduction is made must be of a specified standing (including that of an authorised person). The exclusion does not apply where the arrangements relate to a contract of insurance.

(10) Under article 33A, making arrangements for introducing *persons* to:
(a) an authorised person who has permission to carry on certain regulated activities concerned with home finance transactions; or
(b) an appointed representative who is able to carry on any of those activities without breaching the general prohibition; or
(c) an overseas person who carries on any of those activities;
is excluded from articles 25A(2), 25B(2) and 25C(2) subject to certain conditions related to the receipt of client money and the disclosure of certain information.

(11) Under article 34, a company is not carrying on a regulated activity under article 25(1) or (2) of the Regulated Activities Order (Arranging deals in investments) by arranging for the issue of its own shares or share warrants and a person is not doing so by arranging for the issue of his own debentures or debenture warrants.

(12) Under article 35, a body carrying out international securities business of a specified type can apply to the Treasury for approval as an international securities self-regulating organisation (ISSRO). Arrangements made in order to carry out the functions of an ISSRO are excluded from article 25(1) and (2). The exclusion applies whether the arrangements are made by the ISSRO or by a person acting on its behalf.

(13) The following exclusions from both article 25(1) and (2) (outlined in PERG 2.9) apply in specified circumstances where a *person* makes arrangements:
(a) while acting as trustee or personal representative (see PERG 2.9.3 G);
(b) in connection with the carrying on of a profession or of a business not otherwise consisting of regulated activities (see PERG 2.9.5 G);
(c) in connection with the sale of goods or supply of services (see PERG 2.9.7 G);
(d) in connection with certain transactions by a group member or by a participator in a joint enterprise (see PERG 2.9.9 G);
(e) in connection with the sale of a body corporate (see PERG 2.9.11 G);
(f) in connection with an employee share scheme (see PERG 2.9.13 G);
(g) as an overseas person (see PERG 2.9.15 G);
(h) as an incoming ECA provider (see PERG 2.9.18 G);
(i) as a provider of non-motor goods or services related to travel (see PERG 2.9.19 G);
(j) involving the provision, on an incidental basis, of information to policyholders or potential policyholders about contracts of insurance (see PERG 2.9.19 G);
(k) that involve a contract of insurance covering large risks situated outside the EEA (see PERG 2.9.19 G);
(l) for or with a view to transactions to be entered into by or on behalf of the participants of a business angel-led enterprise capital fund and that person is a body corporate as specified in article 72E(7) of the Regulated Activities Order.

More detailed guidance on the exclusions that relate to contracts of insurance is in PERG 5 (Insurance mediation activities).
The exclusions referred to in (a), (b), (g) and (h) also apply to *arranging* activities related to *home finance transactions*. More detailed *guidance* on the exclusions that relate to *contracts of insurance* is in PERG 5 (Insurance mediation activities).

2.8.6B **[G]** The exclusions referred to in PERG 2.8.6AG(4) and PERG 2.8.6AG(13)(b), (c), (d), (e) and (l) will not be available to *persons* who, when carrying on an *arranging* activity, are *MiFID investment firms* or *third country investment firms* (see PERG 2.5.4G to PERG 2.5.5G (Investment services and activities)).

Managing investments

2.8.7 **[G]** The activities of *persons* appointed under a power of attorney are excluded under article 38 of the *Regulated Activities Order*, from the *regulated activity* of *managing investments*, if specified conditions are satisfied. The exclusion only applies where a *person* is not carrying on *insurance mediation* or *reinsurance mediation* and is subject to further limitations discussed below. In addition, the following exclusions (outlined in PERG 2.9) apply in specified circumstances where a *person* manages assets:
(1) while acting as trustee or personal representative; or
(2) in connection with the sale of goods or supply of services; or
(3) that belong to a *group* member or participator in a *joint enterprise*; or
(4) as an *incoming ECA provider* (see PERG 2.9.18G); or
(5) belonging to the participants of a business angel-led enterprise capital fund and that person is a *body corporate* as specified in article 72E(7) of the *Regulated Activities Order*.

The exclusion in article 38 of the *Regulated Activities Order* and the exclusions referred to in PERG 2.8.7G (2), (3) and (5) will not be available to *persons* who, when carrying on the activity of *managing investments*, are *MiFID investment firms* or *third country investment firms* (see PERG 2.5.4G to PERG 2.5.5G (Investment services and activities)).

Assisting in the administration and performance of a contract of insurance

2.8.7A **[G]** *Assisting in the administration and performance of a contract of insurance* is excluded under article 39B where it is carried on by a *person* acting in the capacity of:
(1) an expert appraiser; or
(2) a loss adjuster acting for a relevant insurer; or
(3) a claims manager acting for a relevant insurer.

The term 'relevant insurer' is defined in article 39B(2).

2.8.7B **[G]** The following exclusions from *assisting in the administration and performance of a contract of insurance* also apply to a *person* in specified circumstances:
(1) while acting as trustee or personal representative (see PERG 2.9.3G); or
(2) in connection with the carrying on of a profession or of a business not otherwise consisting of *regulated activities* (see PERG 2.9.5G); or
(3) as an *incoming ECA provider* (see PERG 2.9.18G); or
(4) as a provider of non-motor goods or services related to travel (see PERG 2.9.19G); or
(5) that involve the provision, on an incidental basis, of information to *policyholders* or potential *policyholders* about *contracts of insurance* (see PERG 2.9.19G(2)); or
(6) that involve a *contract of insurance* covering large risks situated outside the *EEA* (see PERG 2.9.19G).

Safeguarding and administering investments

2.8.8 **[G]** The exclusions from the *regulated activity* of *safeguarding and administering investments* are as follows.

(1) Safeguarding and administration activities carried on by one *person* are excluded if a specified third party undertakes a responsibility for the assets which is no less onerous than it would have been if he were doing the safeguarding and administration himself. The effect of this is that an *authorised person* with *permission* to carry on this *regulated activity* (or in certain circumstances an *exempt person*) can delegate all or part of the activities without the delegate needing to be *authorised* and without loss of protection to the owner of the assets.

(2) Introductions to an *authorised person*, or to an *exempt person* acting within the scope of his exemption and in the course of a business, are excluded from that aspect of this *regulated activity* which consists of *arranging safeguarding and administration of assets* by another *person* (see PERG 2.7.9G).

(2A) Trustees are excluded from arranging for another *person* to safeguard and administer assets where that other *person* is either:

(a) an *authorised person* who has *permission* to *safeguard and administer investments*; or

(b) an *exempt person* whose exemption permits him to *safeguard and administer investments*; or

(c) a *person* to whom (1) applies.

(3) Certain specified activities (such as currency conversion and document handling) are excluded from being the administration of investments. A *person* who safeguards and administers assets will not be carrying on *regulated activities* if these are the only administration activities in which he engages. This is because a *person* must be carrying on both the activity of safeguarding and that of administration, or be arranging for both to be carried on by another, before he requires *authorisation* (see PERG 2.7.9G).

(4) The following exclusions apply in specified circumstances where a *person* safeguards and administers assets (or arranges for another to do so):

(a) while acting as trustee or personal representative (see PERG 2.9.3G);

(b) in connection with the carrying on of a profession or of a business not otherwise consisting of *regulated activities* (see PERG 2.9.5G);

(c) in connection with the sale of goods or supply of services (see PERG 2.9.7G);

(d) which belong to a *group* member or participator in a *joint enterprise* (see PERG 2.9.9G);

(e) in connection with an employee share scheme (see PERG 2.9.13G);

(f) as an *incoming ECA provider* (see PERG 2.9.18G);

(g) that are *contracts of insurance* and, in so doing, provides information to *policyholders* or potential *policyholders* on an incidental basis in the course of his carrying on a business or profession not otherwise consisting of *regulated activities* (see PERG 2.9.19G(2)); and

(h) belonging to the participants in a business angel-led enterprise capital fund, but only where such safeguarding and administration is carried on by a *body corporate* as specified in article 72E(7) of the *Regulated Activities Order*.

Sending dematerialised instructions

2.8.9 **[G]** Exclusions from the *regulated activity* of *sending dematerialised instructions* apply in relation to certain types of instructions sent in the operation of the system maintained under the Uncertificated Securities Regulations 2001 (SI 2001/3755). The various exclusions relate to the roles played by participating issuers, settlement *banks* and network providers (such as Internet service providers) and to instructions sent in connection with takeover offers (as long as specified conditions are met). In addition, the following exclusions (outlined in PERG 2.9) apply in specified circumstances where a *person* sends dematerialised instructions:

(1) while acting as trustee or personal representative (see PERG 2.9.3G);

(2) on behalf of a *group* member (see PERG 2.9.3G);

(3) as an *incoming ECA provider* (see PERG 2.9.18G).

Establishing etc collective investment schemes

2.8.10 **[G]** There are two exclusions from the range of activities specified as being regulated in relation to *collective investment schemes*. These exclusions relate to *incoming ECA providers* (see PERG 2.9.18G) and to business angel-led enterprise capital funds (see PERG 2.9.20G). In other cases, the key issue is whether or not what is being done relates to something that is a *collective investment scheme*. Exclusions exist in relation to that issue (see PERG 2.6.18G).

Establishing etc pension schemes

2.8.11 **[G]** The only exclusion from the range of activities specified as being regulated in relation to *stakeholder pension schemes* and *personal pension schemes* relates to *incoming ECA providers* (see PERG 2.9.18G).

Advising on investments

2.8.12 **[G]** In certain circumstances, advice that takes the form of a regularly updated news or information service and advice which is given in one of a range of different media (for example, newspaper or television) is excluded from the *regulated activities* of:

(1) *advising on investments;*
(2) *advising on regulated mortgage contracts*;
(3) *advising on a home reversion plan*; and
(4) *advising on a home purchase plan.*

See PERG 7 (Periodical publications: news services and broadcasts: applications for certification for further *guidance* on this exclusion.

2.8.12A **[G]** Advice given by an *unauthorised person* in relation to a *home finance transaction* in the circumstances referred to in PERG 2.8.6AG(5)(a) or (b) (Arranging deals in investments and arranging a home finance transaction). In addition:

(1) the following exclusions apply in specified circumstances where a *person* is *advising on investments* or *advising on* a *home finance transaction*:
    (a) while acting as trustee or personal representative (see PERG 2.9.3G);
    (b) in connection with the carrying on of a profession or of a business not otherwise consisting of *regulated activities* (see PERG 2.9.5G); and
    (c) as an *incoming ECA provider* (see PERG 2.9.18G);
(2) the following exclusions apply in specified circumstances where a *person* is *advising on investments*:
    (a) in connection with the sale of goods or supply of services (see PERG 2.9.7G);
    (b) to a *group* member or participator in a *joint enterprise* (see PERG 2.9.9G);
    (c) in connection with the sale of a *body corporate* (see PERG 2.9.11G);
    (d) as an overseas *person* (see PERG 2.9.15G);
    (e) that are limited to certain *contracts of insurance* covering risks to non-motor goods or related to travel (see PERG 2.9.19G);
    (f) that are *contracts of insurance* covering large risks situated outside the *EEA* (see PERG 2.9.19G);
    (g) to be made by or on behalf of the participants of a business angel-led enterprise capital fund, when the advice is given to the participants in that fund and that person is a *body corporate* as specified in article 72E(7) of the *Regulated Activities Order*.

More detailed *guidance* on certain of these exclusions is in PERG 4 (Regulated activities connected with mortgages), PERG 5 (Insurance mediation activities) and PERG 14.3 and PERG 14.4 (Guidance on home reversion and home purchase activities).

2.8.12B **[G]** The exclusions referred to in PERG 2.8.12AG(1)(b) and (2)(a), (b), (c) and (g) will not be available to persons who, when carrying on the activity of *advising on investments* are *MiFID investment firms* or *third country investment firms* (see PERG 2.5.4G to PERG 2.5.5G (Investment services and activities)).

Lloyd's activities

2.8.13 **[G]** *Electronic commerce activities* provided by an *incoming ECA provider* are excluded from the *regulated activities* that relate expressly to business carried on at Lloyd's (see PERG 2.9.18G). Otherwise the only exclusions that apply concern the *regulated activity* of *arranging deals* in its application to business carried on at Lloyd's.

Entering funeral plan contracts

2.8.14 **[G]** *Entering as provider into a funeral plan contract* is not treated as a *regulated activity* where:

(1) the contract is one under which the sums received from the customer will be applied towards a *contract of insurance* on the life of the *person* whose funeral is to be provided or be held on trust for the purpose of providing a funeral; in each case certain specified conditions must be met for the exclusion to apply; or
(2) the customer and the provider intend or expect that the funeral will be provided within one *month* of the contract being entered into; or

(3) it is provided as an *electronic commerce activity* by an *incoming ECA provider* (see PERG 2.9.18G).

Administering regulated mortgage contracts

2.8.14A **[G]** Exclusions from the *regulated activities* that involve *administering a home finance transaction* are provided where an unauthorised *person:*

(1) arranges for administration by an *authorised person* who has *permission* for carrying on that *regulated activity*;

(2) carries out the administration for up to one month after an arrangement of the kind mentioned in (1) comes to an end; or

(3) carries out the administration under an agreement with an *authorised person* who has *permission* for carrying on that *regulated activity.*

These exclusions are subject to certain conditions and are explained in greater detail in PERG 4.8 (Administering a regulated mortgage contract) and PERG 14.3 and PERG 14.4 (Guidance on home reversion and home purchase activities).

2.8.14B **[G]** The following exclusions apply in specified circumstances where a *person* is *administering a home finance plan*:

(1) while acting as trustee or personal representative (see PERG 2.9.3 G);

(2) in connection with the carrying on of a profession or of a business not otherwise consisting of *regulated activities* (see PERG 2.9.5 G); and

(3) as an incoming ECA provider (see PERG 2.9.18 G).

Agreeing

2.8.15 **[G]** A *person* who agrees to carry on certain other *regulated activities* (which is itself a *regulated activity* – see PERG 2.7.21G) does not require *authorisation* where the *person* concerned is an *overseas person* and the agreement is reached as a result of a legitimate approach (see PERG 2.9.12G). For this exclusion to apply, the agreement must be one to arrange deals, *manage investments, assist in the administration and performance of a contract of insurance, safeguard and administer investments* or *send dematerialised instructions.* The provision of *electronic commerce activities* by an *incoming ECA provider* is also excluded from the *regulated activity* of agreeing to carry on certain other *regulated activities* (see PERG 2.7.21G). But this is not the case where the agreement relates to the *regulated activity* of *effecting* or *carrying out contracts of insurance* falling under the *Insurance Directives* (see PERG 2.8.3G). This is still a *regulated activity* when provided as an *electronic commerce activity.*

2.8.16 **[G]** To the extent that an exclusion applies in relation to a *regulated activity*, then 'agreeing' to carry on an activity falling within the exclusion will not be a *regulated activity*. This is the effect of article 4(3) of the *Regulated Activities Order.*

2.9 Regulated activities: exclusions applicable in certain circumstances

2.9.1 **[G]** The various exclusions outlined below deal with a range of different circumstances.

(1) Each set of circumstances described in PERG 2.9.3G to PERG 2.9.17G has some application to several *regulated activities* relating to *securities, relevant investments* or *home finance transactions.* They have no effect in relation to the separate *regulated activities* of *accepting deposits, issuing e-money, effecting* or *carrying out contracts of insurance, advising on syndicate participation at Lloyd's, managing the underwriting capacity of a Lloyd's syndicate as a managing agent at Lloyd's* or *entering as provider into a funeral plan contract.* Within each set of circumstances, the *Regulated Activities Order*, in Chapter XVII of Part II of the Order, makes separate provision for each *regulated activity* affected. This is necessary because each exclusion has to be tailored to reflect the different nature of the *regulated activity* involved and the different language required (for example, some activities involve entering directly into transactions while others relate to the provision of services).

(2) The exclusion described in PERG 2.9.18G relates to *electronic commerce activities* provided by an *incoming ECA provider.* This exclusion applies to all *regulated activities* except *effecting* or *carrying out contracts of insurance.*

2.9.2 **[G]** The exclusions grouped together in the *Regulated Activities Order* are described below in this chapter in general terms. The exact terms of each exclusion will need to be considered by any *person* who is considering whether they need *authorisation.* Each description is accompanied by an indication of which *regulated activities* are affected.

Trustees, nominees or personal representatives

2.9.3 **[G]** This group of exclusions applies, in specified circumstances, to the *regulated activities* of:

(1) *dealing in investments as principal*;

(2) *arranging (bringing about) deals in investments*, and *making arrangements with a view to transactions in investments*;

(2A) *arranging a home finance transaction*;

(3) *managing investments*;

(4) *assisting in the administration and performance of a contract of insurance*;

(5) *safeguarding and administering investments*;

(6) *sending dematerialised instructions*;

(7) *advising on investments* or *advising on a home finance transaction*;

(8) *entering into a home finance transaction*; and

(9) *administering a home finance transaction*.

The exclusion is, however, disapplied where a *person* is carrying on *insurance mediation* or *reinsurance mediation*. This is due to article 4(4A) of the *Regulated Activities Order*. *Guidance* on exclusions relevant to *insurance mediation activities* is in PERG 5 (Insurance mediation activities).

2.9.4 **[G]** A *person* carrying on certain *regulated activities* does not require *authorisation* in specified circumstances if he is acting in a representative capacity. The representative capacities covered by the exclusions depend on the *regulated activity* concerned but, in most cases, the focus is on *persons* who are acting as trustee or personal representative. In broad terms, the exclusions apply to specified transactions, or activities, that are part of the discharge of his general obligations by the trustee or representative when he is acting as such. Many of the exclusions require that the trustee or representative must not hold himself out as providing services consisting of the *regulated activity* in question. In addition, he must not receive remuneration that is additional to any he receives for acting in the representative capacity (although a *person* is not to be regarded as receiving additional remuneration merely because his remuneration as trustee or representative is calculated by reference to time spent). The exclusions for *entering into* a *home finance transaction* and for *administering a home finance transaction*, however, work on a different basis. They apply where the activity relates to a *regulated mortgage contract* under which the borrower, *reversion occupier* or *home purchaser* as the case may be is a beneficiary.

Professions or business not involving regulated activities

2.9.5 **[G]** This group of exclusions applies, in specified circumstances, to the *regulated activities* of:

(1) *dealing in investments as agent*;

(2) *arranging (bringing about) deals in investments* and *making arrangements with a view to transactions in investments*;

(2A) *arranging a home finance transaction*;

(3) *assisting in the administration and performance of a contract of insurance*;

(4) *safeguarding and administering investments*; and *advising on investments* or *advising on a home finance transaction*.

The exclusion is, however, disapplied where a *person* is carrying on *insurance mediation* or *reinsurance mediation*. This is due to article 4(4A) of the *Regulated Activities Order*. *Guidance* on exclusions relevant to *insurance mediation activities* is in PERG 5 (Insurance mediation activities). The exclusion is also disapplied for *persons* who, when carrying on the relevant *regulated activity*, are *MiFID investment firms* or *third country investment firms* (see PERG 2.5.4G to PERG 2.5.5G (Investment services and activities)).

2.9.6 **[G]** The exclusions apply where the *regulated activity* is carried out in the course of a profession or business which does not otherwise consist of the carrying on of *regulated activities* in the *United Kingdom*.

However, activities are only excluded to the extent that they may reasonably be regarded as a necessary part of the other services provided in the course of the profession or business. The exclusion does not apply if separate remuneration is received in respect of any *regulated activity* that is carried on. (See separate *guidance* for *authorised professional firms* in PROF.)

Sale of goods and supply of services

2.9.7 **[G]** This group of exclusions applies, in specified circumstances, to the *regulated activities* of:

(1) *dealing in investments as principal*;

(2) *dealing in investments as agent*;

(3) *arranging (bringing about) deals in investments* and *making arrangements with a view to transactions in investments*;

(4) *managing investments*;

(5) *safeguarding and administering investments*; and
(6) *advising on investments*.

2.9.8 **[G]** Broadly speaking, the exclusions focus on cases where the main business of a *person* is to sell goods or supply services but where certain activities may have to be carried on for the purposes of that business which would otherwise be *regulated activities*. The exclusions are not available where the customer to whom goods are sold or services are supplied is an individual. They are also not available where what is at issue is a transaction entered into, or service provided, in relation to rights under a *contract of insurance* or *units* in a *collective investment scheme* (or rights to, or interests in, either). The exclusions are also disapplied for *persons* who, when carrying on the relevant *regulated activity*, are *MiFID investment firms* or *third country investment firms* (see PERG 2.5.4G to PERG 2.5.5G (Investment services and activities)).

Group and joint enterprises

2.9.9 **[G]** This group of exclusions applies, in specified circumstances, to the *regulated activities* of:
(1) *dealing in investments as principal*;
(2) *dealing in investments as agent*;
(3) *arranging (bringing about) deals in investments* and *making arrangements with a view to transactions in investments*;
(4) *managing investments*;
(5) *safeguarding and administering investments*;
(6) *sending dematerialised instructions*; and
(7) *advising on investments*.

2.9.10 **[G]** These exclusions apply to intra-group dealings and activities and to dealings or activities involving participators in a joint enterprise which take place for the purposes of, or in connection with, the enterprise. The general principle here is that, as long as activities that would otherwise be *regulated activities* take place wholly within a group of companies, then there is no need for *authorisation*. The same principle applies to dealings or activities that take place wholly within a *joint enterprise* entered into for commercial purposes related to the participators' unregulated business. The exclusions in PERG 2.9.9G(2), (3), (4) and (7) are disapplied where they concern a *contract of insurance*. *Guidance* on exclusions relevant to *insurance mediation activities* is in PERG 5 (Insurance mediation activities). The exclusions are also disapplied for *persons* who, when carrying on the relevant *regulated activity*, are *MiFID investment firms* or *third country investment firms* (see PERG 2.5.4G to PERG 2.5.5G (Investment services and activities)).

Sale of body corporate

2.9.11 **[G]** This group of exclusions applies, in specified circumstances, to the *regulated activities* of:
(1) *dealing in investments as principal*;
(2) *dealing in investments as agent*;
(3) *arranging (bringing about) deals in investments* and *making arrangements with a view to transactions in investments*; and
(4) advising on *investments*.

2.9.12 **[G]** The exclusions apply in relation to transactions to *buy* or *sell shares* in a *body corporate* where, in broad terms:
(1) the transaction involves the acquisition or disposal of a least 50 per cent of the voting shares in the *body corporate* and is, or is to be, between certain specified kinds of *person*; or
(2) the object of the transaction may otherwise reasonably be regarded as being the acquisition of day-to-day control of the affairs of the *body corporate*.

These exclusions also apply to transactions that are entered into for the purposes of the above transactions (such as transactions involving the offer of *securities* in the offer or as consideration or part consideration for the sale of the *shares* in the *body corporate*). These exclusions do not have effect in relation to shares in an *open-ended investment company*. The exclusions in PERG 2.9.11G(2), (3) and (4) are disapplied where they concern a *contract of insurance*. *Guidance* on exclusions relevant to *insurance mediation activities* is in PERG 5 (Guidance on insurance mediation activities). The exclusions are also disapplied for *persons* who, when carrying on the relevant *regulated activity*, are *MiFID investment firms or third country investment firms* (see PERG 2.5.4G to PERG 2.5.5G (Investment services and activities)).

2.9.12A **[G]** The Treasury, in its consultative document "Financial Services and Markets Act two year review: Changes to secondary legislation Proposals for change, February 2004" proposed changes to these exclusions aimed primarily at limiting their scope in relation to the objective test referred to in PERG 2.9.12G(2). In its response to the comments received during the consultation, the Treasury announced, in its document "Financial Services and Markets Act two year review: Changes to secondary legislation Government response, November 2004", that it intends to make certain changes to the exclusions in due course.

Part II FSA Handbook Materials

Employee share schemes

2.9.13 **[G]** This group of exclusions applies, in specified circumstance, to the *regulated activities* of:
(1) *dealing in investments as principal*;
(2) *dealing in investments as agent*;
(3) *arranging (bringing about) deals in investments* and *making arrangements with a view to transactions in investments*;
(4) *safeguarding and administering investments*.

2.9.14 **[G]** In broad terms, the exclusions apply to activities which further an employee share scheme, or are carried on in operation of such a scheme. They apply to activities carried on by the *company* whose securities or debentures (which are given an extended meaning for this exclusion) are the subject of the scheme. They also apply to activities of any *company* in the same *group* or of any trustee who holds certain types of securities or debentures under the scheme. They do not apply to the activities of a *person* who is neither such a *company* nor such a trustee (for example, a third party administration service provider).

Overseas persons

2.9.15 **[G]** This group of exclusions applies, in specified circumstances, to the *regulated activities* of:

(1) *dealing in investments as principal*;
(2) *dealing in investments as agent*;
(3) *arranging (bringing about) deals in investments* and *making arrangements with a view to transactions in investments*;
(3A) *arranging a home finance transaction*;
(3B) *operating a multilateral trading facility*;
(4) *advising on investments*;
(5) *entering into a home finance transaction*;
(6) *administering a home finance transaction*; and
(7) *agreeing to carry on the regulated activities* of *managing investments*, *arranging (bringing about) deals in investments*, *making arrangements with a view to transactions in investments*, *assisting in the performance and administration ofa contract of insurance*, *safeguarding and administering investments* or *sending dematerialised instructions*.

2.9.16 **[G]** An *overseas person* is defined as a *person* who carries on what would be *regulated activities* (including any activity that would otherwise be excluded from being a *regulated activity* by virtue of the exclusions for *overseas persons* referred to in PERG 2.9.15G) but who does not do so, or offer to do so, from a permanent place of business maintained by him in the *United Kingdom*. Where a *person* does not have a permanent place of business in the *United Kingdom*, he will not, in any event, need to rely on these exclusions unless what he does is regarded as carried on in the *United Kingdom* (see PERG 2.4). Nor will a *person* be able to rely on the exclusions in PERG 2.9.15G (1) to (4) if when carrying on the relevant *regulated activity* it is a *MiFID investment firm* and its *Home State* is the *United Kingdom*.

2.9.17 **[G]** The exclusions are available, for *regulated activities* other than those that relate to *home finance transactions*, in the two broad cases set out below. For some of these *regulated activities*, the exclusions apply in each case. In others, they apply in only one.
(1) The first case is where the nature of the *regulated activity* requires the direct involvement of another *person* and that *person* is *authorised* or exempt (and acting within the scope of his exemption). For example, this might occur where the *person* with whom an *overseas person* deals is an *authorised person* or where the arrangements he makes are for transactions to be entered into by such a *person*.
(2) The second case is where a particular *regulated activity* is carried on as a result of what is termed a 'legitimate approach'. An approach to an *overseas person* that has not been solicited by him in any way, or has been solicited in a way that does not contravene the restrictions on *financial promotion* in section 21 of the *Act*, is a legitimate approach. An approach that is made by him in a way that does not contravene section 21 of the *Act* is also a legitimate approach. In such circumstances, the *overseas person* can, without requiring *authorisation*, enter into deals with (or on behalf of) a *person* in the *United Kingdom*, give advice in the *United Kingdom* or enter into agreements in the *United Kingdom* to carry on certain *regulated activities*. The exemptions to the *financial promotion* restrictions made by the Treasury under section 21 of the *Act* (Restrictions on financial promotion) will be relevant to the question of whether those restrictions have been contravened (see separate *guidance* on *financial promotion* in PERG 8 (Financial promotion and related activities)).

2.9.17A **[G]** The exclusions for *overseas persons* who carry on certain *regulated activities* related to *home finance transactions* work in a different way. They depend on the residency of the borrower or borrowers, the *reversion occupier* or *reversion occupiers* or the *home purchaser* or *home purchasers* as the case may be. In addition, some of the exclusions also depend on the residency of the reversion provider. *Guidance* on these exclusions is in PERG 4.11 (Link between activities and the United Kingdom) and PERG 14.6 (Guidance on home reversion and home purchase activities).

Incoming ECA providers

2.9.18 **[G]**

(1) In accordance with article 3(2) of the *E-Commerce Directive*, all requirements on *persons* providing *electronic commerce activities* into the *United Kingdom* from the *EEA* are lifted, where these fall within the co-ordinated field and would restrict the freedom of such a firm to provide services. The coordinated field includes any requirement of a general or specific nature concerning the taking up or pursuit of *electronic commerce activities*. *Authorisation* requirements fall within the coordinated field. The services affected are generally those provided electronically, for example through the Internet or solicited e-mail.

(2) The *Regulated Activities Order* was amended by the Financial Services and Markets Act 2000 (Regulated Activities) (Amendment) (Electronic Commerce Directive) Order 2002 (SI 2002/2157). This Order creates a general exclusion from *regulated activities* (except for the *regulated activities* of *effecting* or *carrying out contracts of insurance*). Where activities consist of *electronic commerce activities*, an *incoming ECA provider* will not require *authorisation* for such activities in the *United Kingdom*. This does not extend to the *regulated activity* of *effecting* or *carrying out contracts of insurance* falling under the *Insurance Directives* (see PERG 2.8.3G). However, services provided off-line in the *United Kingdom* (that is, other than as an *electronic commerce activity*) by such a firm which amount to *regulated activities* still require *authorisation*.

(3) *Incoming ECA providers* should note that notification requirements under the *Single Market Directives* still apply (see SUP 13A).

Insurance mediation activities

2.9.19 **[G]** The exclusions in this group apply to certain *regulated activities* involving certain *contracts of insurance*. The exclusions and the *regulated activities* to which they apply are as follows.

(1) The first exclusion of this kind relates to certain activities carried on by a provider of non-motor goods or services related to travel in connection with *general insurance contracts* only. The contracts must be for five years duration or less and have an annual premium of no more than €500. The contract must cover breakdown or loss of or damage to non-motor goods supplied by the provider or loss of or damage to baggage and other risks linked to certain travel services booked with the provider. The travel services must be the hire of an aircraft, vehicle or vessel which does not provide sleeping accommodation, or must relate to attendance at an event organised or managed by the provider. Where the travel services relate to an event, the exclusion does not apply if the party seeking insurance is an individual (acting in his private capacity) or a small business. A small business is a sole trader, *body corporate*, *partnership* or unincorporated association which had a turnover in the last financial year of less than £1,000,000 (but where it is a member of a group, the combined turnover of the group is used). Turnover means the amounts derived from the provision of goods and services falling within the business's ordinary activities, after deduction of trade discounts, value added tax and any other taxes based on those amounts. There must not be any liability risk cover other than where this is ancillary to the main risk covered in a travel policy. The insurance must be complementary to the goods or services being supplied by the provider in the course of his carrying on a business or profession not otherwise consisting of *regulated activities*, and the policy must be in standard form. This exclusion applies where the *regulated activities* concerned are:
   (a) *dealing in investments as agent*;
   (b) *arranging (bringing about) deals in investments* and *making arrangements with a view to transactions in investments*;
   (c) *assisting in the administration and performance of a contract of insurance*; and
   (d) *advising on investments*.

(2) The second exclusion applies where information is provided to a *policyholder* by a *person* on an incidental basis in the course of that *person*'s profession or business that does not otherwise consist of *regulated activities*. This exclusion applies where the *regulated activities* are:
   (a) *arranging (bringing about) deals in investments* and *making arrangements with a view to transactions in investments*;
   (b) *managing investments*;
   (c) *assisting in the administration and performance of a contract of insurance*; and

(d) *safeguarding and administering investments*.

(3) The third exclusion applies to certain *general insurance contracts* covering large risks where the risk is situated outside the *EEA*. This exclusion applies where the *regulated activities* concerned are:

(a) *dealing in investments as agent*;

(b) *arranging (bringing about) deals in investments* and *making arrangements with a view to transactions in investments*;

(c) *assisting in the administration and performance of a contract of insurance*; and

(d) *advising on investments*.

Guidance on these and other exclusions relevant to *insurance mediation activities* is in PERG 5 (Insurance mediation activities).

Business angel-led enterprise capital funds

2.9.20 **[G]** This group of exclusions applies, in specified circumstances, to the *regulated activities* of:

(1) *dealing in investments as agent*;

(2) *arranging (bringing about) deals in investments* and *making arrangements with a view to transactions in investments*;

(3) *managing investments*;

(4) *safeguarding and administering investments*;

(5) establishing, operating or winding up a collective investment scheme; and

(6) advising on investments.

2.9.21 **[G]** The exclusions apply, in general terms:

(1) to a *body corporate* with limited liability:

(a) that is formed in accordance with the law of, and having its registered office, central administration or principal place of business in, an *EEA State*;

(b) that operates a business angel-led enterprise capital fund, being a fund that invests only in *securities* of unlisted *companies* and whose participants are made up solely of *persons* of a specified kind; and

(c) whose members are limited to *persons* of a specified kind.

2.9.21A The exclusions for business angel-led enterprise capital funds are also disapplied for *persons* who, when carrying on the relevant *regulated activity*, are *MiFID investment firms* or *third country investment firms* (see PERG 2.5.4G (Investment services and activities)).

2.9.22 [deleted]

2.10 Persons carrying on regulated activities who do not need authorisation

2.10.1 **[G]** There are various provisions that disapply the *general prohibition* from specific *persons* in relation to the carrying on by them of particular *regulated activities*. There is, however, no general provision for *persons* to apply for an exemption.

2.10.2 **[G]** *Persons* may be exempted from the *general prohibition* in relation to one or more particular *regulated activities*. The extent of any exemption may also be limited to specified circumstances (such as where another *person* who is *authorised* and has relevant *permission* has accepted responsibility for the *regulated activities* in question) or subject to specified conditions (such as a requirement that the activity is not carried on for pecuniary gain).

2.10.3 **[G]** The *Act* provides that *appointed representatives* (see PERG 2.10.5G), *recognised investment exchanges* and *recognised clearing houses* (see PERG 2.10.6G) and certain other *persons* exempt under miscellaneous provisions (see PERG 2.10.7G) are *exempt persons*. Members of Lloyd's and members of the professions are not '*exempt persons*' as such, but the *general prohibition* in section 19 of the *Act* only applies to them in certain circumstances. The distinction is significant in relation to various provisions (such as those in the *Regulated Activities Order*) that apply only to transactions and other activities that involve *exempt persons*.

2.10.4 **[G]** *Appointed representatives* and the *persons* exempt under miscellaneous provisions cannot be exempt in relation to some *regulated activities* and *authorised* in relation to others. If a *person* is already *authorised*, and proposes to carry on additional *regulated activities* in respect of which he would otherwise be exempt as an *appointed representative* or under miscellaneous provisions, he must seek an extension to his existing *permission* to cover those additional activities. A *person* in either of these categories who would otherwise be exempt in relation to particular activities will, if he becomes *authorised*, no longer be able to rely on the exemption.

Appointed representatives

2.10.5 **[G]** A *person* is exempt if he is an *appointed representative* of an *authorised person*. See SUP 12 (Appointed representatives). But where an *appointed representative* carries on *insurance mediation* or *reinsurance mediation* he will not be exempt unless he is included on the register kept by the *FSA* under article 93 of the *Regulated Activities Order* (Duty to maintain a record of unauthorised persons carrying on insurance mediation activities) (see PERG 5.13 (Appointed representatives)).

Recognised Investment Exchanges and Recognised Clearing Houses

2.10.6 **[G]** Investment exchanges and *clearing houses* can apply for recognition under Part XVIII of the *Act* (Recognised investment exchanges and clearing houses.) See REC.

Particular exempt persons

2.10.7 **[G]** Various named *persons* are exempted by Order made by the Treasury under section 38 of the *Act* from the need to obtain *authorisation* (the *Exemption Order*). Some of the exemptions are subject to restrictions as to the circumstances in which they apply. For example, a *person* is only exempt when acting in a particular capacity or for particular purposes.

2.10.8 **[G]** The exemptions apply so as to confer exemption on *persons* from the *general prohibition* in respect of four distinct categories of *regulated activities*.

(1) The first category is carrying on any *regulated activity*, apart from *effecting* or *carrying out contracts of insurance* (or agreeing to do so). *Exempt persons* here are generally supranational bodies of which the *United Kingdom* or another *EEA State* is a member.

(2) The second category is the *regulated activity* of *accepting deposits*. *Exempt persons* here include municipal banks, local authorities, charities and *industrial and provident societies*.

(3) The third category is carrying on any of those *regulated activities* relating to *securities* or *relevant investments* or to 'any property' (or agreeing to do so). *Exempt persons* here include *persons* whose activities are subject to a certain degree of control or oversight by the Government.

(4) The fourth category is carrying on one or more specified *regulated activities* (or agreeing to do so). *Exempt persons* here cover a range of different *persons*.

Members of Lloyd's

2.10.9 **[G]** Several activities carried on in connection with business at Lloyd's are *regulated activities* in respect of which *authorisation* must be obtained. These include the *regulated activities* of *advising on syndicate participation at Lloyd's* or *managing the underwriting capacity of Lloyd's syndicate as a managing agent at Lloyd's* or *arranging (bringing about) deals in investments* or *making arrangements with a view to transactions in investments* for another in relation to such participation or underwriting capacity.

2.10.10 **[G]** But under section 316 of the *Act* (Direction by the FSA) the *general prohibition* does not apply to a *person* who is a member of the *Society* of Lloyd's unless the *FSA* has made a direction that it should apply. The *general prohibition* is disapplied in relation to any *regulated activity* carried on by a member relating to *contracts of insurance* written at Lloyd's. Directions can be made by the *FSA* in relation to individual *members* or the *members* of the *Society* of Lloyd's taken together. Alternatively, instead of being required to obtain *authorisation*, a member of the *Society* of Lloyd's may, as a result of a direction under section 316 of the *Act*, become subject to specific provisions of the *Act* even though he is not an *authorised person*.

2.10.11 **[G]** A *person* who ceased to be an *underwriting member* at any time on or after 24 December 1996 may, without *authorisation*, *carry out contracts of insurance* he has underwritten at Lloyd's. But this is subject to any requirements or *rules* that the *FSA* may impose under sections 320 to 322 of the *Act* (Former underwriting members).

Members of the professions

2.10.12 **[G]** The *general prohibition* does not in certain circumstances apply to a *person* providing professional services that are supervised and regulated by a professional body designated by the Treasury under section 326 of the *Act* (Designation of professional bodies) (see PROF). Certain of the exclusions from *regulated activities* outlined in PERG 2.8 and PERG 2.9 will be relevant to members of *designated professional bodies*. The regime outlined below applies only where no *exclusion applies and a person* will be carrying on a *regulated activity*.

2.10.13 **[G]** Such a *person* may carry on *regulated activities* if the conditions outlined below are met, that is the *person*:

(1) is not affected by an order or direction made by the *FSA* under section 328 or 329 of the *Act* (Directions and orders in relation to the general prohibition) which has the effect of re-imposing the *general prohibition* in any particular case;

(2) is, or is controlled by, a member of a profession;

(3) does not receive any pecuniary reward or other advantage from the *regulated activities* which is given to him by any *person* other than his client (or if he does, he must account to his client for it);

(4) provides any service in the course of carrying on the *regulated activities* in a manner which is incidental to the provision of professional services;
(5) carries on only those *regulated activities* which are permitted by the rules of the professional body or in respect of which they are an *exempt person*; and
(6) is not an *authorised person*.

2.10.14 **[G]** The *regulated activities* that may be carried on in this way are restricted by an Order made by the Treasury under section 327(6) of the *Act* (Exemption from the general prohibition) (the *Non-Exempt Activities Order*). Accordingly, under that section, a *person* may not by way of business carry on any of the following activities without *authorisation*:
(1) *accepting deposits*;
(2) *effecting* or *carrying out contracts of insurance*;
(3) *dealing in investments as principal*;
(4) *establishing, operating or winding up a collective investment scheme*;
(5) *establishing, operating or winding up a stakeholder pension scheme* or a *personal pension scheme*;
(6) *managing the underwriting capacity of a Lloyd's syndicate as a managing agent at Lloyd's*;
(7) *entering as provider into funeral plan contracts*;
(8) agreeing to do certain of the above activities.

2.10.15 **[G]** In addition, there are restrictions on carrying on (or agreeing to carry on) certain other *regulated activities*. These relate to *managing investments, advising on investments, advising on a home finance transaction, advising on syndicate participation at Lloyd's, entering into a home finance transaction* or *administering a home finance transaction*.

2.10.16 **[G]** A *person* carrying on *regulated activities* under the regime for members of the professions will be subject to rules made by the professional body designated by the Treasury. Such bodies are obliged to make rules governing the carrying on by their members of those *regulated activities* that they are able to carry on without *authorisation* under the *Act*. Where such a *person* is carrying on *insurance mediation* or *reinsurance mediation*, he must also be included on the register kept by the *FSA* under article 93 of the *Regulated Activities Order* (Duty to maintain a record of unauthorised persons carrying on insurance mediation activities) (see PERG 5.10 (Exemptions)).

2.11 What to do now?

2.11.1 **[G]** Any *person* who concludes or is advised that he will need to make an application for *Part IV permission* should look at PERG 2 Annex 2G to determine the categories of *specified investment* and *regulated activities* that are relevant to the next step and should then refer to the *FSA* website "How do I get authorised": http://www.fsa.gov.uk/Pages/Doing/how/index.shtml for details of the application process.

2.11.2 **[G]** As part of its application for *Part IV permission*, an applicant may wish to apply for certain *limitations* (details of which are given in the application pack).

2.11.3 **[G]** An example of *limitations* which may be applied for or imposed include a limit on the types of *client* that a *firm* may deal with including:
(1) retail (investment);
(2) professional;
(3) eligible counterparty;

These limitations correspond to the *Glossary* terms *retail client*, *professional client* and *eligible counterparty*.

PERG 2 Annex 1G
Authorisation and regulated activities

Do you need authorisation?

PERG 2 Ann 1 **[G]**

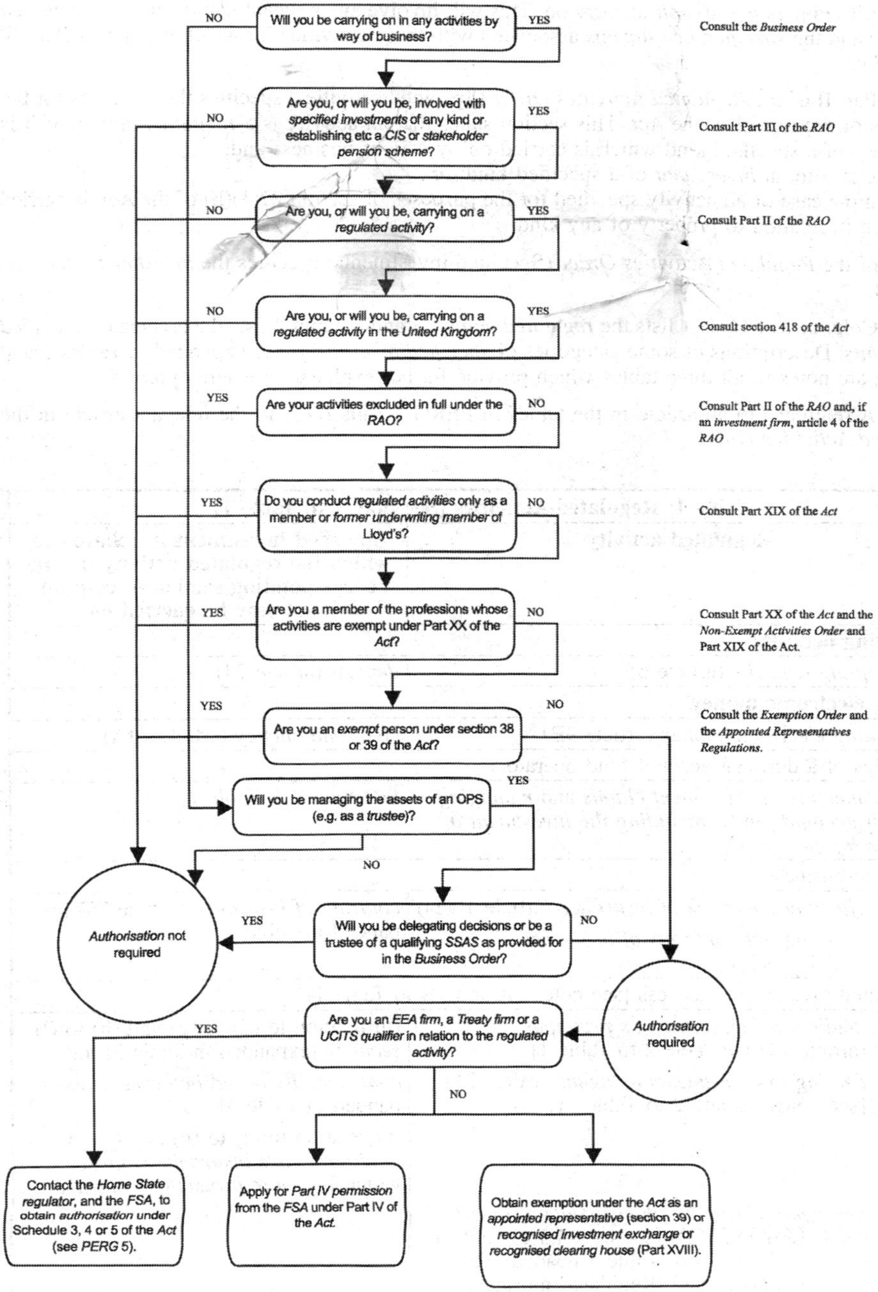

PERG 2 Annex 2G
Regulated activities and the permission regime

PERG 2 Ann 2 **[G]**

1 Table

1.1 **[G]** Table 1 is designed to relate the *permission* regime to *regulated activities*. Section 42(6) of the *Act* gives the *FSA* the power to describe the *regulated activity* or *regulated activities* for which it gives *permission* in such manner as the *FSA* considers appropriate. Table 1 details how the *FSA* has chosen to describe the *regulated activities* and *specified investments* for the purposes of the *permission* regime.

1.2 **[G]** In an application for *Part IV permission*, an applicant will need to state the *regulated activities* it requires *permission* to carry on. This will involve an applicant identifying the *regulated activities* and the *specified investments* associated with those activities for which it requires *Part IV permission*.

1.3 **[G]** Part II of the *Regulated Activities Order* (Specified activities) specifies the activities for the purposes of section 22 of the *Act*. This section states that an activity is a *regulated activity* if it is an activity of a specified kind which is carried on by way of business and:

(1) relates to an *investment* of a specified kind; or

(2) in the case of an activity specified for the purposes of section 22(1)(b) of the *Act*, is carried on in relation to property of any kind.

Part III of the *Regulated Activities Order* (Specified investments) specifies the *investments* referred to in (1).

1.4 **[G]** Column 1 of Table 1 lists the *regulated activities* and column 2 lists the associated *specified investments*. Descriptions of some categories of *specified investments* are expanded in Tables 2 and 3. There are notes to all three tables which provide further explanation where appropriate.

1.5 **[G]** A reference to an article in the tables in PERG 2 Ann 2G is to the relevant article in the *Regulated Activities Order*.

2 Table

Table 1: Regulated Activities [See note 1 to Table 1]	
Regulated activity	**Specified investment in relation to which the regulated activity (in the corresponding section of column one) may be carried on**
Accepting deposits	
(a) *accepting deposits* (article 5)	*deposit* (article 74)
Issuing electronic money	
(aa) *issuing electronic money* (article 9B)	*electronic money* (article 74A)
Activities of a dormant account fund operator	
(ab) the *meeting of repayment claims* and *managing dormant account funds (including the investment of such funds)* (article 63N)	*See Note 8 to Table 1*
Insurance business	
(b) *effecting contracts of insurance* (article 10(1)) (c) *carrying out contracts of insurance* (article 10(2))	*contract of insurance* (article 75) [expanded in Table 2]
Designated investment business [see notes 1A and 1B to Table 1]	
(d) *dealing in investments as principal* (article 14) [see note 2 to Table 1] (e) *dealing in investments as agent* (article 21) [see notes 1B and 2 to Table 1] (f) *arranging (bringing about) deals in investments* (article 25(1)) [see note 1B to Table 1] [also see Sections of Table 1 headed 'The Lloyd's market' and 'Regulated mortgage activity'] (g) *making arrangements with a view to transactions in investments* (article 25(2)) [see note 1B to Table 1] [also see Sections of Table 1 headed 'The Lloyd's market' and 'Regulated mortgage activity']	(in relation to (d) to (g) and (h) to (l)) *security* [expanded in Table 3]; or *contractually based investment* [expanded in Table 3]. (in relation to (e) to (g) and (j) only) a *long-term care insurance contract* which is a *pure protection contract*

Table 1: Regulated Activities [See note 1 to Table 1]

	Regulated activity	Specified investment in relation to which the regulated activity (in the corresponding section of column one) may be carried on
(ga)	*operating a multilateral trading facility* (article 25D) [see note 2A]	*securities* or *contractually based investments* which are *financial instruments* (see PERG 13 Annex 2G Table 2 and note 2A to Table 1]).
(h)	*managing investments* (article 37) [see note 3 to Table 1]	
(i)	*safeguarding and administering investments* (article 40) [see note 3 Table 1] For the purposes of the *permission* regime, this *regulated activity* is subdivided into: (i) *safeguarding and administration of assets (without arranging)*; and (ii) *arranging safeguarding and administration of assets.*	
(j)	*advising on investments* (article 53) [see note 1B to Table 1] [also see Section of Table 1 headed 'Regulated mortgage activity'] For the purposes of the *permission* regime, this *regulated activity*: (i) does not apply to advice given in the course of carrying on the *regulated activity* of *providing basic advice on a stakeholder product*; and (ii) is subdivided into: (A) *advising on investments (except pension transfers and pension opt-outs)*; and (B) *advising on pension transfers and pension opt-outs* [see note 4 to Table 1]	
(k)	*sending dematerialised instructions* (article 45(1))	
(l)	*causing dematerialised instructions to be sent* (article 45(2))	
(m)	*establishing, operating or winding up a collective investment scheme* (article 51) For the purposes of the *permission* regime, this *regulated activity* is subdivided into: (i) *establishing, operating or winding up a regulated collective investment scheme*; and (ii) *establishing, operating or winding up an unregulated collective investment scheme.*	[see note 5 to Table 1]
(n)	*acting as trustee of an authorised unit trust scheme* (article 51)	
(o)	*acting as the depositary or sole director of an open-ended investment company* (article 51)	
(p)	*establishing, operating or winding up a stakeholder pension scheme* (article 52(a))	
(p-a)	*establishing, operating or winding up a personal pension scheme* (article 52(b))	those *specified investments* that are also a *stakeholder product* [see note 7]
(pa)	*providing basic advice on a stakeholder product* (article 52B)	
Insurance mediation activity [see note 5A to Table 1]		
(pb)	*dealing in investments as agent* (article 21)	*life policy* [see note 5B to Table 1]

Table 1: Regulated Activities [See note 1 to Table 1]		
	Regulated activity	**Specified investment in relation to which the regulated activity (in the corresponding section of column one) may be carried on**
(pc)	*arranging (bringing about) deals in investments* (article 25(1))	*non-investment insurance contract*
(pd)	*making arrangements with a view to transactions in investments* (article 25(2))	*rights to or interests in investments* (article 89) in so far as they relate to a *life policy*
(pe)	*assisting in the administration and performance of a contract of insurance* (article 39A)	
(pf)	*advising on investments* (article 53) For the purpose of the *permission* regime, this *regulated activity* is sub-divided into: (i) *advising on investments (except pension transfers or pension opt-outs)*; (ii) *advising on pension transfers or pension opt-outs* [See note 5D to Table 1].	
The Lloyd's market [see note 6 to Table 1]		
(q)	*advising on syndicate participation at Lloyd's* (article 56)	membership of a Lloyd's syndicate (article 86(2))
(r)	*managing the underwriting capacity of a Lloyd's syndicate as a managing agent at Lloyd's* (article 57)	*underwriting capacity of a Lloyd's syndicate* (article 86(1))
(s)	*arranging (bringing about) deals in investments* (article 25(1))	*underwriting capacity of a Lloyd's syndicate* (article 86(1))
(t)	*making arrangements with a view to transactions in investments* (article 25(2))	*membership of a Lloyd's syndicate* (article 86(2)) *rights to or interests in investments* (article 89) in so far as they relate to *underwriting capacity of a Lloyd's syndicate* or *membership of a Lloyd's syndicate*
Funeral plan providers		
(u)	*entering as provider into a funeral plan contract* (article 59) [see note 1A to Table 1]	*funeral plan contract* (article 87)
Regulated home finance activity		
(v)	*arranging (bringing about) regulated mortgage contracts* (article 25A(1))	*regulated mortgage contract* (article 88)
(w)	*making arrangements with a view to regulated mortgage contracts* (article 25A(2))	
(x)	*advising on regulated mortgage contracts* (article 53A)	
(y)	*entering into a regulated mortgage contract* (article 61(1))	
(z)	*administering a regulated mortgage contract* (article 61(2))	
(za)	*arranging (bringing about) a home reversion plan* (article 25B(1))	rights under a *home reversion plan* (article 88A)
(zb)	*making arrangements with a view to a home reversion plan* (article 25B(2))	
(zc)	*advising on a home reversion plan* (article 53B)	
(zd)	*entering into a home reversion plan* (article 63B(1))	
(ze)	*administering a home reversion plan* (article 63B(2))	

Table 1: Regulated Activities [See note 1 to Table 1]		
	Regulated activity	**Specified investment in relation to which the regulated activity (in the corresponding section of column one) may be carried on**
(zf)	*arranging (bringing about) a home purchase plan* (article 25C(1))	rights under a *home purchase plan* (article 88B)
(zg)	*making arrangements with a view to a home purchase plan* (article 25C(2))	
(zh)	*advising on a home purchase plan* (article 53C)	
(zi)	*entering into a home purchase plan* (article 63F(1))	
(zj)	*administering a home purchase plan* (article 63F(2))	

3 Table

Notes to Table 1

Note 1: In addition to the *regulated activities* listed in Table 1, article 64 of the *Regulated Activities Order* specifies that *agreeing to carry on a regulated activity* is itself a *regulated activity* in certain cases. This applies in relation to all the *regulated activities* listed in Table 1 apart from:

- *accepting deposits* (article 5);
- *issuing electronic money* (article 9B);
- *effecting and carrying out contracts of insurance* (article 10);
- *operating a multilateral trading facility* (article 25D);
- *establishing, operating or winding up a collective investment scheme* (article 51(1)(a));
- *acting as trustee of an authorised unit trust scheme* (article 51(1)(b));
- *acting as the sole depositary or sole director of an open-ended investment company* (article 51(1)(c));
- *establishing, operating or winding up a stakeholder pension scheme* or *establishing operating or winding up a personal pension scheme* (article 52); and.
- the *meeting of repayment claims* and/or *managing dormant account funds (including the investment of such funds)* (article 63N).

Permission to carry on the activity of *agreeing to carry on a regulated activity* will be given automatically by the *FSA* in relation to those other *regulated activities* for which an applicant is given *permission* (other than those activities in articles 5, 9B, 10, 51 and 52 detailed above).

Note 1A: *Funeral plan contracts* are *contractually based investments*. Accordingly, the following are *regulated activities* when carried on in relation to a *funeral plan contract*: (a) *arranging (bringing about) deals in investments*, (b) *making arrangements with a view to transactions in investments*, (c) *managing investments*, (d) *safeguarding and administering investments*, (e) *advising on investments*, (f) *sending dematerialised instructions* and (g) *causing dematerialised instructions to be sent* (as well as agreeing to carry on each of the activities listed in (a) to (g)). However, they are not *designated investment business*.

Note 1B: *Life policies* are *contractually based investments*. Where the *regulated activities* listed as *designated investment business* in (e) to (g) and (j) are carried on in relation to a *life policy*, these activities also count as 'insurance mediation activities'. The full list of *insurance mediation activities* is set out in (pb) to (pf). The *regulated activities* of agreeing to carry on each of these activities will, if carried on in relation to a *life policy*, also come within both *designated investment business* and *insurance mediation activities*.

Note 2: For the purposes of the *regulated activities* of *dealing in investments as principal* (article 14) and *dealing in investments as agent* (article 21), the definition *of contractually based investments* [expanded in Table 3] excludes a *funeral plan contract* (article 87) and rights to or interests in *funeral plan contracts*.

Note 2A: PERG 13 Ann 2 Table 2 contains a map indicating which *securities* and *contractually based investments* correspond to *financial instruments*. A *firm's permission* should comprise each of the categories of *security* and *contractually based investment* in relation to which it carries on the activity of *operating a multilateral trading facility*.

Note 3: The *regulated activities* of *managing investments* (article 37) and *safeguarding and administering investments* (article 40) may apply in relation to any assets, in particular circumstances, if the assets being managed or safeguarded and administered include, (or may include), any *security* or *contractually based investment*.

Note 4: For the purposes of the *permission* regime, the activity in (j)(ii) of *advising on pension transfers and pension opt-outs* is carried on in respect of the following *specified investments*:
- *unit* (article 81);
- *stakeholder pension scheme* (article 82(1));
- *personal pension scheme* (article 82(2));
- *life policy* (explained in note 5); and
- *rights to or interests in investments* in so far as they relate to a *unit, a stakeholder pension scheme*, a *personal pension scheme* or a *life policy*.

Note 5: Article 4(2) of *the Regulated Activities Order* specifies the activities (m) to (p) for the purposes of section 22(1)(b) of the *Act*. That is, these activities will be *regulated activities* if carried on in relation to any property and are not expressed as relating to a *specified investment*.

Note 5A: Where they are carried on in relation to a *life policy*, the activities listed as *insurance mediation activities* in (pb) to (pf) (as well as the *regulated activity* of agreeing to carry on those activities) are also *designated investment business*.

Note 5B: In PERG, *life policy* is the term used in the *Handbook* to mean 'qualifying contract of insurance' (as defined in article 3(1) of the *Regulated Activities Order*). For the purpose of the *permission* regime, term also includes a *long term care insurance contract* which is a *pure protection contract* and a *pension term assurance policy*.

Note 5C: '*Non-investment insurance contract*' is the term used in firms' permissions to mean *pure protection contract* or *general insurance contract*. *Pure protection contract* is the term used in the *Handbook* to mean a *long-term insurance contract* which is not a *life policy*. *General insurance contract* is the term used in the *Handbook* to mean *contract of insurance* within column 1 of Table 2.

Note 5D: [deleted]

Note 5E: For the purposes of the *permission* regime, the activity in (pf)(ii) of *advising on pension transfers and pension opt-outs* is carried on in respect of the following *specified investments*:
- *life policy* (explained in note 5A); and
- *rights to or interests in investments* in so far as they relate to a *life policy*.

Note 6: Section 315 of the *Act* (The Society: authorisation and permission) states that the *Society of Lloyd's* has *permission* to carry on the *regulated activities* referred to in that section, one of which is specified in article 58 of the *Regulated Activities Order*. This *permission* is unique to the *Society of Lloyd's*.

Note 7: A *stakeholder product* is defined in the *Glossary* as:
- an investment of a kind specified in the *Stakeholder Regulations*:
- a *stakeholder pension scheme*; and
- a *stakeholder CTF*.

Note 8: Article 4(2) of the *Regulated Activities Order* specifies the activity at (ab) for the purposes of section 22(1)(b) of the *Act*, that is, these activities will be *regulated activities* if carried on in relation to any property and are not expressed as related to a *specified investment*.

4 Table

Table 2: Contracts of insurance		
Contract of insurance (article 75 of the RAO)		
(a) *general insurance contract* (Part I of Schedule 1 to the *Regulated Activities Order*)		(b) *long-term insurance contract* (Part II of Schedule 1 to the *Regulated Activities Order*)
Number		
1	*Accident* (paragraph 1)	*life and annuity* (paragraph I)
2	*Sickness* (paragraph 2)	*marriage or the formation of a civil partnership and birth* (paragraph II)
3	*Land vehicles* (paragraph 3)	*linked long-term* (paragraph III)
4	*Railway rolling stock* (paragraph 4)	*permanent health* (paragraph IV)
5	*Aircraft* (paragraph 5)	*tontines* (paragraph V)
6	*Ships* (paragraph 6)	*capital redemption* (paragraph VI)
7	*Goods in transit* (paragraph 7)	*pension fund management* (paragraph VII)
8	*fire and natural forces* (paragraph 8)	*collective insurance* (paragraph VIII)
9	*damage to property* (paragraph 9)	*social insurance* (paragraph IX)
10	*motor vehicle liability* (paragraph 10)	
11	*aircraft liability* (paragraph 11)	

12	*liability of ships* (paragraph 12)	
13	*general liability* (paragraph 13)	
14	*credit* (paragraph 14)	
15	*suretyship* (paragraph 15)	
16	*miscellaneous financial loss* (paragraph 16)	
17	*legal expenses* (paragraph 17)	
18	*assistance* (paragraph 18)	

Notes to Table 2

Note 1:

See *IPRU(INS)* Ann 10.2 Part II for the groups of *classes of general insurance business* from the Annex to the *First non-Life Directive*.

Note 2:

See *IPRU(INS)* 11.8 and the definition of *ancillary risks* in *IPRU(INS)* for *guidance* on the treatment of supplementary and ancillary provisions in relation to *contracts of insurance*.

5 Table

Table 3: Securities, contractually based investments and relevant investments [see notes 1 and 2 to Table 3]		
Security (article 3(1))	Contractually based investment (article 3(1))	Relevant investments (article 3(1))
share (article 76) *debenture* (article 77) *government and public security* (article 78) *warrant* (article 79) *certificate representing certain security* (article 80) *unit* (article 81) *stakeholder pension scheme* (article 82(1)) *personal pension scheme* (article 82(2)); *rights to or interests in investments* (article 89) in so far as they relate to any of the above categories of *security*	*option* (article 83) For the purposes of the *permission* regime, *option* is subdivided into: (i) *option* (excluding a *commodity option* and an *option* on a *commodity future*); (ii) *commodity option* and *option* on a *commodity* future. *future* (article 84) For the purposes of the *permission* regime, *future* is subdivided into: (i) *future* (excluding a *commodity future* and *a rolling spot forex contract*); (ii) *commodity future*; (iii) *rolling spot forex contract.* *contract for differences* (article 85) For the purposes of the *permission* regime, *contract for differences* is subdivided into: (i) *contract for differences* (excluding a *spread bet* and a *rolling spot forex contract*); (ii) *spread bet*; (iii) *rolling spot forex contract.* *life policy* (but excluding a *long-term care insurance contract* which is a *pure protection contract*) [see note 5B to Table 1]	*contractually based investments* (article 3(1)) *non-investment insurance contract* [see note 5C to Table 1]

Table 3: Securities, contractually based investments and relevant investments [see notes 1 and 2 to Table 3]		
	funeral plan contract (article 87) [see note 1A to Table 1] *rights to or interests in investments* (article 89) in so far as they relate to any of the above categories of *contractually based investment.*	

Notes to Table 3

Note 1:

Security, contractually based investment and *relevant investment* are not, in themselves, *specified investments* they are defined as including a number of *specified investments* as set out in Table 3. *Relevant investments* is the term that is used to cover *contractually based investments* together with rights under a *general insurance contract* and a *pure protection contract.*

Note 2:

For the purposes of the *regulated activities* of *dealing in investments as principal* (article 14) and *dealing in investments as agent* (article 21), the definition *of contractually based investments* excludes a *funeral plan contract* (article 87) and rights to or interests in *funeral plan contracts.*

(*Chapters 3, 4 outside the scope of this work.*)

CHAPTER 5
GUIDANCE ON INSURANCE MEDIATION ACTIVITIES

5.1 Application and purpose

Application

[2221]

5.1.1 **[G]** This chapter applies principally to any *person* who needs to know whether he carries on *insurance mediation activities* and is thereby subject to *FSA* regulation. As such it will be of relevance among others to:

(1) insurance brokers;
(2) insurance advisers;
(3) *insurance undertakings*; and
(4) other *persons* involved in the sale and administration of *contracts of insurance*, even where these activities are secondary to their main business.

Purpose of guidance

5.1.2 to 5.1.5 **[G]** [not used]

5.1.6 **[G]** The purpose of this *guidance* is to help *persons* consider whether they need *authorisation* or a variation of their *Part IV permission*. Businesses new to regulation who act only as introducers of *insurance business* are directed in particular to PERG 5.6.2G (article 25(1): arranging (bringing about) deals in investments) to PERG 5.6.9G (Exclusion: Article 72C (Provision of information on an incidental basis)) and PERG 5.15.6G (Flow chart: Introducers) to help consider whether they require *authorisation*. This *guidance* also explains the availability to *persons* carrying on *insurance mediation activities* of certain exemptions from *FSA* regulation, including the possibility of becoming an *appointed representative* (see PERG 5.13.1G to PERG 5.13.6G (Appointed representatives)).

Effect of guidance

5.1.7 **[G]** This *guidance* is issued under section 157 of the *Act* (Guidance). It is designed to throw light on particular aspects of regulatory requirements, not to be an exhaustive description of a *person*'s obligations. If a *person* acts in line with the *guidance* and the circumstances contemplated by it, then the *FSA* will proceed on the footing that the *person* has complied with aspects of the requirement to which the *guidance* relates.

5.1.8 **[G]** Rights conferred on third parties cannot be affected by *guidance* given by the *FSA*. This *guidance* represents the *FSA's* view, and does not bind the courts, for example, in relation to the enforceability of a contract where there has been a breach of the *general prohibition* on carrying on a *regulated activity* in the *United Kingdom* without *authorisation* (see sections 26 to 29 of the *Act* (Enforceability of Agreements)).

5.1.9 **[G]** A *person* reading this *guidance* should refer to the *Act* and the various Orders that are referred to in this *guidance*. These should be used to find out the precise scope and effect of any particular provision referred to in this *guidance*. A *person* may need to seek his own legal advice.

5.1.10 **[G]** [not used]

Guidance on other activities

5.1.11 **[G]** A *person* may wish to carry on activities related to other forms of *investment* in connection with *contracts of insurance*, such as *advising on* and *arranging regulated mortgage contracts*. Such a *person* should also consult the *guidance* in PERG 2 (Authorisation and Regulated Activities), PERG 4 (Regulated activities connected with mortgages) and PERG 8 (Financial Promotion and Related Activities).

5.2 Introduction

5.2.1 **[G]** This *guidance* is based on the statutory instruments made as part of implementing the *IMD* in the *United Kingdom*. This legislation includes the Financial Services and Markets Act 2000 (Regulated Activities) (Amendment) (No 2) Order 2003 (SI 2003/1476), which amends among others the *Regulated Activities Order*, the Financial Services and Markets *Act* 2000 (Appointed Representatives) Regulations 2001 (SI 2003/1217), the Non-Exempt Activities Order and the Business Order. Other legislation that forms the basis of this *guidance* includes the Financial Services and Markets Act 2000 (Exemption) (Amendment) (No 2) Order 2003 (SI 2003/1675), the Financial Services and Markets Act 2000 (Financial Promotion) (Amendment) Order 2003 (SI 2003/1676) and the Insurance Mediation Directive (Miscellaneous Amendments) Regulations 2003 (SI 2003/1473). For ease of reference, references to the *Regulated Activities Order* below adopt the revised *Regulated Activities Order* numbering indicated in the Financial Services and Markets *Act* 2000 (Regulated Activities) (Amendment) (No 2) Order 2003.

Requirement for authorisation or exemption

5.2.2 **[G]** Any *person* who carries on a *regulated activity* in the *United Kingdom* by way of business must either be an *authorised person* or exempt from the need for *authorisation*. Otherwise, the *person* commits a criminal offence and certain agreements may be unenforceable. PERG 2.2 (Authorisation and regulated activities) has further *guidance* on these consequences.

Questions to be considered to decide if authorisation is required

5.2.3 **[G]** A *person* who is concerned to know whether his proposed *insurance mediation activities* may require *authorisation* will need to consider the following questions (these questions are a summary of the issues to be considered and have been reproduced, in slightly fuller form, in the flow chart in PERG 5.15.2G (Flow chart: regulated activities related to insurance mediation – do you need authorisation?):

(1) will the activities relate to *contracts of insurance* (see PERG 5.3 (Contracts of insurance))?
(2) if so, will I be carrying on any *insurance mediation activities* (see PERG 5.5 (The regulated activities: dealing in contracts as agent) to PERG 5.11 (Other aspects of exclusions))?
(3) if so, will I be carrying on my activities by way of business (see PERG 5.4 (The business test))?
(4) if so, is there the necessary link with the *United Kingdom* (see PERG 5.12 (Link between activities and the United Kingdom))?
(5) if so, will any or all of my activities be excluded (see PERG 5.3.7G (Connected contracts of insurance) to PERG 5.3.8G (Large risks); PERG 5.6.5G (Exclusion: article 72C provision of information on an incidental basis) to PERG 5.6.23G (Other exclusions); PERG 5.7.7G (Exclusions); PERG 5.8.24G (Exclusion: periodical publications, broadcasts and web-sites) to PERG 5.8.26G (Other exclusions); PERG 5.11 (Other aspects of exclusions) and PERG 5.12.9G to PERG 5.12.10G (Overseas persons))?
(6) if it is not the case that all of my activities are excluded, am I a *professional firm* whose activities are exempted under Part XX of the *Act* (see PERG 5.14.1G to PERG 5.14.4G (Professionals))?
(7) if not, am I exempt as an *appointed representative* (see PERG 5.13 (Appointed representatives))?
(8) if not, am I otherwise an exempt *person* (see PERG 5.14.5G (Other exemptions))?

If a *person* gets as far as question (8) and the answer to that question is "no", that *person* requires *authorisation* and should refer to the *FSA* website "How do I get authorised": http://www.fsa.gov.uk/Pages/Doing/how/index.shtml for details of the application process. The order of these questions considers firstly whether a *person* is carrying on *insurance mediation activities* before dealing separately with the questions "will I be carrying on my activities by way of business?" (3) and "if so, will any or all of my activities by excluded?" (5).

5.2.4 **[G]** It is recognised pursuant to section 22 of the *Act* that a *person* will not be carrying on *regulated activities* in the first instance, including *insurance mediation activities*, unless he is carrying on these activities by way of business. Similarly, where a *person's* activities are excluded he cannot, by definition, be carrying on *regulated activities*. To this extent, the content of the

questions above does not follow the scheme of the *Act*. For ease of navigation, however, the questions are set out in an order and form designed to help *persons* consider more easily, and in turn, issues relating to:
(1) the new activities;
(2) the business test; and
(3) the exclusions.

Approach to implementation of the IMD

5.2.5 **[G]** The *IMD* imposes requirements upon *EEA States* relating to the regulation of *insurance* and *reinsurance mediation*. The *IMD* defines "insurance mediation" and "reinsurance mediation" as including the activities of introducing, proposing or carrying out other work preparatory to the conclusion of contracts of insurance and reinsurance, or of concluding such contracts, or of assisting in the administration and performance of such contracts, in particular in the event of a claim (the text of article 2.3 *IMD* is reproduced in full in PERG 5.16.2G (article 2.3 of the Insurance Mediation Directive)).

5.2.6 **[G]** The *United Kingdom's* approach to implementing the *IMD* by domestic legislation is, in part, through secondary legislation, which will apply pre-existing *regulated activities* (slightly amended) in the *Regulated Activities Order* to the component elements of the *insurance mediation* definition in the *IMD* (see PERG 5.2.5G and the text of article 2.3 *IMD* in PERG 5.16.2G (article 2.3 of the Insurance Mediation Directive)).

5.2.7 **[G]** The effect of the *IMD* and its implementation described in PERG 5.2.5G to PERG 5.2.6G is to vary the application of the existing *regulated activities* set out in PERG 5.2.8G (1) to (3), (5) and (6), principally by applying these *regulated activities* to *general insurance contracts* and *pure protection contracts* and by making changes to the application of the various exclusions to these *regulated activities*. These *regulated activities* applied prior to 14 January 2005 to qualifying contracts of insurance (as defined by article 3 of the *Regulated Activities Order* and referred to in the *Handbook* as *life policies* (which includes *pension policies*)). The legislation implementing the *IMD* introduced a new *regulated activity* set out in PERG 5.2.8G (4), which potentially applies to all *contracts of insurance*.

5.2.8 **[G]** It follows that each of the *regulated activities* below potentially apply to any *contract of insurance*:
(1) *dealing in investments as agent* (article 21 (Dealing in investments as agent));
(2) *arranging (bringing about) deals in investments* (article 25(1) (Arranging deals in investments));
(3) *making arrangements with a view to transactions in investments* (article 25(2) (Arranging deals in investments));
(4) *assisting in the administration and performance of a contract of insurance* (article 39A (Assisting in the administration and performance of a contract of insurance));
(5) *advising on investments* (article 53 (Advising on investments));
(6) agreeing to carry on any of the above *regulated activities* (article 64 (Agreeing to carry on specified types of activity)).

5.2.9 **[G]** It is the scope of the *Regulated Activities Order* rather than the *IMD* which will determine whether a *person* requires *authorisation* or exemption. However, the scope of the *IMD* is relevant to the application of certain exclusions under the *Regulated Activities Order* (see, for example, the commentary on article 67 in PERG 5.11.9G (Activities carried on in the course of a profession or non-investment business)).

Financial promotion

5.2.10 **[G]** An *unauthorised person* who intends to carry on activities connected with *contracts of insurance* will need to comply with section 21 of the *Act* (Restrictions on financial promotion). This *guidance* does not cover *financial promotions* that relate to *contracts of insurance*. *Persons* should refer to the general *guidance* on *financial promotion* in PERG 8 (Financial promotion and related activities). (See in particular PERG 8.17A (Financial promotions concerning insurance mediation activities) for information on *financial promotions* that relate to *insurance mediation activities*.)

5.3 Contracts of insurance

5.3.1 **[G]** A *person* who is concerned to know whether his proposed activities may require *authorisation* will wish to consider whether those activities relate to *contracts of insurance* or contracts of *reinsurance*, or to *insurance business* or *reinsurance business*, which is the business of *effecting or carrying out contracts of insurance* or *reinsurance* as *principal*.

Definition

5.3.2 **[G]** The *Regulated Activities Order* does not attempt an exhaustive definition of a 'contract of insurance'. Instead, article 3(1) of the order (Interpretation) makes some specific extensions and limitations to the general common law meaning of the concept. For example, article 3(1) expressly extends the concept to fidelity bonds and similar contracts of guarantee, which are not contracts of insurance at common law, and it excludes certain *funeral plan contracts*, which would generally be contracts of insurance at common law.

5.3.3 **[G]** One consequence of this is that common law judicial decisions about whether particular contracts amount to 'insurance' or their being effected or carried out amounts to 'insurance business' are relevant in defining the regulatory scope of the *Act*.

5.3.4 **[G]** As with any other contract, a *contract of insurance* that is not effected by way of a deed will only be legally binding if, amongst other things, it is entered into for valuable consideration. Determining what amounts to sufficient consideration in any given case is a matter for the courts. In practice, however, the legal definition of consideration is very wide. In particular, just because a *contract of insurance* is 'free' in the colloquial sense does not mean that there is no consideration for it. In the vast majority of cases, therefore, 'free' insurance policies (such as policies that act as loss leaders for an *insurance undertaking*) will be binding contracts and will amount to *specified investments* and therefore be subject to *FSA* regulation.

5.3.5 **[G]** The *Regulated Activities Order* does not define a *reinsurance* contract. The essential elements of the common law description of a *contract of insurance* are also the essential elements of a *reinsurance* contract. Whilst the *IMD* addresses insurance and *reinsurance* separately, throughout this *guidance* the term 'contract of insurance' (italicised or otherwise) also applies to contracts of *reinsurance*.

5.3.6 **[G]** *Guidance* describing how the *FSA* identifies *contracts of insurance* is in PERG 6 (Guidance on the Identification of Contracts of Insurance).

Connected contracts of insurance

5.3.7 **[G]** Article 72B of the *Regulated Activities Order* (Activities carried on by a provider of relevant goods or services) excludes from *FSA* regulation certain *regulated activities* carried on by providers of non-motor goods and services related to travel in relation to *contracts of insurance* that satisfy a number of conditions. Details about the scope of this exclusion can be found at PERG 5.11.13G to PERG 5.11.15G (Activities carried on by a provider of relevant goods or services).

Large risks

5.3.8 **[G]** Large risks situated outside the *EEA* are also excluded (described in more detail at PERG 5.11.16G (Large risks)). The location of the risk or commitment may be determined by reference to the *EEA State* in which the risk is situated, defined in article 2(d) of the Second Non-Life Directive (88/357/EEC) or the *EEA State* of the commitment, defined in article 1(1)(g) of the Consolidated Life Directive (2002/83/EC). Broadly put, this is:

(1) for insurance relating to buildings and/or their contents, the *EEA State* in which the property is situated;

(2) for insurance relating to vehicles, the *EEA State* of registration;

(3) for policies of four months or less duration covering travel or holiday risks, where the *policy* was taken out;

(4) in all other cases (including those determined by reference to the *EEA State* of the commitment), the *EEA State* where the policyholder has his habitual residence, or if the policyholder is a legal person, where his establishment, to which the contract relates, is situated.

Specified investments

5.3.9 **[G]** For an activity to be a *regulated activity*, it must be carried on in relation to 'specified investments' (see section 22 of the Act Regulated activities) and Part III of the Regulated Activities Order (Specified investments)). For the purposes of *insurance mediation activity*, *specified investments* include the following '*relevant investments*' defined in article 3(1) of the *Regulated Activities Order* (Interpretation):

(1) rights under any *contract of insurance* (see article 75 (Contracts of insurance)); and

(2) rights to or interests in rights under *life policies* (see article 89 (Rights to or interests in investments)).

'*Relevant investments*' is the term used in articles 21 (Dealing in investments as agent), 25 (Arranging deals in investments) and 53 (Advising on investments) of the *Regulated Activities Order* to help define the types of investment to which the activities in each of these articles relate.

5.3.10 **[G]** A *person* will have rights under a *contract of insurance* when he is a *policyholder*. The question of whether a *person* has rights under a *contract of insurance* may require careful consideration in the case of group policies (with reference to the *Glossary* definition of *policyholder*). In the case, in particular, of *general insurance contracts* and *pure protection* *contracts*, the existence or otherwise of rights under such policies may be relevant to whether a *person* is carrying on *insurance mediation activities*.

5.3.11 **[G]** A *person* may also have rights to or interests in rights under a *life policy* where he is not a *policyholder*, but this will again depend on the terms of the individual *policy*.

5.4 The business test

5.4.1 **[G]** A *person* will only need *authorisation* or exemption if he is carrying on a *regulated activity* 'by way of business' (see section 22 of the *Act* (Regulated Activities)).

5.4.2 **[G]** There is power in the *Act* for the Treasury to specify the circumstances in which a *person* is or is not to be regarded as carrying on *regulated activities* by way of business. The *Business Order* has been made using this power (partly reflecting differences in the nature of the different activities). As such, the business test for *insurance mediation activity* is distinguished from the standard test for 'investment business' in article 3 of the *Business Order*. Under article 3(4) of the *Business Order*, a *person* is not to be regarded as carrying on by way of business any *insurance mediation activity* unless he takes up or pursues that activity for remuneration. Accordingly, there are two principal elements to the business test in the case of *insurance mediation activities*:

(1) does a *person* receive remuneration for these activities?
(2) if so, does he take up or pursue these activities by way of business?

5.4.3 **[G]** As regards PERG 5.4.2G(1), the *Business Order* does not provide a definition of 'remuneration', but, in the *FSA's* view, it has a broad meaning and covers both monetary and non-monetary rewards. This is regardless of who makes them. For example, where a *person* pays discounted premiums for his own insurance needs in return for bringing other business to an *insurance undertaking*, the discount would amount to remuneration for the purposes of the *Business Order*. Remuneration can also take the form of an economic benefit which the *person* expects to receive as a result of carrying on *insurance mediation activities*. In the *FSA's* view, the remuneration does not have to be provided or identified separately from remuneration for other goods or services provided. Nor is there a minimum level of remuneration.

5.4.4 **[G]** As regards PERG 5.4.2G(2), in the *FSA's* view, for a *person* to take up or pursue *insurance mediation activity* by way of business, he will usually need to be carrying on those activities with a degree of regularity. The *person* will also usually need to be carrying on the activities for commercial purposes. That is to say, he will normally be expecting to gain a direct financial benefit of some kind. Activities carried on out of friendship or for altruistic purposes will not normally amount to a business. However, in the *FSA's* view:

(1) it is not necessarily the case that services provided free of charge will not amount to a business; for example, advice (including advice available on a website) may be provided free of charge to potential *policyholders* but in the course of a business funded by commission payments; and
(2) the 'by way of business' test may very occasionally be satisfied by an activity undertaken on an isolated occasion (provided that the activity would be regarded as done 'by way of business' in other respects, for example, because of the size of reward received or its relevance to other business activities).

5.4.5 **[G]** It follows that whether or not any particular *person* is acting 'by way of business' for these purposes will depend on his individual circumstances. However, a typical example of where the applicable business test would be likely to be satisfied by someone whose main business is not *insurance mediation activities*, is where a *person* recommends or arranges specific insurance *policies* in the course of carrying on that other business and receives a fee or commission for doing so.

5.4.6 **[G]** Some typical examples of where the business test is unlikely to be satisfied, assuming that there is no direct financial benefit to the arranger, include:

(1) arrangements which are carried out by a *person* for himself, or for members of his family;
(2) where employers provide insurance benefits for staff; and
(3) where affinity groups or clubs set up insurance benefits for members.

5.4.7 **[G]** PERG 5.4.8G contains a table that summarises the main issues surrounding the business test as applied to *insurance mediation activities* and that may assist *persons* to determine whether they will need *authorisation* or exemption. The approach taken in the table involves identifying factors that, in the *FSA's* view, are likely to play a part in the analysis. Indicators are then given as to the significance of each factor to the *person's* circumstances. By analysing the indicators as a whole, a picture can be formed of the likely overall position. The table provides separate indicators for the two elements of remuneration and by way of business. As a *person* has to satisfy both elements, a clear overall indication against either element being satisfied should mean that the test is failed. This approach cannot be expected to provide a clear conclusion for everyone. But it should enable *persons* to assess the relevant aspects of their activities and to identify where changes could, if necessary, be made so as to make their position clearer. The *person* to whom the indicators are applied is referred to in the table as 'P'.

5.4.8 **[G]** Table: Carrying on insurance mediation activities 'for remuneration' and 'by way of business'

Carrying on insurance mediation activities 'for remuneration' and 'by way of business'		
'For remuneration'		
Factor	Indicators that P does not carry on activities "for remuneration"	Indicators that P does carry on activities "for remuneration"
Direct remuneration, whether received from the customer or the insurer/broker (cash or benefits in kind such as tickets to the opera, a reduction in other insurance premiums, a remission of a debt or any other benefit capable of being measured in money's worth)	P does not receive any direct remuneration specifically identified as a reward for his carrying on *insurance mediation activities*.	P receives direct remuneration specifically identified as being a reward for his carrying on *insurance mediation activities*.
Indirect remuneration (such as any form of economic benefit as may be explicitly or implicitly agreed between P and the insurer/broker or P's customer – including, for example, through the acceptance of P's terms and conditions or mutual recognition of the economic benefit that is likely to accrue to P). An indirect economic benefit can include expectation of making a profit of some kind as a result of carrying on *insurance mediation activities* as part of other services.	P does not obtain any form of indirect remuneration through an economic benefit other than one which is not likely to have a material effect on P's ability to make a profit from his other activities.	P obtains an economic benefit that: (a) is explicitly or implicitly agreed between P and the insurer/broker or P's customer; and (b) has the potential to go beyond mere cost recovery through fees or other benefits received for providing a package of services that includes *insurance mediation activities* but where no particular part of the fees is attributable to *insurance mediation activities*. This could include where *insurance mediation activities* are likely to: • play a material part in the success of P's other business activities or in P's ability to make a profit from them; or • provide P with a materially increased opportunity to provide other goods or services; or • be a major selling point for P's other business activities; or • be essential for P to provide other goods or services. P charges his customers a greater amount for other goods or services than would be the case if P were not also carrying on *insurance mediation activities* for those customers and this: • is explicitly or implicitly agreed between P and the insurer/broker or P's customer; and • has the potential to go beyond mere cost recovery.

Carrying on insurance mediation activities 'for remuneration' and 'by way of business'		
Recovery of costs	P receives no benefits of any kind (direct or indirect) in respect of his *insurance mediation activities* beyond the reimbursement of his actual costs incurred in carrying on the activity (including receipt by P of a sum equal to the insurance premium that P is to pass on to the *insurer* or broker).	P receives benefits of any kind (direct or indirect) in respect of his *insurance mediation activities* which go beyond the reimbursement of his actual costs incurred in carrying on the activity.
'By way of business'		
Factor	Indicators that P does not carry on activities "by way of business"	Indicators that P does carry on activities "by way of business"
Regularity/frequency	Involvement is one-off or infrequent (for instance, once or twice a year) provided that the transaction(s) is not of such size and importance that it is essential to the success of P's other business activities. Transactions do not result from formal arrangements (for instance, occasional involvement purely as a result of an unsolicited approach).	Involvement is frequent (for instance, once a week) Involvement is infrequent but the transactions are of such size or importance that they are essential to the success of P's other business activities. P has formal arrangements which envisage transactions taking place on a regular basis over time (whether or not such transactions turn out in practice to be regular).
Holding out	P does not hold himself out as providing a professional service that includes *insurance mediation activities* (by professional is meant not the services of a layman).	P holds himself out as providing a professional service that includes *insurance mediation activities*.
Relevance to other activities/business	*Insurance mediation activities*: • have no relevance to P's other activities; or • have some relevance but could easily be ceased without causing P any difficulty in carrying on his main activities; or • would be unlikely to result in a material reduction in income from P's main activities if ceased	*Insurance mediation activities*: • are essential to P in carrying on his main activities; or • would cause a material disruption to P carrying on his main activities if ceased; or • would be likely to reduce P's income by a material amount.
Commercial benefit	P receives no direct or indirect pecuniary or economic benefit. P is a layman and acting in that capacity. P would not obtain materially less income from his main activities if they did not include *insurance mediation activities*.	P receives a direct or indirect pecuniary or economic benefit from carrying on *insurance mediation activities* – such as a fee, a benefit in kind or the likelihood of materially enhanced sales of other goods or services that P provides. P would obtain materially less income from his main activities if they did not include *insurance mediation activities*.

5.5 The regulated activities: dealing in contracts as agent

5.5.1 **[G]** Article 21 of the *Regulated Activities Order* (Dealing in investments as agent) makes dealing in *contracts of insurance* as agent a *regulated activity*. The activity is defined in terms of *buying*, *selling*, subscribing for or underwriting contracts as agent, that is, on behalf of another. Examples include:

(1) where an intermediary, by accepting on the *insurance undertaking's* behalf to provide the insurance, commits an *insurance undertaking* to provide insurance for a prospective policyholder; or

(2) where the intermediary agrees, on behalf of a prospective *policyholder*, to *buy* an insurance *policy*.

5.5.2 **[G]** Intermediaries with delegated authority to bind *insurance undertakings* are likely to be *dealing in investments as agent*. It should be noted, in particular, that this is a *regulated activity*:

(1) whether or not any advice is given (see PERG 5.8 (The regulated activities: advising on contracts of insurance); and

(2) whether or not the intermediary deals through an *authorised person* (for example, where he instructs another agent who is an *authorised person* to enter into a *contract of insurance* on his *client's* behalf).

5.5.3 **[G]** There are also certain exclusions which are relevant to whether a *person* is carrying on the activity of *dealing in investments as agent* (see PERG 5.11 (Other aspects of exclusions)).

5.6 The regulated activities: arranging deals in, and making arrangements with a view to transactions in, contracts of insurance

5.6.1 **[G]** Article 25 of the *Regulated Activities Order* (Arranging deals in investments) describes two types of *regulated activities* concerned with arranging deals in respect of *contracts of insurance*. These are:

(1) *arranging (bringing about) deals in investments* (article 25(1) (Arranging deals in investments)); and

(2) *making arrangements with a view to transactions in investments* (article 25(2) (Arranging deals in investments)).

Article 25(1): arranging (bringing about) deals in investments

5.6.2 **[G]** The activity in article 25(1) is carried on only if the arrangements bring about, or would bring about, the transaction to which the arrangement relates. This is because of the exclusion in article 26 of the *Regulated Activities Order* (Arrangements not causing a deal). Article 26 excludes from article 25(1) arrangements which do not bring about or would not bring about the transaction to which the arrangements relate. In the *FSA's* view, a *person* would bring about a *contract of insurance* if his involvement in the chain of events leading to the *contract of insurance* were important enough that, without it, there would be no policy. Examples of this type of activity would include negotiating the terms of the *contract of insurance* on behalf of the customer with the *insurance undertaking* and vice versa, or assisting in the completion of a proposal form and sending it to the *insurance undertaking*. Other examples include where an *insurance undertaking* enters into a *contract of insurance* as *principal* or an intermediary enters into a *contract of insurance* as agent.

Article 25(2): making arrangements with a view to transactions in investments

5.6.3 **[G]** The activity within article 25(2) contrasts with article 25(1) in that it is not limited by the requirement that the arrangements would bring about the transaction to which they relate.

5.6.4 **[G]** Article 25(2) may, for instance, include activities of *persons* who help potential *policyholders* fill in or check application forms in the context of ongoing arrangements between these *persons* and *insurance undertakings*. A further example of this activity would be a *person* introducing customers to an intermediary either for *advice* or to help arrange an insurance *policy*. The introduction might be oral or written. By contrast, the *FSA* considers that a mere passive display of literature advertising insurance (for example, leaving leaflets advertising insurance in a dentist's or vet's waiting room and doing no more) would not amount to the article 25(2) activity.

Exclusion: article 72C (Provision of information on an incidental basis)

5.6.5 **[G]** The *Regulated Activities Order* provides an important potential exclusion, however, for *persons* whose principal business is other than *insurance mediation activities*.

5.6.6 **[G]** In broad terms, article 72C of the *Regulated Activities Order* excludes from the activities of *arranging* and *assisting in the administration and performance of a contract of insurance* activities that:

(1) consist of the provision of information to the *policyholder* or potential *policyholder*;

(2) are carried on by a *person* carrying on any profession or business which does not otherwise consist of *regulated activities*; and

(3) amount to the provision of information that may reasonably be regarded as being incidental to that profession or business.

5.6.7 **[G]** In the *FSA's* view, 'incidental' in this context means that the activity must arise out of, be complementary to or otherwise be sufficiently closely connected with the profession or business. In other words, there must be an inherent link between the activity and the firm's main business. For example, introducing dental insurance may be incidental to a dentist's activities; introducing pet insurance would not be incidental to his activities. In addition, to be considered 'incidental', in the *FSA's* view, the activity must not amount to the carrying on of a business in its own right.

5.6.8 **[G]** This exclusion applies to a *person* whose profession or business does not otherwise consist of *regulated activities*. In the *FSA's* view, the fact that a *person* may carry on *regulated activities* in the course of the carrying on of a profession or business does not, of itself, mean that the profession or business consists of *regulated activities*. This is provided that the main focus of the profession or business does not involve *regulated activities* and that the *regulated activities* that are carried on arise in a way that is incidental and complementary to the carrying on of the profession or business. So, the exclusion may be of relevance to *exempt professional firms*. It might also, for example, be relied on by doctors, vets and dentists as well as many businesses in the non-financial sector, even if they have *permission* to carry on *regulated activities* or are *appointed representatives*. This is assuming that their activities for which they are seeking to use the exclusion in article 72C are limited to providing information in a way which is incidental to their main profession or business. The exclusion only extends to information given to the *policyholder* or potential *policyholder* and not to the *insurance undertaking* An intermediary who forwards a proposal form to an *insurance undertaking* would not be able to take the benefit of the exclusion. Similarly, where a *person* does more than provide information (for example, by helping a potential *policyholder* fill in an application form), he cannot take the benefit of this exclusion. Nor does it cover the activity of advising a customer under article 53 of the *Regulated Activities Order* (Advising on investments).

5.6.9 **[G]** The exclusion will be of assistance to introducers who would otherwise be carrying on the *regulated activity* of *making arrangements with a view to transactions in investments* (assuming, as mentioned in PERG 5.6.8G, that they provide information only to *policyholders* or potential *policyholders*, and not to the intermediary or *insurance undertaking* to whom they introduce these *policyholders* or potential *policyholders*). In order to assist such *introducers* determine whether or not they are likely to require *authorisation*, a simplified flowchart is included in PERG 5.15.6G (Flow chart: introducers). Introducers may also find the *guidance* at PERG 5.9.2G (The regulated activities: agreeing to carry on a regulated activity) helpful. PERG 5.6.17G (Exclusion from article 25(2) for introducing) has *guidance* to assist *persons* determine whether their introducing activities amount to *making arrangements with a view to transactions in investments*.

Exclusion from article 25(2): arrangements enabling parties to communicate

5.6.10 **[G]** Article 27 of the *Regulated Activities Order* (Enabling parties to communicate) contains an exclusion that applies to arrangements which might otherwise bring within article 25(2) those who merely provide the means by which one party to a transaction (or potential transaction) is able to communicate with other parties. Simply providing the means by which parties to a transaction (or potential transaction) are able to communicate with each other is excluded from article 25(2) only. This will ensure that *persons* such as internet service providers or telecommunications networks are excluded if all they do is provide communication facilities (and these would otherwise be considered to fall within article 25(2)).

5.6.11 **[G]** In the *FSA's* view, the crucial element of the exclusion in article 27 is the inclusion of the word 'merely'. When a publisher, broadcaster or internet website operator goes beyond what is necessary for him to provide his service of publishing, broadcasting or otherwise facilitating the issue of promotions, he may well bring himself within the scope of article 25(2). Further detailed *guidance* relating to the scope of the exclusion in article 27 is contained in PERG 2.8.6G(2) (Arranging deals in investments) and PERG 8.32.6G to PERG 8.32.11G (Arranging deals in investments).

Exclusion from article 25(2): transactions to which the arranger is a party

5.6.12 **[G]** Article 28 of the *Regulated Activities Order* (Arranging transactions to which the arranger is a party) excludes from the *regulated activities* in article 25(1) and 25(2) arrangements made for or with a view to *contracts of insurance* when:
(1) the *person* (P) making the arrangements is the only *policyholder*; or
(2) P, as a result of the transaction, would become the only *policyholder*.

5.6.13 **[G]** Market makers in traded endowment policies may be able to rely on this exclusion to avoid the need to be *authorised*. They must ensure, however, that where they are carrying on the *regulated activity* of *dealing in investments as principal* (article 14) they are also able to rely on the exclusions in articles 15 or 16 (see the *guidance* in PERG 2.8.4G (Dealing in investments as principal)).

5.6.14 **[G]** *Insurance undertakings* do not fall within the terms of this exclusion and so will be *arranging contracts of insurance*, in addition to *effecting* and *carrying out contracts of insurance*.

5.6.15 **[G]** In some cases, a *person* may make arrangements to enter into a *contract of insurance* as *policyholder* on its own behalf and also arrange that another *person* become a *policyholder* under the same *contract of insurance*. If so, the *person* should be aware that the effect of the narrower exclusion in article 28 as part of implementation of the *IMD* is that he may be *arranging* on behalf of the other *policyholder*. This may be relevant, for example, to a *company* which arranges insurance for itself (not *arranging*) as well as other *companies* in a *group* or loan syndicate (potentially *arranging*).

5.6.16 **[G]** The restriction in the scope of article 28 raises an issue where there is a trust with co-trustees, where each trustee will be a *policyholder* with equal rights and obligations. If the activities of one of the trustees include *arranging* in respect of *contracts of insurance*, that trustee could be viewed as *arranging* on behalf of his co-trustees who will also be *policyholders*. Similar issues also arise in respect of trustees *assisting in the administration and performance of a contract of insurance*. The *FSA* is of the view, however, that trustees should not be regarded as carrying on *regulated activities* where they are acting as joint *policyholders* in *arranging* or *assisting in the administration and performance of a contract of insurance*. In this respect, trustees differ from *policyholders* under a group policy, where each *person* covered under the group policy may make claims on the policy in relation to his own risks. In that situation, a *policyholder* who is providing services to other *policyholders* of *arranging* or *assisting in the administration and performance of a contract of insurance* will be carrying on a *regulated activity*.

Exclusion from article 25(2) for introducing

5.6.17 **[G]** Article 33 of the *Regulated Activities Order* (Introducing) excludes arrangements which would otherwise fall under article 25(2) where:

(1) they are arrangements under which *persons* will be introduced to another *person*;

(2) the *person* to whom introductions are to be made is:
- (a) an *authorised person*; or
- (b) an *exempt person* acting in the course of business comprising a *regulated activity* in relation to which he is exempt; or
- (c) a *person* who is not unlawfully carrying on *regulated activities* in the *United Kingdom* and whose ordinary business involves him in engaging in certain activities;

(3) the introduction is made with a view to the provision of independent advice or the independent exercise of discretion in relation to *investments* generally or in relation to any class of *investments* to which the arrangements relate; and

(4) the arrangements do not relate to transactions relating to *contracts of insurance*.

5.6.18 **[G]** The effect of PERG 5.6.17G(4) is that some *persons* who, in making introductions, are *making arrangements with a view to transactions in investments* under article 25(2) of the *Regulated Activities Order*, cannot use the introducing exclusion. This is if, in general terms, the arrangements for making introductions relate to *contracts of insurance* (PERG 5.6.19G has further *guidance* on when arrangements for introductions may be regarded as relating to *contracts of insurance*). However, this does not mean that all introducers whose introductions relate directly or indirectly to *contracts of insurance* will necessarily require *authorisation* if they cannot use the exclusion in article 72C of the *Regulated Activities Order* for merely passing information. For this to be the case, a *person* must first be carrying on the business of *making arrangements with a view to transactions in investments*. In the *FSA's* view, the following points will be relevant in determining whether this is the case.

(1) Article 25(2) applies to ongoing arrangements made with a view to transactions taking place from time to time as a result of *persons* having taken part in the arrangements. So, they will not apply to one-off introductions or introductions that are not part of an ongoing pre-existing arrangement between introducer and introducee. An introducer who merely suggests to a *person* that he seeks advice or assistance from an *authorised person* or an *exempt person* with whom the introducer has no pre-existing agreement that anticipates introductions will be made, will not be making arrangements at all. He will simply be offering general advice or information.

(2) The purpose of the arrangements must be for the *person* who is introduced to, in general terms, enter into a transaction to *buy* or *sell securities* or *relevant investments*. So, arrangements for introducing *persons* for advice only will not be caught (for example, introductions to a financial planner or to the publisher of an investment newsletter). In other cases, it may be likely that transactions will be entered into following the provision of advice. Provided the introducer is completely indifferent as to whether or not a *contract of insurance* may ultimately be bought (or sold) as a result of the advice given to the *person* he has introduced, the introducer will not be *making arrangements with a view to transactions in investments*. This is likely to be the case where the introducer does not receive any pecuniary reward that is linked to the volume of business done as a result of his introductions.

5.6.19 **[G]** Where a *person* is *making arrangements with a view to transactions in investments* by way of making introductions, and he is not completely indifferent to whether or not transactions may result, it may still be the case that the exclusion in article 33 will apply. In the *FSA's* view, this is where:

(1) the introduction is for independent advice on *investments* generally; and
(2) the introducer is indifferent as to whether or not a *contract of insurance* may ultimately be bought (or sold) rather than any other type of *investment*.

This is because the arrangements for making introductions do not specifically relate to a *contract of insurance* or to any other type of *investment* but to *investments* generally. Whether or not a *person* is making arrangements for introductions for the purpose of the provision of independent advice on *investments* generally will depend on the facts in any particular case. But, in the *FSA's* view, it is very unlikely that article 33 could apply where introductions are made to a *person* for the purposes of that *person* giving advice on and then *arranging general insurance*.

5.6.20 **[G]** The table in PERG 5.6.21G has examples of the application of article 33 to arrangements for making introductions.

5.6.21 **[G]** Application of article 33 to arrangements for making introductions. This table belongs to PERG 5.6.20G.

	Type of introduction	Applicability of exclusion
1	Introductions are purely for the purpose of the provision of independent advice – Introducer is completely indifferent to whether or not transactions take place after advice has been given.	Exclusion not relevant as introducer is not *arranging* under article 25(2).
2	Introduction is one-off or otherwise not part of pre-existing ongoing arrangements that envisage such introduction being made.	Exclusion not relevant as introducer is not *arranging* under article 25(2).
3	Introducer is not indifferent to whether or not transactions take place after advice has been given, but is indifferent to whether or not the transactions may involve a *contract of insurance*.	Exclusion will be available provided the introduction was made with a view to the provision of independent advice on *investments* generally.
4	Introducer is not indifferent to whether or not transactions take place after advice has been given (for example, because he expects to receive a percentage of the commission), and introductions specifically relate to *contracts of insurance*.	Exclusion is not available. If introducer is an *unauthorised person*, he will need *authorisation* or exemption as an *appointed representative*. If introducer is an *authorised person* (such as an IFA introducing to a *general insurance* broker), he will need to vary his *Part IV permission* accordingly. If introducer is an *appointed representative*, he will need to ensure that his agreement covers making such arrangements.

Exclusion from article 25(2): arrangements for the provision of finance

5.6.22 **[G]** An *unauthorised person* who makes arrangements with a view to a *person* who participates in the arrangements *buying* or *selling contracts of insurance* may be excluded from article 25(2) by article 32 of the *Regulated Activities Order* (Provision of finance). This is provided the sole purpose of the arrangements is the provision of finance to enable the *person* to *buy* the *contract of insurance*. Premium finance companies may be able to rely on this exclusion provided the arrangements they put in place, taken as a whole, have as their sole purpose the provision of finance to fund premiums.

Other exclusions

5.6.23 **[G]** The *Regulated Activities Order* contains some other exclusions which have the effect of narrowing or limiting the application of *regulated activities* within article 25 by preventing certain activities from amounting to *regulated activities*. These are referred to in PERG 5.11.8G (Exclusions applying to more than one regulated activity).

5.7 The regulated activities: assisting in the administration and performance of a contract of insurance

5.7.1 **[G]** The *regulated activity* of *assisting in the administration and performance of a contract of insurance* (article 39A) relates, in broad terms, to activities carried on by intermediaries after the conclusion of a *contract of insurance* and for or on behalf of *policyholders*, in particular in the event of a claim. Loss assessors acting on behalf of *policyholders* in the event of a claim are, therefore, likely in many cases to be carrying on this *regulated activity*. By contrast, claims management on behalf of certain insurers is not a *regulated activity* (see PERG 5.7.7G (Exclusions)).

5.7.2 **[G]** Neither assisting in the administration nor assisting in the performance of a contract alone will fall within this activity. Generally, an activity will either amount to assisting in the administration or assisting in the performance but not both. Occasionally, however, an activity may amount to both *assisting in the administration and performance of a contract of insurance*. For example, where a *person* assists a claimant in filling in a claims form, in the *FSA's* view this amounts to assisting in the administration of a *contract of insurance*. In some instances, however, this may also amount to assisting in the performance of a *contract of insurance*. In the *FSA's* view, an example of when a *person* may be assisting in the performance of a contract is where a *person* fills in the whole or a significant part of a claims form on behalf of a claimant. This is because, by helping complete a claims form, a *person* may be assisting the *policyholder* to perform his contractual obligation to notify the *insurance undertaking* in the event of a claim and provide details of the claim in the manner and form required by the contract.

5.7.3 **[G]** Put another way, where an intermediary's assistance in filling in a claims form is material to whether performance takes place of the contractual obligation to notify claims, it is more likely to amount to *assisting in the administration and performance of a contract of insurance*. Conversely, in the *FSA's* view, a *person* who merely gives pointers about how to fill in the claims form or merely supplies information in support of a claim will not be assisting in the performance of a *contract of insurance*. Instead, the *person* will only be facilitating rather than assisting in the performance of a *contract of insurance*.

5.7.4 **[G]** More generally, an example of an activity that, in the *FSA's* view, is likely to amount to assisting a *policyholder* in both the administration and the performance of a *contract of insurance* is notifying a claim under a *policy* and then providing evidence in support of the claim, or helping negotiate its settlement on the *policyholder's* behalf. Notifying an *insurance undertaking* of a claim assists the *policyholder* in discharging his contractual obligation to do so (assisting in the performance); providing evidence in support of the claim or negotiating its settlement assists management of the claim (assisting in the administration).

5.7.5 **[G]** On the other hand, where a *person* does no more than advise a *policyholder* generally about making a claim or provide evidence in support of a claim, this is unlikely to amount to both assisting in the administration and performance. Similarly, the mere collection of premiums from *policyholders* is unlikely, without more, to amount to *assisting in the administration and performance of a contract of insurance*. The collection of premiums from customers or clients at the pre-contract stage, however, may amount to *arranging* (see example in PERG 5.15.4G (Types of activity – are they regulated activities and, if so, why?)).

5.7.6 **[G]** Where a *person* receives funds on behalf of a *policyholder* in settlement of a claim, in the *FSA's* view, the act of receipt is likely to amount to assisting in the performance of a contract. By giving valid receipt, the *person* assists the *insurance undertaking* to discharge its contractual obligation to provide compensation to the *policyholder*. He may also be assisting the *policyholder* to discharge any obligations he may have under the contract to provide valid receipt of funds, upon settlement of a claim. Where a *person* provides valid receipt for funds received on behalf of the *policyholder*, he is also likely to be assisting in the administration of a *contract of insurance* (for example, making prior arrangements relating to transmission and receipt of payment).

Exclusions

5.7.7 **[G]** By article 39B of the *Regulated Activities Order* (Claims management on behalf of an insurer etc):

(1) loss adjusting on behalf of a relevant insurer (see PERG 5.7.8G);
(2) expert appraisal; and
(3) managing claims for a relevant insurer;

are also excluded from the *regulated activity* of *assisting in the administration and performance of a contract of insurance*. This is where the activity is carried on in the course of carrying on any profession or business (see also PERG 5.14 (Exemptions)). In determining whether they are carrying on the *regulated activity* of *assisting in the administration and performance of a contract of insurance*, therefore, *persons* should consider whether they are acting on behalf of the relevant insurer and not the *policyholder*.

5.7.8 **[G]** A 'relevant insurer' for the purposes of article 39B means:

(1) an *authorised person* who has *permission* for *effecting and carrying out contracts of insurance*; or
(2) a member of the Society of Lloyd's or the members of the Society of Lloyd's taken together; or
(3) an *EEA firm* that is an *insurer*; or

(4) a reinsurer, being a *person* whose main business consists of accepting risks ceded by a *person* falling under (1), (2) or (3) or a *person* who is established outside the *United Kingdom* and who carries on the activity of *effecting and carrying out contracts of insurance*.

So, a *person* whose activities are excluded under article 12 of the *Regulated Activities Order* (Breakdown insurance) will not be a relevant insurer for these purposes and any *person* who performs loss adjusting or claims management on behalf of such a *person* will not be able to use the exclusion in article 39B.

5.8 The regulated activities: advising on contracts of insurance

5.8.1 **[G]** Article 53 of the *Regulated Activities Order* (Advising on Investments) makes advising on *contracts of insurance* a *regulated activity*. This covers advice which is both:
(1) given to a *person* in his capacity as an insured or potential insured, or as agent for an insured or a potential insured; and
(2) advice on the merits of the insured or his agent:
 (a) *buying*, *selling*, subscribing for or underwriting a particular *contract of insurance*; or
 (b) exercising any right conferred by a *contract of insurance* to *buy*, *sell*, subscribe for or underwrite a *contract of insurance*.

5.8.2 **[G]** For advice to fall within article 53, it must:
(1) relate to a particular *contract of insurance* (that is, one that a *person* may enter into);
(2) be given to a *person* in his capacity as an investor or potential investor;
(3) be advice (that is, not just information); and
(4) relate to the merits of a *person buying*, *selling*, subscribing for or underwriting (or exercising any right to do so) a *contract of insurance* or rights to or interests in *life policies*.

5.8.3 **[G]** Each of these aspects is considered in greater detail in the table in PERG 5.8.5G. Where an activity is identified as not amounting to *advising on investments* it could still form part of another *regulated activity*. This will depend upon whether a *person's* activities, viewed as a whole, amount to *arranging*. Additionally, it should be borne in mind that the provision of advice or information may involve the communication of a *financial promotion* (see PERG 8 (Financial promotion and related activities)).

Advice must relate to a particular contract of insurance

5.8.4 **[G]** Advice about *contracts of insurance* will come within the *regulated activity* in article 53 of the *Regulated Activities Order* only if it relates to a particular *contract of insurance*. So, generic or general advice will not fall under article 53. In particular:
(1) advice would come within article 53 if it took the form of a recommendation that a *person* should *buy* the ABC Insurers motor insurance;
(2) advice would not relate to a particular contract if it consists of a recommendation only that a *person* should take out insurance of a particular class without identifying any particular *insurance undertaking*, or with ABC Insurers provided that the kind of insurance is not specified (either expressly or by implication): a recommendation only that a *person* should *buy* insurance from ABC Insurers could amount to advice if a specific insurance *policy* would be implied from the context;
(3) the table in PERG 5.8.5G identifies several typical recommendations and indicates whether they will be regarded as advice under article 53.

5.8.5 **[G]** Typical recommendations and whether they will be regulated as advice on contracts of insurance under article 53 of the *Regulated Activities Order*. This table belongs to PERG 5.8.4G

Recommendation	Regulated under article 53 or not?
I recommend you take the ABC Insurers motor insurance *policy*	Yes
I recommend that you take out the GHI Insurers life insurance *policy*	Yes
I recommend that you do not take out the ABC Insurers motor insurance *policy*	Yes
I recommend that you do not take out the GHI Insurers life insurance *policy*	Yes
I recommend that you take out either the ABC Insurers motor insurance *policy* or the DEF Insurers motor insurance *policy*	Yes
I recommend that you take out either the GHI Insurers life insurance *policy* or the JKL Insurers life insurance *policy*	Yes

I recommend that you take out (or do not take out) insurance with ABC Insurers	Possibly (depending on whether or not the circumstances relating to the recommendation, including the range of possible products, is such that this amounts to an implied recommendation of a particular *policy*)
I recommend that you take out (or do not take out) contents insurance	No, unless a specific insurance *policy* is implied by the context
I recommend that you take out (or do not take out) life insurance	No, unless a specific insurance *policy* is implied by the context

Advice given to a person in his capacity as an investor or potential investor

5.8.6 **[G]** For the purposes of article 53, advice must be given to a *person* in his capacity as an investor or potential investor (which, in the context of *contracts of insurance*, will mean as *policyholder* or potential *policyholder*). So, article 53 will not apply where advice is given to *persons* who receive it as:

(1) an adviser who will use it only to inform advice given by him to others; or
(2) a journalist or broadcaster who will use it only for journalistic purposes.

5.8.7 **[G]** Advice will still be covered by article 53 even though it may not be given to any particular *policyholder* (for example, advice given in a periodical publication or on a website).

Advice or information

5.8.8 **[G]** In the *FSA's* view, advice requires an element of opinion on the part of the adviser. In effect, it is a recommendation as to a course of action. Information, on the other hand, involves statements of facts or figures.

5.8.9 **[G]** In general terms, simply giving information, without making any comment or value judgement on its relevance to decisions which a *person* may make, is not advice. In this respect, it is irrelevant that a *person* may be providing information on a single *contract of insurance* or on two or more. This means that a *person* may provide information on a single *contract of insurance* without necessarily being regarded as giving advice on it. PERG 5.8.11G has *guidance* on the circumstances in which information can assume the form of advice.

5.8.10 **[G]** In the case of article 53, information relating to *buying* or *selling contracts of insurance* may often involve one or more of the following:

(1) an explanation of the terms and conditions of a *contract of insurance* whether given orally or in writing or by providing leaflets and brochures;
(2) a comparison of the features and benefits of one *contract of insurance* compared to another;
(3) the production of pre-purchase questions for a *person* to use in order to exclude options that would fail to meet his requirements; such questions may often go on to identify a range of *contracts of insurance* with characteristics that appear to meet the *person*'s requirements and to which he might wish to give detailed consideration (pre-purchase questioning is considered in more detail in PERG 5.8.15G to PERG 5.8.19G (Pre-purchase questioning (including decision trees));
(4) tables that compare the costs and other features of different *contracts of insurance*;
(5) leaflets or illustrations that help *persons* to decide which type of *contract of insurance* to take out; and
(6) the provision, in response to a request from a *person* who has identified the main features of the type of *contract of insurance* he seeks, of several leaflets together with an indication that all the *contracts of insurance* described in them have those features.

5.8.11 **[G]** In the *FSA's* opinion, however, such information is likely to take on the nature of advice if the circumstances in which it is provided give it the force of a recommendation. Examples of situations where information provided by a *person* (P) might take the form of advice are given below.

(1) P may provide information on a selected, rather than balanced and neutral, basis that would tend to influence the decision of a *person*. This may arise where P offers to provide information about *contracts of insurance* that contain features specified by the *person*, but then exercises discretion as to which complying *contract of insurance* to offer to that *person*.
(2) P may, as a result of going through the sales process, discuss the merits of one *contract of insurance* over another, resulting in advice to enter into a particular one. In contrast, advice on how to complete an application form, without an explicit or implicit recommendation on the merits of *buying* or *selling* the *contract of insurance* whilst 'advice' in the general sense of the word, is not, in the view of the *FSA*, advice within the meaning of article 53. Such advice may, however, amount to *arranging* (for which see PERG 5.6.1G to PERG 5.6.4G (The regulated activities: arranging deals in, and making arrangements with a view to transactions in, contracts of insurance)).

Advice must relate to the merits (of buying or selling a contract of insurance)

5.8.12 **[G]** Advice under article 53 relates to the advantages and disadvantages of *buying*, *selling*, subscribing for or underwriting a particular *contract of insurance*. It is worth noting that, in this context, '*buying*' and '*selling*' are defined widely under article 3 of the *Regulated Activities Order* (Interpretation). '*Buying*' includes acquiring for valuable consideration, and '*selling*' includes surrendering, assigning or converting rights under a *contract of insurance*.

5.8.13 **[G]** The requirements imposed by the *IMD* (see PERG 5.2.5G (Approach to implementation of the *IMD*)) and the text of article 2.3 *IMD* in PERG 5.16.1G (article 2.3 of the Insurance Mediation Directive) are narrower than the scope of the *Regulated Activities Order* (see PERG 5.2.7G (Approach to implementation of the IMD)). This is that, unlike the *Regulated Activities Order*, they do not relate to the assignment of *contracts of insurance*. This is of relevance to, amongst others, *persons* involved in the 'second-hand' market for *contracts of insurance* such as traded endowment policies and certain viatical instruments (that is, arrangements by which a terminally ill person can obtain value from his *life policy*) (see also PERG 5.6.12G (Exclusion from article 25(2): transactions to which the arranger is a party)). *Persons* advising on or arranging assignments of these *contracts of insurance* are therefore potentially carrying on *regulated activities* although they may be able to take the benefit of article 67 of the *Regulated Activities Order* (Activities carried on in the course of a profession or non-investment business) in certain circumstances (see PERG 5.11.9G to PERG 5.11.12G (Activities carried on in the course of a profession or non-investment business)).

5.8.14 **[G]** Generally speaking, advice on the merits of using a particular *insurance undertaking*, broker or adviser in their capacity as such, does not amount to advice for the purpose of article 53. It is not advice on the merits of *buying* or *selling* a particular *contract of insurance* (unless, in the circumstances, the advice amounts to an implied recommendation of a particular *policy*).

Pre-purchase questioning (including decision trees)

5.8.15 **[G]** Pre-purchase questioning involves putting a sequence of questions in order to extract information from a *person* with a view to facilitating the selection by that *person* of a *contract of insurance* or other product that meets his needs. A decision tree is an example of pre-purchase questioning. The process of going through the questions will usually narrow down the range of options that are available.

5.8.16 **[G]** A key issue for those *firms* proposing to use pre-purchase questioning is whether the specific questioning used may amount to advice. There are two main aspects:

(1) advice must relate to a particular *contract of insurance* (see PERG 5.8.4G (Advice must relate to a particular contract of insurance)); and

(2) the distinction between information and advice (see PERG 5.8.8G to PERG 5.8.11G (Advice or information)).

Whether or not pre-purchase questioning in any particular case is advising on *contracts of insurance* will depend on all the circumstances. The process may involve identifying one or more particular *contracts of insurance*. If so, to avoid advising on *contracts of insurance*, the critical factor is likely to be whether the process is limited to, and likely to be perceived by the *person* as, assisting the *person* to make his own choice of product which has particular features which the *person* regards as important. The questioner will need to avoid providing any judgement on the suitability of one or more products for that *person* and in this respect should have regard to the factors set out in PERG 5.8.2G to PERG 5.8.4G (Advice must relate to a particular contract of insurance) and the table in PERG 5.8.5G. See also PERG 5.8.12G to PERG 5.8.14G (Advice must relate to the merits (of buying or selling a contract of insurance)) for other matters that may be relevant.

5.8.17 **[G]** The potential for variation in the form, content and manner of pre-purchase questioning is considerable, but there are two broad types. The first type involves providing questions and answers which are confined to factual matters (for example, the amount of the cover). In the *FSA's* view, this does not itself amount to advising on *contracts of insurance*, if it involves the provision of information rather than advice. There are various possible scenarios, including the following:

(1) the questioner may go on to identify one or more particular *contracts of insurance* which match features identified by the pre-purchase questioning; provided these are selected in a balanced and neutral way (for example, they identify all the matching *contracts of insurance* available without making a recommendation as to a particular one) this need not involve advising on *contracts of insurance*; and

(2) the questioner may go on to advise a *person* on the merits of one particular *contract of insurance* over another; this would be advising on *contracts of insurance*.

5.8.18 **[G]** The second type of pre-purchase questioning involves providing questions and answers incorporating opinion, judgement or recommendation. There are various possible scenarios, including the following:

(1) the pre-purchase questioning may not lead to the identification of any particular *contract of insurance*; in this case, the questioner has provided advice, but it is generic advice and does not amount to advising on *contracts of insurance*; and

(2) the pre-purchase questioning may lead to the identification of one or more particular *contracts of insurance*; the key issue then is whether the advice can be said to relate to a particular *contract of insurance* (see further PERG 5.8.4G (Advice must relate to a particular contract of insurance)).

5.8.19 **[G]** In the case of PERG 5.8.18G(2) and similar scenarios, the *FSA* considers that it is necessary to look at the process and outcome of pre-purchase questioning as a whole. It may be that the element of advice incorporated in the questioning can properly be viewed as generic advice if it were considered in isolation. But although the actual advice may be generic, the process has ended in identifying one or more particular *contracts of insurance*. The combination of the generic advice and the identification of a particular or several particular *contracts of insurance* to which it leads may well, in the *FSA's* view, cause the questioner to be advising on *contracts of insurance*. Factors that may be relevant in deciding whether the process involves advising on *contracts of insurance* may include:

(1) any representations made by the questioner at the start of the questioning relating to the service he is to provide;
(2) the context in which the questioning takes place;
(3) the stage in the questioning at which the opinion is offered and is significant;
(4) the role played by the questioner who guides a *person* through the pre-purchase questions;
(5) the outcome of the questioning (whether particular *contracts of insurance* are highlighted, how many of them, who provides them, their relationship to the questioner and so on); and
(6) whether the pre-purchase questions and answers have been provided by, and are clearly the responsibility of, an unconnected third party, and all that the questioner has done is help the *person* understand what the questions or options are and how to determine which option applies to his particular circumstances.

Medium used to give advice

5.8.20 **[G]** With the exception of:

(1) periodicals, broadcasts and other news or information services (see PERG 5.8.24G to PERG 5.8.25G (Exclusion: periodical publications, broadcasts and web-sites)); and
(2) situations involving an overseas element (see, generally, PERG 5.12 (Link between activities and the United Kingdom) and, in particular, PERG 5.12.8G (Where is insurance mediation carried on?));

the use of the medium itself to give advice should make no material difference to whether or not the advice is caught by article 53.

5.8.21 **[G]** Advice can be provided in many ways including:

(1) face to face;
(2) orally to a group;
(3) by telephone;
(4) by correspondence (including e-mail);
(5) in a publication, broadcast or web-site; and
(6) through the provision of an interactive software system.

5.8.22 **[G]** Taking electronic commerce as an example, the use of electronic decision trees does not present any novel problem. The same principles apply as with a paper version (see PERG 5.8.15G to PERG 5.8.19G (Pre-purchase questioning (including decision trees))).

5.8.23 **[G]** Advice in publications, broadcasts and web-sites is subject to a special regime (see PERG 5.8.24G (Exclusion: periodical publications, broadcasts and web-sites) and PERG 7 (Periodical publications, news services and broadcasts: applications for certification)).

Exclusion: periodical publications, broadcasts and web-sites

5.8.24 **[G]** An important exclusion from advising on *contracts of insurance* relates to advice given in periodical publications, regularly updated news and information services and broadcasts (article 54 of the *Regulated Activities Order* (Advice given in newspapers etc)). The exclusion applies if the principal purpose of the publication or service taken as a whole (including any advertising content) is neither to give advice of a kind mentioned in article 53 (Advising on investments) or article 53A (Advising on regulated mortgage activities) nor to lead or enable *persons* to *buy*, *sell*, subscribe for or underwrite *relevant investments* or, as borrower, to enter into or vary the terms of a *regulated mortgage contract*.

5.8.25 **[G]** This is explained in greater detail, together with the provisions on the granting of certificates by the *FSA* on the application of the proprietor of a periodical publication or news or information service or broadcast, in PERG 7 (Periodical publications, news services and broadcasts: applications for certification).

Other exclusions

5.8.26 **[G]** The *Regulated Activities Order* contains other limited exclusions which have the effect of preventing certain activities from amounting to advice on *contracts of insurance*. These are referred to in PERG 5.11.8G (Exclusions applying to more than one regulated activity) to PERG 5.11.16G (Large risks).

5.9 The Regulated Activities: agreeing to carry on a regulated activity

5.9.1 **[G]** Under article 64 of the *Regulated Activities Order* (Agreeing to carry on specified kinds of activity), in addition to the *regulated activities* of:
(1) *dealing in investments as agent*;
(2) *arranging (bringing about) deals in investments*;
(3) *making arrangements with a view to transactions in investments;*
(4) *assisting in the administration and performance of a contract of insurance*; and
(5) *advising on investments*;

agreeing to do any of these things is itself a *regulated activity*. In the *FSA's* opinion, this activity concerns the entering into of a legally binding agreement to provide the services to which the agreement relates. So, a *person* is not carrying on a *regulated activity* under article 64 merely because he makes an offer to do so.

5.9.2 **[G]** To the extent that an exclusion applies in relation to a *regulated activity*, 'agreeing' to carry on an activity within the exclusion will not be a *regulated activity*. This is the effect of article 4(3) of the *Regulated Activities Order* (Specified activities: general). So, for example, a vet can, without carrying on a *regulated activity*, enter into an agreement with an *insurance undertaking* to distribute marketing literature provided that the vet can rely on the exclusion in article 72C (Provision of information on an incidental basis) in relation to the activity of distributing the literature (see also PERG 5.6.6G and PERG 5.6.9G (Exclusion: article 72C (Provision of information on an incidental basis))). However, to be able to rely on the exclusion in article 72C, the vet must not be viewed as providing information to the *insurance undertaking*. More specifically, an unauthorised *introducer* can enter into standing arrangements with *insurance undertakings* or brokers to make introductions, provided that these arrangements do not envisage subsequent provision of information to these *insurance undertakings* or brokers with a view to *arranging (bringing about) deals in investments* or *making arrangements with a view to transactions in investments.*

5.10 Renewals

5.10.1 **[G]** It must be emphasised that activities which concern invitations to renew *policies* and the subsequent effecting of renewal of *policies* are likely to fall within *insurance mediation activity*. Those considering the need for *authorisation* or variation of their *permission*s will wish to consider whether a process of tacit renewal operates: that is, where a *policyholder* need take no action if he wishes to maintain his insurance cover by having his *policy* 'renewed'. This process will typically result in the issue of a new *contract of insurance*, not an extension of the period of the existing one. It may involve the activities of *advising on investments*, *arranging* and *dealing in investments as agent*. More specifically, preparing a 'tacit renewal' letter on behalf of an *insurance undertaking* is likely to amount to *arranging*. Where it contains a recommendation to renew existing cover this is likely to constitute *advising on investments* (under article 53 of the *Regulated Activities Order*). If the contract takes effect on the date stipulated in the renewal letter, a contract is concluded with the effect that the letter writer may be *dealing in investments as agent*. The process may also involve a *regulated activity* under article 64 (Agreeing to carry on a regulated activity).

5.11 Other aspects of exclusions

5.11.1 **[G]** This part of the *guidance* deals with:
(1) exclusions which are disapplied where the *regulated activity* relates to *contracts of insurance*;
(2) exclusions which are disapplied where a *person* carries on *insurance mediation*; and
(3) the following exclusions applying to more than one *regulated activity*:
  (a) activities carried on in the course of a profession or non-investment business (article 67 (Activities carried on in the course of a profession or non-investment business));
  (b) activities carried on by a provider of relevant goods or services (article 72B (Activities carried on by a provider of relevant goods or services)); and
  (c) large risks (article 72D (Large risks contracts where risk situated outside the EEA)).

5.11.2 **[G]** There are a number of 'pre-*IMD*' exclusions that have the effect of restricting the scope of the *regulated activities* referred to in this *guidance*. Several of these are disapplied or modified as part of implementation of the *IMD*.

Exclusions disapplied where activities relate to contracts of insurance

5.11.3 **[G]** The exclusions outlined in (1) to (7) were available to intermediaries (and in some cases *insurance undertakings*) acting in connection with *life policies* before 14 January 2005. In essence, however, the following exclusions do not apply if they concern transactions relating to *contracts of insurance*:

(1) *dealing in investments as agent* with or through *authorised persons* (article 22 of the Regulated Activities Order (Deals with or through authorised persons));

(2) *arranging* transactions to which the *arranger* is to be a party, where the *arranger* enters into or is to enter into the transaction:

  (a) as agent for another *person*; or

  (b) as *principal*, unless the *arranger* is the only *policyholder* or will, as a result of the transaction, become the only *policyholder* (article 28 (Arranging transactions to which the arranger is a party));

(3) arranging deals with or through *authorised persons* (article 29 (Arranging deals with or through authorised persons));

(4) introducing (article 33 (Introducing));

(5) activities carried on in connection with the sale of goods and supply of services (article 68 (Activities carried on in connection with the sale of goods and supply of services));

(6) *groups* and *joint enterprises* (article 69 (Groups and joint enterprises)) (see PERG 5.11.6G); and

(7) activities carried on in connection with the sale of a *body corporate* (article 70 (Activities carried on in connection with the sale of a body corporate)).

5.11.4 **[G]** The restrictions placed on the exclusions listed in PERG 5.11.3G on 14 January 2005 have the following effects.

(1) *Unauthorised persons* who:

  (a) introduce clients or customers to an independent financial adviser with a view to a transaction; or

  (b) deal as agent on behalf of their clients or customers with or though an *authorised person*; or

  (c) arrange for their clients or customers to enter into a transaction with or though an *authorised person*;

will not be able to rely on articles 29 or 33 to avoid the need for *authorisation* where the transaction relates to a *contract of insurance*.

(2) *Unauthorised persons* may, however, be able to rely on the exclusion for the provision of information on an incidental basis in article 72C to continue to avoid the need for *authorisation* (see PERG 5.6.5G to PERG 5.6.9G (Exclusion: article 72C (Provision of information on an incidental basis))).

(3) *Authorised persons* who themselves introduce clients or customers to others for the purposes of *buying* or *selling* any kind of *contract of insurance* are likely to require a variation of their *Part IV permission*, as neither article 33 nor generally, article 72C (see PERG 5.6.5G to PERG 5.6.9G (Exclusion: article 72C (Provision of information on an incidental basis))) will apply where this activity amounts to *arranging*.

5.11.5 **[G]** *Insurance undertakings* are referred to MIPRU 5 (Insurance undertakings and mortgage lenders using insurance or mortgage mediation services) as regards their obligations relating to the use of intermediaries generally.

5.11.6 **[G]**

(1) The removal of the exclusion for *groups* and *joint enterprises* in article 69 of the *Regulated Activities Order* (Groups and joint enterprises) may have implications for a *company* providing services for:

  (a) other members of its *group*; or

  (b) other participants in a *joint enterprise* of which it is a participant.

(2) Such *companies* might typically provide risk or treasury management or administration services which may include *regulated activities* relating to a *contract of insurance*. If so, such companies will need *authorisation* or exemption if they conduct the activities by way of business (see PERG 5.4 (The business test) generally and (3) and (4)). This is unless another exclusion applies.

(3) In the *FSA's* view, particular issues arise in applying the by way of business test to group *companies*. Recital 11 of the *Insurance Mediation Directive* states that the Directive should apply to *persons* whose activity consists in providing insurance mediation services to third parties for remuneration. This suggests that the Directive is intended to apply only where the service is provided to a third party. The expression 'third party' is not defined in the Directive. The *FSA* considers that a group *company* that is providing services solely for the benefit of other group *companies* would not normally be regarded as providing services to a third party. The *FSA* also considers that, as a result, a group *company* providing services solely for the benefit of other group *companies* should not normally be regarded as satisfying the requirement that it be remunerated for providing insurance mediation services to third

parties. Were a group *company* to be remunerated other than by another group *company*, however, the situation may be different. For example, if the group *company* receives commission from an insurer or broker, the fact would tend to suggest that the *company* has been rewarded for providing a service to the insurer or broker. In the *FSA's* view, it is appropriate to apply this principle to a *group* as defined in section 421 (Group) of the *Act*.

(4) The *FSA* considers that similar principles to those applied to a group *company* in (2) may be applied to the participants in a *joint enterprise*. This would be where one participant in the *joint enterprise* is providing services solely for the benefit of another participant and for the purposes of the *joint enterprise* and who provides insurance mediation services to one or more participants for the purposes of or in connection with the *joint enterprise*.

Exclusions disapplied in connection with insurance mediation

5.11.7 **[G]** Article 4(4A) of the *Regulated Activities Order* (Specified activities: general) disapplies certain exclusions where a *person*, for remuneration, takes up or pursues *insurance mediation* (as defined in article 2.3 of the *IMD* (see PERG 5.2.5G (Approach to implementation of the IMD) and PERG 5.16.2G (Text of article 2.3 of the Insurance Mediation Directive)) in relation to a risk or commitment located in an *EEA* state. The relevant exclusions which are disapplied are:

(a) arrangements in connection with lending on the security of insurance policies (article 30 of the *Regulated Activities Order* (Arranging transactions in connection with lending on the security of insurance policies));

(b) activities carried on by trustees, nominees and personal representatives (article 66 (Trustees, nominees and personal representatives)); and

(c) activities carried on in the course of a profession or non-investment business (article 67 (Activities carried on in the course of a profession or non-investment business)) (This exclusion is considered in further detail in PERG 5.11.9G to PERG 5.11.12G (Activities carried on in the course of a profession or non-investment business)).

Exclusions applying to more than one regulated activity

5.11.8 **[G]** Chapter XVII of the *Regulated Activities Order* (Exclusions applying to several specified kinds of activity) contains various exclusions applying to several kinds of activity. Three exclusions of relevance in relation to *contracts of insurance* are dealt with in this section and a fourth, *overseas persons*, in PERG 5.12 (Link between activities and the United Kingdom).

Activities carried on in the course of a profession or non-investment business

5.11.9 **[G]** Article 67 excludes from the activities of *dealing as* agent, *arranging (bringing about) deals in investments, making arrangements with a view to transactions in investments, assisting in the administration and performance of a contract of insurance* and *advising on investments*, any activity which:

(1) is carried on in the course of carrying on any profession or business which does not otherwise consist of the carrying on of *regulated activities* in the *United Kingdom*; and

(2) may reasonably be regarded as a necessary part of other services provided in the course of that profession or business.

In the *FSA's* view, the fact that a *person* may carry on *regulated activities* in the course of the carrying on of a profession or business does not, of itself, mean that the profession or business consists of *regulated activities*. This is provided that the main focus of the profession or business does not involve *regulated activities* and that the *regulated activities* that are carried on arise in a way that is incidental and complementary to the carrying on of the profession or business.

5.11.10 **[G]** Although the article 67 exclusion is disapplied (by article 4(4A) of the *Regulated Activities Order* (Specified investments: general)) when a *person* takes up or pursues *insurance mediation* or *reinsurance mediation* as defined by articles 2.3 and 2.5 of the *IMD*, there may be cases where a *person* is not carrying on activities that amount to *insurance mediation*. For example, where a *person*'s activities amount simply to the provision of information on an incidental basis in the context of another professional activity, these may fall outside the scope of article 2.3 of the *IMD* (see PERG 5.16.2G (article 2.3 of the Insurance Mediation Directive)) and the exclusion in article 67 may then operate to exclude these activities. Also, it is possible that a professional *person's* activities may not amount to a *regulated activity* at all. For example, a doctor who provides a medical report to an *insurer* may be regarded as making arrangements with a view to providing an expert medical opinion rather than with a view to transactions in *contracts of insurance*. In such cases, article 67 will not be needed.

5.11.11 **[G]** Article 67 may also apply to activities relating to assignments of insurance *policies*, as, in the *FSA's* view, article 2.3 of the *IMD* applies essentially to the creation of new *contracts of insurance* and not the assignment of rights under existing *policies*. As such, where a solicitor or licensed conveyancer arranges an assignment of a *contract of insurance*, the exclusion in article 67 remains of potential application. For similar reasons, trustees advising on or arranging assignments of *contracts of insurance* may, in certain circumstances, be able to rely on the exclusions in article 66 of the *Regulated Activities Order*.

5.11.12 **[G]** For article 67 to apply in these cases, in addition to PERG 5.11.9G(1) and (2), the activity in question must not be remunerated separately from other services (article 67(2) of the *Regulated Activities Order*).

Activities carried on by a provider of relevant goods or services

5.11.13 **[G]** Article 72B (see also PERG 5.3.7G (Connected contracts of insurance)) may be of relevance to *persons* who supply non-motor goods or provide services related to travel in the course of carrying on a profession or business which does not otherwise consist of carrying on *regulated activities*. In the *FSA's* view, the fact that a *person* may carry on *regulated activities* in the course of the carrying on of a profession or business does not, of itself, mean that the profession or business consists of *regulated activities*. This is provided that the main focus of the profession or business does not involve *regulated activities* and that the *regulated activities* that are carried on arise in a way that is incidental and complementary to the carrying on of the profession or business. For example, a travel agent might carry on *insurance mediation activities* in relation to some *contracts of insurance* that satisfy the conditions of the article 72B and some that do not. The former contracts will be excluded from regulation even though the travel agent must seek *authorisation* or become an *appointed representative* to be permitted to sell the latter contracts. The exclusion applies to *insurance mediation activities* when carried on in relation to 'connected contracts of insurance'. In broad terms, a 'connected contract of insurance' is a *contract of insurance* which:

(1) is not a contract of long-term insurance (as defined by article 3 of the *Regulated Activities Order* (Interpretation));
(2) has a total duration (including rights to *renewal*) of five years or less;
(3) has an annual *premium* (or the equivalent of annual *premium*) of €500 or less;
(4) covers:
    (a) the risk of breakdown, loss of, or damage to, non-motor goods supplied by the provider; or
    (b) travel risks;
(5) does not cover any liability risks (except, in the case of a contract which covers travel risks, where the cover is ancillary to the main cover provided by the contract);
(6) is complementary to the non-motor goods being supplied or service being provided by the provider; and
(7) is of such a nature that the only information that a *person* requires in order to carry on one of the *insurance mediation activities* is the cover provided by the contract.

5.11.13A **[G]**

(1) There are two types of travel risks covered by PERG 5.11.13G(4)(b). The first type covers damage to, or loss of, baggage and other risks linked to the travel booked with the provider where that travel relates to attendance at an event organised or managed by that provider and the party seeking insurance is not an individual (acting in his private capacity) or a small business.
(2) "Small business" means a sole trader, *body corporate*, *partnership* or unincorporated association which had a turnover in the last financial year of less than £1,000,000. But if the small business is a member of a group within the meaning of section 262(1) of the Companies Act 1985 (and after the repeal of that section, within the meaning of section 474(1) of the Companies Act 2006), reference to its turnover means the combined turnover of the group. Turnover means the amounts derived from the provision of goods and services falling within the business's ordinary activities, after deduction of trade discounts, value added tax and any other taxes based on the amounts so derived.
(3) The second type of travel risk is damage to, or loss of, baggage and other risks linked to the hire from the insurance provider of an aircraft, vehicle or vessel which does not provide sleeping accommodation.
(4) PERG 5.11.13G(4)(a) does not apply to the hire of an aircraft, vehicle or vessel but does cover hire purchase and similar agreements.

5.11.14 **[G]** In the *FSA's* view, the liability risks referred to in PERG 5.11.13G(5) cover risks in relation to liabilities that the *policyholder* might have to others (that is, third party claims). Many *policies* will provide this sort of cover and so fall outside the scope of the exclusion. For example, a *policy* that covers the cost of unauthorised calls made when a mobile telephone is stolen includes 'liability risks' and would not be a 'connected contract of insurance'. By contrast, travel *policies* which provide cover in respect of the *policyholder*'s personal liability while travelling may fall within the exclusion by virtue of PERG 5.11.13G(5), where sold as part of a package by event organisers.

5.11.15 **[G]** In the *FSA's* view, the condition in PERG 5.11.13G(7) is likely to be satisfied where the *insurance mediation activities* relate to a standard form *contract of insurance*, the terms of which (other than the cost of the premium) are not subject to negotiation.

Large risks

5.11.16 **[G]** Article 72D (Large risks contracts where risk situated outside the EEA) provides an exclusion for large risks situated outside the *EEA*. Broadly speaking, these are risks relating to:

(1) railway rolling stock, aircraft, ships, goods in transit, aircraft liability and shipping liability;

(2) credit and suretyship where relating to the *policyholder's* commercial or professional liability;

(3) land vehicles, fire and natural forces, property damage, motor vehicle liability where the *policyholder* is a business of a certain size.

For a fuller definition of *contracts of large risks* see the definition in the *Glossary*.

5.12 Link between activities and the United Kingdom

Introduction

5.12.1 **[G]** Section 19 of the *Act* (The general prohibition) provides that the requirement to be *authorised* under the *Act* only applies in relation to *regulated activities* which are carried on 'in the *United Kingdom*'. In many cases, it will be quite straightforward to identify where an activity is carried on. But, when there is a cross-border element, for example because a *customer* is outside the *United Kingdom* or because some other element of the activity happens outside the *United Kingdom*, the question may need careful consideration. PERG 5.15.8G (Flow chart: am I carrying on regulated activities in the United Kingdom?) has a flow chart setting out the questions a *person* needs to consider in determining whether or not his *regulated activities* are carried on 'in the *United Kingdom*'.

5.12.2 **[G]** Even if a *person* concludes that he is not carrying on a *regulated activity* in the *United Kingdom*, he will need to ensure that he does not contravene other provisions of the *Act* that apply to *unauthorised persons*. These include the controls on *financial promotion* (section 21 (Financial promotion) of the *Act*) (see PERG 8 (Financial promotion and related activities)), and on giving the impression that a *person* is *authorised* (section 24 (False claims to be authorised or exempt)).

5.12.3 **[G]** The table in PERG 5.12.4G is a very simplified summary of territorial issues relating to overseas insurance intermediaries carrying on the business of *insurance mediation activities* in or into the *United Kingdom* for remuneration.

5.12.4 **[G]** Table Territorial issues relating to overseas insurance intermediaries carrying on *insurance mediation activities* in or into the *United Kingdom*

	Needs Part IV permission	Schedule 3 EEA passport rights available	Overseas persons exclusion available
Registered *EEA*-based intermediary with *UK* branch (registered office or head office in another *EEA State*)	No	Yes	No
Registered *EEA*-based intermediary with no *UK* branch providing *cross-border* services	No	Yes	Potentially available [see Note]
Third country intermediary operating from branch in the *UK*	Yes	No	No
Third country intermediary providing services in (or into) the *UK*	Yes unless *overseas persons* exclusion applies	No	Potentially available
This does not, however, affect the *firm's authorisation* under Schedule 3 to the *Act* (see PERG 5.12.9G to PERG 5.12.10G (Passporting)).			
For *EEA*-based intermediaries this table assumes that the *insurance mediation activities* are within the scope of the *Insurance Mediation Directive*.			

Where are insurance mediation activities carried on?

5.12.5 **[G]** *Persons* carrying on *insurance mediation activities* from a registered office or head office in the *United Kingdom* will clearly be carrying on *regulated activities* in the *United Kingdom*.

However, a *person* may be considered to be carrying on *regulated activities* in the *United Kingdom* even where not carrying on the activity from a registered office or head office in the *United Kingdom*. This is explained further in PERG 5.12.6G to PERG 5.12.8G.

5.12.6 **[G]** In determining the location of an activity, and hence whether it is carried on in the *United Kingdom*, various factors need to be taken into account in turn, notably:
(1) section 418 of the *Act* (Carrying on regulated activities in the United Kingdom);
(2) the nature of the activity; and
(3) the *overseas persons* exclusion (see PERG 5.12.9G to PERG 5.12.10G (Overseas persons)).

5.12.7 **[G]** Section 418 of the *Act* extends the meaning that 'carry on regulated activity in the United Kingdom' would normally have by setting out additional cases in which a *person* who would not otherwise be regarded as carrying on the activity in the *United Kingdom* is to be regarded as doing so. Each of the following cases thus amounts to carrying on a *regulated activity* in the *United Kingdom*:
(1) where a *UK*-based *person* carries on a *regulated activity* in another *EEA State* in the exercise of rights under a *Single Market Directive*;
(2) where a *UK*-based *person* carries on a *regulated activity* and the day-to-day management of the activity is the responsibility of an establishment in the *United Kingdom*;
(3) where a *regulated activity* is carried on by a *person* who is not based in the *United Kingdom* but is carried on from an establishment maintained by him in the *United Kingdom*; and
(4) where an *electronic commerce activity* is carried on with or for a *person* in an *EEA State* from an establishment in the *United Kingdom*.

In each of these cases it is irrelevant where the *person* with whom the activity is carried on is situated.

5.12.8 **[G]** Otherwise, where the cases in PERG 5.12.7G (1) to (4) do not apply, it is necessary to consider further the nature of the activity in order to determine where *insurance mediation* is carried on. *Persons* that arrange *contracts of insurance* will usually be considered as carrying on the activity of *arranging* in the location where these activities take place. As for dealing activities, the location of the activities will depend on factors such as where the acceptance takes place, which in turn will depend on the method of communication used. In the case of advising, this is generally considered to take place where the advice is received.

Overseas persons

5.12.9 **[G]** Article 72 of the *Regulated Activities Order* (Overseas persons) provides a potential exclusion for *persons* with no permanent place of business in the *United Kingdom* from which *regulated activities* are conducted or offers to conduct *regulated activities* are made. Where these *persons* carry on *insurance mediation activities* in the *United Kingdom*, they may be able to take advantage of the exclusions in article 72 of the *Regulated Activities Order*. In general terms, these apply where the *overseas person* either:
(1) deals or arranges deals with or through *authorised* or *exempt persons* only; or
(2) enters into deals with (or on behalf of) a *person* in the *United Kingdom* or gives advice on investments in the *United Kingdom*, in each case as a result of a 'legitimate approach'.

A 'legitimate approach', for the purposes of (2), is one that results from an unsolicited approach by a *person* (for example, a *customer*) or otherwise is a result of an approach by, or on behalf of, an *overseas person* which complies with the restriction on *financial promotion* under section 21 of the *Act* (see PERG 8.3.1G (Financial promotion)).

5.12.10 **[G]** The *overseas person* exclusion is available to *persons* who do not have a permanent place of business in the *United Kingdom* and so is of relevance to third country intermediaries (that is, non *EEA*-based intermediaries) who carry on *insurance mediation activities* in, or into, the *United Kingdom* (for example with or through *authorised* insurance brokers and insurance *undertakings* operating in the Lloyd's market).

How should persons be authorised?

5.12.11 **[G]** *UK*-based *persons* must obtain *Part IV permission* in relation to their *insurance mediation activities* in the *United Kingdom* as one of the following:
(1) a *body corporate* whose registered office is situated in the *United Kingdom*; or
(2) a *partnership* or unincorporated association whose head office is situated in the *United Kingdom*; or
(3) an individual (that is, a sole trader) whose residence is situated in the *United Kingdom*.

The *United Kingdom* will, in each case, be the *Home State* for the purposes of the *IMD* for insurance or reinsurance intermediaries (see further in connection with the *E-Commerce Directive* in PERG 5.12.15G to PERG 5.12.17G (E-Commerce Directive)).

5.12.12 **[G]** Non-*UK*-based *persons* wishing to carry on *insurance mediation activities* in the *United Kingdom* must:

Part II FSA Handbook Materials

(1) qualify for *authorisation* by exercising passport rights (see section 31 (Authorised persons) and schedule 3 (EEA passport rights) to the Act and PERG 5.12.13G to PERG 5.12.14G (Passporting)); or
(2) make use of the *overseas persons* exclusion (which then has the effect that activities are deemed not to be *regulated activities* carried on in the *United Kingdom*); or
(3) seek *Part IV permission*.

Passporting

5.12.13 **[G]** The effect of the *IMD* is that any *EEA*-based insurance intermediaries doing business within the Directive's scope must first be registered in their home *EEA State* before carrying on *insurance mediation* in that *EEA State* or other *EEA States*. For these purposes, an *EEA*-based insurance intermediary is either:
(1) a legal *person* with its registered office or head office in an *EEA State* other than the *United Kingdom*; or
(2) a natural *person* resident in an *EEA State* other than the *United Kingdom*.

Registered *EEA*-based insurance intermediaries wishing to establish branches in the *United Kingdom* or provide services on a cross-border basis into the *United Kingdom* can do so by notifying their *Home State regulator* which in turn notifies the *FSA*. This enables the intermediary to acquire passporting rights for business within the Directive's scope (so excluding *insurance mediation activities* relating to *connected contracts* or *connected travel insurance contracts*) under Schedule 3 to the *Act* (EEA passporting rights) (see Schedule 3(13) and (14) of the *Act* as amended by the Insurance Mediation Directive (Miscellaneous Amendments) Regulations 2003). SUP 13A (Qualifying for authorisation under the Act) has general *guidance* on the exercise of passporting rights by *EEA firms*.

5.12.14 **[G]** On the other hand, non-*EEA*-based insurance intermediaries wishing to establish a branch in the *UK* for the purpose of carrying on *insurance mediation activities* may only do so with *Part IV permission*.

E-Commerce Directive

5.12.15 **[G]** The *E-Commerce Directive* removes restrictions on the cross-border provision of services by electronic means, introducing a *country of origin* approach to regulation. This requires *EEA States* to impose certain requirements on the outward provision of such services and to lift them from inward providers. The *E-Commerce Directive* defines an e-commerce service (termed an *information society service*) as any service, normally provided for remuneration, at a distance, by electronic means, and at the individual request of the recipient of the service. So, for example, it includes services provided over the internet, by solicited e-mail, and interactive digital television.

5.12.16 **[G]** The *E-Commerce Directive* does not remove the *IMD* requirement for *persons* taking up or pursuing *insurance mediation* for remuneration to be registered in their *Home State*. Nor does it remove the requirement for *EEA*-based intermediaries to acquire passporting rights in order to establish branches in the *United Kingdom* (see PERG 5.12.7G (Where is insurance mediation carried on?) in relation to *electronic commerce activity* carried on from an establishment in the *United Kingdom*) or provide services on a cross–border basis into the *United Kingdom* where the relevant activity is carried on in the *United Kingdom*. An example of *electronic commerce activity* provided on a cross-border basis into the *United Kingdom* could be a recommendation in a (solicited) e-mail from an *EEA*-based intermediary to a *UK*-based customer to *buy* a particular *contract of insurance*.

5.12.17 **[G]** Put shortly, the *E-Commerce Directive* relates to services provided into the *United Kingdom* from other *EEA States* and from the *United Kingdom* into other Member States. In broad terms, such cross-border insurance mediation services provided by an *EEA firm* into the *United Kingdom* (via *electronic commerce activity* or distance means) will generally be subject to *IMD* registration in, and conduct of business regulation of, the intermediary's *EEA State* of origin. By contrast, insurance mediation services provided in the *United Kingdom* will be subject to *UK* conduct of business regulation, although the requirement for registration will again depend upon the intermediary's *EEA State* of origin.

5.13 Appointed representatives

What is an appointed representative?

5.13.1 **[G]** Section 39 of the *Act* (Exemption of appointed representatives) exempts *appointed representatives* from the need to obtain *authorisation*. An *appointed representative* is a *person* who is party to a contract with an *authorised person* which permits or requires him to carry on certain *regulated activities* (see *Glossary* for full definition). SUP 12 (Appointed representatives) contains *rules* and *guidance* relating to *appointed representatives*.

5.13.2 **[G]** A *person* who is an *authorised person* cannot be an *appointed representative* (see section 39(1) of the *Act* (Exemption of appointed representatives)).

Business for which an appointed representative is exempt

5.13.3 **[G]** An *appointed representative* can carry on only those *regulated activities* which are specified in the *Appointed Representatives Regulations*. The *regulated activities* set out in the table in PERG 5.13.4G are included in those regulations. As set out in the table, the *insurance mediation activities* that can be carried on by an *appointed representative* differ depending on the type of *contracts of insurance* in relation to which the activities are carried on.

5.13.4 **[G]** Insurance mediation activities able to be carried on by an appointed representative. This table belongs to PERG 5.13.3G.

Type of contract of insurance	**Regulated activities an appointed representative can carry on**
General insurance contract	• *dealing in investments as agent*; • *arranging*; • *assisting in the administration and performance of a contract of insurance*; • *advising on investments*; and • agreeing to carry on these *regulated activities*.
Pure protection contract	• *dealing in investments as agent* (but only where the contract is not a *long-term care insurance contract*); • *arranging*; • *assisting in the administration and performance of a contract of insurance*; • *advising on investments*; and • agreeing to carry on these *regulated activities*.
Life policy	• *arranging*; • *assisting in the administration and performance of a contract of insurance*; • *advising on investments*; and • agreeing to carry on these *regulated activities*

Persons who are not already appointed representatives

5.13.5 **[G]** A *person* who is not already an *appointed representative* may wish to become one in relation to the *regulated activities* specified in the *Appointed Representatives Regulations* (see table in PERG 5.13.4G). If so, he must be appointed under a written contract by an *authorised person*, who has *permission* to carry on those *regulated activities* and who accepts responsibility for the *appointed representative*'s actions when acting for him. SUP 12.4 (What must a firm do when it appoints an appointed representative?) and SUP 12.5 (Contracts: required terms) set out the detailed requirements that must be met for an appointment to be made. In particular, an *appointed representative* will not be able to commence an *insurance mediation activity* until he is included on the *FSA Register* for such activities.

Persons who are already appointed representatives

5.13.6 **[G]** Where a *person* is already an *appointed representative* and he proposes to carry on any *insurance mediation activities*, he will need to consider the following matters.

(1) He must become *authorised* if his proposed *insurance mediation activities* include activities that do not fall within the table in PERG 5.13.4G (for example, *dealing as agent* in *pure protection contracts*) and he wishes to carry on these activities. The *Act* does not permit any *person* to be exempt for some activities and *authorised* for others. He will, therefore, need to apply for *permission* to cover all the *regulated activities* that he proposes to carry on.

(2) If he proposes to carry on other *regulated activities* specified in the *Appointed Representatives Regulations* in relation to *contracts of insurance* (see the table in PERG 5.13.4G), he may be able to do so as an *appointed representative* bearing in mind the following.

   (a) He will need to be appointed by an *authorised person* prepared to accept responsibility for his *insurance mediation activities* when acting for him. The *authorised person* must have *permission* to carry on these *regulated activities*.

   (b) If these *insurance mediation activities* are to be carried on for the same *authorised person* who has already appointed him for his other *regulated activities*, the contract between them will need to be amended to reflect the additional activities. Other amendments to the contract will be required (see SUP 12.5.6AR).

(c) The effect of amendments to the *Appointed Representatives Regulations* is that an *appointed representative* cannot commence an *insurance mediation activity* until he is included on the *FSA Register* as carrying on such activities.

(d) An *appointed representative* would be entitled to have more than one *principal* subject to certain restrictions. In relation to *non-investment insurance contracts* (*general insurance contracts* and *pure protection contracts*), an *appointed representative* may have an unlimited number of *principals*. In relation to *regulated mortgage contracts* and *designated investment business*, an *appointed representative* is limited in the number of *principals* he may have. In any case where an *appointed representative* has multiple *principals*, those *principals* are required to enter into a multiple-*principal* agreement (see SUP 12.4.5DR to SUP 12.4.5GG (Appointment of an appointed representative (other than an introducer appointed representative)).

(e) If the activities of the *appointed representative* are limited to introducing, he should consider the specific *Handbook* provisions relating to *introducer appointed representatives* (see SUP 12 (What must a firm do when it appoints an appointed representative?)).

5.14 Exemptions

Professionals

5.14.1 **[G]** *Professional firms* (broadly firms of solicitors, accountants and actuaries) may carry on *insurance mediation activities* in the course of their professional activities. *Exempt professional firms* carrying on *insurance mediation activities* may continue to be able to use the *Part XX exemption* to avoid any need for *authorisation*. PROF 2 (Status of exempt professional firm) contains *guidance* on the *Part XX exemption*. They will, however, need to be shown on the *FSA Register* as carrying on *insurance mediation activities*, in order to benefit from this exemption. The task of registration is the responsibility of the *designated professional bodies* who will need to inform the *FSA* both of member firms carrying on *insurance mediation activities* and individuals within firms' management responsible for these activities.

5.14.2 **[G]** *Professional firms* with practices that involve acting for claimants in litigation against *insurance undertakings* are likely to be carrying on the *regulated activity* of *assisting in the administration and performance of a contract of insurance*. *Exempt professional firms* whose practices contain a material element of such activity should consider whether they can continue to take advantage of the *Part XX exemption* to avoid any need for *authorisation*, having regard to the relevant provisions of the *Act*, in particular section 327 (Exemption from the general prohibition) and the *guidance* in PROF 2.1.14G (Exempt regulated activities).

5.14.3 **[G]** *Professional firms* should be aware of the disapplication of the exclusions for trustees (article 66) and activities carried on in the course of a profession or non-investment business (article 67) outlined in PERG 5.11.7G (Exclusions disapplied in connection with insurance mediation) where their activities would amount to *insurance mediation*. Where they do not, they will still be able to rely upon article 67. Otherwise, the *Non-exempt Activities Order* imposes limitations on the extent to which *professional firms* can give advice to individuals. In particular, a *professional firm* cannot recommend to a *private client* that he *buy* a *life policy*, unless he is endorsing a corresponding recommendation given to the *client*. The recommendation he endorses must be one given by an *authorised person* permitted to advise on *life policies*, or an *exempt person* for these purposes. No such restrictions apply, however, in relation to *contracts of insurance* other than *life policies*.

5.14.4 **[G]** As indicated in PERG 5.6.8G, the article 72C exclusion (Provision of information on an incidental basis) is potentially available to *unauthorised professional firms* including *exempt professional firms*. This may be relevant to *professional firms* arranging *contracts of insurance* for *clients* on an individual basis.

5.14.5 **[G]** Other exemptions

In addition to certain named *persons* exempted by the *Exemption Order* from the need to obtain *authorisation*, the following bodies are exempt in relation to *insurance mediation activities* that do not relate to *life policies*:

(1) local authorities but not their subsidiaries;
(2) registered social landlords in England and Wales within the meaning of Part I of the Housing Act 1996 but not their subsidiaries;
(3) registered social landlords in Scotland within the meaning of the Housing (Scotland) Act 2001 but not their subsidiaries;
(4) the Housing Corporation;
(5) Scottish Homes; and
(6) The Northern Ireland Housing Executive.

5.15 Illustrative tables

5.15.1 **[G]** This flow chart sets out the matters a *person* will need to consider to see if he will need *authorisation* for carrying on *insurance mediation activities*. It is referred to in PERG 5.2.3G (Questions to be considered to decide if authorisation is required).

5.15.2 **[G]** Flow chart: regulated activities related to insurance mediation activities – do you need authorisation?

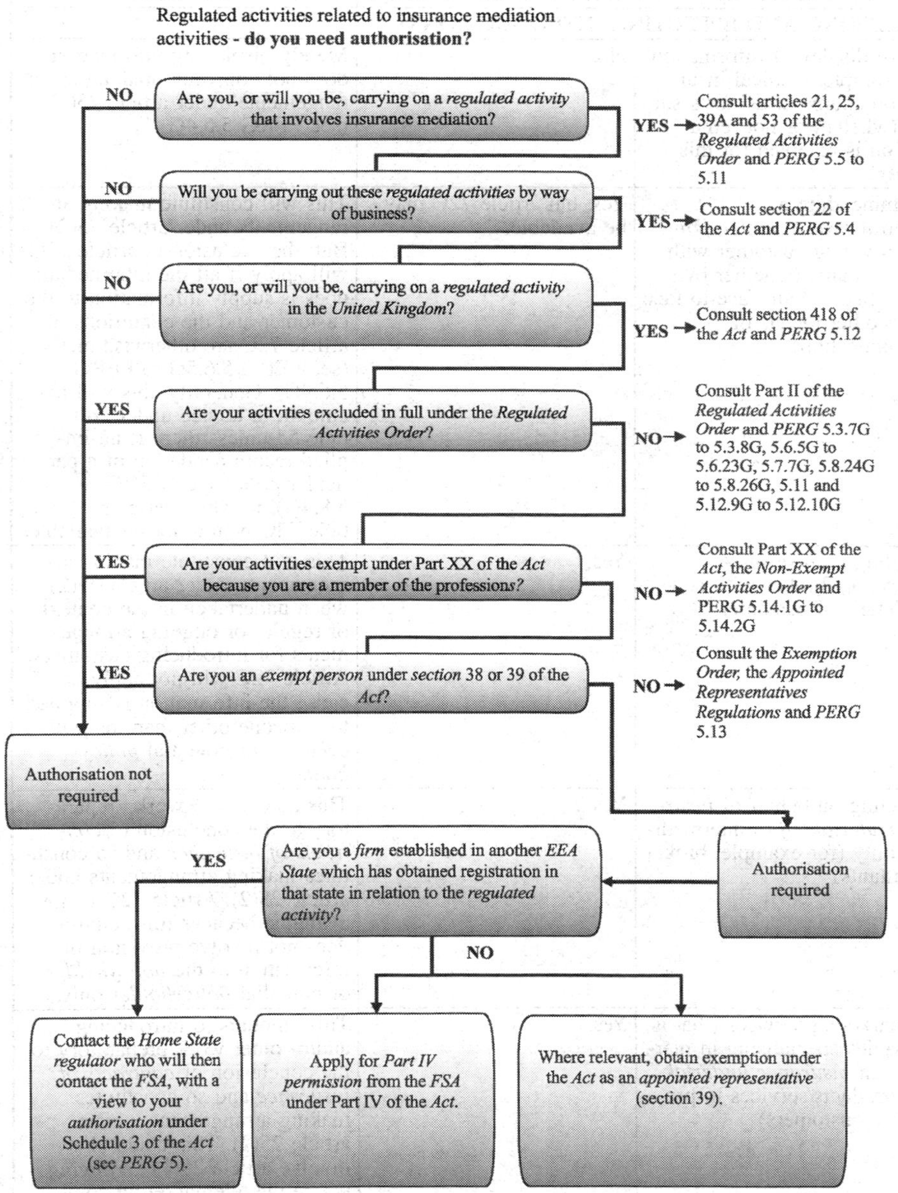
Regulated activities related to insurance mediation activities - do you need authorisation?
Are you, or will you be, carrying on a regulated activity that involves insurance mediation?
NO
YES
Consult articles 21, 25, 39A and 53 of the Regulated Activities Order and PERG 5.5 to 5.11
Will you be carrying out these regulated activities by way of business?
NO
YES
Consult section 22 of the Act and PERG 5.4
Are you, or will you be, carrying on a regulated activity in the United Kingdom?
NO
YES
Consult section 418 of the Act and PERG 5.12
Are your activities excluded in full under the Regulated Activities Order?
YES
NO
Consult Part II of the Regulated Activities Order and PERG 5.3.7G to 5.3.8G, 5.6.5G to 5.6.23G, 5.7.7G, 5.8.24G to 5.8.26G, 5.11 and 5.12.9G to 5.12.10G
Are your activities exempt under Part XX of the Act because you are a member of the professions?
YES
NO
Consult Part XX of the Act, the Non-Exempt Activities Order and PERG 5.14.1G to 5.14.2G
Are you an exempt person under section 38 or 39 of the Act?
YES
NO
Consult the Exemption Order, the Appointed Representatives Regulations and PERG 5.13
Authorisation not required
Authorisation required
Are you a firm established in another EEA State which has obtained registration in that state in relation to the regulated activity?
YES
NO
Contact the Home State regulator who will then contact the FSA, with a view to your authorisation under Schedule 3 of the Act (see PERG 5).
Apply for Part IV permission from the FSA under Part IV of the Act.
Where relevant, obtain exemption under the Act as an appointed representative (section 39).

5.15.3 **[G]** The table in PERG 5.15.4G is designed as a short, user-friendly guide but should be read in conjunction with the relevant sections of the text of this *guidance*. It is not a substitute for consulting the text of this *guidance* or seeking professional advice as appropriate (see PERG 5.1.4G to PERG 5.1.6G on the effect of this *guidance*). References in this table to articles are to articles of the *Regulated Activities Order*. In this table, it is assumed that each of the activities described is carried on by way of business (see PERG 5.4). Save where otherwise indicated, it is assumed that the intermediary is carrying on activities in respect of *policies* where he is not the *policyholder*. Also, that this table does not provide an exhaustive list of all of the exclusions or exemptions that are of relevance to each type of activity. For a full explanation of the exclusions and exemptions under the

Regulated Activities Order and their applicability see generally PERG 5.3.7G to PERG 5.3.8G, PERG 5.6.5G to PERG 5.6.23G, PERG 5.7.7G, PERG 5.8.24G to PERG 5.8.26G, PERG 5.11, PERG 5.12.9G to PERG 5.12.10G, PERG 5.13 and PERG 5.14. This Table is referred to in PERG 5.7.5G (The regulated activities: assisting in the administration and performance of a contract of insurance).

5.15.4 **[G]** Types of activity – are they regulated activities and, if so, why?

Type of activity	Is it a regulated activity?	Rationale
MARKETING AND EFFECTING INTRODUCTIONS		
Passive display of information -for example, medical insurance brochures in doctor's surgery (whether or not remuneration is received for this activity)	No.	Merely displaying information does not constitute making arrangements under article 25(2) (see PERG 5.6.4G).
Recommending a broker/*insurance undertaking* and providing customer with contact details (whether by phone, fax, e-mail, face-to-face or any other means of communication)	Yes, but article 72C may be available.	This will constitute making arrangements under article 25(2). But, the exclusion in article 72C will apply if all the intermediary does is supply information to the customer and the conditions of article 72C are otherwise met (see PERG 5.6.5G to PERG 5.6.9G). Generally, this will not amount to advice under article 53 unless there is an implied recommendation of a particular *policy* (see PERG 5.8.4G), in which case article 72C would not be available.
Providing an *insurance undertaking*/broker with contact details of customer	Yes.	This will constitute making arrangements under article 25(2) when undertaken in the context of regular or ongoing arrangements for introducing customers. Article 72C will not apply because the information is supplied to someone other than the *policyholder* or potential *policyholder*.
Marketing on behalf of *insurance undertaking* to intermediaries only (for example, broker consultants)	Yes.	This amounts to work preparatory to the conclusion of *contracts of insurance* and so constitutes making arrangements under article 25(2). Article 72C is not available because this activity does not involve provision of information to the *policyholder* or potential *policyholder* only.
Telemarketing services (that is, companies specialising in marketing an *insurance undertaking's* products/services to prospective customers)	Yes.	This amounts to introducing and/or other work preparatory to the conclusion of *contracts of insurance* and so constitutes making arrangements under article 25(2). This could also involve article 25(1) *arranging* where the telemarketing company actually *sells* a particular *policy* and could involve *advising on investments*. Article 72C will not be available where the provision of information is more than incidental to the telemarketing company's main business or where the telemarketing company is *advising on investments*.

Type of activity	Is it a regulated activity?	Rationale
PRE-PURCHASE DISCUSSIONS WITH CUSTOMERS AND ADVICE		
Discussion with client about need for insurance generally/need to take out a particular type of insurance	Generally, no. Article 72C available if needed.	Not enough, of itself, to constitute making arrangements under article 25(2), but you should consider whether, viewed as a whole, your activities might amount to *arranging*. If so, article 72C might be of application (see PERG 5.6.5G to PERG 5.6.9G).
Advising on the level of cover needed	Generally, no. Article 72C available if needed.	Not enough, of itself, to constitute making arrangements under article 25(2), but you should consider whether, viewed as a whole, your activities might amount to making arrangements under article 25(2) (see PERG 5.8.3G). If so, article 72C might be of application (see PERG 5.6.5G to PERG 5.6.9G).
Pre-purchase questioning in the context of filtered sales (intermediary asks a series of questions and then suggests several *policies* which suit the answers given)	Yes. Subject to article 72C exclusion where available.	This will constitute *arranging* although article 72C may be of application (see PERG 5.6.5G to PERG 5.6.9G). If there is no express or implied recommendation of a particular *policy*, this activity will not amount to advice under article 53 (see PERG 5.8.15G to PERG 5.8.19G).
Explanation of the terms of a particular *policy* or comparison of the terms of different policies	Possibly. Article 72C available.	This is likely to amount to making arrangements under article 25(2). In certain circumstances, it could involve *advising on investments* (see PERG 5.8.8G (Advice or information)). Where the explanation is provided to the potential *policyholder*, and does not involve *advising on investments*, article 72C may be of application (see PERG 5.6.5G to PERG 5.6.9G), and where information is provided by a professional in the course of a profession, article 67 may apply (see PERG 5.11.9G to PERG 5.11.12G).
Advising that a customer take out a particular *policy*	Yes.	This amounts to advice on the merits of a particular *policy* under article 53 (see PERG 5.8.4G to PERG 5.8.5G).
Advising that a customer does not take out a particular *policy*	Yes.	This amounts to advice on the merits of a particular *policy* under article 53 (see PERG 5.8.4G to PERG 5.8.5G).
Advice by journalists in newspapers, broadcasts etc.	Generally, no because of the article 54 exclusion.	Article 54 provides an exclusion for advice given in newspapers etc (see PERG 5.8.24G to PERG 5.8.25G).

Type of activity	Is it a regulated activity?	Rationale
Giving advice to a customer in relation to his *buying* a consumer product, where insurance is a compulsory secondary purchase and/or a benefit that comes with *buying* the product	Not necessarily but depends on the circumstances.	Where the advice relates specifically to the merits of the consumer product, it is possible that references to the accompanying insurance may be seen to be information and not advice. If, however, the advice relates, in part, to the merits of the insurance element, then it will be *regulated activity*.
ASSISTING CUSTOMERS WITH COMPLETING/SENDING APPLICATION FORMS		
Providing information to customer who fills in application form	Possibly. Subject to article 67 or 72C exclusions where available.	This activity may amount to *arranging* although the exclusions in article 67 (see PERG 5.11.9G to PERG 5.11.12G) and article 72C (see PERG 5.6.5G to PERG 5.6.9G) may be of application.
Helping a potential *policyholder* fill in an application form	Yes.	This activity amounts to *arranging*. Article 72C will not apply because this activity goes beyond the mere provision of information to a *policyholder* or potential *policyholder* (see PERG 5.6.5G to PERG 5.6.9G).
Receiving completed proposal forms for checking and forwarding to an *insurance undertaking* (for example, an administration outsourcing service provider that receives and processes proposal forms)	Yes.	This amounts to *arranging*. Article 72C does not apply because this activity goes beyond the mere provision of information to a *policyholder* or potential *policyholder* (see PERG 5.6.5G to PERG 5.6.9G).
Assisting in completion of proposal form and sending to *insurance undertaking*	Yes.	This activity amounts to *arranging*. Article 72C does not apply because this activity goes beyond the mere provision of information (see PERG 5.6.5G to PERG 5.6.9G).
NEGOTIATING AND CONCLUDING CONTRACTS OF INSURANCE		
Negotiating terms of *policy* on behalf of a customer with the *insurance undertaking*	Yes.	This activity amounts to *arranging* (see PERG 5.6.2G).
Negotiating terms of *policy* on behalf of *insurance undertaking* with the customer and signing proposal form on his behalf	Yes.	These activities amount to both *arranging* and *dealing in investments as agent.*
Concluding a *contract of insurance* on insurance company's behalf, for example, motor dealer who has authority to conclude insurance contract on behalf of *insurance undertaking* when *selling* a car	Yes.	A *person* carrying on this activity will be *dealing in investments as agent*. He will also be *arranging* (as the article 28 exclusion only applies in the limited circumstances envisaged under article 28(3)) (see PERG 5.6.12G).
Agreeing, on behalf of a prospective *policyholder*, to *buy* a *policy*.	Yes.	A *person* who, with authority, enters into a *contract of insurance* on behalf of another is *dealing in investments as agent* under article 21, and will also be *arranging*.

Type of activity	Is it a regulated activity?	Rationale
Providing compulsory insurance as a secondary purchase	Yes. It will amount to *dealing in investments as agent* or *arranging*.	The fact that the insurance is secondary to the primary product does not alter the fact that arranging the package involves *arranging* the insurance.
COLLECTION OF PREMIUMS		
Collection of cheque for premium from the customer at the pre-contract stage.	Yes (as part of *arranging*).	This activity is likely to form part of *arranging*. But the mere collection/receipt of premiums from the customer is unlikely, without more, to amount to *arranging*.
Collection of premiums at post-contract stage	No.	The mere collection of premiums from *policyholders* is unlikely, without more, to amount to *assisting in the administration and performance of a contract of insurance*.
MID-TERM ADJUSTMENTS AND ASSIGNMENTS		
Solicitors or licensed conveyancers discharging client instructions to assign *contracts of insurance*	Not where article 67 applies.	As the assignment of rights under a *contract of insurance* (as opposed to the creation of new *contracts of insurance*) does not fall within the *IMD*, article 67 is of potential application (see PERG 5.11.9G to PERG 5.11.12G).
Making mid-term adjustments to a *policy*, for example, property manager notifies changes to the names of the leaseholders registered as "interested parties" in the *policy* in respect of the property	Yes.	Assuming the freeholder (as *policyholder*) is obliged under the terms of the *policy* to notify the *insurance undertaking* of changes to the identity of the leaseholders, the property manager is likely to be *assisting in the administration and the performance of the contract of insurance*.
TRADED ENDOWMENT POLICIES ("TEPs")		
Making introductions for the purposes of *selling* TEPs	Yes, unless article 72C applies.	Making introductions for these purposes is *arranging* unless article 72C applies (see PERG 5.6.5G to PERG 5.6.9G). The exclusions in article 29 (Arranging deals with or through authorised persons) and 33 (Introducing) no longer apply to arranging *contracts of insurance*.
Market makers in TEPs	Yes, although the exclusion in article 28 may apply.	Unauthorised market makers can continue to make use of the exclusions in articles 15 (Absence of holding out etc.) and 16 (Dealing in contractually based investments), where appropriate. In order to avoid the need for *authorisation* in respect of *arranging* they may be able to rely upon article 28 (see PERG 5.6.12G).
ASSISTING POLICYHOLDER WITH MAKING A CLAIM		

Type of activity	Is it a regulated activity?	Rationale
Merely providing information to the insured to help him complete a claim form	No.	Of itself, this is likely to amount to assisting in the administration but not the performance of a *contract of insurance*. In the *FSA's* view, the provision of information in these circumstances is more akin to facilitating performance of a *contract of insurance* rather than assisting in the performance (see PERG 5.7.3G to PERG 5.7.5G).
Completion of claim form on behalf of insured	Potentially.	This activity amounts to assisting in the administration of a *contract of insurance*. Whether this activity amounts to *assisting in the administration and performance of a contract of insurance* will depend upon whether a *person's* assistance in filling in a claims form is material to whether performance of the contractual obligation to notify a claim takes place (see PERG 5.7.2G to PERG 5.7.3G).
Notification of claim to *insurance undertaking* and helping negotiate its settlement on the *policyholder's* behalf	Yes.	This activity amounts to *assisting in the administration and performance of a contract of insurance* (see PERG 5.7.4G).
ASSISTING INSURANCE UNDERTAKING WITH CLAIMS BY POLICYHOLDERS		
Negotiation of settlement of claims on behalf of an *insurance undertaking*	No.	Claims management on behalf of an *insurance undertaking* does not amount to *assisting in the administration and performance of a contract of insurance* by virtue of the exclusion in article 39B (see PERG 5.7.7G).
Providing information to *an insurance undertaking* in connection with its investigation or assessment of a claim	No.	This activity does not amount to *assisting in the administration and performance of a contract of insurance.*
Loss adjusters and claims management services (for example, by administration outsourcing providers)	Potentially.	These activities may amount to *assisting in the administration and performance of a contract of insurance*. Article 39B excludes these activities, however, when undertaken on behalf of an *insurance undertaking* only (see PERG 5.7.7G).
Providing an expert appraisal of a claim	No.	This activity does not amount to *assisting in the administration and performance of a contract of insurance* whether carried out on behalf of an *insurance undertaking* or otherwise.
Jeweller repairs customer's jewellery pursuant to a *policy* which permits the jeweller to carry out repairs	No.	This activity does not amount to *assisting in the administration and performance of a contract of insurance*. It amounts to managing claims on behalf of an *insurance undertaking* and so falls within the exclusion in article 39B (see PERG 5.7.7G).

5.15.5 **[G]** The flow chart in PERG 5.15.6G sets out the matters a *person* whose introducing activities potentially amount to *making arrangements with a view to transactions in investments* will need to consider if he can use the exclusion in article 72C (Provision of information on an incidental basis). It is referred to in PERG 5.1.6G (Purpose of guidance) and PERG 5.6.9G (Exclusion: article 72C (Provision of information on an incidental basis)).

5.15.6 **[G]** Flow Chart: Introducers.

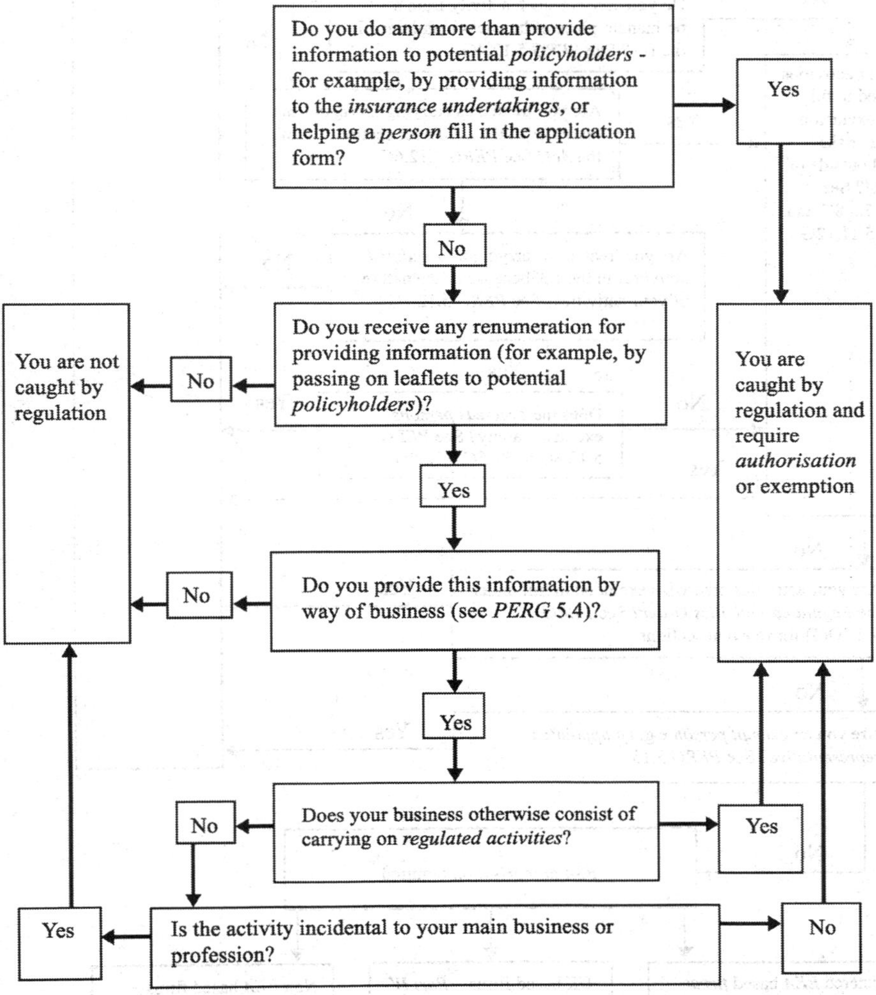

5.15.7 **[G]** The flow chart in PERG 5.15.8G sets out the questions a *person* needs to consider in determining whether or not his *regulated activities* are carried on 'in the *United Kingdom*'.

5.15.8 **[G]** Flow chart: am I carrying on regulated activities in the United Kingdom?

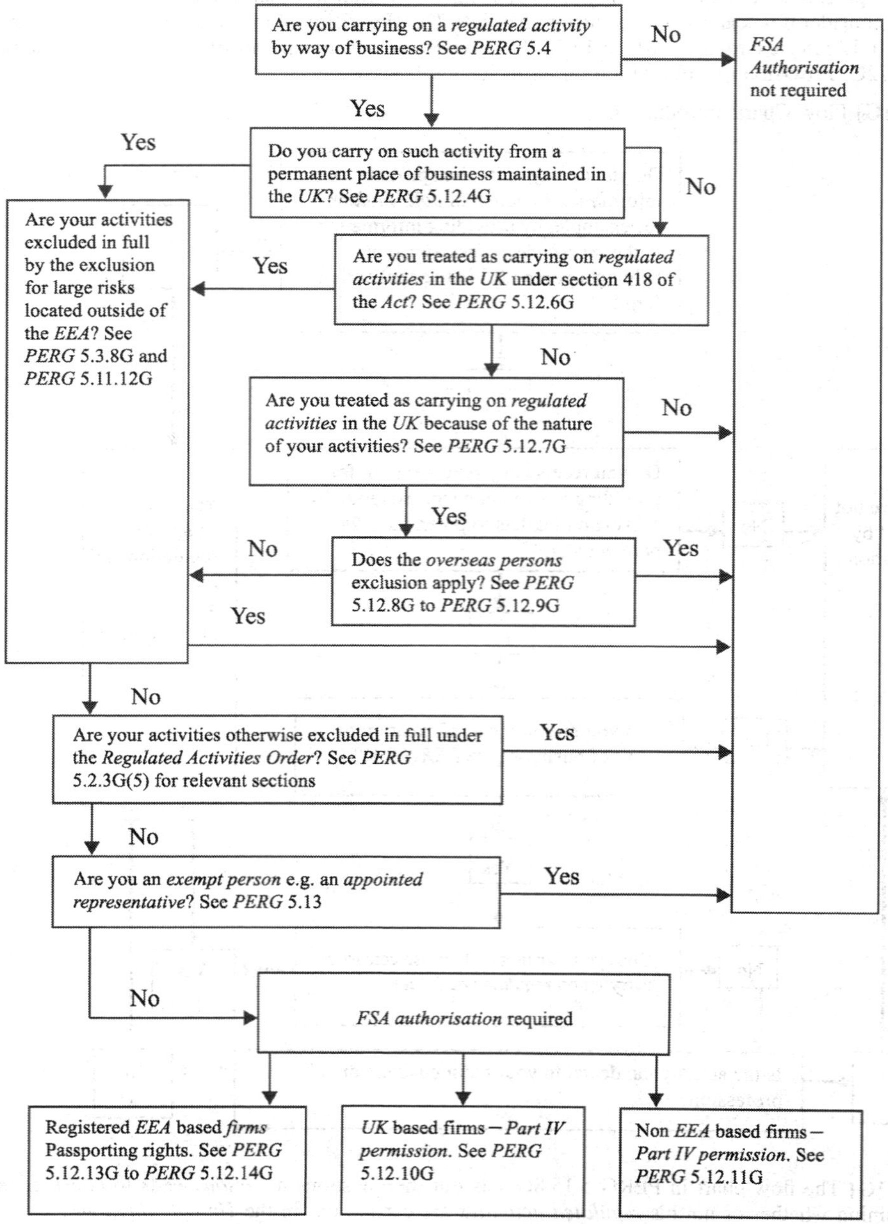

5.16 Meaning of 'insurance mediation'

5.16.1 **[G]** PERG 5.16.2G sets out the text of article 2.3 of the *Insurance Mediation Directive*. It is referred to in PERG 5.2.5G and PERG 5.2.5G (Approach to implementation of the IMD), PERG 5.11.7G (Exclusions disapplied in connection with insurance mediation) and PERG 5.11.10G (Activities carried on in the course of a profession or non-investment business).

5.16.2 **[G]** Text of article 2.3 of the Insurance Mediation Directive

"'Insurance mediation' means the activities of introducing, proposing or carrying out other work preparatory to the conclusion of contracts of insurance, or of concluding such contracts, or of assisting in the administration and performance of such contracts, in particular in the event of a claim.

These activities when undertaken by an insurance undertaking or an employee of an insurance undertaking who is acting under the responsibility of the insurance undertaking shall not be considered as insurance mediation.

The provision of information on an incidental basis in the context of another professional activity provided that the purpose of that activity is not to assist the customer in concluding or performing an insurance contract, the management of claims of an insurance undertaking on a professional basis, and loss adjusting and expert appraisal of claims shall also not be considered as insurance mediation."

CHAPTER 6
GUIDANCE ON THE IDENTIFICATION OF CONTRACTS OF INSURANCE

6.1 Application

[2222]
6.1.1 **[G]** This chapter is relevant to any *person* who needs to know what activities fall within the scope of the *Act*.

6.2 Purpose of guidance

6.2.1 **[G]** The purpose of this *guidance* is to set out:
(1) at PERG 6.5G the general principles; and
(2) at PERG 6.6G the range of specific factors;

that the *FSA* regards as relevant in deciding whether any arrangement is a *contract of insurance*.

6.2.2 **[G]** This *guidance* includes (at PERG 6.7) a number of examples, showing how the factors have been applied to reach conclusions with respect to specific categories of business. Further examples may be published from time-to-time.

6.3 Background

6.3.1 **[G]** The business of *effecting* or *carrying out contracts of insurance* is subject to prior *authorisation* and regulation by the *FSA*. (There are some limited exceptions to this requirement, for example, for breakdown insurance.)

6.3.2 **[G]** The *Regulated Activities Order*, which sets out the activities for which *authorisation* is required, does not attempt an exhaustive definition of a '*contract of insurance*'. Instead, it makes some specific extensions and limitations to the general common law meaning of the concept. For example, it expressly extends the concept to fidelity bonds and similar contracts of guarantee, which are not *contracts of insurance* at common law, and it excludes certain *funeral plan contracts*, which would generally be *contracts of insurance* at common law. Similarly, the *Exemption Order* excludes certain trade union provident business, which would also be insurance at common law. One consequence of this is that common law judicial decisions about whether particular contracts amount to 'insurance' or 'insurance business' are relevant in defining the scope of the *FSA's authorisation* and regulatory activities, as they were under predecessor legislation.

6.3.3 **[G]** The courts have not fully defined the common law meaning of 'insurance' and 'insurance business', since they have, on the whole, confined their decisions to the facts before them. They have, however, given useful guidance in the form of descriptions of *contracts of insurance*.

6.3.4 **[G]** The best established of these descriptions appears in the case of Prudential v. Commissioners of Inland Revenue [1904] 2 KB 658. This case, read with a number of later cases, treats as insurance any enforceable contract under which a 'provider' undertakes:
(1) in consideration of one or more payments;
(2) to pay money or provide a corresponding benefit (including in some cases services to be paid for by the provider) to a 'recipient';
(3) in response to a defined event the occurrence of which is uncertain (either as to when it will occur or as to whether it will occur at all) and adverse to the interests of the recipient.

6.4 Limitations of this guidance

6.4.1 **[G]** Although what appears below is the *FSA's* approach, it cannot state what the law is, as that is a matter for the courts. Accordingly, this *guidance* is not a substitute for adequate legal advice on any transaction.

6.4.2 **[G]** The list of principles and factors is not closed and this *guidance* by no means covers all types of insurance-like business.

6.4.3 **[G]** The *FSA* will consider each case on its facts and on its merits.

6.4.4 **[G]** In some cases transactions with the same commercial purpose or economic effect may be classified differently, ie some as insurance and some as non-insurance.

6.5 General principles

6.5.1 **[G]** The starting point for the identification of a *contract of insurance* is the case of Prudential v. Commissioners of Inland Revenue [1904] 2 KB 658, from which the description set out in PERG 6.3.4G is drawn. Any contracts that fall outside that description are unlikely to be *contracts of insurance*.

6.5.2 **[G]** The *FSA* will interpret and apply the description in PERG 6.3.4G in the light of applicable legislation and common law, including case law.

6.5.3 **[G]** In particular, if the common law is unclear as to whether or not a particular contract is a *contract of insurance*, the *FSA* will interpret and apply the common law in the context of and in a way that is consistent with the purpose of the *Act* as expressed in the *FSA's* statutory objectives.

6.5.4 **[G]** The *FSA* will apply the following principles of construction to determine whether a contract is a *contract of insurance*.

(1) In applying the description in PERG 6.3.4G, more weight attaches to the substance of the contract, than to the form of the contract. The form of the contract is relevant (see PERG 6.6.8G(3) and (4)) but not decisive of whether a contract is a *contract of insurance*: Fuji Finance Inc. v. Aetna Life Insurance Co. Ltd [1997] Ch. 173 (C.A.).

(2) In particular, the substance of the provider's obligation determines the substance of the contract: In re Sentinel Securities [1996] 1 WLR 316. Accordingly, the *FSA* is unlikely to treat the provider's or the customer's intention or purpose in entering into a contract as relevant to its classification.

(3) The contract must be characterised as a whole and not according to its 'dominant purpose' or the relative weight of its 'insurance content': Fuji Finance Inc. v. Aetna Life Insurance Co. Ltd [1997] Ch. 173 (C.A.).

(4) Since only contracts of marine insurance and certain *contracts of insurance* effected without consideration are required to be in writing, a *contract of insurance* may be oral or may be expressed in a number of documents.

6.6 The factors

6.6.1 **[G]** Contracts under which the provider has an absolute discretion as to whether any benefit is provided on the occurrence of the uncertain event, are not *contracts of insurance*. This may be the case even if, in practice, the provider has never exercised its discretion so as to deny a benefit: Medical Defence Union v. Department of Trade and Industry [1979] 2 W.L.R. 686. The degree of discretion required and the matters to which it must relate are illustrated in PERG 6.7.1G (Example 1: discretionary medical schemes).

6.6.2 **[G]** The 'assumption of risk' by the provider is an important descriptive feature of all *contracts of insurance*. The 'assumption of risk' has the meaning in (1) and (3), derived from the case law in (2) and (4) below. The application of the 'assumption of risk' concept is illustrated in PERG 6.7.2G (Example 2: disaster recovery business).

(1) Case law establishes that the provider's obligation under a *contract of insurance* is an enforceable obligation to respond (usually, by providing some benefit in the form of money or services) to the occurrence of the uncertain event. This *guidance* describes the assumption of that obligation as the 'assumption' by the provider of (all or part of) the insured risk. 'Transfer of risk' has the same meaning in this *guidance*.

(2) The case law referred to in (1) is Prudential v. Commissioners of Inland Revenue [1904] 2 KB 658, read with Hampton v. Toxteth Co-operative Provident Society Ltd [1915] 1 Ch. 721 (C.A.), Department of Trade and Industry v. St Christopher Motorists Assoc. Ltd [1974] 1 All E.R. 395, Medical Defence Union v. Department of Trade and Industry [1979] 2 W.L.R. 686 and Wooding v. Monmouthshire and South Wales Mutual Indemnity Soc. Ltd [1939] 4 All E.R. 570 (H.L.).

(3) The *FSA* recognises that there is a line of case law in relation to *long-term insurance business* that establishes that a contract may be a *contract of insurance* even if, having effected that contract, the provider 'trades without any risk'. The *FSA* accepts that the insurer's risk of profit or loss from insurance business is not a relevant descriptive feature of a *contract of insurance*. But in the *FSA's* view that is distinct from and does not undermine the different proposition in (1).

(4) The case law referred to in (3) is Flood v. Irish Provident Assurance Co. Ltd [1912] 2 Ch. 597 (C.A.), Fuji Finance Inc. v. Aetna Life Insurance Co. Ltd [1995] Ch. 122, Re Barrett; Ex parte Young v. NM Superannuation Pty Ltd, (1992) 106 A.L.R. 549, Fuji Finance Inc. v. Aetna Life Insurance Co. Ltd [1997] Ch. 173 (C.A.).

6.6.3 **[G]** Contracts, under which the amount and timing of the payments made by the recipient make it reasonable to conclude that there is a genuine pre-payment for services to be rendered in response to a future contingency, are unlikely to be regarded as insurance. In general, the *FSA* expects that this requirement will be satisfied where there is a commercially reasonable and objectively justifiable relationship between the amount of the payment and the cost of providing the contract benefit.

6.6.4 **[G]** Contracts under which the provider undertakes to provide periodic maintenance of goods or facilities, whether or not any uncertain or adverse event (in the form of, for example, a breakdown or failure) has occurred, are unlikely to be *contracts of insurance*.

6.6.5 **[G]** Contracts under which, in consideration for an initial payment, the provider stands ready to provide services on the occurrence of a future contingency, on condition that the services actually provided are paid for by the recipient at a commercial rate, are unlikely to be regarded as insurance. Contrast PERG 6.7.21G (Example 7: solicitors' retainers) with PERG 6.7.22G (Example 8: time and distance cover).

6.6.6 **[G]** The recipient's payment for a *contract of insurance* need not take the form of a discrete or distinct premium. Consideration may be part of some other payment, for example the purchase price of goods (Nelson v. Board of Trade (1901) 17 T.L.R. 456). Consideration may also be provided in a non-monetary form, for example as part of the service that an employee is contractually required to provide under a contract of employment (Australian Health Insurance Assoc. Ltd v. Esso Australia Pty Ltd (1993) 116 A.L.R. 253).

6.6.7 **[G]** Under most commercial contracts with a *customer*, a provider will assume more than one obligation. Some of these may be insurance obligations, others may not. The *FSA* will apply the principles in PERG 6.5.4G, in the way described in (1) to (3) to determine whether the contract is a *contract of insurance*.

(1) If a provider undertakes an identifiable and distinct obligation that is, in substance an insurance obligation as described in PERG 6.5.4G, then, other things being equal, the *FSA* is likely to find that by undertaking that obligation the provider has effected a *contract of insurance*.

(2) The presence of an insurance obligation will mean that the contract is a *contract of insurance*, whether or not that obligation is 'substantial' in comparison with the other obligations in the contract.

(3) The presence of an insurance obligation will mean that the contract is a *contract of insurance*, whether or not entering into that obligation forms a significant part of the provider's business. The *FSA* generally regards a provider as undertaking an obligation 'by way of business' if he takes on an obligation in connection with or for the purposes of his core business, to realise a commercial advantage or benefit.

6.6.8 **[G]** The following factors are also relevant.

(1) A contract is more likely to be regarded as a *contract of insurance* if the amount payable by the recipient under the contract is calculated by reference to either or both of the probability of occurrence or likely severity of the uncertain event.

(2) A contract is less likely to be regarded as a *contract of insurance* if it requires the provider to assume a speculative risk (ie a risk carrying the possibility of either profit or loss) rather than a pure risk (ie a risk of loss only).

(3) A contract is more likely to be regarded as a *contract of insurance* if the contract is described as insurance and contains terms that are consistent with its classification as a *contract of insurance*, for example, obligations of the utmost good faith.

(4) A contract that contains terms that are inconsistent with obligations of good faith may, therefore, be less likely to be classified as a *contract of insurance*; however, since it is the substance of the provider's rights and obligations under the contract that is more significant, a contract does not cease to be a *contract of insurance* simply because the terms included are not usual insurance terms.

6.7 Examples

Example 1: discretionary medical schemes

6.7.1 **[G]** Medical schemes under which an employer operates or contributes to a fund, from which the employee has a right to a benefit (for example, a payment) on the occurrence of a specified illness or injury, are likely to be insurance schemes. This will be the case whether the employee makes any contribution to the fund, or the scheme is funded by the employer as an emolument. The scheme would not be insurance, however, if the employer has an absolute discretion whether or not to provide any benefit to the employee. Absolute discretion requires, for example, that the employer has an unfettered discretion both as to whether the employee will receive a benefit and as to the amount of that benefit. The absolutely discretionary nature of the benefits should also be clear from the terms of the scheme and any literature published about or in relation to it. If these requirements are met, it may not be relevant that, in practice, the employer has never refused to meet a valid claim under the scheme.

Example 2: disaster recovery business

6.7.2 **[G]** The disaster recovery provider sets up and maintains a range of IT and related facilities (PABX etc). The disaster recovery contracts so far considered by the *FSA* give the recipient, subject to certain conditions including an up front payment, priority access to all or a specified part of these facilities if a 'disaster' causes the failure of a similar business system on which the recipient relies. The provider sells access to the same facilities to a number of different recipients, both for use in response to 'disasters' and, more usually, for use in testing and refining the recipient's ability to switch to alternative systems in the event of a disaster.

6.7.3 **[G]** In principle, a significant part of disaster recovery business could potentially fall within the description of a *contract of insurance* set out in PERG 6.3.4G. The provider undertakes, in consideration of a payment, to provide the recipient with services (alternative facilities) in response to a defined event (a disaster), which is adverse to the interests of the recipient and the occurrence of which is uncertain. The risk dealt with under the disaster recovery contract is a pure risk (see PERG 6.6.8G(2)) and, at least at the commencement of the contract, the provider assumes that risk, within the terms of PERG 6.6.2G.

6.7.4 **[G]** However, the disaster recovery contracts considered by the *FSA* had two key features.

(1) Priority access to facilities in the event of a disaster was expressed to be on a 'first come, first served' basis. The contracts provided expressly that if the facilities needed by recipient A were already in use, following an earlier invocation by recipient B, the provider's obligation to recipient A was reduced to no more than an obligation of 'best endeavours' to meet A's requirements. The entry into additional contracts of this kind did not increase the probability that the provider's existing resources would be inadequate to meet all possible claims. The terms of the contract were such that there was no pattern of claims that would cause the provider to have to pay claims from its own resources.

(2) In general, the contracts were priced so that the total consideration collected from the recipient over the life of the contract bore a reasonable and justifiable relationship to the commercial cost of the services actually provided to the recipient (see PERG 6.6.5G). This was achieved, for example, by post-invocation charges levied according to the actual usage of services.

6.7.5 **[G]** Based on these features, the *FSA* reached the conclusion, with which the other terms of the contracts were consistent (PERG 6.6.8G(3)), that these disaster recovery contracts were not *contracts of insurance*.

6.7.6 **[G]** An important part of the conclusion in PERG 6.7.5G was that, although the provider assumed a risk at the outset of the contract, looking at the contract as a whole and interpreting the common law in the context of the *FSA's* objectives (see PERG 6.5.2G and PERG 6.5.3G) there was no relevant assumption of risk.

(1) The presence or absence of an assumption of risk is an important part of the statutory rationale for the prudential regulation of insurance.

(2) In Medical Defence Union v. Department of Trade and Industry [1979] 2 W.L.R. 686, the court accepted that since there was no common law definition of a *contract of insurance*, the meaning of the term 'fell to be construed in its context according to the general law'. The court recognised that in deciding whether a contract was a *contract of insurance* for the purposes of the Insurance Companies Act 1974, the 'context' included the purpose of the regulatory statute.

(3) Accordingly, when the common law is unclear, the *FSA* will assess the desirability of regulating a particular contract as insurance in the light of the statutory objectives in the *Act*. The *FSA* will use that assessment as an indicator of whether or not a sufficient assumption of risk is present for the contract to be classified as a *contract of insurance* at common law.

(4) In the case of disaster recovery contracts, the fact that there was no pattern of claims that would cause the provider to have to pay claims form its own resources led the *FSA* to conclude that there was no relevant assumption of risk by the disaster recovery provider.

Example 3: manufacturers' and retailers' warranties

6.7.7 **[G]** Under a simple manufacturer's or retailer's warranty the purchase price of the goods includes an amount, in consideration of which the manufacturer undertakes an obligation (the warranty) to respond (without further expense to the purchaser) to specified defects in the product that emerge within a defined time after purchase. When the warranty operates, the manufacturer or retailer provides repairs or replacement products in response to a defined event (the emergence of a latent defect in the product), which is adverse to the interests of the purchaser and the occurrence of which is uncertain. In summary, therefore, a simple manufacturer's or retailer's warranty is an identifiable and distinct obligation that is similar to and capable of being described as an insurance obligation in substance under PERG 6.3.4G.

6.7.8 **[G]** Notwithstanding PERG 6.7.7G, the *FSA's* view is that an obligation that is of the same nature as a seller's or supplier's usual obligations as regards the quality of the goods or services is unlikely to be an insurance obligation in substance.

6.7.9 **[G]** The *FSA* is unlikely to classify a contract containing a simple manufacturer's or retailer's warranty as a *contract of insurance*, if the *FSA* is satisfied that the warranty does no more that crystallise or recognise obligations that are of the same nature as a seller's or supplier's usual obligations as regards the quality of the goods or services.

6.7.10 **[G]** For the purpose of PERG 6.7.9G, an obligation is likely to be of the same nature as the seller's or supplier's usual obligations as regards the quality of goods or services if it is an obligation of the seller to the buyer, assumed by the seller in consideration of the purchase price, which:
(1) implements, or bears a reasonable relationship to, the seller's statutory or common law obligations as regards the quality of goods or services of that kind; or
(2) is a usual obligation relevant to quality or fitness in commercial contracts for the sale of goods or supply of services of that kind.

Example 4: separate warranty transactions and extended warranties

6.7.11 **[G]** It follows from PERG 6.7.10G that the *FSA* is unlikely to be satisfied that an obligation in a contract of sale or supply is of the same nature as the seller's or supplier's usual obligations as regards the quality of goods or services, if that obligation has one or more of the following features:
(1) it is assumed by a person other than the seller or supplier (a 'third party'); or
(2) it is significantly more extensive in content, scope or duration than a seller's usual obligations as to the quality of goods or services of that kind.

6.7.12 **[G]** Other things being equal, the *FSA* is likely to classify a contract of sale containing a warranty that has one or more of the features in PERG 6.7.11G as a *contract of insurance*. The features in PERG 6.7.11G(1) and (2) typically distinguish a 'third party' warranty and an 'extended warranty' from a 'simple' manufacturer's or retailer's warranty.

6.7.13 **[G]** If a warranty is provided by a third party, the *FSA* will usually treat this as conclusive of the fact that there are different transactions and an assumption or transfer of risk. This conclusion would not usually depend on whether the provider is (or is not) a part of the same group of companies as the manufacturer or retailer. But it will be the third party (who assumes the risk) that is potentially effecting a *contract of insurance*.

6.7.14 **[G]** A manufacturer or retailer may undertake a warranty obligation to his customer in a separate contract with the customer, distinct from the contract of sale or supply of goods or services. The *FSA* will examine the separate contract to see if it is a *contract of insurance*. But the mere existence of a separate warranty contract is unlikely to be conclusive by itself.

6.7.15 **[G]** A manufacturer or retailer may undertake an obligation to ensure that the customer becomes a party to a separate *contract of insurance* in respect of the goods sold. This would include, for example, a contract for the sale of a freezer, with a simple warranty in relation to the quality of the freezer, but also providing insurance (underwritten by an *insurer* and in respect of which the customer is the *policyholder*) covering loss of frozen food if the freezer fails. The *FSA* is unlikely to treat a contract containing an obligation of this kind as a *contract of insurance*. However, the manufacturer or retailer may be in the position of an intermediary and may be liable to regulation in that capacity.

6.7.16 **[G]** The *FSA* distinguishes the contract in PERG 6.7.15G from a contract under which the manufacturer or retailer assumes the obligation to provide the customer with an indemnity against loss or damage if the freezer fails, but takes out insurance to cover the cost of having to provide the indemnity to the customer. The obligation to indemnify is of a different nature from the seller's or supplier's usual obligations as regards the quality of goods or services and is an insurance obligation. By assuming it, other things being equal, the manufacturer or retailer effects a *contract of insurance*. The fact that the manufacturer or retailer may take out insurance to cover the cost of having to provide the indemnity is irrelevant

Example 5: typical warranty schemes administered by motor dealers

6.7.17 **[G]** The following are examples of typical warranty schemes operated by motor dealers. Provided that, in each case, the *FSA* is satisfied that the obligations assumed by the dealer are not significantly more extensive in content, scope or duration that a dealer's usual obligations as to the quality of motor vehicles of that kind, the *FSA* would not usually classify the contracts embodying these transactions as *contracts of insurance*.
(a) The dealer gives a verbal undertaking to the purchaser that during a specified period (usually 3 months) he will rectify any fault occurring with the vehicle. No money changes hands, and the dealer is responsible for meeting the warranty obligation.
(b) The dealer undertakes warranty obligations to his customer. The warranty obligations are either included in the contract for the sale of the vehicle or are set out in a separate contract between dealer and customer at the time of sale. The dealer administers his own warranty scheme and does not employ a separate company (for example a subsidiary) to run the scheme. In the event of a fault, the purchaser must contact the dealer, who is responsible for meeting the warranty obligation. The dealer decides whether or not to put money aside to meet potential claims.
(c) The dealer purchases proprietary warranty booklets issued by an administration company. These booklets contain 'terms and conditions' under which the dealer undertakes warranty obligations to the customer. The dealer sells these 'products' to his customer under a separate

contract or inflates the price of the vehicle to include them as part of the sale of the vehicle. The administration company administers any claims that arise. The financial arrangements are that the dealer charges his customer for the warranty, passing a fee to the administration company for the purchase of the booklet and any administration relating to the processing of claims. The dealer retains all monies (less administration fee) received from the sale of the warranties and keeps any surplus after claims have been paid. The dealer is responsible for meeting the warranty obligation.

(d) The dealer undertakes warranty obligations to his customer. The warranty obligations are either included in the contract for the sale of the vehicle or are set out in a separate contract between dealer and customer at the time of sale. The dealer employs an administration company to handle all the claims and associated administrative work. The administration company usually has access to a bank account, funded by the dealer and specifically set aside to meet warranty claims. The administration company authorises and pays warranty claims from the bank account in accordance with the dealer's instructions. The dealer ultimately decides on the amount of claims payable from this account and retains all surplus monies. The dealer is responsible for meeting the warranty obligation.

Example 6: tax investigation schemes

6.7.18 **[G]** When self-assessment for income tax was first introduced, a number of providers set up schemes connected with their tax accounting and tax advisory services. In consideration of an annual fee, the provider undertakes to deal with any enquiries or investigations that HM Revenue and Customs might launch into the self-assessment that the provider completes for the recipient. The event covered by these schemes (an investigation) is both uncertain and adverse to the interests of the recipient, who would, if the scheme were not in place, have to devote resources to dealing with the investigation. Accordingly, these schemes fall within the description of a *contract of insurance* (see PERG 6.3.4G).

6.7.19 **[G]** Some providers argued that these schemes amount to nothing more than a 'manufacturer's warranty' of their own work, within the scope of PERG 6.7.7G (Example 3: manufacturers' and retailers' warranties). However, HM Revenue and Customs is expected to make a significant number of random checks of self-assessment forms, irrespective of the quality of the work done by the provider. These random checks are also covered by the schemes. The *FSA* concluded, therefore, that these schemes were not analogous to manufacturers' warranties and that the better view was that they were *contracts of insurance*.

Example 7: solicitors' retainers

6.7.20 **[G]** A contract under which a provider undertakes, in consideration of an initial payment, to stand ready to provide, or to procure the provision of, legal services on the occurrence of an uncertain event (for example, if the recipient is sued), is capable of being construed as a *contract of insurance* (see PERG 6.3.4G). Indeed, *legal expenses* insurance is commonplace.

6.7.21 **[G]** If, however, a contract of this kind were structured so that the recipient was charged at a commercial rate for any legal services in fact provided, the *FSA's* approach will be to treat the arrangement as non-insurance. This is principally because, by taking on obligations of this kind, the provider does not assume a relevant risk (see PERG 6.7.6G). The position might be different if the solicitor carries the additional obligation to pay for alternative legal services to be provided if the solicitor is unable to act. In that case, the *FSA's* approach will be to examine all the elements of the contract to determine whether the substance of the solicitor's obligation (see PERG 6.5.4G(2)) is to insure, or to give legal advice for a fee.

Example 8: contracts providing for ultimate repayment of any indemnity ('time and distance cover')

6.7.22 **[G]** A contract under which a provider agrees to meet a specified obligation on behalf of the recipient (for example an obligation to pay for the re-purchase of shares or to meet a debt) immediately that obligation falls due, subject to later reimbursement by the recipient, would be a *contract of insurance* if in all other respects it fell within the description of such contract (see PERG 6.3.4G). This is principally because the provider assumes the risk that an immediate payment will be required and, depending on the terms of the contract, may also assume the risk that the recipient will be unable to make future repayments (see PERG 6.6.2G).

(*Chapter 7 outside the scope of this work.*)

CHAPTER 8
FINANCIAL PROMOTION AND RELATED ACTIVITIES

8.1–8.17

(*Outside the scope of this work.*)

8.17A Financial promotions concerning insurance mediation activities

[2223]
8.17A.1 **[G]** The application of section 21 of the *Act* and of exemptions in the *Financial Promotion Order* to invitations or inducements about *insurance mediation activities* will vary depending on the type of activity. The implementation of the *Insurance Mediation Directive* has not led to any changes in the definitions of a *controlled investment* or a *controlled activity* under the *Financial Promotion Order*. So:

(1) rights under any *contract of insurance* are a *controlled investment*;

(2) rights to or interests in rights under *life policies* are *controlled investments* but rights to or interests in rights under other *contracts of insurance* are not;

(3) the activities of:

  (a) *dealing in investments as agent*;

  (b) *arranging (bringing about) deals in investments*;

  (c) *making arrangements with a view to* transactions *in investments*; and

  (d) advising *on investments*;

  where they relate to *contracts of insurance*, are *controlled activities* only where the *contract of insurance* is a *life policy*; and

(4) the activity of *assisting in the administration and performance of a contract of insurance* is not a *controlled activity*.

8.17A.2 **[G]** This means that an *insurance intermediary* will not be *communicating* a *financial promotion*:

(a) where the only activity to which the promotion relates is *assisting in the administration and performance of a contract of insurance*; or

(b) purely by reason of his inviting or inducing *persons* to make use of his advisory or *arranging* services where they relate only to *general insurance contracts* or *pure protection contracts* or both.

But as regards (2), an intermediary will be *communicating* a *financial promotion* if he is also inviting or inducing *persons* to enter into a *contract of insurance*. This is because the making and performance of the contract by the insurer will be a *controlled activity* (of *effecting* and *carrying out a contract of insurance*). *Insurance intermediaries* will, however, be able to use the exemptions in Part V of the *Financial Promotion Order* (see PERG 8.13 (Exemptions applying to financial promotions concerning deposits and certain contracts of insurance) where they promote a *general insurance contract* or a *pure protection contract*. Where an *insurance intermediary* is promoting *life policies*, he will be able to use any exemptions in Part VI of the *Financial Promotion Order* that apply to a *contractually based investment*.

8.18–8.36

(*Outside the scope of this work.*)

(*Chapters 9–14 outside the scope of this work.*)

THE RESPONSIBILITIES OF PROVIDERS AND DISTRIBUTORS FOR THE FAIR TREATMENT OF CUSTOMERS (RPPD)

NOTES

Up to date as at 22 February 2010. For later amendments please see www.fsa.gov.uk.

INTRODUCTION

[2224]

1.1 In this Regulatory Guide ("Guide") we give our view on what the combination of Principles for Businesses ("the Principles") and detailed rules require respectively of providers and distributors in certain circumstances to treat customers fairly. However, it is not, and does not seek to be, a complete exposition of all of a provider's or a distributor's responsibilities to the customer or to each other; nor does it alter, replace or substitute applicable Principles, rules, guidance or law, such as those relating to unfair contract terms (Note (1)).

1.2 A customer's experience should not be affected by whether a product or service was provided and distributed by a single institution or by two or more institutions.

1.3 This Guide is guidance issued under section 157 of the Financial Services and Markets Act 2000 ("the Act"). As such, it is not binding on those to whom the Act and rules apply and need not be followed in order to achieve compliance with rules or other requirements. There is no presumption that departing from this Guide indicates a breach of a rule. However, the Guide may be relevant in an enforcement context, for example to explain the regulatory context. If a person acts in accordance with the Guide in the circumstances contemplated by the Guide, then the FSA will not take action against that person in relation to the aspects of the rules to which the Guide relates. The Guide will also be a useful tool for supervisors, particularly when they deal with TCF issues at firms. Supervisors may use the Guide in their discussions with firms. The issues it covers will continue to be dealt with in our supervision work as they are now, for example in the risk assessment framework we use for supervising firms (ARROW) or in pieces of focused thematic work.

THE APPLICABLE RULES

1.4 Under the Principles (Note (2)), providers and distributors of products and services have various responsibilities that have an impact on customers. Detailed rules within the FSA Handbook further specify what these responsibilities are in certain defined circumstances.

1.5 The Principles apply to all authorised firms. This Guide looks particularly to the following Principles (Note (3)):

- Principle 2 ('A firm must conduct its business with due skill, care and diligence');
- Principle 3 ('A firm must take reasonable care to organise and control its affairs responsibly and effectively, with adequate risk management systems');
- Principle 6 ('A firm must pay due regard to the interests of its customers and treat them fairly'); and
- Principle 7 ('A firm must pay due regard to the information needs of its clients, and communicate information to them in a way which is clear, fair and not misleading').

1.6 What a firm has to do to meet the requirements of a Principle will depend on the circumstances, including the riskiness or complexity of the product or portfolio, who the firm is dealing with (another firm or a customer, for example) and the financial sophistication of the target market (Note (4)). Firms should bear all of these factors in mind in order to interpret the requirements of the Principles in a way that is proportionate. The responsibilities described in this Guide apply to the extent that the Principles themselves apply.

SCOPE

1.7 This Guide is intended to be relevant to all regulated firms involved in the supply of products or services to retail customers. Although we have drafted it to be of particular relevance where there is more than one firm in the supply chain, many of the responsibilities described in the Guide are also relevant where there is only one firm involved in providing and distributing a product or service. Our intention is not to change the existing responsibilities of providers or distributors in delivering fair outcomes for consumers. Rather, it is to articulate the existing regulatory responsibilities. Nor does this Guide seek to determine or change whether or how consumers can seek redress in any individual case or from which firm in the supply chain. This Guide does not determine or change whether or how one firm in a distribution chain may seek redress from another firm; this too will depend on the circumstances of the case.

1.8 The supply chain may not comprise only authorised firms, but this Guide does not deal with the position where an unauthorised firm is involved unless expressly stated otherwise. Where there is a non-UK element to the supply chain, the Guide only applies to the extent that the Principles themselves apply.

1.9 This Guide is not intended to imply that a firm must take on the regulatory responsibilities of other firms in the distribution chain nor that there is a requirement for any firm to 'police' any other firm in the chain.

INTERPRETATION

1.10 In this Guide we use 'must' where an action is required by a Principle or detailed Rule. We use 'should' where we think a firm ought to consider a particular action (not specified in a Principle or Rule) at a reasonably high level to comply with a Principle (not that they should follow a detailed a prescribed course of action). We use 'may' where an action is only one of a number of ways of complying with a Principle.

1.11 Where we refer to the 'customer' in this Guide we use it as a convenient name for the end-customer in the retail supply chain (which may include potential customers). However, it is important to note that the term 'customer' as used in the Principles or detailed rules themselves is a defined term in the FSA Handbook. This Guide does not seek to alter or affect any definitions within the Handbook.

1.12 We use 'provider' to include persons who offer services such as portfolio management (through distributors or otherwise) as well as those who develop, manage or package products such as life insurance, general insurance or investment products or who develop or enter into home finance transactions (i.e. mortgages, home reversion plans and home purchase plans).

1.13 We use 'distributor' to mean those persons who then make up the rest of the supply chain taking the product or service to the customer. This could include, for example, financial advisers, third party administrators, appointed representatives, banks, building societies, and those who sell insurance as a secondary part of their business.

THE RESPONSIBILITIES

1.14 Providers and distributors should consider the impact of their action (or inaction) on the customer in various stages of the product life-cycle, or the various stages of provision of the service (Note (5)). Depending on the precise nature of a firm's business, this could mean addressing the fair treatment of customers at the following stages: design and governance; identifying target markets; marketing and promotion; sales and advice processes; after-sales information and service; and complaints handling. This Guide gives our view of the respective responsibilities of providers and distributors under the Principles during the product life cycle or while the service is provided.

1.15 In this Guide we have distinguished between providers and distributors. While we consider the labels 'provider' and 'distributor' useful for the purposes of this Guide, we recognise that responsibilities flow from the actual roles or functions undertaken in a transaction, and firms should take this into account in considering their responsibilities under the Principles. In considering which responsibilities apply to it, a firm should consider the functions and roles that it undertakes in the product lifecycle. Whether a particular role or function is fulfilled by the distributor or provider (or both) may vary based on the product or service, or particular arrangements in place, and it may be possible for a firm to act as both provider and distributor at the same time in respect of different products or services. For example:

(1) It is possible that a provider creates a product or service to meet criteria or designs specified by a distributor. In such instances, many of the responsibilities fall to the commissioning distributor, as 'retail manufacturer' of the product (Note 6)) or service (Note 7)), rather than the 'pure manufacturer' of the commissioned product or service. Of course, if what the pure manufacturer delivers fails to meet the agreed specification, the retail manufacturer may seek its own redress under the contract between them or the applicable law. That said, the pure manufacturer must act with due skill, care and diligence in accordance with Principle 2 and, where it conducts a regulated activity for the underlying customer (for example, it enters into a contract with a customer), must treat that customer fairly. Other Principles and detailed rules may also apply.

(2) It is also possible that a product manufacturer creates components that are later (and possibly without the component manufacturer's knowledge) subsumed into retail products designed and marketed to customers by 'retail manufacturers'. In such instances, the pure manufacturer may not have a contractual or other relationship with the underlying customer. The pure manufacturer may not be aware (nor is it necessarily the case that it ought to be aware) of whether the retail manufacturer is using the product for itself or for an underlying customer. However, the pure manufacturer should act with due skill, care and diligence in designing its products (Principle 2). The skill, care and diligence that are 'due' under Principle 2 will be determined taking all the circumstances into account. These may include the manufacturer's knowledge of whether the product or service is provided to a firm, rather than an underlying customer, and the information needs of the firm. In addition, the pure manufacturer will normally be obliged to communicate information to the retail manufacturer in a way that is not misleading (Principle 7) (Note (8)).

1.16 Whether providers and distributors can agree between themselves how to apportion responsibilities between themselves will depend on the circumstances. In particular, it depends on the nature of the regulatory responsibility, the extent to which such an agreement would be reasonable, whether the arrangement is clear to both parties and properly recorded and the systems and controls used to monitor whether the agreement continues to be appropriate in the circumstances.

PROVIDER RESPONSIBILITIES (NOTE (9))

1.17 When undertaking product or service design, Principles 2, 3 and 6 are particularly relevant. In particular, a firm:

(1) should identify the target market, namely which types of customer the product or service is likely to be suitable (or not suitable) for;

(2) should stress-test the product or service to identify how it might perform in a range of market environments and how the customer could be affected;

(3) should have in place systems and controls to manage adequately the risks posed by product or service design (Note (10)).

1.18 When providing information to distributors, Principle 2 is particularly relevant. In particular, a firm:

(1) should make clear if that information is not intended for customer use;

(2) should ensure the information is sufficient, appropriate and comprehensible in substance and form, including considering whether it will enable distributors to understand it enough to give suitable advice (where advice is given) and to extract any relevant information and communicate it to the end customer. As part of meeting this standard, the provider may wish to consider, with regard to each distribution channel or type of distributor, what information distributors of that type already have, their likely level of knowledge and understanding, their information needs and what form or medium would best meet those needs (which could include discussions, written material or training as appropriate).

1.19 When providing information to customers (Note (11)), Principles 3, 6 and 7 are particularly relevant. In particular, a firm:

(1) should pay regard to its target market, including its likely level of financial capability;

(2) should take account of what information the customer needs to understand the product or service, its purpose and the risks, and communicate information in a way that is clear, fair and not misleading (Note (12));

(3) should have in place systems and controls to manage effectively the risks posed by providing information to customers.

1.20 When selecting distribution channels, Principles 2, 6 and 7 are particularly relevant. In particular, a firm:

(1) should decide whether this is a product where customers would be wise to seek advice;

(2) should review how what is occurring in practice corresponds to (or deviates from) what was originally planned or envisaged for the distribution of its products or services given the target market. This involves collecting and analysing appropriate Management Information (MI) (Note (13)) such that the firm can detect patterns in distribution as compared with the planned target market, and can assess the performance of the distribution channels through which its products or services are being distributed;

(3) should act when it has concerns, for example by ceasing to use a particular distribution channel.

1.21 In the area of post-sale responsibility, Principles 2, 6 and 7 are particularly important. In particular, a firm:

(1) in supplying information direct to the customer, must ensure that the information is communicated in a way which is clear, fair and not misleading (Note (14));

(2) should periodically review products whose performance may vary materially to check whether the product is continuing to meet the general needs of the target audience that it was designed for, or whether the product's performance will be significantly different from what the provider originally expected and communicated to the distributor or customer at the time of the sale (Note (15)). If this occurs, the provider should consider what action to take, such as whether and how to inform the customer of this (to the extent the customer could not reasonably have been aware) and of their option to seek advice, and whether to cease selling the product;

(3) should communicate to the customer contractual 'breakpoints' such as the end of a long tie-in period that may have a material impact on a customer that the customer cannot reasonably be expected to recall or know about already;

(4) should act fairly and promptly when handling claims or when paying out on a product that has been surrendered or reached maturity. In doing this, the provider should meet any reasonable customer expectations that it may have created with regard to the outcomes or how the process would be handled;

(5) must establish, implement and maintain effective and transparent customer complaint-handling systems.

DISTRIBUTOR RESPONSIBILITIES

1.22 In the area of financial promotions, Principles 3, 6 and 7 are particularly relevant. In particular, a firm:

(1) should have in place systems and controls to manage effectively the risks posed by financial promotions;

(2) in passing on a promotion created by a provider, must act with due skill, care and diligence. A firm will not contravene the financial promotions rules where it communicates a promotion produced by another person provided the firm takes reasonable care to establish that another firm has confirmed compliance with the relevant detailed rules, amongst other matters (Note (16)).

1.23 When providing information at or before the point of sale to a customer, Principles 2, 6 and 7 are particularly relevant. In particular, a firm:

(1) should consider, when passing provider materials to customers, whether it understands the information provided (Note (17));

(2) should ask the provider to supply additional information or training where that seems necessary to understand the product or service adequately;

(3) should not distribute the product or service if it does not understand it sufficiently, especially if it intends to provide advice;

(4) when providing information to another distributor in a distribution chain, should consider how the further distributor will use the information, such as whether it will be given to customers. Firms should consider what information the further distributor requires and the likely level of knowledge and understanding of the further distributor and what medium may suit it best for the transmission of information.

1.24 When advising on selection of a provider, Principles 2 and 6 are particularly relevant (Note (18)). In particular, a firm:

(1) should consider the nature of the products or services offered by the provider and how they fit with the customer's needs and risk appetite;

(2) should consider what impact the selection of a given provider could have on the customer in terms of charges or the financial strength of the provider, or possibly, where information is available to the distributor, how efficiently and reliably the provider will deal with the distributor or customer at the point of sale (or subsequently, such as when queries/complaints arise, claims are made, or a product reaches maturity).

1.25 In the area of post-sale responsibility, Principles 3 and 6 are particularly relevant. In particular, a firm:

(1) should comply with any contractual obligation it has to the customer, for example to provide ongoing advice or periodic reviews. In connection with this, it should also consider its responsibility to maintain adequate systems and controls to deliver on such reviews;

(2) should consider any implied or express representation it made (during meetings, correspondence or promotional material, for example). Where a customer has reasonable expectations based on the prior statements of a distributor, for example that performance will be monitored, the distributor should meet these expectations;

(3) where involved in handling claims or paying out on a product that has been surrendered or reached maturity, should meet any reasonable expectations that the distributor has created in the customer's mind with regard to how the process would be handled;

(4) must establish, implement and maintain effective and transparent customer complaint-handling systems;

(5) should pass any communications received from customers (intended for or suited to providers to act upon) to providers in a timely and accurate way.

NOTES:

(1) The Guide represents our view based on the law, regulation and other circumstances that exist as at the publication date, but also takes into account changes to the Handbook including those to implement the Markets in Financial Instruments Directive (MiFID) that have already been made or consulted on and are due to come into force on 1 November 2007. *(Paragraph 1.1)*

(2) The Principles are set out in PRIN 2. *(Paragraph 1.4)*

(3) Of course, other Principles apply as appropriate. For example, under Principle 9, a firm must take reasonable care to ensure the suitability of its advice and discretionary decisions for any customer who is entitles to rely upon its judgment. *(Paragraph 1.5)*

(4) PRIN 1.2.1G. *(Paragraph 1.6)*

(5) For example, many brokers and investment managers have on-going relationships with intermediaries by virtue of which their services are provided to the intermediary's underlying clients. *(Paragraph 1.14)*

(6) For example, an insurer could be commissioned by a distributor to create a payment protection insurance product where the criteria for the product are specified by the distributor. *(Paragraph 1.15(1))*

(7) For example, a portfolio manager could be commissioned to develop a branded service specifically for a distributor where the criteria for the service are specified by the distributor. *(Paragraph 1.15(1))*

(8) Principle 2 may not apply to a pure manufacturer that is a MiFID investment firm in certain circumstances, for example in relation to eligible counterparty business: see PRIN 4 for further guidance. In some circumstances Principles 6 and 7 will apply even when the retail manufacturer is the only client of the pure manufacturer. *(Paragraph 1.15(2))*

(9) As explained in paragraph 1.15, although we use the terms 'provider' and 'distributor' we recognise that responsibilities flow from the actual roles or functions undertaken by a firm. *(Paragraph 1.17)*

(10) For example, SYSC (Senior Management Arrangements, Systems and Controls). *(Paragraph 1.17(3))*

(11) This includes providing information to distributors for onward transmission to customers. *(Paragraph 1.19)*

(12) For example, COBS 4 (Communicating with clients, including financial promotions); ICOB 3.8 (Form and content of non-investment financial promotions); MCOB 3.6 (Form and content of non-real time qualifying credit promotions); MCOB 3.8A (Form and content of financial promotions of home reversion plans); MCOB 2.2.6AR (Clear, fair and not misleading promotions for home purchase plans). *(Paragraph 1.19)*

(13) See, for example, SYSC 3.2.11–12. See also TCF cluster report on TCF considerations for Management Information: http://www.fsa.gov.uk/pages/Doing/Regulated/tcf/pdf/management_info.pdf *(Paragraph 1.20(2))*

(14) For example, COBS 4 (Communicating with clients, including financial promotions), ICOB 2.2.3R (Clear, fair and not misleading communication), MCOB 2.2.6R (Clear, fair and not misleading communication). *(Paragraph 1.21(1))*

(15) For example, SYSC 3.2.11G (Management information); SYSC 3.2.17G (Business Strategy). *(Paragraph 1.21(2))*

(16) COBS 4.10.10R, ICOB 3.7.5R, MCOB 3.9.5R (Communicating a financial promotion where another firm has confirmed compliance). This exemption is not available in relation to MiFID or equivalent third country business. *(Paragraph 1.22(2))*

(17) For regulated activities other than designated investment business, a firm must take reasonable steps to communicate information in a way that is clear, fair and not misleading (e.g. ICOB 2.2.3R and MCOB 2.2.6R). In doing so, it may be reasonable for a distributor to rely on information produced by a provider unless the distributor is, or ought to be, aware of grounds to question its compliance. For designated investment business, a firm must ensure that any communication to a client is fair, clear and not misleading regardless of whether it has been produced by a provider (COBS 4.2.1R). The standard for designated investment business is an absolute standard, which does not permit reliance unless an exemption applies. *(Paragraph 1.23(1))*

(18) These Principles are also relevant for non-advised sales, where there may be a need to consider a customer's needs and circumstances, for example see COBS 10 (Appropriateness (for non-advised services)), COBS 7.2.4R (Specifying demands and needs), ICOB 4.4 (Statement of demands and needs). *(Paragraph 1.24)*

UNFAIR CONTRACT TERMS REGULATORY GUIDE (UNFCOG)

NOTES

Up to date as at 22 February 2010. For later amendments please see www.fsa.gov.uk.

CONTENTS

1. The Unfair Contract Terms Regulatory Guide . . . . [2225]
2. Statements of Good Practice on fairness of terms in consumer contracts . . . . [2226]

CHAPTER 1

1.1 Application and purpose

[2225]

1.1.1 **[G]** This Guide explains the *FSA's* policy on how it will use its powers under the *Unfair Terms Regulations* (the Regulations)

1.1.2 **[G]** We have agreed with the Office of Fair Trading ('OFT') that the *FSA* will consider the fairness (within the meaning of the Regulations) of financial services contracts for carrying on any *regulated activity*.

1.1.3 **[G]** The OFT will consider the fairness of other financial services contracts which involve activities governed by the Consumer Credit Act 1974. This includes second-charge mortgage loans, buy-to-let mortgages, and non-mortgage personal loans (including credit cards). Also, where the firm concerned is not a *firm* or an *appointed representative*, the OFT may take enforcement action under the Regulations in respect of financial services contracts involving the carrying on of *regulated activities* (see EG 10.16 and 10.17).

1.1.4 **[G]** This Guide applies to:

(1) *firms*;
(2) *appointed representatives*; and
(3) other *persons*, whether or not a *person* with *permission*, who use, or recommend the use of, contracts to carry on *regulated activities*.

1.1.5 **[G]** This Guide uses "firm" to refer to all such persons.

1.2 Introduction

1.2.1 **[G]** This Guide explains the *FSA's* formal powers under the Regulations. It does not contain comprehensive *guidance* on the Regulations themselves, and you should refer to those Regulations for further details.

1.2.2 **[G]** This Guide also provides *guidance* on the approach we take before considering whether to exercise our formal powers under the Regulations.

1.2.3 **[G]** The *FSA* has powers as a qualifying body under the Regulations. The Regulations are not made under the *Act*, but, under the Regulations our functions are treated as functions under the *Act*. This:

(1) makes the *regulatory objectives* relevant to forming policy that governs the discharge of our functions under the Regulations;
(2) means that any complaints about the *FSA's* activities under the Regulations can be referred to the *Complaints Commissioner*;
(3) allows the *FSA* to make full use of its information disclosure powers;
(4) allows the *FSA* to use its power to give *guidance*;
(5) protects the *FSA* against liability in damages in respect of its activities under the Regulations; and
(6) allows the *FSA* to raise fees to fund its activities under the Regulations.

1.2.4 **[G]**

(1) As such, we publish on our website details of cases that result in a change in the contract terms used by the firm. This may happen through either an undertaking by a firm or injunction obtained from the courts.
(2) Under regulation 14 of the Regulations the *FSA* has a duty to pass details of these cases to the OFT.
(3) The OFT also publishes details of cases that it, and other qualifying bodies, have dealt with in accordance with the OFT's duties under regulation 15 of the Regulations.

1.3 The Unfair Terms Regulations

Terms to which the Regulations apply

1.3.1 **[G]**

Part II FSA Handbook Materials

(1) The Regulations apply, with certain exceptions, to terms in contracts concluded between a seller or supplier and a *consumer* which have not been individually negotiated.

(2) Terms cannot be reviewed for fairness within the meaning of the Regulations if they are terms which reflect:
   (a) mandatory statutory or regulatory provisions; or
   (b) the provisions or principles of international conventions to which the *EEA States* or the *EU* as a whole are party.

(3) Terms written in plain, intelligible language cannot be reviewed for fairness within the meaning of the Regulations if the terms relate to:
   - the definition of the main subject matter of the contract; or
   - the adequacy of the price or remuneration, as against the goods or services supplied in exchange.

   However, we can review terms concerning these matters for fairness within the meaning of the Regulations if they are not written in plain, intelligible language. We do not consider that it is enough that a lawyer could understand the term for it to be excluded from such a review. The term must be plain and intelligible to the *consumer*.

When a term is 'unfair' within the meaning of the Regulations

1.3.2 **[G]** Terms are regarded as unfair if, contrary to the requirement of good faith, they cause a significant imbalance in the parties' rights and obligations to the detriment of the *consumer*.

The main powers of the courts and qualifying bodies under the Regulations

1.3.3 **[G]**

(1) Under regulation 13 we have the power to request, for certain purposes:

   '(a) a copy of any document which that person has used or recommended for use, [. . .] as a pre-formulated standard contract in dealings with consumers;
   (b) information about the use, or recommendation for use, by that person of that document or any other such document in dealings with consumers.'

1.3.4 **[G]**

(1) Unless the case is urgent, we will generally first write to a firm to express our concern about the potential unfairness of a term or terms (within the meaning of the Regulations) and will invite the firm to comment on those concerns. If we still believe that the term is unfair, we will normally ask the firm to stop including the term in new contracts and to stop relying on it in any concluded contracts. If the firm either declines to give an undertaking, or gives an undertaking but fails to follow it, the FSA will consider the need to apply to the courts for an injunction under regulation 12.

(2) In deciding whether to ask a firm to undertake to stop including a term in new contracts and to stop relying on it in concluded contracts, we will consider the full circumstances of each case. Several factors may be relevant for this purpose and the following list is not exhaustive, but will give some indication of the sorts of things we consider:
   (a) whether we are satisfied that the contract term may properly be regarded as unfair within the meaning of the Regulations;
   (b) the extent and nature of the detriment to *consumers* resulting from the term or the potential harm which could result from the term;
   (c) whether the firm has fully cooperated with the FSA in resolving our concerns about the fairness of the particular contract term.

1.3.5 **[G]** Regulation 12 states that:

   '(1) The [OFT] or [. . .] any qualifying body may apply for an injunction (including an interim injunction) against any person appearing to them to be using, or recommending the use of, an unfair term drawn up for general use in contracts concluded with consumers'.

   '(3) The court, on an application under this regulation, may grant an *injunction* on such terms as it thinks fit.'

The *FSA* is a qualifying body for the purposes of regulation 12. Our approach to seeking an injunction under the Regulations is set out in Chapter 10 of EG.

1.3.6 **[G]** Regulation 8 states that an unfair term is not binding on the *consumer* but that the contract will continue to bind the parties if it is capable of continuing in existence without the unfair term. Therefore, if the court finds that the term in question is unfair, the firm would have to stop relying on the unfair term in existing contracts governed by the Regulations.

1.4 The Unfair Terms Regulations: the FSA's role and policy

1.4.1 **[G]** The *FSA* may consider the fairness of a contract within the meaning of the Regulations following a complaint from a *consumer* or other person or on its own initiative if the contract is within its scope.

1.4.2 **[G]** There are three main ways in which we might receive a complaint from a *consumer* or other person. These are:
(1) directly; or
(2) from another qualifying body which considers that the *FSA* should deal with the complaint; or
(3) from the OFT.

1.4.3 **[G]**
(1) The main way in which we would act on our own initiative is to undertake a review of contracts in a particular area of business. This might involve looking at the contract terms used by several firms in a particular sector.
(2) We will, for example, consider launching such a review if multiple *consumer* contract complaints or other intelligence lead us to believe that under the Regulations there may be a contractual issue of wider significance to firms and *consumers*.

1.4.4 **[G]** If, following either a complaint or an own-initiative review, we consider that a term in a contract is unfair, we may challenge firms about their use of that term.

Interaction with the FSA's powers under the Act

1.4.5 **[G]**
(1) The *FSA* will consider using its powers under the Regulations in the context of its wider regulatory powers under the *Act*.
(2) In some cases, it might be appropriate for us to use other powers to deal with issues identified under the Regulations. The powers available to the *FSA* under the *Act* may vary depending on the *regulated activities* which the firm carries out. For example, the use of the unfair term might involve a breach of a *Principle* or a *rule* in *COBS*, *MCOB* or *ICOBS*. If so, the *FSA* might also address the issue as a *rule* breach.
(3) We may, in some circumstances, consider treating the matter under our powers in the *Act* itself and also under the Regulations.
(4) However, the use of our powers under the *Act* will not be possible in all cases where a firm has used an unfair term. If we consider using an enforcement power under the *Act*, we will do so in accordance with the policy relating to that power as set out in *EG*.

1.5 Risk Management

1.5.1 **[G]**
(1) Where a firm has given an undertaking or a court has ruled the firm's term unfair, then the *FSA* considers it desirable that the firm should promptly notify clients with whom it has already concluded contracts of the effect the undertaking or ruling will have on their contracts.
(2) The firm should also, as part of its risk management, consider the effect on its own business, including whether there are relevant risks which need mitigation. For example, firms should consider the effect of regulation 8 of the Regulations which provides that an unfair term is not binding on the *consumer*, but that the contract will continue to bind the parties if it is capable of continuing in existence without the unfair term. The mitigation may involve the firm contacting existing customers to ask that they agree to an amended contract, although any such amendment will itself need to avoid unfairness within the meaning of the Regulations and to comply with the law of contract generally.
(3) As part of their risk management, firms that have not themselves given an undertaking or been subject to a court decision should remain alert to undertakings or court decisions about other firms, since these will be of potential value in indicating the likely attitude of the courts, the *FSA*, the OFT or other qualifying bodies to similar terms or to terms with similar effects.

1.6 Redress

1.6.1 **[G]**
(1) The *FSA* does not have the power under the Regulations to grant redress to *consumers* who have suffered loss because of an unfair term. *Consumers* may choose to complain to the firm and to seek redress from it. If the firm does not satisfy the *consumer's* complaint, the *consumer* may choose to refer the complaint to the *Financial Ombudsman Service*, if appropriate.
(2) If the use of an unfair term also amounts to a *rule* breach, and that breach causes loss to *consumers*, the *FSA* can apply to court for restitution or require restitution. The *FSA* will consider whether to use these powers in accordance with the policy in *EG* 11.

CHAPTER 2
STATEMENTS OF GOOD PRACTICE ON FAIRNESS OF TERMS IN CONSUMER CONTRACTS

[2226]–[3000]

2.1. **[G]** In Annexes 1 and 2 you will find 'Statements of Good Practice' where we have set out our views on the likely application of the Regulations in relation to certain types of clause in standard form *consumer* contracts. We will add further Statements of Good Practice relating to the Regulations as and when they are published. Please note that these Statements of Good Practice do not form general *guidance* on rules under the *Act*.

Annex 1

Fairness of terms in consumer contracts: Statement of Good Practice (May 2005)

[link to this Statement on the FSA website at http://www.fsa.gov.uk/pubs/other/good_practice.pdf]

Annex 2

Fairness of terms in consumer contracts: Statement of Good Practice on mortgage exit administration fees (January 2007)

[link to this Statement on the FSA website at http://www.fsa.gov.uk/pubs/other/meaf_goodpractice.pdf]

PART III
STATUTES

LIFE ASSURANCE ACT 1774

(14 Geo 3 c 48)

An Act for regulating Insurances upon Lives, and for prohibiting all such Insurances except in cases where the Persons insuring shall have an Interest in the Life or Death of the Persons insured

NOTES

Short title: given to this Act by the Short Titles Act 1896. The Act is also known as the Gambling Act 1774.

Exemptions: this Act is excluded in relation to insurance by local authorities against accidents to their members and voluntary assistants by the Local Government Act 1972, ss 140(3), 140C(3), and in relation to insurance by internal drainage boards against accidents to their members by the Land Drainage Act 1991, s 1, Sch 2, para 1(3).

Whereas it hath been found by experience that the making insurances on lives or other events wherein the assured shall have no interest hath introduced a mischievous kind of gaming:

[3001]

1 No insurance to be made on lives, etc, by persons having no interest etc

From and after the passing of this Act no insurance shall be made by any person or persons, bodies politick or corporate, on the life or lives of any person or persons, or on any other event or events whatsoever, wherein the person or persons for whose use, benefit, or on whose account such policy or policies shall be made, shall have no interest, or by way of gaming or wagering; and that every assurance made contrary to the true intent and meaning hereof shall be null and void to all intents and purposes whatsoever.

[3002]

2 No policies on lives without inserting the names of persons interested, etc

And . . . it shall not be lawful to make any policy or policies on the life or lives of any person or persons, or other event or events, without inserting in such policy or policies the person or persons name or names interested therein, or for whose use, benefit, or on whose account such policy is so made or underwrote.

NOTES

Words omitted repealed by the Statute Law Revision Act 1888.

Validation of certain group policies: certain group policies are excluded from the effect of this section with retrospective effect, by the Insurance Companies Amendment Act 1973, s 50 at **[3201]**.

[3003]

3 How much may be recovered where the insured hath interest in lives

And . . . in all cases where the insured hath interest in such life or lives, event or events, no greater sum shall be recovered or received from the insurer or insurers than the amount of value of the interest of the insured in such life or lives, or other event or events.

NOTES

Words omitted repealed by the Statute Law Revision Act 1888.

[3004]

4 Not to extend to insurances on ships, goods, etc

Provided, always, that nothing herein contained shall extend or be construed to extend to insurances bona fide made by any person or persons on ships, goods, or merchandises, but every such insurance shall be as valid and effectual in the law as if this Act had not been made.

FIRES PREVENTION (METROPOLIS) ACT 1774

(14 Geo 3 c 78)

An Act . . . for the more effectually preventing Mischiefs by Fire within the Cities of London and Westminster and the Liberties thereof, and other the Parishes, Precincts, and Places within the Weekly Bills of Mortality, the Parishes of Saint Mary-le-bon, Paddington, Saint Pancras and Saint Luke at Chelsea, in the County of Middlesex . . .

NOTES

Short title: given to this Act by the Short Titles Act 1896.

Long title: words omitted repealed by the Statute Law Revision Act 1887. This Act applies to the whole of England.

(*Whole Act, except ss 83, 86, repealed by the Metropolitan Fire Brigade Act 1865, s 34.*)

[3005]
83 Money insured on houses burnt how to be applied
And in order to deter and hinder ill-minded persons from wilfully setting their house or houses or other buildings on fire with a view of gaining to themselves the insurance money, whereby the lives and fortunes of many families may be lost or endangered: Be it further enacted by the authority aforesaid, that it shall and may be lawful to and for the respective governors or directors of the several insurance offices for insuring houses or other buildings against loss by fire, and they are hereby authorised and required, upon the request of any person or persons interested in or intitled unto any house or houses or other buildings which may hereafter be burnt down, demolished or damaged by fire, or upon any grounds of suspicion that the owner or owners, occupier or occupiers, or other person or persons who shall have insured such house or houses or other buildings have been guilty of fraud, or of wilfully setting their house or houses or other buildings on fire, to cause the insurance money to be laid out and expended, as far as the same will go, towards rebuilding, reinstating or repairing such house or houses or other buildings so burnt down, demolished or damaged by fire, unless the party or parties claiming such insurance money shall, within sixty days next after his, her or their claim is adjusted, give a sufficient security to the governors or directors of the insurance office where such house or houses or other buildings are insured, that the same insurance money shall be laid out and expended as aforesaid, or unless the said insurance money shall be in that time settled and disposed of to and amongst all the contending parties, to the satisfaction and approbation of such governors or directors of such insurance office respectively.

[3006]–[3008]
86 No action to lie against a person where the fire accidentally begins
And . . . no action, suit or process whatever shall be had, maintained or prosecuted against any person in whose house, chamber, stable, barn or other building, or on whose estate any fire shall . . . accidentally begin, nor shall any recompence be made by such person for any damage suffered thereby, any law, usage or custom to the contrary notwithstanding: . . . provided that no contract or agreement made between landlord and tenant shall be hereby defeated or made void.

NOTES
Words omitted in the first place repealed by the Statute Law Revision Act 1888; words omitted in the second place repealed by the Statute Law Revision Act 1948; words omitted in the final place repealed by the Statute Law Revision Act 1958 and by virtue of the Statute Law Revision Act 1861.

POLICIES OF ASSURANCE ACT 1867

(30 & 31 Vict c 144)

ARRANGEMENT OF SECTIONS

1 Assignees of life policies, empowered to sue . . . [3009]
2 Defence or reply on equitable grounds . . . [3010]
3 Notice of assignment . . . [3011]
4 Principal place of business to be specified on policies . . . [3012]
5 Mode of assignment . . . [3013]
6 Receipt of notice of assignment . . . [3014]
7 Interpretation . . . [3015]
8 Saving of contracts under 16 & 17 Vict c 45, or 27 & 28 Vict c 43, and of engagements by friendly societies . . . [3016]
9 Short title . . . [3017]

SCHEDULE . . . [3018]

An Act to enable Assignees of Policies of Life Assurance to sue thereon in their own names

[20 August 1867]

(*Preamble repealed by the Statute Law Revision Act 1893.*)

[3009]

1 Assignees of life policies, empowered to sue

Any person or corporation now being or hereafter becoming entitled, by assignment or other derivative title, to a policy of life assurance, and possessing at the time of action brought the right in equity to receive and the right to give an effectual discharge to the assurance company liable under such policy for monies thereby assured or secured, shall be at liberty to sue at law in the name of such person or corporation to recover such monies.

[3010]

2 Defence or reply on equitable grounds

In any action on a policy of life assurance, a defence on equitable grounds, or a reply to such defence on similar grounds, may be respectively pleaded and relied upon in the same manner and to the same extent as in any other personal action.

[3011]

3 Notice of assignment

No assignment made after the passing of this Act of a policy of life assurance shall confer on the assignee therein named, his executors, administrators, or assigns, any right to sue for the amount of such policy, or the monies assured or secured thereby, until a written notice of the date and purport of such assignment shall have been given to the assurance company liable under such policy at their principal place of business for the time being, or in case they have two or more principal places of business, then at some one of such principal places of business, either in England or Scotland or Ireland; and the date on which such notice shall be received shall regulate the priority of all claims under any assignment; and a payment bona fide made in respect of any policy by any assurance company before the date on which such notice shall have been received shall be as valid against the assignee giving such notice as if this Act had not been passed.

[3012]

4 Principal place of business to be specified on policies

Every assurance company shall, on every policy issued by them after the thirtieth day of September one thousand eight hundred and sixty-seven, specify their principal place or principal places of business at which notices of assignment may be given in pursuance of this Act.

[3013]

5 Mode of assignment

Any such assignment may be made either by endorsement on the policy or by a separate instrument in the words or to the effect set forth in the schedule hereto, such endorsement or separate instrument being duly stamped.

[3014]

6 Receipt of notice of assignment

Every assurance company to whom notice shall have been duly given of the assignment of any policy under which they are liable shall, upon the request in writing of any person by whom any such notice was given or signed, or of his executors or administrators, and upon payment in each case of a fee not exceeding [25p] deliver an acknowledgment in writing, under the hand of the manager, secretary, treasurer, or other principal officer of the assurance company, of their receipt of such notice; and every such written acknowledgment, if signed by a person being de jure or de facto the manager, secretary, treasurer, or other principal officer of the assurance company whose acknowledgment the same purports to be, shall be conclusive evidence as against such assurance company of their having duly received the notice to which such acknowledgment relates.

NOTES

Sum in square brackets substituted by virtue of the Decimal Currency Act 1969, s 10(1).

[3015]

7 Interpretation

In the construction and for the purposes of this Act the expression "policy of life assurance" or "policy" shall mean any instrument by which the payment of monies by or out of the funds of an assurance company, on the happening of any contingency depending on the duration of human life, is assured or secured; and the expression "assurance company" shall mean and include every corporation, association, society, or company now or hereafter carrying on the business of assuring lives, or survivorships, either alone or in conjunction with any other object or objects.

[3016]
8 Saving of contracts under 16 & 17 Vict c 45, or 27 & 28 Vict c 43, and of engagements by friendly societies

Provided always, that this Act shall not apply to any policy of assurance granted or to be granted or to any contract for a payment on death entered into or to be entered into in pursuance of the provisions of the Government Annuities Act 1853, and the Government Annuities Act 1864, or either of those Acts, or to any engagement for payment on death by any friendly society.

NOTES

Government Annuities Act 1853 and Government Annuities Act 1864: repealed with savings by the Government Annuities Act 1929, s 66, Sch 2, Pt II, see now Pt II of that Act.

[3017]
9 Short title

For all purposes this Act may be cited as "The Policies of Assurance Act 1867".

SCHEDULE

Section 5

[3018]
I *A.B.*, of, *&c*, in consideration of, *&c*, do hereby assign unto *C.D.*, of, *&c*, his executors, administrators, and assigns, the [within] policy of assurance granted, *&c* [*here describe the policy*].

In witness, *&c*

LLOYD'S ACT 1871

(34 Vict c xxi)

ARRANGEMENT OF SECTIONS

Preamble		[3019]
1	Short title	[3020]
2	Cessor of existing constitution	[3021]
3	Incorporation of Lloyd's	[3022]
4	Property, &c, vested in Society	[3023]
5	Contracts, &c, to remain in force	[3024]
6	Actions, &c, not to abate	[3025]
7	Debts to be paid and received by the Society	[3026]
8	Officers continued	[3027]
9	General saving for rights and liabilities	[3028]
28	Continuance and annulling of existing byelaws	[3030]
30	Application of parts of Companies Clauses Act	[3031]
31	Penalty on imitation of stamp, &c	[3032]
34	Power to undertake recovery of wreck, &c	[3033]
35	Salvage operations as to wreck of Lutine	[3034]
39	Agreements for incorporation of other Societies, &c	[3035]
40	Saving for liability of members, &c	[3036]
41	Saving for rights and powers of Crown, Board of Trade, &c, as to wreck	[3037]
42	Savings respecting exclusion from membership	[3038]
43	Expenses of Act	[3039]

An Act for incorporating the members of the Establishment or Society formerly held at Lloyd's Coffee House in the Royal Exchange in the City of London, for the effecting of Marine Insurance, and generally known as Lloyd's; and for other purposes

[25 May 1871]

NOTES

By virtue of the Contracting Out (Functions in Relation to Insurance) Order 1998, SI 1998/2842, certain functions may now be exercised by, or by employees of, such person (if any) as may be authorised in that behalf by the Treasury.

[3019]
Preamble

Whereas there has long existed in the Royal Exchange in the City of London an Establishment or Society formerly held at Lloyd's Coffee House in the Royal Exchange, for the effecting of marine insurance, and generally known as Lloyd's:

And whereas the Society is regulated by a deed of association, dated on or about the thirtieth day of August one thousand eight hundred and eleven, which deed, or a deed of accession referring thereto, has usually been from time to time executed by the several members of the Society, and the Society is governed by rules or regulations from time to time made under that deed:

And whereas the affairs of the Society, and the business conducted by its members as such, are of large and increasing magnitude and importance, but the constitution of the Society is imperfect, and difficulties arise therefrom in relation to legal proceedings, and the management of the affairs of the Society and the incorporation of its members with proper powers would be of great benefit to the shipping and mercantile interests of the United Kingdom, and it is therefore expedient that they be incorporated, and that provision be made for the government of the Society and the conduct of its affairs:

And whereas by section four hundred and forty-eight of the Merchant Shipping Act 1854, it is enacted to the effect that any receiver of wreck, or in his absence any justice of the peace, shall, as soon as conveniently may be, examine on oath any person belonging to any ship which may be or may have been in distress on the coast of the United Kingdom, or any other person who may be able to give an account thereof or of the cargo or stores thereof, as to the matters in that section specified, and that the receiver or justice shall take the examination down in writing, and shall make two copies of the same, of which he shall send one to the Board of Trade and the other to the Secretary of the Committee for managing the affairs of Lloyd's in London, and such last-mentioned copy shall be placed by the said Secretary in some conspicuous situation for the inspection of persons desirous of examining the same:

And whereas it will be necessary on the incorporation of the Society to secure the continuance of the operation of the said section:

And whereas the capital stock of the Society consisted on the first day of December 1870 of the sum of forty-eight thousand pounds three pounds per centum consolidated annuities standing in the names of four persons being trustees for the Society:

And whereas in or about the year 1799 a vessel of war of the royal navy, named the Lutine, was wrecked on the coast of Holland with a considerable amount of specie on board, insured by underwriters at Lloyd's, being members of the Society, and others, and Holland being then at war with this country the vessel and cargo were captured, and some years afterwards the King of the Netherlands authorised certain undertakers to attempt the further salvage of the cargo on the conditions (among others) that they should pay all expenses, and that one half of all that should be recovered should belong to them, and that the other half should go to the Government of the Netherlands, and subsequently the King of the Netherlands ceded to King George the Fourth on behalf of the Society of Lloyd's, the share in the cargo which had been so reserved to the Government of the Netherlands:

And whereas from time to time operations of salving from the wreck of the Lutine have been carried on, and a portion of the sum recovered, amounting to about twenty-five thousand pounds, is by virtue of the cession aforesaid in the custody or under the control of the Committee for managing the affairs of Lloyd's:

And whereas, by reason of the mode in which the business of insurance has always been carried on by members of the Society, the names of those who underwrite a particular policy cannot, when a considerable time has elapsed, be traced with certainty, if at all, especially as regards policies anterior in date to one thousand eight hundred and thirty-eight, in which year the books and papers relating to the affairs of the Society were lost in the fire which destroyed the Royal Exchange:

And whereas it is expedient that the operations of salving from the wreck of the Lutine be continued, and that provision be made for the application in that behalf, as far as may be requisite, of money that may hereafter be received from those operations, and for the application to public or other purposes of the aforesaid sum of twenty-five thousand pounds, and of the unclaimed residue of money to be hereafter received as aforesaid:

And whereas it is expedient that various powers be conferred on the Society as incorporated, and that its functions be as far as may be defined:

And whereas it is expedient that provision be made for the incorporation, from time to time, by agreement, with the Society, of other societies, associations, companies, or corporations instituted for purposes connected with shipping or marine insurance:

And whereas the objects aforesaid cannot be attained without the authority of Parliament:

May it therefore please Your Majesty that it may be enacted; and be it enacted by the Queen's most Excellent Majesty, by and with the advice and consent of the Lords Spiritual and Temporal, and Commons, in this present Parliament assembled, and by the authority of the same, as follows; (that is to say),

[3020]

1 Short title

This Act may be cited as Lloyd's Act, 1871.

[3021]

2 Cessor of existing constitution

On the passing of this Act, the deed of association, dated on or about the thirtieth day of August one thousand eight hundred and eleven, executed by members of the Establishment or Society of Lloyd's as existing before the passing of this Act, and any deed executed by other members by way of accession thereto, shall be and the same are and each of them is hereby annulled.

[3022]

3 Incorporation of Lloyd's

The Right Honourable George Joachim Goschen, William Simpson, James Leverton Wylie, William Young, Henry Caspar Heintz, Frederic Bernstein Bernard Natusch, James Bischoff, George Dorman Tyser, Michael Wills, William Wilson Saunders, Leonard Charles Wakefield, and Thomas Chapman, and all persons admitted as members of Lloyd's before or after the passing of this Act, are hereby united into a Society and Corporation for the purposes of this Act, and for those purposes are hereby incorporated by the name of Lloyd's and by that name shall be one body corporate, with perpetual succession and a common seal, and with power to purchase, take, hold, and dispose, of lands and other property (which incorporated body is hereafter in this Act referred to as the Society).

[3023]

4 Property, &c, vested in Society

All property and rights of or to which the Committee for managing the affairs of Lloyd's, or any person on their behalf, or any trustee for that Committee, or for the members of Lloyd's, are or is possessed or entitled at law or in equity at the passing of this Act, shall by virtue of this Act belong to the Society to the same extent and for the same estate and interest as the same respectively is and are at the passing of this Act vested in that Committee, person, or trustee, and may be held used, and enjoyed accordingly; and all trustees for the Establishment or Society as it existed before the passing of this Act, or for that Committee, shall be and continue trustees for the Society, as nearly as may be as if this Act had not been passed.

[3024]

5 Contracts, &c, to remain in force

Notwithstanding the annulling by this Act of the aforesaid deeds of association and accession, and the incorporation by this Act of the Society, all deeds of trust, leases, mortgages, bonds, contracts, agreements, securities, transfers, and other acts and things before the passing of this Act made, entered into, executed, or done by or with the Committee for managing the affairs of Lloyd's, or any person or trustee as aforesaid, shall be as good, valid, and effectual to all intents for, against, and with reference to the Society as they would have been for, against, or with reference to such Committee if this Act had not been passed, and may be proceeded on, executed, used, dealt with, and enforced accordingly, the Society being only substituted in or in relation thereto respectively for such Committee.

[3025]

6 Actions, &c, not to abate

Notwithstanding the annulling and incorporation aforesaid, any action, suit, prosecution, or other proceeding instituted before the passing of this Act by or against the Committee for managing the affairs of Lloyd's, or any person or trustee as aforesaid, shall not abate or be discontinued or be prejudicially affected by this Act, but on the contrary, shall continue and take effect both in favour of and against the Society, as it would have done in favour of or against that Committee, or the members thereof, or any of them, or any person or trustee as aforesaid, if this Act had not been passed, the Society being only substituted in or in relation thereto respectively for that Committee or the members thereof, or any one or more of them, or such person or trustee.

[3026]

7 Debts to be paid and received by the Society

All debts due to the Committee for managing the affairs of Lloyd's, or to any person or trustee as aforesaid, with all interest (if any) due or to accrue due thereon, shall be paid to the Society, and shall be recoverable by them, and all debts due by such Committee person, or trustee as aforesaid, with all interest (if any) due or to accrue due thereon, shall be paid by the Society, and shall be recoverable from them.

[3027]
8 Officers continued
All officers of and persons employed by the Committee for managing the affairs of Lloyd's, in office or employment at the passing of this Act, shall continue in their respective offices and employments, according to the tenure of their respective offices and employments, and as if they had been appointed by the Society, and be deemed to be officers of or persons employed by the Society, and they and their respective sureties shall be liable as if they respectively had been appointed by and had become bound to the Society.

[3028]–[3029]
9 General saving for rights and liabilities
Notwithstanding the annulling and incorporation aforesaid, and except as by this Act otherwise expressly provided, everything before the passing of this Act done or suffered by or with reference to the Committee for managing the affairs of Lloyd's, or any person or trustee as aforesaid, shall be as valid as if this Act had not been passed, and the annulling and incorporation aforesaid and this Act respectively shall accordingly be subject and without prejudice to everything so done or suffered, and to all rights, liabilities, claims, and demands, both present and future, which if this Act had not been passed would be incident to and consequent on any and everything so done or suffered, and with respect to all such rights, liabilities, claims and demands the Society shall to all intents represent and be deemed a continuation of the Establishment or Society constituted or regulated by the deeds of association and accession aforesaid, and the generality of this enactment shall not be restricted by any other provision of this Act.

10–27 (*S 10 repealed by the Lloyd's Act 1911, s 4; ss 11, 12, 18–27 repealed by the Lloyd's Act 1982, s 15(1), Sch 3; ss 13–17 repealed by the Lloyd's Act 1925, s 4.*)

[3030]
28 Continuance and annulling of existing byelaws
The general rules and regulations or byelaws for the management of the affairs of Lloyd's, passed at a general meeting of the members of Lloyd's held on the fourth and confirmed at a subsequent meeting held on the eleventh day of January one thousand eight hundred and seventy-one, may be annulled by byelaws under this Act, and, as far as the same are not inconsistent with this Act, the same (except those numbered ninety-three to ninety-nine inclusive) shall continue in force for four months after the passing of this Act (unless sooner so annulled), and no longer, and while so in force shall apply to the Society as incorporated by this Act, and the members thereof; but nothing in this Act shall give any validity or force to any such general rule, regulation, or byelaw as aforesaid, made before the passing of this Act, further or other than it would have had if this Act had not been passed.

29 (*Repealed by the Lloyd's Act 1982, s 15(1), Sch 3.*)

[3031]
30 Application of parts of Companies Clauses Act
Sections ninety-seven to one hundred of The Companies Clauses Consolidation Act, 1845, relating to contracts by and proceedings of and liabilities of directors, are hereby incorporated with this Act, and shall apply to the Committee, and the Society in like manner, mutatis mutandis, as they apply to directors and a company.

[3032]
31 Penalty on imitation of stamp, &c
If any person, without the authority of the Society, or without other lawful excuse (proof whereof respectively shall lie on him) does any of the following things (namely) imitates or copies any stamp, mark, or other thing for the time being used by the Society to distinguish forms of policies of . . . insurance underwritten by members of the Society or offers or utters or uses any form of policy bearing any such stamp, mark, or other thing as aforesaid, he shall for every such offence be liable, on summary conviction before two justices, to a penalty not exceeding [level two on the standard scale].

NOTES
Word omitted repealed by the Lloyd's Act 1911, s 5; words in square brackets substituted by virtue of the Criminal Law Act 1977, s 31 and the Criminal Justice Act 1982, s 46.
Extension: meaning of the word "insurance" extended by the Lloyd's Act 1911, s 5.

32, 33 (*S 32 repealed by the Lloyd's Act 1982, s 15(1), Sch 3; s 33 repealed by the Merchant Shipping Act 1995, s 314(1), Sch 12.*)

[3033]

34 Power to undertake recovery of wreck, &c

The Society may from time to time aid in or undertake in such manner as to them seems fit the discovery, recovery, protection, and restoration or other disposal of property before or after the passing of this Act wrecked, sunk, lost, or abandoned, or found or recovered in, on, or beneath the sea or on the shore, at home or abroad.

[3034]

35 Salvage operations as to wreck of Lutine

The Society may from time to time do or join in doing all such lawful things as they think expedient with a view to further salving from the wreck of the Lutine, and hold, receive and apply for that purpose so much of the money to be received by means of salving therefrom as they from time to time think fit, and the net money produced thereby, and the said sum of twenty-five thousand pounds, shall be applied for purposes connected with shipping or marine insurance, according to a scheme to be prepared by the Society, and confirmed by Order of Her Majesty in Council, on the recommendation of [the Financial Services Authority], after or subject to such public notice to claimants of any part of the money aforesaid to come in, and such investigation of claims, and such barring of claims not made or not proved, and such reservation of rights (if any), as [the Treasury] think fit.

NOTES

Words in square brackets substituted by the Financial Services and Markets Act 2000 (Consequential Amendments and Repeals) Order 2001, SI 2001/3649, art 264(1), (3).

36–38 (*Repealed by the Lloyd's Act 1911, s 6.*)

[3035]

39 Agreements for incorporation of other Societies, &c

The Society, and any other society, association, or corporation instituted for purposes connected with shipping or . . . insurance, may from time to time enter into and carry into effect such agreements as they think fit for the incorporation with the Society of such other society, association, or corporation, and for the transfer to the Society of the property and funds, rights and liabilities, and officers and servants, of such other society, association, or corporation, and for other the incidents and consequences of such incorporation; but no such agreement shall have effect unless and until it is confirmed by Order of Her Majesty in Council, on the recommendation of [the Financial Services Authority], whereupon it shall have the like operation as if the terms thereof had been enacted in this Act; and no such agreement shall be recommended for confirmation as aforesaid if by virtue thereof the Society would acquire any power or authority different from the powers and authorities conferred on the Society by this Act.

NOTES

Word omitted repealed by the Lloyd's Act 1911, s 5; words in square brackets substituted by the Financial Services and Markets Act 2000 (Consequential Amendments and Repeals) Order 2001, SI 2001/3649, art 264(1), (2).

Extension: meaning of the word "insurance" extended by the Lloyd's Act 1911, s 5.

[3036]

40 Saving for liability of members, &c

Nothing in this Act shall confer limited liability on the members of the Society, or in any manner restrict the liability of any member thereof in respect of his individual undertakings, or make any member of the Society as such responsible in any manner for any of the undertakings, debts, or liabilities of any other member of the Society as such, or affect or interfere with or empower the Society or the Committee to interfere with any business whatever other than the business of . . . insurance carried on by any member of the Society.

NOTES

Word omitted repealed by the Lloyd's Act 1911, s 5.

Extension: meaning of the word "insurance" extended by the Lloyd's Act 1911, s 5.

[3037]

41 Saving for rights and powers of Crown, Board of Trade, &c, as to wreck

Nothing in this Act shall take away, abridge, or prejudicially affect any right, title, power, or authority vested in Her Majesty, her heirs or successors, or in any admiral, vice-admiral, or lord of a manor, or in any person or corporation, or in the Board of Trade, or in any receiver of wreck or other officer under The [Merchant Shipping Act 1995], or otherwise in relation to wreck, as defined in The [Merchant Shipping Act 1995], or any interest or right of dealing of any shipowner or other person in or with any property before or after the passing of this Act wrecked, sunk, lost, or abandoned, or found or recovered in, on, or beneath the sea or on the shore, at home or abroad.

NOTES

Words in square brackets substituted by the Merchant Shipping Act 1995, s 314(2), Sch 13, para 3.

[3038]

42 Savings respecting exclusion from membership

Nothing in this Act shall confer on the Society as incorporated by this Act any right or power to exclude, by or under any byelaw or resolution or otherwise, any person from membership of the Society by reason of anything done or omitted before the passing of this Act, or confirm or enlarge any such right or power, if existing at the passing of this Act, in the Establishment or Society of Lloyd's, and on the other hand nothing in this Act shall take away from the Society as incorporated by this Act any such right or power if so existing, or abridge or weaken the same, or prevent the Society as incorporated by this Act from exercising the same, but on the contrary such right or power if and as so existing shall remain in and be exercisable by the Society as incorporated by this Act, in the same cases and in like manner (if any) in which the same would have existed in and been exercisable by the Establishment or Society of Lloyd's if this Act had not been passed, but not further or otherwise.

[3039]

43 Expenses of Act

The costs, charges, and expenses preliminary to and of and incidental to the preparing, applying for, obtaining, and passing of this Act shall be paid by the Society.

(*Schedule repealed by the Lloyd's Act 1982, s 15(1), Sch 3.*)

MARRIED WOMEN'S PROPERTY ACT 1882

(45 & 46 Vict c 75)

An Act to consolidate and amend the Acts relating to the Property of Married Women

[18 August 1882]

Part III Statutes

1–10 (*Ss 1–5 repealed by the Law Reform (Married Women and Tortfeasors) Act 1935, ss 5, 8, Sch 2; ss 6–9 repealed by the Statute Law (Repeals) Act 1969; s 10 outside the scope of this work.*)

[3040]

11 Moneys payable under policy of assurance not to form part of estate of the insured

A married woman may . . . effect a policy upon her own life or the life of her husband for her [own benefit]; and the same and all benefit thereof shall enure accordingly.

A policy of assurance effected by any man on his own life, and expressed to be for the benefit of his wife, or of his children, or of his wife and children, or any of them, or by any woman on her own life, and expressed to be for the benefit of her husband, or of her children, or of her husband and children, or any of them, shall create a trust in favour of the objects therein named, and the moneys payable under any such policy shall not, so long as any object of the trust remains unperformed, form part of the estate of the insured, or be subject to his or her debts: Provided, that if it shall be proved that the policy was effected and the premiums paid with intent to defraud the creditors of the insured, they shall be entitled to receive, out of the moneys payable under the policy, a sum equal to the premiums so paid. The insured may by the policy, or by any memorandum under his or her hand, appoint a trustee or trustees of the moneys payable under the policy, and from time to time appoint a new trustee or new trustees thereof, and may make provision for the appointment of a new trustee or new trustees thereof, and for the investment of the moneys payable under such policy. In default of any such appointment of a trustee, such policy, immediately on its being effected, shall vest in the insured and his or her legal personal representatives, in trust for the purposes aforesaid . . . The receipt of a trustee or trustees duly appointed, or in default of any such appointment, or in default of notice to the insurance office, the receipt of the legal personal representative of the insured shall be a discharge to the office for the sum secured by the policy, or for the value thereof, in whole or in part.

NOTES

Words omitted in the first place repealed and words in square brackets substituted by the Law Reform (Married Women and Tortfeasors) Act 1935, ss 5(1), (2), 8(2), Schs 1, 2; words omitted in the second place repealed by the Statute Law (Repeals) Act 1969.

Children: references in this section to children include illegitimate children in the case of policies effected on or after 1 January 1970; see the Family Law Reform Act 1969, s 19(1), (3).

This section applies in relation to a policy of assurance effected by a civil partner on his own life, and expressed to be for the benefit of his civil partner, or of his children, or of his civil partner and children, or any of them, as it applies in relation to a policy of assurance effected by a husband and expressed to be for the benefit of his wife, or of his children, or of his wife and children, or of any of them: see the Civil Partnership Act 2004, s 70.

12–25 *(S 12 repealed by the Law Reform (Husband and Wife) Act 1962, s 3(2), (5), Schedule, and by the Theft Act 1968, ss 33(3), 36(3), Sch 3, Pt III; s 13 repealed by the Statute Law (Repeals) Act 1969; ss 14, 15 repealed by the Law Reform (Married Women and Tortfeasors) Act 1935, ss 5(2), 8(2), Sch 2; s 16 repealed by the Theft Act 1968, ss 33(3), 36(3), Sch 3, Pt III; ss 17, 24 outside the scope of this work; ss 18, 19, 25 repealed by the Statute Law (Repeals) Act 1969; ss 20, 21 repealed by the Poor Law Act 1927, s 245, Sch 11; s 22 repealed by the Statute Law Revision Act 1898; s 23 repealed by the Law Reform (Husband and Wife) Act 1962, s 3(2), (5), Schedule.)*

[3041]
26 Extent of Act
This Act shall not extend to Scotland.

[3042]
27 Short title
This Act may be cited as the Married Women's Property Act 1882.

LIFE ASSURANCE COMPANIES (PAYMENT INTO COURT) ACT 1896

(59 & 60 Vict c 8)

An Act to enable Life Assurance Companies to pay Money into Court in certain Cases

[21 May 1896]

[3043]
1 Short title
This Act may be cited as the Life Assurance Companies (Payment into Court) Act 1896.

[3044]
2 Interpretation
In this Act—

The expression "life assurance company" means any corporation, company, or society carrying on the business of life assurance, not being a society registered under the Acts relating to friendly societies;

The expression "life policy" includes any policy not foreign to the business of life assurance.

[3045]
3 Power to pay money into court
Subject to rules of court any life assurance company may pay into [the [Senior Courts]] . . . any moneys payable by them under a life policy in respect of which, in the opinion of the board of directors, no sufficient discharge can otherwise be obtained.

NOTES

Words in first (outer) pair of square brackets substituted by the Administration of Justice Act 1965, s 17(1), Sch 1; words in second (inner) pair of square brackets substituted by the Constitutional Reform Act 2005, s 59(5), Sch 11, Pt 2, para 4; words omitted repealed by the Courts Act 1971, s 56, Sch 11, Pt II.

[3046]
4 Receipt of officer sufficient discharge
The receipt or certificate of the proper officer shall be a sufficient discharge to the company for the moneys so paid into court, and such moneys shall, subject to rules of court, be dealt with according to the orders of [the [Senior Courts]] . . .

NOTES

Words in first (outer) pair of square brackets substituted by the Administration of Justice Act 1965, s 17(1), Sch 1; words in second (inner) pair of square brackets substituted by the Constitutional Reform Act 2005, s 59(5), Sch 11, Pt 2, para 4; words omitted repealed by the Courts Act 1971, s 56, Sch 11, Pt II.

[3047]
5 Extent of Act
This Act does not extend to Scotland.

MARINE INSURANCE ACT 1906

(6 Edw 7 c 41)

ARRANGEMENT OF SECTIONS

Marine Insurance

1 Marine insurance defined [3048]
2 Mixed sea and land risks [3049]
3 Marine adventure and maritime perils defined [3050]

Insurable Interest

4 Avoidance of wagering or gaming contracts [3051]
5 Insurable interest defined [3052]
6 When interest must attach [3053]
7 Defeasible or contingent interest [3054]
8 Partial interest [3055]
9 Re-insurance [3056]
10 Bottomry [3057]
11 Master's and seamen's wages [3058]
12 Advance freight [3059]
13 Charges of insurance [3060]
14 Quantum of interest [3061]
15 Assignment of interest [3062]

Insurable Value

16 Measure of insurable value [3063]

Disclosure and Representations

17 Insurance is uberrimae fidei [3064]
18 Disclosure by assured [3065]
19 Disclosure by agent effecting insurance [3066]
20 Representations pending negotiation of contract [3067]
21 When contract is deemed to be concluded [3068]

The Policy

22 Contract must be embodied in policy [3069]
23 What policy must specify [3070]
24 Signature of insurer [3071]
25 Voyage and time policies [3072]
26 Designation of subject-matter [3073]
27 Valued policy [3074]
28 Unvalued policy [3075]
29 Floating policy by ship or ships [3076]
30 Construction of terms in policy [3077]
31 Premium to be arranged [3078]

Double Insurance

32 Double insurance [3079]

Warranties, etc

33 Nature of warranty [3080]
34 When breach of warranty excused [3081]
35 Express warranties [3082]
36 Warranty of neutrality [3083]
37 No implied warranty of nationality [3084]
38 Warranty of good safety [3085]
39 Warranty of seaworthiness of ship [3086]
40 No implied warranty that goods are seaworthy [3087]
41 Warranty of legality [3088]

The Voyage

42 Implied condition as to commencement of risk [3089]
43 Alteration of port of departure [3090]
44 Sailing for different destination [3091]
45 Change of voyage [3092]
46 Deviation [3093]
47 Several ports of discharge [3094]
48 Delay in voyage [3095]
49 Excuses for deviation or delay [3096]

Assignment of Policy

50 When and how policy is assignable [3097]
51 Assured who has no interest cannot assign [3098]

The Premium

52 When premium payable . . . [3099]
53 Policy effected through broker . . . [3100]
54 Effect of receipt on policy . . . [3101]

Loss and Abandonment

55 Included and excluded losses . . . [3102]
56 Partial and total loss . . . [3103]
57 Actual total loss . . . [3104]
58 Missing ship . . . [3105]
59 Effect of transhipment, etc . . . [3106]
60 Constructive total loss defined . . . [3107]
61 Effect of constructive total loss . . . [3108]
62 Notice of abandonment . . . [3109]
63 Effect of abandonment . . . [3110]

Partial Losses (including Salvage and General Average and Particular Charges)

64 Particular average loss . . . [3111]
65 Salvage charges . . . [3112]
66 General average loss . . . [3113]

Measure of Indemnity

67 Extent of liability of insurer for loss . . . [3114]
68 Total loss . . . [3115]
69 Partial loss of ship . . . [3116]
70 Partial loss of freight . . . [3117]
71 Partial loss of goods, merchandise, etc . . . [3118]
72 Apportionment of valuation . . . [3119]
73 General average contributions and salvage charges . . . [3120]
74 Liabilities to third parties . . . [3121]
75 General provisions as to measure of indemnity . . . [3122]
76 Particular average warranties . . . [3123]
77 Successive losses . . . [3124]
78 Suing and labouring clause . . . [3125]

Rights of Insurer on Payment

79 Right of subrogation . . . [3126]
80 Right of contribution . . . [3127]
81 Effect of under insurance . . . [3128]

Return of Premium

82 Enforcement of return . . . [3129]
83 Return by agreement . . . [3130]
84 Return for failure of consideration . . . [3131]

Mutual Insurance

85 Modification of Act in case of mutual insurance . . . [3132]

Supplemental

86 Ratification by assured . . . [3133]
87 Implied obligations varied by agreement or usage . . . [3134]
88 Reasonable time, etc, a question of fact . . . [3135]
89 Slip as evidence . . . [3136]
90 Interpretation of terms . . . [3137]
91 Savings . . . [3138]
94 Short title . . . [3139]

SCHEDULE:

First Schedule —Form of Policy—Rules for construction of policy . . . [3140]

An Act to codify the Law relating to Marine Insurance

[21 December 1906]

NOTES

Marine Insurance Acts 1906 and 1909. By the Marine Insurance (Gambling Policies) Act 1909, s 2 at **[3142]**, that Act and this Act may be cited together by this collective title.

Hovercraft: references in this Act in whatever terms to ships, vessels, boats or activities or places connected therewith include references to hovercraft, etc, by virtue of the Hovercraft (Application of Enactments) Order 1972, SI 1972/971.

Marine Insurance

[3048]

1 Marine insurance defined

A contract of marine insurance is a contract whereby the insurer undertakes to indemnify the assured, in manner and to the extent thereby agreed, against marine losses, that is to say, the losses incident to marine adventure.

[3049]

2 Mixed sea and land risks

(1) A contract of marine insurance may, by its express terms, or by usage of trade, be extended so as to protect the assured against losses on inland waters or on any land risk which may be incidental to any sea voyage.

(2) Where a ship in course of building, or the launch of a ship, or any adventure analogous to a marine adventure, is covered by a policy in the form of a marine policy, the provisions of this Act, in so far as applicable, shall apply thereto; but, except as by this section provided, nothing in this Act shall alter or affect any rule of law applicable to any contract of insurance other than a contract of marine insurance as by this Act defined.

[3050]

3 Marine adventure and maritime perils defined

(1) Subject to the provisions of this Act, every lawful marine adventure may be the subject of a contract of marine insurance.

(2) In particular there is a marine adventure where—

- (a) Any ship goods or other moveables are exposed to maritime perils. Such property is in this Act referred to as "insurable property";
- (b) The earning or acquisition of any freight, passage money, commission, profit, or other pecuniary benefit, or the security for any advances, loan, or disbursements, is endangered by the exposure of insurable property to maritime perils;
- (c) Any liability to a third party may be incurred by the owner of, or other person interested in or responsible for, insurable property, by reason of maritime perils.

"Maritime perils" means the perils consequent on, or incidental to, the navigation of the sea, that is to say, perils of the seas, fire, war perils, pirates, rovers, thieves, captures, seisures, restraints, and detainments of princes and peoples, jettisons, barratry, and any other perils, either of the like kind or which may be designated by the policy.

Insurable Interest

[3051]

4 Avoidance of wagering or gaming contracts

(1) Every contract of marine insurance by way of gaming or wagering is void.

(2) A contract of marine insurance is deemed to be a gaming or wagering contract—

- (a) Where the assured has not an insurable interest as defined by this Act, and the contract is entered into with no expectation of acquiring such an interest; or
- (b) Where the policy is made "interest or no interest," or "without further proof of interest than the policy itself," or "without benefit of salvage to the insurer," or subject to any other like term:

Provided that, where there is no possibility of salvage, a policy may be effected without benefit of salvage to the insurer.

[3052]

5 Insurable interest defined

(1) Subject to the provisions of this Act, every person has an insurable interest who is interested in a marine adventure.

(2) In particular a person is interested in a marine adventure where he stands in any legal or equitable relation to the adventure or to any insurable property at risk therein, in consequence of which he may benefit by the safety or due arrival of insurable property, or may be prejudiced by its loss, or damage thereto, or by the detention thereof, or may incur liability in respect thereof.

[3053]

6 When interest must attach

(1) The assured must be interested in the subject-matter insured at the time of the loss though he need not be interested when the insurance is effected:

Provided that where the subject-matter is insured "lost or not lost," the assured may recover although he may not have acquired his interest until after the loss, unless at the time of effecting the contract of insurance the assured was aware of the loss, and the insurer was not.

(2) Where the assured has no interest at the time of the loss, he cannot acquire interest by any act or election after he is aware of the loss.

[3054]
7 Defeasible or contingent interest
(1) A defeasible interest is insurable, as also is a contingent interest.
(2) In particular, where the buyer of goods has insured them, he has an insurable interest, notwithstanding that he might, at his election, have rejected the goods, or have treated them as at the seller's risk, by reason of the latter's delay in making delivery or otherwise.

[3055]
8 Partial interest
A partial interest of any nature is insurable.

[3056]
9 Re-insurance
(1) The insurer under a contract of marine insurance has an insurable interest in his risk, and may re-insure in respect of it.
(2) Unless the policy otherwise provides, the original assured has no right or interest in respect of such re-insurance.

[3057]
10 Bottomry
The lender of money on bottomry or respondentia has an insurable interest in respect of the loan.

[3058]
11 Master's and seamen's wages
The master or any member of the crew of a ship has an insurable interest in respect of his wages.

[3059]
12 Advance freight
In the case of advance freight, the person advancing the freight has an insurable interest, in so far as such freight is not repayable in case of loss.

[3060]
13 Charges of insurance
The assured has an insurable interest in the charges of any insurance which he may effect.

[3061]
14 Quantum of interest
(1) Where the subject-matter insured is mortgaged, the mortgagor has an insurable interest in the full value thereof, and the mortgagee has an insurable interest in respect of any sum due or to become due under the mortgage.
(2) A mortgagee, consignee, or other person having an interest in the subject-matter insured may insure on behalf and for the benefit of other persons interested as well as for his own benefit.
(3) The owner of insurable property has an insurable interest in respect of the full value thereof, notwithstanding that some third person may have agreed, or be liable, to indemnify him in case of loss.

[3062]
15 Assignment of interest
Where the assured assigns or otherwise parts with his interest in the subject-matter insured, he does not thereby transfer to the assignee his rights under the contract of insurance, unless there be an express or implied agreement with the assignee to that effect.

But the provisions of this section do not affect a transmission of interest by operation of law.

Insurable Value

[3063]
16 Measure of insurable value
Subject to any express provision or valuation in the policy, the insurable value of the subject-matter insured must be ascertained as follows:—

(1) In insurance on ship, the insurable value is the value, at the commencement of the risk, of the ship, including her outfit, provisions and stores for the officers and crew, money advanced for seamen's wages, and other disbursements (if any) incurred to make the ship fit for the voyage or adventure contemplated by the policy, plus the charges of insurance upon the whole:

The insurable value, in the case of a steamship, includes also the machinery, boilers, and coals and engine stores if owned by the assured, and, in the case of a ship engaged in a special trade, the ordinary fittings requisite for that trade:

(2) In insurance on freight, whether paid in advance or otherwise, the insurable value is the gross amount of the freight at the risk of the assured, plus the charges of insurance:

(3) In insurance on goods or merchandise, the insurable value is the prime cost of the property insured, plus the expenses of and incidental to shipping and the charges of insurance upon the whole:

(4) In insurance on any other subject-matter, the insurable value is the amount at the risk of the assured when the policy attaches, plus the charges of insurance.

Disclosure and Representations

[3064]

17 Insurance is uberrimae fidei

A contract of marine insurance is a contract based upon the utmost good faith, and, if the utmost good faith be not observed by either party, the contract may be avoided by the other party.

[3065]

18 Disclosure by assured

(1) Subject to the provisions of this section, the assured must disclose to the insurer, before the contract is concluded, every material circumstance which is known to the assured, and the assured is deemed to know every circumstance which, in the ordinary course of business, ought to be known by him. If the assured fails to make such disclosure, the insurer may avoid the contract.

(2) Every circumstance is material which would influence the judgment of a prudent insurer in fixing the premium, or determining whether he will take the risk.

(3) In the absence of inquiry the following circumstances need not be disclosed, namely:—

- (a) Any circumstance which diminishes the risk;
- (b) Any circumstance which is known or presumed to be known to the insurer. The insurer is presumed to know matters of common notoriety or knowledge, and matters which an insurer in the ordinary course of his business, as such, ought to know;
- (c) Any circumstance as to which information is waived by the insurer;
- (d) Any circumstance which it is superfluous to disclose by reason of any express or implied warranty.

(4) Whether any particular circumstance, which is not disclosed, be material or not is, in each case, a question of fact.

(5) The term "circumstance" includes any communication made to, or information received by, the assured.

[3066]

19

Subject to the provisions of the preceding section as to circumstances which need not be disclosed, where an insurance is effected for the assured by an agent, the agent must disclose to the insurer—

- (a) Every material circumstance which is known to himself, and an agent to insure is deemed to know every circumstance which in the ordinary course of business ought to be known by, or to have been communicated to, him; and
- (b) Every material circumstance which the assured is bound to disclose, unless it come to his knowledge too late to communicate it to the agent.

[3067]

20 Representations pending negotiation of contract

(1) Every material representation made by the assured or his agent to the insurer during the negotiations for the contract, and before the contract is concluded, must be true. If it be untrue the insurer may avoid the contract.

(2) A representation is material which would influence the judgment of a prudent insurer in fixing the premium, or determining whether he will take the risk.

(3) A representation may be either a representation as to a matter of fact, or as to a matter of expectation or belief.

(4) A representation as to matter of fact is true, if it be substantially correct, that is to say, if the difference between what is represented and what is actually correct would not be considered material by a prudent insurer.

(5) A representation as to a matter of expectation or belief is true if it be made in good faith.

(6) A representation may be withdrawn or corrected before the contract is concluded.

(7) Whether a particular representation be material or not is, in each case, a question of fact.

[3068]

21 When contract is deemed to be concluded

A contract of marine insurance is deemed to be concluded when the proposal of the assured is accepted by the insurer, whether the policy be then issued or not; and, for the purpose of showing when the proposal was accepted, reference may be made to the slip or covering note or other customary memorandum of the contract, . . .

NOTES

Words omitted repealed by the Finance Act 1959, s 37(5), Sch 8, Pt II, and the Finance Act (Northern Ireland) 1959, s 17(2), Sch 3, Pt II.

The Policy

[3069]

22 Contract must be embodied in policy

Subject to the provisions of any statute, a contract of marine insurance is inadmissible in evidence unless it is embodied in a marine policy in accordance with this Act. The policy may be executed and issued either at the time when the contract is concluded, or afterwards.

[3070]

23 What policy must specify

A marine policy must specify—

(1) The name of the assured, or of some person who effects the insurance on his behalf:

(2)–(5). . .

NOTES

Sub-ss (2)–(5): repealed by the Finance Act 1959, ss 30(5), (7), 37(5), Sch 8, Pt II, and the Finance Act (Northern Ireland) 1959, ss 5(5), (7), 17(2), Sch 3, Pt II.

[3071]

24 Signature of insurer

(1) A marine policy must be signed by or on behalf of the insurer, provided that in the case of a corporation the corporate seal may be sufficient, but nothing in this section shall be construed as requiring the subscription of a corporation to be under seal.

(2) Where a policy is subscribed by or on behalf of two or more insurers, each subscription, unless the contrary be expressed, constitutes a distinct contract with the assured.

[3072]

25 Voyage and time policies

(1) Where the contract is to insure the subject-matter "at and from", or from one place to another or others, the policy is called a "voyage policy", and where the contract is to insure the subject-matter for a definite period of time the policy is called a "time policy". A contract for both voyage and time may be included in the same policy.

(2) . . .

NOTES

Sub-s (2): repealed by the Finance Act 1959, ss 30(5), (7), 37(5), Sch 8, Pt II, and the Finance Act (Northern Ireland) 1959, ss 5(5), (7), 17(2), Sch 3, Pt II.

[3073]

26 Designation of subject-matter

(1) The subject-matter insured must be designated in a marine policy with reasonable certainty.

(2) The nature and extent of the interest of the assured in the subject-matter insured need not be specified in the policy.

(3) Where the policy designates the subject-matter insured in general terms, it shall be construed to apply to the interest intended by the assured to be covered.

(4) In the application of this section regard shall be had to any usage regulating the designation of the subject-matter insured.

[3074]

27 Valued policy

(1) A policy may be either valued or unvalued.

(2) A valued policy is a policy which specifies the agreed value of the subject-matter insured.

(3) Subject to the provisions of this Act, and in the absence of fraud, the value fixed by the policy is, as between the insurer and assured, conclusive of the insurable value of the subject intended to be insured, whether the loss be total or partial.

(4) Unless the policy otherwise provides, the value fixed by the policy is not conclusive for the purpose of determining whether there has been a constructive total loss.

[3075]
28 Unvalued policy
An unvalued policy is a policy which does not specify the value of the subject-matter insured, but, subject to the limit of the sum insured, leaves the insurable value to be subsequently ascertained, in the manner herein-before specified.

[3076]
29 Floating policy by ship or ships
(1) A floating policy is a policy which describes the insurance in general terms, and leaves the name of the ship or ships and other particulars to be defined by subsequent declaration.
(2) The subsequent declaration or declarations may be made by indorsement on the policy, or in other customary manner.
(3) Unless the policy otherwise provides, the declarations must be made in the order of dispatch or shipment. They must, in the case of goods, comprise all consignments within the terms of the policy, and the value of the goods or other property must be honestly stated, but an omission or erroneous declaration may be rectified even after loss or arrival, provided the omission or declaration was made in good faith.
(4) Unless the policy otherwise provides, where a declaration of value is not made until after notice of loss or arrival, the policy must be treated as an unvalued policy as regards the subject-matter of that declaration.

[3077]
30 Construction of terms in policy
(1) A policy may be in the form in the First Schedule to this Act.
(2) Subject to the provisions of this Act, and unless the context of the policy otherwise requires, the terms and expressions mentioned in the First Schedule to this Act shall be construed as having the scope and meaning in that schedule assigned to them.

[3078]
31 Premium to be arranged
(1) Where an insurance is effected at a premium to be arranged, and no arrangement is made, a reasonable premium is payable.
(2) Where an insurance is effected on the terms that an additional premium is to be arranged in a given event, and that event happens but no arrangement is made, then a reasonable additional premium is payable.

Double Insurance

[3079]
32 Double insurance
(1) Where two or more policies are effected by or on behalf of the assured on the same adventure and interest or any part thereof, and the sums insured exceed the indemnity allowed by this Act, the assured is said to be over-insured by double insurance.
(2) Where the assured is over-insured by double insurance—

- (a) The assured, unless the policy otherwise provides, may claim payment from the insurers in such order as he may think fit, provided that he is not entitled to receive any sum in excess of the indemnity allowed by this Act;
- (b) Where the policy under which the assured claims is a valued policy, the assured must give credit as against the valuation for any sum received by him under any other policy without regard to the actual value of the subject-matter insured;
- (c) Where the policy under which the assured claims is an unvalued policy he must give credit, as against the full insurable value, for any sum received by him under any other policy;
- (d) Where the assured receives any sum in excess of the indemnity allowed by this Act, he is deemed to hold such sum in trust for the insurers, according to their right of contribution among themselves.

Warranties, etc

[3080]
33 Nature of warranty
(1) A warranty, in the following sections relating to warranties, means a promissory warranty, that is to say, a warranty by which the assured undertakes that some particular thing shall or shall not be done, or that some condition shall be fulfilled, or whereby he affirms or negatives the existence of a particular state of facts.
(2) A warranty may be express or implied.
(3) A warranty, as above defined, is a condition which must be exactly complied with, whether it be material to the risk or not. If it be not so complied with, then, subject to any express provision in the policy, the insurer is discharged from liability as from the date of the breach of warranty, but without prejudice to any liability incurred by him before that date.

[3081]
34 When breach of warranty excused
(1) Non-compliance with a warranty is excused when, by reason of a change of circumstances, the warranty ceases to be applicable to the circumstances of the contract, or when compliance with the warranty is rendered unlawful by any subsequent law.
(2) Where a warranty is broken, the assured cannot avail himself of the defence that the breach has been remedied, and the warranty complied with, before loss.
(3) A breach of warranty may be waived by the insurer.

[3082]
35 Express warranties
(1) An express warranty may be in any form of words from which the intention to warrant is to be inferred.
(2) An express warranty must be included in, or written upon, the policy, or must be contained in some document incorporated by reference into the policy.
(3) An express warranty does not exclude an implied warranty, unless it be inconsistent therewith.

[3083]
36 Warranty of neutrality
(1) Where insurable property, whether ship or goods, is expressly warranted neutral, there is an implied condition that the property shall have a neutral character at the commencement of the risk, and that, so far as the assured can control the matter, its neutral character shall be preserved during the risk.
(2) Where a ship is expressly warranted "neutral" there is also an implied condition that, so far as the assured can control the matter, she shall be properly documented, that is to say, that she shall carry the necessary papers to establish her neutrality, and that she shall not falsify or suppress her papers, or use simulated papers. If any loss occurs through breach of this condition, the insurer may avoid the contract.

[3084]
37 No implied warranty of nationality
There is no implied warranty as to the nationality of a ship, or that her nationality shall not be changed during the risk.

[3085]
38 Warranty of good safety
Where the subject-matter insured is warranted "well" or "in good safety" on a particular day, it is sufficient if it be safe at any time during that day.

[3086]
39 Warranty of seaworthiness of ship
(1) In a voyage policy there is an implied warranty that at the commencement of the voyage the ship shall be seaworthy for the purpose of the particular adventure insured.
(2) Where the policy attaches while the ship is in port, there is also an implied warranty that she shall, at the commencement of the risk, be reasonably fit to encounter the ordinary perils of the port.
(3) Where the policy relates to a voyage which is performed in different stages, during which the ship requires different kinds of or further preparation or equipment, there is an implied warranty that at the commencement of each stage the ship is seaworthy in respect of such preparation or equipment for the purposes of that stage.
(4) A ship is deemed to be seaworthy when she is reasonably fit in all respects to encounter the ordinary perils of the seas of the adventure insured.

(5) In a time policy there is no implied warranty that the ship shall be seaworthy at any stage of the adventure, but where, with the privity of the assured, the ship is sent to sea in an unseaworthy state, the insurer is not liable for any loss attributable to unseaworthiness.

[3087]
40 No implied warranty that goods are seaworthy
(1) In a policy on goods or other moveables there is no implied warranty that the goods or moveables are seaworthy.
(2) In a voyage policy on goods or other moveables there is an implied warranty that at the commencement of the voyage the ship is not only seaworthy as a ship, but also that she is reasonably fit to carry the goods or other moveables to the destination contemplated by the policy.

[3088]
41 Warranty of legality
There is an implied warranty that the adventure insured is a lawful one, and that, so far as the assured can control the matter, the adventure shall be carried out in a lawful manner.

The Voyage

[3089]
42 Implied condition as to commencement of risk
(1) Where the subject-matter is insured by a voyage policy "at and from" or "from" a particular place, it is not necessary that the ship should be at that place when the contract is concluded, but there is an implied condition that the adventure shall be commenced within a reasonable time, and that if the adventure be not so commenced the insurer may avoid the contract.
(2) The implied condition may be negatived by showing that the delay was caused by circumstances known to the insurer before the contract was concluded, or by showing that he waived the condition.

[3090]
43 Alteration of port of departure
Where the place of departure is specified by the policy, and the ship instead of sailing from that place sails from any other place, the risk does not attach.

[3091]
44 Sailing for different destination
Where the destination is specified in the policy, and the ship, instead of sailing for that destination, sails for any other destination, the risk does not attach.

[3092]
45 Change of voyage
(1) Where, after the commencement of the risk, the destination of the ship is voluntarily changed from the destination contemplated by the policy, there is said to be a change of voyage.
(2) Unless the policy otherwise provides, where there is a change of voyage, the insurer is discharged from liability as from the time of change, that is to say, as from the time when the determination to change it is manifested; and it is immaterial that the ship may not in fact have left the course of voyage contemplated by the policy when the loss occurs.

[3093]
46 Deviation
(1) Where a ship, without lawful excuse, deviates from the voyage contemplated by the policy, the insurer is discharged from liability as from the time of deviation, and it is immaterial that the ship may have regained her route before any loss occurs.
(2) There is a deviation from the voyage contemplated by the policy—
(a) Where the course of the voyage is specifically designated by the policy, and that course is departed from; or
(b) Where the course of the voyage is not specifically designated by the policy, but the usual and customary course is departed from.
(3) The intention to deviate is immaterial; there must be a deviation in fact to discharge the insurer from his liability under the contract.

[3094]
47 Several ports of discharge
(1) Where several ports of discharge are specified by the policy, the ship may proceed to all or any of them, but, in the absence of any usage or sufficient cause to the contrary, she must proceed to them, or such of them as she goes to, in the order designated by the policy. If she does not there is a deviation.

(2) Where the policy is to "ports of discharge", within a given area, which are not named, the ship must, in the absence of any usage or sufficient cause to the contrary, proceed to them, or such of them as she goes to, in their geographical order. If she does not there is a deviation.

[3095]
48 Delay in voyage
In the case of a voyage policy, the adventure insured must be prosecuted throughout its course with reasonable dispatch, and, if without lawful excuse it is not so prosecuted, the insurer is discharged from liability as from the time when the delay became unreasonable.

[3096]
49 Excuses for deviation or delay
(1) Deviation or delay in prosecuting the voyage contemplated by the policy is excused—
- (a) Where authorised by any special term in the policy; or
- (b) Where caused by circumstances beyond the control of the master and his employer; or
- (c) Where reasonably necessary in order to comply with an express or implied warranty; or
- (d) Where reasonably necessary for the safety of the ship or subject-matter insured; or
- (e) For the purpose of saving human life, or aiding a ship in distress where human life may be in danger; or
- (f) Where reasonably necessary for the purpose of obtaining medical or surgical aid for any person on board the ship; or
- (g) Where caused by the barratrous conduct of the master or crew, if barratry be one of the perils insured against.

(2) When the cause excusing the deviation or delay ceases to operate, the ship must resume her course, and prosecute her voyage, with reasonable dispatch.

Assignment of Policy

[3097]
50 When and how policy is assignable
(1) A marine policy is assignable unless it contains terms expressly prohibiting assignment. It may be assigned either before or after loss.
(2) Where a marine policy has been assigned so as to pass the beneficial interest in such policy, the assignee of the policy is entitled to sue thereon in his own name; and the defendant is entitled to make any defence arising out of the contract which he would have been entitled to make if the action had been brought in the name of the person by or on behalf of whom the policy was effected.
(3) A marine policy may be assigned by indorsement thereon or in other customary manner.

[3098]
51 Assured who has no interest cannot assign
Where the assured has parted with or lost his interest in the subject-matter insured, and has not, before or at the time of so doing, expressly or impliedly agreed to assign the policy, any subsequent assignment of the policy is inoperative:

Provided that nothing in this section affects the assignment of a policy after loss.

The Premium

[3099]
52 When premium payable
Unless otherwise agreed, the duty of the assured or his agent to pay the premium, and the duty of the insurer to issue the policy to the assured or his agent, are concurrent conditions, and the insurer is not bound to issue the policy until payment or tender of the premium.

[3100]
53 Policy effected through broker
(1) Unless otherwise agreed, where a marine policy is effected on behalf of the assured by a broker, the broker is directly responsible to the insurer for the premium, and the insurer is directly responsible to the assured for the amount which may be payable in respect of losses, or in respect of returnable premium.
(2) Unless otherwise agreed, the broker has, as against the assured, a lien upon the policy for the amount of the premium and his charges in respect of effecting the policy; and, where he has dealt with the person who employs him as a principal, he has also a lien on the policy in respect of any balance on any insurance account which may be due to him from such person, unless when the debt was incurred he had reason to believe that such person was only an agent.

[3101]

54 Effect of receipt on policy

Where a marine policy effected on behalf of the assured by a broker acknowledges the receipt of the premium, such acknowledgment is, in the absence of fraud, conclusive as between the insurer and the assured, but not as between the insurer and broker.

Loss and Abandonment

[3102]

55 Included and excluded losses

(1) Subject to the provisions of this Act, and unless the policy otherwise provides, the insurer is liable for any loss proximately caused by a peril insured against, but, subject as aforesaid, he is not liable for any loss which is not proximately caused by a peril insured against.

(2) In particular,—

(a) The insurer is not liable for any loss attributable to the wilful misconduct of the assured, but, unless the policy otherwise provides, he is liable for any loss proximately caused by a peril insured against, even though the loss would not have happened but for the misconduct or negligence of the master or crew;

(b) Unless the policy otherwise provides, the insurer on ship or goods is not liable for any loss proximately caused by delay, although the delay be caused by a peril insured against;

(c) Unless the policy otherwise provides, the insurer is not liable for ordinary wear and tear, ordinary leakage and breakage, inherent vice or nature of the subject-matter insured, or for any loss proximately caused by rats or vermin, or for any injury to machinery not proximately caused by maritime perils.

[3103]

56 Partial and total loss

(1) A loss may be either total or partial. Any loss other than a total loss, as herein-after defined, is a partial loss.

(2) A total loss may be either an actual total loss, or a constructive total loss.

(3) Unless a different intention appears from the terms of the policy, an insurance against total loss includes a constructive, as well as an actual, total loss.

(4) Where the assured brings an action for a total loss and the evidence proves only a partial loss, he may, unless the policy otherwise provides, recover for a partial loss.

(5) Where goods reach their destination in specie, but by reason of obliteration of marks, or otherwise, they are incapable of identification, the loss, if any, is partial, and not total.

[3104]

57 Actual total loss

(1) Where the subject-matter insured is destroyed, or so damaged as to cease to be a thing of the kind insured, or where the assured is irretrievably deprived thereof, there is an actual total loss.

(2) In the case of an actual total loss no notice of abandonment need be given.

[3105]

58 Missing ship

Where the ship concerned in the adventure is missing, and after the lapse of a reasonable time no news of her has been received, an actual total loss may be presumed.

[3106]

59 Effect of transhipment, etc

Where, by a peril insured against, the voyage is interrupted at an intermediate port or place, under such circumstances as, apart from any special stipulation in the contract of affreightment, to justify the master in landing and re-shipping the goods or other moveables, or in transhipping them, and sending them on to their destination, the liability of the insurer continues, notwithstanding the landing or transhipment.

[3107]

60 Constructive total loss defined

(1) Subject to any express provision in the policy, there is a constructive total loss where the subject-matter insured is reasonably abandoned on account of its actual total loss appearing to be unavoidable, or because it could not be preserved from actual total loss without an expenditure which would exceed its value when the expenditure had been incurred.

(2) In particular, there is a constructive total loss—

(i) Where the assured is deprived of the possession of his ship or goods by a peril insured against, and (a) it is unlikely that he can recover the ship or goods, as the case may be, or (b) the cost of recovering the ship or goods, as the case may be, would exceed their value when recovered; or

(ii) In the case of damage to a ship, where she is so damaged by a peril insured against that the cost of repairing the damage would exceed the value of the ship when repaired.

In estimating the cost of repairs, no deduction is to be made in respect of general average contributions to those repairs payable by other interests, but account is to be taken of the expense of future salvage operations and of any future general average contributions to which the ship would be liable if repaired; or

(iii) In the case of damage to goods, where the cost of repairing the damage and forwarding the goods to their destination would exceed their value on arrival.

[3108]
61 Effect of constructive total loss
Where there is a constructive total loss the assured may either treat the loss as a partial loss, or abandon the subject-matter insured to the insurer and treat the loss as if it were an actual total loss.

[3109]
62 Notice of abandonment
(1) Subject to the provisions of this section, where the assured elects to abandon the subject-matter insured to the insurer, he must give notice of abandonment. If he fails to do so the loss can only be treated as a partial loss.
(2) Notice of abandonment may be given in writing, or by word of mouth, or partly in writing and partly by word of mouth, and may be given in terms which indicate the intention of the assured to abandon his insured interest in the subject-matter insured unconditionally to the insurer.
(3) Notice of abandonment must be given with reasonable diligence after the receipt of reliable information of the loss, but where the information is of a doubtful character the assured is entitled to a reasonable time to make inquiry.
(4) Where notice of abandonment is properly given, the rights of the assured are not prejudiced by the fact that the insurer refuses to accept the abandonment.
(5) The acceptance of an abandonment may be either express or implied from the conduct of the insurer. The mere silence of the insurer after notice is not an acceptance.
(6) Where a notice of abandonment is accepted the abandonment is irrevocable. The acceptance of the notice conclusively admits liability for the loss and the sufficiency of the notice.
(7) Notice of abandonment is unnecessary where, at the time when the assured receives information of the loss, there would be no possibility of benefit to the insurer if notice were given to him.
(8) Notice of abandonment may be waived by the insurer.
(9) Where an insurer has re-insured his risk, no notice of abandonment need be given by him.

[3110]
63 Effect of abandonment
(1) Where there is a valid abandonment the insurer is entitled to take over the interest of the assured in whatever may remain of the subject-matter insured, and all proprietary rights incidental thereto.
(2) Upon the abandonment of a ship, the insurer thereof is entitled to any freight in course of being earned, and which is earned by her subsequent to the casualty causing the loss, less the expenses of earning it incurred after the casualty; and, where the ship is carrying the owner's goods, the insurer is entitled to a reasonable remuneration for the carriage of them subsequent to the casualty causing the loss.

Partial Losses (including Salvage and General Average and Particular Charges)

[3111]
64 Particular average loss
(1) A particular average loss is a partial loss of the subject-matter insured, caused by a peril insured against, and which is not a general average loss.
(2) Expenses incurred by or on behalf of the assured for the safety or preservation of the subject-matter insured, other than general average and salvage charges, are called particular charges. Particular charges are not included in particular average.

[3112]
65 Salvage charges
(1) Subject to any express provision in the policy, salvage charges incurred in preventing a loss by perils insured against may be recovered as a loss by those perils.

(2) "Salvage charges" means the charges recoverable under maritime law by a salvor independently of contract. They do not include the expenses of services in the nature of salvage rendered by the assured or his agents, or any person employed for hire by them, for the purpose of averting a peril insured against. Such expenses, where properly incurred, may be recovered as particular charges or as a general average loss, according to the circumstances under which they were incurred.

[3113]
66 General average loss

(1) A general average loss is a loss caused by or directly consequential on a general average act. It includes a general average expenditure as well as a general average sacrifice.
(2) There is a general average act where any extraordinary sacrifice or expenditure is voluntarily and reasonably made or incurred in time of peril for the purpose of preserving the property imperilled in the common adventure.
(3) Where there is a general average loss, the party on whom it falls is entitled, subject to the conditions imposed by maritime law, to a rateable contribution from the other parties interested, and such contribution is called a general average contribution.
(4) Subject to any express provision in the policy, where the assured has incurred a general average expenditure, he may recover from the insurer in respect of the proportion of the loss which falls upon him; and, in the case of a general average sacrifice, he may recover from the insurer in respect of the whole loss without having enforced his right of contribution from the other parties liable to contribute.
(5) Subject to any express provision in the policy, where the assured has paid, or is liable to pay, a general average contribution in respect of the subject insured, he may recover therefor from the insurer.
(6) In the absence of express stipulation, the insurer is not liable for any general average loss or contribution where the loss was not incurred for the purpose of avoiding, or in connexion with the avoidance of, a peril insured against.
(7) Where ship, freight, and cargo, or any two of those interests, are owned by the same assured, the liability of the insurer in respect of general average losses or contributions is to be determined as if those subjects were owned by different persons.

Measure of Indemnity

[3114]
67 Extent of liability of insurer for loss

(1) The sum which the assured can recover in respect of a loss on a policy by which he is insured, in the case of an unvalued policy to the full extent of the insurable value, or, in the case of a valued policy to the full extent of the value fixed by the policy, is called the measure of indemnity.
(2) Where there is a loss recoverable under the policy, the insurer, or each insurer if there be more than one, is liable for such proportion of the measure of indemnity as the amount of his subscription bears to the value fixed by the policy in the case of a valued policy, or to the insurable value in the case of an unvalued policy.

[3115]
68 Total loss

Subject to the provisions of this Act and to any express provision in the policy, where there is a total loss of the subject-matter insured,—

(1) If the policy be a valued policy, the measure of indemnity is the sum fixed by the policy:
(2) If the policy be an unvalued policy, the measure of indemnity is the insurable value of the subject-matter insured.

[3116]
69 Partial loss of ship

Where a ship is damaged, but is not totally lost, the measure of indemnity, subject to any express provision in the policy, is as follows:—

(1) Where the ship has been repaired, the assured is entitled to the reasonable cost of the repairs, less the customary deductions, but not exceeding the sum insured in respect of any one casualty:
(2) Where the ship has been only partially repaired, the assured is entitled to the reasonable cost of such repairs, computed as above, and also to be indemnified for the reasonable depreciation, if any, arising from the unrepaired damage, provided that the aggregate amount shall not exceed the cost of repairing the whole damage, computed as above:

(3) Where the ship has not been repaired, and has not been sold in her damaged state during the risk, the assured is entitled to be indemnified for the reasonable depreciation arising from the unrepaired damage, but not exceeding the reasonable cost of repairing such damage, computed as above.

[3117]
70 Partial loss of freight
Subject to any express provision in the policy, where there is a partial loss of freight, the measure of indemnity is such proportion of the sum fixed by the policy in the case of a valued policy, or of the insurable value in the case of an unvalued policy, as the proportion of freight lost by the assured bears to the whole freight at the risk of the assured under the policy.

[3118]
71 Partial loss of goods, merchandise, etc
Where there is a partial loss of goods, merchandise, or other moveables, the measure of indemnity, subject to any express provision in the policy, is as follows:—

(1) Where part of the goods, merchandise or other moveables insured by a valued policy is totally lost, the measure of indemnity is such proportion of the sum fixed by the policy as the insurable value of the part lost bears to the insurable value of the whole, ascertained as in the case of an unvalued policy:

(2) Where part of the goods, merchandise, or other moveables insured by an unvalued policy is totally lost, the measure of indemnity is the insurable value of the part lost, ascertained as in case of total loss:

(3) Where the whole or any part of the goods or merchandise insured has been delivered damaged at its destination, the measure of indemnity is such proportion of the sum fixed by the policy in the case of a valued policy, or of the insurable value in the case of an unvalued policy, as the difference between the gross sound and damaged values at the place of arrival bears to the gross sound value:

(4) "Gross value" means the wholesale price or, if there be no such price, the estimated value, with, in either case, freight, landing charges, and duty paid beforehand; provided that, in the case of goods or merchandise customarily sold in bond, the bonded price is deemed to be the gross value. "Gross proceeds" means the actual price obtained at a sale where all charges on sale are paid by the sellers.

[3119]
72 Apportionment of valuation
(1) Where different species of property are insured under a single valuation, the valuation must be apportioned over the different species in proportion to their respective insurable values, as in the case of an unvalued policy. The insured value of any part of a species is such proportion of the total insured value of the same as the insurable value of the part bears to the insurable value of the whole, ascertained in both cases as provided by this Act.
(2) Where a valuation has to be apportioned, and particulars of the prime cost of each separate species, quality, or description of goods cannot be ascertained, the division of the valuation may be made over the net arrived sound values of the different species, qualities, or descriptions of goods.

[3120]
73 General average contributions and salvage charges
(1) Subject to any express provision in the policy, where the assured has paid, or is liable for, any general average contribution, the measure of indemnity is the full amount of such contribution, if the subject-matter liable to contribution is insured for its full contributory value; but, if such subject-matter be not insured for its full contributory value, or if only part of it be insured, the indemnity payable by the insurer must be reduced in proportion to the under insurance, and where there has been a particular average loss which constitutes a deduction from the contributory value, and for which the insurer is liable, that amount must be deducted from the insured value in order to ascertain what the insurer is liable to contribute.
(2) Where the insurer is liable for salvage charges the extent of his liability must be determined on the like principle.

[3121]
74 Liabilities to third parties
Where the assured has effected an insurance in express terms against any liability to a third party, the measure of indemnity, subject to any express provision in the policy, is the amount paid or payable by him to such third party in respect of such liability.

[3122]
75 General provisions as to measure of indemnity

(1) Where there has been a loss in respect of any subject-matter not expressly provided for in the foregoing provisions of this Act, the measure of indemnity shall be ascertained, as nearly as may be, in accordance with those provisions, in so far as applicable to the particular case.
(2) Nothing in the provisions of this Act relating to the measure of indemnity shall affect the rules relating to double insurance, or prohibit the insurer from disproving interest wholly or in part, or from showing that at the time of the loss the whole or any part of the subject-matter insured was not at risk under the policy.

[3123]
76 Particular average warranties

(1) Where the subject-matter insured is warranted free from particular average, the assured cannot recover for a loss of part, other than a loss incurred by a general average sacrifice unless the contract contained in the policy be apportionable; but, if the contract be apportionable, the assured may recover for a total loss of any apportionable part.
(2) Where the subject-matter insured is warranted free from particular average, either wholly or under a certain percentage, the insurer is nevertheless liable for salvage charges, and for particular charges and other expenses properly incurred pursuant to the provisions of the suing and labouring clause in order to avert a loss insured against.
(3) Unless the policy otherwise provides, where the subject-matter insured is warranted free from particular average under a specified percentage, a general average loss cannot be added to a particular average loss to make up the specified percentage.
(4) For the purpose of ascertaining whether the specified percentage has been reached, regard shall be had only to the actual loss suffered by the subject-matter insured. Particular charges and the expenses of and incidental to ascertaining and proving the loss must be excluded.

[3124]
77 Successive losses

(1) Unless the policy otherwise provides, and subject to the provisions of this Act, the insurer is liable for successive losses, even though the total amount of such losses may exceed the sum insured.
(2) Where, under the same policy, a partial loss, which has not been repaired or otherwise made good, is followed by a total loss, the assured can only recover in respect of the total loss:
Provided that nothing in this section shall affect the liability of the insurer under the suing and labouring clause.

[3125]
78 Suing and labouring clause

(1) Where the policy contains a suing and labouring clause, the engagement thereby entered into is deemed to be supplementary to the contract of insurance, and the assured may recover from the insurer any expenses properly incurred pursuant to the clause, notwithstanding that the insurer may have paid for a total loss, or that the subject-matter may have been warranted free from particular average, either wholly or under a certain percentage.
(2) General average losses and contributions and salvage charges, as defined by this Act, are not recoverable under the suing and labouring clause.
(3) Expenses incurred for the purpose of averting or diminishing any loss not covered by the policy are not recoverable under the suing and labouring clause.
(4) It is the duty of the assured and his agents, in all cases, to take such measures as may be reasonable for the purpose of averting or minimising a loss.

Rights of Insurer on Payment

[3126]
79 Right of subrogation

(1) Where the insurer pays for a total loss, either of the whole, or in the case of goods of any apportionable part, of the subject-matter insured, he thereupon becomes entitled to take over the interest of the assured in whatever may remain of the subject-matter so paid for, and he is thereby subrogated to all the rights and remedies of the assured in and in respect of that subject-matter as from the time of the casualty causing the loss.
(2) Subject to the foregoing provisions, where the insurer pays for a partial loss, he acquires no title to the subject-matter insured, or such part of it as may remain, but he is thereupon subrogated to all rights and remedies of the assured in and in respect of the subject-matter insured as from the time of the casualty causing the loss, in so far as the assured has been indemnified, according to this Act, by such payment for the loss.

[3127]
80 Right of contribution
(1) Where the assured is over-insured by double insurance, each insurer is bound, as between himself and the other insurers, to contribute rateably to the loss in proportion to the amount for which he is liable under his contract.
(2) If any insurer pays more than his proportion of the loss, he is entitled to maintain an action for contribution against the other insurers, and is entitled to the like remedies as a surety who has paid more than his proportion of the debt.

[3128]
81 Effect of under insurance
Where the assured is insured for an amount less than the insurable value or, in the case of a valued policy, for an amount less than the policy valuation, he is deemed to be his own insurer in respect of the uninsured balance.

Return of Premium

[3129]
82 Enforcement of return
Where the premium or a proportionate part thereof is, by this Act, declared to be returnable,—
(a) If already paid, it may be recovered by the assured from the insurer; and
(b) If unpaid, it may be retained by the assured or his agent.

[3130]
83 Return by agreement
Where the policy contains a stipulation for the return of the premium, or a proportionate part thereof, on the happening of a certain event, and that event happens, the premium, or, as the case may be, the proportionate part thereof, is thereupon returnable to the assured.

[3131]
84 Return for failure of consideration
(1) Where the consideration for the payment of the premium totally fails, and there has been no fraud or illegality on the part of the assured or his agents, the premium is thereupon returnable to the assured.
(2) Where the consideration for the payment of the premium is apportionable and there is a total failure of any apportionable part of the consideration, a proportionate part of the premium is, under the like conditions, thereupon returnable to the assured.
(3) In particular—
(a) Where the policy is void, or is avoided by the insurer as from the commencement of the risk, the premium is returnable, provided that there has been no fraud or illegality on the part of the assured; but if the risk is not apportionable, and has once attached, the premium is not returnable;
(b) Where the subject-matter insured, or part thereof, has never been imperilled, the premium, or, as the case may be, a proportionate part thereof, is returnable:
Provided that where the subject-matter has been insured "lost or not lost" and has arrived in safety at the time when the contract is concluded, the premium is not returnable unless, at such time, the insurer knew of the safe arrival.
(c) Where the assured has no insurable interest throughout the currency of the risk, the premium is returnable, provided that this rule does not apply to a policy effected by way of gaming or wagering;
(d) Where the assured has a defeasible interest which is terminated during the currency of the risk, the premium is not returnable;
(e) Where the assured has over-insured under an unvalued policy, a proportionate part of the premium is returnable;
(f) Subject to the foregoing provisions, where the assured has over-insured by double insurance, a proportionate part of the several premiums is returnable:
Provided that, if the policies are effected at different times, and any earlier policy has at any time borne the entire risk, or if a claim has been paid on the policy in respect of the full sum insured thereby, no premium is returnable in respect of that policy, and when the double insurance is effected knowingly by the assured no premium is returnable.

Mutual Insurance

[3132]
85 Modification of Act in case of mutual insurance
(1) Where two or more persons mutually agree to insure each other against marine losses there is said to be a mutual insurance.

(2) The provisions of this Act relating to the premium do not apply to mutual insurance, but a guarantee, or such other arrangement as may be agreed upon, may be substituted for the premium.
(3) The provisions of this Act, in so far as they may be modified by the agreement of the parties, may in the case of mutual insurance be modified by the terms of the policies issued by the association, or by the rules and regulations of the association.
(4) Subject to the exceptions mentioned in this section, the provisions of this Act apply to a mutual insurance.

Supplemental

[3133]
86 Ratification by assured
Where a contract of marine insurance is in good faith effected by one person on behalf of another, the person on whose behalf it is effected may ratify the contract even after he is aware of a loss.

[3134]
87 Implied obligations varied by agreement or usage
(1) Where any right, duty, or liability would arise under a contract of marine insurance by implication of law, it may be negatived or varied by express agreement, or by usage, if the usage be such as to bind both parties to the contract.
(2) The provisions of this section extend to any right, duty, or liability declared by this Act which may be lawfully modified by agreement.

[3135]
88 Reasonable time, etc, a question of fact
Where by this Act any reference is made to reasonable time, reasonable premium, or reasonable diligence, the question what is reasonable is a question of fact.

[3136]
89 Slip as evidence
Where there is a duly stamped policy, reference may be made, as heretofore, to the slip or covering note, in any legal proceeding.

[3137]
90 Interpretation of terms
In this Act, unless the context or subject-matter otherwise requires,—
"Action" includes counter-claim and set off:
"Freight" includes the profit derivable by a shipowner from the employment of his ship to carry his own goods or moveables, as well as freight payable by a third party, but does not include passage money:
"Moveables" means any moveable tangible property, other than the ship, and includes money, valuable securities, and other documents:
"Policy" means a marine policy.

[3138]
91 Savings
(1) Nothing in this Act, or in any repeal effected thereby, shall affect—
- (a) The provisions of the Stamp Act 1891, or any enactment for the time being in force relating to the revenue;
- (b) The provisions of the Companies Act 1862, or any enactment amending or substituted for the same;
- (c) The provisions of any statute not expressly repealed by this Act.

(2) The rules of the common law including the law merchant, save in so far as they are inconsistent with the express provisions of this Act, shall continue to apply to contracts of marine insurance.

NOTES
Companies Act 1862: That Act was repealed by the Companies (Consolidation) Act 1908; see now the Companies Act 1985.

92, 93 (*Repealed by the Statute Law Revision Act 1927.*)

[3139]

94 Short title

This Act may be cited as the Marine Insurance Act 1906.

SCHEDULES

FIRST SCHEDULE

FORM OF POLICY

Section 30

[3140]

Be it known that as well in own name as for and in the name and names of all and every other person or persons to whom the same doth, may, or shall appertain, in part or in all doth make assurance and cause and them, and every of them, to be insured lost or not lost, at and from

Upon any kind of goods and merchandise, and also upon the body, tackle, apparel, ordnance, munition, artillery, boat, and other furniture, of and in the good ship or vessel called the whereof is master under God, for this present voyage, or whosoever else shall go for master in the said ship, or by whatsoever other name or names the said ship, or the master thereof, is or shall be named or called; beginning the adventure upon the said goods and merchandises from the loading thereof aboard the said ship.

upon the said ship, etc

and so shall continue and endure, during her abode there, upon the said ship, etc

And further, until the said ship, with all her ordnance, tackle, apparel, etc, and goods and merchandises whatsoever shall be arrived at

upon the said ship, etc, until she hath moored at anchor twenty-four hours in good safety; and upon the goods and merchandises, until the same be there discharged and safely landed. And it shall be lawful for the said ship, etc, in this voyage to proceed and sail to and touch and stay at any ports or places whatsoever

without prejudice to this insurance. The said ship, etc, goods and merchandises, etc, for so much as concerns the assured by agreement between the assured and assurers in this policy, are and shall be valued at

Touching the adventures and perils which we the assurers are contented to bear and do take upon us in this voyage: they are of the seas, men of war, fire, enemies, pirates, rovers, thieves, jettisons, letters of mart and countermart, surprisals, takings at sea, arrests, restraints, and detainments of all kings, princes, and people, of what nation, condition, or quality soever, barratry of the master and mariners, and of all other perils, losses, and misfortunes, that have or shall come to the hurt, detriment, or damage of the said goods and merchandises, and ship, etc, or any part thereof. And in case of any loss or misfortune it shall be lawful to the assured, their factors, servants and assigns, to sue, labour, and travel for, in and about the defence, safeguards, and recovery of the said goods and merchandises, and ship, etc, or any part thereof, without prejudice to this insurance; to the charges whereof we, the assurers, will contribute each one according to the rate and quantity of his sum herein assured. And it is especially declared and agreed that no acts of the insurer or insured in recovering, saving, or preserving the property insured shall be considered as a waiver, or acceptance of abandonment. And it is agreed by us, the insurers, that this writing or policy of assurance shall be of as much force and effect as the surest writing or policy of assurance heretofore made in Lombard Street, or in the Royal Exchange, or elsewhere in London. And so we, the assurers, are contented, and do hereby promise and bind ourselves, each one for his own part, our heirs, executors, and goods to the assured, their executors, administrators, and assigns, for the true performance of the premises, confessing ourselves paid the consideration due unto us for this assurance by the assured, at and after the rate of

IN WITNESS whereof we, the assurers, have subscribed our names and sums assured in London.

N.B.—Corn, fish, salt, fruit, flour, and seed are warranted free from average, unless general, or the ship be stranded—sugar, tobacco, hemp, flax, hides and skins are warranted free from average, under five pounds per cent., and all other goods, also the ship and freight, are warranted free from average, under three pounds per cent. unless general, or the ship be stranded.

RULES FOR CONSTRUCTION OF POLICY

The following are the rules referred to by this Act for the construction of a policy in the above or other like form, where the context does not otherwise require:—

1. Where the subject-matter is insured "lost or not lost," and the loss has occurred before the contract is concluded, the risk attaches, unless at such time the assured was aware of the loss, and the insurer was not.

2. Where the subject-matter is insured "from" a particular place, the risk does not attach until the ship starts on the voyage insured.

3.—(a) Where a ship is insured "at and from" a particular place, and she is at that place in good safety when the contract is concluded, the risk attaches immediately.
(b) If she be not at that place when the contract is concluded, the risk attaches as soon as she arrives there in good safety, and, unless the policy otherwise provides, it is immaterial that she is covered by another policy for a specified time after arrival.
(c) Where chartered freight is insured "at and from" a particular place, and the ship is at that place in good safety when the contract is concluded the risk attaches immediately. If she be not there when the contract is concluded, the risk attaches as soon as she arrives there in good safety.
(d) Where freight, other than chartered freight, is payable without special conditions and is insured "at and from" a particular place, the risk attaches pro rata as the goods or merchandise are shipped; provided that if there be cargo in readiness which belongs to the shipowner, or which some other person has contracted with him to ship, the risk attaches as soon as the ship is ready to receive such cargo.

4. Where goods or other moveables are insured "from the loading thereof," the risk does not attach until such goods or moveables are actually on board, and the insurer is not liable for them while in transit from the shore to ship.

5. Where the risk on goods or other moveables continues until they are "safely landed," they must be landed in the customary manner and within a reasonable time after arrival at the port of discharge, and if they are not so landed the risk ceases.

6. In the absence of any further license or usage, the liberty to touch and stay "at any port or place whatsoever" does not authorise the ship to depart from the course of her voyage from the port of departure to the port of destination.

7. The term "perils of the seas" refers only to fortuitous accidents or casualties of the seas. It does not include the ordinary action of the winds and waves.

8. The term "pirates" includes passengers who mutiny and rioters who attack the ship from the shore.

9. The term "thieves" does not cover clandestine theft or a theft committed by any one of the ship's company, whether crew or passengers.

10. The term "arrests, etc, of kings, princes, and people" refers to political or executive acts, and does not include a loss caused by riot or by ordinary judicial process.

11. The term "barratry" includes every wrongful act wilfully committed by the master or crew to the prejudice of the owner, or, as the case may be, the charterer.

12. The term "all other perils" includes only perils similar in kind to the perils specifically mentioned in the policy.

13. The term "average unless general" means a partial loss of the subject-matter insured other than a general average loss, and does not include "particular charges."

14. Where the ship has stranded, the insurer is liable for the excepted losses, although the loss is not attributable to the stranding, provided that when the stranding takes place the risk has attached and, if the policy be on goods, that the damaged goods are on board.

15. The term "ship" includes the hull, materials and outfit, stores and provisions for the officers and crew, and, in the case of vessels engaged in a special trade, the ordinary fittings requisite for the trade, and also, in the case of a steamship, the machinery, boilers, and coals and engine stores, if owned by the assured.

16. The term "freight" includes the profit derivable by a shipowner from the employment of his ship to carry his own goods or moveables, as well as freight payable by a third party, but does not include passage money.

17. The term "goods" means goods in the nature of merchandise, and does not include personal effects or provisions and stores for use on board.

In the absence of any usage to the contrary, deck cargo and living animals must be insured specifically, and not under the general denomination of goods.

(*Sch 2 repealed by the Statue Law Revision Act 1927.*)

MARINE INSURANCE (GAMBLING POLICIES) ACT 1909

(9 Edw 7 c 12)

An Act to prohibit Gambling on Loss by Maritime Perils

[20 October 1909]

[3141]

1 Prohibition of gambling on loss by maritime perils

(1) If—

(a) any person effects a contract of marine insurance without having any bona fide interest, direct or indirect, either in the safe arrival of the ship in relation to which the contract is made or in the safety or preservation of the subject- matter insured, or a bona fide expectation of acquiring such an interest; or

(b) any person in the employment of the owner of a ship, not being a part owner of the ship, effects a contract of marine insurance in relation to the ship, and the contract is made "interest or no interest," or "without further proof of interest than the policy itself," or "without benefit of salvage to the insurer," or subject to any other like term,

the contract shall be deemed to be a contract by way of gambling on loss by maritime perils, and the person effecting it shall be guilty of an offence, and shall be liable, on summary conviction, to imprisonment . . . for a term not exceeding six months or to a fine not exceeding [level 3 on the standard scale], and in either case to forfeit to the Crown any money he may receive under the contract.

(2) Any broker or other person through whom, and any insurer with whom, any such contract is effected shall be guilty of an offence and liable on summary conviction to the like penalties if he acted knowing that the contract was by way of gambling on loss by maritime perils within the meaning of this Act.

(3) Proceedings under this Act shall not be instituted without the consent in England of the Attorney-General, in Scotland of the Lord Advocate, and in Ireland of the Attorney-General for Ireland.

(4) Proceedings shall not be instituted under this Act against a person (other than a person in the employment of the owner of the ship in relation to which the contract was made) alleged to have effected a contract by way of gambling on loss by maritime perils until an opportunity has been afforded him of showing that the contract was not such a contract as aforesaid, and any information given by that person for that purpose shall not be admissible in evidence against him in any prosecution under this Act.

(5) If proceedings under this Act are taken against any person (other than a person in the employment of the owner of the ship in relation to which the contract was made) for effecting such a contract, and the contract was made "interest or no interest," or "without further proof of interest than the policy itself," or "without benefit of salvage to the insurer," or subject to any other like term, the contract shall be deemed to be a contract by way of gambling on loss by maritime perils unless the contrary is proved.

(6) For the purpose of giving jurisdiction under this Act, every offence shall be deemed to have been committed either in the place in which the same actually was committed or in any place in which the offender may be.

(7) Any person aggrieved by an order or decision of a court of summary jurisdiction under this Act, may appeal to [the Crown Court].

(8) For the purposes of this Act the expression "owner" includes charterer.

(9) Subsection (7) of this section shall not apply to Scotland.

NOTES

Sub-s (1): words omitted repealed by virtue of the Criminal Justice Act 1948, s 1(2); reference to a level on the standard scale substituted by virtue of the Criminal Justice Act 1982, ss 38, 46.

Sub-s (7): words in square brackets substituted by the Courts Act 1971, s 56, Sch 9, Pt I.

[3142]

2 Short title

This Act may be cited as the Marine Insurance (Gambling Policies) Act 1909, and the Marine Insurance Act 1906, and this Act may be cited together as the Marine Insurance Acts 1906 and 1909.

LLOYD'S ACT 1911

(1 & 2 Geo V c lxii)

ARRANGEMENT OF SECTIONS

Preamble		[3143]
1	Short and collective titles	[3144]
2	Definition	[3145]
3	Extension of Objects	[3146]
4	Objects of Society	[3147]
5	Amendment of Act of 1871	[3148]
6	Transfer to Society by Trustees of capital stock	[3149]
7	Purposes for which capital stock, &c to be held by Society	[3150]
8	Society may act as Trustee for certain purposes	[3151]
9	Powers to Society with reference to guarantees	[3152]
14	Notices to Members	[3153]
15	Costs of Act	[3154]

An Act to Extend the Objects of and confer Further Powers on Lloyd's and to Amend Lloyd's Act 1871

[18 August 1911]

[3143]
Preamble

WHEREAS by Lloyd's Act 1871 (in this Act referred to as "the Act of 1871") certain persons were united into a Society or Corporation for the purposes of that Act and were incorporated by the name of Lloyd's (which incorporated body was in the Act of 1871 and is in this Act referred to as "the Society") and various powers were conferred on the Society by the said Act:

And whereas by the Act of 1871 the objects of the Society were declared inter alia to be the carrying on of the business of marine insurance by Members of the Society and the protection of the interests of Members of the Society and the collection publication and diffusion of intelligence and information:

And whereas further powers were conferred on the Society and further provisions made with reference to the Society by Lloyd's Act 1888 and Lloyd's Signal Stations Act 1888:

And whereas the Members of the Society have in the past carried on at Lloyd's insurance business other than marine insurance and it is expedient that the objects of the Society should be extended to the carrying on of the business of insurance other than marine insurance by Members of the Society and that further powers should be conferred on the Society and the Committee of Lloyd's as hereinafter in this Act provided:

And whereas by the Act of 1871 it was directed that the capital stock of the Society should be transferred to and kept in the names of four Members of the Society as Trustees for the Members of the Society and such capital stock now stands in the names of certain Members of the Society (hereinafter in this Act called "the Trustees of the capital stock") as Trustees for the Society and its Members as in the said Act mentioned and it is expedient that the capital stock should be transferred to and held by the Society:

And whereas in pursuance of the Assurance Companies Act 1909 or the regulations or requirements for the time being of the Society or the Committee or otherwise Members of the Society furnish security in the form of either a deposit with a trust deed or a guarantee or guarantees or partly in the one form and partly in the other which security is available solely for the purpose of meeting their liabilities in respect of policies underwritten by them or on their account at Lloyd's and the Society have in the past acted as Trustee of certain of such trust deeds and guarantees either solely or jointly with others and doubts have arisen as to the power of the Society to so act and it is expedient that the action of the Society in acting as such Trustee in the past should be confirmed and that the Society should be authorised to act as Trustee of any trust deed or guarantee furnished by any Member of the Society as aforesaid:

And whereas it is expedient that the Society should be authorised itself to act as guarantor either solely or jointly with any other guarantor or guarantors as hereinafter in this Act provided and that the Society should in certain cases be authorised to make good any deficiency arising by reason of the default of any guarantor or the insufficiency of any security furnished by Members of the Society as aforesaid:

And whereas the purposes aforesaid cannot be effected without the authority of Parliament:

MAY IT THEREFORE PLEASE YOUR MAJESTY

That it may be Enacted and be it Enacted by the King's Most Excellent Majesty by and with the advice and consent of the Lords Spiritual and Temporal and Commons in this present Parliament assembled and by the authority of the same as follows:—

[3144]
1 Short and collective titles
This Act may be cited as Lloyd's Act 1911 and the Act of 1871 Lloyd's Signal Stations Act 1888 and this Act may be cited and are hereinafter in this Act referred to as Lloyd's Acts 1871 to 1911.

[3145]
2 Definition
In this Act the expression "the Committee" shall mean the Committee of Lloyd's constituted under the Act of 1871.

[3146]
3 Extension of Objects
The objects of the Society are hereby extended so as to include the carrying on of the business of insurance of every description including guarantee business by Members of the Society and the Act of 1871 shall be read and have effect accordingly.

[3147]
4 Objects of Society
Section 10 of the Act of 1871 and Lloyd's Act 1888 are hereby repealed and in lieu thereof the following provision is hereby enacted and shall have effect accordingly:—

The objects of the Society shall be:—

The carrying on by Members of the Society of the business of insurance of every description including guarantee business;

The advancement and protection of the interests of Members of the Society in connection with the business carried on by them as Members of the Society and in respect of shipping and cargoes and freight and other insurable property or insurable interests or otherwise;

The collection publication and diffusion of intelligence and information;

The doing of all things incidental or conducive to the fulfilment of the objects of the Society.

[3148]
5 Amendment of Act of 1871
Sections 20, 24, 31, 39 and 40 of the Act of 1871 shall be read and have effect as if the word "marine" had been omitted from such sections wherever the same occurs in such sections and as if the word "insurance" where the same occurs in those sections included guarantee business.

[3149]
6 Transfer to Society by Trustees of capital stock
Within six months after the passing of this Act the capital stock of the Society shall be transferred by the Trustees of the capital stock to the Society and such Trustees shall on the request of the Society execute and do all such acts and deeds as may be necessary to effect and carry out such transfer and on such transfer being duly made the said Trustees shall be released and discharged from their trust and cease to act as such Trustees and Sections 36, 37 and 38 of the Act of 1871 shall be repealed.

[3150]
[7 Purposes for which capital stock, &c to be held by Society
The Society shall hold the funds and property of the Society and the income therefrom for all or any of the following purposes:—

(a) for defraying the costs, charges and expenses incurred by the Society, the Council or otherwise in the execution and carrying out of Lloyd's Acts 1871 to 1982;

(b) for furthering the objects of the Society;

(c) for making good any default by any member of the Society under any contract of insurance underwritten at Lloyd's which in the opinion of the Council it is in the interests of the members of the Society to make good;

(d) for guaranteeing or securing, in such manner as the Council think fit, any debt or obligation of or binding on the Society, any of its subsidiaries or any other person;

(e) for such other purposes (if any) as may from time to time be prescribed by byelaw;

and subject thereto for the benefit of the members of the Society jointly.]

NOTES
Substituted by the Lloyd's Act 1982, s 15(1)(b).

[3151]
8 Society may act as Trustee for certain purposes
(1) It shall be lawful and shall be deemed always to have been lawful for the Society to act as trustee either solely or jointly with any other person of any trust deed or guarantee or other document relating to the insurance business carried on at Lloyd's by Members of or Annual Subscribers to the Society.
(2) Any trustee or trustees of any such trust deed or guarantee or other document as aforesaid may transfer any trust fund subject to any such trust deed guarantee or document to the Society and assign to the Society the benefit or advantage to which he or they are entitled under any such trust deed guarantee or document and on the execution of such transfer or deed of assignment the Society shall be entitled to such trust fund and to all benefits and advantages under any such trust deed guarantee or document in the same manner and to the same extent and on the same trusts as such trustees held or were entitled to the same.

NOTES
Repealed by the Lloyd's Act 1951, s 5(3), except in relation to the conditions stated in s 5(4)(a), (b) of that Act at **[3171]**.

[3152]
[9 Powers to Society with reference to guarantees
Without prejudice to the provisions of section 7 of this Act the Society may either by itself or jointly with any other guarantor or guarantors guarantee the payment of claims and demands upon contracts of insurance underwritten at Lloyd's and the Society may for such purposes enter into contracts and may apply the funds and property of the Society and the income therefrom or any part thereof for the purpose of discharging any liabilities of the Society under any guarantees or contracts as aforesaid and the powers conferred on the Society by this section may be exercised by the Council in accordance with byelaws made under Lloyd's Act, 1982.]

NOTES
Substituted by the Lloyd's Act 1982, s 15(1)(c).

10–13 (*Repealed by the Lloyd's Act 1982, s 15(1), Sch 3.*)

[3153]
14 Notices to Members
All notices summoning General Meetings and other notices to Members of the Society under the provisions of Lloyd's Acts 1871 to 1911 or of any byelaws under any of such Acts not specially directed by any such Acts or byelaws thereunder to be otherwise given shall be given by posting the same in the rooms at Lloyd's or in such other manner as may be prescribed by the byelaws of the Society.

[3154]
15 Costs of Act
The costs charges and expenses of and incidental to the preparing applying for obtaining and passing of this Act shall be borne and paid by the Society.

(*Schedule repealed by the Lloyd's Act 1951, s 6(2).*)

Part III Statutes

THIRD PARTIES (RIGHTS AGAINST INSURERS) ACT 1930

(20 & 21 Geo 5 c 25)

ARRANGEMENT OF SECTIONS

1	Rights of third parties against insurers on bankruptcy, etc, of the insured	[3155]
2	Duty to give necessary information to third parties	[3156]
3	Settlement between insurers and insured persons	[3157]
3A	Application to limited liability partnerships	[3158]
4	Application to Scotland	[3159]
5	Short title	[3160]

An Act to confer on third parties rights against insurers of third-party risks in the event of the insured becoming insolvent, and in certain other events

[10 July 1930]

[3155]

1 Rights of third parties against insurers on bankruptcy, etc, of the insured

(1) Where under any contract of insurance a person (hereinafter referred to as the insured) is insured against liabilities to third parties which he may incur, then—

(a) in the event of the insured becoming bankrupt or making a composition or arrangement with his creditors; or

(b) in the case of the insured being a company, in the event of a winding-up order [. . .] being made, or a resolution for a voluntary winding-up being passed, with respect to the company, [or of the company entering administration,] or of a receiver or manager of the company's business or undertaking being duly appointed, or of possession being taken, by or on behalf of the holders of any debentures secured by a floating charge, of any property comprised in or subject to the charge [or of [a voluntary arrangement proposed for the purposes of Part I of the Insolvency Act 1986 being approved under that Part]];

if, either before or after that event, any such liability as aforesaid is incurred by the insured, his rights against the insurer under the contract in respect of the liability shall, notwithstanding anything in any Act or rule of law to the contrary, be transferred to and vest in the third party to whom the liability was so incurred.

(2) Where [the estate of any person falls to be administered in accordance with an order under section [421 of the Insolvency Act 1986]], then, if any debt provable in bankruptcy [in Scotland, any claim accepted in the sequestration] is owing by the deceased in respect of a liability against which he was insured under a contract of insurance as being a liability to a third party, the deceased debtor's rights against the insurer under the contract in respect of that liability shall, notwithstanding anything in [any such order], be transferred to and vest in the person to whom the debt is owing.

(3) In so far as any contract of insurance made after the commencement of this Act in respect of any liability of the insured to third parties purports, whether directly or indirectly, to avoid the contract or to alter the rights of the parties thereunder upon the happening to the insured of any of the events specified in paragraph (a) or paragraph (b) of subsection (1) of this section or upon the [estate of any person falling to be administered in accordance with an order under section [421 of the Insolvency Act 1986]], the contract shall be of no effect.

(4) Upon a transfer under subsection (1) or subsection (2) of this section, the insurer shall, subject to the provisions of section three of this Act, be under the same liability to the third party as he would have been under to the insured, but—

(a) if the liability of the insurer to the insured exceeds the liability of the insured to the third party, nothing in this Act shall affect the rights of the insured against the insurer in respect of the excess; and

(b) if the liability of the insurer to the insured is less than the liability of the insured to the third party, nothing in this Act shall affect the rights of the third party against the insured in respect of the balance.

(5) For the purposes of this Act, the expression "liabilities to third parties", in relation to a person insured under any contract of insurance, shall not include any liability of that person in the capacity of insurer under some other contract of insurance.

(6) This Act shall not apply—

(a) where a company is wound up voluntarily merely for the purposes of reconstruction or of amalgamation with another company; or

(b) to any case to which subsections (1) and (2) of section seven of the Workmen's Compensation Act 1925 applies.

NOTES

Sub-s (1): words omitted from first pair of square brackets inserted by the Insolvency Act 1985, s 235, Sch 8, para 7(2) and repealed by the Enterprise Act 2002 (Insolvency) Order 2003, SI 2003/2096, art 4, Schedule, Pt 1, paras 1, 2(a), except in relation to any case where a petition for an administration order was presented before 15 September 2003; words in second pair of square brackets inserted by SI 2003/2096, art 4, Schedule, Pt 1, paras 1, 2(b), except in relation to any case where a petition for an administration order was presented before 15 September 2003; words in third (outer) pair of square brackets inserted by the Insolvency Act 1985, s 235, Sch 8, para 7(2); words in fourth (inner) pair of square brackets substituted by the Insolvency Act 1986, s 439(2), Sch 14.

Sub-s (2): words in first (outer) and final pairs of square brackets substituted by the Insolvency Act 1985, s 235, Sch 8, para 7(2); words in second (inner) pair of square brackets substituted by the Insolvency Act 1986, s 439(2), Sch 14; words in third pair of square brackets inserted by the Bankruptcy (Scotland) Act 1985, s 75(1), Sch 7, Pt I, para 6(1).

Sub-s (3): words in first (outer) pair of square brackets substituted by the Insolvency Act 1985, s 235, Sch 8, para 7(2); words in second (inner) pair of square brackets substituted by the Insolvency Act 1986, s 439(2), Sch 14.

Workman's Compensation Act 1925: repealed, subject to savings, by the National Insurance (Industrial Injuries) Act 1946, now itself repealed by the Social Security Act 1973, ss 100, 101, Schs 26, 28, Pt I and the Social Security (Consequential Provisions) Act 1975, s 1(2), (5), Sch 1, Pt I.

[3156]

2 Duty to give necessary information to third parties

(1) In the event of any person becoming bankrupt or making a composition or arrangement with his creditors, or in the event of [the estate of any person falling to be administered in accordance with an order under section [421 of the Insolvency Act 1986]], or in the event of a winding-up order [. . .] being made, or a resolution for a voluntary winding-up being passed, with respect to any company [or of the company entering administration] or of a receiver or manager of the company's business or undertaking being duly appointed or of possession being taken by or on behalf of the holders of any debentures secured by a floating charge of any property comprised in or subject to the charge it shall be the duty of the bankrupt, debtor, personal representative of the deceased debtor or company, and, as the case may be, of the trustee in bankruptcy, trustee, liquidator, [administrator,] receiver, or manager, or person in possession of the property to give at the request of any person claiming that the bankrupt, debtor, deceased debtor, or company is under a liability to him such information as may reasonably be required by him for the purpose of ascertaining whether any rights have been transferred to and vested in him by this Act and for the purpose of enforcing such rights, if any, and any contract of insurance, in so far as it purports, whether directly or indirectly, to avoid the contract or to alter the rights of the parties thereunder upon the giving of any such information in the events aforesaid or otherwise to prohibit or prevent the giving thereof in the said events shall be of no effect.

[(1A) The reference in subsection (1) of this section to a trustee includes a reference to the supervisor of a [voluntary arrangement proposed for the purposes of, and approved under, Part I or Part VIII of the Insolvency Act 1986].]

(2) If the information given to any person in pursuance of subsection (1) of this section discloses reasonable ground for supposing that there have or may have been transferred to him under this Act rights against any particular insurer, that insurer shall be subject to the same duty as is imposed by the said subsection on the persons therein mentioned.

(3) The duty to give information imposed by this section shall include a duty to allow all contracts of insurance, receipts for premiums, and other relevant documents in the possession or power of the person on whom the duty is so imposed to be inspected and copies thereof to be taken.

NOTES

Sub-s (1): words in first (outer) pair of square brackets substituted and words in fifth pair of square brackets inserted by the Insolvency Act 1985, s 235, Sch 8, para 7(3)(a); words in second (inner) pair of square brackets substituted by the Insolvency Act 1986, s 439(2), Sch 14; words omitted from third pair of square brackets inserted by the Insolvency Act 1985, s 235, Sch 8, para 7(3)(a) and repealed by the Enterprise Act 2002 (Insolvency) Order 2003, SI 2003/2096, art 4, Schedule, Pt 1, paras 1, 3(a), except in relation to any case where a petition for an administration order was presented before 15 September 2003; words in fourth pair of square brackets inserted by SI 2003/2096, art 4, Schedule, Pt 1, paras 1, 3(b), except in relation to any case where a petition for an administration order was presented before 15 September 2003.

Sub-s (1A): inserted by the Insolvency Act 1985, s 235, Sch 8, para 7(3)(b); words in square brackets substituted by the Insolvency Act 1986, s 439(2), Sch 14.

[3157]

3 Settlement between insurers and insured persons

Where the insured has become bankrupt or where in the case of the insured being a company, a winding-up order [or an administration order] has been made or a resolution for a voluntary winding-up has been passed, with respect to the company, no agreement made between the insurer and the insured after liability has been incurred to a third party and after the commencement of the bankruptcy or winding- up [or the day of the making of the administration order], as the case may be, nor any waiver, assignment, or other disposition made by, or payment made to the insured after the commencement [or day] aforesaid shall be effective to defeat or affect the rights transferred to the third party under this Act, but those rights shall be the same as if no such agreement, waiver, assignment, disposition or payment had been made.

NOTES

Words in square brackets inserted by the Insolvency Act 1985, s 235, Sch 8, para 7(4).

[3158]

[3A Application to limited liability partnerships

(1) This Act applies to limited liability partnerships as it applies to companies.

(2) In its application to limited liability partnerships, references to a resolution for a voluntary winding-up being passed are references to a determination for a voluntary winding-up being made.]

Part III Statutes

NOTES
Inserted by the Limited Liability Partnerships Regulations 2001, SI 2001/1090, reg 9(1), Sch 5, para 2.

[3159]
4 Application to Scotland
In the application of this Act to Scotland—
(a) . . .
(b) any reference to [an estate falling to be administered in accordance with an order under section] [421 of the Insolvency Act 1986], shall be deemed to include a reference to an award of sequestration of the estate of a deceased debtor, and a reference to an appointment of a judicial factor, under section [11A of the Judicial Factors (Scotland) Act 1889], on the insolvent estate of a deceased person.

NOTES
Para (a): repealed by the Bankruptcy (Scotland) Act 1985, s 75(1), (2), Sch 7, para 6(2)(a), Sch 8.
Para (b): words in first pair of square brackets substituted by the Insolvency Act 1985, s 235(1), Sch 8, para 7(5); words in second pair of square brackets substituted by the Insolvency Act 1986, s 439(2), Sch 14; words in third pair of square brackets substituted by the Bankruptcy (Scotland) Act 1985, s 75(1), Sch 7, para 6(2)(b), Sch 8.

[3160]
5 Short title
This Act may be cited as the Third Parties (Rights Against Insurers) Act 1930.

RESTRICTION OF ADVERTISEMENT (WAR RISKS INSURANCE) ACT 1939

(2 & 3 Geo 6 c 120)

ARRANGEMENT OF SECTIONS

1	Restriction of circulars and advertisements relating to insurance against war risks	[3161]
2	Requirements as to carrying on business where permission granted under section 1	[3162]
3	Advisory committee	[3163]
4	Offences	[3164]
6	Interpretation	[3165]
7	Short title and extent	[3166]

An Act to restrict the distribution of circulars, and the publication of advertisements, relating to the insurance of property against war risks, to provide for the imposition of certain conditions and requirements in cases where permission for such distribution or publication is granted, and for purposes connected with the matters aforesaid

[23 November 1939]

[3161]
1 Restriction of circulars and advertisements relating to insurance against war risks
(1) Subject to the provisions of this section, any person who on or after such day as may be fixed by order of [the Treasury]—
(a) distributes or causes to be distributed any circulars containing—
(i) any invitation to persons to insure any property in the United Kingdom in which they are interested against any war risks, or
(ii) any information calculated to lead to the recipient of the information insuring any property in the United Kingdom in which he is interested against any war risks; or
(b) has in his possession for the purpose of distribution any circulars of such a nature as to show that the object or principal object of distributing them would be to communicate such an invitation or such information as aforesaid; or
(c) causes or permits any advertisement to appear which contains such an invitation or such information as aforesaid,

shall, unless permission for the distribution of the circular or the appearance of the advertisement has been granted by [the Treasury] and any conditions imposed by [the Treasury] in relation thereto have been complied with, be guilty of an offence under this Act.
(2) Nothing in this section shall render unlawful—

(a) . . .

[(b) anything done with a view to inducing persons to enter into any contract of insurance, if the [Board of Trade] could, under section one of the Marine and Aviation Insurance (War Risks) Act 1952, lawfully re-insure the person liable under that contract; or]

(c) anything done with a view to inducing persons to enter into any contract of insurance—

(i) of goods consigned for carriage by sea or by air from a place outside the United Kingdom to a place in the United Kingdom, while the goods are in transit between the ship or aircraft and their destination; or

(ii) of goods consigned for carriage by sea or by air from a place in the United Kingdom to a place outside the United Kingdom, while the goods are in transit between the premises from which they are consigned and the ship or aircraft.

NOTES

Sub-s (1): words in square brackets substituted by the Transfer of Functions (Insurance) Order 1997, SI 1997/2781, art 8, Schedule, Pt II, para 95.

Sub-s (2): para (a) repealed by the Statute Law (Repeals) Act 1981; para (b) substituted by the Marine and Aviation Insurance (War Risks) Act 1952, s 8; words in square brackets in para (b) substituted by the Transfer of Functions (Sea Transport etc) Order 1968, SI 1968/2038, art 4(1)(a).

[3162]

2 Requirements as to carrying on business where permission granted under section 1

(1) Where [the Treasury] grant any such permission as is mentioned in subsection (1) of the preceding section, they may, in addition to imposing conditions in relation to the distribution or appearance of the circular or advertisement in question, at the same time by order specify requirements which, if the persons to whom the permission is granted avail themselves thereof, are to be complied with in the carrying on of the business in connection with which the circulars are to be distributed or the advertisements are to appear, being requirements designed to secure that any representations made in the circulars or advertisements are complied with, including, if [the Treasury] think fit—

(a) requirements as to the total or partial separation of the funds respectively available for the payment of claims and the payment of expenses;

(b) requirements as to the proportion of the premiums or other similar payments which is to be allocated to the payment of claims;

(c) requirements as to the manner in which any fund available for the payment of claims is to be maintained and dealt with;

(d) requirements as to the keeping, drawing-up, auditing and publication of accounts.

(2) If the persons to whom permission is granted as aforesaid avail themselves thereof, every person thereafter concerned in carrying on the business shall comply with any requirements specified as aforesaid except so far as [the Treasury] may dispense with compliance therewith, and any person who contravenes the provisions of this subsection shall be guilty of an offence under this Act.

NOTES

Sub-ss (1), (2): words in square brackets substituted by the Transfer of Functions (Insurance) Order 1997, SI 1997/2781, art 8, Schedule, Pt II, para 95.

[3163]

3 Advisory committee

(1) For the purpose of advising them as to the exercise of their functions under this Act, [the Treasury] shall appoint an advisory committee consisting of such persons as [the Treasury] think fit.

(2) Every application for any such permission as is mentioned in subsection (1) of section one of this Act shall be referred by [the Treasury] to the said advisory committee, and [the Treasury] shall not—

(a) grant the permission except on the recommendation of the committee;

(b) if the committee recommend that the permission be granted subject to conditions or that if it is granted requirements should be imposed in relation to the carrying on of the business in question, grant that permission without imposing those conditions or those requirements,

but nothing in this subsection shall be taken to limit the discretion of [the Treasury] to refuse altogether to grant the permission or, if they grant the permission, to impose further conditions or requirements.

(3) The committee shall not recommend the granting of any such permission as aforesaid unless, having regard to all relevant circumstances, and, in particular, to the nature and situation of the property which is proposed to be eligible for insurance, and to the classes of persons whom it is

proposed to invite to insure, the committee are satisfied that the granting of the permission, subject to the imposition of such conditions or requirements, if any, as they may include in their recommendation, would not be contrary to the public interest.

NOTES

Sub-ss (1), (2): words in square brackets substituted by the Transfer of Functions (Insurance) Order 1997, SI 1997/2781, art 8, Schedule, Pt II, para 95.

[3164]

4 Offences

(1) Any person who commits an offence under this Act shall be liable—

(a) on summary conviction, to a fine not exceeding [the prescribed sum] or to imprisonment for a period not exceeding three months, or both to such fine and such imprisonment;

(b) on conviction on indictment, to a fine, or to imprisonment for a period not exceeding two years, or both to a fine and such imprisonment.

(2) Where any offence under this Act committed by a body corporate is proved to have been committed with the consent or connivance of any director, manager, secretary or other officer of the body corporate, he, as well as the body corporate, shall be deemed to be guilty of that offence and shall be liable to be proceeded against and punished accordingly.

(3) No prosecution in respect of an offence under this Act shall, in England or Northern Ireland, be instituted otherwise than with the consent of [the Treasury].

(4) . . .

NOTES

Sub-s (1): reference to the prescribed sum substituted by virtue of the Magistrates' Courts Act 1980, s 32(2).

Sub-s (3): word in square brackets substituted by the Transfer of Functions (Insurance) Order 1997, SI 1997/2781, art 8, Schedule, Pt II, para 95.

Sub-s (4): repealed by the Northern Ireland Act 1962, s 30(2), Sch 4, Pt IV.

5 (*Repealed by the Statute Law (Repeals) Act 1974.*)

[3165]

6 Interpretation

(1) In this Act—

(a) the expression "war risks" means risks arising from action taken by an enemy or from action taken in combating an enemy or in repelling an imagined attack by an enemy;

(b) any reference to the insuring of any property by any person includes a reference to the making by him of any contract or arrangement (not being a contract for the sale or bailment of that property) under which he is, in the event of damage to that property, entitled or eligible, either absolutely or conditionally, to or for any form of indemnification, whether total or partial, and whether by way of a money payment or not, in respect of that damage.

(2) Documents shall not for the purposes of this Act be deemed not to be circulars by reason only that they are in the form of a newspaper, journal, magazine or other periodical publication; but a person shall not be taken to contravene this Act by reason only that he distributes, or causes to be distributed, to purchasers thereof, or has in his possession for the purpose of distribution to purchasers thereof, copies of any newspaper, journal, magazine or other periodical publication of which he is not the publisher.

(3) In the application of subsection (1) of this section to Scotland, the expression "bailment" means delivery of goods, in pursuance of a contract of loan, deposit, pledge, hire, hire purchase, carriage, or location operis faciendi or any other contract which involves delivery by one person to another of the possession of goods for delivery to a third person or re-delivery to the owner when the purpose of the contract is at an end.

[3166]

7 Short title and extent

(1) This Act may be cited as the Restriction of Advertisement (War Risks Insurance) Act 1939.

(2) It is hereby declared that this Act extends to Northern Ireland.

LLOYD'S ACT 1951

(14 & 15 Geo VI c viii)

ARRANGEMENT OF SECTIONS

Preamble		[3167]
1	Short and collective titles	[3168]
2	Interpretation	[3169]
3	Powers of Society to borrow	[3170]
5	Society may act as trustee for certain purposes	[3171]
8	Costs of Act	[3172]

An Act to confer further powers on Lloyd's to amend Lloyd's Acts 1871 to 1925 and for other purposes

[26 April 1951]

[3167]
Preamble

WHEREAS by Lloyd's Act 1871 (in this Act referred to as "the Act of 1871") certain persons were united into a society or corporation for the purposes of that Act and were incorporated by the name of Lloyd's (which incorporated body was in the Act of 1871 and is in this act referred to as "the Society") and various powers were conferred upon the Society by the said Act:

And whereas by Lloyd's Act 1911 the objects of the Society were extended and now include the carrying on by members of the Society of the business of insurance of every description including guarantee business the advancement and protection of the interests of members of the Society in connection with the business carried on by them as members of the Society and in respect of shipping and cargoes and freight and other insurable property or insurable interests or otherwise the collection publication and diffusion of intelligence and information and the doing of all things incidental or conducive to the fulfilment of the objects of the Society:

And whereas further powers were conferred on the Society and further provisions were made with reference to the Society by Lloyd's Signal Stations Act 1888 Lloyd's Act 1911 and Lloyd's Act 1925:

And whereas the number of and the business carried on by members of the Society and the activities of the Society have increased and are increasing and the Society desires to erect and fit up new premises for its accommodation and the accommodation of its members and for other purposes and to borrow money but doubts have arisen as to whether it has power to borrow for that or any other purpose and it is expedient that the provisions of this Act with respect thereto be enacted:

And whereas in addition to members there are annual subscribers to and associates of the Society and others who may be granted admission to the rooms of the Society and who enjoy such privileges as the committee of the Society from time to time determine:

And whereas under section 8 of Lloyd's Act 1911 the Society may act as trustee either solely or jointly with any other person of any trust deed or guarantee or other document furnished to the Society by any member of the Society as security for meeting his liabilities under policies underwritten by him or on his account at Lloyd's and it is expedient to extend the powers of the Society under that section in manner provided by this Act:

And whereas under section 9 of Lloyd's Act 1911 the Society may for the purposes mentioned in that section either by itself or jointly with any other guarantor or guarantors guarantee the payment of claims and demands upon policies of insurance including guarantees underwritten by members of the Society or on their account at Lloyd's subject as mentioned in the said section and it is expedient to extend the powers of the Society under that section in manner provided by this Act:

And whereas it is expedient that the other provisions of this Act be enacted:

And whereas the objects of this Act cannot be effected without the authority of Parliament:

May it therefore please Your Majesty that it may be enacted and be it enacted by the King's most Excellent Majesty by and with the advice and consent of the Lords Spiritual and Temporal and Commons in this present Parliament assembled and by the authority of the same as follows—

[3168]
1 Short and collective titles

(1) This Act may be cited as Lloyd's Act 1951.

(2) Lloyd's Acts 1871 to 1925 and this Act may be cited together as Lloyd's Acts 1871 to 1951.

Part III Statutes

[3169]
2 Interpretation
In this Act unless there is something in the subject or context repugnant to such construction—
"the Act of 1871" means Lloyd's Act 1871;
"the Act of 1911" means Lloyd's Act 1911;
"the committee" means the Committee of Lloyd's constituted under the Act of 1871;
"the society" means the society incorporated by the Act of 1871 by the name of Lloyd's.

[3170]
3 Powers of Society to borrow
(1) The Society may raise or borrow money and secure the same and any interest thereon upon any property of the Society either in order to acquire any land or to develop and turn to account any land acquired by or in which the Society is interested (and in particular by constructing altering pulling down reconstructing decorating furnishing fitting up maintaining and improving buildings and whether the same shall be intended for occupation or part occupation of the Society or its members or subscribers or otherwise) or for any other purpose of the Society.
(2) The powers conferred on the Society by this section may be exercised by the committee: . . .

NOTES
Sub-s (2): words omitted repealed by the Lloyd's Act 1982, s 15(1), Sch 3.

4 (*Repealed by the Lloyd's Act 1982, s 15(1), Sch 3.*)

[3171]
5 Society may act as trustee for certain purposes
(1) It shall be lawful and shall be deemed always to have been lawful for the Society to act as trustee either solely or jointly with any other person of any trust deed or guarantee or other document: . . .
(2) Any trustee or trustees of any such trust deed or guarantee or other document as aforesaid may transfer any trust fund subject to any such trust deed guarantee or document to the Society and assign to the Society the benefit or advantage to which he or they are entitled under any such trust deed guarantee or document and on the execution of such transfer or deed of assignment the Society shall be entitled to such trust fund and to all benefits and advantages under any such trust deed guarantee or document in the same manner and to the same extent and on the same trusts as such trustees held or were entitled to the same.
(3) Section 8 (Society may act as trustee for certain purposes) of the Act of 1911 is hereby repealed.
(4)
(a) Notwithstanding the repeal of the said section 8 any trust deed guarantee document transfer deed of assignment or other instrument of whatsoever nature entered into or made under the powers of that section and in force immediately before the passing of this Act shall continue in full force and effect in every respect and may be enforced as fully and effectually as if that section had not been repealed.
(b) The mention of particular matters in this subsection shall not be held to prejudice or affect the general application of section 38 (Effect of repeal in future Acts) of the Interpretation Act 1889 with regard to the effect of repeals.

NOTES
Sub-s (1): words omitted repealed by the Lloyd's Act 1982, s 15(1)(d).

6, 7 (*S 6 amends the Lloyd's Act 1911, s 9 at* **[3152]**, *and repeals the Lloyd's Act 1911, Schedule; s 7 amends the Lloyd's Act 1871, s 20 (repealed), and the Lloyd's Act 1911, s 10 (repealed).*)

[3172]
8 Costs of Act
The costs charges and expenses of and incidental to the preparing applying for obtaining and passing of this Act shall be paid by the Society.

MARINE AND AVIATION INSURANCE (WAR RISKS) ACT 1952

(15 & 16 Geo 6 & 1 Eliz 2 c 57)

ARRANGEMENT OF SECTIONS

1 Agreements for re-insurance by Minister of Transport of war risks in respect of ships, aircraft and cargoes . . . [3173]
2 Insurance by Minister of Transport of ships, aircraft and cargoes . . . [3174]
3 Transitional provisions for compensation in respect of goods lost or damaged in transit after discharge or before shipment . . . [3175]
4 Liabilities of re-insurer in the event of insurer's insolvency . . . [3176]
5 Establishment of fund for purposes of this Act . . . [3177]
7 Exemption of certain instruments from provisions of Stamp Act 1891 and Marine Insurance Act 1906 . . . [3178]
9 Expenses of the Minister of Transport . . . [3179]
10 Interpretation and savings . . . [3180]
11 Short title, extent and repeal . . . [3181]

An Act to make provision for authorising the Minister of Transport to undertake the insurance of ships, aircraft and certain other goods against war risks and, in certain circumstances, other risks; for the payment by him of compensation in respect of certain goods lost or damaged in transit in consequence of war risks; and for purposes connected with the matters aforesaid

[30 October 1952]

[3173]

1 Agreements for re-insurance by Minister of Transport of war risks in respect of ships, aircraft and cargoes

(1) The Minister of Transport (hereafter in this Act referred to as "the Minister") may, with the approval of the Treasury, enter into agreements with any authorities or persons—

(a) whereby he undertakes the liability of re-insuring any war risks against which a ship or aircraft is for the time being insured; and

(b) whereby he undertakes the liability of re-insuring any war risks against which the cargo carried in a ship or aircraft is for the time being insured:

Provided that the Minister shall not enter into an agreement whereby he undertakes the liability of re-insuring any war risks against which a ship or aircraft not being a British ship or British aircraft is for the time being insured, except in so far as they arise during the continuance of any war or other hostilities in which Her Majesty is engaged or arise after any such war or hostilities in consequence of things done or omitted during the continuance thereof.

(2) A copy of every agreement made in pursuance of this section shall, as soon as may be after the agreement is made, be laid before each House of Parliament; and if either House, within the period of fourteen days beginning with the day on which a copy of such an agreement is laid before it, resolves that the agreement be annulled, the agreement shall thereupon become void except in so far as it confers rights or imposes obligations in respect of things previously done or omitted to be done, without prejudice, however, to the making of a new agreement.

In reckoning for the purposes of this subsection any such period of fourteen days as aforesaid, no account shall be taken of any time during which Parliament is dissolved or prorogued or during which both Houses are adjourned for more than four days.

(3) The reference in paragraph (a) of subsection (1) of this section to a ship or aircraft shall be construed as including a reference to any machinery, tackle, furniture or equipment of a ship or aircraft, and to any goods on board of a ship or aircraft, not being cargo carried therein, and the first reference in the proviso to that subsection to a ship or aircraft shall accordingly be similarly construed.

NOTES

Minister of Transport: the Secretary of State for the Environment Order 1970, SI 1970/1681 abolished the Ministry of Transport and, subject to limited exceptions not relevant to this Act, transferred to the Secretary of State the functions of the Minister of Transport. The Secretary of State for Transport Order 1976, SI 1976/1775 created a separate Department of Transport and all the transport functions of the Secretary of State for the Environment were transferred to the Secretary of State for Transport. In 1979, by virtue of the Minister of Transport Order 1979, SI 1979/571, a Ministry of Transport was again formed and the functions of the Secretary of State for Transport were transferred to the Minister of Transport. This situation continued until 1981, when, by virtue of the Transfer of Functions (Transport) Order 1981, SI 1981/238, the functions of the Minister of Transport were again transferred to the Secretary of State for Transport. The Secretary of State for the Environment, Transport and the Regions Order 1997, SI 1997/2971, arts 3–6, transferred the functions of the Secretary of State for Transport to the Secretary of State for the Environment, Transport and the Regions.

[3174]

2 Insurance by Minister of Transport of ships, aircraft and cargoes

(1) The Minister may, with the approval of the Treasury, carry on business under and in accordance with all or any of the following provisions of this subsection, that is to say:—

(a) at any time when it appears to him that reasonable and adequate facilities for the insurance of British ships or British aircraft against war risks, or any description of such risks, are not available, for the insurance by him of such ships, or as the case may be, such aircraft, against such risks or, as the case may be, that description thereof;

(b) during the continuance of any war or other hostilities in which Her Majesty is engaged, for the insurance by him of ships and aircraft (whether British or not);

(c) at any time when it appears to him that reasonable and adequate facilities for the insurance of cargoes carried in ships or aircraft against war risks, or any description of such risks, are not available, for the insurance by him of such cargoes against such risks or, as the case may be, that description thereof;

(d) during the continuance of any war or other hostilities in which Her Majesty is engaged for the insurance by him of cargoes carried in ships or aircraft;

(e) during the continuance of any such war or hostilities, for the insurance by him of goods consigned for carriage by sea or by air, while the goods are in transit between the premises from which they are consigned and the ship or aircraft or between the ship or aircraft and their destination:

Provided that the Minister shall not, by virtue of paragraph (b), (d) or (e) of this subsection, undertake the insurance of a ship, aircraft or cargo against risks other than war risks unless he is satisfied that, in the interests of the defence of the realm or the efficient prosecution of any such war or hostilities as aforesaid, it is necessary or expedient so to do.

(2) References in paragraphs (a) and (b) of the foregoing subsection to ships of any description and to aircraft of any description shall be construed as including references to any machinery, tackle, furniture or equipment of ships of that description and aircraft of that description respectively and to any goods on board of ships of that description and aircraft of that description respectively, not being cargo carried therein, and the reference in the proviso to that subsection to a ship or aircraft shall accordingly be similarly construed.

(3) In paragraph (e) of subsection (1) of this section the expression "the ship or aircraft", in relation to goods consigned for carriage by sea or by air, does not include a vessel from which the goods are discharged for the purpose of being carried by sea or by air or into which they are discharged for the purpose of being landed.

NOTES

Minister of Transport: see the note to s 1 at **[3173]**.

[3175]

3 Transitional provisions for compensation in respect of goods lost or damaged in transit after discharge or before shipment

(1) Where a person satisfies the Minister with respect to any goods—

(a) that the goods, having been consigned for carriage by sea or by air from a place outside any one of the countries to which this paragraph applies to a place in that country,—

(i) were discharged in that country from the ship or aircraft before the expiration of the period of seven days beginning with such day as the Minister may declare to be the day as from which he will carry on business for the purpose mentioned in paragraph (e) of subsection (1) of the last foregoing section;

(ii) were, after the beginning of that day and before the expiration of the appropriate period, lost or damaged in consequence of a war risk, being one which the Minister was, on that day, prepared to insure under the said paragraph (e); and

(iii) were lost or damaged while in transit between the ship or aircraft and their destination;

or, having been consigned for carriage by sea or by air from a place in any one of the countries to which this paragraph applies to a place outside that country before the expiration of the said period of seven days, were, after the beginning of the said day, lost or damaged in consequence of such a war risk as aforesaid while in transit between the premises from which they were consigned and the ship or aircraft; and

(b) that the goods were not insured against the risk in consequence of which they were lost or damaged; and

(c) that he and his agents exercised all due diligence for securing that no delay occurred while the goods were in such transit as aforesaid; and

(d) that at the time when the loss or damage occurred the property in the goods was vested in him;

the Minister shall pay to him, by way of compensation for that loss or damage, an amount ascertained in accordance with the next following subsection.

(2) The amount of compensation payable under the foregoing subsection shall be—

(a) in the case of lost goods, an amount equal to the insurable value of the goods;

(b) in the case of damaged goods—

(i) where the goods have been delivered at their destination, an amount equal to such proportion of the insurable value of the goods as the difference between the gross sound and damaged values at the place of arrival bears to the gross sound value;

(ii) where the goods have not been so delivered, an amount equal to such proportion of the insurable value of the goods as the difference between the gross sound and damaged values at the premises from which they were consigned bears to the gross sound value.

(3) Where, at a time when the loss or damage for which compensation in respect of any goods has become payable under this section occurred, the goods were subject to a mortgage, charge or other similar obligation, the amount of the compensation shall be deemed to be comprised in that mortgage, charge or other obligation.

(4) The countries to which paragraph (a) of subsection (1) of this section applies are the United Kingdom, the Isle of Man and any of the Channel Islands.

(5) In this section—

(a) the expression "the ship or aircraft", in relation to goods consigned for carriage by sea or by air to or from a country to which paragraph (a) of subsection (1) of this section applies, does not include a vessel into which the goods are discharged at a port or place in that country for the purpose of being landed at that port or place, or from which the goods are discharged for the purpose of being carried by sea or by air from that country, as the case may be;

(b) the expression "the appropriate period" means—

(i) in a case where the destination of the goods is within the port or place at which they were discharged from the ship or aircraft, the period of fifteen days beginning with the day on which they were so discharged; or

(ii) in a case where the destination of the goods is outside the said port or place, the period of thirty days beginning with the day on which they were so discharged; and

(c) the expression "insurable value" means, in relation to goods consigned for carriage by sea or by air, the prime cost of the goods plus the expenses of and incidental to the carriage thereof as aforesaid and the charges of insurance upon the whole;

and for the purposes of this section the gross value of goods shall be taken to be the wholesale price or, if there be no such price, the estimated value, with, in either case, the expenses of and incidental to the carriage of the goods.

[3176]

4 Liabilities of re-insurer in the event of insurer's insolvency

Where a sum becomes payable to a person (hereafter in this section referred to as "the insurer") in respect of any loss or damage arising from a risk against which the insurer has, either originally or by way of re-insurance, insured another person (hereafter in this section referred to as "the assured") and either—

(a) the sum has become payable by the Minister by virtue of an agreement under section one of this Act; or

(b) the sum has become payable under a contract of insurance by some person other than the Minister (hereafter in this section referred to as "the intermediate insurer") and the risk has been re-insured under such an agreement as aforesaid,

then, if before payment of that sum is made by the Minister or the intermediate insurer, the insurer becomes bankrupt or, in a case where the insurer is a company, the company commences to be wound up, or a receiver is appointed on behalf of the holders of any debentures of the company secured by a floating charge or possession is taken by or on behalf of the holders of such debentures of any property comprised in or subject to the charge, that sum shall cease to be payable to the insurer and the amount thereof shall be paid to the assured by the Minister or the intermediate insurer, as the case may be, and the right of the assured to receive payment in respect of the loss or damage from the insurer shall, to the extent to which the risk has been re-insured by the Minister, be extinguished.

[3177]

5 Establishment of fund for purposes of this Act

(1) There shall be established under the control of the Minister a fund, to be called the "marine and aviation insurance (war risks) fund",—

(a) into which shall be paid—

(i) all sums received by the Minister by virtue of this Act;

(ii), (iii) . . .

(b) out of which shall be paid—

(i) all sums required for the fulfilment by the Minister of any of his obligations under this Act; . . .

(ii) . . .

(2) If, at any time when a payment falls to be made out of the marine and aviation insurance (war risks) fund, the sum standing to the credit of that fund is less than the sum required for the making of that payment, an amount equal to the deficiency shall be paid into that fund out of moneys provided by Parliament, but if and so far as that amount is not paid out of such moneys, it shall be charged on and issued out of the Consolidated Fund of the United Kingdom . . . (hereafter in this Act referred to as "the Consolidated Fund").

(3) If, at any time, the amount standing to the credit of the marine and aviation insurance (war risks) fund exceeds the sum which, in the opinion of the Minister and the Treasury, is likely to be required for the making of payments out of that fund, the excess shall be paid into the Exchequer . . .

(4) The Minister shall prepare, in such form and manner as the Treasury may direct, an account of the sums received into and paid out of the marine and aviation insurance (war risks) fund in each financial year, and shall, on or before the thirtieth day of November in each year, transmit the account to the Comptroller and Auditor General, who shall examine and certify the account and lay copies thereof together with copies of his report thereon, before both Houses of Parliament:

Provided that if the Treasury certify that, in the interests of the defence of the realm or the efficient prosecution of any war or other hostilities in which Her Majesty is engaged, it is inexpedient that copies of the account for any year and of the report thereon should be laid before Parliament, a copy of the certificate shall be laid before both Houses of Parliament and, so long as the certificate remains in force, those copies of the account and of the report shall not be so laid.

NOTES

Sub-s (1): words omitted repealed by the Statute Law (Repeals) Act 1981.
Sub-s (2): words omitted repealed by the Statute Law Revision Act 1963.
Sub-s (3): words omitted repealed by the National Loans Act 1968, s 24(2), Sch 6, Pt I.

6 *(Repealed by the National Loans Act 1968, s 24(2), Sch 6, Pt I.)*

[3178]

7 Exemption of certain instruments from provisions of Stamp Act 1891 and Marine Insurance Act 1906

(1) None of the following instruments shall . . . be inadmissible in evidence by reason only that it is not embodied in a marine policy in accordance with the Marine Insurance Act 1906, that is to say:—

(a) an agreement for re-insurance made in pursuance of section one of this Act between the Minister and any other authority or person, and a policy of re-insurance issued by the Minister in pursuance of such an agreement;

(b) an agreement entered into by a body to which this paragraph applies, being an agreement for the re-insurance of a risk insured by another person which may be again re-insured by the Minister, and a policy issued in pursuance of such an agreement, being a policy for the re-insurance only of such a risk as aforesaid;

(c) a contract of insurance entered into by the Minister in exercise of the powers conferred on him by section two of this Act, and a policy of insurance and a certificate of insurance issued by the Minister in connection with any such contract.

(2), (3) . . .

(4) Paragraph (b) of subsection (1) of this section applies to any body of persons for the time being approved for the purposes of this Act by the Minister, being a body the objects of which are or include the carrying on of business by way of the re-insurance of risks which may be re-insured under any agreement for the purpose mentioned in paragraph (b) of subsection (1) of section one of this Act.

NOTES

Section heading: words "Stamp Act 1891" spent consequent on the repeal of sub-s (3).

Sub-s (1): words omitted repealed by the Finance Act 1959, s 37(4), (5), Sch 8, Pt II.

Sub-s (2): repealed by the Finance Act 1970, s 36(7), (8), Sch 8, Pt IV.

Sub-s (3): repealed by the Finance Act 1959, s 37(4), (5), Sch 8, Pt II, and the Finance Act 1970, s 36(8), Sch 8, Pt IV.

8 (*Substitutes the Restriction of Advertisement (War Risks Insurance) Act 1939, s 1(2)(b) at* **[3161]**.)

[3179]

9 Expenses of the Minister of Transport

The expenses incurred for the purposes of this Act by the Minister shall, except in so far as they are required to be defrayed out of the marine and aviation insurance (war risks) fund, be defrayed out of moneys provided by Parliament.

NOTES

Minister of Transport: see the note to s 1 at **[3173]**.

[3180]

10 Interpretation and savings

(1) In this Act, unless the context otherwise requires, the following expressions have the meanings hereby respectively assigned to them, that is to say:—

"British aircraft" means aircraft registered in Her Majesty's dominions;

"goods" includes currency and any securities payable to bearer, not being either bills of exchange or promissory notes;

"war risks" means risks arising from any of the following events, that is to say, hostilities, rebellion, revolution and civil war, from civil strife consequent on the happening of any of those events, or from action taken (whether before or after the outbreak of any hostilities, rebellion, revolution or civil war) for repelling an imagined attack or preventing or hindering the carrying out of any attack, and includes piracy.

(2) The provisions of this Act relating to British ships shall apply also to ships of India and ships of the Republic of Ireland, and references in this Act to British ships shall be construed accordingly.

(3) The provisions of this Act relating to British aircraft shall apply also to aircraft registered in India, the Republic of Ireland, the Federation of Malaya, a protectorate, a protected state, a trust territory or a mandated territory, and references in this Act to British aircraft shall be construed accordingly.

The references in this subsection to a protectorate, a protected state, a trust territory and a mandated territory shall be construed as if they were references contained in the British Nationality Act 1948.

(4) . . .

NOTES

Sub-s (4): repealed by the Statute Law (Repeals) Act 1981.

British Nationality Act 1948: repealed by the British Nationality Act 1981, s 52(8), Sch 9.

[3181]

11 Short title, extent and repeal

(1) This Act may be cited as the Marine and Aviation Insurance (War Risks) Act 1952.

(2) It is hereby declared that this Act extends to Northern Ireland.

(3) . . .

NOTES

Sub-s (3): repealed by the Statute Law (Repeals) Act 1974.

(*Schedule repealed by the Statute Law (Repeals) Act 1974.*)

NUCLEAR INSTALLATIONS ACT 1965

(1965 c 57)

An Act to consolidate the Nuclear Installations Act 1959 and 1965

[5 August 1965]

1–17 (*Outside the scope of this work.*)

Cover for compensation

18 (*Outside the scope of this work.*)

[3182]
19 Special cover for licensee's liability
(1) Subject to section 3(5) of this Act and to subsection (3) of this section, where a nuclear site licence has been granted in respect of any site, the licensee shall make such provision (either by insurance or by some other means) as the Minister may with the consent of the Treasury approve for sufficient funds to be available at all times to ensure that any claims which have been or may be duly established against the licensee as licensee of that site by virtue of section 7 of this Act or any relevant foreign law made for purposes corresponding to those of section 10 of this Act (excluding, but without prejudice to, any claim in respect of interest or costs) are satisfied up to [the required amount] in respect of each severally of the following periods, that is to say—

(a) the current cover period, if any;
(b) any cover period which ended less than ten years before the time in question;
(c) any earlier cover period in respect of which a claim remains to be disposed of, being a claim made—
  (i) within the relevant period within the meaning of section 16 of this Act; and
  (ii) in the case of a claim such as is mentioned in section 15(2) of this Act, also within the period of twenty years so mentioned;

and for the purposes of this section the cover period in respect of which any claim is to be treated as being made shall be that in which the beginning of the relevant period aforesaid fell.
[(1A) In this section "the required amount", in relation to the provision to be made by a licensee in respect of a cover period, means an aggregate amount equal to the amount applicable under section 16(1) of this Act to the licensee, as licensee of the site in question, in respect of an occurrence within that period.]
(2) In this Act, the expression "cover period" means[, subject to the following provisions of this section, the period of the licensee's responsibility;] and for the purposes of this definition the period of the licensee's responsibility shall be deemed to include any time after the expiration of that period during which it remains possible for the licensee to incur any liability by virtue of section 7(2)(b) or (c) of this Act, or by virtue of any relevant foreign law made for purposes corresponding to those of section 10 of this Act.
[(2A) When the amount applicable under section 16(1) of this Act to a licensee of a site changes as a result of—

(a) the coming into force of an order under section 16(1A) or of regulations made for the purposes of section 16(1), or
(b) an alteration relating to the site which brings it within, or takes it outside, the description prescribed by such regulations,

the current cover period relating to him as licensee of that site shall end and a new cover period shall begin.]
[(2B) The current cover period continues to run (and no new cover period begins) on the grant of a new nuclear site licence to the same licensee in respect of a site consisting of or including the site in respect of which his existing nuclear site licence is in force.]
(3) Where in the case of any licensed site the provision required by subsection (1) of this section is to be made otherwise than by insurance and, apart from this subsection, provision would also fall to be so made by the same person in respect of two or more other sites, the requirements of that subsection shall be deemed to be satisfied in respect of each of those sites if funds are available to meet such claims as are mentioned in that subsection in respect of all the sites collectively, and those funds would for the time being be sufficient to satisfy the requirements of that subsection in respect of those two of the sites in respect of which those requirements are highest:

Provided that the Minister may in any particular case at any time direct either that this subsection shall not apply or that the funds available as aforesaid shall be of such amount higher than that provided for by the foregoing provisions of this subsection, but lower than that necessary to satisfy the requirements of the said subsection (1) in respect of all the sites severally, as may be required by the direction.

(4) Where, by reason of the gravity of any occurrence which has resulted or may result in claims such as are mentioned in subsection (1) of this section against a licensee as licensee of a particular licensed site, or having regard to any previous occurrences which have resulted or may result in such claims against the licensee, the Minister thinks it proper so to do, he shall by notice in writing to the licensee direct that a new cover period for the purposes of the said subsection (1) shall begin in respect of that site on such date not earlier than two months after the date of the service of the notice as may be specified therein.

(5) If at any time while subsection (1) of this section applies in relation to any licensed site the provisions of that subsection are not complied with in respect of that site, the licensee shall be guilty of an offence and be liable—

(a) on summary conviction to a fine not exceeding [the prescribed sum] or to imprisonment for a term not exceeding three months, or to both;

(b) on conviction on indictment, to a fine . . . , or to imprisonment for a term not exceeding two years, or to both.

NOTES

Sub-s (1): words in square brackets substituted by the Energy Act 1983, s 27(4).

Sub-ss (1A), (2A): inserted by the Energy Act 1983, s 27(4), (5).

Sub-s (2): words in square brackets substituted with retrospective effect by the Atomic Energy Act 1989, s 4(1)(a).

Sub-s (2B): inserted with retrospective effect by the Atomic Energy Act 1989, s 4(1)(b).

Sub-s (5): words in square brackets in para (a) substituted by virtue of the Magistrates' Courts Act 1980, s 32(2); words omitted from para (b) repealed by virtue of the Criminal Law Act 1977, s 32(1).

Transfer of functions: functions under sub-ss (1), (3) and (4) are transferred, in so far as they are exercisable in or as regards Scotland and, subject to the consent of the Treasury as regards certain matters, to the Scottish Ministers, by the Scotland Act 1998 (Transfer of Functions to the Scottish Ministers etc) Order 1999, SI 1999/1750, art 2, Sch 1.

20, 21 (*Outside the scope of this work.*)

Miscellaneous and general

22–29 (*Outside the scope of this work.*)

[3183]

30 Short title and commencement

(1) This Act may be cited as the Nuclear Installations Act 1965.

(2) This Act shall come into force on such day as Her Majesty may by Order in Council appoint; and a later day may be appointed for the purposes of section 17(5) than that appointed for the purposes of the other provisions of this Act.

NOTES

Orders: the Nuclear Installations Act 1965 (Commencement No 1) Order 1965, SI 1965/1880.

(*Sch 1 outside the scope of this work, Sch 2 repealed, except in relation to Northern Ireland, by the Nuclear Installations Act 1965 etc (Repeals and Modifications) Regulations 1974, SI 1974/2056, reg 2(1)(a), Sch 1.*)

MISREPRESENTATION ACT 1967

(1967 c 7)

An Act to amend the law relating to innocent misrepresentations and to amend sections 11 and 35 of the Sale of Goods Act 1893

[22 March 1967]

[3184]

1 Removal of certain bars to rescission for innocent misrepresentation

Where a person has entered into a contract after a misrepresentation has been made to him, and—

(a) the misrepresentation has become a term of the contract; or

(b) the contract has been performed;

or both, then, if otherwise he would be entitled to rescind the contract with-out alleging fraud, he shall be so entitled, subject to the provisions of this Act, notwithstanding the matters mentioned in paragraphs (a) and (b) of this section.

[3185]
2 Damages for misrepresentation
(1) Where a person has entered into a contract after a misrepresentation has been made to him by another party thereto and as a result thereof he has suffered loss, then, if the person making the misrepresentation would be liable to damages in respect thereof had the misrepresentation been made fraudulently, that person shall be so liable notwithstanding that the misrepresentation was not made fraudulently, unless he proves that he had reasonable ground to believe and did believe up to the time the contract was made that the facts represented were true.
(2) Where a person has entered into a contract after a misrepresentation has been made to him otherwise than fraudulently, and he would be entitled, by reason of the misrepresentation, to rescind the contract, then, if it is claimed, in any proceedings arising out of the contract, that the contract ought to be or has been rescinded, the court or arbitrator may declare the contract subsisting and award damages in lieu of rescission, if of opinion that it would be equitable to do so, having regard to the nature of the misrepresentation and the loss that would be caused by it if the contract were upheld, as well as to the loss that rescission would cause to the other party.
(3) Damages may be awarded against a person under subsection (2) of this section whether or not he is liable to damages under subsection (1) thereof, but where he is so liable any award under the said subsection (2) shall be taken into account in assessing his liability under the said subsection (1).

[3186]
[3 Avoidance of provision excluding liability for misrepresentation
If a contract contains a term which would exclude or restrict—
(a) any liability to which a party to a contract may be subject by reason of any misrepresentation made by him before the contract was made; or
(b) any remedy available to another party to the contract by reason of such a misrepresentation,
that term shall be of no effect except in so far as it satisfies the requirement of reasonableness as stated in section 11(1) of the Unfair Contract Terms Act 1977; and it is for those claiming that the term satisfies that requirement to show that it does.]

NOTES
Substituted by the Unfair Contract Terms Act 1977, s 8(1).

4 (*Repealed by the Sale of Goods Act 1979, s 63(2), Sch 3.*)

[3187]
5 Saving for past transactions
Nothing in this Act shall apply in relation to any misrepresentation or contract of sale which is made before the commencement of this Act.

[3188]
6 Short title, commencement and extent
(1) This Act may be cited as the Misrepresentation Act 1967.
(2) This Act shall come into operation at the expiration of the period of one month beginning with the date on which it is passed.
(3) This Act . . . does not extend to Scotland.
(4) This Act does not extend to Northern Ireland.

NOTES
Sub-s (3): words omitted repealed by the Sale of Goods Act 1979, ss 62, 63, Sch 3.

EMPLOYERS' LIABILITY (COMPULSORY INSURANCE) ACT 1969

(1969 c 57)

ARRANGEMENT OF SECTIONS

1 Insurance against liability for employees . . . . . [3189]
2 Employees to be covered . . . . . [3190]
3 Employers exempted from insurance . . . . . [3191]

4 Certificates of insurance . . . [3192]
5 Penalty for failure to insure . . . [3193]
6 Regulations . . . [3194]
7 Short title, extent and commencement . . . [3195]

An Act to require employers to insure against their liability for personal injury to their employees; and for purposes connected with the matter aforesaid

[22 October 1969]

NOTES

The subject matter of this Act is a "reserved matter" for the purposes of the Scotland Act 1998, which by virtue of s 29(2)(b) of that Act, is outside the legislative competence of the Scottish Parliament; see s 30 of and Sch 5, Pt II, Head H, para H1, Pt III, para 5 to that Act. For restrictions on the ability of the Scottish Parliament to modify the law on reserved matters, see s 29 of and Sch 4, Pt I, paras 2, 3 to that Act.

Exclusions: liability to maintain insurance under this Act is excluded by the Data Protection Act 1998, s 6(7), Sch 5, Pt I, para 4(6).

[3189]

1 Insurance against liability for employees

(1) Except as otherwise provided by this Act, every employer carrying on any business in Great Britain shall insure, and maintain insurance, under one or more approved policies with an authorised insurer or insurers against liability for bodily injury or disease sustained by his employees, and arising out of and in the course of their employment in Great Britain in that business, but except in so far as regulations otherwise provide not including injury or disease suffered or contracted outside Great Britain.

(2) Regulations may provide that the amount for which an employer is required by this Act to insure and maintain insurance shall, either generally or in such cases or classes of case as may be prescribed by the regulations, be limited in such manner as may be so prescribed.

(3) For the purposes of this Act—

(a) "approved policy" means a policy of insurance not subject to any conditions or exceptions prohibited for those purposes by regulations;

[(b) "authorised insurer" means—

(i) a person who has permission under Part 4 of the Financial Services and Markets Act 2000 to effect and carry out contracts of insurance of a kind required by this Act and regulations made under this Act, or

(ii) an EEA firm of the kind mentioned in paragraph 5(d) of Schedule 3 to the Financial Services and Markets Act 2000, which has permission under paragraph 15 of that Schedule to effect and carry out contracts of insurance of a kind required by this Act and regulations made under this Act;]

(c) "business" includes a trade or profession, and includes any activity carried on by a body of persons, whether corporate or unincorporate;

(d) except as otherwise provided by regulations, an employer not having a place of business in Great Britain shall be deemed not to carry on business there.

[(3A) Subsection (3)(b) must be read with—

(a) section 22 of the Financial Services and Markets Act 2000;

(b) any relevant order under that section; and

(c) Schedule 2 to that Act.]

NOTES

Sub-s (3): para (b) substituted by the Financial Services and Markets Act 2000 (Consequential Amendments and Repeals) Order 2001, SI 2001/3649, art 280(1), (2).

Sub-s (3A): added by SI 2001/3649, art 280(1), (3).

Regulations: the Employers' Liability (Compulsory Insurance) Regulations 1998, SI 1998/2573 at **[4180]**.

[3190]

2 Employees to be covered

(1) For the purposes of this Act the term "employee" means an individual who has entered into or works under a contract of service or apprenticeship with an employer whether by way of manual labour, clerical work or otherwise, whether such contract is expressed or implied, oral or in writing.

(2) This Act shall not require an employer to insure—

(a) in respect of an employee of whom the employer is the husband, wife, [civil partner,] father, mother, grandfather, grandmother, step-father, step-mother, son, daughter, grandson, granddaughter, stepson, stepdaughter, brother, sister, half-brother or half-sister; or

(b) except as otherwise provided by regulations, in respect of employees not ordinarily resident in Great Britain.

NOTES

Sub-s (2): words in square brackets inserted by the Civil Partnership Act 2004, s 261(1), Sch 27, para 33.
Regulations: the Employers' Liability (Compulsory Insurance) Regulations 1998, SI 1998/2573 at **[4180]**.

[3191]

3 Employers exempted from insurance

(1) This Act shall not require any insurance to be effected by—

(a) any such authority as is mentioned in subsection (2) below; or

(b) any body corporate established by or under any enactment for the carrying on of any industry or part of an industry, or of any undertaking, under national ownership or control; or

(c) in relation to any such cases as may be specified in the regulations, any employer exempted by regulations.

(2) The authorities referred to in subsection (1)(a) above are

[(a) a health service body, as defined in section 60(7) of the National Health Service and Community Care Act 1990, . . . a National Health Service trust established under [section 25 of the National Health Service Act 2006, section 18 of the National Health Service (Wales) Act 2006] or the National Health Service (Scotland) Act [1978,] [an NHS foundation trust,] [a Primary Care Trust established under [section 18 of the National Health Service Act 2006]] [and a Local Health Board established under [section 11 of the National Health Service (Wales) Act 2006]]; and

(b)] the Common Council of the City of London, . . . , the council of a London borough, the council of a county, . . . or county district in England [the council of a county or county borough in Wales], [the Broads Authority,] [a National Park Authority] [a council constituted under section 2 of the Local Government etc (Scotland) Act 1994 in] Scotland, any joint board or joint committee in England and Wales or joint committee in Scotland which is so constituted as to include among its members representatives of any such council [the Strathclyde Passenger Transport Authority], [. . ., any joint authority established by Part IV of the Local Government Act 1985], [an economic prosperity board established under section 88 of the Local Democracy, Economic Development and Construction Act 2009, a combined authority established under section 103 of that Act,] [an authority established for an area in England by an order under section 207 of the Local Government and Public Involvement in Health Act 2007 (joint waste authorities),] [the London Fire and Emergency Planning Authority,] [and any police authority][; and

(c) the Commission for Equality and Human Rights].

NOTES

Sub-s (2): words from "(a) a health service body" to "(b)" in first pair of square brackets inserted by the National Health Service and Community Care Act 1990, s 60, Sch 8, Pt I; in para (a), word omitted repealed and words in fifth (outer) pair of square brackets inserted, by the Health Act 1999 (Supplementary, Consequential etc Provisions) Order 2000, SI 2000/90, arts 2(3), 3(1), Sch 1, para 9, words in second, sixth (inner) and eighth (inner) pairs of square brackets substituted by the National Health Service (Consequential Provisions) Act 2006, s 2, Sch 1, paras 46, 47, date in third pair of square brackets substituted and words in seventh (outer) pair of square brackets inserted by the National Health Service Reform and Health Care Professions Act 2002, s 6(2), Sch 5, para 3, words in fourth pair of square brackets inserted by the Health and Social Care (Community Health and Standards) Act 2003, s 34, Sch 4, paras 15, 16; in para (b), first words omitted repealed by the Local Government Act 1985, s 102(2), Sch 17, second words omitted repealed by the Local Government Act 1972, s 272(1), Sch 30, words in first pair of square brackets substituted by the Local Government (Wales) Act 1994, s 66(4), Sch 16, para 37, words in second pair of square brackets inserted by the Norfolk and Suffolk Broads Act 1988, s 21, Sch 6, para 7, words in third pair of square brackets inserted by the Environment Act 1995, s 78, Sch 10, para 9, words in fourth pair of square brackets substituted and words in fifth pair of square brackets inserted, in relation to Scotland only, by the Local Government etc (Scotland) Act 1994, s 180(1), Sch 13, para 83, words in sixth pair of square brackets inserted by the Local Government Act 1985, s 84, Sch 14, para 46, words omitted therefrom repealed by the Education Reform Act 1988, s 237(2), Sch 13, Pt I, words in seventh pair of square brackets inserted by the Local Democracy, Economic Development and Construction Act 2009, s 119, Sch 6, para 8, words in eighth pair of square brackets inserted by the Local Government and Public Involvement in Health Act 2007, s 209(2), Sch 13, Pt 2, para 28, words in ninth pair of square brackets inserted by the Greater London Authority Act 1999, s 328(8), Sch 29, Pt I, para 12, words in tenth pair of square brackets substituted by the Criminal Justice and Police Act 2001, s 128(1), Sch 6, Pt 3, para 57; para (c) and word immediately preceding it inserted by the Equality Act 2006, s 2, Sch 1, Pt 2, para 8.

Modification: by the Waste Regulation and Disposal (Authorities) Order 1985, SI 1985/1884, art 10, Sch 3, a reference to a joint authority includes a reference to an authority established by that Order.

Residuary bodies: a residuary body established by the Local Government Act 1985, s 57, and the Residuary Body for Wales are to be treated as a local authority for the purposes of this section; see s 57(7) of, and Sch 13, para 14(b) to, the 1985 Act, and s 39 of, and Sch 13, para 19(d) to, the 1994 Act.

Regulations: the Employers' Liability (Compulsory Insurance) Regulations 1998, SI 1998/2573 at **[4180]**.

[3192]

4 Certificates of insurance

(1) Provision may be made by regulations for securing that certificates of insurance in such form and containing such particulars as may be prescribed by the regulations, are issued by insurers to employers entering into contracts of insurance in accordance with the requirements of this Act and for the surrender in such circumstances as may be so prescribed of certificates so issued.

(2) Where a certificate of insurance is required to be issued to an employer in accordance with regulations under subsection (1) above, the employer (subject to any provision made by the regulations as to the surrender of the certificate) shall during the currency of the insurance and such further period (if any) as may be provided by regulations—

- (a) comply with any regulations requiring him to display copies of the certificate of insurance for the information of his employees;
- (b) produce the certificate of insurance or a copy thereof on demand to any inspector duly authorised by the Secretary of State for the purposes of this Act and produce or send the certificate or a copy thereof to such other persons, at such place and in such circumstances as may be prescribed by regulations;
- (c) permit the policy of insurance or a copy thereof to be inspected by such persons and in such circumstances as may be so prescribed.

(3) A person who fails to comply with a requirement imposed by or under this section shall be liable on summary conviction to a fine not exceeding [level 3 on the standard scale].

NOTES

Sub-s (3): words in square brackets substituted by virtue of the Criminal Justice Act 1982, s 46.

Regulations: the Employers' Liability (Compulsory Insurance) Regulations 1998, SI 1998/2573 at **[4180]**.

[3193]

5 Penalty for failure to insure

An employer who on any day is not insured in accordance with this Act when required to be so shall be guilty of an offence and shall be liable on summary conviction to a fine not exceeding [level 4 on the standard scale]; and where an offence under this section committed by a corporation has been committed with the consent or connivance of, or facilitated by any neglect on the part of, any director, manager, secretary or other officer of the corporation, he, as well as the corporation shall be deemed to be guilty of that offence and shall be liable to be proceeded against and punished accordingly.

NOTES

Words in square brackets substituted by virtue of the Criminal Justice Act 1982, s 46.

[3194]

6 Regulations

(1) The Secretary of State may by statutory instrument make regulations for any purpose for which regulations are authorised to be made by this Act, but any such statutory instrument shall be subject to annulment in pursuance of a resolution of either House of Parliament.

(2) Any regulations under this Act may make different provision for different cases or classes of case, and may contain such incidental and supplementary provisions as appear to the Secretary of State to be necessary or expedient for the purposes of the regulations.

NOTES

Regulations: the Employers' Liability (Compulsory Insurance) Regulations 1998, SI 1998/2573 at **[4180]**.

[3195]

7 Short title, extent and commencement

(1) This Act may be cited as the Employers' Liability (Compulsory Insurance) Act 1969.

(2) This Act shall not extend to Northern Ireland.

(3) This Act shall come into force for any purpose on such date as the Secretary of State may by order contained in a statutory instrument appoint, and the purposes for which this Act is to come into force at any time may be defined by reference to the nature of an employer's business, or to that of an employee's work, or in any other way.

NOTES

Orders: the Employers' Liability (Compulsory Insurance) Act 1969 (Commencement) Order 1971, SI 1971/1116.

LOCAL GOVERNMENT ACT 1972

(1972 c 70)

An Act to make provision with respect to local government and the functions of local authorities in England and Wales; to amend Part II of the Transport Act 1968; to confer rights of appeal in respect of decisions relating to licences under the Home Counties (Music and Dancing) Licensing Act 1926; to make further provision with respect to magistrates' courts committees; to abolish certain inferior courts of record; and for connected purposes

[26 October 1972]

NOTES

Transfer of functions in relation to Wales: as to the transfer of functions under this Act from Ministers of the Crown to the National Assembly for Wales, see the National Assembly for Wales (Transfer of Functions) Order 1999, SI 1999/672.

1–110 (*(Pts I–VI) in so far as unrepealed, outside the scope of this work.*)

PART VII
MISCELLANEOUS POWERS OF LOCAL AUTHORITIES

111–135 (*Outside the scope of this work.*)

Miscellaneous

136–139 (*Outside the scope of this work.*)

[3196]

140 Insurance by local authorities against accidents to members

[(1) A local authority may enter into a contract of [accident insurance] against risks of any member of the authority meeting with a personal accident, whether fatal or not, while engaged on the business of the authority.]

(2) Any sum received by the authority under any such contract shall, after deduction of any expenses incurred in the recovery thereof, be paid by them to, or to the personal representatives of, the member of the authority in respect of an accident to whom that sum is received.

(3) The provisions of the Life Assurance Act 1774 shall not apply to any such contract, . . .

[(3A) References to accident insurance must be read with—

(a) section 22 of the Financial Services and Markets Act 2000;

(b) any relevant order under that section; and

(c) Schedule 2 to that Act.]

(4) In this section, the expression . . . "member of the authority" includes a member of a committee or sub-committee of the authority who is not a member of that authority.

NOTES

Sub-s (1): substituted by the Local Government (Miscellaneous Provisions) Act 1982, s 39(1); words in square brackets therein substituted by the Financial Services and Markets Act 2000 (Consequential Amendments and Repeals) Order 2001, SI 2001/3649, art 282(1), (2).

Sub-s (3): words omitted repealed by the Local Government (Miscellaneous Provisions) Act 1982, ss 39(1), 47, Sch 7, Pt XVI.

Sub-s (3A): inserted by SI 2001/3649, art 282(1), (3).

Sub-s (4): words omitted repealed by the London Regional Transport Act 1984, s 71(3)(b), Sch 7.

Residuary bodies: a residuary body established by the Local Government Act 1985, s 57, and the Residuary Body for Wales are to be treated as a local authority or, as the case may be, a principal council, for the purposes of this section and ss 140A, 140C; see s 57(7) of, and Sch 13, para 12 to, the 1985 Act, and s 39 of, and Sch 13, para 19 to, the 1994 Act.

National Park authorities: are to be treated as a local authority or, as the case may be, a principal council, for the purposes of this section and ss 140A, 140C; see the Environment Act 1995, s 65, Sch 8, para 3(1).

[3197]
[140A Insurance of voluntary assistants of local authorities
(1) A local authority may enter into a contract of insurance of a relevant class against risks of any voluntary assistant of the authority meeting with a personal accident, whether fatal or not, while engaged as such, or suffering from any disease or sickness, whether fatal or not, as the result of being so engaged.
(2) In this section—
"local authority" includes—
(a) a board constituted in pursuance of [section 2 of the Town and Country Planning Act 1990] . . . ;
(b) the Common Council of the City of London; and
(c) the Council of the Isles of Scilly; and
"voluntary assistant" means a person who, at the request of the local authority or an authorised officer of the local authority, performs any service or does anything otherwise than for payment by the local authority (except by way of reimbursement of expenses), for the purposes of, or in connection with, the carrying out of any of the functions of the local authority.]

NOTES
Inserted, together with ss 140B, 140C, by the Local Government (Miscellaneous Provisions) Act 1982, s 39(2).
Sub-s (2): in definition "local authority" words in square brackets substituted by the Planning (Consequential Provisions) Act 1990, s 4, Sch 2, para 28(2), words omitted repealed by the Environment Act 1995, s 120, Sch 24.
Residuary bodies: see the note to s 140 at **[3196]**.
National Park authorities: see the note to s 140 at **[3196]**.

[3198]
[140B Insurance of voluntary assistants of probation committees
(1) A county council . . . may enter into a contract of insurance of a relevant class against risks of any voluntary assistant of a relevant probation committee meeting with a personal accident, whether fatal or not, while engaged as such, or suffering from any disease or sickness, whether fatal or not, as the result of being so engaged.
(2) In this section—
"relevant probation committee" means—
(a) in relation to a county council, a probation committee for a probation area wholly or partly within the county; and
(b) in relation to Greater London, a probation committee for a probation area wholly or partly within an outer London borough (within the meaning of section 1 of the 1963 Act); and
"voluntary assistant" means a person who, at the request of an authorised officer of the probation committee, performs any service or does anything otherwise than for payment by the committee (except by way of reimbursement of expenses), for the purposes of, or in connection with, the carrying out of any of the functions of the committee.
[(3) In relation to Wales—
(a) subsections (1) and (2)(a) above shall have effect as if they referred to a principal council; and
(b) subsection (2)(a) above shall have effect as if it referred to the area of the principal council.]]

NOTES
Inserted as noted to s 140A at **[3197]**.
Sub-s (1): words omitted repealed by the Local Government Act 1985, s 102(2), Sch 17.
Sub-s (3): added by the Local Government (Wales) Act 1994, s 66(5), Sch 15, para 31.

[3199]
[140C Provisions supplementary to sections 140A and 140B
(1) The relevant classes of contracts of insurance for the purposes of sections 140A and 140B above are—
[(a) contracts of permanent health insurance; and
(b) contracts of accident insurance].
[(1A) Subsection (1) must be read with—
(a) section 22 of the Financial Services and Markets Act 2000;
(b) any relevant order under that section; and
(c) Schedule 2 to that Act.]

Part III Statutes

(2) Any sum received under a contract of insurance made by virtue of section 140A or 140B above shall, after deduction of any expenses incurred in the recovery thereof, be paid by the authority receiving it to, or to the personal representatives of, the voluntary assistant who suffered the accident, disease or sickness in respect of which the sum is received or to such other person as the authority consider appropriate having regard to the circumstances of the case; and a sum paid to any person other than the assistant or his personal representatives shall be applied by that person in accordance with any directions given by the authority for the benefit of any dependant of the voluntary assistant.
(3) The provisions of the Life Assurance Act 1774 shall not apply to any such contract.
(4) Section 119 above shall apply to any sum which is due by virtue of subsection (2) above and does not exceed the amount for the time being specified in section 119(1) above.]

NOTES

Inserted as noted to s 140A at **[3197]**.

Sub-s (1): paras (a), (b) substituted by the Financial Services and Markets Act 2000 (Consequential Amendments and Repeals) Order 2001, SI 2001/3649, art 283(1), (2).

Sub-s (1A): inserted by SI 2001/3649, art 283(1), (3).

Residuary bodies: see the note to s 140 at **[3196]**.

National Park authorities: see the note to s 140 at **[3196]**.

141–244 (*Ss 141–146A, ss 147–244A (Pts VIII–XI) outside the scope of this work.*)

PART XII
MISCELLANEOUS AND GENERAL

245–250 (*Outside the scope of this work.*)

General

251–273 (*Outside the scope of this work.*)

[3200]
274 Short title and extent
(1) This Act may be cited as the Local Government Act 1972.
(2) . . . This Act shall not extend to Scotland.
(3) . . . This Act shall not extend to Northern Ireland.

NOTES

Sub-s (2): words omitted repealed by the Statute Law (Repeals) Act 2004.

Sub-s (3): words omitted repealed by the House of Commons Disqualification Act 1875, s 10(2), Sch 3, and the Northern Ireland Assembly Disqualification Act 1975, s 5(2), Sch 3, Pt I.

(*Schs 1–30 outside the scope of this work.*)

INSURANCE COMPANIES AMENDMENT ACT 1973

(1973 c 58)

An Act to amend the law relating to insurance companies and the carrying on of insurance business; and to validate certain group policies

[25 July 1973]

1–35 (*Repealed by the Insurance Companies Act 1974, ss 88(2), 90(3), Sch 2.*)

Miscellaneous

36–49 (*Repealed by the Insurance Companies Act 1974, ss 88(2), 90(3), Sch 2.*)

[3201]
50 Validation of certain group policies
(1) Section 2 of the Life Assurance Act 1774 (policy on life or lives or other event or events not valid unless name or names of assured etc inserted when policy is made) shall not invalidate a policy for the benefit of unnamed persons from time to time falling within a specified class or description if the class or description is stated in the policy with sufficient particularity to make it possible to establish the identity of all persons who at any given time are entitled to benefit under the policy.

(2) This section applies to policies effected before the passing of this Act as well as to policies effected thereafter.

51 (*Repealed by the Financial Services and Markets Act 2000 (Consequential Amendments and Savings) (Industrial Assurance) Order 2001, SI 2001/3647, art 5, Sch 3, Pt I, para 11.*)

Supplementary

52–56 (*Ss 52, 53, 55 repealed by the Insurance Companies Act 1974, ss 88(2), 90(3), Sch 2; s 54 repealed by the Statute Law (Repeals) Act 1993; s 56(1) repealed by the Insurance Companies Act 1980, s 4(3), Sch 5; s 56(2) repealed by the Statute Law (Repeals) Act 1977.*)

[3202]–[3314]

57 Short title, citation and commencement

(1) This Act may be cited as the Insurance Companies Amendment Act 1973.

(2)–(8) . . .

NOTES

Sub-ss (2)–(8): repealed by the Insurance Companies Act 1974, ss 88(2), 90(3), Sch 2.

(*Sch 1 repealed by the Statute Law (Repeals) Act 1993; Sch 2 repealed by the Insurance Companies Act 1974, ss 88(2), 90(3), Sch 2; Schs 3–5 repealed by the Insurance Companies Act 1980, s 4(3), Sch 5.*)

SOLICITORS ACT 1974

(1974 c 47)

An Act to consolidate the Solicitors Acts 1957 to 1974 and certain other enactments relating to solicitors

[31 July 1974]

1–30 (*(Pt I) outside the scope of this work.*)

PART II
PROFESSIONAL PRACTICE, CONDUCT AND DISCIPLINE OF SOLICITORS AND CLERKS

31–34 (*Outside the scope of this work.*)

Intervention in solicitor's practice, Compensation Fund and professional indemnity

35, 36, 36A (*Outside the scope of this work.*)

[3315]

37 Professional indemnity

(1) The [Society] may make rules (in this Act referred to as "indemnity rules") concerning indemnity against loss arising from claims in respect of any description of civil liability incurred—

- (a) by a solicitor or former solicitor in connection with his practice or with any trust of which he is or formerly was a trustee;
- (b) by an employee or former employee of a solicitor or former solicitor in connection with that solicitor's practice or with any trust of which that solicitor or the employee is or formerly was a trustee.

(2) For the purpose of providing such indemnity, indemnity rules—

- (a) may authorise or require the Society to establish and maintain a fund or funds;
- (b) may authorise or require the Society to take out and maintain insurance with authorised insurers;
- (c) may require solicitors or any specified class of solicitors to take out and maintain insurance with authorised insurers.

(3) Without prejudice to the generality of subsections (1) and (2), indemnity rules—

- (a) may specify the terms and conditions on which indemnity is to be available, and any circumstances in which the right to it is to be excluded or modified;
- (b) may provide for the management, administration and protection of any fund maintained by virtue of subsection (2)(a) and require solicitors or any class of solicitors to make payments to any such fund;

(c) may require solicitors or any class of solicitors to make payments by way of premium on any insurance policy maintained by the Society by virtue of subsection (2)(b);
(d) may prescribe the conditions which an insurance policy must satisfy for the purposes of subsection (2)(c);
(e) may authorise the Society to determine the amount of any payments required by the rules, subject to such limits, or in accordance with such provisions, as may be prescribed by the rules;
(f) may specify circumstances in which, where a solicitor for whom indemnity is provided has failed to comply with the rules, the Society or insurers may take proceedings against him in respect of sums paid by way of indemnity in connection with a matter in relation to which he has failed to comply;
(g) may specify circumstances in which solicitors are exempt from the rules;
(h) may empower the [Society] to take such steps as [it considers] necessary or expedient to ascertain whether or not the rules are being[, or have been,] complied with; and
(i) may contain incidental, procedural or supplementary provisions.

(4) If any solicitor fails to comply with indemnity rules, any person may make a complaint in respect of that failure to the Tribunal.

(5) The Society shall have power, without prejudice to any of its other powers, to carry into effect any arrangements which it considers necessary or expedient for the purpose of indemnity under this section.

NOTES

Sub-s (1): word in square brackets substituted by the Legal Services Act 2007, s 177, Sch 16, Pt 1, paras 1, 38(a).

Sub-s (3): in para (h), words in first and second pairs of square brackets substituted, and words in third pair of square brackets inserted, by the Legal Services Act 2007, s 177, Sch 16, Pt 1, paras 1, 38(b).

37A–75 (*Ss 37A–55, ss 56–75 (Pt III) outside the scope of this work.*)

PART IV
MISCELLANEOUS AND GENERAL

76–86 (*Outside the scope of this work.*)

Supplementary

86A–89 (*Outside the scope of this work.*)

[3316]

90 Short title, commencement and extent

(1) This Act may be cited as the Solicitors Act 1974.

(2) This Act shall come into force on such day as the Lord Chancellor may by order made by statutory instrument appoint, not being earlier than the first day on which all the provisions of the Solicitors (Amendment) Act 1974 are in force.

(3) If any order made under section 19(7) of the Solicitors (Amendment) Act 1974 makes any savings from the effect of any provision of that Act which it brings into force, the order under subsection (2) may make corresponding savings from the effect of the corresponding provision of this Act.

(4) The provisions of this Act extend to England and Wales only, with the exception of—
(a) section 4(4) and the repeal of section 5(3) of the Solicitors Act 1957, which extend to Scotland;
(b) section 29 and the repeal of section 1 of the Solicitors (Amendment) Act 1974, which extend to Northern Ireland; and
(c) sections 5(3) and 86, . . . and the repeals of section 5(2) of the Solicitors Act 1957 and paragraphs 1 and 5 of Schedule 2 to the Solicitors (Amendment) Act 1974, all of which extend both to Scotland and to Northern Ireland.

NOTES

Sub-s (4): words omitted repealed by the House of Commons Disqualification Act 1975, s 10(2), Sch 3.
Solicitors (Amendment) Act 1974; Solicitors Act 1957: repealed by s 89(2) of, and Sch 4 to, this Act.
Orders: the Solicitors Act 1974 (Commencement) Order 1975, SI 1975/5334.

(*Schs 1–4 outside the scope of this work.*)

UNFAIR CONTRACT TERMS ACT 1977

(1977 c 50)

ARRANGEMENT OF SECTIONS

PART I
AMENDMENT OF LAW FOR ENGLAND AND WALES AND NORTHERN IRELAND

Introductory

1 Scope of Part I . . . . [3317]

Avoidance of liability for negligence, breach of contract, etc

2 Negligence liability . . . . [3318]
3 Liability arising in contract . . . . [3319]
4 Unreasonable indemnity clauses . . . . [3320]

Liability arising from sale or supply of goods

5 "Guarantee" of consumer goods . . . . [3321]
6 Sale and hire-purchase . . . . [3322]
7 Miscellaneous contracts under which goods pass . . . . [3323]

Other provisions about contracts

9 Effect of breach . . . . [3324]
10 Evasion by means of secondary contract . . . . [3325]

Explanatory provisions

11 The "reasonableness" test . . . . [3326]
12 "Dealing as consumer" . . . . [3327]
13 Varieties of exemption clause . . . . [3328]
14 Interpretation of Part I . . . . [3329]

PART II
AMENDMENT OF LAW FOR SCOTLAND

15 Scope of Part II . . . . [3330]
16 Liability for breach of duty . . . . [3331]
17 Control of unreasonable exemptions in consumer or standard form contracts . . . . [3332]
18 Unreasonable indemnity clauses in consumer contracts . . . . [3333]
19 "Guarantee of consumer goods" . . . . [3334]
20 Obligations implied by law in sale and hire-purchase contracts . . . . [3335]
21 Obligations implied by law in other contracts for the supply of goods . . . . [3336]
22 Consequence of breach . . . . [3337]
23 Evasion by means of secondary contract . . . . [3338]
24 The "reasonableness" test . . . . [3339]
25 Interpretation of Part II . . . . [3340]

PART III
PROVISIONS APPLYING TO WHOLE OF UNITED KINGDOM

Miscellaneous

26 International supply contracts . . . . [3341]
27 Choice of law clauses . . . . [3342]
28 Temporary provision for sea carriage of passengers . . . . [3343]
29 Saving for other relevant legislation . . . . [3344]

General

31 Commencement; amendments; repeals . . . . [3345]
32 Citation and extent . . . . [3346]

SCHEDULES:

Schedule 1—Scope of sections 2 to 4 and 7 . . . . [3347]
Schedule 2—"Guidelines" for Application of Reasonableness Test . . . . [3348]

An Act to impose further limits on the extent to which under the law of England and Wales and Northern Ireland civil liability for breach of contract, or for negligence or other breach of duty, can be avoided by means of contract terms and otherwise, and under the law of Scotland civil liability can be avoided by means of contract terms

[26 October 1977]

PART I
AMENDMENT OF LAW FOR ENGLAND AND WALES AND NORTHERN IRELAND

Introductory

[3317]
1 Scope of Part I

(1) For the purposes of this Part of this Act, "negligence" means the breach—

(a) of any obligation, arising from the express or implied terms of a contract, to take reasonable care or exercise reasonable skill in the performance of the contract;

(b) of any common law duty to take reasonable care or exercise reasonable skill (but not any stricter duty);

(c) of the common duty of care imposed by the Occupiers' Liability Act 1957 or the Occupiers' Liability Act (Northern Ireland) 1957.

(2) This Part of this Act is subject to Part III; and in relation to contracts, the operation of sections 2 to 4 and 7 is subject to the exceptions made by Schedule 1.

(3) In the case of both contract and tort, sections 2 to 7 apply (except where the contrary is stated in section 6(4)) only to business liability, that is liability for breach of obligations or duties arising—

(a) from things done or to be done by a person in the course of a business (whether his own business or another's); or

(b) from the occupation of premises used for business purposes of the occupier;

and references to liability are to be read accordingly [but liability of an occupier of premises for breach of an obligation or duty towards a person obtaining access to the premises for recreational or educational purposes, being liability for loss or damage suffered by reason of the dangerous state of the premises, is not a business liability of the occupier unless granting that person such access for the purposes concerned falls within the business purposes of the occupier].

(4) In relation to any breach of duty or obligation, it is immaterial for any purpose of this Part of this Act whether the breach was inadvertent or intentional, or whether liability for it arises directly or vicariously.

NOTES

Sub-s (3): words in square brackets added by the Occupiers' Liability Act 1984, s 2.

Avoidance of liability for negligence, breach of contract, etc

[3318]
2 Negligence liability

(1) A person cannot by reference to any contract term or to a notice given to persons generally or to particular persons exclude or restrict his liability for death or personal injury resulting from negligence.

(2) In the case of other loss or damage, a person cannot so exclude or restrict his liability for negligence except in so far as the term or notice satisfies the requirement of reasonableness.

(3) Where a contract term or notice purports to exclude or restrict liability for negligence a person's agreement to or awareness of it is not of itself to be taken as indicating his voluntary acceptance of any risk.

[3319]
3 Liability arising in contract

(1) This section applies as between contracting parties where one of them deals as consumer or on the other's written standard terms of business.

(2) As against that party, the other cannot by reference to any contract term—

(a) when himself in breach of contract, exclude or restrict any liability of his in respect of the breach; or

(b) claim to be entitled—

(i) to render a contractual performance substantially different from that which was reasonably expected of him, or

(ii) in respect of the whole or any part of his contractual obligation, to render no performance at all,

except in so far as (in any of the cases mentioned above in this subsection) the contract term satisfies the requirement of reasonableness.

[3320]

4 Unreasonable indemnity clauses

(1) A person dealing as consumer cannot by reference to any contract term be made to indemnify another person (whether a party to the contract or not) in respect of liability that may be incurred by the other for negligence or breach of contract, except in so far as the contract term satisfies the requirement of reasonableness.

(2) This section applies whether the liability in question—

(a) is directly that of the person to be indemnified or is incurred by him vicariously;

(b) is to the person dealing as consumer or to someone else.

Liability arising from sale or supply of goods

[3321]

5 "Guarantee" of consumer goods

(1) In the case of goods of a type ordinarily supplied for private use or consumption, where loss or damage—

(a) arises from the goods proving defective while in consumer use; and

(b) results from the negligence of a person concerned in the manufacture or distribution of the goods,

liability for the loss or damage cannot be excluded or restricted by reference to any contract term or notice contained in or operating by reference to a guarantee of the goods.

(2) For these purposes—

(a) goods are to be regarded as "in consumer use" when a person is using them, or has them in his possession for use, otherwise than exclusively for the purposes of a business; and

(b) anything in writing is a guarantee if it contains or purports to contain some promise or assurance (however worded or presented) that defects will be made good by complete or partial replacement, or by repair, monetary compensation or otherwise.

(3) This section does not apply as between the parties to a contract under or in pursuance of which possession or ownership of the goods passed.

[3322]

6 Sale and hire-purchase

(1) Liability for breach of the obligations arising from—

(a) [section 12 of the Sale of Goods Act 1979] (seller's implied undertakings as to title, etc);

(b) section 8 of the Supply of Goods (Implied Terms) Act 1973 (the corresponding thing in relation to hire-purchase),

cannot be excluded or restricted by reference to any contract term.

(2) As against a person dealing as consumer, liability for breach of the obligations arising from—

(a) [section 13, 14 or 15 of the 1979 Act] (seller's implied undertakings as to conformity of goods with description or sample, or as to their quality or fitness for a particular purpose);

(b) section 9, 10 or 11 of the 1973 Act (the corresponding things in relation to hire-purchase),

cannot be excluded or restricted by reference to any contract term.

(3) As against a person dealing otherwise than as consumer, the liability specified in subsection (2) above can be excluded or restricted by reference to a contract term, but only in so far as the term satisfies the requirement of reasonableness.

(4) The liabilities referred to in this section are not only the business liabilities defined by section 1(3), but include those arising under any contract of sale of goods or hire-purchase agreement.

NOTES

Sub-ss (1), (2): words in square brackets substituted by the Sale of Goods Act 1979, s 63, Sch 2, para 19.

[3323]

7 Miscellaneous contracts under which goods pass

(1) Where the possession or ownership of goods passes under or in pursuance of a contract not governed by the law of sale of goods or hire-purchase, subsections (2) to (4) below apply as regards the effect (if any) to be given to contract terms excluding or restricting liability for breach of obligation arising by implication of law from the nature of the contract.

(2) As against a person dealing as consumer, liability in respect of the goods' correspondence with description or sample, or their quality or fitness for any particular purpose, cannot be excluded or restricted by reference to any such term.

(3) As against a person dealing otherwise than as consumer, that liability can be excluded or restricted by reference to such a term, but only in so far as the term satisfies the requirement of reasonableness.

[(3A) Liability for breach of the obligations arising under section 2 of the Supply of Goods and Services Act 1982 (implied terms about title etc in certain contracts for the transfer of the property in goods) cannot be excluded or restricted by references to any such term.]

(4) Liability in respect of—

(a) the right to transfer ownership of the goods, or give possession; or

(b) the assurance of quiet possession to a person taking goods in pursuance of the contract,

cannot [(in a case to which subsection (3A) above does not apply)] be excluded or restricted by reference to any such term except in so far as the term satisfies the requirement of reasonableness.

(5) . . .

NOTES

Sub-s (3A): inserted by the Supply of Goods and Services Act 1982, s 17(2), (3).

Sub-s (4): words in square brackets inserted by the Supply of Goods and Services Act 1982, s 17(2), (3).

Sub-s (5): repealed by the Regulatory Reform (Trading Stamps) Order 2005, SI 2005/871, art 6, Schedule.

Other provisions about contracts

8 (*Substitutes the Misrepresentation Act 1967, s 3 at* **[3186]**, *and the Misrepresentation Act (Northern Ireland) 1967, s 3.*)

[3324]

9 Effect of breach

(1) Where for reliance upon it a contract term has to satisfy the requirement of reasonableness, it may be found to do so and be given effect accordingly notwithstanding that the contract has been terminated either by breach or by a party electing to treat it as repudiated.

(2) Where on a breach the contract is nevertheless affirmed by a party entitled to treat it as repudiated, this does not of itself exclude the requirement of reasonableness in relation to any contract term.

[3325]

10 Evasion by means of secondary contract

A person is not bound by any contract term prejudicing or taking away rights of his which arise under, or in connection with the performance of, another contract, so far as those rights extend to the enforcement of another's liability which this Part of this Act prevents that other from excluding or restricting.

Explanatory provisions

[3326]

11 The "reasonableness" test

(1) In relation to a contract term, the requirement of reasonableness for the purposes of this Part of this Act, section 3 of the Misrepresentation Act 1967 and section 3 of the Misrepresentation Act (Northern Ireland) 1967 is that the term shall have been a fair and reasonable one to be included having regard to the circumstances which were, or ought reasonably to have been, known to or in the contemplation of the parties when the contract was made.

(2) In determining for the purposes of section 6 or 7 above whether a contract term satisfies the requirement of reasonableness, regard shall be had in particular to the matters specified in Schedule 2 to this Act; but this subsection does not prevent the court or arbitrator from holding, in accordance with any rule of law, that a term which purports to exclude or restrict any relevant liability is not a term of the contract.

(3) In relation to a notice (not being a notice having contractual effect), the requirement of reasonableness under this Act is that it should be fair and reasonable to allow reliance on it, having regard to all the circumstances obtaining when the liability arose or (but for the notice) would have arisen.

(4) Where by reference to a contract term or notice a person seeks to restrict liability to a specified sum of money, and the question arises (under this or any other Act) whether the term or notice satisfies the requirement of reasonableness, regard shall be had in particular (but without prejudice to subsection (2) above in the case of contract terms) to—

(a) the resources which he could expect to be available to him for the purpose of meeting the liability should it arise; and

(b) how far it was open to him to cover himself by insurance.

(5) It is for those claiming that a contract term or notice satisfies the requirement of reasonableness to show that it does.

[3327]
12 "Dealing as consumer"
(1) A party to a contract "deals as consumer" in relation to another party if—
(a) he neither makes the contract in the course of a business nor holds himself out as doing so; and
(b) the other party does make the contract in the course of a business; and
(c) in the case of a contract governed by the law of sale of goods or hire-purchase, or by section 7 of this Act, the goods passing under or in pursuance of the contract are of a type ordinarily supplied for private use or consumption.

[(1A) But if the first party mentioned in subsection (1) is an individual paragraph (c) of that subsection must be ignored.]

[(2) But the buyer is not in any circumstances to be regarded as dealing as consumer—
(a) if he is an individual and the goods are second hand goods sold at public auction at which individuals have the opportunity of attending the sale in person;
(b) if he is not an individual and the goods are sold by auction or by competitive tender.]

(3) Subject to this, it is for those claiming that a party does not deal as consumer to show that he does not.

NOTES
Sub-s (1A): inserted by the Sale and Supply of Goods to Consumers Regulations 2002, SI 2002/3045, reg 14(1), (2).
Sub-s (2): substituted by SI 2002/3045, reg 14(1), (3).

[3328]
13 Varieties of exemption clause
(1) To the extent that this Part of this Act prevents the exclusion or restriction of any liability it also prevents—
(a) making the liability or its enforcement subject to restrictive or onerous conditions;
(b) excluding or restricting any right or remedy in respect of the liability, or subjecting a person to any prejudice in consequence of his pursuing any such right or remedy;
(c) excluding or restricting rules of evidence or procedure;

and (to that extent) sections 2 and 5 to 7 also prevent excluding or restricting liability by reference to terms and notices which exclude or restrict the relevant obligation or duty.

(2) But an agreement in writing to submit present or future differences to arbitration is not to be treated under this Part of this Act as excluding or restricting any liability.

[3329]
14 Interpretation of Part I
In this Part of this Act—

"business" includes a profession and the activities of any government department or local or public authority;
"goods" has the same meaning as in [the Sale of Goods Act 1979];
"hire-purchase agreement" has the same meaning as in the Consumer Credit Act 1974;
"negligence" has the meaning given by section 1(1);
"notice" includes an announcement, whether or not in writing, and any other communication or pretended communication; and
"personal injury" includes any disease and any impairment of physical or mental condition.

NOTES
In definition "goods" words in square brackets substituted by the Sale of Goods Act 1979, s 63, Sch 2, para 20.

PART II
AMENDMENT OF LAW FOR SCOTLAND

[3330]
15 Scope of Part II
(1) This Part of this Act . . . , is subject to Part III of this Act and does not affect the validity of any discharge or indemnity given by a person in consideration of the receipt by him of compensation in settlement of any claim which he has.

(2) Subject to subsection (3) below, sections 16 to 18 of this Act apply to any contract only to the extent that the contract—
(a) relates to the transfer of the ownership or possession of goods from one person to another (with or without work having been done on them);
(b) constitutes a contract of service or apprenticeship;

(c) relates to services of whatever kind, including (without prejudice to the foregoing generality) carriage, deposit and pledge, care and custody, mandate, agency, loan and services relating to the use of land;
(d) relates to the liability of an occupier of land to persons entering upon or using that land;
(e) relates to a grant of any right or permission to enter upon or use land not amounting to an estate or interest in the land.

(3) Notwithstanding anything in subsection (2) above, section 16 to 18—
(a) do not apply to any contract to the extent that the contract—
(i) is a contract of insurance (including a contract to pay an annuity on human life);
(ii) relates to the formation, constitution or dissolution of any body corporate or unincorporated association or partnership;
(b) apply to—
a contract of marine salvage or towage;
a charter party of a ship or hovercraft;
a contract for the carriage of goods by ship or hovercraft; or,
a contract to which subsection (4) below relates,
only to the extent that—
(i) both parties deal or hold themselves out as dealing in the course of a business (and then only in so far as the contract purports to exclude or restrict liability for breach of duty in respect of death or personal injury); or
(ii) the contract is a consumer contract (and then only in favour of the consumer).

(4) This subsection relates to a contract in pursuance of which goods are carried by ship or hovercraft and which either—
(a) specifies ship or hovercraft as the means of carriage over part of the journey to be covered; or
(b) makes no provision as to the means of carriage and does not exclude ship or hovercraft as that means,
in so far as the contract operates for and in relation to the carriage of the goods by that means.

NOTES

Words omitted repealed by the Law Reform (Miscellaneous Provisions) (Scotland) Act 1990, ss 68(2), (6), 74(2), Sch 9.

[3331]

16 Liability for breach of duty

(1) [Subject to subsection (1A) below,] where a term of a contract [, or a provision of a notice given to persons generally or to particular persons,] purports to exclude or restrict liability for breach of duty arising in the course of any business or from the occupation of any premises used for business purposes of the occupier, that term [or provision]—
(a) shall be void in any case where such exclusion or restriction is in respect of death or personal injury;
(b) shall, in any other case, have no effect if it was not fair and reasonable to incorporate the term in the contract [or, as the case may be, if it is not fair and reasonable to allow reliance on the provision].

[(1A) Nothing in paragraph (b) of subsection (1) above shall be taken as implying that a provision of a notice has effect in circumstances where, apart from that paragraph, it would not have effect.]

(2) Subsection (1)(a) above does not affect the validity of any discharge and indemnity given by a person, on or in connection with an award to him of compensation for pneumoconiosis attributable to employment in the coal industry, in respect of any further claim arising from his contracting that disease.

(3) Where under subsection (1) above a term of a contract [or a provision of a notice] is void or has no effect, the fact that a person agreed to, or was aware of, the term [or provision] shall not of itself be sufficient evidence that he knowingly and voluntarily assumed any risk.

NOTES

Sub-ss (1), (3): words in square brackets inserted by the Law Reform (Miscellaneous Provisions) (Scotland) Act 1990, s 68 (3)(a), (c), (6).

Sub-s (1A): inserted by the Law Reform (Miscellaneous Provisions) (Scotland) Act 1990, s 68(3)(b), (6).

[3332]

17 Control of unreasonable exemptions in consumer or standard form contracts

(1) Any term of a contract which is a consumer contract or a standard form contract shall have no effect for the purpose of enabling a party to the contract—

(a) who is in breach of a contractual obligation, to exclude or restrict any liability of his to the consumer or customer in respect of the breach;

(b) in respect of a contractual obligation, to render no performance, or to render a performance substantially different from that which the consumer or customer reasonably expected from the contract;

if it was not fair and reasonable to incorporate the term in the contract.

(2) In this section "customer" means a party to a standard form contract who deals on the basis of written standard terms of business of the other party to the contract who himself deals in the course of a business.

[3333]

18 Unreasonable indemnity clauses in consumer contracts

(1) Any term of a contract which is a consumer contract shall have no effect for the purpose of making the consumer indemnify another person (whether a party to the contract or not) in respect of liability which that other person may incur as a result of breach of duty or breach of contract, if it was not fair and reasonable to incorporate the term in the contract.

(2) In this section "liability" means liability arising in the course of any business or from the occupation of any premises used for business purposes of the occupier.

[3334]

19 "Guarantee of consumer goods"

(1) This section applies to a guarantee—

(a) in relation to goods which are of a type ordinarily supplied for private use or consumption; and

(b) which is not a guarantee given by one party to the other party to a contract under or in pursuance of which the ownership or possession of the goods to which the guarantee relates is transferred.

(2) A term of a guarantee to which this section applies shall be void in so far as it purports to exclude or restrict liability for loss or damage (including death or personal injury)—

(a) arising from the goods proving defective while—

(i) in use otherwise than exclusively for the purposes of a business; or

(ii) in the possession of a person for such use; and

(b) resulting from the breach of duty of a person concerned in the manufacture or distribution of the goods.

(3) For the purposes of this section, any document is a guarantee if it contains or purports to contain some promise or assurance (however worded or presented) that defects will be made good by complete or partial replacement, or by repair, monetary compensation otherwise.

[3335]

20 Obligations implied by law in sale and hire-purchase contracts

(1) Any term of a contract which purports to exclude or restrict liability for breach of the obligations arising from—

(a) section 12 of the Sale of Goods Act [1979] (seller's implied undertakings as to title etc);

(b) section 8 of the Supply of Goods (Implied Terms) Act 1973 (implied terms as to title in hire-purchase agreements),

shall be void.

(2) Any term of a contract which purports to exclude or restrict liability for breach of the obligations arising from—

(a) section 13, 14 or 15 of the said Act of [1979] (seller's implied undertakings as to conformity of goods with description or sample, or as to their quality or fitness for a particular purpose);

(b) section 9, 10 or 11 of the said Act of 1973 (the corresponding provisions in relation to hire-purchase),

shall—

(i) in the case of a consumer contract, be void against the consumer;

(ii) in any other case, have no effect if it was not fair and reasonable to incorporate the term in the contract.

NOTES

Sub-ss (1), (2): dates in square brackets substituted by the Sale of Goods Act 1979, ss 62, 63, Sch 2, para 21.

[3336]

21 Obligations implied by law in other contracts for the supply of goods

(1) Any term of a contract to which this section applies purporting to exclude or restrict liability for breach of an obligation—

(a) such as is referred to in subsection (3)(a) below—

(i) in the case of a consumer contract, shall be void against the consumer, and

(ii) in any other case, shall have no effect if it was not fair and reasonable to incorporate the term in the contract;

(b) such as is referred to in subsection (3)(b) below, shall have no effect if it was not fair and reasonable to incorporate the term in the contract.

(2) This section applies to any contract to the extent that it relates to any such matter as is referred to in section 15(2)(a) of this Act, but does not apply to—

(a) a contract of sale of goods or a hire-purchase agreement; or

(b) a charter party of a ship or hovercraft unless it is a consumer contract (and then only in favour of the consumer).

(3) An obligation referred to in this subsection is an obligation incurred under a contract in the course of a business and arising by implication of law from the nature of the contract which relates—

(a) to the correspondence of goods with description or sample, or to the quality or fitness of goods for any particular purpose; or

(b) to any right to transfer ownership or possession of goods, or to the enjoyment of quiet possession of goods.

(4) . . .

NOTES

Sub-s (4): repealed by the Regulatory Reform (Trading Stamps) Order 2005, SI 2005/871, art 6, Schedule.

[3337]

22 Consequence of breach

For the avoidance of doubt, where any provision of this Part of this Act requires that the incorporation of a term in a contract must be fair and reasonable for that term to have effect—

(a) if that requirement is satisfied, the term may be given effect to notwithstanding that the contract has been terminated in consequence of breach of that contract;

(b) for the term to be given effect to, that requirement must be satisfied even where a party who is entitled to rescind the contract elects not to rescind it.

[3338]

23 Evasion by means of secondary contract

Any term of any contract shall be void which purports to exclude or restrict, or has the effect of excluding or restricting—

(a) the exercise, by a party to any other contract, of any right or remedy which arises in respect of that other contract in consequence of breach of duty, or of obligation, liability for which could not by virtue of the provisions of this Part of this Act be excluded or restricted by a term of that other contract;

(b) the application of the provisions of this Part of this Act in respect of that or any other contract.

[3339]

24 The "reasonableness" test

(1) In determining for the purposes of this Part of this Act whether it was fair and reasonable to incorporate a term in a contract, regard shall be had only to the circumstances which were, or ought reasonably to have been, known to or in the contemplation of the parties to the contract at the time the contract was made.

(2) In determining for the purposes of section 20 or 21 of this Act whether it was fair and reasonable to incorporate a term in a contract, regard shall be had in particular to the matters specified in Schedule 2 to this Act; but this subsection shall not prevent a court or arbiter from holding, in accordance with any rule of law, that a term which purports to exclude or restrict any relevant liability is not a term of the contract.

[(2A) In determining for the purposes of this Part of this Act whether it is fair and reasonable to allow reliance on a provision of a notice (not being a notice having contractual effect), regard shall be had to all the circumstances obtaining when the liability arose of (but for the provision) would have arisen.]

(3) Where a term in a contract [or a provision of a notice] purports to restrict liability to a specified sum of money, and the question arises for the purposes of this Part of this Act whether it was fair and reasonable to incorporate the term in the contract [or whether it is fair and reasonable to allow reliance on the provision], then, without prejudice to subsection (2) above [in the case of a term in a contract], regard shall be had in particular to—

(a) the resources which the party seeking to rely on that term [or provision] could expect to be available to him for the purpose of meeting the liability should it arise;

(b) how far it was open to that party to cover himself by insurance.

(4) The onus of proving that it was fair and reasonable to incorporate a term in a contract [or that it is fair and reasonable to allow reliance on a provision of a notice] shall lie on the party so contending.

NOTES

Sub-s (2A): inserted by the Law Reform (Miscellaneous Provisions) (Scotland) Act 1990, s 68(4)(a), (6).

Sub-ss (3), (4): words in square brackets inserted by the Law Reform (Miscellaneous Provisions) (Scotland) Act 1990, s 68(4)(b), (c), (6).

[3340]

25 Interpretation of Part II

(1) In this Part of this Act—

"breach of duty" means the breach—

(a) of any obligation, arising from the express or implied terms of a contract, to take reasonable care or exercise reasonable skill in the performance of the contract;

(b) of any common law duty to take reasonable care or exercise reasonable skill;

(c) of the duty of reasonable care imposed by section 2(1) of the Occupiers' Liability (Scotland) Act 1960;

"business" includes a profession and the activities of any government department or local or public authority;

"consumer" has the meaning assigned to that expression in the definition in this section of "consumer contract";

"consumer contract" means [subject to subsections (1A) and (1B) below] a contract . . . in which—

(a) one party to the contract deals, and the other party to the contract ("the consumer") does not deal or hold himself out as dealing, in the course of a business, and

(b) in the case of a contract such as is mentioned in section 15(2)(a) of this Act, the goods are of a type ordinarily supplied for private use or consumption;

and for the purposes of this Part of this Act the onus of proving that a contract is not to be regarded as a consumer contract shall lie on the party so contending;

"goods" has the same meaning as in [the Sale of Goods Act 1979];

"hire-purchase agreement" has the same meaning as in section 189(1) of the Consumer Credit Act 1974;

["notice" includes an announcement, whether or not in writing, and any other communication or pretended communication;]

"personal injury" includes any disease and any impairment of physical or mental condition.

[(1A) Where the consumer is an individual, paragraph (b) in the definition of "consumer contract" in subsection (1) must be disregarded.

(1B) The expression of "consumer contract" does not include a contract in which—

(a) the buyer is an individual and the goods are second hand goods sold by public auction at which individuals have the opportunity of attending in person; or

(b) the buyer is not an individual and the goods are sold by auction or competitive tender.]

(2) In relation to any breach of duty or obligation, it is immaterial for any purpose of this Part of this Act whether the act or omission giving rise to that breach was inadvertent or intentional, or whether liability for it arises directly or vicariously.

(3) In this Part of this Act, any reference to excluding or restricting any liability includes—

(a) making the liability or its enforcement subject to any restrictive or onerous conditions;

(b) excluding or restricting any right or remedy in respect of the liability, or subjecting a person to any prejudice in consequence of his pursuing any such right or remedy;

(c) excluding or restricting any rule of evidence or procedure;

(d) . . .

but does not include an agreement to submit any question to arbitration.

(4) . . .

(5) In sections 15 and 16 and 19 to 21 of this Act, any reference to excluding or restricting liability for breach of an obligation or duty shall include a reference to excluding or restricting the obligation or duty itself.

NOTES

Sub-s (1): in definition "consumer contract" words in square brackets inserted and words omitted repealed by the Sale and Supply of Goods to Consumers Regulations 2002, SI 2002/3045, reg 14(1), (4)(a); in definition "goods" words in square brackets substituted by the Sale of Goods Act 1979, ss 62, 63, Sch 2, para 22; definition "notice" inserted by the Law Reform (Miscellaneous Provisions) (Scotland) Act 1990, s 68(5)(a), (6).

Sub-ss (1A), (1B): inserted by SI 2002/3045, reg 14(1), (4)(b).

Sub-s (3): para (d) repealed by the Law Reform (Miscellaneous Provisions) (Scotland) Act 1990, ss 68(5)(b), (6), 74(2), Sch 9.

Sub-s (4): repealed by the Law Reform (Miscellaneous Provisions) (Scotland) Act 1990, ss 68(5)(b), (6), 74(2), Sch 9.

PART III
PROVISIONS APPLYING TO WHOLE OF UNITED KINGDOM

Miscellaneous

[3341]

26 International supply contracts

(1) The limits imposed by this Act on the extent to which a person may exclude or restrict liability by reference to a contract term do not apply to liability arising under such a contract as is described in subsection (3) below.

(2) The terms of such a contract are not subject to any requirement of reasonableness under section 3 or 4: and nothing in Part II of this Act shall require the incorporation of the terms of such a contract to be fair and reasonable for them to have effect.

(3) Subject to subsection (4), that description of contract is one whose characteristics are the following—

(a) either it is a contract of sale of goods or it is one under or in pursuance of which the possession or ownership of goods passes; and

(b) it is made by parties whose places of business (or, if they have none, habitual residences) are in the territories of different States (the Channel Islands and the Isle of Man being treated for this purpose as different States from the United Kingdom).

(4) A contract falls within subsection (3) above only if either—

(a) the goods in question are, at the time of the conclusion of the contract, in the course of carriage, or will be carried, from the territory of one State to the territory of another; or

(b) the acts constituting the offer and acceptance have been done in the territories of different States; or

(c) the contract provides for the goods to be delivered to the territory of a State other than that within whose territory those acts were done.

[3342]

27 Choice of law clauses

(1) Where the [law applicable to] a contract is the law of any part of the United Kingdom only by choice of the parties (and apart from that choice would be the law of some country outside the United Kingdom) sections 2 to 7 and 16 to 21 of this Act do not operate as part [of the law applicable to the contract].

(2) This Act has effect notwithstanding any contract term which applies or purports to apply the law of some country outside the United Kingdom, where (either or both)—

(a) the term appears to the court, or arbitrator or arbiter to have been imposed wholly or mainly for the purpose of enabling the party imposing it to evade the operation of this Act; or

(b) in the making of the contract one of the parties dealt as consumer, and he was then habitually resident in the United Kingdom, and the essential steps necessary for the making of the contract were taken there, whether by him or by others on his behalf.

(3) In the application of subsection (2) above to Scotland, for paragraph (b) there shall be substituted—

"(b) the contract is a consumer contract as defined in Part II of this Act, and the consumer at the date when the contract was made was habitually resident in the United Kingdom, and the essential steps necessary for the making of the contract were taken there, whether by him or by others on his behalf.".

NOTES

Sub-s (1): words in square brackets substituted by the Contracts (Applicable Law) Act 1990, s 5, Sch 4, para 4.

[3343]

28 Temporary provision for sea carriage of passengers

(1) This section applies to a contract for carriage by sea of a passenger or of a passenger and his luggage where the provisions of the Athens Convention (with or without modification) do not have, in relation to the contract, the force of law in the United Kingdom.

(2) In a case where—

(a) the contract is not made in the United Kingdom, and

(b) neither the place of departure nor the place of destination under it is in the United Kingdom,

a person is not precluded by this Act from excluding or restricting liability for loss or damage, being loss or damage for which the provisions of the Convention would, if they had the force of law in relation to the contract, impose liability on him.

(3) In any other case, a person is not precluded by this Act from excluding or restricting liability for that loss or damage—

(a) in so far as the exclusion or restriction would have been effective in that case had the provisions of the Convention had the force of law in relation to the contract; or

(b) in such circumstances and to such extent as may be prescribed, by reference to a prescribed term of the contract.

(4) For the purposes of subsection (3)(a), the values which shall be taken to be the official values in the United Kingdom of the amounts (expressed in gold francs) by reference to which liability under the provisions of the Convention is limited shall be such amounts in sterling as the Secretary of State may from time to time by order made by statutory instrument specify.

(5) In this section,—

(a) the references to excluding or restricting liability include doing any of those things in relation to the liability which are mentioned in section 13 or section 25(3) and (5); and

(b) "the Athens Convention" means the Athens Convention relating to the Carriage of Passengers and their Luggage by Sea, 1974; and

(c) "prescribed" means prescribed by the Secretary of State by regulations made by statutory instrument;

and a statutory instrument containing the regulations shall be subject to annulment in pursuance of a resolution of either House of Parliament.

[3344]

29 Saving for other relevant legislation

(1) Nothing in this Act removes or restricts the effect of, or prevents reliance upon, any contractual provision which—

(a) is authorised or required by the express terms or necessary implication of an enactment; or

(b) being made with a view to compliance with an international agreement to which the United Kingdom is a party, does not operate more restrictively than is contemplated by the agreement.

(2) A contract term is to be taken—

(a) for the purposes of Part I of this Act, as satisfying the requirement of reasonableness; and

(b) for those of Part II, to have been fair and reasonable to incorporate,

if it is incorporated or approved by, or incorporated pursuant to a decision or ruling of, a competent authority acting in the exercise of any statutory jurisdiction or function and is not a term in a contract to which the competent authority is itself a party.

(3) In this section—

"competent authority" means any court, arbitrator or arbiter, government department or public authority;

"enactment" means any legislation (including subordinate legislation) of the United Kingdom or Northern Ireland and any instrument having effect by virtue of such legislation; and

"statutory" means conferred by an enactment.

30 (*Repealed by the Consumer Safety Act 1978, s 10(1), Sch 3.*)

Part III Statutes

[3345]

31 Commencement; amendments; repeals

(1) This Act comes into force on 1st February 1978.

(2) Nothing in this Act applies to contracts made before the date on which it comes into force; but subject to this, it applies to liability for any loss or damage which is suffered on or after that date.

(3) The enactments specified in Schedule 3 to this Act are amended as there shown.

(4) The enactments specified in Schedule 4 to this Act are repealed to the extent specified in column 3 of that Schedule.

[3346]

32 Citation and extent

(1) This Act may be cited as the Unfair Contract Terms Act 1977.

(2) Part I of this Act extends to England and Wales and to Northern Ireland; but it does not extend to Scotland.

(3) Part II of this Act extends to Scotland only.

(4) This Part of this Act extends to the whole of the United Kingdom.

SCHEDULES

SCHEDULE 1

SCOPE OF SECTIONS 2 TO 4 AND 7

Section 1(2)

[3347]

1. Sections 2 to 4 of this Act do not extend to—

(a) any contract of insurance (including a contract to pay an annuity on human life);

(b) any contract so far as it relates to the creation or transfer of an interest in land, or to the termination of such an interest, whether by extinction, merger, surrender, forfeiture or otherwise;

(c) any contract so far as it relates to the creation or transfer of a right or interest in any patent, trade mark, copyright [or design right], registered design, technical or commercial information or other intellectual property, or relates to the termination of any such right or interest;

(d) any contract so far as it relates—

(i) to the formation or dissolution of a company (which means any body corporate or unincorporated association and includes a partnership), or

(ii) to its constitution or the rights or obligations of its corporators or members;

(e) any contract so far as it relates to the creation or transfer of securities or of any right or interest in securities.

2. Section 2(1) extends to—

(a) any contract of marine salvage or towage;

(b) any charterparty of a ship or hovercraft; and

(c) any contract for the carriage of goods by ship or hovercraft;

but subject to this sections 2 to 4 and 7 do not extend to any such contract except in favour of a person dealing as consumer.

3. Where goods are carried by ship or hovercraft in pursuance of a contract which either—

(a) specifies that as the means of carriage over part of the journey to be covered, or

(b) makes no provision as to the means of carriage and does not exclude that means,

then sections 2(2), 3 and 4 do not, except in favour of a person dealing as consumer, extend to the contract as it operates for and in relation to the carriage of the goods by that means.

4. Section 2(1) and (2) do not extend to a contract of employment, except in favour of the employee.

5. Section 2(1) does not affect the validity of any discharge and indemnity given by a person, on or in connection with an award to him of compensation for pneumoconiosis attributable to employment in the coal industry, in respect of any further claim arising from his contracting that disease.

NOTES

Para 1: words in square brackets in sub-para (c) inserted by the Copyright, Designs and Patents Act 1988, s 303(1), Sch 7, para 24.

Modification: references to trade marks or registered trade marks within the meaning of the Trade Marks Act 1938 shall, unless the context otherwise requires, be construed as references to trade marks or registered trade marks within the meaning of the Trade Marks Act 1994; see the Trade Marks Act 1994, Sch 4, para 1.

SCHEDULE 2

"GUIDELINES" FOR APPLICATION OF REASONABLENESS TEST

Sections 11(2), 24(2)

[3348]–[3351]

The matters to which regard is to be had in particular for the purposes of sections 6(3), 7(3) and (4), 20 and 21 are any of the following which appear to be relevant—

- (a) the strength of the bargaining positions of the parties relative to each other, taking into account (among other things) alternative means by which the customer's requirements could have been met;
- (b) whether the customer received an inducement to agree to the term, or in accepting it had an opportunity of entering into a similar contract with other persons, but without having to accept a similar term;
- (c) whether the customer knew or ought reasonably to have known of the existence and extent of the term (having regard, among other things, to any custom of the trade and any previous course of dealing between the parties);
- (d) where the term excludes or restricts any relevant liability if some condition is not complied with, whether it was reasonable at the time of the contract to expect that compliance with that condition would be practicable;
- (e) whether the goods were manufactured, processed or adapted to the special order of the customer.

(*Schs 3, 4 contain amendments and repeals only.*)

LLOYD'S ACT 1982

(1982 c xiv)

ARRANGEMENT OF SECTIONS

Preamble . . . . . [3352]
1 Citation . . . . . [3353]
2 Interpretation . . . . . [3354]
3 The Council . . . . . [3355]
4 The Chairman and Deputy Chairmen of Lloyd's . . . . . [3356]
6 Powers of the Council and of the Committee . . . . . [3358]
7 The Disciplinary Committee and the Appeal Tribunal . . . . . [3359]
8 Insurance business . . . . . [3360]
9 Cessation of membership on bankruptcy . . . . . [3361]
13 Application of certain provisions of Companies Act 1948 . . . . . [3365]
14 Liability of the Society, etc . . . . . [3366]
15 Repeals and amendments . . . . . [3367]
16 Existing byelaws to continue in force . . . . . [3368]
17 Transitional provisions . . . . . [3369]
18 Costs of Act . . . . . [3370]

SCHEDULES:

Schedule 1—Classification of members of the society . . . . . [3371]
Schedule 2—Purposes for which byelaws may be made . . . . . [3372]
Schedule 3—Repeals . . . . . [3373]
Schedule 4—Transitional provisions
Part I—The first members of the Council . . . . . [3374]
Part II—Other transitional provisions . . . . . [3375]

An Act to establish a Council of Lloyd's; to define the functions and powers of the said Council; to amend and repeal certain provisions of Lloyd's Acts 1871 to 1951; and for other purposes

[23 July 1982]

[3352]
Preamble

WHEREAS—

(1) By Lloyd's Act 1871 certain persons were united into a society or corporation for the purposes of that Act and were incorporated by the name of Lloyd's (hereinafter referred to as "the Society") and various powers were conferred upon the Society by the said Act:

(2) By the said Act of 1871 there was established a committee of members of the Society called the Committee of Lloyd's to have the management and superintendence of the affairs of the Society and to exercise all the powers of the Society (except as in the said Act provided), subject to control and regulation by a general meeting of the members of the Society:

(3) By the said Act of 1871 the members of the Society in general meeting were empowered to make byelaws for the purposes provided in that Act and generally for the better execution of the Act and the furtherance of the objects of the Society, and byelaws have from time to time been so made:

(4) Further powers were conferred on the Society and on the members of the Society in general meeting by Lloyd's Act 1911, Lloyd's Act 1925 and Lloyd's Act 1951:

(5) Since 1968 the number of persons resident outside the United Kingdom admitted as members of the Society and the total number of members of the Society have both greatly increased so that it is no longer practical or expedient for the members of the Society to exercise in general meeting the powers reserved to them by the Acts hereinbefore mentioned:

(6) It is expedient in order to enable the Society to regulate the management of its affairs in accordance with both present-day requirements and practice and the interests of Lloyd's policyholders that—

(a) there should be established a Council of Lloyd's to have control over the management and regulation of the affairs of the Society;

(b) the said Council should have power to make byelaws for the purposes of such management and regulation, including byelaws making provision for and regulating the admission, suspension and disciplining of members of the Society, Lloyd's brokers, underwriting agents and others; and

(c) certain provisions in Lloyd's Acts 1871 to 1951 should be amended or repealed:

(7) It is expedient that the other provisions contained in this Act should be enacted:

(8) The purposes of this Act cannot be achieved without the authority of Parliament:

May it therefore please Your Majesty that it may be enacted, and be it enacted, by the Queen's most Excellent Majesty, by and with the advice and consent of the Lords Spiritual and Temporal, and Commons, in this present Parliament assembled, and by the authority of the same, as follows:—

[3353]
1 Citation

(1) This Act may be cited as Lloyd's Act 1982.

(2) Lloyd's Acts 1871 to 1951 and this Act may be cited together as Lloyd's Acts 1871 to 1982.

[3354]
2 Interpretation

(1) In this Act, unless the context otherwise requires—

"the Act of 1871" and "the Act of 1911" mean respectively Lloyd's Act 1871 and Lloyd's Act 1911;

"annual subscriber" means a person admitted to the Room as an annual subscriber;

"Appeal Tribunal" means the appeal tribunal established pursuant to section 7(1)(b) of this Act;

"associate" means a person admitted to the Room as an associate;

. . .

"the Council" means the council constituted by section 3 of this Act;

"director" includes any person occupying the position of director by whatever name called;

"Disciplinary Committee" means a disciplinary committee established pursuant to section 7(1)(a) of this Act;

"external member of the Council" means a member of the Council elected pursuant to section 3(2)(b) of this Act;

"external member of the Society" means a member of the Society who is not a working member of the Society;

["Lloyd's broker" means a partnership or body corporate permitted by the Council to describe itself as a Lloyd's broker;]

"manager" in relation to a Lloyd's broker or underwriting agent, means a person who exercises managerial functions under the immediate authority of the board of directors, or any member thereof, or of the partners, or any one of them, as the case requires, of the Lloyd's broker or underwriting agent;

"member of the Society" means a person admitted to membership of the Society;

"nominated member of the Council" means a member of the Council appointed pursuant to section 3(2)(c) of this Act;

"non-underwriting member" means a member of the Society who is not an underwriting member;

"related company", in relation to any company, means any body corporate—

(a) which is that company's subsidiary; or

(b) of which that company is a subsidiary; or

(c) which is a subsidiary of that company's holding company; and

"holding company" shall have the meaning given by section 154 of the Companies Act 1948 which shall be construed with any necessary modifications where applied to a company incorporated under the law of a country outside the United Kingdom;

"the Room" means the principal room or rooms in the Society's premises in the city of London for the time being designated by the Council for the purposes of underwriting;

"the Society" means the society incorporated by the Act of 1871 by the name of Lloyd's;

"special resolution" means a resolution of the Council passed by separate majorities of both—

(a) all the working members of the Council for the time being; and

(b) all the members for the time being of the Council who are not working members of the Council as aforesaid, that is to say, the external members of the Council and the nominated members of the Council;

"subsidiary" shall have the meaning given by section 154 of the Companies Act 1948 which shall be construed with any necessary modifications where applied to a company incorporated under the law of a country outside the United Kingdom;

"underwriting agent" means a person permitted by the Council to act as an underwriting agent at Lloyd's;

"underwriting member" means a person admitted to the Society as an underwriting member;

"working member of the Council" means a member of the Council elected pursuant to section 3(2)(a) of this Act;

"working member of the Society" means—

(a) a member of the Society who occupies himself principally with the conduct of business at Lloyd's by a Lloyd's broker or underwriting agent; or

(b) a member of the Society who has gone into retirement but who immediately before his retirement so occupied himself.

(2) For the purposes of this Act . . . —

(a) a person controls a partnership or body corporate if—

(i) the partners of the partnership, or the directors of the body corporate, or the directors of another company of which the body corporate is a subsidiary, are accustomed to act in accordance with that person's directions or instructions (otherwise than by reason only that they act on advice given in a professional capacity); or

(ii) in the case of a body corporate that person either alone or with any associate or associates (as defined in section 7(8) of the Insurance Companies Act 1981) is entitled to exercise or control the exercise of one-third or more of the voting power at any general meeting of the body corporate or of another company of which the body corporate is a subsidiary;

(b) a partnership or body corporate is connected with Lloyd's if it is a Lloyd's broker or an underwriting agent, or controls or is controlled by a Lloyd's broker or an underwriting agent, or is owned or controlled by a person who also controls a Lloyd's broker or an underwriting agent.

NOTES

Sub-s (1): definition "the Committee" (omitted) repealed and definition "Lloyd's broker" substituted by the Legislative Reform (Lloyd's) Order 2008, SI 2008/3001, arts 5(1), (2), 9(1), (2), subject to transitional provisions in art 6 of that Order at **[4533]**.

Sub-s (2): words omitted repealed by SI 2008/3001, art 10(2), subject to transitional provisions in art 6 of that Order at **[4533]**.

[3355]

3 The Council

(1) There shall be a Council of Lloyd's.

(2) Subject to subsection (3) below, the members of the Council shall be—

(a) sixteen working members of the Council elected from among the working members of the Society by those members of the Society whose names are shown on Part I of the Register referred to in Schedule 1 to this Act as working members of the Society;

(b) eight external members of the Council elected from among the external members of the Society by those members of the Society whose names are shown on Part II of such Register as external members of the Society;

(c) three nominated members of the Council appointed by the Council by special resolution . . . :

Provided that a person who is a member of the Society or an annual subscriber or an associate shall not be eligible for appointment as a nominated member of the Council.

(3) The Council may by byelaw increase or decrease the number of its members and specify the manner in which such increase or decrease may be effected:

Provided that the number of places available to working members of the Society at any election to the Council shall be such that if filled by such members not more than two-thirds of the members of the Council would be working members of the Council.

(4) The Council may by byelaw limit the number of places which at any election to the Council shall be available to working members of the Society who are—

(a) engaged (as a partner, director or employee) or interested in any way (directly or indirectly) in any one partnership or body corporate which is connected with Lloyd's, and for the purposes of this paragraph and any byelaw made hereunder—

(i) a body corporate which is controlled by a partnership connected with Lloyd's or by any partner or partners therein shall be deemed to form part of that partnership; and

(ii) a related company of a body corporate connected with Lloyd's shall be deemed to form part of that body corporate;

(b) principally occupied with such class or classes of insurance business at Lloyd's or in such capacities as the Council may by byelaw specify.

(5) Subject to the provisions of this section, the Council shall by byelaw regulate—

(a) the conduct of elections of members of the Council, including inter alia the system of voting at any such election;

(b) the number of members of the Council to be elected at each election;

(c) eligibility and nomination for membership of the Council;

(d) the term of office of members of the Council;

(e) any other matter connected with any of the aforesaid matters:

Provided that—

(i) the term of any duly elected or appointed member of the Council shall not be extended during the term of office of such member;

(ii), (iii) . . .

NOTES

Sub-ss (2), (5): words omitted repealed by the Legislative Reform (Lloyd's) Order 2008, SI 2008/3001, art 3, subject to transitional provisions in art 6 of that Order at **[4533]**.

[3356]–[3357]

4 The Chairman and Deputy Chairmen of Lloyd's

[(1)] The Council shall annually elect [by special resolution] from among the . . . members of the Council a Chairman of the Council, who shall be called the "Chairman of Lloyd's", and two or more Deputy Chairmen of the Council, each of whom shall be called a "Deputy Chairman of Lloyd's".

[(2) Subject to subsection (3) a person elected as the Chairman or Deputy Chairman of the Council may, but need not, be a member of the Society.

(3) Where the person elected as Chairman is not a working member of the Society, at least one of the Deputy Chairmen must be elected from among the working members of the Council.]

NOTES

Sub-s (1): numbered as such, words in square brackets inserted and word omitted repealed, by the Legislative Reform (Lloyd's) Order 2008, SI 2008/3001, art 4(1), (2), subject to transitional provisions in art 6 of that Order at **[4533]**.

Sub-ss (2), (3): added by SI 2008/3001, art 4(3), subject to transitional provisions in art 6 of that Order at **[4533]**.

5 (*Repealed by the Legislative Reform (Lloyd's) Order 2008, SI 2008/3001, art 5(1), (3), subject to transitional provisions in art 6 of that Order at* **[4533]**.)

[3358]

6 Powers of the Council . . .

(1) The Council shall have the management and superintendence of the affairs of the Society and the power to regulate and direct the business of insurance at Lloyd's and it may lawfully exercise all the powers of the Society, but all powers so exercised by the Council shall be exercised by it in accordance with and subject to the provisions of Lloyd's Acts 1871 to 1982 and the byelaws made thereunder.

(2) The Council may—

(a) make such byelaws as from time to time seem requisite or expedient for the proper and better execution of Lloyd's Acts 1871 to 1982 and for the furtherance of the objects of the Society, including such byelaws as it thinks fit for any or all of the purposes specified in Schedule 2 to this Act; and

(b) amend or revoke any byelaw made or deemed to have been made hereunder.

(3) Any byelaw made under this Act and any amendment or revocation of any byelaw so made or deemed to have been so made shall be made by special resolution.

(4)

(a) If, within 60 days of the promulgation of any byelaw or the promulgation of any amendment to or revocation of any byelaw, or within such longer period as the Council may determine, a notice in writing signed by not less than 500 members of the Society is served upon the Council requesting that such byelaw, amendment or revocation be submitted to the members of the Society in general meeting, the Council shall convene a general meeting of the Society for that purpose.

(b) If, at a meeting of the members of the Society convened pursuant to paragraph (a) above, a resolution to revoke such byelaw or amendment or to annul such revocation is passed by a majority of members voting in person or by proxy and the number of members voting in favour of such resolution represents at least one-third of the total membership of the Society, such byelaw, amendment or revocation shall thereby be revoked or annulled, as the case may be.

(c) A resolution passed pursuant to paragraph (b) above shall not affect anything done or omitted to be done before the resolution is passed, and in particular—

(i) in the case of a resolution revoking a byelaw or amendment, shall not affect the previous operation of the byelaw or amendment;

(ii) in the case of a resolution annulling the revocation of a byelaw, shall revive the byelaw only from the date of the resolution.

(d) The Council shall by byelaw regulate the calling and conduct of meetings convened pursuant to paragraph (a) above and the system of voting thereat.

(5) Subject to [subsection (10)] of this section, the Council may, by special resolution, delegate the exercise of such of its powers or functions under this Act as are not required to be exercised by special resolution to any one or more of the following that is to say:—

[(a) Committees, subcommittees or other bodies of persons (whose members need not be members of the Society), or

(b) any person (whether or not a member of the Society).]

(c)–(e). . .

[(5A) A delegation under subsection (5) may be made—

(a) to such an extent; and

(b) on such conditions or subject to such restrictions,

as the Council considers appropriate.

(5B) A delegation of the exercise of a power or function made under subsection (5) may authorise the person or body to whom it is delegated to make a further delegation of the exercise of that power or function.]

(6) . . .

(7) Nothing in [subsection (5)] above shall operate to limit the power of the Council . . . to act by persons, committees, sub-committees or other bodies of persons, whose members may include persons who are not members of the Society, or by the employees [or officers] of the Society.

(8), (9) . . .

(10) A delegation [under subsection (5)] [may be amended or revoked] by special resolution of the Council and shall not prevent the exercise of a power or the performance of a function by the Council itself.

(11) No act or proceeding of the Council . . . shall be invalidated in consequence only of there being—

(a) a vacancy or vacancies in the membership of the Council . . . at the time of such act or proceeding being done or taken; or

(b) some defect in the election or appointment of any member of the Council . . .

NOTES

Section heading: words omitted repealed by the Legislative Reform (Lloyd's) Order 2008, SI 2008/3001, art 5(1), (4)(a), subject to transitional provisions in art 6 of that Order at **[4533]**.

Sub-s (5): words in square brackets substituted, and paras (c)–(e) repealed, by SI 2008/3001, arts 5(1), (4)(b), 7(1), (2), subject to transitional provisions in art 6 of that Order at **[4533]**.

Sub-ss (5A), (5B): inserted by SI 2008/3001, art 7(1), (3), subject to transitional provisions in art 6 of that Order at **[4533]**.

Sub-ss (6), (8), (9): repealed by SI 2008/3001, art 5(1), (4)(c), subject, in the case of sub-s (6), to transitional provisions in art 6 of that Order at **[4533]**.

Sub-s (7): words in first pair of square brackets substituted, words omitted repealed, and words in second pair of square brackets inserted, by SI 2008/3001, arts 5(1), (4)(d), 7(1), (4), subject to transitional provisions in art 6 of that Order at **[4533]**.

Sub-s (10): words in square brackets substituted by SI 2008/3001, art 7(1), (5), subject to transitional provisions in art 6 of that Order at **[4533]**.

Sub-s (11): words omitted repealed by SI 2008/3001, art 5(1), (4)(e), subject to transitional provisions in art 6 of that Order at **[4533]**.

[3359]

7 The Disciplinary Committee and the Appeal Tribunal

(1) The Council shall by byelaw—

(a)

(i) establish, provide for the constitution of and define the powers of a Disciplinary Committee or Committees, [provided that the members of any such Disciplinary Committee shall include at least one person who falls within subsection (1A)]; and

(ii) . . . specify the grounds upon which in furtherance of the objects of the Society disciplinary proceedings may be instituted against and penalties or sanctions may be imposed upon any member of the Society, annual subscriber, Lloyd's broker, underwriting agent or such other class of persons as may be so specified;

(b)

(i) establish, provide for the constitution of and define the powers of an Appeal Tribunal to hear and determine appeals (whether or not in the exercise of its disciplinary powers and functions), provided that the President and Deputy President of such Appeal Tribunal, who shall both be appointed by the Council, shall not be members of the Society; and

(ii) specify the class or classes of decisions, findings, orders, acts or omissions against which there shall lie a right of appeal to such Appeal Tribunal.

[(1A) A person falls within this subsection if he is—

(a) a working member of the Society;

(b) a director of a corporate member of the Society;

(c) an officer or employee of an underwriting agent or Lloyd's broker where that officer or employee has been approved by the Financial Services Authority under section 59 of the Financial Services and Markets Act 2000(a);

(d) a person who has gone into retirement, but who immediately before retirement fell within paragraph (b) or (c) above.]

(2) All disciplinary powers and functions of the Council, except the power to confirm, modify or grant dispensation in respect of any penalty or sanction imposed by a Disciplinary Committee or the Appeal Tribunal, shall be exercisable only by a Disciplinary Committee and, in respect of appeals which lie from decisions, findings, orders, acts or omissions of a Disciplinary Committee, only by the Appeal Tribunal.

(3) . . .

(4)

(a) For the purpose of any proceedings before a Disciplinary Committee or the Appeal Tribunal the Disciplinary Committee or the Appeal Tribunal may administer oaths, and any party to the proceedings may sue out writs of subpoena ad testificandum and duces tecum, but no person shall be compelled under any such writ to produce any document which he could not be compelled to produce on the trial of an action.

(b) The provisions of section 36 of the Supreme Court Act 1981 (which provide a special procedure for the issue of such writs so as to be in force throughout the United Kingdom) shall apply in relation to any proceedings before a Disciplinary Committee or the Appeal Tribunal as they apply in relation to causes or matters in the High Court.

(5) Any person other than a member of the Society in respect of whom disciplinary proceedings are taken under this Act shall be deemed for the purposes of paragraph 8 of Part II of the Schedule to the Defamation Act 1952 to be a person who is subject by virtue of a contract to the control of the Society.

NOTES

Sub-s (1): words in square brackets substituted and words omitted repealed by the Legislative Reform (Lloyd's) Order 2008, SI 2008/3001, art 8(1)–(3), subject to transitional provisions in art 6 of that Order at **[4533]**.

Sub-s (1A): inserted by SI 2008/3001, art 8(1), (4), subject to transitional provisions in art 6 of that Order at **[4533]**.

Sub-s (3): repealed by SI 2008/3001, art 5(1), (5), subject to transitional provisions in art 6 of that Order at **[4533]**.

[3360]

8 Insurance business

(1) An underwriting member shall be a party to a contract of insurance underwritten at Lloyd's only if it is underwritten with several liability, each underwriting member for his own part and not one for another, and if the liability of each underwriting member is accepted solely for his own account.

(2) An underwriting member (not being himself an underwriting agent) shall underwrite contracts of insurance at Lloyd's only through an underwriting agent.

(3) . . .

(4) Breach of any of subsections [(1) or (2)] above shall constitute an act or default in respect of which disciplinary proceedings may be brought in accordance with byelaws made under section 7 (The Disciplinary Committee and the Appeal Tribunal) of this Act.

NOTES

Sub-s (3): repealed by the Legislative Reform (Lloyd's) Order 2008, SI 2008/3001, art 9(1), (3), subject to transitional provisions in art 6 of that Order at **[4533]**.

Sub-s (4): words in square brackets substituted by SI 2008/3001, art 9(1), (4), subject to transitional provisions in art 6 of that Order at **[4533]**.

[3361]–[3364]

9 Cessation of membership on bankruptcy

In the event of a member of the Society being adjudicated bankrupt, or being adjudicated or declared insolvent, by the due process of law of a country within the European Economic Community the Council shall forthwith declare his membership to have ceased:

Provided that if such adjudication or declaration is set aside on appeal or otherwise the Council shall take immediate action to cancel its declaration.

10–12 *(Repealed by the Legislative Reform (Lloyd's) Order 2008, SI 2008/3001, art 10, subject to transitional provisions in art 6 of that Order at* **[4533]**.*)*

[3365]

13 Application of certain provisions of Companies Act 1948

(1) Sections 34, 36 and 448 of the Companies Act 1948 (execution of deeds abroad, authentication of documents and relief for the liabilities of officers and auditors of a company) are hereby incorporated in this Act and shall apply to the Society, the Council . . . and officers and auditors of the Society in like manner mutatis mutandis as they apply to a company (as defined by the Companies Act 1948), its officers and auditors.

(2) For the purpose of this Act any member of the Council and any person to whom (whether individually or collectively) any powers or functions are delegated under this Act is to be regarded as an officer of the Society.

NOTES

Sub-s (1): words omitted repealed by the Legislative Reform (Lloyd's) Order 2008, SI 2008/3001, art 5(1), (6), subject to transitional provisions in art 6 of that Order at **[4533]**.

[3366]

14 Liability of the Society, etc

(1) This section shall only exempt the Society from liability in damages at the suit of a member of the Lloyd's community.

(2) For the purposes of this section a member of the Lloyd's community shall be—

- (a) a person who is—
  - (i) a member of the Society;
  - (ii) a Lloyd's broker;
  - (iii) an underwriting agent;
  - (iv) an annual subscriber;
  - (v) an associate;
  - (vi) a director or partner of a Lloyd's broker or an underwriting agent;
  - (vii) a person who works for a Lloyd's broker or underwriting agent as a manager; or
- (b) a person who has been a member of the Lloyd's community in one or more of the capacities listed in paragraph (a) above; or
- (c) a person who is seeking or who has sought to become a member of the Lloyd's community in one or more of the capacities listed in paragraph (a) above.

(3) Subject to subsections (1), (4) and (5) of this section, the Society shall not be liable for damages whether for negligence or other tort, breach of duty or otherwise, in respect of any exercise of or omission to exercise any power, duty or function conferred or imposed by Lloyd's Acts 1871 to 1982 or any byelaw or regulation made thereunder—

- (a) in so far as the underwriting business of any member of the Society or the costs of his membership or the business of any person as a Lloyd's broker or underwriting agent may be affected; or
- (b) in so far as relates to the admission or non-admission to, or the continuance of, or the suspension or exclusion from, membership of the Society; or

(c) in so far as relates to the grant, continuance, suspension, withdrawal or refusal of permission to carry on business at Lloyd's as a Lloyd's broker or an underwriting agent or in any capacity connected therewith; or
(d) in so far as relates to the exercise of, or omission to exercise, disciplinary functions, powers and duties; or
(e) in so far as relates to the exercise of, or omission to exercise, any powers, functions or duties under byelaws made pursuant to paragraphs (21), (22), (23), (24) and (25) of Schedule 2 to this Act;

unless the act or omission complained of—
(i) was done or omitted to be done in bad faith; or
(ii) was that of an employee of the Society and occurred in the course of the employee carrying out routine or clerical duties, that is to say duties which do not involve the exercise of any discretion.

(4) Nothing in this section shall affect any liability of the Society in respect of the death of or personal injury to any person, and for the purposes of this section the expression "personal injury" means bodily injury, any disease and any impairment of a person's physical or mental condition.
(5) Nothing in this section shall exempt the Society from liability for libel or slander.
(6) For the purposes of this section "the Society" means the Society itself and also any of its officers and employees and any person or persons in or to whom (whether individually or collectively) any powers or functions are vested or delegated by or pursuant to Lloyd's Acts 1871 to 1982.

[3367]
15 Repeals and amendments
(1) Subject to the provisions of Schedule 4 to this Act—
(a) the enactments specified in Schedule 3 to this Act are hereby repealed to the extent specified in that Schedule;
(b)–(d). . .

(2) Subject to the provisions of this Act—
(a) any enactment (other than an enactment in this Act) or any other instrument having the effect of law; and
(b) any other document or arrangement whatsoever;

which is in existence before the first meeting of the Council held pursuant to paragraph 7 of Schedule 4 to this Act and which refers or relates to the Society or to the business carried on by persons as members of the Society or as Lloyd's brokers or underwriting agents shall on and after such meeting have effect subject to any necessary modifications as if for any reference however worded and whether express or implied—
(i) to the Committee of Lloyd's constituted by the Act of 1871 there were substituted a reference to the Council; and
(ii) to the Chairman or a Deputy Chairman of that Committee or to the Chairman or a Deputy Chairman of Lloyd's there were substituted a reference to the Chairman of the Council or a Deputy Chairman of the Council, as the case may be:

. . .

NOTES
Sub-s (1): words omitted amend the Lloyd's Acts 1911 and 1951 at **[3143]** and **[3167]**.
Sub-s (2): words omitted repealed by the Legislative Reform (Lloyd's) Order 2008, SI 2008/3001, art 5(1), (7), subject to transitional provisions in art 6 of that Order at **[4533]**.

[3368]
16 Existing byelaws to continue in force
Any byelaw made under Lloyd's Acts 1871 to 1951 shall be deemed to have been made by the Council in the exercise of its power under this Act and subject to the provisions of Schedule 4 to this Act such byelaws shall continue in full force and effect unless and until revoked by the Council pursuant to the said power.

[3369]
17 Transitional provisions
The transitional provisions contained in Schedule 4 to this Act shall have effect.

[3370]
18 Costs of Act
The costs, charges and expenses of and incidental to the preparing, applying for, obtaining and passing of this Act shall be paid by the Society.

SCHEDULES

SCHEDULE 1

CLASSIFICATION OF MEMBERS OF THE SOCIETY

Section 3

[3371]

1. The Council shall keep and maintain a Register to be revised as at the first day of July in each year (or such other day or days as the Council may by byelaw provide) which shall be divided into two parts and shall show in Part I thereof the names of all those members of the Society who were classified as working members of the Society as at that date and in Part II thereof the names of all those members of the Society who were classified as external members of the Society as at that date.

2. A member of the Society may object to his or another member's classification on the Register and the Council shall by byelaw make provision for the determination of such an objection.

3. A member of the Society may appeal against a determination under paragraph 2 above to a committee of the Council consisting of one working member, one external member and one nominated member of the Council whose decision shall be conclusive and the Council shall by byelaw make provision for the hearing and determination of such an appeal.

4. In any election to the Council a member of the Society shall be entitled and only entitled to vote as a working member of the Society or as an external member of the Society according to his classification on the Register on the date on which notice of such election is given.

5. Such Register shall be available for inspection by a member of the Society upon request at the premises of the Society in the city of London, or such other place as the Council shall specify.

SCHEDULE 2

PURPOSES FOR WHICH BYELAWS MAY BE MADE

Section 6

[3372]
Without prejudice to the generality of the powers vested in the Council by subsection (2) of section 6 (Powers of the Council . . .) of this Act, the Council may pursuant to that section make byelaws for the following purposes:—

(1) For regulating the admission to the Society of members as either underwriting members or non-underwriting members, for regulating continuing membership of the Society and for regulating the manner and circumstances in which members may be excluded from membership of the Society, and so that any byelaws made for such purposes may impose or provide for conditions and requirements to be satisfied or complied with on admission or during membership, which conditions and requirements—
- (a) may from time to time be added to, altered or withdrawn;
- (b) may include the requirement to give undertakings;
- (c) may apply to all or any class of underwriting members and as to the whole or any class of their underwriting business; and
- (d) may be imposed notwithstanding any inconsistency therein with any contract subsisting at the commencement of this Act between the Society and any member of the Society:

Provided that, without prejudice to the powers of the Council to require an underwriting member to cease or reduce the level of his underwriting at Lloyd's, a member of the Society shall not be excluded from membership for breach of a byelaw or failure to satisfy a condition, requirement or undertaking where such breach or failure consists solely of his inability to satisfy a financial qualification contained in such byelaw, conditions, requirement or undertaking, which was not applicable on the date he became an underwriting member or, where he has subsequently increased the level of his underwriting, on the date his application to do so was duly accepted;

(2) For requiring an underwriting member to cease to be a member of the Society or to cease underwriting, temporarily or indefinitely, in the event that—

(a) a receiving order in bankruptcy is made against such member by the due process of law of any country; or

(b) such member makes or proposes any composition with his creditors or otherwise acknowledges his insolvency; or

(c) by the due process of law of a country outside the European Economic Community such member is adjudicated bankrupt or is adjudicated or declared insolvent;

and for regulating the procedure to be followed in such event;

(3) For providing for admission to the Room of annual subscribers, associates, and other persons, for enabling the Council to impose conditions and requirements (including the requirement to give undertakings) as to admission and as to continuing right to admission to the Room and for the grant of tickets for the purpose of conducting business in the Room and the renewal and revocation of such tickets;

(4) For regulating the fees, subscriptions and other sums to be paid by members of the Society, annual subscribers, associates, Lloyd's brokers, underwriting agents and others;

(5) For regulating the mode, time and place of summoning and holding general meetings of the Society and the mode of voting and the conduct of proceedings thereat;

(6) For regulating the mode, time and place of summoning and holding meetings of the Council . . . and the quorum and manner of proceedings at meetings of the Council . . . ;

(7) For regulating:—

(a) the manner in which byelaws and the amendment and revocation of byelaws shall be promulgated; . . .

(b) . . .

(8) For regulating the appointment, powers and functions of the Chairman and Deputy Chairmen of Lloyd's . . . ;

(9) For regulating the remuneration and indemnification of all or any of the members of the Council;

(10) For regulating:—

(a) the appointment of other committees of the Council . . . ;

(b) the appointment of any person or body of persons with a duty to report to the Council . . . ;

(c) the inclusion of persons who are not members of the Society, Lloyd's brokers or underwriting agents in such committees, sub-committees or bodies of persons;

(d) the functions of such committees, sub-committees, persons or bodies of persons and the manner in which such functions are to be executed; and

(e) the mode, time and place of summoning, and holding meetings of such committees, sub-committees or bodies of persons, and the quorum and manner of proceedings thereat;

(11) For determining and declaring the grounds upon which and for regulating the mode in which a member of the Council, [any] committee, sub-committee or other body of persons established by or pursuant to this Act shall cease to be a member thereof;

(12) For regulating the grant and renewal of permission to broke insurance business at Lloyd's as a Lloyd's broker, for regulating the continuing right to broke such business and for regulating the manner and circumstances in which such permission may be withdrawn, and so that any byelaws made for such purposes may impose or provide for conditions and requirements to be satisfied or complied with on the grant and during the continuance of such permission, which conditions and requirements—

(a) may from time to time be added to, altered or withdrawn;

(b) may include the requirement to give undertakings;

(c) may apply to all or any class of Lloyd's brokers and as to the whole or any class of their business of broking insurance; and

(d) may have the effect that a partnership or body corporate shall not be permitted after a date to be prescribed by the Council to broke insurance business at Lloyd's so long as it (or any related company)—
  (i) is controlled by such person or class of persons as may be therein specified; or
  (ii) owns any interest in any underwriting agent or an underwriting agent of such class as may be specified by the Council;

[(12A) For regulating the grant and renewal of permission to a partnership or body corporate to describe itself as a Lloyd's broker and regulating the manner and circumstances in which such permission may be withdrawn;]

(13) For regulating the grant and renewal of permission to act as an underwriting agent for underwriting members in carrying on their underwriting business at Lloyd's, for regulating the continuing right to act as such an underwriting agent and for regulating the manner and circumstances in which permission may be withdrawn, and so that any byelaws made for such purposes may impose or provide for conditions and requirements to be satisfied or complied with on the grant and during the continuance of such permission, which conditions and requirements—
(a) may from time to time be added to, altered or withdrawn;
(b) may include the requirement to give undertakings;
(c) may apply to all or any class of underwriting agents and as to the whole or any class of their business as underwriting agents; and
(d) may have the effect that a person shall not be permitted after a date to be prescribed by the Council to act as such agent so long as—
  (i) that person owns any interest in an insurance broker; or
  (ii) where that person is a body corporate, any related company owns any interest in an insurance broker; or
  (iii) where that person is a body corporate or a partnership, it or any related company is controlled by, or any interest in it is owned by, such person or class of person as may be therein specified;

(14) For providing that permission to carry on business at Lloyd's as a Lloyd's broker or as an underwriting agent shall not be granted or renewed and that any such permission may be revoked unless the Council is satisfied as to all or any of the following matters:—
(a) that the person having control of the Lloyd's broker or underwriting agent (being a partnership or body corporate) is, by reason of his character and suitability, a person who should have control of a Lloyd's broker or such an underwriting agent;
(b) that each director or partner of the Lloyd's broker or underwriting agent (being a partnership or body corporate) is, by reason of his character and suitability, a person who should be a director or partner of a Lloyd's broker or such an underwriting agent;
(c) that each person who works for the Lloyd's broker or underwriting agent in such capacity as may be specified by the Council is, by reason of his character and suitability, a person who should work in such capacity for a Lloyd's broker or underwriting agent;

(15) For prescribing or regulating terms which are or are not to be included in agreements between underwriting agents and underwriting members or other underwriting agents;

(16) For requiring that accounts of underwriting syndicates be audited and that reports and audited accounts be furnished to members of the syndicate and for regulating the form and content of such reports and accounts;

(17) For prescribing or regulating information which is to be supplied by underwriting agents to persons applying to become members of the Society;

(18) For empowering the Council to nominate and appoint an underwriting agent (in this paragraph referred to as the "substitute agent") to act as agent or sub-agent for an underwriting member as to the whole or any part of his underwriting business in any case where such member has no underwriting agent for the whole or such part of his underwriting business or where in the opinion of the Council—
(a) such appointment is in the interests of such member; or
(b) it is essential for the proper regulation of the business of insurance at Lloyd's; and to give such directions to any underwriting agent already acting for such member as may be desirable in connection with the appointment of the substitute agent;

(19) For regulating as among and between underwriting members, Lloyd's brokers, underwriting agents and any other person transacting with underwriting members the business of insurance (whether as principal or agent) or interested therein, the mode in which insurance shall be effected with underwriting members and the periods at which settlements in respect of insurances so effected shall be made;

[(19A) For regulating the conditions under which underwriting agents may accept and place business from or through intermediaries other than Lloyd's brokers;

(19B) For regulating the manner and circumstances in which underwriting agents may transact insurance business otherwise than through an intermediary;]

(20) For empowering the Council to take steps and give undertakings required by or under the law of any country in order to secure authorisation for underwriting members to transact insurance business in or emanating from that country and to require underwriting members, Lloyd's brokers and underwriting agents to comply with undertakings so given;

(21) For requiring members of the Society, Lloyd's brokers, underwriting agents, annual subscribers, associates and substitutes, or any director or partner of a Lloyd's broker or underwriting agent or any person who works for a Lloyd's broker or underwriting agent in such capacity as may be specified by the Council to supply such information to the Council as may be so specified;

(22)

(a) For empowering the Council to order any inquiry, including an inquiry concerning the affairs of any member of the Society or syndicate of members or any Lloyd's broker or any underwriting agent;

(b) For requiring any member of the Society or any director or partner of a Lloyd's broker or underwriting agent or any person who works for a Lloyd's broker or underwriting agent in such capacity as may be specified by the Council to give when required such information as may be in his or its possession or to produce such documents and material as may be in his or its possession or under his or its control relating to the subject-matter of the inquiry;

(c) For requiring any person whose affairs have been the subject of any inquiry to pay the costs incurred in connection with the inquiry or to make a contribution thereto;

(23)

(a) For empowering the Council to order that in or in the course of any such inquiry as is referred to in paragraph (22) of this Schedule investigation be made into frauds or crimes, or circumstances having the appearance of frauds or crimes, practised or attempted or intended to be practised in connection with the business of insurance at Lloyd's;

(b) For empowering the Council to take or facilitate the taking of proceedings with a view to the punishment of persons appearing to be responsible for or concerned in any such frauds or crimes;

(c) For empowering the Council to supply to any police constable any information, documents or material in its possession, including any information, documents or material obtained pursuant to byelaws made for the purposes specified in paragraphs (21), (22)(b) and (24) of this Schedule;

(24) For regulating the circumstances in which members of the Society, Lloyd's brokers, underwriting agents, annual subscribers, associates and substitutes, or any director or partner of a Lloyd's broker or underwriting agent or any person who works for a Lloyd's broker or underwriting agent in such capacity as may be specified by the Council may (without being required so to do) give information or produce documents or material to the Council;

(25) For requiring that, save in so far as the same may be used in disciplinary or criminal proceedings, due confidentiality is preserved with respect to any information supplied or documents or material produced pursuant to byelaws made for the purposes specified in paragraphs (21), (22)(b) and (24) of this Schedule, especially in so far as such information, documents or material relate to the affairs of any persons (including principals and clients of Lloyd's brokers and of underwriting agents) other than those supplying or producing such information, documents or material;

(26) For empowering the Council to suspend (for such maximum period as may be specified by byelaw) any of the following from transacting, or being concerned or interested in the transaction of, the business of insurance at Lloyd's or any class or classes of such business, that is to say:—

- (a) a member of the Society;
- (b) a Lloyd's broker;
- (c) an underwriting agent; or
- (d) any person who works for a Lloyd's broker or an underwriting agent in such capacity as may be specified by the Council;

(27) For regulating the grounds on which and the manner in which a member of the Society may by disciplinary proceedings be suspended or excluded from membership or required to cease underwriting temporarily, or indefinitely, or subjected to any lesser penalty prescribed by byelaws, including, but not limited to, a fine and the posting of a notice of censure in the Room;

(28) For regulating the grounds on which and the manner in which permission to broke insurance business at Lloyd's as a Lloyd's broker may by disciplinary proceedings be revoked or suspended, or a Lloyd's broker may be subjected to any lesser penalty prescribed by byelaws, including, but not limited to, a fine and the posting of a notice of censure in the Room;

(29) For regulating the grounds on which and the manner in which permission to act as an underwriting agent may by disciplinary proceedings be revoked or suspended, or an underwriting agent may be subjected to any lesser penalty prescribed by byelaws, including, but not limited to, a fine and the posting of a notice of censure in the Room;

(30) For regulating the grounds on which and the manner in which the right of admission to the Room of an annual subscriber may by disciplinary proceedings be withdrawn or suspended, or an annual subscriber may be subjected to any lesser penalty prescribed by byelaws, including, but not limited to, a fine and the posting of a notice of censure in the Room;

(31) For requiring—

- (a) a partner or director of a Lloyd's broker or underwriting agent; or
- (b) a person who works for a Lloyd's broker or underwriting agent in such capacity as may be specified by byelaw;

to undertake to submit to the jurisdiction of the Council and for regulating the grounds on and the manner in which such persons may by disciplinary proceedings be subjected to any penalty prescribed by byelaws including, but not limited to—

- (i) an order prohibiting or suspending him from being concerned in the conduct of business at Lloyd's;
- (ii) a fine; or
- (iii) the posting of a notice of censure in the Room;

(32) For providing for the recovery of any fine or costs imposed pursuant to byelaws as a civil debt;

(33) For regulating the powers of a Disciplinary Committee and the Appeal Tribunal, including the power to—

- (a) subject to or join in proceedings before a Disciplinary Committee or the Appeal Tribunal and to subject to any penalty prescribed by byelaws, a director or partner of a Lloyd's broker or underwriting agent or a person who works for a Lloyd's broker or underwriting agent in such capacity as may be specified by the Council;
- (b) require any such person as aforesaid (whether or not such person is a party to or otherwise concerned in the proceedings) to appear before a Disciplinary Committee or the Appeal Tribunal to give evidence, or to produce documents and material, or both;
- (c) award costs;

(34) For regulating the procedures of a Disciplinary Committee and the Appeal Tribunal provided that such byelaws shall provide for a right to a hearing and legal representation if so desired for any person upon whom a penalty may be imposed or against whom an order may be made;

(35) For regulating the procedure whereby the Council—

- (a) confirms, modifies or grants dispensation in respect of any penalty imposed by a Disciplinary Committee or the Appeal Tribunal; and
- (b) publishes its decision and any penalty imposed;

(36) For providing for the establishment and constitution of an Arbitration Panel to hear and determine disputes relating to the business of insurance at Lloyd's, for determining the matters to be referred for arbitration to the Arbitration Panel, for requiring parties to such disputes to refer them to the Arbitration Panel for arbitration and for regulating the conduct of any such arbitration proceedings;

(37) For regulating the manner, terms and restrictions in, on and subject to which intelligence and information may be supplied to members of the Society and others;

(38) For providing for the establishment and maintenance of a scheme for the protection of Lloyd's policyholders, underwriting members and others in the event of the default of a Lloyd's broker and for empowering the Council to require Lloyd's brokers and others to be parties to and to contribute to such scheme as a condition or requirement of the grant or renewal of permission to broke insurance business at Lloyd's as a Lloyd's broker or otherwise;

(39) For regulating the use of the Room by members of the Society and others;

(40) For regulating the investment of the funds and other property of the Society;

(41) For regulating the grant and operation of binding authorities, or any other means whereby authority to accept insurance on behalf of underwriting members is delegated;

(42) For regulating the appointments and duties of agents or correspondents of the Society at ports and other places;

(43) For regulating the appointment, terms of employment and remuneration of a Secretary General and other officers and employees of the Society.

NOTES

Opening words, paras (6)–(8), (10): words omitted repealed by the Legislative Reform (Lloyd's) Order 2008, SI 2008/3001, art 5(1), (8)(a)–(f), subject to transitional provisions in art 6 of that Order at **[4533]**.

Para (11): word in square brackets substituted by SI 2008/3001, art 5(1), (8)(g), subject to transitional provisions in art 6 of that Order at **[4533]**.

Paras (12A), (19A), (19B): inserted by SI 2008/3001, art 9(1), (5), subject to transitional provisions in art 6 of that Order at **[4533]**.

SCHEDULE 3

REPEALS

Section 15

[3373]

Chapter	Short Title	Extent of repeal
34 & 35 Vict c xxi	Lloyd's Act 1871.	Sections 11 and 12. Sections 18 to 27. Section 29. The Schedule.
51 & 52 Vict c 29	Lloyd's Signal Stations Act 1888.	The whole Act.
1 & 2 Geo 5 c lxii	Lloyd's Act 1911.	Sections 10 to 13.
15 & 16 Geo 5 c xxvi	Lloyd's Act 1925.	The whole Act.
14 & 15 Geo 6 c viii	Lloyd's Act 1951.	The proviso to section 3(2). Section 4.

SCHEDULE 4

TRANSITIONAL PROVISIONS

Section 17

PART I
THE FIRST MEMBERS OF THE COUNCIL

[3374]

1. Any person who is, immediately prior to the commencement of this Act, a member of the Committee of Lloyd's pursuant to Lloyd's Acts 1871 to 1951 and byelaws made thereunder (in this Schedule referred to as "the Old Committee") shall be a working member of the Council and a member of the Committee established by section 5 of this Act until such time as he would, but for this Act, have ceased to be a member of the Old Committee.

2. The provisions of Schedule 1 to this Act shall be carried into effect by the Old Committee, which shall provide that a member of the Society may object to his or another member's classification on such Register, and for the determination of such objection and for the right to appeal against such determination to a sub-committee of the Old Committee consisting of three members thereof whose decision shall be conclusive, and the election of a person to the Council shall not be challenged or otherwise declared to be invalid by reason of any proceedings pursuant to such provision by the Old Committee not being completed or for any other reason whatsoever.

3. In lieu of the general meeting of members of the Society which would be held in November 1982 but for this Act a ballot to elect four working members of the Council shall be held at that time in accordance with byelaws for the time being in force provided, however, that the four persons to be elected shall be elected from among the working members of the Society by those members whose names are shown on Part I of the Register referred to in Schedule 1 to this Act as working members of the Society. Notwithstanding anything in the byelaws made under Lloyd's Acts 1871 to 1951 the Old Committee shall appoint two or more members as scrutineers to take the vote and report the result.

4. A ballot to elect eight external members of the Council shall be held to which the following provisions shall apply:—

(a) such ballot shall take place within four months of the day on which this Act is passed;

(b) the election shall be by postal ballot of all those members of the Society whose names are shown on Part II of the Register referred to in Schedule 1 to this Act as external members of the Society, and each such member who exercises his right to vote in such ballot shall cast one vote for each of eight of the persons duly nominated for election;

(c) the Old Committee shall give not less than 60 clear days' notice of such ballot by notice in writing to each member of the Society entitled to vote at such ballot, addressed to such member's last known place of business or abode and the notice shall state that the object of the ballot is to elect eight external members of the Council and the date and time by which nominations for such election are to be received in order to be valid;

(d) an external member of the Society shall be nominated for election as an external member by the Council by a requisition signed by not less than sixteen members of the Society entitled to vote at such ballot, which requisition shall be lodged with the Secretary General of Lloyd's or other person duly authorised by the Old Committee at least 42 clear days before the day on which such ballot is to take place;

(e) if the number of persons duly nominated for election as external members of the Council in accordance with sub-paragraph (d) above does not exceed the number to be elected, the nominated candidates shall be declared to be elected and if the number of nominated candidates is reduced by withdrawal or otherwise to no more than that number, the remaining nominated candidates shall be declared to be elected;

(f) not less than 28 clear days before the day on which the ballot is to take place, the Secretary General of Lloyd's or other person duly authorised by the Old Committee shall send to each of the members of the Society entitled to vote at such ballot—

(i) a ballot paper containing the name of each duly nominated candidate and stating that each such member shall cast one vote for each of eight of the candidates and the date and time by which ballot papers are to be received in order to be included in the ballot; and

(ii) particulars of each candidate including any statement he may wish to make concerning his candidature, the form and content of which shall have been approved by the Old Committee;

Part III Statutes

(g) a notice or ballot paper shall be deemed to have been properly sent by the Secretary General of Lloyd's or other person duly authorised by the Old Committee if it is sent to a member at his last known place of business or abode but the result of a ballot under this Schedule shall not be invalidated by any failure by the Secretary General of Lloyd's or other duly authorised person to send a ballot paper to any member of the Society entitled to vote at such ballot or by the non-receipt by any such member of a ballot paper;

(h) a member of the Society entitled to vote at such ballot may exercise his right to vote by posting or delivering his ballot paper duly completed to the Secretary General of Lloyd's or other person duly authorised but only ballot papers received by the Secretary General of Lloyd's or such person on or before the date and time stated on the ballot paper shall be included in the votes counted;

(i) subject to the provisions of any byelaws which may be made pursuant to section 3(5) of this Act four of the persons elected in such ballot shall be external members of the Council until 31st December 1984, and four of the persons so elected shall be external members of the Council until 31st December 1986.

5. Within 28 days after the election pursuant to paragraph 4 of this Schedule, the working members and the external members of the Council shall meet at a place, date and time determined by the Old Committee and shall, by resolution passed by separate majorities of both the working members of the Council and the external members of the Council, appoint the first three nominated members of the Council whose appointments shall be governed mutatis mutandis by the provisions of section 3(2)(c) of this Act.

6. Subject to the provisions of any byelaws which may be made pursuant to section 3(5) of this Act the following provisions shall have effect with respect to the appointments made pursuant to paragraph 5 of this Schedule:—

(a) one of the persons appointed shall hold office until 31st December 1984, one shall hold office until 31st December 1985, and one shall hold office until 31st December 1986 (such persons, in default of agreement among the persons so appointed, to be determined by lot);

(b) no person shall be appointed a nominated member of the Council without his consent.

7. The first meeting of the Council shall take place at such place, date and time not more than 28 days after the meeting referred to in paragraph 5 of this Schedule as may be decided at that meeting.

8. Unless at its first meeting the Council shall otherwise determine, the persons who are immediately prior to such meeting the Chairman of Lloyd's and the Deputy Chairmen of Lloyd's pursuant to Lloyd's Acts 1871 to 1951 and byelaws made thereunder shall be respectively the Chairman of Lloyd's and the Deputy Chairmen of Lloyd's as if appointed under section 4 of this Act and shall continue to hold such positions until the end of the year 1982.

PART II
OTHER TRANSITIONAL PROVISIONS

[3375]

9. Until the first meeting of the Council, Lloyd's Acts 1871 to 1951 shall, subject to the provisions of this Schedule, continue to have effect as though this Act had not been passed.

10. The Council may in preferring any charge against any person refer to, and the Disciplinary Committee in hearing that charge may have regard to and take into account, any act, default or other event which takes place before this Act comes into force.

11. Section 20 (Exclusion from membership for violation of fundamental rules, &c) of the Act of 1871 (including the Schedule to that Act setting out the fundamental rules of the Society), section 12 (Power of Committee to temporarily suspend Members) of the Act of 1911 and byelaw 87 (vi) of the byelaws made pursuant to Lloyd's Acts 1871 to 1951 shall continue to have effect until a Disciplinary Committee shall be established by byelaws made under this Act, and where proceedings have been commenced against any person under either of such sections or under such byelaw, they may be continued in all respects until concluded as if the section or byelaw under which the proceedings had been commenced continued in full force and effect.

COMPANIES ACT 1985

(1985 c 6)

ARRANGEMENT OF SECTIONS

PART VII
ACCOUNTS AND AUDIT

CHAPTER II
EXEMPTIONS, EXCEPTIONS AND SPECIAL PROVISIONS

Banking and insurance companies and groups

255 Special provisions for banking and insurance companies . . . . . [3376]
255A Special provisions for banking and insurance groups . . . . . [3377]

PART VIII
DISTRIBUTION OF PROFITS AND ASSETS

Limits of company's power of distribution

264 Restriction on distribution of assets . . . . . [3378]
265 Other distributions by investment companies . . . . . [3379]
266 Meaning of "investment company" . . . . . [3380]
267 Extension of ss 265, 266 to other companies . . . . . [3381]
268 Realised profits of insurance company with long term business . . . . . [3382]

Supplementary

279 Distributions by banking or insurance companies . . . . . [3383]

PART XXVII
FINAL PROVISIONS

747 Citation . . . . . [3387]

SCHEDULES:

Schedule 9A—Form and Content of Accounts of Insurance Companies and Groups
Part I—Individual Accounts . . . . . [3388]
Part II—Consolidated Accounts . . . . . [3389]
Schedule 11—Modifications of Part VIII where Company's Accounts Prepared in Accordance with Special Provisions for Banking or Insurance Companies . . . . . [3390]

An Act to consolidate the greater part of the Companies Acts

[11 March 1985]

1–220 *((Pt I–VI) in so far as unrepealed, outside the scope of this work.)*

PART VII
ACCOUNTS AND AUDIT

221–245G *((Ch I) in so far as unrepealed, outside the scope of this work.)*

[CHAPTER II
EXEMPTIONS, EXCEPTIONS AND SPECIAL PROVISIONS

246–254 (*In so far as unrepealed, outside the scope of this work.*)

[Banking and insurance companies and groups

[3376]

255 Special provisions for banking and insurance companies

(1) A banking company shall prepare its individual accounts in accordance with Part I of Schedule 9 rather than Schedule 4.

(2) An insurance company [shall] prepare its individual accounts in accordance with Part I of Schedule 9A rather than Schedule 4.

(3) Accounts so prepared shall contain a statement that they are prepared in accordance with the special provisions of this Part relating to banking companies or to insurance companies, as the case may be.

Part III Statutes

(4) In relation to the preparation of individual accounts in accordance with the special provisions of this Part, the references to Schedule 4 in section 226(4) and (5) (relationship between specific requirements and duty to give true and fair view) shall be read as references to the provisions of Part I of Schedule 9, in the case of the accounts of banking companies, or to the provisions of Part I of Schedule 9A, in the case of the accounts of insurance companies.

[(4A) References to Companies Act individual accounts include accounts prepared in accordance with this section.

(4B) This section does not apply to banking companies and insurance companies that prepare IAS individual accounts.]

(5) . . .]

NOTES

Repealed by the Companies Act 2006, s 1295, Sch 16, except in respect of financial years beginning before 6 April 2008.

Substituted, together with preceding cross-heading and ss 255A, 255B for ss 255–255B (as inserted by the Companies Act 1989, s 18(1)), by the Companies Act 1985 (Bank Accounts) Regulations 1991, SI 1991/2705, regs 3, 9.

Sub-s (2): word in square brackets substituted by the Companies Act 1985 (Insurance Companies Accounts) Regulations 1993, SI 1993/3246, reg 2(1), subject to transitional provisions in regs 6, 7 thereof.

Sub-ss (4A), (4B): inserted by the Companies Act 1985 (International Accounting Standards and Other Accounting Amendments) Regulations 2004, SI 2004/2947, reg 3, Sch 1, para 1, 17, in relation to companies' financial years beginning on or after 1 January 2005.

Sub-s (5): repealed by SI 1993/3246, reg 2(2), subject to transitional provisions in regs 6, 7 thereof.

Modification: this section is modified in relation to Lloyd's syndicates by the Insurance Accounts Directive (Lloyd's Syndicate and Aggregate Accounts) Regulations 2004, SI 2004/3219, reg 3(7), Schedule, paras 1, 2 at **[4349]**, **[4364]**.

[3377]

[255A Special provisions for banking and insurance groups

(1) The parent company of a banking group shall prepare group accounts in accordance with the provisions of this Part as modified by Part II of Schedule 9.

(2) The parent company of an insurance group [shall] prepare group accounts in accordance with the provisions of this Part as modified by Part II of Schedule 9A.

(3) Accounts so prepared shall contain a statement that they are prepared in accordance with the special provisions of this Part relating to banking groups or to insurance groups, as the case may be.

[(4) References in this Part to a banking group are to a group where the parent company is a banking company or where—

- *(a) the parent company's principal subsidiary undertakings are wholly or mainly credit institutions, and*
- *(b) the parent company does not itself carry on any material business apart from the acquisition, management and disposal of interests in subsidiary undertakings.*

(5) References in this Part to an insurance group are to a group where the parent company is an insurance company or where—

- *(a) the parent company's principal subsidiary undertakings are wholly or mainly insurance companies, and*
- *(b) the parent company does not itself carry on any material business apart from the acquisition, management and disposal of interests in subsidiary undertakings.*

(5A) For the purposes of subsections (4) and (5) above—

- *(a) a parent company's principal subsidiary undertakings are the subsidiary undertakings of the company whose results or financial position would principally affect the figures shown in the group accounts, and*
- *(b) the management of interests in subsidiary undertakings includes the provision of services to such undertakings.]*

(6) In relation to the preparation of group accounts in accordance with the special provisions of this Part:

- *(a) the references to the provisions of Schedule 4A in [section 227A(4) and (5)] (relationship between specific requirements and duty to give true and fair view) shall be read as references to those provisions as modified by Part II of Schedule 9, in the case of the group accounts of a banking group, or Part II of Schedule 9A, in the case of the group accounts of an insurance group; and*
- *(b) the reference to paragraphs 52 to 57 of Schedule 4 in section 230(2) (relief from obligation to comply with those paragraphs where group accounts prepared) shall be read as a reference to [75 to 77], 80 and 81 of Part I of Schedule 9, in the case of the*

group accounts of a banking group[, and as a reference to paragraphs 73, 74, 79 and 80 of Part I of Schedule 9A, in the case of the group accounts of an insurance group].

[(6A) References to Companies Act group accounts include accounts prepared in accordance with subsections (1) to (3).

(6B) Subsections (1) to (3) and (6) do not apply to parent companies of banking groups or insurance groups that prepare IAS group accounts.]

(7) . . .]

NOTES

Repealed by the Companies Act 2006, s 1295, Sch 16, except in respect of financial years beginning before 6 April 2008.

Substituted as noted to s 255 at **[3376]**.

Sub-s (2): word in square brackets substituted by the Companies Act 1985 (Insurance Companies Accounts) Regulations 1993, SI 1993/3246, reg 3(1), subject to transitional provisions in regs 6, 7 thereof.

Sub-ss (4), (5), (5A): substituted, for original sub-ss (4), (5), by SI 1993/3246, reg 3(2), subject to transitional provisions in regs 6, 7 thereof.

Sub-s (6): words in square brackets in para (a) substituted by the Companies Act 1985 (International Accounting Standards and Other Accounting Amendments) Regulations 2004, SI 2004/2947, reg 3, Sch 1, paras 1, 18(1), (2), in relation to companies' financial years beginning on or after 1 January 2005; words in first pair of square brackets in para (b) substituted, in relation to any financial year ending on or after 2 February 1996, by the Companies Act 1985 (Miscellaneous Accounting Amendments) Regulations 1996, SI 1996/189, regs 15(2), 16(1), subject to a transitional provision in reg 16(2) thereof; words in second pair of square brackets in para (b) added by SI 1993/3246, reg 3(3), subject to transitional provisions in regs 6, 7 thereof.

Sub-ss (6A), (6B): inserted by SI 2004/2947, reg 3, Sch 1, paras 1, 18(1), (3), in relation to companies' financial years beginning on or after 1 January 2005.

Sub-s (7): repealed by SI 1993/3246, reg 3(4), subject to transitional provisions in regs 6, 7 thereof.

For the circumstances in which a controlled foreign company is to be regarded as a member of an insurance group within the meaning of sub-s (5) of this section (subject to modifications in relation to Northern Ireland), see the Income and Corporation Taxes Act 1988, Sch 25, Pt 2, para 11A(6), as inserted by the Finance Act 2003, s 200, Sch 42, paras 1, 4.

255B–262A *(In so far as unrepealed, outside the scope of this work.)*

PART VIII
DISTRIBUTION OF PROFITS AND ASSETS

Limits of company's power of distribution

263 *(Repealed by the Companies Act 2006, s 1295, Sch 16.)*

[3378]
264 Restriction on distribution of assets

(1) A public company may only make a distribution at any time—

- *(a) if at that time the amount of its net assets is not less than the aggregate of its called-up share capital and undistributable reserves, and*
- *(b) if, and to the extent that, the distribution does not reduce the amount of those assets to less than that aggregate.*

This is subject to the provision made by sections 265 and 266 for investment and other companies.

(2) In subsection (1), "net assets" means the aggregate of the company's assets less the aggregate of its liabilities ("liabilities" to include any [provision for liabilities] within paragraph 89 of Schedule 4 [that is made in Companies Act accounts and any provision that is made in IAS accounts]).

(3) A company's undistributable reserves are—

- *(a) the share premium account,*
- *(b) the capital redemption reserve,*
- *(c) the amount by which the company's accumulated, unrealised profits, so far as not previously utilised by capitalisation of a description to which this paragraph applies, exceed its accumulated, unrealised losses (so far as not previously written off in a reduction or reorganisation of capital duly made), and*
- *(d) any other reserve which the company is prohibited from distributing by any enactment (other than one contained in this Part) or by its memorandum or articles;*

and paragraph (c) applies to every description of capitalisation except a transfer of profits of the company to its capital redemption reserve on or after 22nd December 1980.

(4) A public company shall not include any uncalled share capital as an asset in any accounts relevant for purposes of this section.

NOTES

Repealed by the Companies Act 2006, s 1295, Sch 16, as from 6 April 2008, except in relation to distributions made before that date.

Sub-s (2): words in first pair of square brackets substituted and words in second pair of square brackets inserted by the Companies Act 1985 (International Accounting Standards and Other Accounting Amendments) Regulations 2004, SI 2004/2947, regs 3, 15, Sch 1, paras 1, 22, Sch 7, Pt 1, paras 1, 8, in relation to companies' financial years beginning on or after 1 January 2005.

[3379]

265 Other distributions by investment companies

(1) Subject to the following provisions of this section, an investment company (defined in section 266) may also make a distribution at any time out of its accumulated, realised revenue profits, so far as not previously utilised by a distribution or capitalisation, less its accumulated revenue losses (whether realised or unrealised), so far as not previously written off in a reduction or reorganisation of capital duly made—

(a) if at that time the amount of its assets is at least equal to one and a half times the aggregate of its liabilities [to creditors], and

(b) if, and to the extent that, the distribution does not reduce that amount to less than one and a half times that aggregate.

(2) In subsection (1)(a), "liabilities [to creditors]" includes any [provision for liabilities] [to creditors] (within the meaning of paragraph 89 of Schedule 4) [that is made in Companies Act accounts and any provision [for liabilities to creditors] that is made in IAS accounts].

(3) The company shall not include any uncalled share capital as an asset in any accounts relevant for purposes of this section.

(4) An investment company may not make a distribution by virtue of subsection (1) unless—

(a) its shares are listed on a [recognised investment exchange other than an overseas investment exchange . . .], and

(b) during the relevant period it has not—

(i) distributed any of its capital profits [otherwise than by way of the redemption or purchase of any of the company's own shares in accordance with section 160 or 162 in Chapter VII of Part V], or

(ii) applied any unrealised profits or any capital profits (realised or unrealised) in paying up debentures or amounts unpaid on its issued shares.

[(4A) In subsection (4)(a) "recognised investment exchange" and "overseas investment exchange" have the same meaning as in Part 18 of the Financial Services and Markets Act 2000.]

(5) The "relevant period" under subsection (4) is the period beginning with—

(a) the first day of the accounting reference period immediately preceding that in which the proposed distribution is to be made, or

(b) where the distribution is to be made in the company's first accounting reference period, the first day of that period,

and ending with the date of the distribution.

(6) An investment company may not make a distribution by virtue of subsection (1) unless the company gave to the registrar of companies the requisite notice (that is, notice under section 266(1)) of the company's intention to carry on business as an investment company—

(a) before the beginning of the relevant period under subsection (4), or

(b) in the case of a company incorporated on or after 22nd December 1980, as soon as may have been reasonably practicable after the date of its incorporation.

NOTES

Repealed by the Companies Act 2006, s 1295, Sch 16, as from 6 April 2008, except in relation to distributions made before that date.

Sub-s (1): words in square brackets inserted by the Companies Act 1985 (Investment Companies and Accounting and Audit Amendments) Regulations 2005, SI 2005/2280, reg 2(1), (2).

Sub-s (2): words in first, third and fifth (inner) pairs of square brackets inserted by SI 2005/2280, reg 2(1), (3); words in second pair of square brackets substituted and words in fourth (outer) pair of square brackets added by the Companies Act 1985 (International Accounting Standards and Other Accounting Amendments) Regulations 2004, SI 2004/2947, regs 3, 15, Sch 1, paras 1, 23, Sch 7, Pt 1, paras 1, 9, in relation to companies' financial years beginning on or after 1 January 2005.

Sub-s (4): words in square brackets in para (a) substituted by the Financial Services Act 1986, s 212(2), Sch 16, para 19; words omitted from para (a) repealed by the Financial Services and Markets Act 2000 (Consequential Amendments and Repeals) Order 2001, SI 2001/3649, art 17(1), (2); words in square brackets in para (b) inserted by the Companies (Investment Companies) (Distribution of Profits) Regulations 1999, SI 1999/2770, reg 2, subject to a transitional provision in reg 4 thereof.

Sub-s (4A): inserted by SI 2001/3649, art 17(1), (3).

[3380]

266 Meaning of "investment company"

(1) In section 265 "investment company" means a public company which has given notice in the prescribed form (which has not been revoked) to the registrar of companies of its intention to carry on business as an investment company, and has since the date of that notice complied with the requirements specified below.

(2) Those requirements are—

(a) that the business of the company consists of investing its funds mainly in securities, with the aim of spreading investment risk and giving members of the company the benefit of the results of the management of its funds,

(b) that none of the company's holdings in companies (other than those which are for the time being in investment companies) represents more than 15 per cent by value of the investing company's investments,

(c) that [subject to subsection (2A),] distribution of the company's capital profits is prohibited by its memorandum or articles of association,

(d) that the company has not retained, otherwise than in compliance with this Part, in respect of any accounting reference period more than 15 per cent of the income it derives from securities.

[(2A) An investment company need not be prohibited by its memorandum or articles from redeeming or purchasing its own shares in accordance with section 160 or 162 in Chapter VII of Part V out of its capital profits.]

(3) Notice to the registrar of companies under subsection (1) may be revoked at any time by the company on giving notice in the prescribed form to the registrar that it no longer wishes to be an investment company within the meaning of this section; and, on giving such notice, the company ceases to be such a company.

[(4) Subsections (1A) to (3) of section 842 of the Income and Corporation Taxes Act 1988 apply for the purposes of subsection (2)(b) above as for those of subsection (1)(b) of that section.]

NOTES

Repealed by the Companies Act 2006, s 1295, Sch 16, as from 6 April 2008, except in relation to distributions made before that date.

Sub-s (2): words in square brackets inserted by the Companies (Investment Companies) (Distribution of Profits) Regulations 1999, SI 1999/2770, reg 3(a).

Sub-s (2A): inserted by SI 1999/2770, reg 3(b).

Sub-s (4): substituted by the Finance Act 1988, s 117(3), (4), with respect to companies' accounting periods ending after 5 April 1988.

Regulations: the Companies (Forms) Regulations 1985, SI 1985/854.

[3381]

267 Extension of ss 265, 266 to other companies

(1) The Secretary of State may by regulations in a statutory instrument extend the provisions of sections 265 and 266 (with or without modifications) to companies whose principal business consists of investing their funds in securities, land or other assets with the aim of spreading investment risk and giving their members the benefit of the results of the management of the assets.

(2) Regulations under this section—

(a) may make different provision for different classes of companies and may contain such transitional and supplemental provisions as the Secretary of State considers necessary, and

(b) shall not be made unless a draft of the statutory instrument containing them has been laid before Parliament and approved by a resolution of each House.

NOTES

Repealed by the Companies Act 2006, s 1295, Sch 16, as from 6 April 2008, except in relation to distributions made before that date.

[3382]

268 Realised profits of insurance company with long term business

(1) Where [an authorised insurance company] carries on long term business—

[(a) any amount included in the relevant part of the balance sheet of the company which represents a surplus in the fund or funds maintained by it in respect of that business and which has not been allocated to policy holders [or, as the case may be, carried forward unappropriated, in accordance with the asset identification rules made under section 142(2) of the Financial Services and Markets Act 2000], and]

(b) any deficit in that fund or those funds,

are to be (respectively) treated, for purposes of this Part, as a realised profit and a realised loss; and, subject to this, any profit or loss arising in that business is to be left out of account for those purposes.

(2) In subsection (1)—

[(aa) the reference to the relevant part of the balance sheet is

[(i) in the case of Companies Act individual accounts,] to that part of the balance sheet which represents Liabilities item A.V (profit and loss account) in the balance sheet format set out in section B of Chapter I of Part I of Schedule 9A, [and

(ii) in the case of IAS individual accounts, to that part of the balance sheet which represents accumulated profit or loss,]]

(a) the reference to a surplus in any fund or funds of an insurance company is to an excess of the assets representing that fund or those funds over the liabilities of the company attributable to its long term business, as shown by an actuarial investigation, and

(b) the reference to a deficit in any such fund or funds is to the excess of those liabilities over those assets, as so shown.

(3) In this section—

[(a) "actuarial investigation" means—

(i) an investigation made into the financial condition of an authorised insurance company in respect of its long term business, carried out once in every period of twelve months in accordance with rules made under Part 10 of the Financial Services and Markets Act 2000 by an actuary appointed as actuary to that company; or

(ii) an investigation made into the financial condition of an authorised insurance company in respect of its long term business carried out in accordance with a requirement imposed under section 166 of that Act by an actuary appointed as actuary to that company;]

[(b) "long term business" means business which consists of effecting or carrying out contracts of long term insurance.]

[(4) The definition of "long term business" in subsection (3) must be read with—

(a) section 22 of the Financial Services and Markets Act 2000;

(b) any relevant order under that section; and

(c) Schedule 2 to that Act.]

NOTES

Repealed by the Companies Act 2006, s 1295, Sch 16, as from 6 April 2008, except in relation to distributions made before that date.

Sub-s (1): words in first pair of square brackets and words in square brackets in para (a) substituted by the Financial Services and Markets Act 2000 (Consequential Amendments and Repeals) Order 2001, SI 2001/3649, art 18(1), (2); para (a) substituted by the Companies Act 1985 (Miscellaneous Accounting Amendments) Regulations 1996, SI 1996/189, regs 13(1), (2), 16(6), in respect of any distribution made on or after 2 February 1996.

Sub-s (2): para (aa) inserted, in respect of any distribution made on or after 2 February 1996, by SI 1996/189, regs 13(1), (3), 16(6); words in first pair of square brackets in para (aa)(i) and para (aa)(ii) and word "and" immediately preceding it inserted by the Companies Act 1985 (International Accounting Standards and Other Accounting Amendments) Regulations 2004, SI 2004/2947, reg 3, Sch 1, paras 1, 24, in relation to companies' financial years beginning on or after 1 January 2005.

Sub-s (3): paras (a), (b) substituted by SI 2001/3649, art 18(1), (3).

Sub-s (4): added by SI 2001/3649, art 18(1), (4).

269–276 (*Repealed by the Companies Act 2006, s 1295, Sch 16.*)

Supplementary

277, 278 (*Repealed by the Companies Act 2006, s 1295, Sch 16.*)

[3383]–[3386]

[279 Distributions by banking or insurance companies

Where a company's accounts relevant for the purposes of this Part are prepared in accordance with the special provisions of Part VII relating to banking or insurance companies, sections 264 to 275 apply with the modifications shown in Schedule 11.]

NOTES

Repealed by the Companies Act 2006, s 1295, Sch 16, as from 6 April 2008, except in relation to distributions made before that date.

Substituted by the Companies Act 1989, s 23, Sch 10, Pt I, para 8.

280, 281 (*Repealed by the Companies Act 2006, s 1295, Sch 16.*)

282–744A *((Pts IX–XXVI) in so far as unrepealed, outside the scope of this work.)*

PART XXVII
FINAL PROVISIONS

745, 746 *(In so far as unrepealed, outside the scope of this work.)*

[3387]
747 Citation
This Act may be cited as the Companies Act 1985.

(Schs 1–9 in so far as unrepealed, outside the scope of this work.)

SCHEDULES

[SCHEDULE 9A

FORM AND CONTENT OF ACCOUNTS OF INSURANCE COMPANIES AND GROUPS
Sections 255, 255A, 255B

PART I
INDIVIDUAL ACCOUNTS

CHAPTER I
GENERAL RULES AND FORMATS

SECTION A
GENERAL RULES

[3388]

1.—(1) Subject to the following provisions of this Part of this Schedule—

(a) every balance sheet of a company shall show the items listed in the balance sheet format set out below in section B of this Chapter; and

(b) every profit and loss account of a company shall show the items listed in the profit and loss account format so set out,

in either case in the order and under the headings and sub-headings given in the format.

(2) Sub-paragraph (1) above is not to be read as requiring the heading or sub-heading for any item to be distinguished by any letter or number assigned to that item in the format.

2.—(1) Any item required in accordance with paragraph 1 above to be shown in a company's balance sheet or profit and loss account may be shown in greater detail than so required.

(2) A company's balance sheet or profit and loss account may include an item representing or covering the amount of any asset or liability, income or expenditure not specifically covered by any of the items listed in the balance sheet or profit and loss account format set out in section B below, but the following shall not be treated as assets in any company's balance sheet—

(a) preliminary expenses;

(b) expenses of and commission on any issue of shares or debentures; and

(c) costs of research.

(3) Items to which Arabic numbers are assigned in the balance sheet format set out in section B below (except for items concerning technical provisions and the reinsurers' share of technical provisions), and items to which lower case letters in parentheses are assigned in the profit and loss account format so set out (except for items within items I.1 and 4 and II.1, 5 and 6) may be combined in a company's accounts for any financial year if either—

(a) their individual amounts are not material for the purpose of giving a true and fair view; or

(b) the combination facilitates the assessment of the state of affairs or profit or loss of the company for that year;

but in a case within paragraph (b) above the individual amounts of any items so combined shall be disclosed in a note to the accounts and any notes required by this Schedule to the items so combined under that paragraph shall, notwithstanding the combination, be given.

(4) Subject to paragraph 3(3) below, a heading or sub-heading corresponding to an item listed in the format adopted in preparing a company's balance sheet or profit and loss account shall not be included if there is no amount to be shown for that item in respect of the financial year to which the balance sheet or profit and loss account relates.

3.—(1) In respect of every item shown in the balance sheet or profit and loss account, there shall be shown or stated the corresponding amount for the financial year immediately preceding that to which the accounts relate.
(2) Where the corresponding amount is not comparable with the amount to be shown for the item in question in respect of the financial year to which the balance sheet or profit and loss account relates, the former amount [may be adjusted] and [particulars of the non-comparability and of any adjustment] shall be given in a note to the accounts.
(3) Paragraph 2(4) above does not apply in any case where an amount can be shown for the item in question in respect of the financial year immediately preceding that to which the balance sheet or profit and loss account relates, and that amount shall be shown under the heading or sub-heading required by paragraph 1 above for that item.

4. Subject to the provisions of this Schedule, amounts in respect of items representing assets or income may not be set off against amounts in respect of items representing liabilities or expenditure (as the case may be), or vice versa.

5. . . .

6.—[(1)] The provisions of this Schedule which relate to long term business shall apply, with necessary modifications, [to business which consists of effecting or carrying out relevant contracts of general insurance] which—
(a) is transacted exclusively or principally according to the technical principles of long term business, and
(b) is a significant amount of the business of the company.
[(2) For the purposes of paragraph (1), a contract of general insurance is a relevant contract if the risk insured against relates to—
(a) accident; or
(b) sickness.
(3) Sub-paragraph (2) must be read with—
(a) section 22 of the Financial Services and Markets Act 2000;
(b) any relevant order under that section; and
(c) Schedule 2 to that Act.]

[6A. The directors of a company must, in determining how amounts are presented within items in the profit and loss account and balance sheet, have regard to the substance of the reported transaction or arrangement, in accordance with generally accepted accounting principles or practice.]

SECTION B
THE REQUIRED FORMATS FOR ACCOUNTS

Preliminary

7.—(1) References in this Part of this Schedule to the balance sheet format or profit and loss account format are to the balance sheet format or profit and loss account format set out below, and references to the items listed in either of the formats are to those items read together with any of the notes following the formats which apply to any of those items.
(2) The requirement imposed by paragraph 1 to show the items listed in either format in the order adopted in the format is subject to any provision in the notes following the format for alternative positions for any particular items.
(3) Where in respect of any item to which an Arabic number is assigned in either format, the gross amount and reinsurance amount or reinsurers' share are required to be shown, a sub-total of those amounts shall also be given.
(4) Where in respect of any item to which an Arabic number is assigned in the profit and loss account format, separate items are required to be shown, then a separate sub-total of those items shall also be given in addition to any sub-total required by sub-paragraph (3) above.

8. A number in brackets following any item in either of the formats set out below is a reference to the note of that number in the notes following the format.

9.—[(1)] In the profit and loss account format set out below—
(a) the heading "Technical account—General business" is for [business which consists of effecting or carrying out contracts of general insurance]; and
(b) the heading "Technical account—Long term business" is for [business which consists of effecting or carrying out contracts of long term insurance].
[(2) In sub-paragraph (1), references to—
(a) contracts of general or long term insurance; and

(b) the effecting or carrying out of such contracts,

must be read with section 22 of the Financial Services and Markets Act 2000, any relevant order under that section, and Schedule 2 to that Act.]

Balance Sheet Format

ASSETS

A. Called up share capital not paid (1)

B. Intangible assets

1. Development costs

2. Concessions, patents, licences, trade marks and similar rights and assets (2)

3. Goodwill (3)

4. Payments on account

C. Investments

I Land and buildings (4)

II Investments in group undertakings and participating interests

1. Shares in group undertakings

2. Debt securities issued by, and loans to, group undertakings

3. Participating interests

4. Debt securities issued by, and loans to, undertakings in which the company has a participating interest

III Other financial investments

1. Shares and other variable-yield securities and units in unit trusts

2. Debt securities and other fixed income securities (5)

3. Participation in investment pools (6)

4. Loans secured by mortgages (7)

5. Other loans (7)

6. Deposits with credit institutions (8)

7. Other (9)

IV Deposits with ceding undertakings (10)

D. Assets held to cover linked liabilities (11)

Da. Reinsurers' share of technical provisions (12)

1. Provision for unearned premiums

2. Long term business provision

3. Claims outstanding

4. Provisions for bonuses and rebates

5. Other technical provisions

6. Technical provisions for unit-linked liabilities

E. Debtors (13)

I Debtors arising out of direct insurance operations

1. Policy holders

2. Intermediaries

II Debtors arising out of reinsurance operations

III Other debtors

IV Called up share capital not paid (1)

F. Other assets

I Tangible assets

1. Plant and machinery

2. Fixtures, fittings, tools and equipment

3. Payments on account (other than deposits paid on land and buildings) and assets (other than buildings) in course of construction

II Stocks

1. Raw materials and consumables

2. Work in progress

3. Finished goods and goods for resale

4. Payments on account

III Cash at bank and in hand

IV Own shares (14)

V Other (15)

G. Prepayments and accrued income

I Accrued interest and rent (16)

II Deferred acquisition costs (17)

III Other prepayments and accrued income

LIABILITIES

A. Capital and reserves

I Called up share capital or equivalent funds

II Share premium account

III Revaluation reserve

IV Reserves

1. Capital redemption reserve

2. Reserve for own shares

3. Reserves provided for by the articles of association

4. Other reserves

V Profit and loss account

B. Subordinated liabilities (18)

Ba. Fund for future appropriations (19)

C. Technical provisions

1. Provision for unearned premiums (20)

(a) gross amount

(b) reinsurance amount (12)

2. Long term business provision (20) (21) (26)

(a) gross amount

(b) reinsurance amount (12)

3. Claims outstanding (22)

(a) gross amount

(b) reinsurance amount (12)

4. Provision for bonuses and rebates (23)

(a) gross amount

(b) reinsurance amount (12)

5. Equalisation provision (24)

6. Other technical provisions (25)

(a) gross amount

(b) reinsurance amount (12)

D. Technical provisions for linked liabilities (26)

(a) gross amount

(b) reinsurance amount (12)

E. [Provisions for other risks]

1. Provisions for pensions and similar obligations

2. Provisions for taxation

3. Other provisions

F. Deposits received from reinsurers (27)

G. Creditors (28)

I Creditors arising out of direct insurance operations

II Creditors arising out of reinsurance operations

III Debenture loans (29)

IV Amounts owed to credit institutions

V Other creditors including taxation and social security

H. Accruals and deferred income

Notes on the balance sheet format

(1) Called up share capital not paid

(Assets items A and E.IV)

This item may be shown in either of the positions given in the format.

(2) Concessions, patents, licences, trade marks and similar rights and assets

(Assets item B.2)

Amounts in respect of assets shall only be included in a company's balance sheet under this item if either—

(a) the assets were acquired for valuable consideration and are not required to be shown under goodwill; or

(b) the assets in question were created by the company itself.

(3) Goodwill

(Assets item B.3)

Amounts representing goodwill shall only be included to the extent that the goodwill was acquired for valuable consideration.

(4) Land and buildings

(Assets item C.I.)

The amount of any land and buildings occupied by the company for its own activities shall be shown separately in the notes to the accounts.

(5) Debt securities and other fixed income securities

(Assets item C.III.2)

This item shall comprise transferable debt securities and any other transferable fixed income securities issued by credit institutions, other undertakings or public bodies, in so far as they are not covered by Assets item C.II.2 or C.II.4.

Securities bearing interest rates that vary in accordance with specific factors, for example the interest rate on the inter-bank market or on the Euromarket, shall also be regarded as debt securities and other fixed income securities and so be included under this item.

(6) Participation in investment pools

(Assets item C.III.3)

This item shall comprise shares held by the company in joint investments constituted by several undertakings or pension funds, the management of which has been entrusted to one of those undertakings or to one of those pension funds.

(7) Loans secured by mortgages and other loans

(Assets items C.III.4 and C.III.5)

Loans to policy holders for which the policy is the main security shall be included under "Other loans" and their amount shall be disclosed in the notes to the accounts. Loans secured by mortgage shall be shown as such even where they are also secured by insurance policies. Where the amount of "Other loans" not secured by policies is material, an appropriate breakdown shall be given in the notes to the accounts.

(8) Deposits with credit institutions

(Assets item C.III.6)

This item shall comprise sums the withdrawal of which is subject to a time restriction. Sums deposited with no such restriction shall be shown under Assets item F.III even if they bear interest.

(9) Other

(Assets item C.III.7)

This item shall comprise those investments which are not covered by Assets items C.III.1 to 6. Where the amount of such investments is significant, they must be disclosed in the notes to the accounts.

(10) Deposits with ceding undertakings

(Assets item C.IV)

Where the company accepts reinsurance this item shall comprise amounts, owed by the ceding undertakings and corresponding to guarantees, which are deposited with those ceding undertakings or with third parties or which are retained by those undertakings.

These amounts may not be combined with other amounts owed by the ceding insurer to the reinsurer or set off against amounts owed by the reinsurer to the ceding insurer.

Securities deposited with ceding undertakings or third parties which remain the property of the company shall be entered in the company's accounts as an investment, under the appropriate item.

(11) Assets held to cover linked liabilities

(Assets item D)

In respect of long term business, this item shall comprise investments made pursuant to long term policies under which the benefits payable to the policy holder are wholly or partly to be determined by reference to the value of, or the income from, property of any description (whether or not specified in the contract) or by reference to fluctuations in, or in an index of, the value of property of any description (whether or not so specified).

This item shall also comprise investments which are held on behalf of the members of a tontine and are intended for distribution among them.

(12) Reinsurance amounts

(Assets item Da: Liabilities items C.1(b), 2(b), 3(b), 4(b) and 6(b) and D(b))

The reinsurance amounts may be shown either under Assets item Da or under Liabilities items C.1(b), 2(b), 3(b), 4(b) and 6(b) and D(b).

The reinsurance amounts shall comprise the actual or estimated amounts which, under contractual reinsurance arrangements, are deducted from the gross amounts of technical provisions.

As regards the provision for unearned premiums, the reinsurance amounts shall be calculated according to the methods referred to in paragraph 44 above or in accordance with the terms of the reinsurance policy.

(13) Debtors

(Assets item E)

Amounts owed by group undertakings and undertakings in which the company has a participating interest shall be shown separately as sub-items of Assets items E.I, II and III.

(14) Own shares

(Assets item F.IV)

The nominal value of the shares shall be shown separately under this item.

(15) Other

(Assets item F.V)

This item shall comprise those assets which are not covered by Assets items F.I to IV. Where such assets are material they must be disclosed in the notes to the accounts.

(16) Accrued interest and rent

(Assets item G.I)

This item shall comprise those items that represent interest and rent that have been earned up to the balance-sheet date but have not yet become receivable.

(17) Deferred acquisition costs

(Assets item G.II)

This item shall comprise the costs of acquiring insurance policies which are incurred during a financial year but relate to a subsequent financial year ("deferred acquisition costs"), except in so far as—

- *(a) allowance has been made in the computation of the long term business provision made under paragraph 46 below and shown under Liabilities item C2 or D in the balance sheet, for—*
  - *(i) the explicit recognition of such costs, or*
  - *(ii) the implicit recognition of such costs by virtue of the anticipation of future income from which such costs may prudently be expected to be recovered, or*
- *(b) allowance has been made for such costs in respect of general business policies by a deduction from the provision for unearned premiums made under paragraph 44 below and shown under Liabilities item C.I in the balance sheet.*

Deferred acquisition costs arising in general business shall be distinguished from those arising in long term business.

In the case of general business, the amount of any deferred acquisition costs shall be established on a basis compatible with that used for unearned premiums.

There shall be disclosed in the notes to the accounts—

- *(a) how the deferral of acquisition costs has been treated (unless otherwise expressly stated in the accounts), and*
- *(b) where such costs are included as a deduction from the provisions at Liabilities item C.I, the amount of such deduction, or*
- *(c) where the actuarial method used in the calculation of the provisions at Liabilities item C.2 or D has made allowance for the explicit recognition of such costs, the amount of the costs so recognised.*

(18) Subordinated liabilities

(Liabilities item B)

This item shall comprise all liabilities in respect of which there is a contractual obligation that, in the event of winding up or of bankruptcy, they are to be repaid only after the claims of all other creditors have been met (whether or not they are represented by certificates).

(19) Fund for future appropriations

(Liabilities item Ba)

This item shall comprise all funds the allocation of which either to policy holders or to shareholders has not been determined by the end of the financial year.

Transfers to and from this item shall be shown in item II.12a in the profit and loss account.

(20) Provision for unearned premiums

(Liabilities item C.1)

In the case of long term business the provision for unearned premiums may be included in Liabilities item C.2 rather than in this item.

The provision for unearned premiums shall comprise the amount representing that part of gross premiums written which is estimated to be earned in the following financial year or to subsequent financial years.

(21) Long term business provision

(Liabilities item C.2)

This item shall comprise the actuarially estimated value of the company's liabilities (excluding technical provisions included in Liabilities item D), including bonuses already declared and after deducting the actuarial value of future premiums.

This item shall also comprise claims incurred but not reported, plus the estimated costs of settling such claims.

(22) Claims outstanding

(Liabilities item C.3)

This item shall comprise the total estimated ultimate cost to the company of settling all claims arising from events which have occurred up to the end of the financial year (including, in the case of general business, claims incurred but not reported) less amounts already paid in respect of such claims.

(23) Provision for bonuses and rebates

(Liabilities item C.4)

This item shall comprise amounts intended for policy holders or contract beneficiaries by way of bonuses and rebates as defined in Note (5) on the profit and loss account format to the extent that such amounts have not been credited to policy holders or contract beneficiaries or included in Liabilities item Ba or in Liabilities item C.2.

(24) Equalisation provision

(Liabilities item C.5)

[This item shall comprise [the amount of any equalisation reserve maintained in respect of general business by the company, in accordance with rules made by the Financial Services Authority under Part X of the Financial Services and Markets Act 2000].]

This item shall [also] comprise any amounts which, in accordance with Council Directive 87/343/EEC, are required to be set aside by a company to equalise fluctuations in loss ratios in future years or to provide for special risks.

A company which otherwise constitutes reserves to equalise fluctuations in loss ratios in future years or to provide for special risks shall disclose that fact in the notes to the accounts.

(25) Other technical provisions

(Liabilities item C.6)

This item shall comprise, inter alia, the provision for unexpired risks as defined in paragraph 81 below. Where the amount of the provision for unexpired risks is significant, it shall be disclosed separately either in the balance sheet or in the notes to the accounts.

(26) Technical provisions for linked liabilities

(Liabilities item D)

This item shall comprise technical provisions constituted to cover liabilities relating to investment in the context of long term policies under which the benefits payable to policy holders are wholly or partly to be determined by reference to the value of, or the income from, property of any description (whether or not specified in the contract) or by reference to fluctuations in, or in an index of, the value of property of any description (whether or not so specified).

Any additional technical provisions constituted to cover death risks, operating expenses or other risks (such as benefits payable at the maturity date or guaranteed surrender values) shall be included under Liabilities item C.2.

This item shall also comprise technical provisions representing the obligations of a tontine's organiser in relation to its members.

(27) Deposits received from reinsurers

(Liabilities item F)

Where the company cedes reinsurance, this item shall comprise amounts deposited by or withheld from other insurance undertakings under reinsurance contracts. These amounts may not be merged with other amounts owed to or by those other undertakings.

Where the company cedes reinsurance and has received as a deposit securities which have been transferred to its ownership, this item shall comprise the amount owed by the company by virtue of the deposit.

(28) Creditors

(Liabilities item G)

Amounts owed to group undertakings and undertakings in which the company has a participating interest shall be shown separately as sub-items.

(29) Debenture loans

(Liabilities item G.III)

The amount of any convertible loans shall be shown separately.

Special rules for balance sheet format

Additional items

***10.**—(1) Every balance sheet of a company which carries on long term business shall show separately as an additional item the aggregate of any amounts included in Liabilities item A (capital and reserves) which are required not to be treated as realised profits under section 268 of this Act.*

(2) A company which carries on long term business shall show separately, in the balance sheet or in the notes to the accounts, the total amount of assets representing the long term fund valued in accordance with the provisions of this Schedule.

Managed funds

11.—(1) For the purposes of this paragraph "managed funds" are funds of a group pension fund—

[(a) the management of which constitutes long term insurance business, and]

(b) which the company administers in its own name but on behalf of others, and

(c) to which it has legal title.

(2) The company shall, in any case where assets and liabilities arising in respect of managed funds fall to be treated as assets and liabilities of the company, adopt the following accounting treatment: assets and liabilities representing managed funds are to be included in the company's balance sheet, with the notes to the accounts disclosing the total amount included with respect to such assets and liabilities in the balance sheet and showing the amount included under each relevant balance sheet item in respect of such assets or (as the case may be) liabilities.

Deferred acquisition costs

***12.** The costs of acquiring insurance policies which are incurred during a financial year but which relate to a subsequent financial year shall be deferred in a manner specified in Note (17) on the balance sheet format.*

Profit and loss account format

I Technical account—General business

1. Earned premiums, net of reinsurance
  (a) gross premiums written (1)
  (b) outward reinsurance premiums (2)
  (c) change in the gross provision for unearned premiums
  (d) change in the provision for unearned premiums, reinsurers' share

2. Allocated investment return transferred from the non-technical account (item III.6) (10)

2a. Investment income (8) (10)
  (a) income from participating interests, with a separate indication of that derived from group undertakings
  (b) income from other investments, with a separate indication of that derived from group undertakings
    (aa) income from land and buildings
    (bb) income from other investments
  (c) value re-adjustments on investments
  (d) gains on the realisation of investments

3. Other technical income, net of reinsurance

4. Claims incurred, net of reinsurance (4)
  (a) claims paid
    (aa) gross amount
    (bb) reinsurers' share
  (b) change in the provision for claims
    (aa) gross amount
    (bb) reinsurers' share

5. Changes in other technical provisions, net of reinsurance, not shown under other headings

6. Bonuses and rebates, net of reinsurance (5)

7. Net operating expenses
  (a) acquisition costs (6)
  (b) change in deferred acquisition costs
  (c) administrative expenses (7)
  (d) reinsurance commissions and profit participation

8. Other technical charges, net of reinsurance

8a. Investment expenses and charges (8)
  (a) investment management expenses, including interest
  (b) value adjustments on investments
  (c) losses on the realisation of investments

9. Change in the equalisation provision

10. Sub-total (balance on the technical account for general business) (item III.1)

II Technical account—Long term business

1. Earned premiums, net of reinsurance
  (a) gross premiums written (1)
  (b) outward reinsurance premiums (2)
  (c) change in the provision for unearned premiums, net of reinsurance (3)

2. Investment income (8) (10)

(a) income from participating interests, with a separate indication of that derived from group undertakings

(b) income from other investments, with a separate indication of that derived from group undertakings

(aa) income from land and buildings

(bb) income from other investments

(c) value re-adjustments on investments

(d) gains on the realisation of investments

3. Unrealised gains on investments (9)

4. Other technical income, net of reinsurance

5. Claims incurred, net of reinsurance (4)

(a) claims paid

(aa) gross amount

(bb) reinsurers' share

(b) change in the provision for claims

(aa) gross amount

(bb) reinsurers' share

6. Change in other technical provisions, net of reinsurance, not shown under other headings

(a) long term business provision, net of reinsurance (3)

(aa) gross amount

(bb) reinsurers' share

(b) other technical provisions, net of reinsurance

7. Bonuses and rebates, net of reinsurance (5)

8. Net operating expenses

(a) acquisition costs (6)

(b) change in deferred acquisition costs

(c) administrative expenses (7)

(d) reinsurance commissions and profit participation

9. Investment expenses and charges (8)

(a) investment management expenses, including interest

(b) value adjustments on investments

(c) losses on the realisation of investments

10. Unrealised losses on investments (9)

11. Other technical charges, net of reinsurance

11a. Tax attributable to the long term business

12. Allocated investment return transferred to the non-technical account (item III.4)

12a. Transfers to or from the fund for future appropriations

13. Sub-total (balance on the technical account—long term business) (item III.2)

III Non-technical account

1. Balance on the general business technical account—(item I.10)

2. Balance on the long term business technical account—(item II.13)

[2a. Tax credit attributable to balance on the long term business technical account]

3. Investment income (8)

(a) income from participating interests, with a separate indication of that derived from group undertakings

(b) income from other investments, with a separate indication of that derived from group undertakings

(aa) income from land and buildings

(bb) income from other investments

(c) value re-adjustments on investments

(d) gains on the realisation of investments

3a. Unrealised gains on investments (9)

4. Allocated investment return transferred from the long term business technical account (item II.12) (10)

5. Investment expenses and charges (8)

(a) investment management expenses, including interest

(b) value adjustments on investments

(c) losses on the realisation of investments

5a. Unrealised losses on investments (9)

Part III Statutes

6. Allocated investment return transferred to the general business technical account (item I.2) (10)
7. Other income
8. Other charges, including value adjustments
8a. Profit or loss on ordinary activities before tax
9. Tax on profit or loss on ordinary activities
10. Profit or loss on ordinary activities after tax
11. Extraordinary income
12. Extraordinary charges
13. Extraordinary profit or loss
14. Tax on extraordinary profit or loss
15. Other taxes not shown under the preceding items
16. Profit or loss for the financial year

Notes on the profit and loss account format

(1) Gross premiums written

(General business technical account: item I.1.(a)
Long term business technical account: item II.1.(a))

This item shall comprise all amounts due during the financial year in respect of insurance contracts entered into regardless of the fact that such amounts may relate in whole or in part to a later financial year, and shall include inter alia—

(i) premiums yet to be determined, where the premium calculation can be done only at the end of the year;
(ii) single premiums, including annuity premiums, and, in long term business, single premiums resulting from bonus and rebate provisions in so far as they must be considered as premiums under the terms of the contract;
(iii) additional premiums in the case of half-yearly, quarterly or monthly payments and additional payments from policy holders for expenses borne by the company;
(iv) in the case of co-insurance, the company's portion of total premiums;
(v) reinsurance premiums due from ceding and retroceding insurance undertakings, including portfolio entries,

after deduction of cancellations and portfolio withdrawals credited to ceding and retroceding insurance undertakings.

The above amounts shall not include the amounts of taxes or duties levied with premiums.

(2) Outward reinsurance premiums

(General business technical account: item I.1.(b)
Long term business technical account: item II.l.(b))

This item shall comprise all premiums paid or payable in respect of outward reinsurance contracts entered into by the company. Portfolio entries payable on the conclusion or amendment of outward reinsurance contracts shall be added; portfolio withdrawals receivable must be deducted.

(3) Change in the provision for unearned premiums, net of reinsurance

(Long term business technical account: items II.1.(c) and II.6.(a))

In the case of long term business, the change in unearned premiums may be included either in item II.1.(c) or in item II.6.(a) of the long term business technical account.

(4) Claims incurred, net of reinsurance

(General business technical account: item I.4
Long term business technical account: item II.5)

This item shall comprise all payments made in respect of the financial year with the addition of the provision for claims (but after deducting the provision for claims for the preceding financial year).

These amounts shall include annuities, surrenders, entries and withdrawals of loss provisions to and from ceding insurance undertakings and reinsurers and external and internal claims management costs and charges for claims incurred but not reported such as are referred to in paragraphs 47(2) and 49 below.

Sums recoverable on the basis of subrogation and salvage (within the meaning of paragraph 47 below) shall be deducted.

Where the difference between—

(a) the loss provision made at the beginning of the year for outstanding claims incurred in previous years, and
(b) the payments made during the year on account of claims incurred in previous years and the loss provision shown at the end of the year for such outstanding claims,

is material, it shall be shown in the notes to the accounts, broken down by category and amount.

(5) Bonuses and rebates, net of reinsurance

(General business technical account: item I.6
Long term business technical account: item II.7)

Bonuses shall comprise all amounts chargeable for the financial year which are paid or payable to policy holders and other insured parties or provided for their benefit, including amounts used to increase technical provisions or applied to the reduction of future premiums, to the extent that such amounts represent an allocation of surplus or profit arising on business as a whole or a section of business, after deduction of amounts provided in previous years which are no longer required.

Rebates shall comprise such amounts to the extent that they represent a partial refund of premiums resulting from the experience of individual contracts.

Where material, the amount charged for bonuses and that charged for rebates shall be disclosed separately in the notes to the accounts.

(6) Acquisition costs

(General business technical account: item I.7.(a)
Long term business technical account: item II.8.(a))

This item shall comprise the costs arising from the conclusion of insurance contracts. They shall cover both direct costs, such as acquisition commissions or the cost of drawing up the insurance document or including the insurance contract in the portfolio, and indirect costs, such as advertising costs or the administrative expenses connected with the processing of proposals and the issuing of policies.

In the case of long term business, policy renewal commissions shall be included under item II.8.(c) in the long term business technical account.

(7) Administrative expenses

(General business technical account: item I.7.(c)
Long term business technical account: item II.8.(c))

This item shall include the costs arising from premium collection, portfolio administration, handling of bonuses and rebates, and inward and outward reinsurance. They shall in particular include staff costs and depreciation provisions in respect of office furniture and equipment in so far as these need not be shown under acquisition costs, claims incurred or investment charges.

Item II.8.(c) shall also include policy renewal commissions.

(8) Investment income, expenses and charges

(General business technical account: items I.2a and 8a
Long term business technical account: items II.2 and 9
Non-technical account: items III.3 and 5)

Investment income, expenses and charges shall, to the extent that they arise in the long term fund, be disclosed in the long term business technical account. Other investment income, expenses and charges shall either be disclosed in the non-technical account or attributed between the appropriate technical and non-technical accounts. Where the company makes such an attribution it shall disclose the basis for it in the notes to the accounts.

(9) Unrealised gains and losses on investments

(Long term business technical account: items II.3 and 10
Non-technical account: items III.3a and 5a)

In the case of investments attributed to the long term fund, the difference between the valuation of the investments and their purchase price or, if they have previously been valued, their valuation as at the last balance sheet date, may be disclosed (in whole or in part) in item II.3 or II.10 (as the case may be) of the long term business technical account, and in the case of investments shown as assets under Assets item D (assets held to cover linked liabilities) shall be so disclosed.

In the case of other investments, the difference between the valuation of the investments and their purchase price or, if they have previously been valued, their valuation as at the last balance sheet date, may be disclosed (in whole or in part) in item III.3a or III.5a (as the case may require) of the non-technical account.

(10) Allocated investment return

(General business technical account: [item I.2]
Long term business technical account: [item II.12]
Non-technical account: items III.4 and 6)

The allocated return may be transferred from one part of the profit and loss account to another.

Where part of the investment return is transferred to the general business technical account, the transfer from the non-technical account shall be deducted from item III.6 and added to item I.2.

Where part of the investment return disclosed in the long term business technical account is transferred to the non-technical account, the transfer to the non-technical account shall be deducted from item II.12 and added to item III.4.

The reasons for such transfers (which may consist of a reference to any relevant statutory requirement) and the bases on which they are made shall be disclosed in the notes to the accounts.

CHAPTER II
ACCOUNTING PRINCIPLES AND RULES

SECTION A
ACCOUNTING PRINCIPLES

Preliminary

13. *Subject to paragraph 19 below, the amounts to be included in respect of all items shown in a company's accounts shall be determined in accordance with the principles set out in paragraphs 14 to 18 below.*

Accounting principles

14. *The company shall be presumed to be carrying on business as a going concern.*

15. *Accounting policies shall be applied consistently within the same accounts and from one financial year to the next.*

16. *The amount of any item shall be determined on a prudent basis, and in particular—*
- (a) *subject to note (9) on the profit and loss account format, only profits realised at the balance sheet date shall be included in the profit and loss account; and*
- (b) *all liabilities . . . which have arisen . . . in respect of the financial year to which the accounts relate or a previous financial year shall be taken into account, including those which only become apparent between the balance sheet date and the date on which it is signed on behalf of the board of directors in pursuance of section 233 of this Act.*

17. *All income and charges relating to the financial year to which the accounts relate shall be taken into account, without regard to the date of receipt or payment.*

18. *In determining the aggregate amount of any item the amount of each individual asset or liability that falls to be taken into account shall be determined separately.*

Departure from accounting principles

19. *If it appears to the directors of a company that there are special reasons for departing from any of the principles stated above in preparing the company's accounts in respect of any financial year they may do so, but particulars of the departure, the reasons for it and its effect shall be given in a note to the accounts.*

[Valuation

19A.—*(1) The amounts to be included in respect of assets of any description mentioned in paragraph 22 (valuation of assets: general) are determined either—*
- (a) *in accordance with that paragraph and paragraph 24 (but subject to paragraphs 27 to 29); or*
- (b) *so far as applicable to an asset of that description, in accordance with section BA (valuation at fair value).*

(2) The amounts to be included in respect of assets of any description mentioned in paragraph 23 (alternative valuation of fixed-income securities) may be determined—
- (a) *in accordance with that paragraph (but subject to paragraphs 27 to 29); or*
- (b) *so far as applicable to an asset of that description, in accordance with section BA.*

(3) The amounts to be included in respect of assets which—
- (a) *are not assets of a description mentioned in paragraph 22 or 23, but*
- (b) *are assets of a description to which section BA is applicable,*

may be determined in accordance with that section.

(4) Subject to sub-paragraphs (1) to (3), the amounts to be included in respect of all items shown in a company's accounts are determined in accordance with section C.]

SECTION B
CURRENT VALUE ACCOUNTING RULES

Preliminary

20, 21. . . .

Valuation of assets: general

22.—*(1) Subject to paragraph 24 below, investments falling to be included under Assets item C (investments) shall be included at their current value calculated in accordance with paragraphs 25 and 26 below.*

(2) Investments falling to be included under Assets item D (assets held to cover linked liabilities) shall be shown at their current value calculated in accordance with paragraphs 25 and 26 below.

23.—(1) Intangible assets other than goodwill may be shown at their current cost.
(2) Assets falling to be included under Assets items F.I (tangible assets) and F.IV (own shares) in the balance sheet format may be shown at their current value calculated in accordance with paragraphs 25 and 26 below or at their current cost.
(3) Assets falling to be included under Assets item F.II (stocks) may be shown at current cost.

Alternative valuation of fixed-income securities

24.—(1) This paragraph applies to debt securities and other fixed-income securities shown as assets under Assets items C.II (investments in group undertakings and participating interests) and C.III (other financial investments).
(2) Securities to which this paragraph applies may either be valued in accordance with paragraph 22 above or their amortised value may be shown in the balance sheet, in which case the provisions of this paragraph apply.
(3) Subject to sub-paragraph (4) below, where the purchase price of securities to which this paragraph applies exceeds the amount repayable at maturity, the amount of the difference—
(a) shall be charged to the profit and loss account, and
(b) shall be shown separately in the balance sheet or in the notes to the accounts.
(4) The amount of the difference referred to in sub-paragraph (3) above may be written off in instalments so that it is completely written off when the securities are repaid, in which case there shall be shown separately in the balance sheet or in the notes to the accounts the difference between the purchase price (less the aggregate amount written off) and the amount repayable at maturity.
(5) Where the purchase price of securities to which this paragraph applies is less than the amount repayable at maturity, the amount of the difference shall be released to income in instalments over the period remaining until repayment, in which case there shall be shown separately in the balance sheet or in the notes to the accounts the difference between the purchase price (plus the aggregate amount released to income) and the amount repayable at maturity.
(6) Both the purchase price and the current value of securities valued in accordance with this paragraph shall be disclosed in the notes to the accounts.
(7) Where securities to which this paragraph applies which are not valued in accordance with paragraph 22 above are sold before maturity, and the proceeds are used to purchase other securities to which this paragraph applies, the difference between the proceeds of sale and their book value may be spread uniformly over the period remaining until the maturity of the original investment.

Meaning of "current value"

25.—(1) Subject to sub-paragraph (5) below, in the case of investments other than land and buildings, current value shall mean market value determined in accordance with this paragraph.
(2) In the case of listed investments, market value shall mean the value on the balance sheet date or, when the balance sheet date is not a stock exchange trading day, on the last stock exchange trading day before that date.
(3) Where a market exists for unlisted investments, market value shall mean the average price at which such investments were traded on the balance sheet date or, when the balance sheet date is not a trading day, on the last trading day before that date.
(4) Where, on the date on which the accounts are drawn up, listed or unlisted investments have been sold or are to be sold within the short term, the market value shall be reduced by the actual or estimated realisation costs.
(5) Except where the equity method of accounting is applied, all investments other than those referred to in sub-paragraphs (2) and (3) above shall be valued on a basis which has prudent regard to the likely realisable value.

26.—(1) In the case of land and buildings, current value shall mean the market value on the date of valuation, where relevant reduced as provided in sub-paragraphs (4) and (5) below.
(2) Market value shall mean the price at which land and buildings could be sold under private contract between a willing seller and an arm's length buyer on the date of valuation, it being assumed that the property is publicly exposed to the market, that market conditions permit orderly disposal and that a normal period, having regard to the nature of the property, is available for the negotiation of the sale.
(3) The market value shall be determined through the separate valuation of each land and buildings item, carried out at least every five years in accordance with generally recognised methods of valuation.
(4) Where the value of any land and buildings item has diminished since the preceding valuation

under sub-paragraph (3), an appropriate value adjustment shall be made.

(5) The lower value arrived at under sub-paragraph (4) shall not be increased in subsequent balance sheets unless such increase results from a new determination of market value arrived at in accordance with sub-paragraphs (2) and (3).

(6) Where, on the date on which the accounts are drawn up, land and buildings have been sold or are to be sold within the short term, the value arrived at in accordance with sub-paragraphs (2) and (4) shall be reduced by the actual or estimated realisation costs.

(7) Where it is impossible to determine the market value of a land and buildings item, the value arrived at on the basis of the principle of purchase price or production cost shall be deemed to be its current value.

Application of the depreciation rules

27.—(1) Where—

(a) the value of any asset of a company is determined in accordance with paragraph 22 or 23 above, and

(b) in the case of a determination under paragraph 22 above, the asset falls to be included under Assets item C.I,

that value shall be, or (as the case may require) be the starting point for determining, the amount to be included in respect of that asset in the company's accounts, instead of its cost or any value previously so determined for that asset; and paragraphs 31 to 35 and 37 below shall apply accordingly in relation to any such asset with the substitution for any reference to its cost of a reference to the value most recently determined for that asset in accordance with paragraph 22 or 23 above (as the case may be).

(2) The amount of any provision for depreciation required in the case of any asset by paragraph 32 or 33 below as it applies by virtue of sub-paragraph (1) is referred to below in this paragraph as the "adjusted amount", and the amount of any provision which would be required by that paragraph in the case of that asset according to the historical cost accounting rules is referred to as the "historical cost amount".

(3) Where sub-paragraph (1) applies in the case of any asset the amount of any provision for depreciation in respect of that asset included in any item shown in the profit and loss account in respect of amounts written off assets of the description in question may be the historical cost amount instead of the adjusted amount, provided that the amount of any difference between the two is shown separately in the profit and loss account or in a note to the accounts.

Additional information to be provided

28.—(1) This paragraph applies where the amounts to be included in respect of assets covered by any items shown in a company's accounts have been determined in accordance with paragraph 22 or 23 above.

(2) The items affected and the basis of valuation adopted in determining the amounts of the assets in question in the case of each such item shall be disclosed in a note to the accounts.

(3) The purchase price of investments valued in accordance with paragraph 22 above shall be disclosed in the notes to the accounts.

(4) In the case of each balance sheet item valued in accordance with paragraph 23 above either—

(a) the comparable amounts determined according to the historical cost accounting rules (without any provision for depreciation or diminution in value); or

(b) the differences between those amounts and the corresponding amounts actually shown in the balance sheet in respect of that item,

shall be shown separately in the balance sheet or in a note to the accounts.

(5) In sub-paragraph (4) above, references in relation to any item to the comparable amounts determined as there mentioned are references to—

(a) the aggregate amount which would be required to be shown in respect of that item if the amounts to be included in respect of all the assets covered by that item were determined according to the historical cost accounting rules; and

(b) the aggregate amount of the cumulative provisions for depreciation or diminution in value which would be permitted or required in determining those amounts according to those rules.

Revaluation reserve

29.—(1) Subject to sub-paragraph (7) below, with respect to any determination of the value of an asset of a company in accordance with paragraph 22 or 23 above, the amount of any profit or loss arising from that determination (after allowing, where appropriate, for any provisions for depreciation or diminution in value made otherwise than by reference to the value so determined and any adjustments of any such provisions made in the light of that determination) shall be

credited or (as the case may be) debited to a separate reserve ("the revaluation reserve").
(2) The amount of the revaluation reserve shall be shown in the company's balance sheet under Liabilities item A.III, but need not be shown under the name "revaluation reserve".
(3) An amount may be transferred
[(a) from the revaluation reserve—
(i) to the profit and loss account, if the amount was previously charged to that account or represents realised profit, or
(ii) on capitalisation,
(b) to or from the revaluation reserve in respect of the taxation relating to any profit or loss credited or debited to the reserve;]
and the revaluation reserve shall be reduced to the extent that the amounts transferred to it are no longer necessary for the purposes of the valuation method used.
(4) In [sub-paragraph (3)(a)(ii)] "capitalisation", in relation to an amount standing to the credit of the revaluation reserve, means applying it in wholly or partly paying up unissued shares in the company to be allotted to members of the company as fully or partly paid shares.
(5) The revaluation reserve shall not be reduced except as mentioned in this paragraph.
(6) The treatment for taxation purposes of amounts credited or debited to the revaluation reserve shall be disclosed in a note to the accounts.
(7) This paragraph does not apply to the difference between the valuation of investments and their purchase price or previous valuation shown in the long term business technical account or the non-technical account in accordance with note (9) on the profit and loss account format.

[SECTION BA
VALUATION AT FAIR VALUE

Inclusion of financial instruments at fair value

***29A.**—(1) Subject to sub-paragraphs (2) to (4), financial instruments (including derivatives) may be included at fair value.*
(2) Sub-paragraph (1) does not apply to financial instruments which constitute liabilities unless—
(a) they are held as part of a trading portfolio, or
(b) they are derivatives.
(3) Except where they fall to be included under Assets item D (assets held to cover linked liabilities), sub-paragraph (1) does not apply to—
(a) financial instruments (other than derivatives) held to maturity;
(b) loans and receivables originated by the company and not held for trading purposes;
(c) interests in subsidiary undertakings, associated undertakings and joint ventures;
(d) equity instruments issued by the company;
(e) contracts for contingent consideration in a business combination;
(f) other financial instruments with such special characteristics that the instruments, according to generally accepted accounting principles or practice, should be accounted for differently from other financial instruments.
(4) If the fair value of a financial instrument cannot be determined reliably in accordance with paragraph 29B, sub-paragraph (1) does not apply to that financial instrument.
(5) In this paragraph—
"associated undertaking" has the meaning given by paragraph 20 of Schedule 4A; and
"joint venture" has the meaning given by paragraph 19 of that Schedule.

Determination of fair value

***29B.**—(1) The fair value of a financial instrument is determined in accordance with this paragraph.*
(2) If a reliable market can readily be identified for the financial instrument, its fair value is determined by reference to its market value.
(3) If a reliable market cannot readily be identified for the financial instrument but can be identified for its components or for a similar instrument, its fair value is determined by reference to the market value of its components or of the similar instrument.
(4) If neither sub-paragraph (2) nor (3) applies, the fair value of the financial instrument is a value resulting from generally accepted valuation models and techniques.
(5) Any valuation models and techniques used for the purposes of sub-paragraph (4) must ensure a reasonable approximation of the market value.

Inclusion of hedged items at fair value

***29C.** A company may include any assets and liabilities that qualify as hedged items under a fair value hedge accounting system, or identified portions of such assets or liabilities, at the amount required under that system.*

Other assets that may be included at fair value

***29D.**—(1) This paragraph applies to—*

(a) investment property, and

(b) living animals and plants,

that, under international accounting standards, may be included in accounts at fair value.

(2) Such investment property and such living animals and plants may be included at fair value, provided that all such investment property or, as the case may be, all such living animals and plants are so included where their fair value can reliably be determined.

(3) In this paragraph, "fair value" means fair value determined in accordance with relevant international accounting standards.

Accounting for changes in value

***29E.**—(1) This paragraph applies where a financial instrument is valued in accordance with paragraph 29A or 29C or an asset is valued in accordance with paragraph 29D.*

(2) Notwithstanding paragraph 16 in this Part of this Schedule, and subject to sub-paragraphs (3) and (4) below, a change in the value of the financial instrument or of the investment property or living animal or plant must be included in the profit and loss account.

(3) Where—

(a) the financial instrument accounted for is a hedging instrument under a hedge accounting system that allows some or all of the change in value not to be shown in the profit and loss account, or

(b) the change in value relates to an exchange difference arising on a monetary item that forms part of a company's net investment in a foreign entity,

the amount of the change in value must be credited to or (as the case may be) debited from a separate reserve ("the fair value reserve").

(4) Where the instrument accounted for—

(a) is an available for sale financial asset, and

(b) is not a derivative,

the change in value may be credited to or (as the case may be) debited from the fair value reserve.

The fair value reserve

***29F.**—(1) The fair value reserve must be adjusted to the extent that the amounts shown in it are no longer necessary for the purposes of paragraph 29E(3) or (4).*

(2) The treatment for taxation purposes of amounts credited or debited to the fair value reserve shall be disclosed in a note to the accounts.]

SECTION C
HISTORICAL COST ACCOUNTING RULES

Preliminary

***30.** . . .*

Valuation of assets

General rules

***31.** Subject to any provision for depreciation or diminution in value made in accordance with paragraph 32 or 33 below, the amount to be included in respect of any asset in the balance sheet format shall be its cost.*

***32.** In the case of any asset included under Assets item B (intangible assets), C.I (land and buildings), F.I. (tangible assets) or F.II (stocks) which has a limited useful economic life, the amount of—*

(a) its cost; or

(b) where it is estimated that any such asset will have a residual value at the end of the period of its useful economic life, its cost less that estimated residual value,

shall be reduced by provisions for depreciation calculated to write off that amount systematically over the period of the asset's useful economic life.

***33.**—(1) This paragraph applies to any asset included under Assets item B (tangible assets), C (investments), F.I (tangible assets) or F.IV (own shares).*

(2) Where an asset to which this paragraph applies has diminished in value, provisions for diminution in value may be made in respect of it and the amount to be included in respect of it may be reduced accordingly; and any such provisions which are not shown in the profit and loss account shall be disclosed (either separately or in aggregate) in a note to the accounts.

(3) Provisions for diminution in value shall be made in respect of any asset to which this paragraph applies if the reduction in its value is expected to be permanent (whether its useful economic life is limited or not), and the amount to be included in respect of it shall be reduced accordingly; and any such provisions which are not shown in the profit and loss account shall be disclosed (either separately or in aggregate) in a note to the accounts.
(4) Where the reasons for which any provision was made in accordance with sub-paragraph (1) or (2) have ceased to apply to any extent, that provision shall be written back to the extent that it is no longer necessary; and any amounts written back in accordance with this sub-paragraph which are not shown in the profit and loss account shall be disclosed (either separately or in aggregate) in a note to the accounts.

***34.**—(1) This paragraph applies to assets included under Assets items E.I, II and III (debtors) and F.III (cash at bank and in hand) in the balance sheet.*
(2) If the net realisable value of an asset to which this paragraph applies is lower than its cost the amount to be included in respect of that asset shall be the net realisable value.
(3) Where the reasons for which any provision for diminution in value was made in accordance with sub-paragraph (2) have ceased to apply to any extent, that provision shall be written back to the extent that it is no longer necessary.
Development costs

35.—*(1) Notwithstanding that amounts representing "development costs" may be included under Assets item B (intangible assets) in the balance sheet format, an amount may only be included in a company's balance sheet in respect of development costs in special circumstances.*
(2) If any amount is included in a company's balance sheet in respect of development costs the following information shall be given in a note to the accounts—
- *(a) the period over which the amount of those costs originally capitalised is being or is to be written off; and*
- *(b) the reasons for capitalising the development costs in question.*

Goodwill

***36.**—(1) The application of paragraphs 31 to 33 above in relation to goodwill (in any case where goodwill is treated as an asset) is subject to the following provisions of this paragraph.*
(2) Subject to sub-paragraph (3) below, the amount of the consideration for any goodwill acquired by a company shall be reduced by provisions for depreciation calculated to write off that amount systematically over a period chosen by the directors of the company.
(3) The period chosen shall not exceed the useful economic life of the goodwill in question.
(4) In any case where any goodwill acquired by a company is included as an asset in the company's balance sheet the period chosen for writing off the consideration for that goodwill and the reasons for choosing that period shall be disclosed in a note to the accounts.

Miscellaneous and supplemental

Excess of money owed over value received as an asset item

***37.**—(1) Where the amount repayable on any debt owed by a company is greater than the value of the consideration received in the transaction giving rise to the debt, the amount of the difference may be treated as an asset.*
(2) Where any such amount is so treated—
- *(a) it shall be written off by reasonable amounts each year and must be completely written off before repayment of the debt; and*
- *(b) if the current amount is not shown as a separate item in the company's balance sheet it must be disclosed in a note to the accounts.*

Assets included at a fixed amount

38.—*(1) Subject to the following sub-paragraph, assets which fall to be included under Assets item F.I (tangible assets) in the balance sheet format may be included at a fixed quantity and value.*
(2) Sub-paragraph (1) applies to assets of a kind which are constantly being replaced, where—
- *(a) their overall value is not material to assessing the company's state of affairs; and*
- *(b) their quantity, value and composition are not subject to material variation.*

Determination of cost

***39.**—(1) The cost of an asset that has been acquired by the company shall be determined by adding to the actual price paid any expenses incidental to its acquisition.*
(2) The cost of an asset constructed by the company shall be determined by adding to the purchase price of the raw materials and consumables used the amount of the costs incurred by the company which are directly attributable to the construction of that asset.
(3) In addition, there may be included in the cost of an asset constructed by the company—

(a) a reasonable proportion of the costs incurred by the company which are only indirectly attributable to the construction of that asset, but only to the extent that they relate to the period of construction; and

(b) interest on capital borrowed to finance the construction of that asset, to the extent that it accrues in respect of the period of construction;

provided, however, in a case within sub-paragraph (b) above, that the inclusion of the interest in determining the cost of that asset and the amount of the interest so included is disclosed in a note to the accounts.

40.—*(1) Subject to the qualification mentioned below, the cost of any assets which are fungible assets may be determined by the application of any of the methods mentioned in sub-paragraph (2) below in relation to any such assets of the same class.*

The method chosen must be one which appears to the directors to be appropriate in the circumstances of the company.

(2) Those methods are—

(a) the method known as "first in, first out" (FIFO);

(b) the method known as "last in, first out" (LIFO);

(c) a weighted average price; and

(d) any other method similar to any of the methods mentioned above.

(3) Where in the case of any company—

(a) the cost of assets falling to be included under any item shown in the company's balance sheet has been determined by the application of any method permitted by this paragraph; and

(b) the amount shown in respect of that item differs materially from the relevant alternative amount given below in this paragraph;

the amount of that difference shall be disclosed in a note to the accounts.

(4) Subject to sub-paragraph (5) below, for the purposes of sub-paragraph (3)(b) above, the relevant alternative amount, in relation to any item shown in a company's balance sheet, is the amount which would have been shown in respect of that item if assets of any class included under that item at an amount determined by any method permitted by this paragraph had instead been included at their replacement cost as at the balance sheet date.

(5) The relevant alternative amount may be determined by reference to the most recent actual purchase price before the balance sheet date of assets of any class included under the item in question instead of by reference to their replacement cost as at that date, but only if the former appears to the directors of the company to constitute the more appropriate standard of comparison in the case of assets of that class.

Substitution of original amount where price or cost unknown

41. *Where there is no record of the purchase price of any asset acquired by a company or of any price, expenses or costs relevant for determining its cost in accordance with paragraph 39 above, or any such record cannot be obtained without unreasonable expense or delay, its cost shall be taken for the purposes of paragraphs 31 to 36 above to be the value ascribed to it in the earliest available record of its value made on or after its acquisition by the company.*

SECTION D
RULES FOR DETERMINING PROVISIONS

Preliminary

42. *Provisions which are to be shown in a company's accounts shall be determined in accordance with paragraphs 43 to 53 below.*

Technical provisions

43. *The amount of technical provisions must at all times be sufficient to cover any liabilities arising out of insurance contracts as far as can reasonably be foreseen.*

Provision for unearned premiums

44.—*(1) The provision for unearned premiums shall in principle be computed separately for each insurance contract, save that statistical methods (and in particular proportional and flat rate methods) may be used where they may be expected to give approximately the same results as individual calculations.*

(2) Where the pattern of risk varies over the life of a contract, this shall be taken into account in the calculation methods.

Provision for unexpired risks

45. The provision for unexpired risks (as defined in paragraph 81 below) shall be computed on the basis of claims and administrative expenses likely to arise after the end of the financial year from contracts concluded before that date, in so far as their estimated value exceeds the provision for unearned premiums and any premiums receivable under those contracts.

Long term business provision

46.—(1) The long term business provision shall in principle be computed separately for each long term contract, save that statistical or mathematical methods may be used where they may be expected to give approximately the same results as individual calculations.

(2) A summary of the principal assumptions in making the provision under sub-paragraph (1) shall be given in the notes to the accounts.

(3) The computation shall be made annually by a Fellow of the Institute or Faculty of Actuaries on the basis of recognised actuarial methods, with due regard to the actuarial principles laid down in [Directive 2002/83/EC of the European Parliament and of the Council of 5th November 2002 concerning life assurance].

Provisions for claims outstanding

General business

47.—(1) A provision shall in principle be computed separately for each claim on the basis of the costs still expected to arise, save that statistical methods may be used if they result in an adequate provision having regard to the nature of the risks.

(2) This provision shall also allow for claims incurred but not reported by the balance sheet date, the amount of the allowance being determined having regard to past experience as to the number and magnitude of claims reported after previous balance sheet dates.

(3) All claims settlement costs (whether direct or indirect) shall be included in the calculation of the provision.

(4) Recoverable amounts arising out of subrogation or salvage shall be estimated on a prudent basis and either deducted from the provision for claims outstanding (in which case if the amounts are material they shall be shown in the notes to the accounts) or shown as assets.

(5) In sub-paragraph (4) above, "subrogation" means the acquisition of the rights of policy holders with respect to third parties, and "salvage" means the acquisition of the legal ownership of insured property.

(6) Where benefits resulting from a claim must be paid in the form of annuity, the amounts to be set aside for that purpose shall be calculated by recognised actuarial methods, and paragraph 48 below shall not apply to such calculations.

(7) Implicit discounting or deductions, whether resulting from the placing of a current value on a provision for an outstanding claim which is expected to be settled later at a higher figure or otherwise effected, is prohibited.

48.—(1) Explicit discounting or deductions to take account of investment income is permitted, subject to the following conditions:

- *(a) the expected average interval between the date for the settlement of claims being discounted and the accounting date shall be at least four years;*
- *(b) the discounting or deductions shall be effected on a recognised prudential basis;*
- *(c) when calculating the total cost of settling claims, the company shall take account of all factors that could cause increases in that cost;*
- *(d) the company shall have adequate data at its disposal to construct a reliable model of the rate of claims settlements;*
- *(e) the rate of interest used for the calculation of present values shall not exceed a rate prudently estimated to be earned by assets of the company which are appropriate in magnitude and nature to cover the provisions for claims being discounted during the period necessary for the payment of such claims, and shall not exceed either—*
  - *(i) a rate justified by the performance of such assets over the preceding five years, or*
  - *(ii) a rate justified by the performance of such assets during the year preceding the balance sheet date.*

(2) When discounting or effecting deductions, the company shall, in the notes to the accounts, disclose—

- *(a) the total amount of provisions before discounting or deductions,*
- *(b) the categories of claims which are discounted or from which deductions have been made,*
- *(c) for each category of claims, the methods used, in particular the rates used for the estimates referred to in sub-paragraph (1)(d) and (e), and the criteria adopted for*

estimating the period that will elapse before the claims are settled.

Long term business

49. *The amount of the provision for claims shall be equal to the sums due to beneficiaries, plus the costs of settling claims.*

[Equalisation reserves

*[**50.** The amount of any equalisation reserve maintained in respect of general business, in accordance with rules made by the Financial Services Authority under Part X of the Financial Services and Markets Act 2000, shall be determined in accordance with such rules.]]*

Accounting on a non-annual basis

51.—*(1) Either of the methods described in paragraphs 52 and 53 below may be applied where, because of the nature of the class or type of insurance in question, information about premiums receivable or claims payable (or both) for the underwriting years is insufficient when the accounts are drawn up for reliable estimates to be made.*

(2) The use of either of the methods referred to in sub-paragraph (1) shall be disclosed in the notes to the accounts together with the reasons for adopting it.

(3) Where one of the methods referred to in sub-paragraph (1) above is adopted, it shall be applied systematically in successive years unless circumstances justify a change.

(4) In the event of a change in the method applied, the effect on the assets, liabilities, financial position and profit or loss shall be stated in the notes to the accounts.

(5) For the purposes of this paragraph and paragraph 52 below, "underwriting year" means the financial year in which the insurance contracts in the class or type of insurance in question commenced.

52.—*(1) The excess of the premiums written over the claims and expenses paid in respect of contracts commencing in the underwriting year shall form a technical provision included in the technical provision for claims outstanding shown in the balance sheet under Liabilities item C.3.*

(2) The provision may also be computed on the basis of a given percentage of the premiums written where such a method is appropriate for the type of risk insured.

(3) If necessary, the amount of this technical provision shall be increased to make it sufficient to meet present and future obligations.

(4) The technical provision constituted under this paragraph shall be replaced by a provision for claims outstanding estimated in accordance with paragraph 47 above as soon as sufficient information has been gathered and not later than the end of the third year following the underwriting year.

(5) The length of time that elapses before a provision for claims outstanding is constituted in accordance with sub-paragraph (4) above shall be disclosed in the notes to the accounts.

53.—*(1) The figures shown in the technical account or in certain items within it shall relate to a year which wholly or partly precedes the financial year (but by no more than 12 months).*

(2) The amounts of the technical provisions shown in the accounts shall if necessary be increased to make them sufficient to meet present and future obligations.

(3) The length of time by which the earlier year to which the figures relate precedes the financial year and the magnitude of the transactions concerned shall be disclosed in the notes to the accounts.

CHAPTER III
NOTES TO THE ACCOUNTS

Preliminary

*[**54.**—(1) Any information required in the case of any company by the following provisions of this Part of this Schedule shall (if not given in the company's accounts) be given by way of a note to those accounts.*

(2), (3) . . .]

General

Disclosure of accounting policies

55. *The accounting policies adopted by the company in determining the amounts to be included in respect of items shown in the balance sheet and in determining the profit or loss of the company shall be stated (including such accounting policies with respect to the depreciation and diminution in value of assets).*

56. *It shall be stated whether the accounts have been prepared in accordance with applicable accounting standards and particulars of any material departure from those standards and the* *reasons for it shall be given.*

Sums denominated in foreign currencies

57. Where any sums originally denominated in foreign currencies have been brought into account under any items shown in the balance sheet or profit and loss account format, the basis on which those sums have been translated into sterling (or the currency in which the accounts are drawn up) shall be stated.

[Reserves and dividends

57A. There must be stated—

(a) any amount set aside or proposed to be set aside to, or withdrawn or proposed to be withdrawn from, reserves,

(b) the aggregate amount of dividends paid in the financial year (other than those for which a liability existed at the immediately preceding balance sheet date),

(c) the aggregate amount of dividends that the company is liable to pay at the balance sheet date, and

(d) the aggregate amount of dividends that are proposed before the date of approval of the accounts, and not otherwise disclosed under paragraph (b) or (c).]

Information supplementing the balance sheet

Share capital and debentures

58.—(1) The following information shall be given with respect to the company's share capital—

(a) the authorised share capital; and

(b) where shares of more than one class have been allotted, the number and aggregate nominal value of shares of each class allotted.

(2) In the case of any part of the allotted share capital that consists of redeemable shares, the following information shall be given—

(a) the earliest and latest dates on which the company has power to redeem those shares;

(b) whether those shares must be redeemed in any event or are liable to be redeemed at the option of the company or of the shareholder; and

(c) whether any (and, if so, what) premium is payable on redemption.

59. If the company has allotted any shares during the financial year, the following information shall be given—

(a) . . .

(b) the classes of shares allotted; and

(c) as respects each class of shares, the number allotted, their aggregate nominal value and the consideration received by the company for the allotment.

60.—(1) With respect to any contingent right to the allotment of shares in the company the following particulars shall be given—

(a) the number, description and amount of the shares in relation to which the right is exercisable;

(b) the period during which it is exercisable; and

(c) the price to be paid for the shares allotted.

(2) In sub-paragraph (1) above "contingent right to the allotment of shares" means any option to subscribe for shares and any other right to require the allotment of shares to any person whether arising on the conversion into shares of securities of any other description or otherwise.

61.—(1) If the company has issued any debentures during the financial year to which the accounts relate, the following information shall be given—

(a) . . .

(b) the classes of debentures issued; and

(c) as respects each class of debentures, the amount issued and the consideration received by the company for the issue.

(2) . . .

(3) Where any of the company's debentures are held by a nominee of or trustee for the company, the nominal amount of the debentures and the amount at which they are stated in the accounting records kept by the company in accordance with section 221 of this Act shall be stated.

Assets

62.—(1) In respect of any assets of the company included in Assets items B (intangible assets), C.I (land and buildings) and C.II (investments in group undertakings and participating interests) in the company's balance sheet the following information shall be given by reference to each such item—

(a) the appropriate amounts in respect of those assets included in the item as at the date of the beginning of the financial year and as at the balance sheet date respectively;

(b) the effect on any amount included in Assets item B in respect of those assets of—

(i) any determination during that year of the value to be ascribed to any of those assets in accordance with paragraph 23 above;

(ii) acquisitions during that year of any assets;

(iii) disposals during that year of any assets; and

(iv) any transfers of assets of the company to and from the item during that year.

(2) The reference in sub-paragraph (1)(a) to the appropriate amounts in respect of any assets (included in an assets item) as at any date there mentioned is a reference to amounts representing the aggregate amounts determined, as at that date, in respect of assets falling to be included under the item on either of the following bases, that is to say—

(a) on the basis of cost (determined in accordance with paragraphs 39 and 40 above); or

(b) on any basis permitted by paragraph 22 or 23 above,

(leaving out of account in either case any provisions for depreciation or diminution in value).

(3) In addition, in respect of any assets of the company included in any assets item in the company's balance sheet, there shall be stated (by reference to each such item)—

(a) the cumulative amount of provisions for depreciation or diminution in value of those assets included under the item as at each date mentioned in sub-paragraph (1)(a);

(b) the amount of any such provisions made in respect of the financial year;

(c) the amount of any adjustments made in respect of any such provisions during that year in consequence of the disposal of any of those assets; and

(d) the amount of any other adjustments made in respect of any such provisions during that year.

***63.** Where any assets of the company (other than listed investments) are included under any item shown in the company's balance sheet at an amount determined on any basis mentioned in paragraph 22 or 23 above, the following information shall be given—*

(a) the years (so far as they are known to the directors) in which the assets were severally valued and the several values; and

(b) in the case of assets that have been valued during the financial year, the names of the persons who valued them or particulars of their qualifications for doing so and (whichever is stated) the bases of valuation used by them.

***64.** In relation to any amount which is included under Assets item C.I (land and buildings) there shall be stated—*

(a) how much of that amount is ascribable to land of freehold tenure and how much to land of leasehold tenure; and

(b) how much of the amount ascribable to land of leasehold tenure is ascribable to land held on long lease and how much to land held on short lease.

Investments

***65.** In respect of the amount of each item which is shown in the company's balance sheet under Assets item C (investments) there shall be stated—*

(a) how much of that amount is ascribable to listed investments; . . .

(b) . . .

[Information about fair value of assets and liabilities

***65A.**—(1) This paragraph applies where financial instruments have been valued in accordance with paragraph 29A or 29C.*

(2) The items affected and the basis of valuation adopted in determining the amounts of the financial instruments must be disclosed.

(3) The purchase price of the financial instruments must be disclosed.

(4) There must be stated—

(a) where the fair value of the instruments has been determined in accordance with paragraph 29B(4), the significant assumptions underlying the valuation models and techniques used,

(b) for each category of financial instrument, the fair value of the instruments in that category and the changes in value—

(i) included in the profit and loss account, or

(ii) credited to or (as the case may be) debited from the fair value reserve,

in respect of those instruments, and

(c) for each class of derivatives, the extent and nature of the instruments, including significant terms and conditions that may affect the amount, timing and certainty of

future cash flows.

(5) Where any amount is transferred to or from the fair value reserve during the financial year, there must be stated in tabular form—

- *(a) the amount of the reserve as at the date of the beginning of the financial year and as at the balance sheet date respectively;*
- *(b) the amount transferred to or from the reserve during that year; and*
- *(c) the source and application respectively of the amounts so transferred.*

65B. *Where the company has derivatives that it has not included at fair value, there must be stated for each class of such derivatives—*

- *(a) the fair value of the derivatives in that class, if such a value can be determined in accordance with paragraph 29B, and*
- *(b) the extent and nature of the derivatives.*

65C.*—(1) Sub-paragraph (2) applies if—*

- *(a) the company has financial fixed assets that could be included at fair value by virtue of paragraph 29A,*
- *(b) the amount at which those assets are included under any item in the company's accounts is in excess of their fair value, and*
- *(c) the company has not made provision for diminution in value of those assets in accordance with paragraph 33(2) of this Part of this Schedule.*

(2) There must be stated—

- *(a) the amount at which either the individual assets or appropriate groupings of those individual assets are included in the company's accounts,*
- *(b) the fair value of those assets or groupings, and*
- *(c) the reasons for not making a provision for diminution in value of those assets, including the nature of the evidence that provides the basis for the belief that the amount at which they are stated in the accounts will be recovered.*

Information where investment property and living animals and plants included at fair value

65D.*—(1) This paragraph applies where the amounts to be included in a company's accounts in respect of investment property or living animals and plants have been determined in accordance with paragraph 29D.*

(2) The balance sheet items affected and the basis of valuation adopted in determining the amounts of the assets in question in the case of each such item must be disclosed in a note to the accounts.

(3) In the case of investment property, for each balance sheet item affected there must be shown, either separately in the balance sheet or in a note to the accounts—

- *(a) the comparable amounts determined according to the historical cost accounting rules; or*
- *(b) the differences between those amounts and the corresponding amounts actually shown in the balance sheet in respect of that item.*

(4) In sub-paragraph (3) above, references in relation to any item to the comparable amounts determined in accordance with that sub-paragraph are references to—

- *(a) the aggregate amount which would be required to be shown in respect of that item if the amounts to be included in respect of all the assets covered by that item were determined according to the historical cost accounting rules; and*
- *(b) the aggregate amount of the cumulative provisions for depreciation or diminution in value which would be permitted or required in determining those amounts according to those rules.]*

Reserves and provisions

66.*—(1) Where any amount is transferred—*

- *(a) to or from any reserves;*
- *(b) to any [provisions for other risks]; or*
- *(c) from any [provisions for other risks] otherwise than for the purpose for which the provision was established;*

and the reserves or provisions are or would but for paragraph 2(3) above be shown as separate items in the company's balance sheet, the information mentioned in the following sub-paragraph shall be given in respect of the aggregate of reserves or provisions included in the same item.

(2) That information is—

- *(a) the amount of the reserves or provisions as at the date of the beginning of the financial year and as at the balance sheet date respectively;*
- *(b) any amounts transferred to or from the reserves or provisions during that year; and*

(c) the source and application respectively of any amounts so transferred.

(3) Particulars shall be given of each provision included in Liabilities item E.3 (other provisions) in the company's balance sheet in any case where the amount of that provision is material.

Provision for taxation

67. The amount of any provision for deferred taxation shall be stated separately from the amount of any provision for other taxation.

Details of indebtedness

68.—[(1) In respect of each item shown under "creditors" in the company's balance sheet there shall be stated the aggregate of the following amounts, that is to say—

(a) the amount of any debts included under that item which are payable or repayable otherwise than by instalments and fall due for payment or repayment after the end of the period of five years beginning with the day next following the end of the financial year; and

[(b) in the case of any debts so included which are payable or repayable by instalments, the amount of any instalments which fall due for payment after the end of that period.]]

(2) Subject to sub-paragraph (3), in relation to each debt falling to be taken into account under sub-paragraph (1), the terms of payment or repayment and the rate of any interest payable on the debt shall be stated.

(3) If the number of debts is such that, in the opinion of the directors, compliance with sub-paragraph (2) would result in a statement of excessive length, it shall be sufficient to give a general indication of the terms of payment or repayment and the rates of any interest payable on the debts.

(4) In respect of each item shown under "creditors" in the company's balance sheet there shall be stated—

(a) the aggregate amount of any debts included under that item in respect of which any security has been given by the company; and

(b) an indication of the nature of the securities so given.

(5) References above in this paragraph to an item shown under "creditors" in the company's balance sheet include references, where amounts falling due to creditors within one year and after more than one year are distinguished in the balance sheet—

(a) in a case within sub-paragraph (1), to an item shown under the latter of those categories; and

(b) in a case within sub-paragraph (4), to an item shown under either of those categories;

and references to items shown under "creditors" include references to items which would but for paragraph 2(3)(b) above be shown under that heading.

69. If any fixed cumulative dividends on the company's shares are in arrear, there shall be stated—

(a) the amount of the arrears; and

(b) the period for which the dividends or, if there is more than one class, each class of them are in arrear.

Guarantees and other financial commitments

70.—(1) Particulars shall be given of any charge on the assets of the company to secure the liabilities of any other person, including, where practicable, the amount secured.

(2) The following information shall be given with respect to any other contingent liability not provided for (other than a contingent liability arising out of an insurance contract)—

(a) the amount or estimated amount of that liability;

(b) its legal nature;

(c) whether any valuable security has been provided by the company in connection with that liability and if so, what.

(3) There shall be stated, where practicable—

(a) the aggregate amount or estimated amount of contracts for capital expenditure, so far as not provided for; . . .

(b) . . .

(4) Particulars shall be given of—

(a) any pension commitments included under any provision shown in the company's balance sheet; and

(b) any such commitments for which no provision has been made;

and where any such commitment relates wholly or partly to pensions payable to past directors of the company separate particulars shall be given of that commitment so far as it relates to such pensions.

(5) Particulars shall also be given of any other financial commitments, other than commitments arising out of insurance contracts, which—

(a) have not been provided for; and

(b) are relevant to assessing the company's state of affairs.

(6) Commitments within any of the preceding sub-paragraphs undertaken on behalf of or for the benefit of—

(a) any parent undertaking or fellow subsidiary undertaking, or

(b) any subsidiary undertaking of the company,

shall be stated separately from the other commitments within that sub-paragraph, and commitments within paragraph (a) shall also be stated separately from those within paragraph (b).

71. . . .

Miscellaneous matters

72.—(1) Particulars shall be given of any case where the cost of any asset is for the first time determined under paragraph 41 above.

(2) Where any outstanding loans made under the authority of section 153(4)(b), (bb) or (c) or section 155 of this Act (various cases of financial assistance by a company for purchase of its own shares) are included under any item shown in the company's balance sheet, the aggregate amount of those loans shall be disclosed for each item in question.

(3) . . .

Information supplementing the profit and loss account

Separate statement of certain items of income and expenditure

73.—(1) Subject to the following provisions of this paragraph, each of the amounts mentioned below shall be stated.

(2) The amount of the interest on or any similar charges in respect of—

(a) bank loans and overdrafts, . . . and

(b) loans of any other kind made to the company.

This sub-paragraph does not apply to interest or charges on loans to the company from group undertakings, but, with that exception, it applies to interest or charges on all loans, whether made on the security of debentures or not.

(3)–(5) . . .

Particulars of tax

74.—(1) . . .

(2) Particulars shall be given of any special circumstances which affect liability in respect of taxation of profits, income or capital gains for the financial year or liability in respect of taxation of profits, income or capital gains for succeeding financial years.

(3) The following amounts shall be stated—

(a) the amount of the charge for United Kingdom corporation tax;

(b) if that amount would have been greater but for relief from double taxation, the amount which it would have been but for such relief;

(c) the amount of the charge for United Kingdom income tax; and

(d) the amount of the charge for taxation imposed outside the United Kingdom of profits, income and (so far as charged to revenue) capital gains.

Those amounts shall be stated separately in respect of each of the amounts which is shown under the following items in the profit and loss account, that is to say item III.9 (tax on profit or loss on ordinary activities) and item III.14 (tax on extraordinary profit or loss).

Particulars of business

75.—(1) As regards general business a company shall disclose—

(a) gross premiums written,

(b) gross premiums earned,

(c) gross claims incurred,

(d) gross operating expenses, and

(e) the reinsurance balance.

(2) The amounts required to be disclosed by sub-paragraph (1) shall be broken down between direct insurance and reinsurance acceptances, if reinsurance acceptances amount to 10 per cent or more of gross premiums written.

(3) Subject to sub-paragraph (4) below, the amounts required to be disclosed by sub-paragraphs (1) and (2) above with respect to direct insurance shall be further broken down into the following groups of classes—

(a) accident and health,

(b) motor (third party liability),

(c) motor (other classes),

(d) marine, aviation and transport,
(e) fire and other damage to property,
(f) third-party liability,
(g) credit and suretyship,
(h) legal expenses,
(i) assistance, and
(j) miscellaneous,

where the amount of the gross premiums written in direct insurance for each such group exceeds 10 million ECUs.

(4) The company shall in any event disclose the amounts relating to the three largest groups of classes in its business.

76.—(1) As regards long term business, the company shall disclose—

(a) gross premiums written, and
(b) the reinsurance balance.

(2) Subject to sub-paragraph (3) below—

(a) gross premiums written shall be broken down between those written by way of direct insurance and those written by way of reinsurance; and
(b) gross premiums written by way of direct insurance shall be broken down—
  (i) between individual premiums and premiums under group contracts;
  (ii) between periodic premiums and single premiums; and
  (iii) between premiums from non-participating contracts, premiums from participating contracts and premiums from contracts where the investment risk is borne by policy holders.

(3) Disclosure of any amount referred to in sub-paragraph (2)(a) or (2)(b)(i), (ii) or (iii) above shall not be required if it does not exceed 10 per cent of the gross premiums written or (as the case may be) of the gross premiums written by way of direct insurance.

77.—(1) Subject to sub-paragraph (2) below, there shall be disclosed as regards both general and long term business the total gross direct insurance premiums resulting from contracts concluded by the company—

(a) in the member State of its head office,
(b) in the other member States, and
(c) in other countries.

(2) Disclosure of any amount referred to in sub-paragraph (1) above shall not be required if it does not exceed 5 per cent of total gross premiums.

Commissions

78. There shall be disclosed the total amount of commissions for direct insurance business accounted for in the financial year, including acquisition, renewal, collection and portfolio management commissions.

Particulars of staff

79. . . .

Miscellaneous matters

80.—(1) Where any amount relating to any preceding financial year is included in any item in the profit and loss account, the effect shall be stated.

(2) Particulars shall be given of any extraordinary income or charges arising in the financial year.

(3) The effect shall be stated of any transactions that are exceptional by virtue of size or incidence though they fall within the ordinary activities of the company.

CHAPTER IV
INTERPRETATIONS OF PART I

General

81.—(1) The following definitions apply for the purposes of this Part of this Schedule and its interpretation—

. . .

"fungible assets" means assets of any description which are substantially indistinguishable one from another;

["general business" means business which consists of effecting or carrying out contracts of general insurance;]

["investment property" means land held to earn rent or for capital appreciation;]

"lease" includes an agreement for a lease;

"listed investment" means an investment listed on a recognised stock exchange, or on any stock exchange of repute outside Great Britain and the expression "unlisted investment" shall be construed accordingly;

"long lease" means a lease in the case of which the portion of the term for which it was granted remaining unexpired at the end of the financial year is not less than 50 years;

["long term business" means business which consists of effecting or carrying out contracts of long term insurance;]

"long term fund" means the fund or funds maintained by a company in respect of its long term business [in accordance with rules made by the Financial Services Authority under Part X of the Financial Services and Markets Act 2000];

["policy holder" has the meaning given in any relevant order under section 424(2) of the Financial Services and Markets Act 2000;]

"provision for unexpired risks" means the amount set aside in addition to unearned premiums in respect of risks to be borne by the company after the end of the financial year, in order to provide for all claims and expenses in connection with insurance contracts in force in excess of the related unearned premiums and any premiums receivable on those contracts;

"short lease" means a lease which is not a long lease.

(2) In this Part of this Schedule the "ECU" means the unit of account of that name defined in Council Regulation (EEC) No 3180/78 as amended.

The exchange rates as between the ECU and the currencies of the member States to be applied for each financial year shall be the rates applicable on the last day of the preceding October for which rates for the currencies of all the member States were published in the Official Journal of the Communities.

[Financial instruments

***81A.** For the purposes of this Part of this Schedule, references to "derivatives" include commodity-based contracts that give either contracting party the right to settle in cash or some other financial instrument, except when such contracts—*

(a) were entered into for the purpose of, and continue to meet, the company's expected purchase, sale or usage requirements,

(b) were designated for such purpose at their inception, and

(c) are expected to be settled by delivery of the commodity.

***81B.**—(1) The expressions listed in sub-paragraph (2) have the same meaning in Section BA of Chapter 2 and paragraphs 65A to 65C and 81A of this Part of this Schedule as they have in Council Directives 78/660/EEC on the annual accounts of certain types of companies and 91/674/EEC on the annual accounts and consolidated accounts of insurance undertakings, as amended.*

(2) Those expressions are "available for sale financial asset", "business combination", "commodity-based contracts", "derivative", "equity instrument", "exchange difference", "fair value hedge accounting system", "financial fixed asset", "financial instrument", "foreign entity", "hedge accounting", "hedge accounting system", "hedged items", "hedging instrument", "held for trading purposes", "held to maturity", "monetary item", "receivables", "reliable market" and "trading portfolio".]

Loans

***82.** For the purposes of this Part of this Schedule a loan or advance (including a liability comprising a loan or advance) is treated as falling due for repayment, and an instalment of a loan or advance is treated as falling due for payment, on the earliest date on which the lender could require repayment or (as the case may be) payment, if he exercised all options and rights available to him.*

Materiality

***83.** For the purposes of this Part of this Schedule amounts which in the particular context of any provision of this Part are not material may be disregarded for the purposes of that provision.*

Provisions

***84.** For the purposes of this Part of this Schedule and its interpretation—*

(a) references in this Part to provisions for depreciation or diminution in value of assets are to any amount written off by way of providing for depreciation or diminution in value of assets;

(b) any reference in the profit and loss account format or the notes thereto set out in Section B of this Part to the depreciation of, or amounts written off, assets of any description is to any provision for depreciation or diminution in value of assets of that description; and

Part III Statutes

(c) references in this Part to [provisions for other risks] . . . are to any amount retained as reasonably necessary for the purpose of providing for any liability [the nature of which is clearly defined and] which is either likely to be incurred, or certain to be incurred but uncertain as to amount or as to the date on which it will arise.

Scots land tenure

***85.** In the application of this Part of this Schedule to Scotland—*

"land of freehold tenure" means land in respect of which the company is the proprietor of the dominium utile or, in the case of land not held on feudal tenure, is the owner;

"land of leasehold tenure" means land of which the company is the tenant under a lease;

and the reference to ground-rents, rates and other outgoings includes feu-duty and ground annual.

Staff costs

***86.** For the purposes of this Part of this Schedule and its interpretation—*

(a) "Social security costs" means any contributions by the company to any state social security or pension scheme, fund or arrangement;

[(b) "Pension costs" includes any costs incurred by the company in respect of any pension scheme established for the purpose of providing pensions for persons currently or formerly employed by the company, any sums set aside for the future payment of pensions directly by the company to current or former employees and any pensions paid directly to such persons without having first been set aside; and]

(c) any amount stated in respect of [the item "social security costs"] or in respect of the item "wages and salaries" in the company's profit and loss account shall be determined by reference to payments made or costs incurred in respect of all persons employed by the company during the financial year who are taken into account in determining the relevant annual number for the purposes of [section 231A(1)(a)].

NOTES

Repealed by the Companies Act 2006, s 1295, Sch 16, except in respect of financial years beginning before 6 April 2008.

Originally Sch 9, Pts I, II, renumbered as Sch 9A and renamed by the Companies Act 1985 (Bank Accounts) Regulations 1991, SI 1991/2705, reg 5(1), (3); further substituted by the Companies Act 1985 (Insurance Companies Accounts) Regulations 1993, SI 1993/3246, reg 4, Sch 1, subject to transitional provisions contained in regs 6, 7 thereof.

Para 3: words in square brackets substituted by the Companies Act 1985 (Investment Companies and Accounting and Audit Amendments) Regulations 2005, SI 2005/2280, regs 1(3), (4), 10, in relation to companies' financial years which begin on or after 1 January 2005 and end on or after 1 October 2005.

Para 5: repealed by the Companies Act 1985 (International Accounting Standards and Other Accounting Amendments) Regulations 2004, SI 2004/2947, reg 14(5), Sch 6, paras 1, 2, in relation to companies' financial years beginning on or after 1 January 2005.

Para 6: sub-para (1) numbered as such, words in square brackets therein substituted, and sub-paras (2), (3) added by the Financial Services and Markets Act 2000 (Consequential Amendments and Repeals) Order 2001, SI 2001/3649, art 36(1), (2).

Para 6A: inserted by SI 2004/2947, reg 14(5), Sch 6, paras 1, 3, in relation to companies' financial years beginning on or after 1 January 2005.

Para 9: sub-para (1) numbered as such, words in square brackets in sub-paras (1)(a), (b), and second (inner) pair of square brackets in note (24) substituted, and sub-para (2) added by SI 2001/3649, art 36(1), (3), (4); words in square brackets in item "E" under the heading "LIABILITIES" in the balance sheet format substituted by SI 2004/2947, reg 14(5), Sch 6, paras 1, 4, in relation to companies' financial years beginning on or after 1 January 2005; words in first (outer) and third pairs of square brackets in note (24) inserted by the Insurance Companies (Reserves) Act 1995, s 3(1), (2).

Para 11: sub-para (1)(a) substituted by SI 2001/3649, art 36(1), (5).

Para 12: item 2a under head III in the profit and loss account format inserted by SI 1996/189, regs 14(7), 16(5), Sch 5, paras 1, 3, in relation to any annual accounts of a company which are approved by the board of directors on or after 2 February 1996; words in square brackets in note (10) substituted by the Companies Act 1985 (Insurance Companies Accounts) (Minor Amendments) Regulations 1997, SI 1997/2704, reg 2.

Para 16: words omitted repealed by SI 2004/2947, reg 14(5), Sch 6, paras 1, 5, in relation to companies' financial years beginning on or after 1 January 2005.

Para 19A: inserted by SI 2004/2947, reg 14(5), Sch 6, paras 1, 6(1), in relation to companies' financial years beginning on or after 1 January 2005.

Para 20: repealed by SI 2004/2947, reg 14(5), Sch 6, paras 1, 6(2), in relation to companies' financial years beginning on or after 1 January 2005.

Para 21: repealed by SI 1996/189, regs 14(7), 16(5), Sch 5, paras 1, 4, in relation to any annual accounts of a company which are approved by the board of directors on or after 2 February 1996.

Para 29: words in square brackets in sub-paras (3), (4) substituted by SI 1996/189, regs 14(7), 16(1), Sch 5, paras 1, 5, in relation to any financial year ending on or after 2 February 1996, subject to a transitional provision in reg 16(2) of the 1996 Regulations.

Paras 29A–29F: inserted, together with preceding heading, by SI 2004/2947, reg 14(5), Sch 6, paras 1, 7(1), in relation to companies' financial years beginning on or after 1 January 2005.

Para 30: repealed by SI 2004/2947, reg 14(5), Sch 6, paras 1, 7(2), in relation to companies' financial years beginning on or after 1 January 2005.

Para 46: words in square brackets substituted by the Life Assurance Consolidation Directive (Consequential Amendments) Regulations 2004, SI 2004/3379, reg 2(1), (3).

Para 50: substituted by SI 2001/3649, art 36(1), (6).

Para 54: substituted by SI 1996/189, regs 14(7), 16(5), Sch 5, paras 1, 6, in relation to any annual accounts of a company which are approved by the board of directors on or after 2 February 1996; sub-paras (2), (3) repealed by SI 2005/2280, regs 1(3), (4), 11, in relation to companies' financial years which begin on or after 1 January 2005 and end on or after 1 October 2005.

Para 57A: inserted by SI 2004/2947, reg 14(5), Sch 6, paras 1, 8, in relation to companies' financial years beginning on or after 1 January 2005.

Para 59: sub-para (a) repealed, in relation to any financial year ending on or after 2 February 1996, by SI 1996/189, regs 14(7), 16(1), Sch 5, paras 1, 7, subject to a transitional provision in reg 16(2) thereof.

Para 61: sub-paras (1)(a), (2) repealed by SI 1996/189, regs 14(7), 16(1), Sch 5, paras 1, 8, in relation to any financial year ending on or after 2 February 1996, subject to a transitional provision in reg 16(2) thereof.

Para 65: sub-para (b) and the word "and" immediately preceding it repealed by SI 1996/189, regs 14(7), 16(1), Sch 5, paras 1, 9, in relation to any financial year ending on or after 2 February 1996, subject to a transitional provision in reg 16(2) of the 1996 Regulations.

Paras 65A–65D: inserted, together with related cross-headings, by SI 2004/2947, reg 14(5), Sch 6, paras 1, 9, in relation to companies' financial years beginning on or after 1 January 2005.

Para 66: words in square brackets in sub-para (1) substituted by SI 2004/2947, reg 14(5), Sch 6, paras 1, 10, in relation to companies' financial years beginning on or after 1 January 2005.

Para 68: sub-para (1) substituted by SI 1996/189, regs 14(7), 16(1), Sch 5, paras 1, 11, in relation to any financial year ending on or after 2 February 1996, subject to a transitional provision in reg 16(2) thereof; para (b) substituted by the Companies Act 1985 (Accounts of Small and Medium-sized Companies and Minor Accounting Amendments) Regulations 1997, SI 1997/220, reg 7(9), in relation to annual accounts approved by the board of directors on or after 1 March 1997, and to directors' and auditors' reports on such accounts, subject to a transitional provision in reg 1(4) thereof.

Para 70: sub-para (3)(b) and the word "and" immediately preceding it repealed by SI 1996/189, regs 14(7), 16(1), Sch 5, paras 1, 12, in relation to any financial year ending on or after 2 February 1996, subject to a transitional provision in reg 16(2) thereof.

Para 71: repealed by SI 1996/189, regs 14(7), 16(1), Sch 5, paras 1, 13, in relation to any financial year ending on or after 2 February 1996, subject to a transitional provision in reg 16(2) thereof.

Para 72: sub-para (3) repealed by SI 1996/189, regs 14(7), 16(1), Sch 5, paras 1, 14, in relation to any financial year ending on or after 2 February 1996, subject to a transitional provision in reg 16(2) thereof.

Para 73: words omitted from sub-para (2) and sub-paras (3)–(5) repealed by SI 1996/189, regs 14(7), 16(1), Sch 5, paras 1, 15, in relation to any financial year ending on or after 2 February 1996, subject to a transitional provision in reg 16(2) thereof.

Para 74: sub-para (1) repealed by SI 1996/189, regs 14(7), 16(1), Sch 5, paras 1, 16, in relation to any financial year ending on or after 2 February 1996, subject to a transitional provision in reg 16(2) thereof.

Para 79: repealed by SI 2004/2947, reg 3, Sch 1, paras 1, 35(a), in relation to companies' financial years beginning on or after 1 January 2005.

Para 81: definition "the 1982 Act" (omitted) repealed, definitions "general business", "long term business", "policy holder" and words in square brackets in definition "long term fund" substituted by SI 2001/3649, art 36(1), (7); definition "investment property" inserted by SI 2004/2947, reg 14(5), Sch 6, paras 1, 11, in relation to companies' financial years beginning on or after 1 January 2005.

Paras 81A, 81B: inserted by SI 2004/2947, reg 14(5), Sch 6, paras 1, 12, in relation to companies' financial years beginning on or after 1 January 2005.

Para 84: words in square brackets in para (c) substituted by SI 2004/2947, reg 14(5), Sch 6, paras 1, 13, in relation to companies' financial years beginning on or after 1 January 2005; words omitted from para (c) repealed by SI 1996/189, regs 14(7), 16(5), Sch 5, paras 1, 18, in relation to any annual accounts of a company which are approved by the board of directors on or after 2 February 1996.

Para 86: sub-para (b) and words in first pair of square brackets in sub-para (c) substituted by SI 1996/189, regs 14(7), 16(1), Sch 5, paras 1, 19, in relation to any financial year ending on or after 2 February 1996, subject to a transitional provision in reg 16(2) of the 1996 Regulations; words in second pair of square brackets in sub-para (c) substituted by SI 2004/2967, reg 3, Sch 1, paras 1, 35(b), in relation to companies' financial years beginning on or after 1 January 2005.

Modification: this Schedule is modified in relation to Lloyd's syndicates by the Insurance Accounts Directive (Lloyd's Syndicate and Aggregate Accounts) Regulations 2004, SI 2004/3219, reg 3(7), Schedule, paras 1–3, 13.

Council Directive 87/343/EEC: OJ L185, 4.7.1987, p 72.

Directive 2002/83/EC of the European Parliament and of the Council: OJ L345, 19.12.2002, p 1.

Council Regulation (EEC) No 3180/78: OJ L379, 30.12.1978, p 1.

Council Directive 78/660/EEC: OJ L222, 14.8.1978, p 11.

Council Directive 91/674/EEC: OJ L374, 31.12.1991, p 7.

PART II
CONSOLIDATED ACCOUNTS

Schedule 4A to apply Part I of this Schedule with modifications

[3389]

1.—(1) In its application to insurance groups, Schedule 4A shall have effect with the following modifications.

(2) In paragraph 1—

(a) *for the reference in sub-paragraph (1) to the provisions of Schedule 4 there shall be substituted a reference to the provisions of Part I of this Schedule modified as mentioned in paragraph 2 below;*

(b) . . .

(c) *sub-paragraph (3) shall be omitted.*

(3) In paragraph 2(2)(a), for the words "three months" there shall be substituted the words "six months".

(4) In paragraph 3, after sub-paragraph (1) there shall be inserted the following sub-paragraphs—

"(1A) Sub-paragraph (1) shall not apply to those liabilities items the valuation of which by the undertakings included in a consolidation is based on the application of provisions applying only to insurance undertakings, nor to those assets items changes in the values of which also affect or establish policy holders' rights.

(1B) Where sub-paragraph (1A) applies, that fact shall be disclosed in the notes on the consolidated accounts."

(5) For sub-paragraph (4) of paragraph 6 there shall be substituted the following sub-paragraphs—

"(4) Sub-paragraphs (1) and (2) need not be complied with—

(a) where a transaction has been concluded according to normal market conditions and a policy holder has rights in respect of that transaction, or

(b) if the amounts concerned are not material for the purpose of giving a true and fair view.

(5) Where advantage is taken of sub-paragraph (4)(a) above that fact shall be disclosed in the notes to the accounts, and where the transaction in question has a material effect on the assets, liabilities, financial position and profit or loss of all the undertakings included in the consolidation that fact shall also be so disclosed."

(6) In paragraph 17—

(a) *in sub-paragraph (1), for the reference to Schedule 4 there shall be substituted a reference to Part I of this Schedule;*

(b) *in sub-paragraph (2), paragraph (a) and, in paragraph (b), the words "in Format 2" shall be omitted;*

(c) *in sub-paragraph (3), for paragraphs (a) to (d) there shall be substituted the words "between items 10 and 11 in section III";*

(d) *in sub-paragraph (4), for paragraphs (a) to (d) there shall be substituted the words "between items 14 and 15 in section III"; and*

(e) *for sub-paragraph (5) there shall be substituted the following sub-paragraph—*

"(5) Paragraph 2(3) of Part I of Schedule 9A (power to combine items) shall not apply in relation to the additional items required by the foregoing provisions of this paragraph."

(7) In paragraph 18, for the reference to paragraphs 17 to 19 and 21 of Schedule 4 there shall be substituted a reference to paragraphs 31 to 33 and 36 of Part I of this Schedule.

(8) In paragraph 21—

(a) *in sub-paragraph (1), for the reference to Schedule 4 there shall be substituted a reference to Part I of this Schedule; and*

(b) *for sub-paragraphs (2) and (3) there shall be substituted the following sub-paragraphs—*

"(2) In the Balance Sheet Format, Asset item C.II.3 (participating interests) shall be replaced by two items, "Interests in associated undertakings" and "Other participating interests".

(3) In the Profit and Loss Account Format, items II.2(a) and III.3(a) (income from participating interests, with a separate indication of that derived from group undertakings) shall each be replaced by the following items—

(a) "Income from participating interests other than associated undertakings, with a separate indication of that derived from group undertakings", which shall be shown as items II.2(a) and III.3(a), and

(b) "Income from associated undertakings", which shall be shown as items II.2(aa) and III.3(aa)."

(9) In paragraph 22(1), for the reference to paragraphs 17 to 19 and 21 of Schedule 4 there shall be substituted a reference to paragraphs 31 to 33 and 36 of Part I of this Schedule.

Modifications of Part I of this Schedule for purposes of paragraph 1

2.—(1) For the purposes of paragraph 1 above, Part I of this Schedule shall be modified as follows.

(2) The information required by paragraph 10 need not be given.

(3) In the case of general business, investment income, expenses and charges may be disclosed in the non-technical account rather than in the technical account.

(4) In the case of subsidiary undertakings which are not authorised to carry on long term business in Great Britain, notes (8) and (9) to the profit and loss account format shall have effect as if references to investment income, expenses and charges arising in the long term fund or to investments attributed to the long term fund were references to investment income, expenses and charges or (as the case may be) investments relating to long term business.

(5) In the case of subsidiary undertakings which do not have a head office in Great Britain, the computation required by paragraph 46 shall be made annually by an actuary or other specialist in the field on the basis of recognised actuarial methods.

(6) The information required by paragraphs 75 to 78 need not be shown.]

NOTES

Substituted and repealed as noted to Pt I at **[3388]**.

Para 1: sub-para (2)(b) repealed by the Companies Act 1985 (Accounts of Small and Medium-sized Companies and Minor Accounting Amendments) Regulations 1997, SI 1997/220, reg 7(12), in relation to annual accounts approved by the board of directors on or after 1 March 1997, and to directors' and auditors' reports on such accounts, subject to a transitional provision in reg 1(4) thereof.

(Schs 10, 10A repealed by the Companies Act 2006, s 1295, Sch 16.)

SCHEDULE 11

[MODIFICATIONS OF PART VIII WHERE COMPANY'S ACCOUNTS PREPARED IN ACCORDANCE WITH SPECIAL PROVISIONS FOR BANKING OR INSURANCE COMPANIES]

Section 279

[3390]

[1. Paragraphs 2 to 6 below apply where a company has prepared accounts in accordance with the special provisions of Part VII relating to banking companies and paragraphs 7 to 13 below apply where a company has prepared accounts in accordance with the special provisions of Part VII relating to insurance companies.]

2–6. . . .

[Modifications where accounts prepared in accordance with special provisions for insurance companies

[7. Section 264(2) shall apply as if for the words in parentheses there were substituted "("liabilities" to include any provision for other risks and charges within paragraph 84(c) of Part I of Schedule 9A and any amount included under Liabilities items Ba (fund for future appropriations), C (technical provisions) and D (technical provisions for linked liabilities) in a balance sheet drawn up in accordance with the balance sheet format set out in section B of Part I of Schedule 9A)".]

8. Section 269 shall apply as if the reference to paragraph 20 of Schedule 4 in subsection (2)(b) were a reference to paragraph 35 of Part I of Schedule 9A.

[9. Sections 270(2) and 275 shall apply as if the reference to provisions of any of the kinds mentioned in paragraphs 88 and 89 of Schedule 4 were a reference to provisions of any of the kinds mentioned in paragraph 84 of Part I of Schedule 9A and to any amount included under Liabilities items Ba (fund for future appropriations), C (technical provisions) and D (technical provisions for linked liabilities) in a balance sheet drawn up in accordance with the balance sheet format set out in section B of Part I of Schedule 9A.]

10. Sections 272 and 273 shall apply as if the references in section 272(3) to [sections 226, 226A and 226B] and Schedule 4 were references to section 255 and Part I of Schedule 9A.

11. Section 276 shall apply as if the references to paragraphs 12(a) and 34(3)(a) of Schedule 4(d) were references to paragraphs 16(a) and 29(3)(a) of Part I of Schedule 9A.]

NOTES

Repealed by the Companies Act 2006, s 1295, Sch 16, as from 6 April 2008, subject to transitional provisions and savings.

Schedule heading: substituted by the Companies Act 1989, s 23, Sch 10, Pt I, para 21(2).

Para 1: inserted by the Companies Act 1985 (Bank Accounts) Regulations 1991, SI 1991/2705, reg 7, Sch 3, para 1(1), (2).

Paras 2–6: outside the scope of this work.

Paras 7–11: paras 1–7 of this Schedule as originally enacted renumbered as paras 7–13 and cross-heading preceding para 7 inserted by the Companies Act 1985 (Bank Accounts) Regulations 1991, SI 1991/2705, reg 7, Sch 3, para 1(1), (3); paras 7–13 as renumbered and the cross-heading preceding them substituted by paras 7–11 by the Companies Act 1985 (Insurance Companies Accounts) Regulations 1993, SI 1993/3246, reg 5(1), Sch 2, para 8, subject to a transitional provision contained in reg 7 of the 1993 Regulations; paras 7, 9 substituted by the Companies Act 1985 (Miscellaneous Accounting Amendments) Regulations 1996, SI 1996/189, regs 14(8), 16(6), Sch 6, in relation to any distribution made on or after 2 February 1996; words in square brackets in para 9 inserted and words in square brackets in para 10 substituted by the Companies Act 1985 (International Accounting Standards and Other Accounting Amendments) Regulations 2004, SI 2004/2947, reg 3, Sch 1, paras 1, 36(1), (3), (4), in relation to companies' financial years beginning on or after 1 January 2005.

(Schs 12–25 in so far as unrepealed, outside the scope of this work.)

OUTER SPACE ACT 1986

(1986 c 38)

ARRANGEMENT OF SECTIONS

Application of Act

1 Activities to which this Act applies . . . . . [3391]
2 Persons to whom this Act applies . . . . . [3392]

Licensing of activities

3 Prohibition of unlicensed activities . . . . . [3393]
4 Grant of licence . . . . . [3394]
5 Terms of licence . . . . . [3395]

General

15 Short title, commencement and extent . . . . . [3396]

An Act to confer licensing and other powers on the Secretary of State to secure compliance with the international obligations of the United Kingdom with respect to the launching and operation of space objects and the carrying on of other activities in outer space by persons connected with this country

[18 July 1986]

NOTES

Regulation of activities in outer space is a "reserved matter" for the purposes of the Scotland Act 1998, which by virtue of s 29(2)(b) of that Act, is outside the legislative competence of the Scottish Parliament; see s 30 of and Sch 5, Pt II, Head L, para L6 to that Act. For restrictions on the ability of the Scottish Parliament to modify the law on reserved matters, see s 29 of and Sch 4, Pt I, paras 2, 3 to that Act.

Application of Act

[3391]

1 Activities to which this Act applies

This Act applies to the following activities whether carried on in the United Kingdom or elsewhere—

(a) launching or procuring the launch of a space object;
(b) operating a space object;
(c) any activity in outer space.

[3392]

2 Persons to whom this Act applies

(1) This Act applies to United Kingdom nationals, Scottish firms, and bodies incorporated under the law of any part of the United Kingdom.

(2) For this purpose "United Kingdom national" means an individual who is—

(a) a British citizen, a [British overseas territories citizen], a British National (Overseas), or a British Overseas citizen,
(b) a person who under the British Nationality Act 1981 is a British subject, or
(c) a British protected person within the meaning of that Act.

(3) Her Majesty may by Order in Council extend the application of this Act to bodies incorporated under the law of any of the Channel Islands, the Isle of Man or any [British overseas territory].

NOTES

Sub-ss (2), (3): words in square brackets substituted by virtue of the British Overseas Territories Act 2002, ss 1(2), 2(3).

Orders: the Outer Space Act 1986 (Guernsey) Order 1990, SI 1990/248; the Outer Space Act 1986 (Isle of Man) Order 1990, SI 1990/596; the Outer Space Act 1986 (Jersey) Order 1990, SI 1990/597.

Licensing of activities

[3393]

3 Prohibition of unlicensed activities

(1) A person to whom this Act applies shall not, subject to the following provisions, carry on an activity to which this Act applies except under the authority of a licence granted by the Secretary of State.

(2) A licence is not required—

(a) by a person acting as employee or agent of another; or

(b) for activities in respect of which it is certified by Order in Council that arrangements have been made between the United Kingdom and another country to secure compliance with the international obligations of the United Kingdom.

(3) The Secretary of State may by order except other persons or activities from the requirement of a licence if he is satisfied that the requirement is not necessary to secure compliance with the international obligations of the United Kingdom.

(4) An order shall be made by statutory instrument which shall be subject to annulment in pursuance of a resolution of either House of Parliament.

[3394]

4 Grant of licence

(1) The Secretary of State may grant a licence if he thinks fit.

(2) He shall not grant a licence unless he is satisfied that the activities authorised by the licence—

(a) will not jeopardise public health or the safety of persons or property,

(b) will be consistent with the international obligations of the United Kingdom, and

(c) will not impair the national security of the United Kingdom.

(3) The Secretary of State may make regulations—

(a) prescribing the form and contents of applications for licences and other documents to be filed in connection with applications;

(b) regulating the procedure to be followed in connection with applications and authorising the rectification of procedural irregularities;

(c) prescribing time limits for doing anything required to be done in connection with an application and providing for the extension of any period so prescribed;

(d) requiring the payment to the Secretary of State of such fees as may be prescribed.

NOTES

Regulations: the Outer Space Act 1986 (Fees) Regulations 1989, SI 1989/1306.

[3395]

5 Terms of licence

(1) A licence shall describe the activities authorised by it and shall be granted for such period, and may be granted subject to such conditions, as the Secretary of State thinks fit.

(2) A licence may in particular contain conditions—

(a) permitting inspection by the Secretary of State of the licensee's facilities, and inspection and testing by him of the licensee's equipment;

(b) requiring the licensee to provide the Secretary of State as soon as possible with information as to—

(i) the date and territory or location of launch, and

(ii) the basic orbital parameters, including nodal period, inclination, apogee and perigee,

and with such other information as the Secretary of State thinks fit concerning the nature, conduct, location and results of the licensee's activities;

(c) permitting the Secretary of State to inspect and take copies of documents relating to the information required to be given to him;

(d) requiring the licensee to obtain advance approval from the Secretary of State for any intended deviation from the orbital parameters, and to inform the Secretary of State immediately of any unintended deviation;

(e) requiring the licensee to conduct his operations in such a way as to—
 (i) prevent the contamination of outer space or adverse changes in the environment of the earth,
 (ii) avoid interference with the activities of others in the peaceful exploration and use of outer space,
 (iii) avoid any breach of the United Kingdom's international obligations, and
 (iv) preserve the national security of the United Kingdom;

(f) requiring the licensee to insure himself against liability incurred in respect of damage or loss suffered by third parties, in the United Kingdom or elsewhere, as a result of the activities authorised by the licence;

(g) governing the disposal of the payload in outer space on the termination of operations under the licence and requiring the licensee to notify the Secretary of State as soon as practicable of its final disposal; and

(h) providing for the termination of the licence on a specified event.

6–10 (*Outside the scope of this work.*)

General

11–14 (*Outside the scope of this work.*)

[3396]
15 Short title, commencement and extent

(1) This Act may be cited as the Outer Space Act 1986.

(2)–(4) . . .

(5) This Act extends to England and Wales, Scotland and Northern Ireland.

(6) Her Majesty may by Order in Council direct that this Act shall apply, subject to such exceptions and modifications as may be specified in the Order, to the Channel Islands, the Isle of Man or any [British overseas territory].

NOTES

Sub-ss (2)–(4): repealed by the Statute Law (Repeals) Act 2004.

Sub-s (6): words in square brackets substituted by virtue of the British Overseas Territories Act 2002, s 1(2).

Orders: the Outer Space Act 1986 (Commencement) Order 1989, SI 1989/1097; the Outer Space Act 1986 (Guernsey) Order 1990, SI 1990/248; the Outer Space Act 1986 (Isle of Man) Order 1990, SI 1990/596; the Outer Space Act 1986 (Jersey) Order 1990, SI 1990/597; the Outer Space Act 1986 (Gibraltar) Order 1996, SI 1996/1916; the Outer Space Act 1986 (Cayman Islands) Order 1998, SI 1998/2563; the Outer Space Act 1986 (Bermuda) Order 2006, SI 2006/2959.

ROAD TRAFFIC ACT 1988

(1988 c 52)

ARRANGEMENT OF SECTIONS

PART VI
THIRD-PARTY LIABILITIES

Compulsory insurance or security against third-party risks

143 Users of motor vehicles to be insured or secured against third-party risks . . . . [3397]
144 Exceptions from requirement of third party insurance or security . . . . [3398]
144A Offence of keeping vehicle which does not meet insurance requirements . . . . [3398A]
144B Exceptions to section 144A offence . . . . [3398B]
144C Fixed penalty notices . . . . [3398C]
144D Section 144A offence: supplementary . . . . [3398D]
145 Requirements in respect of policies of insurance . . . . [3399]
146 Requirements in respect of securities . . . . [3400]
147 Issue and surrender of certificates of insurance and of security . . . . [3401]
148 Avoidance of certain exceptions to policies or securities . . . . [3402]
149 Avoidance of certain agreements as to liability towards passengers . . . . [3403]
150 Insurance or security in respect of private use of vehicle to cover use under car-sharing arrangements . . . . [3404]
151 Duty of insurers or persons giving security to satisfy judgment against persons insured or secured against third-party risks . . . . [3405]
152 Exceptions to section 151 . . . . [3406]
153 Bankruptcy, etc, of insured or secured persons not to affect claims by third parties . . . . [3407]

154 Duty to give information as to insurance or security where claim made . . . . [3408]

Payments for treatment of traffic casualties

157 Payment for hospital treatment of traffic casualties . . . . [3409]
158 Payment for emergency treatment of traffic casualties . . . . [3410]
159 Supplementary provisions as to payments for treatment . . . . [3411]

General

159A Disclosure of information . . . . [3411A]
160 Regulations . . . . [3412]
161 Interpretation . . . . [3413]
162 Index to Part VI . . . . [3414]

PART VII
MISCELLANEOUS AND GENERAL

Supplementary

197 Short title, commencement and extent . . . . [3415]

SCHEDULES:

Schedule 2A—Offence of Keeping Vehicle which does Not Meet Insurance Requirements: Immobilisation, Removal and Disposal of Vehicles . . . . [3415A]

An Act to consolidate certain enactments relating to road traffic with amendments to give effect to recommendations of the Law Commission and the Scottish Law Commission

[15 November 1988]

NOTES

The subject matter of this Act is a "reserved matter" for the purposes of the Scotland Act 1998, which by virtue of s 29(2)(b) of that Act, is outside the legislative competence of the Scottish Parliament. The reservation does not include ss 39, 40 of this Act (outside the scope of this work); see the Scotland Act 1998, ss 30, 44(2), 56(1)(i), Sch 5, Pt II, Head E, para E1, Pt III, para 5. For restrictions on the ability of the Scottish Parliament to modify the law on reserved matters, see s 29 of and Sch 4, Pt I, paras 2, 3 to that Act.

1–142 *((Pts I–V) outside the scope of this work.)*

PART VI
THIRD-PARTY LIABILITIES

Compulsory insurance or security against third-party risks

[3397]

143 Users of motor vehicles to be insured or secured against third-party risks

(1) Subject to the provisions of this Part of this Act—

(a) a person must not use a motor vehicle on a road [or other public place] unless there is in force in relation to the use of the vehicle by that person such a policy of insurance or such a security in respect of third party risks as complies with the requirements of this Part of this Act, and

(b) a person must not cause or permit any other person to use a motor vehicle on a road [or other public place] unless there is in force in relation to the use of the vehicle by that other person such a policy of insurance or such a security in respect of third party risks as complies with the requirements of this Part of this Act.

(2) If a person acts in contravention of subsection (1) above he is guilty of an offence.

(3) A person charged with using a motor vehicle in contravention of this section shall not be convicted if he proves—

(a) that the vehicle did not belong to him and was not in his possession under a contract of hiring or of loan,

(b) that he was using the vehicle in the course of his employment, and

(c) that he neither knew nor had reason to believe that there was not in force in relation to the vehicle such a policy of insurance or security as is mentioned in subsection (1) above.

(4) This Part of this Act does not apply to invalid carriages.

NOTES

Sub-s (1): words in square brackets substituted by the Motor Vehicles (Compulsory Insurance) Regulations 2000, SI 2000/726, reg 2(1), (2).

[3398]

144 Exceptions from requirement of third party insurance or security

(1) Section 143 of this Act does not apply to a vehicle owned by a person who has deposited and keeps deposited with the Accountant General of the [Senior Courts] the sum of [£500,000], at a time when the vehicle is being driven under the owner's control.

[(1A) The Secretary of State may by order made by statutory instrument substitute a greater sum for the sum for the time being specified in subsection (1) above.

(1B) No order shall be made under subsection (1A) above unless a draft of it has been laid before and approved by resolution of each House of Parliament.]

(2) Section 143 does not apply—

(a) to a vehicle owned—

(i) by the council of a county or county district in England and Wales [the Broads Authority], the Common Council of the City of London, the council of a London borough, [a National Park Authority] the Inner London Education Authority, [the London Fire and Emergency Planning Authority,] [an authority established for an area in England by an order under section 207 of the Local Government and Public Involvement in Health Act 2007 (joint waste authorities)][, a joint authority (other than a police authority) established by Part 4 of the Local Government Act 1985, an economic prosperity board established under section 88 of the Local Democracy, Economic Development and Construction Act 2009 or a combined authority established under section 103 of that Act,]

(ii) by a [council constituted under section 2 of the Local Government etc (Scotland) Act 1994] in Scotland, or

(iii) by a joint board or committee in England or Wales, or joint committee in Scotland, which is so constituted as to include among its members representatives of any such council,

at a time when the vehicle is being driven under the owner's control,

(b) to a vehicle owned by a police authority . . . , at a time when it is being driven under the owner's control, or to a vehicle at a time when it is being driven for police purposes by or under the direction of a constable, or by a person employed by a police authority, . . . or

[(ba) . . .]

(c) to a vehicle at a time when it is being driven on a journey to or from any place undertaken for salvage purposes pursuant to Part IX of the [Merchant Shipping Act 1995],

(d) . . .

[(da) to a vehicle owned by a health service body, as defined in section 60(7) of the National Health Service and Community Care Act 1990 [by a Primary Care Trust established under [section 18 of the National Health Service Act 2006]] [or by a Local Health Board established under section 11 of the National Health Service (Wales) Act 2006], at a time when the vehicle is being driven under the owner's control,

(db) to an ambulance owned by a National Health Service trust established under [section 25 of the National Health Service Act 2006, section 18 of the National Health Service (Wales) Act 2006] or the National Health Service (Scotland) Act 1978, at a time when a vehicle is being driven under the owner's control,]

[(dc) to an ambulance owned by an NHS foundation trust, at a time when the vehicle is being driven under the owner's control,]

(e) to a vehicle which is made available by the Secretary of State [or the Welsh Ministers] to any person, body or local authority in pursuance of [section 12 or 80 of the National Health Service Act 2006, or section 10 or 38 of the National Health Service (Wales) Act 2006,] at a time when it is being used in accordance with the terms on which it is so made available,

(f) to a vehicle which is made available by the Secretary of State to any local authority, education authority or voluntary organisation in Scotland in pursuance of section 15 or 16 of the National Health Service (Scotland) Act 1978 at a time when it is being used in accordance with the terms on which it is so made available,

[(g) to a vehicle owned by [the Care Quality Commission], at a time when the vehicle is being driven under the owner's control].

NOTES

Sub-s (1): words in first pair of square brackets substituted by the Constitutional Reform Act 2005, s 59(5), Sch 11, Pt 2, para 4; sum in second pair of square brackets substituted by the Road Traffic Act 1991, s 20(1), (2).

Sub-ss (1A), (1B): inserted by the Road Traffic Act 1991, s 20(1), (3).

Sub-s (2): in para (a)(i) words in first pair of square brackets inserted by the Norfolk and Suffolk Broads Act 1988, ss 21, 23(2), Sch 6, para 9, words in second pair of square brackets inserted by the Environment Act 1995, s 78, Sch 10, para 29, words in third pair of square brackets inserted by the Greater London Authority Act 1999, s 328(8), Sch 29, Pt I, para 54; words in fourth pair of square brackets inserted by the Local Government and Public Involvement in Health Act 2007, s 209(2), Sch 13, Pt 2, para 45; words in fifth pair of square brackets substituted by the Local Democracy, Economic Development and Construction Act 2009, s 119, Sch 6, para 80; words in square brackets in para (a)(ii) substituted by the Local Government etc (Scotland) Act 1994, s 180(1), Sch 13, para 159(1), (8); words omitted from para (b) repealed by the Greater London Authority Act 1999, ss 325, 423, Sch 27, para 61, Sch 34, Pt VII; para (ba) inserted by the Police Act 1997, s 131(4), Sch 9, para 59 and repealed by the Serious Organised Crime and Police Act 2005, ss 59, 174(2), Sch 4, paras 52, 54, Sch 17, Pt 2; words in square brackets in para (c) substituted by the Merchant Shipping Act 1995, s 314(2), Sch 13, para 85; para (d) repealed by the Armed Forces Act 2006, s 378(2), Sch 17; para (da) inserted by the National Health Service and Community Care Act 1990, s 60, Sch 8, Pt I, para 4, words in first (outer) pair of square brackets inserted by the Health Act 1999 (Supplementary, Consequential etc Provisions) Order 2000, SI 2000/90, art 3(1), Sch 1, para 23, words in second (inner)pair of square brackets substituted by the National Health Service (Consequential Provisions) Act 2006, s 2, Sch 1, paras 121, 122(a)(i), words in third pair of square brackets substituted by the Health and Social Care Act 2008, s 95, Sch 5, Pt 3, para 61(a); para (db) inserted by the National Health Service and Community Care Act 1990, s 60, Sch 8, Pt I, para 4, words in square brackets substituted by the National Health Service (Consequential Provisions) Act 2006, s 2, Sch 1, paras 121, 122(b); para (dc) inserted by the Health and Social Care (Community Health and Standards) Act 2003, s 34, Sch 4, paras 73, 74; in para (e), words in first pair of square brackets inserted and words in second pair of square brackets substituted by the National Health Service (Consequential Provisions) Act 2006, s 2, Sch 1, paras 121, 122(c); para (g) added by SI 2004/2987, art 2(1)(f)(ii) and words in square brackets therein substituted by the Health and Social Care Act 2008, s 95, Sch 5, Pt 3, para 61(b).

[3398A]
[144A Offence of keeping vehicle which does not meet insurance requirements

(1) If a motor vehicle registered under the Vehicle Excise and Registration Act 1994 does not meet the insurance requirements, the person in whose name the vehicle is registered is guilty of an offence.

(2) For the purposes of this section a vehicle meets the insurance requirements if—

(a) it is covered by a such a policy of insurance or such a security in respect of third party risks as complies with the requirements of this Part of this Act, and

(b) either of the following conditions is satisfied.

(3) The first condition is that the policy or security, or the certificate of insurance or security which relates to it, identifies the vehicle by its registration mark as a vehicle which is covered by the policy or security.

(4) The second condition is that the vehicle is covered by the policy or security because—

(a) the policy or security covers any vehicle, or any vehicle of a particular description, the owner of which is a person named in the policy or security or in the certificate of insurance or security which relates to it, and

(b) the vehicle is owned by that person.

(5) For the purposes of this section a vehicle is covered by a policy of insurance or security if the policy of insurance or security is in force in relation to the use of the vehicle.]

NOTES

Commencement: to be appointed.

Inserted, together with ss 144B–144D, by the Road Safety Act 2006, s 22(1), as from a day to be appointed.

[3398B]
[144B Exceptions to section 144A offence

(1) A person ("the registered keeper") in whose name a vehicle which does not meet the insurance requirements is registered at any particular time ("the relevant time") does not commit an offence under section 144A of this Act at that time if any of the following conditions are satisfied.

(2) The first condition is that at the relevant time the vehicle is owned as described—

(a) in subsection (1) of section 144 of this Act, or

(b) in paragraph (a), (b), (da), (db), (dc) or (g) of subsection (2) of that section,

(whether or not at the relevant time it is being driven as described in that provision).

(3) The second condition is that at the relevant time the vehicle is owned with the intention that it should be used as described in paragraph (c), (d), (e) or (f) of section 144(2) of this Act.

(4) The third condition is that the registered keeper—

(a) is not at the relevant time the person keeping the vehicle, and

(b) if previously he was the person keeping the vehicle, he has by the relevant time complied with any requirements under subsection (7)(a) below that he is required to have complied with by the relevant or any earlier time.

(5) The fourth condition is that—

(a) the registered keeper is at the relevant time the person keeping the vehicle,

Part III Statutes

(b) at the relevant time the vehicle is not used on a road or other public place, and
(c) the registered keeper has by the relevant time complied with any requirements under subsection (7)(a) below that he is required to have complied with by the relevant or any earlier time.

(6) The fifth condition is that—
(a) the vehicle has been stolen before the relevant time,
(b) the vehicle has not been recovered by the relevant time, and
(c) any requirements under subsection (7)(b) below that, in connection with the theft, are required to have been complied with by the relevant or any earlier time have been complied with by the relevant time.

(7) Regulations may make provision—
(a) for the purposes of subsection (4)(b) and (5)(c) above, requiring a person in whose name a vehicle is registered to furnish such particulars and make such declarations as may be prescribed, and to do so at such times and in such manner as may be prescribed, and
(b) for the purposes of subsection (6)(c) above, as to the persons to whom, the times at which and the manner in which the theft of a vehicle is to be notified.

(8) Regulations may make provision amending this section for the purpose of providing for further exceptions to section 144A of this Act (or varying or revoking any such further exceptions).

(9) A person accused of an offence under section 144A of this Act is not entitled to the benefit of an exception conferred by or under this section unless evidence is adduced that is sufficient to raise an issue with respect to that exception; but where evidence is so adduced it is for the prosecution to prove beyond reasonable doubt that the exception does not apply.]

NOTES

Commencement: to be appointed.

Inserted as noted to s 144A at **[3398A]**.

[3398C]

[144C Fixed penalty notices

(1) Where on any occasion the Secretary of State has reason to believe that a person has committed an offence under section 144A of this Act, the Secretary of State may give the person a notice offering him the opportunity of discharging any liability to conviction for that offence by payment of a fixed penalty to the Secretary of State.

(2) Where a person is given a notice under this section in respect of an offence under section 144A of this Act—
(a) no proceedings may be instituted for that offence before the end of the period of 21 days following the date of the notice, and
(b) he may not be convicted of that offence if he pays the fixed penalty before the end of that period.

(3) A notice under this section must give such particulars of the circumstances alleged to constitute the offence as are necessary for giving reasonable information of the offence.

(4) A notice under this section must also state—
(a) the period during which, by virtue of subsection (2) above, proceedings will not be taken for the offence,
(b) the amount of the fixed penalty, and
(c) the person to whom and the address at which the fixed penalty may be paid.

(5) Without prejudice to payment by any other method, payment of the fixed penalty may be made by pre-paying and posting a letter containing the amount of the penalty (in cash or otherwise) to the person mentioned in subsection (4)(c) above at the address so mentioned.

(6) Where a letter is sent in accordance with subsection (5) above payment is to be regarded as having been made at the time at which that letter would be delivered in the ordinary course of post.

(7) Regulations may make provision as to any matter incidental to the operation of this section, and in particular—
(a) as to the form of a notice under this section,
(b) as to the information to be provided in such a notice by virtue of this section, and
(c) as to any further information to be provided in a such notice.

(8) The fixed penalty payable under this section is, subject to subsection (9) below, £100.

(9) Regulations may substitute a different amount for the amount for the time being specified in subsection (8) above.

(10) Regulations may make provision for treating a fixed penalty payable under this section as having been paid if a lesser amount is paid before the end of a prescribed period.

(11) In any proceedings a certificate which—
(a) purports to be signed by or on behalf of the Secretary of State, and

(b) states that payment of a fixed penalty was or was not received by a date specified in the certificate,

is evidence of the facts stated.]

NOTES

Commencement: to be appointed.
Inserted as noted to s 144A at **[3398A]**.

[3398D]

[144D Section 144A offence: supplementary

(1) Schedule 2A makes provision about the immobilisation of vehicles as regards which it appears that an offence under section 144A of this Act is being committed and about their removal and disposal.

(2) A person authorised by the Secretary of State for the purposes of this subsection may on behalf of the Secretary of State conduct and appear in any proceedings by or against the Secretary of State in connection with the enforcement of an offence under section 144A of this Act or under regulations made under section 160 of this Act by virtue of Schedule 2A to this Act—

(a) in England and Wales, in a magistrates' court, and

(b) in Scotland, in any court other than the High Court of Justiciary or the Court of Session.]

NOTES

Commencement: to be appointed.
Inserted as noted to s 144A at **[3398A]**.

[3399]

145 Requirements in respect of policies of insurance

(1) In order to comply with the requirements of this Part of this Act, a policy of insurance must satisfy the following conditions.

(2) The policy must be issued by an authorised insurer.

(3) Subject to subsection (4) below, the policy—

(a) must insure such person, persons or classes of persons as may be specified in the policy in respect of any liability which may be incurred by him or them in respect of the death of or bodily injury to any person or damage to property caused by, or arising out of, the use of the vehicle on a road [or other public place] in Great Britain, and

[(aa) must, in the case of a vehicle normally based in the territory of another member State, insure him or them in respect of any civil liability which may be incurred by him or them as a result of an event related to the use of the vehicle in Great Britain if,—

(i) according to the law of that territory, he or they would be required to be insured in respect of a civil liability which would arise under that law as a result of that event if the place where the vehicle was used when the event occurred were in that territory, and

(ii) the cover required by that law would be higher than that required by paragraph (a) above, and]

(b) must[, in the case of a vehicle normally based in Great Britain,] insure him or them in respect of any liability which may be incurred by him or them in respect of the use of the vehicle and of any trailer, whether or not coupled, in the territory other than Great Britain and Gibraltar of each of the member States of the Communities according to

[(i) the law on compulsory insurance against civil liability in respect of the use of vehicles of the State in whose territory the event giving rise to the liability occurred; or

(ii) if it would give higher cover, the law which would be applicable under this Part of this Act if the place where the vehicle was used when that event occurred were in Great Britain; and]

(c) must also insure him or them in respect of any liability which may be incurred by him or them under the provisions of this Part of this Act relating to payment for emergency treatment.

(4) The policy shall not, by virtue of subsection (3)(a) above, be required—

(a) to cover liability in respect of the death, arising out of and in the course of his employment, of a person in the employment of a person insured by the policy or of bodily injury sustained by such a person arising out of and in the course of his employment, or

Part III Statutes

(b) to provide insurance of more than [£1,000,000] in respect of all such liabilities as may be insured in respect of damage to property caused by, or arising out of, any one accident involving the vehicle, or
(c) to cover liability in respect of damage to the vehicle, or
(d) to cover liability in respect of damage to goods carried for hire or reward in or on the vehicle or in or on any trailer (whether or not coupled) drawn by the vehicle, or
(e) to cover any liability of a person in respect of damage to property in his custody or under his control, or
(f) to cover any contractual liability.

[(4A) In the case of a person—
(a) carried in or upon a vehicle, or
(b) entering or getting on to, or alighting from, a vehicle,

the provisions of paragraph (a) of subsection (4) above do not apply unless cover in respect of the liability referred to in that paragraph is in fact provided pursuant to a requirement of the Employers' Liability (Compulsory Insurance) Act 1969.]

[(5) "Authorised insurer" has the same meaning as in section 95.]

(6) If any person or body of persons ceases to be a member of the Motor Insurers' Bureau, that person or body shall not by virtue of that cease to be treated as an authorised insurer for the purposes of this Part of this Act [. . .]—
(a) in relation to any policy issued by the insurer before ceasing to be such a member, or
(b) in relation to any obligation (whether arising before or after the insurer ceased to be such a member) which the insurer may be called upon to meet under or in consequence of any such policy or under section 157 of this Act [. . .] by virtue of making a payment in pursuance of such an obligation.

NOTES

Sub-s (3): words in square brackets in para (a) substituted by the Motor Vehicles (Compulsory Insurance) Regulations 2000, SI 2000/726, reg 2(1), (3); para (aa) inserted, in para (b) words in first pair of square brackets inserted and words in second pair of square brackets substituted, by the Motor Vehicles (Compulsory Insurance) Regulations 1992, SI 1992/3036, reg 2(1), (2).

Sub-s (4): sum in square brackets in para (b) substituted by the Motor Vehicles (Compulsory Insurance) Regulations 2007, SI 2007/1426, reg 2(1), (2).

Sub-s (4A): inserted by the Motor Vehicles (Compulsory Insurance) Regulations 1992, SI 1992/3036, reg 2(3).

Sub-s (5): substituted by the Financial Services and Markets Act 2000 (Consequential Amendments and Repeals) Order 2001, SI 2001/3649, art 313.

Sub-s (6): words omitted inserted by the Road Traffic (NHS Charges) Act 1999, s 18(1) and repealed by the Health and Social Care (Community Health and Standards) Act 2003, s 196, Sch 14, Pt 3.

[3400]

146 Requirements in respect of securities

(1) In order to comply with the requirements of this Part of this Act, a security must satisfy the following conditions.

(2) The security must be given either by an authorised insurer or by some body of persons which carries on in the United Kingdom the business of giving securities of a like kind and has deposited and keeps deposited with the Accountant General of the [Senior Courts] the sum of £15,000 in respect of that business.

(3) Subject to subsection (4) below, the security must consist of an undertaking by the giver of the security to make good, subject to any conditions specified in it, any failure by the owner of the vehicle or such other persons or classes of persons as may be specified in the security duly to discharge any liability which may be incurred by him or them, being a liability required under section 145 of this Act to be covered by a policy of insurance.

(4) In the case of liabilities arising out of the use of a motor vehicle on a road [or other public place] in Great Britain the amount secured need not exceed—
(a) in the case of an undertaking relating to the use of public service vehicles (within the meaning of the Public Passenger Vehicles Act 1981), £25,000,
(b) in any other case, £5,000.

NOTES

Sub-s (2): words in square brackets substituted by the Constitutional Reform Act 2005, s 59(5), Sch 11, Pt 2, para 4.

Sub-s (4): words in square brackets substituted by the Motor Vehicles (Compulsory Insurance) Regulations 2000, SI 2000/726, reg 2(1), (4).

[3401]

147 Issue and surrender of certificates of insurance and of security

(1) A policy of insurance shall be of no effect for the purposes of this Part of this Act unless and until there is delivered by the insurer to the person by whom the policy is effected a certificate (in this Part of this Act referred to as a "certificate of insurance") in the prescribed form and containing such particulars of any conditions subject to which the policy is issued and of any other matters as may be prescribed.

(2) A security shall be of no effect for the purposes of this Part of this Act unless and until there is delivered by the person giving the security to the person to whom it is given a certificate (in this Part of this Act referred to as a "certificate of security") in the prescribed form and containing such particulars of any conditions subject to which the security is issued and of any other matters as may be prescribed.

(3) Different forms and different particulars may be prescribed for the purposes of subsection (1) or (2) above in relation to different cases or circumstances.

(4) Where a certificate has been delivered under this section and the policy or security to which it relates is cancelled by mutual consent or by virtue of any provision in the policy or security, the person to whom the certificate was delivered must, within seven days from the taking effect of the cancellation—

- (a) surrender the certificate to the person by whom the policy was issued or the security was given, or
- (b) if the certificate has been lost or destroyed, make a statutory declaration to that effect.

(5) A person who fails to comply with subsection (4) above is guilty of an offence.

NOTES

Regulations: no regulations have been made for the purposes of sub-ss (1), (2) above, but by virtue of the Road Traffic (Consequential Provisions) Act 1988, s 2(2), and the Interpretation Act 1978, s 17(2)(b), the Motor Vehicles (Third Party Risks) Regulations 1972, SI 1972/1217 at **[4020]** have effect as if made under this section.

[3402]

148 Avoidance of certain exceptions to policies or securities

(1) Where a certificate of insurance or certificate of security has been delivered under section 147 of this Act to the person by whom a policy has been effected or to whom a security has been given, so much of the policy or security as purports to restrict—

- (a) the insurance of the persons insured by the policy, or
- (b) the operation of the security,

(as the case may be) by reference to any of the matters mentioned in subsection (2) below shall, as respects such liabilities as are required to be covered by a policy under section 145 of this Act, be of no effect.

(2) Those matters are—

- (a) the age or physical or mental condition of persons driving the vehicle,
- (b) the condition of the vehicle,
- (c) the number of persons that the vehicle carries,
- (d) the weight or physical characteristics of the goods that the vehicle carries,
- (e) the time at which or the areas within which the vehicle is used,
- (f) the horsepower or cylinder capacity or value of the vehicle,
- (g) the carrying on the vehicle of any particular apparatus, or
- (h) the carrying on the vehicle of any particular means of identification other than any means of identification required to be carried by or under [the Vehicle Excise and Registration Act 1994].

(3) Nothing in subsection (1) above requires an insurer or the giver of a security to pay any sum in respect of the liability of any person otherwise than in or towards the discharge of that liability.

(4) Any sum paid by an insurer or the giver of a security in or towards the discharge of any liability of any person which is covered by the policy or security by virtue only of subsection (1) above is recoverable by the insurer or giver of the security from that person.

(5) A condition in a policy or security issued or given for the purposes of this Part of this Act providing—

- (a) that no liability shall arise under the policy or security, or
- (b) that any liability so arising shall cease,

in the event of some specified thing being done or omitted to be done after the happening of the event giving rise to a claim under the policy or security, shall be of no effect in connection with such liabilities as are required to be covered by a policy under section 145 of this Act.

(6) Nothing in subsection (5) above shall be taken to render void any provision in a policy or security requiring the person insured or secured to pay to the insurer or the giver of the security any sums which the latter may have become liable to pay under the policy or security and which have been applied to the satisfaction of the claims of third parties.
(7) Notwithstanding anything in any enactment, a person issuing a policy of insurance under section 145 of this Act shall be liable to indemnify the persons or classes of persons specified in the policy in respect of any liability which the policy purports to cover in the case of those persons or classes of persons.

NOTES

Sub-s (2): words in square brackets substituted by the Vehicle Excise and Registration Act 1994, s 63, Sch 3, para 24(1).

[3403]
149 Avoidance of certain agreements as to liability towards passengers
(1) This section applies where a person uses a motor vehicle in circumstances such that under section 143 of this Act there is required to be in force in relation to his use of it such a policy of insurance or such a security in respect of third-party risks as complies with the requirements of this Part of this Act.
(2) If any other person is carried in or upon the vehicle while the user is so using it, any antecedent agreement or understanding between them (whether intended to be legally binding or not) shall be of no effect so far as it purports or might be held—
- (a) to negative or restrict any such liability of the user in respect of persons carried in or upon the vehicle as is required by section 145 of this Act to be covered by a policy of insurance, or
- (b) to impose any conditions with respect to the enforcement of any such liability of the user.

(3) The fact that a person so carried has willingly accepted as his the risk of negligence on the part of the user shall not be treated as negativing any such liability of the user.
(4) For the purposes of this section—
- (a) references to a person being carried in or upon a vehicle include references to a person entering or getting on to, or alighting from, the vehicle, and
- (b) the reference to an antecedent agreement is to one made at any time before the liability arose.

[3404]
150 Insurance or security in respect of private use of vehicle to cover use under car-sharing arrangements
(1) To the extent that a policy or security issued or given for the purposes of this Part of this Act—
- (a) restricts the insurance of the persons insured by the policy or the operation of the security (as the case may be) to use of the vehicle for specified purposes (for example, social, domestic and pleasure purposes) of a non-commercial character, or
- (b) excludes from that insurance or the operation of the security (as the case may be)—
  - (i) use of the vehicle for hire or reward, or
  - (ii) business or commercial use of the vehicle, or
  - (iii) use of the vehicle for specified purposes of a business or commercial character,

then, for the purposes of that policy or security so far as it relates to such liabilities as are required to be covered by a policy under section 145 of this Act, the use of a vehicle on a journey in the course of which one or more passengers are carried at separate fares shall, if the conditions specified in subsection (2) below are satisfied, be treated as falling within that restriction or as not falling within that exclusion (as the case may be).
(2) The conditions referred to in subsection (1) above are—
- (a) the vehicle is not adapted to carry more than eight passengers and is not a motor cycle,
- (b) the fare or aggregate of the fares paid in respect of the journey does not exceed the amount of the running costs of the vehicle for the journey (which for the purposes of this paragraph shall be taken to include an appropriate amount in respect of depreciation and general wear), and
- (c) the arrangements for the payment of fares by the passenger or passengers carried at separate fares were made before the journey began.

(3) Subsections (1) and (2) above apply however the restrictions or exclusions described in subsection (1) are framed or worded.
(4) In subsections (1) and (2) above "fare" and "separate fares" have the same meaning as in section 1(4) of the Public Passenger Vehicles Act 1981.

[3405]

151 Duty of insurers or persons giving security to satisfy judgment against persons insured or secured against third-party risks

(1) This section applies where, after a certificate of insurance or certificate of security has been delivered under section 147 of this Act to the person by whom a policy has been effected or to whom a security has been given, a judgment to which this subsection applies is obtained.

(2) Subsection (1) above applies to judgments relating to a liability with respect to any matter where liability with respect to that matter is required to be covered by a policy of insurance under section 145 of this Act and either—

- (a) it is a liability covered by the terms of the policy or security to which the certificate relates, and the judgment is obtained against any person who is insured by the policy or whose liability is covered by the security, as the case may be, or
- (b) it is a liability, other than an excluded liability, which would be so covered if the policy insured all persons or, as the case may be, the security covered the liability of all persons, and the judgment is obtained against any person other than one who is insured by the policy or, as the case may be, whose liability is covered by the security.

(3) In deciding for the purposes of subsection (2) above whether a liability is or would be covered by the terms of a policy or security, so much of the policy or security as purports to restrict, as the case may be, the insurance of the persons insured by the policy or the operation of the security by reference to the holding by the driver of the vehicle of a licence authorising him to drive it shall be treated as of no effect.

(4) In subsection (2)(b) above "excluded liability" means a liability in respect of the death of, or bodily injury to, or damage to the property of any person who, at the time of the use which gave rise to the liability, was allowing himself to be carried in or upon the vehicle and knew or had reason to believe that the vehicle had been stolen or unlawfully taken, not being a person who—

- (a) did not know and had no reason to believe that the vehicle had been stolen or unlawfully taken until after the commencement of his journey, and
- (b) could not reasonably have been expected to have alighted from the vehicle.

In this subsection the reference to a person being carried in or upon a vehicle includes a reference to a person entering or getting on to, or alighting from, the vehicle.

(5) Notwithstanding that the insurer may be entitled to avoid or cancel, or may have avoided or cancelled, the policy or security, he must, subject to the provisions of this section, pay to the persons entitled to the benefit of the judgment—

- (a) as regards liability in respect of death or bodily injury, any sum payable under the judgment in respect of the liability, together with any sum which, by virtue of any enactment relating to interest on judgments, is payable in respect of interest on that sum,
- (b) as regards liability in respect of damage to property, any sum required to be paid under subsection (6) below, and
- (c) any amount payable in respect of costs.

(6) This subsection requires—

- (a) where the total of any amount paid, payable or likely to be payable under the policy or security in respect of damage to property caused by, or arising out of, the accident in question does not exceed [£1,000,000], the payment of any sum payable under the judgment in respect of the liability, together with any sum which, by virtue of any enactment relating to interest on judgments, is payable in respect of interest on that sum,
- (b) where that total exceeds [£1,000,000], the payment of either—
  - (i) such proportion of any sum payable under the judgment in respect of the liability as [£1,000,000] bears to that total, together with the same proportion of any sum which, by virtue of any enactment relating to interest on judgments, is payable in respect of interest on that sum, or
  - (ii) the difference between the total of any amounts already paid under the policy or security in respect of such damage and [£1,000,000], together with such proportion of any sum which, by virtue of any enactment relating to interest on judgments is payable in respect of interest on any sum payable under the judgment in respect of the liability as the difference bears to that sum,

whichever is the less, unless not less than [£1,000,000] has already been paid under the policy or security in respect of such damage (in which case nothing is payable).

(7) Where an insurer becomes liable under this section to pay an amount in respect of a liability of a person who is insured by a policy or whose liability is covered by a security, he is entitled to recover from that person—

- (a) that amount, in a case where he became liable to pay it by virtue only of subsection (3) above, or

(b) in a case where that amount exceeds the amount for which he would, apart from the provisions of this section, be liable under the policy or security in respect of that liability, the excess.

(8) Where an insurer becomes liable under this section to pay an amount in respect of a liability of a person who is not insured by a policy or whose liability is not covered by a security, he is entitled to recover the amount from that person or from any person who—

(a) is insured by the policy, or whose liability is covered by the security, by the terms of which the liability would be covered if the policy insured all persons or, as the case may be, the security covered the liability of all persons, and

(b) caused or permitted the use of the vehicle which gave rise to the liability.

(9) In this section—

(a) "insurer" includes a person giving a security,

(b) . . .

(c) "liability covered by the terms of the policy or security" means a liability which is covered by the policy or security or which would be so covered but for the fact that the insurer is entitled to avoid or cancel, or has avoided or cancelled, the policy or security.

(10) In the application of this section to Scotland, the words "by virtue of any enactment relating to interest on judgments" in subsections (5) and (6) (in each place where they appear) shall be omitted.

NOTES

Sub-s (6): sums in square brackets substituted by the Motor Vehicles (Compulsory Insurance) Regulations 2007, SI 2007/1426, reg 2(1), (3).

Sub-s (9): para (b) repealed by the Road Traffic Act 1991, s 83, Sch 8.

[3406]

152 Exceptions to section 151

(1) No sum is payable by an insurer under section 151 of this Act—

(a) in respect of any judgment unless, before or within seven days after the commencement of the proceedings in which the judgment was given, the insurer had notice of the bringing of the proceedings, or

(b) in respect of any judgment so long as execution on the judgment is stayed pending an appeal, or

(c) in connection with any liability if, before the happening of the event which was the cause of the death or bodily injury or damage to property giving rise to the liability, the policy or security was cancelled by mutual consent or by virtue of any provision contained in it, and also—

(i) before the happening of that event the certificate was surrendered to the insurer, or the person to whom the certificate was delivered made a statutory declaration stating that the certificate had been lost or destroyed, or

(ii) after the happening of that event, but before the expiration of a period of fourteen days from the taking effect of the cancellation of the policy or security, the certificate was surrendered to the insurer, or the person to whom it was delivered made a statutory declaration stating that the certificate had been lost or destroyed, or

(iii) either before or after the happening of that event, but within that period of fourteen days, the insurer has commenced proceedings under this Act in respect of the failure to surrender the certificate.

(2) Subject to subsection (3) below, no sum is payable by an insurer under section 151 of this Act if, in an action commenced before, or within three months after, the commencement of the proceedings in which the judgment was given, he has obtained a declaration—

(a) that, apart from any provision contained in the policy or security, he is entitled to avoid it on the ground that it was obtained—

(i) by the non-disclosure of a material fact, or

(ii) by a representation of fact which was false in some material particular, or

(b) if he has avoided the policy or security on that ground, that he was entitled so to do apart from any provision contained in it

[and, for the purposes of this section, "material" means of such a nature as to influence the judgment of a prudent insurer in determining whether he will take the risk and, if so, at what premium and on what conditions.]

(3) An insurer who has obtained such a declaration as is mentioned in subsection (2) above in an action does not by reason of that become entitled to the benefit of that subsection as respects any judgment obtained in proceedings commenced before the commencement of that action unless

before, or within seven days after, the commencement of that action he has given notice of it to the person who is the plaintiff (or in Scotland pursuer) in those proceedings specifying the non-disclosure or false representation on which he proposes to rely.

(4) A person to whom notice of such an action is so given is entitled, if he thinks fit, to be made a party to it.

NOTES

Sub-s (2): words in square brackets added by the Road Traffic Act 1991, s 48, Sch 4, para 66.

[3407]

153 Bankruptcy, etc, of insured or secured persons not to affect claims by third parties

(1) Where, after a certificate of insurance or certificate of security has been delivered under section 147 of this Act to the person by whom a policy has been effected or to whom a security has been given, any of the events mentioned in subsection (2) below happens, the happening of that event shall, notwithstanding anything in the Third Parties (Rights Against Insurers) Act 1930, not affect any such liability of that person as is required to be covered by a policy of insurance under section 145 of this Act.

(2) In the case of the person by whom the policy was effected or to whom the security was given, the events referred to in subsection (1) above are—

(a) that he becomes bankrupt or makes a composition or arrangement with his creditors or that his estate is sequestrated or he grants a trust deed for his creditors,

(b) that he dies and—

(i) his estate falls to be administered in accordance with an order under section 421 of the Insolvency Act 1986,

(ii) an award of sequestration of his estate is made, or

(iii) a judicial factor is appointed to administer his estate under section 11A of the Judicial Factors (Scotland) Act 1889,

(c) that if that person is a company—

(i) a winding-up order . . . is made with respect to the company [or the company enters administration],

(ii) a resolution for a voluntary winding-up is passed with respect to the company,

(iii) a receiver or manager of the company's business or undertaking is duly appointed, or

(iv) possession is taken, by or on behalf of the holders of any debentures secured by a floating charge, of any property comprised in or subject to the charge.

(3) Nothing in subsection (1) above affects any rights conferred by the Third Parties (Rights Against Insurers) Act 1930 on the person to whom the liability was incurred, being rights so conferred against the person by whom the policy was issued or the security was given.

NOTES

Sub-s (2): in para (c)(i) words omitted repealed and words in square brackets added by the Enterprise Act 2002 (Insolvency) Order 2003, SI 2003/2096, art 4, Schedule, Pt 1, paras 1, 14, except in relation to any case where a petition for an administration order was presented before 15 September 2003.

[3408]

154 Duty to give information as to insurance or security where claim made

(1) A person against whom a claim is made in respect of any such liability as is required to be covered by a policy of insurance under section 145 of this Act must, on demand by or on behalf of the person making the claim—

(a) state whether or not, in respect of that liability—

(i) he was insured by a policy having effect for the purposes of this Part of this Act or had in force a security having effect for those purposes, or

(ii) he would have been so insured or would have had in force such a security if the insurer or, as the case may be, the giver of the security had not avoided or cancelled the policy or security, and

(b) if he was or would have been so insured, or had or would have had in force such a security—

(i) give such particulars with respect to that policy or security as were specified in any certificate of insurance or security delivered in respect of that policy or security, as the case may be, under section 147 of this Act, or

(ii) where no such certificate was delivered under that section, give the following particulars, that is to say, the registration mark or other identifying particulars of the vehicle concerned, the number or other identifying particulars of the insurance policy issued in respect of the vehicle, the name of the insurer and the period of the insurance cover.

(2) If without reasonable excuse, a person fails to comply with the provisions of subsection (1) above, or wilfully makes a false statement in reply to any such demand as is referred to in that subsection, he is guilty of an offence.

155, 156 *(Outside the scope of this work.)*

Payments for treatment of traffic casualties

[3409]

157 Payment for hospital treatment of traffic casualties

(1) Subject to subsection (2) below, where—

(a) a payment, other than a payment under section 158 of this Act, is made (whether or not with an admission of liability) in respect of the death of, or bodily injury to, any person arising out of the use of a motor vehicle on a road or *in a place to which the public have a right of access*, and

(b) the payment is made—

(i) by an authorised insurer, the payment being made under or in consequence of a policy issued under section 145 of this Act, or

(ii) by the owner of a vehicle in relation to the use of which a security under this Part of this Act is in force, or

(iii) by the owner of a vehicle who has made a deposit under this Part of this Act, and

(c) the person who has so died or been bodily injured has to the knowledge of the insurer or owner, as the case may be, received treatment at a hospital, whether as an in-patient or as an out-patient, in respect of the injury so arising,

the insurer or owner must pay the expenses reasonably incurred by the hospital in affording the treatment, after deducting from the expenses any moneys actually received in payment of a specific charge for the treatment, not being moneys received under any contributory scheme.

(2) The amount to be paid shall not exceed [£2,949.00] for each person treated as an in-patient or [£295.00] for each person treated as an out-patient.

(3) For the purposes of this section "expenses reasonably incurred" means—

(a) in relation to a person who receives treatment at a hospital as an in-patient, an amount for each day he is maintained in the hospital representing the average daily cost, for each in-patient, of the maintenance of the hospital and the staff of the hospital and the maintenance and treatment of the in-patients in the hospital, and

(b) in relation to a person who receives treatment at a hospital as an out-patient, reasonable expenses actually incurred.

NOTES

Sub-s (1): for the words in italics there are substituted the words "in some other public place", in relation to Scotland only, by the Community Care and Health (Scotland) Act 2002, s 20(1).

Sub-s (2): sums in square brackets substituted by the Road Traffic Accidents (Payments for Treatment) Order 1995, SI 1995/889, art 2.

[3410]

158 Payment for emergency treatment of traffic casualties

(1) Subsection (2) below applies where—

(a) medical or surgical treatment or examination is immediately required as a result of bodily injury (including fatal injury) to a person caused by, or arising out of, the use of a motor vehicle on a road [or in some other public place], and

(b) the treatment or examination so required (in this Part of this Act referred to as "emergency treatment") is effected by a legally qualified medical practitioner.

(2) The person who was using the vehicle at the time of the event out of which the bodily injury arose must, on a claim being made in accordance with the provisions of section 159 of this Act, pay to the practitioner (or, where emergency treatment is effected by more than one practitioner, to the practitioner by whom it is first effected)—

(a) a fee of [£21.30] in respect of each person in whose case the emergency treatment is effected by him, and

(b) a sum, in respect of any distance in excess of two miles which he must cover in order—

(i) to proceed from the place from which he is summoned to the place where the emergency treatment is carried out by him, and

(ii) to return to the first mentioned place,

equal to [41 pence] for every complete mile and additional part of a mile of that distance.

(3) Where emergency treatment is first effected in a hospital, the provisions of subsections (1) and (2) above with respect to payment of a fee shall, so far as applicable, but subject (as regards the recipient of a payment) to the provisions of section 159 of this Act, have effect with the substitution of references to the hospital for references to a legally qualified medical practitioner.

(4) Liability incurred under this section by the person using a vehicle shall, where the event out of which it arose was caused by the wrongful act of another person, be treated for the purposes of any claim to recover damage by reason of that wrongful act as damage sustained by the person using the vehicle.

NOTES

Sub-s (1): words in square brackets inserted in relation to Scotland only, by the Community Care and Health (Scotland) Act 2002, s 20(2).

Sub-s (2): sums in square brackets substituted by the Road Traffic Accidents (Payments for Treatment) Order 1995, SI 1995/889, art 3.

[3411]

159 Supplementary provisions as to payments for treatment

(1) A payment falling to be made under section 157 or 158 of this Act in respect of treatment in a hospital must be made [to the hospital].

(2) A claim for a payment under section 158 of this Act may be made at the time when the emergency treatment is effected, by oral request to the person who was using the vehicle, and if not so made must be made by request in writing served on him within seven days from the day on which the emergency treatment was effected.

(3) Any such request in writing—

- (a) must be signed by the claimant or, in the case of a hospital, by an executive officer of [the hospital claiming the payment],
- (b) must state the name and address of the claimant, the circumstances in which the emergency treatment was effected, and that it was first effected by the claimant or, in the case of a hospital, in the hospital, and
- (c) may be served by delivering it to the person who was using the vehicle or by sending it in a prepaid registered letter, or the recorded delivery service, addressed to him at his usual or last known address.

(4) A payment made under section 158 of this Act shall operate as a discharge, to the extent of the amount paid, of any liability of the person who was using the vehicle, or of any other person, to pay any sum in respect of the expenses or remuneration of the practitioner or hospital concerned of or for effecting the emergency treatment.

(5) A chief officer of police must, if so requested by a person who alleges that he is entitled to claim a payment under section 158 of this Act, provide that person with any information at the disposal of the chief officer—

- (a) as to the identification marks of any motor vehicle which that person alleges to be a vehicle out of the use of which the bodily injury arose, and
- (b) as to the identity and address of the person who was using the vehicle at the time of the event out of which it arose.

NOTES

Sub-ss (1), (3): words in square brackets substituted by the Road Traffic (NHS Charges) Act 1999, s 18(2).

Transfer of functions: as to the transfer of functions under this section to the National Assembly for Wales, see the National Assembly for Wales (Transfer of Functions) Order 1999, SI 1999/672, art 2, Sch 1.

General

[3411A]

[159A Disclosure of information

(1) Regulations may make provision for and in connection with requiring MIIC to make information available to any prescribed person for the purposes of the exercise of any of that person's functions in connection with the enforcement of an offence under this Part of this Act or under regulations made under section 160 of this Act.

(2) In this section—

"MIIC" means the Motor Insurers' Information Centre (a company limited by guarantee and incorporated under the Companies Act 1985 on 8th December 1998), and

"information" means information held in any form.]

NOTES

Commencement: to be appointed.

Inserted by the Road Safety Act 2006, s 22(2), as from a day to be appointed.

[3412]

160 Regulations

(1) The Secretary of State may make regulations for any purpose for which regulations may be made under this Part of this Act and for prescribing anything which may be prescribed under this Part of this Act and generally for the purpose of carrying this Part of this Act into effect.

In this Part of this Act "regulations" means regulations under this section and "prescribed" means prescribed by regulations.

(2) In particular, but without prejudice to the generality of subsection (1) above, the regulations may make provision—

(a) as to forms to be used for the purposes of this Part of this Act,

(b) as to applications for and the issue of certificates of insurance and certificates of security and any other documents which may be prescribed, and as to the keeping of records of documents and the providing of particulars of them or the giving of information with respect to them to the Secretary of State or a chief officer of police,

(c) as to the issue of copies of any such certificates or other documents which are lost or destroyed,

(d) as to the custody, production, cancellation and surrender of any such certificates or other documents, and

(e) for providing that any provisions of this Part of this Act shall, in relation to vehicles brought into Great Britain by persons making only a temporary stay in Great Britain, have effect subject to such modifications and adaptations as may be prescribed.

NOTES

Regulations: by virtue of the Road Traffic (Consequential Provisions) Act 1988, s 2(2), and the Interpretation Act 1978, s 17(2)(b), the following regulations partly have effect under this section: the Motor Vehicles (International Motor Insurance Card) Regulations 1971, SI 1971/792 at **[4012]**; the Motor Vehicles (Third Party Risks) Regulations 1972, SI 1972/1217 at **[4020]**; the Motor Vehicles (Third-Party Risks Deposits) Regulations 1992, SI 1992/1284 at **[4042]**.

[3413]

161 Interpretation

(1) In this Part of this Act—

["hospital" means any institution which provides medical or surgical treatment for in-patients, other than—

(a) a health service hospital within the meaning of [the National Health Service Act 2006 or the National Health Service (Wales) Act 2006] or the National Health Service (Scotland) Act 1978,

(b) . . . or

(c) any institution carried on for profit,]

"policy of insurance" includes a covering note,

"salvage" means the preservation of a vessel which is wrecked, stranded or in distress, or the lives of persons belonging to, or the cargo or apparel of, such a vessel, and

"under the owner's control" means, in relation to a vehicle, that it is being driven by the owner or by a servant of the owner in the course of his employment or is otherwise subject to the control of the owner.

(2) In any provision of this Part of this Act relating to the surrender, or the loss or destruction, of a certificate of insurance or certificate of security, references to such a certificate—

(a) shall, in relation to policies or securities under which more than one certificate is issued, be construed as references to all certificates, and

(b) shall, where any copy has been issued of any certificate, be construed as including a reference to that copy.

(3) In this Part of this Act, any reference to an accident includes a reference to two or more causally related accidents.

(4) This section is affected by Schedule 5 to the Road Traffic (Consequential Provisions) Act 1988 (transitory modifications).

NOTES

Sub-s (1): definition "hospital" substituted by the Road Traffic (NHS Charges) Act 1999, s 18(3), words in square brackets in para (a) of that definition substituted by the National Health Service (Consequential Provisions) Act 2006, s 2, Sch 1, paras 121, 123, and para (b) thereof repealed by the Health and Social Care (Community Health and Standards) Act 2003, s 196, Sch 14, Pt 3.

[3414]

162 Index to Part VI

The expressions listed in the left-hand column below are respectively defined or (as the case may be) fall to be construed in accordance with the provisions of this Part of this Act listed in the right-hand column in relation to those expressions.

Expression	*Relevant provision*
Accident	Section 161(3)
[Authorised insurer	Section 145(5)]
Certificate of insurance	Sections 147(1) and 161(2)
Certificate of security	Sections 147(2) and 161(2)
Hospital	Section 161(1)
Policy of insurance	Section 161(1)
Prescribed	Section 160(1)
Regulations	Section 160(1)
Salvage	Section 161(1)
Under the owner's control	Section 161(1)

NOTES

Entry "Authorised insurer" substituted by the Financial Services and Markets Act 2000 (Consequential Amendments and Repeals) Order 2001, SI 2001/3649, art 314.

PART VII
MISCELLANEOUS AND GENERAL

163–194 (*Outside the scope of this work.*)

Supplementary

195, 196 (*Outside the scope of this work.*)

[3415]

197 Short title, commencement and extent

(1) This Act may be cited as the Road Traffic Act 1988.

(2) This Act shall come into force, subject to the transitory provisions in Schedule 5 to the Road Traffic (Consequential Provisions) Act 1988, at the end of the period of six months beginning with the day on which it is passed.

(3) This Act, except section 80 and except as provided by section 184, does not extend to Northern Ireland.

(*Schs 1, 2 outside the scope of this work.*)

[SCHEDULE 2A

OFFENCE OF KEEPING VEHICLE WHICH DOES NOT MEET INSURANCE REQUIREMENTS: IMMOBILISATION, REMOVAL AND DISPOSAL OF VEHICLES

Section 144D

Immobilisation

[3415A]–[3540]

1.—(1) Regulations may make provision with respect to any case where an authorised person has reason to believe that, on or after such date as may be prescribed, an offence under section 144A of this Act is being committed as regards a vehicle which is stationary on a road or other public place.

(2) The regulations may provide that the authorised person or a person acting under his direction may—

- (a) fix an immobilisation device to the vehicle while it remains in the place where it is stationary, or
- (b) move it from that place to another place on the same or another road or public place and fix an immobilisation device to it in that other place.

(3) The regulations may provide that on any occasion when an immobilisation device is fixed to a vehicle in accordance with the regulations the person fixing the device must also fix to the vehicle a notice—

Part III Statutes

(a) indicating that the device has been fixed to the vehicle and warning that no attempt should be made to drive it or otherwise put it in motion until it has been released from the device,

(b) specifying the steps to be taken to secure its release, and

(c) giving such other information as may be prescribed.

(4) The regulations may provide that a vehicle to which an immobilisation device has been fixed in accordance with the regulations—

(a) may only be released from the device by or under the direction of an authorised person, but

(b) subject to that, must be released from the device if the first and second requirements specified below are met.

(5) The first requirement is that such charge in respect of the release as may be prescribed is paid in any manner specified in the immobilisation notice.

(6) The second requirement is that, in accordance with instructions specified in the immobilisation notice, there is produced such evidence as may be prescribed establishing—

(a) that any person who proposes to drive the vehicle away will not in doing so be guilty of an offence under section 143 of this Act, and

(b) that the person in whose name the vehicle is registered under the Vehicle Excise and Registration Act 1994 is not guilty of an offence under section 144A of this Act as regards the vehicle.

(7) The regulations may provide that they do not apply in relation to a vehicle if—

(a) a current disabled person's badge is displayed on the vehicle, or

(b) such other conditions as may be prescribed are fulfilled,

and "disabled person's badge" means a badge issued, or having effect as if issued, under any regulations for the time being in force under section 21 of the Chronically Sick and Disabled Persons Act 1970.

(8) The regulations may provide that an immobilisation notice is not to be removed or interfered with except by or on the authority of a person falling within a prescribed description.

Offences connected with immobilisation

2.—(1) The regulations may provide that a person contravening provision made under paragraph 1(8) above is guilty of an offence.

(2) The regulations may provide that a person who, without being authorised to do so in accordance with provision made under paragraph 1 above, removes or attempts to remove an immobilisation device fixed to a vehicle in accordance with the regulations is guilty of an offence.

(3) The regulations may provide that where they would apply in relation to a vehicle but for provision made under paragraph 1(7)(a) above and the vehicle was not, at the time it was stationary, being used—

(a) in accordance with regulations under section 21 of the Chronically Sick and Disabled Persons Act 1970, and

(b) in circumstances falling within section 117(1)(b) of the Road Traffic Regulation Act 1984 (use where a disabled person's concession would be available),

the person in charge of the vehicle at that time is guilty of an offence.

(4) The regulations may provide that where—

(a) a person makes a declaration with a view to securing the release of a vehicle from an immobilisation device purported to have been fixed in accordance with the regulations,

(b) the declaration is that no offence under section 144A of this Act is or was being committed as regards the vehicle, and

(c) the declaration is to the person's knowledge either false or in any material respect misleading,

he is guilty of an offence.

Removal and disposal of vehicles

3.—(1) The regulations may make provision with respect to any case where—

(a) an authorised person has reason to believe that an offence under section 144A of this Act is being committed as regards a vehicle which is stationary on a road or other public place, and such conditions as may be prescribed are fulfilled, or

(b) an authorised person has reason to believe that such an offence was being committed as regards a vehicle at a time when an immobilisation device which is fixed to the vehicle was fixed to it in accordance with the regulations, and such conditions as may be prescribed are fulfilled.

(2) The regulations may provide that the authorised person, or a person acting under his direction, may remove the vehicle and deliver it into the custody of a person—

(a) who is identified in accordance with prescribed rules, and
(b) who agrees to accept delivery in accordance with arrangements agreed between that person and the Secretary of State,

and the arrangements may include provision as to the payment of a sum to the person into whose custody the vehicle is delivered.

(3) The regulations may provide that the person into whose custody the vehicle is delivered may dispose of it, and may in particular make provision as to—
(a) the time at which the vehicle may be disposed of, and
(b) the manner in which it may be disposed of.

(4) The regulations may make provision allowing a person to take possession of the vehicle if—
(a) he claims it before it is disposed of, and
(b) any prescribed conditions are fulfilled.

(5) The regulations may provide for a sum of an amount arrived at under prescribed rules to be paid to a person if—
(a) he claims after the vehicle's disposal to be or to have been its owner,
(b) the claim is made within a prescribed time of the disposal, and
(c) any other prescribed conditions are fulfilled.

(6) The regulations may provide that—
(a) the Secretary of State, or
(b) a person into whose custody the vehicle is delivered under the regulations,

may recover from the vehicle's owner (whether or not a claim is made under provision made under sub-paragraph (4) or (5) above) such charges as may be prescribed in respect of all or any of the following, namely its release, removal, custody and disposal; and "owner" means the person who was the owner when the vehicle was removed.

(7) The conditions prescribed under sub-paragraph (4) above may include conditions as to—
(a) satisfying the person with custody that the claimant is the vehicle's owner,
(b) the payment of prescribed charges in respect of the vehicle's release, removal and custody,
(c) the production of such evidence as may be prescribed establishing that in driving the vehicle away the claimant will not be guilty of an offence under section 143 of this Act, and
(d) the production of such evidence as may be prescribed establishing that the person in whose name the vehicle is registered under the Vehicle Excise and Registration Act 1994 is not guilty of an offence under section 144A of this Act as regards the vehicle.

(8) The regulations may in particular include provision for purposes corresponding to those of sections 101 and 102 of the Road Traffic Regulation Act 1984 (disposal and charges) subject to such additions, omissions or other modifications as the Secretary of State thinks fit.

Offences as to securing possession of vehicles

4. The regulations may provide that where—
(a) a person makes a declaration with a view to securing possession of a vehicle purported to have been delivered into the custody of a person in accordance with provision made under paragraph 3 above,
(b) the declaration is that no offence under section 144A of this Act is or was being committed as regards the vehicle, and
(c) the declaration is to the person's knowledge either false or in any material respect misleading,

he is guilty of an offence.

Disputes

5. The regulations may make provision about the proceedings to be followed where a dispute occurs as a result of the regulations, and may in particular make provision—
(a) for an application to be made to a magistrates' court or (in Scotland) to the sheriff, or
(b) for a court to order a sum to be paid by the Secretary of State.

Authorised persons

6. As regards anything falling to be done under the regulations (such as receiving payment of a charge or other sum) the regulations may provide that it may be done—
(a) by an authorised person, or
(b) by an authorised person or a person acting under his direction.

Application of Road Traffic Offenders Act 1988

7. The regulations may make provision for the application of any or all of sections 1, 6, 11 and 12(1) of the Road Traffic Offenders Act 1988 to an offence for which provision is made by the regulations.

Interpretation

8.—(1) The regulations may make provision as to the meaning for the purposes of the regulations of "owner" as regards a vehicle.

(2) In particular, the regulations may provide that for the purposes of the regulations the owner of a vehicle is taken to be the person in whose name it is then registered under the Vehicle Excise and Registration Act 1994.

9.—(1) The regulations may make provision as to the meaning in the regulations of "authorised person".

(2) In particular, the regulations may provide that—
- (a) references to an authorised person are to a person authorised by the Secretary of State for the purposes of the regulations,
- (b) an authorised person may be a local authority or an employee of a local authority or a member of a police force or some other person, and
- (c) different persons may be authorised for the purposes of different provisions of the regulations.

10. In this Schedule—
- (a) references to an immobilisation device are to a device or appliance which is an immobilisation device for the purposes of section 104 of the Road Traffic Regulation Act 1984 (immobilisation of vehicles illegally parked), and
- (b) references to an immobilisation notice are to a notice fixed to a vehicle in accordance with the regulations.]

NOTES

Commencement: to be appointed.
Inserted by the Road Safety Act 2006, s 22(3), Sch 5, as from a day to be appointed.

(Second Sch 2A (as inserted by SI 2006/1892, regs 2, 5), Schs 3, 4 outside the scope of this work.)

TRANSPORT AND WORKS ACT 1992

(1992 c 42)

An Act to provide for the making of orders relating to, or to matters ancillary to, the construction or operation of railways, tramways, trolley vehicle systems, other guided transport systems and inland waterways, and orders relating to, or to matters ancillary to, works interfering with rights of navigation; to make further provision in relation to railways, tramways, trolley vehicle systems and other guided transport systems; to amend certain enactments relating to harbours; and for connected purposes

[16 March 1992]

1–25 *((Pt I) outside the scope of this work.)*

PART II
SAFETY OF RAILWAYS ETC

26–39 *((Ch I) outside the scope of this work.)*

CHAPTER II
OTHER SAFETY PROVISIONS

General

40–45 *(S 40 repealed by the Serious Organised Crime and Police Act 2005, s 174(2), Sch 17, Pt 2; ss 41, 45 outside the scope of this work; s 42 repealed by the Railway Safety (Miscellaneous Provisions) Regulations 1997, SI 1997/553, reg 12, Schedule, Pt I; ss 43, 44 repealed by the Reporting of Injuries, Diseases and Dangerous Occurrences Regulations 1995, SI 1995/3163, reg 14(1).)*

[3541]
46 Directions requiring insurance
(1) The Secretary of State may give a direction under this section to an operator of a railway, tramway, trolley vehicle system or system using any other mode of guided transport.
(2) A direction under this section may require the person to whom it is given to ensure that there are at all times in force such policies of insurance against liability in respect of death or personal injury as comply with the requirements of the direction.
(3) Before giving a direction under this section, the Secretary of State shall consult the person to whom he proposes to give it.
(4) If a direction under this section is contravened, the person to whom the direction was given shall be guilty of an offence.
(5) A person guilty of an offence under this section shall be liable on summary conviction to a fine not exceeding level 5 on the standard scale.

47–59 (*Ss 47–49, 51–59 outside the scope of this work; s 50 repealed by the Statute Law (Repeals) Act 2004.*)

PART III
MISCELLANEOUS AND GENERAL

60–65 (*Outside the scope of this work.*)

General

66–71 (*Outside the scope of this work.*)

[3542]
72 Short title
This Act may be cited as the Transport and Works Act 1992.

(*Schs 1–4 outside the scope of this work.*)

REINSURANCE (ACTS OF TERRORISM) ACT 1993

(1993 c 18)

An Act to provide for the payment out of money provided by Parliament or into the Consolidated Fund of sums referable to reinsurance liabilities entered into by the Secretary of State in respect of loss or damage to property resulting from or consequential upon acts of terrorism and losses consequential on such loss or damage

[27 May 1993]

Part III Statutes

[3543]
1 Financing of reinsurance obligations of the [Treasury]
(1) There shall be paid out of money provided by Parliament such sums as may be necessary to enable the [Treasury] to meet [their] obligations under—
- (a) any agreement of reinsurance which . . . is entered into (whether before or after the passing of this Act) pursuant to arrangements to which this Act applies, or
- (b) any guarantee which . . . is entered into (whether before or after that passing) pursuant to any such agreement.

(2) As soon as practicable after the passing of this Act or, if it is later, after [they enter] into the agreement or guarantee, the [Treasury] shall lay before each House of Parliament a copy of any agreement or guarantee falling within subsection (1) above.
(3) There shall be paid into the Consolidated Fund any sums received by the [Treasury] pursuant to any arrangements to which this Act applies.

NOTES
Section heading: word in square brackets substituted by the Transfer of Functions (Insurance) Order 1997, SI 1997/2781, art 8, Schedule, para 121.
Sub-ss (1)–(3): words in square brackets substituted and words omitted repealed by SI 1997/2781, art 8, Schedule, paras 120–122.

[3544]
2 Reinsurance arrangements to which this Act applies
(1) This Act applies to arrangements under which the [Treasury] . . . [undertake] to any extent the liability of reinsuring risks against—

(a) loss of or damage to property in Great Britain resulting from or consequential upon acts of terrorism; and

(b) any loss which is consequential on loss or damage falling within paragraph (a) above;

and to the extent that the arrangements relate to events occurring before as well as after an agreement of reinsurance comes into being, the reference in section 1(1) above to the obligations of the [Treasury] shall be construed accordingly.

(2) In this section "acts of terrorism" means acts of persons acting on behalf of, or in connection with, any organisation which carries out activities directed towards the overthrowing or influencing, by force or violence, of Her Majesty's government in the United Kingdom or any other government de jure or de facto.

(3) In subsection (2) above "organisation" includes any association or combination of persons.

NOTES

Sub-s (1): words in square brackets substituted, and words omitted repealed, by the Transfer of Functions (Insurance) Order 1997, SI 1997/2781, art 8, Schedule, paras 120, 121, 123.

[3545]–[3547]

3 Citation and extent

(1) This Act may be cited as the Reinsurance (Acts of Terrorism) Act 1993.

(2) This Act does not extend to Northern Ireland.

FINANCE ACT 1994

(1994 c 9)

ARRANGEMENT OF SECTIONS

PART III
INSURANCE PREMIUM TAX

The basic provisions

48 Insurance premium tax [3548]
49 Charge to tax [3549]
50 Chargeable amount [3550]
51 Rate of tax [3551]
51A Premiums liable to tax at the higher rate [3552]
52 Liability to pay tax [3553]
52A Certain fees to be treated as premiums under higher rate contracts [3554]

Administration

53 Registration of insurers [3555]
53AA Registration of taxable intermediaries [3556]
53A Information required to keep register up to standard [3557]
54 Accounting for tax and time for payment [3558]
55 Credit [3559]
56 Power to assess [3560]

Review and appeal

59 Appeals [3563]
59A Offer of review [3563A]
59B Right to require review [3563B]
59C Review by HMRC [3563C]
59D Extensions of time [3563D]
59E Review out of time [3563E]
59F Nature of review etc [3563F]
59G Bringing of appeals [3563G]
60 Further provisions relating to appeals [3564]
61 Review and appeal: commencement [3565]

Miscellaneous

62 Partnership, bankruptcy, transfer of business, etc [3566]
63 Groups of companies [3567]
64 Information, powers, penalties, etc [3568]
65 Liability of insured in certain cases [3569]
66 Directions as to amounts of premiums [3570]
67 Deemed date of receipt of certain premiums [3571]
67A Announced increase in rate of tax: certain premiums treated as received on date of increase [3572]
67B Announced increase in rate of tax: certain contracts treated as made on date of increase [3573]
67C Announced increase in rate of tax: exceptions and apportionments [3574]
68 Special accounting schemes [3575]
69 Charge to tax where different rates of tax apply [3576]

Supplementary

70 Interpretation: taxable insurance contracts [3577]
71 Taxable insurance contracts: power to change definition [3578]
72 Interpretation: premium [3579]
73 Interpretation: other provisions [3580]
74 Orders and regulations [3581]

PART VIII
MISCELLANEOUS AND GENERAL

General

257 Interpretation and construction [3582]
259 Short title [3583]

SCHEDULES:

Schedule 6A—Premiums liable to tax at the higher rate
Part I—Interpretation [3584]
Part II—Descriptions of premium [3585]
Schedule 7—Insurance premium tax

Part III Statutes

Part I—Information . . . . . [3586]
Part II—Powers . . . . . [3587]
Part III—Recovery . . . . . [3588]
Part IV—Penalties . . . . . [3589]
Part V—Interest . . . . . [3590]
Part VI—Miscellaneous . . . . . [3591]
Schedule 7A—Insurance Premium Tax: Contracts that are not Taxable
Part I—Descriptions of Contract . . . . . [3592]
Part II—Interpretation . . . . . [3593]

An Act to grant certain duties, to alter other duties, and to amend the law relating to the National Debt and the Public Revenue, and to make further provision in connection with Finance

[3 May 1994]

1–47 *((Pts I, II) outside the scope of this work.)*

PART III
INSURANCE PREMIUM TAX

The basic provisions

[3548]
48 Insurance premium tax

(1) A tax, to be known as insurance premium tax, shall be charged in accordance with this Part.

(2) The tax shall be under the care and management of the Commissioners of Customs and Excise.

[3549]
49 Charge to tax

Tax shall be charged on the receipt of a premium by an insurer if the premium is received—

(a) under a taxable insurance contract, and

(b) on or after 1st October 1994.

[3550]
50 Chargeable amount

(1) Tax shall be charged by reference to the chargeable amount.

(2) For the purposes of this Part, the chargeable amount is such amount as, with the addition of the tax chargeable, is equal to the amount of the premium.

(3) [Subsections (1) and (2)] above shall have effect subject to section 69 below.

NOTES

Sub-s (3): words in square brackets substituted in relation to a premium which falls to be regarded for the purposes of this Part as received under a taxable insurance contract by an insurer on or after 1 April 1997, by the Finance Act 1997, ss 23(2), 24(1); for further provision as to the effect of this amendment see s 24(2)–(4) of the 1997 Act at **[3612]**.

[3551]
[51 Rate of tax

(1) Tax shall be charged—

(a) at the higher rate, in the case of a premium which is liable to tax at that rate; and

(b) at the standard rate, in any other case.

(2) For the purposes of this Part—

(a) the higher rate is 17.5 per cent; and

(b) the standard rate is [5 per cent].]

NOTES

Substituted, in relation to a premium which falls to be regarded for the purposes of this Part as received under a taxable insurance contract by an insurer on or after 1 April 1997, by the Finance Act 1997, ss 21(1), 24(1); for further provision as to the effect of this amendment see s 24(2)–(4) of the 1997 Act at **[3612]**.

Sub-s (2): in para (b) words in square brackets substituted by the Finance Act 1999, s 125(1), with effect in relation to a premium which falls to be regarded for the purposes of Pt III of this Act as received under a taxable insurance contract by an insurer on or after 1 July 1999: see the Finance Act 1999, s 125(2); for further provision as to the effect of this amendment see s 125(3)–(5) thereof.

[3552]
[51A Premiums liable to tax at the higher rate

(1) A premium received under a taxable insurance contract by an insurer is liable to tax at the higher rate if it falls within one or more of the paragraphs of Part II of Schedule 6A to this Act.

(2) Part I of Schedule 6A to this Act shall have effect with respect to the interpretation of that Schedule.
(3) Provision may be made by order amending Schedule 6A as it has effect for the time being.
(4) This section is subject to section 69 below.]

NOTES

Inserted, in relation to a premium which falls to be regarded for the purposes of this Part as received under a taxable insurance contract by an insurer on or after 1 April 1997, by the Finance Act 1997, ss 22(1), 24(1); for further provision as to the effect of this amendment see s 24(2)–(4) of the 1997 Act at **[3612]**.

[3553]
52 Liability to pay tax
(1) Tax shall be payable by the person who is the insurer in relation to the contract under which the premium is received.
(2) Subsection (1) above shall have effect subject to any regulations made under section 65 below.

[3554]
[52A Certain fees to be treated as premiums under higher rate contracts
(1) This section applies where—
(a) at or about the time when a higher rate contract is effected, and
(b) in connection with that contract,
a fee in respect of an insurance-related service is charged by a taxable intermediary to a person who is or becomes the insured (or one of the insured) under the contract or to a person who acts for or on behalf of such a person.
(2) Where this section applies—
(a) a payment in respect of the fee shall be treated for the purposes of this Part as a premium received under a taxable insurance contract by an insurer, and
(b) that premium—
(i) shall be treated for the purposes of this Part as so received at the time when the payment is made, and
(ii) shall be chargeable to tax at the higher rate.
(3) Tax charged by virtue of subsection (2) above shall be payable by the taxable intermediary as if he were the insurer under the contract mentioned in paragraph (a) of that subsection.
(4) For the purposes of this section, a contract of insurance is a "higher rate contract" if—
(a) it is a taxable insurance contract; and
(b) the whole or any part of a premium received under the contract by the insurer is (apart from this section) liable to tax at the higher rate.
(5) For the purposes of this Part a "taxable intermediary" is a person falling within subsection (6) [or (6A)] below who—
(a) at or about the time when a higher rate contract is effected, and
(b) in connection with that contract,
charges a fee in respect of an insurance-related service to a person who is or becomes the insured (or one of the insured) under the contract or to a person who acts for or on behalf of such a person.
[(6) A person falls within this subsection if the higher rate contract mentioned in subsection (1) above falls within paragraph 2 or 3 of Schedule 6A to this Act (motor cars or motor cycles, or relevant goods) and the person is—
(a) within the meaning of the paragraph in question, a supplier of motor cars or motor cycles or, as the case may be, of relevant goods; or
(b) a person connected with a person falling within paragraph (a) above; or
(c) a person who in the course of his business pays—
(i) the whole or any part of the premium received under that contract, or
(ii) a fee connected with the arranging of that contract,
to a person falling within paragraph (a) or (b) above.
(6A) A person falls within this subsection if the higher rate contract mentioned in subsection (1) above falls within paragraph 4 of Schedule 6A to this Act (travel insurance) and the person is—
(a) the insurer under that contract; or
(b) a person through whom that contract is arranged in the course of his business; or
(c) a person connected with the insurer under that contract; or
(d) a person connected with a person falling within paragraph (b) above; or
(e) a person who in the course of his business pays—
(i) the whole or any part of the premium received under that contract, or
(ii) a fee connected with the arranging of that contract,
to a person falling within any of paragraphs (a) to (d) above.]

(8) For the purposes of this section, any question whether a person is connected with another shall be determined in accordance with section 839 of the Taxes Act 1988.

(9) In this section—

"insurance-related service" means any service which is related to, or connected with, insurance;

. . .]

NOTES

Inserted, in relation to payments in respect of fees charged on or after 19 March 1997, by the Finance Act 1997, s 25.

Sub-s (5): words in square brackets inserted by the Finance Act 1998, s 147(2), (5), with effect in relation to payments in respect of fees charged on or after 1 August 1998.

Sub-ss (6), (6A): substituted for original sub-ss (6), (7) by the Finance Act 1998, s 147(3), (5), with effect in relation to payments in respect of fees charged on or after 1 August 1998.

Sub-s (9): definitions omitted repealed by the Finance Act 1998, s 147(4), (5), 165, Sch 27, Pt V(1), with effect in relation to payments in respect of fees charged on or after 1 August 1998.

Administration

[3555]

53 Registration of insurers

(1) A person who—

(a) receives, as insurer, premiums in the course of a taxable business, and

(b) is not registered,

is liable to be registered.

[(1A) The register kept under this section may contain such information as the Commissioners think is required for the purposes of the care and management of the tax.]

(2) A person who—

(a) at any time forms the intention of receiving, as insurer, premiums in the course of a taxable business, and

(b) is not already receiving, as insurer, premiums in the course of another taxable business,

shall notify the Commissioners of those facts.

(3) A person who at any time—

(a) ceases to have the intention of receiving, as insurer, premiums in the course of a taxable business, and

(b) has no intention of receiving, as insurer, premiums in the course of another taxable business,

shall notify the Commissioners of those facts.

(4) Where a person is liable to be registered by virtue of subsection (1) above the Commissioners shall register him with effect from the time when he begins to receive premiums in the course of the business concerned; and it is immaterial whether or not he notifies the Commissioners under subsection (2) above.

(5) Where a person—

(a) notifies the Commissioners under subsection (3) above, [and]

(b) satisfies them of the facts there mentioned, . . .

(c) . . .

the Commissioners shall cancel his registration with effect from the earliest practicable time after he ceases to receive, as insurer, premiums in the course of any taxable business.

[(5A) In a case where—

(a) the Commissioners are satisfied that a person has ceased to receive, as insurer, premiums in the course of any taxable business, but

(b) he has not notified them under subsection (3) above,

they may cancel his registration with effect from the earliest practicable time after he so ceased.]

(6) For the purposes of this section regulations may make provision—

(a) as to the time within which a notification is to be made;

(b) as to the circumstances in which premiums are to be taken to be received in the course of a taxable business;

(c) as to the form and manner in which any notification is to be made and as to the information to be contained in or provided with it;

(d) requiring a person who has made a notification to notify the Commissioners if any information contained in or provided in connection with it is or becomes inaccurate;

(e) as to the correction of entries in the register.

(7) References in this section to receiving premiums are to receiving premiums on or after 1st October 1994.

NOTES

Sub-s (1A): inserted by the Finance Act 1995, s 34, Sch 5, para 3.

Sub-s (5): word in square brackets inserted and words omitted repealed by the Finance Act 1995, ss 34, 162, Sch 5, paras 1, 2(1), (2), (4), Sch 29, Pt VII.

Sub-s (5A): inserted by the Finance Act 1995, s 34, Sch 5, paras 1, 2(1), (3).

Regulations: the Insurance Premium Tax Regulations 1994, SI 1994/1774 at **[4075]**.

[3556]

[53AA Registration of taxable intermediaries

(1) A person who—

(a) is a taxable intermediary, and

(b) is not registered,

is liable to be registered.

(2) The register kept under this section may contain such information as the Commissioners think is required for the purposes of the care and management of the tax.

(3) A person who—

(a) at any time forms the intention of charging taxable intermediary's fees, and

(b) is not already charging such fees in the course of another business,

shall notify the Commissioners of those facts.

(4) A person who at any time—

(a) ceases to have the intention of charging taxable intermediary's fees in the course of his business, and

(b) has no intention of charging such fees in the course of another business of his,

shall notify the Commissioners of those facts.

(5) Where a person is liable to be registered by virtue of subsection (1) above, the Commissioners shall register him with effect from the time when he begins to charge taxable intermediary's fees in the course of the business concerned; and it is immaterial whether or not he notifies the Commissioners under subsection (3) above.

(6) Where a person—

(a) notifies the Commissioners under subsection (4) above, and

(b) satisfies them of the facts there mentioned,

the Commissioners shall cancel his registration with effect from the earliest practicable time after he ceases to charge taxable intermediary's fees in the course of any business of his.

(7) In a case where—

(a) the Commissioners are satisfied that a person has ceased to charge taxable intermediary's fees in the course of any business of his, but

(b) he has not notified them under subsection (4) above,

they may cancel his registration with effect from the earliest practicable time after he so ceased.

(8) For the purposes of this section regulations may make provision—

(a) as to the time within which a notification is to be made;

(b) as to the form and manner in which any notification is to be made and as to the information to be contained in or provided with it;

(c) requiring a person who has made a notification to notify the Commissioners if any information contained in or provided in connection with it is or becomes inaccurate;

(d) as to the correction of entries in the register.

(9) In this Part "taxable intermediary's fees" means fees which, to the extent of any payment in respect of them, are chargeable to tax by virtue of section 52A above.]

NOTES

Inserted by the Finance Act 1997, s 26.

[3557]

[53A Information required to keep register up to date

(1) Regulations may make provision requiring a registrable person to notify the Commissioners of particulars which—

(a) are of changes in circumstances relating to the registrable person or any business carried on by him,

(b) appear to the Commissioners to be required for the purpose of keeping the register kept under section 53 [or 53AA] above up to date, and

(c) are of a prescribed description.

(2) Regulations may make provision—

(a) as to the time within which a notification is to be made;

(b) as to the form and manner in which a notification is to be made;

Part III Statutes

(c) requiring a person who has made a notification to notify the Commissioners if any information contained in it is inaccurate.]

NOTES

Inserted by the Finance Act 1995, s 34, Sch 5, paras 1, 4.

Sub-s (1): words in square brackets in para (b) inserted by the Finance Act 1997, s 27(1), (2).

[3558]

54 Accounting for tax and time for payment

Regulations may provide that a registrable person shall—

(a) account for tax by reference to such periods (accounting periods) as may be determined by or under the regulations;

(b) make, in relation to accounting periods, returns in such form as may be prescribed and at such times as may be so determined;

(c) pay tax at such times and in such manner as may be so determined.

NOTES

Regulations: the Insurance Premium Tax Regulations 1994, SI 1994/1774 at **[4075]**.

[3559]

55 Credit

(1) Regulations may provide that where an insurer [or taxable intermediary] has paid tax and all or part of the premium [or taxable intermediary's fee (as the case may be)] is repaid, the insurer [or taxable intermediary] shall be entitled to credit of such an amount as is found in accordance with prescribed rules.

(2) Regulations may provide that where—

(a) by virtue of regulations made under section 68 below tax is charged in relation to a premium which is shown in the accounts of an insurer as due to him,

(b) that tax is paid, and

(c) it is shown to the satisfaction of the Commissioners that the premium, or part of it, will never actually be received by or on behalf of the insurer,

the insurer shall be entitled to credit of such an amount as is found in accordance with prescribed rules.

(3) Regulations may make provision as to the manner in which an insurer [or taxable intermediary] is to benefit from credit, and in particular may make provision—

(a) that an insurer [or taxable intermediary] shall be entitled to credit by reference to accounting periods;

(b) that an insurer [or taxable intermediary] shall be entitled to deduct an amount equal to his total credit for an accounting period from the total amount of tax due from him for the period;

(c) that if no tax is due from an insurer [or taxable intermediary] for an accounting period but he is entitled to credit for the period, the amount of the credit shall be paid to him by the Commissioners;

(d) that if the amount of credit to which an insurer [or taxable intermediary] is entitled for an accounting period exceeds the amount of tax due from him for the period, an amount equal to the excess shall be paid to him by the Commissioners;

(e) for the whole or part of any credit to be held over to be credited for a subsequent accounting period;

(f) as to the manner in which a person who has ceased to be registrable [(whether under section 53 or section 53AA)] is to benefit from credit.

(4) Regulations under subsection (3)(c) or (d) above may provide that where at the end of an accounting period an amount is due to an insurer [or taxable intermediary] who has failed to submit returns for an earlier period as required by this Part, the Commissioners may withhold payment of the amount until he has complied with that requirement.

(5) Regulations under subsection (3)(e) above may provide for credit to be held over either on the insurer's [or taxable intermediary's] application or in accordance with general or special directions given by the Commissioners from time to time.

(6) Regulations may provide that—

(a) no deduction or payment shall be made in respect of credit except on a claim made in such manner and at such time as may be determined by or under regulations;

(b) payment in respect of credit shall be made subject to such conditions (if any) as the Commissioners think fit to impose, including conditions as to repayment in specified circumstances;

(c) deduction in respect of credit shall be made subject to such conditions (if any) as the Commissioners think fit to impose, including conditions as to the payment to the Commissioners, in specified circumstances, of an amount representing the whole or part of the amount deducted.

(7) Regulations may require a claim by an insurer [or taxable intermediary] to be made in a return required by provision made under section 54 above.

(8) Regulations may provide that where—

(a) all or any of the tax payable in respect of a premium [or taxable intermediary's fee] has not been paid, and

(b) the circumstances are such that a person would be entitled to credit if the tax had been paid,

prescribed adjustments shall be made as regards any amount of tax due from any person.

NOTES

Sub-ss (1), (3)–(5), (7), (8): words in square brackets inserted by the Finance Act 1997, s 27(1), (3).

Regulations: the Insurance Premium Tax Regulations 1994, SI 1994/1774 at **[4075]**.

[3560]–[3562]

56 Power to assess

(1) In a case where—

(a) a person has failed to make any returns required to be made under this Part,

(b) a person has failed to keep any documents necessary to verify returns required to be made under this Part,

(c) a person has failed to afford the facilities necessary to verify returns required to be made under this Part, or

(d) it appears to the Commissioners that returns required to be made by a person under this Part are incomplete or incorrect,

the Commissioners may assess the amount of tax due from the person concerned to the best of their judgment and notify it to him.

(2) Where a person has for an accounting period been paid an amount to which he purports to be entitled under regulations made under section 55 above, then, to the extent that the amount ought not to have been paid or would not have been paid had the facts been known or been as they later turn out to be, the Commissioners may assess the amount as being tax due from him for that period and notify it to him accordingly.

(3) Where a person is assessed under subsections (1) and (2) above in respect of the same accounting period the assessments may be combined and notified to him as one assessment.

(4) Where the person failing to make a return, or making a return which appears to the Commissioners to be incomplete or incorrect, was required to make the return as a personal representative, trustee in bankruptcy, trustee in sequestration, receiver, liquidator or person otherwise acting in a representative capacity in relation to another person, subsection (1) above shall apply as if the reference to tax due from him included a reference to tax due from that other person.

(5) An assessment under subsection (1) or (2) above of an amount of tax due for an accounting period shall not be made after the later of the following—

(a) two years after the end of the accounting period;

(b) one year after evidence of facts, sufficient in the Commissioners' opinion to justify the making of the assessment, comes to their knowledge;

but where further such evidence comes to their knowledge after the making of an assessment under subsection (1) or (2) above another assessment may be made under the subsection concerned in addition to any earlier assessment.

(6) In a case where—

(a) as a result of a person's failure to make a return for an accounting period the Commissioners have made an assessment under subsection (1) above for that period,

(b) the tax assessed has been paid but no proper return has been made for the period to which the assessment related, and

(c) as a result of a failure to make a return for a later accounting period, being a failure by the person referred to in paragraph (a) above or a person acting in a representative capacity in relation to him, as mentioned in subsection (4) above, the Commissioners find it necessary to make another assessment under subsection (1) above,

then, if the Commissioners think fit, having regard to the failure referred to in paragraph (a) above, they may specify in the assessment referred to in paragraph (c) above an amount of tax greater than that which they would otherwise have considered to be appropriate.

(7) Where an amount has been assessed and notified to any person under subsection (1) or (2) above it shall be deemed to be an amount of tax due from him and may be recovered accordingly unless, or except to the extent that, the assessment has subsequently been withdrawn or reduced.
(8) For the purposes of this section notification to—
(a) a personal representative, trustee in bankruptcy, trustee in sequestration, receiver or liquidator, or
(b) a person otherwise acting in a representative capacity in relation to another person,
shall be treated as notification to the person in relation to whom the person mentioned in paragraph (a) above, or the first person mentioned in paragraph (b) above, acts.

57, 58 *(Repealed by the Finance Act 2008, s 142(1)(a).)*

Review and appeal

[3563]
59 [Appeals]
[(1) Subject to section 60, an appeal shall lie to an appeal tribunal from any person who is or will be affected by any decision of HMRC with respect to the any of the following matters—]
(a) the registration or cancellation of registration of any person under this Part;
(b) whether tax is chargeable in respect of a premium or how much tax is chargeable;
[(bb) whether a payment falls to be treated under section 52A(2) above as a premium received under a taxable insurance contract by an insurer and chargeable to tax at the higher rate;]
(c) whether a person is entitled to credit by virtue of regulations under section 55 above or how much credit a person is entitled to or the manner in which he is to benefit from credit;
(d) an assessment [falling within subsection (1A) below] or the amount of such an assessment;
(e) any refusal of an application under section 63 below;
(f) whether a notice may be served on a person by virtue of regulations made under section 65 below;
(g) an assessment under regulations made under section 65 below or the amount of such an assessment;
(h) whether a scheme established by regulations under section 68 below applies to an insurer as regards an accounting period;
(i) the requirement of any security under paragraph 24 of Schedule 7 to this Act or its amount;
(j) any liability to a penalty under paragraphs 12 to 19 of Schedule 7 to this Act;
(k) the amount of any penalty or interest specified in an assessment under paragraph 25 of Schedule 7 to this Act;
(l) a claim for the repayment of an amount under paragraph 8 of Schedule 7 to this Act;
(m) any liability of the Commissioners to pay interest under paragraph 22 of Schedule 7 to this Act or the amount of the interest payable.
[(1A) An assessment falls within this subsection if it is an assessment under section 56 above in respect of an accounting period in relation to which a return required to be made by virtue of regulations under section 54 above has been made.]
(2)–(8) . . .

NOTES

Section heading: substituted by the Transfer of Tribunal Functions and Revenue and Customs Appeals Order 2009, SI 2009/56, art 3(1), Sch 1, para 205(1), (2), subject to savings and transitional provisions in art 6 of, and Sch 3 to, that Order.

Sub-s (1): opening para substituted by SI 2009/56, art 3(1), Sch 1, para 205(1), (3), subject to savings and transitional provisions in art 6 of, and Sch 3 to, that Order; para (bb) inserted by the Finance Act 1997, s 27(1), (6); words in square brackets in para (d) substituted by the Finance Act 1995, s 34, Sch 5, para 5(1), (2), (4).

Sub-s (1A): inserted by the Finance Act 1995, s 34, Sch 5, para 5(1), (3), (4).

Sub-ss (2)–(8): repealed by SI 2009/56, art 3(1), Sch 1, para 205(1), (4), subject to savings and transitional provisions in art 6 of, and Sch 3 to, that Order.

[3563A]
[59A Offer of review
(1) HMRC must offer a person (P) a review of a decision that has been notified to P if an appeal lies under section 59 in respect of the decision.
(2) The offer of the review must be made by notice given to P at the same time as the decision is notified to P.
(3) This section does not apply to the notification of the conclusions of a review.]

NOTES

Commencement: 1 April 2009.

Inserted, together with ss 59B–59G, by the Transfer of Tribunal Functions and Revenue and Customs Appeals Order 2009, SI 2009/56, art 3(1), Sch 1, para 206, subject to savings and transitional provisions in art 6 of, and Sch 3 to, that Order.

[3563B]

[59B Right to require review

(1) Any person (other than P) who has the right of appeal under section 59 against a decision may require HMRC to review that decision if that person has not appealed to the appeal tribunal under section 59G.

(2) A notification that such a person requires a review must be made within 30 days of that person becoming aware of the decision.]

NOTES

Commencement: 1 April 2009.

Inserted as noted to s 59A at **[3563A]**.

[3563C]

[59C Review by HMRC

(1) HMRC must review a decision if—

(a) they have offered a review of the decision under section 59A, and

(b) P notifies HMRC accepting the offer within 30 days from the date of the document containing the notification of the offer.

(2) But P may not notify acceptance of the offer if P has already appealed to the appeal tribunal under section 59G.

(3) HMRC must review a decision if a person other than P notifies them under section 59B.

(4) HMRC shall not review a decision if P, or another person, has appealed to the appeal tribunal under section 59G in respect of the decision.]

NOTES

Commencement: 1 April 2009.

Inserted as noted to s 59A at **[3563A]**.

[3563D]

[59D Extensions of time

(1) If under section 59A HMRC have offered P a review of a decision, HMRC may within the relevant period notify P that the relevant period is extended.

(2) If under section 59B another person may require HMRC to review a matter, HMRC may within the relevant period notify the other person that the relevant period is extended.

(3) If notice is given the relevant period is extended to the end of 30 days from—

(a) the date of the notice, or

(b) any other date set out in the notice or a further notice.

(4) In this section "relevant period" means—

(a) the period of 30 days referred to in—

(i) section 59C(1)(b) (in a case falling within subsection (1)), or

(ii) section 59B(2) (in a case falling within subsection (2)), or

(b) if notice has been given under subsection (1) or (2), that period as extended (or as most recently extended) in accordance with subsection (3).]

NOTES

Commencement: 1 April 2009.

Inserted as noted to s 59A at **[3563A]**.

[3563E]

[59E Review out of time

(1) This section applies if—

(a) HMRC have offered a review of a decision under section 59A and P does not accept the offer within the time allowed under section 59C(1)(b) or 59D(3); or

(b) a person who requires a review under section 59B does not notify HMRC within the time allowed under that section or section 59D(3).

(2) HMRC must review the decision under section 59C if—

(a) after the time allowed, P, or the other person, notifies HMRC in writing requesting a review out of time,

Part III Statutes

(b) HMRC are satisfied that P, or the other person, had a reasonable excuse for not accepting the offer or requiring review within the time allowed, and

(c) HMRC are satisfied that P, or the other person, made the request without unreasonable delay after the excuse had ceased to apply.

(3) HMRC shall not review a decision if P, or another person, has appealed to the appeal tribunal under section 59G in respect of the decision.]

NOTES

Commencement: 1 April 2009.
Inserted as noted to s 59A at **[3563A]**.

[3563F]
[59F Nature of review etc

(1) This section applies if HMRC are required to undertake a review under section 59C or 59E.

(2) The nature and extent of the review are to be such as appear appropriate to HMRC in the circumstances.

(3) For the purpose of subsection (2), HMRC must, in particular, have regard to steps taken before the beginning of the review—

(a) by HMRC in reaching the decision, and

(b) by any person in seeking to resolve disagreement about the decision.

(4) The review must take account of any representations made by P, or the other person, at a stage which gives HMRC a reasonable opportunity to consider them.

(5) The review may conclude that the decision is to be—

(a) upheld,

(b) varied, or

(c) cancelled.

(6) HMRC must give P, or the other person, notice of the conclusions of the review and their reasoning within—

(a) a period of 45 days beginning with the relevant date, or

(b) such other period as HMRC and P, or the other person, may agree.

(7) In subsection (6) "relevant date" means—

(a) the date HMRC received P's notification accepting the offer of a review (in a case falling within section 59A), or

(b) the date HMRC received notification from another person requiring review (in a case falling within section 59B), or

(c) the date on which HMRC decided to undertake the review (in a case falling within section 59E).

(8) Where HMRC are required to undertake a review but do not give notice of the conclusions within the time period specified in subsection (6), the review is to be treated as having concluded that the decision is upheld.

(9) If subsection (8) applies, HMRC must notify P or the other person of the conclusion which the review is treated as having reached.]

NOTES

Commencement: 1 April 2009.
Inserted as noted to s 59A at **[3563A]**.

[3563G]
[59G Bringing of appeals

(1) An appeal under section 59 is to be made to the appeal tribunal before—

(a) the end of the period of 30 days beginning with—

(i) in a case where P is the appellant, the date of the document notifying the decision to which the appeal relates, or

(ii) in a case where a person other than P is the appellant, the date that person becomes aware of the decision, or

(b) if later, the end of the relevant period (within the meaning of section 59D).

(2) But that is subject to subsections (3) to (5).

(3) In a case where HMRC are required to undertake a review under section 59C—

(a) an appeal may not be made until the conclusion date, and

(b) any appeal is to be made within the period of 30 days beginning with the conclusion date.

(4) In a case where HMRC are requested to undertake a review by virtue of section 59E—

(a) an appeal may not be made—

(i) unless HMRC have decided whether or not to undertake a review, and
(ii) if HMRC decide to undertake a review, until the conclusion date; and
(b) any appeal is to be made within the period of 30 days beginning with—
(i) the conclusion date (if HMRC decide to undertake a review), or
(ii) the date on which HMRC decide not to undertake a review.

(5) In a case where section 59F(8) applies, an appeal may be made at any time from the end of the period specified in section 59F(6) to the date 30 days after the conclusion date.

(6) An appeal may be made after the end of the period specified in subsection (1), (3)(b), (4)(b) or (5) if the appeal tribunal gives permission to do so.

(7) In this section "conclusion date" means the date of the document notifying the conclusion of the review.]

NOTES

Commencement: 1 April 2009.
Inserted as noted to s 59A at **[3563A]**.

[3564]

60 [Further provisions relating to appeals]

(1) . . .

(2) Without prejudice to paragraph 13 of Schedule 7 to this Act, nothing in [section 59] above shall be taken to confer on a tribunal any power to vary an amount assessed by way of penalty or interest except in so far as it is necessary to reduce it to the amount which is appropriate under paragraphs 12 to 21 of that Schedule.

(3) . . .

[(4) Subject to subsections (4A) and (4B), where the appeal is against the decisions with respect to any of the matters mentioned in section 59(1)(b) and (d), it shall not be entertained unless the amount which HMRC have determined to be payable as tax has been paid or deposited with them.

(4A) In a case where the amount determined to be payable as tax has not been paid or deposited an appeal shall be entertained if—
(a) HMRC are satisfied (on the application of the appellant), or
(b) the appeal tribunal decides (HMRC not being so satisfied and on the application of the appellant),

that the requirement to pay or deposit the amount determined would cause the appellant to suffer hardship.

(4B) Notwithstanding the provisions of sections 11 and 13 of the Tribunals, Courts and Enforcement Act 2007, the decision of the appeal tribunal as to the issue of hardship is final.]

(5) Where on an appeal against a decision with respect to any of the matters mentioned in section 59(1)(d) above—
(a) it is found that the amount specified in the assessment is less than it ought to have been, and
(b) the tribunal gives a direction specifying the correct amount,

the assessment shall have effect as an assessment of the amount specified in the direction and that amount shall be deemed to have been notified to the appellant.

(6) Where on an appeal under this section it is found that the whole or part of any amount paid or deposited in pursuance of subsection (4) above is not due, so much of that amount as is found not to be due shall be repaid with interest [at the rate applicable under section 197 of the Finance Act 1996].

(7) Where on an appeal under this section it is found that the whole or part of any amount due to the appellant by virtue of regulations under section 55(3)(c) or (d) or (f) above has not been paid, so much of that amount as is found not to have been paid shall be paid with interest [at the rate applicable under section 197 of the Finance Act 1996].

(8) Where an appeal under this section has been entertained notwithstanding that an amount determined by [HMRC] to be payable as tax has not been paid or deposited and it is found on the appeal that that amount is due [it shall be paid with interest at the rate applicable under section 197 of the Finance Act 1996].

[(8A) Interest under subsection (8) shall be paid without any deduction of income tax.]

(9) On an appeal against an assessment to a penalty under paragraph 12 of Schedule 7 to this Act, the burden of proof as to the matters specified in paragraphs (a) and (b) of sub-paragraph (1) of paragraph 12 shall lie upon [HMRC].

[(10) Sections 85 and 85B of the Value Added Tax Act 1994 (settling of appeals by agreement and payment of tax where there is a further appeal) shall have effect as if—
(a) the references to section 83 of that Act included references to section 59 above, and
(b) the references to value added tax included references to insurance premium tax.]

Part III Statutes

NOTES

Section heading: substituted by the Transfer of Tribunal Functions and Revenue and Customs Appeals Order 2009, SI 2009/56, art 3(1), Sch 1, para 207(1), (2), subject to savings and transitional provisions in art 6 of, and Sch 3 to, that Order.

Sub-ss (1), (3): repealed by SI 2009/56, art 3(1), Sch 1, para 207(1), (3), (5), subject to savings and transitional provisions in art 6 of, and Sch 3 to, that Order.

Sub-s (2): words in square brackets substituted by SI 2009/56, art 3(1), Sch 1, para 207(1), (4), subject to savings and transitional provisions in art 6 of, and Sch 3 to, that Order.

Sub-ss (4)–(4B): substituted for original sub-s (4) by SI 2009/56, art 3(1), Sch 1, para 207(1), (6), subject to savings and transitional provisions in art 6 of, and Sch 3 to, that Order.

Sub-ss (6)–(8): words in square brackets substituted by SI 2009/56, art 3(1), Sch 1, para 207(1), (7)–(9), subject to savings and transitional provisions in art 6 of, and Sch 3 to, that Order.

Sub-s (8A): inserted by SI 2009/56, art 3(1), Sch 1, para 207(1), (10), subject to savings and transitional provisions in art 6 of, and Sch 3 to, that Order.

Sub-s (9): reference in square brackets substituted by SI 2009/56, art 3(1), Sch 1, para 207(1), (11), subject to savings and transitional provisions in art 6 of, and Sch 3 to, that Order.

Sub-s (10): substituted by SI 2009/56, art 3(1), Sch 1, para 207(1), (12), subject to savings and transitional provisions in art 6 of, and Sch 3 to, that Order.

[3565]

61 Review and appeal: commencement

Sections 59 and 60 above shall come into force on such day as may be appointed by order.

NOTES

Orders: the Finance Act 1994 (Appointed Day) Order 1994, SI 1994/1773.

Miscellaneous

[3566]

62 Partnership, bankruptcy, transfer of business, etc

(1) Regulations may make provision for determining by what persons anything required by this Part to be done by an insurer [or taxable intermediary] is to be done where the business concerned is carried on in partnership or by another unincorporated body.

(2) The registration under this Part of an unincorporated body other than a partnership may be in the name of the body concerned; and in determining whether premiums are received by such a body no account shall be taken of any change in its members.

(3) Regulations may make provision for determining by what person anything required by this Part to be done by an insurer is to be done in a case where insurance business is carried on by persons who are underwriting members of Lloyd's and are members of a syndicate of such underwriting members.

(4) Regulations may—

- (a) make provision for the registration for the purposes of this Part of a syndicate of underwriting members of Lloyd's;
- (b) provide that for purposes prescribed by the regulations no account shall be taken of any change in the members of such a syndicate;

and regulations under paragraph (a) above may modify section 53 above.

(5) As regards any case where a person carries on a business of an insurer [or taxable intermediary] who has died or become bankrupt or incapacitated or been sequestrated, or of an insurer [or taxable intermediary] which is in liquidation or receivership or [administration], regulations may—

- (a) require the person to inform the Commissioners of the fact that he is carrying on the business and of the event that has led to his carrying it on;
- (b) make provision allowing the person to be treated for a limited time as if he were the insurer [or taxable intermediary];
- (c) make provision for securing continuity in the application of this Part where a person is so treated.

(6) Regulations may make provision for securing continuity in the application of this Part in cases where a business carried on by a person is transferred to another person as a going concern.

(7) Regulations under subsection (6) above may in particular provide—

- (a) for liabilities and duties under this Part of the transferor to become, to such extent as may be provided by the regulations, liabilities and duties of the transferee;
- (b) for any right of either of them to repayment or credit in respect of tax to be satisfied by making a repayment or allowing a credit to the other;

but the regulations may provide that no such provision as is mentioned in paragraph (a) or (b) of this subsection shall have effect in relation to any transferor and transferee unless an application in that behalf has been made by them under the regulations.

NOTES

Sub-s (1): words in square brackets inserted by the Finance Act 1997, s 27(1), (7).

Sub-s (5): words in first, second and fourth pairs of square brackets inserted by the Finance Act 1997, s 27(1), (7); word in third pair of square brackets substituted by the Enterprise Act 2002 (Insolvency) Order 2003, SI 2003/2096, art 4, Schedule, Pt 1, paras 1, 23, except in relation to any case where a petition for an administration order was presented before 15 September 2003.

Regulations: the Insurance Premium Tax Regulations 1994, SI 1994/1774 at **[4075]**.

[3567]

63 Groups of companies

(1) Where under the following provisions of this section any bodies corporate are treated as members of a group, for the purposes of this Part—

- (a) any taxable business carried on by a member of the group shall be treated as carried on by the representative member,
- [(aa) any business carried on by a member of the group who is a taxable intermediary shall be treated as carried on by the representative member,]
- (b) the representative member shall be taken to be the insurer in relation to any taxable insurance contract as regards which a member of the group is the actual insurer,
- [(bb) the representative member shall be taken to be the taxable intermediary in relation to any taxable intermediary's fees as regards which a member of the group is the actual taxable intermediary,]
- (c) any receipt by a member of the group of a premium under a taxable insurance contract shall be taken to be a receipt by the representative member, and
- (d) all members of the group shall be jointly and severally liable for any tax due from the representative member.

(2) Two or more bodies corporate are eligible to be treated as members of a group if each of them falls within subsection (3) below and—

- (a) one of them controls each of the others,
- (b) one person (whether a body corporate or an individual) controls all of them, or
- (c) two or more individuals carrying on a business in partnership control all of them.

(3) A body falls within this subsection if it is resident in the United Kingdom or it has an established place of business in the United Kingdom.

(4) Where an application to that effect is made to the Commissioners with respect to two or more bodies corporate eligible to be treated as members of a group, then—

- (a) from the beginning of an accounting period they shall be so treated, and
- (b) one of them shall be the representative member,

unless the Commissioners refuse the application; and the Commissioners shall not refuse the application unless it appears to them necessary to do so for the protection of the revenue.

(5) Where any bodies corporate are treated as members of a group and an application to that effect is made to the Commissioners, then, from the beginning of an accounting period—

- (a) a further body eligible to be so treated shall be included among the bodies so treated,
- (b) a body corporate shall be excluded from the bodies so treated,
- (c) another member of the group shall be substituted as the representative member, or
- (d) the bodies corporate shall no longer be treated as members of a group,

unless the application is to the effect mentioned in paragraph (a) or (c) above and the Commissioners refuse the application.

(6) The Commissioners may refuse an application under subsection (5)(a) or (c) above only if it appears to them necessary to do so for the protection of the revenue.

(7) Where a body corporate is treated as a member of a group as being controlled by any person and it appears to the Commissioners that it has ceased to be so controlled, they shall, by notice given to that person, terminate that treatment from such date as may be specified in the notice.

(8) An application under this section with respect to any bodies corporate must be made by one of those bodies or by the person controlling them and must be made not less than 90 days before the date from which it is to take effect, or at such later time as the Commissioners may allow.

(9) For the purposes of this section a body corporate shall be taken to control another body corporate if it is empowered by statute to control that body's activities or if it is that body's holding company within the meaning of section [1159 of and Schedule 6 to] the Companies Act [2006]; and an individual or individuals shall be taken to control a body corporate if he or they, were he or they a company, would be that body's holding company within the meaning of [those provisions].

NOTES

Sub-s (1): paras (aa), (bb) inserted by the Finance Act 1997, s 27(1), (8).

Sub-s (9): words in square brackets substituted by the Companies Act 2006 (Consequential Amendments) (Taxes and National Insurance) Order 2009, SI 2009/1890, art 4(1)(b).

[3568]

64 Information, powers, penalties, etc

Schedule 7 to this Act (which contains provisions relating to information, powers, penalties and other matters) shall have effect.

[3569]

65 Liability of insured in certain cases

(1) Regulations may make provision under this section with regard to any case where at any time [the insurer—

(a) does not have any business establishment or other fixed establishment in the United Kingdom, and

(b) is established in a country or territory in respect of which it appears to the Commissioners that the condition in subsection (1A) below is met].

[(1A) The condition mentioned in subsection (1)(b) above is that—

(a) the country or territory is neither a member State nor a part of a member State, and

(b) there is no provision for mutual assistance between the United Kingdom and the country or territory similar in scope to the assistance provided for between the United Kingdom and each other member State by the mutual assistance provisions.

(1B) In subsection (1A) above "the mutual assistance provisions" means—

(a) section 134 of, and Schedule 39 to, the Finance Act 2002 (recovery of taxes etc due in other member States), and

(b) section 197 of the Finance Act 2003 (exchange of information between tax authorities of member States).]

(2) Regulations may make provision allowing notice to be served in accordance with the regulations on—

(a) the person who is insured under a taxable insurance contract, if there is one insured person, or

(b) one or more of the persons who are insured under a taxable insurance contract, if there are two or more insured persons;

and a notice so served is referred to in this section as a liability notice.

(3) Regulations may provide that if a liability notice has been served in accordance with the regulations—

(a) the Commissioners may assess to the best of their judgment the amount of any tax due in respect of premiums received by the insurer under the contract concerned after the material date and before the date of the assessment, and

(b) that amount shall be deemed to be the amount of tax so due.

(4) The material date is—

(a) where there is one person on whom a liability notice has been served in respect of the contract, the date when the notice was served or such later date as may be specified in the notice;

(b) where there are two or more persons on whom liability notices have been served in respect of the contract, the date when the last of the notices was served or such later date as may be specified in the notices.

(5) Regulations may provide that where—

(a) an assessment is made in respect of a contract under provision included in the regulations by virtue of subsection (3) above, and

(b) the assessment is notified to the person, or each of the persons, on whom a liability notice in respect of the contract has been served,

the persons mentioned in subsection (6) below shall be jointly and severally liable to pay the tax assessed, and that tax shall be recoverable accordingly.

(6) The persons are—

(a) the person or persons mentioned in subsection (5)(b) above, and

(b) the insurer.

(7) Where regulations make provision under subsection (5) above they must also provide that any provision made under that subsection shall not apply if, or to the extent that, the assessment has subsequently been withdrawn or reduced.

(8) Regulations may make provision as to the time within which, and the manner in which, tax which has been assessed is to be paid.

(9) Where any amount is recovered from an insured person by virtue of regulations made under this section, the insurer shall be liable to pay to the insured person an amount equal to the amount recovered; and regulations may make provision requiring an insurer to pay interest where this subsection applies.

(10) Regulations may make provision for adjustments to be made of a person's liability in any case where—

(a) an assessment is made under section 56 above in relation to the insurer, and

(b) an assessment made by virtue of regulations under this section relates to premiums received (or assumed for the purposes of the assessment to be received) within a period which corresponds to any extent with the accounting period to which the assessment under section 56 relates.

(11) Regulations may make provision as regards a case where—

(a) an assessment made in respect of a contract by virtue of regulations under this section relates to premiums received (or assumed for the purposes of the assessment to be received) within a given period, and

(b) an amount of tax is paid by the insurer in respect of an accounting period which corresponds to any extent with that period;

and the regulations may include provision for determining whether, or how much of, any of the tax paid as mentioned in paragraph (b) above is attributable to premiums received under the contract in the period mentioned in paragraph (a) above.

(12) Regulations may—

(a) make provision requiring the Commissioners, in prescribed circumstances, to furnish prescribed information to an insured person;

(b) make provision requiring any person on whom a liability notice has been served to keep records, to furnish information, or to produce documents for inspection or cause documents to be produced for inspection;

(c) make such provision as the Commissioners think is reasonable for the purpose of facilitating the recovery of tax from the persons having joint and several liability (rather than from the insurer alone);

(d) modify the effect of any provision of this Part.

(13) Regulations may provide for an insured person to be liable to pay tax assessed by virtue of the regulations notwithstanding that he has already paid an amount representing tax as part of a premium.

NOTES

Sub-s (1): words in square brackets substituted by the Finance Act 2008, ss 142(1)(b), 143(1), (2).

Sub-ss (1A), (1B): inserted by the Finance Act 2008, s 143(1), (3).

Regulations: the Insurance Premium Tax Regulations 1994, SI 1994/1774 at **[4075]**.

[3570]

66 Directions as to amounts of premiums

(1) This section applies where—

(a) anything is received by way of premium under a taxable insurance contract, and

(b) the amount of the premium is less than it would be if it were received under the contract in open market conditions.

(2) The Commissioners may direct that the amount of the premium shall be taken for the purposes of this Part to be such amount as it would be if it were received under the contract in open market conditions.

(3) A direction under subsection (2) above shall be given by notice in writing to the insurer, and no direction may be given more than three years after the time of the receipt.

(4) Where the Commissioners make a direction under subsection (2) above in the case of a contract they may also direct that if—

(a) anything is received by way of premium under the contract after the giving of the notice or after such later date as may be specified in the notice, and

(b) the amount of the premium is less than it would be if it were received under the contract in open market conditions,

the amount of the premium shall be taken for the purposes of this Part to be such amount as it would be if it were received under the contract in open market conditions.

(5) For the purposes of this section a premium is received in open market conditions if it is received—

(a) by an insurer standing in no such relationship with the insured person as would affect the premium, and

(b) in circumstances where there is no other contract or arrangement affecting the parties.

(6) For the purpose of this section it is immaterial whether what is received by way of premium is money or something other than money or both.

[3571]
67 Deemed date of receipt of certain premiums

(1) In a case where—

(a) a premium under a contract of insurance is received by the insurer after 30th November 1993 and before 1st October 1994, and

(b) the period of cover for the risk begins on or after 1st October 1994,

for the purposes of this Part the premium shall be taken to be received on 1st October 1994.

(2) Subsection (3) below applies where—

(a) a premium under a contract of insurance is received by the insurer after 30th November 1993 and before 1st October 1994,

(b) the period of cover for the risk begins before 1st October 1994 and ends after 30th September 1995, and

(c) the premium, or any part of it, is attributable to such of the period of cover as falls after 30th September 1995.

(3) For the purposes of this Part—

(a) so much of the premium as is attributable to such of the period of cover as falls after 30th September 1995 shall be taken to be received on 1st October 1994;

(b) so much as is so attributable shall be taken to be a separate premium.

(4) If a contract relates to more than one risk subsection (1) above shall have effect as if the reference in paragraph (b) to the risk were to any given risk.

(5) If a contract relates to more than one risk, subsections (2) and (3) above shall apply as follows—

(a) so much of the premium as is attributable to any given risk shall be deemed for the purposes of those subsections to be a separate premium relating to that risk;

(b) those subsections shall then apply separately in the case of each given risk and the separate premium relating to it;

and any further attribution required by those subsections shall be made accordingly.

(6) Subsections (1) and (4) above do not apply in relation to a contract if the contract belongs to a class of contract as regards which the normal practice is for a premium to be received by or on behalf of the insurer before the date when cover begins.

(7) Subsections (2), (3) and (5) above do not apply in relation to a contract if the contract belongs to a class of contract as regards which the normal practice is for cover to be provided for a period exceeding twelve months.

(8) Any attribution under this section shall be made on such basis as is just and reasonable.

[3572]
[67A Announced increase in rate of tax: certain premiums treated as received on date of increase

(1) This section applies in any case where a proposed increase is announced by a Minister of the Crown in the rate at which tax is to be charged on a premium if it is received by the insurer on or after a date specified in the announcement ("the date of the change").

(2) In a case where—

(a) a premium under a contract of insurance is received by the insurer on or after the date of the announcement but before the date of the change, and

(b) the period of cover for the risk begins on or after the date of the change,

for the purposes of this Part the premium shall be taken to be received on the date of the change.

(3) Subsection (4) below applies where—

(a) a premium under a contract of insurance is received by the insurer on or after the date of the announcement but before the date of the change;

(b) the period of cover for the risk begins before the date of the change and ends on or after the first anniversary of the date of the change; and

(c) the premium, or any part of it, is attributable to such of the period of cover as falls on or after the first anniversary of the date of the change.

(4) For the purposes of this Part—

(a) so much of the premium as is attributable to such of the period of cover as falls on or after the first anniversary of the date of the change shall be taken to be received on the date of the change; and

(b) so much as is so attributable shall be taken to be a separate premium.

(5) In determining whether the condition in subsection (2)(a) or (3)(a) above is satisfied, the provisions of regulations made by virtue of subsection (3) or (7) of section 68 below apply as they would apart from this section; but, subject to that, where subsection (2) or (4) above applies—

(a) that subsection shall have effect notwithstanding anything in section 68 below or regulations made under that section; and

(b) any regulations made under that section shall have effect as if the entry made in the accounts of the insurer showing the premium as due to him had been made as at the date of the change.

(6) Any attribution under this section shall be made on such basis as is just and reasonable.

(7) In this section—

"increase", in relation to the rate of tax, includes the imposition of a charge to tax by adding to the descriptions of contract which are taxable insurance contracts;

"Minister of the Crown" has the same meaning as in the Ministers of the Crown Act 1975.]

NOTES

Inserted, together with ss 67B, 67C, by the Finance Act 1997, s 29(1), (3), with effect from 26 November 1996; for provision as to the application of these sections in relation to the increases in insurance premium tax effected by Part II of that Act, see s 29(2) of the 1997 Act at **[3613]**.

[3573]

[67B Announced increase in rate of tax: certain contracts treated as made on date of increase

(1) This section applies in any case where—

(a) an announcement falling within section 67A(1) above is made; but

(b) a proposed exception from the increase in question is also announced by a Minister of the Crown; and

(c) the proposed exception is to apply in relation to a premium only if the conditions described in subsection (2) below are satisfied in respect of the premium.

(2) Those conditions are—

(a) that the premium is in respect of a contract made before the date of the change;

(b) that the premium falls, by virtue of regulations under section 68 below, to be regarded for the purposes of this Part as received under the contract by the insurer before such date ("the concessionary date") as is specified for the purpose in the announcement.

(3) In a case where—

(a) a premium under a contract of insurance is received by the insurer on or after the date of the announcement but before the concessionary date, and

(b) the period of cover for the risk begins on or after the date of the change,

the rate of tax applicable in relation to the premium shall be determined as if the contract had been made on the date of the change.

(4) Subsection (5) below applies where—

(a) a premium under a contract of insurance is received by the insurer on or after the date of the announcement but before the concessionary date;

(b) the period of cover for the risk begins before the date of the change and ends on or after the first anniversary of the date of the change; and

(c) the premium, or any part of it, is attributable to such of the period of cover as falls on or after the first anniversary of the date of the change.

(5) Where this subsection applies—

(a) the rate of tax applicable in relation to so much of the premium as is attributable to such of the period of cover as falls on or after the first anniversary of the date of the change shall be determined as if the contract had been made on the date of the change; and

(b) so much of the premium as is so attributable shall be taken to be a separate premium.

(6) Any attribution under this section shall be made on such basis as is just and reasonable.

(7) In this section—

"the date of the change" has the same meaning as in section 67A above;

"Minister of the Crown" has the same meaning as in section 67A above.]

NOTES

Inserted as noted to s 67A at **[3572]**.

[3574]

[67C Announced increase in rate of tax: exceptions and apportionments

(1) Sections 67A(2) and 67B(3) above do not apply in relation to a premium if the risk to which that premium relates belongs to a class of risk as regards which the normal practice is for a premium to be received by or on behalf of the insurer before the date when cover begins.

(2) Sections 67A(3) and (4) and 67B(4) and (5) above do not apply in relation to a premium if the risk to which that premium relates belongs to a class of risk as regards which the normal practice is for cover to be provided for a period exceeding twelve months.
(3) If a contract relates to more than one risk, then, in the application of section 67A(2), 67A(3) and (4), 67B(3) or 67B(4) and (5) above—

(a) the reference in section 67A(2)(b) or (3)(b) or 67B(3)(b) or (4)(b), as the case may be, to the risk shall be taken as a reference to any given risk,

(b) so much of the premium as is attributable to any given risk shall be taken for the purposes of section 67A(2), 67A(3) and (4), 67B(3) or 67B(4) and (5) above, as the case may be, to be a separate premium relating to that risk,

(c) those provisions shall then apply separately in the case of each given risk and the separate premium relating to it, and

(d) any further attribution required by section 67A(3) and (4) or 67B(4) and (5) above shall be made accordingly,

and subsections (1) and (2) above shall apply accordingly.
(4) Any attribution under this section shall be made on such basis as is just and reasonable.]

NOTES

Inserted as noted to s 67A at **[3572]**.

[3575]
68 Special accounting schemes
(1) Regulations may make provision establishing a scheme in accordance with the following provisions of this section; and in this section "a relevant accounting period", in relation to an insurer, means an accounting period as regards which the scheme applies to the insurer.
(2) Regulations may provide that if an insurer notifies the Commissioners that the scheme should apply to him as regards accounting periods beginning on or after a date specified in the notification and prescribed conditions are fulfilled, then, subject to any provision made under subsection (9) below, the scheme shall apply to the insurer as regards accounting periods beginning on or after that date.
(3) Regulations may provide that where—

(a) an entry is made in the accounts of an insurer showing a premium under a taxable insurance contract as due to him, and

(b) the entry is made as at a particular date which falls within a relevant accounting period,

then (whether or not that date is one on which the premium is actually received by the insurer or on which the premium would otherwise be treated for the purposes of this Part as received by him) the premium shall for the purposes of this Part be taken to be received by the insurer on that date or, in prescribed circumstances, to be received by him on a different date determined in accordance with the regulations.
(4) Where regulations make provision under subsection (3) above they may also provide that, for the purposes of this Part, the amount of the premium shall be taken to be the amount which the entry in the accounts treats as its amount.
(5) Regulations may provide that provision made under subsections (3) and (4) above shall apply even if the premium, or part of it, is never actually received by the insurer or on his behalf; and the regulations may include provision that, where the premium is never actually received because the contract under which it would have been received is never entered into or is terminated, the premium is nonetheless to be taken for the purposes of this Part to be received under a taxable insurance contract.
(6) Regulations may provide that any provision made under subsection (4) above shall be subject to any directions made under section 66 above.
(7) Regulations may provide that where a premium is treated as received on a particular date by virtue of provision made under subsection (3) above and there is another date on which the premium—

(a) is actually received by the insurer, or

(b) would, apart from the regulations, be treated for the purposes of this Part as received by him,

the premium shall be taken for the purposes of this Part not to be received by him on that other date.
(8) Regulations may provide that provision made under subsection (7) above shall apply only to the extent that there is no excess of the actual amount of the premium over the amount which, by virtue of regulations under this section or of a direction under section 66 above, is to be taken for the purposes of this Part to be its amount; and the regulations may include provision that where

there is such an excess, the excess amount shall be taken for the purposes of this Part to be a separate premium and to be received by the insurer on a date determined in accordance with the regulations.

(9) Regulations may provide that if a notification has been given in accordance with provision made under subsection (2) above and subsequently—

(a) the insurer gives notice to the Commissioners that the scheme should not apply to him as regards accounting periods beginning on or after a date specified in the notice, or

(b) the Commissioners give notice to the insurer that the scheme is not to apply to him as regards accounting periods beginning on or after a date specified in the notice,

then, if prescribed conditions are fulfilled, the scheme shall not apply to the insurer as regards an accounting period beginning on or after the date specified in the notice mentioned in paragraph (a) or (b) above unless the circumstances are such as may be prescribed.

(10) Regulations may include provision—

(a) enabling an insurer to whom the scheme applies as regards an accounting period to account for tax due in respect of that period on the assumption that the scheme will apply to him as regards subsequent accounting periods;

(b) designed to secure that, where the scheme ceases to apply to an insurer, any tax which by virtue of provision made under paragraph (a) above has not been accounted for is accounted for and paid.

(11) Regulations may provide that where—

(a) an entry in the accounts of an insurer shows a premium as due to him,

(b) the entry is made as at a date falling before 1st October 1994,

(c) tax in respect of the receipt of the premium would, apart from the regulations, be charged by reference to a date (whether or not the date on which the premium is actually received by the insurer) falling on or after 1st October 1994,

(d) the date by reference to which tax would be charged falls within a relevant accounting period, and

(e) prescribed conditions are fulfilled,

the premium, or such part of it as may be found in accordance with prescribed rules, shall be taken for the purposes of this Part to have been received by the insurer before 1st October 1994.

(12) Without prejudice to subsection (13) below, regulations may include provision modifying any provision made under this section so as to secure the effective operation of the provision in a case where a premium consists wholly or partly of anything other than money.

(13) Regulations may modify the effect of any provision of this Part.

(14) The reference in subsection (3)(a) above to a premium under a taxable insurance contract includes a reference to anything that, although not actually received by or on behalf of the insurer, would be such a premium if it were so received.

NOTES

Regulations: the Insurance Premium Tax Regulations 1994, SI 1994/1774 at **[4075]**.

[3576]

[69 Charge to tax where different rates of tax apply

(1) This section applies for the purpose of determining the chargeable amount in a case where a contract provides cover falling within any one of the following paragraphs, that is to say—

(a) cover for one or more exempt matters,

(b) cover for one or more standard rate matters, or

(c) cover for one or more higher rate matters,

and also provides cover falling within another of those paragraphs.

(2) In the following provisions of this section "the non-exempt premium" means the difference between—

(a) the amount of the premium; and

(b) such part of the premium as is attributable to any exempt matter or matters or, if no part is so attributable, nil.

(3) If the contract provides cover for one or more exempt matters and also provides cover for either—

(a) one or more standard rate matters, or

(b) one or more higher rate matters,

the chargeable amount is such amount as, with the addition of the tax chargeable at the standard rate or (as the case may be) the higher rate, is equal to the non-exempt premium.

(4) If the contract provides cover for both—

(a) one or more standard rate matters, and

(b) one or more higher rate matters,

the higher rate element and the standard rate element shall be found in accordance with the following provisions of this section.

(5) For the purposes of this section—

(a) "the higher rate element" is such portion of the non-exempt premium as is attributable to the higher rate matters (including tax at the higher rate); and

(b) "the standard rate element" is the difference between—

(i) the non-exempt premium; and

(ii) the higher rate element.

(6) In a case falling within subsection (4) above, tax shall be charged separately—

(a) at the standard rate, by reference to the standard rate chargeable amount, and

(b) at the higher rate, by reference to the higher rate chargeable amount,

and the tax chargeable in respect of the premium is the aggregate of those amounts of tax.

(7) For the purposes of this section—

"the higher rate chargeable amount" is such amount as, with the addition of the tax chargeable at the higher rate, is equal to the higher rate element;

"the standard rate chargeable amount" is such amount as, with the addition of the tax chargeable at the standard rate, is equal to the standard rate element.

(8) References in this Part to the chargeable amount shall, in a case falling within subsection (4) above, be taken as referring separately to the standard rate chargeable amount and the higher rate chargeable amount.

(9) In applying subsection (2)(b) above, any amount that is included in the premium as being referable to tax (whether or not the amount corresponds to the actual amount of tax payable in respect of the premium) shall be taken to be wholly attributable to the non-exempt matter or matters.

(10) In applying subsection (5)(a) above, any amount that is included in the premium as being referable to tax at the higher rate (whether or not the amount corresponds to the actual amount of tax payable at that rate in respect of the premium) shall be taken to be wholly attributable to the higher rate element.

(11) Subject to subsections (9) and (10) above, any attribution under subsection (2)(b) or (5)(a) above shall be made on such basis as is just and reasonable.

(12) For the purposes of this section—

(a) an "exempt matter" is any matter such that, if it were the only matter for which the contract provided cover, the contract would not be a taxable insurance contract;

(b) a "non-exempt matter" is a matter which is not an exempt matter;

(c) a "standard rate matter" is any matter such that, if it were the only matter for which the contract provided cover, tax at the standard rate would be chargeable on the chargeable amount;

(d) a "higher rate matter" is any matter such that, if it were the only matter for which the contract provided cover, tax at the higher rate would be chargeable on the chargeable amount.

(13) If the contract relates to a lifeboat and lifeboat equipment, the lifeboat and the equipment shall be taken together in applying this section.

(14) For the purposes of this section "lifeboat" and "lifeboat equipment" have the same meaning as in paragraph 6 of Schedule 7A to this Act.]

NOTES

Substituted, in relation to a premium which falls to be regarded for the purposes of this Part as received under a taxable insurance contract by an insurer on or after 1 April 1997, by the Finance Act 1997, ss 23(1), 24(1); for further provision as to the effect of this amendment see s 24(2)–(4) of the 1997 Act at **[3612]**.

Supplementary

[3577]

70 Interpretation: taxable insurance contracts

(1) Subject to [subsection (1A) below], any contract of insurance is a taxable insurance contract.

[(1A) A contract is not a taxable insurance contract if it falls within one or more of the paragraphs of Part I of Schedule 7A to this Act.

(1B) Part II of Schedule 7A to this Act (interpretation of certain provisions of Part I) shall have effect.]

(2)–(10) . . .

(11) This section has effect subject to section 71 below.

(12) This section and section 71 below have effect for the purposes of this Part.

NOTES

Sub-s (1): words in square brackets substituted by the Insurance Premium Tax (Taxable Insurance Contracts) Order 1994, SI 1994/1698, art 4(a).

Sub-ss (1A), (1B): inserted by SI 1994/1698, art 4(b).

Sub-ss (2)–(10): repealed by SI 1994/1698, art 4(c).

[3578]

71 Taxable insurance contracts: power to change definition

(1) Provision may be made by order that—

(a) a contract of insurance that would otherwise not be a taxable insurance contract shall be a taxable insurance contract if it falls within a particular description;

(b) a contract of insurance that would otherwise be a taxable insurance contract shall not be a taxable insurance contract if it falls within a particular description.

(2) A description referred to in subsection (1) above may be by reference to the nature of the insured or by reference to such other factors as the Treasury think fit.

(3) Provision under this section may be made in such way as the Treasury think fit, and in particular may be made by amending this Part.

(4) An order under this section may amend or modify the effect of section 69 above in such way as the Treasury think fit.

NOTES

Orders: the Insurance Premium Tax (Taxable Insurance Contracts) Order 1994, SI 1994/1698; the Insurance Premium Tax (Taxable Insurance Contracts) Order 1996, SI 1996/2955; the Insurance Premium Tax (Taxable Insurance Contracts) Order 1997, SI 1997/1627.

[3579]

72 Interpretation: premium

(1) In relation to a taxable insurance contract, a premium is any payment received under the contract by the insurer, and in particular includes any payment wholly or partly referable to—

(a) any risk,

(b) costs of administration,

(c) commission,

(d) any facility for paying in instalments or making deferred payment (whether or not payment for the facility is called interest), or

(e) tax.

[(1A) Where an amount is charged to the insured by any person in connection with a taxable insurance contract, any payment in respect of that amount is to be regarded as a payment received under that contract by the insurer unless—

(a) the payment is chargeable to tax at the higher rate by virtue of section 52A above; or

(b) the amount is charged under a separate contract and is identified in writing to the insured as a separate amount so charged.]

[(1B) Where—

(a) an amount is charged (to the insured or any other person) in respect of the acquisition of a right (whether of the insured or any other person) to require the insurer to provide, or offer to provide, any of the cover included in a taxable insurance contract, and

(b) any payment in respect of that amount is not regarded as a payment received under that contract by the insurer by virtue of subsection (1A) above,

the payment is to be regarded as a payment received under that contract by the insurer unless it is chargeable to tax at the higher rate by virtue of section 52A above.]

(2) A premium may consist wholly or partly of anything other than money, and references to payment in subsection (1) above shall be construed accordingly.

(3) Where a premium is to any extent received in a form other than money, its amount shall be taken to be—

(a) an amount equal to the value of whatever is received in a form other than money, or

(b) if money is also received, the aggregate of the amount found under paragraph (a) above and the amount received in the form of money.

(4) The value to be taken for the purposes of subsection (3) above is open market value at the time of the receipt by the insurer.

(5) The open market value of anything at any time shall be taken to be an amount equal to such consideration in money as would be payable on a sale of it at that time to a person standing in no such relationship with any person as would affect that consideration.

(6) Where (apart from this subsection) anything received under a contract by the insurer would be taken to be an instalment of a premium, it shall be taken to be a separate premium.

(7) Where anything is received by any person on behalf of the insurer—

(a) it shall be treated as received by the insurer when it is received by the other person, and

(b) the later receipt of the whole or any part of it by the insurer shall be disregarded.

[(7A) Where any person is authorised by or on behalf of an employee to deduct from anything due to the employee under his contract of employment an amount in respect of a payment due under a taxable insurance contract, subsection (7) above shall not apply to the receipt on behalf of the insurer by the person so authorised of the amount deducted.]

(8) In a case where—

(a) a payment under a taxable insurance contract is made to a person (the intermediary) by or on behalf of the insured, and

(b) the whole or part of the payment is referable to commission to which the intermediary is entitled,

in determining for the purposes of subsection (7) above whether, or how much of, the payment is received by the intermediary on behalf of the insurer any of the payment that is referable to that commission shall be regarded as received by the intermediary on behalf of the insurer notwithstanding the intermediary's entitlement.

[(8A) Where, by virtue of subsection (7A) above, subsection (7) above does not apply to the receipt of an amount by a person and the whole or part of the amount is referable to commission to which he is entitled—

(a) if the whole of the amount is so referable, the amount shall be treated as received by the insurer when it is deducted by that person; and

(b) otherwise, the part of the amount that is so referable shall be treated as received by the insurer when the remainder of the payment concerned is or is treated as received by him.]

(9) References in subsection (8) above to a payment include references to a payment in a form other than money.

(10) This section has effect for the purposes of this Part.

NOTES

Sub-s (1A): inserted, in relation to payments received in respect of amounts charged on or after 1 April 1997, by the Finance Act 1997, s 28(1).

Sub-s (1B): inserted in relation to amounts charged on or after 22 March 2007, by the Finance Act 2007, s 101.

Sub-ss (7A), (8A): inserted, in relation to amounts deducted on or after 19 March 1997, by the Finance Act 1997, s 30.

[3580]

73 Interpretation: other provisions

(1) Unless the context otherwise requires—

"accounting period" shall be construed in accordance with section 54 above;

"appeal tribunal" means [the First-tier Tribunal or, where determined by or under Tribunal Procedure Rules, the Upper Tribunal;]

"authorised person" means any person acting under the authority of the Commissioners;

"the Commissioners" means the Commissioners of Customs and Excise;

"conduct" includes any act, omission or statement;

["the higher rate" shall be construed in accordance with section 51 above;]

["HMRC" means Her Majesty's Revenue and Customs;]

["insurance business" means a business which consists of or includes the provision of insurance;]

"insurer" means a person or body of persons (whether incorporated or not) carrying on insurance business;

"legislation relating to insurance premium tax" means this Part (as defined by subsection (9) below), any other enactment (whenever passed) relating to insurance premium tax, and any subordinate legislation made under any such enactment;

"prescribed" means prescribed by an order or regulations under this Part;

["the standard rate" shall be construed in accordance with section 51 above;]

"tax" means insurance premium tax;

. . .

"taxable business" means a business which consists of or includes the provision of insurance under taxable insurance contracts;

"taxable insurance contract" shall be construed in accordance with section 70 above.

["taxable intermediary" shall be construed in accordance with section 52A above;]

["taxable intermediary's fees" has the meaning given by section 53AA(9) above.]

(2) . . .

(3) [Subject to subsection (3A) below,] a registrable person is a person who—
  (a) is registered under section 53 above, or
  (b) is liable to be registered under that section.

[(3A) References in sections 53A and 54 above and paragraphs 1, 9 and 12 of Schedule 7 to this Act to a registrable person include a reference to a person who—
  (a) is registered under section 53AA above; or
  (b) is liable to be registered under that section.]

(4)–(8) . . .

(9) A reference to this Part includes a reference to any order or regulations made under it and a reference to a provision of this Part includes a reference to any order or regulations made under the provision, unless otherwise required by the context or any order or regulations.

(10) This section has effect for the purposes of this Part.

NOTES

Sub-s (1): words in square brackets in definition "appeals tribunal" substituted and definition "HMRC" inserted by the Transfer of Tribunal Functions and Revenue and Customs Appeals Order 2009, SI 2009/56, art 3(1), Sch 1, para 208, subject to savings and transitional provisions in art 6 of, and Sch 3 to, that Order; definition "insurance business" inserted by the Finance Act 1995, s 34, Sch 5, paras 1, 6; definition "tax representative" (omitted) repealed by the Finance Act 2008, s 142(1)(c); definitions "taxable intermediary" and "taxable intermediary's fees" inserted, and definitions "the higher rate" and "the standard rate" added in relation to a premium which falls to be regarded for the purposes of this Part as received under a taxable insurance contract by an insurer on or after 1 April 1997, by the Finance Act 1997, ss 21(2), 24(1), 27(1), (9), for further provision as to the effect of this amendment see s 24(2)–(4) of the 1997 Act at **[3612]**.

Sub-ss (2), (4)–(8): repealed by the Insurance Premium Tax (Taxable Insurance Contracts) Order 1994, SI 1994/1698, art 6.

Sub-s (3): words in square brackets inserted by the Finance Act 1997, s 27(1), (10).

Sub-s (3A): inserted by the Finance Act 1997, s 27(1), (10).

[3581]

74 Orders and regulations

(1) The power to make an order under section 61 above shall be exercisable by the Commissioners, and the power to make an order under any other provision of this Part shall be exercisable by the Treasury.

(2) Any power to make regulations under this Part shall be exercisable by the Commissioners.

(3) Any power to make an order or regulations under this Part shall be exercisable by statutory instrument.

(4) An order under section [51A or] 71 above shall be laid before the House of Commons; and unless it is approved by that House before the expiration of a period of 28 days beginning with the date on which it was made it shall cease to have effect on the expiration of that period, but without prejudice to anything previously done under the order or to the making of a new order.

(5) In reckoning any such period as is mentioned in subsection (4) above no account shall be taken of any time during which Parliament is dissolved or prorogued or during which the House of Commons is adjourned for more than four days.

(6) A statutory instrument containing an order or regulations under this Part (other than an order under section [51A or] 71 above) shall be subject to annulment in pursuance of a resolution of the House of Commons.

(7) Any power to make an order or regulations under this Part—
  (a) may be exercised as regards prescribed cases or descriptions of case;
  (b) may be exercised differently in relation to different cases or descriptions of case.

(8) An order or regulations under this Part may include such supplementary, incidental, consequential or transitional provisions as appear to the Treasury or the Commissioners (as the case may be) to be necessary or expedient.

(9) No specific provision of this Part about an order or regulations shall prejudice the generality of subsections (7) and (8) above.

NOTES

Sub-ss (4), (6): words in square brackets inserted, in relation to a premium which falls to be regarded for the purposes of this Part as received under a taxable insurance contract by an insurer on or after 1 April 1997, by the Finance Act 1997, ss 22(2), 24(1); for further provision as to the effect of these amendments see s 24(2)–(4) of the 1997 Act at **[3612]**.

75–248 *((Pts IV–VII) outside the scope of this work.)*

PART VIII
MISCELLANEOUS AND GENERAL

249–256 *(Outside the scope of this work.)*

General

[3582]

257 Interpretation and construction

(1) In this Act "the Taxes Act 1988" means the Income and Corporation Taxes Act 1988.

(2), (3) *(Outside the scope of this work.)*

258 *(Outside the scope of this work.)*

[3583]

259 Short title

This Act may be cited as the Finance Act 1994.

(Schs 1–6 outside the scope of this work.)

SCHEDULES

[SCHEDULE 6A

PREMIUMS LIABLE TO TAX AT THE HIGHER RATE

Section 51A

PART I
INTERPRETATION

[3584]

1.—(1) In this Schedule—

"insurance-related service" means any service which is related to, or connected with, insurance;

"supply" includes all forms of supply; and "supplier" shall be construed accordingly.

(2) For the purposes of this Schedule, any question whether a person is connected with another shall be determined in accordance with section 839 of the Taxes Act 1988.]

NOTES

Inserted, in relation to a premium which falls to be regarded for the purposes of this Part as received under a taxable insurance contract by an insurer on or after 1 April 1997, by the Finance Act 1997, ss 22(3), 24(1), Sch 4; for further provision as to the effect of this amendment see s 24(2)–(4) of the 1997 Act at **[3612]**.

[PART II
DESCRIPTIONS OF PREMIUM

Insurance relating to motor cars or motor cycles

[3585]

2.—(1) A premium under a taxable insurance contract relating to a motor car or motor cycle falls within this paragraph if—

(a) the contract is arranged through a person falling within sub-paragraph (2) below, or

(b) the insurer under the contract is a person falling within that sub-paragraph,

unless the insurance is provided to the insured free of charge.

(2) A person falls within this sub-paragraph if—

(a) he is a supplier of motor cars or motor cycles;

(b) he is connected with a supplier of motor cars or motor cycles; or

(c) he pays—

(i) the whole or any part of the premium received under the taxable insurance contract, or

(ii) a fee connected with the arranging of that contract,

to a supplier of motor cars or motor cycles or to a person who is connected with a supplier of motor cars or motor cycles.

[(2A) A premium does not fall within this paragraph if it is—

(a) payable under a taxable insurance contract relating to a motor car or motor cycle which is supplied by way of sale, and

(b) attributable to cover of the kind generally known as—
(i) fully comprehensive,
(ii) third party, fire and theft, or
(iii) third party.]

(3) Where a taxable insurance contract relating to a motor car or motor cycle is arranged through a person who is connected with a supplier of motor cars or motor cycles, the premium does not fall within this paragraph by virtue only of sub-paragraph (2)(b) above except to the extent that the premium is attributable to cover for a risk which relates to a motor car or motor cycle supplied by a supplier of motor cars or motor cycles with whom that person is connected.

(4) Where the insurer under a taxable insurance contract relating to a motor car or motor cycle is connected with a supplier of motor cars or motor cycles, the premium does not fall within this paragraph by virtue only of sub-paragraph (2)(b) above except to the extent that the premium is attributable to cover for a risk which relates to a motor car or motor cycle supplied by a supplier of motor cars or motor cycles with whom the insurer is connected.

(5) For the purposes of this paragraph, the cases where insurance is provided to the insured free of charge are those cases where no charge (whether by way of premium or otherwise) is made—
(a) in respect of the taxable insurance contract, or
(b) at or about the time when the taxable insurance contract is made and in connection with that contract, in respect of any insurance-related service,

by any person falling within sub-paragraph (2) above to any person who is or becomes the insured (or one of the insured) under the contract or to any person who acts, otherwise than in the course of a business, for or on behalf of such a person.

(6) In this paragraph—
"motor car" and "motor cycle" have the meaning given—
(a) by section 185(1) of the Road Traffic Act 1988; or
(b) in Northern Ireland, by Article 3(1) of the Road Traffic (Northern Ireland) Order 1995;

["sale", in relation to a motor car or motor cycle, means—
(a) a sale under which title to the motor car or motor cycle passes to the purchaser immediately on purchase, or
(b) a sale pursuant to a hire purchase agreement (within the meaning of the Consumer Credit Act 1974) under which it is intended at the outset of the agreement that the title to the motor car or motor cycle is to pass to the purchaser, whether on conclusion of the agreement or at the end of a period specified in the agreement.]

"supplier" does not include an insurer who supplies a car or motor cycle as a means of discharging liabilities arising by reason of a claim under an insurance contract.

Insurance relating to domestic appliances etc

3.—(1) A premium under a taxable insurance contract relating to relevant goods falls within this paragraph if—
(a) the contract is arranged through a person falling within sub-paragraph (2) below, or
(b) the insurer under the contract is a person falling within that sub-paragraph,

unless the insurance is provided to the insured free of charge.

(2) A person falls within this sub-paragraph if—
(a) he is a supplier of relevant goods;
(b) he is connected with a supplier of relevant goods; or
(c) he pays—
(i) the whole or any part of the premium received under the taxable insurance contract, or
(ii) a fee connected with the arranging of that contract,

to a supplier of relevant goods or to a person who is connected with a supplier of relevant goods.

(3) Where a taxable insurance contract relating to relevant goods is arranged through a person who is connected with a supplier of relevant goods, the premium does not fall within this paragraph by virtue only of sub-paragraph (2)(b) above except to the extent that the premium is attributable to cover for a risk which relates to relevant goods supplied by a supplier of relevant goods with whom that person is connected.

(4) Where the insurer under a taxable insurance contract relating to relevant goods is connected with a supplier of relevant goods, the premium does not fall within this paragraph by virtue only of sub-paragraph (2)(b) above except to the extent that the premium is attributable to cover for a risk which relates to relevant goods supplied by a supplier of relevant goods with whom the insurer is connected.

(5) For the purposes of this paragraph, the cases where insurance is provided to the insured free of charge are those cases where no charge (whether by way of premium or otherwise) is made—

(a) in respect of the taxable insurance contract, or

(b) at or about the time when the taxable insurance contract is made and in connection with that contract, in respect of any insurance-related service,

by any person falling within sub-paragraph (2) above to any person who is or becomes the insured (or one of the insured) under the contract or to any person who acts, otherwise than in the course of a business, for or on behalf of such a person.

(6) In this paragraph—

"relevant goods" means any electrical or mechanical appliance of a kind—

(a) which is ordinarily used in or about the home; or

(b) which is ordinarily owned by private individuals and used by them for the purposes of leisure, amusement or entertainment;

"supplier" does not include an insurer who supplies relevant goods as a means of discharging liabilities arising by reason of a claim under an insurance contract.

(7) In sub-paragraph (6) above—

"appliance" includes any device, equipment or apparatus;

"the home" includes any private garden and any private garage or private workshop appurtenant to a dwelling.

[Insurance provided by divided company

[3A.—(1) A premium under a taxable insurance contract relating to a motor car or motor cycle also falls within paragraph 2 above if—

(a) the insurance to be provided under the contract is provided by a divided company, and

(b) any division of that company would, if it were a separate company, be a person connected with a supplier of motor cars or motor cycles.

(2) A premium under a taxable insurance contract relating to relevant goods also falls within paragraph 3 above if—

(a) the insurance to be provided under the contract is provided by a divided company, and

(b) any division of that company would, if it were a separate company, be a person connected with a supplier of relevant goods.

(3) Sub-paragraph (1) or (2) above does not apply if the insurance is provided to the insured free of charge.

(4) A premium falls within paragraph 2 above by virtue of this paragraph only to the extent that it is attributable to cover for a risk which relates to a motor car or motor cycle supplied by a supplier of motor cars or motor cycles with whom the division in question would, if it were a separate company, be connected.

(5) A premium falls within paragraph 3 above by virtue of this paragraph only to the extent that it is attributable to cover for a risk which relates to relevant goods supplied by a supplier of relevant goods with whom the division would, if it were a separate company, be connected.

(6) For the purposes of this paragraph—

(a) a company is a "divided company" if under the law under which the company is formed, under the company's constitution or under arrangements entered into by or in relation to the company-

(i) some or all of the assets of the company are available primarily, or only, to meet particular liabilities of the company, and

(ii) some or all of the members of the company, and some or all of its creditors, have rights primarily, or only, in relation to particular assets of the company;

(b) a "division" of such a company means an identifiable part of it (by whatever name known) that carries on distinct business activities and to which particular assets and liabilities of the company are primarily or wholly attributable.

(7) In this paragraph "provided to the insured free of charge" has the meaning given by sub-paragraph (5) of paragraph 2 or 3 above.

In determining for this purpose whether a divided company by whom insurance is provided is a person falling within sub-paragraph (2) of paragraph 2 or 3 above, the company shall be treated as connected with any person with whom a division of that company would be connected if it were a separate company.

(8) Other expressions defined for the purposes of paragraph 2 or 3 above have the same meaning in this paragraph.]

[Travel insurance

4.—(1) A premium under a taxable insurance contract falls within this paragraph if it is in respect of the provision of cover against travel risks for a person travelling.

(2) Where—

(a) a contract of insurance provides cover against both travel risks and risks other than travel risks,

(b) the premium attributable to the cover against travel risks does not exceed 10 per cent. of the total premium payable under the contract, and

(c) the contract does not provide cover for a person travelling against travel risks falling within two or more of the paragraphs of sub-paragraph (3) below,

the premium, so far as attributable to the cover against travel risks, does not fall within this paragraph by virtue of sub-paragraph (1) above.

(3) The travel risks mentioned in sub-paragraph (2)(c) above are—

(a) liability in respect of cancellation of travel or of accommodation arranged in connection with travel;

(b) delayed or missed departure;

(c) curtailment of travel or of the use of accommodation arranged in connection with travel;

(d) loss or delayed arrival of baggage;

(e) personal injury or illness or expenses of repatriation.

(4) A premium does not fall within this paragraph by virtue of sub-paragraph (1) above if it is payable under a taxable insurance contract relating to a motor vehicle and is attributable to cover of the kind generally known as—

(a) fully comprehensive,

(b) third party, fire and theft,

(c) third party, or

(d) roadside assistance,

or if it is payable under a taxable insurance contract relating to a caravan, boat or aircraft and is attributable to cover of a description broadly corresponding to any of those set out in paragraphs (a) to (d) above (so far as applicable) provided in respect of the caravan, boat or aircraft for a period of at least one month for the person travelling.

(5) In this paragraph—

"person travelling" includes a person intending to travel;

"travel risks" means risks associated with, or related to, travel or intended travel-

(a) outside the United Kingdom,

(b) by air within the United Kingdom,

(c) within the United Kingdom in connection with travel falling within paragraph (a) or (b) above, or

(d) which involves absence from home for at least one night,

or risks to which a person travelling may be exposed during, or at any place at which he may be in the course of, any such travel.]]

NOTES

Inserted as noted to Pt I at **[3584]**.

Para 2: sub-para (2A) and definition "sale" in sub-para (6) inserted by the Insurance Premium Tax (Amendment of Schedule 6A to the Finance Act 1994) Order 2009, SI 2009/219, art 2, in relation to taxable insurance contracts made or coming into operation on or after 1 April 2009.

Para 3A: inserted, together with preceding cross-heading, by the Finance Act 2003, s 194(1), in relation to a premium that falls to be regarded for the purposes of Part 3 of this Act as received under a taxable insurance contract by an insurer on or after 10 July 2003.

Para 4: substituted, together with preceding cross-heading, by the Finance Act 1998, s 146(1), in relation to a premium which falls to be regarded for the purposes of Part III of this Act as received under a taxable insurance contract by an insurer on or after 1 August 1998; for transitional provision see s 146(4) of the 1998 Act.

SCHEDULE 7

INSURANCE PREMIUM TAX

Section 64

PART I
INFORMATION

Records

[3586]

1.—(1) Regulations may require registrable persons to keep records.

(2) Regulations under sub-paragraph (1) above may be framed by reference to such records as may be specified in any notice published by the Commissioners in pursuance of the regulations and

not withdrawn by a further notice.
(3) Regulations may[—
(a)] require any records kept in pursuance of the regulations to be preserved for such period not exceeding six years as may be specified in the regulations.
[(b) authorise the Commissioners to direct that any such records need only be preserved for a shorter period than that specified in the regulations, and
(c) authorise a direction to be made so as to apply generally or in such cases as the Commissioners may stipulate].
(4) Any duty under regulations to preserve records may be discharged by the preservation of the information contained in them by such means as the Commissioners may approve; and where that information is so preserved a copy of any document forming part of the records shall (subject to the following provisions of this paragraph) be admissible in evidence in any proceedings, whether civil or criminal, to the same extent as the records themselves.
(5) The Commissioners may, as a condition of approving under sub-paragraph (4) above any means of preserving information contained in any records, impose such reasonable requirements as appear to them necessary for securing that the information will be as readily available to them as if the records themselves had been preserved.
(6) A statement contained in a document produced by a computer shall not by virtue of sub-paragraph (4) above be admissible in evidence—
(a), (b) . . .
(c) in civil proceedings in Scotland, except in accordance with sections 5 and 6 of the Civil Evidence (Scotland) Act 1988;
(d) in criminal proceedings in Scotland, except in accordance with [Schedule 8 to the Criminal Procedure (Scotland) Act 1995];
(e), (f) . . .

2, 3. . . .

NOTES

Para 1: words in square brackets inserted by the Finance Act 2009, s 98(1), Sch 50, para 1(1), (2), as from a day to be appointed; sub-para (6)(a) repealed by the Civil Evidence Act 1995, s 15(2), Sch 2; sub-para (6)(b) repealed by the Criminal Justice Act 2003, s 332, Sch 37, Pt 6; words in square brackets in sub-para (6)(d) substituted by the Criminal Procedure (Consequential Provisions) (Scotland) Act 1995, s 5, Sch 4, para 89(4)(a); sub-para (6)(e) repealed by the Civil Evidence (Northern Ireland) Order 1997, SI 1997/2983, art 13(2), Sch 2, subject to a saving; sub-para (6)(f) repealed, in relation to criminal proceedings begun before 3 April 2006, by the Criminal Justice (Evidence) (Northern Ireland) Order 2004, SI 2004/1501, art 46(2), Sch 2; sub-paras (4)–(6) substituted by new sub-para (4) by the Finance Act 2009, s 98(1), Sch 50, para 1(1), (3), as from a day to be appointed, as follows:

"(4) A duty under the regulations to preserve records may be discharged—
(a) by preserving them in any form and by any means, or
(b) by preserving the information contained in them in any form and by any means, subject to any conditions or exceptions specified in writing by the Commissioners.".

Paras 2, 3: repealed by the Finance Act 2009, Section 96 and Schedule 48 (Appointed Day, Savings and Consequential Amendments) Order 2009, SI 2009/3054, art 3, Schedule, para 6(a).
Regulations: the Insurance Premium Tax Regulations 1994, SI 1994/1774 at **[4075]**.

PART II
POWERS

Entry, arrest, etc

[3587]

4. . . .

[Order for access to recorded information etc

4A.—(1) Where, on an application by an authorised person, a justice of the peace or, in Scotland, a justice (within the meaning of section 462 of the Criminal Procedure (Scotland) Act 1975) is satisfied that there are reasonable grounds for believing—
(a) that an offence in connection with tax is being, has been or is about to be committed, and
(b) that any recorded information (including any document of any nature whatsoever) which may be required as evidence for the purpose of any proceedings in respect of such an offence is in the possession of any person,

he may make an order under this paragraph.
(2) An order under this paragraph is an order that the person who appears to the justice to be in possession of the recorded information to which the application relates shall—

(a) give an authorised person access to it, and
(b) permit an authorised person to remove and take away any of it which he reasonably considers necessary,

no later than the end of the period of 7 days beginning on the date of the order or the end of such longer period as the order may specify.

(3) The reference in sub-paragraph (2)(a) above to giving an authorised person access to the recorded information to which the application relates includes a reference to permitting the authorised person to take copies of it or to make extracts from it.

(4) Where the recorded information consists of information [stored in any electronic form], an order under this paragraph shall have effect as an order to produce the information in a form in which it is visible and legible [or from which it can readily be produced in a visible and legible form] and, if the authorised person wishes to remove it, in a form in which it can be removed.

(5) This paragraph is without prejudice to paragraphs 3 and 4 above.]

Removal of documents etc

5.—(1) An authorised person who removes anything in the exercise of a power conferred by or under paragraph 4 [or 4A] above shall, if so requested by a person showing himself—
(a) to be the occupier of premises from which it was removed, or
(b) to have had custody or control of it immediately before the removal,

provide that person with a record of what he removed.

(2) The authorised person shall provide the record within a reasonable time from the making of the request for it.

(3) Subject to sub-paragraph (7) below, if a request for permission to be allowed access to anything which—
(a) has been removed by an authorised person, and
(b) is retained by the Commissioners for the purposes of investigating an offence,

is made to the officer in overall charge of the investigation by a person who had custody or control of the thing immediately before it was so removed or by someone acting on behalf of such a person, the officer shall allow the person who made the request access to it under the supervision of an authorised person.

(4) Subject to sub-paragraph (7) below, if a request for a photograph or copy of any such thing is made to the officer in overall charge of the investigation by a person who had custody or control of the thing immediately before it was so removed, or by someone acting on behalf of such a person, the officer shall—
(a) allow the person who made the request access to it under the supervision of an authorised person for the purpose of photographing it or copying it, or
(b) photograph or copy it, or cause it to be photographed or copied.

(5) Subject to sub-paragraph (7) below, where anything is photographed or copied under sub-paragraph (4)(b) above the officer shall supply the photograph or copy, or cause it to be supplied, to the person who made the request.

(6) The photograph or copy shall be supplied within a reasonable time from the making of the request.

(7) There is no duty under this paragraph to allow access to, or to supply a photograph or copy of, anything if the officer in overall charge of the investigation for the purposes of which it was removed has reasonable grounds for believing that to do so would prejudice—
(a) that investigation,
(b) the investigation of an offence other than the offence for the purposes of the investigation of which the thing was removed, or
(c) any criminal proceedings which may be brought as a result of the investigation of which he is in charge or any such investigation as is mentioned in paragraph (b) above.

(8) Any reference in this paragraph to the officer in overall charge of the investigation is a reference to the person whose name and address are endorsed on the warrant concerned as being the officer so in charge.

6.—(1) Where, on an application made as mentioned in sub-paragraph (2) below, the appropriate judicial authority is satisfied that a person has failed to comply with a requirement imposed by paragraph 5 above, the authority may order that person to comply with the requirement within such time and in such manner as may be specified in the order.

(2) An application under sub-paragraph (1) above shall be made—
(a) in the case of a failure to comply with any of the requirements imposed by sub-paragraphs (1) and (2) of paragraph 5 above, by the occupier of the premises from which the thing in question was removed or by the person who had custody or control of it immediately before it was so removed, and

(b) in any other case, by the person who had such custody or control.
(3) In this paragraph "the appropriate judicial authority" means—
(a) in England and Wales, a magistrates' court;
(b) in Scotland, the sheriff;
(c) in Northern Ireland, a court of summary jurisdiction, as defined in Article 2(2)(a) of the Magistrates' Court (Northern Ireland) Order 1981.
(4) In England and Wales and Northern Ireland, an application for an order under this paragraph shall be made by way of complaint; and sections 21 and 42(2) of the Interpretation Act (Northern Ireland) 1954 shall apply as if any reference in those provisions to any enactment included a reference to this paragraph.

NOTES

Para 4: sub-para (1) repealed by the Finance Act 2009, Section 96 and Schedule 48 (Appointed Day, Savings and Consequential Amendments) Order 2009, SI 2009/3054, art 3, Schedule, para 6(a); sub-paras (2)–(7) repealed by the Finance Act 2007, ss 84(4), 114, Sch 22, Pt 2, paras 3, 9, Sch 27, Pt 5(1).

Para 4A: inserted, together with preceding cross-heading, by the Finance Act 1995, s 34, Sch 5, paras 1, 8(1); in sub-para (4) words in first pair of square brackets substituted and words in second pair of square brackets inserted by the Criminal Justice and Police Act 2001, s 70, Sch 2, Pt 2, para 13(1), (2)(g).

Para 5: words in square brackets in sub-para (1) inserted by the Finance Act 1995, s 34, Sch 5, paras 1, 8(2).

PART III
RECOVERY

Recovery of tax etc

[3588]

7.—(1) Tax due from any person shall be recoverable as a debt due to the Crown.
(2)–(12) . . .

Recovery of overpaid tax

8.—(1) Where a person has paid an amount to the Commissioners by way of tax which was not tax due to them, they shall be liable to repay the amount to him.
(2) The Commissioners shall only be liable to repay an amount under this paragraph on a claim being made for the purpose.
(3) It shall be a defence, in relation to a claim under this paragraph, that repayment of an amount would unjustly enrich the claimant.
[(4) The Commissioners shall not be liable, on a claim made under this paragraph, to repay any amount paid to them more than *three years* before the making of the claim.]
(6) A claim under this paragraph shall be made in such form and manner and shall be supported by such documentary evidence as may be prescribed by regulations.
(7) Except as provided by this paragraph, the Commissioners shall not be liable to repay an amount paid to them by way of tax by virtue of the fact that it was not tax due to them.

NOTES

Para 7: sub-para (2) repealed by the Enterprise Act 2002, s 278(2), Sch 26; sub-paras (3)–(5) amend the Bankruptcy (Scotland) Act 1985, Sch 3; sub-para (6) repealed by the Insolvency (Northern Ireland) Order 2005, SI 2005/1455, art 31, Sch 9; sub-para (7), sub-paras (8)–(12) (as substituted, for original sub-para (8), by the Finance Act 1995, s 34, Sch 5, para 9), repealed by the Finance Act 1997, s 113, Sch 18, Pt V(2).

Para 8: sub-para (4) substituted, for original sub-paras (4), (5), by the Finance Act 1997, s 50, Sch 5, para 5(2); for the words in italics in sub-para (4) there are substituted the words "4 years" by the Finance Act 2009, s 99(1), Sch 51, paras 1, 2, as from a day to be appointed.

Regulations: the Insurance Premium Tax Regulations 1994, SI 1994/1774 at **[4075]**.

PART IV
PENALTIES

Criminal offences

[3589]

9.—(1) A person is guilty of an offence if—
(a) being a registrable person, he is knowingly concerned in, or in the taking of steps with a view to, the fraudulent evasion of tax by him or another registrable person, or
(b) not being a registrable person, he is knowingly concerned in, or in the taking of steps with a view to, the fraudulent evasion of tax by a registrable person.
(2) Any reference in sub-paragraph (1) above to the evasion of tax includes a reference to the obtaining of a payment under regulations under section 55(3)(c) or (d) or (f) of this Act.
(3) A person is guilty of an offence if with the requisite intent—

(a) he produces, furnishes or sends, or causes to be produced, furnished or sent, for the purposes of this Part of this Act any document which is false in a material particular, or

(b) he otherwise makes use for those purposes of such a document;

and the requisite intent is intent to deceive or to secure that a machine will respond to the document as if it were a true document.

(4) A person is guilty of an offence if in furnishing any information for the purposes of this Part of this Act he makes a statement which he knows to be false in a material particular or recklessly makes a statement which is false in a material particular.

(5) A person is guilty of an offence by virtue of this sub-paragraph if his conduct during any specified period must have involved the commission by him of one or more offences under the preceding provisions of this paragraph; and the preceding provisions of this sub-paragraph apply whether or not the particulars of that offence or those offences are known.

(6) A person is guilty of an offence if—

(a) he enters into a taxable insurance contract, or

(b) he makes arrangements for other persons to enter into a taxable insurance contract,

with reason to believe that tax in respect of the contract will be evaded.

(7) A person is guilty of an offence if he enters into taxable insurance contracts without giving security (or further security) he has been required to give under paragraph 24 below.

Criminal penalties

10.—(1) A person guilty of an offence under paragraph 9(1) above shall be liable—

(a) on summary conviction, to a penalty of the statutory maximum or of three times the amount of the tax, whichever is the greater, or to imprisonment for a term not exceeding six months or to both;

(b) on conviction on indictment, to a penalty of any amount or to imprisonment for a term not exceeding seven years or to both.

(2) The reference in sub-paragraph (1) above to the amount of the tax shall be construed, in relation to tax itself or a payment falling within paragraph 9(2) above, as a reference to the aggregate of—

(a) the amount (if any) falsely claimed by way of credit, and

(b) the amount (if any) by which the gross amount of tax was falsely understated.

(3) A person guilty of an offence under paragraph 9(3) or (4) above shall be liable—

(a) on summary conviction, to a penalty of the statutory maximum or, where sub-paragraph (4) below applies, to the alternative penalty there specified if it is greater, or to imprisonment for a term not exceeding six months or to both;

(b) on conviction on indictment, to a penalty of any amount or to imprisonment for a term not exceeding seven years or to both.

(4) In a case where—

(a) the document referred to in paragraph 9(3) above is a return required under this Part of this Act, or

(b) the information referred to in paragraph 9(4) above is contained in or otherwise relevant to such a return,

the alternative penalty is a penalty equal to three times the aggregate of the amount (if any) falsely claimed by way of credit and the amount (if any) by which the gross amount of tax was understated.

(5) A person guilty of an offence under paragraph 9(5) above shall be liable—

(a) on summary conviction, to a penalty of the statutory maximum or (if greater) three times the amount of any tax that was or was intended to be evaded by his conduct, or to imprisonment for a term not exceeding six months or to both;

(b) on conviction on indictment, to a penalty of any amount or to imprisonment for a term not exceeding seven years or to both;

and paragraph 9(2) and sub-paragraph (2) above shall apply for the purposes of this sub-paragraph as they apply respectively for the purposes of paragraph 9(1) and sub-paragraph (1) above.

(6) A person guilty of an offence under paragraph 9(6) above shall be liable on summary conviction to a penalty of level 5 on the standard scale or three times the amount of the tax, whichever is the greater.

(7) A person guilty of an offence under paragraph 9(7) above shall be liable on summary conviction to a penalty of level 5 on the standard scale.

(8) In this paragraph—

(a) "credit" means credit for which provision is made by regulations under section 55 of this Act;

(b) "the gross amount of tax" means the total amount of tax due before taking into account any deduction for which provision is made by regulations under section 55(3) of this Act.

Criminal proceedings etc

11. Sections 145 to 155 of the Customs and Excise Management Act 1979 (proceedings for offences, mitigation of penalties and certain other matters) shall apply in relation to offences under paragraph 9 above and penalties imposed under paragraph 10 above as they apply in relation to offences and penalties under the customs and excise Acts as defined in that Act.

Civil penalties

12–14. . . .

15.—(1) This paragraph applies if a person fails to comply with—

(a) a requirement imposed by regulations made under section 54 of this Act to pay the tax due in respect of any period within the time required by the regulations, or

(b) a requirement imposed by regulations made under that section to furnish a return in respect of any period within the time required by the regulations;

and sub-paragraphs (2) and (3) below shall have effect subject to sub-paragraphs (5) and (6) below and paragraph 25(7) below.

(2) The person shall be liable to a penalty equal to 5 per cent of the tax due or, if it is greater, to a penalty of £250.

(3) The person—

(a) shall be liable, in addition to an initial penalty under sub-paragraph (2) above, to a penalty of £20 for every relevant day when he fails to pay the tax or furnish the return, but

(b) shall not in respect of the continuation of the failure be liable to further penalties under sub-paragraph (2) above;

and a relevant day is any day falling after the time within which the tax is required to be paid or the return is required to be furnished.

(4) For the purposes of sub-paragraph (2) above the tax due—

(a) shall, if the person concerned has furnished a return, be taken to be the tax shown in the return as that for which he is accountable in respect of the period in question, and

(b) shall, in any other case, be taken to be such tax as has been assessed for that period and notified to him under section 56(1) of this Act.

(5) A failure falling within sub-paragraph (1) or (3) above shall not give rise to liability to a penalty under this paragraph if the person concerned satisfies the Commissioners or, on appeal, an appeal tribunal that there is a reasonable excuse for the failure.

(6) Where, by reason of a failure falling within sub-paragraph (1) or (3) above—

(a) a person is convicted of an offence (whether under this Part of this Act or otherwise), or

(b) a person is assessed to a penalty under paragraph 12 above [or to a penalty for a deliberate inaccuracy under Schedule 24 to the Finance Act 2007 (penalties for errors)],

that failure shall not also give rise to liability to a penalty under this paragraph.

(7) If it appears to the Treasury that there has been a change in the value of money since the passing of this Act or, as the case may be, the last occasion when the power conferred by this sub-paragraph was exercised, they may by order substitute for the sums for the time being specified in sub-paragraphs (2) and (3) above such other sums as appear to them to be justified by the change.

(8) An order under sub-paragraph (7) above shall not apply in relation to a failure which began before the date on which the order comes into force.

16.—(1) This paragraph applies where—

(a) by virtue of regulations made under section 65 of this Act a liability notice (within the meaning of that section) is served on an insured person,

(b) by virtue of such regulations that person is liable to pay an amount of tax which has been assessed in accordance with the regulations, and

(c) that tax is not paid within the time required by the regulations;

and sub-paragraphs (2) and (3) below shall have effect subject to sub-paragraphs (4) and (5) below and paragraph 25(7) below.

(2) The person shall be liable to a penalty equal to 5 per cent of the tax assessed as mentioned in sub-paragraph (1) above or, if it is greater, to a penalty of £250.

(3) The person—

(a) shall be liable, in addition to an initial penalty under sub-paragraph (2) above, to a penalty of £20 for every relevant day when the tax is unpaid, but

(b) shall not in respect of the continuation of the non-payment of the tax be liable to further penalties under sub-paragraph (2) above;

and a relevant day is any day falling after the time within which the tax is required to be paid.

(4) A person shall not be liable to a penalty by virtue of this paragraph if he satisfies the Commissioners or, on appeal, an appeal tribunal that he took all reasonable steps to ensure that the tax mentioned in sub-paragraph (1)(b) above was paid within the time required by the regulations.
(5) Where, by reason of a failure to pay tax, a person is convicted of an offence (whether under this Part of this Act or otherwise), that failure shall not also give rise to liability to a penalty under this paragraph.
(6) If it appears to the Treasury that there has been a change in the value of money since the passing of this Act or, as the case may be, the last occasion when the power conferred by this sub-paragraph was exercised, they may by order substitute for the sums for the time being specified in sub-paragraphs (2) and (3) above such other sums as appear to them to be justified by the change.
(7) An order under sub-paragraph (6) above shall not apply in relation to any failure to pay tax that was required to be paid before the date on which the order comes into force.

17.—(1) If a person fails to comply with—
- (a) section 53(3) of this Act,
- . . . or
- (c) a requirement imposed by any regulations made under this Part of this Act, other than a requirement falling within sub-paragraph (2) below,

he shall be liable to a penalty of £250; but this is subject to sub-paragraphs (3) and (4) below.
(2) A requirement falls within this sub-paragraph if it is—
- (a) a requirement imposed by regulations made under section 54 of this Act to pay the tax due in respect of any period within the time required by the regulations,
- (b) a requirement imposed by regulations made under that section to furnish a return in respect of any period within the time required by the regulations,
- (c) a requirement imposed by regulations made under section 65 of this Act to pay tax within the time required by the regulations, or
- (d) a requirement specified for the purposes of this sub-paragraph by regulations.

(3) A failure falling within sub-paragraph (1) above shall not give rise to liability to a penalty under this paragraph if the person concerned satisfies the Commissioners or, on appeal, an appeal tribunal that there is a reasonable excuse for the failure.
(4) Where by reason of a failure falling within sub-paragraph (1) above—
- (a) a person is convicted of an offence (whether under this Part of this Act or otherwise), or
- (b) a person is assessed to a penalty under paragraph 12 above [or to a penalty for a deliberate inaccuracy under Schedule 24 to the Finance Act 2007 (penalties for errors)],

that failure shall not also give rise to liability to a penalty under this paragraph.
(5) If it appears to the Treasury that there has been a change in the value of money since the passing of this Act or, as the case may be, the last occasion when the power conferred by this sub-paragraph was exercised, they may by order substitute for the sum for the time being specified in sub-paragraph (1) above such other sum as appears to them to be justified by the change.
(6) An order under sub-paragraph (5) above shall not apply in relation to a failure which began before the date on which the order comes into force.

18. . . .

[18A.—*(1) This paragraph applies where an enforcement agent acting under the power conferred by section 51(A1) of the Finance Act 1997 (power to use the procedure in Schedule 12 to the Tribunals, Courts and Enforcement Act 2007) has entered into a controlled goods agreement with the person against whom the power is exercisable ("the person in default").*
(2) In this paragraph, "controlled goods agreement" has the meaning given by paragraph 13(4) of that Schedule.
(3) Subject to sub-paragraph (4) below, if the person in default removes or disposes of goods (or permits their removal or disposal) in breach of the controlled goods agreement, he is liable to a penalty equal to half of the tax or other amount recoverable under section 51(A1) of the Finance Act 1997.
(4) The person in default shall not be liable to a penalty under sub-paragraph (3) above if he satisfies the Commissioners or, on appeal, an appeal tribunal, that there is a reasonable excuse for the breach in question.
(5) This paragraph extends only to England and Wales.]

19.—(1) This paragraph applies where—
- (a) in accordance with regulations under [section 51 of the Finance Act 1997 (enforcement by distress)] a distress is authorised to be levied on the goods and chattels of a person (a

person in default) who has refused or neglected to pay any tax due from him or any amount recoverable as if it were tax due from him, and
- (b) the person levying the distress and the person in default have entered into a walking possession agreement.

(2) For the purposes of this paragraph a walking possession agreement is an agreement under which, in consideration of the property distrained upon being allowed to remain in the custody of the person in default and of the delaying of its sale, the person in default—
- (a) acknowledges that the property specified in the agreement is under distraint and held in walking possession, and
- (b) undertakes that, except with the consent of the Commissioners and subject to such conditions as they may impose, he will not remove or allow the removal of any of the specified property from the premises named in the agreement.

(3) Subject to sub-paragraph (4) below, if the person in default is in breach of the undertaking contained in a walking possession agreement, he shall be liable to a penalty equal to half of the tax or other amount referred to in sub-paragraph (1)(a) above.

(4) The person in default shall not be liable to a penalty under sub-paragraph (3) above if he satisfies the Commissioners or, on appeal, an appeal tribunal that there is a reasonable excuse for the breach in question.

(5) This paragraph does not extend to Scotland.

20. For the purposes of paragraphs 14(3), 15(5), 17(3) . . . and 19(4) above—
- (a) an insufficiency of funds available for paying any amount is not a reasonable excuse, and
- (b) where reliance is placed on any other person to perform any task, neither the fact of that reliance nor any conduct of the person relied upon is a reasonable excuse.

NOTES

Paras 12, 13: repealed by the Finance Act 2008, s 122(1), Sch 40, para 21(d)(ii).

Para 14: repealed by the Finance Act 2008, s 123(1), Sch 41, para 25(e)(iii).

Para 15: words in square brackets in sub-para (6)(b) inserted by SI 2009/571, art 8, Sch 1, para 11(1), (3).

Para 17: words omitted from sub-para (1) repealed by the Finance Act 2009, Section 96 and Schedule 48 (Appointed Day, Savings and Consequential Amendments) Order 2009, SI 2009/3054, art 3, Schedule, para 6(b); words in square brackets in sub-para (4)(b) inserted by SI 2009/571, art 8, Sch 1, para 11(1), (4).

Para 18: repealed by the Finance Act 2008, s 142(1)(d).

Para 18A: inserted by the Tribunals, Courts and Enforcement Act 2007, s 62(3), Sch 13, paras 113, 116(1), (2), as from a day to be appointed; repealed by the Finance Act 2008, s 129(1), Sch 43, Pt 1, paras 3(1), (3), as from a day to be appointed.

Para 19: words in square brackets in sub-para (1) substituted by the Finance Act 1997, s 53(5); sub-para (5) substituted by the Tribunals, Courts and Enforcement Act 2007, s 62(3), Sch 13, paras 113, 116(1), (3), as from a day to be appointed, as follows—

"(5) This paragraph extends only to Northern Ireland.".

Para 20: reference omitted repealed by the Finance Act 2008, s 142(2).

PART V
INTEREST

Interest on tax etc

[3590]

21.—(1) Where an assessment is made under any provision of section 56 of this Act, the whole of the amount assessed shall carry interest at [the rate applicable under section 197 of the Finance Act 1996] from the reckonable date until payment; but this is subject to sub-paragraph (2) and paragraph 25(7) below.

(2) Sub-paragraph (1) above shall not apply in relation to an assessment under section 56(1) of this Act unless at least one of the following conditions is fulfilled, namely—
- (a) that the assessment relates to an accounting period in respect of which either a return has previously been made, or an earlier assessment has already been notified to the person concerned;
- (b) that the assessment relates to an accounting period which exceeds three months and begins on the date with effect from which the person was, or was required to be, registered under this Part of this Act.

(3) In a case where—
- (a) the circumstances are such that a relevant assessment could have been made, but
- (b) before such an assessment was made the tax due or other amount concerned was paid (so that no such assessment was necessary),

the whole of the amount paid shall carry interest at [the rate applicable under section 197 of the Finance Act 1996] from the reckonable date until the date on which it was paid; and for the purposes of this sub-paragraph a relevant assessment is an assessment in relation to which sub-paragraph (1) above would have applied if the assessment had been made.

(4) The references in sub-paragraphs (1) and (3) above to the reckonable date shall be construed as follows—

(a) where the amount assessed or paid is such an amount as is referred to in subsection (2) of section 56 of this Act, the reckonable date is the seventh day after the day on which a written instruction was issued by the Commissioners directing the making of the payment of the amount which ought not to have been paid to the person concerned;

(b) in all other cases the reckonable date is the latest date on which (in accordance with regulations under this Part of this Act) a return is required to be made for the accounting period to which the amount assessed or paid relates;

and interest under this paragraph shall run from the reckonable date even if that date is a non-business day, within the meaning of section 92 of the Bills of Exchange Act 1882.

(5) . . .

(6) Interest under this paragraph shall be paid without any deduction of income tax.

Interest payable by Commissioners

22.—(1) Where, due to an error on the part of the Commissioners, a person—

(a) has paid to them by way of tax an amount which was not tax due and which they are in consequence liable to repay to him,

(b) has failed to claim payment of an amount to the payment of which he was entitled in pursuance of provision made under section 55(3)(c), (d) or (f) of this Act, or

(c) has suffered delay in receiving payment of an amount due to him from them in connection with tax,

then, if and to the extent that they would not be liable to do so apart from this paragraph, they shall (subject to the following provisions of this paragraph) pay interest to him on that amount for the applicable period.

[(1A) In sub-paragraph (1) above—

(a) the reference in paragraph (a) to an amount which the Commissioners are liable to repay in consequence of the making of a payment that was not due is a reference to only so much of that amount as is the subject of a claim that the Commissioners are required to satisfy or have satisfied; and

(b) the amounts referred to in paragraph (c) do not include any amount payable under this paragraph.]

(2) Interest under this paragraph shall be payable at [the rate applicable under section 197 of the Finance Act 1996].

(3) The applicable period, in a case falling within sub-paragraph (1)(a) above, is the period—

(a) beginning with the date on which the payment is received by the Commissioners, and

(b) ending with the date on which they authorise payment of the amount on which the interest is payable.

(4) The applicable period, in a case falling within sub-paragraph (1)(b) or (c) above, is the period—

(a) beginning with the date on which, apart from the error, the Commissioners might reasonably have been expected to authorise payment of the amount on which the interest is payable, and

(b) ending with the date on which they in fact authorise payment of that amount.

[(5) In determining the applicable period for the purposes of this paragraph there shall be left out of account any period by which the Commissioners' authorisation of the payment of interest is delayed by the conduct of the person who claims the interest.

(5A) The reference in sub-paragraph (5) above to a period by which the Commissioners' authorisation of the payment of interest is delayed by the conduct of the person who claims it includes, in particular, any period which is referable to—

(a) any unreasonable delay in the making of the claim for interest or in the making of any claim for the payment or repayment of the amount on which interest is claimed;

(b) any failure by that person or a person acting on his behalf or under his influence to provide the Commissioners—

(i) at or before the time of the making of a claim, or

(ii) subsequently in response to a request for information by the Commissioners,

with all the information required by them to enable the existence and amount of the claimant's entitlement to a payment or repayment, and to interest on that payment or repayment, to be determined; and

(c) the making, as part of or in association with either—
(i) the claim for interest, or
(ii) any claim for the payment or repayment of the amount on which interest is claimed,
of a claim to anything to which the claimant was not entitled.

(6) In determining for the purposes of sub-paragraph (5A) above whether any period of delay is referable to a failure by any person to provide information in response to a request by the Commissioners, there shall be taken to be so referable, except so far as may be provided for by regulations, any period which—
(a) begins with the date on which the Commissioners require that person to provide information which they reasonably consider relevant to the matter to be determined; and
(b) ends with the earliest date on which it would be reasonable for the Commissioners to conclude—
(i) that they have received a complete answer to their request for information;
(ii) that they have received all that they need in answer to that request; or
(iii) that it is unnecessary for them to be provided with any information in answer to that request.]

(8) The Commissioners shall only be liable to pay interest under this paragraph on a claim made in writing for that purpose.

[(9) A claim under this paragraph shall not be made more than *three years* after the end of the applicable period to which it relates.]

[(10) References in this paragraph to the authorisation by the Commissioners of the payment of any amount include references to the discharge by way of set-off of the Commissioners' liability to pay that amount.]

23.—(1) In a case where—
(a) any interest is payable by the Commissioners to a person on a sum due to him under this Part of this Act, and
(b) he is a person to whom regulations under section 55 of this Act apply,
the interest shall be treated as an amount to which he is entitled by way of credit in pursuance of the regulations.

(2) Sub-paragraph (1) above shall be disregarded for the purpose of determining a person's entitlement to interest or the amount of interest to which he is entitled.

NOTES

Para 21: words in square brackets in sub-paras (1), (3) substituted and sub-para (5) repealed by the Finance Act 1996, ss 197(6)(b), (7), 205, Sch 41, Part VIII(1), in relation to interest running from before, as well as interest running from, or from after, 1 April 1997.

Para 22: sub-para (1A) inserted with retrospective effect, and sub-paras (9), (10) substituted with retrospective effect, by the Finance Act 1997, s 50, Sch 5, para 9; words in square brackets in sub-para (2) substituted by the Finance Act 1996, ss 197(6)(c), (7); sub-paras (5), (5A), (6) substituted, for original sub-paras (5)–(7), in relation to any period beginning on or after 19 March 1997 is left out of account, by the Finance Act 1997, s 50, Sch 5, para 10; for the words in italics in sub-para (9) there are substituted the words "4 years" by the Finance Act 2009, s 99(1), Sch 51, paras 1, 3, as from a day to be appointed.

See further, in relation to the recovery of excess payment under this Schedule: the Finance Act 1997, Sch 5, paras 15–19.

PART VI
MISCELLANEOUS

Security for tax

[3591]

24. Where it appears to the Commissioners requisite to do so for the protection of the revenue they may require a registrable person, as a condition of his entering into taxable insurance contracts, to give security (or further security) of such amount and in such manner as they may determine for the payment of any tax which is or may become due from him.

Assessments to penalties etc

25.—(1) Where a person is liable—
(a) to a penalty under any of paragraphs 12 to 19 above, or
(b) for interest under paragraph 21 above,
the Commissioners may, subject to sub-paragraph (2) below, assess the amount due by way of penalty or interest (as the case may be) and notify it to him accordingly; and the fact that any conduct giving rise to a penalty under any of paragraphs 12 to 19 above may have ceased before an assessment is made under this paragraph shall not affect the power of the Commissioners to make

such an assessment.

(2) In the case of the penalties and interest referred to in the following paragraphs of this sub-paragraph, the assessment under this paragraph shall be of an amount due in respect of the accounting period which in the paragraph concerned is referred to as the relevant period—

(a) in the case of a penalty under paragraph 12 above relating to the evasion of tax, the relevant period is the accounting period for which the tax evaded was due;

(b) in the case of a penalty under paragraph 12 above relating to the obtaining of a payment under regulations under section 55(3)(c) or (d) or (f) of this Act, the relevant period is the accounting period in respect of which the payment was obtained;

(c) in the case of interest under paragraph 21 above, the relevant period is the accounting period in respect of which the tax (or amount assessed as tax) was due.

(3) In a case where the amount of any penalty or interest falls to be calculated by reference to tax which was not paid at the time it should have been and that tax cannot be readily attributed to any one or more accounting periods, it shall be treated for the purposes of this Part of this Act as tax due for such period or periods as the Commissioners may determine to the best of their judgment and notify to the person liable for the tax and penalty or interest.

(4) Where a person is assessed under this paragraph to an amount due by way of any penalty or interest falling within sub-paragraph (2) above and is also assessed under subsection (1) or (2) of section 56 of this Act for the accounting period which is the relevant period under sub-paragraph (2) above, the assessments may be combined and notified to him as one assessment, but the amount of the penalty or interest shall be separately identified in the notice.

(5) Sub-paragraph (6) below applies in the case of—

(a) an amount due by way of penalty under paragraph 15 or 16 above;

(b) an amount due by way of interest under paragraph 21 above.

(6) Where this sub-paragraph applies in the case of an amount—

(a) a notice of assessment under this paragraph shall specify a date, being not later than the date of the notice, to which the aggregate amount of the penalty or, as the case may be, the amount of interest which is assessed is calculated, and

(b) if the penalty or interest continues to accrue after that date, a further assessment or further assessments may be made under this paragraph in respect of amounts which so accrue.

(7) If, within such period as may be notified by the Commissioners to the person liable to the penalty under paragraph 15 or 16 above or for the interest under paragraph 21 above—

(a) a failure falling within paragraph 15(3) above is remedied,

(b) the tax referred to in paragraph 16(1) above is paid, or

(c) the amount referred to in paragraph 21(1) above is paid,

it shall be treated for the purposes of paragraph 15, 16 or 21 above (as the case may be) as remedied or paid on the date specified as mentioned in sub-paragraph (6)(a) above.

(8) Where an amount has been assessed and notified to any person under this paragraph it shall be recoverable as if it were tax due from him unless, or except to the extent that, the assessment has subsequently been withdrawn or reduced.

(9) Subsection (8) of section 56 of this Act shall apply for the purposes of this paragraph as it applies for the purposes of that section.

Assessments: time limits

26.—(1) Subject to the following provisions of this paragraph, an assessment under—

(a) any provision of section 56 of this Act, or

(b) paragraph 25 above,

shall not be made more than *[three years] after the end of the accounting period concerned or, in the case of an assessment under paragraph 25 above of an amount due by way of a penalty which is not a penalty referred to in sub-paragraph (2) of that paragraph, [three years] after the event giving rise to the penalty.*

[(1A) In this paragraph "the relevant event", in relation to an assessment, means—

(a) the end of the accounting period concerned, or

(b) in the case of an assessment under paragraph 25 of an amount due by way of a penalty other than a penalty referred to in paragraph 25(2), the event giving rise to the penalty.]

(2) An assessment under paragraph 25 above of—

(a) an amount due by way of any penalty referred to in sub-paragraph (2) of that paragraph, or

(b) an amount due by way of interest,

may be made at any time before the expiry of the period of two years beginning with the time when the amount of tax due for the accounting period concerned has been finally determined.

(3) In relation to an assessment under paragraph 25 above, any reference in *sub-paragraph (1)* or (2) above to the accounting period concerned is a reference to that period which, in the case of the penalty or interest concerned, is the relevant period referred to in sub-paragraph (2) of that paragraph.

(4) If tax has been lost—

(a) as a result of conduct falling within paragraph 12(1) above or for which a person has been convicted of fraud, or

(b) in circumstances giving rise to liability to a penalty under paragraph 14 above,

an assessment may be made as if, in sub-paragraph (1) above, each reference to [three years] were a reference to twenty years.

Supplementary assessments

27. If, section 56 of this Act, it appears to the Commissioners that the amount which ought to have been assessed in an assessment under any provision of that section or under paragraph 25 above exceeds the amount which was so assessed, then—

(a) under the like provision as that assessment was made, and

(b) on or before the last day on which that assessment could have been made,

the Commissioners may make a supplementary assessment of the amount of the excess and shall notify the person concerned accordingly.

Disclosure of information

28.—(1) Notwithstanding any obligation not to disclose information that would otherwise apply, the Commissioners may disclose information—

(a) to the Secretary of State, or

(b) to an authorised officer of the Secretary of State,

for the purpose of assisting the Secretary of State in the performance of his duties.

(2) Notwithstanding any such obligation as is mentioned in sub-paragraph (1) above—

(a) the Secretary of State, or

(b) an authorised officer of the Secretary of State,

may disclose information to the Commissioners or to an authorised officer of the Commissioners for the purpose of assisting the Commissioners in the performance of duties in relation to tax.

(3) Information that has been disclosed to a person by virtue of this paragraph shall not be disclosed by him except—

(a) to another person to whom (instead of him) disclosure could by virtue of this paragraph have been made, or

(b) for the purpose of any proceedings connected with the operation of any provision of, or made under, any enactment in relation to insurance or to tax.

(4) References in the preceding provisions of this paragraph to an authorised officer of the Secretary of State are to any person who has been designated by the Secretary of State as a person to and by whom information may be disclosed under this paragraph.

(5) The Secretary of State shall notify the Commissioners in writing of the name of any person designated under sub-paragraph (4) above.

[28A.—(1) Notwithstanding any obligation not to disclose information that would otherwise apply, the Commissioners may disclose information—

(a) to the Treasury, or

(b) to an authorised officer of the Treasury,

for the purpose of assisting the Treasury in the performance of their duties.

(2) Notwithstanding any such obligation as is mentioned in sub-paragraph (1) above—

(a) the Treasury, or

(b) an authorised officer of the Treasury,

may disclose information to the Commissioners or to an authorised officer of the Commissioners for the purpose of assisting the Commissioners in the performance of duties in relation to tax.

(3) Information that has been disclosed to a person by virtue of this paragraph shall not be disclosed by him except—

(a) to another person to whom (instead of him) disclosure could by virtue of this paragraph have been made, or

(b) for the purpose of any proceedings connected with the operation of any provision of, or made under, any enactment in relation to insurance or to tax,

(4) References in the preceding provisions of this paragraph to an authorised officer of the Treasury are to any person who has been designated by the Treasury as a person to and by whom information may be disclosed under this paragraph.

(5) The Treasury shall notify the Commissioners in writing of the name of any person designated under sub-paragraph (4) above.]

[28B.—(1) Notwithstanding any obligation not to disclose information that would otherwise apply, the Commissioners may disclose information to the Financial Services Authority ("the Authority") for the purpose of assisting the Authority in the performance of its functions.
(2) Information that has been disclosed to the Authority pursuant to this paragraph shall not be disclosed by the Authority except for the purpose of any proceedings connected with the operation of any provision of, or made under, any enactment in relation to insurance or to tax.]

Evidence by certificate

29.—(1) A certificate of the Commissioners—
(a) that a person was or was not at any time registered under section 53 of this Act, [or]
(b) that any return required by regulations under section 54 of this Act has not been made or had not been made at any time, . . .
(c) . . .
shall be sufficient evidence of that fact until the contrary is proved.
(2) Any document purporting to be a certificate under sub-paragraph (1) above shall be taken to be such a certificate until the contrary is proved.

Service of notices etc

30. Any notice, notification or requirement to be served on, given to or made of any person for the purposes of this Part of this Act may be served, given or made by sending it by post in a letter addressed to that person or his tax representative at the last or usual residence or place of business of that person or representative.

31, 32. . . .

Provisional collection of tax

33. . . .

34.—(1) In a case where—
(a) by virtue of a resolution having effect under the Provisional Collection of Taxes Act 1968 tax has been paid at a rate specified in the resolution, and
(b) by virtue of section 1(6) or (7) or 5(3) of that Act any of that tax is repayable in consequence of the restoration in relation to the premium concerned of a lower rate,
the amount repayable shall be the difference between the tax paid by reference to the actual chargeable amount at the rate specified in the resolution and the tax that would have been payable by reference to the actual chargeable amount at the lower rate.
(2) In sub-paragraph (1) above the "actual chargeable amount" means the chargeable amount by reference to which tax was paid.
(3) In a case where—
(a) by virtue of a resolution having effect under the Provisional Collection of Taxes Act 1968 tax is chargeable at a rate specified in the resolution, but
(b) before the tax is paid it ceases to be chargeable at that rate in consequence of the restoration in relation to the premium concerned of a lower rate,
the tax chargeable at the lower rate shall be charged by reference to the same chargeable amount as that by reference to which tax would have been chargeable at the rate specified in the resolution.

Adjustment of contracts

35.—(1) Where, after the making of a contract of insurance and before a given premium is received by the insurer under the contract, there is a change in the tax chargeable on the receipt of the premium, then, unless the contract otherwise provided, there shall be added to or deducted from the amount payable as the premium an amount equal to the difference between—
(a) the tax chargeable had the change not been made, and
(b) the tax in fact chargeable.
(2) References in sub-paragraph (1) above to a change in the tax chargeable include references to a change to or from no tax being chargeable.
(3) Where this paragraph applies, the amount of the premium shall not be treated as altered for the purposes of calculating tax.

NOTES

Para 26: words in square brackets in sub-paras (1), (4) substituted by the Finance Act 1997, s 50, Sch 5, para 6; for the words in italics in sub-para (1) there are substituted the words "4 years after the relevant event", sub-para (1A) inserted, for the words in italics in sub-para (3) there are substituted the words "sub-paragraph (1A)", and sub-para (4) substituted by new sub-paras (4), (5), by the Finance Act 2009, s 99(1), Sch 51, paras 1, 4, as from a day to be appointed, as follows:

"(4) An assessment of an amount due from a person in a case involving a loss of tax—
(a) brought about deliberately by the person (or by another person acting on that person's behalf), or
(b) attributable to a failure by the person to comply with an obligation under section 53(1) or (2) or 53AA(1) or (3), may be made at any time not more than 20 years after the relevant event.
(5) In sub-paragraph (4)(a) the reference to a loss brought about deliberately by the person includes a loss brought about as a result of a deliberate inaccuracy in a document given to Her Majesty's Revenue and Customs by or on behalf of that person.".

Para 28A: inserted by the Transfer of Functions (Insurance) Order 1997, SI 1997/2781, art 8, Schedule, para 124.

Para 28B: inserted by the Financial Services and Markets Act 2000 (Consequential Amendments) Order 2004, SI 2004/355, art 4.

Para 29: word in square brackets in sub-para (1)(a) inserted and words omitted repealed by the Finance Act 2008, s 138(2), Sch 44, para 5.

Para 31: amends the Income and Corporation Taxes Act 1988, s 827.

Para 32: repealed by the Commissioners for Revenue and Customs Act 2005, ss 50(6), 52(2), Sch 4, para 53, Sch 5.

Para 33: amends the Provisional Collection of Taxes Act 1968, s 1.

[SCHEDULE 7A

INSURANCE PREMIUM TAX: CONTRACTS THAT ARE NOT TAXABLE

Section 70(1A), (1B)

PART I
DESCRIPTIONS OF CONTRACT

Contracts of reinsurance

[3592]

1. A contract falls within this paragraph if it is a contract of reinsurance.

Contracts constituting long term business

2.—(1) [Subject to sub-paragraph (3) below, a contract falls] within this paragraph [if it is exclusively a contract of long-term insurance].

[(2) In deciding whether a contract is exclusively a contract of long-term insurance, as is mentioned in sub-paragraph (1) above, where—
(a) the contract includes cover for risks relating to accident or sickness;
(b) the contract contains related and subsidiary provisions such that it might also be regarded as a contract of general insurance, but is treated as a contract of long-term insurance for the purposes of any relevant order made under section 22 of the Financial Services and Markets Act 2000; and
(c) the contract was not entered into after 30th November 1993,
the inclusion of such cover shall be ignored.]

[(3) A contract which would otherwise fall within this paragraph does not do so if it is for medical insurance.

(4) Subject to sub-paragraph (5) below, for the purposes of this paragraph a contract is a contract for medical insurance if it provides one or more of the following benefits, whether or not their provision is subject to conditions or limitations—
(a) medical, dental or optical, consultation, diagnosis or treatment;
(b) alternative or complementary medical treatment or therapy;
(c) convalescent care;
(d) goods or services related to any of the above;
(e) payment or reimbursement of, or a grant towards, the whole or part of the cost of any of the above;
(f) payment of a specified sum for optical, dental or medical appointments;
(g) payment of a specified sum for each specified period of treatment as a hospital in-patient;
(h) payment of a specified sum for each specified period of convalescent care; or
(i) payment of a specified sum, except one to which sub-paragraph (6) below applies, when a person is diagnosed as requiring or has undergone a specified medical procedure.

(5) A benefit which would apart from this sub-paragraph fall within sub-paragraph (4) above shall not do so if, before he can become entitled to the benefit, the insured is required—
(a) to be suffering from a disability which so impairs his ability to carry out normal activities of daily living that he requires long term care, supervision or assistance; and

(b) to have been suffering from the disability for a continuous period of not less than 4 weeks.

(6) This sub-paragraph applies to a payment of a specified sum if the contract under which it is payable provides that only one such payment in relation to each specified medical procedure will be made in respect of each person in relation to whom benefit is payable under the contract.]

Contracts relating to motor vehicles for use by handicapped persons

3.—(1) A contract falls within this paragraph if it relates only to a motor vehicle and the conditions mentioned in sub-paragraph (2) below are satisfied.

(2) The conditions referred to in sub-paragraph (1) above are that—

(a) the vehicle is used, or intended for use, by a handicapped person in receipt of a disability living allowance by virtue of entitlement to the mobility component or of a mobility supplement;

(b) the insured lets such vehicles on hire to such persons in the course of a business consisting predominantly of the provision of motor vehicles to such persons; and

(c) the insured does not in the course of the business let such vehicles on hire to such persons on terms other than qualifying terms.

(3) For the purposes of sub-paragraph (2)(c) above a vehicle is let on qualifying terms to a person (the lessee) if the consideration for the letting consists wholly or partly of sums paid to the insured by—

[(a) the Department for Work and Pensions;]

(b) the Department of Health and Social Services for Northern Ireland; or

(c) the Ministry of Defence,

on behalf of the lessee in respect of the disability living allowance or mobility supplement to which the lessee is entitled.

(4) For the purposes of this paragraph—

(a) "handicapped" means chronically sick or disabled;

(b) "disability living allowance" means a disability living allowance within the meaning of section 71 of the Social Security Contributions and Benefits Act 1992 or section 71 of the Social Security Contributions and Benefits (Northern Ireland) Act 1992;

(c) "mobility supplement" means a mobility supplement within the meaning of article 26A of the Naval, Military and Air Forces etc (Disablement and Death) Service Pensions Order 1983, article 25A of the Personal Injuries (Civilians) Scheme 1983, article 3 of the Motor Vehicles (Exemption from Vehicles Excise Duty) Order 1985 or article 3 of the Motor Vehicles (Exemption from Vehicles Excise Duty) (Northern Ireland) Order 1985.

Contracts relating to commercial ships

4.—(1) A contract falls within this paragraph if it relates only to a commercial ship and is [a contract of general insurance of a relevant class].

[(2) For the purposes of this paragraph, a contract of general insurance is of a relevant class if it insures against risks arising from or in relation to—

(a) accidents,

(b) ships, or

(c) liabilities of ships,

(and no other risks).]

(3) For the purposes of this paragraph a commercial ship is a ship which is—

(a) of a gross tonnage of 15 tons or more; and

(b) not designed or adapted for use for recreation or pleasure.

Contracts relating to lifeboats and lifeboat equipment

5.—(1) A contract falls within this paragraph if it relates only to a lifeboat and is [a contract of general insurance of a relevant class].

[(2) For the purposes of this paragraph, a contract of general insurance is of a relevant class if it insures against risks arising from or in relation to—

(a) accidents,

(b) ships, or

(c) liabilities of ships,

(and no other risks).]

(3) For the purposes of this paragraph a lifeboat is a vessel used or to be used solely for rescue or assistance at sea.

6.—(1) A contract falls within this paragraph if it relates only to a lifeboat and lifeboat equipment and is such that, if it related only to a lifeboat, it would fall within paragraph 5 above.

(2) In deciding whether a contract relates to lifeboat equipment the nature of the risks concerned is immaterial, and they may (for example) be risks of dying or sustaining injury or of loss or damage.

(3) For the purposes of this paragraph—

(a) "lifeboat" has the meaning given by paragraph 5(3) above; and

(b) "lifeboat equipment" means anything used or to be used solely in connection with a lifeboat.

Contracts relating to commercial aircraft

7.—(1) A contract falls within this paragraph if it relates only to a commercial aircraft and is [a contract of general insurance of a relevant class].

[(2) For the purposes of this paragraph, a contract of general insurance is of a relevant class if it insures against risks arising from or in relation to—

(a) accidents,

(b) aircraft, or

(c) aircraft liability,

(and no other risks).]

(3) For the purposes of this paragraph a commercial aircraft is an aircraft which is—

(a) of a weight of 8,000 kilogrammes or more; and

(b) not designed or adapted for use for recreation or pleasure.

Contracts relating to risks outside the United Kingdom

8.—(1) A contract falls within this paragraph if it relates only to a risk which is situated outside the United Kingdom.

[(2) The question of whether a risk is situated in the United Kingdom shall be determined in accordance with regulations made under section 424(3) of the Financial Services and Markets Act 2000; but in determining that question as respects a contract which relates to a building it shall be irrelevant whether or not the contract also covers the contents of the building.]

Contracts relating to foreign or international railway rolling stock

9.—(1) A contract falls within this paragraph if it relates only to foreign or international railway rolling stock and is [a contract of general insurance of a relevant class].

[(2) For the purposes of this paragraph, a contract of general insurance is of a relevant class if it insures against risks arising from or in relation to—

(a) railway rolling stock, or

(b) general liability to third parties,

(and no other risks).]

(3) For the purposes of this paragraph foreign or international railway rolling stock is railway rolling stock used principally for journeys taking place wholly or partly outside the United Kingdom.

Contracts relating to the Channel tunnel

10.—(1) A contract falls within this paragraph if it relates only to the Channel tunnel system and is [a contract of general insurance of a relevant class].

[(2) For the purposes of this paragraph, a contract of general insurance is of a relevant class if it insures against risks arising from or in relation to—

(a) fire or natural forces,

(b) damage to property, or

(c) general liability to third parties,

(and no other risks).]

(3) For the purposes of this paragraph "the Channel tunnel system" means—

(a) the tunnels described in section 1(7)(a) of the Channel Tunnel Act 1987;

(b) the control towers situated in the terminal areas described in section 1(7)(b) of that Act; and

(c) the shuttle crossovers, wherever situated.

11.—(1) A contract falls within this paragraph if it relates only to relevant Channel tunnel equipment and is [a contract of general insurance of a relevant class].

[(2) For the purposes of this paragraph, a contract of general insurance is of a relevant class if it insures against risks arising from or in relation to—

(a) fire or natural forces,

(b) damage to property, or

(c) general liability to third parties,

(and no other risks).]
(3) For the purposes of this paragraph "the Channel tunnel system" has the meaning given by paragraph 10(3) above.
(4) For the purposes of this paragraph "relevant Channel tunnel equipment" means, subject to sub-paragraph (5) below, the fixed or movable equipment needed for the operation of the Channel tunnel system or for the operation of trains through any tunnel forming part of it and in particular includes—
- (a) any ventilation, cooling or electrical plant used or to be used in connection with any such operation; and
- (b) any safety, signalling and control equipment which is or is to be so used.

(5) Equipment which consists of or forms part of—
- (a) roads, bridges, platforms, ticket offices and other facilities for the use of passengers or motor vehicles;
- (b) administrative buildings and maintenance facilities; and
- (c) railway track or signalling equipment which is not situated in any part of the Channel tunnel system,

is not relevant Channel tunnel equipment for the purposes of this paragraph.

Contracts relating to goods in foreign or international transit

12.—(1) A contract falls within this paragraph if it relates only to loss of or damage to goods in foreign or international transit and the insured enters into the contract in the course of a business carried on by him.
(2) For the purposes of this paragraph goods in foreign or international transit are goods in transit, and any container in which they are carried, where their carriage—
- (a) begins and ends outside the United Kingdom;
- (b) begins outside but ends in the United Kingdom; or
- (c) ends outside but begins in the United Kingdom.

(3) For the purposes of sub-paragraph (2) above "container" has the same meaning as in regulation 38(3) of the Value Added Tax (General) Regulations 1985.

Contracts relating to credit

13.—(1) A contract falls within this paragraph if it relates only to credit granted in relation to goods or services supplied under a relevant contract by a person carrying on business in the United Kingdom.
(2) For the purposes of this paragraph a relevant contract is—
- (a) a contract to make a relevant supply of goods, or a supply of services, or both, to an overseas customer;
- (b) a contract to supply goods to a person who is to—
  - (i) export those goods; or
  - (ii) incorporate those goods in other goods which he is to export,

  where the condition mentioned in sub-paragraph (3) below is satisfied;
- (c) a contract to supply to a person who is to export goods services consisting of the valuation or testing of, or other work carried out on, those goods where the condition mentioned in sub-paragraph (3) below is satisfied;
- (d) a contract to supply services to a person in order that he may comply with a legally binding obligation to make a supply of services to an overseas customer.

(3) The condition referred to in sub-paragraph (2)(b) and (c) above is that the goods to be exported are to be exported in order that the person exporting them may comply with a legally binding obligation to make a relevant supply of goods to an overseas customer.
(4) For the purposes of this paragraph—
- (a) "export" means export from the United Kingdom and cognate expressions shall be construed accordingly; and
- (b) any reference to a person who is to export goods shall be taken as including a reference to a person at whose direction the insured is to export them and the reference in sub-paragraph (3) above to the person exporting goods shall be construed accordingly.

(5) Where a contract relates to—
- (a) credit of the description in sub-paragraph (1) above; and
- (b) loss resulting from the insured or any third party being required to pay the amount of any bond or guarantee against non-performance by the insured of the contract which involves him making the supply,

the contract shall be treated for the purposes of sub-paragraph (1) above as if it did not relate to loss of the description in paragraph (b) above.

Contracts relating to exchange losses

14.—(1) A contract falls within this paragraph if—
(a) it relates only to loss resulting from a change in the rate at which the price for a supply which is or may be made by the insured may be exchanged for another currency; and
(b) the conditions mentioned in sub-paragraph (2) below are satisfied.
(2) The conditions referred to in sub-paragraph (1) above are that—
(a) the insured is a person carrying on business in the United Kingdom;
(b) the contract of insurance concerns a contract to make a relevant supply of goods, or a supply of services, or both, to an overseas customer (whether or not the contract to make the supply is one into which the insured has entered, or one for which he has tendered or intends to tender); and
(c) the period of cover for the risk expires no later than the date by which the whole of the price for the supply is to be paid or, where the contract has not been entered into, would be required to be paid.
(3) Where the contract relates to—
(a) loss of the description in sub-paragraph (1)(a) above; and
(b) loss relating from a change in the rate at which the price of goods which the insured imports into the United Kingdom for the purpose of enabling him to make the supply concerned may be exchanged for another currency,

the contract shall be treated for the purposes of sub-paragraphs (1) and (2) above as if it did not relate to loss of the description in paragraph (b) above.

Contracts relating to the provision of financial facilities

15.—(1) A contract falls within this paragraph if it relates only to the provision of a relevant financial facility and the conditions mentioned in sub-paragraph (2) below are satisfied.
(2) The conditions referred to in sub-paragraph (1) above are that—
(a) the person to whom the relevant financial facility is provided is an overseas customer;
(b) it is provided in order that he may comply with a legally binding obligation to receive a relevant supply of goods, or a supply of services, or both, from a person carrying on business . . . ; and
[(c) the contract of insurance insures against risks arising from or in relation to either or both—
(i) credit,
(ii) suretyship.]
(3) For the purposes of this paragraph a relevant financial facility is—
(a) the making of an advance;
(b) the issue of a letter of credit or acceptance of a bill of exchange;
(c) the giving of a guarantee or bond; or
(d) any other similar transaction entered into in order to provide a customer with the means to pay, or a supplier with the right to call upon a third party for, the consideration for goods or services.

NOTES

Inserted by the Insurance Premium Tax (Taxable Insurance Contracts) Order 1994, SI 1994/1698, art 5.

Para 2: words in first pair of square brackets in sub-para (1) substituted, and sub-paras (3)–(6) added, by the Insurance Premium Tax (Taxable Insurance Contracts) Order 1997, SI 1997/1627, art 2; words in second pair of square brackets in sub-para (1) and sub-para (2) substituted by the Financial Services and Markets Act 2000 (Consequential Amendments and Repeals) Order 2001, SI 2001/3649, art 346(1)–(3).

Para 3: sub-para (3)(a) substituted by the Secretaries of State for Education and Skills and for Work and Pensions Order 2002, SI 2002/1397, art 12, Schedule, Pt I, para 10.

Para 4, 5, 7–11: words in square brackets substituted by SI 2001/3649, art 346(1), (4)–(10).

Para 15: words omitted from sub-para (2)(b) repealed by the Insurance Premium Tax (Taxable Insurance Contracts) Order 1996, SI 1996/2955, art 2; sub-para (2)(c) substituted by SI 2001/3649, art 346(1), (11).

PART II
INTERPRETATION

[3593]–[3596]

16.—(1) This Part of this Schedule applies for the purposes of Part I of this Schedule.
(2) A relevant supply of goods is any supply of goods where the supply is to be made outside the United Kingdom or where the goods are to be exported from the United Kingdom.
(3) An overseas customer, in relation to a supply of goods or services, is a person who—

(a) does not have any business establishment in the United Kingdom but has such an establishment elsewhere;

(b) has such establishments both in the United Kingdom and elsewhere, provided that the establishment at which, or for the purposes of which, the goods or services which are to be supplied to him are most directly to be used is not in the United Kingdom; or

(c) has no such establishment in any place and does not have his usual place of residence in the United Kingdom.]

[16A. Paragraphs 2, 4, 5, 7, 8, 9, 10, 11 and 15 must be read with—

(a) section 22 of the Financial Services and Markets Act 2000;

(b) any relevant order under that section; and

(c) Schedule 2 to that Act.]

NOTES

Inserted as noted to Pt I at **[3592]**.

Para 16A: added by the Financial Services and Markets Act 2000 (Consequential Amendments and Repeals) Order 2001, SI 2001/3649, art 346(1), (12).

(Schs 8–26 outside the scope of this work.)

BRITISH WATERWAYS ACT 1995

(1995 c i)

An Act to confer powers on the British Waterways Board to enter land and repair or maintain, or carry out other operations with respect to, the waterways owned or managed by them and other works; to confer further powers on the Board for the regulation and management of their waterways and in relation to their undertaking; to amend or repeal statutory provisions relating to the Board or their undertaking; and for other purposes

[16 January 1995]

PART I
PRELIMINARY

[3597]

1 Short and collective titles

(1) This Act may be cited as the British Waterways Act 1995.

(2) The British Waterways Acts 1963 to 1988 and this Act may be cited together as the British Waterways Acts 1963 to 1995.

2–15 *(S 2, ss 3–15 (Pt II) outside the scope of this work.)*

PART III
REGULATION AND MANAGEMENT OF INLAND WATERWAYS

16 *(Outside the scope of this work.)*

[3598]

17 Conditions as to certificates and licences

(1) In this section—

"houseboat certificate" means a houseboat certificate issued under Act of 1971;

"insurance policy" means an insurance policy complying with Part I of Schedule 2 to this Act;

"licence" means a licence issued by the Board in respect of any vessel allowing the use of the vessel on any inland waterways;

"pleasure boat certificate" means a pleasure boat certificate issued under the Act of 1971;

"relevant consent" means a houseboat certificate, a licence or a pleasure boat certificate; and

"standards" means standards for the construction and equipment of vessels prescribed under this section and Part II of the said Schedule 2.

(2) Part I of Schedule 2 to this Act shall have effect with respect to insurance policies and Part II of that Schedule shall have effect with respect to standards.

(3) Notwithstanding anything in any enactment but subject to subsection (7) below, the Board may refuse a relevant consent in respect of any vessel unless—

(a) the applicant for the relevant consent satisfies the Board that the vessel complies with the standards applicable to that vessel;

(b) an insurance policy is in force in respect of the vessel and a copy of the policy, or evidence that it exists and is in force, has been produced to the Board; and

(c) either—

(i) the Board are satisfied that a mooring or other place where the vessel can reasonably be kept and may lawfully be left will be available for the vessel, whether on an inland waterway or elsewhere; or

(ii) the applicant for the relevant consent satisfies the Board that the vessel to which the application relates will be used bona fide for navigation throughout the period for which the consent is valid without remaining continuously in any one place for more than 14 days or such longer period as is reasonable in the circumstances.

(4) If—

(a) (subject to subsection (6) below) the vessel does not comply with the standards applicable to the vessel on the date when the consent was granted; or

(b) an insurance policy is not in force in respect of the vessel; or

(c) either—

(i) (in the case of a vessel in respect of which a relevant consent is issued pursuant to subsection (3)(c)(i) above) it appears to the Board that a mooring or other place such as is referred to in subsection (3)(c)(i) above is not available for the vessel; or

(ii) (in the case of a vessel in respect of which a relevant consent is issued pursuant to subsection (3)(c)(ii) above) the vessel has not in fact been used bona fide for navigation in accordance with the said subsection (3)(c)(ii);

the Board may give notice requiring the holder of the relevant consent to remedy the default within such time as may be reasonable (not being less than 28 days).

(5) If the holder of the relevant consent does not comply with any notice served pursuant to subsection (4) above then the relevant consent shall determine on the date the notice expires.

(6) Where prior to the grant of a relevant consent a certificate ("the boat safety certificate") has been issued by a person authorised by the Board so to do in respect of a vessel confirming that the vessel complies with the standards applicable to it at the date upon which the boat safety certificate is issued, subsection (4)(a) above shall have effect throughout the period for which the boat safety certificate is expressed to be valid as if for reference to the date when the consent was granted there were substituted reference to the date when the boat safety certificate was issued.

(7)

(a) In this subsection—

"designated vessel" means any vessel in respect of which a relevant consent has been in force at any time during the qualifying period other than—

(i) a houseboat registered under the Act of 1971 for the first time after 31st December 1979; or

(ii) any hire pleasure boat, that is, any pleasure boat which is let, lent, hired or engaged for gift, pay, hire or reward or promise of payment or carries or conveys passengers for a charge or payment; or

(iii) any pleasure boat (not being a hire pleasure boat) adapted or used for the carriage or conveyance of passengers, being a vessel in respect of which the Board are satisfied that a multi-user licence would be appropriate; and

"the qualifying period" means the period commencing twelve months before the date of the passing of this Act and ending six months before the date of the passing of this Act.

(b) The Board shall not—

(i) before the first anniversary of the passing of this Act, in the case of any designated vessel constructed after 31st December 1970; or

(ii) before the second anniversary of the passing of this Act, in the case of any designated vessel constructed before 1st January 1971;

refuse or withdraw a relevant consent in respect of the vessel on the grounds that the vessel does not or has ceased to comply with the standards applicable to it.

(8) The Board shall not within the period expiring at the end of the sixth month after the month current at the date of the passing of this Act refuse or withdraw a relevant consent in respect of any vessel on the grounds that a mooring or other place such as is referred to in subsections (3)(c)(i) and (4)(c)(i) above is not available for the vessel.

(9) Nothing in this section shall affect any power of the Board under any other enactment to refuse or withdraw a relevant consent.

(10) Section 3 (Construction and equipment of vessels) of the Act of 1983 shall cease to have effect.

(11)
(a) The refusal or withdrawal by the Board of a relevant consent in respect of any vessel on the grounds that the vessel does not comply with the standards applicable to that vessel shall not preclude the movement or use of the vessel with the consent of the Board (which shall not be unreasonably withheld) and subject to such reasonable conditions (if any) as they may determine.
(b) Without prejudice to the generality of paragraph (a) above, the Board shall not withhold their consent under this subsection to the movement or use of a vessel for the purpose of taking it to a place where it may be repaired or modified so as to comply with the standards applicable to it, or for the purpose of taking the vessel to be destroyed, unless such movement or use would give rise to the risk of obstruction or danger to navigation or to persons or property.
(c) Nothing in this section shall affect the operation of section 7 (Control of unsafe vessels) of the Act of 1983.

NOTES
Act of 1971: British Waterways Act 1971.
Act of 1983: British Waterways Act 1983.

18–37 *(Ss 18–21, ss 22–37 (Pt IV) outside the scope of this work.)*

(Sch 1 outside the scope of this work.)

SCHEDULES

SCHEDULE 2

Section 17

PART I
INSURANCE POLICIES AS TO VESSELS

[3599]

1. An insurance policy must be issued by an insurer authorised under the Insurance Companies Act 1982 to carry on in Great Britain or in Northern Ireland insurance business of a relevant class or who has corresponding permission under the law of another member state of the European Community.

2. The policy must insure the owner of the vessel and such other person, persons or classes of persons (if any) as is or as are authorised by the owner to have control of the vessel, in respect of any liability (other than a liability specified in paragraph 3 below) which may be incurred by the owner or any such other person resulting from the presence of the vessel on any inland waterway in respect of the death of or bodily injury to any person or any damage to property.

3. The policy shall not by virtue of this Act be required—
(a) to cover liability in respect of the death, arising out of and in the course of his employment, of a person in the employment of a person insured by the policy or of bodily injury sustained by such a person arising out of and in the course of his employment;
(b) to cover liability in respect of damage to the vessel to which the policy relates;
(c) to cover liability in respect of goods carried on or in the vessel to which the policy relates, or any vessel drawn or propelled by such vessel;
(d) to cover any liability of a person in respect of damage to property in his custody or under his control;
(e) to cover any contractual liability; or
(f) to provide cover in respect of any one accident for a sum in excess of such sum as may for the time being be prescribed by the Board for the purposes of this paragraph.

(Sch 2, Pt II, Sch 3 outside the scope of this work.)

MERCHANT SHIPPING ACT 1995

(1995 c 21)

ARRANGEMENT OF SECTIONS

PART VI
PREVENTION OF POLLUTION

CHAPTER III
LIABILITY FOR OIL POLLUTION

Compulsory insurance

163 Compulsory insurance against liability for pollution . . . . [3600]
163A Compulsory insurance against liability for pollution from bunker oil . . . . [3600A]
164 Issue of certificate by Secretary of State . . . . [3601]
165 Rights of third parties against insurers . . . . [3602]

CHAPTER IV
INTERNATIONAL OIL POLLUTION COMPENSATION FUND

Supplemental

181 Interpretation . . . . [3603]

PART VII
LIABILITY OF SHIPOWNERS AND OTHERS

Regulations requiring insurance or security

192A Compulsory insurance or security . . . . [3604]

PART XIII
SUPPLEMENTAL

Final provisions

316 Short title and commencement . . . . [3605]

SCHEDULE:

Schedule 5A—Text of international convention on liability and compensation for damage in connection with the carriage of hazardous and noxious substances by sea . . . . [3606]

An Act to consolidate the Merchant Shipping Acts 1894 to 1994 and other enactments relating to merchant shipping

[19 July 1995]

NOTES

The subject matter of this Act is a "reserved matter" for the purposes of the Scotland Act 1998, which by virtue of s 29(2)(b) of that Act, is outside the legislative competence of the Scottish Parliament; see s 30 of and Sch 5, Pt II, Head E, para E3, Pt III, paras 4, 5 to that Act. The regulation of sea fishing (except in relation to Scottish fishing boats) and oil and gas pollution from ships outside controlled waters are reserved separately under Sch 5, Pt II, Head C, para C6 and Head D, para D2. For restrictions on the ability of the Scottish Parliament to modify the law on reserved matters, see s 29 of and Sch 4, Pt I, paras 2, 3 to that Act.

1–127 *((Pts I–V) outside the scope of this work.)*

PART VI
PREVENTION OF POLLUTION

128–151 *((Chs I, IA, II) outside the scope of this work.)*

CHAPTER III
LIABILITY FOR OIL POLLUTION

152–162 *(Outside the scope of this work.)*

Compulsory insurance

[3600]

163 Compulsory insurance against liability for pollution

(1) Subject to the provisions of this Chapter relating to Government ships, subsection (2) below shall apply to any ship carrying in bulk a cargo of more than 2,000 tons of oil of a description specified in regulations made by the Secretary of State.

(2) The ship shall not enter or leave a port in the United Kingdom or arrive at or leave a terminal in the territorial sea of the United Kingdom nor, if the ship is a United Kingdom ship, a port in any other country or a terminal in the territorial sea of any other country, unless there is in force a certificate complying with the provisions of subsection (3) below and showing that there is in force in respect of the ship a contract of insurance or other security satisfying the requirements of Article VII of the Liability Convention (cover for owner's liability).

(3) The certificate must be—

(a) if the ship is a United Kingdom ship, a certificate issued by the Secretary of State;

(b) if the ship is registered in a Liability Convention country other than the United Kingdom, a certificate issued by or under the authority of the government of the other Liability Convention country; and

(c) if the ship is registered in a country which is not a Liability Convention country, a certificate issued by the Secretary of State or by or under the authority of the government of any Liability Convention country other than the United Kingdom.

(4) Any certificate required by this section to be in force in respect of a ship shall be carried in the ship and shall, on demand, be produced by the master to any officer of customs and excise or of the Secretary of State and, if the ship is a United Kingdom ship, to any proper officer.

(5) If a ship enters or leaves, or attempts to enter or leave, a port or arrives at or leaves, or attempts to arrive at or leave, a terminal in contravention of subsection (2) above, the master or *owner* shall be liable on conviction on indictment to a fine, or on summary conviction to a fine not exceeding £50,000.

(6) If a ship fails to carry, or the master of a ship fails to produce, a certificate as required by subsection (4) above, the master shall be liable on summary conviction to a fine not exceeding level 4 on the standard scale.

(7) If a ship attempts to leave a port in the United Kingdom in contravention of this section the ship may be detained.

NOTES

Sub-s (5): for the word in italics there are substituted the words "registered owner" by the Merchant Shipping (Oil Pollution) (Bunkers Convention) Regulations 2006, SI 2006/1244, regs 2, 16, as from a day to be appointed.

Regulations: the Oil Pollution (Compulsory Insurance) Regulations 1997, SI 1997/1820 at **[4167]**.

[3600A]

[163A Compulsory insurance against liability for pollution from bunker oil

(1) Subject to the provisions of this Chapter relating to Government ships, subsection (2) below shall apply to any ship having a gross tonnage greater than 1,000 tons calculated in the manner prescribed by an order made by the Secretary of State under paragraph 5(2) of Part II of Schedule 7.

(2) The ship shall not enter or leave a port in the United Kingdom or arrive at or leave a terminal in the territorial sea of the United Kingdom nor, if the ship is a United Kingdom ship, a port in any other country or a terminal in the territorial sea of any other country, unless there is in force—

(a) a contract of insurance or other security in respect of the ship satisfying the requirements of Article 7 of the Bunkers Convention; and

(b) a certificate complying with the provisions of subsection (3) showing that there is in force in respect of the ship a contract of insurance or other security satisfying those requirements.

(3) The certificate must be—

(a) if the ship is a United Kingdom ship, a certificate issued by the Secretary of State;

(b) if the ship is registered in a Bunkers Convention country other than the United Kingdom, a certificate issued by or under the authority of the government of the other Bunkers Convention country; and

(c) if the ship is registered in a country which is not a Bunkers Convention country, a certificate issued by the Secretary of State or by or under the authority of the government of any Bunkers Convention country other than the United Kingdom.

(4) Any certificate required by this section to be in force in respect of a ship shall be carried in the ship and shall, on demand, be produced by the master to any officer of Revenue and Customs or of the Secretary of State and, if the ship is a United Kingdom ship, to any proper officer.

(5) If a ship enters or leaves, or attempts to enter or leave, a port or arrives at or leaves, or attempts to arrive at or leave, a terminal in contravention of subsection (2) by reason of there being no certificate in force as mentioned in that subsection, the master or registered owner shall be liable on conviction on indictment to a fine, or on summary conviction to a fine not exceeding the statutory maximum.

(6) If a ship fails to carry, or the master of a ship fails to produce, a certificate as required by subsection (4), the master shall be liable on summary conviction to a fine not exceeding level 5 on the standard scale.

(7) If a ship attempts to leave a port in the United Kingdom in contravention of subsection (2), the ship may be detained.

(8) Any document required or authorised, by virtue of any statutory provision, to be served on a foreign company for the purposes of the institution of (or otherwise in connection with) proceedings for an offence under subsection (5) against the company as registered owner of the ship shall be treated as duly served on the company if the document is served on the master of the ship.

[In this subsection "foreign company" means a company or body which is not one to which section 1139 of the Companies Act 2006 applies so as to authorise service of the document in question].

(9) Any person authorised to serve any document for the purposes of the institution of (or otherwise in connection with) the institution of proceedings for an offence under this section shall, for that purpose, have the right to go on board the ship in question.

(10) In the case of a ship of which, at any relevant time, the tonnage has not been and cannot be ascertained in the manner set out in subsection (1), the best available evidence shall be used in calculating the tonnage of the ship in accordance with any order under paragraph 5(2) of Part II of Schedule 7.]

NOTES

Commencement: to be appointed.

Inserted by the Merchant Shipping (Oil Pollution) (Bunkers Convention) Regulations 2006, SI 2006/1244, regs 2, 17, as from a day to be appointed.

Sub-s (8): words in square brackets substituted by the Companies Act 2006 (Consequential Amendments, Transitional Provisions and Savings) Order 2009, SI 2009/1941, art 2(1), Sch 1, para 152(1), (3).

[3601]

164 Issue of certificate by Secretary of State

(1) Subject to subsection (2) below, if the Secretary of State is satisfied, on the application for such a certificate as is mentioned in *section 163* in respect of a United Kingdom ship or a ship registered in any country which is not a Liability Convention country, that there will be in force in respect of the ship, throughout the period for which the certificate is to be issued, a contract of insurance or other security satisfying the requirements of Article VII of the Liability Convention, the Secretary of State shall issue such a certificate to the *owner*.

[(1A) Subject to subsection (2) below, if the Secretary of State is satisfied, on the application for such a certificate as is mentioned in section 163A(2) in respect of a United Kingdom ship or a ship registered in any country which is not a Bunkers Convention country, that there will be in force in respect of the ship, throughout the period for which the certificate is to be issued, a contract of insurance or other security satisfying the requirements of Article 7 of the Bunkers Convention, the Secretary of State shall issue such a certificate to the registered owner.]

(2) If the Secretary of State is of opinion that there is a doubt whether the person providing the insurance or other security will be able to meet his obligations thereunder, or whether the insurance or other security will cover the owner's liability under section 153 in all circumstances, he may refuse the certificate.

(3) The Secretary of State may make regulations providing for the cancellation and delivery up of a certificate under this section in such circumstances as may be prescribed by the regulations.

(4) If a person required by regulations under subsection (3) above to deliver up a certificate fails to do so he shall be liable on summary conviction to a fine not exceeding level 4 on the standard scale.

(5) The Secretary of State shall send a copy of any certificate issued by him under this section in respect of a United Kingdom ship to the Registrar General of Shipping and Seamen, and the Registrar shall make the copy available for public inspection.

NOTES

Sub-s (1): for the first words in italics there are substituted the words "section 163(2)" and for the second word in italics there are substituted the words "registered owner" by the Merchant Shipping (Oil Pollution) (Bunkers Convention) Regulations 2006, SI 2006/1244, regs 2, 18(1), (2), as from a day to be appointed.

Sub-s (1A): inserted by SI 2006/1244, regs 2, 18(1), (3), as from 15 July 2006 (for the purposes of enabling certificates under this sub-s to be issued before the day on which the International Convention on Civil Liability for Bunker Oil Pollution Damage 2001 comes into force in respect of the United Kingdom) and as from a day to be appointed (otherwise).

Sub-s (2): substituted by SI 2006/1244, regs 2, 18(1), (4), as from 15 July 2006 (for the purposes of enabling certificates under this sub-s to be issued before the day on which the International Convention on Civil Liability for Bunker Oil Pollution Damage 2001 comes into force in respect of the United Kingdom) and as from a day to be appointed (otherwise), as follows—

"(2) The Secretary of State may refuse the certificate if he is of the opinion that there is a doubt whether—

(a) the person providing the insurance or other security will be able to meet his obligations thereunder; or

(b) the insurance or other security will cover the registered owner's liability under section 153, or the owner's liability under section 153A, as the case may be.".

Regulations: the Oil Pollution (Compulsory Insurance) Regulations 1997, SI 1997/1820 at **[4167]**.

[3602]

165 Rights of third parties against insurers

(1) Where it is alleged that the *owner* of a ship has incurred a liability under section 153 as a result of any discharge or escape of oil occurring, or as a result of any relevant threat of contamination arising, while there was in force a contract of insurance or other security to which such a certificate as is mentioned in section *163* related, proceedings to enforce a claim in respect of the liability may be brought against the person who provided the insurance or other security *(in the following provisions of this section referred to as "the insurer")*.

[(1A) Where it is alleged that the owner of a ship has incurred a liability under section 153A as a result of any discharge or escape of bunker oil occurring, or as a result of any relevant threat of contamination arising, while there was in force a contract of insurance or other security to which such a certificate as is mentioned in section 163A(2) related, proceedings to enforce a claim in respect of the liability may be brought against the person who provided the insurance or other security.

(1B) In the following provisions of this section, "the insurer" means the person who provided the insurance or other security referred to in subsection (1) or subsection (1A), as the case may be.]

(2) In any proceedings brought against the insurer by virtue of this section [in respect of liability under section 153] it shall be a defence (in addition to any defence affecting the *owner's* liability) to prove that the discharge or escape, or (as the case may be) the threat of contamination, was due to the wilful misconduct of the *owner* himself.

(3) The insurer may limit his liability in respect of claims [in respect of liability under section 153 which are] made against him by virtue of this section in like manner and to the same extent as the *owner* may limit his liability [under section 157] but the insurer may do so whether or not the discharge or escape, or (as the case may be) the threat of contamination, resulted from anything done or omitted to be done by the *owner* as mentioned in section 157(3).

(4) Where the *owner* and the insurer each apply to the court for the limitation of his liability [(in relation to liability under section 153)] any sum paid into court in pursuance of either application shall be treated as paid also in pursuance of the other.

[(4A) In any proceedings brought against the insurer by virtue of this section in respect of liability under section 153A it shall be a defence (in addition to any defence affecting the owner's liability) to prove that the discharge or escape, or (as the case may be) the threat of contamination, was due to the wilful misconduct of the owner himself.

(4B) The insurer may limit his liability in respect of claims in respect of liability under section 153A which are made against him by virtue of this section in like manner and to the same extent as the owner may limit his liability by virtue of section 185; but the insurer may do so whether or not the discharge or escape, or (as the case may be) the threat of contamination, resulted from any act or omission mentioned in Article 4 of the Convention set out in Part I of Schedule 7.

(4C) Where the owner and the insurer each apply to the court for the limitation of his liability (in relation to liability under section 153A) any sum paid into court in pursuance of either application shall be treated as paid also in pursuance of the other.]

(5) The Third Parties (Rights against Insurers) Act 1930 and the Third Parties (Rights against Insurers) Act (Northern Ireland) 1930 shall not apply in relation to any contract of insurance to which such a certificate as is mentioned in section 163 [or 163A] relates.

NOTES

Sub-s (1): for the first word in italics there are substituted the words "registered owner", for the figure in italics there is substituted "163(2)" and final words in italics repealed by the Merchant Shipping (Oil Pollution) (Bunkers Convention) Regulations 2006, SI 2006/1244, regs 2, 19(1), (2), as from a day to be appointed.

Sub-ss (1A), (1B): inserted by SI 2006/1244, regs 2, 19(1), (3), as from a day to be appointed.

Sub-s (2): words in square brackets inserted and for the first and second words in italics there are substituted the words "registered owner's" and "registered owner" respectively by SI 2006/1244, regs 2, 19(1), (4), as from a day to be appointed.

Sub-s (3): words in square brackets inserted and for the word in italics in both places it appears there are substituted the words "registered owner" by SI 2006/1244, regs 2, 19(1), (5), as from a day to be appointed.

Sub-s (4): for the word in italics there are substituted the words "registered owner" and words in square brackets inserted by SI 2006/1244, regs 2, 19(1), (6), as from a day to be appointed.

Sub-ss (4A)–(4C): inserted by SI 2006/1244, regs 2, 19(1), (7), as from a day to be appointed.

Sub-s (5): words in square brackets inserted by SI 2006/1244, regs 2, 19(1), (8), as from a day to be appointed.

166–171 *(Outside the scope of this work.)*

CHAPTER IV
INTERNATIONAL OIL POLLUTION COMPENSATION FUND

172–176B *(Outside the scope of this work.)*

Supplemental

177–180 *(Outside the scope of this work.)*

[3603]

181 Interpretation

(1) In this Chapter, unless the context otherwise requires—

"damage" includes loss;

"discharge or escape", in relation to pollution damage, means the discharge or escape of oil from the ship;

"guarantor" means any person providing insurance or other financial security to cover the owner's liability of the kind described in section 163;

"incident" means any occurrence, or series of occurrences having the same origin, resulting in a discharge or escape of oil from a ship or in a relevant threat of contamination;

"oil", except in sections 173 and 174, means persistent hydrocarbon mineral oil;

"owner" means the person or persons registered as the owner of the ship or, in the absence of registration, the person or persons owning the ship, except that, in relation to a ship owned by a State which is operated by a person registered as the ship's operator, it means the person registered as its operator;

"pollution damage" means—

(a) damage caused outside a ship by contamination resulting from a discharge or escape of oil from the ship,

(b) the cost of preventive measures, and

(c) further damage caused by preventive measures,

but does not include any damage attributable to any impairment of the environment except to the extent that any such damage consists of—

(i) any loss of profits, or

(ii) the cost of any reasonable measures of reinstatement actually taken or to be taken;

"preventive measures" means any reasonable measures taken by any person to prevent or minimise pollution damage, being measures taken—

(a) after an incident has occurred, or

(b) in the case of an incident consisting of a series of occurrences, after the first of those occurrences;

"relevant threat of contamination" means a grave and imminent threat of damage being caused outside a ship by contamination resulting from a discharge or escape of oil from the ship; and

"ship" means any ship (within the meaning of Chapter III of this Part) to which section 153 applies.

(2) For the purposes of this Chapter—

(a) references to a discharge or escape of oil from a ship are references to such a discharge or escape wherever it may occur, and whether it is of oil carried in a cargo tank or of oil carried in a bunker fuel tank; and

(b) where more than one discharge or escape results from the same occurrence or from a series of occurrences having the same origin, they shall be treated as one.

(3) References in this Chapter to the territory of any country shall be construed in accordance with section 170(4) reading the reference to a Liability Convention country as a reference to a Fund Convention country [or a Supplementary Fund Protocol country (as the case may be)].

NOTES

Sub-s (3): words in square brackets inserted by the Merchant Shipping (Oil Pollution) (Supplementary Fund Protocol) Order 2006, SI 2006/1265, arts 2, 11.

182–182C *(Outside the scope of this work.)*

PART VII
LIABILITY OF SHIPOWNERS AND OTHERS

183–192 *(Outside the scope of this work.)*

[Regulations requiring insurance or security

[3604]

192A Compulsory insurance or security

(1) Subject to subsections (2) and (3) below, the Secretary of State may make regulations requiring that, in such cases as may be prescribed by the regulations, while a ship is in United Kingdom waters, there must be in force in respect of the ship—

(a) a contract of insurance insuring such person or persons as may be specified by the regulations against such liabilities as may be so specified and satisfying such other requirements as may be so specified, or

(b) such other security relating to those liabilities as satisfies requirements specified by or under the regulations.

(2) Regulations under this section shall not apply in relation to—

(a) a qualifying foreign ship while it is exercising—

(i) the right of innocent passage, or

(ii) the right of transit passage through straits used for international navigation,

(b) any warship, or

(c) any ship for the time being used by the government of any State for other than commercial purposes.

(3) Regulations under this section may not require insurance or security to be maintained in respect of a ship in relation to any liability in any case where an obligation to maintain insurance or security in respect of that ship in relation to that liability is imposed by section 163 or by or under an Order in Council under section 182B.

(4) Regulations under this section may require that, where a person is obliged to have in force in respect of a ship a contract of insurance or other security, such documentary evidence as may be specified by or under the regulations of the existence of the contract of insurance or other security must be carried in the ship and produced on demand, by such persons as may be specified in the regulations, to such persons as may be so specified.

(5) Regulations under this section may provide—

(a) that in such cases as are prescribed a ship which contravenes the regulations shall be liable to be detained and that section 284 shall have effect, with such modifications (if any) as are prescribed by the regulations, in relation to the ship,

(b) that a contravention of the regulations shall be an offence punishable on summary conviction by a fine of an amount not exceeding £50,000, or such less amount as is prescribed by the regulations, and on conviction on indictment by a fine, and

(c) that any such contravention shall be an offence punishable only on summary conviction by a fine of an amount not exceeding £50,000, or such less amount as is prescribed by the regulations.

(6) Regulations under this section may—

(a) make different provision for different cases,

(b) make provision in terms of any document which the Secretary of State or any person considers relevant from time to time, and

(c) include such incidental, supplemental and transitional provision as appears to the Secretary of State to be expedient for the purposes of the regulations.]

NOTES

Inserted, together with preceding cross-heading, by the Merchant Shipping and Maritime Security Act 1997, s 16.

Regulations: the Merchant Shipping (Compulsory Insurance: Ships Receiving Trans-shipped Fish) Regulations 1998, SI 1998/209.

193–291 *((Pts VIII–XII) in so far as unrepealed, outside the scope of this work.)*

Part III Statutes

PART XIII
SUPPLEMENTAL

292–312 *(Outside the scope of this work.)*

Final provisions

313–315 *(Outside the scope of this work.)*

[3605]
316 Short title and commencement
(1) This Act may be cited as the Merchant Shipping Act 1995.
(2) This Act shall come into force on 1st January 1996.

(Schs 1–5, 5ZA outside the scope of this work.)

SCHEDULES

[SCHEDULE 5A

TEXT OF INTERNATIONAL CONVENTION ON LIABILITY AND COMPENSATION FOR DAMAGE IN CONNECTION WITH THE CARRIAGE OF HAZARDOUS AND NOXIOUS SUBSTANCES BY SEA

Section 182A(2)

[3606]–[3607]
The States parties to the present Convention,

Conscious of the dangers posed by the world-wide carriage by sea of hazardous and noxious substances,

Convinced of the need to ensure that adequate, prompt and effective compensation is available to persons who suffer damage caused by incidents in connection with the carriage by sea of such substances,

Desiring to adopt uniform international rules and procedures for determining questions of liability and compensation in respect of such damage,

Considering that the economic consequences of damage caused by the carriage by sea of hazardous and noxious substances should be shared by the shipping industry and the cargo interests involved,

Have agreed as follows—

Articles 1–6

((Ch 1) outside the scope of this work.)

CHAPTER II
LIABILITY

Articles 7–11

(Outside the scope of this work.)

Compulsory insurance of the owner

Article 12

1. The owner of a ship registered in a State Party and actually carrying hazardous and noxious substances shall be required to maintain insurance or other financial security, such as the guarantee of a bank or similar financial institution, in the sums fixed by applying the limits of liability prescribed in article 9, paragraph 1, to cover liability for damage under this Convention.

2. A compulsory insurance certificate attesting that insurance or other financial security is in force in accordance with the provisions of this Convention shall be issued to each ship after the appropriate authority of a State Party has determined that the requirements of paragraph 1 have been complied with. With respect to a ship registered in a State Party such compulsory insurance certificate shall be issued or certified by the appropriate authority of the State of the ship's registry; with respect to a ship not registered in a State Party it may be issued or certified by the appropriate authority of any State Party. This compulsory insurance certificate shall be in the form of the model set out in Annex I and shall contain the following particulars—

(a) name of the ship, distinctive number or letters and port of registry;
(b) name and principal place of business of the owner;
(c) IMO ship identification number;

(d) type and duration of security;
(e) name and principal place of business of insurer or other person giving security and, where appropriate, place of business where the insurance or security is established; and
(f) period of validity of certificate, which shall not be longer than the period of validity of the insurance or other security.

3. The compulsory insurance certificate shall be in the official language or languages of the issuing State. If the language used is neither English, nor French nor Spanish, the text shall include a translation into one of these languages.

4. The compulsory insurance certificate shall be carried on board the ship and a copy shall be deposited with the authorities who keep the record of the ship's registry or, if the ship is not registered in a State Party, with the authority of the State issuing or certifying the certificate.

5. An insurance or other financial security shall not satisfy the requirements of this article if it can cease, for reasons other than the expiry of the period of validity of the insurance or security specified in the certificate under paragraph 2, before three months have elapsed from the date on which notice of its termination is given to the authorities referred to in paragraph 4, unless the compulsory insurance certificate has been issued within the said period. The foregoing provisions shall similarly apply to any modification which results in the insurance or security no longer satisfying the requirements of this article.

6. The State of the ship's registry shall, subject to the provisions of this article, determine the conditions of issue and validity of the compulsory insurance certificate.

7. Compulsory insurance certificates issued or certified under the authority of a State Party in accordance with paragraph 2 shall be accepted by other States Parties for the purposes of this Convention and shall be regarded by other States Parties as having the same force as compulsory insurance certificates issued or certified by them even if issued or certified in respect of a ship not registered in a State Party. A State Party may at any time request consultation with the issuing or certifying State should it believe that the insurer or guarantor named in the compulsory insurance certificate is not financially capable of meeting the obligations imposed by this Convention.

8. Any claim for compensation for damage may be brought directly against the insurer or other person providing financial security for the owner's liability for damage. In such case the defendant may, even if the owner is not entitled to limitation of liability, benefit from the limit of liability prescribed in accordance with paragraph 1. The defendant may further invoke the defences (other than the bankruptcy or winding up of the owner) which the owner would have been entitled to invoke. Furthermore, the defendant may invoke the defence that the damage resulted from the wilful misconduct of the owner, but the defendant shall not invoke any other defence which the defendant might have been entitled to invoke in proceedings brought by the owner against the defendant. The defendant shall in any event have the right to require the owner to be joined in the proceedings.

9. Any sums provided by insurance or by other financial security maintained in accordance with paragraph 1 shall be available exclusively for the satisfaction of claims under this Convention.

10. A State Party shall not permit a ship under its flag to which this article applies to trade unless a certificate has been issued under paragraph 2 or 12.

11. Subject to the provisions of this article, each State Party shall ensure, under its national law, that insurance or other security in the sums specified in paragraph 1 is in force in respect of any ship, wherever registered, entering or leaving a port in its territory, or arriving at or leaving an offshore facility in its territorial sea.

12. If insurance or other financial security is not maintained in respect of a ship owned by a State Party, the provisions of this article relating thereto shall not be applicable to such ship, but the ship shall carry a compulsory insurance certificate issued by the appropriate authorities of the State of the ship's registry stating that the ship is owned by that State and that the ship's liability is covered within the limit prescribed in accordance with paragraph 1. Such a compulsory insurance certificate shall follow as closely as possible the model prescribed by paragraph 2.

Articles 13–54

((Chs III–VI) outside the scope of this work.)]

NOTES

Inserted by the Merchant Shipping and Maritime Security Act 1997, s 14(2), Sch 3.

(Schs 6–8, 10–14 outside the scope of this work; Sch 9 repealed by the Merchant Shipping and

Maritime Security Act 1997, s 29(1), (2), Sch 6, para 9, Sch 7, Pt I.)

DISABILITY DISCRIMINATION ACT 1995

(1995 c 50)

An Act to make it unlawful to discriminate against disabled persons in connection with employment, the provision of goods, facilities and services or the disposal or management of premises; to make provision about the employment of disabled persons; and to establish a National Disability Council.

[8 November 1995]

NOTES

The subject matter of this Act is a "reserved matter" for the purposes of the Scotland Act 1998, which by virtue of s 29(2)(b) of that Act, is outside the legislative competence of the Scottish Parliament; see s 30 of and Sch 5, Pt II, Head L, para L2, Pt III, para 5 to that Act. For restrictions on the ability of the Scottish Parliament to modify the law on reserved matters, see s 29 of and Sch 4, Pt I, paras 2, 3 to that Act.

1–18E *(Ss 1–3 (Pt I) outside the scope of this work; ss 3A–18E (Pt II) in so far as unrepealed outside the scope of this work.)*

PART III
DISCRIMINATION IN OTHER AREAS

Goods, facilities and services

[3608]

19 Discrimination in relation to goods, facilities and services

(1) It is unlawful for a provider of services to discriminate against a disabled person—

(a) in refusing to provide, or deliberately not providing, to the disabled person any service which he provides, or is prepared to provide, to members of the public;

(b) in failing to comply with any duty imposed on him by section 21 in circumstances in which the effect of that failure is to make it impossible or unreasonably difficult for the disabled person to make use of any such service;

(c) in the standard of service which he provides to the disabled person or the manner in which he provides it to him; or

(d) in the terms on which he provides a service to the disabled person.

(2) For the purposes of this section and sections 20 [to 21ZA]—

(a) the provision of services includes the provision of any goods or facilities;

(b) a person is "a provider of services" if he is concerned with the provision, in the United Kingdom, of services to the public or to a section of the public; and

(c) it is irrelevant whether a service is provided on payment or without payment.

(3) The following are examples of services to which this section and sections 20 and 21 apply—

(a) access to and use of any place which members of the public are permitted to enter;

(b) access to and use of means of communication;

(c) access to and use of information services;

(d) accommodation in a hotel, boarding house or other similar establishment;

(e) facilities by way of banking or insurance or for grants, loans, credit or finance;

(f) facilities for entertainment, recreation or refreshment;

(g) facilities provided by employment agencies or under section 2 of the Employment and Training Act 1973;

(h) the services of any profession or trade, or any local or other public authority.

(4) In the case of an act which constitutes discrimination by virtue of section 55, this section also applies to discrimination against a person who is not disabled.

[(4A) Subsection (1) does not apply to anything that is governed by Regulation (EC) No 1107/2006 of the European Parliament and of the Council of 5 July 2006 concerning the rights of disabled persons and persons with reduced mobility when travelling by air.]

[(5) Regulations may provide for subsection (1) and section 21(1), (2) and (4) not to apply, or to apply only to a prescribed extent, in relation to a service of a prescribed description.]

[(5A) Nothing in this section or sections 20 to 21A applies to the provision of a service in relation to which discrimination is unlawful under Part 4.]

(6) . . .

NOTES

Sub-s (2): words in square brackets substituted by the Disability Discrimination Act 2005, s 19(1), Sch 1, Pt 1, paras 1, 13(1), (2), and in relation to Northern Ireland by the Disability Discrimination (Northern Ireland) Order 2006, SI 2006/312, art 19(1), Sch 1, paras 1, 12(1), (2).

Sub-s (4A): inserted by the Civil Aviation (Access to Air Travel for Disabled Persons and Persons with Reduced Mobility) Regulations 2007, SI 2007/1895, reg 8.

Sub-s (5): substituted by the Disability Discrimination Act 2005, s 19(1), Sch 1, Pt 1, paras 1, 13(1), (3), and in relation to Northern Ireland by SI 2006/312, art 19(1), Sch 1, paras 1, 12(1), (3).

Sub-s (5A): inserted by the Special Educational Needs and Disability Act 2001, s 38(1), (6); substituted by the Disability Discrimination Act 2005, s 19(1), Sch 1, Pt 1, paras 1, 13(1), (4).

Sub-s (6): repealed by the Special Educational Needs and Disability Act 2001, ss 38(1), (5)(b), 42(6), Sch 9.

20–59A *(Ss 20–28, ss 28A–59A (Pts IV–VII) outside the scope of this work.)*

PART VIII
MISCELLANEOUS

60–69 *(Outside the scope of this work.)*

[3609]

70 Short title, commencement, extent etc

(1) This Act may be cited as the Disability Discrimination Act 1995.

(2) This section (apart from subsections (4), (5) and (7)) comes into force on the passing of this Act.

[(2A) . . .]

(3) The other provisions of this Act come into force on such day as the Secretary of State may by order appoint and different days may be appointed for different purposes.

(4), (5), [(5A), (5B)] . . .

(6) [Subject to subsections (5A) and (5B), this Act extends to England and Wales, Scotland and Northern Ireland;] but in their application to Northern Ireland the provisions of this Act mentioned in Schedule 8 shall have effect subject to the modifications set out in that Schedule.

(7) . . .

(8) Consultations which are required by any provision of this Act to be held by the Secretary of State may be held by him before the coming into force of that provision.

NOTES

Sub-ss (2A), (4), (5), (5A), (5B): outside the scope of this work.

Sub-s (6): words in square brackets substituted by the Disability Discrimination Act 1995 (Amendment) Regulations 2003, SI 2003/1673, regs 3(1), 28(b).

Sub-s (7): amends the House of Commons Disqualification Act 1975, Sch 1, Pt II, and the Northern Ireland Assembly Disqualification Act 1975, Sch 1, Pt II; repealed in part by the Disability Rights Commission Act 1999, s 14(2), Sch 5.

Orders: the Disability Discrimination Act 1995 (Commencement No 1) Order 1995, SI 1995/3330; the Disability Discrimination Act 1995 (Commencement No 2) Order 1996, SI 1SI 1996/1336; the Disability Discrimination Act 1995 (Commencement No 3 and Saving and Transitional Provisions) Order 1996, SI 1996/1474; the Disability Discrimination Act 1995 (Commencement No 4) Order 1996, SI 1996/3003; the Disability Discrimination Act 1995 (Commencement Order No 5) Order 1998, SI 1998/1282; the Disability Discrimination Act 1995 (Commencement Order No 6) Order 1999, SI 1999/1190; the Disability Discrimination Act 1995 (Commencement No 7) Order 2000, SI 2000/1969; the Disability Discrimination Act 1995 (Commencement No 9) Order 2001, SI 2001/2030; the Disability Discrimination Act 1995 (Commencement No 10) (Scotland) Order 2003, SI 2003/215; the Disability Discrimination Act 1995 (Commencement No 11) Order 2005, SI 2005/1122.

(Schs 1–8 outside the scope of this work.)

EMPLOYMENT RIGHTS ACT 1996

(1996 c 18)

An Act to consolidate enactments relating to employment rights

[22 May 1996]

NOTES

The subject matter of this Act is a "reserved matter" for the purposes of the Scotland Act 1998, which by virtue of s 29(2)(b) of that Act, is outside the legislative competence of the Scottish Parliament; see s 30 of and

Sch 5, Pt II, Head H, para H1, Pt III, para 5 to that Act. For restrictions on the ability of the Scottish Parliament to modify the law on reserved matters, see s 29 of and Sch 4, Pt I, paras 2, 3 to that Act.

1–190 *((Pts I–XII) outside the scope of this work.)*

PART XIII
MISCELLANEOUS

191–201 *((Ch I) outside the scope of this work.)*

CHAPTER II
OTHER MISCELLANEOUS MATTERS

202 *(Outside the scope of this work.)*

Contracting out etc and remedies

[3610]

203 Restrictions on contracting out

(1) Any provision in an agreement (whether a contract of employment or not) is void in so far as it purports—

(a) to exclude or limit the operation of any provision of this Act, or

(b) to preclude a person from bringing any proceedings under this Act before an [employment tribunal].

(2) Subsection (1)—

(a)–(e) *(outside the scope of this work.)*

(f) does not apply to any agreement to refrain from instituting or continuing . . . any proceedings within [the following provisions of section 18(1) of the Employment Tribunals Act 1996 (cases where conciliation available)—

(i) paragraph (d) (proceedings under this Act),

(ii) paragraph (h) (proceedings arising out of the Part-time Workers (Prevention of Less Favourable Treatment) Regulations 2000),]

[(iii) paragraph (i) (proceedings arising out of the Fixed-term Employees (Prevention of Less Favourable Treatment) Regulations 2002),

(iv) paragraph (j) (proceedings under those Regulations),]

if the conditions regulating compromise agreements under this Act are satisfied in relation to the agreement.

(3) For the purposes of subsection (2)(f) the conditions regulating compromise agreements under this Act are that—

(a)–(c) *(Outside the scope of this work.)*

(d) there must be in force, when the adviser gives the advice, a [contract of insurance, or an indemnity provided for members of a professional body,] covering the risk of a claim by the employee or worker in respect of loss arising in consequence of the advice,

(e), (f) *(Outside the scope of this work.)*

[(3A)–(4)], [(5)] *(Outside the scope of this work.)*

NOTES

Sub-ss (1), (3): words in square brackets substituted by the Employment Rights (Dispute Resolution) Act 1998, ss 1(2)(a), 10(1), (2)(e).

Sub-s (2): words omitted repealed by the Employment Rights (Dispute Resolution) Act 1998, s 15, Sch 2; words in first pair of square brackets in para (f) substituted by the Part-time Workers (Prevention of Less Favourable Treatment) Regulations 2001, SI 2001/1107, reg 3; para (f)(iii), (iv) added by the Fixed-term Employees (Prevention of Less Favourable Treatment) Regulations 2002, SI 2002/2034, reg 11, Sch 2, Pt 1, para 3(1), (17)(b).

Orders: the Compromise Agreements (Description of Person) Order 2004, SI 2004/754.

204–235 *(Ss 204–209, ss 210–235 (Pt XIV) outside the scope of this work.)*

PART XV
GENERAL AND SUPPLEMENTARY

236–239 *(Outside the scope of this work.)*

Final provisions

240–244 *(Outside the scope of this work.)*

[3611]

245 Short title

This Act may be cited as the Employment Rights Act 1996.

(Schs 1–3 outside the scope of this work.)

FINANCE ACT 1997

(1997 c 16)

An Act to grant certain duties, to alter other duties, and to amend the law relating to the National Debt and the Public Revenue, and to make further provision in connection with Finance

[19 March 1997]

1–20 *((Pt I) outside the scope of this work.)*

PART II
INSURANCE PREMIUM TAX

New rates of tax

21–23 *(Substitute the Finance Act 1994, ss 51, 69, at* **[3551]**, **[3576]**, *insert s 51A, Sch 6A, at* **[3552]**, **[3584]**, *and amend ss 50, 73, 74 of that Act at* **[3550]**, **[3580]**, **[3581]**.*)*

[3612]

24 Commencement of sections 21 to 23

(1) Except as provided by subsection (2) below, sections 21 to 23 above have effect in relation to a premium which falls to be regarded for the purposes of Part III of the Finance Act 1994 as received under a taxable insurance contract by an insurer on or after 1st April 1997.

(2) Sections 21 to 23 above do not have effect in relation to a premium if the premium—

- (a) is in respect of a contract made before 1st April 1997; and
- (b) falls, by virtue of regulations under section 68 of the Finance Act 1994 (special accounting scheme), to be regarded for the purposes of Part III of that Act as received under the contract by the insurer on a date before 1st August 1997.

(3) Subsection (2) above does not apply in relation to a premium if the premium—

- (a) is an additional premium under the contract;
- (b) falls as mentioned in subsection (2)(b) above to be regarded as received under the contract by the insurer on or after 1st April 1997; and
- (c) is in respect of a risk which was not covered by the contract before 1st April 1997.

(4) Without prejudice to the generality of subsections (1) to (3) above, those subsections shall be construed in accordance with sections 67A to 67C of the Finance Act 1994 (which are inserted by section 29 below).

25–27 *(Ss 25, 26 insert the Finance Act 1994, s 52A, 53AA at* **[3554]**, **[3556]**; *s 27 amends ss 53A, 55, 59, 62, 63, 73, Sch 7 of that Act at* **[3557]**, **[3559]**, **[3563]**, **[3566]**, **[3567]**, **[3580]**, **[3586]** *and is repealed in part by the Finance Act 2008, ss 123(1), 142(2), Sch 41, para 25(i).)*

Miscellaneous

28 *(Inserts the Finance Act 1994, s 72(1A) at* **[3579]**.*)*

[3613]

29 Prevention of pre-emption

(1) . . .

(2) In the application of sections 67A to 67C of the Finance Act 1994 in relation to the increases in insurance premium tax effected by this Part and the exceptions from those increases—

- (a) the announcement relating to those increases, as described in section 67A(1), and to those exceptions, as described in section 67B(1), shall be taken to have been made on 26th November 1996;
- (b) "the date of the change" is 1st April 1997; and
- (c) "the concessionary date" is 1st August 1997.

(3) The amendment made by subsection (1) above has effect on and after 26th November 1996.

NOTES

Sub-s (1): inserts the Finance Act 1994, ss 67A–67C at **[3572]–[3574]**.

30 *(Inserts the Finance Act 1994, s 72(7A), (8A) at* **[3579]***.)*

31–106 *((Pts III–VII) Outside the scope of this work.)*

PART VIII
MISCELLANEOUS AND SUPPLEMENTAL

107–111 *(Outside the scope of this work.)*

Supplemental

112, 113 *(Outside the scope of this work.)*

[3614]
114 Short title
This Act may be cited as the Finance Act 1997.

(Schs 1–3, 5–18 in so far as unrepealed, outside the scope of this work, Sch 4 inserts the Finance Act 1994, Sch 6A at **[3584]***.)*

DATA PROTECTION ACT 1998

(1998 c 29)

ARRANGEMENT OF SECTIONS

PART I
PRELIMINARY

1 Basic interpretative provisions . . . . [3615]
2 Sensitive personal data . . . . [3616]
3 The special purposes . . . . [3617]
4 The data protection principles . . . . [3618]
5 Application of Act . . . . [3619]
6 The Commissioner . . . . [3620]

PART II
RIGHTS OF DATA SUBJECTS AND OTHERS

7 Right of access to personal data . . . . [3621]
8 Provisions supplementary to section 7 . . . . [3622]
10 Right to prevent processing likely to cause damage or distress . . . . [3623]
11 Right to prevent processing for purposes of direct marketing . . . . [3624]
12 Rights in relation to automated decision-taking . . . . [3625]
13 Compensation for failure to comply with certain requirements . . . . [3626]
14 Rectification, blocking, erasure and destruction . . . . [3627]
15 Jurisdiction and procedure . . . . [3628]

PART III
NOTIFICATION BY DATA CONTROLLERS

16 Preliminary . . . . [3629]
17 Prohibition on processing without registration . . . . [3630]
18 Notification by data controllers . . . . [3631]
19 Register of notifications . . . . [3632]
20 Duty to notify changes . . . . [3633]
21 Offences . . . . [3634]
22 Preliminary assessment by Commissioner . . . . [3635]
23 Power to make provision for appointment of data protection supervisors . . . . [3636]
24 Duty of certain data controllers to make certain information available . . . . [3637]
25 Functions of Commissioner in relation to making of notification regulations . . . . [3638]
26 Fees regulations . . . . [3639]

PART IV
EXEMPTIONS

27 Preliminary . . . . [3640]
28 National security . . . . [3641]
29 Crime and taxation . . . . [3642]
31 Regulatory activity . . . . [3642AA]
33 Research, history and statistics . . . . [3642AB]
34 Information available to the public by or under enactment . . . . [3642AC]
35 Disclosures required by law or made in connection with legal proceedings etc . . . . [3642AD]
35A Parliamentary privilege . . . . [3642AE]
36 Domestic purposes . . . . [3642AF]

37 Miscellaneous exemptions . . . . . [3642AG]
38 Powers to make further exemptions by order . . . . . [3642AH]
39 Transitional relief . . . . . [3642AI]

PART V
ENFORCEMENT

40 Enforcement notices . . . . . [3642AJ]
41 Cancellation of an enforcement notice . . . . . [3642AK]
41A Assessment notices . . . . . [3642AKA]
41B Assessment notices: limitations . . . . . [3642AKB]
41C Code of practice about assessment notices . . . . . [3642AKC]
42 Request for assessment . . . . . [3642AL]
43 Information notices . . . . . [3642AM]
44 Special information notices . . . . . [3642AN]
45 Determination by Commissioner as to the special purposes . . . . . [3642AO]
46 Restriction on enforcement in case of processing for the special purposes . . . . . [3642AP]
47 Failure to comply with notice . . . . . [3642AQ]
48 Rights of appeal . . . . . [3642AR]
49 Determination of appeals . . . . . [3642AS]
50 Powers of entry and inspection . . . . . [3642AT]

PART VI
MISCELLANEOUS AND GENERAL

Functions of Commissioner

51 General duties of Commissioner . . . . . [3642AU]
52 Reports and codes of practice to be laid before Parliament . . . . . [3642AV]
52A Data-sharing code . . . . . [3642AVA]
52B Data-sharing code: procedure . . . . . [3642AVB]
52C Alteration or replacement of data-sharing code . . . . . [3642AVC]
52D Publication of data-sharing code . . . . . [3642AVD]
52E Effect of data-sharing code . . . . . [3642AVE]
53 Assistance by Commissioner in cases involving processing for the special purposes . . . . . [3642AW]
54 International co-operation . . . . . [3642AX]

Unlawful obtaining etc of personal data

55 Unlawful obtaining etc of personal data . . . . . [3642AY]

Monetary penalties

55A Power of Commissioner to impose monetary penalty . . . . . [3642AZ]
55B Monetary penalty notices: procedural rights . . . . . [3642BA]
55C Guidance about monetary penalty notices . . . . . [3642BB]
55D Monetary penalty notices: enforcement . . . . . [3642BC]
55E Notices under sections 55A and 55B: supplemental . . . . . [3642BD]

Records obtained under data subject's right of access

56 Prohibition of requirement as to production of certain records . . . . . [3642BE]
57 Avoidance of certain contractual terms relating to health records . . . . . [3642BF]

Information provided to Commissioner or Tribunal

58 Disclosure of information . . . . . [3642BG]

General provisions relating to offences

60 Prosecutions and penalties . . . . . [3642BH]
61 Liability of directors etc . . . . . [3642BI]

General

64 Transmission of notices etc by electronic or other means . . . . . [3642BJ]
65 Service of notices by Commissioner . . . . . [3642BK]
66 Exercise of rights in Scotland by children . . . . . [3642BL]
67 Orders, regulations and rules . . . . . [3642BM]
68 Meaning of "accessible record" . . . . . [3642BN]
70 Supplementary definitions . . . . . [3642BO]
71 Index of defined expressions . . . . . [3642BP]
72 Modifications of Act . . . . . [3642BQ]
73 Transitional provisions and savings . . . . . [3642BR]
74 Minor and consequential amendments and repeals and revocations . . . . . [3642BS]
75 Short title, commencement and extent . . . . . [3642BT]

SCHEDULES:

Schedule 1—The Data Protection Principles
Part I—The Principles . . . . . [3642BU]
Part II—Interpretation of the Principles in Part I . . . . . [3642BV]
Schedule 2—Conditions Relevant for Purposes of the First Principle: Processing of any Personal Data . . . . . [3642BW]
Schedule 3—Conditions Relevant for Purposes of the First Principle: Processing of

Part III Statutes

Sensitive Personal Data . . . . [3642BX]
Schedule 4—Cases where the Eighth Principle does not Apply . . . . [3642BY]
Schedule 5—The Information Commissioner
Part I—The Commissioner . . . . [3642BZ]
Schedule 6—Appeal Proceedings . . . . [3642CA]
Schedule 7—Miscellaneous Exemptions . . . . [3642CB]
Schedule 8—Transitional Relief
Part I—Interpretation of Schedule . . . . [3642CC]
Part II—Exemptions Available Before 24th October 2001 . . . . [3642CD]
Part III—Exemptions Available After 23rd October 2001 but Before 24th October 2007 . . . . [3642CE]
Part V—Exemption from Section 22 . . . . [3642CF]
Schedule 9—Powers of Entry and Inspection . . . . [3642CG]
Schedule 10—Further Provisions Relating to Assistance under Section 53 . . . . [3642CH]
Schedule 14—Transitional Provisions and Savings . . . . [3642CI]

An Act to make new provision for the regulation of the processing of information relating to individuals, including the obtaining, holding, use or disclosure of such information

[16 July 1998]

PART I
PRELIMINARY

[3615]

1 Basic interpretative provisions

(1) In this Act, unless the context otherwise requires—

"data" means information which—

(a) is being processed by means of equipment operating automatically in response to instructions given for that purpose,

(b) is recorded with the intention that it should be processed by means of such equipment,

(c) is recorded as part of a relevant filing system or with the intention that it should form part of a relevant filing system, . . .

(d) does not fall within paragraph (a), (b) or (c) but forms part of an accessible record as defined by section 68, [or

(e) is recorded information held by a public authority and does not fall within any of paragraphs (a) to (d);]

"data controller" means, subject to subsection (4), a person who (either alone or jointly or in common with other persons) determines the purposes for which and the manner in which any personal data are, or are to be, processed;

"data processor", in relation to personal data, means any person (other than an employee of the data controller) who processes the data on behalf of the data controller;

"data subject" means an individual who is the subject of personal data;

"personal data" means data which relate to a living individual who can be identified—

(a) from those data, or

(b) from those data and other information which is in the possession of, or is likely to come into the possession of, the data controller,

and includes any expression of opinion about the individual and any indication of the intentions of the data controller or any other person in respect of the individual;

"processing", in relation to information or data, means obtaining, recording or holding the information or data or carrying out any operation or set of operations on the information or data, including—

(a) organisation, adaptation or alteration of the information or data,

(b) retrieval, consultation or use of the information or data,

(c) disclosure of the information or data by transmission, dissemination or otherwise making available, or

(d) alignment, combination, blocking, erasure or destruction of the information or data;

["public authority" means a public authority as defined by the Freedom of Information Act 2000 or a Scottish public authority as defined by the Freedom of Information (Scotland) Act 2002;]

"relevant filing system" means any set of information relating to individuals to the extent that, although the information is not processed by means of equipment operating automatically in response to instructions given for that purpose, the set is structured, either by reference to individuals or by reference to criteria relating to individuals, in such a way that specific information relating to a particular individual is readily accessible.

(2) In this Act, unless the context otherwise requires—

(a) "obtaining" or "recording", in relation to personal data, includes obtaining or recording the information to be contained in the data, and

(b) "using" or "disclosing", in relation to personal data, includes using or disclosing the information contained in the data.

(3) In determining for the purposes of this Act whether any information is recorded with the intention—

(a) that it should be processed by means of equipment operating automatically in response to instructions given for that purpose, or

(b) that it should form part of a relevant filing system,

it is immaterial that it is intended to be so processed or to form part of such a system only after being transferred to a country or territory outside the European Economic Area.

(4) Where personal data are processed only for purposes for which they are required by or under any enactment to be processed, the person on whom the obligation to process the data is imposed by or under that enactment is for the purposes of this Act the data controller.

[(5) In paragraph (e) of the definition of "data" in subsection (1), the reference to information "held" by a public authority shall be construed in accordance with section 3(2) of the Freedom of Information Act 2000 [or section 3(2), (4) and (5) of the Freedom of Information (Scotland) Act 2002].

(6) Where

[(a)] section 7 of the Freedom of Information Act 2000 prevents Parts I to V of that Act [or

(b) section 7(1) of the Freedom of Information (Scotland) Act 2002 prevents that Act,]

from applying to certain information held by a public authority, that information is not to be treated for the purposes of paragraph (e) of the definition of "data" in subsection (1) as held by a public authority.]

NOTES

Sub-s (1): in definition "data" word omitted from para (c) repealed, and para (e) and word immediately preceding it inserted by the Freedom of Information Act 2000, ss 68(1), (2)(a), 86, Sch 8, Pt III; definition "public authority" inserted by the Freedom of Information Act 2000, s 68(1), (2)(b), substituted by the Freedom of Information (Scotland) Act 2002 (Consequential Modifications) Order 2004, SI 2004/3089, art 2(1), (2)(a).

Sub-s (5): added, together with sub-s (6), by the Freedom of Information Act 2000, s 68(1), (3); words in square brackets inserted by SI 2004/3089, art 2(1), (2)(b).

Sub-s (6): added as noted to sub-s (5); para (a) numbered as such and para (b) and the word immediately preceding it inserted by SI 2004/3089, art 2(1), (2)(c).

[3616]

2 Sensitive personal data

In this Act "sensitive personal data" means personal data consisting of information as to—

(a) the racial or ethnic origin of the data subject,

(b) his political opinions,

(c) his religious beliefs or other beliefs of a similar nature,

(d) whether he is a member of a trade union (within the meaning of the Trade Union and Labour Relations (Consolidation) Act 1992,

(e) his physical or mental health or condition,

(f) his sexual life,

(g) the commission or alleged commission by him of any offence, or

(h) any proceedings for any offence committed or alleged to have been committed by him, the disposal of such proceedings or the sentence of any court in such proceedings.

[3617]

3 The special purposes

In this Act "the special purposes" means any one or more of the following—

(a) the purposes of journalism,

(b) artistic purposes, and

(c) literary purposes.

[3618]

4 The data protection principles

(1) References in this Act to the data protection principles are to the principles set out in Part I of Schedule 1.

(2) Those principles are to be interpreted in accordance with Part II of Schedule 1.

(3) Schedule 2 (which applies to all personal data) and Schedule 3 (which applies only to sensitive personal data) set out conditions applying for the purposes of the first principle; and Schedule 4 sets out cases in which the eighth principle does not apply.
(4) Subject to section 27(1), it shall be the duty of a data controller to comply with the data protection principles in relation to all personal data with respect to which he is the data controller.

[3619]
5 Application of Act
(1) Except as otherwise provided by or under section 54, this Act applies to a data controller in respect of any data only if—
- (a) the data controller is established in the United Kingdom and the data are processed in the context of that establishment, or
- (b) the data controller is established neither in the United Kingdom nor in any other EEA State but uses equipment in the United Kingdom for processing the data otherwise than for the purposes of transit through the United Kingdom.

(2) A data controller falling within subsection (1)(b) must nominate for the purposes of this Act a representative established in the United Kingdom.
(3) For the purposes of subsections (1) and (2), each of the following is to be treated as established in the United Kingdom—
- (a) an individual who is ordinarily resident in the United Kingdom,
- (b) a body incorporated under the law of, or of any part of, the United Kingdom,
- (c) a partnership or other unincorporated association formed under the law of any part of the United Kingdom, and
- (d) any person who does not fall within paragraph (a), (b) or (c) but maintains in the United Kingdom—
  - (i) an office, branch or agency through which he carries on any activity, or
  - (ii) a regular practice;

and the reference to establishment in any other EEA State has a corresponding meaning.

[3620]
6 The Commissioner . . .
[(1) For the purposes of this Act and of the Freedom of Information Act 2000 there shall be an officer known as the Information Commissioner (in this Act referred to as "the Commissioner").]
(2) The Commissioner shall be appointed by Her Majesty by Letters Patent.
(3)–(6) . . .
(7) Schedule 5 has effect in relation to the Commissioner . . .

NOTES
Section heading: words omitted repealed by the Transfer of Tribunal Functions Order 2010, SI 2010/22, art 5(1), Sch 2, paras 24, 25(a), subject to transitional provisions and savings in Sch 5 thereto.
Sub-s (1): substituted by the Freedom of Information Act 2000, s 18(4), Sch 2, Pt I, para 13.
Sub-ss (3)–(6): repealed by SI 2010/22, art 5(1), Sch 2, paras 24, 25(b), subject to transitional provisions and savings in Sch 5 thereto.
Sub-s (7): words omitted repealed by SI 2010/22, art 5(1), Sch 2, paras 24, 25(c), subject to transitional provisions and savings in Sch 5 thereto.

PART II
RIGHTS OF DATA SUBJECTS AND OTHERS

[3621]
7 Right of access to personal data
(1) Subject to the following provisions of this section and to [sections 8, 9 and 9A], an individual is entitled—
- (a) to be informed by any data controller whether personal data of which that individual is the data subject are being processed by or on behalf of that data controller,
- (b) if that is the case, to be given by the data controller a description of—
  - (i) the personal data of which that individual is the data subject,
  - (ii) the purposes for which they are being or are to be processed, and
  - (iii) the recipients or classes of recipients to whom they are or may be disclosed,
- (c) to have communicated to him in an intelligible form—
  - (i) the information constituting any personal data of which that individual is the data subject, and
  - (ii) any information available to the data controller as to the source of those data, and
- (d) where the processing by automatic means of personal data of which that individual is the data subject for the purpose of evaluating matters relating to him such as, for example,

his performance at work, his creditworthiness, his reliability or his conduct, has constituted or is likely to constitute the sole basis for any decision significantly affecting him, to be informed by the data controller of the logic involved in that decision-taking.

(2) A data controller is not obliged to supply any information under subsection (1) unless he has received—

(a) a request in writing, and

(b) except in prescribed cases, such fee (not exceeding the prescribed maximum) as he may require.

[(3) Where a data controller—

(a) reasonably requires further information in order to satisfy himself as to the identity of the person making a request under this section and to locate the information which that person seeks, and

(b) has informed him of that requirement,

the data controller is not obliged to comply with the request unless he is supplied with that further information.]

(4) Where a data controller cannot comply with the request without disclosing information relating to another individual who can be identified from that information, he is not obliged to comply with the request unless—

(a) the other individual has consented to the disclosure of the information to the person making the request, or

(b) it is reasonable in all the circumstances to comply with the request without the consent of the other individual.

(5) In subsection (4) the reference to information relating to another individual includes a reference to information identifying that individual as the source of the information sought by the request; and that subsection is not to be construed as excusing a data controller from communicating so much of the information sought by the request as can be communicated without disclosing the identity of the other individual concerned, whether by the omission of names or other identifying particulars or otherwise.

(6) In determining for the purposes of subsection (4)(b) whether it is reasonable in all the circumstances to comply with the request without the consent of the other individual concerned, regard shall be had, in particular, to—

(a) any duty of confidentiality owed to the other individual,

(b) any steps taken by the data controller with a view to seeking the consent of the other individual,

(c) whether the other individual is capable of giving consent, and

(d) any express refusal of consent by the other individual.

(7) An individual making a request under this section may, in such cases as may be prescribed, specify that his request is limited to personal data of any prescribed description.

(8) Subject to subsection (4), a data controller shall comply with a request under this section promptly and in any event before the end of the prescribed period beginning with the relevant day.

(9) If a court is satisfied on the application of any person who has made a request under the foregoing provisions of this section that the data controller in question has failed to comply with the request in contravention of those provisions, the court may order him to comply with the request.

(10) In this section—

"prescribed" means prescribed by the [Secretary of State] by regulations;

"the prescribed maximum" means such amount as may be prescribed;

"the prescribed period" means forty days or such other period as may be prescribed;

"the relevant day", in relation to a request under this section, means the day on which the data controller receives the request or, if later, the first day on which the data controller has both the required fee and the information referred to in subsection (3).

(11) Different amounts or periods may be prescribed under this section in relation to different cases.

NOTES

Sub-s (1): words in square brackets substituted by the Freedom of Information Act 2000, s 69(1).

Sub-s (3): substituted by the Freedom of Information Act 2000, s 73, Sch 6, para 1.

Sub-s (10): in definition "prescribed" words in square brackets substituted by the Secretary of State for Constitutional Affairs Order 2003, SI 2003/1887, art 9, Sch 2, para 9(1)(a).

Regulations: the Data Protection (Subject Access) (Fees and Miscellaneous Provisions) Regulations 2000, SI 2000/191. See also, for further exemptions from this section, the Data Protection (Miscellaneous Subject Access Exemptions) Order 2000, SI 2000/419; the Data Protection (Subject Access Modification) (Health) Order 2000, SI 2000/413; the Data Protection (Subject Access Modification) (Education) Order 2000,

SI 2000/414; the Data Protection (Subject Access Modification) (Social Work) Order 2000, SI 2000/415, which modify s 7 in relation to data to which the respective orders apply.

[3622]
8 Provisions supplementary to section 7
(1) The [Secretary of State] may by regulations provide that, in such cases as may be prescribed, a request for information under any provision of subsection (1) of section 7 is to be treated as extending also to information under other provisions of that subsection.
(2) The obligation imposed by section 7(1)(c)(i) must be complied with by supplying the data subject with a copy of the information in permanent form unless—

(a) the supply of such a copy is not possible or would involve disproportionate effort, or
(b) the data subject agrees otherwise;

and where any of the information referred to in section 7(1)(c)(i) is expressed in terms which are not intelligible without explanation the copy must be accompanied by an explanation of those terms.
(3) Where a data controller has previously complied with a request made under section 7 by an individual, the data controller is not obliged to comply with a subsequent identical or similar request under that section by that individual unless a reasonable interval has elapsed between compliance with the previous request and the making of the current request.
(4) In determining for the purposes of subsection (3) whether requests under section 7 are made at reasonable intervals, regard shall be had to the nature of the data, the purpose for which the data are processed and the frequency with which the data are altered.
(5) Section 7(1)(d) is not to be regarded as requiring the provision of information as to the logic involved in any decision-taking if, and to the extent that, the information constitutes a trade secret.
(6) The information to be supplied pursuant to a request under section 7 must be supplied by reference to the data in question at the time when the request is received, except that it may take account of any amendment or deletion made between that time and the time when the information is supplied, being an amendment or deletion that would have been made regardless of the receipt of the request.
(7) For the purposes of section 7(4) and (5) another individual can be identified from the information being disclosed if he can be identified from that information, or from that and any other information which, in the reasonable belief of the data controller, is likely to be in, or to come into, the possession of the data subject making the request.

NOTES

Sub-s (1): words in square brackets substituted by the Secretary of State for Constitutional Affairs Order 2003, SI 2003/1887, art 9, Sch 2, para 9(1)(a).

Regulations: the Data Protection (Subject Access) (Fees and Miscellaneous Provisions) Regulations 2000, SI 2000/191.

9, 9A *(Outside the scope of this work.)*

[3623]
10 Right to prevent processing likely to cause damage or distress
(1) Subject to subsection (2), an individual is entitled at any time by notice in writing to a data controller to require the data controller at the end of such period as is reasonable in the circumstances to cease, or not to begin, processing, or processing for a specified purpose or in a specified manner, any personal data in respect of which he is the data subject, on the ground that, for specified reasons—

(a) the processing of those data or their processing for that purpose or in that manner is causing or is likely to cause substantial damage or substantial distress to him or to another, and
(b) that damage or distress is or would be unwarranted.

(2) Subsection (1) does not apply—

(a) in a case where any of the conditions in paragraphs 1 to 4 of Schedule 2 is met, or
(b) in such other cases as may be prescribed by the [Secretary of State] by order.

(3) The data controller must within twenty-one days of receiving a notice under subsection (1) ("the data subject notice") give the individual who gave it a written notice—

(a) stating that he has complied or intends to comply with the data subject notice, or
(b) stating his reasons for regarding the data subject notice as to any extent unjustified and the extent (if any) to which he has complied or intends to comply with it.

(4) If a court is satisfied, on the application of any person who has given a notice under subsection (1) which appears to the court to be justified (or to be justified to any extent), that the data controller in question has failed to comply with the notice, the court may order him to take such steps for complying with the notice (or for complying with it to that extent) as the court thinks fit.

(5) The failure by a data subject to exercise the right conferred by subsection (1) or section 11(1) does not affect any other right conferred on him by this Part.

NOTES

Sub-s (2): words in square brackets in para (b) substituted by the Secretary of State for Constitutional Affairs Order 2003, SI 2003/1887, art 9, Sch 2, para 9(1)(a).

[3624]

11 Right to prevent processing for purposes of direct marketing

(1) An individual is entitled at any time by notice in writing to a data controller to require the data controller at the end of such period as is reasonable in the circumstances to cease, or not to begin, processing for the purposes of direct marketing personal data in respect of which he is the data subject.

(2) If the court is satisfied, on the application of any person who has given a notice under subsection (1), that the data controller has failed to comply with the notice, the court may order him to take such steps for complying with the notice as the court thinks fit.

[(2A) This section shall not apply in relation to the processing of such data as are mentioned in paragraph (1) of regulation 8 of the Telecommunications (Data Protection and Privacy) Regulations 1999 (processing of telecommunications billing data for certain marketing purposes) for the purposes mentioned in paragraph (2) of that regulation.]

(3) In this section "direct marketing" means the communication (by whatever means) of any advertising or marketing material which is directed to particular individuals.

NOTES

Sub-s (2A): inserted by the Telecommunications (Data Protection and Privacy) Regulations 1999, SI 1999/2093, reg 3(3), Sch 1, Pt II, para 3.

[3625]

12 Rights in relation to automated decision-taking

(1) An individual is entitled at any time, by notice in writing to any data controller, to require the data controller to ensure that no decision taken by or on behalf of the data controller which significantly affects that individual is based solely on the processing by automatic means of personal data in respect of which that individual is the data subject for the purpose of evaluating matters relating to him such as, for example, his performance at work, his creditworthiness, his reliability or his conduct.

(2) Where, in a case where no notice under subsection (1) has effect, a decision which significantly affects an individual is based solely on such processing as is mentioned in subsection (1)—

(a) the data controller must as soon as reasonably practicable notify the individual that the decision was taken on that basis, and

(b) the individual is entitled, within twenty-one days of receiving that notification from the data controller, by notice in writing to require the data controller to reconsider the decision or to take a new decision otherwise than on that basis.

(3) The data controller must, within twenty-one days of receiving a notice under subsection (2)(b) ("the data subject notice") give the individual a written notice specifying the steps that he intends to take to comply with the data subject notice.

(4) A notice under subsection (1) does not have effect in relation to an exempt decision; and nothing in subsection (2) applies to an exempt decision.

(5) In subsection (4) "exempt decision" means any decision—

(a) in respect of which the condition in subsection (6) and the condition in subsection (7) are met, or

(b) which is made in such other circumstances as may be prescribed by the [Secretary of State] by order.

(6) The condition in this subsection is that the decision—

(a) is taken in the course of steps taken—

(i) for the purpose of considering whether to enter into a contract with the data subject,

(ii) with a view to entering into such a contract, or

(iii) in the course of performing such a contract, or

(b) is authorised or required by or under any enactment.

(7) The condition in this subsection is that either—

(a) the effect of the decision is to grant a request of the data subject, or

(b) steps have been taken to safeguard the legitimate interests of the data subject (for example, by allowing him to make representations).

(8) If a court is satisfied on the application of a data subject that a person taking a decision in respect of him ("the responsible person") has failed to comply with subsection (1) or (2)(b), the court may order the responsible person to reconsider the decision, or to take a new decision which is not based solely on such processing as is mentioned in subsection (1).

(9) An order under subsection (8) shall not affect the rights of any person other than the data subject and the responsible person.

NOTES

Sub-s (5): words in square brackets in para (b) substituted by the Secretary of State for Constitutional Affairs Order 2003, SI 2003/1887, art 9, Sch 2, para 9(1)(a).

[3626]

13 Compensation for failure to comply with certain requirements

(1) An individual who suffers damage by reason of any contravention by a data controller of any of the requirements of this Act is entitled to compensation from the data controller for that damage.

(2) An individual who suffers distress by reason of any contravention by a data controller of any of the requirements of this Act is entitled to compensation from the data controller for that distress if—

(a) the individual also suffers damage by reason of the contravention, or

(b) the contravention relates to the processing of personal data for the special purposes.

(3) In proceedings brought against a person by virtue of this section it is a defence to prove that he had taken such care as in all the circumstances was reasonably required to comply with the requirement concerned.

[3627]

14 Rectification, blocking, erasure and destruction

(1) If a court is satisfied on the application of a data subject that personal data of which the applicant is the subject are inaccurate, the court may order the data controller to rectify, block, erase or destroy those data and any other personal data in respect of which he is the data controller and which contain an expression of opinion which appears to the court to be based on the inaccurate data.

(2) Subsection (1) applies whether or not the data accurately record information received or obtained by the data controller from the data subject or a third party but where the data accurately record such information, then—

(a) if the requirements mentioned in paragraph 7 of Part II of Schedule 1 have been complied with, the court may, instead of making an order under subsection (1), make an order requiring the data to be supplemented by such statement of the true facts relating to the matters dealt with by the data as the court may approve, and

(b) if all or any of those requirements have not been complied with, the court may, instead of making an order under that subsection, make such order as it thinks fit for securing compliance with those requirements with or without a further order requiring the data to be supplemented by such a statement as is mentioned in paragraph (a).

(3) Where the court

(a) makes an order under subsection (1), or

(b) is satisfied on the application of a data subject that personal data of which he was the data subject and which have been rectified, blocked, erased or destroyed were inaccurate,

it may, where it considers it reasonably practicable, order the data controller to notify third parties to whom the data have been disclosed of the rectification, blocking, erasure or destruction.

(4) If a court is satisfied on the application of a data subject—

(a) that he has suffered damage by reason of any contravention by a data controller of any of the requirements of this Act in respect of any personal data, in circumstances entitling him to compensation under section 13, and

(b) that there is a substantial risk of further contravention in respect of those data in such circumstances,

the court may order the rectification, blocking, erasure or destruction of any of those data.

(5) Where the court makes an order under subsection (4) it may, where it considers it reasonably practicable, order the data controller to notify third parties to whom the data have been disclosed of the rectification, blocking, erasure or destruction.
(6) In determining whether it is reasonably practicable to require such notification as is mentioned in subsection (3) or (5) the court shall have regard, in particular, to the number of persons who would have to be notified.

[3628]
15 Jurisdiction and procedure
(1) The jurisdiction conferred by sections 7 to 14 is exercisable by the High Court or a county court or, in Scotland, by the Court of Session or the sheriff.
(2) For the purpose of determining any question whether an applicant under subsection (9) of section 7 is entitled to the information which he seeks (including any question whether any relevant data are exempt from that section by virtue of Part IV) a court may require the information constituting any data processed by or on behalf of the data controller and any information as to the logic involved in any decision-taking as mentioned in section 7(1)(d) to be made available for its own inspection but shall not, pending the determination of that question in the applicant's favour, require the information sought by the applicant to be disclosed to him or his representatives whether by discovery (or, in Scotland, recovery) or otherwise.

PART III
NOTIFICATION BY DATA CONTROLLERS

[3629]
16 Preliminary
(1) In this Part "the registrable particulars", in relation to a data controller, means—
(a) his name and address,
(b) if he has nominated a representative for the purposes of this Act, the name and address of the representative,
(c) a description of the personal data being or to be processed by or on behalf of the data controller and of the category or categories of data subject to which they relate,
(d) a description of the purpose or purposes for which the data are being or are to be processed,
(e) a description of any recipient or recipients to whom the data controller intends or may wish to disclose the data,
(f) the names, or a description of, any countries or territories outside the European Economic Area to which the data controller directly or indirectly transfers, or intends or may wish directly or indirectly to transfer, the data,
[(ff) where the data controller is a public authority, a statement of that fact,] *and*
(g) in any case where—
(i) personal data are being, or are intended to be, processed in circumstances in which the prohibition in subsection (1) of section 17 is excluded by subsection (2) or (3) of that section, and
(ii) the notification does not extend to those data,
a statement of that fact [, and
(h) such information about the data controller as may be prescribed under section 18(5A).]
(2) In this Part—
"fees regulations" means regulations made by the [Secretary of State] under section 18(5) or 19(4) or (7);
"notification regulations" means regulations made by the [Secretary of State] under the other provisions of this Part;
"prescribed", except where used in relation to fees regulations, means prescribed by notification regulations.
(3) For the purposes of this Part, so far as it relates to the addresses of data controllers—
(a) the address of a registered company is that of its registered office, and
(b) the address of a person (other than a registered company) carrying on a business is that of his principal place of business in the United Kingdom.

NOTES
Sub-s (1): para (ff) inserted by the Freedom of Information Act 2000, s 71; word in italics in para (ff) repealed and para (h) inserted together with word preceding it, by the Coroners and Justice Act 2009, ss 175, 178, Sch 20, Pt 1, para 1, Sch 23, Pt 8, as from a day to be appointed.
Sub-s (2): in definitions "fees regulations", "notification regulations" words in square brackets substituted by the Secretary of State for Constitutional Affairs Order 2003, SI 2003/1887, art 9, Sch 2, para 9(1)(a).

[3630]

17 Prohibition on processing without registration

(1) Subject to the following provisions of this section, personal data must not be processed unless an entry in respect of the data controller is included in the register maintained by the Commissioner under section 19 (or is treated by notification regulations made by virtue of section 19(3) as being so included).

(2) Except where the processing is assessable processing for the purposes of section 22, subsection (1) does not apply in relation to personal data consisting of information which falls neither within paragraph (a) of the definition of "data" in section 1(1) nor within paragraph (b) of that definition.

(3) If it appears to the [Secretary of State] that processing of a particular description is unlikely to prejudice the rights and freedoms of data subjects, notification regulations may provide that, in such cases as may be prescribed, subsection (1) is not to apply in relation to processing of that description.

(4) Subsection (1) does not apply in relation to any processing whose sole purpose is the maintenance of a public register.

NOTES

Sub-s (3): words in square brackets substituted by the Secretary of State for Constitutional Affairs Order 2003, SI 2003/1887, art 9, Sch 2, para 9(1)(a).

Regulations: the Data Protection (Notification and Notification Fees) Regulations 2000, SI 2000/188.

[3631]

18 Notification by data controllers

(1) Any data controller who wishes to be included in the register maintained under section 19 shall give a notification to the Commissioner under this section.

(2) A notification under this section must specify in accordance with notification regulations—

(a) the registrable particulars, and

(b) a general description of measures to be taken for the purpose of complying with the seventh data protection principle.

(3) Notification regulations made by virtue of subsection (2) may provide for the determination by the Commissioner, in accordance with any requirements of the regulations, of the form in which the registrable particulars and the description mentioned in subsection (2)(b) are to be specified, including in particular the detail required for the purposes of section 16(1)(c), (d), (e) and (f) and subsection (2)(b).

(4) Notification regulations may make provision as to the giving of notification—

(a) by partnerships, or

(b) in other cases where two or more persons are the data controllers in respect of any personal data.

(5) The notification must be accompanied by such fee as may be prescribed by fees regulations.

[(5A) Notification regulations may prescribe the information about the data controller which is required for the purpose of verifying the fee payable under subsection (5).]

(6) Notification regulations may provide for any fee paid under subsection (5) or section 19(4) to be refunded in prescribed circumstances.

NOTES

Sub-s (5A): inserted by the Coroners and Justice Act 2009, s 175, Sch 20, Pt 1, para 2.

Regulations: the Data Protection (Notification and Notification Fees) Regulations 2000, SI 2000/188.

[3632]

19 Register of notifications

(1) The Commissioner shall—

(a) maintain a register of persons who have given notification under section 18, and

(b) make an entry in the register in pursuance of each notification received by him under that section from a person in respect of whom no entry as data controller was for the time being included in the register.

(2) Each entry in the register shall consist of—

(a) the registrable particulars notified under section 18 or, as the case requires, those particulars as amended in pursuance of section 20(4), and

(b) such other information as the Commissioner may be authorised or required by notification regulations to include in the register.

(3) Notification regulations may make provision as to the time as from which any entry in respect of a data controller is to be treated for the purposes of section 17 as having been made in the register.

(4) No entry shall be retained in the register for more than the relevant time except on payment of such fee as may be prescribed by fees regulations.
(5) In subsection (4) "the relevant time" means twelve months or such other period as may be prescribed by notification regulations; and different periods may be prescribed in relation to different cases.
(6) The Commissioner—
- (a) shall provide facilities for making the information contained in the entries in the register available for inspection (in visible and legible form) by members of the public at all reasonable hours and free of charge, and
- (b) may provide such other facilities for making the information contained in those entries available to the public free of charge as he considers appropriate.

(7) The Commissioner shall, on payment of such fee, if any, as may be prescribed by fees regulations, supply any member of the public with a duly certified copy in writing of the particulars contained in any entry made in the register.
[(8) Nothing in subsection (6) or (7) applies to information which is included in an entry in the register only by reason of it falling within section 16(1)(h).]

NOTES

Sub-s (8): added by the Coroners and Justice Act 2009, s 175, Sch 20, Pt 1, para 3.
Regulations: the Data Protection (Fees under section 19(7)) Regulations 2000, SI 2000/187; the Data Protection (Notification and Notification Fees) Regulations 2000, SI 2000/188; the Data Protection (Notification and Notification Fees) (Amendment) Regulations 2001, SI 2001/3214.

[3633]
20 Duty to notify changes
(1) For the purpose specified in subsection (2), notification regulations shall include provision imposing on every person in respect of whom an entry as a data controller is for the time being included in the register maintained under section 19 a duty to notify to the Commissioner, in such circumstances and at such time or times and in such form as may be prescribed, such matters relating to the registrable particulars and measures taken as mentioned in section 18(2)(b) as may be prescribed.
(2) The purpose referred to in subsection (1) is that of ensuring, so far as practicable, *that at any time*—
- (a) [that at any time] the entries in the register maintained under section 19 contain current names and addresses and describe the current practice or intentions of the data controller with respect to the processing of personal data,
- [(aa) that the correct fee is paid under section 19(4),] and
- (b) [that at any time] the Commissioner is provided with a general description of measures currently being taken as mentioned in section 18(2)(b).

(3) Subsection (3) of section 18 has effect in relation to notification regulations made by virtue of subsection (1) as it has effect in relation to notification regulations made by virtue of subsection (2) of that section.
(4) On receiving any notification under notification regulations made by virtue of subsection (1), the Commissioner shall make such amendments of the relevant entry in the register maintained under section 19 as are necessary to take account of the notification.

NOTES

Sub-s (2): words in italics repealed and words in square brackets inserted by the Coroners and Justice Act 2009, ss 175, 178, Sch 20, Pt 1, para 4, Sch 23, Pt 8, as from a day to be appointed.
Regulations: the Data Protection (Notification and Notification Fees) Regulations 2000, SI 2000/188.

[3634]
21 Offences
(1) If section 17(1) is contravened, the data controller is guilty of an offence.
(2) Any person who fails to comply with the duty imposed by notification regulations made by virtue of section 20(1) is guilty of an offence.
(3) It shall be a defence for a person charged with an offence under subsection (2) to show that he exercised all due diligence to comply with the duty.

[3635]
22 Preliminary assessment by Commissioner
(1) In this section "assessable processing" means processing which is of a description specified in an order made by the [Secretary of State] as appearing to him to be particularly likely—
- (a) to cause substantial damage or substantial distress to data subjects, or
- (b) otherwise significantly to prejudice the rights and freedoms of data subjects.

(2) On receiving notification from any data controller under section 18 or under notification regulations made by virtue of section 20 the Commissioner shall consider—

(a) whether any of the processing to which the notification relates is assessable processing, and

(b) if so, whether the assessable processing is likely to comply with the provisions of this Act.

(3) Subject to subsection (4), the Commissioner shall, within the period of twenty-eight days beginning with the day on which he receives a notification which relates to assessable processing, give a notice to the data controller stating the extent to which the Commissioner is of the opinion that the processing is likely or unlikely to comply with the provisions of this Act.

(4) Before the end of the period referred to in subsection (3) the Commissioner may, by reason of special circumstances, extend that period on one occasion only by notice to the data controller by such further period not exceeding fourteen days as the Commissioner may specify in the notice.

(5) No assessable processing in respect of which a notification has been given the Commissioner as mentioned in subsection (2) shall be carried on unless either—

(a) the period of twenty-eight days beginning with the day on which the notification is received by the Commissioner (or, in a case falling within subsection (4), that period as extended under that subsection) has elapsed, or

(b) before the end of that period (or that period as so extended) the data controller has received a notice from the Commissioner under subsection (3) in respect of the processing.

(6) Where subsection (5) is contravened, the data controller is guilty of an offence.

(7) The [Secretary of State] may by order amend subsections (3), (4) and (5) by substituting for the number of days for the time being specified there a different number specified in the order.

NOTES

Sub-ss (1), (7): words in square brackets substituted by the Secretary of State for Constitutional Affairs Order 2003, SI 2003/1887, art 9, Sch 2, para 9(1)(a).

[3636]

23 Power to make provision for appointment of data protection supervisors

(1) The [Secretary of State] may by order—

(a) make provision under which a data controller may appoint a person to act as a data protection supervisor responsible in particular for monitoring in an independent manner the data controller's compliance with the provisions of this Act, and

(b) provide that, in relation to any data controller who has appointed a data protection supervisor in accordance with the provisions of the order and who complies with such conditions as may be specified in the order, the provisions of this Part are to have effect subject to such exemptions or other modifications as may be specified in the order.

(2) An order under this section may—

(a) impose duties on data protection supervisors in relation to the Commissioner, and

(b) confer functions on the Commissioner in relation to data protection supervisors.

NOTES

Sub-s (1): words in square brackets substituted by the Secretary of State for Constitutional Affairs Order 2003, SI 2003/1887, art 9, Sch 2, para 9(1)(a).

[3637]

24 Duty of certain data controllers to make certain information available

(1) Subject to subsection (3), where personal data are processed in a case where—

(a) by virtue of subsection (2) or (3) of section 17, subsection (1) of that section does not apply to the processing, and

(b) the data controller has not notified the relevant particulars in respect of that processing under section 18,

the data controller must, within twenty-one days of receiving a written request from any person, make the relevant particulars available to that person in writing free of charge.

(2) In this section "the relevant particulars" means the particulars referred to in paragraphs (a) to (f) of section 16(1).

(3) This section has effect subject to any exemption conferred for the purposes of this section by notification regulations.

(4) Any data controller who fails to comply with the duty imposed by subsection (1) is guilty of an offence.

(5) It shall be a defence for a person charged with an offence under subsection (4) to show that he exercised all due diligence to comply with the duty.

[3638]

25 Functions of Commissioner in relation to making of notification regulations

(1) As soon as practicable after the passing of this Act, the Commissioner shall submit to the Secretary of State proposals as to the provisions to be included in the first notification regulations.

(2) The Commissioner shall keep under review the working of notification regulations and may from time to time submit to the [Secretary of State] proposals as to amendments to be made to the regulations.

(3) The [Secretary of State] may from time to time require the Commissioner to consider any matter relating to notification regulations and to submit to him proposals as to amendments to be made to the regulations in connection with that matter.

(4) Before making any notification regulations, the [Secretary of State] shall—

(a) consider any proposals made to him by the Commissioner under [subsection (2) or (3)], and

(b) consult the Commissioner.

NOTES

Sub-ss (2), (3): words in square brackets substituted by the Secretary of State for Constitutional Affairs Order 2003, SI 2003/1887, art 9, Sch 2, para 9(1)(a).

Sub-s (4): words in first pair of square brackets substituted by SI 2003/1887, art 9, Sch 2, para 9(1)(a); words in square brackets in para (a) substituted by the Transfer of Functions (Miscellaneous) Order 2001, SI 2001/3500, art 8, Sch 2, Pt I, para 6(2).

[3639]

26 Fees regulations

(1) Fees regulations prescribing fees for the purposes of any provision of this Part may provide for different fees to be payable in different cases.

(2) In making any fees regulations, the [Secretary of State] shall have regard to the desirability of securing that the fees payable to the Commissioner are sufficient to offset—

[(a) the expenses incurred by the Commissioner in discharging his functions under this Act and any expenses of the Secretary of State in respect of the Commissioner so far as attributable to those functions; and]

(b) to the extent that the [Secretary of State] considers appropriate—

(i) any deficit previously incurred (whether before or after the passing of this Act) in respect of the expenses mentioned in paragraph (a), and

(ii) expenses incurred or to be incurred by the [Secretary of State] in respect of the inclusion of any officers or staff of the Commissioner in any scheme under section 1 of the Superannuation Act 1972.

NOTES

Sub-s (2): words in first pair of square brackets and words in square brackets in para (b) substituted by the Secretary of State for Constitutional Affairs Order 2003, SI 2003/1887, art 9, Sch 2, para 9(1)(a); para (a) substituted by the Transfer of Tribunal Functions Order 2010, SI 2010/22, art 5(1), Sch 2, paras 24, 26, subject to transitional provisions and savings in Sch 5 thereto.

Regulations: the Data Protection (Notification and Notification Fees) Regulations 2000, SI 2000/188.

PART IV
EXEMPTIONS

[3640]

27 Preliminary

(1) References in any of the data protection principles or any provision of Parts II and III to personal data or to the processing of personal data do not include references to data or processing which by virtue of this Part are exempt from that principle or other provision.

(2) In this Part "the subject information provisions" means—

(a) the first data protection principle to the extent to which it requires compliance with paragraph 2 of Part II of Schedule 1, and

(b) section 7.

(3) In this Part "the non-disclosure provisions" means the provisions specified in subsection (4) to the extent to which they are inconsistent with the disclosure in question.

(4) The provisions referred to in subsection (3) are—

(a) the first data protection principle, except to the extent to which it requires compliance with the conditions in Schedules 2 and 3,

(b) the second, third, fourth and fifth data protection principles, and

(c) sections 10 and 14(1) to (3).

(5) Except as provided by this Part, the subject information provisions shall have effect notwithstanding any enactment or rule of law prohibiting or restricting the disclosure, or authorising the withholding, of information.

[3641]
28 National security
(1) Personal data are exempt from any of the provisions of—
- (a) the data protection principles,
- (b) Parts II, III and V, and
- (c) [sections 54A and] 55,

if the exemption from that provision is required for the purpose of safeguarding national security.
(2) Subject to subsection (4), a certificate signed by a Minister of the Crown certifying that exemption from all or any of the provisions mentioned in subsection (1) is or at any time was required for the purpose there mentioned in respect of any personal data shall be conclusive evidence of that fact.
(3) A certificate under subsection (2) may identify the personal data to which it applies by means of a general description and may be expressed to have prospective effect.
(4) Any person directly affected by the issuing of a certificate under subsection (2) may appeal to the Tribunal against the certificate.
(5) If on an appeal under subsection (4), the Tribunal finds that, applying the principles applied by the court on an application for judicial review, the Minister did not have reasonable grounds for issuing the certificate, the Tribunal may allow the appeal and quash the certificate.
(6) Where in any proceedings under or by virtue of this Act it is claimed by a data controller that a certificate under subsection (2) which identifies the personal data to which it applies by means of a general description applies to any personal data, any other party to the proceedings may appeal to the Tribunal on the ground that the certificate does not apply to the personal data in question and, subject to any determination under subsection (7), the certificate shall be conclusively presumed so to apply.
(7) On any appeal under subsection (6), the Tribunal may determine that the certificate does not so apply.
(8) A document purporting to be a certificate under subsection (2) shall be received in evidence and deemed to be such a certificate unless the contrary is proved.
(9) A document which purports to be certified by or on behalf of a Minister of the Crown as a true copy of a certificate issued by that Minister under subsection (2) shall in any legal proceedings be evidence (or, in Scotland, sufficient evidence) of that certificate.
(10) The power conferred by subsection (2) on a Minister of the Crown shall not be exercisable except by a Minister who is a member of the Cabinet or by the Attorney General or the [Advocate General for Scotland].
(11) No power conferred by any provision of Part V may be exercised in relation to personal data which by virtue of this section are exempt from that provision.
(12) Schedule 6 shall have effect in relation to appeals under subsection (4) or (6) and the proceedings of the Tribunal in respect of any such appeal.

NOTES

Sub-s (1): words in square brackets in para (c) substituted by the Crime (International Co-operation) Act 2003, s 91(1), Sch 5, paras 68, 69.

Sub-s (10): words in square brackets substituted by virtue of the Transfer of Functions (Lord Advocate and Advocate General for Scotland) Order 1999, SI 1999/679, art 2, Schedule.

[3642]
29 Crime and taxation
(1) Personal data processed for any of the following purposes—
- (a) the prevention or detection of crime,
- (b) the apprehension or prosecution of offenders, or
- (c) the assessment or collection of any tax or duty or of any imposition of a similar nature,

are exempt from the first data protection principle (except to the extent to which it requires compliance with the conditions in Schedules 2 and 3) and section 7 in any case to the extent to which the application of those provisions to the data would be likely to prejudice any of the matters mentioned in this subsection.
(2) Personal data which—
- (a) are processed for the purpose of discharging statutory functions, and
- (b) consist of information obtained for such a purpose from a person who had it in his possession for any of the purposes mentioned in subsection (1),

are exempt from the subject information provisions to the same extent as personal data processed for any of the purposes mentioned in that subsection.

(3) Personal data are exempt from the non-disclosure provisions in any case in which—

(a) the disclosure is for any of the purposes mentioned in subsection (1), and

(b) the application of those provisions in relation to the disclosure would be likely to prejudice any of the matters mentioned in that subsection.

(4) Personal data in respect of which the data controller is a relevant authority and which—

(a) consist of a classification applied to the data subject as part of a system of risk assessment which is operated by that authority for either of the following purposes—

(i) the assessment or collection of any tax or duty or any imposition of a similar nature, or

(ii) the prevention or detection of crime, or apprehension or prosecution of offenders, where the offence concerned involves any unlawful claim for any payment out of, or any unlawful application of, public funds, and

(b) are processed for either of those purposes,

are exempt from section 7 to the extent to which the exemption is required in the interests of the operation of the system.

(5) In subsection (4)—

"public funds" includes funds provided by any Community institution;

"relevant authority" means—

(a) a government department,

(b) a local authority, or

(c) any other authority administering housing benefit or council tax benefit.

30 *(Outside the scope of this work.)*

[3642AA]

31 Regulatory activity

(1) Personal data processed for the purposes of discharging functions to which this subsection applies are exempt from the subject information provisions in any case to the extent to which the application of those provisions to the data would be likely to prejudice the proper discharge of those functions.

(2) Subsection (1) applies to any relevant function which is designed—

(a) for protecting members of the public against—

(i) financial loss due to dishonesty, malpractice or other seriously improper conduct by, or the unfitness or incompetence of, persons concerned in the provision of banking, insurance, investment or other financial services or in the management of bodies corporate,

(ii) financial loss due to the conduct of discharged or undischarged bankrupts, or

(iii) dishonesty, malpractice or other seriously improper conduct by, or the unfitness or incompetence of, persons authorised to carry on any profession or other activity,

(b) for protecting charities [or community interest companies] against misconduct or mismanagement (whether by trustees[, directors] or other persons) in their administration,

(c) for protecting the property of charities [or community interest companies] from loss or misapplication,

(d) for the recovery of the property of charities [or community interest companies],

(e) for securing the health, safety and welfare of persons at work, or

(f) for protecting persons other than persons at work against risk to health or safety arising out of or in connection with the actions of persons at work.

(3) In subsection (2) "relevant function" means—

(a) any function conferred on any person by or under any enactment,

(b) any function of the Crown, a Minister of the Crown or a government department, or

(c) any other function which is of a public nature and is exercised in the public interest.

(4) Personal data processed for the purpose of discharging any function which—

(a) is conferred by or under any enactment on—

(i) the Parliamentary Commissioner for Administration,

(ii) the Commission for Local Administration in England [. . .] . . . ,

(iii) the Health Service Commissioner for England [. . .] . . . ,

[(iv) the Public Services Ombudsman for Wales,]

(v) the Assembly Ombudsman for Northern Ireland, . . .

(vi) the Northern Ireland Commissioner for Complaints, [or]

[(vii) the Scottish Public Services Ombudsman, and]

(b) is designed for protecting members of the public against—
(i) maladministration by public bodies,
(ii) failures in services provided by public bodies, or
(iii) a failure of a public body to provide a service which it was a function of the body to provide,

are exempt from the subject information provisions in any case to the extent to which the application of those provisions to the data would be likely to prejudice the proper discharge of that function.

[(4A) Personal data processed for the purpose of discharging any function which is conferred by or under Part XVI of the Financial Services and Markets Act 2000 on the body established by the Financial Services Authority for the purposes of that Part are exempt from the subject information provisions in any case to the extent to which the application of those provisions to the data would be likely to prejudice the proper discharge of the function.]

[(4B) Personal data processed for the purposes of discharging any function of the Legal Services Board are exempt from the subject information provisions in any case to the extent to which the application of those provisions to the data would be likely to prejudice the proper discharge of the function.

(4C) Personal data processed for the purposes of the function of considering a complaint under the scheme established under Part 6 of the Legal Services Act 2007 (legal complaints) are exempt from the subject information provisions in any case to the extent to which the application of those provisions to the data would be likely to prejudice the proper discharge of the function.]

(5) Personal data processed for the purpose of discharging any function which—
(a) is conferred by or under any enactment on [the Office of Fair Trading], and
(b) is designed—
(i) for protecting members of the public against conduct which may adversely affect their interests by persons carrying on a business,
(ii) for regulating agreements or conduct which have as their object or effect the prevention, restriction or distortion of competition in connection with any commercial activity, or
(iii) for regulating conduct on the part of one or more undertakings which amounts to the abuse of a dominant position in a market,

are exempt from the subject information provisions in any case to the extent to which the application of those provisions to the data would be likely to prejudice the proper discharge of that function.

[(5A) Personal data processed by a CPC enforcer for the purpose of discharging any function conferred on such a body by or under the CPC Regulation are exempt from the subject information provisions in any case to the extent to which the application of those provisions to the data would be likely to prejudice the proper discharge of that function.

(5B) In subsection (5A)—
(a) "CPC enforcer" has the meaning given to it in section 213(5A) of the Enterprise Act 2002 but does not include the Office of Fair Trading;
(b) "CPC Regulation" has the meaning given to it in section 235A of that Act.]

[(6) Personal data processed for the purpose of the function of considering a complaint under [section 14 of the NHS Redress Act 2006,] section 113(1) or (2) or 114(1) or (3) of the Health and Social Care (Community Health and Standards) Act 2003, or section 24D, 26 . . . or 26ZB of the Children Act 1989, are exempt from the subject information provisions in any case to the extent to which the application of those provisions to the data would be likely to prejudice the proper discharge of that function.]

[(7) Personal data processed for the purpose of discharging any function which is conferred by or under Part 3 of the Local Government Act 2000 on—
(a) the monitoring officer of a relevant authority,
(b) an ethical standards officer, or
(c) the Public Services Ombudsman for Wales,

are exempt from the subject information provisions in any case to the extent to which the application of those provisions to the data would be likely to prejudice the proper discharge of that function.

(8) In subsection (7)—
(a) "relevant authority" has the meaning given by section 49(6) of the Local Government Act 2000, and
(b) any reference to the monitoring officer of a relevant authority, or to an ethical standards officer, has the same meaning as in Part 3 of that Act.]

NOTES

Sub-s (2): words in square brackets inserted by the Companies (Audit, Investigations and Community Enterprise) Act 2004, s 59(3).

Sub-s (4): in para (a)(ii), (iii) first word omitted inserted by the Scottish Public Services Ombudsman Act 2002 (Consequential Provisions and Modifications) Order 2004, SI 2004/1823, art 19(a)(i), (b)(i) and repealed by the Public Services Ombudsman (Wales) Act 2005, s 39, Sch 6, para 60, Sch 7; in para (a)(iii) first word omitted inserted and final words omitted repealed, word omitted from para (a)(v) repealed, word in square brackets in para (a)(vi) substituted and para (a)(vii) inserted by SI 2004/1823, art 19(a)(ii), (b)(ii), (c)–(e); sub-para (a)(iv) substituted by the Public Services Ombudsman (Wales) Act 2005, s 39(1), Sch 6, para 60(c).

Sub-s (4A): inserted by the Financial Services and Markets Act 2000, s 233.

Sub-ss (4B), (4C): inserted by the Legal Services Act 2007, ss 153, 170.

Sub-s (5): words in square brackets in para (a) substituted by the Enterprise Act 2002, s 278(1), Sch 25, para 37.

Sub-ss (5A), (5B): inserted by the Enterprise Act 2002 (Amendment) Regulations 2006, SI 2006/3363, reg 29.

Sub-s (6): added by the Health and Social Care (Community Health and Standards) Act 2003, s 119; words in square brackets inserted by the NHS Redress Act 2006, s 14(10), as from a day to be appointed; reference omitted repealed by the Education and Inspections Act 2006, ss 157, 184, Sch 14, para 32, Sch 18, Pt 5.

Sub-ss (7), (8): added by the Local Government and Public Involvement in Health Act 2007, s 200.

32 *(Outside the scope of this work.)*

[3642AB]

33 Research, history and statistics

(1) In this section—

"research purposes" includes statistical or historical purposes;

"the relevant conditions", in relation to any processing of personal data, means the conditions—

(a) that the data are not processed to support measures or decisions with respect to particular individuals, and

(b) that the data are not processed in such a way that substantial damage or substantial distress is, or is likely to be, caused to any data subject.

(2) For the purposes of the second data protection principle, the further processing of personal data only for research purposes in compliance with the relevant conditions is not to be regarded as incompatible with the purposes for which they were obtained.

(3) Personal data which are processed only for research purposes in compliance with the relevant conditions may, notwithstanding the fifth data protection principle, be kept indefinitely.

(4) Personal data which are processed only for research purposes are exempt from section 7 if—

(a) they are processed in compliance with the relevant conditions, and

(b) the results of the research or any resulting statistics are not made available in a form which identifies data subjects or any of them.

(5) For the purposes of subsections (2) to (4) personal data are not to be treated as processed otherwise than for research purposes merely because the data are disclosed—

(a) to any person, for research purposes only,

(b) to the data subject or a person acting on his behalf,

(c) at the request, or with the consent, of the data subject or a person acting on his behalf, or

(d) in circumstances in which the person making the disclosure has reasonable grounds for believing that the disclosure falls within paragraph (a), (b) or (c).

33A *(Outside the scope of this work.)*

[3642AC]

34 Information available to the public by or under enactment

Personal data are exempt from—

(a) the subject information provisions,

(b) the fourth data protection principle and section 14(1) to (3), and

(c) the non-disclosure provisions,

if the data consist of information which the data controller is obliged by or under any enactment [other than an enactment contained in the Freedom of Information Act 2000] to make available to the public, whether by publishing it, by making it available for inspection, or otherwise and whether gratuitously or on payment of a fee.

NOTES

Words in square brackets inserted by the Freedom of Information Act 2000, s 72.

[3642AD]
35 Disclosures required by law or made in connection with legal proceedings etc
(1) Personal data are exempt from the non-disclosure provisions where the disclosure is required by or under any enactment, by any rule of law or by the order of a court.
(2) Personal data are exempt from the non-disclosure provisions where the disclosure is necessary—
- (a) for the purpose of, or in connection with, any legal proceedings (including prospective legal proceedings), or
- (b) for the purpose of obtaining legal advice,

or is otherwise necessary for the purposes of establishing, exercising or defending legal rights.

[3642AE]
[35A Parliamentary privilege
Personal data are exempt from—
- (a) the first data protection principle, except to the extent to which it requires compliance with the conditions in Schedules 2 and 3,
- (b) the second, third, fourth and fifth data protection principles,
- (c) section 7, and
- (d) sections 10 and 14(1) to (3),

if the exemption is required for the purpose of avoiding an infringement of the privileges of either House of Parliament.]

NOTES
Inserted by the Freedom of Information Act 2000, s 73, Sch 6, para 2.

[3642AF]
36 Domestic purposes
Personal data processed by an individual only for the purposes of that individual's personal, family or household affairs (including recreational purposes) are exempt from the data protection principles and the provisions of Parts II and III.

[3642AG]
37 Miscellaneous exemptions
Schedule 7 (which confers further miscellaneous exemptions) has effect.

[3642AH]
38 Powers to make further exemptions by order
(1) The [Secretary of State] may by order exempt from the subject information provisions personal data consisting of information the disclosure of which is prohibited or restricted by or under any enactment if and to the extent that he considers it necessary for the safeguarding of the interests of the data subject or the rights and freedoms of any other individual that the prohibition or restriction ought to prevail over those provisions.
(2) The [Secretary of State] may by order exempt from the non-disclosure provisions any disclosures of personal data made in circumstances specified in the order, if he considers the exemption is necessary for the safeguarding of the interests of the data subject or the rights and freedoms of any other individual.

NOTES
Words in square brackets substituted by the Secretary of State for Constitutional Affairs Order 2003, SI 2003/1887, art 9, Sch 2, para 9(1)(a).
Orders: the Data Protection (Miscellaneous Subject Access Exemptions) Order 2000, SI 2000/419.

[3642AI]
39 Transitional relief
Schedule 8 (which confers transitional exemptions) has effect.

PART V
ENFORCEMENT

[3642AJ]
40 Enforcement notices
(1) If the Commissioner is satisfied that a data controller has contravened or is contravening any of the data protection principles, the Commissioner may serve him with a notice (in this Act referred to as "an enforcement notice") requiring him, for complying with the principle or principles in question, to do either or both of the following—
- (a) to take within such time as may be specified in the notice, or to refrain from taking after such time as may be so specified, such steps as are so specified, or

(b) to refrain from processing any personal data, or any personal data of a description specified in the notice, or to refrain from processing them for a purpose so specified or in a manner so specified, after such time as may be so specified.

(2) In deciding whether to serve an enforcement notice, the Commissioner shall consider whether the contravention has caused or is likely to cause any person damage or distress.

(3) An enforcement notice in respect of a contravention of the fourth data protection principle which requires the data controller to rectify, block, erase or destroy any inaccurate data may also require the data controller to rectify, block, erase or destroy any other data held by him and containing an expression of opinion which appears to the Commissioner to be based on the inaccurate data.

(4) An enforcement notice in respect of a contravention of the fourth data protection principle, in the case of data which accurately record information received or obtained by the data controller from the data subject or a third party, may require the data controller either—

(a) to rectify, block, erase or destroy any inaccurate data and any other data held by him and containing an expression of opinion as mentioned in subsection (3), or

(b) to take such steps as are specified in the notice for securing compliance with the requirements specified in paragraph 7 of Part II of Schedule 1 and, if the Commissioner thinks fit, for supplementing the data with such statement of the true facts relating to the matters dealt with by the data as the Commissioner may approve.

(5) Where—

(a) an enforcement notice requires the data controller to rectify, block, erase or destroy any personal data, or

(b) the Commissioner is satisfied that personal data which have been rectified, blocked, erased or destroyed had been processed in contravention of any of the data protection principles,

an enforcement notice may, if reasonably practicable, require the data controller to notify third parties to whom the data have been disclosed of the rectification, blocking, erasure or destruction; and in determining whether it is reasonably practicable to require such notification regard shall be had, in particular, to the number of persons who would have to be notified.

(6) An enforcement notice must contain—

(a) a statement of the data protection principle or principles which the Commissioner is satisfied have been or are being contravened and his reasons for reaching that conclusion, and

(b) particulars of the rights of appeal conferred by section 48.

(7) Subject to subsection (8), an enforcement notice must not require any of the provisions of the notice to be complied with before the end of the period within which an appeal can be brought against the notice and, if such an appeal is brought, the notice need not be complied with pending the determination or withdrawal of the appeal.

(8) If by reason of special circumstances the Commissioner considers that an enforcement notice should be complied with as a matter of urgency he may include in the notice a statement to that effect and a statement of his reasons for reaching that conclusion; and in that event subsection (7) shall not apply but the notice must not require the provisions of the notice to be complied with before the end of the period of seven days beginning with the day on which the notice is served.

(9) Notification regulations (as defined by section 16(2)) may make provision as to the effect of the service of an enforcement notice on any entry in the register maintained under section 19 which relates to the person on whom the notice is served.

(10) This section has effect subject to section 46(1).

[3642AK]

41 Cancellation of an enforcement notice

(1) If the Commissioner considers that all or any of the provisions of an enforcement notice need not be complied with in order to ensure compliance with the data protection principle or principles to which it relates, he may cancel or vary the notice by written notice to the person on whom it was served.

(2) A person on whom an enforcement notice has been served may, at any time after the expiry of the period during which an appeal can be brought against that notice, apply in writing to the Commissioner for the cancellation or variation of that notice on the ground that, by reason of a change of circumstances, all or any of the provisions of that notice need not be complied with in order to ensure compliance with the data protection principle or principles to which that notice relates.

[3642AKA]
[41A Assessment notices

(1) The Commissioner may serve a data controller within subsection (2) with a notice (in this Act referred to as an "assessment notice") for the purpose of enabling the Commissioner to determine whether the data controller has complied or is complying with the data protection principles.

(2) A data controller is within this subsection if the data controller is—

(a) a government department,

(b) a public authority designated for the purposes of this section by an order made by the Secretary of State, or

(c) a person of a description designated for the purposes of this section by such an order.

(3) An assessment notice is a notice which requires the data controller to do all or any of the following—

(a) permit the Commissioner to enter any specified premises;

(b) direct the Commissioner to any documents on the premises that are of a specified description;

(c) assist the Commissioner to view any information of a specified description that is capable of being viewed using equipment on the premises;

(d) comply with any request from the Commissioner for—

(i) a copy of any of the documents to which the Commissioner is directed;

(ii) a copy (in such form as may be requested) of any of the information which the Commissioner is assisted to view;

(e) direct the Commissioner to any equipment or other material on the premises which is of a specified description;

(f) permit the Commissioner to inspect or examine any of the documents, information, equipment or material to which the Commissioner is directed or which the Commissioner is assisted to view;

(g) permit the Commissioner to observe the processing of any personal data that takes place on the premises;

(h) make available for interview by the Commissioner a specified number of persons of a specified description who process personal data on behalf of the data controller (or such number as are willing to be interviewed).

(4) In subsection (3) references to the Commissioner include references to the Commissioner's officers and staff.

(5) An assessment notice must, in relation to each requirement imposed by the notice, specify—

(a) the time at which the requirement is to be complied with, or

(b) the period during which the requirement is to be complied with.

(6) An assessment notice must also contain particulars of the rights of appeal conferred by section 48.

(7) The Commissioner may cancel an assessment notice by written notice to the data controller on whom it was served.

(8) Where a public authority has been designated by an order under subsection (2)(b) the Secretary of State must reconsider, at intervals of no greater than 5 years, whether it continues to be appropriate for the authority to be designated.

(9) The Secretary of State may not make an order under subsection (2)(c) which designates a description of persons unless—

(a) the Commissioner has made a recommendation that the description be designated, and

(b) the Secretary of State has consulted—

(i) such persons as appear to the Secretary of State to represent the interests of those that meet the description;

(ii) such other persons as the Secretary of State considers appropriate.

(10) The Secretary of State may not make an order under subsection (2)(c), and the Commissioner may not make a recommendation under subsection (9)(a), unless the Secretary of State or (as the case may be) the Commissioner is satisfied that it is necessary for the description of persons in question to be designated having regard to—

(a) the nature and quantity of data under the control of such persons, and

(b) any damage or distress which may be caused by a contravention by such persons of the data protection principles.

(11) Where a description of persons has been designated by an order under subsection (2)(c) the Secretary of State must reconsider, at intervals of no greater than 5 years, whether it continues to be necessary for the description to be designated having regard to the matters mentioned in subsection (10).

(12) In this section—

"public authority" includes any body, office-holder or other person in respect of which—

(a) an order may be made under section 4 or 5 of the Freedom of Information Act 2000, or

(b) an order may be made under section 4 or 5 of the Freedom of Information (Scotland) Act 2002;

"specified" means specified in an assessment notice.]

NOTES

Commencement: to be appointed.

Inserted, together with ss 41B, 41C, by the Coroners and Justice Act 2009, s 173.

[3642AKB]

[41B Assessment notices: limitations

(1) A time specified in an assessment notice under section 41A(5) in relation to a requirement must not fall, and a period so specified must not begin, before the end of the period within which an appeal can be brought against the notice, and if such an appeal is brought the requirement need not be complied with pending the determination or withdrawal of the appeal.

(2) If by reason of special circumstances the Commissioner considers that it is necessary for the data controller to comply with a requirement in an assessment notice as a matter of urgency, the Commissioner may include in the notice a statement to that effect and a statement of the reasons for that conclusion; and in that event subsection (1) applies in relation to the requirement as if for the words from "within" to the end there were substituted "of 7 days beginning with the day on which the notice is served".

(3) A requirement imposed by an assessment notice does not have effect in so far as compliance with it would result in the disclosure of—

(a) any communication between a professional legal adviser and the adviser's client in connection with the giving of legal advice with respect to the client's obligations, liabilities or rights under this Act, or

(b) any communication between a professional legal adviser and the adviser's client, or between such an adviser or the adviser's client and any other person, made in connection with or in contemplation of proceedings under or arising out of this Act (including proceedings before the Tribunal) and for the purposes of such proceedings.

(4) In subsection (3) references to the client of a professional legal adviser include references to any person representing such a client.

(5) Nothing in section 41A authorises the Commissioner to serve an assessment notice on—

(a) a judge,

(b) a body specified in section 23(3) of the Freedom of Information Act 2000 (bodies dealing with security matters), or

(c) the Office for Standards in Education, Children's Services and Skills in so far as it is a data controller in respect of information processed for the purposes of functions exercisable by Her Majesty's Chief Inspector of Education, Children's Services and Skills by virtue of section 5(1)(a) of the Care Standards Act 2000.

(6) In this section "judge" includes —

(a) a justice of the peace (or, in Northern Ireland, a lay magistrate),

(b) a member of a tribunal, and

(c) a clerk or other officer entitled to exercise the jurisdiction of a court or tribunal;

and in this subsection "tribunal" means any tribunal in which legal proceedings may be brought.]

NOTES

Commencement: to be appointed.

Inserted as noted to s 41A at **[3642AKA]**.

[3642AKC]

[41C Code of practice about assessment notices

(1) The Commissioner must prepare and issue a code of practice as to the manner in which the Commissioner's functions under and in connection with section 41A are to be exercised.

(2) The code must in particular—

(a) specify factors to be considered in determining whether to serve an assessment notice on a data controller;

(b) specify descriptions of documents and information that—

(i) are not to be examined or inspected in pursuance of an assessment notice, or

(ii) are to be so examined or inspected only by persons of a description specified in the code;

Part III Statutes

(c) deal with the nature of inspections and examinations carried out in pursuance of an assessment notice;
(d) deal with the nature of interviews carried out in pursuance of an assessment notice;
(e) deal with the preparation, issuing and publication by the Commissioner of assessment reports in respect of data controllers that have been served with assessment notices.

(3) The provisions of the code made by virtue of subsection (2)(b) must, in particular, include provisions that relate to—
(a) documents and information concerning an individual's physical or mental health;
(b) documents and information concerning the provision of social care for an individual.

(4) An assessment report is a report which contains—
(a) a determination as to whether a data controller has complied or is complying with the data protection principles,
(b) recommendations as to any steps which the data controller ought to take, or refrain from taking, to ensure compliance with any of those principles, and
(c) such other matters as are specified in the code.

(5) The Commissioner may alter or replace the code.

(6) If the code is altered or replaced, the Commissioner must issue the altered or replacement code.

(7) The Commissioner may not issue the code (or an altered or replacement code) without the approval of the Secretary of State.

(8) The Commissioner must arrange for the publication of the code (and any altered or replacement code) issued under this section in such form and manner as the Commissioner considers appropriate.

(9) In this section "social care" has the same meaning as in Part 1 of the Health and Social Care Act 2008 (see section 9(3) of that Act).]

NOTES

Commencement: 1 February 2010.
Inserted as noted to s 41A at **[3642AKA]**.

[3642AL]

42 Request for assessment

(1) A request may be made to the Commissioner by or on behalf of any person who is, or believes himself to be, directly affected by any processing of personal data for an assessment as to whether it is likely or unlikely that the processing has been or is being carried out in compliance with the provisions of this Act.

(2) On receiving a request under this section, the Commissioner shall make an assessment in such manner as appears to him to be appropriate, unless he has not been supplied with such information as he may reasonably require in order to—
(a) satisfy himself as to the identity of the person making the request, and
(b) enable him to identify the processing in question.

(3) The matters to which the Commissioner may have regard in determining in what manner it is appropriate to make an assessment include—
(a) the extent to which the request appears to him to raise a matter of substance,
(b) any undue delay in making the request, and
(c) whether or not the person making the request is entitled to make an application under section 7 in respect of the personal data in question.

(4) Where the Commissioner has received a request under this section he shall notify the person who made the request—
(a) whether he has made an assessment as a result of the request, and
(b) to the extent that he considers appropriate, having regard in particular to any exemption from section 7 applying in relation to the personal data concerned, of any view formed or action taken as a result of the request.

[3642AM]

43 Information notices

(1) If the Commissioner—
(a) has received a request under section 42 in respect of any processing of personal data, or
(b) reasonably requires any information for the purpose of determining whether the data controller has complied or is complying with the data protection principles,

he may serve the data controller with a notice (in this Act referred to as "an information notice") requiring the data controller, *within such time as is specified in the notice, to furnish the Commissioner, in such form as may be so specified, with such information relating to the request or to compliance with the principles as is so specified.*

[(1A) In subsection (1) "specified information" means information—

(a) specified, or described, in the information notice, or

(b) falling within a category which is specified, or described, in the information notice.

(1B) The Commissioner may also specify in the information notice—

(a) the form in which the information must be furnished;

(b) the period within which, or the time and place at which, the information must be furnished.]

(2) An information notice must contain—

(a) in a case falling within subsection (1)(a), a statement that the Commissioner has received a request under section 42 in relation to the specified processing, or

(b) in a case falling within subsection (1)(b), a statement that the Commissioner regards the specified information as relevant for the purpose of determining whether the data controller has complied, or is complying, with the data protection principles and his reasons for regarding it as relevant for that purpose.

(3) An information notice must also contain particulars of the rights of appeal conferred by section 48.

(4) Subject to subsection (5), *the time specified in an information notice shall not expire* before the end of the period within which an appeal can be brought against the notice and, if such an appeal is brought, the information need not be furnished pending the determination or withdrawal of the appeal.

(5) If by reason of special circumstances the Commissioner considers that the information is required as a matter of urgency, he may include in the notice a statement to that effect and a statement of his reasons for reaching that conclusion; and in that event subsection (4) shall not apply, but the notice shall not require the information to be furnished before the end of the period of seven days beginning with the day on which the notice is served.

(6) A person shall not be required by virtue of this section to furnish the Commissioner with any information in respect of—

(a) any communication between a professional legal adviser and his client in connection with the giving of legal advice to the client with respect to his obligations, liabilities or rights under this Act, or

(b) any communication between a professional legal adviser and his client, or between such an adviser or his client and any other person, made in connection with or in contemplation of proceedings under or arising out of this Act (including proceedings before the Tribunal) and for the purposes of such proceedings.

(7) In subsection (6) references to the client of a professional legal adviser include references to any person representing such a client.

(8) A person shall not be required by virtue of this section to furnish the Commissioner with any information if the furnishing of that information would, by revealing evidence of the commission of any offence *other than an offence under this Act*, expose him to proceedings for that offence.

[(8A) The offences mentioned in subsection (8) are—

(a) an offence under section 5 of the Perjury Act 1911 (false statements made otherwise than on oath),

(b) an offence under section 44(2) of the Criminal Law (Consolidation) (Scotland) Act 1995 (false statements made otherwise than on oath), or

(c) an offence under Article 10 of the Perjury (Northern Ireland) Order 1979 (false statutory declarations and other false unsworn statements).

(8B) Any relevant statement provided by a person in response to a requirement under this section may not be used in evidence against that person on a prosecution for any offence under this Act (other than an offence under section 47) unless in the proceedings—

(a) in giving evidence the person provides information inconsistent with it, and

(b) evidence relating to it is adduced, or a question relating to it is asked, by that person or on that person's behalf.

(8C) In subsection (8B) "relevant statement", in relation to a requirement under this section, means—

(a) an oral statement, or

(b) a written statement made for the purposes of the requirement.]

(9) The Commissioner may cancel an information notice by written notice to the person on whom it was served.

(10) This section has effect subject to section 46(3).

NOTES

Sub-s (1): for the words in italics there are substituted the words "to furnish the Commissioner with specified information relating to the request or to compliance with the principles." by the Coroners and Justice Act 2009, s 175, Sch 20, Pt 3, para 8(1), (2), as from a day to be appointed.

Sub-ss (1A), (1B): inserted by the Coroners and Justice Act 2009, s 175, Sch 20, Pt 3, para 8(1), (3), as from a day to be appointed.

Sub-s (4): for the words in italics there are substituted the words "a period specified in an information notice under subsection (1B)(b) must not end, and a time so specified must not fall," by the Coroners and Justice Act 2009, s 175, Sch 20, Pt 3, para 8(1), (4), as from a day to be appointed.

Sub-s (8): for the words in italics there are substituted the words ", other than an offence under this Act or an offence within subsection (8A)," by the Coroners and Justice Act 2009, s 175, Sch 20, Pt 4, para 10(1), (2), as from a day to be appointed.

Sub-ss (8A)–(8C): inserted by the Coroners and Justice Act 2009, s 175, Sch 20, Pt 4, para 10(1), (3), as from a day to be appointed.

[3642AN]

44 Special information notices

(1) If the Commissioner—

(a) has received a request under section 42 in respect of any processing of personal data, or

(b) has reasonable grounds for suspecting that, in a case in which proceedings have been stayed under section 32, the personal data to which the proceedings relate—

(i) are not being processed only for the special purposes, or

(ii) are not being processed with a view to the publication by any person of any journalistic, literary or artistic material which has not previously been published by the data controller,

he may serve the data controller with a notice (in this Act referred to as a "special information notice") requiring the data controller, *within such time as is specified in the notice, to furnish the Commissioner, in such form as may be so specified, with such information as is so specified for the purpose specified in subsection (2).*

[(1A) In subsection (1) "specified information" means information—

(a) specified, or described, in the special information notice, or

(b) falling within a category which is specified, or described, in the special information notice.

(1B) The Commissioner may also specify in the special information notice—

(a) the form in which the information must be furnished;

(b) the period within which, or the time and place at which, the information must be furnished.]

(2) That purpose is the purpose of ascertaining—

(a) whether the personal data are being processed only for the special purposes, or

(b) whether they are being processed with a view to the publication by any person of any journalistic, literary or artistic material which has not previously been published by the data controller.

(3) A special information notice must contain—

(a) in a case falling within paragraph (a) of subsection (1), a statement that the Commissioner has received a request under section 42 in relation to the specified processing, or

(b) in a case falling within paragraph (b) of that subsection, a statement of the Commissioner's grounds for suspecting that the personal data are not being processed as mentioned in that paragraph.

(4) A special information notice must also contain particulars of the rights of appeal conferred by section 48.

(5) Subject to subsection (6), *the time specified in a special information notice shall not expire* before the end of the period within which an appeal can be brought against the notice and, if such an appeal is brought, the information need not be furnished pending the determination or withdrawal of the appeal.

(6) If by reason of special circumstances the Commissioner considers that the information is required as a matter of urgency, he may include in the notice a statement to that effect and a statement of his reasons for reaching that conclusion; and in that event subsection (5) shall not apply, but the notice shall not require the information to be furnished before the end of the period of seven days beginning with the day on which the notice is served.

(7) A person shall not be required by virtue of this section to furnish the Commissioner with any information in respect of—

(a) any communication between a professional legal adviser and his client in connection with the giving of legal advice to the client with respect to his obligations, liabilities or rights under this Act, or

(b) any communication between a professional legal adviser and his client, or between such an adviser or his client and any other person, made in connection with or in contemplation of proceedings under or arising out of this Act (including proceedings before the Tribunal) and for the purposes of such proceedings.

(8) In subsection (7) references to the client of a professional legal adviser include references to any person representing such a client.

(9) A person shall not be required by virtue of this section to furnish the Commissioner with any information if the furnishing of that information would, by revealing evidence of the commission of any offence *other than an offence under this Act*, expose him to proceedings for that offence.

[(9A) The offences mentioned in subsection (9) are—

(a) an offence under section 5 of the Perjury Act 1911 (false statements made otherwise than on oath),

(b) an offence under section 44(2) of the Criminal Law (Consolidation) (Scotland) Act 1995 (false statements made otherwise than on oath), or

(c) an offence under Article 10 of the Perjury (Northern Ireland) Order 1979 (false statutory declarations and other false unsworn statements).

(9B) Any relevant statement provided by a person in response to a requirement under this section may not be used in evidence against that person on a prosecution for any offence under this Act (other than an offence under section 47) unless in the proceedings—

(a) in giving evidence the person provides information inconsistent with it, and

(b) evidence relating to it is adduced, or a question relating to it is asked, by that person or on that person's behalf.

(9C) In subsection (9B) "relevant statement", in relation to a requirement under this section, means—

(a) an oral statement, or

(b) a written statement made for the purposes of the requirement.]

(10) The Commissioner may cancel a special information notice by written notice to the person on whom it was served.

NOTES

Sub-s (1): for the words in italics there are substituted the words "to furnish the Commissioner with specified information for the purpose specified in subsection (2)." by the Coroners and Justice Act 2009, s 175, Sch 20, Pt 3, para 9(1), (2), as from a day to be appointed.

Sub-ss (1A), (1B): inserted by the Coroners and Justice Act 2009, s 175, Sch 20, Pt 3, para 9(1), (3), as from a day to be appointed.

Sub-s (5): for the words in italics there are substituted the words "a period specified in a special information notice under subsection (1B)(b) must not end, and a time so specified must not fall," by the Coroners and Justice Act 2009, s 175, Sch 20, Pt 3, para 9(1), (4), as from a day to be appointed.

Sub-s (9): for the words in italics there are substituted the words ", other than an offence under this Act or an offence within subsection (9A)," by the Coroners and Justice Act 2009, s 175, Sch 20, Pt 4, para 11(1), (2), as from a day to be appointed.

Sub-ss (9A)–(9C): inserted by the Coroners and Justice Act 2009, s 175, Sch 20, Pt 4, para 11(1), (3), as from a day to be appointed.

[3642AO]

45 Determination by Commissioner as to the special purposes

(1) Where at any time it appears to the Commissioner (whether as a result of the service of a special information notice or otherwise) that any personal data—

(a) are not being processed only for the special purposes, or

(b) are not being processed with a view to the publication by any person of any journalistic, literary or artistic material which has not previously been published by the data controller,

he may make a determination in writing to that effect.

(2) Notice of the determination shall be given to the data controller; and the notice must contain particulars of the right of appeal conferred by section 48.

(3) A determination under subsection (1) shall not take effect until the end of the period within which an appeal can be brought and, where an appeal is brought, shall not take effect pending the determination or withdrawal of the appeal.

[3642AP]

46 Restriction on enforcement in case of processing for the special purposes

(1) The Commissioner may not at any time serve an enforcement notice on a data controller with respect to the processing of personal data for the special purposes unless—

(a) a determination under section 45(1) with respect to those data has taken effect, and

(b) the court has granted leave for the notice to be served.

(2) The court shall not grant leave for the purposes of subsection (1)(b) unless it is satisfied—

(a) that the Commissioner has reason to suspect a contravention of the data protection principles which is of substantial public importance, and

(b) except where the case is one of urgency, that the data controller has been given notice, in accordance with rules of court, of the application for leave.

(3) The Commissioner may not serve an information notice on a data controller with respect to the processing of personal data for the special purposes unless a determination under section 45(1) with respect to those data has taken effect.

[3642AQ]

47 Failure to comply with notice

(1) A person who fails to comply with an enforcement notice, an information notice or a special information notice is guilty of an offence.

(2) A person who, in purported compliance with an information notice or a special information notice—

(a) makes a statement which he knows to be false in a material respect, or

(b) recklessly makes a statement which is false in a material respect,

is guilty of an offence.

(3) It is a defence for a person charged with an offence under subsection (1) to prove that he exercised all due diligence to comply with the notice in question.

[3642AR]

48 Rights of appeal

(1) A person on whom an enforcement notice[, an assessment notice], an information notice or a special information notice has been served may appeal to the Tribunal against the notice.

(2) A person on whom an enforcement notice has been served may appeal to the Tribunal against the refusal of an application under section 41(2) for cancellation or variation of the notice.

(3) Where an enforcement notice[, an assessment notice], an information notice or a special information notice contains a statement by the Commissioner in accordance with section 40(8)[, 41B(2)] 43(5) or 44(6) then, whether or not the person appeals against the notice, he may appeal against—

(a) the Commissioner's decision to include the statement in the notice, or

(b) the effect of the inclusion of the statement as respects any part of the notice.

(4) A data controller in respect of whom a determination has been made under section 45 may appeal to the Tribunal against the determination.

(5) Schedule 6 has effect in relation to appeals under this section and the proceedings of the Tribunal in respect of any such appeal.

NOTES

Sub-ss (1), (3): words and figure in square brackets inserted by the Coroners and Justice Act 2009, s 175, Sch 20, Pt 2, para 5, as from a day to be appointed.

[3642AS]

49 Determination of appeals

(1) If on an appeal under section 48(1) the Tribunal considers—

(a) that the notice against which the appeal is brought is not in accordance with the law, or

(b) to the extent that the notice involved an exercise of discretion by the Commissioner, that he ought to have exercised his discretion differently,

the Tribunal shall allow the appeal or substitute such other notice or decision as could have been served or made by the Commissioner; and in any other case the Tribunal shall dismiss the appeal.

(2) On such an appeal, the Tribunal may review any determination of fact on which the notice in question was based.

(3) If on an appeal under section 48(2) the Tribunal considers that the enforcement notice ought to be cancelled or varied by reason of a change in circumstances, the Tribunal shall cancel or vary the notice.

(4) On an appeal under subsection (3) of section 48 the Tribunal may direct—

(a) that the notice in question shall have effect as if it did not contain any such statement as is mentioned in that subsection, or

(b) that the inclusion of the statement shall not have effect in relation to any part of the notice,

and may make such modifications in the notice as may be required for giving effect to the direction.

(5) On an appeal under section 48(4), the Tribunal may cancel the determination of the Commissioner.

(6), (7) . . .

NOTES

Sub-ss (6), (7): repealed by the Transfer of Tribunal Functions Order 2010, SI 2010/22, art 5(1), Sch 2, paras 24, 27, subject to transitional provisions and savings in Sch 5 thereto.

[3642AT]

50 Powers of entry and inspection

Schedule 9 (powers of entry and inspection) has effect.

PART VI
MISCELLANEOUS AND GENERAL

Functions of Commissioner

[3642AU]

51 General duties of Commissioner

(1) It shall be the duty of the Commissioner to promote the following of good practice by data controllers and, in particular, so to perform his functions under this Act as to promote the observance of the requirements of this Act by data controllers.

(2) The Commissioner shall arrange for the dissemination in such form and manner as he considers appropriate of such information as it may appear to him expedient to give to the public about the operation of this Act, about good practice, and about other matters within the scope of his functions under this Act, and may give advice to any person as to any of those matters.

(3) Where—

(a) the [Secretary of State] so directs by order, or

(b) the Commissioner considers it appropriate to do so,

the Commissioner shall, after such consultation with trade associations, data subjects or persons representing data subjects as appears to him to be appropriate, prepare and disseminate to such persons as he considers appropriate codes of practice for guidance as to good practice.

(4) The Commissioner shall also—

(a) where he considers it appropriate to do so, encourage trade associations to prepare, and to disseminate to their members, such codes of practice, and

(b) where any trade association submits a code of practice to him for his consideration, consider the code and, after such consultation with data subjects or persons representing data subjects as appears to him to be appropriate, notify the trade association whether in his opinion the code promotes the following of good practice.

(5) An order under subsection (3) shall describe the personal data or processing to which the code of practice is to relate, and may also describe the persons or classes of persons to whom it is to relate.

[(5A) In determining the action required to discharge the duties imposed by subsections (1) to (4), the Commissioner may take account of any action taken to discharge the duty imposed by section 52A (data-sharing code).]

(6) The Commissioner shall arrange for the dissemination in such form and manner as he considers appropriate of—

(a) any Community finding as defined by paragraph 15(2) of Part II of Schedule 1,

(b) any decision of the European Commission, under the procedure provided for in Article 31(2) of the Data Protection Directive, which is made for the purposes of Article 26(3) or (4) of the Directive, and

(c) such other information as it may appear to him to be expedient to give to data controllers in relation to any personal data about the protection of the rights and freedoms of data subjects in relation to the processing of personal data in countries and territories outside the European Economic Area.

(7) The Commissioner may, with the consent of the data controller, assess any processing of personal data for the following of good practice and shall inform the data controller of the results of the assessment.

(8) The Commissioner may charge such sums as he may with the consent of the [Secretary of State] determine for any services provided by the Commissioner by virtue of this Part.

(9) In this section—

"good practice" means such practice in the processing of personal data as appears to the Commissioner to be desirable having regard to the interests of data subjects and others, and includes (but is not limited to) compliance with the requirements of this Act;

"trade association" includes any body representing data controllers.

NOTES

Sub-ss (3), (8): words in square brackets substituted by the Secretary of State for Constitutional Affairs Order 2003, SI 2003/1887, art 9, Sch 2, para 9(1)(a).

Sub-s (5A): inserted by the Coroners and Justice Act 2009, s 174(2).

[3642AV]

52 Reports and codes of practice to be laid before Parliament

(1) The Commissioner shall lay annually before each House of Parliament a general report on the exercise of his functions under this Act.

(2) The Commissioner may from time to time lay before each House of Parliament such other reports with respect to those functions as he thinks fit.

(3) The Commissioner shall lay before each House of Parliament any code of practice prepared under section 51(3) for complying with a direction of the [Secretary of State], unless the code is included in any report laid under subsection (1) or (2).

NOTES

Sub-s (3): words in square brackets substituted by the Secretary of State for Constitutional Affairs Order 2003, SI 2003/1887, art 9, Sch 2, para 9(1)(a).

[3642AVA]

[52A Data-sharing code

(1) The Commissioner must prepare a code of practice which contains—

(a) practical guidance in relation to the sharing of personal data in accordance with the requirements of this Act, and

(b) such other guidance as the Commissioner considers appropriate to promote good practice in the sharing of personal data.

(2) For this purpose "good practice" means such practice in the sharing of personal data as appears to the Commissioner to be desirable having regard to the interests of data subjects and others, and includes (but is not limited to) compliance with the requirements of this Act.

(3) Before a code is prepared under this section, the Commissioner must consult such of the following as the Commissioner considers appropriate—

(a) trade associations (within the meaning of section 51);

(b) data subjects;

(c) persons who appear to the Commissioner to represent the interests of data subjects.

(4) In this section a reference to the sharing of personal data is to the disclosure of the data by transmission, dissemination or otherwise making it available.]

NOTES

Commencement: 1 February 2010.

Inserted, together with ss 52B–52E, by the Coroners and Justice Act 2009, s 174(1).

[3642AVB]

[52B Data-sharing code: procedure

(1) When a code is prepared under section 52A, it must be submitted to the Secretary of State for approval.

(2) Approval may be withheld only if it appears to the Secretary of State that the terms of the code could result in the United Kingdom being in breach of any of its Community obligations or any other international obligation.

(3) The Secretary of State must—

(a) if approval is withheld, publish details of the reasons for withholding it;

(b) if approval is granted, lay the code before Parliament.

(4) If, within the 40-day period, either House of Parliament resolves not to approve the code, the code is not to be issued by the Commissioner.

(5) If no such resolution is made within that period, the Commissioner must issue the code.

(6) Where—

(a) the Secretary of State withholds approval, or

(b) such a resolution is passed,

the Commissioner must prepare another code of practice under section 52A.

(7) Subsection (4) does not prevent a new code being laid before Parliament.

(8) A code comes into force at the end of the period of 21 days beginning with the day on which it is issued.
(9) A code may include transitional provision or savings.
(10) In this section "the 40-day period" means the period of 40 days beginning with the day on which the code is laid before Parliament (or, if it is not laid before each House of Parliament on the same day, the later of the 2 days on which it is laid).
(11) In calculating the 40-day period, no account is to be taken of any period during which Parliament is dissolved or prorogued or during which both Houses are adjourned for more than 4 days.]

NOTES
Commencement: 1 February 2010.
Inserted as noted to s 52A at **[3642AVA]**.

[3642AVC]
[52C Alteration or replacement of data-sharing code
(1) The Commissioner—
(a) must keep the data-sharing code under review, and
(b) may prepare an alteration to that code or a replacement code.
(2) Where, by virtue of a review under subsection (1)(a) or otherwise, the Commissioner becomes aware that the terms of the code could result in the United Kingdom being in breach of any of its Community obligations or any other international obligation, the Commissioner must exercise the power under subsection (1)(b) with a view to remedying the situation.
(3) Before an alteration or replacement code is prepared under subsection (1), the Commissioner must consult such of the following as the Commissioner considers appropriate—
(a) trade associations (within the meaning of section 51);
(b) data subjects;
(c) persons who appear to the Commissioner to represent the interests of data subjects.
(4) Section 52B (other than subsection (6)) applies to an alteration or replacement code prepared under this section as it applies to the code as first prepared under section 52A.
(5) In this section "the data-sharing code" means the code issued under section 52B(5) (as altered or replaced from time to time).]

NOTES
Commencement: 1 February 2010.
Inserted as noted to s 52A at **[3642AVA]**.

[3642AVD]
[52D Publication of data-sharing code
(1) The Commissioner must publish the code (and any replacement code) issued under section 52B(5).
(2) Where an alteration is so issued, the Commissioner must publish either—
(a) the alteration, or
(b) the code or replacement code as altered by it.]

NOTES
Commencement: 1 February 2010.
Inserted as noted to s 52A at **[3642AVA]**.

[3642AVE]
[52E Effect of data-sharing code
(1) A failure on the part of any person to act in accordance with any provision of the data-sharing code does not of itself render that person liable to any legal proceedings in any court or tribunal.
(2) The data-sharing code is admissible in evidence in any legal proceedings.
(3) If any provision of the data-sharing code appears to—
(a) the Tribunal or a court conducting any proceedings under this Act,
(b) a court or tribunal conducting any other legal proceedings, or
(c) the Commissioner carrying out any function under this Act,

to be relevant to any question arising in the proceedings, or in connection with the exercise of that jurisdiction or the carrying out of those functions, in relation to any time when it was in force, that provision of the code must be taken into account in determining that question.
(4) In this section "the data-sharing code" means the code issued under section 52B(5) (as altered or replaced from time to time).]

NOTES

Commencement: 1 February 2010.

Inserted as noted to s 52A at **[3642AVA]**.

[3642AW]

53 Assistance by Commissioner in cases involving processing for the special purposes

(1) An individual who is an actual or prospective party to any proceedings under section 7(9), 10(4), 12(8) or 14 or by virtue of section 13 which relate to personal data processed for the special purposes may apply to the Commissioner for assistance in relation to those proceedings.

(2) The Commissioner shall, as soon as reasonably practicable after receiving an application under subsection (1), consider it and decide whether and to what extent to grant it, but he shall not grant the application unless, in his opinion, the case involves a matter of substantial public importance.

(3) If the Commissioner decides to provide assistance, he shall, as soon as reasonably practicable after making the decision, notify the applicant, stating the extent of the assistance to be provided.

(4) If the Commissioner decides not to provide assistance, he shall, as soon as reasonably practicable after making the decision, notify the applicant of his decision and, if he thinks fit, the reasons for it.

(5) In this section—

- (a) references to "proceedings" include references to prospective proceedings, and
- (b) "applicant", in relation to assistance under this section, means an individual who applies for assistance.

(6) Schedule 10 has effect for supplementing this section.

[3642AX]

54 International co-operation

(1) The Commissioner—

- (a) shall continue to be the designated authority in the United Kingdom for the purposes of Article 13 of the Convention, and
- (b) shall be the supervisory authority in the United Kingdom for the purposes of the Data Protection Directive.

(2) The [Secretary of State] may by order make provision as to the functions to be discharged by the Commissioner as the designated authority in the United Kingdom for the purposes of Article 13 of the Convention.

(3) The [Secretary of State] may by order make provision as to co-operation by the Commissioner with the European Commission and with supervisory authorities in other EEA States in connection with the performance of their respective duties and, in particular, as to—

- (a) the exchange of information with supervisory authorities in other EEA States or with the European Commission, and
- (b) the exercise within the United Kingdom at the request of a supervisory authority in another EEA State, in cases excluded by section 5 from the application of the other provisions of this Act, of functions of the Commissioner specified in the order.

(4) The Commissioner shall also carry out any data protection functions which the [Secretary of State] may by order direct him to carry out for the purpose of enabling Her Majesty's Government in the United Kingdom to give effect to any international obligations of the United Kingdom.

(5) The Commissioner shall, if so directed by the [Secretary of State], provide any authority exercising data protection functions under the law of a colony specified in the direction with such assistance in connection with the discharge of those functions as the [Secretary of State] may direct or approve, on such terms (including terms as to payment) as the [Secretary of State] may direct or approve.

(6) Where the European Commission makes a decision for the purposes of Article 26(3) or (4) of the Data Protection Directive under the procedure provided for in Article 31(2) of the Directive, the Commissioner shall comply with that decision in exercising his functions under paragraph 9 of Schedule 4 or, as the case may be, paragraph 8 of that Schedule.

(7) The Commissioner shall inform the European Commission and the supervisory authorities in other EEA States—

- (a) of any approvals granted for the purposes of paragraph 8 of Schedule 4, and
- (b) of any authorisations granted for the purposes of paragraph 9 of that Schedule.

(8) In this section—

"the Convention" means the Convention for the Protection of Individuals with regard to Automatic Processing of Personal Data which was opened for signature on 28th January 1981;

"data protection functions" means functions relating to the protection of individuals with respect to the processing of personal information.

NOTES

Sub-ss (2)–(5): words in square brackets substituted by the Secretary of State for Constitutional Affairs Order 2003, SI 2003/1887, art 9, Sch 2, para 9(1)(a).

Orders: the Data Protection (Functions of Designated Authority) Order 2000, SI 2000/186; the Data Protection (International Co-operation) Order 2000, SI 2000/190.

54A *(Outside the scope of this work.)*

Unlawful obtaining etc of personal data

[3642AY]

55 Unlawful obtaining etc of personal data

(1) A person must not knowingly or recklessly, without the consent of the data controller—

(a) obtain or disclose personal data or the information contained in personal data, or

(b) procure the disclosure to another person of the information contained in personal data.

(2) Subsection (1) does not apply to a person who shows—

(a) that the obtaining, disclosing or procuring—

(i) was necessary for the purpose of preventing or detecting crime, or

(ii) was required or authorised by or under any enactment, by any rule of law or by the order of a court,

(b) that he acted in the reasonable belief that he had in law the right to obtain or disclose the data or information or, as the case may be, to procure the disclosure of the information to the other person,

(c) that he acted in the reasonable belief that he would have had the consent of the data controller if the data controller had known of the obtaining, disclosing or procuring and the circumstances of it,

[(ca) that he acted—

(i) for the special purposes,

(ii) with a view to the publication by any person of any journalistic, literary or artistic material, and

(iii) in the reasonable belief that in the particular circumstances the obtaining, disclosing or procuring was justified as being in the public interest,] or

(d) that in the particular circumstances the obtaining, disclosing or procuring was justified as being in the public interest.

(3) A person who contravenes subsection (1) is guilty of an offence.

(4) A person who sells personal data is guilty of an offence if he has obtained the data in contravention of subsection (1).

(5) A person who offers to sell personal data is guilty of an offence if—

(a) he has obtained the data in contravention of subsection (1), or

(b) he subsequently obtains the data in contravention of that subsection.

(6) For the purposes of subsection (5), an advertisement indicating that personal data are or may be for sale is an offer to sell the data.

(7) Section 1(2) does not apply for the purposes of this section; and for the purposes of subsections (4) to (6), "personal data" includes information extracted from personal data.

(8) References in this section to personal data do not include references to personal data which by virtue of section 28 [or 33A] are exempt from this section.

NOTES

Sub-s (2): para (ca) inserted by the Criminal Justice and Immigration Act 2008, s 78, as from a day to be appointed, subject to transitional provisions and savings in s 148(2) of, and Sch 27, Pt 5, para 28 to, that Act.

Sub-s (8): words in square brackets inserted by the Freedom of Information Act 2000, s 70(2).

[Monetary penalties

[3642AZ]

55A Power of Commissioner to impose monetary penalty

(1) The Commissioner may serve a data controller with a monetary penalty notice if the Commissioner is satisfied that—

(a) there has been a serious contravention of section 4(4) by the data controller,

(b) the contravention was of a kind likely to cause substantial damage or substantial distress, and
(c) subsection (2) or (3) applies.

(2) This subsection applies if the contravention was deliberate.

(3) This subsection applies if the data controller—
(a) knew or ought to have known—
(i) that there was a risk that the contravention would occur, and
(ii) that such a contravention would be of a kind likely to cause substantial damage or substantial distress, but
(b) failed to take reasonable steps to prevent the contravention.

[(3A) The Commissioner may not be satisfied as mentioned in subsection (1) by virtue of any matter which comes to the Commissioner's attention as a result of anything done in pursuance of—
(a) an assessment notice;
(b) an assessment under section 51(7).]

(4) A monetary penalty notice is a notice requiring the data controller to pay to the Commissioner a monetary penalty of an amount determined by the Commissioner and specified in the notice.

(5) The amount determined by the Commissioner must not exceed the prescribed amount.

(6) The monetary penalty must be paid to the Commissioner within the period specified in the notice.

(7) The notice must contain such information as may be prescribed.

(8) Any sum received by the Commissioner by virtue of this section must be paid into the Consolidated Fund.

(9) In this section—
"data controller" does not include the Crown Estate Commissioners or a person who is a data controller by virtue of section 63(3);
"prescribed" means prescribed by regulations made by the Secretary of State.]

NOTES

Commencement: 1 October 2009 (sub-ss (4), (5), (7), (9)); to be appointed (otherwise).

Inserted, together with the preceding cross-heading and ss 55B–55E, by the Criminal Justice and Immigration Act 2008, s 144(1).

Sub-s (3A): inserted by the Coroners and Justice Act 2009, s 175, Sch 20, Pt 5, para 13, as from a day to be appointed.

[3642BA]

[55B Monetary penalty notices: procedural rights

(1) Before serving a monetary penalty notice, the Commissioner must serve the data controller with a notice of intent.

(2) A notice of intent is a notice that the Commissioner proposes to serve a monetary penalty notice.

(3) A notice of intent must—
(a) inform the data controller that he may make written representations in relation to the Commissioner's proposal within a period specified in the notice, and
(b) contain such other information as may be prescribed.

(4) The Commissioner may not serve a monetary penalty notice until the time within which the data controller may make representations has expired.

(5) A person on whom a monetary penalty notice is served may appeal to the Tribunal against—
(a) the issue of the monetary penalty notice;
(b) the amount of the penalty specified in the notice.

(6) In this section, "prescribed" means prescribed by regulations made by the Secretary of State.]

NOTES

Commencement: 1 October 2009 (sub-ss (2), (3)(b), (6)); to be appointed (otherwise).

Inserted as noted to s 55A at **[3642AZ]**.

Regulations: the Data Protection (Monetary Penalties) (Maximum Penalty and Notices) Regulations 2010, SI 2010/31.

[3642BB]

[55C Guidance about monetary penalty notices

(1) The Commissioner must prepare and issue guidance on how he proposes to exercise his functions under sections 55A and 55B.

(2) The guidance must, in particular, deal with—
(a) the circumstances in which he would consider it appropriate to issue a monetary penalty notice, and
(b) how he will determine the amount of the penalty.

(3) The Commissioner may alter or replace the guidance.
(4) If the guidance is altered or replaced, the Commissioner must issue the altered or replacement guidance.
(5) The Commissioner may not issue guidance under this section without the approval of the Secretary of State.
(6) The Commissioner must lay any guidance issued under this section before each House of Parliament.
(7) The Commissioner must arrange for the publication of any guidance issued under this section in such form and manner as he considers appropriate.
(8) In subsections (5) to (7), "guidance" includes altered or replacement guidance.]

NOTES
Commencement: 1 October 2009.
Inserted as noted to s 55A at **[3642AZ]**.

[3642BC]
[55D Monetary penalty notices: enforcement
(1) This section applies in relation to any penalty payable to the Commissioner by virtue of section 55A.
(2) In England and Wales, the penalty is recoverable—
(a) if a county court so orders, as if it were payable under an order of that court;
(b) if the High Court so orders, as if it were payable under an order of that court.
(3) In Scotland, the penalty may be enforced in the same manner as an extract registered decree arbitral bearing a warrant for execution issued by the sheriff court of any sheriffdom in Scotland.
(4) In Northern Ireland, the penalty is recoverable—
(a) if a county court so orders, as if it were payable under an order of that court;
(b) if the High Court so orders, as if it were payable under an order of that court.]

NOTES
Commencement: to be appointed.
Inserted as noted to s 55A at **[3642AZ]**.

[3642BD]
[55E Notices under sections 55A and 55B: supplemental
(1) The Secretary of State may by order make further provision in connection with monetary penalty notices and notices of intent.
(2) An order under this section may in particular—
(a) provide that a monetary penalty notice may not be served on a data controller with respect to the processing of personal data for the special purposes except in circumstances specified in the order;
(b) make provision for the cancellation or variation of monetary penalty notices;
(c) confer rights of appeal to the Tribunal against decisions of the Commissioner in relation to the cancellation or variation of such notices;
(d) . . .
(e) make provision for the determination of [appeals made by virtue of paragraph (c)].
(f) . . .
(3) An order under this section may apply any provision of this Act with such modifications as may be specified in the order.
(4) An order under this section may amend this Act.]

NOTES
Commencement: 1 October 2009.
Inserted as noted to s 55A at **[3642AZ]**.
Sub-s (2): paras (d), (f) repealed and words in square brackets in para (e) substituted by the Transfer of Tribunal Functions Order 2010, SI 2010/22, art 5(1), Sch 2, paras 24, 28, subject to transitional provisions and savings in Sch 5 thereto.

Records obtained under data subject's right of access

[3642BE]
56 Prohibition of requirement as to production of certain records
(1) A person must not, in connection with—
(a) the recruitment of another person as an employee,
(b) the continued employment of another person, or
(c) any contract for the provision of services to him by another person,

Part III Statutes

require that other person or a third party to supply him with a relevant record or to produce a relevant record to him.

(2) A person concerned with the provision (for payment or not) of goods, facilities or services to the public or a section of the public must not, as a condition of providing or offering to provide any goods, facilities or services to another person, require that other person or a third party to supply him with a relevant record or to produce a relevant record to him.

(3) Subsections (1) and (2) do not apply to a person who shows—

(a) that the imposition of the requirement was required or authorised by or under any enactment, by any rule of law or by the order of a court, or

(b) that in the particular circumstances the imposition of the requirement was justified as being in the public interest.

(4) Having regard to the provisions of Part V of the Police Act 1997 (certificates of criminal records etc), the imposition of the requirement referred to in subsection (1) or (2) is not to be regarded as being justified as being in the public interest on the ground that it would assist in the prevention or detection of crime.

(5) A person who contravenes subsection (1) or (2) is guilty of an offence.

(6) In this section "a relevant record" means any record which—

(a) has been or is to be obtained by a data subject from any data controller specified in the first column of the Table below in the exercise of the right conferred by section 7, and

(b) contains information relating to any matter specified in relation to that data controller in the second column,

and includes a copy of such a record or a part of such a record.

TABLE

Data controller		***Subject-matter***	
1 Any of the following persons—		(a)	Convictions.
(a)	a chief officer of police of a police force in England and Wales.	(b)	Cautions.
(b)	a chief constable of a police force in Scotland.		
(c)	the [Chief Constable of the Police Service of Northern Ireland].		
[(d)	the Director General of the Serious Organised Crime Agency.]		
2 The Secretary of State.		(a)	Convictions.
		(b)	Cautions.
		(c)	His functions under [section 92 of the Powers of Criminal Courts (Sentencing) Act 2000], section 205(2) or 208 of the Criminal Procedure (Scotland) Act 1995 or section 73 of the Children and Young Persons Act (Northern Ireland) 1968 in relation to any person sentenced to detention.
		(d)	His functions under the Prison Act 1952, the Prisons (Scotland) Act 1989 or the Prison Act (Northern Ireland) 1953 in relation to any person imprisoned or detained.
		(e)	His functions under the Social Security Contributions and Benefits Act 1992, the Social Security Administration Act 1992 or the Jobseekers Act 1995.
		(f)	His functions under Part V of the Police Act 1997.
		[(g)	His functions under the Safeguarding Vulnerable Groups Act 2006 [or the Safeguarding Vulnerable Groups (Northern Ireland) Order 2007]].

Data controller	*Subject-matter*
3 The Department of Health and Social Services for Northern Ireland.	Its functions under the Social Security Contributions and Benefits (Northern Ireland) Act 1992, the Social Security Administration (Northern Ireland) Act 1992 or the Jobseekers (Northern Ireland) Order 1995.
[4 The [Independent Safeguarding Authority].	Its functions under the Safeguarding Vulnerable Groups Act 2006 [or the Safeguarding Vulnerable Groups (Northern Ireland) Order 2007]].

[(6A) A record is not a relevant record to the extent that it relates, or is to relate, only to personal data falling within paragraph (e) of the definition of "data" in section 1(1).]

(7) In the Table in subsection (6)—

"caution" means a caution given to any person in England and Wales or Northern Ireland in respect of an offence which, at the time when the caution is given, is admitted;

"conviction" has the same meaning as in the Rehabilitation of Offenders Act 1974 or the Rehabilitation of Offenders (Northern Ireland) Order 1978.

(8) The [Secretary of State] may by order amend—

(a) the Table in subsection (6), and

(b) subsection (7).

(9) For the purposes of this section a record which states that a data controller is not processing any personal data relating to a particular matter shall be taken to be a record containing information relating to that matter.

(10) In this section "employee" means an individual who—

(a) works under a contract of employment, as defined by section 230(2) of the Employment Rights Act 1996, or

(b) holds any office,

whether or not he is entitled to remuneration; and "employment" shall be construed accordingly.

NOTES

Commencement: 16 Jul 1998 (sub-s (8) in so far as conferring power to make subordinate legislation); 7 July 2008 (in so far as relating to the entries in sub-s (6) which relate to the functions of the Secretary of State or the Independent Safeguarding Authority under the Safeguarding Vulnerable Groups Act 2006 or SI 2007/1351 (NI 11)); to be appointed (otherwise).

Sub-s (6): Table: in entry numbered 1(c) words in square brackets substituted by the Police (Northern Ireland) Act 2000, s 78(2)(a); entry numbered 1(d) substituted, for entries 1(d), (e) as originally enacted, by the Serious Organised Crime and Police Act 2005, Sch 4, para 112; in entry numbered 2 column 2, para (c) words in square brackets substituted by the Powers of Criminal Courts (Sentencing) Act 2000, s 165(1), Sch 9, para 191; in entry numbered 2 in column 2 para (g) inserted by the Safeguarding Vulnerable Groups Act 2006, s 63(1), Sch 9, Pt 2, para 15(1), (2)(a), words in square brackets inserted by the Safeguarding Vulnerable Groups (Northern Ireland) Order 2007, SI 2007/1351, art 60(1), Sch 7, para 4(1), as from a day to be appointed; entry numbered 4 inserted by the Safeguarding Vulnerable Groups Act 2006, s 63(1), Sch 9, Pt 2, para 15(1), (2)(b), in entry numbered 4 in column 1 words in square brackets substituted by the Policing and Crime Act 2009, s 81(2), (3)(i), in entry numbered 4 in column 2 words in square brackets inserted by SI 2007/1351, art 60(1), Sch 7, para 4(1), as from a day to be appointed.

Sub-s (6A): inserted by the Freedom of Information Act 2000, s 68(4).

Sub-s (8): words in square brackets substituted by the Secretary of State for Constitutional Affairs Order 2003, SI 2003/1887, art 9, Sch 2, para 9(1)(a).

[3642BF]
57 Avoidance of certain contractual terms relating to health records

(1) Any term or condition of a contract is void in so far as it purports to require an individual—

(a) to supply any other person with a record to which this section applies, or with a copy of such a record or a part of such a record, or

(b) to produce to any other person such a record, copy or part.

(2) This section applies to any record which—

(a) has been or is to be obtained by a data subject in the exercise of the right conferred by section 7, and

(b) consists of the information contained in any health record as defined by section 68(2).

Information provided to Commissioner or Tribunal

[3642BG]
58 Disclosure of information

No enactment or rule of law prohibiting or restricting the disclosure of information shall preclude a person from furnishing the Commissioner or the Tribunal with any information necessary for the discharge of their functions under this Act [or the Freedom of Information Act 2000].

NOTES

Words in square brackets inserted by the Freedom of Information Act 2000, s 18(4), Sch 2, Pt II, para 18.

59 *(Outside the scope of this work.)*

General provisions relating to offences

[3642BH]

60 Prosecutions and penalties

(1) No proceedings for an offence under this Act shall be instituted—

(a) in England or Wales, except by the Commissioner or by or with the consent of the Director of Public Prosecutions;

(b) in Northern Ireland, except by the Commissioner or by or with the consent of the Director of Public Prosecutions for Northern Ireland.

(2) A person guilty of an offence under any provision of this Act other than [section 54A and] paragraph 12 of Schedule 9 is liable—

(a) on summary conviction, to a fine not exceeding the statutory maximum, or

(b) on conviction on indictment, to a fine.

(3) A person guilty of an offence under [section 54A and] paragraph 12 of Schedule 9 is liable on summary conviction to a fine not exceeding level 5 on the standard scale.

(4) Subject to subsection (5), the court by or before which a person is convicted of—

(a) an offence under section 21(1), 22(6), 55 or 56,

(b) an offence under section 21(2) relating to processing which is assessable processing for the purposes of section 22, or

(c) an offence under section 47(1) relating to an enforcement notice,

may order any document or other material used in connection with the processing of personal data and appearing to the court to be connected with the commission of the offence to be forfeited, destroyed or erased.

(5) The court shall not make an order under subsection (4) in relation to any material where a person (other than the offender) claiming to be the owner of or otherwise interested in the material applies to be heard by the court, unless an opportunity is given to him to show cause why the order should not be made.

NOTES

Sub-ss (2), (3): words in square brackets inserted by the Crime (International Co-operation) Act 2003, s 91(1), Sch 5, paras 68, 70.

[3642BI]

61 Liability of directors etc

(1) Where an offence under this Act has been committed by a body corporate and is proved to have been committed with the consent or connivance of or to be attributable to any neglect on the part of any director, manager, secretary or similar officer of the body corporate or any person who was purporting to act in any such capacity, he as well as the body corporate shall be guilty of that offence and be liable to be proceeded against and punished accordingly.

(2) Where the affairs of a body corporate are managed by its members subsection (1) shall apply in relation to the acts and defaults of a member in connection with his functions of management as if he were a director of the body corporate.

(3) Where an offence under this Act has been committed by a Scottish partnership and the contravention in question is proved to have occurred with the consent or connivance of, or to be attributable to any neglect on the part of, a partner, he as well as the partnership shall be guilty of that offence and shall be liable to be proceeded against and punished accordingly.

62 *(Outside the scope of this work.)*

General

63, 63A *(Outside the scope of this work.)*

[3642BJ]

64 Transmission of notices etc by electronic or other means

(1) This section applies to

(a) a notice or request under any provision of Part II,

(b) a notice under subsection (1) of section 24 or particulars made available under that subsection, or

(c) an application under section 41(2),

but does not apply to anything which is required to be served in accordance with rules of court.

(2) The requirement that any notice, request, particulars or application to which this section applies should be in writing is satisfied where the text of the notice, request, particulars or application—

(a) is transmitted by electronic means,

(b) is received in legible form, and

(c) is capable of being used for subsequent reference.

(3) The [Secretary of State] may by regulations provide that any requirement that any notice, request, particulars or application to which this section applies should be in writing is not to apply in such circumstances as may be prescribed by the regulations.

NOTES

Sub-s (3): words in square brackets substituted by the Secretary of State for Constitutional Affairs Order 2003, SI 2003/1887, art 9, Sch 2, para 9(1)(a).

[3642BK]

65 Service of notices by Commissioner

(1) Any notice authorised or required by this Act to be served on or given to any person by the Commissioner may—

(a) if that person is an individual, be served on him—

(i) by delivering it to him, or

(ii) by sending it to him by post addressed to him at his usual or last-known place of residence or business, or

(iii) by leaving it for him at that place;

(b) if that person is a body corporate or unincorporate, be served on that body—

(i) by sending it by post to the proper officer of the body at its principal office, or

(ii) by addressing it to the proper officer of the body and leaving it at that office;

(c) if that person is a partnership in Scotland, be served on that partnership—

(i) by sending it by post to the principal office of the partnership, or

(ii) by addressing it to that partnership and leaving it at that office.

(2) In subsection (1)(b) "principal office", in relation to a registered company, means its registered office and "proper officer", in relation to any body, means the secretary or other executive officer charged with the conduct of its general affairs.

(3) This section is without prejudice to any other lawful method of serving or giving a notice.

[3642BL]

66 Exercise of rights in Scotland by children

(1) Where a question falls to be determined in Scotland as to the legal capacity of a person under the age of sixteen years to exercise any right conferred by any provision of this Act, that person shall be taken to have that capacity where he has a general understanding of what it means to exercise that right.

(2) Without prejudice to the generality of subsection (1), a person of twelve years of age or more shall be presumed to be of sufficient age and maturity to have such understanding as is mentioned in that subsection.

[3642BM]

67 Orders, regulations and rules

(1) Any power conferred by this Act on the [Secretary of State] to make an order, regulations or rules shall be exercisable by statutory instrument.

(2) Any order, regulations or rules made by the [Secretary of State] under this Act may—

(a) make different provision for different cases, and

(b) make such supplemental, incidental, consequential or transitional provision or savings as the [Secretary of State] considers appropriate;

and nothing in section 7(11), 19(5), 26(1) or 30(4) limits the generality of paragraph (a).

(3) Before making—

(a) an order under any provision of this Act other than section 75(3),

(b) any regulations under this Act other than notification regulations (as defined by section 16(2)),

the [Secretary of State] shall consult the Commissioner.

(4) A statutory instrument containing (whether alone or with other provisions) an order under—

section 10(2)(b),
section 12(5)(b),
section 22(1),
section 30,
section 32(3),

section 38,
[section 41A(2)(c),]
[section 55E(1),]
section 56(8),
paragraph 10 of Schedule 3, or
paragraph 4 of Schedule 7,

shall not be made unless a draft of the instrument has been laid before and approved by a resolution of each House of Parliament.

(5) A statutory instrument which contains (whether alone or with other provisions)—

(a) an order under—

section 22(7),
section 23,
[section 41A(2)(b),]
section 51(3),
section 54(2), (3) or (4),
paragraph 3, 4 or 14 of Part II of Schedule 1,
paragraph 6 of Schedule 2,
paragraph 2, 7 or 9 of Schedule 3,
paragraph 4 of Schedule 4,
paragraph 6 of Schedule 7,

(b) regulations under section 7 which—
(i) prescribe cases for the purposes of subsection (2)(b),
(ii) are made by virtue of subsection (7), or
(iii) relate to the definition of "the prescribed period",

(c) regulations under section 8(1) [, 9(3) or 9A(5)],

[(ca) regulations under section 55A(5) or (7) or 55B(3)(b),]

(d) regulations under section 64,

(e) notification regulations (as defined by section 16(2)), or

(f) rules under paragraph 7 of Schedule 6,

and which is not subject to the requirement in subsection (4) that a draft of the instrument be laid before and approved by a resolution of each House of Parliament, shall be subject to annulment in pursuance of a resolution of either House of Parliament.

(6) A statutory instrument which contains only—

(a) regulations prescribing fees for the purposes of any provision of this Act, or

(b) regulations under section 7 prescribing fees for the purposes of any other enactment,

shall be laid before Parliament after being made.

NOTES

Sub-ss (1)–(3): words in square brackets substituted by the Secretary of State for Constitutional Affairs Order 2003, SI 2003/1887, art 9, Sch 2, para 9(1)(a).

Sub-s (4): words in first pair of square brackets inserted by the Coroners and Justice Act 2009, s 175, Sch 20, Pt 2, para 6(a), as from a day to be appointed; words in second pair of square brackets inserted by the Criminal Justice and Immigration Act 2008, s 144(2)(a).

Sub-s (5): words in square brackets in para (a) inserted by the Coroners and Justice Act 2009, s 175, Sch 20, Pt 2, para 6(b), as from a day to be appointed; words in square brackets in para (c) substituted by the Freedom of Information Act 2000, s 69(3); para (ca) inserted by the Criminal Justice and Immigration Act 2008, s 144(2)(b).

[3642BN]

68 Meaning of "accessible record"

(1) In this Act "accessible record" means—

(a) a health record as defined by subsection (2),

(b) an educational record as defined by Schedule 11, or

(c) an accessible public record as defined by Schedule 12.

(2) In subsection (1)(a) "health record" means any record which—

(a) consists of information relating to the physical or mental health or condition of an individual, and

(b) has been made by or on behalf of a health professional in connection with the care of that individual.

69 *(Outside the scope of this work.)*

[3642BO]

70 Supplementary definitions

(1) In this Act, unless the context otherwise requires—

"business" includes any trade or profession;

"the Commissioner" means [the Information Commissioner];

"credit reference agency" has the same meaning as in the Consumer Credit Act 1974;

"the Data Protection Directive" means Directive 95/46/EC on the protection of individuals with regard to the processing of personal data and on the free movement of such data;

"EEA State" means a State which is a contracting party to the Agreement on the European Economic Area signed at Oporto on 2nd May 1992 as adjusted by the Protocol signed at Brussels on 17th March 1993;

"enactment" includes an enactment passed after this Act [and any enactment comprised in, or in any instrument made under, an Act of the Scottish Parliament];

"government department" includes a Northern Ireland department and any body or authority exercising statutory functions on behalf of the Crown;

"Minister of the Crown" has the same meaning as in the Ministers of the Crown Act 1975;

"public register" means any register which pursuant to a requirement imposed—

(a) by or under any enactment, or

(b) in pursuance of any international agreement,

is open to public inspection or open to inspection by any person having a legitimate interest;

"pupil"—

(a) in relation to a school in England and Wales, means a registered pupil within the meaning of the Education Act 1996,

(b) in relation to a school in Scotland, means a pupil within the meaning of the Education (Scotland) Act 1980, and

(c) in relation to a school in Northern Ireland, means a registered pupil within the meaning of the Education and Libraries (Northern Ireland) Order 1986;

"recipient", in relation to any personal data, means any person to whom the data are disclosed, including any person (such as an employee or agent of the data controller, a data processor or an employee or agent of a data processor) to whom they are disclosed in the course of processing the data for the data controller, but does not include any person to whom disclosure is or may be made as a result of, or with a view to, a particular inquiry by or on behalf of that person made in the exercise of any power conferred by law;

"registered company" means a company registered under the enactments relating to companies for the time being in force in the United Kingdom;

"school"—

(a) in relation to England and Wales, has the same meaning as in the Education Act 1996,

(b) in relation to Scotland, has the same meaning as in the Education (Scotland) Act 1980, and

(c) in relation to Northern Ireland, has the same meaning as in the Education and Libraries (Northern Ireland) Order 1986;

"teacher" includes—

(a) in Great Britain, head teacher, and

(b) in Northern Ireland, the principal of a school;

"third party", in relation to personal data, means any person other than—

(a) the data subject,

(b) the data controller, or

(c) any data processor or other person authorised to process data for the data controller or processor;

["the Tribunal", in relation to any appeal under this Act, means—

(a) the Upper Tribunal, in any case where it is determined by or under Tribunal Procedure Rules that the Upper Tribunal is to hear the appeal; or

(b) the First-tier Tribunal, in any other case].

(2) For the purposes of this Act data are inaccurate if they are incorrect or misleading as to any matter of fact.

NOTES

Sub-s (1): in definition "the Commissioner" words in square brackets substituted by the Freedom of Information Act 2000, s 18(4), Sch 2, Pt I, para 14(a); in definition "enactment" words in square brackets inserted by the Scotland Act 1998 (Consequential Modifications) (No 2) Order 1999, SI 1999/1820, art 4, Sch 2, Pt I, para 133; definition "the Tribunal" substituted by the Transfer of Tribunal Functions Order 2010, SI 2010/22, art 5(1), Sch 2, paras 24, 29, subject to transitional provisions and savings in Sch 5 thereto; definition "government department" substituted by the Coroners and Justice Act 2009, s 175, Sch 20, Pt 2, para 7, as from a day to be appointed, as follows:

""government department" includes—

(a) any part of the Scottish Administration;
(b) a Northern Ireland department;
(c) the Welsh Assembly Government;
(d) any body or authority exercising statutory functions on behalf of the Crown.".

[3642BP]
71 Index of defined expressions

The following Table shows provisions defining or otherwise explaining expressions used in this Act (other than provisions defining or explaining an expression only used in the same section or Schedule)—

accessible record	section 68
address (in Part III)	section 16(3)
Business	section 70(1)
the Commissioner	section 70(1)
credit reference agency	section 70(1)
Data	section 1(1)
data controller	sections 1(1) and (4) and 63(3)
data processor	section 1(1)
the Data Protection Directive	section 70(1)
data protection principles	section 4 and Schedule 1
data subject	section 1(1)
disclosing (of personal data)	section 1(2)(b)
EEA State	section 70(1)
Enactment	section 70(1)
enforcement notice	section 40(1)
fees regulations (in Part III)	section 16(2)
government department	section 70(1)
health professional	section 69
inaccurate (in relation to data)	section 70(2)
information notice	section 43(1)
Minister of the Crown	section 70(1)
the non-disclosure provisions (in Part IV)	section 27(3)
notification regulations (in Part III)	section 16(2)
Obtaining (of personal data)	section 1(2)(a)
personal data	section 1(1)
prescribed (in Part III)	section 16(2)
processing (of information or data)	section 1(1) and paragraph 5 of Schedule 8
[public authority	section 1(1)]
public register	section 70(1)
publish (in relation to journalistic, literary or artistic material)	section 32(6)
pupil (in relation to a school)	section 70(1)
recipient (in relation to personal data)	section 70(1)
Recording (of personal data)	section 1(2)(a)
registered company	section 70(1)
registrable particulars (in Part III)	section 16(1)
relevant filing system	section 1(1)
School	section 70(1)
Sensitive personal data	section 2
special information notice	section 44(1)
the special purposes	section 3
the subject information provisions (in Part IV)	section 27(2)
Teacher	section 70(1)

third party (in relation to processing of personal data)	section 70(1)
the Tribunal	section 70(1)
using (of personal data)	section 1(2)(b).

NOTES

Table: entry "public authority" inserted by the Freedom of Information Act 2000, s 68(5).

[3642BQ]

72 Modifications of Act

During the period beginning with the commencement of this section and ending with 23rd October 2007, the provisions of this Act shall have effect subject to the modifications set out in Schedule 13.

[3642BR]

73 Transitional provisions and savings

Schedule 14 (which contains transitional provisions and savings) has effect.

[3642BS]

74 Minor and consequential amendments and repeals and revocations

(1) Schedule 15 (which contains minor and consequential amendments) has effect.

(2) The enactments and instruments specified in Schedule 16 are repealed or revoked to the extent specified.

[3642BT]

75 Short title, commencement and extent

(1) This Act may be cited as the Data Protection Act 1998.

(2) The following provisions of this Act—

- (a) sections 1 to 3,
- (b) section 25(1) and (4),
- (c) section 26,
- (d) sections 67 to 71,
- (e) this section,
- (f) paragraph 17 of Schedule 5,
- (g) Schedule 11,
- (h) Schedule 12, and
- (i) so much of any other provision of this Act as confers any power to make subordinate legislation,

shall come into force on the day on which this Act is passed.

(3) The remaining provisions of this Act shall come into force on such day as the [Secretary of State] may by order appoint; and different days may be appointed for different purposes.

(4) The day appointed under subsection (3) for the coming into force of section 56 must not be earlier than the first day on which sections 112, 113 and 115 of the Police Act 1997 (which provide for the issue by the Secretary of State of criminal conviction certificates, criminal record certificates and enhanced criminal record certificates) are all in force.

[(4A) Subsection (4) does not apply to section 56 so far as that section relates to a record containing information relating to—

- (a) the Secretary of State's functions under the Safeguarding Vulnerable Groups Act 2006 [or the Safeguarding Vulnerable Groups (Northern Ireland) Order 2007], or
- (b) the [Independent Safeguarding Authority's] functions under that Act [or that Order].]

(5) Subject to subsection (6), this Act extends to Northern Ireland.

(6) Any amendment, repeal or revocation made by Schedule 15 or 16 has the same extent as that of the enactment or instrument to which it relates.

NOTES

Sub-s (3): words in square brackets substituted by the Secretary of State for Constitutional Affairs Order 2003, SI 2003/1887, art 9, Sch 2, para 9(1)(a).

Sub-s (4A): inserted by the Safeguarding Vulnerable Groups Act 2006, s 63(1), Sch 9, Pt 2, para 15(1), (3); words in first and third pairs of square brackets inserted by the Safeguarding Vulnerable Groups (Northern Ireland) Order 2007, SI 2007/1351, art 60(1), Sch 7, para 4(2), as from a day to be appointed; words in second pair of square brackets substituted by the Policing and Crime Act 2009, s 81(2), (3)(i).

Orders: the Data Protection Act 1998 (Commencement) Order 2000, SI 2000/183; the Data Protection Act 1998 (Commencement No 2) Order 2008, SI 2008/1592.

SCHEDULE 1

THE DATA PROTECTION PRINCIPLES

Section 4(1) and (2)

PART I
THE PRINCIPLES

[3642BU]

1. Personal data shall be processed fairly and lawfully and, in particular, shall not be processed unless—

(a) at least one of the conditions in Schedule 2 is met, and

(b) in the case of sensitive personal data, at least one of the conditions in Schedule 3 is also met.

2. Personal data shall be obtained only for one or more specified and lawful purposes, and shall not be further processed in any manner incompatible with that purpose or those purposes.

3. Personal data shall be adequate, relevant and not excessive in relation to the purpose or purposes for which they are processed.

4. Personal data shall be accurate and, where necessary, kept up to date.

5. Personal data processed for any purpose or purposes shall not be kept for longer than is necessary for that purpose or those purposes.

6. Personal data shall be processed in accordance with the rights of data subjects under this Act.

7. Appropriate technical and organisational measures shall be taken against unauthorised or unlawful processing of personal data and against accidental loss or destruction of, or damage to, personal data.

8. Personal data shall not be transferred to a country or territory outside the European Economic Area unless that country or territory ensures an adequate level of protection for the rights and freedoms of data subjects in relation to the processing of personal data.

PART II
INTERPRETATION OF THE PRINCIPLES IN PART I

The first principle

[3642BV]

1.—(1) In determining for the purposes of the first principle whether personal data are processed fairly, regard is to be had to the method by which they are obtained, including in particular whether any person from whom they are obtained is deceived or misled as to the purpose or purposes for which they are to be processed.

(2) Subject to paragraph 2, for the purposes of the first principle data are to be treated as obtained fairly if they consist of information obtained from a person who—

(a) is authorised by or under any enactment to supply it, or

(b) is required to supply it by or under any enactment or by any convention or other instrument imposing an international obligation on the United Kingdom.

2.—(1) Subject to paragraph 3, for the purposes of the first principle personal data are not to be treated as processed fairly unless—

(a) in the case of data obtained from the data subject, the data controller ensures so far as practicable that the data subject has, is provided with, or has made readily available to him, the information specified in sub-paragraph (3), and

(b) in any other case, the data controller ensures so far as practicable that, before the relevant time or as soon as practicable after that time, the data subject has, is provided with, or has made readily available to him, the information specified in sub-paragraph (3).

(2) In sub-paragraph (1)(b) "the relevant time" means—

(a) the time when the data controller first processes the data, or

(b) in a case where at that time disclosure to a third party within a reasonable period is envisaged—

(i) if the data are in fact disclosed to such a person within that period, the time when the data are first disclosed,

(ii) if within that period the data controller becomes, or ought to become, aware that the data are unlikely to be disclosed to such a person within that period, the time when the data controller does become, or ought to become, so aware, or

(iii) in any other case, the end of that period.

(3) The information referred to in sub-paragraph (1) is as follows, namely—

(a) the identity of the data controller,

(b) if he has nominated a representative for the purposes of this Act, the identity of that representative,

(c) the purpose or purposes for which the data are intended to be processed, and

(d) any further information which is necessary, having regard to the specific circumstances in which the data are or are to be processed, to enable processing in respect of the data subject to be fair.

3.—(1) Paragraph 2(1)(b) does not apply where either of the primary conditions in sub-paragraph (2), together with such further conditions as may be prescribed by the [Secretary of State] by order, are met.

(2) The primary conditions referred to in sub-paragraph (1) are—

(a) that the provision of that information would involve a disproportionate effort, or

(b) that the recording of the information to be contained in the data by, or the disclosure of the data by, the data controller is necessary for compliance with any legal obligation to which the data controller is subject, other than an obligation imposed by contract.

4.—(1) Personal data which contain a general identifier falling within a description prescribed by the [Secretary of State] by order are not to be treated as processed fairly and lawfully unless they are processed in compliance with any conditions so prescribed in relation to general identifiers of that description.

(2) In sub-paragraph (1) "a general identifier" means any identifier (such as, for example, a number or code used for identification purposes) which—

(a) relates to an individual, and

(b) forms part of a set of similar identifiers which is of general application.

The second principle

5. The purpose or purposes for which personal data are obtained may in particular be specified—

(a) in a notice given for the purposes of paragraph 2 by the data controller to the data subject, or

(b) in a notification given to the Commissioner under Part III of this Act.

6. In determining whether any disclosure of personal data is compatible with the purpose or purposes for which the data were obtained, regard is to be had to the purpose or purposes for which the personal data are intended to be processed by any person to whom they are disclosed.

The fourth principle

7. The fourth principle is not to be regarded as being contravened by reason of any inaccuracy in personal data which accurately record information obtained by the data controller from the data subject or a third party in a case where—

(a) having regard to the purpose or purposes for which the data were obtained and further processed, the data controller has taken reasonable steps to ensure the accuracy of the data, and

(b) if the data subject has notified the data controller of the data subject's view that the data are inaccurate, the data indicate that fact.

The sixth principle

8. A person is to be regarded as contravening the sixth principle if, but only if—

(a) he contravenes section 7 by failing to supply information in accordance with that section,

(b) he contravenes section 10 by failing to comply with a notice given under subsection (1) of that section to the extent that the notice is justified or by failing to give a notice under subsection (3) of that section,

(c) he contravenes section 11 by failing to comply with a notice given under subsection (1) of that section, or

(d) he contravenes section 12 by failing to comply with a notice given under subsection (1) or (2)(b) of that section or by failing to give a notification under subsection (2)(a) of that section or a notice under subsection (3) of that section.

The seventh principle

9. Having regard to the state of technological development and the cost of implementing any measures, the measures must ensure a level of security appropriate to—

(a) the harm that might result from such unauthorised or unlawful processing or accidental loss, destruction or damage as are mentioned in the seventh principle, and

(b) the nature of the data to be protected.

10. The data controller must take reasonable steps to ensure the reliability of any employees of his who have access to the personal data.

11. Where processing of personal data is carried out by a data processor on behalf of a data controller, the data controller must in order to comply with the seventh principle—

(a) choose a data processor providing sufficient guarantees in respect of the technical and organisational security measures governing the processing to be carried out, and

(b) take reasonable steps to ensure compliance with those measures.

12. Where processing of personal data is carried out by a data processor on behalf of a data controller, the data controller is not to be regarded as complying with the seventh principle unless—

(a) the processing is carried out under a contract—

(i) which is made or evidenced in writing, and

(ii) under which the data processor is to act only on instructions from the data controller, and

(b) the contract requires the data processor to comply with obligations equivalent to those imposed on a data controller by the seventh principle.

The eighth principle

13. An adequate level of protection is one which is adequate in all the circumstances of the case, having regard in particular to—

(a) the nature of the personal data,

(b) the country or territory of origin of the information contained in the data,

(c) the country or territory of final destination of that information,

(d) the purposes for which and period during which the data are intended to be processed,

(e) the law in force in the country or territory in question,

(f) the international obligations of that country or territory,

(g) any relevant codes of conduct or other rules which are enforceable in that country or territory (whether generally or by arrangement in particular cases), and

(h) any security measures taken in respect of the data in that country or territory.

14. The eighth principle does not apply to a transfer falling within any paragraph of Schedule 4, except in such circumstances and to such extent as the [Secretary of State] may by order provide.

15.—(1) Where—

(a) in any proceedings under this Act any question arises as to whether the requirement of the eighth principle as to an adequate level of protection is met in relation to the transfer of any personal data to a country or territory outside the European Economic Area, and

(b) a Community finding has been made in relation to transfers of the kind in question,

that question is to be determined in accordance with that finding.

(2) In sub-paragraph (1) "Community finding" means a finding of the European Commission, under the procedure provided for in Article 31(2) of the Data Protection Directive, that a country or territory outside the European Economic Area does, or does not, ensure an adequate level of protection within the meaning of Article 25(2) of the Directive.

NOTES

Para 3, 4, 14: words in square brackets substituted by the Secretary of State for Constitutional Affairs Order 2003, SI 2003/1887, art 9, Sch 2, para 9(1)(b).

Orders: the Data Protection (Conditions under Paragraph 3 of Part II of Schedule 1) Order 2000, SI 2000/185.

SCHEDULE 2

CONDITIONS RELEVANT FOR PURPOSES OF THE FIRST PRINCIPLE: PROCESSING OF ANY PERSONAL DATA

Section 4(3)

[3642BW]

1. The data subject has given his consent to the processing.

2. The processing is necessary—
- (a) for the performance of a contract to which the data subject is a party, or
- (b) for the taking of steps at the request of the data subject with a view to entering into a contract.

3. The processing is necessary for compliance with any legal obligation to which the data controller is subject, other than an obligation imposed by contract.

4. The processing is necessary in order to protect the vital interests of the data subject.

5. The processing is necessary—
- (a) for the administration of justice,
- [(aa) for the exercise of any functions of either House of Parliament,]
- (b) for the exercise of any functions conferred on any person by or under any enactment,
- (c) for the exercise of any functions of the Crown, a Minister of the Crown or a government department, or
- (d) for the exercise of any other functions of a public nature exercised in the public interest by any person.

6.—(1) The processing is necessary for the purposes of legitimate interests pursued by the data controller or by the third party or parties to whom the data are disclosed, except where the processing is unwarranted in any particular case by reason of prejudice to the rights and freedoms or legitimate interests of the data subject.

(2) The [Secretary of State] may by order specify particular circumstances in which this condition is, or is not, to be taken to be satisfied.

NOTES

Para 5: sub-para (aa) inserted by the Freedom of Information Act 2000, s 73, Sch 6, para 4.

Para 6: words in square brackets substituted by the Secretary of State for Constitutional Affairs Order 2003, SI 2003/1887, art 9, Sch 2, para 9(1)(b).

SCHEDULE 3

CONDITIONS RELEVANT FOR PURPOSES OF THE FIRST PRINCIPLE: PROCESSING OF SENSITIVE PERSONAL DATA

Section 4(3)

[3642BX]

1. The data subject has given his explicit consent to the processing of the personal data.

2.—(1) The processing is necessary for the purposes of exercising or performing any right or obligation which is conferred or imposed by law on the data controller in connection with employment.

(2) The [Secretary of State] may by order—
- (a) exclude the application of sub-paragraph (1) in such cases as may be specified, or
- (b) provide that, in such cases as may be specified, the condition in subparagraph (1) is not to be regarded as satisfied unless such further conditions as may be specified in the order are also satisfied.

3. The processing is necessary—
- (a) in order to protect the vital interests of the data subject or another person, in a case where—
  - (i) consent cannot be given by or on behalf of the data subject, or
  - (ii) the data controller cannot reasonably be expected to obtain the consent of the data subject, or
- (b) in order to protect the vital interests of another person, in a case where consent by or on behalf of the data subject has been unreasonably withheld.

Part III Statutes

4. The processing—
(a) is carried out in the course of its legitimate activities by any body or association which—
(i) is not established or conducted for profit, and
(ii) exists for political, philosophical religious or trade-union purposes,
(b) is carried out with appropriate safeguards for the rights and freedoms of data subjects,
(c) relates only to individuals who either are members of the body or association or have regular contact with it in connection with its purposes, and
(d) does not involve disclosure of the personal data to a third party without the consent of the data subject.

5. The information contained in the personal data has been made public as a result of steps deliberately taken by the data subject.

6. The processing—
(a) is necessary for the purpose of, or in connection with, any legal proceedings (including prospective legal proceedings),
(b) is necessary for the purpose of obtaining legal advice, or
(c) is otherwise necessary for the purposes of establishing, exercising or defending legal rights.

7.—(1) The processing is necessary—
(a) for the administration of justice,
[(aa) for the exercise of any functions of either House of Parliament,]
(b) for the exercise of any functions conferred on any person by or under an enactment, or
(c) for the exercise of any functions of the Crown, a Minister of the Crown or a government department.
(2) The [Secretary of State] may by order—
(a) exclude the application of sub-paragraph (1) in such cases as may be specified, or
(b) provide that, in such cases as may be specified, the condition in subparagraph (1) is not to be regarded as satisfied unless such further conditions as may be specified in the order are also satisfied.

[**7A.**—(1) The processing—
(a) is either—
(i) the disclosure of sensitive personal data by a person as a member of an anti-fraud organisation or otherwise in accordance with any arrangements made by such an organisation; or
(ii) any other processing by that person or another person of sensitive personal data so disclosed; and
(b) is necessary for the purposes of preventing fraud or a particular kind of fraud.
(2) In this paragraph "an anti-fraud organisation" means any unincorporated association, body corporate or other person which enables or facilitates any sharing of information to prevent fraud or a particular kind of fraud or which has any of these functions as its purpose or one of its purposes.]

8.—(1) The processing is necessary for medical purposes and is undertaken by—
(a) a health professional, or
(b) a person who in the circumstances owes a duty of confidentiality which is equivalent to that which would arise if that person were a health professional.
(2) In this paragraph "medical purposes" includes the purposes of preventative medicine, medical diagnosis, medical research, the provision of care and treatment and the management of healthcare services.

9.—(1) The processing—
(a) is of sensitive personal data consisting of information as to racial or ethnic origin,
(b) is necessary for the purpose of identifying or keeping under review the existence or absence of equality of opportunity or treatment between persons of different racial or ethnic origins, with a view to enabling such equality to be promoted or maintained, and
(c) is carried out with appropriate safeguards for the rights and freedoms of data subjects.
(2) The [Secretary of State] may by order specify circumstances in which processing falling within sub-paragraph (1)(a) and (b) is, or is not, to be taken for the purposes of sub-paragraph (1)(c) to be carried out with appropriate safeguards for the rights and freedoms of data subjects.

10. The personal data are processed in circumstances specified in an order made by the [Secretary of State] for the purposes of this paragraph

NOTES

Para 2, 9, 10: words in square brackets substituted by the Secretary of State for Constitutional Affairs Order 2003, SI 2003/1887, art 9, Sch 2, para 9(1)(b).

Para 7: sub-para (1)(aa) inserted by the Freedom of Information Act 2000, s 73, Sch 6, para 5; words in square brackets in sub-para (2) substituted by SI 2003/1887, art 9, Sch 2, para 9(1)(b).

Para 7A: inserted by the Serious Crime Act 2007, s 72.

Orders: the Data Protection (Processing of Sensitive Personal Data) Order 2000, SI 2000/417; the Data Protection (Processing of Sensitive Personal Data) (Elected Representatives) Order 2002, SI 2002/2905; the Data Protection (Processing of Sensitive Personal Data) Order 2006, SI 2006/2068; the Data Protection (Processing of Sensitive Personal Data) Order 2009, SI 2009/1811.

SCHEDULE 4

CASES WHERE THE EIGHTH PRINCIPLE DOES NOT APPLY

Section 4(3)

[3642BY]

1. The data subject has given his consent to the transfer.

2. The transfer is necessary—

(a) for the performance of a contract between the data subject and the data controller, or

(b) for the taking of steps at the request of the data subject with a view to his entering into a contract with the data controller.

3. The transfer is necessary—

(a) for the conclusion of a contract between the data controller and a person other than the data subject which—

(i) is entered into at the request of the data subject, or

(ii) is in the interests of the data subject, or

(b) for the performance of such a contract.

4.—(1) The transfer is necessary for reasons of substantial public interest.

(2) The [Secretary of State] may by order specify—

(a) circumstances in which a transfer is to be taken for the purposes of subparagraph (1) to be necessary for reasons of substantial public interest, and

(b) circumstances in which a transfer which is not required by or under an enactment is not to be taken for the purpose of sub-paragraph (1) to be necessary for reasons of substantial public interest.

5. The transfer—

(a) is necessary for the purpose of, or in connection with, any legal proceedings (including prospective legal proceedings),

(b) is necessary for the purpose of obtaining legal advice, or

(c) is otherwise necessary for the purposes of establishing, exercising or defending legal rights.

6. The transfer is necessary in order to protect the vital interests of the data subject.

7. The transfer is of part of the personal data on a public register and any conditions subject to which the register is open to inspection are complied with by any person to whom the data are or may be disclosed after the transfer.

8. The transfer is made on terms which are of a kind approved by the Commissioner as ensuring adequate safeguards for the rights and freedoms of data subjects.

9. The transfer has been authorised by the Commissioner as being made in such a manner as to ensure adequate safeguards for the rights and freedoms of data subjects.

NOTES

Para 4: words in square brackets substituted by the Secretary of State for Constitutional Affairs Order 2003, SI 2003/1887, art 9, Sch 2, para 9(1)(b).

SCHEDULE 5

[THE INFORMATION COMMISSIONER] . . .

Section 6(7)

PART I
THE COMMISSIONER

[3642BZ]

1–3. . . .

Officers and staff

4.—(1)–(5) . . .

(6) The Employers' Liability (Compulsory Insurance) Act 1969 shall not require insurance to be effected by the Commissioner.

Authentication of seal of the Commissioner

6. The application of the seal of the Commissioner shall be authenticated by his signature or by the signature of some other person authorised for the purpose.

Presumption of authenticity of documents issued by the Commissioner

7. Any document purporting to be an instrument issued by the Commissioner and to be duly executed under the Commissioner's seal or to be signed by or on behalf of the Commissioner shall be received in evidence and shall be deemed to be such an instrument unless the contrary is shown.

8–11. . . .

NOTES

Schedule title: words in square brackets substituted by virtue of the Freedom of Information Act 2000, s 18(4), Sch 2, Pt I, para 1(1); words omitted repealed by the Transfer of Tribunal Functions Order 2010, SI 2010/22, art 5(1), Sch 2, paras 24, 30(a), subject to transitional provisions and savings in Sch 5 thereto.

Para 1–3, 8–11: outside the scope of this work.

Para 4: sub-paras (1)–(5) outside the scope of this work.

(Pt II repealed by the Transfer of Tribunal Functions Order 2010, SI 2010/22, art 5(1), Sch 2, paras 24, 30(b), subject to transitional provisions and savings in Sch 5 thereto; Pt III outside the scope of this work.)

SCHEDULE 6

APPEAL PROCEEDINGS

Sections 28(12), 48(5)

[3642CA]

1–6. . . .

[Tribunal Procedure Rules]

7.—[(1) Tribunal Procedure Rules may make provision for regulating the exercise of the rights of appeal conferred—

(a) by sections 28(4) and (6) and 48 of this Act, and

(b) by sections 47(1) and (2) and 60(1) and (4) of the Freedom of Information Act 2000.

(2) In the case of appeals under this Act and the Freedom of Information Act 2000, Tribunal Procedure Rules may make provision—

(a) for securing the production of material used for the processing of personal data;

(b) for the inspection, examination, operation and testing of any equipment or material used in connection with the processing of personal data;

(c) for hearing an appeal in the absence of the appellant or for determining an appeal without a hearing.]

(3) . . .

Obstruction etc

8.—(1) If any person is guilty of any act or omission in relation to proceedings before the Tribunal which, if those proceedings were proceedings before a court having power to commit for contempt, would constitute contempt of court, the Tribunal may certify the offence to the High Court or, in Scotland, the Court of Session.

(2) Where an offence is so certified, the court may inquire into the matter and, after hearing any witness who may be produced against or on behalf of the person charged with the offence, and after hearing any statement that may be offered in defence, deal with him in any manner in which it could deal with him if he had committed the like offence in relation to the court.

NOTES

Paras 1–6: repealed by the Transfer of Tribunal Functions Order 2010, SI 2010/22, art 5(1), Sch 2, paras 24, 31(a), subject to transitional provisions and savings in Sch 5 thereto.

Para 7: cross heading preceding this para and sub-paras (1), (2) substituted and sub-para (3) repealed by SI 2010/22, art 5(1), Sch 2, paras 24, 31(b), subject to transitional provisions and savings in Sch 5 thereto.

Rules: the Data Protection Tribunal (National Security Appeals) (Telecommunications) Rules 2000, SI 2000/731; the Information Tribunal (National Security Appeals) Rules 2005, SI 2005/13; the Information Tribunal (Enforcement Appeals) Rules 2005, SI 2005/14.

SCHEDULE 7

MISCELLANEOUS EXEMPTIONS

Section 37

Confidential references given by the data controller

[3642CB]

1. Personal data are exempt from section 7 if they consist of a reference given or to be given in confidence by the data controller for the purposes of—

(a) the education, training or employment, or prospective education, training or employment, of the data subject,

(b) the appointment, or prospective appointment, of the data subject to any office, or

(c) the provision, or prospective provision, by the data subject of any service.

2–4. . . .

Management forecasts etc

5. Personal data processed for the purposes of management forecasting or management planning to assist the data controller in the conduct of any business or other activity are exempt from the subject information provisions in any case to the extent to which the application of those provisions would be likely to prejudice the conduct of that business or other activity.

Corporate finance

6.—(1) Where personal data are processed for the purposes of, or in connection with, a corporate finance service provided by a relevant person—

(a) the data are exempt from the subject information provisions in any case to the extent to which either—

(i) the application of those provisions to the data could affect the price of any instrument which is already in existence or is to be or may be created, or

(ii) the data controller reasonably believes that the application of those provisions to the data could affect the price of any such instrument, and

(b) to the extent that the data are not exempt from the subject information provisions by virtue of paragraph (a), they are exempt from those provisions if the exemption is required for the purpose of safeguarding an important economic or financial interest of the United Kingdom.

(2) For the purposes of sub-paragraph (1)(b) the [Secretary of State] may by order specify—

(a) matters to be taken into account in determining whether exemption from the subject information provisions is required for the purpose of safeguarding an important economic or financial interest of the United Kingdom, or

(b) circumstances in which exemption from those provisions is, or is not, to be taken to be required for that purpose.

(3) In this paragraph—

"corporate finance service" means a service consisting in—

(a) underwriting in respect of issues of, or the placing of issues of, any instrument,

(b) advice to undertakings on capital structure, industrial strategy and related matters and advice and service relating to mergers and the purchase of undertakings, or

(c) services relating to such underwriting as is mentioned in paragraph (a);

"instrument" means any instrument listed in [section C of Annex I to Directive 2004/39/EC of the European Parliament and of the Council of 21 April 2004 on markets in financial instruments] . . . ;

"price" includes value;

"relevant person" means—

[(a) any person who, by reason of any permission he has under Part IV of the Financial Services and Markets Act 2000, is able to carry on a corporate finance service without contravening the general prohibition, within the meaning of section 19 of that Act,

(b) an EEA firm of the kind mentioned in paragraph 5(a) or (b) of Schedule 3 to that Act which has qualified for authorisation under paragraph 12 of that Schedule, and may lawfully carry on a corporate finance service,

(c) any person who is exempt from the general prohibition in respect of any corporate finance service—

(i) as a result of an exemption order made under section 38(1) of that Act, or

(ii) by reason of section 39(1) of that Act (appointed representatives),

(cc) any person, not falling within paragraph (a), (b) or (c) who may lawfully carry on a corporate finance service without contravening the general prohibition,]

(d) any person who, in the course of his employment, provides to his employer a service falling within paragraph (b) or (c) of the definition of "corporate finance service", or

(e) any partner who provides to other partners in the partnership a service falling within either of those paragraphs.

Negotiations

7. Personal data which consist of records of the intentions of the data controller in relation to any negotiations with the data subject are exempt from the subject information provisions in any case to the extent to which the application of those provisions would be likely to prejudice those negotiations.

8, 9. . . .

Legal professional privilege

10. Personal data are exempt from the subject information provisions if the data consist of information in respect of which a claim to legal professional privilege [or, in Scotland, to confidentiality of communications] could be maintained in legal proceedings.

Self-incrimination

11.—(1) A person need not comply with any request or order under section 7 to the extent that compliance would, by revealing evidence of the commission of any offence *other than an offence under this Act*, expose him to proceedings for that offence.

[(1A) The offences mentioned in sub-paragraph (1) are—

(a) an offence under section 5 of the Perjury Act 1911 (false statements made otherwise than on oath),

(b) an offence under section 44(2) of the Criminal Law (Consolidation) (Scotland) Act 1995 (false statements made otherwise than on oath), or

(c) an offence under Article 10 of the Perjury (Northern Ireland) Order 1979 (false statutory declarations and other false unsworn statements).]

(2) Information disclosed by any person in compliance with any request or order under section 7 shall not be admissible against him in proceedings for an offence under this Act.

NOTES

Paras 2–4, 8, 9: outside the scope of this work.

Para 6: words in square brackets in sub-para (2) substituted by the Secretary of State for Constitutional Affairs Order 2003, SI 2003/1887, art 9, Sch 2, para 9(1)(e); in sub-para (3) in definition "instrument" words in square brackets substituted by the Financial Services and Markets Act 2000 (Markets in Financial Instruments) Regulations 2007, SI 2007/126, reg 3(6), Sch 6, Pt 1, para 12; in sub-para (3) in definition "instrument" words omitted repealed and in definition "relevant person" paras (a)–(c), (cc) substituted, for original paras (a)–(c), by the Financial Services and Markets Act 2000 (Consequential Amendments) Order 2002, SI 2002/1555, art 25.

Para 10: words in square brackets substituted by the Freedom of Information Act 2000, s 73, Sch 6, para 7.

Para 11: for the words in italics in sub-para (1) there are substituted the words ", other than an offence under this Act or an offence within sub-paragraph (1A)," and sub-para (1A) inserted by the Coroners and Justice Act 2009, s 175, Sch 20, Pt 4, para 12, as from a day to be appointed.

Orders: the Data Protection (Corporate Finance Exemption) Order 2000, SI 2000/184; the Data Protection (Crown Appointments) Order 2000, SI 2000/416.

SCHEDULE 8

TRANSITIONAL RELIEF

Section 39

PART I
INTERPRETATION OF SCHEDULE

[3642CC]

1.—(1) For the purposes of this Schedule, personal data are "eligible data" at any time if, and to the extent that, they are at that time subject to processing which was already under way immediately before 24th October 1998.

(2) In this Schedule—

"eligible automated data" means eligible data which fall within paragraph (a) or (b) of the definition of "data" in section 1(1);

"eligible manual data" means eligible data which are not eligible automated data;

"the first transitional period" means the period beginning with the commencement of this Schedule and ending with 23rd October 2001;

"the second transitional period" means the period beginning with 24th October 2001 and ending with 23rd October 2007.

PART II
EXEMPTIONS AVAILABLE BEFORE 24TH OCTOBER 2001

Manual data

[3642CD]

2.—(1) Eligible manual data, other than data forming part of an accessible record, are exempt from the data protection principles and Parts II and III of this Act during the first transitional period.

(2) This paragraph does not apply to eligible manual data to which paragraph 4 applies.

3.—(1) This paragraph applies to—

(a) eligible manual data forming part of an accessible record, and

(b) personal data which fall within paragraph (d) of the definition of "data" in section 1(1) but which, because they are not subject to processing which was already under way immediately before 24th October 1998, are not eligible data for the purposes of this Schedule.

(2) During the first transitional period, data to which this paragraph applies are exempt from—

(a) the data protection principles, except the sixth principle so far as relating to sections 7 and 12A,

(b) Part II of this Act, except—

(i) section 7 (as it has effect subject to section 8) and section 12A, and

(ii) section 15 so far as relating to those sections, and

(c) Part III of this Act.

4.—(1) This paragraph applies to eligible manual data which consist of information relevant to the financial standing of the data subject and in respect of which the data controller is a credit reference agency.

(2) During the first transitional period, data to which this paragraph applies are exempt from—

(a) the data protection principles, except the sixth principle so far as relating to sections 7 and 12A,

(b) Part II of this Act, except—

(i) section 7 (as it has effect subject to sections 8 and 9) and section 12A, and

(ii) section 15 so far as relating to those sections, and

(c) Part III of this Act.

Processing otherwise than by reference to the data subject

5. During the first transitional period, for the purposes of this Act (apart from paragraph 1), eligible automated data are not to be regarded as being "processed" unless the processing is by reference to the data subject.

Payrolls and accounts

6.—(1) Subject to sub-paragraph (2), eligible automated data processed by a data controller for one or more of the following purposes—

Part III Statutes

(a) calculating amounts payable by way of remuneration or pensions in respect of service in any employment or office or making payments of, or of sums deducted from, such remuneration or pensions, or

(b) keeping accounts relating to any business or other activity carried on by the data controller or keeping records of purchases, sales or other transactions for the purpose of ensuring that the requisite payments are made by or to him in respect of those transactions or for the purpose of making financial or management forecasts to assist him in the conduct of any such business or activity,

are exempt from the data protection principles and Parts II and III of this Act during the first transitional period.

(2) It shall be a condition of the exemption of any eligible automated data under this paragraph that the data are not processed for any other purpose, but the exemption is not lost by any processing of the eligible data for any other purpose if the data controller shows that he had taken such care to prevent it as in all the circumstances was reasonably required.

(3) Data processed only for one or more of the purposes mentioned in subparagraph (1)(a) may be disclosed—

(a) to any person, other than the data controller, by whom the remuneration or pensions in question are payable,

(b) for the purpose of obtaining actuarial advice,

(c) for the purpose of giving information as to the persons in any employment or office for use in medical research into the health of, or injuries suffered by, persons engaged in particular occupations or working in particular places or areas,

(d) if the data subject (or a person acting on his behalf) has requested or consented to the disclosure of the data either generally or in the circumstances in which the disclosure in question is made, or

(e) if the person making the disclosure has reasonable grounds for believing that the disclosure falls within paragraph (d).

(4) Data processed for any of the purposes mentioned in sub-paragraph (1) may be disclosed—

(a) for the purpose of audit or where the disclosure is for the purpose only of giving information about the data controller's financial affairs, or

(b) in any case in which disclosure would be permitted by any other provision of this Part of this Act if sub-paragraph (2) were included among the non-disclosure provisions.

(5) In this paragraph "remuneration" includes remuneration in kind and "pensions" includes gratuities or similar benefits.

Unincorporated members' clubs and mailing lists

7. Eligible automated data processed by an unincorporated members' club and relating only to the members of the club are exempt from the data protection principles and Parts II and III of this Act during the first transitional period.

8. Eligible automated data processed by a data controller only for the purposes of distributing, or recording the distribution of, articles or information to the data subjects and consisting only of their names, addresses or other particulars necessary for effecting the distribution, are exempt from the data protection principles and Parts II and III of this Act during the first transitional period.

9. Neither paragraph 7 nor paragraph 8 applies to personal data relating to any data subject unless he has been asked by the club or data controller whether he objects to the data relating to him being processed as mentioned in that paragraph and has not objected.

10. It shall be a condition of the exemption of any data under paragraph 7 that the data are not disclosed except as permitted by paragraph 11 and of the exemption under paragraph 8 that the data are not processed for any purpose other than that mentioned in that paragraph or as permitted by paragraph 11, but—

(a) the exemption under paragraph 7 shall not be lost by any disclosure in breach of that condition, and

(b) the exemption under paragraph 8 shall not be lost by any processing in breach of that condition,

if the data controller shows that he had taken such care to prevent it as in all the circumstances was reasonably required.

11. Data to which paragraph 10 applies may be disclosed—

(a) if the data subject (or a person acting on his behalf) has requested or consented to the disclosure of the data either generally or in the circumstances in which the disclosure in question is made,

(b) if the person making the disclosure has reasonable grounds for believing that the disclosure falls within paragraph (a), or

(c) in any case in which disclosure would be permitted by any other provision of this Part of this Act if paragraph 10 were included among the non-disclosure provisions.

Back-up data

12. Eligible automated data which are processed only for the purpose of replacing other data in the event of the latter being lost, destroyed or impaired are exempt from section 7 during the first transitional period.

Exemption of all eligible automated data from certain requirements

13.—(1) During the first transitional period, eligible automated data are exempt from the following provisions—

(a) the first data protection principle to the extent to which it requires compliance with—

(i) paragraph 2 of Part II of Schedule 1,

(ii) the conditions in Schedule 2, and

(iii) the conditions in Schedule 3,

(b) the seventh data protection principle to the extent to which it requires compliance with paragraph 12 of Part II of Schedule 1;

(c) the eighth data protection principle,

(d) in section 7(1), paragraphs (b), (c)(ii) and (d),

(e) sections 10 and 11,

(f) section 12, and

(g) section 13, except so far as relating to—

(i) any contravention of the fourth data protection principle,

(ii) any disclosure without the consent of the data controller,

(iii) loss or destruction of data without the consent of the data controller, or

(iv) processing for the special purposes.

(2) The specific exemptions conferred by sub-paragraph (1)(a), (c) and (e) do not limit the data controller's general duty under the first data protection principle to ensure that processing is fair.

PART III
EXEMPTIONS AVAILABLE AFTER 23RD OCTOBER 2001 BUT BEFORE 24TH OCTOBER 2007

[3642CE]

14.—(1) This paragraph applies to—

(a) eligible manual data which were held immediately before 24th October 1998, and

(b) personal data which fall within paragraph (d) of the definition of "data" in section 1(1) but do not fall within paragraph (a) of this subparagraph,

but does not apply to eligible manual data to which the exemption in paragraph 16 applies.

(2) During the second transitional period, data to which this paragraph applies are exempt from the following provisions—

(a) the first data protection principle except to the extent to which it requires compliance with paragraph 2 of Part II of Schedule 1,

(b) the second, third, fourth and fifth data protection principles, and

(c) section 14(1) to (3).

[14A.—(1) This paragraph applies to personal data which fall within paragraph (e) of the definition of "data" in section 1(1) and do not fall within paragraph 14(1)(a), but does not apply to eligible manual data to which the exemption in paragraph 16 applies

(2) During the second transitional period, data to which this paragraph applies are exempt from—

(a) the fourth data protection principle, and

(b) section 14(1) to (3).]

NOTES

Para 14A: inserted by the Freedom of Information Act 2000, s 70(3).

(Pt IV outside the scope of this work.)

PART V
EXEMPTION FROM SECTION 22

[3642CF]

19. Processing which was already under way immediately before 24th October 1998 is not assessable processing for the purposes of section 22.

SCHEDULE 9

POWERS OF ENTRY AND INSPECTION

Section 50

Issue of warrants

[3642CG]

1.—(1) If a circuit judge [or a District Judge (Magistrates' Courts)] is satisfied by information on oath supplied by the Commissioner that there are reasonable grounds for suspecting—

(a) that a data controller has contravened or is contravening any of the data protection principles, or

(b) that an offence under this Act has been or is being committed,

and that evidence of the contravention or of the commission of the offence is to be found on any premises specified in the information, he may, subject to subparagraph (2) and paragraph 2, grant a warrant to the Commissioner.

[(1A) Sub-paragraph (1B) applies if a circuit judge or a District Judge (Magistrates' Courts) is satisfied by information on oath supplied by the Commissioner that a data controller has failed to comply with a requirement imposed by an assessment notice.

(1B) The judge may, for the purpose of enabling the Commissioner to determine whether the data controller has complied or is complying with the data protection principles, grant a warrant to the Commissioner in relation to any premises that were specified in the assessment notice; but this is subject to sub-paragraph (2) and paragraph 2.]

(2) A judge shall not issue a warrant under this Schedule in respect of any personal data processed for the special purposes unless a determination by the Commissioner under section 45 with respect to those data has taken effect.

(3) A warrant issued under *sub-paragraph (1)* shall authorise the Commissioner or any of his officers or staff at any time within seven days of the date of the warrant *to enter the premises, to search them, to inspect, examine, operate and test any equipment found there which is used or intended to be used for the processing of personal data and to inspect and seize any documents or other material found there which may be such evidence as is mentioned in that sub-paragraph.*

2.—(1) A judge shall not issue a warrant under this Schedule unless he is satisfied—

(a) that the Commissioner has given seven days' notice in writing to the occupier of the premises in question demanding access to the premises, and

(b) that either—

   (i) access was demanded at a reasonable hour and was unreasonably refused, or

   (ii) although entry to the premises was granted, the occupier unreasonably refused to comply with a request by the Commissioner or any of the Commissioner's officers or staff to permit the Commissioner or the officer or member of staff to do any of the things referred to in paragraph 1(3), and

(c) that the occupier, has, after the refusal, been notified by the Commissioner of the application for the warrant and has had an opportunity of being heard by the judge on the question whether or not it should be issued.

[(1A) In determining whether the Commissioner has given an occupier the seven days' notice referred to in sub-paragraph (1)(a) any assessment notice served on the occupier is to be disregarded.]

(2) Sub-paragraph (1) shall not apply if the judge is satisfied that the case is one of urgency or that compliance with those provisions would defeat the object of the entry.

3. A judge who issues a warrant under this Schedule shall also issue two copies of it and certify them clearly as copies.

Execution of warrants

4. A person executing a warrant issued under this Schedule may use such reasonable force as may be necessary.

5. A warrant issued under this Schedule shall be executed at a reasonable hour unless it appears to the person executing it that there are grounds for suspecting that the *evidence in question would not be found* if it were so executed.

6. If the person who occupies the premises in respect of which a warrant is issued under this Schedule is present when the warrant is executed, he shall be shown the warrant and supplied with a copy of it; and if that person is not present a copy of the warrant shall be left in a prominent place on the premises.

7.—(1) A person seizing anything in pursuance of a warrant under this Schedule shall give a receipt for it if asked to do so.

(2) Anything so seized may be retained for so long as is necessary in all the circumstances but the person in occupation of the premises in question shall be given a copy of anything that is seized if he so requests and the person executing the warrant considers that it can be done without undue delay.

Matters exempt from inspection and seizure

8. The powers of inspection and seizure conferred by a warrant issued under this Schedule shall not be exercisable in respect of personal data which by virtue of section 28 are exempt from any of the provisions of this Act.

9.—(1) Subject to the provisions of this paragraph, the powers of inspection and seizure conferred by a warrant issued under this Schedule shall not be exercisable in respect of—

(a) any communication between a professional legal adviser and his client in connection with the giving of legal advice to the client with respect to his obligations, liabilities or rights under this Act, or

(b) any communication between a professional legal adviser and his client, or between such an adviser or his client and any other person, made in connection with or in contemplation of proceedings under or arising out of this Act (including proceedings before the Tribunal) and for the purposes of such proceedings.

(2) Sub-paragraph (1) applies also to—

(a) any copy or other record of any such communication as is there mentioned, and

(b) any document or article enclosed with or referred to in any such communication if made in connection with the giving of any advice or, as the case may be, in connection with or in contemplation of and for the purposes of such proceedings as are there mentioned.

(3) This paragraph does not apply to anything in the possession of any person other than the professional legal adviser or his client or to anything held with the intention of furthering a criminal purpose.

(4) In this paragraph references to the client of a professional legal adviser include references to any person representing such a client.

10. If the person in occupation of any premises in respect of which a warrant is issued under this Schedule objects to the inspection or seizure under the warrant of any material on the grounds that it consists partly of matters in respect of which those powers are not exercisable, he shall, if the person executing the warrant so requests, furnish that person with a copy of so much of the material as is not exempt from those powers.

Return of warrants

11. A warrant issued under this Schedule shall be returned to the court from which it was issued—

(a) after being executed, or

(b) if not executed within the time authorised for its execution;

and the person by whom any such warrant is executed shall make an endorsement on it stating what powers have been exercised by him under the warrant.

Offences

12. Any person who—

(a) intentionally obstructs a person in the execution of a warrant issued under this Schedule, *or*

(b) fails without reasonable excuse to give any person executing such a warrant such assistance as he may reasonably require for the execution of the warrant,

[(c) makes a statement in response to a requirement under paragraph (e) or (f) of paragraph 1(3) which that person knows to be false in a material respect, or

(d) recklessly makes a statement in response to such a requirement which is false in a material respect,]

is guilty of an offence.

Vessels, vehicles etc

13. In this Schedule "premises" includes any vessel, vehicle, aircraft or hovercraft, and references to the occupier of any premises include references to the person in charge of any vessel, vehicle, aircraft or hovercraft.

Scotland and Northern Ireland

14. In the application of this Schedule to Scotland—

(a) for any reference to a circuit judge there is substituted a reference to the sheriff,

(b) for any reference to information on oath there is substituted a reference to evidence on oath, and

(c) for the reference to the court from which the warrant was issued there is substituted a reference to the sheriff clerk.

15. In the application of this Schedule to Northern Ireland—

(a) for any reference to a circuit judge there is substituted a reference to a county court judge, and

(b) for any reference to information on oath there is substituted a reference to a complaint on oath.

[Self-incrimination

16. An explanation given, or information provided, by a person in response to a requirement under paragraph (e) or (f) of paragraph 1(3) may only be used in evidence against that person—

(a) on a prosecution for an offence under—

(i) paragraph 12,

(ii) section 5 of the Perjury Act 1911 (false statements made otherwise than on oath),

(iii) section 44(2) of the Criminal Law (Consolidation) (Scotland) Act 1995 (false statements made otherwise than on oath), or

(iv) Article 10 of the Perjury (Northern Ireland) Order 1979 (false statutory declarations and other false unsworn statements), or

(b) on a prosecution for any other offence where—

(i) in giving evidence that person makes a statement inconsistent with that explanation or information, and

(ii) evidence relating to that explanation or information is adduced, or a question relating to it is asked, by that person or on that person's behalf.]

NOTES

Para 1: words in square brackets in sub-para (1) inserted by the Courts Act 2003, s 65, Sch 4, para 8, as from a day to be appointed; sub-paras (1A), (1B) inserted, for the first words in italics in sub-para (3) there are substituted the words "this Schedule" and for the second words in italics there are substituted the following words, by the Coroners and Justice Act 2009, s 175, Sch 20, Pt 6, para 14(1)–(3), as from a day to be appointed: "—

(a) to enter the premises;

(b) to search the premises;

(c) to inspect, examine, operate and test any equipment found on the premises which is used or intended to be used for the processing of personal data;

(d) to inspect and seize any documents or other material found on the premises which—

(i) in the case of a warrant issued under sub-paragraph (1), may be such evidence as is mentioned in that paragraph;

(ii) in the case of a warrant issued under sub-paragraph (1B), may enable the Commissioner to determine whether the data controller has complied or is complying with the data protection principles;

(e) to require any person on the premises to provide an explanation of any document or other material found on the premises;

(f) to require any person on the premises to provide such other information as may reasonably be required for the purpose of determining whether the data controller has contravened, or is contravening, the data protection principles.".

Para 2: sub-para (1A) inserted by the Coroners and Justice Act 2009, s 175, Sch 20, Pt 6, para 14(1), (4), as from a day to be appointed.

Para 5: for the words in italics there are substituted the words "object of the warrant would be defeated" by the Coroners and Justice Act 2009, s 175, Sch 20, Pt 6, para 14(1), (5), as from a day to be appointed.

Para 12: word in italics in sub-para (a) repealed and sub-paras (c), (d) inserted by the Coroners and Justice Act 2009, ss 175, 178, Sch 20, Pt 6, para 14(1), (6), Sch 23, Pt 8, as from a day to be appointed.

Para 16: inserted, together with preceding cross heading by the Coroners and Justice Act 2009, s 175, Sch 20, Pt 6, para 14(1), (7), as from a day to be appointed.

SCHEDULE 10

FURTHER PROVISIONS RELATING TO ASSISTANCE UNDER SECTION 53

Section 53(6)

[3642CH]

1. In this Schedule "applicant" and "proceedings" have the same meaning as in section 53.

2. The assistance provided under section 53 may include the making of arrangements for, or for the Commissioner to bear the costs of—

(a) the giving of advice or assistance by a solicitor or counsel, and

(b) the representation of the applicant, or the provision to him of such assistance as is usually given by a solicitor or counsel—

(i) in steps preliminary or incidental to the proceedings, or

(ii) in arriving at or giving effect to a compromise to avoid or bring an end to the proceedings.

3. Where assistance is provided with respect to the conduct of proceedings—

(a) it shall include an agreement by the Commissioner to indemnify the applicant (subject only to any exceptions specified in the notification) in respect of any liability to pay costs or expenses arising by virtue of any judgment or order of the court in the proceedings,

(b) it may include an agreement by the Commissioner to indemnify the applicant in respect of any liability to pay costs or expenses arising by virtue of any compromise or settlement arrived at in order to avoid the proceedings or bring the proceedings to an end, and

(c) it may include an agreement by the Commissioner to indemnify the applicant in respect of any liability to pay damages pursuant to an undertaking given on the grant of interlocutory relief (in Scotland, an interim order) to the applicant.

4. Where the Commissioner provides assistance in relation to any proceedings, he shall do so on such terms, or make such other arrangements, as will secure that a person against whom the proceedings have been or are commenced is informed that assistance has been or is being provided by the Commissioner in relation to them.

5. In England and Wales or Northern Ireland, the recovery of expenses incurred by the Commissioner in providing an applicant with assistance (as taxed or assessed in such manner as may be prescribed by rules of court) shall constitute a first charge for the benefit of the Commissioner—

(a) on any costs which, by virtue of any judgment or order of the court, are payable to the applicant by any other person in respect of the matter in connection with which the assistance is provided, and

(b) on any sum payable to the applicant under a compromise or settlement arrived at in connection with that matter to avoid or bring to an end any proceedings.

6. In Scotland, the recovery of such expenses (as taxed or assessed in such manner as may be prescribed by rules of court) shall be paid to the Commissioner, in priority to other debts—

(a) out of any expenses which, by virtue of any judgment or order of the court, are payable to the applicant by any other person in respect of the matter in connection with which the assistance is provided, and

(b) out of any sum payable to the applicant under a compromise or settlement arrived at in connection with that matter to avoid or bring to an end any proceedings.

(Schs 11–13 outside the scope of this work.)

SCHEDULE 14

TRANSITIONAL PROVISIONS AND SAVINGS

Section 73

Interpretation

[3642CI]

1. In this Schedule—

"the 1984 Act" means the Data Protection Act 1984;

"the old principles" means the data protection principles within the meaning of the 1984 Act;

"the new principles" means the data protection principles within the meaning of this Act.

Effect of registration under Part II of 1984 Act

2.—(1) Subject to sub-paragraphs (4) and (5) any person who, immediately before the commencement of Part III of this Act—

(a) is registered as a data user under Part II of the 1984 Act, or

(b) is treated by virtue of section 7(6) of the 1984 Act as so registered,

is exempt from section 17(1) of this Act until the end of the registration period . . .

(2) In sub-paragraph (1) "the registration period", in relation to a person, means—

(a) where there is a single entry in respect of that person as a data user, the period at the end of which, if section 8 of the 1984 Act had remained in force, that entry would have fallen to be removed unless renewed, and

(b) where there are two or more entries in respect of that person as a data user, the period at the end of which, if that section had remained in force, the last of those entries to expire would have fallen to be removed unless renewed.

(3) Any application for registration as a data user under Part II of the 1984 Act which is received by the Commissioner before the commencement of Part III of this Act (including any appeal against a refusal of registration) shall be determined in accordance with the old principles and the provisions of the 1984 Act.

(4) If a person falling within paragraph (b) of sub-paragraph (1) receives a notification under section 7(1) of the 1984 Act of the refusal of his application, sub-paragraph (1) shall cease to apply to him—

(a) if no appeal is brought, at the end of the period within which an appeal can be brought against the refusal, or

(b) on the withdrawal or dismissal of the appeal.

(5) If a data controller gives a notification under section 18(1) at a time when he is exempt from section 17(1) by virtue of sub-paragraph (1), he shall cease to be so exempt.

(6) The Commissioner shall include in the register maintained under section 19 an entry in respect of each person who is exempt from section 17(1) by virtue of sub-paragraph (1); and each entry shall consist of the particulars which, immediately before the commencement of Part III of this Act, were included (or treated as included) in respect of that person in the register maintained under section 4 of the 1984 Act.

(7) Notification regulations under Part III of this Act may make provision modifying the duty referred to in section 20(1) in its application to any person in respect of whom an entry in the register maintained under section 19 has been made under sub-paragraph (6).

(8) Notification regulations under Part III of this Act may make further transitional provision in connection with the substitution of Part III of this Act for Part II of the 1984 Act (registration), including provision modifying the application of provisions of Part III in transitional cases.

Rights of data subjects

3.—(1) The repeal of section 21 of the 1984 Act (right of access to personal data) does not affect the application of that section in any case in which the request (together with the information referred to in paragraph (a) of subsection (4) of that section and, in a case where it is required, the consent referred to in paragraph (b) of that subsection) was received before the day on which the repeal comes into force.

(2) Sub-paragraph (1) does not apply where the request is made by reference to this Act.

(3) Any fee paid for the purposes of section 21 of the 1984 Act before the commencement of section 7 in a case not falling within sub-paragraph (1) shall be taken to have been paid for the purposes of section 7.

4. The repeal of section 22 of the 1984 Act (compensation for inaccuracy) and the repeal of section 23 of that Act (compensation for loss or unauthorised disclosure) do not affect the application of those sections in relation to damage or distress suffered at any time by reason of anything done or omitted to be done before the commencement of the repeals.

5. The repeal of section 24 of the 1984 Act (rectification and erasure) does not affect any case in which the application to the court was made before the day on which the repeal comes into force.

6. Subsection (3)(b) of section 14 does not apply where the rectification, blocking, erasure or destruction occurred before the commencement of that section.

Enforcement and transfer prohibition notices served under Part V of 1984 Act

7.—(1) If, immediately before the commencement of section 40—

(a) an enforcement notice under section 10 of the 1984 Act has effect, and

(b) either the time for appealing against the notice has expired or any appeal has been determined,

then, after that commencement, to the extent mentioned in sub-paragraph (3), the notice shall have effect for the purposes of sections 41 and 47 as if it were an enforcement notice under section 40.

(2) Where an enforcement notice has been served under section 10 of the 1984 Act before the commencement of section 40 and immediately before that commencement either—

(a) the time for appealing against the notice has not expired, or

(b) an appeal has not been determined,

the appeal shall be determined in accordance with the provisions of the 1984 Act and the old principles and, unless the notice is quashed on appeal, to the extent mentioned in sub-paragraph (3) the notice shall have effect for the purposes of sections 41 and 47 as if it were an enforcement notice under section 40.

(3) An enforcement notice under section 10 of the 1984 Act has the effect described in sub-paragraph (1) or (2) only to the extent that the steps specified in the notice for complying with the old principle or principles in question are steps which the data controller could be required by an enforcement notice under section 40 to take for complying with the new principles or any of them.

8.—(1) If, immediately before the commencement of section 40—

(a) a transfer prohibition notice under section 12 of the 1984 Act has effect, and

(b) either the time for appealing against the notice has expired or any appeal has been determined,

then, on and after that commencement, to the extent specified in sub-paragraph (3), the notice shall have effect for the purposes of sections 41 and 47 as if it were an enforcement notice under section 40.

(2) Where a transfer prohibition notice has been served under section 12 of the 1984 Act and immediately before the commencement of section 40 either—

(a) the time for appealing against the notice has not expired, or

(b) an appeal has not been determined,

the appeal shall be determined in accordance with the provisions of the 1984 Act and the old principles and, unless the notice is quashed on appeal, to the extent mentioned in sub-paragraph (3) the notice shall have effect for the purposes of sections 41 and 47 as if it were an enforcement notice under section 40.

(3) A transfer prohibition notice under section 12 of the 1984 Act has the effect described in sub-paragraph (1) or (2) only to the extent that the prohibition imposed by the notice is one which could be imposed by an enforcement notice under section 40 for complying with the new principles or any of them.

Notices under new law relating to matters in relation to which 1984 Act had effect

9. The Commissioner may serve an enforcement notice under section 40 on or after the day on which that section comes into force if he is satisfied that, before that day, the data controller contravened the old principles by reason of any act or omission which would also have constituted a contravention of the new principles if they had applied before that day.

10. Subsection (5)(b) of section 40 does not apply where the rectification, blocking, erasure or destruction occurred before the commencement of that section.

11. The Commissioner may serve an information notice under section 43 on or after the day on which that section comes into force if he has reasonable grounds for suspecting that, before that day, the data controller contravened the old principles by reason of any act or omission which would also have constituted a contravention of the new principles if they had applied before that day.

12. Where by virtue of paragraph 11 an information notice is served on the basis of anything done or omitted to be done before the day on which section 43 comes into force, subsection (2)(b) of that section shall have effect as if the reference to the data controller having complied, or complying, with the new principles were a reference to the data controller having contravened the old principles by reason of any such act or omission as is mentioned in paragraph 11.

Self-incrimination, etc

13.—(1) In section 43(8), section 44(9) and paragraph 11 of Schedule 7, any reference to an offence under this Act includes a reference to an offence under the 1984 Act.

(2) In section 34(9) of the 1984 Act, any reference to an offence under that Act includes a reference to an offence under this Act.

Warrants issued under 1984 Act

14. The repeal of Schedule 4 to the 1984 Act does not affect the application of that Schedule in any case where a warrant was issued under that Schedule before the commencement of the repeal.

Complaints under section 36(2) of 1984 Act and requests for assessment under section 42

15. The repeal of section 36(2) of the 1984 Act does not affect the application of that provision in any case where the complaint was received by the Commissioner before the commencement of the repeal.

16. In dealing with a complaint under section 36(2) of the 1984 Act or a request for an assessment under section 42 of this Act, the Commissioner shall have regard to the provisions from time to time applicable to the processing, and accordingly—

(a) in section 36(2) of the 1984 Act, the reference to the old principles and the provisions of that Act includes, in relation to any time when the new principles and the provisions of this Act have effect, those principles and provisions, and

(b) in section 42 of this Act, the reference to the provisions of this Act includes, in relation to any time when the old principles and the provisions of the 1984 Act had effect, those principles and provisions.

Applications under Access to Health Records Act 1990 or corresponding Northern Ireland legislation

17.—(1) The repeal of any provision of the Access to Health Records Act 1990 does not affect—

(a) the application of section 3 or 6 of that Act in any case in which the application under that section was received before the day on which the repeal comes into force, or

(b) the application of section 8 of that Act in any case in which the application to the court was made before the day on which the repeal comes into force.

(2) Sub-paragraph (1)(a) does not apply in relation to an application for access to information which was made by reference to this Act.

18.—(1) The revocation of any provision of the Access to Health Records (Northern Ireland) Order 1993 does not affect—

(a) the application of Article 5 or 8 of that Order in any case in which the application under that Article was received before the day on which the repeal comes into force, or

(b) the application of Article 10 of that Order in any case in which the application to the court was made before the day on which the repeal comes into force.

(2) Sub-paragraph (1)(a) does not apply in relation to an application for access to information which was made by reference to this Act.

Applications under regulations under Access to Personal Files Act 1987 or corresponding Northern Ireland legislation

19.—(1) The repeal of the personal files enactments does not affect the application of regulations under those enactments in relation to—

(a) any request for information,

(b) any application for rectification or erasure, or

(c) any application for review of a decision,

which was made before the day on which the repeal comes into force.

(2) Sub-paragraph (1)(a) does not apply in relation to a request for information which was made by reference to this Act.

(3) In sub-paragraph (1) "the personal files enactments" means—

(a) in relation to Great Britain, the Access to Personal Files Act 1987, and

(b) in relation to Northern Ireland, Part II of the Access to Personal Files and Medical Reports (Northern Ireland) Order 1991.

20. . . .

NOTES

Para 2: words omitted from sub-para (1) repealed by the Freedom of Information Act 2000, ss 73, 86, Sch 6, para 8, Sch 8, Pt I.

Para 20: outside the scope of this work.

Regulations: the Data Protection (Notification and Notification Fees) Regulations 2000, SI 2000/188.

(Schs 15, 16 outside the scope of this work.)

ACCESS TO JUSTICE ACT 1999

(1999 c 22)

An Act to establish the Legal Services Commission, the Community Legal Service and the Criminal Defence Service; to amend the law of legal aid in Scotland; to make further provision about legal services; to make provision about appeals, courts, judges and court proceedings; to amend the law about magistrates and magistrates' courts; and to make provision about immunity from action and costs and indemnities for certain officials exercising judicial functions

[27 July 1999]

1–26 *((Pt I) outside the scope of this work.)*

PART II
OTHER FUNDING OF LEGAL SERVICES

27, 28 *(Outside the scope of this work.)*

Costs

[3643]
29 Recovery of insurance premiums by way of costs
Where in any proceedings a costs order is made in favour of any party who has taken out an insurance policy against the risk of incurring a liability in those proceedings, the costs payable to him may, subject in the case of court proceedings to rules of court, include costs in respect of the premium of the policy.

[3644]
30 Recovery where body undertakes to meet costs liabilities
(1) This section applies where a body of a prescribed description undertakes to meet (in accordance with arrangements satisfying prescribed conditions) liabilities which members of the body or other persons who are parties to proceedings may incur to pay the costs of other parties to the proceedings.
(2) If in any of the proceedings a costs order is made in favour of any of the members or other persons, the costs payable to him may, subject to subsection (3) and (in the case of court proceedings) to rules of court, include an additional amount in respect of any provision made by or on behalf of the body in connection with the proceedings against the risk of having to meet such liabilities.
(3) But the additional amount shall not exceed a sum determined in a prescribed manner; and there may, in particular, be prescribed as a manner of determination one which takes into account the likely cost to the member or other person of the premium of an insurance policy against the risk of incurring a liability to pay the costs of other parties to the proceedings.
(4) In this section "prescribed" means prescribed by regulations made by the [Lord Chancellor] by statutory instrument; and a statutory instrument containing such regulations shall be subject to annulment in pursuance of a resolution of either House of Parliament.
(5) Regulations under subsection (1) may, in particular, prescribe as a description of body one which is for the time being approved by the [Lord Chancellor] or by a prescribed person.

NOTES

Sub-ss (4), (5): words in square brackets substituted by the Transfer of Functions (Lord Chancellor and Secretary of State) Order 2005, SI 2005/3429, art 8, Schedule, para 4(c).

Regulations: the Access to Justice (Membership Organisation) Regulations 2005, SI 2005/2306.

31–104 *(Ss 31–34, 35–104 (Pts III–VI) outside the scope of this work.)*

PART VII
SUPPLEMENTARY

105–109 *(Outside the scope of this work.)*

[3645]
110 Short title
This Act may be cited as the Access to Justice Act 1999.

(Schs 1–15 outside the scope of this work.)

CONTRACTS (RIGHTS OF THIRD PARTIES) ACT 1999

(1999 c 31)

ARRANGEMENT OF SECTIONS

1	Right of third party to enforce contractual term	[3646]
2	Variation and rescission of contract	[3647]
3	Defences etc available to promisor	[3648]
4	Enforcement of contract by promisee	[3649]
5	Protection of promisor from double liability	[3650]
6	Exceptions	[3651]
7	Supplementary provisions relating to third party	[3652]
8	Arbitration provisions	[3653]
10	Short title, commencement and extent	[3654]

An Act to make provision for the enforcement of contractual terms by third parties

[11 November 1999]

[3646]

1 Right of third party to enforce contractual term

(1) Subject to the provisions of this Act, a person who is not a party to a contract (a "third party") may in his own right enforce a term of the contract if—

(a) the contract expressly provides that he may, or

(b) subject to subsection (2), the term purports to confer a benefit on him.

(2) Subsection (1)(b) does not apply if on a proper construction of the contract it appears that the parties did not intend the term to be enforceable by the third party.

(3) The third party must be expressly identified in the contract by name, as a member of a class or as answering a particular description but need not be in existence when the contract is entered into.

(4) This section does not confer a right on a third party to enforce a term of a contract otherwise than subject to and in accordance with any other relevant terms of the contract.

(5) For the purpose of exercising his right to enforce a term of the contract, there shall be available to the third party any remedy that would have been available to him in an action for breach of contract if he had been a party to the contract (and the rules relating to damages, injunctions, specific performance and other relief shall apply accordingly).

(6) Where a term of a contract excludes or limits liability in relation to any matter references in this Act to the third party enforcing the term shall be construed as references to his availing himself of the exclusion or limitation.

(7) In this Act, in relation to a term of a contract which is enforceable by a third party—

"the promisor" means the party to the contract against whom the term is enforceable by the third party, and

"the promisee" means the party to the contract by whom the term is enforceable against the promisor.

[3647]

2 Variation and rescission of contract

(1) Subject to the provisions of this section, where a third party has a right under section 1 to enforce a term of the contract, the parties to the contract may not, by agreement, rescind the contract, or vary it in such a way as to extinguish or alter his entitlement under that right, without his consent if—

(a) the third party has communicated his assent to the term to the promisor,

(b) the promisor is aware that the third party has relied on the term, or

(c) the promisor can reasonably be expected to have foreseen that the third party would rely on the term and the third party has in fact relied on it.

(2) The assent referred to in subsection (1)(a)—

(a) may be by words or conduct, and

(b) if sent to the promisor by post or other means, shall not be regarded as communicated to the promisor until received by him.

(3) Subsection (1) is subject to any express term of the contract under which—

(a) the parties to the contract may by agreement rescind or vary the contract without the consent of the third party, or

(b) the consent of the third party is required in circumstances specified in the contract instead of those set out in subsection (1)(a) to (c).

(4) Where the consent of a third party is required under subsection (1) or (3), the court or arbitral tribunal may, on the application of the parties to the contract, dispense with his consent if satisfied—

(a) that his consent cannot be obtained because his whereabouts cannot reasonably be ascertained, or

(b) that he is mentally incapable of giving his consent.

(5) The court or arbitral tribunal may, on the application of the parties to a contract, dispense with any consent that may be required under subsection (1)(c) if satisfied that it cannot reasonably be ascertained whether or not the third party has in fact relied on the term.

(6) If the court or arbitral tribunal dispenses with a third party's consent, it may impose such conditions as it thinks fit, including a condition requiring the payment of compensation to the third party.

(7) The jurisdiction conferred on the court by subsections (4) to (6) is exercisable by both the High Court and a county court.

[3648]

3 Defences etc available to promisor

(1) Subsections (2) to (5) apply where, in reliance on section 1, proceedings for the enforcement of a term of a contract are brought by a third party.

(2) The promisor shall have available to him by way of defence or set-off any matter that—

(a) arises from or in connection with the contract and is relevant to the term, and

(b) would have been available to him by way of defence or set-off if the proceedings had been brought by the promisee.

(3) The promisor shall also have available to him by way of defence or set-off any matter if—

(a) an express term of the contract provides for it to be available to him in proceedings brought by the third party, and

(b) it would have been available to him by way of defence or set-off if the proceedings had been brought by the promisee.

(4) The promisor shall also have available to him—

(a) by way of defence or set-off any matter, and

(b) by way of counterclaim any matter not arising from the contract,

that would have been available to him by way of defence or set-off or, as the case may be, by way of counterclaim against the third party if the third party had been a party to the contract.

(5) Subsections (2) and (4) are subject to any express term of the contract as to the matters that are not to be available to the promisor by way of defence, set-off or counterclaim.

(6) Where in any proceedings brought against him a third party seeks in reliance on section 1 to enforce a term of a contract (including, in particular, a term purporting to exclude or limit liability), he may not do so if he could not have done so (whether by reason of any particular circumstances relating to him or otherwise) had he been a party to the contract.

[3649]

4 Enforcement of contract by promisee

Section 1 does not affect any right of the promisee to enforce any term of the contract.

[3650]

5 Protection of party promisor from double liability

Where under section 1 a term of a contract is enforceable by a third party, and the promisee has recovered from the promisor a sum in respect of—

(a) the third party's loss in respect of the term, or

(b) the expense to the promisee of making good to the third party the default of the promisor,

then, in any proceedings brought in reliance on that section by the third party, the court or arbitral tribunal shall reduce any award to the third party to such extent as it thinks appropriate to take account of the sum recovered by the promisee.

[3651]

6 Exceptions

(1) Section 1 confers no rights on a third party in the case of a contract on a bill of exchange, promissory note or other negotiable instrument.

(2) Section 1 confers no rights on a third party in the case of any contract binding on a company and its members under [section 33 of the Companies Act 2006 (effect of company's constitution)].

[(2A) Section 1 confers no rights on a third party in the case of any incorporation document of a limited liability partnership [or any agreement (express or implied) between the members of a limited liability partnership, or between a limited liability partnership and its members, that determines the mutual rights and duties of the members and their rights and duties in relation to the limited liability partnership].]

(3) Section 1 confers no right on a third party to enforce—

(a) any term of a contract of employment against an employee,

(b) any term of a worker's contract against a worker (including a home worker), or

(c) any term of a relevant contract against an agency worker.

(4) In subsection (3)—

(a) "contract of employment", "employee", "worker's contract", and "worker" have the meaning given by section 54 of the National Minimum Wage Act 1998,

(b) "home worker" has the meaning given by section 35(2) of that Act,

(c) "agency worker" has the same meaning as in section 34(1) of that Act, and

(d) "relevant contract" means a contract entered into, in a case where section 34 of that Act applies, by the agency worker as respects work falling within subsection (1)(a) of that section.

(5) Section 1 confers no rights on a third party in the case of—

(a) a contract for the carriage of goods by sea, or

(b) a contract for the carriage of goods by rail or road, or for the carriage of cargo by air, which is subject to the rules of the appropriate international transport convention,

except that a third party may in reliance on that section avail himself of an exclusion or limitation of liability in such a contract.

(6) In subsection (5) "contract for the carriage of goods by sea" means a contract of carriage—

(a) contained in or evidenced by a bill of lading, sea waybill or a corresponding electronic transaction, or

(b) under or for the purposes of which there is given an undertaking which is contained in a ship's delivery order or a corresponding electronic transaction.

(7) For the purposes of subsection (6)—

(a) "bill of lading", "sea waybill" and "ship's delivery order" have the same meaning as in the Carriage of Goods by Sea Act 1992, and

(b) a corresponding electronic transaction is a transaction within section 1(5) of that Act which corresponds to the issue, indorsement, delivery or transfer of a bill of lading, sea waybill or ship's delivery order.

(8) In subsection (5) "the appropriate international transport convention" means—

(a) in relation to a contract for the carriage of goods by rail, the Convention which has the force of law in the United Kingdom under [regulation 3 of the Railways (Convention on International Carriage by Rail) Regulations 2005],

(b) in relation to a contract for the carriage of goods by road, the Convention which has the force of law in the United Kingdom under section 1 of the Carriage of Goods by Road Act 1965, and

(c) in relation to a contract for the carriage of cargo by air—

(i) the Convention which has the force of law in the United Kingdom under section 1 of the Carriage by Air Act 1961, or

(ii) the Convention which has the force of law under section 1 of the Carriage by Air (Supplementary Provisions) Act 1962, or

(iii) either of the amended Conventions set out in Part B of Schedule 2 or 3 to the Carriage by Air Acts (Application of Provisions) Order 1967.

NOTES

Sub-s (2): words in square brackets substituted by the Companies Act 2006 (Consequential Amendments, Transitional Provisions and Savings) Order 2009, SI 2009/1941, art 2(1), Sch 1, para 179(1), (2)(a).

Sub-s (2A): inserted by the Limited Liability Partnerships Regulations 2001, SI 2001/1090, reg 9, Sch 5, para 20; words in square brackets substituted by SI 2009/1941, art 2(1), Sch 1, para 179(1), (2)(b).

Sub-s (8): words in square brackets in para (a) substituted by the Railways (Convention on International Carriage by Rail) Regulations 2005, SI 2005/2092, reg 9(2), Sch 3, para 3.

[3652]

7 Supplementary provisions relating to third party

(1) Section 1 does not affect any right or remedy of a third party that exists or is available apart from this Act.

(2) Section 2(2) of the Unfair Contract Terms Act 1977 (restriction on exclusion etc of liability for negligence) shall not apply where the negligence consists of the breach of an obligation arising from a term of a contract and the person seeking to enforce it is a third party acting in reliance on section 1.
(3) In sections 5 and 8 of the Limitation Act 1980 the references to an action founded on a simple contract and an action upon a specialty shall respectively include references to an action brought in reliance on section 1 relating to a simple contract and an action brought in reliance on that section relating to a specialty.
(4) A third party shall not, by virtue of section 1(5) or 3(4) or (6), be treated as a party to the contract for the purposes of any other Act (or any instrument made under any other Act).

[3653]
8 Arbitration provisions
(1) Where—
(a) a right under section 1 to enforce a term ("the substantive term") is subject to a term providing for the submission of disputes to arbitration ("the arbitration agreement"), and
(b) the arbitration agreement is an agreement in writing for the purposes of Part I of the Arbitration Act 1996,

the third party shall be treated for the purposes of that Act as a party to the arbitration agreement as regards disputes between himself and the promisor relating to the enforcement of the substantive term by the third party.
(2) Where—
(a) a third party has a right under section 1 to enforce a term providing for one or more descriptions of dispute between the third party and the promisor to be submitted to arbitration ("the arbitration agreement"),
(b) the arbitration agreement is an agreement in writing for the purposes of Part I of the Arbitration Act 1996, and
(c) the third party does not fall to be treated under subsection (1) as a party to the arbitration agreement,

the third party shall, if he exercises the right, be treated for the purposes of that Act as a party to the arbitration agreement in relation to the matter with respect to which the right is exercised, and be treated as having been so immediately before the exercise of the right.

9 *(Applies to Northern Ireland only.)*

[3654]
10 Short title, commencement and extent
(1) This Act may be cited as the Contracts (Rights of Third Parties) Act 1999.
(2) This Act comes into force on the day on which it is passed but, subject to subsection (3), does not apply in relation to a contract entered into before the end of the period of six months beginning with that day.
(3) The restriction in subsection (2) does not apply in relation to a contract which—
(a) is entered into on or after the day on which this Act is passed, and
(b) expressly provides for the application of this Act.
(4) This Act extends as follows—
(a) section 9 extends to Northern Ireland only;
(b) the remaining provisions extend to England and Wales and Northern Ireland only.

ELECTRONIC COMMUNICATIONS ACT 2000

(2000 c 7)

ARRANGEMENT OF SECTIONS

PART II
FACILITATION OF ELECTRONIC COMMERCE, DATA STORAGE, ETC

7 Electronic signatures and related certificates . . . . [3655]
8 Power to modify legislation . . . . [3656]
9 Section 8 orders . . . . [3657]
10 Modifications in relation to Welsh matters . . . . [3658]

PART III
MISCELLANEOUS AND SUPPLEMENTAL

Supplemental

13 Ministerial expenditure etc . . . . . [3659]
14 Prohibition on key escrow requirements . . . . . [3660]
15 General interpretation . . . . . [3661]
16 Short title, commencement, extent . . . . . [3662]

An Act to make provision to facilitate the use of electronic communications and electronic data storage; to make provision about the modification of licences granted under section 7 of the Telecommunications Act 1984; and for connected purposes

[25 May 2000]

1–6 *(Pt I repealed by virtue of s 16(4) of this Act.)*

PART II
FACILITATION OF ELECTRONIC COMMERCE, DATA STORAGE, ETC

[3655]
7 Electronic signatures and related certificates

(1) In any legal proceedings—
(a) an electronic signature incorporated into or logically associated with a particular electronic communication or particular electronic data, and
(b) the certification by any person of such a signature,

shall each be admissible in evidence in relation to any question as to the authenticity of the communication or data or as to the integrity of the communication or data.

(2) For the purposes of this section an electronic signature is so much of anything in electronic form as—
(a) is incorporated into or otherwise logically associated with any electronic communication or electronic data; and
(b) purports to be so incorporated or associated for the purpose of being used in establishing the authenticity of the communication or data, the integrity of the communication or data, or both.

(3) For the purposes of this section an electronic signature incorporated into or associated with a particular electronic communication or particular electronic data is certified by any person if that person (whether before or after the making of the communication) has made a statement confirming that—
(a) the signature,
(b) a means of producing, communicating or verifying the signature, or
(c) a procedure applied to the signature,

is (either alone or in combination with other factors) a valid means of establishing the authenticity of the communication or data, the integrity of the communication or data, or both.

[3656]
8 Power to modify legislation

(1) Subject to subsection (3), the appropriate Minister may by order made by statutory instrument modify the provisions of—
(a) any enactment or subordinate legislation, or
(b) any scheme, licence, authorisation or approval issued, granted or given by or under any enactment or subordinate legislation,

in such manner as he may think fit for the purpose of authorising or facilitating the use of electronic communications or electronic storage (instead of other forms of communication or storage) for any purpose mentioned in subsection (2).

(2) Those purposes are—
(a) the doing of anything which under any such provisions is required to be or may be done or evidenced in writing or otherwise using a document, notice or instrument;
(b) the doing of anything which under any such provisions is required to be or may be done by post or other specified means of delivery;
(c) the doing of anything which under any such provisions is required to be or may be authorised by a person's signature or seal, or is required to be delivered as a deed or witnessed;
(d) the making of any statement or declaration which under any such provisions is required to be made under oath or to be contained in a statutory declaration;

(e) the keeping, maintenance or preservation, for the purposes or in pursuance of any such provisions, of any account, record, notice, instrument or other document;

(f) the provision, production or publication under any such provisions of any information or other matter;

(g) the making of any payment that is required to be or may be made under any such provisions.

(3) The appropriate Minister shall not make an order under this section authorising the use of electronic communications or electronic storage for any purpose, unless he considers that the authorisation is such that the extent (if any) to which records of things done for that purpose will be available will be no less satisfactory in cases where use is made of electronic communications or electronic storage than in other cases.

(4) Without prejudice to the generality of subsection (1), the power to make an order under this section shall include power to make an order containing any of the following provisions—

(a) provision as to the electronic form to be taken by any electronic communications or electronic storage the use of which is authorised by an order under this section;

(b) provision imposing conditions subject to which the use of electronic communications or electronic storage is so authorised;

(c) provision, in relation to cases in which any such conditions are not satisfied, for treating anything for the purposes of which the use of such communications or storage is so authorised as not having been done;

(d) provision, in connection with anything so authorised, for a person to be able to refuse to accept receipt of something in electronic form except in such circumstances as may be specified in or determined under the order;

(e) provision, in connection with any use of electronic communications so authorised, for intermediaries to be used, or to be capable of being used, for the transmission of any data or for establishing the authenticity or integrity of any data;

(f) provision, in connection with any use of electronic storage so authorised, for persons satisfying such conditions as may be specified in or determined under the regulations to carry out functions in relation to the storage;

(g) provision, in relation to cases in which the use of electronic communications or electronic storage is so authorised, for the determination of any of the matters mentioned in subsection (5), or as to the manner in which they may be proved in legal proceedings;

(h) provision, in relation to cases in which fees or charges are or may be imposed in connection with anything for the purposes of which the use of electronic communications or electronic storage is so authorised, for different fees or charges to apply where use is made of such communications or storage;

(i) provision, in relation to any criminal or other liabilities that may arise (in respect of the making of false or misleading statements or otherwise) in connection with anything for the purposes of which the use of electronic communications or electronic storage is so authorised, for corresponding liabilities to arise in corresponding circumstances where use is made of such communications or storage;

(j) provision requiring persons to prepare and keep records in connection with any use of electronic communications or electronic storage which is so authorised;

(k) provision requiring the production of the contents of any records kept in accordance with an order under this section;

(l) provision for a requirement imposed by virtue of paragraph (j) or (k) to be enforceable at the suit or instance of such person as may be specified in or determined in accordance with the order;

(m) any such provision, in relation to electronic communications or electronic storage the use of which is authorised otherwise than by an order under this section, as corresponds to any provision falling within any of the preceding paragraphs that may be made where it is such an order that authorises the use of the communications or storage.

(5) The matters referred to in subsection (4)(g) are—

(a) whether a thing has been done using an electronic communication or electronic storage;

(b) the time at which, or date on which, a thing done using any such communication or storage was done;

(c) the place where a thing done using such communication or storage was done;

(d) the person by whom such a thing was done; and

(e) the contents, authenticity or integrity of any electronic data.

(6) An order under this section—

(a) shall not (subject to paragraph (b)) require the use of electronic communications or electronic storage for any purpose; but

(b) may make provision that a period of notice specified in the order must expire before effect is given to a variation or withdrawal of an election or other decision which—
   (i) has been made for the purposes of such an order; and
   (ii) is an election or decision to make use of electronic communications or electronic storage.

(7) The matters in relation to which provision may be made by an order under this section do not include any matter under the care and management of the Commissioners of Inland Revenue or any matter under the care and management of the Commissioners of Customs and Excise.

(8) In this section references to doing anything under the provisions of any enactment include references to doing it under the provisions of any subordinate legislation the power to make which is conferred by that enactment.

NOTES

Orders: the Local Government and Housing Act 1989 (Electronic Communications) (England) Order 2000, SI 2000/3056; the Companies Act 1985 (Electronic Communications) Order 2000, SI 2000/3373; the Local Government and Housing Act 1989 (Electronic Communications) (Wales) Order 2001, SI 2001/605; the Unsolicited Goods and Services Act 1971 (Electronic Communications) Order 2001, SI 2001/2778; the National Health Service (Charges for Drugs and Appliances) (Electronic Communications) Order 2001, SI 2001/2887; the National Health Service (Pharmaceutical Services) and (Misuse of Drugs) (Electronic Communications) Order 2001, SI 2001/2888; the Housing (Right to Acquire) (Electronic Communications) (England) Order 2001, SI 2001/3257; the Public Records Act 1958 (Admissibility of Electronic Copies of Public Records) Order 2001, SI 2001/4058; the Building Societies Act 1986 (Electronic Communications) Order 2003, SI 2003/404; the Patents Act 1977 (Electronic Communications) Order 2003, SI 2003/512; the Town and Country Planning (Electronic Communications) (England) Order 2003, SI 2003/956; the Council Tax and Non-Domestic Rating (Electronic Communications) (England) Order 2003, SI 2003/2604; the Social Security (Electronic Communications) (Carer's Allowance) Order 2003, SI 2003/2800; the Council Tax and Non-Domestic Rating (Electronic Communications) (England) (No 2) Order 2003, SI 2003/3052; the Town and Country Planning (Electronic Communications) (Scotland) Order 2004, SSI 2004/332; the Education Act 1996 (Electronic Communications) Order 2004, SI 2004/2521; the Town and Country Planning (Electronic Communications) (Wales) (No 1) Order 2004, SI 2004/3156; the Town and Country Planning (Electronic Communications) (Wales) (No 2) Order 2004, SI 2004/3157; the Town and Country Planning (Electronic Communications) (Wales) (No 3) Order 2004, SI 2004/3172; the Consumer Credit Act 1974 (Electronic Communications) Order 2004, SI 2004/3236; the Social Security (Electronic Communications) (Miscellaneous Benefits) Order 2005, SI 2005/3321; the Non-Domestic Rating and Council Tax (Electronic Communications) (England) Order 2006, SI 2006/237; the Registered Designs Act 1949 and Patents Act 1977 (Electronic Communications) Order 2006, SI 2006/1229; the Transport Security (Electronic Communications) Order 2006, SI 2006/2190; the Registration of Births and Deaths (Electronic Communications and Electronic Storage) Order 2006, SI 2006/2809; the Housing Benefit and Council Tax Benefit (Electronic Communications) Order 2006, SI 2006/2968; the Council Tax (Electronic Communications) (Scotland) Order 2006, SSI 2006/67; the Non-Domestic Rating (Electronic Communications) (Scotland) Order 2006, SSI 2006/201; the Electronic Communications (Scotland) Order 2006, SSI 2006/367; the Automated Registration of Title to Land (Electronic Communications) (Scotland) Order 2006, SSI 2006/491; the Valuation Appeal Committee (Electronic Communications) (Scotland) Order 2007, SSI 2007/124; the Council Tax (Electronic Communications) (England) Order 2008, SI 2008/316; the Building (Electronic Communications) Order 2008, SI 2008/2334; the Adults with Incapacity (Electronic Communications) (Scotland) Order 2008, SSI 2008/380; the Police Act 1997 (Criminal Records) (Electronic Communications) Order 2009, SI 2009/203; the Unit Trusts (Electronic Communications) Order 2009, SI 2009/555; the Council Tax and Non-Domestic Rating (Electronic Communications) (Wales) Order 2009, SI 2009/2706; the Registration of Marriages etc (Electronic Communications and Electronic Storage) Order 2009, SI 2009/2821; the Health and Social Care Act 2008 (Commencement No 13, Transitory and Transitional Provisions and Electronic Communications) Order 2009, SI 2009/3023.

[3657]

9 Section 8 orders

(1) In this Part "the appropriate Minister" means (subject to subsections (2) and (7) and section 10(1))—
   (a) in relation to any matter with which a department of the Secretary of State is concerned, the Secretary of State;
   (b) in relation to any matter with which the Treasury is concerned, the Treasury; and
   (c) in relation to any matter with which any Government department other than a department of the Secretary of State or the Treasury is concerned, the Minister in charge of the other department.

(2) Where in the case of any matter—
   (a) that matter falls within more than one paragraph of subsection (1),
   (b) there is more than one such department as is mentioned in paragraph (c) of that subsection that is concerned with that matter, or
   (c) both paragraphs (a) and (b) of this subsection apply,

references, in relation to that matter, to the appropriate Minister are references to any one or more of the appropriate Ministers acting (in the case of more than one) jointly.

(3) Subject to subsection (4) and section 10(6), a statutory instrument containing an order under section 8 shall be subject to annulment in pursuance of a resolution of either House of Parliament.
(4) Subsection (3) does not apply in the case of an order a draft of which has been laid before Parliament and approved by a resolution of each House.
(5) An order under section 8 may—
   (a) provide for any conditions or requirements imposed by such an order to be framed by reference to the directions of such persons as may be specified in or determined in accordance with the order;
   (b) provide that any such condition or requirement is to be satisfied only where a person so specified or determined is satisfied as to specified matters.
(6) The provision made by such an order may include—
   (a) different provision for different cases;
   (b) such exceptions and exclusions as the person making the order may think fit; and
   (c) any such incidental, supplemental, consequential and transitional provision as he may think fit;

and the provision that may be made by virtue of paragraph (c) includes provision modifying any enactment or subordinate legislation or any scheme, licence, authorisation or approval issued, granted or given by or under any enactment or subordinate legislation.
(7) In the case of any matter which is not one of the reserved matters within the meaning of the Scotland Act 1998 or in respect of which functions are, by virtue of section 63 of that Act, exercisable by the Scottish Ministers instead of by or concurrently with a Minister of the Crown, this section and section 8 shall apply to Scotland subject to the following modifications—
   (a) subsections (1) and (2) of this section are omitted;
   (b) any reference to the appropriate Minister is to be read as a reference to the Secretary of State;
   (c) any power of the Secretary of State, by virtue of paragraph (b), to make an order under section 8 may also be exercised by the Scottish Ministers with the consent of the Secretary of State; and
   (d) where the Scottish Ministers make an order under section 8—
      (i) any reference to the Secretary of State (other than a reference in this subsection) shall be construed as a reference to the Scottish Ministers; and
      (ii) any reference to Parliament or to a House of Parliament shall be construed as a reference to the Scottish Parliament.

[3658]
10 Modifications in relation to Welsh matters
(1) For the purposes of the exercise of the powers conferred by section 8 in relation to any matter the functions in respect of which are exercisable by the National Assembly for Wales, the appropriate Minister is the Secretary of State.
(2) Subject to the following provisions of this section, the powers conferred by section 8, so far as they fall within subsection (3), shall be exercisable by the National Assembly for Wales, as well as by the appropriate Minister.
(3) The powers conferred by section 8 fall within this subsection to the extent that they are exercisable in relation to—
   (a) the provisions of any subordinate legislation made by the National Assembly for Wales;
   (b) so much of any other subordinate legislation as makes provision the power to make which is exercisable by that Assembly;
   (c) any power under any enactment to make provision the power to make which is so exercisable;
   (d) the giving, sending or production of any notice, account, record or other document or of any information to or by a body mentioned in subsection (4); or
   (e) the publication of anything by a body mentioned in subsection (4).
(4) Those bodies are—
   (a) the National Assembly for Wales;
   (b) any body specified in Schedule 4 to the Government of Wales Act 1998 (Welsh public bodies subject to reform by that Assembly);
   (c) any other such body as may be specified for the purposes of this section by an order made by the Secretary of State with the consent of that Assembly.
(5) The National Assembly for Wales shall not make an order under section 8 except with the consent of the Secretary of State.
(6) Section 9(3) shall not apply to any order made under section 8 by the National Assembly for Wales.

(7) Nothing in this section shall confer any power on the National Assembly for Wales to modify any provision of the Government of Wales Act 1998.

(8) The power of the Secretary of State to make an order under subsection (4)(c)—

(a) shall include power to make any such incidental, supplemental, consequential and transitional provision as he may think fit; and

(b) shall be exercisable by statutory instrument subject to annulment in pursuance of a resolution of either House of Parliament.

NOTES

Orders: the Council Tax and Non-Domestic Rating (Electronic Communications) (Wales) Order 2009, SI 2009/2706.

PART III
MISCELLANEOUS AND SUPPLEMENTAL

11, 12 *(Repealed by the Communications Act 2003, s 406(7), Sch 19(1).)*

Supplemental

[3659]

13 Ministerial expenditure etc

There shall be paid out of money provided by Parliament—

(a) any expenditure incurred by the Secretary of State for or in connection with the carrying out of his functions under this Act; and

(b) any increase attributable to this Act in the sums which are payable out of money so provided under any other Act.

[3660]

14 Prohibition on key escrow requirements

(1) Subject to subsection (2), nothing in this Act shall confer any power on any Minister of the Crown, on the Scottish Ministers, on the National Assembly for Wales or on any person appointed under section 3—

(a) by conditions of an approval under Part I, or

(b) by any regulations or order under this Act,

to impose a requirement on any person to deposit a key for electronic data with another person.

(2) Subsection (1) shall not prohibit the imposition by an order under section 8 of—

(a) a requirement to deposit a key for electronic data with the intended recipient of electronic communications comprising the data; or

(b) a requirement for arrangements to be made, in cases where a key for data is not deposited with another person, which otherwise secure that the loss of a key, or its becoming unusable, does not have the effect that the information contained in a record kept in pursuance of any provision made by or under any enactment or subordinate legislation becomes inaccessible or incapable of being put into an intelligible form.

(3) In this section "key", in relation to electronic data, means any code, password, algorithm, key or other data the use of which (with or without other keys)—

(a) allows access to the electronic data, or

(b) facilitates the putting of the electronic data into an intelligible form;

and references in this section to depositing a key for electronic data with a person include references to doing anything that has the effect of making the key available to that person.

[3661]

15 General interpretation

(1) In this Act, except in so far as the context otherwise requires—

"document" includes a map, plan, design, drawing, picture or other image;

"communication" includes a communication comprising sounds or images or both and a communication effecting a payment;

"electronic communication" means a communication transmitted (whether from one person to another, from one device to another or from a person to a device or vice versa)—

(a) by means of [an electronic communications network]; or

(b) by other means but while in an electronic form;

"enactment" includes—

(a) an enactment passed after the passing of this Act,

(b) an enactment comprised in an Act of the Scottish Parliament, and

(c) an enactment contained in Northern Ireland legislation,

but does not include an enactment contained in Part I or II of this Act;

"modification" includes any alteration, addition or omission, and cognate expressions shall be construed accordingly;

"record" includes an electronic record; and

"subordinate legislation" means—

(a) any subordinate legislation (within the meaning of the Interpretation Act 1978);

(b) any instrument made under an Act of the Scottish Parliament; or

(c) any statutory rules (within the meaning of the Statutory Rules (Northern Ireland) Order 1979).

(2) In this Act—

(a) references to the authenticity of any communication or data are references to any one or more of the following—

(i) whether the communication or data comes from a particular person or other source;

(ii) whether it is accurately timed and dated;

(iii) whether it is intended to have legal effect;

and

(b) references to the integrity of any communication or data are references to whether there has been any tampering with or other modification of the communication or data.

(3) References in this Act to something's being put into an intelligible form include references to its being restored to the condition in which it was before any encryption or similar process was applied to it.

NOTES

Sub-s (1): in definition "electronic communication" words in square brackets in para (a) substituted by the Communications Act 2003, s 406(1), Sch 17, para 158.

[3662]

16 Short title, commencement, extent

(1) This Act may be cited as the Electronic Communications Act 2000.

(2) Part I of this Act and sections 7, 11 and 12 shall come into force on such day as the Secretary of State may by order made by statutory instrument appoint; and different days may be appointed under this subsection for different purposes.

(3) An order shall not be made for bringing any of Part I of this Act into force for any purpose unless a draft of the order has been laid before Parliament and approved by a resolution of each House.

(4) If no order for bringing Part I of this Act into force has been made under subsection (2) by the end of the period of five years beginning with the day on which this Act is passed, that Part shall, by virtue of this subsection, be repealed at the end of that period.

(5) This Act extends to Northern Ireland.

NOTES

Orders: the Electronic Communications Act 2000 (Commencement No 1) Order 2000, SI 2000/1798.

HEALTH AND SOCIAL CARE (COMMUNITY HEALTH AND STANDARDS) ACT 2003

(2003 c 43)

An Act to amend the law about the National Health Service; to make provision about quality and standards in the provision of health and social care, including provision establishing the Commission for Healthcare Audit and Inspection and the Commission for Social Care Inspection; to amend the law about the recovery of NHS costs from persons making compensation payments; to provide for the replacement of the Welfare Food Schemes; to make provision about appointments to health and social care bodies; and for connected purposes

[20 November 2003]

1–149 *((Pts 1, 2) outside the scope of this work.)*

PART 3
RECOVERY OF NHS CHARGES

150–162 *(Outside the scope of this work.)*

Miscellaneous and general

163 *(Outside the scope of this work.)*

[3663]

164 Liability of insurers

(1) If a compensation payment is made in a case where—

(a) a person is liable to any extent in respect of the injury, and

(b) the liability is covered to any extent by a policy of insurance,

the policy is also to be treated as covering any liability of that person under section 150(2).

(2) Liability imposed on the insurer by subsection (1) cannot be excluded or restricted.

(3) For that purpose excluding or restricting liability includes—

(a) making the liability or its enforcement subject to restrictive or onerous conditions,

(b) excluding or restricting any right or remedy in respect of the liability, or subjecting a person to any prejudice in consequence of his pursuing any such right or remedy, or

(c) excluding or restricting rules of evidence or procedure.

(4) Regulations may in prescribed cases limit the amount of the liability imposed on the insurer by subsection (1).

(5) This section applies in relation to policies of insurance issued before (as well as those issued after) the date on which it comes into force.

(6) References in this section to policies of insurance and their issue include references to contracts of insurance and their making.

NOTES

Commencement: 20 November 2003 (in so far as confers power to make orders or regulations); 29 January 2007 (otherwise).

Regulations: the Personal Injuries (NHS Charges) (General) (Scotland) Regulations 2006, SSI 2006/592.

165–192 *(Ss 165–169, ss 170–192 (Pts 4, 5) outside the scope of this work.)*

PART 6
FINAL PROVISIONS

193–201 *(Outside the scope of this work.)*

[3664]

202 Extent

(1) The amendment or repeal of any provision by this Act has the same extent as the provision being amended or repealed (subject to any express limitation contained in this Act).

(2) Subject to that and except as provided below this Act extends to England and Wales only.

(3) The following provisions also extend to Scotland—

(a) *(outside the scope of this work.)*

(b) Part 3, except for section 163(3);

(c) *(outside the scope of this work.)*

(d) this Part.

(4) The following provisions also extend to Northern Ireland—

(a)–(c) *(outside the scope of this work.)*

(d) this Part.

[3665]

203 Short title

This Act may be cited as the Health and Social Care (Community Health and Standards) Act 2003.

(Schs 1–14 outside the scope of this work.)

COMPANIES ACT 2006

(2006 c 46)

ARRANGEMENT OF SECTIONS

PART 10
A COMPANY'S DIRECTORS

Chapter 7
Directors' Liabilities

232 Provisions protecting directors from liability . . . . [3666]
233 Provision of insurance . . . . [3667]
234 Qualifying third party indemnity provision . . . . [3668]
235 Qualifying pension scheme indemnity provision . . . . [3669]

PART 23
DISTRIBUTIONS

Chapter 3
Supplementary Provisions

843 Realised profits and losses of long-term insurance business . . . . [3670]

PART 38
COMPANIES: INTERPRETATION

Other definitions

1165 Meaning of "insurance company" and related expressions . . . . [3671]

PART 47
FINAL PROVISIONS

1298 Short title . . . . [3672]
1299 Extent . . . . [3673]
1300 Commencement . . . . [3674]

SCHEDULE:

Schedule 10—Recognised Supervisory Bodies
Part 2—Requirements for Recognition of a Supervisory Body . . . . [3675]

An Act to reform company law and restate the greater part of the enactments relating to companies; to make other provision relating to companies and other forms of business organisation; to make provision about directors' disqualification, business names, auditors and actuaries; to amend Part 9 of the Enterprise Act 2002; and for connected purposes.

[8 November 2006]

1–153 *((Pts 1–9) Outside the scope of this work.)*

PART 10
A COMPANY'S DIRECTORS

154–231 *((Chs 1–6) Outside the scope of this work.)*

CHAPTER 7
DIRECTORS' LIABILITIES

[3666]
232 Provisions protecting directors from liability

(1) Any provision that purports to exempt a director of a company (to any extent) from any liability that would otherwise attach to him in connection with any negligence, default, breach of duty or breach of trust in relation to the company is void.

(2) Any provision by which a company directly or indirectly provides an indemnity (to any extent) for a director of the company, or of an associated company, against any liability attaching to him in connection with any negligence, default, breach of duty or breach of trust in relation to the company of which he is a director is void, except as permitted by—

(a) section 233 (provision of insurance),
(b) section 234 (qualifying third party indemnity provision), or
(c) section 235 (qualifying pension scheme indemnity provision).

Part III Statutes

(3) This section applies to any provision, whether contained in a company's articles or in any contract with the company or otherwise.
(4) Nothing in this section prevents a company's articles from making such provision as has previously been lawful for dealing with conflicts of interest.

NOTES

Commencement: 1 October 2007 (applies to any provision made on or after that date; see the Companies Act 2006 (Commencement No 3, Consequential Amendments, Transitional Provisions and Savings) Order 2007, SI 2007/2194, art 9, Sch 3, para 15).

Disapplication: this section is disapplied in relation to proceedings against directors of Northern Rock, by the Northern Rock plc Transfer Order 2008, SI 2008/432, art 11(1), (3), in relation to Bradford & Bingley by the Bradford & Bingley plc Transfer of Securities and Property etc Order 2008, SI 2008/2546, art 12(3), in relation to Heritable and Deposits Management (Heritable) by the Heritable Bank plc Transfer of Certain Rights and Liabilities Order 2008, SI 2008/2644, arts 2, 30, and in relation to Kaupthing Singer & Friedlander by the Kaupthing Singer & Friedlander Limited Transfer of Certain Rights and Liabilities Order 2008, SI 2008/2674, arts 2, 32.

[3667]

233 Provision of insurance

Section 232(2) (voidness of provisions for indemnifying directors) does not prevent a company from purchasing and maintaining for a director of the company, or of an associated company, insurance against any such liability as is mentioned in that subsection.

NOTES

Commencement: 1 October 2007 (applies to any provision made on or after that date; see the Companies Act 2006 (Commencement No 3, Consequential Amendments, Transitional Provisions and Savings) Order 2007, SI 2007/2194, art 9, Sch 3, para 15).

[3668]

234 Qualifying third party indemnity provision

(1) Section 232(2) (voidness of provisions for indemnifying directors) does not apply to qualifying third party indemnity provision.
(2) Third party indemnity provision means provision for indemnity against liability incurred by the director to a person other than the company or an associated company.

Such provision is qualifying third party indemnity provision if the following requirements are met.

(3) The provision must not provide any indemnity against—
- (a) any liability of the director to pay—
  - (i) a fine imposed in criminal proceedings, or
  - (ii) a sum payable to a regulatory authority by way of a penalty in respect of non-compliance with any requirement of a regulatory nature (however arising); or
- (b) any liability incurred by the director—
  - (i) in defending criminal proceedings in which he is convicted, or
  - (ii) in defending civil proceedings brought by the company, or an associated company, in which judgment is given against him, or
  - (iii) in connection with an application for relief (see subsection (6)) in which the court refuses to grant him relief.

(4) The references in subsection (3)(b) to a conviction, judgment or refusal of relief are to the final decision in the proceedings.
(5) For this purpose—
- (a) a conviction, judgment or refusal of relief becomes final—
  - (i) if not appealed against, at the end of the period for bringing an appeal, or
  - (ii) if appealed against, at the time when the appeal (or any further appeal) is disposed of; and
- (b) an appeal is disposed of—
  - (i) if it is determined and the period for bringing any further appeal has ended, or
  - (ii) if it is abandoned or otherwise ceases to have effect.

(6) The reference in subsection (3)(b)(iii) to an application for relief is to an application for relief under—

section 661(3) or (4) (power of court to grant relief in case of acquisition of shares by innocent nominee), or

section 1157 (general power of court to grant relief in case of honest and reasonable conduct).

NOTES

Commencement: 1 October 2007 (applies to any provision made on or after that date; see the Companies Act 2006 (Commencement No 3, Consequential Amendments, Transitional Provisions and Savings) Order 2007,

SI 2007/2194, art 9, Sch 3, para 15).

[3669]

235 Qualifying pension scheme indemnity provision

(1) Section 232(2) (voidness of provisions for indemnifying directors) does not apply to qualifying pension scheme indemnity provision.

(2) Pension scheme indemnity provision means provision indemnifying a director of a company that is a trustee of an occupational pension scheme against liability incurred in connection with the company's activities as trustee of the scheme.

Such provision is qualifying pension scheme indemnity provision if the following requirements are met.

(3) The provision must not provide any indemnity against—

- (a) any liability of the director to pay—
  - (i) a fine imposed in criminal proceedings, or
  - (ii) a sum payable to a regulatory authority by way of a penalty in respect of non-compliance with any requirement of a regulatory nature (however arising); or
- (b) any liability incurred by the director in defending criminal proceedings in which he is convicted.

(4) The reference in subsection (3)(b) to a conviction is to the final decision in the proceedings.

(5) For this purpose—

- (a) a conviction becomes final—
  - (i) if not appealed against, at the end of the period for bringing an appeal, or
  - (ii) if appealed against, at the time when the appeal (or any further appeal) is disposed of; and
- (b) an appeal is disposed of—
  - (i) if it is determined and the period for bringing any further appeal has ended, or
  - (ii) if it is abandoned or otherwise ceases to have effect.

(6) In this section "occupational pension scheme" means an occupational pension scheme as defined in section 150(5) of the Finance Act 2004 (c 12) that is established under a trust.

NOTES

Commencement: 1 October 2007 (applies to any provision made on or after that date; see the Companies Act 2006 (Commencement No 3, Consequential Amendments, Transitional Provisions and Savings) Order 2007, SI 2007/2194, art 9, Sch 3, para 15).

236–828 *(Ss 236–239, ss 240–259 (Chs 8, 9), ss 260–828 (Pts 11–22) outside the scope of this work.)*

PART 23
DISTRIBUTIONS

829–840 *((Chs 1, 2) outside the scope of this work.)*

CHAPTER 3
SUPPLEMENTARY PROVISIONS

841, 842 *(Outside the scope of this work.)*

[3670]

843 Realised profits and losses of long-term insurance business

(1) The provisions of this section have effect for the purposes of this Part as it applies in relation to an authorised insurance company[, other than an insurance special purpose vehicle,] carrying on long-term business.

(2) An amount included in the relevant part of the company's balance sheet that—

- (a) represents a surplus in the fund or funds maintained by it in respect of its long-term business, and
- (b) has not been allocated to policy holders or, as the case may be, carried forward unappropriated in accordance with asset identification rules made under section 142(2) of the Financial Services and Markets Act 2000 (c 8),

is treated as a realised profit.

(3) For the purposes of subsection (2)—

- (a) the relevant part of the balance sheet is that part of the balance sheet that represents accumulated profit or loss;

(b) a surplus in the fund or funds maintained by the company in respect of its long-term business means an excess of the assets representing that fund or those funds over the liabilities of the company attributable to its long-term business, as shown by an actuarial investigation.

(4) A deficit in the fund or funds maintained by the company in respect of its long-term business is treated as a realised loss.

For this purpose a deficit in any such fund or funds means an excess of the liabilities of the company attributable to its long-term business over the assets representing that fund or those funds, as shown by an actuarial investigation.

(5) Subject to subsections (2) and (4), any profit or loss arising in the company's long-term business is to be left out of account.

(6) For the purposes of this section an "actuarial investigation" means an investigation made into the financial condition of an authorised insurance company in respect of its long-term business—

(a) carried out once in every period of twelve months in accordance with rules made under Part 10 of the Financial Services and Markets Act 2000, or

(b) carried out in accordance with a requirement imposed under section 166 of that Act,

by an actuary appointed as actuary to the company.

(7) In this section "long-term business" means business that consists of effecting or carrying out contracts of long-term insurance.

This definition must be read with section 22 of the Financial Services and Markets Act 2000, any relevant order under that section and Schedule 2 to that Act.

[(8) In this section "insurance special purpose vehicle" means a special purpose vehicle within the meaning of Article 2.1(p) of Directive 2005/68/EC of the European Parliament and of the Council of 16 November 2005 on reinsurance and amending Council Directives 73/239/EEC, 92/49/EEC as well as Directives 98/78/EC and 2002/83/EC.]

NOTES

Commencement: 6 April 2008 (applies to distributions made on or after 6 April 2008; ss 263–281 of the Companies Act 1985 Act continue to apply to distributions made before that date; see the Companies Act 2006 (Commencement No 5, Transitional Provisions and Savings) Order 2007, SI 2007/3495, art 9, Sch 4, Pt 1, para 33).

Sub-s (1): words in square brackets inserted by the Reinsurance Directive Regulations 2007, SI 2007/3253, reg 2(3), Sch 3, para 2(1)(a).

Sub-s (8): added by SI 2007/3253, reg 2(3), Sch 3, para 2(1)(b).

844–1157 *(Ss 844–853, ss 854–1157 (Pts 24–37) outside the scope of this work.)*

PART 38
COMPANIES: INTERPRETATION

1158–1162 *(Outside the scope of this work.)*

Other definitions

1163, 1164 *(Outside the scope of this work.)*

[3671]

1165 Meaning of "insurance company" and related expressions

(1) This section defines "insurance company", "authorised insurance company", "insurance group" and "insurance market activity" for the purposes of the Companies Acts.

(2) An "authorised insurance company" means a person (whether incorporated or not) who has permission under Part 4 of the Financial Services and Markets Act 2000 (c 8) to effect or carry out contracts of insurance.

(3) An "insurance company" means—

(a) an authorised insurance company, or

(b) any other person (whether incorporated or not) who—

(i) carries on insurance market activity, or

(ii) may effect or carry out contracts of insurance under which the benefits provided by that person are exclusively or primarily benefits in kind in the event of accident to or breakdown of a vehicle.

(4) Neither expression includes a friendly society within the meaning of the Friendly Societies Act 1992 (c 40).

(5) References to an insurance group are to a group where the parent company is an insurance company or where—

(a) the parent company's principal subsidiary undertakings are wholly or mainly insurance companies, and

(b) the parent company does not itself carry on any material business apart from the acquisition, management and disposal of interests in subsidiary undertakings.

"Group" here means a parent undertaking and its subsidiary undertakings.

(6) For the purposes of subsection (5)—

(a) a parent company's principal subsidiary undertakings are the subsidiary undertakings of the company whose results or financial position would principally affect the figures shown in the group accounts, and

(b) the management of interests in subsidiary undertakings includes the provision of services to such undertakings.

(7) "Insurance market activity" has the meaning given in section 316(3) of the Financial Services and Markets Act 2000.

(8) References in this section to contracts of insurance and to the effecting or carrying out of such contracts must be read with section 22 of that Act, any relevant order under that section and Schedule 2 to that Act.

NOTES

Commencement: 6 April 2008.

1166–1297 *(Ss 1166–1174, ss 1175–1297 (Pts 39–46) outside the scope of this work.)*

PART 47
FINAL PROVISIONS

[3672]

1298 Short title

The short title of this Act is the Companies Act 2006.

NOTES

Commencement: 8 November 2006.

[3673]

1299 Extent

Except as otherwise provided (or the context otherwise requires), the provisions of this Act extend to the whole of the United Kingdom.

NOTES

Commencement: 8 November 2006.

[3674]

1300 Commencement

(1) The following provisions come into force on the day this Act is passed—

(a)–(c) *(outside the scope of this work.)*

(d) this Part.

(2) The other provisions of this Act come into force on such day as may be appointed by order of the Secretary of State or the Treasury.

NOTES

Commencement: 8 November 2006.

Orders: the Companies Act 2006 (Commencement No 1, Transitional Provisions and Savings) Order 2006, SI 2006/3428; the Companies Act 2006 (Commencement No 2, Consequential Amendments, Transitional Provisions and Savings) Order 2007, SI 2007/1093; the Companies Act 2006 (Commencement No 3, Consequential Amendments, Transitional Provisions and Savings) Order 2007, SI 2007/2194; the Companies Act 2006 (Commencement No 4 and Commencement No 3 (Amendment)) Order 2007, SI 2007/2607; the Companies Act 2006 (Commencement No 5, Transitional Provisions and Savings) Order 2007, SI 2007/3495; the Companies Act 2006 (Commencement No 7, Transitional Provisions and Savings) Order 2008, SI 2008/1886; the Companies Act 2006 (Commencement No 8, Transitional Provisions and Savings) Order 2008, SI 2008/2860.

(Schs 1–9 outside the scope of this work.)

SCHEDULE 10

RECOGNISED SUPERVISORY BODIES

(Pt 1 outside the scope of this work.)

PART 2
REQUIREMENTS FOR RECOGNITION OF A SUPERVISORY BODY

[3675]–[4000]

6–16A. . . .

Meeting of claims arising out of audit work

17.—(1) The body must have adequate rules or arrangements designed to ensure that persons eligible under its rules for appointment as a statutory auditor take such steps as may reasonably be expected of them to secure that they are able to meet claims against them arising out of statutory audit work.

(2) This may be achieved by professional indemnity insurance or other appropriate arrangements.

18–20A. . . .

NOTES

Commencement: 6 April 2008.

Paras 6–16A, 18–20A: outside the scope of this work.

(Sch 10, Pt 3, Schs 11–16 outside the scope of this work.)

PART IV
STATUTORY INSTRUMENTS

INDUSTRIAL ASSURANCE (INDIVIDUAL TRANSFER) REGULATIONS 1928

(SR & O 1928/580)

NOTES

Made: 26 July 1928.
Authority: Industrial Assurance Act 1923, s 43.
Commencement: 1 September 1928.

[4001]

1 The Industrial Assurance (Individual Transfer) Regulations, 1923, dated 11th December, 1923, are hereby rescinded.

[4002]

2 The form of consent and document annexed thereto required by Section 26 of the above-named Act shall be that set out in the Schedule hereto.

[4003]

3 If the Society or Company to which the transfer is to be made requires any information to enable it properly to complete the said form, it shall apply to the Society or Company from which the transfer is to be made, and it shall be the duty of the latter Society or Company to supply such information, on payment, if demanded, of a sum not exceeding [5p] for each policy in respect of which such information is required.

NOTES

Sum in square brackets substituted by virtue of the Decimal Currency Act 1969, s 10(1).

[4004]

4 These Regulations may be cited as the Industrial Assurance (Individual Transfer) Regulations, 1928, and shall come into operation on September 1st, 1928.

SCHEDULE
INDUSTRIAL ASSURANCE ACT 1923

Section 26

Prescribed Form of Consent and Annexed Document

[4005]

Name of the Society or Company which issued the existing* policy . . . .

Policy No . . . . Date of policy . . . .

Name and address of the collector or agent to whom the last premium under the policy was paid . . . .
. . . .

STATEMENT OF THE TERMS OF AND RIGHTS UNDER THE ABOVE-MENTIONED POLICY AND THE PROPOSED NEW POLICY RESPECTIVELY

Particulars as to which information must be given	Information with regard to existing* policy	Information with regard to proposed new policy
(1) Name of member or person assured	(1)	(1)
(2) Name of the person whose life is assured	(2)	(2)
(3) Amount of premium	(3)	(3)
(4) Interval at which premiums are payable	(4)	(4)
(5) Ultimate sum or sums assured (including any bonus now attaching)—	(5)	(5)
(a) on death	(a)	(a)
(b) on other event or events	(b)	(b)
(6) The date at which full benefit is payable	(6)	(6)
(7) Event or events other than death, on which the said sum or sums become payable	(7)	(7)
(8) Whether the policy is with or without profits	(8)	(8)

(9) Any other benefits, including relief from premiums	(9)	(9)
(10) The earliest date on which—	(10)	(10)
(a) a free policy	(a)	(a)
(b) a surrender value	(b)	(b)
can be claimed, and the amount		

* "Existing" policy includes a policy discontinued or allowed to be forfeited with intent to effect a transfer within the meaning of the section.

The consideration, if any, which has been or is to be paid for the transfer . . . .

The full names and address of any person to whom such consideration has been or will be paid . . . .

This document is furnished by the . . . .

. . . .

the society or company by which the new policy is to be issued.

Signed on behalf of the society or company.

Signature . . . .
Description . . . .
Date . . . .

CONSENT TO TRANSFER

I, the undersigned, being the member or person** assured by the existing policy above described, have read the above statement containing the terms of and rights under the said policy and the proposed new policy. I understand that I shall cease to have any rights whatever under my existing policy and I do hereby give my consent to the transfer.

	Signed by the said . . . . }	
	in the presence of . . . . }	Signature . . . .
Witness's	Signature . . . . }	Address . . . .
"	Address . . . . }	Date . . . .
"	Occupation or Description . . . . }	

** If the member or person assured is an infant this consent must be signed by the parent or other guardian and a statement of the relationship added.

INDUSTRIAL ASSURANCE (PREMIUM RECEIPT BOOKS) REGULATIONS 1948

(SI 1948/2770)

NOTES

Made: 17 December 1948.

Authority: Industrial Assurance and Friendly Societies Act 1948, s 8(2) (repealed by the Financial Services and Markets Act 2000, ss 416(1)(a), 432(3), Sch 22; for savings and modifications in relation to existing policies of industrial assurance see the Financial Services and Markets Act 2000 (Consequential Amendments and Savings) (Industrial Assurance) Order 2001, SI 2001/3647, art 3(2), Sch 1, Pt II, paras 19, 20.) These Regulations now have effect (except in relation to the Channel Islands) as rules made under the Financial Services and Markets Act 2000, s 138 at **[111]**.

Commencement: 5 January 1949.

[4006]

1 A premium receipt book provided for use in respect of any policy or policies effected on or after the 5th day of July, 1949, shall contain the following particulars in respect of each such policy to which the book relates:—

(a) the number (if any) and date of the policy;

[(b) the name of the life assured as stated in the proposal or the life assured's present name, and his age as stated in the proposal or such corrected age as may have been entered in the book with the authority of the owner of the policy;

(c) the name of the proposer as stated in the proposal or the proposer's present name;] and

(d) the amount of the premium and the interval at which it is payable.

NOTES

Paras (b), (c): substituted by the Industrial Assurance (Premium Receipt Books) (Amendment) Regulations 1961, SI 1961/597, reg 1.

[4007]

2 An entry relating to a policy proposed by any person and effected on or after the 5th day of July, 1949, shall not be made in any book containing an entry (other than an entry made in accordance with the proviso to this Regulation) relating to any policy not proposed by that person:

Provided that this Regulation shall not prohibit the making in a book in respect of any policy proposed by that person of an entry relating to a policy the proposer of which is a child, stepchild or grandchild of that person and is under sixteen years of age when the entry is made, or is the spouse [or civil partner] of that person.

NOTES

Words in square brackets inserted by the Civil Partnership Act 2004 (Amendments to Subordinate Legislation) Order 2005, SI 2005/2114, art 2(16), Sch 16, Pt 3, para 13.

[4008]

3 Any collector who receives a payment in respect of a policy or policies shall enter in a appropriate book the amount of the payment and shall initial the entry.

[4009]

4— (1) An entry relating to a policy on which none of the premium payments is in arrear shall not be made in a book relating to a policy on which a premium payment is in arrear, unless the book contains a previous entry relating to the first-mentioned policy.

(2) An entry relating to a policy on which a premium payment is in arrear shall not be made in a book relating to a policy or policies on none of which a premium payment is in arrear, unless the book contains a previous entry relating to the first-mentioned policy.

(3) For the purposes of this Regulation two books, one of which has been provided to replace or continue the other, shall be deemed to be the same book, and in the case of any books divided into sections containing separate entries in respect of one or more policies, each such section shall be deemed to be a separate book.

[4010]

5 A Society or a Company or a collector shall not cause or permit a premium receipt book to be provided or any entry to be made therein which does not comply with any of the provisions of these Regulations.

[4011]

6— (1) The Interpretation Act, 1889, shall apply to the interpretation of these Regulations as it applies to the interpretation of an Act of Parliament.

(2) In these Regulations—

(a) "premium receipt book" or "book" means a premium receipt book provided for the purposes of Section 8(1) of the Industrial Assurance and Friendly Societies Act, 1948;

(b) "policy" means a policy of industrial assurance;

(c) "society" and "company" means a collecting society and an industrial assurance company respectively;

(d) "proposer" includes a person on whose behalf a policy has been proposed and does not include a person who has proposed a policy on behalf of another, and the word "proposed" shall be construed accordingly; and

(e) "name" means surname together with the initial letter or letters of any christian name or names.

[(f) "the amount of the premium" in relation to a policy to which the prescribed scheme, or an approved scheme which provides for payment of net premiums, applies means the amount of the net premium; and

(g) "the prescribed scheme", "an approved scheme" and "net premium" have the meanings assigned in paragraph (1) of regulation 2 of the Industrial Assurance (Life Assurance Premium Relief) Regulations 1977.]

(3) These Regulations may be cited as the Industrial Assurance (Premium Receipt Books) Regulations, 1948, and shall come into operation on the 5th day of January, 1949.

NOTES

Para (2): sub-paras (f), (g) added by the Friendly Societies (Life Assurance Premium Relief) Regulations 1977, SI 1977/1353, reg 2.

MOTOR VEHICLES (INTERNATIONAL MOTOR INSURANCE CARD) REGULATIONS 1971

(SI 1971/792)

NOTES

Made: 10 May 1971.

Authority: Road Traffic Act 1960, ss 211, 215 (repealed), insofar as they were made under ss 211, 215 of the 1960 Act, they then took effect as if made under the Road Traffic Act 1972, ss 153, 157 (repealed), and now have effect as if made under the Road Traffic Act 1988, ss 156, 160; Vehicles (Excise) Act 1971, s 37(1) (repealed), insofar as they were made under s 37(1) of the 1971 Act, they now have effect as if made under the Vehicle Excise and Registration Act 1994, s 57(1).

Commencement: 10 June 1971.

ARRANGEMENT OF REGULATIONS

1 Title and commencement . . . . . [4012]
3 Interpretation . . . . . [4013]
4 Validity of insurance card . . . . . [4014]
5 Third party risks arising out of the use of motor vehicles by visitors . . . . . [4015]
6 . . . . . [4016]
8 Production of insurance card on application for excise license . . . . . [4017]
10 Special provision for motor vehicles from Northern Ireland . . . . . [4018]

SCHEDULE:

Schedule 1—Particulars to be shown in pages of Insurance Card . . . . . [4019]

[4012]

1 Title and commencement

These Regulations may be cited as the Motor Vehicles (International Motor Insurance Card) Regulations 1971 and shall come into operation on the 10th June 1971.

2 *(Revokes the Motor Vehicles (International Motor Insurance Card) Regulations 1969, SI 1969/668.)*

[4013]

3 Interpretation

(1) In these Regulations—

"the Act" means the Road Traffic Act 1960;

"authorised insurer" has the same meaning as in Part VI of the Act;

"British Bureau" means the Motor Insurers' Bureau incorporated under the Companies Act 1929, and having its registered office at Aldermary House, Queen Street, London, EC4;

. . .

"Foreign Bureau" means a central organisation set up by motor insurers in any country outside the United Kingdom, the Isle of Man and the Channel Islands for the purpose of giving effect to international arrangements for the insurance of motorists against third-party risks when entering countries where insurance against such risks is compulsory, and with which organisation the British Bureau has entered into such an arrangement;

"hired motor vehicle" means a motor vehicle which is:—

(a) designed for private use and with seats for not more than eight persons excluding the driver, and

(b) specified in an insurance card, and

(c) last brought into Great Britain by a person making only a temporary stay therein, and

(d) owned and let for hire by a person whose business includes the letting of vehicles for hire and whose principal place of business is outside the United Kingdom;

"hiring visitor" means a person to whom a hired motor vehicle is let on hire, who is making only a temporary stay in Great Britain and is named as the insured or user of that vehicle in the insurance card in which that vehicle is specified;

["insurance card" means an international motor insurance card issued under the authority of a Foreign Bureau or of the British Bureau which is green in colour and—

(a) is either in English or a foreign language containing the particulars specified in, and set out in two pages as shown in, Schedule 1 to these Regulations; or

(b) until 31st December 1977, is either in English or a foreign language in the form specified in Schedule 2 of these Regulations;]

"the Secretary of State" means the [Secretary of State for the Environment, Transport and the Regions];

"trade licence" has the same meaning as in the Vehicles (Excise) Act 1971;

"visitor" means a person bringing a motor vehicle into Great Britain, making only a temporary stay therein and named in an insurance card as the insured or user of the vehicle, and includes a hiring visitor who brings a hired motor vehicle into Great Britain, but no other hiring visitor.

(2) Any reference in these Regulations to any provision in an Act of Parliament or in subordinate legislation shall be construed as a reference to that provision as amended by any other such provision.

(3) The Interpretation Act 1889 shall apply for the interpretation of these Regulations as it applies for the interpretation of an Act of Parliament and as if for the purposes of section 38 of that Act these Regulations were an Act of Parliament and the Regulations revoked by Regulation 2 of these Regulations were an Act of Parliament thereby repealed.

NOTES

Para (2): definitions omitted revoked, and definition "insurance card" substituted, by the Motor Vehicles (International Motor Insurance Card) (Amendment) Regulations 1977, SI 1977/895, reg 3; in definition "the Secretary of State" words in square brackets substituted by virtue of the Secretary of State for the Environment, Transport and the Regions Order 1997, SI 1997/2971, art 6.

Road Traffic Act 1960, Pt VI: see now Road Traffic Act 1988, Pt VI.

Interpretation Act 1889: see now the Interpretation Act 1978.

[4014]

4 Validity of insurance card

(1) An insurance card shall be valid for the purposes of these Regulations only if—

(a) the motor vehicle specified in the card is brought into the United kingdom during the period of validity so specified;

(b) the application of the card in Great Britain is indicated thereon;

(c) all relevant information provided for in the card has been inscribed therein;

(d) the card has been duly signed by the visitor, by the insurer named in the card and, in the case of a hired motor vehicle, by every hiring visitor who is named in the card as the insured or user thereof; and

(e) in the case of a card [in the form specified in] Schedule 2 to these Regulations, the card bears on page 1 thereof the name of the Foreign Bureau or the British Bureau, as the case may be, under whose authority the card was issued.

(2) The information required to be inscribed in paragraphs 2, 7 and 8 in the page of the card shown in Schedule 1 to these Regulations and marked "original" and in paragraphs 2, 3 and 8 on page 3 of the card in the form in Schedule 2 to these Regulations is:—

(a) in the said paragraph 2, the name of the Foreign Bureau or the British Bureau, as the case may be, under whose authority the card was issued; and

(b) in the said paragraph 3 or 7, the name and address of the insured visitor and of every person who is, as respects a hired motor vehicle, a hiring visitor; and

(c) in the said paragraph 8, the name and address of the insurer authorised to issue the card by the Foreign Bureau or the British Bureau, as the case may be, and by whom the card was issued.

NOTES

Para (1): words in square brackets in sub-para (e) substituted by the Motor Vehicles (International Motor Insurance Card) (Amendment) Regulations 1977, SI 1977/895, reg 4.

[4015]

5 Third-party risks arising out of the use of motor vehicles by visitors

(1) As respects the use on a road of a motor vehicle specified in a valid insurance card, being use by the visitor to whom the card was issued, or by any hiring visitor named therein, or by any other person on the order or with the permission of the said visitor or of any such hiring visitor, section 201 of the Act shall have effect as though the said card were a policy of insurance complying with the requirements of and having effect for the purposes of Part VI of the Act in relation to such use;

Provided that where the said motor vehicle remains in the United Kingdom after the expiry of the period of validity specified in the card, then as respects any period whilst it so remains during which the vehicle is in Great Britain the said card shall not be regarded as having ceased to be in force for the purposes of the said section 201 by reason only of effluxion of the period of validity specified in the card.

For the purposes of this paragraph a motor vehicle shall be deemed not to have left the United Kingdom whilst it is only in transit between different parts of the United Kingdom.

(2) Any reference in this Regulation and in [the next following Regulation] to the use on a road of a motor vehicle shall not include any use of the vehicle for the purpose of delivering it to or for the visitor at some place other than the place of entry of the vehicle into Great Britain, which is authorised under a trade licence.

NOTES

Para (2): words in square brackets substituted by the Motor Vehicles (International Motor Insurance Card) (Amendment) Regulations 1977, SI 1977/895, reg 5.

Section 201 of the Act: see now the Road Traffic Act 1988, s 143 at **[3397]**.

[4016]

6— (1) For the purposes of sections 226, 230 and 231 of the Act, a valid insurance card shall have effect as though it were a certificate of insurance issued by an authorised insurer and in relation to any claim in respect of any such liability as is required to be covered by a policy of insurance under section 203 of the Act and arising out of the use on a road of a motor vehicle specified in such a card by the visitor to whom it was issued, by any hiring visitor named therein, or by any other person on the order or with the permission of the said visitor or of any such hiring visitor, the person against whom the claim is made shall in lieu of making the statement and giving the particulars referred to in section 209(1) of the Act, give to the person making the claim, on his demand, the serial letter or letters (if any) and serial number shown in the card, the name of the Bureau under whose authority it was issued and the name and address of the person specified therein as the insured.

(2) Any person making or intending to make any such claim as is mentioned in the preceding paragraph of this Regulation shall give notice of the claim in writing to the British Bureau as soon as practicable after the happening of the event out of which the claim arose specifying the nature of the claim and against whom it is made or intended to be made.

(3) . . .

NOTES

Para (3): revoked by the Motor Vehicles (International Motor Insurance Card) (Amendment) Regulations 1977, SI 1977/895, reg 5(ii).

Sections 203, 209(1), 226, 230 and 231 of the Act: see now the Road Traffic Act 1988, ss 145, 154(1), 165, 170(5)–(7), 171 respectively.

7 *(Revoked by the Motor Vehicles (International Motor Insurance Card) (Amendment) Regulations 1977, SI 1977/895, reg 5(ii).)*

[4017]

8 Production of insurance card on application for excise licence

Any visitor or hiring visitor applying for a licence under the Vehicles (Excise) Act 1971 for a motor vehicle specified in a valid insurance card in which he is named as the insured may, during the period of validity specified in the card, in lieu of producing to the licensing authority such evidence as is required by Regulation 9 of the Motor Vehicles (Third Party Risks) Regulations 1961, as amended, produce such a card to the licensing authority.

NOTES

Vehicles (Excise) Act 1971: see now the Vehicle Excise and Registration Act 1994.

Motor Vehicles (Third Party Risks) Regulations 1961, SI 1961/1465, reg 9: see now the Motor Vehicles (Third Party Risks) Regulations 1972, SI 1972/1217, reg 9.

9 *(Revoked by the Motor Vehicles (International Motor Insurance Card) (Amendment) Regulations 1977, SI 1977/895, reg 5(ii).)*

[4018]

10 Special provision for motor vehicles from Northern Ireland

In the case of a motor vehicle brought from Northern Ireland into Great Britain by a person making only a temporary stay in Great Britain, a policy of insurance or a security which complies with the Road Traffic Act (Northern Ireland) 1970 and which covers the driving of the motor vehicle in Great Britain and any certificate of insurance or certificate of security issued in pursuance of that Act and the Regulations made thereunder in respect of such policy or security shall have effect as a policy of insurance or a security or a certificate of insurance or certificate of security respectively for the purposes of Part VI of the Act, and of the Motor Vehicles (Third Party Risks) Regulations 1961, as amended.

NOTES

Road Traffic Act (Northern Ireland) 1970: repealed with savings by the Road Traffic (Northern Ireland) Order 1981, SI 1981/154.

Motor Vehicles (Third Party Risks) Regulations 1961, SI 1961/1465: see now the Motor Vehicles (Third Party Risks) Regulations 1972, SI 1972/1217.

SCHEDULES

[SCHEDULE 1

PARTICULARS TO BE SHOWN IN PAGES OF INSURANCE CARD

(See Regulation 3)

[4019]

ORIGINAL

1. INTERNATIONAL MOTOR INSURANCE CARD

2. ISSUED UNDER THE AUTHORITY OF (NATIONAL INSURER'S BUREAU)

3. VALID						4. Serial and Policy Numbers
FROM			TO			
Day	Month	Year	Day	Month	Year	
(Both Dates Inclusive)						
5. Registration Number (or if none) Chassis or engine number						6. Category and make of Vehicle*

(Cancel Country inapplicable)								A	B	L	NL	CH	CS	D	DK	N	S	SF	E	F	GB
GR	H	I	IL	IRL	IS	MA	P	PL	R	TN	TR	YU									

7. Name and Address of Insured (or User of the Vehicle)

8. This Card has been Issued by— (Name and Address of Insurer)	9. Signature of Insurer

* For details of Letter-Code for Category of Vehicle, see next page.

INTERNATIONAL MOTOR INSURANCE CARD
CARTE INTERNATIONALE D'ASSURANCE AUTOMOBILE

(1) In each country visited, the Bureau of that country assumes, in respect of the use of the vehicle referred to herein, the liability of an Insurer in accordance with the laws relating to compulsory insurance in that country.

(2) After the date of expiry of this Card, liability is assumed by the Bureau of the country visited, if so required by the law of such country or by any agreement with its Government. In such case, the within-mentioned insured undertakes to pay the premium due for the duration of the stay after the date for which the Insurance Card is valid has passed.

(3) I, the within-mentioned insured, hereby authorise the Motor Insurer's Bureau and the Bureaux of any mentioned countries, to which it may delegate such powers, to accept service of legal proceedings, to handle and eventually settle, on my behalf, any claim for damages in respect of liability to third parties required to be covered under the compulsory insurance laws of the country or countries specified herein, which may arise from the use of the vehicle in that country (those countries).

(4) Signature of the Insured	(5) For visitors to Great Britain and Northern Ireland only. Signature of any other persons who may use the vehicle.
. . . .	. . . .

(This Insurance Card is only valid when signed by the Insured).

Cards applicable to the following country must contain detachable copies of the form on the preceding page—

Switzerland

***CATEGORY OF VEHICLE (CODE)**

A. CAR	C. LORRY OR TRACTOR	E. BUS
B. MOTORCYCLE	D. CYCLE FITTED WITH AUXILIARY ENGINE	F. TRAILER]

NOTES

Substituted by the Motor Vehicles (International Motor Insurance Card) (Amendment) Regulations 1977, SI 1977/895, reg 6.

(Sch 2 spent.)

MOTOR VEHICLES (THIRD PARTY RISKS) REGULATIONS 1972

(SI 1972/1217)

NOTES

Made: 1 August 1972.

Authority: Road Traffic Act 1972, ss 147, 157, 162 (repealed), insofar as they were made under ss 147, 157, 162 of the 1972 Act, they now have effect as if made under the Road Traffic Act 1988, ss 147, 160(1), (2), 165; Vehicles (Excise) Act 1971, s 37 (repealed), insofar as they were made under s 37 of the 1971 Act, they now have effect as if made under the Vehicle Excise and Registration Act 1994, s 57.

Commencement: 1 November 1972.

ARRANGEMENT OF REGULATIONS

1 Citation and commencement . . . . . [4020]
3 Temporary use of existing forms . . . . . [4021]
4 Interpretation . . . . . [4022]
5 Issue of certificates of insurance or security . . . . . [4023]
6 . . . . . [4024]
7 Production of evidence as alternatives to certificates . . . . . [4025]
8 . . . . . [4026]
9 Production of evidence of insurance or security on application for excise licences . . . . . [4027]
10 Keeping of records by companies . . . . . [4028]

Part IV Statutory Instruments

11	Notification to the Secretary of State of ineffective policies or securities	[4029]
12	Return of certificates to issuing company	[4030]
13	Issue of fresh certificates	[4031]

SCHEDULE

Part 1	[4032]
Part 2	[4033]

[4020]
1 Commencement and citation

These Regulations shall come into operation on 1st November 1972 and may be cited as the Motor Vehicles (Third Party Risks) Regulations 1972.

2 *(Revokes the Motor Vehicles (Third Party Risks) Regulations 1961, SI 1961/1465 and the Motor Vehicles (Third Party Risks) (Amendment) Regulations 1969, SI 1969/1733.)*

[4021]
3 Temporary use of existing forms

Nothing in these Regulations shall affect the validity of any certificate which has been issued before these Regulations came into force in a form prescribed by the Motor Vehicles (Third Party Risks) Regulations 1961, as amended by the Motor Vehicles (Third Party Risks) (Amendment) Regulations 1969, as in force immediately before the coming into operation of these Regulations, and any certificate in such a form may continue to be issued until the expiration of three years from the coming into force of these Regulations.

[4022]
4 Interpretation

(1) In these Regulations, unless the context otherwise requires, the following expressions have the meanings hereby respectively assigned to them:—

"the Act" means the Road Traffic Act 1972;

"company" means an authorised insurer within the meaning of Part VI of the Act or a body of persons by whom a security may be given in pursuance of the said Part VI;

["Motor Insurers' Bureau" means the company referred to in section 145(5) of the Road Traffic Act 1988;]

"motor vehicle" has the meaning assigned to it by sections 190, 192 and 193 of the Act, but excludes any invalid carriage, tramcar or trolley vehicle to which Part VI of the Act does not apply;

"policy" means a policy of insurance in respect of third party risks arising out of the use of motor vehicles which complies with the requirements of Part VI of the Act and includes a covering note;

"security" means a security in respect of third party risks arising out of the use of motor vehicles which complies with the requirements of Part VI of the Act;

"specified body" means—

(a) any of the local authorities referred to in paragraph (a) of section 144(2) of the Act; or

(b) a Passenger Transport Executive established under an order made under section 9 of the Transport Act 1968, or a subsidiary of that Executive, being an Executive or subsidiary to whose vehicles section 144(2)(a) of the Act has been applied; or

(c) the London Transport Executive or a wholly-owned subsidiary of that Executive referred to in paragraph (e) of section 144(2) of the Act.

(2) Any reference in these Regulations to a certificate in Form A, B, C, D, E or F shall be construed as a reference to a certificate in the form so headed and set out in Part 1 of the Schedule to these Regulations which has been duly made and completed subject to and in accordance with the provisions set out in Part 2 of the said Schedule.

(3) Any reference in these Regulations to any enactment shall be construed as a reference to that enactment as amended by any subsequent enactment.

(4) The Interpretation Act 1889 shall apply for the interpretation of these Regulations as it applies for the interpretation of an Act of Parliament, and as if for the purposes of section 38 of that Act these Regulations were an Act of Parliament and the Regulations revoked by Regulation 2 of these Regulations were Acts of Parliament thereby repealed.

NOTES

Para (1): definition "Motor Insurers' Bureau" inserted by the Motor Vehicles (Third Party Risks) (Amendment) Regulations 2001, SI 2001/2266, reg 2(1), (2).

Road Traffic Act 1972, ss 144(2)(a), 190, 192, 193: see now the Road Traffic Act 1988, ss 144(2)(a), 185, 188, 189 respectively.
Interpretation Act 1889: see now the Interpretation Act 1978.

[4023]
5 Issue of certificates of insurance or security

(1) A company shall issue to every holder of a security or of a policy other than a covering note issued by the company:—

(a) in the case of a policy or security relating to one or more specified vehicles a certificate of insurance in Form A or a certificate of security in Form D in respect of each such vehicle;

(b) in the case of a policy or security relating to vehicles other than specified vehicles such number of certificates in Form B or Form D as may be necessary for the purpose of complying with the requirements of section 162(1) of the Act and of these Regulations as to the production of evidence that a motor vehicle is not being driven in contravention of section 143 of the Act—

[Provided that where a security is intended to cover the use of more than ten motor vehicles at one time the company by whom it was issued may issue one certificate only and the holder of the security may issue duplicate copies of such certificate duly authenticated by him.]

(2) Notwithstanding the foregoing provisions of this Regulation, where as respects third party risks a policy or security relating to a specified vehicle extends also to the driving by the holder of other motor vehicles, not being specified vehicles, the certificate may be in Form A or Form D, as the case may be, containing a statement in either case that the policy or security extends to such driving of other motor vehicles. Where such a certificate is issued by a company they may, and shall in accordance with a demand made to them by the holder, issue to him a further such certificate or a certificate in Form B.

(3) Every policy in the form of a covering note issued by a company shall have printed thereon or on the back thereof a certificate of insurance in Form C.

NOTES

Para (1): words in square brackets substituted by the Motor Vehicles (Third Party Risks) (Amendment) Regulations 1997, SI 1997/97, reg 2(1), (2).
Sections 143 and 162(1) of the Act: see now the Road Traffic Act 1988, s 143 at **[3397]**, and s 165(1)–(3), respectively.

[4024]
6 Every certificate of insurance or certificate of security shall be issued not later than four days after the date on which the policy or security to which it relates is issued or renewed.

[4025]
7 Production of evidence as alternatives to certificates

The following evidence that a motor vehicle is not or was not being driven in contravention of section 143 of the Act may be produced in pursuance of section 162 of the Act as an alternative to the production of a certificate of insurance or a certificate of security:—

(1) a duplicate copy of a certificate of security issued in accordance with the proviso to sub-paragraph (b) of paragraph (1) of Regulation 5 of these Regulations;

(2) in the case of a motor vehicle of which the owner has for the time being deposited with the Accountant-General of the Supreme Court [the sum for the time being specified in section 144(1) of the Road Traffic Act 1988], a certificate in Form E signed by the owner of the motor vehicle or by some person authorised by him in that behalf that such sum is on deposit;

(3) in the case of a motor vehicle owned by a specified body, a police authority or the Receiver for the metropolitan police district, a certificate in Form F signed by some person authorised in that behalf by such specified body, police authority or Receiver as the case may be that the said motor vehicle is owned by the said specified body, police authority or Receiver.

[(4) in the case of a vehicle normally based [in the territory other than the United Kingdom and Gibraltar of a member State of the Communities or of [Austria, Czechoslovakia, Finland, the German Democratic Republic, Hungary, Norway, Sweden or Switzerland]], a document issued by the insurer of the vehicle which indicates the name of the insurer, the number or other identifying particulars of the insurance policy issued in respect of the vehicle and the period of the insurance cover. In this paragraph the territory of the state in which a vehicle is normally based is—

(a) the territory of the state in which the vehicle is registered, or

(b) in cases where no registration is required for the type of vehicle, but the vehicle bears an insurance plate or distinguishing sign analogous to a registration plate, the territory of the state in which the insurance plate or the sign is issued, or

(c) in cases where neither registration plate nor insurance plate nor distinguishing sign is required for the type of vehicle, the territory of the state in which the keeper of the vehicle is permanently resident.]

NOTES

Para (2): words in square brackets substituted by the Motor Vehicles (Third-Party Risks) (Amendment) Regulations 1992, SI 1992/1283, reg 2(a).

Para (4): added by the Motor Vehicles (Third Party Risks) (Amendment) Regulations 1973, SI 1973/1821, reg 2; words in first (outer) pair of square brackets substituted by the Motor Vehicles (Third-Party Risks) (Amendment) Regulations 1974, SI 1974/792, reg 2; words in second (inner) pair of square brackets substituted by the Motor Vehicles (Third Party Risks) (Amendment) (No 2) Regulations 1974, SI 1974/2187, reg 2.

Sections 143 and 162 of the Act: see now the Road Traffic Act 1988, s 143 at **[3397]**, and s 165 respectively.

[4026]

8 Any certificate issued in accordance with paragraph (2) or (3) of the preceding Regulation shall be destroyed by the owner of the vehicle to which it relates before the motor vehicle is sold or otherwise disposed of.

[4027]

9 Production of evidence of insurance or security on application for excise licences

(1) Any person applying for a vehicle licence under the Vehicles (Excise) Act 1971 shall, except as hereinafter provided and subject to the provisions of Regulation 8 of the Motor Vehicles (International Motor Insurance Card) Regulations 1971, produce to the Secretary of State either:—

(a) a certificate of insurance, certificate of security or duplicate copy of a certificate of security issued in accordance with these Regulations indicating that on the date when the licence comes into operation there will be in force the necessary policy or the necessary security in relation to the user of the motor vehicle by the applicant or by other persons on his order or with his permission and such further evidence as may be necessary to establish that the certificate relates to such user; or

(b) in the case where the motor vehicle is one of more than ten motor vehicles owned by the same person in respect of which a policy or policies of insurance have been obtained by him from the same authorised insurer, a statement duly authenticated by the authorised insurer to the effect that on the date when the licence becomes operative an insurance policy which complies with Part VI of the Act will be in force in relation to the user of the motor vehicle; or

(c) evidence that section 143 of the Act does not apply to the motor vehicle at a time when it is being driven under the owner's control, in accordance with the following provisions—

(i) in the case of a motor vehicle of which the owner has for the time being deposited with the Accountant-General of the Supreme Court [the sum for the time being specified in section 144(1) of the Road Traffic Act 1988], a certificate in Form E signed by the owner of the motor vehicle or by some person authorised by him in that behalf that such sum is on deposit;

(ii) in the case of a motor vehicle owned by a specified body, a police authority or by the Receiver for the metropolitan police district, a certificate in Form F signed by some person authorised in that behalf by such specified body, police authority or Receiver as the case may be that the vehicle in respect of which the application for a licence is made is owned by the said specified body, police authority or Receiver.

(2) A person engaged in the business of letting motor vehicles on hire shall not, when applying for a licence under the Vehicles (Excise) Act 1971, be required to comply with the provisions of paragraph (1) of this Regulation if the motor vehicle in respect of which the licence is applied for is intended to be used solely for the purpose of being let on hire and driven by the person by whom the motor vehicle is hired or by persons under his control.

[(3) A person shall not, when applying for a licence under the Vehicle Excise and Registration Act 1994, be required to comply with the provisions of paragraph (1) of this regulation if–

(a) the motor vehicle in respect of which the licence is applied for is part of a fleet of not less than 250 motor vehicles owned by one person;

(b) the person who applies for the licence manages the fleet of motor vehicles on behalf of the owner of the fleet under a contract, and

(c) the contract under which the person manages the fleet contains a requirement that all the motor vehicles in the fleet be insured in accordance with the Road Traffic Act 1988.]

[(4) A person applying for a vehicle licence for a vehicle under the Vehicle Excise and Registration Act 1994 shall not be required to comply with the provisions of paragraph (1) if—

(a) on the date when the licence is to come into operation there will be in force the necessary policy in relation to the use of the vehicle by the applicant or by other persons on his order or with his permission;

(b) the policy has been issued by an insurer which has entered into an agreement with the Secretary of State for the purposes of this paragraph of this regulation;

(c) in pursuance of that agreement the insurer has either—

(i) made available for inspection by the Secretary of State an electronic data base maintained by it, on which there are recorded sufficient particulars of the policy to enable the Secretary of State to satisfy himself that condition (a) is satisfied; or

(ii) confirmed to the Secretary of State that condition (a) is satisfied.]

NOTES

Para (1): words in square brackets in sub-para (c) substituted by the Motor Vehicles (Third Party Risks) (Amendment) Regulations 1992, SI 1992/1283, reg 2(a).

Para (3): added by the Motor Vehicles (Third Party Risks) (Amendment) Regulations 1997, SI 1997/97, reg 2(1), (3).

Para (4): added by the Motor Vehicles (Third Party Risks) (Amendment) Regulations 1999, SI 1999/2392, regs 2, 3.

Vehicles (Excise) Act 1971: see now the Vehicle Excise and Registration Act 1994.

Pt VI and s 143 of the 1972 Act: see now the Road Traffic Act 1988, Pt VI and s 143 at **[3397]**, respectively.

[4028]

10 Keeping of records by companies

[(1) Every company by whom a policy or security is issued must keep a record of the following particulars relating to that policy or security and which are either contained therein or specified in a certificate of insurance or security issued in respect thereof—

(a) the number of the policy or security;

(b) the name and address of the person to whom the policy or security is issued;

(c) either—

(i) the name of every person whose liability is covered by the policy or security, or

(ii) (where it is not reasonably possible for the company to keep a record of those names) a description of the persons whose liability is covered by the policy or security;

(d) in respect of vehicles the use of which is covered by the policy or security—

(i) the registration number of every vehicle specifically identified by that number in the policy or security (a "specified vehicle"), and

(ii) a description of every other vehicle or class of vehicles which are identified in the policy or security other than by reference to a registration number;

(e) a description of every specified vehicle sufficient to enable it to be identified by a police officer;

(f) the date on which the policy or security comes into force and the date on which it expires;

(g) in the case of a policy, the conditions subject to which the person or persons whose liability is covered will be indemnified by the insurer;

(h) in the case of a security, the conditions subject to which the undertaking by the giver of the security will be implemented.]

(2) Every specified body shall keep a record of the motor vehicles owned by them in respect of which a policy or a security has not been obtained, and of any certificates issued by them under these Regulations in respect of such motor vehicles, and of the withdrawal or destruction of any such certificates.

(3) Any person who has deposited and keeps deposited with the Accountant-General of the Supreme Court [the sum for the time being specified in section 144(1) of the Road Traffic Act 1988] shall keep a record of the motor vehicles owned by him and of any certificates issued by him or on his behalf under these Regulations in respect of such motor vehicles and of the withdrawal or destruction of any such certificates.

[(4) Records which are required to be kept under paragraph (1) shall be preserved by the company keeping them for a period of seven years commencing on the expiry of the relevant policy or security.

(5) Every company, specified body and other person required by this regulation to keep records—

(a) shall furnish, without charge, to the Secretary of State or a chief officer of police upon request any particulars contained in those records, and

(b) may provide copies of those records to the Motor Insurers' Bureau or, if the Bureau so requests, to a subsidiary company nominated by it but where copies are provided they must be provided in electronic form.

(6) Where a copy of any record has been provided to the Motor Insurers' Bureau or its nominated subsidiary under paragraph (5)(b), the Bureau or its subsidiary shall—

(a) in the case of a record which is required to be kept under paragraph (1), preserve that copy record for a period of seven years from the date of expiry of the relevant policy or security, and

(b) furnish, without charge, to the Secretary of State or a chief officer of police upon request any particulars which it holds by virtue of this regulation.]

NOTES

Para (1): substituted by the Motor Vehicles (Third Party Risks) (Amendment) Regulations 2001, SI 2001/2266, reg 2(1), (3).

Para (3): words in square brackets substituted by the Motor Vehicles (Third-Party Risks) (Amendment) Regulations 1992, SI 1992/1283, reg 2(a).

Paras (4)–(6): substituted for original para (4) by SI 2001/2266, reg 2(1), (4).

[4029]

11 Notification to the Secretary of State of ineffective policies or securities

Where to the knowledge of a company a policy or security issued by them ceases to be effective without the consent of the person to whom it was issued, otherwise than by effluxion of time or by reason of his death, the company shall forthwith notify the Secretary of State of the date on which the policy or security ceased to be effective—

Provided that such notification need not be made if the certificate relating to the policy or security has been received by the company from the person to whom the certificate was issued on or before the date on which the policy or security ceases to be effective.

[4030]

12 Return of certificates to issuing company

(1) The following provisions shall apply in relation to the transfer of a policy or security with the consent of the holder to any other person:—

(a) the holder shall, before the policy or security is transferred, return any relative certificates issued for the purposes of these Regulations to the company by whom they were issued; and

(b) the policy or security shall not be transferred to any other person unless and until the certificates have been so returned or the company are satisfied that the certificates have been lost or destroyed.

(2) In any case where with the consent of the person to whom it was issued a policy or security is suspended or ceases to be effective, otherwise than by effluxion of time, in circumstances in which the provisions of section 147(4) of the Act (relating to the surrender of certificates) do not apply, the holder of the policy or security shall within seven days from the date when it is suspended or ceases to be effective return any relative certificates issued for the purposes of these Regulations to the company by whom they were issued and the company shall not issue a new policy or security to the said holder in respect of the motor vehicle or vehicles to which the said first mentioned policy or security related unless and until the certificates have been returned to the company or the company are satisfied that they have been lost or destroyed.

(3) Where a policy or security is cancelled by mutual consent or by virtue of any provision in the policy or security, any statutory declaration that a certificate has been lost or destroyed made in pursuance of section 147(4) (which requires any such declaration to be made within a period of seven days from the taking effect of the cancellation) shall be delivered forthwith after it has been made to the company by whom the policy was issued or the security given.

(4) The provisions of the last preceding paragraph shall be without prejudice to the provisions of paragraph (c) of subsection (2) of section 149 of the Act as to the effect for the purposes of that subsection of the making of a statutory declaration within the periods therein stated.

NOTES

Sections 147(4) and 149(2)(c) of the 1972 Act: see now the Road Traffic Act 1988, ss 147(4), (5) and 152(1)(c) respectively at **[3401]**, **[3406]**.

[4031]

13 Issue of fresh certificates

Where any company by whom a certificate of insurance or a certificate of security has been issued are satisfied that the certificate has become defaced or has been lost or destroyed they shall, if they are requested to do so by the person to whom the certificate was issued, issue to him a fresh certificate. In the case of a defaced certificate the company shall not issue a fresh certificate unless the defaced certificate is returned to the company.

SCHEDULE

PART 1

[4032]

NOTES

This Schedule contains forms which are not themselves reproduced in this work, but their numbers and titles are listed below.

Form No	***Title***
A	Certificate of Motor Insurance.
B	Certificate of Motor Insurance.
C	Certificate of Motor Insurance.
D	Certificate of Security.
E	Certificate of Deposit (amended by SI 1992/1283).
F	Certificate of Ownership.

PART 2

PROVISIONS RELATING TO THE FORMS AND COMPLETION OF CERTIFICATES

[4033]

[**1.** Every certificate shall be printed and completed in black [on a white background]. This provision shall not prevent the reproduction of a seal or monogram or similar device referred to in paragraph 2 of this Part of this Schedule, or the presence of a background pattern (of whatever form and whether coloured or not) on the face of the form which does not materially affect the legibility of the certificate.

2. No certificate shall contain any advertising matter, either on the face or on the back thereof—

Provided that the name and address of the company by whom the certificate is issued, or a reproduction of the seal of the company or any monogram or similar device of the company, or the name and address of an insurance broker, shall not be deemed to be advertising matter for the purposes of this paragraph if it is printed or stamped at the foot or on the back of such certificate, or if it forms, or forms part of, any such background pattern as is referred to in the foregoing paragraph.]

3. The whole of each form as set out in Part 1 of this Schedule shall in each case appear on the face of the form, the items being in the order so set out and the certification being set out at the end of the form.

4. The particulars to be inserted on the said forms shall so far as possible appear on the face of the form, but where in the case of any of the numbered headings in Forms A, B, or D, this cannot conveniently be done, any part of such particulars may be inserted on the back of the form, provided that their presence on the back is clearly indicated under the relevant heading.

5. The particulars to be inserted on any of the said forms shall not include particulars relating to any exceptions purporting to restrict the insurance under the relevant policy or the operation of the relevant security which are by subsection (1) of section 148 of the Act rendered of no effect as respects the third party liabilities required by sections 145 and 146 of the Act to be covered by a policy or security.

6.—(1) In any case where it is intended that a certificate of insurance, certificate of security or a covering note shall be effective not only in Great Britain, but also in any of the following territories, that is to say Northern Ireland, the Isle of Man, the Island of Guernsey, the Island of Jersey or the Island of Alderney, Forms A, B, C and D may be modified by the addition thereto, where necessary, of a reference to the relevant legal provisions of such of those territories as may be appropriate.

(2) A certificate of insurance or a certificate of security may contain either on the face or on the back of the certificate a statement as to whether or not the policy or security to which it relates satisfies the requirements of the relevant law in any of the territories referred to in this paragraph.

7. Every certificate of insurance or certificate of security shall be duly authenticated by or on behalf of the company by whom it is issued.

8. A certificate in Form F issued by a subsidiary of a Passenger Transport Executive or by a wholly-owned subsidiary of the London Transport Executive shall indicate under the signature that the issuing body is such a subsidiary of an Executive, which shall there be specified.

NOTES

Para 1: substituted by the Motor Vehicles (Third Party Risks) (Amendment) Regulations 1981, SI 1981/1567, reg 2; words in square brackets substituted by the Motor Vehicles (Third Party Risks) (Amendment) Regulations 1992, SI 1992/1283, reg 2(b).

Para 2: substituted by SI 1981/1567, reg 2.

MOTOR VEHICLES (COMPULSORY INSURANCE) (NO 2) REGULATIONS 1973

(SI 1973/2143)

NOTES

Made: 18 December 1973.
Authority: European Communities Act 1972, s 2(2).
Commencement: 1 January 1973.

[4034]

1— (1) These Regulations shall come into operation on 1st January 1974 and may be cited as the Motor Vehicles (Compulsory Insurance) (No 2) Regulations 1973.

(2) . . .

NOTES

Para 2: revokes the Motor Vehicles (Compulsory Insurance) Regulations 1973, SI 1973/1820.

[4035]

2— (1) In these Regulations "vehicle" means any motor vehicle intended for travel on land and propelled by mechanical power, but not running on rails, and any trailer, whether or not coupled [and references to a relevant foreign state are references to [Austria, Czechoslovakia, Finland, the German Democratic Republic, Hungary, Norway, Sweden or Switzerland]].

(2) For the purposes of these Regulations the territory in which a vehicle is normally based is—

(a) the territory of the state [of which the vehicle bears a registration plate] or

(b) in cases where no registration is required for the type of vehicle, but the vehicle bears an insurance plate or distinguishing sign analogous to a registration plate, the territory of the state in which the insurance plate or the sign is issued, or

(c) in cases where neither registration plate nor insurance plate nor distinguishing sign is required for the type of vehicle, the territory of the state in which the keeper of the vehicle is permanently resident.

(3) The Interpretation Act 1889 shall apply for the interpretation of these Regulations as it applies for the interpretation of an Act of Parliament.

NOTES

Para (1): words in first (outer) pair of square brackets added by the Motor Vehicles (Compulsory Insurance) (No 2) (Amendment) Regulations 1974, SI 1974/791, reg 3; words in second (inner) pair of square brackets substituted by Motor Vehicles (Compulsory Insurance) (No 2) (Amendment) (No 2) Regulations 1974, SI 1974/2186, reg 2.

Para (2): words in square brackets in sub-para (a) substituted by the Motor Vehicles (Compulsory Insurance) Regulations 1987, SI 1987/2171, reg 6.

Interpretation Act 1889: see now the Interpretation Act 1978.

3, 4 (*Revoked by the Road Traffic (Consequential Provisions) Act 1988, s 3(1), Sch 1, Pt II.*)

[4036]

5— (1) It shall be an offence for a person to use a specified motor vehicle registered in Great Britain, or any trailer kept by a person permanently resident in Great Britain, whether or not coupled, in the territory other than Great Britain and Gibraltar of any of the member states of the Communities, unless a policy of insurance is in force in relation to the person using that vehicle which insures him in respect of any liability which may be incurred by him in respect of the use of the vehicle in such territory according to the law on compulsory insurance against civil liability in respect of the use of vehicles of the state where the liability may be incurred.

(2) In this Regulation "specified motor vehicle" means a motor vehicle which is exempted from the provisions of section 143 of the Road Traffic Act 1972 (users of motor vehicles to be insured or secured against third-party risks) by virtue of section 144 of that Act.

(3) A person guilty of an offence under this Regulation shall be liable on summary conviction to a fine not exceeding [the statutory maximum] or to imprisonment for a term not exceeding three months, or to both such fine and such imprisonment.

(4) Proceedings for an offence under this Regulation may be taken, and the offence may for all incidental purposes be treated as having been committed in any place in Great Britain.

(5) Sections 180 (time within which summary proceedings for certain offences must be commenced) and 181 (evidence by certificate) of the Road Traffic Act 1972 shall apply for the purposes of an offence under this Regulation as if such an offence were an offence under that Act to which those sections had been applied by column 7 of Part I of Schedule 4 to that Act.

NOTES

Para (3): words in square brackets substituted by virtue of the Criminal Justice Act 1988, s 51.

Road Traffic Act 1972, ss 143, 144, 180, 181, Sch 4, Pt I: see now the Road Traffic Act 1988, ss 143, 144 at **[3397]**, **[3398]**, and the Road Traffic Offenders Act 1988, ss 6(1)–(4), (6), 11, Sch 1, Table respectively.

[4037]

6— (1) Any person appointed by the Secretary of State for the purpose (in this Regulation referred to as an "appointed person") may require a person having custody of any vehicle, being a vehicle which is normally based in the territory of a state [(other than a relevant foreign state)] which is not a member of the Communities or in the non-European territory of a member state or in Gibraltar, when entering Great Britain to produce evidence that any loss or injury which may be caused by such a vehicle is covered throughout the territory in which the treaty establishing the European Economic Community is in force, in accordance with the requirements of the laws of the various member states on compulsory insurance against civil liability in respect of the use of vehicles.

(2) An appointed person may, if no such evidence is produced or if he is not satisfied by such evidence, prohibit the use of the vehicle in Great Britain.

(3) Where an appointed person prohibits the use of a vehicle under this Regulation, he may also direct the driver to remove the vehicle to such place and subject to such conditions as are specified in the direction; and the prohibition shall not apply to the removal of the vehicle in accordance with the direction.

(4) Any person who—

(a) uses a vehicle or causes or permits a vehicle to be used in contravention of a prohibition imposed under paragraph (2) of this Regulation, or

(b) refuses, neglects or otherwise fails to comply in a reasonable time with a direction given under paragraph (3) of this Regulation,

shall be guilty of an offence and shall be liable on summary conviction to a fine not exceeding £50.

(5) Section 181 of the Road Traffic Act 1972 shall apply for the purposes of an offence under this Regulation as if such an offence were an offence under that Act to which that section had been applied by column 7 of Part 1 of Schedule 4 to that Act.

(6) A prohibition under paragraph (2) of this Regulation may be removed by an appointed person if he is satisfied that appropriate action has been taken to remove or remedy the circumstances in consequence of which the prohibition was imposed.

NOTES

Para (1): words in square brackets inserted by Motor Vehicles (Compulsory Insurance) (No 2) (Amendment) Regulations 1974, SI 1974/791, reg 4.

Road Traffic Act 1972, s 181, Sch 4, Pt I: see now the Road Traffic Offenders Act 1988, s 11, Sch 1, Table.

[4038]

7— (1) Where a constable in uniform has reasonable cause to suspect the driver of a vehicle of having committed an offence under the preceding Regulation, the constable may detain the vehicle, and for that purpose may give a direction, specifying an appropriate person and directing the vehicle to be removed by that person to such place and subject to such conditions as are specified in the direction; and the prohibition shall not apply to the removal of the vehicle in accordance with that direction.

(2) Where under paragraph (1) of this Regulation a constable—

(a) detains a motor vehicle drawing a trailer, or

(b) detains a trailer drawn by a motor vehicle,

then, for the purpose of securing the removal of the trailer, he may also (in a case falling within sub-paragraph (a) above) detain the trailer or (in a case falling within sub-paragraph (b) above) detain the motor vehicle; and a direction under paragraph (1) of this Regulation may require both the motor vehicle and the trailer to be removed to the place specified in the direction.

(3) A vehicle which, in accordance with a direction given under paragraph (1) of this Regulation, is removed to a place specified in the direction shall be detained in that place, or in any other place to which it is removed in accordance with a further direction given under that paragraph, until a constable (or, if that place is in the occupation of the Secretary of State, the Secretary of State) authorises the vehicle to be released on being satisfied—

(a) that the prohibition (if any) imposed in respect of the vehicle under the preceding Regulation has been removed, or that no such prohibition was imposed, or

(b) that appropriate arrangements have been made for removing or remedying the circumstances in consequence of which any such prohibition was imposed, or

(c) that the vehicle will be taken forthwith to a place from which it will be taken out of Great Britain to a place not in the European territory other than Gibraltar of a member state of the Communities [and not in the territory of a relevant foreign state].

(4) Any person who—

(a) drives a vehicle in accordance with a direction given under this Regulation, or

(b) is in charge of a place at which a vehicle is detained under this Regulation,

shall not be liable for any damage to, or loss in respect of, the vehicle or its load unless it is shown that he did not take reasonable care of the vehicle while driving it or, as the case may be, did not, while the vehicle was detained in that place, take reasonable care of the vehicle or (if the vehicle was detained there with its load) did not take reasonable care of its load.

(5) In this Regulation "appropriate person"—

(a) in relation to a direction to remove a motor vehicle, other than a motor vehicle drawing a trailer, means a person licensed to drive vehicles of the class to which the vehicle belongs, and

(b) in relation to a direction to remove a trailer, or to remove a motor vehicle drawing a trailer, means a person licensed to drive vehicles of a class which, when the direction is complied with, will include the motor vehicle drawing the trailer in accordance with that direction.

NOTES

Para (3): words in square brackets in sub-para (c) added by Motor Vehicles (Compulsory Insurance) (No 2) (Amendment) Regulations 1974, SI 1974/791, reg 5.

[4039]–[4041]

8 Nothing in section 145(2) (policies to be issued by authorised insurers) and section 147(1) (policies to be of no effect unless certificates issued) of the Road Traffic Act 1972 shall apply in the case of an insurance policy which is issued elsewhere than in the United Kingdom in respect of a vehicle normally based [in the territory other than the United Kingdom and Gibraltar of a member State of the Communities or of a relevant foreign state].

NOTES

Words in square brackets substituted by Motor Vehicles (Compulsory Insurance) (No 2) (Amendment) Regulations 1974, SI 1974/791, reg 6.

Road Traffic Act 1972, ss 145(2), 147(1): see now the Road Traffic Act 1988, ss 145(2), (5) and 147(1) respectively at **[3399]**, **[3401]**.

9 *(Revoked by the Road Traffic (Consequential Provisions) Act 1988, s 3(1), Sch 1, Pt II.)*

MOTOR VEHICLES (THIRD-PARTY RISKS DEPOSITS) REGULATIONS 1992

(SI 1992/1284)

NOTES

Made: 3 June 1992.
Authority: Insurance Companies Act 1958, s 20(1).
Commencement: 1 July 1992.

ARRANGEMENT OF REGULATIONS

1 Commencement and citation [4042]
3 Interpretation [4043]
4 Deposits [4044]
5 Investment [4045]
6 Withdrawal of deposits [4046]
7 Warrants [4047]
8 Application of Court Funds Rules [4048]

[4042]

1 Commencement and citation

These Regulations may be cited as the Motor Vehicles (Third-Party Risks Deposits) Regulations 1992, and shall come into force on 1st July 1992.

2 (*Revokes the Motor Vehicles (Third-Party Risks Deposits) Regulations 1967, SI 1967/1326.*)

[4043]

3 Interpretation

In these Regulations, except where the context otherwise requires, the following expressions have the meanings hereby respectively assigned to them—

"the Act" means the Road Traffic Act 1988;

"the Accountant General" means the Accountant General of the Supreme Court;

"basic account" means a deposit account bearing interest;

"the court" means the High Court;

"the depositor" has the meaning assigned thereto in regulation 4 of these Regulations;

"permitted securities" means the securities specified in Part I, paragraphs 1 to 10A and 12 of Part II, and paragraphs 2 and 3 of Part III, of Schedule 1 to the Trustee Investments Act 1961, as supplemented by Part IV of that Schedule;

"the prescribed sum" means the sum for the time being specified in section 144(1) of the Act; and

"the Secretary of State" means the [Secretary of State for the Environment, Transport and the Regions].

NOTES

In definition "the Secretary of State" words in square brackets substituted by virtue of the Secretary of State for the Environment, Transport and the Regions Order 1997, SI 1997/2971, art 6.

Interpretation Act 1889: see now the Interpretation Act 1978.

[4044]

4 Deposits

Any person wishing to deposit with the Accountant General the prescribed sum, or to increase the deposit already made to the prescribed sum, or any person wishing to deposit with the Accountant General the sum of £15,000 in pursuance of section 146(2) of the Act, may apply to the Secretary of State for a warrant which shall be a sufficient authority for the Accountant General to issue a direction for lodgment into court by the person named in the warrant (hereinafter referred to as "the depositor") of the said prescribed sum, or of sufficient sum to increase the deposit already made to the prescribed sum, or the said sum of £15,000, which shall be credited in the books of the Accountant General to an account entitled ex parte the depositor, in respect of the Act—

Provided that in lieu, wholly or in part, of the deposit of money the depositor may deposit an equivalent amount of securities in which cash under the control of or subject to the order of the court may for the time being be invested (the value thereof being taken at a price as near as may be to, but not exceeding, the current market price) and in that case the Secretary of State shall vary his warrant accordingly.

[4045]
5 Investment

(1) Any money deposited shall be—

(a) invested by the Accountant General in such permitted securities as the depositor may in writing request, or

(b) in the absence of such request, placed to a basic account.

(2) Any interest, dividend or income accruing due on money or securities deposited with the court under the last preceding regulation shall, subject to any order of the court, be paid to the depositor at his request.

(3) This regulation shall apply to any deposit made, or having effect as if made, in pursuance of sections 144(1) or 146(2) of the Act, whether under these Regulations or any preceding Rules or Regulations.

[4046]
6 Withdrawal of deposits

In any case where it may be just and equitable so to do, and in particular in any of the following cases, that is to say—

(a) where a person who has made a deposit in pursuance of section 144(1) of the Act, or having effect as if made in pursuance of that section, complies, or satisfies the Accountant General that he intends to comply, in some other manner, whether by way of insurance or otherwise, with the provisions of Part VI of the Act,

(b) where—

(i) a person who has made such a deposit as aforesaid ceases to own, or to control the use of, a motor vehicle, or

(ii) a person who has made a deposit in pursuance of section 146(2) of the Act, or having effect as if made in pursuance of that section, has ceased altogether to carry on in the United Kingdom the business of giving securities under Part VI of the Act,

and in either case all liabilities in respect of which money or securities were deposited in court have been satisfied or otherwise provided for,

the Secretary of State may, on the application of any such person, authorise the Accountant General to pay or transfer any money or securities deposited with him to such person as aforesaid or otherwise as the Accountant General may direct.

[4047]
7 Warrants

The issue of any warrant under regulation 4 of these Regulations or any error in any such warrant, or in relation thereto, shall not render the Secretary of State or the person signing the warrant on his behalf, in any manner liable for or in respect of any money or security deposited in court, or any securities for the time being representing the same, or the interest, dividends or income accruing due thereon.

[4048]–[4066]
8 Application of Court Funds Rules

Subject to the foregoing Regulations, the relevant provisions of the Court Funds Rules 1987 shall apply to deposits made, or having effect as if made, in pursuance of section 144(1) or section 146(2) of the Act, whether under these Regulations or any preceding Rules or Regulations.

INSURANCE ACCOUNTS DIRECTIVE (MISCELLANEOUS INSURANCE UNDERTAKINGS) REGULATIONS 1993

(SI 1993/3245)

NOTES

Made: 18 December 1993.
Authority: European Communities Act 1972, s 2(2).
Commencement: 19 December 1993.

ARRANGEMENT OF REGULATIONS

1	Citation, commencement and extent	[4067]
2	Interpretation	[4068]
3	Preparation of accounts by qualifying bodies	[4069]
5	Publication of accounts	[4070]

6 Penalties for non-compliance . . . . . [4071]
7 Industrial and provident societies . . . . . [4072]
8 Transitional provisions . . . . . [4073]

SCHEDULE

Modifications of certain enactments in their application to Industrial and Provident Societies . . . . . [4074]

[4067]

1 Citation, commencement and extent

(1) These Regulations may be cited as the Insurance Accounts Directive (Miscellaneous Insurance Undertakings) Regulations 1993.

(2) These Regulations shall come into force on the day after the day on which they are made.

(3) These Regulations do not extend to Northern Ireland.

NOTES

These Regulations were revoked by the Insurance Accounts Directive (Miscellaneous Insurance Undertakings) Regulations 2008, SI 2008/565, reg 16 at **[4473]**, in relation to any financial year of an insurance undertaking beginning on or after 6 April 2008 and are replaced by the 2008 Regulations at **[4459]**.

[4068]

2 Interpretation

(1) In these Regulations—

"the 1985 Act" means the Companies Act 1985;

"director" includes, in the case of a body which is not a company, any corresponding officer of that body;

"enactment" includes any subordinate legislation within the meaning of section 21(1) of the Interpretation Act 1978, other than these Regulations;

["friendly society" has the same meaning as in the Financial Services and Markets Act 2000;]

"industrial and provident society" means a registered society within the meaning given by section 74 of the Industrial and Provident Societies Act 1965;

"qualifying body" shall be construed in accordance with paragraphs (2) and (3) below;

and other expressions shall have the meanings ascribed to them by the 1985 Act.

(2) Subject to paragraph (3) below, a body incorporated in or formed under the law of any part of Great Britain is a qualifying body for the purposes of these Regulations if it—

(a) is incorporated by or registered under any public general Act of Parliament,

[(b) requires permission under Part 4 of the Financial Services and Markets Act 2000 to effect or carry out contracts of insurance without contravening the prohibition imposed by section 19 of that Act, and]

(c) is not required by any enactment to prepare accounts under Part VII of the 1985 Act (accounts and audit).

(3) A body is not a qualifying body for the purposes of these Regulations if it—

(a) is excluded from the scope of Council Directive 73/239/EEC by Article 3 of that Directive, or

(b) is referred to in [Article 3(2) to (6) of Directive 2002/83/EC of the European Parliament and of the Council of 5th November 2002 concerning life assurance][,

(c) is a friendly society].

(4) Any reference in these Regulations to the accounts required by or prepared under regulation 3 below are references to the annual accounts, the annual report and the auditors' report required by or prepared under paragraph (1) of that regulation.

[(5) Paragraph 2(b) must be read with—

(a) section 22 of the Financial Services and Markets Act 2000;

(b) any relevant order under that section;

(c) Schedule 2 to that Act.]

NOTES

Revoked as noted to reg 1 at **[4067]**.

Para (1): definition "friendly society" inserted by the Financial Services and Markets Act 2000 (Consequential Amendments and Repeals) Order 2001, SI 2001/3649, art 450(1), (2).

Para (2): sub-para (b) substituted by SI 2001/3649, art 450(1), (3).

Para (3): words in square brackets in sub-para (b) substituted by the Life Assurance Consolidation Directive (Consequential Amendments) Regulations 2004, SI 2004/3379, reg 8; sub-para (c) inserted by SI 2001/3649, art 450(1), (4).

Para (5): added by SI 2001/3649, art 450(1), (5).

Council Directive 73/239/EEC: OJ L228, 16.8.1973, p 3.

Directive 2002/83/EC of the European Parliament and of the Council: OJ L345, 19.12.2002, p 1.

[4069]

3 Preparation of accounts by qualifying bodies

(1) The directors of a qualifying body shall in respect of each financial year of the body—

(a) prepare the like annual accounts and annual report, and

(b) cause to be prepared such an auditors' report,

as would be required under the provisions mentioned in paragraph (3) below if the body were an insurance company formed and registered under the 1985 Act.

(2) The accounts required by this regulation—

(a) shall be prepared within the period of 7 months beginning immediately after the end of the body's financial year,

(b) shall state that they are prepared under this regulation, and

(c) shall comply with such of the requirements of the provisions mentioned in paragraph (3) below as relate to the contents of accounts or reports subject, where the qualifying body is unincorporated, to any necessary modifications to take account of that fact.

(3) The provisions referred to in paragraphs (1) and (2) above are the following provisions of Part VII of the 1985 Act, namely—

(a) sections 226 to 237 (annual accounts and reports),

(b) section 242B (delivery and publication of accounts in ECUs),

(c) sections 255 and 255A (banking and insurance companies and groups),

(d) [where Companies Act group accounts are prepared,] Schedule 4A (form and content of group accounts), as modified by Part II of Schedule 9A other than paragraphs [13(3) and (5)], 14 and 15,

(e) Schedule 5 (disclosure of information: related undertakings) other than [paragraphs 4 and 12],

(f) Schedule 6 (disclosure of information: emoluments and other benefits of directors and others) other than [paragraphs 2], 8 and 9,

(g) [paragraphs 5A and 6] of Schedule 7 (matters to be included in directors' report), and

(h) [where Companies Act individual accounts are prepared,] Schedule 9A other than paragraphs 10, 56, 61, 63, 64, 65, . . . 72(2), 73 and 74, and, in paragraph 2(2), the words from "but the following" to the end.

(4) For the purposes of those provisions as applied to accounts prepared under this regulation, these Regulations shall be regarded as part of the requirements of the 1985 Act.

(5) Part II of the Companies Act 1989 (eligibility for appointment as auditors) shall apply to auditors appointed for the purposes of this regulation subject, where the body concerned is unincorporated, to any necessary modifications to take account of that fact.

(6) In this regulation "financial year", in relation to a qualifying body, means—

(a) any period in respect of which a profit and loss account, or in the case of an industrial and provident society, an annual return, of the body is required to be made up by or in accordance with its constitution or by any enactment (whether that period is a year or not); or

(b) failing any such requirement, each period of 12 months beginning with 1st April.

NOTES

Revoked as noted to reg 1 at **[4067]**.

Para (3): in sub-para (d) words in first pair of square brackets inserted and words in second pair of square brackets substituted, in sub-paras (e)–(g) words in square brackets substituted, and in sub-para (h) words in square brackets inserted and words omitted revoked, by the Insurance Accounts Directive (Miscellaneous Insurance Undertakings) (Amendment) Regulations 2005, SI 2005/1985, reg 2(1), (2), as respects financial years beginning on or after 1 January 2005 and ending on or after 1 October 2005.

4 *(Revoked by the Insurance Accounts Directive (Lloyd's Syndicate and Aggregate Accounts) Regulations 2004, SI 2004/3219, reg 18(1).)*

[4070]

5 Publication of accounts

(1) A qualifying body shall—

(a) make available the latest accounts prepared under regulation 3 above for inspection by any person, without charge and during business hours, at the body's head office in Great Britain; and

(b) supply to any person upon request a copy of those accounts (or such part of those accounts as may be requested) at a price not exceeding the administrative cost of making the copy.

(2) . . .

(3) In the case of industrial and provident societies which are qualifying bodies, the obligation in paragraph (1)(b) above is subject to the provisions of section 39(5) of the Industrial and Provident Societies Act 1965.

NOTES

Revoked as noted to reg 1 at **[4067]**.

Para (2): revoked by the Insurance Accounts Directive (Lloyd's Syndicate and Aggregate Accounts) Regulations 2004, SI 2004/3219, reg 18(1).

[4071]

6 Penalties for non-compliance

(1) If—

(a) the directors of a qualifying body fail to comply with paragraph (1) of regulation 3 above within the period referred to in paragraph (2) of that regulation . . .

(b) . . .

every person who, immediately before the end of that period, was a director of the body . . . is guilty of an offence and liable on summary conviction to a fine not exceeding level 5 on the standard scale.

(2) If—

(a) accounts which are made available for inspection under regulation 5(1) above do not comply with the requirements of regulation 3 above . . .

(b) . . .

every person who, at the time when the accounts were or the account was first made available for inspection, was a director of the qualifying body . . . is guilty of an offence and liable on summary conviction to a fine not exceeding level 5 on the standard scale.

(3) If—

(a) a qualifying body fails to comply with regulation 5(1) above . . .

(b) . . .

the body . . . and every person who, at the time when the failure takes place, is a director of the body . . . is guilty of an offence and liable on summary conviction to a fine not exceeding level 5 on the standard scale.

(4) It is a defence for a person charged with an offence under this regulation to show that he took all reasonable steps for securing that the requirements in question would be complied with.

(5) The following provisions of the 1985 Act, namely—

(a) section 731 (summary proceedings),

(b) section 733 (offences by bodies corporate), and

(c) section 734 (criminal proceedings against unincorporated bodies),

shall apply to an offence under this regulation.

NOTES

Revoked as noted to reg 1 at **[4067]**.

Paras (1), (2): words omitted in the first place revoked by the Insurance Accounts Directive (Miscellaneous Insurance Undertakings) (Amendment) Regulations 2005, SI 2005/1985, reg 3(1)–(3), as respects financial years beginning on or after 1 January 2005 and ending on or after 1 October 2005; words omitted in the second and third places revoked by the Insurance Accounts Directive (Lloyd's Syndicate and Aggregate Accounts) Regulations 2004, SI 2004/3219, reg 18.

Para (3): words omitted in the first and third places revoked by SI 2005/1985, reg 3(1), (4), as respects financial years beginning on or after 1 January 2005 and ending on or after 1 October 2005; words omitted in the second and fourth places revoked by SI 2004/3219, reg 18(1), (2).

[4072]

7 Industrial and provident societies

(1) The Schedule to these Regulations shall have effect for the purpose of modifying—

(a) the Industrial and Provident Societies Act 1965; and

(b) the Friendly and Industrial and Provident Societies Act 1968,

in their application to industrial and provident societies which prepare accounts under the provisions of these Regulations.

(2) The Industrial and Provident Societies (Group Accounts) Regulations 1969 shall not apply to industrial and provident societies which prepare accounts under the provisions of these Regulations.

NOTES

Revoked as noted to reg 1 at **[4067]**.

[4073]

8 *Transitional provisions*

(1) The directors of a qualifying body need not prepare accounts in accordance with regulation 3 with respect to a financial year of the body commencing before 23rd December 1994.

(2) Where advantage is taken of paragraph (1), regulation 5 shall not apply to the body.

NOTES

Revoked as noted to reg 1 at **[4067]**.

SCHEDULE
MODIFICATIONS OF CERTAIN ENACTMENTS IN THEIR APPLICATION TO INDUSTRIAL AND PROVIDENT SOCIETIES

Regulation 7

[4074]

[1. *In its application to industrial and provident societies which prepare accounts under the provisions of these Regulations, the Friendly and Industrial and Provident Societies Act 1968 shall have effect subject to the modifications made by paragraphs 3 to 7 below.]*

2. . . .

3. *The following provisions of the Friendly and Industrial and Provident Societies Act 1968 shall not apply—*

- *(a) section 3 (general provisions as to accounts and balance sheets of societies),*
- *(b) section 4(2) to (8) (exemptions from audit for small societies),*
- *(c) section 7 (qualified auditors),*
- *(d) section 8 (restrictions on appointment of auditors),*
- *(e) section 9(1) to (4) and (6) (auditors' report),*
- *(f) section 13(1) to (5) (group accounts of societies),*
- *(g) section 14 (exemption from requirements in respect of group accounts), and*
- *(h) section 15 (meaning of "subsidiary").*

4.—*(1) In paragraph (a) of subsection (2) of section 11 of that Act (annual returns of societies), the reference to the revenue account or accounts of the society shall be construed as a reference to the profit and loss account required to be prepared by section 226 of the 1985 Act as applied by regulation 3 of these Regulations.*

(2) For paragraph (b) of that subsection there shall be substituted the following paragraph—

> *"(b) shall not contain any other accounts.".*

5.—*(1) In subsection (1) of section 12 of that Act (rules by societies), after the words "of this Act" in both places where they occur, there shall be inserted "or of the Insurance Accounts Directive (Miscellaneous Insurance Undertakings) Regulations 1993".*

(2) After subsection (2) of that section there shall be inserted the following subsection—

> *"(2A) For the purposes of subsection (1) the appropriate period after the commencement of the Insurance Accounts Directive (Miscellaneous Insurance Undertakings) Regulations 1993 shall be the period of one year beginning with the date of coming into force of those Regulations.".*

6. *In section 21(1) of that Act (interpretation)—*

(a) there shall be inserted at the appropriate places the following definitions—

> *""accounts" means the profit and loss account required to be prepared by section 226 of the Companies Act 1985 as applied by regulation 3 of the Insurance Accounts Directive (Miscellaneous Insurance Undertakings) Regulations 1993;*
>
> *"qualified auditor" means a person eligible for appointment as an auditor of the society under Part II of the Companies Act 1989 as applied by paragraph 3 of Schedule 9 to those Regulations;"; and*

(*b*) *for the definition of "group accounts" there shall be substituted the following definition—*

""group accounts" means the accounts required to be prepared by section 227 of the Companies Act 1985 as applied by regulation 3 of the Insurance Accounts Directive (Miscellaneous Insurance Undertakings) Regulations 1993.".

[**7.** *In section 3A of the Friendly and Industrial and Provident Societies Act 1968, for subsections (2) to (12) substitute—*

"(2) If a society publishes any of its statutory accounts, they must be accompanied by the relevant auditors' report under the Insurance Accounts Directive (Miscellaneous Insurance Undertakings) Regulations 1993.

(3) A society which is required to prepare group accounts for a financial year shall not publish its statutory individual accounts for that year without also publishing with them its statutory group accounts.

(4) If a society publishes non-statutory accounts, it shall publish with them a statement indicating—

(*a*) *that they are not the society's statutory accounts,*

(*b*) *whether statutory accounts dealing with any financial year with which the non-statutory accounts purport to deal have been delivered to the Authority,*

(*c*) *whether the society's auditors have made a report under the Insurance Accounts Directive (Miscellaneous Insurance Undertakings) Regulations 1993,*

(*d*) *whether any such auditors' report—*

(*i*) *was qualified or unqualified, or included a reference to any matters to which the auditors drew attention by way of emphasis without qualifying the report, or*

(*ii*) *contained a statement under section 237(2) or (3) of the Companies Act 1985 as applied to industrial and provident societies by the Insurance Accounts Directive (Miscellaneous Insurance Undertakings) Regulations 1993 (accounting records or returns inadequate, accounts not agreeing with records and returns or failure to obtain necessary information and explanations),*

and it shall not publish with the non-statutory accounts any auditors' report under the Insurance Accounts Directive (Miscellaneous Insurance Undertakings) Regulations 1993.

(5) For the purposes of this section a society shall be regarded as publishing a document if it publishes, issues or circulates it or otherwise generally makes it available for public inspection in a manner calculated to invite members of the public generally, or any class of members of the public, to read it.

(6) References in this section to a society's statutory accounts are to its individual or group accounts for a financial year as required to be prepared by the Insurance Accounts Directive (Miscellaneous Insurance Undertakings) Regulations 1993; and references to the publication by a society of "non-statutory accounts" are to the publication of—

(*a*) *any balance sheet or profit and loss account relating to, or purporting to deal with, a financial year of the society, or*

(*b*) *an account in any form purporting to be a balance sheet or profit and loss account for the group consisting of the society and its subsidiary undertakings relating to, or purporting to deal with, a financial year of the society,*

otherwise than as part of the society's statutory accounts."]

NOTES

Revoked as noted to reg 1 at **[4067]**.

Para 1: substituted by the Insurance Accounts Directive (Miscellaneous Insurance Undertakings) (Amendment) Regulations 2005, SI 2005/1985, reg 4(1), (2), as respects financial years beginning on or after 1 January 2005 and ending on or after 1 October 2005.

Para 2: revoked by SI 2005/1985, reg 4(1), (3), as respects financial years beginning on or after 1 January 2005 and ending on or after 1 October 2005.

Para 7: added by SI 2005/1985, reg 4(1), (4), as respects financial years beginning on or after 1 January 2005 and ending on or after 1 October 2005.

INSURANCE PREMIUM TAX REGULATIONS 1994

(SI 1994/1774)

NOTES

Made: 6 July 1994.

Authority: Finance Act 1994, ss 53(6), 54, 55(1)–(8), 57(15), 58(2), (4), 62(1), (3)–(7), 65(1)–(3), (5), (7)–(13), 68(1)–(11), 74(2), (7), (8), Sch 7, paras 1(1)–(3), 7(7), (8), 8(6).
Commencement: 1 August 1994.

ARRANGEMENT OF REGULATIONS

PART I
PRELIMINARY

1 Citation and commencement . . . [4075]
2 Interpretation . . . [4076]
3 Requirement, direction, demand or approval . . . [4077]

PART II
REGISTRATION AND PROVISIONS FOR SPECIAL CASES

4 Notification of liability to register . . . [4078]
4A Notification of liability to register—taxable intermediaries . . . [4079]
5 Changes in particulars . . . [4080]
6 Notification of liability to be de-registered . . . [4081]
6A Notification of liability to be de-registered—taxable intermediaries . . . [4082]
7 Transfer of a going concern . . . [4083]
8 Registration of Lloyd's syndicates . . . [4084]
9 Representation of Lloyd's syndicates . . . [4085]
10 Representation of unincorporated body . . . [4086]
11 Death, bankruptcy or incapacity of registrable persons . . . [4087]

PART III
ACCOUNTING, PAYMENT AND RECORDS

12 Making of returns . . . [4088]
13 Correction of errors . . . [4089]
14 Claims for overpaid tax . . . [4090]
15 Payment of tax . . . [4091]
16 Records . . . [4092]

PART IV
CLAIMS IN RESPECT OF CREDIT

17 Scope . . . [4093]
18 Claims in returns . . . [4094]
19 Payments in respect of credit . . . [4095]

PART IVA
REIMBURSEMENT ARRANGEMENTS

19A Interpretation of Part IVA . . . [4096]
19B Reimbursement arrangements—general . . . [4097]
19C Reimbursement arrangements—provisions to be included . . . [4098]
19D Repayments to the Commissioners . . . [4099]
19E Records . . . [4100]
19F Production of records . . . [4101]
19G Undertakings . . . [4102]
19H Reimbursement arrangements made before 11th February 1998 . . . [4103]

PART V
SPECIAL ACCOUNTING SCHEME

20 Interpretation . . . [4104]
21 Notification by insurer that scheme to apply . . . [4105]
22 Relevant accounting periods . . . [4106]
23 Premiums treated as received on premium written date . . . [4107]
24 Amount of premium . . . [4108]
25 Credit . . . [4109]
26 Withdrawal from the scheme . . . [4110]
27 Expulsion from the scheme . . . [4111]
28 Tax to be accounted for on cessation . . . [4112]

PART VI
TAX REPRESENTATIVES

29 Notification in certain cases . . . [4113]
30 Registration . . . [4114]
31 Liability to notify . . . [4115]

PART VII
LIABILITY OF INSURED PERSONS

32 Interpretation . . . [4116]
33 Scope . . . [4117]
34 Liability notices . . . [4118]

35 Power to assess tax due . . . . . [4119]
36 Persons liable for tax assessed . . . . . [4120]
37 Adjustment of assessments . . . . . [4121]
38 Time for payment . . . . . [4122]
39 Interest on reimbursements . . . . . [4123]
40 Allocation of payments . . . . . [4124]
41 Records . . . . . [4125]

PART VIII
DISTRESS AND DILIGENCE

A42 . . . . . [4126]
43 Diligence . . . . . [4127]

SCHEDULE . . . . . [4128]

PART I
PRELIMINARY

[4075]

1 Citation and commencement

These Regulations may be cited as the Insurance Premium Tax Regulations 1994 and shall come into force on 1st August 1994.

[4076]

2 Interpretation

(1) In these Regulations—

"accounting period" means—

(a) in the case of a registered person, each period of three months ending on the dates notified to him by the Commissioners, whether by means of a certificate of registration issued by them or otherwise;

(b) in the case of a registrable person who is not registered, each quarter; or

(c) in the case of any registrable person, such other period in relation to which he is required by or under regulation 12 to make a return;

and, in every case, the first accounting period of a registrable person shall commence on the effective date determined in accordance with section 53 [or 53AA] of the Act upon which the person was or should have been registered;

"the Act" means Part III of the Finance Act 1994;

"Collector" means a Collector, Deputy Collector or Assistant Collector of Customs and Excise;

"Lloyd's" means the society incorporated by section 3 of Lloyd's Act 1871;

"managing agent" has the same meaning as in section 12(1) of Lloyd's Act 1982;

"registered person" means a person who is registered under section 53 [or 53AA] of the Act and, except in regulation 30, "register" and "registration" shall be construed accordingly;

"registration number" means the unique identifying number allocated to a registered person and notified to him by the Commissioners;

"return" means a return which is required to be made in accordance with regulation 12;

["taxable intermediary's fees" means fees which, to the extent of any payment in respect of them, are chargeable to tax by virtue of section 52A of the Finance Act 1994 and references in these regulations to "fee" or "fees" shall be construed accordingly;]

"underwriting member" has the same meaning as in section 2(1) of Lloyd's Act 1982.

(2) Any reference in these Regulations to "this Part" is a reference to the Part of these Regulations in which that reference is made.

(3) Any reference in these Regulations to a form prescribed in the Schedule to these Regulations shall include a reference to a form which the Commissioners are satisfied is a form to the like effect.

NOTES

Para (1): words in square brackets in definitions "accounting period" and "registered person" and definition "taxable intermediary's fees" inserted by the Insurance Premium Tax (Amendment) Regulations 1997, SI 1997/1157, reg 3.

[4077]

3 Requirement, direction, demand or approval

Any requirement, direction, demand or approval by the Commissioners under or for the purposes of these Regulations shall be made or given by a notice in writing.

PART II
REGISTRATION AND PROVISIONS FOR SPECIAL CASES

[4078]
4 Notification of liability to register

(1) A person who is required by section 53(2) of the Act to notify the Commissioners of the facts there mentioned shall do so on the form numbered 1 in the Schedule to these Regulations.

(2) Where the notification referred to in this regulation is made by a partnership, it shall include the particulars set out on the form numbered 2 in the Schedule to these Regulations.

(3) The notification referred to in this regulation shall be made within thirty days of the earliest date after 31st July 1994 on which the person either forms or continues to have the intention to receive premiums in the course of a taxable business.

[4079]
[4A Notification of liability to register—taxable intermediaries

(1) A person who is required by section 53AA(3) of the Act to notify the Commissioners of the facts there mentioned shall do so on the form numbered 1 in the Schedule to these Regulations.

(2) Where the notification referred to in this regulation is made by a partnership, it shall include the particulars set out on the form numbered 2 in the Schedule to these Regulations.

(3) The notification referred to in this regulation shall be made within thirty days of the earliest date after 30th April 1997 on which the person either forms or continues to have the intention to charge taxable intermediary's fees in the course of any business of his.]

NOTES

Inserted by the Insurance Premium Tax (Amendment) Regulations 1997, SI 1997/1157, reg 4.

[4080]
[5 Changes in particulars

(1) A person who has made a notification under regulation 4 [or 4A], whether or not it was made in accordance with paragraph (3) [of regulation 4 or 4A above], shall, within thirty days of—
- (a) discovering any inaccuracy in; or
- (b) any change occurring which causes to become inaccurate,

any information contained in or provided with the notification, notify the Commissioners in writing and furnish them with full particulars thereof.

(2) Without prejudice to paragraph (1) above, a registrable person shall, within thirty days of any change occurring in any of the circumstances referred to in paragraph (4) below, notify the Commissioners in writing and furnish them with particulars of—
- (a) the change; and
- (b) the date on which the change occurred.

(3) A registrable person who discovers that any information contained in or provided with a notification under paragraph (2) above is inaccurate shall, within thirty days of his discovering the inaccuracy, notify the Commissioners and furnish them with particulars of—
- (a) the inaccuracy;
- (b) the date on which the inaccuracy was discovered;
- (c) why the information was inaccurate; and
- (d) the correct information.

(4) The circumstances mentioned in paragraph (2) above are the following circumstances relating to the registrable person[, any insurance business carried on by him or any business in the course of which he charges taxable intermediary's fees]—
- (a) his name, his trading name (if different) and address;
- (b) the name, the trading name (if different) and address of his tax representative;
- (c) his status, namely whether he carries on business as a sole proprietor, body corporate, partnership or other unincorporated body;
- (d) in the case of a partnership, the name and address of the partners;
- (e) in the case of a syndicate of underwriting members of Lloyd's which has been registered as such, the number or other identifying feature by reference to which it is registered.

(5) Where in relation to a registrable person the Commissioners are satisfied that any of the information recorded in the register kept under section 53 [or 53AA] of the Act is or has become inaccurate they may correct the register accordingly.

(6) For the purposes of paragraph (5) above it is immaterial whether or not the registrable person has made any notification he was required to make under this regulation.]

NOTES

Substituted by the Insurance Premium Tax (Amendment) Regulations 1995, SI 1995/1587, reg 3.

Para (1): words in first pair of square brackets inserted, and words in second pair of square brackets substituted, by the Insurance Premium Tax (Amendment) Regulations 1997, SI 1997/1157, reg 5(a).

Para (4): words in square brackets substituted by SI 1997/1157, reg 5(b).

Para (5): words in square brackets inserted by SI 1997/1157, reg 5(c).

[4081]

6 Notification of liability to be de-registered

A person who is required by section 53(3) of the Act to notify the Commissioners of the facts there mentioned shall, within thirty days of his having ceased to have the intention to receive premiums in the course of any taxable business, notify the Commissioners in writing and shall therein inform them of—

(a) the date on which he ceased to have the intention of receiving premiums in the course of any taxable business; and

(b) if different, the date on which the last such premium was received.

[4082]

[6A Notification of liability to be de-registered—taxable intermediaries

A person who is required by section 53AA(4) of the Act to notify the Commissioners of the facts there mentioned shall, within thirty days of his having ceased to have the intention of charging taxable intermediary's fees, give notice to the Commissioners in writing—

(a) of the date on which he ceased to charge taxable intermediary's fees in the course of any business of his; and

(b) if different, the date on which the last such fee was received.]

NOTES

Inserted by the Insurance Premium Tax (Amendment) Regulations 1997, SI 1997/1157, reg 6.

[4083]

7 Transfer of a going concern

(1) Where—

(a) a taxable business is transferred as a going concern;

(b) the registration of the transferor has not already been cancelled;

(c) as a result of the transfer of the business the registration of the transferor is to be cancelled and the transferee becomes liable to be registered; and

(d) an application is made on the form numbered 3 in the Schedule to these Regulations by both the transferor and the transferee,

the Commissioners may with effect from the date of the transfer cancel the registration of the transferor and register the transferee with the registration number previously allocated to the transferor.

(2) An application under paragraph (1) above shall be treated as the notification referred to in regulation 6.

(3) Where the transferee of a business has been registered under paragraph (1) above with the registration number previously allocated to the transferor—

(a) any liability of the transferor existing at the date of the transfer to make a return or account for or pay any tax under Part III of these Regulations shall become the liability of the transferee;

(b) any entitlement of the transferor, whether or not existing at the date of the transfer, to credit or payment under Part IV of these Regulations shall become the entitlement of the transferee.

(4) In addition to the provisions set out in paragraph (3) above, where the transferee of a business has been registered under paragraph (1) above with the registration number previously allocated to the transferor during an accounting period subsequent to that in which the transfer took place (but with effect from the date of the transfer) and any—

(a) return has been made;

(b) tax has been accounted for; or

(c) entitlement to credit has been claimed,

by either the transferor or the transferee, it shall be treated as having been done by the transferee.

(5) Where—

(a) a taxable business is transferred as a going concern;

(b) the transferee makes a payment to a person which represents the repayment of any premium or part of a premium received in the course of that business; and

(c) the transferor has paid tax on that premium or part,

then, whether or not the transferee has been registered under paragraph (1) above with the registration number previously allocated to the transferor, any entitlement to credit under Part IV of these Regulations shall become the entitlement of the transferee.

[4084]

8 Registration of Lloyd's syndicates

(1) Where a taxable business is carried on by persons who are underwriting members of Lloyd's who are members of a syndicate of such underwriting members the registration of those persons for the purposes of the Act may be by reference to the syndicate; and, where such a syndicate is not known by any name, the registration may be by reference to any number or other identifying feature of the syndicate.

(2) In determining whether premiums are received by any syndicate which has been registered in the manner described in paragraph (1) above no account shall be taken of any change in the members of the syndicate.

[4085]

9 Representation of Lloyd's syndicates

(1) Anything required to be done by or under the Act (whether by these Regulations or otherwise) by or on behalf of a syndicate of underwriting members of Lloyd's shall be the joint and several responsibility of the persons mentioned in paragraph (2) below; but if it is done by any of those persons it shall be sufficient compliance with any such requirement.

(2) The persons are—

(a) the underwriting members of the syndicate;

(b) the managing agent of the syndicate; and

(c) as regards any accounting period for which it is required by paragraph (3) below to act as the syndicate's representative, Lloyd's.

(3) Where a syndicate of underwriting members of Lloyd's has made an election that Lloyd's shall act as its representative Lloyd's shall so act in relation to any accounting period as regards which—

(a) that election has effect;

(b) the syndicate is registered as described in regulation 8; and

(c) the scheme established by Part V of these Regulations applies to the syndicate.

(4) An election under paragraph (3) above shall be made in writing and shall specify the first accounting period of the syndicate in respect of which the election is to have effect, being an accounting period beginning on or after the date the election is made.

(5) Subject to paragraphs (6) and (7) below, an election under paragraph (3) above shall have effect for the accounting period specified in the election and all subsequent accounting periods.

(6) An election under paragraph (3) above shall not have effect unless written notification of the election is given to the Commissioners before the beginning of the accounting period specified in the election.

(7) An election under paragraph (3) above shall cease to have effect with effect from the accounting period specified in any notice in writing given by the syndicate to the Commissioners for this purpose, being an accounting period beginning after the date the notice is given.

[4086]

10 Representation of unincorporated body

(1) Where anything is required to be done by or under the Act (whether by these Regulations or otherwise) by or on behalf of an unincorporated body other than a partnership, it shall be the joint and several responsibility of—

(a) every member holding office as president, chairman, treasurer, secretary or any similar office; or

(b) if there is no such office, every member holding office as a member of a committee by which the affairs of the body are managed; or

(c) if there is no such office or committee, every member;

but, subject to paragraph (2) below, if it is done by any of the persons referred to above that shall be sufficient compliance with any such requirement.

(2) Where an unincorporated body other than a partnership is required to make any notification such as is referred to in regulations 4 to 6, it shall not be sufficient compliance unless the notification is made by a person upon whom a responsibility for making it is imposed by paragraph (1) above.

(3) Where anything is required to be done by or under the Act (whether by these Regulations or otherwise) by or on behalf of a partnership, it shall be the joint and several responsibility of every partner; but if it is done by one partner or, in the case of a partnership whose principal place of business is in Scotland, by any other person authorised by the partnership with respect thereto that shall be sufficient compliance with any such requirement.

[4087]

11 Death, bankruptcy or incapacity of registrable persons

(1) If a registrable person dies or becomes bankrupt or incapacitated, the Commissioners may, from the date on which he died or became bankrupt or incapacitated, as the case may be, treat as a registrable person any person carrying on any taxable business of his [or any business in the course of which he charged taxable intermediary's fees]; and any legislation relating to insurance premium tax shall apply to any person so treated as though he were a registered person.

(2) Any person carrying on such business as aforesaid shall, within thirty days of commencing to do so, inform the Commissioners in writing of that fact and of the date of the death or bankruptcy or of the nature of the incapacity and the date on which it began.

(3) Where the Commissioners have treated a person carrying on a business as a registrable person under paragraph (1) above, they shall cease so to treat him if—

(a) the registration of the registrable person is cancelled, whether or not any other person is registered with the registration number previously allocated to him;

(b) the bankruptcy is discharged or the incapacity ceases; or

(c) he ceases carrying on the business of the registrable person.

(4) In relation to a registrable person which is a company, the references in this regulation to the registrable person becoming incapacitated shall be construed as references to its going into liquidation or receivership or to [entering administration]; and references to the incapacity ceasing shall be construed accordingly.

NOTES

Para (1): words in square brackets inserted by the Insurance Premium Tax (Amendment) Regulations 1997, SI 1997/1157, reg 7.

Para (4): words in square brackets substituted by the Enterprise Act 2002 (Insolvency) Order 2003, SI 2003/2096, art 5, Schedule, Pt 2, para 54, except in relation to any case where a petition for an administration order was presented before 15 September 2003.

PART III
ACCOUNTING, PAYMENT AND RECORDS

[4088]

12 Making of returns

(1) Subject to paragraphs (2) and (4) below and save as the Commissioners may otherwise allow, a registrable person shall, in respect of each accounting period, make a return to the Controller, Central Collection Unit (IPT) on the form numbered 4 in the Schedule to these Regulations.

(2) Lloyd's may, in respect of any two or more syndicates of underwriting members of Lloyd's for which it is required by regulation 9(3) to act as representative as regards an accounting period which, as regards each such syndicate, begins on the same date and ends on the same date, make a return on the form numbered 5 in the Schedule to these Regulations; and, provided it is accompanied by a summary schedule on the form numbered 6 in the Schedule to these Regulations, the making of a return under this paragraph shall be treated as sufficient compliance with paragraph (1) above in relation to the accounting period of each of the syndicates concerned.

(3) Subject to paragraph (4) below, a registrable person shall make each return not later than the last day of the month next following the end of the period to which it relates.

(4) Where the Commissioners consider it necessary in the circumstances of any particular case, they may—

(a) vary the length of any accounting period or the date on which it begins or ends or by which any return must be made;

(b) allow or direct the registrable person to make a return in accordance with sub-paragraph (a) above;

(c) allow or direct a registrable person to make returns to a specified address;

and any person to whom the Commissioners give any direction such as is referred to in this regulation shall comply therewith.

[4089]

13 Correction of errors

(1) In this regulation—

"credit" means credit to which a person is entitled under Part IV of these Regulations;

"overdeclaration" means, in relation to any return, the amount (if any) which was wrongly treated as tax due for the accounting period concerned and which caused either the amount of tax which was payable to be overstated or the entitlement to a payment under regulation 19(1) to be understated or both or would have caused such an overstatement or understatement were it not for the existence of an underdeclaration in relation to that return;

"underdeclaration" means, in relation to any return, the aggregate of—

(a) the amount (if any) of tax due for the accounting period concerned which was not taken into account; and

(b) the amount (if any) which was wrongly deducted as credit,

and which caused either the amount of tax which was payable to be understated or the entitlement to a payment under regulation 19(1) to be overstated or both or would have caused such an understatement or overstatement were it not for the existence of an overdeclaration in relation to that return.

(2) This regulation applies where a registrable person has made a return which was inaccurate as the result of an overdeclaration or underdeclaration.

(3) Where, in relation to any overdeclarations or underdeclarations that are discovered by the registrable person in an accounting period—

(a) the total of the overdeclarations discovered does not exceed [£50,000], he may enter that total in [Boxes 6 to 8 (overdeclarations), as appropriate,] in the return for that accounting period;

(b) the total of the underdeclarations discovered does not exceed [£50,000], he may enter that total in [Boxes 3 and 4 (underdeclarations), as appropriate,] in the return for that accounting period;

and, where he does so, he shall calculate the tax payable by him or the payment to which he is entitled accordingly.

[But if Box 10 of the registrable person's return for the accounting period requires an entry for net value of taxable premiums (excluding tax) that is less than £5,000,000 (see regulation 12 and Forms 4 and 5 in the Schedule), the total mentioned in sub-paragraph (a) or (b) must not for these purposes exceed 1% of that net value unless the respective total is [£10,000 or less].]

(4) Where the return for the accounting period in which the overdeclaration or underdeclaration was discovered is made by Lloyd's in accordance with regulation 12(2), paragraph (3) above shall apply as if the references to the totals of the overdeclarations or underdeclarations . . . were references to each such total for each syndicate in respect of which the return is made . . .

(5) No amount shall be entered in any return in respect of any overdeclaration or underdeclaration except in accordance with this regulation.

(6) Where any amount has been entered in a return in accordance with this regulation, that return shall be regarded as correcting any earlier return to which that amount relates.

NOTES

Para (3): words and sums in square brackets in sub-paras (a), (b) substituted and words in fifth (outer) pair of square brackets added by the Value Added Tax, etc (Correction of Errors, etc) Regulations 2008, SI 2008/1482, reg 3(1), in relation to accounting periods beginning on or after 1 July 2008; words in sixth (inner) pair of square brackets substituted by the Amusement Machine Licence Duty, etc (Amendments) Regulations 2008, SI 2008/2693, reg 4(1)(a), in relation to a discovery first made on or after 1 November 2008.

Para (4): words omitted revoked by SI 2008/1482, reg 3(2), in relation to accounting periods beginning on or after 1 July 2008.

[4090]

14 Claims for overpaid tax

Except where the amount to which the claim relates has been entered in a return in accordance with regulation 13 or is included in an amount so entered, any claim under paragraph 8 of Schedule 7 to the Act shall be made in writing to the Commissioners and shall, by reference to such documentary evidence as is in the possession of the claimant, state the amount of the claim and the method by which that amount was calculated.

[4091]

15 Payment of tax

Save as the Commissioners may otherwise allow or direct, any person required to make a return shall pay to the Controller, Central Collection Unit (IPT) such amount of tax as is payable by him in respect of the accounting period to which the return relates no later than the last day on which he was required to make the return.

[4092]

16 Records

(1) Every registrable person shall, for the purpose of accounting for tax, keep and preserve the following—

(a) his business and accounting records;

(b) policy documents, cover notes, endorsements and similar documents, and copies of such documents that are issued by him;

(c) copies of all invoices, renewal notices and similar documents issued by him;

(d) all credit or debit notes or other documents received by him which evidence an increase or decrease in the amount of any premium [or fee], and copies of such documents that are issued by him;

(e) such other records as the Commissioners may specify in a notice published by them and not withdrawn by them.

(2) Every registrable person shall keep and preserve the records specified in paragraph (1) above for a period of six years.

(3) The reference in paragraph (1)(d) above to any premium shall be construed for the purposes of that paragraph as it would be construed for the purposes of Part V of these Regulations.

NOTES

Para (1): words in square brackets inserted by the Insurance Premium Tax (Amendment) Regulations 1997, SI 1997/1157, reg 8.

PART IV
CLAIMS IN RESPECT OF CREDIT

[4093]

17 Scope

[(1) This Part applies where—

(a) an insurer has paid tax and all or part of the premium on which the tax was charged is repaid; or

(b) a taxable intermediary has paid tax and all or part of the fee on which the tax was charged is repaid.

(2) Where—

(a) an insurer receives a premium in an accounting period and repays that premium or part of it in that accounting period; or

(b) a taxable intermediary receives a fee in an accounting period and repays that fee or part of it in that accounting period,

this Part shall apply as if the tax on the premium or fee (as the case may be) had already been paid by him.]

(3) This Part applies subject to regulation 7.

NOTES

Paras (1), (2): substituted by the Insurance Premium Tax (Amendment) Regulations 1997, SI 1997/1157, reg 9.

[4094]

18 Claims in returns

(1) Where this Part applies, the insurer [or, as the case may be, taxable intermediary] shall be entitled to credit of an amount which represents the difference between the amount of tax paid by him and the amount of tax he would have been liable to pay had the premium [or fee] received by him been reduced or extinguished, as the case may be, by the amount of the repayment.

(2) Subject to paragraph (3) below, an insurer [or taxable intermediary] who is entitled to credit under this Part may claim it by deducting its amount from any tax due from him for the accounting period in which the premium [or fee] was repaid or any subsequent accounting period and, where he does so, he shall make his return for that accounting period accordingly.

(3) Where the Commissioners have given a special or general direction under section 55(5) of the Act prescribing rules according to which any credit may or shall be held over to an accounting period subsequent to that in which the [premium or fee, or part of such premium or fee] was repaid, that credit, subject to any subsequent such direction varying or withdrawing the rules, may only be claimed in accordance with those rules.

NOTES

Paras (1), (2): words in square brackets inserted by the Insurance Premium Tax (Amendment) Regulations 1997, SI 1997/1157, reg 10(a), (b).

Para (3): words in square brackets substituted by SI 1997/1157, reg 10(c).

[4095]

19 Payments in respect of credit

(1) Subject to paragraph (5) below, where the total credit claimed by the insurer [or taxable intermediary] in accordance with this Part exceeds the total of the tax due from him for the accounting period, the Commissioners shall pay to him an amount equal to the excess.

(2) Where the Commissioners have cancelled the registration of an insurer [or taxable intermediary] in accordance with section 53(5) [or 53AA(6) of the Act], and he is not a registrable person, he shall make any claim in respect of credit to which this Part applies by making an application in writing.

(3) An insurer [or taxable intermediary] making an application under paragraph (2) above shall furnish to the Commissioners full particulars in relation to the credit claimed, including (but not restricted to)—

(a) the return in which the relevant tax was accounted for;

(b) the date and manner of payment of that tax;

(c) the date of the repayment of the [premium or fee, or part of such premium or fee]; and

(d) the amounts of both the tax which was paid and the repayment.

(4) Subject to paragraph (5) below, where the Commissioners are satisfied that the insurer [or taxable intermediary as the case may be,] is entitled to credit as claimed by him, and that he has not previously had the benefit of that credit, they shall pay to him an amount equal to the credit.

(5) The Commissioners shall not be liable to make any payment under this regulation unless and until the insurer [or taxable intermediary] has made all the returns which he was required to make.

NOTES

Paras (1), (2), (4), (5): words in square brackets inserted by the Insurance Premium Tax (Amendment) Regulations 1997, SI 1997/1157, reg 11(a), (b), (d), (e).

Para (3): words in first pair of square brackets inserted, and words in second pair of square brackets substituted, by SI 1997/1157, reg 11(c).

Note: there appears to be a drafting error with regard to the amendment of para (2), the effect of which is to duplicate the words "of the Act". This has been corrected in the interests of clarity.

[PART IVA
REIMBURSEMENT ARRANGEMENTS

[4096]

19A Interpretation of Part IVA

In this Part—

"claim" means a claim made (irrespective of when it was made) under paragraph 8 of Schedule 7 to the Act for repayment of an amount paid to the Commissioners by way of tax which was not tax due to them; and "claimed" and "claimant" shall be construed accordingly;

"reimbursement arrangements" means any arrangements (whether made before, on or after 30th January 1998) for the purposes of a claim which—

(a) are made by a claimant for the purpose of securing that he is not unjustly enriched by the repayment of any amount in pursuance of the claim; and

(b) provide for the reimbursement of persons (consumers) who have, for practical purposes, borne the whole or any part of the cost of the original payment of that amount to the Commissioners;

"relevant amount" means that part (which may be the whole) of the amount of a claim which the claimant has reimbursed or intends to reimburse to consumers.]

NOTES

Part IVA (regs 19A–19H) inserted by the Insurance Premium Tax (Amendment) Regulations 1998, SI 1998/60, reg 2.

[4097]

[19B Reimbursement arrangements—general

Without prejudice to regulation 19H below, for the purposes of paragraph 8(3) of Schedule 7 to the Act (defence by the Commissioners that repayment by them of an amount claimed would unjustly enrich the claimant) reimbursement arrangements made by a claimant shall be disregarded except where they—

(a) include the provisions described in regulation 19C below; and

(b) are supported by the undertakings described in regulation 19G below.]

NOTES

Inserted as noted to reg 19A at **[4096]**.

[4098]

[19C Reimbursement arrangements—provisions to be included

The provisions referred to in regulation 19B(a) above are that—

(a) reimbursement for which the arrangements provide will be completed by no later than 90 days after the repayment to which it relates;

(b) no deduction will be made from the relevant amount by way of fee or charge (howsoever expressed or effected);

(c) reimbursement will be made only in cash or by cheque;

(d) any part of the relevant amount that is not reimbursed by the time mentioned in paragraph (a) above will be repaid by the claimant to the Commissioners;

(e) any interest paid by the Commissioners on any relevant amount repaid by them will also be treated by the claimant in the same way as the relevant amount falls to be treated under paragraphs (a) and (b) above; and

(f) the records described in regulation 19E below will be kept by the claimant and produced by him to the Commissioners, or to an officer of theirs in accordance with regulation 19F below.]

NOTES

Inserted as noted to reg 19A at **[4096]**.

[4099]

[19D Repayments to the Commissioners

The claimant shall, without prior demand, make any repayment to the Commissioners that he is required to make by virtue of regulation 19C(d) and (e) above within 14 days of the expiration of the period of 90 days referred to in regulation 19C(a) above.

NOTES

Inserted as noted to reg 19A at **[4096]**.

[4100]

[19E Records

The claimant shall keep records of the following matters—

(a) the names and addresses of those consumers whom he has reimbursed or whom he intends to reimburse;

(b) the total amount reimbursed to each such consumer;

(c) the amount of interest included in each total amount reimbursed to each consumer;

(d) the date that each reimbursement is made.]

NOTES

Inserted as noted to reg 19A at **[4096]**.

[4101]

[19F Production of records

(1) Where a claimant is given notice in accordance with paragraph (2) below, he shall, in accordance with such notice produce to the Commissioners, or to an officer of theirs, the records that he is required to keep pursuant to regulation 19E above.

(2) A notice given for the purposes of paragraph (1) above shall—

(a) be in writing;

(b) state the place and time at which, and the date on which the records are to be produced; and

(c) be signed and dated by the Commissioners, or by an officer of theirs,

and may be given before or after, or both before and after the Commissioners have paid the relevant amount to the claimant.]

NOTES

Inserted as noted to reg 19A at **[4096]**.

[4102]
[19G Undertakings

(1) Without prejudice to regulation 19H(b) below, the undertakings referred to in regulation 19B(b) above shall be given to the Commissioners by the claimant no later than the time at which he makes the claim for which the reimbursement arrangements have been made.

(2) The undertakings shall be in writing, shall be signed and dated by the claimant, and shall be to the effect that—

(a) at the date of the undertakings he is able to identify the names and addresses of those consumers whom he has reimbursed or whom he intends to reimburse;

(b) he will apply the whole of the relevant amount repaid to him, without any deduction by way of fee or charge or otherwise, to the reimbursement in cash or by cheque, of such consumers by no later than 90 days after his receipt of that amount (except insofar as he has already so reimbursed them);

(c) he will apply any interest paid to him on the relevant amount repaid to him wholly to the reimbursement of such consumers by no later than 90 days after his receipt of that interest;

(d) he will repay to the Commissioners without demand the whole or such part of the relevant amount repaid to him or of any interest paid to him as he fails to apply in accordance with the undertakings mentioned in sub-paragraphs (b) and (c) above;

(e) he will keep the records described in regulation 19E above; and

(f) he will comply with any notice given to him in accordance with regulation 19F above concerning the production of such records.]

NOTES

Inserted as noted to reg 19A at **[4096]**.

[4103]
[19H Reimbursement arrangements made before 11th February 1998

Reimbursement arrangements made by a claimant before 11th February 1998 shall not be disregarded for the purposes of paragraph 8(3) of Schedule 7 to the Act if, not later than 11th March 1998—

(a) he includes in those arrangements (if they are not already included) the provisions described in regulation 19C above; and

(b) gives the undertakings described in regulation 19G above.]

NOTES

Inserted as noted to reg 19A at **[4096]**.

PART V
SPECIAL ACCOUNTING SCHEME

[4104]
20 Interpretation

(1) In this Part—

"date of receipt", in relation to any premium, means the date on which apart from the operation of the scheme the premium is received or taken to be received by the provisions of the Act;

"initial period" means the first of the accounting periods which begin on or after the date specified in a notification made under regulation 1(1);

"premium written date", in relation to any premium, means the date as at which the insurer makes an entry in his accounts showing the premium as due to him.

(2) Any reference in this Part to the accounts of any person shall be construed as a reference to—

(a) the books, accounts or other similar records which he maintains in whatever form for the purpose of enabling him to show the premiums receivable by him in the revenue account he is required to prepare [in accordance with rules made under Part 10 of the Financial Services and Markets Act 2000]; and "premiums receivable" has the same meaning as [in those rules]; or

(b) where he is not required to prepare the revenue account referred to in sub-paragraph (a) above, any books, accounts or other records which would enable him to prepare one.

(3) Any reference in this Part to a premium shall be construed as including a reference to anything that, although not actually received by or on behalf of an insurer, would be a premium if it were so received.

(4) In deciding whether and (if it does) how the scheme applies to an accounting period of an insurer to whom the scheme has previously applied as regards one or more accounting periods ending before the beginning of the initial period specified in a notification he has made under regulation 21(1), the fact of such previous application of the scheme shall be ignored.

NOTES

Para (2): words in square brackets in para (a) substituted by the Financial Services and Markets Act 2000 (Consequential Amendments and Repeals) Order 2001, SI 2001/3649, art 462.

[4105]

21 Notification by insurer that scheme to apply

(1) An insurer who is a registrable person and—

(a) is required to prepare the revenue account referred to in regulation 20(2)(a); or

(b) not being required to prepare such a revenue account, keeps accounts as described in regulation 20(2)(b),

may notify the Commissioners in writing that the scheme should apply to him as regards accounting periods beginning on or after a date specified in the notification, being a date falling after the date the notification is made.

(2) An insurer who has made a notification under paragraph (1) above may notify the Commissioners in writing that he wishes to withdraw the notification and, provided he makes the notification referred to in this paragraph no later than the last day by which he is required to make the return for the initial period and before he has made that return, the scheme shall not apply to him as regards any accounting period.

(3) The fact that an insurer has on a previous occasion withdrawn or been expelled from the scheme under regulation 26 or 27 or withdrawn a notification under paragraph (2) above shall not prevent him making a notification under paragraph (1) above.

[4106]

22 Relevant accounting periods

Subject to regulations 21(2), 26 and 27, the scheme shall apply as regards all the accounting periods of an insurer who has made a notification under regulation 21(1) with effect from the initial period.

[4107]

23 Premiums treated as received on premium written date

(1) Subject to paragraph (8) below, any premium in relation to which—

(a) an insurer has made an entry in his accounts showing the premium as due to him;

(b) the premium written date falls within a relevant accounting period; and

(c) the date of receipt does not fall within an accounting period which is earlier than the initial period and which is not a relevant accounting period,

shall be treated for the purposes of the Act as received by the insurer on the premium written date; and the insurer shall account for tax due in respect of the relevant accounting period concerned accordingly.

(2) Paragraph (1) above shall apply even if the premium or any part of it is never actually received by the insurer; and, where it is never actually received because the contract under which it is or would have been received is terminated or is not entered into, the premium shall nonetheless be taken for the purposes of the Act to have been received under the contract (including, where appropriate, a taxable insurance contract) under which the insurer treated it as due.

(3) Where in relation to any premium to which paragraph (1) above applies the premium written date is a date other than the date of receipt, the premium shall be treated for the purposes of the Act as not having been received by the insurer on the date of receipt; but this is subject to paragraph (4) below.

(4) Paragraph (3) above shall not apply to any excess which falls to be treated as a separate premium in accordance with regulation 24(2).

(5) An insurer to whom the scheme applies as regards an accounting period may assume that the scheme will apply as regards all subsequent accounting periods and account for tax due in respect of that period accordingly.

(6) Subject to paragraph (7) below, where in relation to a premium—

(a) the premium written date falls before 1st October 1994;

(b) the premium was actually received by the insurer on or after 1st October 1994; and

(c) the contract under which the premium was received is not a contract to which, if the premium had actually been received on the premium written date, section 67(3) of the Act would have applied,

the premium shall be treated for the purposes of the Act as received before 1st October 1994 and the insurer shall accordingly not account for any tax on that premium.

(7) Paragraph (6) above shall not apply to any premium where—

(a) the contract under which the premium was received relates to a risk the period of cover for which begins on or after 1st October 1994; and

(b) it is not the normal practice as regards the class of contract to which that contract belongs for an insurer to make an entry in his accounts showing the premium as due as at a date before the period of cover begins.

(8) Where the initial period begins on 1st October 1994, nothing in this regulation shall be taken as requiring a premium—

(a) which was actually received by the insurer before 1st October 1994;

(b) in respect of which the premium written date falls within a relevant accounting period;

(c) which is not taken by virtue of section 67 of the Act to be received on 1st October 1994; and

(d) which was received under a contract which relates to a risk the period of cover for which begins before 1st October 1994,

to be treated as received on a date other than the date of receipt.

(9) Where in relation to any premium—

(a) an insurer has made an entry in his accounts showing the premium as due to him;

(b) the entry was made on a date falling within a relevant accounting period; and

(c) the premium written date would, apart from this paragraph, fall in a relevant accounting period which is earlier than the accounting period referred to in paragraph (b) above,

the insurer shall be treated for the purposes of this regulation as if he had made the entry showing the premium as due to him as at the date on which the entry was made and that date (and no other date) shall be the premium written date accordingly.

[4108]

24 Amount of premium

(1) Subject to any direction made under section 66 of the Act, where in relation to any premium to which regulation 23(1) applies the amount which is entered in the accounts as due (the initial amount) is not the amount which is or would be found apart from the operation of the scheme to be the amount of the premium in accordance with the provisions of the Act the amount of the premium shall be taken to be the initial amount.

(2) Where paragraph (1) above applies and the amount of the premium which is received exceeds the initial amount, the excess shall be treated as a separate premium and shall be treated as received on a date determined in accordance with paragraphs (3) and (4) below.

(3) Where an amount of premium is treated as a separate premium in accordance with paragraph (2) above and—

(a) the initial amount is not less than the amount which has been agreed with the insured by the insurer or his agent as the amount which, as at the date the entry is made, is due under the contract; and

(b) the insurer makes an entry in his accounts showing the excess as due, it shall be treated as received on the date he makes that entry in his accounts.

(4) In any case where an amount of premium is treated as a separate premium in accordance with paragraph (2) above and paragraph (3) above does not apply, the excess shall be treated as received on the date as at which the initial amount is entered in the accounts as due.

(5) An insurer who intends to enter in his accounts as due any excess over the initial amount of any premium which, if he were to make such an entry, would be treated as received on a date determined in accordance with paragraph (3) above may assume that it will be so treated until such time as he ceases to have that intention.

(6) Where in relation to an amount of premium which is treated as a separate premium in accordance with paragraph (2) above the date of receipt is a date other than the date determined in accordance with paragraphs (3) and (4) above, it shall be treated as not having been received by the insurer on the date of receipt.

[4109]

25 Credit

(1) Subject to paragraph (2) below, where tax has been paid—

(a) in respect of a premium to which regulation 24(1) applies and the initial amount exceeds the amount which is or would be found apart from the operation of the scheme to be the amount of the premium in accordance with the provisions of the Act; or

(b) in respect of a premium or part of a premium which has not been received, then, if it is shown to the satisfaction of the Commissioners that that excess, premium or part, as the case may be, will never actually be received, the amount of that excess, premium or part shall be treated as an amount of premium which the insurer has repaid on the date upon which the Commissioners are so satisfied and he shall be entitled to credit for the amount concerned in accordance with Part IV of these Regulations.

(2) It shall be a condition of any claim being made by an insurer in reliance upon paragraph (1) above that, if the excess, premium or part (as the case may be) or any part thereof is in fact received by the insurer, he shall pay to the Commissioners an amount equal to the tax chargeable on the amount received; and any amount which the insurer is liable to pay under this paragraph shall be treated as tax due for the accounting period in which the amount of excess or premium was received.

[4110]

26 Withdrawal from the scheme

(1) An insurer may notify the Commissioners in writing that the scheme should not apply to him as regards accounting periods beginning on or after a date specified in the notification (being a date falling after the date the notification is made) and the scheme shall cease to apply to him accordingly.

(2) The scheme shall nonetheless continue to apply to an insurer who has made a notification under paragraph (1) above unless and until—

(a) he has made all the returns which he was required to make;

(b) he has paid all the tax which was payable in respect of the accounting periods for which he was required to make those returns; and

(c) the scheme has applied as regards such number of relevant accounting periods as is required in order for the scheme to have applied to him for a period of not less than twelve consecutive months beginning with the first day of the initial period;

and, when he has complied with sub-paragraphs (a) to (c) above and with any requirement to make returns or pay tax arising since the date the notification was made, the scheme shall cease to apply with effect from the first of his accounting periods which begin on or after the date of such compliance.

[4111]

27 Expulsion from the scheme

(1) In any case where the Commissioners consider it necessary for the protection of the revenue, including (but not restricted to) a case where the revenue is prejudiced by reason of the premium written date in relation to premiums falling in accounting periods later than those in which falls the date of receipt, they may give notice to an insurer who has made the notification under regulation 21(1) that the scheme is not to apply to him; and the scheme shall accordingly not apply or cease to apply, as the case may be.

(2) Where a notice is given under paragraph (1) above before the last day of the initial period, the scheme shall not apply to any of the accounting periods of the insurer.

(3) Where a notice is given under paragraph (1) above on or after the last day of the initial period, the notice shall specify the accounting period of the insurer with effect from which the scheme is not to apply to him, being an accounting period the last day of which falls after the date the notice is given.

[4112]–[4115]

28 Tax to be accounted for on cessation

(1) Where the scheme has ceased to apply to an insurer by virtue of regulation 26 or 27, he shall account for and pay any tax chargeable on premiums in relation to which the date of receipt falls within a relevant accounting period and for which he has not accounted and which he has not paid in reliance upon the assumption referred to in regulation 23(5) as if the premiums were received in the accounting period with effect from which the scheme has ceased to apply to him.

(2) Where the Commissioners have cancelled the registration of an insurer and the last of his accounting periods is a relevant accounting period, paragraph (1) above shall apply as if—

(a) the scheme had ceased to apply to him by virtue of regulation 26 or 27; and

(b) the reference to the accounting period with effect from which the scheme has ceased to apply to him were a reference to the last of his accounting periods.

29–31 *((Pt VI) revoked by the Insurance Premium Tax (Amendment) Regulations 2008, SI 2008/1945, regs 2, 3.)*

PART VII
LIABILITY OF INSURED PERSONS

[4116]
32 Interpretation

In this Part—

"contract" means a taxable insurance contract;

"liability notice" means a notice served under regulation 34;

"material date" has the same meaning as in section 65(4) of the Act;

"tax debt" means a liability to pay an amount which is tax or is deemed to be or recoverable as if it were tax which, at the time of any payment, has not been discharged.

[4117]
[33 Scope

This Part applies where an insurer who is a registrable person—

(a) does not have any business establishment or other fixed establishment in the United Kingdom, and

(b) is established in a country or territory in respect of which it appears to the Commissioners that the condition in section 65(1A) of the Act is met.]

NOTES

Commencement: 1 September 2008.

Substituted by the Insurance Premium Tax (Amendment) Regulations 2008, SI 2008/1945, regs 2, 4.

[4118]
34 Liability notices

Where this Part applies, the Commissioners may serve a notice on the person who is insured under a contract or, where there are two or more such persons, one or more of them.

[4119]
35 Power to assess tax due

(1) This regulation applies where—

(a) the Commissioners have served a liability notice or notices; and

(b) the insurer—

(i) has failed to make any return he was required to make or any such return appears to the Commissioners to be incomplete or incorrect; or

(ii) has failed to pay any tax or amount deemed to be tax, including an amount which he was liable to pay by virtue of this Part.

(2) Where this regulation applies—

(a) the Commissioners may assess to the best of their judgment the amount of any tax due in respect of premiums received by the insurer under the contract after the material date and before the date of the assessment; and

(b) the amount so assessed shall be deemed to be the amount of tax due in respect of that contract for the period by reference to which the assessment is made.

[4120]
36 Persons liable for tax assessed

(1) Where the Commissioners make an assessment under regulation 35 and notify it to the insured person, or each of the insured persons, on whom a liability notice in respect of the contract has been served—

(a) the insurer; and

(b) the insured persons mentioned in this regulation,

shall be jointly and severally liable to pay the amount of tax assessed, to the extent that the assessment has not subsequently been reduced or withdrawn, and that tax shall be recoverable accordingly.

(2) An insured person who has been notified of an assessment made under regulation 35 shall be liable in accordance with this regulation to pay the tax so assessed notwithstanding that he has already paid an amount representing that tax or any part of it as part of a premium.

[4121]
37 Adjustment of assessments

(1) Where—

(a) an amount of tax has been assessed under regulation 35; and

(b) the amount of that tax, or any part of it, has also been assessed under section 56 of the Act and notified to the insurer,

the assessment which has been made under regulation 35 shall be treated as reduced to the extent that the amount referred to in sub-paragraph (b) above has been included in the amount thereof.

(2) Where an assessment such as is referred to in paragraph (1)(a) or (b) above is subsequently withdrawn, that paragraph shall not apply; and where the assessment is reduced, it shall apply as if any reference to the amount of tax which has been assessed were a reference to the reduced amount.

[4122]
38 Time for payment

Any insured person who is liable to pay an amount of tax which has been assessed under regulation 35 shall do so no later than thirty days after the date on which it was notified to him.

[4123]
39 Interest on reimbursements

(1) Where an insurer is liable by virtue of section 65(9) of the Act to pay to an insured person an amount equal to the amount which has been recovered from him, then, if and to the extent that the insurer would not be liable to do so apart from this regulation, he shall pay interest to him.

(2) The interest payable under paragraph (1) above shall be paid at the rate of 8 per cent per annum for the period beginning with the date on which the amount was recovered from the insured person and ending with the date the insurer paid to him an amount equal to that amount.

[4124]
40 Allocation of payments

(1) This regulation applies where an insurer pays an amount of tax to the Commissioners and—

- (a) at the time of the payment there exists a tax debt of his by virtue of his being liable to pay tax which has been assessed under regulation 35;
- (b) at the time of the payment there exists a tax debt of his which—
  - (i) is not within sub-paragraph (a) above; and
  - (ii) relates to an accounting period which corresponds to any extent with the period by reference to which the assessment referred to in sub-paragraph (a) above was made; and
- (c) the amount of the payment is not sufficient to satisfy all his tax debts in full.

(2) Where this regulation applies and the payment would not otherwise be applied as described in this paragraph, the payment shall be applied to reduce or extinguish the tax debt within paragraph (1)(a) above before it is applied to any other tax debt.

(3) Where—

- (a) this regulation applies;
- (b) there are two or more tax debts within paragraph (1)(a) above; and
- (c) the payment is not sufficient to satisfy those tax debts in full,

there shall be applied to each such tax debt such proportion of the payment as bears the same relationship to the whole of the payment as does the tax debt to the total of those tax debts.

[4125]
41 Records

(1) Where—

- (a) an insured person has been served with a liability notice;
- (b) he is carrying on a business; and
- (c) the contract provides cover for any matter associated with that business,

the insured person shall keep and preserve the records specified in paragraph (2) below.

(2) The records which an insured person shall keep and preserve are such of the following as relate to the contract—

- (a) his business and accounting records;
- (b) policy documents, cover notes, endorsements and similar documents;
- (c) all invoices, renewal notices and similar documents issued to him;
- (d) all credit or debit notes or other documents received by him which evidence an increase or decrease in the premium, and copies of such documents that are issued by him.

(3) Every insured person who is required to keep and preserve records by paragraph (1) above shall do so for a period of six years.

(4) The reference in paragraph (2)(d) above to any premium shall be construed for the purposes of that paragraph as it would be construed for the purposes of Part V of these Regulations.

PART VIII
DISTRESS AND DILIGENCE

[4126]

[A42 In this Part—

"Job Band" followed by a number between "1" and "12" means the band for the purposes of pay and grading in which the job an officer performs is ranked in the system applicable to Customs and Excise.]

NOTES

Inserted by the Insurance Premium Tax (Amendment) Regulations 1996, SI 1996/2099, regs 2, 3.

42 (*Revoked by the Distress for Customs and Excise Duties and Other Indirect Taxes Regulations 1997, SI 1997/1431, reg 3(1), Sch 3.*)

[4127]

[43 Diligence

In Scotland, the following provisions shall have effect—

(a) where the Commissioners are empowered to apply to the sheriff for a warrant to authorise a sheriff officer to recover any amount of tax or sum recoverable as if it were tax remaining due and unpaid, any application, and any certificate required to accompany that application, may be made on their behalf by a Collector or an officer of rank not below that of [Job Band 7];

(b) where, during the course of [an attachment] the Commissioners are entitled as a creditor to do any act, then any such act, with the exception of the exercise of the power contained in [section 30(4) of the Debt Arrangement and Attachment (Scotland) Act (asp 17)], may be done on their behalf by a Collector or an officer of rank not below that of [Job Band 7].]

NOTES

Substituted by the Insurance Premium Tax (Amendment) Regulations 1995, SI 1995/1587, reg 4.

Words in first and fourth pairs of square brackets substituted by the Insurance Premium Tax (Amendment) Regulations 1996, SI 1996/2099, regs 2, 4; words in second and third pairs of square brackets substituted by the Debt Arrangement and Attachment (Scotland) Act 2002, s 61, Sch 3, Pt 2, para 34.

SCHEDULE

[4128]–[4131]

NOTES

This Schedule contains forms which are not themselves reproduced in this work, but their numbers and titles are listed below.

Form No	*Title*
1–3	Application for insurance premium tax registration (Form 1 substituted by SI 2008/1945).
4	Insurance premium tax return (substituted by SI 2008/1482 in relation to accounting periods beginning on or after 1 July 2008).
5	Lloyd's composite IPT return for syndicates (substituted by SI 2008/1482 in relation to accounting periods beginning on or after 1 July 2008).
6	Lloyd's composite return—schedule of participating syndicates (substituted by SI 1997/1157).

COMPANIES (SUMMARY FINANCIAL STATEMENT) REGULATIONS 1995

(SI 1995/2092)

NOTES

Made: 4 August 1995.

Authority: Companies Act 1985, ss 245(3), (4), 251(1), (2), (3).

Commencement: 1 September 1995.

These Regulations were revoked by the Companies (Summary Financial Statement) Regulations 2008, SI 2008/374, reg 12(1), as from 6 April 2008, subject to transitional provisions and savings in reg 12(2)–(4) thereof relating to financial years beginning before that date.

1–6 *((Pts I, II) outside the scope of this work.)*

PART III
FORM AND CONTENT OF SUMMARY FINANCIAL STATEMENT

7–9 (*Outside the scope of this work.*)

[4132]

10 Insurance companies and groups

(1) [Subject to regulation 10A,] the summary financial statement of a . . . company which is in relation to the financial year in question an insurance company the directors of which are not required to prepare group accounts under Part VII of the 1985 Act, shall be in the form, and contain the information, required by Schedule 3 to these Regulations, so far as applicable to such a company.

(2) [Subject to regulation 10A,] the summary financial statement of a . . . company which is the parent company of an insurance group shall be in the form, and contain the information, required by Schedule 3 to these Regulations, so far as applicable to such a company.

NOTES

Revoked as noted at the beginning of these Regulations.

Paras (1), (2): words in square brackets inserted and words omitted revoked by the Companies (Summary Financial Statement) (Amendment) Regulations 2005, SI 2005/2281, reg 10.

[4132A]

[10A *The summary financial statement of a company that is required to prepare group accounts and prepares IAS group accounts or, in the case of a company that is not required to prepare group accounts, prepares IAS individual accounts, must be in the form and contain the information required by Schedule 3A to these Regulations, so far as applicable to such a company.]*

NOTES

Commencement: 1 October 2005.

Inserted by the Companies (Summary Financial Statement) (Amendment) Regulations 2005, SI 2005/2281, reg 11.

Revoked as noted at the beginning of these Regulations.

11, 12 *((Pt IV) outside the scope of this work.)*

(Schs 1, 2 outside the scope of this work.)

SCHEDULE 3

FORM AND CONTENT OF SUMMARY FINANCIAL STATEMENT OF INSURANCE COMPANIES AND GROUPS

Regulation 10

[4133]

1 . . .

2 Form of summary financial statement

(1) The summary financial statement shall contain the information prescribed by the following paragraphs of this Schedule, in such order and under such headings as the directors consider appropriate, together with any other information necessary to ensure that the summary financial statement is consistent with the full accounts and reports for the financial year in question.

(2) Nothing in this Schedule shall be construed as prohibiting the inclusion in the summary financial statement of any additional information derived from the company's annual accounts[, the directors' remuneration report (if any) . . .] and the directors' report.

3 . . .

[3A Summary of paragraph 1(1) of Schedule 6 to the 1985 Act and of the directors' remuneration report

The summary financial statement shall contain the whole of, or a summary of—

- *(a) that portion of the notes to the accounts for the year in question which set out the information required by paragraph 1(1) of Part I of Schedule 6 to the 1985 Act (Aggregate amount of directors' emoluments etc); and*
- *(b) to the extent that the company is required to produce a directors' remuneration report, those portions of the directors' remuneration report for the year in question which set*

Part IV Statutory Instruments

out the matters required by paragraphs 3 (Statement of company's policy on directors' remuneration) and 4 (Performance graph) of Schedule 7A to the 1985 Act.]

4 Summary profit and loss account: companies not required to prepare group accounts

(1) The summary financial statement shall contain, in the case of a company the directors of which are not required to prepare group accounts for the financial year, a summary profit and loss account showing, in so far as they may be derived from the full profit and loss account, the items, or combinations of items, listed in sub-paragraph (3) below, in the order set out in that sub-paragraph.

(2) The items or combinations of items listed in sub-paragraph (3) below may appear under such headings as the directors consider appropriate.

(3) The items, or combinations of items, referred to in sub-paragraph (1) above are—

(a) gross premiums written—general business—
— *item I 1(a);*

(b) gross premiums written—long term business—
— *item II 1(a);*

(c) balance on the technical account for general business—
— *item I 10;*

(d) balance on the technical account for long term business—
— *item II 13;*

(e) other income and charges: the net figure resulting from the combination of the following items—
— *item III 3*
— *item III 3a*
— *item III 4*
— *item III 5*
— *item III 5a*
— *item III 6*
— *item III 7*
— *item III 8;*

(f) the profit or loss on ordinary activities before tax—
— *item III 8a;*

(g) tax on profit or loss on ordinary activities—
— *item III 9;*

(h) profit or loss on ordinary activities after tax—
— *item III 10;*

(i) extraordinary profit or loss after tax—
— *the net figure resulting from the combination of items III 13 and 14;*

(j) other taxes—
— *item III 15;*

(k) profit or loss for the financial year—
— *item III 16; and*

(l) . . .

(4) . . .

*[4A **Dividends***

The summary financial statement shall also contain the information concerning recognised and proposed dividends included in the full accounts and reports.]

5 Summary profit and loss account: companies required to prepare group accounts

(1) The summary financial statement shall contain, in the case of a company the directors of which are required to prepare group accounts for the financial year, a summary consolidated profit and loss account showing the items, or combinations of items, required by paragraph 4 above, in the order required by that paragraph and under such headings as the directors consider appropriate, but with the modifications specified in sub-paragraph (2) below[, and shall also contain the information required by paragraph 4A above].

(2) The modifications referred to in sub-paragraph (1) above are as follows—

(a) between the information required by paragraph 4(3)(e) and that required by paragraph 4(3)(f) there shall in addition be shown, under such heading as the directors consider appropriate, the item "Income from associated undertakings" required to be shown in the Schedule 9A formats by paragraph 21(3)(b) of Schedule 4A to the 1985 Act, as adapted by paragraph 1(8) of Part II of Schedule 9A to that Act;

(b) *between the information required by paragraph 4(3)(h) and that required by paragraph 4(3)(i) there shall in addition be shown, under such heading as the directors consider appropriate, the item "Minority interests" required to be shown in the Schedule 9A formats by paragraph 17(3) of Schedule 4A to the 1985 Act as adapted by paragraph 1(6)(c) of Part II of Schedule 9A to that Act; and*

(c) *the figures required by paragraph 4(3)(i) and (j) shall each be shown after the deduction or the addition (as the case may be) of the item "Minority interests" required to be shown in the Schedule 9A formats by paragraph 17(4) of Schedule 4A to the 1985 Act as adapted by paragraph 1(6)(d) of Part II of Schedule 9A to that Act.*

6 Summary balance sheet: companies not required to prepare group accounts

(1) The summary financial statement shall contain, in the case of a company the directors of which are not required to prepare group accounts for the financial year, a summary balance sheet which shall show, in so far as they may be derived from the full balance sheet, the items, or combinations of items, set out in sub-paragraph (2) below in the order of that sub-paragraph and under such headings as the directors consider appropriate.

(2) The items, or combinations of items, referred to in sub-paragraph (1) above are—

(a) *investments—*
— *the aggregate of items C and D under the heading "ASSETS";*

(b) *reinsurers' share of technical provisions—*
— *item Da under the heading "ASSETS";*

(c) *other assets—*
— *the aggregate of items A or E(IV), B, E(I) to (III), F and G under the heading "ASSETS";*

(d) *total assets under the heading "ASSETS";*

(e) *capital and reserves—*
— *item A under the heading "LIABILITIES";*

(f) *subordinated liabilities—*
— *item B under the heading "LIABILITIES";*

(g) *fund for future appropriations—*
— *item Ba under the heading "LIABILITIES";*

(h) *gross technical provisions—*
— *the aggregate of items C.1(a), C.2(a), C.3(a), C.4(a), C.5, C.6(a) and D(a) under the heading "LIABILITIES";*

(i) *technical provisions—reinsurance amounts—*
— *the aggregate of items C.1(b), C.2(b), C.3(b), C.4(b), C.6(b) and D(b) under the heading "LIABILITIES";*

(j) *other liabilities—*
— *the aggregate of items E, F, G and H under the heading "LIABILITIES"; and*

(k) *total liabilities under the heading "LIABILITIES".*

7 Summary balance sheet: companies required to prepare group accounts

(1) The summary financial statement shall contain, in the case of a company the directors of which are required to prepare group accounts for the financial year, a summary consolidated balance sheet which shall show the items required by paragraph 6 above, in the order required by that paragraph and under such headings as the directors consider appropriate, but with the addition of the item specified in sub-paragraph (2) below.

(2) Between the items required by paragraph 6(2)(d) and (e) above, there shall in addition be shown under an appropriate heading the item "Minority interests" required to be shown in the Schedule 9A format by paragraph 17(2) of Schedule 4A to the 1985 Act, as adapted by paragraph 1(6)(b) of Part II of Schedule 9A to the 1985 Act.

8 Corresponding amounts

In respect of every item shown in the summary profit and loss account or summary consolidated profit and loss account (as the case may be) or in the summary balance sheet or summary consolidated balance sheet (as the case may be) the corresponding amount shall be shown for the immediately preceding financial year; for this purpose "the corresponding amount" is the amount shown in the summary financial statement for that year or which would have been so shown had such a statement been prepared for that year, [taking account of any adjustments to corresponding amounts made in the full accounts and reports].

9–12 . . .

NOTES

Revoked as noted at the beginning of these Regulations.

Paras 1, 3, 9–12: revoked by the Companies (Summary Financial Statement) (Amendment) Regulations 2005, SI 2005/2281, regs 14(1), (3), 17(b).

Para 2: words in square brackets inserted by SI 2005/2281, reg 14(1), (2); words omitted revoked by the Companies Act 1985 (Operating and Financial Review) (Repeal) Regulations 2005, SI 2005/3442, reg 2(2)(b), Sch 2, para 2(1), (6).

Para 3A: inserted by the Companies (Summary Financial Statement) Amendment Regulations 2002, SI 2002/1780, reg 7(1), in relation to companies' financial years ending on or after 31 December 2002.

Para 4: sub-para (3)(l) revoked by SI 2005/2281, reg 14(1), (4); sub-para (4) revoked by SI 2002/1780, reg 7(2), in relation to companies' financial years ending on or after 31 December 2002.

Para 4A: inserted by SI 2005/2281, reg 14(1), (5).

Para 5: words in square brackets inserted by SI 2005/2281, reg 14(1), (6).

Para 8: words in square brackets substituted by SI 2005/2281, reg 14(1), (7).

[SCHEDULE 3A

FORM AND CONTENT OF SUMMARY FINANCIAL STATEMENT OF COMPANIES AND GROUPS PREPARING ACCOUNTS IN ACCORDANCE WITH INTERNATIONAL ACCOUNTING STANDARDS

Regulation 10A

[4133A]–[4157]

1 Form of summary financial statement

(1) The summary financial statement shall contain the information prescribed by the following paragraphs of this Schedule in such order, and under such headings, as the directors consider appropriate.

(2) The summary financial statement shall contain any other information necessary to ensure that the statement is consistent with the full accounts and reports for the year in question.

(3) Nothing in this Schedule shall be construed as prohibiting the inclusion in the summary financial statement of any additional information derived from the company's annual accounts, directors' report, directors' remuneration report (if any) or operating and financial review (if any).

2 Summary of paragraph 1(1) of Schedule 6 to the 1985 Act and of the directors' remuneration report

The summary financial statement shall contain the whole of, or a summary of—

(a) that portion of the notes to the accounts for the year in question which set out the information required by paragraph 1(1) of Part 1 of Schedule 6 to the 1985 Act (aggregate amount of directors' emoluments etc); and

(b) to the extent that the company is required to produce a directors' remuneration report, those portions of the directors' remuneration report for the year in question which set out the matters required by paragraphs 3 (statement of company's policy on directors' remuneration) and 4 (performance graph) of Schedule 7A to the 1985 Act.

3 Summary profit loss and account: companies not required to prepare group accounts

(1) The summary financial statement shall contain, in the case of a company the directors of which are not required to prepare group accounts for the financial year, a summary profit and loss account showing either—

(a) each of the headings and sub-totals included in the full profit and loss account in accordance with international accounting standards, or

(b) where the directors consider it appropriate, a combination of such headings and sub-totals where they are of a similar nature.

(2) The summary financial statement shall also contain the information concerning recognised and proposed dividends included in the full accounts and reports.

(3) In this paragraph, and in paragraphs 4 to 6 below, the expressions "headings" and "subtotals" have the same meaning as in international accounting standard 1 on the presentation of financial statements.

4 Summary profit and loss account: companies required to prepare group accounts

(1) The summary financial statement shall contain, in the case of a company the directors of which are required to prepare group accounts for the financial year, a summary consolidated profit and loss account showing either—

(a) each of the headings and sub-totals included in the full consolidated profit and loss account in accordance with international accounting standards, or

(b) where the directors consider it appropriate, a combination of such headings and sub-totals where they are of a similar nature.

(2) The summary financial statement shall also contain the information concerning recognised and proposed dividends included in the full accounts and reports.

5 Summary balance sheet: companies not required to prepare group accounts

The summary financial statement shall contain, in the case of a company the directors of which are not required to prepare group accounts for the financial year, a summary balance sheet showing either—

(a) each of the headings and sub-totals included in the full balance sheet in accordance with international accounting standards, or

(b) where the directors consider it appropriate, a combination of such headings and sub-totals where they are of a similar nature.

6 Summary balance sheet: companies required to prepare group accounts

The summary financial statement shall contain, in the case of a company the directors of which are required to prepare group accounts for the financial year, a summary consolidated balance sheet showing either—

(a) each of the headings and sub-totals included in the full consolidated balance sheet in accordance with international accounting standards, or

(b) where the directors consider it appropriate, a combination of such headings and sub-totals where they are of a similar nature.

7 Corresponding amounts

(1) In respect of every item shown in the summary profit and loss account or summary consolidated profit and loss account (as the case may be), or in the summary balance sheet or summary consolidated balance sheet (as the case may be), the corresponding amount must be shown for the immediately preceding financial year.

(2) For the purposes of sub-paragraph (1), "the corresponding amount" is the amount shown in the summary financial statement for that year or which would have been so shown had such a statement been prepared for that year, taking account of any adjustments to corresponding amounts made in the full accounts and reports.]

NOTES

Commencement: 1 October 2005.

Inserted by the Companies (Summary Financial Statement) (Amendment) Regulations 2005, SI 2005/2281, reg 15, Schedule.

Revoked as noted at the beginning of these Regulations.

LIFE ASSURANCE AND OTHER POLICIES (KEEPING OF INFORMATION AND DUTIES OF INSURERS) REGULATIONS 1997

(SI 1997/265)

NOTES

Made: 10 February 1997.

Authority: Income and Corporation Taxes Act 1988, s 552(4A)(b), (4B), (4C).

Commencement: 1 April 1997.

[4158]

1 Citation and commencement

These Regulations may be cited as the Life Assurance and Other Policies (Keeping of Information and Duties of Insurers) Regulations 1997 and shall come into force on 1st April 1997.

[4159]

2 Interpretation

(1) In these Regulations unless the context otherwise requires—

"the Board" means the Commissioners [for Her Majesty's Revenue and Customs];

"relevant records", in respect of a policy or contract, means the books, documents and records specified in regulation 3;

"Schedule 15" means Schedule 15 to the Taxes Act;

"section 552" means section 552 of the Taxes Act [and a reference to that section without more includes, where necessary, a reference to section 552ZA of the Taxes Act];

"the Taxes Act" means the Income and Corporation Taxes Act 1988.

(2) For the purposes of these Regulations, an "insurer"—

(a) in a case where the obligations under any policy or contract of the body that issued, entered into or effected it ("the original insurer") are at any time the obligations of

Part IV Statutory Instruments

another body ("the transferee") to whom there has been a transfer of the whole or any part of a business previously carried on by the original insurer, means the transferee, and

(b) in any other case, means the body by or with whom the policy or contract was issued, entered into or effected.

(3) For the purposes of these Regulations and in relation to an insurer, a policy or contract is a relevant policy or contract if, on the happening of a chargeable event within the meaning of [Chapter 9 of Part 4 of the Income Tax (Trading and Other Income) Act 2005] in relation to the policy or contract, the insurer is under the duty to deliver a certificate pursuant to section 552; and, for the purposes of this paragraph, [the words "unless satisfied that no gain is to be treated as arising by reason of the event" in subsection (1)(a) shall be disregarded].

(4) For the purposes of these Regulations and in respect of any policy or contract, any reference to books, documents and records includes books, documents and records (including material prepared for the purposes of advertising or publicity) which contain information—

(a) relating to the terms of the policy or contract, or

(b) required for the purposes of a certificate to be delivered under section 552.

NOTES

Para (1): in definition "the Board" words in square brackets substituted by the Life Assurance and Other Policies (Keeping of Information and Duties of Insurers) (Amendment) Regulations 2008, SI 2008/2628, reg 2(1), (2)(a); in definition "section 552" words in square brackets added by the Life Assurance and Other Policies (Keeping of Information and Duties of Insurers) (Amendment) Regulations 2002, SI 2002/444, reg 3(1), (2).

Para (3): words in first pair of square brackets substituted by SI 2008/2628, reg 2(1), (2)(b); words in second pair of square brackets substituted by SI 2002/444, reg 3(1), (3).

[4160]

3 Keeping of records—general

An insurer shall, in respect of each relevant policy or contract, keep sufficient books, documents and records to enable the Board—

(a) to ascertain the terms of the policy or contract,

(b) to ascertain whether there has been or is likely to be any contravention of the requirements of section 552, and

(c) to verify any certificate delivered under that section.

[4161]

4 Period for which records to be kept

(1) Subject to paragraph (2), an insurer shall, in respect of each relevant policy or contract, keep the relevant records for a period of three years after the termination of the policy or contract.

(2) In any case where—

(a) a relevant policy is connected with another policy for the purposes of paragraph 13 or 14 of Schedule 15, or

(b) in relation to a relevant policy under which a single premium only is payable, liability for that payment is discharged in accordance with paragraph 15(2) of Schedule 15, or

(c) a relevant policy is issued in substitution for, or on the maturity of and in consequence of an option conferred by, another policy,

an insurer shall, in respect of each policy, keep the relevant records for a period of three years after the termination of the final policy which is in force.

Transfers of records

[4162]

5— (1) This regulation applies in any case where the obligations under any policy or contract of the body that issued, entered into or effected it ("the original insurer") are at any time the obligations of another body ("the transferee") to whom there has been a transfer of the whole or any part of a business previously carried on by the original insurer.

(2) The original insurer shall, in respect of that policy or contract, deliver the relevant records to the transferee within the period of three months after the transfer.

(3) This regulation has effect in relation to transfers on or after 1st April 1997.

[4163]

6— (1) This regulation applies in any case where each of the three conditions specified in paragraphs (2) to (4) is fulfilled.

(2) The first condition is that one policy (the "new policy") is issued in substitution for another policy (the "old policy").

(3) The second condition is that the new policy is issued in substitution for an old policy issued by an insurance company (the "old insurer") which was resident outside the United Kingdom at the time the old policy was issued.

(4) The third condition is that the new policy is issued by an insurance company (the "new insurer") pursuant to arrangements made between the old insurer and the new insurer for the issue of policies in substitution for ones held by persons becoming resident in the United Kingdom.

(5) The new insurer shall, in respect of the old policy, obtain the relevant records from the old insurer within the period of three months after the issue of the new policy.

(6) This regulation has effect in relation to any new policy where the insurance for that new policy is made, and that new policy is issued, on or after 1st April 1997.

[4164]

7— (1) This regulation applies in any case where each of the conditions specified in paragraphs (2) and (3) is fulfilled.

(2) The first condition is that one policy ("the new policy") is issued in substitution for, or on the maturity of and in consequence of an option conferred by, another policy ("the old policy").

(3) The second condition is that, at the time the new policy is issued, the insurance company issuing the new policy ("the new insurer") and the insurance company which issued the old policy ("the old insurer") are both members of a group of companies.

(4) For the purposes of paragraph (3) two companies are members of a group of companies if one is the 51 per cent subsidiary of the other or both are 51 per cent subsidiaries of a third company.

(5) The original insurer shall, in respect of the old policy, deliver the relevant records to the new insurer within the period of three months beginning with the date on which the new policy was substituted for the old policy or, as the case may be, the date of the exercise of the option on the maturity of the old policy.

(6) This regulation has effect in relation to any new policy where the insurance for that new policy is made, and that new policy is issued, on or after 1st April 1997.

[4165]

8 Information to be provided to the Board

(1) The Board may by notice require any person to whom premiums under any policy are or have at any time been payable, within such period as may be specified in the notice, to furnish them with such information as they may reasonably require to enable them—

(a) to ascertain whether there has been or is likely to be any contravention of the requirements of section 552, and

(b) to verify any certificate delivered under that section.

(2) The period specified in a notice given under paragraph (1) shall be a period of not less than 14 days beginning with the date on which the notice is given.

[4166]

9 Inspection of records by officer of the Board

(1) The Board may by notice require any person to whom premiums under any policy are or have at any time been payable, to make available for inspection by an officer of the Board authorised for that purpose, at such time as that officer may reasonably require, all such books, documents and records as are in that person's possession or under that person's control and are such as may be required by the Board under regulation 8.

(2) The time specified in a notice given under paragraph (1) shall not fall within the period of 14 days beginning with the date on which the notice is given.

OIL POLLUTION (COMPULSORY INSURANCE) REGULATIONS 1997

(SI 1997/1820)

NOTES

Made: 23 July 1997.

Authority: Merchant Shipping Act 1995, ss 163(1), 164(3), 302.

Commencement: 1 September 1997.

[4167]
1 Citation, commencement and interpretation

(1) These Regulations may be cited as the Oil Pollution (Compulsory Insurance) Regulations 1997 and shall come into force on 1st September 1997.

(2) In these Regulations "the Act" means the Merchant Shipping Act 1995.

2 *(Revokes the Oil Pollution (Compulsory Insurance) Regulations 1981 and the Oil Pollution (Compulsory Insurance) (Amendment) (No 2) Regulations 1990.)*

[4168]
3 Definition

For the purposes of section 163(1) of the Act, "oil" means any persistent hydrocarbon mineral oil such as crude oil, fuel oil, heavy diesel oil and lubricating oil, but excluding any oil which at the time of shipment, consists of hydrocarbon fractions—

(a) at least 50% of which, by volume, distil at a temperature of 340°C, and

(b) at least 95% of which, by volume, distil at a temperature of 370°C,

when tested by the ASTM Method D86/78 published by the American Society for Testing and Materials.

[4169]
4 Cancellation and delivery up of certificates

(1) Where, at any time while a certificate under section 164 of the Act is in force, the person to whom the certificate has been issued ceases to be the owner of the ship to which the certificate relates, he shall forthwith deliver up the certificate to the Secretary of State or to a proper officer and in such a case the certificate shall be cancelled by the Secretary of State.

(2) Where, at any time while a certificate under the said section 164 is in force, it is established in any legal proceedings that the contract of insurance or other security in respect of which the certificate was issued is or may be treated as invalid, the certificate may be cancelled by the Secretary of State and, if so cancelled, shall on demand forthwith be delivered up to him by the person to whom it was issued.

(3) Where, at any time while a certificate under the said section 164 is in force, circumstances arise in relation to the insurer or guarantor named in the certificate (or, where more than one is so named, to any of them) such that, if the certificate were applied for at that time, the Secretary of State would be entitled to refuse the application under subsection (2) of that section the certificate may be cancelled by the Secretary of State and, if so cancelled, shall on demand forthwith be delivered up to him by the person to whom it was issued.

5 *(Revoked by the Merchant Shipping (Fees) Regulations 2006, SI 2006/2055, reg 7, Sch 2.)*

MERCHANT SHIPPING (COMPULSORY INSURANCE: SHIPS RECEIVING TRANS-SHIPPED FISH) REGULATIONS 1998

(SI 1998/209)

NOTES

Made: 3 February 1998.
Authority: Merchant Shipping Act 1995, s 192A(1), (4), (5), (6).
Commencement: 6 April 1998.

[4170]
1 Citation and commencement

These Regulations may be cited as the Merchant Shipping (Compulsory Insurance: Ships Receiving Trans-shipped Fish) Regulations 1998 and shall come into force on 6th April 1998.

[4171]
2 Interpretation

In these Regulations—

"the Act" means the Merchant Shipping Act 1995;

"Merchant Shipping Notice No MSN 1711" means the Notice described as such, issued by the Secretary of State, and includes a reference to any document amending or replacing it which is considered by the Secretary of State to be relevant from time to time;

"trans-shipment licence" means a licence under section 4A of the Sea Fish (Conservation) Act 1967.

[4172]

3 Application

These Regulations apply to ships in respect of which trans-shipment licences are in force, while in United Kingdom waters.

[4173]

4 Insurance or security to be in force

(1) Subject to paragraphs (2) and (3) below the owner, charterer and master of a ship shall ensure that there is in force in respect of the ship a contract of insurance complying with regulation 6 below insuring the owner against the liabilities mentioned in regulation 5.

(2) In place of a contract of insurance there may be in force such other form of security as complies with regulation 6 below which will enable the owner to meet the liabilities mentioned in regulation 5.

(3) Paragraphs (1) and (2) are without prejudice to any entitlement to limit liability provided by section 185 of the Act and contracts of insurance and security may be limited accordingly.

[4174]

5 Liability to be covered

The liabilities to be covered are—

(a) any liability under section 154 of the Act;

(b) any liability for the costs of any operation to remove or render harmless the ship, or any article which had been on the ship, taken under the powers conferred by sections 252 or 253 of the Act or under corresponding powers under any statutory provision of local application;

(c) any liability for payment of salvage awards under Article 12 or 13, and special compensation under Article 14, of the International Convention on Salvage 1989; and

(d) any liability for the cost of providing relief to, and of repatriating, seamen left behind or shipwrecked.

[4175]

6 Contracts of insurance and other security

A contract of insurance or other security shall be sufficient for the purpose of these Regulations only if it satisfies all requirements (whether as to the person issuing it, the amount of compensation available, or for any other reason) as is specified in Merchant Shipping Notice No MSN 1711.

[4176]

7 Documents

(1) Where a person is required under these Regulations to ensure that there is in force a contract of insurance or other security, documentary evidence of compliance with this requirement shall be carried in the ship. Such documentary evidence shall be in the form specified in Merchant Shipping Notice No MSN 1711.

(2) The master and any other officer on the ship shall produce on demand such documentary evidence to any person mentioned in paragraph (a), (b) or (c) of section 258(1) of the Act.

[4177]

8 Penalties

(1) If there is any contravention of regulation 4, the owner, charterer and master shall each be guilty of an offence punishable on summary conviction by a fine not exceeding £50,000.

(2) Any contravention of regulation 7 shall be an offence by any person required to produce documentary evidence punishable on summary conviction by a fine not exceeding level 4 on the standard scale.

(3) It shall be a defence for a person charged with an offence under paragraph (1) or (2) of this regulation to show that he took all reasonable precautions and exercised all due diligence to avoid the commission of the offence.

[4178]–[4179]

9 Power to detain

In any case where a ship does not comply with the requirements of these Regulations, the ship shall be liable to be detained and section 284 of the Act (which relates to the detention of a ship) shall have effect in relation to the ship, subject to the modification that as if for the words "this Act", wherever they appear, there were substituted "the Merchant Shipping (Compulsory Insurance: Ships Receiving Trans-shipped Fish) Regulations 1998".

EMPLOYERS' LIABILITY (COMPULSORY INSURANCE) REGULATIONS 1998

(SI 1998/2573)

NOTES

Made: 13 October 1998.

Authority: Employers' Liability (Compulsory Insurance) Act 1969, ss 1(2), 1(3)(a), 2(2), 3(1)(c), 4(1), (2) and 6.

Commencement: 1 January 1999.

ARRANGEMENT OF REGULATIONS

1	Citation, commencement and interpretation	[4180]
2	Prohibition of certain conditions in policies of insurance	[4181]
3	Limit of amount of compulsory insurance	[4182]
4	Issue of certificates of insurance	[4183]
5	Display and production of copies of certificates of insurance	[4184]
6	Production of certificates of insurance to an Inspector	[4185]
7	Inspection of policies of insurance	[4186]
8	Production by inspectors of evidence of authority	[4187]
9	Employers exempted from insurance	[4188]
10	Revocations and transitional	[4189]

SCHEDULES:

Schedule 1—Certificate of Employers' Liability Insurance	[4190]
Schedule 2—Employers Exempted from Insurance	[4191]

[4180]

1 Citation, commencement and interpretation

(1) These Regulations may be cited as the Employers' Liability (Compulsory Insurance) Regulations 1998 and shall come into force on 1st January 1999.

(2) In these Regulations—

"the 1969 Act" means the Employers' Liability (Compulsory Insurance) Act 1969;

"associated structure" means, in relation to an offshore installation, a vessel, aircraft or hovercraft attendant on the installation or any floating structure used in connection with the installation;

"company" has the same meaning as in section 735 of the Companies Act 1985;

"inspector" means an inspector duly authorised by the Secretary of State under section 4(2)(b) of the 1969 Act;

"offshore installation" has the same meaning as in the Offshore Installations and Pipeline Works (Management and Administration) Regulations 1995;

"relevant employee" means an employee—

(a) who is ordinarily resident in the United Kingdom; or

(b) who, though not ordinarily resident in the United Kingdom, has been employed on or from an offshore installation or associated structure for a continuous period of not less than 7 days; or

(c) who, though not ordinarily resident in Great Britain, is present in Great Britain in the course of employment for a continuous period of not less than 14 days; and

"subsidiary" has the same meaning as in section 736 of the Companies Act 1985.

[4181]

2 Prohibition of certain conditions in policies of insurance

(1) For the purposes of the 1969 Act, there is prohibited in any contract of insurance any condition which provides (in whatever terms) that no liability (either generally or in respect of a particular claim) shall arise under the policy, or that any such liability so arising shall cease, if—

(a) some specified thing is done or omitted to be done after the happening of the event giving rise to a claim under the policy;

(b) the policy holder does not take reasonable care to protect his employees against the risk of bodily injury or disease in the course of their employment;

(c) the policy holder fails to comply with the requirements of any enactment for the protection of employees against the risk of bodily injury or disease in the course of their employment; or

(d) the policy holder does not keep specified records or fails to provide the insurer with or make available to him information from such records.

(2) For the purposes of the 1969 Act there is also prohibited in a policy of insurance any condition which requires—

(a) a relevant employee to pay; or

(b) an insured employer to pay the relevant employee,

the first amount of any claim or any aggregation of claims.

(3) Paragraphs (1) and (2) above do not prohibit for the purposes of the 1969 Act a condition in a policy of insurance which requires the employer to pay or contribute any sum to the insurer in respect of the satisfaction of any claim made under the contract of insurance by a relevant employee or any costs and expenses incurred in relation to any such claim.

[4182]

3 Limit of amount of compulsory insurance

(1) Subject to paragraph (2) below, the amount for which an employer is required by the 1969 Act to insure and maintain insurance in respect of relevant employees under one or more policies of insurance shall be, or shall in aggregate be not less than £5 million in respect of—

(a) a claim relating to any one or more of those employees arising out of any one occurrence; and

(b) any costs and expenses incurred in relation to any such claim.

(2) Where an employer is a company with one or more subsidiaries, the requirements of paragraph (1) above shall be taken to apply to that company with any subsidiaries together, as if they were a single employer.

[4183]

4 Issue of certificates of insurance

(1) Every authorised insurer who enters into a contract of insurance with an employer in accordance with the 1969 Act shall issue the employer with a certificate of insurance in the form, and containing the particulars, set out in Schedule 1 to these Regulations.

(2) The certificate shall be issued by the insurer not later than thirty days after the date on which the insurance commences or is renewed.

(3) Where a contract of insurance for the purposes of the 1969 Act is entered into together with one or more other contracts of insurance which jointly provide insurance cover of no less than £5 million, the certificate shall specify both—

(a) the amount in excess of which insurance cover is provided by the policy; and

(b) the maximum amount of that cover.

(4), (5) . . .

(6) In any case where it is intended that a contract of insurance for the purposes of the 1969 Act is to be effective, not only in Great Britain, but also—

(a) in Northern Ireland, the Isle of Man, the Island of Guernsey, the Island of Jersey or the Island of Alderney;

(b) in any waters outside the United Kingdom to which the 1969 Act may have been applied by any enactment,

the form set out in Schedule 1 to these Regulations may be modified by a reference to the relevant law which is applicable and a statement that the policy to which it relates satisfies the requirements of that law.

NOTES

Paras (4), (5): revoked by the Employers' Liability (Compulsory Insurance) (Amendment) Regulations 2008, SI 2008/1765, reg 2(1), (2).

[4184]

5 Display and production of copies of certificates of insurance

[(1) An employer who has been issued with a certificate under regulation 4 must display one or more copies of it at each place of business at which he employs any relevant employee of the class or description to which such certificate relates.

(2) The requirements in paragraph (1) will be satisfied if the certificate is made available in electronic form and each relevant employee to whom it relates has reasonable access to it in that form.]

(3) Copies of a certificate which are required to be displayed in accordance with paragraph (1) above shall be kept on display until the date of expiry or earlier termination of the approved policy mentioned in the certificate.

(4) The requirements of paragraphs (1), (2) and (3) above do not apply where an employer employs a relevant employee on or from an offshore installation or associated structure, but in such a case the employer shall produce, at the request of that employee and within the period of ten days from such request, a copy of the certificate which relates to that employee.

NOTES

Paras (1), (2): substituted by the Employers' Liability (Compulsory Insurance) (Amendment) Regulations 2008, SI 2008/1765, reg 2(1), (3).

[4185]

6 Production of certificates of insurance to an Inspector

An employer who is required by a written notice issued by an inspector to do so shall produce or send to any person specified in the notice, at the address and within the time specified in the notice—

(a) either the original or a copy of every certificate issued to him under regulation 4 above which relates to a period of insurance current at the date of issue of the notice;

(b) either the original or a copy of every certificate issued to him under regulation 4 above . . .

NOTES

Words omitted revoked by the Employers' Liability (Compulsory Insurance) (Amendment) Regulations 2008, SI 2008/1765, reg 2(1), (4).

[4186]

7 Inspection of policies of insurance

Where a certificate is required to be issued to an employer in accordance with regulation 4 above, the employer shall during the currency of the insurance permit the policy of insurance or a copy of it to be inspected by an inspector—

(a) at such reasonable time as the inspector may require;

(b) at such place of business of the employer (which, in the case of an employer who is a company, may include its registered office) as the inspector may require.

[4187]

8 Production by inspectors of evidence of authority

Any inspector shall, if so required when visiting any premises for the purposes of the 1969 Act, produce to an employer or his agent some duly authenticated document showing that he is authorised by the Secretary of State under section 4(2)(b) of the 1969 Act.

[4188]

9 Employers exempted from insurance

(1) The employers specified in Schedule 2 to these Regulations are exempted from the requirement of the 1969 Act to insure and maintain insurance.

(2) The exemption applies to all cases to which that requirement would otherwise apply, except that for the employers specified in paragraphs 1, 12, 13 and 14 it applies only so far as is mentioned in those paragraphs.

[4189]

10 Revocations and transitional

(1) Subject to paragraphs (2) and (3) below, the instruments specified in column 1 of Schedule 3 to these Regulations are hereby revoked to the extent specified in column 3 of that Schedule.

(2) Subject to paragraphs (4) and (5) below, in the case of an insurance policy commenced before, and current at, 1st January 1999, regulations 2 to 6 of, and the Schedule to, the 1971 Regulations shall continue to apply, instead of regulations 2 to 6 of, and Schedule 1 to, these Regulations, until the expiry or renewal of the policy or until 1st January 2000, whichever is the earlier.

(3) The certificate required to be issued by regulation 4(1) of these Regulations in respect of insurance commenced or renewed on or after 1st January 1999 but before 1st April 1999 may, instead of being in the prescribed form, be in the form and contain the particulars specified in the Schedule to the 1971 Regulations.

(4) Every authorised insurer who has issued a certificate in the form, and containing the particulars, specified in the Schedule to the 1971 Regulations in respect of insurance current at 1st April 2000 shall replace it by that date with a certificate in the prescribed form and the replacement shall then be the relevant certificate for the purposes of regulation 5 of these Regulations.

(5) The certificates to which regulation 4(4) of these Regulations applies include any certificate of which a copy is required to be displayed or maintained by regulation 6(1) of the 1971 Regulations immediately before 1st January 1999, and any such certificate shall be treated for the purposes of regulation 6 of these Regulations as having been issued under regulation 4 of these Regulations.

(6) Regulation 7 of these Regulations applies where a certificate is required, in accordance with paragraph (2) above, to be issued in accordance with the 1971 Regulations as it applies where a certificate is required to be issued in accordance with regulation 4 of these Regulations.

(7) In this regulation—

"in the prescribed form" means in the form, and containing the particulars, required by regulation 4(1) and (3) of, and Schedule 1 to, these Regulations;

"the 1971 Regulations" means the Employers' Liability (Compulsory Insurance) General Regulations 1971 as in force on 31st December 1998, including those Regulations as applied by the Employers' Liability (Compulsory Insurance) (Offshore Installations) Regulations 1975.

SCHEDULE 1

Regulation 4

"CERTIFICATE OF EMPLOYERS' LIABILITY INSURANCE

(Where required by regulation 5 of the Employers' Liability (Compulsory Insurance) Regulations 1998 (the Regulations), one or more copies of this certificate must be displayed at each place of business at which the policy holder employs persons covered by the policy)

Policy No . . . .

1. Name of policy holder.
2. Date of commencement of insurance policy.
3. Date of expiry of insurance policy.

We hereby certify that subject to paragraph 2:—

1. the policy to which this certificate relates satisfies the requirements of the relevant law applicable in [Great Britain]; and
2.
   (a) the minimum amount of cover provided by this policy is no less than £5 million; or

   (b) the cover provided under this policy relates to claims in excess of [£] but not exceeding [£].

Signed on behalf of . . . . (Authorised Insurer)

. . . . Signature

Notes

(a) *Where the employer is a company to which regulation 3(2) of the Regulations applies, the certificate shall state in a prominent place, either that the policy covers the holding company and all its subsidiaries, or that the policy covers the holding company and all its subsidiaries except any specifically excluded by name, or that the policy covers the holding company and only the named subsidiaries.*

(b) *Specify applicable law as provided for in regulation 4(6) of the Regulations.*

(c) *See regulation 3(1) of the Regulations and delete whichever of paragraphs 2(a) or 2(b) does not apply. Where 2(b) is applicable, specify the amount of cover provided by the relevant policy."*

SCHEDULE 2

EMPLOYERS EXEMPTED FROM INSURANCE

Regulation 9

[4191]–[4192]

1. A person who for the time being holds a current certificate issued by a government department [or the Scottish Ministers] [or the National Assembly for Wales] stating that claims established against that person in respect of any liability to such employees of the kind mentioned in section 1(1) of the 1969 Act as are mentioned in the certificate will, to any extent to which they are incapable of being satisfied by that person, be satisfied out of money provided by Parliament [or, in

Part IV Statutory Instruments

the case of a certificate issued by the Scottish Ministers, out of the Scottish Consolidated Fund] [or, in the case of a certificate issued by the National Assembly for Wales, out of monies provided by that Assembly]; but only in respect of employees covered by the certificate.

2. The Government of any foreign state or Commonwealth country.

3. Any inter-governmental organisation which by virtue of any enactment is to be treated as a body corporate.

4. Any subsidiary of any such body as is mentioned in section 3(1)(b) of the 1969 Act (which exempts any body corporate established by or under any enactment for the carrying on of any industry or part of an industry, or of any undertaking, under national ownership or control) and any company of which two or more such bodies are members and which would, if those bodies were a single corporate body, be a subsidiary of that body corporate.

5. Any Passenger Transport Executive and any subsidiary thereof.

[**6.** Transport for London or any of its subsidiaries (within the meaning of the Greater London Authority Act 1999).]

7. . . .

8. The Qualifications and Curriculum Authority.

9. Any voluntary management committee of an approved bail or approved probation hostel within the meaning of the Probation Service Act 1993.

10. Any magistrates' courts committee established under the Justices of the Peace Act 1997.

11. Any probation committee established under the Probation Service Act 1993.

12. Any employer who is a member of a mutual insurance association of shipowners or of shipowners and others, in respect of any liability to an employee of the kind mentioned in section 1(1) of the 1969 Act against which the employer is insured for the time being with that association for an amount not less than that required by the 1969 Act and regulations under it, being an employer who holds a certificate issued by that association to the effect that he is so insured in relation to that employee.

13. Any licensee within the meaning of the Nuclear Installations Act 1965, in respect of any liability to pay compensation under that Act to any of his employees in respect of a breach of duty imposed on him by virtue of section 7 of that Act.

14. Any employer to the extent he is required to insure and maintain insurance by subsection (1) of section 1 of the 1969 Act against liability for bodily injury sustained by his employee when the employee is—

(i) carried in or upon a vehicle; or

(ii) entering or getting on to, or alighting from, a vehicle,

in the circumstances specified in that subsection and where that bodily injury is caused by or, arises out of, the use by the employer of a vehicle on a road; and the expression "road", "use" and "vehicle" have the same meanings as in Part VI of the Road Traffic Act 1988.

[**15.** Any employer which is a company that has only one employee and that employee also owns fifty per cent or more of the issued share capital in that company.]

NOTES

Para 1: words in first and third pairs of square brackets inserted by the Scotland Act 1998 (Consequential Modifications) (No 2) Order 1999, SI 1999/1820, art 4, Sch 2, Pt II, para 165; words in second and final pairs of square brackets inserted by the National Assembly for Wales (Transfer of Functions) Order 2000, SI 2000/253, art 7, Sch 5, para 8.

Para 6: substituted by the Transport for London (Consequential Provisions) Order 2003, SI 2003/1615, art 2, Sch 1, Pt 3, para 53.

Para 7: revoked by the Abolition of the Commission for the New Towns and the Urban Regeneration Agency (Appointed Day and Consequential Amendments) Order 2009, SI 2009/801, art 3(2).

Para 15: added by the Employers' Liability (Compulsory Insurance) (Amendment) Regulations 2004, SI 2004/2882, reg 2.

Transfer of functions: the National Assembly for Wales (Transfer of Functions) Order 2000, SI 2000/253, art 2(1), Sch 1 provides that the function under para 1 of this Schedule shall be exercisable by the National Assembly for Wales concurrently with any Minister of the Crown by whom it is exercisable.

(Sch 3 revokes the Employers' Liability (Compulsory Insurance) General Regulations 1971, SI 1971/1117, the Employers' Liability (Compulsory Insurance) Exemption Regulations 1971, SI 1971/1933, the Employers' Liability (Compulsory Insurance) (Amendment) Regulations 1974, SI 1974/208, the Employers' Liability (Compulsory Insurance) (Amendment) Regulations 1975,

SI 1975/194, the Employers' Liability (Compulsory Insurance) (Offshore Installations) Regulations 1975, SI 1975/1443, the Employers' Liability (Compulsory Insurance) (Amendment) Regulations 1981, SI 1981/1489, the Employers' Liability (Compulsory Insurance) Exemption (Amendment) Regulations 1992, SI 1992/3172, the Employers' Liability (Compulsory Insurance) Exemption (Amendment) Regulations 1994, SI 1994/520, and the Employers' Liability (Compulsory Insurance) General (Amendment) Regulations 1994, SI 1994/3301.)

UNFAIR TERMS IN CONSUMER CONTRACTS REGULATIONS 1999

(SI 1999/2083)

NOTES

Made: 22 July 1999.
Authority: European Communities Act 1972, s 2(2).
Commencement: 1 October 1999.

ARRANGEMENT OF REGULATIONS

1 Citation and commencement [4193]
3 Interpretation [4194]
4 Terms to which these Regulations apply [4195]
5 Unfair Terms [4196]
6 Assessment of unfair terms [4197]
7 Written contracts [4198]
8 Effect of unfair term [4199]
9 Choice of law clauses [4200]
10 Complaints—consideration by OFT [4201]
11 Complaints—consideration by qualifying bodies [4202]
12 Injunctions to prevent continued use of unfair terms [4203]
13 Powers of the OFT and qualifying bodies to obtain documents and information [4204]
14 Notification of undertakings and orders to OFT [4205]
15 Publication, information and advice [4206]
16 The functions of the Financial Services Authority [4207]

SCHEDULES:

Schedule 1—Qualifying Bodies
Part One [4208]
Part Two [4209]
Schedule 2—Indicative and Non-Exhaustive List of Terms which may be Regarded as Unfair [4210]

[4193]
1 Citation and commencement

These Regulations may be cited as the Unfair Terms in Consumer Contracts Regulations 1999 and shall come into force on 1st October 1999.

2 *(Revokes the Unfair Terms in Consumer Contracts Regulations 1994, SI 1994/3159.)*

[4194]
3 Interpretation

(1) In these Regulations—

"the Community" means the European Community;

"consumer" means any natural person who, in contracts covered by these Regulations, is acting for purposes which are outside his trade, business or profession;

"court" in relation to England and Wales and Northern Ireland means a county court or the High Court, and in relation to Scotland, the Sheriff or the Court of Session;

"[OFT]" means [the Office of Fair Trading];

"EEA Agreement" means the Agreement on the European Economic Area signed at Oporto on 2nd May 1992 as adjusted by the protocol signed at Brussels on 17th March 1993;

"Member State" means a State which is a contracting party to the EEA Agreement;

"notified" means notified in writing;

"qualifying body" means a person specified in Schedule 1;

"seller or supplier" means any natural or legal person who, in contracts covered by these Regulations, is acting for purposes relating to his trade, business or profession, whether publicly owned or privately owned;

"unfair terms" means the contractual terms referred to in regulation 5.

[(1A) The references—

(a) in regulation 4(1) to a seller or a supplier, and

(b) in regulation 8(1) to a seller or supplier,

include references to a distance supplier and to an intermediary.

(1B) In paragraph (1A) and regulation 5(6)—

"distance supplier" means—

(a) a supplier under a distance contract within the meaning of the Financial Services (Distance Marketing) Regulations 2004, or

(b) a supplier of unsolicited financial services within regulation 15 of those Regulations; and

"intermediary" has the same meaning as in those Regulations.]

(2) In the application of these Regulations to Scotland for references to an "injunction" or an "interim injunction" there shall be substituted references to an "interdict" or "interim interdict" respectively.

NOTES

Para (1): in definition "OFT" (originally "Director") words in square brackets substituted by virtue of the Enterprise Act 2002, s 2.

Paras (1A), (1B): inserted by the Financial Services (Distance Marketing) Regulations 2004, SI 2004/2095, reg 24(1), (2).

[4195]

4 Terms to which these Regulations apply

(1) These Regulations apply in relation to unfair terms in contracts concluded between a seller or a supplier and a consumer.

(2) These Regulations do not apply to contractual terms which reflect—

(a) mandatory statutory or regulatory provisions (including such provisions under the law of any Member State or in Community legislation having effect in the United Kingdom without further enactment);

(b) the provisions or principles of international conventions to which the Member States or the Community are party.

[4196]

5 Unfair Terms

(1) A contractual term which has not been individually negotiated shall be regarded as unfair if, contrary to the requirement of good faith, it causes a significant imbalance in the parties' rights and obligations arising under the contract, to the detriment of the consumer.

(2) A term shall always be regarded as not having been individually negotiated where it has been drafted in advance and the consumer has therefore not been able to influence the substance of the term.

(3) Notwithstanding that a specific term or certain aspects of it in a contract has been individually negotiated, these Regulations shall apply to the rest of a contract if an overall assessment of it indicates that it is a pre-formulated standard contract.

(4) It shall be for any seller or supplier who claims that a term was individually negotiated to show that it was.

(5) Schedule 2 to these Regulations contains an indicative and non-exhaustive list of the terms which may be regarded as unfair.

[(6) Any contractual term providing that a consumer bears the burden of proof in respect of showing whether a distance supplier or an intermediary complied with any or all of the obligations placed upon him resulting from the Directive and any rule or enactment implementing it shall always be regarded as unfair.

(7) In paragraph (6)—

"the Directive" means Directive 2002/65/EC of the European Parliament and of the Council of 23 September 2002 concerning the distance marketing of consumer financial services and amending Council Directive 90/619/EEC and Directives 97/7/EC and 98/27/EC; and

"rule" means a rule made by the Financial Services Authority under the Financial Services and Markets Act 2000 or by a designated professional body within the meaning of section 326(2) of that Act.]

NOTES

Paras (6), (7): added by the Financial Services (Distance Marketing) Regulations 2004, SI 2004/2095, reg 24(1), (3).

Directive 2002/65/EC of the European Parliament and of the Council: OJ L271, 9.10.2002, p 16.

Council Directive 90/619/EEC: OJ L330, 29.11.1990, p 50.

Council Directive 97/7/EC: OJ L144, 4.6.1997, p 19.

Council Directive 98/27/EC: OJ L166, 11.6.1998, p 51.

[4197]

6 Assessment of unfair terms

(1) Without prejudice to regulation 12, the unfairness of a contractual term shall be assessed, taking into account the nature of the goods or services for which the contract was concluded and by referring, at the time of conclusion of the contract, to all the circumstances attending the conclusion of the contract and to all the other terms of the contract or of another contract on which it is dependent.

(2) In so far as it is in plain intelligible language, the assessment of fairness of a term shall not relate—

(a) to the definition of the main subject matter of the contract, or

(b) to the adequacy of the price or remuneration, as against the goods or services supplied in exchange.

[4198]

7 Written contracts

(1) A seller or supplier shall ensure that any written term of a contract is expressed in plain, intelligible language.

(2) If there is doubt about the meaning of a written term, the interpretation which is most favourable to the consumer shall prevail but this rule shall not apply in proceedings brought under regulation 12.

[4199]

8 Effect of unfair term

(1) An unfair term in a contract concluded with a consumer by a seller or supplier shall not be binding on the consumer.

(2) The contract shall continue to bind the parties if it is capable of continuing in existence without the unfair term.

[4200]

9 Choice of law clauses

These Regulations shall apply notwithstanding any contract term which applies or purports to apply the law of a non-Member State, if the contract has a close connection with the territory of the Member States.

[4201]

10 Complaints—consideration by [OFT]

(1) It shall be the duty of the [OFT] to consider any complaint made to [it] that any contract term drawn up for general use is unfair, unless—

the complaint appears to the [OFT] to be frivolous or vexatious; or

a qualifying body has notified the [OFT] that it agrees to consider the complaint.

(2) The [OFT] shall give reasons for [its] decision to apply or not to apply, as the case may be, for an injunction under regulation 12 in relation to any complaint which these Regulations require [it] to consider.

(3) In deciding whether or not to apply for an injunction in respect of a term which the [OFT] considers to be unfair, [it] may, if [it] considers it appropriate to do so, have regard to any undertakings given to [it] by or on behalf of any person as to the continued use of such a term in contracts concluded with consumers.

NOTES

Provision heading: words in square brackets substituted by virtue of the Enterprise Act 2002, s 2.

Paras (1)–(3): words in square brackets substituted by virtue of the Enterprise Act 2002, s 2.

[4202]

11 Complaints—consideration by qualifying bodies

(1) If a qualifying body specified in Part One of Schedule 1 notifies the [OFT] that it agrees to consider a complaint that any contract term drawn up for general use is unfair, it shall be under a

duty to consider that complaint.

(2) Regulation 10(2) and (3) shall apply to a qualifying body which is under a duty to consider a complaint as they apply to the [OFT].

NOTES

Paras (1), (2): words in square brackets substituted by virtue of the Enterprise Act 2002, s 2.

[4203]

12 Injunctions to prevent continued use of unfair terms

(1) The [OFT] or, subject to paragraph (2), any qualifying body may apply for an injunction (including an interim injunction) against any person appearing to the [OFT] or that body to be using, or recommending use of, an unfair term drawn up for general use in contracts concluded with consumers.

(2) A qualifying body may apply for an injunction only where—

- (a) it has notified the [OFT] of its intention to apply at least fourteen days before the date on which the application is made, beginning with the date on which the notification was given; or
- (b) the [OFT] consents to the application being made within a shorter period.

(3) The court on an application under this regulation may grant an injunction on such terms as it thinks fit.

(4) An injunction may relate not only to use of a particular contract term drawn up for general use but to any similar term, or a term having like effect, used or recommended for use by any person.

NOTES

Paras (1), (2): words in square brackets substituted by virtue of the Enterprise Act 2002, s 2.

[4204]

13 Powers of the [OFT] and qualifying bodies to obtain documents and information

(1) The [OFT] may exercise the power conferred by this regulation for the purpose of—

- (a) facilitating [its] consideration of a complaint that a contract term drawn up for general use is unfair; or
- (b) ascertaining whether a person has complied with an undertaking or court order as to the continued use, or recommendation for use, of a term in contracts concluded with consumers.

(2) A qualifying body specified in Part One of Schedule 1 may exercise the power conferred by this regulation for the purpose of—

- (a) facilitating its consideration of a complaint that a contract term drawn up for general use is unfair; or
- (b) ascertaining whether a person has complied with—
  - (i) an undertaking given to it or to the court following an application by that body, or
  - (ii) a court order made on an application by that body,

as to the continued use, or recommendation for use, of a term in contracts concluded with consumers.

(3) The [OFT] may require any person to supply to [it], and a qualifying body specified in Part One of Schedule 1 may require any person to supply to it—

- (a) a copy of any document which that person has used or recommended for use, at the time the notice referred to in paragraph (4) below is given, as a pre-formulated standard contract in dealings with consumers;
- (b) information about the use, or recommendation for use, by that person of that document or any other such document in dealings with consumers.

(4) The power conferred by this regulation is to be exercised by a notice in writing which may—

- (a) specify the way in which and the time within which it is to be complied with; and
- (b) be varied or revoked by a subsequent notice.

(5) Nothing in this regulation compels a person to supply any document or information which he would be entitled to refuse to produce or give in civil proceedings before the court.

(6) If a person makes default in complying with a notice under this regulation, the court may, on the application of the [OFT] or of the qualifying body, make such order as the court thinks fit for requiring the default to be made good, and any such order may provide that all the costs or expenses of and incidental to the application shall be borne by the person in default or by any officers of a company or other association who are responsible for its default.

NOTES

Provision heading: reference in square brackets substituted by virtue of the Enterprise Act 2002, s 2.
Paras (1), (3), (6): words in square brackets substituted by virtue of the Enterprise Act 2002, s 2.

[4205]

14 Notification of undertakings and orders to [OFT]

A qualifying body shall notify the [OFT]—

(a) of any undertaking given to it by or on behalf of any person as to the continued use of a term which that body considers to be unfair in contracts concluded with consumers;
(b) of the outcome of any application made by it under regulation 12, and of the terms of any undertaking given to, or order made by, the court;
(c) of the outcome of any application made by it to enforce a previous order of the court.

NOTES

References in square brackets substituted by virtue of the Enterprise Act 2002, s 2.

[4206]

15 Publication, information and advice

(1) The [OFT] shall arrange for the publication in such form and manner as [it] considers appropriate, of—

(a) details of any undertaking or order notified to [it] under regulation 14;
(b) details of any undertaking given to [it] by or on behalf of any person as to the continued use of a term which the [OFT] considers to be unfair in contracts concluded with consumers;
(c) details of any application made by [it] under regulation 12, and of the terms of any undertaking given to, or order made by, the court;
(d) details of any application made by the [OFT] to enforce a previous order of the court.

(2) The [OFT] shall inform any person on request whether a particular term to which these Regulations apply has been—

(a) the subject of an undertaking given to the [OFT] or notified to [it] by a qualifying body; or
(b) the subject of an order of the court made upon application by [it] or notified to [it] by a qualifying body;

and shall give that person details of the undertaking or a copy of the order, as the case may be, together with a copy of any amendments which the person giving the undertaking has agreed to make to the term in question.

(3) The [OFT] may arrange for the dissemination in such form and manner as [it] considers appropriate of such information and advice concerning the operation of these Regulations as may appear to [it] to be expedient to give to the public and to all persons likely to be affected by these Regulations.

NOTES

Paras (1)–(3): words in square brackets substituted by virtue of the Enterprise Act 2002, s 2.

[4207]

[16 The functions of the Financial Services Authority

The functions of the Financial Services Authority under these Regulations shall be treated as functions of the Financial Services Authority under the [Financial Services and Markets Act 2000].]

NOTES

Added by the Unfair Terms in Consumer Contracts (Amendment) Regulations 2001, SI 2001/1186, reg 2(a).
Words in square brackets substituted by the Financial Services and Markets Act 2000 (Consequential Amendments and Repeals) Order 2001, SI 2001/3649, art 583.

SCHEDULE 1

QUALIFYING BODIES

Regulation 3

PART ONE

[4208]

[1 The Information Commissioner.

2 The Gas and Electricity Markets Authority.

3 The Director General of Electricity Supply for Northern Ireland.

4 The Director General of Gas for Northern Ireland.

5 [The Office of Communications].

6 [The Water Services Regulation Authority].

7 [The Office of Rail Regulation].

8 Every weights and measures authority in Great Britain.

9 The Department of Enterprise, Trade and Investment in Northern Ireland.

10 The Financial Services Authority.]

NOTES

Substituted by the Unfair Terms in Consumer Contracts (Amendment) Regulations 2001, SI 2001/1186, reg 2(b).

Para 5: words in square brackets substituted by the Communications Act 2003 (Consequential Amendments No 2) Order 2003, SI 2003/3182, art 2.

Para 6: words in square brackets substituted by the Unfair Terms in Consumer Contracts (Amendment) and Water Act 2003 (Transitional Provision) Regulations 2006, SI 2006/523, reg 2, subject to transitional provisions in reg 3 thereof.

Para 7: words in square brackets substituted by virtue of the Railways and Transport Safety Act 2003, s 16(4), (5), Sch 3, para 4; for savings see s 16 of, and Sch 3 to, that Act.

PART TWO

[4209]

11 Consumers' Association.

SCHEDULE 2

INDICATIVE AND NON-EXHAUSTIVE LIST OF TERMS WHICH MAY BE REGARDED AS UNFAIR

Regulation 5(5)

[4210]–[4211]

1. Terms which have the object or effect of—

(a) excluding or limiting the legal liability of a seller or supplier in the event of the death of a consumer or personal injury to the latter resulting from an act or omission of that seller or supplier;

(b) inappropriately excluding or limiting the legal rights of the consumer vis-à-vis the seller or supplier or another party in the event of total or partial non-performance or inadequate performance by the seller or supplier of any of the contractual obligations, including the option of offsetting a debt owed to the seller or supplier against any claim which the consumer may have against him;

(c) making an agreement binding on the consumer whereas provision of services by the seller or supplier is subject to a condition whose realisation depends on his own will alone;

(d) permitting the seller or supplier to retain sums paid by the consumer where the latter decides not to conclude or perform the contract, without providing for the consumer to receive compensation of an equivalent amount from the seller or supplier where the latter is the party cancelling the contract;

(e) requiring any consumer who fails to fulfil his obligation to pay a disproportionately high sum in compensation;

(f) authorising the seller or supplier to dissolve the contract on a discretionary basis where the same facility is not granted to the consumer, or permitting the seller or supplier to retain the sums paid for services not yet supplied by him where it is the seller or supplier himself who dissolves the contract;

(g) enabling the seller or supplier to terminate a contract of indeterminate duration without reasonable notice except where there are serious grounds for doing so;

(h) automatically extending a contract of fixed duration where the consumer does not indicate otherwise, when the deadline fixed for the consumer to express his desire not to extend the contract is unreasonably early;

(i) irrevocably binding the consumer to terms with which he had no real opportunity of becoming acquainted before the conclusion of the contract;

(j) enabling the seller or supplier to alter the terms of the contract unilaterally without a valid reason which is specified in the contract;

(k) enabling the seller or supplier to alter unilaterally without a valid reason any characteristics of the product or service to be provided;

(l) providing for the price of goods to be determined at the time of delivery or allowing a seller of goods or supplier of services to increase their price without in both cases giving the consumer the corresponding right to cancel the contract if the final price is too high in relation to the price agreed when the contract was concluded;

(m) giving the seller or supplier the right to determine whether the goods or services supplied are in conformity with the contract, or giving him the exclusive right to interpret any term of the contract;

(n) limiting the seller's or supplier's obligation to respect commitments undertaken by his agents or making his commitments subject to compliance with a particular formality;

(o) obliging the consumer to fulfil all his obligations where the seller or supplier does not perform his;

(p) giving the seller or supplier the possibility of transferring his rights and obligations under the contract, where this may serve to reduce the guarantees for the consumer, without the latter's agreement;

(q) excluding or hindering the consumer's right to take legal action or exercise any other legal remedy, particularly by requiring the consumer to take disputes exclusively to arbitration not covered by legal provisions, unduly restricting the evidence available to him or imposing on him a burden of proof which, according to the applicable law, should lie with another party to the contract.

2. Scope of paragraphs 1(g), (j) and (l).

(a) Paragraph 1(g) is without hindrance to terms by which a supplier of financial services reserves the right to terminate unilaterally a contract of indeterminate duration without notice where there is a valid reason, provided that the supplier is required to inform the other contracting party or parties thereof immediately.

(b) Paragraph 1(j) is without hindrance to terms under which a supplier of financial services reserves the right to alter the rate of interest payable by the consumer or due to the latter, or the amount of other charges for financial services without notice where there is a valid reason, provided that the supplier is required to inform the other contracting party or parties thereof at the earliest opportunity and that the latter are free to dissolve the contract immediately.

Paragraph 1(j) is also without hindrance to terms under which a seller or supplier reserves the right to alter unilaterally the conditions of a contract of indeterminate duration, provided that he is required to inform the consumer with reasonable notice and that the consumer is free to dissolve the contract.

(c) Paragraphs 1(g), (j) and (l) do not apply to:

— transactions in transferable securities, financial instruments and other products or services where the price is linked to fluctuations in a stock exchange quotation or index or a financial market rate that the seller or supplier does not control;

— contracts for the purchase or sale of foreign currency, traveller's cheques or international money orders denominated in foreign currency.

(d) Paragraph 1(1) is without hindrance to price indexation clauses, where lawful, provided that the method by which prices vary is explicitly described.

INSURERS (WINDING UP) RULES 2001

(SI 2001/3635)

1 Citation, commencement and revocation . . . . . [4212]
2 Interpretation . . . . . [4213]
3 Application . . . . . [4214]
4 Appointment of liquidator . . . . . [4215]
5 Maintenance of separate financial records for long-term and other business in winding up . . . . . [4216]
6 Valuation of general business policies . . . . . [4217]

7 Valuation of long-term policies . . . [4218]
8 . . . [4219]
9 Attribution of liabilities to company's long-term business . . . [4220]
10 Attribution of assets to company's long-term business . . . [4221]
11 Excess of long-term business assets . . . [4222]
12 Actuarial advice . . . [4223]
13 Utilisation of excess of assets . . . [4224]
14 . . . [4225]
15 Custody of assets . . . [4226]
16 Maintenance of accounting, valuation and other records . . . [4227]
17 Additional powers in relation to long-term business . . . [4228]
18 Accounts and audit . . . [4229]
19 Security by the liquidator and special manager . . . [4230]
20 Proof of debts . . . [4231]
21 Failure to pay premiums . . . [4232]
22 Notice of valuation of policy . . . [4233]
23 Dividends to creditors . . . [4234]
24 Meetings of creditors . . . [4235]
25 Remuneration of liquidator carrying on long-term business . . . [4236]
26 Apportionment of costs payable out of the assets . . . [4237]
27 Notice of stop order . . . [4238]

SCHEDULES:

Schedule 1—Rules for valuing general business policies . . . [4239]
Schedule 2—Rules for valuing non-linked life policies, non-linked deferred annuity policies, non-linked annuities in payment, unitised non-linked policies and capital redemption policies . . . [4240]
Schedule 3—Rules for valuing life policies and deferred annuity policies which are linked policies . . . [4241]
Schedule 4—Rules for valuing long-term policies which are not dealt with in Schedules 2 or 3 . . . [4242]
Schedule 5—Rules for valuing long-term policies where a stop order has been made . . . [4243]
Schedule 6—Forms . . . [4244]

NOTES

Made: 9 November 2001
Authority: Insolvency Act 1986, ss 411, 413; Financial Services and Markets Act 2000, s 379.
Commencement: 1 December 2001.

[4212]

1 Citation, commencement and revocation

(1) These Rules may be cited as the Insurers (Winding Up) Rules 2001 and come into force on 1st December 2001.

(2) The Insurance Companies (Winding Up) Rules 1985 are revoked.

[4213]

2 Interpretation

(1) In these Rules, unless the context otherwise requires—

"the 1923 Act" means the Industrial Assurance Act 1923;

"the 1985 Act" means the Companies Act 1985;

"the 1986 Act" means the Insolvency Act 1986;

"the 2000 Act" means the Financial Services and Markets Act 2000;

"the Authority" means the Financial Services Authority;

"company" means an insurer which is being wound up;

"contract of general insurance" and "contract of long-term insurance" have the meaning given by article 3(1) of the Financial Services and Markets Act 2000 (Regulated Activities) Order 2001;

"excess of the long-term business assets" means the amount, if any, by which the value of the assets representing the fund or funds maintained by the company in respect of its long-term business as at the liquidation date exceeds the value as at that date of the liabilities of the company attributable to that business;

"excess of the other business assets" means the amount, if any, by which the value of the assets of the company which do not represent the fund or funds maintained by the company in respect of its long-term business as at the liquidation date exceeds the value as at that date of the liabilities of the company (other than liabilities in respect of share capital) which are not attributable to that business;

"Financial Services Compensation Scheme" means the scheme established under section 213 of the 2000 Act;

"general business" means the business of effecting or carrying out a contract of general insurance;

"the general regulations" means the Insolvency Regulations 1994;

"the Industrial Assurance Acts" means the 1923 Act and the Industrial Assurance and Friendly Societies Act 1948;

"insurer" has the meaning given by article 2 of the Financial Services and Markets Act 2000 (Insolvency) (Definition of "Insurer") Order 2001;

"linked liability" means any liability under a policy the effecting of which constitutes the carrying on of long-term business the amount of which is determined by reference to—

(a) the value of property of any description (whether or not specified in the policy),

(b) fluctuations in the value of such property,

(c) income from any such property, or

(d) fluctuations in an index of the value of such property;

"linked policy" means a policy which provides for linked liabilities and a policy which when made provided for linked liabilities is deemed to be a linked policy even if the policy holder has elected to convert his rights under the policy so that at the liquidation date there are no longer linked liabilities under the policy;

"liquidation date" means the date of the winding-up order or the date on which a resolution for the winding up of the company is passed by the members of the company (or the policyholders in the case of a mutual insurance company) and, if both a winding-up order and winding-up resolution have been made, the earlier date;

"long-term business" means the business of effecting or carrying out any contract of long-term insurance;

"non-linked policy" means a policy which is not a linked policy;

"other business", in relation to a company carrying on long-term business, means such of the business of the company as is not long-term business;

"the principal rules" means the Insolvency Rules 1986;

"stop order", in relation to a company, means an order of the court, made under section 376(2) of the 2000 Act, ordering the liquidator to stop carrying on the long-term business of the company;

"unit" in relation to a policy means any unit (whether or not described as a unit in the policy) by reference to the numbers and value of which the amount of the liabilities under the policy at any time is measured.

(2) Unless the context otherwise requires, words or expressions contained in these Rules bear the same meaning as in the principal rules, the general regulations, the 1986 Act, the 2000 Act or any statutory modification thereof respectively.

[4214]

3 Application

(1) These Rules apply to proceedings for the winding up of an insurer which commence on or after the date on which these Rules come into force.

(2) These Rules supplement the principal rules and the general regulations which continue to apply to the proceedings in the winding up of an insurer under the 1986 Act as they apply to proceedings in the winding up of any company under that Act; but in the event of a conflict between these Rules and the principal rules or the general regulations these Rules prevail.

[4215]

4 Appointment of liquidator

Where the court is considering whether to appoint a liquidator under—

(a) section 139(4) of the 1986 Act (appointment of liquidator where conflict between creditors and contributories), or

(b) section 140 of the 1986 Act (appointment of liquidator following administration or voluntary arrangement),

the manager of the Financial Services Compensation Scheme may appear and make representations to the court as to the person to be appointed.

[4216]

[5 Maintenance of separate financial records for long-term and other business in winding up

(1) This rule applies in the case of a company carrying on long-term business in whose case no stop order has been made.

(2) The liquidator shall prepare and keep separate financial records in respect of the long-term

business and the other business of the company.

(3) Paragraphs (4) and (5) apply in the case of a company to which this rule applies which also carries on permitted general business ('a hybrid insurer').

(4) Where, before the liquidation date, a hybrid insurer has, or should properly have, apportioned the assets and liabilities attributable to its permitted general business to its long term business for the purposes of any accounts, those assets and liabilities must be apportioned to its long term business for the purposes of complying with paragraph (2) of this rule.

(5) Where, before the liquidation date, a hybrid insurer has, or should properly have, apportioned the assets and liabilities attributable to its permitted general business other than to its long term business for the purposes of any accounts, those assets and liabilities must be apportioned to its other business for the purposes of complying with paragraph (2) of this rule.

(6) Regulation 10 of the general regulations (financial records) applies only in relation to the company's other business.

(7) In relation to the long-term business, the liquidator shall, with a view to the long-term business of the company being transferred to another insurer, maintain such accounting, valuation and other records as will enable such other insurer upon the transfer being effected to comply with the requirements of any rules made by the Authority under Part X of the 2000 Act relating to accounts and statements of insurers.

(8) In paragraphs (4) and (5)—

(a) "accounts" means any accounts or statements maintained by the company in compliance with a requirement under the Companies Act 1985 or any rules made by the Authority under Part X of the 2000 Act;

(b) "permitted general business" means the business of effecting or carrying out a contract of general insurance where the risk insured against relates to either accident or sickness.]

NOTES

Substituted by the Insurers (Reorganisation and Winding Up) Regulations 2003, SI 2003/1102, regs 52, 53(1).

[4217]

6 Valuation of general business policies

Except in relation to amounts which have fallen due for payment before the liquidation date and liabilities referred to in paragraph 2(1)(b) of Schedule 1, the holder of a general business policy shall be admitted as a creditor in relation to his policy without proof for an amount equal to the value of the policy and for this purpose the value of a policy shall be determined in accordance with Schedule 1.

[4218]

7 Valuation of long-term policies

(1) This rule applies in relation to a company's long-term business where no stop order has been made.

(2) In relation to a claim under a policy which has fallen due for payment before the liquidation date, a policy holder shall be admitted as a creditor without proof for such amount as appears from the records of the company to be due in respect of that claim.

(3) In all other respects a policy holder shall be admitted as a creditor in relation to his policy without proof for an amount equal to the value of the policy and for this purpose the value of a policy of any class shall be determined in the manner applicable to policies of that class provided by Schedules 2, 3 and 4.

(4) This rule applies in relation to a person entitled to apply for a free paid-up policy under section 24 of the 1923 Act (provisions as to forfeited policies) and to whom no such policy has been issued before the liquidation date (whether or not it was applied for) as if such a policy had been issued immediately before the liquidation date—

(a) for the minimum amount determined in accordance with section 24(2) of the 1923 Act, or

(b) if the liquidator is satisfied that it was the practice of the company during the five years immediately before the liquidation date to issue policies under that section in excess of the minimum amounts so determined, for the amount determined in accordance with that practice.

[4219]

8— (1) This rule applies in relation to a company's long-term business where a stop order has been made.

(2) In relation to a claim under a policy which has fallen due for payment on or after the liquidation date and before the date of the stop order, a policy holder shall be admitted as a creditor without proof for such amount as appears from the records of the company and of the liquidator to be due in respect of that claim.

(3) In all other respects a policy holder shall be admitted as a creditor in relation to his policy without proof for an amount equal to the value of the policy and for this purpose the value of a policy of any class shall be determined in the manner applicable to policies of that class provided by Schedule 5.

(4) Paragraph (4) of rule 7 applies for the purposes of this rule as if references to the liquidation date (other than that in sub-paragraph (b) of that paragraph) were references to the date of the stop order.

[4220]

9 Attribution of liabilities to company's long-term business

(1) This rule applies in the case of a company carrying on long-term business if at the liquidation date there are liabilities of the company in respect of which it is not clear from the accounting and other records of the company whether they are or are not attributable to the company's long-term business.

(2) The liquidator shall, in such manner and according to such accounting principles as he shall determine, identify the liabilities referred to in paragraph (1) as attributable or not attributable to a company's long-term business and those liabilities shall for the purposes of the winding-up be deemed as at the liquidation date to be attributable or not as the case may be.

(3) For the purposes of paragraph (2) the liquidator may—

(a) determine that some liabilities are attributable to the company's long-term business and that others are not (the first method); or

(b) determine that a part of a liability shall be attributable to the company's long-term business and that the remainder of the liability is not (the second method),

and he may use the first method for some of the liabilities and the second method for the remainder of them.

(4) Notwithstanding anything in the preceding paragraphs of this rule, the court may order that the determination of which (if any) of the liabilities referred to in paragraph (1) are attributable to the company's long-term business and which (if any) are not shall be made in such manner and by such methods as the court may direct or the court may itself make the determination.

[4221]

10 Attribution of assets to company's long-term business

(1) This rule applies in the case of a company carrying on long-term business if at the liquidation date there are assets of the company in respect of which—

(a) it is not clear from the accounting and other records of the company whether they do or do not represent the fund or funds maintained by the company in respect of its long-term business, and

(b) it cannot be inferred from the source of the income out of which those assets were provided whether they do or do not represent those funds.

(2) Subject to paragraph (6) the liquidator shall determine which (if any) of the assets referred to in paragraph (1) are attributable to those funds and which (if any) are not and those assets shall, for the purposes of the winding up, be deemed as at the liquidation date to represent those funds or not in accordance with the liquidator's determination.

(3) For the purposes of paragraph (2) the liquidator may—

(a) determine that some of those assets shall be attributable to those funds and that others of them shall not (the first method); or

(b) determine that a part of the value of one of those assets shall be attributable to those funds and that the remainder of that value shall not (the second method),

and he may use the first method for some of those assets and the second method for others of them.

(4)

(a) In making the attribution the liquidator's objective shall in the first instance be so far as possible to reduce any deficit that may exist, at the liquidation date and before any attribution is made, either in the company's long-term business or in its other business.

(b) If there is a deficit in both the company's long-term business and its other business the attribution shall be in the ratio that the amount of the one deficit bears to the amount of the other until the deficits are eliminated.

(c) Thereafter the attribution shall be in the ratio which the aggregate amount of the liabilities attributable to the company's long-term business bears to the aggregate amount of the liabilities not so attributable.

(5) For the purposes of paragraph (4) the value of a liability of the company shall, if it falls to be valued under rule 6 or 7, have the same value as it has under that rule but otherwise it shall have such value as would have been included in relation to it in a balance sheet of the company prepared in accordance with the 1985 Act as at the liquidation date; and, for the purpose of determining the ratio referred to in paragraph (4) but not for the purpose of determining the amount of any deficit therein referred to, the net balance of shareholders' funds shall be included in the liabilities not attributable to the company's long-term business.

(6) Notwithstanding anything in the preceding paragraphs of this rule, the court may order that the determination of which (if any) of the assets referred to in paragraph (1) are attributable to the fund or funds maintained by the company in respect of its long-term business and which (if any) are not shall be made in such manner and by such methods as the court may direct or the court may itself make the determination.

[4222]

11 Excess of long-term business assets

(1) Where the company is one carrying on long-term business [and in whose case no stop order has been made], for the purpose of determining the amount, if any, of the excess of the long-term business assets, there shall be included amongst the liabilities of the company attributable to its long-term business an amount determined by the liquidator in respect of liabilities and expenses likely to be incurred in connection with the transfer of the company's long-term business as a going concern to another insurance company being liabilities not included in the valuation of the long-term policies made in pursuance of rule 7.

(2) Where the liquidator is carrying on the long-term business of an insurer with a view to that business being transferred as a going concern to a person or persons ("transferee") who may lawfully carry out those contracts (or substitute policies being issued by another insurer), the liquidator may, in addition to any amounts paid by the Financial Services Compensation Scheme for the benefit of the transferee to secure such a transfer or to procure substitute policies being issued, pay to the transferee or other insurer all or part of such funds or assets as are attributable to the long-term business being transferred or substituted.

NOTES

Para (1): words in square brackets substituted by the Insurers (Reorganisation and Winding Up) Regulations 2003, SI 2003/1102, regs 52, 54.

[4223]

12 Actuarial advice

(1) Before doing any of the following, that is to say—

(a) determining the value of a policy in accordance with Schedules 1 to 5 (other than paragraph 3 of Schedule 1);

(b) identifying long-term liabilities and assets in accordance with rules 9 and 10;

(c) determining the amount (if any) of the excess of the long-term business assets in accordance with rule 11;

(d) determining the terms on which he will accept payment of overdue premiums under rule 21(1) or the amount and nature of any compensation under rule 21(2);

the liquidator shall obtain and consider advice thereon (including an estimate of any value or amount required to be determined) from an actuary.

(2) Before seeking, for the purpose of valuing a policy, the direction of the court as to the assumption of a particular rate of interest or the employment of any rates of mortality or disability, the liquidator shall obtain and consider advice thereon from an actuary.

[4224]

13 Utilisation of excess of assets

(1) Except at the direction of the court, no distribution may be made out of and no transfer to another insurer may be made of—

(a) any part of the excess of the long-term business assets which has been transferred to the other business; or

(b) any part of the excess of the other business assets, which has been transferred to the long-term business.

(2) Before giving a direction under paragraph (1) the court may require the liquidator to advertise the proposal to make a distribution or a transfer in such manner as the court shall direct.

[4225]

14 In the case of a company carrying on long-term business in whose case no stop order has been made, regulation 5 of the general regulations (payments into the Insolvency Services Account) applies only in relation to the company's other business.

[4226]

15 Custody of assets

(1) The Secretary of State may, in the case of a company carrying on long-term business in whose case no stop order has been made, require that the whole or a specified proportion of the assets representing the fund or funds maintained by the company in respect of its long-term business shall be held by a person approved by him for the purpose as trustee for the company.

(2) No assets held by a person as trustee for a company in compliance with a requirement imposed under this rule shall, so long as the requirement is in force, be released except with the consent of the Secretary of State but they may be transposed by the trustee into other assets by any transaction or series of transactions on the written instructions of the liquidator.

(3) The liquidator may not grant any mortgage or charge of assets which are held by a person as trustee for the company in compliance with a requirement imposed under this rule except with the consent of the Secretary of State.

[4227]

16 Maintenance of accounting, valuation and other records

(1) In the case of a company carrying on long-term business in whose case no stop order has been made, regulation 10 of the general regulations (financial records) applies only in relation to the company's other business.

(2) The liquidator of such company shall, with a view to the long-term business of the company being transferred to another insurer, maintain such accounting, valuation and other records as will enable such other insurer upon the transfer being effected to comply with the requirements of any rules made by the Authority under Part X of the 2000 Act relating to accounts and statements of insurers.

[4228]

17 Additional powers in relation to long-term business

(1) In the case of a company carrying on long-term business in whose case no stop order has been made, regulation 9 of the general regulations (investment or otherwise handling of funds in winding up of companies and payment of interest) applies only in relation to the company's other business.

(2) The liquidator of a company carrying on long-term business shall, so long as no stop order has been made, have power to do all such things as may be necessary to the performance of his duties under section 376(2) of the 2000 Act (continuation of contracts of long-term insurance where insurer in liquidation) but the Secretary of State may require him—

(a) not to make investments of a specified class or description,

(b) to realise, before the expiration of a specified period, the whole or a specified proportion of investments of a specified class or description held by the liquidator.

[4229]

18 Accounts and audit

(1) In the case of a company carrying on long-term business in whose case no stop order has been made, regulation 12 of the general regulations (liquidator carrying on business) applies only in relation to the company's other business.

(2) The liquidator of such a company shall supply the Secretary of State, at such times or intervals as he may specify, with such accounts as he may specify and audited in such manner as he may require and with such information about specified matters and verified in such specified manner as he may require.

(3) The liquidator of such a company shall, if required to do so by the Secretary of State, instruct an actuary to investigate the financial condition of the company's long-term business and to report thereon in such manner as the Secretary of State may specify.

[4230]

19 Security by the liquidator and special manager

In the case of a company carrying on long-term business in whose case no stop order has been made, rule 4.207 of the principal rules (security) applies separately to the company's long-term business and to its other business.

[4231]

20 Proof of debts

(1) This rule applies in the case of a company carrying on long-term business [in whose case no stop order has been made].

(2) The liquidator may in relation to the company's long-term business and to its other business fix different days on or before which the creditors of the company who are required to prove their debts or claims are to prove their debts or claims and he may fix one of those days without at the same time fixing the other.

(3) In submitting a proof of any debt a creditor may claim the whole or any part of such debt as attributable to the company's long-term business or to its other business or he may make no such attribution.

(4) When he admits any debt, in whole or in part, the liquidator shall state in writing how much of what he admits is attributable to the company's long-tem business and how much to the company's other business.

NOTES

Para (1): words in square brackets added by the Insurers (Reorganisation and Winding Up) Regulations 2003, SI 2003/1102, regs 52, 55.

[4232]

21 Failure to pay premiums

(1) The liquidator may in the course of carrying on the company's long-term business and on such terms as he thinks fit accept payment of a premium even though the payment is tendered after the date on which under the terms of the policy it was finally due to be paid.

(2) The liquidator may in the course of carrying on the company's long-term business, and having regard to the general practice of insurers, compensate a policy holder whose policy has lapsed in consequence of a failure to pay any premium by issuing a free paid-up policy for reduced benefits or otherwise as the liquidator thinks fit.

[4233]

22 Notice of valuation of policy

(1) Before paying a dividend respect of claims other than under contracts of long-term insurance, the liquidator shall give notice of the value of each general business policy, as determined by him in accordance with rule 6, to the persons appearing from the records of the company or otherwise to be entitled to an interest in that policy and he shall do so in such manner as the court may direct.

(2) Before paying a dividend in respect of claims under contracts of long-term insurance and where a stop order has not been made in relation to the company, the liquidator shall give notice to the persons appearing from the records of the company or otherwise to be entitled to a payment under or to an interest in a long- term policy of the amount of that payment or the value of that policy as determined by him in accordance with rule 7(2) or (3), as the case may be.

(3) If a stop order is made in relation to the company, the liquidator shall give notice to all the persons appearing from the records of the company or otherwise to be entitled to a payment under or to an interest in a long-term policy of the amount of that payment or the value of that policy as determined by him in accordance with rule 8(2) or (3), as the case may be, and he shall give that notice in such manner as the court may direct.

(4) Any person to whom notice is so given shall be bound by the value so determined unless and until the court otherwise orders.

(5) Paragraphs (2) and (3) of this rule have effect as though references therein to persons appearing to be entitled to an interest in a long-term policy and to the value of that policy included, respectively, references to persons appearing to be entitled to apply for a free paid-up policy under section 24 of the 1923 Act and to the value of that entitlement under rule 7 (in the case of paragraph (2) of this rule) or under rule 8 (in the case of paragraph (3) of this rule).

(6) Where the liquidator summons a meeting of creditors in respect of liabilities of the company [attributable to either or both] its long-tem business or other business, he may adopt any valuation carried out in accordance with rules 6, 7 or 8 as the case may be or, if no such valuation has been carried out by the time of the meeting, he may conduct the meeting using such estimates of the value of policies as he thinks fit.

NOTES

Para (6): words in square brackets substituted by the Insurers (Reorganisation and Winding Up) Regulations 2003, SI 2003/1102, regs 52, 56.

[4234]

23 Dividends to creditors

(1) This rule applies in the case of a company carrying on long-term business.

(2) Part II of the principal rules applies separately in relation to the two separate companies assumed for the purposes of rule 5 above.

(3) The court may, at any time before the making of a stop order, permit a dividend to be declared and paid on such terms as thinks fit in respect only of debts which fell due to payment before the liquidation date or, in the case of claims under long-term policies, which have fallen due for payment on or after the liquidation date.

[4235]

24 Meetings of creditors

[(1) In the case of a company carrying on long-term business in whose case no stop order has been made, the creditors entitled to participate in creditors' meetings may be—

(a) in relation to the long-term business assets of the company, only those who are creditors in respect of liabilities attributable to the long-term business of the company; and

(b) in relation to the other business assets of the company, only those who are creditors in respect of liabilities attributable to the other business of the company.

(1A) In a case where separate general meetings of the creditors are summoned by the liquidator pursuant to—

(a) paragraph (1) above; or

(b) [regulation 29 of the Insurers (Reorganisation and Winding Up) Regulations 2004] (composite insurers: general meetings of creditors),

chapter 8 of Part 4 and Part 8 of the principal rules apply to each such separate meeting.]

(2) In relation to any such separate meeting—

(a) rule 4.61(3) of the principal rules (expenses of summoning meetings) has effect as if the reference therein to assets were a reference to the assets available under the above-mentioned Regulations for meeting the liabilities of the company owed to the creditors summoned to the meeting, and

(b) rule 4.63 of the principal rules (resolutions) applies as if the reference therein to value in relation to a creditor who is not, by virtue of rule 6, 7 or 8 above, required to prove his debt, were a reference to the value most recently notified to him under rule 22 above or, if the court has determined a different value in accordance with rule 22(4), as if it were a reference to that different value.

[(3) In paragraph (1)—

"long-term business assets" means the assets representing the fund or funds maintained by the company in respect of its long-term business;

"other business assets" means any assets of the company which are not long-term business assets.]

NOTES

Para (1): substituted, together with para (1A) for original para (1), by the Insurers (Reorganisation and Winding Up) Regulations 2003, SI 2003/1102, regs 52, 57(1), (2).

Para (1A): substituted, together with para (1), for original para (1) by SI 2003/1102, regs 52, 57(1), (2); words in square brackets in para (b) substituted by the Insurers (Reorganisation and Winding Up) Regulations 2004, SI 2004/353, reg 51(1), (2) (as amended by the Insurers (Reorganisation and Winding Up) (Amendment) Regulations 2004, SI 2004/546, reg 2(1), (6)).

Para (3): added by SI 2003/1102, regs 52, 57(1), (3).

[4236]

25 Remuneration of liquidator carrying on long-term business

(1) So long as no stop order has been made in relation to a company carrying on long-term business, the liquidator is entitled to receive remuneration for his services as such in relation to the carrying on of that business provided for in this rule.

(2) The remuneration shall be fixed by the liquidation committee by reference to the time properly given by the liquidator and his staff in attending to matters arising in the winding up.

(3) If there is no liquidation committee or the committee does not make the requisite determination, the liquidator's remuneration may be fixed (in accordance with paragraph (2)) by a resolution of a meeting of creditors.

(4) If not fixed as above, the liquidator's remuneration shall be in accordance with the scale laid down for the Official Receiver by the general regulations.

(5) If the liquidator's remuneration has been fixed by the liquidation committee, and the liquidator considers the amount to be insufficient, he may request that it be increased by resolution of the creditors.

[4237]

26 Apportionment of costs payable out of the assets

(1) [Where no stop order has been made in relation to a company, rule 4.218] of the principal rules (general rule as to priority) applies separately to the assets of the company's long-term business and to the assets of the company's other business.

(2) But where any fee, expense, cost, charge, disbursement or remuneration does not relate exclusively to the assets of the company's long-tem business or to the assets of the company's other business, the liquidator shall apportion it amongst those assets in such manner as he shall determine.

NOTES

Para (1): words in square brackets substituted by the Insurers (Reorganisation and Winding Up) Regulations 2003, SI 2003/1102, regs 52, 58(1).

[4238]

27 Notice of stop order

(1) When a stop order has been made in relation to the company, the court shall, on the same day send to the Official Receiver a notice informing him that the stop order has been made.

(2) The notice shall be in Form No 1 set out in Schedule 6 with such variation as circumstances may require.

(3) Three copies of the stop order sealed with the seal of the court shall forthwith be sent by the court to the Official Receiver.

(4) The Official Receiver shall cause a sealed copy of the order to be served upon the liquidator by prepaid letter or upon such other person or persons, or in such other manner as the court may direct, and shall forward a copy of the order to the registrar of companies.

(5) The liquidator shall forthwith on receipt of a sealed copy of the order—

- (a) cause notice of the order in Form 2 set out in Schedule 6 to be gazetted, and
- (b) advertise the making of the order in the newspaper in which the liquidation date was advertised, by notice in Form No 3 set out in Schedule 6.

SCHEDULE 1

RULES FOR VALUING GENERAL BUSINESS POLICIES

Rule 6

[4239]

1.—(1) This paragraph applies in relation to periodic payments under a general business policy which fall due for payment after the liquidation date where the event giving rise to the liability to make the payments occurred before the liquidation date.

(2) The value to be attributed to such periodic payments shall be determined on such actuarial principles and assumptions in regard to all relevant factors as the court shall direct.

2.—(1) This paragraph applies in relation to liabilities under a general business policy which arise from events which occurred before the liquidation date but which have not—

- (a) fallen due for payment before the liquidation date; or
- (b) been notified to the company before the liquidation date.

(2) The value to be attributed to such liabilities shall be determined on such actuarial principles and assumptions in regard to all relevant factors as the court shall direct.

3.—(1) This paragraph applies in relation to liabilities under a general business policy not dealt with by paragraphs 1 or 2.

(2) The value to be attributed to those liabilities shall—

- (a) if the terms of the policy provide for a repayment of premium upon the early termination of the policy or the policy is expressed to run from one definite date to another or the policy may be terminated by any of the parties with effect from a definite date, be the greater of the following two amounts:
  - (i) the amount (if any) which under the terms of the policy would have been repayable on early termination of the policy had the policy terminated on the liquidation date, and

(ii) where the policy is expressed to run from one definite date to another or may be terminated by any of the parties with effect from a definite date, such proportion of the last premium paid as is proportionate to the unexpired portion of the period in respect of which that premium was paid; and

(b) in any other case, be a just estimate of that value.

SCHEDULE 2

RULES FOR VALUING NON-LINKED LIFE POLICIES, NON-LINKED DEFERRED ANNUITY POLICIES, NON-LINKED ANNUITIES IN PAYMENT, UNITISED NON-LINKED POLICIES AND CAPITAL REDEMPTION POLICIES

Rule 7

[4240]

1 General

In valuing a policy—

(a) where it is necessary to calculate the present value of future payments by or to the company, interest shall be assumed at such fair and reasonable rate or rates as the court may direct;

(b) where relevant, the rates of mortality and the rates of disability to be employed shall be such rates as the court considers appropriate after taking into account:

(i) relevant published tables of rates of mortality and rates of disability, and

(ii) the rates of mortality and the rates of disability experienced in connection with similar policies issued by the company;

(c) there shall be determined:

(i) the present value of the ordinary benefits,

(ii) the present value of additional benefits;

(iii) the present value of options, and

(iv) if further premiums fall to be paid under the policy on or after the liquidation date, the present value of the premiums;

and for the purposes of this Schedule if the ordinary benefits only take into account premiums paid to date, the present value of future premiums shall be taken as nil.

2 Present value of the ordinary benefits

(1) Ordinary benefits are the benefits which will become payable to the policy holder on or after the liquidation date without his having to exercise any option under the policy (including any bonus or addition to the sum assured or the amount of annuity declared before the liquidation date) and for this purpose "option" includes a right to surrender the policy.

(2) Subject to sub-paragraph (3), the present value of the ordinary benefits shall be the value at the liquidation date of the reversion in the ordinary benefits according to the contingency upon which those benefits are payable calculated on the basis of the rates of interest, mortality and disability referred to in paragraph 1.

(3) For accumulating with profits policies—

(a) where the benefits are not expressed in the form of units in a with-profits fund, the value of the ordinary benefits is the amount that would have been payable, excluding any discretionary additions, if the policyholder had been able to exercise a right to terminate the policy at the liquidation date; and

(b) where the benefits are expressed in the form of units in a with-profits fund, the value of the ordinary benefits is the number of units held by the policy holder at the liquidation date valued at the unit price in force at that time or, if that price is not calculated on a daily basis, such price as the court may determine having regard to the last published unit price and any change in the value of assets attributable to the fund since the date of the last published unit price.

(4) Where—

(a) sub-paragraph (3) applies, and

(b) paragraph 3(1) of Schedule 3 applies to the calculation of the unit price (or as the case may be) the fund value,

the value shall be adjusted on the basis set out in paragraph 3(3) to (5) of Schedule 3.

(5) Where sub-paragraph (3) applies, the value may be further adjusted by reference to the value of the assets underlying the unit price (or as the case may be) the value of the fund, if the liquidator considers such an adjustment to be necessary.

3 Present value of additional benefits

(1) Where under the terms of the policy or on the basis of the company's established practice the policy holder has a right to receive or an expectation of receiving benefits additional to the minimum benefits guaranteed under those terms, the court shall determine rates of interest, bonus (whether reversionary, terminal or any other type of bonus used by the company), mortality and disability to provide for the present value (if any) of that right or expectation.

(2) In determining what (if any) value to attribute to any such expectations the court shall have regard to the premium payable in relation to the minimum guaranteed benefits and the amount (if any) an insurer is required to provide in respect of those expectations in any rules made by the Authority under Part X of the 2000 Act.

4 Present value of options

The amount of the present value of options shall be the amount which, in the opinion of the liquidator, is necessary to be provided at the liquidation date (in addition to the amount of the present value of the ordinary benefits) to cover the additional liabilities likely to arise upon the exercise on or after that date by the policy holder of any option conferred upon him by the terms of the policy or, in the case of an industrial assurance policy, by the Industrial Assurance Acts other than an option whereby the policy holder can secure a guaranteed cash payment within the period of 12 months beginning with that date.

5 Present value of premiums

The present value of the premiums shall be the value at the liquidation date of the premiums which fall due to be paid by the policy holder after the liquidation date calculated on the basis of the rates of interest, mortality and disability referred to in paragraph 1.

6 Value of the policy

(1) Subject to sub-paragraph (2)—

- (a) if no further premiums fall due to be paid under the policy on or after the liquidation date, the value of the policy shall be the aggregate of:
  - (i) the present value of the ordinary benefits;
  - (ii) the present value of options; and
  - (iii) the present value of additional benefits;
- (b) if further premiums fall due to be so paid and the aggregate value referred to in sub-paragraph (a) exceeds the present value of the premiums, the value of the policy shall be the amount of that excess; and
- (c) if further premiums fall due to be so paid and that aggregate does not exceed the present value of the premiums, the policy shall have no value.

(2) Where the policy holder has a right conferred upon him by the terms of the policy or by the Industrial Assurance Acts whereby the policy holder can secure a guaranteed cash payment within the period of 12 months beginning with the liquidation date, the liquidator shall determine the amount which in his opinion it is necessary to provide at that date to cover the liabilities which will accrue when that option is exercised (on the assumption that it will be exercised) and the value of the policy shall be that amount if it exceeds the value of the policy (if any) determined in accordance with sub-paragraph (1).

SCHEDULE 3

RULES FOR VALUING LIFE POLICIES AND DEFERRED ANNUITY POLICIES WHICH ARE LINKED POLICIES

Rule 7

[4241]

1.—(1) Subject to sub-paragraph (2) the value of the policy shall be the aggregate of the value of the linked liabilities (calculated in accordance with paragraphs 2 or 4) and the value of other than linked liabilities (calculated in accordance with paragraph 5) except where that aggregate is a negative amount it which case the policy shall have no value.

(2) Where the terms of the policy include a right whereby the policy holder can secure a guaranteed cash payment within the period of 12 months beginning with the liquidation date then, if the amount which in the opinion of the liquidator is necessary to be provided at that date to cover any liabilities which will accrue when that option is exercised (on the assumption that it will be exercised) is greater than the value determined under sub-paragraph (1) of this paragraph, the value of the policy shall be that greater amount.

2.—(1) Where the linked liabilities are expressed in terms of units the value of those liabilities shall, subject to paragraph 3, be the amount arrived at by taking the product of the number of units of each class of units allocated to the policy on the liquidation date and the value of each such unit on that date and then adding those products.

(2) For the purposes of sub-paragraph (1)—

(a) where under the terms of the policy the value of a unit at any time falls to be determined by reference to the value at that time of the assets of a particular fund maintained by the company in relation to that and other policies, the value of a unit on the liquidation date shall be determined by reference to the net realisable value of the assets credited to that fund on that date (after taking account of disposal costs, any tax liabilities resulting from the disposal of assets insofar as they have not already been provided for by the company and any other amounts which under the terms of those policies are chargeable to the fund), and

(b) in any other case, the value of a unit on the liquidation date shall be the value which would have been ascribed to each unit credited to the policy holder, after any deductions which may be made under the terms of the policy, for the purpose of

determining the benefits payable under the policy on the liquidation date had the policy matured on that date.

3.—(1) This paragraph applies where—

(a) paragraph 2(2)(a) applies and the company has a right under the terms of the policy either to make periodic withdrawals from the fund referred to in that paragraph or to retain any part of the income accruing in respect of the assets of that fund,

(b) paragraph 2(2)(b) applies and the company has a right under the terms of the policy to receive the whole or any part of any distributions made in respect of the units referred to in that paragraph, or

(c) paragraph 2(2)(a) or paragraph 2(2)(b) applies and the company has a right under the terms of the policy to make periodic cancellations of a proportion of the number of units credited to the policy.

(2) Where this paragraph applies, the value of the linked liabilities calculated in accordance with paragraph 2(1) shall be reduced by an amount calculated in accordance with sub-paragraph (3) of this paragraph.

(3) The said amount is—

(a) where this paragraph applies by virtue of head (a) or (b) of sub-paragraph (1), the value as at the liquidation date, calculated on actuarial principles, of the future income of the company in respect of the units in question arising from the rights referred to in head (a) or (b) of sub-paragraph (1) as the case may be, or

(b) where this paragraph applies by virtue of head (c) of sub-paragraph (1), the value as at the liquidation date, calculated on actuarial principles, of the liabilities of the company in respect of the units which fall to be cancelled in the future under the right referred to in head (c) of sub-paragraph (1).

(4) In calculating any amount in accordance with sub-paragraph (3) there shall be disregarded—

(a) such part of the rights referred to in the relevant head of sub-paragraph (1) which in the opinion of the liquidator constitutes appropriate provision for future expenses and mortality risks, and

(b) such part of those rights (if any) which the court considers to constitute appropriate provision for any right or expectation of the policy holder to receive benefits additional to the benefits guaranteed under the terms of the policy.

(5) In determining the said amount—

(a) interest shall be assumed at such rate or rates as the court may direct, and

(b) where relevant, the rates of mortality and the rates of disability to be employed shall be such rates as the court considers appropriate after taking into account:

(i) relevant published tables of rates of mortality and rates of disability, and

(ii) the rates of mortality and the rates of disability experienced in connection with similar policies issued by the company.

4. Where the linked liabilities are not expressed in terms of units the value of those liabilities shall be the value (subject to adjustment for any amounts which would have been deducted for taxation) which would have been ascribed to those liabilities had the policy matured on the liquidation date.

5.—(1) The value of any liabilities other than linked liabilities including reserves for future expenses, options and guarantees shall be determined on actuarial principles and appropriate assumptions in regard to all relevant factors including the assumption of such rate or rates of interest, mortality and disability as the court may direct.

(2) In valuing liabilities under this paragraph credit shall be taken for those parts of future premiums which do not fall to be applied in the allocation of further units to the policy and for any rights of the company which have been disregarded under paragraph 3(4)(a) in valuing the linked liabilities.

SCHEDULE 4

RULES FOR VALUING LONG-TERM POLICIES WHICH ARE NOT DEALT WITH IN SCHEDULES 2 OR 3

Rule 7

[4242]

The value of a long-term policy not covered by Schedule 2 or 3 shall be the value of the benefits due to the policy holder determined on such actuarial principles and assumptions in regard to all relevant factors as the court shall determine.

SCHEDULE 5

RULES FOR VALUING LONG-TERM POLICIES WHERE A STOP ORDER HAS BEEN MADE

Rule 8

[4243]

1. Subject to paragraphs 2 and 3, in valuing a policy Schedules 2, 3 or 4 shall apply according to the class of that policy as if those Schedules were herein repeated but with a view to a fresh valuation of each policy on appropriate assumptions in regard to all relevant factors and subject to the following modifications—

(a) references to the stop order shall be substituted for references to the liquidation date,

(b) in paragraph 4 of Schedule 2 for the words "whereby the policy holder can secure a guaranteed cash payment within the period of 12 months beginning with that date" there shall be substituted the words "to surrender the policy which can be exercised on that date",

(c) paragraph 6(2) of Schedule 2 shall be deleted, and

(d) paragraph 1(2) of Schedule 3 shall be deleted.

2.—(1) This paragraph applies where the policy holder has a right conferred upon him under the terms of the policy or by the Industrial Assurance Acts to surrender the policy and that right is exercisable on the date of the stop order.

(2) Where this paragraph applies and the amount required at the date of the stop order to provide for the benefits payable upon surrender of the policy (on the assumption that the policy is surrendered on the date of the stop order) is greater than the value of the policy determined in accordance with paragraph 1, the value of the policy shall, subject to paragraph 3, be the said amount so required.

(3) Where any part of the surrender value is payable after the date of the stop order, sub-paragraph (2) shall apply but the value therein referred to shall be discounted at such a rate of interest as the court may direct.

3.—(1) This paragraph applies in the case of a linked policy where—

(a) the terms of the policy include a guarantee that the amount assured will on maturity of the policy be worth a minimum amount calculable in money terms, or

(b) the terms of the policy include a right on the part of the policy holder to surrender the policy and a guarantee that the payment on surrender will be worth a minimum amount calculable in money terms and that right is exercisable on or after the date of the stop order.

(2) Where this paragraph applies the value of the policy shall be the greater of the following two amounts—

(a) the value the policy would have had at the date of the stop order had the policy been a non-linked policy, that is to say, had the linked liabilities provided by the policy not been so provided but the policy had otherwise been on the same terms, and

(b) the value the policy would have had at the date of the stop order had the policy not included any guarantees of payments on maturity or surrender worth a minimum amount calculable in money terms.

SCHEDULE 6

FORMS

Rule 27

FORM NO 1

[4244]–[4246]
Notification to Official Receiver of order made under section 376(2) of the Financial Services and Markets Act 2000

(Title)

To the Official Receiver of the Court

(Address)
Order made this day by the Honourable Mr Justice (or, *as the case may be*) that the liquidator or (insert name of company) shall not carry on the long-term business of the company.

FORM NO 2

Notice for London Gazette
Notice of order made under section 376(2) of the Financial Services and Markets Act 2000 for cessation of long-term business
Name of Company . . . . Address of Registered Office . . . .
Court . . . . Number of Matter . . . . Date of Order. . . . .
Date of liquidation date . . . .

FORM NO 3

Notice for Newspaper
Notice of order made under section 376(2) of the Financial Services and Markets Act 2000 for cessation of long-term business
Name of Company . . . .
Date of Liquidation date . . . .
Date of Order . . . .
[Liquidator] . . . .

EUROPEAN COMMUNITIES (RIGHTS AGAINST INSURERS) REGULATIONS 2002

(SI 2002/3061)

NOTES
Made: 10 December 2002.
Authority: European Communities Act 1972, s 2(2).
Commencement: 19 January 2003.

[4247]
1 Citation and commencement
These Regulations may be cited as the European Communities (Rights against Insurers) Regulations 2002 and shall come into force on 19th January 2003.

[4248]
2 Interpretation
(1) In these Regulations—
"the 1981 Order" means the Road Traffic (Northern Ireland) Order 1981;
"the 1988 Act" means the Road Traffic Act 1988;
"accident" means an accident on a road or other public place in the United Kingdom caused by, or arising out of, the use of any insured vehicle;
"entitled party" means any person who is—
(a) a resident of a Member State; or

Part IV Statutory Instruments

(b) a resident of any other State which is a Contracting Party to the Agreement on the European Economic Area signed at Oporto on 2nd May 1992 and the Protocol adjusting the Agreement signed at Brussels on 17th March 1993;

"insured person" means a person insured under a policy of insurance satisfying the conditions set out in paragraph (3) of this regulation;

"vehicle" means any motor vehicle intended for travel on land and propelled by mechanical power, but not running on rails, and any trailer whether or not coupled, which is normally based (within the meaning of paragraph (2) of this regulation) in the United Kingdom.

(2) The territory in which a vehicle is normally based is—

(a) the territory of the State of which the vehicle bears a registration plate; or

(b) in cases where no registration is required for the type of vehicle, but the vehicle bears an insurance plate or a distinguishing sign analogous to a registration plate, the territory of the State in which the insurance plate or the sign is issued; or

(c) in cases where neither registration plate nor insurance plate nor distinguishing sign is required for the type of vehicle, the territory of the State in which the keeper of the vehicle is permanently resident.

(3) For the purposes of these Regulations, a vehicle is insured if there is in force in relation to the use of that vehicle on a road or other public place in the United Kingdom by the insured person a policy of insurance (including a covering note) which fulfils the requirements of section 145 of the 1988 Act or article 92 of the 1981 Order.

[4249]
3 Right of action

(1) Paragraph (2) of this regulation applies where an entitled party has a cause of action against an insured person in tort or (as the case may be) delict, and that cause of action arises out of an accident.

(2) Where this paragraph applies, the entitled party may, without prejudice to his right to issue proceedings against the insured person, issue proceedings against the insurer which issued the policy of insurance relating to the insured vehicle, and that insurer shall be directly liable to the entitled party to the extent that he is liable to the insured person.

MOTOR VEHICLES (COMPULSORY INSURANCE) (INFORMATION CENTRE AND COMPENSATION BODY) REGULATIONS 2003

(SI 2003/37)

NOTES

Made: 10 January 2003.
Authority: European Communities Act 1972, s 2(2).
Commencement: 19 January 2003.

ARRANGEMENT OF REGULATIONS

1 Citation and commencement [4250]
2 Interpretation [4251]

The information centre

3 The information centre for the United Kingdom and its duties [4252]
4 The specified information [4253]
5 Maintenance and supply of information by insurers [4254]
6 Maintenance and supply of information by policyholders [4255]
7 Maintenance and supply of information by others [4256]
8 Information held by Secretary of State [4257]
9 Supply of information by the information centre [4258]

The compensation body

10 Compensation body for the United Kingdom [4259]
11 Entitlement to compensation where the insurer is identified [4260]
12 Response from the compensation body [4261]
13 Entitlement to compensation where vehicle or insurer is not identified [4262]
14 Reimbursement of foreign compensation body where insurer is identified [4263]
15 Reimbursement of foreign compensation body where insurer is unidentified [4264]

Miscellaneous

16 Civil liability [4265]

17 Enforcement . . . . . . [4266]

SCHEDULE

Part 1—Information to be Recorded by Insurers . . . . . . [4267]
Part 2—Information to be Recorded by Policyholders . . . . . . [4268]
Part 3—Information to be Recorded by Users Taking Advantage of the Derogation Provided in Article 4(a) of the First Motor Insurance Directive . . . . . . [4269]

[4250]

1 Citation and commencement

These Regulations may be cited as the Motor Vehicles (Compulsory Insurance) (Information Centre and Compensation Body) Regulations 2003 and shall come into force on 19th January 2003.

[4251]

2 Interpretation

(1) In these Regulations—

"claims representative" means, in the case of an insurer carrying on the business of effecting or carrying out a UK insurance policy, the person appointed to act as such by that insurer in each EEA State other than the United Kingdom with responsibility and authority for handling and settling claims arising from accidents of the kind mentioned in Article 1(2) of the fourth motor insurance directive;

"compensation body" means the body named in regulation 9;

"EEA State" means a State which is a Contracting Party to the Agreement on the European Economic Area signed at Oporto on 2nd May 1992 and the Protocol adjusting the Agreement signed at Brussels on 17th March 1993;

"European insurance policy" means an insurance policy issued in an EEA State fulfilling the requirements of Article 3 of the first motor insurance directive where the territory in which the vehicle the use of which is insured is normally based is an EEA State other than the United Kingdom;

"first motor insurance directive" means Council Directive 72/166/EEC of 24 April 1972 on the approximation of the laws of the Member States relating to insurance against civil liability in respect of the use of motor vehicles, and to the enforcement of the obligation to insure against such liability;

"fourth motor insurance directive" means the Directive of the European Parliament and the Council of 16 May 2000 on the approximation of the laws of the Member States relating to insurance against civil liability in respect of the use of motor vehicles and amending Council Directives 73/239/EEC and 88/357/EEC (No 2000/26/EC);

"foreign compensation body" means a person or body established or approved (by virtue of Article 6(1) of the fourth motor insurance directive) in an EEA State other than the United Kingdom to fulfil like functions to the compensation body;

"foreign information centre" means a person or body established or approved as an information centre in an EEA State other than the United Kingdom by virtue of Article 5(1) of the fourth motor insurance directive;

. . .

"information centre" means the body named in regulation 3(1);

"injured party" means a person resident in an EEA State claiming to be entitled to compensation in respect of any loss or injury resulting from an accident caused by or arising out of the use of a vehicle;

"registered keeper" in relation to a vehicle means the person who is registered as the keeper under the Vehicle Excise and Registration Act 1994 or, in the case of vehicles in the public service of the Crown which are not registered under that Act, the person who has charge of the vehicle;

"MIB" means the Motor Insurers' Bureau (a company limited by guarantee and incorporated under the Companies Act 1929 on 14th June 1946);

"MIIC" means the Motor Insurers' Information Centre (a company limited by guarantee and incorporated under the Companies Act 1985 on 8th December 1998);

"open cover contract" means a UK insurance policy where the vehicles covered are not specifically identified in the contract or the covering note;

"second motor insurance directive" means the Second Council Directive 84/5/EEC of 30 December 1983 on the approximation of the laws of the Member States relating to insurance against civil liability in respect of the use of motor vehicles;

"specified information" means the information referred to in regulation 4;

"standard contract" means a UK insurance policy where every vehicle covered is specifically identified in the contract or the covering note;

"subscribing State" means a State other than an EEA State whose national insurer's bureau as defined in Article 1(3) of the first motor insurance directive has joined the Green Card System;

"UK insurance policy" means a policy of insurance (including a covering note) covering the use of a vehicle on a road or other public place in the United Kingdom which—

(a) fulfils the requirements of section 145 of the Road Traffic Act 1988, or article 92 of the Road Traffic (Northern Ireland) Order 1981, and

(b) in the case of a policy of insurance complying with article 92 of the 1981 Order, is issued by an insurer within the meaning of article 12 of that Order;

"vehicle" means any motor vehicle intended for travel on land and propelled by mechanical power, but not running on rails, and any trailer, whether or not coupled.

(2) In these Regulations a reference (however phrased) to a place where a vehicle is normally based is a reference to—

(a) the territory of the state of which the vehicle bears a registration plate, or

(b) in cases where no registration is required for the type of vehicle but the vehicle bears an insurance plate or a distinguishing sign analogous to a registration plate, the territory of the state in which the insurance plate or the sign is issued, or

(c) in cases where neither registration plate nor insurance plate nor distinguishing sign is required for the type of vehicle, the territory of the state in which the keeper of the vehicle is permanently resident.

NOTES

Para (1): definition "guarantee fund" (omitted) revoked by the Motor Vehicles (Compulsory Insurance) (Information Centre and Compensation Body) (Amendment) Regulations 2007, SI 2007/2982, reg 2.

Council Directive 72/166/EEC: OJ L103, 2.5.1972, p 1.

Directive of the European Parliament and the Council 2000/26/EC: OJ L181, 20.7.2000, p 65.

Council Directive 73/239/EEC: OJ L228, 16.8.1973, p 3.

Council Directive 88/357/EEC: OJ L172, 4.7.1988, p 1.

Second Council Directive 84/5/EEC: OJ L8, 11.1.1984, p 17.

The information centre

[4252]

3 The information centre for the United Kingdom and its duties

(1) MIIC is approved as the information centre for the United Kingdom for the purposes of the fourth motor insurance directive.

(2) The information centre shall establish a means of access to the specified information in a manner whereby it can co-ordinate and disseminate that information for the purposes of these Regulations.

(3) The information centre shall retain access to the specified information for a period of not less than seven years commencing on—

(a) in the case of the information specified in regulation 4(a), (c) and (d), the date on which the vehicle ceases to be registered under the Vehicle Excise and Registration Act 1994, and

(b) in the case of the information specified in regulation 4(b), the day immediately following the date of expiry of the policy of insurance to which that information relates.

(4) Where the information necessary to enable the information centre to respond to a request from a person under regulation 9 does not form part of the specified information, the information centre shall obtain from the foreign information centre of the territory in which the vehicle is normally based such information as may from time to time be required so as to enable the information centre to comply with regulation 9.

(5) Where the information centre is satisfied that a valid request for the name and address of the registered keeper of a vehicle has been made to it pursuant to regulation 9 it shall immediately seek the information from the Secretary of State.

(6) The information centre shall co-operate with every foreign information centre to the extent necessary to enable those centres to discharge their functions under the fourth motor insurance directive.

[4253]

4 The specified information

The specified information is—

(a) a list of all vehicles normally based in the United Kingdom the names and addresses of their registered keepers and the registration marks assigned to them by the Secretary of State;

(b) the following information in relation to every UK insurance policy under which the use of any such vehicle is insured—
(i) the number of the policy,
(ii) the name of the policyholder,
(iii) the name and address of the insurer,
(iv) the names and addresses of that insurer's claims representatives, and
(v) the period during which the use of the vehicle is insured under that contract;
(c) a list of all vehicles which take advantage of the derogation provided in Article 4(a) of the first motor insurance directive (so that they may lawfully be used on a road or other public place in the United Kingdom without there being in force any policy of insurance), and the registration marks assigned to them;
(d) the name and address of the person or body designated as responsible for compensating an injured party (in cases where the procedure provided for in the first indent of Article 2(2) of the first motor insurance directive is not applicable) if an accident is caused by or arises out of the use of a vehicle named in the list kept under sub-paragraph (c).

[4254]
5 Maintenance and supply of information by insurers
(1) Every insurer shall maintain a record of the information set out in Part 1 of the Schedule to these Regulations for the period specified in regulation 3(3).
(2) Where the information centre so requests an insurer shall supply to it immediately such of that information as may be specified in that request in respect of any UK insurance policy to which that insurer is or was a party.
(3) The information requested—
(a) shall be supplied in the manner specified in the request, or
(b) where no manner of supply is specified in the request, may be supplied in any manner except orally.
(4) An insurer shall not be obliged by virtue of this regulation to maintain a record or to supply information if he has used his best endeavours to obtain such information from his insured and the insured has failed or refused to supply the information to the insurer.
(5) Where the information centre so requests, an insurer shall immediately supply to it the name and address of every policyholder to whom it has issued an open cover contract in respect of such period as may be specified in that request.

[4255]
6 Maintenance and supply of information by policyholders
(1) Every policyholder who has entered into an open cover contract with an insurer shall maintain in respect of that contract a record of the information set out in Part 2 of the Schedule to these Regulations for the period specified in regulation 3(3).
(2) Where the information centre so requests, any such policyholder shall supply to it immediately so much of the information set out in Part 2 of the Schedule as may be specified in that request in respect of any open cover contract to which he is or was a party.
(3) Every policyholder who has entered into an open cover contract of the type specified in Part 1 of the Schedule with an insurer shall immediately supply to that insurer the information described in Part 1 of the Schedule.
(4) Where any detail of the information set out in Part 1 of the Schedule to these Regulations changes in respect of any open cover contract, the policyholder shall notify the insurer of the changed details immediately.
(5) Any information requested under this regulation—
(a) shall be supplied in the manner specified in the request, or
(b) where no manner of supply is specified in the request, may be supplied in any manner except orally.

[4256]
7 Maintenance and supply of information by others
(1) Every person who takes advantage of the derogation provided in Article 4(a) of the first motor insurance directive in respect of any vehicle normally based in the United Kingdom shall maintain a record of the information set out in Part 3 of the Schedule for the period specified in regulation 3(3).
(2) Every such person shall supply immediately to the information centre the information set out in Part 3 of the Schedule in respect of any vehicle for which that person is or was the user for more

than 14 days.

(3) Where the information centre so requests, every such person shall supply to it immediately so much of the information set out in Part 3 of the Schedule as may be specified in that request in respect of any vehicle which that person is or was the user.

[4257]

8 Information held by Secretary of State

(1) The Secretary of State shall immediately notify the information centre in writing of any alteration in the information specified in regulation 4(d).

(2) Where the information centre so requests, the Secretary of State shall without delay supply in writing to the information centre the name and address of the registered keeper of any vehicle specified in that request which is normally based in the UK.

[4258]

9 Supply of information by the information centre

(1) This regulation applies where—

(a) an accident, caused by or arising out of the use of a vehicle which is normally based in an EEA State, occurs in the United Kingdom;

(b) an accident, caused by or arising out of the use of a vehicle, occurs on the territory of—

(i) an EEA State other than the United Kingdom, or

(ii) a subscribing state,

and that vehicle is normally based in the United Kingdom;

(c) an accident, caused by or arising out of the use of a vehicle which is normally based in an EEA State, occurs on the territory of—

(i) an EEA State other than the United Kingdom, or

(ii) a subscribing state,

and an injured party resides in the United Kingdom.

(2) Where this regulation applies, an injured party may request the information centre to provide to him the information described in paragraph (4) in respect of every vehicle involved in the accident which is normally based in an EEA State.

(3) The information centre shall provide the information requested if the request is—

(a) made in writing,

(b) received by the information centre no later than seven years after the date of the accident, and

(c) contains sufficient information to identify the vehicle in respect of which the information is being sought.

(4) The information which may be requested in respect of a vehicle is—

(a) the name and address of any insurer who has issued a UK insurance policy or European insurance policy covering the use of that vehicle at the time the accident occurred;

(b) the number of that policy;

(c) the name and address of that insurer's claims representative in the state of residence of the injured party; and

(d) where the information centre is satisfied that the injured party has a legitimate interest in obtaining that information, the name and address of the registered keeper of the vehicle or, where the territory in which the vehicle is normally based is an EEA State other than the United Kingdom, the person having custody of the vehicle.

(5) Where an injured party has requested information in respect of a vehicle which may lawfully be used on a road or other public place in the United Kingdom without there being in force a UK insurance policy, the information centre shall provide the injured party with the name and address of the person or body designated as responsible for compensating injured parties and referred to in regulation 4(d).

(6) The information centre shall provide information pursuant to this regulation in writing immediately after it receives the request.

(7) The information centre may charge a fee of not more than £10.00 for providing that information.

The compensation body

[4259]

10 Compensation body for the United Kingdom

MIB is approved as the compensation body for the United Kingdom for the purposes of the fourth motor insurance directive.

[4260]

11 Entitlement to compensation where the insurer is identified

(1) This regulation and regulation 12 apply in a case where—

(a) an injured party is resident in the United Kingdom,

(b) that person claims to be entitled to compensation in respect of an accident occurring in an EEA State other than the United Kingdom or in a subscribing state, and

(c) the loss or injury to which the claim relates has been caused by or arises out of the use of a vehicle which is—

(i) normally based in an EEA State other than the United Kingdom, and

(ii) insured though an establishment in an EEA State other than the United Kingdom.

(2) Where this regulation applies, the injured party may make a claim for compensation from the compensation body if—

(a) he has not commenced legal proceedings against the insurer of the vehicle the use of which caused the accident, and

(b) either of the conditions set out in paragraph (3) is fulfilled.

(3) The conditions are—

(a) that the injured party has claimed compensation from the insurer of the vehicle or the insurer's claims representative and neither the insurer nor the claims representative has provided a reasoned reply to the claim within the period of three months after the date it was made;

(b) that the insurer has failed to appoint a claims representative in the United Kingdom, and the injured party has not claimed compensation directly from that insurer.

[4261]

12 Response from the compensation body

(1) Upon receipt of a claim for compensation under regulation 11, the compensation body shall immediately notify—

(a) the insurer of the vehicle the use of which is alleged to have caused the accident, or that insurer's claims representative;

(b) the foreign compensation body in the EEA State in which that insurer's establishment is situated; and

(c) if known, the person who is alleged to have caused the accident,

that it has received a claim from the injured party and that it will respond to that claim within two months from the date on which the claim was received.

(2) The compensation body shall respond to a claim for compensation within two months of receiving the claim.

(3) If the injured party satisfies the compensation body as to the matters specified in paragraph (4), the compensation body shall indemnify the injured party in respect of the loss and damage described in paragraph (4)(b).

(4) The matters referred to in paragraph (3) are—

(a) that a person whose liability for the use of the vehicle is insured by the insurer referred to in regulation 11(1)(c) is liable to the injured party in respect of the accident which is the subject of the claim, and

(b) the amount of loss and damage (including interest) that is properly recoverable in consequence of that accident by the injured party from that person under the laws applying in that part of the United Kingdom in which the injured party resided at the date of the accident.

(5) The compensation body shall cease forthwith to act in respect of a claim as soon as it becomes aware that—

(a) the insurer referred to in regulation 11(1)(c), or the claims representative of that insurer, has made a reasoned response to the claim, or

(b) the injured party has commenced legal proceedings against the insurer.

[4262]

13 Entitlement to compensation where vehicle or insurer is not identified

(1) This regulation applies where—

(a) an accident, caused by or arising out of the use of a vehicle which is normally based in an EEA State, occurs on the territory of—

(i) an EEA State other than the United Kingdom, or

(ii) a subscribing State,

and an injured party resides in the United Kingdom,

(b) that injured party has made a request for information under regulation 9(2), and

(c) it has proved impossible—
  (i) to identify the vehicle the use of which is alleged to have been responsible for the accident, or
  (ii) within a period of two months after the date of the request, to identify an insurance undertaking which insures the use of the vehicle.

(2) Where this regulation applies—
  (a) the injured party may make a claim for compensation from the compensation body, and
  (b) the compensation body shall compensate the injured party in accordance with the provisions of Article 1 of the second motor insurance directive as if it were the body authorised under paragraph 4 of that Article and the accident had occurred in Great Britain.

[4263]
14 Reimbursement of foreign compensation body where insurer is identified

(1) Where—
  (a) an injured party is resident in an EEA State other than the United Kingdom,
  (b) that person has been compensated in respect of an accident by the foreign compensation body of the State where he resides,
  (c) the foreign compensation body has paid the compensation to that person under a provision corresponding to regulation 12(3),
  (d) the accident in respect of which compensation has been paid was caused by, or arose out of, the use of a vehicle the use of which is insured under a UK insurance policy by an insurer established in the United Kingdom, and
  (e) the place where the vehicle is normally based is an EEA State other than the State in which the injured party resides,

the compensation body shall be liable to indemnify the foreign compensation body.

(2) Where the compensation body has indemnified the foreign compensation body under paragraph (1), it is subrogated to the rights of the injured party against the person who caused the accident or that person's insurer to the extent that it has indemnified the foreign compensation body.

(3) All similar rights of subrogation as provided for in other EEA States are hereby acknowledged to the extent required under Article 6(2) of the fourth motor insurance directive.

[4264]
15 Reimbursement of foreign compensation body where insurer is unidentified

(1) This regulation applies where—
  (a) an injured party is resident in an EEA State other than the United Kingdom, and
  (b) that person has been compensated by the foreign compensation body of the State where he resides.

(2) Where this regulation applies, the MIB shall be liable to indemnify the foreign compensation body in the following cases—
  (a) where the accident took place in the United Kingdom and it was caused by or arose from the use of—
    (i) an unidentified vehicle, or
    (ii) a vehicle normally based in a territory which is not an EEA State or a subscribing state or part of any such state;
  (b) where the accident was caused by, or arose from the use of, a vehicle normally based in the United Kingdom but it has proved impossible to identify the insurer of that vehicle within 2 months from the date when the request for compensation was lodged with the foreign compensation body.

Miscellaneous

[4265]
16 Civil Liability

Any sum due and owing pursuant to these Regulations shall be recoverable as a civil debt.

[4266]
17 Enforcement

If any person fails or refuses to maintain any record or supply any information for the purposes of these regulations, or if in giving any information for the purposes of these Regulations, makes any statement which he knows to be false in a material particular, or recklessly makes any statement which is false in a material particular, he is guilty of an offence and shall be liable on summary conviction to a fine not exceeding level 5 on the standard scale.

SCHEDULE

Regulations 5, 6 and 7

PART 1
INFORMATION TO BE RECORDED BY INSURERS

[4267]

1. In respect of every standard contract to which the insurer is a party—

(a) the number of the policy,

(b) the name of the policyholder,

(c) the registration mark of every vehicle the use of which is covered by the policy, and

(d) the period during which the use of each of those vehicles is (or has been) covered under the policy.

2. In respect of every open cover contract other than a contract in respect of an excepted vehicle to which the insurer is a party—

(a) the number of the policy,

(b) the name of the policyholder,

(c) the registration mark of every vehicle, other than an excepted vehicle, the use of which is from time to time covered under that contract, and

(d) the period during which the use of each of those vehicles is (or has been) covered under the policy.

3. In this Schedule an "excepted vehicle" is a vehicle the use of which is covered under the open cover contract for a period of less than 15 days.

PART 2
INFORMATION TO BE RECORDED BY POLICYHOLDERS

[4268]

In respect of every excepted vehicle insured under an open cover contract to which the policyholder is a party—

(a) the number of the policy under which the use of the vehicle is insured,

(b) the registration mark of the vehicle, and

(c) the period during which the use of the vehicles is (or has been) covered under the policy.

PART 3
INFORMATION TO BE RECORDED BY USERS TAKING ADVANTAGE OF THE DEROGATION PROVIDED IN ARTICLE 4(A) OF THE FIRST MOTOR INSURANCE DIRECTIVE

[4269]

In respect of every vehicle the use of which on a road or other public place in the United Kingdom is authorised without insurance by virtue of Article 4(a) of the first motor insurance directive—

(a) the registration mark of the vehicle; and

(b) the period during which the use of the vehicle is or was authorised by virtue of that derogation.

INSURERS (REORGANISATION AND WINDING UP) REGULATIONS 2004

(SI 2004/353)

NOTES

Made: 12 February 2004.
Authority: European Communities Act 1972, s 2(2).
Commencement: 18 February 2004.

ARRANGEMENT OF REGULATIONS

PART I
GENERAL

1 Citation and commencement [4270]
2 Interpretation [4271]
3 Scope [4272]

PART II
INSOLVENCY MEASURES AND PROCEEDINGS:
JURISDICTION IN RELATION TO INSURERS

4 Prohibition against winding up etc EEA insurers in the United Kingdom [4273]
5 Schemes of arrangement: EEA insurers [4274]
6 Reorganisation measures and winding up proceedings in respect of EEA insurers effective in the United Kingdom [4275]
7 Confirmation by the court of a creditors' voluntary winding up [4276]

PART III
MODIFICATIONS OF THE LAW OF INSOLVENCY:
NOTIFICATION AND PUBLICATION

8 Modifications of the law of insolvency [4277]
9 Notification of relevant decision to the Authority [4278]
10 Notification of relevant decision to EEA regulators [4279]
11 Publication of voluntary arrangement, administration order, winding up order or scheme of arrangement [4280]
12 Notification to creditors: winding up proceedings [4281]
13 Submission of claims by EEA creditors [4282]
14 Reports to creditors [4283]
15 Service of notices and documents [4284]
16 Disclosure of confidential information received from an EEA regulator [4285]

PART IV
PRIORITY OF PAYMENT OF INSURANCE CLAIMS IN WINDING UP ETC

17 Interpretation of this Part [4286]
18 Application of regulations 19 to 27 [4287]
19 Application of this Part: assets subject to a section 425 or Article 418 compromise or arrangement [4288]
20 Preferential debts: disapplication of section 175 of the 1986 Act or Article 149 of the 1989 Order [4289]
21 Preferential debts: long term insurers and general insurers [4290]
22 Composite insurers: preferential debts attributable to long term and general business [4291]
23 Preferential debts: long term business of a non-transferring composite insurer [4292]
24 Preferential debts: general business of a composite insurer [4293]
25 Insufficiency of long term business assets and general business assets [4294]
26 Composite insurers: excess of long term business assets and general business assets [4295]
27 Composite insurers: application of other assets [4296]
28 Composite insurers: proof of debts [4297]
29 Composite insurers: general meetings of creditors [4298]
30 Composite insurers: apportionment of costs payable out of the assets [4299]
31 Summary remedy against liquidators [4300]
32 Priority of subrogated claims by the Financial Services Compensation Scheme [4301]
33 Voluntary arrangements: treatment of insurance debts [4302]

PART V
REORGANISATION OR WINDING UP OF UK INSURERS:
RECOGNITION OF EEA RIGHTS

34 Application of this Part [4303]
35 Application of this Part: assets subject to a section 425 or Article 418 compromise or arrangement [4304]
36 Interpretation of this Part [4305]
37 EEA rights: applicable law in the winding up of a UK insurer [4306]

38 Employment contracts and relationships . . . [4307]
39 Contracts in connection with immovable property . . . [4308]
40 Registrable rights . . . [4309]
41 Third parties' rights in rem . . . [4310]
42 Reservation of title agreements etc . . . [4311]
43 Creditors' rights to set off . . . [4312]
44 Regulated markets . . . [4313]
45 Detrimental acts pursuant to the law of an EEA State . . . [4314]
46 Protection of third party purchasers . . . [4315]
47 Lawsuits pending . . . [4316]

PART VI
THIRD COUNTRY INSURERS

48 Interpretation of this Part . . . [4317]
49 Application of these Regulations to a third country insurer . . . [4318]
50 Disclosure of confidential information: third country insurers . . . [4319]

PART VII
REVOCATION AND AMENDMENTS

53 Revocation and transitional . . . [4320]

PART I
GENERAL

[4270]
1 Citation and Commencement

These Regulations may be cited as the Insurers (Reorganisation and Winding Up) Regulations 2004, and come into force on 18th February 2004.

[4271]
2 Interpretation

(1) In these Regulations—

"the 1985 Act" means the Companies Act 1985;

"the 1986 Act" means the Insolvency Act 1986;

"the 2000 Act" means the Financial Services and Markets Act 2000;

"the 1989 Order" means the Insolvency (Northern Ireland) Order 1989;

"administrator" has the meaning given by paragraph 13 of Schedule B1[, or by paragraph 14 of Schedule B1 to the 1989 Order];

"Article 418 compromise or arrangement" means a compromise or arrangement sanctioned by the court in relation to a UK insurer under Article 418 of the Companies Order, but does not include a compromise or arrangement falling within Article 420 or Articles 420A of that Order (reconstruction and amalgamations);

"the Authority" means the Financial Services Authority;

"branch", in relation to an EEA or UK insurer has the meaning given by Article 1(b) of the life insurance directive or the third non-life insurance directive;

"claim" means a claim submitted by a creditor of a UK insurer in the course of—

(a) a winding up,

(b) an administration, or

(c) a voluntary arrangement,

with a view to recovering his debt in whole or in part, and includes a proof of debt, within the meaning of Rule 4.73(4) of the Insolvency Rules, Rule 4.079(4) of the Insolvency Rules (Northern Ireland) or in Scotland a claim made in accordance with rule 4.15 of the Insolvency (Scotland) Rules;

"the Companies Order" means the Companies (Northern Ireland) Order 1986;

"creditors' voluntary winding up" has the meaning given by section 90 of the 1986 Act or Article 76 of the 1989 Order;

"debt"—

(a) in England and Wales and Northern Ireland—

(i) in relation to a winding up or administration of a UK insurer, has the meaning given by Rule 13.12 of the Insolvency Rules or Article 5 of the 1989 Order, and

(ii) in a case where a voluntary arrangement has effect, in relation to a UK insurer, means a debt which would constitute a debt in relation to the winding up of that insurer, except that references in paragraph (1) of Rule 13.12 or paragraph (1) of Article 5 of the 1989 Order to the date on which the company goes into liquidation are to be read as references to the date on which the voluntary arrangement has effect;

(b) in Scotland—

(i) in relation to a winding up of a UK insurer, shall be interpreted in accordance with Schedule 1 to the Bankruptcy (Scotland) Act 1985 as applied by Chapter 5 of Part 4 of the Insolvency (Scotland) Rules, and

(ii) in a case where a voluntary arrangement has effect in relation to a UK insurer, means a debt which would constitute a debt in relation to the winding up of that insurer, except that references in Chapter 5 of Part 4 of the Insolvency (Scotland) Rules to the date of commencement of winding up are to be read as references to the date on which the voluntary arrangement has effect;

"directive reorganisation measure" means a reorganisation measure as defined in Article 2(c) of the reorganisation and winding-up directive which was adopted or imposed on or after 20th April 2003;

"directive winding up proceedings" means winding up proceedings as defined in Article 2(d) of the reorganisation and winding-up directive which were opened on or after 20th April 2003;

"EEA creditor" means a creditor of a UK insurer who—

(a) in the case of an individual, is ordinarily resident in an EEA State, and

(b) in the case of a body corporate or unincorporated association of persons, has its head office in an EEA State;

"EEA insurer" means an undertaking, other than a UK insurer, pursuing the activity of direct insurance (within the meaning of Article 1 of the first life insurance directive or the first non-life insurance directive) which has received authorisation under Article 6 from its home state regulator;

"EEA regulator" means a competent authority (within the meaning of Article 1(1) of the life insurance directive or Article 1(k) of the third non-life insurance directive, as the case may be) of an EEA State;

["EEA State" has the meaning given by Schedule 1 to the Interpretation Act 1978;]

"the first non-life insurance directive" means the Council Directive (73/239/EEC) of 24 July 1973 on the co-ordination of laws, regulations and administrative provisions relating to the taking up and pursuit of the business of direct insurance other than life assurance;

"home state regulator", in relation to an EEA insurer, means the relevant EEA regulator in the EEA State where its head office is located;

"the Insolvency Rules" means the Insolvency Rules 1986;

"the Insolvency Rules (Northern Ireland)" means the Insolvency Rules (Northern Ireland) 1991;

"the Insolvency (Scotland) Rules" means the Insolvency (Scotland) Rules 1986;

"insurance claim" means any claim in relation to an insurance debt;

"insurance creditor" means a person who has an insurance claim against a UK insurer (whether or not he has claims other than insurance claims against that insurer);

"insurance debt" means a debt to which a UK insurer is, or may become liable, pursuant to a contract of insurance, to a policyholder or to any person who has a direct right of action against that insurer, and includes any premium paid in connection with a contract of insurance (whether or not that contract was concluded) which the insurer is liable to refund;

"life insurance directive" means the Directive (2002/83/EC) of the European Parliament and of the Council concerning life assurance;

"officer", in relation to a company, has the meaning given by section 744 of the 1985 Act or Article 2 of the Companies Order;

"official language" means a language specified in Article 1 of Council Regulation No 1 of 15th April 1958 determining the languages to be used by the European Economic Community (Regulation 1/58/EEC), most recently amended by paragraph (a) of Part XVIII of Annex I to the Act of Accession 1994 (194 N);

"policyholder" has the meaning given by the Financial Services and Markets Act 2000 (Meaning of "Policy" and "Policyholder") Order 2001;

"the reorganisation and winding-up directive" means the Directive (2001/17/EC) of the European Parliament and of the Council of 19 March 2001 on the reorganisation and winding-up of insurance undertakings;

"Schedule B1" means Schedule B1 to the 1986 Act as inserted by section 248 of the Enterprise Act 2002[, unless specified otherwise];

"section 425 compromise or arrangement" means a compromise or arrangement sanctioned by the court in relation to a UK insurer under section 425 of the 1985 Act, but does not include a compromise or arrangement falling within section 427 or section 427A of that Act (reconstructions or amalgamations);

"section 425 or Article 418 compromise or arrangement" means a section 425 compromise or arrangement or an Article 418 compromise or arrangement;

"supervisor" has the meaning given by section 7 of the 1986 Act or Article 20 of the 1989 Order;

"the third non-life insurance directive" means the Council Directive (92/49/EEC) of 18th June 1992 on the co-ordination of laws, etc, and amending directives 73/239/EEC and 88/357/EEC);

"UK insurer" means a person who has permission under Part IV of the 2000 Act to effect or carry out contracts of insurance, but does not include a person who, in accordance with that permission, carries on that activity exclusively in relation to reinsurance contracts;

"voluntary arrangement" means a voluntary arrangement which has effect in relation to a UK insurer in accordance with section 4A of the 1986 Act or Article 17A of the 1989 Order; and

"winding up" means—

(a) winding up by the court, or

(b) a creditors' voluntary winding up.

(2) In paragraph (1)—

(a) for the purposes of the definition of "directive reorganisation measure", a reorganisation measure is adopted or imposed at the time when it is treated as adopted or imposed by the law of the relevant EEA State; and

(b) for the purposes of the definition of "directive winding up proceedings", winding up proceedings are opened at the time when they are treated as opened by the law of the relevant EEA State,

and in this paragraph "relevant EEA State" means the EEA State under the law of which the reorganisation is adopted or imposed, or the winding up proceedings are opened, as the case may be.

(3) In these Regulations, references to the general law of insolvency of the United Kingdom include references to every provision made by or under the 1986 Act or the 1989 Order; and in relation to friendly societies or to industrial and provident societies references to the law of insolvency or to any provision of the 1986 Act or the 1989 Order are to that law as modified by the Friendly Societies Act 1992 or by the Industrial and Provident Societies Act 1965 or the Industrial and Provident Societies Act (Northern Ireland) 1969 (as the case may be).

(4) References in these Regulations to a "contract of insurance" must be read with—

(a) section 22 of the 2000 Act;

(b) any relevant order made under that section; and

(c) Schedule 2 to that Act,

but for the purposes of these Regulations a contract of insurance does not include a reinsurance contract.

(5) Functions imposed or falling on the Authority by or under these Regulations shall be deemed to be functions under the 2000 Act.

NOTES

Para (1): words in square brackets in definitions "administrator" and "Schedule B1" inserted by the Insurers (Reorganisation and Winding Up) (Amendment) Regulations 2007, SI 2007/851, reg 2(1), (2); definition "EEA State" substituted by the Financial Services (EEA State) Regulations 2007, SI 2007/108, reg 8.

Council Directive 73/239/EEC: OJ L228, 16.8.1973, p 3.

Directive 2002/83/EC of the European Parliament and of the Council: OJ L345, 19.12.2002, p 1.

Council Regulation 1/58/EEC: OJ 17, 6.10.1958, p 385.

Directive 2001/17/EC of the European Parliament and of the Council: OJ L110, 20.4.2001, p 28.

Council Directive 92/49/EEC: OJ L228, 11.8.1992, p 1.

Council Directive 88/357/EEC: OJ L172, 4.7.1988, p 1.

[4272]

3 Scope

For the purposes of these Regulations, neither the Society of Lloyd's nor the persons specified in section 316(1) of the 2000 Act are UK insurers.

PART II
INSOLVENCY MEASURES AND PROCEEDINGS: JURISDICTION IN RELATION TO INSURERS

[4273]

4 Prohibition against winding up etc EEA insurers in the United Kingdom

(1) On or after the relevant date a court in the United Kingdom may not, in relation to an EEA insurer or any branch of an EEA insurer—

- (a) make a winding up order pursuant to section 221 of the 1986 Act or Article 185 of the 1989 Order;
- (b) appoint a provisional liquidator;
- (c) make an administration order.

(2) Paragraph (1)(a) does not prevent—

- (a) the court from making a winding up order after the relevant date in relation to an EEA insurer if—
  - (i) a provisional liquidator was appointed in relation to that insurer before the relevant date, and
  - (ii) that appointment continues in force until immediately before that winding up order is made;
- (b) the winding up of an EEA insurer after the relevant date pursuant to a winding up order which was made, and has not been discharged, before that date.

(3) Paragraph (1)(b) does not prevent a provisional liquidator of an EEA insurer appointed before the relevant date from acting in relation to that insurer after that date.

(4) Paragraph (1)(c) does not prevent an administrator appointed before the relevant date from acting after that date in a case in which the administration order under which he or his predecessor was appointed remains in force after that date.

(5) An administrator may not, in relation to an EEA insurer, be appointed under paragraphs 14 or 22 of Schedule B1 [or paragraph 15 or 23 of Schedule B1 to the 1989 Order].

(6) A proposed voluntary arrangement shall not have effect in relation to an EEA insurer if a decision, under section 4 of the 1986 Act or Article 17 of the 1989 Order, with respect to the approval of that arrangement was made after the relevant date.

(7) Section 377 of the 2000 Act (reducing the value of contracts instead of winding up) does not apply in relation to an EEA insurer.

[(8) An order under section 254 of the Enterprise Act 2002 (application of insolvency law to a foreign company) or under Article 9 of the Insolvency (Northern Ireland) Order 2005 (application of insolvency law to company incorporated outside Northern Ireland) may not provide for any of the following provisions of the 1986 Act or of the 1989 Order to apply in relation to an EEA insurer—

- (a) Part I of the 1986 Act or Part II of the 1989 Order (company voluntary arrangements);
- (b) Part II of the 1986 Act or Part III of the 1989 Order (administration);
- (c) Chapter VI of Part IV of the 1986 Act (winding up by the Court) or Chapter VI of Part V of the 1989 Order (winding up by the High Court).]

(9) In this regulation and regulation 5, "relevant date" means 20th April 2003.

NOTES

Para (5): words in square brackets inserted by the Insurers (Reorganisation and Winding Up) (Amendment) Regulations 2007, SI 2007/851, reg 2(1), (3).

Para (8): substituted by SI 2007/851, reg 2(1), (4).

[4274]

5 Schemes of arrangement: EEA insurers

(1) For the purposes of section 425(6)(a) of the 1985 Act or Article 418(5)(a) of the Companies Order, an EEA insurer or a branch of an EEA insurer is to be treated as a company liable to be wound up under the 1986 Act or the 1989 Order if it would be liable to be wound up under that Act or Order but for the prohibition in regulation 4(1)(a).

(2) But a court may not make a relevant order under section 425(2) of the 1985 Act or Article 418(2) of the Companies Order in relation to an EEA insurer which is subject to a directive reorganisation measure or directive winding up proceedings, or a branch of an EEA insurer which is subject to such a measure or proceedings unless the conditions set out in paragraph (3) are satisfied.

(3) Those conditions are—

(a) the person proposing the section 425 or Article 418 compromise or arrangement ("the proposal") has given—
(i) the administrator or liquidator, and
(ii) the relevant competent authority,
reasonable notice of the details of that proposal; and
(b) no person notified in accordance with sub-paragraph (a) has objected to the proposal.

(4) Nothing in this regulation invalidates a compromise or arrangement which was sanctioned by the court by an order made before the relevant date.

(5) For the purposes of paragraph (2), a relevant order means an order sanctioning a section 425 or Article 418 compromise or arrangement which—
(a) is intended to enable the insurer, and the whole or any part of its undertaking, to survive as a going concern and which affects the rights of persons other than the insurer or its contributories; or
(b) includes among its purposes a realisation of some or all of the assets of the EEA insurer to which the order relates and the distribution of the proceeds to creditors, with a view to terminating the whole or any part of the business of that insurer.

(6) For the purposes of this regulation—
(a) "administrator" means an administrator, as defined by Article 2(i) of the reorganisation and winding up directive, who is appointed in relation to the EEA insurer in relation to which the proposal is made;
(b) "liquidator" means a liquidator, as defined by Article 2(j) of the reorganisation and winding up directive, who is appointed in relation to the EEA insurer in relation to which the proposal is made;
(c) "competent authority" means the competent authority, as defined by Article 2(g) of the reorganisation and winding up directive, which is competent for the purposes of the directive reorganisation measure or directive winding up proceedings mentioned in paragraph (2).

[4275]

6 Reorganisation measures and winding up proceedings in respect of EEA insurers effective in the United Kingdom

(1) An EEA insolvency measure has effect in the United Kingdom in relation to—
(a) any branch of an EEA insurer,
(b) any property or other assets of that insurer,
(c) any debt or liability of that insurer
as if it were part of the general law of insolvency of the United Kingdom.

(2) Subject to paragraph (4)—
(a) a competent officer who satisfies the condition mentioned in paragraph (3); or
(b) a qualifying agent appointed by a competent officer who satisfies the condition mentioned in paragraph (3),
may exercise in the United Kingdom, in relation to the EEA insurer which is subject to an EEA insolvency measure, any function which, pursuant to that measure, he is entitled to exercise in relation to that insurer in the relevant EEA State.

(3) The condition mentioned in paragraph (2) is that the appointment of the competent officer is evidenced—
(a) by a certified copy of the order or decision by a judicial or administrative authority in the relevant EEA State by or under which the competent officer was appointed; or
(b) by any other certificate issued by the judicial or administrative authority which has jurisdiction in relation to the EEA insolvency measure,
and accompanied by a certified translation of that order, decision or certificate (as the case may be).

(4) In exercising functions of the kind mentioned in paragraph (2), the competent officer or qualifying agent—
(a) may not take any action which would constitute an unlawful use of force in the part of the United Kingdom in which he is exercising those functions;
(b) may not rule on any dispute arising from a matter falling within Part V of these Regulations which is justiciable by a court in the part of the United Kingdom in which he is exercising those functions; and
(c) notwithstanding the way in which functions may be exercised in the relevant EEA State, must act in accordance with relevant laws or rules as to procedure which have effect in the part of the United Kingdom in which he is exercising those functions.

(5) For the purposes of paragraph (4)(c), "relevant laws or rules as to procedure" mean—

(a) requirements as to consultation with or notification of employees of an EEA insurer;
(b) law and procedures relevant to the realisation of assets;
(c) where the competent officer is bringing or defending legal proceedings in the name of, or on behalf of, an EEA insurer, the relevant rules of court.

(6) In this regulation—

"competent officer" means a person appointed under or in connection with an EEA insolvency measure for the purpose of administering that measure;

"qualifying agent" means an agent validly appointed (whether in the United Kingdom or elsewhere) by a competent officer in accordance with the relevant law in the relevant EEA State;

"EEA insolvency measure" means, as the case may be, a directive reorganisation measure or directive winding up proceedings which has effect in relation to an EEA insurer by virtue of the law of the relevant EEA State;

"relevant EEA State", in relation to an EEA insurer, means the EEA State in which that insurer has been authorised in accordance with Article 4 of the life insurance directive or Article 6 of the first non-life insurance directive.

[4276]
7 Confirmation by the court of a creditors' voluntary winding up

(1) Rule 7.62 of the Insolvency Rules or Rule 7.56 of the Insolvency Rules (Northern Ireland) applies in relation to a UK insurer with the modification specified in paragraph (2) or (3).

(2) In Rule 7.62 paragraph (1), after the words "the Insurers (Reorganisation and Winding Up) Regulations 2003" insert the words "or the Insurers (Reorganisation and Winding Up) Regulations 2004".

(3) In Rule 7.56 of the Insolvency Rules (Northern Ireland) paragraph (1), after the words "the Insurers (Reorganisation and Winding Up) Regulations 2003" insert the words "or the Insurers (Reorganisation and Winding Up) Regulations 2004".

PART III
MODIFICATIONS OF THE LAW OF INSOLVENCY: NOTIFICATION AND PUBLICATION

[4277]
8 Modifications of the law of insolvency

The general law of insolvency has effect in relation to UK insurers subject to the provisions of this Part.

[4278]
9 Notification of relevant decision to the Authority

(1) Where on or after [3rd March 2004] the court makes a decision, order or appointment of any of the following kinds—

(a) an administration order under paragraph 13 of Schedule B1[, or paragraph 14 of Schedule B1 to the 1989 Order];
(b) a winding up order under section 125 of the 1986 Act or Article 105 of the 1989 Order;
(c) the appointment of a provisional liquidator under section 135(1) of the 1986 Act or Article 115(1) of the 1989 Order;
(d) an interim order under paragraph 13(1)(d) of Schedule B1 [or paragraph 14(1)(d) of Schedule B1 to the 1989 Order];
(e) a decision to reduce the value of one or more of the insurer's contracts, in accordance with section 377 of the 2000 Act,

it must immediately inform the Authority, or cause the Authority to be informed of the decision, order or appointment which has been made.

(2) Where a decision with respect to the approval of a voluntary arrangement has effect, and the arrangement which is the subject of that decision is a qualifying arrangement, the supervisor must forthwith inform the Authority of the arrangement.

(3) Where a liquidator is appointed as mentioned in section 100 of the 1986 Act, paragraph 83 of Schedule B1[, paragraph 84 of Schedule B1 to the 1989 Order] or Article 86 of the 1989 Order (appointment of liquidator in a creditors' voluntary winding up), the liquidator must inform the Authority forthwith of his appointment.

(4) Where in the case of a members' voluntary winding up, section 95 of the 1986 Act (effect of company's insolvency) or Article 81 of the 1989 Order applies, the liquidator must inform the Authority forthwith that he is of that opinion.

(6) Paragraphs (1), (2) and (3) do not apply in any case where the Authority was represented at all hearings in connection with the application in relation to which the decision, order or appointment

is made.

(7) For the purposes of paragraph (2), a "qualifying arrangement" means a voluntary arrangement which—

(a) varies the rights of creditors as against the insurer and is intended to enable the insurer, and the whole or any part of its undertaking, to survive as a going concern; or

(b) includes a realisation of some or all of the assets of the insurer and distribution of the proceeds to creditors, with a view to terminating the whole or any part of the business of that insurer.

(8) An administrator, supervisor or liquidator who fails without reasonable excuse to comply with paragraph (2), (3), or (4) (as the case may be) commits an offence and is liable on summary conviction to a fine not exceeding level 3 on the standard scale.

NOTES

Para (1): words in first pair of square brackets substituted by the Insurers (Reorganisation and Winding Up) (Amendment) Regulations 2004, SI 2004/546, reg 2(1), (2); words in square brackets in sub-paras (a), (d) inserted by the Insurers (Reorganisation and Winding Up) (Amendment) Regulations 2007, SI 2007/851, reg 2(1), (5).

Para (3): words in square brackets inserted by SI 2007/851, reg 2(1), (6).

Modification: this regulation is applied, with modifications in respect of the Lloyd's of London insurance market, by the Insurers (Reorganisation and Winding Up) (Lloyd's) Regulations 2005, SI 2005/1998, regs 32, 33 at **[4429]**, **[4430]**.

[4279]

10 Notification of relevant decision to EEA regulators

(1) Where the Authority is informed of a decision, order or appointment in accordance with regulation 9, the Authority must as soon as is practicable inform the EEA regulators in every EEA State—

(a) that the decision, order or appointment has been made; and

(b) in general terms, of the possible effect of a decision, order or appointment of that kind on—

(i) the business of an insurer, and

(ii) the rights of policyholders under contracts of insurance effected and carried out by an insurer.

(2) Where the Authority has been represented at all hearings in connection with the application in relation to which the decision, order or appointment has been made, the Authority must inform the EEA regulators in every EEA State of the matters mentioned in paragraph (1) as soon as is practicable after that decision, order or appointment has been made.

NOTES

Modification: this regulation is applied, with modifications in respect of the Lloyd's of London insurance market, by the Insurers (Reorganisation and Winding Up) (Lloyd's) Regulations 2005, SI 2005/1998, regs 32, 34 at **[4429]**, **[4431]**.

[4280]

11 Publication of voluntary arrangement, administration order, winding up order or scheme of arrangement

(1) This regulation applies where a qualifying decision has effect, or a qualifying order or qualifying appointment is made, in relation to a UK insurer on or after 20th April 2003.

(2) For the purposes of this regulation—

(a) a qualifying decision means a decision with respect to the approval of a proposed voluntary arrangement, in accordance with section 4A of the 1986 Act or Article 17A of the 1989 Order;

(b) a qualifying order means—

(i) an administration order under paragraph 13 of Schedule B1 [or under paragraph 14 of Schedule B1 to the 1989 Order],

(ii) an order appointing a provisional liquidator in accordance with section 135 of the 1986 Act or Article 115 of the 1989 Order, or

(iii) a winding up order made by the court under Part IV of the 1986 Act or Part V of the 1989 Order.

(c) a qualifying appointment means the appointment of a liquidator as mentioned in section 100 of the 1986 Act or Article 86 of the 1989 Order (appointment of liquidator in a creditors' voluntary winding up).

(3) Subject to paragraph (8), as soon as is reasonably practicable after a qualifying decision has effect, or a qualifying order or a qualifying appointment has been made, the relevant officer must publish, or cause to be published, in the Official Journal of the European Communities the information mentioned in paragraph (4) and (if applicable) paragraphs (5), (6) or (7).

(4) That information is—

(a) a summary of the terms of the qualifying decision or qualifying appointment or the provisions of the qualifying order (as the case may be);

(b) the identity of the relevant officer; and

(c) the statutory provisions in accordance with which the qualifying decision has effect or the qualifying order or appointment has been made or takes effect.

(5) In the case of a qualifying appointment falling within paragraph (2)(c), that information includes the court to which an application under section 112 of the 1986 Act (reference of questions to the court) or Article 98 of the 1989 Order (reference of questions to the High Court) may be made.

(6) In the case of a qualifying decision, that information includes the court to which an application under section 6 of the 1986 Act or Article 19 of the 1989 Order (challenge of decisions) may be made.

(7) Paragraph (3) does not apply where a qualifying decision or qualifying order falling within paragraph (2)(b)(i) affects the interests only of the members, or any class of members, or employees of the insurer (in their capacity as members or employees).

(8) This regulation is without prejudice to any requirement to publish information imposed upon a relevant officer under any provision of the general law of insolvency.

(9) A relevant officer who fails to comply with paragraph (3) of this regulation commits an offence and is liable on summary conviction to a fine not exceeding level 3 on the standard scale.

(10) A qualifying decision, qualifying order or qualifying appointment is not invalid or ineffective if the relevant official fails to comply with paragraph (3) of this regulation.

(11) In this regulation, "relevant officer" means—

(a) in the case of a voluntary arrangement, the supervisor;

(b) in the case of an administration order or the appointment of an administrator, the administrator;

(c) in the case of a creditors' voluntary winding up, the liquidator;

(d) in the case of winding up order, the liquidator;

(e) in the case of an order appointing a provisional liquidator, the provisional liquidator.

NOTES

Para (2): words in square brackets in sub-para (b) inserted by the Insurers (Reorganisation and Winding Up) (Amendment) Regulations 2007, SI 2007/851, reg 2(1), (7).

Modification: this regulation is applied, with modifications in respect of the Lloyd's of London insurance market, by the Insurers (Reorganisation and Winding Up) (Lloyd's) Regulations 2005, SI 2005/1998, regs 32, 35 at **[4429]**, **[4432]**.

[4281]

12 Notification to creditors: winding up proceedings

(1) When a relevant order or appointment is made, or a relevant decision is taken, in relation to a UK insurer on or after 20th April 2003, the appointed officer must as soon as is reasonably practicable—

(a) notify all known creditors of that insurer in writing of—

(i) the matters mentioned in paragraph (4), and

(ii) the matters mentioned in paragraph (5); and

(b) notify all known insurance creditors of that insurer in writing of the matters mentioned in paragraph 6,

in any case.

(2) The appointed officer may comply with the requirement in paragraph (1)(a)(i) and the requirement in paragraph (1)(a)(ii) by separate notifications.

(3) For the purposes of this regulation—

(a) "relevant order" means—

(i) an administration order made under section 8 of the 1986 Act before 15th September 2003, or made on or after that date under paragraph 13 of Schedule B1 in the prescribed circumstances [or under paragraph 14 of Schedule B1 to the 1989 Order in the prescribed circumstances],

(ii) a winding up order under section 125 of the 1986 Act (powers of the court on hearing a petition) or Article 105 of the 1989 Order (powers of High Court on hearing of petition),

(iii) the appointment of a liquidator in accordance with section 138 of the 1986 Act (appointment of a liquidator in Scotland), and

(iv) an order appointing a provisional liquidator in accordance with section 135 of that Act or Article 115 of the 1989 Order;

(b) "relevant appointment" means the appointment of a liquidator as mentioned in section 100 of the 1986 Act or Article 86 of the 1989 Order (appointment of liquidator in a creditors' voluntary winding up); and

(c) "relevant decision" means a decision as a result of which a qualifying voluntary arrangement has effect.

(4) The matters which must be notified to all known creditors in accordance with paragraph (1)(a)(i) are as follows—

(a) that a relevant order or appointment has been made, or a relevant decision taken, in relation to the UK insurer; and

(b) the date from which that order, appointment or decision has effect.

(5) The matters which must be notified to all known creditors in accordance with paragraph (1)(a)(ii) are as follows—

(a) if applicable, the date by which a creditor must submit his claim in writing;

(b) the matters which must be stated in a creditor's claim;

(c) details of any category of debt in relation to which a claim is not required;

(d) the person to whom any such claim or any observations on a claim must be submitted; and

(e) the consequences of any failure to submit a claim by any specified deadline.

(6) The matters which must be notified to all known insurance creditors, in accordance with paragraph (1)(b), are as follows—

(a) the effect which the relevant order, appointment or decision will, or is likely, to have on the kind of contract of insurance under, or in connection with, which that creditor's insurance claim against the insurer is founded; and

(b) the date from which any variation (resulting from the relevant order or relevant decision) to the risks covered by, or the sums recoverable under, that contract has effect.

(7) Subject to paragraph (8), where a creditor is notified in accordance with paragraph (1)(a)(ii), the notification must be headed with the words "Invitation to lodge a claim: time limits to be observed", and that heading must be given in—

(a) the official language, or one of the official languages, of the EEA State in which that creditor is ordinarily resident; or

(b) every official language.

(8) Where a creditor notified in accordance with paragraph (1) is—

(a) an insurance creditor; and

(b) ordinarily resident in an EEA State,

the notification must be given in the official language, or one of the official languages, of that EEA State.

(9) The obligation under paragraph (1)(a)(ii) may be discharged by sending a form of proof in accordance with Rule 4.74 of the Insolvency Rules, Rule 4.080 of the Insolvency Rules (Northern Ireland) or Rule 4.15(2) of the Insolvency (Scotland) Rules as applicable in cases where any of those rules applies, provided that the form of proof complies with paragraph (7) or (8) (whichever is applicable).

[(10) The prescribed circumstances are where the administrator includes in the statement required under Rule 2.3 of the Insolvency Rules or under Rule 2.003 of the Insolvency Rules (Northern Ireland) a statement to the effect that the objective set out in paragraph 3(1)(a) of Schedule B1 or in paragraph 4(1)(a) of Schedule B1 to the 1989 Order is not reasonably likely to be achieved.]

(11) Where, after the appointment of an administrator, the administrator concludes that it is not reasonably practicable to achieve the objective specified in paragraph 3(1)(a) of Schedule B1 [or in paragraph 4(1)(a) of Schedule B1 to the 1989 Order], he shall inform the court and the Authority in writing of that conclusion and upon so doing the order by which he was appointed shall be a relevant order for the purposes of this regulation and the obligation under paragraph (1) shall apply as from the date on which he so informs the court and the Authority.

(12) An appointed officer commits an offence if he fails without reasonable excuse to comply with an applicable requirement under this regulation, and is liable on summary conviction to a fine not exceeding level 3 on the standard scale.

(13) For the purposes of this regulation—

(a) "appointed officer" means—

(i) in the case of a relevant order falling within paragraph (3)(a)(i) or a relevant appointment falling within paragraph (3)(b)(i), the administrator,

(ii) in the case of a relevant order falling within paragraph (3)(a)(ii) or (iii) or a relevant appointment falling within paragraph (3)(b)(ii), the liquidator,

(iii) in the case of a relevant order falling within paragraph (3)(a)(iv), the provisional liquidator, or

(iv) in the case of a relevant decision, the supervisor; and

(b) a creditor is a "known" creditor if the appointed officer is aware, or should reasonably be aware of—

(i) his identity,

(ii) his claim or potential claim, and

(iii) a recent address where he is likely to receive a communication.

(14) For the purposes of paragraph (3), and of regulations 13 and 14, a voluntary arrangement is a qualifying voluntary arrangement if its purposes include a realisation of some or all of the assets of the UK insurer to which the order relates and a distribution of the proceeds to creditors, with a view to terminating the whole or any part of the business of that insurer.

NOTES

Para (3): words in square brackets inserted by the Insurers (Reorganisation and Winding Up) (Amendment) Regulations 2007, SI 2007/851, reg 2(1), (8).

Para (10): substituted by SI 2007/851, reg 2(1), (9).

Para (11): words in square brackets inserted by SI 2007/851, reg 2(1), (10).

Modification: this regulation is applied, with modifications in respect of the Lloyd's of London insurance market, by the Insurers (Reorganisation and Winding Up) (Lloyd's) Regulations 2005, SI 2005/1998, regs 32, 36 at **[4429]**, **[4433]**.

[4282]

13 Submission of claims by EEA creditors

(1) An EEA creditor who on or after 20th April 2003 submits a claim or observations relating to his claim in any relevant proceedings (irrespective of when those proceedings were commenced or had effect) may do so in his domestic language, provided that the requirements in paragraphs (3) and (4) are complied with.

(2) For the purposes of this regulation, "relevant proceedings" means—

(a) a winding up;

(b) a qualifying voluntary arrangement;

(c) administration.

(3) Where an EEA creditor submits a claim in his domestic language, the document must be headed with the words "Lodgement of claim" (in English).

(4) Where an EEA creditor submits observations on his claim (otherwise than in the document by which he submits his claim), the observations must be headed with the words "Submission of observations relating to claims" (in English).

(5) Paragraph (3) does not apply where an EEA creditor submits his claim using—

(a) in the case of a winding up, a form of proof supplied by the liquidator in accordance with Rule 4.74 of the Insolvency Rules, Rule 4.080 of the Insolvency Rules (Northern Ireland) or rule 4.15(2) of the Insolvency (Scotland) Rules as the case may be;

(b) in the case of a qualifying voluntary arrangement, a form approved by the court for that purpose.

(6) In this regulation—

(a) "domestic language", in relation to an EEA creditor, means the official language, or one of the official languages, of the EEA State in which he is ordinarily resident or, if the creditor is not an individual, in which the creditor's head office is located; and

(b) "qualifying voluntary arrangement" has the meaning given by regulation 12(12).

NOTES

Modification: this regulation is applied, with modifications in respect of the Lloyd's of London insurance market, by the Insurers (Reorganisation and Winding Up) (Lloyd's) Regulations 2005, SI 2005/1998, regs 32, 37 at **[4429]**, **[4434]**.

[4283]

14 Reports to creditors

(1) This regulation applies where, on or after 20th April 2003—

Part IV Statutory Instruments

(a) a liquidator is appointed in accordance with section 100 of the 1986 Act or Article 86 of the 1989 Order (creditors' voluntary winding up: appointment of liquidator) or, on or after 15th September 2003, paragraph 83 of Schedule B1 [or paragraph 84 of Schedule B1 to the 1989 Order] (moving from administration to creditors' voluntary liquidation);

(b) a winding up order is made by the court;

(c) a provisional liquidator is appointed; or

(d) [an administrator is appointed under paragraph 13 of Schedule B1] [or under paragraph 14 of Schedule B1 to the 1989 Order.]

(2) The liquidator or provisional liquidator (as the case may be) must send to every known creditor a report once in every 12 months beginning with the date when his appointment has effect.

(3) The requirement in paragraph (2) does not apply where a liquidator or provisional liquidator is required by order of the court to send a report to creditors at intervals which are more frequent than those required by this regulation.

(4) This regulation is without prejudice to any requirement to send a report to creditors, imposed by the court on the liquidator or provisional liquidator, which is supplementary to the requirements of this regulation.

(5) A liquidator or provisional liquidator commits an offence if he fails without reasonable excuse to comply with an applicable requirement under this regulation, and is liable on summary conviction to a fine not exceeding level 3 on the standard scale.

(6) For the purposes of this regulation—

(a) "known creditor" means—

(i) a creditor who is known to the liquidator or provisional liquidator, and

(ii) in a case falling within paragraph (1)(b) or (c), a creditor who is specified in the insurer's statement of affairs (within the meaning of section 131 of the 1986 Act or Article 111 of the 1989 Order); and

(b) "report" means a written report setting out the position generally as regards the progress of the winding up or provisional liquidation (as the case may be).

NOTES

Para (1): words in square brackets in sub-para (a) and words in second pair of square brackets in sub-para (d) inserted by the Insurers (Reorganisation and Winding Up) (Amendment) Regulations 2007, SI 2007/851, reg 2(1), (11); words in first pair of square brackets in sub-para (d) substituted by the Insurers (Reorganisation and Winding Up) (Amendment) Regulations 2004, SI 2004/546, reg 2(1), (3).

Modification: this regulation is applied, with modifications in respect of the Lloyd's of London insurance market, by the Insurers (Reorganisation and Winding Up) (Lloyd's) Regulations 2005, SI 2005/1998, regs 32, 38 at **[4429]**, **[4435]**.

[4284]

15 Service of notices and documents

(1) This regulation applies to any notification, report or other document which is required to be sent to a creditor of a UK insurer by a provision of this Part ("a relevant notification").

(2) A relevant notification may be sent to a creditor by either of the following methods—

(a) posting it to the proper address of the creditor;

(b) transmitting it electronically, in accordance with paragraph (4).

(3) For the purposes of paragraph (2)(a), the proper address of a creditor is any current address provided by that creditor as an address for service of a relevant notification or, if no such address is provided—

(a) the last known address of that creditor (whether his residence or a place where he carries on business);

(b) in the case of a body corporate, the address of its registered or principal office; or

(c) in the case of an unincorporated association, the address of its principal office.

(4) A relevant notification may be transmitted electronically only if it is sent to—

(a) an electronic address notified to the relevant officer by the creditor for this purpose; or

(b) if no such address has been notified, an electronic address at which the relevant officer reasonably believes the creditor will receive the notification.

(5) Any requirement in this part to send a relevant notification to a creditor shall also be treated as satisfied if—

(a) the creditor has agreed with—

(i) the UK insurer which is liable under the creditor's claim, or

(ii) the relevant officer,

that information which is required to be sent to him (whether pursuant to a statutory or contractual obligation, or otherwise) may instead be accessed by him on a web site;

(b) the agreement applies to the relevant notification in question;

(c) the creditor is notified of—

(i) the publication of the relevant notification on a web site,

(ii) the address of that web site,

(iii) the place on that web site where the relevant notification may be accessed, and how it may be accessed; and

(d) the relevant notification is published on that web site throughout a period of at least one month beginning with the date on which the creditor is notified in accordance with sub-paragraph (c):

(6) Where, in a case in which paragraph (5) is relied on for compliance with a requirement of regulation 12 or 14—

(a) a relevant notification is published for a part, but not all, of the period mentioned in paragraph (5)(d); but

(b) the failure to publish it throughout that period is wholly attributable to circumstances which it would not be reasonable to have expected the relevant officer to prevent or avoid,

no offence is committed under regulation 12(10) or regulation 14(5) (as the case may be) by reason of that failure.

(7) In this regulation—

(a) "electronic address" includes any number or address used for the purposes of receiving electronic communications;

(b) "electronic communication" means an electronic communication within the meaning of the Electronic Communications Act 2000 the processing of which on receipt is intended to produce writing; and

(c) "relevant officer" means (as the case may be) an administrator, liquidator, provisional liquidator or supervisor who is required to send a relevant notification to a creditor by a provision of this Part.

NOTES

Modification: this regulation is applied, with modifications in respect of the Lloyd's of London insurance market, by the Insurers (Reorganisation and Winding Up) (Lloyd's) Regulations 2005, SI 2005/1998, regs 32, 39 at **[4429]**, **[4436]**.

[4285]

16 Disclosure of confidential information received from an EEA regulator

(1) This regulation applies to information ("insolvency information") which—

(a) relates to the business or affairs of any other person; and

(b) is supplied to the Authority by an EEA regulator acting in accordance with Articles 5, 8 or 30 of the reorganisation and winding up directive.

(2) Subject to paragraphs (3) and (4), sections 348, 349 and 352 of the 2000 Act apply in relation to insolvency information in the same way as they apply in relation to confidential information within the meaning of section 348(2) of the 2000 Act.

(3) Insolvency information is not subject to the restrictions on disclosure imposed by section 348(1) of the 2000 Act (as it applies by virtue of paragraph (2)) if it satisfies any of the criteria set out in section 348(4) of the 2000 Act.

(4) The Disclosure Regulations apply in relation to insolvency information as they apply in relation to single market directive information (within the meaning of those Regulations).

(5) In this regulation, "the Disclosure Regulations" means the Financial Services and Markets Act 2000 (Disclosure of Confidential Information) Regulations 2001.

PART IV
PRIORITY OF PAYMENT OF INSURANCE CLAIMS IN WINDING UP ETC

[4286]

17 Interpretation of this Part

(1) For the purposes of this Part—

"composite insurer" means a UK insurer who is authorised to carry on both general business and long term business, in accordance with article 18(2) of the life insurance directive;

"floating charge" has the meaning given by section 251 of the 1986 Act or paragraph (1) of Article 5 of the 1989 Order;

"general business" means the business of effecting or carrying out a contract of general insurance;

"general business assets" means the assets of a composite insurer which are, or should properly be, apportioned to that insurer's general business, in accordance with the requirements of Article 18(3) of the life insurance directive (separate management of long term and general business of a composite insurer);

"general business liabilities" means the debts of a composite insurer which are attributable to the general business carried on by that insurer;

"general insurer" means a UK insurer who carries on exclusively general business;

"long term business" means the business of effecting or carrying out a contract of long term insurance;

"long term business assets" means the assets of a composite insurer which are, or should properly be, apportioned to that insurer's long term business, in accordance with the requirements of Article 18(3) of the first life insurance directive (separate management of long term and general business of a composite insurer);

"long term business liabilities" means the debts of a composite insurer which are attributable to the long term business carried on by that insurer;

"long term insurer" means a UK insurer who—

(a) carries on long term business exclusively, or

(b) carries on long term business and permitted general business;

"non-transferring composite insurer" means a composite insurer the long term business of which has not been, and is not to be, transferred as a going concern to a person who may lawfully carry out those contracts, in accordance with section 376(2) of the 2000 Act;

"other assets" means any assets of a composite insurer which are not long term business assets or general business assets;

"other business", in relation to a composite insurer, means such of the business (if any) of the insurer as is not long term business or general business;

"permitted general business" means the business of effecting or carrying out a contract of general insurance where the risk insured against relates to either accident or sickness;

"preferential debt" means a debt falling into any of categories 4 or 5 of the debts listed in Schedule 6 to the 1986 Act or Schedule 4 to the 1989 Order, that is—

(a) contributions to occupational pension schemes, etc, and

(b) remuneration etc of employees;

"society" means—

(a) a friendly society incorporated under the Friendly Societies Act 1992,

(b) a society which is a friendly society within the meaning of section 7(1)(a) of the Friendly Societies Act 1974, and registered within the meaning of that Act, or

(c) an industrial and provident society registered or deemed to be registered under the Industrial and Provident Societies Act 1965 or the Industrial and Provident Societies Act (Northern Ireland) 1969.

(2) In this Part, references to assets include a reference to proceeds where an asset has been realised, and any other sums representing assets.

(3) References in paragraph (1) to a contract of long term or of general insurance must be read with—

(a) section 22 of the 2000 Act;

(b) any relevant order made under that section; and

(c) Schedule 2 to that Act.

NOTES

Modification: this regulation is applied, with modifications in respect of the Lloyd's of London insurance market, by the Insurers (Reorganisation and Winding Up) (Lloyd's) Regulations 2005, SI 2005/1998, regs 32, 40(1)–(4), 43 at **[4429]**, **[4437]**, **[4440]**.

[4287]

18 Application of regulations 19 to 27

(1) Subject to paragraph (2), regulations 19 to 27 apply in the winding up of a UK insurer where—

(a) in the case of a winding up by the court, the winding up order is made on or after 20th April 2003; or

(b) in the case of a creditors' voluntary winding up, the liquidator is appointed, as mentioned in section 100 of the 1986 Act, paragraph 83 of Schedule B1[, paragraph 84 of Schedule B1 to the 1989 Order] or Article 86 of the 1989 Order, on or after 20th April 2003.

(2) Where a relevant section 425 or Article 418 compromise or arrangement is in place,
- (a) no winding up proceedings may be opened without the permission of the court, and
- (b) the permission of the court is to be granted only if required by the exceptional circumstances of the case.

(3) For the purposes of paragraph (2), winding up proceedings include proceedings for a winding up order or for a creditors' voluntary liquidation with confirmation by the court.

(4) Regulations 20 to 27 do not apply to a winding up falling within paragraph (1) where, in relation to a UK insurer—
- (a) an administration order was made before 20th April 2003, and that order is not discharged until the commencement date; or
- (b) a provisional liquidator was appointed before 20th April 2003, and that appointment is not discharged until the commencement date.

(5) For purposes of this regulation, "the commencement date" means the date when a UK insurer goes into liquidation within the meaning given by section 247(2) of the 1986 Act or Article 6(2) of the 1989 Order.

NOTES

Para (1): words in square brackets in sub-para (b) inserted by the Insurers (Reorganisation and Winding Up) (Amendment) Regulations 2007, SI 2007/851, reg 2(1), (12).

Modification: this regulation is applied, with modifications in respect of the Lloyd's of London insurance market, by the Insurers (Reorganisation and Winding Up) (Lloyd's) Regulations 2005, SI 2005/1998, regs 32, 40(1)–(4), 43 at **[4429]**, **[4437]**, **[4440]**.

[4288]

19 Application of this Part: assets subject to a section 425 or Article 418 compromise or arrangement

(1) For the purposes of this Part, the insolvent estate of a UK insurer shall not include any assets which at the commencement date are subject to a relevant section 425 or Article 418 compromise or arrangement.

(2) In this regulation—
- (a) "assets" has the same meaning as "property" in section 436 of the 1986 Act or Article 2(2) of the 1989 Order;
- (b) "commencement date" has the meaning given in [regulation 18(5)];
- (c) "insolvent estate"—
  - (i) in England, Wales and Northern Ireland has the meaning given by Rule 13.8 of the Insolvency Rules or Rule 0.2 of the Insolvency Rules (Northern Ireland), and
  - (ii) in Scotland means the company's assets;
- (d) "relevant section 425 or Article 418 compromise or arrangement" means
  - (i) a section 425 or Article 418 compromise or arrangement which was sanctioned by the court before 20th April 2003, or
  - (ii) any subsequent section 425 or Article 418 compromise or arrangement sanctioned by the court to amend or replace a compromise or arrangement of a kind mentioned in paragraph (i).

NOTES

Para (2): words in square brackets substituted by the Insurers (Reorganisation and Winding Up) (Lloyd's) Regulations 2005, SI 2005/1998, reg 49.

Modification: this regulation is applied, with modifications in respect of the Lloyd's of London insurance market, by the Insurers (Reorganisation and Winding Up) (Lloyd's) Regulations 2005, SI 2005/1998, regs 32, 40(1)–(4), 43 at **[4429]**, **[4437]**, **[4440]**.

[4289]

20 Preferential debts: disapplication of section 175 of the 1986 Act or Article 149 of the 1989 Order

Except to the extent that they are applied by regulation 27, section 175 of the 1986 Act or Article 149 of the 1989 Order (preferential debts (general provision)) does not apply in the case of a winding up of a UK insurer, and instead the provisions of regulations 21 to 26 have effect.

NOTES

Modification: this regulation is applied, with modifications in respect of the Lloyd's of London insurance market, by the Insurers (Reorganisation and Winding Up) (Lloyd's) Regulations 2005, SI 2005/1998, regs 32, 40(1)–(5), 43 at **[4429]**, **[4437]**, **[4440]**.

[4290]
21 Preferential debts: long term insurers and general insurers

(1) This regulation applies in the case of a winding up of—

(a) a long term insurer;
(b) a general insurer;
(c) a composite insurer, where the long term business of that insurer has been or is to be transferred as a going concern to a person who may lawfully carry out the contracts in that long term business in accordance with section 376(2) of the 2000 Act.

(2) Subject to paragraph (3), the debts of the insurer must be paid in the following order of priority—

(a) preferential debts;
(b) insurance debts;
(c) all other debts.

(3) Preferential debts rank equally among themselves [after the expenses of the winding up] and must be paid in full, unless the assets are insufficient to meet them, in which case they abate in equal proportions.

(4) Insurance debts rank equally among themselves and must be paid in full, unless the assets available after the payment of preferential debts are insufficient to meet them, in which case they abate in equal proportions.

(5) Subject to paragraph (6), so far as the assets of the insurer available for the payment of unsecured creditors are insufficient to meet the preferential debts, those debts (and only those debts) have priority over the claims of holders of debentures secured by, or holders of, any floating charge created by the insurer, and must be paid accordingly out of any property comprised in or subject to that charge.

(6) The order of priority specified in paragraph (2)(a) and (b) applies for the purposes of any payment made in accordance with paragraph (5).

(7) Section 176A of the 1986 Act [and Article 150A of the 1989 Order] [have] effect with regard to an insurer so that insurance debts must be paid out of the prescribed part in priority to all other unsecured debts.

NOTES

Para (3): words in square brackets inserted by the Insurers (Reorganisation and Winding Up) (Amendment) Regulations 2004, SI 2004/546, reg 2(1), (4).

Para (7): words in first pair of square brackets inserted and word in second pair of square brackets substituted by the Insurers (Reorganisation and Winding Up) (Amendment) Regulations 2007, SI 2007/851, reg 2(1), (13).

Modification: this regulation is applied, with modifications in respect of the Lloyd's of London insurance market, by the Insurers (Reorganisation and Winding Up) (Lloyd's) Regulations 2005, SI 2005/1998, regs 32, 40(1)–(4), (6), 43 at **[4429]**, **[4437]**, **[4440]**.

[4291]
22 Composite insurers: preferential debts attributable to long term and general business

(1) This regulation applies in the case of the winding up of a non-transferring composite insurer.

(2) Subject to the payment of costs in accordance with regulation 30, the long term business assets and the general business assets must be applied separately in accordance with paragraphs (3) and (4).

(3) Subject to paragraph (6), the long term business assets must be applied in discharge of the long term business preferential debts in the order of priority specified in regulation 23(1).

(4) Subject to paragraph (8), the general business assets must be applied in discharge of the general business preferential debts in the order of priority specified in regulation 24(1).

(5) Paragraph (6) applies where the value of the long term business assets exceeds the long term business preferential debts and the general business assets are insufficient to meet the general business preferential debts.

(6) Those long term business assets which represent the excess must be applied in discharge of the outstanding general business preferential debts of the insurer, in accordance with the order of priority specified in regulation 24(1).

(7) Paragraph (8) applies where the value of the general business assets exceeds the general business preferential debts, and the long term business assets are insufficient to meet the long term business preferential debts.

(8) Those general business assets which represent the excess must be applied in discharge of the outstanding long term business preferential debts of the insurer, in accordance with the order of priority specified in regulation 23(1).

(9) For the purposes of this regulation and regulations 23 and 24—

"long term business preferential debts" means those debts mentioned in regulation 23(1) and, unless the court orders otherwise, any expenses of the winding up which are apportioned to the long term business assets in accordance with regulation 30;

"general business preferential debts" means those debts mentioned in regulation 24(1) and, unless the court orders otherwise, any expenses of the winding up which are apportioned to the general business assets in accordance with regulation 30.

(10) For the purposes of paragraphs (6) and (8)—

"outstanding long term business preferential debts" means those long term business preferential debts, if any, which remain unpaid, either in whole or in part, after the application of the long term business assets, in accordance with paragraph (3);

"outstanding general business preferential debts" means those general business preferential debts, if any, which remain unpaid, either in whole or in part, after the application of the general business assets, in accordance with paragraph (3).

NOTES

Modification: this regulation is applied, with modifications in respect of the Lloyd's of London insurance market, by the Insurers (Reorganisation and Winding Up) (Lloyd's) Regulations 2005, SI 2005/1998, regs 32, 40(1)–(4), 43 at **[4429]**, **[4437]**, **[4440]**.

[4292]

23 Preferential debts: long term business of a non-transferring composite insurer

(1) For the purpose of compliance with the requirement in regulation 22(3), the long term business assets of a non-transferring composite insurer must be applied in discharge of the following debts and in the following order of priority—

(a) relevant preferential debts;

(b) long term insurance debts.

(2) Relevant preferential debts rank equally among themselves, unless the long term business assets, any available general business assets and other assets (if any) applied in accordance with regulation 24 are insufficient to meet them, in which case they abate in equal proportions.

(3) Long term insurance debts rank equally among themselves, unless the long term business assets available after the payment of relevant preferential debts and any available general business assets and other assets (if any) applied in accordance with regulation 25 are insufficient to meet them, in which case they abate in equal proportions.

(4) So far as the long term business assets, and any available general business assets, which are available for the payment of unsecured creditors are insufficient to meet the relevant preferential debts, those debts (and only those debts) have priority over the claims of holders of debentures secured by, or holders of, any floating charge created by the insurer over any of its long term business assets, and must be paid accordingly out of any property comprised in or subject to that charge.

(5) The order of priority specified in paragraph (1) applies for the purposes of any payment made in accordance with paragraph (4).

(6) For the purposes of this regulation—

"available general business assets" means those general business assets which must be applied in discharge of the insurer's outstanding long term business preferential debts, in accordance with regulation 22(8);

"long term insurance debt" means an insurance debt which is attributable to the long term business of the insurer;

"relevant preferential debt" means a preferential debt which is attributable to the long term business of the insurer.

NOTES

Modification: this regulation is applied, with modifications in respect of the Lloyd's of London insurance market, by the Insurers (Reorganisation and Winding Up) (Lloyd's) Regulations 2005, SI 2005/1998, regs 32, 40(1)–(4), 43 at **[4429]**, **[4437]**, **[4440]**.

[4293]

24 Preferential debts: general business of a composite insurer

(1) For the purpose of compliance with the requirement in regulation 22(4), the long term business assets of a non-transferring composite insurer must be applied in discharge of the following debts and in the following order of priority—

(a) relevant preferential debts;

(b) general insurance debts.

(2) Relevant preferential debts rank equally among themselves, unless the general business assets, any available long term business assets, and other assets (if any) applied in accordance with regulation 25 are insufficient to meet them, in which case they abate in equal proportions.

(3) General insurance debts rank equally among themselves, unless the general business assets available after the payment of relevant preferential debts, any available long term business assets, and other assets (if any) applied in accordance with regulation 26 are insufficient to meet them, in which case they abate in equal proportions.

(4) So far as the other business assets and available long term assets of the insurer which are available for the payment of unsecured creditors are insufficient to meet relevant preferential debts, those debts (and only those debts) have priority over the claims of holders of debentures secured by, or holders of, any floating charge created by the insurer, and must be paid accordingly out of any property comprised in or subject to that charge.

(5) The order of priority specified in paragraph (1) applies for the purposes of any payment made in accordance with paragraph (4).

(6) For the purposes of this regulation—

"available long term business assets" means those long term business assets which must be applied in discharge of the insurer's outstanding general business preferential debts, in accordance with regulation 22(6);

"general insurance debt" means an insurance debt which is attributable to the general business of the insurer;

"relevant preferential debt" means a preferential debt which is attributable to the general business of the insurer.

NOTES

Modification: this regulation is applied, with modifications in respect of the Lloyd's of London insurance market, by the Insurers (Reorganisation and Winding Up) (Lloyd's) Regulations 2005, SI 2005/1998, regs 32, 40(1)–(4), 43 at **[4429]**, **[4437]**, **[4440]**.

[4294]

25 Insufficiency of long term business assets and general business assets

(1) This regulation applies in the case of the winding up of a non-transferring composite insurer where the long term business assets and the general business assets, applied in accordance with regulation 22, are insufficient to meet in full the preferential debts and insurance debts.

(2) In a case in which this regulation applies, the other assets (if any) of the insurer must be applied in the following order of priority—

(a) outstanding preferential debts;
(b) unattributed preferential debts;
(c) outstanding insurance debts;
(d) all other debts.

(3) So far as the long term business assets, and any available general business assets, which are available for the payment of unsecured creditors are insufficient to meet the outstanding preferential debts and the unattributed preferential debts, those debts (and only those debts) have priority over the claims of holders of debentures secured by, or holders of, any floating charge created by the insurer over any of its other assets, and must be paid accordingly out of any property comprised in or subject to that charge.

(4) For the purposes of this regulation—

"outstanding insurance debt" means any insurance debt, or any part of an insurance debt, which was not discharged by the application of the long term business assets and the general business assets in accordance with regulation 22;

"outstanding preferential debt" means any preferential debt attributable either to the long term business or the general business of the insurer which was not discharged by the application of the long term business assets and the general business assets in accordance with regulation 23;

"unattributed preferential debt" means a preferential debt which is not attributable to either the long term business or the general business of the insurer.

NOTES

Modification: this regulation is applied, with modifications in respect of the Lloyd's of London insurance market, by the Insurers (Reorganisation and Winding Up) (Lloyd's) Regulations 2005, SI 2005/1998, regs 32, 40(1)–(4), 43 at **[4429]**, **[4437]**, **[4440]**.

[4295]

26 Composite insurers: excess of long term business assets and general business assets

(1) This regulation applies in the case of the winding up of a non-transferring composite insurer where the value of the long term business assets and the general business assets, applied in accordance with regulation 22, exceeds the value of the sum of the long term business preferential debts and the general business preferential debts.

(2) In a case to which this regulation applies, long term business assets or general business assets which have not been applied in discharge of long term business preferential debts or general business preferential debts must be applied in accordance with regulation 27.

(3) In this regulation, "long term business preferential debts" and "general business preferential debts" have the same meaning as in regulation 22.

NOTES

Modification: this regulation is applied, with modifications in respect of the Lloyd's of London insurance market, by the Insurers (Reorganisation and Winding Up) (Lloyd's) Regulations 2005, SI 2005/1998, regs 32, 40(1)–(4), 43 at **[4429]**, **[4437]**, **[4440]**.

[4296]

27 Composite insurers: application of other assets

(1) This regulation applies in the case of the winding up of a non-transferring composite insurer where regulation 25 does not apply.

(2) The other assets of the insurer, together with any outstanding business assets, must be paid in discharge of the following debts in accordance with section 175 of the 1986 Act or Article 149 of the 1989 Order—

(a) unattributed preferential debts;

(b) all other debts.

(3) In this regulation—

"unattributed preferential debt" has the same meaning as in regulation 25;

"outstanding business assets" means assets of the kind mentioned in regulation 26(2).

NOTES

Modification: this regulation is applied, with modifications in respect of the Lloyd's of London insurance market, by the Insurers (Reorganisation and Winding Up) (Lloyd's) Regulations 2005, SI 2005/1998, regs 32, 40(1)–(4), (7), 43 at **[4429]**, **[4437]**, **[4440]**.

[4297]

28 Composite insurers: proof of debts

(1) This regulation applies in the case of the winding up of a non-transferring composite insurer in compliance with the requirement in regulation 23(2).

(2) The liquidator may in relation to the insurer's long term business assets and its general business assets fix different days on or before which the creditors of the company who are required to prove their debts or claims are to prove their debts or claims, and he may fix one of those days without at the same time fixing the other.

(3) In submitting a proof of any debt a creditor may claim the whole or any part of such debt as is attributable to the company's long term business or to its general business, or he may make no such attribution.

(4) When he admits any debt, in whole or in part, the liquidator must state in writing how much of what he admits is attributable to the company's long term business, how much is attributable to the company's general business, and how much is attributable to its other business (if any).

(5) Paragraph (2) does not apply in Scotland.

NOTES

Modification: this regulation is applied, with modifications in respect of the Lloyd's of London insurance market, by the Insurers (Reorganisation and Winding Up) (Lloyd's) Regulations 2005, SI 2005/1998, regs 32, 40(1)–(4), 43 at **[4429]**, **[4437]**, **[4440]**.

[4298]

29 Composite insurers: general meetings of creditors

(1) This regulation applies in the same circumstances as regulation 28.

(2) The creditors mentioned in section 168(2) of the 1986 Act, Article 143(2) of the 1989 Order or rule 4.13 of the Insolvency (Scotland) Rules (power of liquidator to summon general meetings of creditors) are to be—

(a) in relation to the long term business assets of that insurer, only those who are creditors in respect of long term business liabilities; and
(b) in relation to the general business assets of that insurer, only those who are creditors in respect of general business liabilities,

and, accordingly, any general meetings of creditors summoned for the purposes of that section, Article or rule are to be separate general meetings of creditors in respect of long term business liabilities and general business liabilities.

NOTES

Modification: this regulation is applied, with modifications in respect of the Lloyd's of London insurance market, by the Insurers (Reorganisation and Winding Up) (Lloyd's) Regulations 2005, SI 2005/1998, regs 32, 40(1)–(4), (8), 43 at **[4429]**, **[4437]**, **[4440]**.

[4299]

30 Composite insurers: apportionment of costs payable out of the assets

(1) In the case of the winding up of a non-transferring composite insurer, Rule 4.218 of the Insolvency Rules or Rule 4.228 of the Insolvency Rules (Northern Ireland) (general rules as to priority) or rule 4.67 (order of priority of expenses of liquidation) of the Insolvency (Scotland) Rules applies separately to long-term business assets and to the general business assets of that insurer.

(2) But where any fee, expense, cost, charge, or remuneration does not relate exclusively to the long-term business assets or to the general business assets of that insurer, the liquidator must apportion it amongst those assets in such manner as he shall determine.

NOTES

Modification: this regulation is applied, with modifications in respect of the Lloyd's of London insurance market, by the Insurers (Reorganisation and Winding Up) (Lloyd's) Regulations 2005, SI 2005/1998, regs 32, 40(1)–(4), (9), 43 at **[4429]**, **[4437]**, **[4440]**.

[4300]

31 Summary remedy against liquidators

Section 212 of the 1986 Act or Article 176 of the 1989 Order (summary remedy against delinquent directors, liquidators etc) applies in relation to a liquidator who is required to comply with regulations 21 to 27, as it applies in relation to a liquidator who is required to comply with section 175 of the 1986 Act or Article 149 of the 1989 Order.

NOTES

Modification: this regulation is applied, with modifications in respect of the Lloyd's of London insurance market, by the Insurers (Reorganisation and Winding Up) (Lloyd's) Regulations 2005, SI 2005/1998, regs 32, 40(1)–(4), (10), 43 at **[4429]**, **[4437]**, **[4440]**.

[4301]

32 Priority of subrogated claims by the Financial Services Compensation Scheme

(1) This regulation applies where an insurance creditor has assigned a relevant right to the scheme manager ("a relevant assignment").

(2) For the purposes of regulations 21, 23 and 24, where the scheme manager proves for an insurance debt in the winding up of a UK insurer pursuant to a relevant assignment, that debt must be paid to the scheme manager in the same order of priority as any other insurance debt.

(3) In this regulation—

"relevant right" means any direct right of action against a UK insurer under a contract of insurance, including the right to prove for a debt under that contract in a winding up of that insurer;

"scheme manager" has the meaning given by section 212(1) of the 2000 Act.

NOTES

Modification: this regulation is applied, with modifications in respect of the Lloyd's of London insurance market, by the Insurers (Reorganisation and Winding Up) (Lloyd's) Regulations 2005, SI 2005/1998, regs 32, 40(1)–(4), 43 at **[4429]**, **[4437]**, **[4440]**.

[4302]

33 Voluntary arrangements: treatment of insurance debts

(1) The modifications made by paragraph (2) apply where a voluntary arrangement is proposed under section 1 of the 1986 Act or Article 14 of the 1989 Order in relation to a UK insurer, and that arrangement includes—

(a) a composition in satisfaction of any insurance debts; and

(b) a distribution to creditors of some or all of the assets of that insurer in the course of, or with a view to, terminating the whole or any part of the business of that insurer.

(2) Section 4 of the 1986 Act (decisions of meetings) has effect as if—

(a) after subsection (4) there were inserted—

"(4A) A meeting so summoned and taking place on or after 20th April 2003 shall not approve any proposal or modification under which any insurance debt of the company is to be paid otherwise than in priority to such of its debts as are not insurance debts or preferential debts.

(4B) Paragraph (4A) does not apply where—

(a) a winding up order made before 20th April 2003 is in force; or

(b) a relevant insolvency appointment made before 20th April 2003 has effect, in relation to the company.";

(b) for subsection (7) there were substituted—

"(7) References in this section to preferential debts mean debts falling into any of categories 4 and 5 of the debts listed in Schedule 6 to this Act; and references to preferential creditors are to be construed accordingly."; and

(c) after subsection (7) as so substituted there were inserted—

"(8) For the purposes of this section—

(a) "insurance debt" has the meaning it has in the Insurers (Reorganisation and Winding up) Regulations 2004; and

(b) "relevant insolvency measure" means—

(i) the appointment of a provisional liquidator, or

(ii) the appointment of an administrator,

where an effect of the appointment will be, or is intended to be, a realisation of some or all of the assets of the insurer and the distribution of the proceeds to creditors, with a view to terminating the whole or any part of the business of that insurer.".

(3) Article 17 of the 1989 Order (decisions of meetings) has effect as if—

(a) after paragraph (4) there were inserted—

"(4A) A meeting so summoned and taking place on or after 20th April 2003 shall not approve any proposal or modification under which any insurance debt of the company is to be paid otherwise than in priority to such of its debts as are not insurance debts or preferential debts.

(4B) Paragraph (4A) does not apply where—

(a) a winding up order made before 20th April 2003 is in force; or

(b) a relevant insolvency appointment made before 20th April 2003 has effect, in relation to the company.";

(b) for paragraph (7) there were substituted—

"(7) References in this Article to preferential debts mean debts falling into any of categories 4 and 5 of the debts listed in Schedule 4 to this Order, and references to preferential creditors are to be construed accordingly."; and

(c) after paragraph (7) as so substituted there were inserted—

"(8) For the purposes of this section—

(a) "insurance debt" has the meaning it has in the Insurers (Reorganisation and Winding Up) Regulations 2004 and

(b) "relevant insolvency measure" means—

(i) the appointment of a provisional liquidator, or

(ii) the appointment of an administrator,

where an effect of the appointment will be, or is intended to be, a realisation of some or all of the assets of the insurer and the distribution of the proceeds to creditors, with a view to terminating the whole or any part of the business of that insurer.".

NOTES

Modification: this regulation is applied, with modifications in respect of the Lloyd's of London insurance market, by the Insurers (Reorganisation and Winding Up) (Lloyd's) Regulations 2005, SI 2005/1998, regs 32,

40(1)–(4), (11), 43 at **[4429]**, **[4437]**, **[4440]**.

PART V
REORGANISATION OR WINDING UP OF UK INSURERS: RECOGNITION OF EEA RIGHTS

[4303]

34 Application of this Part

(1) This Part applies—

(a) where a decision with respect to the approval of a proposed voluntary arrangement having a qualifying purpose is made under section 4A of the 1986 Act or Article 17A of the 1989 Order on or after 20th April 2003 in relation to a UK insurer;

(b) where an administration order made under section 8 of the 1986 Act on or after 20th April 2003 or, on or after 15th September 2003, made under paragraph 13 of Schedule B1 [or under paragraph 14 of Schedule B1 to the 1989 Order] is in force in relation to a UK insurer;

(c) where on or after 20th April 2003 the court reduces the value of one or more of the contracts of a UK insurer under section 377 of the 2000 Act or section 24(5) of the Friendly Societies Act 1992;

(d) where a UK insurer is subject to a relevant winding up;

(e) where a provisional liquidator is appointed in relation to a UK insurer on or after 20th April 2003.

(2) For the purposes of paragraph (1)(a), a voluntary arrangement has a qualifying purpose if it—

(a) varies the rights of the creditors as against the insurer and is intended to enable the insurer, and the whole or any part of its undertaking, to survive as a going concern; or

(b) includes a realisation of some or all of the assets of the insurer to which it relates and the distribution of the proceeds to creditors, with a view to terminating the whole or any part of the business of that insurer.

(3) For the purposes of paragraph (1)(d), a winding up is a relevant winding up if—

(a) in the case of a winding up by the court, the winding up order is made on or after 20th April 2003; or

(b) in the case of a creditors' voluntary winding up, the liquidator is appointed in accordance with section 100 of the 1986 Act, paragraph 83 of Schedule B1[, paragraph 84 of Schedule B1 to the 1989 Order] or Article 86 of the 1989 Order on or after 20th April 2003.

NOTES

Para (1): words in square brackets in sub-para (b) inserted by the Insurers (Reorganisation and Winding Up) (Amendment) Regulations 2007, SI 2007/851, reg 2(1), (14).

Para (3): words in square brackets in sub-para (b) inserted by SI 2007/851, reg 2(1), (15).

Application: this regulation is applied in respect of the Lloyd's of London insurance market, by the Insurers (Reorganisation and Winding Up) (Lloyd's) Regulations 2005, SI 2005/1998, regs 45, 47 at **[4442]**, **[4444]**.

[4304]

35 Application of this Part: assets subject to a section 425 or Article 418 compromise or arrangement

(1) For the purposes of this Part, the insolvent estate of a UK insurer shall not include any assets which at the commencement date are subject to a relevant section 425 or Article 418 compromise or arrangement.

(2) In this regulation—

(a) "assets" has the same meaning as "property" in section 436 of the 1986 Act or Article 2(2) of the 1989 Order;

(b) "commencement date" has the meaning given in regulation 18(4);

(c) "insolvent estate" in England and Wales and Northern Ireland has the meaning given by Rule 13.8 of the Insolvency Rules or Rule 0.2 of the Insolvency Rules (Northern Ireland) and in Scotland means the company's assets;

(d) "relevant section 425 or Article 418 compromise or arrangement" means—

(i) a section 425 or Article 418 compromise or arrangement which was sanctioned by the court before 20th April 2003, or

(ii) any subsequent section 425 or Article 418 compromise or arrangement sanctioned by the court to amend or replace a compromise or arrangement of the kind mentioned in paragraph (i).

[4305]
36 Interpretation of this Part

(1) For the purposes of this Part—

(a) "affected insurer" means a UK insurer which is the subject of a relevant reorganisation or a relevant winding up;

(b) "relevant reorganisation or a relevant winding up" means any voluntary arrangement, administration order, winding up, or order referred to in regulation 34(1)(d) t o which this Part applies; and

(c) "relevant time" means the date of the opening of a relevant reorganisation or a relevant winding up.

(2) In this Part, references to the opening of a relevant reorganisation or a relevant winding up mean—

(a) in the case of winding up proceedings—

(i) in the case of a winding up by the court, the date on which the winding up order is made, or

(ii) in the case of a creditors' voluntary winding up, the date on which the liquidator is appointed in accordance with section 100 of the 1986 Act, paragraph 83 of Schedule B1 or Article 86 of the 1989 Order [or paragraph 84 of Schedule B1 to the 1989 Order];

(b) in the case of a voluntary arrangement, the date when a decision with respect to that voluntary arrangement has effect in accordance with section 4A(2) of the 1986 Act or Article 17A(2) of the 1989 Order;

(c) in a case where an administration order under paragraph 13 of Schedule B1 [or under paragraph 14 of Schedule B1 to the 1989 Order] is in force, the date of the making of that order;

(d) in a case where an administrator is appointed under paragraphs 14 or 22 of Schedule B1 [or under paragraph 15 or 23 of Schedule B1 to the 1989 Order,] the date on which that appointment takes effect;

(e) in a case where the court reduces the value of one or more of the contracts of a UK insurer under section 377 of the 2000 Act or section 24(5) of the Friendly Societies Act 1992, the date the court exercises that power; and

(f) in a case where a provisional liquidator has been appointed, the date of that appointment,

and references to the time of an opening must be construed accordingly.

NOTES

Para (2): words in square brackets in sub-paras (a), (c), (d) inserted by the Insurers (Reorganisation and Winding Up) (Amendment) Regulations 2007, SI 2007/851, reg 2(1), (16).

Modification: this regulation is applied, with modifications in respect of the Lloyd's of London insurance market, by the Insurers (Reorganisation and Winding Up) (Lloyd's) Regulations 2005, SI 2005/1998, regs 45, 46(1), (3), 47 at **[4442]–[4444]**.

[4306]
37 EEA rights: applicable law in the winding up of a UK insurer

(1) This regulation is subject to the provisions of regulations 38 to 47.

(2) In a relevant winding up, the matters mentioned in paragraph (3) in particular are to be determined in accordance with the general law of insolvency of the United Kingdom.

(3) Those matters are—

(a) the assets which form part of the estate of the affected insurer;

(b) the treatment of assets acquired by, or devolving on, the affected insurer after the opening of the relevant winding up;

(c) the respective powers of the affected insurer and the liquidator or provisional liquidator;

(d) the conditions under which set-off may be revoked;

(e) the effects of the relevant winding up on current contracts to which the affected insurer is a party;

(f) the effects of the relevant winding up on proceedings brought by creditors;

(g) the claims which are to be lodged against the estate of the affected insurer;

(h) the treatment of claims against the affected insurer arising after the opening of the relevant winding up;

(i) the rules governing—

(i) the lodging, verification and admission of claims,

(ii) the distribution of proceeds from the realisation of assets,

(iii) the ranking of claims,

(iv) the rights of creditors who have obtained partial satisfaction after the opening of the relevant winding up by virtue of a right in rem or through set-off;

(j) the conditions for and the effects of the closure of the relevant winding up, in particular by composition;

(k) the rights of creditors after the closure of the relevant winding up;

(l) who is to bear the cost and expenses incurred in the relevant winding up;

(m) the rules relating to the voidness, voidability or unenforceability of legal acts detrimental to all the creditors.

(4) In this regulation, "relevant winding up" has the meaning given by regulation 34(3).

NOTES

Modification: this regulation is applied, with modifications in respect of the Lloyd's of London insurance market, by the Insurers (Reorganisation and Winding Up) (Lloyd's) Regulations 2005, SI 2005/1998, regs 45, 46(1), (4), 47 at **[4442]–[4444]**.

[4307]

38 Employment contracts and relationships

(1) The effects of a relevant reorganisation or a relevant winding up on any EEA employment contract and any EEA employment relationship are to be determined in accordance with the law of the EEA State to which that contract or that relationship is subject.

(2) In this regulation, an employment contract is an EEA employment contract, and an employment relationship is an EEA employment relationship, if it is subject to the law of an EEA State.

NOTES

Application: this regulation is applied, in respect of the Lloyd's of London insurance market, by the Insurers (Reorganisation and Winding Up) (Lloyd's) Regulations 2005, SI 2005/1998, regs 45, 47 at **[4442]**, **[4444]**.

[4308]

39 Contracts in connection with immovable property

The effects of a relevant reorganisation or a relevant winding up on a contract conferring the right to make use of or acquire immovable property situated within the territory of an EEA State are to be determined in accordance with the law of that State.

NOTES

Application: this regulation is applied, in respect of the Lloyd's of London insurance market, by the Insurers (Reorganisation and Winding Up) (Lloyd's) Regulations 2005, SI 2005/1998, regs 45, 47 at **[4442]**, **[4444]**.

[4309]

40 Registrable rights

The effects of a relevant reorganisation or a relevant winding up on rights of the affected insurer with respect to—

(a) immovable property,

(b) a ship, or

(c) an aircraft

which is subject to registration in a public register kept under the authority of an EEA State are to be determined in accordance with the law of that State.

NOTES

Application: this regulation is applied, in respect of the Lloyd's of London insurance market, by the Insurers (Reorganisation and Winding Up) (Lloyd's) Regulations 2005, SI 2005/1998, regs 45, 47 at **[4442]**, **[4444]**.

[4310]

41 Third parties' rights in rem

(1) A relevant reorganisation or a relevant winding up shall not affect the rights in rem of creditors or third parties in respect of tangible or intangible, movable or immovable assets (including both specific assets and collections of indefinite assets as a whole which change from time to time) belonging to the affected insurer which are situated within the territory of an EEA State at the relevant time.

(2) The rights in rem referred to in paragraph (1) shall in particular include—

(a) the right to dispose of the assets in question or have them disposed of and to obtain satisfaction from the proceeds of or the income from those assets, in particular by virtue of a lien or a mortgage;

(b) the exclusive right to have a claim met out of the assets in question, in particular a right guaranteed by a lien in respect of the claim or by assignment of the claim by way of guarantee;

(c) the right to demand the assets in question from, or to require restitution by, any person having possession or use of them contrary to the wishes of the party otherwise entitled to the assets;

(d) a right in rem to the beneficial use of assets.

(3) A right, recorded in a public register and enforceable against third parties, under which a right in rem within the meaning of paragraph (1) may be obtained, is also to be treated as a right in rem for the purposes of this regulation.

(4) Paragraph (1) does not preclude actions for voidness, voidability or unenforceability of legal acts detrimental to creditors under the general law of insolvency of the United Kingdom, as referred to in regulation 37(3)(m).

NOTES

Application: this regulation is applied, in respect of the Lloyd's of London insurance market, by the Insurers (Reorganisation and Winding Up) (Lloyd's) Regulations 2005, SI 2005/1998, regs 45, 47 at **[4442]**, **[4444]**.

[4311]

42 Reservation of title agreements etc

(1) The opening of a relevant reorganisation or a relevant winding up in relation to an insurer purchasing an asset shall not affect the seller's rights based on a reservation of title where at the time of that opening the asset is situated within the territory of an EEA State.

(2) The opening of a relevant reorganisation or a relevant winding up in relation to an insurer selling an asset, after delivery of the asset, shall not constitute grounds for rescinding or terminating the sale and shall not prevent the purchaser from acquiring title where at the time of that opening the asset sold is situated within the territory of an EEA State.

(3) Paragraphs (1) and (2) do not preclude actions for voidness, voidability or unenforceability of legal acts detrimental to creditors under the general law of insolvency of the United Kingdom, as referred to in regulation 37(3)(m).

NOTES

Modification: this regulation is applied, with modifications in respect of the Lloyd's of London insurance market, by the Insurers (Reorganisation and Winding Up) (Lloyd's) Regulations 2005, SI 2005/1998, regs 45, 46(1), (5), 47 at **[4442]–[4444]**.

[4312]

43 Creditors' rights to set off

(1) A relevant reorganisation or a relevant winding up shall not affect the right of creditors to demand the set-off of their claims against the claims of the affected insurer, where such a set-off is permitted by the applicable EEA law.

(2) In paragraph (1), "applicable EEA law" means the law of the EEA State which is applicable to the claim of the affected insurer.

(3) Paragraph (1) does not preclude actions for voidness, voidability or unenforceability of legal acts detrimental to creditors under the general law of insolvency of the United Kingdom, as referred to in regulation 37(3)(m).

NOTES

Application: this regulation is applied, in respect of the Lloyd's of London insurance market, by the Insurers (Reorganisation and Winding Up) (Lloyd's) Regulations 2005, SI 2005/1998, regs 45, 47 at **[4442]**, **[4444]**.

[4313]

44 Regulated markets

(1) Without prejudice to regulation 40, the effects of a relevant reorganisation measure or winding up on the rights and obligations of the parties to a regulated market operating in an EEA State must be determined in accordance with the law applicable to that market.

(2) Paragraph (1) does not preclude actions for voidness, voidability or unenforceability of legal acts detrimental to creditors under the general law of insolvency of the United Kingdom, as referred to in regulation 37(3)(m).

(3) For the purposes of this regulation, "regulated market" has the meaning given by [Article 4.1.14 of Directive 2004/39/EC of the European Parliament and of the Council of 21 April 2004 on markets in financial instruments].

NOTES

Para (3): words in square brackets substituted by the Financial Services and Markets Act 2000 (Markets in Financial Instruments) Regulations 2007, SI 2007/126, reg 3(6), Sch 6, Pt 2, para 17.

Application: this regulation is applied, in respect of the Lloyd's of London insurance market, by the Insurers (Reorganisation and Winding Up) (Lloyd's) Regulations 2005, SI 2005/1998, regs 45, 47 at **[4442]**, **[4444]**.

Directive 2004/39/EC of the European Parliament and of the Council: OJ L145, 30.4.2004, p 1.

[4314]

45 Detrimental acts pursuant to the law of an EEA State

(1) In a relevant reorganisation or a relevant winding up, the rules relating to detrimental transactions shall not apply where a person who has benefited from a legal act detrimental to all the creditors provides proof that—

(a) the said act is subject to the law of an EEA State; and

(b) that law does not allow any means of challenging that act in the relevant case.

(2) For the purposes of paragraph (1), "the rules relating to detrimental transactions" means any provisions of the general law of insolvency relating to the voidness, voidability or unenforceability of legal acts detrimental to all the creditors, as referred to in regulation 37(3)(m).

NOTES

Application: this regulation is applied, in respect of the Lloyd's of London insurance market, by the Insurers (Reorganisation and Winding Up) (Lloyd's) Regulations 2005, SI 2005/1998, regs 45, 47 at **[4442]**, **[4444]**.

[4315]

46 Protection of third party purchasers

(1) This regulation applies where, by an act concluded after the opening of a relevant reorganisation or a relevant winding up, an affected insurer disposes for a consideration of—

(a) an immovable asset situated within the territory of an EEA State;

(b) a ship or an aircraft subject to registration in a public register kept under the authority of an EEA State; or

(c) securities whose existence or transfer presupposes entry into a register or account laid down by the law of an EEA State or which are placed in a central deposit system governed by the law of an EEA State.

(2) The validity of that act is to be determined in accordance with the law of the EEA State within whose territory the immovable asset is situated or under whose authority the register, account or system is kept, as the case may be.

NOTES

Application: this regulation is applied, in respect of the Lloyd's of London insurance market, by the Insurers (Reorganisation and Winding Up) (Lloyd's) Regulations 2005, SI 2005/1998, regs 45, 47 at **[4442]**, **[4444]**.

[4316]

47 Lawsuits pending

(1) The effects of a relevant reorganisation or a relevant winding up on a relevant lawsuit pending in an EEA State shall be determined solely in accordance with the law of that EEA State.

(2) In paragraph (1), "relevant lawsuit" means a lawsuit concerning an asset or right of which the affected insurer has been divested.

NOTES

Application: this regulation is applied, in respect of the Lloyd's of London insurance market, by the Insurers (Reorganisation and Winding Up) (Lloyd's) Regulations 2005, SI 2005/1998, regs 45, 47 at **[4442]**, **[4444]**.

PART VI
THIRD COUNTRY INSURERS

[4317]

48 Interpretation of this Part

(1) In this Part—

(a) "relevant measure", in relation to a third country insurer, means

(i) a winding up;

(ii) an administration order made under paragraph 13 of Schedule B1 [or under paragraph 14 of Schedule B1 to the 1989 Order]; or

(iii) a decision of the court to reduce the value of one or more of the insurer's contracts, in accordance with section 377 of the 2000 Act;

(b) "third country insurer" means a person—
(i) who has permission under the 2000 Act to effect or carry out contracts of insurance; and
(ii) whose head office is not in the United Kingdom or an EEA State.

(2) In paragraph (1), the definition of "third country insurer" must be read with—
(a) section 22 of the 2000 Act;
(b) any relevant order made under that section; and
(c) Schedule 2 to that Act.

NOTES

Para (1): words in square brackets in sub-para (a) inserted by the Insurers (Reorganisation and Winding Up) (Amendment) Regulations 2007, SI 2007/851, reg 2(1), (17).

[4318]

49 Application of these Regulations to a third country insurer

Parts III, IV and V of these Regulations apply where a third country insurer is subject to a relevant measure, as if references in those Parts to a UK insurer included a reference to a third country insurer.

[4319]

50 Disclosure of confidential information: third country insurers

(1) This regulation applies to information ("insolvency practitioner information") which—
(a) relates to the business or other affairs of any person; and
(b) is information of a kind mentioned in paragraph (2).

(2) Information falls within paragraph (1)(b) if it is supplied to—
(a) the Authority by an EEA regulator; or
(b) an insolvency practitioner by an EEA administrator or liquidator,
in accordance with or pursuant to Article 30 of the reorganisation and winding up directive.

(3) Subject to paragraphs (4), (5) and (6), sections 348, 349 and 352 of the 2000 Act apply in relation to insolvency practitioner information in the same way as they apply in relation to confidential information within the meaning of section 348(2) of that Act.

(4) For the purposes of this regulation, sections 348, 349 and 352 of the 2000 Act and the Disclosure Regulations have effect as if the primary recipients specified in subsection (5) of section 348 of the 2000 Act included an insolvency practitioner.

(5) Insolvency practitioner information is not subject to the restrictions on disclosure imposed by section 348(1) of the 2000 Act (as it applies by virtue of paragraph (3)) if it satisfies any of the criteria set out in section 348(4) of the 2000 Act.

(6) The Disclosure Regulations apply in relation to insolvency practitioner information as they apply in relation to single market directive information (within the meaning of those Regulations).

(7) In this regulation—

"the Disclosure Regulations" means the Financial Services and Markets Act 2000 (Disclosure of Confidential Information) Regulations 2001;

"EEA administrator" and "EEA liquidator" mean respectively an administrator or liquidator within the meaning of the reorganisation and winding up directive;

"insolvency practitioner" means an insolvency practitioner, within the meaning of section 388 of the 1986 Act or Article 3 of the 1989 Order, who is appointed or acts in relation to a third country insurer.

PART VII
REVOCATION AND AMENDMENTS

51, 52 (*Art 51 amends the Insurers (Winding Up) Rules 2001, SI 2001/3635, r 24 and the Insurers (Winding Up) (Scotland) Rules 2001, SI 2001/4040, r 24; art 52 amends the Financial Services and Markets Act 2000 (Administration Orders Relating to Insurers) Order 2002, SI 2002/1242, reg 3 at* **[853]**.)

[4320]

53 Revocation and Transitional

(1) Except as provided in this regulation, the Insurers (Reorganisation and Winding Up) Regulations 2003 are revoked.

(2) Subject to (3), the provisions of Parts III and IV shall continue in force in respect of decisions orders or appointments referred to therein and made before the coming into force of these Regulations.

(3) Where an administrator has been appointed in respect of a UK insurer on or after 15th September 2003, he shall be treated as being so appointed on the date these regulations come into force.

FINANCIAL SERVICES (DISTANCE MARKETING) REGULATIONS 2004

(SI 2004/2095)

NOTES

Made: 4 August 2004.
Authority: European Communities Act 1972, s 2(2).
Commencement: 31 October 2004.

ARRANGEMENT OF REGULATIONS

1 Citation, commencement and extent . . . . [4321]
2 Interpretation . . . . [4322]
3 Scope of these Regulations . . . . [4323]
4 . . . . [4324]
5 . . . . [4325]
6 Financial services marketed by an intermediary . . . . [4326]
7 Information required prior to the conclusion of the contract . . . . [4327]
8 Written and additional information . . . . [4328]
9 Right to cancel . . . . [4329]
10 Cancellation period . . . . [4330]
11 Exceptions to the right to cancel . . . . [4331]
12 Automatic cancellation of an attached distance contract . . . . [4332]
13 Payment for services provided before cancellation . . . . [4333]
15 Unsolicited services . . . . [4335]
16 Prevention of contracting-out . . . . [4336]
17 Enforcement authorities . . . . [4337]
18 Consideration of complaints . . . . [4338]
19 Injunctions to secure compliance with these Regulations . . . . [4339]
20 Notification of undertakings and orders to the OFT . . . . [4340]
21 Publication, information and advice . . . . [4341]
22 Offences . . . . [4342]
23 Functions of the Authority . . . . [4343]
29 Transitional provisions . . . . [4344]

SCHEDULES:

Schedule 1—Information Required Prior to the Conclusion of the Contract . . . . [4345]
Schedule 2—Information Required in the Case of Voice Telephone Communications . . . . [4346]

[4321]
1 Citation, commencement and extent

These Regulations may be cited as the Financial Services (Distance Marketing) Regulations 2004 and come into force on 31st October 2004.

[4322]
2 Interpretation

(1) In these Regulations—

"the 1974 Act" means the Consumer Credit Act 1974;

"the 2000 Act" means the Financial Services and Markets Act 2000;

"the Authority" means the Financial Services Authority;

"appointed representative" has the same meaning as in section 39(2) of the 2000 Act (exemption of appointed representatives);

"authorised person" has the same meaning as in section 31(2) of the 2000 Act (authorised persons);

"breach" means a contravention by a supplier of a prohibition in, or a failure by a supplier to comply with a requirement of, these Regulations;

"business" includes a trade or profession;

"consumer" means any individual who, in contracts to which these Regulations apply, is acting for purposes which are outside any business he may carry on;

"court" in relation to England and Wales and Northern Ireland means a county court or the High Court, and in relation to Scotland means the Sheriff Court or the Court of Session;

"credit" includes a cash loan and any other form of financial accommodation, and for this purpose "cash" includes money in any form;

"designated professional body" has the same meaning as in section 326(2) of the 2000 Act (designation of professional bodies);

"the Directive" means Directive 2002/65/EC of the European Parliament and of the Council of 23 September 2002 concerning the distance marketing of consumer financial services and amending Council Directive 90/619/EEC and Directives 97/7/EC and 98/27/EC;

"distance contract" means any contract concerning one or more financial services concluded between a supplier and a consumer under an organised distance sales or service-provision scheme run by the supplier or by an intermediary, who, for the purpose of that contract, makes exclusive use of one or more means of distance communication up to and including the time at which the contract is concluded;

"durable medium" means any instrument which enables a consumer to store information addressed personally to him in a way accessible for future reference for a period of time adequate for the purposes of the information and which allows the unchanged reproduction of the information stored;

"EEA supplier" means a supplier who is a national of an EEA State, or a company or firm (within the meaning of Article 48 of the Treaty establishing the European Community) formed in accordance with the law of an EEA State;

["EEA State" has the meaning given by Schedule 1 to the Interpretation Act 1978;]

"exempt regulated activity" has the same meaning as in section 325(2) of the 2000 Act;

"financial service" means any service of a banking, credit, insurance, personal pension, investment or payment nature;

"means of distance communication" means any means which, without the simultaneous physical presence of the supplier and the consumer, may be used for the marketing of a service between those parties;

"the OFT" means the Office of Fair Trading;

"regulated activity" has the same meaning as in section 22 of the 2000 Act (the classes of activity and categories of investment);

"Regulated Activities Order" means the Financial Services and Markets Act 2000 (Regulated Activities) Order 2001;

"rule" means a rule—

(a) made by the Authority under the 2000 Act, or

(b) made by a designated professional body, and approved by the Authority, under section 332 of the 2000 Act,

as the context requires;

"supplier" means any person who, acting in his commercial or professional capacity, is the contractual provider of services.

(2) In these Regulations, subject to paragraph (1), any expression used in these Regulations which is also used in the Directive has the same meaning as in the Directive.

NOTES

Para (1): definition "EEA State" substituted by the Financial Services (EEA State) Regulations 2007, SI 2007/108, reg 10.

Directive 2002/65/EC of the European Parliament and of the Council: OJ L271, 9.10.2002, p 16.

Council Directive 90/619/EEC: OJ L330, 29.11.1990, p 50.

Directive 97/7/EC: OJ L144, 4.6.1997, p 19.

Directive 98/27/EC: OJ L166, 11.6.1998, p 51.

[4323]

3 Scope of these Regulations

(1) Regulations 7 to 14 apply, subject to regulations 4 and 5, in relation to distance contracts made on or after 31st October 2004.

(2) Regulation 15 applies in relation to financial services supplied on or after 31st October 2004 under an organised distance sales or service-provision scheme run by the supplier or by an intermediary, who, for the purpose of that supply, makes exclusive use of one or more means of distance communication up to and including the time at which the financial services are supplied.

[4324]

4— (1) Where an EEA State, other than the United Kingdom, has transposed the Directive or has obligations in its domestic law corresponding to those provided for in the Directive—

(a) regulations 7 to 14 do not apply in relation to any contract made between an EEA supplier contracting from an establishment in that EEA State and a consumer in the United Kingdom, and

(b) regulation 15 does not apply to any supply of financial services by an EEA supplier from an establishment in that EEA State to a consumer in the United Kingdom,

if the provisions by which that State has transposed the Directive, or the obligations in the domestic law of that State corresponding to those provided for in the Directive, as the case may be, apply to that contract or that supply.

(2) Subject to paragraph (5) and regulation 6(3) and (4)—

(a) regulations 7 to 11 do not apply in relation to any contract made by a supplier who is an authorised person, the making or performance of which constitutes or is part of a regulated activity carried on by him;

(b) regulation 15 does not apply to any supply of financial services by a supplier who is an authorised person, where that supply constitutes or is part of a regulated activity carried on by him.

(3) Subject to regulation 6(3) and (4)—

(a) regulations 7 and 8 do not apply in relation to any contract made by a supplier who is an appointed representative, the making or performance of which constitutes or is part of a regulated activity (other than an exempt regulated activity) carried on by him;

(b) regulation 15 does not apply to any supply of financial services by a supplier who is an appointed representative, where that supply constitutes or is part of a regulated activity (other than an exempt regulated activity) carried on by him.

(4) Subject to regulation 6(3) and (4)—

(a) regulations 7 and 8 do not apply in relation to any contract where—

(i) the supplier is bound, or is controlled or managed by one or more persons who are bound, by rules of a designated professional body which are equivalent to those regulations, and

(ii) the making or performance of that contract constitutes or is part of an exempt regulated activity carried on by the supplier;

(b) regulation 15 does not apply to any supply of financial services where—

(i) the supplier is bound, or is controlled or managed by one or more persons who are bound, by rules of a designated professional body which are equivalent to that regulation, and

(ii) that supply constitutes or is part of an exempt regulated activity carried on by the supplier.

(5) Paragraph (2) does not apply in relation to any contract or supply of financial services made by a supplier who is the operator, trustee or depositary of a scheme which is a recognised scheme by virtue of section 264 of the 2000 Act (schemes constituted in other EEA States), where the making or performance of the contract or the supply of the financial services constitutes or is part of a regulated activity for which he has permission in that capacity.

(6) In paragraph (5)—

"the operator", "trustee" and "depositary" each has the same meaning as in section 237(2) of the 2000 Act (other definitions); and

"permission" has the same meaning as in section 266 of that Act (disapplication of rules).

[4325]

5— (1) Where a consumer and a supplier enter an initial service agreement and—

(a) successive operations of the same nature, or

(b) a series of separate operations of the same nature,

are subsequently performed between them over time and within the framework of that agreement, then, if any of regulations 7 to 14 apply, they apply only to the initial service agreement.

(2) Where a consumer and a supplier do not enter an initial service agreement and—

(a) successive operations of the same nature, or

(b) a series of separate operations of the same nature,

are performed between them over time, then, if regulations 7 and 8 apply, they apply only—

(i) when the first operation is performed, and

(ii) to any operation which is performed more than one year after the previous operation.

(3) For the purposes of this regulation, "initial service agreement" includes, for example, an agreement for the provision of—

(a) a bank account;

(b) a credit card; or

(c) portfolio management services.

(4) For the purposes of this regulation, "operations" includes, for example—

(a) deposits to or withdrawals from a bank account;
(b) payments by a credit card;
(c) transactions carried out within the framework of an initial service agreement for portfolio management services; and
(d) subscriptions to new units of the same collective investment fund,

but does not include adding new elements to an existing initial service agreement, for example adding the possibility of using an electronic payment instrument together with an existing bank account.

[4326]

6 Financial services marketed by an intermediary

(1) This regulation applies where a financial service is marketed by an intermediary.

(2) These Regulations have effect as if—

(a) each reference to a supplier in the definition of "breach" in regulation 2(1) were a reference to a supplier or an intermediary;
(b) the reference to the supplier in the definition of "means of distance communication" in regulation 2(1), each reference to the supplier in regulations 7, 8(1) and (2), 10 and 11(3)(b), and the first reference to the supplier in regulation 8(4), were a reference to the intermediary;
(c) the reference to the supplier in regulation 8(3) were a reference to the supplier or the intermediary;
(d) for regulation 11(2) there were substituted—

"(2) Paragraph (1) does not apply to a distance contract if the intermediary has not complied with regulation 8(1) (and the supplier has not done what the intermediary was required to do by regulation 8(1)), unless—

(a) the circumstances fall within regulation 8(1)(b); and
(b) either—
(i) the intermediary has complied with regulation 7(1) and (2) or, if applicable, regulation 7(4)(b), and with regulation 7(5), or
(ii) the supplier has done what the intermediary was required to do by regulation 7(1) and (2) or, if applicable, regulation 7(4)(b), and by regulation 7(5).";

(e) the reference to a supplier in regulation 22(1) were a reference to an intermediary; and
(f) each reference to the supplier in paragraphs 2, 4, 5 and 19 of Schedule 1 were a reference to the supplier and the intermediary.

(3) Notwithstanding paragraphs (2) to (4) of regulation 4, regulations 7 and 8 apply in relation to the intermediary unless—

(a) the intermediary is an authorised person and the marketing of the financial service constitutes or is part of a regulated activity carried on by him;
(b) the intermediary is an appointed representative and the marketing of the financial service constitutes or is part of a regulated activity (other than an exempt regulated activity) carried on by him; or
(c) the intermediary is not an authorised person, but—
(i) he is bound, or is controlled or managed by one or more persons who are bound, by rules of a designated professional body which are equivalent to regulations 7 and 8, and
(ii) the marketing of the financial service constitutes or is part of an exempt regulated activity carried on by him.

(4) Notwithstanding paragraphs (2) to (4) of regulation 4, regulation 15 applies to the intermediary unless—

(a) the intermediary is an authorised person and is acting in the course of a regulated activity carried on by him;
(b) the intermediary is an appointed representative and is acting in the course of a regulated activity (other than an exempt regulated activity) carried on by him; or
(c) the intermediary is not an authorised person, but—
(i) he is bound, or is controlled or managed by one or more persons who are bound, by rules of a designated professional body which are equivalent to regulation 15, and
(ii) he is acting in the course an exempt regulated activity carried on by him.

[4327]
7 Information required prior to the conclusion of the contract

(1) Subject to [paragraph (1A) and (4)], in good time prior to the consumer being bound by any distance contract, the supplier shall provide to the consumer the information specified in Schedule 1.

[(1A) Where a distance contract to which paragraph (1) applies is also a contract for payment services to which the Payment Services Regulations 2009 apply, the supplier is required to provide to the consumer only the information specified in paragraphs 8 to 13, 16, 17 and 21 of Schedule 1.]

(2) The supplier shall provide the information specified in Schedule 1 in a clear and comprehensible manner appropriate to the means of distance communication used, with due regard in particular to the principles of good faith in commercial transactions and the principles governing the protection of those who are unable to give their consent such as minors.

(3) Subject to paragraph (4), the supplier shall make clear his commercial purpose when providing the information specified in Schedule 1.

(4) In the case of a voice telephone communication—

- (a) the supplier shall make clear his identity and the commercial purpose of any call initiated by him at the beginning of any conversation with the consumer; and
- (b) if the consumer explicitly consents, only the information specified in Schedule 2 need be given.

(5) The supplier shall ensure that the information he provides to the consumer pursuant to this regulation, regarding the contractual obligations which would arise if the distance contract were concluded, accurately reflects the contractual obligations which would arise under the law presumed to be applicable to that contract.

NOTES

Para (1): words in square brackets there are substituted by the Payment Services Regulations 2009, SI 2009/209, reg 126, Sch 6, Pt 2, para 5(a)(i).

Para (1A): inserted by SI 2009/209, reg 126, Sch 6, Pt 2, para 5(a)(ii).

[4328]
8 Written and additional information

(1) [Subject to paragraph (1A),] the supplier under a distance contract shall communicate to the consumer on paper, or in another durable medium which is available and accessible to the consumer, all the contractual terms and conditions and the information specified in Schedule 1, either—

- (a) in good time prior to the consumer being bound by that distance contract; or
- (b) immediately after the conclusion of the contract, where the contract has been concluded at the consumer's request using a means of distance communication which does not enable provision in accordance with sub-paragraph (a) of the contractual terms and conditions and the information specified in Schedule 1.

[(1A) Where a distance contract to which paragraph (1) applies is also a contract for payment services to which the Payment Services Regulations 2009 apply, the supplier is required to communicate to the consumer all the contractual terms and conditions and the information specified in paragraphs 8 to 13, 16, 17 and 21 of Schedule 1.]

(2) The supplier shall communicate the contractual terms and conditions to the consumer on paper, if the consumer so requests at any time during their contractual relationship.

(3) Paragraph (2) does not apply if the supplier has already communicated the contractual terms and conditions to the consumer on paper during that contractual relationship, and those terms and conditions have not changed since they were so communicated.

(4) The supplier shall change the means of distance communication with the consumer if the consumer so requests at any time during his contractual relationship with the supplier, unless that is incompatible with the distance contract or the nature of the financial service provided to the consumer.

NOTES

Para (1): words in square brackets inserted by the Payment Services Regulations 2009, SI 2009/209, reg 126, Sch 6, Pt 2, para 5(b)(i).

Para (1A): inserted by SI 2009/209, reg 126, Sch 6, Pt 2, para 5(b)(ii).

[4329]
9 Right to cancel

(1) Subject to regulation 11, if within the cancellation period set out in regulation 10 notice of cancellation is properly given by the consumer to the supplier, the notice of cancellation shall

operate to cancel the distance contract.

(2) Cancelling the contract has the effect of terminating the contract at the time at which the notice of cancellation is given.

(3) For the purposes of these Regulations, a notice of cancellation is a notification given—

- (a) orally (where the supplier has informed the consumer that notice of cancellation may be given orally),
- (b) in writing, or
- (c) in another durable medium available and accessible to the supplier,

which, however expressed, indicates the intention of the consumer to cancel the contract by that notification.

(4) Notice of cancellation given under this regulation by a consumer to a supplier is to be treated as having been properly given if the consumer—

- (a) gives it orally to the supplier (where the supplier has informed the consumer that notice of cancellation may be given orally);
- (b) leaves it at the address of the supplier last known to the consumer and addressed to the supplier by name (in which case it is to be taken to have been given on the day on which it was left);
- (c) sends it by post to the address of the supplier last known to the consumer and addressed to the supplier by name (in which case it is to be taken to have been given on the day on which it was posted);
- (d) sends it by facsimile to the business facsimile number of the supplier last known to the consumer (in which case it is to be taken to have been given on the day on which it was sent);
- (e) sends it by electronic mail to the business electronic mail address of the supplier last known to the consumer (in which case it is to be taken to have been given on the day on which it is sent); or
- (f) by other electronic means—
  - (i) sends it to an internet address or web-site which the supplier has notified the consumer may be used for the purpose, or
  - (ii) indicates it on such a web-site in accordance with instructions which are on the web-site or which the supplier has provided to the consumer,

  (in which case it is to be taken to have been given on the day on which it is sent to that address or web-site or indicated on that web-site).

(5) The references in paragraph (4)(b) and (c) to the address of the supplier shall, in the case of a supplier which is a body corporate, be treated as including a reference to the address of the secretary or clerk of that body.

(6) The references in paragraph (4)(b) and (c) to the address of the supplier shall, in the case of a supplier which is a partnership, be treated as including a reference to the address of a partner or a person having control or management of the partnership business.

(7) In this regulation—

- (a) every reference to the supplier includes a reference to any other person previously notified by or on behalf of the supplier to the consumer as a person to whom notice of cancellation may be given;
- (b) the references to giving notice of cancellation orally include giving such notice by voice telephone communication, where the supplier has informed the consumer that notice of cancellation may be given in that way; and
- (c) "electronic mail" has the same meaning as in regulation 2(1) of the Privacy and Electronic Communications (EC Directive) Regulations 2003 (interpretation).

[4330]

10 Cancellation period

(1) For the purposes of regulation 9, the cancellation period begins on the day on which the distance contract is concluded ("conclusion day") and ends as provided for in paragraphs (2) to (5).

(2) Where the supplier complies with regulation 8(1) on or before conclusion day, the cancellation period ends on the expiry of fourteen calendar days beginning with the day after conclusion day.

(3) Where the supplier does not comply with regulation 8(1) on or before conclusion day, but subsequently communicates to the consumer on paper, or in another durable medium which is available and accessible to the consumer, all the contractual terms and conditions and the information required under regulation 8(1), the cancellation period ends on the expiry of fourteen calendar days beginning with the day after the day on which the consumer receives the last of those terms and conditions and that information.

(4) In the case of a distance contract relating to life insurance, for the references to conclusion day in paragraphs (2) and (3) there are substituted references to the day on which the consumer is informed that the distance contract has been concluded.

(5) In the case of a distance contract relating to life insurance or a personal pension, for the references to fourteen calendar days in paragraphs (2) and (3) there are substituted references to thirty calendar days.

[4331]
11 Exceptions to the right to cancel

(1) Subject to paragraphs (2) and (3), regulation 9 does not confer on a consumer a right to cancel a distance contract which is—

(a) a contract for a financial service where the price of that service depends on fluctuations in the financial market outside the supplier's control, which may occur during the cancellation period, such as services related to—
  (i) foreign exchange,
  (ii) money market instruments,
  (iii) transferable securities,
  (iv) units in collective investment undertakings,
  (v) financial-futures contracts, including equivalent cash-settled instruments,
  (vi) forward interest-rate agreements,
  (vii) interest-rate, currency and equity swaps,
  (viii) options to acquire or dispose of any instruments referred to in sub-paragraphs (i) to (vii), including cash-settled instruments and options on currency and on interest rates;

(b) a contract whose performance has been fully completed by both parties at the consumer's express request before the consumer gives notice of cancellation;

(c) a contract which—
  (i) is a connected contract of insurance within the meaning of article 72B(1) of the Regulated Activities Order (activities carried on by a provider of relevant goods or services),
  (ii) covers travel risks within the meaning of article 72B(1)(d)(ii) of that Order, and
  (iii) has a total duration of less than one month;

(d) a contract under which a supplier provides credit to a consumer and the consumer's obligation to repay is secured by a legal mortgage on land;

(e) a credit agreement cancelled under regulation 15(1) of the Consumer Protection (Distance Selling) Regulations 2000 (automatic cancellation of a related credit agreement);

(f) a credit agreement cancelled under section 6A of the Timeshare Act 1992 (automatic cancellation of timeshare credit agreement); or

(g) a restricted-use credit agreement (within the meaning of the 1974 Act) to finance the purchase of land or an existing building, or an agreement for a bridging loan in connection with the purchase of land or an existing building.

(2) Paragraph (1) does not apply to a distance contract if the supplier has not complied with regulation 8(1), unless—

(a) the circumstances fall within regulation 8(1)(b); and

(b) the supplier has complied with regulation 7(1) and (2) or, if applicable, regulation 7(4)(b), and with regulation 7(5).

(3) Where—

(a) the conditions in sub-paragraphs (a) and (b) of paragraph (2) are satisfied in relation to a distance contract falling within paragraph (1),

(b) the supplier has not complied with regulation 8(1), and

(c) the consumer has not, by the end of the sixth day after the day on which the distance contract is concluded, received all the contractual terms and conditions and the information required under regulation 8(1),

the consumer may cancel the contract under regulation 9 during the period beginning on the seventh day after the day on which the distance contract is concluded and ending when he receives the last of the contractual terms and conditions and the information required under regulation 8(1).

[4332]

12 Automatic cancellation of an attached distance contract

(1) For the purposes of this regulation, where there is a distance contract for the provision of a financial service by a supplier to a consumer ("the main contract") and there is a further distance contract ("the secondary contract") for the provision to that consumer of a further financial service by—

(a) the same supplier, or

(b) a third party, the further financial service being provided pursuant to an agreement between the third party and the supplier under the main contract,

then the secondary contract (referred to in these Regulations as an "attached contract") is attached to the main contract if any of the conditions in paragraph (2) are satisfied.

(2) The conditions referred to in paragraph (1) are—

(a) the secondary contract is entered into in compliance with a term of the main contract;

(b) the main contract is, or is to be, financed by the secondary contract;

(c) the main contract is a debtor-creditor-supplier agreement within the meaning of the 1974 Act, and the secondary contract is, or is to be, financed by the main contract;

(d) the secondary contract is entered into by the consumer to induce the supplier to enter into the main contract;

(e) performance of the secondary contract requires performance of the main contract.

(3) Where a main contract is cancelled by a notice of cancellation given under regulation 9—

(a) the cancellation of the main contract also operates to cancel, at the time at which the main contract is cancelled, any attached contract which is not a contract or agreement of a type listed in regulation 11(1); and

(b) the supplier under the main contract shall, if he is not the supplier under the attached contract, forthwith on receipt of the notice of cancellation inform the supplier under the attached contract.

(4) Paragraph (3)(a) does not apply to an attached contract if, at or before the time at which the notice of cancellation in respect of the main contract is given, the consumer has given and not withdrawn a notice to the supplier under the main contract that cancellation of the main contract is not to operate to cancel that attached contract.

(5) Where a main contract made by an authorised person, the making or performance of which constitutes or is part of a regulated activity carried on by him, is cancelled under rules made by the Authority corresponding to regulation 9—

(a) the cancellation of the main contract also operates to cancel, at the time at which the main contract is cancelled, any attached contract which is not a contract or agreement of a type listed in regulation 11(1); and

(b) the supplier under the main contract shall, if he is not the supplier under the attached contract, inform the supplier under the attached contract forthwith on receiving notification of the consumer's intention to cancel the main contract by that notification.

(6) Paragraph (5)(a) does not apply to an attached contract if, at or before the time at which the consumer gives notification of his intention to cancel the main contract by that notification, the consumer has given and not withdrawn a notice to the supplier under the main contract that cancellation of the main contract is not to operate to cancel that attached contract.

[4333]–[4334]

13 Payment for services provided before cancellation

(1) This regulation applies where a cancellation event occurs in relation to a distance contract.

(2) In this regulation, "cancellation event" means the cancellation of a distance contract under regulation 9 or 12.

(3) The supplier shall refund any sum paid by or on behalf of the consumer under or in relation to the contract to the person by whom it was paid, less any charge made in accordance with paragraph (6), as soon as possible and in any event within a period not exceeding 30 calendar days beginning with—

(a) the day on which the cancellation event occurred; or

(b) if the supplier proves that this is later—

(i) in the case of a contract cancelled under regulation 9, the day on which the supplier in fact received the notice of cancellation, or

(ii) in the case of an attached contract under which the supplier is not the supplier under the main contract, the day on which, pursuant to regulation 12(3)(b) or (5)(b), he was in fact informed by the supplier under the main contract of the cancellation of the main contract.

(4) The reference in paragraph (3) to any sum paid on behalf of the consumer includes any sum paid by any other person ("the creditor"), who is not the supplier, under an agreement between the consumer and the creditor by which the creditor provides the consumer with credit of any amount.

(5) Where any security has been provided in relation to the contract, the security (so far as it has been provided) shall, on cancellation under regulation 9 or 12, be treated as never having had effect; and any property lodged solely for the purposes of the security as so provided shall be returned forthwith by the person with whom it is lodged.

(6) Subject to paragraphs (7), (8) and (9), the supplier may make a charge for any service actually provided by the supplier in accordance with the contract.

(7) The charge shall not exceed an amount which is in proportion to the extent of the service provided to the consumer prior to the time at which the cancellation event occurred (including the service of arranging to provide the financial service) in comparison with the full coverage of the contract, and in any event shall not be such that it could be construed as a penalty.

(8) The supplier may not make any charge unless he can prove on the balance of probabilities that the consumer was informed about the amount payable in accordance with—

- (a) regulation 7(1) and paragraph 13 of Schedule 1,
- (b) regulation 7(4) and paragraph 5 of Schedule 2, or
- (c) rules corresponding to those provisions,

as the case may be.

(9) The supplier may not make any charge if, without the consumer's prior request, he commenced performance of the contract prior to the expiry of the relevant cancellation period.

(10) In paragraph (9), the relevant cancellation period is the cancellation period which—

- (a) in the case of a main contract, is applicable to that contract, or
- (b) in the case of an attached contract, would be applicable to that contract if that contract were a main contract,

under regulation 10, or under rules corresponding to that regulation, as the case may be.

(11) The consumer shall, as soon as possible and in any event within a period not exceeding 30 calendar days beginning with the day on which the cancellation event occurred—

- (a) refund any sum paid by or on behalf of the supplier under or in relation to that contract to the person by whom it was paid; and
- (b) either restore to the supplier any property of which he has acquired possession under that contract, or deliver or send that property to any person to whom, under regulation 9, a notice of cancellation could have been given in respect of that contract.

(12) Breach of a duty imposed by paragraph (11) on a consumer is actionable as a breach of statutory duty.

14 *(Revoked by the Payment Services Regulations 2009, SI 2009/209, reg 126, Sch 6, Pt 2, para 5(c).)*

[4335]

15 Unsolicited services

(1) A person ("the recipient") who receives unsolicited financial services for purposes other than those of his business from another person who supplies those services in the course of his business, shall not thereby become subject to any obligation (to make payment, or otherwise).

(2), (3) . . .

(4) In this regulation, "unsolicited" means, in relation to financial services supplied to any person, that they are supplied without any prior request made by or on behalf of that person.

(5)–(7) . . .

(8) This regulation is without prejudice to any right a supplier may have at any time, by contract or otherwise, to renew a distance contract with a consumer without any request made by or on behalf of that consumer prior to the renewal of that contract.

NOTES

Paras (2), (3), (5)–(7): revoked by the Consumer Protection from Unfair Trading Regulations 2008, SI 2008/1277, reg 30(1), (3), Sch 2, Pt 2, para 110(1), (2), Sch 4, Pt 2.

[4336]

16 Prevention of contracting-out

(1) A term contained in any contract is void if, and to the extent that, it is inconsistent with the application of a provision of these Regulations to a distance contract or the application of regulation 15 to a supply of unsolicited financial services.

(2) Where a provision of these Regulations specifies a duty or liability of the consumer in certain circumstances, a term contained in a contract is inconsistent with that provision if it purports to impose, directly or indirectly, an additional or greater duty or liability on him in those circumstances.

(3) These Regulations apply notwithstanding any contract term which applies or purports to apply the law of a State which is not an EEA State if the contract or supply has a close connection with the territory of an EEA State.

[4337]

17 Enforcement authorities

(1) For the purposes of regulations 18 to 21—

(a) in relation to any alleged breach concerning a specified contract, the Authority is the enforcement authority;

(b) in relation to any alleged breach concerning a contract under which the supplier is a local authority, but which is not a specified contract, the OFT is the enforcement authority;

(c) in relation to any other alleged breach—

(i) the OFT, and

(ii) in Great Britain every local weights and measures authority, and in Northern Ireland the Department of Enterprise, Trade and Investment,

is an enforcement authority.

(2) For the purposes of paragraph (1) and regulation 22(6), each of the following is a specified contract—

(a) a contract the making or performance of which constitutes or is part of a regulated activity carried on by the supplier;

(b) a contract for the provision of a debit card;

(c) a contract relating to the issuing of electronic money by a supplier to whom the Authority has given a certificate under article 9C of the Regulated Activities Order (persons certified as small issuers etc);

(d) a contract the effecting or carrying out of which is excluded from article 10(1) or (2) of the Regulated Activities Order (effecting and carrying out contracts of insurance) by article 12 of that order (breakdown insurance), where the supplier is a person who does not otherwise carry on an activity of the kind specified by article 10 of that order;

(e) a contract under which a supplier provides credit to a consumer and the obligation of the consumer to repay is secured by a first legal mortgage on land;

(f) a contract, made before 14th January 2005, for insurance mediation activity other than in respect of a contract of long-term care insurance.

(3) For the purposes of the application of this regulation and regulations 18 to 22 in relation to breaches of, and offences under, regulation 15, "contract"—

(a) wherever it appears in this regulation other than in the expression "contract of long-term care insurance", and

(b) in regulation 22(6),

is to be taken to mean "supply of financial services".

(4) For the purposes of this regulation—

"contract of long-term care insurance" has the same meaning as in the Financial Services and Markets Act 2000 (Regulated Activities) (Amendment) (No 2) Order 2003;

"insurance mediation activity" means any activity which is not a regulated activity at the time the contract is made but will be a regulated activity of the kind specified by article 21, 25(1) or (2), 39A or 53 of the Regulated Activities Order when the amendments to that order made by the Financial Services and Markets Act 2000 (Regulated Activities) (Amendment) (No 2) Order 2003 come into force;

"local authority" means—

(a) in England and Wales, a local authority within the meaning of the Local Government Act 1972, the Greater London Authority, the Common Council of the City of London or the Council of the Isles of Scilly,

(b) in Scotland, a council constituted under section 2 of the Local Government etc (Scotland) Act 1994, and

(c) in Northern Ireland, a district council within the meaning of the Local Government Act (Northern Ireland) 1972.

[4338]
18 Consideration of complaints

(1) An enforcement authority shall consider any complaint made to it about a breach unless—

(a) the complaint appears to that authority to be frivolous or vexatious; or

(b) that authority is aware that another enforcement authority has notified the OFT that it agrees to consider the complaint.

(2) If an enforcement authority notifies the OFT that it agrees to consider a complaint made to another enforcement authority, the first mentioned authority shall be under a duty to consider the complaint.

[4339]
19 Injunctions to secure compliance with these Regulations

(1) Subject to paragraph (2), an enforcement authority may apply for an injunction (including an interim injunction) against any person who appears to that authority to be responsible for a breach.

(2) An enforcement authority, other than the OFT or the Authority, may apply for an injunction only where—

(a) that authority has notified the OFT, at least fourteen days before the date on which the application is to be made, of its intention to apply; or

(b) the OFT consents to the application being made within a shorter period.

(3) On an application made under this regulation, the court may grant an injunction on such terms as it thinks fit to secure compliance with these Regulations.

(4) An enforcement authority which has a duty under regulation 18 to consider a complaint shall give reasons for its decision to apply or not to apply, as the case may be, for an injunction.

(5) In deciding whether or not to apply for an injunction in respect of a breach, an enforcement authority may, if it considers it appropriate to do so, have regard to any undertaking as to compliance with these Regulations given to it or to another enforcement authority by or on behalf of any person.

(6) In the application of this regulation to Scotland, for references to an "injunction" or an "interim injunction" there are substituted references to an "interdict" or an "interim interdict" respectively.

[4340]
20 Notification of undertakings and orders to the OFT

An enforcement authority, other than the OFT and the Authority, shall notify the OFT of—

(a) any undertaking given to it by or on behalf of any person who appears to it to be responsible for a breach;

(b) the outcome of any application made by it under regulation 19 and the terms of any undertaking given to, or order made by, the court; and

(c) the outcome of any application made by it to enforce a previous order of the court.

[4341]
21 Publication, information and advice

(1) The OFT shall arrange for the publication, in such form and manner as it considers appropriate, of details of any undertaking or order notified to it under regulation 20.

(2) Each of the OFT and the Authority shall arrange for the publication in such form and manner as it considers appropriate of—

(a) details of any undertaking as to compliance with these Regulations given to it by or on behalf of any person;

(b) details of any application made by it under regulation 19, and of the terms of any undertaking given to, or order made by, the court; and

(c) details of any application made by it to enforce a previous order of the court.

(3) Each of the OFT and the Authority may arrange for the dissemination, in such form and manner as it considers appropriate, of such information and advice concerning the operation of these Regulations as may appear to it to be expedient to give to the public and to all persons likely to be affected by these Regulations.

[4342]
22 Offences

(1) A supplier under a distance contract who fails to comply with regulation 7(3) or (4)(a) or regulation 8(2) or (4) is guilty of an offence and liable, on summary conviction, to a fine not exceeding level 3 on the standard scale.

(2) If an offence under paragraph (1) . . . committed by a body corporate is shown—

(a) to have been committed with the consent or connivance of any director, manager, secretary or other similar officer of the body corporate, or any person who was purporting to act in any such capacity, or

(b) to be attributable to any neglect on his part,

he as well as the body corporate is guilty of the offence and liable to be proceeded against and punished accordingly.

(3) If the affairs of a body corporate are managed by its members, paragraph (2) applies in relation to the acts and defaults of a member in connection with his functions of management as if he were a director of the body.

(4) If an offence under paragraph (1) . . . committed by a partnership is shown—

(a) to have been committed with the consent or connivance of any partner, or any person who was purporting to act as a partner, or

(b) to be attributable to any neglect on his part,

he as well as the partnership is guilty of an offence and liable to be proceeded against and punished accordingly.

(5) If an offence under paragraph (1) . . . committed by an unincorporated association (other than a partnership) is shown—

(a) to have been committed with the consent or connivance of an officer of the association or a member of its governing body, or any person who was purporting to act in any such capacity, or

(b) to be attributable to any neglect on his part,

he as well as the association is guilty of an offence and liable to be proceeded against and punished accordingly.

(6) Except in Scotland—

(a) the Authority may institute proceedings for an offence under these Regulations which relates to a specified contract;

(b) the OFT, and—

(i) in Great Britain, every local weights and measures authority,

(ii) in Northern Ireland, the Department of Enterprise, Trade and Investment,

may institute proceedings for any other offence under these Regulations.

NOTES

Paras (2), (4), (5): words omitted revoked by the Consumer Protection from Unfair Trading Regulations 2008, SI 2008/1277, reg 30(1), (3), Sch 2, Pt 2, para 110(1), (3), Sch 4, Pt 2.

[4343]

23 Functions of the Authority

The functions conferred on the Authority by these Regulations shall be treated as if they were conferred by the 2000 Act.

24–28 (*Reg 24 amends the Unfair Terms in Consumer Contracts Regulations 1999, SI 1999/2083, regs 3, 5 at* **[4194]**, **[4196]**; *reg 25 amends the Consumer Protection (Distance Selling) Regulations 2000, SI 2000/2334, regs 3, 5, 6 and revokes Sch 2 to those Regulations; regs 26–28 outside the scope of this work.*)

[4344]

29 Transitional provisions

(1) In relation to any contract made before 31st May 2005 which is a consumer credit agreement within the meaning of the 1974 Act and a regulated agreement within the meaning of that Act—

(a) regulations 7, 8, 10 and 11 apply subject to the modifications in paragraphs (2) to (5); and

(b) references in these Regulations to regulations 7, 8, 10 and 11 or to provisions contained in them shall be construed accordingly.

(2) In regulation 7—

(a) in paragraphs (1) to (3), before "Schedule 1" at each place where it occurs insert "paragraph 13 of"; and

(b) in paragraph (4)(b), before "Schedule 2" insert "paragraph 5 of".

(3) In regulation 8(1), for "contractual terms and conditions and the information specified in" at each place where it occurs substitute "information specified in paragraph 13 of".

(4) In regulation 10(3), omit—

(a) "the contractual terms and conditions and"; and

(b) "those terms and conditions and".

(5) In regulation 11(3), omit "the contractual terms and conditions and" at each place where it occurs.

SCHEDULE 1

INFORMATION REQUIRED PRIOR TO THE CONCLUSION OF THE CONTRACT

Regulations 7(1) and 8(1)

[4345]

1. The identity and the main business of the supplier, the geographical address at which the supplier is established and any other geographical address relevant to the consumer's relations with the supplier.

2. Where the supplier has a representative established in the consumer's State of residence, the identity of that representative and the geographical address relevant to the consumer's relations with him.

3. Where the consumer's dealings are with any professional other than the supplier, the identity of that professional, the capacity in which he is acting with respect to the consumer, and the geographical address relevant to the consumer's relations with that professional.

4. Where the supplier is registered in a trade or similar public register, the particulars of the register in which the supplier is entered and his registration number or an equivalent means of identification in that register.

5. Where the supplier's activity is subject to an authorisation scheme, the particulars of the relevant supervisory authority.

6. A description of the main characteristics of the financial service.

7. The total price to be paid by the consumer to the supplier for the financial service, including all related fees, charges and expenses, and all taxes paid via the supplier or, where an exact price cannot be indicated, the basis for the calculation of the price enabling the consumer to verify it.

8. Where relevant, notice indicating that: (i) the financial service is related to instruments involving special risks related to their specific features or the operations to be executed or whose price depends on fluctuations in the financial markets outside the supplier's control; and (ii) historical performances are no indicators for future performances.

9. Notice of the possibility that other taxes or costs may exist that are not paid via the supplier or imposed by him.

10. Any limitations of the period for which the information provided is valid.

11. The arrangements for payment and for performance.

12. Any specific additional cost for the consumer of using the means of distance communication, if such additional cost is charged.

13. Whether or not there is a right of cancellation and, where there is a right of cancellation, its duration and the conditions for exercising it, including information on the amount which the consumer may be required to pay in accordance with regulation 13, as well as the consequences of not exercising that right.

14. The minimum duration of the distance contract in the case of financial services to be performed indefinitely or recurrently.

15. Information on any rights the parties may have to terminate the distance contract early or unilaterally by virtue of the terms of the contract, including any penalties imposed by the contract in such cases.

16. Practical instructions for exercising the right to cancel in accordance with regulation 9 indicating, among other things, the address at which the notice of cancellation should be left or to which it should be sent by post, and any facsimile number or electronic mail address to which it should be sent.

17. The EEA State or States whose laws are taken by the supplier as a basis for the establishment of relations with the consumer prior to the conclusion of the distance contract.

18. Any contractual clause on the law applicable to the distance contract or on the competent court.

19. In which language, or languages: (i) the contractual terms and conditions, and the prior information specified in this Schedule, are supplied; and (ii) the supplier, with the agreement of the consumer, undertakes to communicate during the duration of the distance contract.

20. Whether or not there is an out-of-court complaint and redress mechanism for the consumer and, if so, the methods for having access to it.

21. The existence of guarantee funds or other compensation arrangements, except to the extent that they are required by Directive 94/19/EC of the European Parliament and of the Council of 30 May 1994 on deposit guarantee schemes or Directive 97/9/EC of the European Parliament and of the Council of 3 March 1997 on investor compensation schemes.

NOTES

Directive 94/19/EC of the European Parliament and of the Council: OJ L135, 31.5.1994, p 5.
Directive 97/9/EC of the European Parliament and of the Council: OJ L84, 26.3.1997, p 22.

SCHEDULE 2

INFORMATION REQUIRED IN THE CASE OF VOICE TELEPHONE COMMUNICATIONS

Regulation 7(4)(b)

[4346]

1. The identity of the person in contact with the consumer and his link with the supplier.

2. A description of the main characteristics of the financial service.

3. The total price to be paid by the consumer to the supplier for the financial service including all taxes paid via the supplier or, if an exact price cannot be indicated, the basis for the calculation of the price enabling the consumer to verify it.

4. Notice of the possibility that other taxes or costs may exist that are not paid via the supplier or imposed by him.

5. Whether or not there is a right to cancel and, where there is such a right, its duration and the conditions for exercising it, including information on the amount which the consumer may be required to pay in accordance with regulation 13, as well as the consequences of not exercising that right.

6. That other information is available on request and the nature of that information.

INSURANCE ACCOUNTS DIRECTIVE (LLOYD'S SYNDICATE AND AGGREGATE ACCOUNTS) REGULATIONS 2004

(SI 2004/3219)

NOTES

Made: 8 December 2004.
Authority: European Communities Act 1972, s 2(2).
Commencement: 31 December 2004.

ARRANGEMENT OF REGULATIONS

PART 1
GENERAL

1 Citation and commencement . . . [4347]
2 Interpretation . . . [4348]

PART 2
SYNDICATE ACCOUNTS

3 Preparation of syndicate annual accounts . . . [4349]
4 Preparation of syndicate underwriting year accounts . . . [4350]
5 Accounts to be sent to syndicate members, the Council and the Authority . . . [4351]
6 Publication of syndicate accounts . . . [4352]
7 Penalties for non-compliance . . . [4353]

PART 3
AGGREGATE ACCOUNTS

8 Preparation of aggregate accounts by Council of Lloyd's . . . [4354]
9 Approval and signing of aggregate accounts . . . [4355]

10 Preparation of annual report by the Council of Lloyd's . . . . . [4356]
11 Approval and signing of annual report . . . . . [4357]
12 Auditors' report . . . . . [4358]
13 Signature of auditors' report . . . . . [4359]
14 Appointment of and duties of auditors . . . . . [4360]
15 Aggregate accounts and annual report of Council to be delivered to the Authority and published . . . . . [4361]

PART 4
REGULATION BY THE FINANCIAL SERVICES AUTHORITY

16 Functions of the Financial Services Authority . . . . . [4362]

PART 5
TRANSITIONAL AND CONSEQUENTIAL PROVISIONS

17 Transitional provisions . . . . . [4363]

SCHEDULE

Modification of Part 7 of the 1985 Act for Syndicate Accounts . . . . . [4364]

PART 1
GENERAL

[4347]

1 Citation and commencement

These Regulations may be cited as the Insurance Accounts Directive (Lloyd's Syndicate and Aggregate Accounts) Regulations 2004 and come into force on 31st December 2004.

NOTES

These Regulations are revoked by the Insurance Accounts Directive (Lloyd's Syndicate and Aggregate Accounts) Regulations 2008, SI 2008/1950, reg 30 at **[4523]**, in relation to financial years beginning on or after 1 January 2009, subject to savings in relation to financial years beginning on or before 1 January 2008, and are replaced by the 2008 Regulations at **[4494]**.

[4348]

2 Interpretation

(1) In these Regulations—

"the 1985 Act" means the Companies Act 1985;

"the Authority" means the Financial Services Authority;

"the Council of Lloyd's" means the Council constituted by section 3 of the Lloyd's Act 1982;

"financial year" means the period of 12 months beginning on 1st January;

"Lloyd's byelaws" means the byelaws made under the Lloyd's Acts 1871 to 1982;

"managing agent" means a person who is permitted by the Council of Lloyd's, in the conduct of his business as an underwriting agent, to perform, for a member of Lloyd's, one or more of the following functions—

(a) underwriting contracts of insurance at Lloyd's;

(b) reinsuring such contracts in whole or in part;

(c) paying claims on such contracts;

"syndicate" means one or more persons, to whom a syndicate number has been assigned by or under the authority of the Council of Lloyd's, carrying out or effecting contracts of insurance written at Lloyd's.

(2) In these Regulations any reference to the accounts required by or prepared under regulation 3 is a reference to the annual accounts, annual report and auditors' report required by or prepared under paragraph (2) of that regulation.

(3) In these Regulations an underwriting year of account is closed—

(a) at the time when a contract of reinsurance to close that year of account, which complies with the requirements in the Lloyd's byelaws, takes effect; or

(b) in the case of a syndicate which consists of a single corporate member, at the time when an amount representing the provision for all known and unknown liabilities attributable to the closing year of account, is included in the underwriting account for the following underwriting year.

(4) Other expressions used in these Regulations have the meanings ascribed to them by the 1985 Act.

NOTES

Revoked as noted to reg 1 at **[4347]**.

PART 2
SYNDICATE ACCOUNTS

[4349]

3 Preparation of syndicate annual accounts

(1) Managing agents must prepare or cause to be prepared the accounts and reports required by paragraph (2), in respect of—

- *(a) each syndicate that they manage on 31st December; and*
- *(b) any syndicate that they were the last managing agent to manage during the preceding year and which has no managing agent on 31st December.*

(2) Managing agents must, for the financial year preceding 31st December, in respect of each syndicate—

- *(a) prepare the annual accounts and annual report; and*
- *(b) cause to be prepared such an auditors' report,*

as would be required under the provisions listed in paragraph (4) below if the syndicate were an insurance company formed and registered under the 1985 Act.

(3) The accounts required by this regulation must—

- *(a) be prepared within a period of 3 months beginning immediately after the end of the syndicate's financial year;*
- *(b) state that they are prepared under this regulation; and*
- *(c) comply with such of the requirements of the provisions in paragraph (4) as relate to the contents of the required accounts or reports, subject to the modifications in the Schedule to these Regulations.*

(4) The provisions referred to in paragraphs (2) and (3) the provisions are the following provisions of the 1985 Act—

- *(a) sections 226(1) and (2)(a),226A, 231 to 234, 234A, 235 to 237, 240, 242B, 255;*
- *(b) paragraphs 11 and 12 of Schedule 5;*
- *(c) paragraph 6 of Schedule 7;*
- *(d) Schedule 9A other than—*
    - *(i) paragraphs 10(2), 61, 64, 65, 72(2), 73;*
    - *(ii) in paragraph 2(2) the words from "but the following" to the end of that paragraph; and*
    - *(iii) Part 2 of that Schedule.*

(5) For the purposes of the provisions listed in paragraph (4) as applied to accounts prepared under this regulation, these Regulations shall be regarded as part of the requirements of the 1985 Act.

(6) Part 2 of the Companies Act 1989 (eligibility for appointment as auditors) applies to auditors appointed for the purposes of this regulation subject to any necessary modifications to take account of the fact that the syndicate is unincorporated.

(7) The Schedule to these Regulations has effect for the purpose of modifying the provisions of the 1985 Act listed in paragraph (4), in their application to syndicates.

NOTES

Revoked as noted to reg 1 at **[4347]**.

Note that para (4) is printed as it appears in the Queen's Printer version. It is thought that the words "the provisions" where they appear for the second time should be deleted.

[4350]

4 Preparation of syndicate underwriting year accounts

(1) Managing agents must, in respect of each syndicate for which Regulation 3(1) requires them to ensure the preparation of accounts and reports, prepare or cause to be prepared underwriting year accounts in accordance with paragraph (2), unless—

- *(a) no underwriting year of that syndicate has been closed in the preceding financial year or is being closed at the end of that financial year; or*
- *(b) the members of the syndicate for each underwriting year included in the underwriting year accounts, agree unanimously, in writing, that no underwriting year accounts shall be prepared in respect of that syndicate.*

(2) The underwriting year accounts must be an account which—

(a) *is prepared on an underwriting year basis; and*

(b) *gives a true and fair view of the result of that underwriting year at closure.*

(3) The accounts required by this regulation must—

(a) *be prepared within a period of 3 months beginning immediately after the end of the syndicate's financial year; and*

(b) *state that they are prepared under this regulation.*

(4) Managing agents must cause to be prepared an auditors' report on the underwriting year accounts required by this regulation stating whether a true and fair view is given of the result of the underwriting year at closure.

(5) Part 2 of the Companies Act 1989 (eligibility for appointment as auditors) applies to auditors appointed for the purposes of this regulation subject to any necessary modifications to take account of the fact that the syndicate is unincorporated.

NOTES

Revoked as noted to reg 1 at **[4347]**.

[4351]

5 Accounts to be sent to syndicate members, the Council and the Authority

(1) The managing agent responsible for the preparation of the accounts of a syndicate must send a copy of the accounts prepared under regulations 3 and 4 to every member of Lloyd's who participates in that syndicate and to the Council of Lloyd's, within 3 months from the end of the financial year.

(2) The managing agent responsible for the preparation of the accounts of a syndicate must send a copy of the accounts prepared under regulations 3 and 4 to the Authority within 6 months from the end of the financial year.

(3) References in this regulation to sending, include references to using electronic communications for sending copies of those documents to such address as may for the time being be notified to the managing agent by that person for that purpose.

NOTES

Revoked as noted to reg 1 at **[4347]**.

[4352]

6 Publication of syndicate accounts

Where a managing agent has sent accounts to the Council of Lloyd's under regulation 5, the Council must—

(a) *make available, on reasonable notice, those accounts for inspection by any person without charge and during business hours at the Council's head office for a period of three years from the date of signature of each document;*

(b) *supply to any person upon request a copy of those accounts (or such part of those accounts as may be requested) at a price not exceeding the administrative cost of making the copy, for a period of three years from the date of signature of each document.*

NOTES

Revoked as noted to reg 1 at **[4347]**.

[4353]

7 Penalties for non-compliance

(1) If the managing agent of a Lloyd's syndicate fails to comply with paragraph (1) of regulation 3, within the period referred to in paragraph (3) of that regulation, the managing agent and every person who was a director or partner of it immediately before the end of that period, is guilty of an offence and liable on summary conviction to a fine not exceeding level 5 on the standard scale.

(2) If the managing agent of a Lloyd's syndicate fails to comply with paragraph (1) of regulation 4, within the period referred to in paragraph (3) of that regulation, the managing agent and every person who was a director or partner of it immediately before the end of that period, is guilty of an offence and liable on summary conviction to a fine not exceeding level 5 on the standard scale.

(3) If accounts which are supplied under regulation 5, do not comply with the requirements of regulations 3 and 4, the managing agent of the Lloyd's syndicate and every person who was a director or partner of it at the time when the accounts were first made available for inspection or supplied, is guilty of an offence and liable on summary conviction to a fine not exceeding level 5 on the standard scale.

(4) If a managing agent fails to comply with regulation 5(1), it and every person who was a director or partner of it at the time when the failure took place is guilty of an offence and liable on summary conviction to a fine not exceeding level 5 on the standard scale.

(5) If a managing agent fails to comply with regulation 5(2), it and every person who was a director or partner of it at the time when the failure took place is guilty of an offence and liable on summary conviction to a fine not exceeding level 5 on the standard scale.

(6) It is a defence for a person charged with an offence under this regulation to show that he took all reasonable steps for securing that the requirements in question would be complied with.

(7) Section 731 of the 1985 Act applies to any offence under this regulation.

NOTES

Revoked as noted to reg 1 at **[4347]**.

PART 3
AGGREGATE ACCOUNTS

[4354]

8 Preparation of aggregate accounts by Council of Lloyd's

(1) The members of the Council of Lloyd's must prepare aggregate accounts in respect of each financial year by cumulating all the syndicate annual accounts prepared in accordance with regulation 3 for that year.

(2) The aggregate accounts must consist of—

- *(a) an aggregate balance sheet as at the last day of the year; and*
- *(b) an aggregate profit and loss account.*

Those accounts are referred to in these Regulations as the "aggregate accounts".

(3) The aggregate accounts must—

- *(a) be prepared within the period of 6 months beginning immediately after the end of the financial year; and*
- *(b) state that they are prepared under these Regulations.*

(4) The aggregate accounts must comply with the provisions of Schedule 9A to the 1985 Act as to the form and content of the aggregate balance sheet and aggregate profit and loss account, and additional information to be provided by way of notes to the accounts, apart from the provisions set out in paragraph (5).

(5) The provisions are the following—

- *(a) paragraphs 10(2), 61, 64, 65, 68, 70, 72(2), 73;*
- *(b) in paragraph 2(2) the words from "but the following" to the end; and*
- *(c) Part 2 of that Schedule.*

NOTES

Revoked as noted to reg 1 at **[4347]**.

[4355]

9 Approval and signing of aggregate accounts

(1) The aggregate accounts must be approved by the Council of Lloyd's and signed on behalf of the Council by a member of the Council.

(2) The signature must be on the aggregate balance sheet.

(3) Every copy of the aggregate balance sheet which is circulated, published or issued must state the name of the person who signed it on behalf of the Council.

(4) The copy of the aggregate balance sheet which is delivered to the Authority must be signed on behalf of the Council by a member of the Council.

NOTES

Revoked as noted to reg 1 at **[4347]**.

[4356]

10 Preparation of annual report by the Council of Lloyd's

(1) The members of the Council of Lloyd's must prepare an annual report on the insurance business carried on by the members of Lloyd's containing—

(a) a fair review of the insurance business carried on by the members of Lloyd's during the financial year, and of the position of the Lloyd's market at the end of it, consisting of a balanced and comprehensive analysis of the development and performance of the business of the members of Lloyd's; and

(b) a description of the principal risks and uncertainties facing the Lloyd's market.

(2) The business review in the Council of Lloyd's' annual report must include, to the extent necessary for an understanding of the development, performance or position of the insurance business of the members of Lloyd's—

(a) analysis using financial key performance indicators; and

(b) where appropriate, analysis using other key performance indicators.

(3) The review must, where appropriate, include references to and additional explanations of amounts included in the aggregate accounts.

(4) In this regulation "key performance indicators" means factors by reference to which the development, performance or position of the insurance business of the members of Lloyd's can be measured most effectively.

NOTES

Revoked as noted to reg 1 at **[4347]**.

[4357]

11 Approval and signing of annual report

(1) The annual report prepared under regulation 10 above must be approved by the Council of Lloyd's and signed on behalf of the Council by a member of the Council.

(2) Every copy of the annual report which is circulated, published or issued, must state the name of the person who signed it on behalf of the Council.

(3) The copy of the annual report which is delivered to the Authority must be signed on behalf of the Council by a member of the Council.

NOTES

Revoked as noted to reg 1 at **[4347]**.

[4358]

12 Auditors' report

(1) The members of the Council of Lloyd's must obtain an auditors' report on the aggregate accounts.

(2) The auditors' report shall include—

(a) an introduction identifying the aggregate accounts that are the subject of the report and the financial reporting framework that has been applied in their preparation;

(b) a description of the scope of the review carried out by the auditors and identifying the standards in accordance with which the review was conducted;

(c) a clear statement as to whether, in their opinion, the aggregate accounts have been properly prepared in accordance with the requirements of these Regulations and whether those accounts are correctly aggregated.

(3) The auditors' report—

(a) must be either unqualified or qualified; and

(b) must include a reference to any matters to which the auditors wish to draw attention by way of emphasis without qualifying the report.

(4) The auditors' report must state whether, in their opinion, the annual report of the Council of Lloyd's—

(a) is consistent with the aggregate accounts for the same financial year; and

(b) has been prepared in accordance with these Regulations.

NOTES

Revoked as noted to reg 1 at **[4347]**.

[4359]

13 Signature of auditors' report

(1) The auditors' report must state the names of the auditors and be signed and dated by them.

(2) Every copy of the auditors' report which is circulated, published or issued must state the names of the auditors.

(3) The copy of the auditors' report which is delivered to the Authority must state the names of the auditors and be signed and dated by them.

(4) References in this regulation to signature by the auditors are, where the office of auditor is held by a body corporate or partnership, to signature in the name of the body corporate or partnership by a person authorised to sign on its behalf.

NOTES

Revoked as noted to reg 1 at **[4347]**.

[4360]

14 Appointment of and duties of auditors

(1) Part 2 of the Companies Act 1989 (eligibility for appointment as auditors) applies to auditors appointed by the Council of Lloyd's to report on the aggregate accounts.

(2) The auditors of the aggregate accounts must, in preparing their report, carry out such investigations as will enable them to form an opinion as to whether the aggregate accounts are properly prepared and a correct aggregation of the syndicate accounts which have been cumulated to prepare them.

(3) If those auditors are of the opinion that the aggregate accounts are not properly prepared or not a correct aggregation of the syndicate accounts which have been cumulated to prepare them, the auditors must state that fact in their report.

(4) If those auditors fail to obtain all the information and explanations which, to the best of their knowledge and belief, are necessary for the purposes of their report, they must state that fact in their report.

NOTES

Revoked as noted to reg 1 at **[4347]**.

[4361]

15 Aggregate accounts and annual report of Council to be delivered to the Authority and published

(1) The Council of Lloyd's must deliver to the Authority a copy of the aggregate accounts and its annual report on each financial year within a period of 6 months from the end of that year.

(2) The Council of Lloyd's must—

- *(a) make available, on reasonable notice, the latest aggregate accounts and its latest annual report for inspection by any person, without charge and during business hours, at the Council's head office; and*
- *(b) supply to any person upon request a copy of those accounts or that report (or such part of them as may be requested) at a price not exceeding the administrative cost of making the copy.*

NOTES

Revoked as noted to reg 1 at **[4347]**.

PART 4
REGULATION BY THE FINANCIAL SERVICES AUTHORITY

[4362]

16 Functions of the Financial Services Authority

(1) The Authority has responsibility for administering the system of regulation of Lloyd's syndicates and the Council of Lloyd's provided for by these Regulations.

(2) Proceedings for an offence under these Regulations may be instituted only—

- *(a) by the Authority or the Secretary of State; or*
- *(b) by or with the consent of the Director of Public Prosecutions.*

(3) In exercising its power to institute proceedings for an offence under these Regulations, the Authority must comply with any conditions or restrictions imposed in writing by the Treasury.

(4) The Authority may increase any fee which it charges managing agents under the Financial Services and Markets Act 2000 to take account of the expenses incurred in carrying out its functions under these Regulations.

NOTES

Revoked as noted to reg 1 at **[4347]**.

PART 5
TRANSITIONAL AND CONSEQUENTIAL PROVISIONS

[4363]

17 Transitional provisions

(1) The managing agent of a syndicate need not prepare accounts in accordance with regulations 3 and 4 with respect to a financial year of the syndicate commencing on or before 31st December 2004.

(2) Where advantage is taken of paragraph (1), regulation 7 does not apply to the managing agent.

(3) The members of the Council of Lloyd's need not—

(a) prepare aggregate accounts in accordance with regulation 8;

(b) prepare an annual report in accordance with regulation 10; or

(c) obtain an auditors' report in accordance with regulation 12

with respect to a financial year commencing on or before 31st December 2004.

(4) Nothing in this regulation exempts a managing agent or the Council of Lloyd's from any requirement to include corresponding amounts from previous financial years in syndicate or aggregate accounts prepared in accordance with these Regulations.

NOTES

Revoked as noted to reg 1 at **[4347]**.

18 *(Revokes the Insurance Accounts Directive (Miscellaneous Insurance Undertakings) Regulations 1993, SI 1993/3245, reg 4(2), and amends regs 5, 6 thereof at* **[4070]**, **[4071]**; *revoked as noted to reg 1 at* **[4347]**.)

SCHEDULE
MODIFICATION OF PART 7 OF THE 1985 ACT FOR SYNDICATE ACCOUNTS

Regulation 3

[4364]

1. The accounts prepared under regulation 3 must comply with the provisions of the 1985 Act set out in paragraph (4) of that regulation subject to any necessary modifications to take account of the fact that syndicates are unincorporated.

2. Where any of the provisions of the 1985 Act set out in regulation 3(4) impose a duty on the directors of a company, that provision shall, in the case of a syndicate, impose the same duty upon the managing agent of the syndicate.

3. The following sections of the 1985 Act are modified in their application to syndicates as follows.

4. Section 226 (duty to prepare individual accounts) is modified as follows—

(a) in subsection 226(2) for the word "may" substitute "must"; and

(b) at the end of subsection 226(2)(a), "or" is omitted;

5. Section 231 (disclosure required in notes to accounts: related undertakings) is modified so that subsection (7) is omitted.

6.—(1) Section 232 (disclosure required in notes to accounts: emoluments and other benefits of directors and others) is modified as follows—

(a) For subsection (1) there shall be substituted the following—

"(1) The information specified in subsection (2) must be given in notes to the syndicate's annual accounts.";

(b) For subsection (2) substitute the following—

"(2) That information is—

(a) the aggregate amount charged to a syndicate by its managing agent, in respect of emoluments paid to the managing agents' directors, the active underwriter and (where applicable) the run-off manager of the syndicate, in the last financial year;

(b) the specific amount charged to a syndicate by its managing agent in respect of emoluments paid to the syndicate's active underwriter and (where applicable) its run-off manager in the last financial year.";

(c) for subsection (3) substitute the following—

"(3) In this section "emoluments"—

(a) includes salaries, fees and bonuses, sums paid by way of expenses allowance (so far as they are chargeable to United Kingdom income tax) and, subject to paragraph (b), the estimated money value of any other benefits received by him otherwise than in cash; but

(b) does not include any of the following, namely—

(i) the value of any share options granted or the amount of any gains made on the exercise of any such options;

(ii) any contributions paid, or treated as paid, in respect of him under any pension scheme or any benefits to which he is entitled under any such scheme; or

(iii) any money or other assets paid, received or receivable under any long term incentive scheme."; and

(d) subsection (4) is omitted.

(2) In this paragraph—

"active underwriter" means, in relation to a syndicate, the individual at or deemed by the Council to be at, the underwriting box with principal authority to accept risks on behalf of the members of the syndicate;

"run-off manager" means, in relation to a run-off syndicate, the person who has principal authority to negotiate or place contracts of reinsurance or negotiate and settle the payment of claims on contracts of insurance or reinsurance on behalf of the members of a syndicate;

"run-off syndicate" means a syndicate which no longer accepts new or renewal insurance business (other than the variation or extension of risks previously underwritten, or reinsurance to close of an earlier year of account of that syndicate).

7. *Section 233 (approval and signing of accounts) is modified as follows—*

(a) for subsection (1) substitute the following—

"(1) A syndicate's accounts shall be approved and signed by the syndicate's managing agent and where the managing agent is a body corporate or a partnership the accounts must be signed by a director or partner of the managing agent, authorised to sign on its behalf.";

(b) for subsection (3) substitute the following—

"(3) Every copy of the balance sheet which is circulated published, issued or delivered to the Authority must state the name of the person who signed the balance sheet on behalf of the syndicate's managing agent."; and

(c) subsection (5) is omitted.

8. *Section 234 (duty to prepare directors' report) is modified as follows—*

(a) in subsection (1), omit paragraph (b);

(b) in subsection (2) omit "the names of the persons who, at any time during the financial year were directors of the company, and";

(c) subsections (5) and (6) are omitted.

9. *Section 234A (approval and signing of directors' report) is modified as follows—*

(a) for subsection (1) substitute the following—

"(1) The directors' report shall be approved and signed by the syndicate's managing agent and where the managing agent is a body corporate or a partnership, the report shall be signed by a director or partner of the managing agent, authorised to sign on its behalf.";

(b) for subsection (2) there shall be substituted the following—

"(2) Every copy of the report which is circulated, published, issued or delivered to the Authority shall state the name of the person who signed the balance sheet on behalf of the syndicate's managing agent."; and

(c) subsections (3) and (4) are omitted.

10. *Section 235 (auditors' report) is modified so that subsection (1) is substituted as follows—*

"(1) A syndicate's auditors shall make a report to the syndicate's members on all annual accounts of the syndicate of which copies are to be sent to the syndicate members during the auditors' tenure of office.".

11. *Section 236 (signature of auditors report) is modified as follows—*

(a) for subsection (2) substitute the following—

"(2) Every copy of the auditors' report which is circulated, published, issued or delivered to the Authority shall state the names of the auditors and be signed by them."; and

(b) subsections (3) and (4) are omitted.

12. *Section 240 (requirements in connections with publication of accounts) is modified as follows—*

(a) in subsection (5), for "as required to be delivered to the registrar under section 242" substitute "as required to be sent to the Authority under regulation 5(2) of the Insurance Accounts Directive (Lloyd's Syndicate and Aggregate Accounts) Regulations 2004";

(b) subsection (6) is omitted.

13. *Schedule 9A (form and content of accounts of insurance companies and groups) is modified by the insertion of the following paragraph after paragraph 72—*

*"**72A.** A description, which need not include particulars of funds held by members of the syndicate, must be given of funds which members are required to hold at Lloyd's.".*

NOTES

Revoked as noted to reg 1 at **[4347]**.

INSURERS (WINDING-UP) RULES (NORTHERN IRELAND) 2005

(SR 2005/399)

NOTES

Made: 18 August 2005.

Authority: Financial Services and Markets Act 2000, s 379; Insolvency (Northern Ireland) Order 1989, art 359.

Commencement: 19 September 2005.

ARRANGEMENT OF RULES

1 Citation, commencement and revocation [4365]
2 Interpretation [4366]
3 Application [4367]
4 Appointment of liquidator [4368]
5 Maintenance of separate financial records for long-term and other business in winding-up [4369]
6 Valuation of general business policies [4370]
7 Valuation of long-term policies [4371]
8 [4372]
9 Attribution of liabilities to company's long-term business [4373]
10 Attribution of assets to company's long-term business [4374]
11 Excess of long-term business assets [4375]
12 Actuarial advice [4376]
13 Utilisation of excess of assets [4377]
14 [4378]
15 Custody of assets [4379]
16 Maintenance of accounting, valuation and other records [4380]
17 Additional powers in relation to long-term business [4381]
18 Accounts and audit [4382]
19 Security by the liquidator and special manager [4383]
20 Proof of debts [4384]
21 Failure to pay premiums [4385]
22 Notice of valuation of policy [4386]
23 Dividends to creditors [4387]
24 Meetings of creditors [4388]
25 Remuneration of liquidator carrying on long-term business [4389]
26 Apportionment of costs payable out of the assets [4390]
27 Notice of stop order [4391]

SCHEDULES:

Schedule 1—Rules for valuing general business policies . . . [4392]
Schedule 2—Rules for valuing non-linked life policies, non-linked deferred annuity policies, non-linked annuities in payment, unitised non-linked policies and capital redemption policies . . . [4393]
Schedule 3—Rules for valuing life policies and deferred annuity policies which are linked policies . . . [4394]
Schedule 4—Rules for valuing long-term policies which are not dealt with in Schedules 2 or 3 . . . [4395]
Schedule 5—Rules for valuing long-term policies where a stop order has been made . . . [4396]
Schedule 6—Forms . . . [4397]

[4365]

1 Citation, commencement and revocation

(1) These Rules may be cited as the Insurers (Winding-Up) Rules (Northern Ireland) 2005 and shall come into operation on 19th September 2005.

(2) The Insurance Companies (Winding-Up) Rules (Northern Ireland) 1992 are hereby revoked.

NOTES

Commencement: 19 September 2005.

[4366]

2 Interpretation

(1) In these Rules—

"the 2000 Act" means the Financial Services and Markets Act 2000;

"the Authority" means the Financial Services Authority;

"company" means an insurer which is being wound up;

"contract of general insurance" and "contract of long-term insurance" have the meaning given by Article 3(1) of the Financial Services and Markets Act 2000 (Regulated Activities) Order 2001;

"the Department" means the Department of Enterprise, Trade and Investment;

"excess of the long-term business assets" means the amount, if any, by which the value of the assets representing the fund or funds maintained by the company in respect of its long-term business as at the liquidation date exceeds the value as at that date of the liabilities of the company attributable to that business;

"excess of the other business assets" means the amount, if any, by which the value of the assets of the company which do not represent the fund or funds maintained by the company in respect of its long-term business as at the liquidation date exceeds the value as at that date of the liabilities of the company (other than liabilities in respect of share capital) which are not attributable to that business;

"Financial Services Compensation Scheme" means the scheme established under section 213 of the 2000 Act;

"general business" means the business of effecting or carrying out a contract of general insurance;

"the general regulations" means the Insolvency Regulations (Northern Ireland) 1996;

"insurer" has the meaning given by Article 2 of the Financial Services and Markets Act 2000 (Insolvency) (Definition of "Insurer") Order 2001;

"linked liability" means any liability under a policy the effecting of which constitutes the carrying on of long-term business the amount of which is determined by reference to—

(a) the value of property of any description (whether or not specified in the policy),

(b) fluctuations in the value of such property,

(c) income from any such property, or

(d) fluctuations in an index of the value of such property;

"linked policy" means a policy which provides for linked liabilities and a policy which when made provided for linked liabilities is deemed to be a linked policy even if the policy holder has elected to convert his rights under the policy so that at the liquidation date there are no longer linked liabilities under the policy;

"liquidation date" means the date of the winding-up order or the date on which a resolution for the winding-up of the company is passed by the members of the company (or the policy holders in the case of a mutual insurance company) and, if both a winding-up order and winding-up resolution have been made, the earlier date;

"long-term business" means the business of effecting or carrying out any contract of long-term insurance;

"non-linked policy" means a policy which is not a linked policy;
"the 1979 Order" means the Industrial Assurance (Northern Ireland) Order 1979;
"the 1986 Order" means the Companies (Northern Ireland) Order 1986;
"the 1989 Order" means the Insolvency (Northern Ireland) Order 1989;
"other business", in relation to a company carrying on long-term business, means such of the business of the company as is not long-term business;
"the principal Rules" means the Insolvency Rules (Northern Ireland) 1991;
"stop order", in relation to a company, means an order of the High Court made under section 376(2) of the 2000 Act, ordering the liquidator to stop carrying on the long-term business of the company;
"unit" in relation to a policy means any unit (whether or not described as a unit in the policy) by reference to the numbers and value of which the amount of the liabilities under the policy at any time is measured.

(2) Unless the context otherwise requires, words or expressions contained in these Rules bear the same meaning as in the principal Rules, the general regulations, the 1989 Order, the 2000 Act or any statutory modification thereof respectively.

(3) The Interpretation Act (Northern Ireland) 1954 shall apply to these Rules as it applies to an Act of the Northern Ireland Assembly.

NOTES

Commencement: 19 September 2005.

[4367]

3 Application

(1) These Rules apply to proceedings for the winding-up of an insurer which commence on or after the date on which these Rules come into operation.

(2) These Rules supplement the principal Rules and the general regulations which continue to apply to the proceedings in the winding-up of an insurer under the 1989 Order as they apply to proceedings in the winding-up of any company under that Order; but in the event of a conflict between these Rules and the principal Rules or the general regulations these Rules prevail.

NOTES

Commencement: 19 September 2005.

[4368]

4 Appointment of liquidator

Where the High Court is considering whether to appoint a liquidator under—

(a) Article 118(4) of the 1989 Order (appointment of liquidator where conflict between creditors and contributories), or

(b) Article 119 of the 1989 Order (appointment of liquidator following administration or voluntary arrangement),

the manager of the Financial Services Compensation Scheme may appear and make representations to the Court as to the person to be appointed.

NOTES

Commencement: 19 September 2005.

[4369]

5 Maintenance of separate financial records for long-term and other business in winding-up

(1) This rule applies in the case of a company carrying on long-term business in whose case no stop order has been made.

(2) The liquidator shall prepare and keep separate financial records in respect of the long-term business and the other business of the company.

(3) Paragraphs (4) and (5) apply in the case of a company to which this rule applies which also carries on permitted general business ("a hybrid insurer").

(4) Where, before the liquidation date, a hybrid insurer has, or should properly have, apportioned the assets and liabilities attributable to its permitted general business to its long-term business for the purposes of any accounts, those assets and liabilities must be apportioned to its long-term business for the purposes of complying with paragraph (2) of this rule.

(5) Where, before the liquidation date, a hybrid insurer has, or should properly have, apportioned the assets and liabilities attributable to its permitted general business other than to its long-term business for the purposes of any accounts, those assets and liabilities must be apportioned to its other business for the purposes of complying with paragraph (2) of this rule.

(6) Regulation 10 of the general regulations (financial records) applies only in relation to the company's other business.

(7) In relation to the long-term business, the liquidator shall, with a view to the long-term business of the company being transferred to another insurer, maintain such accounting, valuation and other records as will enable such other insurer upon the transfer being effected to comply with the requirements of any rules made by the Authority under Part X of the 2000 Act relating to accounts and statements of insurers.

(8) In paragraphs (4) and (5)—

(a) "accounts" means any accounts or statements maintained by the company in compliance with a requirement under the 1986 Order or any rules made by the Authority under Part X of the 2000 Act;

(b) "permitted general business" means the business of effecting or carrying out a contract of general insurance where the risk insured against relates to either accident or sickness.

NOTES

Commencement: 19 September 2005.

[4370]

6 Valuation of general business policies

Except in relation to amounts which have fallen due for payment before the liquidation date and liabilities referred to in paragraph 2(1)(b) of Schedule 1, the holder of a general business policy shall be admitted as a creditor in relation to his policy without proof for an amount equal to the value of the policy and for this purpose the value of a policy shall be determined in accordance with Schedule 1.

NOTES

Commencement: 19 September 2005.

[4371]

7 Valuation of long-term policies

(1) This Rule applies in relation to a company's long-term business where no stop order has been made.

(2) In relation to a claim under a policy which has fallen due for payment before the liquidation date, a policy holder shall be admitted as a creditor without proof for such amount as appears from the records of the company to be due in respect of that claim.

(3) In all other respects a policy holder shall be admitted as a creditor in relation to his policy without proof for an amount equal to the value of the policy and for this purpose the value of a policy of any class shall be determined in the manner applicable to policies of that class provided by Schedules 2, 3 and 4.

(4) This Rule applies in relation to a person entitled to apply for a free paid-up policy under Article 30 of the 1979 Order (provisions as to forfeited policies) and to whom no such policy has been issued before the liquidation date (whether or not it was applied for) as if such a policy had been issued immediately before the liquidation date—

(a) for the minimum amount determined in accordance with Article 30(2) and (3) of the 1979 Order, or

(b) if the liquidator is satisfied that it was the practice of the company during the five years immediately before the liquidation date to issue policies under Article 30 of that Order in excess of the minimum amounts so determined, for the amount determined in accordance with that practice.

NOTES

Commencement: 19 September 2005.

[4372]

8— (1) This Rule applies in relation to a company's long-term business where a stop order has been made.

(2) In relation to a claim under a policy which has fallen due for payment on or after the liquidation date and before the date of the stop order, a policy holder shall be admitted as a creditor without proof for such amount as appears from the records of the company and of the liquidator to be due in respect of that claim.

(3) In all other respects a policy holder shall be admitted as a creditor in relation to his policy without proof for an amount equal to the value of the policy and for this purpose the value of a policy of any class shall be determined in the manner applicable to policies of that class provided

by Schedule 5.

(4) Rule 7(4) applies for the purposes of this Rule as if references to the liquidation date (other than that in sub-paragraph (b) of that paragraph) were references to the date of the stop order.

NOTES

Commencement: 19 September 2005.

[4373]

9 Attribution of liabilities to company's long-term business

(1) This Rule applies in the case of a company carrying on long-term business if at the liquidation date there are liabilities of the company in respect of which it is not clear from the accounting and other records of the company whether they are or not attributable to the company's long-term business.

(2) The liquidator shall, in such manner and according to such accounting principles as he shall determine, identify the liabilities referred to in paragraph (1) as attributable or not attributable to a company's long-term business and those liabilities shall for the purpose of the winding-up be deemed as at the liquidation date to be attributable or not as the case may be.

(3) For the purpose of paragraph (2) the liquidator may—

(a) determine that some liabilities are attributable to the company's long-term business and that others are not (the first method); or

(b) determine that a part of a liability shall be attributable to the company's long-term business and that the remainder of the liability is not (the second method),

and he may use the first method for some of the liabilities and the second method for the remainder of them.

(4) Notwithstanding anything in paragraph (1) to (3), the High Court may order that the determination of which (if any) of the liabilities referred to in paragraph (1) are attributable to the company's long-term business and which (if any) are not shall be made in such manner and by such methods as the Court may direct or the Court may itself make the determination.

NOTES

Commencement: 19 September 2005.

[4374]

10 Attribution of assets to company's long-term business

(1) This Rule applies in the case of a company carrying on long-term business if at the liquidation date there are assets of the company in respect of which—

(a) it is not clear from the accounting and other records of the company whether they do or do not represent the fund or funds maintained by the company in respect of its long-term business, and

(b) it cannot be inferred from the source of the income out of which those assets were provided whether they do or do not represent those funds.

(2) Subject to paragraph (6) the liquidator shall determine which (if any) of the assets referred to in paragraph (1) are attributable to those funds and which (if any) are not and those assets shall, for the purpose of the winding-up, be deemed as at the liquidation date to represent those funds or not in accordance with the liquidator's determination.

(3) For the purpose of paragraph (2) the liquidator may—

(a) determine that some of those assets shall be attributable to those funds and that others of them shall not (the first method); or

(b) determine that a part of the value of one of those assets shall be attributable to those funds and that the remainder of that value shall not (the second method),

and he may use the first method for some of those assets and the second method for others of them.

(4)

(a) In making the attribution the liquidator's objective shall in the first instance be so far as possible to reduce any deficit that may exist, at the liquidation date and before any attribution is made, either in the company's long-term business or in its other business.

(b) If there is a deficit in both the company's long-term business and its other business the attribution shall be in the ratio that the amount of the one deficit bears to the amount of the other until the deficits are eliminated.

(c) Thereafter the attribution shall be in the ratio which the aggregate amount of the liabilities attributable to the company's long-term business bears to the aggregate amount of the liabilities not so attributable.

(5) For the purpose of paragraph (4) the value of a liability of the company shall, if it falls to be valued under Rule 6 or 7, have the same value as it has under that Rule but otherwise it shall have such valued as would have been included in relation to it in a balance sheet of the company prepared in accordance with the 1986 Order as at the liquidation date; and for the purpose of determining the ratio referred to in paragraph (4) but not for the purpose of determining the amount of any deficit therein referred to, the net balance of shareholders' funds shall be included in the liabilities not attributable to the company's long-term business.

(6) Notwithstanding anything in paragraphs (1) to (5), the High Court may order that the determination of which (if any) of the assets referred to in paragraph (1) are attributable to the fund or funds maintained by the company in respect of its long-term business and which (if any) are not shall be made in such manner and by such methods as the Court may direct or the Court may itself make the determination.

NOTES

Commencement: 19 September 2005.

[4375]

11 Excess of long-term business assets

(1) Where the company is one carrying on long-term business and in whose case no stop order has been made, for the purpose of determining the amount, if any, of the excess of the long-term business assets, there shall be included amongst the liabilities of the company attributable to its long-term business an amount determined by the liquidator in respect of liabilities and expenses likely to be incurred in connection with the transfer of the company's long-term business as a going concern to another insurance company being liabilities not included in the validation of the long-term policies made in pursuance of Rule 7.

(2) Where the liquidator is carrying on the long-term business of an insurer with a view to that business being transferred as a going concern to a person or persons ("transferee") who may lawfully carry out those contracts (or substitute policies being issued by another insurer), the liquidator may, in addition to any amounts paid by the Financial Services Compensation Scheme for the benefit of the transferee to secure such a transfer or to procure substitute policies being issued, pay to the transferee or other insurer all or part of such funds or assets as are attributable to the long-term business being transferred or substituted.

NOTES

Commencement: 19 September 2005.

[4376]

12 Actuarial advice

(1) Before doing any of the following, that is to say—

- (a) determining the value of a policy in accordance with Schedules 1 to 5 (other than paragraph 3 of Schedule 1);
- (b) identifying long-term liabilities and assets in accordance with Rules 9 and 10;
- (c) determining the amount (if any) of the excess of the long-term business assets in accordance with Rule 11;
- (d) determining the terms on which he will accept payment of overdue premiums under Rule 21(1) or the amount and nature of any compensation under Rule 21(2);

the liquidator shall obtain and consider advice thereon (including an estimate of any value or amount required to be determined) from an actuary.

(2) Before seeking, for the purpose of valuing a policy, the direction of the High Court as to the assumption of a particular rate of interest or the employment of any rates of mortality or disability, the liquidator shall obtain and consider advice thereon from an actuary.

NOTES

Commencement: 19 September 2005.

[4377]

13 Utilisation of excess of assets

(1) Except at the direction of the High Court, no distribution may be made out of and no transfer to another insurer may be made of—

- (a) any part of the excess of the long-term business assets which has been transferred to the other business; or
- (b) any part of the excess of the other business assets, which has been transferred to the long-term business.

(2) Before giving a direction under paragraph (1) the High Court may require the liquidator to advertise the proposal to make a distribution or a transfer in such manner as the Court shall direct.

NOTES

Commencement: 19 September 2005.

[4378]

14 In the case of a company carrying on long-term business in whose case no stop order has been made, Regulation 5 of the general regulations (payments into the Insolvency Account) applies only in relation to the company's other business.

NOTES

Commencement: 19 September 2005.

[4379]

15 Custody of assets

(1) The Department may, in the case of a company carrying on long-term business in whose case no stop order has been made, require that the whole or a specified proportion of the assets representing the fund or funds maintained by the company in respect of its long-term business shall be held by a person approved by it for the purpose as trustee for the company.

(2) No assets held by a person as trustee for a company in compliance with a requirement imposed under this Rule shall, so long as the requirement is in force, be released except with the consent of the Department but they may be transposed by the trustee into other assets by any transaction or series of transactions on the written instructions of the liquidator.

(3) The liquidator may not grant any mortgage or charge of assets which are held by a person as trustee for the company in compliance with a requirement imposed under this Rule except with the consent of the Department.

NOTES

Commencement: 19 September 2005.

[4380]

16 Maintenance of accounting, valuation and other records

(1) In the case of a company carrying on long-term business in whose case no stop order has been made, Regulation 10 of the general regulations (financial records) applies only in relation to the company's other business.

(2) The liquidator of such a company shall, with a view to the long-term business of the company being transferred to another insurer, maintain such accounting, valuation and other records as will enable such other insurer upon the transfer being effected to comply with the requirements of any rules made by the Authority under Part X of the 2000 Act relating to accounts and statements of insurers.

NOTES

Commencement: 19 September 2005.

[4381]

17 Additional powers in relation to long-term business

(1) In the case of a company carrying on long-term business in whose case no stop order has been made, Regulation 9 of the general regulations (interest) applies only in relation to the company's other business.

(2) The liquidator of a company carrying on long-term business shall, so long as no stop order has been made, have power to do all such things as may be necessary to the performance of his duties under section 376(2) of the 2000 Act (continuation of contracts of long-term insurance where insurer in liquidation) but the Department may require him—

(a) not to make investments of a specified class or description,

(b) to realise, before the expiration of a specified period, the whole or a specified proportion of investments of a specified class or description held by the liquidator.

NOTES

Commencement: 19 September 2005.

[4382]
18 Accounts and audit

(1) In the case of a company carrying on long-term business in whose case no stop order has been made, Regulation 12 of the general regulations (liquidator carrying on business) applies only in relation to the company's other business.

(2) The liquidator of such a company shall supply the Department, at such times or intervals as it may specify, with such accounts as it may specify and audited in such manner as it may require and with such information about specified matters and verified in such specified manner as it may require.

(3) The liquidator of such a company shall, if required to do so by the Department, instruct an actuary to investigate the financial condition of the company's long-term business and to report thereon in such manner as the Department may specify.

NOTES

Commencement: 19 September 2005.

[4383]
19 Security by the liquidator and special manager

In the case of a company carrying on long-term business in whose case no stop order has been made, Rule 4.217 of the principal Rules (security) applies separately to the company's long-term business and to its other business.

NOTES

Commencement: 19 September 2005.

[4384]
20 Proof of debts

(1) This Rule applies in the case of a company carrying on long-term business and in whose case no stop order has been made.

(2) The liquidator may in relation to the company's long-term business and to its other business fix different days on or before which the creditors of the company who are required to prove their debts or claims are to prove their debts or claims and he may fix one of those days without at the same time fixing the other.

(3) In submitting a proof of any debt a creditor may claim the whole or any part of such debt as attributable to the company's long-term business or to its other business or he may make no such attribution.

(4) When he admits any debt, in whole or in part, the liquidator shall state in writing how much of what he admits is attributable to the company's long-term business and how much to the company's other business.

NOTES

Commencement: 19 September 2005.

[4385]
21 Failure to pay premiums

(1) The liquidator may in the course of carrying on the company's long-term business and on such terms as he thinks fit accept payment of a premium even though the payment is tendered after the date on which under the terms of the policy it was finally due to be paid.

(2) The liquidator may in the course of carrying on the company's long-term business, and having regard to the general practice of insurers, compensate a policy holder whose policy has lapsed in consequence of a failure to pay any premium by issuing a free paid-up policy for reduced benefits or otherwise as the liquidator thinks fit.

NOTES

Commencement: 19 September 2005.

[4386]
22 Notice of valuation of policy

(1) Before paying a dividend in respect of claims other than under contracts of long-term insurance, the liquidator shall give notice of the value of each general business policy, as determined by him in accordance with Rule 6, to the persons appearing from the records of the company or otherwise to be entitled to an interest in that policy and he shall do so in such manner as the High Court may direct.

(2) Before paying a dividend in respect of claims under contracts of long-term insurance and where a stop order has not been made in relation to the company, the liquidator shall give notice to the persons appearing from the records of the company or otherwise to be entitled to a payment under or to an interest in a long-term policy of the amount of that payment or the value of that policy as determined by him in accordance with Rule 7(2) or (3), as the case may be.

(3) If a stop order is made in relation to the company, the liquidator shall give notice to all the persons appearing from the records of the company or otherwise to be entitled to a payment under or to an interest in a long-term policy of the amount of that payment or the value of that policy as determined by him in accordance with Rule 8(2) or (3), as the case may be, and he shall give that notice in such manner as the High Court may direct.

(4) Any person to whom notice is so given shall be bound by the value so determined unless and until the High Court otherwise orders.

(5) Paragraphs (2) and (3) have effect as though references therein to persons appearing to be entitled to an interest in a long-term policy and to the value of that policy included, respectively, references to persons appearing to be entitled to apply for a free paid-up policy under Article 30 of the 1979 Order and to the value of that entitlement under Rule 7 (in the case of paragraph (2)) or under Rule 8 (in the case of paragraph (3)).

(6) Where the liquidator summons a meeting of creditors in respect of liabilities of the company attributable to either or both its long-term business or other business, he may adopt any valuation carried out in accordance with Rules 6, 7 or 8 as the case may be or, if no such valuation has been carried out by the time of the meeting, he may conduct the meeting using such estimates of the value of policies as he thinks fit.

NOTES

Commencement: 19 September 2005.

[4387]

23 Dividends to creditors

(1) This Rule applies in the case of a company carrying on long-term business.

(2) Part 11 of the principal Rules applies separately in relation to the two separate companies assumed for the purposes of Rule 5.

(3) The High Court may, at any time before the making of a stop order, permit a dividend to be declared and paid on such terms as it thinks fit in respect only of debts which fell due to payment before the liquidation date or, in the case of claims under long-term policies, which have fallen due for payment on or after the liquidation date.

NOTES

Commencement: 19 September 2005.

[4388]

24 Meetings of creditors

(1) In the case of a company carrying on long-term business in whose case no stop order has been made, the creditors entitled to participate in creditor's meetings may be—

(a) in relation to the long-term business assets of the company, only those who are creditors in respect of liabilities attributable to the long-term business of the company; and

(b) in relation to the other business assets of the company, only those who are creditors in respect of liabilities attributable to the other business of the company.

(1A) In a case where separate general meetings of the creditors are summoned by the liquidator pursuant to—

(a) paragraph (1); or

(b) regulation 29 of the Insurers (Reorganisation and Winding-Up) Regulations 2004 (composite insurers: general meetings of creditors),

chapter 8 of Part 4 and Part 8 of the principal Rules apply to each such separate meeting.

(2) In relation to any such separate meeting—

(a) Rule 4.068(3) of the principal Rules (expenses of summoning meetings) has effect as if the reference therein to assets were a reference to the assets available under the above mentioned Regulations for meeting the liabilities of the company owed to the creditors summoned to the meeting, and

(b) Rule 4.070 of the principal Rules (resolutions) applies as if the reference therein to value in relation to a creditor who is not, by virtue of Rule 6, 7 or 8, required to prove his debt, were a reference to the value most recently notified to him under Rule 22 or, if the High Court has determined a different value in accordance with Rule 22(4), as if it were a reference to that different value.

(3) In paragraph (1)—

"long-term business assets" means the assets representing the fund or funds maintained by the company in respect of its long-term business;

"other business assets" means any assets of the company which are not long-term business assets.

[4389]

25 Remuneration of liquidator carrying on long-term business

(1) So long as no stop order has been made in relation to a company carrying on long-term business, the liquidator is entitled to receive remuneration for his services as such in relation to the carrying on of that business as provided for in this Rule.

(2) The remuneration shall be fixed by the liquidation committee by reference to the time properly given by the liquidator and his staff in attending to matters arising in the winding-up.

(3) If there is no liquidation committee or the committee does not make the requisite determination, the liquidator's remuneration may be fixed (in accordance with paragraph (2)) by a resolution of a meeting of creditors.

(4) If not fixed in paragraphs (2) and (3), the liquidator's remuneration shall be in accordance with the scale laid down for the official receiver by the general regulations.

(5) If the liquidator's remuneration has been fixed by the liquidation committee, and the liquidator considers the amount to be insufficient, he may request that it be increased by resolution of the creditors.

NOTES

Commencement: 19 September 2005.

[4390]

26 Apportionment of costs payable out of the assets

(1) Where no stop order has been made in relation to a company, Rule 4.228 of the principal Rules (general rule as to priority) applies separately to the assets of the company's long-term business and to the assets of the company's other business.

(2) But where any fee, expense, cost, charge, disbursement or remuneration does not relate exclusively to the assets of the company's long-term business or to the assets of the company's other business, the liquidator shall apportion it amongst those assets in such manner as he shall determine.

NOTES

Commencement: 19 September 2005.

[4391]

27 Notice of stop order

(1) When a stop order has been made in relation to the company, the High Court shall, on the same day, send to the official receiver a notice informing him that the stop order has been made.

(2) The notice shall be in Form No. 1 set out in Schedule 6 with such variation as circumstances may require.

(3) Three copies of the stop order sealed with the seal of the High Court shall forthwith be sent by the Court to the official receiver.

(4) The official receiver shall cause a sealed copy of the order to be served upon the liquidator by prepaid letter or upon such other person or persons, or in such other manner as the High Court may direct, and shall forward a copy of the order to the registrar of companies.

(5) The liquidator shall forthwith on receipt of a sealed copy of the order—

(a) cause notice of the order in Form 2 set out in Schedule 6 to be gazetted, and

(b) advertise the making of the order in the newspaper in which the liquidation date was advertised, by notice in Form 3 set out in Schedule 6.

NOTES

Commencement: 19 September 2005.

SCHEDULE 1

RULES FOR VALUING GENERAL BUSINESS POLICIES

Rule 6

[4392]

1.—(1) This paragraph applies in relation to periodic payments under a general business policy which fall due for payment after the liquidation date where the event giving rise to the liability to make the payments occurred before the liquidation date.
(2) The value to be attributed to such periodic payments shall be determined on such actuarial principles and assumptions in regard to all relevant factors as the High Court shall direct.

2.—(1) This paragraph applies in relation to liabilities under a general business policy which arise from events which occurred before the liquidation date but which have not—
(a) fallen due for payment before the liquidation date; or
(b) been notified to the company before the liquidation date.
(2) The value to be attributed to such liabilities shall be determined on such actuarial principles and assumptions in regard to all relevant factors as the High Court shall direct.

3.—(1) This paragraph applies in relation to liabilities under a general business policy not dealt with by paragraphs 1 or 2.
(2) The value to be attributed to those liabilities shall—
(a) if the terms of the policy provide for a repayment of premium upon the early termination of the policy or the policy is expressed to run from one definite date to another or the policy may be terminated by any of the parties with effect from a definite date, be the greater of the following two amounts:
(i) the amount (if any) which under the terms of the policy would have been repayable on early termination of the policy had the policy terminated on the liquidation date, and
(ii) where the policy is expressed to run from one definite date to another or may be terminated by any of the parties with effect from a definite date, such proportion of the last premium paid as is proportionate to the unexpired portion of the period in respect of which that premium was paid; and
(b) in any other case, be a just estimate of that value.

NOTES
Commencement: 19 September 2005.

SCHEDULE 2

RULES FOR VALUING NON-LINKED LIFE POLICIES, NON-LINKED DEFERRED ANNUITY POLICIES, NON-LINKED ANNUITIES IN PAYMENT, UNITISED NON-LINKED POLICIES AND CAPITAL REDEMPTION POLICIES

Rule 7(3)

[4393]

1 General
In valuing a policy—
(a) where it is necessary to calculate the present value of future payments by or to the company, interest shall be assumed at such fair and reasonable rate or rates as the High Court may direct;
(b) where relevant, the rates of mortality and the rates of disability to be employed shall be such rates as the High Court considers appropriate after taking into account:
(i) relevant published tables of rates of mortality and rates of disability, and
(ii) the rates of mortality and the rates of disability experienced in connection with similar policies issued by the company;
(c) there shall be determined:
(i) the present value of the ordinary benefits;
(ii) the present value of additional benefits;
(iii) the present value of options; and
(iv) if further premiums fall to be paid under the policy on or after the liquidation date, the present value of the premiums;
and for the purposes of this Schedule if the ordinary benefits only take into account

premiums paid to date, the present value of future premiums shall be taken as nil.

2 Present value of the ordinary benefits

(1) Ordinary benefits are the benefits which will become payable to the policy holder on or after the liquidation date without his having to exercise any option under the policy (including any bonus or addition to the sum assured or the amount of annuity declared before the liquidation date) and for this purpose "option" includes a right to surrender the policy.

(2) Subject to sub-paragraph (3), the present value of the ordinary benefits shall be the value at the liquidation date of the reversion in the ordinary benefits according to the contingency upon which those benefits are payable calculated on the basis of the rates of interest, mortality and disability referred to in paragraph 1.

(3) For accumulating with-profits policies—

(a) where the benefits are not expressed in the form of units in a with-profits fund, the value of the ordinary benefits is the amount that would have been payable, excluding any discretionary additions, if the policy holder had been able to exercise a right to terminate the policy at the liquidation date; and

(b) where the benefits are expressed in the form of units in a with-profits fund, the value of the ordinary benefits is the number of units held by the policy holder at the liquidation date valued at the unit price in force at that time or, if that price is not calculated on a daily basis, such price as the High Court may determine having regard to the last published unit price and any change in the value of assets attributable to the fund since the date of the last published unit price.

(4) Where—

(a) sub-paragraph (3) applies, and

(b) paragraph 3(1) of Schedule 3 applies to the calculation of the unit price (or as the case may be) the fund value,

the value shall be adjusted on the basis set out in paragraph 3(3) to (5) of Schedule 3.

(5) Where sub-paragraph (3) applies, the value may be further adjusted by reference to the value of the assets underlying the unit price (or as the case may be) the value of the fund, if the liquidator considers such an adjustment to be necessary.

3 Present value of additional benefits

(1) Where under the terms of the policy or on the basis of the company's established practice the policy holder has a right to receive or an expectation of receiving benefits additional to the minimum benefits guaranteed under those terms, the High Court shall determine rates of interest, bonus (whether reversionary, terminal or any other type of bonus used by the company), mortality and disability to provide for the present value (if any) of that right or expectation.

(2) In determining what (if any) value to attribute to any such expectations the High Court shall have regard to the premium payable in relation to the minimum guaranteed benefits and the amount (if any) an insurer is required to provide in respect of those expectations in any rules made by the Authority under Part X of the 2000 Act.

4 Present value of options

The amount of the present value of options shall be the amount which, in the opinion of the liquidator, is necessary to be provided at the liquidation date (in addition to the amount of the present value of the ordinary benefits) to cover the additional liabilities likely to arise upon the exercise on or after that date by the policy holder of any option conferred upon him by the terms of the policy or, in the case of an industrial assurance policy, by the 1979 Order other than an option whereby the policy holder can secure a guaranteed cash payment within the period of 12 months beginning with that date.

5 Present value of premiums

The present value of the premiums shall be the value at the liquidation date of the premiums which fall due to be paid by the policy holder after the liquidation date calculated on the basis of the rates of interest, mortality and disability referred to in paragraph 1.

6 Value of the policy

(1) Subject to sub-paragraph (2)—

(a) if no further premiums fall due to be paid under the policy on or after the liquidation date, the value of the policy shall be the aggregate of:

(i) the present value of the ordinary benefits;

(ii) the present value of options; and

(iii) the present value of additional benefits;

(b) if further premiums fall due to be so paid and the aggregate value referred to in head (a) exceeds the present value of the premiums, the value of the policy shall be the amount of that excess; and

(c) if further premiums fall due to be so paid and that aggregate does not exceed the present value of the premiums, the policy shall have no value.

(2) Where the policy holder has a right conferred upon him by the terms of the policy or by the 1979 Order whereby the policy holder can secure a guaranteed cash payment within the period of 12 months beginning with the liquidation date, the liquidator shall determine the amount which in his opinion it is necessary to provide at that date to cover the liabilities which will accrue when that option is exercised (on the assumption that it will be exercised) and the value of the policy shall be that amount if it exceeds the value of the policy (if any) determined in accordance with sub-paragraph (1).

NOTES

Commencement: 19 September 2005.

SCHEDULE 3

RULES FOR VALUING LIFE POLICIES AND DEFERRED ANNUITY POLICIES WHICH ARE LINKED POLICIES

Rule 7(3)

[4394]

1.—(1) Subject to sub-paragraph (2) the value of the policy shall be the aggregate of the value of the linked liabilities (calculated in accordance with paragraphs 2 or 4) and the value of other than linked liabilities (calculated in accordance with paragraph 5) except where that aggregate is a negative amount in which case the policy shall have no value.

(2) Where the terms of the policy include a right whereby the policy holder can secure a guaranteed cash payment within the period of 12 months beginning with the liquidation date then, if the amount which in the opinion of the liquidator is necessary to be provided at that date to cover any liabilities which will accrue when that option is exercised (on the assumption that it will be exercised) is greater than the value determined under sub-paragraph (1), the value of the policy shall be that greater amount.

2.—(1) Where the linked liabilities are expressed in terms of units the value of those liabilities shall, subject to paragraph 3, be the amount arrived at by taking the product of the number of units of each class of units allocated to the policy on the liquidation date and the value of each such unit on that date and then adding those products.

(2) For the purposes of sub-paragraph (1)—

(a) where under the terms of the policy the value of a unit at any time falls to be determined by reference to the value at that time of the assets of a particular fund maintained by the company in relation to that and other policies, the value of a unit on the liquidation date shall be determined by reference to the net realisable value of the assets credited to that fund on that date (after taking account of disposal costs, any tax liabilities resulting from the disposal of assets insofar as they have not already been provided for by the company and any other amounts which under the terms of those policies are chargeable to the fund), and

(b) in any other case, the value of a unit on the liquidation date shall be the value which would have been ascribed to each unit credited to the policy holder, after any deductions which may be made under the terms of the policy, for the purpose of determining the benefits payable under the policy on the liquidation date had the policy matured on that date.

3.—(1) This paragraph applies where—

(a) paragraph 2(2)(a) applies and the company has a right under the terms of the policy either to make periodic withdrawals from the fund referred to in that paragraph or to retain any part of the income accruing in respect of the assets of that fund,

(b) paragraph 2(2)(b) applies and the company has a right under the terms of the policy to receive the whole or any part of any distributions made in respect of the units referred to in that paragraph, or

(c) paragraph 2(2)(a) or paragraph 2(2)(b) applies and the company has a right under the terms of the policy to make periodic cancellations of a proportion of the number of units credited to the policy.

(2) Where this paragraph applies, the value of the linked liabilities calculated in accordance with paragraph 2(1), shall be reduced by an amount calculated in accordance with sub-paragraph (3).

(3) The amount referred to in sub-paragraph (2) is—

(a) where this paragraph applies by virtue of head (a) or (b) of sub-paragraph (1), the value as at the liquidation date, calculated on actuarial principles, of the future income of the company in respect of the units in question arising from the rights referred to in head (a) or (b) of sub-paragraph (1) as the case may be, or

(b) where this paragraph applies by virtue of head (c) of sub-paragraph (1), the value as at the liquidation date, calculated on actuarial principles, of the liabilities of the company in respect of the units which fall to be cancelled in the future under the right referred to in head (c) of sub-paragraph (1).

(4) In calculating any amount in accordance with sub-paragraph (3) there shall be disregarded—

(a) such part of the rights referred to in the relevant head of sub-paragraph (1) which in the opinion of the liquidator constitutes appropriate provision for future expenses and mortality risks, and

(b) such part of those rights (if any) which the High Court considers to constitute appropriate provision for any right or expectation of the policy holder to receive benefits additional to the benefits guaranteed under the terms of the policy.

(5) In determining the amount referred to in sub-paragraph (2)—

(a) interest shall be assumed at such rate or rates as the High Court may direct, and

(b) where relevant, the rates of mortality and the rates of disability to be employed shall be such rates as the Court considers appropriate after taking into account:

(i) relevant published tables of rates of mortality and rates of disability, and

(ii) the rates of mortality and the rates of disability experienced in connection with similar policies issued by the company.

4. Where the linked liabilities are not expressed in terms of units the value of those liabilities shall be the value (subject to adjustment for any amounts which would have been deducted for taxation) which would have been ascribed to those liabilities had the policy matured on the liquidation date.

5.—(1) The value of any liabilities other than linked liabilities including reserves for future expenses, options and guarantees shall be determined on actuarial principles and appropriate assumptions in regard to all relevant factors including the assumption of such rate or rates of interest, mortality and disability as the High Court may direct.

(2) In valuing liabilities under this paragraph credit shall be taken for those parts of future premiums which do not fall to be applied in the allocation of further units to the policy and for any rights of the company which have been disregarded under paragraph 3(4)(a) in valuing the linked liabilities.

NOTES

Commencement: 19 September 2005.

SCHEDULE 4

RULES FOR VALUING LONG-TERM POLICIES WHICH ARE NOT DEALT WITH IN SCHEDULES 2 OR 3

Rule 7(3)

[4395]

The value of a long-term policy not covered by Schedule 2 or 3 shall be the value of the benefits due to the policy holder determined on such actuarial principles and assumptions in regard to all relevant factors as the High Court shall determine.

NOTES

Commencement: 19 September 2005.

SCHEDULE 5

RULES FOR VALUING LONG-TERM POLICIES WHERE A STOP ORDER HAS BEEN MADE

Rule 8(3)

[4396]

1. Subject to paragraphs 2 and 3, in valuing a policy Schedules 2, 3 or 4 shall apply according to the class of that policy as if those Schedules were herein repeated but with a view to a fresh valuation of each policy on appropriate assumptions in regard to all relevant factors and subject to the following modifications—

(a) references to the stop order shall be substituted for references to the liquidation date,

(b) in paragraph 4 of Schedule 2 for the words "whereby the policy holder can secure a guaranteed cash payment within the period of 12 months beginning with that date" there shall be substituted the words "to surrender the policy which can be exercised on that date",

(c) paragraph 6(2) of Schedule 2 shall be deleted, and

(d) paragraph 1(2) of Schedule 3 shall be deleted.

2.—(1) This paragraph applies where the policy holder has a right conferred upon him under the terms of the policy or by the 1979 Order to surrender the policy and that right is exercisable on the date of the stop order.

(2) Where this paragraph applies and the amount required at the date of the stop order to provide for the benefits payable upon surrender of the policy (on the assumption that the policy is surrendered on the date of the stop order) is greater than the value of the policy determined in accordance with paragraph 1 the value of the policy shall, subject to paragraph 3, be the said amount so required.

(3) Where any part of the surrender value is payable after the date of the stop order, sub-paragraph (2) shall apply but the value therein referred to shall be discounted at such a rate of interest as the High Court may direct.

3.—(1) This paragraph applies in the case of a linked policy where—

(a) the terms of the policy include a guarantee that the amount assured will on maturity of the policy be worth a minimum amount calculable in money terms, or

(b) the terms of the policy include a right on the part of the policy holder to surrender the policy and a guarantee that the payment on surrender will be worth a minimum amount calculable in money terms and that right is exercisable on or after the date of the stop order.

(2) Where this paragraph applies the value of the policy shall be the greater of the following two amounts—

(a) the value the policy would have had at the date of the stop order had the policy been a non-linked policy, that is to say, had the linked liabilities provided by the policy not been so provided but the policy had otherwise been on the same terms, and

(b) the value the policy would have had at the date of the stop order had the policy not included any guarantees of payments on maturity or surrender worth a minimum amount calculable in money terms.

NOTES

Commencement: 19 September 2005.

SCHEDULE 6

FORMS

Rules 27(2) and (5)

FORM NO 1

[4397]

Notification to Official Receiver of order made under section 376(2) of the Financial Services and Markets Act 2000

(Title)

To the Official Receiver

(Address)

Order made this day by the Honourable Mr Justice (or, *as the case may be*) that the liquidator or (*insert name of company*) shall not carry on the long-term business of the company.

FORM NO 2

Notice for Belfast Gazette

Notice of order made under section 376(2) of the Financial Services and Markets Act 2000 for cessation of long-term business

Name of Company . . . . Address of Registered Office . . . .

Court . . . . Number of Matter . . . . Date of Order. . . . .

Date of liquidation date . . . .

FORM NO 3

Notice for Newspaper

Notice of order made under section 376(2) of the Financial Services and Markets Act 2000 for cessation of long-term business

Name of Company . . . .

Date of Liquidation date . . . .

Date of Order . . . .

[Liquidator] . . . .

NOTES

Commencement: 19 September 2005.

INSURERS (REORGANISATION AND WINDING UP) (LLOYD'S) REGULATIONS 2005

(SI 2005/1998)

NOTES

Made: 19 July 2005.
Authority: European Communities Act 1972, s 2(2).
Commencement: 10 August 2005.

ARRANGEMENT OF REGULATIONS

PART 1
GENERAL

1 Citation and commencement . . . . . [4398]
2 Interpretation . . . . . [4399]

PART 2
LLOYD'S MARKET REORGANISATION ORDER

3 Lloyd's market reorganisation order . . . . . [4400]
4 Condition for making order . . . . . [4401]
5 Objectives of a Lloyd's market reorganisation order . . . . . [4402]
6 Application for a Lloyd's market reorganisation order . . . . . [4403]
7 Powers of the court . . . . . [4404]
8 Moratorium . . . . . [4405]
9 Reorganisation controller . . . . . [4406]
10 Announcement of appointment of controller . . . . . [4407]
11 Market reorganisation plan . . . . . [4408]
12 Remuneration of the reorganisation controller . . . . . [4409]
13 Treatment of members . . . . . [4410]
14 Revocation of an order under regulation 13 . . . . . [4411]
15 Reorganisation controller's powers: voluntary arrangements in respect of a member . . . . . [4412]
16 Reorganisation controller's powers: individual voluntary arrangements in respect of a member . . . . . [4413]
17 Reorganisation controller's powers: trust deeds for creditors in Scotland . . . . . [4414]
18 Powers of reorganisation controller: section 425 or Article 418 compromise or arrangement . . . . . [4415]
19 Appointment of an administrator, receiver or interim trustee in relation to a member . . . . . [4416]
20 Reorganisation controller's powers: administration orders in respect of members . . . . . [4417]
21 Reorganisation controller's powers: receivership in relation to members . . . . . [4418]
22 Syndicate set-off . . . . . [4419]
23 Voluntary winding up of members: consent of reorganisation controller . . . . . [4420]
24 Voluntary winding up of members: powers of reorganisation controller . . . . . [4421]
25 Petition for winding up of a member by reorganisation controller . . . . . [4422]
26 Winding up of a member: powers of reorganisation controller . . . . . [4423]
27 Petition for bankruptcy of a member by reorganisation controller . . . . . [4424]
28 Bankruptcy of a member: powers of reorganisation controller . . . . . [4425]
29 Petition for winding up of the Society by reorganisation controller . . . . . [4426]
30 Winding up of the Society: service of petition etc on reorganisation controller . . . . . [4427]
31 Payments from central funds . . . . . [4428]

PART 3
MODIFICATION OF LAW OF INSOLVENCY:
NOTIFICATION AND PUBLICATION

32 Application of Parts 3 and 4 . . . [4429]
33 Notification of relevant decision to Authority . . . [4430]
34 Notification of relevant decision to EEA Regulators . . . [4431]
35 Application of certain publication requirements in the principal Regulations to members . . . [4432]
36 Notification to creditors: winding up proceedings relating to members . . . [4433]
37 Submission of claims by EEA creditor . . . [4434]
38 Reports to creditors . . . [4435]
39 Service of notices and documents . . . [4436]

PART 4
APPLICATION OF PARTS 4 AND 5 OF THE PRINCIPAL REGULATIONS

40 Priority for insurance claims . . . [4437]
41 Treatment of liabilities arising in connection with a contract subject to reinsurance to close . . . [4438]
42 Assets of members . . . [4439]
43 Application of Part 4 of the principal Regulations: protection of settlements . . . [4440]
44 Challenge by reorganisation controller to conduct of insolvency practitioner . . . [4441]
45 Application of Part 5 of the principal Regulations . . . [4442]
46 Modification of provisions in Part 5 of the principal Regulations . . . [4443]
47 Application of Part 5 of the principal Regulations: protection of dispositions etc made before a Lloyd's market reorganisation order comes into force . . . [4444]
48 Non-EEA countries . . . [4445]

PART 1
GENERAL

[4398]

1 Citation and commencement

These Regulations may be cited as the Insurers (Reorganisation and Winding Up) (Lloyd's) Regulations 2005, and come into force on 10 August 2005.

NOTES

Commencement: 10 August 2005.

[4399]

2 Interpretation

(1) In these Regulations—

"the Administration for Insurers Order" means the Financial Services and Markets Act 2000 (Administration Orders Relating to Insurers) Order 2002 [and the "Administration for Insurers (Northern Ireland) Order" means the Financial Services and Markets Act 2000 (Administration Relating to Insurers) (Northern Ireland) Order 2007];

"affected market participant" means any member, former member, managing agent, members' agent, Lloyd's broker, approved run-off company or coverholder to whom the Lloyd's market reorganisation order applies;

"approved run-off company" means a company with the permission of the Society to perform executive functions, insurance functions or administrative and processing functions on behalf of a managing agent;

"the association of underwriters known as Lloyd's" has the meaning it has for the purposes of the First Council Directive of 24 July 1973 on the coordination of laws, regulations and administrative provisions relating to the taking and pursuit of the business of direct insurance other than life assurance (73/239/EEC) and Directive 2002/83/EC of the European Parliament and of the Council of 5 November 2002 concerning life assurance;

"central funds" means the New Central Fund as provided for in the New Central Fund Byelaw (No 23 of 1996) and the Central Fund as provided for in the Central Fund Byelaw (No 4 of 1986);

"company" means a company within the meaning of section 735 of the 1985 Act or Article 3 of the Companies Order or a company incorporated elsewhere than in Great Britain that is a member of Lloyd's;

"corporate member" means a company admitted to membership of Lloyd's as an underwriting member;

"coverholder" means a company or partnership authorised by a managing agent to enter into, in accordance with the terms of a binding authority, a contract or contracts of insurance to be underwritten by the members of a syndicate managed by that managing agent;

"former member" means a person who has ceased to be a member, whether by resignation or otherwise, in accordance with Lloyd's Act 1982 and any byelaw made under it or in accordance with the provisions of Lloyd's Acts 1871–1982 then in force at the time the person ceased to be a member;

"Gazette" means the London Gazette, the Edinburgh Gazette and the Belfast Gazette;

"individual member" means a member or former member who is an individual;

"insurance market activity" has the meaning given by section 316(3) of the 2000 Act;

"insurance market debt" means an insurance debt under or in connection with a contract of insurance written at Lloyd's;

"Lloyd's Acts 1871–1982" means Lloyd's Act 1871, Lloyd's Act 1911, Lloyd's Act 1951 and Lloyd's Act 1982;

"Lloyd's broker" has the meaning given by section 2(1) of Lloyd's Act 1982;

"managing agent" has the meaning given by article 3(1) of the Financial Services and Markets Act 2000 (Regulated Activities) Order 2001;

"member" means an underwriting member of the Society;

"members' agent" means a person who carries out the activity of advising a person to become, or continue or cease to be, a member of a particular Lloyd's syndicate;

"overseas business regulatory deposit" means a deposit provided or maintained in respect of the overseas insurance and reinsurance business carried on by members in accordance with binding legal or regulatory requirements from time to time in force in the country or territory in which the deposit is held;

"overseas insurance business" means insurance business and reinsurance business transacted by members in a country or territory that is not or is not part of an EEA State;

"the principal Regulations" means the Insurers (Reorganisation and Winding Up) Regulations 2004;

"relevant trust fund" means any funds held on trust under a trust deed entered into by the member in accordance with the requirements of the Authority and the Byelaws of the Society for the payment of an obligation arising in connection with insurance market activity carried on by the member or for the establishment of a Lloyd's deposit and includes funds held on further trusts declared by the Society or the trustee of such a trust deed in respect of any class of insurance market activity;

"the Room" has the meaning given by section 2(1) of Lloyd's Act 1982;

"the Society" means the Society incorporated by Lloyd's Act 1871;

"subsidiary of the Society" means a company that is a subsidiary of the Society within the meaning of section 736 of the 1985 Act or Article 4 of the Companies Order;

"syndicate" has the meaning given by article 3(1) of the Financial Services and Markets Act 2000 (Regulated Activities) Order 2001.

(2) Subject to paragraph (3), words and phrases used in these Regulations have the same meaning as in the principal Regulations except where otherwise specified or where the context requires otherwise.

(3) For the purposes of these Regulations, "UK insurer" is to be treated as including a member or a former member.

(4) These Regulations have effect notwithstanding the provisions of section 360 of the 2000 Act.

NOTES

Commencement: 10 August 2005.

Para (1): words in square brackets in definition "the Administration for Insurers Order" inserted by the Insurers (Reorganisation and Winding Up) (Amendment) Regulations 2007, SI 2007/851, reg 3(1), (2).

Directive 2002/83/EC of the European Parliament and of the Council: OJ L345, 19.12.2002, p 1.

PART 2
LLOYD'S MARKET REORGANISATION ORDER

[4400]

3 Lloyd's market reorganisation order

(1) In these Regulations "Lloyd's market reorganisation order" means an order which—

(a) is made by the court in relation to the association of underwriters known as Lloyd's;

(b) appoints a reorganisation controller; and

(c) on the making of which there comes into force a moratorium on the commencement of—

(i) proceedings, or

(ii) other legal processes

set out in regulation 8 in respect of affected market participants, the Society and subsidiaries of the Society.

(2) A Lloyd's market reorganisation order applies to—

(a) every member, former member, managing agent, members' agent, Lloyd's broker and approved run-off company who has not been excluded from the order in accordance with regulation 7;

(b) every coverholder who has been included in the order in accordance with regulation 7;

(c) the Society; and

(d) subsidiaries of the Society.

NOTES

Commencement: 10 August 2005.

[4401]

4 Condition for making order

(1) The court may make a Lloyd's market reorganisation order if it is satisfied that—

(a) any regulatory solvency requirement is not, or may not be, met; and

(b) an order is likely to achieve one or both of the objectives in regulation 5.

(2) In paragraph (1), "regulatory solvency requirement" means a requirement to maintain adequate financial resources in respect of insurance business at Lloyd's, imposed under the 2000 Act, whether on a member or former underwriting member, either singly or together with other members or former underwriting members, or on the Society and includes a requirement to maintain a margin of solvency.

(3) In paragraph (2), "former underwriting member" has the meaning given by section 324(1) of the 2000 Act.

NOTES

Commencement: 10 August 2005.

[4402]

5 Objectives of a Lloyd's market reorganisation order

The objectives of a Lloyd's market reorganisation order are—

(a) to preserve or restore the financial situation of, or market confidence in, the association of underwriters known as Lloyd's in order to facilitate the carrying on of insurance market activities by members at Lloyd's;

(b) to assist in achieving an outcome that is in the interests of creditors of members, and insurance creditors in particular.

NOTES

Commencement: 10 August 2005.

[4403]

6 Application for a Lloyd's market reorganisation order

(1) An application for a Lloyd's market reorganisation order may be made by the Authority or by the Society, or by both.

(2) If the application is made by only one of those bodies it must inform the other body of its intention to make the application as soon as possible, and in any event before the application is lodged at the court.

(3) The Authority and the Society are entitled to be heard at the hearing of the application, regardless of which body makes the application.

(4) An application must clearly designate—

(a) any member, former member, managing agent, members' agent, Lloyd's broker, or approved run-off company to whom the order should not apply; and

(b) every coverholder to whom the order should apply.

(5) The applicant must give notice of the application by—

(a) ensuring the posting of a copy in the Room,

(b) displaying a copy on its website, and

(c) publishing a copy

(i) in the Gazette, and

(ii) in such newspaper or newspapers within the United Kingdom and elsewhere as the applicant considers appropriate to bring the application to the attention of those likely to be affected by it.

(6) The notice must be given as soon as reasonably practicable after the making of the application, unless the court orders otherwise.

NOTES
Commencement: 10 August 2005.

[4404]
7 Powers of the court

(1) On hearing an application for a Lloyd's market reorganisation order, the court may make—
- (a) a Lloyd's market reorganisation order, and
- (b) any other order in addition to a Lloyd's market reorganisation order which the court thinks appropriate for the attainment of either or both of the objectives in regulation 5.

(2) A Lloyd's market reorganisation order comes into force—
- (a) at the time appointed by the court; or
- (b) if no time is so appointed, when the order is made

and remains in force until revoked by the court.

(3) The court may on an application made by the Authority or the Society at the same time as an application under regulation 6 or the reorganisation controller, the Authority, the Society, a subsidiary of the Society or any affected market participant at any time while the Lloyd's market reorganisation order is in force, amend or vary a Lloyd's market reorganisation order so that it—
- (a) does not apply to—
  - (i) particular assets, or
  - (ii) particular members, former members, member's agents, managing agents, Lloyd's brokers, approved run-off companies or subsidiaries of the Society,

  specified in the order; and
- (b) does apply to any coverholder specified in the order.

(4) The court—
- (a) must appoint one or more persons to be the reorganisation controller;
- (b) must specify the powers and duties of the reorganisation controller;
- (c) may establish or approve the respective duties and functions of two or more persons appointed to be the reorganisation controller, including specifying that one of them shall have precedence; and
- (d) may from time to time vary the powers of a reorganisation controller.

(5) An application made under paragraph (3) other than at the time of the application under regulation 6 shall be served on the reorganisation controller and the Authority who shall each be entitled to attend and be heard at a hearing of such an application.

NOTES
Commencement: 10 August 2005.

[4405]
8 Moratorium

(1) Except with the permission of the court, for the period during which a Lloyd's market reorganisation order is in force, no proceedings or other legal process may be commenced or continued against:
- (a) an affected market participant;
- (b) the Society; or
- (c) a subsidiary of the Society to which the order applies.

(2) In paragraph (1),
- (a) "court" means in England and Wales the High Court, in Northern Ireland the High Court and in Scotland the Court of Session; and
- (b) "proceedings" means proceedings of every description and includes:
  - (i) a petition under section 124 or 124A of the 1986 Act or Article 104 or 104A of the 1989 Order for the appointment of a liquidator or provisional liquidator;
  - (ii) an application under section 252 of the 1986 Act or Article 226 of the 1989 Order for an interim order;
  - (iii) a petition for a bankruptcy order under Part 9 of the 1986 Act or Part 9 of the 1989 Order; and
  - (iv) a petition for sequestration under section 5 or 6 of the Bankruptcy (Scotland) Act, but

  does not include prosecution for a criminal offence.

(3) Except with the permission of the court, for the period during which a Lloyd's market reorganisation order is in force, no execution may be commenced or continued, no security may be enforced, and no distress may be levied, against (or against the assets of or in the possession of):

(a) any person specified in paragraph (1);
(b) a relevant trust fund (or the trustees of a relevant trust fund); and
(c) an overseas business regulatory deposit.

(4) Paragraph (3) does not prevent the enforcement of—
(a) approved security granted to secure payment of approved debts of a member incurred in connection with an overseas regulatory deposit arrangement; or
(b) security granted by a Lloyd's broker over assets not being assets constituting or representing assets received or held by the Lloyd's broker as intermediary in respect of any contract of insurance or reinsurance written at Lloyd's or any contract of reinsurance reinsuring a member of Lloyd's in respect of a contract or contracts of insurance or reinsurance written by that member at Lloyd's.

(5) In the application of paragraph (3) to Scotland, references to execution being commenced or continued include references to diligence being carried out or continued, and references to distress being levied shall be omitted.

(6) For the period during which a Lloyd's market reorganisation order is in force, no action or step may be taken in respect of any of the persons specified in paragraph (1) by any person who is or may be entitled—
(a) under any provision in Schedule B1 [or in Schedule B1 to the 1989 Order] to appoint an administrator;
(b) to appoint an administrative receiver or receiver;
(c) under section 425 of the 1985 Act or Article 418 of the Companies Order to propose a compromise or arrangement,

unless he has complied with paragraph (7).

(7) A person intending to take any such action or step shall give notice [in writing] to the reorganisation controller before doing so.

(8) Where a person fails to comply with paragraph (7),
(a) an appointment to which sub-paragraph (6)(a) or (b) applies shall be void, and
(b) no application under section 425 or Article 418 may be entertained by the court,

except where the court, having heard the reorganisation controller, orders otherwise.

(9) Every application pursuant to paragraph (1) or paragraph (3) must be served on the reorganisation controller.

(10) For the period during which a Lloyd's market reorganisation order is in force, an affected market participant in Scotland may not grant a trust deed for his creditors without the consent of the reorganisation controller.

(11) Where a person who is subject to a Lloyd's market reorganisation order is, at the date of the order, in administration or liquidation or has been adjudged bankrupt or is a person whose estate is being sequestrated or who has granted a trust deed for his creditors—
(a) any application to the court for permission to take any action that would be subject to a moratorium arising in those earlier proceedings shall be served on the reorganisation controller and the reorganisation controller shall be entitled to be heard on the application; and
(b) the court shall take into account the achievement of the objectives for which the Lloyd's market reorganisation order was made.

(12) In this regulation—
(a) "approved debt" means a debt approved by the Society at the time it is incurred;
(b) "approved security" means security approved by the Society at the time it is granted over or in respect of assets comprised in the member's premiums trust funds or liable in the future to become comprised therein;
(c) "overseas regulatory deposit arrangement" means an arrangement approved by the Society and notified to the Authority whose purpose is to facilitate funding of any overseas business regulatory deposit.

NOTES

Commencement: 10 August 2005.

Para (6): words in square brackets in sub-para (a) inserted by the Insurers (Reorganisation and Winding Up) (Amendment) Regulations 2007, SI 2007/851, reg 3(1), (3)(a).

Para (7): words in square brackets inserted by SI 2007/851, reg 3(1), (3)(b).

[4406]

9 Reorganisation controller

(1) The reorganisation controller is an officer of the court.

(2) A person may be appointed as reorganisation controller only if he is qualified to act as an insolvency practitioner under Part 13 of the 1986 Act [or under Part 12 of the 1989 Order] and the court considers that he has appropriate knowledge, expertise and experience.

(3) On an application by the reorganisation controller, the court may appoint one or more additional reorganisation controllers to act jointly or severally with the first reorganisation controller on such terms as the court sees fit.

NOTES

Commencement: 10 August 2005.

Para (2): words in square brackets inserted by the Insurers (Reorganisation and Winding Up) (Amendment) Regulations 2007, SI 2007/851, reg 3(1), (4).

[4407]

10 Announcement of appointment of controller

(1) This regulation applies when the court makes a Lloyd's market reorganisation order.

(2) As soon as is practicable after the order has been made, the Authority must inform the EEA regulators in every EEA State—

(a) that the order has been made; and

(b) in general terms, of the possible effect of a Lloyd's market reorganisation order on—

(i) the effecting or carrying out of contracts of insurance at Lloyd's, and

(ii) the rights of policyholders under or in respect of contracts of insurance written at Lloyd's.

(3) As soon as is reasonably practicable after a person becomes the reorganisation controller, he must—

(a) procure that notice of his appointment is posted—

(i) in the Room,

(ii) on the Society's website, and

(iii) on the Authority's website; and

(b) publish a notice of his appointment—

(i) once in the Gazette, and

(ii) once in such newspapers as he thinks most appropriate for securing so far as possible that the Lloyd's market reorganisation order comes to the notice of those who may be affected by it.

NOTES

Commencement: 10 August 2005.

[4408]

11 Market reorganisation plan

(1) The reorganisation controller may require any affected market participant, and any Lloyd's broker, approved run-off company, coverholder, the Society, subsidiary of the Society or trustee of a relevant trust fund—

(a) to provide him with any information he considers useful to him in the achievement of the objectives set out in regulation 5; and

(b) to carry out such work as may be necessary to prepare or organise information as the reorganisation controller may consider useful to him in the achievement of those objectives.

(2) As soon as is reasonably practicable and in any event by such date as the court may require, the reorganisation controller must prepare a plan ("the market reorganisation plan") for achieving the objectives of the Lloyd's market reorganisation order.

(3) The reorganisation controller must send a copy of the market reorganisation plan to the Authority and to the Society.

(4) Before the end of a period of one month beginning with the day on which it receives the market reorganisation plan, the Authority must notify the reorganisation controller and the Society in writing of its decision to—

(a) approve the plan;

(b) reject the plan; or

(c) approve the plan provisionally, subject to modifications set out in the notification.

(5) Where the Authority rejects the plan, the notification must—

(a) give reasons for its decision; and

(b) specify a date by which the reorganisation controller may submit a new market reorganisation plan.

(6) Where the reorganisation controller submits a new market reorganisation plan, he must send a copy to the Authority and to the Society.

(7) Before the end of a period of one month beginning with the day on which the Authority receives that plan, the Authority must—

(a) accept it;
(b) reject it; or
(c) accept it provisionally subject to modifications.

(8) Before the end of a period of one month beginning with the day on which he receives the notification from the Authority of the modifications required by it, the reorganisation controller must—

(a) accept the plan as modified by the Authority; or
(b) reject the plan as so modified.

(9) The reorganisation controller must—

(a) file with the court the market reorganisation plan that has been approved by him and the Authority, and
(b) send a copy of it to—
 (i) every member, former member, managing agent and member's agent who requests it, and
 (ii) every other person who requests it, on payment of a reasonable charge.

(10) Paragraph (11) applies if—

(a) the Authority rejects the market reorganisation plan and the reorganisation controller decides not to submit a new market reorganisation plan;
(b) the Authority rejects the new market reorganisation plan submitted by the reorganisation controller; or
(c) the reorganisation controller rejects the modifications made by the Authority to a new market reorganisation plan.

(11) As soon as is reasonably practicable after any such rejection, the reorganisation controller must apply to the court for directions.

(12) The Authority or the reorganisation controller as the case may be may apply to the court for an extension of the period specified in paragraph (4), (7) or (8) by a period of not more than one month. The court may not grant more than one such extension in respect of each period.

(13) Where any person is under an obligation to publish anything under this regulation, that obligation is subject to the provisions of sections 348 and 349 of the 2000 Act.

NOTES

Commencement: 10 August 2005.

[4409]

12 Remuneration of the reorganisation controller

(1) The reorganisation controller shall be entitled to receive remuneration and to recover expenses properly incurred in connection with the performance of his functions under or in connection with a Lloyd's market reorganisation order.

(2) Subject to paragraph (3), the remuneration so charged is payable by—

(a) members,
(b) former members,
(c) the Society, and
(d) managing agents.

(3) The court must give directions as to the payment of the remuneration and expenses of the reorganisation controller and in particular may provide for—

(a) apportionment of the amounts so charged between the classes of persons set out in paragraph (2) and between groups of persons within those classes; and
(b) payment of such remuneration and expenses out of relevant trust funds.

(4) Amounts of such remuneration and expenses paid by any of the persons described in paragraph (2) are to be treated as payments of the expenses of a liquidator, administrator, trustee in bankruptcy or in Scotland an interim or permanent trustee.

(5) The reorganisation controller may pay the reasonable charges of those to whom he has addressed a request for assistance or information under regulation 11 or anyone else from whom he has requested assistance in the performance of his functions.

(6) The provision of such information or assistance in good faith does not constitute a breach of

(a) any duty owed by any person involved in its preparation or delivery to any company or partnership of which he is an officer, member or employee,

(b) any duty owed by an agent to his principal, or
(c) any duty of confidence, subject to sections 348 and 349 of the 2000 Act.

NOTES

Commencement: 10 August 2005.

[4410]

13 Treatment of members

(1) Paragraph (2) applies where, after the making of a Lloyd's market reorganisation order, any of the following occurs pursuant to the 1986 Act, the 1989 Order or the Bankruptcy (Scotland) Act—

(a) a person seeks to exercise an entitlement to appoint an administrator,
(b) an application is made to the court for the appointment of an administrator,
(c) a petition for the winding up of a corporate member is presented to the court,
(d) a petition for a bankruptcy order or sequestration is presented to the court,

in respect of a member.

(2) These Regulations, the principal Regulations[, the Administration for Insurers Order and the Administration for Insurers (Northern Ireland) Order] shall apply to the member and—

(a) for the purposes of the principal Regulations (notwithstanding regulation 3 of those Regulations), the member shall be treated as if it, he or she were a UK insurer; and
(b) for the purposes of the Administration for Insurers Order [or the Administration for Insurers (Northern Ireland) Order], a member that is a company shall be treated as if it were an insurance company.

(3) Paragraph (2) does not apply where the court so orders, on the application of the administrator, liquidator, provisional liquidator, receiver or trustee in bankruptcy, the Accountant in Bankruptcy or trustee under a trust deed for creditors or the person referred to in paragraph (1)(b) or (c) seeking the appointment or presenting the petition.

(4) A person who exercises an entitlement, makes an application or submits a petition to which paragraph (1) applies shall—

(a) if he intends to make an application under paragraph (3) make the application before doing any of those things; and
(b) include in any statement to be made under Schedule B1 [or in Schedule B1 to the 1989 Order], or in any application or petition, a statement as to whether an order under paragraph (3) has been made in respect of the member concerned.

(5) An application under paragraph (3) must be notified [in writing] to the reorganisation controller.

(6) The court must take account of any representation made by the reorganisation controller in relation to the application.

(7) The court may not make an order under paragraph (3) unless the court considers it likely that the insurance market debts of the member will be satisfied.

(8) In this regulation and regulation 14, references to a member include references to a former member.

NOTES

Commencement: 10 August 2005.

Para (2): words in first pair of square brackets substituted and words in second pair of square brackets inserted by the Insurers (Reorganisation and Winding Up) (Amendment) Regulations 2007, SI 2007/851, reg 3(1), (5)(a), (b).

Paras (4), (5): words in square brackets inserted by SI 2007/851, reg 3(1), (5)(c), (d).

[4411]

14 Revocation of an order under regulation 13

(1) This regulation applies in the case of a member in respect of whom an order has been made under regulation 13(3).

(2) If the Society does not meet any request for payment of a cash call made by or on behalf of such a member, it must so inform the reorganisation controller, the Authority and the court.

(3) If it appears to the reorganisation controller that, in respect of any such member, the insurance market debts of the member are not likely to be satisfied, he must apply to the court for the revocation of that order.

(4) If the court revokes an order made under regulation 13(3), the provisions of these Regulations, the principal Regulations and the Administration for Insurers Order [or the Administration for Insurers (Northern Ireland) Order] apply to the member and from the date of the revocation a relevant officer is to be treated as having been appointed by the court.

(5) For the purposes of paragraph (4), a relevant officer means—

(a) an administrator,

(b) a liquidator,

(c) a receiver,

(d) a trustee in bankruptcy, or

(e) in Scotland, an interim or permanent trustee,

as the case may be.

(6) For the purposes of this regulation, a "cash call" means a request or demand made by a managing agent to a member of a syndicate to make payments to the trustees of any relevant trust fund to be held for the purpose of discharging or providing for the liabilities incurred by that member as a member of the syndicate.

NOTES

Commencement: 10 August 2005.

Para (4): words in square brackets inserted by the Insurers (Reorganisation and Winding Up) (Amendment) Regulations 2007, SI 2007/851, reg 3(1), (6).

[4412]

15 Reorganisation controller's powers: voluntary arrangements in respect of a member

(1) The directors of a corporate member or former corporate member may make a proposal for a voluntary arrangement under Part 1 of the 1986 Act (or Part 2 of the 1989 Order) in relation to the member only if the reorganisation controller consents to the terms of that arrangement.

(2) Section 1A of that Act or Article 14A of that Order do not apply to a corporate member or former corporate member if—

(a) a Lloyd's market reorganisation order applies to it; and

(b) there is no order under regulation 13(3) in force in relation to it.

(3) The reorganisation controller is entitled to be heard at any hearing of an application relating to the arrangement.

NOTES

Commencement: 10 August 2005.

[4413]

16 Reorganisation controller's powers: individual voluntary arrangements in respect of a member

(1) The reorganisation controller is entitled to be heard on an application under section 253 of the 1986 Act (or Article 227 of the 1989 Order) by an individual member or former member.

(2) When considering such an application the court shall have regard to the objectives of the Lloyd's market reorganisation order.

(3) Paragraphs (4) to (7) apply if an interim order is made on the application of such a person.

(4) The reorganisation controller, or a person appointed by him for that purpose, may attend any meeting of creditors of the member or former member summoned under section 257 of the 1986 Act (or Article 231 of the 1989 Order) (summoning of creditors meeting).

(5) Notice of the result of a meeting so summoned must be given [in writing] to the reorganisation controller by the chairman of the meeting.

(6) The reorganisation controller may apply to the court under section 262 (challenge of meeting's decision) or 263 (implementation and supervision of approved voluntary arrangement) of the 1986 Act (or Article 236 or 237 or the 1989 Order).

(7) If a person other than the reorganisation controller makes an application to the court under any provision mentioned in paragraph (6), the reorganisation controller is entitled to be heard at any hearing relating to the application.

NOTES

Commencement: 10 August 2005.

Para (5): words in square brackets inserted by the Insurers (Reorganisation and Winding Up) (Amendment) Regulations 2007, SI 2007/851, reg 3(1), (7).

[4414]

17 *Reorganisation controller's* powers: trust deeds for creditors in Scotland

(1) This regulation applies to the granting at any time by a debtor who is a member or former member of a trust deed for creditors.

(2) The debtor must inform the person who is or is proposed to be the trustee at or before the time that the trust deed is granted that he is a member or former member of Lloyd's.

(3) As soon as practicable after the making of the Lloyd's market reorganisation order the trustee must send to the reorganisation controller—

(a) in every case, a copy of the trust deed;

(b) where any other document or information is sent to every creditor known to the trustee in pursuance of paragraph 5(1)(c) of Schedule 5 to the Bankruptcy (Scotland) Act 1985, a copy of such document or information.

(4) If the debtor or the trustee fails without reasonable excuse to comply with any obligation in paragraph (2) or (3) he shall be guilty of an offence and shall be liable on summary conviction to a fine not exceeding level 5 on the statutory scale or to imprisonment for a term not exceeding 3 months or both.

(5) Paragraph 7 of that Schedule applies to the reorganisation controller as if he were a qualified creditor who has not been sent a copy of the notice as mentioned in paragraph 5(1)(c) of the Schedule.

(6) The reorganisation controller must be given the same notice as the creditors of any meeting of creditors held in relation to the trust deed.

(7) The reorganisation controller, or a person appointed by him for the purpose, is entitled to attend and participate in (but not to vote at) any such meeting of creditors as if the reorganisation controller were a creditor under the deed.

(8) Expressions used in this regulation and in the Bankruptcy (Scotland) Act 1985 have the same meaning in this regulation as in that Act.

NOTES

Commencement: 10 August 2005.

[4415]

18 Powers of reorganisation controller: section 425 or Article 418 compromise or arrangement

(1) The reorganisation controller may apply to the court for an order that a meeting or meetings be summoned under section 425(1) of the 1985 Act or Article 418(1) of the Companies Order (power of company to compromise with creditors and members) in connection with a compromise or arrangement in relation to a member or former member.

(2) Where a member, its creditors or members make an application under section 425(1) or Article 418 the reorganisation controller is entitled to attend and be heard at any hearing.

(3) Where a meeting is summoned under section 425(1) or Article 418(1), the reorganisation controller is entitled to attend the meeting so summoned and to participate in it (but not to vote at it).

NOTES

Commencement: 10 August 2005.

[4416]

19 Appointment of an administrator, receiver or interim trustee in relation to a member

(1) Where a Lloyd's market reorganisation order is in force, the following appointments may be made in relation to a member or former member only where an order has been made under regulation 13(3) and has not been revoked and shall be notified to the reorganisation controller—

(a) the appointment of an administrator under paragraph 14 of Schedule B1 [or under paragraph 15 of Schedule B1 to the 1989 Order];

(b) the appointment of an administrator under paragraph 22 of Schedule B1 [or under paragraph 23 of Schedule B1 to the 1989 Order];

(c) the appointment of an administrative receiver;

(d) the appointment of an interim receiver; and

(e) the appointment of an interim trustee, within the meaning of the Bankruptcy (Scotland) Act 1985.

(2) The notification to the reorganisation controller under paragraph (1) must be in writing.

(3) If the requirement to notify the reorganisation controller in paragraph (1) is not complied with the administrator, administrative receiver, interim receiver or interim trustee is guilty of an offence and is liable on conviction to a fine not exceeding level 3 on the standard scale.

NOTES

Commencement: 10 August 2005.

Para (1): words in square brackets in sub-paras (a), (b) inserted by the Insurers (Reorganisation and Winding Up) (Amendment) Regulations 2007, SI 2007/851, reg 3(1), (8).

[4417]
20 Reorganisation controller's powers: administration orders in respect of members

(1) The reorganisation controller may make an administration application under paragraph 12 of Schedule B1 [or under paragraph 13 of Schedule B1 to the 1989 Order] in respect of a member or former member.

(2) Paragraphs (3) to (5) apply if—

(a) a person other than the reorganisation controller makes an administration application under Schedule B1[, or under Schedule B1 to the 1989 Order,] in relation to a member or former member; and

(b) an order under regulation 13(3) is not in force in respect of that member.

(3) The reorganisation controller is entitled to be heard—

(a) at the hearing of the administration application; and

(b) at any other hearing of the court in relation to the member under Schedule B1 [or under Schedule B1 to the 1989 Order].

(4) Any notice or other document required to be sent to a creditor of the member must also be sent to the reorganisation controller.

(5) The reorganisation controller, or a person appointed by him for the purpose, may—

(a) attend any meeting of creditors of the member summoned under any enactment;

(b) attend any meeting of a committee established under paragraph 57 of Schedule B1 [or under paragraph 58 of Schedule B1 to the 1989 Order]; and

(c) make representations as to any matter for decision at such a meeting.

(6) If, during the course of the administration of a member, a compromise or arrangement is proposed between the member and its creditors, or any class of them, the reorganisation controller may apply to court under section 425 of the 1985 Act (or Article 418 of the Companies Order).

NOTES

Commencement: 10 August 2005.

Paras (1), (2): words in square brackets inserted by the Insurers (Reorganisation and Winding Up) (Amendment) Regulations 2007, SI 2007/851, reg 3(1), (9)(a), (b).

Para (3): words in square brackets substituted by SI 2007/851, reg 3(1), (9)(c).

Para (5): words in square brackets inserted by SI 2007/851, reg 3(1), (9)(d).

[4418]
21 Reorganisation controller's powers: receivership in relation to members

(1) This regulation applies if a receiver has been appointed in relation to a member or former member.

(2) The reorganisation controller may be heard on an application made under section 35 or 63 of the 1986 Act (or Article 45 of the 1989 Order).

(3) The reorganisation controller may make an application under section 41(1)(a) or 69(1)(a) of the 1986 Act (or Article 51(1)(a) of the 1989 Order).

(4) A report under section 48(1) or 67(1) of the 1986 Act (or Article 58(1) of the 1989 Order) must be sent by the person making it to the reorganisation controller.

(5) The reorganisation controller, or a person appointed by him for the purpose, may—

(a) attend any meeting of creditors of the member or former member summoned under any enactment;

(b) attend any meeting of a committee established under section 49 or 68 of the 1986 Act (or [Article 59] of the 1989 Order);

(c) attend any meeting of a committee of creditors of a member or former member in Scotland; and

(d) make representations as to any matter for decision at such a meeting.

(6) Where an administration application is made in respect of a member by the reorganisation controller (and there is an administrative receiver, or in Scotland a receiver, of that member), paragraph 39 of Schedule B1 [or paragraph 40 of Schedule B1 to the 1989 Order] does not require the court to dismiss the application if it thinks that—

(a) the objectives of the Lloyd's market reorganisation order are more likely to be achieved by the appointment of an administrator than by the appointment or continued appointment of a receiver in respect of that member, and

(b) the interests of the person by or on behalf of whom the receiver was appointed will be adequately protected.

NOTES

Commencement: 10 August 2005.

Para (5): words in square brackets in sub-para (b) substituted by the Insurers (Reorganisation and Winding Up) (Amendment) Regulations 2007, SI 2007/851, reg 3(1), (10)(a).
Para (6): words in square brackets inserted by SI 2007/851, reg 3(1), (10)(b).

[4419]
22 Syndicate set-off

(1) This regulation applies where—
   (a) a member ("the debtor") is subject to a relevant insolvency proceeding; and
   (b) no order under regulation 13(3) is in effect in relation to the debtor.

(2) In the application of section 323 of the 1986 Act or Article 296 of the 1989 Order, Rule 2.85 and Rule 4.90 of the Insolvency Rules or [Rule 2.086 and] R4.096 of the Insolvency Rules (Northern Ireland) to the debtor, the following paragraphs apply in relation to each syndicate of which the debtor is a member, and for that purpose each reference to the debtor is to the debtor as a member of that syndicate only.

(3) Subject to paragraphs (4) and (5), where there have been mutual credits, mutual debts or other mutual dealings between the debtor in the course of his business as a member of the syndicate ("syndicate A") and a creditor, an account shall be taken of what is due from the debtor to that creditor, and of what is due from that creditor to the debtor, such account to be taken in respect of business transacted by the debtor as a member of syndicate A only and the sums due from one party shall be set off against the sums due from the other.

(4) Where the creditor is a member (whether or not a member of syndicate A) and there have been mutual credits, mutual debts or other mutual dealings between the debtor as a member of syndicate A and the creditor in the course of the creditor's business as a member of syndicate A or of another syndicate of which he is a member, paragraph (5) applies.

(5) A separate account must be taken in relation to each syndicate of which the creditor is a member of what is due from the debtor to the creditor, and of what is due from the creditor to the debtor, in respect only of business transacted between the debtor as a member of syndicate A and the creditor as a member of the syndicate in question (and not in respect of business transacted by the creditor as a member of any other syndicate or otherwise), and the sums due from one party shall be set off against the sums due from the other.

(6) In this regulation—
   (a) references to a member include references to a former member; and
   (b) "relevant insolvency proceedings" means proceedings in respect of an application or petition referred to in regulation 13(1).

NOTES

Commencement: 10 August 2005.
Para (2): words in square brackets inserted by the Insurers (Reorganisation and Winding Up) (Amendment) Regulations 2007, SI 2007/851, reg 3(1), (11).

[4420]
23 Voluntary winding up of members: consent of reorganisation controller

(1) During any period in which a Lloyd's market reorganisation order is in force, a member or former member that is a company may not be wound up voluntarily without the consent of the reorganisation controller.

(2) Before a member or former member passes a resolution for voluntary winding up it must give written notice to the reorganisation controller.

(3) Where notice is given under paragraph (2), a resolution for voluntary winding up may be passed only—
   (a) after the end of a period of five business days beginning with the day on which the notice was given, if the reorganisation controller has not refused his consent, or
   (b) if the reorganisation controller has consented in writing to the passing of the resolution.

(4) A copy of a resolution for the voluntary winding up of a member forwarded to the registrar of companies in accordance with section 380 of the 1985 Act (or Article 388 of the Companies Order) must be accompanied by a certificate issued by the reorganisation controller stating that he consents to the voluntary winding up of the member.

(5) If paragraph (4) is complied with, the voluntary winding up is to be treated as having commenced at the time the resolution was passed.

(6) If paragraph (4) is not complied with, the resolution has no effect.

NOTES

Commencement: 10 August 2005.

[4421]

24 Voluntary winding up of members: powers of reorganisation controller

(1) This regulation applies in relation to a member or former member that is a company and which is being wound up voluntarily with the consent of the reorganisation controller.

(2) The reorganisation controller may apply to the court under section 112 of the 1986 Act (reference of questions to court) (or Article 98 of the 1989 Order) in respect of the member.

(3) The reorganisation controller is entitled to be heard at any hearing of the court in relation to the voluntary winding up of the member.

(4) Any notice or other document required to be sent to a creditor of the member must also be sent to the reorganisation controller.

(5) The reorganisation controller, or a person appointed by him for the purpose, is entitled—

(a) to attend any meeting of creditors of the member summoned under any enactment;

(b) to attend any meeting of a committee established under section 101 of the 1986 Act (or Article 87 of the 1989 Order); and

(c) to make representations as to any matter for decision at such a meeting.

(6) If, during the course of the winding up of the member, a compromise or arrangement is proposed between the member and its creditors, or any class of them, the reorganisation controller may apply to court under section 425 of the 1985 Act (or Article 418 of the Companies Order).

NOTES

Commencement: 10 August 2005.

[4422]

25 Petition for winding up of a member by reorganisation controller

(1) The reorganisation controller may present a petition to the court for the winding up of a member or former member that is a company.

(2) The petition is to be treated as made under section 124 of the 1986 Act or Article 104 of the 1989 Order.

(3) Section 122(1) of the 1986 Act, or [Article 102] of the 1989 Order must, in the case of an application made by the reorganisation controller be read as if they included the following grounds—

(a) the member is in default of an obligation to pay an insurance market debt which is due and payable; or

(b) the court considers that the member is or is likely to be unable to pay insurance market debts as they fall due; and

(c) in the case of either (a) or (b), the court thinks that the winding up of the member is necessary or desirable for achieving the objectives of the Lloyd's market reorganisation order.

NOTES

Commencement: 10 August 2005.

Para (3): words in square brackets substituted by the Insurers (Reorganisation and Winding Up) (Amendment) Regulations 2007, SI 2007/851, reg 3(1), (12).

[4423]

26 Winding up of a member: powers of reorganisation controller

(1) This regulation applies if a person other than the reorganisation controller presents a petition for the winding up of a member or former member that is a company.

(2) Any notice or other document required to be sent to a creditor of the member must also be sent to the reorganisation controller.

(3) The reorganisation controller may be heard—

(a) at the hearing of the petition; and

(b) at any other hearing of the court in relation to the member under or by virtue of Part 4 or 5 of the 1986 Act (or Part 5 or 6 of the 1989 Order).

(4) The reorganisation controller, or a person appointed by him for the purpose, may—

(a) attend any meeting of the creditors of the member;

(b) attend any meeting of a committee established for the purposes of Part 4 or 5 of the 1986 Act under section 101 of that Act or under section 141 or 142 of that Act;

(c) attend any meeting of a committee established for the purposes of Part 5 or 6 of the 1989 Order under Article 87 or Article 120 of that Order;

(d) make representations as to any matter for decision at such a meeting.

(5) If, during the course of the winding up of a member, a compromise or arrangement is proposed between the member and its creditors, or any class of them, the reorganisation controller may apply to the court under section 425 of the 1985 Act (or Article 418 of the Companies Order).

NOTES

Commencement: 10 August 2005.

[4424]

27 Petition for bankruptcy of a member by reorganisation controller

(1) The reorganisation controller may present a petition to the court for a bankruptcy order to be made against an individual member or, in Scotland, for the sequestration of the estate of an individual.

(2) The application shall be treated as made under section 264 of the 1986 Act (or Article 238 of the 1989 Order) or in Scotland under section 5 or 6 of the Bankruptcy (Scotland) Act 1985.

(3) On such a petition, the court may make a bankruptcy order or in Scotland an award of sequestration if (and only if)—

- (a) the member is in default of an obligation to pay an insurance market debt which is due and payable; and
- (b) the court thinks that the making of a bankruptcy order or award of sequestration in respect of that member is necessary or desirable for achieving the objectives of the Lloyd's market reorganisation order.

NOTES

Commencement: 10 August 2005.

[4425]

28 Bankruptcy of a member: powers of reorganisation controller

(1) This regulation applies if a person other than the reorganisation controller presents a petition to the court—

- (a) under section 264 of the 1986 Act (or Article 238 of the 1989 Order) for a bankruptcy order to be made against an individual member;
- (b) under section 5 of the Bankruptcy (Scotland) Act 1985 for the sequestration of the estate of an individual member; or
- (c) under section 6 of that Act for the sequestration of the estate belonging to or held for or jointly by the members of an entity mentioned in subsection (1) of that section.

(2) The reorganisation controller is entitled to be heard—

- (a) at the hearing of the petition, and
- (b) at any other hearing in relation to the individual member or entity under—
  - (i) Part 9 of the 1986 Act,
  - (ii) Part 9 of the 1989 Order; or
  - (iii) the Bankruptcy (Scotland) Act 1985.

(3) A copy of the report prepared under section 274 of the 1986 Act (or Article 248 of the 1989 Order) must also be sent to the reorganisation controller.

(4) The reorganisation controller, or a person appointed by him for the purpose, is entitled—

- (a) to attend any meeting of the creditors of the individual member or entity;
- (b) to attend any meeting of a committee established under section 301 of the 1986 Act (or Article 274 of the 1989 Order);
- (c) to attend any meeting of commissioners held under paragraph 17 or 18 of Schedule 6 to the Bankruptcy (Scotland) Act; and
- (d) to make representations as to any matter for decision at such a meeting.

(5) In this regulation—

- (a) references to an individual member include references to a former member who is an individual;
- (b) "entity" means an entity which is a member or a former member.

NOTES

Commencement: 10 August 2005.

[4426]

29 Petition for winding up of the Society by reorganisation controller

(1) The reorganisation controller may present a petition to the court for the winding up of the Society in the circumstances set out in section 221(5) (winding up of unregistered companies) of the 1986 Act.

(2) Section 221(1) of that Act shall apply in respect of a petition presented by the reorganisation controller.

NOTES

Commencement: 10 August 2005.

[4427]

30 Winding up of the Society: service of petition etc on reorganisation controller

(1) This regulation applies if a person other than the reorganisation controller presents a petition for the winding up of the Society.

(2) The petitioner must serve a copy of the petition on the reorganisation controller.

(3) Any notice or other document required to be sent to a creditor of the Society must also be sent to the reorganisation controller.

(4) The reorganisation controller is entitled to be heard—

(a) at the hearing of the petition; and

(b) at any other hearing of the court in relation to the Society under or by virtue of Part 5 of the 1986 Act (winding up of unregistered companies).

(5) The reorganisation controller, or a person appointed by him for the purpose, is entitled—

(a) to attend any meeting of the creditors of the Society;

(b) to attend any meeting of a committee established for the purposes of Part 5 of the 1986 Act under section 101 of that Act (appointment of liquidation committee);

(c) to make representations as to any matter for decision at such a meeting.

(6) If, during the course of the winding up of the Society, a compromise or arrangement is proposed between the Society and its creditors, or any class of them, the reorganisation controller may apply to the court under section 425 of the 1985 Act.

NOTES

Commencement: 10 August 2005.

[4428]

31 Payments from central funds

(1) Unless otherwise agreed in writing between the Society, the reorganisation controller and the Authority, before making a payment from central funds during the period of the Lloyd's market reorganisation order, the Society must give 5 working days [written] notice to the reorganisation controller.

(2) Notice under paragraph (1) must specify—

(a) the amount of the proposed payment;

(b) the purpose for which it is proposed to be made;

(c) the recipient of the proposed payment.

(3) An agreement under paragraph (1) may in particular provide for payments—

(a) to a specified person;

(b) to a specified class of person;

(c) for a specified purpose;

(d) for a specified class of purposes,

to be made without the notice provided for in paragraph (1)

(4) If before the end of the period of 5 working days from the date on which he receives the notice under paragraph (1) the reorganisation controller considers that the payment should not be made, he must within that period—

(a) apply to the court for a determination that the payment not be made; and

(b) give notice [in writing] of his application to the Society and the Authority on or before the making of the application,

and the Society must not make payment without the permission of the court.

(5) The Society and the Authority may be heard at any hearing in connection with any such application.

(6) Where the reorganisation controller makes an application under paragraph (4), the Society commits an offence if it makes a payment from central funds without the permission of the court.

(7) If an offence under paragraph (6) is shown to have been committed with the consent or connivance of an officer of the Society, the officer as well as the Society is guilty of the offence.

(8) A person guilty of an offence under this regulation is liable—

(a) on summary conviction, to a fine not exceeding the statutory maximum;

(b) on conviction on indictment, to a fine.

(9) In this regulation "working day" means any day other than a Saturday, a Sunday, Christmas Day, Good Friday or a day which is a bank holiday under the Banking and Financial Dealings Act 1971 in any part of the United Kingdom.

(10) In paragraph (7), "officer", in relation to the Society, means the Chairman of Lloyd's, a Deputy Chairman of Lloyd's, the Chairman of the Committee established by section 5 of Lloyd's Act 1982, a deputy Chairman of the Committee, or a member of the Council established by section 3 of that Act.

NOTES

Commencement: 10 August 2005.

Paras (1), (4): words in square brackets inserted by the Insurers (Reorganisation and Winding Up) (Amendment) Regulations 2007, SI 2007/851, reg 3(1), (13).

PART 3
MODIFICATION OF LAW OF INSOLVENCY: NOTIFICATION AND PUBLICATION

[4429]

32 Application of Parts 3 and 4

Parts 3 and 4 of these Regulations apply where a Lloyd's market reorganisation order is in force and in respect of a member or former member in relation to whom no order under regulation 13(3) is in force.

NOTES

Commencement: 10 August 2005.

[4430]

33 Notification of relevant decision to Authority

(1) Regulation 9 of the principal Regulations applies to a member or former member in the circumstances set out in paragraph (2) and has effect as if the modifications set out in paragraphs (3) and (4) were included in it as regards members or former members.

(2) The circumstances are where—

(a) the member or former member is subject to a Lloyd's market reorganisation order which remains in force; and

(b) no order has been made in respect of that member or former member under regulation 13(3) of these Regulations and has not been revoked.

(3) In paragraph (1) of regulation 9 of the principal Regulations, insert—

(a) after sub-paragraph (b)—

"(ba) a bankruptcy order under section 264 of the 1986 Act or under [Article 238] of the 1989 Order;

(bb) an award of sequestration under the Bankruptcy (Scotland) Act 1985;";

(b) after paragraph (c)—

"(ca) the appointment of an interim trustee under section 286 or 287 of the 1986 Act or under Article 259 or 260 of the 1989 Order;

(cb) the appointment of a trustee in bankruptcy under sections 295, 296 or 300 of that Act or under Articles 268, 269 or 273 of that Order;

(cc) the appointment of an interim or permanent trustee under the Bankruptcy (Scotland) Act 1985;".

(4) In paragraph (2) of that regulation after "voluntary arrangement", insert "or individual voluntary arrangement" and after "supervisor" insert "or nominee (as the case may be)".

(5) In paragraph (7) of that regulation, in the definition of "qualifying arrangement",

(a) after "voluntary arrangement" insert "or individual voluntary arrangement"; and

(b) for "insurer", wherever appearing substitute "member or former member".

(6) In paragraph (8), after "supervisor" insert ", nominee, trustee in bankruptcy, trustee under a trust deed for creditors".

NOTES

Commencement: 10 August 2005.

Para (3): words in square brackets substituted by the Insurers (Reorganisation and Winding Up) (Amendment) Regulations 2007, SI 2007/851, reg 3(1), (14).

[4431]

34 Notification of relevant decision to EEA Regulators

Regulation 10 of the principal Regulations applies as if—

(a) in paragraph (1)(b)(i) for "the business of an insurer" there were substituted "the insurance business of a member or former member"; and

(b) in paragraph (1)(b)(ii) for "an insurer" there were substituted "a member or former member".

NOTES

Commencement: 10 August 2005.

[4432]

35 Application of certain publication requirements in the principal Regulations to members

(1) Regulation 11 of the principal Regulations (publication of voluntary arrangement, administration order, winding up order or scheme of arrangement) applies, with the following, where a qualifying decision has effect, or a qualifying order or appointment is made, in relation to a member or former member.

(2) References in regulation 11(2) to a "qualifying decision", a "qualifying order" and a "qualifying appointment" have the same meaning as in that regulation, subject to the modifications set out in paragraphs (3) and (5).

(3) Regulation 11(2)(a) has effect as if a qualifying decision included a decision with respect to the approval of a proposed individual voluntary arrangement in relation to a member in accordance with section 258 of the 1986 Act or Article 232 of the 1989 Order (decisions of creditors' meeting: individual voluntary arrangements) or in Scotland the grant of a trust deed (within the meaning of the Bankruptcy (Scotland) Act 1985).

(4) In the case of a qualifying decision of a kind mentioned in paragraph (3) above, regulation 11(4) has effect as if the information mentioned therein included the court to which an application under sections 262 (challenge of the meeting's decision) and 263(3) (implementation and supervision of approved voluntary arrangement) of the 1986 Act may be made or Articles 236 (challenge of the meeting's decision) and 237(3) (implementation and supervision of approved voluntary arrangement) of the 1989 Order, or in Scotland under paragraph 12 of Schedule 5 to the Bankruptcy (Scotland) Act 1985.

(5) Regulation 11(2)(b) has effect as if a qualifying order included in relation to a member or former member a bankruptcy order under Part 9 of the 1986 Act or Part 9 of the 1989 Order, or in Scotland, an award of sequestration under the Bankruptcy (Scotland) Act.

(6) In the case of a qualifying order of the kind mentioned in paragraph (5) above, regulation 11(4) has effect as if the information mentioned therein included the court to which an application may be made under section 303 or 375 of the 1986 Act or Article 276 of the 1989 Order, or in Scotland included the court having jurisdiction to sequestrate.

(7) Regulation 11(11) has effect as if the meaning of "relevant officer" included—

(a) in the case of a voluntary arrangement under Part 9 of the 1986 Act or Part 9 of the 1989 Order, the nominee;

(b) in the case of a bankruptcy order, the trustee in bankruptcy;

(c) in Scotland,

(i) the trustee acting under a trust deed;

(ii) in the case of an award of sequestration, the interim or permanent trustee, as the case may be.

NOTES

Commencement: 10 August 2005.

[4433]

36 Notification to creditors: winding up proceedings relating to members

(1) Regulation 12 of the principal Regulations (notification to creditors: winding up proceedings) applies, with the following modifications, where a relevant order or appointment is made, or a relevant decision is taken, in relation to a member or former member.

(2) References in paragraph (3) of that regulation to a "relevant order", a "relevant appointment" and a "relevant decision" have the meaning they have in that regulation, subject to the modifications set out in paragraphs (3) and (7).

(3) Paragraph (3) of that regulation has effect, for the purposes of this regulation, as if—

(a) a relevant order included a bankruptcy order made in relation to a member or former member under Part 9 of the 1986 Act or Part 9 of the 1989 Order or an award of sequestration under the Bankruptcy (Scotland) Act 1985; and

(b) a relevant decision included a decision as a result of which a qualifying individual voluntary arrangement in relation to a member or former member has effect in accordance with section 258 of the 1986 Act or Article 232 of the 1989 Order (decisions of creditors' meeting: individual voluntary arrangements) or in Scotland the grant of a qualifying trust deed.

(4) Paragraph (4)(a) of that regulation has effect as if the reference to a UK insurer included a reference to a member or former member who is to be treated as a UK insurer for the purposes of the application of the principal Regulations.

(5) Paragraph (9) of that regulation has effect as if, in a case where a bankruptcy order is made in relation to a member or former member, it permitted the obligation under paragraph (1)(a)(ii) of that regulation to be discharged by sending a form of proof in accordance with rule 6.97 of the Insolvency Rules or Rule 6.095 of the Insolvency Rules (Northern Ireland) or submitting a claim in accordance with section 48 of the Bankruptcy (Scotland) Act 1985, provided that the form of proof or submission of claim complies with paragraph (7) or (8) of that regulation (whichever is applicable).

(6) Paragraph (13)(a) of that regulation has effect as if the meaning of "appointed officer" included—

(a) in the case of a qualifying individual voluntary arrangement approved in relation to a member or former member, the nominee;

(b) in the case of a bankruptcy order in relation to an individual member or former member, the trustee in bankruptcy;

(c) in Scotland in the case of a sequestration, the interim or permanent trustee; and

(d) in Scotland in the case of a relevant decision, the trustee.

(7) For the purposes of paragraph (3) of that regulation, an individual voluntary arrangement approved in relation to an individual member or former member is a qualifying individual voluntary arrangement and a trust deed within section 5(4A) of the Bankruptcy (Scotland) Act 1985 is a qualifying trust deed if its purposes or objects, as the case may be, include a realisation of some or all of the assets of that member or former member and a distribution of the proceeds to creditors, with a view to terminating the whole or any part of the business of that member carried on or formerly carried on in connection with contracts of insurance written at Lloyd's.

NOTES

Commencement: 10 August 2005.

[4434]

37 Submission of claims by EEA creditor

(1) Regulation 13 of the principal Regulations (submission of claims by EEA creditors) applies, with the modifications set out in paragraphs (3) to (6) below, in the circumstances set out in paragraph (2) below, in the same way as it applies where an EEA creditor submits a claim or observations in the circumstances set out in paragraph (1) of that regulation.

(2) Those circumstances are where, after the date these Regulations come into force an EEA creditor submits a claim or observations relating to his claim in any relevant proceedings in respect of a member or former member (irrespective of when those proceedings were commenced or had effect).

(3) Paragraph (2) of that regulation has effect as if the "relevant proceedings" included—

(a) bankruptcy or sequestration; or

(b) a qualifying individual voluntary arrangement or in Scotland a qualifying trust deed for creditors.

(4) Paragraph (5) of that regulation has effect as if it also provided that paragraph (3) of that regulation does not apply where an EEA creditor submits his claim using—

(a) in a case of a bankruptcy or an award of sequestration of a member or former member, a form of proof in accordance with Rule 6.97 of Insolvency Rules or Rule 4.080 of the Insolvency Rules (Northern Ireland) or section 48 of the Bankruptcy (Scotland) Act 1985;

(b) in the case of a qualifying trust deed, the form prescribed by the trustee; and

(c) in the case of a qualifying individual voluntary arrangement, a form approved by the court for that purpose.

(5) For the purposes of that regulation (as applied in the circumstances set out in paragraph (2) above), an individual voluntary arrangement approved in relation to an individual member is a qualifying individual voluntary arrangement and a trust deed for creditors within section 5(4A) of the Bankruptcy (Scotland) Act 1985 is a qualifying trust deed for creditors if its purposes or objects as the case may be include a realisation of some or all of the assets of that member or former member and a distribution of the proceeds to creditors including insurance creditors, with a view to terminating the whole or any part of the business of that member carried on in connection with effecting or carrying out contracts of insurance written at Lloyd's.

NOTES

Commencement: 10 August 2005.

[4435]

38 Reports to creditors

(1) Regulation 14 of the principal Regulations (reports to creditors) applies with the modifications set out in paragraphs (2) to (4) where—

- (a) a liquidator is appointed in respect of a member or former member in accordance with—
  - (i) section 100 of the 1986 Act or Article 86 of the 1989 Order (creditors' voluntary winding up: appointment of a liquidator), or
  - (ii) paragraph 83 of Schedule B1 [or paragraph 84 of Schedule B1 to the 1989 Order] (moving from administration to creditors' voluntary liquidation);
- (b) a winding up order is made by the court in respect of a member or former member;
- (c) a provisional liquidator is appointed in respect of a member or former member;
- [(d) an administrator (within the meaning given by paragraph 1(1) of Schedule B1 or paragraph 2(1) of Schedule B1 to the 1989 Order) of a member or former member includes in the statement required by Rule 2.3 of the Insolvency Rules or by Rule 2.003 of the Insolvency Rules (Northern Ireland) a statement to the effect that the objective set out in paragraph 3(1)(a) of Schedule B1 or paragraph 4(1)(a) of Schedule B1 to the 1989 Order is not reasonably likely to be achieved;] or
- (e) a bankruptcy order or award of sequestration is made in respect of a member or former member.

(2) Paragraphs (2) to (5) of that regulation have effect as if they each included a reference to—

- (a) an administrator who has made a statement to the effect that the objective set out in paragraph 3(1)(a) of Schedule B1 [or in paragraph 4(1)(a) of Schedule B1 to the 1989 Order] is not reasonably likely to be achieved;
- (b) the official receiver or a trustee in bankruptcy; and
- (c) in Scotland, an interim or permanent trustee.

(3) Paragraph (6)(a) of that regulation has effect as if the meaning of "known creditor" included—

- (a) a creditor who is known to the administrator, the trustee in bankruptcy or the trustee, as the case may be;
- (b) in a case where a bankruptcy order is made in respect of a member or former member, a creditor who is specified in a report submitted under section 274 of the 1986 Act or [Article 248] of the 1989 Order or a statement of affairs submitted under section 288 or Article 261 in respect of the member or former member;
- (c) in a case where an administrator of a member has made a statement to the effect that the objective set out in paragraph 3(1)(a) of Schedule B1 [or in paragraph 4(1)(a) of Schedule B1 to the 1989 Order] is not reasonably likely to be achieved, a creditor who is specified in the statement of the member's affairs required by the administrator under paragraph 47(1) of [Schedule B1 or under paragraph 48(1) of Schedule B1 to the 1989 Order];
- (d) in a case where a sequestration has been awarded, a creditor who is specified in a statement of assets and liabilities under section 19 of the Bankruptcy (Scotland) Act 1985.

(4) Paragraph (6)(b) of that regulation has effect as if "report" included a written report setting out the position generally as regards the progress of—

- (a) the bankruptcy or sequestration; or
- (b) the administration.

NOTES

Commencement: 10 August 2005.

Para (1): words in square brackets in sub-para (a) inserted and sub-para (d) substituted by the Insurers (Reorganisation and Winding Up) (Amendment) Regulations 2007, SI 2007/851, reg 3(1), (15)(a), (b).

Para (2): words in square brackets in sub-para (a) inserted by SI 2007/851, reg 3(1), (15)(c).

Para (3): words in square brackets in sub-para (b) and words in second pair of square brackets in sub-para (c) substituted, and words in first pair of square brackets in sub-para (c) inserted by SI 2007/851, reg 3(1), (15)(d), (e).

[4436]

39 Service of notices and documents

(1) Regulation 15 of the principal Regulations (service of notices and documents) applies, with the modifications set out in paragraphs (2) and (3) below, to any notification, report or other document which is required to be sent to a creditor of a member or former member by a provision of Part III of those Regulations as applied and modified by regulations 33 to 35 above.

(2) Paragraph 15(5)(a)(i) of that regulation has effect as if the reference to the UK insurer which is liable under the creditor's claim included a reference to the member or former member who or which is liable under the creditor's claim.

(3) Paragraph (7)(c) of that regulation has effect as if "relevant officer" included a trustee in bankruptcy, nominee, receiver or, in Scotland, an interim or permanent trustee under a trust deed within the meaning of section 5(4A) of the Bankruptcy (Scotland) Act who is required to send a notification to a creditor by a provision of Part III of the principal Regulations as applied and modified by regulations 33 to 37 above.

NOTES

Commencement: 10 August 2005.

PART 4
APPLICATION OF PARTS 4 AND 5 OF THE PRINCIPAL REGULATIONS

[4437]

40 Priority for insurance claims

(1) Part 4 of the principal Regulations applies with the modifications set out in paragraphs (2) to (11).

(2) References, in relation to a UK insurer, to a winding up by the court have effect as if they included a reference to the bankruptcy or sequestration of a member or former member.

(3) References to the making of a winding up order in relation to a UK insurer have effect as if they included a reference to the making of a bankruptcy order or, in Scotland, an award of sequestration in relation to an individual member or a member or former member that is a Scottish limited partnership.

(4) References to an administration order in relation to a UK insurer have effect as if they included a reference to an individual voluntary arrangement in relation to an individual member and a trust deed for creditors within the meaning of section 5(4A) of the Bankruptcy (Scotland) Act.

(5) Regulation 20 (preferential debts: disapplication of section 175 of the 1986 Act or Article 149 of the 1989 Order) has effect as if the references to section 175 of the 1986 Act and Article 149 of the 1989 Order included a reference to section 328 of that Act, Article 300 of that Order and section 51(1)(d) to (h) of the Bankruptcy (Scotland) Act 1985.

(6) Regulation 21(3) (preferential debts: long term insurers and general insurers) has effect as if after the words "rank equally among themselves" there were inserted the words "after the expenses of the bankruptcy or sequestration".

(7) Regulation 27 (composite insurers: application of other assets) has effect as if the reference to section 175 of the 1986 Act or Article 149 of the 1989 Order included a reference to section 328 of that Act, Article 300 of that Order and section 51(1) (e) to (h) of the Bankruptcy (Scotland) Act.

(8) Regulation 29 (composite insurers: general meetings of creditors) has effect as if after paragraph (2) there were inserted—

> "(3) If the general meeting of the bankrupt's creditors proposes to establish a creditors' committee pursuant to section 301(1) of the 1986 Act or Article 274(1) of the 1989 Order, it must establish separate committees of creditors in respect of long-term business liabilities and creditors in respect of general business liabilities.
>
> (4) The committee of creditors in respect of long-term business liabilities may exercise the functions of a creditors' committee under the 1986 Act or the 1989 Order in relation to long term business liabilities only.
>
> (5) The committee of creditors in respect of general business liabilities may exercise the functions of a creditors' committee under the 1986 Act or the 1989 Order in relation to general business liabilities only.

(6) If, in terms of section 30(1) of the Bankruptcy (Scotland) Act 1985, at the statutory meeting or any subsequent meeting of creditors it is proposed to elect one or more commissioners (or new or additional commissioners) in the sequestration, it shall elect separate commissioners in respect of the long-term business liabilities and the general business liabilities.

(7) Any commissioner elected in respect of the long-term business liabilities shall exercise his functions under the Bankruptcy (Scotland) Act 1985 in respect of the long-term business liabilities only.

(8) Any commissioner elected in respect of the general business liabilities shall exercise his functions under the Bankruptcy (Scotland) Act 1985 in respect of the general business liabilities only.".

(9) Regulation 30 (composite insurers: apportionment of costs payable out of the assets) has effect as if in its application to members or former members who are individuals or Scottish limited partnerships—

(a) in England and Wales, the reference to Rule 4.218 of the Insolvency Rules (general rule as to priority) included a reference to Rule 6.224 of the Insolvency Rules (general rule as to priority (bankruptcy));

(b) in Northern Ireland, the reference to Rule 4.228 of the Insolvency Rules (Northern Ireland) (general rule as to priority) included a reference to Rule 6.222 of the Insolvency Rules (Northern Ireland) (general rule as to priority (bankruptcy)); and

(c) in Scotland, the reference to Rule 4.67 of the Insolvency (Scotland) Rules includes reference to—

(i) any finally determined outlays or remuneration in a sequestration within the meaning of section 53 of the Bankruptcy (Scotland) Act 1985 and shall be calculated and applied separately in respect of the long-term business assets and the general business assets of that member; and

(ii) the remuneration and expenses of a trustee under a trust deed for creditors within the meaning of the Bankruptcy (Scotland) Act 1985,

and references to a liquidator include references to a trustee in bankruptcy, interim or permanent trustee, trustee under a trust deed for creditors, Accountant in Bankruptcy or Commissioners where appropriate.

(10) Regulation 31 (summary remedies against liquidators) has effect as if—

(a) the reference to section 212 of the 1986 Act or Article 176 of the 1989 Order included a reference to section 304 of that Act or Article 277 of that Order (liability of trustee);

(b) the references to a liquidator included a reference to a trustee in bankruptcy in respect of a qualifying insolvent member; and

(c) the reference to section 175 of the 1986 Act or Article 149 of the 1989 Order included a reference to section 328 of that Act or Article 300 of that Order.

(11) Regulation 33 (voluntary arrangements: treatment of insurance debts) has effect as if after paragraph (3) there were inserted—

"(4) The modifications made by paragraph (5) apply where an individual member proposes an individual voluntary arrangement in accordance with Part 8 of the 1986 Act or Part 8 of the 1989 Order, and that arrangement includes—

(a) a composition in satisfaction of any insurance debts; and

(b) a distribution to creditors of some or all of the assets of that member in the course of, or with a view to, terminating the whole or any part of the insurance business of that member carried on at Lloyd's.

(5) Section 258 of the 1986 Act (decisions of creditors' meeting) has effect as if—

(a) after subsection (5) there were inserted—

"(5A) A meeting so summoned in relation to an individual member and taking place when a Lloyd's market reorganisation order is in force shall not approve any proposal or modification under which any insurance debt of that member is to be paid otherwise than in priority to such of his debts as are not insurance debts or preferential debts.";

(b) after subsection (7) there were inserted—

"(8) For the purposes of this section—

(a) "insurance debt" has the meaning it has in the Insurers (Reorganisation and Winding Up) Regulations 2004;

(b) "Lloyd's market reorganisation order" and "individual member" have the meaning they have in the Insurers (Reorganisation and Winding Up) (Lloyd's)

Regulations 2005.".

(6) Article 232 of the 1989 Order (Decisions of creditors' meeting) has effect as if—

(a) after paragraph (6) there were inserted—

"(6A) A meeting so summoned in relation to an individual member and taking place when a Lloyd's market reorganisation order is in force shall not approve any proposal or modification under which any insurance debt of that member is to be paid otherwise than in priority to such of his debts as are not insurance debts or preferential debts.";

(b) after paragraph (9) there were inserted—

"(10) For the purposes of this Article—

(a) "insurance debt" has the meaning it has in the Insurers (Reorganisation and Winding Up) Regulations 2004;

(b) "Lloyd's market reorganisation order" and "individual member" have the meaning they have in the Insurers (Reorganisation and Winding Up) (Lloyd's) Regulations 2005.".

(7) In Scotland, where a member or former member grants a trust deed for creditors, Schedule 5 to the Bankruptcy (Scotland) Act 1985 shall be read as if after paragraph 4 there were included paragraphs 4A and 4B as follows—

"4A. Whether or not provision is made in any trust deed, where such a trust deed includes a composition in satisfaction of any insurance debts of a member or former member and a distribution to creditors of some or all of the assets of that member or former member in the course of or with a view to meeting obligations of his insurance business carried on at Lloyd's, the trustee may not provide for any insurance debt to be paid otherwise than in priority to such of his debts as are not insurance debts or preferred debts within the meaning of section 51(2).

4B. For the purposes of paragraph 4A,

(a) "insurance debt" has the meaning it has in the Insurance (Reorganisation and Winding Up) Regulations 2004; and

(b) "member" and "former member" have the meaning given in regulation 2(1) of the Insurers (Reorganisation and Winding Up) (Lloyd's) Regulations 2005.".".

(12) The power to apply to court in section 303 of the 1986 Act or Article 276 of the 1989 Order or section 63 of the Bankruptcy (Scotland) Act (general control of trustee by court) may be exercised by the reorganisation controller if it appears to him that any act, omission or decision of a trustee of the estate of a member contravenes the provisions of Part 4 of the principal Regulations (as applied by this regulation).

NOTES

Commencement: 10 August 2005.

[4438]

41 Treatment of liabilities arising in connection with a contract subject to reinsurance to close

(1) Where in respect of a member or former member who is subject to a Lloyd's market reorganisation order any of the events specified in paragraph (2)(a) have occurred, for the purposes of the application of Part 4 of the principal Regulations to that member (and only for those purposes), an obligation of that member under a reinsurance to close contract in respect of a debt due or treated as due under a contract of insurance written at Lloyd's is to be treated as an insurance debt.

(2) For the purposes of this regulation—

(a) The events are—

(i) in respect of a member which is a corporation the appointment of a liquidator, provisional liquidator or administrator;

(ii) in respect of an individual member, the appointment of a receiver or trustee in bankruptcy; and

(iii) in respect of a member in Scotland being either an individual or a Scottish limited partnership, the making of a sequestration order or the appointment of an interim or permanent trustee;

(b) "reinsurance to close contract" means a contract under which, in accordance with the rules or practices of Lloyd's, underwriting members ("the reinsured members") who are members of a syndicate for a year of account ("the closed year") agree with underwriting members who constitute that or another syndicate for a later year of account ("the reinsuring members") that the reinsuring members will indemnify the reinsured members against all known and unknown liabilities of the reinsured members arising out of the insurance business underwritten through that syndicate and allocated to the closed year (including liabilities under any reinsurance to close contract underwritten by the reinsured members).

NOTES

Commencement: 10 August 2005.

[4439]

42 Assets of members

(1) This regulation applies where a member or former member is treated as a UK insurer in accordance with regulations 13 and 40 above.

(2) Subject to paragraphs (3) and (4), the undistributed assets of the member are to be treated as assets of the insurer for the purposes of the application of Part 4 of the principal Regulations in accordance with regulation 43 below.

(3) For the purposes of this regulation, the undistributed assets of the member so treated do not include any asset held in a relevant trust fund.

(4) But any asset released from a relevant trust fund and received by such a member is to be treated as an asset of the insurer for the purposes of the application of Part 4 of the principal Regulations.

NOTES

Commencement: 10 August 2005.

[4440]

43 Application of Part 4 of the principal Regulations: protection of settlements

(1) This regulation applies where a member or former member is subject to an insolvency measure mentioned in paragraph (4) at the time that a Lloyd's market reorganisation order comes into force.

(2) Nothing in these Regulations or Part 4 of the principal Regulations affects the validity of any payment or disposition made, or any settlement agreed, by the relevant officer before the date when the Lloyd's market reorganisation order came into force.

(3) For the purposes of the application of Part 4 of the principal Regulations, the insolvent estate of the member or former member shall not include any assets which are subject to a relevant section 425 or Article 418 compromise or arrangement, a relevant individual voluntary arrangement, or a relevant trust deed for creditors.

(4) In paragraph (2) "relevant officer" means—
- (a) where the insolvency measure is a voluntary arrangement, the nominee;
- (b) where the insolvency measure is administration, the administrator;
- (c) where the insolvency measure is the appointment of a provisional liquidator, the provisional liquidator;
- (d) where the insolvency measure is a winding up, the liquidator;
- (e) where the insolvency measure is an individual voluntary arrangement, the nominee or supervisor;
- (f) where the insolvency measure is bankruptcy, the trustee in bankruptcy;
- (g) where the insolvency measure is sequestration, the interim or permanent trustee; and
- (h) where the insolvency measure is a trust deed for creditors, the trustee.

(5) For the purposes of paragraph (3)—
- (a) "assets" has the same meaning as "property" in section 436 of the 1986 Act or Article 2(2) of the 1989 Order;
- (b) "insolvent estate" in England and Wales and Northern Ireland has the meaning given by Rule 13.8 of the Insolvency Rules or Rule 0.2 of the Insolvency Rules (Northern Ireland), and in Scotland means the whole estate of the member;
- (c) "a relevant section 425 or Article 418 compromise or arrangement" means—
  - (i) a section 425 or Article 418 compromise or arrangement which was sanctioned by the court before the date on which an application for a Lloyd's market reorganisation order was made, or
  - (ii) any subsequent section 425 or Article 418 compromise or arrangement sanctioned by the court to amend or replace a compromise or arrangement of the kind mentioned in paragraph (i);

(d) "a relevant individual voluntary arrangement" and "a relevant trust deed for creditors" mean an individual voluntary arrangement or trust deed for creditors which was sanctioned by the court or entered into before the date on which an application for a Lloyd's market reorganisation order was made.

NOTES

Commencement: 10 August 2005.

[4441]

44 Challenge by reorganisation controller to conduct of insolvency practitioner

(1) The reorganisation controller may apply to the court claiming that a relevant officer is acting, has acted, or proposes to act in a way that fails to comply with a requirement of Part 4 of the principal Regulations.

(2) The reorganisation controller must send a copy of an application under paragraph (1) to the relevant officer in respect of whom the application is made.

(3) In the case of a relevant officer who is acting in respect of a member or former member subject to the jurisdiction of a Scottish court, the application must be made to the Court of Session.

(4) The court may—

(a) dismiss the application;

(b) make an interim order;

(c) make any other order it thinks appropriate.

(5) In particular, an order under this regulation may—

(a) regulate the relevant officer's exercise of his functions;

(b) require that officer to do or not do a specified thing;

(c) make consequential provision.

(6) An order may not be made under this regulation if it would impede or prevent the implementation of—

(a) a voluntary arrangement approved under Part 1 of the 1986 Act or Part 2 of the 1989 Order before the date when the Lloyd's market reorganisation order was made;

(b) an individual voluntary arrangement approved under Part 8 of that Act or Part 8 of that Order before the date when the Lloyd's market reorganisation order was made; or

(c) a section 425 or Article 418 compromise or arrangement which was sanctioned by the court before the date when the Lloyd's market reorganisation order was made.

(7) In this regulation "relevant officer" means—

(a) a liquidator,

(b) a provisional liquidator,

(c) an administrator

(d) the official receiver or a trustee in bankruptcy, or

(e) in Scotland, an interim or permanent trustee or a trustee for creditors,

who is appointed in relation to a member or former member.

NOTES

Commencement: 10 August 2005.

[4442]

45 Application of Part 5 of the principal Regulations

(1) Part 5 of the principal Regulations (reorganisation or winding up of UK insurers: recognition of EEA rights) applies with the modifications set out in regulation 46 where, on or after the date that a Lloyd's market reorganisation order comes into force, a member or former member is or becomes subject to a reorganisation or insolvency measure.

(2) For the purposes of this regulation a "reorganisation or insolvency measure" means—

(a) a voluntary arrangement, having a qualifying purpose, approved in accordance with section 4A of the 1986 Act or Article 17A of the 1989 Order;

(b) administration pursuant to an order under paragraph 13 of Schedule B1 [or under paragraph 14 of Schedule B1 to the 1989 Order];

(c) the reduction by the court of the value of one or more relevant contracts of insurance under section 377 of the 2000 Act or section 24(5) of the Friendly Societies Act 1992;

(d) winding up;

(e) the appointment of a provisional liquidator in accordance with section 135 of the 1986 Act or Article 115 of the 1989 Order;

(f) an individual voluntary arrangement, having a qualifying purpose, approved in accordance with section 258 of the 1986 Act or Article 232 of the 1989 Order;

(g) in Scotland a qualifying trust deed for creditors within the meaning of section 5(4A) of the Bankruptcy (Scotland) Act 1985;
(h) bankruptcy, in accordance with Part 9 of the 1986 Act or Part 9 of the 1989 Order; or
(i) sequestration under the Bankruptcy (Scotland) Act 1985.

(3) A measure imposed under the law of a State or country other than the United Kingdom is not a reorganisation or insolvency measure for the purposes of this regulation.

(4) For the purposes of sub-paragraphs (a), (f) and (g) of paragraph (2), a voluntary arrangement or individual voluntary arrangement has a qualifying purpose and a trust deed is a qualifying trust deed if it—
(a) varies the rights of creditors as against the member and is intended to enable the member to continue to carry on an insurance market activity at Lloyd's; or
(b) includes a realisation of some or all of the assets of the member and the distribution of proceeds to creditors, with a view to terminating the whole or any part of that member's business at Lloyd's.

NOTES

Commencement: 10 August 2005.

Para (2): words in square brackets in sub-para (b) inserted by the Insurers (Reorganisation and Winding Up) (Amendment) Regulations 2007, SI 2007/851, reg 3(1), (16).

[4443]

46 Modification of provisions in Part 5 of the principal Regulations

(1) The modifications mentioned in regulation 45(1) are as follows.

(2) Regulation 35 is disapplied.

(3) Regulation 36 (interpretation of Part 5) has effect as if—
(a) in paragraph (1)—
(i) the meaning of "affected insurer" included a member or former member who, on or after the date that a Lloyd's market reorganisation order comes into force, is or becomes subject to a reorganisation or insolvency measure within the meaning given by regulation 44(2)of these Regulations;
(ii) the meaning of "relevant reorganisation or relevant winding up" included any reorganisation or insolvency measure, in respect of a member or former member, to which Part 5 of the principal Regulations applies by virtue of regulation 45(1) of these Regulations;
(iii) in the case of sequestration, the date of sequestration within the meaning of section 12 of the Bankruptcy (Scotland) Act 1985; and
(b) in paragraph (2) references to the opening of a relevant reorganisation or a relevant winding up meant (in addition to the meaning in the cases set out in that paragraph)—
(i) in the case of an individual voluntary arrangement, the date when a decision with respect to that arrangement has effect in accordance with section 258 of the 1986 Act or Article 232 of the 1989 Order;
(ii) in the case of bankruptcy, the date on which the bankruptcy order is made under Part 9 of the 1986 Act or Part 9 of the 1989 Order;
(iii) in the case of a trust deed for creditors under the Bankruptcy (Scotland) Act 1985 the date when the trust deed was granted.

(4) Regulation 37 of the principal Regulations (EEA rights: applicable law in the winding up of a UK insurer) has effect as if—
(a) references to a relevant winding up included (in each case) a reference to a reorganisation or insolvency measure within the meaning given by sub-paragraphs (d), (g) (h) and (i) of regulation 45(2) of these Regulations (winding up and bankruptcy) in respect of a member or former member; and
(b) the reference in paragraph (3)(c) to the liquidator included a reference to the trustee in bankruptcy or in Scotland to the interim or permanent trustee.

(5) Regulation 42 (reservation of title agreements etc) has effect as if the reference to an insurer in paragraphs (1) and (2) included a reference to a member or former member.

NOTES

Commencement: 10 August 2005.

[4444]

47 Application of Part 5 of the principal Regulations: protection of dispositions etc made before a Lloyd's market reorganisation order comes into force

(1) This regulation applies where—

(a) a member or former member is subject to a reorganisation or insolvency measure on the date when a Lloyd's market reorganisation order comes into force; and

(b) Part 5 of the principal Regulations applies in relation to that reorganisation or insolvency measure by virtue of regulation 45 above.

(2) Nothing in Part 5 of the principal Regulations affects the validity of any payment or disposition made, or any settlement agreed, by the relevant officer before the date when the Lloyd's market reorganisation order came into force.

(3) For the purposes of the application of Part 5 of the principal Regulations, the insolvent estate of the member does not include any assets which are subject to a relevant section 425 or Article 418 compromise or arrangement, a relevant individual voluntary arrangement, or a relevant trust deed for creditors.

(4) In paragraph (2) "relevant officer" means—

(a) where the member is subject to a voluntary arrangement in accordance with section 4A of the 1986 Act or Article 17A of the 1989 Order, the supervisor;

(b) where the member is in administration in accordance with Schedule B1 [or with Schedule B1 to the 1989 Order], the administrator;

(c) where a provisional liquidator has been appointed in relation to a member in accordance with section 135 of the 1986 Act or Article 115 of the 1989 Order, the provisional liquidator;

(d) where the member is being wound up under Part 4 of the 1986 Act or Part 5 of the 1989 Order, the liquidator;

(e) where the member has made a voluntary arrangement in accordance with Part 8 of the 1986 Act or Part 8 of the 1989 Order, the nominee;

(f) where the member is bankrupt within the meaning of Part 9 of the 1986 Act or Part 9 of the 1989 Order, the official receiver or trustee in bankruptcy;

(g) where the member is being sequestrated, the interim or permanent trustee; and

(h) where a trust deed for creditors has been granted, the trustee.

(5) For the purposes of paragraph (3)—

(a) "assets" has the same meaning as "property" in section 436 of the 1986 Act or Article 2(2) of the 1989 Order, except in relation to relevant trust deeds;

(b) "insolvent estate" in England and Wales and Northern Ireland has the meaning given by Rule 13.8 of the Insolvency Rules or Rule 0.2 of the Insolvency Rules (Northern Ireland), and in Scotland means the assets of the member;

(c) "relevant section 425 or Article 418 compromise or arrangement" means—

(i) a section 425 or Article 418 compromise or arrangement which was sanctioned by the court before the date when the Lloyd's market reorganisation order came into force, or

(ii) any subsequent section 425 or Article 418 compromise or arrangement sanctioned by the court to amend or replace a compromise or arrangement of the kind mentioned in paragraph (i);

(d) "relevant individual voluntary arrangement" means—

(i) an individual voluntary arrangement approved under Part 8 of the 1986 Act [or Part 8 of the 1989 Order] before the date when a Lloyd's market reorganisation order came in to force, and

(ii) any subsequent individual voluntary arrangement sanctioned by the court to amend or replace an arrangement of the kind mentioned in paragraph (i); and

(e) "relevant trust deed" means a trust deed granted by a member or former member before the date when the Lloyd's market reorganisation order entered into force.

NOTES

Commencement: 10 August 2005.

Para (4): words in square brackets in sub-para (b) inserted by the Insurers (Reorganisation and Winding Up) (Amendment) Regulations 2007, SI 2007/851, reg 3(1), (17)(a).

Para (5): words in square brackets in sub-para (d) inserted by SI 2007/851, reg 3(1), (17)(b).

[4445]

48 Non-EEA countries

In respect of a member or former member who is established in a country outside the EEA, the court or the Authority may, subject to sections 348 and 349 of the 2000 Act, make such disclosures as each considers appropriate to a court or to a regulator with a role equivalent to that of the Authority for the purpose of facilitating the work of the reorganisation controller.

NOTES

Commencement: 10 August 2005.

49 (*Amends the Insurers (Reorganisation and Winding Up) Regulations 2004, SI 2004/353, reg 19(2)(b) at* **[4288]**.)

COMPANIES (SUMMARY FINANCIAL STATEMENT) REGULATIONS 2008

(SI 2008/374)

NOTES

Made: 19 February 2008.
Authority: Companies Act 2006, ss 426(1), (3), 427(2), (5), 428(2), (5), 1292(1).
Commencement: 6 April 2008.

1–8 *((Pts 1, 2) outside the scope of this work.)*

PART 3
FORM AND CONTENT OF SUMMARY FINANCIAL STATEMENT

9, 10 *(Outside the scope of this work.)*

[4446]
11 Contents of summary financial statements

(1)–(3) *(Outside the scope of this work.)*

(4) The summary financial statement of an insurance company the directors of which—

(a) do not prepare group accounts under Part 15 of the 2006 Act, and

(b) prepare Companies Act individual accounts under section 396 of the 2006 Act,

must comply with Schedule 3 to these Regulations.

(5), (6) *(Outside the scope of this work.)*

(7) The summary financial statement of the parent company of an insurance group the directors of which prepare Companies Act group accounts under section 403 of the 2006 Act, must comply with Schedule 6 to these Regulations.

(8), (9) *(Outside the scope of this work.)*

NOTES

Commencement: 6 April 2008.

12 *((Pt 4) outside the scope of this work.)*

SCHEDULES

(Schs 1, 2 outside the scope of this work.)

SCHEDULE 3

FORM AND CONTENT OF SUMMARY FINANCIAL STATEMENT OF INSURANCE COMPANY PREPARING COMPANIES ACT INDIVIDUAL ACCOUNTS

Regulation 11(4)

[4447]

1. Summary profit and loss account

(1) The summary financial statement must contain a summary profit and loss account showing, in so far as they may be derived from the full profit and loss account, the items, or combinations of items, listed in sub-paragraph (3), in the order set out in that sub-paragraph.

(2) The items or combinations of items listed in sub-paragraph (3) may appear under such headings as the directors consider appropriate.

(3) The items, or combinations of items referred to in sub-paragraph (1) are—

(a) gross premiums written-general business—
item I 1(a);

(b) gross premiums written-long term business—
item II 1(a);

(c) balance on the technical account for general business—
item I 10;

(d) balance on the technical account for long term business—
item II 13;

(e) other income and charges; the net figure resulting from the combination of the following items—

(i) item III 3

(ii) item III 3a
(iii) item III 4
(iv) item III 5
(v) item III 5a
(vi) item III 6
(vii) item III 7
(viii) item III 8;

(f) the profit or loss on ordinary activities before tax—
item III 8a;

(g) tax on profit or loss on ordinary activities—
item III 9;

(h) profit or loss on ordinary activities after tax—
item III 10;

(i) extraordinary profit or loss after tax—
the net figure resulting from the combination of items III 13 and 14;

(j) other taxes—
item III 15; and

(k) profit or loss for the financial year—
item III 16.

2. Dividends

The summary financial statement must also contain the information concerning recognized and proposed dividends included in the full accounts and reports.

3. Summary balance sheet

(1) The summary financial statement must contain a summary balance sheet which must show, in so far as they may be derived from the full balance sheet, the items, or combinations of items, set out in sub-paragraph (2) in the order of that sub-paragraph and under such headings as the directors consider appropriate.

(2) The items, or combinations of items, referred to in sub-paragraph (1) are—

(a) investments—
the aggregate of items C and D under the heading "ASSETS";

(b) reinsurers' share of technical provisions—
item Da under the heading "ASSETS";

(c) other assets—
the aggregate of items A or E(IV), B, E(I) to (III), F and G under the heading "ASSETS";

(d) total assets under the heading "ASSETS";

(e) capital and reserves—
item A under the heading "LIABILITIES";

(f) subordinated liabilities—
item B under the heading "LIABILITIES";

(g) fund for future appropriations—
item Ba under the heading "LIABILITIES";

(h) gross technical provisions—
the aggregate of items C1(a), C2(a), C3(a), C4(a), C5, C6(a) and D(a) under the heading "LIABILITIES";

(i) technical provisions-reinsurance amounts—
the aggregate of items C1(b), C2(b), C3(b), C4(b), C6(b) and D(b) under the heading "LIABILITIES";

(j) other liabilities—
the aggregate of items E, F, G and H under the heading "LIABILITIES"; and

(k) total liabilities under the heading "LIABILITIES".

4. Corresponding amounts

(1) In respect of every item shown in the summary profit and loss account, or in the summary balance sheet, the corresponding amount must be shown for the immediately preceding financial year.

(2) For the purposes of sub-paragraph (1), "the corresponding amount" is the amount shown in the summary financial statement for that year or which would have been so shown had such a statement been prepared for that year, taking account of any adjustments to corresponding amounts made in the full accounts and reports.

NOTES

Commencement: 6 April 2008.

(*Schs 4, 5 outside the scope of this work.*)

SCHEDULE 6

FORM AND CONTENT OF SUMMARY FINANCIAL STATEMENT OF PARENT COMPANY OF INSURANCE GROUP PREPARING COMPANIES ACT GROUP ACCOUNTS

Regulation 11(7)

[4448]

1. Summary profit and loss account

(1) The summary financial statement must contain a summary consolidated profit and loss account showing the items, or combinations of items, required by paragraph 1 of Schedule 3 to these Regulations, in the order required by that paragraph and under such headings as the directors consider appropriate, but with the modifications specified in sub-paragraph (3).

(2) The summary financial statement must also contain the information required by paragraph 2 of that Schedule.

(3) The modifications referred to in sub-paragraph (1) are as follows—

(a) between the information required by paragraph 1(3)(e) and that required by paragraph 1(3)(f) of Schedule 3 to these Regulations there must in addition be shown, under such heading as the directors consider appropriate, the item "Income from associated undertakings" required to be shown in the profit and loss account formats in Schedule 3 to the Large and Medium-sized Companies Accounts Regulations (insurance companies: Companies Act individual accounts) by paragraph 20(3)(b) of Schedule 6 to those Regulations as substituted by paragraph 37 of Schedule 6 to those Regulations;

(b) between the information required by paragraph 1(3)(h) and that required by paragraph 1(3)(i) of Schedule 3 to these Regulations there must in addition be shown, under such heading as the directors consider appropriate, the item required to be shown in the profit and loss account formats in Schedule 3 to the Large and Medium-sized Companies Accounts Regulations by paragraph 17(3)(a) of Schedule 6 to those Regulations (minority interests) as applied by paragraph 36 of Schedule 6 to those Regulations; and

(c) the figures required by paragraph 1(3)(i) and (j) of Schedule 3 to these Regulations must each be shown after the deduction or the addition (as the case may be) of the item required to be shown in the profit and loss account formats in Schedule 3 to the Large and Medium-sized Companies Accounts Regulations by paragraph 17(3)(b) of Schedule 6 to those Regulations (minority interests) as applied by paragraph 36 of Schedule 6 to those Regulations.

2. Summary balance sheet

(1) The summary financial statement must contain a summary consolidated balance sheet showing the items required by paragraph 3 of Schedule 3 to these Regulations, in the order required by that paragraph and under such headings as the directors consider appropriate, but with the addition of the item specified in sub-paragraph (2).

(2) Between the items required by paragraph 3(2)(d) and (e) of Schedule 3 to these Regulations, there must in addition be shown under an appropriate heading the item required to be shown in the balance sheet format in Schedule 3 to the Large and Medium-sized Companies Accounts Regulations by paragraph 17(2) of Schedule 6 to those Regulations (minority interests), as applied by paragraph 36 of Schedule 6 to those Regulations.

3. Corresponding amounts

(1) In respect of every item shown in the summary consolidated profit and loss account, or in the summary consolidated balance sheet, the corresponding amount must be shown for the immediately preceding financial year.

(2) For the purposes of sub-paragraph (1), "the corresponding amount" is the amount shown in the summary financial statement for that year or which would have been so shown had such a statement been prepared for that year, taking account of any adjustments to corresponding amounts made in the full accounts and reports.

NOTES

Commencement: 6 April 2008.

(*Schs 7, 8 outside the scope of this work.*)

LARGE AND MEDIUM-SIZED COMPANIES AND GROUPS (ACCOUNTS AND REPORTS) REGULATIONS 2008

(SI 2008/410)

NOTES

Made: 19 February 2008.

Authority: Companies Act 2006, ss 396(3), 404(3), 409(1)–(3), 412(1)–(3), 416(4), 421(1), (2), 445(3)(a), (b), 677(3)(a), 712(2)(b)(i), 831(3)(a), 832(4)(a), 836(1)(b)(i), 1292(1)(a), (c).

Commencement: 6 April 2008 (with effect in relation to financial years beginning on or after that date).

ARRANGEMENT OF REGULATIONS

PART 2
FORM AND CONTENT OF ACCOUNTS

6 Companies Act individual accounts: insurance companies . . . . . [4449]

SCHEDULES:

Schedule 3—Insurance Companies: Companies Act Individual Accounts
Part 1—General Rules and Formats . . . . . [4450]
Part 2—Accounting Principles and Rules . . . . . [4451]
Part 3—Notes to the Accounts . . . . . [4452]
Part 4— Interpretation of this Schedule . . . . . [4453]
Schedule 6—Insurance Companies: Companies Act Individual Accounts
Part 1—General Rules . . . . . [4454]
Part 3—Modifications for Insurance Groups . . . . . [4455]
Schedule 9—Interpretation of Term "Provisions"
Part 1—Meaning for Purposes of these Regulations . . . . . [4456]
Part 2—Meaning for Purposes of Parts 18 and 23 of the 2006 Act . . . . . [4457]
Schedule 10—General Interpretation . . . . . [4458]

1, 2 *((Pt 1) outside the scope of this work.)*

PART 2
FORM AND CONTENT OF ACCOUNTS

3–5 *(Outside the scope of this work.)*

[4449]

6 Companies Act individual accounts: insurance companies

(1) The directors of a company—

(a) for which they are preparing Companies Act individual accounts under section 396 of the 2006 Act, and

(b) which is an insurance company,

must comply with the provisions of Schedule 3 to these Regulations as to the form and content of the balance sheet and profit and loss account, and additional information to be provided by way of notes to the accounts.

(2) The profit and loss account of a company that falls within section 408 of the 2006 Act (individual profit and loss account where group accounts prepared) need not contain the information specified in paragraphs 83 to 89 of Schedule 3 to these Regulations (information supplementing the profit and loss account).

(3) Accounts prepared in accordance with this regulation must contain a statement that they are prepared in accordance with the provisions of these Regulations relating to insurance companies.

NOTES

Commencement: 6 April 2008 (with effect in relation to financial years beginning on or after that date).

7–9 *(Outside the scope of this work.)*

10–13 *((Pts 3–15) outside the scope of this work.)*

(Schs 1, 2 outside the scope of this work.)

SCHEDULE 3

INSURANCE COMPANIES: COMPANIES ACT INDIVIDUAL ACCOUNTS

Regulation 6(1)

PART 1
GENERAL RULES AND FORMATS

SECTION A
GENERAL RULES

[4450]

1.—(1) Subject to the following provisions of this Schedule—

(a) every balance sheet of a company must show the items listed in the balance sheet format in Section B of this Part, and

(b) every profit and loss account must show the items listed in the profit and loss account format in Section B.

(2) References in this Schedule to the items listed in any of the formats in Section B are to those items read together with any of the notes following the formats which apply to those items.

(3) The items must be shown in the order and under the headings and sub-headings given in the particular format, but—

(a) the notes to the formats may permit alternative positions for any particular items, and

(b) the heading or sub-heading for any item does not have to be distinguished by any letter or number assigned to that item in the format used.

2.—(1) Any item required to be shown in a company's balance sheet or profit and loss account may be shown in greater detail than required by the particular format.

(2) The balance sheet or profit and loss account may include an item representing or covering the amount of any asset or liability, income or expenditure not specifically covered by any of the items listed in the formats set out in Section B, save that none of the following may be treated as assets in any balance sheet—

(a) preliminary expenses,

(b) expenses of, and commission on, any issue of shares or debentures, and

(c) costs of research.

3.—(1) The directors may combine items to which Arabic numbers are given in the balance sheet format set out in Section B (except for items concerning technical provisions and the reinsurers' share of technical provisions), and items to which lower case letters in parentheses are given in the profit and loss account format so set out (except for items within items I.1 and 4 and II.1, 5 and 6) if—

(a) their individual amounts are not material for the purpose of giving a true and fair view, or

(b) the combination facilitates the assessment of the state of affairs or profit or loss of the company for the financial year in question.

(2) Where sub-paragraph (1)(b) applies—

(a) the individual amounts of any items which have been combined must be disclosed in a note to the accounts, and

(b) any notes required by this Schedule to the items so combined must, notwithstanding the combination, be given.

4.—(1) Subject to sub-paragraph (2), the directors must not include a heading or sub-heading corresponding to an item in the balance sheet or profit and loss account format used if there is no amount to be shown for that item for the financial year to which the balance sheet or profit and loss account relates.

(2) Where an amount can be shown for the item in question for the immediately preceding financial year that amount must be shown under the heading or sub-heading required by the format for that item.

5.—(1) For every item shown in the balance sheet or profit and loss account the corresponding amount for the immediately preceding financial year must also be shown.

(2) Where that corresponding amount is not comparable with the amount to be shown for the item in question in respect of the financial year to which the balance sheet or profit and loss account relates, the former amount may be adjusted, and particulars of the non-comparability and of any adjustment must be disclosed in a note to the accounts.

6. Subject to the provisions of this Schedule, amounts in respect of items representing assets or income may not be set off against amounts in respect of items representing liabilities or expenditure (as the case may be), or vice versa.

7.—(1) The provisions of this Schedule which relate to long-term business apply, with necessary modifications, to business which consists of effecting or carrying out relevant contracts of general insurance which—

(a) is transacted exclusively or principally according to the technical principles of long-term business, and

(b) is a significant amount of the business of the company.

(2) For the purposes of paragraph (1), a contract of general insurance is a relevant contract if the risk insured against relates to—

(a) accident, or

(b) sickness.

(3) Sub-paragraph (2) must be read with—

(a) section 22 of the Financial Services and Markets Act 2000,

(b) the Financial Services and Markets Act 2000 (Regulated Activities) Order 2001, and

(c) Schedule 2 to that Act.

8. The company's directors must, in determining how amounts are presented within items in the profit and loss account and balance sheet, have regard to the substance of the reported transaction or arrangement, in accordance with generally accepted accounting principles or practice.

SECTION B
THE REQUIRED FORMATS

9.—(1) Where in respect of any item to which an Arabic number is assigned in the balance sheet or profit and loss account format, the gross amount and reinsurance amount or reinsurers' share are required to be shown, a sub-total of those amounts must also be given.

(2) Where in respect of any item to which an Arabic number is assigned in the profit and loss account format, separate items are required to be shown, then a separate sub-total of those items must also be given in addition to any sub-total required by sub-paragraph (1).

10.—(1) In the profit and loss account format set out below—

(a) the heading "Technical account—General business" is for business which consists of effecting or carrying out contracts of general business; and

(b) the heading "Technical account—Long-term business" is for business which consists of effecting or carrying out contracts of long-term insurance.

(2) In sub-paragraph (1), references to—

(a) contracts of general or long-term insurance, and

(b) the effecting or carrying out of such contracts,

must be read with section 22 of the Financial Services and Markets Act 2000, the Financial Services and Markets Act 2000 (Regulated Activities) Order 2001, and Schedule 2 to that Act.

Balance sheet format

ASSETS

A Called up share capital not paid *(1)*

B Intangible assets

- 1 Development costs
- 2 Concessions, patents, licences, trade marks and similar rights and assets *(2)*
- 3 Goodwill *(3)*
- 4 Payments on account

C Investments

- I Land and buildings *(4)*
- II Investments in group undertakings and participating interests
  - 1 Shares in group undertakings
  - 2 Debt securities issued by, and loans to, group undertakings
  - 3 Participating interests
  - 4 Debt securities issued by, and loans to, undertakings in which the company has a participating interest
- III Other financial investments
  - 1 Shares and other variable-yield securities and units in unit trusts
  - 2 Debt securities and other fixed-income securities *(5)*
  - 3 Participation in investment pools *(6)*

4 Loans secured by mortgages *(7)*
5 Other loans *(7)*
6 Deposits with credit institutions *(8)*
7 Other *(9)*
IV Deposits with ceding undertakings *(10)*
D Assets held to cover linked liabilities *(11)*
Da Reinsurers' share of technical provisions *(12)*
1 Provision for unearned premiums
2 Long-term business provision
3 Claims outstanding
4 Provisions for bonuses and rebates
5 Other technical provisions
6 Technical provisions for unit-linked liabilities
E Debtors *(13)*
I Debtors arising out of direct insurance operations
1 Policyholders
2 Intermediaries
II Debtors arising out of reinsurance operations
III Other debtors
IV Called up share capital not paid *(1)*
F Other assets
I Tangible assets
1 Plant and machinery
2 Fixtures, fittings, tools and equipment
3 Payments on account (other than deposits paid on land and buildings) and assets (other than buildings) in course of construction
II Stocks
1 Raw materials and consumables
2 Work in progress
3 Finished goods and goods for resale
4 Payments on account
III Cash at bank and in hand
IV Own shares *(14)*
V Other *(15)*
G Prepayments and accrued income
I Accrued interest and rent *(16)*
II Deferred acquisition costs *(17)*
III Other prepayments and accrued income
LIABILITIES
A Capital and reserves
I Called up share capital or equivalent funds
II Share premium account
III Revaluation reserve
IV Reserves
1 Capital redemption reserve
2 Reserve for own shares
3 Reserves provided for by the articles of association
4 Other reserves
V Profit and loss account
B Subordinated liabilities *(18)*
Ba Fund for future appropriations *(19)*
C Technical provisions
1 Provision for unearned premiums *(20)*
(a) gross amount
(b) reinsurance amount *(12)*
2 Long-term business provision *(20) (21) (26)*
(a) gross amount
(b) reinsurance amount *(12)*
3 Claims outstanding *(22)*
(a) gross amount
(b) reinsurance amount *(12)*
4 Provision for bonuses and rebates *(23)*

Part IV Statutory Instruments

(a) gross amount
(b) reinsurance amount *(12)*
5 Equalisation provision *(24)*
6 Other technical provisions *(25)*
(a) gross amount
(b) reinsurance amount *(12)*
D Technical provisions for linked liabilities *(26)*
(a) gross amount
(b) reinsurance amount *(12)*
E Provisions for other risks
1 Provisions for pensions and similar obligations
2 Provisions for taxation
3 Other provisions
F Deposits received from reinsurers *(27)*
G Creditors *(28)*
I Creditors arising out of direct insurance operations
II Creditors arising out of reinsurance operations
III Debenture loans *(29)*
IV Amounts owed to credit institutions
V Other creditors including taxation and social security
H Accruals and deferred income

Notes on the balance sheet format

(1) Called up share capital not paid
(Assets items A and E.IV)
This item may be shown in either of the positions given in the format.
(2) Concessions, patents, licences, trade marks and similar rights and assets
(Assets item B.2)
Amounts in respect of assets are only to be included in a company's balance sheet under this item if either—
(a) the assets were acquired for valuable consideration and are not required to be shown under goodwill, or
(b) the assets in question were created by the company itself.
(3) Goodwill
(Assets item B.3)
Amounts representing goodwill are only to be included to the extent that the goodwill was acquired for valuable consideration.
(4) Land and buildings
(Assets item CI)
The amount of any land and buildings occupied by the company for its own activities must be shown separately in the notes to the accounts.
(5) Debt securities and other fixed-income securities
(Assets item CIII.2)
This item is to comprise transferable debt securities and any other transferable fixed-income securities issued by credit institutions, other undertakings or public bodies, in so far as they are not covered by assets item CII.2 or CII.4.
Securities bearing interest rates that vary in accordance with specific factors, for example the interest rate on the inter-bank market or on the Euromarket, are also to be regarded as debt securities and other fixed-income securities and so be included under this item.
(6) Participation in investment pools
(Assets item CIII.3)
This item is to comprise shares held by the company in joint investments constituted by several undertakings or pension funds, the management of which has been entrusted to one of those undertakings or to one of those pension funds.
(7) Loans secured by mortgages and other loans
(Assets items CIII.4 and CIII.5)
Loans to policyholders for which the policy is the main security are to be included under "Other loans" and their amount must be disclosed in the notes to the accounts. Loans secured by mortgage are to be shown as such even where they are also secured by insurance policies. Where the amount of "Other loans" not secured by policies is material, an appropriate breakdown must be given in the notes to the accounts.
(8) Deposits with credit institutions
(Assets item CIII.6)

This item is to comprise sums the withdrawal of which is subject to a time restriction. Sums deposited with no such restriction must be shown under assets item F.III even if they bear interest.

(9) Other

(Assets item CIII.7)

This item is to comprise those investments which are not covered by assets items CIII.1 to 6. Where the amount of such investments is significant, they must be disclosed in the notes to the accounts.

(10) Deposits with ceding undertakings

(Assets item CIV)

Where the company accepts reinsurance this item is to comprise amounts, owed by the ceding undertakings and corresponding to guarantees, which are deposited with those ceding undertakings or with third parties or which are retained by those undertakings.

These amounts may not be combined with other amounts owed by the ceding insurer to the reinsurer or set off against amounts owed by the reinsurer to the ceding insurer.

Securities deposited with ceding undertakings or third parties which remain the property of the company must be entered in the company's accounts as an investment, under the appropriate item.

(11) Assets held to cover linked liabilities

(Assets item D)

In respect of long-term business, this item is to comprise investments made pursuant to long-term policies under which the benefits payable to the policyholder are wholly or partly to be determined by reference to the value of, or the income from, property of any description (whether or not specified in the contract) or by reference to fluctuations in, or in an index of, the value of property of any description (whether or not so specified).

This item is also to comprise investments which are held on behalf of the members of a tontine and are intended for distribution among them.

(12) Reinsurance amounts

(Assets item Da: liabilities items C1(b), 2(b), 3(b), 4(b) and 6(b) and D(b))

The reinsurance amounts may be shown either under assets item Da or under liabilities items C1(b), 2(b), 3(b), 4(b) and 6(b) and D(b).

The reinsurance amounts are to comprise the actual or estimated amounts which, under contractual reinsurance arrangements, are deducted from the gross amounts of technical provisions.

As regards the provision for unearned premiums, the reinsurance amounts must be calculated according to the methods referred to in paragraph 50 below or in accordance with the terms of the reinsurance policy.

(13) Debtors

(Assets item E)

Amounts owed by group undertakings and undertakings in which the company has a participating interest must be shown separately as sub-items of assets items E.I, II and III.

(14) Own shares

(Assets item F.IV)

The nominal value of the shares must be shown separately under this item.

(15) Other

(Assets item F.V)

This item is to comprise those assets which are not covered by assets items F.I to IV. Where such assets are material they must be disclosed in the notes to the accounts.

(16) Accrued interest and rent

(Assets item G.I)

This item is to comprise those items that represent interest and rent that have been earned up to the balance-sheet date but have not yet become receivable.

(17) Deferred acquisition costs

(Assets item G.II)

This item is to comprise the costs of acquiring insurance policies which are incurred during a financial year but relate to a subsequent financial year ("deferred acquisition costs"), except in so far as—

(a) allowance has been made in the computation of the long-term business provision made under paragraph 52 below and shown under liabilities item C2 or D in the balance sheet, for—

  (i) the explicit recognition of such costs, or

  (ii) the implicit recognition of such costs by virtue of the anticipation of future income from which such costs may prudently be expected to be recovered, or

(b) allowance has been made for such costs in respect of general business policies by a deduction from the provision for unearned premiums made under paragraph 50 below and shown under liabilities item CI in the balance sheet.

Deferred acquisition costs arising in general business must be distinguished from those arising in long-term business.

In the case of general business, the amount of any deferred acquisition costs must be established on a basis compatible with that used for unearned premiums.

There must be disclosed in the notes to the accounts—

(c) how the deferral of acquisition costs has been treated (unless otherwise expressly stated in the accounts), and

(d) where such costs are included as a deduction from the provisions at liabilities item CI, the amount of such deduction, or

(e) where the actuarial method used in the calculation of the provisions at liabilities item C2 or D has made allowance for the explicit recognition of such costs, the amount of the costs so recognised.

(18) Subordinated liabilities

(Liabilities item B)

This item is to comprise all liabilities in respect of which there is a contractual obligation that, in the event of winding up or of bankruptcy, they are to be repaid only after the claims of all other creditors have been met (whether or not they are represented by certificates).

(19) Fund for future appropriations

(Liabilities item Ba)

This item is to comprise all funds the allocation of which either to policyholders or to shareholders has not been determined by the end of the financial year.

Transfers to and from this item must be shown in item II.12a in the profit and loss account.

(20) Provision for unearned premiums

(Liabilities item C1)

In the case of long-term business the provision for unearned premiums may be included in liabilities item C2 rather than in this item.

The provision for unearned premiums is to comprise the amount representing that part of gross premiums written which is estimated to be earned in the following financial year or to subsequent financial years.

(21) Long-term business provision

(Liabilities item C2)

This item is to comprise the actuarially estimated value of the company's liabilities (excluding technical provisions included in liabilities item D), including bonuses already declared and after deducting the actuarial value of future premiums.

This item is also to comprise claims incurred but not reported, plus the estimated costs of settling such claims.

(22) Claims outstanding

(Liabilities item C3)

This item is to comprise the total estimated ultimate cost to the company of settling all claims arising from events which have occurred up to the end of the financial year (including, in the case of general business, claims incurred but not reported) less amounts already paid in respect of such claims.

(23) Provision for bonuses and rebates

(Liabilities item C4)

This item is to comprise amounts intended for policyholders or contract beneficiaries by way of bonuses and rebates as defined in Note *(5)* on the profit and loss account format to the extent that such amounts have not been credited to policyholders or contract beneficiaries or included in liabilities item Ba or in liabilities item C2.

(24) Equalisation provision

(Liabilities item C5)

This item is to comprise the amount of any equalisation reserve maintained in respect of general business by the company, in accordance with the rules in section 1.4 of the Prudential Sourcebook for Insurers made by the Financial Services Authority under Part 10 of the Financial Services and Markets Act 2000.

This item is also to comprise any amounts which, in accordance with Council Directive 87/343/EEC of 22nd June 1987, are required to be set aside by a company to equalise fluctuations in loss ratios in future years or to provide for special risks.

A company which otherwise constitutes reserves to equalise fluctuations in loss ratios in future years or to provide for special risks must disclose that fact in the notes to the accounts.

(25) Other technical provisions

(Liabilities item C6)

This item is to comprise, inter alia, the provision for unexpired risks as defined in paragraph 91 below. Where the amount of the provision for unexpired risks is significant, it must be disclosed separately either in the balance sheet or in the notes to the accounts.

(26) Technical provisions for linked liabilities
(Liabilities item D)

This item is to comprise technical provisions constituted to cover liabilities relating to investment in the context of long-term policies under which the benefits payable to policyholders are wholly or partly to be determined by reference to the value of, or the income from, property of any description (whether or not specified in the contract) or by reference to fluctuations in, or in an index of, the value of property of any description (whether or not so specified).

Any additional technical provisions constituted to cover death risks, operating expenses or other risks (such as benefits payable at the maturity date or guaranteed surrender values) must be included under liabilities item C2.

This item must also comprise technical provisions representing the obligations of a tontine's organiser in relation to its members.

(27) Deposits received from reinsurers
(Liabilities item F)

Where the company cedes reinsurance, this item is to comprise amounts deposited by or withheld from other insurance undertakings under reinsurance contracts. These amounts may not be merged with other amounts owed to or by those other undertakings.

Where the company cedes reinsurance and has received as a deposit securities which have been transferred to its ownership, this item is to comprise the amount owed by the company by virtue of the deposit.

(28) Creditors
(Liabilities item G)

Amounts owed to group undertakings and undertakings in which the company has a participating interest must be shown separately as sub-items.

(29) Debenture loans
(Liabilities item G.III)

The amount of any convertible loans must be shown separately.

Additional items

11.—(1) Every balance sheet of a company which carries on long-term business must show separately as an additional item the aggregate of any amounts included in liabilities item A (capital and reserves) which are required not to be treated as realised profits under section 843 of the 2006 Act.

(2) A company which carries on long-term business must show separately, in the balance sheet or in the notes to the accounts, the total amount of assets representing the long-term fund valued in accordance with the provisions of this Schedule.

Managed funds

12.—(1) For the purposes of this paragraph "managed funds" are funds of a group pension fund—

(a) the management of which constitutes long-term insurance business, and
(b) which the company administers in its own name but on behalf of others, and
(c) to which it has legal title.

(2) The company must, in any case where assets and liabilities arising in respect of managed funds fall to be treated as assets and liabilities of the company, adopt the following accounting treatment: assets and liabilities representing managed funds are to be included in the company's balance sheet, with the notes to the accounts disclosing the total amount included with respect to such assets and liabilities in the balance sheet and showing the amount included under each relevant balance sheet item in respect of such assets or (as the case may be) liabilities.

Deferred acquisition costs

13. The costs of acquiring insurance policies which are incurred during a financial year but which relate to a subsequent financial year must be deferred in a manner specified in Note *(17)* on the balance sheet format.

Profit and loss account format

I Technical account—General business

1 Earned premiums, net of reinsurance
  (a) gross premiums written *(1)*
  (b) outward reinsurance premiums *(2)*
  (c) change in the gross provision for unearned premiums
  (d) change in the provision for unearned premiums, reinsurers' share

2 Allocated investment return transferred from the non-technical account (item III.6) *(10)*

2a Investment income *(8) (10)*
- (a) income from participating interests, with a separate indication of that derived from group undertakings
- (b) income from other investments, with a separate indication of that derived from group undertakings
  - (aa) income from land and buildings
  - (bb) income from other investments
- (c) value re-adjustments on investments
- (d) gains on the realisation of investments

3 Other technical income, net of reinsurance

4 Claims incurred, net of reinsurance *(4)*
- (a) claims paid
  - (aa) gross amount
  - (bb) reinsurers' share
- (b) change in the provision for claims
  - (aa) gross amount
  - (bb) reinsurers' share

5 Changes in other technical provisions, net of reinsurance, not shown under other headings

6 Bonuses and rebates, net of reinsurance *(5)*

7 Net operating expenses
- (a) acquisition costs *(6)*
- (b) change in deferred acquisition costs
- (c) administrative expenses *(7)*
- (d) reinsurance commissions and profit participation

8 Other technical charges, net of reinsurance

8a Investment expenses and charges *(8)*
- (a) investment management expenses, including interest
- (b) value adjustments on investments
- (c) losses on the realisation of investments

9 Change in the equalisation provision

10 Sub-total (balance on the technical account for general business) (item III.1)

II Technical account—Long-term business

1 Earned premiums, net of reinsurance
- (a) gross premiums written *(1)*
- (b) outward reinsurance premiums *(2)*
- (c) change in the provision for unearned premiums, net of reinsurance *(3)*

2 Investment income *(8) (10)*
- (a) income from participating interests, with a separate indication of that derived from group undertakings
- (b) income from other investments, with a separate indication of that derived from group undertakings
  - (aa) income from land and buildings
  - (bb) income from other investments
- (c) value re-adjustments on investments
- (d) gains on the realisation of investments

3 Unrealised gains on investments *(9)*

4 Other technical income, net of reinsurance

5 Claims incurred, net of reinsurance *(4)*
- (a) claims paid
  - (aa) gross amount
  - (bb) reinsurers' share
- (b) change in the provision for claims
  - (aa) gross amount
  - (bb) reinsurers' share

6 Change in other technical provisions, net of reinsurance, not shown under other headings
- (a) Long-term business provision, net of reinsurance *(3)*
  - (aa) gross amount
  - (bb) reinsurers' share

(b) other technical provisions, net of reinsurance
7 Bonuses and rebates, net of reinsurance *(5)*
8 Net operating expenses
(a) acquisition costs *(6)*
(b) change in deferred acquisition costs
(c) administrative expenses *(7)*
(d) reinsurance commissions and profit participation
9 Investment expenses and charges *(8)*
(a) investment management expenses, including interest
(b) value adjustments on investments
(c) losses on the realisation of investments
10 Unrealised losses on investments *(9)*
11 Other technical charges, net of reinsurance
11a Tax attributable to the long-term business
12 Allocated investment return transferred to the non-technical account (item III.4)
12a Transfers to or from the fund for future appropriations
13 Sub-total (balance on the technical account—long-term business) (item III.2)

III Non-technical account
1 Balance on the general business technical account (item I.10)
2 Balance on the long-term business technical account (item II.13)
2a Tax credit attributable to balance on the long-term business technical account
3 Investment income *(8)*
(a) income from participating interests, with a separate indication of that derived from group undertakings
(b) income from other investments, with a separate indication of that derived from group undertakings
(aa) income from land and buildings
(bb) income from other investments
(c) value re-adjustments on investments
(d) gains on the realisation of investments
3a Unrealised gains on investments *(9)*
4 Allocated investment return transferred from the long-term business technical account (item II.12) *(10)*
5 Investment expenses and charges *(8)*
(a) investment management expenses, including interest
(b) value adjustments on investments
(c) losses on the realisation of investments
5a Unrealised losses on investments *(9)*
6 Allocated investment return transferred to the general business technical account (item I.2) *(10)*
7 Other income
8 Other charges, including value adjustments
8a Profit or loss on ordinary activities before tax
9 Tax on profit or loss on ordinary activities
10 Profit or loss on ordinary activities after tax
11 Extraordinary income
12 Extraordinary charges
13 Extraordinary profit or loss
14 Tax on extraordinary profit or loss
15 Other taxes not shown under the preceding items
16 Profit or loss for the financial year

Notes on the profit and loss account format

(1) Gross premiums written
(General business technical account: item I.1.(a)
Long-term business technical account: item II.1.(a))

This item is to comprise all amounts due during the financial year in respect of insurance contracts entered into regardless of the fact that such amounts may relate in whole or in part to a later financial year, and must include inter alia—

(i) premiums yet to be determined, where the premium calculation can be done only at the end of the year;

(ii) single premiums, including annuity premiums, and, in long-term business, single premiums resulting from bonus and rebate provisions in so far as they must be considered as premiums under the terms of the contract;
(iii) additional premiums in the case of half-yearly, quarterly or monthly payments and additional payments from policyholders for expenses borne by the company;
(iv) in the case of co-insurance, the company's portion of total premiums;
(v) reinsurance premiums due from ceding and retroceding insurance undertakings, including portfolio entries,

after deduction of cancellations and portfolio withdrawals credited to ceding and retroceding insurance undertakings.

The above amounts must not include the amounts of taxes or duties levied with premiums.

(2) Outward reinsurance premiums

(General business technical account: item I.1.(b)
Long-term business technical account: item II.1.(b))

This item is to comprise all premiums paid or payable in respect of outward reinsurance contracts entered into by the company. Portfolio entries payable on the conclusion or amendment of outward reinsurance contracts must be added; portfolio withdrawals receivable must be deducted.

(3) Change in the provision for unearned premiums, net of reinsurance

(Long-term business technical account: items II.1.(c) and II.6.(a))

In the case of long-term business, the change in unearned premiums may be included either in item II.1.(c) or in item II.6.(a) of the long-term business technical account.

(4) Claims incurred, net of reinsurance

(General business technical account: item I.4.
Long-term business technical account: item II.5)

This item is to comprise all payments made in respect of the financial year with the addition of the provision for claims (but after deducting the provision for claims for the preceding financial year).

These amounts must include annuities, surrenders, entries and withdrawals of loss provisions to and from ceding insurance undertakings and reinsurers and external and internal claims management costs and charges for claims incurred but not reported such as are referred to in paragraphs 53(2) and 55 below.

Sums recoverable on the basis of subrogation and salvage (within the meaning of paragraph 53 below) must be deducted.

Where the difference between—
(a) the loss provision made at the beginning of the year for outstanding claims incurred in previous years, and
(b) the payments made during the year on account of claims incurred in previous years and the loss provision shown at the end of the year for such outstanding claims,

is material, it must be shown in the notes to the accounts, broken down by category and amount.

(5) Bonuses and rebates, net of reinsurance

(General business technical account: item I.6.
Long-term business technical account: item II.7)

Bonuses are to comprise all amounts chargeable for the financial year which are paid or payable to policyholders and other insured parties or provided for their benefit, including amounts used to increase technical provisions or applied to the reduction of future premiums, to the extent that such amounts represent an allocation of surplus or profit arising on business as a whole or a section of business, after deduction of amounts provided in previous years which are no longer required.

Rebates are to comprise such amounts to the extent that they represent a partial refund of premiums resulting from the experience of individual contracts.

Where material, the amount charged for bonuses and that charged for rebates must be disclosed separately in the notes to the accounts.

(6) Acquisition costs

(General business technical account: item I.7.(a).
Long-term business technical account: item II.8.(a))

This item is to comprise the costs arising from the conclusion of insurance contracts. They must cover both direct costs, such as acquisition commissions or the cost of drawing up the insurance document or including the insurance contract in the portfolio, and indirect costs, such as advertising costs or the administrative expenses connected with the processing of proposals and the issuing of policies.

In the case of long-term business, policy renewal commissions must be included under item II.8.(c) in the long-term business technical account.

(7) Administrative expenses

(General business technical account: item I.7.(c).
Long-term business technical account: item II.8.(c))

This item must include the costs arising from premium collection, portfolio administration, handling of bonuses and rebates, and inward and outward reinsurance. They must in particular include staff costs and depreciation provisions in respect of office furniture and equipment in so far as these need not be shown under acquisition costs, claims incurred or investment charges.

Item II.8.(c) must also include policy renewal commissions.

(8) Investment income, expenses and charges

(General business technical account: items I.2a and 8a.

Long-term business technical account: items II.2 and 9.

Non-technical account: items III.3 and 5)

Investment income, expenses and charges must, to the extent that they arise in the long-term fund, be disclosed in the long-term business technical account. Other investment income, expenses and charges must either be disclosed in the non-technical account or attributed between the appropriate technical and non-technical accounts. Where the company makes such an attribution it must disclose the basis for it in the notes to the accounts.

(9) Unrealised gains and losses on investments

(Long-term business technical account: items II.3 and 10.

Non-technical account: items III.3a and 5a)

In the case of investments attributed to the long-term fund, the difference between the valuation of the investments and their purchase price or, if they have previously been valued, their valuation as at the last balance sheet date, may be disclosed (in whole or in part) in item II.3 or II.10 (as the case may be) of the long-term business technical account, and in the case of investments shown as assets under assets item D (assets held to cover linked liabilities) must be so disclosed.

In the case of other investments, the difference between the valuation of the investments and their purchase price or, if they have previously been valued, their valuation as at the last balance sheet date, may be disclosed (in whole or in part) in item III.3a or III.5a (as the case may require) of the non-technical account.

(10) Allocated investment return

(General business technical account: item I.2.

Long-term business technical account: item II.2.

Non-technical account: items III.4 and 6)

The allocated return may be transferred from one part of the profit and loss account to another.

Where part of the investment return is transferred to the general business technical account, the transfer from the non-technical account must be deducted from item III.6 and added to item I.2.

Where part of the investment return disclosed in the long-term business technical account is transferred to the non-technical account, the transfer to the non-technical account shall be deducted from item II.12 and added to item III.4.

The reasons for such transfers (which may consist of a reference to any relevant statutory requirement) and the bases on which they are made must be disclosed in the notes to the accounts.

NOTES

Commencement: 6 April 2008 (with effect in relation to financial years beginning on or after that date).

Council Directive 87/343/EEC: OJ L185, 4.7.1987, p 72.

PART 2
ACCOUNTING PRINCIPLES AND RULES

SECTION A
ACCOUNTING PRINCIPLES

Preliminary

[4451]

14. The amounts to be included in respect of all items shown in a company's accounts must be determined in accordance with the principles set out in this Section.

15. But if it appears to the company's directors that there are special reasons for departing from any of those principles in preparing the company's accounts in respect of any financial year they may do so, in which case particulars of the departure, the reasons for it and its effect must be given in a note to the accounts.

Accounting principles

16. The company is presumed to be carrying on business as a going concern.

17. Accounting policies must be applied consistently within the same accounts and from one financial year to the next.

18. The amount of any item must be determined on a prudent basis, and in particular—
(a) subject to note (9) on the profit and loss account format, only profits realised at the balance sheet date are to be included in the profit and loss account, and
(b) all liabilities which have arisen in respect of the financial year to which the accounts relate or a previous financial year must be taken into account, including those which only become apparent between the balance sheet date and the date on which it is signed on behalf of the board of directors in accordance with section 414 of the 2006 Act (approval and signing of accounts).

19. All income and charges relating to the financial year to which the accounts relate are to be taken into account, without regard to the date of receipt or payment.

20. In determining the aggregate amount of any item, the amount of each individual asset or liability that falls to be taken into account must be determined separately.

Valuation

21.—(1) The amounts to be included in respect of assets of any description mentioned in paragraph 22 (valuation of assets: general) must be determined either—
(a) in accordance with that paragraph and paragraph 24 (but subject to paragraphs 27 to 29), or
(b) so far as applicable to an asset of that description, in accordance with Section C (valuation at fair value).
(2) The amounts to be included in respect of assets of any description mentioned in paragraph 24 (alternative valuation of fixed-income securities) may be determined—
(a) in accordance with that paragraph (but subject to paragraphs 27 to 29), or
(b) so far as applicable to an asset of that description, in accordance with Section C
(3) The amounts to be included in respect of assets which—
(a) are not assets of a description mentioned in paragraph 22 or 23, but
(b) are assets of a description to which Section C is applicable,
may be determined in accordance with that Section.
(4) Subject to sub-paragraphs (1) to (3), the amounts to be included in respect of all items shown in a company's accounts are determined in accordance with Section C

SECTION B
CURRENT VALUE ACCOUNTING RULES

Valuation of assets: general

22.—(1) Subject to paragraph 24, investments falling to be included under assets item C (investments) must be included at their current value calculated in accordance with paragraphs 25 and 26.
(2) Investments falling to be included under assets item D (assets held to cover linked liabilities) must be shown at their current value calculated in accordance with paragraphs 25 and 26.

23.—(1) Intangible assets other than goodwill may be shown at their current cost.
(2) Assets falling to be included under assets items F.I (tangible assets) and F.IV (own shares) in the balance sheet format may be shown at their current value calculated in accordance with paragraphs 25 and 26 or at their current cost.
(3) Assets falling to be included under assets item F.II (stocks) may be shown at current cost.

Alternative valuation of fixed-income securities

24.—(1) This paragraph applies to debt securities and other fixed-income securities shown as assets under assets items CII (investments in group undertakings and participating interests) and CIII (other financial investments).
(2) Securities to which this paragraph applies may either be valued in accordance with paragraph 22 or their amortised value may be shown in the balance sheet, in which case the provisions of this paragraph apply.
(3) Subject to sub-paragraph (4), where the purchase price of securities to which this paragraph applies exceeds the amount repayable at maturity, the amount of the difference—
(a) must be charged to the profit and loss account, and
(b) must be shown separately in the balance sheet or in the notes to the accounts.
(4) The amount of the difference referred to in sub-paragraph (3) may be written off in instalments so that it is completely written off when the securities are repaid, in which case there must be shown separately in the balance sheet or in the notes to the accounts the difference between the purchase price (less the aggregate amount written off) and the amount repayable at maturity.

(5) Where the purchase price of securities to which this paragraph applies is less than the amount repayable at maturity, the amount of the difference must be released to income in instalments over the period remaining until repayment, in which case there must be shown separately in the balance sheet or in the notes to the accounts the difference between the purchase price (plus the aggregate amount released to income) and the amount repayable at maturity.
(6) Both the purchase price and the current value of securities valued in accordance with this paragraph must be disclosed in the notes to the accounts.
(7) Where securities to which this paragraph applies which are not valued in accordance with paragraph 22 are sold before maturity, and the proceeds are used to purchase other securities to which this paragraph applies, the difference between the proceeds of sale and their book value may be spread uniformly over the period remaining until the maturity of the original investment.

Meaning of "current value"

25.—(1) Subject to sub-paragraph (5), in the case of investments other than land and buildings, current value means market value determined in accordance with this paragraph.
(2) In the case of listed investments, market value means the value on the balance sheet date or, when the balance sheet date is not a stock exchange trading day, on the last stock exchange trading day before that date.
(3) Where a market exists for unlisted investments, market value means the average price at which such investments were traded on the balance sheet date or, when the balance sheet date is not a trading day, on the last trading day before that date.
(4) Where, on the date on which the accounts are drawn up, listed or unlisted investments have been sold or are to be sold within the short term, the market value must be reduced by the actual or estimated realisation costs.
(5) Except where the equity method of accounting is applied, all investments other than those referred to in sub-paragraphs (2) and (3) must be valued on a basis which has prudent regard to the likely realisable value.

26.—(1) In the case of land and buildings, current value means the market value on the date of valuation, where relevant reduced as provided in sub-paragraphs (4) and (5).
(2) Market value means the price at which land and buildings could be sold under private contract between a willing seller and an arm's length buyer on the date of valuation, it being assumed that the property is publicly exposed to the market, that market conditions permit orderly disposal and that a normal period, having regard to the nature of the property, is available for the negotiation of the sale.
(3) The market value must be determined through the separate valuation of each land and buildings item, carried out at least every five years in accordance with generally recognised methods of valuation.
(4) Where the value of any land and buildings item has diminished since the preceding valuation under sub-paragraph (3), an appropriate value adjustment must be made.
(5) The lower value arrived at under sub-paragraph (4) must not be increased in subsequent balance sheets unless such increase results from a new determination of market value arrived at in accordance with sub-paragraphs (2) and (3).
(6) Where, on the date on which the accounts are drawn up, land and buildings have been sold or are to be sold within the short term, the value arrived at in accordance with sub-paragraphs (2) and (4) must be reduced by the actual or estimated realisation costs.
(7) Where it is impossible to determine the market value of a land and buildings item, the value arrived at on the basis of the principle of purchase price or production cost is deemed to be its current value.

Application of the depreciation rules

27.—(1) Where—
(a) the value of any asset of a company is determined in accordance with paragraph 22 or 23, and
(b) in the case of a determination under paragraph 22, the asset falls to be included under assets item CI,

that value must be, or (as the case may require) must be the starting point for determining, the amount to be included in respect of that asset in the company's accounts, instead of its cost or any value previously so determined for that asset.
Paragraphs 36 to 41 and 43 apply accordingly in relation to any such asset with the substitution for any reference to its cost of a reference to the value most recently determined for that asset in accordance with paragraph 22 or 23 (as the case may be).

(2) The amount of any provision for depreciation required in the case of any asset by paragraph 37 or 38 as it applies by virtue of sub-paragraph (1) is referred to below in this paragraph as the adjusted amount, and the amount of any provision which would be required by that paragraph in the case of that asset according to the historical cost accounting rules is referred to as the historical cost amount.
(3) Where sub-paragraph (1) applies in the case of any asset the amount of any provision for depreciation in respect of that asset included in any item shown in the profit and loss account in respect of amounts written off assets of the description in question may be the historical cost amount instead of the adjusted amount, provided that the amount of any difference between the two is shown separately in the profit and loss account or in a note to the accounts.

Additional information to be provided

28.—(1) This paragraph applies where the amounts to be included in respect of assets covered by any items shown in a company's accounts have been determined in accordance with paragraph 22 or 23.
(2) The items affected and the basis of valuation adopted in determining the amounts of the assets in question in the case of each such item must be disclosed in a note to the accounts.
(3) The purchase price of investments valued in accordance with paragraph 22 must be disclosed in the notes to the accounts.
(4) In the case of each balance sheet item valued in accordance with paragraph 23 either—
(a) the comparable amounts determined according to the historical cost accounting rules (without any provision for depreciation or diminution in value), or
(b) the differences between those amounts and the corresponding amounts actually shown in the balance sheet in respect of that item,

must be shown separately in the balance sheet or in a note to the accounts.
(5) In sub-paragraph (4), references in relation to any item to the comparable amounts determined as there mentioned are references to—
(a) the aggregate amount which would be required to be shown in respect of that item if the amounts to be included in respect of all the assets covered by that item were determined according to the historical cost accounting rules, and
(b) the aggregate amount of the cumulative provisions for depreciation or diminution in value which would be permitted or required in determining those amounts according to those rules.

Revaluation reserve

29.—(1) Subject to sub-paragraph (7), with respect to any determination of the value of an asset of a company in accordance with paragraph 22 or 23, the amount of any profit or loss arising from that determination (after allowing, where appropriate, for any provisions for depreciation or diminution in value made otherwise than by reference to the value so determined and any adjustments of any such provisions made in the light of that determination) must be credited or (as the case may be) debited to a separate reserve ("the revaluation reserve").
(2) The amount of the revaluation reserve must be shown in the company's balance sheet under liabilities item A.III, but need not be shown under the name "revaluation reserve".
(3) An amount may be transferred—
(a) from the revaluation reserve—
(i) to the profit and loss account, if the amount was previously charged to that account or represents realised profit, or
(ii) on capitalisation,
(b) to or from the revaluation reserve in respect of the taxation relating to any profit or loss credited or debited to the reserve.

The revaluation reserve must be reduced to the extent that the amounts transferred to it are no longer necessary for the purposes of the valuation method used.
(4) In sub-paragraph (3)(a)(ii) "capitalisation", in relation to an amount standing to the credit of the revaluation reserve, means applying it in wholly or partly paying up unissued shares in the company to be allotted to members of the company as fully or partly paid shares.
(5) The revaluation reserve must not be reduced except as mentioned in this paragraph.
(6) The treatment for taxation purposes of amounts credited or debited to the revaluation reserve must be disclosed in a note to the accounts.
(7) This paragraph does not apply to the difference between the valuation of investments and their purchase price or previous valuation shown in the long-term business technical account or the non-technical account in accordance with note (9) on the profit and loss account format.

SECTION C
VALUATION AT FAIR VALUE

Inclusion of financial instruments at fair value

30.—(1) Subject to sub-paragraphs (2) to (5), financial instruments (including derivatives) may be included at fair value.

(2) Sub-paragraph (1) does not apply to financial instruments that constitute liabilities unless—

- (a) they are held as part of a trading portfolio,
- (b) they are derivatives, or
- (c) they are financial instruments falling within paragraph (4).

(3) Except where they fall within paragraph (4), or fall to be included under assets item D (assets held to cover linked liabilities), sub-paragraph (1) does not apply to—

- (a) financial instruments (other than derivatives) held to maturity,
- (b) loans and receivables originated by the company and not held for trading purposes,
- (c) interests in subsidiary undertakings, associated undertakings and joint ventures,
- (d) equity instruments issued by the company,
- (e) contracts for contingent consideration in a business combination, or
- (f) other financial instruments with such special characteristics that the instruments, according to generally accepted accounting principles or practice, should be accounted for differently from other financial instruments.

(4) Financial instruments that, under international accounting standards adopted by the European Commission on or before 5th September 2006 in accordance with the IAS Regulation, may be included in accounts at fair value, may be so included, provided that the disclosures required by such accounting standards are made.

(5) If the fair value of a financial instrument cannot be determined reliably in accordance with paragraph 31, sub-paragraph (1) does not apply to that financial instrument.

(6) In this paragraph—

"associated undertaking" has the meaning given by paragraph 19 of Schedule 6 to these Regulations; and

"joint venture" has the meaning given by paragraph 18 of that Schedule.

Determination of fair value

31.—(1) The fair value of a financial instrument is its value determined in accordance with this paragraph.

(2) If a reliable market can readily be identified for the financial instrument, its fair value is determined by reference to its market value.

(3) If a reliable market cannot readily be identified for the financial instrument but can be identified for its components or for a similar instrument, its fair value is determined by reference to the market value of its components or of the similar instrument.

(4) If neither sub-paragraph (2) nor (3) applies, the fair value of the financial instrument is a value resulting from generally accepted valuation models and techniques.

(5) Any valuation models and techniques used for the purposes of sub-paragraph (4) must ensure a reasonable approximation of the market value.

Hedged items

32. A company may include any assets and liabilities, or identified portions of such assets or liabilities, that qualify as hedged items under a fair value hedge accounting system at the amount required under that system.

Other assets that may be included at fair value

33.—*(1) This paragraph applies to*—

- (a) investment property, and
- (b) living animals and plants,

that, under international accounting standards, may be included in accounts at fair value.

(2) Such investment property and such living animals and plants may be included at fair value, provided that all such investment property or, as the case may be, all such living animals and plants are so included where their fair value can reliably be determined.

(3) In this paragraph, "fair value" means fair value determined in accordance with relevant international accounting standards.

Accounting for changes in value

34.—(1) This paragraph applies where a financial instrument is valued in accordance with paragraph 30 or 32 or an asset is valued in accordance with paragraph 33.
(2) Notwithstanding paragraph 18 in this Part of this Schedule, and subject to sub-paragraphs (3) and (4), a change in the value of the financial instrument or of the investment property or living animal or plant must be included in the profit and loss account.
(3) Where—
(a) the financial instrument accounted for is a hedging instrument under a hedge accounting system that allows some or all of the change in value not to be shown in the profit and loss account, or
(b) the change in value relates to an exchange difference arising on a monetary item that forms part of a company's net investment in a foreign entity,

the amount of the change in value must be credited to or (as the case may be) debited from a separate reserve ("the fair value reserve").
(4) Where the instrument accounted for—
(a) is an available for sale financial asset, and
(b) is not a derivative,

the change in value may be credited to or (as the case may be) debited from the fair value reserve.

The fair value reserve

35.—(1) The fair value reserve must be adjusted to the extent that the amounts shown in it are no longer necessary for the purposes of paragraph 34(3) or (4).
(2) The treatment for taxation purposes of amounts credited or debited to the fair value reserve must be disclosed in a note to the accounts.

SECTION D
HISTORICAL COST ACCOUNTING RULES

VALUATION OF ASSETS

General rules

36.—(1) The rules in this Section are "the historical cost accounting rules".
(2) Subject to any provision for depreciation or diminution in value made in accordance with paragraph 37 or 38, the amount to be included in respect of any asset in the balance sheet format is its cost.

37. In the case of any asset included under assets item B (intangible assets), CI (land and buildings), F.I (tangible assets) or F.II (stocks) which has a limited useful economic life, the amount of—
(a) its cost, or
(b) where it is estimated that any such asset will have a residual value at the end of the period of its useful economic life, its cost less that estimated residual value,

must be reduced by provisions for depreciation calculated to write off that amount systematically over the period of the asset's useful economic life.

38.—(1) This paragraph applies to any asset included under assets item B (intangible assets), C (investments), F.I (tangible assets) or F.IV (own shares).
(2) Where an asset to which this paragraph applies has diminished in value, provisions for diminution in value may be made in respect of it and the amount to be included in respect of it may be reduced accordingly.
(3) Provisions for diminution in value must be made in respect of any asset to which this paragraph applies if the reduction in its value is expected to be permanent (whether its useful economic life is limited or not), and the amount to be included in respect of it must be reduced accordingly.
(4) Any provisions made under sub-paragraph (2) or (3) which are not shown in the profit and loss account must be disclosed (either separately or in aggregate) in a note to the accounts.

39.—(1) Where the reasons for which any provision was made in accordance with paragraph 38 have ceased to apply to any extent, that provision must be written back to the extent that it is no longer necessary.
(2) Any amounts written back in accordance with sub-paragraph (1) which are not shown in the profit and loss account must be disclosed (either separately or in aggregate) in a note to the accounts.

40.—(1) This paragraph applies to assets included under assets items E.I, II and III (debtors) and F.III (cash at bank and in hand) in the balance sheet.
(2) If the net realisable value of an asset to which this paragraph applies is lower than its cost the amount to be included in respect of that asset is the net realisable value.
(3) Where the reasons for which any provision for diminution in value was made in accordance with sub-paragraph (2) have ceased to apply to any extent, that provision must be written back to the extent that it is no longer necessary.

Development costs

41.—(1) Notwithstanding that amounts representing "development costs" may be included under assets item B (intangible assets) in the balance sheet format, an amount may only be included in a company's balance sheet in respect of development costs in special circumstances.
(2) If any amount is included in a company's balance sheet in respect of development costs the following information must be given in a note to the accounts—
(a) the period over which the amount of those costs originally capitalised is being or is to be written off, and
(b) the reasons for capitalising the development costs in question.

Goodwill

42.—(1) The application of paragraphs 36 to 39 in relation to goodwill (in any case where goodwill is treated as an asset) is subject to the following.
(2) Subject to sub-paragraph (3), the amount of the consideration for any goodwill acquired by a company must be reduced by provisions for depreciation calculated to write off that amount systematically over a period chosen by the directors of the company.
(3) The period chosen must not exceed the useful economic life of the goodwill in question.
(4) In any case where any goodwill acquired by a company is included as an asset in the company's balance sheet, there must be disclosed in a note to the accounts—
(a) the period chosen for writing off the consideration for that goodwill, and
(b) the reasons for choosing that period.

Miscellaneous and supplementary provisions

Excess of money owed over value received as an asset item

43.—(1) Where the amount repayable on any debt owed by a company is greater than the value of the consideration received in the transaction giving rise to the debt, the amount of the difference may be treated as an asset.
(2) Where any such amount is so treated—
(a) it must be written off by reasonable amounts each year and must be completely written off before repayment of the debt, and
(b) if the current amount is not shown as a separate item in the company's balance sheet, it must be disclosed in a note to the accounts.

Assets included at a fixed amount

44.—(1) Subject to sub-paragraph (2), assets which fall to be included under assets item F.I (tangible assets) in the balance sheet format may be included at a fixed quantity and value.
(2) Sub-paragraph (1) applies to assets of a kind which are constantly being replaced where—
(a) their overall value is not material to assessing the company's state of affairs, and
(b) their quantity, value and composition are not subject to material variation.

Determination of cost

45.—(1) The cost of an asset that has been acquired by the company is to be determined by adding to the actual price paid any expenses incidental to its acquisition.
(2) The cost of an asset constructed by the company is to be determined by adding to the purchase price of the raw materials and consumables used the amount of the costs incurred by the company which are directly attributable to the construction of that asset.
(3) In addition, there may be included in the cost of an asset constructed by the company—
(a) a reasonable proportion of the costs incurred by the company which are only indirectly attributable to the construction of that asset, but only to the extent that they relate to the period of construction, and
(b) interest on capital borrowed to finance the construction of that asset, to the extent that it accrues in respect of the period of construction,

provided, however, in a case within paragraph (b), that the inclusion of the interest in determining the cost of that asset and the amount of the interest so included is disclosed in a note to the accounts.

46.—(1) The cost of any assets which are fungible assets may be determined by the application of any of the methods mentioned in sub-paragraph (2) in relation to any such assets of the same class, provided that the method chosen is one which appears to the directors to be appropriate in the circumstances of the company.

(2) Those methods are—

(a) the method known as "first in, first out" (FIFO),

(b) the method known as "last in, first out" (LIFO),

(c) a weighted average price, and

(d) any other method similar to any of the methods mentioned above.

(3) Where in the case of any company—

(a) the cost of assets falling to be included under any item shown in the company's balance sheet has been determined by the application of any method permitted by this paragraph, and

(b) the amount shown in respect of that item differs materially from the relevant alternative amount given below in this paragraph,

the amount of that difference must be disclosed in a note to the accounts.

(4) Subject to sub-paragraph (5), for the purposes of sub-paragraph (3)(b), the relevant alternative amount, in relation to any item shown in a company's balance sheet, is the amount which would have been shown in respect of that item if assets of any class included under that item at an amount determined by any method permitted by this paragraph had instead been included at their replacement cost as at the balance sheet date.

(5) The relevant alternative amount may be determined by reference to the most recent actual purchase price before the balance sheet date of assets of any class included under the item in question instead of by reference to their replacement cost as at that date, but only if the former appears to the directors of the company to constitute the more appropriate standard of comparison in the case of assets of that class.

Substitution of original amount where price or cost unknown

47.—(1) This paragraph applies where—

(a) there is no record of the purchase price of any asset acquired by a company or of any price, expenses or costs relevant for determining its cost in accordance with paragraph 45, or

(b) any such record cannot be obtained without unreasonable expense or delay.

(2) In such a case, the cost of the asset must be taken, for the purposes of paragraphs 36 to 42, to be the value ascribed to it in the earliest available record of its value made on or after its acquisition by the company.

SECTION E
RULES FOR DETERMINING PROVISIONS

Preliminary

48. Provisions which are to be shown in a company's accounts are to be determined in accordance with this Section.

Technical provisions

49. The amount of technical provisions must at all times be sufficient to cover any liabilities arising out of insurance contracts as far as can reasonably be foreseen.

Provision for unearned premiums

50.—(1) The provision for unearned premiums must in principle be computed separately for each insurance contract, save that statistical methods (and in particular proportional and flat rate methods) may be used where they may be expected to give approximately the same results as individual calculations.

(2) Where the pattern of risk varies over the life of a contract, this must be taken into account in the calculation methods.

Provision for unexpired risks

51. The provision for unexpired risks (as defined in paragraph 91) must be computed on the basis of claims and administrative expenses likely to arise after the end of the financial year from contracts concluded before that date, in so far as their estimated value exceeds the provision for unearned premiums and any premiums receivable under those contracts.

Long-term business provision

52.—(1) The long-term business provision must in principle be computed separately for each long-term contract, save that statistical or mathematical methods may be used where they may be expected to give approximately the same results as individual calculations.
(2) A summary of the principal assumptions in making the provision under sub-paragraph (1) must be given in the notes to the accounts.
(3) The computation must be made annually by a Fellow of the Institute or Faculty of Actuaries on the basis of recognised actuarial methods, with due regard to the actuarial principles laid down in Directive 2002/83/EC of the European Parliament and of the Council of 5th November 2002 concerning life assurance.

Provisions for claims outstanding

General business

53.—(1) A provision must in principle be computed separately for each claim on the basis of the costs still expected to arise, save that statistical methods may be used if they result in an adequate provision having regard to the nature of the risks.
(2) This provision must also allow for claims incurred but not reported by the balance sheet date, the amount of the allowance being determined having regard to past experience as to the number and magnitude of claims reported after previous balance sheet dates.
(3) All claims settlement costs (whether direct or indirect) must be included in the calculation of the provision.
(4) Recoverable amounts arising out of subrogation or salvage must be estimated on a prudent basis and either deducted from the provision for claims outstanding (in which case if the amounts are material they must be shown in the notes to the accounts) or shown as assets.
(5) In sub-paragraph (4), "subrogation" means the acquisition of the rights of policy holders with respect to third parties, and "salvage" means the acquisition of the legal ownership of insured property.
(6) Where benefits resulting from a claim must be paid in the form of annuity, the amounts to be set aside for that purpose must be calculated by recognised actuarial methods, and paragraph 54 does not apply to such calculations.
(7) Implicit discounting or deductions, whether resulting from the placing of a current value on a provision for an outstanding claim which is expected to be settled later at a higher figure or otherwise effected, is prohibited.

54.—(1) Explicit discounting or deductions to take account of investment income is permitted, subject to the following conditions—

(a) the expected average interval between the date for the settlement of claims being discounted and the accounting date must be at least four years;
(b) the discounting or deductions must be effected on a recognised prudential basis;
(c) when calculating the total cost of settling claims, the company must take account of all factors that could cause increases in that cost;
(d) the company must have adequate data at its disposal to construct a reliable model of the rate of claims settlements;
(e) the rate of interest used for the calculation of present values must not exceed a rate prudently estimated to be earned by assets of the company which are appropriate in magnitude and nature to cover the provisions for claims being discounted during the period necessary for the payment of such claims, and must not exceed either—
    (i) a rate justified by the performance of such assets over the preceding five years, or
    (ii) a rate justified by the performance of such assets during the year preceding the balance sheet date.

(2) When discounting or effecting deductions, the company must, in the notes to the accounts, disclose—

(a) the total amount of provisions before discounting or deductions,
(b) the categories of claims which are discounted or from which deductions have been made,

(c) for each category of claims, the methods used, in particular the rates used for the estimates referred to in sub-paragraph (1)(d) and (e), and the criteria adopted for estimating the period that will elapse before the claims are settled.

Long-term business

55. The amount of the provision for claims must be equal to the sums due to beneficiaries, plus the costs of settling claims.

Equalisation reserves

56. The amount of any equalisation reserve maintained in respect of general business by the company, in accordance with the rules in section 1.4 of the Prudential Sourcebook for Insurers made by the Financial Services Authority under Part 10 of the Financial Services and Markets Act 2000, must be determined in accordance with such rules.

Accounting on a non-annual basis

57.—(1) Either of the methods described in paragraphs 58 and 59 may be applied where, because of the nature of the class or type of insurance in question, information about premiums receivable or claims payable (or both) for the underwriting years is insufficient when the accounts are drawn up for reliable estimates to be made.
(2) The use of either of the methods referred to in sub-paragraph (1) must be disclosed in the notes to the accounts together with the reasons for adopting it.
(3) Where one of the methods referred to in sub-paragraph (1) is adopted, it must be applied systematically in successive years unless circumstances justify a change.
(4) In the event of a change in the method applied, the effect on the assets, liabilities, financial position and profit or loss must be stated in the notes to the accounts.
(5) For the purposes of this paragraph and paragraph 58, "underwriting year" means the financial year in which the insurance contracts in the class or type of insurance in question commenced.

58.—(1) The excess of the premiums written over the claims and expenses paid in respect of contracts commencing in the underwriting year shall form a technical provision included in the technical provision for claims outstanding shown in the balance sheet under liabilities item C3.
(2) The provision may also be computed on the basis of a given percentage of the premiums written where such a method is appropriate for the type of risk insured.
(3) If necessary, the amount of this technical provision must be increased to make it sufficient to meet present and future obligations.
(4) The technical provision constituted under this paragraph must be replaced by a provision for claims outstanding estimated in accordance with paragraph 53 as soon as sufficient information has been gathered and not later than the end of the third year following the underwriting year.
(5) The length of time that elapses before a provision for claims outstanding is constituted in accordance with sub-paragraph (4) must be disclosed in the notes to the accounts.

59.—(1) The figures shown in the technical account or in certain items within it must relate to a year which wholly or partly precedes the financial year (but by no more than 12 months).
(2) The amounts of the technical provisions shown in the accounts must if necessary be increased to make them sufficient to meet present and future obligations.
(3) The length of time by which the earlier year to which the figures relate precedes the financial year and the magnitude of the transactions concerned must be disclosed in the notes to the accounts.

NOTES

Commencement: 6 April 2008 (with effect in relation to financial years beginning on or after that date).
Directive 2002/83/EC of the European Parliament and of the Council: OJ L345, 19.12.2002, p 1.

PART 3
NOTES TO THE ACCOUNTS

Preliminary

[4452]

60. Any information required in the case of any company by the following provisions of this Part of this Schedule must (if not given in the company's accounts) be given by way of a note to the accounts.

General

Disclosure of accounting policies

61. The accounting policies adopted by the company in determining the amounts to be included in respect of items shown in the balance sheet and in determining the profit or loss of the company must be stated (including such policies with respect to the depreciation and diminution in value of assets).

62. It must be stated whether the accounts have been prepared in accordance with applicable accounting standards and particulars of any material departure from those standards and the reasons for it must be given.

Sums denominated in foreign currencies

63. Where any sums originally denominated in foreign currencies have been brought into account under any items shown in the balance sheet or profit and loss account format, the basis on which those sums have been translated into sterling (or the currency in which the accounts are drawn up) must be stated.

Reserves and dividends

64. There must be stated—

(a) any amount set aside or proposed to be set aside to, or withdrawn or proposed to be withdrawn from, reserves,

(b) the aggregate amount of dividends paid in the financial year (other than those for which a liability existed at the immediately preceding balance sheet date),

(c) the aggregate amount of dividends that the company is liable to pay at the balance sheet date, and

(d) the aggregate amount of dividends that are proposed before the date of approval of the accounts, and not otherwise disclosed under sub-paragraph (b) or (c).

Information Supplementing the Balance Sheet

Share capital and debentures

65.—(1) Where shares of more than one class have been allotted, the number and aggregate nominal value of shares of each class allotted must be given.

(2) In the case of any part of the allotted share capital that consists of redeemable shares, the following information must be given—

(a) the earliest and latest dates on which the company has power to redeem those shares,

(b) whether those shares must be redeemed in any event or are liable to be redeemed at the option of the company or of the shareholder, and

(c) whether any (and, if so, what) premium is payable on redemption.

66. If the company has allotted any shares during the financial year, the following information must be given—

(a) the classes of shares allotted, and

(b) as respects each class of shares, the number allotted, their aggregate nominal value and the consideration received by the company for the allotment.

67.—(1) With respect to any contingent right to the allotment of shares in the company the following particulars must be given—

(a) the number, description and amount of the shares in relation to which the right is exercisable,

(b) the period during which it is exercisable, and

(c) the price to be paid for the shares allotted.

(2) In sub-paragraph (1) "contingent right to the allotment of shares" means any option to subscribe for shares and any other right to require the allotment of shares to any person whether arising on the conversion into shares of securities of any other description or otherwise.

68.—(1) If the company has issued any debentures during the financial year to which the accounts relate, the following information must be given—

(a) the classes of debentures issued, and

(b) as respects each class of debentures, the amount issued and the consideration received by the company for the issue.

(2) Where any of the company's debentures are held by a nominee of or trustee for the company, the nominal amount of the debentures and the amount at which they are stated in the accounting records kept by the company in accordance with section 386 of the 2006 Act (duty to keep accounting records) must be stated.

Assets

69.—(1) In respect of any assets of the company included in assets items B (intangible assets), CI (land and buildings) and CII (investments in group undertakings and participating interests) in the company's balance sheet the following information must be given by reference to each such item—

(a) the appropriate amounts in respect of those assets included in the item as at the date of the beginning of the financial year and as at the balance sheet date respectively,

(b) the effect on any amount included in assets item B in respect of those assets of—

(i) any determination during that year of the value to be ascribed to any of those assets in accordance with paragraph 23,

(ii) acquisitions during that year of any assets,

(iii) disposals during that year of any assets, and

(iv) any transfers of assets of the company to and from the item during that year.

(2) The reference in sub-paragraph (1)(a) to the appropriate amounts in respect of any assets (included in an assets item) as at any date there mentioned is a reference to amounts representing the aggregate amounts determined, as at that date, in respect of assets falling to be included under the item on either of the following bases—

(a) on the basis of cost (determined in accordance with paragraphs 45 and 46), or

(b) on any basis permitted by paragraph 22 or 23,

(leaving out of account in either case any provisions for depreciation or diminution in value).

(3) In addition, in respect of any assets of the company included in any assets item in the company's balance sheet, there must be stated (by reference to each such item)—

(a) the cumulative amount of provisions for depreciation or diminution in value of those assets included under the item as at each date mentioned in sub-paragraph (1)(a),

(b) the amount of any such provisions made in respect of the financial year,

(c) the amount of any adjustments made in respect of any such provisions during that year in consequence of the disposal of any of those assets, and

(d) the amount of any other adjustments made in respect of any such provisions during that year.

70. Where any assets of the company (other than listed investments) are included under any item shown in the company's balance sheet at an amount determined on any basis mentioned in paragraph 22 or 23, the following information must be given—

(a) the years (so far as they are known to the directors) in which the assets were severally valued and the several values, and

(b) in the case of assets that have been valued during the financial year, the names of the persons who valued them or particulars of their qualifications for doing so and (whichever is stated) the bases of valuation used by them.

71. In relation to any amount which is included under assets item CI (land and buildings) there must be stated—

(a) how much of that amount is ascribable to land of freehold tenure and how much to land of leasehold tenure, and

(b) how much of the amount ascribable to land of leasehold tenure is ascribable to land held on long lease and how much to land held on short lease.

Investments

72. In respect of the amount of each item which is shown in the company's balance sheet under assets item C (investments) there must be stated how much of that amount is ascribable to listed investments.

Information about fair value of assets and liabilities

73.—(1) This paragraph applies where financial instruments have been valued in accordance with paragraph 30 or 32.

(2) The items affected and the basis of valuation adopted in determining the amounts of the financial instruments must be disclosed.

(3) The purchase price of the financial instruments must be disclosed.

(4) There must be stated—

(a) the significant assumptions underlying the valuation models and techniques used, where the fair value of the instruments has been determined in accordance with paragraph 31(4),

(b) for each category of financial instrument, the fair value of the instruments in that category and the changes in value—

(i) included in the profit and loss account, or

(ii) credited to or (as the case may be) debited from the fair value reserve,

in respect of those instruments, and

(c) for each class of derivatives, the extent and nature of the instruments, including significant terms and conditions that may affect the amount, timing and certainty of future cash flows.

(5) Where any amount is transferred to or from the fair value reserve during the financial year, there must be stated in tabular form—

(a) the amount of the reserve as at the date of the beginning of the financial year and as at the balance sheet date respectively,

(b) the amount transferred to or from the reserve during that year, and

(c) the source and application respectively of the amounts so transferred.

74. Where the company has derivatives that it has not included at fair value, there must be stated for each class of such derivatives—

(a) the fair value of the derivatives in that class, if such a value can be determined in accordance with paragraph 31, and

(b) the extent and nature of the derivatives.

75.—(1) This paragraph applies if—

(a) the company has financial fixed assets that could be included at fair value by virtue of paragraph 30,

(b) the amount at which those assets are included under any item in the company's accounts is in excess of their fair value, and

(c) the company has not made provision for diminution in value of those assets in accordance with paragraph 38(2) of this Schedule.

(2) There must be stated—

(a) the amount at which either the individual assets or appropriate groupings of those individual assets are included in the company's accounts,

(b) the fair value of those assets or groupings, and

(c) the reasons for not making a provision for diminution in value of those assets, including the nature of the evidence that provides the basis for the belief that the amount at which they are stated in the accounts will be recovered.

Information where investment property and living animals and plants included at fair value

76.—(1) This paragraph applies where the amounts to be included in a company's accounts in respect of investment property or living animals and plants have been determined in accordance with paragraph 33.

(2) The balance sheet items affected and the basis of valuation adopted in determining the amounts of the assets in question in the case of each such item must be disclosed in a note to the accounts.

(3) In the case of investment property, for each balance sheet item affected there must be shown, either separately in the balance sheet or in a note to the accounts—

(a) the comparable amounts determined according to the historical cost accounting rules, or

(b) the differences between those amounts and the corresponding amounts actually shown in the balance sheet in respect of that item.

(4) In sub-paragraph (3), references in relation to any item to the comparable amounts determined in accordance with that sub-paragraph are to—

(a) the aggregate amount which would be required to be shown in respect of that item if the amounts to be included in respect of all the assets covered by that item were determined according to the historical cost accounting rules, and

(b) the aggregate amount of the cumulative provisions for depreciation or diminution in value which would be permitted or required in determining those amounts according to those rules.

Reserves and provisions

77.—(1) This paragraph applies where any amount is transferred—

(a) to or from any reserves,

(b) to any provisions for other risks, or
(c) from any provisions for other risks otherwise than for the purpose for which the provision was established,

and the reserves or provisions are or would but for paragraph 3(1) be shown as separate items in the company's balance sheet.
(2) The following information must be given in respect of the aggregate of reserves or provisions included in the same item—
(a) the amount of the reserves or provisions as at the date of the beginning of the financial year and as at the balance sheet date respectively,
(b) any amounts transferred to or from the reserves or provisions during that year, and
(c) the source and application respectively of any amounts so transferred.
(3) Particulars must be given of each provision included in liabilities item E.3 (other provisions) in the company's balance sheet in any case where the amount of that provision is material.

Provision for taxation

78. The amount of any provision for deferred taxation must be stated separately from the amount of any provision for other taxation.

Details of indebtedness

79.—(1) In respect of each item shown under "creditors" in the company's balance sheet there must be stated the aggregate of the following amounts—
(a) the amount of any debts included under that item which are payable or repayable otherwise than by instalments and fall due for payment or repayment after the end of the period of five years beginning with the day next following the end of the financial year, and
(b) in the case of any debts so included which are payable or repayable by instalments, the amount of any instalments which fall due for payment after the end of that period.
(2) Subject to sub-paragraph (3), in relation to each debt falling to be taken into account under sub-paragraph (1), the terms of payment or repayment and the rate of any interest payable on the debt must be stated.
(3) If the number of debts is such that, in the opinion of the directors, compliance with sub-paragraph (2) would result in a statement of excessive length, it is sufficient to give a general indication of the terms of payment or repayment and the rates of any interest payable on the debts.
(4) In respect of each item shown under "creditors" in the company's balance sheet there must be stated—
(a) the aggregate amount of any debts included under that item in respect of which any security has been given by the company, and
(b) an indication of the nature of the securities so given.
(5) References above in this paragraph to an item shown under "creditors" in the company's balance sheet include references, where amounts falling due to creditors within one year and after more than one year are distinguished in the balance sheet—
(a) in a case within sub-paragraph (1), to an item shown under the latter of those categories, and
(b) in a case within sub-paragraph (4), to an item shown under either of those categories.

References to items shown under "creditors" include references to items which would but for paragraph 3(1)(b) be shown under that heading.

80. If any fixed cumulative dividends on the company's shares are in arrear, there must be stated—
(a) the amount of the arrears, and
(b) the period for which the dividends or, if there is more than one class, each class of them are in arrear.

Guarantees and other financial commitments

81.—(1) Particulars must be given of any charge on the assets of the company to secure the liabilities of any other person, including, where practicable, the amount secured.
(2) The following information must be given with respect to any other contingent liability not provided for (other than a contingent liability arising out of an insurance contract)—
(a) the amount or estimated amount of that liability,
(b) its legal nature, and
(c) whether any valuable security has been provided by the company in connection with that liability and if so, what.
(3) There must be stated, where practicable, the aggregate amount or estimated amount of

contracts for capital expenditure, so far as not provided for.

(4) Particulars must be given of—

(a) any pension commitments included under any provision shown in the company's balance sheet, and

(b) any such commitments for which no provision has been made,

and where any such commitment relates wholly or partly to pensions payable to past directors of the company separate particulars must be given of that commitment so far as it relates to such pensions.

(5) Particulars must also be given of any other financial commitments, other than commitments arising out of insurance contracts, that—

(a) have not been provided for, and

(b) are relevant to assessing the company's state of affairs.

(6) Commitments within any of the preceding sub-paragraphs undertaken on behalf of or for the benefit of—

(a) any parent undertaking or fellow subsidiary undertaking, or

(b) any subsidiary undertaking of the company,

must be stated separately from the other commitments within that sub-paragraph, and commitments within paragraph (a) must also be stated separately from those within paragraph (b).

Miscellaneous matters

82.—(1) Particulars must be given of any case where the cost of any asset is for the first time determined under paragraph 47.

(2) Where any outstanding loans made under the authority of section 682(2)(b), (c) or (d) of the 2006 Act (various cases of financial assistance by a company for purchase of its own shares) are included under any item shown in the company's balance sheet, the aggregate amount of those loans must be disclosed for each item in question.

Information supplementing the profit and loss account

Separate statement of certain items of income and expenditure

83.—(1) Subject to sub-paragraph (2), there must be stated the amount of the interest on or any similar charges in respect of—

(a) bank loans and overdrafts, and

(b) loans of any other kind made to the company.

(2) Sub-paragraph (1) does not apply to interest or charges on loans to the company from group undertakings, but, with that exception, it applies to interest or charges on all loans, whether made on the security of debentures or not.

Particulars of tax

84.—(1) Particulars must be given of any special circumstances which affect liability in respect of taxation of profits, income or capital gains for the financial year or liability in respect of taxation of profits, income or capital gains for succeeding financial years.

(2) The following amounts must be stated—

(a) the amount of the charge for United Kingdom corporation tax,

(b) if that amount would have been greater but for relief from double taxation, the amount which it would have been but for such relief,

(c) the amount of the charge for United Kingdom income tax, and

(d) the amount of the charge for taxation imposed outside the United Kingdom of profits, income and (so far as charged to revenue) capital gains.

Those amounts must be stated separately in respect of each of the amounts which is shown under the following items in the profit and loss account, that is to say item III.9 (tax on profit or loss on ordinary activities) and item III.14 (tax on extraordinary profit or loss).

Particulars of business

85.—(1) As regards general business a company must disclose—

(a) gross premiums written,

(b) gross premiums earned,

(c) gross claims incurred,

(d) gross operating expenses, and

(e) the reinsurance balance.

(2) The amounts required to be disclosed by sub-paragraph (1) must be broken down between direct insurance and reinsurance acceptances, if reinsurance acceptances amount to 10 per cent or more of gross premiums written.

(3) Subject to sub-paragraph (4), the amounts required to be disclosed by sub-paragraphs (1) and (2) with respect to direct insurance must be further broken down into the following groups of classes—

(a) accident and health,
(b) motor (third party liability),
(c) motor (other classes),
(d) marine, aviation and transport,
(e) fire and other damage to property,
(f) third-party liability,
(g) credit and suretyship,
(h) legal expenses,
(i) assistance, and
(j) miscellaneous,

where the amount of the gross premiums written in direct insurance for each such group exceeds 10 million Euros.

(4) The company must in any event disclose the amounts relating to the three largest groups of classes in its business.

86.—(1) As regards long-term business, the company must disclose—

(a) gross premiums written, and
(b) the reinsurance balance.

(2) Subject to sub-paragraph (3)—

(a) gross premiums written must be broken down between those written by way of direct insurance and those written by way of reinsurance, and
(b) gross premiums written by way of direct insurance must be broken down—
  (i) between individual premiums and premiums under group contracts,
  (ii) between periodic premiums and single premiums, and
  (iii) between premiums from non-participating contracts, premiums from participating contracts and premiums from contracts where the investment risk is borne by policyholders.

(3) Disclosure of any amount referred to in sub-paragraph (2)(a) or (2)(b)(i), (ii) or (iii) is not required if it does not exceed 10 per cent of the gross premiums written or (as the case may be) of the gross premiums written by way of direct insurance.

87.—(1) Subject to sub-paragraph (2), there must be disclosed as regards both general and long-term business the total gross direct insurance premiums resulting from contracts concluded by the company—

(a) in the member State of its head office,
(b) in the other member States, and
(c) in other countries.

(2) Disclosure of any amount referred to in sub-paragraph (1) is not required if it does not exceed 5 per cent of total gross premiums.

Commissions

88. There must be disclosed the total amount of commissions for direct insurance business accounted for in the financial year, including acquisition, renewal, collection and portfolio management commissions.

Miscellaneous matters

89.—(1) Where any amount relating to any preceding financial year is included in any item in the profit and loss account, the effect must be stated.

(2) Particulars must be given of any extraordinary income or charges arising in the financial year.

(3) The effect must be stated of any transactions that are exceptional by virtue of size or incidence though they fall within the ordinary activities of the company.

Related party transactions

90.—(1) Particulars may be given of transactions which the company has entered into with related parties, and must be given if such transactions are material and have not been concluded under normal market conditions.

(2) The particulars of transactions required to be disclosed by sub-paragraph (1) must include—

(a) the amount of such transactions,
(b) the nature of the related party relationship, and
(c) other information about the transactions necessary for an understanding of the financial

position of the company.

(3) Information about individual transactions may be aggregated according to their nature, except where separate information is necessary for an understanding of the effects of related party transactions on the financial position of the company.

(4) Particulars need not be given of transactions entered into between two or more members of a group, provided that any subsidiary undertaking which is a party to the transaction is wholly-owned by such a member.

(5) In this paragraph, "related party" has the same meaning as in international accounting standards.

NOTES

Commencement: 6 April 2008 (with effect in relation to financial years beginning on or after that date).

PART 4
INTERPRETATION OF THIS SCHEDULE

Definitions for this Schedule

[4453]

91. The following definitions apply for the purposes of this Schedule and its interpretation—

"general business" means business which consists of effecting or carrying out contracts of general insurance;

"long-term business" means business which consists of effecting or carrying out contracts of long-term insurance;

"long-term fund" means the fund or funds maintained by a company in respect of its long-term business in accordance with rule 1.5.22 in the Prudential Sourcebook for Insurers made by the Financial Services Authority under Part 10 of the Financial Services and Markets Act 2000;

"policyholder" has the meaning given by article 3 of the Financial Services and Markets Act 2000 (Meaning of "Policy" and "Policyholder") Order 2001;

"provision for unexpired risks" means the amount set aside in addition to unearned premiums in respect of risks to be borne by the company after the end of the financial year, in order to provide for all claims and expenses in connection with insurance contracts in force in excess of the related unearned premiums and any premiums receivable on those contracts.

NOTES

Commencement: 6 April 2008 (with effect in relation to financial years beginning on or after that date).

(*Schs 4, 5 outside the scope of this work.*)

SCHEDULE 6

COMPANIES ACT GROUP ACCOUNTS

Regulation 9

PART 1
GENERAL RULES

General rules

[4454]

1.—(1) Group accounts must comply so far as practicable with the provisions of Schedule 1 to these Regulations as if the undertakings included in the consolidation ("the group") were a single company (*see Parts 2 and 3 of this Schedule for modifications for banking and insurance groups*).

(2) Where the parent company is treated as an investment company for the purposes of Part 5 of Schedule 1 (special provisions for investment companies) the group must be similarly treated.

2.—(1) The consolidated balance sheet and profit and loss account must incorporate in full the information contained in the individual accounts of the undertakings included in the consolidation, subject to the adjustments authorised or required by the following provisions of this Schedule and to such other adjustments (if any) as may be appropriate in accordance with generally accepted accounting principles or practice.

(2) If the financial year of a subsidiary undertaking included in the consolidation does not end with that of the parent company, the group accounts must be made up—

(a) from the accounts of the subsidiary undertaking for its financial year last ending before the end of the parent company's financial year, provided that year ended no more than three months before that of the parent company, or
(b) from interim accounts prepared by the subsidiary undertaking as at the end of the parent company's financial year.

3.—(1) Where assets and liabilities to be included in the group accounts have been valued or otherwise determined by undertakings according to accounting rules differing from those used for the group accounts, the values or amounts must be adjusted so as to accord with the rules used for the group accounts.
(2) If it appears to the directors of the parent company that there are special reasons for departing from sub-paragraph (1) they may do so, but particulars of any such departure, the reasons for it and its effect must be given in a note to the accounts.
(3) The adjustments referred to in this paragraph need not be made if they are not material for the purpose of giving a true and fair view.

4. Any differences of accounting rules as between a parent company's individual accounts for a financial year and its group accounts must be disclosed in a note to the latter accounts and the reasons for the difference given.

5. Amounts that in the particular context of any provision of this Schedule are not material may be disregarded for the purposes of that provision.

Elimination of group transactions

6.—(1) Debts and claims between undertakings included in the consolidation, and income and expenditure relating to transactions between such undertakings, must be eliminated in preparing the group accounts.
(2) Where profits and losses resulting from transactions between undertakings included in the consolidation are included in the book value of assets, they must be eliminated in preparing the group accounts.
(3) The elimination required by sub-paragraph (2) may be effected in proportion to the group's interest in the shares of the undertakings.
(4) Sub-paragraphs (1) and (2) need not be complied with if the amounts concerned are not material for the purpose of giving a true and fair view.

Acquisition and merger accounting

7.—(1) The following provisions apply where an undertaking becomes a subsidiary undertaking of the parent company.
(2) That event is referred to in those provisions as an "acquisition", and references to the "undertaking acquired" are to be construed accordingly.

8. An acquisition must be accounted for by the acquisition method of accounting unless the conditions for accounting for it as a merger are met and the merger method of accounting is adopted.

9.—(1) The acquisition method of accounting is as follows.
(2) The identifiable assets and liabilities of the undertaking acquired must be included in the consolidated balance sheet at their fair values as at the date of acquisition.
(3) The income and expenditure of the undertaking acquired must be brought into the group accounts only as from the date of the acquisition.
(4) There must be set off against the acquisition cost of the interest in the shares of the undertaking held by the parent company and its subsidiary undertakings the interest of the parent company and its subsidiary undertakings in the adjusted capital and reserves of the undertaking acquired.
(5) The resulting amount if positive must be treated as goodwill, and if negative as a negative consolidation difference.

10.—(1) The conditions for accounting for an acquisition as a merger are—
(a) that at least 90% of the nominal value of the relevant shares in the undertaking acquired (excluding any shares in the undertaking held as treasury shares) is held by or on behalf of the parent company and its subsidiary undertakings,
(b) that the proportion referred to in paragraph (a) was attained pursuant to an arrangement providing for the issue of equity shares by the parent company or one or more of its subsidiary undertakings,

(c) that the fair value of any consideration other than the issue of equity shares given pursuant to the arrangement by the parent company and its subsidiary undertakings did not exceed 10% of the nominal value of the equity shares issued, and

(d) that adoption of the merger method of accounting accords with generally accepted accounting principles or practice.

(2) The reference in sub-paragraph (1)(a) to the "relevant shares" in an undertaking acquired is to those carrying unrestricted rights to participate both in distributions and in the assets of the undertaking upon liquidation.

11.—(1) The merger method of accounting is as follows.

(2) The assets and liabilities of the undertaking acquired must be brought into the group accounts at the figures at which they stand in the undertaking's accounts, subject to any adjustment authorised or required by this Schedule.

(3) The income and expenditure of the undertaking acquired must be included in the group accounts for the entire financial year, including the period before the acquisition.

(4) The group accounts must show corresponding amounts relating to the previous financial year as if the undertaking acquired had been included in the consolidation throughout that year.

(5) There must be set off against the aggregate of—

(a) the appropriate amount in respect of qualifying shares issued by the parent company or its subsidiary undertakings in consideration for the acquisition of shares in the undertaking acquired, and

(b) the fair value of any other consideration for the acquisition of shares in the undertaking acquired, determined as at the date when those shares were acquired,

the nominal value of the issued share capital of the undertaking acquired held by the parent company and its subsidiary undertakings.

(6) The resulting amount must be shown as an adjustment to the consolidated reserves.

(7) In sub-paragraph (5)(a) "qualifying shares" means—

(a) shares in relation to which any of the following provisions applies (merger relief), and in respect of which the appropriate amount is the nominal value—

(i) section 131 of the Companies Act 1985,

(ii) Article 141 of the Companies (Northern Ireland) Order 1986, or

(iii) section 612 of the 2006 Act, or

(b) shares in relation to which any of the following provisions applies (group reconstruction relief), and in respect of which the appropriate amount is the nominal value together with any minimum premium value within the meaning of that section—

(i) section 132 of the Companies Act 1985,

(ii) Article 142 of the Companies (Northern Ireland) Order 1986, or

(iii) section 611 of the 2006 Act.

12.—(1) Where a group is acquired, paragraphs 9 to 11 apply with the following adaptations.

(2) References to shares of the undertaking acquired are to be construed as references to shares of the parent undertaking of the group.

(3) Other references to the undertaking acquired are to be construed as references to the group; and references to the assets and liabilities, income and expenditure and capital and reserves of the undertaking acquired must be construed as references to the assets and liabilities, income and expenditure and capital and reserves of the group after making the set-offs and other adjustments required by this Schedule in the case of group accounts.

13.—(1) The following information with respect to acquisitions taking place in the financial year must be given in a note to the accounts.

(2) There must be stated—

(a) the name of the undertaking acquired or, where a group was acquired, the name of the parent undertaking of that group, and

(b) whether the acquisition has been accounted for by the acquisition or the merger method of accounting;

and in relation to an acquisition which significantly affects the figures shown in the group accounts, the following further information must be given.

(3) The composition and fair value of the consideration for the acquisition given by the parent company and its subsidiary undertakings must be stated.

(4) Where the acquisition method of accounting has been adopted, the book values immediately prior to the acquisition, and the fair values at the date of acquisition, of each class of assets and liabilities of the undertaking or group acquired must be stated in tabular form, including a statement of the amount of any goodwill or negative consolidation difference arising on the acquisition, together with an explanation of any significant adjustments made.

(5) In ascertaining for the purposes of sub-paragraph (4) the profit or loss of a group, the book values and fair values of assets and liabilities of a group or the amount of the assets and liabilities of a group, the set-offs and other adjustments required by this Schedule in the case of group accounts must be made.

14.—(1) There must also be stated in a note to the accounts the cumulative amount of goodwill resulting from acquisitions in that and earlier financial years which has been written off otherwise than in the consolidated profit and loss account for that or any earlier financial year.
(2) That figure must be shown net of any goodwill attributable to subsidiary undertakings or businesses disposed of prior to the balance sheet date.

15. Where during the financial year there has been a disposal of an undertaking or group which significantly affects the figure shown in the group accounts, there must be stated in a note to the accounts—
(a) the name of that undertaking or, as the case may be, of the parent undertaking of that group, and
(b) the extent to which the profit or loss shown in the group accounts is attributable to profit or loss of that undertaking or group.

16. The information required by paragraph 13, 14 or 15 need not be disclosed with respect to an undertaking which—
(a) is established under the law of a country outside the United Kingdom, or
(b) carries on business outside the United Kingdom,
if in the opinion of the directors of the parent company the disclosure would be seriously prejudicial to the business of that undertaking or to the business of the parent company or any of its subsidiary undertakings and the Secretary of State agrees that the information should not be disclosed.

Minority interests

17.—(1) The formats set out in Schedule 1 to these Regulations have effect in relation to group accounts with the following additions.
(2) In the balance sheet formats there must be shown, as a separate item and under an appropriate heading, the amount of capital and reserves attributable to shares in subsidiary undertakings included in the consolidation held by or on behalf of persons other than the parent company and its subsidiary undertakings.
(3) In the profit and loss account formats there must be shown, as a separate item and under an appropriate heading—
(a) the amount of any profit or loss on ordinary activities, and
(b) the amount of any profit or loss on extraordinary activities,
attributable to shares in subsidiary undertakings included in the consolidation held by or on behalf of persons other than the parent company and its subsidiary undertakings.
(4) For the purposes of paragraph 4(1) and (2) of Schedule 1 (power to adapt or combine items)—
(a) the additional item required by sub-paragraph (2) above is treated as one to which a letter is assigned, and
(b) the additional items required by sub-paragraph (3)(a) and (b) above are treated as ones to which an Arabic number is assigned.

Joint ventures

18.—(1) Where an undertaking included in the consolidation manages another undertaking jointly with one or more undertakings not included in the consolidation, that other undertaking ("the joint venture") may, if it is not—
(a) a body corporate, or
(b) a subsidiary undertaking of the parent company,
be dealt with in the group accounts by the method of proportional consolidation.
(2) The provisions of this Schedule relating to the preparation of consolidated accounts apply, with any necessary modifications, to proportional consolidation under this paragraph.

Associated undertakings

19.—(1) An "associated undertaking" means an undertaking in which an undertaking included in the consolidation has a participating interest and over whose operating and financial policy it exercises a significant influence, and which is not—
(a) a subsidiary undertaking of the parent company, or
(b) a joint venture dealt with in accordance with paragraph 18.
(2) Where an undertaking holds 20% or more of the voting rights in another undertaking, it is

presumed to exercise such an influence over it unless the contrary is shown.

(3) The voting rights in an undertaking means the rights conferred on shareholders in respect of their shares or, in the case of an undertaking not having a share capital, on members, to vote at general meetings of the undertaking on all, or substantially all, matters.

(4) The provisions of paragraphs 5 to 11 of Schedule 7 to the 2006 Act (parent and subsidiary undertakings: rights to be taken into account and attribution of rights) apply in determining for the purposes of this paragraph whether an undertaking holds 20% or more of the voting rights in another undertaking.

20.—(1) The formats set out in Schedule 1 to these Regulations have effect in relation to group accounts with the following modifications.

(2) In the balance sheet formats replace the items headed "Participating interests", that is—

- (a) in format 1, item B.III.3, and
- (b) in format 2, item B.III.3 under the heading "ASSETS",

by two items: "Interests in associated undertakings" and "Other participating interests".

(3) In the profit and loss account formats replace the items headed "Income from participating interests", that is—

- (a) in format 1, item 8,
- (b) in format 2, item 10,
- (c) in format 3, item B.4, and
- (d) in format 4, item B.6,

by two items: "Income from interests in associated undertakings" and "Income from other participating interests".

21.—(1) The interest of an undertaking in an associated undertaking, and the amount of profit or loss attributable to such an interest, must be shown by the equity method of accounting (including dealing with any goodwill arising in accordance with paragraphs 17 to 20 and 22 of Schedule 1 to these Regulations).

(2) Where the associated undertaking is itself a parent undertaking, the net assets and profits or losses to be taken into account are those of the parent and its subsidiary undertakings (after making any consolidation adjustments).

(3) The equity method of accounting need not be applied if the amounts in question are not material for the purpose of giving a true and fair view.

Related party transactions

22. Paragraph 72 of Schedule 1 to these Regulations applies to transactions which the parent company, or other undertakings included in the consolidation, have entered into with related parties, unless they are intra group transactions.

NOTES

Commencement: 6 April 2008 (with effect in relation to financial years beginning on or after that date).

Modification: these Regulations are applied, with modifications, to the preparation of accounts of qualifying partnerships for financial years beginning on or after 6 April 2008, by the Partnerships (Accounts) Regulations 2008, SI 2008/569, reg 4, Schedule, Pt 1, paras 1, 2(2), (3).

See further, in relation to the disapplication of paras 13(3), (4), 14, 15 above, with regards to the preparation of accounts of qualifying banks for financial years beginning on or after 6 April 2008 and auditors appointed in respect of those financial years: the Bank Accounts Directive (Miscellaneous Banks) Regulations 2008, SI 2008/567, reg 4, Schedule, paras 7, 11, 12.

(Pt 2 outside the scope of this work.)

PART 3
MODIFICATIONS FOR INSURANCE GROUPS

General application of provisions applicable to individual accounts

[4455]

31. In its application to insurance groups, Part 1 of this Schedule has effect with the following modifications.

32. In paragraph 1 of this Schedule—

- (a) the reference in sub-paragraph (1) to the provisions of Schedule 1 to these Regulations is to be construed as a reference to the provisions of Schedule 3 to these Regulations, and
- (b) sub-paragraph (2) is to be omitted.

Financial years of subsidiary undertakings

33. In paragraph 2(2)(a), for "three months" substitute "six months".

Assets and liabilities to be included in group accounts

34. In paragraph 3, after sub-paragraph (1) insert—

"(1A) Sub-paragraph (1) is not to apply to those liabilities items the valuation of which by the undertakings included in a consolidation is based on the application of provisions applying only to insurance undertakings, nor to those assets items changes in the values of which also affect or establish policyholders' rights.

(1B) Where sub-paragraph (1A) applies, that fact must be disclosed in the notes to the consolidated accounts.".

Elimination of group transactions

35. For sub-paragraph (4) of paragraph 6 substitute—

"(4) Sub-paragraphs (1) and (2) need not be complied with—

(a) where a transaction has been concluded according to normal market conditions and a policyholder has rights in respect of the transaction, or

(b) if the amounts concerned are not material for the purpose of giving a true and fair view.

(5) Where advantage is taken of sub-paragraph (4)(a) that fact must be disclosed in the notes to the accounts, and where the transaction in question has a material effect on the assets, liabilities, financial position and profit or loss of all the undertakings included in the consolidation that fact must also be so disclosed.".

Minority interests

36. In paragraph 17—

(a) in sub-paragraph (1), for the reference to Schedule 1 to these Regulations, substitute a reference to Schedule 3, and

(b) for sub-paragraph (4) substitute—

"(4) Paragraph 3(1) of Schedule 3 to these Regulations (power to combine items) does not apply in relation to the additional items required by the above provisions of this paragraph.".

Associated undertakings

37. In paragraph 20—

(a) in sub-paragraph (1), for the reference to Schedule 1 to these Regulations substitute a reference to Schedule 3 to these Regulations, and

(b) for sub-paragraphs (2) and (3) substitute—

"(2) In the balance sheet format, replace asset item CII.3 (participating interests) with two items, "Interests in associated undertakings" and "Other participating interests".

(3) In the profit and loss account format, replace items II.2.(a) and III.3.(a) (income from participating interests, with a separate indication of that derived from group undertakings) with—

(a) "Income from participating interests other than associated undertakings, with a separate indication of that derived from group undertakings", to be shown as items II.2.(a) and III.3.(a), and

(b) "Income from associated undertakings", to be shown as items II.2.(aa) and III.3.(aa).".

38. In paragraph 21(1) of this Schedule, for the references to paragraphs 17 to 20 and 22 of Schedule 1 to these Regulations, substitute references to paragraphs 36 to 39 and 42 of Schedule 3 to these Regulations.

Related party transactions

39. In paragraph 22 of this Schedule, for the reference to paragraph 72 of Schedule 1 to these Regulations substitute a reference to paragraph 90 of Schedule 3 to these Regulations.

Modifications of Schedule 3 to these Regulations for purposes of paragraph 31

40.—(1) For the purposes of paragraph 31 of this Schedule, Schedule 3 to these Regulations is to be modified as follows.

(2) The information required by paragraph 11 (additional items) need not be given.

(3) In the case of general business, investment income, expenses and charges may be disclosed in the non-technical account rather than in the technical account.
(4) In the case of subsidiary undertakings which are not authorised to carry on long-term business in the United Kingdom, notes (8) and (9) to the profit and loss account format have effect as if references to investment income, expenses and charges arising in the long-term fund or to investments attributed to the long-term fund were references to investment income, expenses and charges or (as the case may be) investments relating to long-term business.
(5) In the case of subsidiary undertakings which do not have a head office in the United Kingdom, the computation required by paragraph 52 must be made annually by an actuary or other specialist in the field on the basis of recognised actuarial methods.
(6) The information required by paragraphs 85 to 88 need not be shown.

NOTES

Commencement: 6 April 2008 (with effect in relation to financial years beginning on or after that date).

(Schs 7, 8 outside the scope of this work.)

SCHEDULE 9

INTERPRETATION OF TERM "PROVISIONS"

Regulation 12

PART 1
MEANING FOR PURPOSES OF THESE REGULATIONS

Definition of "Provisions"

[4456]

1.—(1) In these Regulations, references to provisions for depreciation or diminution in value of assets are to any amount written off by way of providing for depreciation or diminution in value of assets.
(2) Any reference in the profit and loss account formats or the notes to them set out in Schedule 1, 2 or 3 to these Regulations to the depreciation of, or amounts written off, assets of any description is to any provision for depreciation or diminution in value of assets of that description.

2. References in these Regulations to provisions for liabilities or, in the case of insurance companies, to provisions for other risks are to any amount retained as reasonably necessary for the purpose of providing for any liability the nature of which is clearly defined and which is either likely to be incurred, or certain to be incurred but uncertain as to amount or as to the date on which it will arise.

NOTES

Commencement: 6 April 2008 (with effect in relation to financial years beginning on or after that date).

PART 2
MEANING FOR PURPOSES OF PARTS 18 AND 23 OF THE 2006 ACT

Financial assistance for purchase of own shares

[4457]

3. The specified provisions for the purposes of section 677(3)(a) of the 2006 Act (Companies Act accounts: relevant provisions for purposes of financial assistance) are provisions within paragraph 2 of this Schedule.

Redemption or purchase by private company out of capital

4. The specified provisions for the purposes of section 712(2)(b)(i) of the 2006 Act (Companies Act accounts: relevant provisions to determine available profits for redemption or purchase out of capital) are provisions of any of the kinds mentioned in paragraphs 1 and 2 of this Schedule.

Net asset restriction on public companies distributions

5. The specified provisions for the purposes of section 831(3)(a) of the 2006 Act (Companies Act accounts: net asset restriction on public company distributions) are—
(a) provisions within paragraph 2 of this Schedule, and

(b) in the case of an insurance company, any amount included under liabilities items Ba (fund for future appropriations), C (technical provisions) and D (technical provisions for linked liabilities) in a balance sheet drawn up in accordance with Schedule 3 to these Regulations.

Distributions by investment companies

6. The specified provisions for the purposes of section 832(4)(a) of the 2006 Act (Companies Act accounts: investment companies distributions) are provisions within paragraph 2 of this Schedule.

Justification of distribution by references to accounts

7. The specified provisions for the purposes of section 836(1)(b)(i) of the 2006 Act (Companies Act accounts: relevant provisions for distribution purposes)—

(a) are provisions of any of the kinds mentioned in paragraphs 1 and 2 of this Schedule, and

(b) in the case of an insurance company, any amount included under liabilities items Ba (fund for future appropriations), C (technical provisions) and D (technical provisions for linked liabilities) in a balance sheet drawn up in accordance with Schedule 3 to these Regulations.

[8. Realised losses

The specified provisions for the purposes of section 841(2)(a) of the 2006 Act (Companies Act accounts: treatment of provisions as realised losses) are provisions of any of the kinds mentioned in paragraphs 1 and 2 of this Schedule.]

NOTES

Commencement: 6 April 2008 (with effect in relation to financial years beginning on or after that date).

Para 8: added by the Companies Act 2006 (Accounts, Reports and Audit) Regulations 2009, SI 2009/1581, reg 12(1), (4), in relation to financial years beginning on or after 6 April 2008 which have not ended before 27 June 2009.

SCHEDULE 10

GENERAL INTERPRETATION

Regulation 13

Capitalisation

[4458]

1. "Capitalisation", in relation to work or costs, means treating that work or those costs as a fixed asset.

Financial instruments

2. Save in Schedule 2 to these Regulations, references to "derivatives" include commodity-based contracts that give either contracting party the right to settle in cash or in some other financial instrument, except where such contracts—

(a) were entered into for the purpose of, and continue to meet, the company's expected purchase, sale or usage requirements,

(b) were designated for such purpose at their inception, and

(c) are expected to be settled by delivery of the commodity (for banking companies, see the definition in paragraph 94 of Schedule 2 to these Regulations).

3.—(1) Save in Schedule 2 to these Regulations, the expressions listed in sub-paragraph (2) have the same meaning as they have in Council Directive 78/660/EEC on the annual accounts of certain types of companies and 91/674/EEC on the annual accounts and consolidated accounts of insurance undertakings (for banking companies, see the definition in paragraph 96 of Schedule 2 to these Regulations).

(2) Those expressions are "available for sale financial asset", "business combination", "commodity-based contracts", "derivative", "equity instrument", "exchange difference", "fair value hedge accounting system", "financial fixed asset", "financial instrument", "foreign entity", "hedge accounting", "hedge accounting system", "hedged items", "hedging instrument", "held for trading purposes", "held to maturity", "monetary item", "receivables", "reliable market" and "trading portfolio".

Fixed and current assets

4. "Fixed assets" means assets of a company which are intended for use on a continuing basis in the company's activities, and "current assets" means assets not intended for such use.

Fungible assets

5. "Fungible assets" means assets of any description which are substantially indistinguishable one from another.

Historical cost accounting rules

6. References to the historical cost accounting rules are to be read in accordance with paragraph 30 of Schedule 1, paragraph 38 of Schedule 2 and paragraph 36(1) of Schedule 3 to these Regulations.

Leases

7.—(1) "Long lease" means a lease in the case of which the portion of the term for which it was granted remaining unexpired at the end of the financial year is not less than 50 years.
(2) "Short lease" means a lease which is not a long lease.
(3) "Lease" includes an agreement for a lease.

Listed investments

8.—(1) "Listed investment" means an investment as respects which there has been granted a listing on—

(a) a recognised investment exchange other than an overseas investment exchange, or
(b) a stock exchange of repute outside the United Kingdom.

(2) "Recognised investment exchange" and "overseas investment exchange" have the meaning given in Part 18 of the Financial Services and Markets Act 2000.

Loans

9. A loan or advance (including a liability comprising a loan or advance) is treated as falling due for repayment, and an instalment of a loan or advance is treated as falling due for payment, on the earliest date on which the lender could require repayment or (as the case may be) payment, if he exercised all options and rights available to him.

Materiality

10. Amounts which in the particular context of any provision of Schedules 1, 2 or 3 to these Regulations are not material may be disregarded for the purposes of that provision.

Participating interests

11.—(1) A "participating interest" means an interest held by an undertaking in the shares of another undertaking which it holds on a long-term basis for the purpose of securing a contribution to its activities by the exercise of control or influence arising from or related to that interest.
(2) A holding of 20% or more of the shares of the undertaking is to be presumed to be a participating interest unless the contrary is shown.
(3) The reference in sub-paragraph (1) to an interest in shares includes—

(a) an interest which is convertible into an interest in shares, and
(b) an option to acquire shares or any such interest,

and an interest or option falls within paragraph (a) or (b) notwithstanding that the shares to which it relates are, until the conversion or the exercise of the option, unissued.
(4) For the purposes of this regulation an interest held on behalf of an undertaking is to be treated as held by it.
(5) In the balance sheet and profit and loss formats set out in Schedules 1, 2 and 3 to these Regulations, "participating interest" does not include an interest in a group undertaking.
(6) For the purpose of this regulation as it applies in relation to the expression "participating interest"—

(a) in those formats as they apply in relation to group accounts, and
(b) in paragraph 19 of Schedule 6 (group accounts: undertakings to be accounted for as associated undertakings),

the references in sub-paragraphs (1) to (4) to the interest held by, and the purposes and activities of, the undertaking concerned are to be construed as references to the interest held by, and the purposes and activities of, the group (within the meaning of paragraph 1 of that Schedule).

Purchase price

12. "Purchase price", in relation to an asset of a company or any raw materials or consumables used in the production of such an asset, includes any consideration (whether in cash or otherwise) given by the company in respect of that asset or those materials or consumables, as the case may be.

Realised profits and realised losses

13. "Realised profits" and "realised losses" have the same meaning as in section 853(4) and (5) of the 2006 Act.

Staff costs

14.—(1) "Social security costs" means any contributions by the company to any state social security or pension scheme, fund or arrangement.

(2) "Pension costs" includes—

(a) any costs incurred by the company in respect of any pension scheme established for the purpose of providing pensions for persons currently or formerly employed by the company,

(b) any sums set aside for the future payment of pensions directly by the company to current or former employees, and

(c) any pensions paid directly to such persons without having first been set aside.

(3) Any amount stated in respect of the item "social security costs" or in respect of the item "wages and salaries" in the company's profit and loss account must be determined by reference to payments made or costs incurred in respect of all persons employed by the company during the financial year under contracts of service.

Scots land tenure

15. In the application of these Regulations to Scotland, "land of freehold tenure" means land in respect of which the company is the owner; "land of leasehold tenure" means land of which the company is the tenant under a lease.

NOTES

Commencement: 6 April 2008 (with effect in relation to financial years beginning on or after that date).
Council Directive 78/660/EEC: OJ L222, 14.8.1978, p 11.
Council Directive 91/674/EEC: OJ L374, 31.12.1991, p 7.

INSURANCE ACCOUNTS DIRECTIVE (MISCELLANEOUS INSURANCE UNDERTAKINGS) REGULATIONS 2008

(SI 2008/565)

NOTES

Made: 26 February 2008.
Authority: European Communities Act 1972, s 2(2).
Commencement: 6 April 2008.

ARRANGEMENT OF REGULATIONS

PART 1
INTRODUCTION

1 Citation, commencement and application . . . [4459]
2 Interpretation . . . [4460]

PART 2
ACCOUNTS

3 Preparation of accounts by insurance undertakings . . . [4461]
4 Publication of accounts . . . [4462]
5 Penalties for non-compliance (accounts) . . . [4463]

PART 3
AUDITORS

6 Appointment of auditors . . . [4464]
7 Functions of auditor . . . [4465]
8 Signature of auditor's report . . . [4466]
9 Removal of auditors on improper grounds . . . [4467]
10 Duty of auditor to notify appropriate audit authority . . . [4468]
11 Duty of insurance undertaking to notify appropriate audit authority . . . [4469]

12 Penalties for non-compliance (notification of appropriate audit authority) . . . . [4470]

PART 4
FINAL PROVISIONS

13 Summary proceedings: venue and time limit . . . . [4471]
14 Industrial and provident societies . . . . [4472]
16 Revocation . . . . [4473]

SCHEDULES:

Schedule 1—Modification of the Friendly and Industrial and Provident Societies Act 1968 . . . . . [4474]

PART 1
INTRODUCTION

[4459]
1 Citation, commencement and application

(1) These Regulations may be cited as the Insurance Accounts Directive (Miscellaneous Insurance Undertakings) Regulations 2008.

(2) These Regulations come into force on 6th April 2008 and apply in relation to—
- (a) insurance undertakings' financial years beginning on or after that date, and
- (b) auditors appointed in respect of those financial years.

NOTES

Commencement: 6 April 2008.

[4460]
2 Interpretation

(1) In these Regulations—

"the Companies Accounts Regulations" means the Large and Medium-sized Companies and Groups (Accounts and Reports) Regulations 2008;

"the appropriate audit authority" means—
- (a) the Secretary of State, or
- (b) if the Secretary of State has delegated functions under section 1252 of the Companies Act 2006 to a body whose functions include receiving the equivalent notice under section 522 or 523 of that Act, that body;

"the Authority" means the Financial Services Authority;

"director" includes, in the case of an undertaking which is not a company, any corresponding officer of that body;

"enactment" includes—
- (a) an enactment contained in subordinate legislation, other than these Regulations,
- (b) an enactment contained in, or in an instrument made under, an Act of the Scottish Parliament,
- (c) an enactment contained in, or in an instrument made under, Northern Ireland legislation, and
- (d) an enactment contained in, or in an instrument made under, a Measure or Act of the National Assembly for Wales;

"friendly society" has the same meaning as in the Financial Services and Markets Act 2000;

"industrial and provident society" means a registered society within the meaning of either section 74 of the Industrial and Provident Societies Act 1965 or section 101 of the Industrial and Provident Societies Act (Northern Ireland) 1969;

"insurance undertaking" shall be construed in accordance with paragraphs (2) and (3).

(2) Subject to paragraph (3), a body incorporated in or formed under the law of any part of the United Kingdom is an insurance undertaking for the purposes of these Regulations if it—
- (a) is incorporated by or registered under any public general Act of Parliament,
- (b) requires permission under Part 4 of the Financial Services and Markets Act 2000 to effect or carry out contracts of insurance without contravening the prohibition imposed by section 19 of that Act, and
- (c) is not required by any enactment to prepare accounts under Part 15 of the Companies Act 2006 (accounts and reports).

(3) Paragraph (2)(b) must be read with—
- (a) section 22 of the Financial Services and Markets Act 2000,
- (b) the Financial Services and Markets Act 2000 (Regulated Activities) Order 2001,

(c) Schedule 2 to that Act.

(4) A body is not an insurance undertaking for the purposes of these Regulations if it—

(a) is excluded from the scope of Council Directive 73/239/EEC by Article 3 of that Directive,

(b) is referred to in Article 3(2) to (6) of Directive 2002/83/EC of the European Parliament and of the Council of 5th November 2002 concerning life assurance, or

(c) is a friendly society.

(5) Any reference in these Regulations to the accounts required by or prepared under regulation 3 are references to the annual accounts, the directors' report and the auditor's report required by or prepared under paragraph (1) of that regulation.

(6) Any reference in these Regulations to "financial year" in relation to an insurance undertaking means—

(a) any period in respect of which a profit and loss account, or in the case of an industrial and provident society, an annual return, of that undertaking is required to be made up by or in accordance with its constitution or by any enactment (whether that period is a year or not), or

(b) failing any such requirement, each period of 12 months beginning with 1st April.

(7) Except as otherwise provided in these Regulations, words and expressions used in the Companies Act 2006 have the same meaning in these Regulations as they have in that Act.

NOTES

Commencement: 6 April 2008.

Council Directive 73/239/EEC: OJ L228, 16.8.1973, p 3.

Directive 2002/83/EC of the European Parliament and of the Council: OJ L345, 19.12.2002, p 1.

PART 2
ACCOUNTS

[4461]

3 Preparation of accounts by insurance undertakings

(1) The directors of an insurance undertaking must in respect of each financial year of the undertaking—

(a) prepare the like annual accounts and directors' report, and

(b) cause to be prepared such an auditor's report,

as would be required under the provisions mentioned in paragraph (3) if the undertaking were a company which is an insurance company or the parent company of an insurance group.

(2) The accounts required by this regulation must—

(a) be prepared within the period of 6 months beginning immediately after the end of the undertaking's financial year,

(b) state that they are prepared under this regulation, and

(c) comply with such of the requirements of the provisions mentioned in paragraph (3) as relate to the contents of accounts or reports subject, where the insurance undertaking is unincorporated, to any necessary modifications to take account of that fact.

(3) The provisions referred to in paragraphs (1) and (2) are the following provisions of the Companies Act 2006 and the Companies Accounts Regulations—

(a) Chapters 4 and 5 of Part 15 of the Companies Act 2006 (accounts and reports),

(b) sections 433 (name of signatory to be stated in published copies of accounts and reports) and 436 (meaning of "publication" in relation to accounts and reports) of that Act as far as the latter section has effect for the purposes of section 433,

(c) section 469 of that Act (preparation and filing of accounts in euros),

(d) sections 475(1) (requirement for audited accounts), 495 (auditor's report on annual accounts), 496 (auditor's report on directors' report), 498 (duties of auditor), 503 (signature of auditor's report) and 505 (names to be stated in published copies of auditor's report) of that Act,

(e) where Companies Act individual accounts are prepared, Schedule 3 to the Companies Accounts Regulations (insurance companies: Companies Act individual accounts) other than paragraphs 11, 62, 68, 70, 71, 72, 82(2), 83 and 84 and, in paragraph 2(2), the words from "save that none of the following" to the end,

(f) Schedule 4 to those Regulations (information on related undertakings required whether preparing Companies Act or IAS accounts) other than paragraphs 9 and 12,

(g) Schedule 5 to those Regulations (information about benefits of directors) other than paragraphs 2, 4 and 5,

(h) where Companies Act group accounts are prepared, Part 1 of Schedule 6 to the Companies Accounts Regulations (Companies Act group accounts: general rules) (as modified by Part 3 of that Schedule (modifications for insurance groups)) other than paragraphs 13(3) and (4), 14 and 15,

(i) paragraphs 6 and 7 of Schedule 7 to those Regulations (directors' report).

(4) For the purposes of those provisions as applied to accounts prepared under this regulation, these Regulations are to be regarded as part of the requirements of the Companies Act 2006 and the Companies Accounts Regulations.

(5) Regulations 5 and 6 of the Companies (Disclosure of Auditor Remuneration and Liability Limitation Agreements) Regulations 2008 apply in relation to the accounts required by this regulation as they apply in relation to the annual accounts of a company or group which is not a small or medium-sized company or group.

NOTES

Commencement: 6 April 2008.

[4462]

4 Publication of accounts

(1) An insurance undertaking must—

(a) make available the latest accounts and reports prepared under regulation 3 for inspection by any person, without charge and during business hours, at the undertaking's head office in the United Kingdom, and

(b) supply to any person upon request a copy of those accounts (or such part of those accounts as may be requested) at a price not exceeding the administrative cost of making the copy.

(2) In the case of industrial and provident societies which are insurance undertakings, the obligation in paragraph (1)(b) is subject to the provisions of section 39(5) of the Industrial and Provident Societies Act 1965 or section 48(6) of the Industrial and Provident Societies Act (Northern Ireland) 1969, as the case may be.

NOTES

Commencement: 6 April 2008.

[4463]

5 Penalties for non-compliance (accounts)

(1) If the directors of an insurance undertaking fail to comply with paragraph (1) of regulation 3 within the period referred to in paragraph (2) of that regulation, an offence is committed by every person who, immediately before the end of that period, was a director of the undertaking.

(2) If accounts and reports which are made available for inspection under regulation 4(1) do not comply with the requirements of regulation 3, an offence is committed by every person who, at the time when the accounts and reports were or the account was first made available for inspection, was a director of the insurance undertaking.

(3) If an insurance undertaking fails to comply with regulation 4(1) an offence is committed by—

(a) the insurance undertaking, and

(b) every director of the insurance undertaking who is in default.

(4) Where the affairs of an insurance undertaking are managed by its members, any reference in this regulation to a director of the insurance undertaking shall be read as referring to a member of the undertaking.

(5) In proceedings for an offence under this section it is a defence for the person charged to show that he took all reasonable steps and exercised all due diligence to avoid the commission of the offence.

(6) A person guilty of an offence under this regulation is liable on summary conviction to a fine not exceeding level 5 on the standard scale.

(7) Section 1130 of the Companies Act 2006 (proceedings against unincorporated bodies) applies to an offence under paragraph (3) as it does to an offence under section 519 of that Act (statement by auditor to be deposited with company).

NOTES

Commencement: 6 April 2008.

PART 3
AUDITORS

[4464]

6 Appointment of auditors

(1) Sections 485 (appointment of auditors of private company: general), 486 (appointment of auditors of private company: default power of Secretary of State), 487 (term of office of auditors of private company) and 488 (prevention by members of deemed re-appointment of auditor) of the Companies Act 2006 apply in relation to the appointment of auditors of an insurance undertaking subject—

(a) where the undertaking concerned is unincorporated, to any necessary modifications to take account of that fact,

(b) to the modifications made by paragraph (2), and

(c) to paragraph (3).

(2) The modifications are—

(a) in section 485(2)(a), the reference to "the time allowed for sending out copies of the company's annual accounts and reports" is to be construed as a reference to the time allowed under regulation 3(2)(a) of these Regulations for preparing the accounts required by regulation 3;

(b) in section 485(2)(b), the reference to "the day on which copies of the company's annual accounts and reports for the previous financial year are sent out under section 423" is to be construed as a reference to the day on which the accounts required by regulation 3 are prepared;

(c) in section 487(3), the reference to "the provisions of this Part as to removal and resignation of auditors" is to be construed as a reference to provisions in these Regulations, and to any public general Act governing an insurance undertaking, as to removal and resignation of auditors;

(d) in section 488(3)(c), the reference to "the accounting reference period" is to be construed as a reference to the financial year.

(3) Sections 1121 (liability of officer in default), 1122 (liability of company as officer in default), 1123 (application to bodies other than companies) and 1130 (proceedings against unincorporated bodies) of the Companies Act 2006 apply in relation to an offence committed under section 486(3) of that Act as applied by this regulation.

(4) This regulation does not apply in relation to industrial and provident societies which prepare accounts under the provisions of these Regulations.

NOTES

Commencement: 6 April 2008.

[4465]

7 Functions of auditor

(1) The following provisions of the Companies Act 2006 apply to the auditor of an insurance undertaking as they apply to an auditor of a company—

(a) section 495 (auditor's report on company's annual accounts);

(b) section 498 (duties of auditor);

(c) section 499 (auditor's general right to information).

(2) The auditor of an insurance undertaking must supply the directors of that undertaking with such information as is necessary to enable the disclosure required by regulation 3(5) to be made.

(3) This regulation does not apply in relation to industrial and provident societies which prepare accounts under the provisions of these Regulations.

NOTES

Commencement: 6 April 2008.

[4466]

8 Signature of auditor's report

(1) Sections 503 to 506 of the Companies Act 2006 (signature of auditor's report) apply in relation to the auditor's report required by regulation 3(1)(b), subject to—

(a) any necessary modifications to take account of the fact that the insurance undertaking is unincorporated, and

(b) the modifications made by paragraph (2).

(2) The modifications are—

(a) in section 505(1)(b) and section 506(2)(b), the references to the Secretary of State are to be construed as references to the Authority, and

(b) in section 506(1)(b), the reference to the copy of the report delivered to the registrar under Chapter 10 of Part 15 (filing of accounts and reports) is to be construed as a reference to any copy of the report made available for inspection by, or supplied to, the Authority.

(3) The reference to section 505 of the Companies Act 2006 in regulation 3(3)(d) is to be construed in accordance with this regulation.

NOTES

Commencement: 6 April 2008.

[4467]

9 Removal of auditors on improper grounds

(1) Where the auditor of an insurance undertaking is removed from office an application may be made to the High Court under this regulation.

(2) The persons who may make such an application are—

(a) any member of the insurance undertaking who was also a member at the time of the removal, and

(b) the Authority.

(3) If the court is satisfied that the removal was—

(a) on grounds of divergence of opinion on accounting treatments or audit procedures, or

(b) on any other improper grounds,

it may make such order as it thinks fit for giving relief in respect of the removal.

(4) The court may, in particular—

(a) declare that any resolution of the insurance undertaking removing an auditor, or appointing a new auditor in his place, is void;

(b) require the directors of the insurance undertaking to re-appoint the dismissed auditor until the next general meeting of the insurance undertaking;

(c) give directions as to the conduct of the insurance undertaking's affairs in the future.

(5) In the application of this regulation to an insurance undertaking whose principal place of business is in Scotland or Northern Ireland, references to the High Court are to be read as references to the Court of Session or, as the case may be, the High Court in Northern Ireland.

NOTES

Commencement: 6 April 2008.

[4468]

10 Duty of auditor to notify appropriate audit authority

(1) Where an auditor of an insurance undertaking ceases for any reason to hold office, he must notify the appropriate audit authority.

(2) The notice must—

(a) inform the appropriate audit authority that he has ceased to hold office, and

(b) if the auditor resigns, be accompanied by a copy of any notice of resignation and a statement of the reasons for his resignation.

(3) The auditor must comply with this regulation—

(a) if he resigns, at the same time as he deposits his notice of resignation at the head office of the insurance undertaking or otherwise informs it of his resignation;

(b) in any other case, not later than the end of the period of 14 days beginning with the date on which he ceases to hold office.

NOTES

Commencement: 6 April 2008.

[4469]

11 Duty of insurance undertaking to notify appropriate audit authority

(1) Where an auditor of an insurance undertaking ceases to hold office before the end of his term of office, the undertaking must notify the appropriate audit authority.

(2) The notice must—

(a) inform the appropriate audit authority that the auditor has ceased to hold office, and

(b) be accompanied by—

(i) a statement by the undertaking of the reasons for his ceasing to hold office, or

(ii) if the auditor has resigned and he has given the insurance undertaking a statement of the reasons for his resignation, a copy of that statement.

(3) The insurance undertaking must give notice under this paragraph—

(a) if the auditor resigns, not later than the end of the period of 14 days beginning with the date on which the auditor first informs the insurance undertaking of his resignation (whether by notice deposited at its head office or otherwise);

(b) in any other case, not later than the end of the period of 14 days beginning with the date on which the auditor ceases to hold office.

NOTES

Commencement: 6 April 2008.

[4470]

12 Penalties for non-compliance (notification of appropriate audit authority)

(1) If an auditor fails to comply with regulation 10, an offence is committed by—

(a) the auditor, and

(b) if the auditor is a firm, every officer of the firm who is in default.

(2) If an insurance undertaking fails to comply with regulation 11, an offence is committed by—

(a) the insurance undertaking, and

(b) every director of the insurance undertaking who is in default.

(3) Where the affairs of an insurance undertaking are managed by its members, any reference in this regulation to a director of the insurance undertaking shall be read as referring to a member of the undertaking.

(4) In proceedings for an offence under this section it is a defence for the person charged to show that he took all reasonable steps and exercised all due diligence to avoid the commission of the offence.

(5) A person guilty of an offence under this regulation is liable—

(a) on conviction on indictment, to a fine, and

(b) on summary conviction, to a fine not exceeding the statutory maximum.

(6) Sections 1121 (liability of officer in default), 1122 (liability of company as officer in default), 1123 (application to bodies other than companies) and 1130 (proceedings against unincorporated bodies) of the Companies Act 2006 apply to an offence under paragraphs (1) and (2) as they apply to an offence under section 519 of that Act (statement by auditor to be deposited with company).

NOTES

Commencement: 6 April 2008.

PART 4
FINAL PROVISIONS

[4471]

13 Summary proceedings: venue and time limit

Sections 1127 (summary proceedings: venue) and 1128 (summary proceedings: time limit for proceedings) of the Companies Act 2006 apply in relation to summary proceedings for any offence under these Regulations as they apply in relation to such proceedings for any offence under that Act.

NOTES

Commencement: 6 April 2008.

[4472]

14 Industrial and provident societies

(1) Schedule 1 to these Regulations makes provision for the modification of the Friendly and Industrial and Provident Societies Act 1968 in its application to industrial and provident societies that are insurance undertakings for the purposes of these Regulations.

(2) Schedule 2 makes provision for the modification of the Industrial and Provident Societies (Northern Ireland) Act 1969 in its application to industrial and provident societies that are insurance undertakings for the purposes of these Regulations.

(3) The Industrial and Provident Societies (Group Accounts) Regulations 1969 and the Industrial and Provident Societies Act (Group Accounts) Regulations (Northern Ireland) 1969 do not apply to industrial and provident societies that are insurance undertakings for the purposes of these Regulations.

(4) Notwithstanding anything in the rules of the society, the committee of an industrial and provident society that is an insurance undertaking for the purposes of these Regulations may by resolution passed before 1st April 2009 make such amendments of the rules of the society as may be consequential on the provisions of these Regulations.

(5) The Authority is not required to register any amendment of the rules of such a society unless such consequential amendments of the rules of the society as are mentioned in paragraph (4) either have been made before the application for registration of that amendment or are to be effected by that amendment.

NOTES

Commencement: 6 April 2008.

15 (*Amends the Companies Act 2006, s 1210, the Friendly and Industrial and Provident Societies Act 1968, s 4A(3) and the Industrial and Provident Societies (Northern Ireland) Act 1969, s 38A.*)

[4473]

16 Revocation

(1) The Insurance Accounts Directive (Miscellaneous Insurance Undertakings) Regulations 1993 and the Insurance Accounts Directive (Miscellaneous Insurance Undertakings) Regulations (Northern Ireland) 1994 are revoked.

(2) The regulations specified in paragraph (1) continue to apply to any financial year of an insurance undertaking beginning before 6th April 2008.

NOTES

Commencement: 6 April 2008.

SCHEDULE 1

MODIFICATION OF THE FRIENDLY AND INDUSTRIAL AND PROVIDENT SOCIETIES ACT 1968

Regulation 14(1)

[4474]

1. In its application to industrial and provident societies that are insurance undertakings for the purposes of these Regulations, the Friendly and Industrial and Provident Societies Act 1968 has effect subject to the following modifications.

2. Section 3 (general provisions as to accounts and balance sheets of societies) does not apply.

3. In section 3A (publication of accounts and balance sheets of societies), for subsections (2) to (12), substitute—

> "(2) If a society publishes any of its statutory accounts, they must be accompanied by the relevant auditors' report under the Insurance Accounts Directive (Miscellaneous Insurance Undertakings) Regulations 2008.
>
> (3) A society which is required to prepare group accounts for a financial year shall not publish its statutory individual accounts for that year without also publishing with them its statutory group accounts.
>
> (4) If a society publishes non-statutory accounts, it shall publish with them a statement indicating—
>
> (a) that they are not the society's statutory accounts,
>
> (b) whether statutory accounts dealing with any financial year with which the non-statutory accounts purport to deal have been delivered to the Authority,
>
> (c) whether the society's auditors have made a report under the Insurance Accounts Directive (Miscellaneous Insurance Undertakings) Regulations 2008,
>
> (d) whether any such auditors' report—
>
> (i) was qualified or unqualified, or included a reference to any matters to which the auditors drew attention by way of emphasis without qualifying the report, or
>
> (ii) contained a statement under section 498(2) or (3) of the Companies Act 2006 as applied to industrial and provident societies by the Insurance Accounts Directive (Miscellaneous Insurance Undertakings) Regulations 2008 (accounting records or returns inadequate, accounts not agreeing with records and returns or failure to obtain necessary information and explanations),
>
> and it shall not publish with the non-statutory accounts any auditors' report under the Insurance Accounts Directive (Miscellaneous Insurance Undertakings)

Regulations 2008.

(5) For the purposes of this section a society shall be regarded as publishing a document if it publishes, issues or circulates it or otherwise generally makes it available for public inspection in a manner calculated to invite members of the public generally, or any class of members of the public, to read it.

(6) References in this section to a society's statutory accounts are to its individual or group accounts for a financial year as required to be prepared by the Insurance Accounts Directive (Miscellaneous Insurance Undertakings) Regulations 2008; and references to the publication by a society of "non-statutory accounts" are to the publication of—

(a) any balance sheet or profit and loss account relating to, or purporting to deal with, a financial year of the society, or

(b) an account in any form purporting to be a balance sheet or profit and loss account for the group consisting of the society and its subsidiary undertakings relating to, or purporting to deal with, a financial year of the society,

otherwise than as part of the society's statutory accounts.".

4. Sections 4 and 4A (appointment of auditors) do not apply.

5. In section 5 (re-appointment and removal of auditors)—

(a) in subsection (1), at the end of paragraph (d) insert—

", or

(e) he was appointed by the committee, or

(f) the society's rules require actual re-appointment, or

(g) the re-appointment is prevented by the members under section 5A".

(b) after subsection (2) insert—

"(3) A person who is not automatically re-appointed as auditor by virtue of subsection (1)(e) of this subsection may be re-appointed by the committee for the current year of account and for any subsequent year of account commencing before the next general meeting of the society.

However, he may only be re-appointed for any year of account commencing on or after the date of that general meeting by a resolution of the society at that meeting.".

6. After section 5, insert—

"5A Prevention by members of automatic re-appointment of auditor

(1) An auditor of a society is not automatically re-appointed under section 5 of this Act if the society has received notices under this section from members representing at least the requisite percentage of the total voting rights of all members who would be entitled to vote on a resolution that the auditor should not be re-appointed.

(2) The "requisite percentage" is 5%, or such lower percentage as is specified for this purpose in the society's rules.

(3) A notice under this section—

(a) may be in hard copy or electronic form,

(b) must be authenticated by the person or persons giving it, and

(c) must be received by the society before the end of the year of account immediately preceding the year of account for which the automatic re-appointment would have effect.".

7. For section 7 (qualified auditors) substitute—

"7 Qualified auditors

References in this Act to a qualified auditor, in relation to a society, are to a person who—

(a) is eligible for appointment as a statutory auditor under Part 42 of the Companies Act 2006, and

(b) is not prohibited from acting as statutory auditor of the society by virtue of section 1214 of that Act (independence requirement).".

8. Section 8 (restrictions on appointment of auditors) does not apply.

9. In section 9 (auditors' report and rights), only subsection (5) (auditors' rights of access to books and to require information and explanations) applies.

10. Sections 9A to 9C (reporting accountant procedure) do not apply.

11. In section 10 (remuneration of auditors), the following do not apply—

(a) in subsection (1), the words from "or for the making of a report" to the end;

(b) in subsection (2), the words "or reporting accountant";
(c) subsection (3).

12. In section 11 (annual returns)—
(a) in subsection (2)(a), for "the revenue account or accounts of the society prepared in accordance with section 3(2) of this Act" substitute "the profit and loss account required to be prepared by section 396 of the Companies Act 2006 as applied by regulation 3 of the Insurance Accounts Directive (Miscellaneous Insurance Undertakings) Regulations 2008";
(b) for subsection (2)(b) substitute—

"(b) shall not contain any other accounts.";

(c) subsection (5A) does not apply.

13. In section 13 (group accounts)—
(a) subsections (1) to (5) do not apply;
(b) in subsection (6) for "under the last preceding subsection" substitute "on those accounts".

14. Section 14 (exemption from requirements in respect of group accounts) does not apply.

15. Section 15 (meaning of "subsidiary") does not apply.

16. In section 18 (offences), the words from "or any direction" to "section 9C(1) of this Act" do not apply.

17. In section 19(2) (regulations), the words "section 4 or" do not apply.

18. In section 21(1) (interpretation)—
(a) insert at the appropriate place—

""accounts" means the profit and loss account required to be prepared by section 396 of the Companies Act 2006 as applied by regulation 3 of the Insurance Accounts Directive (Miscellaneous Insurance Undertakings) Regulations 2008;";

(b) for the definition of "group accounts" substitute—

""group accounts" means the accounts required to be prepared by section 404 of the Companies Act 2006 as applied by regulation 3 of the Insurance Accounts Directive (Miscellaneous Insurance Undertakings) Regulations 2008;";

(c) the definition of "subsidiary" does not apply.

NOTES
Commencement: 6 April 2008.

(*Sch 2 outside the scope of this work.*)

CONSUMER PROTECTION FROM UNFAIR TRADING REGULATIONS 2008

(SI 2008/1277)

NOTES
Made: 8 May 2008.
Authority: European Communities Act 1972, s 2(2).
Commencement: 26 May 2008.

ARRANGEMENT OF REGULATIONS

PART 1
GENERAL

1 Citation and commencement . . . . . [4475]
2 Interpretation . . . . . [4476]

PART 2
PROHIBITIONS

3 Prohibition of unfair commercial practices . . . . . [4477]
4 Prohibition of the promotion of unfair commercial practices . . . . . [4478]

5 Misleading actions . . . [4479]
6 Misleading omissions . . . [4480]
7 Aggressive commercial practices . . . [4481]

PART 3
OFFENCES

8 Offences relating to unfair commercial practices . . . [4482]
9 . . . [4483]
10 . . . [4484]
11 . . . [4485]
12 . . . [4486]
13 Penalty for offences . . . [4487]
14 Time limit for prosecution . . . [4488]
15 Offences committed by bodies of persons . . . [4489]
16 Offence due to the default of another person . . . [4490]
17 Due diligence defence . . . [4491]
18 Innocent publication of advertisement defence . . . [4492]

SCHEDULES:

Schedule 1—Commercial Practices Which are in All Circumstances Considered Unfair . . . [4493]

PART 1
GENERAL

[4475]
1 Citation and commencement

These Regulations may be cited as the Consumer Protection from Unfair Trading Regulations 2008 and shall come into force on 26th May 2008.

NOTES

Commencement: 26 May 2008.

[4476]
2 Interpretation

(1) In these Regulations—

"average consumer" shall be construed in accordance with paragraphs (2) to (6);

"business" includes a trade, craft or profession;

"code of conduct" means an agreement or set of rules (which is not imposed by legal or administrative requirements), which defines the behaviour of traders who undertake to be bound by it in relation to one or more commercial practices or business sectors;

"code owner" means a trader or a body responsible for—

(a) the formulation and revision of a code of conduct; or

(b) monitoring compliance with the code by those who have undertaken to be bound by it;

"commercial practice" means any act, omission, course of conduct, representation or commercial communication (including advertising and marketing) by a trader, which is directly connected with the promotion, sale or supply of a product to or from consumers, whether occurring before, during or after a commercial transaction (if any) in relation to a product;

"consumer" means any individual who in relation to a commercial practice is acting for purposes which are outside his business;

"enforcement authority" means the OFT, every local weights and measures authority in Great Britain (within the meaning of section 69 of the Weights and Measures Act 1985) and the Department of Enterprise, Trade and Investment in Northern Ireland;

"goods" includes ships, aircraft, animals, things attached to land and growing crops;

"invitation to purchase" means a commercial communication which indicates characteristics of the product and the price in a way appropriate to the means of that commercial communication and thereby enables the consumer to make a purchase;

"materially distort the economic behaviour" means in relation to an average consumer, appreciably to impair the average consumer's ability to make an informed decision thereby causing him to take a transactional decision that he would not have taken otherwise;

"OFT" means the Office of Fair Trading;

"premises" includes any place and any stall, vehicle, ship or aircraft;

"product" means any goods or service and includes immovable property, rights and obligations;

"professional diligence" means the standard of special skill and care which a trader may reasonably be expected to exercise towards consumers which is commensurate with either—
(a) honest market practice in the trader's field of activity, or
(b) the general principle of good faith in the trader's field of activity;

"ship" includes any boat and any other description of vessel used in navigation;

"trader" means any person who in relation to a commercial practice is acting for purposes relating to his business, and anyone acting in the name of or on behalf of a trader;

"transactional decision" means any decision taken by a consumer, whether it is to act or to refrain from acting, concerning—
(a) whether, how and on what terms to purchase, make payment in whole or in part for, retain or dispose of a product; or
(b) whether, how and on what terms to exercise a contractual right in relation to a product.

(2) In determining the effect of a commercial practice on the average consumer where the practice reaches or is addressed to a consumer or consumers account shall be taken of the material characteristics of such an average consumer including his being reasonably well informed, reasonably observant and circumspect.

(3) Paragraphs (4) and (5) set out the circumstances in which a reference to the average consumer shall be read as in addition referring to the average member of a particular group of consumers.

(4) In determining the effect of a commercial practice on the average consumer where the practice is directed to a particular group of consumers, a reference to the average consumer shall be read as referring to the average member of that group.

(5) In determining the effect of a commercial practice on the average consumer—
(a) where a clearly identifiable group of consumers is particularly vulnerable to the practice or the underlying product because of their mental or physical infirmity, age or credulity in a way which the trader could reasonably be expected to foresee, and
(b) where the practice is likely to materially distort the economic behaviour only of that group,

a reference to the average consumer shall be read as referring to the average member of that group.

(6) Paragraph (5) is without prejudice to the common and legitimate advertising practice of making exaggerated statements which are not meant to be taken literally.

NOTES

Commencement: 26 May 2008.

PART 2
PROHIBITIONS

[4477]

3 Prohibition of unfair commercial practices

(1) Unfair commercial practices are prohibited.

(2) Paragraphs (3) and (4) set out the circumstances when a commercial practice is unfair.

(3) A commercial practice is unfair if—
(a) it contravenes the requirements of professional diligence; and
(b) it materially distorts or is likely to materially distort the economic behaviour of the average consumer with regard to the product.

(4) A commercial practice is unfair if—
(a) it is a misleading action under the provisions of regulation 5;
(b) it is a misleading omission under the provisions of regulation 6;
(c) it is aggressive under the provisions of regulation 7; or
(d) it is listed in Schedule 1.

NOTES

Commencement: 26 May 2008.

[4478]

4 Prohibition of the promotion of unfair commercial practices

The promotion of any unfair commercial practice by a code owner in a code of conduct is prohibited.

NOTES
Commencement: 26 May 2008.

[4479]
5 Misleading actions

(1) A commercial practice is a misleading action if it satisfies the conditions in either paragraph (2) or paragraph (3).

(2) A commercial practice satisfies the conditions of this paragraph—
- (a) if it contains false information and is therefore untruthful in relation to any of the matters in paragraph (4) or if it or its overall presentation in any way deceives or is likely to deceive the average consumer in relation to any of the matters in that paragraph, even if the information is factually correct; and
- (b) it causes or is likely to cause the average consumer to take a transactional decision he would not have taken otherwise.

(3) A commercial practice satisfies the conditions of this paragraph if—
- (a) it concerns any marketing of a product (including comparative advertising) which creates confusion with any products, trade marks, trade names or other distinguishing marks of a competitor; or
- (b) it concerns any failure by a trader to comply with a commitment contained in a code of conduct which the trader has undertaken to comply with, if—
  - (i) the trader indicates in a commercial practice that he is bound by that code of conduct, and
  - (ii) the commitment is firm and capable of being verified and is not aspirational,

and it causes or is likely to cause the average consumer to take a transactional decision he would not have taken otherwise, taking account of its factual context and of all its features and circumstances.

(4) The matters referred to in paragraph (2)(a) are—
- (a) the existence or nature of the product;
- (b) the main characteristics of the product (as defined in paragraph 5);
- (c) the extent of the trader's commitments;
- (d) the motives for the commercial practice;
- (e) the nature of the sales process;
- (f) any statement or symbol relating to direct or indirect sponsorship or approval of the trader or the product;
- (g) the price or the manner in which the price is calculated;
- (h) the existence of a specific price advantage;
- (i) the need for a service, part, replacement or repair;
- (j) the nature, attributes and rights of the trader (as defined in paragraph 6);
- (k) the consumer's rights or the risks he may face.

(5) In paragraph (4)(b), the "main characteristics of the product" include—
- (a) availability of the product;
- (b) benefits of the product;
- (c) risks of the product;
- (d) execution of the product;
- (e) composition of the product;
- (f) accessories of the product;
- (g) after-sale customer assistance concerning the product;
- (h) the handling of complaints about the product;
- (i) the method and date of manufacture of the product;
- (j) the method and date of provision of the product;
- (k) delivery of the product;
- (l) fitness for purpose of the product;
- (m) usage of the product;
- (n) quantity of the product;
- (o) specification of the product;
- (p) geographical or commercial origin of the product;
- (q) results to be expected from use of the product; and
- (r) results and material features of tests or checks carried out on the product.

(6) In paragraph (4)(j), the "nature, attributes and rights" as far as concern the trader include the trader's—
- (a) identity;

(b) assets;
(c) qualifications;
(d) status;
(e) approval;
(f) affiliations or connections;
(g) ownership of industrial, commercial or intellectual property rights; and
(h) awards and distinctions.

(7) In paragraph (4)(k) "consumer's rights" include rights the consumer may have under Part 5A of the Sale of Goods Act 1979 or Part 1B of the Supply of Goods and Services Act 1982.

NOTES

Commencement: 26 May 2008.

[4480]

6 Misleading omissions

(1) A commercial practice is a misleading omission if, in its factual context, taking account of the matters in paragraph (2)—

(a) the commercial practice omits material information,
(b) the commercial practice hides material information,
(c) the commercial practice provides material information in a manner which is unclear, unintelligible, ambiguous or untimely, or
(d) the commercial practice fails to identify its commercial intent, unless this is already apparent from the context,

and as a result it causes or is likely to cause the average consumer to take a transactional decision he would not have taken otherwise.

(2) The matters referred to in paragraph (1) are—

(a) all the features and circumstances of the commercial practice;
(b) the limitations of the medium used to communicate the commercial practice (including limitations of space or time); and
(c) where the medium used to communicate the commercial practice imposes limitations of space or time, any measures taken by the trader to make the information available to consumers by other means.

(3) In paragraph (1) "material information" means—

(a) the information which the average consumer needs, according to the context, to take an informed transactional decision; and
(b) any information requirement which applies in relation to a commercial communication as a result of a Community obligation.

(4) Where a commercial practice is an invitation to purchase, the following information will be material if not already apparent from the context in addition to any other information which is material information under paragraph (3)—

(a) the main characteristics of the product, to the extent appropriate to the medium by which the invitation to purchase is communicated and the product;
(b) the identity of the trader, such as his trading name, and the identity of any other trader on whose behalf the trader is acting;
(c) the geographical address of the trader and the geographical address of any other trader on whose behalf the trader is acting;
(d) either—
    (i) the price, including any taxes; or
    (ii) where the nature of the product is such that the price cannot reasonably be calculated in advance, the manner in which the price is calculated;
(e) where appropriate, either—
    (i) all additional freight, delivery or postal charges; or
    (ii) where such charges cannot reasonably be calculated in advance, the fact that such charges may be payable;
(f) the following matters where they depart from the requirements of professional diligence—
    (i) arrangements for payment,
    (ii) arrangements for delivery,
    (iii) arrangements for performance,
    (iv) complaint handling policy;
(g) for products and transactions involving a right of withdrawal or cancellation, the existence of such a right.

NOTES
Commencement: 26 May 2008.

[4481]
7 Aggressive commercial practices

(1) A commercial practice is aggressive if, in its factual context, taking account of all of its features and circumstances—
- (a) it significantly impairs or is likely significantly to impair the average consumer's freedom of choice or conduct in relation to the product concerned through the use of harassment, coercion or undue influence; and
- (b) it thereby causes or is likely to cause him to take a transactional decision he would not have taken otherwise.

(2) In determining whether a commercial practice uses harassment, coercion or undue influence account shall be taken of—
- (a) its timing, location, nature or persistence;
- (b) the use of threatening or abusive language or behaviour;
- (c) the exploitation by the trader of any specific misfortune or circumstance of such gravity as to impair the consumer's judgment, of which the trader is aware, to influence the consumer's decision with regard to the product;
- (d) any onerous or disproportionate non-contractual barrier imposed by the trader where a consumer wishes to exercise rights under the contract, including rights to terminate a contract or to switch to another product or another trader; and
- (e) any threat to take any action which cannot legally be taken.

(3) In this regulation—
- (a) "coercion" includes the use of physical force; and
- (b) "undue influence" means exploiting a position of power in relation to the consumer so as to apply pressure, even without using or threatening to use physical force, in a way which significantly limits the consumer's ability to make an informed decision.

NOTES
Commencement: 26 May 2008.

PART 3
OFFENCES

[4482]
8 Offences relating to unfair commercial practices

(1) A trader is guilty of an offence if—
- (a) he knowingly or recklessly engages in a commercial practice which contravenes the requirements of professional diligence under regulation 3(3)(a); and
- (b) the practice materially distorts or is likely to materially distort the economic behaviour of the average consumer with regard to the product under regulation 3(3)(b).

(2) For the purposes of paragraph (1)(a) a trader who engages in a commercial practice without regard to whether the practice contravenes the requirements of professional diligence shall be deemed recklessly to engage in the practice, whether or not the trader has reason for believing that the practice might contravene those requirements.

NOTES
Commencement: 26 May 2008.

[4483]
9 A trader is guilty of an offence if he engages in a commercial practice which is a misleading action under regulation 5 otherwise than by reason of the commercial practice satisfying the condition in regulation 5(3)(b).

NOTES
Commencement: 26 May 2008.

[4484]
10 A trader is guilty of an offence if he engages in a commercial practice which is a misleading omission under regulation 6.

NOTES

Commencement: 26 May 2008.

[4485]

11 A trader is guilty of an offence if he engages in a commercial practice which is aggressive under regulation 7.

NOTES

Commencement: 26 May 2008.

[4486]

12 A trader is guilty of an offence if he engages in a commercial practice set out in any of paragraphs 1 to 10, 12 to 27 and 29 to 31 of Schedule 1.

NOTES

Commencement: 26 May 2008.

[4487]

13 Penalty for offences

A person guilty of an offence under regulation 8, 9, 10, 11 or 12 shall be liable—

(a) on summary conviction, to a fine not exceeding the statutory maximum; or

(b) on conviction on indictment, to a fine or imprisonment for a term not exceeding two years or both.

NOTES

Commencement: 26 May 2008.

[4488]

14 Time limit for prosecution

(1) No proceedings for an offence under these Regulations shall be commenced after—

(a) the end of the period of three years beginning with the date of the commission of the offence, or

(b) the end of the period of one year beginning with the date of discovery of the offence by the prosecutor,

whichever is earlier.

(2) For the purposes of paragraph (1)(b) a certificate signed by or on behalf of the prosecutor and stating the date on which the offence was discovered by him shall be conclusive evidence of that fact and a certificate stating that matter and purporting to be so signed shall be treated as so signed unless the contrary is proved.

(3) Notwithstanding anything in section 127(1) of the Magistrates' Courts Act 1980, an information relating to an offence under these Regulations which is triable by a magistrates' court in England and Wales may be so tried if it is laid at any time before the end of the period of twelve months beginning with the date of the commission of the offence.

(4) Notwithstanding anything in section 136 of the Criminal Procedure (Scotland) Act 1995 summary proceedings in Scotland for an offence under these Regulations may be commenced at any time before the end of the period of twelve months beginning with the date of the commission of the offence.

(5) For the purposes of paragraph (4), section 136(3) of the Criminal Procedure (Scotland) Act 1995 shall apply as it applies for the purposes of that subsection.

(6) Notwithstanding anything in Article 19(1) of the Magistrates' Courts (Northern Ireland) Order 1981 a complaint charging an offence under these Regulations which is triable by a magistrates' court in Northern Ireland may be so tried if it is made at any time before the end of the period of twelve months beginning with the date of the commission of the offence.

NOTES

Commencement: 26 May 2008.

[4489]

15 Offences committed by bodies of persons

(1) Where an offence under these Regulations committed by a body corporate is proved—

(a) to have been committed with the consent or connivance of an officer of the body, or

(b) to be attributable to any neglect on his part,

the officer as well as the body corporate is guilty of the offence and liable to be proceeded against and punished accordingly.

(2) In paragraph (1) a reference to an officer of a body corporate includes a reference to—

(a) a director, manager, secretary or other similar officer; and

(b) a person purporting to act as a director, manager, secretary or other similar officer.

(3) Where an offence under these Regulations committed by a Scottish partnership is proved—

(a) to have been committed with the consent or connivance of a partner, or

(b) to be attributable to any neglect on his part,

the partner as well as the partnership is guilty of the offence and liable to be proceeded against and punished accordingly.

(4) In paragraph (3) a reference to a partner includes a person purporting to act as a partner.

NOTES

Commencement: 26 May 2008.

[4490]

16 Offence due to the default of another person

(1) This regulation applies where a person "X"—

(a) commits an offence under regulation 9, 10, 11 or 12, or

(b) would have committed an offence under those regulations but for a defence under regulation 17 or 18,

and the commission of the offence, or of what would have been an offence but for X being able to rely on a defence under regulation 17 or 18, is due to the act or default of some other person "Y".

(2) Where this regulation applies Y is guilty of the offence, subject to regulations 17 and 18, whether or not Y is a trader and whether or not Y's act or default is a commercial practice.

(3) Y may be charged with and convicted of the offence by virtue of paragraph (2) whether or not proceedings are taken against X.

NOTES

Commencement: 26 May 2008.

[4491]

17 Due diligence defence

(1) In any proceedings against a person for an offence under regulation 9, 10, 11 or 12 it is a defence for that person to prove—

(a) that the commission of the offence was due to—

(i) a mistake;

(ii) reliance on information supplied to him by another person;

(iii) the act or default of another person;

(iv) an accident; or

(v) another cause beyond his control; and

(b) that he took all reasonable precautions and exercised all due diligence to avoid the commission of such an offence by himself or any person under his control.

(2) A person shall not be entitled to rely on the defence provided by paragraph (1) by reason of the matters referred to in paragraph (ii) or (iii) of paragraph (1)(a) without leave of the court unless—

(a) he has served on the prosecutor a notice in writing giving such information identifying or assisting in the identification of that other person as was in his possession; and

(b) the notice is served on the prosecutor at least seven clear days before the date of the hearing.

NOTES

Commencement: 26 May 2008.

[4492]

18 Innocent publication of advertisement defence

(1) In any proceedings against a person for an offence under regulation 9, 10, 11 or 12 committed by the publication of an advertisement it shall be a defence for a person to prove that—

(a) he is a person whose business it is to publish or to arrange for the publication of advertisements;

(b) he received the advertisement for publication in the ordinary course of business; and

(c) he did not know and had no reason to suspect that its publication would amount to an offence under the regulation to which the proceedings relate.

(2) In paragraph (1) "advertisement" includes a catalogue, a circular and a price list.

19–30 (*Pts 4, 5 outside the scope of this work.*)

SCHEDULE 1

COMMERCIAL PRACTICES WHICH ARE IN ALL CIRCUMSTANCES CONSIDERED UNFAIR

Regulation 3(4)(d)

[4493]

1. Claiming to be a signatory to a code of conduct when the trader is not.

2. Displaying a trust mark, quality mark or equivalent without having obtained the necessary authorisation.

3. Claiming that a code of conduct has an endorsement from a public or other body which it does not have.

4. Claiming that a trader (including his commercial practices) or a product has been approved, endorsed or authorised by a public or private body when the trader, the commercial practices or the product have not or making such a claim without complying with the terms of the approval, endorsement or authorisation.

5. Making an invitation to purchase products at a specified price without disclosing the existence of any reasonable grounds the trader may have for believing that he will not be able to offer for supply, or to procure another trader to supply, those products or equivalent products at that price for a period that is, and in quantities that are, reasonable having regard to the product, the scale of advertising of the product and the price offered (bait advertising).

6. Making an invitation to purchase products at a specified price and then—

(a) refusing to show the advertised item to consumers,

(b) refusing to take orders for it or deliver it within a reasonable time, or

(c) demonstrating a defective sample of it,

with the intention of promoting a different product (bait and switch).

7. Falsely stating that a product will only be available for a very limited time, or that it will only be available on particular terms for a very limited time, in order to elicit an immediate decision and deprive consumers of sufficient opportunity or time to make an informed choice.

8. Undertaking to provide after-sales service to consumers with whom the trader has communicated prior to a transaction in a language which is not an official language of the EEA State where the trader is located and then making such service available only in another language without clearly disclosing this to the consumer before the consumer is committed to the transaction.

9. Stating or otherwise creating the impression that a product can legally be sold when it cannot.

10. Presenting rights given to consumers in law as a distinctive feature of the trader's offer.

11. Using editorial content in the media to promote a product where a trader has paid for the promotion without making that clear in the content or by images or sounds clearly identifiable by the consumer (advertorial).

12. Making a materially inaccurate claim concerning the nature and extent of the risk to the personal security of the consumer or his family if the consumer does not purchase the product.

13. Promoting a product similar to a product made by a particular manufacturer in such a manner as deliberately to mislead the consumer into believing that the product is made by that same manufacturer when it is not.

14. Establishing, operating or promoting a pyramid promotional scheme where a consumer gives consideration for the opportunity to receive compensation that is derived primarily from the introduction of other consumers into the scheme rather than from the sale or consumption of products.

15. Claiming that the trader is about to cease trading or move premises when he is not.

16. Claiming that products are able to facilitate winning in games of chance.

17. Falsely claiming that a product is able to cure illnesses, dysfunction or malformations.

18. Passing on materially inaccurate information on market conditions or on the possibility of finding the product with the intention of inducing the consumer to acquire the product at conditions less favourable than normal market conditions.

19. Claiming in a commercial practice to offer a competition or prize promotion without awarding the prizes described or a reasonable equivalent.

20. Describing a product as 'gratis', 'free', 'without charge' or similar if the consumer has to pay anything other than the unavoidable cost of responding to the commercial practice and collecting or paying for delivery of the item.

21. Including in marketing material an invoice or similar document seeking payment which gives the consumer the impression that he has already ordered the marketed product when he has not.

22. Falsely claiming or creating the impression that the trader is not acting for purposes relating to his trade, business, craft or profession, or falsely representing oneself as a consumer.

23. Creating the false impression that after-sales service in relation to a product is available in an EEA State other than the one in which the product is sold.

24. Creating the impression that the consumer cannot leave the premises until a contract is formed.

25. Conducting personal visits to the consumer's home ignoring the consumer's request to leave or not to return, except in circumstances and to the extent justified to enforce a contractual obligation.

26. Making persistent and unwanted solicitations by telephone, fax, e-mail or other remote media except in circumstances and to the extent justified to enforce a contractual obligation.

27. Requiring a consumer who wishes to claim on an insurance policy to produce documents which could not reasonably be considered relevant as to whether the claim was valid, or failing systematically to respond to pertinent correspondence, in order to dissuade a consumer from exercising his contractual rights.

28. Including in an advertisement a direct exhortation to children to buy advertised products or persuade their parents or other adults to buy advertised products for them.

29. Demanding immediate or deferred payment for or the return or safekeeping of products supplied by the trader, but not solicited by the consumer, except where the product is a substitute supplied in accordance with regulation 19(7) of the Consumer Protection (Distance Selling) Regulations 2000 (inertia selling).

30. Explicitly informing a consumer that if he does not buy the product or service, the trader's job or livelihood will be in jeopardy.

31. Creating the false impression that the consumer has already won, will win, or will on doing a particular act win, a prize or other equivalent benefit, when in fact either—

(a) there is no prize or other equivalent benefit, or

(b) taking any action in relation to claiming the prize or other equivalent benefit is subject to the consumer paying money or incurring a cost.

NOTES

Commencement: 26 May 2008.

(*Schs 2–4 outside the scope of this work.*)

INSURANCE ACCOUNTS DIRECTIVE (LLOYD'S SYNDICATE AND AGGREGATE ACCOUNTS) REGULATIONS 2008

(SI 2008/1950)

NOTES

Made: 22 July 2008.

Authority: European Communities Act 1972, s 2(2).

Commencement: 15 August 2008.

ARRANGEMENT OF REGULATIONS

PART 1
GENERAL

1 Citation, commencement and application . . . [4494]
2 Interpretation . . . [4495]
3 Senior Statutory Auditor . . . [4496]
4 Summary proceedings . . . [4497]

PART 2
SYNDICATE ACCOUNTS

5 Preparation of syndicate's annual accounts . . . [4498]
6 Preparation of syndicate underwriting year accounts . . . [4499]
7 Approval and signing of accounts . . . [4500]
8 Accounts to be sent to syndicate members, the Council of Lloyd's and the Authority . . . [4501]
9 Publication of syndicate accounts and reports . . . [4502]
10 Auditor's report . . . [4503]
11 Duties of auditors . . . [4504]
12 Signature of auditor's report . . . [4505]
13 Names to be stated in copies of auditor's report published or filed . . . [4506]
14 Circumstances in which names may be omitted . . . [4507]
15 Requirements in connection with publication of statutory accounts . . . [4508]
16 Delivery and publication of accounts in euros . . . [4509]
17 Penalties for non-compliance . . . [4510]

PART 3
AGGREGATE ACCOUNTS

18 Preparation of aggregate accounts by Council of Lloyd's . . . [4511]
19 Approval and signing of aggregate accounts . . . [4512]
20 Preparation of annual report by the Council of Lloyd's . . . [4513]
21 Approval and signing of annual report . . . [4514]
22 Auditor's report . . . [4515]
23 Signature of auditor's report . . . [4516]
24 Names to be stated in copies of auditor's report published or filed . . . [4517]
25 Circumstances in which names may be omitted . . . [4518]
26 Duties of auditors . . . [4519]
27 Aggregate accounts and annual report of Council to be delivered to the Authority and published . . . [4520]
28 Penalties for non-compliance . . . [4521]

PART 4
REGULATION BY THE AUTHORITY

29 Functions of the Authority . . . [4522]

PART 5
REVOCATION AND CONSEQUENTIAL PROVISION

30 Revocation . . . [4523]
31 Consequential amendment . . . [4524]

SCHEDULES:

Schedule 1—Syndicate Accounts
Part 1—General Provisions . . . [4525]
Part 2—Managing Agent's Report . . . [4526]
Part 3—Auditors . . . [4527]
Schedule 2—Auditor's Remuneration . . . [4528]
Schedule 3—Provisions Applying to Aggregate Accounts
Part 1—General Provisions and Annual Report . . . [4529]
Part 2—Auditors . . . [4530]

PART 1
GENERAL

[4494]

1 Citation, commencement and application

(1) These Regulations may be cited as the Insurance Accounts Directive (Lloyd's Syndicate and Aggregate Accounts) Regulations 2008.

(2) These Regulations come into force on 15th August 2008 and apply in relation to financial years beginning on or after 1st January 2009.

NOTES

Commencement: 15 August 2008.

[4495]

2 Interpretation

(1) In these Regulations—

"the 2006 Act" means the Companies Act 2006;

"the 2008 Regulations" means the Large and Medium-sized Companies and Groups (Accounts and Reports) Regulations 2008;

"appropriate audit authority" means—

- (a) the Secretary of State, or
- (b) if the Secretary of State has delegated functions under section 1252 of the Companies Act 2006 (delegation of the Secretary of State's functions) to a body whose functions include receiving notice that an auditor of a syndicate or of the aggregate accounts has ceased to hold office, that body;

"the Authority" means the Financial Services Authority;

"the Council of Lloyd's" means the Council constituted by section 3 of Lloyd's Act 1982 (the Council);

"financial year" means the period of 12 months beginning on 1st January;

"Lloyd's byelaws" means the byelaws made under Lloyd's Acts 1871 to 1982;

"managing agent" means a person who is permitted by the Council of Lloyd's, in the conduct of his business as an underwriting agent, to perform, for a member of Lloyd's, one or more of the following functions—

- (a) underwriting contracts of insurance at Lloyd's;
- (b) reinsuring such contracts in whole or in part;
- (c) paying claims on such contracts;

"syndicate" means one or more persons, to whom a syndicate number has been assigned by or under the authority of the Council of Lloyd's, carrying out or effecting contracts of insurance written at Lloyd's;

"syndicate's annual accounts" means the accounts prepared in accordance with regulation 5(2)(a) of these Regulations.

(2) In these Regulations any reference to a person being "in default" in relation to a requirement of these Regulations means a person who authorises or permits, participates in, or fails to take all reasonable steps to prevent, a contravention of that requirement.

(3) For the purposes of these Regulations an underwriting year of account is closed—

- (a) at the time when a contract of reinsurance to close that year of account, which complies with the requirements in the Lloyd's byelaws, takes effect; or
- (b) in the case of a syndicate which consists of a single corporate member, at the time when an amount representing the provision for all known and unknown liabilities attributable to the closing year of account, is included in the underwriting account for the following underwriting year.

(4) Except as otherwise provided in these Regulations, words and expressions used in the 2006 Act have the same meaning in these Regulations as they have in that Act.

NOTES

Commencement: 15 August 2008.

[4496]

3 Senior Statutory Auditor

(1) In these Regulations, "senior statutory auditor" means the individual identified by a firm as senior statutory auditor in relation to an audit in accordance with the standards or guidance mentioned in section 504(1) of the 2006 Act (senior statutory auditor).

(2) The person identified as senior statutory auditor must be eligible for appointment as auditor of the syndicate in question under Chapter 2 of Part 42 of the 2006 Act (statutory auditors: individuals and firms).

(3) The senior statutory auditor is not, by reason of being named or identified as senior statutory auditor or by reason of his or her having signed the auditor's report, subject to any civil liability to which he or she would not otherwise be subject.

NOTES

Commencement: 15 August 2008.

[4497]

4 Summary proceedings

Sections 1127 and 1128 of the 2006 Act (summary proceedings: venue and time limit for proceedings) apply to an offence under these Regulations as they apply to an offence under the Companies Acts (as defined by section 2(1) of the 2006 Act).

NOTES

Commencement: 15 August 2008.

PART 2
SYNDICATE ACCOUNTS

[4498]

5 Preparation of syndicate's annual accounts

(1) Managing agents must prepare or cause to be prepared the accounts and reports required by paragraph (2), in respect of—

(a) each syndicate that they manage on 31st December; and

(b) any syndicate that they were the last managing agent to manage during the preceding year and which has no managing agent on 31st December.

(2) Managing agents must, for the financial year preceding 31st December, in respect of each syndicate—

(a) prepare annual accounts;

(b) prepare an annual report; and

(c) cause to be prepared an auditor's report.

(3) The accounts and annual report required by paragraph (2) must—

(a) be prepared within a period of 3 months beginning immediately after the end of the syndicate's financial year;

(b) state that they are prepared under this regulation; and

(c) comply with the requirements in Schedule 1 to these Regulations.

(4) The accounts required by paragraph (2)(a) must also contain the information on auditor remuneration required by Schedule 2 to these Regulations.

(5) Schedules 1 and 2 to these Regulations have effect.

NOTES

Commencement: 15 August 2008.

[4499]

6 Preparation of syndicate underwriting year accounts

(1) Managing agents must, in respect of each syndicate to which regulation 5(1) refers, prepare or cause to be prepared underwriting year accounts in accordance with paragraph (2), unless—

(a) no underwriting year of that syndicate has been closed in the preceding financial year or is being closed at the end of that financial year; or

(b) the members of the syndicate for each underwriting year included in the underwriting year accounts, agree unanimously, in writing, that no underwriting year accounts shall be prepared in respect of that syndicate.

(2) The underwriting year accounts must be an account which—

(a) is prepared on an underwriting year basis; and

(b) gives a true and fair view of the result of that underwriting year at closure.

(3) The accounts required by this regulation must—

(a) be prepared within a period of 3 months beginning immediately after the end of the syndicate's financial year; and

(b) state that they are prepared under this regulation.

(4) Managing agents must cause to be prepared an auditor's report on the underwriting year accounts required by this regulation stating whether a true and fair view is given of the result of the underwriting year at closure.

(5) Part 42 of the 2006 Act (statutory auditors) applies to an auditor appointed for the purposes of this regulation subject to any necessary modifications to take account of the fact that the syndicate is unincorporated, as it applies to the person appointed for the purposes of regulation 5 or the person appointed to report on the aggregate accounts under section 1210 of the 2006 Act (meaning of "statutory auditor").

NOTES

Commencement: 15 August 2008.

[4500]

7 Approval and signing of accounts

(1) A syndicate's annual accounts must be approved and signed by the syndicate's managing agent and, where the managing agent is a body corporate or a partnership, the accounts must be approved by the board of directors or partners and signed by a director or partner of the managing agent, authorised to sign on its behalf.

(2) The signature must be on the syndicate's balance sheet.

(3) Every copy of the balance sheet which is circulated, published, issued or delivered to the Authority must state the name of the person who signed it on behalf of the syndicate's managing agent.

NOTES

Commencement: 15 August 2008.

[4501]

8 Accounts to be sent to syndicate members, the Council of Lloyd's and the Authority

(1) The managing agent responsible for the preparation of the accounts of a syndicate must send a copy of the accounts and reports prepared under regulations 5 and 6 to every member of Lloyd's who participates in that syndicate and to the Council of Lloyd's, within 3 months from the end of the financial year.

(2) The managing agent responsible for the preparation of the accounts of a syndicate must send a copy of the accounts and reports prepared under regulations 5 and 6 to the Authority within 6 months from the end of the financial year.

(3) References in this regulation to sending documents to a person include references to using electronic communications for sending copies of those documents to such address as may for the time being be notified to the managing agent by that person for that purpose.

NOTES

Commencement: 15 August 2008.

[4502]

9 Publication of syndicate accounts and reports

Where a managing agent has sent accounts and reports to the Council of Lloyd's under regulation 8, the Council must—

(a) make available, on reasonable notice, those accounts and reports for inspection by any person without charge and during business hours at the Council's head office for a period of three years from the date of signature of each document; and

(b) supply to any person upon request a copy of those accounts and reports (or such part of those accounts and reports as may be requested) at a price not exceeding the administrative cost of making the copy, for a period of three years from the date of signature of each document.

NOTES

Commencement: 15 August 2008.

[4503]

10 Auditor's report

(1) A syndicate's auditor must make a report to the syndicate's members on all annual accounts of the syndicate of which copies are to be sent to the syndicate members during the auditor's tenure of office.

(2) The auditor's report must include—

(a) an introduction identifying the annual accounts that are the subject of the audit and the financial reporting framework that has been applied in their preparation; and

(b) a description of the scope of the audit identifying the auditing standards in accordance with which the audit was conducted.

(3) The report must state clearly whether, in the auditor's opinion, the annual accounts—

(a) give a true and fair view—

(i) in the case of an individual balance sheet, of the state of affairs of the syndicate as at the end of the financial year; and

(ii) in the case of an individual profit and loss account, of the profit or loss of the syndicate for the financial year;

(b) have been properly prepared in accordance with the relevant financial reporting framework; and

(c) have been prepared in accordance with the requirements of these Regulations.

(4) The report on the syndicate's annual accounts must also state whether in the auditor's opinion the information given in the managing agent's report for the financial year for which the annual accounts are prepared is consistent with those accounts.

(5) The auditor's report—

(a) must be unqualified or qualified; and

(b) must include a reference to any matters to which the auditor wishes to draw attention by way of emphasis without qualifying the report.

NOTES

Commencement: 15 August 2008.

[4504]

11 Duties of auditors

(1) A syndicate's auditor, in preparing the audit report, must carry out such investigations as will enable the auditor to form an opinion as to—

(a) whether adequate accounting records have been kept on behalf of the syndicate; and

(b) whether the syndicate's annual accounts are in agreement with the accounting records.

(2) If the auditor is of the opinion—

(a) that adequate accounting records have not been kept; or

(b) that the syndicate's annual accounts are not in agreement with the accounting records,

the audit report shall state that fact.

(3) If the auditor fails to obtain all the information and explanations which, to the best of the auditor's knowledge and belief, are necessary for the purposes of the audit, the audit report shall state that fact.

(4) If the requirements of paragraph 5 of Schedule 1 are not complied with in the annual accounts the audit report must include, so far as the auditor is reasonably able to do so, a statement giving the required particulars.

NOTES

Commencement: 15 August 2008.

[4505]

12 Signature of auditor's report

(1) The syndicate's auditor's report on the syndicate's annual accounts required under regulation 5(2), and on the underwriting year accounts required by regulation 6, must state the name of the auditor and be signed and dated.

(2) Where the auditor is an individual, the report must be signed by that individual.

(3) Where the auditor is a firm, the report must be signed by the senior statutory auditor in his or her own name, for and on behalf of the auditor.

NOTES

Commencement: 15 August 2008.

[4506]

13 Names to be stated in copies of auditor's report published or filed

(1) Every copy of the syndicate's auditor's report that is published by or on behalf of the syndicate or the Council of Lloyd's or which is sent to the Authority under regulation 8(2) must—

(a) state the name of the auditor and (where the auditor is a firm) the name of the person who signed it as senior statutory auditor; or

(b) if the conditions in regulation 14 are met, state that a resolution has been passed and notified to the Authority in accordance with regulation 14(2)(b).

(2) For the purposes of this regulation, the syndicate (or the Council) is regarded as publishing the report if it publishes, issues, circulates or otherwise makes it available for public inspection in a manner calculated to invite members of the public generally, or any class of members of the public, to read it.

NOTES

Commencement: 15 August 2008.

[4507]

14 Circumstances in which names may be omitted

(1) The auditor's name, and (where the auditor is a firm) the name of the person who signed the report as senior statutory auditor, may be omitted from copies of the report circulated, published, issued or delivered where the conditions in paragraph (2) are met.

(2) The conditions referred to in paragraph (1) are that the managing agent responsible for preparing the syndicate's accounts—

- (a) considering on reasonable grounds that statement of the name would create or be likely to create a serious risk that the auditor or senior statutory auditor, or any other person, would be subject to violence or intimidation, has resolved that the name should not be stated; and
- (b) has given notice of the resolution to the Authority, stating—
  - (i) the name and number of the syndicate;
  - (ii) the year to which the report relates; and
  - (iii) the name of the auditor and (where the auditor is a firm) the name of the person who signed the report as senior statutory auditor.

NOTES

Commencement: 15 August 2008.

[4508]

15 Requirements in connection with publication of statutory accounts

(1) If a managing agent publishes any of the statutory accounts of a syndicate, they must be accompanied by the auditor's report on those accounts.

(2) If a managing agent publishes non-statutory accounts of a syndicate, it must publish with them a statement indicating—

- (a) that they are not the syndicate's statutory accounts;
- (b) whether statutory accounts dealing with any financial year with which the non-statutory accounts purport to deal have been sent to the Authority under regulation 8(2) of these Regulations; and
- (c) whether an auditor's report has been made on the syndicate's accounts for any such financial year, and if so whether the report—
  - (i) was qualified or unqualified, or included a reference to any matters to which the auditor drew attention by way of emphasis without qualifying the report; or
  - (ii) contained a statement under regulation 11(2), (3) or (4).

(3) The managing agent must not publish the auditor's report on the syndicate's statutory accounts with non-statutory accounts.

(4) References in this paragraph to the publication by a managing agent of "non-statutory accounts" are to the publication of any balance sheet or profit and loss account relating to, or purporting to deal with, a financial year of the syndicate or an underwriting year of the syndicate otherwise than as part of the syndicate's statutory accounts.

(5) A syndicate's "statutory accounts" are its accounts for a financial year specified in regulations 5(2)(a) and 6 (1) and required to be sent to the Authority under regulation 8(2).

NOTES

Commencement: 15 August 2008.

[4509]

16 Delivery and publication of accounts in euros

(1) The amounts set out in the syndicate's annual accounts may also be shown in the same accounts translated into euros.

(2) When complying with regulation 8(2) the managing agent may send to the Authority an additional copy of the syndicate's annual accounts in which the amounts have been translated into euros.

(3) In both cases—

- (a) the amounts must have been translated at the exchange rate prevailing on the date to which the balance sheet is made up; and
- (b) that rate must be disclosed in the notes to the accounts.

(4) For the purposes of regulation 15 any additional copy of the syndicate's annual accounts sent to the Authority under paragraph (2) above shall be treated as statutory accounts of the syndicate.

(5) In the case of such a copy, references in regulation 15 to the auditor's report on the syndicate's annual accounts must be read as references to the auditor's report on the annual accounts of which it is a copy.

NOTES

Commencement: 15 August 2008.

[4510]

17 Penalties for non-compliance

(1) If the managing agent of a Lloyd's syndicate fails to comply with regulation 5(1), within the period referred to in regulation 5(3), the managing agent and every person who was a director or partner of it immediately before the end of that period, is guilty of an offence and liable on summary conviction to a fine not exceeding level 5 on the standard scale.

(2) If the managing agent of a Lloyd's syndicate fails to comply with regulation 6(1), within the period referred to in regulation 6(3), the managing agent and every person who was a director or partner of it immediately before the end of that period, is guilty of an offence and liable on summary conviction to a fine not exceeding level 5 on the standard scale.

(3) If accounts which are approved under regulation 7 do not comply with the requirements of these Regulations, the managing agent of the Lloyd's syndicate and every person who was a director or partner of the managing agent at the time when the accounts were approved who—

(a) knew that they did not comply, or was reckless as to whether they complied, and

(b) failed to take reasonable steps to secure compliance with those requirements or, as the case may be, to prevent the accounts from being approved,

is guilty of an offence and liable on conviction on indictment, to a fine, and on summary conviction to a fine not exceeding the statutory maximum.

(4) If an annual report which is approved under paragraph 12 of Schedule 1 does not comply with the requirements of these Regulations, the managing agent of the Lloyd's syndicate and every person who was a director or partner of the managing agent at the time when the accounts were approved who—

(a) knew that they did not comply, or was reckless as to whether they complied, and

(b) failed to take reasonable steps to secure compliance with those requirements or, as the case may be, to prevent the accounts from being approved,

is guilty of an offence and liable on conviction on indictment to a fine, and on summary conviction to a fine not exceeding the statutory maximum.

(5) If a managing agent fails to comply with regulation 8(1), it and every person who was a director or partner of the managing agent at the time when the failure took place is guilty of an offence and liable on summary conviction to a fine not exceeding level 5 on the standard scale.

(6) If a managing agent fails to comply with regulation 8(2), it and every person who was a director or partner of the managing agent at the time when the failure took place is guilty of an offence and liable on summary conviction to a fine not exceeding level 5 on the standard scale.

(7) If a copy of the syndicate auditor's report is sent to the Authority or published without the statement required by regulation 13, the managing agent, and every person who was a director or partner of the managing agent at the time when the failure took place is guilty of an offence and liable on summary conviction to a fine not exceeding level 3 on the standard scale.

(8) If a managing agent contravenes any provision of regulation 15, the managing agent and every person who was a director or partner of the managing agent at the time when the contravention took place, is guilty of an offence and liable on summary conviction to a fine not exceeding level 3 on the standard scale.

(9) It is a defence for a person charged with an offence under this regulation to show that he or she took all reasonable steps for securing that the requirements in question would be complied with.

NOTES

Commencement: 15 August 2008.

PART 3
AGGREGATE ACCOUNTS

[4511]

18 Preparation of aggregate accounts by Council of Lloyd's

(1) The members of the Council of Lloyd's must prepare aggregate accounts for each financial year by cumulating all the syndicate annual accounts prepared in accordance with regulation 5 for that year.

(2) The aggregate accounts must consist of—
(a) an aggregate balance sheet as at the last day of the financial year; and
(b) an aggregate profit and loss account.

Those accounts are referred to in these Regulations as the "aggregate accounts".

(3) The aggregate accounts must—
(a) be prepared within the period of 6 months beginning immediately after the end of the financial year; and
(b) state that they are prepared under these Regulations.

(4) The aggregate accounts must comply with the provisions of Schedule 3 to the 2008 Regulations (insurance companies: Companies Act individual accounts), other than the provisions (or parts of provisions) set out in paragraph (5) as to—
(a) the form and content of the aggregate balance sheet and aggregate profit and loss account; and
(b) additional information to be provided by way of notes to the accounts.

(5) The provisions are the following—
(a) paragraphs 11(2), 68, 71, 72, 79, 81, 82(2), 83; and
(b) in paragraph 2(2) the words from "save that none" to the end of that sub-paragraph.

(6) The aggregate accounts must also contain the information on auditor remuneration required in Schedule 2 to these Regulations and comply with the provisions set out in paragraph 1 of Schedule 3 to these Regulations.

(7) Schedule 3 to these Regulations has effect.

NOTES

Commencement: 15 August 2008.

[4512]

19 Approval and signing of aggregate accounts

(1) The aggregate accounts must be approved by the Council of Lloyd's and signed on behalf of the Council by a member of the Council.

(2) The signature must be on the aggregate balance sheet.

(3) Every copy of the aggregate balance sheet which is circulated, published or issued must state the name of the person who signed it on behalf of the Council.

(4) The copy of the aggregate balance sheet which is delivered to the Authority must be signed on behalf of the Council by a member of the Council.

NOTES

Commencement: 15 August 2008.

[4513]

20 Preparation of annual report by the Council of Lloyd's

The members of the Council of Lloyd's must prepare an annual report on the insurance business carried on by the members of Lloyd's which complies with the requirements set out in paragraphs 2 to 4 of Schedule 3.

NOTES

Commencement: 15 August 2008.

[4514]

21 Approval and signing of annual report

(1) The annual report prepared under regulation 20 must be approved by the Council of Lloyd's and signed on behalf of the Council by a member of the Council.

(2) Every copy of the annual report which is circulated, published or issued, must state the name of the person who signed it on behalf of the Council.

(3) The copy of the annual report which is delivered to the Authority must be signed on behalf of the Council by a member of the Council.

NOTES

Commencement: 15 August 2008.

[4515]

22 Auditor's report

(1) The members of the Council of Lloyd's must obtain an auditor's report on the aggregate accounts.

(2) The auditor's report shall include—

(a) an introduction identifying the aggregate accounts that are the subject of the report and the financial reporting framework that has been applied in their preparation;

(b) a description of the scope of the review carried out by the auditor and identifying the standards in accordance with which the review was conducted; and

(c) a clear statement as to whether, in the auditor's opinion, the aggregate accounts have been properly prepared in accordance with the requirements of these Regulations, and whether those accounts are correctly aggregated.

(3) The auditor's report must state whether, in the auditor's opinion, the annual report of the Council of Lloyd's—

(a) is consistent with the aggregate accounts for the same financial year; and

(b) has been prepared in accordance with these Regulations.

(4) The auditor's report—

(a) must be either unqualified or qualified; and

(b) must include a reference to any matters to which the auditor wishes to draw attention by way of emphasis without qualifying the report.

NOTES

Commencement: 15 August 2008.

[4516]

23 Signature of auditor's report

(1) The auditor's report must state the name of the auditor and be signed and dated.

(2) Where the auditor is an individual, the report must be signed by that individual.

(3) Where the auditor is a firm, the report must be signed by the senior statutory auditor in his own name, for and on behalf of the auditor.

NOTES

Commencement: 15 August 2008.

[4517]

24 Names to be stated in copies of auditor's report published or filed

(1) Every copy of the auditor's report which is published by or on behalf of the Council of Lloyd's must—

(a) state the name of the auditor and (where the auditor is a firm) the name of the person who signed it as senior statutory auditor; or

(b) if the conditions in regulation 25 are met, state that a resolution has been passed and notified to the Authority in accordance with regulation 25(2)(b).

(2) The copy of the auditor's report delivered to the Authority must be signed and dated by the auditor.

(3) For the purposes of this regulation, the Council is regarded as publishing the report if it publishes, issues, circulates or otherwise makes it available for public inspection in a manner calculated to invite members of the public generally, or any class of members of the public, to read it.

NOTES

Commencement: 15 August 2008.

[4518]

25 Circumstances in which names may be omitted

(1) The auditor's name, and (where the auditor is a firm) the name of the person who signed the report as senior statutory auditor, may be omitted from copies of the report circulated, published, issued or delivered where the conditions in paragraph (2) are met.

(2) The conditions referred to in paragraph (1) are that the Council of Lloyd's—

(a) considering on reasonable grounds that statement of the name would create or be likely to create a serious risk that the auditor, senior statutory auditor, or any other person, would be subject to violence or intimidation, has resolved that the name should not be stated; and

(b) has given notice of the resolution to the Authority, stating—

(i) the year to which the report relates; and

(ii) the name of the auditor and (where the auditor is a firm) the name of the person who signed the report as senior statutory auditor.

NOTES
Commencement: 15 August 2008.

[4519]
26 Duties of auditors

(1) The auditor of the aggregate accounts must, in preparing the auditor's report, carry out such investigations as will enable the auditor to form an opinion as to whether the aggregate accounts are properly prepared and a correct aggregation of the syndicate accounts which have been cumulated to prepare them.

(2) If the auditor is of the opinion that the aggregate accounts are not properly prepared or not a correct aggregation of the syndicate accounts which have been cumulated to prepare them, that fact must be stated in the auditor's report.

(3) If the auditor fails to obtain all the information and explanations which, to the best of the auditor's knowledge and belief, are necessary for the purposes of the auditor's report, that fact must be stated in the auditor's report.

NOTES
Commencement: 15 August 2008.

[4520]
27 Aggregate accounts and annual report of Council to be delivered to the Authority and published

(1) The Council of Lloyd's must deliver to the Authority a copy of the aggregate accounts and its annual report on each financial year within 6 months from the end of that year.

(2) The Council of Lloyd's must—

(a) make available, on reasonable notice, the latest aggregate accounts and its latest annual report for inspection by any person, without charge and during business hours, at the Council's head office; and

(b) supply to any person upon request a copy of those accounts or that report (or such part of them as may be requested) at a price not exceeding the administrative cost of making the copy.

NOTES
Commencement: 15 August 2008.

[4521]
28 Penalties for non-compliance

(1) If the members of the Council of Lloyd's fail to comply with the requirement in regulation 18(1) within the period referred to in regulation 18(3) to prepare aggregate accounts, every person who was a member of the Council of Lloyd's immediately before the end of that period is guilty of an offence and liable on summary conviction to a fine not exceeding level 5 on the standard scale.

(2) If aggregate accounts which are approved under regulation 19 do not comply with the requirements of these Regulations, every member of the Council of Lloyd's who—

(a) knew that they did not comply, or was reckless as to whether they complied, and

(b) failed to take reasonable steps to secure compliance with those requirements or, as the case may be, to prevent the accounts from being approved,

is guilty of an offence and liable on conviction on indictment to a fine, and on summary conviction to a fine not exceeding the statutory maximum.

(3) In the case of failure to comply with the requirement in regulation 20 to prepare an annual report, every person who was a member of the Council of Lloyd's immediately before the end of the period referred to in regulation 27(1) is guilty of an offence and liable on conviction on indictment to a fine, and on summary conviction to a fine not exceeding the statutory maximum.

(4) If an annual report which is approved under regulation 21 does not comply with the requirements of these Regulations, every member of the Council of Lloyd's who—

(a) knew it did not comply, or was reckless as to whether it complied; and

(b) failed to take reasonable steps to secure compliance with those requirements or, as the case may be, to prevent the report from being approved,

is guilty of an offence and liable on conviction on indictment to a fine, and on summary conviction to a fine not exceeding the statutory maximum.

(5) If a copy of the auditor's report is sent to the Authority or published without the statement required by regulation 24, every person who was a member of the Council of Lloyd's at the time when the failure took place is guilty of an offence and liable on summary conviction to a fine not exceeding level 3 on the standard scale.

(6) In the event of failure to deliver a copy of the aggregate accounts and the report of the Council of Lloyd's to the Authority under regulation 27, every person who was a member of the Council of Lloyd's at the time when the failure took place is guilty of an offence and liable on conviction on indictment to a fine, and on summary conviction to a fine not exceeding the statutory maximum.

(7) It is a defence for a person charged with an offence under this regulation to show that he or she took all reasonable steps for securing that the requirements in question would be complied with.

NOTES

Commencement: 15 August 2008.

PART 4
REGULATION BY THE AUTHORITY

[4522]

29 Functions of the Authority

(1) The Authority has responsibility for administering the system of regulation of Lloyd's syndicates and the Council of Lloyd's provided for by these Regulations.

(2) Proceedings for an offence under these Regulations may be instituted only—

- (a) by the Authority or the Secretary of State; or
- (b) by or with the consent of the Director of Public Prosecutions.

(3) In exercising its power to institute proceedings for an offence under these Regulations, the Authority must comply with any conditions or restrictions imposed in writing by the Treasury.

(4) The Authority may increase any fee which it charges managing agents under the Financial Services and Markets Act 2000 to take account of the expenses incurred in carrying out its functions under these Regulations.

NOTES

Commencement: 15 August 2008.

PART 5
REVOCATION AND CONSEQUENTIAL PROVISION

[4523]

30 Revocation

The Insurance Accounts Directive (Lloyd's Syndicate and Aggregate Accounts) Regulations 2004 are revoked, but continue to apply to financial years beginning on or before 1 January 2008.

NOTES

Commencement: 15 August 2008.

[4524]

31 Consequential amendment

(1) . . .

(2) In relation to financial years beginning on or before 1st January 2008, subsection (1)(e) of that section is to continue to have effect without the substitution made by paragraph (1).

NOTES

Commencement: 15 August 2008.
Sub-s (1): substitutes the Companies Act 2006, s 1210(1)(e).

SCHEDULE 1

SYNDICATE ACCOUNTS

Regulation 5(3) and (5)

PART 1
GENERAL PROVISIONS

Syndicate's annual accounts

[4525]

1.—(1) A syndicate's annual accounts must be prepared in accordance with this paragraph.
(2) Annual accounts must comprise—
 (a) a balance sheet as at the last day of the financial year; and
 (b) a profit and loss account.
(3) The accounts must—
 (a) in the case of the balance sheet, give a true and fair view of the state of affairs of the syndicate as at the end of the financial year; and
 (b) in the case of the profit and loss account, give a true and fair view of the profit or loss of the syndicate for the financial year.
(4) Subject to sub-paragraph (5) the accounts must comply with the provisions of Schedule 3 to the 2008 Regulations, other than the provisions (or parts of provisions) set out in sub-paragraph (7) as to—
 (a) the form and content of the balance sheet and profit and loss account; and
 (b) additional information to be provided by way of notes to the accounts.
(5) The information required by paragraph 90 of Schedule 3 to the 2008 Regulations must be given by the managing agent in relation to any transactions entered into by the managing agent on behalf of the syndicate and must in addition—
 (a) identify any related party who is an insurance or reinsurance intermediary within the meaning of Article 2 of Directive 2002/92/EC of the European Parliament and of the Council on insurance mediation; and
 (b) include particulars of the amount of any material transactions concluded otherwise than under normal market conditions with any related party within paragraph (a).
(6) Where the managing agent has related parties within the meaning of sub-paragraph (5)(a), but there have been no transactions with them which require disclosure under paragraph 90 of Schedule 3 to the 2008 Regulations, the accounts must contain a statement to that effect, and identify any such related parties.
(7) The provisions in Schedule 3 to the 2008 Regulations referred to in sub-paragraph (4) are—
 (a) paragraphs 11(2), 68, 71, 72, 82(2), 83; and
 (b) in paragraph 2(2) the words from "save that none of the following" to the end of that sub-paragraph.
(8) The syndicate's annual accounts must also include a description of funds which members are required to hold at Lloyd's.
(9) The description of funds referred to in sub-paragraph (8) need not include particulars of funds held by members of the syndicate.

Compliance with Regulations

2.—(1) Where compliance with—
 (a) Schedule 3 to the 2008 Regulations; and
 (b) these Regulations,

would not be sufficient to give a true and fair view, the additional information necessary to achieve this must be given in the accounts or in a note to them.
(2) If in special circumstances compliance with any of the provisions referred to in sub-paragraph (1) is inconsistent with the requirement to give a true and fair view, the managing agent must depart from that provision to the extent necessary to give a true and fair view.
(3) Particulars of any such departure, the reasons for it and its effect must be given in a note to the accounts.

Information about related undertakings

3. The syndicate's annual accounts must comply with the requirements of regulation 7 of the 2008 Regulations (including the application of Schedule 4 to those Regulations) as to information about related undertakings of the managing agent to be given in notes to the syndicate's accounts.

Information about employee numbers and staff

4.—(1) Subject to sub-paragraph (2), the syndicate's annual accounts must comply with the requirements of section 411 (information about employee numbers and costs) of the 2006 Act in relation to the syndicate as if references in it to a company were treated as references to the managing agent.

(2) Information about employee numbers and costs need only be given under sub-paragraph (1) in relation to employees of the managing agent who have spent any part of their time during the year in question working on behalf of that syndicate.

Information about emoluments of managing agents and other benefits of managing and others

5.—(1) The information specified in sub-paragraph (2) must be given in notes to the syndicate's annual accounts.

(2) The information is—

(a) the aggregate amount charged to a syndicate by its managing agent, in respect of emoluments paid to the managing agent's directors, the active underwriter and (where applicable) the run-off manager of the syndicate, in the financial year to which the accounts relate; and

(b) the specific amounts charged to a syndicate by its managing agent in respect of emoluments paid to the syndicate's active underwriter and (where applicable) its run-off manager in that financial year.

(3) In this paragraph, "emoluments"—

(a) includes salaries, fees and bonuses, sums paid by way of expenses allowance (so far as they are chargeable to United Kingdom income tax) and, subject to paragraph (b), the estimated money value of any other benefits received by the person concerned otherwise than in cash; but

(b) does not include any of the following, namely—

(i) the value of any share options granted or the amount of any gains made on the exercise of any such options;

(ii) any contributions paid, or treated as paid, in respect of the person concerned under any pension scheme or any benefits to which that person is entitled under any such scheme; or

(iii) any money or other assets paid, received or receivable under any long term incentive scheme.

(4) In this paragraph—

"active underwriter" means, in relation to a syndicate, the individual at or deemed by the Council to be at, the underwriting box with principal authority to accept risks on behalf of the members of the syndicate;

"run-off manager" means, in relation to a run-off syndicate, the person who has principal authority to negotiate or place contracts of reinsurance or negotiate and settle the payment of claims on contracts of insurance or reinsurance on behalf of the members of the syndicate;

"run-off syndicate" means a syndicate which no longer accepts new or renewal insurance business (other than the variation or extension of risks previously underwritten, or reinsurance to close of an earlier year of account of that syndicate).

Information about directors' benefits: advances and credit

6.—(1) The information specified in sub-paragraph (2) must be given in notes to the syndicate's annual accounts.

(2) The information is—

(a) details of any advance or credit granted by the managing agent to its directors, or, where the managing agent is a partnership, to its partners, and charged to the syndicate by the managing agent, namely—

(i) the amount of the advance or credit;

(ii) an indication of the interest rate;

(iii) its main conditions; and

(iv) any amounts repaid;

(b) the totals of the amounts stated under paragraph (a)(i) and (iv).

(3) References in this paragraph to the directors or partners of the managing agent are to the persons who were a director or a partner at any time in the financial year to which the accounts relate.

(4) The requirements of this section apply in relation to every advance or credit subsisting at any time in the financial year to which the accounts relate—

(a) whenever it was entered into;

(b) whether or not the person concerned was a director or partner of the managing agent in question at the time it was entered into.

Off-balance sheet arrangements

7.—(1) If in any financial year—

(a) a syndicate is or has been party to an arrangement that is not reflected in its balance sheet; and

(b) at the balance sheet date the risks or benefits arising from that arrangement are material,

the information required by this paragraph must be given in notes to the syndicate's annual accounts.

(2) The information required is—

(a) the nature and business purpose of the arrangement; and

(b) the financial impact of the arrangement on the syndicate.

(3) The information need only be given to the extent necessary for enabling the financial position of the syndicate to be assessed.

NOTES

Commencement: 15 August 2008.

Directive 2002/92/EC of the European Parliament and of the Council: OJ L9, 15.1.2003, p 3.

PART 2
MANAGING AGENT'S REPORT

Managing agent's report: general requirements

[4526]

8.—(1) The managing agent's report for a financial year must state—

(a) the names of the persons who at any time during the financial year were directors or partners of the managing agent; and

(b) the principal activities of the syndicate in the course of the year and any significant change to those activities in the year.

(2) The managing agent's report must contain—

(a) particulars of any important events affecting the syndicate which have occurred since the end of the financial year;

(b) an indication of likely future developments in the business of the syndicate; and

(c) an indication of the activities (if any) of the syndicate in the field of research and development.

Managing agent's report: business review

9.—(1) The managing agent's report must contain a business review.

(2) The business review must contain—

(a) a fair review of the business of the syndicate; and

(b) a description of the principal risks and uncertainties facing the syndicate.

(3) The review required is a balanced and comprehensive analysis of—

(a) the development and performance of the syndicate's business during the financial year; and

(b) the position of the syndicate's business at the end of that year,

consistent with the size and complexity of the business.

(4) The review must include to the extent necessary for an understanding of the development, performance or position of the insurance business of the syndicate—

(a) analysis using financial key performance indicators; and

(b) where appropriate, analysis using other key performance indicators, including information relating to environmental matters and employee matters.

(5) In sub-paragraph (4), "key performance indicators" means factors by reference to which the development, performance or position of the insurance business of the syndicate can be measured effectively.

(6) The review must, where appropriate, include references to and additional explanations of amounts included in the syndicate accounts.

(7) Nothing in this paragraph requires the disclosure of information about impending developments or matters in the course of negotiation if the disclosure would, in the opinion of the managing agent, be seriously prejudicial to the interests of the syndicate.

Financial instruments

10.—(1) In relation to the use of financial instruments by a syndicate, the managing agent's report must contain an indication of—

(a) the financial risk management objectives and policies of the syndicate, including the policy for hedging each major type of forecasted transaction for which hedge accounting is used; and

(b) the exposure of the syndicate to price risk, credit risk, liquidity risk and cash flow risk,

unless such information is not material for the assessment of the assets, liabilities, financial position and profit or loss of the syndicate.

(2) In sub-paragraph (1) the expressions "hedge accounting", "price risk", "credit risk", "liquidity risk" and "cash flow risk" have the same meaning as they have in Council Directive 78/660/EEC on the annual accounts of certain types of companies, and in Council Directive 83/349/EEC on consolidated accounts.

Statement as to disclosure of information to auditors

11.—(1) The managing agent's report must contain a statement to the effect that, in the case of each of the persons who are directors, or, where the managing agent is a partnership, of each of the persons who are partners, of the managing agent at the time the report is approved—

(a) so far as the director or partner is aware, there is no relevant audit information of which the syndicate's auditor is unaware; and

(b) the director or partner has taken all the steps that he or she ought to have taken as a director or partner to become aware of any relevant audit information and to establish that the syndicate's auditor is aware of that information.

(2) In sub-paragraph (1) "relevant audit information" means information needed by the syndicate's auditor in connection with preparing the auditor's report.

(3) For the purposes of sub-paragraph (1), a director or partner of the managing agent is regarded as having taken all the steps that he or she ought to have taken as a director or partner in order to do the things mentioned in sub-paragraph (1)(b) if the director or partner has—

(a) made such enquiries of fellow directors or partners and of the syndicate's auditors for that purpose; and

(b) taken such other steps (if any) for that purpose,

as were required by his or her duty as a director or partner of the managing agent of the syndicate to exercise due care, skill and diligence.

(4) Where the managing agent's report containing the statement required by this paragraph is approved but the statement is false, every director or partner of the managing agent who—

(a) knew that the statement was false, or was reckless as to whether it was false; and

(b) failed to take reasonable steps to prevent the report from being approved,

commits an offence.

(5) A person guilty of an offence under sub-paragraph (4) is liable—

(a) on conviction on indictment, to imprisonment for a term not exceeding two years or to a fine, or both;

(b) on summary conviction, to imprisonment for a term not exceeding three months or to a fine not exceeding the statutory maximum, or both.

Approval and signing of managing agent's report

12.—(1) The managing agent's report must be approved and signed by the syndicate's managing agent and, where the managing agent is a body corporate or a partnership, the report must be approved by the board of directors or by the partners and signed by a director or partner of the managing agent, authorised to sign on its behalf.

(2) Every copy of the managing agent's report which is circulated, published, or issued shall state the name of the person who signed the balance sheet on behalf of the syndicate's managing agent.

(3) Every copy of the managing agent's report which is delivered to the Authority must be signed on behalf of the managing agent by a director or partner of the managing agent, authorised to sign on its behalf.

NOTES

Commencement: 15 August 2008.

Council Directive 78/660/EEC: OJ L222, 14.8.1978, p 11.

Council Directive 83/349/EEC: OJ L193, 18.7.1983, p 1

PART 3
AUDITORS

Appointment of syndicate auditors

[4527]

13.—(1) Subject to sub-paragraph (3), the members of Lloyd's who participate in a syndicate must appoint its auditor for each financial year, unless the auditor is deemed to be re-appointed in accordance with paragraph 14(2).
(2) For each financial year for which the auditor is to be appointed, the appointment must be made before the end of the period of 28 days beginning with—
- (a) the end of the time allowed under regulation 8(1) for sending out the accounts and reports required by regulation 5 for the previous financial year; or
- (b) if earlier, the day on which copies of the accounts and reports prepared under regulation 5 for the previous financial year are sent out under regulation 8(1).

This is the "period for appointing auditors" for the purposes of this Part of this Schedule.
(3) The managing agent of the syndicate may appoint an auditor for the syndicate—
- (a) at any time before the syndicate's first period for appointing auditors; or
- (b) to fill a casual vacancy in the office of auditor.

(4) Where no appointment has been made under paragraph (1) by the end of the period for appointing auditors, and the auditor in office is not deemed to be re-appointed under paragraph 14(2)—
- (a) the managing agent must within one week from the end of that period give notice in writing to the Authority of that fact; and
- (b) the Authority must appoint an auditor of the syndicate to fill the vacancy as soon as possible.

(5) If the managing agent fail to give the notice required by this paragraph, an offence is committed by—
- (a) the managing agent; and
- (b) every director or partner of the managing agent who was in default.

(6) A person guilty of an offence under this paragraph is liable on summary conviction to a fine not exceeding level 3 on the standard scale and, for continued contravention, a daily default fine not exceeding one-tenth of level 3 on the standard scale.

Term of office of auditors of syndicate

14.—(1) An auditor of a syndicate holds office in accordance with the terms of his or her appointment, subject to the requirements that—
- (a) the auditor does not take office until any previous auditor ceases to hold office; and
- (b) the auditor ceases to hold office at the end of the next period for appointing auditors unless re-appointed.

(2) Where no auditor has been appointed by the end of the next period for appointing auditors, any auditor in office immediately before that time is deemed to be re-appointed at that time, unless—
- (a) Lloyd's byelaws require actual re-appointment;
- (b) the deemed re-appointment is prevented by the members of the syndicate under paragraph 15; or
- (c) the members of the syndicate have resolved that the auditor should not be re-appointed.

Prevention by members of deemed re-appointment of auditor

15.—(1) An auditor of a syndicate is not deemed to be re-appointed under paragraph 14(2) if the managing agent has received notices under this paragraph from members of the syndicate representing at least the requisite percentage of the total voting rights of all members of the syndicate who would be entitled to vote on a resolution that the auditor should not be re-appointed.
(2) The "requisite percentage" is 5%, or such lower percentage as is specified for this purpose in Lloyd's byelaws.
(3) A notice under this paragraph—
- (a) may be in hard copy or electronic form;
- (b) must be authenticated by the person or persons giving it; and
- (c) must be received by the managing agent before the end of the financial year immediately preceding the time when the deemed re-appointment would have effect.

Removal of auditor on improper grounds

16.—(1) Where an auditor of a syndicate is removed from office an application may be made to the High Court under this paragraph.

(2) The persons who may make such an application are—
- (a) any member of the syndicate who was a member at the time the auditor was removed;
- (b) the Society of Lloyd's; or
- (c) the Authority.

(3) If the Court is satisfied that the removal was—
- (a) on grounds of divergence of opinion on accounting treatments or audit procedures; or
- (b) on any other improper grounds,

it may make such order as it thinks fit for giving relief in respect of the removal.

(4) The Court may, in particular—
- (a) declare that any decision to remove an auditor, or to appoint a new auditor in place of the auditor, is void;
- (b) require the members of the syndicate to re-appoint the auditor; and
- (c) give directions as to the conduct of the syndicate's affairs in the future.

Duty of auditor to notify appropriate audit authority

17.—(1) Where the auditor of the syndicate ceases to hold office before the end of his or her term of office, the auditor must notify in writing the appropriate audit authority.

(2) The notice must—
- (a) inform the appropriate audit authority that the auditor has ceased to hold office; and
- (b) be accompanied by a statement of the reasons for the auditor's ceasing to hold office.

(3) The auditor must give notice under this paragraph—
- (a) if the auditor resigns, at the same time as the auditor first informs the managing agent of the syndicate of his or her resignation (whether by notice or otherwise); and
- (b) in any other case, not later than the end of the period of fourteen days beginning with the date on which the auditor ceases to hold office.

(4) A person ceasing to hold office as auditor who fails to comply with this paragraph commits an offence.

(5) If that person is a firm an offence is committed by—
- (a) the firm; and
- (b) every officer of the firm who is in default.

(6) A person guilty of an offence under this paragraph is liable—
- (a) on conviction on indictment, to a fine;
- (b) on summary conviction, to a fine not exceeding the statutory maximum.

(7) In proceedings for an offence under this paragraph it is a defence for the person charged to show that he or she took all reasonable steps and exercised all due diligence to avoid the commission of the offence.

Duty of managing agent to notify appropriate audit authority

18.—(1) Where the auditor of the syndicate ceases to hold office before the end of his or her term of office, the managing agent of the syndicate must notify in writing the appropriate audit authority.

(2) The notice must—
- (a) inform the appropriate audit authority that the auditor has ceased to hold office; and
- (b) be accompanied by a statement of the reasons for the auditor's ceasing to hold office.

(3) The managing agent must give notice under this paragraph—
- (a) if the auditor resigns, not later than the end of the period of fourteen days beginning with the date on which the auditor first informs the managing agent of his or her resignation (whether by notice or otherwise); and
- (b) in any other case, not later than the end of the period of fourteen days beginning with the date on which the auditor ceases to hold office.

(4) If the managing agent fails to comply with this paragraph, an offence is committed by—
- (a) the managing agent; and
- (b) every director or partner of the managing agent who was in default.

(5) A person guilty of an offence under this paragraph is liable—
- (a) on conviction on indictment, to a fine;
- (b) on summary conviction, to a fine not exceeding the statutory maximum.

(6) In proceedings for an offence under this paragraph it is a defence for the person charged to show that he or she took all reasonable steps and exercised all due diligence to avoid the commission of the offence.

NOTES

Commencement: 15 August 2008.

SCHEDULE 2

AUDITOR'S REMUNERATION

Regulations 5(4) and (5) and 18(6)

Disclosure required in notes to accounts

[4528]

1.—(1) The following information must be disclosed in—

(a) the notes to a syndicate's annual accounts; and

(b) the notes to the aggregate accounts.

(2) In this Schedule "the auditor" refers to the syndicate's auditor in the case of a syndicate's annual accounts, and to the auditor of the aggregate accounts in the case of the aggregate accounts.

2.—(1) There must be disclosed in a note to a syndicate's annual accounts and to the aggregate accounts—

(a) the amount of any remuneration receivable by the auditor for the auditing of the syndicate's annual accounts, or the aggregate accounts, as the case may be; and

(b) the amount of any remuneration receivable in respect of the financial year by—

(i) the auditor; or

(ii) any person who was, at any time during that financial year, an associate of the auditor,

for the supply of other services to the syndicate or to the managing agent of the syndicate (in the case of the syndicate's annual accounts), or to the Society or the Council of Lloyd's (in the case of the aggregate accounts).

(2) Where the remuneration includes benefits in kind, the nature and estimated money-value of those benefits must also be disclosed in a note.

(3) Separate disclosure is required in respect of the auditing of the accounts in question and of each type of service specified in paragraph 3, but not in respect of each service falling within a type of service.

(4) Separate disclosure is required in respect of services supplied to—

(a) the syndicate or the Society or the Council of Lloyd's; and

(b) associated pension schemes.

(5) Where more than one person has been appointed as auditor in respect of the financial year, separate disclosure is required in respect of the remuneration of each such person and his associates.

(6) Disclosure is not required of remuneration receivable for the supply of services falling within paragraph 3(j) supplied by a distant associate of the auditor where the total remuneration receivable for all those services supplied by that associate does not exceed either—

(a) £10,000; or

(b) 1% of the total audit remuneration received by the auditor in the most recent financial year of the auditor which ended no later than the end of the financial year of the syndicate or syndicates to which the syndicate accounts or aggregate accounts relate.

(7) In this paragraph—

"associate" and "direct associate" have the meaning given by paragraph 4;

"financial year of the auditor" means—

(a) the period of not more than 18 months in respect of which the auditor's profit and loss account is required to be made up (whether by law or in accordance with the auditor's constitution (if any)); or

(b) failing any such requirement, the period of 12 months beginning with 1st April;

"remuneration" includes payments in respect of expenses and benefits in kind.

"total audit remuneration received" means the total remuneration received for the auditing pursuant to legislation (including that of countries and territories outside the United Kingdom) of any accounts of any person.

Disclosure of types of service

3.—(1) The types of service in respect of which disclosure is required are—

(a) either—

(i) the auditing of accounts of associates of the managing agent responsible for managing the syndicate pursuant to legislation (including that of countries and territories outside the United Kingdom), in the case of the syndicate's annual accounts; or

(ii) the auditing of accounts of associates of the Society of Lloyd's pursuant to legislation (including that of countries and territories outside the United Kingdom), in the case of the aggregate accounts;

(b) other services supplied pursuant to such legislation;

(c) other services relating to taxation;

(d) services relating to information technology;

(e) internal audit services;

(f) valuation and actuarial services;

(g) services relating to litigation;

(h) services relating to recruitment and remuneration;

(i) services relating to corporate finance transactions entered into or proposed to be entered into on behalf of the managing agent or any of its associates, or the Society of Lloyd's or any of its associates;

(j) all other services.

(2) References in sub-paragraph (1) to an associate of the managing agent are to—

(a) any subsidiary of the managing agent, other than a subsidiary in respect of which severe long-term restrictions substantially hinder the exercise of rights of the managing agent over the assets or management of that subsidiary; or

(b) any associated pension scheme.

(3) An "associated pension scheme", in relation to a managing agent, means a scheme for the provision of benefits for or in respect of directors or employees (or former directors or employees) of the managing agent or any subsidiary of the managing agent where—

(a) the benefits consist of or include any pension, lump sum, gratuity or other like benefit given or to be given on retirement or on death or in anticipation of retirement or, in connection with past service, after retirement or death; and

(b) either—

(i) a majority of the trustees are appointed by, or by a person acting on behalf of, the managing agent or a subsidiary of the managing agent; or

(ii) the managing agent, or a subsidiary of the managing agent, exercises a dominant influence over the appointment of the auditor (if any) of the scheme.

(4) References in sub-paragraph (1) to an associate of the Society of Lloyd's are to—

(a) any subsidiary of the Society of Lloyd's, other than a subsidiary in respect of which severe long-term restrictions substantially hinder the exercise of rights of the society over the assets or management of that subsidiary; or

(b) any associated pension scheme.

(5) An "associated pension scheme", in relation to the Society of Lloyd's, means a scheme for the provision of benefits for or in respect of members of the Council or employees (or former members of the Council or employees) of the Society or any subsidiary of the Society where—

(a) the benefits consist of or include any pension, lump sum, gratuity or other like benefit given or to be given on retirement or on death or in anticipation of retirement or, in connection with past service, after retirement or death; and

(b) either—

(i) a majority of the trustees are appointed by, or by a person acting on behalf of, the Society or a subsidiary of the Society; or

(ii) the Society, or a subsidiary of the Society, exercises a dominant influence over the appointment of the auditor (if any) of the scheme.

(6) In this paragraph "subsidiary" means a subsidiary undertaking that is a body corporate.

Meaning of "associate of auditor" and "distant associate"

4.—(1) This paragraph defines what is meant in paragraph 2 by an "associate" of the auditor.

(2) The following are associates of the auditor—

(a) any person controlled by the auditor or by any associate of the auditor (whether alone or through two or more persons acting together to secure or exercise control), but only if that control does not arise solely by virtue of the auditor or any associate of the auditor acting—

(i) as an insolvency practitioner in relation to any person;

(ii) in the capacity of a receiver, or a receiver or manager, of the property (or part of the property) of the Society of Lloyd's, a syndicate, a managing agent or other body corporate; or

(iii) as a judicial factor on the estate of any person;

(b) any person who, or group of persons acting together which, has control of the auditor;

(c) any person using a trading name which is the same as or similar to a trading name used by the auditor, but only if the auditor uses that trading name with the intention of creating the impression of a connection between the auditor and that other person; or

(d) any person who is party to an arrangement with the auditor, with or without any other person, under which costs, profits, quality control, business strategy or significant professional resources are shared.

(3) Where the auditor is a partnership, the following shall also be regarded as associates of the auditor—

(a) any other partnership which has a partner in common with the auditor;

(b) any partner in the auditor;

(c) any body corporate which is in the same group as a body corporate which is a partner in the auditor;

(d) any body corporate which is in the same group as a body corporate which is a partner in a partnership which has a partner in common with the auditor; or

(e) any body corporate of which a partner in the auditor is a director.

(4) Where an auditor is a body corporate (other than one which is also a partnership as defined in sub-paragraph (6)(d)), each of the following shall also be regarded as an associate of the auditor—

(a) any other body corporate which has a director in common with the auditor;

(b) any director of the auditor;

(c) any body corporate which is in the same group as a body corporate which is a director of the auditor;

(d) any body corporate which is in the same group as a body corporate which has a director in common with the auditor;

(e) any partnership in which a director of the auditor is a partner;

(f) any body corporate which is in the same group as the auditor;

(g) any partnership in which any such body corporate which is in the same group as the auditor is a partner.

(5) A distant associate of an auditor is a person who is an associate of that auditor by reason only that that person is an associate within one or more of—

(a) paragraph 4(2)(a) where the person in question is controlled by a distant associate of the auditor but not by the auditor or by an associate who is not a distant associate;

(b) paragraph 4(3)(a), (d) or (e);

(c) paragraph 4(4)(a), (d) or (e).

(6) For the purposes of this paragraph—

(a) "acting as an insolvency practitioner" shall be construed in accordance with section 388 of the Insolvency Act 1986 or Article 3 of the Insolvency (Northern Ireland) Order 1989;

(b) "director" includes any person occupying the position of director, by whatever name called;

(c) "partner" includes a member of a limited liability partnership;

(d) "partnership" includes a limited liability partnership and a partnership constituted under the law of a country or a territory outside the United Kingdom;

(e) a person able, directly or indirectly to control or materially to influence the operating and financial policy of another person shall be treated as having control of that other person; and

(f) a body corporate is in the same group as another body corporate if one is a subsidiary of the other.

(7) In this paragraph "subsidiary" means a subsidiary undertaking that is a body corporate.

Duty of auditor to supply information

5.—(1) The auditor of a syndicate must supply the managing agent of the syndicate with such information as is necessary to enable the disclosure required by paragraph 2(1)(b) to be made.

(2) The auditor of the aggregate accounts must supply the Council of Lloyd's with such information as is necessary to enable the disclosure required by paragraph 2(1)(b) to be made.

NOTES

Commencement: 15 August 2008.

SCHEDULE 3

PROVISIONS APPLYING TO AGGREGATE ACCOUNTS

Regulations 18(6), (7) and 20

PART 1
GENERAL PROVISIONS AND ANNUAL REPORT

Disclosure required in notes to accounts: off-balance sheet arrangements

[4529]

1.—(1) If for any financial year—

(a) a syndicate has noted in its annual accounts that it is or has been party to an arrangement that is not reflected in its balance sheet; and

(b) at the balance sheet date the risks or benefits arising from that arrangement are material,

the information required by this paragraph must be given in notes to the aggregate accounts.

(2) The information required is—

(a) the nature and business purpose of the arrangement; and

(b) the financial impact of the arrangement on the syndicate.

(3) The information need only be given to the extent necessary for enabling the financial position of the Lloyd's market to be assessed.

Annual report: general requirements

2.—(1) The annual report on a financial year required by regulation 20 must state—

(a) the names of the persons who at any time during the financial year were members of the Council of Lloyd's; and

(b) the principal activities of the Lloyd's market in the course of the year and any significant change to those activities in the year.

(2) The annual report must contain—

(a) particulars of any important events affecting the Lloyd's market which have occurred since the end of the financial year;

(b) an indication of likely future developments in the business of the Lloyd's market; and

(c) an indication of the activities (if any) of the members of Lloyd's in the field of research and development.

Annual report: business review

3.—(1) The annual report must contain a business review.

(2) The business review must contain—

(a) a fair review of the business of the Lloyd's market; and

(b) a description of the principal risks and uncertainties facing the Lloyd's market.

(3) The review required is a balanced and comprehensive analysis of—

(a) the development and performance of the insurance business carried on by the members of Lloyd's during the financial year; and

(b) the position of the insurance business of the members of Lloyd's at the end of that year,

consistent with the size and complexity of the Lloyd's market.

(4) The review must include to the extent necessary for an understanding of the development, performance or position of the insurance business of the members of Lloyd's—

(a) analysis using financial key performance indicators; and

(b) where appropriate, analysis using other key performance indicators, including information relating to environmental matters and employee matters.

(5) In sub-paragraph (4), "key performance indicators" means factors by reference to which the development, performance or position of the insurance business of the members of Lloyd's can be measured effectively.

(6) The review must, where appropriate, include references to and additional explanations of amounts included in the aggregate accounts.

(7) Nothing in this paragraph requires the disclosure of information about impending developments or matters in the course of negotiation if the disclosure would, in the opinion of the Council of Lloyd's, be seriously prejudicial to the interests of the members of Lloyd's.

Statement as to disclosure of information to auditors

4.—(1) The annual report must contain a statement to the effect that, in the case of each of the persons who are members of the Council of Lloyd's at the time the report is approved—

(a) so far as the Council member is aware, there is no relevant audit information of which the auditor of the aggregate accounts is unaware; and

(b) the Council member has taken all the steps that he or she ought to have taken as a member of the Council to become aware of any relevant audit information and to establish that the auditor of the aggregate accounts is aware of that information.

(2) In sub-paragraph (1) "relevant audit information" means information needed by the auditor of the aggregate accounts in connection with preparing the auditor's report.

(3) For the purposes of sub-paragraph (1) the Council member is regarded as having taken all the steps that he or she ought to have taken as a member of the Council in order to do the things mentioned in sub-paragraph (1)(b) if he or she has—

(a) made such enquiries of fellow Council members and of the auditors of the aggregate accounts for that purpose; and

(b) taken such other steps (if any) for that purpose,

as were required by his or her duty as a member of the Council of Lloyd's to exercise due care, skill and diligence.

(4) Where the annual report containing the statement required by this paragraph is approved but the statement is false, every member of the Council who—

(a) knew that the statement was false, or was reckless as to whether it was false; and

(b) failed to take reasonable steps to prevent the report from being approved,

commits an offence.

(5) A person guilty of an offence under sub-paragraph (4) is liable—

(a) on conviction on indictment, to imprisonment for a term not exceeding two years or to a fine, or both;

(b) on summary conviction to imprisonment for a term not exceeding three months or to a fine not exceeding the statutory maximum, or both.

NOTES

Commencement: 15 August 2008.

PART 2
AUDITORS

Appointment of auditor for aggregate accounts

[4530]

5.—(1) Subject to sub-paragraph (3), the members of the Society of Lloyd's must appoint the auditor for the aggregate accounts for each financial year, unless the auditor is deemed to be re-appointed in accordance with paragraph 6(2).

(2) For each financial year for which the auditor is to be appointed, the appointment must be made before the end of the period of 28 days beginning with the end of the time allowed under regulation 18(3)(a) for preparing the accounts required by regulation 18. This is the "period for appointing auditors" for the purposes of this Part of this Schedule.

(3) The Council of Lloyd's may appoint an auditor for the aggregate accounts to fill a casual vacancy in the office of auditor.

(4) Where no appointment has been made under paragraph (1) by the end of the period for appointing auditors, and the auditor in office is not deemed to be re-appointed under paragraph 6(2)—

(a) the Council of Lloyd's must within one week from the end of that period give notice in writing to the Authority of that fact; and

(b) the Authority must appoint an auditor for the aggregate accounts to fill the vacancy as soon as possible.

(5) If the Council of Lloyd's fail to give the notice required by this paragraph, an offence is committed by—

(a) the Society of Lloyd's; and

(b) every member of the Council who was in default.

(6) A person guilty of an offence under this paragraph is liable on summary conviction to a fine not exceeding level 3 on the standard scale and, for continued contravention, a daily default fine not exceeding one-tenth of level 3 on the standard scale.

Term of office of auditors of the aggregate accounts

6.—(1) An auditor of the aggregate accounts holds office in accordance with the terms of his or her appointment, subject to the requirements that—

(a) the auditor does not take office until any previous auditor ceases to hold office; and

(b) the auditor ceases to hold office at the end of the next period for appointing auditors unless re-appointed.

(2) Where no auditor has been appointed by the end of the next period for appointing auditors, any auditor in office immediately before that time is deemed to be re-appointed at that time, unless—

(a) Lloyd's byelaws require actual re-appointment; or

(b) the deemed re-appointment is prevented by the members of the Society of Lloyd's under paragraph 7; or

(c) the members of the Society of Lloyd's have resolved that the auditor should not be re-appointed.

Prevention by members of deemed re-appointment of auditor

7.—(1) An auditor of the aggregate accounts is not deemed to be re-appointed under paragraph 6(2) if the Council of Lloyd's has received notices under this paragraph from members of the Society of Lloyd's representing at least the requisite percentage of the total voting rights of all members of the Society who would be entitled to vote on a resolution that the auditor should not be re-appointed.

(2) The "requisite percentage" is 5%, or such lower percentage as is specified for this purpose in Lloyd's byelaws.

(3) A notice under this paragraph—

(a) may be in hard copy or electronic form;

(b) must be authenticated by the person or persons giving it; and

(c) must be received by the managing agent before the end of the financial year immediately preceding the time when the deemed re-appointment would have effect.

Removal of auditors on improper grounds

8.—(1) Where an auditor of the aggregate accounts is removed from office, an application may be made to the High Court under this paragraph.

(2) The persons who may make such an application are—

(a) any member of the Society of Lloyd's; or

(b) the Authority.

(3) Where the Court is satisfied that the removal was—

(a) on grounds of divergence of opinion on accounting treatments or audit procedures; or

(b) on any other improper grounds,

it may make such order as it thinks fit for giving relief in respect of the removal.

(4) The Court may, in particular—

(a) declare that any decision to remove an auditor, or to appoint a new auditor in place of the auditor, is void;

(b) require the members of the Society of Lloyd's to re-appoint the auditor; or

(c) give directions as to the conduct of the Council of Lloyd's affairs in the future.

Duty of auditor to notify appropriate audit authority

9.—(1) Where the auditor of the aggregate accounts ceases to hold office before the end of his or her term of office, the auditor must notify in writing the appropriate audit authority.

(2) The notice must—

(a) inform the appropriate audit authority that the auditor has ceased to hold office; and

(b) be accompanied by a statement of the reasons for the auditor's ceasing to hold office.

(3) The auditor must give notice under this paragraph—

(a) if the auditor resigns, at the same time as the auditor informs the Council of Lloyd's of his or her resignation (whether by notice or otherwise);

(b) in any other case, not later than the end of the period of fourteen days beginning with the date on which the auditor ceases to hold office.

(4) A person ceasing to hold office as auditor who fails to comply with this paragraph commits an offence.

(5) If that person is a firm an offence is committed by—

(a) the firm; and

(b) every officer of the firm who is in default.

(6) A person guilty of an offence under this paragraph is liable—

(a) on conviction on indictment, to a fine;

(b) on summary conviction, to a fine not exceeding the statutory maximum.

(7) In proceedings for an offence under this paragraph it is a defence for the person charged to show that he or she took all reasonable steps and exercised all due diligence to avoid the commission of the offence.

Duty of Council of Lloyd's to notify the appropriate audit authority

10.—(1) Where the auditor of the aggregate accounts ceases to hold office before the end of his or her term of office, the Council of Lloyd's must notify in writing the appropriate audit authority.

(2) The notice must—

(a) inform the appropriate audit authority that the auditor has ceased to hold office; and

(b) be accompanied by a statement of the reasons for the auditor's ceasing to hold office.

(3) The Council of Lloyd's must give notice under this paragraph—

(a) if the auditor resigns, not later than the end of the period of fourteen days beginning with the date on which the auditor first informs the Council of his or her resignation (whether by notice or otherwise); and

(b) in any other case, not later than the end of the period of fourteen days beginning with the date on which the auditor ceases to hold office.

(4) If the Council of Lloyd's fails to comply with this paragraph, an offence is committed by—

(a) the Society of Lloyd's; and

(b) every member of the Council who was in default.

(5) A person guilty of an offence under this paragraph is liable—

(a) on conviction on indictment, to a fine;

(b) on summary conviction, to a fine not exceeding the statutory maximum.

(6) In proceedings for an offence under this paragraph it is a defence for the person charged to show that he or she took all reasonable steps and exercised all due diligence to avoid the commission of the offence.

NOTES

Commencement: 15 August 2008.

LEGISLATIVE REFORM (LLOYD'S) ORDER 2008

(SI 2008/3001)

NOTES

Made: 18 November 2008.
Authority: Legislative and Regulatory Reform Act 2006, s 1.
Commencement: 19 November 2008.

[4531]

1 Citation and commencement

This Order may be cited as the Legislative Reform (Lloyd's) Order 2008 and shall come into force on the day after the day on which it is made.

NOTES

Commencement: 19 November 2008.

[4532]

2 Interpretation

In this Order "the Act" means Lloyd's Act 1982.

NOTES

Commencement: 19 November 2008.

3–5 (*Amend the Lloyd's Act 1982, ss 2–4, 6, 7, 13, 15, Sch 2 at* **[3354]–[3356]**, **[3358]**, **[3359]**, **[3365]**, **[3367]**, **[3372]** *and repeal s 5 at* **[3357]**, *subject to transitional provisions in art 6 hereof of this Order.*)

[4533]

6— (1) In this article, "Committee" means the Committee constituted by section 5 of the Act (as in force immediately before the coming into force of this Order), and "Council" means the Council constituted by section 3 of the Act.

(2) Any regulation made by the Committee in the exercise of powers delegated to it under section 6(6)(a)(i) of the Act (as in force immediately before the coming into force of this Order) shall be deemed to have been made by the Council in the exercise of its powers under the Act, and shall continue in full force and effect unless and until revoked by the Council.

(3) Anything required or authorised to be done by the Committee under the provisions of any enactment, subordinate legislation, instrument, trust deed, or other document may after this Order comes into force be done by the Council.

NOTES

Commencement: 19 November 2008.

7–10 (*Amend the Lloyd's Act 1982, ss 2, 6–8, Sch 2 at* **[3354]**, **[3358]–[3360]**, **[3372]** *and repeal ss 10–12, subject to transitional provisions in art 6 of this Order.*)

MUTUAL SOCIETIES (TRANSFERS) ORDER 2009

(SI 2009/509)

NOTES

Made: 4 March 2009.

Authority: Building Societies (Funding) and Mutual Societies (Transfers) Act 2007, ss 3, 4.

Commencement: 5 March 2009.

This Order relates to the transfer of a building society's business to the subsidiary of another mutual society. Its significance in an insurance context arises because the transferee (but not the transferor) can now be the subsidiary of an insurance mutual (with membership conferred on the former members of the transferring business in the holding mutual insurer). Section 3 of the Building Societies (Funding) and Mutual Societies (Transfers) Act 2007 contemplates that secondary legislation may be passed allowing the transfer of the business of an insurance mutual to the subsidiary of another mutual society but to date, no such legislation has yet been promulgated.

ARRANGEMENT OF ARTICLES

PART 1

INTRODUCTORY

1 Citation and commencement [4534]
2 Interpretation [4535]

PART 2

BUILDING SOCIETIES

3 Application of Part 2 [4536]
4 Interpretation of the transfer provisions [4537]
5 The transfer resolution [4538]
6 Formation of the successor company [4539]
7 Distribution of funds of building society or holding mutual [4540]
8 Distribution of funds: regulated term [4541]
9 Confirmation of the transfer [4542]
10 Modified application of section 100 (distributions and share rights) [4543]
11 Membership of the holding mutual [4544]
12 Restrictions on further transfer [4545]
13 Modified application of sections 102B and 102C of the 1986 Act [4546]
14 Issue of statement or summary to members [4547]
15 [4548]
16 [4549]
17 [4550]
18 Issue of statement or summary to members: powers of Financial Services Authority [4551]

PART 3

SUPPLEMENTARY

19 EEA mutual society [4552]

Part IV Statutory Instruments

PART 1
INTRODUCTORY

[4534]
1 Citation and commencement

(1) This Order may be cited as the Mutual Societies (Transfers) Order 2009.

(2) It comes into force on the day after the day on which it is made.

NOTES
Commencement: 5 March 2009.

[4535]
2 Interpretation

In this Order—

"the 1986 Act" means the Building Societies Act 1986;

"the 1998 Regulations" means the Building Societies (Transfer of Business) Regulations 1998;

"the 2007 Act" means the Building Societies (Funding) and Mutual Societies (Transfers) Act 2007.

NOTES
Commencement: 5 March 2009.

PART 2
BUILDING SOCIETIES

[4536]
3 Application of Part 2

(1) This Part applies to a transfer of the whole of the business of a building society incorporated or deemed to be incorporated under the 1986 Act to the subsidiary of another mutual society where the transfer agreement contains a statement that it so applies.

(2) A transfer to which this Part applies is referred to in this Part as a "relevant transfer".

(3) The transfer provisions of the 1986 Act and the 1998 Regulations apply in relation to a relevant transfer with the modifications made by this Part.

(4) In this article "transfer agreement" has the same meaning as in section 97 of the 1986 Act (transfer of business to commercial company).

NOTES
Commencement: 5 March 2009.

[4537]
4 Interpretation of the transfer provisions

(1) Section 97(12) of the 1986 Act applies in relation to a relevant transfer with the following modifications.

(2) At the appropriate places insert—

""the 2007 Act" means the Building Societies (Funding) and Mutual Societies (Transfers) Act 2007;";

""the 2009 Order" means the Mutual Societies (Transfers) Order 2009;";

""holding mutual" means the mutual society of which the successor is a subsidiary;";

""mutual society" has the same meaning as in section 3 of the 2007 Act;";

""parent undertaking" has the same meaning as in the Companies Acts (see section 1162 of, and Schedule 7 to, the Companies Act 2006);";

""subsidiary" (except in the term "subsidiary undertaking") has the same meaning as in section 3 of the 2007 Act;".

NOTES
Commencement: 5 March 2009.

[4538]
5 The transfer resolution

Paragraph 30 of Schedule 2 to the 1986 Act (transfer resolutions) applies in relation to a relevant transfer with the following modifications—

(a) in sub-paragraph (1)(b), for "("the requisite shareholders' resolution") is passed in accordance with sub-paragraphs (2) to (5) below", substitute "is passed as a shareholding members' resolution";

(b) omit sub-paragraphs (2) to (8).

NOTES

Commencement: 5 March 2009.

[4539]

6 Formation of the successor company

Section 97 of the 1986 Act applies in relation to a relevant transfer with the following modifications—

(a) in subsection (3), after "formed by the society" insert "or by the holding mutual";

(b) in subsection (12), in the definition of "company", after "formed by a building society" insert "or by the holding mutual".

NOTES

Commencement: 5 March 2009.

[4540]

7 Distribution of funds of building society or holding mutual

(1) Section 4 of the 2007 Act (transfers to subsidiaries: distribution of funds) has effect in relation to a relevant transfer.

(2) The terms of a relevant transfer may include provision for part of the funds of the transferor building society or of the holding mutual (or both) to be distributed to members of the transferor or of the holding mutual (or both) in consideration of the transfer, in accordance with section 4 of the 2007 Act and this article.

(3) The limit referred to in section 4(3) and (4) of the 2007 Act, in relation to a distribution made by a transferor building society, is—

(a) five per cent of the value of that society's total assets, or

(b) if less, the sum calculated in accordance with paragraph (4).

(4) The sum referred to in paragraph (3)(b) is calculated by deducting the value of the transferor society's fixed assets, both tangible and intangible, from the aggregate of that society's general reserves and, if any, revaluation and other reserves.

(5) For the purposes of paragraphs (3) and (4), the value of any assets, liabilities or reserves of a building society is their value as given in the most recent annual accounts of the society sent to the Financial Services Authority in accordance with section 81(2) of the 1986 Act (laying and furnishing accounts, etc, to members and the Authority).

(6) The limit referred to in section 4(3) and (4) of the 2007 Act, in relation to a distribution made by the holding mutual, is five per cent of the holding mutual's total assets as shown in the most recent audited accounts of the holding mutual.

(7) The resolution referred to in section 4(3)(a) of the 2007 Act, in the case of the holding mutual, is—

(a) where the transfer is approved by a resolution of the members of the holding mutual, that resolution, or

(b) where the transfer is approved by the board of directors or committee of management of the holding mutual, a resolution of the members of the holding mutual.

(8) Any terms of a transfer of business to which section 4(3) of the 2007 Act and paragraphs (3) to (7) above apply are regulated terms for the purposes of section 97 of the 1986 Act.

(9) In this article—

"annual accounts" has the same meaning as in Part 8 of the 1986 Act (see section 81B of that Act (interpretation of Part 8));

"transfer of business" and "regulated terms" have the same meaning as in section 97 of the 1986 Act.

NOTES

Commencement: 5 March 2009.

[4541]

8 Distribution of funds: regulated term

Section 97 of the 1986 Act applies in relation to a relevant transfer with the following modifications—

(a) in subsection (4)(b), after "transfer regulations" insert ", and with section 4 of the 2007 Act and article 7 of the 2009 Order";

(b) in subsection (12), in the definition of "regulated terms", after "section 102" insert "or under article 7 of the 2009 Order".

NOTES
Commencement: 5 March 2009.

[4542]
9 Confirmation of the transfer
(1) Section 98 of the 1986 Act (transfers of business: supplementary provisions) applies in relation to a relevant transfer with the following modifications.
(2) In subsection (3)(d), for "this Act" substitute "an applicable enactment".
(3) In subsection (4), for "this Act" substitute "an applicable enactment".
(4) In subsection (7), for "this Act" substitute "an applicable enactment".
(5) For subsection (8), substitute—

"(8) In this section—
"applicable enactment" means the applicable provisions of this Act (as modified by the 2009 Order), section 4 of the 2007 Act and article 7 of the 2009 Order; and
"relevant requirement", with reference to an applicable enactment or the rules of a society, means a requirement of an applicable enactment or of any rules prescribing the procedure to be followed by the society in approving the transfer and its terms.".

NOTES
Commencement: 5 March 2009.

[4543]
10 Modified application of section 100 (distributions and share rights)
(1) Section 100 of the 1986 Act (regulated terms etc: distributions and share rights) applies in relation to a relevant transfer with the following modifications.
(2) For subsection (1) substitute—

"(1) Subject to subsections (8) and (10) below, the terms of a transfer of business by a building society to the company which is to be its successor may include provision for rights in relation to shares in the successor to be conferred on members of the society in consideration of the transfer.".

(3) Omit subsection (9).
(4) For subsection (10) substitute—

"(10) The following restriction applies to any conferring of rights in relation to shares in connection with the transfer of its business from the society to its successor where the successor is a company specially formed by the society or the holding mutual.
Where negotiable instruments acknowledging rights to shares are issued by the successor within the period of two years beginning with the vesting date, no such instruments shall be issued to former members of the society unless they are also issued, and on the same terms, to all other members of the company.".

NOTES
Commencement: 5 March 2009.

[4544]
11 Membership of the holding mutual
(1) The transfer provisions apply in relation to a relevant transfer as if after section 100 of the 1986 Act there were inserted—

"100A Regulated terms: membership of the holding mutual

(1) The terms of a transfer of business by a building society to the company which is to be its successor must include provision for making membership of the holding mutual available to every qualifying member of the building society and to every person who, after the transfer, becomes a customer of the company.
(2) The membership made available pursuant to that provision must be on terms no less favourable than those enjoyed by existing members of the holding mutual.
(3) Subsection (1) above does not apply where the terms of the transfer of business include provision for making membership of any parent undertaking of the holding mutual available to the persons mentioned in that subsection on terms no less favourable than those enjoyed by existing members of the parent undertaking.

(4) Any terms of a transfer of business to which subsections (1) and (2) above apply are regulated terms for the purposes of section 97.
(5) For the purposes of this section, any member of the building society who, on the day immediately preceding the vesting date, is a shareholding or borrowing member of the society, is a qualifying member.".

(2) Section 97 of the 1986 Act applies in relation to a relevant transfer with the following modifications—

(a) in subsection (2), after "section 100," insert "section 100A,";
(b) in subsection (4)(b), after "section 100" insert ", section 100A";
(c) in subsection (12), in the definition of "regulated terms", after "section 100" insert ", section 100A".

NOTES

Commencement: 5 March 2009.

[4545]

12 Restrictions on further transfer

(1) Section 101 (protective provisions for specially formed successors) applies in relation to a relevant transfer with the following modifications—

(a) in subsection (1), after "other than the society" insert "or the holding mutual";
(b) in subsection (4), omit paragraph (b);
(c) in subsection (6)—
   (i) in the definition of "the protective period", for "five years" substitute "three years";
   (ii) omit the definition of "the requisite majority".

(2) The transfer provisions apply in relation to a relevant transfer as if after section 101 of the 1986 Act there were inserted—

"101A Protective provisions where successor is an existing company

(1) Section 101 (as modified by the 2009 Order) applies in relation to a successor of a building society which is an existing company as it applies in relation to a successor which is a specially formed company, with the following modification.
(2) In subsection (6), for the definition of "the protective period" substitute—

""the protective period" is the period beginning with the date of any alterations to the company's articles made to comply with subsection (2) above or, if no alterations are made, beginning with the vesting date, and ending three years after the vesting date or, if this section ceases to apply to the company, ending on the date on which it so ceases".".

(3) In section 97—

(a) in subsection (2), after "section 101," insert "section 101A,";
(b) in subsection (4), for paragraph (a) substitute—

"(a) secure that the successor company's articles of association include the requisite protective provisions;";

(c) in subsection (12), for the definition of "the requisite protective provisions" substitute—

""the requisite protective provisions", in relation to a specially formed company, means the provisions required to be made by section 101(2), and in relation to an existing company, means the provisions required to be made by section 101(2) as applied by section 101A.".

NOTES

Commencement: 5 March 2009.

[4546]

13 Modified application of sections 102B and 102C of the 1986 Act

(1) Section 102B of the 1986 Act (protection of interests of beneficiaries in the case of trustee account holders) applies in relation to a relevant transfer with the following modifications—

(a) in subsection (2), for paragraph (a) substitute—

"(a) a distribution among members of the society of part of the funds of the society or the holding mutual made in accordance with section 4 of the 2007 Act and article 7 of the 2009 Order, but not a distribution within section 100(2)(b), or";

(b) in subsection (3), for "and its successor" substitute ", its successor and the holding mutual";

(c) in subsection (6), for "and its successor" substitute ", its successor and the holding mutual".

(2) Section 102C of the 1986 Act (consequences of false declaration) applies in relation to a relevant transfer with the following modifications—

(a) in subsection (1)(b)(i), after "the society's successor" insert "or the holding mutual";

(b) in subsection (2), after "the successor", in each place where it occurs, insert "or the holding mutual";

(c) in subsection (4), after "the successor", in each place where it occurs, insert "or the holding mutual".

NOTES

Commencement: 5 March 2009.

[4547]

14 Issue of statement or summary to members

Regulation 2 of the 1998 Regulations (interpretation) applies in relation to a relevant transfer with the following modifications—

(a) in the definition of "group", before "shall be construed" insert "(except in the term "immediate group")";

(b) after the definition of "group" insert—

""immediate group", in relation to a successor company, means the immediate parent undertaking of that company and any subsidiary undertakings of that immediate parent undertaking, but does not include any parent undertaking of that immediate parent undertaking.".

NOTES

Commencement: 5 March 2009.

[4548]

15—(1) Regulation 3 of the 1998 Regulations (transfer statements) applies in relation to a relevant transfer with the following modification.

(2) After paragraph (1) insert—

"(1A) Any such transfer statement shall also give particulars of the matters specified in Part 5 of Schedule 1 to these Regulations.".

NOTES

Commencement: 5 March 2009.

[4549]

16—(1) Schedule 1 to the 1998 Regulations (prescribed matters for transfer statements) applies in relation to a relevant transfer with the following modifications.

(2) In Part 1 (matters of which particulars are to be included in the case of any transfer)—

(a) for paragraph 4 substitute—

"**4.** The financial position of the society and its connected undertakings at the most recent reasonably practicable date and of any material change in that position since that date.";

(b) in paragraph 9, for "any group" substitute "the immediate group";

(c) in paragraph 21, at the end insert "and of any change to be made in connection with the transfer in the terms governing outstanding loans made by the society which are secured on land".

(3) In Part 2 (matters of which particulars are to be included in the case of a transfer to an existing company)—

(a) in paragraph 2, for "any group" substitute "the immediate group";

(b) for paragraph 3 substitute—

"**3.** The consolidated financial position of the successor company and the immediate group to which it belongs at the most recent reasonably practicable date and of any material change in that position since that date.";

(c) in paragraph 4, for "any group" substitute "the immediate group";

(d) for paragraph 5 substitute—

"**5.** The last three summary financial statements prepared by the directors of the society.";

(e) omit paragraph 6;

(f) for paragraph 11 substitute—

"**11—** (1) An explanation by the board of the society of the reasons for the transfer and the choice of successor company.

(2) The board's assessment of—

(a) the advantages and disadvantages of the transfer for members and employees of the society;

(b) any other issues which, in the board's view, are relevant to the transfer.";

(g) omit paragraph 12;

(h) at the end insert—

"**13.** The protective provisions for existing companies applied by section 101A of the Act (inserted by the Mutual Societies (Transfers) Order 2009).".

(4) In Part 3 (matters of which particulars are to be included in the case of a transfer to a specially formed company)—

(a) after paragraph 1 insert—

"**1A.** The structure and activities of the immediate group to which the successor company belongs.";

(b) in paragraph 5, at the end insert "(as modified by the Mutual Societies (Transfers) Order 2009)".

(5) After Part 4 (matters of which particulars are to be included in a case where shares or rights in relation to shares are to be offered in connection with a transfer) insert—

"PART 5
MATTERS OF WHICH PARTICULARS ARE TO BE INCLUDED IN A CASE TO WHICH PART 2 OF THE MUTUAL SOCIETIES (TRANSFERS) ORDER 2009 APPLIES

1. As a result of the transfer, the members of the society will no longer be members of a building society.

2. The following information in relation to the membership rights that will be made available to members of the building society in accordance with section 100A of the Act (inserted by the Mutual Societies (Transfers) Order 2009)—

(a) the membership rights that will be made available;

(b) the entity in which membership rights will be made available, including its legal form;

(c) the procedure by which members of the building society may become members of that entity.

3. A comparison of the rights members enjoy as members of a building society and the membership rights that will be made available to them referred to in paragraph 2 above.

4. Every person who, after the transfer, becomes a customer of the successor company will be able to obtain similar membership rights to those referred to in paragraph 2.

5. An explanation of the following statutory requirements relating to the business of a building society and that they will not apply in relation to the successor company—

(a) the purpose or principal purpose of a building society (section 5 of the Act);

(b) the lending limit (section 6 of the Act);

(c) the funding limit (section 7 of the Act);

(d) the restrictions in sections 9A and 9B of the Act.

6. That the transfer may be approved by a borrowing members' resolution and a shareholding members' resolution and an explanation of the requirements for a resolution to be passed as a shareholding members' resolution and a borrowing members' resolution.

7. Part 2 of the Mutual Societies (Transfers) Order 2009 will apply to the transfer.".

NOTES

Commencement: 5 March 2009.

[4550]
17 Schedule 2 to the 1998 Regulations (specified information for transfer summaries) applies in relation to a relevant transfer with the following modifications—

(a) in paragraph 2, for "paragraphs 1, 2, 3, 5, 6, 10 and 11" substitute "paragraphs 1, 2, 3, 5, 10, 11 and 13";
(b) in paragraph 3, for "paragraphs 1 and 4" substitute "paragraphs 1, 1A, 4 and 5";
(c) at the end insert—

"**5.** Where the proposed transfer of business is one to which Part 2 of the Mutual Societies (Transfers) Order 2009 will apply, information comprising particulars of all the matters described in Part 5 of Schedule 1 to these Regulations.".

NOTES
Commencement: 5 March 2009.

[4551]
18 Issue of statement or summary to members: powers of Financial Services Authority

The modifications to the application of the 1998 Regulations made by articles 14 to 17 are without prejudice to the powers of the Financial Services Authority in paragraph 3 of Schedule 17 to the 1986 Act to require particulars of any other matters to be provided in the case of a particular transfer, including without limitation any matters omitted by those modifications.

NOTES
Commencement: 5 March 2009.

PART 3
SUPPLEMENTARY

[4552]–[5000]
19 EEA mutual society

(1) A mutual insurer is an EEA mutual society for the purposes of section 3 of the 2007 Act (transfers to subsidiaries of other mutuals).

(2) A mutual insurer is a body corporate which—
(a) is a cooperative or mutual undertaking;
(b) is established or operates in accordance with the laws of an EEA state or any of the Channel Islands or the Isle of Man;
(c) has no share capital;
(d) is not a wholly-owned subsidiary within the meaning of section 1159(2) of the Companies Act 2006; and
(e) is an insurer.

(3) In paragraph (2) "insurer" means—
(a) an undertaking authorised under Article 4 of the life assurance consolidation directive or Article 6 of the first non-life insurance directive, or
(b) an undertaking which—
(i) is incorporated in any of the Channel Islands or the Isle of Man, and
(ii) would satisfy the requirements for authorisation under either of the directives mentioned in sub-paragraph (a) if it had its registered office (or if it does not have a registered office, its head office) in an EEA state.

(4) In paragraph (3)—
"the first non-life insurance directive" means First Council Directive 73/239/EEC on the coordination of laws, Regulations and administrative provisions relating to the taking-up and pursuit of the business of direct insurance other than life assurance;
"the life assurance consolidation directive" means Directive 2002/83/EC of the European Parliament and of the Council concerning life assurance.

NOTES
Commencement: 5 March 2009.

PART V
OTHER MATERIALS

A. PROFESSIONAL INDEMNITY OF SOLICITORS

SOLICITORS (SCOTLAND) PROFESSIONAL INDEMNITY INSURANCE RULES 2005

Rules dated 29 April 2005 made by the Council of the Law Society of Scotland with the concurrence of the Lord President of the Court of Session under section 44 of the Solicitors (Scotland) Act 1980.

[5001]

Citation, commencement, revocation and transitional provisions

1.—(1) These Rules may be cited as the Solicitors (Scotland) Professional Indemnity Insurance Rules 2005.

(2) These Rules shall come into operation on 1 June 2005.

(3) The Solicitors (Scotland) Professional Indemnity Insurance Rules 1995 (the "1995 Rules") are hereby revoked.

(4) All acts done under or pursuant to the 1995 Rules shall be treated as having been done under or pursuant to these Rules, except insofar as they are inconsistent with these Rules.

Definitions and interpretation

2.—(1) In these Rules, unless the context otherwise requires:—

"the Act" means the Solicitors (Scotland) Act 1980;

"acceptable alternative insurer" means a person so designated by the Council in terms of rule 8;

"authorised insurer" means any person permitted under the Financial Services and Markets Act 2000 to carry on liability insurance business or pecuniary loss insurance business;

"brokers" means the brokers from time to time appointed by the Council to act on behalf of the Society and its members in relation to any master policy entered into by the Society in terms of these Rules;

"the Council" means the Council of the Society;

"principal place of business" means the principal place of business of a multi-national practice determined in accordance with the Solicitors (Scotland) (MNP Principal Place of Business) Practice Rules 2005;

"the Society" means the Law Society of Scotland; and

"solicitor" means a solicitor holding a practising certificate under the Act and includes a firm of solicitors and an incorporated practice, and also includes registered foreign lawyers and multi-national practices.

(2) The Interpretation Act 1978 applies to the interpretation of these Rules as it applies to the interpretation of an Act of Parliament.

Application

3. These Rules apply to every solicitor who is, or is held out to the public as, a principal in private practice in Scotland.

Principals in private practice

4.—(1) For the purposes of these Rules, a solicitor who is a sole practitioner, a partner of a firm of solicitors, a member or director of an incorporated practice or a member of a multi-national practice having its principal place of business in Scotland is a principal in private practice in Scotland.

(2) A solicitor shall not be deemed to be a principal in private practice or to be held out as such by reason only—

(a) that he is a member of a multi-national practice having its principal place of business outwith Scotland; or

(b) that he practises only as consultant or associate to another solicitor provided that if his name appears on the name-plate or letter paper of such other solicitor it is accompanied by the designation "Consultant" or "Associate"; or

(c) in the case of a solicitor employed by another solicitor that the former in carrying out work for his employer uses his own name.

Master policy

5.—(1) The Society shall take out and maintain with authorised insurers to be determined from time to time by the Council a master policy in terms to be approved by the Council to provide indemnity against such classes of professional liability as the Council may decide. The Council at its discretion may amend the terms of the master policy from time to time.

(2) Subject to rule 7, the master policy shall provide indemnity for all solicitors to whom these Rules apply and for such former solicitors and other parties as may be mentioned in the master policy.

(3) The limits of indemnity and the self-insured amounts under the master policy shall be as may be determined from time to time by the Council.

(4) Nothing in these Rules shall prohibit any solicitor from arranging with the insurers to extend the cover provided by the master policy if and on such terms as the insurers may agree.

Obligation to be insured under master policy

6. Subject to rule 7, every solicitor to whom these Rules apply shall be obliged to be insured under the master policy and—

- (a) to comply with the terms of the master policy and of any certificate of insurance issued to him thereunder; and
- (b) to produce along with each application for a practising certificate a certificate from the brokers certifying that the solicitor in question is insured under the master policy for the practice year then commencing or the part thereof still to run as the case may be, or such other evidence of such insurance as may be acceptable to the Council.

Exceptions

7.—(1) The master policy need not provide indemnity for any solicitor to whom these Rules apply who is a member of a multi-national practice.

(2) Where in terms of paragraph (1) no indemnity is provided by the master policy in respect of a solicitor to whom these Rules apply—

- (a) that solicitor shall not be obliged to comply with rule 6, and
- (b) that solicitor shall be obliged to be insured with an acceptable alternative insurer, in terms equivalent to the terms of the master policy or acceptable to the Council and—
  - (i) shall comply with the terms of that insurance policy and of any certificate of insurance issued to him thereunder; and
  - (ii) shall produce along with each application for a practising certificate (or, if he is a registered foreign lawyer, registration certificate) a certificate certifying that he is insured for the practice year in question or the part thereof still to run as the case may be, or such other evidence of such insurance as may be acceptable to the Council.

Acceptable alternative insurer

8. The Council shall designate an authorised insurer or authorised insurers as an acceptable alternative insurer or as acceptable alternative insurers for the purposes of rule 7.

Waiver

9. The Council shall have power in any case or class of case to waive any of the provisions of these Rules and to revoke any such waiver.

Additional powers

10. The Council is hereby empowered to take such steps as it may consider expedient in order to—

- (a) ascertain whether or not these Rules are being complied with; or
- (b) satisfy itself with regard to any matters arising out of the master policy or any insurance policy taken out in accordance with rule 7(2)(b).

Professional practice

11. Failure to comply with these Rules may be treated as professional misconduct for the purposes of Part IV of the Act.

SOLICITORS' INDEMNITY (ENACTMENT) RULES 2007
SOLICITORS' INDEMNITY RULES 2007

Rules in force from 1 October 2007 (amended 31 March 2009)

NOTES

SOLICITORS' INDEMNITY (ENACTMENT) RULES 2007

[5002]

Rules made under section 37 of the Solicitors Act 1974 and section 9 of the Administration of Justice Act 1985 with the concurrence of the Master of the Rolls on 5 June 2007.

1. The Solicitors' Indemnity Rules 1987 as amended from time to time shall be further amended with effect from 1 October 2007 and shall continue in force thereafter in the form annexed hereto in which form they may be known as the Solicitors' Indemnity Rules 2007.

2. The Solicitors' Indemnity (Incorporated Practice) Rules 1991 as amended from time to time shall continue in force only in respect of the Indemnity Periods commencing on 1 September 1991 and 1 September 1992.

3. The contributions payable in respect of the Indemnity Periods commencing prior to 1 September 1996 shall remain unaltered.

4. In respect of any Indemnity Periods commencing on or after 1 September 1996 the Society shall retain the power under Rule 35 of the Solicitors' Indemnity Rules 1996 to determine Supplementary Contributions in respect of any such period.

5. The indemnity available in respect of the Indemnity Periods commencing prior to 1 October 2007 shall remain unaltered.

ANNEX: SOLICITORS' INDEMNITY RULES 2007

Part I General provisions and definitions

1 Authority

[5003]

1.1 These Rules are made by the Council with the concurrence of the Master of the Rolls under section 37 of the Solicitors Act 1974 and section 9 of the Administration of Justice Act 1985.

1.2 These Rules regulate indemnity provision in respect of the practices of solicitors, recognised bodies, registered European lawyers, registered foreign lawyers and certain other European lawyers carried on wholly or in part in England and Wales.

2 Citation

2.1 These Rules may be cited as the Solicitors' Indemnity Rules 2007.

3 Definitions and interpretation

3.1 For the purposes of these Rules:

Contributions means contributions previously made to the Fund in accordance with Part IV of the Solicitors' Indemnity Rules 2006 (or any earlier corresponding provisions), and any additional sums paid in accordance with Rule 16

Fund means the fund maintained in accordance with these Rules

Foreign Lawyer means an individual who is not a solicitor but is a member, and entitled to practise as such, of a legal profession regulated within a jurisdiction outside England and Wales

Indemnity Period means the period of one year commencing on 1 September in any calendar year from 1987 to 2002 inclusive, the period of 13 calendar months commencing on 1 September 2003, and the period of one year commencing on 1 October in any subsequent calendar year, unless and until otherwise determined by future Rules; and the **Relevant Indemnity Period** in relation to Contributions or indemnity means that Indemnity Period in respect of which such Contributions are payable or such indemnity is to be provided in accordance with these Rules

Master Policies and **Master Policy Certificates** means the policies and certificates referred to in Rule 4.3 and **Master Policy Insurers** means the insurers thereunder

A **Member** of a practice means any principal therein; any officer thereof in the case of a Recognised Body which is a company; any member thereof in the case of a Recognised Body which is a limited liability partnership; any Recognised Body which is a partner or held out to be a partner therein and any officer of such Recognised Body which is a company, or any member of such Recognised Body which is a limited liability partnership; any person employed in connection therewith (including any trainee solicitor); any solicitor or registered European lawyer who is a consultant to or associate in the practice; any foreign lawyer who is not a registered European lawyer and who is a consultant or associate in the practice; and any solicitor or foreign lawyer who is working in the practice as an agent or locum tenens, whether he or she is so working under a contract of service or contract for services; and the estate and/or personal representative(s) of any such persons

A **non-registered European lawyer** means a member of a legal profession which is covered by the Establishment of Lawyers Directive 98/5/EC, but who is not:
(a) a solicitor, registered European lawyer or registered foreign lawyer,
(b) a barrister of England and Wales, Northern Ireland or the Irish Republic, or
(c) a Scottish advocate

Overseas means outside England and Wales

An **Overseas Practice** means a Practice carried on wholly from an Overseas office or offices, including a Practice deemed to be a Separate Practice by virtue of paragraph (b) of the definition of Separate Practice

Partner and **partnership** (except in the phrase "limited liability partnership") refer to an unincorporated Practice, and not to a Practice incorporated as a limited liability partnership

Practice means a practice to the extent that it carries on Private Practice providing professional services as a sole solicitor or registered European lawyer or as a partnership of a type referred to in Rule 6.1(d) to 6.1(f) and consisting of or including one or more solicitors and/or registered European lawyers, and shall include the business or practice carried on by a Recognised Body in the providing of professional services such as are provided by individuals practising in Private Practice as solicitors and/or registered European lawyers or by such individuals in partnership with registered foreign lawyers, whether such Practice is carried on by the Recognised Body alone or in partnership with one or more solicitors, registered European lawyers and/or other recognised bodies

Private Practice shall be deemed to include:
(a) the acceptance and performance of obligations as trustees;
(b) notarial practice where a solicitor notary operates such notarial practice in conjunction with a solicitor's practice, whether or not the notarial fees accrue to the benefit of the solicitor's practice;

but does not include:
(c) practice to the extent that any fees or other income accruing do not accrue to the benefit of the Practice carrying on such practice (except as provided by paragraph (b) in this definition);
(d) practice by a solicitor or registered European lawyer in the course of his or her employment with an employer other than a solicitor, registered European lawyer, Recognised Body, or partnership such as is referred to in Rule 6.1(d) to 6.1(f); in which connection and for the avoidance of doubt:
    (i) any such solicitor or registered European lawyer does not carry on Private Practice when he or she acts in the course of his or her employment for persons other than his or her employer;
    (ii) any such solicitor or registered European lawyer does not carry on Private Practice merely because he or she uses in the course of his or her employment a style of stationery or description which appears to hold him or her out as a principal or solicitor or foreign lawyer in Private Practice;
    (iii) any practice carried on by such a solicitor outside the course of his or her employment will constitute Private Practice;
(e) discharging the functions of the following offices:
    (i) judicial office;
    (ii) Under Sheriffs;
    (iii) members and clerks of such tribunals, committees, panels and boards as the Council may from time to time designate but including those subject to the Tribunals and Inquiries Act 1992, the Competition Commission, Legal Services Commission Review Panels and Parole Boards;
    (iv) Justices' Clerks;
    (v) Superintendent Registrars and Deputy Superintendent Registrars of Births, Marriages and Deaths and Registrars of Local Crematoria;
    (vi) such other offices as the Council may from time to time designate

Previous Practice means any practice which shall have ceased to exist as such (for whatever reason, including by reason of (a) any death, retirement or addition of principals or (b) any split or cession of the whole or part of its practice to another without any change of principals)

Principal means:

(a) a solicitor or registered European lawyer who is a partner or sole practitioner, or a registered foreign lawyer or non-registered European lawyer who is a partner, and includes any solicitor, registered European lawyer, registered foreign lawyer or non-registered European lawyer held out as a principal; and

(b) additionally in relation to a Practice carried on by a Recognised Body alone, or a Practice in which a Recognised Body is or is held out to be a partner:

(i) a solicitor, registered European lawyer, registered foreign lawyer or non-registered European lawyer who:

(A) beneficially owns the whole or any part of a share in such Recognised Body (where it is a company with a share capital); or

(B) is a member of such Recognised Body (where it is a company without a share capital or a limited liability partnership or a partnership with legal personality); or

(ii) a solicitor, registered European lawyer, registered foreign lawyer or non-registered European lawyer who is

(A) the ultimate beneficial owner of the whole or any part of a share in such Recognised Body (where the Recognised Body is a company with a share capital); or

(B) the ultimate owner of a member or any part of a member of such Recognised Body (where the Recognised Body is a company without a share capital or a limited liability partnership or a partnership with legal personality)

A **Recognised Body** means a body for the time being recognised under section 9 of the Administration of Justice Act 1985

A **registered European lawyer** means an individual registered with the Society under regulation 17 of the European Communities (Lawyer's Practice) Regulations 2000

A **registered foreign lawyer** means an individual registered with the Society under section 89 of the Courts and Legal Services Act 1990

A **Separate Practice** means

(a) A Practice in which the number and identity of the Principals is not the same as the number and identity of the Principals in any other Practice. When the same Principals in number and identity carry on practice under more than one name or style, there is only one Practice.

(b) In the case of a Practice of which more than 25% of the Principals are foreign lawyers, any Overseas offices shall be deemed to form a Separate Practice from the offices in England and Wales.

(c) In the case of an Overseas office of a Practice, the fact that a Principal or a limited number of Principals represent all the Principals in the Practice on a local basis shall not of itself cause that Overseas office to be a Separate Practice provided that any fee or other income arising out of that office accrues to the benefit of the Practice.

(d) In the case of a Recognised Body the fact that all of the shares in the Recognised Body are beneficially owned by only some of the Principals in another Practice, shall not, of itself, cause such a Recognised Body to be a Separate Practice provided that any fee or other income arising out of the Recognised Body accrues to the benefit of that other Practice

The terms **Society** and **Council** have the meanings assigned to them by the Solicitors Act 1974

A **solicitor** means a person who has been admitted as a solicitor of the Supreme Court of England and Wales and whose name is on the roll kept by the Society under section 6 of the Solicitors Act 1974.

3.2 In these Rules, unless the context otherwise requires:

(a) the singular includes the plural, and vice versa;

(b) a reference to a person includes a body corporate, partnerships, and other unincorporated associations or bodies of persons;

(c) a reference to a Rule is to a Rule forming part of these Rules;

(d) a reference to any statute, statutory provision, or regulation includes:

(i) any subordinate legislation (as defined by section 21(1) of the Interpretation Act 1978) made under it; and

(ii) any provision which it has superseded or re-enacted (with or without modification) or amended, and any provision superseding it or re-enacting it (with or without modification) or amending it either before, or at the date of the commencement of these Rules, or after the date of the commencement of these Rules;

(e) references to the Society and to the Council include the Solicitors Regulation Authority and the Legal Complaints Service, and any body or person which succeeds in whole or in part to the functions of the Society, the Council, the Solicitors Regulation Authority or the Legal Complaints Service, and any delegate of the Society, the Council, the Solicitors Regulation Authority, the Legal Complaints Service or any such body or person;

(f) headings are for ease of reference only and shall not affect the interpretation of these Rules; and

(g) the Schedule to these Rules forms part of these Rules.

3.3 These Rules will be governed by and interpreted in accordance with English law.

4 Establishment and maintenance of Fund

4.1 The Society shall maintain the Fund in accordance with these Rules.

4.2 The purpose of the Fund is to provide indemnity against loss as mentioned in section 37 of the Solicitors Act 1974 as extended by section 9 of the Administration of Justice Act 1985, Schedule 4 paragraph 1(3) of the European Communities (Lawyer's Practice) Regulations 2000 and section 89 of the Courts and Legal Services Act 1990 in the circumstances, to the extent and subject to the conditions and exclusions specified by the Solicitors' Indemnity Rules 1987 as the same have been and are in force and amended and applied from time to time and by any future Rules continuing, amending, adding to, applying or re-enacting such or other Rules to provide such indemnity in respect of annual Indemnity Periods (starting in 1987) unless and until otherwise determined by future Rules.

4.3 The Fund shall be maintained by Contributions previously made by or on behalf of solicitors, recognised bodies, registered European lawyers and registered foreign lawyers in respect of each Indemnity Period in accordance with Part IV of the Solicitors' Indemnity Rules 2006 (or any earlier corresponding provisions), and by any additional Contributions in accordance with Rule 16.

4.4 The Society may maintain the Fund as a single continuous Fund, and any deficiency in respect of one Indemnity Period may be met in whole or part from Contributions in respect of another Period or Periods and any balance in respect of one Period may be applied to the benefit of any other Period or Periods.

4.5 The Fund shall be held, managed and administered in accordance with Part IV of these Rules by Solicitors Indemnity Fund Limited, a company set up by the Society for this purpose, or by such other person or persons (including the Society itself) as the Society may designate for such purpose, in place of Solicitors Indemnity Fund Limited. References in these Rules to Solicitors Indemnity Fund Limited shall include any such other person or persons.

5 Indemnity Periods before 1 September 1987

The Master Policies taken out and maintained and the certificates issued by the Society pursuant to the Solicitors' Indemnity Rules 1975 to 1986 shall continue to provide cover subject to and in accordance with their terms in respect of their respective periods up to and including 31 August 1987. They shall not provide cover in respect of any subsequent period.

6 Application of the Rules

6.1 These Rules shall apply to a Practice carried on by:

(a) a sole solicitor;
(b) a registered European lawyer practising as a sole practitioner;
(c) a Recognised Body;
(d) a partnership consisting of one or more solicitors and/or registered European lawyers and/or recognised bodies;
(e) a partnership consisting of one or more solicitors and/or registered European lawyers, together with one or more registered foreign lawyers; and
(f) a partnership consisting of one or more registered European lawyers with or without one or more registered foreign lawyers, together with one or more non-registered European lawyers practising from one or more offices in any state to which the Establishment of Lawyers Directive 98/5/EC applies, but outside England and Wales.

7 Scope of indemnity

7.1 The following persons, namely:

(a) solicitors, former solicitors, registered European lawyers, persons formerly practising as registered European lawyers, registered foreign lawyers practising in partnership with solicitors or registered European lawyers, persons formerly practising as registered foreign lawyers in partnership with solicitors or registered European lawyers, non-registered European lawyers practising in partnership with registered European lawyers, and persons formerly practising as non-registered European lawyers in partnership with registered European lawyers;
(b) employees and former employees of the above;
(c) *recognised bodies and former* recognised bodies; and
(d) officers and employees and former officers and employees of recognised bodies and former recognised bodies,

shall be provided with indemnity out of the Fund against loss arising from claims in respect of civil liability incurred in Private Practice in their aforesaid capacities or former capacities in the manner set out in Rule 10 and in the circumstances, to the extent and subject to the conditions and exclusions set out in Part II of these Rules and not otherwise.

Part II Indemnity cover

8 Indemnity

Indemnity for ceased Practices

[5004]
8.1 Any Member of a Previous Practice which ceased on or before 31 August 2000 who has at any time been either:

8.1.1 an Assured as a result of the issue of a certificate under one or more of the Master Policies, or

8.1.2 a person entitled to be indemnified by virtue of the issue of a receipt under the Solicitors' Indemnity Rules 1987–1990 or a payment of Contribution and Value Added Tax thereon as stated in the Solicitors' Indemnity Rules 1991–1999,

and who is not, at the time during the Indemnity Period when a claim is first made or intimated against him or her or when circumstances which might give rise to such a claim are first notified by him or her to Solicitors Indemnity Fund Limited a person entitled or required to be indemnified in respect of claims arising from that Previous Practice by a policy of Qualifying Insurance or otherwise under the Solicitors' Indemnity Insurance Rules 2000 or any rules subsequent thereto, and the Previous Practice

shall be entitled to indemnity out of the Fund in the manner, to the extent and subject to the conditions and exclusions set out in these Rules against:

(a) all loss (including liability for third party claimants' costs) incurred by the Previous Practice or any Member thereof at any time arising directly from:
  (i) any claim(s) first made or intimated against the Previous Practice or any Member thereof during the Indemnity Period in respect of any description of civil liability whatsoever which may have been incurred in Private Practice by the Previous Practice or by a Member as a Member of such Previous Practice;
  (ii) any claim in respect of any such description of civil liability as aforesaid made or intimated against the Previous Practice or any Member thereof whether during or subsequent to the Indemnity Period arising out of circumstances notified to Solicitors Indemnity Fund Limited during the Indemnity Period as circumstances which might give rise to such a claim; and

(b) all costs and expenses incurred with the consent of Solicitors Indemnity Fund Limited (such consent not to be unreasonably withheld) in the defence or settlement or compromise of any such claim as aforesaid.

Eligible Former Principals

8.2 Rule 8.1 shall apply in addition in respect of any Principal of a Previous Practice where:
(a) that Previous Practice ceased on or before 31 August 2000; and
(b) a claim is made on or after 1 September 2000 against a "Successor Practice" (as defined in Appendix 1 to the Solicitors' Indemnity Insurance Rules 2000 or any rules subsequent thereto (the "**SIIR**") to that Previous Practice (a "**Relevant Successor Practice**") in respect of any matter which would have given rise to an entitlement to that Principal to indemnity out of the Fund under the Solicitors' Indemnity Rules 1999 had the claim been notified to Solicitors Indemnity Fund Limited on 31 August 2000 (a "**Relevant Claim**"); and
(c) he or she has not at any time been a "Principal" of the Relevant Successor Practice ("Principal" having the meaning set out in Rule 3 of the SIIR); and
(d) at the time that the Relevant Claim is made he or she is not a principal in private practice ("Principal" and "Private Practice" having the meanings set out in Rule 3 of the SIIR)

(an "**Eligible Former Principal**").

8.3 In respect of any claim referred to in Rule 8.2 made by an Eligible Former Principal, the extent of the indemnity (if any) to be provided by Solicitors Indemnity Fund Limited shall be limited to an amount equal to the lesser of:
(a) the Due Proportion of the Deductible (excluding any Penalty Deductible) in respect of the Eligible Former Principal that would have been disregarded by Solicitors Indemnity Fund Limited in relation to the claim had it been made under the Solicitors' Indemnity Rules 1999; and
(b) such amount if any which the Relevant Successor Practice is entitled to and seeks to recover from the Eligible Former Principal in relation to the claim.

8.4 For the purposes of Rule 8.3, "**Due Proportion**", "**Deductible**" and "**Penalty Deductible**" shall have the meanings respectively given to them by the Solicitors' Indemnity Rules 1999, as set out in Schedule 1 to these Rules.

Expired Run-off Claims

8.5 Any firm or person shall be entitled to indemnity out of the Fund in the manner, to the extent and subject to the conditions and exclusions set out in this Rule 8.5, in relation to an Expired Run-off Claim, provided that:

(a) such claim is first notified to Solicitors Indemnity Fund Limited at any time between 1 September 2007 and 30 September 2017; and
(b) there is no Preceding Qualifying Insurance which provides cover for such claim; and
(c) such claim does not relate to or arise out of any Claim first made against an Insured or Circumstances first notified to the provider of such Preceding Qualifying Insurance, in either case at a time when such Preceding Qualifying Insurance was required to provide cover in respect thereof; and
(d) such person was an Insured under the relevant Preceding Qualifying Insurance.

Notwithstanding any other provision of these Rules:

(i) the obligations of the Fund and/or any Insured in respect of an Expired Run-off Claim shall be in accordance with, and limited to, the Expired Run-off Cover; and
(ii) any obligation owed by any insured under the Preceding Qualifying Insurance to the qualifying insurer which issued such insurance shall be deemed to be owed to Solicitors Indemnity Fund Limited in place of such qualifying insurer, unless and to the extent that Solicitors Indemnity Fund Limited in its absolute discretion otherwise agrees.

8.6 In Rule 8.5:

"**Expired Run-off Claim**" means any claim made against the Fund for indemnity under these Rules in respect of which no Preceding Qualifying Insurance remains in force to cover such claim, by reason only of:

(a) the run-off cover provided or required to be provided under the policy having been activated; and
(b) the sixth anniversary of the date on which cover under such Qualifying Insurance would have ended but for the activation of such run-off cover having passed; or
(c) (in the case of a Firm In Default or a Run-off Firm) the period of run-off cover provided or required to be provided under arrangements made to cover such claim through the Assigned Risks Pool having expired

"**Expired Run-off Cover**" means either:

(a) (unless (b) below applies) the terms of the ARP Policy/Assigned Risks Pool Policy in force at the time immediately prior to the date on which run-off cover was triggered under the Preceding Qualifying Insurance, excluding clause 5 (Run-off cover), as if it were a contract between Solicitors Indemnity Fund Limited and the firm or person making an Expired Run-off Claim; or
(b) where they are provided to Solicitors Indemnity Fund Limited prior to payment of the Claim, the terms of the Preceding Qualifying Insurance, provided that:
    (i) references in the Preceding Qualifying Insurance to the qualifying insurer that issued such insurance shall be read as references to Solicitors Indemnity Fund Limited;
    (ii) any obligation owed by any insured under the Preceding Qualifying Insurance to the qualifying insurer which issued such insurance shall be deemed to be owed to Solicitors Indemnity Fund Limited in place of such qualifying insurer, unless and to the extent that Solicitors Indemnity Fund Limited in its absolute discretion otherwise agrees;
    (iii) the obligations of the Fund and/or any Insured in respect of an Expired Run-off Claim shall neither exceed nor be less than the requirements of the Minimum Terms and Conditions which, in accordance with the applicable SIIR, such Preceding Qualifying Insurance included or was required to include.

Solicitors Indemnity Fund Limited shall be under no obligation to take any steps to obtain the terms of any such Preceding Qualifying Insurance, which for these purposes includes the terms on which it was written in respect of the insured firm or person in question, and not merely a standard policy wording

"**Preceding Qualifying Insurance**" means, in the case of any firm or person who makes an Expired Run-off Claim, the policy of Qualifying Insurance which previously provided run-off cover in respect of that firm or person, or which was required to provide such cover, or (in the case of a Firm In Default or a Run-off Firm) arrangements to provide such run-off cover through the Assigned Risks Pool

"**ARP Policy**", "**Assigned Risks Pool**", "**Assigned Risks Pool Policy**", "**Claim**", "**Circumstances**", "**Firm In Default**", "**Minimum Terms and Conditions**", "**Qualifying Insurance**" and "**Run-off Firm**" each have the meaning respectively given to such expressions in the SIIR in force at the time immediately prior to the date on which run-off cover was triggered under the Preceding Qualifying Insurance.

9 Exclusions from cover

9.1 The Fund shall not afford any indemnity in respect of any loss arising out of any claim:

(a) for death, bodily injury, physical loss or physical damage to property of any kind whatsoever (other than property in the care, custody and control of the Previous Practice or Member thereof in connection with its, his or her Private Practice for which it, he or she is responsible, not being property occupied or used by it, him or her for the purposes of the Previous Practice);

(b) for any alleged breach or other relief in respect of any partnership or partnership agreement between the Principals in the Previous Practice or between any Principal therein and any other person as Principals in any other Previous Practice;

(c) for wrongful dismissal or termination of articles of clerkship or training contract or any other alleged breach or any other relief by either party in respect of any contract of employment by the Previous Practice or any Member thereof; and/or for wrongful termination or any other alleged breach or any other relief by either party in respect of any contract for supply to or use by the Previous Practice or any Member thereof of services and/or materials and/or equipment and/or other goods;

(d) for the payment of a trading debt incurred by the Previous Practice or any Member thereof;

(e) in respect of any undertaking given by any Principal in the Previous Practice or by a Recognised Body or on his, her or its behalf (whether in his, her or its own name or in the name of the Previous Practice) to any person in connection with the provision of finance, property, assistance or other advantage whatsoever to or for the benefit of such Principal or any other Principal or of his or her or any other Principal's spouse or children or of such Recognised Body or of any business, firm, company, enterprise, association or venture owned or controlled by him, her or it or any other Principal or in a beneficial capacity whether alone or in concert with others, EXCEPT to the extent that the person seeking indemnity shall establish that he, she or it was unaware that the undertaking was or was likely to be connected with the provision of any such finance, property, assistance or other advantage;

(f) in respect of any dishonest or fraudulent act or omission, but nothing in this exclusion shall prevent any particular Member of the Previous Practice who was not concerned in such dishonesty or fraud being indemnified in accordance with these Rules in respect of any loss arising out of any claim in respect of any dishonest or fraudulent act or omission by any other such Member;

(g) in respect of any liability incurred in connection with an Overseas Practice. In relation to a Previous Practice having any Overseas offices deemed by paragraph (b) of the definition of Separate Practice in Rule 3.1 to form a Separate Practice, a liability shall be deemed to have been incurred in connection with the office where or from which the major part of the work out of which the loss arose in respect of which indemnity is sought was being done. In the event of doubt as to which (if any) office satisfies this requirement, the liability shall be deemed to have been incurred in connection with the office to which the person who accepted the initial instructions was most closely connected;

(h) in respect of any liability incurred in connection with a Previous Practice in relation to which the obligation to pay Contribution has been exempted under Rule 27 of the Solicitors' Indemnity Rules 2006 (or any earlier corresponding Rule) or, unless otherwise provided by the terms of the waiver, waived by the Council under Rule 19 (or under any corresponding earlier Rule);

(i) arising out of any circumstances or occurrences which have been notified under the Master Policy or any certificate issued under the Master Policy or any other insurance existing prior to 1 September 1987;

(j) in respect of any adjustment by way of claims loading or loss of discount which may at any future date or in respect of any future period be made by reference to any claim or claims first made or intimated during any Indemnity Period;

(k) in respect of any liability incurred by any person in his, her or its capacity as a shareholder or beneficial owner of a share in a Recognised Body notwithstanding the definition of Principal in Rule 3.1;

(l) in respect of any act or omission on the part of any Principal whilst acting on behalf of the Previous Practice or any Member thereof in connection with any matter affecting the business of the Previous Practice provided that at the time of such act or omission such Principal was a Principal in the Previous Practice;

(m) where the Previous Practice or any Member thereof is entitled to indemnity under any insurance except in respect of any amount greater than the amount which would have been payable under such insurance in the absence of the indemnity provided by the Fund.

9.2 For the avoidance of doubt, any claim or claims by any Member or former Member of any Previous Practice against any Member or former Member of any such Previous Practice for the payment of the whole or any part of the deductible paid or due in respect of a claim already notified or made under these Rules or any previous Rules is not a loss arising within the meaning of Rule 8 and shall in no event be recoverable hereunder.

9.3 The exclusions set out in this Rule 9 shall not apply in relation to an Expired Run-Off Claim, in respect of which the provisions of Rule 8.5 shall apply.

10 Manner of indemnity

10.1 Such indemnity shall be provided, according to the decision of Solicitors Indemnity Fund Limited as set out in Rule 10.2, in any one or any combination of the following ways:

(a) by payment, in or towards satisfaction of the claim and/or claimant's costs and expenses, to or to the order of the claimant making the claim;

(b) by payment, in respect of the claim and/or claimant's costs and expenses and/or costs and expenses incurred in respect of the defence or settlement or compromise of the claim, to or to the order of the person against whom the claim is made;

(c) by payment, in or towards discharge of costs and expenses incurred in respect of the defence or settlement or compromise of the claim, to or to the order of the legal advisers, adjusters or other persons by whom or in respect of whose services such costs and expenses were incurred;

(d) by payment to any firm or person in relation to an Expired Run-off Claim who was an Insured under the relevant Preceding Qualifying Insurance.

10.2 Solicitors Indemnity Fund Limited shall in any particular case, and notwithstanding the insolvency or bankruptcy of any person for whom indemnity is provided, have the sole and absolute right to decide in which way or combination of ways indemnity is provided.

11 Source of indemnity

11.1 Any such indemnity shall be provided and any claim thereto shall lie and be made exclusively out of and against the Fund.

11.2 Solicitors Indemnity Fund Limited shall have no obligation to provide indemnity save to the extent that the same can be provided out of the Fund.

11.3 In no circumstances shall any claim to indemnity lie or be made against the Society or the Council.

11.4 Save as provided in Rule 21, the Fund shall be available exclusively for the purpose specified in Rule 4.2.

11.5 In no circumstances shall the Fund or any part thereof be available or be treated by any person as available (whether by virtue of any claim, attachment, execution or proceeding or otherwise howsoever) for or in connection with any other purpose.

12 Maximum liability of the Fund

12.1 The liability of the Fund as stated in Rule 8.1.2(a) shall in no event exceed in respect of each such claim the Indemnity Limit for the Relevant Indemnity Period.

12.2 All claims arising from the same act or omission (whether or not made or intimated or arising out of circumstances notified during the same Indemnity Period and whether or not involving the same or any number of different Practices or Previous Practices and/or Members of such Practices or Previous Practices) shall be regarded as one claim.

12.3 If a payment exceeding the Indemnity Limit is made to dispose of any such claim (or, in circumstances within Rule 12.2, claims) for loss (including claimants' costs) such as stated in Rule 8.1.2(a), then any liability of the Fund for costs and expenses under Rule 8.1.2(b) shall be limited to such proportion of such costs and expenses as the Indemnity Limit bears to the amount of the payment so made.

12.4 The provisions of this Rule 12 shall not apply in relation to an Expired Run-Off Claim, in respect of which the provisions of Rule 8.5 shall apply.

13 Indemnity Limit

13.1 Save in relation to an Expired Run-Off Claim, in respect of which the provisions of Rule 8.5 shall apply, the Indemnity Limit shall be £1,000,000 each and every claim (including claimants' costs).

14 Conditions

14.1 The Previous Practice and each Member thereof shall procure that notice to Solicitors Indemnity Fund Limited shall be given in writing as soon as practicable of:

(a) any claim(s) the subject of Rule 8 made or intimated during the Relevant Indemnity Period against it, him or her of any claim for or likely to be for more than £500;

(b) the receipt by it, him or her of notice of any intention to make any such claim(s).

14.2 The Previous Practice and any Member thereof may also give notice in writing to Solicitors Indemnity Fund Limited of any circumstances of which it, he or she shall become aware which may (whether during or after the Relevant Indemnity Period) give rise to any such claim(s).

14.3 Any notice given under Rule 14.2, will be effective only if, at the date when such notice was given, the circumstances known to and notified by the Previous Practice and/or Member thereof, represent sufficient ground for a genuine and reasonable supposition on the part of the Previous Practice or Member that those circumstances may give rise to a claim the subject of indemnity under Rule 8.

14.4 If notice is given to Solicitors Indemnity Fund Limited under Rule 14.1(b) or 14.2, any claim subsequently made (whether during or after the Relevant Indemnity Period) pursuant to such an intention to claim or arising from circumstances so notified shall be deemed to have been made at the date when such notice was given.

14.5 The Previous Practice and each Member thereof shall not admit liability for, or settle, any claim falling within Rule 8 or incur any costs or expenses in connection therewith without the prior consent of Solicitors Indemnity Fund Limited (such consent not to be unreasonably withheld).

14.6 Subject to Rule 14.7:

(a) the Previous Practice and each Member thereof shall procure that Solicitors Indemnity Fund Limited shall be entitled at the Fund's own expense at any time to take over the conduct in the name of the Previous Practice or Member of the defence or settlement of any such claim, including any claim in respect of which the Previous Practice or Member may become entitled to partial indemnity under any insurance with any insurers; and

(b) Solicitors Indemnity Fund Limited may after taking over the defence or settlement of any such claim conduct the same as it may in its absolute discretion think fit notwithstanding any dispute or difference, whether or not referred to arbitration under Rule 15, which may exist or arise between it and the Previous Practice or Member.

14.7 No Previous Practice or Member thereof shall be required to contest any legal proceedings unless a Queen's Counsel (to be mutually agreed upon or failing agreement to be appointed by the President of the Society for the time being) shall advise that such proceedings should be contested.

14.8 Without prejudice to Rules 14.5, 14.6 and 14.7, the Previous Practice and each Member thereof shall keep Solicitors Indemnity Fund Limited informed in writing at all times, whether or not Solicitors Indemnity Fund Limited shall specifically so request, as to the development and handling of any claim, intimated claim, notice or circumstances the subject of or arising subsequent to any notice given to Solicitors Indemnity Fund Limited under Rule 14.1 or 14.2; and shall consult and co-operate with Solicitors Indemnity Fund Limited in relation thereto as Solicitors Indemnity Fund Limited may request, whether or not Solicitors Indemnity Fund Limited shall take over the conduct thereof.

14.9 The Fund waives any rights of subrogation against any Member of the Previous Practice save where those rights arise in connection with

(a) a dishonest or criminal act by that Member; or

(b) the provision of indemnity under the exception to Rule 9.1(e); or

(c) a claim to indemnity in circumstances where that Member has received a net benefit to which he or she was not entitled as a consequence of another Member being provided with indemnity out of the Fund;

and save as otherwise expressly provided in these Rules.

14.10 If the Previous Practice or any Member thereof shall prefer any claim to indemnity out of the Fund knowing the same to be false or fraudulent as regards amount or otherwise, it, he or she shall forfeit any claim to any such indemnity in respect of any claim or future claim against the Previous Practice or Member to which the false or fraudulent claim to indemnity out of the Fund may have related or relate.

14.11 Where there has been a failure to pay any instalment of any Contribution due or any Value Added Tax payable in accordance with the Solicitors' Indemnity Rules 1987 to 1999 and a claim has been made or intimated against the Previous Practice or any Member thereof in respect of which such Previous Practice or Member would otherwise have been entitled to be provided with indemnity, Solicitors Indemnity Fund Limited shall provide such indemnity by payment (up to the Indemnity Limit) in or towards satisfying, or enabling the Previous Practice or Member concerned to satisfy, the claim and claimants' costs and such Previous Practice shall thereafter upon request reimburse to Solicitors Indemnity Fund Limited on behalf of the Fund the whole or such part as Solicitors Indemnity Fund Limited may request of any payment so made and of any costs and expenses incurred in its defence, settlement or compromise, and each Principal therein shall be jointly and severally responsible to Solicitors Indemnity Fund Limited for such reimbursement accordingly. Provided always that Solicitors Indemnity Fund Limited shall require such reimbursement only to the extent of (a) any increase which in its opinion may have occurred in the total payable out of the Fund (including costs and expenses) as a result of such failure, together with (b) such amount as may be necessary to satisfy any unpaid Contribution and Value Added Tax and interest thereon at the rate of 4% above Barclays Bank base rate with quarterly rests or at such other rate as the Society may from time to time publish in the Law Society's Gazette.

14.12 Where non-compliance with any provision of these Rules by any Previous Practice or any Member thereof claiming to be entitled to indemnity out of the Fund has resulted in prejudice to the handling or settlement of any claim in respect of which such Previous Practice or Member is entitled to indemnity hereunder, such Previous Practice or Member shall reimburse to Solicitors Indemnity Fund Limited on behalf of the Fund the difference between the sum payable out of the Fund in respect of that claim and the sum which would have been payable in the absence of such prejudice. Provided always that it shall be a condition precedent of the right of the Fund to such reimbursement that it shall first have provided full indemnity for such Previous Practice or Member by payment (up to the Indemnity Limit) in or towards satisfying, or enabling such Previous Practice or Member to satisfy, the claim and claimants' costs in accordance with the terms hereof.

14.13 In respect of any loss arising from any claim or claims as described by Rule 8.1.2(a) arising out of any dishonest or fraudulent act or omission of any Member of the Previous Practice, the Fund shall nonetheless be available to afford indemnity in accordance with these Rules to the Previous Practice and any Member thereof, other than and excluding in each case the particular Member concerned in such dishonesty or fraud. Provided always that at the request of Solicitors Indemnity Fund Limited, the Previous Practice or Member being indemnified shall:

(a) take or procure to be taken at the Fund's expense all reasonable steps to obtain reimbursement for the benefit of the Fund from or from the personal representatives of any such Member concerned in such dishonesty or fraud, and

(b) procure that any reimbursement so obtained together with any monies which but for such fraud or dishonesty would be due to such Member concerned in such dishonesty or fraud shall be paid to the Fund up to but not exceeding the amounts paid by the Fund in respect of such claim together with any expenditure reasonably incurred by the Fund in obtaining such reimbursement.

14.14 In the event of indemnity being afforded under the exception to Rule 9.1(e), the Previous Practice or Member being indemnified shall take or procure to be taken at the Fund's expense all reasonable steps to obtain reimbursement for the benefit of the Fund from any person to whom any benefit arising from the giving of any undertaking accrues in the circumstances set out in Rule 9.1(e). Provided always that such reimbursement shall not exceed:

(a) the amount paid by the Fund by way of indemnity together with any expenditure reasonably incurred by the Fund in obtaining such reimbursement, or

(b) the amount of any benefit accruing to such person,

whichever is the lesser.

14.15 In respect of any claim to indemnity, Solicitors Indemnity Fund Limited may appoint solicitors (**Panel Solicitors**) to act on its behalf and on behalf of the Previous Practice or any Member thereof, and Panel Solicitors shall:

(a) act at the sole direction of the Fund for any purpose falling within the scope of these Rules, including acting on the Court record for the Previous Practice or any Member thereof, and

(b) disclose to Solicitors Indemnity Fund Limited as required any statement or information given to or which becomes known to Panel Solicitors in the course of so acting, and such disclosure shall be treated as having been made directly to Solicitors Indemnity Fund Limited by the Previous Practice or Member.

14.16 The provisions of this Rule 14 shall not apply in relation to an Expired Run-Off Claim, in respect of which the provisions of Rule 8.5 shall apply.

15 Arbitration

Any dispute or difference concerning any claim or the quantum of any claim to be provided with indemnity in accordance with these Rules, or concerning any payment under Rule 22, shall be referred to the sole arbitrament, which shall be final and binding, of a person to be appointed on the application of either party in default of agreement by the President of the Society for the time being. Any such arbitration shall take place and be conducted between, on the one hand, the person for whom indemnity is provided, the party to the dispute or difference and, on the other hand, Solicitors Indemnity Fund Limited for and in respect of the Fund.

Part III Contributions

16 Power to require Contributions

[5005]

16.1 The Society shall have power to require Principals to make Contributions of such amount and on such basis as the Society may from time to time determine. Value Added Tax, to the extent chargeable on any relevant supply which takes or may be treated as taking place under or by virtue of these Rules, will be charged and payable in addition to and at the same time as any Contributions payable hereunder.

16.2 Solicitors Indemnity Fund Limited may at any time give to any Practice written notice correcting any inaccuracy in the calculation of any Contribution under these Rules. Any reimbursement or any payment of Contribution hereby required shall be made forthwith upon, respectively, issue or receipt of such a notice, together with any Value Added Tax applicable and (in the case of any amount payable to Solicitors Indemnity Fund Limited upon correction of an inaccuracy in calculation) interest at a rate of 4% above Barclays Bank base rate with quarterly rests or at such other rate as the Society may from time to time determine and publish in the Law Society's Gazette.

16.3 Solicitors Indemnity Fund Limited may at any time, to the extent that it is reasonably practicable for it to do so, recalculate any claims adjustment applicable to any Practice under the Solicitors' Indemnity Rules 2006 (or any earlier corresponding Rules) as a result of the receipt by Solicitors Indemnity Fund Limited of any sum from any third party relating to any indemnity provided to that Practice out of the Fund under these Rules or any earlier corresponding Rules, after deduction of the reasonable costs and expenses incurred by Solicitors Indemnity Fund Limited.

16.4 Solicitors Indemnity Fund Limited shall not be entitled, at any time after 30 September 2008, to require any Practice to make any Contribution under the Solicitors' Indemnity Rules 2006 (or any earlier corresponding Rules) which would otherwise be payable by reason of an inaccuracy in calculation, unless that inaccuracy is attributable to a failure to provide information or to a material inaccuracy in information provided by or on behalf of that Practice under Part III of the Solicitors' Indemnity Rules 2006 (or any earlier corresponding Rules).

16.5 The Society's decision shall be final and binding on all affected on any question arising as to:
(a) any obligation to make a Contribution; or
(b) any sum due to any person out of the Fund;

under this Rule 16.

Part IV Management and administration of the fund

17 Powers of the Society

[5006]
17.1 Solicitors Indemnity Fund Limited shall hold, and have full power to manage and administer, the Fund, subject only to:
(a) such directions, conditions and/or requirements as the Society may from time to time issue to or impose upon it expressly pursuant to this provision, and/or
(b) such further detailed arrangements as the Society may from time to time agree with it.

17.2 Without limiting the generality of Rule 17.1, the management and administration of the Fund shall include power to:
(a) collect and recover Contributions due to the Fund in accordance with these Rules;
(b) deposit or invest in such manner as Solicitors Indemnity Fund Limited may determine all or any part of the Fund, including any interest, dividends, profits, gains or other assets accruing to or acquired by the Fund;
(c) arrange such insurances as Solicitors Indemnity Fund Limited may determine in respect of the Fund and/or its assets and/or the Fund's liability under these Rules to afford indemnity in respect of claims and costs and expenses; and to handle all aspects of any such insurances, including the payment of premiums thereon out of the Fund and the making and recovery of claims thereunder;
(d) receive, investigate and handle claims to indemnity and other notices prescribed to be given to Solicitors Indemnity Fund Limited by these Rules, including settlement and compromise and making of ex gratia payments out of the Fund in respect thereof and conduct of any dispute or difference referred to arbitration under Rule 15;
(e) receive, investigate and handle any claim made or intimated against any person in respect of which they are or may be entitled to be provided with indemnity out of the Fund (whether or not a claim to indemnity hereunder has been made) and/or in respect of which the conduct is by these Rules assigned to Solicitors Indemnity Fund Limited, including settlement and compromise and making of ex gratia payments and conduct of any proceedings arising in respect of such claim;
(f) claim and recover reimbursement in respect of any sums paid by way of indemnity in any circumstances in which such reimbursement may under these Rules be claimed;
(g) exercise any right of subrogation save where such rights are waived in accordance with these Rules;
(h) maintain full and proper records and statistics (which subject to Rule 18, shall at all reasonable times be available on request to the Society for inspection and copying) as to the Fund and all aspects of its management and administration;
(i) make to and review with the Council of the Society annually and at any other time that the Council may require, written and (if the Council so requires) oral reports as to the Fund and, subject to Rule 18, its management and administration, including inter alia recommendations as to the Contributions which are or may be required in respect of past, present and/or future Indemnity Periods and the circumstances in which, extent to which and conditions and exclusions subject to which indemnity should in any future Indemnity Period be afforded out of the Fund;

(j) engage the assistance of any third party in respect of all or any aspect(s) of the management and administration of the Fund;
(k) delegate to any third party all or any aspect(s) of the management and administration of the Fund;
(l) institute and/or conduct such proceedings as it may consider necessary or appropriate for the due management and administration of the Fund in its own name or (subject to prior consent of the Society) in the name of the Society;
(m) disburse and/or reimburse out of the Fund all administrative and legal and other costs, overheads, fees and other expenses and liabilities incurred in respect of the Fund, including without prejudice to the generality of the foregoing any such costs, overheads, fees and other expenses and liabilities incurred by the Society in respect of the establishment or maintenance, or the management, administration or protection, of the Fund;
(n) disburse and/or reimburse out of the Fund payments for any educational, charitable or other useful purpose which in its opinion is likely directly or indirectly to lead to the reduction or prevention of claims on the Fund or otherwise to further the purpose or interests of the Fund;
(o) disburse and/or reimburse out of the Fund the costs, fees and expenses of the handling after 31 August 1987 of claims and potential claims against Assureds notified under the Master Policies and Master Policy Certificates;
(p) effect out of the Fund or by arrangement with third parties the funding pending reimbursement by Master Policy Insurers of such claims and potential claims and to bear out of the Fund the costs, fees and expenses incurred thereby.

18 Use of information

18.1 Without prejudice to the Society's power under Rule 4.5 to designate itself as the person responsible for holding, managing and administering the Fund, information and documents obtained by Solicitors Indemnity Fund Limited about any particular Practice or Member thereof in the course of investigating and handling any claim made or intimated or any circumstances notified as mentioned in Rule 21, may be utilised by Solicitors Indemnity Fund Limited for the purpose of preparation of general records, statistics, reports and recommendations (not identifying the particular Practice or Member) for or to the Society.

18.2 Solicitors Indemnity Fund Limited may bring to the attention of the Society (including, in the case of the matters referred to in Rule 18.2(f), the Legal Complaints Service) at any time and without notice to the Practice or person concerned:
(a) any failure to provide information in respect of any Practice as required by Part III of the Solicitors' Indemnity Rules 2006 (or any earlier corresponding provisions) or any material omission or inaccuracy in such information;
(b) any failure to pay any Contribution or other sum due when required to do so under these Rules (or any earlier corresponding Rules) or to reimburse any amount due by way of a Deductible, Due Proportion or Penalty Deductible, or (in the case of an Expired Run-off Claim) which falls within a policy excess;
(c) a material inaccuracy in any proposal form submitted by or on behalf of a Practice;
(d) (in the case of an Expired Run-off Claim) any matter or circumstances that would permit the Expired Run-off Cover to be avoided or but for the provisions of clause 4.1 of the Minimum Terms and Conditions (and/or the corresponding of the Expired Run-off Cover);
(e) any dishonesty or fraud suspected on the part of any in relation to any Practice or Member thereof, or any other person subject to these Rules or any earlier corresponding Rules, or any Insured (as defined in the Minimum Terms and Conditions); and
(f) any claim of inadequate professional services of which it becomes aware made against any such Practice, Member or person or any Insured.

18.3 Such information and documents shall not otherwise be disclosed or available to the Society without the prior consent of the Practice (or any subsequent or successor Practice thereto) or Member concerned, except where Solicitors Indemnity Fund Limited or the Society have reason to suspect dishonesty on the part of any Practice, Previous, subsequent or successor Practice or any Member or former Member thereof, or Insured.

18.4 Any information and documents held by Solicitors Indemnity Fund Limited about a particular Practice or Member thereof may be disclosed or available to the Society without the prior consent of the Practice (or any subsequent or successor practice thereto) or Member concerned where the Society has been requested by any Practice, subsequent or successor Practice or Member thereof to grant, amend or revoke any waiver under Rule 19 or to make a determination under Rule 20.

18.5 Solicitors Indemnity Fund Limited may pass to the Society the name of any Practice (including any subsequent, successor or Previous Practice) or any Member or former Member thereof in circumstances where Solicitors Indemnity Fund Limited has cause for concern having regard to:
(a) the nature, incidence or value of paid and/or reserved claims in respect of any such Practice or Member; or
(b) the existence of circumstances which are considered by the Fund to create an increased risk of claims occurring in respect of that Practice or Member; or

(c) failure on the part of a Practice or Member thereof, or any Insured (as defined in the Minimum Terms and Conditions), to comply with their obligations under these Rules (or any earlier corresponding Rules);

and for the purposes of paragraphs (b) and (c) above Solicitors Indemnity Fund Limited shall have the power to determine criteria which would indicate the likelihood of an increased risk of claims occurring and to specify those obligations in respect of which a failure to comply could form the basis for Solicitors Indemnity Fund Limited to pass on information.

18.6 In the exercise of the powers set out in Rule 18.5 Solicitors Indemnity Fund Limited may give details to the Society of the reasons for the decision to pass the name of the Practice or Member thereof to the Society including, in appropriate cases, releasing documentary information provided that no such documentary information will be released which could breach the general duty of confidentiality owed by a Practice or Member thereof to a client or former client.

18.7 The Legal Complaints Service of the Society may pass such information as it in its absolute discretion sees fit to any other department or office of the Society, and to Solicitors Indemnity Fund Limited, in relation to any complaint of inadequate professional services against a Practice of which it becomes aware.

18.8 In respect of any information that may be brought to the attention of the Society in accordance with Rules 18.1 to 18.7:

(a) the Society shall keep all such information confidential;

(b) the Society shall not (except where and to the extent required by law or in the proper performance by the Society of its regulatory functions) at any time reveal any such information to any person other than a duly authorised employee of the Society or any of its subsidiaries; and

(c) any privilege attaching to such information shall not be regarded as having been waived whether by virtue of such information having been provided to the Society or otherwise;

but the provisions of this Rule 18.8 shall not prevent the Society from making use of any such information for the purpose of bringing disciplinary proceedings against any person.

19 Waivers

19.1 The Society shall have power in any case or class of cases to waive in writing prospectively or retrospectively any obligation on any solicitor, Recognised Body or foreign lawyer under these Rules and to amend or revoke any such waiver.

19.2 Any application by any person for:

(a) a waiver of any obligation under these Rules or under the Solicitors' Indemnity Rules 2001 or any Rules subsequent thereto; or

(b) a correction or recalculation of any sum paid or payable to the Fund under these Rules, or under the Solicitors' Indemnity Rules 2001 or any Rules subsequent thereto;

must be made in writing to the Society no later than 3 calendar months from the date on which the relevant obligation has effect in relation to that person, or the date on which that person is notified thereof by Solicitors Indemnity Fund Limited, whichever is the earlier.

19.3 No application by any person for:

(a) a waiver of any obligation under the Solicitors' Indemnity Rules 2000 or any Rules made prior thereto; or

(b) a correction or recalculation of any sum paid or payable to the Fund under the Solicitors' Indemnity Rules 2000 or any Rules made prior thereto;

may be considered unless it was made in writing to the Society as soon as practicable, and in any event no later than 28 February 2002.

19.4 Any appeal against any decision made by the Society in respect of any application for a waiver of any obligation under these Rules or any previous Rules, or in respect of any correction or recalculation of any sum paid or payable to the Fund under these Rules or any previous Rules, must be made in writing to the Society within 21 days from the date of the decision.

19.5 An application for a waiver as contemplated by this Rule 19 or the making of an appeal against any decision made by the Society in respect of such application shall not relieve any person from any obligation under these Rules or any previous Rules pending the determination of any such application or appeal.

20 Decisions by the Society

20.1 The Society shall have power to treat any person as complying with any provision of these Rules for the purposes of the Solicitors Act 1974 notwithstanding that the person has failed to comply with any provision of these Rules where such non-compliance is regarded by the Society in a particular case or cases as being insignificant.

Part V Maintenance and termination of the fund

21 Maintenance and termination of the Fund

[5007]

21.1 The Fund shall continue to be held, managed and administered by Solicitors Indemnity Fund Limited for so long as and to the extent that the Society, in the light of the reports made to it by Solicitors Indemnity Fund Limited, may consider necessary or appropriate for the purpose of providing indemnity in respect of any claim(s) made or intimated during any Indemnity Period and/or during or subsequent to any Indemnity Period arising out of circumstances notified during any Indemnity Period as circumstances which might give rise to such claim(s).

21.2 As and when the Society no longer considers it necessary or appropriate that all or any part of the Fund should be so held, managed and administered, the Society may require all or any part of the Fund not so required to be released to the Society which shall apply the same if and to the extent the Society considers it reasonably practicable for the purpose of providing indemnity in any other way permitted by section 37(2) of the Solicitors Act 1974 and otherwise for the overall benefit of the solicitors' profession in such manner as it may decide.

22 Return of surplus relating to specific Indemnity Periods

22.1 If directed to do so by the Society, Solicitors Indemnity Fund Limited shall return Relevant Contributions by way of payment to Recipient Practices or otherwise in accordance with this Rule 22.

22.2 In this Rule 22:

Applicable Principals means Principals who have made or caused to be made Relevant Contributions

Relevant Contributions means Initial Contributions paid in respect of the Indemnity Periods 2001–2002 and/or 2002–2003 under the Solicitors' Indemnity Rules 2001 and 2002 respectively, but does not include interest or any sum in respect of interest thereon, and does not include any sum charged in accordance with Rule 37 of the Solicitors' Indemnity Rules 2001 or 2002

Recipient Practice means a Practice in respect of which Relevant Contributions were made, whether or not, on the date of any payment under this Rule 22, any Principal of the Practice is an Applicable Principal.

22.3 Solicitors Indemnity Fund Limited may return Relevant Contributions by making payment to each Recipient Practice.

22.4 Solicitors Indemnity Fund Limited may require Recipient Practices and/or Applicable Principals to provide it with such information as it may reasonably require to enable it to determine entitlement to any payment to be made under this Rule 22 or to enable such payment to be made. Solicitors Indemnity Fund Limited may require, as a condition precedent to payment of any sum under this Rule 22, the provision to Solicitors Indemnity Fund Limited of an indemnity in such form as Solicitors Indemnity Fund Limited may reasonably require from the person or Practice to which payment is to be made.

22.5 Where payment cannot be made in accordance with Rule 22.3, Solicitors Indemnity Fund Limited may take such steps as it considers in its absolute discretion to be appropriate to identify and make payment to persons whom Solicitors Indemnity Fund Limited believes to be Applicable Principals, including the estates of deceased Applicable Principals, on such basis as it considers fair in all the circumstances of the case.

22.6 Solicitors Indemnity Fund Limited may deduct from any payments due under this Rule 22 to a Recipient Practice or to any Applicable Principal any sums due from that Recipient Practice or Applicable Principal under these Rules or any previous Rules.

22.7 Solicitors Indemnity Fund Limited may make payments under this Rule 22 in such manner as it sees fit and on the basis of the information in its records at the relevant time or as provided to it by any person having apparent authority to do so. Solicitors Indemnity Fund Limited shall not be required to verify or seek confirmation of such information.

22.8 The repayment by Solicitors Indemnity Fund Limited of a Relevant Contribution to a Recipient Practice in accordance with Rule 22.3 or otherwise in accordance with Rule 22.5 shall constitute a good discharge of any obligations of Solicitors Indemnity Fund Limited in respect of that Relevant Contribution, and Solicitors Indemnity Fund Limited shall have no obligation as to its distribution or allocation to Applicable Principals (within a Recipient Practice or otherwise) or to any other person or Practice.

22.9 The obligation of Solicitors Indemnity Fund Limited to make payments in accordance with this Rule 22 shall cease on 1 October 2008. Any Relevant Contributions which Solicitors Indemnity Fund Limited has not paid by that date and in respect of which no valid claim in respect of an

Applicable Principal has been made to Solicitors Indemnity Fund Limited shall cease to be payable under this Rule 22 and shall be regarded as part of the Fund available for release to the Society in accordance with Rule 21.

Schedule 1: Extract from the Solicitors' Indemnity Rules 1999

[5008]
The definitions set out below are provided for convenience only. For the purposes of these Rules, the full text of the Solicitors' Indemnity Rules 1999 prevails and should be consulted when interpreting the extracts contained in this Schedule.

21 Deductibles

21.1 For the purposes of these Rules:

(a) the "Deductible" means in respect of any claim either:

- (i) the sum calculated by reference to the total number of Relevant Principals and shall be the amount set out in Table I which corresponds to a Practice with the same number of Principals as there are Relevant Principals; or
- (ii) the amount of the increased deductible under Rule 22.2 applicable to the Practice in which the majority of Relevant Principals practise at the Date of Notification;

(b) a "Relevant Principal" means a Principal or former Principal who is liable for the claim by virtue of having been a Principal in the Practice which was concerned with the matters giving rise to the claim at the date when such matters occurred;

(c) "Due Proportion of the Deductible" means a sum equal to the amount of the Deductible divided by the number of Relevant Principals except where the number of Relevant Principals exceeds fifty when it means a sum equal to the amount of the Deductible divided by the number of Relevant Principals still in practice as Principals at the Date of Notification (provided such number still exceeds fifty);

(d) the "Date of Notification" means either the date of receipt by Solicitors Indemnity Fund Limited of the first of any notices given under either Rule 19.1 or 19.2, or the date of receipt by Solicitors Indemnity Fund Limited of any claim or intimation of claim in respect of which there is or may be an entitlement to indemnity out of the Fund, whichever is the earlier. Provided however that if in either case such date is subsequent to the Relevant Indemnity Period, the Date of Notification shall be deemed to be the date any claim was first made or intimated against the Practice or any Member thereof;

(e) the "Aggregate Deductible" is the amount set out in Table II corresponding to the number of Principals in the Practice as at 1st September 1999 or, where applicable, the date of commencement given in any notice required to be delivered under either Rule 26 or 27 during the Relevant Indemnity Period or the amount of the amended aggregate effected under Rule 22.2.

22 Amending the deductible or aggregate deductible

22.1 In respect of any claim not yet made or intimated and not arising from circumstances already known to the Practice or any Member thereof or notified to Solicitors Indemnity Fund Limited:

(a) the Deductible applicable to the Practice in accordance with Table I may be reduced to 50% or to nil (such reduction also having the effect of reducing the Aggregate Deductible applicable to the Practice in accordance with Table II to 50% or to nil);

(b) the Aggregate Deductible applicable to the Practice in accordance with Table II may be reduced as follows:

- (i) to one third or two thirds;
- (ii) to one third or two thirds, of any aggregate calculated in accordance with Rule 22.1(a);

in each case upon payment by the Practice to the Fund of an additional Contribution in an amount calculated on a scale approved by the Society from time to time taking into account the claims record of such Practice and of any other Practice(s) in which any Principal therein was previously a Member.

22.2 In respect of any claim not yet made or intimated and not arising from circumstances already notified to Solicitors Indemnity Fund Limited, the Deductible and Aggregate Deductible applicable to the Practice may be increased specifically to sums of:

- (i) £250,000 subject to an aggregate of two or three times;
- (ii) £500,000 subject to an aggregate of one, two or three times;
- (iii) £750,000 subject to an aggregate of one, two or three times;
- (iv) £1,000,000 subject to an aggregate of one, two or three times

by any Practice in respect of which Gross Fees in excess of £15 million have been disclosed in the Certificate or Notice of Succession, whichever may be appropriate, delivered under Rule 27 save that the amount of the Aggregate Deductible after amendment shall not exceed 3% of the said Gross

Fees, in return for a reduced Contribution or repayment by the Fund of any part of any Contribution paid, in an amount determined by the Society either generally or in respect of the particular Practice or any Successor Practice.

22.3 Without prejudice to Rule 22.1, where a claim arises out of circumstances known to the Practice or any Member thereof but not notified prior to the Relevant Indemnity Period and an amendment to the Deductible or Aggregate Deductible was in force during the Indemnity Period when such knowledge was acquired, Solicitors Indemnity Fund Limited may apply the benefit of any Deductible or Aggregate Deductible amendment effected for the Relevant Indemnity Period under Rule 22.1 to any such claim, but shall not be required to do so in any circumstances.

TABLE I
Deductible (Rule 21.1(a))

Number of Principals in Practice	Amount per Practice (£)	Number of Principals in Practice	Amount per Practice (£)
1	3,000	27	74,250
2	3,000	28	77,000
3	4,500	29	79,750
4	6,000	30	82,500
5	7,500	31	93,000
6	10,500	32	96,000
7	12,250	33	99,000
8	14,000	34	102,000
9	18,000	35	105,000
10	20,000	36	108,000
11	22,000	37	111,000
12	24,000	38	114,000
13	26,000	39	117,000
14	28,000	40	120,000
15	30,000	41	123,000
16	32,000	42	126,000
17	36,000	43	129,000
18	40,000	44	132,000
19	44,000	45	135,000
20	48,000	46	138,000
21	52,000	47	141,000
22	56,000	48	144,000
23	60,000	49	147,000
24	64,000	50	150,000
25	68,000	Over 50	150,000
26	71,500		

TABLE II
Aggregate Deductible (Rule 21.1(e))

Number of Principals in Practice	Amount per Practice (£)	Number of Principals in Practice	Amount per Practice (£)
1	9,000	27	222,750
2	9,000	28	231,000
3	13,500	29	239,250
4	18,000	30	247,500
5	22,500	31	279,000
6	31,500	32	288,000
7	36,750	33	297,000
8	42,000	34	306,000
9	54,000	35	315,000
10	60,000	36	324,000

TABLE II
Aggregate Deductible (Rule 21.1(e))

Number of Principals in Practice	Amount per Practice (£)	Number of Principals in Practice	Amount per Practice (£)
11	66,000	37	333,000
12	72,000	38	342,000
13	78,000	39	351,000
14	84,000	40	360,000
15	90,000	41	369,000
16	96,000	42	378,000
17	108,000	43	387,000
18	120,000	44	396,000
19	132,000	45	405,000
20	144,000	46	414,000
21	156,000	47	423,000
22	168,000	48	432,000
23	180,000	49	441,000
24	192,000	50	450,000
25	204,000	Over 50	450,000
26	214,500		

23 Penalty deductibles

23.1 For the purposes of these Rules:

(a) the "Penalty Deductible" means in respect of any claim arising out of the circumstances referred to in Rule 23.2 such sum as is equal to 50% of the amount set out in Table I which corresponds to a Practice with the same number of Principals as there are Relevant Principals;

(b) "Due Proportion of the Penalty Deductible" means a sum equal to the amount of the Penalty Deductible divided by the number of Relevant Principals except where the number of Relevant Principals exceeds fifty when it means a sum equal to the amount of the Penalty Deductible divided by the number of Relevant Principals still in practice as Principals at the Date of Notification (provided such number still exceeds fifty);

(c) the "Aggregate Penalty Deductible" is the sum equivalent to 50% of the amount set out in Table II corresponding to the number of Principals in the Practice as at 1st September 1999 or, where applicable, the date of commencement given in any notice required to be delivered under either Rule 26 or 27 during the Relevant Indemnity Period.

23.2 Each and every claim that

(a) arises from a failure to:

(i) commence proceedings within the time permitted under sections 2, 5 or 11 of the Limitation Act 1980 or any statutory re-enactment thereof;

(ii) commence proceedings within the time permitted under section 111 of the Employment Rights Act 1996 or any statutory re-enactment thereof;

(iii) serve civil proceedings within the time permitted under Part 7.5 of the Civil Procedure Rules 1998 or any statutory re-enactment thereof;

(iv) serve a notice or issue an application within the periods permitted under Part II of the Landlord and Tenant Act 1954 or any statutory re-enactment thereof;

(v) register at Companies House a charge against the assets of a company within the time permitted by section 395 of the Companies Act 1985 or any statutory re-enactment thereof;

(vi) apply to register a protected transaction within the priority period afforded under the Land Registration (Official Searches) Rules 1993 or any statutory re-enactment thereof;

(vii) execute a Deed of Variation within the two years permitted under section 142(1) of the Inheritance Tax Act 1984 and/or to give written notice to the Inland Revenue within the six months permitted under section 142(2) or any statutory re-enactment thereof; or

(b) falls within Rule 19.15(c);

shall, in addition to any Deductible applicable, be subject to a Penalty Deductible in respect of which the Fund shall not afford indemnity under Rule 13(a) PROVIDED THAT such failure occurred on or after 1st September 1996.

23.3 Each Relevant Principal shall be liable for a Due Proportion of the Penalty Deductible PROVIDED THAT:

(a) in the case of any Relevant Principal practising in the same Practice as any other Relevant Principal(s) at the Date of Notification such Relevant Principal shall be jointly and severally liable for such sum as is equal to the total sum of the Due Proportions of the Penalty Deductible payable by all Relevant Principals in that Practice.

(b) Solicitors Indemnity Fund Limited shall disregard the Due Proportion(s) of the Penalty Deductible payable by:

(i) any insolvent or bankrupt Relevant Principal;

(ii) any Relevant Principal in a Practice where the total sum of Penalty Deductible payments in respect of claims to which the Relevant Indemnity Period applies is equal to that Practice's Aggregate Penalty Deductible;

(iii) any Relevant Principal who as at the Date of Notification has ceased to be a Principal in any Practice and who does not become a Principal in any Practice within 12 months of that date;

PROVIDED ALWAYS THAT where the number of Relevant Principals exceeds fifty, the definition in Rule 23.1(b) shall apply and (i) and (iii) above shall not apply unless the number of Principals in practice as Principals at the Date of Notification is fifty or less.

(c) Where an increased Deductible under Rule 22.2 is applicable to the Practice in which the majority of Relevant Principals practise at the Date of Notification, the Principals in such Practice shall be jointly and severally liable for the whole of any Penalty Deductible due PROVIDED ALWAYS THAT if the number of Principals in the Originating Practice is not more than ten then any Penalty Deductible payable shall be due and payable in such Due Proportions as would apply in the absence of any increased Deductible under Rule 22.2.

(d) Solicitors Indemnity Fund Limited may pay, or include in any payment made, out of the Fund in respect of any claim, the whole or any part of any Penalty Deductible applicable thereto, and in that event the Penalty Deductible or any Due Proportion of the Penalty Deductible shall be reimbursed forthwith to the Fund by the appropriate Relevant Principal(s) in accordance with Rule 23.3(a).

23.4 Every Practice shall have an Aggregate Penalty Deductible.

SOLICITORS (SCOTLAND) PROFESSIONAL INDEMNITY INSURANCE CONTINGENCY FUND RULES 2007

Rules dated 29th June 2007 made by the Council of the Law Society of Scotland with the concurrence of the Lord President of the Court of Session under section 44 of the Solicitors (Scotland) Act 1980.

[5009]

Citation and Commencement

1.—(1) These Rules may be cited as the Solicitors (Scotland) Professional Indemnity Insurance Contingency Fund Rules 2007.

(2) These Rules shall come into operation on 1st September 2007.

Definitions and Interpretation

2.—(1) In these Rules

"the Act" means the Solicitors (Scotland) Act 1980;

"contingency fund" means the fund which was established in terms of Rule 6(2) of the Solicitors (Scotland) Professional Indemnity Insurance Rules 1995 for the purpose of refunding to practice units such portion of the premiums paid by them as was attributable to circumstances intimated in accordance with the master policy if and when the brokers were satisfied that no claim would result from such circumstances;

"contingency fund monies" means the monies which remain in the contingency fund as at the date specified in Rule 1(2);

"professional indemnity purpose" means any purpose concerning indemnity for solicitors, former solicitors of the Society against any class of professional liability which is not *otherwise funded*—

(a) in terms of rules made under section 44 of the Act, or

(b) by the Society in terms of arrangements for such indemnity in respect of its activities;

"the Society" means the Law Society of Scotland; and

"solicitors" means solicitors holding practising certificates under the Act and includes firms of solicitors and incorporated practices, and also includes registered foreign lawyers and multi-national practices; and "former solicitors" shall be construed accordingly.

(2) The Interpretation Act 1978 applies to the interpretation of these Rules as it applies to the interpretation of an Act of Parliament.

Contingency Fund Monies

3.—(1) The Society shall manage and administer the contingency fund monies.

(2) The Society may use the contingency fund monies for any professional indemnity purpose.

(3) The Society may use the contingency fund monies to pay costs and expenses reasonably incurred in connection with the management and administration of those monies or with their use for any professional indemnity purpose.

INDEMNITY INSURANCE DISCLOSURE GUIDELINES

9 December 2008

NOTES

OBLIGATIONS UNDER THE SOLICITORS' INDEMNITY INSURANCE RULES

[5009A]

Under Rule 18 of the Solicitors' Indemnity Insurance Rules (SIIR), a firm and its principals are required, upon request, to provide their insurance details to any person (or their representative) asserting a claim, whether or not such a claim would or may be upheld. In the case of a ceased firm, the obligation rests with the principals in the firm immediately before it ceased. If a firm fails to provide the information requested, under delegated powers the Solicitors Regulation Authority (SRA) can, under Rule 17.5, exercise its discretion and provide that information.

However, such discretion is only usually exercised when the SRA has confirmation that the information has been requested from the firm in question and that the claim being asserted relates to matters within the scope of the Minimum Terms and Conditions of Professional Indemnity Insurance.

THE IMPORTANCE OF THE DATE THE CLAIM IS NOTIFIED, OR THE DATE THE INSURER IS NOTIFIED, BY THE FIRM OF CIRCUMSTANCES THAT MAY GIVE RISE TO A CLAIM

Professional indemnity insurance operates on a "claims made" basis rather than a "losses occurring" basis. This means that responsibility for handling a claim lies with the insurer on risk at the time the claim is made against the firm, or when circumstances that may give rise to a claim are notified to the insurer by the firm, rather than with the company who was on cover when the alleged negligent act took place.

WHAT IF A PRACTICE HAS CEASED?

Where a practice has ceased and there is a successor practice, as defined in the Minimum Terms and Conditions appended to the SIIR, claims arising after the cessation will be dealt with by the qualifying insurer providing cover for the successor practice at the time the claim is made, or when the insurer is notified of circumstances that may give rise to a claim.

Where a practice has ceased and there is no successor practice, the qualifying insurer on cover at the date of closure of the practice will be liable to provide 6 years' run-off cover from the date of expiry of the policy. Any claims or circumstances notified after the firm has closed will be handled by the qualifying insurer providing this run-off cover.

How do I find out if there is a successor practice?

The SRA cannot make a declaration or a ruling as to which is, or is not, a successor practice in any particular situation as it depends on the precise circumstances at the time. However, using the SRA's records and any other information we are provided with, we will offer guidance.

What the SRA will do if a firm or their successor practice refuses to provide a potential claimant with their insurance details

- We will check if the information has been requested from the appropriate firm and that a claim has been asserted. We require evidence of both the assertion of a claim and request for insurance details, such as a letter before action.
- If the information has not been requested we will write to advise what action should be taken.

- If the information has been requested, we will write to the firm outlining their obligations under the SIIR and the potential consequences of failing to comply with those obligations. We will give them a time limit in which to respond (usually 7–10 days). At the same time we will write to the claimant (or their representative) with a copy of the letter asking them to inform us if they do not receive a response.
- If no response is received from the firm, we will exercise our discretion and provide the relevant information.
- The firm's failure to comply with the requirements of the SIIR will be passed onto the Regulatory Investigations Unit of the SRA for consideration.

If the firm has ceased

- The Client Protection Policy Unit will consider if there is a successor practice and, if so, direct the potential claimant to that firm. The claimant will then have to assert the claim against that firm as successor practice.
- If there is no successor practice we will disclose the details of the relevant insurer if we are satisfied there is a claim that may be covered by the Minimum Terms and Conditions of Professional Indemnity Insurance SIIR.

All queries for insurance disclosure should be directed to

Client Protection Policy Unit, SRA, Ipsley Court, Berrington Close, Ipsley, Redditch, Worcestershire, B98 0TD

or DX 19114 – Redditch

Email: professionalindemnity@sra.org.uk

Telephone: + 44 (0) 1527 504422

SOLICITORS' INDEMNITY INSURANCE RULES 2009

NOTES

The commentary provided with these Rules does not form part of the Rules, is provided for guidance only, and does not affect the meaning or interpretation of the Rules in any way.

PART 1: GENERAL

1 Authority and commencement

[5010]

1.1 These Rules are made by the Solicitors Regulation Authority Board under sections 31, 37, 79 and 80 of the Solicitors Act 1974 and section 9 of the Administration of Justice Act 1985 with the concurrence of the Master of the Rolls under sections 31 and 37 of the Solicitors Act 1974, and paragraph 16 of the Legal Services Act 2007 and the concurrence of the Lord Chancellor under paragraph 16 of Schedule 22 of the Legal Services Act 2007.

1.2 These Rules come into force on 1 October 2009.

1.3 These Rules require Solicitors, Registered European Lawyers, Registered Foreign Lawyers and Recognised Bodies and their managers in Private Practice in England and Wales to take out and maintain professional indemnity insurance with Qualifying Insurers with effect from 1 October 2009.

Commentary: These Rules apply to:

- Solicitors
- Registered European Lawyers
- Registered Foreign Lawyers and
- Recognised Bodies and their managers

carrying on Private Practice in England and Wales as a Firm at any time after 1 October 2009. Refer to the definitions in Rule 3 for guidance on the exact meanings of these terms.

1.4 These Rules will apply to any Indemnity Period beginning on or after 1 October 2009.

Commentary: Before 1 September 2000, Firms were required to take out insurance with the Solicitors Indemnity Fund. Since 1 September 2000, Firms have been required to take out insurance in accordance with the Solicitors' Indemnity Insurance Rules. From 1 October 2009, Firms must take out insurance in accordance with these Rules with one or more Qualifying Insurers. Continuing arrangements dealing with past claims on the Solicitors Indemnity Fund are covered in the Solicitors' Indemnity Rules.

1.5 The Solicitors Indemnity Insurance Rules 2008 shall not apply in respect of any Indemnity Period beginning on or after 1 October 2009, but they shall remain in force in respect of the Indemnity Period from 1 October 2007 to 30 September 2008 inclusive (as amended by the Solicitors' Indemnity Insurance (Amendment) Rules 2009 with effect from 31 March 2009)subject to the provisions of Rules 19.1(a), 19.1(b), 19.1(c) and 19.1(d) below.

Commentary: You should refer to previous Solicitors' Indemnity Insurance Rules in relation to earlier Indemnity Periods since 1 September 2000. However, you should refer to Rules 19.1(a) to 19.1(d) in relation to time limits in respect of an application for a waiver of the provisions of the Solicitors' Indemnity Insurance Rules 2000 to 2009.

2 Citation

2.1 These Rules may be cited as the Solicitors' Indemnity Insurance Rules 2009.

3 Definitions and interpretation

3.1 In these Rules, unless the context otherwise requires:

Appointed Person means any person who is designated as a fee-earner in accordance with any arrangements made from time to time between the Firm and the Legal Services Commission pursuant to the provisions of the Access to Justice Act 1999, regardless of whether the services performed for the Firm by that person in accordance with Rule 4.1 are performed pursuant to such arrangements or otherwise, and who is engaged by the Firm under a contract for services in the course of the Private Practice of the Firm.

Commentary: Under Rule 4, work carried out by a designated fee-earner may be covered under the Qualifying Insurance of the Firm for which they do that work.

Approved Regulator means a body listed in the first column of the table in paragraph 1 of Schedule 4 to the Legal Services Act 2007 (whether or not that paragraph has been brought into force), or designated as an approved regulator by an order under Part 2 of that Schedule.

Assigned Risks Pool means the arrangements by which an Eligible Firm may obtain professional indemnity insurance against civil liability by means of an ARP Policy on the terms set out in Part 3 of these Rules.

Commentary: The Assigned Risks Pool is designed to ensure that professional indemnity insurance will be available to all Eligible Firms. However, it is important to note that premiums payable to the Assigned Risks Pool are intended to be high. Refer to Appendix 2 to the Rules for the method of calculation of the ARP Premium.

ARP Manager means the manager of the Assigned Risks Pool being any person from time to time appointed by the Society to carry out all or any particular functions of the ARP Manager or the Society and any such person.

ARP Policy means a contract of professional indemnity insurance issued by the ARP Manager on behalf of Qualifying Insurers to an Eligible Firm in the Assigned Risks Pool including where the context permits a Policy provided to a Firm in Default.

Commentary: A copy of the standard-form ARP Policy is available on the website of the Solicitors Regulation Authority at www.sra.org.uk, and is also available from the Solicitors Regulation Authority. Contact details appear at the end of the introductory commentary.

ARP Premium means the premium calculated in accordance with Part 1 of Appendix 2 to these Rules, ARP Default Premium means the premium calculated in accordance with Part 2 of Appendix 2 to these Rules and ARP Run-off Premium means the premium calculated in accordance with Part 3 of Appendix 2 to these Rules.

ARP Run-off Policy means a contract of professional indemnity insurance issued by the ARP Manager on behalf of Qualifying Insurers to a Run-off Firm in the Assigned Risks Pool.

Authorised Insurer means:

(a) a person who has permission under Part IV of the Financial Services and Markets Act 2000 to effect or carry out contracts of insurance of a relevant class;

(b) a person who carries on an insurance market activity, within the meaning of section 316(3) of that Act;

(c) an EEA Firm of the kind mentioned in paragraph 5(d) of Schedule 3 to that Act, which has permission under paragraph 15 of that Schedule (as a result of qualifying for authorisation under paragraph 12 of that Schedule) to effect or carry out contracts of insurance of a relevant class; or

(d) a person who does not fall within paragraph (i), (ii) or (iii) and who may lawfully effect or carry out contracts of insurance of a relevant class in a member state other than the United Kingdom

where relevant class has the meaning set out in section 87(1B) of the Solicitors Act 1974 and provided that this definition must be read with section 22 of the Financial Services and Markets Act 2000, any relevant order under that section and Schedule 2 to that Act.

Commentary: Under the Solicitors Act 1974, it is only permitted to enter into arrangements with authorised insurers (including relevant Lloyd's syndicates), as defined under section 87(1A) of that Act. A Qualifying Insurer must be authorised to write new business on the date on which a Policy incepts, but the Policy will remain a Policy of Qualifying Insurance until it expires, even if the Qualifying Insurer then ceases to write, or be authorised to write, new insurance business.

Council means the Council of the Society.

Difference In Conditions Policy means a contract of professional indemnity insurance, made between one or more Qualifying Insurers and a Firm, which provides cover including the Minimum Terms and Conditions as modified in accordance with paragraph 2 of Appendix 3 to these Rules.

Eligible Firm means any Firm which is eligible to be in the Assigned Risks Pool, being any Firm other than:

(a) a Firm that has been in the Assigned Risks Pool for twenty four months or more (or twenty five months or more in the case of a Firm which was in the Assigned Risks Pool for the whole of the Indemnity Period from 1 September 2003 to 30 September 2004) in the four Indemnity Periods immediately prior to the date from which cover is sought, without the prior written approval of the Council; or

(b) a Firm determined by the Council not to be an Eligible Firm by reason of its being treated as one single Firm with one or more other Firms already in the Assigned Risks Pool for the purposes of Rule 12.5 or Rule 12.6; or

(c) subject to Rule 12.3, a Firm that at the end of any Indemnity Period to which these Rules apply is in Policy Default; or

(d) a Firm which, at the time it applies to enter the Assigned Risks Pool, already has in place Qualifying Insurance outside the Assigned Risks Pool for the Indemnity Period in which that Firm requests cover through the Assigned Risks Pool to commence.

Commentary: Firms cannot remain insured through the Assigned Risks Pool indefinitely. For example, a Firm which has been insured through the Assigned Risks Pool for the 2005/06 and 2006/07 Indemnity Periods will not be eligible to be insured through the Assigned Risks Pool for the 2009/10 Indemnity Period. Subject to any waiver granted under Rule 19, any Firm which no longer fulfils the definition of an Eligible Firm is therefore required to obtain Qualifying Insurance from a Qualifying Insurer outside the Assigned Risks Pool, or to cease Practice.

In addition, a Firm is not eligible to join the Assigned Risks Pool if it has already obtained Qualifying Insurance from a Qualifying Insurer outside the Assigned Risks Pool for the relevant Indemnity Period.

Firm means:

(a) Recognised Sole Practitioner; or

(b) any Recognised Body (as constituted from time to time); or

(c) any solicitor or Registered European Lawyer who is a sole practitioner, unless that sole practitioner is a Non-SRA Firm; or

(d) any Partnership (as constituted from time to time) which is eligible to become a Recognised Body and which meets the requirements applicable to Recognised Bodies set out in rules 14.01, 14.03 and 14.04 of the Solicitors' Code of Conduct 2007, unless that Partnership is a Non-SRA Firm,

whether before or during any relevant Indemnity Period

Commentary: If you are unsure whether you or your business fall within this definition, you should consult the Solicitors Regulation Authority. Contact details appear at the end of the introductory commentary.

Firm in Default means a Firm that has failed to obtain Qualifying Insurance outside the Assigned Risks Pool and which,

(a) in the case of an Eligible Firm, has failed to apply in accordance with these Rules to be admitted into the Assigned Risks Pool before either the start of any Indemnity Period to which these Rules apply or the start of its Practice, whichever is the later; or

(b) in the case of a Firm which is not an Eligible Firm, is a Firm which is carrying on or continuing to carry on a Practice without Qualifying Insurance outside the Assigned Risks Pool; or

(c) in the case of a Run-off Firm, is a Run-off Firm which has failed to make an application in manner prescribed by these Rules to be issued with an ARP Run-off Policy; or

(d) is a Firm which is a Firm in Default by virtue of Rule 10.4,

or a Firm which, having previously obtained Qualifying Insurance, has failed to obtain alternative Qualifying Insurance when required to do so in accordance with Rule 6.

Commentary: A Firm In Default, and each Principal in that Firm, will be required to pay the ARP Default Premium, and/or the ARP Run-Off Premium to the Assigned Risks Pool, and each Principal in that Firm will have committed a disciplinary offence by having breached these Rules. Refer to Part 4 of these Rules for the provisions that apply to a Firm In Default.

Indemnity Period means the period of one year starting on 1 September 2000, 2001 or 2002, the period of 13 calendar months starting on 1 September 2003, or the period of one year starting on 1 October in any subsequent calendar year.

Commentary: Under the Qualifying Insurer's Agreement, each Policy is required to expire at the end of an Indemnity Period. It is envisaged that any change to these Rules or to the Minimum Terms and Conditions would take effect from the start of an Indemnity Period, so that at any one time, all Policies in force comply with the same version of these Rules and the Minimum Terms and Conditions.

Qualifying Insurers are permitted under the Qualifying Insurer's Agreement to issue a Policy covering more than one Indemnity Period, provided that the Policy expires at the end of a subsequent Indemnity Period, and provided that the terms of the Policy are amended if required to reflect any change in the Rules or the Minimum Terms and Conditions while the Policy is in force.

Insolvency Event means in relation to a Qualifying Insurer:

(a) the appointment of a provisional liquidator, administrator, receiver or an administrative receiver; or

(b) the approval of a voluntary arrangement under Part 1 of the Insolvency Act 1986 or the making of any other form of arrangement, composition or compounding with its creditors generally; or

(c) the passing of a resolution for voluntary winding up where the winding up is or becomes a creditors' voluntary winding up under Part IV of the Insolvency Act 1986; or

(d) the making of a winding up order by the court; or

(e) the making of an order by the court reducing the value of one or more of the Qualifying Insurer's contracts under section 377 of the Financial Services and Markets Act 2000; or

(f) the occurrence of any event analogous to any of the foregoing insolvency events in any jurisdiction outside England and Wales.

Limited Liability Partnership *means a limited liability partnership incorporated under the Limited* Liability Partnerships Act 2000.

Manager means:

(a) a Partner in a Partnership;

(b) a member of a Limited Liability Partnership; or

(c) a director of a company.

Minimum Terms and Conditions means the minimum terms and conditions with which a Policy of Qualifying Insurance is required by these Rules to comply a copy of which is annexed as Appendix 1 to these Rules.

Commentary: All Qualifying Insurers agree under the Qualifying Insurer's Agreement to issue Policies which comply with the Minimum Terms and Conditions. However, under Rule 4 it remains the duty of each Firm and each Principal within that Firm to ensure that the Policy issued to it is issued by an insurer which is a Qualifying Insurer for the Indemnity Period in question, and that it complies with the Minimum Terms and Conditions. The SRA does not approve Qualifying Insurers, nor does it review their policy terms.

The standard form ARP Policy does comply with the Minimum Terms and Conditions.

In addition, each Firm should satisfy itself that the professional indemnity insurance that it has in place is sufficient. This may mean that the Firm takes out additional insurance over and above that provided under the Minimum Terms and Conditions. Any such "top-up" cover is outside the scope of these Rules, and does not have to be taken out with a Qualifying Insurer.

Most recognised bodies are required to obtain cover complying with the minimum terms and conditions and with a sum insured of £3 million, rather than £2 million for other Firms. The definition of "Relevant Recognised Body" in clause 8.2 of the Minimum Terms and Conditions indicates which recognised bodies this requirement applies to.

Non-SRA Firm means a sole practitioner, Partnership, Limited Liability Partnership or company which is not authorised to practise by the Solicitors Regulation Authority, and which is either:
(a) authorised or capable of being authorised to practise by another Approved Regulator; or
(b) not capable of being authorised to practise by any Approved Regulator.

Partnership means an unincorporated Firm in which persons are or are held out as partners and does not include a Firm incorporated as a Limited Liability Partnership and Partner means a person who is or is held out to be a partner in a Partnership.

Commentary: A limited liability partnership is treated for these purposes as a Recognised Body, rather than as a partnership.

Period Of Default means in relation to a Firm in Default the period starting with the date when such Firm first became a Firm in Default and ending with the date when it ceased to be a Firm in Default.

Policy means a contract of professional indemnity insurance made between one or more persons, each of which is a Qualifying Insurer, and a Firm, including where the context permits an ARP Policy and an ARP Run-off Policy.

Policy Default means a failure on the part of a Firm or any Principal of that Firm:
(a) to pay for more than two months after the due date for payment all or any part of the premium or any other sum due in respect of a Policy (including without limitation any payment due under Rule 14.1); or
(b) to pay for more than two months after the due date for payment all or any part of any ARP Premium, any ARP Default Premium, or any ARP Run-Off Premium, or any instalment payable in relation thereto whether payable to the ARP Manager or otherwise; or
(c) to reimburse within two months a Qualifying Insurer (including the ARP Manager on behalf of Qualifying Insurers) in respect of any amount falling within a Firm's Policy excess which has been paid on an insured's behalf to a claimant by a Qualifying Insurer or by the ARP Manager.

For the purposes of this definition, the due date for payment means, in respect of any Policy or any payment to be made under any Policy:
(i) the date on which such payment fell due under the terms of the Policy or any related agreement or arrangement; or
(ii) if a Firm was first required under these or any previous Rules to effect such a Policy prior to the date on which it did so, the date if earlier on which such payment would have fallen due had such Policy been effected by the Firm when it was first required to do so under these Rules or any previous rules.

Commentary: Principals are committing a disciplinary offence if they or their Firm is in Policy Default, whether as a result of failing to pay premium when demanded or as a result of failing to take out a Policy when required to do so. In addition, their Firm will cease to be an Eligible Firm for the purpose of taking out or renewing an ARP Policy.

Practice means the whole or such part of the Private Practice of a Firm as is carried on from one or more offices in England and Wales.

Commentary: The Rules require Firms to take out Policies which include cover in accordance with the Minimum Terms and Conditions for that part of their Practice carried on from offices located in England and Wales. They do not apply to any part of the Practice of the Firm carried on from offices outside England and Wales (although rule 15.26 of the Solicitors' Code of Conduct 2007 does apply in such cases). However, the cover in relation to the Practice carried on from offices located in England and Wales must extend to acts or omissions wherever in the world they occur, and would therefore include, for example, a Principal based in a Firm's London office who travels to Paris to advise a client.

If you are unsure whether you or your business fall within this definition, you should consult the Solicitors Regulation Authority. Contact details appear at the end of the introductory commentary.

Principal means:

(a) where the Firm is or was:

- (i) a sole practitioner - that practitioner;
- (ii) a Partnership - each Partner;
- (iii) a company with a share capital - each director of that company and any solicitor, Registered European Lawyer or Registered Foreign Lawyer who:
  - (A) is held out as a director; or
  - (B) beneficially owns the whole or any part of a share in the company; or
  - (C) is the ultimate beneficial owner of the whole or any part of a share in the company.
- (iv) a company without a share capital - each director of that company and any solicitor, Registered European Lawyer or Registered Foreign Lawyer who:
  - (A) is held out as a director; or
  - (B) is a member of the company; or
  - (C) is the ultimate owner of the whole or any part of a body corporate or other legal person which is a member of the company;
- (v) a Limited Liability Partnership - each member of that Limited Liability Partnership, and any solicitor, Registered European Lawyer or Registered Foreign Lawyer who is the ultimate owner of the whole or any part of a body corporate or other legal person which is member of the Limited Liability Partnership.

(b) where a body corporate or other legal person is a Partner in the Firm, all solicitors, Registered European Lawyers or Registered Foreign Lawyers who are within paragraph (a)(iii) of this definition (including sub paragraphs (A) and (C) thereof), paragraph (a)(iv) of this definition (including sub paragraphs (A) and (C) thereof), or paragraph a(v) of this definition.

Commentary: It is the duty of each Principal, under Rule 4, to ensure that the Firm has Qualifying Insurance at all times.

Private Practice includes without limitation all the professional services provided by a Firm including acting as a personal representative, trustee, attorney, notary, insolvency practitioner or in any other role in conjunction with a Practice, and includes services provided pro bono publico, but does not include:

(a) Practice carried on by a Solicitor or Registered European Lawyer in the course of employment with an employer other than a Firm; or

(b) Practice carried on through a Non-SRA Firm; or

(c) discharging the functions of any of the following offices or appointments:

- (i) judicial office;
- (ii) Under Sheriffs;
- (iii) members and clerks of such tribunals, committees, panels and boards as the Council may from time to time designate but including those subject to the Tribunals and Inquiries Act 1992, the Competition Commission, Legal Services Commission Review Panels and Parole Boards;
- (iv) Justices' Clerks;
- (v) Superintendent Registrars and Deputy Superintendent Registrars of Births, Marriages and Deaths and Registrars of Local Crematoria;
- (vi) such other offices as the Council may from time to time designate; or

(d) Practice consisting only of:

- (i) providing professional services without remuneration for friends, relatives, or companies wholly owned by the solicitor or Registered European Lawyer's family, or registered charities; or
- (ii) administering oaths and taking affidavits.

Commentary: If you are unsure whether you or your Practice fall within this definition, you should consult the Solicitors Regulation Authority. Contact details appear at the end of the introductory commentary.

Qualifying Insurance means a single Policy which includes the Minimum Terms and Conditions, or more than one Policy which, taken together, include the Minimum Terms and Conditions, and each of which includes the Minimum Terms and Conditions except only in relation to the Sum Insured (as defined in the Minimum Terms and Conditions).

Commentary: All Firms are required to take out and maintain, as a minimum, Qualifying Insurance. This may take the form of a single policy, or policies written by more than one Qualifying Insurer which together provide the minimum cover required under these Rules.

Qualifying Insurer means an Authorised Insurer which has entered into a Qualifying Insurer's agreement with the Society which remains in force for the purposes of underwriting new business at the date on which the relevant contract of Qualifying Insurance is made.

Commentary: A list of all Qualifying Insurers appears on the website of the Solicitors Regulation Authority at www.sra.org.uk, and is also available from the Solicitors Regulation Authority. Contact details appear at the end of the introductory commentary.

Qualifying Insurer's Agreement means an agreement in such terms as the Society may from time to time prescribe setting out the terms and conditions on which a Qualifying Insurer may provide professional indemnity insurance to solicitors and others in Private Practice in England and Wales.

Commentary: A copy of this standard form agreement, which each Qualifying Insurer is required to enter into, is available on request from the Solicitors Regulation Authority. Contact details appear at the end of the introductory commentary.

Recognised Body means a body for the time being recognised by the Solicitors Regulation Authority under section 9 of the Administration of Justice Act 1985 and the SRA Recognised Bodies Regulations 2009.

Recognised Sole Practitioner means a solicitor or Registered European Lawyer authorised by the Solicitors Regulation Authority under section 1B of the Solicitors Act 1974 to practise as a sole practitioner.

Registered European Lawyer means an individual registered with the Society under regulation 17 of the European Communities (Lawyer's Practice) Regulations 2000.

Registered Foreign Lawyer means an individual registered with the Society under section 89 of the Courts and Legal Services Act 1990.

Rules means these rules as from time to time modified or amended.

Run-off Firm means a Firm or former Firm which has ceased to practise in circumstances where, in accordance with paragraph 5.1 of the Minimum Terms and Conditions, run-off cover is not required to be provided by any Qualifying Insurer.

Society means the Law Society of England and Wales.

Solicitor means a person who has been admitted as a solicitor and whose name is on the roll (within the meaning of the Solicitors Act 1974) and who practises as a solicitor whether or not he or she has in force a practising certificate as referred to in that Act and also includes practice under home title of a former Registered European Lawyer who has become a solicitor.

Solicitors Regulation Authority means the Solicitors Regulation Authority carrying out regulatory functions assigned to the Law Society as an Approved Regulator.

Special Measures means such measures as the Council may from time to time require with a view to reducing the risk of claims being made against a Firm in the future or with a view to enabling a Firm in the future to obtain Qualifying Insurance outside the Assigned Risks Pool.

Supplementary Run-off Cover means run-off cover provided by the Solicitors Indemnity Fund following the expiry of run-off cover provided to a Firm in accordance with these Rules or otherwise under a Policy (but subject to compliance with the Minimum Terms and Conditions).

3.2 Interpretation

In these Rules, unless the context otherwise requires:
(a) the singular includes the plural, and vice versa;

(b) a reference to a person includes a body corporate, partnerships, and other unincorporated associations or bodies of persons;
(c) a reference to a Rule is to a Rule forming part of these Rules;
(d) a reference to any statute, statutory provision, code or regulation includes:
 (i) any subordinate legislation (as defined by section 21(1) of the Interpretation Act 1978) made under it; and
 (ii) any provision which it has superseded or re-enacted (with or without modification) or amended, and any provision superseding it or re-enacting it (with or without modification) or amending it either before, or at the date of the commencement of these Rules, or after the date of the commencement of these Rules;
(e) references to the Society and to the Council include the Solicitors Regulation Authority and the Legal Complaints Service, and any body or person which succeeds in whole or in part to the functions of the Society, the Council, the Solicitors Regulation Authority or the Legal Complaints Service, and any delegate of the Society, the Council, the Solicitors Regulation Authority, the Legal Complaints Service or any such body or person;
(f) headings are for ease of reference only and shall not affect the interpretation of these Rules;
(g) explanatory notes and commentary shall be ignored in interpreting these Rules; and
(h) the appendices to these Rules form part of these Rules.

These Rules will be governed by and interpreted in accordance with English law.

PART 2: RESPONSIBILITY AND MONITORING

4 Obligation to effect insurance

[5011]
4.1 All Firms carrying on a Practice during any Indemnity Period beginning on or after 1 October 2009 must take out and maintain Qualifying Insurance under these Rules.

4.2 A solicitor or Registered European Lawyer is not required to take out and maintain Qualifying Insurance under these Rules in respect of work done as an employee or whilst otherwise directly engaged in the Practice of another Firm (including without limitation as an Appointed Person), where that Firm is required by these Rules to take out and maintain Qualifying Insurance.

4.3 Run-off Firm must apply in accordance with these Rules to be issued with an ARP Run-off Policy.

Commentary: Under these Rules, Firms have a continuing obligation to ensure that they have Qualifying Insurance in place at all times with effect from 1 October 2009. Refer to the definitions of Practice, amongst others, to establish whether a Firm falls within the scope of these Rules. Firms should also check that any insurance that they take out in order to comply with these Rules (as opposed to any "top-up" cover) is taken out with a Qualifying Insurer. A list of Qualifying Insurers appears on the website of the Solicitors Regulation Authority at www.sra.org.uk, and is also available from the Solicitors Regulation Authority. Contact details appear at the end of the introductory commentary.

Firms should note in particular that work carried out by an Appointed Person for that Firm may be covered by the Firm's Policy, whether that person is engaged as an employee or on a contract for services.

If a Firm cannot obtain a Policy from a Qualifying Insurer it should apply to join the Assigned Risks Pool in accordance with Part 3 of the Rules, if it is an Eligible Firm. If it is not an Eligible Firm, it must cease Practice.

Note that, under the Minimum Terms and Conditions, a Policy, once taken out, cannot be cancelled before the end of an Indemnity Period unless:

(1) the Policy is an ARP Policy and the Firm has replaced it with a Policy of Qualifying Insurance outside the Assigned Risks Pool; or

(2) the Firm merges with another Firm and a Policy of Qualifying Insurance is in place for the merged Firm; or

(3) it subsequently transpires that the Firm was not in fact required to take out and maintain a Policy under these Rules; or

(4) in the case of an ARP Policy, it subsequently transpires that the Firm was not was not, or has ceased to be, an Eligible Firm; or the Qualifying Insurer which issues the Policy becomes the subject of an Insolvency Event, and the Firm has replaced the Policy with another Policy of Qualifying Insurance.

The effect of cancellation in the circumstances described in (3) or (4) above is that the Firm ceases to have Qualifying Insurance in place with effect from the cancellation, and would therefore be in breach of Rule 4.1 if it were to carry on a Practice thereafter without taking out a new Policy.

Most Recognised Bodies are required to obtain cover complying with the Minimum Terms and Conditions and with a sum insured of £3 million, rather than £2 million for other Firms. The definition of "Relevant Recognised Body" in clause 8.2 of the Minimum Terms and Conditions indicates which Recognised Bodies this requirement applies to.

4.4 The provisions of this Rule 4 shall be without prejudice to the ability of Firms to include as insureds on a Policy persons not required under these Rules to be insured.

5 Responsibility

5.1 Each Firm carrying on a Practice during any Indemnity Period beginning on or after 1 October 2009, and any person who is a Principal of such a Firm, must ensure:

(a) that the Firm has in place and maintains Qualifying Insurance outside the Assigned Risks Pool during any such Indemnity Period;

or, in the case of an Eligible Firm,

(b) that the Firm has applied to enter the Assigned Risks Pool in accordance with the procedure set out in Rule 10;

in either case before the start of any relevant Indemnity Period or the start of Practice whichever is later.

Commentary: Note that the duty to ensure that Qualifying Insurance is in place rests not just on the Firm as a whole, but also on every Principal within that Firm.

5.2 A Run-off Firm, and any person who was a Principal of that Run-off Firm immediately prior to it becoming a Run-off Firm, must ensure that the Run-off Firm has applied to enter the Assigned Risks Pool in accordance with the procedure set out in Rule 13.4(a). Making such an application does not absolve any Firm or person from any breach of Rule 5.1.

Commentary: A Firm which has continued to practise without Qualifying Insurance immediately prior to closing down is required to apply for Run-Off Cover through the Assigned Risks Pool, but the Firm and any Principal of the Firm may still face action for a breach of Rule 5.1 for practising without Qualifying Insurance.

6 Insolvency of Qualifying Insurer

6.1 If a Firm is carrying on a Practice which is being provided with Qualifying Insurance by a Qualifying Insurer (whether alone or together with other Qualifying Insurers) and that Qualifying Insurer is the subject of an Insolvency Event then, subject to any waiver under Rule 19.1, the Firm and any person who is a Principal of the Firm must ensure:

(a) that the Firm has in place Qualifying Insurance with another Qualifying Insurer which must be arranged as soon as may be reasonably practicable and in any event within four weeks of such an Insolvency Event;

or, in the case of an Eligible Firm,

(b) that the Firm applies within that period of four weeks to enter the Assigned Risks Pool in accordance with the procedure set out in Rule 10.

Commentary: It is important to be aware that the arrangements for professional indemnity insurance put in place by the Solicitors Regulation Authority do not seek to protect Firms against the insolvency of a Qualifying Insurer. If an Insolvency Event occurs in respect of an insurer, that insurer will cease to be a Qualifying Insurer for the purposes of these Rules. This is because, in such circumstances, the insurer may not be in a position to pay claims in full. Any Firm which has qualifying insurance with a Qualifying Insurer which is the subject of an Insolvency Event must therefore obtain replacement cover as soon as possible, and in any event within four weeks of the Insolvency Event occurring. Having done so, a Firm should cancel the policy with the insolvent insurer and, if entitled to do so, seek a return of the premium relating to the balance of the Indemnity Period from the insurer which has become the subject of the Insolvency Event.

7 Monitoring

The Council may require from a Firm or any Principal in a Firm carrying on, or reasonably believed by the Council to be carrying on, a Practice such information and evidence as it may reasonably require to satisfy itself that such a Firm has in place Qualifying Insurance.

8 Registered European Lawyers

8.1 The special provisions contained in Appendix 3 to these Rules shall apply to a Firm that has at least one Principal who is a Registered European Lawyer.

PART 3: THE ASSIGNED RISKS POOL

9 Operation of the Assigned Risks Pool

[5012]

The Assigned Risks Pool shall be managed by the ARP Manager.

10 Applying to the Assigned Risks Pool

10.1 Where a Firm carrying on a Practice has not obtained Qualifying Insurance outside the Assigned Risks Pool in respect of any Indemnity Period or part thereof to which these Rules apply it must, if an Eligible Firm, apply in accordance with the procedure set out in this Rule 10 to enter the Assigned Risks Pool, subject to Rule 10.2, before the start of the relevant Indemnity Period.

Commentary: A Firm which for any reason does not have Qualifying Insurance in place should apply to the Assigned Risks Pool before the start of the relevant Indemnity Period if it is an Eligible Firm. However, it is important to note that premiums payable to the Assigned Risks Pool are intended to be high, and Firms would therefore be prudent to seek quotations from Qualifying Insurers outside the Assigned Risks Pool before the start of an Indemnity Period.

An ARP Policy can be cancelled if it is replaced by a Policy with a Qualifying Insurer. A return premium may be payable to a Firm which cancels an ARP Policy in these circumstances – refer to Appendix 2 for the basis on which the ARP Premium and any return premium is calculated.

Firms should also be aware of the other consequences of being insured through the Assigned Risks Pool set out in this part of the Rules, including the need to comply with any Special Measures under Rule 10, and the limitations on eligibility set out in the definition of "Eligible Firm".

10.2 A Firm about to start carrying on a Practice which has not already obtained Qualifying Insurance outside the Assigned Risks Pool may, if an Eligible Firm, apply to enter the Assigned Risks Pool after the start of any relevant Indemnity Period. A Firm must not start carrying on a Practice without either having obtained Qualifying Insurance outside the Assigned Risks Pool or, alternatively, in the case of an Eligible Firm, without having applied in accordance with the procedure set out in this Rule 10 to enter the Assigned Risks Pool.

Commentary: Any Firm wishing to start up a new Practice must obtain Qualifying Insurance, whether in the open market with a Qualifying Insurer or through the Assigned Risks Pool, before starting Practice. Subject to this requirement, a new Firm may start Practice at any time during an Indemnity Period.

10.3 By applying to enter the Assigned Risks Pool, the Firm and any person who is a Principal of that Firm agrees to, and (if the Firm is admitted to the Assigned Risks Pool) the Firm and any person who is a Principal of that Firm shall be jointly and severally liable to:

(a) pay the ARP Premium in accordance with these Rules, together with any other sums due to the ARP Manager under the ARP Policy; and

(b) submit to such investigation and monitoring and to pay the Society's costs and expenses as referred to in Rule 11.2; and

(c) pay any costs and expenses incurred by the Society or the ARP Manager incurred as a result of any failure or delay by the Firm in complying with these Rules;

and shall be required to implement at the expense of the Firm any Special Measures.

Commentary: Firms within the Assigned Risks Pool may be subject to a range of Special Measures. The appointed inspectors (in the first instance, the Forensic Investigations Unit of the Compliance Directorate) will visit a Firm insured through the Assigned Risks Pool to carry out investigation and monitoring of the Firm. This is in order to determine what Special Measures are appropriate for that Firm, and to ensure that those measures are fully implemented. It should be noted that the costs of investigation and monitoring by the Inspection & Investigation Directorate, costs and expenses incurred through any failure or delay by the Firm to comply, and the implementation of the Special Measures will be payable by the Firm concerned (and by any Principal of that Firm), in addition to paying the ARP Premium.

10.4 Any material misrepresentation made in an application for admission to the Assigned Risks Pool shall, subject to any waiver under Rule 19.1, render the Firm a Firm in Default for the purposes of Part 4 of these Rules. The provisions of that Part shall apply to the Firm as if that Firm had not been admitted to the Assigned Risks Pool but neither the Firm nor any Principal of the Firm shall be entitled to the refund of any ARP Premium paid to the ARP Manager. Any amount so paid shall be credited against any sums payable under Part 4 of these Rules.

Commentary: Although an ARP Policy, once issued, cannot be cancelled (unless and until a replacement Policy with a Qualifying Insurer is issued to that Firm), a Firm which makes a material misrepresentation in its application to be admitted to the Assigned Risks Pool will be nevertheless treated in the same way as a Firm in Default.

10.5 The application for admission to the Assigned Risks Pool must be made to the ARP Manager on the proposal form provided by the ARP Manager.

10.6 The applicant must state on the proposal form the date from which cover is sought. This date must not be earlier than the date on which the application is made for admission to the Assigned Risks Pool. The applicant must also provide such other information as the ARP Manager requires for the purposes of setting a premium.

10.7 If the applicant is a Firm in Default it must state on the proposal form that it is a Firm in Default and give the date of the start of the Period of Default from which retrospective cover is sought.

Commentary: The ARP Premium is calculated in accordance with a formula set out in Appendix 2, and is linked to the gross fees of the Firm concerned. It is important to note that, under Rule 15, any material misrepresentation in an application will result in the Firm being treated in the same way as a Firm In Default, including being liable to pay the ARP Default Premium.

10.8 The Firm, together with each Principal of the Firm, must ensure that the Firm's application has been made and must provide the ARP Manager with all information it reasonably requires to process the application.

Commentary: It is in the interests of the Firm and each of the Principals of that Firm to verify that the application to enter the Assigned Risks Pool has been received and that the Firm is insured. An application should be made before the start of an Indemnity Period. Failure to comply with the requirements of this Rule and Rules 13 to 15 will result in the Firm becoming a Firm in Default.

10.9 If a Firm has not received a written acknowledgement of its application from the ARP Manager 30 days after making the application, or within such other period as is stated on the proposal form, the Firm and any person who is a Principal of the Firm must seek written confirmation that the Firm's application has been received by the ARP Manager. If that written confirmation is not obtained within seven days after the end of the 30 days, or within seven days after such other period specified on the proposal form, the application shall be deemed not to have been made.

10.10 An applicant whose first application is deemed under Rule 10.9 not to have been made must, within seven days of the day when under Rule 10.9 the first application is deemed not to have been made, make a fresh application. The Firm and any person who is a Principal of the Firm must ensure that the Firm is in a position to prove to the reasonable satisfaction of the Society that the Firm's fresh application was delivered within those seven days to the ARP Manager at the address specified on the proposal form. Provided the Firm's fresh application was so delivered, the application shall be treated as having been made at the date when the Firm's first application was made. A Firm that is not in a position to prove to the reasonable satisfaction of the Society that its fresh application was so delivered shall be deemed not to have made any application.

10.11 Provided that an application or, if necessary, a fresh application, has been made in accordance with Rules 10.5 to 10.10, a Firm which is an Eligible Firm will be covered in the terms of the ARP Policy to be issued to it from the start of the relevant Indemnity Period or, in the case of a Firm to which Rule 10.2 applies, the date specified in the application, being the date specified in accordance with Rule 10.6, until whichever is the earlier of:

(a) the end of the relevant Indemnity Period; or

(b) the date on which the Firm obtains Qualifying Insurance outside the Assigned Risks Pool; or

(c) the date when the Firm ceases to be an Eligible Firm.

Commentary: An Eligible Firm which should have applied to the Assigned Risks Pool before the start of an Indemnity Period but fails to do so will have breached these Rules by failing to take out a Policy from the start of the Indemnity Period. It may make a later application, but will be liable to pay the ARP Default Premium for the Indemnity Period in question. Each Principal in an Eligible Firm which fails to make an application in time commits a disciplinary offence.

10.12 Any Firm in the Assigned Risks Pool, and any person who is a Principal of that Firm, is liable to pay to the ARP Manager the ARP Premium in respect of that Firm within thirty days of such premium being notified to it by the ARP Manager.

Commentary: It is a disciplinary offence for a Firm and for any Principal of that Firm to fail to pay the ARP Premium (including the ARP Run-off Premium) to the ARP Manager within the required 30 day period. A Firm may enter into arrangements with, for example, a premium funding company (whether offered by the ARP Manager or arranged independently) to enable it to make payments by instalments, provided that the premium is received in full by the ARP Manager from the premium funding company within the required 30 day period.

11 Special Measures

11.1 An Eligible Firm that has applied to enter the Assigned Risks Pool in accordance with the procedure set out in Rule 10 will be issued with an ARP Policy by the ARP Manager.

Commentary: A copy of the standard-form ARP Policy is available on the website of the Solicitors Regulation Authority at www.sra.org.uk and is also available from the Solicitors Regulation Authority. Contact details appear at the end of the introductory commentary.

11.2 A Firm in the Assigned Risks Pool must if and to the extent required by the Council submit to investigation and monitoring by the Society and/or its agents, including investigation and monitoring:

(a) to determine the reasons why Qualifying Insurance outside the Assigned Risks Pool was not obtained;

(b) to ascertain what Special Measures should be taken by the Firm.

The Society's costs and expenses of the investigation and monitoring and the Society's costs and expenses of ascertaining what Special Measures should be taken and of monitoring them shall be met by the Firm and by any person who is a Principal of that Firm. The amount of such costs and expenses shall be determined by the Society which shall not be required to give any detailed breakdown thereof.

Commentary: The appointed inspectors (in the first instance, the Forensic Investigations Department of the Inspection & Investigation Directorate) will visit a Firm insured through the Assigned Risks Pool to carry out investigation and monitoring. This is in order to determine what Special Measures should be taken and are appropriate for that Firm, and to ensure that those measures are fully implemented. It should be noted that the costs and expenses of investigation and monitoring by the Inspection & Investigation Directorate and the implementation of the Special Measures (together with VAT if applicable) will be payable by the Firm concerned (including each Principal of that Firm), in addition to paying the ARP Premium.

12 Time in the Assigned Risks Pool

12.1 A Firm may leave the Assigned Risks Pool at any time after it has satisfied the ARP Manager that the Firm has obtained Qualifying Insurance outside the Assigned Risks Pool at least until the expiry of the relevant Indemnity Period.

Commentary: Refer to Appendix 2 to determine whether any return premium will be payable on leaving the Assigned Risks Pool.

12.2 Subject to Rule 12.7, a Firm may only remain in the Assigned Risks Pool so long as it is an Eligible Firm, or if it becomes a Run-off Firm.

Commentary: Firms cannot remain insured through the Assigned Risks Pool for more than 24 months in any five year period, and should therefore seek insurance in the open market with a Qualifying Insurer as soon as practicable. A Firm which is no longer an Eligible Firm (because, for example, it has already been insured through the Assigned Risks Pool for 24 months in the last five years) must either obtain Qualifying Insurance on the open market or cease carrying on Practice.

12.3 Subject to Rule 12.7(b), a Firm in Policy Default at the end of an Indemnity Period shall be deemed to be a Firm in Default for the purposes of Part 4 of these Rules and shall not be an Eligible Firm. This Rule shall not apply in any case where the Council is satisfied that there exists a genuine dispute between the Firm and a Qualifying Insurer or the ARP Manager which makes it unreasonable for the Firm to be deemed to be a Firm in Default pending the resolution of that dispute.

Commentary: A Firm in Policy Default must remedy that default before the start of an Indemnity Period if it wishes to obtain insurance through the Assigned Risks Pool at any time during that Indemnity Period. Alternatively, it must either obtain Qualifying Insurance in the open market, or cease carrying on Practice. If a Firm believes that there is a genuine dispute which justifies that Firm not being deemed to be a Firm in Default, it should apply to the Solicitors Regulation Authority as soon as possible before the start of the next Indemnity Period. Contact details appear at the end of the introductory commentary.

12.4 A Firm that is no longer an Eligible Firm must either have Qualifying Insurance outside the Assigned Risks Pool or forthwith cease carrying on Practice.

12.5 Where the Practice of a Firm (the **Original Firm**) which has at any time been in the Assigned Risks Pool is split between two or more Firms (the **Successor Firms**), the Council may in its absolute discretion treat the Successor Firms or any of them and the Original Firm as being a single Firm for the purposes of determining whether the Successor Firms or any of them are or remain an Eligible Firm.

12.6 Where the Practice of a Firm (the **Original Firm**) which has at any time been in the Assigned Risks Pool is merged with, acquired, absorbed, or by any other means taken over by a Firm (the **Successor Firm**) the Council may in its absolute discretion treat the Successor Firm and the Original Firm as being a Single Firm for the purposes of determining whether the Successor Firm is or remains an Eligible Firm.

Commentary: The purpose of this Rule is to ensure that the time limit on participation in the Assigned Risks Pool cannot be avoided by a merger or reconstitution of that Firm. A Firm which was not previously eligible to join the Assigned Risks Pool will not necessarily become an Eligible Firm by virtue of changes in the composition of a Firm. Firms which are unsure about their eligibility following any such change should consult the Solicitors Regulation Authority. Contact details appear at the end of the introductory commentary.

12.7 The Council shall have power in any particular case or cases:

(a) to allow a Firm to remain in or to re-enter the Assigned Risks Pool after any date when the Firm would otherwise cease to be an Eligible Firm; and

(b) to permit a Firm to be admitted into or remain in or to re-enter the Assigned Risks Pool notwithstanding that the Firm is in Policy Default on such terms and conditions as the Council may prescribe including the taking of steps by the Firm by a specified date or dates to remedy the Policy Default;

and when such power is exercised the Firm shall continue to be an Eligible Firm for so long as the Council may from time to time permit and provided that it complies with any such terms and conditions.

Commentary: It is envisaged that these powers would be exercised only in exceptional circumstances. Any application seeking the exercise of this power should be made to the Solicitors Regulation Authority at least three months before the Firm in question would otherwise cease to be an Eligible Firm.

PART 4: FIRMS IN DEFAULT

13 Eligibility of Firms in Default

[5013]

13.1 At any time during the Period of Default a Firm in Default is entitled to be admitted to the Assigned Risks Pool and to be issued with an ARP Policy in accordance with Rule 13.2, subject to the provisions of this Rule 13.

13.2 A Firm in Default is entitled to be admitted to the Assigned Risks Pool if:

(a) it was an Eligible Firm at the start of the Period of Default;

(b) had it been admitted to the Assigned Risks Pool at the start of the Period of Default, its admission at that time would not have rendered it ineligible to be admitted to the Assigned Risks Pool for any part of any subsequent Indemnity Period in which it was in fact admitted to the Assigned Risks Pool;

(c) it has applied to join the Assigned Risks Pool in accordance with Rule 10;

(d) the Firm discharges in full the ARP Default Premium calculated for the whole of the Indemnity Period or Indemnity Periods for which cover is sought within 30 days of such premium being notified to it by the ARP Manager or such longer period as the Council may allow;

(e) the Firm will be subject to and company with Rules 10.3(b) (other than Rule 10.3(a)) and 11.2.

Commentary: If a Firm fails to make an application to the Assigned Risks Pool at the start of an Indemnity Period, and does not have any other Policy of Qualifying Insurance in force for that Indemnity Period, it may still be eligible to be issued with an ARP Policy provided that it meets all of the requirements of Rule 13.2. However, each Principal of the Firm will have committed a disciplinary offence, and the Firm and each Principal of that Firm will be liable to pay the ARP Default Premium under any ARP Policy issued.

13.3 An ARP Policy issued under this Rule may afford cover retrospectively from the start of the Period of Default until the earlier of:

(a) the end of the then current Indemnity Period or;

(b) the date on which the Firm in Default would have ceased to be an Eligible Firm, ignoring for these purposes any failure to pay the ARP Premium or the ARP Default Premium; or

(c) the date on which, had the Firm in Default been admitted to the Assigned Risks Pool at the start of the Period of Default, its being covered by the Assigned Risks Pool from that time would have first caused it to have been ineligible to be admitted to the Assigned Risks Pool for any part of any subsequent Indemnity Period in which it was in fact admitted to the Assigned Risks Pool.

13.4 A Run-off Firm shall be entitled at any time following the date on which it first becomes a Run-off Firm to be admitted to the Assigned Risks Pool and to be issued with an ARP Run-off Policy, subject to the following conditions:

(a) the Run-off Firm has made an application to join the Assigned Risks Pool in manner provided by Rule 10.5 stating on the proposal form that it is a Run-off Firm and giving the date from which cover under an ARP Run-off Policy is sought;

(b) the ARP Run-off Premium is discharged in full within thirty days of such premium being notified by the ARP Manager to the Firm or such longer period as the Council may allow; and

(c) the Firm, and any person who is a Principal of that Firm, will be subject to and comply with Rule 10.3(c).

Commentary: A Run-off Firm will be eligible to be issued with an ARP Policy if it meets all of the requirements of Rule 13.4. However, each Principal of the Firm will have committed a disciplinary offence for failing to make an application to the Assigned Risks Pool for run-off cover in accordance with Rule 5.2, and the Firm and each Principal of the Firm will be required to pay the ARP Run-off Premium under any ARP Run-off Policy issued.

13.5 An ARP Run-off Policy shall provide run-off cover to a Run-off Firm retrospectively from the date on which it became a Run-off Firm until the end of the day immediately prior to the sixth anniversary of:

(a) the start of the Indemnity Period in which it became a Run-off Firm; or

(b) if applicable, the start of the last Indemnity Period, prior to it becoming a Run-off Firm, in which it both ceased to be an Eligible Firm and was a Firm in Default and continued as such until the date on which it became a Run-off Firm,

whichever is the earlier.

Commentary: Run-off Firms which are issued with an ARP Run-off Policy obtain six years' run-off cover either from the start of the Indemnity Period in which their Practice ceased, or the date on which they ceased to be eligible to apply for an ARP Policy while practising uninsured.

13.6 Rule 12.7 shall apply so as to enable the Council to extend the period in Rule 13.3(b) for which a Firm in Default may be issued with an ARP Policy.

Commentary: It is envisaged that this power would be exercised only in exceptional circumstances.

13.7 Any Firm that has been admitted to the Assigned Risks Pool under Rule 13.1 shall for the purposes of computing its continuing eligibility to remain in the Assigned Risks Pool be deemed to have been admitted to the Assigned Risks Pool at start of the Period of Default and to have remained continuously in the Assigned Risks Pool until the end of the Indemnity Period current at the date of its application.

13.8 Rule 15.2 shall not apply to a Firm which has under Rule 13 been admitted to the Assigned Risks Pool and which has been issued with an ARP Policy or an ARP Run-off Policy, the liability of the Firm and of any person who is a Principal of that Firm being limited in those circumstances to the excess payable under the terms of the Policy.

Commentary: If a Firm is eligible to be issued with an ARP Policy under Rule 13.1, or an ARP Run-off Policy under Rule 13.4 then, provided that it complies with the relevant requirements under Rule 13 and is issued with an ARP Policy or an ARP Run-off Policy, the Firm and the Principals of that Firm will be required to pay to the ARP Manager only the relevant premium and the excess in the event of any claim.

14 Firms which fail to apply to the Assigned Risks Pool

14.1 A Firm in Default which is entitled to be admitted to the Assigned Risks Pool and to be issued with an ARP Policy in accordance with Rule 13.1 but which does not make an application to join the Assigned Risks Pool shall, notwithstanding, be liable, together with any person who is a Principal of that Firm, to pay to the Society an amount equivalent to the ARP Default Premium calculated for the whole of the Period of Default.

14.2 A Firm in Default which is entitled to be admitted to the Assigned Risks Pool and to be issued with an ARP Run-off Policy in accordance with Rules 13.4 and 13.5 but which does not make an application to join the Assigned Risks Pool shall, notwithstanding, be liable, together with any person who is a Principal of that Firm, to pay to the Society an amount equivalent to the ARP Run-off Premium calculated for the whole of the period equivalent to that which would be provided by an ARP Run-off Policy in accordance with Rule 13.5, or, if shorter and if it can be ascertained, the Period of Default.

14.3 Any amount payable in accordance with Rules 14.1 or 14.2 shall be determined by the ARP Manager on the basis of such assumption as to the Firm's gross fees and other matters as the ARP Manager shall in its absolute discretion determine, and may be reviewed from time to time by the ARP Manager in its absolute discretion on the basis of any further information provided to it. Any such amount paid under Rule 14.1 or 14.2 shall be deducted from any amount payable pursuant to Rule 15.2. The ARP Manager may and is hereby authorised to recover all sums due under Rules 14.1 or 14.2 on behalf of the Society.

Commentary: If a Firm fails to make an application to the Assigned Risks Pool, but carries on Practice without having obtained Qualifying Insurance, each Principal in that Firm will have committed a disciplinary offence. The same is true if a Run-off Firm fails to apply to be issued wit an ARP Run-off Policy. In each case, that Firm, and each Principal in that Firm, will also be liable under these Rules to:

pay an amount to the Society equivalent to the ARP Default Premium calculated for the whole of the Period of Default; and reimburse to the Society in full under Rule 15 the amount of any claim (together with defence costs) made against the Firm and relating to the period when it did not have Qualifying Insurance in force, less any amount due under this Rule.

15 Arrangements in relation to uninsured Firms

15.1 The ARP Manager on behalf of the Society shall make arrangements with Qualifying Insurers to cover any Claim (as defined in the Minimum Terms and Conditions) against:

(a) a Firm in Default; and
(b) a Run-off Firm

including any Defence Costs (as defined in the Minimum Terms and Conditions) relating to a Claim, in like manner and to the like extent as the Claim and the Defence Costs would have been covered had that Firm during the Period of Default been in the Assigned Risks Pool and been issued with an ARP Policy and/or, as the case may require, an ARP Run-off Policy.

15.2 Subject to Rule 13.8, Rule 14.1 and Rule 14.2, the Society on behalf of Qualifying Insurers shall be entitled to recover from each and every Principal in the Firm in Default during the Period of Default all amounts paid in or towards the discharge of a Claim and Defence Costs pursuant to Rule 15 together with interest thereon at Barclays Bank Plc base rate plus three per cent from the date when such amounts were respectively paid. The ARP Manager may and is hereby authorised to recover all sums due under this Rule on behalf of the Society.

15.3 A Firm shall not be deemed to have been admitted to the Assigned Risks Pool or to be covered in accordance with Rule 15 solely by virtue of the fact that the ARP Manager may conduct or settle any claim made against that Firm under the terms of any agreement between the Society and any Qualifying Insurer.

Commentary: If a Firm fails to make an application to the Assigned Risks Pool, but carries on Practice without having obtained Qualifying Insurance, each Principal in that Firm will have committed a disciplinary offence. The same is true if a Run-off Firm fails to apply to be issued wit an ARP Run-off Policy. In each case, that Firm, and each Principal in that Firm, will also be liable under these Rules to:

reimburse to the Society in full the amount paid pursuant to Rule 15.1 in respect of any claim (together with defence costs) made against the Firm and relating to the period when it did not have Qualifying Insurance in force, less any amount due under Rule 14 (where applicable);

and pay an amount under Rule 14 (where applicable) to the Society equivalent to the ARP Default Premium calculated for the whole of the Period of Default.

However, if a Firm in these circumstances is eligible under Rule 13.1 to be issued with an ARP Policy, then, provided that it complies with Rule 13.1 and is issued with an ARP Policy, the liability of the Firm and the Principals of that Firm will be limited, from that point on, to the ARP Default Premium and the excess payable under the terms of the ARP Policy.

PART 5: DISCIPLINARY OFFENCES AND REPORTING

16 Disciplinary consequences of failure to comply with these Rules

[5014]

16.1 The provisions in Part 4 of the Rules are made without prejudice to the powers of the Council or the Society under the Solicitors Act 1974, the Administration of Justice Act 1985, the Courts and Legal Services Act 1990 or the European Communities (Lawyer's Practice) Regulations 2000, or rules made under any of them, to bring disciplinary proceedings against any Firm that has failed to comply with these Rules or any person who is or was a Principal in such a Firm or to intervene in a Practice carried on by such a Firm.

Commentary: Payment of the ARP Default Premium and/or the ARP Run-off Premium does not detract from the fact that the Firm in question, and each Principal of that Firm, has committed a breach of these Rules as a result of the Firm being a Firm in Default. If a Firm in Default is not an Eligible Firm, it must either obtain Qualifying Insurance in the open market, or cease carrying on Practice and make an application to the Assigned Risks Pool for run-off cover in accordance with Rule 5.2.

16.2 Without prejudice to any other disciplinary offence which may arise under these Rules, it shall be a disciplinary offence for any Firm or any person who is at the relevant time a Principal in a Firm to be in Policy Default, or to fail to implement any Special Measures to the satisfaction of the Society.

Commentary: Policy Default and Special Measures are defined in Rule 3.1. Note that a Firm that is carrying on a Practice while in Policy Default will also not be an Eligible Firm for the purpose of seeking further cover through the Assigned Risks Pool.

17 Use of information

17.1 Any Qualifying Insurer (including the ARP Manager) may, in relation to any Firm which applies to it for Qualifying Insurance, and in the case of the ARP Manager any Run-off Firm or Firm in Default, whether or not that Firm applies to enter the Assigned Risks Pool, bring to the attention of the Society (including, in the case of the matters referred to in Rule 17.1(f), the Legal Complaints Service and/or the Office for Legal Complaints) at any time and without notice to the Firm concerned:

(a) any failure on the part of the Firm or any person who is a Principal of that Firm to pay any sum, including an ARP Premium, ARP Default Premium or ARP Run-off Premium, on or before the date specified in these Rules or to reimburse any amount falling within a Policy excess which has been paid out by a Qualifying Insurer to a claimant;

(b) a material inaccuracy in any proposal form submitted by or on behalf of the Firm;

(c) the fact that the Firm has become or is believed to have become a Run-off Firm;

(d) any matter or circumstances that would entitle the Firm's Qualifying Insurer to avoid or repudiate a Policy but for the provisions of clause 4.1 of the Minimum Terms and Conditions (and/or the corresponding of the Policy);

(e) any dishonesty or fraud suspected by a Qualifying Insurer on the part of any Insured as defined in the Minimum Terms and Conditions; and

(f) any claim of inadequate professional services made against the Firm or any Insured of that Firm of which it becomes aware.

Commentary: All Firms, whether they obtain their Qualifying Insurance on the open market or through the Assigned Risks Pool, or whether, having failed to obtain Qualifying Insurance, they are subject to the provisions of Part 4 of these Rules, are deemed to have consented to their Qualifying Insurer or the ARP Manager bringing to the attention of the Solicitors Regulation Authority any of the matters referred to Rule 17.1 that may be applicable to the Firm. Any such information is subject to the confidentiality provisions of Rule 17.4.

17.2 The Legal Complaints Service of the Society and/or the Office for Legal Complaints may pass such information as it in its absolute discretion sees fit to any department or office of the Society, and to any Qualifying Insurer, including the ARP Manager, in relation to any complaint of inadequate professional services against a Firm of which it becomes aware.

17.3 The Council may require any Qualifying Insurer or the ARP Manager to bring to the attention of the Society any of the matters referred to in Rule 17.1 where it reasonably believes there are matters which ought to be brought to the attention of the Society in accordance with Rule 17.1.

17.4 In respect of any information that may be brought to the attention of the Society in accordance with Rules 17.1 to 17.3:

(a) the Society shall keep all such information confidential;

(b) the Society shall not (except where and to the extent required by law or in the proper performance by the Society of its regulatory functions) at any time reveal any such information to any person other than a duly authorised employee of the Society or any of its subsidiaries; and

(c) any privilege attaching to such information shall not be regarded as having been waived whether by virtue of such information having been provided to the Society or otherwise.

17.5 The provisions of Rule 17.4 shall not prevent the Society from:

(a) making use of any information referred to in that Rule for the purpose of bringing disciplinary proceedings against any person; or

(b) in relation to information about a Firm's Policy under Rule 18, disclosing that information, where and to the extent that the Society in its absolute discretion considers it appropriate, to any person entitled to such information, and to any other department or office of the Society, including without limitation to the Legal Complaints Service and/or the Office for Legal Complaints.

18 Details of Qualifying Insurer

18.1 If a person (a **Claimant**) asserts a claim against a Firm or any person insured under that Firm's Policy, and where such claim relates to any matter within the scope of cover of the Minimum Terms and Conditions (whether or not such claim would or may be upheld), the Firm and any person who is at the relevant time (or, in the case of a Firm which has ceased Practice, any person who was immediately before that Firm ceased Practice) a Principal in that Firm shall be required, upon being so requested by that Claimant, by any person insured under that Firm's Policy, or by any other person with a legitimate interest, to provide to that person the following details in relation to that Firm's Policy:

(a) the name of the Qualifying Insurer(s) who issued the policy; and

(b) the policy number; and

(c) the address and contact details of the Qualifying Insurer(s) for the purpose of making a claim under the policy;

in each case in respect of the Policy which it is reasonably believed to be the relevant Policy to respond to the claim, or, if applicable, the fact that the Firm or person against whom the claim is asserted is covered by Supplementary Run-off Cover.

Commentary: A Firm, and each Principal in that Firm, is required to provide details of that Firm's policy of Qualifying Insurance to any person who asserts a claim against anyone insured under that Firm's Policy. Under Rule 17, the Solicitors Regulation Authority has the power to disclose information regarding a Firm's Qualifying Insurer where it considers it appropriate to do so.

PART 6: GENERAL POWERS OF THE COUNCIL

19 Waiver powers

[5015]

19.1 The Council shall have power on such terms and conditions as it shall think fit to waive any Rule or part of any Rule in a particular case or cases including extending the time, either prospectively or retrospectively, for the doing of any act under any Rule.

(a) Any application by any person for a waiver of any Rule or part of any Rule under the Solicitors' Indemnity Insurance Rules 2001 to 2009 must be made in writing to the Society as soon as reasonably practicable, and in any event no later than the relevant date set out below:

Solicitors' Indemnity Insurance Rules 2001

Relevant date - whichever is the later of:

30 November 2001; or

3 calendar months from the occurrence of any event or circumstances first giving rise to the obligation on that person under the relevant Rule or part of any Rule in respect of which the waiver application is or was made, but in any event no later than 30 November 2002.

Solicitors' Indemnity Insurance Rules 2002

Relevant date - whichever is the later of:

30 November 2002; or

3 calendar months from the occurrence of any event or circumstances first giving rise to the obligation on that person under the relevant Rule or part of any Rule in respect of which the waiver application is or was made, but in any event no later than 30 November 2003.

Solicitors' Indemnity Insurance Rules 2003

Relevant date - whichever is the later of:

30 November 2003; or

3 calendar months from the occurrence of any event or circumstances first giving rise to the obligation on that person under the relevant Rule or part of any Rule in respect of which the waiver application is or was made, but in any event no later than 31 December 2004.

Solicitors' Indemnity Insurance Rules 2004

Relevant date - whichever is the later of:

31 December 2004; or

3 calendar months from the occurrence of any event or circumstances first giving rise to the obligation on that person under the relevant Rule or part of any Rule in respect of which the waiver application is or was made, but in any event no later than 31 December 2005.

Solicitors' Indemnity Insurance Rules 2005

Relevant date - whichever is the later of:

31 December 2005; or

3 calendar months from the occurrence of any event or circumstances first giving rise to the obligation on that person under the relevant Rule or part of any Rule in respect of which the waiver application is or was made, but in any event no later than 31 December 2006.

Solicitors' Indemnity Insurance Rules 2006

Relevant date - whichever is the later of:

31 December 2006; or

3 calendar months from the occurrence of any event or circumstances first giving rise to the obligation on that person under the relevant Rule or part of any Rule in respect of which the waiver application is or was made, but in any event no later than 31 December 2007.

Solicitors' Indemnity Insurance Rules 2007

Relevant date - whichever is the later of:

31 December 2007; or

3 calendar months from the occurrence of any event or circumstances first giving rise to the obligation on that person under the relevant Rule or part of any Rule in respect of which the waiver application is or was made, but in any event no later than 31 December 2008.

Solicitors' Indemnity Insurance Rules 2008

Relevant date - whichever is the later of:

31 December 2008; or

3 calendar months from the occurrence of any event or circumstances first giving rise to the obligation on that person under the relevant Rule or part of any Rule in respect of which the waiver application is or was made, but in any event no later than 31 December 2009.

Solicitors' Indemnity Insurance Rules 2009

Relevant date - whichever is the later of:

31 December 2009; or

3 calendar months from the occurrence of any event or circumstances first giving rise to the obligation on that person under the relevant Rule or part of any Rule in respect of which the waiver application is or was made, but in any event no later than 31 December 2010.

(b) No application by any person for a waiver of any Rule or part of any Rule under the Solicitors' Indemnity Insurance Rules 2000 may be considered unless it was made in writing to the Society as soon as reasonably practicable and in any event no later than 28 February 2002.

(c) Any appeal against any decision made by the Society in respect of any application for a waiver of any Rule or part of any Rule under the Solicitors' Indemnity Insurance Rules 2000 to 2009) must be made in writing to the Society within 21 days from the date of the decision.

(d) An application for a waiver as contemplated by this Rule 19.1 or the making of an appeal against any decision made by the Society in respect of such application shall not relieve any person from any obligation under the Solicitors' Indemnity Insurance Rules 2000 to 2009 pending the determination of any such application or appeal.

Commentary: It is envisaged that Rules will be waived only in exceptional circumstances. Anyone who wishes to apply for a waiver, or to appeal against an initial decision, must do so in accordance with the time limits set out in this Rule. Contact details appear at the end of the introductory commentary. The Panel of Adjudicators Sub Committee has adopted a waiver policy, which is available on request. Unless and until any waiver is granted, the person concerned must comply with the requirements of these Rules in full. A waiver may be granted subject to conditions, and may be revoked without notice.

19.2 The Council shall have power to treat any Firm as complying with any Rule or Rules for the purposes of the Solicitors Act 1974 notwithstanding that the Firm has failed to comply with a Rule or Rules where such non-compliance is regarded by the Council in a particular case or cases as being insignificant.

19.3 For the purposes of the Solicitors Act 1974 (including without limitation section 10 of that Act), any person who is in breach of any Rule or part of any Rule under the Solicitors' Indemnity Insurance Rules 2000 to 2009 shall be deemed, for so long as he remains in breach, not to be complying with these Rules.

Commentary: The effect of this general power is that, for example, a practising certificate may be issued to a person notwithstanding a technical and insignificant breach by that person or a Firm of any provision of these Rules.

PART 7: OTHER OBLIGATIONS

20 Accountants' reports

[5016]
Any accountant's report which a solicitor or Registered European Lawyer or registered foreign lawyer who is a Principal in a Practice or a Recognised Body is required to deliver to the Society under section 34 of the Solicitors Act 1974 or paragraph 8 of Schedule 14 to the Courts and Legal Services Act 1990 containing such information as is prescribed by rule 35 of the Solicitors' Accounts Rules 1998 must contain a statement certifying (if it is the case) for the whole period covered by the report (excluding any part of that period falling before 1 September 2000) either that the Firm has one or more certificates of Qualifying Insurance outside the Assigned Risks Pool or that the Firm has been issued with one or more policies by the ARP Manager.

Commentary: Firms are required to provide evidence to their accountants that a Policy of Qualifying Insurance is in place. Each Qualifying Insurer is required under the Qualifying Insurer's agreement to provide a certificate of Qualifying Insurance to each Firm within 20 working days of the start of the period covered by the Policy. Producing the relevant certificate(s) to the reporting accountant will satisfy the requirement of this Rule.

APPENDIX 1: MINIMUM TERMS AND CONDITIONS OF PROFESSIONAL INDEMNITY INSURANCE FOR SOLICITORS AND REGISTERED EUROPEAN LAWYERS IN ENGLAND AND WALES

1 Scope of cover

1.1 Civil liability

[5017]
The insurance must indemnify each Insured against civil liability to the extent that it arises from Private Legal Practice in connection with the Insured Firm's Practice, provided that a Claim in respect of such liability:

(a) is first made against an Insured during the Period of Insurance; or
(b) is made against an Insured during or after the Period of Insurance and arising from Circumstances first notified to the Insurer during the Period of Insurance.

1.2 Defence Costs

The insurance must also indemnify the Insured against Defence Costs in relation to:

(a) any Claim referred to in clause 1.1, 1.4 or 1.6; or
(b) any Circumstances first notified to the Insurer during the Period of Insurance; or
(c) any investigation, inquiry or disciplinary proceeding during or after the Period of Insurance arising from any Claim referred to in clause 1.1, 1.4 or 1.6 or from Circumstances first notified to the Insurer during the Period of Insurance.

1.3 The Insured

For the purposes of the cover contemplated by clause 1.1, the Insured must include:

(a) the Insured Firm; and
(b) each service, administration, trustee or nominee company owned as at the date of occurrence of relevant Circumstances by the Insured Firm and/or the Principals of the Insured Firm; and
(c) each Principal, each former Principal and each person who becomes a Principal during the Period of Insurance of the Insured Firm or a company referred to in paragraph (b); and
(d) each Employee, each former Employee and each person who becomes during the Period of Insurance an Employee of the Insured Firm or a company referred to in paragraph (b); and

(e) the estate or legal personal representative of any deceased or legally incapacitated person referred to in paragraph (c) or (d).

1.4 Prior Practice

The insurance must indemnify each Insured against civil liability to the extent that it arises from Private Legal Practice in connection with a Prior Practice, provided that a Claim in respect of such liability is first made against an Insured:

(a) during the Period of Insurance; or

(b) during or after the Period of Insurance and arising from Circumstances first notified to the Insurer during the Period of Insurance.

1.5 The Insured - Prior Practice

For the purposes of the cover contemplated by clause 1.4, the Insured must include:

(a) each Partnership or Recognised Body which, or Sole Practitioner who, carried on the Prior Practice; and

(b) each service, administration, trustee or nominee company owned as at the date of occurrence of relevant Circumstances by the Partnership or Recognised Body which, or Sole Practitioner who, carried on the Prior Practice and/or the Principals of such Partnership or Recognised Body; and

(c) each Principal and former Principal of each Partnership or Recognised Body referred to in paragraph (a) or company referred to in paragraph (b); and

(d) each Employee and former Employee of the Partnership, Recognised Body or Sole Practitioner referred to in paragraph (a) or company referred to in paragraph (b); and

(e) the estate or legal personal representative of any deceased or legally incapacitated Sole Practitioner referred to in paragraph (a) or person referred to in paragraph (c) or (d).

1.6 Successor Practice

The insurance must indemnify each Insured against civil liability to the extent that it arises from Private Legal Practice in connection with a Successor Practice to the Insured Firm's Practice (where succession is as a result of one or more separate mergers, acquisitions, absorptions or other transitions), provided that a Claim in respect of such liability is first made against an Insured:

(a) during the Period of Insurance; or

(b) during or after the Period of Insurance and arising from Circumstances first notified to the Insurer during the Period of Insurance.

1.7 The Insured - Successor Practice

For the purposes of the cover contemplated by clause 1.6, the Insured must include:

(a) each Partnership or Recognised Body which, or Sole Practitioner who, carries on the Successor Practice during the Period of Insurance; and

(b) each service, administration, trustee or nominee company owned as at the date of occurrence of relevant Circumstances by the Partnership or Recognised Body which, or Sole Practitioner who, carries on the Successor Practice and/or the Principals of such Partnership or Recognised Body; and

(c) each Principal, each former Principal and each person who becomes during the Period of Insurance a Principal of any Partnership or Recognised Body referred to in paragraph (a) or company referred to in paragraph (b); and

(d) each Employee, each former Employee and each person who becomes during the Period of Insurance an Employee of the Partnership, Recognised Body or Sole Practitioner referred to in paragraph (a) or company referred to in paragraph (b); and

(e) the estate or legal personal representative of any deceased or legally incapacitated Sole Practitioner referred to in paragraph (a) or person referred to in paragraph (c) or (d).

1.8 Award by regulatory authority

The insurance must indemnify each Insured against any amount paid or payable in accordance with the recommendation of the Legal Services Ombudsman, the Legal Complaints Service, the Office for Legal Complaintsor any other regulatory authority to the same extent as it indemnifies the Insured against civil liability.

2 Limit of insurance cover

2.1 Any one Claim

The Sum Insured for any one Claim (exclusive of Defence Costs) must be, where the Insured Firm is a Relevant Recognised Body, at least £3 million, and in all other cases, at least £2 million.

2.2 No limit on Defence Costs

There must be no monetary limit on the cover for Defence Costs.

2.3 Proportionate limit on Defence Costs

Notwithstanding clauses 2.1 and 2.2, the insurance may provide that liability for Defence Costs in relation to a Claim which exceeds the Sum Insured is limited to the proportion that the Sum Insured bears to the total amount paid or payable to dispose of the Claim.

2.4 No other limit

The insurance must not limit liability to any monetary amount (whether by way of an aggregate limit or otherwise) except as contemplated by clauses 2.1 and 2.3.

2.5 One Claim

The insurance may provide that, when considering what may be regarded as one Claim for the purposes of the limits contemplated by clauses 2.1 and 2.3:

(a) all Claims against any one or more Insured arising from:
   (i) one act or omission;
   (ii) one series of related acts or omissions;
   (iii) the same act or omission in a series of related matters or transactions;
   (iv) similar acts or omissions in a series of related matters or transactions

   and

(b) all Claims against one or more Insured arising from one matter or transaction

will be regarded as one Claim.

2.6 Multiple underwriters

2.6.1 The insurance may be underwritten by more than one insurer, each of which must be a Qualifying Insurer, provided that the insurance may provide that the Insurer shall be severally liable only for its respective proportion of liability in accordance with the terms of the insurance.

2.6.2 Where the insurance is underwritten jointly by more than one insurer:

(a) the insurance must state which Qualifying Insurer shall be the Lead Insurer; and

(b) in addition to any proportionate limit on Defence Costs in accordance with clause 2.3, the insurance may provide that each Insurer's liability for Defence Costs is further limited to the extent or the proportion of that Insurer's liability (if any) in relation to the relevant Claim.

[Note: under clause 2.6 of the Qualifying Insurer's Agreement, a Policy may be issued on an excess of loss basis only in the layers set out in that clause.]

3 Excesses

3.1 The Excess

The insurance may be subject to an Excess of such monetary amount and on such terms as the Insurer and the Insured Firm agree. Subject to clause 3.4, the Excess may be "self-insured" or partly or wholly insured without regard to these minimum terms and conditions.

3.2 No deductibles

The insurance must provide that the Excess does not reduce the limit of liability contemplated by clause 2.1.

3.3 Excess not to apply to Defence Costs

The Excess must not apply to Defence Costs.

3.4 *Funding of the Excess*

The insurance must provide that, if an Insured fails to pay to a Claimant any amount which is within the Excess within 30 days of it becoming due for payment, the Claimant may give notice of the Insured's default to the Insurer, whereupon the Insurer is liable to remedy the default on the Insured's behalf. The insurance may provide that any amount paid by the Insurer to remedy such a default erodes the Sum Insured.

3.5 One Claim

The insurance may provide for multiple Claims to be treated as one Claim for the purposes of an Excess contemplated by clause 3.1 on such terms as the Insured Firm and the Insurer agree.

3.6 Excess layers

In the case of insurance written on an excess of loss basis, there shall be no Excess except in relation to the primary layer.

4 Special conditions

4.1 No avoidance or repudiation

The insurance must provide that the Insurer is not entitled to avoid or repudiate the insurance on any grounds whatsoever including, without limitation, non-disclosure or misrepresentation, whether fraudulent or not.

4.2 No adjustment or denial

The insurance must provide that the Insurer is not entitled to reduce or deny its liability under the insurance on any grounds whatsoever including, without limitation, any breach of any term or condition of the insurance, except to the extent that one of the exclusions contemplated by clause 6 applies.

4.3 No cancellation

The insurance must provide that it cannot be cancelled except (in the case of (a), (b) or (c) below) by the agreement of both the Insured Firm and the Insurer, and in any event only in circumstances where:

(a) the Insured Firm's Practice is merged into a Successor Practice, provided that there is insurance complying with these minimum terms and conditions in relation to that Successor Practice, in which case cancellation shall have effect no earlier than the date of such merger; or

(b) replacement insurance complying with these minimum terms and conditions commences, but only where, in the case of insurance not provided wholly or partly by the Assigned Risks Pool, the replacement insurance is not provided wholly or partly by the Assigned Risks Pool, in which case cancellation shall have effect no earlier than the date on which such replacement insurance commences; or

(c) it subsequently transpires that the Insured Firm is not required under the Solicitors Indemnity Insurance Rules 2009 to effect a policy of Qualifying Insurance, in which case cancellation shall have effect from the later of (a) the start of the relevant Indemnity Period and (b) the date on which the Insured Firm ceased to be required to effect a policy of Qualifying Insurance, or such later date as the Insured Firm and the Insurer may agree; or

(d) in the case of an ARP Policy, it subsequently transpires that the Insured Firm was not or has ceased to be an Eligible Firm, in which case cancellation shall have effect from the date on which it ceased to be an Eligible Firm.

Cancellation must not affect the rights and obligations of the parties accrued under the insurance prior to the date from which cancellation has effect.

4.4 No set-off

The insurance must provide that any amount payable by the Insurer to indemnify an Insured against civil liability to a Claimant will be paid only to the Claimant, or at the Claimant's direction, and that the Insurer is not entitled to set-off against any such amount any payment due to it by any Insured including, without limitation, any payment of premium or to reimburse the Insurer.

4.5 No "other insurance" provision

The insurance must not provide that the liability of the Insurer is reduced or excluded by reason of the existence or availability of any other insurance other than as contemplated by clause 6.1. For the avoidance of doubt, this requirement is not intended to affect any right of the Insurer to claim contribution from any other insurer which is also liable to indemnify any Insured.

4.6 No retroactive date

The insurance must not exclude or limit the liability of the Insurer in respect of Claims arising from incidents, occurrences, facts, matters, acts and/or omissions which occurred prior to a specified date.

4.7 Successor Practice - "double insurance"

The insurance may provide that, if the Insured Firm's Practice is succeeded during the Period of Insurance and, as a result, a situation of "double insurance" exists between two or more insurers of the Successor Practice, contribution between insurers is to be determined in accordance with the relative numbers of Principals of the owners of the constituent Practices immediately prior to succession.

4.8 Advancement of Defence Costs

The insurance must provide that the Insurer will meet Defence Costs as and when they are incurred, including Defence Costs incurred on behalf of an Insured who is alleged to have committed or condoned dishonesty or a fraudulent act or omission, provided that the Insurer is not liable for Defence Costs incurred on behalf of that Insured after the earlier of:

(a) that Insured admitting to the Insurer the commission or condoning of such dishonesty, act or omission; or

(b) a court or other judicial body finding that that Insured was in fact guilty of such dishonesty, act or omission.

4.9 Resolution of disputes

The insurance must provide that, if there is a dispute as to whether a Practice is a Successor Practice for the purposes of clauses 1.4, 1.6 or 5.3, the Insured and the Insurer will take all reasonable steps (including, if appropriate, referring the dispute to arbitration) to resolve the dispute in conjunction with any related dispute between any other party which has insurance complying with these minimum terms and conditions and that party's insurer.

4.10 Conduct of a Claim pending dispute resolution

The insurance must provide that, pending resolution of any coverage dispute and without prejudice to any issue in dispute, the Insurer will, if so directed by the Society, conduct any Claim, advance Defence Costs and, if appropriate, compromise and pay the Claim. If the Society is satisfied that:

(a) the party requesting the direction has taken all reasonable steps to resolve the dispute with the other party/ies; and

(b) there is a reasonable prospect that the coverage dispute will be resolved or determined in the Insured's favour; and

(c) it is fair and equitable in all the circumstances for such direction to be given;

it may in its absolute discretion make such a direction.

4.11 Minimum terms and conditions to prevail

The insurance must provide that:

(a) the insurance is to be construed or rectified so as to comply with the requirements of these minimum terms and conditions; and

(b) any provision which is inconsistent with these minimum terms and conditions is to be severed or rectified to comply.

4.12 Period of Insurance

The Period of Insurance must not expire prior to 30 September 2010.

5 Run-off cover

5.1 Cessation of the Insured Firm's Practice

The insurance must provide that, if the Insured Firm's Practice ceases during or on expiry of the Period of Insurance and the Insured Firm has not obtained succeeding insurance in compliance with these minimum terms and conditions (a Cessation), the insurance will provide run-off cover.

For these purposes, an Insured Firm's Practice shall (without limitation) be regarded as ceasing if (and with effect from the date upon which) the Insured Firm becomes a Non-SRA Firm.

5.2 Scope of run-off cover

The run-off cover referred to in clause 5.1 must indemnify each Insured in accordance with clauses 1.1 to 1.8 (but subject to the limits, exclusions and conditions of the insurance which are in accordance with these minimum terms and conditions) on the basis that the Period of Insurance extends for an additional six years (ending on the sixth anniversary of the date upon which, but for this requirement, it would have ended).

5.3 Succession

The insurance must provide that run-off cover is not activated if there is a Successor Practice to the ceased Practice, provided that there is insurance complying with these minimum terms and conditions in relation to that Successor Practice.

5.4 Suspended Practices

The insurance must provide that, where run-off cover has been activated in accordance with this clause 5, but where the Insured Firm's Practice restarts, the Insurer may (but shall not be obliged to) cancel such run-off cover, on such terms as may be agreed, provided that:

(a) there is insurance complying with these minimum terms and conditions in relation to that Insured Firm in force on the date of cancellation;

(b) the Qualifying Insurer providing such insurance confirms in writing to the Insured Firm and the Insurer (if different) that:
  (i) it is providing insurance complying with these minimum terms and conditions in relation to that Insured Firm for the then current Indemnity Period; and
  (ii) it is doing so on the basis that the Insured Firm's Practice is regarded as being a continuation of the Insured Firm's Practice prior to Cessation and that accordingly it is liable for Claims against the Insured Firm arising from incidents, occurrences, facts, matters, acts and/or omissions which occurred prior to Cessation.

6 Exclusions

The insurance must not exclude or limit the liability of the Insurer except to the extent that any Claim or related Defence Costs arise from the matters set out in this clause 6.

6.1 Prior cover

Any Claim in respect of which the Insured is entitled to be indemnified by the Solicitors Indemnity Fund (**SIF**) or under a professional indemnity insurance contract for a period earlier than the Period of Insurance, whether by reason of notification of Circumstances to SIF or under the earlier contract or otherwise.

6.2 Death or bodily injury

Any liability of any Insured for causing or contributing to death or bodily injury, except that the insurance must nonetheless cover liability for psychological injury or emotional distress which arises from a breach of duty in the performance of (or failure to perform) legal work.

6.3 Property damage

Any liability of any Insured for causing or contributing to damage to, or destruction or physical loss of, any property (other than property in the care, custody or control of any Insured in connection with the Insured Firm's Practice and not occupied or used in the course of the Insured Firm's Practice), except that the insurance must nonetheless cover liability for such damage, destruction or loss which arises from breach of duty in the performance of (or failure to perform) legal work.

6.4 Partnership disputes

Any actual or alleged breach of the Insured Firm's Partnership or shareholder agreement or arrangements, including any equivalent agreement or arrangement where the Insured Firm is a Limited Liability Partnership or a company without a share capital.

6.5 Employment breaches, discrimination, etc.

Wrongful dismissal, repudiation or breach of an employment contract or arrangement, termination of a training contract, harassment, discrimination or like conduct in relation to any Partnership or shareholder agreement or arrangement or the equivalent where the Insured Firm is a Limited Liability Partnership or a company without a share capital, or in relation to any employment or training agreement or arrangement.

6.6 Debts and trading liabilities

Any:

(a) trading or personal debt of any Insured; or

(b) breach by any Insured of the terms of any contract or arrangement for the supply to, or use by, any Insured of goods or services in the course of the Insured Firm's Practice; or

(c) guarantee, indemnity or undertaking by any particular Insured in connection with the provision of finance, property, assistance or other benefit or advantage directly or indirectly to that Insured.

6.7 Fines, penalties, etc

Any:

(a) fine or penalty; or

(b) award of punitive, exemplary or like damages under the law of the United States of America or Canada, other than in respect of defamation; or

(c) order or agreement to pay the costs of a complainant, regulator, investigator or prosecutor of any professional conduct complaint against, or investigation into the professional conduct of, any Insured.

6.8 Fraud or dishonesty

The insurance may exclude liability of the Insurer to indemnify any particular person to the extent that any civil liability or related Defence Costs arise from dishonesty or a fraudulent act or omission committed or condoned by that person, except that:

(a) the insurance must nonetheless cover each other Insured; and

(b) the insurance must provide that no dishonesty, act or omission will be imputed to a body corporate unless it was committed or condoned by, in the case of a company, all directors of that company, or, in the case of a Limited Liability Partnership, all members of that Limited Liability Partnership.

6.9 Directors' or officers' liability

The insurance may exclude liability of the Insurer to indemnify any natural person in their capacity as a director or officer of a body corporate (other than a Recognised Body or a service, administration, trustee or nominee company referred to in clauses 1.3(b), 1.5 (b) or 1.7(b)) except that:

(a) the insurance must nonetheless cover any liability of that person which arises from a breach of duty in the performance of (or failure to perform) legal work; and

(b) the insurance must nonetheless cover each other Insured against any vicarious or joint liability.

6.10 War and Terrorism, and Asbestos

The Insurance may exclude, by way of an exclusion or endorsement, liability of the Insurer to indemnify any Insured in respect of, or in any way in connection with:

(a) terrorism, war or other hostilities; and/or

(b) asbestos, or any actual or alleged asbestos-related injury or damage involving the use, presence, existence, detection, removal, elimination or avoidance of asbestos or exposure to asbestos,

provided that any such exclusion or endorsement does not exclude or limit any liability of the Insurer to indemnify any Insured against civil liability or related Defence Costs arising from any actual or alleged breach of duty in the performance of (or failure to perform) legal work or failure to discharge or fulfil any duty incidental to the Insured Firm's Practice or to the conduct of Private Legal Practice.

7 General conditions

7.1 As agreed

The insurance may contain such general conditions as are agreed between the Insurer and the Insured Firm, but the insurance must provide that the special conditions required by clause 4 prevail to the extent of any inconsistency.

7.2 Reimbursement

The insurance may provide that each Insured who:

(a) committed; or

(b) condoned (whether knowingly or recklessly):

  (i) non-disclosure or misrepresentation; or

  (ii) any breach of the terms or conditions of the insurance; or

  (iii) dishonesty or any fraudulent act or omission,

will reimburse the Insurer to the extent that is just and equitable having regard to the prejudice caused to the Insurer's interests by such non-disclosure, misrepresentation, breach, dishonesty, act or omission, provided that no Insured shall be required to make any such reimbursement to the extent that any such breach of the terms or conditions of the insurance was in order to comply with any applicable rules or codes laid down from time to time by the Society, or in the Society publication Your Clients - Your Business, as amended from time to time.

The insurance must provide that no non-disclosure, misrepresentation, breach, dishonesty, act or omission will be imputed to a body corporate unless it was committed or condoned by, in the case of a company, all directors of that company, or, in the case of a Limited Liability Partnership, all members of that Limited Liability Partnership. The insurance must provide further that any right of reimbursement contemplated by this clause 7.2 against any person referred to in clauses 1.3(d), 1.5(d) or 1.7(d) (or against the estate or legal personal representative of any such person if they die or become legally incapacitated) is limited to the extent that is just and equitable having regard to the prejudice caused to the Insurer's interests by that person having committed or condoned (whether knowingly or recklessly) dishonesty or any fraudulent act or omission.

7.3 Reimbursement of Defence Costs

The insurance may provide that each Insured will reimburse the Insurer for Defence Costs advanced on that Insured's behalf which the Insurer is not ultimately liable to pay.

7.4 Reimbursement of the Excess

The insurance may provide for those persons who are at any time during the Period of Insurance Principals of the Insured Firm, together with, in relation to a Sole Practitioner, any person held out as a Partner of that practitioner, to reimburse the Insurer for any Excess paid by the Insurer on an Insured's behalf. The Sum Insured must be reinstated to the extent of reimbursement of any amount which eroded it as contemplated by clause 3.4.

7.5 Reimbursement of moneys paid pending dispute resolution

The insurance may provide that each Insured will reimburse the Insurer following resolution of any coverage dispute for any amount paid by the Insurer on that Insured's behalf which, on the basis of the resolution of the dispute, the Insurer is not ultimately liable to pay.

7.6 Withholding assets or entitlements

The insurance may require the Insured Firm to account to the Insurer for any asset or entitlement of any person who committed or condoned any dishonesty or fraudulent act or omission, provided that the Insured Firm is legally entitled to withhold that asset or entitlement from that person.

7.7 Premium

The premium may be calculated on such basis as the Insurer determines and the Insured Firm accepts including, without limitation, a basis which recognises Claims history, categories of work performed by the Insured Firm, numbers of Principals and Employees, revenue derived from the Insured Firm's Practice and other risk factors determined by the Insurer.

7.8 Co-operation and assistance

The insurance (except in the case of an ARP Policy) must provide that, if the ARP Manager is appointed to conduct any Claim, each Insured will give the ARP Manager and any investigators or solicitors appointed by it all information and documents they reasonably require, and full co-operation and assistance in the investigation, defence, settlement, avoidance or reduction of any actual or possible Claim or any related proceeding.

8 Definitions and interpretation

8.1 General

8.1.1 In these minimum terms and conditions, unless the context otherwise requires:

(a) the singular includes the plural, and vice versa; and

(b) the male gender includes the female and neuter genders; and

(c) a reference to a person includes a body corporate, partnerships, and other unincorporated associations or bodies of persons;

(d) a reference to any statute, statutory provision, code or regulation includes:

- (i) any subordinate legislation (as defined by section 21(1) of the Interpretation Act 1978) made under it; and
- (ii) (ii) a reference to any provision which it has superseded or re-enacted (with or without modification) or amended, and any provision superseding it or re-enacting it (with or without modification) or amending it either before, or at or after the date of these minimum terms and conditions;

(e) references to the Society include the Solicitors Regulation Authority and the Legal Complaints Service, and any body or person which succeeds in whole or in part to the functions of the Society, the Solicitors Regulation Authority or the Legal Complaints Service, and any delegate of the Society, the Solicitors Regulation Authority, the Legal Complaints Service or any such body or person;

(f) headings are for ease of reference only and shall not affect the interpretation of these minimum terms and conditions;

(g) explanatory notes and commentary shall be ignored in interpreting these minimum terms and conditions;

(h) a reference to a director includes a member of a Limited Liability Partnership; and

(i) words and expressions which begin with a capital letter in these minimum terms and conditions have the meaning set out in this clause 8; and

(j) words and expressions in these minimum terms and conditions are to be construed consistently with the same or similar words or expressions in the Solicitors' Indemnity Insurance Rules 2008.

8.1.2 These minimum terms and conditions shall be, and the insurance shall be expressed to be, governed by and interpreted in accordance with English law.

8.2 Defined terms

In these minimum terms and conditions:

Circumstances means an incident, occurrence, fact, matter, act or omission which may give rise to a Claim in respect of civil liability

Claim means a demand for, or an assertion of a right to, civil compensation or civil damages or an intimation of an intention to seek such compensation or damages. For these purposes, an obligation on an Insured Firm and/or any Insured to remedy a breach of the Solicitors' Accounts Rules 1998 (as amended from time to time), or any rules which replace the Solicitors' Accounts Rules 1998 in whole or in part, shall be treated as a Claim, and the obligation to remedy such breach shall be treated as a civil liability for the purposes of clause 1, whether or not any person makes a demand for, or an assertion of a right to, civil compensation or civil damages or an intimation of an intention to seek such compensation or damages as a result of such breach, except where any such obligation may arise as a result of the insolvency of a bank (as defined in section 87 of the Solicitors Act 1974) or a building society (within the meaning of the Building Societies Act 1986) which holds client money in a client account of the Insured Firm or the failure of such bank or building society generally to repay monies on demand.

Claimant means a person or entity which has made or may make a Claim including a Claim for contribution or indemnity.

Defence Costs means legal costs and disbursements and investigative and related expenses reasonably and necessarily incurred with the consent of the Insurer in:

(a) defending any proceedings relating to a Claim; or
(b) conducting any proceedings for indemnity, contribution or recovery relating to a Claim; or
(c) investigating, reducing, avoiding or compromising any actual or potential Claim; or
(d) acting for any Insured in connection with any investigation, inquiry or disciplinary proceeding.

Defence Costs do not include any internal or overhead expenses of the Insured Firm or the Insurer or the cost of any Insured's time.

Employee means any person other than a Principal:

(a) employed or otherwise engaged in the Insured Firm's Practice (including under a contract for services) including, without limitation, as a solicitor, lawyer, trainee solicitor or lawyer, consultant, associate, locum tenens, agent, appointed person (as defined in the Solicitors' Indemnity Insurance Rules 2009), office or clerical staff member or otherwise;
(b) seconded to work in the Insured Firm's Practice; or
(c) seconded by the Insured Firm to work elsewhere.

Employee does not include any person who is engaged by the Insured Firm under a contract for services in respect of any work where that person is required, whether under the Solicitors' Indemnity Insurance Rules 2009 or under the rules of any other professional body, to take out or to be insured under separate professional indemnity insurance in respect of that work.

Excess means the first amount of a Claim which is not covered by the insurance.

Insured means each person and entity named or described as a person to whom the insurance extends and includes, without limitation, those referred to in clause 1.3 and, in relation to Prior and Successor Practices respectively, those referred to in clauses 1.5 and 1.7.

Insured Firm means the Firm (as defined for the purposes of the Solicitors Indemnity Insurance Rules 2008) which contracted with the Insurer to provide the insurance.

Insured Firm's Practice means:

(a) the legal Practice carried on by the Insured Firm as at the commencement of the Period of Insurance; and
(b) the continuous legal Practice preceding and succeeding the Practice referred to in paragraph (a) (irrespective of changes in ownership of the Practice or in the composition of any Partnership which owns or owned the Practice).

Insurer means the underwriter(s) of the insurance.

Lead Insurer means the insurer named as such in the contract of insurance, or, if no Lead Insurer is named as such, the first-named insurer on the relevant certificate of insurance

Limited Liability Partnership means a limited liability partnership incorporated under the Limited Liability Partnerships Act 2000.

Partnership means an unincorporated Insured Firm in which persons are or are held out as partners, and does not include an Insured Firm incorporated as a Limited Liability Partnership, and Partner means a person who is or is held out to be a partner in a Partnership.

Period of Insurance means the period for which the insurance operates.

Principal means:

(a) where the Insured Firm is or was:
  (i) a sole practitioner - that practitioner;

(ii) (ii) a Partnership - each Partner;

(iii) a company with a share capital each director of that company and any solicitor, Registered European Lawyer or Registered Foreign Lawyer who:

(A) is held out as a director; or

(B) beneficially owns the whole or any part of a share in the company; or

(C) is the ultimate beneficial owner of the whole or any part of a share in the company.

(iv) a company without a share capital - each director of that company and any solicitor, Registered European Lawyer or Registered Foreign Lawyer who:

(A) is held out as a director; or

(B) is a member of the company; or

(C) is the ultimate owner of the whole or any part of a body corporate or other legal person which is a member of the company;

(v) a Limited Liability Partnership - each member of that Limited Liability Partnership, and any solicitor, Registered European Lawyer or Registered Foreign Lawyer who is the ultimate owner of the whole or any part of a body corporate or other legal person which is member of the Limited Liability Partnership.

(b) where a body corporate or other legal person is a Partner in the Insured Firm, all solicitors, Registered European Lawyers or Registered Foreign Lawyers who are within paragraph (a)(iii) of this definition (including sub paragraphs (A) and (C) thereof), paragraph (a)(iv) of this definition (including sub paragraphs (A) and (C) thereof), or paragraph a(v) of this definition.

Prior Practice means each Practice to which the Insured Firm's Practice is ultimately a Successor Practice by way of one or more mergers, acquisitions, absorptions or other transitions.

Private Legal Practice means the provision of services in private Practice as a solicitor or Registered European Lawyer including, without limitation:

(a) providing such services in England, Wales or anywhere in the world, whether alone or with other lawyers in a Partnership permitted to practice in England and Wales by rule 12 of the Solicitors' Code of Conduct 2007; and

(b) the provision of such services as a secondee of the Insured Firm; and

(c) any Insured acting as a personal representative, trustee, attorney, notary, insolvency practitioner or in any other role in conjunction with a Practise; and

(d) the provision of such services by any Employee; and

(e) (e) the provision of such services pro bono publico.

Private Legal Practice does not include:

(i) practising as an Employee of an employer other than a solicitor, a registered European lawyer, a Partnership permitted to practice in England and Wales by rule 12 of the Solicitors' Code of Conduct 2007, or a Recognised Body; or

(ii) discharging the functions of any of the following offices or appointments:

(A) judicial office;

(B) Under Sheriffs;

(C) members and clerks of such tribunals, committees, panels and boards as the Council may from time to time designate but including those subject to the Tribunals and Inquiries Act 1992, the Competition Commission, Legal Services Commission Review Panels and Parole Boards;

(D) Justices' Clerks; or

(E) Superintendent Registrars and Deputy Superintendent Registrars of Births, Marriages and Deaths and Registrars of Local Crematoria.

Recognised Body means a body for the time being recognised by the Solicitors Regulation Authority under Section 9 of the Administration of Justice Act 1985 and the SRA Recognised Bodies Regulations 2009.

Relevant Recognised Body means a Recognised Body other than:

(a) an unlimited company, or an overseas company whose members' liability for the company's debts is not limited by its constitution or by the law of its country of incorporation; or

(b) a nominee company only, holding assets for clients of another Practice; and

(i) it can act only as agent for the other Practice; and

(ii) all the individuals who are Principals of the Recognised Body are also Principals of the other Practice; and

any fee or other income arising out of the Recognised Body accrues to the benefit of the other Practice; or

(c) a partnership in which none of the partners is a limited company, a Limited Liability Partnership or a legal person whose members have limited liability.

Sole Practitioner means a solicitor or registered European lawyer who is a sole practitioner, and includes a Recognised Sole Practitioner.

Successor Practice means a Practice identified in this definition as "B", where:

(a) "A" is the Practice to which B succeeds; and
(b) "A's owner" is the owner of A immediately prior to transition; and
(c) "B's owner" is the owner of B immediately following transition; and
(d) "transition" means merger, acquisition, absorption or other transition which results in A no longer being carried on as a discrete legal Practice.

B is a Successor Practice to A where:

(i) B is or was held out, expressly or by implication, by B's owner as being the successor of A or as incorporating A, whether such holding out is contained in notepaper, business cards, form of electronic communications, publications, promotional material or otherwise, or is contained in any statement or declaration by B's owner to any regulatory or taxation authority; and/or
(ii) (where A's owner was a Sole Practitioner and the transition occurred on or before 31 August 2000) - the Sole Practitioner is a Principal of B's owner; and/or
(iii) (where A's owner was a Sole Practitioner and the transition occurred on or after 1 September 2000) - the Sole Practitioner is a Principal or Employee of B's owner; and/or
(iv) (where A's owner was a Recognised Body) - that body is a Principal of B's owner; and/or
(v) (where A's owner was a Partnership) - the majority of the Principals of A's owner have become Principals of B's owner; and/or
(vi) (where A's owner was a Partnership and the majority of Principals of A's owner did not become Principals of the owner of another legal Practice as a result of the transition) - one or more of the Principals of A's owner have become Principals of B's owner and:
    (A) B is carried on under the same name as A or a name which substantially incorporates the name of A (or a substantial part of the name of A); and/or
    (B) B is carried on from the same premises as A; and/or
    (C) the owner of B acquired the goodwill and/or assets of A; and/or
    (D) the owner of B assumed the liabilities of A; and/or
    (E) the majority of staff employed by A's owner became employees of B's owner.

Notwithstanding the foregoing, B is not a Successor Practice to A under paragraph (ii), (iii), (iv) (v) or (vi) if another Practice is or was held out by the owner of that other Practice as the successor of A or as incorporating A, provided that there is insurance complying with these minimum terms and conditions in relation to that other Practice.

Sum Insured means the aggregate limit of liability of each Insurer under the insurance.

APPENDIX 2: RATING SCHEDULE FOR 2009/2010

1 Method for calculation of the ARP Premium

[5018]

1.1 The annual ARP Premium is calculated by identifying the fee band appropriate to the Gross Fees (as defined below) of the Insured Firm. For a £2 million primary policy (£3 million in the case of Relevant Recognised Bodies), where the Gross Fees are £500,000 or less, the ARP Premium is calculated at a rate of 271/2% of the fees declared (30% in the case of Relevant Recognised Bodies). Where the Gross Fees of the Insured Firm are £500,001 or more, the ARP Premium is the sum of:

- the Maximum Premium for the previous Fee Band; plus
- the Marginal Rate on Fees applied to the amount of fees that exceed the ceiling of the previous Fee Band.

There is a minimum premium of £1,500 irrespective of the level of Gross Fees, or the period of time spent in the Assigned Risks Pool during an Indemnity Period.

1.2 Firms other than Relevant Recognised Bodies (£2 million indemnity limit)

Fee Band 1: £0 to £500,000	
Marginal rate on fees	27.5%
Calculation of maximum premium for fee band (Calculation of example premium)	27.5% × £500,000 = £137,500
Maximum premium for fee band	£137,500
Minimum rate on fee for fee band	27.50%
Fee Band 2: £500,001 to £1,500,000	
Marginal rate on fees	22%
Calculation of maximum premium for fee band (Calculation of example premium)	£137,500 (maximum premium for fee band 1) plus 22% × £1,000,000 = £220,000 = £357,000
Maximum premium for fee band	£357,000

Minimum rate on fee for fee band	23.826%
Example	e.g. if fees £1,000,000 £137,500 plus (22% × £500,000 = £110,000) = £247,500
Fee Band 3: £1,500,001 to £3,000,000	
Marginal rate on fees	16.5%
Calculation of maximum premium for fee band (Calculation of example premium)	16.5% × £1,500,000 = £247,500 plus £357,000 (maximum premium for fee band 2) = £605,000
Maximum premium for fee band	£605,000
Minimum rate on fee for fee band	20.163%
Example	e.g. if fees £2,250,000 £357,000 plus (16.5% × £750,000 = £123,750) = £481,250
Fee Band 4: £3,000,001 to £5,000,000	
Marginal rate on fees	13.2%
Calculation of maximum premium for fee band (Calculation of example premium)	13.2% × £2,000,000 = £264,000 plus £605,000 (maximum premium for fee band 3) = £869,000
Maximum premium for fee band	£869,000
Minimum rate on fee for fee band	17.38%
Example	e.g. if fees £4,000,000 £605,000 plus (13.2% × £1,000,000 = £132,000) = £737,000
Fee Band 5: £5,000,001 to £20,000,000	
Marginal rate on fees	11%
Calculation of maximum premium for fee band (Calculation of example premium)	11% × £15,000,000 = £1,650,000 plus £869,000 (maximum premium for fee band 4) = £2,519,000
Maximum premium for fee band	£2,519,000
Minimum rate on fee for fee band	12.595%
Example	e.g. if fees £10,000,000 £869,000 plus (11% × £5,000,000 = £550,000) = £1,419,000
Fee Band 6: £20,000,001 +	
Marginal rate on fees	5.5%
Calculation of maximum premium for fee band (Calculation of example premium)	5.5% × (actual fees — £20,000,000) plus £2,519,000 (maximum premium for fee band 5) = (annual premium)
Maximum premium for fee band	—
Minimum rate on fee for fee band	—
Example	e.g. if fees £30,000,000 £2,519,000 plus (5.5% × £10,000,000) = £550,000 = £3,069,000 or if fees £50,000,000 £2,519,000 plus (5.5% × £30,000,000 = £1,650,000) = £4,169,000

1.3 Relevant Recognised Bodies (£3 million indemnity limit)

Fee Band 1: £0 to £500,000	
Marginal rate on fees	30%
Calculation of maximum premium for fee band (Calculation of example premium)	30% × £500,000 = £150,000
Maximum premium for fee band	£150,000
Minimum rate on fee for fee band	30.00%
Fee Band 2: £500,001 to £1,500,000	
Marginal rate on fees	24%
Calculation of maximum premium for fee band (Calculation of example premium)	£150,000 (maximum premium for fee band 1) plus 24% × £1,000,000 = £200,000 = £390,000
Maximum premium for fee band	£390,000
Minimum rate on fee for fee band	25.992%
Example	e.g. if fees £1,000,000 £150,000 plus (24% × £500,000 = £120,000) = £270,000

Fee Band 3: £1,500,001 to £3,000,000	
Marginal rate on fees	18%
Calculation of maximum premium for fee band (Calculation of example premium)	18% × £1,500,000 = £270,000 plus £390,000 (maximum premium for fee band 2) = £660,000
Maximum premium for fee band	£660,000
Minimum rate on fee for fee band	24.196%
Example	e.g. if fees £2,250,000 £390,000 plus (18% × £750,000 = £135,000) = £525,000
Fee Band 4: £3,000,001 to £5,000,000	
Marginal rate on fees	14.4%
Calculation of maximum premium for fee band (Calculation of example premium)	14.4% × £2,000,000 = £288,000 plus £660,000 (maximum premium for fee band 3)= £948,000
Maximum premium for fee band	£948,000
Minimum rate on fee for fee band	18.96%
Example	e.g. if fees £4,000,000 £660,000 plus (14.4% × £1,000,000 = £144,000) = £804,000
Fee Band 5: £5,000,001 to £20,000,000	
Marginal rate on fees	12%
Calculation of maximum premium for fee band (Calculation of example premium)	12% × £15,000,000 = £1,800,000 plus £948,000 (maximum premium for fee band 4) = £2,748,000
Maximum premium for fee band	£2,748,000
Minimum rate on fee for fee band	13.74%
Example	e.g. if fees £10,000,000 £948,000 plus (12% × £5,000,000 = £600,000) = £1,548,000
Fee Band 6: £20,000,001 +	
Marginal rate on fees	6%
Calculation of maximum premium for fee band (Calculation of example premium)	6% × (actual fees — £20,000,000) plus £2,748,000 (maximum premium for fee band 5) = (annual premium)
Maximum premium for fee band	—
Minimum rate on fee for fee band	—
Example	e.g. if fees £30,000,000 £2,748,000 plus (6% × £10,000,000) = £600,000 = £3,348,000 or if fees £50,000,000 £2,748,000 plus (6% × £30,000,000 = £1,800,000) = £4,548,000

1.4 Primary layer rates

Where an ARP Policy is written as a primary layer of £1 million, with excess layer(s) provided by a Qualifying Insurer, the premium due to the Assigned Risks Pool in respect of that policy shall be an amount calculated in accordance with the table below:

Fee Band 1: £0 to £500,000	
Marginal rate on fees	25%
Calculation of maximum premium for fee band (Calculation of example premium)	25% × £500,000 = £125,000
Maximum premium for fee band	£125,000
Minimum rate on fee for fee band	25.00%
Fee Band 2: £500,001 to £1,500,000	
Marginal rate on fees	20%
Calculation of maximum premium for fee band (Calculation of example premium)	£125,000 (Maximum Premium for fee band 1) plus 20% × £1,000,000 = £200,000 = £325,000
Maximum premium for fee band	£325,000
Minimum rate on fee for fee band	21.66%
Example	e.g. if fees £1,000,000 £125,000 plus (20% × £500,000 = £100,000) = £225,000

Fee Band 3: £1,500,001 to £3,000,000	
Marginal rate on fees	15%
Calculation of maximum premium for fee band (Calculation of example premium	15% × £1,500,000 = £225,000 plus £325,000 (Maximum Premium for fee band 2) = £550,000
Maximum premium for fee band	£550,000
Minimum rate on fee for fee band	18.33%
Example	e.g. if fees £2,250,000 £325,000 plus (15% × £750,000 = £112,500) = £437,500
Fee Band 4: £3,000,001 to £5,000,000	
Marginal rate on fees	12%
Calculation of maximum premium for fee band (Calculation of example premium)	12% × £2,000,000 = £240,000 plus £550,000 (Maximum Premium for fee band 3) = £790,000
Maximum premium for fee band	£790,000
Minimum rate on fee for fee band	15.80%
Example	e.g. if fees £4,000,000 £550,000 plus (12% × £1,000,000 = £120,000) = £670,000
Fee Band 5: £5,000,001 to £20,000,000	
Marginal rate on fees	10%
Calculation of maximum premium for fee band (Calculation of example premium)	10% × £15,000,000 = £1,500,000 plus £790,000 (Maximum Premium for fee band 4) = £2,290,000
Maximum premium for fee band	£2,290,000
Minimum rate on fee for fee band	11.45%
Example	e.g. if fees £10,000,000 £790,000 plus (10% × £5,000,000 = £500,000) = £1,290,000
Fee Band 6: £20,000,001 +	
Marginal rate on fees	5%
Calculation of maximum premium for fee band (Calculation of example premium)	5% × (actual fees — £20,000,000) plus £2,290,000 (Maximum Premium for fee band 5) = (annual premium)
Maximum premium for fee band	—
Minimum rate on fee for fee band	—
Example	e.g. if fees £30,000,000 £2,290,000 plus (5% × £10,000,000) = £500,000 = £2,790,000 or if fees £50,000,000 £2,290,000 plus (5% × £30,000,000 = £1,500,000) = £3,790,000

1.5 Excess layer rates

Where an ARP Policy is written as an excess layer and the primary layer is provided by a Qualifying Insurer, the premium due to the Assigned Risks Pool in respect of that policy shall be an amount equal to the percentage set out below of the primary layer rate calculated in accordance with the information above:

Excess layer	Percentage of primary layer rate
£1 million excess of £1 million (or any part thereof)	10%
£2 million excess of £1 million (or any part thereof)	20%
£1 million excess of £2 million (or any part thereof)	10%

1.6 Co-insurance

Where an ARP Policy is written as co-insurance, on the basis that one or more other Qualifying Insurers are liable in respect of a proportion only of the Sum Insured, the premium due to the *Assigned Risks Pool in respect* of that policy shall be an amount equal to **T × P**, where:

T= the total premium (including any default charge in accordance with Part 2) that would have been due to the Assigned Risks Pool in relation to that policy if the Assigned Risks Pool was the only insurer

P= the proportion, expressed as a percentage, in respect of which the Assigned Risks Pool is liable in relation to that policy

1.7 Definition of Gross Fees

For the purposes of the Assigned Risks Pool rating, Gross Fees means all professional fees of the Insured Firm for the latest complete financial year including remuneration, retained commission, and income of any sort whatsoever of the Insured Firm and notarial fees where a solicitor notary operates a notarial Practice in conjunction with a solicitor's Practice, but excluding only:

(a) interest;
(b) the reimbursement of disbursements;
(c) any amount charged in respect of value added tax;
(d) remuneration derived from any office excluded from the definition of private Practice by these Rules;
(e) dividends;
(f) rents received by the Insured Firm;
(g) income and capital profits from reserved funds established or other investments made by the Insured Firm.

Where the Insured Firm has been in existence for less than 12 months, the Gross Fees for ARP rating purposes shall be the Insured Firm's best estimate of the Gross Fees likely to be received during its first 12 months of trading. However, where the expiry date of the Indemnity Period precedes the completion date of the first 12 months of trading, the Gross Fees for Assigned Risks Pool rating purposes shall be the Insured Firm's best estimate of the Gross Fees likely to be received during the period commencing with the starting date of the Practice and ending with the expiry date of the Indemnity Period.

In the event that the estimated amount of Gross Fees differs from the actual amount of Gross Fees for the relevant period, the Assigned Risks Pool premium shall be adjusted by reference to the actual amount of Gross Fees.

1.8 New Firms

In the case of a new Firm which commences Practice during the course of an Indemnity Period, the ARP Premium payable in relation to that Insured Firm shall be reduced pro rata according to the number of days elapsed in the relevant Indemnity Period prior to that Insured Firm commencing Practice.

1.9 Firms with limited eligibility

In the case of a Firm which will cease to be an Eligible Firm during the course of an Indemnity Period, the ARP Premium or ARP Default Premium (but not any ARP Run-off Premium) which would otherwise be payable in relation to that Insured Firm shall be reduced in accordance with the table below:

Point in Indemnity Period when Firm ceases to be an Eligible Firm	Reduction applied to ARP Premium payable
First calendar month	80 per cent
Second or third calendar month	60 per cent
Fourth, fifth or sixth calendar month	30 per cent
Seventh, eighth or ninth calendar month	15 per cent
Tenth, eleventh or twelfth calendar month	Nil

1.10 Premium payment

The ARP Premium shall be paid to the ARP Manager within 30 days of such premium being notified to the Insured Firm by the ARP Manager.

1.11 Cancellation

Where a Firm enters the Assigned Risks Pool during any Indemnity Period, but subsequently arranges Qualifying Insurance outside the Assigned Risks Pool before the end of that Indemnity Period, a return premium shall become due to the Insured Firm concerned. The return premium shall be calculated in accordance with the Short Period Scale shown below.

1.12 Short Period Scale

Cancellation effective in which calendar month of the Indemnity Period	Percentage of ARP Premium to be returned
First calendar month	80%
Second or third calendar month	60%
Fourth, fifth or sixth calendar month	30%
Seventh, eighth or ninth calendar month	15%
Tenth, eleventh or twelfth calendar month	Nil

However, there shall be no return premium due to the Insured Firm in the event that any claims, or circumstances that may give rise to claims, have been notified to the ARP Manager during the Indemnity Period concerned. Furthermore, in the event that the Assigned Risks Pool insurers are called upon to deal with a claim that was first made against the Insured Firm during the Indemnity Period concerned, but which claim the Insured Firm failed to notify to the ARP Manager, the amount of the return premium shall be repaid to the ARP Manager. The ARP Manager may set off any return premium due to the Insured Firm against any part of the ARP Premium which is due in respect of that Insured Firm but which remains unpaid.

1.13 Run-off premium

If an Insured Firm ceases to carry on a Practice during the course of any Indemnity Period in circumstances where the Assigned Risks Pool is required to provide run-off cover in respect of that Insured Firm under the terms of an ARP Policy issued to that Insured Firm, no return premium shall be payable to that Insured Firm in respect of that ARP Policy.

In addition, in such circumstances the Insured Firm and every Principal of that Insured Firm (including, for these purposes, every person held out as a partner of a sole practitioner) shall be required to pay to the Assigned Risks Pool an additional premium equal to:

- 12/13 of the full annual ARP Premium (or, if applicable, the full annual ARP Default Premium and, for the avoidance of doubt, prior to any reduction applied under paragraph 1.9 above) payable in respect of that Insured Firm in relation to the last Indemnity Period for which such premium was payable, where such Indemnity Period was the period from 1 September 2003 to 30 September 2004; or
- 100 per cent of the full annual ARP premium (or, if applicable, the full annual ARP Default Premium and, for the avoidance of doubt, prior to any reduction applied under paragraph 1.9 above) payable in respect of that Insured Firm in relation to the last Indemnity Period for which such premium was payable, in the case of any other Indemnity Period.

Such additional premium shall be payable to the ARP Manager within 30 days of such premium being notified to the Insured Firm by the ARP Manager.

1.14 Suspended Practices

If:

- an Insured Firm ceases to carry on a Practice during the course of any Indemnity Period in circumstances where the Assigned Risks Pool is required to provide run-off cover in respect of that Insured Firm under the terms of an ARP Policy issued to that Insured Firm; and
- that Insured Firm's Practice subsequently restarts; and
- the ARP Manager agrees to cancel such run-off cover

the Insured Firm shall be entitled to such reimbursement of premium (if any), as the ARP Manager considers appropriate.

If, in addition, the ARP Manager agrees to provide continuing cover in accordance with paragraph 5.4(b)(ii) of the Minimum Terms and Conditions, the Insured Firm and every Principal of that Insured Firm (including, for these purposes, every person held out as a partner of a Sole Practitioner) shall be liable to pay such additional premium (if any) as the ARP Manager considers appropriate.

1.15 Self-Insured excesses for 2009/2010

The Self-Insured excess for each and every claim shall be calculated by multiplying the relevant number of Principals by £4,500, subject to a maximum of £225,000 each claim. The relevant number of Principals is the number of Principals (including, for these purposes, every person held out as a *partner of a Sole Practitioner*) as at the inception date of the Policy.

2 Method for calculation of the ARP Default Premium

The ARP Default Premium shall be an amount equal to the ARP Premium calculated in accordance with Part 1 above, plus an additional default charge of 20% of the amount concerned.

3 Method for calculation of the ARP Run-off Premium

The ARP Run-off Premium shall be an amount equal to **A + B – C**, where:

A= The amount that would have been payable as the ARP Default Premium calculated in accordance with Part 2 above in relation to each Indemnity Period in which the Firm has failed to obtain Qualifying Insurance prior to it becoming a Runoff Firm (including the Indemnity Period in which it ceased to practise)

B= A further amount equal to that which would have been payable as the ARP Default Premium calculated in accordance with Part 2 above in relation to the Indemnity Period during which the Firm ceased to practise

C= Any sum due under Rule 14.2

APPENDIX 3: SPECIAL PROVISIONS FOR REGISTERED EUROPEAN LAWYERS

[5019]–[5020]

1 If:

(a) one or more of the Principals of an Insured Firm are Registered European Lawyers who claim that professional indemnity insurance, or a professional indemnity fund, under their home professional rules provides the Insured Firm's Practice with professional indemnity cover in all respects equivalent in its conditions and extent to that which would be provided under the Minimum Terms and Conditions (Full Home State Cover); and

(b) the Council is so satisfied, (including, without limitation, by reason of any provider of the Full Home State Cover entering into such agreement as the Council may require from time to time but provided that the Council shall not be so satisfied if more than 25% of the Principals are Solicitors),

the Insured Firm and its Principals shall for so long as such cover continues (and, where the Council has required such agreement, for so long as such agreement remains in force and its requirements are complied with by the provider(s) of the Full Home State Cover that are party to it) be exempted from the obligation to take out and maintain Qualifying Insurance.

2 If on an application by one or more Registered European Lawyers who are Principals in an Insured Firm, the Council is satisfied that the Insured Firm's Practice has professional indemnity cover under home professional rules but that the equivalence is only partial (Partial Home State Cover) (including, without limitation, by reason of the provider of the Partial Home State Cover entering into such agreement as the Council may require from time to time), the Insured Firm and its Principals shall for so long as such cover continues (and, where the Council has required such agreement, for so long as such agreement remains in force and its requirements are complied with by the provider(s) of the Partial Home State Cover that are party to it) be exempted from the obligation to take out and maintain Qualifying Insurance, on condition that they take out and maintain a Difference In Conditions Policy, which shall provide cover including the Minimum Terms and Conditions as modified by the following changes (but not otherwise):

(a) Clause 4.5 shall be deleted and replaced with the following:

4.5 No "other insurance" provision

The insurance must not provide that the liability of the Insurer is reduced or excluded by reason of the existence or availability of any other insurance other than as contemplated by clauses 6.2 or 6.12. For the avoidance of doubt, this requirement is not intended to affect any right of the Insurer to claim contribution from any other insurer which is also liable to indemnify any Insured.

(b) Clause 4.9 shall be deleted and replaced with the following:

4.9 Resolution of disputes

The insurance must provide that, if there is a dispute as to whether a Practice is a Successor Practice for the purposes of clauses 1.4, 1.6 or 5.3, the Insured and the Insurer will take all reasonable steps (including, if appropriate, referring the dispute to arbitration) to resolve the dispute in conjunction with any related dispute between any other party which has insurance complying with these minimum terms and conditions and that party's insurer, and in conjunction with the provider of the Partial Home State Cover.

(c) Clause 4.10 shall be deleted and replaced with the following:

4.10 Conduct of a Claim pending dispute resolution

The insurance must provide that, pending resolution of any coverage dispute and without prejudice to any issue in dispute, the Insurer will, if so directed by the Society, conduct any Claim, advance Defence Costs and, if appropriate, compromise and pay the Claim (whether alone or in conjunction with the provider of the Partial Home State Cover). If the Society is satisfied that:

(a) the party requesting the direction has taken all reasonable steps to resolve the dispute with the other party/ies; and

(b) there is a reasonable prospect that the coverage dispute will be resolved or determined in the Insured's favour; and

(c) it is fair and equitable in all the circumstances for such direction to be given;

it may in its absolute discretion make such a direction.

(d) Clause 4.12 shall be deleted and replaced with the following:

4.12 Period of Insurance

The Period of Insurance must not expire prior to the earlier of:

(a) 30 September 2010; or

(b) the date with effect on which the Partial Home State Cover expires or is avoided.

(e) The following clause shall be added:

6.11 Partial Home State Cover

The insurance may exclude any liability of the Insurer to the extent that any such liability is covered under the terms of the Partial Home State Cover irrespective of whether recovery is actually made in respect of such liability.

and in clause 8.2 the following definition shall be added:

Partial Home State Cover has the meaning given in Appendix 3 to the Solicitors' Indemnity Insurance Rules 2009.

3 In the event of an Insured Firm which has the benefit of an exemption under paragraph 1 or paragraph 2 of this Appendix ceasing for whatever reason to enjoy that exemption but continuing to carry on a Practice it shall be treated for all the purposes of these Rules as though it had commenced the Practice on the date when such exemption ceased.

4 Rule 6 (Insolvency Event) shall apply to an Insured Firm which has the benefit of an exemption under paragraph 1 or paragraph 2 of this Appendix in like manner as though the insurance company or entity or fund providing professional indemnity cover under its home professional rules, on the basis of which exemption or partial exemption was granted, was a Qualifying Insurer.

5 In the case of an Insured Firm which has the benefit of an exemption under paragraph 2 of this Appendix all the provisions of these Rules shall apply to the additional professional indemnity insurance required under that paragraph to be taken out with a Qualifying Insurer.

B. MOTOR INSURERS' BUREAU AGREEMENTS

MOTOR INSURERS' BUREAU
A. COMPENSATION OF VICTIMS OF UNTRACED DRIVERS

(14 February 2003, amended 30 December 2008)

THIS AGREEMENT is made the seventh day of February 2003 between the **Secretary of State for Transport** (hereinafter referred to as "the Secretary of State") and the **Motor Insurers' Bureau**, whose registered office is at Linford Wood House 6–12 Capital Drive Linford Wood Milton Keynes MK14 6XT (hereinafter referred to as "MIB").

IT IS HEREBY AGREED AS FOLLOWS:—

INTERPRETATION

General interpretation

[5021]
1

(1) In this Agreement, unless the context otherwise requires, the following expressions have the following meanings—

"1988 Act" means the Road Traffic Act 1988;

"1996 Agreement" means the Agreement made on 14 June 1996 between the Secretary of State for Transport and MIB providing for the compensation of victims of untraced drivers;

"1999 Agreement" means the Agreement dated 13th August 1999 made between the Secretary of State for the Environment, Transport and the Regions and MIB providing for the compensation of victims of uninsured drivers;

"applicant" means the person who has applied for compensation in respect of a death, bodily injury or damage to property (or the person on whose behalf such an application has been made) and "application" means an application made by or on behalf of an applicant;

"arbitrator", where the arbitration takes place under Scottish law, includes an arbiter;

"award" means the aggregate of the sums which MIB is obliged to pay under this Agreement;

"bank holiday" means a day which is, or is to be observed as, a bank holiday under the Banking and Financial Dealings Act 1971;

"judgement" means, in relation to a court in Scotland, a court decree;

"property" means any property whether (in England and Wales) real or personal, or (in Scotland) heritable or moveable;

"relevant proceedings" means civil proceedings brought by the applicant (whether or not pursuant to a requirement made under this Agreement) against a person other than the unidentified person in respect of an event described in clause 4(1);

"specified excess" means £300 or such other sum as may from time to time be agreed in writing between the Secretary of State and MIB;

"unidentified person" means a person who is, or appears to be, wholly or partly liable in respect of the death, injury or damage to property to which an application relates and who cannot be identified.

(2) Save as otherwise herein provided, the Interpretation Act 1978 shall apply for the interpretation of this Agreement as it applies for the interpretation of an Act of Parliament.

(3) Where, under this Agreement, something is required to be done within a specified period after a date or the happening of a particular event, the period begins on the day after the happening of that event.

(4) Where, apart from this paragraph, the period in question, being a period of 7 days or less, would include a Saturday, Sunday, bank holiday, Christmas Day or Good Friday, that day shall be excluded.

(5) Save where expressly otherwise provided, a reference in this Agreement to a numbered clause is a reference to the clause bearing that number in this Agreement and a reference to a numbered paragraph is a reference to a paragraph bearing that number in the clause or schedule in which the reference occurs.

(6) In this Agreement—

(a) a reference (however framed) to the doing of any act or thing by or the happening of any event in relation to the applicant includes a reference to the doing of that act or thing by or the happening of that event in relation to a Solicitor or other person acting on his behalf, and

(b) a requirement to give notice or send documents to MIB shall, where MIB has appointed a Solicitor to act on its behalf in relation to the application, be satisfied by the giving of the notice or the sending of the documents, in the manner herein provided for, to that Solicitor.

Applicants' representatives

2 Where, under and in accordance with this Agreement—

(a) any notice or other document is given to or by a Solicitor or other person acting on behalf of an applicant,

(b) any act or thing is done by or in respect of such Solicitor or other person,

(c) any decision is made by or in respect of such Solicitor or other person, or

(d) any payment is made to such Solicitor or other person,

then, whatever may be the age or other circumstances affecting the capacity of the applicant, that act, thing, decision or payment shall be treated as if it had been done to or by, or made to or in respect of an applicant of full age and capacity.

APPLICATION OF AGREEMENT

Duration of Agreement

[5022]

3

(1) This Agreement shall come into force on 14 February 2003.

(2) This Agreement may be determined by the Secretary of State or by MIB giving to the other not less than twelve months notice in writing to that effect.

(3) Notwithstanding the giving of notice of determination under paragraph (2) this Agreement shall continue to operate in respect of any application made in respect of death, bodily injury or damage to property arising from an event occurring on or before the date of termination specified in the notice.

Scope of Agreement

4

(1) Save as provided in clause 5, this Agreement applies where—

(a) the death of, or bodily injury to, a person or damage to any property of a person has been caused by, or arisen out of, the use of a motor vehicle on a road or other public place in Great Britain, and

(b) the event giving rise to the death, bodily injury or damage to property occurred on or after fourteenth day February 2003, and

(c) the death, bodily injury or damage to property occurred in circumstances giving rise to liability of a kind which is required to be covered by a policy of insurance or a security under Part VI of the 1988 Act, and

(d) it is not possible for the applicant—

(i) to identify the person who is, or appears to be, liable in respect of the death, injury or damage, or

(ii) (where more than one person is or appears to be liable) to identify any one or more of those persons,

and

(e) the applicant has made an application in writing to MIB for the payment of an award in respect of such death, bodily injury or damage to property (and in a case where they are applicable the requirements of paragraph (2) are satisfied), and

(f) the conditions specified in paragraph (3), or such of those conditions as are relevant to the application, are satisfied.

(2) Where an application is signed by a person who is neither the applicant nor a Solicitor acting on behalf of the applicant MIB may refuse to accept the application (and shall incur no liability under this Agreement) until it is reasonably satisfied that, having regard to the status of the signatory and his relationship with the applicant, the applicant is fully aware of the content and effect of the application but subject thereto MIB shall not refuse to accept an application by reason only of the fact that it is signed by a person other than the applicant or his Solicitor.

(3) The conditions referred to in paragraph (1)(f) are that—

(a) [the application must have been within—]

[(i) subject to paragraph (a)(ii), the time limits provided for the victims of traced drivers bringing actions in tort by the Limitation Act 1980 (with regards to England and Wales) or the Prescription and Limitation (Scotland) Act 1973 (with regard to Scotland) in the case of a claim for compensation for death or bodily injury (whether or not damage to property has also arisen from the same event); but]

(ii) nine months after the date of that event in the case of a claim for compensation for damage to property (whether or not death or bodily injury has also arisen from the same event);

(b) in a case where the applicant could not reasonably have been expected to have become aware of the existence of bodily injury or damage to property, the

application must have been made as soon as practicable after he did become (or ought reasonably to have become) aware of it and in any case not later than—

(i) fifteen years after the date of the event which is the subject of the application in the case of a claim for compensation for death or bodily injury (whether or not damage to property has also arisen from the same event), or

(ii) two years after the date of that event in the case of a claim for compensation for damage to property (whether or not death or bodily injury has also arisen from the same event);

[(b)] the applicant, or a person acting on the applicant's behalf, must have reported that event to the police—

(i) in the case of an event from which there has arisen a death or bodily injury alone, not later than 14 days after its occurrence, and

(ii) in the case of an event from which there has arisen property damage (whether or not a death or bodily injury has also arisen from it), not later than 5 days after its occurrence,

but where that is not reasonably possible the event must have been reported as soon as reasonably possible;

[(c)] the applicant must produce satisfactory evidence of having made the report required under sub-paragraph (c) in the form of an acknowledgement from the relevant force showing the crime or incident number under which that force has recorded the matter;

[(d)] after making, or authorising the making of, a report to the police the applicant must have co-operated with the police in any investigation they have made into the event.

(4) Where both death or bodily injury and damage to property have arisen from a single event nothing contained in this clause shall require an applicant to make an application in respect of the death or bodily injury on the same occasion as an application in respect of the damage to property and where two applications are made in respect of one event the provisions of this Agreement shall apply separately to each of them.

Exclusions from Agreement

5

(1) This Agreement does not apply where an application is made in any of the following circumstances (so that where an application is made partly in such circumstances and partly in other circumstances, it applies only to the part made in those other circumstances)—

(a) where the applicant makes no claim for compensation in respect of death or bodily injury and the damage to property in respect of which compensation is claimed has been caused by, or has arisen out of, the use of an unidentified vehicle;

(b) where the death, bodily injury or damage to property in respect of which the application is made has been caused by or has arisen out of the use of a motor vehicle which at the time of the event giving rise to such death, injury or damage was owned by or in the possession of the Crown, unless at that time some other person had undertaken responsibility for bringing into existence a policy of insurance or security satisfying the requirements of the 1988 Act;

(c) where, at the time of the event in respect of which the application is made the person suffering death, injury or damage to property was voluntarily allowing himself to be carried in the responsible vehicle and before the commencement of his journey in the vehicle (or after such commencement if he could reasonably be expected to have alighted from the vehicle) he knew or ought to have known that the vehicle—

(i) had been stolen or unlawfully taken, or

(ii) was being used without there being in force in relation to its use a contract of insurance or security which complied with the 1988 Act; or

(iii) was being used in the course or furtherance of crime; or

(iv) was being used as a means of escape from or avoidance of lawful apprehension;

(d) where the death, bodily injury or damage to property was caused by, or in the course of, an act of terrorism;

(e) where property damaged as a result of the event giving rise to the application is insured against such damage and the applicant has recovered the full amount of his loss from the insurer on or before the date of the application (but without prejudice to the application of the Agreement in the case of any other claim for compensation made in respect of the same event);

(f) where a claim is made for compensation in respect of damage to a motor vehicle (or losses arising therefrom) and, at the time when the damage to it was sustained—

(i) there was not in force in relation to the use of that vehicle such a contract of insurance as is required by Part VI of the 1988 Act, and
(ii) the person suffering damage to property either knew or ought to have known that was the case

(but without prejudice to the application of the Agreement in the case of any other claim for compensation made in respect of the same event);

(g) where the application is made neither by a person suffering injury or property damage nor by the personal representative of such a person nor by a dependant claiming in respect of the death of another person but is made in any of the following circumstances, namely—
(i) where a cause of action or a judgment has been assigned to the applicant, or
(ii) where the applicant is acting pursuant to a right of subrogation or a similar contractual or other right belonging to him.

(2) The burden of proving that the person suffering death, injury or damage to property knew or ought to have known of any matter set out in paragraph (1)(c) shall be on MIB but, in the absence of evidence to the contrary, proof by MIB of any of the following matters shall be taken as proof of his knowledge of the matter set out in paragraph (1)(c)(ii)—
(a) that he was the owner or registered keeper of the vehicle or had caused or permitted its use;
(b) that he knew the vehicle was being used by a person who was below the minimum age at which he could be granted a licence authorising the driving of a vehicle of that class;
(c) that he knew that the person driving the vehicle was disqualified for holding or obtaining a driving licence;
(d) that he knew that the user of the vehicle was neither its owner nor registered keeper nor an employee of the owner or registered keeper nor the owner or registered keeper of any other vehicle.
(e) Where—
(a) the application includes a claim for compensation both in respect of death or bodily injury and also in respect of damage to property, and
(b) the death or injury and the property damage has been caused by, or has arisen out of, the use of an unidentified vehicle,

the Agreement does not apply to the claim for compensation in respect of the damage to property.

(3) For the purposes of paragraphs (1) and (2)—
(a) references to a person being carried in a vehicle include references to his being carried in or upon, or entering or getting on to or alighting from the vehicle;
(b) knowledge which a person has or ought to have for the purposes of sub-paragraph (c) includes knowledge of matters which he could reasonably be expected to have been aware of had he not been under the self-induced influence of drink or drugs;
(c) "crime" does not include the commission of an offence under the Traffic Acts, except an offence under section 143 (use of a motor vehicle on a road without there being in force a policy of insurance), and "Traffic Acts" means the Road Traffic Regulation Act 1984, the Road Traffic Act 1988 and the Road Traffic Offenders Act 1988;
(d) "responsible vehicle" means the vehicle the use of which caused (or through the use of which there arose) the death, bodily injury or damage to property which is the subject of the application;
(e) "terrorism" has the meaning given in section 1 of the Terrorism Act 2000;
(f) "dependant" has the same meaning as in section 1(3) of the Fatal Accidents Act 1976.

Limitation on application of Agreement

6

(1) This clause applies where an applicant receives compensation or other payment in respect of the death, bodily injury or damage to property otherwise than in the circumstances described in clause 5(1)(e) from any of the following persons—
(a) an insurer or under an insurance policy (other than a life assurance policy) or arrangement between the applicant or his employer and the insurer, or
(b) a person who has given a security pursuant to the requirements of 1988 Act under an agreement between the applicant and the security giver, or
(c) any other source other than a person who is an identified person for the purposes of clauses 13 to 15 or an insurer of, or a person who has given a security on behalf of, such a person.

(2) Where the compensation or other payment received is equal to or greater than the amount which MIB would otherwise be liable to pay under the provisions of clauses 8 and 9 MIB shall have no liability under those provisions (to the intent that this Agreement shall immediately cease to apply except to the extent that the applicant is entitled to a contribution to his legal costs under clause 10).

(3) Where the compensation or other payment received is less than the amount which MIB would otherwise be liable to pay under the provisions of clauses 8 and 9 MIB's liability under those provisions shall be reduced by an amount equal to that compensation or payment.

NOTES

Clause 4: words in square brackets in para (3)(a) substituted for the words "except in a case to which sub-paragraph (b) applies, the application must have been made not later than—", para (3)(a)(i) substituted, para (3)(b) in italics repealed and original para (3)(c)–(e) renumbered as para (3)(b)–(d) by the Supplementary Agreement between the Secretary of State for Transport and the Motor Insurers' Bureau, dated 30 December 2008, clause 4(a)–(c), in relation to accidents occurring after midnight on 1 February 2009. Original para (3)(a)(i) read as follows—

"(i) three years after the date of the event which is the subject of the application in the case of a claim for compensation for death or bodily injury (whether or not damage to property has also arisen from the same event), or".

PRINCIPAL TERMS AND CONDITIONS

MIB's obligation to investigate claims and determine amount of award

[5023]
7

(1) MIB shall, at its own cost, take all reasonable steps to investigate the claim made in the application and–
- (a) if it is satisfied after conducting a preliminary investigation that the case is not one to which this Agreement applies and the application should be rejected, it shall inform the applicant accordingly and (subject to the following provisions of this Agreement) need take no further action, or
- (b) in any other case, it shall conduct a full investigation and shall as soon as reasonably practicable having regard to the availability of evidence make a report on the applicant's claim.

(2) Subject to the following paragraphs of this clause, MIB shall, on the basis of the report and, where applicable, any relevant proceedings—
- (a) reach a decision as to whether it must make an award to the applicant in respect of the death, bodily injury or damage to property, and
- (b) where it decides to make an award, determine the amount of that award.

(3) Where MIB reaches a decision that the Agreement applies and that it is able to calculate the whole amount of the award the report shall be treated as a full report and the award shall (subject to the following provisions of this Agreement) be treated as a full and final award.

(4) Where MIB reaches a decision that the Agreement applies and that it should make an award but further decides that it is not at that time able to calculate the final amount of the award (or a part thereof), it may designate the report as an interim report and where it does so–
- (a) it may, as soon as reasonably practicable, make one or more further interim reports, but
- (b) it must, as soon as reasonably practicable having regard to the availability of evidence, make a final report.

(5) Where it makes an interim or final report MIB shall, on the basis of that report and, where applicable, any relevant proceedings—
- (a) in the case of an interim report, determine the amount of any interim award it wishes to make, and
- *(b) in the case of its final report*, determine the whole amount of its award which shall (subject to the following provisions of this Agreement) be treated as a full and final award.

(6) MIB shall be under an obligation to make an award only if it is satisfied, on the balance of probabilities, that the death, bodily injury or damage to property was caused in such circumstances that the unidentified person would (had he been identified) have been held liable to pay damages to the applicant in respect of it.

(7) MIB shall determine the amount of its award in accordance with the provisions of clauses 8 to 10 and (in an appropriate case) clauses 12 to 14 but shall not thereby be under a duty to calculate the exact proportion of the award which represents compensation, interest or legal costs.

Compensation

8

(1) MIB shall include in its award to the applicant, by way of compensation for the death, bodily injury or damage to property, a sum equivalent to the amount which a court—

(a) applying the law of England and Wales, in a case where the event giving rise to the death, injury or damage occurred in England or Wales, or

(b) applying the law of Scotland, in a case where that event occurred in Scotland,

would have awarded to the applicant (where applying English law) as general and special damages or (where applying the law of Scotland) as solatium and patrimonial loss if the applicant had brought successful proceedings to enforce a claim for damages against the unidentified person.

(2) In calculating the sum payable under paragraph (1), MIB shall adopt the same method of calculation as the court would adopt in calculating damages but it shall be under no obligation to include in that calculation an amount in respect of loss of earnings suffered by the applicant to the extent that he has been paid wages or salary (or any sum in lieu of them) whether or not such payments were made subject to an agreement or undertaking on his part to repay the same in the event of his recovering damages for the loss of those earnings.

(3) Where an application includes a claim in respect of damage to property, MIB's liability in respect of that claim shall be limited in accordance with the following rules–

(a) if the loss incurred by an applicant in respect of any one event giving rise to a claim does not exceed the specified excess, MIB shall incur no liability to that applicant in respect of that event;

(b) if the aggregate of all losses incurred by both the applicant and other persons in respect of any one event giving rise to a claim ("the total loss") exceeds the specified excess but does not exceed £250,000—

(i) MIB's liability to an individual applicant shall be the amount of the claim less the specified excess, and

(ii) MIB's total liability to applicants in respect of claims arising from that event shall be the total loss less a sum equal to the specified excess multiplied by the number of applicants who have incurred loss through damage to property;

(c) if the total loss exceeds £250,000—

(i) MIB's liability to an individual applicant shall not exceed the amount of the claim less the specified excess, and

(ii) MIB's total liability to applicants in respect of claims arising from that event shall be £250,000 less a sum equal to the specified excess multiplied by the number of applicants who have incurred loss due to property damage.

(4) MIB shall not be liable to pay compensation to an appropriate authority in respect of any loss incurred by that authority as a result of its failure to recover a charge for the recovery, storage or disposal of an abandoned vehicle under a power contained in the Refuse Disposal (Amenity) Act 1978 or Part VIII of the Road Traffic Regulation Act 1984 (and in this paragraph "appropriate authority" has the meaning given in the Act under which the power to recover the charge was exercisable).

Interest

9

(1) MIB shall in an appropriate case also include in the award a sum representing interest on the compensation payable under clause 8 at a rate equal to that which a court—

(a) applying the law of England and Wales, in a case where the event giving rise to the death, bodily injury or damage to property occurred in England or Wales, or

(b) applying the law of Scotland, in a case where that event occurred in Scotland,

would have awarded to a successful applicant.

(2) MIB is not required by virtue of paragraph (1) to pay a sum representing interest in respect of the period before the date which is one month after the date on which MIB receives the police report (but, where MIB has failed to seek and obtain that report promptly after the date of the application, interest shall run from the date which falls one month after the date on which it would have received it had it acted promptly).

Contribution towards legal costs

10

(1) MIB shall, in a case where it has decided to make a compensation payment under clause 8, also include in the award a sum by way of contribution towards the cost of obtaining legal advice from a Solicitor, Barrister or Advocate in respect of—

(a) the making of an application under this Agreement;

(b) the correctness of a decision made by MIB under this Agreement; or

(c) the adequacy of an award (or a part thereof) offered by MIB under this Agreement

that sum to be determined in accordance with the Schedule to this Agreement.

(2) MIB shall not be under a duty to make a payment under paragraph (1) unless it is satisfied that the applicant did obtain legal advice in respect of any one or more of the matters specified in that paragraph.

Conditions precedent to MIB's obligations

11

(1) The applicant must—
- (a) make his application in such form,
- (b) provide in support of the application such statements and other information (whether in writing or orally at interview), and
- (c) give such further assistance,

as may reasonably be required by MIB or by any person acting on MIB's behalf to enable an investigation to be carried out under clause 7 of this Agreement.

(2) The applicant must provide MIB with written authority to take all such steps as may be reasonably necessary in order to carry out a proper investigation of the claim.

(3) The applicant must, if MIB reasonably requires him to do so before reaching a decision under clause 7, provide MIB with a statutory declaration, made by him, setting out to the best of his knowledge and belief all the facts and circumstances upon which his application is based or such facts and circumstances in relation to the application as MIB may reasonably specify.

(4) The applicant must, if MIB reasonably requires him to do so before it reaches a decision or determination under clause 7 and subject to the following provisions of this clause—
- (a) at MIB's option (and subject to paragraph (5)) either—
  - (i) bring proceedings against any person or persons who may, in addition or alternatively to the unidentified person, be liable to the applicant in respect of the death, bodily injury or damage to property (by virtue of having caused or contributed to that death, injury or damage, by being vicariously liable in respect of it or having failed to effect third party liability insurance in respect of the vehicle in question) and co-operate with MIB in taking such steps as are reasonably necessary to obtain judgement in those proceedings, or
  - (ii) authorise MIB to bring such proceedings and take such steps in the applicant's name;
- (b) at MIB's expense, provide MIB with a transcript of any official shorthand or recorded note taken in those proceedings of any evidence given or judgement delivered therein;
- (c) assign to MIB or to its nominee the benefit of any judgement obtained by him (whether or not obtained in proceedings brought under sub-paragraph (a) above) in respect of the death, bodily injury or damage to property upon such terms as will secure that MIB or its nominee will be accountable to the applicant for any amount by which the aggregate of all sums recovered by MIB or its nominee under the judgement (after deducting all reasonable expenses incurred in effecting recovery) exceeds the award made by MIB under this Agreement in respect of that death, injury or damage;
- (d) undertake to assign to MIB the right to any sum which is or may be due from an insurer, security giver or other person by way of compensation for, or benefit in respect of, the death, bodily injury or damage to property and which would (if payment had been made before the date of the award) have excluded or limited MIB's liability under the provisions of clause 6.

(5) If, pursuant to paragraph (4)(a), MIB requires the applicant to bring proceedings or take steps against any person or persons (or to authorise MIB to bring such proceedings or take such steps in his name) MIB shall indemnify the applicant against all costs and expenses reasonably incurred by him in complying with that requirement.

(6) Where the applicant, without having been required to do so by MIB, has commenced proceedings against any person described in paragraph (4)(a)—
- (a) the applicant shall as soon as reasonably possible notify MIB of such proceedings and provide MIB with such further information about them as MIB may reasonably require, and
- (b) the applicant's obligations in paragraph (4)(a) to (c) shall apply in respect of such proceedings as if they had been brought at MIB's request.

JOINT AND SEVERAL LIABILITY

Joint and several liability: interpretation

[5024]

12 In clauses 13 to 15—

"identified person" includes an identified employer or principal of a person who is himself unidentified;

"original judgement" means a judgement obtained against an identified person at first instance in relevant proceedings;

"three month period" means the period of three months specified in clause 13(3); and

"unidentified person's liability" means—

(a) the amount of the contribution which (if not otherwise apparent) would, on the balance of probabilities, have been be recoverable from the unidentified person in an action brought—
   (i) in England and Wales, under the Civil Liability (Contribution) Act 1978, or
   (ii) in Scotland, under the Law Reform (Miscellaneous Provisions) (Scotland) Act 1940,
   by an identified person who had been held liable in full in an earlier action brought by the applicant, and
(b) where a court has awarded the applicant interest or costs in addition to damages, an appropriate proportion of that interest or those costs.

MIB's liability where wrongdoer is identified
13
(1) This clause applies where the death, bodily injury or damage to property in respect of which the application is made is caused, or appears on the balance of probabilities to have been caused—
   (a) partly by an unidentified person and partly by an identified person, or
   (b) partly by an unidentified person and partly by another unidentified person whose employer or principal is identified,
   in circumstances making (or appearing to make) the identified person liable, or vicariously liable, to the applicant in respect of the death, injury or damage.
(2) Where this clause applies, MIB's liability under this Agreement shall not exceed the unidentified person's liability and the following provisions shall apply to determine MIB's liability in specific cases.
(3) Where the applicant has obtained a judgement in relevant proceedings in respect of the death, injury or damage which has not been satisfied in full by or on behalf of the identified person within the period of three months after the date on which the applicant became entitled to enforce it—
   (a) if that judgement is wholly unsatisfied within the three month period MIB shall make an award equal to the unidentified person's liability;
   (b) if the judgement is satisfied in part only within the three month period, MIB shall make an award equal to—
      (i) the unsatisfied part, if it does not exceed the unidentified person's liability; and
      (ii) the unidentified person's liability, if the unsatisfied part exceeds the unidentified person's liability.
(4) A judgment given in any relevant proceedings against an identified person shall be conclusive as to any issue determined in those proceedings which is relevant to the determination of MIB's liability under this Agreement.
(5) Where the applicant has not obtained (or been required by MIB to obtain) a judgement in respect of the death, injury or damage against the identified person but has received an agreed payment from the identified person in respect of the death, bodily injury or damage to property, that payment shall be treated for the purposes of this Agreement as a full settlement of the applicant's claim and MIB shall be under no liability under this Agreement in respect thereof.
(6) Where the applicant has not obtained (or been required by MIB to obtain) a judgement in respect of the death, injury or damage against the identified person nor received any payment by way of compensation in respect thereof from the identified person MIB shall make an award equal to the unidentified person's liability.

Appeals by identified persons
14
(1) This clause applies where an appeal against, or other proceeding to set aside, the original judgement is commenced within the three month period.
(2) If, as a result of the appeal or other proceeding—
   (a) the applicant ceases to be entitled to receive any payment in respect of the death, bodily injury or damage to property from any identified person, clause 13 shall apply as if he had neither obtained nor been required by MIB to obtain a judgement against that person;
   (b) the applicant becomes entitled to recover an amount different from that which he was entitled to recover under the original judgement the provisions of clause 13(3) shall apply, but as if for each of the references therein to the original judgement there were substituted a reference to the judgement in that appeal or other proceeding;

(c) the applicant remains entitled to enforce the original judgement the provisions of clause 13(3) shall apply, but as if for each of the references therein to the three month period there were substituted a reference to the period of three months after the date on which the appeal or other proceeding was disposed of.

(3) Where the judgement in the appeal or other proceeding is itself the subject of a further appeal or similar proceeding the provisions of this clause shall apply in relation to that further appeal or proceeding in the same manner as they apply in relation to the first appeal or proceeding.

(4) Nothing in this clause shall oblige MIB to make a payment to the applicant until the appeal or other proceeding has been determined.

Compensation recovered under Uninsured Drivers Agreements

15

(1) Where, in a case to which clause 13 applies, judgement in the relevant proceedings is given against an identified person in circumstances which render MIB liable to satisfy that judgement under any of the Uninsured Drivers Agreements, MIB shall not be under any liability under this Agreement in respect of the event to which the relevant proceedings relate.

(2) In this clause "Uninsured Drivers Agreements" means—

(a) the Agreement dated 21st December 1988 made between the Secretary of State for Transport and MIB providing for the compensation of victims of uninsured drivers,

(b) the 1999 Agreement, and

(c) any agreement made between the Secretary of State and MIB (or their respective successors) which supersedes (whether immediately or otherwise) the 1999 Agreement.

NOTIFICATION OF DECISION AND PAYMENT OF AWARD

Notification of decision

[5025]

16 MIB shall give the applicant notice of a decision or determination under clause 7 in writing and when so doing shall provide him—

(a) if the application is rejected because a preliminary investigation has disclosed that it is not one made in a case to which this Agreement applies, with a statement to that effect;

(b) if the application has been fully investigated, with a statement setting out—

(i) all the evidence obtained during the investigation, and

(ii) MIB's findings of fact from that evidence which are relevant to the decision;

(c) if it has decided to make an interim award on the basis of an interim report under clause 7(4), with a copy of the report and a statement of the amount of the interim award;

(d) if it has decided to make a full report under clause 7(3) or a final report under clause 7(4)(b), with a copy of the report and a statement of the amount of the full and final award;

(e) in a case to which clause 13 applies, with a statement setting out the way in which the amount of the award has been computed under the provisions of that clause; and

(f) in every case, with a statement of its reasons for making the decision or determination.

Acceptance of decision and payment of award

17

(1) Subject to the following paragraphs of this clause, if MIB gives notice to the applicant that it has decided to make an award to him, it shall pay him that award—

(a) in the case of an interim award made pursuant to clause 7(5)(a), as soon as reasonably practicable after the making of the interim report to which the award relates;

(b) in the case of a full and final award made pursuant to clause 7(3) or (5)(b)—

(i) where the applicant notifies MIB in writing that he accepts the offer of the award unconditionally, not later than 14 days after the date on which MIB receives that acceptance, or

(ii) where the applicant does not notify MIB of his acceptance in accordance with sub-paragraph (a) but the period during which he may give notice of an appeal under clause 19 has expired without such notice being given, not later than 14 days after the date of expiry of that period,

and that payment shall discharge MIB from all liability under this Agreement in respect of the death, bodily injury or damage to property for which the award is made.

(2) MIB may, upon notifying an applicant of its decision to make an award, offer to pay the award in instalments in accordance with a structure described in the decision letter (the "structured settlement") and if the applicant notifies MIB in writing of his acceptance of the offer—

(a) the first instalment of the payment under the structured settlement shall be made not later than 14 days after the date on which MIB receives that acceptance, and

(b) subsequent payments shall be made in accordance with the agreed structure.

(3) Where an applicant has suffered bodily injury and believes either that there is a risk that he will develop a disease or condition other than that in respect of which he has made a claim or that a disease or condition in respect of which he has made a claim will deteriorate, he may—

(a) by notice given in his application, or

(b) by notice in writing received by MIB before the date on which MIB issues notification of its full or (as the case may be) final report under clause 16,

state that he wishes MIB to make a provisional award and if he does so paragraphs (4) and (5) shall apply.

(4) The applicant must specify in the notice given under paragraph (3)—

(a) each disease and each type of deterioration which he believes may occur, and

(b) the period during or within which he believes it may occur.

(5) Where MIB receives a notice under paragraph (3) it shall, not later than 14 days after the date of such receipt (or within such longer period as the applicant may agree)—

(a) accept the notice and confirm that any award it makes (other than an interim award made pursuant to clause 7(5)(a)) is to be treated as a provisional award, or

(b) reject the notice and inform the applicant that it is not willing to make a provisional award.

(6) Where MIB has notified the applicant that it accepts the notice, an award which would otherwise be treated a full or final award under this Agreement shall be treated as a provisional award only and the applicant may make a supplementary application under this Agreement but—

(a) only in respect of a disease or a type of deterioration of his condition specified in his notice, and

(b) not later than the expiration of the period specified in his notice.

(7) Where MIB has notified the applicant that it rejects the notice, subject to any decision to the contrary made by an arbitrator, no award which MIB makes shall be treated as a provisional award.

APPEALS AGAINST MIB'S DECISION

Right of appeal

[5026]

18 Where an applicant is not willing to accept—

(a) a decision or determination made by MIB under clause 7 or a part thereof, or

(b) a proposal for a structured settlement or a rejection of the applicant's request for a provisional award under clause 17,

he may give notice (a "notice of appeal") that he wishes to submit the matter to arbitration in accordance with the provisions of clauses 19 to 25.

Notice of appeal

19

(1) A notice of appeal shall be given in writing to MIB at any time before the expiration of a period of 6 weeks from—

(a) the date on which the applicant receives notice of MIB's decision under clause 16;

(b) where he disputes a notification given under clause 17(5)(b), the date when such notification is given;

(c) in any other case, the date on which he is given notification of the decision, determination or requirement.

(2) The notice of appeal—

(a) shall state the grounds on which the appeal is made,

(b) shall contain the applicant's observations on MIB's decision,

(c) may be accompanied by such further evidence in support of the appeal as the applicant thinks fit, and

(d) shall contain an undertaking that (subject, in the case of an arbitration to be conducted England and Wales, to his rights under sections 67 and 68 of the Arbitration Act 1996) the applicant will abide by the decision of the arbitrator made under this Agreement.

Procedure following notice of appeal

20

(1) Not later than 7 days after receiving the notice of appeal MIB shall—

(a) apply to the Secretary of State for the appointment of a single arbitrator, or

(b) having notified the applicant of its intention to do so, cause an investigation to be made into any further evidence supplied by the applicant and report to the applicant upon that investigation and of any change in its decision which may result from it.

(2) Where the only ground stated in the notice of appeal is that the award is insufficient (including a ground contesting the degree of contributory negligence attributed to the applicant or, as the case may be, the person in respect of whose death the application is made), MIB may give notice to the applicant of its intention, if the appeal proceeds to arbitration, to ask the arbitrator to decide whether its award exceeds what a court would have awarded or whether the case is one in which it would make an award at all and shall in that notice set out such observations on that matter as MIB considers relevant to the arbitrator's decision.

(3) Where MIB has made a report under paragraph (1)(b) or given to the applicant notice under paragraph (2), the applicant may, not later than 6 weeks after the date on which the report or (as the case may be) the notice was given to him—

(a) notify MIB that he wishes to withdraw the appeal, or

(b) notify MIB that he wishes to continue with the appeal and send with that notification—

(i) any observations on the report made under paragraph (1)(b) which he wishes to have drawn to the attention of the arbitrator,

(ii) any observations on the contents of the notice given under paragraph (2), including any further evidence not previously made available to MIB and relevant to the matter, which he wishes to have drawn to the attention of the arbitrator.

(4) Where the applicant notifies MIB under paragraph (3)(b) of his wish to continue the appeal, or if the applicant fails within the specified period of 6 weeks to give notification of his wish either to withdraw or to continue with the appeal, MIB shall, not later than 7 days after receiving the notification or 7 days after the expiry of the said period (as the case may be)—

(a) apply to the Secretary of State for the appointment of an arbitrator, or

(b) having notified the applicant of its intention to do so, cause a further investigation to be made into the further evidence sent under paragraph (3)(b)(ii).

(5) Where MIB has caused an investigation to be made into any further evidence supplied by the applicant under paragraph (3)(b)(ii), it shall report to the applicant upon that investigation and of any change in a decision or determination made under clause 7 which may result from it and the applicant may, not later than 6 weeks after the date on which he receives the report—

(a) notify MIB that he wishes to withdraw the appeal, or

(b) notify MIB that he wishes to continue with the appeal.

(6) Where the applicant notifies MIB under paragraph (5)(b) of his wish to continue the appeal, or if the applicant fails within the specified period of 6 weeks to give notification of his wish either to withdraw or to continue with the appeal, MIB shall not later than 7 days after receiving the notification or 7 days after the expiry of the said period (as the case may be) apply to the Secretary of State for the appointment of an arbitrator.

(7) When applying to the Secretary of State for the appointment of an arbitrator MIB may send with the application such written observations as it wishes to make upon the applicant's notice of appeal but must at the same time send a copy of those observations to the applicant.

Appointment of arbitrator

21

(1) In the event of MIB neither applying to the Secretary of State for the appointment of an arbitrator in accordance with the provisions of clause 20 nor taking such further steps as it may at its discretion take in accordance with that clause, the applicant may apply to the Secretary of State for the appointment of an arbitrator.

(2) For the purposes of the Arbitration Act 1996 (where the arbitration is to be conducted in England and Wales) the arbitral proceedings are to be regarded as commencing on the date of the making of the application by the Secretary of State or the applicant (as the case may be).

(3) The Secretary of State shall, upon the making of an application for the appointment of an arbitrator to hear the appeal, appoint the first available member, by rotation, of a panel of Queen's Counsel appointed for the purpose of determining appeals under this Agreement (where the event giving rise to the death, bodily injury or damage to property occurred in England and Wales) by the Lord Chancellor or (where the event giving rise to the death, bodily injury or damage to property occurred in Scotland) by the Lord Advocate and shall forthwith notify the applicant and MIB of the appointment.

Arbitration procedure

22

(1) Upon receiving notification from the Secretary of State of the appointment of an arbitrator, MIB shall send to the arbitrator—

(a) the notice of appeal,

(b) (if appropriate) its request for a decision as to whether its award exceeds what a court would have awarded or whether the case is one in which it would make an award at all,

(c) copies of—

(i) the applicant's application,

(ii) its decision; and

(iii) all statements, declarations, notices, reports, observations and transcripts of evidence made or given under this Agreement by the applicant or MIB.

(2) The arbitrator may, if it appears to him to be necessary or expedient for the purpose of resolving any issue, ask MIB to make a further investigation and to submit a written report of its findings to him for his consideration and in such a case—

(a) MIB shall undertake the investigation and send copies of the report to the arbitrator and the applicant,

(b) the applicant may, not later than 4 weeks after the date on which a copy of the report is received by him, submit written observations on it to the arbitrator and if he does so he shall send a copy of those observations to MIB.

(3) The arbitrator shall, after considering the written submissions referred to in paragraphs (1) and (2), send to the applicant and MIB a preliminary decision letter setting out the decision he proposes to make under clause 23 and his reasons for doing so.

(4) Not later than 28 days after the date of sending of the preliminary decision letter (or such later date as the applicant and MIB may agree) the applicant and MIB may, by written notification given to the arbitrator and copied to the other, either—

(a) accept the preliminary decision, or

(b) submit written observations upon the preliminary decision or the reasons or both, or

(c) request an oral hearing,

and if either of them should within that period fail to do any of those things (including a failure to provide the other person with a copy of his notification) he or it shall be treated as having accepted the decision.

(5) If the applicant submits new evidence with any written observations under paragraph (4)(b) MIB may at its discretion, but within 28 days or such longer period as the arbitrator may allow, do any of the following–

(a) make an investigation into that evidence,

(b) submit its own written observations on that evidence, and

(c) if it has not already done so, request an oral hearing,

and, except where an oral hearing has been requested, the arbitrator shall (in exercise of his powers under section 34 of the Arbitration Act 1996 if the arbitration is being conducted in England and Wales) determine whether, and if so how, such evidence shall be admitted and tested.

(6) If both the applicant and MIB accept the reasoned preliminary decision that decision shall be treated as his final decision for the purposes of clause 23 (so that clause 23(2) shall not then apply) but if either of them submits observations on that decision the arbitrator must take those observations into account before making a final decision.

(7) If the applicant or MIB requests an oral hearing, the arbitrator shall determine the appeal in that manner and in such a case—

(a) the hearing shall be held in public unless the applicant requests that it (or any part of it) be heard in private;

(b) the hearing shall take place at a location—

(i) in England or Wales, where the event giving rise to the death, bodily injury or damage to property occurred in England or Wales and the applicant is resident in England or Wales,

(ii) in Scotland, where the event giving rise to the death, bodily injury or damage to property occurred in Scotland and the applicant is resident in Scotland, or

(iii) in England, Wales or Scotland in any other case,

which in the opinion of the arbitrator (after consultation with each of them) is convenient for both MIB and the applicant as well as for himself;

(c) a party to the hearing may be represented by a lawyer or other person of that party's choosing;

(d) a party to the hearing shall be entitled to address the arbitrator, to call witnesses and to put questions to those witnesses and any other person called as a witness.

Arbitrator's decision

23

(1) The arbitrator, having regard to the subject matter of the proceedings, may in an appropriate case–

(a) determine whether or not the case is one to which this Agreement applies;

(b) remit the application to MIB for a full investigation and a decision in accordance with the provisions of this Agreement;

(c) determine whether MIB should make an award under this Agreement and if so what that award should be;

(d) determine such other questions as have been referred to him as he thinks fit;

(e) (subject to the provisions of paragraph (4) of this clause and clause 24) order that the costs of the proceedings shall be paid by one party or allocated between the parties in such proportions as he thinks fit;

(f) [determine, in like manner as a court, whether it would be equitable to allow the case to proceed having regard to the circumstances envisaged by section 33 of the Limitation Act 1980 (with regard to England and Wales) or section 19A of the Prescription and Limitation (Scotland) Act 1973 (with regard to Scotland);]

and where the arbitrator makes a determination under sub-paragraph (a) that the case is one to which this Agreement applies, all the provisions of this Agreement shall apply as if the case were one to which clause 7(1)(b) applies.

(2) The arbitrator shall notify MIB and the applicant of his decision in writing.

(3) MIB shall pay to the applicant any amount which the arbitrator has decided shall be awarded to him, and that payment shall discharge MIB from all liability under this Agreement in respect of the death, bodily injury or damage to property in respect of which that decision is given.

(4) Where an oral hearing has taken place at the request of the applicant and the arbitrator is satisfied that it was unnecessary and that the matter could have been decided on the basis of the written submissions referred to in clause 22(1) and (2) he shall take that into account when making an order under paragraph (1)(e).

Payment of arbitrator's fee and costs of legal representation

24

(1) Subject to paragraph (2), MIB shall upon being notified of the decision of the arbitrator pay the arbitrator a fee approved by the Lord Chancellor or the Lord Advocate, as the case may be, after consultation with MIB.

(2) In a case where it appears to the arbitrator that, having regard to all the surrounding circumstances of the case, there were no reasonable grounds for making the appeal or bringing the question before him, the arbitrator may, in his discretion, order–

(a) the applicant or,

(b) where he considers it appropriate to do so, any Solicitor or other person acting on behalf of the applicant,

to reimburse MIB the fee it has paid to the arbitrator or any part thereof.

(3) Where, pursuant to paragraph (2), the arbitrator orders–

(a) the applicant to reimburse MIB, MIB may deduct an amount equal to the fee from any amount which it pays to the applicant to discharge its liability under this Agreement;

(b) a Solicitor or other person to reimburse MIB, MIB may deduct an amount equal to the fee from any amount which it pays to that Solicitor or other person to discharge its liability to the applicant under this Agreement.

(4) Where there is an oral hearing and the applicant secures an award of compensation greater than that previously offered, then (unless the arbitrator orders otherwise) MIB shall make a contribution of £500 per half day towards the cost incurred by the applicant in respect of representation by a Solicitor, Barrister or Advocate.

Applicants under a disability

25

(1) If in any case it appears to MIB that, by reason of the applicant being a minor or of any other circumstance affecting his capacity to manage his affairs, it would be in the applicant's interest that all or some part of the award should be administered for him by an appropriate representative, MIB may establish for that purpose a trust of the whole or part of the award (such trust to take effect for such period and under such provisions as appears to MIB to be appropriate in the circumstances of the case) or, as the case may be, initiate or cause any other person in initiate the proceedings necessary to have the award administered by an appropriate representative and otherwise cause any amount payable under the award to be paid to and administered by the appropriate representative.

(2) In this clause "appropriate representative" means—

(a) in England and Wales—

(i) the Family Welfare Association, or a similar body or person, as trustee of the trust, or
(ii) the Court of Protection; and
(b) in Scotland—
(i) a Judicial Factor, or
(ii) a guardian under the Adults with Incapacity (Scotland) Act 2000, or
(iii) (where the applicant is a child) the tutor or curator of the child or a person having parental responsibilities under the Children (Scotland) Act 1995.

NOTES

Clause 23: para (1)(f) added by the Supplementary Agreement between the Secretary of State for Transport and the Motor Insurers' Bureau, dated 30 December 2008, clause 4(d), in relation to accidents occurring after midnight on 1 February 2009.

ACCELERATED PROCEDURE

Instigation of accelerated procedure

[5027]
26

(1) In any case where, after making a preliminary investigation under clause 7, MIB has decided that—
(a) the case is one to which this Agreement applies, and
(b) it is not one to which clause 13, applies,
MIB may notify the applicant of that decision and, instead of causing a full investigation and report to be made under clause 7, may make to the applicant an offer to settle his claim by payment of an award specified in the offer representing compensation assessed in accordance with clause 8 together, in an appropriate case, with interest thereon assessed in accordance with clause 9 and a contribution towards the cost of obtaining legal advice in respect of the making of the application.

(2) Where an offer is made under paragraph (1), MIB shall send to the applicant a statement setting out–
(a) the relevant evidence it has collected disclosing the circumstances in which the death, bodily injury or damage to property occurred, and
(b) its reasons for the assessment of the award.

Settlement by accelerated procedure

27

(1) The applicant shall not later than 6 weeks after he receives an offer under clause 26 notify MIB of his acceptance or rejection thereof.

(2) Where the applicant notifies MIB of his acceptance of the offer–
(a) MIB shall not later than 14 days after receipt of the acceptance pay to the applicant the amount of the award, and
(b) MIB shall be discharged from all liability under this Agreement in respect of the death, bodily injury or damage to property for which that payment is made.

(3) In the event of the applicant failing to accept the offer within the specified period, the application shall be treated as one to which clause 7(1)(b) applies.

MISCELLANEOUS

Referral of disputes to arbitrator

[5028]–[5029]
28

(1) Any dispute between the applicant and MIB concerning a decision, determination or requirement made by MIB under the terms of this Agreement, other than a dispute relating to MIB's decision for which provision is made by clause 18, shall be referred to and determined by an arbitrator.

(2) Where an applicant wishes to refer such a dispute to arbitration, he shall not later than 4 weeks after the decision, determination or requirement is communicated to him, give notice to MIB that he wishes the matter to be so resolved.

(3) For the purposes of the Arbitration Act 1996 (where the arbitration is to be conducted in England and Wales) the arbitral proceedings are to be regarded as commencing on the date of such application.

(4) Upon receipt of the applicant's notice MIB shall apply immediately to the Secretary of State for the appointment of an arbitrator and in the event of MIB failing to do so the applicant may make the application.

(5) The Secretary of State shall, upon receiving the application for the appointment of an arbitrator to hear the appeal, appoint the first available member, by rotation, of a panel of Queen's Counsel appointed for the purpose of determining appeals under this Agreement (where the event giving rise to the death, bodily injury or damage to property occurred in England and Wales) by the Lord Chancellor or (where the event giving rise to the death, bodily injury or damage to property occurred in Scotland) by the Lord Advocate and shall forthwith notify the applicant and MIB of the appointment.

(6) The applicant and MIB shall, not later than 4 weeks after receiving notification of the appointment of the arbitrator, submit to him a written statement of their respective cases with supporting documentary evidence where available.

(7) Subject to paragraphs (8) to (10), the arbitrator shall decide the appeal on the documents submitted to him under paragraph (6) and no further evidence shall be produced to him.

(8) The applicant may, by notice in writing given to the arbitrator and MIB not later than the date on which he submits the statement of his case, ask the arbitrator to determine the appeal by means of an oral hearing and shall submit to the arbitrator and MIB a written statement, with supporting documentary evidence where appropriate, in support of that request.

(9) The arbitrator shall in such a case seek the view of MIB on the need for an oral hearing and MIB may submit to the arbitrator and the applicant a written statement, with supporting documentary evidence where appropriate, in support of its view.

(10) If, after considering those written submissions, the arbitrator decides that an oral hearing is necessary to determine the dispute–

- (a) the hearing shall be held in public unless the applicant requests that it (or any part of it) be heard in private;
- (b) the hearing shall take place at a location—
  - (i) in England or Wales, where the event giving rise to the death, bodily injury or damage to property occurred in England or Wales and the applicant is resident in England or Wales,
  - (ii) in Scotland, where the event giving rise to the death, bodily injury or damage to property occurred in Scotland and the applicant is resident in Scotland, or
  - (iii) in England, Wales or Scotland in any other case,

  which in the opinion of the arbitrator (after consultation with each of them) is convenient for both MIB and the applicant as well as for himself;
- (c) a party to the hearing may be represented by a lawyer or other person of that party's choosing;
- (d) a party to the hearing shall be entitled to address the arbitrator, to call witnesses and to put questions to those witnesses and any other person called as a witness.

(11) The arbitrator may, having regard to the subject matter of the proceedings and in an appropriate case, order that his fee or the costs of the proceedings (as determined according to clause 10(1)(b) of, and the Schedule to, this Agreement) or both his fee and those costs shall be paid by one party or allocated between the parties in such proportions as he thinks fit.

(12) Unless otherwise agreed, the decision, determination or requirement in respect of which notice is given under paragraph (2) shall stand unless reversed by the arbitrator.

Services of notices, etc, on MIB

29 Any notice required to be served on or any other notification or document required to be given or sent to MIB under the terms of this Agreement shall be sufficiently served or given sent by fax or by Registered or Recorded Delivery post to MIB's registered office and delivery shall be proved by the production of a fax report produced by the sender's fax machine or an appropriate postal receipt.

Agents

30 MIB may perform any of its obligations under this Agreement by agents.

Contracts (Rights of Third Parties) Act 1999

31

(1) For the purposes of the Contracts (Rights of Third Parties) Act 1999 the following provisions shall apply.

(2) This Agreement may be—

- (a) varied or rescinded without the consent of any person other than the parties hereto, and
- (b) determined under clause 3(2) without the consent of any such person.

(3) Save for the matters specified in paragraph (4), MIB shall not have available to it against an applicant any matter by way of counterclaim or set-off which would have been available to it if the applicant rather than the Secretary of State had been a party to this Agreement.

(4) The matters referred to in paragraph (3) are any counterclaim or set-off arising by virtue of the provisions of—

(a) this Agreement;
(b) the 1996 Agreement;
(c) the 1999 Agreement;
(d) either of the agreements which were respectively superseded by the 1996 Agreement and the 1999 Agreement.

(5) This agreement, being made for the purposes of Article 1(4) of Council Directive 84/5/EEC of 30th December 1983–
(a) is intended to confer a benefit on an applicant but on no other person, and
(b) to confer such benefit subject to the terms and conditions set out herein.

Enforcement against MIB

32 If MIB fail to pay compensation in accordance with the provisions of this agreement the applicant is entitled to enforce payment through the courts.

Transitional provisions

33 The 1996 Agreement shall cease to have effect after the 13 February 2003 but shall continue in force in relation to any claim arising out of an event occurring on or before that date.

IN WITNESS whereof the Secretary of State has caused his Corporate Seal to be hereunto affixed and the Motor Insurer's Bureau has caused its Common Seal to be hereunto affixed the day and year first above written.

SCHEDULE
MIB'S CONTRIBUTION TOWARDS APPLICANT'S LEGAL COSTS

(1) Subject to paragraph 4, MIB shall pay a contribution towards the applicant's costs of obtaining legal advice determined in accordance with paragraph 2,

(2) That amount shall be the aggregate of–
(a) the fee specified in column (2) of the table below in relation to the amount of the award specified in column (1) of that table,
(b) the amount of value added tax charged on that fee,
(c) where the applicant has opted for an oral hearing under clause and
(d) reasonable disbursements.

Amount of the award (1)	Specified fee (2)
Not exceeding £150,000	15% of the amount of the award, subject to a minimum of £500 and a maximum of £3000
Exceeding £150,000	2% of the amount of the award

(3) For the purposes of paragraph 2—
"amount of the award" means the aggregate of the sum awarded by way of compensation and interest under clauses 8 and 9, before deduction of any reimbursement due to be paid to the Secretary of State for Work and Pensions through the Compensation Recovery Unit (CRU) of his Department (or to any successor of that unit), but excluding the amount of any payment due in respect of benefits and hospital charges.
"reasonable disbursements" means reasonable expenditure incurred on the applicant's behalf and agreed between the applicant and MIB before it is incurred (MIB's agreement not having been unreasonably withheld) but includes Counsel's fees only where the applicant is a minor or under a legal disability.

(4) The foregoing provisions of this Schedule are without prejudice to MIB's liability under the provisions of this Agreement to pay the costs of arbitration proceedings or an arbitrator's fee.

MOTOR INSURERS' BUREAU
B. COMPENSATION OF VICTIMS OF UNINSURED DRIVERS

(13 August 1999, amended 7 November 2008)

Text of an Agreement dated the 13th August 1999 between the Secretary of State for the Environment, Transport and the Regions and Motor Insurers' Bureau together with some notes on its scope and purpose

THIS AGREEMENT is made the thirteenth day of August 1999 between the SECRETARY OF STATE FOR THE ENVIRONMENT, TRANSPORT AND THE REGIONS (hereinafter referred to as "the Secretary of State") and the MOTOR INSURERS' BUREAU, whose registered office is at 152 Silbury Boulevard, Milton Keynes MK9 1NB (hereinafter referred to as "MIB") and is SUPPLEMENTAL to an Agreement (hereinafter called "the Principal Agreement") made the 31st Day of December 1945 between the Minister of War Transport and the insurers transacting compulsory motor insurance business in Great Britain by or on behalf of whom the said Agreement was signed and in pursuance of paragraph 1 of which MIB was incorporated.

IT IS HEREBY AGREED AS FOLLOWS—

INTERPRETATION

1 General definitions

[5030]–[5031]

In this Agreement, unless the context otherwise requires, the following expressions have the following meanings—

"1988 Act" means the Road Traffic Act 1988;

"1988 Agreement" means the Agreement made on 21 December 1988 between the Secretary of State for Transport and MIB;

"bank holiday" means a day which is, or is to be observed as, a bank holiday under the Banking and Financial Dealings Act 1971;

"claimant" means a person who has commenced or who proposes to commence relevant proceedings and has made an application under this Agreement in respect thereof;

"contract of insurance" means a policy of insurance or a security covering a relevant liability;

"insurer" includes the giver of a security;

"MIB's obligation" means the obligation contained in clause 5;

"property" means any property whether real, heritable or personal;

"relevant liability" means a liability in respect of which a contract of insurance must be in force to comply with Part VI of the 1988 Act;

"relevant proceedings" means proceedings in respect of a relevant liability (and "commencement", in relation to such proceedings means, in England and Wales, the date on which a Claim Form or other originating process is issued by a Court or, in Scotland, the date on which the originating process is served on the Defender);

"relevant sum" means a sum payable or remaining payable under an unsatisfied judgment, including—

(a) an amount payable or remaining payable in respect of interest on that sum, and

(b) either the whole of the costs (whether taxed or not) awarded by the Court as part of that judgment or, where the judgment includes an award in respect of a liability which is not a relevant liability, such proportion of those costs as the relevant liability bears to the total sum awarded under the judgment;

"specified excess" means £300 or such other sum as may from time to time be agreed in writing between the Secretary of State and MIB;

"unsatisfied judgment" means a judgment or order (by whatever name called) in respect of a relevant liability which has not been satisfied in full within seven days from the date upon which the claimant became entitled to enforce it.

2 Meaning of references

(1) Save as otherwise herein provided, the Interpretation Act 1978 shall apply for the interpretation of this Agreement as it applies for the interpretation of an Act of Parliament.

(2) Where, under this Agreement, something is required to be done—

- (a) within a specified period after or from the happening of a particular event, the period begins on the day after the happening of that event;
- (b) within or not less than a specified period before a particular event, the period ends on the day immediately before the happening of that event.

(3) Where, apart from this paragraph, the period in question, being a period of seven days or less, would include a Saturday, Sunday or bank holiday or Christmas Day or Good Friday, that day shall be excluded.

(4) Save where expressly otherwise provided, a reference in this Agreement to a numbered clause is a reference to the clause bearing that number in this Agreement and a reference to a numbered paragraph is a reference to a paragraph bearing that number in the clause in which the reference occurs.

(5) In this Agreement—

- (a) a reference (however framed) to the doing of any act or thing by or the happening of any event in relation to the claimant includes a reference to the doing of that act or thing by or the happening of that event in relation to a Solicitor or other person acting on his behalf, and
- (b) a requirement to give notice to, or to serve documents upon, MIB or an insurer mentioned in clause 9(1)(a) shall be satisfied by the giving of the notice to, or the service of the documents upon, a Solicitor acting on its behalf in the manner provided for.

3 Claimants not of full age or capacity

Where, under and in accordance with this Agreement—

(a) any act or thing is done to or by a Solicitor or other person acting on behalf of a claimant,

(b) any decision is made by or in respect of a Solicitor or other person acting on behalf of a claimant, or

(c) any sum is paid to a Solicitor or other person acting on behalf of a claimant,

then, whatever may be the age or other circumstances affecting the capacity of the claimant, that act, thing, decision or sum shall be treated as if it had been done to or by, or made in respect of or paid to a claimant of full age and capacity.

NOTES

Clause 1: definition "specified excess" repealed by the Supplementary Agreement between the Secretary of State for Transport and the Motor Insurers' Bureau, dated 7 November 2008, clause 3(a), in relation to accidents occurring after midnight on 7 November 2008.

PRINCIPAL TERMS

4 Duration of Agreement

(1) This Agreement shall come into force on 1st October 1999 in relation to accidents occurring on or after that date and, save as provided by clause 23, the 1988 Agreement shall cease and determine immediately before that date.

(2) This Agreement may be determined by the Secretary of State or by MIB giving to the other not less than twelve months' notice in writing but without prejudice to its continued operation in respect of accidents occurring before the date of termination.

5 MIB's obligation to satisfy compensation claims

(1) Subject to clauses 6 to 17, if a claimant has obtained against any person in a Court in Great Britain a judgment which is an unsatisfied judgment then MIB will pay the relevant sum to, or to the satisfaction of, the claimant or will cause the same to be so paid.

(2) paragraph (1) applies whether or not the person liable to satisfy the judgment is in fact covered by a contract of insurance and whatever may be the cause of his failure to satisfy the judgment.

EXCEPTIONS TO AGREEMENT

[5032]–[5034]

6

(1) Clause 5 does not apply in the case of an application made in respect of a claim of any of the following descriptions (and, where part only of a claim satisfies such a description, clause 5 does not apply to that part)—

- (a) a claim arising out of a relevant liability incurred by the user of a vehicle owned by or in the possession of the Crown, unless—
  - (i) responsibility for the existence of a contract of insurance under Part VI of the 1988 Act in relation to that vehicle had been undertaken by some other person (whether or not the person liable was in fact covered by a contract of insurance), or
  - (ii) the relevant liability was in fact covered by a contract of insurance;
- (b) a claim arising out of the use of a vehicle which is not required to be covered by a contract of insurance by virtue of section 144 of the 1988 Act, unless the use is in fact covered by such a contract;
- (c) a claim by, or for the benefit of, a person ("the beneficiary") other than the person suffering death, injury or other damage which is made either—
  - (i) in respect of a cause of action or a judgment which has been assigned to the beneficiary, or
  - (ii) pursuant to a right of subrogation or contractual or other right belonging to the beneficiary;
- (d) a claim in respect of damage to a motor vehicle or losses arising therefrom where, at the time when the damage to it was sustained—
  - (i) there was not in force in relation to the use of that vehicle such a contract of insurance as is required by Part VI of the 1988 Act, and
  - (ii) the claimant either knew or ought to have known that that was the case;
- (e) a claim which is made in respect of a relevant liability described in paragraph (2) by a claimant who, at the time of the use giving rise to the relevant liability was voluntarily allowing himself to be carried in the vehicle and, either before the commencement of his journey in the vehicle or after such commencement if he could reasonably be expected to have alighted from it, knew or ought to have known that—
  - (i) the vehicle had been stolen or unlawfully taken,

(ii) the vehicle was being used without there being in force in relation to its use such a contract of insurance as would comply with Part VI of the 1988 Act,
(iii) the vehicle was being used in the course or furtherance of a crime, or
(f) the vehicle was being used as a means of escape from, or avoidance of, lawful apprehension.

(2) The relevant liability referred to in paragraph (1)(e) is a liability incurred by the owner or registered keeper or a person using the vehicle in which the claimant was being carried.

(3) The burden of proving that the claimant knew or ought to have known of any matter set out in paragraph (1)(e) shall be on MIB but, in the absence of evidence to the contrary, proof by MIB of any of the following matters shall be taken as proof of the claimant's knowledge of the matter set out in paragraph (1)(e)(ii)—
(a) that the claimant was the owner or registered keeper of the vehicle or had caused or permitted its use;
(b) that the claimant knew the vehicle was being used by a person who was below the minimum age at which he could be granted a licence authorising the driving of a vehicle of that class;
(c) that the claimant knew that the person driving the vehicle was disqualified for holding or obtaining a driving licence;
(d) that the claimant knew that the user of the vehicle was neither its owner nor registered keeper nor an employee of the owner or registered keeper nor the owner or registered keeper of any other vehicle.

(4) Knowledge which the claimant has or ought to have for the purposes of paragraph (1)(e) includes knowledge of matters which he could reasonably be expected to have been aware of had he not been under the self-induced influence of drink or drugs.

(5) For the purposes of this clause—
(a) a vehicle which has been unlawfully removed from the possession of the Crown shall be taken to continue in that possession whilst it is kept so removed,
(b) references to a person being carried in a vehicle include references to his being carried upon, entering, getting on to and alighting from the vehicle, and
(c) "owner", in relation to a vehicle which is the subject of a hiring agreement or a hire-purchase agreement, means the person in possession of the vehicle under that agreement.

CONDITIONS PRECEDENT TO MIB'S OBLIGATION

7 Form of application

(1) MIB shall incur no liability under MIB's obligation unless an application is made to the person specified in clause 9(1)—
(a) in such form,
(b) giving such information about the relevant proceedings and other matters relevant to this Agreement, and
(c) accompanied by such documents as MIB may reasonably require.

(2) Where an application is signed by a person who is neither the claimant nor a Solicitor acting on his behalf MIB may refuse to accept the application (and shall incur no liability under MIB's obligation) until it is reasonably satisfied that, having regard to the status of the signatory and his relationship to the claimant, the claimant is fully aware of the contents and effect of the application but subject thereto MIB shall not refuse to accept such an application by reason only that it is signed by a person other than the claimant or his Solicitor.

8 Service of notices etc

Any notice required to be given or documents to be supplied to MIB pursuant to clauses 9 to 12 of this Agreement shall be sufficiently given or supplied only if sent by facsimile transmission or by Registered or Recorded Delivery post to MIB's registered office for the time being and delivery shall be proved by the production of a facsimile transmission report produced by the sender's facsimile machine or an appropriate postal receipt.

9 Notice of relevant proceedings

(1) MIB shall incur no liability under MIB's obligation unless proper notice of the bringing of the relevant proceedings has been given by the claimant not later than fourteen days after the commencement of those proceedings—
(a) in the case of proceedings in respect of a relevant liability which is covered by a contract of insurance with an insurer whose identity can be ascertained, to that insurer;
(b) in any other case, to MIB.

(2) In this clause "proper notice" means, except in so far as any part of such information or any copy document or other thing has already been supplied under clause 7—

(a) notice in writing that proceedings have been commenced by Claim Form, Writ, or other means,
(b) a copy of the sealed Claim Form, Writ or other official document providing evidence of the commencement of the proceedings and, in Scotland, a statement of the means of service,
(c) a copy or details of any insurance policy providing benefits in the case of the death, bodily injury or damage to property to which the proceedings relate where the claimant is the insured party and the benefits are available to him,
(d) copies of all correspondence in the possession of the claimant or (as the case may be) his Solicitor or agent to or from the Defendant or the Defender or (as the case may be) his Solicitor, insurers or agent which is relevant to—
  (i) the death, bodily injury or damage for which the Defendant or Defender is alleged to be responsible, or
  (ii) any contract of insurance which covers, or which may or has been alleged to cover, liability for such death, injury or damage the benefit of which is, or is claimed to be, available to Defendant or Defender,
(e) subject to paragraph (3), a copy of the Particulars of Claim whether or not indorsed on the Claim Form, Writ or other originating process, and whether or not served (in England and Wales) on any Defendant or (in Scotland) on any Defender, and
(f) a copy of all other documents which are required under the appropriate rules of procedure to be served on a Defendant or Defender with the Claim Form, Writ or other originating process or with the Particulars of Claim,
(g) such other information about the relevant proceedings as MIB may reasonably specify.

(3) If, in the case of proceedings commenced in England or Wales, the Particulars of Claim (including any document required to be served therewith) has not yet been served with the Claim Form or other originating process paragraph (2)(e) shall be sufficiently complied with if a copy thereof is served on MIB not later than seven days after it is served on the Defendant.

10 Notice of service of proceedings

(1) This clause applies where the relevant proceedings are commenced in England or Wales.
(2) MIB shall incur no liability under MIB's obligation unless the claimant has, not later than the appropriate date, given notice in writing to the person specified in clause 9(1) of the date of service of the Claim Form or other originating process in the relevant proceedings.
(3) In this clause, "the appropriate date" means the day falling—
(a) seven days after—
  (i) the date when the claimant receives notification from the Court that service of the Claim Form or other originating process has occurred,
  (ii) the date when the claimant receives notification from the Defendant that service of the Claim Form or other originating process has occurred, or
  (iii) the date of personal service, or
(b) fourteen days after the date when service is deemed to have occurred in accordance with the Civil Procedure Rules,

whichever of those days occurs first.

11 Further information

(1) MIB shall incur no liability under MIB's obligation unless the claimant has, not later than seven days after the occurrence of any of the following events, namely—
(a) the filing of a defence in the relevant proceedings,
(b) any amendment to the Particulars of Claim or any amendment of or addition to any schedule or other document required to be served therewith, and
(c) either—
  (i) the setting down of the case for trial, or
  (ii) where the court gives notice to the claimant of the trial date, the date when that notice is received,

given notice in writing of the date of that event to the person specified in clause 9(1) and has, in the case of the filing of a defence or an amendment of the Particulars of Claim or any amendment of or addition to any schedule or other document required to be served therewith, supplied a copy thereof to that person.

(2) MIB shall incur no liability under MIB's obligation unless the claimant furnishes to the person specified in clause 9(1) within a reasonable time after being required to do so such further information and documents in support of his claim as MIB may reasonably require notwithstanding that the claimant may have complied with clause 7(1).

12 Notice of intention to apply for judgment

(1) MIB shall incur no liability under MIB's obligation unless the claimant has, after commencement of the relevant proceedings and not less than thirty-five days before the appropriate date, given notice in writing to the person specified in clause 9(1) of his intention to apply for or to sign judgment in the relevant proceedings.

(2) In this clause, "the appropriate date" means the date when the application for judgment is made or, as the case may be, the signing of judgment occurs.

13 Section 154 of the 1988 Act

MIB shall incur no liability under MIB's obligation unless the claimant has as soon as reasonably practicable—

(a) demanded the information and, where appropriate, the particulars specified in section 154(1) of the 1988 Act, and

(b) if the person of whom the demand is made fails to comply with the provisions of that subsection—

(i) made a formal complaint to a police officer in respect of such failure, and

(ii) used all reasonable endeavours to obtain the name and address of the registered keeper of the vehicle.

or, if so required by MIB, has authorised MIB to take such steps on his behalf.

14 Prosecution of proceedings

MIB shall incur no liability under MIB's obligation—

(a) unless the claimant has, if so required by MIB and having been granted a full indemnity by MIB as to costs, taken all reasonable steps to obtain judgment against every person who may be liable (including any person who may be vicariously liable) in respect of the injury or death or damage to property, or

(b) if the claimant, upon being requested to do so by MIB, refuses to consent to MIB being joined as a party to the relevant proceedings.

15 Assignment of judgment and undertakings

MIB shall incur no liability under MIB's obligation unless the claimant has—

(a) assigned to MIB or its nominee the unsatisfied judgment, whether or not that judgment includes an amount in respect of a liability other than a relevant liability, and any order for costs made in the relevant proceedings, and

(b) undertaken to repay to MIB any sum paid to him—

(i) by MIB in discharge of MIB's obligation if the judgment is subsequently set aside either as a whole or in respect of the part of the relevant liability to which that sum relates;

(ii) by any other person by way of compensation or benefit for the death, bodily injury or other damage to which the relevant proceedings relate, including a sum which would have been deductible under the provisions of clause 17 if it had been received before MIB was obliged to satisfy MIB's obligation.

LIMITATIONS ON MIB'S LIABILITY

16 Compensation for damage to property

(1) Where a claim under this Agreement includes a claim in respect of damage to property, MIB's obligation in respect of that part of the relevant sum which is awarded for such damage and any losses arising therefrom (referred to in this clause as "the property damage compensation") is limited in accordance with the following [paragraph].

(2) Where the property damage compensation does not exceed the specified excess, MIB shall incur no liability.

(3) Where the property damage compensation in respect of any one accident exceeds the specified excess but does not exceed £250,000, MIB shall incur liability only in respect of the property damage compensation less the specified excess.

[(2) Where the property damage compensation in respect of any one accident exceeds £1 million MIB's liability is limited to the sum of £1 million.]

NOTES

Clause 16: word "paragraph" in square brackets in para (1) substituted for the word "paragraphs", paras (2), (3) in italics repealed and original para (4) substituted by new para (2) in square brackets, by the Supplementary Agreement between the Secretary of State for Transport and the Motor Insurers' Bureau, dated 7 November 2008, clause 3(b)–(e), in relation to accidents occurring after midnight on 7 November 2008. Original para (4) read as follows—

"(4) Where the property damage compensation in respect of any one accident exceeds £250,000, MIB shall incur liability only in respect of the sum of £250,000 less the specified excess.".

17 Compensation received from other sources

Where a claimant has received compensation from—
(a) the Policyholders Protection Board under the Policyholders Protection Act 1975, or
(b) an insurer under an insurance agreement or arrangement, or
(c) any other source,

in respect of the death, bodily injury or other damage to which the relevant proceedings relate and such compensation has not been taken into account in the calculation of the relevant sum MIB may deduct from the relevant sum, *in addition to any sum deductible under clause 16,* an amount equal to that compensation.

NOTES

Words in italics repealed by the Supplementary Agreement between the Secretary of State for Transport and the Motor Insurers' Bureau, dated 7 November 2008, clause 3(f), in relation to accidents occurring after midnight on 7 November 2008.

MISCELLANEOUS

18 Notifications of decisions by MIB

[5035]

Where a claimant—
(a) has made an application in accordance with clause 7, and
(b) has given to the person specified in clause 9(1) proper notice of the relevant proceedings in accordance with clause 9(2),

MIB shall—
(i) give a reasoned reply to any request made by the claimant relating to the payment of compensation in pursuance of MIB's obligation, and
(ii) as soon as reasonably practicable notify the claimant in writing of its decision regarding the payment of the relevant sum, together with the reasons for that decision.

19 Reference of disputes to the Secretary of State

(1) In the event of any dispute as to the reasonableness of a requirement made by MIB for the supply of information or documentation or for the taking of any step by the claimant, it may be referred by the claimant or MIB to the Secretary of State whose decision shall be final.
(2) Where a dispute is referred to the Secretary of State—
  (a) MIB shall supply the Secretary of State and, if it has not already done so, the claimant with notice in writing of the requirement from which the dispute arises, together with the reasons for that requirement and such further information as MIB considers relevant, and
  (b) where the dispute is referred by the claimant, the claimant shall supply the Secretary of State and, if he has not already done so, MIB with notice in writing of the grounds on which he disputes the reasonableness of the requirement.

20 Recoveries

Nothing in this Agreement shall prevent an insurer from providing by conditions in a contract of insurance that all sums paid by the insurer or by MIB by virtue of the Principal Agreement or this Agreement in or towards the discharge of the liability of the insured shall be recoverable by them or by MIB from the insured or from any other person.

21 Apportionment of damages, etc

(1) Where an unsatisfied judgment which includes an amount in respect of a liability other than a relevant liability has been assigned to MIB or its nominee in pursuance of clause 15 MIB shall—
  (a) apportion any sum it receives in satisfaction or partial satisfaction of the judgment according to the proportion which the damages awarded in respect of the relevant liability bear to the damages awarded in respect of the other liability, and
  (b) account to the claimant in respect of the moneys received properly apportionable to the other liability.
(2) Where the sum received includes an amount in respect of interest or an amount awarded under an order for costs, the interest or the amount received in pursuance of the order shall be dealt with in the manner provided in paragraph (1).

22 Agents

MIB may perform any of its obligations under this Agreement by agents.

23 Transitional provisions

(1) The 1988 Agreement shall continue in force in relation to claims arising out of accidents occurring before 1st October 1999 with the modifications contained in paragraph (2).

(2) In relation to any claim made under the 1988 Agreement after this Agreement has come into force, the 1988 Agreement shall apply as if there were inserted after clause 6 thereof—

> "6A Where any person in whose favour a judgment in respect of a relevant liability has been made has—
>
> (a) made a claim under this Agreement, and
>
> (b) satisfied the requirements specified in clause 5 hereof,
>
> MIB shall, if requested to do so, give him a reasoned reply regarding the satisfaction of that claim.".

IN WITNESS whereof the Secretary of State has caused his Corporate Seal to be hereunto affixed and the Motor Insurer's Bureau has caused its Common Seal to be hereunto affixed the day and year first above written.

THE CORPORATE SEAL of the Secretary of State FOR THE ENVIRONMENT, TRANSPORT AND THE REGIONS hereunto affixed is authenticated by:—

Richard Jones

Authorised by the Secretary of State

THE COMMON SEAL of THE MOTOR INSURERS' BUREAU was hereunto affixed in the presence of:—

James Arthur Read

Roger Merer Jones

Directors of the Board of Management

Byford Louisy

Secretary

NOTES FOR THE GUIDANCE OF VICTIMS OF ROAD TRAFFIC ACCIDENTS

[5036]–[5040]

The following notes are for the guidance of anyone who may have a claim on the Motor Insurers' Bureau under this Agreement and their legal advisers. They are not part of the Agreement, their purpose being to deal in ordinary language with the situations which most readily occur. They are not in any way a substitute for reading and applying the terms of this or any other relevant Agreement.

At the request of the Secretary of State, these notes have been revised with effect from 15th April 2002 and in their revised form have been agreed and approved by MIB, the Law Society of England and Wales, the Law Society of Scotland, the Motor Accident Solicitors' Society and the Association of Personal Injury Lawyers. Any application made under the Agreement after this date (unless proceedings have already been issued) will be handled by MIB in accordance with these notes.

Where proceedings have been issued in Scotland, for the words "Claimant" and "Defendant" there shall be substituted in these Notes where appropriate the words "Pursuer" and "Defender" respectively.

Enquiries, requests for application forms and general correspondence In connection with the Agreement should be addressed to:—

Motor Insurers Bureau
Linford Wood House
6–12 Capital Drive
MILTON KEYNES MK14 6XT DX: 142620 Milton Keynes
Tel: 01908 830001
Fax: 01908 671681

1. Introduction—MIB's role and application of the Agreement

1.1 The role of MIB under this Agreement is to provide a safety net for innocent victims of drivers who have been identified but are uninsured. MIB's funds for this purpose are obtained from levies charged upon insurers and so come from the premiums which are charged by those insurers to members of the public.

1.2 MIB has entered into a series of Agreements with the Secretary of State and his predecessors in office. Under each Agreement MIB undertakes obligations to pay defined compensation in specific circumstances. There are two sets of Agreements, one relating to victims of uninsured drivers (the "Uninsured Drivers" Agreements) and the other concerned with victims of hit and run or otherwise untraceable drivers (the "Untraced Drivers" Agreements). These Notes are addressed specifically to the procedures required to take advantage of the rights granted by the Uninsured Drivers Agreements. However, it is not always certain which of the Agreements applies. For guidance in such cases please see the note on Untraced Drivers at paragraph 11 below.

1.3 In order to determine which of the Uninsured Drivers Agreements is applicable to a particular victim's claim, regard must be had to the date of the relevant accident. This Agreement only applies in respect of claims arising on or after 1st October 1999. Claims arising earlier than that are covered by the following Agreements:—

1.3.1 Claims arising in respect of an incident occurring between 1st July 1946 and 28th February 1971 are governed by the Agreement between the Minister of Transport and the Bureau dated 17th June 1946.

1.3.2 Claims arising in respect of an incident occurring between 1st March 1971 and 30th November 1972 are governed by the Agreement between the Secretary of State for the Environment and the Bureau dated 1st February 1971.

1.3.3 Claims arising in respect of an incident occurring between 1st December 1972 and 30th December 1988 are governed by the Agreement between the Secretary of State and the Bureau dated 22nd November 1972.

1.3.4 Claims arising in respect of an incident occurring between 31st December 1988 and 30th September 1999 are governed by the Agreement between the Secretary of State and the Bureau dated 21st December 1988.

2. MIB's obligation

2.1 MIB's basic obligation (see clause 5) is to satisfy judgments which fall within the terms of this Agreement and which, because the Defendant to the proceedings is not insured, are not satisfied.

2.2 This obligation is, however, not absolute. It is subject to certain exceptions where MIB has no liability (see clause 6), there are a number of pre- conditions which the claimant must comply with (see clauses 7 to 15) and there are some limitations on MIB's liability (see clauses 16 and 17).

2.3 Nothing in the Agreement is intended to vary the limitation rules applying to claimants not of full age or capacity. Limitation for personal injury remains 3 years from the date of full age or capacity.

2.4 MIB does not have to wait for a judgment to be given; it can become party to the proceedings or negotiate and settle the claim if it wishes to do so.

3. Claims which MIB is not obliged to satisfy

MIB is not liable under the Agreement in the case of the following types of claim.

3.1 A claim made in respect of an unsatisfied judgment which does not concern a liability against which Part VI of the Road Traffic Act 1988 requires a vehicle user to insure (see section 145 of the Act). An example would be a case where the accident did not occur in a place specified in the Act. See the definitions of "unsatisfied judgment" and "relevant liability" in clause 1.

3.2 A claim in respect of loss or damage caused by the use of a vehicle owned by or in the possession of the Crown (that is the Civil Service, the armed forces and so on) to which Part VI does not apply. If the responsibility for motor insurance has been undertaken by someone else or the vehicle is in fact insured, this exception does not apply. See clause 6(1)(a).

3.3 A claim made against any person who is not required to insure by virtue of section 144 of the Road Traffic Act 1988. See clause 6(1)(b).

3.4 A claim (commonly called subrogated) made in the name of a person suffering damage or injury but which is in fact wholly or partly for the benefit of another who has indemnified, or is liable to indemnify that person. See clause 6(1)(c).

It is not the intention of this Clause to exclude claims for the gratuitous provision of care, travel expenses by family members or friends, or miscellaneous expenses incurred on behalf of the Claimant, where the claimant is entitled to include such claims in his claim for damages.

3.5 A claim in respect of damage to a motor vehicle or losses arising from such damage where the use of the damaged vehicle was itself not covered by a contract of insurance as required by law. See clause 6(1)(d).

3.6 A claim made by a passenger in a vehicle where the loss or damage has been caused by the user of that vehicle if:—

3.6.1 the use of the vehicle was not covered by a contract of insurance; and

3.6.2 the claimant knew or could be taken to have known that the vehicle was being used without insurance, had been stolen or unlawfully taken or was being used in connection with crime.

See clause 6(1)(e), (2), (3) and (4).

For an interpretation of "knew or ought to have known" refer to the House of Lords judgment in White v White of 1st March 2001.

3.7 A claim in respect of property damage amounting to £300 or less, £300 being the "specified excess". See clause 16(2).

3.8 Where the claim is for property damage, the first £300 of the loss and so much of it as exceeds £250,000. See clause 16(3) and (4).

4. Procedure after the accident and before proceedings

4.1 The claimant must take reasonable steps to establish whether there is in fact any insurance covering the use of the vehicle which caused the injury or damage. First, a claimant has statutory rights under section 154 of the Road Traffic Act 1988 to obtain relevant particulars which he must take steps to exercise even if that involves incurring expense and MIB will insist that he does so. See clause 13(a).

MIB accept that if the MIB application form is sufficiently completed and signed by the Claimant, the Claimant will have complied with this Clause of the Agreement.

4.2 Other steps will include the following:

4.2.1 The exchange of names, addresses and insurance particulars between those involved either at the scene of the accident or afterwards.

4.2.2 Corresponding with the owner or driver of the vehicle or his representatives. He will be obliged under the terms of his motor policy to inform his insurers and a letter of claim addressed to him will commonly be passed to the insurers who may reply on his behalf. See clause 9(2)(d).

4.2.3 Where only the vehicle's number is known, enquiry of the Driver and Vehicle Licensing Agency at Swansea SA99 1BP as to the registered keeper of the vehicle is desirable so that through him the identity of the owner or driver can be established or confirmed.

4.2.4 Enquiries of the police (see clause 13(b) and Note 4.1 above).

4.3 If enquiries show that there is an insurer who is obliged to accept and does accept the obligation to handle the claim against the user of the vehicle concerned, even though the relevant liability may not be covered by the policy in question, then the claim should be pursued with such insurer.

4.4 If, however, enquiries disclose that there is no insurance covering the use of the vehicle concerned or if the insurer cannot be identified or the insurer asserts that it is under no obligation to handle the claim or if for any other reason it is clear that the insurer will not satisfy any judgment, the claim should be directed to MIB itself.

5. When proceedings are commenced or contemplated

5.1 As explained above, MIB does not have to wait for a judgment to be obtained before intervening. Claimants may apply to MIB before the commencement of proceedings. MIB will respond to any claim which complies with clause 7 and must give a reasoned reply to any request for compensation in respect of the claim (see clause 18) although normally a request for compensation will not be met until MIB is satisfied that it is properly based. Interim compensation payments are dealt with at paragraph 8 below.

Application Forms are available from MIB's office or their website: www.mib.org.uk.

Where a claim is made by the Claimant in person, who has not received legal advice, then if the claim is first made within 14 days prior to expiry of the limitation period, MIB will require the completed application form within the 21 days after the issue of proceedings.

5.2 It is important that wherever possible claims should be made using MIB's application form, fully completed and accompanied by documents supporting the claim, as soon as possible to avoid unnecessary delays. See clause 7(1). Copies of the form can be obtained on request made by post, telephone, fax or the DX or on personal application to MIB's offices.

5.3 The claimant must give MIB notice in writing that he has commenced legal proceedings. The notice, the completed application form (if appropriate) and all necessary documents must be received by MIB no later than 14 days after the date of commencement of proceedings. See clause 9(1) and (2)(a). The date of commencement is determined in accordance with the definitions of "relevant proceedings" and "commencement" given in clause 1.

When it is decided to commence legal proceedings, MIB should be joined as a defendant (unless there is good reason not to do so). Once MIB is a defendant, the Court will advise the relevant events direct and clauses 9(3),11 and 12 will no longer apply.

The form of words set out below should be used for the joinder of MIB as second defendant:

(1) The Second Defendant is a Company limited by guarantee under the Companies Act. Pursuant to an Agreement with the Secretary of State for the Environment Transport and the Regions dated 13th August 1999, the Second Defendant provides compensation in certain circumstances to persons suffering injury or damage as a result of the negligence of uninsured motorists.

(2) The Claimant has used all reasonable endeavours to ascertain the liability of an insurer for the First Defendant and at the time of the commencement of these proceedings verily believes that the First Defendant is not insured.

(3) The Claimant accepts that only if a final judgment is obtained against the First Defendant (which judgment is not satisfied in full within seven days from the date upon which the Claimant became entitled to enforce it) can the Second Defendant be required to satisfy the judgement and then only if the terms and conditions set out in the Agreement are satisfied. Until that time, any liability of the Second Defendant is only contingent.

(4) To avoid the Second Defendant having later to apply to join itself to this action (which the Claimant must consent to in any event, pursuant to Clause 14(b) of the Agreement) the Claimant seeks to include the Second Defendant from the outset recognising fully the Second Defendant's position as reflected in 3 above and the rights of the Second Defendant fully to participate in the action to protect its position as a separate party to the action.

(5) With the above in mind, the Claimant seeks a declaration of the Second Defendant's contingent liability to satisfy the claimant's judgment against the First Defendant.

5.4 This notice must have with it the following:

5.4.1 a copy of the document originating the proceedings, usually in England and Wales a Claim Form and in Scotland a Sheriff Court Writ or Court of Session Summons (see clause 9(2)(b));

5.4.2 normally the Particulars of Claim endorsed on or served with the Claim Form or Writ (see clause 9(2)(e), although this document may be served later in accordance with clause 9(3) if that applies);

5.4.3 in any case the documents required by the relevant rules of procedure (see clause 9(2)(f).

Provided that the documents referred to above are forwarded to MIB, it is not necessary to enclose the Response Pack or the Notice of Issue.

5.5 In addition, other items as mentioned in clause 9(2), e.g. correspondence with the Defendant (or Defender) or his representatives, need to be supplied where appropriate.

5.6 It is for the claimant to satisfy himself that the notice has in fact been received by MIB. However, where the Claimant proves that service by DX, First Class Post, Personal Service or any other form of service allowed by the Civil Procedure Rules, was effected, MIB will accept that such notice has been served in the same circumstances in which a party to litigation would be obliged to accept that he had been validly served by such means.

5.7 It should be noted that when MIB has been given notice of a claim, it may elect to require the claimant to bring proceedings and attempt to secure a judgment against the party whom MIB alleges to be wholly or partly responsible for the loss or damage or who may be contracted to indemnify the claimant. In such a case MIB must indemnify the claimant against the costs of such proceedings. Subject to that, however, MIB's obligation to satisfy the judgment in the action will only arise if the claimant commences the proceedings and takes all reasonable steps to obtain a judgment. See clause 14(a).

6. Service of proceedings

6.1 If proceedings are commenced in England or Wales the claimant must inform MIB of the date of service (see clause 10(1) and (2)).

6.2 If service of the Claim Form is effected by the Court, notice should be given within 7 days from the earliest of the dates listed in clause 10(3)(a)(i) or (ii) or within 14 days from the date mentioned in clause 10(3)(b) (the date of deemed service under the court's rules of procedure). Claimants are advised to take steps to ensure that the court or the defendant's legal representatives inform them of the date of service as soon as possible. Although a longer period is allowed than in other cases, service may be deemed to have occurred without a Claimant knowing of it until some time afterwards.

6.3 Where proceedings are served personally, notice should be given 7 days from the date of personal service (clause 10(3)(a)(iii)).

6.4 However, by concession MIB will accept the notice referred to in note 6.1 above if it is received by MIB within 14 days from the dates referred to in notes 6.2 and 6.3.

6.5 In Scotland, proceedings are commenced at the date of service (see clause 1) so notice should already have been given under clause 9 and clause 10 does not apply there.

7. After service and before judgment

See Note 5.3 above.

7.1 Notice of the filing of a defence, of an amendment to the Statement or Particulars of Claim, and the setting down of the case for trial should be given not later than 7 days after the occurrence of such events and a copy of the document must be supplied (clause 11(1)).

7.2 However, by concession MIB will accept the notice referred to in note 7.1 above if it is received by MIB within 14 days after the proven date on which it was received by the claimant

7.3 MIB may request further information and documents to support the claim where it is not satisfied that the documents supplied with the application form are sufficient to enable it to assess its liability under the Agreement (see clause 11(2)).

7.4 If the claimant intends to sign or apply for judgment he must give MIB notice of the fact before doing so. This notice must be given at least 35 days before the application is to be made or the date when judgment is to be signed (see clause 12).

The 35 days notice does not apply where the court enters judgment of its own motion.

7.5 At no time must the claimant oppose MIB if it wishes to be joined as a party to proceedings and he must if requested consent to any application by MIB to be joined. Conflicts may arise between a Defendant and MIB which require MIB to become a Defendant or, in Scotland, a party Minuter if a defence is to be filed on its behalf (see clause 14(b)).

8. Interim payments

In substantial cases, the claimant may wish to apply for an interim payment. MIB will consider such applications on a voluntary basis but otherwise the claimant has the right to apply to the court for an interim payment order which, if granted, will be met by MIB.9. After judgment

9.1 MIB's basic obligation normally arises if a judgment is not satisfied within 7 days after the claimant has become entitled to enforce it (see clause 1). However, that judgment may in certain circumstances be set aside and with it MIB's obligation to satisfy it. Sometimes MIB wishes to apply to set aside a judgment either wholly or partially. If MIB decides not to satisfy a judgment it will notify the claimant as soon as possible. Where a judgment is subsequently set aside, MIB will require the claimant to repay any sum previously paid by MIB to discharge its obligation under the Agreement (see clause 15(b)).

9.2 MIB is not obliged to satisfy a judgment unless the claimant has in return assigned the benefit to MIB or its nominee (see clause 15(a)). If such assignment is effected and if the subject matter of the judgment includes claims in respect of which MIB is not obliged to meet any judgment and if MIB effects any recovery on the judgment, the sum recovered will be divided between MIB and the claimant in proportion to the liabilities which were and which were not covered by MIB's obligation (see clause 21).

10. Permissible deductions from payments by MIB

10.1 Claims for loss and damage for which the claimant has been compensated or indemnified, e.g. under a contract of insurance or under the Policyholders Protection Act 1975, and which has not been taken into account in the judgment, may be deducted from the sum paid in settlement of MIB's obligation (see clause 17).

10.2 If there is a likelihood that the claimant will receive payment from such a source after the judgment has been satisfied by MIB, MIB will require him to undertake to repay any sum which duplicates the compensation assessed by the court (see clause 15(b)).

11. Untraced drivers

11.1 Where the owner or driver of a vehicle cannot be identified application may be made to MIB under the relevant Untraced Drivers Agreement. This provides, subject to specified conditions, for the payment of compensation for personal injury. It does not provide for compensation in respect of damage to property.

11.2 In those cases where it is unclear whether the owner or driver of a vehicle has been correctly identified it is sensible for the claimant to register a claim under both this Agreement and the Untraced Drivers Agreement following which MIB will advise which Agreement will, in its view, apply in the circumstances of the particular case.

C. ASSOCIATION OF BRITISH INSURERS STATEMENTS, CODES AND GUIDELINES

NOTES
Additional statements and codes can be found on the ABI website at www.abi.org.uk

GENERAL INSURANCE CODES AND GUIDANCE NOTES

ASSOCIATION OF BRITISH INSURERS STATEMENT OF PRINCIPLES FOR TRADE CREDIT INSURANCE

(April 2009)

NOTES

1. BACKGROUND

[5041]
1.1 The primary objective of credit insurance is to protect policyholders against unexpected credit losses generally caused by the default or insolvency of their own customers (i.e. buyers).

1.2 This is achieved by setting a credit limit for the policyholder on its customers, and using expertise to actively manage that limit for the duration of the policy. In the event of an adverse event or information, preventative action is taken to reduce or stop cover for future trade.

1.3 Where a credit loss arises due to the unexpected default of the policyholder's customer, a claim is paid. It is in both the insurer's and its policyholder's interests to avoid a claim being paid since both parties share in the risk.

1.4 It is always in the interest of credit insurers and their customers to support trade on credit terms wherever reasonable and possible. As a matter of principle, it is only where prudent risk management dictates that cover must be reduced or stopped for the protection of policyholders that such action is taken.

1.5 Credit insurance is a risk management tool to help companies manage and reduce the risks involved in trade credit transactions through the provision of cover on insurable risks as well as risk prevention and debt collection services. Credit insurers change their view on insurable risks from time to time in line with financial and other developments. Credit insurers provide an indemnity against losses incurred by companies. Policyholders should act just as prudently as they would if they were uninsured and it is not an unconditional guarantee that companies can continue to trade irrespective of the risks involved. Unlike banks or other financial partners, they are normally unsecured creditors in any trade transaction.

1.6 In order to formalise and reinforce the position set out above, and to make transparent the procedures described, the ABI has produced this Statement of Principles. It should be noted that many insurers have already been following these principles for some time and in some cases insurers will go beyond this minimum standard.

1.7 In some instances credit insurers will be bound by duties of confidentiality which may limit their ability to share with companies all the background reasons for their decisions. Credit insurers will always fully comply with their obligations under such agreements.

2. SCOPE

2.1 This statement of principles applies to credit insurance companies underwriting cancellable limits for whole turnover class policies in the UK. The whole turnover class, where companies include all of the insurable turnover within a policy, accounts for the majority of policies underwritten in the UK.

2.2 This document does not form part of any contract with any credit insurer. It is a statement of principles and is not legally binding. Customers should ensure that any contract they enter into satisfies their requirements. In the unlikely event of a conflict between this document and any insurance policy or regulatory or legal requirements, the latter will always take precedence.

3. STATEMENT OF PRINCIPLES

Maintenance of Cover

3.1 UK credit insurers will continue to support the UK economy to the greatest extent possible, by maintaining levels of credit insurance, insofar as consistent with prudent trade credit risk management and their obligations to all stakeholders, including their shareholders and customers.

Fair Assessment of Risk

3.2 Like any insurer, individual UK credit insurers must retain absolute discretion to assess and underwrite risk. However, they will base decisions regarding appropriate levels of credit insurance cover to be granted to their insured customers in respect of any individual UK buyer on a robust underwriting analysis of the fullest relevant financial information relating to that entity. Decisions on individual credit limits will not normally be based solely on the situation of the particular trade sector in which the relevant entity operates. Decisions are based on various types of information, public and confidential, financial and non-financial, which constitute a credit insurer's unique source of value.

3.3 In order to perform an informed risk assessment, UK credit insurers may require, from time to time, that companies provide them with additional information in respect of their business. Whilst credit insurers recognise they have no direct contract relationships with the buyers they assess, they expect companies to provide them with the necessary level of disclosure and transparency.

3.4 To facilitate the provision of such information, credit insurers will — if necessary — enter into suitable confidentiality or non-disclosure agreements with the companies involved. A company's failure to provide adequate transparency in its financial position may impair the ability of credit insurers to assess the risks they take on behalf of their clients and may lead to insurance cover being reduced or stopped to an extent that may not have been necessary had information that satisfied the insurer been provided.

Notice of Decisions

3.5 UK credit insurers will give as much notice as is reasonably possible to a customer of a decision to stop or substantially reduce credit insurance cover in respect of that entity. The purpose of the notice period is to enable the customer to make representations to the credit insurer and/or allow sufficient time for alternative supply arrangements to be made. However, credit insurers must retain the right to withdraw or reduce cover with immediate effect where necessary.

Reasons for Decisions

3.6 UK credit insurers will at the request of a customer provide reasons for their decision to stop or substantially reduce credit insurance cover in respect of a UK entity.

3.7 UK credit insurers will make an effort to provide explanations to companies where cover has been altered or stopped. However, credit insurers have no direct contractual obligation to these companies and will provide such explanations upon request and subject to compliance with existing confidentiality agreements.

Treating Customers Fairly

3.8 UK credit insurers will consider any appeal or representations made by an affected policyholder in response to an actual or intended withdrawal or substantial reduction of cover. Credit insurers will normally provide general guidance on the information needed to review decisions made. Taking into account the information provided by the trading entity, insurers will maintain, amend or rescind their decision when they believe such action to be justified. Any such appeal against a particular risk management decision will receive a formal response without undue delay.

Relations with Insured Customers

3.9 UK credit insurers will maintain open communications with their insured customers in relation to decisions relating to levels of cover, and will provide explanations for or enter into dialogue with their insured customers regarding such decisions.

Co-operation with Banks and other Trade Financiers

3.10 Credit insurers will work collaboratively with banks, companies or any other parties and take such steps as are prudent and practicable to maximise the potential for a UK entity to continue to trade as a viable business. Where appropriate, this may involve entering into suitable arrangements, including undertakings from credit insurers to maintain certain levels of cover in return for assurances or security provided by the company or its banks.

4. PARTICIPATING CREDIT INSURERS

4.1 The following UK credit insurers have agreed to follow this Statement of Principles:

AIG UK
Atradius Credit Insurance
Coface UK
Credit Indemnity & Financial Services (CIFS)
Euler Hermes UK
HCC International Insurance Company
QBE European Operations
Zurich

April 2009

ENSURING POSITIVE CUSTOMER EXPERIENCES OF BUYING INSURANCE ONLINE

A Good Practice Guide

(December 2009)

NOTES

FOREWORD

[5042]

Recent years have seen significant growth in both the number of general insurance comparison websites, and the number of customers using them. The scale and pace of this expansion have put comparison websites under the regulatory and media spotlights, with examples of good and bad practice being identified.

But while it is the scrutiny of comparison websites that led to the development of this guidance, this is also relevant to other online distributors. All customers are entitled to receive high levels of service regardless of how they buy their insurance, whether direct from the insurer, through a broker or via a comparison website.

This guidance therefore sets out a series of high-level aims that all organisations who sell general insurance to retail consumers should seek to achieve. Our goal is to ensure that, regardless of which online distribution channel customers use, they can be confident that they are able to identify and purchase the insurance product most appropriate to their needs.

INTRODUCTION

The purpose of the guidance

The guidance sets out a series of high-level standards insurers, brokers, comparison websites and software houses should seek to achieve in order to ensure customers have positive experiences when purchasing general insurance products online.

There are already a number of principles and rules (e.g. Insurance Conduct of Business Sourcebook and the Direct Marketing Directive) applied to insurers, brokers and comparison websites by virtue of regulation by the Financial Services Authority (FSA). FSA regulation requires that:

- A firm must pay due regard to the interests of its customers and treat them fairly (Principle 6), and
- A firm must pay due regard to the information needs of its customers, and communicate information to them in a way which is clear, fair and not misleading.

This guidance is intended to strengthen existing practices in these areas; but it is not a definitive guide.

The status of the guidance

This is not FSA-confirmed guidance. This is a voluntary good practice guide for insurers, brokers, software houses and insurance comparison websites.

Authors of the guidance

The guidance has been developed by:

- Association of British Insurers (ABI)
- British Insurance Brokers' Association (BIBA)
- Confused
- GoCompare
- Moneysupermarket
- Beat that Quote
- Tescocompare
- Swinton
- CDL
- Which?
- UNLOCK.

Background

The last decade has seen a significant change in the way people buy general insurance products. In 2007, more than two-thirds of customers used the internet to identify suitable motor insurance policies. Many of these searches were conducted via insurance comparison websites.

Comparison websites can help customers compare different product features in order to find the policy most suited to their needs; however, concerns have been raised about the way information is sometimes presented.

In 2008, the FSA conducted a review of comparison websites to determine the extent to which they treat customers fairly and, in particular, whether the information they provide to consumers is clear, fair and not misleading. It found examples of good and bad practice.

While many comparison websites took action to improve information to customers following the FSA's review, a number of stakeholders continued to express concerns. In June 2009, the ABI held a forum on comparison websites to identify where further improvements were needed. The forum was attended by a range of stakeholders including insurers, brokers, software houses, comparison websites, the FSA, and consumer groups, the output of which was an agreement to work together to ensure positive customer experiences of online insurance purchases.

A further forum was held in October 2009 to agree aims that online insurance distributors should work towards. This guidance has been developed as a result of that discussion.

Implementation

This guidance will be available to all general insurers, brokers, software houses and comparison websites from December 2009. We urge stakeholders to implement the necessary changes as soon as possible.

Review and update

While the guidance is voluntary, it is important that online distributors seek to achieve the high-level standards it sets out. The ABI will therefore carry out regular reviews to establish how widely it is being implemented, and to identify any new issues that need to be incorporated into it, after consultation with stakeholders.

Format of the guide

The guidance establishes standards in the following areas

- Excess levels
- Add-ons
- Total price disclosure
- Accurate data
- Guaranteed prices
- Policy information
- Referrals and signposting.

EXCESS LEVELS

Aim: customers should understand what an excess payment is, and how much they will be expected to pay towards any claim against the policy

How to achieve the aim

What	Who
Provide customers with clear information about what excesses are— • websites should display text explaining what voluntary, compulsory and total excess means. Language should meet the requirements of the FSA's Principle 7.[1]	All online distributors
Ensure customers understand what the different components of their excess are— • the results page should breakdown the excess into voluntary, compulsory and total components. — as a minimum, total excess should be displayed.	All online distributors
• the results page should display excesses for all people to be covered by the policy, not just the policyholder (e.g. a young named driver may incur a higher compulsory excess). — as a minimum, if another person to be covered by the policy incurs a different excess this must be highlighted to the customer in the detail of the quote. This should not be displayed as 'help text' as some customers may not click to view it.	All online distributors

• insurers and brokers should provide comparison websites with sufficient information to allow them to comply with the good practice on excess levels identified above.	Brokers & insurers
Ensure all returned quotes match the customer's requested criteria—	
• only display quotes which state the level of excess (i.e. do not display quotes which refer the customer to the insurer).	Comparison websites
• quotes should not be returned which include a significantly different excess from the one the customer has requested. Where the excess differs from that requested, the difference must be reasonable and clearly highlighted.	Comparison websites
Be clear about what is and what isn't covered by the policy—	
• it should be clear where there are different levels of excess for different components of cover (e.g. windscreen cover in a motor policy).	All online distributors

1 FSA Principles of Business, Principle 7: Communications with customers A firm must pay due regard to the information needs of its customers, and communicate information to them in a way which is clear, fair and not misleading.

ADD-ONS

Aim: customers should only be provided with quotes which are consistent with the type of cover they have requested

How to achieve the aim

What	Who
Ensure quotes are consistent with the customer's request—	
• quotes should only be returned that include all the add-ons the customer has requested.	All online distributors
— if comparison websites are unable to return quotes from at least 25% of their panel, they might want to consider providing quotes that do not offer the customers with all the add-ons that they have requested. However, any differences between what has been requested and what is returned must be reasonable and clearly highlighted.	
• any additional add-ons that are returned as part of the quote should be highlighted to the customer.	All online distributors
Be clear about what cover is provided as standard—	
• it should be made clear to the customer which features are provided as part of the standard policy and which are being sold as an add-on.	All distributors
• it should be made clear to the customer what level of cover each add-on provides ad cover may differ between providers (e.g. home emergency cover from one insurer could be quite different from that of another insurer).	All online distributors
• practice on excess levels identified above.	
Customer preferences should be passed from the comparison websites to the provider's site so the customer need not reselect.	All online distributors & software houses

TOTAL PRICE DISCLOSURE

Aim: customers should understand the total price of the policy

How to achieve the aim

What	Who
Display the total price of the policy—	
• all returned quotes should display the total price of the premium. Where a customer opts to pay in instalments, the total price of all instalments — including any APR — should be displayed.	All online distributors

Insurers and brokers should provide comparison websites with all the information needed for them to comply with the good practice around total price disclosure set out above.	Insurers & brokers

ACCURATE DATA

Aim: all returned quotes should be based on accurate data about the customer

How to achieve the aim

What	Who
Encourage customers to enter accurate data about their risk—	
• be careful that 'helpful hints' (see Annex B) do not encourage customers to enter inaccurate data to achieve a cheaper quote.	Comparison websites
• make customers aware of the consequences of entering inaccurate data, e.g. through the use of warning triangles.	All online distributors
• require customers to provide answers to every question — default answers should be avoided.	All online distributors
— as a minimum, it should be made clear to customers where answers have been defaulted and the defaults should be reasonable.	
Be clear where any assumptions have been made about anyone to be covered by the policy—	
• tell the customer early in the buying process what, if any, assumptions you have made about them or anyone to be covered by the policy.	All online distributors
• require customers to explicitly state that any assumptions made are accurate.	All online distributors & software houses

GUARANTEED PRICES

Aim: customers should know how long a quote is valid for

How to achieve the aim

What	Who
All quotes returned should state how long they are valid for.	All online distributors

POLICY INFORMATION

Aim: customers should be able to review key features of their selected policy before they commit to buy

How to achieve the aim

What	Who
Ensure that customers are able to review sufficient information before they make an informed decision to purchase the policy (before the customer is transferred to the selected insurer/broker site)—	
• identify the key features of each policy.	Insurers
• key features information should be displayed on the selected insurer's website before the customer makes a payment.	Insurers & brokers
• provide more detail on key /significant exclusions in order for customers to make informed decisions.	Insurers & brokers

REFERRALS AND SIGNPOSTING

Aim: non-standard customers should be helped to find cover

How to achieve the aim

What	Who
Help customers with non-standard needs to find cover— • where online distributors are unable to provide the customer with a quote, they should point the customer to alternative sources of help. — consider setting up referral arrangements with distributors who provide cover to customers with non-standard needs, or — signpost the customer to other organisations able to help (see Annex A for more information)	All online distributors
Be clear when you may pass customer details onto a third-party— • ask customers to opt in to allowing their details to be passed to a third party. — as a minimum, highlight to the customer that their details can/have been transferred to a third party.	All online distributors

GLOSSARY

Add-ons

Additional coverage to a standard insurance policy. Examples of add-ons include personal accident cover and legal expenses cover.

Excess levels

The contribution a policyholder must pay in the event of a claim against their policy. It has two components:

- **Compulsory excess** — the amount up to which the policyholder has to pay towards the cost of a claim
- **Voluntary excess** — the maximum amount over and above the compulsory excess that the policyholder agrees to pay in the event of a claim.

Non-standard customers

Customers whose circumstances and/or needs make it difficult to obtain insurance.

ANNEX A

Customers with non-standard circumstances and/or needs sometimes struggle to find suitable cover through mainstream online distributors. Where an insurer, broker or comparison websites is unable to return quotes for a customer, they should aim to point the customer in the direction of someone who can help. Non-standard risks might include:

- High-risk flood areas
- Unspent[2] convictions
- Older customers
- Pre-existing medical conditions

UNLOCK, the National Association of Reformed Offenders, has developed a list of insurers who are able to provide cover to people with unspent convictions: They can be contacted on: Tel: 01634 247350; Website: www.unlock.org.uk

BIBA operates a service which puts customers in touch with suitable brokers. They can be contacted on: Tel: 0870 950 1790; Website: www.biba.org.uk

[2] The Rehabilitation of Offenders Act (1974) sets a time period, based on the sentence given, during which past convictions must be declared to employers or insurers. Until this period passes, the conviction is defined in law as *unspent.*

ANNEX B

The following are examples of unacceptable helpful hints as they can encourage the customer to purchase the wrong type of policy:

- Highlighting that adding additional drivers can lower the premium

- Encouraging manipulation of occupation or employer's business
- Suggesting that changing where the vehicle is kept overnight can lower the premium
- Encouraging customers to enter lower mileage
- Encouraging customers to switch the main driver (fronting).

LIFE AND SAVINGS CODES AND GUIDANCE NOTES

ABI WITH-PROFITS BONDS BEST PRACTICE GUIDE

Note of Industry Best Practice Drawn up by a Working Group of Life Offices for With Profit Bonds Promotional Material

(revised December 2002)

[5043]

NOTES

OBJECTIVE

To set out prevailing good industry practice in respect of aspects of promotional material for with-profit bonds (including bonds offering both with-profits and unit linked funds ie all pre-sale literature and website information) so that investors might better understand the product and make better informed choices.

To enhance investor understanding by ensuring that the terms, advantages and disadvantages of the with-profit bond are promoted in a clear and unambiguous manner.

To reflect the impact of a shift in the economy to a low inflation environment and at times of relative stock market under performance, by promoting with-profit bonds to investors in a balanced manner allowing reasonable policyholder expectations to be set.

IMPLEMENTATION

All providers of with-profits promotional material are encouraged to have reviewed their material against these standards, and where necessary improved their material so that it meets these industry standards as revised in October 2002 as soon as is practical.

Nothing in this document prevents providers of promotional material exceeding the standards set out in it. The standards will be reviewed in the light of developments in the market and operational experience of them, and changes and additions made if necessary.

RELATIONSHIP OF INDUSTRY STANDARDS WITH EXISTING REGULATION

These standards are intended to complement and supplement as appropriate the Regulator's existing rules and guidance.

PRINCIPLES

All investor materials will be expressed in plain, consistent language. Jargon will be minimised and explained where used. The content will not mislead investors.

All points made will be expressed as clearly and concisely as possible. Figures will be kept to the minimum necessary.

There will be a logical order, structure and format to all consumer materials. Small print will not be used.

THE PROPOSED STANDARDS OF BEST PRACTICE

1. High "Headline" First Year Returns

Few participants in the with-profit bonds market still use advertisements quoting a rate of return in the first year designed to attract attention. Those that do will give equal prominence to the fact that there are charges/expenses to be deducted from the return, and what is and what is not guaranteed both in respect of the first year and thereafter.

There are many ways of creating the headline rates. An explanation should be given to investors as to how exactly the rate is comprised and how likely it is to be sustained throughout the duration of the contract.

Promotional material should make explicitly clear which part of the bonus is:

— the regular (reversionary) bonus;

— a "one-off" bonus applicable for a limited period of the contract – an early declaration of terminal bonus.

For example, where first year bonus rates are achieved through a combination of reversionary bonus rates and an increased allocation rate this should be spelt out clearly for investors.

The exact nature of any "special offer" rates should also be made clear and include an explanation of what happens to the bonus rate after the offer period.

Where the level of bonus to be applied is dependent on the size of the initial investment, promotional material should explain to investors the level of investment required and state clearly the level of bonus available for smaller investments.

2. The Impact of Charges

All charges that could apply throughout the term of the contract should be made clear to consumers.

Where a contract contains a bid-offer spread the promotional material should explain, where applicable, that it applies both to the whole fund value and to the first year rate.

Similarly, where set up, early surrender or other charges apply, promotional material must clearly explain the nature and impact of these charges on the investor's investment.

The promotional material will sign-post from its general information about yield and charges to the specific key features/illustration that will give detailed figures and explanation.

3. Term of the Investment

The promotional material will make clear to investors that with-profit bonds should be viewed as long-term investments, not usually for less than five years. Where early surrender penalties apply these must be spelt out to investors.

Reductions that can be made to the policy pay-out

Investors should be told clearly if a market value reduction (MVR) or any other type of adjustment may be applied to the contract. The reasons for each of the possible adjustments should be explained with a description given of the circumstances when each might be applied. These explanations should be given due prominence in the literature.

Product Positioning

Care must be taken to ensure promotional material gives a balanced description of the "risk and return" relationship within the contract. It should also be made clear that with-profit bonds are a stock-market related investment.

Promotional material should not describe a with-profit bond as "the best of both worlds" implying that investors will benefit from **all** of the security of a deposit account combined with all the growth potential of stock market investments. Clearly, full equivalent benefits cannot be offered in both respects.

The security of an investor's capital should be made clear to the investor.

In explaining the concept of smoothed returns promotional material should cover the relationship between the performance of underlying assets and the declared bonus rate.

Presentation of Tax Benefits

Promotional literature must make clear the differences in tax benefit for higher rate and lower rate taxpayers. Tax benefits should not be presented as being equally applicable regardless of the rate the investor pays. Promotional literature should not focus on tax at the expense of the overall suitability of the product to meet the investor's needs.

ABI MORTGAGE ENDOWMENT POLICY REVIEWS CODE OF PRACTICE

(1 June 2004)

[5044]

NOTES

INTRODUCTION

1. Members of the Association have undertaken, as a condition of membership, to implement this code of practice concerning reviews of mortgage endowment life policies and to follow the guidance to the code.

2. This code should be read in conjunction with the model reprojection letters and the code guidance, which are attached to it.

OBJECTIVE

3. To ensure that all investors with mortgage endowment policies bought with the intention to pay off all or part of a mortgage and who are still paying premiums, are kept regularly informed of the progress of such life policies in meeting this intention by means of regular policy reviews.

IMPLEMENTATION

4. This revised code comes into force on 1 June 2004. It replaces the earlier version of the Code that was in force from 1 July 2001 to 31 May 2004.

TIMING OF POLICY REVIEWS

5. Policies should be reviewed at least every 2 years, except:
— The first review can be issued up to 3 years after the start of the policy; and
— For policies in force before 2000, the gap between the first and second review can be up to 3 years, in accordance with the guidance issued by the ABI at the time.

6. Where an investor requests a policy review at a time other than those stipulated above, insurers will provide such a review within a reasonable time. A further review need not be provided within 12 months of a review taking place.

COMMUNICATING THE REVIEW

7. The overall aim of the reviews is to give consumers timely, accurate and appropriate information that can be easily understood.

8. Companies must comply with the model re-projection letters and Plan Updates provided by the ABI as far as possible.

9. There is a general duty not to mislead an investor in any investor communication and should any insurer wish to depart from the ABI model communication, any departure will need to be justified by testing to ensure that the change will reduce the risk of the investor being misled

10. Policy review materials sent to investors will conform to the following principles:
— All investor materials will be expressed in plain English. Jargon will be minimised and explained where used. The content will not mislead investors.
— Small print will not be used. It is unlikely that a font size below 11 will be easily read. Clarity is most important.

11. No non-related material will be enclosed with the policy review communication. The only exceptions to this principle are where:
— A policyholder receives a re-projection letter under a contractual obligation instead of a letter required by this code; or
— An insurer combines re-projection with the annual bonus (or similar) statement; or
— An insurer combines re-projection with any annual renewal information.

12. Other than as expressly permitted by this Code, no selling activity will be directly connected with this exercise.

GENERAL

13. Reasonable efforts will be made to trace customers for whom the company does not have an up-to-date address, in line with normal procedures operated by the insurer for other purposes.

14. Helpline staff will be trained to a suitable standard to be able to deal with enquiries arising from re-projection letters in an effective and courteous manner.

SCOPE

15. This code covers endowment life policies still in force and for which premiums are being paid and which are being, or might be used to repay, all or part of a mortgage. It applies to all policies except:
— Full or without profits endowments;
— Policies where the sum assured and reversionary (ie annual) bonuses already exceed the target sum;
— Policies where a guarantee to pay the target sum has been given by the insurer. (Any doubts in this area to be resolved by reference to the FSA);
— Policies where a mortality or morbidity claim is in hand that will terminate the policy;
— Policies that have previously had a review showing no shortfall and which are guaranteed to continue to maturity with no shortfall;
— Lapsed or paid-up policies;

— Policies where the insurer knows that the policy is no longer being used for the purpose of repaying a mortgage or part of the mortgage;
— Traded, or second-hand, endowment policies;
— Policies within six months of maturity;
— Non-UK-regulated international business.

16. The requirements of this code do not override any rights investors may have under their endowment contract of insurance to periodic premium reviews. However, to the extent that it is feasible, insurers will apply the requirements of the code to contractual reviews.

17. Where policies contain contractual premium policy reviews and guarantee payment of the sum assured/death benefit on maturity or earlier death if the policyholder follows the insurer's review recommendations, the implications of taking one of the other options rather than following the review recommendations must be clearly explained in the letter.

18. Nothing in this code prevents insurers exceeding the minimum requirements of this code if they wish.

MONITORING

19. Compliance with this code will be checked by the Chief Executive of each firm signing an annual statement confirming his or her office's compliance.

MORTGAGE ENDOWMENT POLICY REVIEWS GUIDANCE FOR INSURERS COMPLYING WITH THE ABI CODE OF PRACTICE

(1 June 2004)

[5045]

NOTES

1. This guidance accompanies the ABI Mortgage Endowment Policy Reviews code of practice, which came into force on 1 June 2004.

CURRENT AND FUTURE RE-PROJECTION MAILINGS

2. The ABI's Mortgage Endowment Working Party, whose members include all leading mortgage endowment providers, has led the work of developing the model letters and updates and is keen that all possible steps should be taken by members to provide a consistent message to policyholders by following the model letters as closely as possible. This will help ensure that the different messages contained in the red, amber and green letters and updates are properly received and understood by policyholders. It is important to remember above all that the purpose of the re-projection letter is to tell customers two key things:
— 'this is a series of illustrations of what your policy might produce at maturity, though the eventual pay out may be more or less than the figures shown'; and
— 'these are things you might like to consider doing if you are unhappy about any projected shortfall'.

Other information should not detract from these key messages.

3. For green letters, it is now optional to include some of the 'action you could take' information. Companies are free to decide whether to include this or not, although it is highly recommended: even green letters do not guarantee that there will not be an eventual shortfall and consumers may wish to be aware of the options open to them if they wish to have a contingency plan. It might be advantageous to include information with green letters about what people can do if they are concerned about the possibility of a shortfall in the future, particularly if you think there may be a realistic possibility of reductions in annual and terminal bonuses or weakness in investment markets.

4. The 'action you can take' information, and information on the complaints process (as set out in paragraph 5), will not, however, be appropriate for 'super green' cases. 'Super green' refers to policies that are guaranteed to pay at least the target sum, usually because the basic sum assured plus guaranteed bonuses to date already exceed the target sum. There is no requirement in the Code for letters to be sent to 'super green' cases, but many companies wish to include them for completeness and good customer relations.

ENCLOSURES

5. Companies must ensure that all policyholders receive all the FSA factsheets referred to in the Annex. In particular you must not omit the phase of sending the phase 2 factsheet 'Your mortgage endowment – time to decide'. For phase 3 and beyond, the 1 page factsheets 'Your mortgage endowment – have you acted yet?' and 'Your endowment mortgage – making a complaint' must be sent with all future re-projection letters until such time as FSA decide new factsheets are needed. Firms do not need to include the information on complaints in cases where customers are already time barred. These factsheets can be obtained from FSA or you can print them yourselves in-house if you wish, provided you abide by the FSA's strict print requirements including the requirement to print in colour. These can be established by contacting the FSA direct. A suitable period to change over to any new factsheet will always be agreed.

RE-PROJECTION LETTERS

6. Templates for the model re-projection letters have been circulated to ABI members and can be accessed from the members' section of the ABI website, where there is a dedicated section providing information on mortgage endowments. Everyone who works for an ABI member company can access this section of the website by requesting a password in the public section of the site.

7. When possible, details of multiple policy holdings with one insurer should be sent together so that the investor can ascertain the overall position with that insurer. If it is possible to consolidate multiple holdings in one letter, surpluses and shortfalls may be set off against one another so the investor can see the overall position.

8. Companies must comply with the model re-projection letters and plan updates provided by the ABI as far as possible. Any departure will need to be justified by testing to ensure that the change will reduce the risk of the investor being misled. ABI recommends that you bear in mind the following factors:

— Ideally the letter should fit on to two pages, as should the plan update.

— The most important part of the communication is to update customers on the progress of the investment and to let them know whether or not they should be considering taking any action. This will mean that the letter should be the top document when the envelope is opened and the contents removed (and unfolded from A5 size if folded).

— Companies must consider whether red ink or a similarly striking colour should be used to highlight the importance of the information contained in the letter.

— The warning box identifying the exact nature of the conclusion of the review should be in the top half of page one of the letter so as to be visible immediately the letter is taken out of the envelope. The warning box should also be highlighted in some way, for example shaded. The heading 'RED ALERT: HIGH RISK OF SHORTFALL', 'AMBER ALERT: SIGNIFICANT RISK OF SHORTFALL' or 'GREEN LETTER: PLAN ON TRACK' should also be clearly written above the highlighted box. The warning box should also be in the top half of the first page of the Plan Update. The wording for this should not be altered without careful consideration.

— There should be a further warning box on the second page of the letter including information on how to complain. This should be highlighted in the same way as the warning box on page one. For firms who are implementing time bars (see paragraphs 9–13) it should also include the time a customer has left to complain. The model letter provides the wording that should be used. The whole box can be omitted in letters where a customer has been timed out.

— Neither the letter nor the plan update should mislead the policyholder, and any changes needed to avoid misleading should be made.

— Plain language should be used. There should be minimal use of figure work, percentages etc.

— Technical terms should be avoided. Any that are unavoidable should be explained clearly and in plain language.

— No selling material or other enclosures should be included, with two exceptions only:

  — There may be contractual obligations to include quotations to increase premiums to keep the policy on track. These need careful handling – see paragraphs 17–20 below.

  — Companies may enclose annual bonus notices and annual statements with the re-projection letters.

  — There is a template for a combined re-projection letter and annual statement/bonus notice that meets Raising Standards requirements. This gives more scope for individual tailoring.

TIME BARS

9. Companies who are enforcing time bars in accordance with FSA rules[1] need to:

— Explain clearly to customers how time barring may impact on their right to make a complaint and to make sure they explain how the time bars are being implemented. They must follow the FSA rules in including information on the time limits for individual customers in their re-projection letters.

— Calculate either the exact amount of time that a customer has before their right to complain runs out or use a general figure for a larger group of customers, so long as that figure provides at least as much time as any of the customers would have had individually.

— Include the information on time bars in all future correspondence until the customers right to complain runs out.

10. Insurers do not have to implement time bars, but they should have regard to the position of any intermediaries who will be affected by their decision.

11. Where the insurer both produced the product and sold it to the customer, the company can determine for themselves not to include information on time bars in the re-projection letters.

12. However companies should be aware that where they are not planning to implement a time bar, intermediaries against whom a complaint might be made may wish to do so. In these circumstances customers need to be informed of the fact that they are still subject to a time bar. As a result, companies who do not wish to implement time bars and where there is an intermediary involved must contact the intermediary to achieve one of the following:

— Obtain a written agreement with the intermediary who sold the product that neither wish to implement time limits.

— Make reasonable efforts to provide any intermediary who does wish to impose a time bar with the information they need in order for them to directly contact the customers affected by their (the intermediary's) decision to impose time limitations.

13. In either of the cases above the company does not need to include information on time bars in the re-projection letters. If a company can do neither of the above, a time limit must be included in the re-projection letters.

CUSTOMERS FOR WHOM THE COMPANY DOES NOT HAVE AN UP-TO-DATE ADDRESS

14. The code requires reasonable efforts to be made to trace customers for whom the company does not have an up-to-date address in line with normal procedures operated by the insurer for other purposes. It would not be acceptable for no action to be taken to trace them; 'reasonable efforts' requires some action to be taken.

15. If companies are aware that they are unable to trace their policyholder, with reasonable efforts having been fruitless, re-projections should still be prepared with the usual regularity. These can be sent to the last known address or kept on the paper or computer file. When the policyholder is eventually traced, copies of outstanding (ie unreceived) re-projections should be available on request.

PROJECTION RATES – WHAT RATES TO USE?

16. FSA currently mandate projection rates, and re-projections should be done in accordance with FSA rules. These rules also mandate that lower rates must be used if you, the insurer, expect the rates in the tables within the FSA's handbook to overstate the investment potential of a contract.[2] FSA wrote a "Dear CEO" letter on 23 June 2003 reminding firms of this rule.[3] Examples of cases where you may need to consider using lower rates than the standard might include where the policyholder is invested in:

— a with-profits fund that is likely to have a significantly reduced equity exposure for the foreseeable future; or

— a cash fund, or other fund where the long-term return is likely to be significantly lower than the range of FSA projection rates, with no option to switch or reasonable likelihood of switching.

17. The above points are illustrative only. The decision on the projection rates to use is one that must be considered and made by each company for its own funds.

18. In making this decision, companies will need to consider how to handle funds where there are options to switch between higher and lower risk funds, with higher and lower likely long-term returns. It is important that the re-projection letter does not become a detailed explanation of the different funds on offer, or the risk rating applicable to each. If customers would benefit from this sort of information regularly it should be provided separately.

19. Where a company does use their own projection rates, they can adjust the relevant wording on the template plan update accordingly.

DATE OF FUND VALUATION

20. It is important that consumers are told the date of any fund valuation used in calculating the re-projection if it is not a fairly current valuation. No direct provision is made in the models for *insertion of this information* as it is ABI understanding that most companies use up-to-date valuations in re-projection letters. But if you do use older data, for example if you use end of year fund values for the following 12 months for with-profits policies, it is vital that this is made clear in the letters.

21. Firms may wish to include a current value figure in the plan update. This is entirely optional. If firms do wish to include this figure it should be included in the table relating to 'Your Plan now'. The figure should also be clearly explained as a footnote under the table.

CONTRACTUAL REVIEWS

22. Many policies contain contractual conditions whereby you the insurer are bound to carry out a review of the policy at regular intervals and to tell the customer the outcome and perhaps offer certain options and guarantees. Clearly you must comply with these contractual conditions and the ABI code does not require you to do otherwise. The letters must be changed as necessary to ensure compliance. But do bear in mind the need for simplicity of language and the overriding message about possible outcomes and "action you can take".

23. Some contracts give policyholders the opportunity to increase their premiums in exchange for a guarantee for a certain period that the target sum will be met. Other policies do not have such a guarantee. Others again contain automatic premium increases when needed. It is vital that you explain their own situation clearly to your customers. If there is a guarantee, this should be clearly explained, together with the effect of the additional premium not being paid and no guarantee being activated. It is also useful to explain that once the guarantee period has expired the next review may again require additional premium or may show that the target sum might be exceeded, depending on investment returns in the meantime.

24. It is also important that you set out clearly whether or not the policyholder is compelled by the policy terms to increase the premium, or whether you will automatically increase the direct debit unless you hear to the contrary. It would be helpful to include some words explaining that the policy is likely on current projections to fall short of the target sum without a premium increase. But the language should also be clear that there are other ways of addressing projected shortfalls to ensure that any linked mortgage can be paid off at maturity. These letters should not be capable of being read as compelling the payment of additional premium where this is not the case. Where it is the case because of the contractual conditions this should also be clear.

25. The regularity of the contractual reviews may not match the regularity with which the ABI code requires re-projections or the regularity with which you choose to issue re-projections. For example, many contracts require reviews every five years, whereas the ABI code requires re-projections every two years. Many companies choose to issue re-projections every year. This raises difficulties in presentation of regular letters with differing status. ABI believe it is most helpful for consumers to see similar letters each time, and to be able to compare the information provided from one letter to the next. Companies are therefore encouraged to make the contractual review letters and the code re-projection letters as similar as possible, without breaching or exceeding the contractual requirements. For example, if the contract allows you to increase the direct debit automatically every five years to address any projected shortfall, you should not do so at more frequent intervals without the policyholder's agreement.

TOP UPS

26. Although the ABI does not issue any guidance on charges and commissions, members will be aware of concerns surrounding the sales of top ups. Firms are encouraged to take this into account when considering how to handle top ups. Firms should make clear that if consumers choose to top up, there is still no guarantee that the policy will deliver the target sum.

GENERAL ADVICE

27. The general approach to calls from policyholders should be to see what you, the insurer, can do to help your customer. Companies should be prepared to try to leave customers with a further identified route to explore rather than sending them away empty handed.

28. If the customer does not have an IFA you could, for instance, suggest that they can find details of the IFAs in their area at www.ifap.org.uk or can call 0800 085 3250.

HANDLING CUSTOMER COMPLAINTS

29. The general approach to complaints from policyholders should be to see what you, the insurer, can do to help your customer. You should ensure that you make consumers aware of the Financial Ombudsman Service (FOS) and the free availability of that service to nearly all consumers if you are having to refer the complaint on to someone else such as an IFA in order to try and help customers avoid them to using complaints handling firms.

30. If consumers complain that they cannot approach the FOS or the Financial Services Compensation Scheme (FSCS), perhaps because they bought from a defunct IFA before 'A day' in 1988 when the Financial Services Act came into force, you should explain why this is and that regrettably there is no formal route available for redress for the consumer. You should go on to consider how else you might be able to help. This will vary according to the qualifications of the person dealing with the consumer, but for instance might include stressing the need for action to address any projected shortfall and referring to the FSA's material as a source of information on the options for achieving this, or reference to a qualified company representative or to an IFA (or IFA Promotions) for advice on the issues involved. If you are also the mortgage provider, or if you are able to offer mortgage advice, you might be able to offer assistance in addressing the projected shortfall. You might also be in a position to help if the customer is considering surrendering the policy or wishes to take out replacement term life cover.

31. If a customer makes a complaint, you should try to manage their expectations from the start. Explain in your acknowledgement letter the process you will be following in dealing with their complaint and roughly how long you expect it to take before they hear further from you. The letter could also remind customers that they should still consider taking action even while their complaint is being dealt with because there is no guarantee that their complaint will be upheld or that they will receive compensation. Companies who are enforcing time bars need to explain clearly to customers the effect time barring may have on how their complaint may be handled.

32. Regular updates should then be sent, keeping the customer advised as to the progress of their complaint. Research has shown that customers find the combination of the delay and not being told what is happening to be one of the most irritating aspects of the complaints process – more irritating than having the complaint turned down.

33. It is worth reviewing the wording of your standard complaint letters frequently to ensure they are properly managing customers' expectations of the complaints process. Your workload and timings are likely to change, so the letters should reflect the current situation.

REDRESS LETTERS

34. There is no template for a model redress letter. However in the drafting of your letters, the ABI recommends that you bear in the mind the following:

— Plain language should be used as much as possible.

— The letter should explain how the redress calculations are done. Companies can refer to the FSA's rules on 'Handling Mortgage Endowment Complaints'[4] but only to reassure customers that an approved procedure is being followed. The steps need to be set out in each case and the letter should also make clear whether it includes a full or simplified calculation.

— If the redress amount consists of two separately calculated sums, the total amount of redress money should be clearly highlighted at the end of the letter. This will ensure that customers clearly understand the total amount they will receive.

— Companies should explain to customers that they can use their redress money to repay some or all of their outstanding mortgage. The following wording in the offer letter has been agreed by the Council of Mortgage Lenders:

> 'The endowment was originally designed to repay your mortgage. You should consider using your compensation payment to repay your outstanding debt. If you do not do this, you will need to think of alternative methods for repaying your mortgage'.

— Companies should make the process as simple and easy as possible. Companies should consider using the following wording in this regard which has also been agreed with the Council of Mortgage Lenders:

> 'The compensation can be paid directly to your mortgage lender, to reduce the sum owing on your mortgage. Please fill in the name and address of your lender and your mortgage account number on the acceptance form and we will send the payment direct to them. Your mortgage lender will contact you when they have received the payment.
>
> If you wish for the payment to be directly credited to your bank account/via a cheque you do not need to fill out the details below. You will be contacted when this has been done'.

— Where companies already know the name and address of the customer's lender and mortgage account number they may want to pre-fill in these details on the acceptance form.

— Where a company knows that a customer no longer has a mortgage or has made suitable arrangements to pay off their outstanding debt, they are not required to explain this process.

FURTHER QUERIES?

35. If you have further queries about how to ensure you comply with the ABI code please contact us. Please remember that here at ABI we are not experts on the FSA rulebook and you should seek advice on that from your own compliance department or your FSA supervisors. There are many decisions that you will need to make and review in connection with the mortgage endowment re-projection exercise, and there is rarely one right answer that will apply for all companies in all cases. It can help to think 'what will this look like to the consumer?', 'how can I explain this simply to consumers?', 'what will consumers do or think when they get this?', 'will the consumer understand it as I intend it?', 'will this volume of papers confuse consumers?'. It can be helpful sometimes to show a draft to a non-technical person in your office to see if they understand or how they react. Often here at ABI we need to see a draft of what you are proposing, so that we can see how it will look. We can then consider how consumers might react. It is often worth you trying that first.

ANNEX: BACKGROUND

The code of practice was initially introduced in September 1999 and required re-projections to be carried out every five years after the first one. It was withdrawn later in 1999 when it became clear that a general mailing would have to take place to all endowment policyholders and that more frequent regular updates would be required. A revised code was issued in November 2000, in advance of the completion of the first phase of mailings. It came into force in July 2001 and lasted until 31 May 2004 when it was replaced by the current version.

In early 2000 companies wrote to all endowment policyholders telling them that the re- projection exercise was taking place and that they would be receiving individual re- projection letters in due course. They had to enclose with this "warm-up" letter the FSA factsheet called "Your endowment mortgage – what you need to know".

The first phase of re-projection mailings took place from April 2000 to June 2001. A re- projection was sent to each policyholder (within the definitions of the code – eg it is not necessary to send re-projections to certain classes of policyholder). Companies enclosed with the red and amber letters their own company booklet called "Mortgage endowments – reviewing your needs". ABI supplied the model text for this, which left room for free text in many areas. Companies were encouraged to mail policyholders nearest to maturity first, as they would have the least time to take action if any were needed.

The second re-projection letter had to be sent to policyholders within three years of the first, with subsequent letters being sent at least every two years. The reason for permitting an initial three year gap was to allow companies to align their re-projections to a suitable timetable for them to follow from then on. Some companies prefer to mail on policy anniversary dates, some to mail all letters at once, some to mail at the same time as bonus notices are issued and others to set up a genius regular and permanent programme of mailings throughout the year.

The second re-projection letters enclosed the FSA factsheet "Your endowment mortgage – time to decide". This had to be sent with all letters, whether red, amber or green.

---

1 See Dispute Resolution Sourcebook: http://www.fsa.gov.uk/vhb/html/disp/DISPtoc.html

2 See Conduct of Business sourcebook section 6.6

3 See FSA website: http://www.fsa.gov.uk/pubs/press/2003/064.html

4 http://www.fsa.gov.uk/handbook/BL4DISPpp/DISP/Appendix_2.pdf

---

ASSOCIATION OF BRITISH INSURERS
A GUIDE OF GOOD PRACTICE FOR UNIT LINKED FUNDS

NOTES

1. FOREWORD

[5046]

1.0.1 This Guide establishes standards that the ABI believes all companies managing unit linked funds should aspire to and work toward. The Guide sets out requirements in the following areas:

Governance

Documenting the scope and exercise of discretion

Disclosure

Pricing

Valuation

Transaction processing

Box management

Rounding

Error correction

1.0.2 It is acknowledged that existing practices may not meet all of these standards and that in some cases products sold in the past may not ever fully meet these good practice guidelines owing to the materiality of the issues, the disproportionate costs, or contractual constraints.

1.0.3 Nevertheless, where firms do not meet these guidelines, it will be incumbent on them to *explain* the reasons for this to their supervisors.

1.0.4 Following adoption of this Guide by the ABI, firms will need to review their existing policies and processes and make adjustments where appropriate.

1.0.5 By 31 December 2006 firms should have undertaken a high level gap analysis against the standards set out in this Guide and begun making progress towards the changes needed to meet these standards. In some cases significant changes to systems and processes may be required which will have a longer timeframe for completion. However, a clear plan should be in place by end-2006 to achieve the necessary changes.

1.1 Introduction

1.1.1 This document is intended to provide a 'Guide of Good Practice' for insurance companies operating unit linked funds.

1.1.2 It has been prepared recognising that there is not currently a detailed set of rule requirements placed on Unit Linked fund managers. Instead, the FSA set out a framework of principles for business which senior management must apply and interpret, coupled with some specific requirements in particular areas, such as permitted links for investments.

1.1.3 The guiding principle throughout this document is that firms must act in accordance with the concept of Treating Customers Fairly (TCF) as set out by the FSA in a number of publications[1] and in their Principles for Business, which form part of the FSA Handbook. TCF incorporates a number of elements including 'Policyholders' Reasonable Expectations' (PRE) but is a much broader concept. Where appropriate, we have also drawn upon the ABI's own work in our *Customer Impact* scheme[2].

1.1.4 This Guide has been prepared by a working group of the Association of British Insurers (ABI) to provide more specific guidance to firms looking to understand what TCF means in the context of unit linked fund governance. The FSA has also indicated that it will take account of the standards set out in this Guide in their supervision of unit linked life offices.

1.1.5 It is recognised that some funds will have either a significant, or exclusively institutional investor base, which may influence how the standards in this document are applied. Wholesale fund parameters will differ in some areas and in these cases firms will rightly depart from the standards indicated as appropriate to retail customers.

1.1.6 There is also a distinction to be drawn between closed funds, which have a finite lifetime and revenue stream, and those funds continuing to accept new customers. In the former case, complex or expensive systems changes may not be financially viable and an appropriate balance will need to be struck between raising standards and sustaining the business in run off.

1.1.7 However, even for closed funds it is likely that there will be additional premiums paid, or switches or surrenders of policies beyond 31 December 2006. Accordingly, firms operating closed funds should still review their existing practices and work towards the standards in this Guide unless such change would have a disproportionate cost or the changes would be immaterial to their policyholders.

1.2 Status of the Guide and Implementation

1.2.1 This Guide was endorsed as a statement of Good Practice by the ABI Board on (17 May 2006). The ABI consulted with the FSA in developing the standards in this document, however this Guide does not constitute guidance from the FSA. In the event of conflict between the Guide and the FSA Handbook, the FSA's Handbook text prevails. Ultimately, interpretation of the law is a matter for the courts.

1.2.2 However, this Guide does establish standards that the ABI believes all companies selling unit linked policies should meet within a reasonable period, taking into account the results of their gap analysis and their financial and other circumstances[3]. The FSA supports this initiative, which will inform its approach to the supervision of unit linked life offices.

1.2.3 It is acknowledged that in some cases firms may adopt a policy or approach at variance with that set down in the Guide. Where this occurs, a firm should be able to explain why they are adopting a different approach and to demonstrate how this approach is at least as effective in securing TCF. Alternatively, if they cannot meet the standard set out in the Guide, (or an equivalent) they should be able to explain why such a standard would not be appropriate to their circumstances – for instance on grounds of materiality or disproportionate cost.

1.2.4 The ABI have prepared this Guide of Good Practice to assist firms in meeting the FSA's regulatory requirements as set out in their high-level 'Principles for Business'. It is intended to assist both firms and supervisors in interpreting these principles by providing a more detailed framework of good practice standards.

1.2.5 The FSA recognise the potential of the Guide to assist firms in meeting their regulatory obligations and have taken account of its anticipated implementation when considering their priorities for regulatory reform going forward. They will also take into account firms' compliance with the standards in this Guide in their supervision of unit linked life offices.

Implementation

1.2.6 Subject to the constraints outlined, we would expect firms to have reviewed their own policies and begun implementation of the necessary changes to meet these standards by 31 December 2006. However, we do not expect firms to make retrospective adjustments to transactions already completed[4].

1.2.7 It is acknowledged that existing practice in firms will not meet all of these standards and that in some cases products sold in the past may never fully meet the requirements set out in these guidelines for new business owing to contractual constraints, disproportionate costs or materiality considerations.

1.2.8 In other areas, where substantial investment in IT or systems change is required this may also entail a longer timescale, but a clear plan and timescale for implementation should be established by the firm.

Review and update of the Guide

1.2.9 This Guide represents a new initiative by the industry, which for the first time provides a framework to record good practice and will help firms to interpret the application of the 'Treating Customers Fairly' principle in the context of unit linked life products.

1.2.10 This is intended to be a living document, more flexible than a rule-book based solution and able to adapt to recognise emerging thinking and good practice. Accordingly we would expect a periodic review of the content and standards in the Guide to ensure that they remained appropriate and up to date, with any new material added where this was considered to be of benefit.

1.2.11 The focus of the work to date has been on pricing and related issues of governance and control. In the future it may be appropriate to extend the scope of the guidance.

1.2.12 Specifically, following the expected completion of the gap analysis exercise by the end of 2006, it may be appropriate to update the Guide in the light of these findings. This would draw upon both the experience of firms in beginning to apply the standards and the FSA in using the Guide to inform its approach to the supervision of unit linked life companies.

---

1 See FSA's original discussion Paper, June 2001: http://www.fsa.gov.uk/pubs/discussion/dp7.pdf and their recent consumer research paper June 2005: http://www.fsa.gov.uk/pubs/consumer-research/crpr38.pdf.

2 This is initiative sets out standards to improve customer service, building on the original 'Raising Standards' scheme.

3 By 31 December 2006 a plan should be developed by the firm setting out the measures it intends to adopt and the proposed timetable, taking account of the findings of the gap analysis, including the economic factors and any other circumstances affecting the nature and timing of the proposed changes.

4 We do not expect firms to re-price past transactions according to these new standards, but this should not preclude the correction of errors where existing contracts were incorrectly priced under the standards prevailing at the time the transaction was undertaken.

---

2. FUND GOVERNANCE

[5047]

2.1.1 Insurance companies operating in the unit linked field will generally have a number of funds in existence. Their structure and policy conditions will vary according to the legacy of their creation and with a number of mergers and consolidations in the sector, differences will exist between funds even with the same insurer.

2.1.2 However, the governance structure will typically include:

The Board

2.1.3 *The Board carries ultimate responsibility for the oversight and management of the fund.*

A General Management Committee

2.1.4 *A management committee may be appointed by the Board and delegated to perform a day-to-day management role. This may include monitoring and management of the risk management process.*

A Pricing and Actuarial Committee/Function

2.1.5 *A committee (or an individual) may be appointed by the Board with delegated responsibility to oversee the fund's pricing arrangements, ensuring targets for accuracy are met, and fairness to customer in the application of pricing policies.*

The Actuarial Function holder

2.1.6 *The actuarial function holder must fulfil a range of responsibilities set out in the FSA Handbook*[5] *to advise the Board on the management of the fund, including any risks run by the fund in meeting their liabilities, issues of capital adequacy, etc.*

Internal audit/compliance

2.1.7 *Internal audit and compliance provide an essential function in defining and monitoring appropriate standards for the operation of the fund, reporting these findings ultimately to the Board.*

2.1.8 The Board may choose to out-source certain functions to third parties. Where this is the case, the Board must ensure that they have appropriate systems and controls in place, including regular and reliable management information, to ensure that they can fulfil their responsibilities to policyholders. Further specific requirements in this area are set out in the FSA Handbook.[6]

2.1.9 Whilst this Guide[7] provides a high-level framework, the individual policy conditions should define in more detail the boundaries within which a company has agreed to operate its unit-linked funds. This should cover:

- How and when value is assigned to each asset.
- Deductions that can be made from the funds, including charges and allowance for taxes and how they are calculated.
- The basis on which the company can create or cancel units in a fund.
- The calculation of fund prices, including allowance for selling and buying costs.
- The basis of transacting with policyholders.

2.1.10 Where this information has not been set out in individual policy conditions, then firms must ensure that they make such information readily available to their customers[8]. Firms should ensure that in addition to any summarised customer information, further explanation and more detailed information is clearly sign-posted and provided on request.

2.1.11 Taken together, all the information provided (or made available) to customers should enable them to understand how the firm operates the fund and manages their investments. It will also provide the FSA with a clear statement of the standards applied to the fund, offering a criterion against which to review the fund's operation.

---

5 See SUP 4.3.

6 See SYSC 3A.9.

7 In conjunction with the relevant rules and principles for business contained within the FSA Handbook.

8 The principal terms and features of the policy should appear either in policy conditions or some other policy document provided to new retail customers. For existing customers, where such information has never been provided, the firm should consider how best to draw this information to attention, for instance by publication on the firm's website and/or inclusion of a reference in an annual statement or other customer mailing, with an offer to provide details on request.

---

3. USE OF DISCRETION IN MANAGING THE FUND

[5048]

3.1.1 Where discretion is exercised in the management of the fund, it is very important to ensure that the firm treats its customers fairly.

3.1.2 Where possible, and as set out in this guide, funds should be operated according to published criteria and standards. Specifically, the scope of the firm's discretion in managing the fund and the limits to that discretion should be documented and disclosed to policyholders and other relevant parties[9].

3.1.3 This codification provides a clear point of reference against which to review any decisions taken, helping to provide clarity and certainty for all parties.

3.1.4 The scope of discretion should be confirmed annually with a more significant review every three to five years, or upon a significant change to the fund or the investor base.

3.1.5 Robust and effective reporting structures should be in place to allow the Board[10] to monitor the exercise of this discretion on an on-going basis, to ensure that policyholder interests are safeguarded.

3.1.6 Subject to the terms of the original policy conditions, areas where discretion may be applied include:

- Launching funds and seeding with shareholder capital
- Allowing for dealing costs
- Unit Price rounding[11]
- Application of annual management charges and any ability to alter the definition or level of the charge
- Tax (eg how actual charges or credits for tax are calculated, when they are taken from fund or credited to fund, how deferred tax provisions are calculated)
- Introducing charges for new or unforeseen types of expense which may not be described or covered under existing policy terms
- Criteria for moving funds between bid and offer bases[12]
- Merging funds
- Internal deals between two unit linked funds
- Ability to defer switches/surrenders (eg in adverse market conditions)
- Ability to defer transactions by customers seeking to exploit market timing opportunities
- Ability to close a fund to new business or switches in

- Basis for valuing assets – especially where market prices do not exist
- Determining, if applicable, distribution rates for income
- Choice of pricing point
- Frequency and time of pricing
- Addressing breaches of policy conditions or other customer commitments and dispute resolution

---

9 For general policyholder communications a significantly abridged and simplified description of the scope and effect of the use of discretion would normally be provided. A full, technical account of these powers should then be made available to the regulator and others where appropriate.

10 Either directly or through a delegated body.

11 See later section on rounding.

12 Which has potential to dilute or concentrate the fund.

---

4. OPERATING STANDARDS

[5049]
4.0.1 Openness and transparency are fundamental concepts that underpin the principle of Treating Customers Fairly. The standards set out in this Guide strongly support this open and transparent approach. Wherever possible processes and decisions should be documented by the firm with relevant information made available both to the regulator and to policyholders, according to their respective needs and requirements.

4.0.2 However, this should not imply large amounts of new, unsolicited, printed material being sent to every policyholder. Instead, it is anticipated firms should adopt a combination of measures to meet the requirements set out in this Guide, to increase the scope and quality of information available to policyholders. Some of this information may go into new and existing customer literature, some may be published on a website or in other mass-media formats and some information is likely to be of interest only to the regulator, intermediaries and large institutional investors.

4.0.3 Firms must ensure that they make it easy for customers to access information relevant to their investment decisions. Customer literature must distil those key elements which are essential to enable retail investors to make effective and informed choices, whilst more detailed information should be clearly sign-posted and made available on request[13].

4.0.4 In short, it is about empowering ordinary policyholders with concise and relevant information, not swamping them with a mass of technical, abstract disclosures that they are unlikely to need, read or ever understand.

4.1 Pricing Issues – Overview

4.1.1 Unit prices should be calculated in a fair and transparent manner, which means:
(1) Cross-subsidy among policyholders or individual funds should be avoided as far as reasonably possible.
(2) The pricing mechanism should not be used as a deliberate means of extracting value from the fund or from policyholders[14].

4.1.2 In particular, unit prices will be calculated so as to treat policyholders fairly, in accordance with policy provisions, legislation, insurance regulations, and FSA rules and guidance[15] where appropriate.

4.1.3 Expenses, income and taxation should be recognised appropriately in the price, being accrued in a timely and accurate fashion so that the unit price properly reflects the value of the underlying assets.

4.2 Pricing models

4.2.1 Whilst there are many possible permutations in the method for calculating prices, at its simplest there are two different approaches[16]:
(1) Forward pricing. This involves calculating the price at which the transaction is undertaken after the deal is done, so as to establish the 'true' value of the units at the time of purchase or disposal.
(2) Historic pricing. Transactions are undertaken on the basis of a known, quoted price at the time the deal is done, based on an existing (ie historic) valuation of the assets in the fund.

4.2.2 Each approach has advantages and disadvantages. The firm must carefully consider the effect of its chosen pricing model on its customers, particularly retail customers, who are unlikely to have the knowledge or expertise to question the firm on its approach and so must rely on the firm to safeguard their interests.

4.2.3 A historic pricing model has the attraction of allowing customers to deal at a known price, rather than having to wait until after the deal is done to establish the exact terms of settlement (ie the price at which the units were bought or sold). The administration of historic pricing may also prove to be simpler, easier and cheaper, particularly where a substantial proportion of transactions are pre-determined regular investments[17].

4.2.4 Whereas, in its purest form, a 'forward pricing' approach should ensure that the price at which a customer's order is transacted precisely matches the value of the underlying investments backing those units. This eliminates the risk of any potential mis-match between the dealing price and the value of the underlying investments. Where such a mis-match does occur, this can be exploited by sophisticated and well-informed customers to the disadvantage of other investors in the fund[18].

4.2.5 Where the firm itself is dealing with the fund, rather than with customers, (for example for internal reconciliation) this would usually be on a forward-price basis and should not normally be based on historic prices.

4.3 **<u>Pricing Frequency and unit transaction timing</u>**

4.3.1 The timing of unit transactions such as allocation to policyholders, creation and cancellation of units will be determined according to events such as the receipt of policyholder instructions. The following objectives should be taken into account when determining pricing frequency and unit transaction timing:

- Avoiding any losses to policyholders through market timing and other 'strategic dealing activity'.
- Maintaining, within defined tolerances, appropriate levels of liquidity in the fund to avoid any significant, unintended gearing effects.
- Ensuring that funds designed to track the performance of an underlying asset, for example an OEIC, do so within defined tolerances avoiding the risk of any significant distortion or deviation.
- Avoiding any material loss to the fund or policyholders by ensuring a good match between net policyholder unit transactions and the related asset purchase or disposal[19].
- Avoiding any material loss to the fund or policyholders by ensuring there is no undue delay between receipt of a trading instruction from a policyholder and the resulting unit transaction.

4.3.2 To help firms apply this approach and meet the overall requirements of TCF, the following standards are recommended as good practice[20].

Pricing Frequency

4.3.3 Funds will typically be valued and priced on each working day. Where the price is updated at a fixed time during the working day, or pricing is scheduled to occur less frequently than once per day, this will be disclosed to policyholders[21].

Pricing basis: switching between bid and offer pricing

4.3.4 The firm should keep the pricing basis of the fund under regular review, so as to avoid any significant dilution where the net flow of investment (either into or out of the fund) changes. It may be appropriate to switch the pricing basis quite frequently where material changes in the flow of funds occurs, in order to protect the interests of continuing policyholders.

4.3.5 Where the fund uses a single price and applies a dilution levy, a similar principle applies. The purpose should be to ensure broad neutrality between new and continuing policyholders, so as to avoid any material concentration or dilution of the fund arising from customer transactions.

Historic pricing

4.3.6 As discussed above, any pricing model which relies on past data to determine the unit price of the fund will carry the risk of mis-match between the quoted price and the underlying value of the units.

4.3.7 Whilst fully prospective pricing and valuation of assets would be unrealistic in most cases, given the delays to settlement this could imply[22], firms should seek to ensure that the price and valuation information used is as up-to-date as possible.

4.3.8 Where a firm uses a historic price model and identifies a significant movement in asset values[23] based on interim price information or proxy data since the last pricing point, the firm should consider whether, in the interests of its customers, it should continue to execute orders at the historic price, or move to update the price/unit valuation in advance of the next scheduled pricing point.

Market timing

4.3.9 Where the firm's pricing model relies to any extent on historic prices or valuations, then certain additional safeguards should be considered, both to protect against strategic dealing activity and to ensure fairness to new and existing policyholders[24].

4.3.10 Responses may include:

- Deferring execution of deals
- Temporarily suspending the right to deal for customers believed to be engaged in market timing activity
- Moving to a 'Fair Value' model of pricing
- Moving to a forward pricing model

4.3.11 The extent of any response needed will depend upon movements in the underlying asset markets and the pattern of customer transactions with the fund.

Transaction processing

4.3.12 The firm should ensure that transactions are processed and settled in a timely manner. Where delays do occur the firm will make good any loss suffered by the policyholder or the fund as a consequence of the delay. Large, unplanned backlogs not only impede efficient and effective administration, compromising customer service standards, they can also result in unintended additional risks for the firm. Wherever possible such backlogs should be avoided but where, exceptionally, they do occur, every effort should be made to address the backlog and return to normal operating conditions as quickly as possible.

Box Management

4.3.13 It is acknowledged that maintaining a Box may be helpful in providing an interface between customers' transactions, buying and selling units on an almost instant basis, with the subsequent underlying asset transactions in the fund. It allows the two processes to be de-coupled to a limited extent so that the fund manager has time to adjust the underlying portfolio to match the overall unit investment base[25].

4.3.14 Shareholders (or owners of the business) put up risk capital to cover these units (or liabilities in the event of a negative box) and can expect to earn a return. However, in accordance with the principle of Treating Customers Fairly, the firm should not exploit the information at its disposal to profit[26] from the fund through strategic management of the box.

4.3.15 In the absence of proper safeguards firms can have a material impact on unit prices as a result of their actions in creating/cancelling units, in transacting switches across funds and in their management of the box. In order to safeguard policyholders, the following considerations should apply[27]:

- The company must hold assets whose value matches the total unit liability as closely as possible[28].
- The firm should set clear limits for the operation of the box with close monitoring and regular reconciliation to the firm's administrative systems.
- Any deviation from the box limits should be recorded and justified.
- Unit creations/cancellations by the box manager, and inter-fund cross-holding transactions should be carried out on a basis that will meet TCF requirements.

Cash transaction timing

4.3.16 Firms should ensure that the timing of cash transactions (eg applying management charges and tax payments) between the fund and the company do not give rise to an undue gearing effect on policyholder returns.

4.4 Valuations

4.4.1 Where possible assets will be valued at current, recognised and independently assessed prices. Any reliance upon 'stale' prices significantly increases the risk of strategic dealing activity (market timing) and may discriminate unfairly against either new or existing policyholders.

4.4.2 Prices for securities should be derived from recognised sources including Bloomberg, Reuters, Ex-share, IBOX, Bridge, FT Interactive, stockbrokers or other appropriate sources, including unit trust/OEIC managers, at the relevant pricing point[29]. Where a price used is not obtained from an independent party, the firm will need to consider whether any additional steps are required to validate the price obtained.

4.4.3 Where no market valuation is possible then the Board is responsible for ensuring that clear, defined procedures exist and are applied to ensure a *fair value* is assigned to the relevant assets[30].

4.4.4 Where a transaction occurs between the firm and a connected party, this should be on a 'fair value' basis. Details of such transactions should be recorded and disclosed to the regulator on request.

Unit price rounding

4.4.5 Rounding is a necessary process used to simplify the pricing of unit-linked funds.

4.4.6 Firms will have an established approach to rounding, which should be clearly defined and monitored. The approach to rounding will typically be driven by IT systems and the other processes used to obtain underlying asset prices and to calculate the final unit price. Change to these systems, particularly IT-related change, will often be complex and expensive to achieve and will require significant lead times.

4.4.7 However, as a matter of good practice:

- Rounding should be kept to a minimum and should not normally exceed 0.5% of the unit price.
- Rounding should be undertaken on a neutral basis[31].
- Rounding should not be used as a method of levying a charge on the fund.

4.4.8 *Rounding limited to the 4th significant figure (or a maximum of 0.1% of the unit price[32]) is recognised as best practice for firms to work towards. The pace at which firms can achieve this goal will depend upon a number of factors, including IT and systems constraints as identified above.*

4.4.9 In some cases, policy conditions will define the extent to which prices derived from the offer or the bid value of the fund may be increased or decreased (respectively) by a rounding factor to arrive at the published price. This may constrain the extent and pace of change possible, particularly in the case of older policies.

4.5 Charges

4.5.1 Charges should match their description in the policy conditions and other published material provided to policyholders[33].

Management Charges

4.5.2 Management Charges should be clearly defined and disclosed to policyholders[34].

4.5.3 Firms should be aware of the possible impact of double-charging. Where a fund invests in another in-house fund the firm should reduce or refund the additional charges either by rebates or by investing in a nil charge share class[35]. Where the firm chooses to pass on additional fees to policyholders for externally managed funds, these should be clearly signalled in marketing literature.

4.5.4 All charges made to the fund, including the annual management charge and any other additional fees or investment management costs, will be subject to disclosure and illustration through the required approaches[36].

Dealing Costs

4.5.5 Dealing costs will typically be charged to the fund and this should be clearly disclosed to policyholders. This should include taxes on dealing (such as SDRT[37]). Dealing costs should be subject to review where significant changes in the market occur – for instance where there are changes to the rate of SDRT.

4.5.6 Allowance for such costs are often made in unit pricing. For instance, allowances may be added to the offer prices or deducted from the bid prices of the securities held. Any charges applied should reflect known or expected dealing costs and transaction terms[38].

4.5.7 Where dealing cost allowances are used they should be reviewed at least once per year and any changes implemented in a timely manner.

Other charges

4.5.8 Where any other charges are levied on the fund (for example custody costs) these must be in accordance with the relevant policy conditions and unless otherwise specified and disclosed should be charged on the basis of actual costs incurred.

Tax

4.5.9 Where the fund is subject to tax the following principles should apply:

- Policyholders should be treated fairly.
- The firm's approach to tax should, as far as possible, be consistent with any information or commitments given in marketing literature or policy documents.
- The basis of taxation chosen should aim to achieve broad equity between generations of policyholders and fairness between the company and the fund, supported by appropriate reconciliation to help ensure that a fair outcome has been achieved[39].

4.5.10 The scope and nature of the taxation of unit linked life funds may be subject to change over time, but wherever possible announcements of future changes should be taken into account in any tax calculations.

4.6 Error Correction

Overview

4.6.1 Pricing errors arise, typically, from a mistake in administration or processing. However, an adjustment to a unit price does not necessarily mean there has been an error, but instead may reflect a change from an estimated asset value included in a unit price, which is later adjusted when the actual value becomes known. Neither the price quoted before the change, nor the price derived after the change is in error, provided that these prices were arrived at using soundly-based policies, consistently applied[40].

4.6.2 Where such a change is to be made to a unit price, the change should be made as quickly as possible and should not be phased over time.

4.6.3 However, where errors do occur, these should be quickly identified and any systemic issues rectified. Where a complaint is made by a policyholder, it should be investigated fairly and resolved without undue delay. Compensation should be paid where appropriate[41].

Pricing Errors

4.6.4 Set out below is a suggested criteria for investigating and resolving pricing errors:

Price error	***Action***
Below 0.1%:	Errors are recorded but not normally investigated[42].
Between 0.1% and 0.5%:	Errors are recorded and investigated for possible wider implications. Compensation may be considered but not normally required[43].
0.5% or above:	Errors are recorded, corrected and investigated for possible wider implications. Compensation would normally be paid.

4.6.5 The Board must, at all times, be satisfied that appropriate and reliable systems and controls are in place. Any review of the wider implications of a pricing error must consider any possible systems and controls failings.

4.6.6 The Board are responsible for providing oversight[44] to this process to ensure that any significant or recurring failings are swiftly and effectively remedied.

Reporting to the FSA

4.6.7 Pricing errors may be significant in themselves but may also be symptomatic of other process or control weaknesses. Accordingly, where significant or persistent failings have occurred it is likely to be appropriate to share this information with the FSA. The FSA Handbook sets out a number of requirements in respect of those matters having 'a serious regulatory impact'[45], although firms may wish to go beyond this basic requirement to disclose all non-trivial pricing errors.

Speed of correction

4.6.8 Where an error is identified in the quoted fund price, the price should be corrected and implemented as soon as possible. There should be no phasing or 'smoothing' over a number of days (or pricing points) between the incorrect price and the correct price.

De minimis criteria

4.6.9 It may be appropriate to apply de minimis criteria to compensation payments, where the error has resulted in an immaterial loss to the investor. The threshold of immateriality will depend on a number of factors including:

- Whether it is a retail or wholesale customer who is affected.
- The scale of investment.
- The relative costs of providing redress against the scale of compensation due.

4.6.10 Clearly, the outcome to be avoided is one where costs for the wholesale policyholder in processing the compensation exceed the value of the compensation. It may be possible to make redress in forms other than cash, eg by allocation of extra units or reduced collection of a future premium. This may attract lower costs and be more practical for small amounts and so preferred by the investor.

4.6.11 For retail customers, even where compensation is by means of a cash payment, compensation should normally be paid where the amount due is greater than £10, or such other amount as agreed by the Board[46].

4.6.12 For wholesale customers arrangements will vary according to a number of factors and may be governed by specific terms in the customer's agreement. Where there is any doubt, the *assumption must* be *one of* disclosing the errors with an offer of payment of compensation.

4.6.13 Where a pricing error has resulted in overpayment to a customer, the firm will need to carefully consider whether it is appropriate to seek recovery of the overpaid sum. It is likely that a higher disregard threshold will apply in such cases, taking account of the costs and inconvenience to the customer. However, in all cases the firm will put right any loss to the fund.

Timely payment of compensation

4.6.14 Firms are reminded of the importance of making timely compensation payments. Excessive delays should be avoided wherever possible. Firms are reminded of the requirements set out in the FSA Handbook for the resolution of complaints, which include a number of relevant time limits[47].

4.7 Emergency situations/Disaster Recovery

4.7.1 There may be occasions where exceptional circumstances prevail – in times of crisis or disaster. In such circumstances it may be appropriate to use additional powers or discretions to secure the longer-term interests of the fund. This may include, but is not limited to:

- Temporary suspension of trading.
- Temporary suspension of unit price.
- Diverging from stated investment strategy (eg % equity invested).

4.7.2 Firms should document the scope of these powers and discretions reserved for emergency use. However, it is recognised that not all circumstances and not all possible responses can be foreseen in advance.

4.7.3 The overarching principle must be that emergency powers will be used only to the minimum extent necessary to secure policyholder protection and will be time-limited. Beyond any reporting requirements in the FSA Handbook, where significant breaches to normal policyholder conditions occur and this has a material impact on policyholders, the firm will review the impact of its decisions and consider additional disclosures to the regulator, and where appropriate, policyholders.

---

13 This is an approach that the FSA are particularly keen to promote and firms' success in meeting this requirement will inform the FSA's view of the need to take further action in this area, in particular to consider formal new rules and guidance on disclosure for unit linked funds.

14 This is not intended to cover incidental or unintentional flows which may arise on a limited scale, nor prevent the proper application of disclosed management charges and fees.

15 The CIS Sourcebook provides useful context in this area – see in particular CIS Ch 7 Annex 1G.

16 Whilst this is a simplification, the actual pricing model used by the firm will normally exhibit characteristics of either 'forward pricing' or 'historic pricing'.

17 The potential distortion between historic prices and current underlying asset value may in practice be largely eliminated where the firm can anticipate and synchronise planned customer orders with unit creation/cancellation.

18 A sophisticated investor may use knowledge of a significant movement in the value of the fund's underlying assets to purchase or dispose of units in the fund at the historic price, based on earlier asset valuation. Accordingly, this sophisticated investor accrues a risk-free profit to himself at the cost of the fund's underlying investors, or to the shareholders of the firm managing the fund where a box or other mechanism is used to by the firm to protect the fund from this risk.

19 In some cases, for example property funds, asset acquisition or disposal may lag behind buy/sell orders in the fund, resulting in the potential for excess liquidity or excess exposure. Unless precluded under existing policy conditions, firms should consider delaying significant policyholder transactions where these cannot be synchronised with purchase or sale of the necessary assets. In extreme cases, new business into that fund may need to be restricted.

20 These standards represent good practice, but firms may in some cases apply an alternative approach – for instance to meet existing policy conditions. The firm should be able to demonstrate that their own approach can meet the same standards of TCF.

21 This information may be set out in the policy conditions or otherwise made publicly available.

22 For unquoted assets such as property, formal valuation may occur relatively infrequently. Even for quoted securities there may be a compounding of delays where one fund invests in another fund – especially in overseas markets.

23 The firm would typically define a specific review threshold, to reflect the considerations set out in this section on pricing frequency and unit transaction timing.

24 In some instances, existing policy conditions would limit the firm's ability to take such action.

25 A 'box' is just one means of managing customer transactions with underlying asset movements in the fund. There should be no presumption that a box is necessary or required to secure fair dealing for customers.

26 *It is acknowledged that* some firms hold their own reserves as units in the fund. This can clearly be distinguished from short-term strategic 'arbitrage trading' by the firm.

27 These considerations are not intended to prevent cross holdings by one unit linked fund in another, or significant holdings of units by with-profits funds.

28 This is necessary to meet the matching requirements for policyholder liabilities set out in the EU Consolidated Life Directive and see also the FSA Handbook: PRU 4.2.57R.

29 This may be derived from quoted bid and offer prices or based on quoted mid-prices.

30 Useful references include: IFRS Application Guidance for IAS39 – 2006 (AG74 to AG81), FSA's CIS Sourcebook (Ch. 4.8 *Valuation*) & COLL Sourcebook (Ch 6.3 *Valuation and pricing*) and the IMA's Guide to Fair Value Pricing – September 2004 (See: http://www.investmentuk.org/news/standards/Fairvaluepricing.pdf).

31 ie mathematical rounding to the nearest unit of price, rather than systematic rounding up or down of all 'odd amounts'.

32 The 4th significant figure (SF) test gives rise to a large cliff-edge effect. For instance, where the price of a fund dips from £1 to 99.9p a 4SF requirement would need an extra decimal on the pricing system. But a system accurate to 1 decimal place with 'natural rounding' would still result in a maximum rounding error of 0.05% at 99.9p and under 0.1% down to a price of 50.1p.

33 For some unit series (eg stakeholder) a cap on charges may apply and so some adjustments, such as a small deduction from the annual management charge may be needed to ensure that the cap is not inadvertently breached.

34 This should include disclosure of how the asset value is calculated for charging purposes (eg whether based on net or gross assets under management).

35 For existing funds that incorporate double-charging on in-house investments, firms should review previous disclosures and consider whether the existing arrangements meet the requirements of TCF.

36 Typically Reduction-in-Yield calculations.

37 Stamp Duty Reserve Tax.

38 This may be most pertinent to Unit Trust and OEIC transactions where terms and costs may vary.

39 Without perfect foresight it will not be possible to achieve perfect equity, but the goal should be to balance the interests of different generations of policyholder and achieve a fair allocation of the burden of tax between the firm and the fund, recognising the tax relief which may be claimed on management expenses.

40 However, firms will need to consider carefully how they respond to *incorrect* price or valuation information provided by third parties. In particular, where investors have lost out it may be appropriate to provide compensation (regardless of whether the firm intends to take action against the third party).

41 Further rule requirements and guidance on complaints handling may be found in the FSA handbook, in chapters 1 and 2 of *DISP* – the Dispute Resolution Complaints Sourcebook.

42 However, consideration should be given to the possibility that the error is evidence of wider failings which would merit investigation.

43 Except where the firm identifies a widespread, systemic error likely to have resulted in losses above £50 for individual retail investors.

44 Whilst the day to day monitoring may be delegated to a management committee or other function holder, the Board retains ultimate responsibility.

45 See SUP 15.3.1R.

46 Firms should carefully consider their approach to redress and where the firm's systems allow for easy and cost-effective redress for retail investors then it may be appropriate to compensate for the loss in some form, even where the amount concerned is below the suggested £10 threshold for cash payments.

47 See DISP Ch 1.4.

INDIVIDUAL CAPITAL ASSESSMENT (ICA) A GUIDE TO THE ICA PROCESS FOR INSURERS

2 February 2007

1. FOREWORD

[5050]
This Guide to the ICA Process for Insurers is intended to complement the FSA's new Handbook material[1] on ICA, which came into effect on 31 December 2006.

It is structured around the nine main requirements set out by the FSA under three 'sub-principles for ICAS', which may be summarised as:

(1) The firm's assessment of the adequacy of its capital resources
(2) Comparability to a 99.5% / 1 year probability that the value of the firm's assets will exceed the value of their liabilities
(3) Model methodology: documenting the firm's reasoning and judgement underlying the ICA assessment

This Guide provides a commentary to these requirements. It has been prepared by the Association of British Insurers (ABI), in conjunction with the International Underwriting Association (IUA), the Investment & Life Assurance Group (ILAG), Lloyd's and the Lloyd's Market Association (LMA).

1.1 Status of the Guide and implementation

This Guide is intended to provide advice to companies in developing their ICA submission. It describes a variety of established approaches companies currently use to meet the ICA requirements, as well as emerging thinking in the industry on how to prepare the ICA. Accordingly, the Guide does not try to suggest a one-size-fits-all approach to ICA, since the range of risks captured and the narrative provided in the ICA submission will depend upon the specific circumstances of the firm and the nature of the business it is writing.

The Guide is not a replacement for the FSA's own rules and guidance for ICA. Whilst the FSA were consulted during the development of this document, this Guide does not constitute guidance from the FSA, and the advice and approaches outlined here are not binding on firms. In the event of conflict between the Guide and the FSA Handbook, the FSA's Handbook text prevails. Ultimately, interpretation of the law is a matter for the courts.

Instead, this Guide complements the FSA's ICA rules and guidance with advice on the approaches that firms may wish to use in meeting the FSA's requirements. Firms are not bound to follow this advice and there may be circumstances where it is appropriate to adopt different techniques.

This Guide has been published by the leading trade bodies for the insurance industry to draw together in a single document a wide range of advice and good practice that has been developed for ICA.

This Guide also provides an opportunity for the industry to share with the FSA, in an open and transparent way, emerging good practice. Through our dialogue with firms, and with the FSA, we can record and disseminate information relating to potential concerns or obstacles that firms may face in preparing their ICA along with, we hope, suggestions as to how these might be overcome.

1.2 Definition of terms

The terms used in this document will normally have the same meaning as they would have in the appropriate section of the FSA Handbook to which our advice refers. Where FSA do not provide a definition, and unless we provide our own specific definition, then it should be assumed that a term or word is being used with its normal, natural meaning relevant to the context of the sentence.

1.3 Period for comment and publication of final version

We first published this Guide on 25 September 2006 as a draft for comment, with a deadline of 31 October to receive those comments. We have incorporated appropriate revisions based on this feedback. This final draft has been approved for publication by the ABI's Board and the other sponsoring associations, to complement the FSA's new rules and guidance for ICA which came into effect on 31 December 2006.

1.4 Review and update of the Guide

We believe this Guide provides a more appropriate place than the FSA Handbook to publish good practice for ICA, offering greater flexibility to record and update our advice on the ICA process. Accordingly, we intend to review the Guide at least annually, in consultation with firms, trade associations and the FSA, to ensure it remains appropriate and up to date. In doing so, we will draw upon the experience of firms in applying the FSA's new rules and guidance for ICA, and of the FSA in reviewing the ICA assessments.

---

[1] As set out in CP 06/16 (issued September 2006), PS 06/14 (issued December 2006) and the Prudential Requirements for Insurers (Amendment) Instrument approved by the FSA Board on 15 December 2006

---

2. FSA'S 'LCA SUB-PRINCIPLES'

[5051]

Sub-Principle 1*: Methodology of capital resources assessment*
(INSPRU 7.1.15R)

Where a firm is carrying out an assessment of the adequacy of its overall financial resources in accordance with GENPRU 1.2, the assessment of the adequacy of the firm's capital resources must:

(1) *reflect the firm's assets, liabilities, intra-group arrangements and future plans;*
(2) *be consistent with the firm's management practice, systems and controls;*
(3) *consider all material risks that may have an impact on the firm's ability to meet its liabilities to policyholders; and*
(4) *use a valuation basis that is consistent throughout the assessment.*

Sub-Principle 2*: ICA submitted to FSA: confidence level*
(INSPRU 7.1.42R)

Where the FSA requests a firm to submit to it a written record of the firm's assessments of the adequacy of its capital resources carried out in accordance with INSPRU 7.1.15R, those assessments must include an assessment comparable to a 99.5% confidence level over a one-year timeframe that the value of assets exceeds the value of liabilities, whether or not this is the confidence level otherwise used in the firm's own assessments.

Sub-Principle 3*: Documenting ICAs submitted to the FSA*
(INSPRU 7.1.49R)

The written record of a firm's individual capital assessments carried out in accordance with INSPRU 7.1.15R submitted by the firm to the FSA must:

(1) *in relation to the assessment comparable to a 99.5% confidence level over a one year timeframe that the value of assets exceeds the value of liabilities, document the reasoning and judgements underlying that assessment and, in particular, justify:*
   (a) *the assumptions used;*
   (b) *the appropriateness of the methodology used; and*
   (c) *the results of the assessment; and*

(2) *identify the major differences between that assessment and any other assessments carried out by the firm using a different confidence level.*

3. ADVICE AND GUIDANCE MATERIAL

[5052]
FSA ICA SUB-PRINCIPLE 1.1 [INSPRU 7.1.15R]

Where a firm is carrying out an assessment of the adequacy of its overall financial resources in accordance with GENPRU 1.2, the assessment of the adequacy of the firm's capital resources must reflect the firm's assets, liabilities, intra-group arrangements and future plans.

Context and FSA Guidance

FSA Guidance explains that the capital assessment should reflect both the insurer's desire to fulfil their business objectives and its responsibility to meet its liabilities to policyholders. Accordingly, the capital assessment should demonstrate that the firm holds sufficient capital to be able to make planned investments and take on new business (within an appropriate planning horizon). It should also ensure that if the firm had to close to new business it would be able to meet its existing commitments. Similarly, for closed firms, the capital assessment should demonstrate that the firm can meet its existing liabilities.

The definition of 'new business' is important in this context. FSA Guidance explains that where an obligation exists on the insurer to renew an insurance contract, this business should be considered as part of the firm's existing liabilities, and not treated as new business. This would include multi-year general insurance contracts and the exercise of options by long-term policyholders.

In *GENPRU* 1.2.30R – 1.2.41G FSA set out a number of review requirements relating to the key areas of risk described in the ICA. FSA guidance states that firms should carry out these assessments at least annually, or more frequently if changes in the business, strategy, nature or scale of its activities or operational environment suggest that the current level of financial resources is no longer adequate.

Industry Guidance

Below we discuss three points: review and update of the ICA, the treatment of new business where there is no obligation to renew, and allowing for a notice period before an underwriting agent employed by the firm stops writing new business.

Review and update of the ICA

FSA's rules and guidance, in particular *GENPRU 1.2.40G*, make clear that the ICA should be updated at least annually and more frequently when other changes demand it. We would suggest that the senior management of firms think about their ICA whenever a major strategic decision is made, to consider whether any new course of action will affect the assumptions made in the ICA. Accordingly, it may be sensible to include review of the ICA within the business planning cycle. The frequency with which the formal ICA is renewed and re-published would depend on the materiality of any changes made to the business plan. It would also depend on whether there was any significant divergence between actual experience and those assumptions originally made in the business plan, but only those changes or divergences that are substantial would suggest the need for a new ICA in advance of the annual review.

The ICA process should form an integral part of the board's management of risk within the organisation. Clear records and documentation[2] of the ICA process will help to demonstrate how this has been achieved.

New Business

FSA Guidance makes explicit an expectation that insurance contracts, including an obligation on the insurer to renew, should be treated as part of existing liabilities. However, where there is no such obligation, we would suggest that firms treat as new business the renewal of all policies where there is no express legal or contractual obligation on the firm to renew.

Capital should be held to cover all planned underwriting activity. New business should always be assumed to increase the aggregate net capital requirement. A one-year time period may be considered reasonable in most circumstances, although a firm might consider less than one year of new business if it can justify the assumption that it could react to emerging experience more rapidly, for example by increasing premium rates, reducing volumes, changing business mix or raising further capital.

In some circumstances, it may be appropriate to consider more than one year of new business. For example, the firm may be unable or unwilling to change its new business strategy in the light of adverse experience. Alternatively, a firm may consider several years' new business to help understand risks that cannot otherwise be captured easily in the capital model. Examples of such risks include trends in market profitability, risks that will only be known after the balance sheet date, and uncertainty over management actions. Firms should justify their rationale for the selection of their new business period, with reference to the nature of the firm.

Use of underwriting agents

Where a firm has delegated authority to an underwriting agent to take on new business, we suggest that the firm would need to consider how a closure to new business might be achieved. Specifically, the firm may need to allow appropriately for the new business that may be written by the underwriting agent during the notice period under the contract between the insurer and the underwriting agent. The firm would also need to consider any penalties due on early termination.

FSA ICA SUB-PRINCIPLE 1.2 [INSPRU 7.1.15R]

Where a firm is carrying out an assessment of the adequacy of its overall financial resources in accordance with GENPRU 1.2, the assessment of the adequacy of the firm's capital resources must be consistent with the firm's management practice, systems and controls.

Context and FSA Guidance

FSA Guidance explains that whilst the firm's capital assessment should reflect the firm's ability to react to events as they occur, there are a number of constraints on a firm's ability to take 'management actions'.

Industry Guidance

Below we discuss two points, constraints on management actions – especially relating to employment of staff and, the run-off of liabilities and how this might be modelled.

Constraints on Management Actions

Firms need to take a realistic and practical assessment of the scope to take management actions. For example, whilst the firm may have the legal authority to make workers redundant, it must consider how to maintain an effective business operation. The firm needs staff to meet its commitments to customers[3], for example to handle claims and make payments.

Similarly, the firm may have the right to alter pay and benefits for employees or contract workers, but if the firm cannot maintain competitive remuneration workers will leave, often in an unpredictable fashion, which may jeopardise the effective running of the business. There may also be a number of management actions that a firm could take to reduce the overall cost of the pension scheme obligation at a time of stress, but the firm will need to be able to explain its choice of assumptions about the method and timing of funding for any emerging deficit.

For life firms in particular, it may be necessary to consider the likely impact of management actions against the commitments made in its Principles and Practices of Financial Management (PPFM) documents. (See also advice under principle 3.1 in this Guide).

Modelling the run-off of liabilities

A firm's capital assessment would normally reflect the circumstances in which it might expect the existing liabilities to be discharged. Factors typically taken into account in this part of the assessment include:

(a) closure to new business;
(b) the management of the run-off (eg out-sourcing, commutations, transfer of portfolio);
(c) the costs that can be removed if new business is no longer being written;
(d) the one-off costs that might be associated with removing these new business costs;
(e) the loss of economies of scale if new business is no longer written;
(f) the possible changes in the asset portfolio;
(g) other management actions that might be taken to reduce costs or to minimise risks, while not reducing the protection of policyholder liabilities, or conflicting with TCF; and
(h) any constraints on moving capital from ring-fenced funds such as with-profits funds.

FSA ICA SUB-PRINCIPLE 1.3 [INSPRU 7.1.15R]

Where a firm is carrying out an assessment of the adequacy of its overall financial resources in accordance with GENPRU 1.2, the assessment of the adequacy of the firm's capital resources must consider all material risks that may have an impact on the firm's ability to meet its liabilities to policyholders.

Context and FSA Guidance

FSA Guidance indicates that the firm's capital assessment should demonstrate, to the required level of confidence, that the firm's liabilities to policyholders will be paid. The assessment should also consider all material risks that may arise before these liabilities are met.

Industry Guidance

We have advice for firms on the method for assessing such changes in longer-term risks, taking account of the requirement for a defined level of confidence in meeting policyholder liabilities. We also describe a number of the primary, generic risk types that may feature in the firm's capital assessment. Naturally, the range of risks captured in the assessment and the extent of any supporting narrative and analysis will depend upon the specific circumstances of the firm and the nature of the business it is writing.

Assessing risk and demonstrating the required level of confidence in meeting policyholder liabilities

We consider that a value-at-risk (VaR) approach or the use of sudden changes in conditions may provide a suitable method to meet the FSA's requirement to demonstrate that policyholder liabilities will be met to the required level of confidence.

For example, the risk of a fall in the value of assets could be quantified as either:

(i) a sudden change in conditions with a revaluation of the assets and liabilities on a best estimate basis (consistent with a return to more benign conditions); or

(ii) a fall in the value of assets over an extended period.

In this context, it is helpful to refer to FSA Guidance (INSPRU 7.1.31G) which indicates that firms may exclude from their capital assessment risks which have an immaterial effect on the firm's financial position or only occur with an extreme probability.

Major risk types pertinent to ICA

In *GENPRU 1.2.30R* FSA provide a list of generic risk types that may be relevant to a firm's ICA, depending on the size and nature of its business.

Drawing on this list, we discuss below many of the major risks firms are likely to consider in their capital assessment. Not all of these risks will be relevant to every firm, but it is likely that many will. We also set out advice on the approaches that may be used to analyse these risks and describe factors that firms may wish to take into account in assessing the adequacy of their capital resources:

Insurance Risk

Insurance risk typically refers to fluctuations in the timing, frequency and severity of insured events, relative to the expectations of the firm at the time of underwriting. Insurance risk may also refer to fluctuations in the timing and amount of claim settlements. For general insurance business, examples of insurance risk include variations in the amount or frequency of claims or the unexpected occurrence of multiple claims arising from a single cause. For life insurance business, examples include variations in the mortality and persistency rates of policyholders, or the possibility that guarantees could acquire a value that adversely affects the finances of a firm and its ability to treat all its policyholders fairly, whilst adhering to the firm's contractual obligations. More generally, insurance risk includes the potential for expense overruns relative to pricing or provisioning assumptions.

It may also be appropriate to consider the extent to which variations in insurance costs may arise as a result of catastrophe events, including both risk and event losses; the cost of reinstatement premiums any possible reinsurance exhaustion; unexpected claim types including latent liabilities, court awards, contract disputes; trends in costs over a period of time; and the effect of loss ratios being higher than planned (in other words, worse than would be suggested by analysing historic loss ratio experience and volatility).

Consideration might also be given to the extent to which competitive pressures can limit the firm's ability to charge adequate premiums for renewals and new business.

In deciding whether, and to what extent, a firm allows for new business in its capital assessment it may also be appropriate to consider changes in the volume and mix of new business. Some further areas to consider in developing Insurance Risk scenarios might include:

Underwriting Risk, (General and Life):

- the adequacy of the firm's pricing, taking the insurance premium cycle into account and the high level of uncertainty in pricing in new or emerging markets;
- the uncertainty of claims experience;
- the dependence on intermediaries for a disproportionate share of the premium income;
- geographical or jurisdictional concentrations;
- the appropriateness of policy wordings;
- the risk of mis-selling, for example, the number of complaints or disputed claims; and
- the tolerance for expense reserve variations or variations in expenses (including indirect costs).

Underwriting Risk (General):

- the length of tail of the claims development and latent claims; and
- the effects of rapid growth or decline in the volume of the underwriting portfolio.

Underwriting Risk (Life):

- the uncertainty of future investment returns;
- the effects of rapid growth or decline in the volume and nature of new business written; and
- the ability of firms to adjust premium rates or charges for some products.

Reserving and Claims Risks (General and Life)

- the frequency and size of large claims;
- possible outcomes relating to any disputed claims, particularly where the outcome is subject to legal proceedings;
- the ability of the firm to withstand catastrophic events, increases in unexpected exposures, latent claims or aggregation of claims;
- the possible exhaustion of reinsurance arrangements, both on a per risk and per event basis;
- social and societal factors driving an increase in the propensity to claim and to sue; and
- other social, economic and technological changes.

Reserving and Claims Risks (General):

- the adequacy and uncertainty of the technical claims provisions, such as outstanding claims, IBNR and claims handling expense reserves;
- the adequacy of other underwriting provisions, such as the provisions for unearned premium and unexpired risk reserves;
- the appropriateness of catastrophe models and underlying assumptions used, such as possible maximum loss (PML) factors used;
- unanticipated legal judgements and legal change with retrospective effect specifically with regard to the claims reserves; and
- the effects of inflation.

Reserving and Claims Risks (Life):

- the adequacy and sensitivity of the mathematical reserves to variations in future experience, including:
  (1) the risk that investment returns differ from those assumed in the reserving assumptions;
  (2) the risk of variations in mortality, morbidity and persistency experience and in the exercise of options under contracts;
  (3) the rates of taxation applied, in particular where there is uncertainty over the tax treatment; and
- unanticipated legal judgements and legal change with retrospective effect specifically with regard to the impact on mathematical reserves.

Credit Risk

Credit risk typically refers to any risk in an insurer's ability to recover money owed by third parties. This includes all counterparties, including reinsurance firms, intermediaries, policyholders, banks and issuers of investments.

We suggest that firms should not only consider default, but also partial impairment, delay in settlement and the risk that credit ratings may be downgraded or credit spreads widen within the time horizon of the assessment (which may reduce the value of the debt instrument). Other relevant considerations include the risks arising from concentration of relationships with individual counterparties, lack of contract certainty and contract disputes.

These risks can emerge not only in connection with external parties but may also arise within a group.

Some further areas to consider in developing the credit risk stress tests and scenario analyses might include:

- the adequacy of the reinsurance programme and whether it is appropriate for the risks selected by the firm and adequately takes account of the underwriting and business plans;
- the collapse of a reinsurer or several reinsurers on the firm's reinsurance programme and the subsequent impact this may have on the firm's outstanding reinsurance recoveries and IBNR recoveries;
- the prospect of reinsurance rates increasing substantially or reinsurance being unavailable;
- any existing or possible future disputes relating to reinsurance contracts on a pessimistic basis, to the extent that they are not already reflected in the value attributed to the reinsurances;
- greater losses from bad debts than anticipated;
- deterioration in the extent and quality of collateral; and
- guarantees given by the insurer of the performance of others, whether under contracts of insurance or otherwise.

Market Risk

Market risk typically refers to the risk that arises from fluctuations in the values of or income from assets, from interest rates or exchange rates.

It will usually be appropriate to consider both increases and decreases in the market value of different asset classes, taking into account the possibility that opposing movements in the value of different asset classes may be more onerous than movement of all values in the same direction.

It may be inappropriate to assume that matching of liabilities or the use of hedging strategies can completely eliminate exposure to market risks. Firms may need to allow for the potential costs of replacing short-term hedges or the costs associated with rebalancing their portfolio of assets where (perhaps under stressed conditions) there is a material risk that the matching/hedging strategy may have a flaw or the individual instruments may be subject to default.

Firms may also need to consider their exposure to changes in the shape of yield curves, which can produce quite different results to a parallel shift.

Firms with assets or liabilities in currencies other than sterling may also need to allow for shifts in asset values relative to liability values arising from currency fluctuations.

Some further areas to consider in developing the market risk scenario might include:

- the possibility of a severe economic or market downturn or upturn leading to adverse interest rate movements affecting the firm's investment position;
- unanticipated losses and defaults of issuers;
- price shifts in asset classes, and their impact on the entire portfolio;
- inadequate valuation of assets;
- the direct impact on the portfolio of currency devaluation, as well as the effect on related markets and currencies;
- the extent of any mismatch of assets and liabilities, including reinvestment risk;
- the impact on the portfolio value of a dramatic change in the spread between a market index of interest rates and the risk-free interest rates; and
- the extent to which market moves could have non-linear effects on values, such as derivatives.

Liquidity Risk

Liquidity risk typically refers to the risk that a firm reaches a position where, although total assets exceed the value of liabilities, the firm does not have sufficient financial resources available in cash to enable it to meet its obligations as they fall due, or can secure such resources only at prohibitive cost.

When assessing liquidity risk, a firm would usually consider the extent of mismatch between assets and liabilities and the value of assets held in highly liquid, marketable forms that may be realised should unexpected cashflows lead to a liquidity problem. This may include consideration of the effect on cashflows of the exercise of options by policyholders and the consequent rapid disposal of assets that may mean that best prices cannot be achieved. Where the firm has to rely on finance facilities to provide liquidity, firms may need to consider the cost and continuity of this finance.

Some further areas to consider in developing the liquidity risk scenario might include:

- any mismatching between expected asset and liability cash flows;
- the inability to sell assets quickly;
- the extent to which the firm's assets have been pledged;
- the cash-flow positions generally of the firm and its ability to withstand sharp, unexpected outflows of funds via claims, or an unexpected drop in the inflow of premiums; and
- the possible need to reduce large asset positions at different levels of market liquidity, and the related potential costs and timing constraints.

Operational Risk

Operational risk can be defined as the risk of an incident occurring which leads to or could lead to the actual outcome of a business process to differ from the expected outcome due to inadequate or failed processes, people, systems, or external factors.

Examples of some issues that a firm might want to consider include:

- the likelihood of fraudulent activity occurring that may impact upon the financial or operational aspects of the firm;
- the technology risks that the firm may be exposed to regarding its operations. For example, risks relating to both the hardware systems and the software utilised to run those systems;
- the reputation risks to which the firm is exposed. For example, the impact on the firm if the firm's brand is damaged resulting in a loss of policyholders from the underwriting portfolio;
- the marketing and distribution risks that the firm may be exposed to. For example, the dependency on intermediary business or a firm's own sales force;
- the impact of legal risks. For example a non-insurance related legal action being pursued against the firm;
- the management of employees – for instance: withdraw of goodwill by dissatisfied staff, staff strikes, fraud or other acts which could give rise to a loss of reputation;
- the resourcing of key functions including risk management, ensuring there are a sufficient number of staff with an appropriate mix of skills in areas such as underwriting, claims handling, accounting, actuarial and legal expertise.

A firm may consider that investigation of operational weaknesses and corrective action is a better response than holding capital and may believe that a certain degree of operational risk is within its pre-defined risk tolerance. However, until the firm accurately identifies and corrects any deficiencies it should consider capital as an interim response to the risk.

It is often the case that operational loss data is limited for an individual firm or even for the insurance industry as a whole[4]. So it is unlikely to be appropriate to rely solely on the firm's own experience when assessing the capital impact of operational risk.

Along with the application of tools specific to the individual firm, industry and sector data as well as expert judgement will always be required when assessing and managing operational risk. Firms will need to document their underlying thinking, to explain how the capital calculations relate to the firm's day-to-day risk management approach. Consideration may also need to be given to the management of previous loss events both from within the firm and externally.

Where risks are identified which overlap with operational risk (eg expenses) firms would typically want to ensure that these risks are included in one of the categories of the assessment (and not missed or double counted).

Firms would also normally want to ensure that their assessment of operational risk capital relates to their own business, systems and controls and management, rather than simply rely on applying a loading to other elements of its risk capital, premium income or provisions. Set out below are some of the key issues raised by the FSA in the context of operational risk:

Cross-cutting risks (eg mis-selling)

It is important to consider the broad economic context and likely changes in financial markets. Unplanned or unexpected costs may arise in a number of different ways, for example from possible mis-selling, either from past business or from future new business. The firm should also be aware of the possibility that outstanding projects and risk mitigation programmes may not be completed on time or may not deliver the expected benefits.

Specific risks (eg outsourcing)

It should not generally be assumed that an outsourcing arrangement isolates the firm from all risks, even if contractual terms place obligations on the outsourcer in this area. Where a firm has outsourced aspects of its business it should be able to justify the extent to which it has assumed that outsourcing reduces the risk of increases in future expenses by reference, for example, to the credit rating of the outsourcer and relevant contractual factors.

Where outsourcing services are provided by a company within the same group, the firm should consider both the risks that the group company is taking and the extent to which capital to mitigate these risks is likely to come from the insurer's own resources. Where the service company does not hold capital of its own or does not have the right to call on additional capital when required, then typically the capital for the outsourcer's risks should be held by the insurer.

Group Risk

Group risk typically refers to the risks a firm is exposed to as a member of a group. In many cases, being a member of a group can provide significant advantages in terms of financial strength, technical expertise and management experience. However, there may be group risks external to the individual entity that may deplete or divert financial resources held by the individual firm to meet liabilities arising from the parent or another entity in the group.

Accordingly, entities that are members of a group may need to consider, within their entity specific ICA:

(i) The accumulation of risk arising from one counterparty where several different entities within the group may undertake separate transactions with the same counterparty (eg significant investments in a third party by several members of the group or multiple reinsurance contracts across the group with a single reinsurer); and

(ii) The risk that reputation damage to one firm will have knock-on effects to other entities within the group (ie brand failure).

FSA guidance (INSPRU 7.1.22G – INSPRU 7.1.24G) provides further specific recommendations on the treatment of intra-group capital arrangements.

Other potential risks include:

Pension Schemes

Where a material deficit has arisen, it would normally be appropriate to allow for a realistic assessment of the additional costs of reducing the deficit as part of the firm's ICA. The costs should take into account senior management's views of the suitable time period and contribution rates that the firm can practically make. The regulatory constraints currently applying, and realistically expected to apply in the future, should also be considered.

Indeed, it may be appropriate to take into account the risks associated with a defined benefit scheme which covers the employees of a service company used by the firm, to the extent that the costs of operating the service function is met from the fees paid by the insurer.

Many of the risks affecting the pension scheme will be common to the risks affecting the firm's insurance business, so the firm would need to be able to justify any significant differences in the assumptions and scenarios used for the pension scheme as compared to its insurance business.

Tax considerations

A firm will need to be able to explain the key tax assumptions made and the extent to which it is taking credit within its assessment for tax assets.

While it will often be impractical to model with precision the tax regime that applies to the firm, the ICA should include an allowance for the material features of the tax regime, since these may have a significant impact on the capital requirements. Surplus assets not required to meet the firm's ICA should normally be shown on the balance sheet net of any tax[5] that would arise on the realisation of unrealised gains or recognition of unrecognised profits, such as the valuation of in-force business or release of reserving margins.

In the extreme loss events being considered in the ICA, there may be opportunities for firms to realise tax assets that would not be recognised in normal circumstances. Where such credit is taken, firms should consider the possibility of permanent impairment of tax assets or material reductions in their value, for example, owing to timing issues or dependency on profit streams outside the business, which may not emerge in those stressed circumstances.

FSA ICA SUB-PRINCIPLE 1.4 [INSPRU 7.1.15R]

Where a firm is carrying out an assessment of the adequacy of its overall financial resources in accordance with GENPRU 1.2, the assessment of the adequacy of the firm's capital resources must use a valuation basis that is consistent throughout the assessment.

Context and FSA Guidance

FSA Guidance suggests that the valuation approach should not contain margins for risk nor should the approach be optimistic. The guidance indicates that firms should carry out a broad reconciliation of the key parts of any balance sheet used in the capital assessment with any corresponding entry from audited results.

Industry Guidance

We believe this is a useful validation and cross-reference. It will help firms to identify:

- the main differences in methodology;
- any changes in the underlying assumptions; and
- different regulatory constraints such as the admissibility rules, explicit valuation margins and discounting for anticipated investment returns.

Valuation of assets and liabilities

The valuation of traded assets would normally be based on the actual market price[6] of the portfolio of assets at the relevant valuation date. For most insurance liabilities and some assets there is no liquid market with published price data, so the market price is more difficult to determine. In these cases, the valuation would normally be based on the firm's best estimate of:

(i) the realisable value of the assets on the open market; and

(ii) an expected present value of the liabilities, allowing for the time value of money.

Where a firm is unable to use a realistic approach as described, there are alternatives that may be used, such as valuations derived from company accounts. In such cases, the firm would need to demonstrate that this valuation could reasonably be expected to result in total available resources no greater than would be calculated under a realistic approach.

Examples of such evidence would include:

(i) demonstration that the liability valuation approach makes less allowance for the time-value of money than it would under a realistic valuation; and

(ii) demonstration that the book value of traded assets is no higher than the market value of the same assets.

Inclusion of dividends

A firm would normally include, within its capital assessment, at least an allowance for future dividend payments to the extent that these have been declared and represent a current liability. Likewise, declared dividend payments to be received from intra-group companies may also be included in the ICA.

FSA ICA SUB-PRINCIPLE 2 [INSPRU 7.1.42R]

Where the FSA requests a firm to submit to it a written record of the firm's assessments of the adequacy of its capital resources carried out in accordance with INSPRU 7.1.15R, those assessments must include an assessment comparable to a 99.5% probability over a one-year timeframe that the value of assets exceeds the value of liabilities, whether or not this is the confidence level otherwise used in the firm's own assessments.

Context and FSA Guidance

In this principle the FSA define a criteria against which they will judge capital assessments. Their Guidance makes clear that firms are not bound by the 99.5% / 1 year test, but that the firm should be able to justify its choice of a longer time horizon and explain how the confidence interval chosen by the firm is comparable to the 99.5% /1 year standard.

Industry Guidance

Whilst the FSA have a clear interest in establishing a common point of reference for ICA assessments across the industry, a firm's management will determine their own risk appetite and select a risk measure they consider appropriate to the on-going management of their business.

FSA have emphasised that the capital assessment should be owned by the firm and driven by business need, rather than engineered as a tool of regulatory compliance. It is the use and ownership by all parts of the business of this assessment that make it a valuable mechanism for managing and controlling risk and hence to determine the appropriate level, quality and allocation of capital.

FSA ICA SUB-PRINCIPLE 3.1 [INSPRU 7.1.49R (1)]

The written record of a firm's individual capital assessments carried out in accordance with INSPRU 7.1.15R submitted by the firm to the FSA must in relation to the assessment comparable to a 99.5% confidence level over a one year timeframe that the value of assets exceeds the value of liabilities, document the reasoning and judgements underlying that assessment and, in particular, justify the assumptions used.

Context and FSA Guidance

FSA Guidance provides a clear link between this sub-principle and the requirements in *GEN-PRU 1.2*, that a firm must maintain its own assessment of the adequacy of its financial resources. In essence, this requires a firm to document the reasoning and judgements underlying its ICA, justifying the assumptions and methodology used, and to explain any major differences between its ICA and the firm's own assessment, where this is different from the ICA.

FSA set out a number of requirements covering:
(i) the choice of assumptions;
(ii) the evidence required to support these assumptions; and
(iii) the regular review of assumptions.

We set out below some further advice on these points.

Industry Guidance

The main categories of assumptions firms may need to consider are:

- Expected outcomes for the key risks;
- Variability and/or possible extreme outcomes for the key risks;
- The way that the risks aggregate, in particular assumptions about lack of correlation or dependency between risks; and
- The way that the business responds to the risk factors, including the actions of management, policyholders and other stakeholders whose behaviour can affect the firm's financial position.

Specific justification of each *individual* assumption would not usually be required, but a firm would normally document the approach it has used to derive sets of similar assumptions.

To illustrate the point we set out a number of examples below:

Examples for life insurers:

(i) When setting a best estimate lapse assumption, a firm would normally consider an analysis of its lapse experience over recent years showing variation by:
  - type of contract;
  - length of the contract term or duration of contract since issue[7];

  Firms would not necessarily assume that all contracts experience a rise or fall in lapse experience if variation in experience would be more onerous, but the assumptions used should be appropriate to the circumstances of the firm. Firms will also want to consider:
  - how fluctuations in recent experience are dealt with in determining best estimate assumptions for future experience; and
  - the relevance and reliability of the data from which the experience analysis has been drawn.

(ii) When considering the best estimate assumption for future expenses for each homogeneous risk group, a firm would typically prepare an analysis of expenses across the business, and then consider direct expenses allocated to each specific risk group. Future expenses such as renewal and other maintenance expenses would reflect the expected ongoing expense levels required to manage the in-force business (including investment in systems required to support that business and allowing for future inflation). Overheads must be covered by the business and may be allocated between new and in-force business to reflect current business plans and future expectations. All expected expense overruns, including holding company operating expenses, overhead costs and development costs such as those incurred in start-up operations, would also need to be allowed for.

Examples for non-life insurers:

(i) When considering the effect of the underwriting cycle, a firm would normally explain how their ICA reflects the external pressures of lower premium rates and in particular the risk that premium rates will be lower than those anticipated in their business plan.
(ii) When assessing claims variability, firms would normally analyse their underwriting risk split by attritional, large and catastrophe claims. This split should enable firms to apply the results for other business decision purposes, for instance, to evaluate and construct a suitable reinsurance programme.

Use of Prudent Assumptions

Wherever a firm has used an assumption that it regards as prudent (ie would tend to give a higher capital requirement than the corresponding best estimate assumption), it should distinguish between:
(i) a loading intended to compensate for parameter or model error; and
(ii) prudence intended to address another concern, for example, a known weakness elsewhere in the ICA.

Where a firm believes areas of prudence in the ICA could compensate for other areas of optimism, it should quantify the impact and the extent to which one offsets the other.

While it is acceptable for firms to use prudent assumptions to compensate for a more approximate modelling approach, this prudence should not also be taken as compensation for areas of optimism elsewhere in the model.

Evidence to support the choice of assumptions

FSA Guidance makes clear that firms need to be able to support their choice of assumptions, whether through the use of data or by expert judgement. In addition to the Guidance provided by the FSA, we would suggest that firms may wish to consider the following points:

(i) Where possible and appropriate, mathematical assumptions are justified by the use of back-testing.

(ii) Where a scenario generator has been used, the rationale for choosing the particular statistical distribution should be explained, particularly where limited data is used to calibrate models that make use of the 'distribution tail'.

(iii) Firms demonstrate how they have satisfied themselves that the calibration of their model is appropriate and suited to their business.

(iv) Firms should consider different periods of historical market data as part of the overall calibration process. This helps to justify the final selection of assumptions, and to understand likely parameter estimation error.

Regular review of assumptions

FSA Guidance indicates that firms should regularly review the key parameters underpinning the model. We set out below some suggestions covering the nature and scope of this review.

The review of the parameters may include a degree of back-testing. The nature and extent of this back-testing would depend on the nature of each assumption. Some assumptions, such as the expectation of certain distributions, may be derived entirely from one year's experience; for these assumptions, comparison of the most recent year's experience with previous expectations can help inform future capital assessments.

For other assumptions, most commonly those relating to the variance of a distribution and/or stressed outcomes, the relative importance of one year's experience is much more limited.

For all assumptions, it may be appropriate to consider how emerging experience might change the firm's view of the assumptions to be used.

The selection of parameters in the calibration of the firm's capital assessment carries some uncertainty, even where a substantial quantity of data is available. The most common source of uncertainty is a lack of credible and relevant data on which to base the main assumptions. Firms will need to understand the strength and reliability of the information available both for the best estimate assumptions and for the risk distributions and dependencies assumed in the calculation of the ICA. A firm might also need to consider the potential risk of selecting the wrong value for a parameter and the impact that this might have on their capital assessment.

In addition, appropriate weighting may need to be given to the greater uncertainty attaching to new business, new or changed products and changes in administration and distribution.

Management Actions

Management actions are likely to underpin many of the assumptions in the model and so it may be necessary to describe in some detail the extent of any significant management actions assumed, and the extent to which these management actions have been used in the past, or since the previous assessment.

As part of the practical process of building models, firms may usefully include dynamic rules within a stochastic model to quantify the impact of management actions. Firms will typically want to consider whether the nature and magnitude of the actions within the model have been carefully tested as part of the model validation process and that the impact of the primary management actions for key scenarios has been considered by senior management before signing off the overall results. This will help to ensure that senior management has a clear understanding of the management actions the ICA assumes they will take. As a key aspect of management control it is vital that the assumed management actions are not obscured within the complexities of a model.

Firms will want to ensure that the quantification of all significant management actions, whether calculated within a stochastic model or as a separate exercise, appropriately reflects the stressed environment that will apply when the action is taken. In such circumstances there are likely to be a greater number of constraints than would be the case in normal conditions. Care is also required when management actions or stresses are considered in combination, for example:

(i) If more than one management action could be used as a mitigant of the same stress, the assessment should normally allow for the combination that would actually be used;

(ii) The assessment should normally consider the combined effect of using several management actions simultaneously, which may be different from the result achieved when each is used individually; and

(iii) If the same management action could be used in different circumstances as a mitigant of more than one type stress, care will be required to ensure that the effect of that management action is not double-counted.

Firms will also, typically, need to consider the potential reaction of other stakeholders in the business, including policyholders, reinsurance partners, outsourcers and providers of capital, to any management actions that the firm takes. The financial implications of any potential actions taken by these stakeholders would usually be taken account of within the assessment.

> ***FSA ICA SUB-PRINCIPLE 3.2 [INSPRU 7.1.49R (1)]***
>
> The written record of a firm's individual capital assessment, as carried out in accordance with INSPRU 7.1.15R submitted by the firm to the FSA must in relation to the assessment comparable to a 99.5% confidence level over a one year timeframe that the value of assets exceeds the value of liabilities, document the reasoning and judgements underlying that assessment and, in particular, justify the appropriateness of the methodology used.

Context and FSA Guidance

FSA Guidance [INSPRU 7.1.65G – 7.1.67G] provides further explanation of the 'appropriateness requirement' for the methodology used in the capital assessment. The Guidance indicates firms should apply a methodology that allows them to quantify the financial effect of material risks, to the required confidence level. The methodology should also reflect the nature of the firm's business and be consistent with the way in which the firm identifies and manages risk.

FSA also provide Guidance on the use of stress tests, aggregation and scenario testing.

We have some advice for firms that may assist them in fulfilling these requirements.

Industry Guidance

Proportionality and Model Sophistication

As with all statistical models, a balance needs to be struck between the homogeneity of individual model components, for example types of business or types of loss, and the credibility of any data or analysis available for each component.

As FSA guidance indicates, larger firms would be expected to take a more sophisticated approach to capital modelling than smaller firms. However, a more sophisticated approach does not automatically imply that the firm's model should be a fully-integrated, simulation-based model office. Increased sophistication does typically imply both a greater number of individual risk components and a deeper analysis of each risk component.

Approaches to identifying Financial Risk

In identifying financial risk, firms will typically use either:

(i) **a 'balance sheet' approach**, meaning that they measure capital requirements with reference to the variability in the value of assets and liabilities at different time points; or

(ii) **a 'cashflow' or 'run-off' approach**, meaning that they measure capital requirements from the projected cashflows arising from the business.

In some cases it may be appropriate to use a combination of these approaches. When calculating future balance sheet values, firms may use simulation models with transformed probability assumptions ('risk neutral' models).

Where a firm uses a balance sheet approach and a time horizon of more than one year, then actual balance sheet assessments at future dates could result in a position where assessed liabilities exceed assets even if, after this balance sheet date, the business would later be able to meet all its policyholder liabilities (due to favourable experience after one or more of the interim balance sheet dates during the projected time horizon). Such a position, where a firm's liabilities exceed the value of assets, is unlikely to provide confidence in the financial position of the firm and could result in a winding up of the business and a requirement to buy-out some, or all, of the remaining policyholder liabilities. Accordingly, it may be appropriate for the firm to set their capital requirements so as to ensure that assets exceed assessed liabilities on a balance sheet basis at all future balance sheet dates.

Where a firm is using a 'run-off' or cashflow approach, the firm would normally select a time horizon long enough to project the discharge of all, or a significant proportion of, the policyholder obligations. If the time horizon is not sufficient to project the discharge of all obligations, then an appropriate approximation should be made at the end of the time horizon to allow for the assumed cost of the residual liability.

Whether using a 'balance sheet' or a 'run-off' approach, firms would normally want to be able to demonstrate that the value of assets will exceed the value of liabilities on a continuous basis. However, a sensible and pragmatic alternative is to calculate an assessment at regular intervals, for example annual future balance sheets. More frequent balance sheet checks may be considered where this is appropriate to the business.

Aggregation, Stress Tests and Scenario Investigations

Aggregation of risks can be achieved in a number of ways: from relatively simple mathematical combinations to simulation models that replicate the relationships between all risks and the overall capital requirement.

Stress tests and scenario analysis are both useful and powerful tools:

Stress testing, quantifying the effect of a change on a single parameter, is useful for understanding the potential impact of individual risks in isolation.

Scenario testing, quantifying the effect of a change on multiple parameters, is useful for considering the combined effect of a number of risks and the cumulative impact of several different mitigating actions all occurring at the same time.

In *GENPRU 1.2.42R*, FSA require firms to undertake stress and scenario analyses for each of the major sources of risk identified in its ICA. Stress testing can also provide a useful link between the risk register (or other risk identification tool) and the complete capital model. Stress tests may be deterministic but they are often developed with probability distributions in mind.

In designing scenarios, firms should consider potential cause and effect relationships between risks. Such relationships may be better modelled using deterministic relationships rather than relying on statistical correlations.

Assumptions about the Aggregation of Risk

Firms will typically use one or a combination of the following approaches to assessing the aggregate risk:

(i) the **'correlation matrix'** approach: deterministic stress tests applied to individual risks, aggregated using a mathematical approach to allow for diversification between risks;
(ii) the **'scenario'** approach: deterministic scenario tests applied to combinations of risks; and
(iii) the **'stochastic'** approach: simulation models that consider a collection of risks together and test their inter-dependencies and interactions directly.

Firms may also choose to use a correlation matrix to combine the results of both deterministic stress tests and the output from stochastic models.

Correlation Matrix

Firms may wish to consider the possibility that each risk is correlated with every other. In many models this could result in a large number of parameters and so it may not practicable to correlate every risk with every other. In such cases firms may want to identify the most material correlations and pay less attention to those where the outcome is less sensitive. However, where an assumption of less than one is assumed implicitly or explicitly, the firm will need to be able to explain that assumption.

It may be appropriate to use a number of correlation matrices to aggregate similar types of risk and then use a final high-level matrix to aggregate the capital amounts from each of the broad risk areas. However, firms will want to be satisfied that this does not result in missing out interactions between individual risks across categories.

Firms may find it necessary to invest a considerable amount of time establishing which correlations are most important to their business and selecting and challenging these key assumptions. Often there is very little or no data available and firms will need to use general reasoning.

Where the correlation assumptions have been derived indirectly, firms may need to consider a number of scenarios and possible 'cause and effect' event chains to satisfy themselves that their correlation assumptions are appropriate.

They may also need to consider the external factors that can influence the experience of several risks at once: for example economic factors or the behaviour of the law courts.

When presenting an ICA, firms will typically be expected to provide a full commentary on the selection of correlation assumptions, including the sources of data where relevant, the external factors considered and a discussion of the rationale for the final selection of each parameter to include any adjustments for non-linearity.

Scenario approach

Firms that do not consider combination scenarios as inputs to their capital assessments are likely to need strong arguments to justify this approach.

One reason why the aggregation of individual scenarios may prove inadequate without adjustment is that some risk events may combine to give much heavier losses than implied even by the sum of the impacts of the individual risk scenarios. This 'non-linearity' of risk impacts can increase the importance of certain combinations of risks dramatically.

For example, there may be several unconnected risks, each of which in isolation can be successfully mitigated by the same mechanism (for example by raising prices). However, where each of these risks occurs together, this mechanism may not be able to fully mitigate the cumulative impact of all of these risks. This outcome may only be revealed when these combinations of losses are tested. Alternatively, the impact of one risk may be exacerbated by the impact of another. Discretionary policyholder behaviour is often a factor in such cases, while in others the interaction can be accidental.

It is generally easy to predict the direction of the effect on capital of a single risk (for example a fall in equity values leading to a fall, rather than a rise, in capital). However, when more than one risk is considered, these simple relationships can break down and it is far more difficult to predict which combinations of risk losses give rise to an overall loss of the expected magnitude. Assuming that the risks are not fully correlated, firms may find it is reasonable to test combination scenarios where the individual impact of each risk is lower than the appropriate percentile for that risk in isolation. However, in selecting combination tests, firms will want to consider the likely to need to demonstrate that they have considered the impact of different combinations of the main risks identified in their ICA to satisfy themselves that they are making a reasonable estimate of the required confidence level for their ICA.

Stochastic Models

Whilst firms may rely on third parties for aspects of their modelling and assumptions (for example economic scenario generators), the firm remains responsible for the reliability of the underlying assumptions – this responsibility cannot be passed on to a third party. Where a firm uses proprietary components within its overall ICA it may be asked to explain how it has satisfied itself that these components are suitable for its business, including the choice of any discretionary assumptions and inputs with those components.

A firm using a stochastic model incorporating several risks may be able to spend relatively less effort identifying the important combinations of risk events, but will still need to ensure that the assumed relationships between risks and their respective impacts on the business are appropriate.

Aggregation of Risk under Extreme Conditions

In their capital assessment firms will need to give reasonable consideration to the possibility that one risk event may increase the likelihood of other risk events. This may be the result of factors external or internal to the firm. Under a 'correlation matrix' approach, firms may choose to use 'correlation' assumptions that are intended to be stronger than might be expected or observed in normal circumstances. Under a 'scenario' approach, firms may investigate more closely the cause-and-effect relationships between risk events. Using a stochastic model, firms may be able to do both, perhaps employing more sophisticated mathematical techniques to model the effect of the dependencies.

FSA ICA SUB-PRINCIPLE 3.3 [INSPRU 7.1.49R (1)]

The written record of a firm's individual capital assessment, as carried out in accordance with INSPRU 7.1.15R submitted by the firm to the FSA must in relation to the assessment comparable to a 99.5% confidence level over a one year timeframe that the value of assets exceeds the value of liabilities, document the reasoning and judgements underlying that assessment and, in particular, justify the results of the assessment.

Context and FSA Guidance

FSA guidance indicates that firms should consider the full range of possible outcomes (not only those below the 99.5%/1yr confidence level), however unlikely any one single outcome might be, to ensure capital is set to provide appropriate protection against all but the most extreme losses. FSA also suggest that checks should be made as to the reasonableness of the outcomes, with consideration given to a range of scenarios that could give rise to the scale of loss envisaged in the capital assessment[8].

Industry Guidance

We have some advice on how these reasonableness checks might be achieved:

- test the scenarios for plausibility, for example by comparison with actual historical events;
- consider how well the scenarios represent the extreme probabilities that the capital assessment is intended to address; and
- ensure that a reasonable range or permutation of scenarios is identified to allow for the possibility of more extreme aggregate losses that are still within the required confidence level for the capital assessment.

Such analysis is important for checking the reasonableness of risk assumptions – particularly assumptions about the way that risks and prospective management actions aggregate.

> ***FSA ICA SUB-PRINCIPLE 3.4 [INSPRU 7.1.49R (2)]***
> The written record of a firm's individual capital assessments as carried out in accordance with INSPRU 7.1.15R submitted by the firm to the FSA must identify the major differences between that assessment and any other assessments carried out by the firm using a different confidence level.

Context and FSA Guidance

FSA guidance indicates that whilst a firm is required to submit an assessment comparable to a 99.5% probability over a one-year time horizon that the value of assets exceeds liabilities, it may be the case that for its own assessment the firm will use a different confidence level. For example, this may be because the firm:

- has a different view of its capital adequacy
- is seeking to meet the demands of ratings agencies to secure a given rating
- seeks to distinguish itself from competitors when describing its financial strength to policyholders

Where the firm does use a different confidence level, the FSA require the submission of a comparison between the firm's own assessment and the prescribed 99.5% confidence level. This would include any major differences in the definition of assets or liabilities, the management actions used, the risks considered or the valuation methodology.

Industry Guidance

FSA make clear that firms only need to make this comparison where they have chosen to adopt a separate confidence level.

Whether a firm chooses to use a separate confidence level in its own assessment will depend on many factors, including those listed in the FSA Guidance (see INSPRU 7.1.53G). Firms will want to ensure that they have a clear and logical explanation that reconciles these differences.

Whilst the FSA's Guidance confirms that a firm's own assessment, which applies a different confidence level, will not be part of the submission to the FSA, the FSA wish to understand the connections between the two.

Firms will want to ensure that the FSA has a clear understanding of the reasons for the different confidence levels being applied in the two assessments. This should reduce the risk that the ICA assessment becomes perceived by the FSA as divorced from the day-to-day management of the business, which may give the regulator concern and prompt further responses from the FSA.

2 For example, version numbers and dates at which Boards have accepted the ICA should be recorded in the ICA document

3 Including the obligations deriving from FSA's High Level Principle 6: 'Treating Customers Fairly'

4 However, ABI's ORIC initiative is seeking to address this, see http://www.abioric.com/

5 Or if assets are shown gross then an appropriate deterred tax liability should be established

6 Typically the bid price

7 Or other risk classification as appropriate to a firm's business

8 For example, through a combination of connected events that might separately be beyond the 99.5% / 1 year probability assuming each risk event were considered in isolation.

ANNEX 1: ICA FOR SMALLER FIRMS

[5053]

This annex provides a qualitative example of how a small firm could undertake its stress and scenario analysis without this being disproportionate to the size and complexity of its business, in accordance with GENPRU 1.2. There are likely to be other approaches that are equally appropriate and the approach we describe is provided for the purposes of advice and illustration. We do not give any quantitative guidance as we believe this would be impractical given the diverse nature of each firm's individual circumstances.

The areas discussed are not exhaustive and it is likely that in practice a firm will need to consider a range of other issues.

The scenarios that the firm generates as part of its analysis should aim to reflect the degree of risk in a variety of areas. How extreme these scenarios are will influence the ultimate level of capital required by the firm. The firm should not necessarily develop scenarios based on the current trading or economic conditions, but on possible trading or economic conditions that could occur during the next three to five years.

In addition to examining its event scenarios, a firm should also be able to meet any individual risk (however unlikely) that it has accepted (or proposes to accept through its business plan) from policyholders. It therefore should analyse its exposures and ensure that it has sufficient capital or available reinsurance to cover its largest individual risks and accumulations.

Worked example

Background

The firm used for this example is an insurer carrying on general insurance business within a large group, writing predominantly personal lines, household and motor policies of approximately £25m gross written premium. This business has a reasonable geographical spread, sourced significantly from within the United Kingdom. The firm has purchased appropriate reinsurance cover from a variety of reinsurers and has a demonstrated record of utilising this cover. Its settlement pattern for claims averages three years, however, there is a small element of the account with longer tail liability claims. The firm's investments and IT support are outsourced.

Insurance risk

The risk of incorrect or inaccurate pricing of business over the scenario period can be addressed by examining typical uncertainties within the pricing basis and the volatility of claims experience.

In examining the adequacy of its pricing, the firm establishes its underwriting and claims trend over a ten-year base period by reviewing profit and loss accounts (particularly underwriting profit). In particular it examines the following:
(i) the volatility of losses in a particular line of business;
(ii) whether the loss ratio exceeded 100% in any line of business; and
(iii) whether the deferred acquisition cost (DAC) amount had been written down; eg whether an unexpired risk provision (URP) was necessary.

The firm also examines whether its premiums over the last ten years have been:
(i) reasonably stable;
(ii) responsive enough to changes in claim exposures (so that profitability is maintained);
(iii) providing adequately for contingencies (such as major losses eg hail, earthquake etc);
(iv) encouraging loss control (through the use of deductibles, no claim bonuses etc);

The firm also reviews its method of pricing. The firm considers and performs:
(i) a review of acceptable rates, eg premiums being charged by competitors for similar products;
(ii) an examination of whether there have been any difficulties in the past with delegated authorities in relation to pricing including the ability and experience of staff members setting or recommending premium prices;
(iii) an examination of whether the firm has the appropriate mechanisms in place regarding premium rate changes (that is, who makes these decisions, frequency, and on what basis?); and
(iv) a benchmark price assessment (eg the ability to provide adequate competitive premium rates). For example, indicative rates being determined through the use of industry statistics, competitor statistics and the firm's own analysis for all classes.

Other factors the firm would consider are:
(i) changes in environment (eg legislation, social, economic etc);
(ii) changes in policy conditions and deductibles; and
(iii) impact of market segments (eg the effects of different claim frequencies and costs impacting the price charged).

Having completed its analysis, the firm makes the following assumptions to define its underwriting risk:
(i) claims costs. The firm assumes these are X% higher than in the premium basis;
(ii) claims inflation. The firm assumes a X% claims inflation over the scenario period, compared to Y% in the pricing basis;
(iii) policy expenses (fixed and variable) are X% higher than anticipated in the pricing basis;
(iv) reinsurance charges are X% higher than anticipated in the pricing basis; and
(v) investment income is X% lower than anticipated in the pricing basis.

As a result of the above analysis on a per risk basis, the firm considers that capital of between £X and £Y would cover the possibility of material deviations to projected results.

Allowing for catastrophes

The allowance for catastrophic events within the insurance risk scenario should reflect both the severity and the frequency of these events.

After considering the catastrophe reinsurance programme it may be clear that the upper limit is set at a level unlikely to be breached eg a 1 in 200 year event. Thus, for the purposes of the capital assessment, it would not be necessary to assume losses in excess of this retention.

However, it may be determined that there is possible exhaustion of free reinstatements or of horizontal cover in total. For example, if there were a significant chance of three catastrophic losses in any one period but the reinsurance allowed only one free reinstatement, then the assessment may be to hold two retentions and the entire gross loss for the third event.

As a result of the above analysis, the firm considers it appropriate to hold capital sufficient to absorb three catastrophic losses: one European windstorm of £X, one UK flood of £Y, and one large man made explosion of £Z.

The reinsurance structure in place allows for X number of reinstatements at full premium.

Deterioration of reserves

The firm considers the adequacy of its claims reserves by focussing on the liability valuation.

The liability valuation may contain a range of answers that might indicate possible reserve variability. Also, the valuation will contain areas where judgement has been applied and assumptions formulated which are subjective. These areas are considered and stressed as appropriate.

The firm also reviews the historic level of claims reserves and subsequent level of settlements to help determine the size of any historic levels of under and over reserving.

Reinsurance arrangements are considered and the extent to which these arrangements protect against reserve deterioration is assessed.

For unearned premium, where losses have yet to occur, the firm considers that the level of uncertainty is greater and considers similar factors to those relating to underwriting risk in addition to those discussed above.

As a result of the above analysis, the firm considers it appropriate to apply a X% loading to the outstanding claims provision, a Y% loading to the unearned premium provision and Z% to all other liability values. The firm considers that capital of between £X and £Y would adequately cover reserve deterioration.

Credit risk

Credit risk relates to the risk of default by counterparties. The firm believes its exposure to credit risk results from financial transactions with counterparties including issuers, debtors, borrowers, brokers, policyholders, reinsurers and guarantors.

When assessing credit risk the firm makes an assessment of the creditworthiness of counterparties to the assets of the firm.

The assessment includes an evaluation of the credit risk associated with loans and investment portfolios; the quality of on and off balance sheet assets; the ongoing management of the loans and investment portfolios; as well as loss provisions and reserves.

The firm believes its exposure to credit risk also arises due to its exposure to its reinsurers. In this regard, the firm uses the credit ratings assigned to particular counterparties as a measure of credit risk, most notably Standard & Poor's, Moody's Investors Service and AM Best's (particularly for reinsurers).

When forming an opinion on credit risk the firm considers:

Reinsurance

The firm's strategy is to manage its concentration risk in reinsurance by setting limits for the lead and subsidiary reinsurers. In this case the firm chooses to limit exposure to a single lead reinsurer to less than 30%, with other participants holding no more than 15%[9]. In all cases, the panel of reinsurers would need to meet a specified minimum rating. The firm has no prior experience of disputes, and their working relationship with the panel may be excellent, and thus the firm does not envisage any future difficulties arising in this regard.

Bond default rates could then be used to assess a likely credit risk figure for reinsurance recoveries (including IBNR recoveries).

The firm considers that capital of between £X and £Y would cover reinsurance defaults, with no additional allowance for disputes.

Overseas financial institutions and banks

The firm investigates its business relationships with overseas financial institution counterparties including banks, and decides no additional allowance is required.

Quality of counterparties and trends in counterparty risk

The firm assesses the level and age of debtors, focussing particularly upon unpaid premiums, especially those greater than three months old, and reviews the level and trend of contingent liabilities. For example, the firm estimates that the credit risk scenario equates to taking a 10% reduction in the asset value of debtors, based on bond default rates and age of debt.

The firm considers that capital of between £X and £Y would cover credit risk to counterparties.

Off-balance sheet transactions

The firm investigates any unfunded commitments, credit derivatives, commercial or standby letters of credit. Where these exist the possibility of a loss on these instruments is considered in relation to the requirement of the credit risk scenario.

The firm considers that no additional capital is necessary.

Market risk

Market risk encompasses an adverse movement in the value of the assets as a consequence of market movements such as interest rates, foreign exchange rates, equity prices, etc which is not matched by a corresponding movement in the value of the liabilities.

In examining possible market risks, the firm considers its sensitivity to market risk by evaluating the degree to which changes in interest rates, foreign exchange rates, equity prices, or other areas can adversely affect the firm's earnings or capital.

The firm believes its assets and liabilities are approximately matched eg there are no large unmatched or unhedged currency positions; short tail business is backed by cash/fixed interest assets of suitable term and long tail business is backed by assets affording an appropriate hedge for inflation, which may include shares and property. If mismatching does exist this should be allowed for within the estimate.

In developing the scenario the firm estimates the effect of an X% increase in interest rates on bond values.

Similarly, the firm estimates the effect on equity values of a major recession to estimate the possible reduction in the value of equity capital[10]. Also, it uses a suitable equity index to determine the size of historical falls in equity values and indicate possible future falls.

Counterparty risk might be allowed for by assuming one or several major corporate bond holding defaults.

For all investments, the stability of trading revenues should be examined to determine the volatility of investment.

From the above analysis, the firm considers that capital of between £X and £Y would be appropriate to protect it against adverse movement in market risk.

Liquidity risk

When assessing liquidity risk, the firm considers the extent of mismatch between assets and liabilities and the amount of assets held in a highly liquid, marketable form should unexpected cashflows lead to a liquidity crunch.

The price concession of liquidating assets is a prime concern when assessing liquidity risk and is built into the scenario.

In examining the liquidity risk, the firm examines the following:

Marketability, quality and liquidity of assets

The firm considers the assets held and makes an assessment regarding the quality and liquidity of these assets. Even though the assets matched the liabilities, residual risk remains given that timings are uncertain and there is a possibility that assets will be realised at unfavourable times. This is allowed for by assuming a 2.5% reduction in the market value of assets at realisation compared to the current market value.

The firm considers that capital of between £X and £Y would cover timing risk to counterparties.

Reliance on new business income

The firm relies partially upon new business cash flows to meet current liabilities as they fall due. The firm analyses the sensitivity of future cash flow projections and new business assumptions and considers the effect of a reduced level of new business.

The firm finds that it did not have immediate alternatives in place in case these expected new business cash flows were reduced. In this regard, it considers that these sources should be stressed by X%.

The firm considers that capital of between £X and £Y would cover possible effects of adjusting the asset portfolio to switch to more liquid assets.

The firm also examines the volatility and cost of on- and off-balance sheet funding sources. The firm is satisfied that no concerns need to be raised and that there should not be any impact on its liquidity position.

The firm believes it is well placed to manage unplanned changes in funding sources as well as react to changes in market conditions that affect its ability to quickly liquidate assets with minimal loss. The firm assesses that it has reasonable access to money markets and other sources of funding such as lines of credit.

The firm has no previous problems or delays in meeting obligations (or accessing external funding).

Overall, from the above analysis, the firm considers that capital of between £X and £Y would be necessary to withstand the effects of deterioration in liquidity.

Governance Risk

Governance risk relates to the risk associated with the board and/or senior management of the firm not effectively performing their respective roles.

The existence and level of directors and officers insurance in place is investigated compared to known incidence of claims of this type.

The firm assesses whether the current level of governance is appropriate for the firm, and the likelihood that the firm's practices may result in the board and/or senior management not adequately undertaking their roles. The cost of altering and strengthening the current board structure is considered.

In this regard, the firm makes an assessment that it may be reliant on only a few senior executives, and may be exposed if they experience any misadventure.

The firm considers that capital of between £X and £Y would cover governance risk.

Strategic Risk

Strategic risk arises from an inability to implement appropriate business plans and strategies, make decisions, allocate resources or adapt to changes in the business environment.

The firm therefore assesses the prudence and appropriateness of its business strategy in the context of the firm's competitive and economic environment. In particular the assumptions, forecasting and projections are assessed considering the possibility of a fundamental market change due, for example, to higher numbers of competitors, changes in sales channels, new forms of insurance or changes in legislation. This review includes whether the reinsurance programme is appropriate for the risks selected by the firm and whether it adequately takes account of the underwriting and business plans of the firm generally.

The firm considers the likelihood of a fundamental strategic shift too remote to include within the scenario given the maturity of the market in which they operate.

Operational risks

In reviewing the operational risk exposures, the firm has examined its administration, compliance, event, fraud, governance, strategic and technological risks.

Administration

The firm considers the risk of error or failure associated with the administrative aspects of the operation of its business. In this regard, the firm considers likelihood of financial loss and reputation harm due to failure or errors occurring and the likely size of these losses.

None of the firm's administration is out-sourced to service providers.

In undertaking the assessment, the firm considers the history of failure or error from transaction processing or control within the firm. Exception reports are produced on a quarterly basis. Past reports highlighted past administrative deficiencies. The biggest event in the past 10 years related to a situation where claim-handling staff shared access codes to the claims administration system. This resulted in an overpayment to some clients.

The firm also examines the nature and extent of centralised and decentralised functions within the firm. Three branches report regularly to the central office and an appropriate system is in place to record financial information, handle complaints etc.

The firm also reviews the segregation of duties between staff. It is satisfied that an adequate segregation of duties between underwriting claims and payments divisions exist in terms of acceptance, authorisation and payments. It is also satisfied that sufficient interaction between the front, middle and back offices exist in terms of financial control and risk management. For example, it is confident that its guidelines for accepting risks are adequate and that any breach would be picked up by exception reporting.

The firm also investigates the level of staff expertise and training to administer its product range/services.

The firm considers that capital of between £X and £Y would cover the risk of future administration issues.

Compliance Risk

The firm believes its main compliance risk relates to the risk of non-adherence to legislative and internal firm requirements.

An investigation into compliance over the last 10 years finds no history of non-compliance with firm policy and control systems nor have there been any reported areas of non-compliance with legislation or other requirements.

Regulatory reforms including corporate and consumer law are considered and it is assumed that expenses costs will rise as a result of developments in the next 5 years. As a result an additional X% of premium income was assumed for the expense ratio.

The firm considers that capital of between £X and £Y would cover the risk of future compliance issues.

Event risk

Event risk relates to risks associated with the potential impact of significant events (eg, financial system crisis, major change in fiscal system, natural disaster) on the operations of the firm.

The definition of event risk is not intended to cover events that are directly associated with products and services offered, for example, events which may directly impact on the general insurance business.

The firm concludes that no additional specific allocation is required.

Fraud Risk

Fraud risk relates to the risk associated with intentional misappropriation of funds, undertaken with the objective of personal benefit at the expense of the firm.

In assessing fraud risk, the firm considers the possibility of fraudulent acts occurring within the firm and the extent of controls which management has established to mitigate such acts.

The firm examines fraud issues over a period of 10 years and finds one major incident where it was subject to a fraudulent activity. This involved fraudulent payments being made by a member of staff which resulted in a loss for the firm of £Xm. Based on this previous incident and allowing for improvements in controls, the company assessed a financial figure that it believes is consistent with the probability for this scenario.

The firm considers that capital of between £X and £Y would cover the risk of future fraud.

Technology Risk

The firm considers the risk of error or failure associated with the technological aspects (IT systems) of its operations. Specifically, technology risk refers to both the hardware systems and the software utilised to run those systems.

In relation to the firm's information systems, the firm assesses the past reliability and future functionality and believes them to be adequate. It does not have any future plans to either replace its systems or make major systems modifications.

Concerning business continuity management and disaster recovery planning (and testing of plans), the firm reviews these plans regularly and tests them quarterly. A full back-up site exists with full recovery capabilities. Costs associated with utilising the site and associated business interruption insurance was estimated.

The firm considers that capital of between £X and £Y would cover technology risk.

Group risk

The size of the group risk element within operational risk will depend on the ownership structure of the firm and how it is funded by the parent.

The firm considers the likelihood and financial consequences of both insolvency and credit downgrading of its parent. Given the firm shares the parent's name there is a large risk of association.

The firm considers it within the scope of the scenario to allow for a single downgrade of the parent's credit rating from AA to A. It does not believe the chance of insolvency great enough to allow for directly.

The firm estimates the effect on its business plan and profit margins of the downgrade. It estimates the amount of business lost and the increase in marketing costs required to maintain the client base. It also allows for a change in the pricing basis to incorporate a reduced profit margin (with knock on impacts on the business volume and loss ratios).

From the above analysis, the firm considers that capital of between £X and £Y would be required to cover group risks.

Overall assessment

After individually assessing each risk area, the firm considers the capital that it has estimated might be absorbed under each scenario. In aggregate the range of capital absorbed is between £X and £Y. It considers how many of these scenarios might reasonably occur within a period and the extent to which it could replace capital within that period. It takes into account scenarios which might reasonably be linked, the difficulty with which capital might be replaced if the scenarios occurred, and the changes in strategy which might need to be adopted if the scenarios occurred.

The firm decides that the worst realistic combination of circumstances that might arise would absorb capital of between £A and £B.

---

9 These limits are purely illustrative and in determining its approach a firm would need to consider their own circumstances, including the nature of their insurance liabilities and the quality and availability of reinsurance cover

10 The firm should also consider any effect on the value of its liabilities

---

ANNEX 2: FURTHER READING

[5054]

Archer-Lock, Philip R; Gillott, et al.

"Stress and scenario analysis – risk assessment and quantification and use in the determination of capital", *2004 General Insurance Convention, (2004) loA Library Ref: 34722*

URL: http://www.actuaries.org.uk/files/pdf/proceedings/giro2004/Shaw.pdf

Brown, David.

"Risk appraisal – a multidisciplinary approach" (1994), *The Actuary, January/February 1994 p32–33; loA Library Ref: 15969*

URL: Can be ordered from the loA Library: http://ioa.soutron.com/ioa/library/default.htm

Bruce, Daniel H.

"ICAS – The challenge ahead", (2006), *The Actuary, April 2006 p28–29 loA Library Ref: 36326*

URL: http://www.the-actuary.org.uk/pdfs/06_04_03.pdf

Brooke-Taylor, Tony.

"Internal capital assessment", (2003), *The Actuary, October 2003*

URL: http://www.the-actuary.org.uk/pdfs/03_10_03.pdf

Clark, Karen M.

"A formal approach to catastrophe risk assessment and management", *Proceedings of the Casualty Actuarial Society, 73 (1986) loA Library Ref: 30886*

URL: http://www.casact.org/pubs/proceed/proceed86/index.htm

Eaton, Philip; Kipling, Michael R.

"The FSA Arrow risk assessment process" (Nov 2003), *(copies of slides), loA Library Ref: 34112*

URL: http://www.actuaries.org.uk/files/pdf/proceedings/life2003/Eaton.pdf (PDF File)
Alternatively: http://www.actuaries.org.uk/files/pdf/proceedings/life2003/Eaton.ppt (Powerpoint File)

Exley, Jon.

"The implications of the individual capital assessment applied to life companies' pension liabilities" (2005), *Finance & Investment Conference. 2005. loA Library Ref: 35984*

URL: Can be ordered from the loA Library: http://ioa.soutron.com/ioa/library/default.htm

Financial Services Authority (FSA)

"ICAS one year on" (2005), *Insurance Sector Briefing, November 2005.*

URL: http://www.fsa.gov.uk/pubs/other/isb_icas.pdf

Leigh, Julian CT; Lee-Tsang-Tan, Laurence; Rowland, John.

"Doing an ICA" (Copies of slides from the Killarney Convention), *General Insurance Convention 2004, IoA Library Ref: 35338*

URL: http://www.actuaries.org.uk/Display_Page.cgi?url=/proceedings/giro2004/index.html

Lloyd's of London

"Risk-based capital: The risk assessment approach: Consultative document" (1996). *IoA Library Ref: 18584.*

URL: Can be ordered from the IoA Library: http://ioa.soutron.com/ioa/library/default.htm (Cost £4.80)

Lloyd's of London

"Guide to the risk assessment framework". (1997) *IoA Library Ref: 18514*

URL: Can be ordered from the IoA Library: http://ioa.soutron.com/ioa/library/default.htm (Cost £8.00)

Lloyd's of London

"ICA: 2007 Guidance and instructions", *Lloyd's of London (2006)*

URL: http://www.lloyds.com/NR/rdonlyres/5D2C3B8D-E2A8-4BB0-944F-EA16776F2DD8/0/2007GuidanceandinstructionsMarch2006.pdf

Ryan, John P; Archer-Lock, Philip R; et al.

"Financial condition assessment" (2001), *British Actuarial Journal, Vol 7:4; IoA Library Ref: 23672.*

URL: http://www.actuaries.org.uk/Display_Page.cgi?url=/maintained/resource_centre/baj.html

Train, Mark C; Guijarro, Philippe.

"Embedding risk based capital in an organisation: practical lessons" (2003) (copies of slides), *The 2003 Life Convention. IoA Library Ref: 34139*

URL: Can be ordered from the IoA Library: http://ioa.soutron.com/ioa/library/default.htm

ASSOCIATION OF BRITISH INSURERS GOOD PRACTICE GUIDE: IMPROVING CUSTOMERS' RETIREMENT EXPERIENCES

July 2008

NOTES

INTRODUCTION

[5055]

The aim of this Good Practice Guide is to support companies in improving the service experienced by customers as they approach retirement.

The guide describes ways in which a company can achieve this aim. It gives examples of ways in which the desired outcomes can be achieved, but recognises that the results depend on the circumstances of each case. The guide is intended to help improve customers' experience when deciding what to do with their pension fund (or funds) and to help companies in meeting their objectives in relation to the FSA's Treating Customers Fairly requirements.

The guide is intended as a practical tool on which companies can draw, depending on their own circumstances. It is not intended to be a rigid process checklist, and there is no assumption that the contents of this guide describe the only valid approach. The guide is intended to stand alone, but cross-refers to other ABI guidance and key regulations as appropriate.

This guide replaces all previous ABI Statements of Best Practice (SoBP) for pensions maturities and transfers and the template letters contained within the SoBP.

GUIDE CONTENTS

[5056]

The guide contains the following elements:

1. Approaches to key pre-retirement events

The guidance section of the guide is structured as follows:

- Principles
  The outcomes each company should work to achieve.
- Good practice
  Some effective ways of achieving the desired outcomes.
- Possible approaches
  Examples of different approaches to achieving good practice and meeting customers' expectations. Some but not all of these may be contained in existing FSA guidance.
- Example Key Performance Indicators (KPIs)
  Intended to help companies identify suitable ways of measuring whether customers are experiencing the outcomes expected. Practical examples are provided which are not intended to prescriptive. Wherever possible, the use of relevant and readily available management information to produce robust KPIs is described.

2. Pre-retirement 'wake-up' packs

- Background to the ABI template content.
- Appendix A: Suggested template content.

1. APPROACHES TO KEY PRE-RETIREMENT EVENTS

[5057]

Principle	Good practice	Possible Approaches	Example KPI
Supply information for customers which is accurate, consistent, easily understandable and not misleading.	• Write in language which is clear to the customer.	• Communicate using active verbs and personalise (*we, you*) wherever possible. Cross-refer to the Customer Impact Clear Language and Layout Good Practice Guide. • Think about your intended reader, include only information that is appropriate to their circumstances or is required by regulation. • Use customer research, previous feedback, complaints and any other feedback to shape the design and content of communications.	Measure customer satisfaction with: • communications received during the claims / payment process. • the use of plain English rather than jargon. • customer research surveys.
	• Minimise the use of jargon and abbreviations.	• Use clear language. Where use of jargon is unavoidable, explain what it means, possibly using signposting or margin commentary.	
	• Set out the information in a logical structure, order and format.	• Develop effective internal processes and a consistent style guide.	
	• Show key information prominently.	• Highlight the value of the benefits payable – usually the most important figure for the customer. • Highlight risks of not taking benefits immediately.	
	• Customer details and illustrated benefits must be accurate.	• Take care to maintain the integrity of your / the relevant customer database and coding of the illustration systems.	

Make it easy for the customer to take their benefits and get help.	• Prominently display customer telephone helpline numbers and opening times in communications.	• Offer customers a range of contact channels eg mail, email and telephone. • Show helpline numbers in larger font clearly on the front page of customer communications.	• Measure customer satisfaction with the simplicity of the process.
	• Encourage customers to seek further information or financial advice from an intermediary and explain why it is important.	• Clearly signpost in communications that the customer may wish to consider seeking further information or financial advice, for example TPAS. • Explain this need not necessarily involve payment by fee, and that a commission payment only option may be available.	
Draw the customer's attention to product features and terms and conditions that may significantly affect benefits.	• In quoting all available options draw the customer's attention in good time to particular options that may be to their advantage. • Explain the risks of each option clearly to the customer.	• Regardless of whether the information is provided to the customer or IFA, draw attention to options, for example: – the Open Market Option – any MVR-free period • Annuity options – any available guaranteed annuity rate – Joint life / single life – Indexed / escalating / guaranteed – Enhanced / impaired – Other retirement income products	Measure customer satisfaction with: • the simplicity of the process. • the use of plain English rather than jargon.
	• Draw the customer's attention to exit charges or penalties which may reduce the benefits.	• Draw the customer's attention to features such as: – any MVR on early / deferred retirement for with-profits funds – any product exit charges	

Help customers make an informed decision.	At four / six months before retirement: • Send a 'wake-up' pack to the customer, well in advance of the selected retirement date; to get the customer to select their chosen benefit options.	• Aim to issue the 'wake-up' pack four months before the selected retirement date. In the case of Occupational Scheme members send the 'wake-up' pack at least six months before the selected retirement date.	Measure customer satisfaction with: • the simplicity of the process.
	• Use the template content below as the basis of your 'wake-up' pack.	• Ask the customer to advise if they do not intend to retire / take benefits on the selected retirement date.	• any communication received during the claims / payment process. • the use of plain English instead of jargon.
		• Include a summary timetable of what will happen next. • Include the FSA fact sheet *Just the facts about your pension – it's time to choose* or a firm's-own version. • Include a summary of the types of options the customer will have to choose from between nearer to retirement. • Advise customers of the benefits of a joint life annuity. • Explain the options / potential benefits of: – The Open Market Option. – The benefits of annuities. – Include projected benefits and options available (and how to get alternative quotes). – The availability of different types of annuities such as index-linked annuities, joint-life annuities, enhanced / impaired annuities, and other retirement income products. – Health and lifestyle conditions likely to provide an increased income. – The option to defer taking benefits.	• the ease of understanding correspondence.

		– Features such as any MVR on early / deferred retirement for with-profits funds. – The option to take a tax-free lump sum and that this option expires 12 months after the chosen pension date. – The option to defer taking the annuity. – The option, if the total of all pension funds is trivial (explain what this means), to take as a lump sum. – The ability to take an unsecured pension. • Clearly signpost in communications that the customer may wish to consider seeking further information or financial advice, for example TPAS. • Request outstanding information / documentation needed to release benefits. • Take reasonable steps to contact customers who do not respond. Cross-refer to the Customer Impact Managing Unclaimed Policies Good Practice Guide.	
	At six weeks before retirement: • Send a follow-up pack to the customer closer to the actual retirement date, from which the customer can select their chosen benefit options. • Ensure follow-up pack material fits with four / six month 'wake-up' pack.	• Aim to issue the retirement / maturity options pack six weeks before the selected retirement date to allow the customer to make an informed decision and to enable them to act. • Include projected benefits and options available (and how to get alternative quotes). For example: – The Open Market Option. Emphasise the timescale for exercising this and encourage early action, if appropriate. – The benefits of annuities. – Include projected benefits and options available (and how to get alternative quotes).	Measure customer satisfaction with: • the simplicity of the process. • any communication received during the claims / payment process. • the use of plain English instead of jargon. • the ease of understanding of correspondence.

		– The availability of different types of annuities such as index-linked annuities, joint-life annuities, enhanced / impaired annuities, and other retirement income products. – That health and lifestyle conditions are likely to provide them with the opportunity to increase their income. – The option to defer taking benefits. – Features such as any MVR on early / deferred retirement for with-profits funds. – The option to take a tax-free lump sum and that this option expires 12 months after the chosen pension date. – The option to defer taking the annuity. – The option, if the total of all pension funds is trivial (explain what this means), to take as a lump sum. – The availability to take an unsecured pension. • Ask the customer to make their choice of benefits from the available options. • Ask for any outstanding information / documentation that you need to release the benefits.	
Pay out benefits with the minimum of bureaucracy / delay. *NB The timescales assume that the company has all the information it needs to complete the claim and is in direct control of the process.*	• Review what documentary evidence is required to support the payment of benefits.	• Only ask for documentation that is essential. • Set out internal service standards at initial contact.	Measure customer satisfaction with: • The simplicity of the process.
	• Develop a flexible process that recognises that customers don't always have documents available.	• Consider whether it is reasonable to expect the customer to have retained all documents. • For essential documents establish a mitigation plan to help customers gain the relevant information.	• The speed with which the claim was paid. • The number of days taken to pay benefits, from acceptance of the quotation.

	• Set and maintain service performance targets.	• Set and maintain targets, even if only internally.	• The number of days taken to pay benefits, from the point of receipt of all documents.
	• Monitor the meeting of customer expectations.	• Use regular customer feedback mechanisms (eg the Customer Impact Survey) to monitor progress.	• The average time taken to pay benefits.
	• Calculate the tax-free lump sum accurately and pay it out promptly.	• Aim to pay any tax-free lump sum on the selected retirement date or explain any delay to the customer.	• The number of Open Market Option enquiries.
	Where the customer purchases a pension from their pension company: • Accurately set up the chosen pension annuity option and start payments in a reasonable timescale. • Issue a confirmation of the selected benefit options promptly after the selected retirement date (including pension tax basis and lifetime allowance / charge details).	• Aim to set up annuity and start payments on the selected retirement date or explain any delay to the customer. • When relevant, issue confirmation of the benefits paid immediately after the selected retirement date. • Consider paying interest if the payment is late.	• The number of Open Market Options taken.
	• In the event of a pensions annuity being bought from another company: – pass the remaining pension fund (after any tax-free lump sum) to the new provider promptly. – the company receiving Open Market Option funds and supporting information / documentation should issue a quotation and set up / confirm benefits promptly.	• Aim to pay out tax-free sum on the selected retirement date and pass the remaining pension fund to the new provider or explain any delay to the customer. • Make payment to the product provider and supply all required documentation promptly. • Issue quotations for the Open Market Option and set up / confirm benefits in a timely manner following receipt of full requirements. • When relevant, issue a confirmation of the benefits paid immediately after the selected retirement date. • Pay interest if the payment is late, when the delay has been solely within the company's control.	

	• Where the customer opts to transfer funds between companies this should be achieved with the minimum of bureaucracy.	• Accept electronic documentation. • Minimise the number of separate forms / declarations for the customer to sign (eg by accepting combined application and authorisation forms). • Ensure that correspondence with third party companies is suitably referenced (client name, policy or scheme number etc). • Use electronic payment transfers where both parties can accept this. • Where some or all of the transfer payment includes contracted out benefits, the transferring scheme should complete and return the relevant contributions agency form within the required timescales.	
Keep the customer, or their representative, informed about any delays in the process.	• Advise the customer, or their representative, if the handling of the claim has been, or will be, delayed (eg where a task directly in your company's control is taking longer than a customer should reasonably expect or where the total elapsed time since receipt of instruction by the transferring scheme is becoming excessive).	• Use the telephone for ease / speed wherever possible. • Encourage staff to ask for telephone numbers and preferred hours of contact. • Use the telephone to seek additional information if claim documentation is incomplete.	Measure customer satisfaction with the speed with which the payment was made once the claim was settled. The number of days taken to pay claims, from point of receipt of all documents.
	• Give the reason for the delay and the next steps to resolve it.		
	• Pay compensation / interest on payments that are paid after the due date when the delay has been solely within the company's control.	• Implement a consistent approach to compensation across the business. Refer to standard FSA guidance for late payments.	

2. GUIDANCE ON PRE-RETIREMENT 'WAKE-UP' PACKS

Introduction to the template content

[5058]
The remainder of this document contains template content for the pre-retirement 'wake-up' cover letter sent to customers in firm's four-month 'wake-up' packs. It complements the ABI Good Practice Guide on Handling Customer Claims and has been developed with ABI members, drawing on contributions from key external stakeholders including the Government, FSA and consumer groups.

Objective

This guidance has been produced to help firms improve customer communications and, specifically, to ensure customers receive information on their pension fund and retirement options that is clear, concise and easily understood. The full content consists of several paragraphs, highlighting the Open Market Option and other key issues to consider in choosing a retirement income product. This forms a menu from which firms can select paragraphs as appropriate to their customers.

Use of the template content

Firms should use the template content when drafting 'wake-up' packs and deciding the content, tone and style of their own cover letters. Naturally, firms will want to tailor the text to fit their and their customers' circumstances, so we do not envisage this content will be standardised or reproduced exactly as it appears in this guide, nor will the paragraphs follow in the same order. Firms may also produce different versions of their cover letters for different customers to ensure relevant information is provided.

Customers may ignore or be intimidated by a long cover letter. Firms' cover letters should therefore be as short as possible to encourage customers to read the information given. Firms do not need to include all of the paragraphs outlined in this guidance and should aim to keep cover letters within three pages.

The cover letter should:

- inform the customer that a better alternative to their own product(s) may be available under the Open Market Option;
- recommend they seek financial advice if unsure of their options; and
- signpost additional sources of information that will help them make an informed decision.

This guidance includes key paragraphs for firms to consider when drafting their own wake-up packs. These cover the crucial issues customers must consider when deciding what to do with their pension fund, including:

- Headline message
- An introduction
- The Open Market Option
- The tax-free lump sum option
- Commutation
- Guaranteed annuity rates (where applicable)
- Types of annuities
- Protected rights (where applicable)
- Taking benefits at a later date
- Market Value Reductions (where applicable)
- The Lifetime Allowance
- Timeline
- Additional sources of information

Prominence of the OMO

Firms may alter the order in which the key issues above are covered, with the exception of the headline message. This should appear prominently at the top of the letter to instruct the reader of the potential benefit of shopping around.

Firms must always include the headline message and paragraph three (Types of annuities). Otherwise firms can consider for themselves which of the template paragraphs should be used. A firm may omit, for example, the paragraph explaining trivial commutation where the pension fund value is above the trivial commutation limit, or the MVR paragraph where this does not apply.

Where a customer is eligible for a guaranteed annuity rate (GAR), firms should always make this prominent and explain the benefits – and the circumstances in which these may be lost.

Enclosures and signposting

Firms should enclose either the FSA booklet *Just the facts about your retirement – it's time to choose* [www.moneymadeclear.fsa.gov.uk/pdfs/pensions_choose.pdf], or their own version of this booklet in their 'wake-up' packs. The combined effect should be to inform the customer of the key issues within the cover letter itself, then signpost the reader to the additional information available in the enclosed booklet. Firms are encouraged to signpost to the specific booklet page numbers where possible.

Occupational schemes

These are subject to specific rules, set by the DWP, which must be reflected in the timing and content of communications issued by firms. Under the DWP's disclosure of information regulations, trustees of an occupational scheme are required to tell members about the OMO no later than six months before retirement.

Firms must adhere to this timeframe for occupational scheme members, and include a copy of the Pensions Regulator's *Your Retirement Choices* booklet instead of the FSA *Just the facts about your retirement – it's time to choose* booklet. Alternatively, firms should ensure details sent to occupational scheme members comply with the DWP's disclosure requirements. For details of the timeframe for occupational scheme communications go to www.thepensionsregulator.gov.uk/guidance/dcScheme/retirementOptions/process.aspx.

Advice and further information

Firms should highlight the various sources of information and advice, including details of IFA Promotions, the Pensions Advisory Service online annuity planner, and the FSA annuity tables. Wake-up packs should encourage customers to seek advice if they are unsure of their options, and should also include firms' own customer services details as appropriate.

Management information relating to pre-retirement packs

Firms should consider what management information they should collect in relation to their wake-up packs. This may include:

- the number of retirement income products bought by internal and external customers – ie those who saved with the firm itself, and those transferring funds from another provider.
- the number (and nature) of enquiries and complaints received in relation to communications.
- feedback from customers on their experience, and whether they used the OMO to compare their product with those offered by other firms.
- checks on transfer applications to other providers where a GAR is in place, to confirm the customer understands the implications.

Additional guidance is available in the ABI's '*Management information relating to good customer outcomes*' guide www.customerimpact.org/main/guides/managementinformationcustomeroutcomes.aspx.

Customer testing

Firms should ensure wake-up packs are tested on consumers. This will help ensure key messages are understood, identify where improvements may be required and allow for continual improvement of firms' customer communications. Firms may also wish to submit their wake-up packs for assessment by the Plain English Campaign or similar kite-mark schemes.

The ABI will be working with firms to collect key data on OMO usage and customer views on firms' wake-up packs. This will help improve customer experiences and form part of the industry's broader engagement with the OMO Review.

Association of British Insurers
July 2008

APPENDIX A: TEMPLATE CONTENT FOR FOUR OR SIX MONTH 'WAKE-UP' LETTER

[1 – Headline message]

[5059]
Please read this letter carefully. By shopping around you may improve the income you receive in retirement.

[2 – Introduction]

Dear x,

We know you are approaching your selected retirement date and this could mean big changes. Sorting out your pension can be daunting and we want to make it as easy as possible for you.

The pension fund you have built up with us won't automatically pay you an income when you retire. You will need to buy a retirement income product that provides you with that income. And to make the most of the money in your pension fund, you should shop around.

This letter contains important information on how you do this. Please read it and keep it safe. The enclosed booklet has more details on the various products that can provide an income in retirement.

[3] Shopping around – buying an annuity

An annuity is a retirement income product whereby you use some or all of the money in your pension fund to provide you with an annual income in retirement. It is the most popular way in which people ensure they have enough to live on for the rest of their lives. If you have built up several pension funds with separate pension companies, you can usually combine them when buying an annuity.

You do not have to buy an annuity from us. The Open Market Option (OMO) is your right to compare what we can offer you with what other pension companies can provide. If you move to another provider you might get a higher income. This is not always the case, but it is always worth checking before you buy.

Once you know what type of annuity interests you, you can then compare the varying levels of income offered by other pension companies. A financial adviser can help you with this. You can also use the Financial Services Authority's free online annuity tables – www.fsa.gov.uk/tables. See page 8 of the attached booklet for more details.

[4] Types of annuities

There are many different types of annuity, each designed to suit personal circumstances such as your health and lifestyle, and whether you want to provide an income for your family or other dependants.

You don't have to buy a retirement income product now. You can leave your pension fund with us or move it to another pension company. You are required by law to secure a retirement income by age 75, or take an alternatively secured pension. See page 9 of the attached booklet for more on these options.

If you do plan to buy an annuity, you should consider the following questions:

Are you married or do you have a partner? Will they need an income if you die first?

If so, you may want a 'joint-life' or 'guaranteed' annuity. Make sure you discuss this with your spouse or partner.

Do you have a recognised medical condition? Are you a smoker?

If so, you may be able to buy an annuity that pays more because of these factors. They are known as 'enhanced' or 'impaired' annuities.

Do you want your income to increase over time, or adjust to rises in inflation?

If you do, think about an 'escalating', or 'index-linked' annuity. These start with a lower income but increase over time.

Details of these and other types of annuities are explained in the enclosed booklet, pages 6–7. The flow chart on page 15 will give you an idea of the type of annuity that might suit you best. A financial adviser will be able to help you decide.

You should also use the online annuity planner www.pensionsadvisoryservice.org.uk. This free service helps you with the decision-making process for converting your pension fund into an income. Alternatively, you can call the Pensions Advisory Service on 0845 601 2923.

[5] Tax-free lump sum option

You can usually take up to a quarter of your total pension fund as a lump sum. This is tax-free. The rest of your pension fund must then be used to buy an annuity or another form of income, with income taxed as you receive it.

The lump sum must usually be taken at the same time you buy your retirement income product, but this may depend on which product you choose. If you don't do so by your 75th birthday, you will lose your right to the tax-free lump sum.

[6] Options for smaller pension funds – 'commutation' [*Only to be used where this is likely to be an option, ie pots less than £16,500*]

If the total value of all your pension savings is less than £16,500 (2008/09), you may be able to take it all as a cash lump sum. If you wish to do this, you have to take all payments from all your pension funds within a 12-month period, between the ages of 60 and 75.

See page 13 of the enclosed booklet for further information. If this interests you, please ask us for further details.

[7] Your Guaranteed Annuity Rate (GAR) [*Where applicable*]

Your pension fund has a Guaranteed Annuity Rate option attached to it. This is a valuable option since it often means you would get a higher income from us than you would from another pension company.

There are some conditions that go with your Guaranteed Annuity Rate option. Details of these conditions will be provided to you shortly.

[8] Contracted-out pension restrictions [*Where applicable*]

If you have used your pension to replace the additional state pension (by 'contracting out'), there are some restrictions on the type of annuity, and the tax-free lump sum, you can take. Further details are given in the enclosed booklet, page 4.

[9] Other pension options

If you don't want to secure an income with your pension fund now, there are other options. These include short-term annuities, income withdrawal, investment-linked annuities, phased retirement, and alternatively secured pensions. The enclosed booklet provides details, on page 9.

You should consider taking financial advice if you are planning to delay buying a retirement income product.

[10] What is a Market Value Reduction (MVR)? [*Where applicable*]

If you invested in a 'with-profits' pension fund, the profits you receive depend on your policy reaching maturity. Every person who removes money from a with-profits fund before it reaches maturity reduces the overall profit available to other customers also invested in the fund. Consequently, a penalty may apply if you take money out before the policy matures. This penalty is known as a Market Value Reduction (MVR).

We only use an MVR if the with-profit fund has not performed well enough to cover the bonuses and increases we've already added to your pension fund.

[Firm to detail circumstances when an MVR is applicable]

[11] The Lifetime Allowance [*To be included where firms are unable to confirm the pension funds are unlikely to be near LTA limit*]

If the total value of **all** your pension funds is more than £1.65 million (2008/09), we have to apply a 'Lifetime Allowance' charge set by the Government. We strongly recommend that you take financial advice if your total pension funds exceed or are close to this amount.

[12] Timeline – what happens next? [*Firms may use illustrations to convey their process*]

[x] weeks before your retirement date . . .

We will write to you [x–x] weeks before your retirement date to give you an estimate of the value of your pension fund. We will include some forms for you to fill in and return to us so that we know which options interest you, or if you wish to transfer your pension fund to a different pension company.

Within [x] weeks of your retirement date . . .

We will give you final details of the value of your pension fund, but you will need to return the forms mentioned above to confirm what you want to do with your pension fund. If you choose to move to another company, we will send you details of the amount we have passed to them.

[13] Getting help and advice

We recognise that this is a big decision, and we strongly recommend you seek financial advice if you feel you need help. This need not involve a fee – many advisers will offer a commission-only service, with no up-front fee. Details of where to go for impartial advice are given on page 20 of the enclosed booklet.

Alternately contact us at . . . ***[Firm to add contact details for further enquiries]***

HEALTH AND PROTECTION CODES AND GUIDANCE NOTES

ABI STATEMENT OF BEST PRACTICE FOR INCOME PROTECTION INSURANCE

August 2003 (amended 14 January 2005)

NOTES

Income Protection Statement of Best Practice – changes for regulation from 14 January 2005

1) Insurers need to include details of "How to contact us in the event of a claim" within their IP Key Features document (KFD). This information should be inserted after the "The deadline for claiming" text within the "When will the policy pay out?" section.

2) If insurers want to adopt the Policy Summary approach rather than retain the current KFD format they will need to drop the Aim, Your commitment and Risk factors sections of the current KFD. Also, any content they provide in their KFD that doesn't meet the requirements of the Retail Customer Policy Summary table detailed in ICOB 5 – 5.5.5 should be removed.

1. INTRODUCTION

[5060]

1.1 The Association of British Insurers is the trade association for insurance companies in the United Kingdom. Of its more than 400 members around 200 transact long-term insurance business and they account for almost 100% of the life insurance and pension business written in the United Kingdom.

1.2 This revised Statement of Best Practice falls under the ABI Life Insurance (Non Investment Business) Selling Code of Practice, and covers the following:

— The description of Income Protection Cover in a Key Features Document
— Guidance notes for certain policy terms and conditions
— Generic Terms
— The review process.

1.3 The Statement updates part of the industry's response to the second report by the Office of Fair Trading (OFT) on Health Insurance, published in May 1998. It was developed by the ABI's Income Protection Working Party, which produced their original proposals following research to discover what consumers would find most useful as an aid to understanding and comparing income protection products. These proposals were validated by further consumer research and have been subject to wide consultation across the industry and with key external partners such as the OFT, the Financial Ombudsman Service (FOS), and others.

2. GENERAL PRINCIPLES

Applicability

2.1 The Statement applies to income protection providers who are members of the ABI. From 29 February 2000, compliance with the Statement of Best Practice has been a condition of ABI membership.

2.2 This Statement applies to individual income protection policies. It is not intended for group income protection policies. However best practice for group income protection is being developed by Group Risk Development (GRID) insurance industry contributors – see their website www.grouprisk.org.uk.

Is Income Protection the right product for the applicant?

2.3 Before a potential applicant gets to the stage of applying for an income protection policy and, for example, comparing key features of different companies products they need to decide if income protection is the right type of insurance policy for them. A model leaflet, which companies may wish to adopt to help their customers come to an informed decision, has been issued at the same time as this Statement.

Products Covered by the Income Protection Model Key Features Document (KFD)

2.4 If the product is primarily income protection (which may or may not include waiver of premium) then the model KFD should be used. A similar format should apply to the following contracts with appropriate amendments:

— Housepersons policies (ie policies for housewives, househusbands etc);
— Expenditure related (eg mortgage) protection plans.

2.5 The Statement does not address policies which incorporate more than one health-related benefit (eg critical illness, private medical insurance or long term care insurance in addition to income protection). Nevertheless we recommend that insurers comply with the spirit of the Income Protection KFD when they print their product literature in respect of such policies in addition to the Statements of Best Practice that apply to these products. Protection plans classified as short term under the Insurance Companies Act are not included in the above. Combinations of income protection and unemployment insurance are covered by these provisions, but creditor insurance is not.

2.6 The Statement is based on the following concepts.

CLARITY

2.7 Wherever possible to aid consumer understanding, the preferred wording of the Key Features Document will be in "Plain English" provided that this does not dilute or conflict with the meaning.

2.8 The intention behind the guidance notes is that policy terms/conditions should be as robust as possible in differentiating between what is, and is not, covered to:

2.8.1 Create a clear expectation of the scope and limitations of the cover.

2.8.2 Allow valid claims to be paid promptly.

2.8.3 Minimise the number of disputed claims to avoid disappointment.

KEY FEATURES DOCUMENT

2.9 The requirements of the Key Features Document included in this Statement are in addition to (and, in the event of a conflict, are overruled by) any regulatory, legal, 3rd Life Directive and product specific requirements for Key Features.

2.10 The Key Features format is intended to ensure that income protection is described in a way that allows consumers to compare the income protection cover of different providers.

Providers should give Key Features Documents to enquirers and potential customers (via intermediaries as appropriate) at the earliest opportunity to allow them to make meaningful product comparisons before purchase. They may also wish to issue their version of the model leaflet to consumers. The KFD should be issued in addition to the company's marketing and quotation materials.

IMPLEMENTATION

[5061]

2.11 The provisions apply to new policies effected on or after the implementation date adopted by the provider. An increment or increase to an existing policy effected after that date as a new policy may be excluded if it mirrors the original contract.

2.12 Companies are currently required to apply the 1999 Statement of Best Practice together with the revised 2001 Key Features document. The timetable for implementing the revised 2003 Statement of Best Practice and Key Features Document is **1 January 2004**.

3. USE OF THE KEY FEATURES DOCUMENT

General

[5062]

3.1 The model Key Features Document reproduced at Appendix A represents an industry standard template, and should be used taking the points below into account:

3.1.1 the front page and the left hand side (headings and subheadings) of the subsequent pages are mandated;

3.1.2 the right hand side – the answers – on the second and subsequent pages are an example text. We recommend that you use this, subject to the qualifications that:

3.1.2.a the wording accurately describes your product;

3.1.2.b material in square brackets should only be used if it applies to your product;

3.1.2.c amendments to the text can also be made to meet PPIAB or other guidelines on plain language. We have tried to incorporate the spirit of these guidelines in the Key Features Document, but brands may amend the text if this is necessary to gain PPIAB or other accreditation;

3.2 Sections should only be omitted where they are inappropriate to the product (eg no relation of benefit to earnings on Housepersons products);

3.3 Providers should ensure that the wording they use accurately describes the limitation of benefits. This may involve changes to the mandated wordings.

3.4 Providers are permitted to use any presentational or print style as long as the order of the questions is the same.

Front Page Headings

3.5 The front page headings ("Its Aims", "Your Commitment" and "Risk Factors") are already mandated for regulated business. This is extended under this Statement of Best Practice to non-regulated business.

"Questions and Answers"

3.6 A brief guide to the key features of the product are given in the form of answers to questions. The questions provided in the Model Key Features Document should be adopted as standard.

3.7 Additional questions and answers may be included to describe any material features not covered by the standard questions and answers. Alternatively, such features can be included in the sections headed "What other benefits can I choose?" and "What other features are there?"

4. USE OF THE GUIDANCE NOTES ON POLICY TERMS AND CONDITIONS

[5063]
4.1 The guidance notes cover ten of the most important policy terms and conditions:

- Definition of Incapacity – Own Occupation (Appendix B1a)
- Definition of Incapacity – Any Occupation (Appendix B1b)
- Limitation of Benefit (Appendix B2)
- Proportionate/Rehabilitation Benefits (Appendix B3)
- Change of Occupation (Appendix B4)
- Claims Notification Period (Appendix B5)
- Deferred Period (Appendix B6)
- Waiver of Premium (Appendix B7)
- Pregnancy Clause (Appendix B8)
- Linked Claims (Appendix B9)

4.2 For each condition, the Guidance Note describes its purpose, the main features that should typically be covered by the policy wording, the insurer's obligations to the consumer in describing their practice, and recommendations as to how the wordings should be applied.

4.3 For each term or condition included in a policy, the insurer should give proper consideration to the relevant guidance note. The practice of the insurer should be consistent with the guidance unless there is a good business case against such consistency, in which case the actual practice should be clearly explained.

4.4 Insurers should adopt these guidance notes when they next review the wording in their policy conditions. Insurers may choose to enhance cover retrospectively for customers with existing policies, but they are not obliged to do so.

5. GENERIC TERMS

[5064]
5.1 When generic terms are used, they should have the meanings shown and other terms should not be used in their place. This is to ensure that the terms always have the same meanings.

5.2 The generic terms are as follows:

Deferred Period

5.3 The meaning of this term is: "The period of incapacity before any benefit is paid." Please note that terms such as "waiting period" and "elimination period" should not be used.

Incapacity

5.4 The term "incapacity" should be used instead of the term "disability", in particular as regards the definition of disability clause in the policy contract, which should be called the definition of *incapacity clause.*

Generic Product Name

5.5 The terms "Income Protection Cover" and "Income Protection" apply to this type of cover. Providers are free to use marketing names for their products and cover, provided that the cover is described either as: "Income Protection Cover" or by using the words "Income Protection".

Model Exclusions

5.6 The following model exclusion wordings have been created for use by Income Protection and Critical Illness insurers.

5.7 Income Protection providers are free to omit or amend any of the model exclusions and may include additional exclusions.

5.8 The heading forms part of the model wording.

5.9 All exclusions and limitations (not only model exclusions) should be contained in one section of the policy (and key features, as set out above).

5.10 Providers should state which exclusions apply to which conditions in their policy (and other benefits as appropriate, eg Waiver of Premium Benefit) and should use an introductory policy wording to suit their individual policy style (see the example below).

Example introductory wording for policy exclusions
"We will not pay an Income Protection claim if it is caused directly or indirectly from any of the following:"

Aviation

Taking part in any flying activity, other than as a passenger in a commercially licensed aircraft.

Criminal Acts

Taking part in a criminal act.

Drug Abuse

Alcohol or solvent abuse, or the taking of drugs except under the direction of a registered medical practitioner.

Hazardous Sports and Pastimes

Taking part in (or practising for) [boxing, caving, climbing, horse-racing, jet skiing, martial arts, mountaineering, off piste skiing, pot-holing, power boat racing, under water diving, yacht racing or any race, trial or timed motor sport.]

HIV/AIDS

Infection with Human Immunodeficiency Virus (HIV) or conditions due to any Acquired Immune Deficiency Syndrome (AIDS).

Self-inflicted Injury

Intentional self-inflicted injury.

War & Civil Commotion

War, invasion, hostilities, (whether war is declared or not), civil war, rebellion, revolution or taking part in a riot or civil commotion.

6. REVIEW PROCESS

[5065]
6.1 This Statement of Best Practice, the Key Features Document and the Guidance Notes will be reviewed regularly to ensure they continue to reflect current legislative and regulatory requirements and market practice. The next review will take place, at the latest, by February 2004, subject to FSA proposals on regulating this product. It could, however, take place earlier if this proves necessary.

6.2 Changes to any of these documents which are recommended as a result of a review will only be made following consultation with the industry and interested parties.

APPENDIX A
INCOME PROTECTION MODEL KEY FEATURES DOCUMENT

[5066]
This key features document gives you the main points about the income protection plan you're considering. It should be read with any quotation. Please read it carefully and keep it with your other plan documents.

This key features document follows the Association of British Insurers Statement of Best Practice for Income Protection Insurance.

Aims

— To give you a regular benefit if you suffer illness or injury leading to a loss of earnings. Your benefit can [replace some of the earnings you lose][maintain key items of expenditure][or, if you don't work, it can meet additional expenditure].

Your commitment

— To give us all the [medical and other] information we ask for when applying for your plan and when claiming benefit. If you don't do this we may not pay your benefit.
— To make all the regular premium payments we need for the length of the plan.
— [To tell us if you change your [occupation/job/duties] – or if you become unemployed – as required by company – see Change of Occupation].
— To tell us of any claim within the time limits we set.
— To select an appropriate level of cover and review it regularly to make sure you have enough for your needs but not more than we'll pay.

Risk factors

— You won't be covered if you stop paying premiums. [However, premiums are not payable when you're receiving benefit having made a claim].
— The cover may be less than you need if you don't review it regularly to keep it in line with your earnings. On the other hand if your income does not support your chosen cover, then your benefit will have to be reduced. We won't give you back any of your premium payments if this happens.
— The benefit we pay under the plan may affect your claim to some means tested State Benefits. Your entitlement to State Incapacity Benefit won't be affected.
— The benefit we pay under this plan may affect your claim to benefits under other income protection policies.
— State Benefit rules may change.
— The present tax-free treatment of the plan's benefits may change.
— [In future we may change the premium payments for people covered by these plans because of factors such as our claims costs and interest rates, but this won't happen for at least x years and we'll tell you beforehand.]
— [Certain causes of claim won't be covered (see When will the plan not pay out?)]

Questions and answers

What is a [Company] Income Protection Plan?

It is a plan designed to give you a regular benefit if you suffer illness or injury leading to loss of earnings. You select the features of the plan to make sure the cover is right for you.

— You decide:
  — the amount of benefit you require
  — how soon you need the benefit to start
  — [for how long you need the benefit to be paid,] and
  — for how long you want the cover to last.

— You pay regular premiums to keep the cover in force.
— We provide cover until your policy ends no matter how many claims you make.
— You tell us when illness or injury has stopped you working.
— We pay you a [monthly] income for as long as the claim is valid.

How do I select the plan's features so that it meets my needs?

This section deals with the choices you make when setting up your plan.

The amount of benefit that can be paid	You choose the amount of benefit you'll need. Remember that tax and national insurance are deducted from your normal earnings but not from the benefits we pay you. This means that you should not need benefit which is more than [50%] of your pre-incapacity earnings. This is the maximum percentage of your earnings which we'll pay out. [We'll never provide benefit of more than [£ insert amount and terms and conditions], regardless of your earnings.] See also the section "Other income which may reduce your benefit".
The earnings upon which to base your cover	When choosing your cover, remember that if you claim, we'll pay benefit based on your pre-incapacity earnings:

	— *If you're employed*, these are your pre-tax earnings for PAYE assessment purposes [excluding benefits in kind] in the [insert number] months before you became unable to work; — *If you're self-employed*, these are your share of pre-tax profit from your trade, profession or vocation after deduction of trading expenses, as described in Schedule D Case I and II of the Income and Corporation Taxes Act 1988, in the [number] months before you become unable to work. [Explain treatment of fluctuating income if company specific.] [We'll ask for evidence of your earnings.] Income received from savings and investments isn't taken into account.
Increasing your cover	You may choose to increase your cover [company specific wording on contractual and forward underwriting options allowed] when you take out this plan. See also the section "the amount of benefit that can be paid". An appropriate premium increase will apply when your cover increases. [Explain company specific effect of declining an increase.]
Automatic increases to your benefit payments	You may choose at the start of your plan for your benefit to increase each year [by a set percentage] [or] [in line with inflation] from the date on which any claim becomes payable.
When benefit payments start	There will be a period when you're first unable to work for which we don't pay benefit. This is known as the deferred period. You can choose between [1, 3, 6 and 12 months]. The longer the deferred period, the cheaper your policy will be. Benefit is paid (monthly) in arrears. Your choice should allow for any earnings which you expect to continue after you stop working, such as sick pay, or how long you're prepared to live on your savings.
How long the benefits can be paid	[company specific text to explain limited payment periods] Until the plan ends.
How long the cover should last	You choose for your plan to end when you think you would no longer need the benefits but no later than your planned retirement date.
Medical and other details we may need	Your application will include questions about your medical history, earnings, occupation and other personal circumstances. We may request additional medical evidence to support your application at our expense. [give details of Pre Existing Conditions/moratorium if applicable]
[What other benefits can I choose?]	[describe any optional company specific benefits]

How flexible is it?

This section deals with choices you can make once your plan has started

Regular review of your cover	You should consider how your earnings and living costs have changed since you last reviewed your cover.

If you wish to increase your cover [by more than any automatic options provided by your plan], please contact us. It will be subject to a fresh assessment of your health, earnings, occupation and other personal circumstances.

Your premium payments to us will increase.

[company specific guidance for reduction in cover]

Suspending your cover

[Company specific rules to suspend/reinstate plans eg career and maternity breaks.]

Change of occupation

[You don't need to tell us if you change your occupation after the plan starts.]

[If notification needed, state requirements and consequences of not doing so.]

When will the plan pay out?

When to claim

When you're unable to work, because of illness or injury, resulting in a loss of earnings.

The deadline for claiming

Tell us as soon as possible but [for deferred periods of 3 months or more] no later than [8 weeks from when you're first incapacitated].

The extent of incapacity

Our usual definition of incapacity is [company definition].

We'll tell you when you apply if we wish to use a different definition.

How we assess your claim

We'll look at the duties of your occupation, your ability to do them, [and whether adjustments can be made to help you do them].

We'll ask for evidence of your loss of earnings.

[State also any other evidence required.]

We'll then consider your ability to work in an alternative occupation.

You'll qualify for benefit if you're unable to [perform the essential duties of your occupation] [and any occupation to which you are suited by education, training or experience] resulting in a loss of earnings, and are not doing any other work.

How long the claim is paid for

Your benefit will be paid until the first of the following happens:

— you recover and are no longer incapacitated

— you no longer suffer a loss of earnings

— the term of the plan ends

— [the benefit payment period ends – *company specific*]

— you die.

Claiming again after returning to work

There is no limit to the number of claims you can make.

You must restart premium payment when your claim ends so your cover is maintained.

If you need to claim again for the same cause within [6] months of returning to work then the deferred period won't apply.

Returning to part time or less well paid work

In addition to the money you earn we'*ll* pay you a reduced benefit, which takes account of your lost earnings.

[Company specific: explain if this has to follow a period of full incapacity, any time limits on the benefit payments and if the formula is inflation proofed.]

How benefits are paid

Benefits are payable [at the end of each month] from the end of the deferred period.

Premium payments when claiming

You should continue to pay premiums until we accept your claim. [However, you don't need to pay premiums to us while benefit is being paid.]

Other income which is likely to reduce your benefit

We'll reduce the benefit we pay if any of the following take you over the maximum allowable (which is explained in "The amount of benefit that can be paid"):

— Continuing payments from your employment – such as sick pay

— Pension payments – unless you were entitled to them while still working

— Other insurance benefits – if they arise because of your incapacity and either result in regular payments to you or make regular payments on your behalf – such as mortgage payments [or company specific wording]

— [Incapacity benefit from Social Security – company specific]

— If your benefit is reduced we don't refund any of your premium payments to us and your cover remains unchanged unless you choose to reduce it.

We won't reduce your benefit if you receive:

— [Incapacity benefit from Social Security – company specific]

— Income support or other means tested state benefits. However, benefit payment from your plan may affect your eligibility for means tested state benefits

— Investment income.

When will the plan not pay out?

Benefit won't be paid because of: [company specific conditions]

— [incapacity, due to or arising from, HIV or AIDS except when contracted in the course of your normal job]

— [normal pregnancy]

— [war and civil commotion]

— [self-inflicted injury]

— [criminal acts]

— [drug abuse]

— [failure to follow medical advice].

We may add other conditions in some cases. If so we'll tell you before you start your plan.

[If you claim and live outside of the [British Isles] benefits will only be paid for 26 weeks – company specific.]

[You cannot claim just because you become unemployed. If you become unemployed your cover can continue – company specific.]

[You cannot claim if you are not in [full-time] employment when you become incapacitated.]

What other features are there?

[describe any non-optional company specific benefits]

What will my premium payments be?

Your illustration will show the normal cost of the cover you have chosen.

	Your premium payments depend upon your age, sex, occupation, smoking habits, medical history, other personal circumstances and upon the level and features of the cover you choose. We'll tell you the actual cost you'll pay once we have assessed your application.
	Payments to us are by [yearly cheque or monthly direct debit].
[Changes to your premium payments in the future]	[In future we may change the premium payments for people covered by these plans because of factors such as our claims costs and interest rates, but this won't happen for at least x years and you'll be told beforehand.]
[Where are my premiums invested?]	[*company specific for investment-linked plans*]
What happens to the plan if I die?	[Your plan will end and no premium refund will be paid.] [Company wording about death benefits.]
What are the charges?	The premium payments shown in your illustration include all the costs of administration, underwriting, claim and selling expenses [commission] and the fees payable for any medical examinations, which we ask you to attend.
What if I stop paying premiums?	Your plan and cover will end. [You won't get any money back.]
Does the plan have a cash-in value?	[Your plan has no cash-in value at any time.] [investment return if applicable with a warning that it will be a lot less than premiums paid]
What about tax?	Present UK tax law and Inland Revenue practice means you don't — get tax relief on premiums — pay tax or national insurance contributions on your benefits. This may change in the future.
Can I change my mind?	After [we accept your application *or company specific*] we'll send you a Cancellation Notice. If you don't want the plan, you will have [30] days to send this Notice back.
How to contact us	[Remember your financial adviser will normally be your first point of contact. We won't be able to give you financial advice.] If you have any questions at any time, you can phone, or send a fax or e-mail, or you can write to us. Call us on 0000 000 0000 during the following times: Monday to Friday 0 am – 0 pm Saturday 0 am – 0 pm We may monitor calls to improve our service. 24 hour answerphone number – 0000 000 0000 Fax number – 0000 000 0000 e-mail address – insurance@somewhere.co.uk Office address Insurance Company, XYZ Street, Anytown, Somewhere, SW1 1SW
Other information	
How to complain	If you ever need to complain, first write to us at the above address. If you're not satisfied with our response, you can complain to: **Financial Ombudsman Service**

South Quay Plaza
183 Marsh Wall
London
E14 9SR

Complaining to the Ombudsman won't affect your legal rights.

Terms and Conditions

These Key Features give a summary of the <company name> Income Protection Plan. They don't include all the definitions, exclusions, terms and conditions.

If you'd like a copy of the full terms and conditions, please [ask your financial adviser or] contact us direct.

[We have the right to change some of the terms and conditions. We'll write and explain if this happens. We'll also send you a copy of anything that's changed. – *if applicable*]

Law

The law [and courts] of [England and Wales] will decide any dispute.

Compensation

The UK Financial Services and Markets Act 2000 covers your plan. It is designed to protect you if we become insolvent.

APPENDIX B1A
GUIDANCE NOTE ON DEFINITION OF INCAPACITY – OWN OCCUPATION

Purpose

[5067]
The definition of incapacity clause is a key factor in determining the validity of any claim. As such it will be examined by the discerning consumer to determine the product that will be purchased.

Typical wording content

Typical wording

Totally unable by reason of illness or injury to follow their own occupation(s) (as stated herein) and is not following any other occupation.

Key words/phrases

(1) *Totally*
(2) *Illness or injury*
(3) *Own occupation(s)*
(4) *(as stated herein)*
(5) *any other occupation*

Insurers' Obligations

The insurer should make clear to the policyholder in Key Features Documents the principal characteristics of the definition of incapacity and the criteria on which it will be based.

Guidelines

The following practices are recommended:

1. ***Totally***

Traditional industry practice has been to use the word "totally", not in its literal sense (ie 100%) but to make it clear that partial incapacity is not covered. Previous Ombudsman guidance and case law supports this view.

Where "totally" is used by the insurer, the Key Features Document should explain that the purpose is to distinguish this from partial incapacity and that a reasonable, non-literal interpretation will apply.

Some insurers have clarified the basis on which the person will be assessed by referring to the "material and substantial" or "essential" duties of a person's occupation. This is recommended where appropriate.

2. ***Illness or injury***

The phrase "illness or injury" or "sickness or accident" helps the consumer in understanding that unemployment/redundancy or normal pregnancy are not covered conditions within the policy wording.

3. ***Own occupation***

There are two potential interpretations of the word "occupation": the generic duties of a trade or profession, or the specific duties currently being performed. Insurers should make it clear which interpretation they will apply.

4. ***Stated Herein***

Some insurers use the words "stated herein" in their policies. If they do so, and the policy does not contain a change of occupation provision, clear guidelines should be given about the occupation(s) against which claims will be assessed if the claimant has changed jobs in the interim.

5. ***And is not following any other occupation***

The purpose of this phrase is to ensure that a claimant who is unable to perform his own occupation does not receive benefit if he finds alternative employment and suffers no reduction in earnings.

Insurers should note the importance of the word "and", as to use "or" would change the meaning to an "any occupation" wording.

There may be difficulty in assessing whether the claimant's "new occupation" can be regarded as real work or is voluntary work, therapeutic work or even a hobby from which some income results. Insurers should be clear what criteria they will apply (ie would the work normally merit profit, pay or reward?).

Additional factors

If there are any supplementary claims conditions governing the validity of a claim (eg a requirement to participate in rehabilitation, a requirement to co-operate with reasonable workplace adjustment under the Disability Discrimination Act, or a requirement for continued medical supervision) this should be made clear.

Insurers should make clear in the Key Features Document that the availability of suitable employment is not a factor in assessing the claimant's ability to work.

APPENDIX B1B
GUIDANCE NOTE ON DEFINITION OF INCAPACITY – ANY OCCUPATION

Purpose

[5068]
The definition of incapacity clause is a key factor in determining the validity of any claim. As such it will be examined by the discerning consumer to determine the product that will be purchased.

The "Inability to follow Any Occupation" definition of incapacity carries with it stricter criteria for claiming than the other occupational based definitions. Policies with this wording are usually issued to policyholders who would find it impossible or prohibitively expensive to obtain insurance on one of the other, occupationally based, definitions of incapacity.

Typical wording content

Typical Wording

In July 2001 the ABI recommended the following specimen wording to reflect the work carried out by the Income Protection Working Party.

"Totally unable by reason of illness or injury to follow any occupation. This means that if after that injury or the onset of that illness there is an occupation that you are able to perform, irrespective of whether or not you do so, you will not receive payment".

Key words/phrases

1. *Totally*

2. *Illness or injury*

3. *Any*

Insurers' Obligations

The Insurance Ombudsman has stated that, as with other definitions of incapacity, the insurer should make clear the principal characteristics of the definition of incapacity and the criteria on which it will be based.

Ombudsmen have expressed concern about this particular definition of incapacity as being the one most capable of being misunderstood by the proposer. There seems little doubt that the Ombudsman will find against insurers who fail to spell out the restrictive nature of this wording in their KFD or other documentation.

The "Inability to follow Any Occupation" definition of incapacity may be offered to a proposer who originally applied for another definition which the insurer, for underwriting reasons, is not prepared to offer. In such circumstances the proposer will often have read a KFD describing another definition of incapacity. It is the insurer's responsibility therefore to draft its counter-offer such that the restrictive nature of this wording is explained.

Guidelines

The use of this wording must be interpreted and applied reasonably. Severely disabled people can often show tremendous resilience and motivation going to extraordinary lengths to perform an occupation. People who are virtually totally paralysed but who, perhaps, can type by using a specially designed typewriter that enables them to select the letter by use of their mouth, is such an example. It would be regarded as unreasonable to deny a claim under this definition in such circumstances.

The ability to work only in a sheltered working environment, limited to disabled people, is not a reason to deny a claim.

Similarly, a claimant who is severely disabled but could do an hour or so employment a day would nevertheless satisfy this definition of incapacity.

It is the ability to perform the occupation rather than the availability of that occupation that is the criterion that needs to be satisfied.

It is the responsibility of insurers to clearly state **credible** alternative occupation(s) that the claimant could perform, having determined his/her physical and mental capabilities. In some circumstances the insurer may consider it appropriate to offer help in the form of vocational assessment, re-training and preparation to return to work and this is likely to be viewed positively should any dispute arise over the claimant's ability to work.

Meanings

1. ***Totally***

Traditional industry practice has been to use the word "totally", not in its literal sense (ie 100%) but to make it clear that partial incapacity is not covered. Previous Ombudsman guidance and case law supports this view.

Where "totally" is used by the insurer, the Key Features Document should explain that the purpose is to distinguish this from partial incapacity and that a reasonable, non-literal interpretation will apply.

2. ***"Illness or injury"***

The phrases "sickness or accident" or "illness or injury" help the consumer in understanding that unemployment/redundancy or normal pregnancy are not covered conditions within the policy wording.

3. ***"Any"***

The specimen wording is consistent with ABI guidance of 7 November 1997, which emphasised the need to clarify the context when the word "any" was used in policies defining disability.

Additional factors

If there are any supplementary claims conditions governing the validity of a claim (eg a requirement to participate in rehabilitation, a requirement to co-operate with reasonable workplace adjustment under the Disability Discrimination Act, or a requirement for continued medical supervision) this should be made clear.

APPENDIX B2
GUIDANCE NOTE ON LIMITATION OF BENEFIT

Purpose

[5069]
Insurers limit the level of benefit paid to claimants to a stated percentage of their pre-incapacity earnings and/or a maximum monetary amount. This is to ensure that the claimant is not better off financially on claim than in work (or, in the case of monetary maxima for housepersons, to restrict the benefit to a figure which meets the reasonable needs of the claimant), thereby preserving an incentive to return to former duties.

Percentages and benefit maxima vary considerably and are key factors influencing consumer choice. Higher percentage maxima may be accompanied by a greater tendency to offset other sources of income such as State benefits.

Typical wording content

Wordings stipulate that the benefit stated in the policy (as adjusted by any subsequent increases) will be subject to a maximum percentage of the claimant's pre-incapacity earnings and/or a maximum monetary amount. The basis upon which "pre-incapacity earnings" are calculated is shown, and other sources of continuing income that may be offset against this by the insurer are listed.

Insurers' Obligations

This is a key clause that will influence the consumer's choice of product and determine the benefit they will receive in the event of a claim. As such, a full explanation of this clause must be given in the Key Features Document. In particular, clear information needs to be provided to the consumer on the following:

(a) the percentage and monetary maxima applied;
(b) how these maxima are affected by any subsequent benefit increases through indexation or increase options;
(c) what constitutes "pre-incapacity earnings";
(d) what other forms of income might reduce the benefit paid and a warning to the applicant that if they have a policy with different benefit formula and intend to keep it in force they should consult the first insurer before taking out the new policy to clarify the potential impact of the second policy on their benefit entitlement and ensure that they are properly protected;
(e) the tax basis used in the calculation of "pre-incapacity earnings";
(f) the tax basis on which benefit is paid;
(g) what happens in the event of over-insurance (ie benefit limitation/any return of premiums).

Guidelines

Monetary Maxima

The following practices are recommended:

(1) It should be clearly stated that any monetary maximum applies to the aggregate of all Income Protection policies (including group policies) effected for the benefit of the policyholder with all insurers.
(2) If the insurer wishes to take into account other forms of insurance (eg short term Personal Accident and Sickness, Critical Illness or Waiver of Premium) the policy classes in question should be clearly set out.
(3) Insurers should liaise to achieve a fair and reasonable outcome for policyholders who are over-insured in a way that reflects the product design and pricing of the two or more products.
(4) It should be made clear whether such maxima are adjusted or are subject to review in the light of inflation.

Percentage Limitations

The following practices are recommended:

(1) The definition of "pre-incapacity earnings" should include:
    (a) the basis for the assessment of earnings for the employed and the self-employed. The recommended practice is:
        — Employed: earnings for PAYE purposes;
        — Self-employed: share of profit for the purposes of Schedule D Case I and II of the Income and Corporation Taxes Act 1988 (ie share of profit after deduction of trading expenses).
    (b) whether the earnings calculation is based upon pre-tax or net income.
    (c) the status of benefits in kind, bonuses, commission, drawings and dividend payments in the calculation.
    (d) the period over which earnings are assessed and averaged.
(2) A clear statement regarding the effect on benefit of:
    (a) State benefits (Incapacity Benefit, disability related awards such as Industrial Injuries Benefit and Disability Living Allowance and means tested benefits such as Income Support). Insurers offsetting Incapacity Benefit should clearly state what rate is used ie short term or long term, single person's (and whether this includes age allowances) or full benefit (including dependants allowances). It should also be clear whether any Incapacity Benefit deduction is automatic or only applied if the claimant actually receives it. Finally, it should be clear how any subsequent change in State benefit payments would affect the claim (eg cost of living adjustments, withdrawal of an existing benefit or receipt of a new benefit).

(b) ongoing payments from the claimant's employer or business (including salary, commissions, bonuses and dividend payments etc).
(c) pension payments.
(d) other insurance payments (what forms of insurance are covered, lump sum or income and whether this includes benefits such as creditor insurance or waiver where no payment is received by the claimant).
(e) compensation payments and court awards.
(f) income from savings or investments.

(3) An indication of the evidence normally required as initial proof of claim, eg P60, audited accounts etc.

APPENDIX B3
GUIDANCE NOTE ON PROPORTIONATE/REHABILITATION BENEFITS

Purpose

[5070]
The purpose is to motivate claimants to return to work in a reduced capacity or to take up a new occupation. This is in the interests of both insurer and insured.

As a general rule, the expression "proportionate benefit" applies to claimants who take up a new occupation, while "rehabilitation benefit" applies to claimants who return to their own job. However, not all insurers differentiate between these two categories. It is also common for a number of insurers to restrict the period during which "rehabilitation benefit" is payable.

As a general rule, policies using an "own occupation" definition of incapacity would contain such provisions. However, those containing an "any occupation" definition of incapacity are unlikely to contain such a wording as, *prima facie*, being able to return to work in any capacity would result in the definition of incapacity not being met.

Typical wording content

The wording will vary from insurer to insurer but the main features will be as follows:

After being on full benefit

Most insurers require the claimant to have been in receipt of full benefit before he is able to claim for a Proportionate/Rehabilitation Benefit. Others require there to be a period of "full time" absence from work within the deferred period whilst some allow the benefit even if there has been no "full time" absence from work.

When proportionate/rehabilitation benefits might apply

There are a number of different scenarios where a proportionate/rehabilitation benefit may be allowed because of continuing incapacity. These scenarios would include:

(a) A return to work in the claimant's previous occupation but where there is some limiting factor, eg number of hours worked.
(b) A return to work in a different occupation but with the same employer.
(c) A return to work in a different occupation with a different employer. The latter would include becoming self employed or vice versa.
(d) A therapeutic return to work or into sheltered employment where the objective is to provide rehabilitation back into the work place in the longer term.

Suffer a reduction in earnings

In order to qualify for payment as a valid claim, all claimants must be both medically unable to work to their normal capacity and demonstrate a financial loss. To qualify for proportionate or rehabilitation benefits, the claimant must continue to demonstrate a reduction in earnings. However many, if not most, insurers would allow some form of inflation proofing before applying this rule.

Proportionate/rehabilitation benefit claims can reduce to zero where, even though the claimant has been unable to fully resume their former occupation, their level of earnings is comparable to their pre-incapacity earnings. In these circumstances, most insurers would be happy to leave the claim open for a period equal to their linked claims period, to ensure that, should the claimant be unable to sustain this level of earnings due to the same or related cause of claim the claim can be re-activated without the need to serve a further deferred period. This is subject to any overriding time limitation on the rehabilitation benefit.

Calculation Formula

Some insurers give only the most general description of the way that proportionate or rehabilitation benefits will be calculated. Others give a detailed and prescribed formula.

Insurers' Obligations

The insurer has certain obligations as set out below:

(1) Insurers should bring the policyholder's attention to the proportionate/rehabilitation benefits in the Key Features Document.

(2) The word "partial" should not be used, as it may imply payment of benefit when a person is partially incapacitated but still able to undertake his normal occupation.

(3) Insurers who place a time limit on payment of proportionate/rehabilitation benefits should state clearly in the Key Features document the period of time for which the benefit may be payable.

(4) Insurers who use a "switched" definition of incapacity should make it clear in the Key Features document whether eligibility for proportionate benefit is affected once the new definition is applied.

(5) Insurers should make it clear in the Key Features document whether it is possible to be in receipt of proportionate benefit without having previously been in receipt of full benefit.

(6) Those insurers who allow "inflation proofing" of benefits should state in the policy documentation the method, and index, used to make the calculations.

(7) Insurers should state, in the policy documentation, whether the proportionate benefit will be adjusted to take account of any loss of State Benefits on returning to work in a reduced capacity.

(8) Insurers should state in the policy documentation for how long they will keep open claims without the need to serve a further deferred period, where the claimant is still not working to their former capacity but no payment is due because of the level of earnings being received.

Guidelines

This is one area where it is very difficult to provide guidelines that suit all likely circumstances. It is recommended that:

(1) The Key Features Document should describe in what circumstances the policy provides for payment of proportionate/rehabilitation benefit.

(2) The policy documentation should clearly set out how these benefits are calculated and in what circumstances they are payable.

(3) As proportionate/rehabilitation benefits offer encouragement to return to the workplace, which reflects an important strand of government policy, insurers should consider these benefits when reviewing or redesigning their policies.

(4) Recognising that it is in their own (and their policyholders') long term interest to facilitate a return to employment in some form, insurers should be prepared to adopt a flexible approach to proportionate or rehabilitation benefits in order to reach a financial agreement with the claimant to this end.

(5) Subject to any time limitation on the payment of rehabilitation benefit, insurers should be prepared to keep open claims where the claimant is not yet working to their full capacity but no payment is due because of their level of earnings, for a period equal to their linked claims period, in order to avoid the claimant needing to serve a further deferred period where such earnings are not sustained due to the same or a related cause.

APPENDIX B4
GUIDANCE NOTE ON CHANGE OF OCCUPATION

Purpose

[5071]
Some insurers have a requirement that policyholders notify them of any change of occupation (or in some cases change of occupational duties) during the currency of the policy. Any claim submitted by the policyholder will be at risk of being declined or reduced if the occupational risk category has changed and the insurer has not confirmed that cover continues.

Typical wording content

The wording will vary from insurer to insurer, and will range from those who require notification following a change of occupation, to those who require notification of any change of duty within the occupation declared at the outset.

Insurers may also vary in their attitude to stating the policyholder's normal occupation in the policy document.

Insurers' Obligations

The insurer has certain obligations as set out below:

Key Features Document

Those insurers who require notification of a change of occupation must make this requirement clear in the Key Features Document.

In particular there needs to be clarity over what constitutes "change" and how "occupation" is defined. For example, does the insurer need to know about a change to a job for which the original occupational title is no longer appropriate, a change of duties within the same occupation, a change of employer, or periods of unemployment?

The insurer should make clear the consequences to the policyholder of any change in occupation. In this context those insurers who change the definition of incapacity, regardless of whether they have a Change of Occupation clause within their policy, upon the policyholder becoming unemployed or taking up the role of a houseperson should set out such details.

Notifying the Policyholder of his obligations to advise Changes of Occupation

As income protection tends to be written on a long term basis, often without the need for the insurer to notify the policyholder of changes of premium and conditions on an annual basis, it is unreasonable to expect the insurer to periodically remind the policyholder of his obligation to notify changes of occupation.

However, where the insurer periodically writes to the policyholder because of the need to review premium rates or to increase premiums or benefits, it should bring to the policyholder's attention his duty to notify any change of occupation.

Guidelines

Re-underwriting during the Currency of the Policy

The insurer has the right to re-underwrite the risk upon receiving notification of change of occupation. However, such re-underwriting should be confined to the circumstances arising as a result of the change of occupation/duties and should not seek to address any change in other risk features (eg health status) of which the insurer may have become aware.

For those insurers who only require notification of change of occupation (as opposed to changes of duties), any changes to duties, change of location or change of employer should not result in re-underwriting.

Those insurers who require notification of change of duties, and who have brought this to the policyholder's attention, may re-underwrite as above on changes of duty but such insurers should have internal procedure notes to ensure a fair and consistent approach.

When determining whether an additional premium is payable or indeed whether cover can continue, the insurer should look to the occupational class that the "new" occupation would have been placed in at the inception of the policy. Insurers should not change premiums or alter cover merely because their underwriting approach to a particular occupation has moved it from one class to another since the policy commenced.

If the insurer requires notification of change of occupation to be done within a certain period, the guidance note on Claims Notification Periods should be followed.

Claims without a prior notification of a change of occupation

Insurers should follow these guidelines in the event that the first notification of a change in occupation (or occupational duties) is made at the claim stage:

(1) If the change of occupation is one that is unacceptable to the insurer, it has the right to refuse the claim.

(2) If the change of occupation is one that would only be acceptable to the insurer on a "harsher" definition of incapacity, then that "harsher" definition will be applied.

(3) If the change of occupation is such that the policyholder remains in the same occupational class as before then cover and level of premiums should continue unchanged.

(4) If the insured has changed from one occupation class to a "worse risk" occupational class, the amount payable will be determined by the application of the principle of proportionality: namely that proportion of the annual benefit otherwise payable as the premiums paid bear to the premiums that should have been paid. The insurer must determine the premium basis to be used, eg gross premium, risk premium, etc.

(5) If the policy states that the definition of incapacity shall change because the policyholder has become, for example, unemployed or a houseperson then the insurer shall adjudicate the claim against the changed definition.

All the above shall be subject to satisfactory proof of claim to the insurer and to any restrictions in payment that may be imposed because of the application of another policy clause such as a Limitation of Benefits clause.

Premiums in respect of claims without a prior notification of change of occupation

The following guidelines should be followed:

(1) If cover is declined, the insurer should refund the premiums from the date of the change of occupation.

(2) Similarly, if the insured has moved from an occupational class to a "better" occupational class, he shall be entitled to a refund of any "excess" premiums paid.

(3) However, in the event that the policyholder has changed to a "worse risk" occupational class, it is not appropriate that he should be asked to pay any additional premiums with effect from the date of change of occupation. The remedy is, as described above, a proportionate reduction in the benefit that might be payable.

(4) In all of the above, interest is not payable (although this is at the insurer's discretion).

APPENDIX B5
GUIDANCE NOTE ON CLAIMS NOTIFICATION PERIOD

Purpose

[5072]

In order to improve claims handling effectiveness, insurers ask for notification of a potential claim prior to the date on which the claim becomes eligible for payment. Traditionally, claims notification was requested shortly before the expiry of the deferred period, allowing sufficient time for the necessary claims administration procedures to be completed prior to the determination of the claim. In recent years, however, insurers have requested earlier notification, in order both to be proactive in assisting the claimant to return to work, where possible, and to ensure that valid claims are paid without delay.

Typical wording content

Such policy wordings have the following main features:

(a) A stipulation as to how the claim should be notified (eg in writing).

(b) A time limit for notification of the claim. This may be fixed by reference to:
  (i) a designated period from the onset of incapacity, or
  (ii) a designated period prior to the expiry of the deferred period.

(c) A time limit may also be stipulated for the return of a claims form following the initial notification.

(d) A description of the consequences of not observing these time limits, eg failure may postpone the claimant's eligibility to claim by the length of the delay unless the office is satisfied that failure to do so was no fault of the claimant.

Insurers' Obligations

The claims notification period should be included in the Key Features Document. Additional product literature must also be clear about the time limits to be applied by the insurer and the consequences of their not being followed.

Guidelines

The ABI Statement of Long Term Insurance Practice states: "Under any circumstances regarding a time limit for notification of a claim, the claimant will not be asked to do more than report a claim as soon as reasonably possible."

It is therefore recommended that the following guidance be given to policyholders as to when notification of a potential claim should be given:

"Please notify us as soon as you believe that you may wish to claim, but in any event:

(a) within a claims notification period of 8 weeks from when first unable to work for deferred periods of 13 weeks or more;

(b) within a claims notification period of 4 weeks from when first unable to work for a deferred period of 8 weeks;

(c) within a claims notification period of 2 weeks from when first unable to work for a deferred period of 4 weeks."

The claim should be paid from the end of the deferred period if the policyholder is able to satisfy the insurer that, in the circumstances, the delay was not unreasonable.

APPENDIX B6
GUIDANCE NOTE ON DEFERRED PERIOD

Purpose

[5073]
The purpose of a deferred period is to both reduce claims costs to the insurer and premiums for the insured by eliminating claims during the deferred period. The period chosen may be influenced by any occupational sick pay arrangements.

This reduction in costs results in a smaller premium as the policyholder effectively self funds for his sickness needs during the deferred period.

Typical wording content

There are two ways of approaching such wording with the majority of insurers using the first:
(a) To make it a requirement that the absence from work during the deferred period must be continuous.
(b) To express the deferred period as a total of X weeks' absence during Y weeks.

Using the second format, the claimant has the opportunity of adding together a series of absences over the stated period and, once he reaches a certain figure, he may make a claim.

Insurers' Obligations

Insurers should include in their Key Features Documents the choice of deferred periods available with a clear explanation of how the wording works. The explanation should include information as to when claim payments are made and, if incapacity does not need to be continuous, the qualification criteria (eg X weeks in Y weeks) should be explained. Insurers should explain when benefit becomes payable after the deferred period.

Guidelines

Possibilities for claims disputes include the following scenarios:
(a) The claimant makes an attempt to return to work during the deferred period, is unsuccessful, and in consequence potentially fails the requirement for the absence to be continuous.
Generally it is unfair and unreasonable for the insurer to penalise a claimant for an unsuccessful but genuine attempt to return to work.
(b) There may be a requirement that a single cause of incapacity precludes the claimant's ability to work. This may occur particularly in conjunction with the approach outlined at (b) under "Typical wording content" above.
The insurer should apply a test of reasonableness. Two distinct causes of incapacity may well strictly fail such a requirement but illnesses can be interconnected and diagnoses can be imprecise on occasions.

Name of Clause

Insurers currently have different names for the clause described in this guidance note. However, when comparing products across the healthcare range, consumers can be confused where one clause can have different meanings, or where several terms have the same meaning. The expression "deferred period" should therefore be used for the purpose described in this guidance note and for no other purpose. Other terms, such as "waiting period" or "elimination period" should no longer be used to describe this clause.

APPENDIX B7
GUIDANCE NOTE ON WAIVER OF PREMIUM

Purpose

[5074]
As a further contribution towards supporting the policyholder in times of financial difficulty, most insurers agree to waive premium payments during periods of incapacity. The main exceptions to this rule are the Friendly Societies who instead provide profit sharing schemes for their members. In addition, some insurers provide a facility whereby premiums can be waived for career break purposes (a maximum period may be stipulated).

Typical wording content

Such policy wordings have the following main features:
(a) A definition of incapacity governing eligibility for Waiver.
(b) The length of the deferred period before becoming eligible for Waiver.
(c) The level of premium waived. There are two main alternative approaches:
  (i) any premium falling due whilst the main benefit is being paid is waived; or

(ii) a refund of premiums is made proportionate to the period of claim.

Insurers' Obligations

The insurer has certain obligations as set out below:

(1) The availability of Waiver should be included in the Key Features Document. Additional product literature must be clear about the level of premium waived, particularly whether any of the benefit criteria differ from those applying to the payment of the main benefit and whether the clause will continue to operate during periods of proportionate or rehabilitation benefits.

(2) The insurer must make it clear in the policy document, in respect of policies with increasing or reviewable premiums, the level of premium that will be waived.

Guidelines

The definition of incapacity for waiver should be no stricter than that applying to the main benefit.

For guidance on "definition of incapacity" and "deferred period" see elsewhere in these guidance notes.

APPENDIX B8
GUIDANCE NOTE ON PREGNANCY CLAUSE

Purpose

[5075]
Some insurers operate a pregnancy exclusion. This has two main purposes. It first of all emphasises that pregnancy in itself is not a valid cause for claim. Incapacity must be related to illness or injury. Secondly, it defines normal pregnancy as including a recovery period after birth or other termination.

Typical wording content

Practice varies considerably but can be summarised as follows:

— Some insurers have no pregnancy exclusion.
— Some insurers exclude only the term of the pregnancy itself (not the recovery period).
— Some insurers exclude both the pregnancy and the recovery period (which is generally 3 months but can be up to 6 months).
— Some insurers extend the exclusion to cover "complications of pregnancy" as well as the pregnancy itself. The effect of this is that anyone with medical incapacity arising from complications of pregnancy has to go through the recovery period and then the normal deferred period before they become eligible for benefit.
— Some insurers will not cover complications of pregnancy at all.

Insurers' Obligations

The presence of a pregnancy exclusion should be brought to the applicant's attention in the Key Features Document.

Guidelines

Whilst there may be some merit in excluding normal pregnancy (to avoid any misunderstanding over what is or is not covered), it is recommended that any medical complications should be covered.

In considering this recommendation, insurers should be aware of the 1998 Equal Opportunities Commission (EOC) ruling regarding similar exclusions on Creditor Insurance policies, where the Commission deemed the blanket exclusion of pregnancy claims to be discriminatory to women under the Sex Discrimination Act.

The EOC did not dispute that insurers needed to exclude claims arising from normal pregnancy. However, they were concerned that claims relating to complications arising from pregnancy should be covered. As a result of this, Creditor insurers agreed a new exclusion clause with EOC allowing claims for "complications arising from pregnancy, subject to the policy's general conditions relating to payment of benefits, which are diagnosed as such by a doctor, or consultant, who specialises in obstetrics". The "general conditions" referred to above effectively state that cover is only provided where the person is working or, where applicable, on statutory maternity leave.

Consequently, it is recommended that insurers should:

(a) cover claims arising from complications of pregnancy diagnosed by a doctor, or consultant, who specialises in obstetrics.

(b) cover such complications from the date on which they become incapacitating ie without any extension of the standard deferred period.

APPENDIX B9
GUIDANCE NOTES ON LINKED CLAIMS

Principle

[5076]
The Linked Claims Clause is intended to encourage claimants to attempt to return to work by eliminating the need for a second deferred period if they suffer from the same disability within a specified period. It is designed to apply to the period following a full time return to work but similar arrangements may apply to some proportionate/rehabilitation claims (see Appendix B3).

Construction of the wording

A typical wording will cover the following points:
— Subsequent period(s) of incapacity must result from the same or a related cause.
— The Linked Claim period commences on the first day of return to work and will be effective for typically six or twelve months.
— The number of occurrences which can be linked for the purposes of a claim.

Insurers' Obligations

A Linked Claims Clause is a valuable safety net for claimants who attempt to return to work. Insurers should make it clear in their Key Features Documents how it works and its relevance to claimants.

If this clause is not offered, the Key Features Document must state that a further deferred period will apply.

Guidelines
— The insurer should remind the policyholder of the Linked Claims Clause when a claim is first assessed, periodically thereafter and, most importantly, if rehabilitation is undertaken.
— Usually, the Linked Claims Clause will require that subsequent periods of incapacity must result from the same or related condition. It is recommended that proper regard should be had to appropriate medical opinion when determining whether conditions are related.
— Rehabilitation is an increasingly important part of claims management, potentially reducing claims costs and returning the claimant to active employment and a better level of income. The insurer should not penalise the claimant financially by assessing the benefit on the level of earnings immediately prior to the linked claim and should also give regard to the claimant's earnings before the initial period of incapacity.

CONCORDAT AND MORATORIUM ON GENETICS AND INSURANCE

14 March 2005

If you would like more copies of this document, please contact:

Department of Health
652C Skipton House
80 London Road
LONDON SE1 6LH
Tel: 020 7972 1518
Fax: 020 7972 1717

INTRODUCTION

[5077]
1. The Government and the insurance industry recognise and wish to respond to understandable concerns about the potential use of personal genetic data by insurance companies. They consider that the relationship between medical data and insurance underwriting should be proportionate and based on sound evidence. They also accept the commercial principle that, unless otherwise agreed, insurance companies should have access to all relevant information to enable them to assess and price risk fairly in the interest of all their customers.

2. They agree to:
(i) create a policy framework ("Concordat") for cooperation that provides that insurers' use of genetic information is transparent, fair and subject to independent oversight, building on existing voluntary codes of practice;
(ii) extend the existing voluntary Moratorium on insurers' use of predictive genetic test results by five years to 1 November 2011, and to review this Concordat in 2008.

3. This document provides a single high-level policy agreement on the use of genetic test results in insurance underwriting practices. It is informed by discussions between the Association of British

Insurers, its member companies and the Government, the Genetics and Insurance Committee (GAIC), the Human Genetics Commission (HGC), patient groups and other interested parties.

BACKGROUND

4. Genetic testing is in its infancy and its long term implications for insurance, preventative medicine or treatment is indeterminate. The majority of genetic tests confirm diagnoses of ill health and inform treatments. Such diagnostic testing falls into the same category as other clinical technologies. The Concordat is concerned only with the far smaller number of tests used to predict future illness. Only in recent years has it become possible to design tests that examine genetic material for changes that may predict future disease. Even with such advances, very few tests can predict with any certainty when an illness might begin, or how severe it might be. There remain concerns that a minority of patients might be deterred from taking predictive genetic tests, if they fear that insurance companies may discriminate against them unfairly on the basis of the test results. The Concordat addresses those fears.

5. The Concordat preserves the principle that, unless otherwise agreed, insurance companies should have access to all relevant information to enable them to assess and price risk fairly in the interest of all their customers. So, if a customer for life insurance knows (from medical information, family history or tests) of a specific risk to his or her health, it should in all normal circumstances be disclosed. If the risk is not disclosed, the insurance company may face more, and more costly, claims than it was able to assume in setting the price of its insurance policies. This could potentially affect the future pricing or availability of insurance cover to all.

6. The current approach works in practice because the number of policies affected by non-disclosure of predictive genetic test results is low. The moratorium allows customers who have had adverse predictive genetic test results to obtain significant levels of cover, whilst protecting the customers of individual insurers from the consequences of extremely high claims, which have not been priced for.

PURPOSE

7. The Concordat establishes a robust and flexible framework for cooperation between the Government and the Association of British Insurers and its members, and builds on the voluntary Code of Practice already implemented by the Association. It is designed to balance societal concerns with the need for a commercially viable, long term and fair insurance market. The Concordat sets out the policy on how predictive genetic tests may be used and creates strict arrangements for their use by:

— requiring higher standards of evidence of increased risk than apply to other forms of medical information used by insurers;

— subjecting the evidence to scrutiny and approval by a Government appointed independent committee;

— creating a rigorous compliance process beyond the statutory and regulatory requirements; and

— creating an independent mechanism for handling any complaints that fall outside the jurisdiction of the Financial Ombudsman Service.

The Concordat and Moratorium protect the interests of both customers and insurers, by preserving customers' access to insurance, and insurers' right of equal access to information about risks.

PARTIES

8. The parties to this Concordat are the Government of the United Kingdom and Devolved Administrations ("the Government"), and the Association of British Insurers ("the ABI"). The ABI is the trade association for Britain's insurance industry. Its more than 400 member companies provide over 97% of the insurance business in the UK. The Government is represented by the Secretaries of State for Health and Trade & Industry and the Chancellor of the Exchequer.

9. Adoption of the Concordat is voluntary and is intended to be binding in honour only. It is a statement of intent and does not create legal obligations between the parties. However, some aspects, including the Moratorium, are in practice considered to be binding on all member companies of the ABI, via its Code of Practice.

10. Nothing in this Concordat should be construed as conflicting with statutory requirements or with other professional duties and obligations.

GENERAL PRINCIPLES

11. The parties to this Concordat agree the following principles:

— Insurers should not treat customers who have an adverse predictive genetic test result less favourably than others without justification;

— The technical, clinical and actuarial relevance of predictive genetic test results should be subject to independent oversight through GAIC;

— Customers should receive clear explanations of their rights. They should have access to a free, independent service for resolving complaints;
— Insurers and customers should have equal access to information that is material and relevant for insurance underwriting, except as provided for by the Concordat and the Moratorium on access to predictive genetic tests by insurers.

PREDICTIVE GENETIC TESTS

12. This agreement applies to predictive genetic tests, which examine the structure of chromosomes (cytogenetic tests) or detect abnormal patterns in the DNA of specific genes (molecular tests). It does not apply to non-genetic medical tests, for example blood or urine tests for cholesterol, prostate cancer, liver function or diabetes.

13. GAIC has said that it will consider applications to approve the use of predictive genetic test results by insurers for conditions that are:
– Monogenic (single gene disorders that are inherited in a simple fashion);
– Late-onset (symptoms are delayed until adult ages); and of
– High penetrance (a high probability that those with the gene will develop the disorder).

POLICY ON THE USE OF PREDICTIVE AND DIAGNOSTIC GENETIC TEST RESULTS

14. Insurers have agreed a set of measures intended to reassure patients so that they are not deterred from taking a predictive genetic test by fear of potential insurance consequences. The measures cover:
— the nature and detail of information sought from customers;
— how insurers will handle information provided voluntarily by customers; and
— the use made of that information.

15. The ABI will continue to work with GAIC, patient interest groups and industry stakeholders to examine methods of improving access to insurance for people with genetic diseases through, for example, development of standardised information about rare genetic conditions to give a common evidence base to underpin underwriting decisions.

INFORMATION SOUGHT FROM CUSTOMERS

16. Insurers agree that:
(i) Customers will not be asked to, nor be put under any pressure to, undergo a predictive genetic test in order to obtain insurance.
(ii) Customers will not be asked to disclose another person's predictive test results, such as a blood relative's test.
(iii) Customers will not be asked to disclose any predictive or diagnostic genetic test results acquired as part of clinical research.
(iv) Customers will not be required to disclose any predictive genetic test results that are made available after their policy has started, for as long as that policy is in force.
(v) Customers who have taken a predictive genetic test before the date of this Concordat will be treated in the same way as customers taking tests under the terms of the Concordat.
(vi) Insurers are permitted to seek, with customers' consent, access to certain family medical history, diagnostic (but not predictive) genetic test results, and to reports from GPs in order to accurately price the additional risk from any health problems an applicant discloses.
(vii) Customers can be asked by insurers to disclose the adverse results of predictive genetic tests approved by GAIC under specific conditions, when they apply for insurance policies over the financial limits of the moratorium.
(viii) Insurers have stringent procedures for seeking access to relevant medical information held by a GP or other clinician, agreed between the ABI and the British Medical Association.
(ix) Insurers will protect personal medical information in accordance with ABI Genetics Code.
(x) Insurers will destroy medical evidence when it is no longer relevant to them.

HANDLING OF INFORMATION PROVIDED VOLUNTARILY

17. Insurers agree that:
(i) Customers may choose to disclose predictive genetic test results that are in their favour in order to over-ride family history information. Individual insurance companies will publish information about the way they will use such test results to inform their underwriting decisions.
(ii) Most insurance companies will take into account the result of such a voluntarily disclosed genetic test, even if it has not been approved by GAIC, provided that the result is from a reputable source.

USE OF INFORMATION

18. Insurers agree that:

(i) They will not use information from predictive genetic test results to underwrite travel insurance, private medical insurance, or any other one-off or annual policy, or for long term care policies.

(ii) The broad classes of insurance for which genetic test results may be relevant are confined to the following products:
- life;
- critical illness; and
- income protection.

(iii) Where they make use of the results of GAIC approved tests to impose special terms or conditions, they will not impose unjustified exclusions from cover, or other special terms or conditions, which have the effect of preventing a policyholder from making a claim for a condition that is not related to the genetic condition identified by an approved test.

(iv) If a predictive genetic test is disclosed by mistake, insurers will ignore it.

THE MORATORIUM

19. The Moratorium on insurers' use of predictive tests is a key part of the overall Concordat. It makes an exception to the principle of disclosure. It allows patients who have taken a predictive genetic test to obtain significant levels of cover without disclosing the results of that test. Insurers have been prepared to bear the risks and costs of non-disclosure, which are spread across the broad pool of policyholders, because the number of policies affected by non-disclosure of predictive genetic tests is low. Accordingly the insurance industry and Government have agreed that the Moratorium should be extended.

20. The terms of the Moratorium are as follows:

(i) Customers will not be required to disclose the results of predictive genetic tests for policies up to £500,000 of life insurance, or £300,000 for critical illness insurance, or paying annual benefits of £30,000 for income protection insurance (the "financial limits"). More than 97% of policies issued in 2004 were below these limits in each category.

(ii) When the cumulative value of insurance exceeds the financial limits, insurers may seek information about, and customers must disclose, tests approved by GAIC for use for a particular insurance product, subject to the restrictions in the Concordat.

(iii) The Moratorium will expire on 1 November 2011, unless it is explicitly renewed through the Concordat.

COMPLIANCE

21. The ABI will continue to run an annual exercise assessing the compliance of its member companies with the ABI Code of Practice and the Moratorium, the results of which are published. GAIC will continue to comment on this compliance report. Government and ABI will explore further and consult GAIC and the HGC on the detailed aspects of the compliance and complaints system, in conjunction with the revision of the ABI Code of Practice.

CODE OF PRACTICE

22. The ABI will consult on and publish an updated Code of Practice ("the Code") laying down the standards that insurers should meet. Compliance with the Code is a condition of membership of the ABI. The new Code will update the detailed arrangements for the internal handling of genetic test results by nominated genetics underwriters and Chief Medical Officers within companies. It will also set strict standards for security and confidentiality of medical information. The ABI will revise and reissue the Code from time to time.

RESOLUTION OF DISPUTES AND COMPLAINTS

23. Customers have the right to ask an insurer to provide information on whether, and if so, how, a predictive test result has contributed to an underwriting decision. They have the right of appeal against an underwriting decision and a right to have a complaint heard fairly.

24. An insurer must tell a customer that they have the right to complain about a decision where a predictive test result has been disclosed and a customer believes that they have been unfairly treated. An insurer must explain the complaints process and adjudication system. It must investigate a complaint and give the customer a written decision as soon as is practicable and within the time limits set for authorised insurers by the Financial Services Authority.

25. Where a dispute is unresolved after this process, a complaint may be made:

(i) under the terms of the Financial Ombudsman Service, if a complainant believes that they have suffered or may suffer financial loss, material distress or material inconvenience as a result of an insurer's wrongful act or omission. The service, which is available to customers once a contract is signed, is free to customers and decisions are binding on insurers and complainants, subject to the right of insurers to seek judicial review or complainants to go to Court in the normal way; or

(ii) to the ABI, who will look again at all the material facts and decide whether a breach of the Code, Concordat or Moratorium has occurred. The service is free to customers and is binding on insurers.

26. The ABI may refer cases to GAIC if it is unable to resolve them or if it believes that the case has wider implications concerning genetic testing. Customers may also appeal to GAIC if the ABI is unable to resolve a complaint to the customer's satisfaction about the way that an insurer has dealt with their case.

27. The Committee will adjudicate on the use and interpretation of predictive genetic tests by insurers. It may review the material evidence and may seek further information before reaching a decision. The service is free to customers and Insurers agree to be bound by decisions taken by GAIC. However, the Committee will not be able to give personal advice about insurance, or to deal with complaints about the ABI process, about firms which are not insurance companies or members of the ABI, the operation of an insurance policy, or an insurer's proper use of its commercial judgement.

28. If a customer receives a final decision from GAIC or from the ABI, with which they are not satisfied, they may ask the ABI to convene an independent tribunal under the terms of its Code of Practice. The tribunal will be authorised to fine companies and compensate customers, normally within six months. The tribunal service is free to customers and is binding on insurers.

29. In every case a customer's legal rights are unimpaired. They remain free to take court proceedings against an insurer at any time.

THE GENETICS AND INSURANCE COMMITTEE (GAIC)

30. GAIC has developed and published the technical, clinical, and actuarial criteria for evaluating predictive genetic tests, their application to particular conditions and their reliability and relevance to particular types of insurance. GAIC's core duty will remain that of evaluating predictive genetic tests against those criteria and publicising its findings.

31. GAIC will provide independent, wide-ranging oversight of how insurers are using predictive genetic tests. It will continue to report to Health, Treasury, and Department of Trade and Industry Ministers on proposals it receives from insurance providers and the subsequent level of compliance by the industry. GAIC will publish an annual report containing details of tests reviewed and of insurers' compliance with the Concordat, Moratorium and ABI Code of Practice.

32. GAIC will liaise with the clinical genetics community, patient groups and experts in insurance and actuarial sciences. GAIC will monitor and publish trends on the nature and volume of NHS predictive genetic testing for late-onset, high penetrance single gene conditions, such as Huntington's Disease. It will also work with HGC to provide a horizon-scanning capability for potential future developments relevant to genetics and insurance.

THE HUMAN GENETICS COMMISSION

33. HGC will continue to advise Ministers on the ethical, legal and social implications of wider developments in genetics and their implications for healthcare and the adequacy of the regulatory framework that applies to human genetics. It will work closely with GAIC where these considerations relate to genetics and insurance.

DURATION AND REVIEW

34. The Concordat comes into effect on 14 March 2005. It may be updated in the light of experience, research findings and developments in genetic technology, and clinical practice.

35. The Moratorium on insurers' use of predictive genetic tests dating from 1 November 2001 will be extended by an extra five years until 1 November 2011.

36. There will be a review of the operation of this Concordat and Moratorium in 2008.

ASSOCIATION OF BRITISH INSURERS STATEMENT OF BEST PRACTICE FOR CRITICAL ILLNESS COVER

12 April 2006

NOTES

INTRODUCTION AND CONTENTS

[5078]

This Statement of Best Practice for Critical Illness Cover aims to help protect consumers and help them understand and compare critical illness policies through the following:

- Having a common format for the way Critical Illness Cover is described to potential buyers at the point of purchase
- The use of common Generic Terms
- The use of Model Wordings for Critical Illnesses and Exclusions which meet appropriate minimum standards

This latest version of the Statement of Best Practice for Critical Illness Cover has been produced as a result of a Full Review – see section 7. This Statement replaces the previous version published in August 2004. Insurers should adopt the changes as soon as is practical but must do so by no later than the end of April 2007.

The main changes to the previous Statement are:
- The introduction of a generic description of critical illness cover to improve consumer understanding.
- The use of more descriptive headings for critical illnesses in marketing material to improve clarity about what is, and is not, covered.
- Changes to the model critical illness definitions to help reduce the need for future changes and to improve consistency.
- Extending the number of conditions for which a model definition is available to improve clarity and make it easier for consumers to compare policies.
- Removing the categories of "core" and "additional" conditions – these are no longer relevant and can cause confusion.
- Extending the use of generic terms to include terms that can be used as part of the critical illness definitions or as part of a glossary to improve consistency and clarity.

This Statement of Best Practice is mandated for members of the Association of British Insurers (ABI) offering critical illness cover.

The Association of British Insurers is the trade association for insurance companies in the United Kingdom. We represent over 400 insurance companies, which provide over 96% of the insurance business in the UK. We represent insurance companies to the Government, and to regulatory and other agencies, and provide a wide range of services to our members.

1 GENERAL PRINCIPLES

[5079]
1.1 This Statement of Best Practice applies to critical illness cover offered by insurers who are members of the ABI and is based on the following principles.

1.2 Critical illness cover means insurance which pays out on meeting the policy definition of a specified critical illness and where all of the following are included:

1.2.1 **Cancer** – *excluding less advanced cases*

1.2.2 **Heart attack** – *of specified severity*

1.2.3 **Stroke** – *resulting in permanent symptoms*

Clarity

1.3 Wherever possible to aid consumer understanding, "Plain English" should always be used in product information, provided that this does not dilute or conflict with the meaning.

1.4 The headings form part of the model wordings. If an insurer includes an optional age limit in a particular condition, this should appear in the heading of the condition.

1.5 All model wordings should be as robust as possible in differentiating between what is, and is not, covered to:

1.5.1 Create a clear expectation of the scope and limitations of the cover.

1.5.2 Allow valid claims to be paid promptly.

1.5.3 Minimise the number of disputed claims to avoid disappointment.

1.6 All conditions should be listed in alphabetical order to help consumers compare products.

Generic terminology

1.7 For clarity, the generic terminology should be used in all cases where the appropriate generic terms apply. This is to ensure that insurers use common language to describe critical illness product features to help consumers compare different policies. Other terms to describe these features should not be used.

1.8 Insurers may use the descriptions of generic terms given in this Statement as definitions – for example, if a generic term is used in a critical illness definition, insurers may wish to add precision and clarity by defining that generic term as a "sub-definition". Alternatively, insurers may use the generic terms without defining them providing the terms are used in the appropriate context.

Product information

1.9 Critical illness cover is required by regulations to be described in a Policy Summary document carrying the FSA "Key Facts" logo or a Key Features document, depending on the underlying product type, for example, whether it is an investment or a pure protection product for the purposes of regulation. In this statement, we refer to these documents generically as the "product information".

1.10 The product information requirements set out in this document are in addition to (and, in the event of a conflict, are overruled by) any other regulatory or legal requirements.

1.11 The product information requirements in this Statement are intended to ensure that critical illness cover is described in the same way, regardless of the underlying product type. This is intended to allow consumers to compare the critical illness cover of different insurers, accepting that the underlying products may be different.

1.12 Insurers should give the product information to enquirers and potential customers (via intermediaries as appropriate) at the earliest opportunity to allow them to make meaningful product comparisons before purchase.

1.13 The product information requirements in this Statement apply to all individual long-term products featuring critical illness cover with guaranteed or reviewable premiums. This includes (but is not limited to) the following product types where critical illness cover is included as a standard feature or as an optional benefit:

1.13.1 Endowment

1.13.2 Whole of Life

1.13.3 Term Assurance

1.14 The format is based on the principle that critical illness cover is not usually a product in its own right, but is more frequently a benefit added to an underlying product type.

Group critical illness cover

1.15 Insurers offering group critical illness cover should follow the provisions relating to Generic Terminology and model wordings for critical illness definitions and exclusions. The other provisions of this Statement do not apply.

Implementation

1.16 The provisions apply to new policies effected on or after the implementation date adopted by the insurer.

1.17 An increment or increase to an existing policy effected after that date as a new policy may be excluded if it mirrors the original contract.

1.18 Insurers cannot normally apply revised definitions to existing in-force policies unless the policy specifically allows this.

Model wordings

1.19 Model wordings for medical conditions, surgical procedures, disabilities and policy exclusions are collectively referred to as the "model critical illness definitions" and "model exclusions". The constituents will be determined at each full review (and subsequently published) based on the following:

1.19.1 "Model critical illnesses" are the conditions for which there is a model wording available. They will normally be any existing model critical illnesses and additionally those conditions included in the policy of at least 75% of critical illness policies on the market at the time of the review.

1.19.2 "Model exclusions" are the policy exclusions and limitations where a model wording is available. These will normally be any existing model exclusions and additionally any exclusions and limitations included in the policy of at least 50% of critical illness policies on the market at the time of the review.

Basis of standard for new model wordings

1.20 All model wordings are on the basis of an "appropriate minimum standard". Insurers are free to offer additional cover by including other conditions or by offering additional cover as described in Principle 1.22 below.

Use of model wordings

1.21 Insurers are free to omit any condition (other than those listed in 1.2 above) or exclusion and may include any other conditions or exclusions as they see fit. While insurers are free to decide on the conditions and exclusions applicable to their products, where a model wording is available, it should be used.

1.22 Insurers will be deemed to be using the model wording (for a condition or exclusion) where it is modified to provide at least equivalent cover in the following ways:

1.22.1 By using the model wording and showing separately the additional cover offered.

1.22.2 By omitting a specific limitation or exclusion contained within the model wording for any condition or exclusion, while leaving the remaining words unchanged. For example, this could be by omitting the words "off-piste skiing" from the Hazardous sports & pastimes exclusion to cover incidents that would otherwise be excluded.

1.22.3 By using or omitting specified optional age limits.

1.23 Insurers should set out any additional specific claim requirements in their policy, for example in a general heading along the following lines:

> Example Policy Condition
>
> All diagnoses and medical opinions must be given by a medical specialist who:
>
> - is a Consultant at a hospital in the UK;
> - is acceptable to our Chief Medical Officer; and
> - is a specialist in an area of medicine appropriate to the cause of the claim.

Reviews of existing model wordings

1.24 No changes should be made to any existing agreed wordings without both the following:

1.24.1 A clear issue that has resulted (or is expected to result) in industry-wide problems for customers and/or insurers.

1.24.2 Agreement that the proposed change will address the issue.

2 GENERIC TERMS

[5080]

2.1 When generic terms are used they should have the meanings shown and other terms should not be used in their place. This is to ensure that the terms always have the same meaning.

2.2 Not all the terms will apply to the critical illness cover contained in all products. Insurers should only use those terms that are applicable.

2.3 The Generic Terms and associated descriptions as set out below are intended to establish the context in which each term should be used. Insurers are free to use them as definitions or as part of a glossary of terms.

Critical illness cover

2.4 Critical illness cover

Insurance which pays out on meeting the policy definition of a specified critical illness and where all of the following are included:

- **Cancer** – *excluding less advanced cases*
- **Heart attack** – *of specified severity*
- **Stroke** – *resulting in permanent symptoms*

Product features

2.5 Assessment period

The period during which we will assess a condition before we make a decision on whether or not to accept a claim. The assessment period will typically start on receipt of the claim and will not normally be longer than 12 months, as long as we have all the evidence we need. Also, the assessment period should only apply to claims for the conditions which must be permanent for cover to apply.

2.6 Deferred period

The period during which an insured person must be ill or disabled before we will pay any benefit.

2.7 Model critical illnesses

The critical illnesses for which model wordings are available.

2.8 Model exclusions

The exclusions to cover for which model wordings are available.

2.9 Survival period

The period after an insured event that the insured person has to survive before a claim becomes valid. A survival period normally applies to stand-alone critical illness cover or where the death benefit is a different amount from the critical illness benefit.

Terms that are used in definitions

2.12 Irreversible

Cannot be reasonably improved upon by medical treatment and/or surgical procedures used by the National Health Service in the UK at the time of the claim.

2.13 Occupation

A trade, profession or type of work undertaken for profit or pay. It is not a specific job with any particular employer and is independent of location.

2.14 Permanent

Expected to last throughout the insured person's life, irrespective of when the cover ends or the insured person retires.

2.15 Permanent neurological deficit with persisting clinical symptoms

Symptoms of dysfunction in the nervous system that are present on clinical examination and expected to last throughout the insured person's life.

Symptoms that are covered include numbness, hyperaesthesia (increased sensitivity), paralysis, localised weakness, dysarthria (difficulty with speech), aphasia (inability to speak), dysphagia (difficulty in swallowing), visual impairment, difficulty in walking, lack of coordination, tremor, seizures, lethargy, dementia, delirium and coma.

The following are not covered:

- An abnormality seen on brain or other scans without definite related clinical symptoms
- Neurological signs occurring without symptomatic abnormality, eg brisk reflexes without other symptoms
- Symptoms of psychological or psychiatric origin.

3 MODEL CRITICAL ILLNESSES

[5081]

3.1 For each condition, a heading, an extended heading (where applicable) and a definition are given.

3.2 The extended headings (including the descriptions given in italics after a "–") should be used where the critical illnesses are listed without the accompanying full definitions, for example in marketing material.

Marketing Material Examples: how headings should be used in marketing material:

- **Blindness** – *permanent and irreversible*
- **Cancer** – *excluding less advanced cases*
- **Heart attack** – *of specified severity*
- **Parkinson's disease before age 60** – *resulting in permanent symptoms*
- **Stroke** – *resulting in permanent symptoms*
- **Terminal illness**

3.3 Where the full definition is given, for example in policy documents, the descriptions associated with the headings may be omitted.

Policy Document Example: how headings may be presented with their definitions in policy documents:

Blindness

Permanent and irreversible loss of sight to the extent that even when tested with the use of visual aids, vision is measured at 3/60 or worse in the better eye using a Snellen eye chart.

or

Blindness – *permanent and irreversible*

Permanent and irreversible loss of sight to the extent that even when tested with the use of visual aids, vision is measured at 3/60 or worse in the better eye using a Snellen eye chart.

3.4 In this section, the use of [square brackets] means that the wording shown may vary as follows:

3.4.1 The age limits for Alzheimer's disease, motor neurone disease and Parkinson's disease are optional. However, if an age limit is included in the definition, it should also be included in the heading (as shown in the policy, product information and other material).

3.4.2 If insurers cover HIV, they should include any geographical limits and eligible occupations as appropriate.

The model critical illness definitions

3.5 Alzheimer's disease [before age x] – *resulting in permanent symptoms*

A definite diagnosis of Alzheimer's disease [before age x] by a Consultant Neurologist, Psychiatrist or Geriatrician. There must be permanent clinical loss of the ability to do all of the following:

- remember;
- reason; and
- perceive, understand, express and give effect to ideas.

For the above definition, the following are not covered:

- Other types of dementia.

3.6 Aorta graft surgery – *for disease*

The undergoing of surgery for disease to the aorta with excision and surgical replacement of a portion of the diseased aorta with a graft.

The term aorta includes the thoracic and abdominal aorta but not its branches.

For the above definition, the following are not covered:

- Any other surgical procedure, for example the insertion of stents or endovascular repair.
- Surgery following traumatic injury to the aorta.

3.7 Benign brain tumour – *resulting in permanent symptoms*

A non-malignant tumour or cyst in the brain, cranial nerves or meninges within the skull, resulting in permanent neurological deficit with persisting clinical symptoms.

For the above definition, the following are not covered:

- Tumours in the pituitary gland.
- Angiomas.

3.8 Blindness – *permanent and irreversible*

Permanent and irreversible loss of sight to the extent that even when tested with the use of visual aids, vision is measured at 3/60 or worse in the better eye using a Snellen eye chart.

3.9 Cancer – *excluding less advanced cases*

Any malignant tumour positively diagnosed with histological confirmation and characterised by the uncontrolled growth of malignant cells and invasion of tissue.

The term malignant tumour includes leukaemia, lymphoma and sarcoma.

For the above definition, the following are not covered:

- All cancers which are histologically classified as any of the following:
  - pre-malignant;
  - non-invasive;
  - cancer in situ;
  - having either borderline malignancy; or
  - having low malignant potential.
- All tumours of the prostate unless histologically classified as having a Gleason score greater than 6 or having progressed to at least clinical TNM classification T2N0M0.
- Chronic lymphocytic leukaemia unless histologically classified as having progressed to at least Binet Stage A.

- Any skin cancer other than malignant melanoma that has been histologically classified as having caused invasion beyond the epidermis (outer layer of skin).

3.10 Coma – *resulting in permanent symptoms*

A state of unconsciousness with no reaction to external stimuli or internal needs which:
- requires the use of life support systems for a continuous period of at least 96 hours; and
- results in permanent neurological deficit with persisting clinical symptoms.

For the above definition, the following is not covered:
- Coma secondary to alcohol or drug abuse.

3.11 Coronary artery by-pass grafts – *with surgery to divide the breastbone*

The undergoing of surgery requiring median sternotomy (surgery to divide the breastbone) on the advice of a Consultant Cardiologist to correct narrowing or blockage of one or more coronary arteries with by-pass grafts.

3.12 Deafness – *permanent and irreversible*

Permanent and irreversible loss of hearing to the extent that the loss is greater than 95 decibels across all frequencies in the better ear using a pure tone audiogram.

3.13 Heart attack – *of specified severity*

Death of heart muscle, due to inadequate blood supply, that has resulted in all of the following evidence of acute myocardial infarction:
- Typical clinical symptoms (for example, characteristic chest pain).
- New characteristic electrocardiographic changes.
- The characteristic rise of cardiac enzymes or Troponins recorded at the following levels or higher;
  - — Troponin T > 1.0 ng/ml
  - — AccuTnl > 0.5 ng/ml or equivalent threshold with other Troponin I methods.

The evidence must show a definite acute myocardial infarction.

For the above definition, the following are not covered:
- Other acute coronary syndromes including but not limited to angina.

3.14 Heart valve replacement or repair – *with surgery to divide the breastbone*

The undergoing of surgery requiring median sternotomy (surgery to divide the breastbone) on the advice of a Consultant Cardiologist to replace or repair one or more heart valves.

3.15 HIV infection – *caught [in the UK] from a blood transfusion, a physical assault or at work in an eligible occupation*

Infection by Human Immunodeficiency Virus resulting from:
- a blood transfusion given as part of medical treatment;
- a physical assault; or
- an incident occurring during the course of performing normal duties of employment [from the eligible occupations listed below][1];

after the start of the policy and satisfying all of the following:
- The incident must have been reported to appropriate authorities and have been investigated in accordance with the established procedures.
- Where HIV infection is caught through a physical assault or as a result of an incident occurring during the course of performing normal duties of employment, the incident must be supported by a negative HIV antibody test taken within 5 days of the incident.
- There must be a further HIV test within 12 months confirming the presence of HIV or antibodies to the virus.
- [The incident causing infection must have occurred in the UK][2].

For the above definition, the following is not covered:
- HIV infection resulting from any other means, including sexual activity or drug abuse.

3.16 Kidney failure – *requiring dialysis*

Chronic and end stage failure of both kidneys to function, as a result of which regular dialysis is necessary.

3.17 Loss of speech – *permanent and irreversible*

Total permanent and irreversible loss of the ability to speak as a result of physical injury or disease.

3.18 Loss of hands or feet – *permanent physical severance*

Permanent physical severance of any combination of 2 or more hands or feet at or above the wrist or ankle joints.

3.19 Major organ transplant

The undergoing as a recipient of a transplant of bone marrow or of a complete heart, kidney, liver, lung, or pancreas, or inclusion on an official UK waiting list for such a procedure.

For the above definition, the following is not covered:
- Transplant of any other organs, parts of organs, tissues or cells.

3.20 Motor neurone disease [before age x] – *resulting in permanent symptoms*

A definite diagnosis of motor neurone disease [before age x] by a Consultant Neurologist. There must be permanent clinical impairment of motor function.

3.21 Multiple sclerosis – *with persisting symptoms*

A definite diagnosis of Multiple Sclerosis by a Consultant Neurologist. There must be current clinical impairment of motor or sensory function, which must have persisted for a continuous period of at least 6 months.

3.22 Paralysis of limbs – *total and irreversible*

Total and irreversible loss of muscle function to the whole of any 2 limbs.

3.23 Parkinson's disease [before age x] – *resulting in permanent symptoms*

A definite diagnosis of Parkinson's disease [before age x] by a Consultant Neurologist. There must be permanent clinical impairment of motor function with associated tremor, rigidity of movement and postural instability.

For the above definition, the following is not covered:
- Parkinson's disease secondary to drug abuse.

3.24 Stroke – *resulting in permanent symptoms*

Death of brain tissue due to inadequate blood supply or haemorrhage within the skull resulting in permanent neurological deficit with persisting clinical symptoms.

For the above definition, the following are not covered:
- Transient ischaemic attack.
- Traumatic injury to brain tissue or blood vessels.

3.25 Terminal illness

Advanced or rapidly progressing incurable illness where, in the opinions of an attending Consultant and our Chief Medical Officer, the life expectancy is no greater than 12 months.

3.26 Third degree burns – *covering 20% of the body's surface area*

Burns that involve damage or destruction of the skin to its full depth through to the underlying tissue and covering at least 20% of the body's surface area.

3.27 Traumatic head injury – *resulting in permanent symptoms*

Death of brain tissue due to traumatic injury resulting in permanent neurological deficit with persisting clinical symptoms.

---

1 Note: include specified occupations if applicable

2 Note: include geographic limits as applicable

---

4 MODEL EXCLUSIONS

[5082]

4.1 Insurers are free to omit any of the model exclusions and may include additional exclusions.

4.2 Insurers may offer additional cover whilst still being deemed to use the model wordings, subject to doing so as set out above (see General Principles section 1.22).

4.3 The headings form part of the model wording.

4.4 All exclusions and limitations (not only model exclusions) should be contained in one section in the policy and marketing literature.

4.5 Insurers may define European Union as a list of EU Countries as at the start of the contract.

4.6 Insurers should state which exclusions apply to which conditions in their policy (and other benefits as appropriate, eg waiver of premium benefit) and should use an introductory policy wording to suit their individual policy wording style (see the example below).

Example introductory wording for model exclusions

We will not pay a critical illness claim if it is caused directly or indirectly from any of the following:

The model exclusions

4.7 Alcohol or drug abuse

Inappropriate use of alcohol or drugs, including but not limited to the following:

- Consuming too much alcohol.
- Taking an overdose of drugs, whether lawfully prescribed or otherwise.
- Taking Controlled Drugs (as defined by the Misuse of Drugs Act 1971) otherwise than in accordance with a lawful prescription.

4.8 Criminal acts

Taking part in a criminal act.

4.9 Flying

Taking part in any flying activity, other than as a passenger in a commercially licensed aircraft.

4.10 Hazardous sports and pastimes

Taking part in (or practising for) boxing, caving, climbing, horse-racing, jet skiing, martial arts, mountaineering, off-piste skiing, pot-holing, power-boat racing, under-water diving, yacht racing or any race, trial or timed motor sport.

4.11 HIV/AIDS

Infection with Human Immunodeficiency Virus (HIV) or conditions due to any Acquired Immune Deficiency Syndrome (AIDS).

4.12 Living abroad

Living outside of the European Union for more than 13 consecutive weeks in any 12 months.

4.13 Self-inflicted injury

Intentional self-inflicted injury.

4.14 Unreasonable failure to follow medical advice

Unreasonable failure to seek or follow medical advice.

4.15 War and civil commotion

War, invasion, hostilities (whether war is declared or not), civil war, rebellion, revolution or taking part in a riot or civil commotion.

5 HOW CRITICAL ILLNESS INSURANCE SHOULD BE DESCRIBED

[5083]

5.1 These provisions are intended to supplement the regulatory disclosure requirements which, for example, already require insurers to disclose significant or unusual exclusions. In the event of a conflict, any legal or regulatory requirement would take precedence.

5.2 In the following guidelines, the text shown in [square brackets] and in the examples is illustrative and may be omitted or amended from that shown. Otherwise, the actual wording shown should be used. Insurers are free to adopt any layout for their product information documents to suit their corporate style (eg 2 columns).

Description of critical illness cover

5.3 To help consumers get a consistent, accurate description of the cover, including when accelerated benefits pay out only once, insurers should always include the following generic description in all marketing material, adapted depending on the type of cover offered:

"[Life and critical illness cover] pays out [a lump sum/a monthly income until the end of the policy term] if you [either die or] are diagnosed with a critical illness that meets our policy definition [and then survive for at least x days]. We only cover the critical illnesses we define in our policy and no others."

Examples:

Stand-alone cover

Critical illness cover pays out a lump sum if you are diagnosed with a critical illness that meets our policy definition and then survive for at least 28 days. We only cover the critical illnesses we define in our policy and no others.

Accelerated cover

Life and critical illness cover pays out a lump sum if you either die or are diagnosed with a critical illness that meets our policy definition, We only cover the critical illnesses we define in our policy and no others.

Explanation of critical illness cover

5.4 In product information, insurers should list the critical illnesses covered. The following guidelines apply:

5.4.1 The opening question should refer to what is included in "critical illness [insurance/cover]".

5.4.2 It must be unambiguous that the list of conditions covered is exhaustive.

Phrases such as "We cover the following:" and "The following are included:" should not be used.

5.4.3 Insurers should state:

"The complete list of conditions we cover is set out below. These headings are only a guide to what is covered. The full definitions of the illnesses covered and the circumstances in which you can claim are given in the policy. These typically use medical terms to describe the illnesses but in some cases the cover may be limited. For example:

- Some types of cancer are not covered.
- To make a claim for some illnesses, you need to have permanent symptoms.

[Please let us know if you would like to see a copy of the policy. The definitions are also available on our website at www.abc-insurance.co.uk/ci-definitions.]"

5.4.4 Insurers should list all the conditions covered in alphabetical order to help consumers compare products.

5.4.5 If an insurer includes age limits in certain conditions, these should be shown in the heading of the condition.

Example: How critical illness cover might be described in product information

What conditions does critical illness insurance cover?

The complete list of conditions we cover is set out below. These headings are only a guide to what is covered. The full definitions of the illnesses covered and the circumstances in which you can claim are given in the policy. These typically use medical terms to describe the illnesses but in some cases the cover may be limited. For example:

- Some types of cancer are not covered.
- To make a claim for some illnesses, you need to have permanent symptoms.

Please let us know if you would like to see a copy of the policy. The definitions are also available on our website at www.abc-insurance.co.uk/ci-definitions.

- **Alzheimer's disease before age 60** – *resulting in permanent symptoms*
- **Aorta graft surgery** – *for disease*
- **Benign brain tumour** – *resulting in permanent symptoms*
- **Blindness** – *permanent and irreversible*
- **Cancer** – *excluding less advanced cases*
- **Coma** – *resulting in permanent symptoms*
- **Coronary artery by-pass grafts** – *with surgery to divide the breastbone*
- **Deafness** – *permanent and irreversible*
- **Heart attack** – *of specified severity*
- **Heart valve replacement or repair** – *with surgery to divide the breastbone*
- **HIV infection** – *caught in the UK from a blood transfusion, a physical assault or at work in an eligible occupation**
- **Kidney failure** – *requiring dialysis*
- **Loss of hands or feet** – *permanent physical severance*
- **Loss of speech** – *permanent and irreversible*
- **Major organ transplant**
- **Motor neurone disease before age 60** – *resulting in permanent symptoms*
- **Multiple sclerosis** – *with persisting symptoms*
- **Paralysis of limbs** – *total and irreversible*
- **Parkinson's disease before age 60** – *resulting in permanent symptoms*
- **Stroke** – *resulting in permanent symptoms*
- **Terminal illness**
- **Third degree burns** – *covering 20% of the body's surface area*
- **Traumatic head injury** – *resulting in permanent symptoms*

*The eligible occupations for HIV caught at work are:

- The emergency services – police, fire, ambulance
- The medical profession – including administrators, cleaners, dentists, doctors, nurses and porters
- The armed forces

General information about critical illness cover

5.5 Any obligations on the customer should be stated, together with the consequences of not meeting the obligation. For example:

5.5.1 To answer all questions on the application form carefully, to the best of the applicant's knowledge and belief

Note: See the ABI guidance "Application Form Design for Life and Health Protection Insurances" for examples.

5.5.2 To tell the insurer about health and occupation changes that happen between completing the application form and the policy starting.

Note: See the ABI guidance "Application Form Design for Life and Health Protection Insurances" for examples.

5.5.3 To maintain premiums

> Example: If you stop paying your monthly premium, your cover will end 28 days after the due date of the last premium you paid.

5.5.4 To tell the insurer about any changes in personal circumstances (for example, changes in smoking status, residence or occupation).

> Examples:
>
> You must tell us if you change your job. This could change your cover and/or your premium.
>
> You must tell us if you start living abroad. This could change your cover.

Further information

5.6 The product information should inform customers of the availability of the ABI Guide to Critical illness cover, which may be obtained from the insurer or the ABI.

5.7 Insurers should state that their product information complies with this Statement of Best Practice.

6 TOTAL PERMANENT DISABILITY

[5084]

6.1 There are a number of definitions used for Total Permanent Disability. For example, "total disability" may be measured by assessing the person's ability to perform certain of the following:

6.1.1 The insured person's "own occupation".

6.1.2 "Suited occupations".

6.1.3 "Any occupation" whatsoever.

6.1.4 A number of specified activities – for example, activities of daily living or functional ability tests.

Change of occupation

6.2 Depending on whether the definition used relies on the occupation of the person covered, this occupation may be disclosed and underwritten at the outset of the policy. Where this applies, subsequent changes of occupation may vary the initial underwriting assessment. Insurers normally deal with this issue in one or a combination of the following ways:

6.2.1 Notification is required. The new occupation is re-underwritten and the terms of the contract are adjusted if necessary. The customer's ability to perform an occupation (or one that is suited, depending on the definition) is judged against the occupation most recently notified (if all changes have been notified as required).

6.2.2 Notification is not required. The customer's ability to perform an occupation (or one that is suited, depending on the definition) is judged against the occupation being followed immediately before the claim. In this case, the insurer accepts the risk of changes in occupation.

6.2.3 Alternatively, the insurer judges the claim against the occupation declared in the application, regardless of subsequent changes.

Guidelines

6.3 Insurers are free to use any one or more definitions of disability they wish, including but not limited to those shown in 6.1 above.

6.4 Insurers should make it clear in their product information which procedure is adopted in relation to change of occupation together with the potential consequences.

6.5 If insurers require notification of changes in occupation, they should periodically remind the policyholder.

7 REVIEW PROCESS

[5085]

7.1 Industry-wide provisions, such as the product information format set out in this document, and model wordings based on market practice, legislation and medical science should be reviewed regularly to ensure that they remain up to date. The ABI will therefore make provision for reviews as follows.

Types of review

7.2 There will be 2 types of review:

7.2.1 Full Reviews (normally every 3 years); and

7.2.2 Intermediate Reviews.

7.3 The ABI will arrange to carry out all Full and Intermediate Reviews.

Full reviews

7.4 Full Reviews will be carried out every 3 years unless the ABI decides not to carry out the Full Review in which case it will be deferred for up to 1 year.

7.5 At a Full Review, the scope will be to review the product information format and all model wordings in line with the principles set out above. This will take into account changes in medical science, relevant "events" (such as changes in legislation since the last Full or Intermediate Review), experience, available research, and current market practice. The process should use the expertise of ABI members and appropriate liaisons.

7.6 At a Full Review, the recommendations will include a recommended process for implementing any changes and the review process itself should be reviewed and any changes put forward for the next review.

Intermediate reviews

7.7 An Intermediate Review may be held where a compelling issue is raised that is, for example, of a legal or regulatory nature. Less compelling issues will normally be dealt with at a Full Review.

7.8 The scope of Intermediate Reviews will be limited to the agreed impact of the issue raised and recommendations for implementing any changes. Other issues will be outside the scope of the Intermediate Review.

7.9 The normal process for establishing an Intermediate Review will be:

7.9.1 An issue is raised with the ABI.

7.9.2 The ABI decides on whether to carry out the Intermediate Review – otherwise the issue is recorded for the next Full Review.

EXAMPLE A – POLICY SUMMARY FOR CRITICAL ILLNESS COVER

Key facts
about our Term Assurance Plan
[5086]
ABC
Life Assurance Company Limited

ABC Life Assurance Company Limited is registered in England No 01234567. The company is authorised and regulated by the Financial Services Authority and has its registered office at Our Road, Any Town, County AB1 2CD.

What is a Term Assurance Plan?

A Term Assurance Plan is a long term insurance policy which can be tailored to meet your needs by allowing you to choose:

- **The type of cover you need** – your plan can include one of the following:
  - **Life cover** – pays out a lump sum if you die; or
  - **Critical illness cover** – pays out a lump sum if you are diagnosed with a critical illness that meets our policy definition and then survive for at least 28 days. We only cover the critical illnesses we define in our policy and no others; or
  - **Life and critical illness cover** – pays out a lump sum if you either die or are diagnosed with a critical illness that meets our policy definition. We only cover the critical illnesses we define in our policy and no others.
- **The level of cover you need** – the amount of the lump sum we pay out after a valid claim
- **How long the cover lasts** – the period of cover can be from 5 to 25 years provided the cover ends before age 70

After the lump sum is paid, your policy ends and you pay no more premiums.

The full list of critical illnesses we cover is shown on page 2 overleaf. There are also some circumstances when the plan will not pay out – these are shown on page 3 below.

How much does the plan cost?

You pay a premium every month by direct debit to keep your cover in force.

Your premium depends on the following:

- Your personal circumstances – for example, your age, health, sex, occupation and whether you smoke.
- The amount and type of cover you choose.
- How long you decide you want the cover to last.

If you stop paying your monthly premiums, your cover will end 30 days after the due date of the last premium you paid. The plan has no cash-in value at any time.

How much does the plan pay out?

The plan pays out a lump sum. You decide how much you would like this to be when you take the plan out.

Other than critical illness payments for children which do not affect your cover, the plan only pays out the main benefit once and then all cover ends. The attached personal illustration shows the period of cover, the type and amount of cover you have chosen and your monthly premium.

Who can the plan cover?

You can apply for the plan to cover:

- you alone;
- you and another person; or
- one or two people not including you.

If the plan covers two people it will only pay out once if either an insured person dies or has a valid critical illness claim during the period of cover, whichever is first – depending on the cover you choose.

Can children have critical illness cover?

If you choose critical illness cover, the children of each insured person also have critical illness cover, as long as the policy remains in force. The cover for each child starts when the child is three years old and ends when they become 18.

The amount we pay for a child meeting our definition of a critical illness is £10,000.

We will only pay one claim for each child. If we pay a claim for a child being diagnosed with a critical illness, cover for that child will end. However, cover will continue for the insured person and their other children (if any).

What conditions are covered by critical illness cover?

The complete list of conditions we cover is set out below. These headings are only a guide to what is covered. The full definitions of the illnesses covered and the circumstances in which you can claim are given in the policy. These typically use medical terms to describe the illnesses but in some cases the cover may be limited. For example:

- Some types of cancer are not covered.
- To make a claim for some illnesses, you need to have permanent symptoms.

Please let us know if you would like to see a copy of the policy. The definitions are also available on our website at www.abc-insurance.co.uk/ci-definitions.

- **Alzheimer's disease before age 60** – *resulting in permanent symptoms*
- **Aorta graft surgery** – *for disease*
- **Benign brain tumour** – *resulting in permanent symptoms*
- **Blindness** – *permanent and irreversible*
- **Cancer** – *excluding less advanced cases*
- **Coma** – *resulting in permanent symptoms*
- **Coronary artery by-pass grafts** – *with surgery to divide the breastbone*
- **Deafness** – *permanent and irreversible*
- **Heart attack** – *of specified severity*
- **Heart valve replacement or repair** – *with surgery to divide the breastbone*
- **HIV infection** – *caught in the UK from a blood transfusion, a physical assault or at work in an eligible occupation**
- **Kidney failure** – *requiring dialysis*
- **Loss of hands or feet** – *permanent physical severance*
- **Loss of speech** – *permanent and irreversible*
- **Major organ transplant**
- **Motor neurone disease before age 60** – *resulting in permanent symptoms*
- **Multiple sclerosis** – *with persisting symptoms*
- **Paralysis of limbs** – *total and irreversible*
- **Parkinson's disease before age 60** – *resulting in permanent symptoms*
- **Stroke** – *resulting in permanent symptoms*
- **Terminal illness**
- **Third degree burns** – *covering 20% of the body's surface area*
- **Traumatic head injury** – *resulting in permanent symptoms*

* The eligible occupations for HIV caught at work are:

- The emergency services – police, fire, ambulance
- The medical profession – including administrators, cleaners, dentists, doctors, nurses and porters
- The armed forces

When will the plan not pay out?

We will not pay a claim for life cover or for critical illness cover and all cover under the plan may be cancelled:

- If you do not disclose relevant information we ask for when you take out your plan. You should not assume that we will write to your doctor, it is your responsibility to complete the application form properly.
- If you do not tell us about any of the following changes that happen between completing the application form and when your plan starts[1]:
    - Your health
    - Family history
    - Occupation
    - Travel or residence
    - Hazardous pastimes
    - Alcohol consumption
    - Start smoking
    - Use of drugs (for example, cocaine or heroin)

We will not pay a claim for life cover:

- If an insured person commits suicide in the first year of the policy.

We will not pay a claim for critical illness cover:

- If you have an illness that does not meet our definition of one of the critical illnesses we cover. For example, some types of cancer are not covered.
- If your plan is for critical illness cover only and you die within 28 days of meeting our definition of the critical illness.
- If your claim arises within three months of reinstating a plan that has previously ended.
- If the cause of the claim results from alcohol or drug abuse, criminal acts, flying, hazardous sports and pastimes, HIV/AIDS, self-inflicted injury, unreasonable failure to follow medical advice or war and civil commotion.

- If the claim is for children's critical illness cover and:
  - — the condition was present at birth; or
  - — the symptoms first arose before the child was covered; or
  - — if the child dies within 28 days of meeting our definition of the critical illness.

Full details of what is covered, and any standard exclusions and restrictions to the cover are given in sections 2 and 4 respectively of the policy document. You can ask us for a sample copy of the policy document.

We may apply specific exclusions when we accept your policy. These will be shown in your acceptance letter and policy schedule.

What other options are available?

You can choose to include Waiver of Premium Benefit. This benefit pays your premiums if you are too ill to work for six months or more as a result of illness or injury. Full details of this extra benefit are given in section 6 of the policy document. You can ask us for a copy of this.

Your personal illustration shows whether Waiver of Premium Benefit is included in your plan and, if so, the cost.

How do I take out a plan?

You can take out a Term Assurance Plan by sending us a filled in application form.

After the plan starts, is there anything I need to do?

If your plan includes critical illness cover, you must tell us if you do any of the following or your plan will not pay out:

- Change your job. This could change your cover and your premium.
- Start living abroad. This could change your cover.

Further Information

Your cancellation rights

When we accept your application for the plan, we will send you a notice explaining your right to cancel. You will then have 30 days in which you can cancel the policy. If you do this, we will refund any premiums you have paid.

Making a claim

To make a claim, you should contact our Claims Department at:

ABC Life
Our Road
Any Town
County
AB1 2CD

Phone: 01234 56789

Complaints

If you have any complaint about this plan, or about any part of our service, contact our Customer Service Manager at:

ABC Life
Our Road
Any Town
County AB1 2CD
Phone: 01234 56789

If you are not satisfied with the way we deal with your complaint, you can contact the Financial Ombudsman Service at:

ABC Life
Our Road
Any Town
County AB1 2CD
Phone: 01234 56789

Making a complaint will not affect your right to take legal action. You can ask us for details of our compensation arrangements.

Law

The Law of England applies to this plan.

The Financial Services Compensation Scheme (FSCS)

The plan is covered by the FSCS. You may be entitled to compensation from the scheme if we cannot meet our obligations. This depends on the type of business and the circumstances of the claim. You can get more details from us or from the Financial Services Authority.

Tax

The proceeds from this plan are free from UK income tax and capital gains tax. However, if we pay the proceeds after the death of an insured person, inheritance tax may be due on the benefit paid. You may be able to avoid inheritance tax by using an appropriate trust. Ask your financial adviser for more details.

The Government may change the tax position described above.

A Guide to Critical illness cover

The ABI (Association of British Insurers) give general information about critical illness cover in their booklet 'A Guide to Critical illness cover'. You can ask us for a copy or you can get a copy at www.abi.org.uk or by writing to:

The Association of British Insurers
51 Gresham St
London EC2V 7HQ.

Please Note

This leaflet complies with the ABI Statement of Best Practice for Critical illness cover. It is a guide to our Term Assurance Plan and is based on our understanding of current laws and tax rules. Further details are given in the plan schedule and the policy document. You should get expert advice about the legal and tax information in this leaflet.

ABC Life is registered in England no 01234567.
The registered office is ABC Life, Our Road, Any Town, County AB1 2CD.
ABC Life is authorised and regulated by the Financial Services Authority.

---

1 See ABI guidance "Application Form Design for Life and Health Protection Insurances"

EXAMPLE B – KEY FEATURES FOR CRITICAL ILLNESS COVER

Key facts
Key Features of the Term Assurance Plan

[5087]
ABC
Life Assurance Company Limited

Its aims

The plan aims to do the following.

- To provide the amount of cover you choose.
- To provide cover for the period you choose.
- To provide the type of cover you choose. Your plan can include one of the following:
  - **Life cover** – pays out a lump sum if you die; or
  - **Critical illness cover** – pays out a lump sum if you are diagnosed with a critical illness that meets our policy definition and then survive for at least 28 days. We only cover the critical illnesses we define in our policy and no others; or
  - **Life and critical illness cover** – pays out a lump sum if you either die or are diagnosed with a critical illness that meets our policy definition. We only cover the critical illnesses we define in our policy and no others.
- After the lump sum is paid, your policy ends and you pay no more premiums.
- The full list of critical illnesses we cover is shown on page 3 overleaf. There are also some circumstances when the plan will not pay out – these are shown on page 3 below.

Your commitment

You must do the following.

- Disclose relevant information we ask for when you take out your plan. If you do not do this, it could mean your plan will not pay out. You should not assume that we will write to your doctor – it is your responsibility to complete the application form properly.
- Tell us about any of the following changes that happen between completing the application form and when your plan starts[2]:
  - Your health
  - Family history
  - Occupation
  - Travel or residence
  - Hazardous pastimes
  - Alcohol consumption
  - Start smoking
  - Use of drugs (for example, cocaine or heroin)

  If you do not do this, it could mean your plan will not pay out.
- Pay the premium by direct debit every month during the period of cover.

Risk factors

The plan carries the following risks.

- If you stop paying your monthly premiums your cover will end 30 days after due date of the last premium you paid.
- We will not pay out in the circumstances described under "When will the plan not pay out" on page 3.
- The plan has no cash-in value at any time.

What is a Term Assurance Plan?

A Term Assurance Plan is a long term insurance policy which can be tailored to meet your needs by allowing you to choose:

- **The type of cover you need** – your plan can include one of the following:
  - **Life cover** – pays out a lump sum if you die; or
  - **Critical illness cover** – pays out a lump sum if you are diagnosed with a critical illness that meets our policy definition and then survive for at least 28 days. We only cover the critical illnesses we define in our policy and no others; or
  - **Life and critical illness cover** – pays out a lump sum if you either die or are diagnosed with a critical illness that meets our policy definition. We only cover the critical illnesses we define in our policy and no others.
- **The level of cover you need** – the amount of the lump sum we pay out after a valid claim
- **How long the cover lasts** – the period of cover can be from 5 to 25 years provided the cover ends before age 70

After the lump sum is paid, your policy ends and you pay no more premiums.

The full list of critical illnesses we cover is shown on page 2 below. There are also some circumstances when the plan will not pay out – these are shown on page 3 below.

How much does the plan cost?

You pay a premium every month by direct debit to keep your cover in force.

Your premium depends on the following:

- Your personal circumstances – for example, your age, health, sex, occupation and whether you smoke.
- The amount and type of cover you choose.
- How long you decide you want the cover to last.

If you stop paying your monthly premiums, your cover will end 30 days after the due date of the last premium you paid. The plan has no cash-in value at any time.

How much does the plan pay out?

The plan pays out a lump sum. You decide how much you would like this to be when you take the plan out.

Other than critical illness payments for children which do not affect your cover, the plan only pays out the main benefit once and then all cover ends. The attached personal illustration shows the period of cover, the type and amount of cover you have chosen and your monthly premium.

Who can the plan cover?

You can apply for the plan to cover:

- you alone;
- you and another person; or

- one or two people not including you.

If the plan covers two people it will only pay out once if either an insured person dies or has a valid critical illness claim during the period of cover, whichever is first – depending on the cover you choose.

Can children have critical illness cover?

If you choose critical illness cover, the children of each insured person also have critical illness cover, as long as the policy remains in force. The cover for each child starts when the child is three years old and ends when they become 18.

The amount we pay for a child meeting our definition of a critical illness is £10,000.

We will only pay one claim for each child. If we pay a claim for a child being diagnosed with a critical illness, cover for that child will end. However, cover will continue for the insured person and their other children (if any).

What conditions are covered by critical illness cover?

The complete list of conditions we cover is set out below. These headings are only a guide to what is covered. The full definitions of the illnesses covered and the circumstances in which you can claim are given in the policy. These typically use medical terms to describe the illnesses but in some cases the cover may be limited. For example:

- Some types of cancer are not covered.
- To make a claim for some illnesses, you need to have permanent symptoms.

Please let us know if you would like to see a copy of the policy. The definitions are also available on our website at www.abc-insurance.co.uk/ci-definitions.

- **Alzheimer's disease before age 60** – *resulting in permanent symptoms*
- **Aorta graft surgery** – *for disease*
- **Benign brain tumour** – *resulting in permanent symptoms*
- **Blindness** – *permanent and irreversible*
- **Cancer** – *excluding less advanced cases*
- **Coma** – *resulting in permanent symptoms*
- **Coronary artery by-pass grafts** – *with surgery to divide the breastbone*
- **Deafness** – *permanent and irreversible*
- **Heart attack** – *of specified severity*
- **Heart valve replacement or repair** – *with surgery to divide the breastbone*
- **HIV infection** – *caught in the UK from a blood transfusion, a physical assault or at work in an eligible occupation**
- **Kidney failure** – *requiring dialysis*
- **Loss of hands or feet** – *permanent physical severance*
- **Loss of speech** – *permanent and irreversible*
- **Major organ transplant**
- **Motor neurone disease before age 60** – *resulting in permanent symptoms*
- **Multiple sclerosis** – *with persisting symptoms*
- **Paralysis of limbs** – *total and irreversible*
- **Parkinson's disease before age 60** – *resulting in permanent symptoms*
- **Stroke** – *resulting in permanent symptoms*
- **Terminal illness**
- **Third degree burns** – *covering 20% of the body's surface area*
- **Traumatic head injury** – *resulting in permanent symptoms*

* The eligible occupations for HIV caught at work are:

- The emergency services – police, fire, ambulance
- The medical profession – including administrators, cleaners, dentists, doctors, nurses and porters
- The armed forces

When will the plan not pay out?

We will not pay a claim for life cover or for critical illness cover and all cover under the plan may be cancelled:

- If you do not disclose relevant information we ask for when you take out your plan. You should not assume that we will write to your doctor, it is your responsibility to complete the application form properly.
- If you do not tell us about any of the following changes that happen between completing the application form and when your plan starts[3]:
  - Your health
  - Family history
  - Occupation

- Travel or residence
- Hazardous pastimes
- Alcohol consumption
- Start smoking
- Use of drugs (for example, cocaine or heroin)

We will not pay a claim for life cover:

- If an insured person commits suicide in the first year of the policy.

We will not pay a claim for critical illness cover:

- If you have an illness that does not meet our definition of one of the critical illnesses we cover. For example, some types of cancer are not covered.
- If your plan is for critical illness cover only and you die within 28 days of meeting our definition of the critical illness.
- If your claim arises within three months of reinstating a plan that has previously ended.
- If the cause of the claim results from alcohol or drug abuse, criminal acts, flying, hazardous sports and pastimes, HIV/AIDS, self-inflicted injury, unreasonable failure to follow medical advice or war and civil commotion.
- If the claim is for children's critical illness cover and:
  — the condition was present at birth; or
  — the symptoms first arose before the child was covered; or
  — if the child dies within 28 days of meeting our definition of the critical illness.

Full details of what is covered, and any standard exclusions and restrictions to the cover are given in sections 2 and 4 respectively of the policy document. You can ask us for a sample copy of the policy document.

We may apply specific exclusions when we accept your policy. These will be shown in your acceptance letter and policy schedule.

What other options are available?

You can choose to include Waiver of Premium Benefit. This benefit pays your premiums if you are too ill to work for six months or more as a result of illness or injury. Full details of this extra benefit are given in section 6 of the policy document. You can ask us for a copy of this.

Your personal illustration shows whether Waiver of Premium Benefit is included in your plan and, if so, the cost.

After the plan starts, is there anything I need to do?

If your plan includes critical illness cover, you must tell us if you do any of the following or your plan will not pay out:

- Change your job. This could change your cover and your premium.
- Start living abroad. This could change your cover.

Further Information

Your cancellation rights

When we accept your application for the plan, we will send you a notice explaining your right to cancel. You will then have 30 days in which you can cancel the policy. If you do this, we will refund any premiums you have paid.

Making a claim

To make a claim, you should contact our Claims Department at:

ABC Life
Our Road
Any Town
County AB1 2CD
Phone: 01234 56789

Complaints

If you have any complaint about this plan, or about any part of our service, contact our Customer Service Manager at:

ABC Life
Our Road
Any Town
County AB1 2CD

Phone: 01234 56789

If you are not satisfied with the way we deal with your complaint, you can contact the Financial Ombudsman Service at:

South Quay Plaza
183 Marsh Wall
London E14 9SR
Phone: 020 7964 1000

Making a complaint will not affect your right to take legal action. You can ask us for details of our compensation arrangements.

Law

The Law of England applies to this plan.

The Financial Services Compensation Scheme (FSCS)

The plan is covered by the FSCS. You may be entitled to compensation from the scheme if we cannot meet our obligations. This depends on the type of business and the circumstances of the claim. You can get more details from us or from the Financial Services Authority.

Tax

The proceeds from this plan are free from UK income tax and capital gains tax. However, if we pay the proceeds after the death of an insured person, inheritance tax may be due on the benefit paid. You may be able to avoid inheritance tax by using an appropriate trust. Ask your financial adviser for more details.

The Government may change the tax position described above.

A Guide to Critical illness cover

The ABI (Association of British Insurers) give general information about critical illness cover in their booklet 'A Guide to Critical illness cover'. You can ask us for a copy or you can get a copy at www.abi.org.uk or by writing to:

The Association of British Insurers
51 Gresham St
London EC2V 7HQ.

Please Note

This leaflet complies with the ABI Statement of Best Practice for Critical illness cover. It is a guide to our Term Assurance Plan and is based on our understanding of current laws and tax rules. Further details are given in the plan schedule and the policy document. You should get expert advice about the legal and tax information in this leaflet.

ABC Life is registered in England no 01234567.
The registered office is ABC Life, Our Road, Any Town, County AB1 2CD.
ABC Life is authorised and regulated by the Financial Services Authority.

---

2 See ABI guidance "Application Form Design for Life and Health Protection Insurances"

3 See ABI guidance "Application Form Design for Life and Health Protection Insurances"

ABI STATEMENT OF BEST PRACTICE FOR THE SELLING OF PRIVATE MEDICAL INSURANCE COVER

October 2007

NOTES

INTRODUCTION

[5088]

1. This Statement has been prepared to ensure that the particular information needs of individual customers are met when buying a private medical insurance (PMI) policy.

2. This Statement was revised in 2006 following consultation with members and stakeholder groups. Its primary focus remains the information-needs of individual customers when they are choosing between the variety of PMI policies on the market.

3. The common definitions were revised in 2007 following consultation with members and stakeholder groups, to improve clarity and further explain the approach to cover for cancer. The ABI appreciates the need for insurers to control and manage their portfolios in accordance with their own approach to risk. Guidance on the common definitions was published in October 2007.

4. This Statement is mandated for members of the Association of British Insurers (ABI) offering PMI cover and is recommended to those members of AMEI who are not members of the ABI. It replaces all previous versions, including the one published by ABI in January 2004, and the General Insurance Standards Council (GISC) Practice Requirement for Private Medical Insurance. The Statement is based on previous work done by the industry that had been adopted by the GISC. ABI took over this wording because GISC's regulatory function passed to the FSA on 14 January 2005.

5. Members should implement the revised Statement and Common Definitions as soon as possible, but in any event the Statement by 31st December 2007 and the Common Definitions by 31st December 2008.

6. The Association of British Insurers is the trade association for insurance companies in the United Kingdom. We represent over 400 insurance companies, which provide over 96% of the insurance business in the UK. We represent insurance companies to the Government and to regulatory and other agencies, and provide a wide range of services to our members.

EXPLANATION TO CUSTOMERS

7. There are particular aspects of PMI contracts which need especially careful explanation to retail customers. Under FSA regulation, the significant features and benefits of the product, and also any significant and unusual exclusions or limitation must be explained to the customer before conclusion of the PMI contract.

8. Companies should provide customers with a full and clear explanation of the following points (A–E) at an appropriate time, but no later than the point at which the terms and conditions are provided to the customer:

(A) The benefits payable under the policy (ie the benefit table), any significant medical or technical exclusions or restrictions applying, which are included in and imposed by the standard terms and conditions; the underwriting of the individual application which will affect the scope of the cover or benefits.

(B) The company's definitions of any words or phrases used in the policy documents may differ from clear English definitions, or may be used differently by different companies. This is in line with the FSA's Treating Customers Fairly initiative that states that policies should be clear, fair and not misleading.

(C) The cover available (or otherwise) for pre-existing conditions.

(a) Where no medical history is asked for (moratorium)

- A clear explanation that any pre-existing and related medical conditions will not be covered for an initial period;
- When any such conditions may become eligible for cover after there has been a continuous period, stipulated by the insurer, during which time there has not been treatment, symptoms, medication, tests and or advice for that condition (or a related one). Retail customers must be advised not to forego medical treatment in an attempt to achieve this;
- That some conditions, eg chronic conditions which require continuous treatment and or monitoring, are not likely to be eligible for such delayed cover because of the need to remain free of treatment, medication, tests and advice;
- That full medical underwriting (FMU) is an alternative. **NB Any company offering a moratorium MUST also offer FMU.**

(b) Where medical history is asked for (medical underwriting)

- An explanation that possible exclusions specific to the individual or extra premium relating to a pre-existing medical condition(s) that is (are) likely to recur and that this might include any conditions related to it.

(c) Switches (insurers should explain the underwriting terms they use for switches)

- If the customer is moving from one provider of PMI to another or transferring from one type of PMI policy to another the customer should be informed that policy conditions and benefits may vary. The customer should also be given sufficient information concerning the new product to enable them to compare the two products and make an informed decision whether to move.

(D) Arrangements for making and paying claims, including whether payment is made directly to the provider of services or to the insured.

(E) The fact that premiums and coverage may vary for all policyholders. The fact that premiums are likely to rise above the rate of inflation on renewal and those premiums will generally increase with age. Against this any discounts and the operation and effects of any excess will be explained.

9. In addition, the customer should be given or be directed to the ABI Guide 'Are you buying PMI' and, for moratorium sales, the insurer's leaflet 'How you can apply for cover'.

CUSTOMER INFORMATION

10. In addition to the requirements set out in the FSA regulations, there are specific requirements relating to the information provided by PMI providers resulting from industry agreements.

11. Documents (i), (ii) and (iii) should be provided to the customer no later than the information required by FSA rules (ICOB 5.3.1.R – 5.3.8R). The information contained in these documents must be provided in a durable medium but may be contained within other documentation. This will usually be before conclusion of contract, although certain exemptions apply. The FSA's Insurance Conduct of Business (ICOB) rules are available at www.fsa.gov.uk.

(i) ABI Guide 'Are you buying PMI?'
This Guide is produced by the ABI and must be given to any UK based individual (retail) customers who enquire about purchasing PMI. It clarifies various aspects of PMI policies such as premium increases and the consequences of changing product or insurer. This guide is available from the ABI.

(ii) 'How you can apply for cover'
This guide has a specified format to enable every insurer offering a moratorium to explain how different conditions will be affected by their moratorium, as opposed to being fully underwritten. The examples are specified so that a prospective purchaser can compare how different companies' moratoriums will affect the same conditions (see Appendix A).

(iii) 'Your PMI Cover for *xxx*[1] condition(s)' or 'Chronic Conditions Explained'
This information has a prescribed format that companies must use to explain any cover they provide for chronic conditions. This must be provided where a product excludes cover for chronic conditions. Using a generic title would enable companies to include information on other areas of cover. Companies must make clear how they define their approach to cancer and include Example 3 of Appendix B (see Appendices B and C).

(iv) Common Definitions
There are ten industry agreed Common Definitions, which should be used in policy or other documents that describe the cover. The Common Definitions are not designed to describe the scope of the cover provided by the product, but to ensure that in whatever context the words or phrases so defined are used, they will have the same meaning (see Appendix C).

PROCESSING OF INFORMATION

12. As information collected in relation to the selling of PMI policies is often medical information, insurers will ensure that all information obtained from customers is treated as confidential and in accordance with the Access to Medical Reports Act 1988 and Access to Health Records Act 1990.

13. In addition, the Association issues guidance to its members including PMI providers to assist their compliance with legislation. This includes the Disability Discrimination Act 1995 and the Data Protection Act 1998, in which information relating to someone's physical or mental health is defined as 'sensitive personal data', and is subject to additional safeguards under Schedule 3 of the Act.

[1] eg '. . . for chronic conditions and cancer'

APPENDIX A

How you can apply for cover

The purpose of Private Medical Insurance

[5089]

Insurance policies provide cover against an unexpected event happening after the start of the policy. In health Insurance this means cover for the cost of private medical treatment for unforeseen medical conditions arising after your policy starts.

Your policy is not intended to cover conditions that you already have before your policy starts – these are called 'pre-existing conditions'. Conditions that are related to pre-existing conditions are also not usually covered. A related condition is one that is caused by, or could be the cause of, another condition.

Your policy will not cover all medical treatments. You should check your policy carefully to see which treatments are covered and which are not.

Your PMI underwriting options

Underwriting is the process by which an insurer decides on what terms it will accept a person for cover based on the information they supply. This leaflet is designed to explain the two most common methods by which you can apply for cover, so that you can decide which one best suits your requirements.

Your choices

You have a choice between two ways of applying for the cover (*insurer's name/product*) provides.

1. Full medical underwriting

This is based on your completing a health questionnaire (also called a Medical History Declaration)

If you choose this option, you will be asked a number of questions about your health. These will enable us to understand your medical history (and that of any member of your family whom you wish to insure). It is important that you consider the questions carefully, for each person to be covered, and answer them fully. We will review your details and decide the basis on which we can accept you for cover. If necessary, we may need to ask your doctor for any further information we need to help us to do this.

If you have a pre-existing condition that may need treatment in the future, we will usually exclude it from the cover along with any conditions related to it. We will show any exclusions on the policy schedule you receive from us when we have processed your application. (The same process will also apply for any members of your family included in your application.)

If we exclude treatment for a pre-existing condition at the time when your policy starts we will, in some cases, review the exclusion in future should you wish us to do so.

Of course, any new medical conditions arising after the start of your policy will be covered immediately subject to the policy terms and conditions.

Note: You must ensure that you provide full and accurate information in answer to the questionnaire. Failure to do so may mean that we cannot cover a claim or even that your policy is void. If you are unsure whether we would want to know about a particular condition, you should tell us about it.

What is the advantage of full medical underwriting?

Although this option involves more of your time when completing your application, it does mean that, when you receive your policy documentation, you will know which conditions are excluded from cover.

2. Moratorium

With this option you do not need to fill in a health statement. Instead, we automatically exclude any pre-existing conditions for which you (and any family member included in your application) have received treatment and/or medication, or asked advice on, or had symptoms of (whether or not diagnosed), during the (usually) five years immediately before your PMI cover started.

However, if you do not have any symptoms, treatment, medication, or advice for those pre-existing conditions, and any directly related conditions, for (usually) two continuous years after your policy starts, then we will reinstate cover for those conditions.

You should understand that long-term medical conditions, which are likely to continue to need regular or periodic treatment, medication or medical advice, will never be covered by your policy.

You should not delay seeking medical advice or treatment for a pre-existing condition simply to obtain cover under your policy.

Of course, as with full medical underwriting, new medical conditions arising after the start of your policy will be covered immediately subject to the policy terms and conditions.

What is the advantage of moratorium underwriting?

If you choose this option you will only be asked to provide basic information about you and any members of your family you wish to insure. You will not be asked to disclose details of your medical history, but it relies on you to understand that if you have any medical conditions these will be excluded from cover. Also, if you can satisfy the criteria (usually two years) outlined in the above section, for a pre-existing condition, then treatment for that condition will automatically be covered should it later recur, subject to the policy terms and conditions.

Examples of how both options work:

Example 1

I had an operation on my right knee recently. Will I be covered for any further treatment to it after my policy starts?

Insurer's response, FMU

Insurer's response, Moratorium

Example 2

Some time after my cover begins, I go to the doctor for a routine visit. A heart condition is diagnosed and it must have started to develop before my policy began. What is the position?

Insurer's response, FMU

Insurer's response, Moratorium

Example 3

What if I suspect I am suffering from a condition (for example, I have a lump) but have not seen a doctor about it, nor received any firm diagnosis before my cover starts? Will I be covered if I need to have any investigations or treatment for the condition once my policy has started?

Insurer's response, FMU

Insurer's response, Moratorium

For Moratorium Option only – Example 4

How do regular check-ups affect the moratorium?

Insurer's response, Moratorium

Please note:

This leaflet is intended as a general guide only. The policy gives full details of the cover provided. It is important that you read your schedules together with your policy document. If you have any questions, ask the person arranging your PMI cover or phone our Helpline on [XXXXXX] and our staff will be pleased to assist you. A specimen copy of the policy is available on request should you wish to see this before making your decision. You will also have xx days from the time you receive your policy documents to review them. If, during this period, you decide to change your mind, you will receive a full refund of any premiums you have paid, providing that you have not already made a claim.

APPENDIX B

[5090]
'Your PMI Cover for *xxx*[2] condition(s)' or 'Chronic Conditions Explained'

This information is intended to explain to retail customers any cover that is provided for chronic conditions and other areas of cover.

The explanation should be provided to the retail customers at the point of sale. It is recommended that members also send it to existing retail customers.

Members may choose to produce this information in the form of a leaflet or leaflets or to incorporate it within their other point of sale material. Only those examples relevant to the product need be used. (This information does not apply to international products that include cover for chronic conditions).

Member firms must make clear how they define their approach to cancer and include Example 3 in the relevant literature (also see 'Explanation of Cancer Cover' below).

> **Note: The words "or leaflets" have been added to make it clear to members that they are free to provide additional information on specific conditions where they believe that their customers would find this helpful.** Some insurers produce separate leaflets giving details of their coverage of particular conditions, for example cancer. The Statement of Best Practice is designed to permit this flexible approach.

Members should use the following prescribed format:

- The explanation should include an introductory paragraph stating its purpose.
- First Heading: **'What is a chronic condition?'** This should start with the agreed Common Definition followed by a general description of the insurers' own approach to covering these.
- Second Heading: **'What does this mean in practice?'** This should explain the process undertaken by the insurer to establish whether or not a condition is, or has become, chronic and the subsequent actions arising from this. **Retail customers should be warned if cover will stop once a condition is deemed to be chronic and the implications of this.**
- Third Heading: **'What if your condition gets worse?'** This should explain what happens when a condition that has been deemed chronic subsequently has an acute flare-up.
- Fourth Heading: **'Examples of chronic conditions'** The following examples should be worded exactly as they are shown below, with each insurer explaining how they would respond in the circumstances described. Where the example relates to a benefit which is not included in the product it need not be used, eg Example 5 relates to treatment by an osteopath, if osteopathy is not covered under the policy this example should not be used. The examples are: angina and heart disease; asthma; cancer; diabetes; hip pain.

Example 1 – Angina and Heart Disease

Alan has been with *insurer's name* for many years. He develops chest pains and is referred by his GP to a specialist. He has a number of investigations and is diagnosed as suffering from angina. Alan is placed on medication to control his symptoms.

Insurer's response (to be included here)

Two years later, Alan's chest pain recurs more severely and his specialist recommends that he have a heart by-pass operation.

Insurer's response (to be included here)

Example 2 – Asthma

Eve has been with *insurer's name* for five years when she develops breathing difficulties. Her GP refers her to a specialist who arranges for a number of tests. These reveal that Eve has asthma. Her specialist puts her on medication and recommends a follow-up consultation in three months, to see if her condition has improved. At that consultation Eve states that her breathing has been much better, so the specialist suggests she have check-ups every four months.

Insurer's response (to be included here)

Eighteen months later, Eve has a bad asthma attack.

Insurer's response (to be included here)

Example 3 – Cancer

Beverley has been with *insurer's name* for five years when she is diagnosed with breast cancer. Following discussion with her specialist she decides to have the breast removed followed by breast reconstruction. Her specialist also recommends a course of radiotherapy and chemotherapy. In addition she is to have hormone therapy tablets for several years. Will her insurance cover this treatment plan and are there any limits to the cover?

Insurer's response (to be included here)

Cara has previously had a breast cancer which was previously treated by lumpectomy, radiotherapy and chemotherapy under her existing policy. She now has a recurrence in her other breast and has decided to have a mastectomy, radiotherapy and chemotherapy. Will her insurance cover this and are there any limits to the cover?

Insurer's response (to be included here)

Monica, who was previously treated for breast cancer under her existing policy, has a recurrence which has unfortunately spread to other parts of the body. Her specialist has recommended the following treatment plan:

- A course of six cycles of chemotherapy aimed at destroying cancer cells to be given over the next six months.
- Monthly infusions of a drug to help protect the bones against pain and fracture. This infusion is to be given for as long as it is working (hopefully years).
- Weekly infusions of a drug to suppress the growth of the cancer. These infusions are to be given for as long as they are working (hopefully years).

Will her insurance cover this treatment plan and are there any limits to the cover?

Insurer's response (to be included here)

Sharon would like to be admitted to a hospice for care aimed solely at relieving symptoms. Will her insurance cover this and are there any limits to the cover?

Insurer's response (to be included here)

Example 4 – Diabetes

Deidre has been with *insurer's name* for two years when she develops symptoms that indicate she may have diabetes. Her GP refers her to an endocrinology specialist who organises a series of investigations to confirm the diagnosis, and she then starts on oral medication to control the diabetes. After several months of regular consultations and some adjustments made to her medication regime, the specialist confirms the condition is now well controlled and explains he would like to see her every four months to review the condition.

Insurer's response (to be included here)

One year later, Deidre's diabetes becomes unstable and her GP arranges for her to go into hospital for treatment.

Insurer's response (to be included here)

Example 5 – Hip Pain

Bob has been with *insurer's name* for three years when he develops hip pain. His GP refers him to an osteopath who treats him every other day for two weeks and then recommends that he return once a month for additional treatment to prevent a recurrence of his original symptoms.

Insurer's response (to be included here)

Explanation of cancer cover

Firms must have a distinct section in their policy documents to explain the cover for cancer. To allow for flexibility in approach, firms may consider having a separate leaflet, or a separate section in a leaflet, to explain the cover for cancer. The explanation of the cover for cancer must be available at point of sale.

Where appropriate, firms should explain clearly what would be covered, including limits on time periods, cycles of treatment, maximum payments, and circumstances in which firms would not provide cover.

Example of a section to explain the cover for cancer:

Firms may or may not choose to use this format. Firms may choose to provide separate information that is specific to a type of cancer. The example template contains prompts that may be added to or revised, when explaining the terms and what is covered, including clarifying when cover starts and ends:

Recommended topics	Prompts for recommended topics
Place of treatment	• hospice • hospital • at home
Diagnostic	• consultation • test • scan • genetics
Surgery	
Preventative	• screening • surgery • vaccines
Drug therapy	What types do you cover? • chemotherapy • to maintain remission • maintenance therapy • biological therapy
Radiotherapy	• including when given for pain relief
Palliative	• maintenance therapy
Terminal	• maintenance therapy
Monitoring	
Other	Is there a level of cover that is specific to cancer? • experimental treatment/advanced therapy/pre-licensed/NICE appraisal • clinical trials

When referring to cancer, firms may wish to use terms such as 'preventative', 'maintenance', and 'palliative'. In order to increase clarity, firms should avoid using the common definitions 'acute condition' or 'chronic condition' within this explanation of cover for cancer. Use of a generic leaflet to explain PMI cover would not prevent firms from providing a cancer specific leaflet, if they so choose.

2 eg ' . . . for chronic conditions and cancer'

APPENDIX C

Common definitions

[5091]

The common definitions set out in this section should be used in policy or other documents (with the exception of those relating to international products). Information should be provided to the customer as required by the FSA rules (ICOB 5.3.1R – 5.3.8R). The common definitions are not designed to describe the scope of cover provided by a product. Their purpose is to ensure that in whatever context the defined word or phrases are used they will have the same meaning.

Members may use additional information or support material to describe the extent, or otherwise, of cover provided.

1.1 Acute condition

A disease, illness or injury that is likely to respond quickly to treatment which aims to return you to the state of health you were in immediately before suffering the disease, illness or injury, or which leads to your full recovery.

1.2 Cancer

A malignant tumour, tissues or cells, characterised by the uncontrolled growth and spread of malignant cells and invasion of tissue.

1.3 Chronic condition

A disease, illness, or injury that has one or more of the following characteristics:
- it needs ongoing or long-term monitoring through consultations, examinations, check-ups, and/or tests
- it needs ongoing or long-term control or relief of symptoms
- it requires your rehabilitation or for you to be specially trained to cope with it
- it continues indefinitely
- it has no known cure
- it comes back or is likely to come back

1.4 Day patient

A patient who is admitted to a hospital or day patient unit because they need a period of medically supervised recovery but does not occupy a bed overnight.

1.5 Diagnostic tests

Investigations, such as X-rays or blood tests, to find or to help to find the cause of your symptoms.

1.6 Inpatient

A patient who is admitted to hospital and who occupies a bed overnight or longer, for medical reasons.

1.7 Nurse

A qualified nurse who is on the register of the Nursing and Midwifery Council (NMC) and holds a valid NMC personal identification number.

1.8 Out patient

A patient who attends a hospital, consulting room, or outpatient clinic and is not admitted as a day patient or an inpatient.

1.9 Pre-existing condition

Any disease, illness or injury for which:
- you have received medication, advice or treatment; or
- you have experienced symptoms;

whether the condition has been diagnosed or not in the xxx years before the start of your cover.

(the same period is not common to all insurers)

1.10 Treatment

Surgical or medical services (including **diagnostic tests**) that are needed to diagnose, relieve or cure a disease, illness or injury.

It is recognised that some firms use the term 'active treatment'. This has the potential to confuse customers given the current agreed definition of treatment. If firms do use the term it must be accompanied by a specific definition.

ASSOCIATION OF BRITISH INSURERS CODE OF PRACTICE FOR GENETIC TESTS

June 2008

NOTES

1 INTRODUCTION

[5092]

1.1 The Association of British Insurers (ABI) is the trade association for the UK insurance industry.

1.2 The Code of Practice for Genetic Tests (the Code) governs insurers' use of predictive genetic test results. Compliance with the Code is a condition of ABI membership. It identifies a standard that ABI member companies must meet, and upon which companies may wish to build.

1.3 The Code was originally introduced in 1997 and, following the latest review, is scheduled to last until 2014 with the next planned review in 2011.

1.4 This edition of the Code acknowledges the dispute resolution arbitration service and the option for direct communication with the applicant where they know about their condition. This edition came into effect on 13 June 2008 and will be revised in 2011. It supersedes and replaces all previous editions.

2 DEFINITION OF GENETIC TESTS

2.1 A *genetic test* is defined as a test that examines the structure of chromosomes (cytogenetic tests) or detects abnormal patterns in the DNA of specific genes (molecular tests). A genetic test can be predictive or diagnostic:

- a *predictive* genetic test is taken prior to the appearance of any symptoms of the condition in question
- a *diagnostic* genetic test is taken to confirm a diagnosis based on existing symptoms

3 WHAT THE CODE OF PRACTICE COVERS

3.1 The Code is applicable to insurance where an applicant may disclose a predictive genetic test result.

3.2 The broad classes of insurance for which genetic test results may be relevant are confined to the following products:

- Life
- Critical Illness
- Income Protection

3.3 Insurers will not use information from predictive genetic test results to underwrite Travel insurance, Private Medical Insurance, or any other one-off or annual policy, or for long-term care policies.

4 WHO THE CODE OF PRACTICE APPLIES TO

4.1 The Code applies to all companies that are members of the ABI. Compliance with the provisions of the Code is a mandatory requirement of ABI membership.

5 CONCORDAT AND MORATORIUM ON GENETICS AND INSURANCE

5.1 The 'Concordat and Moratorium on Genetics and Insurance' is a policy agreement between the ABI and the Government on the use of genetic test results in insurance underwriting practices.[1]

5.2 The Concordat and Moratorium set out the policy on how predictive genetic tests may be used and the insurers' agreement not to use specified genetic tests.

5.3 The Code must be implemented in conjunction with the Concordat and Moratorium on Genetics and Insurance. Compliance with the Code is overseen by the government's advisory body, the Genetics and Insurance Committee (GAIC).

6 PRINCIPLES ON WHICH THE CODE IS BASED

1 Applicants will not be asked to, nor be put under any pressure to, undergo a predictive genetic test in order to obtain insurance.

2 Insurers may only take into account adverse results of those predictive genetic tests that the government's advisory body, GAIC, has decided are technically, clinically and actuarially relevant.

3 There must be no increase in the premium or worsening in the terms an insurer offers, arising from such a test, unless GAIC has decided that an adverse predictive genetic test result is technically, clinically and actuarially relevant for insurance purposes.

4 A predictive genetic test result, indicating the absence or mitigation of a genetic risk factor, may alter the effects of a family history of a genetic condition, and so avoid the need for a loading. Insurers should publish their policy in respect of normal (negative) or mitigating genetic test results.

5 Insurers must not offer individuals lower than standard premiums on the basis of their predictive genetic test results: that is, genetic test results cannot be used as a trigger for allowing preferred life underwriting terms. Insurers may use a normal (negative) predictive genetic test result to reduce the impact of loading which would otherwise have applied due to the applicant's known medical or family history.

6 Written reasons for any increase in premium or rejection of an application due to a genetic test result must be provided on request.

7 Insurers must monitor their staff's compliance with this Code and must take action where there has been a breach.

8 The insurance company's Chief Executive must certify insurers' compliance with the Code annually to the ABI. Insurers must also complete the data return associated with the compliance exercise.

STANDARDS

7 Compliance and reporting

7.1 Insurers must maintain a log of the details of all applications where a genetic test result is disclosed, and the underwriting decision made on them. This information will be provided to the ABI through the annual compliance exercise. The content of the log is directed by GAIC.

7.2 The ABI reports annually to GAIC on compliance with the Code and moratorium. The report includes information on any non-compliance under the Code. GAIC reports to government on insurers' compliance with the Code and moratorium. The ABI will publish the results of its annual compliance exercise.

8 Information to applicants

8.1 The applicant should be advised that they must answer an insurer's questions carefully, accurately and to the best of their knowledge and belief and provide all information requested, as outlined in section 8.3.

8.2 The insurer must obtain the applicant's prior, explicit, informed consent to the handling of personal information.

8.3 Before the application form is completed, the insurer must make the following clear to the applicant:

(a) Diagnostic genetic test results do need to be disclosed.

(b) Predictive or diagnostic genetic test results acquired as part of clinical research do not need to be disclosed.

(c) Predictive genetic test results do not need to be disclosed in applications for insurance below the financial limits set out in the moratorium. Guidance to General Practitioners is in the Medical Information and Insurance guidelines available at www.abi.org.uk and www.b-ma.org.uk.

(d) Predictive genetic test results must only be disclosed in applications for insurance above the financial limits set out in the concordat and moratorium, if the tests have been approved by GAIC. Approved tests are listed at www.doh.gov.uk/genetics and www.abi.org.uk. This list should be made available to applicants on request.

9 Applicant obligations and rights

9.1 Applicants are under no obligation to:

(a) Take a genetic test.

(b) Disclose the results of a predictive genetic test undertaken by another person (such as a blood relative).

(c) Disclose the results of a genetic test acquired as part of clinical research.

(d) To find out medical information not known to him/her to complete the application form.

(e) To consent to disclosure of identifiable personal information to another party outside of the insurance company unless they are directly involved in assessing or managing the application or claim, or in reinsuring the risk.

(f) Reveal the results of any future predictive genetic test to the insurer.

9.2 All applicants have the right to:

(a) Change their mind about proceeding with the application for insurance.

(b) Apply to another insurer.

(c) Expect the insurer to assess an insurance application fairly, based solely on relevant evidence.

(d) See a medical report prepared by their doctor before it is sent to the insurer, and to amend or add comments to it, under the Access to Medical Reports Act 1988 (or equivalent legislation in Northern Ireland).
(e) Ask the insurer to provide a clear explanation of whether and (if so) to what extent, a predictive genetic test result contributed to the underwriting decision.
(f) Ask the insurer to review any adverse underwriting decision based on a relevant predictive genetic test result.
(g) Complain about any alleged breach of this Code. The complaints procedure is set out in section 15.
(h) To find out what personal, including medical, information the insurer has on file about themselves other than in specific circumstances, under the data protection legislation.

10 Underwriting

10.1 Insurers must not use information from predictive genetic test results to underwrite unless:
(a) The predictive test is approved by the government's Genetics and Insurance Committee as clinically reliable and actuarially relevant and the application for insurance is above the financial limits set out in the moratorium.
(b) A favourable test result is disclosed by the applicant to nullify a potential rating or exclusion that would have been applied due to family history.

10.2 An applicant may choose to disclose a predictive genetic test result that is in their favour in order to over-ride family history information. Insurers must publish information about the way they will use such test results to inform the underwriting decision. For example, a favourable (negative) result may be taken into account if it is relevant and could prevent a loading that would otherwise have been applied because of the applicant's family history. An adverse (positive) result may only be taken into account if it is favourable to the applicant (see Principle 4).

10.3 A predictive genetic test result declared by an applicant will not be linked to, or taken into account during, the assessment of an application for insurance from another person.

10.4 Applicants will not be required to disclose the results of a predictive genetic test undertaken by another person (such as a blood relative). If such information is received it must it must be ignored unless taking the result into account will produce a decision in the applicant's favour.

11 Internal handling of genetic test results

The role of the Nominated Genetics Underwriter (NGU) and the Chief Medical Officer (CMO)

11.1 Insurers must nominate an underwriter with sufficient seniority in the company (and each subsidiary). This person is to be known as the Nominated Genetics Underwriter (NGU). Their responsibilities are described in Annex 1. A deputy nominated genetics underwriter must also be identified, to cover absences of the NGU.

11.2 Insurers must pass all applications containing a genetic test result (whether predictive, diagnostic, carrier, or unknown) to the NGU for a decision on insurability, and to ensure the secure handling of the test result.

11.3 When the NGU receives an application involving complex[2] genetic information, the NGU must consult a medical practitioner, normally the insurance company's Chief Medical Officer (CMO) before reaching a decision. The responsibilities of the CMO are described in Annex 2.

11.4 If the NGU, or the CMO, has evidence and is certain that an applicant *does* know the result of their genetic test, the NGU or the CMO may communicate the decision to the applicant directly, without going through the applicant's medical adviser.

11.5 If the NGU, or the CMO, believes that an applicant *does not* know the result of a genetic test[3] (or if this is unclear) and the applicant's consent has been obtained, the NGU or the CMO will contact the applicant's medical adviser before informing the applicant of a decision to increase the premium or decline the application. This may slow down the process of obtaining cover, but it ensures that the applicant can be given relevant medical information by his/her medical adviser. In these circumstances, insurers will not communicate medical information to clients.

12 Security and confidentiality of medical information

12.1 Each company must have a Confidentiality Policy in place governing the security, handling, transfer and storage of medical and other sensitive information. The insurer should be able to demonstrate that its practices are secure. The guidelines in Annex 3 may be used as a benchmark.

12.2 The Chief Executive is responsible for the Confidentiality Policy, upon which the CMO must be consulted. The Chief Executive may delegate the responsibility to the CMO, if he/she occupies a senior position within the company, or another senior member of management.

12.3 Insurers must ensure that as few staff as are necessary will have access to sensitive information, including genetic test results. Details of how this is to be achieved must be contained in each company's Confidentiality Policy.

12.4 The insurer must obtain the applicant's prior, explicit, informed consent to:
(a) Handle personal information. This includes any genetic test result.
(b) Request information relating to the applicant, including any genetic test result from the applicant's medical adviser. Details are available in the joint ABI/BMA guidance 'Medical Information and Insurance' and from ABI's guidance on General Practitioner Report forms.
(c) Share any information obtained about an applicant with other insurance companies, reinsurers or third party administrators.

12.5 The insurer must fully specify the purposes for which the data are required. The data may be used and kept by the insurer only for these purposes. The insurer must comply with the Data Protection Act and not retain out of date and/or irrelevant personal data about an applicant.

13 Education and training

13.1 Insurers must take steps to ensure that as few staff as practicable are involved in the handling and interpretation of genetic test results.

13.2 A contact point (the NGU) must be provided for internal enquiries concerning genetic issues.

13.3 Insurers must provide their employees and any third party (for example, an administrator who acts on their behalf) with sufficient information and training so that they can reasonably be expected to understand the content and meaning of:
(a) The Code and the moratorium and concordat in so far as they relate to their particular jobs and responsibilities under it.
(b) Other relevant industry codes of practice, and legislation such as the Data Protection Act and the Disability Discrimination Act.

13.4 If a breach of this Code occurs insurers must take appropriate action. This may include, for example, informing/apologising to the applicant that a breach has taken place, taking disciplinary action, retraining staff, and/or amending procedures.

13.5 Insurers will keep themselves informed of wider developments in genetics likely to affect insurance and risk assessment, including treatment or lifestyle choices, by appropriate means; for example, through observing the information and advice in ABI circulars, reinsurers' circulars, general publications, relevant websites, or validated research results. Staff working in this area will be encouraged to attend relevant seminars and conferences.

13.6 Insurers must incorporate into their procedures new information that affects the way certain genetic diseases are underwritten as quickly as is practicable.

14 Research

14.1 Insurers will support research initiatives where practicable (and lawful), for example by sharing aggregate, anonymous data with those involved in research, with geneticists, and with the Continuous Mortality Investigation Committee at the Faculty and Institute of Actuaries.

14.2 Insurers will consider applications for funding for genetic research projects that are relevant to insurance.

15 Complaints

15.1 Where an applicant believes that they have been treated unfairly on the basis of a disclosed genetic test result, whether predictive or diagnostic, the insurer must provide:
(a) Details of the complaints process.
(b) The applicant's rights and obligations under it.
(c) On request, a copy of this Code, in order to explain what the Code covers.

This does not affect the applicant's rights to use alternative complaints mechanisms.

15.2 Insurers must investigate and deal with any complaint made under the Code promptly and in accordance with the Financial Services Authority (FSA) regulations handbook at: www.fsahandbook.info/FSA/html/handbook/DISP. The ABI good practice guide on complaint handling is at: www.customerimpact.org.

15.3 If, at the end of the complaints process, the insurer does not resolve the complaint, the insurer must notify the customer in writing that they have the right to complain under this Code to the free[4] independent Arbitration Service, administered by the Chartered Institute of Arbitrators (www.**arbitrators**.org), that will look at all underwriting complaints including decisions. This does not affect their rights to use existing alternative complaints mechanisms, such as the Financial Ombudsman's Service[5] (www.financial-ombudsman.org.uk) that may look at other underwriting matters, or the courts.

15.4 The timeframes[6] stated in the FSA handbook apply to accessing the arbitration service (www.fsahandbook.info/FSA/html/handbook/DISP/1/6). In exceptional cases, such as when the complainant has been or is incapacitated, applicants may be allowed to begin the complaints procedure after the stated time.

15.5 Insurers can assess their complaint management systems through the ABI customer impact annual benchmarking exercise. The ABI customer impact survey is at: www.customerimpact.org.

1 Copies can be obtained from the Department of Health at www.dh.gov.uk

2 Such as, the interaction of different genes along with environmental effects, eg smoking or diet

3 Predictive, diagnostic, carrier, unknown

4 This service is free to customers

5 This service is free to customers

6 Dispute Resolution DISP 1.6 time limit rules

ANNEX 1
DUTIES AND RESPONSIBILITIES OF THE NOMINATED GENETICS UNDERWRITER

[5093]
A1.1 Each insurer will nominate a central reference point within the company for each application in which a genetic test result is disclosed. This person will be a senior underwriter, who will be known as the Nominated Genetics Underwriter (NGU).

A1.2 The NGU's responsibilities include the following:

(a) To be registered with the ABI as the company's NGU.

(b) To ensure that a deputy NGU is available to cover their absences.

(c) To hold, and to have a thorough knowledge of, an up to date copy of the Code of Practice.

(d) To keep up to date with relevant developments in genetic science and technology. Helpful sources of information will include ABI circulars and briefings, industry updates, conferences and seminars, and the internet.

(e) To consult a medical practitioner, normally the insurance company's CMO, on any application involving complex genetic medical evidence.

(f) To base all decisions on the facts, on expert medical and genetic opinion, and on his or her own professional judgement.

(g) To disregard any test where it is not clear whether it is covered by the moratorium or not.

(h) To ensure that where an application involving a genetic test result is too great a risk to insure the insurer must consider offering alternative terms, where practicable, such as excluding the genetic risk whilst providing cover for other risks. This is in line with insurers' responsibilities under the Disability Discrimination Act 1998. The potential to offer alternative terms will depend on the type of insurance and the legal requirements to which it is subject; it will be more practical with Critical Illness cover, for example, than with Life insurance.

(i) To record the decision making process and the underlying rationale clearly, so that for cases involving a genetic test result, a full explanation can be given upon request.

(j) To assist with, and contribute to, the insurer's internal monitoring mechanisms, where appropriate.

(k) To report any breach of the Code to the person responsible for compliance, and to assist in implementing any corrective action.

(l) To contribute to, or maintain, a log of all applications where any genetic test result is disclosed.

(m) To assist with, and where appropriate provide, education and training for relevant staff.

(n) To ensure that genetic information disclosed when an insured person makes a claim, and that was not disclosed at application stage, is treated in accordance with the moratorium, concordat and Code. For instance:

- If a policy is taken out during the moratorium and a claim arises post-moratorium, the insured person's non-disclosure at point of application will be treated in accordance with the moratorium and concordat which existed at the time the policy was taken out.
- Predictive genetic tests results that are not disclosed until the point of claim will not impact on payment of the claim unless the conditions of the moratorium and concordat, applicable at policy inception, allow this (ie GAIC approved tests and policy values above the moratorium financial limits).

ANNEX 2 DUTIES AND RESPONSIBILITIES OF THE CHIEF MEDICAL OFFICER

[5094]
A2.1 The nominated genetics underwriter in each insurer must consult the company's Chief Medical Officer (CMO) on each application in which a complex genetic issue is disclosed. The CMO's responsibilities in such cases are set out below.

Insurance companies offering long-term insurances

A2.2 UK insurance companies selling long-term insurance products (such as Life, Critical Illness and Income Protection) employ (often on a part-time basis) a Chief Medical Officer to act as their medical adviser. Whether these doctors are Consultant Physicians or GPs, they are accountable to the General Medical Council for their professional conduct.

The CMO's duties include:

(a) Contributing to the development of the company's underwriting philosophy and practice.

(b) Advising the Chief Executive and Chief Underwriter in relation to the company's policy on confidentiality and security of clinical information. This will include advising that only staff with a business need to handle medical evidence, as directed by the CMO, should have access to that evidence.

(c) Liaising with medical examiners, medical advisers and other relevant disciplines.

(d) Providing medical training for underwriters.

(e) Providing expert advice to the underwriter on complex cases and where necessary consulting a genetics specialist.

(f) Providing expert advice on medical documentation to the insurer.

(g) Keeping the insurer abreast of major medical advances, including those in the areas of genetic science and technology.

(h) Providing expert medical advice on claims, when there is a dispute, or when irregularities are suspected.

(i) Exercising his or her judgement on issues of medical ethics.

ANNEX 3 CONFIDENTIALITY GUIDANCE

A3.1 Introduction

[5095]

A3.1.1 The ABI Code of Practice on Predictive Genetic Testing requires companies to have a documented set of practices in place to ensure that confidential information, including medical information, about their customers is held, and transferred, securely. Companies should be able to demonstrate that confidentiality practices are secure. These practices must conform to the provisions of the Data Protection Act 1998 (DPA 98).

A3.1.2 The Chief Executive is responsible for the confidentiality of all information, but the Chief Medical Officer (CMO) has a key role to play in the Confidentiality Policy for medical information. The CMO's duties are set out in Annex 2 to the Code of Practice.

A3.1.3 These guidelines form a benchmark against which companies can review their existing Confidentiality Policy. Some companies may wish to build on this benchmark.

A3.1.4 Insurers must take steps to ensure that all staff are aware of their Confidentiality Policy and that appropriate staff have their own copy of it. Insurers should make it clear to staff that breaching the policy will be treated as misconduct and that deliberate or reckless communication of confidential information will be treated as serious misconduct.

A3.2 Confidentiality within the Sales Process

A3.2.1 The Confidentiality Policy should apply to all those involved in the sales process (eg the company's own sales force and telesales units), as follows:

A3.2.2 The seller should explain to the customer that all evidence given by the customer, or received from third parties such as doctors, would be kept strictly confidential.

A3.2.3 The seller should explain to the customer his or her rights under the Access to Medical Reports Act (or equivalent legislation).

A3.2.4 The applicant may exercise his/her right to complete medical questionnaires in private and seal them in an envelope addressed to the CMO and marked "Private and Confidential". The envelope will be opened only by the CMO, or by the staff to whom he/she has delegated authority according to the company's confidentiality policy.

A3.2.5 Members of sales forces should have no access to medical information received from third parties or given to the CMO (or delegated staff) in confidence by the customer.

A3.3 Confidentiality and Administration

A3.3.1 The Confidentiality Policy should cover all administrative staff within head offices, regional offices and branch offices.

A3.3.2 All medical reports and information posted to the company should be addressed to the CMO in an envelope marked "Private and Confidential".

A3.3.3 All medical reports and information should be opened only by the CMO or those members of staff authorised by the CMO. Such authorisation should be agreed in discussion with the Chief Underwriter or other relevant senior official of the company.

A3.3.4 Only staff with a business need to handle medical evidence, as directed by the CMO, should have access to such evidence. However, other staff, such as those involved in claims, policy servicing, imaging, filing, internal audit or those on helpdesks, have a need to handle the files containing sensitive information in the course of their duties. Therefore, all relevant staff need to have a thorough understanding of the company's Confidentiality Policy.

A3.3.5 The access of temporary staff to sensitive data needs to be carefully considered and, if practicable, avoided. If access for temporary staff is unavoidable, a process must be adopted for ensuring their knowledge of, and compliance with, the company's Confidentiality Policy.

A3.3.6 There must be no discussion of confidential medical information by staff with any person who does not have "a need to know" this information for their job. Staff who cannot have "a need to know" include members of the sales force, other sellers, and other customers. It must be stressed to all authorised staff that discussions of a casual nature with other members of staff or with anyone else that include confidential details relating to identifiable individuals, are prohibited.

A3.3.7 All files containing medical evidence should be securely stored, particularly outside normal working hours, to prevent unauthorised access.

A3.4 Confidentiality and External Bodies

Special considerations apply when dealing with external bodies:

A3.4.1 Subject to the applicant's or policyholder's explicit and informed consent having been obtained, medical information may be shared with or shown to people outside the company if this is necessary for the conduct of business. This may include reinsurers and third party providers and may be necessary to process the individual's application and policy; to handle a complaint; to satisfy audit requirements; or to prevent fraudulent applications.

A3.4.2 Medical information should always be sent to the CMO of the external organisation.

A3.4.3 The CMO, or his/her nominee, will satisfy themselves that the recipient has an appropriate confidentiality policy in place, before any sensitive information is sent.

A3.4.4 If companies have reason to believe that information they are legitimately releasing could be harmful to the customer then they should ensure that the recipient of this information understands this. An example might be where medical information has been received that the customer is, unknowingly, suffering from a terminal illness.

A3.4.5 The applicant/policyholder's medical adviser may be given medical information if this would be helpful in the treatment of the patient, as long as the applicant/policyholder does not object.

A3.4.6 Medical information and/or reasons for underwriting decisions should not be given to an employer without the employee's permission.

A3.5 Methods of Communication

The following guidelines apply to communications:

A3.5.1 Any evidence sent by post or courier should be in sealed envelopes, addressed to the CMO or to a named doctor.

A3.5.2 Medical information should only be given over the telephone (for example, to a doctor) after the identity and *bona fides* of the caller have been established.

A3.5.3 Facsimile or electronic data transmissions of medical evidence should only be made or received by authorised staff within a secure environment. Electronic communications may require encryption or password protection to ensure security. Inward and outward facsimile transmissions should only be made when there is an authorised person available to receive them. Ideally, subject identifiers should be sent separately from their data.

A3.6 Storage of Confidential Information

Guidelines for the storage of confidential information are:

A3.6.1 Medical information should only be accessed by authorised staff who have a business need for such information.

A3.6.2 Access to files containing medical or other confidential information should be limited to those individuals who have a proper business reason. Once the file has been accessed, staff should be made aware that they should only read that part of the file that is relevant to the task being performed.

A3.6.3 Copies of imaged electronic confidential information should only be taken by, and, should be controlled by authorised staff.

A3.6.4 All personal information should be destroyed as soon as it is no longer relevant. Facilities should be in place to ensure all confidential information no longer required is disposed of by shredding or by a similar method.

ANNEX 4 ARBITRATION SCHEME

[5096]
The Chartered Institute of Arbitrators (CIArb) will provide an arbitration scheme for the resolution of disputes under the Code. The following criterion will be used in the arbitration scheme:

A4.1 Efficiency – complaints should be dealt with within given time limits

A4.1.1 There will be published deadlines within the arbitration scheme developed to resolve disputes under the Code. Parties will be required to comply with time limits that will be strictly enforced by the arbitrator.

A4.2 Proportional costs

A4.2.1 A procedure with a high maintenance cost would not be appropriate. The two complaints received since 1997 were dealt with without having to set up the independent tribunal that was a feature of the previous arrangements.

A4.2.2 A suitable and proportionate one-off development fee has been agreed with the CIArb for the creation of this service. The development fee incorporates fees paid to external experts such as Sir Michael Wright, a retired judge and Chairman of the Thalidomide Trust.

A4.3 Confidentiality – especially given the sensitivity of the personal medical information involved

A4.3.1 Confidentiality is key to the business of the CIArb. They have published complaints procedures and a Code of Ethics for their members. CIArb staff are experienced in dealing with a wide range of confidential information, including personal medical records and the CIArb's Subject Information Statement covers this subject.

A4.4 Fairness/impartiality – it must be independent of the industry

A4.4.1 Any arbitrator nominated for appointment must disclose any potential conflicts of interest before accepting an appointment. This is included in the Code of Ethics for CIArb members.

A4.5 Clarity – the procedure must be written in plain English

A4.5.1 Any rules or guidance notes relating to the scheme will be sent to the Plain English Campaign and it is hoped that they will achieve the Crystal Mark for clarity. However, sometimes legal documents are not eligible for the Crystal Mark due to the need for certain legal terms and it is possible that only the guidance notes will receive PEC award.

A4.6 Use of experts

A4.6.1 Genetic science is changing all the time; insurance practice is relatively little understood. The procedure must be able to take account of specialist knowledge, including specialist knowledge about insurance.

A4.6.2 The CIArb will identify arbitrators with relevant experience. Due to the nature of the disputes and the potential for judicial awards of unlimited damages, arbitrators will be drawn from a panel of retired judges. The CIArb can seek expert scientific knowledge through government advisory bodies and academic institutions, such as the Human Genetics Commission, Genetics Knowledge Parks, PHG Foundation, and the Genetics and Insurance Committee.

A4.7 Ease of access/free to consumers at the point of use

A4.7.1 Applications to the scheme can be made online and there will be facilities for individuals with disabilities. Rules will be converted in to relevant languages and made available in Braille.

A4.8 Informative – both the company and the ABI should able to draw conclusions from the result to improve our systems

A4.8.1 All awards will be reasoned. This means that the parties will be given the history of the dispute and how it arose, the decision of the arbitrator him or herself, and the full reasons for the decision.

A4.9 Remedies available to CIArb

A4.9.1 The arbitrators within the scheme will have the power under the rules to impose financial penalties against companies and grant awards to complainants in the event of the service finding a breach of the concordat, moratorium or Code.

A4.10 Findings are binding on disputing parties

A4.10.1 Arbitration awards are binding on the parties – more so than if they were made in court by a judge. These additional binding powers make awards very difficult to overturn with limited grounds of appeal in the High Court. Arbitration awards are legally binding and enforceable in more than 130 countries signed to the New York Convention, 1958.

A4.11 Findings are confidential to disputing parties

A4.11.1 Arbitration is held in a private session. The findings can be made available with (prior or post) agreement of the parties and the arbitrator, but the information provided to the arbitrator in reaching his or her decision remains confidential. Thus, the claimant's identify is protected as is the company's intellectual property. It is understood that there will be extensive press interest in any dispute referred to arbitration under the Code and with this in mind it is again important that the arbitrators being nominated for appointment are strong characters with experience in dealing with the press.

A4.12 Other comments

A4.12.1 Complainants remain free to take court proceedings against an insurer.

ASSOCIATION OF BRITISH INSURERS STATEMENT OF BEST PRACTICE FOR HIV AND INSURANCE

July 2008

NOTES

1. INTRODUCTION

What is the purpose of this Statement?

[5097]

1.1 The issue of how HIV, and HIV testing, is dealt with by insurers has long been a subject of public interest. This document makes it clear that insurers do not ask questions about an applicant's sexual orientation or request an HIV test be taken solely because of perceived sexual orientation, and will not take into account sexual orientation in assessing an application if it is inadvertently revealed by an applicant. Insurers are allowed to ask questions about HIV risk, including about risky sexual behaviour, and about travel to or origin from areas of the world with high levels of HIV.

1.2 This Statement is intended to help insurers selling long-term insurance products[1] to adopt best practice. It sets out requirements on, and guidance for, insurance industry professionals, for use when dealing with applications for insurance where HIV may be an issue. HIV is an issue of major concern to public policymakers, the insurance industry and the general public.

1.3 The Health Protection Agency's 2007 Report on HIV and Other Sexually Transmitted Infections in the UK[2] stated the number of new diagnoses reported to end June 2007 had increased 157% since 1997. Among all newly diagnosed individuals 3,727 (59%) were heterosexual and 2,301 (36%) were men who had sex with men (MSM). Most of the heterosexual infections were acquired abroad. The Report estimated there were 73,000 people living with HIV in the UK in 2006 (both diagnosed and undiagnosed). Of these an estimated 69,400 people were aged 15–59 years with 43% being MSM, 31% heterosexual women, 21% heterosexual men and 4% injecting drug users (IDU). African-born men and women accounted for 35% of the total number of adults and 31% of all those unaware of their infection. When only heterosexually acquired infections were considered, African born men and women accounted for 68% of the total and 61% of those unaware of their infection.

NOTES

There is no paragraph 1.4 in the original.

Who should read the Statement?

1.5 This Statement is intended primarily for insurance underwriters. Some aspects of it will also be relevant to others working in insurance companies, and staff should be made aware of it, including Chief Medical Officers, sales personnel and those working in customer services or complaints departments.

1.6 The Statement is also intended to explain to external stakeholders the way that the insurance industry deals with issues surrounding HIV. It will therefore be of interest to doctors, patient support groups, policymakers and interested individuals.

1.7 A consumer guide to HIV and Insurance is available at: www.abi.org.uk.

What status does the Statement have?

1.8 The Statement is an ABI arrangement with members.

How was the Statement developed?

1.9 The Medical Underwriting Committee developed the Statement. The ABI HIV Expert Working Party, the Terence Higgins Trust and Pinkfinance.com made significant contributions to the Statement. There was a wide response from insurers, reinsurers, insurance brokers and external interest groups to the consultation exercises that resulted in the Statement.

1.10 This Statement replaces all previous versions of the ABI Statement of Best Practice on HIV and Insurance, first published in 1994 and revised in 1997 and 2004. The 2008 Statement will be reviewed in 2011.

1.11 The Statement draws on ABI publications in related areas available at www.abi.org.uk. These are:

- An Insurer's Guide to the Disability Discrimination Act
- Statement of Best Practice for Critical Illness Cover
- Statement of Best Practice for Income Protection Insurance

Implementation

1.12 The content of the Statement was revised to incorporate the implementation of the Civil Partnership legislation in April 2008. There are no other changes to the content of the Statement and on this basis the 2008 Statement of Best Practice will take immediate effect.

---

1 The insurance products covered by this guide are income protection, critical illness, term life, long term care and the life insurance element of whole life and endowments.

2 http://www.hpa.org.uk/web/HPAweb&HPAwebStandard/HPAweb_C/1203084355941

---

2. KEY PRINCIPLES

[5098]

2.1 The key principles that underpin this Statement of Best Practice are:

- **Principle 1 – Underwriting approach** – take decisions on a case-by-case basis and assess premiums fairly
- **Principle 2 – Collection of information** – don't ask for excessive, speculative or irrelevant information
- **Principle 3 – Use of information** – take account of all relevant factors
- **Principle 4 – Accuracy of information** – stay up to date with developments and statistics
- **Principle 5 – Company policy on HIV and underwriting** – have an agreed policy on dealing with HIV which is updated at least every three years

2.2 The following paragraphs explain briefly what each principle is intended to cover. The other sections of the Statement expand upon the principles in greater detail.

Principle 1 – Underwriting approach

2.3 The primary duty of insurers is to assess insurance applications fairly according to the degree of risk that the applicant brings to the insurance pool. Insurers should consider each application for insurance on a case-by-case basis, based solely on the best available relevant evidence, in accordance with the guidelines in this Statement. An individual's occupation is no guide to HIV risk. Being, for example, a cabin crew member, ballet dancer or hairdresser cannot of itself justify an HIV rating.

Principle 2 – Collection of information

2.4 Insurers will not request information that is unnecessary or irrelevant to the risk being insured, such as speculative questions that rely on inference and assumption on the part of the underwriter, for example house co-purchasing arrangements. Insurers must not differentiate between customers in civil partnerships and married couples.

Principle 3 – Use of information

2.5 In reaching a decision on a particular application, the underwriter will take account of all relevant information and will be able to explain the reason for the underwriting decision.

Principle 4 – Accuracy of information

2.6 Insurers should continually review HIV incidence rates and statistics, with a view to updating company policy on HIV/AIDS every three years (see Annex A for evidence sources). Reinsurers should update their manuals in respect of HIV every three years.

2.7 The development of policy is informed by a group of multidisciplinary HIV experts from the insurance and reinsurance industry and stakeholder groups who would consider issues such as:

- The evidence base for HIV risk

- Cultural attitudes and encouraging responsible behaviour
- Rational and respectful decision making
- Fair policy and procedures

Principle 5 – Company policy on HIV and underwriting

2.8 Each member company of ABI should have a clear policy on how it deals with applications where HIV status may be an issue, and their practice on exclusions, to ensure that it reflects current knowledge as in Annex A. Insurers should review and if appropriate update this policy at least every three years.

3. ACTION AT THE APPLICATION STAGE

[5099]
3.1 Insurers are bound by the Civil Partnership Act 2004 and must not differentiate between customers in civil partnerships and married couples when setting HIV testing limits.

Communicating with the applicant's GP

3.2 Care should be exercised when communicating with an applicant's GP. Prior explicit written permission **must be obtained** from the applicant before writing to the doctor with any information or questions that could directly or indirectly reveal the sexuality of the applicant to the GP. It is highly unlikely that insurers would know such information given the wording of the questions on HIV risk in this Statement.

3.3 The ABI/British Medical Association (BMA) agreed General Practitioner Report form (GPR) and the Guidance on Medical Information and Insurance advises GPs that they should inform insurers if the applicant is HIV positive or is awaiting an HIV test result or if the applicant has had one or more episodes of a sexually transmitted infection that has long term health implications.

3.4 The GPR does not include questions on applicant sexuality and this information, even if known, must not be disclosed to insurers. If it is inadvertently disclosed it should be ignored by insurers.

Medical Examiner's Report or Health Screening Report

3.5 Some insurers ask applicants to have a medical examination (unrelated to HIV risk), or use tele-underwriting, and repeat some of the questions contained on the application form. Where this is done, the same principles about consent and not passing on information about sexuality apply.

Asking about the applicant's HIV status and risk

3.6 Since publication of the ABI Statement of Best Practice on Underwriting Life Insurance for HIV in July 1994, insurers have not asked whether an applicant had undergone counselling about HIV, or had taken an HIV test. Instead, insurers ask whether the applicant had tested positive for HIV, or was awaiting the results of an HIV test.

3.7 Insurers that use "short" application forms (which have a minimum of medical questions) may choose to incorporate these questions in a separate questionnaire. ABI members should use the following questions (in bold type):

(A) HIV, hepatitis B or hepatitis C status

"Have you ever tested positive for HIV, hepatitis B, or hepatitis C, or are you awaiting the results of such a test?

Note: If the result is negative, the fact of having an HIV test will not, of itself, have any effect on your acceptance terms for insurance"

(B) HIV risk – potential sexual transmission

3.9 There are five main infection routes:
- People who have unprotected sex[3]
- *People who have been resident* or travelled in or to countries with high HIV prevalence who caught HIV there
- People who inject non-prescription drugs
- People who have had blood transfusions or blood products, or surgery, outside the EU
- Mother-to-baby-transmission

3.10 Being gay does not necessarily mean a person is at higher risk of HIV infection. The person concerned may be celibate, or always have protected sex. Insurers and the medical profession, who have dealt with this issue for some time (for example, for blood donors), ask specific questions about personal behaviour. Questions must be directed at personal behaviour. Whereas people might not be sure of what constitutes safe sexual behaviour, most people are aware of what constitutes **unsafe** sexual behaviour. We therefore recommend the following question—

"Within the last five years have you been exposed to the risk of HIV infection?"

3.11 Insurers can ask questions on injecting drug use, blood transfusions carried out outside the EU and travel or residence abroad separately. Insurers may also wish to include in the question above examples of increased risk of HIV. Asking if a person is gay would not be acceptable. However the following are:

"(this can be caught through unsafe sex, intravenous drug abuse, or blood transfusions or surgery undertaken outside the EU)"

3.12 If insurers wish to explain unsafe or safe sex they may do so but the explanation must be related to individual personal behaviour, for example, unprotected sex and not to a person's sexuality.

3.13 It is **optional** for insurers to invite applicants to give information that they think may mean that they are less at risk of HIV infection. The question would need to be "open" to avoid asking leading or intrusive questions. We propose the following:

"Have you anything to add to your declaration, which in your view, means that you are (or are not) at risk of HIV?"

(C) Other sexually transmitted diseases/infections (STDs/STIs)

3.14 Insurers can ask applicants if they have had other sexually transmitted infections. This is to identify whether applicants have serious STIs (like syphilis) and because repeated infections may indicate an increased risk of HIV.

3.15 GPs only disclose STDs with long-term health implications, in accordance with the joint BMA-ABI guidance on medical information and insurance. Whether an STD has a long-term health implication is, in many cases, more dependent on how it was acquired rather than the type of infection – for example if acquired through injecting drug use. Members of the public cannot be asked to make judgements as to what infection may or may not have long-term health implications. This is something that would almost certainly be outside their normal or expected knowledge range. From an underwriting standpoint the key issues would depend upon the stage to which it had progressed at the time of diagnosis and how it had been acquired.

Insurers continue to have the option of asking the following question:

"Within the last five years have you tested positive or been treated for any disease, which was transmitted sexually?"

(D) Intravenous drug use

3.16 Information on drug use is not always related to HIV or hepatitis C risk. Insurers can ask about the use of recreational drugs such as cocaine. A typical question to obtain information about injecting drug use is:

"Have you ever injected non-prescription drugs?"

(E) Blood transfusions or surgery

3.17 Insurers can ask for information about blood transfusions or surgery from outside the EU. There may be issues concerning some countries in the enlarged EU. An option would be to narrow the question to countries outside the UK (see residence in paragraph 3.18). There is no recommendation either way as this is a matter for continued policy development.

(F) Residence and travel outside the UK

3.18 Insurers should maintain a list of countries or areas of high HIV prevalence as part of their policy on when to ask for HIV tests and should make this available on request to applicants (see Annex A for evidence sources). Countries with high HIV prevalence are generally those where at least 1% of the population has HIV. This prevalence is considered as "high" because at this level insurers would usually need to take account of the increased risk for individuals from those countries when compared to the UK.

(G) Supplementary questions

3.19 Adoption of the questions in the previous paragraphs means that the practice of asking additional supplementary questions is obsolete. Insurers can choose to ask any of the above questions or not but they may not ask additional supplementary questions – for example about monogamy, number of sexual partners, and length of relationships.

3 *anal, oral or vaginal sex*

4. COMPANY POLICY ON ASKING AN APPLICANT TO TAKE AN HIV TEST [5100]

4.1 Insurers must have a clear policy on asking an applicant to take an HIV test, as set out in principle 5, and make this available on request to applicants. As with all requests for all other medical tests, requests for HIV tests should have a clear reason, which is evidence based and can be explained to the applicant for example:

- Answering "yes" to the question about exposure to risk of HIV, for example through unsafe sex
- Having being diagnosed with (a) sexually transmitted disease(s) with long-term health implications
- Being resident or visiting in a non-UK country with high HIV prevalence (see 3.18; a list of countries should be available for applicants)
- Applying for a relatively large amount of insurance
- Injecting drug use
- Blood transfusions or surgery

5. ARRANGING AN HIV TEST

Detailed Guidance

[5101]
5.1 The guidance note at Annex B explains the points that insurers should consider when arranging for an applicant to be tested for HIV. It gives guidance on:

- The choice of test method and provider
- Customer discussion and consent
- Recommended clinical procedures

Annex C and Annex D contain:

- Model pre-testing leaflet and consent letters to the applicant
- An example HIV protocol for health professionals

Before the test – pre-testing leaflet and consent issues

5.2 It is particularly important that applicants are made fully aware of the purpose of the HIV test before they are asked to consent to being tested. To this end, a HIV pre-testing leaflet letter and a consent form must be issued directly to every applicant who is asked to have an HIV test. These must not be sent via the sales intermediary.

5.3 Applicants should receive their pre-test information before the test takes place. The testing centres must ensure that the applicant has read the pre-testing leaflet before consent to a test is given. This is part of the protocol between the insurer and the centre (see Annex D). The consent form is part of the pre-test information and must be completed at the time of the test. The test cannot happen unless consent has been given. Consent forms should be signed in accordance with the procedures in Annex B of the Statement.

5.4 The pre-testing leaflet explains that the applicant should take the unsigned consent form with them to the test centre where, if they are willing to take the test, they should sign it and have their signature witnessed. As part of the consent process they should nominate a professional contact that they wish to be notified by the insurer in the unlikely event of a positive HIV test result. Options include their own GP, or a named Genitourinary Medicine (GUM) clinic or professional HIV counselling service. If they are unable or unwilling to nominate one of these it should be explained that the test centre (if it offers appropriate services) or their own GP would be the point of contact. The insurer **must** satisfy itself that, should the applicant refuse to provide written consent, the health professional will not proceed with a test.

All test results

5.5 The insurer must ensure that the applicant (or nominee) is told the result as quickly as possible to relieve uncertainty. In the rare cases of positive results this is even more important so that arrangements can be made for counselling and future care.

5.6 Wherever possible, the salesperson should not be aware that an HIV test has been requested. Whether they are or not, however, the salesperson **must not** be told the result of the test.

Negative test results

5.7 Negative test results should be communicated as soon as possible to relieve applicant uncertainty. The insurer should also explain that the negative test had no effect on the applicant's insurance rating. This is particularly important where premiums are rated or exclusions applied as applicants may be under the misapprehension that negative tests have an impact on insurance.

Positive test results

5.8 In those rare cases where an HIV test returns a positive result, indicating that the individual has contracted HIV, the insurer **must** ensure that the applicant is told the result – by the person they have nominated on their consent form or the test centre or their own GP – as quickly as possible, so that arrangements for counselling and future care can be discussed.

5.9 If the Chief Underwriter or Underwriting Manager receives the test result, they should communicate it to their Chief Medical Officer (CMO) immediately. Once the CMO is aware of a positive test result, they **must** contact the person nominated on the applicant's consent form, or the test centre, as quickly as possible.

5.10 The applicant's nominee or test centre should be asked to advise the CMO when the counselling meeting has taken place. Only once this confirmation has been received should the insurer issue a letter, signed by the CMO or the Chief Underwriter, to the applicant giving the underwriting decision. Care must be taken to ensure that the decision letter is **not** issued until after the applicant has been counselled.

5.11 The applicant's HIV status must not be referred to in any oral or written communications with third parties, unless the applicant has given written consent. Insurers have no role in notifying partners of applicants with positive test results. Responsibility for partner notification lies with the infected person, or their nominee or the test centre or their own GP if there are grounds to believe that the partner will not be told. Under these circumstances, the General Medical Council (GMC) advises that the doctor *may* disclose information to a person who is at risk of HIV infection. Insurer CMOs should receive positive test results. If any ethical dilemmas arise they should be dealt with by CMOs in accordance with the GMC guidelines on Serious Communicable Diseases at www.gmc-uk.org/standards/serious.htm.

Invalid test results

5.12 Occasionally, the test laboratory may not be able to obtain a clear result from the applicant's sample. This may be due to the sample being insufficient, contaminated, or being mislaid. In these circumstances the applicant should be told that the test was inconclusive and the reasons for this (if known). In these cases we recommend that another test be arranged. Some insurers in these circumstances waive the requirement for a further test. This raises serious ethical issues – particularly if the applicant were to assume that this meant the test was negative.

6. CONFIDENTIALITY

Insurance company confidentiality – ABI guidelines

[5102]
6.1 Insurers recognise the importance of ensuring the confidentiality and privacy of sensitive personal information of the kind disclosed on insurance application forms. They are also fully aware of their responsibilities under data protection and other legislation. To assist member companies in fulfilling their obligations, the ABI has produced a set of confidentiality guidelines published in the ABI Code of Practice on Genetic Testing.

Group/corporate insurance polices

6.2 This Statement refers in general to the "applicant" for insurance. However, the contract is between the policyholder and the insurer and, in some circumstances, for example, group insurance policies, the insured person and the policyholder is not the same person. For group insurance policies, for example, the policyholder is the employer, not the employee.

6.3 When dealing with such cases, insurers **must** ensure that they communicate directly with the "insured person", rather than the policyholder (where they are different), on all personal, sensitive and medical issues. The policyholder must not be informed of any enquiries the insurer makes about the insured person's risk of HIV infection. Should the insured person be HIV positive it is not for the insurer to give this information to the policyholder. As in paragraph 5.11, the GMC Guidelines apply and any ethical issues should be dealt with by the insurer's CMO.

Confidentiality and joint life applications

6.4 Where an applicant is asked to complete a supplementary questionnaire, it is important to recognise that the information disclosed is confidential to that person. In particular, when underwriting applications for joint life insurance, insurers **must** protect the confidentiality of such information. They must ensure that the "ignorant" party to a joint life application cannot infer any confidential information from the underwriting result (but see also paragraph 5.11).

Security of electronic communications

6.5 Insurers should ensure, in their dealings with doctors and laboratories that positive test results are only sent by post. Negative test results should normally be sent by post but secure fax is acceptable for negative results from medical test centres. All test results must be sent promptly.

7. COMPLAINTS

[5103]
7.1 Insurers should ensure that their complaints procedure takes account of this Statement. Where

a complaint is received that falls within the area covered by this Statement, the complaint handler should consult the insurer's Chief Underwriter or Underwriting Manager and, if necessary, the Chief Medical Officer.

8. FURTHER INFORMATION

References:

[5104]

ABI Code of Practice on genetic testing

Civil Partnership Act 2004

ABI/BMA joint guidelines: "Medical information and insurance"

ABI "An Insurer's Guide to the Disability Discrimination Act, January 2003"

ABI "Consumer guide for gay men on HIV and insurance"

ABI "Consumer guide – countries with high HIV prevalence"

ABI/BMA agreed wording to request a General Practitioner's Report

Health Protection Agency Annual Report on HIV and other Sexually Transmitted Infections in the United Kingdom (see) www.hpa.org.uk

Contact:

Association of British Insurers, 51 Gresham Street, London EC2V 7HQ

020 7600 3333

www.abi.org.uk

ANNEX A

Guidance: underwriting – evidence and exclusions

Evidence

[5105]

A1. Insurers should review their underwriting practice and approach regularly to ensure that it is up to date. Annual reviews are recommended for evidence. Insurer policies should be reviewed at least every three years in the light of this evidence. Data sources are:

- Statistics in the UK – insurers should monitor regularly the data collected by the Health Protection Agency (www.hpa.org.uk/infections) and their own death claims, and consider whether these suggest the need for changes in policy or practice;
- Higher risk countries – underwriters should have up to date information on the situation in those countries where the incidence of HIV infection is high. The World Health Organisation collates HIV data from specific countries:
  - WHO web address www.who.int
  - statistics and maps www.who.int/globalatlas/default.asp
  - global atlas of infectious diseases www.who.int/emc-hiv/fact_sheets/All_countries.html
  - World maps showing HIV prevalence www.gamapserver.who.int/mapLibrary/app/searchResults.aspx
  - Other useful sources of information are the EU Commission's epidemiological surveillance site www.eurosurveillance.org the Joint United Nations Programme on HIV/AIDS www.unaids.org www.ceses.org

Excluding HIV/AIDS as a cause of claim

A2. Life insurance policies do not normally exclude AIDS. However, HIV/AIDS exclusions are more common with other long-term health products such as critical illness (CI) and income protection (IP) insurance. The ABI's Statements of Best Practice for CI and for IP insurance require that any general exclusions (for example, "drug abuse") and any specific conditions, such as HIV/AIDS, that are not covered by the policy are shown prominently in the Key Features Document given to the customer as part of the sales process, so that the scope of the cover is clear.

A3. Where an exclusion for HIV/AIDS is applied, the model wording which is recommended is:

'We will not pay a claim if it is caused directly or indirectly by infection with Human Immunodeficiency Virus (HIV) or by conditions due to any Acquired Immune Deficiency Syndrome (AIDS).'

A4. Exclusions worded in this way ensure that, while HIV and AIDS are not included in the scope of cover, someone who has been diagnosed with HIV or AIDS is not prevented from claiming on their policy if they suffer an unrelated condition such as a heart attack.

A5. The ABI document "An Insurer's Guide to the Disability Discrimination Act 1995" makes clear (section 2.8.2) that insurers "must not use general exclusions that have the effect of preventing a person from claiming for a condition that is not related to the excluded condition. General exclusions that have this effect are not lawful as they would be regarded as both unfair contract terms . . . and discriminatory". The Guide then gives, as an example of an unlawful HIV/AIDS exclusion, the following: "we will not pay a claim if the insured person has HIV or AIDS".

A6. When imposing exclusions on policies, insurers should pay particular attention to the following points:

- If the exclusion means that the questions (Paragraphs 3.12–3.14) about a person's **risk** of HIV infection are irrelevant the questions should NOT be asked. This is particularly likely to be the case for stand-alone income protection and critical illness policies because it should usually be relatively simple to establish whether or not HIV/AIDS is the cause of the claim. In the case of menu/multi benefit products (for example CI and term life), if any part of the policy does **not** include an HIV exclusion, the HIV risk questions may be asked. Insurers may still ask for details of positive HIV tests as to do otherwise would be to offer an unfair contract to those already infected;
- Problems arising from, for example, the limitations of old computer systems should be solved, through manual administration if necessary. Individuals should not be declined a policy simply because the system cannot impose a particular exclusion;
- The policy should state clearly whether the exclusion relates to the whole contract, to some part of it, or to one or more of the benefits;
- Where HIV/AIDS is excluded, name the occupations (if any) where the exclusion will be waived – for example, medical or emergency workers where HIV/AIDS is contracted through normal occupational duties;
- Documents should include the full names for HIV and AIDS:
  - HIV = Human Immunodeficiency Virus;
  - AIDS = Acquired Immune Deficiency Syndrome;
- Where definitions are required, suggested forms are:
  - HIV – a viral infection, caused by the human immunodeficiency virus, that gradually destroys the immune system;
  - AIDS – the most serious stage of HIV infection characterised by symptoms of severe immune deficiency.

ANNEX B

Guidance: arranging an HIV test

[5106]

B.1 This guidance note details the points that insurers should consider when arranging for an applicant to be tested for HIV.

Choice of test method and provider

B.2 When deciding whether to employ blood or saliva or OMT (oral mucosal transudate) tests, and when deciding which testing centres and laboratories to use, insurers may wish to consider:

- The quality of pre-test discussion and care given to applicants
- The robustness of individual laboratories' protocols
- The testing kits used – in particular their reliability and whether they are customer-friendly. If saliva tests are used, whether this is sufficiently accurate to give a positive result
- The service standards of each laboratory
- The cost of the testing procedure
- Any customer requirements

B.3 Insurers will want to undertake regular reviews to ensure that the chosen testing centres and laboratories continue to be reliable and effective providers of test services.

Customer pre-testing leaflet and consent

B.4 A pre-testing leaflet and a consent form **must** be issued directly to every applicant who is asked to have an HIV test. They should be sent by first class post, and the name and address should be carefully checked prior to posting.

B.5 Recommended text for the pre-testing leaflet and the consent form are reproduced at the end of this annex.

Recommended procedures for the insurer

B.6 If an HIV test is to be requested, it will need to be carried out by a clinician. The insurer should inform the applicant that a test is being requested and at which testing centre it will be carried out. If the applicant wishes the test to be carried out by their own doctor or by another centre this should be treated on its merits. The applicant should also be told to take the leaflet and consent form with them to the testing centre.

B.7 If an insurer "approved" testing centre is **not** to be used, the surgery or centre that is used should be asked to provide the insurer with a copy of the protocol used by their health professionals. The insurer will want to be satisfied that the professional who will carry out the test has clear instructions covering:

- The content of the discussion to be given prior to obtaining consent for the test and confirmation that they will check that the applicant has read and understood the pre-testing leaflet;
- The need to obtain the applicant's written consent to a tissue sample being taken, and to obtain the contact details of the applicant's nominee who the insurer will contact if the test result is positive;
- The need to refuse to proceed further if the applicant does not provide consent.

ANNEX C

HIV Pre-testing leaflet

[5107]
As you are probably aware, the Acquired Immune Deficiency Syndrome (AIDS) is caused by infection with a virus known as Human Immunodeficiency Virus (HIV).

When insurers consider an application for life or health protection insurance, they sometimes require additional information about your risk of HIV. This assessment of HIV risk is designed to protect the funds held for both existing and future policyholders. Your insurance company has asked you to undergo an HIV antibody test. This could be because of answers you gave on your application form which revealed that you could be at risk of HIV, or it could be because you have applied for a relatively large amount of insurance.

The nurse/doctor will take a sample of blood/saliva (delete as appropriate). The test will form a routine part of your medical examination and the sample will be sent to a specialist laboratory. Your test will be protected by a strict code of confidentiality, and will only be disclosed if you give your written consent to the disclosure. Your insurer asks you to consent to your test result being released to your local GP, GUM clinic or HIV counselling service, as insurers are unable to provide adequate post-test support if your test proves to be positive.

A positive test would mean that you have been exposed to HIV and have developed antibodies. You should be aware of the possible consequences of testing positive. It would, however, enable you to access effective treatments earlier. If you decide not to have the test at this time, please sign the appropriate section of the enclosed declaration and ask the doctor/nurse to return it to the insurance company. You will, of course, understand that this will mean that we cannot proceed further with your application. Your decision not to test will not be held against you for any future applications.

If you have no objections to this test being performed, please sign the declaration and consent in the nurse's presence.

Your Full Name: . . . .

Details and address of person nominated to receive a test result if it is positive

. . . .

. . . .

. . . .

. . . .

Signature: . . . .

Date: . . . .

Witnessed by (Nurse): . . . .

Insurance Company: . . . .

Reference Number: . . . .

Refusal to be tested form

REFUSAL TO BE TESTED
I am unwilling to undergo testing for HIV antibodies. I understand that, as a result, my application for life assurance will be cancelled.

Signature: ....
Date: ....
Witnessed by (Nurse): ....

ANNEX D

Example text for HIV protocol

[5108]
To: The health professional providing HIV discussion and test services

We would be grateful if you could please follow the procedures below when dealing with individuals who have applied for insurance with us, and whom we have asked to take an HIV test. This will help to ensure that a consistent and thorough approach is maintained.

(1) Ensure that the person to be tested has read and understood the HIV pre-testing leaflet that has been sent to them
(2) Carry out the pre-test discussion
(3) Ask the applicant if they are willing to take the HIV test
(4) If they are, ensure they complete the written consent form for the HIV test, including nominating another individual apart from themselves (normally their GP or GUM clinic) who the insurer will contact if the test result is positive. In the event of the applicant being unwilling or unable to make a nomination confirm (and obtain their agreement to) yourselves being the contact point. (If the centre is not able to provide suitable support the default option would be the applicant's own GP)
(5) Witness their signature on the consent form
(6) Take a sample of blood or saliva, as directed by the insurer
(7) Send the sample to the analysing laboratory on the same day
(8) Return the completed consent form to the insurer with the medical examiner's report.

[Insurance company sign off.]

MEDICAL INFORMATION AND INSURANCE

Joint guidelines from the British Medical Association and the Association of British Insurers

July 2008

1. INTRODUCTION

[5109]
This joint guidance has been drawn up by the British Medical Association (BMA) and the Association of British Insurers (ABI) to set out best practice and practical advice on the use of medical information in insurance. It is primarily designed for providers of primary medical services who have a registered list of patients and hold their long-term records, and other doctors who are asked to provide medical information to, or who work with, insurance companies.

Some of the issues covered in the guidance are the subject of more detailed advice from the BMA and the ABI. Any such sources of advice are referenced and are available on the relevant website. Information about changes affecting this guidance will be made available on the BMA and ABI websites. Contact details are given at the end of this booklet. This guidance will be reviewed every three years. The next revision of this guidance is planned for 2011.

2. MEDICAL FACTORS IN INSURANCE

2.1 Why do insurance companies need medical information?

[5110]
The insurance industry bases the premiums it charges for life and health-related products on the mortality and morbidity rates of the insured population. The basic rates for an insurance product are set by a company's actuarial department. These rates are calculated using mortality and morbidity tables and claims experience, and take into account the company's target market. This is why the same type of cover on the same life may cost differing amounts depending on the insurance company.

Individuals' lives are underwritten at the company's standard rate if their potential mortality or morbidity is not significantly greater than average for their age. Insured people who represent a risk that is worse than that of a standard life pay an extra premium or have restrictions imposed on their policies. The terms that the underwriter quotes need to be as far as possible commensurate with the extra risk and information about the applicant's health may be helpful in evaluating this risk.

The insurance industry also sometimes needs medical information when assessing insurance claims. Typically this happens when the payout on a claim is triggered by an insured person having a particular medical condition.

2.2 How is medical information collected?

If an insurance company wants information about a person's health before deciding whether, or at what premium, to offer insurance, the company can obtain this information in several ways:

- direct from the applicant him or herself
- from the applicant's general practitioner or other doctor, through a general practitioner's report (GPR)
- from an independent medical practitioner who examines the applicant specifically for the purpose of assessing medical risk factors
- from a medical examination by their general practitioner; and/or
- through the results of a health screening or blood test.

Often more than one source of information is used. A GPR is often commissioned where the company wants more information about, or investigation of, conditions identified by the applicant. Independent examinations are used for particular products, amounts of benefit or if the applicant is over a certain age. Such examinations are helpful in identifying conditions or illnesses, for example hypertension, which have not previously been diagnosed.

Although an insurance company may rely on factual information about an applicant's health in its underwriting decisions, it must not discriminate unfairly against any applicant, including people with disabilities. Guidance on the circumstances in which insurers may offer less favourable terms to people with disabilities is given in the ABI's An insurer's guide to the Disability Discrimination Act 1995.[1]

The insurance contract is between the policyholder and the insurance company. Applicants must provide answers to questions asked by the insurer carefully, accurately and to the best of their knowledge and belief. Failure to do so could invalidate a policy. Provided the applicant has given valid consent, the doctor's duty is to respond to the questions he or she is asked based on information acquired or held in a professional capacity as the applicant's doctor.

2.3 Information required for different insurance products

There are various types of insurance products providing life, health and disability cover, and different underwriting considerations for each of these types of cover. Insurance companies only need information that is relevant to the type of insurance, and should make unambiguously clear to doctors what information they require. It is worth noting that some applicants apply for more than one type of cover at a time.

Some insurance policies require the insured person who has been diagnosed with a condition that may be subject to dispute, such as mental illness or back pain, to have been diagnosed by and be under the care of a consultant or GP, who is a specialist in the insured person's condition. Neither the BMA nor the ABI wish to see NHS resources used inappropriately, and would not want to encourage an NHS GP to make a referral solely to satisfy the conditions of an insurance policy. If the insured person's NHS GP does not consider that a referral for specialist care is necessary, and an insurance company requires a specialist opinion, the payment of a private specialist opinion would need to be agreed between the insured person and the company concerned.

Appendix 1 provides an overview of the types of cover provided and the types of medical information that a company's chief medical officer (CMO) and underwriter will find useful in the medical assessment of an application or a claim. Insurance companies may find it helpful to provide information of this nature to doctors they are asking to write reports.

3. MEDICAL REPORTS

[5111]
Insurance companies generally prefer to ask the applicant's GP to write a report rather than arrange an independent examination. A GP is likely to be able to provide an overall picture of the applicant's health instead of just the snapshot seen by an independent examiner. A GPR can, for example, validate the information that the applicant has provided or clarify whether an applicant's condition is being controlled. Some applicants also prefer this option as it may be more convenient than having an independent examination.

Some general practitioners have expressed concerns about this process, however, as they believe that it endangers the open, trusting nature of the doctor-patient relationship. There is anecdotal evidence to show that some patients do not share information with their GP or avoid going to their GP for advice or treatment because they think the information will not be kept confidential. They may believe that it will jeopardise their employment prospects, their chances of getting insurance at standard rates or of obtaining insurance cover at all. The BMA is concerned about the effects on the health of the individual and the public of information being withheld from doctors providing care. The scale of this problem is not known, but the ABI and the BMA suggest that, should such fears arise, insurers should explain to their clients the reasons why the information is needed, their confidentiality safeguards, and applicants' rights under the Data Protection and Access to Medical Reports Acts. Insurers should not submit GPRs to general practitioners without the applicant's consent obtained in accordance with the principles set out in this document.

It may, however, be the case in the future that, for example, with the introduction of polyclinics and expansion of private general practice, patients will not be registered with a traditional GP practice. Furthermore, how patient health information is stored and accessed looks set to change with the introduction of national care record systems. The ABI and BMA will monitor these developments and revise this guidance accordingly as the situation changes.

4. GENERAL PRACTITIONER REPORTS

[5112]

The ABI and BMA have developed a standard GPR form, which is available on the ABI and BMA websites (www.abi.org.uk and www.bma.org.uk) and is widely used.

Only relevant information should be provided and it is ethically unacceptable to provide extraneous information. Doctors must not send originals, photocopies or printouts of full medical records in lieu of medical reports and ABI members should not accept them. The full records are not necessary and will very probably include information that is not relevant to the insurance being applied for. Insurance companies only need information that is relevant to the policy. Disclosure or other processing of information that is released without the consent of the applicant or insured person is likely to breach the Data Protection Act 1998, and may compromise a doctor's registration.

4.1 Consent for disclosure

Doctors' professional, ethical and legal duties require them not to disclose information about their patients without consent. This is true in all but the most exceptional of circumstances.[2]

4.1.1 Proof of consent

Doctors must not release information about patients simply because another person requests it. They must be able to justify any decision to disclose information to an insurance company. Except where the disclosure is about a deceased person (see section 10), that justification is evidence of their patients' valid consent. The GMC requires doctors to:

> "Obtain, or have seen, written consent to the disclosure from the patient or a person properly authorised to act on the patient's behalf."[3]

Similarly, BMA policy states that doctors should refuse to complete insurance reports unless a copy of the applicant's written consent has been provided for the doctor's retention. The consent form should make clear what the applicant is agreeing to. Doctors should not rely on an electronic copy of the applicant's signed consent form unless satisfied that the company has in place robust mechanisms for verifying that the document has not been altered in any way.

4.1.2 Validity of consent

Consent for disclosure of information is valid only where applicants understand the nature and extent of the information that is being requested, and the use to which it will be put. If doctors are in any doubt about whether valid consent has been given, they should check with the applicant. The GMC requires doctors to:

> "Be satisfied that the patient has been told at the earliest opportunity about the purpose of the examination and/or disclosure, the extent of the information to be disclosed and the fact that relevant information cannot be concealed or withheld. You might wish to show the form to the patient before you complete it to ensure the patient understands the scope of the information requested."[4]

The insurance company or agent is responsible for ensuring that the consent is competently given and is based on a full understanding of the request. There is anecdotal evidence that, in the past, the subjects of GPRs have not always been aware of the extent of the information that is requested. To minimise the potential for misunderstanding, insurance companies, or their agents, could give applicants a copy of the questions their doctor will be asked, with time for the information to be read and understood, as part of the application process or the process of seeking consent.

4.2 Access to GPRs

All doctors who write medical reports should be prepared to discuss the content of reports with the patient. The GMC advises doctors to check with insurance applicants whether they wish to see their report, unless it has been clearly and specifically stated that they do not.[5]

In addition, the Access to Medical Reports Act 1988 gives insurance applicants rights in respect of reports written about them. It covers reports written by the applicant's GP, a specialist, or any other registered health care professional who has provided care. Reports written by an independent medical examiner are not covered (see section 5).

The administrative requirements of the Act fall mainly upon insurance companies. Companies must inform applicants of their rights under the Act:

- to withhold permission for the company to seek a medical report (that is, to refuse consent to the release of information)
- to have access to the medical report after completion by the doctor either before it is sent to the company or up to six months after it is sent
- if seeing the report before it is sent, to instruct the doctor not to send the report; and
- to request the amendment of inaccuracies in the report.

The applicant must be notified in writing of these rights.

If an applicant indicates a wish to see the report before it is sent, the insurance company must tell the doctor and explain the applicant's rights.

The applicant has 21 days from the time of notification to exercise the right to see the report. It is the applicant's responsibility to contact the doctor regarding arrangements for obtaining access. If the report is not seen within 21 days, the doctor may send the completed report to the insurance company. If the applicant sees the report and withdraws consent for it to be released, it must not be dispatched and the doctor should inform the company.

If the applicant believes that there are factual inaccuracies in the report, he or she may seek their correction. If the doctor agrees that a factual error has been made, the report must be amended accordingly. If the doctor does not agree that there is an error, he or she must append a note to the report regarding the disputed information.

Doctors cannot comply with applicants' or insured people's requests to leave out relevant information from reports. If an applicant or an insured person refuses to give permission for certain relevant information to be included, the doctor should indicate to the insurance company that he or she cannot write a report, taking care not to reveal any information the applicant or insured person did not want revealed.

Doctors and insurance companies should ensure that they are familiar with the provisions of the Access to Medical Reports Act. Detailed guidance for doctors is available from the BMA.[6]

5. INDEPENDENT MEDICAL REPORTS

[5113]

This section covers reports that are written by a doctor who examines the applicant solely for the purpose of writing a medical report, and has had no other professional relationship with the applicant.

5.1 Consent

Insurance companies asking applicants to be examined by an independent doctor should explain the nature and purpose of the examination, together with the necessary practical details. As part of this, applicants could be provided with a copy of the questions the doctor will be asked to answer, and must be provided with a copy on request.

The examining doctor also has responsibilities to ensure that he or she has valid consent to undertake the examination and that the applicant understands the nature and implications of any tests involved. Consent is also needed before information about the applicant may be disclosed to the insurance company. The General Medical Council says that doctors must:

> "Be satisfied that the patient has been told at the earliest opportunity about the purpose of the examination and/or disclosure, the extent of the information to be disclosed and the fact that relevant information cannot be concealed or withheld. You might wish to show the form to the patient before you complete it to ensure the patient understands the scope of the information requested."[7]

If during the course of, or as part of, an examination the examining doctor detects some significant abnormality or other feature of the applicant's health that requires investigation or treatment, and of which the applicant may not be aware, the doctor has an ethical responsibility to ensure that either the applicant or, with the applicant's consent, his or her GP, is informed promptly. The examining doctor should usually undertake this task. If this is not possible, the company's CMO might need to be involved. The purpose of informing the GP is to give people the opportunity to discuss with their own GP their health management if they have a medical condition that needs attention. The GP has an ethical obligation to discuss with his or her patient that patient's management and care. Examining doctors may find it helpful to ascertain the applicant's views on disclosure to his or her GP before the examination, and to obtain permission to liaise with the GP and CMO, if the need arises.

5.2 Access to independent medical reports

All doctors who write medical reports should be prepared to discuss the content of reports with the applicant. The GMC advises doctors to check with insurance applicants whether they wish to see their report.[8]

In addition, the Data Protection Act gives people rights to see and have copies of health records which:

- are about them and from which they can be identified (either directly or in conjunction with other information the person holding the record has or is likely to have)
- consist of information relating to their physical or mental health or condition; and
- have been made by or on behalf of a health professional in connection with their care.

The ABI and the BMA believe that this includes reports written by doctors who examine people for the sole purpose of writing a report and who have no other clinical relationship with the person. The Data Protection Act also gives certain rights for inaccurate information to be corrected. Detailed advice for doctors about the Act, and the fees that may be charged for providing access to and copies of records, is available from the BMA.[9]

6. CONTENT OF REPORTS

[5114]
This section gives general guidance on completing medical reports. Insurance companies must ensure that they only ask for information that is relevant to the insurance product. Similarly doctors must ensure that they disclose only information that is relevant to the request and should be aware of their obligations of confidentiality to other patients, particularly the applicant's family (see section 6.5).

Medical reports are about clinical facts and the doctor's opinion about the applicant's medical condition. Doctors should not be asked to give an opinion about whether an applicant's condition merits the application of a 'normal' or 'increased' rate of insurance. In cases where doctors consider it inappropriate to answer a question they should indicate this on the form.

6.1 Sexually transmitted infections

The ABI and the BMA are aware that the possibility that information about sexually transmitted infections (STIs) will be revealed to another party, such as an insurance company, might discourage some people from approaching their GP about this area of their health. The problem of information being withheld from the GP is particularly pronounced in this area since genitourinary medicine (GUM) is an area of specialist medical care that patients can access without a referral from their GP. Anecdotal evidence suggests that patients sometimes seek services direct from GUM clinics because they prefer to retain anonymity in this area, or in order to conceal from their GP information that they believe may affect their chance of obtaining insurance at standard rate, or at all.

The BMA and the ABI are concerned about the health implications of patients not seeking advice and testing for HIV and other STIs, and of patients' refusal to allow their GP to be kept informed about certain aspects of their health care. There is evidence to suggest that the actuarial implications of withholding information about isolated or non-serious STIs from insurance reports would be negligible. Such negligible impact on insurance companies, coupled with the potential to overcome some patients' disincentive to seek advice and testing regarding STIs, makes a strong medical and public health argument for this information being excluded from insurance reports.

The BMA and the ABI therefore believe that insurers should not request, and doctors should not reveal, information about an isolated incident of an STI that has no long-term health implications, or even multiple episodes of non-serious STIs, again where there are no long-term health implications. Other incidents of STIs may have actuarial or underwriting significance and should be revealed in accordance with the consent guidelines in this document.

6.2 HIV, Hepatitis B and C

Insurance companies should not ask whether an applicant for insurance has taken an HIV or Hepatitis B or C test, had counselling in connection with such a test, or received a negative test result. Doctors should not reveal this information when writing reports and insurance companies will not expect this information to be provided. Insurers may ask only whether someone has had a positive test result, or is receiving treatment for HIV/AIDS, or Hepatitis B or C.

For large value policies or where there is a need to clarify the level of risk, insurers may send applicants a supplementary questionnaire and/or request that they are tested for HIV, or Hepatitis B or C. A test will only be administered after the applicant has: been notified of the test procedure; given valid consent in writing; nominated a doctor or clinic to receive the results if the test is positive; and received an appropriate pre-test discussion before the test is undertaken. In the rare cases of a positive result it is important that the nominee is told the result as quickly as possible so the applicant can be informed and arrangements made for future care.

Existing life insurance policies will not be affected in any way by taking an HIV test, even if the result is positive. Providing that the applicant did not withhold any material facts when the life policy was taken out, life insurers will meet all valid claims whatever the cause of death, including AIDS-related diseases. Material facts the applicant might need to reveal include information about activities that increase the risk of HIV infection.

The ABI has published a statement of best practice on HIV and insurance.[10]

6.3 Lifestyle questions

Doctors are expert in clinical matters and can only give professional advice about those issues upon which they are expert. Nevertheless doctors often do hold information about patients' lifestyle, such as smoking, alcohol intake, drug use or sexual behaviour. The applicant might want his/her GP to provide any information about his/her lifestyle held in the GP record or the applicant might want to be the source of this information him/herself. Only the applicant has accurate information about lifestyle. Medical conditions that have arisen as a result of a patient's lifestyle choice are legitimate areas for doctors to comment on with, of course, appropriate consent.

6.4 Genetic information

The use of the results of genetic tests by insurers is tightly controlled. A genetic test is defined as

> "a test that examines the structure of chromosomes (cytogenetic tests) or detects abnormal patterns in the DNA of specific genes (molecular tests). A genetic test can be predictive or diagnostic:
>
> - a *predictive* genetic test is taken prior to the appearance of any symptoms of the condition in question
> - a *diagnostic* genetic test is taken to confirm a diagnosis based on existing symptoms"

The details of the arrangements are set out in the ABI's code of practice on genetic testing.[11]

Key points include:

- Applicants must not be asked or put under any pressure to undergo a predictive genetic test in order to obtain insurance.
- Insurance companies may not ask for predictive genetic test results from applicants for insurance policies up to £500,000 for life insurance or £300,000 for critical illness or paying annual benefits of £30,000 for income protection. Doctors must not give insurers predictive genetic test results that fall outside these levels and have not been approved for use by the Genetics and Insurance Committee.
- Above these levels, insurers may only take into account the results of genetic tests which have been approved for this purpose by the government's Genetics and Insurance Committee (GAIC) which assesses whether the tests and their results are relevant for insurance purposes.[12]
- Applicants may wish to volunteer favourable genetic test results that demonstrate that they have not inherited a condition in their family. Insurers may take these into account in underwriting. In this case an insurer may wish to seek confirmation from the GP, or geneticist, of the interpretation of the test result with the patient's consent.
- Insurance companies have been asked to publicise their policy on the use of favourable genetic test results on their websites.

6.5 Family history

Many companies ask an applicant to provide details if parents or siblings have suffered from or died of conditions with an inherited component. These usually include heart disease, stroke, MS, diabetes and cancer. GPR forms also often ask doctors to provide any information from the applicant's own medical record which shows that the applicant is aware of a family history of inherited conditions.

Requesting information about family history from an applicant's doctor presents ethical and practical difficulties. Information on GP records about a genetic risk may have come from a number of sources, including direct from the patient or from the GP's knowledge of other family members, and it is not always apparent which. Clearly patients can only give valid consent for the disclosure of information when they are aware of the nature and extent of the information being disclosed.

In order to ensure that there is no breach of family members' confidentiality, doctors may choose not to complete this section of the GPR if they wish. Doctors should, however, report the results of any tests or investigations they have undertaken on applicants because of their family history, whilst bearing in mind the limited moratorium on the use of genetic information in insurance (see section 6.4). This information may be useful in confirming or counteracting information about family history provided by the patient. For example if the applicant had mentioned a family history of breast cancer, it may be helpful for the doctor to report that the applicant had undergone tests, such as BRCA testing, which revealed a reduced risk of developing cancer (subject to the restrictions under 6.4 regarding disclosure of genetic test results). Under no circumstances should doctors reveal information about an insurance applicant's family if the information did not come from the applicant him or herself.

7. EXPLANATIONS

[5115]
Insurance companies must provide written reasons for any higher than standard premium, rejection of an application, exclusion, rejection of a claim or cancellation of a policy to applicants or insured people, on request. They must not ask applicants' doctors to explain their actuarial and underwriting decisions. If the company is concerned that the applicant is not aware of a health condition that has influenced the underwriting, or if it believes that further care or treatment may be beneficial, a medical officer of the company should discuss the best way to proceed with the applicant's GP promptly. Any health concerns that the insurance company has brought to the attention of the GP should be discussed (if the GP felt necessary) in a normal NHS consultation.

8. RELEASE OF INFORMATION TO VERIFY CLAIMS

8.1 Information about the insured person

[5116]
Consent is needed before information is disclosed to insurance companies for the purpose of verifying claims, for example before a company organises repatriation of an insured person taken ill abroad. In such cases, the company must approach the insured person for permission to release sufficient information to verify the claim. Evidence of that consent must be provided to the insured person's doctors in the usual way (see section 4.1.1). If the insured person is not competent to give consent, doctors may release information necessary to satisfy the claim provided that doing so is in the person's best interests and not contrary to his or her previously stated wishes (see in addition section 9).

8.2 Information about third parties

Sometimes insurance companies need information about people other than the holder of the policy. This is most often the case with travel insurance, for example where a close relative of the insured person becomes ill and the insured person has to curtail a holiday and return home urgently. In such cases insurance companies will want to confirm that the illness of the relative was sudden and unexpected and occurred at the time the insured person claimed. Depending on the particular nature of the policy, the company may also want to confirm that the seriousness of the condition was such that the insured person was urgently required to attend the relative. If competent to give it, the sick relative's consent is needed before doctors can release information to verify the claim. If the relative is not competent, doctors may disclose relevant information to the company provided this is not contrary to their patient's wishes or interests (see in addition section 9). The insurance company will explain what information is required in each case.

9. ADULTS WHO LACK CAPACITY

[5117]
Although ordinarily disclosures of health information require consent, where adults lack the capacity to consent on their own behalf to disclosures of their information, in certain circumstances, disclosure can still take place. Both the Adults With Incapacity (Scotland) Act (2000), and the Mental Capacity Act 2005 for England and Wales contain powers to nominate individuals to make health and welfare decisions on behalf of incapacitated adults. Where these proxy decision makers require access to health information that is necessary to carry out their functions, that information should ordinarily be provided. These individuals can also be asked to consent for disclosure to third parties. Where there are no nominated individuals, requests for access to information relating to incapacitated adults can usually be granted where there is both a legitimate need for the information, and releasing the information would be in the best interests of the incapacitated adult. In all cases, only such information as is necessary to achieve the purpose or purposes for which disclosure has been requested should be released.

10. DECEASED PEOPLE

[5118]
Doctors have an ethical obligation to keep personal information confidential after a person dies. In 2006 the Information Commissioner also ruled that, other than the limited rights of access under the Access to Health legislation, legally, a duty of confidence attaches to medical records of the deceased under section 41 of the Freedom of Information Act 2000.

Insurance companies request information about deceased people in order to assess claims. Such requests are known as 'duration certificates'. It is preferable that risks are properly assessed before a company agrees to offer cover. The contract between insurer and insured person is one of good faith and doctors should not be asked to provide guarantees against fraudulent claims. It is recognised, however, that the law does, in certain circumstances, give people with a claim arising from the death of an individual statutory rights of access to information necessary to satisfy the claim. Insurance companies should exercise those rights only where there are reasonable grounds to believe that relevant information may have been withheld at the time the policy was taken out. In the case of life insurance, this may be for example, where the insured person dies, apparently unexpectedly, say within six months of taking out the policy or where an insured person has died of heart disease although the application made no mention of the condition.

Requests for information after a person's death are made under the Access to Health Records Act 1990, that covers manual health records made since 1 November 1991, and in Northern Ireland the Access to Health Records (Northern Ireland) Order 1993, that covers manual records since 30 May 1994. Access to information recorded before these dates may only be given where this is necessary to make any later part of the records intelligible. Rights of access are limited to information necessary to satisfy the claim. Insurance companies must not ask for full records to be released, and doctors must not provide any information that is not relevant to the claim. There are three further categories of information that must not be released:

- information that the deceased made known they did not want released
- information that identifies a third party who is not a health professional
- information that, if disclosed, is likely to cause serious mental or physical harm to somebody's health.

Doctors may wish to counsel their patients about the possibility of disclosure after their death and solicit their views if it is apparent that there may be some sensitivity. People's views and wishes should be recorded in their health records. It also follows that insurance companies must explain to applicants if there is a chance that information will be sought following their death. Insurance application forms contain a clause asking applicants to agree to information about them being disclosed after their death in the event that a claim is made. Although this agreement may have been given a significant time before disclosure is actually sought, it does give doctors an indication of the applicant's wishes at the time the policy was taken out. Before disclosing any information, doctors should consider their obligations under the Access to Health Records Act.

11. FEES

[5119]
Reports and medical examinations undertaken at the request of insurance companies are not part of the terms of service of either NHS GPs or hospital doctors. Doctors may therefore charge the company a fee for this work. Fees are covered in an agreement between the BMA and the ABI. The agreement covers GPRs, supplementary reports, medical examinations undertaken by an applicant's own GP, quality of work by GPs and the process for reviewing the agreement should this prove necessary in the future. Information about agreed fees is available on the BMA website.

NHS GPs are reminded that they cannot charge their NHS patients for consultations that arise from this process, such as the discussion of health concerns that have come to light during the course of applying for insurance.

There is no agreement, as yet, on fees for HIV testing for insurance purposes. Fees for this work should be fully reflective of the time and expertise needed for pre- and post-test discussions.

12. RETURN AND QUALITY OF REPORTS

[5120]
Doctors are encouraged to return reports as quickly as possible. If proper professional fees are to be charged, high quality reports should be produced and processed quickly, normally within 20 working days of receipt of the request. If a delay is expected, doctors should make this clear to their patients and indicate when they expect to be able to complete the report. Reports must be legible and authorised by the doctor.

It should be noted, however, that some of these reports are covered by the Access to Medical Reports Act (see section 4.2). Under this Act, if an applicant indicates that he or she wishes to see the report before it is dispatched, the GP should refrain from sending it for 21 days from the receipt of the request for the report. It may be advisable to inform the insurance company if a request to see the report has been made. Once the applicant has seen the report he or she may decide to withdraw consent for it to be sent. In such circumstances the insurance company will still pay the appropriate fee.

13. FURTHER INFORMATION

[5121]
For further information about these guidelines BMA members may contact:
*ask*BMA on 0870 60 60 828 or
British Medical Association
Department of Medical Ethics, BMA House
Tavistock Square, London WC1H 9JP
Tel: 020 7383 6286
Fax: 020 7383 6233
Email: ethics@bma.org.uk

Further information for BMA members about fees
is available from the BMA's website and *ask*BMA 0870 60 60 828.

Non-members may contact:
British Medical Association
Public Affairs Department, BMA House
Tavistock Square, London WC1H 9JP
Tel: 020 7387 4499
Fax: 020 7383 6400
Email: info.public@bma.org.uk

Health and Protection
Association of British Insurers
51 Gresham Street
London EC2V 7HQ
Tel: 020 7600 3333
Fax: 020 7696 8999
Email: info@abi.org.uk
Web: www.abi.org.uk

APPENDIX 1
MEDICAL INFORMATION IN THE ASSESSMENT OF RISK

[5122]
This appendix provides an overview of some of the types of insurance cover that are provided and the medical information that a company's chief medical officer (CMO) and underwriter will find useful in the medical assessment of an application.

Life insurance

Many products fall within the general description of life insurance. The most common types are:

- **Term insurance**: the simplest form of life insurance. The policy is limited to a definite term with the sum insured payable only on death within that term.
- **Whole of life insurance**: pays the sum insured upon the death of the insured person whenever that should occur.
- **Endowments**: combine life cover and an investment element. The sum insured is paid at the end of a fixed term or on the prior death of the insured person.

Other products include:

- **Impaired Life Annuity** – pays a guaranteed income in return for a capital sum to someone with a significant impairment that reduces his/her life expectancy. An impaired annuity pays out a higher regular amount than a normal annuity.
- **Discounted Gift Scheme** – enables a person to donate a gift to a trust while keeping the right to get an income from the gift. Under these arrangements, the value deemed to be transferred for tax purposes depends, among other things, on the life expectancy of the person making the gift.

Terminal illness benefit is frequently included in life insurance policies. This benefit means that the policy pays out in full if the insured person is diagnosed as having an illness or injury from which he or she is expected to die within a time specified in the policy.

Information required

A life insurance underwriter must calculate the actuarial risk of the applicant dying before the end of the term. Thus the underwriter is interested in the diagnosis, treatment, severity and prognosis of a medical condition that will predictably result in premature death, not the applicant's quality of life. Non-life threatening conditions/illnesses are not relevant in the assessment of life insurance. Examples are colds, flu, routine vaccinations, wisdom teeth, uncomplicated pregnancies, contraception, minor breaks and sprains, common childhood complaints where there have been no sequelae, or a single episode of a sexually transmitted infection.

Critical illness insurance

Critical illness policies typically pay out a lump sum if the insured person either dies or is diagnosed with a critical illness that meets the insurer's policy. Policies usually cover cancer, coronary artery bypass surgery, heart attack, kidney failure, major organ transplant, multiple sclerosis and stroke, and may specify other conditions. There are model wordings for the most common conditions. While insurers are free to decide on the conditions or exclusions applicable to their products, where a model wording is available, it should be used.[13]

Critical illness insurance can be marketed as additional cover on a life insurance product or as a stand-alone policy. In addition to the specified critical illnesses, policies can also include cover for total and permanent incapacity.

Information required

The underwriter is concerned with the possibility of one of the covered critical illnesses occurring. Information is therefore needed about the existence of any of the conditions covered, and other health factors that affect the likelihood of the conditions covered developing. The ABI Statement of Best Practice for Critical Illness defines the conditions that are covered.

Total incapacity can be covered in critical illness cover, and in such cases the underwriter is also interested in medical conditions that, whilst not on the list of conditions, mean that the insured person is permanently unable to carry out any part of his or her occupation.

Income protection plans/permanent health insurance

Income protection cover protects the insured person against the loss of earned income resulting from illness or accident. The income continues to be paid until the insured person is fit to return to work, or the policy ends. Benefits are paid after the insured person has been unable to work because of an illness or injury for an agreed period – typically three or six months but other periods are available. With health and disability cover it is the morbidity of an applicant that is relevant in the medical assessment. Therefore whilst life-threatening conditions are of importance, conditions which could possibly lead to chronic health and disability problems are of equal concern when assessing the medical information. The nature of the applicant's occupation may affect the significance of certain conditions.

Information required

The underwriter needs the insured person's diagnosis, the date the problem was first noted, dates of subsequent problems, details about the care being received (including treatment and investigations), severity of the condition, prognosis and the amount of time the insured person has had off work due to the condition. If a part of the body is affected, it is important to specify whether it is the right or left side.

Waiver of contribution

This optional benefit means that the insured person does not have to pay the premiums on the policy while the insured person is too ill to work. For example waiver of contribution taken out with a pension plan covers the payment of the premium if the insured person is unable to carry on working due to ill-health or disability beyond a pre-defined period, usually six months.

Information required

The risk being assessed is similar to that of income protection/permanent health insurance therefore the same medical information and considerations are relevant.

Long-term care

Long-term care benefit is payable if the insured person becomes physically or mentally disabled as a result of illness, accident or old age, and requires routine care for an extended period of time. It is payable to insured people who are unable to carry out specific activities of daily living, as set out in the policy. Activities of daily living (ADLs) include bathing, dressing and feeding.

Information required

The vast majority of applicants for long-term care insurance are retired. The underwriter is looking for chronic and progressive mental and physical conditions/illnesses that could lead to the applicant being unable to perform the activities of daily living.

APPENDIX 2
CONFIDENTIALITY OF MEDICAL REPORTS

[5123]
The insurance company's chief executive is responsible for the confidentiality of medical information that the company holds. The chief executive must take advice from the chief medical officer (CMO) or other medical adviser in respect of medical information.[14]

The information companies hold about individuals may only be used for the purposes for which the information is supplied. If an applicant applies to the same company for a different product, consent is needed for the information already held to be used for this new purpose. Under no circumstances is it acceptable for insurance companies to use information gained about one person in actuarial assessment of his or her relatives.

Insurance companies requesting medical reports must supply doctors with envelopes, pre-addressed to the CMO or senior medical adviser. Reports should be returned in these envelopes and marked 'confidential – medical report'. Administrative duties in respect of these reports may be delegated to non-medical staff, but the CMO or senior medical adviser remains ultimately responsible for confidentiality. Similarly, the CMO or senior medical adviser is ultimately responsible for medical decision-making relevant to requests for medical information about applicants or insured people.

The Data Protection Act 1998 and the Financial Services Authority regulations apply to all those involved in the sales process, including the company's own salesforce, appointed representatives, telesales units, and all administrative staff within head offices, regional offices and branch offices. The Data Protection Guidance[15] sets out how medical reports and other information should be handled within the company. Only staff with a business need to handle medical evidence, as directed by the CMO, should have access to such evidence and efforts should be made to ensure that staff with no need to know do not come into contact with health information. All staff working in an environment where sensitive information is handled must have a thorough understanding of the company's confidentiality policy.

Special considerations apply to confidentiality and external bodies. Subject to the applicant's or insured person's explicit and informed consent, medical information may be shared with or shown to people outside the company if this is necessary for the conduct of business. This may be necessary to process the individual's application and policy; to handle a complaint; and to satisfy audit requirements, or to prevent fraudulent applications.

The Data Protection Guidance also covers methods of communication and the storage of confidential information.

NOTES AND REFERENCES

1 Association of British Insurers (2003) *An insurer's guide to the Disability Discrimination Act 1995*. London: ABI. Available on the ABI's website: www.abi.org.uk.

2 Detailed advice about confidentiality and the situations in which it may be breached are given in: British Medical Association (2008) *Confidentiality and disclosure of health information tool kit*. London: BMA. Available on the BMA's website: www.bma.org.uk.

3 General Medical Council (2004) *Confidentiality: protecting and providing information: frequently asked questions*, qu 13. London: GMC.

4 Ibid.

5 Ibid.

6 British Medical Association (2007) *Guidelines on the Access to Medical Reports Act 1988*. London: BMA. Available on the BMA's website: www.bma.org.uk.

7 General Medical Council (2004) *Confidentiality: protecting and providing information: frequently asked questions*, qu 13. London: GMC.

8 Ibid.

9 British Medical Association (2007) *Access to health records by patients*. London: BMA. Available on the BMA's website: www.bma.org.uk.

10 Association of British Insurers (2004) *Statement of best practice on HIV and insurance*. London: ABI. Available on the ABI's website at: www.abi.org.uk.

11 The terms of the ABI's moratorium and *Genetic testing – ABI code of practice* are available on the ABI's genetics and insurance website at: www.abi.org.uk.

12 A current list is available on the ABI website at: www.abi.org.uk/consumer2/disclosure.htm.

13 The full list of model wordings for assessing claims on critical illness policies can be found in the ABI's *Statement of best practice for critical illness insurance*, available on the ABI website at: www.abi.org.uk.

14 The BMA issues general guidance on confidentiality for doctors: British Medical Association (2008) *Confidentiality and disclosure of health information tool kit*. London: BMA. Available on the BMA's website: www.bma.org.uk.

15 The financial services area, Association of British Insurers, Association of Unit Trusts and Investment Funds, British Bankers Association, Consumer Credit Trade Association, Council of Mortgage Lenders, and Finance & Leasing Association joint guidance on the Data Protection Act, including confidentiality guidelines available at www.bba.org.uk reference ISBN 1-874185-16-6.

ABI CODE OF PRACTICE
MANAGING CLAIMS FOR INDIVIDUAL AND GROUP LIFE, CRITICAL ILLNESS AND INCOME PROTECTION INSURANCE PRODUCTS

Non-Disclosure and Treating Customers Fairly

January 2009

1 SCOPE

[5124]

1.1 This ABI code covers the continuing fair treatment of claims for UK individual and group life, critical illness, income protection and other long-term protection insurance contracts in the light of evolving industry practice, FSA regulations and the treating customers fairly (TCF) regime and experience. It covers individual policies and individually underwritten benefits within group schemes, but does not apply to any non-disclosure by scheme owners.

1.2 For the purposes of this ABI code, any reference to non-disclosure includes both the omission and misrepresentation of material information that the insurer has asked for.

1.3 This code covers the fair treatment of non-disclosure occurring during the application process and discovered at the point of claim.

1.4 This code replaces previous guidance issued by ABI dealing with non-disclosure discovered at the point of claim.

1.5 ABI believes that this code goes beyond the current legal position in many aspects. However, insurers should note that it does not purport in any way to replace the Law.

2 THE THREE CATEGORIES OF NON-DISCLOSURE AND ASSOCIATED OUTCOMES

2.1 The three high level categories of non-disclosure and outcomes are set out in the table below.

Category	Explanation	Outcome
Innocent	• The customer has acted honestly and reasonably in all of the circumstances, including the customer's individual circumstances but only where these were known to the insurer. • In the circumstances, a reasonable person would have considered that the information was not relevant to the insurer. • The non-disclosure would have resulted in a different underwriting outcome.	Pay the claim in full
Negligent	• Applies where the non-disclosure resulted from insufficient care – the failure to exercise reasonable care. This includes anything from an understandable oversight or an inadvertent mistake to serious negligence. • In the circumstances, a reasonable person would have known that the information given was incorrect and was relevant to the insurer. • The non-disclosure would have resulted in a different underwriting outcome.	Apply a proportionate remedy
Deliberate or without any care	• Only applies where the non-disclosure was deliberate or without any care. • In the circumstances, on the balance of probabilities, the customer knew, or must have known, that the information given was both incorrect and relevant to the insurer, or the customer acted without any care as to whether it was either correct or relevant to the insurer. • The non-disclosure would have resulted in a different underwriting outcome.	Avoid the policy (decline the claim and cancel the policy from inception)

2.2 The overall principle is that the severe remedy of avoiding a policy from outset should be confined to the most serious cases of non-disclosure. See section 8 below.

3 ASSESSING CLAIMS

3.1 Customers cannot be expected to provide information that they are unaware of. In these circumstances, there is no lack of utmost good faith and therefore no non-disclosure.

3.2 In assessing claims, insurers should consider all of the circumstances, including:

3.2.1 How clear and concise the relevant questions were. Where the insurer has asked a clear question, there will be a presumption that the customer realised that it would be relevant to the insurer. Insurers can expect customers to answer clear questions carefully, accurately and to the best of their knowledge and belief. However, not much weight should be given to 'catch all' or 'memory test questions'.

3.2.2 The sales process and its effect on the customer – for example:

3.2.2.1 Whether or not an intermediary was involved (see 3.4 below).

3.2.2.2 Whether or not the customer had the opportunity to check their answers.

3.2.3 The warnings given and whether these were adequately prominent.

3.3 As far as possible, insurers should always try to understand the reasons for non-disclosure. Where possible, insurers should ask the customer (or the potential beneficiary) about the reasons why the information was incomplete or incorrect before making any judgement about the category of non-disclosure.

Intermediated sales

3.4 Insurers should always try to establish the facts and credibility of allegations that non-disclosure arose as a consequence of failures during the sales process and their effect on the customer, paying special regard to those parts of the process for which the insurer, or those acting for the insurer, is responsible. In particular, where the allegations are supported by credible evidence:

3.4.1 If the intermediary was acting on behalf of the insurer, and information was properly disclosed to that intermediary, then the insurer cannot claim that the information was not disclosed to it.

3.4.2 Whether an intermediary was acting as an insurer's agent in a transaction will depend on the facts and circumstances in each case.

3.4.3 The insurer will always benefit from being able to provide an audit trail – regardless of whether the sale was intermediated – to show that clear questions were asked and understood, and that the customer had the opportunity to check and confirm the accuracy of their answers.

3.4.4 If the intermediary was clearly acting on behalf of the customer, for example, an independent financial adviser, the intermediary (as opposed to the insurer) should be accountable for any non-disclosure resulting directly from the intermediary's action or omission.

Collecting medical information

3.5 Insurers are fully entitled to ask for any medical or other information needed to properly assess a claim.

3.6 However, insurers should have a legitimate reason for requesting medical information at the point of claim and should apply the principles set out in the joint BMA/ABI guidance, 'Medical Information and Insurance', on gathering medical information at the point of claim.

3.7 Accordingly, insurers should only ask for medical information beyond that needed to assess whether the insured event has occurred, or to case manage a disability claim, to the extent that the circumstances of the claim reasonably prompt the insurer to believe that there might have been non-disclosure by the customer. In particular, insurers should:

3.7.1 Keep an audit trail of the reasons for requesting medical records (the Financial Ombudsman Service, FOS, will be concerned at the use of medical evidence clearly obtained without an appropriate reason).

3.7.2 Note that an early claim is not a reason by itself (although it may be a relevant supporting factor).

3.7.3 Carefully consider the time period for which it is appropriate to request information and the relevant areas that should be investigated.

3.7.4 Ensure that claims investigations are consistent with the timely collation of evidence and the need to make claims decisions promptly.

See Annex, example cases 1 to 5 — asking for appropriate medical information

4 A PROPORTIONATE REMEDY

4.1 A proportionate remedy means that, as far as possible, the insurer will seek to put the customer back to the same position as an identical customer who had accurately disclosed the omitted information and who paid the same premium for the same type of policy.

4.2 The outcome will therefore depend on what the underwriting decision would have been if the omitted information had been accurately disclosed at the time the customer took out the policy, as follows:

4.2.1 **The premium would have been rated** – the insurer will work out how much cover the total premium paid by the customer would have bought, and pay that amount.

See Annex, example case 6 – applying a proportionate remedy where the premium would have been rated

4.2.2 **An exclusion would have been applied to the cover** – in this case, the insurer will assess the claim as though the exclusion had been applied when the cover started. If the exclusion applies to the claim, no payment will be made. If the exclusion does not apply to the claim, a payment will be made (note: the amount paid may still be less than the full sum assured in cases where a premium rating would also have applied as above).

4.2.3 **The term would have been restricted** – in this case, the claim will be paid only if it arose within the restricted term (note: the amount paid may still be less than the full sum assured in cases where a premium rating would also have applied as above).

4.2.4 **The application would have been declined** – in this case, had the information been disclosed, there would have been no policy at all so the claim will result in no payment. However, the premiums will be returned.

4.2.5 **The underwriting decision would have been deferred** – In cases where the underwriting decision would have been deferred, or where the decision to defer the cover would have been made. As far as possible, insurers should try to determine what the ultimate underwriting decision would have been (that is, at the end of the deferred period or when the investigation was complete) and apply the appropriate remedy as above. If it is not possible to work out whether the insurer would have offered any cover, or if the deferral decision would have required the customer to re-apply at a future date, then this should be treated as a decline in 4.2.4 above.

See Annex, example cases 7 to 9 – deferred decisions

4.3 Important considerations:

4.3.1 In applying a proportionate remedy, in principle, no customer should be better off than any other customer who had disclosed all the requested information.

4.3.2 For the purpose of determining the appropriate amount to pay when a higher premium would have applied, proportionality applies at the policy level, for example where the policy covers more than one person or multiple types of benefit.

See Annex, example case 10 – applying a proportionate remedy to a multi-benefit policy

For a joint life policy see Annex, example case 6 – applying a proportionate remedy where the premium would have been rated

5 NON-DISCLOSURE AND INDUCEMENT

5.1

5.1.1 A higher premium would have applied to the policy for the same sum assured;

5.1.2 A lower sum assured would have applied to the policy for the same premium;

5.1.3 Part of the cover would have been excluded for the relevant life assured;

5.1.4 The term of the policy would have been restricted;

5.1.5 The application would have been deferred, for example, pending the outcome of a medical investigation; or

5.1.6 The application would have been declined.

6 MENU AND MULTI-BENEFIT POLICIES — SEVERABLE BENEFITS AND NON-DISCLOSURE THAT IS DELIBERATE OR WITHOUT ANY CARE

6.1 Insurers may not decline a claim as a result of non-disclosure if the omitted information was material only to a severable benefit which is not the subject of the claim.

6.2 For this purpose, for combinations of critical illness and/or income protection and/or life cover benefits in a single policy, the severable benefit types are limited to Total Permanent Disability and Waiver of Premium Benefit.

See Annex, example case 11 — a claim with non-disclosure that relates only to a severable benefit

6.3 When considering non-disclosure, insurers should take into account the risk warnings given and whether these were adequately prominent — see section 3.2.3 above.

7 NOTES ON INNOCENT NON-DISCLOSURE OR MISREPRESENTATION

7.1 Typical characteristics:

7.1.1 The question was not clear enough – any ambiguous wording should be construed in favour of the customer.

7.1.2 The question did not apply clearly to the facts in question.

7.1.3 It was reasonable for the customer to have overlooked the omitted information – for example, a minor childhood ailment.

7.2 It is irrelevant whether or not there is a link between the non-disclosure and the cause of the claim.

8 NOTES ON NON-DISCLOSURE THAT IS DELIBERATE OR WITHOUT ANY CARE

8.1 The overall principle is that the severe remedy of avoiding a policy from outset should be confined to the most serious cases of non-disclosure.

8.2 The insurer has the initial burden of establishing whether any case falls into this category on the balance of probabilities. Accordingly, insurers need clear evidence to show this applies.

8.3 This category does not apply where:

8.3.1 Having investigated the matter, the customer has a credible explanation supported by the facts for having omitted information and/or there are other credible mitigating circumstances.

8.3.2 The degree of materiality associated with the non-disclosure is relatively low and, in cases where a premium rating would have applied, the underlying risk premium rating resulting from the non-disclosed information in aggregate would not have been more than +50% (or £1/mil) for the applicable life assured.

8.4 Typical characteristics:

8.4.1 **Deliberate** – in the circumstances, the customer knew, or must have known, that the representation they made in answer to a question was incorrect, and knew, or must have known, that the information was relevant to the insurer (that is, they intended to omit the information).

8.4.2 **Without any care** – it is clear that the customer had a complete disregard for the question or the accuracy of the answer when completing the application and must have understood that the information was relevant to the insurer.

8.4.3 **Medical information** – in cases where the omitted information was about the customer's medical history or family medical history (as opposed to, for example, about occupation, time spent abroad, the use of tobacco products, alcohol or drugs) insurers should take into account that in some circumstances consumers may not have a full understanding of their medical history. Accordingly, this category is more likely to apply in the following situations:

8.4.3.1 The omitted information is widely known by consumers to be important to the risk of a claim being made (for example, cancer, heart disease, diabetes or, for income protection, periods of time off work as a result of incapacity).

8.4.3.2 The omitted information concerns recent or ongoing treatment, specialist consultations and/or medical investigations about matters that a reasonable consumer would have understood to be important to their health.

8.4.3.3 The customer has specialist knowledge – for example, someone in the medical profession or relevant parts of the insurance industr y.

See Annex, example cases 12 & 13 – non-disclosure of medical information

8.4.4 **Lifestyle information** – since lifestyle information is usually more familiar and easier for customers to understand, it follows that customers will need to give a particularly credible and convincing explanation for clearly evidenced non-disclosure not to be classified as deliberate or without any care.

See Annex, example cases 14 & 15 – where smoking is not disclosed

8.4.5 **Continuing duty of disclosure** – insurers will need to have a particularly robust case for classifying non-disclosure occurring after the application was completed as deliberate or without any care (that is, when the non-disclosure results from a change of health or other circumstances after the application was completed but before the cover starts).

8.5 Returning premiums — when avoiding a policy, insurers will normally return the premiums paid. Insurer will only keep the premiums in cases where there is clear evidence of fraud, or if the non-disclosure has been proved fraudulent in a court of law.

9 NOTES ON NEGLIGENT NON-DISCLOSURE OR MISREPRESENTATION

9.1 Includes all cases between innocent and deliberate or without any care.

10 NOTES ON THE APPLICATION OF THIS CODE FOR GROUP SCHEMES

10.1 This code only applies to non-disclosure by individual members of group schemes. It does not apply to any non-disclosure by employers, trustees or other group scheme owners.

10.2 Any non-disclosure by an individual group scheme member should not affect that member's entitlement to benefits up to the amount of any free cover limit applicable to that member at the time of joining the scheme.

10.3 Any non-disclosure by an individual scheme member should not affect any other scheme member's entitlement to receive benefits from the scheme.

11 FLOWCHART FOR ASSESSING NON-DISCLOSURE DISCOVERED AT THE POINT OF CLAIM

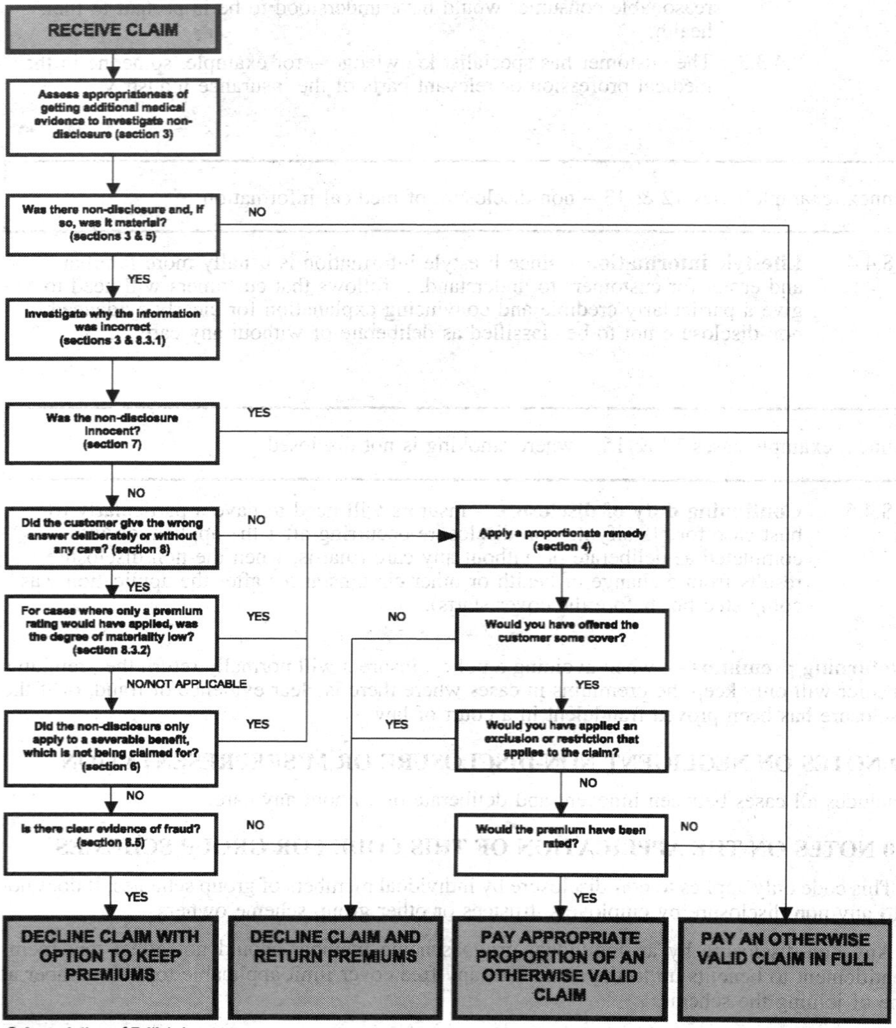
RECEIVE CLAIM
Assess appropriateness of getting additional medical evidence to investigate non-disclosure (section 3)
Was there non-disclosure and, if so, was it material? (sections 3 & 5)
NO
YES
Investigate why the information was incorrect (sections 3 & 8.3.1)
Was the non-disclosure innocent? (section 7)
YES
NO
Did the customer give the wrong answer deliberately or without any care? (section 8)
NO
Apply a proportionate remedy (section 4)
YES
For cases where only a premium rating would have applied, was the degree of materiality low? (section 8.3.2)
YES
NO
Would you have offered the customer some cover?
NO/NOT APPLICABLE
YES
Did the non-disclosure only apply to a severable benefit, which is not being claimed for? (section 6)
YES
YES
Would you have applied an exclusion or restriction that applies to the claim?
NO
NO
Is there clear evidence of fraud? (section 8.5)
NO
Would the premium have been rated?
NO
YES
YES
DECLINE CLAIM WITH OPTION TO KEEP PREMIUMS
DECLINE CLAIM AND RETURN PREMIUMS
PAY APPROPRIATE PROPORTION OF AN OTHERWISE VALID CLAIM
PAY AN OTHERWISE VALID CLAIM IN FULL

ANNEX — ILLUSTRATIVE EXAMPLES

Case 1 — asking for appropriate medical information for a benign brain tumour claim

[5125]

A 42 year old woman makes a critical illness insurance claim for a benign brain tumour after her policy has been in force for a year. The insurer's medical advice is that there is a reasonable likelihood that the woman experienced related symptoms before the policy started.

In addition to asking for all the details relating to the need to assess whether the benign brain tumour definition is met, the insurer asks her GP for a report that includes details of all consultations concerning neurological and related symptoms in the two years before the woman took out the policy. The insurer explains that it is interested in all relevant symptoms including loss of coordination or motor control, hemiparesis, numbness, speech difficulties, hearing loss, impairment of vision, intellectual impairment, headache, epilepsy, vomiting. The insurer makes it clear that it wants a copy of the original medical records, referral letters, etc that relate to any such consultations. This is so that it can get the most accurate picture of what underwriting terms, if any, it would have offered.

If the claim had been for cancer, depending on the site, the potential early symptoms might be too wide in scope for the insurer to list for the GP. Therefore, it would be appropriate for the insurer to ask for a copy of the original medical records over a time period appropriate to the likely onset of the cancer.

Case 2 — asking for appropriate medical information in an accidental death claim

A man takes out life insurance and dies less than two years later. The information on the interim certificate of the fact of death leaves the insurer with reason to believe that the customer might have committed suicide, been the victim of an unlawful killing, suffered an accident with no contributory medical factor or suffered an accident with a contributory medical factor. The insurer is at first unable to get further credible information from the Coroner or other sources.

The insurer is keen to avoid delaying settlement of the claim. It wishes to avoid repeated requests for additional information or evidence; especially for evidence that the customer could reasonably say that the insurer was able to ask for earlier in its consideration of the claim.

In some of the potential scenarios, it is likely that the customer would have experienced undisclosed symptoms of a contributing medical condition before the policy started. However, this could involve a wide range of relevant medical conditions or symptoms. In these circumstances, it is therefore reasonable for the insurer to request from the GP sight of the medical records over a time period appropriate to the medical conditions that it has reason to believe may have existed.

Before receiving this medical information, and before the Inquest has been held, the Coroner is able to inform the insurer that there is no evidence to suggest anything other than that the customer was the innocent victim of a road traffic collision and the customer had no contributory medical condition. The insurer should pay the claim and inform the GP that it no longer needs sight of the medical information.

Case 3 — asking for appropriate medical information in an accidental death claim with an underlying medical cause

A man takes out life insurance and dies less than a year later. The circumstances of his death are such that the insurer believes that he has died in a road traffic collision. The Coroner and post-mortem indicate that the man suffered a heart attack at the wheel of his car.

The insurer therefore has reason to believe that not all questions about the customer's cardiovascular history, and related factors such as family history, weight and smoking history were correctly answered. This includes coronary heart disease, congenital and valvular heart disease, cardiac arrhythmias, hypertension and other circulatory disorders, and their related symptoms, tests and treatment. The insurer writes accordingly to the GP.

The information received from the GP shows that the customer did not disclose a history of angina, related treatment and a relevant family history. However, the information doesn't enable the insurer to determine whether the non-disclosure was deliberate or precisely what terms it might have offered if there had been full disclosure at outset. Accordingly, the insurer asks the doctor for further clarification of the matters that were not disclosed.

Case 4 — asking for appropriate additional medical information for an income protection claim

A 40 year old woman makes a claim for chronic fatigue syndrome under her income protection policy which she took out six years ago. The insurer asks her GP and her Consultant Neurologist for the full medical reports on her current condition.

The GP report confirms that she is currently incapacitated. The Consultant's report suggests that a neurological investigation revealed no adverse findings. However, this report also refers to episodes of anxiety and depression when she was in her late 20's and early 30's. These episodes were not disclosed when she took out the policy, despite being the subject of clear questions in the application.

The insurer therefore asks the GP for a copy of her medical records since the age of 25. These records show recurrent episodes of depression, irritable bowel syndrome, stress at work, reports of being tired all the time, treatment with fluoxetine and prozac, as well as time off work for depression in the year before she took out the policy.

Accordingly, the insurer asks her why she did not disclose this information as the next first step in assessing her claim.

Case 5 — asking for appropriate medical information for a death claim caused by liver failure

A man dies of liver failure three years after taking out life insurance. The circumstances are such that the insurer has reason to suspect that the claim might be related to a history of heavy alcohol consumption or drug use that started before the policy was taken out, but was not disclosed.

Accordingly, the insurer asks the customer's GP for information, including a copy of the original medical records, relating to the use of alcohol and drugs in the period before the policy started, together with details of any history of liver disorder such as hepatitis or cirrhosis, or of any metabolic disorder. The insurer also asks for details of any consultations and treatment regarding the customer's mental health. The time period asked about is appropriate to the development of the conditions that the insurer has reason to be concerned about.

Case 6 — applying a proportionate remedy where the premium would have been rated

When assessing a man's critical illness claim, an insurer finds that he had incorrectly answered a question about his medical history when he took out the policy, jointly with his wife, several years before. They paid a premium of £50 a month for joint cover of £100,000. The insurer assesses the non-disclosure in accordance with this code and concludes that he had been negligent.

If he had given the correct information, using the premium rates that applied when the policy was taken out, the insurer works out that the premium of £50 a month would only have bought joint cover of £75,000.

As the claim is otherwise valid and a proportionate remedy is appropriate, the insurer pays out £75,000.

Case 7 — where the underwriting decision would have been deferred pending an investigation

A man takes out critical illness insurance and subsequently claims for cancer. In assessing the claim, the insurer discovers that when he took out the policy he failed to disclose that he was waiting for the results of a test for the malignancy of a mole. The insurer assesses the non-disclosure in accordance with this code and concludes that he had been negligent.

If the insurer had known about this, it would have deferred the underwriting decision until the result of the test was known. However, on this occasion the test showed that the mole was perfectly normal with no signs of malignancy. In these circumstances, the insurer would have accepted the application on standard terms. Accordingly, in applying a proportionate remedy, the insurer pays the claim in full.

Case 8 — where the underwriting decision would have been deferred subject to a fresh application at an unspecified time in the future

A woman takes out life insurance and subsequently dies of a heart attack. In assessing the claim, the insurer discovers that she failed to disclose that, shortly before she took out the policy, she had made a failed suicide attempt after a significant life event and she was taking treatment for depression. The insurer assesses the non-disclosure in accordance with this code and concludes that she had been negligent.

If the insurer had known this, it would have deferred the underwriting decision indefinitely, but would have been prepared to consider a new application for life insurance when she has been free from treatment for at least a year.

In these circumstances, the insurer would not have offered any cover at all at the time of her application, nor in the foreseeable future. Accordingly, the insurer applies a proportionate remedy meaning that it declines the claim, cancels the policy from inception and returns her premiums in full.

Case 9 — where the insurer would have asked for specific tests

A man takes out life insurance and subsequently dies in the early years of the policy. In assessing the claim, the insurer discovers that he failed to disclose GP consultations six months before he took out the policy. At these consultations he reported alcohol-related symptoms, including early morning tremors and a jaundiced appearance. However, there is no evidence that shows the amount of alcohol he was consuming in the period immediately before he took out the policy, nor can the insurer establish with certainty that he was advised to stop or reduce his drinking on medical grounds. The insurer assesses the non-disclosure in accordance with this code and concludes that he had been negligent. If the insurer had known about these GP consultations, it would have deferred the underwriting decision until he had taken a liver function test.

Depending on what the outcome of the liver function test would have been (if one had been performed) the underwriting decision might have been any of the following:

- Application accepted at normal rates.
- Application accepted with a higher premium (where the amount of the extra premium would have depended on the actual test result).
- Application declined.

In a case where his medical history while the policy was in-force is consistent with continuing excessive alcohol consumption (for example, death from liver cirrhosis), the insurer concludes that the most likely result of the liver function test would have meant that using the underwriting guidelines applicable at that time they would not have offered insurance when he applied for the policy. In these circumstances, the insurer would have declined his application and, accordingly, in applying a proportionate remedy the insurer declines the claim.

However, in a case where there is evidence of only moderate alcohol consumption after the initial GP consultations, the insurer might conclude on the balance of probabilities that the test result would have allowed the insurer to accept the case on rated terms. Accordingly, in these circumstances, in applying a proportionate remedy the insurer will apply their expert judgement as to the terms that are most likely to have been offered and makes the appropriate payment.

Case 10 — applying a proportionate remedy to a multi-benefit policy

A man takes out a multi-benefit policy with £100,000 critical illness insurance (CI) and £1000 a month income protection (IP). The premium he pays is £80 a month. When he took out the policy he incorrectly answered a specific question about his occupation.

Some time later, he makes an otherwise valid critical illness claim for testicular cancer. After a review of the circumstances of the non-disclosure, the insurer concludes that the misrepresentation was negligent and applies a proportionate remedy.

Using the premium rates that would have applied at the time the policy was taken out, the insurer works out that, if he had correctly disclosed his occupation, the premium for the whole policy would have been £100 a month. By applying the same proportion to all benefits, a premium of £80 a month would have provided £80,000 CI and £800 a month IP. As the CI claim is otherwise valid, the insurer pays out £80,000.

Under the terms of the policy, cover for CI ends with the payment of a claim, and the premium for this part of the cover stops. However, as IP is a continuing benefit, the insurer reduces the ongoing IP cover to £800 a month and notifies the customer.

Case 11 — a claim with non-disclosure that relates only to a severable benefit

A woman takes out a policy for critical illness insurance (CI) with total permanent disability (TPD) benefit where cover for one of the benefits continues after a successful claim on the other. When she took out the policy she knowingly answered a specific question incorrectly, deliberately concealing an ongoing history of serious back problems. She then makes an otherwise valid CI claim for breast cancer.

The insurer does not decline the claim because the outcome of the underwriting would only have changed the terms offered for TPD, and not for the main CI benefit being claimed for.

If the back problems had been disclosed, the insurer would have issued the policy at standard premium rates but with an exclusion for back problems for TPD. As this exclusion does not apply to breast cancer, the insurer pays the CI claim in full.

However, as there was deliberate non-disclosure relating to TPD, the insurer avoids the remaining TPD benefit.

Case 12 — finding out why medical information was not disclosed

A man aged 42 takes out a critical illness (CI) policy for £100,000 for a premium of £40 a month. Some time later he makes a claim for a heart attack.

In assessing the claim, the insurer finds that when he took out the policy he had for several years been taking tablets daily to control hypertension. However, he incorrectly answered a clear question about high blood pressure and a clear question about ongoing treatment. He answered the remaining questions in the application correctly. If he had disclosed his high blood pressure and treatment, the insurer would have charged a premium of £80 a month.

The insurer asks him why he wrongly answered the questions. He explains that he did not consider himself to have had high blood pressure as his pills were effectively controlling it. Further, his doctor had told him that the treatment was "routine" and that his condition was very common for a man of his age and that it was "nothing to worry about". He did not therefore consider this to be relevant.

The insurer decides that his explanation for the incorrect answer is credible because it fits his medical records and the other circumstances of the case. However, the representation was incorrect and the omission was material.

Taking into account all the circumstances, the insurer gives him the benefit of the doubt. That is, on the balance of probabilities, although he must have known about his condition and treatment, the insurer cannot say that he must have known that his condition was relevant to the insurer or that he acted with complete disregard to the truth of his answers. Accordingly, the insurer does not classify the non-disclosure as deliberate or without any care.

Given the questions asked, the insurer concludes that a reasonable person ought to have known that the representation given was relevant to the insurer. In the circumstances, the customer's answer to the question about ongoing treatment was not reasonable. Accordingly, the insurer treats his misrepresentation as negligent having concluded that it was not innocent.

Using the premium rates that applied when the policy started, the insurer works out that a premium of £40 a month would have provided cover of £48,500. As a proportionate remedy applies and the claim is otherwise valid, the insurer pays out £48,500.

Case 13 — where non-disclosure of medical information is deliberate or without any care

A man aged 47 takes out critical illness insurance for £100,000. Two years later he makes a claim for a heart attack.

In assessing the claim, the insurer finds out that when he took out the policy, for a continuous period of three years he had been taking a combination of three types of medication for hypertension. His medical records show that, despite the treatment, his blood pressure had been significantly raised during this period and that he had been to see his doctor at regular intervals to monitor his blood pressure and renew his prescription for treatment. However, he wrongly answered two clear questions in the application about high blood pressure and ongoing treatment. If he had disclosed his high blood pressure and treatment, using the underwriting manual applicable when he took out the policy, the insurer would have applied a risk premium rating of +100%.

The insurer asks him why his answers to the questions were incorrect. He explains that, because he had been taking treatment for many years, he did not consider his condition or the treatment to be important, and that his blood pressure was controlled by the treatment.

However, contrary to his explanation, the evidence in his medical records shows that his GP had repeatedly warned him about his uncontrolled high blood pressure. Therefore, the insurer concludes that:

- he must have known that his answers were incorrect; and
- he must have known they were relevant to the insurer.

If he had correctly disclosed his condition and treatment, the underwriting outcome would have been a risk premium rating of more than +50%. Accordingly, the insurer classifies the non-disclosure as deliberate or without any care. The insurer therefore avoids the policy and refunds the premiums.

Case 14 — where smoking is negligently not disclosed

A woman takes out a combined (accelerated) life and critical illness insurance policy and declares that she is a non-smoker. Following an otherwise valid claim for cancer, the insurer finds that her medical records show that she was a smoker six months before she took out the policy, and she was also a smoker at the time of the claim.

The insurer asks her why she declared herself to be a non-smoker. She explained that her reason for buying the policy was because she was starting a family. She said she had given up smoking since finding out she was pregnant which was when she took out the policy. The evidence supports this. Her adviser, an employee of the insurer, filled in her application on-line. She recalls that her adviser had only asked her if she was a smoker and not whether she had used tobacco within the preceding 12 months as asked in the application. She accepted that she should have been more careful in checking the copy of the completed application sent to her to review.

In the circumstances, the insurer accepts her explanation as credible given the evidence of the pregnancy as mitigating circumstances and does not avoid the policy. It therefore treats the non-disclosure as negligent (as opposed to deliberate or without any care) and applies a proportionate remedy. Based on the smoker rates that applied when she took out the policy, the insurer works out how much cover her premium would have provided and pays that amount.

If she had not been asked to check the application, as she answered the question asked by the adviser (acting on behalf of the insurer) to the best of her knowledge and belief, there would have been no non-disclosure and the claim should be paid in full.

Case 15 — where smoking is deliberately not disclosed

A man applies for critical illness insurance and declares that he is a non-smoker. Following a claim for cancer, the insurer finds that his medical records show that he was a heavy smoker three months before he took out the policy and also after the start of the policy.

The insurer asks why he had declared himself to be a non-smoker but he fails to offer any plausible mitigating explanation. In the circumstances, the insurer concludes that either:

- he must have known that he was a smoker and, given the question in the application, must have known that this was relevant; or
- he showed no care at all in answering the question about whether he had smoked.

Accordingly, on the balance of probabilities, the insurer concludes that the non-disclosure was deliberate or without any care. The insurer therefore avoids the policy and refunds the premiums.

OTHER

ABI STATEMENT OF RECOMMENDED PRACTICE ON ACCOUNTING FOR INSURANCE BUSINESS (SORP)

December 2005 (as amended in December 2006)

NOTES

STATEMENT BY THE ACCOUNTING STANDARDS BOARD

[5126]

The aims of the Accounting Standards Board (the ASB) are to establish and improve standards of financial accounting and reporting, for the benefit of users, preparers, and auditors of financial information. To this end, the ASB issues accounting standards that are primarily applicable to general purpose company financial statements. In particular industries or sectors, further guidance may be required in order to implement accounting standards effectively. This guidance is issued, in the form of Statements of Recommended Practice (SORPs), by bodies recognised for the purpose by the ASB.

The Association of British Insurers (ABI) has confirmed that it shares the ASB's aims of advancing and maintaining standards of financial reporting in the public interest and has been recognised by the ASB for the purpose of issuing SORPs. As a condition of recognition, the ABI has agreed to follow the ASB's code of practice for bodies recognised for issuing SORPs.

The code of practice sets out procedures to be followed in the development of SORPs. These procedures do not include a comprehensive review of the proposed SORP by the ASB, but a review of limited scope is performed.

On the basis of its review, the ASB has concluded that the SORP has been developed in accordance with the ASB's code of practice.

The ASB's review also considers whether the SORP appears to contain any fundamental points of principle that are unacceptable in the context of present accounting practice or to conflict with an accounting standard or the ASB's plans for future standards. Because the SORP reflects an interplay between general accounting practice, the requirements of Schedule 9A of the Companies Act 1985 and detailed regulatory requirements (the FSA Rules) there are aspects of insurance accounting that do not align with other accounting practice. These include: the deferral of acquisition costs as assets; the inclusion of both equity and liabilities in the Fund for Future Appropriations; the measurement of provisions for liabilities to policyholders on a regulatory, solvency basis rather than at the best estimate of the expenditure required to settle them; and the measurement of such liabilities using discount rates based on asset yields, which is consistent with the FSA Rules but is inconsistent with guidance in FRS 12 'Provisions, Contingent Liabilities and Contingent Assets', FRS 17 'Retirement Benefits' and FRS 19 'Deferred Tax'.

December 2005

Association of British Insurers
51 Gresham Street,
London EC2V 7HQ
Tel: 0207 600 3333
Fax: 0207 696 8999
Web site http://www.abi.org.uk

PART 1 – PREFACE

Introduction

[5127]

1 The recommendations in this Statement only apply directly to insurance companies and groups that are subject to the requirements of Schedule 9A to the Companies Act 1985 ("the CA 85") and UK generally accepted accounting principles (UK GAAP). The Statement does not address alternative methods of accounting for shareholders' profits from long term insurance business such as the European Embedded Values Principles, which have been developed by the CFO Forum.

2 This SORP has no direct application to entities that are required or choose to adopt international accounting standards (IAS) as the basis for financial reporting. These entities however are encouraged to have regard to its provisions insofar as this is compatible with the requirements of IAS.

3 The recommendations in this statement are made in the context of the deferral and matching accounting methodology and the modified statutory solvency basis for life business and within the constraints imposed by Schedule 9A to the Companies Act 1985 ("the CA85"). Within those limitations, they should be regarded as laying down best practice on accounting for insurance business in the United Kingdom.

4 The EU Commission has issued a Regulation requiring all listed entities within its jurisdiction to prepare their consolidated accounts for accounting periods beginning on or after 1 January 2005 in accordance with IFRS to the extent that they have been endorsed by the Commission. In the United Kingdom, listed parent companies in their own financial statements, and unlisted companies and groups, have the option to adopt IFRS from that date. The International Accounting Standards Board (IASB) has published an international financial reporting standard (IFRS 4) on insurance contracts as phase I of a longer term project on accounting for insurance contracts.

5 FRS 26 (Financial Instruments: Measurement) applies to those entities preparing accounts under UK GAAP that are either listed or prepare their financial statements in accordance with the fair value accounting rules in the CA 85*. Under this standard, an entity must not account for financial instruments as an insurance contract unless they are rights and obligations under an "insurance contract" as defined in Appendix C of FRS 26, which is taken from IFRS 4, or contain a discretionary participation feature as defined in that Appendix. In particular, FRS 26 will apply to unlisted insurers that hold derivative instruments measured at fair value as this treatment is now governed by the fair value accounting rules.

6 FRS 26 requires contracts previously accounted for as insurance but which do not meet the conditions set out above, to be accounted for as investment contracts.

7 FRS 26 is effective for listed entities with effect from accounting periods beginning on or after 1 January 2005 and for unlisted entities adopting the fair value accounting rules in the CA 85 for accounting periods beginning on or after 1 January 2006, although voluntary compliance is permitted for accounting periods beginning on or after 1 January 2005 but not earlier.

8 With effect from accounting periods ending on or after 23 December 2005, reporting entities that include a business which is a life assurance business (including reinsurance business) are required to comply with FRS 27 (Life Assurance) but early adoption of all or part of this standard is permitted. FRS 27 amends some of the provisions of this SORP and in addition imposes further disclosure requirements (see paragraph **18**.)

Objectives

9 The principal objectives of this Statement are:

(i) to set out recommended accounting practice for UK insurance entities within the framework of the CA 85 (and equivalent Northern Ireland legislation) in order to narrow the range of accounting practices and thereby enhance the usefulness of published accounting information; and

(ii) to provide guidance on certain provisions of the CA85 and ASB Financial Reporting Standards relating to the financial statements of insurance undertakings where the Wording of these provisions requires clarification, or is insufficient in it to ensure a uniform interpretation of the requirements, or would result in an inappropriate diversity of accounting practices.

(iii) In particular to provide guidance on:

- Some aspects of the accounting for contracts issued by insurance undertakings which are subject to FRS 26 and do not satisfy the definition of an "insurance contract" or contain a "discretionary participation feature" as those terms are defined in FRS 26; and
- The implementation of certain aspects of FRS 27 ("Life Assurance").

Reporting Framework

10 This Statement should be read in conjunction with the requirements of the CA85 applicable to insurance undertakings and, in particular, with Schedule 9A to the CA85.

11 Financial Reporting Standards (FRSs) issued by, and Statements of Standard Accounting Practice (SSAPs) adopted by, the Accounting Standards Board (ASB) together with "Abstracts" of the Urgent Issues Task Force of the ASB (UITF) are applicable to all financial statements which are intended to give a true and fair view of an undertaking's financial performance during an accounting period and of its financial position at the end of the period. Accordingly, all insurance undertakings to which this Statement applies are expected to follow these unless in special circumstances the requirement to give a true and fair view requires a departure from accounting standards. In such circumstances, the requirements of the accounting standard should be departed from only to the extent necessary to give a true and fair view and explanatory disclosures given in accordance with FRS 18 (Accounting Policies).

12 The SORP takes into account all relevant UK accounting standards and other pronouncements that were extant at 31 March 2005. The references to FSA rules are to those rules applicable at 31 October 2005.

General Insurance Business Accounting

13 This Statement generally requires the annual basis of accounting to be used for general insurance business. Under this method, the underwriting result disclosed in the financial statements comprises the result for the current accounting period and any adjustments during the current accounting period to estimates made in prior accounting periods.

Long Term Insurance Business Accounting

14 UK insurance companies are regulated by the Financial Services Authority (the FSA) through the granting by the FSA of permission to carry on the regulated activities of effecting and carrying out contracts of insurance. The regulations made by the FSA, pursuant to the Financial Services and Markets Act 2000, are contained in the FSA Handbook of Rules and Guidance (the FSA Handbook). Under the FSA Principles for Businesses as amplified by FSA rules, insurance companies carrying on long term insurance business must:

- Maintain its long term insurance fund(s) separately;
- keep adequate records to enable assets and liabilities attributable to the fund or funds to be identified;
- use the assets of the fund only for the purposes of that business; and
- make transfers out of the fund, other than reimbursements, only out of surplus ascertained after carrying out an actuarial investigation.

15 There is no requirement for financial statements prepared under the CA85 to be on the basis required for regulatory returns by the FSA rules. In consequence, CA85 accounts exhibit a number of differences in both form and content from the regulatory returns. In practice, however, before the implementation in the United Kingdom of the EU Insurance Accounts Directive, the transfer to shareholders from the long term business fund as determined in accordance with the FSA rules was also taken as the after tax result in the CA85 financial statements. This method of financial reporting came to be known as the "statutory solvency basis".

16 For the purpose of preparing financial statements in accordance with Schedule 9A to the CA85 for contracts issued by insurance undertakings other than contracts which are required to be accounted for as investment contracts under FRS 26, two significant adjustments need to be made to the statutory solvency basis:

(a) Firstly, to defer new business acquisition costs incurred where the benefit of such costs will be obtained in subsequent accounting periods; and

(b) Secondly, to consider the treatment of investment reserves, or reserves in respect of general contingencies or the specific contingency that the fund will be closed to new business, where such items are held within the long term business fund. These amounts, to the extent that they should be regarded as reserves rather than provisions, should be included as appropriate within shareholders' capital and reserves or the fund for future appropriations.

17 The basis described in paragraph **16** is referred to as the "modified statutory solvency basis" (MSSB).

18 FRS 27 (Life Assurance) forms part of UK GAAP with effect from accounting periods ending on or after 23 December 2005. The main provisions of this standard are summarised below:

- Policyholder liabilities for with-profits life assurance business subject to the FSA realistic capital regime to be measured at their realistic value with no deferral of acquisition costs;
- Adjustments from the MSSB to meet the above requirements to be included in the profit and loss account with a transfer to or from the fund for future appropriations of the net amount of such adjustments;
- Except where it arises from non-participating business written in a with-profits fund and is taken into account in the determination of the realistic liabilities of that fund, or is an amount recognised as an intangible asset as part of the allocation of fair values under acquisition accounting in accordance with FRS 7 "Fair values in acquisition accounting" which are subject to the measurement requirements under that standard, the value of in-force life assurance business can only be recognised as an asset if it is an entity's existing accounting policy to recognise it as an asset (or deduction from a liability) and it excludes any value attributable to future investment margins;
- Certain disclosures are required in relation to policyholders' options and guarantees; and
- A capital statement to be presented with associated disclosures.

Interpretation

19 Paragraphs **82** to **312** should be read in the context of the Objectives as set out in paragraph **9** and the definitions set out in paragraphs **20** to **81**.

---

* The ASB is considering proposals to extend the scope of FRS 26 with effect from accounting periods beginning on or after 1 January 2007 to all financial statements that are intended to give a true and fair view of a reporting entity's financial position and profit or loss except those applying the FRSSE.

PART 2 – DEFINITIONS

[5128]
The following definitions apply in this Statement.

Acquisition Costs

20 Schedule 9A to the CA85 defines acquisition costs as costs arising from the conclusion of insurance contracts including direct costs such as acquisition, commission or the cost of drawing up the insurance document or including the insurance contract in the portfolio, and indirect costs such as advertising costs or the administrative expenses connected with the processing of proposals and the issuing of policies. Policy renewal commission in the case of long term insurance business should be included under administrative expenses.

Administrative Expenses

21 Schedule 9A to the CA85 defines administrative expenses as costs of an administrative nature including those arising from premium collection, portfolio administration, handling of bonuses and rebates, and inward and outward reinsurance, including in particular staff costs and depreciation provisions in respect of office furniture and equipment insofar as these need not be shown under acquisition costs, claims incurred or investment charges.

Amortised Cost

22 The purchase price of a redeemable debt security or other fixed income security adjusted by any increase or decrease in value representing the proportion of any difference between the purchase price and the final redemption proceeds of the investment having regard to the period for which the investment has been held and the period remaining until the redemption date, or the assumed redemption date where a range of such dates exists.

Annual Basis of Accounting

23 A basis of accounting for general insurance business whereby a result is determined at the end of the accounting period reflecting the profit or loss from providing insurance cover during that period (including the anticipation of losses arising on cover to be provided in subsequent periods in respect of commitments entered into prior to the end of the accounting period) and any adjustments to the profit or loss of providing insurance cover during earlier accounting periods.

Balance Sheet Format

24 The balance sheet presented in the format required by Section B of Chapter I of Part I of Schedule 9A to the CA85. References to balance sheet asset and liability items are to the asset and liability items as specified in that format.

Bonuses

25 Amounts allocated to policyholders under with-profits contracts whose existence but not size is specified in the contract. Subject to any promises or guarantees given under the contract, bonus size and timing are at the discretion of the insurer and are determined in the light of a number of factors including past and expected investment performance during the contract. Bonuses may be regular, occasional or terminal.

Category of Business

26 Groupings of general insurance business with similar characteristics (Such as patterns of risk, claims incurrence and settlement patterns, and setting of premiums).

Claim

27 The amount payable under a contract of insurance arising from the occurrence of an insured event.

Claims Handling Expenses

28 Expenses incurred in connection with the negotiation and settlement of claims. They include all internal and external expenses incurred in the handling of claims. Internal expenses include all direct expenses of the claims department and any part of the general administration expenses attributable to the claims function.

Claims Incurred

29 A claim is incurred when the event giving rise to the claim occurs. Claims incurred include paid claims and movements in outstanding claims.

Claims Incurred But Not Reported (IBNR)

30 Claims arising out of events, which have occurred by the balance sheet date but have not been reported to the undertaking at that date.

Claims Outstanding General Business

31 The amounts provided to cover the estimated ultimate cost of settling claims arising out of events which have occurred by the balance sheet date, including IBNR claims and claims handling expenses, less amounts already paid in respect of those claims.

Claims Outstanding Long Term Business

32 The amount provided to cover the estimated ultimate cost of settling claims arising out of events, which have been notified by the balance sheet date being the sums due to beneficiaries together with claims handling expenses, less amounts already paid in respect of those claims.

Coinsurance

33 An arrangement whereby two or more insurance undertakings enter into a single contract with the insured to cover a risk in agreed proportions at a specified premium.

Current Value of Investments

34 Current value means the market value determined in accordance with paragraph 25 (or, in the case of land and buildings, paragraph 26) of Part 1 of Schedule 9A to the CA85.

Deferred Acquisition Costs – General Business

35 Acquisition costs relating to the unexpired period of risk of contracts in force at the balance sheet date which are carried forward from one accounting period to subsequent accounting periods.

Deferred Acquisition Costs – Long Term Business

36 Acquisition costs relating to contracts in-force at the balance sheet date, which are carried forward from one accounting period to subsequent accounting periods in the expectation that they will be recoverable out of future margins within insurance contracts after providing for contractual liabilities.

Discounting

37 The reduction to present value at a given date of future cash flows at an assumed date by the application of an appropriate discount factor reflecting the time value of money.

Earned Premium

38 In the case of general insurance business, earned premium is the proportion of written premiums (including where relevant those of prior accounting periods) attributable to the risks borne by the insurer during the accounting period.

Financial Reinsurance

39 Where a reinsurance contract is intended, either in whole or in part, to mitigate the requirement to establish prudent provisions, and/or to provide an element of financing, the identifiable elements of the contract which do not transfer significant insurance risk are considered to be financial reinsurance.

General Insurance Business

40 Contracts of insurance (including reinsurance) falling within one of the classes of insurance specified in Part I of Schedule 1 to the Regulated Activities Order.

Gross Premium Valuation

41 A form of actuarial valuation of liabilities arising under long term insurance contracts where the premiums brought into account are the full amounts receivable under the contract. The method includes explicit estimates of cash flows for:

- premiums, adjusted for renewals and lapses;
- expected claims and for with-profits business future regular but not occasional or terminal bonuses
- costs of maintaining contracts; and
- future renewal expenses

Cash flows are discounted at the valuation interest rate. The methodology for UK companies is included in FSA rules. The discount rate is based on the expected return on the assets deemed to back the liabilities as prescribed by the FSA rules. This may be further constrained by a maximum rate set by the regulator. This will be adjusted to reflect any further risks although, under this method, most of the key risks will be reflected in the modelling of the cash flows. For linked business, allowance may be made for the purchase of future units required by the contract terms and credit is taken for future charges permitted under those terms.

Inception of Risk

42 In relation to general insurance business, the time at which the period of cover commences under a policy or contract of insurance.

Insurance Risk

43 Uncertainty over the likelihood of an insured event occurring, the quantum of the claim, or the time when claims payments will fall due.

Investment Return

44 Investment return comprises all investment income, realised investment gains and losses and movements in unrealised investment gains and losses. It also includes investment expenses and charges and, if appropriate, interest payable.

Linked Business

45 Long term insurance business where the benefits payable to policyholders are wholly or partly to be determined by reference to the value of, or the income from, property of any description or by reference to fluctuations in, or in an index of, the value of property of any description.

Long Term Fund

46 The fund or funds maintained by an undertaking in respect of its long-term business in accordance with the FSA rules.

Long Term Insurance Business

47 Contracts of insurance (including reinsurance) falling within one of the classes of insurance specified in Part II of Schedule 1 to the Regulated Activities Order.

Longer Term Rate of Investment Return

48 The longer term rate of investment return is an estimate of the long term trend investment return for the relevant category of investments having regard to past performance, current trends and future expectations.

Net Premium Method

49 An actuarial valuation of liabilities arising under long term insurance contracts where the premium brought into account at any valuation date is that which, on the valuation assumptions regarding interest, mortality and disability, will exactly provide for the benefits guaranteed. A variation of the net premium method involves zillmerisation (see paragraph **81**). Under the net premium method, no explicit allowance is made for the future costs of maintaining the policy but these are taken into account, if necessary, by adjusting downwards the amount of future premiums included in the calculation. For with-profits policies, vested bonuses are included in the cash flows assessed but future allocations of bonuses are not included explicitly, although they may be taken into account as a downwards adjustment to the discount rate used. The discount rate before adjustment for risk and items not explicitly included in the cash flows assessed is based on the return available on suitable investments. The detailed methodology for UK companies is included in regulations contained in the FSA rules.

Non-Participating Business

50 Long term insurance business where policyholders are not entitled to share in the surplus of the relevant long-term fund.

Non-Proportional Reinsurance

51 Contracts of reinsurance whereby the reinsurer accepts the whole or a proportion of the liability for an individual claim or group of claims incurred by the cedent in excess of an agreed amount, normally also subject to an upper limit.

Non-Technical Account

52 The section of the profit and loss account prescribed by Section B of Chapter 1 of Part 1 of Schedule 9A to the CA85 in addition to the technical accounts for general and long term insurance business.

Participating Business

53 Long term insurance business where policyholders are contractually entitled to share in the surplus of the relevant long-term fund.

Pipeline Premiums

54 Premiums written but not reported to the undertaking by the balance sheet date.

Portfolio Claims Payments

55 Amounts payable by one insurance undertaking to another in consideration for a contract whereby the latter agrees to assume responsibility for the unpaid claims incurred by the former prior to a date specified in the contract.

Portfolio Premiums Payments

56 Amounts payable by an insurer to another insurer in consideration for a contract whereby the latter agrees to assume responsibility for the claims arising on a portfolio of in-force business written by the former from a future date until the expiry of the policies.

Present Value of Future Profits ("PVFP")

57 The value determined in accordance with Rule 7.4.37 of the FSA Integrated Prudential Sourcebook and related guidance.

Present Value of In-force Business ("PVIF")

58 The net present value of the shareholders' interest in the expected after tax cash flows from long term insurance business, on the assumption that all assets backing the business will be distributed over time to in-force policyholders and/or shareholders. The calculation of PVIF should allow for uncertainties associated with the assessment of future cashflows, as well as for the time value of money. PVIF includes both the shareholders' interest which is expected to arise in the form of cash flows over the lifetime of current in-force contracts and the interest in the surplus assets which, in practice, is not expected to be distributed over this period. This distinction is of importance when considering the application of paragraph **198**.

Proportional Reinsurance

59 A contract of reinsurance under which, in return for a proportion of the original premium, the reinsurer accepts liability for the same proportion of each related claim against the cedent.

Profit and Loss Account Format

60 The profit and loss account set out in the format required by Section B of Chapter I of Part I of Schedule 9A to the CA85. References to items in the profit and loss account are to those items as specified in that format.

Purchase Price of Investments

61 The consideration for the purchase of investments, including related acquisition costs (eg stamp duty and brokerage) except where they are restricted by FRS 26, but excluding accrued interest included in the purchase price of interest bearing stocks. Accrued interest should be separately identified and accounted for.

Realised Investment Gains/Losses

62

(a) For investments included in the financial statements at current value, the difference between the net proceeds on disposal and their purchase price.

(b) For investments included at amortised cost, the difference between the net proceeds on disposal and the latest carrying value (or if acquired after the last balance sheet date the purchase price).

Realistic value of Liabilities

63 The realistic value of liabilities being that element of the amount defined by rule 7.4.40 in the FSA's integrated prudential sourcebook, excluding current liabilities falling within the definition in rule 7.4.190, that are recognised separately on the entity's balance sheet.

Reinsurance

64 An arrangement whereby one party (the reinsurer), in consideration for a premium, agrees to indemnify another party (the cedent) against part or all of the liability assumed by the cedent under a policy or policies of insurance.

Reinsurance Inwards

65 The acceptance of risks under a contract of reinsurance.

Reinsurance Outwards

66 The placing of risks under a contract of reinsurance.

Retrocession

67 The reinsurance outwards of risks previously accepted by an insurer as reinsurance inwards. The recipient is known as the retrocessionaire. References in this Statement to reinsurance include retrocession.

Run-Off Deviation

68 For general insurance business, the difference (before any reduction in respect of discounting) between:

- the provisions made at the beginning of the accounting period for outstanding claims incurred in previous accounting periods, and
- the payments made during the accounting period on account of claims incurred in previous accounting periods and the claims provision at the end of the accounting period for such outstanding claims.

Sale Proceeds of Investments

69 The consideration for the sale of investments after deducting the related costs of sale. In the case of interest bearing securities, the consideration should exclude any interest accrued at the date of sale.

Structured Settlements

70 Arrangements by consent between the parties concerned or under a Court Order whereby damages in the form of a lump sum are replaced by a smaller lump sum and a series of periodic payments.

Technical Account for General Business

71 The section of the profit and loss account for recording insurance business within the classes specified in Part I of Schedule 1 to the Regulated Activities Order which must be prepared in accordance with the format prescribed in Section B of Chapter I of Part 1 of Schedule 9A to the CA85.

Technical Account for Long Term Business

72 The section of the profit and loss account for recording insurance business within the classes specified in Part II of Schedule 1 to the Regulated Activities Order, which must be prepared in accordance with the format prescribed in Section B of Chapter I of Part I of Schedule 9A to the CA85.

Transaction costs (FRS 26)

73 Incremental costs that are directly attributable to the acquisition, issue or disposal of a financial instrument. An incremental cost is one that would not have been incurred if the entity had not acquired, issued or disposed of the financial instrument.

Transfer of Insurance Risk

74 A transfer of insurance risk, which may involve underwriting risk or timing risk or both, between the insured and insurer as a result of which, having regard to the commercial substance of the contract or contracts being evaluated, there are a number of reasonably possible outcomes some of which may present the insurer with the possibility of suffering a material loss.

Unearned Premiums Provision

75 This usually relates to general business and is the proportion of written premiums relating to periods of risk after the accounting date, which are deferred to subsequent accounting periods.

Underwriting Year

76 The accounting period in which a contract of general insurance incepts.

Unexpired Risks Provision

77 The excess of the estimated value of claims and expenses likely to arise after the end of the financial year from contracts concluded before that date, insofar as their estimated value exceeds the provision for unearned premiums (after deduction of any acquisition costs deferred), and any premiums receivable under those contracts.

Unrealised Investment Gains/Losses

78 The difference between the current value at the balance sheet date of investments held on that date and their purchase price. Movements in unrealised investment gains/losses comprise:

- the increase/decrease in the accounting period in the value of investments held at the balance sheet date; and
- the reversal of unrealised investment gains/losses recognised in earlier accounting periods in respect of investment disposals of the current period.

Written Premiums – General Business

79 Premiums, which an insurer is contractually entitled to receive from the insured in relation to contracts of insurance. These are premiums on contracts entered into during the accounting period and adjustments arising in the accounting period to premiums receivable in respect of contracts entered into in prior accounting periods.

Written Premiums – Long Term Business

80 Premiums to which the insurer is contractually entitled becoming due for payment in the accounting period.

Zillmerisation

81 A variation of the net premium method (see paragraph **49**) which increases the future premiums valued to take account of acquisition costs incurred.

PART 3 – GENERAL INSURANCE BUSINESS

Basis of Accounting

[5129]

82 Paragraphs **83** to **143** apply to general insurance contracts falling within the scope of this Statement, except those contracts, which do not satisfy the definition of an insurance contract in FRS 26 and which, in consequence, are required to be accounted for in accordance with paragraph 162 below.

83 Underwriting results should be determined on an **annual basis**, notwithstanding that this will normally require some estimation to be made at the balance sheet date, particularly with regard to outstanding claims.

Gross Written Premiums

84 **Written premiums** should comprise the total premiums receivable for the whole period of cover provided by the contracts entered into during the accounting period, regardless of whether these are wholly due for payment in the accounting period, together with any adjustments arising in the accounting period to such premiums receivable in respect of business written in prior accounting periods.

85 A common arrangement in general insurance is for premiums to be remitted by intermediaries on a net of commission basis to the insurer, even though the insurer is contractually entitled to the full amount. Alternatively the intermediary may remit the whole of the premium to the insurer and receive the commission as a payment. In both situations grossing up for the commission should be applied, if necessary on an estimated basis, as this correctly reflects the contractual arrangements in force, This also applies where the premiums are determined by an intermediary, Where, however, policies are issued to intermediaries on a wholesale basis and they are themselves responsible for setting the final amount payable by the insured without reference to the insurer, the written premium will normally comprise the premium payable to the insurer and grossing-up will be inappropriate unless it reflects the contractual position.

86 Where premiums are receivable by instalments during the period of risk covered by contracts, any outstanding amount at the balance sheet date to which the insurer is contractually entitled should be treated as a debtor.

87 Written premiums should include **pipeline premiums**. Contracts may have been entered into which provide for intermediaries to accept business on the insurance undertaking's behalf (for example binding covers and line-slip arrangements). The details of these policies may not be notified to the insurer until some time after the balance sheet date and may embrace business incepting both before and after the balance sheet date. The estimate of pipeline premiums should relate only to those underlying contracts of insurance where the period of cover has commenced prior to the balance sheet date.

88 Where an insurer has offered renewal and is therefore contractually liable to pay claims if renewal is subsequently confirmed by the policyholder, it should recognise the renewal premium, subject to making a provision for anticipated lapses.

89 Under some policies written premiums may be adjusted retrospectively in the light of claims experience or where the risk covered cannot be assessed accurately at the commencement of cover. Where written premiums are subject to an increase retrospectively, recognition of potential increases should be deferred until the additional amount can be ascertained with reasonable certainty.

Recognition of such amounts should be commensurate with the degree to which related provisions for claims have been established. Where written premiums are subject to a reduction, an adjustment for such a reduction should be made as soon as it can be foreseen.

90 Additional or return premiums should be treated as adjustments to the initial premium. Where a claims event causes a reinstatement premium to be paid, the recognition of the reinstatement premium and the effect on the initial premium should reflect the respective incidence of risk attaching to those premiums in determining under the annual accounting basis that proportion earned and unearned at the balance sheet date.

91 Written premiums should be recognised as **earned premiums** over the period of the policy having regard to the incidence of risk. Time apportionment of the premium is normally appropriate if the incidence of risk is the same throughout the period of cover. If there is a marked unevenness in the incidence of risk over the period of cover, a basis which reflects the profile of risk should be used. The proportion of the written premiums relating to the unexpired period of these policies will be carried forward as an **unearned premiums** provision at the balance sheet date.

Disclosure

92 The method of calculating the unearned premiums provision should be disclosed.

Insurance Premium Taxes

93 Insurance premium taxes should not be included within written premiums in the technical account. Unpaid premium taxes should be dealt with in the balance sheet within balance sheet liabilities item GV (Other creditors including taxation and social security).

Claims – Annual Basis

94 Provision should be made at the balance sheet date for the expected ultimate cost of settlement of all **claims incurred** in respect of events up to that date, whether reported or not, together with related claims handling expenses, less amounts already paid. There may be a considerable degree of uncertainty as to the eventual outcome of some insurance contract with a wide range of possible outcomes, and time delays in claims notifications which in some cases can exceed 25 years. If a liability is known to exist but there is uncertainty as to its eventual amount, a provision should nevertheless be made, consistent with paragraph 25 of FRS12 which deals with the role of estimates. Provision should also be made, usually on an estimated basis, for claims events which have occurred but have not yet been reported, using appropriate statistical and other techniques to address any uncertainty arising.

95 The level of claims provisions should be set such that no adverse **run-off deviation** is envisaged. This is consistent with the requirement of paragraph 43 of Part I of Schedule 9A to the CA85 that technical provisions should be sufficient at all times to cover any liabilities arising out of insurance contracts so far as can reasonably be foreseen. However, given the uncertainty in establishing a provision for outstanding claims, it is likely that the final outcome will prove to be different from the original liability established. In setting the provision, consideration should be given to the probability and magnitude of future experience being more adverse than assumed.

Where there is considerable uncertainty concerning future events a degree of caution will be necessary in the exercise of the judgement required for setting provisions such that liabilities are not understated.

96 In determining the sufficiency of evidence and the ability to measure claims costs, an insurance undertaking should take all reasonable steps to ensure that it has appropriate information with regard to its claims exposures.

97 Paragraphs **238** to **247** set out in more detail the requirements relating to estimation techniques, uncertainty and contingent liabilities.

98 Anticipated salvage or subrogation recoveries, where material, should be disclosed under assets item EIII (Other debtors) and not deducted from claims provisions. In accordance with Note 4 to the profit and loss account format, they should be deducted from claims incurred in the technical account for general business.

Claims Handling Expenses

99 Provision should be made at the end of the accounting period for all **claims handling expenses** to cover the anticipated future costs of negotiating and settling claims which have been incurred – whether reported or not – up to the balance sheet date. Separate provisions should be assessed for *each category of business*.

100 In determining the provision for claims handling expenses, unless clear evidence is available to the contrary, it should be assumed that the activity of the claims handling department will remain at its current level and therefore that the contribution to its costs from future new business will remain at the same level.

101 The provision for claims handling expenses should be included within the provision for claims outstanding but need not be separately disclosed. Claims handling expenses incurred should be included within claims incurred in the technical account for general business.

Disclosure

102 Disclosure should be made in the notes to the financial statements to provide an understanding of the main principles underlying the establishment of the claims provisions and, where relevant, any changes from previous accounting periods in the procedures adopted for establishing claims provisions, and the reasons for them. In particular there should be disclosure of the policies adopted and bases used with regard to:

- reported claims;
- **claims incurred but not reported**;
- claims handling expenses; and
- salvage and other recoveries.

103 In accordance with Note 4 to the profit and loss account format in Part 1 of Schedule 9A to the CA 85, and consistent with the requirements of FRS 12 (Provisions, contingent liabilities and contingent assets), where **run-off deviations** arise, the amounts should, if material, be shown in the notes to the financial statements, broken down by category. For this purpose, materiality is in relation to the insurance business as a whole and not to individual categories of insurance business.

Discounting

104 Paragraph 47(7) of Part I of Schedule 9A to the CA85 prohibits implicit **discounting** of claims provisions. Explicit discounting of claims provisions to recognise the time value of money is permissible only if the preconditions laid down in Paragraph 48 of Part I of Schedule 9A to the CA85 are satisfied, and the disclosures required by that paragraph are made. Explicit discounting will not affect the total charge to the technical account over time, but will affect the timing of the recognition of that charge.

105 Paragraph 48(1)(a) of Part I of Schedule 1 to Schedule 9A to the CA85 requires that explicit discounting may only be applied where the expected average interval between the date for the settlement of claims being discounted and the accounting date is at least four years. The four-year test should be applied by reference to the end of each accounting period in respect of all claims outstanding at that time, and not just once in the accounting period in which the claims were incurred.

106 Where applied, explicit discounting should normally be adopted by reference to **categories** of claims (with similar characteristics but not solely by length of settlement pattern) rather than to individual claims.

107 The calculation of the average interval referred to in paragraph **105** above should be weighted on the basis of expected claims before any deduction for reinsurance.

108 Discounting should be considered only if there is adequate data available to construct a reliable model of the rate of claims settlement. The principal factors to be considered are the amount of future claims settlements, the timing of future cash flows and the discount rate. A cautious approach should be taken to ensure a sufficient level of reliability in the construction of the claims settlement pattern. Procedures should be undertaken to assess the accuracy of the claims settlement pattern predicted by the model in previous periods and the current model should be adjusted, as appropriate, to reflect the out-turn and conclusions of analyses in the previous period. Cash flows should be modelled gross and net of reinsurance as reinsurance recoveries may arise later than the related claims payments.

109 As required by law, discounting should be applied only where assets (excluding those attributable to shareholders' funds) are available which are appropriate in magnitude and nature to cover the liabilities discounted. The discount rate must comply with the requirement of Paragraph 48(1)(e) of Part I of Schedule 9A to the CA85. In particular, it should not exceed a rate expected to be earned by assets of the undertaking which are appropriate in magnitude and nature to cover the provisions for claims being discounted during the period necessary for the payment of such claims and should not exceed either:

- a rate justified by the performance of such assets over the preceding five years; or
- a rate justified by the performance of such assets during the year preceding the balance sheet date.

110 For the purpose of determining an appropriate discount rate, justification requires a consideration of the returns achieved over the period in question to the extent that this is relevant to the future.

111 When discounting is applied, the following disclosures should be made in the notes to the financial statements:

- the total amount of the provisions before discounting;
- the categories of claims in relation to which discounting has been applied; and

- for each category of claims where discounting has been applied, the methods used, the assumed average period to claims settlement, the rate of investment return used to determine the discounted value of claims provisions, and the criteria adopted for estimating the period that will elapse before the claims are settled.

112 The effect of the unwinding of discounted claims provisions during an accounting period should be disregarded in considering whether material adverse run-off deviations have arisen requiring disclosure under Note 4 to the Profit and Loss Account format in Section B of Chapter 1 of Part I of Schedule 9A to the CA85. (See paragraph **103** above).

113 Investment return associated with any unwinding of the discount on general insurance business claims provisions in an accounting period should be recorded under the headings for investment income or gains in the appropriate sections of the profit and loss account and should not be credited directly to claims incurred. Separate disclosure should then be made, where material, of the amount of the investment return which corresponds to the unwinding of the discount.

Claims Provisions on Acquisition

114 FRS 7 (Fair values in acquisition accounting) requires that, for acquisition accounting, the identifiable assets and liabilities of an acquired undertaking should be included in the acquirer's balance sheet at their fair value at the date of acquisition. In calculating the fair value of claims provisions on acquisition, consideration should be given to the amounts expected to be paid reflecting the uncertain quantum and timing of future payments.

115 The adjustment for the timing of payment applied in calculating the fair value of claims arising on acquisition should be treated as an element of goodwill and amortised on an appropriate basis over the run-off period of the claims arising from the portfolio of business acquired. This element of goodwill should be separately identified in the notes to the financial statements and described as "goodwill on acquired claims provisions". A review for impairment should be undertaken consistent with the requirements of FRS 11 (Impairment of fixed assets and goodwill).

116 The amortisation should be described as "Amortisation of goodwill on acquired claims provisions" and included under item I.8 (Other technical charges, net of reinsurance) in the technical account for general insurance business where an allocation of investment return has been made to that account from the non-technical account. Where no such allocation has been made, the amortisation should be included in item III.8 (Other charges, including value adjustments) in the non-technical account.

Unexpired Risks Provision

117 Subject to paragraph **122** below, where the estimated value of claims and expenses attributable to the unexpired periods of policies in force at the balance sheet date exceeds the unearned premiums provision in relation to such policies after deduction of any acquisition costs deferred, an **unexpired risks provision** should be established. If material, this provision should be disclosed separately either in the balance sheet or in the notes to the financial statements. This is consistent with the requirements of FRS 12 on onerous contracts.

118 An assessment of whether an unexpired risks provision is necessary should be made for each grouping of business, which is managed together with any unexpired risks surpluses and deficits within that grouping being offset. For this purpose "managed together" is to be construed in accordance with paragraph **119** below.

119 Business should only be regarded as being managed together where no constraints exist on the ability to use assets held in relation to such business to meet any of the associated liabilities and either:

(i) There are significant common characteristics, which are relevant to the assessment of risk and setting of premiums for the business lines in question; or

(ii) the lines of business are written together as separate parts of the same insurance contracts.

120 For binding authorities, where the insurer is unable to influence the terms on which policies are issued, a provision should be established at the balance sheet date for any anticipated losses arising on policies incepting in the period after the balance sheet date during which the binding authority entered into before that date remains in force.

121 The assessment of whether an unexpired risks provision is required and if so its quantum should be based on information available at the balance sheet date which may include evidence of relevant previous claims experience on similar contracts as adjusted for known differences, events not expected to recur and, where appropriate, the normal level of seasonal claims if the previous accounting period was not typical in this respect. The assessment should not however take into account any new claims events occurring after the balance sheet date as, these are non-adjusting events. Exceptional claims events, however, occurring between the balance sheet date and the date on which the financial statements are approved by the board of directors should be disclosed in the notes to the financial statements together with an estimate of their financial effect. The amount of any unexpired risks provision should be determined having regard to paragraph 43 of Schedule 9A to the

CA85 which requires technical provisions to be sufficient at all times to over any liabilities arising out of insurance contracts so far as can reasonably be foreseen. Where there is considerable uncertainty concerning future events, a degree of caution will be necessary in the exercise of the judgement required for setting provisions such that liabilities are not understated.

122 In calculating the estimated value of future claims in relation to the unexpired periods of risk on policies in force at the balance sheet date, the future investment return arising on investments supporting the unearned premiums provision and the unexpired risks provision may be taken into account. For the purposes of calculating this provision, the deferred acquisition costs should be deducted from the unearned premiums provision. The investment return will be that expected to be earned by the investments held until the future claims are settled.

123 Acquisition costs to which the provisions of Schedule 9A to the CA85 on deferral apply, should not be written off in whole or in part to the profit and loss account as being irrecoverable for the purpose of reducing or eliminating the need for an unexpired risks provision.

124 Disclosure should be made of the method of assessing any requirement for an unexpired risks provision and, in particular, the practice with regard to recognising future investment return, offsetting surpluses and deficits and the extent to which post balance sheet events are taken into account.

Equalisation Reserves

125 Disclosure should be made in the accounting policies section of the financial statements where an equalisation reserve has been established in accordance with Chapter 6 of FSA rules. Where, in accordance with Note 24 to the balance sheet format in Schedule 9A to the CA 85, equalisation reserves are included under balance sheet liabilities item C.5 (Equalisation provision), the following disclosures should be made in the notes to the financial statements:

- the amounts provided are not liabilities because they are in addition to the provisions required to meet the anticipated ultimate cost of settlement of outstanding claims at the balance sheet date; and
- notwithstanding this, they are required by Schedule 9A to the CA 85 to be included within technical provisions.

126 In addition, there should be disclosure of the impact of equalisation reserves on shareholders' funds and the effect of movements in the reserves on the results of the accounting period. Where earnings per share figures are disclosed, consideration should be given to disclosure of an alternative earnings per share figure disregarding equalisation reserves.

Portfolio Premiums and Claims

127 **Portfolio premiums** payable should be included within premiums for reinsurance outwards in the financial statements of the transferor undertaking but deferred to subsequent accounting periods as appropriate in respect of any unexpired period of risk at the balance sheet date. In the financial statements of the transferee undertaking they should be included with written premiums with any amount unearned at the balance sheet date being carried forward in the unearned premiums provision.

128 **Portfolio claims** transfers should be accounted for in the financial statements of the transferor undertaking as payments in settlement of the claims transferred in accordance with the requirements of Note 4 to the profit and loss account format.

129 For the same reason, the consideration receivable by the transferee undertaking should be credited to claims payable in the balance sheet.

130 Disclosure should be made in notes to the financial statements of any claims portfolio transfers, which materially affect the transferee undertaking's exposure to risk.

Structured Settlements

131 Where, pursuant to a **structured settlement** arrangement falling within one of the cases referred to in Section 329AA of the Income and Corporation Taxes Act 1988, either:

- an annuity is purchased by a general insurance undertaking under which the structured settlement beneficiary is the annuitant; or
- an annuity previously purchased by a general insurance undertaking for its own account to fund the periodic payments under a structured settlement agreement is assigned to the structured settlement beneficiary;

the general insurance company will normally remain liable to the policyholder should the annuity provider fail. Unless this is not the case, this liability should continue to be recognised in the balance sheet. An annuity, paid by an annuity provider, which exactly matches the amount and timing of this liability should be recognised as an asset and measured at the same amount as the related obligation.

Deferred Acquisition Costs

132 **Acquisition costs** should be deferred commensurate with the unearned premiums provision. The acquisition costs to be deferred will be that proportion of the total acquisition costs which the unearned premiums provision bears to gross written premiums for the class of business in question. For this purpose acquisition expenses should be allocated to classes of business. This may not always be possible for reinsurance business inwards since the ceding enterprise, when advising the reinsurer of the unearned premium provision, may include in that provision an amount for deferred acquisition expenses. In these circumstances, an estimate should be made.

133 Advertising costs should not be deferred unless they directly relate to the acquisition of new business.

134 **Deferred acquisition costs** should be shown separately in the balance sheet under assets item GII (Deferred acquisition costs).

135 Related reinsurance commissions deferred should not be netted against deferred acquisition costs but should be shown under balance sheet liabilities item H (Accruals and deferred income).

Insurance Business in Run off

136 The provisions of FRS 3 (Reporting financial performance) should be applied where a decision has been taken to cease writing the whole, or a material category, of the insurance business. For this purpose a material category must constitute a discrete segment of the insurance business.

137 Subject to paragraph **138**, provision should be made for the full amount of any costs associated with running off the insurance business no longer being written. Full provision for these additional costs should be made in the accounting period in which the decision to cease writing new business is taken. No part of this additional expenditure should be charged in future accounting periods against the results of other new business.

138 In setting any additional provision for the costs of running off the insurance business no longer being written, the amount provided should comply with the FRS 3 requirement that obligations that have been incurred should be recognised to the extent that they are not expected to be covered by the future profits of the operation. Thus, expected future investment return not already recognised in calculating technical provisions should be taken account of (except to the extent that an asset would be created) with separate disclosure in the notes to the financial statements of the full amount of the additional provision required and of the expected future investment return which has been offset against it. Investment Return should be recognised as that which is expected to be earned on the assets of the business prior to settlement in future accounting periods of the undiscounted claims liabilities and expense provisions of the business no longer being written.

139 The principles to be applied in providing for claims are unaltered by a partial or complete cessation of writing new business. The provision will need to include any additional claims handling costs arising as a result of ceasing wholly or partly to write new business (for instance, the costs where relevant of scaling down or closing the claims handling department). Other significant additional costs may include redundancy and similar payments (other than in relation to claims handling staff), continuing administrative costs and the additional costs of making recoveries under reinsurance contracts.

Deferred Taxation (Section 107 Finance Act 2000)

140 Where general insurance claims provisions recorded in tax computations exceed the amount that would have been provided on the basis of full foresight, and discounting at the rate required by tax legislation, HM Revenue and Customs (HMRC) may raise an additional charge to compensate it for the deferral of any tax payment arising as a result.

141 The additional charge referred to above is raised through the tax charge to compensate HMRC for receiving tax later than would have been the case if the circumstances in paragraph **140** had not applied. It should therefore be regarded as a permanent difference and recorded as part of the tax charge for the accounting period to which it relates.

142 Where non-life insurance technical provisions included in tax computations are less than the amount of the related claims when determined under Section 107 Finance Act 2000, that section requires HMRC to make an adjustment in favour of the taxpayer calculated by reference to that difference. Where in the accounting period there is an excess of this credit ("finance credit") over any charge ("finance charge") referred to in paragraph **140** above, this should be treated as a permanent difference and credited to the tax charge.

143 Where general insurance technical provisions disclosed in the financial statements exceed the amount used for tax computational purposes, a deferred tax asset should be established, as taxable profits will exceed accounting profits. This asset will be recognised subject to compliance with the relevant accounting standard.

PART 4 – LONG TERM INSURANCE BUSINESS

Scope

[5130]

144 Except in the case of contracts issued by insurance undertakings falling within the scope of

FRS 26 which do not satisfy the definition of an insurance contract or contain a discretionary participation feature and with-profits life insurance business which, by virtue of falling within the scope of the FSA realistic capital regime, is subject to paragraph 4 of FRS 27, paragraphs **163** to **217** will apply in full.

145 Where and to the extent that an insurance undertaking carries on with-profits life insurance business falling within the scope of FRS 27, the following provisions of the SORP are superseded by the requirements of FRS 27:

- Paragraph **170** to **177** (deferred acquisition costs)
- Paragraphs **180** to **183** (determination of the long term business provision)
- Paragraph **185** (allowance for future bonuses) insofar as future bonuses are recognised in the calculation of the realistic liabilities
- Paragraph **186** (net premium method)
- Paragraph **196** (exclusion of certain regulatory margins from the long term business provision).

146 However, non-participating life insurance contracts written within, or by a subsidiary or associate of, a with-profits fund subject to FRS 27 will be subject to paragraphs **163** to **217** of this statement if they fall to be accounted for as insurance contracts, and paragraphs **158** to **162** will apply if under FRS 26 they are required to be accounted for as investment contracts.

147 Paragraphs **148** to **157** apply to the measurement of the with-profits liabilities and related assets of with-profits contracts falling within the scope of FRS 27.

FRS 27

148 Paragraph 4(a) of FRS 27 requires that 'for with-profits funds falling within the scope of the FSA realistic capital regime, liabilities to policyholders arising from with-profits life assurance business shall be stated at the amount of the realistic value of liabilities adjusted to exclude the shareholders' share of projected future bonuses'. The amount deducted should not exceed the amount included in the liability. The FSA's realistic capital regime permits insurers to use a range of approaches when calculating liabilities within the realistic balance sheet. Some of these incorporate explicit projection of bonuses and the corresponding shareholder transfers whilst others rely on retrospective calculations of amounts earned by with profits policyholders. However, independent of the mechanism used to calculate the liabilities, the philosophy underpinning the FSA's approach is that these liabilities should represent the value of the fund's total liabilities for with profits business, including the value of future transfers to shareholders, calculated using financial assumptions consistent with the market pricing of financial instruments.

149 To ensure consistency with this, the shareholders' share of projected future bonuses deducted in accordance with Para 4(a) should be calculated as the value of future transfers to shareholders calculated using market consistent financial assumptions, and assuming that transfers take place at a level consistent with the assumptions within the FSA realistic balance sheet. Where an explicit assumption is not required in order to calculate the liabilities under the FSA's approach then continuation of the current profit sharing arrangements should be assumed unless the firm has plans to change this approach. Non-economic projection assumptions should be consistent with those used elsewhere in the realistic balance sheet. The amount deducted in accordance with this paragraph should be taken to the fund for future appropriations. If shareholders transfers have been included as part of the FSA realistic liability (or otherwise included in liabilities) then the amount of such transfers should be taken out of liabilities and included in the FFA, together with any related tax liability. If shareholders transfers have not been set up as part of the FSA realistic liability or elsewhere, no adjustment is required.

150 Paragraph 4(b) of FRS 27 (acquisition costs not to be deferred) does not apply to insurance funds falling outside the scope of the FSA realistic capital regime.

151 Paragraph 4(d) of FRS 27 permits an amount to be recognised for the **present value of future profits** (PVFP) on non-participating business written in a with profits fund when the non-participating business is: (i) measured on this basis for the purposes of the regulatory returns made under the FSA realistic capital regime, (ii) the value of the PVFP is calculated on the basis used in the FSA's realistic capital regime and (iii) the determination of the realistic value of liabilities takes account of this value either directly or indirectly. As explained in paragraph 13 of FRS 27 in determining whether the PVFP of non-participating business has been taken into account in determining the realistic liabilities it is not necessary that there is a direct link between the value of the realistic liabilities and the value of the PVFP. Where with profits policyholders are entitled to a share of the profits on non-participating business it would generally be expected that the determination of the realistic liabilities would take account, directly or indirectly, of the value of future profits on this business.

152 Paragraph 4 of FRS 27 requires that the value of the PVFP asset recognised should be determined in accordance with the FSA's realistic capital regime requirements. Paragraph 15 of FRS 27 explains that the value calculated under the realistic capital regime requirements must be adjusted to ensure consistency where adjustments have been made onto the MSSB measurement basis in relation to non-participating contracts. The measurement of the PVFP asset recognised in accordance with the FSA's realistic regime may take into account the release of capital requirements for non-participating business. It would not be appropriate to recognise this release of capital requirements within the PVFP asset presented in the accounts because the MSSB liabilities do not include an allowance for capital. Therefore the amount of the PVFP asset determined for the purposes of the FSA's realistic capital regime should be adjusted accordingly.

153 For entities within the scope of FRS 26 the profit recognition profile for non-participating contracts which do not satisfy FRS 26's definition of an insurance contract or contain a discretionary participation feature will be determined by the requirements of that Standard and the guidance relating thereto in paragraphs **159** to **162** of this Statement. Where these contracts are written in a with profits fund, paragraph **151** will apply but the PVFP value recognised for such contracts for the purposes of the FSA's realistic capital regime should be adjusted to reflect the difference in the profit recognition bases between the basis used to determine the PVFP value used in the FSA's realistic capital regime and the profit recognition profile determined by FRS 26 and FRS 5.

154 Paragraph 4(e) of FRS 27 permits that where a with profits fund has an interest in a subsidiary or associated entity that is valued for FSA regulatory purposes at an amount in excess of the net amounts that would be included in the entity's consolidated accounts, an amount may be recognised representing this excess if the determination of the realistic value of liabilities to with-profits policyholders takes account of this value. As explained in Paragraph 16 of FRS 27 this situation could arise where the subsidiary or associated entity writes non-participating business and the value of the subsidiary or associated entity recognised for FSA reporting purposes incorporates the PVFP of non-participating business written in the subsidiary or associated entity. The value of the subsidiary or associated entity recognised for FSA reporting purposes is reduced by the subsidiary's or associate's capital requirement as noted in rule 7.4.33(3) of the FSA's integrated prudential sourcebook. When preparing both consolidated and non-consolidated accounts, the excess value that may be recognised should therefore be taken as the excess before deduction of the subsidiary or associated entity's capital requirement.

155 Paragraph 5 of FRS 27 permits a number of options for how the amounts recognised in paragraphs **152** to **154** should be presented. In order to comply with the requirements of CA 85 Schedule 9A the option in 5(a) should be adopted but if this is not feasible, the option in 5(c) should be applied.

156 Paragraph 56(a) of FRS 27 requires disclosure of the effect of changes in assumptions used to measure life assurance liabilities. The effect of each change in assumptions having a material effect on the group must be shown separately subject to paragraph 59 which permits the impact of changes in assumptions which have a common cause to be grouped together. The impact of changes in assumptions which individually do not have a material effect on the group may be disclosed in aggregate. A narrative description of these should be provided. Where it is not practicable to refer to each change in assumption individually, this should analyse the impact in a way that meets the objective of the disclosure and is appropriate for the entity's particular circumstances.

157 Where an assumption is linked to a defined external variable, for example base rates, a change in that variable will not constitute a change in assumptions. Its impact should therefore be categorised under paragraph 56(c) of FRS 27 as a change resulting from external development.

FRS 26

158 Paragraphs **159** to **162** apply to contracts issued by insurance undertakings that fall to be accounted for as investment contracts under FRS 26.

159 Where the consideration for the investment contract issued comprises both a fee for the origination of a financial instrument and an ongoing charge for the provision of investment management services, the insurance undertaking should record the origination fee as turnover on the date on which it becomes entitled to it where it can be demonstrated that the undertaking has no further obligations in respect of the fee.

160 Subject to this, origination fees and charges for managing investments should be recognised as revenue where and to the extent that the insurance undertaking has obtained the right to consideration through its performance.

161 Incremental costs that is directly attributable to securing an investment management contract are recognised as an asset if they can be identified separately and measured reliably and if it is probable that they will be recovered. An incremental cost is one that would not have been incurred if the entity had not secured the investment management contract. The asset represents the entity's contractual right to benefit from providing investment management services and is amortised as the entity recognises the related revenue. If the entity has a portfolio of investment management contracts, it may assess their recoverability on a portfolio basis.

162 As noted in Paragraph C26 of Appendix C to FRS 26, deposit accounting should be adopted for investment contracts. This involves the following:

(a) One party recognises the consideration received as a liability rather than as revenue.

(b) The other party recognises the consideration paid as a financial asset rather than as an expense.

Gross Premiums Written

163 Premiums, including those for inwards reinsurance business, should be accounted for when due for payment. Where the amount due is Not known, for example with certain pensions business, estimates should be used. For unit-linked business the due date for payment may be taken as the date when the liability is established.

Reinsurance Outwards

164 **Reinsurance outwards** premiums should be accounted for when paid or payable.

Disclosure

165 The basis of premium recognition should be disclosed in the financial statements.

Claims Recognition

166 Claims payable on maturity should be accounted for when the claim becomes due for payment and claims payable on death should be accounted for on notification. Where a claim is payable and the policy or contract remains in force, the relevant instalments should be accounted for when due for payment. In all cases there should be consistent treatment between the recognition of the claim in the technical account for long-term business and the calculation of the long-term business provision and/or the provision for linked liabilities as appropriate. In accordance with Note 21 to the balance sheet format, provision for claims incurred but not reported (IBNR), including related claims handling expenses, should be included within balance sheet liabilities item C2(a) (Long term business provision). Any element of the claims payable which represents bonus allocated in anticipation of the surplus arising from the actuarial valuation at the balance sheet date should be included in line 5(a) (Claims paid) of the technical account for long term business.

Surrenders

167 Surrenders should be included within claims incurred and accounted for either when paid or at the earlier date on which, following notification, the policy ceases to be included within the calculation of the long term business provision and/or the provision for linked liabilities. Any element of surrenders payable which represents bonus allocated in anticipation of the surplus arising from the actuarial valuation at the balance sheet date should be included in item 5(a) (Claims paid) of the technical account for long term business.

Claims Handling Expenses

168 Claims incurred should include related internal and external claims handling expenses.

Disclosures

169 The basis of claims recognition should be disclosed.

Deferred Acquisition Costs

170 Paragraph 12 of Part I of Schedule 9A to the CA85 requires costs associated with the acquisition of new business incurred in an accounting period but relating to subsequent accounting periods to be deferred. Acquisition costs should be deferred explicitly. The deferred acquisition costs asset may be calculated in whole or in part by means of an actuarial method, which enables the costs so deferred to be separately identified.

171 Advertising costs should not be deferred unless they directly relate to the acquisition of new business.

172 The full amount of the deferred acquisition costs should be included in balance sheet assets item GII (Deferred acquisition costs), after adjusting, where appropriate, for any deferred tax liability recognised automatically in the actuarial valuation. A deferred tax provision should be established where appropriate in accordance with the requirements of current accounting standards. The long-term business provision should be adjusted appropriately to reflect the inclusion of the deferred acquisition costs asset and any corresponding deferred tax liability.

173 The movement in the accounting period in deferred acquisition costs disclosed, as an asset should be included under item 8(b) (Change in deferred acquisition costs) of the technical account for long-term business.

174 Deferred acquisition costs, which are carried forward, should be amortised over a period no longer than that in which, net of any related deferred tax provision, they are expected to be recoverable out of margins in matching revenues in relation to the related insurance contracts in force at the balance sheet date, at a rate, which is commensurate with the pattern of such margins.

175 Acquisition costs should not be deferred to the extent that:

- the costs in question have already been recovered (for example where the design of the policy provides for the recovery of costs as incurred);
- the net present value of margins within the insurance contracts is not expected to be sufficient to cover deferred acquisition costs after providing for contractual liabilities to policyholders and expenses; or
- the receipt of future premiums or the achievement of future margins is insufficiently certain based on estimates of future expected discontinuance rates or other experience.

176 Deferred acquisition costs should be reviewed by category of business at the end of each accounting period. Where circumstances which have justified the deferral of such costs no longer apply or are considered doubtful, the costs to the extent to which they are considered to be irrecoverable, should be written off to the long-term business technical account.

177 The basis of amortising acquisition costs should be disclosed in the notes to the financial statements.

Technical Provisions

178 Under Schedule 9A to the CA85, technical provisions in respect of long term business are analysed as follows:—

- Long term business provision;
- Technical provisions for linked liabilities; and
- Claims outstanding.

Balance sheet liabilities item C4 (Provision for bonuses and rebates) and line II.7 (Bonuses and rebates, net of reinsurance) in the technical account for long-term business should not be used. Bonuses attributable to the accounting period, other than those included within claims paid in accordance with paragraphs **166** and **167**, should be included in line II.6(a) (Change in other technical provisions – long term business provision) and in Balance Sheet Liabilities item C.2 (Long term business provision).

Long Term Business Provision

179 Paragraph 46(3) of Part I of Schedule 9A to the CA85 requires the computation of the LTBP of UK business to be made annually by a Fellow of the Institute or Faculty of Actuaries on the basis of recognized methods, with due regard to the actuarial principles laid down in the EU Third Life Directive (92/96/EEC).

180 The **gross premium method** should be used for every class of insurance business except those for which the net premium method is used in the related regulatory returns, but policyholder liabilities of overseas subsidiaries may be computed on a local basis subject to paragraph **202.**

181 The method of valuation used for each principal category of insurance business should be disclosed in the notes to the accounts together with a summary of the principal assumptions made in accordance with paragraph **184**. In the case of overseas subsidiaries, the computation shall be prepared by an actuary or other specialists using recognized actuarial methods. Guidance on the extent to which the local bases of reporting can be incorporated in group accounts is contained in paragraph **202**. Paragraph 43 of Part I of Schedule 9A to the CA85 requires the long term business provision to be at all times sufficient to cover any liabilities arising out of insurance contracts as far as can reasonably be foreseen.

182 Liabilities should be assessed on a basis consistent with the bases adopted for valuing the corresponding assets. In determining the long-term business provision and the technical provision for linked liabilities, no policy may have an overall negative provision except as allowed by FSA rules or a provision, which is less than any guaranteed surrender or transfer value.

183 Having regard to the adjustment referred to in paragraph **172** and the need for consistency in paragraph **182**, the long term business provision may be calculated on the basis used for reporting under FSA rules subject to:

- Reassessment of the provisions and reserves included in the statutory liabilities for solvency purposes to consider the extent to which they should be included in the long-term business provision. This will require the exclusion of the appropriate proportion of reserves (such as investment reserves, reserves to cover general contingencies and reserves to cover the specific contingency of the fund being closed to new business). Any amount in excess of the necessary provision should be disclosed in the financial statements as a reserve or in the fund for future appropriations as appropriate;
- The reversal of any reduction in policyholder liabilities in the regulatory returns where these liabilities already implicitly take account of a pension fund surplus through future expense assumptions, which reflect, lower expected contributions.

184 Paragraph 46(2) of Part I of Schedule 9A to the CA85 requires that a summary of the principal assumptions underlying the long-term business provision should be given. This would include for each principal category of business the more significant assumptions relating to the following:

- premiums;
- persistency;
- mortality and morbidity;
- interest rates;
- the discount rates used with, if relevant, explanation of the basis of reflecting risk margins; and
- if applicable, any other significant factors.

There should be a brief discussion (which may be qualitative) of:

- any changes in significant assumptions or bases of preparation; and
- the sensitivity of the amount reported with respect to changes in the principal assumptions or bases of preparation.

(See also the disclosure requirements in paragraph **240**.)

185 For each significant class of with-profits insurance business, the insurer should disclose the extent to which the basis of preparation of the long-term business provision incorporates allowance for future bonuses. For example, it should be stated (if it is the case) that explicit provision is made only for vested bonuses (including those vesting following the current valuation) and that no such provision is made for future regular or terminal bonuses. If practical, and it can be done without undue cost, insurers should disclose the amount that has been included explicitly in the long-term business provision in relation to future bonuses. If the valuation method makes implicit allowance for future bonuses by adjusting the discount rate used or by another method, this fact should be stated together with a broad description of the means by which such allowance is made.

186 Where the valuation is performed using a net premium method, bonuses should be included in the long-term business provision only if they have vested or have been declared as a result of the current valuation.

187 The aggregate of the bonuses added to policies in the accounting period should be disclosed by way of note to the financial statements.

188 Where the long-term business provision has been determined on an actuarial basis that, in assessing the future net cash flows, has regard to the timing of tax relief where assumed expenses exceed attributable income, the entity should ensure that such tax relief is excluded from the determination of any deferred taxation requirement.

189 Where the technical provision for linked liabilities has regard to the timing of the tax obligation, the effect of this should be excluded from the determination of any deferred tax requirement.

Technical Provisions for Linked Liabilities

190 The relevant provision for any contract should not be less than the element of any surrender or transfer value which is calculated by reference to the relevant fund or funds or index.

191 The net assets held to cover linked liabilities at the balance sheet date may differ from the technical provisions for linked liabilities. The reasons for any significant mismatching should be disclosed. In practice this should apply only to overseas companies included in group financial statements because of the requirements of PRU 4.2.57 of the FSA rules.

Claims Outstanding

192 Amounts included under balance sheet liabilities item C3 (claims outstanding) should include claims in relation to both linked and non-linked business.

Fund for Future Appropriations

193 Note 19 to the balance sheet format defines the fund for future appropriations as an item comprising all funds the allocation of which either to policyholders or to shareholders has not been determined by the end of the financial year.

194 In the case of funds where there is reasonable certainty over the allocation to policyholders or to shareholders of all items recognised in the technical account for long term business, it is inappropriate to establish a fund for future appropriations. However, certain long-term business funds of proprietary insurers are established in such a way that segmentation between shareholders' reserves and policyholders' liabilities is not clear cut.

195 Where a fund for future appropriations is established, the notes to the financial statements should indicate the reasons for its use and the nature of the funds involved.

Reserves Relating to Long Term Business

196 Investment reserves (realised and unrealised investment gains and exchange gains), surpluses carried forward, resilience and similar reserves, contingency and closed fund reserves which may be included in the statutory liabilities for solvency purposes under the FSA rules, should be considered to assess the extent to which they should be included in the long term business provision (see paragraph **183**).

197 The investment return (which includes movements in realised and unrealised investment gains and losses) and related tax charges on assets representing reserves which are held within the long term fund for solvency purposes under the FSA rules should be credited to the technical account for long term business. Allocations may then be made as appropriate to the non-technical account in accordance with paragraphs **292** and **293** or to the fund for future appropriations.

Present Value of Acquired In-Force (PVIF) Business

198 Consistent with FRS 6 (Acquisitions and mergers) and FRS 7 (Fair values in acquisition accounting), the PVIF arising from the acquisition of a portfolio of long term insurance business should be recognised in the balance sheet as an asset. Subject to paragraph **201** below, the relevant element of the asset should be amortised and the discount unwound over the anticipated lives of the related contracts in the portfolio on a systematic basis. The relevant element is that part of PVIF which will be recognised as profit over the remaining lifetime of the in-force policies. The carrying value of the asset should be tested annually for impairment, as per paragraph **115**.

199 Internally generated PVIF should not be recognised.

200 The amortisation should be included in the technical account for long-term business under item II.11 (Other technical charges, net of reinsurance) and the amount of the PVIF asset and the amortisation for the accounting period should be disclosed separately. Disclosure should also be made of the method of amortisation employed.

201 Where a group reconstruction occurs and the new group carries on substantially the same insurance business as the group which it replaces (for example where a demutualisation is effected through the establishment of a proprietary company to acquire the business of an existing mutual insurer), any PVIF which would be regarded as internally-generated under the former group structure should continue to be treated as such in the new group.

Overseas Subsidiaries

202 Paragraph 40 of FRS2 requires uniform accounting policies to be used in determining the amounts to be included in consolidated financial statements, if necessary by making consolidation adjustments of amounts reported by subsidiaries. However policyholder liabilities of overseas subsidiaries incorporated into group financial statements may be computed on a local basis (either on a regulatory basis or in accordance with generally accepted accounting principles) provided the principles outlined in this SORP are followed and this is not inconsistent with paragraph 40 of FRS 2. Disclosure of that fact should be made in the notes to the group financial statements.

203 Paragraph 41 of FRS 2 recognises that in exceptional cases different accounting policies may be used when consolidating subsidiaries. Where the directors of the parent undertaking depart from the CA85 general requirement to use the same group accounting rules, or otherwise determine the assets or liabilities to be included in the consolidated financial statements, the CA85 requires disclosure of the particulars, which would include the different accounting policies used.

Deferred Tax

204 Deferred tax provisions, including deferred tax provided in relation to unrealised investment gains, should be shown separately under liabilities item E2 (Provisions for other risks and charges – provision for taxation) of the balance sheet format. Any net deferred tax asset should be shown as a separate sub-heading within assets EIII (Debtors – other debtors).

205 In the case of a composite insurance company or group, any policy to discount deferred tax should be applied to the whole of the insurer's business, including both the long term insurance business and the general insurance business and other shareholders' interests.

206 Timing differences can arise between the recognition of profits in the accounts and the emergence of surplus on the basis required by the FSA rules on which the taxation of the profits of life assurance business is currently based. In respect of such timing differences, the general incremental liability principle underlying FRS19 should be applied and deferred tax should be recognised as a liability or asset only if the transactions or events that give the insurer an obligation to pay more tax in future or a right to pay less tax in future have occurred by the balance sheet date.

207 It follows that where payment of incremental tax in the future depends upon a specific future event under the undertaking's control no event giving rise to the need to provide deferred tax has occurred. An example of this may be where an insurer has made arrangements under which part of the long-term fund is identified as being referable solely to shareholders resulting in the amount attributed and the movement thereon being recognised in the profit and loss account. In these circumstances no additional deferred tax should be recognised if the reversal of the timing difference is dependent solely on the discretion of the undertaking in bringing an amount into account as an increase or decrease in the value of non-linked assets in the revenue account required by Rule 9.14(b) of FSA rules. However, the amount of any deferred tax not recognised on such a timing difference should be disclosed in the notes to the accounts in accordance with paragraph 64(e) of FRS 19. This amount should be determined using the incremental rate of tax applicable to additional surplus in future years using enacted tax rates and legislation, but otherwise assuming that the existing basis of taxation of the undertaking is maintained.

208 The reconciliation required by paragraph 64(a) of FRS19 should apply only to the tax charge borne by shareholders through the non-technical account.

Disclosure of Tax Provisions

209 To the extent that they are not allowed for in the computation of the long term technical provision or the provision for linked liabilities, tax provisions should be included within liabilities item GV (Creditors – other creditors including taxation and social security) of the balance sheet format and disclosed either as a separate sub-category of that item or in the notes to the financial statements.

Grossing-up for Tax

210 Where the shareholders' profit from long term business is computed on an after-tax basis, it should be grossed-up to the pre-tax level for presentation in the non-technical account section of the profit and loss account. This grossing-up should be at the effective rate in accordance with FRS16 (Current tax). Uniquely, for life insurance business there is a single tax charge which integrates tax on both shareholders' profits and policyholders' investment return. Any disclosure of an amount as tax on shareholders' profits alone is therefore notional. Accordingly, for this business it will normally be appropriate to take the full rate of corporation tax as the appropriate rate to be attributed to shareholders' profits for the accounting period in question provided this does not result in material mis-statement of the profit before tax for the year.

211 Where shareholders' profits from long term business are computed at the pre-tax level, no grossing-up is required although, where transfers from the fund are partly on this basis and partly on an after-tax basis, the after-tax figure should be grossed up.

212 Tax attributable to the long-term business should be shown at line 11a (Tax attributable to long term business) of the technical account for long-term business. The tax attributable to the balance on the long-term business technical account should be included in line 2a (Tax credit attributable to balance on long term business technical account) of the non-technical account. The tax charge in line 9 of the non technical account (Tax on profit or loss on ordinary activities) will then comprise the shareholders' tax charge on all activities carried on by the undertaking.

Segmental Reporting

213 In the case of long term insurance business, segmental analysis should be provided of gross new business premiums and, if materially different, new business premiums net of reinsurance. New annual and single premiums should be disclosed separately in the financial statements together with an explanation of the basis adopted for recognising premiums as either annual or single premiums. New annual premiums should be shown as the premiums payable in a full year ie annual equivalent premium.

214 For the purpose of paragraph **213** above, new life insurance premiums must be defined in accordance with the following principles:

'Single premium contracts shall consist of those contracts under which there is no expectation of continuing premiums being paid at regular intervals. Additional single premiums paid in respect of existing individual contracts shall be included.

Regular premium contracts shall include those contracts under which premiums are payable at regular intervals during the policy year, including repeated or recurrent single premiums where the level of premiums is defined'.

The words in quotation marks are taken from paragraphs 2 and 3 of the instructions for completing Form 47 in the FSA rules.

215 In addition, FSA guidance states that:

'It is typical of regular premium business that the office will issue a renewal notice for the expected amount of the premium, albeit that the policyholder may have a contractual right to pay a different amount, or nothing at all. Another characteristic might be that premiums collection is by direct debit or other payment order'.

216 DSS rebates received on certain pensions contracts should be treated as single premiums.

217 Internal transfers between products where open market options are available should be counted as new business. If no open market option exists, the transfer should not be treated as new business.

PART 5 – GENERAL AND LONG TERM INSURANCE BUSINESS

Commission

[5131]

218 Paragraph 78 of Part I of Schedule 9A to the CA85 requires disclosure of the total amount of commissions for direct business including acquisition, renewal, collection and portfolio management. For this purpose, commission should exclude payments made to employees of the undertaking.

Exchange Gains and Losses

219 Where SSAP 20 (Foreign currency translation), or FRS 23 (The Effects of Changes in Foreign Currency Exchange Rates) insofar as it applies to entities writing insurance business, require companies to include exchange differences within the profit and loss account, these differences should be dealt with through the non-technical account except for long term insurance business where exchange differences should be recorded in the technical account for long term business. Where the assets and liabilities of an insurance enterprise are denominated mainly in a foreign currency, SSAP 20/FRS 23 requires that the closing rate/net investment method of translating the local currency financial statements should normally be used. Under the closing rate/net investment method of foreign exchange translation, exchange differences arising from the retranslation of the opening net investment in a foreign enterprise at the closing rate of exchange should be recorded as a movement in reserves except where, in the case of the long term insurance business, it is more appropriate to take them to the fund for future appropriations.

Segmental Reporting

220 For individual financial statements (but not group financial statements), the disclosures required by paragraphs 75 to 77 of Part 1 of Schedule 9A to the CA85 should be made. Segmented analysis should also conform with the requirements of SSAP25 (Segmental Reporting).

Guarantee Fund Levies Based on Premium Income

221 Levies based on premium income represent a charge on the Insurance undertaking even if they are passed on to policyholders in higher premiums. They should therefore be included in the profit and loss account as an expense and not as a deduction from written premiums. General business levies raised by the Financial Services Compensation Scheme (FSCS) and levies raised by the Motor Insurers' Bureau should be included within item 7(c) (Administrative expenses) in the technical account for general business. Long term business levies raised by the FSCS should be included within item 8(c) (Administrative expenses) in the technical account for long term business. FSCS levies are raised by reference to "financial years" of the Scheme ending on 31 March and are based on the leviable premium income of the calendar year ending immediately before the beginning of the Scheme's financial year, so for example a levy raised in the Scheme's financial year ending 31 March 2003 would be based on the leviable premium of the 2001 calendar year.

222 In deciding whether a provision for guarantee fund levies should be made, it will be necessary in accordance with FRS 12 to determine whether:

- the entity has a present obligation as a result of a past event;
- it is probable that a transfer of economic benefits will be required to settle the obligation; and
- a reliable estimate can be made of the amount of the obligation.

223 Where it is unclear whether there is a present obligation, a past event is deemed to give rise to a present obligation if, taking account of all available evidence, it is more likely than not that a present obligation exists at the balance sheet date. For the purpose of this paragraph, the past event is the recognition in the financial statements of the premium by reference to which the levy is calculated. The declaration of a levy by the guarantee fund will clearly constitute sufficient evidence but, in addition consideration may need to be given to any statement of intent by the guarantee fund to raise further levies based on premium income already recognised in the financial statements, or any consistent trend in the amount and timing of levies in previous periods. Where the conditions for establishing a provision are not present, it will be necessary to consider whether the possibility of future levies should be disclosed in the notes to the financial statements as a contingent liability.

224 In relation to long term insurance business, it is appropriate to provide for levies related to future premium receipts (in respect of in-force business) within the long term business provision, unless those levies can be charged against assets held to cover linked liabilities.

Profit and Loss Account

225 Where the amounts of general or long-term business are not material, the results should be disclosed as "other technical income, net of reinsurance" or "other technical charges, net of reinsurance" in the technical account for the business, which is material. Appropriate additional disclosure should be made in the notes to the financial statements in relation to the business accounted for in this way.

226 On consolidation, the result of any non-insurance entity belonging to the long-term fund may be included directly in the technical account for long-term business under item II.4 (Other technical income) or II.11 (Other technical charges) as appropriate. Where material, more detailed disclosure should be provided in the notes to the financial statements. Where an entity carrying on general insurance business is owned by the long-term fund, the result of this business should be transferred from the non-technical account to the technical account for long-term business using new lines for this purpose.

227 In the case of mutual insurance undertakings, no balance on the technical account for long-term business (item II.13) will normally arise as any surpluses or deficits on this account will be fully offset by transfers to or from the fund for future appropriations.

228 Paragraph 14 of FRS 3 requires that, where not shown on the face of the profit and loss account, an analysis between continuing operations, acquisitions (as a component of continuing operations) and discontinued operations of each of the other statutory profit and loss account format items between turnover and operating profit should be given by way of note. The analysis for insurance undertakings should only include the income and expenditure headings assigned with Arabic numerals in the profit and loss account format prescribed by Schedule 9A to the CA85 where the amounts concerned are material. More detailed information denoted by lower case letters in parenthesis need not be shown.

FRS17 – Retirement Benefits

229 For defined contribution schemes the contribution payable for the accounting period, and for defined benefit schemes the current service cost and any past service costs (including gains and losses on settlement and curtailments), should be included under the appropriate headings in the profit and loss account.

230 In relation to insurance business, the difference between the interest cost (ie the unwind of the discount on the pension liabilities) and the expected investment return on pension fund assets should be included as appropriate in the technical account for long-term insurance business or the non-technical account as a new line within Investment Income, or Investment Charges. These amounts should be disclosed separately in the notes to the financial statements.

231 Actuarial gains/losses, that is to say:

- Differences between the expected return on the scheme assets and the actual return;
- the impact of experience variations on the scheme liabilities and the effect of changes in assumptions; and
- adjustments because of limits on the amount that can be recognized as a pension fund asset in the balance sheet,

should be disclosed in the Statement of Total Recognised Gains and Losses (STRGL) where these gains and losses are attributable to shareholders.

232 Any movement in actuarial gains or losses (as defined in paragraph **231**) which is not attributable to shareholders should be treated as an amount, the allocation of which either to policyholders or to shareholders has not been determined by the end of the financial year. It should be included as a separate line in the technical account for long-term insurance business immediately above the line for transfer to or from the fund for future appropriations, and reflected in that transfer. This is consistent with paragraph 27 of FRS3 (Reporting Financial Performance) which states that the components of the STRGL should be the gains and losses that are recognised in the period in so far as they are attributable to shareholders.

233 A pension asset or liability should be shown as the last item of the assets or liabilities section as appropriate. A subtotal of assets or liabilities should be disclosed immediately before the pension fund asset or liability.

234 Where the Fund for Future Appropriations is determined after taking account of a pension asset or a pension liability, the impact should be disclosed separately in the notes to the accounts.

235 The methodology adopted for calculating the longer term rate of investment return on pension scheme assets should be consistent with any method used for determining the longer term rate of return on investments held for the purpose of the insurance business.

236 In some group defined benefit schemes, it may not be possible for the individual companies in the group to identify their share of a pension asset or a pension liability. In these circumstances, individual group entities may account for the scheme as a defined contribution scheme but must in addition disclose:

(a) The fact that the scheme is a defined benefit scheme but that the employer is unable to identify its share of the underlying assets and liabilities; and

(b) any available information about the existence of the surplus or deficit in the scheme and the implications of that surplus or deficit for the employer.

237 However, in the consolidated accounts it will be necessary to account for the group scheme as a defined benefit scheme. The allocation of the defined benefit scheme surplus/deficit between that attributable to shareholders and that attributable to funds the allocation of which to policyholders or to shareholders has not been determined by the end of the financial year should reflect the extent to which each benefits (in the case of a surplus) or is disadvantaged (in the case of a deficit). Sufficient disclosure should be made to enable the accounting treatment to be understood.

Estimation Techniques, Uncertainty and Contingent Liabilities

238 The purpose of this section is to give guidance on the disclosure of uncertainties and estimation techniques required by FRS 18 (Accounting policies). In addition, it introduces the requirement to give disclosure on contingent liabilities arising from insurance contracts in certain circumstances.

239 Uncertainties arising from insurance contracts can be classified for financial reporting purposes as follows:

(a) General uncertainties arising where the range of outcomes for provisioning purposes is within a 'normal' range;

(b) Specific uncertainties which are material and subject to an unusually wide range of outcomes;

(c) Uncertainties in areas where FRS12 does not require a provision to be established but where that standard may require contingent liability disclosures.

240 There is inherent uncertainty in estimating many of the technical provisions in respect of liabilities arising from insurance business. Compliance with FRS 18 requires the following disclosures in the notes to the financial statements:

- A broad description of the factors giving rise to uncertainty;
- A description of those items to which significant estimation techniques have been applied;
- A description of the estimation techniques used;
- Details of the significant assumptions made and information used in forming the estimates; and
- A note of those factors to which the estimation technique is particularly sensitive.

241 Some disclosure relating to long-term business technical provisions is already required by paragraphs **184** to **187** of the SORP. These disclosures may need to be enhanced to include the matters referred to above.

242 Where a specific material uncertainty results in the possibility of a range of outcomes outside the 'normal range', separate disclosure should be made. Disclosures should include the circumstances giving rise to this level of uncertainty, an indication of the uncertainties relating to the amount and timing of the outflows and the possibility of any related reimbursements.

243 Under FRS 18, estimates techniques are significant if the range of reasonable monetary outcomes is so large that the use of a different estimation technique could materially affect the view shown by the entity's financial statements. The description of a significant estimation technique will include details of those underlying assumptions to which the monetary amount is particularly sensitive.

244 FRS 18 also requires disclosure of the impact of significant changes to estimation techniques. Companies should consider those techniques and assumptions which have changed from year to year and where practicable make appropriate disclosure of the effect of significant changes in accordance with paragraph 55(d) of FRS 18.

245 Provisions, contingent liabilities and contingent assets arising from insurance contracts with policyholders are exempt from the requirements of FRS 12 (Provisions, contingent liabilities and contingent assets). Notwithstanding this, however, insurers should apply the principles of paragraph 91 of FRS12 in certain circumstances.

246 Where provision has been made for liabilities and any contingency arises solely because those provisions are subject to a degree of uncertainty because estimation techniques have been used in their determination, the disclosure required by paragraph **238** to **242** above will be sufficient to alert users of financial statements to the fact that the amounts at which liabilities are settled may exceed the provisions recorded in the financial statements. In some cases, there will be considerable uncertainty concerning future events. In these circumstances, a degree of caution will be necessary in the exercise of the judgment required for setting provisions such that liabilities are not understated.

247 Where a specific material contingent liability arises in respect of an item for which no provision has been made in the financial statements, and the prospect of this resulting in a transfer of economic benefits is more than remote, the disclosure set out in paragraph 91 of FRS12 should be given. It should be noted that nothing in this paragraph should be read to suggest that a provision need not be made even where there is material uncertainty. As explained in paragraph 91 of FRS 12, the level of provision should be assessed having regard to the range of uncertainty as to the eventual outcome for the category of business in question.

Reporting the Substance of Reinsurance Transactions – General Principles

248 Paragraphs **250** to **255** and **258** to **261** below do not apply to rights and obligations under reinsurance contracts that do not satisfy the definition of an insurance contract in Appendix C of FRS 26, where FRS 26 has been adopted.

249 In accordance with FRS 5, the economic substance of a reinsurance transaction should be reflected in the result for the year and the balance sheet.

250 A key characteristic of reinsurance is the transfer and assumption of significant insurance risk. There will be no transfer of insurance risk where the contract provides for the reinsurer to receive no more than a lender's rate of return under all reasonably possible scenarios. The assessment as to whether there has been a significant transfer of risk should be made having regard to the timing of all cash flows anticipated under the contract and any related contract.

251 The insurance risks relating to a long term reassurance contract include mortality, morbidity, investment, persistency and expenses risks.

252 The insurance risks relating to a general reinsurance contract may consist of either or both of underwriting risk and timing risk.

253 In considering whether or not a significant transfer of insurance risk has taken place, the entity should consider first whether it is reasonably possible that the reinsurer may realise a significant loss from the contract and secondly whether there is reasonable possibility of a significant range of outcomes from the contract. Insurance risk will not have transferred unless both of these conditions exist. 'Significant' should be assessed in the context of the commercial substance of the contract or contracts being evaluated as a whole, and should be judged with reference to the range of outcomes that would reasonably be expected to occur in practice.

254 The assessment as to whether significant insurance risk is transferred should be made prospectively at the time the contract is entered into. The method of accounting should be followed consistently over the whole period of the contract. If there has been a material change in contract terms during the period of the contract, the entity should perform a new assessment of whether or not a significant transfer of insurance risk has occurred.

255 Any reinsurance contract should be accounted for in two parts where elements can be identified that do not result in the transfer of significant insurance risk.

256 A reinsurance contract can create new assets (eg a right to reinsurance recoveries) and liabilities (eg an obligation to pay premiums for the reinsurance) in the financial statements of the cedent. It cannot lead to assets and liabilities arising from the underlying reinsured business ceasing to be recognised.

257 To determine whether or not an asset and/or a liability has been created, a three stage process should be followed:

- consideration of the transaction in conjunction with any other where this is necessary to obtain an understanding of the overall commercial effect;
- determination of the reasonably possible outcomes of the transaction having regard to its commercial effect, uncertainty and the intentions of the parties to the transaction insofar as these assist in determining its substance; and
- assessment of whether assets and/or liabilities have been created based on the above stages.

258 Where a reinsurance contract covers more than one accounting period, the reinsured should remeasure future entitlements and liabilities under the contract at each balance sheet date. This remeasurement should have regard to experience under the contract up to the balance sheet date and the amount, and for financial reinsurance the timing, of expected future cash flows.

259 A provision should be made for any shortfall in value (eg any anticipated inability on the part of the reinsurer to meet its obligations to the cedent, when they are expected to fall due).

260 Assets created by reinsurance transactions should normally be valued on the same basis as the related reinsured liabilities except in the circumstances covered in paragraph **259**.

261 Where material, any financial reinsurance element should not result in a **net** credit to the profit and loss account at inception. The measurement of any asset created at inception through financial reinsurance should not exceed the corresponding liability to the reinsurer. To achieve this result an additional provision should be established. This provision should be released to the technical account for long-term or general insurance business on a systematic and rational basis over the period of the contract.

Presentation and Disclosure – Reinsurance Contracts

262 Reinsurance should be dealt with in the technical account for general business or the technical account for long-term business as appropriate provided the contract is one which may be accounted for as a reinsurance contract in accordance with paragraphs **250** to **255**. In accordance with FRS5, the economic substance of all reinsurance contracts must be reflected in the results for the year and the balance sheet. The presentation and disclosure of reinsurance contracts should be such as to enable a clear understanding of their effect on the results. Where or to the extent that, the application of FRS5 principles does not permit a reinsurance contract to be accounted for as insurance, the accounting treatment and disclosure should be appropriate to the nature of the contract.

263 Reinsurance recoveries should be accounted for in the same accounting period as the related claim, and included in the balance sheet as an asset under Assets item Da3 (Reinsurers' share of technical provisions: claims outstanding). Although permitted under Schedule 9A to the CA85, the alternative method of showing reinsurance recoveries as a disclosed deduction from technical provisions is not permitted by the offset rule in FRS 5.

Reinsurance Balance

264 For the purpose of the disclosure required under paragraphs 75 and 76 of Part 1 of Schedule 9A to the CA85, the "**reinsurance balance**" means for general business the aggregate total of all those items included in the technical account for general business which relate to reinsurance outwards transactions including items recorded under item 1.7(d) (Reinsurance Commission and Profit Participations) and for long-term insurance business the corresponding items in the technical account for long-term business including items recorded under item 11.8(d) (Reinsurance Commissions and Profit Participations).

PART 6 – ACCOUNTING FOR INVESTMENTS

FRS 26 (Financial Instruments: Measurement)

[5132]
265 The guidance in this section applies in full to insurance undertakings that are not subject to the provisions of FRS 26 relating to financial assets. Where, and to the extent that an entity is subject to those provisions, paragraphs **266**, **268** and **279–290** are not applicable.

Valuation of Investments Other than non-linked Land and buildings

266 Investments included under asset items CII, CIII and CIV should be stated in the balance sheet at their **current value** except for redeemable fixed income securities where the **amortised cost** basis of valuation has been adopted as permitted by paragraph 24 of Schedule 9A to the CA85. Assets held to cover linked liabilities should be stated in the balance sheet under assets item D at their current value at the balance sheet date. This paragraph and the provisions set out in paragraphs **285–298** do not apply to PVIF whether accounted for as an investment or otherwise.

Valuation of land and buildings excluding those held to cover linked liabilities

267 Land and buildings, excluding those held to cover linked liabilities, should be included under assets item CI. Investment properties as defined by SSAP19 should, in accordance with that Standard, be included in the balance sheet at their open market value and should not be subject to any periodic charge for depreciation. Self-occupied properties should be shown in the balance sheet at current value and, where material, a charge for depreciation should be made in accordance with FRS15. The book value of self-occupied properties included under assets item CI should be disclosed in the notes to the financial statements in accordance with Schedule 9A to the CA85.

Anticipated cost of realisation

268 Where, in accordance with paragraphs 25(4) and 26(6) of Part I of Schedule 9A to the CA85, the valuation takes into account the anticipated costs of realisation of investments subsequent to the balance sheet date, no allowance should be made for any reduction in the value of such investments subsequent to the balance sheet date.

Group companies

269 Shares in group undertakings (asset item CII.1) should be accounted for at current value in the parent company's individual balance sheet.

270 In the consolidated financial statements, subject to paragraph **271** below, interests in group companies should be consolidated on a line by line basis as required by law, having regard also to paragraph **226** above.

271 In the case of an interest in a group company belonging to the long term business fund, changes in the value of which affect or establish policyholders' rights, paragraph 3(1A) of Schedule 4A to the CA85 prohibits any adjustment to the related insurance liabilities in the consolidated accounts. Where this necessitates the inclusion of an additional asset or liability in the balance sheet reflecting the difference between the current value and the net assets consolidated, the additional items should be included using a new line for this purpose.

Associates and Joint Ventures

272 Interests in associates and joint ventures which form part of an investment portfolio within the meaning of paragraph 50 of FRS 9 should be accounted for as investments according to the method of accounting applied to other investments within the same portfolio rather than as associates or joint ventures. Other interests in associates and joint ventures should be accounted for in accordance with paragraphs **273** and **274**.

273 Interests in associates and joint ventures should be shown under asset item C.II.3 (Investments in group undertakings and participating interests: participating interests) in the parent company and consolidated financial statements. In the parent company's financial statements, they should be valued at current value.

274 In the consolidated financial statements, the equity or gross equity method of accounting should be adopted as required by FRS 9.

275 The provisions of paragraph **271** will apply as appropriate to interests in associates and joint ventures.

276 The layout of the profit and loss account specified in Schedule 9A to the CA 85 is incompatible with the FRS 9 requirement to disclose the share of the operating results of associates and joint ventures immediately after group operating profit. Insurers should therefore comply with the FRS 9 disclosure requirement by including the amounts in the profit and loss account under Investment Income: income from participating interests (item 2(a) in the technical account for long-term insurance business and 3(a) in the non-technical account) and disclosing as a memorandum item in the non-technical account the amount of the group operating result attributable to the share of operating results of associates and joint ventures.

277 It is envisaged that insurers will not normally enter into joint arrangements that are not an entity. For this reason no guidance is given in this Statement on the appropriate accounting treatment. Insurers entering into this type of arrangement should follow the provisions of FRS 9.

Valuation Movements

278 Movements in the value of interests in group companies, associates and joint ventures shown in the balance sheet at current value are not covered by the guidance on investment return set out in paragraphs **285** to **298**. Valuation movements on interests attributable to the long-term business (including the additional asset referred to in paragraph **271**) should be taken to the technical account for long-term business. Valuation movements on interests not attributable to the long-term business should be taken to revaluation reserve except where the interests form part of an investment portfolio in which case the valuation movements should be taken to the non-technical account.

Valuation at Amortised cost

279 Use of the amortised cost basis of valuation is appropriate for redeemable fixed income securities which are part of a portfolio of such securities intended to be held on an ongoing basis in the activities of the insurance undertaking.

280 The amortised cost basis of valuation is inappropriate for irredeemable fixed interest stocks and accordingly these should be accounted for at current value.

281 Where redeemable fixed income securities are valued at amortised cost, any excess of the purchase price over the amount repayable at maturity should be charged to the profit and loss account by instalments so that it is completely written off when the securities are redeemed. Any excess of maturity value over purchase price should be released to profit and loss account by instalments over the period remaining until repayment.

282 Where, in relation to a security which has been valued at amortised cost, there is a choice of redemption dates, and the amortised cost should be computed on the basis of the redemption date, which would give the lowest yield measured from the date of purchase.

283 The amortised cost should be reduced if necessary to take account of any permanent diminution in value arising from potential default losses.

284 In respect of investments valued at amortised cost the following disclosures should be made, analysed between investments attributable to the long term business and other investments:

- the aggregate totals of the purchase price, the amortised cost and current value; and
- the net excess/deficit of the amounts payable at maturity over the amortised cost.

Accounting Treatment of Investment Return

285 Whilst insurance companies have the option under Schedule 9A to take unrealised **investment gains and losses** to revaluation reserve (and the statement of total recognised gains and losses), the distinction between realised and unrealised gains and losses on readily marketable investments is largely irrelevant. Accordingly, (subject to paragraph **278** above) all such realised and unrealised gains and losses should be taken to the profit and loss account.

286 In accordance with Notes 8 and 9 to the profit and loss account format in Part I of Schedule 9A to the CA 85, the **investment return** arising during the accounting period in relation to investments which are directly connected with the carrying on of long term insurance business should initially be included in the technical account for long term business. These investments comprise those arising in, or attributed to, the long-term fund including the fund for future appropriations together with such directly connected investments where the return accrues to shareholders whether held within or outside the long-term business fund.

287 The investment return arising in relation to all other investments including realised and unrealised investment gains and losses should initially be taken to the non-technical account.

288 Amortisation amounts, which are charged or released to the profit and loss account in accordance with paragraph **281** above should be disclosed as investment income in item III.3(b)(bb) of the non-technical account (Income from other investments) or item II.2(b)(bb) of the long-term business technical account (Income from other investments) as appropriate.

289 Where redeemable fixed income securities valued in the balance sheet at amortised cost are disposed of, the difference between the net sale proceeds and carrying value should be recognised in full in the profit and loss account of the period in which the disposal takes place. This is notwithstanding that the proceeds may be used to purchase other debt securities and fixed income securities which are also valued at amortised cost.

290 However, for the purpose of calculating the longer term rate of investment return, it may be appropriate to spread these realised gains or losses over the period to maturity (or deemed maturity) of the investments sold. (See paragraph **303**).

Allocation of Investment Return

291 In assessing the performance and financial position of their operations, insurers will usually consider the longer term investment performance to be more important than the investment return arising in the accounting period. Therefore, this SORP permits, but does not require, a form of presentation which enables the reader to identify operating results based on the longer term rate of investment return. This return may be recorded within the general business and long-term business technical accounts and may also be disclosed separately as part of the total operating profit.

292 Where investment return is allocated, it should be on one of the following bases:

- The longer term rate of return basis (see paragraphs **295** to **298**); or
- an allocation of the actual investment return on investments supporting the general insurance technical provisions and associated shareholders' funds should be made from the non-technical account to the technical account for general business.

293 To ensure consistency of treatment in the case of an insurance company or group transacting both general and long term insurance business:

- where the longer term rate basis of allocation is used, it must be applied to both the general and long term insurance business; and
- where an allocation of the actual investment return on investments supporting the general business technical provisions and associated shareholders' funds is made from the non-technical account to the technical account for general business, no allocation of investment return should be made from the technical account for long term business to the non-technical account.

294 The reasons for making allocations of investment return within the profit and loss account and the bases on which they are made should be disclosed in the notes to the accounts.

Longer Term Rate Allocation Basis

295 The allocation of investment return from item II.12 (Allocated investment return transferred to the non-technical account) of the technical account for long-term business to item III.4 (Allocated investment return transferred from the long term business technical account) of the non-technical account should be such that the investment return remaining in the technical account for long term business on investments directly attributable to shareholders reflects the longer term rate of return on these investments. For this purpose, the investments directly attributable to shareholders are those supporting the long-term business other than assets supporting

(i) the long term business provision,
(ii) he fund for future appropriations; and
(iii) the technical provision for linked liabilities.

296 The allocation from item III.6 (Allocated investment return transferred to the general business technical account) of the non-technical account to item I.2 (Allocated investment return transferred from the non-technical account) of the technical account for general business should be based on the longer term rate of investment return on investments supporting the general insurance technical provisions and all the relevant shareholders' funds. The technical account for general business will then include the longer-term investment return relating to the investments attributable to the general insurance business.

297 Where it is necessary for the purpose of reflecting the longer term rate of investment return in the technical account for general business, the allocation referred to in paragraph **296** above may exceed the actual investment return of the accounting period on the corresponding investments. Similarly, the allocation referred to in paragraph **295** above may be of a negative amount which increases rather than decreases the amount of investment return included in the long term business technical account.

298 The allocation referred to in paragraph **295** above should be included in line II.12 of the long-term business technical account and in item III.4 of the non-technical account gross of any attributable tax. The tax attributable to the allocated investment return should be deducted from the tax attributable to long-term business in item II.11a of the long term business technical account and added to the tax on profit or loss on ordinary activities in item III.9 of the non-technical account.

The Longer Term Rate of Investment Return

Equities and Properties

299 The longer term investment return on equities and properties should be determined using one of the following methods:

- grossing-up actual income earned for each asset class by a factor representing the longer term rate of investment return divided by an assumed long term dividend or rental yield (based on the assumption that income will reflect the mix of assets held during the accounting period). Adjustments will be required for special factors which may distort the underlying yields of the portfolio such as (in the case of equities), special or stock dividends and share buy-backs; or
- applying the longer term rate of return to investible assets held during the period (taking account of new money invested and changes in portfolio mix) by reference to the quarterly or monthly weighted average of each group of assets after excluding the effect of short term market movements.

300 The longer-term rate of return should be determined separately for equities and property and for each material currency in which relevant investments are held.

301 Taking into account the investment policy followed by the undertaking, the longer-term rate of investment return should reflect a combination of historical experience and current market expectations for each geographical area and each category of investments. The rates chosen should be best estimates based on historical market real rates of return and current inflation expectations, having regard, where appropriate, to the following factors:

- comparison of the business's actual returns and market returns over the previous five years or such longer period as may be appropriate;
- longer-term rates of return currently used in the business for other purposes, for example, product pricing, with profits bonus policy, and pensions funding;
- the rate used for the purpose of achieved profits method reporting;
- consensus economic and investment market forecasts of investment returns; and
- any political and economic factors which may influence current returns.

302 Rates of return should be set with a view to ensuring that longer-term returns credited to operating results do not consistently exceed or fall below actual returns being earned. Any downturn in expectations of longer-term returns should be recognised immediately by reducing the assumed rate of return. Rates used should be reviewed at least annually although changes would be expected to be infrequent.

Fixed Income Securities

303 In the case of redeemable fixed income securities, the longer term rate of return may be determined by using either a redemption yield calculated on principles similar to that defined in paragraph **281** or the amortised cost basis with realised gains and losses subject to continuing amortisation over the remaining period to the maturity date. However, it may be based on interest earned where the net effect of amortisation would be immaterial. In the case of irredeemable fixed interest securities and short-term assets, the allocated longer-term rate of investment return should be the interest income receivable in respect of the financial year.

Derivatives

304 Where derivatives have a material effect and are used to adjust exposure to the various classes of investments, the calculation of the longer term rate of return set out in paragraphs **299** to **302** should be adjusted to reflect the underlying economic exposure.

Disclosure

305 Where technical results are disclosed which reflect the longer term rate of investment return the following disclosures should be made in the notes to the financial statements:

- The methodology used to determine the longer-term rate of return for each investment category;
- For each investment category and material currency, both the longer term rates of return and, if applicable, the long term dividend and rental yields used to calculate the grossing-up factor for equities and property;
- A comparison over a longer term (at least five years) of the actual return achieved with the return allocated using the longer term rate of return analysed between returns relating to *general business, long term* business and other; and
- The sensitivity of the longer-term investment return to a 1% decrease and a 1% increase in the longer-term rate of investment return.

Disclosure of Total Operating Profit

306 Where technical results are determined taking into account longer term levels of investment return, supplementary disclosure may be provided by way of a memorandum item in the non-technical account of:

- the operating profit based on the longer term level of investment return; and
- the difference between the actual and longer term levels of investment return arising in the accounting period as a result of short term fluctuations in investment return.

307 An alternative earnings per share figure reflecting the result based on the longer term rate of investment return may also be shown.

Segmental Reporting

308 Where allocations of investment return are made, the profit before tax of each segment shown in the segmental analysis should be based on the longer-term investment returns. The segmental results should be reconciled to the total of the actual result before tax disclosed in the non-technical account.

Aggregation of Investment Gains/Losses

309 The headings for realised and unrealised investment gains/losses in the profit and loss account should include the overall gains net of losses or losses net of gains as a single figure. It is not necessary to disclose separately the aggregate investment gains and aggregate investment losses.

Investment Income

310 Rents and interest income should be recognised on an accruals basis. Dividends receivable should be recognised in the financial statements on the date on which the price of the investment is quoted "ex-dividend".

Investments in Unit Trusts/Open Ended Investment Companies (OEICs)

311 Except for investments held to cover linked liabilities shown under assets item D, all investments in unit trusts and OEICs should be included in the balance sheet under assets item CIII.1 (Shares and other variable yield securities and units in unit trusts) regardless of the nature of the underlying assets of the unit trusts.

FRS 25

312 The presentation requirements of FRS 25 (Financial Instruments: Disclosure and Presentation) will apply with effect from accounting periods beginning on or after 1 January 2005. Financial instruments that are rights and obligations under an insurance contract as defined in Appendix C of FRS 26 are outside the scope of FRS 25. The disclosure requirements of FRS 25 will apply insofar as entities are subject to FRS 26 with effect from no later than the accounting period in which FRS 26 is given effect by the entity.

PART 8 – EFFECTIVE DATE

[5133]

313 This statement, which replaces the statement issued in November 2003 applies to financial statements for accounting periods beginning on or after 1 January 2005. In accordance with paragraph 58 of FRS 18 (Accounting Policies), entities should state in relation to their financial statements commencing in 2005 whether they have complied with this statement.

PART 9 – LEGAL REQUIREMENTS

Great Britain

[5134]

314 The provisions of the EU Insurance Accounts Directive have been implemented in Great Britain by the Companies Act 1985 (Insurance Companies Accounts) Regulations 1993 and, for insurance undertakings not formed and registered under the CA85, by the Insurance Accounts Directive (Miscellaneous Insurance Undertakings) Regulations 1993.

315 Under these regulations, the old Schedule 9A to the CA85 was replaced by a new Schedule 9A. In consequence, the disclosure exemptions available to insurers in the old Schedule 9A have been withdrawn. Moreover, the financial statements of insurance undertakings are now required to show a true and fair view. The references in this Part are to the new Schedule 9A.

316 Insurance undertakings have been required to comply with the new Schedule 9A to the CA85 in financial statements for financial years commencing on or after 23 December 1994.

Chapter I of Part I

317 Section A lays down general rules on the layout of insurers' financial statements and the extent to which items appearing under separate headings may be combined in the accounts, although separate disclosure may be required in the notes. In particular, paragraph 4 provides that, subject to the provisions of Schedule 9A, amounts in respect of items representing assets or income may not be set off against amounts in respect of items representing liabilities or expenditure (as the case may be) or vice versa.

318 Section B lays down required formats for the balance sheet and profit and loss account of an insurance undertaking. The notes to the accounting formats define certain items appearing in the financial statements and in some cases prescribe the accounting treatment to be applied. In particular Note 17 to the balance sheet format includes provisions governing the accounting treatment of deferred acquisition costs and Note 19 defines the fund for future appropriations. The long-term business provision is defined in Note 21 and the technical provision for linked liabilities is defined in Note 26. Acquisition costs and administrative expenses are defined in Notes 6 and 7 to the profit and loss account formats respectively. Notes 8 and 9 prescribe the accounting treatment of investment income, expenses and charges, and unrealised gains and losses on investments. Note 10 permits certain allocations of investment return to be made between the technical and non-technical accounts.

319 Paragraph 10 requires every balance sheet of a company which carries on long term business to show separately as an additional item the aggregate of any amounts included in balance sheet liabilities item A (capital and reserves) which are required not to be treated as realised profits under Section 268 of the CA85. A company which carries on long term business shall show separately, in the balance sheet or in the notes to the accounts, the total amount of assets representing the long term fund valued in accordance with the provision of Schedule 9A to the CA85.

Chapter II of Part I

320 Section A lays down general accounting principles in relation to insurers' financial statements. In particular, paragraph 15 requires accounting policies to be applied consistently within the same accounts and from one financial year to another. Paragraph 19 provides that, if it appears to the directors that there are special reasons for departing from any of the principles stated in Section A in preparing the company's accounts in respect of any financial year they may do so, but particulars of the departure, the reasons for it and its effect shall be given in a note to the accounts.

321 Section B lays down current value accounting rules for assets. In particular paragraph 22 requires investments included under assets items C and D in the required balance sheet format to be disclosed in the balance sheet at current value. Paragraph 28 requires the purchase price of these investments to be disclosed in the notes to the accounts.

322 Paragraphs 25 and 26 lay down requirements for determining respectively the current value of investments (other than land and buildings) and land and buildings.

323 Paragraph 24 permits debt securities and other fixed income securities shown as assets under Assets item CII (investments in group undertakings and participating interests) and CIII (other financial investments) to be included in the balance sheet at amortised cost. Both the purchase price and current value of securities valued at amortised cost in the balance sheet must be disclosed in the notes to the accounts.

324 Paragraph 32 in Section C requires assets included under Assets item CI (land and buildings) to be depreciated but paragraph 27 in Section B provides that in this case the depreciation is to be calculated by reference to the most recently determined current value. Paragraph 10 of SSAP 19 (accounting for investment properties) provides however that investment properties should not be subject to periodic charges for depreciation except for properties held on lease which should be depreciated on the basis set out in FRS 15 at least over the period when the unexpired term is 20 years or less.

325 Section D lays down rules for determining insurance technical provisions. Paragraph 43 sets out the general requirement for the amounts of technical provisions and paragraphs 46 and 47 contain rules governing respectively the computation of the long-term business provision, and general business outstanding claims. Paragraph 47(7) prohibits implicit discounting of claims provisions in relation to general business. Paragraph 48 permits explicit discounting of general business claims provisions subject to certain conditions being satisfied while paragraphs 51–53 describe the two methods permitted for accounting on a non-annual basis.

Chapter III of Part I of Schedule 9A

326 This sets out the information which insurance undertakings are required to include in the notes to their accounts. Paragraphs 75–78, however, apply only to individual insurance undertakings and the information, which they require, need not be given in the financial statements of insurance groups, which do not include entity profit and loss accounts.

Chapter IV of Part I of Schedule 9A

327 Paragraph 81 includes certain definitions of terms referred to in the Schedule 9A. In particular, the "long term fund" is defined as the fund or funds maintained by a company in respect of its long term business in accordance with the provisions of the Insurance Companies Act 1982.

Part II of Schedule 9A

328 This provides for the application of Schedule 4A to the CA85 to insurance groups with certain modifications. In particular, consolidated accounts of insurance groups must comply so far as practicable with the provisions of Part I of Schedule 9A as if the undertakings included in the consolidation were a single company.

329 For this purpose, section 255A(5) of the CA85 defines an insurance group as one where the parent company is an insurance company or where:

(a) the parent company's principal subsidiary undertakings are wholly or mainly insurance companies, and

(b) the parent company does not itself carry on any material business apart from the acquisition, management and disposal of interests in subsidiary undertakings.

330 Paragraph 1(4) provides that sub-paragraph (1) of paragraph 3 of Schedule 4A to the CA85 shall not apply to those liabilities items the valuation of which by the undertakings included in a consolidation is based on the application of provisions applying only to insurance undertakings, nor to those assets items changes in the values of which also affect or establish policyholder's rights.

331 Paragraph 1(5) provides that sub-paragraphs (1) and (2) of paragraph 6 of Schedule 4A to the CA85 need not be complied with:

(i) where a transaction has been concluded according to normal market conditions and a policyholder has rights in respect of that transaction, or

(ii) if the amounts concerned are not material for the purpose of giving a true and fair view.

Northern Ireland

332 The Insurance Accounts Directive is implemented in Northern Ireland by the Companies (1986 Order) (Insurance Companies Accounts) Regulations 1994.

Recent EU Legislation

333 For each financial year starting on or after 1 January 2005, Regulation (EC) No 1606/2002 of the European Parliament and of the Council requires the consolidated accounts of publicly traded companies to be prepared in conformity with such IAS as have been endorsed by the EU Commission for application in Europe. Member states may permit or require a listed parent company and unlisted groups and companies to prepare their financial statements in accordance with such IAS.

334 The Companies Act 1985 (International Accounting Standards and Other Accounting Amendments) Regulations 2004 amend the CA 85 to permit but not require listed parent companies and unlisted groups and companies to prepare their financial statements in accordance with EU endorsed IAS. Section 227C(1) of the CA 85 as amended requires the directors of a parent company to secure that the individual accounts of (a) the parent company and (b) each of its subsidiary undertakings falling within the scope of the Act are all prepared using the same financial reporting framework, except to the extent that in their opinion there are good reasons for not doing so. However, where the directors of a parent company prepare IAS group accounts, section 227C(5) permits the individual accounts of the parent company to be prepared under IAS, and the requirement of section 227C(1) then only applies to each of the subsidiaries falling within the scope of the CA85.

335 The Regulations also insert a new Section BA into Schedule 9A of the CA85 to implement the provisions of the EU "Fair Value Directive" (2001/65/EEC). This provides inter alia that certain financial instruments (including derivatives) may be included in the financial statements at fair value.

ABI GUIDELINES ON THE INSTRUCTION AND USE OF PRIVATE INVESTIGATORS AND TRACING AGENTS

5 July 2007

NOTES

FOREWORDS

Richard Thomas, Information Commissioner

[5135]

Respect for privacy is one of the foundation stones of the modern democratic state. Failure to respect an individual's privacy can lead to distress and in some circumstances cause that individual real damage, mentally, physically and financially. In my report 'What price privacy?' I brought to light evidence of an illegal trade in confidential personal information and identified a role for professional bodies to help stamp out that trade. I called on them to take a strong line and influence the industries in which they operate. I welcome these guidelines as a positive step by the insurance industry towards raising awareness and tackling an area where insurers or their agents could be drawn into the illegal trade in personal information.

Stephen Haddrill, Director-General, Association of British Insurers [ABI]

People rightly wish to ensure that their privacy is protected. At the same time they do not want to pay more for their insurance because others are getting away with fraud. Insurers have to strike the right balance, respecting privacy whilst stopping cheating policyholders who add nearly £40 to the average premium.

To protect the interests of our policyholders, it is sometimes necessary for an insurer to use a private investigator to check whether or not a claim is genuine. When this step is taken, it must be taken with care. It is simply not enough to employ a PI company just because it 'gets results' – any organisation that fails to check the credentials and working practices of a PI runs the risk of falling foul of the law and facing prosecution.

It isn't just about finding the cheats. Insurers will also use tracing agents to find beneficiaries who are due windfalls from long-forgotten policies. Insurers will expect the same high standards to apply to tracing agents, as they do to PIs.

Insurers should also remember that they too can be the victims of deception. So staff, particularly those in call centres, should be suitably trained.

The ABI has worked with the Information Commissioner and the PI industry in developing this guidance. I hope it will provide insurers with the information and tools they need to help track down the cheats while respecting the right to privacy. Insurers who follow it can act safe in the knowledge that PIs working for them will operate to high standards within the parameters set by the law.

SCOPE

[5136]

These guidelines apply to the instruction of private investigators and tracing agents by insurers in the United Kingdom. They are intended to provide a framework for insurers to devise their own procedures for investigating potential frauds in relation to claims from policyholders and third parties. The guidelines encourage insurers to instruct only private investigators (PIs) who operate within the confines of the law and to high ethical standards, without unduly hindering insurers' efforts to combat fraud.

The guidelines are in two parts. The first, more detailed part, relates to private investigators and the second to tracing agents. Investigations involving PIs tend to be of a more intrusive nature than those involving tracing agents, though the same considerations should apply when the instruction of either is contemplated.

Adoption of the guidelines is voluntary and entirely at the discretion of each individual insurer.

BACKGROUND

Investigation of insurance claims

[5137]

The vast majority of insurance claims are not subject to investigation. Of the few that are, most are conducted by in-house investigators, covered by FSA regulation, or chartered loss adjusters who are subject to their own professional standards. Most investigations are carried out with the knowledge of the claimant and will often involve standard checks against industry databases, which the customer has been told about at inception of the policy.

It is sometimes necessary to conduct covert investigations. These occur in two main instances: first, where an insurer has good grounds to suspect that a customer is inventing or exaggerating a claim and cannot reasonably accept the evidence that the customer presents; and second, where organised fraud is suspected and alerting the suspected fraudster might prejudice other investigations, including those conducted by the police.

The views of the Information Commissioner and the Government

In May 2006, the Information Commissioner published 'What price privacy?' This report highlighted the existence of a widespread trade devoted to illegally buying and selling personal information causing significant distress, intrusion and harm to individuals. The report identified the insurance industry as one of the sectors with an apparent incentive to acquire confidential personal data, particularly in respect of suspect claims. While these activities already constitute offences under Section 55 of the Data Protection Act (the Act), the report proposed a substantial increase in penalties, including custodial sanctions.

In December 2006 the Information Commissioner published a further report, 'What price privacy now?' that set out the reactions from the media, the security industry, financial bodies and the Government to the initial report. Many organisations have taken positive steps to raise awareness and tighten security. The report explicitly acknowledged the work that the Association of British Insurers (ABI) has undertaken. The FSA has stated that compliance with all relevant legislation is necessary in order to meet the authorisation threshold criteria for firms to act in a fit and proper way. The Information Commissioner's Office (ICO) will be making the FSA aware of any regulated firms that are convicted of Section 55 offences. A conviction or a caution for a Section 55 offence may also be grounds for refusing or withdrawing a PI's licence, when the scheme run by the Security Industry Authority becomes operational.

In early 2007, following a consultation by the Department for Constitutional Affairs, the Government confirmed that it will legislate to introduce custodial sanctions for Section 55 offences as soon as Parliamentary time permits.

Regulation of the private investigator sector

Insurance fraud is a problem that costs the industry's customers around £1.6bn a year. The vast majority of policyholders are honest and insurers will do all they can to protect their interests and may reasonably investigate suspect claims. However, they will not tolerate illegal access to personal information by those acting for them. Insurers expect the highest ethical and professional standards from private investigators and those acting for them. The ABI has supported regulation of the private investigation sector. Although this will raise costs for insurers, the industry accepts that it is key to raising standards and shutting out a rogue element in that industry.

Under the Private Security Act 2001, PIs will be licensed and regulated by the Security Industry Authority. Licensing is likely to come into effect in late 2008 and will help to ensure that PIs are fit and proper individuals that are competent to carry out their instructions. The competency criteria will not be insurance-specific, so the ABI is issuing these sector-specific guidelines to foster high standards among PIs. This will help to ensure that insurers are able to identify and take action on fraudulent claims swiftly, benefiting the insured population as a whole.

PRIVATE INVESTIGATORS (PIS)

Considering the use of a PI

[5138]
Surveillance is likely to be an intrusion into that individual's privacy. So a PI should only be employed where there is reasonable suspicion that the claim might be fraudulent and the information they can obtain is necessary to dispute it. When an insurer is considering whether or not to instruct a PI to investigate an individual, it should assess whether information gathering by the PI is required or whether it would be more suitable to investigate using other sources of information already available to the insurer.

The purpose of surveillance, as recognised by the courts, is to obtain independent, objective evidence in order to prove, disprove or validate a claim. Properly authorised surveillance is often the only method of securing the evidence necessary for a fair trial.

There might be circumstances where the use of a PI might not be an appropriate way of confirming the validity of a claim, for example, because an individual is alleging an illness that could not be verified through surveillance of that individual. So the insurer should consider what alternative courses of action might be appropriate in the particular circumstances of the case. For example, there are a number of research tools available to the insurer that can play an important role in the claims validation process. These include underwriting and anti-fraud databases such as the Claims and Underwriting Exchange (CUE), CIFAS (the UK's financial fraud prevention service), and credit reference agency databases.

In some cases the information that may impact upon a claim cannot be obtained by surveillance of the individual, but is held securely by another organisation for its own purposes. Obtaining personal information knowingly and recklessly without the consent of the organisation that holds it, either by deception or bribery, is a criminal offence under Section 55 of the Act. An insurer instructing a PI to gather information that could only reasonably be obtained by these means may be committing a criminal offence, as will the PI.

Where another organisation holds information that is necessary for the insurer to investigate a fraud, and is not available from other legitimate sources, it should be approached directly by the insurer or its agent. It will then be for that organisation to decide whether or not to disclose the relevant information to the insurer or their agent. The organisation approached would have to be satisfied that they had a legitimate basis for the disclosure.

Before a PI is employed, an impact assessment should be completed, documented and retained. Suggested areas to be assessed include:

What are the insurer's grounds for suspicion?

The insurer should state why it believes that the claim might not be genuine.

What means have been explored, other than the use of a PI, to verify the insurer's suspicions?

A PI should only be used where there is reasonable suspicion that the claim is not genuine. The insurer should always consider what information it already has at its disposal, or may gain access to, before instructing a PI.

What information needs to be disclosed to the PI so that he can fulfil his instructions?

Only the minimum information necessary to allow the PI to perform their task should be provided to them. It may be inappropriate to inform the PI of the ailment that the claimant is suffering, particularly where this would involve disclosing sensitive data such as an actual illness. The insurer should instead generalise. For example, it should use descriptive terms such as 'restricted mobility', 'ability to drive', etc. But if the insurer is aware that the individual under investigation could endanger the PI, then the PI should be forewarned.

In some circumstances, it would be necessary to inform the PI of the illness, for example in cases of depression, panic attacks, chronic fatigue, incontinence or agoraphobia.

With personal injury cases, it is often necessary to disclose the location on the human body of the injury so that video footage is properly focused on the areas and activity relevant to the claim.

What information would be required from the PI to verify suspicion?

The insurer should only request the PI to obtain information that is reasonably necessary to establish the status of the claim and should not request information that could only be obtained by deception or bribery. As part of its impact assessment the insurer should consider what information is required and why it is justified.

This might include:

(1) **Verification of the claimant's address** – the PI will usually need to verify where the individual lives, and that the person lives at the address supplied. This might be obtained by cross checking against the electoral roll. But remember that those most likely to consider making a fraudulent claim are those least likely to register on the roll. Moreover, it is not uncommon for individuals intent on defrauding insurers to deliberately provide a false address or register at the address of a friend, neighbour or relative in a determined attempt to avoid surveillance. Not knowing the subject's address might lead to the privacy of an innocent person being breached if the wrong information is supplied.

(2) **Photographic evidence** – the insurer should consider whether photographic evidence is required for positive verification.

(3) **Video evidence** – this might, for example, demonstrate the claimant's level of mobility or that the claimant is working. The original video tape should be from virgin stock (ie new and unused). If the insurer has a specific preference as to how it wants the video evidence edited, the insurer should stipulate this at the time of instruction.

(4) **PI Report** – this might be required, for example, to register the claimant's movements.

(5) **Other physical evidence** – such as advertisements offering services, invoices or receipts.

Entering into a relationship with a PI

The insurer should ensure that it chooses a PI that will act in an appropriate manner, both in compliance with the law and with standards of ethics and explicitly require the PI to do so.

It is strongly recommended that there is an appropriate written agreement between the insurer and the PI. It is difficult to see how without this an insurer could limit any additional use of the information, confine its disclosure and ensure its secure destruction at an appropriate time. Without such an arrangement the insurer could find it difficult to justify its compliance with the security requirements placed on it by the Act. At the very least the insurer should ensure that the PI adheres to a code of conduct. However, a code will be non-binding and provides less protection than a legal contract. The advantages of a formal agreement include that it:

(1) Protects the insurer from financial liability in the event of the insurer being sued and risk to reputation.

(2) Provides certainty as to the extent of the PI's remit.

(3) Provides guidelines for the security of documents and information.

(4) Forms a basis for recovering damages against the PI in the event of improper conduct by the PI

It should be noted that if a PI, when acting on behalf of an insurer, knowingly and recklessly obtains personal information without the consent of the organisation that holds it, this may be an offence under Section 55 of the Act. In these circumstances, the Information Commissioner will investigate both the PI and the insurer with a view to prosecution. For this reason, it is important that the insurer leaves the PI in no doubt that they are to obtain information by legal means only. It should do this in its instructions and any ongoing contact around the investigation of the case.

Where PIs are operating only on the basis of insurers' instructions, they will ordinarily be data processors for those purposes. Their status will, however, depend on the particular circumstances of the service they provide the insurer. Where a controller-processor relationship exists, it should be documented in a contract. This could be part of the agreement referred to above. PIs will of course be data controllers in their own right.

The insurer should consider including the following provisions in any agreement entered into with the PI:

(1) The PI company's employees engaged in the provision of the services should be suitably qualified, skilled, experienced, and trained. Many PIs would be involved in activities that are unconnected to claims investigations. So the insurer should ensure that the PI fully understands what is required of him in the particular case. The insurer might wish to establish what checks the PI company undertakes of staff prior to recruitment and should consider seeking references and specimen reports.

(2) The PI company and its employees should hold any licences required by local legislation.

(3) The PI company and its employees should act in accordance with all applicable laws, rules, regulations and codes of practice (hereinafter referred to generically as 'The Act') relevant to the services provided.

(4) The PI company should hold adequate professional indemnity insurance. This reduces the risk borne by the insurer and provides a degree of comfort that the PI company has demonstrated a level of professionalism.

(5) The PI should complete only the provision of services requested and retain the personal information involved for no other purpose.

(6) The PI company should obtain agreement from the insurer before sub-contracting to an agent in fulfilling the provision of the service.

(7) The PI company should take appropriate steps to ensure that if it sub-contracts to other agents in the provision of services to the insurer, those agents are bound by the same requirements as the PI. This should include full awareness training about the Act and the legal obligations that arise from it.

(8) The PI company should take appropriate steps to ensure that its employees comply with the Act when obtaining, using and disclosing the data.

(9) The PI company should take appropriate steps to ensure that neither it or any of its employees or agents shall use any data other than in connection with the provision of services as instructed by the insurer

(10) The PI company should have an entry on the register maintained by the Information Commissioner.

(11) The PI company should hold all data in strict confidence and take all actions, and put in place appropriate security measures, necessary to protect that data from:

- Any unauthorised or unlawful access; and
- Any accidental loss, destruction or damage
- Onward use and disclosure not associated with the investigation

The PI company should also return or ensure the secure destruction of the data when it is no longer required for the investigation, defence of the claim or potential further legal action. The PI company should notify the insurer of those measures on request. These might include steps that the PI company takes to maintain a clear chain of evidence, to store securely all original evidence and to safely dispose of evidence at the appropriate time.

(12) The PI company should allow the insurer, on request, to carry out an audit of its procedures in respect of the data gathered under this agreement. This might be conducted at the premises of the PI company.

(13) The insurer has the right to remove from the investigation employees of the PI company or sub-contractors, if they are found to be acting inappropriately or if there are reasonable grounds for suspecting that they may be acting inappropriately. Without prejudice to the insurer's right to pursue damages against the PI company in the event of improper conduct by the PI company, the insurer might also seek recovery of any interim fee payments made.

(14) The PI company should inform the insurer, as soon as reasonably practicable, following receipt of a subject access request from a claimant and should assist the insurer in satisfying that subject access request.

(15) On completion of the provision of services or on the renewal of the Service Agreement or after a set and agreed period, the PI should return all case material that is not active to the insurer.

(16) The PI company should not transfer the data, or any part of it, to a country or territory outside the European Economic Area except with the explicit consent of the insurer.

(17) The PI company should inform the insurer as soon as it becomes aware of any breach of the terms of the Act and advise the insurer of the steps that it intends to take to remedy that breach. The PI company should agree to keep the insurer apprised as to the progress and completion of those steps. The parties should agree that if the insurer considers the breach to be a material breach of the Act, the insurer is entitled to terminate any agreement that it has with the PI company by notice in writing. Any outstanding instructions at the time of receipt of that notice should be regarded as cancelled.

(18) There should be a time limit to the Service Agreement.

Where there is reinsurance in place, the insurer should also consider whether the agreement should also reflect any conditions imposed by the reinsurer.

The insurer should also consider whether the PI has ever given evidence in court or at a tribunal hearing in connection with an investigated claim. It is worth remembering that evidence might not be heard for several years. So the PI should be asked what measures are taken to ensure that the evidence can be supported several years after the investigation eg maintaining a surveillance log. Evidence contained within signed contemporaneous surveillance logs is acceptable in court in circumstances where there is no independent video evidence, for example, if a video tape is defective or where an evidential incident may have occurred which could not be documented by video footage.

Fair processing wording

The 1st Data Protection Principle requires data to be fairly and lawfully processed. This would ordinarily require the insurer to disclose to the customer all sources, uses and disclosures of personal data.

A PI will be instructed in order to verify an insurer's reasonable suspicions of fraud. Where PIs are not routinely instructed, a generic reference to the processing of data, including disclosures to third parties, for the *prevention, detection and investigation* of crime (including fraud/attempted fraud) might be sufficient. This information should be included in the notification given to customers. The customer would have the right to be informed of the identity of the third parties should they make an enquiry of the insurer.

Where PIs are instructed routinely, the insurer should make that clear to customers in its fair processing notice. The insurer should inform the applicant/policyholder at the earliest stage that a PI might be used.

This might be in the:

(1) Application form
(2) Claim form eg a group contract where the insurer would not receive any personal data until the claims stage
(3) Supporting documentation at the proposal stage

A third party claimant, for example, an employee claiming under a group policy or a third party motor accident claimant, should be notified in the initial letter from the insurer following receipt of the claim.

Instruction to the PI

The insurer should decide on the most appropriate medium for issuing instructions.

Sending information via facsimile transmission might be insecure and telephone instructions could be open to interpretation and lack any form of documentation. So it might be prudent for any instructions to a PI to be given in writing and sent securely (eg sent by recorded delivery). Alternatively, the insurer could send an email, with the instructions contained in an attachment that is suitably protected against unauthorised access (eg by encryption or, at the very least, password protected).

The instructions to the PI must be explicit and transparent, with the subject matter clearly documented. The insurer should request the minimum amount of information needed to gather evidence to support the insurer's suspicions.

The insurer should provide the PI with sufficient information as is necessary to ensure that the investigation focuses on the correct individual. The information provided to the PI should only be that which is necessary and relevant to identify the subject of their investigation and inform them of what type of investigation is required. This might include:

(1) The claimant's name
(2) The claimant's sex
(3) The claimant's address (on file) [which the PI may be asked to verify]
(4) The claimant's date of birth
(5) The description of the claimant (this might be obtained, for example, from the nurses' report or other medical report)
(6) Family circumstances
(7) A description of the type of data required:
   - Photographs
   - Video recording
   - PI report
   - Original signed surveillance logs
   - Any other information that is reasonably required (and justified) in order to help the insurer resolve the case. If the insurer is in any doubt as to whether further information is required or is justifiable, the insurer's data protection officer should be consulted.
(8) Instructions on what to look for:
   - The PI should not ordinarily be informed of the medical condition that the claimant alleges they are suffering from. The instructions should instead advise the PI to assess the way in which the claimant acts and may ask for evidence of particular activity. For example, the claimant might have difficulty lifting objects or should not be driving.

The claims handler and the PI might hold regular review meetings. This would help to ensure consistent standards of work, a mutual understanding of what is required from the investigation and provides a forum for providing feedback on the PI's work.

Access to data collected by a PI

The insurer should establish appropriate procedures to ensure that access to the information collected is restricted to relevant employees.

But there might also be a number of organisations that the insurer needs to consult in connection with the claim (eg to gather evidence) and this might involve disclosure of some of the information obtained by the PI. These include:

(1) The ***reinsurer*** who underwrites a proportion of the risk, and may be consulted on the appointment of a PI and as to whether the claim should continue following receipt of the PI's evidence.
(2) The ***employer*** who, as the policyholder on a group policy, might have the right to ascertain whether a claim should continue.
(3) The ***legal advisers*** who might be involved in advising on whether the claim should be repudiated, involved in subsequent legal action or in advising on legislative requirements.
(4) The ***medical advisers*** who might need, for example, to give an expert opinion as to whether certain behaviour or activity might be possible if the claimant is suffering from the condition claimed.

Retention of data collected by the PI

The insurer should consider the length of time that it might need to hold the data provided by the PI. The 5th Data Protection Principle states that personal data processed for any purpose or purposes shall *not be kept for longer than is necessary for that purpose* or those purposes. FSA guidance on systems and controls similarly provides that the general principle is that records should be retained for as long as is relevant for the purposes for which they are made.

For evidential purposes, in line with the Limitation Act 1980, it might be prudent to hold data for 6 years following the cancellation of the policy or repudiation of the claim. It is vital that the insurer notifies the PI when a claim has been settled/closed so that the PI can then take steps to dispose of the data securely. The insurer should allow sufficient time for an appeal to be lodged or disposed of.

TRACING AGENTS

[5139]

Many of the requirements that would apply to employing a PI apply equally in respect of tracing agents. Most tracing agents are employed to find the beneficiaries of wills and do not involve insurers. However, insurers might trace 'gone aways' who are the beneficiaries of life policies.

When contemplating instructing a tracing agent, the insurer should follow the same process as when instructing a PI. The following steps should be considered:

(1) An impact assessment should be undertaken to establish whether it is necessary to use a tracing agent.
(2) If a tracing agent is to be instructed, the parties should enter into a written agreement including provisions that are similar to those involving an arrangement with a PI.
(3) The instruction to the tracing agent should be secure, precise and specify exactly what information is to be obtained.
(4) The insurer should apply the same considerations to a tracing agent who wished to sub contract as they would in respect of a PI.
(5) The insurer should be the only party other than the tracing agent who has access to the data.
(6) The tracing agent should destroy data that it has accumulated from its investigation within 3 months of providing the insurer with its findings. This would provide sufficient time to deal with any enquiries.

GLOSSARY

[5140]

Blagging: A form of deception by which the 'blagger' pretends to be someone they are not in order to wheedle out the information they are seeking, usually by way of a series of telephone calls. Information that is obtained illegally is then sold on.

Data controller (Data Protection Act): A person who determines the purposes for which, and the manner in which, personal information is to be processed. This may be an individual or an organisation and the processing may be carried out jointly or in common with other persons.

Data processor (Data Protection Act): A person, who processes personal information on a data controller's behalf. Anyone responsible for the disposal of confidential waste is also included under this definition.

Data protection principles: There are eight principles of data protection – these form the core around which much of the Data Protection Act is written. All data controllers must generally comply with all eight, even if they are exempt from notification. The principles are enforceable by the Information Commissioner.

Encryption: The process of obscuring information to make it unreadable without special knowledge, so that the information remains private and secure.

Fair and lawful processing: The first data protection principle requires data to be processed fairly and lawfully. For processing to be considered fair, individuals must be provided with certain information including the controller's identity, the reasons that their information is being collected and any third parties it will be disclosed to. In addition, it is necessary that all personal data processing must comply with at least one of six threshold conditions. Where sensitive personal data is processed, including information about the health or the commission or alleged commission of an offence, additional considerations for processing must be met. For insurers, this will often be that the individual has provided explicit consent.

'Gone aways': A person who has left his/her given address since their data was added to the insurer's customer contact database and their current whereabouts is not recorded.

Notification (Data Protection Act): The process by which a data controller's processing details are added to the Information Commissioner's register. Under the Data Protection Act, every data controller who is processing personal information needs to notify unless they are exempt. Failure to notify is a criminal offence. Even if a data controller is exempt from notification, they must still comply with the data protection principles. The Commissioner maintains a public register of data controllers at www.ico.gov.uk. A register entry only shows what a data controller has told the Commissioner about the type of data being processed. It does not name the people about whom information is held.

Personal data: Information held in electronic and some highly structured paper files about a living individual who can be identified from that information and other information which is in, or likely to come into, the data controller's possession.

Private investigator: A person privately hired to do investigatory work, for example, to investigate suspicious insurance claims.

Processing (Data Protection Act): Obtaining, recording or holding the data or carrying out any operation or set of operations on data.

Subject access request (Data Protection Act): Under the Data Protection Act, individuals can ask for a copy of information about themselves that is held on computer and in some paper records. If an individual wants to exercise this subject access right, they should write to the person or organisation that they believe is processing the data.

A subject access request must be made in writing and accompanied by the appropriate fee. In most cases, the maximum fee will be £10, but this can vary. A request must include enough information to enable the person or organisation to whom the subject is writing to satisfy itself as to their identity and to find the information.

The request must be fulfilled within 40 days as long as the necessary fee has been paid. A data controller should act promptly in requesting the fee or any further information necessary to fulfil the request. If a data controller is not processing personal information of which this individual is the data subject, the data controller must reply saying so.

Surveillance log: Records or logs of incidents and activities carried out at specific times that serve as memory refreshing documents. They are used by private investigators when giving evidence and should be made on the understanding that that they may be produced in evidence.

Tracing agent: Insurers may employ tracing agents to find people or assets, for example, beneficiaries under life insurance policies.

ABI/GOVERNMENT STATEMENT ON FLOODING AND INSURANCE FOR ENGLAND

[5141]–[5142]

1. The Government and the Association of British Insurers (ABI) agree on the importance of managing the risk from flooding to people and property. As the floods of 2007 demonstrated, flooding can have devastating impacts: it can cause loss of life, displace thousands of people, and can cause major economic and social dislocation.

2. While flood defences, effective surface water management, flood warnings and other policies can reduce the risk from flooding, this risk can never be completely eliminated. In the UK, unlike in most other countries, insurance against the impact of flooding has been a standard feature of household and many small business insurance policies since the early 1960s. This enables households and small businesses to plan for and minimise the financial cost of flooding while insurers provide effective and efficient claims services and repair teams if flooding does occur.

3. The ABI and the Government both want to ensure that the risk from flooding is managed effectively and that flood insurance remains as affordable and widely available as possible so that consumers and small businesses continue to be able to protect themselves from the financial cost of flooding. Since 2000, this has been achieved through a 'statement of principles on flood insurance': in the short term this commits insurers to continue to provide flood insurance under certain scenarios and the Government to manage the risk from flooding. However, we recognise that the statement of principles may distort the market, hinder the development of specialist flood insurance for the more difficult cases and limit incentives for the uptake of cost-effective resilience measures to protect individual properties.

4. The ABI and the Government have agreed to work together to provide a long-term solution that will enable flood insurance to continue to be as widely available as possible without distorting the market. To achieve this, we have identified the following measures that must be taken:

- improve our understanding of flood risk through assessing both the probability and consequences of flooding from all sources including surface water;
- put in place a long-term strategy to reduce flood risk; set out the Government's short, medium and long term strategic flood prevention aims; assess funding needs; and ensure effective and prioritised allocation of resources and delivery over the medium and long term in line with future Government spending rounds;
- ensure that the planning system prevents inappropriate development in flood risk areas, and that any essential new development in high flood-risk areas is flood resistant and/or resilient;
- raise awareness in areas where flood risks are significant, encourage actions to mitigate and minimise the risks and costs of being flooded; and provide information about how to obtain flood insurance; and
- promote access to insurance for low-income households.

5. The ABI and the Government agree that implementing these measures over the next five years should ensure that flood insurance continues to be as widely available as possible without the need for the statement of principles from 1 July 2013. Until that date, subject to annual reviews to confirm continuing progress and to update commitments as necessary, the ABI and Government have agreed that the statement of principles will remain in force.

6. The revised statement of principles, published on the ABI website, will apply from 1 August 2008. It remains subject to additional review in the event of any significant external shocks, such as a withdrawal of flood reinsurance. The statement of principles will not apply to any property built after 1 January 2009.

HM Government

Association of British Insurers

July 2008

AREAS OF CONTINUING WORK FOR COMPLETION OVER NEXT 12 MONTHS

Improving flood risk assessment

- Establish timetable for incorporation of the EU Floods Directive into law.
- Establish how to streamline arrangements for providing available flood risk data from the Environment Agency to insurers in an appropriate format under agreed licensing and charging arrangements that enable insurers to use the data for assessing risk, underwriting, pricing and administering insurance.

Reducing flood risk

- Produce the first version of modelling of flood and coastal erosion risk management scenarios for a 25-year period, to inform the Government's Long-Term Investment Strategy. These will be published in Spring 2009 and show the impact, outcomes and funding implications of a range of policy options.
- Establish how flooding from surface water will be better managed in the future, including necessary progress on who will lead this work, how this will be funded, the responsibilities and powers that will be needed, and ensuring an appropriate regulatory environment for those responsible to encourage flood management measures: this will feed into the Government's Floods and Water Bill to be published in draft in Spring 2009.
- Establish and complete a review of outcome measures for the Environment Agency, assessing in particular the case for including measures for the protection of commercial property.

Development planning policy and building design

- Establish if any policy reforms are needed following the evaluation of the planning policy framework for flood risk.
- Establish how to improve building design in flood risk areas; and how to encourage homeowners to take steps to protect their homes (consultation expected in 2008).

GOVERNMENT COMMITMENTS ON FLOOD RISK MANAGEMENT

[5143]

The Government has agreed the following as part of the joint statement on flooding and insurance for England:

Improving flood risk assessment

- Environment Agency to provide a more accurate National Flood Risk Assessment for river and coastal flooding by January 2009 and to undertake an annual review thereafter: a work plan for delivery of the above and further supporting information to facilitate better communication of flood risk to the public and insurers is summarised in a separate note.
- Environment Agency to develop effective means to make its flood risk assessments publicly accessible, including for surface water flood risk.

Reducing flood risk

- Government to prepare a detailed response to the Pitt report with a prioritised action plan in Autumn 2008.
- Environment Agency to provide data to identify locations that are expected to benefit from improved flood defences against flooding from main rivers and the sea within the next five years by January 2009 and to update this annually thereafter: data to be included is summarised in a separate note.
- Government to publish a draft Floods and Water Bill in spring 2009. This follows from both the Pitt Review into the 2007 floods and the Government's Water Strategy, *Future Water.*
- Government to set out a long-term investment strategy to reduce river and coastal flood risk prior to the next spending review, based on the Environment Agency's scenarios modelling work of flood and coastal risk management to be published in spring 2009. This will set out Government's short, medium and long term strategic flood prevention aims; assess funding needs and ensure effective and prioritised allocation of resources and delivery over the medium and long term.
- Government to set outcome measures for effective flood and coastal erosion risk management over spending review periods in consultation with stakeholders.

Development planning policy and building design

- Government to publish an initial evaluation of the planning policy framework for flood risk by March 2009, including the quality of Strategic Flood Risk Assessments, the number of planning applications approved against Environment Agency advice, and the use and extent of call-in powers.

July 2008

REVISED STATEMENT OF PRINCIPLES ON THE PROVISION OF FLOOD INSURANCE

[5144]
The Government and the insurance industry have agreed that the conditions should be in place to enable the insurance market to be able to provide flood insurance to the vast majority of households and small businesses efficiently and without the specific commitments below from 1 July 2013. Thereafter, the industry will continue to work with existing customers to explore insurance options for domestic property and small business customers where the flood risk is significant and no public plans are in place to defend the property.

Until 30 June 2013, ABI members commit to:

- Continue to make flood insurance for domestic properties and small businesses available as a feature of standard household and small business policies if the flood risk is not significant (this is generally defined as no worse than a 1.3% or 1 in 75 annual probability of flooding).
- Continue to offer flood cover to existing domestic property and small business customers at significant flood risk providing the Environment Agency has announced plans and notified the ABI of its intention to reduce the risk for those customers below significant within five years. The commitment to offer cover will extend to the new owner of any applicable property subject to satisfactory information about the new owner.

It is important to note that:

- The premiums charged and policy terms will reflect the level of risk presented and are not affected by this commitment.
- This commitment does not apply to any new property built after 1 January 2009: the ABI encourages developers and customers purchasing a property in a new development to ensure that it is insurable for flooding. The ABI intends to publish guidance on insurance for new developments in autumn 2008.

This commitment is subject to annual review that will consider progress in resolving the areas of continuing work and implementing the Government's commitments and to additional review in the event of any significant external shocks, such as a reduction in the availability of flood reinsurance or major changes in the UK insurance market.

July 2008

ABI/SCOTTISH GOVERNMENT – JOINT STATEMENT ON THE PROVISION OF FLOOD INSURANCE

(December 2008)

ABI/GOVERNMENT STATEMENT ON FLOODING AND INSURANCE FOR SCOTLAND

[5145]
1. The Scottish Government and the Association of British Insurers (ABI) agree on the importance of managing the risk from flooding to people and property. As previous floods in Perth, Glasgow and Moray have demonstrated, flooding can have devastating impacts: it can cause loss of life, displace thousands of people, and can cause major economic and social dislocation.

2. While flood defences, effective surface water management, flood warnings and other policies can reduce the risk from flooding, this risk can never be completely eliminated. In the UK, unlike in most other countries, insurance against the impact of flooding has been a standard feature of household and many small business insurance policies since the early 1960s. This enables households and small businesses to plan for and minimise the financial cost of flooding while insurers provide effective and efficient claims services and repair teams if flooding does occur.

3. The ABI and the Scottish Government both want to ensure that the risk from flooding is managed effectively and that flood insurance remains as affordable and widely available as possible so that consumers and small businesses continue to be able to protect themselves from the financial cost of flooding. Since 2000, this has been achieved through a 'statement of principles on flood insurance': in the short term this commits insurers to continue to provide flood insurance under certain scenarios and the Scottish Government to manage the risk from flooding. However, we recognise that the statement of principles may distort the market, hinder the development of specialist flood insurance for the more difficult cases and limit incentives for the uptake of cost-effective resilience measures to protect individual properties.

4. The ABI and the Scottish Government have agreed to work together to provide a long-term solution that will enable flood insurance to continue to be as widely available as possible without distorting the market. To achieve this, we have identified the following measures that must be taken:

- improve our understanding of flood risk through assessing both the probability and consequences of flooding from all sources including surface water;
- work towards putting in place a long-term (25+ years) strategy to reduce flood risk; which will set out the Scottish Government's objectives and measures at a national level, ensuring effective and prioritised allocation of resource across six year planning cycles, backed by local plans with realistic and deliverable objectives and measures and agreed outline spending plans that are aligned with funding arrangements for all responsible authorities;
- retain national planning policy so that planning authorities should prevent inappropriate development in flood risk areas, and that any essential new development in medium to high flood-risk areas is flood resistant and/or resilient as appropriate;
- raise awareness in areas where flood risks are significant, encourage actions to mitigate and minimise the risks and costs of being flooded, including reinstatement of flood damaged property in a more resilient way; and provide information about how to obtain flood insurance; and
- promote access to insurance for low-income households.

5. The ABI and the Scottish Government agree that implementing these measures over the next five years should ensure that flood insurance continues to be as widely available as possible without the need for the statement of principles from 1 July 2013. Until that date, subject to annual reviews to confirm continuing progress and to update commitments as necessary, the ABI and Scottish Government have agreed that the statement of principles will remain in force.

6. The revised statement of principles, published on the ABI website, will apply from 1 January 2009. It remains subject to additional review in the event of any significant external shocks, such as a withdrawal of flood reinsurance. The statement of principles will not apply to any property built after 1 January 2009.

Scottish Government

Association of British Insurers

December 2008

SCOTTISH GOVERNMENT COMMITMENTS ON FLOOD RISK MANAGEMENT

[5146]–[5147]
The Scottish Government has agreed the following as part of the joint statement on flooding and insurance for Scotland:

Improving flood risk assessment

- Establish how to streamline arrangements for providing available flood risk data from the Scottish Environment Protection Agency to insurers in an appropriate format under agreed licensing and charging arrangements that enable insurers to use the data for assessing risk, underwriting, pricing and administering insurance.
- Scottish Environment Protection Agency to prepare Flood Hazard and Flood Risk Maps covering flood risk from all sources with appropriate arrangements for communicating this effectively to the public and insurers in a convenient administrative format that provides as accurate and specific data as possible whilst recognising the appropriate degree of uncertainty that attaches to the data.
- A work plan for delivery of the commitments under this section, covering the period through until 2013, will be agreed by end of March 2009 with early release to insurers of maps currently available on river and coastal flooding.

Reducing flood risk

- Scottish Government to ensure that Scotland benefits from the lessons learned in England and the action points identified in the Pitt report, wherever they are relevant.
- Scottish Government to provide data to identify locations that are expected to benefit from improved flood defences against flooding from main rivers and the sea within the next five years by January 2009 and to update this annually thereafter, data to be included is to be agreed by March 2009.
- Take forward a new Flood Risk Management Bill that ensures an appropriate regulatory environment and establishes the responsibilities and powers needed for those responsible to ensure the maximum possible social and economic resilience against all forms of flooding, covering assessment of flood risk from all sources and preparation of flood risk management plans, including transposing the EU Floods Directive.
- Scottish Government to work towards putting in place a long-term (25+ years) strategy to reduce flood risk; which sets out the Scottish Government's objectives and measures at a national level, ensuring effective and prioritised allocation of resource across six year planning cycles, backed by local plans with realistic and deliverable objectives and measures; agree outline spending plans that are aligned with funding arrangements for all responsible authorities; report annually on progress towards developing and implementing the plans.
- Produce the first version of long-term (25+ years) objectives and measures for managing flood risk at a national level in 2015, prioritised over six year planning cycles, based on available information about flood risk.
- Ensure local authorities publish local flood risk management plans, that include realistic and deliverable measures that align with national plans over the current planning cycle.

Development planning policy and building design

- Scottish Government to review the planning policy framework for flood risk to ensure that it aligns with the new Flood Risk Management (Scotland) Bill and continues to prevent inappropriate development in flood risk areas.
- Establish how to improve building design in flood risk areas; and how to encourage homeowners to take steps to protect their homes.

December 2008

ABI STATEMENT OF PRINCIPLES ON THE PROVISION OF FLOOD INSURANCE

- The Scottish Government and the insurance industry have agreed that the conditions should be in place to enable the insurance market to be able to provide flood insurance to the vast majority of households and small businesses efficiently and without the specific commitments below from 1 July 2013. Thereafter, the industry will continue to work with existing customers to explore insurance options for domestic property and small business customers where the flood risk is significant and no public plans are in place to defend the property. Throughout this period, ABI members commit to making advice available to customers which will encourage them to increase the resilience of their property as part of its reinstatement, following flood damage.

Until 30 June 2013, ABI members commit to:

- Continue to make flood insurance for domestic properties and small businesses available as a feature of standard household and small business policies if the flood risk is not significant (this is generally defined as no worse than a 1.3% or 1 in 75 annual probability of flooding).
- Continue to offer flood cover to existing domestic property and small business customers at significant flood risk providing the local authority has announced plans and notified the ABI of its intention to reduce the risk for those customers below significant within five years. The commitment to offer cover will extend to the new owner of any applicable property subject to satisfactory information about the new owner.

It is important to note that:

- The premiums charged and policy terms will reflect the level of risk presented and are not affected by this commitment.
- This commitment does not apply to any new property built after 1 January 2009: the ABI encourages developers and customers purchasing a property in a new development to ensure that it is insurable for flooding. The ABI intends to publish guidance on insurance for new developments later this year.

This commitment is subject to annual review that will consider progress in resolving the areas of continuing work and implementing the Scottish Government's commitments and to additional review in the event of any significant external shocks, such as a reduction in the availability of flood reinsurance or major changes in the UK insurance market.

December 2008

D. CODE OF PRACTICE FOR TRACING EMPLOYERS' LIABILITY INSURANCE POLICIES

CODE OF PRACTICE FOR TRACING EMPLOYERS' LIABILITY INSURANCE POLICIES

MINISTERIAL FOREWORD

I am very pleased that this new Code of Practice is being launched. Its appearance honours a commitment given by my predecessor, to work with the insurance industry to tackle a problem which prevents certain employees from seeking compensation from their employer for an industrial injury or disease.

The recent review of the Employers' Liability (Compulsory Insurance) Act 1969 found that some employees suffering from industrial diseases which took a long time to develop, could not trace their employer's insurance policy. This was most likely to happen where the employer had ceased to trade by the time a disease became apparent. The Government views with concern instances where proceedings are unable to be taken only for this reason. It therefore wants to see improvements in the tracing of such policies. That is what this voluntary Code aims to achieve.

The Code sets out the procedures which insurers will follow, and the standards they will meet, when dealing with enquiries from employees or their representatives. There are some gaps in insurers' records which it is now too late to fill. But this Code commits insurers to keep, and do their best to search, those employers' liability policy records which do exist. And to keep future policy records in ways which will make it much easier to answer future enquiries from employees.

The Code has been developed by DETR[1] and the insurance industry, working together in full co-operation. I am grateful to all of those who contributed to its preparation, and to those who responded to a public consultation earlier this year on a draft version.

I know that some would have liked the Government to take a more regulatory approach. But I believe that the industry deserves a chance to show what it can do to solve this problem. Its commitment to the Code is evident in the Statement by the Association of British Insurers and the Non-Marine Association at Lloyd's, which appears in this document.

Arrangements for monitoring the effectiveness of the Code have been put in place—insurers' performance will be subject to independent review. The Review Body includes representatives of an employees' organisation and the legal profession, bodies which can reflect the views of those the Code is designed to help. The Review Body's Annual Statement on how well the Code is working, will be published by DETR.

I hope very much that by improving the identification of relevant policies, this Code will be of real help to those employees who need to seek compensation.

Lord Whitty

Parliamentary Under-Secretary of State

---

1 The functions of the Department of the Environment, Transport and the Regions in relation to this Code of Practice are now carried out by the Department for Work and Pensions.

STATEMENT BY THE INSURANCE INDUSTRY

The growth of the "compensation culture" in the UK has had a huge impact on insurers. But one group of potential claimants has been held back, through no fault of their own. These are the victims of industrial injury and illness, whose condition may not have developed until many years after they left the job which caused it.

The business they worked for may no longer exist and, even if it does, may not have kept a record of its insurance arrangements. If the details of the employers' liability insurer who covered their employer during the appropriate time cannot be traced, a compensation claim has a reduced chance of being satisfied.

Insurers and the Government have, quite rightly, become increasingly concerned about this problem. Although the number of people affected is small, it is wrong that they cannot be compensated where a liability exists in law.

Working with the Government, insurers have been looking at how arrangements could be put into place to resolve the difficulties, and provide easy and quick access for claimants. We are pleased to launch today the Codes of Practice for Tracing Employers' Liability Insurance Policies to meet this objective.

The whole of the insurance industry—insurers, Lloyd's syndicates and insurance brokers—are committed to working together so that we can respond more effectively to compensation claims from ill and injured employees.

Code of Practice for Tracing Employers' Liability Insurance Policies: Contacting the ABI, NMA or DWP

1. The Association of British Insurers (ABI)

Employers' Liability Enquiry Unit,
Association of British Insurers,
51, Gresham Street,
London EC2V 7HQ
Fax: [020 7]367 8612
email: info@abi.org.uk
Website: http://www.abi.org.uk

2. Non-marine Association (NMA)

Lloyd's of London
One Lime Street
London EC3M 7DQ
Tel: 020 7327 4931
Fax: 020 7623 9390
email: nma@lloyds.com
Website: http://www.nma.org.uk

3. Department for Work and Pensions (DWP) (from February 2003)

Health, Safety and Occupational Compensation Division (HSOCD)
The Adelphi
Level 2
1–11 John Adam Street
London WC2N 8HT
Tel: Peter Schutterlin on 020 7712 2082 or Freda Ali on 020 7712 2745
Fax: 020 7962 8524
Website: http://www.dwp.gsi.gov.uk

The Code can be downloaded from the DWP website.

The electronic enquiries for Tracing Employers' Liability Compulsory Insurance (ELCI) can be obtained on-line from the ABI websites on www.abi.org.uk.

PART 1
DWP GUIDANCE NOTES

A. Introduction

Background

[5148]
In law, an employer may be liable to pay compensation to an employee who suffers injury or disease sustained during their employment.[1]

Employers are required by law to insure against this potential liability. The current relevant legislation is the Employers' Liability (Compulsory Insurance) Act 1969—which came into force on 1 January 1972—and associated Regulations.[2] The aim of the 1969 Act is to ensure that funds are available to pay any compensation for which an employer is liable. The Act does not guarantee an employee compensation for injury or disease sustained during their employment—they would need to prove the employer's liability. But it is intended to protect employees.

An employee claiming damages from their employer, will normally need to trace the insurance policy their employer held at the relevant time. A recent review of the Act showed that this can be a problem, particularly for employees suffering from industrial diseases which have taken a long time to develop. The greatest difficulties are experienced where the relevant employer is no longer in business. (The employee may need to trace a policy for a period before 1972; many employers had such insurance in earlier decades.) There are also instances where relevant insurance records have been lost, or have not been retained, by an employer who is still trading.[3] In all of these cases, the only surviving information about a policy may be that held by the insurer.

An employee who cannot identify their employer's insurance policy, may be unable to seek compensation.[4] The Government is concerned about this unsatisfactory situation. It wants insurers to do everything practicable to help employees to trace policies.

The press release accompanying the new Employers' Liability (Compulsory Insurance) Regulations announced on 27 October 1998, that this Department would work with the insurance industry to draw up a Code of Practice to help in tracing employers' liability policies. This Code has been developed by DETR (DWP will have responsibility from February 2003) and the industry in consultation with each other; its evolution was greatly assisted by the comments received on a draft version, which was distributed during Spring 1999 to those with an interest—employees' and employers' organisations, the legal profession and the different parts of the insurance industry.

---

1 The employee would need to show that the employer had been negligent, or in breach of their statutory duty of care.

2 The Employers' Liability (Compulsory Insurance) Regulations 1998, SI 1998/2573, which came into force on 1 January 1999.

3 An employer who is required by law to be insured, is now required to retain for 40 years any certificate of insurance issued to him on/after 1 January 1999; also the certificate for any previous policy which was current on 31 December 1998 or January 1999.

4 Inability to trace an insurance policy can also be a problem for an employer. If they cannot establish their right to be indemnified, claims will have to be met from their own resources.

Purpose of the Code

Its purpose is two-fold: to help employees needing to trace insurance policies taken out by employers in the past; and to ensure that insurers keep future records in ways which will make tracing such policies much easier. The Code should help employees and their representatives—normally it is the employee's solicitor who will try to identify the employer's insurance policy.

Legal Status

This is a voluntary Code entered into by insurance companies and Syndicates at Lloyd's. It does not provide potential claimants, or employers, with any rights which do not already exist in law. This is not a statutory code.

Content

This Code sets out the procedures insurers will follow, and the standards they will meet, if they are asked to help trace an employer's insurance policy. It also contains commitments on record keeping.

Two Parts of the Code

An employer may buy employers' liability insurance from—

(i) an insurance company, or

(ii) an underwriting Syndicate at Lloyd's.

Because these two types of organisation operate in different ways, there are two parts to this Code: the ABI Code, and the NMA Code. But each has the **same** purpose, approach and standards.

Most insurance companies in the United Kingdom belong to the Association of British Insurers (the ABI), a trade association. **The ABI's Code** for its members is **Part 2** of this document.

Lloyd's is a marketplace in which many Syndicates transact various kinds of business; some Syndicates underwrite the insurance of employers' liability risks.[1] Most Syndicates belong to the Non-Marine Association (the NMA), a trade association. **The NMA's Code** for its members is **Part 3** of this document.[2]

---

1 Lloyd's itself is not an insurer.

2 Neither the ABI nor the NMA are insurers.

Scope

The purpose of the Code is to improve the tracing of employers' insurance policies.

Whether a particular employer was liable for an injury or disease suffered by an employee, is a separate issue—which should be pursued in the normal way. There is no provision under the Code for accepting claims for compensation, or for evaluating or negotiating such claims.[1]

---

1 A claim for compensation should be made against **the employer**, whose responsibility it is to deal with such claims. The employer will then involve its insurers. They will take over control of the claim, investigate the circumstances, and—where there is a liability upon the employer—negotiate a settlement of the claim with the employee or their representative.

Compulsory policies and voluntary policies

Employers who are not obliged by law to have employers' liability insurance, may nevertheless choose to buy this type of cover—for instance, some public sector employers do so. Insurers will follow the Code in dealing with enquiries about voluntary employers' liability policies, in the same way as for they would for policies taken out in order to comply with the law.

Effective date

This Code was launched in November 1999.

B. Making an Enquiry

Do you need to ask an insurer for information?

Before putting forward an enquiry under this Code, you should make every effort to trace your employer and submit a claim to them. The Code is really intended to help those who cannot obtain information about a relevant insurance policy from their employer or former employer.

Questions which insurers may ask

You may conclude that you need to put an enquiry to an insurer. Under the Code, insurers undertake to search their records when given a minimum amount of information. This minimum is described in **paragraph 2(ii)** of each Code.[1]

You may be asked to provide more information than this—an insurer may ask you to complete an enquiry form like the one at the end of this document. You are not obliged to provide this information. But if you do, the prospects of a policy being traced could be significantly improved.

For instance, telling the insurer where your employer was located, may enable the insurer to identify their branch office which dealt with the insurance. Insurers' historical records are often held by intermediaries rather than by the insurers themselves; some intermediaries specialise in dealing with particular types of trades or businesses. So telling the insurer about your employer's business, or about the nature of your injury or disease, may enable the insurer to identify the relevant intermediary.

Another possible problem could be that a relevant policy was held in a name which is not the name of your employer. For instance, you may have worked for a subsidiary company of the main policyholder. A search made by an insurer using your employer's name, might not identify this policy. Insurers appreciate that you may not know the name in which a policy was held, but you should provide any information you can on this. For instance, Companies House records might help in tracing parent company and subsidiary relationships. Or if an employer has been taken over or merged with another organisation, they might help to identify the company which is now responsible for past trading.

Providing as much information as you possibly can could therefore help the insurer to help you.

1 See Part 2 and Part 3 of this document.

Contacting the right person

Contact an insurer

The insurance broker who arranged your employer's insurance is **not** the insurer who provided the insurance policy. Your enquiry needs to be addressed to an insurer.

Which insurer?

— *If you think you know which insurance company or Syndicate at Lloyd's provided the insurance, submit your enquiry directly to them.*

If you know the name of the insurance company, you can get its address from the ABI. Information on how to contact the ABI is at the front of this document.

An enquiry to a Lloyd's Syndicate should be sent to:

[Syndicate name]

Lloyd's
One Lime Street
London EC3M 7HA.

— If you think the insurance was provided by a Syndicate at Lloyd's but do not know which one, send your enquiry to the Non-Marine Association at Lloyd's (NMA) whose contact details are at the front of this document.

— If there are no clues as to who the insurer might have been, submit your enquiry to the Association of British Insurers (ABI), whose contact details are at the front of this document. They will circulate your request for information to all their members who provide this type of insurance. They will also copy it on your behalf to the Non-Marine Association at Lloyd's, for circulation to relevant Syndicates there.

C. How Insurers Will Deal with Enquiries

Most of the information about this is in the ABI and NMA Codes—**Parts 2 and 3** of this document. These Notes provide additional background.

Insurers' ability to search records

Advances in technology mean that insurers now find it simple and cost-effective to maintain permanent policy records, which can be readily searched to identify whether an employers' liability insurance policy was in force at a particular time.

However, when such record keeping systems were developed, it was not always possible to capture data on policies which had lapsed earlier, and some records had already been destroyed. So the database which each insurer has at present, is not necessarily a complete record of the policies they have issued. Progressively, it will become a complete record.

Surviving paper records for earlier periods can be difficult and time-consuming to search effectively: for instance, where they are arranged according to the date when the policy expired, or by policy number.

The situation will vary from insurer to insurer so—as **section 4** of the ABI and NMA Codes explains—each will draw up a statement about what historical data they have, and how they can search it. These statements will be made available on request. Historic record statements will be covered in the ABI and NMA Annual Reports on their members' performance under the Code.

Information held by insurance brokers etc

Information which can help to identify a policy may be held by an intermediary— such as an insurance broker—rather than by the insurer. Insurers will make suitable arrangements, so that when they receive a query they can obtain relevant data from intermediaries. The British Insurance Brokers Association (BIBA) will bring this Code to the attention of its members.

D. Independent Review Body

Composition

The Review Body is chaired by the Department of Work and Pensions from February 2003. It has members drawn from the insurance industry, organisations representing employees and employers, and members of the legal profession who specialise in personal injury work and dealing with insurance claims.

Functions

At the end of each year, the Review Body will receive an Annual Report from the Association of British Insurers (ABI), giving an overview of all aspects of insurers' performance under the Code during that period. A parallel report will be provided by the Non-Marine Association at Lloyd's (NMA), covering the performance of relevant Lloyd's Syndicates.

Following its consideration of these reports, the Review Body will draw up an Annual Statement commenting on the insurance industry's performance under the Code. DWP will publish the Annual Statement, which will include the Annual Reports from the ABI and NMA.

E. Complaints to DWP (from February 2003)

The complaints system

If you need to make a complaint about the performance of an insurer or Syndicate under the Code, **Section 7** in the ABI and NMA Codes (**Parts 2 and 3** of this document) explains what to do. Consideration of a complaint by DWP is the final stage of the complaints process.

DWP will only consider a complaint, if—

— in the case of an insurer, the insurer and the Association of British Insurers, or

— in the case of a Lloyd's Syndicate, the Syndicate and Lloyd's Complaints Department,

have first been given the opportunity to resolve it.

Contacting DWP (effective from February 2003)

Complaints should be sent to:

Department for Work and Pensions (DWP)

Code of Practice on Tracing EL Insurers
Health, Safety and Occupational Compensation Division (HSOCD)
The Adelphi
Level 2
1–11 John Adam Street
London WC1N 2HT.
Tel: 020 7712 2082 (direct) or 020 7712 2745 (switchboard).
Fax: 020 7962 8524

You may wish to contact us for information before sending in a complaint. **But the complaint itself must be submitted in writing.**

How Your Complaint Will Be Dealt with

DWP will acknowledge the complaint within 5 working days of receipt.

DWP will decide if the insurer or Syndicate acted in accordance with the Code or not, on the basis of written evidence from the complainant[1] and the insurer. The complainant should state clearly what aspect of the Code they believe has not been observed, and provide supporting evidence. The insurer or Syndicate will be asked to explain their view of the case and provide relevant supporting evidence.

1 This can be the potential claimant or their representative.

Where DWP concludes that a complaint is justified

It will inform the insurer or Syndicate in writing (with a copy to the ABI or Lloyd's Complaints Department as appropriate), giving the reasons for its decision. DWP will give the insurer or Syndicate one calendar month in which to rectify the situation.

If the insurer or Syndicate does not do so, DWP's report to the Review Body on the complaints it has received that year will highlight the case, and recommend that the Review Body should draw attention to it in its published Annual Statement— naming the insurer or Syndicate concerned.[1]

DWP will inform the complainant of its final decision on their complaint, and the reasons for this.

1 DWP will report to the Review Body each year on the number of complaints which have been referred to it and their nature, the numbers which were found to be justified, and the numbers which were not justified.

Where DWP concludes that a complaint is unjustified

It will inform the complainant and the relevant insurer or Syndicate (with a copy to the ABI or Lloyd's Complaints Department as appropriate), and give reasons for its conclusion.

F. Sanctions

DWP will report to the Review Body on any complaint which it has found to be justified, and where the insurer or Syndicate has failed to provide a remedy within one calendar month of being notified of DWP's view.

DWP will recommend that the Review Body draw attention to the case in its next Annual Statement, and that it name the insurer or Syndicate concerned. The Review Body's Annual Statement will be published by DWP.

PART 2
ASSOCIATION OF BRITISH INSURERS (ABI) CODE OF PRACTICE FOR THE TRACING OF EMPLOYERS' LIABILITY COMPULSORY INSURANCE POLICIES

1. Introduction

[5149]
This Code of Practice applies in respect of potential claims made against employers who hold, or may have held, employers' liability insurance at the time of an injury, or during the period of exposure to a cause of occupational illness or disease.

The intention of this Code is to—
(i) help current claimants to trace past employers' insurers more effectively;
(ii) ensure future claimants (those at work now who may need to claim in the future) have access to insurers' details, particularly where the employer goes out of business.

The Code is applicable to all members of the Association of British Insurers ("ABI") which transact employers' liability business or have transacted such insurance in previous years.

Guidance Notes on its application, issued by the Department of Work and Pensions (DWP), can be found in **Part 1** of this document.

2. Procedural Steps to Be Taken On an Enquiry Being Made to an Insurer

(i) On receipt of an enquiry from a potential claimant or their representative, it will be referred to a central contact point within the Insurer.

(ii) The enquirer must provide the following minimum information for the Insurer to undertake a search—
- — name of employee;
- — name and address (including postcode) of employer and/or the policyholder;
- — type of injury and when caused, or type of illness/disease and period of exposure which caused that illness/disease.

(iii) The Insurer may ask the enquirer for additional information such as:
- — whether the employer is still in existence;
- — whether the enquirer is aware of the employer's insurers;
- — whether enquiries have been made of the employer regarding insurance arrangements (including details of any broker involvement).

If the Insurer does ask for such additional information, they will explain that it is being sought in order to increase the likelihood of a record of insurance being traced.

(iv) The Insurer will make every practical effort within reasonable bounds to try to establish whether they were on risk at the time of the injury or during the period of exposure.

(v) The Insurer will respond to the enquirer within 20 working days of receipt of the enquiry, irrespective of whether or not any search has found a successful match.

(vi) If—having made extensive enquiries of their own records and exhausted other avenues of enquiry—the Insurer is unable to trace any record of relevant insurance, they will advise the enquirer that the matter will be referred to ABI. The Insurer must advise the enquirer of all steps that it has taken during the course of its search and of all relevant information that has been discovered.

3. Procedural Steps to Be Taken On an Enquiry Being Referred to ABI

(i) On referral of an enquiry to ABI by an Insurer, or on receipt of an enquiry directly from a potential claimant or their representative, a designated contact point at ABI will confirm to the enquirer within 5 working days of receipt of the enquiry that the matter is being dealt with.

(ii) ABI will circulate details of referred and directly received enquiries every 20 working days (by e-mail or fax) to all Insurers participating in this Code, for them to investigate the enquiry in accordance with the procedures set out in Section 2 above. Details will also be sent to the Non-Marine Association at Lloyd's at the same time.

(iii) Each Insurer will respond to ABI within 20 working days of receipt of the e-mail/fax circular, irrespective of whether or not any search has found a successful match.

(iv) When an Insurer(s) has been found, ABI will inform the enquirer within 5 working days of being notified by the Insurer(s), giving the name, address and telephone number of the designated contact at the Insurers(s).

(v) In the event that no Insurer can be traced within 20 working days of receipt of the e-mail/fax circular, ABI will contact the enquirer within 5 working days of being notified by the Insurers(s), explaining all the steps that have been taken, including all Insurers contacted.

4. Record Keeping

(i) Historical Data

On becoming a signatory to the Code, each Insurer will make a statement as to the date from and the manner in which they can search historical data.

(ii) Current/future Data

On becoming a signatory to the Code, each Insurer will undertake to record and maintain all current and future policies for a period of 60 years in a form that facilitates ready searches, ie by name of employer and/or policyholder (after the start date of the Code).

In the event of an Insurer acquiring a new subsidiary, the Insurer must use best endeavours to ensure that all future Employers' Liability records of that subsidiary comply with the terms of the Code.

5. Training

Each Insurer will undertake to train all relevant staff in the procedures for handling Employers' Liability Code enquiries. All enquiries must be handled in an efficient and courteous manner.

6. Independent Review

(i) The ABI will produce an annual report giving an overview of the performance of the Code, including details of complaints received under the complaints procedure.

(ii) The report will be subject to an independent review. The Review Body will be chaired by the Department of Work and Pensions (DWP). Further information about the Review Body is given in **section D of DWP Guidance Notes**, which are in **Part 1** of this document.

7. Complaints Procedure

If an enquirer has a complaint about the conduct of a particular Insurer in relation to their operation of the Code, this should in the first instance be referred in writing to that Insurer.

Action by the Insurer

The Insurer must acknowledge a written complaint within 5 working days of receipt, giving details of its complaints handling procedure. A definitive response will be provided within 40 working days.

If the enquirer is not satisfied with the explanation provided
They may refer the complaint in writing to ABI, who will take up the matter with the company concerned.

Action by ABI
A complaint which is referred to ABI, will be acknowledged within 5 working days of receipt. ABI will forward correspondence to the senior management of the Insurer concerned, for their review and action as appropriate.

If the enquirer is not satisfied with the explanation provided
They may refer the complaint in writing to the Department of Work and Pensions (DWP).

Action by DWP

Information on this stage of the complaints process is given in **section E of DWP Guidance Notes**, which are in **Part 1** of this document.

8. Sanctions

See **section F of DWP's Guidance Notes**, which are in **Part 1** of this document.

PART 3
UNDERWRITERS AT LLOYD'S: NMA CODE OF PRACTICE FOR THE TRACING OF RECORDS OF EMPLOYERS' LIABILITY INSURANCES POLICIES

1. Introduction

[5150]
This Code of Practice applies in respect of potential claims made against employers, who hold or may have held employers' liability insurance at the time of an injury or during a period of exposure to a cause of occupational illness or disease.

The intention of this Code is to:
(i) help current claimants to trace past employers' insurers more effectively
(ii) ensure future claimants (those at work now who may need to claim in the future) have access to insurers' details, particularly where the employer goes out of business.

This code is applicable to all Syndicates at Lloyd's which transact employers' liability insurance or which have transacted such insurance in previous years.

Your attention is drawn to the guidance notes in Part 1 of this document, which have been issued by the Department of Work and Pensions.

2. Procedural Steps to be Taken on receipt of an enquiry by a Syndicate

(i) On receipt of an enquiry from a potential claimant or their representative, it will be referred to a central contact within the Syndicate.

(ii) The enquirer must provide the following minimum information for the Syndicate to commence a search:
   (a) name of the employee
   (b) name of the employer and/or the policyholder (if different)
   (c) type of injury and when caused or the type of illness/disease and the period of exposure which caused that illness/disease

(iii) The Syndicate may ask for further information or may ask the enquirer to complete an Enquiry Form. In doing so, the Syndicate should explain to the enquirer that this additional information is being requested in order to increase the likelihood of a record being traced.

(iv) The Syndicate will make every effort within reasonable bounds to establish whether it was the insurer on risk at the time of the injury or exposure.

(v) The Syndicate will respond to the enquirer within twenty (20) working days of receipt of the enquiry, irrespective of the result of the search.

(vi) If, after having made extensive enquiries of their own records and exhausted any other avenues of enquiry, the Syndicate is unable to trace any record of a relevant insurance, the Syndicate must inform the enquirer and tell the enquirer that the enquiry is being referred to the NMA. In doing so, the Syndicate must tell the enquirer of all steps which were taken during the course of their search and of all relevant information which has been discovered.

3. Procedural Steps to be Taken on referral of an enquiry to the NMA (or on receipt of an enquiry directly by the NMA)

(i) On referral of an enquiry by a Syndicate to the NMA, or on receipt of an enquiry directly by the NMA, a designated contact point at the NMA will confirm to the enquirer within five (5) working days of receipt of the enquiry that their enquiry is being dealt with.

(ii) Each twenty (20) working days the NMA will circulate details of all referred or received enquiries to all Syndicates participating in this Code who will undertake a search of their records in accordance with the procedures outlined in 2. above.

(iii) Each Syndicate will respond to the NMA within twenty (20) working days of the receipt of the circular, irrespective of the result of the search.

(iv) When a Syndicate is found to be the relevant insurer, the NMA will inform the enquirer within five (5) working days giving the name, address and telephone number of the designated contact at the Syndicate.

(v) In the event that no insurer can be traced within twenty (20) working days of the date of receipt of the circular, the NMA will contact the enquirer within five (5) working days explaining the steps which have been taken.

4. Record Keeping

(i) Historical Data

On becoming a signatory to the Code, each Syndicate will make a statement as to the date from and manner in which they can search historical data.

(ii) Current and Future Data

On becoming a signatory to the Code, each Syndicate will undertake to record and maintain all current and new policies for a period of sixty (60) years in a form which facilitates ready searches (ie a search by employer's/policyholder's name).

In the event of a Syndicate acquiring the business of another employers' liability insurer, the Syndicate must use its best endeavours to ensure that the records of such business comply with the provisions of this Code.

5. Training

Each Syndicate will undertake to train all relevant staff in the procedures for handling enquiries under the Code. All enquiries must be handled in an efficient and courteous manner.

6. Independent Review

The NMA will produce an annual report giving an overview of the performance of the Code, including details of complaints received under the Complaints procedure.

The report will be subject to an independent review. The Review Body will be chaired by the Department of Work and Pensions (DWP).

7. Complaints Procedure

Any complaint made by an enquirer about the conduct of a particular Syndicate subscribing to the Code should, in the first instance, be referred in writing to that Syndicate. Every Syndicate at Lloyd's is required to have written procedures to enable the prompt and proper handling of complaints.

If it is felt a Syndicate has failed to resolve the matter, the dispute can be referred to Lloyd's Complaints Department.

Correspondence should be addressed to:

The Manager
Lloyd's Complaints Department
Lloyd's
One Lime Street
London EC3M 7HA

The Lloyd's Complaints Department will acknowledge the complaint within 5 days of receipt, and will initially refer the matter to a senior representative of the Syndicate concerned and allow them a final 14 working days to review the matter. Lloyd's Complaints Department can be asked to investigate the matter if it still remains unresolved after that time.

In the unlikely event that the matter remains unresolved after investigation by Lloyd's Complaints Department, the dispute may be referred to the Department of Work and Pensions (DWP). **The Guidance Notes in Part 1E** of this document explain how DWP would deal with such a complaint.

8. Sanctions

See the **Guidance Notes in Part 1F** of this document.

CODE OF PRACTICE FOR THE TRACING OF EMPLOYERS' LIABILITY INSURANCE POLICIES
ENQUIRY FORM

[5151]–[6000]
This service is offered on-line by the ABI

The ABI declines all enquiries sent in by letter, email or fax. As the tracing service is fully automated the ABI cannot accept queries to chase up or track the progress of a search. Responses from insurers will be sent via email so it is essential you correctly enter a contact email address.

If you would like advice on how to use this form or if you have any questions about your completed search, please call Briony Krikorian on 020 7216 7492.

Please provide as much information as possible to help insurers trace the relevant policy record for the employer. Mandatory fields marked with an * must be completed. If you have no information to input into non-mandatory fields, leave them blank; do not write N/A or N/K. The form should be checked thoroughly for any mistakes, including spelling and typing errors.

On clicking the 'Submit Enquiry' button you will receive an immediate acknowledgement message on your screen, with a reference number for your enquiry. If you have filled in any mandatory fields incorrectly a red message will appear at the top of the form to inform you of the changes which need to be made. Until all mandatory fields are completed correctly, the form will not submit.

1. Information about the Enquirer			
*Name:			
*Name of Organisation:			
Address:			
*Telephone Number:		Fax Number:	
*Email:			
*Confirm Email:			
*Relationship to claimant:		Other:	
Solicitor's Reference:			

2. Information about the Employer		
This Code should be used where the employer has ceased trading. If the employer is still trading, any claim should be initially addressed directly to the employer. In extreme circumstances, an enquiry can be made for a trading company by ticking the 'still trading' box below. If the employer is a company, the Companies House website may provide the information on its trading status.		
*Name at time of employment:		
*Company designation:		
*Company No:		
*First line of address		
**City; if not known, Region:*		
Postcode:		
*Nature of business		Other:

*Trading status:	Ceased trading/dissolved/in liquidation Date . . . . MM/YY If you do not know the specific month, January will be selected for you.	Still trading/active
3. Information about the Employee		
This Code applies only in respect of claims made by employees harmed at work (not for public or any other liability claims). If your claim does not fall within this definition, the Code <u>will not</u> be able to assist with your enquiry.		
*Employee	*First name:	*Surname:
Claimant (if different to above	First name:	Surname:
	Age:	
Period spent working for the employer:	*From: . . . . MM/YY	*To: . . . . MM/YY
	If you do not know the specific months, January and December will be selected automatically for you as the start and end points.	
Disease or injury type:		
Mesothelioma		
OR		
Disease or injury type:		
Other:		
For Mesothelioma and disease claims only		
Period of exposure:	*From: . . . . MM/YY	*To: . . . . MM/YY
OR		
For accident claims only:		
Date of accident:	. . . . DD/MM/YY	
	If you do not know the specific months, January and December will be selected automatically for you as the start and end points.	
4. Information about Insurers		
Please give any information you have about insurers e.g. name of insurer, policy numbers, policy dates. Please also give any details of correspondence you have had with insurance companies or syndicates.		
5. Other Information		
Please provide any other information about the employer, including variation in name or address, parent companies, and mergers and takeovers, that you think might help with this enquiry. Do not submit multiple forms for the same claimant and the same employer. Any duplicate enquires will be ignored.		

PART VI
EUROPEAN MATERIALS

A. GENERAL

[TREATY ON THE FUNCTIONING OF THE EUROPEAN UNION] (FORMERLY TREATY ESTABLISHING THE EUROPEAN COMMUNITY) (TREATY OF ROME)

[25 March 1957]

NOTES

The provisions of the Treaty reproduced below are set out as consolidated in OJ C325, 24.12.2002, p 1, and further amended by the Treaty of Lisbon (OJ C306 17.12.2007, p 1) which entered into force on 1 December 2009.

Title in square brackets substituted for original title "Treaty Establishing the European Community" (Treaty of Rome) by the Treaty of Lisbon, art 2(1).

PART THREE
[POLICIES AND INTERNAL ACTIONS OF THE UNION]

NOTES

Words in square brackets substituted by the Treaty of Lisbon, arts 2(39), 5(1), Annex.

[TITLE IV]
FREE MOVEMENT OF PERSONS, SERVICES AND CAPITAL

NOTES

Title renumbered (formerly Title III) by the Treaty of Lisbon, art 5(1), Annex.

CHAPTER 3
SERVICES

[6001]
[Article 56] (ex Article 49)
Within the framework of the provisions set out below, restrictions on freedom to provide services within the [Union] shall be prohibited in respect of nationals of Member States who are established in a [Member State] other than that of the person for whom the services are intended.

[The European Parliament and the Council, acting in accordance with the ordinary legislative procedure, may, extend] the provisions of this Chapter to nationals of a third country who provide services and who are established within the [Union].

NOTES

Article renumbered by the Treaty of Lisbon, art 5(1), Annex.
Words in square brackets substituted by the Treaty of Lisbon, art 2(2)(a), (56).

[6002]
[Article 57] (ex Article 50)
Services shall be considered to be "services" within the meaning of [the Treaties] where they are normally provided for remuneration, insofar as they are not governed by the provisions relating to freedom of movement for goods, capital and persons.

"Services" shall in particular include—

(a) activities of an industrial character;
(b) activities of a commercial character;
(c) activities of craftsmen;
(d) activities of the professions.

Without prejudice to the provisions of the Chapter relating to the right of establishment, the person providing a service may, in order to do so, temporarily pursue his activity in [the Member State] where the service is provided, under the same conditions as are imposed by that State on its own nationals.

NOTES

Article renumbered by the Treaty of Lisbon, art 5(1), Annex.
Words in square brackets substituted by the Treaty of Lisbon, art 2(2)(b), (57).

[6003]
[Article 58] (ex Article 51)
1. Freedom to provide services in the field of transport shall be governed by the provisions of the Title relating to transport.
2. The liberalisation of banking and insurance services connected with movements of capital shall be effected in step with the liberalisation of movement of capital.

NOTES
Article renumbered by the Treaty of Lisbon, art 5(1), Annex.

[6004]
[Article 59] (ex Article 52)
1. In order to achieve the liberalisation of a specific service, [the European Parliament and the Council, acting in accordance with the ordinary legislative procedure and after consulting the Economic and Social Committee, shall issue] directives . . .
2. As regards the directives referred to in paragraph 1, priority shall as a general rule be given to those services which directly affect production costs or the liberalisation of which helps to promote trade in goods.

NOTES
Article renumbered by the Treaty of Lisbon, art 5(1), Annex.
Para 1: words in square brackets substituted and words omitted repealed by the Treaty of Lisbon, art 2(2)(d), (58).

[6005]
[Article 60] (ex Article 53)
The Member States [shall endeavour to] undertake the liberalisation of services beyond the extent required by the directives issued pursuant to [Article 59(1)], if their general economic situation and the situation of the economic sector concerned so permit.
To this end, the Commission shall make recommendations to the Member States concerned.

NOTES
Article renumbered by the Treaty of Lisbon, art 5(1), Annex.
Words in square brackets substituted by the Treaty of Lisbon, arts 2(59), 5(1), Annex.

[6006]
[Article 61] (ex Article 54)
As long as restrictions on freedom to provide services have not been abolished, each Member State shall apply such restrictions without distinction on grounds of nationality or residence to all persons providing services within the meaning of the first paragraph of [Article 56].

NOTES
Article renumbered and words in square brackets substituted by the Treaty of Lisbon, art 5(1), Annex.

[6007]
[Article 62] (ex Article 55)
The provisions of [Articles 51 to 54] shall apply to the matters covered by this Chapter.

NOTES
Article renumbered and words in square brackets substituted by the Treaty of Lisbon, art 5(1), Annex.

CHAPTER 4
CAPITAL AND PAYMENTS

[6008]
[Article 63] (ex Article 56)
1. Within the framework of the provisions set out in this Chapter, all restrictions on the movement of capital between Member States and between Member States and third countries shall be prohibited.
2. Within the framework of the provisions set out in this Chapter, all restrictions on payments between Member States and between Member States and third countries shall be prohibited.

NOTES
Article renumbered by the Treaty of Lisbon, art 5(1), Annex.

[6009]
[Article 64] (ex Article 57)
1. The provisions of Article 63 shall be without prejudice to the application to third countries of any restrictions which exist on 31 December 1993 under national or [Union] law adopted in respect of the movement of capital to or from third countries involving direct investment—including in real estate—establishment, the provision of financial services or the admission of securities to capital markets.
2. Whilst endeavouring to achieve the objective of free movement of capital between Member States and third countries to the greatest extent possible and without prejudice to the other Chapters of [the Treaties], [the European Parliament and the Council, acting in accordance with the ordinary legislative procedure, shall adopt the measures] on the movement of capital to or from third countries involving direct investment—including investment in real estate—establishment, the provision of financial services or the admission of securities to capital markets.
[3. Notwithstanding paragraph 2, only the Council, acting in accordance with a special legislative procedure, may unanimously, and after consulting the European Parliament, adopt measures which constitute a step backwards in Union law as regards the liberalisation of the movement of capital to or from third countries.]

NOTES
Article renumbered by the Treaty of Lisbon, art 5(1), Annex.
Para 1: words in square brackets substituted by the Treaty of Lisbon, arts 2(2)(a), 5(1), Annex.
Para 2: words in square brackets substituted by the Treaty of Lisbon, art 2(2)(b), (60).
Para 3: substituted for words originally in para 2 by the Treaty of Lisbon, art 2(60).

[6010]
[Article 65] (ex Article 58)
1. The provisions of [Article 63] shall be without prejudice to the right of Member States—
(a) to apply the relevant provisions of their tax law which distinguish between taxpayers who are not in the same situation with regard to their place of residence or with regard to the place where their capital is invested;
(b) to take all requisite measures to prevent infringements of national law and regulations, in particular in the field of taxation and the prudential supervision of financial institutions, or to lay down procedures for the declaration of capital movements for purposes of administrative or statistical information, or to take measures which are justified on grounds of public policy or public security.
2. The provisions of this Chapter shall be without prejudice to the applicability of restrictions on the right of establishment which are compatible with [the Treaties].
3. The measures and procedures referred to in paragraphs 1 and 2 shall not constitute a means of arbitrary discrimination or a disguised restriction on the free movement of capital and payments as defined in [Article 63].
[4. In the absence of measures pursuant to [Article 64(3)], the Commission or, in the absence of a Commission decision within three months from the request of the Member State concerned, the Council, may adopt a decision stating that restrictive tax measures adopted by a Member State concerning one or more third countries are to be considered compatible with the Treaties insofar as they are justified by one of the objectives of the Union and compatible with the proper functioning of the internal market. The Council shall act unanimously on application by a Member State.]

NOTES
Article renumbered by the Treaty of Lisbon, art 5(1), Annex.
Para 1: words in square brackets substituted by the Treaty of Lisbon, art 5(1), Annex.
Para 2: words in square brackets substituted by the Treaty of Lisbon, art 2(2)(b).
Para 3: words in square brackets substituted by the Treaty of Lisbon, art 5(1), Annex.
Para 4: added and words in square brackets therein substituted by the Treaty of Lisbon, arts 2(61), 5(1), Annex.

[6011]–[6012]
[Article 66] (ex Article 59)
Where, in exceptional circumstances, movements of capital to or from third countries cause, or threaten to cause, serious difficulties for the operation of economic and monetary union, the Council, . . . on a proposal from the Commission and after consulting the [European Central Bank], may take safeguard measures with regard to third countries for a period not exceeding six months if such measures are strictly necessary.

NOTES
Article renumbered by the Treaty of Lisbon, art 5(1), Annex.
Words in square brackets substituted and words omitted repealed by the Treaty of Lisbon, art 2(2)(d), (j).

[TITLE VII]
COMMON RULES ON COMPETITION, TAXATION AND APPROXIMATION OF LAWS

NOTES
Title renumbered (formerly Title VI) by the Treaty of Lisbon, art 5(1), Annex.

CHAPTER 1
RULES ON COMPETITION

SECTION 1
RULES APPLYING TO UNDERTAKINGS

[6013]
[Article 101] (ex Article 81)
1. The following shall be prohibited as incompatible with the [internal market]: all agreements between undertakings, decisions by associations of undertakings and concerted practices which may affect trade between Member States and which have as their object or effect the prevention, restriction or distortion of competition within the [internal market], and in particular those which—
(a) directly or indirectly fix purchase or selling prices or any other trading conditions;
(b) limit or control production, markets, technical development, or investment;
(c) share markets or sources of supply;
(d) apply dissimilar conditions to equivalent transactions with other trading parties, thereby placing them at a competitive disadvantage;
(e) make the conclusion of contracts subject to acceptance by the other parties of supplementary obligations which, by their nature or according to commercial usage, have no connection with the subject of such contracts.
2. Any agreements or decisions prohibited pursuant to this Article shall be automatically void.
3. The provisions of paragraph 1 may, however, be declared inapplicable in the case of—
— any agreement or category of agreements between undertakings;
— any decision or category of decisions by associations of undertakings;
— any concerted practice or category of concerted practices;
which contributes to improving the production or distribution of goods or to promoting technical or economic progress, while allowing consumers a fair share of the resulting benefit, and which does not:
(a) impose on the undertakings concerned restrictions which are not indispensable to the attainment of these objectives;
(b) afford such undertakings the possibility of eliminating competition in respect of a substantial part of the products in question.

NOTES
Article renumbered by the Treaty of Lisbon, art 5(1), Annex.
Para 1: words in square brackets substituted by the Treaty of Lisbon, art 2(2)(g).

COUNCIL DIRECTIVE

(71/86/EEC)

of 1 February 1971

on harmonisation of the basic provisions in respect of guarantees for short-term transactions (political risks) with public buyers or with private buyers

NOTES
Date of publication in OJ: OJ L36, 13.2.1971, p 14.

[6014]
THE COUNCIL OF THE EUROPEAN COMMUNITIES,
Having regard to the Treaty establishing the European Economic Community;
Having regard to the proposal from the Commission;
Whereas export credit is of primary importance in international trade and is an important instrument of commercial policy;
Whereas the various systems of export credit insurance in force in the Member States may give rise to distortions in competition between Community undertakings in markets in third countries;

Whereas harmonisation of the various systems of export credit insurance could facilitate co-operation between undertakings in the various Member States;

Whereas harmonisation can be achieved, according to the different types of transaction, either by means of common policies or by means of common provisions relating to those elements which are basic as far as competition is concerned;

Whereas at present guaranteed transactions represent, by and large, a smaller percentage of exports in the short-term field than they do in the medium-term field;

Whereas, moreover, this is a sector in which private credit insurance companies operate, and whereas it therefore seems appropriate to confine harmonisation solely to cover of political risks;

Whereas it therefore seems appropriate to reject the idea of drawing up a common policy and to confine harmonisation to those elements which are basic as far as competition is concerned;

HAS ADOPTED THIS DIRECTIVE—

Part VI European Materials

[6015]
Article 1

Subject to the provisions of Annex D to Council Directives Nos 70/509/EEC and 70/510/EEC[1] of 27 October 1970, Member States shall adopt such measures by law, regulation or administrative action as may be necessary to put into force the harmonised provisions on short-term transactions set out in the Annex to this Directive.

NOTES

[1] OJ L254, 23.10.1970, pp 1, 26.

[6016]
Article 2

Member States shall ensure that credit insurance organisations guaranteeing for the account or with the support of the State insure transactions that fall within the scope of the harmonised provisions, in accordance with the terms laid down in those provisions and such specific rules as are adopted by the Council.

[6017]
Article 3

1. Whatever the type of policy used, the harmonised provisions shall apply to transactions which:
   - include either a credit risk of less than twenty-four months, or a credit risk and a guaranteed manufacturing risk where the cumulative period is less than twenty-four months; the manufacturing risk, however, must be of less than twelve months;
   - are concluded with a public buyer or with a private buyer;
   - are on a supplier credit basis.

2. The provisions harmonised by this Directive concern only the guarantee in respect of political risks.

3. The definitions of "public buyer" and "private buyer" contained in Article 3 of Directive No 70/509/EEC and in Article 4 of Directive No 70/510/EEC respectively shall apply.

[6018]
Article 4

The Advisory Committee for Export Credit Insurance, set up under Article 4 of Directive No 70/509/EEC, may be consulted by the Commission on any problem relating to the uniform application of this Directive.

[6019]
Article 5

This Directive is addressed to the Member States.

Done at Brussels, 1 February 1971.

ANNEX

HARMONISED PROVISIONS CONCERNING GUARANTEES FOR SHORT-TERM TRANSACTIONS (POLITICAL RISKS) WITH PUBLIC BUYERS OR WITH PRIVATE BUYERS

[6020]

Article 1 Definition of the credit risk

The definition to be included in policies must not provide for a qualifying period for claims shorter than six months.

Article 2 List of events constituting a cause of loss

The basic list shall comprise events C to H inclusive as set out in Article 3 of the Common Policies for Medium- and Long-Term Transactions with Public Buyers and with Private Buyers, and, in the case of public buyers, includes also event B of Article 3 of the Common Policy for Medium- and Long-Term Transactions with Public Buyers.

The basic list may, however, be amended by the credit insurance organisation provided such amendment does not involve an extension of the cover beyond that afforded under the above-mentioned list.

Article 3 Extent of the guarantee

The guarantee shall apply to the amount owed to the insured in principal and interest, excluding interest on arrears, penalties and damages payable by the debtor.

Article 4 Percentage guaranteed

The insured himself shall retain exclusively for his own account responsibility for the portion not guaranteed by the credit insurance organisation.

Article 5 General principles of indemnification

The following principles must be observed:

(a) The insured shall be required as regards the conclusion and performance of the guaranteed transaction to exercise all reasonable and usual care, skill and forethought; this requirement shall apply equally to the conduct of his agents, co-contractors or sub-contractors;

(b) The insured shall be responsible for obtaining the necessary authorisations and for completing the legal formalities (including those which are incumbent upon the debtor until the entry into force of the contract);

(c) Invalid debts shall not be indemnified.

Article 6 General principles for the appropriation of payments received and of proceeds from the realisation of securities

Policies shall include such rules for appropriation as will ensure that any payments or recoveries whatsoever received by the insured will not be appropriated to unguaranteed debts in priority to guaranteed debts.

Article 7 General principles for recoveries

Policies shall observe the principle that recoveries are shared between the credit insurance organisation and the insured.

COUNCIL REGULATION

(2155/91/EEC)

of 20 June 1991

laying down particular provisions for the application of Articles 37, 39 and 40 of the Agreement between the European Economic Community and the Swiss Confederation on direct insurance other than life assurance

NOTES

Date of publication in OJ: OJ L205, 27.7.91, p 1.

[6021]

THE COUNCIL OF THE EUROPEAN COMMUNITIES,

Having regard to the Treaty establishing the European Economic Community, and in particular the last sentence of Article 57(2) and Article 235 thereof,

Having regard to the proposal from the Commission,[1]

In cooperation with the European Parliament,[2]

Having regard to the opinion of the Economic and Social Committee,[3]

Whereas an Agreement between the European Economic Community and the Swiss Confederation on direct insurance other than life assurance was signed at Luxembourg on 10 October 1989;

Whereas under that Agreement a Joint Committee is to be set up to administer the Agreement, ensure that it is properly implemented and take decisions in the circumstances provided for therein; whereas the Community's representatives on the Joint Committee have to be designated and particular provisions have to be adopted concerning the determination of the Community's positions in the Committee;

NOTES

1 OJ C53, 5.3.90, p 46.

2 OJ C72, 18.3.91, p 175, and Decision of 12 June 1991 (not yet published in the Official Journal).

3 OJ C56, 7.3.90, p 27.

HAS ADOPTED THIS REGULATION—

[6022]
Article 1

The Community shall be represented on the Joint Committee provided for in Article 37 of the Agreement by the Commission, assisted by representatives of the Member States.

[6023]
Article 2

The Community's position in the Joint Committee shall be adopted by the Council acting by a qualified majority on a proposal from the Commission.

With regard to the adoption of decisions to be taken by the Joint Committee pursuant to Articles 37, 39 and 40 of the Agreement, the Commission shall submit proposals to the Council, which shall act by a qualified majority.

[6024]
Article 3

This Regulation shall enter into force on the day following that of its publication in the *Official Journal of the European Communities.*

This Regulation shall be binding in its entirety and directly applicable in all Member States.

Done at Luxembourg, 20 June 1991.

COUNCIL DECISION

(91/370/EEC)

of 20 June 1991

on the conclusion of the Agreement between the European Economic Community and the Swiss Confederation concerning direct insurance other than life assurance

NOTES

Date of publication in OJ: OJ L205, 27.7.91, p 2.

[6025]

THE COUNCIL OF THE EUROPEAN COMMUNITIES,

Having regard to the Treaty establishing the European Economic Community, and in particular the last sentence of Article 57(2) and Article 235 thereof,

Having regard to the proposal from the Commission,[1]

In cooperation with the European Parliament,[2]

Having regard to the opinion of the Economic and Social Committee,[3]

Whereas it is desirable to approve the Agreement with Switzerland concerning direct insurance other than life assurance, signed at Luxembourg on 10 October 1989,

NOTES

[1] OJ C53, 5.3.90, p 1.

[2] OJ C72, 18.3.91, p 175, and Decision of 12 June 91 (not yet published in the Official Journal).

[3] OJ C56, 7.3.90, p 27.

HAS DECIDED AS FOLLOWS—

[6026]
Article 1

The Agreement between the European Economic Community and the Swiss Confederation concerning direct insurance other than life assurance is hereby approved on behalf of the Community.

The text of the Agreement is attached to this Decision.

[6027]
Article 2

The President of the Council shall take the measures necessary for the exchange of instruments provided for in Article 44 of the Agreement.[1]

Done at Luxembourg, 20 June 1991.

NOTES

[1] The date of entry into force of the Agreement will be published in the *Official Journal of the European Communities* by the General-Secretariat of the Council.

AGREEMENT

Between the European Economic Community and the Swiss Confederation On Direct Insurance Other Than Life Assurance

CONTENTS
OF THE AGREEMENT BETWEEN THE EUROPEAN ECONOMIC COMMUNITY AND THE SWISS CONFEDERATION ON DIRECT INSURANCE OTHER THAN LIFE ASSURANCE

1.	Principal agreement	
	Preamble	
	Section I:	Basic provisions (Articles 1 to 6)
	Section II:	Conditions governing admission (Articles 7 to 14)
	Section III:	Conditions governing the pursuit of business (Articles 15 to 26)
	Section IV:	Withdrawal of authorisation (Articles 27 to 29)
	Section V:	Collaboration between supervisory authorities (Articles 30 to 33)
	Section VI:	General and final provisions (Articles 34 to 44)
2.	Annex No 1:	Classes of insurance subject to the Agreement
3.	Annex No 2:	Kinds of insurance, operations and undertakings not subject to the Agreement
4.	Annex No 3:	Listing of acceptable legal forms
5.	Annex No 4:	Particular provisions for certain Member States of the Community
6.	Annex No 5:	Methods of calculating the equalisation reserve for the credit insurance class and conditions governing exemption from the obligation to set up such a reserve
7.	Protocol No 1:	Solvency margin
8.	Protocol No 2:	Scheme of operations
9.	Protocol No 3:	Relationship between the ecu and the Swiss franc
10.	Protocol No 4:	Agencies and branches of undertakings whose head office is situated outside the territories to which this Agreement applies
11.	Exchange of Letters No 1:	Principle of non-discrimination
12.	Exchange of Letters No 2:	Scope of authorisation
13.	Exchange of Letters No 3:	Authorised agent

14.	Exchange of Letters No 4:	Assignment to the Swiss Securities Fund of immovable property directly owned by insurance undertakings
15.	Exchange of Letters No 5:	Principles governing investment
16.	Exchange of Letters No 6:	Swiss list of classes of insurance
17.	Exchange of Letters No 7:	The capital of insurance undertakings
18.	Exchange of Letters No 8:	Transitional arrangements for assistance
19.	Exchange of Letters No 9:	Transitional arrangements for the large risks referred to in paragraph 2.1 of Protocol No 2
20.	Joint Declaration by the Contracting Parties concerning the period between the date of signature and the date of entry into force of the Agreement	
21.	Final Act	

PREAMBLE THE EUROPEAN ECONOMIC COMMUNITY OF THE ONE PART THE SWISS CONFEDERATION OF THE OTHER PART

CONSIDERING the close relations which exist between Switzerland and the Community;

DESIRING to avail themselves of the occasion offered by the establishment of a unified Community insurance market to consolidate existing economic relations between the two Parties in this field, and to promote, under fair conditions of competition, the harmonious development of these relations by ensuring protection for insured persons;

RESOLVED to that end to remove obstacles to the taking-up and pursuit of the business of direct insurance, other than life assurance, on a reciprocal and non-discriminatory basis safeguarded by the necessary legal conditions in respect of supervision, and thus to introduce between themselves freedom of establishment in this field;

EMPHASISING that this in no way affects their power to legislate subject to limits set by public international law;

ENDEAVOURING to do everything in their power to see that their domestic legal orders in this field evolve in a mutually compatible manner;

OBSERVING that it is in the interest of their economies to develop and strengthen their relations in this way in a field which up to now has not been governed by contractual rules, and to contribute thus to the coordination of economic law between the two Parties;

DECLARE themselves ready to consider in the light of any relevant factor, and particularly of the evolution of Community insurance law, the possibility of concluding other agreements in respect of private insurance;

HAVE AGREED in pursuit of these aims to conclude the present Agreement and to this end have designated as their Plenipotentiaries:

The European Economic Community; The Swiss Confederation . . .

HAVE AGREED AS FOLLOWS—

SECTION I
BASIC PROVISIONS

[6028]
Article 1
Object of the Agreement

The object of the Agreement is to lay down, on a reciprocal basis, the conditions which are necessary and sufficient to enable agencies and branches of undertakings whose head office is situated in the territory of one of the Contracting Parties and which wish to become established in the territory of the other Contracting Party, or are established there, to take up or pursue the self-employed activity of direct insurance other than life assurance.

[6029]
Article 2
Scope

The classes of insurance which are subject to this Agreement are set out in Annex 1.

[6030]
Article 3
Exceptions to the scope

The kinds of insurance, operations and undertakings which are not subject to this Agreement are listed in Annex 2.

Part VI European Materials

[6031]
Article 4
Application of domestic law
The law in force in each Contracting Party shall apply—
— to points which are not governed by this Agreement, and
— to questions relating to points governed by this Agreement, in so far as such questions are not regulated by the Agreement.

[6032]
Article 5
Principle of non-discrimination
The Contracting Parties undertake to apply the principle of non-discrimination when introducing and applying the provisions of this Agreement.

[6033]
Article 6
Supervisory authority
For the purposes of this Agreement, the supervisory authority shall, in the case of the Community, be the competent authority of the Member State in whose territory the head office of the undertaking is situated or in whose territory an agency or branch takes up or pursues the business of direct insurance.

SECTION II
CONDITIONS GOVERNING ADMISSION

[6034]
Article 7
Compulsory authorisation
7.1 Each Contracting Party shall make the taking-up of the business of direct insurance in its territory by an undertaking which establishes its head office there subject to authorisation by the supervisory authority.
7.2 Each Contracting Party shall, furthermore, make the opening in its territory of an agency or branch of an undertaking whose head office is situated in the territory of the other Contracting Party subject to authorisation by the supervisory authority.
7.3 In addition, it shall make the opening in its territory of an agency or branch of an undertaking whose head office is situated outside the territories to which this Agreement applies, as laid down in Article 43, subject to authorisation by the supervisory authority.

[6035]
Article 8
Scope of authorisation
8.1 An authorisation shall be valid for the covering of risks situated in the entire territory in which the supervisory authority granting the authorisation is competent unless, and in so far as the legislation applicable permits, the applicant seeks permission to carry on his business only in a part of that territory.
8.2 A risk is situated in the territory in which a supervisory authority is competent—
— in the case of insurance relating either to buildings or to buildings and their contents, in so far as the contents are covered by the same insurance policy, where the property is situated in that territory;
— in the case of insurance relating to vehicles of any type, where the vehicle is registered in that territory;
— in the case of policies of a duration of four months or less covering travel or holiday risks, whatever the class concerned, where the policy-holder took out the policy in that territory;
— in all cases not explicitly covered by the foregoing indents, where the policy-holder has his habitual residence in that territory or, if the policy-holder is a legal person, where the latter's establishment, to which the contract relates, is situated in that territory.
8.3 Authorisation shall be granted in respect of a particular class of insurance. It shall cover the entire class, unless the applicant wishes to cover only part of the risks pertaining to such class, as classified under Part A of Annex 1.
However—
— it shall be open to the supervisory authority to grant authorisation for any group of classes classified under Part B of Annex 1, provided that it attaches to such authorisation the appropriate denomination specified therein;

— authorisation granted for one class or group of classes shall also be valid for the purpose of covering ancillary risks included in another class if the conditions specified under Part C of Annex 1 are fulfilled.

[6036]
Article 9
Legal form

The legal forms which may be assumed by an undertaking whose head office is situated in the territory of a Contracting Party are listed in Annex 3.

[6037]
Article 10
Conditions of authorisation

10.1 Each Contracting Party shall require that an undertaking whose head office is situated in the territory of the other Contracting Party and which seeks an authorisation to open in its territory an agency or branch shall satisfy the following conditions—

(a) it shall submit its statutes and a list of its directors and managers;

(b) it shall produce a certificate issued by the supervisory authority of the Contracting Party in whose territory its head office is situated, attesting—

— that the applicant undertaking is constituted in one of the legal forms listed in Annex 3,

— that the applicant undertaking limits its business activities to the business of insurance and to operations directly arising therefrom to the exclusion of all other commercial business,

— the classes of insurance which the undertaking is entitled to transact,

— that it possesses the minimum guarantee fund referred to in paragraph 3.2 of Protocol No 1 or, where appropriate, the minimum solvency margin calculated in accordance with paragraph 2.2 of that Protocol if the minimum solvency margin is higher than the minimum guarantee fund,

— the risks which it actually covers,

— the existence of the financial resources referred to in paragraph 1(f) of Protocol No 2;

(c) it shall submit a scheme of operations drawn up in accordance with Protocol No 2, accompanied by the balance sheet and profit and loss account of the undertaking for each of the past three financial years.

However, where an undertaking has existed for fewer than three financial years, it shall submit such documents only for the financial years that have closed, if—

— it is a new undertaking created as a result of a merger between existing undertakings, or

— it is a new undertaking created by one or more existing undertakings for the purpose of transacting a specific class of insurance, previously pursued by one of the undertakings in question;

(d) it shall designate an authorised agent having his permanent residence and abode in the territory in which the supervisory authority of the Contracting Party in question is competent and possessing sufficient powers to bind the undertaking in relation to third parties and to represent it in relations with the authorities and courts of that Contracting Party.

Where the legal provisions of a Contracting Party permit the authorised agent to have legal personality, it shall have its head office in the territory of that Contracting Party and in turn designate a natural person to represent it who satisfies the above conditions.

10.2 This Agreement shall not prevent the Contracting Parties from enforcing provisions requiring for all insurance undertakings, at the time of granting of the authorisation, approval of the general and special policy conditions, scales of premiums and any other documents necessary for the normal exercise of supervision.

However, with regard to the risks referred to in paragraph 2.1 of Protocol No 2, the Contracting Parties shall not lay down provisions requiring the approval or systematic notification of general and special policy conditions, scales of premiums, or forms and other printed documents which the undertaking intends to use in its dealings with policy holders. They may require only non-systematic notification of these conditions and other documents, for the purpose of verifying compliance with laws, regulations and administrative provisions in respect of such risks, and this requirement may not constitute a prior condition for an undertaking to be able to carry on its activities.

For the purposes of this Agreement, general and special policy conditions shall not include specific conditions intended to meet, in an individual case, the particular circumstances of the risk to be covered.

This Agreement shall likewise not prevent the Contracting Parties from subjecting undertakings requesting authorisation for class 18 in Part A of Annex 1 to checks on their direct or indirect resources in staff and equipment, including the qualification of their medical teams and the quality of the equipment, available to the undertakings to meet their commitments arising from this class of insurance.

[6038]
Article 11
Granting of authorisation

11.1 Each Contracting Party undertakes to grant authorisation provided the conditions laid down in Article 10 are met and further provided that the other provisions governing undertakings with their head offices in its territory are observed.

11.2 The Contracting Parties shall not make authorisation subject to the lodging of a deposit or the provision of security.

11.3 The Contracting Parties undertake furthermore that no application for an authorisation shall be examined in the light of the economic requirements of the market.

11.4 The designated authorised agent may be challenged by the supervisory authority only on grounds relating to his good repute or technical qualifications.

[6039]
Article 12
Extension of the scope of an authorisation

12.1 Each Contracting Party shall make any extension of the business for which an initial authorisation was granted pursuant to Articles 7 and 8 subject to a new authorisation.

12.2 Each Contracting Party shall require that, for the purpose of extending the business of an agency or branch either to other classes or in the circumstances referred to in paragraph 8.1, the applicant for the authorisation shall submit a scheme of operations in accordance with Protocol 2 and produce the certificate referred to in paragraph 10.1(b).

[6040]
Article 13
Authorisation procedure

13.1 Authorisation shall be sought from the supervisory authority by the undertaking whose head office is situated in the territory of the other Contracting Party.

13.2 The scheme of operations drawn up in accordance with Protocol No 2, together with the observations of the supervisory authority responsible for granting authorisation, shall be forwarded by the latter to the supervisory authority of the Contracting Party in whose territory the head office is situated.

The latter shall make known its opinion to the former within three months following receipt of the documents. If no opinion has been received upon the expiry of that period, it shall be deemed to be favourable.

13.3 The supervisory authority from whom authorisation has been sought shall forward to the applicant undertaking its decision on the application not later than six months following receipt of the application for authorisation.

[6041]
Article 14
Refusal of authorisation

14.1 Any decision to refuse an authorisation shall be accompanied by the grounds on which it is based and shall be notified to the undertaking in question.

14.2 Each Contracting Party shall make provision for a right of recourse to the courts in the event of any refusal of authorisation. Provision shall also be made for such right in regard to cases where the supervisory authority has not given a decision on an application for authorisation upon the of a period of six months from the date of its receipt.

SECTION III
CONDITIONS GOVERNING THE PURSUIT OF BUSINESS

[6042]
Article 15
Choice of assets

The Contracting Parties shall not prescribe any rules as to the choice of assets in excess of those representing the technical reserves referred to in Articles 19 to 23. Subject to the provisions of paragraph 18.2, Articles 20, 21 and 23 and paragraphs 29.2 and 29.3, the Contracting Parties shall not restrict the free disposal of movable or immovable property forming part of the assets of undertakings.

[6043]
Article 16
Establishment of solvency margin

16.1 Each Contracting Party shall require every undertaking whose head office is situated in its territory to establish an adequate solvency margin in respect of its entire business.

16.2 The definition of the solvency margin and the manner in which it is to be calculated and represented, and the minimum guarantee fund fixed, are set out in Protocol No 1.

[6044]
Article 17
Verification of the state of solvency

17.1 The supervisory authority of the Contracting Party in whose territory the head office of the undertaking is situated shall verify the state of solvency of the undertaking with respect to its entire business.

17.2 The supervisory authority of the other Contracting Party shall, where it has granted the said undertaking authorisation to open an agency or branch, provide the abovementioned authority with all the information necessary to enable such verification to be carried out.

17.3 Each Contracting Party shall require undertakings whose head office is situated in its territory to produce an annual account, covering all their transactions, of their situation and solvency, and, as regards cover for risks listed under class 18 in Part A of Annex No 1, of the other resources available to them for meeting their liabilities, where its laws provide for supervision of such resources.

[6045]
Article 18
Restoration of financial situation

18.1 For the purpose of restoring the financial situation of an undertaking whose solvency margin has fallen below the minimum required under paragraph 2.2 of Protocol No 1, the supervisory authority of the Contracting Party in whose territory the head office is situated shall require a plan for the restoration of a sound financial situation to be submitted for its approval.

18.2 If the solvency margin falls below the guarantee fund defined in Article 3 of Protocol No 1, the supervisory authority of the Contracting Party in whose territory the head office of the undertaking is situated shall require the latter to submit a short-term financing plan for its approval.

It may also restrict or prohibit the free disposal of the assets of the undertaking. It shall inform the supervisory authority of the Contracting Party in whose territory authorised agencies or branches of the undertaking are situated of any such measures. If they are requested by the former authority, the latter authority shall take the same measures.

The supervisory authority may, furthermore, take all measures necessary to safeguard the interests of insured persons should the situation envisaged in this paragraph arise.

[6046]
Article 19
Establishment of technical reserves

19.1 Each Contracting Party in whose territory an undertaking carries on business shall require that undertaking to establish sufficient technical reserves.

19.2 The amount of such reserves shall be determined in accordance with the rules laid down in each Contracting Party, or, in the absence of such rules, in accordance with the established practices in each Contracting Party.

19.3 Each Contracting Party shall furthermore require undertakings established in its territory and underwriting risks listed under class 14 in Part A of Annex 1 (credit insurance) to set up an equalisation reserve for the purpose of offsetting any technical deficit or above average claims ratio arising in that class for a financial year.

The methods of calculating the equalisation reserve and the conditions governing exemption from the obligation to make such a reserve are set out in Annex No 5.

The equalisation reserve must be calculated, under the rules laid down by each Contracting Party, in accordance with one of the four methods set out in Annex 5, which shall be regarded as being equivalent. Up to the amount calculated in accordance with those methods, the equalisation reserve shall be disregarded for purposes of calculating the solvency margin.

Undertakings shall make available to the supervisory authority accounts showing both the technical results and the technical reserves relating to this business.

[6047]
Article 20
Matching assets and localisation of assets constituting technical reserves

20.1 Technical reserves shall be represented by equivalent and matching assets localised in the territory in which the supervisory authority of each Contracting Party is respectively competent. Each Contracting Party may, however, permit relaxations of the rules on matching assets and the localisation of assets.

20.2 "Matching assets" means the representation of underwriting liabilities expressed in a particular currency by assets expressed or realisable in the same currency.

20.3 "Localisation of assets" means the existence of movable or immovable assets in the territory in which the supervisory authority of the Contracting Party concerned is competent, but shall not be construed as involving a requirement that movable property be deposited or that immovable property be made subject to restrictive measures such as the registration of a mortgage. Assets represented by claims against debtors shall be regarded as localised in the territory in which the supervisory authority of the Contracting Party where they are to be realised is competent.

Subject to the above, localisation shall be governed by the respective rules in force in the Contracting Parties.

[6048]
Article 21
Nature of technical reserves

21.1 The rules in force in each Contracting Party in whose territory an undertaking pursues its business shall determine the nature of the assets and, where appropriate, the extent to which they may be used for the purpose of representing the technical reserves, and shall also determine the rules for valuing such assets.

21.2 The expression "nature of the assets" refers to the various categories of movable and immovable assets and their specific characteristics, such as those relating to the debtor in the case of a claim forming part of the representation of the technical reserves.

21.3 If a Contracting Party allows any technical reserves to be represented by claims against re-insurers, it shall fix the percentage so allowed or shall make provision for it to be fixed. In such case, notwithstanding the provisions of paragraph 20.1, it may not require the assets representing such claims to be localised.

[6049]
Article 22
Balance sheet

The supervisory authority of the Contracting Party in whose territory the head office of an undertaking is situated shall verify that the undertaking's balance sheet shows in respect of the technical reserves assets equivalent to the underwriting liabilities assumed in all the countries in which it carries on business.

[6050]
Article 23
Non-compliance with the requirements relating to technical reserves

If an agency or branch does not comply with the provisions laid down in Articles 19 to 21, the supervisory authority of the Contracting Party in whose territory it carries on business may prohibit the free disposal of assets localised in its territory after having informed the supervisory authority of the Contracting Party in whose territory the head office is situated that it intends to take such action.

The supervisory authority of the Contracting Party in whose territory such agency or branch carries on business may, furthermore, take any measure necessary to safeguard the interests of insured persons.

[6051]
Article 24
Transfer of portfolio
24.1 Under the conditions laid down by the legal provisions in force in the Contracting Party in question, the supervisory authority shall authorise undertakings which are established in the territory for which it is responsible to transfer all or part of their portfolios of contracts to an accepting office established in the same territory as the transferring undertaking, if the supervisory authority of the Contracting Party in whose territory the head office of the accepting office is situated certifies that the latter possesses the necessary margin of solvency after taking the transfer into account.
24.2 A transfer authorised in accordance with paragraph 24.1 shall be published in the territory in which the supervisory authority of the Contracting Party in which the transferring undertaking and the accepting office are established is competent, under the conditions laid down by the legal provisions in force in each Contracting Party in question. Such transfer shall be automatically valid against the policy-holders, the insured persons and any other person having rights and obligations arising out of the contracts transferred. However, this paragraph shall not preclude the existence in each of the Contracting Parties of provisions providing policy-holders with the option of cancelling the contract within a given period after the transfer.

[6052]
Article 25
Approval of conditions and scales of premiums
25.1 This Agreement shall not prevent the Contracting Parties from enforcing provisions requiring of all undertakings and in respect of all classes of insurance, during the pursuit of business, approval of the general and special policy conditions, scales of premiums and any other documents necessary for the normal exercise of supervision.

However, with regard to the risks referred to in paragraph 2.1 of Protocol No 2, the Contracting Parties shall not lay down provisions requiring the approval or systematic notification of general and special policy conditions, scales of premiums, forms and other printed documents which the undertaking intends to use in its dealings with policy-holders. They may require only non-systematic notification of these conditions and other documents, for the purpose of verifying compliance with laws, regulations and administrative provisions in respect of such risks.

With regard to the same risks, the Contracting Parties may not retain or introduce prior notification or approval of proposed increases in scales of premiums except as part of a general price control system.
25.2 This Agreement shall likewise not prevent the Contracting Parties from subjecting undertakings which have obtained authorisation for class 18 in Part A of Annex 1 to checks on their direct or indirect resources in staff and equipment, including the qualification of their medical teams and the quality of the equipment, available to the undertakings to meet their commitments arising from this class of insurance.
25.3 For the purposes of this Agreement, general and special policy conditions shall not include specific conditions intended to meet, in an individual case, the particular circumstances of the risk to be covered.

[6053]
Article 26
Documentation
The Contracting Parties shall require undertakings carrying on business in their territory to produce the documents, including statistical documents, necessary for the exercise of supervision and, as regards cover for risks listed under class 18 in Part A of Annex 1, to indicate the resources available to them for meeting their liabilities, where their laws provide for supervision of such resources.

SECTION IV
WITHDRAWAL OF AUTHORISATION

[6054]
Article 27
Withdrawal conditions
The supervisory authority of a Contracting Party may withdraw from an undertaking whose head office is situated in the territory of the other Contracting Party the authorisation which it granted to open an agency or branch, where such agency or branch—
- (a) no longer fulfils the conditions for admission, or
- (b) fails seriously to fulfil its obligations under the rules applicable to it, in particular with respect to the establishment of technical reserves.

[6055]
Article 28
Withdrawal procedure

28.1 Before withdrawing authorisation, the supervisory authority shall consult the supervisory authority of the Contracting Party in whose territory the head office of the undertaking is situated.

If the former authority deems it necessary to suspend the business of the agency or branch referred to in Article 27 before consultation is concluded, it shall immediately advise the latter authority thereof.

28.2 Any decision to withdraw an authorisation or to order the suspension of business shall state the reasons on which it is based and shall be notified to the undertaking in question.

28.3 Each Contracting Party shall make provision for a right of recourse to the courts against such a decision.

[6056]
Article 29
Withdrawal of the authorisation granted to the head office

29.1 Where the supervisory authority of a Contracting Party in whose territory the head office is situated withdraws the authorisation which it has granted to the undertaking, it shall notify such action to the supervisory authority of the other Contracting Party if the latter has granted the undertaking authorisation to open an agency or branch. The latter authority shall also withdraw its authorisation.

29.2 In the case referred to in paragraph 1, the supervisory authority of the Contracting Party in whose territory the head office is situated shall, in conjunction with the supervisory authority of the other Contracting Party, take all measures necessary to safeguard the interests of insured persons and shall, in particular, restrict the free disposal of the assets of the undertaking, if this measure has not already been taken, pursuant to paragraph 18.2 and Article 23.

29.3 Paragraph 29.1 and, where relevant, 29.2 shall likewise apply where the undertaking surrenders of its own accord the authorisation granted to it.

SECTION V
COLLABORATION BETWEEN SUPERVISORY AUTHORITIES

[6057]
Article 30
Conditions of collaboration

The Contracting Parties shall take all necessary measures to enable their supervisory authorities to collaborate closely in the implementation of this Agreement.

[6058]
Article 31
Objectives of collaboration

31.1 The supervisory authorities shall collaborate in verifying the provisions by undertakings of financial guarantees as defined in Articles 16 and 19 to 21 and, in particular, in applying the measures provided for in Articles 18 and 23.

31.2 Where the undertakings in question are authorised to cover the risks listed under class 18 in Part A of Annex No 1, the supervisory authorities shall also collaborate in supervising the resources available to those undertakings for carrying out the assistance operations they have undertaken to perform, where their laws provide for supervision of such resources.

[6059]
Article 32
Exchange of information

The supervisory authorities shall furnish each other with all documents and information necessary for exercising supervision.

[6060]
Article 33
Requirements of secrecy

33.1 Articles 30 to 32 shall under no circumstances be interpreted as requiring any supervisory authority to furnish information which would disclose commercial secrets of an undertaking or information the communication of which would be contrary to public policy.

33.2 Nevertheless, the secrecy rules to which the supervisory authorities are subject shall not hinder collaboration between those authorities and the mutual assistance provided for by this Agreement.

33.3 The information exchanged shall be used by such authorities solely for the pupose of carrying out their supervisory duties.

SECTION VI
GENERAL AND FINAL PROVISIONS

[6061]
Article 34
Particular provisions and undertakings of third countries
34.1 Particular provisions applicable to certain Member States of the Community are set out in Annex 4.
34.2 The provisions applicable to agencies and branches of undertakings whose head office is situated outside the territories to which this Agreement applies pursuant to Article 43 thereof are set out in Protocol No 4.

[6062]
Article 35
Integral parts of the Agreement
The Annexes, Protocols and Exchanges of Letters annexed to this Agreement shall form an integral part thereof.

[6063]
Article 36
Failure to fulfil obligations
36.1 The Contracting Parties shall refrain from taking any measures which might jeopardise the attainment of the objectives of the Agreement.
36.2 They shall take all general or special measures necessary to ensure fulfilment of the obligations arising from this Agreement.

If either Contracting Party considers that the other Contracting Party has failed to fulfil an obligation arising from this Agreement, the procedure preferred to in paragraph 37.2 shall apply.

[6064]
Article 37
Joint Committee
37.1 A Joint Committee, composed of representatives of Switzerland and representatives of the Community, is hereby established, which shall be responsible for the administration of the Agreement and its proper implementation and for taking decisions in the circumstances provided for therein. Its decisions shall be taken by mutual agreement.
37.2 For the purpose of the proper implementation of the Agreement, the contracting Parties shall exchange information and, at the request of either Party, shall hold consultations within the Joint Committee. The exercise of supervision, referred to in Section V, shall not come within its powers.
37.3 The Joint Committee shall adopt its own rules of procedure.
37.4 The Joint Committee shall be chaired in turn by each of the ContractingParties in accordance with detailed arrangements to be laid down in its rules of procedure. At the request of either Contracting Party, in accordance with conditions to be laid down in its rules of procedure, it shall be convened by its Chairman whenever special circumstances so require.

The Joint Committee may decide to set up any working party needed to assist it in carrying out its tasks.

[6065]
Article 38
Settlement of disputes
38.1 If a dispute arises between the Contracting Parties concerning the operation of this Agreement and in particular its interpretation or implementation and such dispute cannot be resolved either through collaboration between the supervisory authorities referred to in Section V or by the Joint Committee referred to in Article 37, the Contracting Parties shall consult each other through diplomatic channels.
38.2 If it has not been possible to resolve the dispute by means of the procedure provided for in paragraph 38.1, it shall be referred, at the request of either of the Parties, to an arbitration tribunal consisting of three members. Reference may be made to this tribunal at the earliest after a period of two years following the first reference to the Joint Committee referred to in Article 37, unless the Parties agree jointly to refer their dispute to the said tribunal before the end of that period. Each Party shall appoint an arbitrator. The two arbitrators appointed shall appoint an umpire who shall be a national neither of Switzerland nor of a Member State of the Community.

38.3 Where one of the Contracting Parties does not appoint its arbitrator and has not complied with the request made by the other Party to make such appointment within two months, the arbitrator shall be appointed, at the request of that other Party, by the President of the International Court of Justice.
38.4 Where after a period of two months following their appointment the two arbitrtors are unable to agree on the choice of an umpire, the latter shall be appointed at the request of one of the Parties by the President of the International Court of Justice.
38.5 Where, in the case provided for in paragraphs 38.3 and 38.4, the President ofthe International Court of Justice is unable to act, or is a national of Switzerland or of a Member State of the Community, the appointments shall be made by the Vice-President. If the latter is unable to act or is a national of Switzerland or of a Member State of the Community, the appointments shall be made by the oldest member of the Court who is not a national either of Switzerland or of a Member State of the Community.
38.6 Save as otherwise provided by the Contracting Parties, the tribunal shall lay down its own rules of procedure. It shall take its decision by majority vote.
38.7 The decisions of the tribunal shall be binding on the Contracting Parties.

[6066]
Article 39
Evolution of the domestic legislation of the Contracting Parties
39.1 The Agreement shall be without prejudice to the right of each Contracting Party, subject to compliance with the principle of non-discrimination and the provisions of this Article, unilaterally to amend its domestic legislation on a point regulated by this Agreement.
39.2 As soon as a Contracting Party has initiated the process for adopting a draft amendment of its domestic legislation concerning the conditions for taking up and pursuing, by means of establishment, the activity of direct insurance other than life assurance, it shall inform the other Contracting Party via the Joint Committee referred to in Article 37. The Joint Committee shall hold an exchange of views on the implications of such an amendment for the proper functioning of the Agreement.
39.3 As soon as the amended legislation has been adopted, and eight days after adotion at the latest, the Contracting Party concerned shall notify the text of the new provisions to the other Contracting Party.
39.4 In order to guarantee legal certainty, a period of at least 12 months rom the date of adoption of the amended legislation must be laid down by the Contracting Party concerned for the implementation of any amendment of legislation which deviates from the provisions of the Agreement.
39.5 Any amendment of legislation which has been the subject of the procedures referred to in paragraphs 39.2 and 39.3 and which, in the opinion of either Contracting Party, deviates from the provisions of the Agreement, shall be referred to the Joint Committee. The Joint Committee shall meet at the latest six weeks after the notification laid down in paragraph 39.3.
39.6 The Joint Committee shall—

- — either adopt a decision revising the provisions of the Agreement so as to integrate therein, if necessary on a basis of reciprocity, the amendments made to the legislation in question,
- — or, as long as the insured person is guaranteed equivalent protection to tat provided for under the Agreement, adopt a decision to the effect that the amendments to the legislation in question shall be regarded as in accordance with the Agreement,
- — or decide any other measure to safeguard the proper functioning of the Agreement.

39.7 The decisions of the Joint Committee shall be published in the Official Compendium of Federal Laws *(Recueil Officiel des lois fédérales)* and in the *Official Journal of the European Communities*. Each decision shall state the date of its implementation in the two Contracting Parties and any other information likely to concern economic operators. The decisions shall be submitted as necessary for ratification or approval by the Contracting Parties in accordance with their own procedures.

The Contracting Parties shall notify each other of the completion of this formality. If upon the expiry of the period provided for in paragraph 39.4 such notification has not taken place, the decisions of the Joint Committee shall be implemented provisionally pending their ratification or approval by the Contracting Parties. If either Contracting Party notifies the non-ratification or non-approval of a decision of the Joint Committee, paragraph 39.8 shall apply *mutatis mutandis* from the time of such notification.

39.8 If the Joint Committee does not reach agreement on the decisions to be taken within six months of the date of referral pursuant to paragraph 39.5, the Agreement shall be regarded as ended on the day the legislation in question is implemented, pursuant to paragraph 39.4; in that event the provisions of Article 38 are not applicable. The provisions of paragraph 42.2 shall apply *mutatis mutandis.*

[6067]
Article 40
Revision of the Agreement

40.1 If a Contracting Party wishes that this Agreement be revised, it shall request the other Contracting Party to open negotiations to that end. Such request shall be made through diplomatic channels.

40.2 Amendments to this Agreement shall enter into force in accordance with the procedure set out in Article 44.

40.3 Nevertheless, amendments to the Annexes, Protocols and Exchanges of Letters annexed to this Agreement shall be adopted by the Joint Committee referred to in Article 37, which shall determine the date of their entry into force.

[6068]
Article 41
Matters not covered by the Agreement

41.1 Where a Contracting Party considers that it would be useful in the interests of both Contracting Parties to develop the relations established by this Agreement by extending them to private insurance activities not covered thereby, it shall propose to the other Contracting Party that negotiations be opened to that end.

41.2 Agreements resulting from negotiations referred to in paragraph 41.1 shall be subject to ratification or approval by the Contracting Parties in accordance with their own procedures.

[6069]
Article 42
Denunciation

42.1 Either Contracting Party may denounce this Agreement at any time by notifying the other Contracting Party to that effect. The Agreement shall cease to be in force 12 months after the date of such notification.

42.2 In the event of denunciation, the Contracting Parties shall jointly agree on rules governing the situation of undertakings which have obtained authorisation in accordance with paragraph 11.1. In the absence of agreement upon expiry of the period of 12 months referred to in paragraph 42.1, those undertakings shall be made subject to the rules applicable to those of third countries. Nevertheless, the Contracting Parties hereby undertake that the authorisation obtained in accordance with paragraph 11.1 shall not be withdrawn in the light of the economic requirements of the market for a period of at least five years from the date on which this Agreement ceases to be in force.

[6070]
Article 43
Territorial scope

This Agreement shall apply, on the one hand, to the territory of the Swiss Confederation and, on the other hand, to the territories in which the Treaty establishing the European Economic Community is applied and under the conditions laid down in that Treaty.

[6071]
Article 44
Entry into force

44.1 This Agreement was negotiated in French and drawn up in duplicate in the Danish, Dutch, English, French, German, Italian, Portuguese and Spanish languages, each of these texts being equally authentic.

44.2 This Agreement shall be ratified or approved by the Contracting Parties in accordance with their own procedures.

44.3 This Agreement shall enter into force on the first day of the calendar year following the exchange of instruments of ratification or approval on condition that such exchange takes place not later than one month before that date.

Nevertheless, the Contracting Parties may, on exchanging instruments of ratification or approval, jointly agree on another date for the entry into force of this Agreement; in that case, the date shall be published forthwith.

ANNEX 1

CLASSES OF INSURANCE SUBJECT TO THE AGREEMENT

[6072]

A. Classification of risks according to classes of insurance

1. *Accident (including industrial injury and occupational diseases)*
   - fixed pecuniary benefits,
   - benefits in the nature of indemnity,
   - combinations of the two,
   - injury to passengers.
2. *Sickness*
   - fixed pecuniary benefits,
   - benefits in the nature of indemnity,
   - combinations of the two.
3. *Land vehicles (other than railway rolling stock)*

   All damage to or loss of—
   - land motor vehicles,
   - land vehicles other than motor vehicles.
4. *Railway rolling stock*

   All damage to or loss of railway rolling stock.
5. *Aircraft*

   All damage to or loss of aircraft.
6. *Ships (sea, lake and river and canal vessels)*

   All damage to or loss of—
   - river and canal vessels,
   - lake vessels,
   - sea vessels.
7. *Goods in transit (including merchandise, baggage and all other goods)*

   All damage to or loss of goods in transit or baggage, irrespective of the form of transport.
8. *Fire and natural forces*

   All damage to or loss of property (other than property included in classes 3, 4, 5, 6 and 7) due to—
   - fire,
   - explosion,
   - storm,
   - natural forces other than storm,
   - nuclear energy,
   - land subsidence.
9. *Other damage to property*

   All damage to or loss of property (other than property included in classes 3, 4, 5, 6 and 7) due to hail or frost, and any event such as theft, other than those mentioned under 8.
10. *Motor vehicle liability*

    All liability arising out of the use of motor vehicles operating on land (including carrier's liability).
11. *Aircraft liability*

    All liability arising out of the use of aircraft (including carrier's liability).
12. *Liability for ships (sea, lake and river and canal vessels)*

    All liability arising out of the use of ships, vessels or boats on the sea, lakes, rivers or canals (including carrier's liability).
13. *General liability*

    All liability other than those forms mentioned under Nos 10, 11 and 12.
14. *Credit*
    - insolvency (general),
    - export credit,
    - instalment credit,
    - mortgages,
    - agricultural credit.
15. *Suretyship*
    - suretyship (direct),
    - suretyship (indirect).
16. *Miscellaneous financial loss*
    - employment risks,

— insufficiency of income (general),
— bad weather,
— loss of profits,
— continuing general expenses,
— unforeseen trading expenses,
— loss of market value,
— loss of rent or revenue,
— indirect trading losses other than those mentioned above,
— other financial loss (non-trading),
— other forms of financial loss.

17. *Legal expenses*

Legal expense and costs of litigation.

18. *Tourist assistance*

Assistance for persons who get into difficulties while travelling, while away from home or while away from their permanent residence.

The risks included in a class may not be included in any other class except in the cases referred to in Part C.

B. Description of authorisations granted simultaneously for more than one class of insurance

Where the authorisation simultaneously covers—

(a) classes Nos 1 and 2, it shall be named "Accident and Health Insurance";
(b) classes Nos 1 (fourth indent), 3, 7 and 10, it shall be named "Motor Insurance";
(c) classes Nos 1 (fourth indent), 4, 6, 7 and 12, it shall he named "Marine and Transport Insurance";
(d) classes Nos 1 (fourth indent), 5, 7 and 11, it shall be named "Aviation Insurance";
(e) classes Nos 8 and 9, it shall be named "Insurance against Fire and other Damage to Property";
(f) classes Nos 10, 11, 12 and 13, it shall be named "Liability Insurance";
(g) classes Nos 14 and 15, it shall be named "Credit and Suretyship Insurance";
(h) all classes, it shall have the name or names chosen by the Contracting Party in question, which shall notify the other Contracting Party of its choice(s).

C. Ancillary risks

An undertaking obtaining an authorisation for a principal risk belonging to one class or a group of classes may also insure risks included in another class without an authorisation being necessary for them if they—

— are connected with the principal risk,
— concern the object which is covered against the principal risk, and
— are covered by the contract insuring the principal risk.

However, the risks included in classes 14, 15 and 17 may not be regarded as risks ancillary to other classes.

Nonetheless, the risk included in class 17 (legal expenses insurance) may be regarded as an ancillary risk of class 18 where the conditions laid down in the first subparagraph of Part C of this Annex are fulfilled, and where the main risk relates solely to the assistance provided for persons who fall into difficulties while travelling, while away from home or while away from their permanent residence.

Legal expenses insurance may also be regarded as an ancillary risk under the conditions set out in the first subparagraph of Part C of this Annex where it concerns disputes or risks arising out of, or in connection with, the use of sea-going vessels.

D. Assistance

1. The assistance activity shall be the assistance provided for persons who get into difficulties while travelling, while away from home or while away from their permanent residence. It shall consist in undertaking, against the prior payment of a premium, to make aid immediately available to the beneficiary under an assistance contract where that person is in difficulties following the occurrence of a chance event, in the cases and under the conditions set out in the contract.

The aid may consist in the provision of benefits in cash or in kind. The provision of benefits in kind may also be effected by means of the staff and equipment of the person providing them.

The assistance activity does not cover servicing, maintenance, after-sales service or the mere indication or provision of aid as an intermediary.

2. Either Contracting Party may, in its territory, make the provision of assistance to persons who get into difficulties in circumstances other than those referred to in 1 subject to the arrangements introduced by this Agreement. If a Contracting Party makes use of this possibility it shall, for the purposes of applying these arrangements, treat such activity as if it were listed under class 18 in Part A of this Annex, without prejudice to Part C thereof.

This shall in no way affect the possibilities for classification laid down in this Annex for activities which clearly come under other classes.

It shall not be possible to refuse authorisation sought for an agency or branch by an undertaking whose head office is situated in the territory of the other Contracting Party solely on the grounds that the activity covered by this point is classified differently in the Contracting Party, in the territory of which the head office of the undertaking is situated.

ANNEX 2

KINDS OF INSURANCE, OPERATIONS AND UNDERTAKINGS NOT SUBJECT TO THE AGREEMENT

[6073]

A. Kinds of insurance excluded

This Agreement does not apply to—

1. life assurance, that is to say the class of insurance which comprises, in particular, assurance on survival to a stipulated age only, assurance on death only, assurance on survival to a stipulated age or on earlier death, life assurance with return of premiums, tontines, marriage assurance and birth assurance;
2. annuities;
3. supplementary insurance carried on by life assurance undertakings, that is to say, insurance against personal injury including incapacity for employment, insurance against death resulting from an accident, and insurance against disability resulting from an accident or sickness, where these various kinds of insurance are underwritten in addition to life assurance;
4. *in Switzerland*—
   insurance forming part of a statutory system of social security, except where such insurance is written by authorised undertakings;
   in the Community—
   insurance forming part of a statutory system of social security;
5. the type of insurance existing in Ireland and the United Kingdom known as "permanent health insurance not subject to cancellation".

B. Operations excluded

This Agreement does not apply to—

1. capital redemption operations, as defined by the law in each Contracting Party;
2. operations of provident and mutual benefit institutions whose benefits vary according to the resources available and in which the contributions of members are determined on a flat rate basis;
3. operations carried out by organisations not having legal personality with the purpose of providing mutual cover for their members without there being any payment of premiums or constitution of technical reserves;
4. export credit insurance operations for the account of or guaranteed by the State, or where the State is the insurer;
5. the assistance activity in which liability is limited to the following operations provided in the event of an accident or breakdown involving a road vehicle which normally occurs in the territory in which the supervisory authority of the Contracting Party in which the undertaking providing cover is established is competent—
   — an on-the-spot breakdown service for which the undertaking providing cover uses, in most circumstances, its own staff and equipment,
   — the conveyance of the vehicle to the nearest or the most appropriate locationat which repairs may be carried out and the possible accompaniment, normally by the same means of assistance, of the driver and passengers to the nearest location from where they may continue their journey by other means,
   — if provided for by the provisions in force in the territory in which the supervisory authority of the Contracting Party in which the undertaking providing cover is

established is competent, the conveyance of the vehicle, possibly accompanied by the driver and passengers, to their home, point of departure or original destination within the same territory,

unless such operations are carried out by an undertaking subject to the Agreement.

In the cases referred to in the first two indents, the condition that the accident or breakdown must have happened in the territory in which the supervisory authority of the Contracting Party, in which the undertaking providing cover is established, is competent—

(a) shall not apply where the latter is a body of which the beneficiary is a member and the breakdown service or conveyance of the vehicle is provided simply on presentation of a membership card, without any additional premium being paid, by a similar body in the same or the other Contracting Party on the basis of a reciprocal agreement;

(b) shall not preclude the provision of such assistance in Ireland and the United Kingdom by a single body operating in both States.

In the circumstances referred to in the third indent, where the accident or the breakdown has occurred in the territory of Ireland or, in the case of the United Kingdom, in the territory of Northern Ireland, the vehicle, possibly accompanied by the driver and passengers, may be conveyed to their home, point of departure or original destination within either territory.

Moreover, the Agreement does not concern assistance operations carried out on the occasion of an accident to or the breakdown of a road vehicle and consisting in conveying the vehicle which has been involved in an accident or has broken down outside the territory of the Grand Duchy of Luxembourg, possibly accompanied by the driver and passengers, to their home, where such operations are carried out by the Automobile Club of the Grand Duchy of Luxembourg.

Undertakings subject to the Agreement may engage in the activity referred to under this point only if they have received authorisation for class 18 in Part A of Annex 1 without prejudice to Part C of the said Annex. In that event the Agreement shall apply to the operations in question.

C. Exclusion of undertakings occupying special positions

This Agreement does not apply—

1. to undertakings which fulfil the following conditions—
   — the undertaking does not pursue any activity falling within the scope of the Agreement other than the one described in class 18 in Part A of Annex No 1,
   — the activity is carried out exclusively on a local basis and consists only of benefits in kind, and
   — the total annual income collected in respect of the activity of assistance to persons who get into difficulties does not exceed ECU 200 000.
2. in the case of undertakings whose head office is situated in Switzerland, to—
   undertakings whose annual premium income for the activities covered by the Agreement does not exceed the sum of three million Swiss francs on the date of entry into force of this Agreement and whose activities extend only to Swiss territory for such time as they satisfy these conditions. Once it has become subject to the rules of the Agreement an undertaking may no longer rely on this exception even if it satisfies the two abovementioned conditions.
3. in the case of undertakings whose head office is situated in the Community, to—
   mutual associations in so far as they fulfil all the following conditions—
   — the articles of association contain provisions for calling up additional contributions or reducing their benefits,
   — their business does not cover liability risks—unless the latter constitute ancillary cover within the meaning of Part C of Annex 1—or credit and suretyship risks,
   — the annual contribution income from the activities covered by this Agreement does not exceed ECU 1 million, and
   — at least half of the contribution income from the activities covered by this Agreement comes from persons who are members of the mutual association.

   Mutual associations which have concluded with another undertaking of the same nature an agreement which provides for the full reinsurance of the insurance contracts concluded by them or under which the concessionary undertaking is to meet the liabilities arising out of such contracts in the place of the ceding undertaking.

   In such a case, the concessionary undertaking shall be subject to this Agreement.

D. Exclusion of specific undertakings

This Agreement shall not apply to the undertakings listed under 1 and 2 unless their articles of association are amended as regards capacity.

However, the territorial capacity of the undertakings referred to in 1 and 2(b) shall not be regarded as modified in the case of a merger between or division of such undertakings which has the effect of maintaining for the benefit of the new undertaking or undertakings the territorial capacity of the undertaking which has divided or the undertakings which have merged, nor shall capacity as to the classes of insurance be regarded as modified if one of these undertakings takes over in respect of the same territory one or more of the classes of another such undertaking.

1. *in Switzerland*

The following cantonal institutions under public law, enjoying a monopoly—

(a) Aargau: Aargauisches Versicherungsamt, Aarau;
(b) Appenzell Ausser-Roden: Brand und Elementarschadenversicherung Appenzell AR, Herisau;
(c) Basel Land: Basellandschaftliche Gebäudeversicherung, Liestal;
(d) Basel Stadt: Gebàudeversicherung des Kantons Basel Stadt, Basel;
(e) Bern/Berne: Gebäudeversicherung des Kantons Bern, Bern, Assurance immobilière du canton de Berne, Berne;
(f) Fribourg/Freiburg: Etablissement cantonal d'assurance des bâtiments du canton de Fribourg, Fribourg/Kantonale Gebäudeversicherungsanstalt Freiburg, Freiburg;
(g) Glarus: Kantonale Sachversicherung Glarus, Glarus;
(h) Graubünden/Grigioni/Grischun: Gebäudeversicherungsanstalt des Kantons Graubünden, Chur/Istituto d'assicurazione fabbricati del cantone dei Grigioni, Coira/Institut dil cantun Grischun per assicuranzas da baghetgs, Cuera;
(i) Jura: Assurance immobilière de la République et canton du Jura, Saignelégier;
(j) Luzern: Gebäudeversicherung des Kantons Luzern, Luzern;
(k) Neuchâtel: Etablissement cantonal d'assurance immobilière contre l'incendie, Neuchâtel;
(l) Nidwalden: Kantonale Brandversicherungsanstalt Nidwalden, Stans;
(m) Schaffhausen: Gebäudeversicherung des Kantons Schaffhausen, Schaffhausen;
(n) Solothurn: Solothurnische Gebäudeversicherung, Solothurn;
(o) St Gallen: Gebäudeversicherungsanstalt des Kantons St Gallen, St Gallen;
(p) Thurgau: Gebäudeversicherung des Kantons Thurgau, Frauenfeld;
(q) Vaud: Etablissement d'assurance contre l'incendie et les éléments naturels du canton de Vaud, Lausanne;
(r) Zug: Gebäudeversicherung des Kantons Zug, Zug;
(s) Zürich: Gebäudeversicherung des Kantons Zürich, Zürich;

2. *in the Community*

(a) in Denmark
Falcks Redningskorps A/S, København;
(b) in Germany
— the following institutions under public law enjoying a monopoly (Monopolanstalten)—
(aa) Badische Gebäudeversicherungsanstalt, Karlsruhe;
(bb) Bayerische Landesbrandversicherungsanstalt, München;
(cc) Bayerische Landestierversicherungsanstalt, Schlachtviehversicherung, München;
(dd) Braunschweigische Landesbrandversicherungsanstalt, Braunschweig;
(ee) Hamburger Feuerkasse, Hamburg;
(ff) Hessische Brandversicherungsanstalt (Hessische Brandversicherungskammer), Darmstadt;
(gg) Hessische Brandversicherungsanstalt, Kassel;
(hh) Lippische Landesbrandversicherungsanstalt, Detmold;
(ii) Nassauische Brandversicherungsanstalt, Wiesbaden;
(jj) Oldenburgische Landesbrandkasse, Oldenburg;
(kk) Ostfriesische Landschaftliche Brandkasse, Aurich;
(ll) Feuersozietät Berlin, Berlin;
(mm) Württembergische Gebäudebrandversicherungsanstalt, Stuttgart,
— the following semi-public institutions—
(na) Postbeamtenkrankenkasse;
(oo) Krankenversorgung der Bundesbahnbeamten;
(c) in Spain
— the following public institutions—
(aa) Comisariá de Seguro Obligatorio de Viajeros;
(bb) Consorcio de Compensación de Seguros;

(cc) Fondo Nacional de Garantiá de Riesgos de Ia Circulación;

(d) in France

— the following institutions—

(aa) Caisse départementale des incendiés des Ardennes;

(bb) Caisse départementale des incendiés le la Côte d'Or;

(cc) Caisse départementale des incendiés de la Marne;

(dd) Caisse départementale des incendiés le la Meuse;

(ee) Caisse départementale des incendiés de la Somme;

(e) in Ireland

Voluntary Health Insurance Board;

(f) in Italy

la Cassa di Previdenza per l'assicurazione degli sportivi (Sportass);

(g) in the United Kingdom

the Crown Agents.

ANNEX 3

LISTING OF ACCEPTABLE LEGAL FORMS

[6074]

An undertaking whose head office is situated in the territory of a Contracting Party shall be constituted in one of the forms listed below.

The Contracting Parties may also set up, where appropriate, undertakings under any form governed by public law provided that such institutions have as their object insurance transactions under conditions equivalent to those of undertakings governed by private law.

A. In Switzerland

— Aktiengesellschaft/société anonyme/società per azioni

— Genossenschaft/coopérative/cooperativa

B. In the Community

1. *in Belgium*

— société anonyme/naamloze vennootschap,

— société en commandite par actions/vennootschap bij wijze van geldschieting op aandelen,

— association d'assurance mutuelle/onderlinge verzekeringsmaatschappij,

— Societé coopérative/coöperatieve vennootschap;

2. *in Denmark*

— aktieselskaber,

— gensidige selskaber;

3. *in Germany*

— Aktiengesellschaft,

— Versicherungsverein auf Gegenseitigkeit,

— öffentflich-rechtliche Wettbewerbs-Versicherungsunternehmen;

4. *in France*

— société anonyme,

— société à forme mutuelle,

— mutuelle,

— union de mutuelles;

5. *in Spain*

— sociedad anónima,

— sociedad mutua,

— sociedad cooperativa;

6. *in Greece*

— Ανωνυμος Εταιρια,

— ΑλληλασΦαλιστικος Συνεταιρισμος;

7. *in Ireland*

— incorporated companies limited by shares or by guarantee or unlimited;

8. *in Italy*

— società per azioni,

— società cooperativa,

— mutua di assicurazione;

9. *in Luxembourg*

— société anonyme,

— société en commandite par actions,
— association d'assurances mutuelles,
— société coopérative;

10. *in the Netherlands*
— naamloze vennootschap,
— onderlinge waarborgmaatschappij;

11. *in Portugal*
— sociedade anónima,
— mútua de seguros;

12. *in the United Kingdom*
— incorporated companies limited by shares or by guarantee or unlimited,
— societies registered under the Industrial and Provident Societies Acts,
— societies registered under the Friendly Societies Act,
— the association of underwriters known as Lloyd's.

ANNEX 4

PARTICULAR PROVISIONS FOR CERTAIN MEMBER STATES OF THE COMMUNITY

[6075]

By way of derogation from the provisions of this Agreement, the following special provisions shall apply in certain Member States of the Community—

1. in Denmark

re Article 15—

Denmark may retain in force its legislation restricting the free disposal of assets built up by insurance undertakings to cover pensions payable under compulsory insurance against industrial accidents;

2. in Germany

re paragraph 8.2—

Germany may maintain the provision prohibiting the simultaneous undertaking in its territory of health insurance with other classes;

re Article 15—

Germany may maintain, with respect to health insurance within the meaning of paragraph 2.3 of Protocol No 1, the restrictions imposed on the free disposal of assets in so far as the free disposal of assets covering mathematical reserves is subject to the agreement of a "Treuhänder";

3. in Luxembourg

re paragraphs 20.1 and 20.3—

Luxembourg may retain the system of guarantees for technical reserves existing at the time of entry into force of this Agreement;

4. in the United Kingdom

re paragraph 10.1(c)—

with regard to the association of underwriters known as Lloyd's, submission of the balance sheet and the profit and loss account shall be replaced by the compulsory presentation of overall annual trading accounts covering the insurance operations, and accompanied by an affidavit certifying that auditors' certificates have been supplied in respect of each insurer and showing that the liabilities incurred as a result of those operations are wholly covered by the assets. These documents must allow the supervisory authorities to form a comparable view of the state of solvency of the Association;

re paragraph 10.1(d)—

with regard to the association of underwriters known as Lloyd's, in the event of any litigation in the host country resulting from underwritten commitments, insured persons must not be less favourably treated than if the litigation had been brought against a business of a more conventional type. The authorised agent must, therefore, possess sufficient powers to enable proceedings to be instituted against him and must in that capacity be able to bind the Lloyd's underwriters concerned.

ANNEX 5

METHODS OF CALCULATING THE EQUALISATION RESERVE FOR THE CREDIT INSURANCE CLASS AND CONDITIONS GOVERNING EXEMPTION FROM THE OBLIGATION TO SET UP SUCH A RESERVE

[6076]

A Methods

Method No 1

1.1 In respect of the risks listed under class 14 in Part A of Annex 1 (credit insurance), the undertaking shall set up an equalisation reserve to which shall be charged any technical deficit arising in that class for a financial year.

1.2 Such reserve shall in each financial year receive 75% of any technical surplus arising on credit insurance business, subject to a limit of 12% of the net premiums or contributions until the reserve has reached 150% of the highest annual amount of net premiums or contributions received during the previous five financial years.

Method No 2

2.1 In respect of the risks listed under class 14 in Part A of Annex 1 (credit insurance), the undertaking shall set up an equalisation reserve to which shall be charged any technical deficit arising in that class for a financial year.

2.2 The minimum amount of the equalisation reserve shall be 134% of the average of the premiums or contributions received annually during the previous five financial years after subtraction of the cessions and addition of the reinsurance acceptances.

2.3 Such reserve shall in each of the successive financial years receive 75% of any technical surplus arising in that class until the reserve is at least equal to the minimum calculated in accordance with point 2.2 of this Annex.

2.4 The Contracting Parties may lay down special rules for the calculation of the amount of the reserve and/or the amount of the annual levy in excess of the minimum amounts laid down in points 2.2 and 2.3 of this Annex.

Method No 3

3.1 An equalisation reserve shall be formed for class 14 in Part A of Annex 1 (credit insurance) for the purpose of offsetting any above average claims ratio for a financial year in that class of insurance.

3.2 The equalisation reserve shall be calculated on the basis of the method set out below.

All calculations shall relate to income and expenditure for the insurer's own account.

An amount in respect of any claims shortfall for each financial year shall be placed to the equalisation reserve until it has reached, or is restored to, the required amount.

There shall be deemed to be a claims shortfall if the claims ratio for a financial year is lower than the average claims ratio for the reference period. The amount in respect of the claims shortfall shall be arrived at by multiplying the difference between the two ratios by the earned premiums for the financial year.

The required amount shall be equal to six times the standard deviation of the claims ratios in the reference period from the average claims ratio, multiplied by the earned premium for the financial year.

Where claims for any financial year are in excess, an amount in respect thereof shall be taken from the equalisation reserve. Claims shall be deemed to be in excess if the claims ratio for the financial year is higher than the average claims ratio. The amount in respect of the excess claims shall be arrived at by multiplying the difference between the two ratios by the earned premiums for the financial year.

Irrespective of claims experience, 3.5% of the required amount of the equalisation reserve shall be first placed to that reserve each financial year until its required amount has been reached or restored.

The length of the reference period shall be not less than 15 years and not more than 30 years. No equalisation reserve need be formed if no underwriting loss has been noted during the reference period.

The required amount of the equalisation reserve and the amount to be taken from it may be reduced if the average claims ratio for the reference period in conjunction with the expenses ratio show that the premiums include a safety margin.

Method No 4

4.1 An equalisation reserve shall be formed for class 14 in Part A of Annex 1 (credit insurance) for the purpose of offsetting any above average claims ratio for a financial year in that class of insurance.

4.2 This equalisation reserve shall be calculated on the basis of the method set out below.

Part VI European Materials

All calculations shall relate to income and expenditure for the insurer's own account.

An amount in respect of any claims shortfall for each financial year shall be placed to the equalisation reserve until it has reached the maximum required amount.

There shall be deemed to be a claims shortfall if the claims ratio for a financial year is lower than the average claims ratio for the reference period. The amount in respect of the claims shortfall shall be arrived at by multiplying the difference between the two ratios by the earned premiums for the financial year.

The maximum required amount shall be equal to six times the standard deviation of the claims ratio in the reference period from the average claims ratio, multiplied by the earned premiums for the financial year.

Where claims for any financial year are in excess, an amount in respect thereof shall be taken from the equalisation reserve until it has reached the minimum required amount. Claims shall be deemed to be in excess if the claims ratio for the financial year is higher than the average claims ratio. The amount in respect of the excess claims shall be arrived at by multiplying the difference between the two ratios by the earned premiums for the financial year.

The minimum required amount shall be equal to three times the standard deviation of the claims ratio in the reference period from the average claims ratio multiplied by the earned premiums for the financial year.

The length of the reference period shall be not less than 15 years and not more than 30 years. No equalisation reserve need be formed if no underwriting loss has been noted during the reference period.

Both required amounts of the equalisation reserve and the amount to be placed to it or the amount to be taken from it may be reduced if the average claims ratio for the reference period in conjunction with the expenses ratio show that the premiums include a safety margin and that safety margin is more than one and a half times the standard deviation of the claims ratio in the reference period. In such a case the amounts in question shall be multiplied by the quotient of one and a half times the standard deviation and the safety margin.

B. Exemption

Each Contracting Party may exempt head offices, agencies or branches from the obligation to set up an equalisation reserve for credit insurance business where the premiums or contributions receivable in respect of credit insurance are less than 4% of the total premiums or contributions receivable by them and less than ECU 2 500 000.

The relationship between the ecu and the Swiss franc and the procedures necessary for defining that relationship for the purposes of this Annex are laid down in Protocol No 3.

PROTOCOL NO 1
SOLVENCY MARGIN

[6077]

Article 1 Definition of the solvency margin

The solvency margin shall correspond to the assets of the undertaking, free of all foreseeable liabilities, less any intangible items. In particular the following shall be considered—

- the paid up share capital or, in the case of a mutual concern, the effective initial fund,
- one half of the share capital or the initial fund which is not yet paid up, once the paid up part reaches 25% of this capital or fund,
- reserves (statutory reserves and free reserves) not corresponding to underwriting liabilities,
- any carry forward of profits,
- in the case of a mutual or mutual type association with variable contributions, any claim which it has against its members by way of a call for supplementary contribution, within the financial year, up to one half of the difference between the maximum contributions and the contributions actually called in, and subject to a overriding limit of 50% of the margin,
- at the request of, and upon proof being shown by the undertaking, and with the agreement of the concerned supervisory authorities of the Contracting Parties in whose territory the undertaking carries on its business, any hidden reserves resulting from under-estimation of assets or over-estimation of liabilities in the balance sheet, in so far as such hidden reserves are not of an exceptional nature.

Over-estimation of technical reserves shall be determined relation to their amount calculated by the undertaking conformity with national rules; however, an amount equivalent to 75% of the difference between the amount of the reserve for outstanding risks calculated at a flat rate by the undertaking by application of a minimum percentage in relation to premiums and the amount that would have been obtained by calculating the reserve contract by contract where the national law in question gives an option between the two methods, can be taken into account in the solvency margin up to 20%.

Article 2 Relationship between the solvency margin and the amount of premiums or the burden of claims

2.1 The solvency margin shall be determined on the basis either of the annual amount of premiums or contributions, or the average burden of claims for the past three financial years. In the case, however, of undertakings which essentially underwrite only one or more of the risks of credit, storm, hail and frost, the last seven years shall be taken as the period of reference for the average burden of claims.

2.2 Subject to the provisions of Article 3 of this Protocol, the amount of the solvency margin shall be equal to the higher of the following two results—

First Result (premium basis)—

— the premiums or contributions (inclusive of charges ancillary to premiums or contributions) due in respect of all direct business in the last financial year for all financial years, shall be aggregated,

— to this aggregate there shall be added the amount of premiums accepted for all reinsurance in the last financial year,

— from this sum there shall then be deducted the total amount of premiums or contributions cancelled in the last financial year, as well as the total amount of taxes and levies pertaining to the premiums or contributions entering into the aggregate.

The amount so obtained shall be divided into two portions, the first portion extending up to ECU 10 million, the second comprising the excess; 18% and 16% of these portions respectively shall be calculated and added together.

The first result shall be obtained by multiplying the sum so calculated by the ratio existing in respect of the last financial year between the amount of claims remaining to be borne by the undertaking after deduction of transfers for reinsurance and the gross amount of claims; this ratio may in no case be less than 50%.

Second result (claims basis)—

— the amounts of claims paid in respect of direct business (without any deduction of claims borne by reinsurers and retrocessionnaires) in the periods specified in paragraph 2.1 of this Protocol shall be aggregated,

— to this aggregate there shall be added the amount of claims paid in respect of reinsurances or retrocessions accepted during the same periods,

— to this sum there shall be added the amount of provisions or reserves for outstanding claims established at the end of the last financial year both for direct business and for reinsurance acceptances,

— from this sum there shall be deducted the amount of recoveries effected during the periods specified in paragraph 2.1 of this Protocol,

— from the sum then remaining, there shall be deducted the amount of provisions or reserves for outstanding claims established at the commencement of the second financial year preceding the last financial year for which there are accounts, both for direct business and for reinsurance acceptances.

One-third, or one-seventh, of the amount so obtained, according to the period of reference established in paragraph 2.1 of this Protocol, shall be divided into two portions, the first extending up to ECU 7 million, and the second comprising the excess; 26% and 23% of these portions respectively shall be calculated and added together.

The second result shall be obtained by multiplying the sum so obtained by the ratio existing in respect of the last financial year between the amount of claims remaining to be borne by the business after transfers for reinsurance and the gross amount of claims; this ratio may in no case be less than 50%.

2.3 The fractions applicable to the portions referred to in paragraph 2.2 of this Protocol shall each be reduced to a third in the case of health insurance practised on a similar technical basis to that of life assurance, if

— the premiums paid are calculated on the basis of sickness tables according to the mathematical method applied in insurance,

— a reserve is set up for increasing age,

— an additional premium is collected in order to set up a safety margin of an appropriate amount,

— the insurer may only cancel the contract before the end of the third year of insurance at the latest,

— the contract provides for the possibility of increasing premiums or reducing payments even for current contracts.

2.4 In the case of the association of underwriters known as Lloyd's, the calculation of the first result in respect of premiums, referred to in paragraph 2.2 of this Protocol, shall be made on the basis of net premiums, which shall be multiplied by a flat rate percentage fixed annually by the supervisory authority of the Contracting Party in whose territory the head office of the undertaking is situated. This flat rate percentage must be calculated on the basis of the most recent statistical data on commissions paid.

The details, together with the relevant calculations, shall be sent to the supervisory authority of Switzerland if the association of underwriters known as Lloyd's is established there.

2.5 In the case of the risks listed under class 18 in Part A of Annex 1, the amount of claims paid used to calculate the second result (claims basis) shall be the costs borne by the undertaking in respect of assistance given. Such costs shall be calculated in accordance with the provisions of the Contracting Party in whose territory the head office of the undertaking is situated.

Article 3 Guarantee fund

3.1 One-third of the solvency margin shall constitute the guarantee fund.

3.2 The guarantee fund may not, however, be less than—

— ECU 1 400 000 in the case where all or some of the risks included in the class listed in Part A of Annex 1 under No 14 are covered. This provision shall apply to every undertaking for which the annual amount of premiums or contributions due in this class for each of the last three financial years exceeded ECU 2 500 000 or 4% of the total amount of premiums or contributions receivable by the undertaking concerned,

— ECU 400 000 in the case where all or some of the risks included in one of the classes listed in Part A of Annex 1 under Nos 10, 11, 12, 13 and 15 and, in so far as the first indent does not apply, No 14, are covered,

— ECU 300 000 in the case where all or some of the risks included in one of the classes listed in Part A of Annex 1 under Nos 1, 2, 3, 4, 5, 6, 7, 8, 16 and 18 are covered,

— ECU 200 000 in the case where all or some of the risks included in one of the classes listed in Part A of Annex 1 under Nos 9 and 17 are covered.

3.3 If the business carried on by the undertaking covers several classes or several risks, only that class or risk for which the highest amount is required shall be taken into account.

3.4 Each Contracting Party may provide for a one-fourth reduction of the minimum guarantee fund in the case of mutual associations and mutual type associations.

3.5 Where an undertaking has, in accordance with the first indent of paragraph 3.2 of this Protocol, to increase the guarantee fund to ECU 1 400 000, the Contracting Party in question shall allow such undertaking—

— a period of three years in which to bring the fund up to ECU 1 000 000,

— a period of five years in which to bring the fund up to ECU 1 200 000,

— a period of seven years in which to bring the fund up to ECU 1 400 000.

These periods shall run from the date from which the conditions referred to in the first indent of paragraph 3.2 of this Protocol are fulfilled.

Article 4 Relationship between the ecu and the Swiss franc

The relationship between the ecu and the Swiss franc and the procedures necessary for defining that relationship for the purposes of this Protocol are laid down in Protocol No 3.

PROTOCOL NO 2
SCHEME OF OPERATIONS

[6078]

Article 1 Content

The scheme of operations of the agency or branch shall contain the following particulars or proofs concerning—

(a) the nature of the risks which the undertaking proposes to cover;

(b) the general and special policy conditions which it proposes to use;

(c) the scales of premiums which the undertaking proposes to apply or each category of business;

(d) the guiding principles as to reinsurance;

(e) the state of the solvency margin of the undertaking, referred to in Protocol No 1;

(f) estimates relating to the expenses of installing the administrative services and the organisation for securing business; the financial resources intended to cover them, and, where the risks to be covered are listed under class 18 in Part A of Annex No 1, the resources available to the undertaking for providing the promised assistance; and, in addition, for the first three financial years,

(g) estimates relating to expenses of management;
(h) estimates relating to premiums or contributions and to claims in respect of the new business;
(i) the forecast balance sheet for the agency for branch.

Article 2 Exceptions
2.1 The particulars referred to in (b) and (c) of Article 1 of this Protocol shall not be required with regard to the following risks (large risks)—
(a) risks listed under classes 4, 5, 6, 7, 11 and 12 in Part A of Annex 1;
(b) risks listed under classes 14 and 15 in Part A of Annex No 1, where the policy holder is engaged professionally in an industrial or commercial activity or in one of the liberal professions, and the risks relate to such activity;
(c) risks listed under classes 8, 9, 13 and 16 in Part A of Annex 1 in so far as the policy holder exceeds the limits of at least two of the following three criteria.

First stage: until 31 December 1992—
— balance sheet total: ECU 12.4 million,
— net turnover: ECU 24 million,
— average number of employees during the financial year: 500.

Second stage: from 1 January 1993—
— balance sheet total: ECU 6.2 million,
— net turnover: ECU 12.8 million,
— average number of employees during the financial year: 250.

If the policy holder belongs to a group of undertakings for which consolidated accounts are drawn up in accordance with the law in force in the Contracting Party to whose jurisdiction the group is subject, the criteria mentioned above shall be applied on the basis of the consolidated accounts.

Each Contracting Party may add to the category mentioned under (c) risks insured by professional associations, joint ventures or temporary groupings.

2.2 However, in Switzerland the particulars referred to in (b) and (c) of Article 1 of this Protocol may be required with regard to the risks listed under No 12 in Part A of Annex 1 where the vessels involved are lake or river vessels.

PROTOCOL NO 3
RELATIONSHIP BETWEEN THE ECU AND THE SWISS FRANC

[6079]

Article 1 Ecu
For the purposes of this Agreement, "ecu" means the ecu as defined by the competent Community authorities.

Article 2 Relationship between national currencies and the ecu
2.1 In so far as amounts expressed in ecus in this Agreement have to be converted into national currencies to enable the supervisory authorities to apply the Agreement's provisions directly, the conversion shall be effected in accordance with the provisions of paragraphs 2.2 and 2.3 of this Protocol.
2.2 With regard to the conversion of amounts expressed in ecus into the national currencies of the Member States of the Community, the rules laid down by the competent Community authorities shall apply.
2.3 With regard to the equivalent in Swiss francs of amounts expressed in ecus, the exchange value of one ecu shall, for the purposes of this Agreement, be . . . . Swiss francs.

Article 3 Alteration of the relationship between the ecu and the Swiss franc
3.1 The relationship between the ecu and the Swiss franc referred to in paragraph 2.3 shall be reviewed annually on the basis of the following: where the exchange value of the ecu in terms of Swiss francs as fixed by the Swiss National Bank for the last working day in October differs by more than 10% on either side of the value in force for the purposes of this Agreement, that value shall be adjusted accordingly with effect from 1 January of the following year.
3.2 The Joint Committee referred to in Article 37 may make such other adjustments as may be necessary.

PROTOCOL NO 4
AGENCIES AND BRANCHES OF UNDERTAKINGS WHOSE HEAD OFFICE IS SITUATED OUTSIDE THE TERRITORIES TO WHICH THIS AGREEMENT APPLIES

[6080]

Article 1 Conditions for authorisation
Each Contracting Party may grant to an undertaking whose head office is situated outside the territories to which this Agreement applies under Article 43 thereof, authorisation to open an agency or branch in its territory, if the applicant undertaking fulfils at least the following conditions—

(a) it is entitled to undertake insurance business under its national law;
(b) it establishes an agency or branch in the territory of the Contracting Party in question;
(c) it undertakes to establish at the place of management of the agency or branch accounts specific to the business which it undertakes there, and to keep there all the records relating to the business transacted;
(d) it designates an authorised agent, to be approved by the supervisory authority;
(e) it possesses in the country in which it carries on its business assets of an amount equal to at least one-half of the minimum amount prescribed in paragraph 3.2 of Protocol No 1, in respect of the guarantee fund, and deposits one-quarter of the minimum amount as security;
(f) it undertakes to keep a solvency margin in accordance with Article 3 of this Protocol;
(g) it submits a scheme of operations in accordance with the provisions of paragraph 10.1(c) of the Agreement and Protocol No 2. Each Contracting Party may, if the legal provisions in force therein so permit, require an undertaking which has been in existence for fewer than three financial years to supply the balance sheet and profit and loss account which must accompany the scheme of operations only in respect of the financial years which have closed.

Article 2 Technical reserves
Under this Protocol, each Contracting Party shall apply to agencies or branches set up in its territory rules regarding technical reserves which may not be more favourable than those provided for in Articles 19, 20 and 21. By way of derogation from the second sentence of paragraph 20.1 it shall require assets representing technical reserves to be localised in the territory in which the supervisory authority of the Contracting Party concerned is competent.

Article 3 Solvency margin
3.1 Under this Protocol, each Contracting Party shall require for agencies or branches established in its territory a solvency margin consisting of assets free of all foreseeable liabilities, less any intangible items. The solvency margin shall be calculated in accordance with paragraphs 2.2 and 2.3 of Protocol No 1. However, for the purpose of calculating this margin, account shall be taken only of the premiums or contributions and claims pertaining to the business effected by the agency or branch concerned.
3.2 One-third of the solvency margin shall constitute the guarantee fund. The guarantee fund may not be less than one-half of the minimum required under paragraph 3.2 of Protocol No 1. The initial security lodged in accordance with paragraph 1(e) of this Protocol shall be counted towards such guarantee fund.
3.3 The assets representing the solvency margin shall be localised in the territory in which the supervisory authority of the Contracting Party concerned is competent.
3.4 The Community may allow these rules to be relaxed in the case of undertakings with agencies or branches in various Member States in order to facilitate their supervision.

Article 4 Verification and restoration of financial situation
The provisions of paragraph 17.3 and Article 18 shall apply *mutatis mutandis* in relation to agencies and branches of undertakings to which this Protocol applies.

Article 5 Agreements with third countries
Each Contracting Party may, by means of agreements concluded with one or more third countries, agree to the application of provisions different from those provided for in this Protocol on condition that its insured persons are adequately protected under conditions of reciprocity.

Exchange of letters No 1

[6081]

Principle of non-discrimination

Delegation of the Commission
of the European Communities

Brussels, 26 July 1989

Sir,

With reference to the Agreement between the Community and Switzerland, initialled today, I have the honour to confirm that the obligation of non-discrimination referred to in Article 5 thereof exclusively concerns the taking up and pursuit of the activity of direct insurance in the territory in which the supervisory authority which grants authorisation is competent and also applies to the Member States of the Community in the exercise of their power to legislate in the areas covered by the said Agreement.

I would ask you to take note of this communication, and to accept, Sir, the assurance of my high consideration.

Head of the Delegation of the
Commission of the European Communities
(s. Geoffrey FITCHEW)

Franz Blankart, Esq
State Secretary

Head of the Swiss Delegation

Berne

Swiss Delegation

Berne, 26 July 1989

Sir,

I have the honour to acknowledge receipt of your letter of today's date, worded as follows—

"With reference to the Agreement between the Community and Switzerland, initialled today, I have the honour to confirm that the obligation of non-discrimination referred to in Article 5 thereof exclusively concerns the taking up and pursuit of the activity of direct insurance in the territory in which the supervisory authority which grants authorisation is competent and also applies to the Member States of the Community in the exercise of their power to legislate in the areas covered by the said Agreement."

I have taken note of this communication, and in turn ask you to accept, Sir, the assurance of my high consideration.

Head of the Swiss Delegation
(s. Franz BLANKART)

Geoffrey Fitchew, Esq
Director General

Head of the Delegation of the
Commission of the European Communities

Brussels

Exchange of letters No 2

[6082]

Scope of authorisation

Delegation of the Commission
of the European Communities

Brussels, 26 July 1989

Sir,

With reference to the Agreement between the Community and Switzerland, initialled today, I have the honour to remind you of our understanding that paragraph 8.1 does not affect the provisions in force in each Contracting Party concerning the possibility for an insurance undertaking to cover risks situated outside the territory in which the supervisory authority which granted it authorisation is competent.

I would ask you to kindly confirm the above, and to accept, Sir, the assurance of my high consideration.

Head of the Delegation of the
Commission of the European Communities

(s. Geoffrey FITCHEW)

Franz Blankart, Esq
State Secretary

Head of the Swiss Delegation

Berne

Swiss Delegation

Berne, 26 July 1989

Sir,

I have the honour to acknowledge receipt of your letter of today's date, worded as follows—

"With reference to the Agreement between the Community and Switzerland, initialled today, I have the honour to remind you of our understanding that paragraph 8.1 does not affect the provisions in force in each Contracting Party concerning the possibility for an insurance undertaking to cover risks situated outside the territory in which the supervisory authority which granted it authorisation is competent."

I have taken note of this communication, and in turn ask you to accept, Sir, the assurance of my high consideration.

Head of the Swiss Delegation

(s. Franz BLANKART)

Geoffrey Fitchew, Esq
Director General

Head of the Delegation of the
Commission of the European Communities

Brussels

Exchange of letters No 3

[6083]

Authorised agent

Swiss Delegation

Berne, 25 June 1982

Sir,

With reference to the Agreement between Switzerland and the Community, initialled today, I have the honour to state that it does not preclude the authorised agent referred to in paragraphs 10.1(d) and 11.4 thereof and in paragraph 1(d) of Protocol No 4 being required to assume effective management of the agency or branch in respect of all the business activities the latter intends carrying on in the territory in which the supervisory authority from which authorisation is sought is competent.

I would ask you to kindly confirm the above, and to accept, Sir, the assurance of my high consideration.

Head of the Swiss Delegation

(s. Franz BLANKART)

Gérard Imbert, Esq
Director

Head of the Delegation of the
Commission of the European Communities

Brussels

Delegation of the Commission
of the European Communities

Brussels, 25 June 1982

Sir,

I have the honour to acknowledge receipt of your letter of today's date, worded as follows—

"With reference to the Agreement between Switzerland and the Community, initialled today, I have the honour to state that it does not preclude the authorised agent referred to in paragraphs 10.1(d) and 11.4 thereof and in paragraph 1(d) of Protocol No 4 being required to assume effective management of the agency or branch in respect of all the business activities the latter intends carrying on in the territory in which the supervisory authority from which authorisation is sought is competent."

I hereby confirm the above, and in turn ask you to accept, Sir, the assurance of my high consideration.

Head of the Delegation of the
Commission of the European Communities
(s. Gérard IMBERT)

Franz Blankart, Esq Ambassador

Head of the Swiss Delegation

Berne

Exchange of letters No 4

[6084]

Assignment to the Swiss Securities Fund of immovable property directly owned by insurance undertakings

Swiss Delegation

Berne, 25 June 1982

Sir,

With reference to the Agreement between Switzerland and the Community, initialled today, I have the honour to inform you that Switzerland reserves the right, with regard to the assignment to the securities fund of immovable property directly owned by insurance undertakings, to have the said immovable property registered in the securities fund register maintained by the undertaking and to have included in the land register a note relating there to restricting the right to dispose freely of such property which, under Swiss law, does not constitute registration of a mortgage.

I would ask you to confirm that you are also of the opinion that such a procedure is not contrary to paragraphs 11.2 and 20.3 of the said Agreement.

Please accept, Sir, the assurance of my high consideration.

Head of the Swiss Delegation
(Franz BLANKART)

Gérard Imbert, Esq
Director

Head of the Delegation of the
Commission of the European Communities

Brussels

Delegation of the Commission
of the European Communities

Brussels, 25 June 1982

Sir,

I have the honour to acknowledge receipt of your letter of today's date, worded as follows—

"With reference to the Agreement between Switzerland and the Community, initialled today, I have the honour to inform you that Switzerland reserves the right, with regard to the assignment to the securities fund of immovable property directly owned by insurance undertakings, to have the said immovable property registered in the securities fund register

Part VI European Materials

maintained by the undertaking and to have included in the land register a note relating thereto restricting the right to dispose freely of such property which, under Swiss law, does not constitute registration of a mortgage."

I hereby confirm that I am also of the opinion that such a procedure is not contrary to paragraphs 11.2 and 20.3 of the said Agreement.

Please accept, Sir, the assurance of my high consideration.

Head of the Delegation of the
Commission of the European Communities
(Gérard IMBERT)

Franz Blankart, Esq Ambassador

Head of the Swiss Delegation

Berne

Exchange of letters No 5

[6085]

Principles governing investment

Swiss Delegation

Berne, 25 June 1982

Sir,

With reference to the Agreement between Switzerland and the Community, initialled today, I have the honour to state with regard to the assets referred to in Article 15 that the said Agreement does not preclude the supervisory authority from taking action in specific cases where the choice of assets is likely to place the financial security of an undertaking in serious jeopardy or diminish its degree of liquidity.

I would ask you to kindly confirm the above, and to accept, Sir, the assurance of my high consideration.

Head of the Swiss Delegation
(s. Franz BLANKART)

Gérard Imbert, Esq
Director

Head of the Delegation of the
Commission of the European Communities

Brussels

Delegation of the Commission
of the European Communities

Brussels, 25 June 1982

Sir,

I have the honour to acknowledge receipt of your letter of today's date, worded as follows—

"With reference to the Agreement between Switzerland and the Community, initialled today, I have the honour to state with regard to the assets referred to in Article 15 that the said Agreement does not preclude the supervisory authority from taking action in specific cases where the choice of assets is likely to place the financial security of an undertaking in serious jeopardy or diminish its degree of liquidity."

I hereby confirm the above, and in turn ask you to accept, Sir, the assurance of my high consideration.

Head of the Delegation of the
Commission of the European Communities
(s. Gérard IMBERT)

Franz Blankart, Esq
Ambassador

Head of the Swiss Delegation

Berne

Exchange of letters No 6

[6086]

Swiss List of classes of insurance

Swiss Delegation

Berne, 25 June 1982

Sir,

With reference to the Agreement between Switzerland and the Community, initialled today, I have the honour to inform you that Switzerland will continue to apply to head office, agencies and branches established in its territory its "List of classes of insurance" for the purposes of submission of accounts and statistics. This will also be the case with regard to the report of the Federal Office for Private Insurance on "Private insurance undertakings in Switzerland". However, the "Classification of risks according to classes of insurance", set out in Part A of Annex 1 to the said Agreement, will apply for the purposes of the specification of classes in applications for authorisation and assessment of the need to approve the general and special conditions of insurance policies and scales of premiums.

This does not preclude examination by Switzerland, at a later date, of the possibility of applying the abovementioned "Classification" in its entirety. A decision to that effect would be notified to the Community through diplomatic channels.

Is it agreed that the scope of the "List of classes of insurance" is the same as that of the "Classification of risks according to classes of insurance". Comparability as between the two types of classification is as follows—

Swiss list of classes of insurance	***Classes of insurance according to the classification in Annex 1***
1. Accident	A.1
2. Liability	A.10, 11, 12, 13
3. Fire and natural forces	A.8
4. Transport	A.4, 6, 7
5. Vehicles	A.3, 5
6. Hail	A.9
7. Animals	A.9
8. Theft	A.9
9. Breakage of glass	A.9
10. Damage by water	A.9
11. Machinery	A.9
12. Jewellery	A.9
13. Suretyship	A.15
14. Credit	A.14
15. Legal expenses	A.17
16. Health	A.2
17. Rain	A.2
18. Special policies	A.16, 18

I would ask you to take note of this communication, and to accept, Sir, the assurance of my high consideration.

Head of the Swiss Delegation

(s. Franz BLANKART)

Gérard Imbert

Head of the Delegation
of the Commission of the European Communities

Brussels

Delegation of the Commission
of the European Communities

Brussels, 25 June 1982

Sir,

I have the honour to acknowledge receipt of your letter of today's date, worded as follows—

"With reference to the Agreement between Switzerland and the Community, initialled today, I have the honour to inform you that Switzerland will continue to apply to head offices, agencies and branches established in its territory its "List of classes of insurance" for the purposes of submission of accounts and statistics. This will also be the case with regard to the report of the Federal Office for Private Insurance on "Private insurance undertakings in Switzerland". However, the "Classification of risks according to classes of insurance", set out in Part A of Annex No 1 to the said Agreement, will apply for the purposes of the specification of classes in applications for authorisation and assessment of the need to approve the general and special conditions of insurance policies and scales of premiums.

This does not preclude examination by Switzerland, at a later date, of the possibility of applying the abovementioned "Classification" in its entirety. A decision to that effect would be notified to the Community through diplomatic channels.

It is agreed that the scope of the "List of classes of insurance" is the same as that of the "Classification of risks according to classes of insurance". Comparability as between the two types of classification is as follows—

Swiss list of classes of insurance	***Classes of insurance according to the classification in Annex 1***
1. Accident	A.1
2. Liability	A.10, 11, 12, 13
3. Fire and natural forces	A.8
4. Transport	A.4, 6, 7
5. Vehicles	A.3, 5
6. Hail	A.9
7. Animals	A.9
8. Theft	A.9
9. Breakage of glass	A.9
10. Damage by water	A.9
11. Machinery	A.9
12. Jewellery	A.9
13. Suretyship	A.15
14. Credit	A.14
15. Legal expenses	A.17
16. Health	A.2
17. Rain	A.2
18. Special policies	A.16, 18".

I have taken note of this communication, and in turn ask you to accept, Sir, the assurance of my high consideration.

Head of the Delegation of the
Commission of the European Communities

(s. Gérard IMBERT)

Franz Blankart, Esq
Ambassador

Head of the Swiss Delegation

Berne

[6087]

Exchange of letters No 7

The capital of insurance undertakings

Swiss Delegation

Berne, 25 June 1982

Sir,

With reference to the Agreement between Switzerland and the Community, initialled today, I have the honour to remind you of our understanding that the provisions concerning the minimum solvency margin calculated in accordance with paragraph 2.2 of Protocol No 1, and the minimum guarantee fund, referred to in paragraph 3.2 of that Protocol, have no bearing on the laws or practices of the Contracting Parties regarding the requirements relating to the capital of undertakings.

I would ask you to kindly confirm the above, and to accept, Sir, the assurance of my high consideration.

Head of the Swiss Delegation
(s. Franz BLANKART)

Gérard Imbert, Esq
Director

Head of the Delegation of the
Commission of the European Communities

Brussels

Delegation of the Commission
of the European Communities

Brussels, 25 June 1982

Sir,

I have the honour to acknowledge receipt of your letter of today's date, worded as follows—

> "With reference to the Agreement between Switzerland and the Community, initialled today, I have the honour to remind you of our understanding that the provisions concerning the minimum solvency margin calculated in accordance with paragraph 2.2 of Protocol No 1, and the minimum guarantee fund, referred to in paragraph 3.2 of that Protocol, have no bearing on the laws or practices of the Contracting Parties regarding the requirements relating to the capital of undertakings."

I hereby confirm the above, and in turn ask you to accept, Sir, the assurance of my high consideration.

Head of the Delegation of the
Commission of the European Communities
(s. Gérard IMBERT)

Franz Blankart, Esq
Ambassador

Head of the Swiss Delegation

Berne

[6088]

Exchange of letters No 8

Transitional Arrangements for Assistance

Delegation of the Commission
of the European Communities

Brussels, 26 July 1989

Sir,

Part VI European Materials

With reference to the Agreement between the Community and Switzerland, initialled today, I have the honour to remind you of our understanding that the Member States of the Community may allow undertakings which, on 12 December 1984, provided only assistance in their territory a period of five years from that date in order to comply with the requirements set out in Article 16 of this Agreement.

The Member States of the Community may allow any undertakings referred to above which, upon expiry of the five year period, have not fully established the solvency margin a further period not exceeding two years in which to do so provided that such undertakings have, in accordance with Article 18 of this Agreement, submitted for the approval of the supervisory authority the measures which they propose to take for that purpose.

Any undertaking referred to above which wishes to extend its business to other classes or, in the case referred to in paragraph 8.1 of this Agreement, to another part of the territory, may do so only on condition that it complies forthwith with this Agreement.

Moreover, until 12 December 1992, the condition specified in point 5 of Part B of Annex 2 to this Agreement, namely that the accident or break down must have happened in the territory of the Contracting Party in which the undertaking providing cover is established, shall not apply to the operations referred to in the third indent of the abovementioned point where these operations are carried out by the ELPA (Automobile and Touring Club of Greece).

I would ask you to kindly confirm the above, and to accept, Sir, the assurance of my high consideration.

Head of the Delegation of the
Commission of the European Communities
(s. Geoffrey FITCHEW)

Franz Blankart Esq
State Secretary

Head of the Swiss Delegation

Berne

Swiss Delegation

Berne, 26 July 1989

Sir,

I have the honour to acknowledge receipt of your letter of today's date, worded as follows—

> "With reference to the Agreement between the Community and Switzerland, initialled today, I have the honour to remind you of our understanding that the Member States of the Community may allow undertakings which, on 12 December 1984, provided only assistance in their territory a period of five years from that date in order to comply with the requirements set out in Article 16 of the Agreement.
>
> The Member States of the Community may allow any undertakings referred to above which, upon expiry of the five year period, have not fully established the solvency margin a further period not exceeding two years in which to do so provided that such undertakings have, in accordance with Article 18 of this Agreement, submitted for the approval of the supervisory authority the measures which they propose to take for that purpose.
>
> Any undertaking referred to above which wishes to extend its business to other classes or, in the case referred to in paragraph 8.1 of this Agreement, to another part of the territory, may do so only on condition that it complies forthwith with this Agreement.
>
> Moreover, until 12 December 1992, the condition specified in point 5 of Part B of Annex 2 to this Agreement, namely that the accident or breakdown must have happened in the territory of the Contracting Party in which the undertaking providing cover is established, shall not apply to the operations referred to in the third indent of the abovementioned point where these operations are carried out by the ELPA (Automobile and Touring Club of Greece)."

I hereby confirm the above, and in turn ask you to accept, Sir, the assurance of my high consideration.

Head of the Swiss Delegation
(s. Franz BLANKART)

Geoffrey Fitchew, Esq
Director General

Head of the Delegation of the Commission
of the European Communities

Brussels

Exchange of letters No 9

[6089]

Transitional arrangements for the large risks referred to in paragraph 2.1 of protocol No 2

Delegation of the Commission
of the European Communities

Brussels, 26 July 1989

Sir,

With reference to the Agreement between the Community and Switzerland, initialled today, I have the honour to remind you of our understanding that Greece, Ireland, Portugal and Spain benefit from the following transitional arrangements in respect of the large risks referred to in paragraph 2.1 of Protocol No 2 to this Agreement—

(a) until 31 December 1992, they may apply, to all risks, the regime other than that for risks referred to in paragraph 2.1 of Protocol No 2 to this Agreement;

(b) from 1 January 1993 to 31 December 1994, the regime for large risks shall apply to risks referred to in paragraph 2.1(a) and (b) of Protocol No 2 to this Agreement; for risks referred to under (c) of the same paragraph, these Member States shall fix the thresholds to apply therefor;

(c) Spain—

— from 1 January 1995 to 31 December 1996, the thresholds of the first stage fixed in paragraph 2.1(c) of Protocol No 2 to this Agreement shall apply,

— from 1 January 1997, the thresholds of the second stage shall apply;

(d) Greece, Ireland and Portugal—

— from 1 January 1995 to 31 December 1998, the thresholds of the first stage fixed in paragraph 2.1(c) of Protocol No 2 to this Agreement shall apply,

— from 1 January 1999, the thresholds of the second stage shall apply.

The derogation allowed from 1 January 1995 shall only apply to contracts covering risks classified under classes 8, 9, 13 and 16 in Part A of Annex 1 situated exclusively in one of the four Member States of the Community benefiting from these provisions.

I would ask you to kindly confirm the above, and to accept, Sir, the assurance of my high consideration.

Head of the Delegation of the
Commission of the European Communities
(s. Geoffrey FITCHEW)

Franz Blankart, Esq State Secretary

Head of the Swiss Delegation

Berne

Swiss Delegation

Berne, 26 July 1989

Sir,

I have the honour to acknowledge receipt of your letter of today's date, worded as follows—

"With reference to the Agreement between the Community and Switzerland, initialled today, I have the honour to remind you of our understanding that Greece, Ireland, Portugal and Spain benefit from the following transitional arrangements in respect of the large risks referred to in paragraph 2.1 of Protocol No 2 to this Agreement—

(a) until 31 December 1992, they may apply, to all risks, the regime other than that for risks referred to in paragraph 2.1 of Protocol No 2 to this Agreement;

(b) from 1 January 1993 to 31 December 1994, the regime for large risks shall apply to risks referred to in paragraph 2.1(a) and (b) of Protocol No 2 to this Agreement; for risks referred to under (c) of the same paragraph, these Member States shall fix the thresholds to apply therefor;

(c) Spain—

— from 1 January 1995 to 31 December 1996, the thresholds of the first stage fixed in paragraph 2.1(c) of Protocol No 2 to this Agreement shall apply,

— from 1 January 1997, the thresholds of the second stage shall apply;

(d) Greece, Ireland and Portugal—

— from 1 January 1995 to 31 December 1998, the thresholds of the first stage fixed in paragraph 2.1(c) of Protocol No 2 to this Agreement shall apply,

— from 1 January 1999, the thresholds of the second stage shall apply.

The derogation allowed from 1 January 1995 shall only apply to contracts covering risks classified under classes 8, 9, 13 and 16 in Part A of Annex No 1 situated exclusively in one of the four Member States of the Community benefiting from these provisions."

I hereby confirm the above, and in turn ask you to accept, Sir, the assurance of my high consideration.

Head of the Swiss Delegation
(s. Franz BLANKART)

Geoffrey Fitchew, Esq
Director General

Head of the Delegation of the
Commission of the European Communities

Brussels

[6090]
Joint Declaration by the Contracting Parties concerning the period between the date of signature and the date of entry into force of the Agreement

During the period between the date of signature and the date of entry into force of this Agreement, referred to in paragraph 44.3 thereof, each Contracting Party hereby declares that it will not introduce any new provisions on supervision which are liable to be repealed under this Agreement concerning agencies and branches belonging to undertakings whose head office is situated in the territory of the other Contracting Party and which wish to become established in its territory, or are established there, for the purpose of taking up or pursuing the self-employed activity of direct insurance other than life assurance.

The Contracting Parties further undertake to initiate without delay the procedures necessary to amend their national laws in accordance with this Agreement.

FINAL ACT

The representatives of

THE EUROPEAN ECONOMIC COMMUNITY,

AND THE SWISS CONFEDERATION,
assembled in Luxembourg on 10 October 1989,

on the occasion of the signature of the Agreement between the European Economic Community and the Swiss Confederation on direct insurance other than life assurance,

have, at the time of signature of this Agreement—

— taken note of the Exchanges of Letters annexed to the abovementioned Agreement—

Exchange of Letters No 1:	Principle of non-discrimination
Exchange of Letters No 2:	Scope of authorisation
Exchange of Letters No 3:	Authorised agent
Exchange of Letters No 4:	Assignment to the Swiss Securities Fund of immovable property directly owned by insurance undertakings
Exchange of Letters No 5:	Principles governing investment
Exchange of Letters No 6:	Swiss list of classes of insurance
Exchange of Letters No 7:	The capital of insurance undertakings
Exchange of Letters No 8:	Transitional arrangements for assistance
Exchange of Letters No 9:	Transitional arrangements for the large risks referred to in paragraph 2.1 of Protocol No 2,

— adopted the following Declaration which is annexed to the above Agreement—

Joint Declaration by the Contracting Parties concerning the period between the date of signature and the date of entry into force of the Agreement.

Done at Luxembourg on the tenth day of October in the year one thousand nine hundred and eighty-nine.

COUNCIL DIRECTIVE

(91/371/EEC)

of 20 June 1991

on the implementation of the Agreement between the European Economic Community and the Swiss Confederation concerning direct insurance other than life assurance

NOTES

Date of publication in OJ: OJ L205, 27.7.91, p 48.

[6091]

THE COUNCIL OF THE EUROPEAN COMMUNITIES,

Having regard to the Treaty establishing the European Economic Community, and in particular the last sentence of Article 57(2) and Article 235 thereof,

Having regard to the proposal from the Commission,[1]

In cooperation with the European Parliament,[2]

Having regard to the opinion of the Economic and Social Committee,[3]

Whereas an Agreement between the European Economic Community and the Swiss Confederation concerning direct insurance other than life assurance was signed at Luxembourg on 10 October 1989;

Whereas one of the effects of that Agreement is to impose, in relation to insurance undertakings which have their head offices in Switzerland, legal rules different from those applicable, under Title III of Council Directive 73/239/EEC of 24 July 1973 on the coordination of laws, regulations and administrative provisions relating to the taking up and pursuit of the business of direct insurance other than life assurance,[4] to agencies and branches established within the Community of undertakings whose head offices are outside the Community;

Whereas the coordinated rules relating to the pursuit of these activities within the Community by the Swiss undertakings subject to the provisions of the said Agreement must take effect on the same date in all the Member States of the Community; whereas that Agreement will not come into force until the first day of the calendar year following the date on which the instruments of approval are exchanged,

NOTES

1 OJ C53, 5.3.90, p 45.

2 OJ C72, 18.3.91, p 175, and Decision of 2 June 1991 (not yet published in the Official Journal).

3 OJ C5, 7.3.90, p 27.

4 OJ L228, 16.8.73, p 3.

HAS ADOPTED THIS DIRECTIVE—

[6092]

Article 1

The Member States shall amend their national provisions to comply with the Agreement between the European Economic Community and the Swiss Confederation within a period of 24 months following the notification of this Directive. They shall immediately inform the Commission thereof.

When Member States adopt these measures, they shall contain a reference to this Directive or shall be accompanied by such reference on the occasion of their official publication. The methods of making such a reference shall be laid down by the Member States.

[6093]

Article 2

The Member States shall specify in their national provisions that the amendments thereto made pursuant to the Agreement shall not come into force until the date on which the Agreement enters into force.

[6094]
Article 3
This Directive is addressed to the Member States.
Done at Luxembourg, 20 June 1991.

COUNCIL DIRECTIVE

(91/675/EEC)

of 19 December 1991

setting up a [European Insurance and Occupational Pensions Committee]

NOTES
Date of publication in OJ: OJ L374, 31.12.91, p 32.
Title: words in square brackets substituted by European Parliament and Council Directive 2005/1/EC, art 5(1).

[6095]
THE COUNCIL OF THE EUROPEAN COMMUNITIES,

Having regard to the Treaty establishing the European Economic Community, and in particular the third sentence of Article 57(2) thereof,

Having regard to the proposal from the Commission,[1]

In cooperation with the European Parliament,[2]

Having regard to the Opinion of the Economic and Social Committee,[3]

Whereas the Council shall confer on the Commission powers for the implementation of the rules which the Council lays down;

Whereas implementing measures are necessary for the application of Council Directives on non-life insurance and life assurance; whereas, in particular, technical adaptations may from time to time be necessary to take account of developments in the insurance sector; whereas it is appropriate that these measures shall be taken in accordance with the procedure laid down in Article 2, procedure III, variant (b), of Council Decision 87/373/EEC of 13 July 1987 laying down the procedures for the exercise of implementing powers conferred on the Commission;[4]

Whereas it is necessary for this purpose to set up an Insurance Committee;

Whereas the establishment of an Insurance Committee does not rule out other forms of cooperation between authorities which supervise the taking up and pursuit of the business of insurance undertakings, and in particular cooperation within the Conference on Insurance Supervisory Authorities, which is in particular competent for the drafting of protocols implementing Community Directives; whereas close cooperation between the Committee and the Conference would be particularly useful;

Whereas the examination of problems arising in non-life insurance and life assurance makes cooperation desirable between the competent authorities and the Commission; whereas it is appropriate to confer this task on the Insurance Committee; whereas it should furthermore be ensured that there is smooth coordination of the activities of this Committee with those of other committees of a similar nature set up by Community acts,

NOTES

1 OJ C230, 15.9.90, p 5.

2 OJ C240, 16.9.91, p 117 and OJ C305, 25.11.91.

3 OJ C102, 18.4.91, p 11.

4 OJ L197, 18.7.87, p 33.

HAS ADOPTED THIS DIRECTIVE—

[6096]
[Article 1
1. The Commission shall be assisted by the European Insurance and Occupational Pensions Committee established by Commission Decision 2004/9/EC of 5 November 2003[1] (hereinafter the Committee).

2. The chairperson of the Committee of European Insurance and Occupational Pensions Supervisors established by Commission Decision 2004/6/EC[2] shall participate at the meetings of the Committee as an observer.

3. The Committee may invite experts and observers to attend its meetings.

4. The secretariat of the Committee shall be provided by the Commission.]

NOTES

Substituted by European Parliament and Council Directive 2005/1/EC, art 5(2).

[1] OJ L3, 7.1.2004, p 34.

[2] OJ L3, 7.1.2004, p 30.

[6097]

[Article 2

Where reference is made to this Article, Article 5a(1) to (4) and Article 7 of Decision 1999/468/EC[1] shall apply, having regard to the provisions of Article 8 thereof.]

NOTES

Substituted by European Parliament and Council Directive 2008/21/EC, art 1(1).

[1] OJ L184, 17.7.1999, p 23. Decision as amended by Decision 2006/512/EC (OJ L200, 22.7.2006, p 11).

[6097A]

[Article 2A

Where reference is made to this Article, Articles 5 and 7 of Decision 1999/468/EC shall apply, having regard to the provisions of Article 8 thereof.

The period laid down in Article 5(6) of Decision 1999/468/EC shall be set at three months.]

NOTES

Inserted by European Parliament and Council Directive 2008/21/EC, art 1(2).

Articles 3, 4 (*Repealed by European Parliament and Council Directive 2005/1/EC, art 5(4).*)

[6098]

Article 5

This Directive is addressed to the Member States.

Done at Brussels, 19 December 1991.

EUROPEAN PARLIAMENT AND COUNCIL REGULATION

(593/2008/EC)

of 17 June 2008

on the law applicable to contractual obligations (Rome I)

NOTES

Date of publication in OJ: OJ L177, 4.7.2008, p 6.

Application to the United Kingdom: Commission Decision 2009/26/EC of 22 December 2008 (OJ L10, 15.1.2009, p 22) provides that:

"Article 1

Regulation (EC) No 593/2008 shall apply to the United Kingdom in accordance with Article 2.

Article 2

Regulation (EC) No 593/2008 shall enter into force in the United Kingdom from the date of notification of this Decision. It shall apply from 17 December 2009, except for Article 26 which shall apply from 17 June 2009.".

[6098AA]

THE EUROPEAN PARLIAMENT AND THE COUNCIL OF THE EUROPEAN UNION,

Having regard to the Treaty establishing the European Community, and in particular Article 61(c) and the second indent of Article 67(5) thereof,

Having regard to the proposal from the Commission,

Having regard to the opinion of the European Economic and Social Committee,[1]

Acting in accordance with the procedure laid down in Article 251 of the Treaty,[2]

Whereas:

(1) The Community has set itself the objective of maintaining and developing an area of freedom,

security and justice. For the progressive establishment of such an area, the Community is to adopt measures relating to judicial cooperation in civil matters with a cross-border impact to the extent necessary for the proper functioning of the internal market.

(2) According to Article 65, point (b) of the Treaty, these measures are to include those promoting the compatibility of the rules applicable in the Member States concerning the conflict of laws and of jurisdiction.

(3) The European Council meeting in Tampere on 15 and 16 October 1999 endorsed the principle of mutual recognition of judgments and other decisions of judicial authorities as the cornerstone of judicial cooperation in civil matters and invited the Council and the Commission to adopt a programme of measures to implement that principle.

(4) On 30 November 2000 the Council adopted a joint Commission and Council programme of measures for implementation of the principle of mutual recognition of decisions in civil and commercial matters.[3] The programme identifies measures relating to the harmonisation of conflict-of-law rules as those facilitating the mutual recognition of judgments.

(5) The Hague Programme,[4] adopted by the European Council on 5 November 2004, called for work to be pursued actively on the conflict-of-law rules regarding contractual obligations (Rome I).

(6) The proper functioning of the internal market creates a need, in order to improve the predictability of the outcome of litigation, certainty as to the law applicable and the free movement of judgments, for the conflict-of-law rules in the Member States to designate the same national law irrespective of the country of the court in which an action is brought.

(7) The substantive scope and the provisions of this Regulation should be consistent with Council Regulation (EC) No 44/2001 of 22 December 2000 on jurisdiction and the recognition and enforcement of judgments in civil and commercial matters[5] (Brussels I) and Regulation (EC) No 864/2007 of the European Parliament and of the Council of 11 July 2007 on the law applicable to non-contractual obligations (Rome II).[6]

(8) Family relationships should cover parentage, marriage, affinity and collateral relatives. The reference in Article 1(2) to relationships having comparable effects to marriage and other family relationships should be interpreted in accordance with the law of the Member State in which the court is seised.

(9) Obligations under bills of exchange, cheques and promissory notes and other negotiable instruments should also cover bills of lading to the extent that the obligations under the bill of lading arise out of its negotiable character.

(10) Obligations arising out of dealings prior to the conclusion of the contract are covered by Article 12 of Regulation (EC) No 864/2007. Such obligations should therefore be excluded from the scope of this Regulation.

(11) The parties' freedom to choose the applicable law should be one of the cornerstones of the system of conflict-of-law rules in matters of contractual obligations.

(12) An agreement between the parties to confer on one or more courts or tribunals of a Member State exclusive jurisdiction to determine disputes under the contract should be one of the factors to be taken into account in determining whether a choice of law has been clearly demonstrated.

(13) This Regulation does not preclude parties from incorporating by reference into their contract a non-State body of law or an international convention.

(14) Should the Community adopt, in an appropriate legal instrument, rules of substantive contract law, including standard terms and conditions, such instrument may provide that the parties may choose to apply those rules.

(15) Where a choice of law is made and all other elements relevant to the situation are located in a country other than the country whose law has been chosen, the choice of law should not prejudice the application of provisions of the law of that country which cannot be derogated from by agreement. This rule should apply whether or not the choice of law was accompanied by a choice of court or tribunal. Whereas no substantial change is intended as compared with Article 3(3) of the 1980 Convention on the Law Applicable to Contractual Obligations[7] (the Rome Convention), the wording of this Regulation is aligned as far as possible with Article 14 of Regulation (EC) No 864/2007.

(16) To contribute to the general objective of this Regulation, legal certainty in the European judicial area, the conflict-of-law rules should be highly foreseeable. The courts should, however, retain a degree of discretion to determine the law that is most closely connected to the situation.

(17) As far as the applicable law in the absence of choice is concerned, the concept of 'provision of services' and 'sale of goods' should be interpreted in the same way as when applying Article 5 of Regulation (EC) No 44/2001 in so far as sale of goods and provision of services are covered by that Regulation. Although franchise and distribution contracts are contracts for services, they are the subject of specific rules.

(18) As far as the applicable law in the absence of choice is concerned, multilateral systems

should be those in which trading is conducted, such as regulated markets and multilateral trading facilities as referred to in Article 4 of Directive 2004/39/EC of the European Parliament and of the Council of 21 April 2004 on markets in financial instruments,[8] regardless of whether or not they rely on a central counterparty.

(19) Where there has been no choice of law, the applicable law should be determined in accordance with the rule specified for the particular type of contract. Where the contract cannot be categorised as being one of the specified types or where its elements fall within more than one of the specified types, it should be governed by the law of the country where the party required to effect the characteristic performance of the contract has his habitual residence. In the case of a contract consisting of a bundle of rights and obligations capable of being categorised as falling within more than one of the specified types of contract, the characteristic performance of the contract should be determined having regard to its centre of gravity.

(20) Where the contract is manifestly more closely connected with a country other than that indicated in Article 4(1) or (2), an escape clause should provide that the law of that other country is to apply. In order to determine that country, account should be taken, inter alia, of whether the contract in question has a very close relationship with another contract or contracts.

(21) In the absence of choice, where the applicable law cannot be determined either on the basis of the fact that the contract can be categorised as one of the specified types or as being the law of the country of habitual residence of the party required to effect the characteristic performance of the contract, the contract should be governed by the law of the country with which it is most closely connected. In order to determine that country, account should be taken, inter alia, of whether the contract in question has a very close relationship with another contract or contracts.

(22) As regards the interpretation of contracts for the carriage of goods, no change in substance is intended with respect to Article 4(4), third sentence, of the Rome Convention. Consequently, single-voyage charter parties and other contracts the main purpose of which is the carriage of goods should be treated as contracts for the carriage of goods. For the purposes of this Regulation, the term 'consignor' should refer to any person who enters into a contract of carriage with the carrier and the term 'the carrier' should refer to the party to the contract who undertakes to carry the goods, whether or not he performs the carriage himself.

(23) As regards contracts concluded with parties regarded as being weaker, those parties should be protected by conflict-of-law rules that are more favourable to their interests than the general rules.

(24) With more specific reference to consumer contracts, the conflict-of-law rule should make it possible to cut the cost of settling disputes concerning what are commonly relatively small claims and to take account of the development of distance-selling techniques. Consistency with Regulation (EC) No 44/2001 requires both that there be a reference to the concept of directed activity as a condition for applying the consumer protection rule and that the concept be interpreted harmoniously in Regulation (EC) No 44/2001 and this Regulation, bearing in mind that a joint declaration by the Council and the Commission on Article 15 of Regulation (EC) No 44/2001 states that 'for Article 15(1)(c) to be applicable it is not sufficient for an undertaking to target its activities at the Member State of the consumer's residence, or at a number of Member States including that Member State; a contract must also be concluded within the framework of its activities'. The declaration also states that 'the mere fact that an Internet site is accessible is not sufficient for Article 15 to be applicable, although a factor will be that this Internet site solicits the conclusion of distance contracts and that a contract has actually been concluded at a distance, by whatever means. In this respect, the language or currency which a website uses does not constitute a relevant factor.'.

(25) Consumers should be protected by such rules of the country of their habitual residence that cannot be derogated from by agreement, provided that the consumer contract has been concluded as a result of the professional pursuing his commercial or professional activities in that particular country. The same protection should be guaranteed if the professional, while not pursuing his commercial or professional activities in the country where the consumer has his habitual residence, directs his activities by any means to that country or to several countries, including that country, and the contract is concluded as a result of such activities.

(26) For the purposes of this Regulation, financial services such as investment services and activities and ancillary services provided by a professional to a consumer, as referred to in sections A and B of Annex I to Directive 2004/39/EC, and contracts for the sale of units in collective investment undertakings, whether or not covered by Council Directive 85/611/EEC of 20 December 1985 on the coordination of laws, regulations and administrative provisions relating to undertakings for collective investment in transferable securities (UCITS),[9] should be subject to Article 6 of this Regulation. Consequently, when a reference is made to terms and conditions governing the issuance or offer to the public of transferable securities or to the subscription and redemption of units in collective investment undertakings, that reference should include all aspects binding the issuer or the offeror to the consumer, but should not include those aspects involving the provision of financial services.

(27) Various exceptions should be made to the general conflict-of-law rule for consumer contracts. Under one such exception the general rule should not apply to contracts relating to rights in rem in immovable property or tenancies of such property unless the contract relates to the right to use

immovable property on a timeshare basis within the meaning of Directive 94/47/EC of the European Parliament and of the Council of 26 October 1994 on the protection of purchasers in respect of certain aspects of contracts relating to the purchase of the right to use immovable properties on a timeshare basis.[10]

(28) It is important to ensure that rights and obligations which constitute a financial instrument are not covered by the general rule applicable to consumer contracts, as that could lead to different laws being applicable to each of the instruments issued, therefore changing their nature and preventing their fungible trading and offering. Likewise, whenever such instruments are issued or offered, the contractual relationship established between the issuer or the offeror and the consumer should not necessarily be subject to the mandatory application of the law of the country of habitual residence of the consumer, as there is a need to ensure uniformity in the terms and conditions of an issuance or an offer. The same rationale should apply with regard to the multilateral systems covered by Article 4(1)(h), in respect of which it should be ensured that the law of the country of habitual residence of the consumer will not interfere with the rules applicable to contracts concluded within those systems or with the operator of such systems.

(29) For the purposes of this Regulation, references to rights and obligations constituting the terms and conditions governing the issuance, offers to the public or public take-over bids of transferable securities and references to the subscription and redemption of units in collective investment undertakings should include the terms governing, inter alia, the allocation of securities or units, rights in the event of over-subscription, withdrawal rights and similar matters in the context of the offer as well as those matters referred to in Articles 10, 11, 12 and 13, thus ensuring that all relevant contractual aspects of an offer binding the issuer or the offeror to the consumer are governed by a single law.

(30) For the purposes of this Regulation, financial instruments and transferable securities are those instruments referred to in Article 4 of Directive 2004/39/EC.

(31) Nothing in this Regulation should prejudice the operation of a formal arrangement designated as a system under Article 2(a) of Directive 98/26/EC of the European Parliament and of the Council of 19 May 1998 on settlement finality in payment and securities settlement systems.[11]

(32) Owing to the particular nature of contracts of carriage and insurance contracts, specific provisions should ensure an adequate level of protection of passengers and policy holders. Therefore, Article 6 should not apply in the context of those particular contracts.

(33) Where an insurance contract not covering a large risk covers more than one risk, at least one of which is situated in a Member State and at least one of which is situated in a third country, the special rules on insurance contracts in this Regulation should apply only to the risk or risks situated in the relevant Member State or Member States.

(34) The rule on individual employment contracts should not prejudice the application of the overriding mandatory provisions of the country to which a worker is posted in accordance with Directive 96/71/EC of the European Parliament and of the Council of 16 December 1996 concerning the posting of workers in the framework of the provision of services.[12]

(35) Employees should not be deprived of the protection afforded to them by provisions which cannot be derogated from by agreement or which can only be derogated from to their benefit.

(36) As regards individual employment contracts, work carried out in another country should be regarded as temporary if the employee is expected to resume working in the country of origin after carrying out his tasks abroad. The conclusion of a new contract of employment with the original employer or an employer belonging to the same group of companies as the original employer should not preclude the employee from being regarded as carrying out his work in another country temporarily.

(37) Considerations of public interest justify giving the courts of the Member States the possibility, in exceptional circumstances, of applying exceptions based on public policy and overriding mandatory provisions. The concept of 'overriding mandatory provisions' should be distinguished from the expression 'provisions which cannot be derogated from by agreement' and should be construed more restrictively.

(38) In the context of voluntary assignment, the term 'relationship' should make it clear that Article 14(1) also applies to the property aspects of an assignment, as between assignor and assignee, in legal orders where such aspects are treated separately from the aspects under the law of obligations. However, the term 'relationship' should not be understood as relating to any relationship that may exist between assignor and assignee. In particular, it should not cover preliminary questions as regards a voluntary assignment or a contractual subrogation. The term should be strictly limited to the aspects which are directly relevant to the voluntary assignment or contractual subrogation in question.

(39) For the sake of legal certainty there should be a clear definition of habitual residence, in particular for companies and other bodies, corporate or unincorporated. Unlike Article 60(1) of Regulation (EC) No 44/2001, which establishes three criteria, the conflict-of-law rule should proceed on the basis of a single criterion; otherwise, the parties would be unable to foresee the law applicable to their situation.

(40) A situation where conflict-of-law rules are dispersed among several instruments and where there are differences between those rules should be avoided. This Regulation, however, should not exclude the possibility of inclusion of conflict-of-law rules relating to contractual obligations in provisions of Community law with regard to particular matters.

This Regulation should not prejudice the application of other instruments laying down provisions designed to contribute to the proper functioning of the internal market in so far as they cannot be applied in conjunction with the law designated by the rules of this Regulation. The application of provisions of the applicable law designated by the rules of this Regulation should not restrict the free movement of goods and services as regulated by Community instruments, such as Directive 2000/31/EC of the European Parliament and of the Council of 8 June 2000 on certain legal aspects of information society services, in particular electronic commerce, in the Internal Market (Directive on electronic commerce).[13]

(41) Respect for international commitments entered into by the Member States means that this Regulation should not affect international conventions to which one or more Member States are parties at the time when this Regulation is adopted. To make the rules more accessible, the Commission should publish the list of the relevant conventions in the *Official Journal of the European Union* on the basis of information supplied by the Member States.

(42) The Commission will make a proposal to the European Parliament and to the Council concerning the procedures and conditions according to which Member States would be entitled to negotiate and conclude, on their own behalf, agreements with third countries in individual and exceptional cases, concerning sectoral matters and containing provisions on the law applicable to contractual obligations.

(43) Since the objective of this Regulation cannot be sufficiently achieved by the Member States and can therefore, by reason of the scale and effects of this Regulation, be better achieved at Community level, the Community may adopt measures, in accordance with the principle of subsidiarity as set out in Article 5 of the Treaty. In accordance with the principle of proportionality, as set out in that Article, this Regulation does not go beyond what is necessary to attain its objective.

(44) In accordance with Article 3 of the Protocol on the position of the United Kingdom and Ireland, annexed to the Treaty on European Union and to the Treaty establishing the European Community, Ireland has notified its wish to take part in the adoption and application of the present Regulation.

(45) In accordance with Articles 1 and 2 of the Protocol on the position of the United Kingdom and Ireland, annexed to the Treaty on European Union and to the Treaty establishing the European Community, and without prejudice to Article 4 of the said Protocol, the United Kingdom is not taking part in the adoption of this Regulation and is not bound by it or subject to its application.

(46) In accordance with Articles 1 and 2 of the Protocol on the position of Denmark, annexed to the Treaty on European Union and to the Treaty establishing the European Community, Denmark is not taking part in the adoption of this Regulation and is not bound by it or subject to its application,

NOTES

1 OJ C318, 23.12.2006, p 56.

2 Opinion of the European Parliament of 29 November 2007 (not yet published in the Official Journal) and Council Decision of 5 June 2008.

3 OJ C12, 15.1.2001, p 1.

4 OJ C53, 3.3.2005, p 1.

5 OJ L12, 16.1.2001, p 1. Regulation as last amended by Regulation (EC) No 1791/2006 (OJ L363, 20.12.2006, p 1).

6 OJ L199, 31.7.2007, p 40.

7 OJ C334, 30.12.2005, p 1.

8 OJ L145, 30.4.2004, p 1. Directive as last amended by Directive 2008/10/EC (OJ L76, 19.3.2008, p 33).

9 OJ L375, 31.12.1985, p 3. Directive as last amended by Directive 2008/18/EC of the European Parliament and of the Council (OJ L76, 19.3.2008, p 42).

10 OJ L280, 29.10.1994, p 83.

11 OJ L166, 11.6.1998, p 45.

12 OJ L18, 21.1.1997, p 1.

13 OJ L178, 17.7.2000, p 1.

HAVE ADOPTED THIS REGULATION:

CHAPTER I
SCOPE

[6098AB]
Article 1
Material scope

1. This Regulation shall apply, in situations involving a conflict of laws, to contractual obligations in civil and commercial matters.

It shall not apply, in particular, to revenue, customs or administrative matters.

2. The following shall be excluded from the scope of this Regulation:

(a) questions involving the status or legal capacity of natural persons, without prejudice to Article 13;

(b) obligations arising out of family relationships and relationships deemed by the law applicable to such relationships to have comparable effects, including maintenance obligations;

(c) obligations arising out of matrimonial property regimes, property regimes of relationships deemed by the law applicable to such relationships to have comparable effects to marriage, and wills and succession;

(d) obligations arising under bills of exchange, cheques and promissory notes and other negotiable instruments to the extent that the obligations under such other negotiable instruments arise out of their negotiable character;

(e) arbitration agreements and agreements on the choice of court;

(f) questions governed by the law of companies and other bodies, corporate or unincorporated, such as the creation, by registration or otherwise, legal capacity, internal organisation or winding-up of companies and other bodies, corporate or unincorporated, and the personal liability of officers and members as such for the obligations of the company or body;

(g) the question whether an agent is able to bind a principal, or an organ to bind a company or other body corporate or unincorporated, in relation to a third party;

(h) the constitution of trusts and the relationship between settlors, trustees and beneficiaries;

(i) obligations arising out of dealings prior to the conclusion of a contract;

(j) insurance contracts arising out of operations carried out by organisations other than undertakings referred to in Article 2 of Directive 2002/83/EC of the European Parliament and of the Council of 5 November 2002 concerning life assurance[1] the object of which is to provide benefits for employed or self-employed persons belonging to an undertaking or group of undertakings, or to a trade or group of trades, in the event of death or survival or of discontinuance or curtailment of activity, or of sickness related to work or accidents at work.

3. This Regulation shall not apply to evidence and procedure, without prejudice to Article 18.

4. In this Regulation, the term 'Member State' shall mean Member States to which this Regulation applies. However, in Article 3(4) and Article 7 the term shall mean all the Member States.

---

[1] OJ L345, 19.12.2002, p 1. Directive as last amended by Directive 2008/19/EC (OJ L76, 19.3.2008, p 44).

[6098AC]
Article 2
Universal application

Any law specified by this Regulation shall be applied whether or not it is the law of a Member State.

CHAPTER II
UNIFORM RULES

[6098AD]
Article 3
Freedom of choice

1. A contract shall be governed by the law chosen by the parties. The choice shall be made expressly or clearly demonstrated by the terms of the contract or the circumstances of the case. By their choice the parties can select the law applicable to the whole or to part only of the contract.

2. The parties may at any time agree to subject the contract to a law other than that which previously governed it, whether as a result of an earlier choice made under this Article or of other provisions of this Regulation. Any change in the law to be applied that is made after the conclusion of the contract shall not prejudice its formal validity under Article 11 or adversely affect the rights of third parties.
3. Where all other elements relevant to the situation at the time of the choice are located in a country other than the country whose law has been chosen, the choice of the parties shall not prejudice the application of provisions of the law of that other country which cannot be derogated from by agreement.
4. Where all other elements relevant to the situation at the time of the choice are located in one or more Member States, the parties' choice of applicable law other than that of a Member State shall not prejudice the application of provisions of Community law, where appropriate as implemented in the Member State of the forum, which cannot be derogated from by agreement.
5. The existence and validity of the consent of the parties as to the choice of the applicable law shall be determined in accordance with the provisions of Articles 10, 11 and 13.

[6098AE]
Article 4
Applicable law in the absence of choice

1. To the extent that the law applicable to the contract has not been chosen in accordance with Article 3 and without prejudice to Articles 5 to 8, the law governing the contract shall be determined as follows:
   (a) a contract for the sale of goods shall be governed by the law of the country where the seller has his habitual residence;
   (b) a contract for the provision of services shall be governed by the law of the country where the service provider has his habitual residence;
   (c) a contract relating to a right in rem in immovable property or to a tenancy of immovable property shall be governed by the law of the country where the property is situated;
   (d) notwithstanding point (c), a tenancy of immovable property concluded for temporary private use for a period of no more than six consecutive months shall be governed by the law of the country where the landlord has his habitual residence, provided that the tenant is a natural person and has his habitual residence in the same country;
   (e) a franchise contract shall be governed by the law of the country where the franchisee has his habitual residence;
   (f) a distribution contract shall be governed by the law of the country where the distributor has his habitual residence;
   (g) a contract for the sale of goods by auction shall be governed by the law of the country where the auction takes place, if such a place can be determined;
   (h) a contract concluded within a multilateral system which brings together or facilitates the bringing together of multiple third-party buying and selling interests in financial instruments, as defined by Article 4(1), point (17) of Directive 2004/39/EC, in accordance with non-discretionary rules and governed by a single law, shall be governed by that law.
2. Where the contract is not covered by paragraph 1 or where the elements of the contract would be covered by more than one of points (a) to (h) of paragraph 1, the contract shall be governed by the law of the country where the party required to effect the characteristic performance of the contract has his habitual residence.
3. Where it is clear from all the circumstances of the case that the contract is manifestly more closely connected with a country other than that indicated in paragraphs 1 or 2, the law of that other country shall apply.
4. Where the law applicable cannot be determined pursuant to paragraphs 1 or 2, the contract shall be governed by the law of the country with which it is most closely connected.

[6098AF]
Article 5
Contracts of carriage

1. To the extent that the law applicable to a contract for the carriage of goods has not been chosen in accordance with Article 3, the law applicable shall be the law of the country of habitual residence of the carrier, provided that the place of receipt or the place of delivery or the habitual residence of the consignor is also situated in that country. If those requirements are not met, the law of the country where the place of delivery as agreed by the parties is situated shall apply.

2. To the extent that the law applicable to a contract for the carriage of passengers has not been chosen by the parties in accordance with the second subparagraph, the law applicable shall be the law of the country where the passenger has his habitual residence, provided that either the place of departure or the place of destination is situated in that country. If these requirements are not met, the law of the country where the carrier has his habitual residence shall apply.

The parties may choose as the law applicable to a contract for the carriage of passengers in accordance with Article 3 only the law of the country where:

(a) the passenger has his habitual residence; or
(b) the carrier has his habitual residence; or
(c) the carrier has his place of central administration; or
(d) the place of departure is situated; or
(e) the place of destination is situated.

3. Where it is clear from all the circumstances of the case that the contract, in the absence of a choice of law, is manifestly more closely connected with a country other than that indicated in paragraphs 1 or 2, the law of that other country shall apply.

[6098AG]
Article 6
Consumer contracts

1. Without prejudice to Articles 5 and 7, a contract concluded by a natural person for a purpose which can be regarded as being outside his trade or profession (the consumer) with another person acting in the exercise of his trade or profession (the professional) shall be governed by the law of the country where the consumer has his habitual residence, provided that the professional:

(a) pursues his commercial or professional activities in the country where the consumer has his habitual residence, or
(b) by any means, directs such activities to that country or to several countries including that country,

and the contract falls within the scope of such activities.

2. Notwithstanding paragraph 1, the parties may choose the law applicable to a contract which fulfils the requirements of paragraph 1, in accordance with Article 3. Such a choice may not, however, have the result of depriving the consumer of the protection afforded to him by provisions that cannot be derogated from by agreement by virtue of the law which, in the absence of choice, would have been applicable on the basis of paragraph 1.

3. If the requirements in points (a) or (b) of paragraph 1 are not fulfilled, the law applicable to a contract between a consumer and a professional shall be determined pursuant to Articles 3 and 4.

4. Paragraphs 1 and 2 shall not apply to:

(a) a contract for the supply of services where the services are to be supplied to the consumer exclusively in a country other than that in which he has his habitual residence;
(b) a contract of carriage other than a contract relating to package travel within the meaning of Council Directive 90/314/EEC of 13 June 1990 on package travel, package holidays and package tours;[1]
(c) a contract relating to a right in rem in immovable property or a tenancy of immovable property other than a contract relating to the right to use immovable properties on a timeshare basis within the meaning of Directive 94/47/EC;
(d) rights and obligations which constitute a financial instrument and rights and obligations constituting the terms and conditions governing the issuance or offer to the public and public take-over bids of transferable securities, and the subscription and redemption of units in collective investment undertakings in so far as these activities do not constitute provision of a financial service;
(e) a contract concluded within the type of system falling within the scope of Article 4(1)(h).

NOTES

[1] OJ L158, 23.6.1990, p 59.

[6098AH]
Article 7
Insurance contracts

1. This Article shall apply to contracts referred to in paragraph 2, whether or not the risk covered is situated in a Member State, and to all other insurance contracts covering risks situated inside the territory of the Member States. It shall not apply to reinsurance contracts.

2. An insurance contract covering a large risk as defined in Article 5(d) of the First Council Directive 73/239/EEC of 24 July 1973 on the coordination of laws, regulations and administrative provisions relating to the taking-up and pursuit of the business of direct insurance other than life assurance[1] shall be governed by the law chosen by the parties in accordance with Article 3 of this Regulation.

To the extent that the applicable law has not been chosen by the parties, the insurance contract shall be governed by the law of the country where the insurer has his habitual residence. Where it is clear from all the circumstances of the case that the contract is manifestly more closely connected with another country, the law of that other country shall apply.

3. In the case of an insurance contract other than a contract falling within paragraph 2, only the following laws may be chosen by the parties in accordance with Article 3:

(a) the law of any Member State where the risk is situated at the time of conclusion of the contract;

(b) the law of the country where the policy holder has his habitual residence;

(c) in the case of life assurance, the law of the Member State of which the policy holder is a national;

(d) for insurance contracts covering risks limited to events occurring in one Member State other than the Member State where the risk is situated, the law of that Member State;

(e) where the policy holder of a contract falling under this paragraph pursues a commercial or industrial activity or a liberal profession and the insurance contract covers two or more risks which relate to those activities and are situated in different Member States, the law of any of the Member States concerned or the law of the country of habitual residence of the policy holder.

Where, in the cases set out in points (a), (b) or (e), the Member States referred to grant greater freedom of choice of the law applicable to the insurance contract, the parties may take advantage of that freedom.

To the extent that the law applicable has not been chosen by the parties in accordance with this paragraph, such a contract shall be governed by the law of the Member State in which the risk is situated at the time of conclusion of the contract.

4. The following additional rules shall apply to insurance contracts covering risks for which a Member State imposes an obligation to take out insurance:

(a) the insurance contract shall not satisfy the obligation to take out insurance unless it complies with the specific provisions relating to that insurance laid down by the Member State that imposes the obligation. Where the law of the Member State in which the risk is situated and the law of the Member State imposing the obligation to take out insurance contradict each other, the latter shall prevail;

(b) by way of derogation from paragraphs 2 and 3, a Member State may lay down that the insurance contract shall be governed by the law of the Member State that imposes the obligation to take out insurance.

5. For the purposes of paragraph 3, third subparagraph, and paragraph 4, where the contract covers risks situated in more than one Member State, the contract shall be considered as constituting several contracts each relating to only one Member State.

6. For the purposes of this Article, the country in which the risk is situated shall be determined in accordance with Article 2(d) of the Second Council Directive 88/357/EEC of 22 June 1988 on the coordination of laws, regulations and administrative provisions relating to direct insurance other than life assurance and laying down provisions to facilitate the effective exercise of freedom to provide services[2] and, in the case of life assurance, the country in which the risk is situated shall be the country of the commitment within the meaning of Article 1(1)(g) of Directive 2002/83/EC.

NOTES

1 OJ L228, 16.8.1973, p 3. Directive as last amended by Directive 2005/68/EC of the European Parliament and of the Council (OJ L323, 9.12.2005, p 1).

2 OJ L172, 4.7.1988, p 1. Directive as last amended by Directive 2005/14/EC of the European Parliament and of the Council (OJ L149, 11.6.2005, p 14).

[6098AI]
Article 8
Individual employment contracts

1. An individual employment contract shall be governed by the law chosen by the parties in accordance with Article 3. Such a choice of law may not, however, have the result of depriving the employee of the protection afforded to him by provisions that cannot be derogated from by agreement under the law that, in the absence of choice, would have been applicable pursuant to paragraphs 2, 3 and 4 of this Article.

2. To the extent that the law applicable to the individual employment contract has not been chosen by the parties, the contract shall be governed by the law of the country in which or, failing that, from which the employee habitually carries out his work in performance of the contract. The country where the work is habitually carried out shall not be deemed to have changed if he is temporarily employed in another country.
3. Where the law applicable cannot be determined pursuant to paragraph 2, the contract shall be governed by the law of the country where the place of business through which the employee was engaged is situated.
4. Where it appears from the circumstances as a whole that the contract is more closely connected with a country other than that indicated in paragraphs 2 or 3, the law of that other country shall apply.

[6098AJ]
Article 9
Overriding mandatory provisions
1. Overriding mandatory provisions are provisions the respect for which is regarded as crucial by a country for safeguarding its public interests, such as its political, social or economic organisation, to such an extent that they are applicable to any situation falling within their scope, irrespective of the law otherwise applicable to the contract under this Regulation.
2. Nothing in this Regulation shall restrict the application of the overriding mandatory provisions of the law of the forum.
3. Effect may be given to the overriding mandatory provisions of the law of the country where the obligations arising out of the contract have to be or have been performed, in so far as those overriding mandatory provisions render the performance of the contract unlawful. In considering whether to give effect to those provisions, regard shall be had to their nature and purpose and to the consequences of their application or non-application.

[6098AK]
Article 10
Consent and material validity
1. The existence and validity of a contract, or of any term of a contract, shall be determined by the law which would govern it under this Regulation if the contract or term were valid.
2. Nevertheless, a party, in order to establish that he did not consent, may rely upon the law of the country in which he has his habitual residence if it appears from the circumstances that it would not be reasonable to determine the effect of his conduct in accordance with the law specified in paragraph 1.

[6098AL]
Article 11
Formal validity
1. A contract concluded between persons who, or whose agents, are in the same country at the time of its conclusion is formally valid if it satisfies the formal requirements of the law which governs it in substance under this Regulation or of the law of the country where it is concluded.
2. A contract concluded between persons who, or whose agents, are in different countries at the time of its conclusion is formally valid if it satisfies the formal requirements of the law which governs it in substance under this Regulation, or of the law of either of the countries where either of the parties or their agent is present at the time of conclusion, or of the law of the country where either of the parties had his habitual residence at that time.
3. A unilateral act intended to have legal effect relating to an existing or contemplated contract is formally valid if it satisfies the formal requirements of the law which governs or would govern the contract in substance under this Regulation, or of the law of the country where the act was done, or of the law of the country where the person by whom it was done had his habitual residence at that time.
4. Paragraphs 1, 2 and 3 of this Article shall not apply to contracts that fall within the scope of Article 6. The form of such contracts shall be governed by the law of the country where the consumer has his habitual residence.
5. Notwithstanding paragraphs 1 to 4, a contract the subject matter of which is a right in rem in immovable property or a tenancy of immovable property shall be subject to the requirements of form of the law of the country where the property is situated if by that law:
   (a) those requirements are imposed irrespective of the country where the contract is concluded and irrespective of the law governing the contract; and
   (b) those requirements cannot be derogated from by agreement.

[6098AM]
Article 12
Scope of the law applicable

1. The law applicable to a contract by virtue of this Regulation shall govern in particular:
   (a) interpretation;
   (b) performance;
   (c) within the limits of the powers conferred on the court by its procedural law, the consequences of a total or partial breach of obligations, including the assessment of damages in so far as it is governed by rules of law;
   (d) the various ways of extinguishing obligations, and prescription and limitation of actions;
   (e) the consequences of nullity of the contract.

2. In relation to the manner of performance and the steps to be taken in the event of defective performance, regard shall be had to the law of the country in which performance takes place.

[6098AN]
Article 13
Incapacity

In a contract concluded between persons who are in the same country, a natural person who would have capacity under the law of that country may invoke his incapacity resulting from the law of another country, only if the other party to the contract was aware of that incapacity at the time of the conclusion of the contract or was not aware thereof as a result of negligence.

[6098AO]
Article 14
Voluntary assignment and contractual subrogation

1. The relationship between assignor and assignee under a voluntary assignment or contractual subrogation of a claim against another person (the debtor) shall be governed by the law that applies to the contract between the assignor and assignee under this Regulation.

2. The law governing the assigned or subrogated claim shall determine its assignability, the relationship between the assignee and the debtor, the conditions under which the assignment or subrogation can be invoked against the debtor and whether the debtor's obligations have been discharged.

3. The concept of assignment in this Article includes outright transfers of claims, transfers of claims by way of security and pledges or other security rights over claims.

[6098AP]
Article 15
Legal subrogation

Where a person (the creditor) has a contractual claim against another (the debtor) and a third person has a duty to satisfy the creditor, or has in fact satisfied the creditor in discharge of that duty, the law which governs the third person's duty to satisfy the creditor shall determine whether and to what extent the third person is entitled to exercise against the debtor the rights which the creditor had against the debtor under the law governing their relationship.

[6098AQ]
Article 16
Multiple liability

If a creditor has a claim against several debtors who are liable for the same claim, and one of the debtors has already satisfied the claim in whole or in part, the law governing the debtor's obligation towards the creditor also governs the debtor's right to claim recourse from the other debtors. The other debtors may rely on the defences they had against the creditor to the extent allowed by the law governing their obligations towards the creditor.

[6098AR]
Article 17
Set-off

Where the right to set-off is not agreed by the parties, set-off shall be governed by the law applicable to the claim against which the right to set-off is asserted.

[6098AS]
Article 18
Burden of proof

1. The law governing a contractual obligation under this Regulation shall apply to the extent that, in matters of contractual obligations, it contains rules which raise presumptions of law or determine the burden of proof.

2. A contract or an act intended to have legal effect may be proved by any mode of proof recognised by the law of the forum or by any of the laws referred to in Article 11 under which that contract or act is formally valid, provided that such mode of proof can be administered by the forum.

CHAPTER III
OTHER PROVISIONS

[6098AT]
Article 19
Habitual residence
1. For the purposes of this Regulation, the habitual residence of companies and other bodies, corporate or unincorporated, shall be the place of central administration.

The habitual residence of a natural person acting in the course of his business activity shall be his principal place of business.

2. Where the contract is concluded in the course of the operations of a branch, agency or any other establishment, or if, under the contract, performance is the responsibility of such a branch, agency or establishment, the place where the branch, agency or any other establishment is located shall be treated as the place of habitual residence.

3. For the purposes of determining the habitual residence, the relevant point in time shall be the time of the conclusion of the contract.

[6098AU]
Article 20
Exclusion of *renvoi*
The application of the law of any country specified by this Regulation means the application of the rules of law in force in that country other than its rules of private international law, unless provided otherwise in this Regulation.

[6098AV]
Article 21
Public policy of the forum
The application of a provision of the law of any country specified by this Regulation may be refused only if such application is manifestly incompatible with the public policy (*ordre public*) of the forum.

[6098AW]
Article 22
States with more than one legal system
1. Where a State comprises several territorial units, each of which has its own rules of law in respect of contractual obligations, each territorial unit shall be considered as a country for the purposes of identifying the law applicable under this Regulation.

2. A Member State where different territorial units have their own rules of law in respect of contractual obligations shall not be required to apply this Regulation to conflicts solely between the laws of such units.

[6098AX]
Article 23
Relationship with other provisions of Community law
With the exception of Article 7, this Regulation shall not prejudice the application of provisions of Community law which, in relation to particular matters, lay down conflict-of-law rules relating to contractual obligations.

[6098AY]
Article 24
Relationship with the Rome Convention
1. This Regulation shall replace the Rome Convention in the Member States, except as regards the territories of the Member States which fall within the territorial scope of that Convention and to which this Regulation does not apply pursuant to Article 299 of the Treaty.

2. In so far as this Regulation replaces the provisions of the Rome Convention, any reference to that Convention shall be understood as a reference to this Regulation.

[6098AZ]
Article 25
Relationship with existing international conventions

1. This Regulation shall not prejudice the application of international conventions to which one or more Member States are parties at the time when this Regulation is adopted and which lay down conflict-of-law rules relating to contractual obligations.

2. However, this Regulation shall, as between Member States, take precedence over conventions concluded exclusively between two or more of them in so far as such conventions concern matters governed by this Regulation.

[6098BA]
Article 26
List of Conventions

1. By 17 June 2009, Member States shall notify the Commission of the conventions referred to in Article 25(1). After that date, Member States shall notify the Commission of all denunciations of such conventions.

2. Within six months of receipt of the notifications referred to in paragraph 1, the Commission shall publish in the *Official Journal of the European Union*:

(a) a list of the conventions referred to in paragraph 1;
(b) the denunciations referred to in paragraph 1.

[6098BB]
Article 27
Review clause

1. By 17 June 2013, the Commission shall submit to the European Parliament, the Council and the European Economic and Social Committee a report on the application of this Regulation. If appropriate, the report shall be accompanied by proposals to amend this Regulation. The report shall include:

(a) a study on the law applicable to insurance contracts and an assessment of the impact of the provisions to be introduced, if any; and
(b) an evaluation on the application of Article 6, in particular as regards the coherence of Community law in the field of consumer protection.

2. By 17 June 2010, the Commission shall submit to the European Parliament, the Council and the European Economic and Social Committee a report on the question of the effectiveness of an assignment or subrogation of a claim against third parties and the priority of the assigned or subrogated claim over a right of another person. The report shall be accompanied, if appropriate, by a proposal to amend this Regulation and an assessment of the impact of the provisions to be introduced.

[6098BC]
Article 28
Application in time

This Regulation shall apply to contracts concluded after 17 December 2009.

CHAPTER IV
FINAL PROVISIONS

[6098BD]
Article 29
Entry into force and application

This Regulation shall enter into force on the 20th day following its publication in the *Official Journal of the European Union*.

It shall apply from 17 December 2009 except for Article 26 which shall apply from 17 June 2009.

This Regulation shall be binding in its entirety and directly applicable in the Member States in accordance with the Treaty establishing the European Community.

Done at Strasbourg, 17 June 2008.

B. REGULATION AND SOLVENCY

COUNCIL REGULATION

(1534/91/EEC)
of 31 May 1991

on the application of Article 85(3) of the Treaty to certain categories of agreements, decisions and concerted practices in the insurance sector

NOTES
Date of publication in OJ: OJ L143, 7.6.91, p 1.

[6099]
THE COUNCIL OF THE EUROPEAN COMMUNITIES,

Having regard to the Treaty establishing the European Economic Community, and in particular Article 87 thereof,

Having regard to the proposal from the Commission,[1]

Having regard to the opinion of the European Parliament,[2]

Having regard to the opinion of the Economic and Social Committee,[3]

Whereas Article 85(1) of the Treaty may, in accordance with Article 85(3), be declared inapplicable to categories of agreements, decisions and concerted practices which satisfy the requirements of Article 85(3);

Whereas the detailed rules for the application of Article 85(3) of the Treaty must be adopted by way of a Regulation based on Article 87 of the Treaty;

Whereas cooperation between undertakings in the insurance sector is, to a certain extent, desirable to ensure the proper functioning of this sector and may at the same time promote consumers' interests;

Whereas the application of Council Regulation (EEC) No 4064/89 of 21 December 1989 on the control of concentrations between undertakings[4] enables the Commission to exercise close supervision on issues arising from concentrations in all sectors, including the insurance sector;

Whereas exemptions granted under Article 85(3) of the Treaty cannot themselves affect Community and national provisions safeguarding consumers' interests in this sector;

Whereas agreements, decisions and concerted practices serving such aims may, in so far as they fall within the prohibition contained in Article 85(1) of the Treaty, be exempted therefrom under certain conditions; whereas this applies in particular to agreements, decisions and concerted practices relating to the establishment of common risk premium tariffs based on collectively ascertained statistics or the number of claims, the establishment of standard policy conditions, common coverage of certain types of risks, the settlement of claims, the testing and acceptance of security devices, and registers of, and information on, aggravated risks;

Whereas in view of the large number of notifications submitted pursuant to Council Regulation No 17 of 6 February 1962: First Regulation implementing Articles 85 and 86 of the Treaty,[5] as last amended by the Act of Accession of Spain and Portugal, it is desirable that in order to facilitate the Commission's task, it should be enabled to declare, by way of Regulation, that the provisions of Article 85(1) of the Treaty are inapplicable to certain categories of agreements, decisions and concerted practices;

Whereas it should be laid down under which conditions the Commission, in close and constant liaison with the competent authorities of the Member States, may exercise such powers;

Whereas, in the exercise of such powers, the Commission will take account not only of the risk of competition being eliminated in a substantial part of the relevant market and of any benefit that might be conferred on policyholders resulting from the agreements, but also of the risk which the proliferation of restrictive clauses and the operation of accommodation companies would entail for policyholders;

Whereas the keeping of registers and the handling of information on aggravated risks should be carried out subject to the proper protection of confidentiality;

Whereas, under Article 6 of Regulation No 17, the Commission may provide that a decision taken in accordance with Article 85(3) of the Treaty shall apply with retroactive effect; whereas the Commission should also be able to adopt provisions to such effect in a Regulation;

Whereas, under Article 7 of Regulation No 17, agreements, decisions and concerted practices may, by decision of the Commission, be exempted from prohibition, in particular if they are modified in such manner that they satisfy the requirements of Article 85(3) of the Treaty; whereas it is desirable that the Commission be enabled to grant by Regulation like exemption to such agreements, decisions and concerted practices if they are modified in such manner as to fall within a category defined in an exempting Regulation;

Whereas it cannot be ruled out that, in specific cases, the conditions set out in Article 85(3) of the Treaty may not be fulfilled; whereas the Commission must have the power to regulate such cases pursuant to Regulation No 17 by way of a Decision having effect for the future,

NOTES

1 OJ C16, 23.1.90, p 13.

2 OJ C260, 15.10.90, p 57.

3 OJ C182, 23.7.90, p 27.

4 OJ L395, 30.12.89, p 1.

5 OJ 13, 21.2.62, p 204/62.

HAS ADOPTED THIS REGULATION—

[6100]
Article 1

1. Without prejudice to the application of Regulation No 17, the Commission may, by means of a Regulation and in accordance with Article 85(3) of the Treaty, declare that Article 85(1) shall not apply to categories of agreements between undertakings, decisions of associations of undertakings and concerted practices in the insurance sector which have as their object cooperation with respect to—

(a) the establishment of common risk premium tariffs based on collectively ascertained statistics or the number of claims;
(b) the establishment of common standard policy conditions;
(c) the common coverage of certain types of risks;
(d) the settlement of claims;
(e) the testing and acceptance of security devices;
(f) registers of, and information on, aggravated risks, provided that the keeping of these registers and the handling of this information is carried out subject to the proper protection of confidentiality.

2. The Commission Regulation referred to in paragraph 1, shall define the categories of agreements, decisions and concerted practices to which it applies and shall specify in particular—

(a) the restrictions or clauses which may, or may not, appear in the agreements, decisions and concerted practices;
(b) the clauses which must be contained in the agreements, decisions and concerted practices or the other conditions which must be satisfied.

[6101]
Article 2

Any Regulation adopted pursuant to Article 1 shall be of limited duration.

It may be repealed or amended where circumstances have changed with respect to any of the facts which were essential to its being adopted; in such case, a period shall be fixed for modification of the agreements, decisions and concerted practices to which the earlier Regulation applies.

[6102]
Article 3

A Regulation adopted pursuant to Article 1 may provide that it shall apply with retroactive effect to agreements, decisions and concerted practices to which, at the date of entry into force of the said Regulation, a Decision taken with retroactive effect pursuant to Article 6 of Regulation No 17 would have applied.

[6103]
Article 4

1. A Regulation adopted pursuant to Article 1 may provide that the prohibition contained in Article 85(1) of the Treaty shall not apply, for such period as shall be fixed in that Regulation, to agreements, decisions and concerted practices already in existence on 13 March 1962 which do not satisfy the conditions of Article 85(3) where—

— within six months from the entry into force of the said Regulation, they are so modified as to satisfy the said conditions in accordance with the provisions of the said Regulation and

— the modifications are brought to the notice of the Commission within the time limit fixed by the said Regulation.

The provisions of the first subparagraph shall apply in the same way to those agreements, decisions and concerted practices existing at the date of accession of new Member States to which Article 85(1) of the Treaty applies by virtue of accession and which do not satisfy the conditions of Article 85(3).

2. Paragraph 1 shall apply to agreements, decisions and concerted practices which had to be notified before 1 February 1963, in accordance with Article 5 of Regulation No 17, only where they have been so notified before that date.

Paragraph 1 shall not apply to agreements, decisions and concerted practices existing at the date of accession of new Member States to which Article 85(1) of the Treaty applies by virtue of accession and which had to be notified within six months from the date of accession in accordance with Articles 5 and 25 of Regulation No 17, unless they have been so notified within the said period.

3. The benefit of provisions adopted pursuant to paragraph 1 may not be invoked in actions pending at the date of entry into force of a Regulation adopted pursuant to Article 1; neither may it be invoked as grounds for claims for damages against third parties.

[6104]
Article 5

Where the Commission proposes to adopt a Regulation, it shall publish a draft thereof to enable all persons and organisations concerned to submit to it their comments within such time limit, being not less than one month, as it shall fix.

[6105]
Article 6

1. The Commission shall consult the Advisory Committee on Restrictive Practices and Monopolies—

(a) before publishing a draft Regulation;

(b) before adopting a Regulation.

2. Article 10(5) and (6) of Regulation No 17, relating to consultation of the Advisory Committee, shall apply. However, joint meetings with the Commission shall take place not earlier than one month after dispatch of the notice convening them.

Article 7 (*Repealed by Council Regulation 1/2003/EC, art 40.*)

[6106]
Article 8

Not later than six years after the entry into force of the Commission Regulation provided for in Article 1, the Commission shall submit to the European Parliament and the Council a report on the functioning of this Regulation, accompanied by such proposals for amendments to this Regulation as may appear necessary in the light of experience.

This Regulation shall be binding in its entirety and directly applicable in all Member States.

Done at Brussels, 31 May 1991.

DIRECTIVE OF THE EUROPEAN PARLIAMENT AND OF THE COUNCIL

(98/78/EC)

of 27 October 1998

[on the supplementary supervision of insurance and reinsurance undertakings in an insurance or reinsurance group]

NOTES

Date of publication in OJ: OJ L330, 5.12.98, p 1.

Title: substituted by European Parliament and Council Directive 2005/68/EC, art 59(1).

This Directive is repealed by European Parliament and Council Directive 2009/138/EC on the taking-up and pursuit of the business of Insurance and Reinsurance (Solvency II) at **[6153]** et seq, with effect from 1 November 2012 (see art 310 thereof at **[6462]**).

[6107]

THE EUROPEAN PARLIAMENT AND THE COUNCIL OF THE EUROPEAN UNION,

Having regard to the Treaty establishing the European Community, and in particular Article 57(2) thereof,

Having regard to the proposal from the Commission,[1]

Having regard to the opinion of the Economic and Social Committee,[2]

Acting in accordance with the procedure laid down in Article 189b of the Treaty,[3]

(1) Whereas the first Council Directive 73/239/EEC of 24 July 1973 on the coordination of laws, regulations and administrative provisions relating to the taking up and pursuit of the business of direct insurance other than life assurance[4] *and the first Council Directive 79/267/EEC of 5 March 1979 on the coordination of laws, regulations and administrative provisions relating to the taking up and pursuit of the business of direct life assurance*[5] *require insurance undertakings to have solvency margins;*

(2) Whereas, under Council Directive 92/49/EEC of 18 June 1992 on the coordination of laws, regulations and administrative provisions relating to direct insurance other than life assurance and amending Directives 73/239/EEC and 88/357/EEC[6] *and Council Directive 92/96/EEC of 10 November 1992 on the coordination of laws, regulations and administrative provisions relating to direct life assurance and amending Directives 79/267/EEC and 90/619/EEC*[7] *the taking up and the pursuit of the business of insurance are subject to the granting of a single official authorisation issued by the authorities of the Member State in which an insurance undertaking has its registered office (home Member State); whereas such authorisation allows an undertaking to carry on business throughout the Community, under either the right of establishment or the freedom to provide services; whereas the competent authorities of home Member States are responsible for monitoring the financial health of insurance undertakings, including their solvency;*

(3) Whereas measures concerning the supplementary supervision of insurance undertakings in an insurance group should enable the authorities supervising an insurance undertaking to form a more soundly based judgment of its financial situation; whereas such supplementary supervision should take into account certain undertakings which are not at present subject to supervision under Community Directives; whereas this Directive does not in any way imply that Member States are required to undertake supervision of those undertakings considered individually;

(4) Whereas insurance undertakings in a common insurance market engage in direct competition with each other and the rules concerning capital requirements must therefore be equivalent; whereas, to that end, the criteria applied to determine supplementary supervision must not be left solely to the discretion of Member States; whereas the adoption of common basic rules will be in the best interests of the Community in that it will prevent distortions of competition; whereas it is necessary to eliminate certain divergences between the laws of the Member States as regards the prudential rules to which insurance undertakings that are part of an insurance group are subject;

(5) Whereas the approach adopted consists in bringing about such harmonisation as is essential, necessary and sufficient to achieve the mutual recognition of prudential control systems in this field; whereas the aim of this Directive is in particular to protect the interests of insured persons;

(6) Whereas certain provisions of this Directive define minimum standards; whereas a home Member State may lay down stricter rules for insurance undertakings authorised by its own competent authorities;

(7) Whereas this Directive provides for the supplementary supervision of any insurance company which is a participating undertaking in at least one insurance undertaking, reinsurance undertaking or non-member-country insurance undertaking and, under different rules, for the supplementary supervision of any insurance company whose parent undertaking is an insurance holding company, a reinsurance undertaking, a non-member-country insurance undertaking or a mixed-activity insurance holding company; whereas the supervision of individual insurance undertakings by the competent authorities remains the essential principle of insurance supervision;

(8) Whereas it is necessary to calculate an adjusted solvency situation for insurance undertakings forming part of an insurance group; whereas different methods are applied by the competent authorities in the Community to take into account the effects on the financial situation of an insurance undertaking attributable to the fact that it belongs to an insurance group; whereas this Directive lays down three methods to effect that calculation; whereas the principle is accepted that these methods are prudentially equivalent;

(9) Whereas the solvency of a related subsidiary insurance undertaking of an insurance holding company, reinsurance undertaking or non-member-country insurance undertaking may be affected by the financial resources of the group of which it is a part and by the distribution of financial resources within that group; whereas the competent authorities should be provided with the means of exercising supplementary supervision and of taking appropriate measures at the level of the insurance undertaking where its solvency is or may be jeopardised;

(10) Whereas the competent authorities should have access to all the information relevant to the exercise of supplementary supervision; whereas cooperation between the authorities responsible for the supervision of insurance undertakings as well as between those authorities and the authorities responsible for the supervision of other financial sectors should be established;

(11) Whereas intra-group transactions can affect the financial position of an insurance under-

taking; whereas the competent authorities should be in a position to exercise general supervision over certain types of such intra-group operations and take appropriate measures at the level of the insurance undertaking where its solvency is or may be jeopardised,

NOTES

Repealed as noted at the beginning of this Directive.

1 OJ C341, 19.12.1995, p 16, and OJ C108, 7.4.1998, p 48.

2 OJ C174, 17.6.1996, p 16.

3 Opinion of the European Parliament of 23 October 1997 (OJ C339, 10.11.1997, p 136), Council common position of 30 March 1998 (OJ C204, 30.6.1998, p 1), Decision of the European Parliament of 16 September 1998 (OJ C313, 12.10.1998) and Council Decision of 13 October 1998.

4 OJ L228, 16.8.1973, p 3. Directive as last amended by Directive 95/26/EC (OJ L168, 18.7.1995, p 7).

5 OJ L63, 13.3.1979, p 1. Directive as last amended by Directive 95/26/EC.

6 OJ L228, 11.8.1992, p 1. Directive as amended by Directive 95/26/EC.

7 OJ L360, 9.12.1992, p 1. Directive as amended by Directive 95/26/EC.

HAVE ADOPTED THIS DIRECTIVE—

[6108]
Article 1
Definitions

For the purposes of this Directive—

(a) *insurance undertaking means an undertaking which has received official authorisation in accordance with Article 6 of Directive 73/239/EEC or Article 6 of Directive 79/267/EEC;*

(b) *non-member-country insurance undertaking means an undertaking which would require authorisation in accordance with Article 6 of Directive 73/239/EEC or Article 6 of Directive 79/267/EEC if it had its registered office in the Community;*

[(c) *reinsurance undertaking means an undertaking, which has received official authorisation in accordance with Article 3 of Directive 2005/68/EC of the European Parliament and of the Council of 16 November 2005 on reinsurance;*[1]]

(d) *parent undertaking means a parent undertaking within the meaning of Article 1 of Directive 83/349/EEC*[2] *and any undertaking which, in the opinion of the competent authorities, effectively exercises a dominant influence over another undertaking;*

(e) *subsidiary undertaking means a subsidiary undertaking within the meaning of Article 1 of Directive 83/349/EEC and any undertaking over which, in the opinion of the competent authorities, a parent undertaking effectively exercises a dominant influence. All subsidiaries of subsidiary undertakings shall also be considered subsidiaries of the parent undertaking which is at the head of those undertakings;*

(f) *participation means participation within the meaning of Article 17, first sentence, of Directive 78/660/EEC*[3] *or the holding, directly or indirectly, of 20% or more of the voting rights or capital of an undertaking;*

[(g) *participating undertaking shall mean an undertaking which is either a parent undertaking or other undertaking which holds a participation, or an undertaking linked with another undertaking by a relationship within the meaning of Article 12(1) of Directive 83/349/EEC;*

(h) *related undertaking shall mean either a subsidiary or other undertaking in which a participation is held, or an undertaking linked with another undertaking by a relationship within the meaning of Article 12(1) of Directive 83/349/EEC;*]

[(i) *insurance holding company means a parent undertaking, the main business of which is to acquire and hold participations in subsidiary undertakings, where those subsidiary undertakings are exclusively or mainly insurance undertakings, reinsurance undertakings or non-member country insurance undertakings or non-member country reinsurance undertakings, at least one of such subsidiary undertakings being an insurance undertaking, or a reinsurance undertaking and which is not a mixed financial holding company within the meaning of Directive 2002/87/EC of the European Parliament and of the Council of 16 December 2002 on the supplementary supervision of credit institutions, insurance undertakings and investment firms in a financial conglomerate;*[4]

(j) *mixed-activity insurance holding company means a parent undertaking, other than an insurance undertaking, a non-member country insurance undertaking, a reinsurance undertaking, a non-member country reinsurance undertaking, an insurance holding*

Part VI European Materials

company or a mixed financial holding company within the meaning of Directive 2002/87/EC, which includes at least one insurance undertaking or a reinsurance undertaking among its subsidiary undertakings;

(k) *competent authorities means the national authorities which are empowered by law or regulation to supervise insurance undertakings or reinsurance undertakings;]*

[(l) *non-member country reinsurance undertaking means an undertaking which would require authorisation in accordance with Article 3 of Directive 2005/68/EC if it had its head office in the Community.]*

NOTES

Repealed as noted at the beginning of this Directive.

Paras (c), (i)–(k) substituted and para (l) added by European Parliament and Council Directive 2005/68/EC, art 59(2); paras (g), (h) substituted by European Parliament and Council Directive 2002/87/EC, art 28(1).

1 OJ L323, 9.12.2005, p 1.

2 Seventh Council Directive 83/349/EEC of 13 June 1983 based on Article 54(3)(g) of the Treaty on consolidated accounts (OJ L193, 18.7.1983, p 1). Directive as last amended by the 1994 Act of Accession.

3 Fourth Council Directive 78/660/EEC of 25 July 1978 based on Article 54(3)(g) of the Treaty on the annual accounts of certain types of companies (OJ L222, 14.8.1978, p 11). Directive as last amended by the 1994 Act of Accession.

4 OJ L35, 11.2.2003, p 1. Directive as amended by Directive 2005/1/EC (OJ L79, 24.3.2005, p 9).

[6109]

[Article 2

Cases of application of supplementary supervision of insurance undertakings and reinsurance undertakings

1. In addition to the provisions of Directive 73/239/EEC, Directive 2002/83/EC of the European Parliament and of the Council of 5 November 2002 concerning life assurance[1] and Directive 2005/68/EC, which lay down the rules for the supervision of insurance undertakings and reinsurance undertakings, Member States shall provide supervision of any insurance undertaking or any reinsurance undertaking, which is a participating undertaking in at least one insurance undertaking, reinsurance undertaking, non-member-country insurance undertaking or non-member country reinsurance undertaking, shall be supplemented in the manner prescribed in Articles 5, 6, 8 and 9 of this Directive.

2. Every insurance undertaking or reinsurance undertaking the parent undertaking of which is an insurance holding company, a non-member country insurance or a non-member country reinsurance undertaking shall be subject to supplementary supervision in the manner prescribed in Articles 5(2), 6, 8 and 10.

3. Every insurance undertaking or reinsurance undertaking the parent undertaking of which is a mixed-activity insurance holding company shall be subject to supplementary supervision in the manner prescribed in Articles 5(2), 6 and 8.]

NOTES

Substituted, together with arts 3, 4, by European Parliament and Council Directive 2005/68/EC, art 59(3).
Repealed as noted at the beginning of this Directive.

1 OJ L345, 19.12.2002, p 1. Directive as last amended by Directive 2005/1/EC.

[6110]

[Article 3

Scope of supplementary supervision

1. The exercise of supplementary supervision in accordance with Article 2 shall in no way imply that the competent authorities are required to play a supervisory role in relation to the non-member country insurance undertaking, the non-member country reinsurance undertaking, insurance holding company or mixed-activity insurance holding company taken individually.

2. The supplementary supervision shall take into account the following undertakings referred to in Articles 5, 6, 8, 9 and 10:

- *related undertakings of the insurance undertaking or of the reinsurance undertaking,*
- *participating undertakings in the insurance undertaking or in the reinsurance undertaking,*
- *related undertakings of a participating undertaking in the insurance undertaking or in the reinsurance undertaking.*

3. Member States may decide not to take into account in the supplementary supervision referred to in Article 2 undertakings having their registered office in a non-member country where there are legal impediments to the transfer of the necessary information, without prejudice to the provisions of Annex I, point 2.5, and of Annex II, point 4.

Furthermore, the competent authorities responsible for exercising supplementary supervision may in the cases listed below decide on a case-by-case basis not to take an undertaking into account in the supplementary supervision referred to in Article 2:

- *if the undertaking which should be included is of negligible interest with respect to the objectives of the supplementary supervision of insurance undertakings or reinsurance undertakings;*
- *if the inclusion of the financial situation of the undertaking would be inappropriate or misleading with respect to the objectives of the supplementary supervision of insurance undertakings or reinsurance undertakings.]*

NOTES

Substituted as noted to art 2 at **[6109]**.

Repealed as noted at the beginning of this Directive.

[6111]
[Article 4
Competent authorities for exercising supplementary supervision

1. Supplementary supervision shall be exercised by the competent authorities of the Member State in which the insurance undertaking or the reinsurance undertaking has received official authorisation under Article 6 of Directive 73/239/EEC or Article 4 of Directive 2002/83/EC or Article 3 of Directive 2005/68/EC.

2. Where insurance undertakings or reinsurance undertakings authorised in two or more Member States have as their parent undertaking the same insurance holding company, non-member country insurance undertaking, non-member country reinsurance undertaking or mixed-activity insurance holding company, the competent authorities of the Member States concerned may reach agreement as to which of them will be responsible for exercising supplementary supervision.

3. Where a Member State has more than one competent authority for the prudential supervision of insurance undertakings and reinsurance undertakings, such Member State shall take the requisite measures to organise coordination between those authorities.]

NOTES

Substituted as noted to art 2 at **[6109]**.

Repealed as noted at the beginning of this Directive.

[6112]
Article 5
Availability and quality of information

[1. Member States shall prescribe that the competent authorities are to require that every insurance undertaking or reinsurance undertaking subject to supplementary supervision shall have adequate internal control mechanisms in place for the production of any data and information relevant for the purposes of such supplementary supervision.]

2. Member States shall take the appropriate steps to ensure that there are no legal impediments within their jurisdiction preventing the undertakings that are subject to the supplementary supervision and their related undertakings and participating undertakings from exchanging among themselves any information relevant for the purposes of such supplementary supervision.

NOTES

Repealed as noted at the beginning of this Directive.

Para 1: substituted by European Parliament and Council Directive 2005/68/EC, art 59(4).

[6113]
[Article 6
Access to information

1. Member States shall provide that their competent authorities responsible for exercising supplementary supervision are to have access to any information which would be relevant for the purpose of supervision of an insurance undertaking or a reinsurance undertaking subject to such supplementary supervision. The competent authorities may address themselves directly to the relevant undertakings referred to in Article 3(2) to obtain the necessary information only if such information has been requested from the insurance undertaking or the reinsurance undertaking and has not been supplied by it.

2. Member States shall provide that their competent authorities may carry out within their territory, themselves or through the intermediary of persons whom they appoint for that purpose, on-the-spot verification of the information referred to in paragraph 1 at:

- *the insurance undertaking subject to supplementary supervision,*
- *the reinsurance undertaking subject to supplementary supervision,*
- *subsidiary undertakings of that insurance undertaking,*
- *subsidiary undertakings of that reinsurance undertaking,*
- *parent undertakings of that insurance undertaking,*
- *parent undertakings of that reinsurance undertaking,*
- *subsidiary undertakings of a parent undertaking of that insurance undertaking.*
- *subsidiary undertakings of a parent undertaking of that reinsurance undertaking.*

3. Where, in applying this Article, the competent authorities of one Member State wish in specific cases to verify important information concerning an undertaking situated in another Member State which is a related insurance undertaking, a related reinsurance undertaking, a subsidiary undertaking, a parent undertaking or a subsidiary of a parent undertaking of the insurance undertaking or of the reinsurance undertaking subject to supplementary supervision, they must ask the competent authorities of that other Member State to have that verification carried out. The authorities which receive such a request must act on it within the limits of their jurisdiction by carrying out the verification themselves, by allowing the authorities making the request to carry it out or by allowing an auditor or expert to carry it out.

The competent authority which made the request may, if it so wishes, participate in the verification when it does not carry out the verification itself.]

NOTES

Substituted, together with arts 7, 8, by European Parliament and Council Directive 2005/68/EC, art 59(5).

Repealed as noted at the beginning of this Directive.

[6114]
[Article 7
Cooperation between competent authorities

1. Where insurance undertakings or reinsurance undertakings established in different Member States are directly or indirectly related or have a common participating undertaking, the competent authorities of each Member State shall communicate to one another on request all relevant information which may allow or facilitate the exercise of supervision pursuant to this Directive and shall communicate on their own initiative any information which appears to them to be essential for the other competent authorities.

2. Where an insurance undertaking or a reinsurance undertaking and either a credit institution as defined in Directive 2000/12/EC of the European Parliament and of the Council of 20 March 2000 relating to the taking up and pursuit of the business of credit institutions[1] or an investment firm as defined in Council Directive 93/22/EEC of 10 May 1993 on investment services in the securities field,[2] or both, are directly or indirectly related or have a common participating undertaking, the competent authorities and the authorities with public responsibility for the supervision of those other undertakings shall cooperate closely. Without prejudice to their respective responsibilities, those authorities shall provide one another with any information likely to simplify their task, in particular within the framework of this Directive.

3. Information received pursuant to this Directive and, in particular, any exchange of information between competent authorities which is provided for in this Directive shall be subject to the obligation of professional secrecy defined in Article 16 of Council Directive 92/49/EEC of 18 June 1992 on the coordination of laws, regulations and administrative provisions relating to direct insurance other than life assurance (third non-life insurance Directive)[3] and Article 16 of Directive 2002/83/EC and Articles 24 to 30 of Directive 2005/68/EC.]

NOTES

Substituted as noted to art 6 at **[6113]**.

Repealed as noted at the beginning of this Directive.

[1] OJ L126, 26.5.2000, p 1. Directive as last amended by Directive 2005/1/EC.

[2] OJ L141, 11.6.1993, p 27. Directive as last amended by Directive 2002/87/EC.

[3] OJ L228, 11.8.1992, p 1. Directive as last amended by Directive 2005/1/EC.

[6115]
[Article 8
Intra-group transactions

1. Member States shall provide that the competent authorities exercise general supervision over transactions between:

(a) an insurance undertaking or a reinsurance undertaking and:
(i) a related undertaking of the insurance undertaking or of the reinsurance undertaking;
(ii) a participating undertaking in the insurance undertaking or in the reinsurance undertaking;
(iii) a related undertaking of a participating undertaking in the insurance undertaking or in the reinsurance undertaking;

(b) an insurance undertaking or a reinsurance undertaking and a natural person who holds a participation in:
(i) the insurance undertaking, the reinsurance undertaking or any of its related undertakings;
(ii) a participating undertaking in the insurance undertaking or in the reinsurance undertaking;
(iii) a related undertaking of a participating undertaking in the insurance undertaking or in the reinsurance undertaking.

These transactions concern in particular:

— *loans,*
— *guarantees and off-balance-sheet transactions,*
— *elements eligible for the solvency margin,*
— *investments,*
— *reinsurance and retrocession operations,*
— *agreements to share costs.*

2. Member States shall require insurance undertakings and reinsurance undertakings to have in place adequate risk management processes and internal control mechanisms, including sound reporting and accounting procedures, in order to identify, measure, monitor and control transactions as provided for in paragraph 1 appropriately. Member States shall also require at least annual reporting by insurance undertakings and reinsurance undertakings to the competent authorities of significant transactions. These processes and mechanisms shall be subject to overview by the competent authorities.

If, on the basis of this information, it appears that the solvency of the insurance undertaking or the reinsurance undertaking is, or may be, jeopardised, the competent authority shall take appropriate measures at the level of the insurance undertaking or of the reinsurance undertaking.]

NOTES

Substituted as noted to art 6 at **[6113]**.
Repealed as noted at the beginning of this Directive.

[6116]
Article 9
Adjusted solvency requirement

1. In the case referred to in Article 2(1), Member States shall require that an adjusted solvency calculation be carried out in accordance with Annex I.

2. Any related undertaking, participating undertaking or related undertaking of a participating undertaking shall be included in the calculation referred to in paragraph 1.

[3. If the calculation referred to in paragraph 1 demonstrates that the adjusted solvency is negative, the competent authorities shall take appropriate measures at the level of the insurance undertaking or the reinsurance undertaking in question.]

NOTES

Repealed as noted at the beginning of this Directive.
Para 3: substituted by European Parliament and Council Directive 2005/68/EC, art 59(6).

[6117]
Article 10
[Insurance holding companies, non-member country insurance undertakings and non-member country reinsurance undertakings]

1. In the case referred to in Article 2(2), Member States shall require the method of supplementary supervision to be applied in accordance with Annex II.

[2. In the case referred to in Article 2(2), the calculation shall include all related undertakings of the insurance holding company, the non-member country insurance undertaking or the non-member country reinsurance undertaking, in the manner provided for in Annex II.

3. If, on the basis of that calculation, the competent authorities conclude that the solvency of a subsidiary insurance undertaking or a reinsurance undertaking of the insurance holding company, the non-member country insurance undertaking or the non-member country reinsurance undertaking is, or may be, jeopardised, they shall take appropriate measures at the level of that insurance undertaking or reinsurance undertaking.]

NOTES

Repealed as noted at the beginning of this Directive.

Heading: substituted by European Parliament and Council Directive 2005/68/EC, art 59(7)(a).

Paras 2, 3: substituted by European Parliament and Council Directive 2005/68/EC, art 59(7)(b).

[6118]

[Article 10a

Cooperation with third countries' competent authorities

1. The Commission may submit proposals to the Council, either at the request of a Member State or on its own initiative, for the negotiation of agreements with one or more third countries regarding the means of exercising supplementary supervision over—

- *(a) insurance undertakings which have, as participating undertakings, undertakings within the meaning of Article 2 which have their head office situated in a third country; and*
- *[(b) reinsurance undertakings which have, as participating undertakings, undertakings within the meaning of Article 2 which have their head office situated in a third country;*
- *(c) non-member country insurance undertakings or non-member country reinsurance undertakings which have, as participating undertakings, undertakings within the meaning of Article 2 which have their head office in the Community.]*

[2. The agreements referred to in paragraph 1 shall in particular seek to ensure both—

- *(a) that the competent authorities of the Member States are able to obtain the information necessary for the supplementary supervision of insurance undertakings and reinsurance undertakings which have their head office in the Community and which have subsidiaries or hold participations in undertakings outside the Community; and*
- *(b) that the competent authorities of third countries are able to obtain the information necessary for the supplementary supervision of insurance undertakings and reinsurance undertakings which have their head office in their territories and which have subsidiaries or hold participations in undertakings in one or more Member States.]*

[3. Without prejudice to Article 300(1) and (2) of the Treaty, the Commission shall, with the assistance of the European Insurance and Occupational Pensions Committee, examine the outcome of the negotiations referred to in paragraph 1 and the resulting situation.]]

NOTES

Inserted, together with art 10b, by European Parliament and Council Directive 2002/87/EC, art 28(4).

Repealed as noted at the beginning of this Directive.

Para 1: words in square brackets substituted by European Parliament and Council Directive 2005/68/EC, art 59(8)(a).

Para 2: substituted by European Parliament and Council Directive 2005/68/EC, art 59(8)(b).

Para 3: substituted by European Parliament and Council Directive 2005/1/EC, art 7(1).

[6119]

[Article 10b

Management body of insurance holding companies

The Member States shall require that persons who effectively direct the business of an insurance holding company are of sufficiently good repute and have sufficient experience to perform these duties.]

NOTES

Inserted as noted to art 10a at **[6118]**.

Repealed as noted at the beginning of this Directive.

[6120]

Article 11

Implementation

1. Member States shall adopt not later than 5 June 2000 the laws, regulations and administrative provisions necessary to comply with this Directive. They shall immediately inform the Commission thereof.

2. Member States shall provide that the provisions referred to in paragraph 1 shall first apply to the supervision of accounts for financial years beginning on 1 January 2001 or during that calendar year.

3. When Member States adopt the measures referred to in paragraph 1, they shall contain a reference to this Directive or shall be accompanied by such reference on the occasion of their official publication. The methods of making such reference shall be laid down by Member States.

4. Member States shall communicate to the Commission the main provisions of national law which they adopt in the field covered by this Directive.

[5. Not later than 1 January 2006 the Commission shall issue a report on the application of this Directive and, if necessary, on the need for further harmonisation.]

NOTES

Repealed as noted at the beginning of this Directive.

Para 5: substituted by European Parliament and Council Directive 2005/1/EC, art 7(2).

[6121]
Article 12
Entry into force

This Directive shall enter into force on the day of its publication in the Official Journal of the European Communities.

NOTES

Repealed as noted at the beginning of this Directive.

[6122]
Article 13
Addressees

This Directive is addressed to the Member States.

NOTES

Repealed as noted at the beginning of this Directive.

Done at Luxembourg, 27 October 1998.

[ANNEX I

CALCULATION OF THE ADJUSTED SOLVENCY OF INSURANCE UNDERTAKINGS AND REINSURANCE UNDERTAKINGS

[6123]

***1.* Choice of calculation method and general principles**

A. Member States shall provide that the calculation of the adjusted solvency of insurance undertakings and reinsurance undertakings referred to in Article 2(1) shall be carried out according to one of the methods described in point 3. A Member State may, however, provide for the competent authorities to authorise or impose the application of a method set out in point 3 other than that chosen by the Member State.

B. Proportionality

The calculation of the adjusted solvency of an insurance undertaking or a reinsurance undertaking shall take account of the proportional share held by the participating undertaking in its related undertakings.

"Proportional share" means either, where method 1 or method 2 described in point 3 is used, the proportion of the subscribed capital that is held, directly or indirectly, by the participating undertaking or, where method 3 described in point 3 is used, the percentages used for the establishment of the consolidated accounts.

However, whichever method is used, when the related undertaking is a subsidiary undertaking and has a solvency deficit, the total solvency deficit of the subsidiary has to be taken into account.

However, where, in the opinion of the competent authorities, the responsibility of the parent undertaking owning a share of the capital is limited strictly and unambiguously to that share of the capital, such competent authorities may give permission for the solvency deficit of the subsidiary undertaking to be taken into account on a proportional basis.

Where there are no capital ties between some of the undertakings in an insurance group or a reinsurance group, the competent authority shall determine which proportional share will have to be taken account of.

C. Elimination of double use of solvency margin elements

C.1. General treatment of solvency margin elements

Regardless of the method used for the calculation of the adjusted solvency of an insurance undertaking or a reinsurance undertaking, the double use of elements eligible for the solvency margin among the different insurance undertakings or reinsurance undertakings taken into account in that calculation must be eliminated.

For that purpose, when calculating the adjusted solvency of an insurance undertaking or a reinsurance undertaking and where the methods described in point 3 do not provide for it, the following amounts shall be eliminated:

— *the value of any asset of that insurance undertaking or reinsurance undertaking which represents the financing of elements eligible for the solvency margin of one of its related insurance undertakings or related reinsurance undertakings,*
— *the value of any asset of a related insurance undertaking or a related reinsurance undertaking of that insurance undertaking or reinsurance undertaking which represents the financing of elements eligible for the solvency margin of that insurance undertaking or reinsurance undertaking,*
— *the value of any asset of a related insurance undertaking or related reinsurance undertaking of that insurance undertaking or reinsurance undertaking which represents the financing of elements eligible for the solvency margin of any other related insurance undertaking or related reinsurance undertaking of that insurance undertaking or reinsurance undertaking.*

C.2. Treatment of certain elements

Without prejudice to the provisions of Section C.1:

— *profit reserves and future profits arising in a related life assurance undertaking or a related life reinsurance undertaking of the insurance undertaking or reinsurance undertaking for which the adjusted solvency is calculated, and*
— *any subscribed but not paid-up capital of a related insurance undertaking or a related reinsurance undertaking of the insurance undertaking or of reinsurance undertaking for which the adjusted solvency is calculated,*

may only be included in the calculation in so far as they are eligible for covering the solvency margin requirement of that related undertaking. However, any subscribed but not paid-up capital which represents a potential obligation on the part of the participating undertaking shall be entirely excluded from the calculation.

Any subscribed but not paid-up capital of the participating insurance undertaking or the participating reinsurance undertaking which represents a potential obligation on the part of a related insurance undertaking or of a related reinsurance undertaking shall also be excluded from the calculation.

Any subscribed but not paid-up capital of a related insurance undertaking or a reinsurance undertaking which represents a potential obligation on the part of another related insurance undertaking or reinsurance undertaking of the same participating insurance undertaking or reinsurance undertaking shall be excluded from the calculation.

C.3. Transferability

If the competent authorities consider that certain elements eligible for the solvency margin of a related insurance undertaking or a related reinsurance undertaking other than those referred to in Section C.2 cannot effectively be made available to cover the solvency margin requirement of the participating insurance undertaking or the participating reinsurance undertaking for which the adjusted solvency is calculated, those elements may be included in the calculation only in so far as they are eligible for covering the solvency margin requirement of the related undertaking.

C.4. The sum of the elements referred to in Sections C.2 and C.3 may not exceed the solvency margin requirement of the related insurance undertaking or the related reinsurance undertaking.

D. Elimination of the intra-group creation of capital

When calculating adjusted solvency, no account shall be taken of any element eligible for the solvency margin arising out of reciprocal financing between the insurance undertaking or the reinsurance undertaking and:

— *a related undertaking,*
— *a participating undertaking,*
— *another related undertaking of any of its participating undertakings.*

Furthermore, no account shall be taken of any element eligible for the solvency margin of a related insurance undertaking or a related reinsurance undertaking of the insurance undertaking or reinsurance undertaking for which the adjusted solvency is calculated when the element in question arises out of reciprocal financing with any other related undertaking of that insurance undertaking or reinsurance undertaking.

In particular, reciprocal financing exists when an insurance undertaking or a reinsurance undertaking, or any of its related undertakings, holds shares in, or makes loans to, another undertaking which, directly or indirectly, holds an element eligible for the solvency margin of the first undertakings.

E. The competent authorities shall ensure that the adjusted solvency is calculated with the same frequency as that laid down by Directives 73/239/EEC, 91/674/EEC, 2002/83/EC and 2005/68/EC for calculating the solvency margin of insurance undertakings or reinsurance undertakings. The value of the assets and liabilities shall be assessed in accordance with the relevant provisions of Directives 73/239/EEC, 91/674/EEC, 2002/83/EC and 2005/68/EC.

2. Application of the calculation methods

2.1. Related insurance undertakings and related reinsurance undertakings.

The adjusted solvency calculation shall be carried out in accordance with the general principles and methods set out in this Annex.

In the case of all methods, where the insurance undertaking or reinsurance undertaking has more than one related insurance undertaking or related reinsurance undertaking the adjusted solvency calculation shall be carried out by integrating each of these related insurance undertakings or related reinsurance undertakings.

In cases of successive participations (for example, where an insurance undertaking or a reinsurance undertaking is a participating undertaking in another insurance undertaking or reinsurance undertaking which is also a participating undertaking in an insurance undertaking or a reinsurance undertaking), the adjusted solvency calculation shall be carried out at the level of each participating insurance undertaking or reinsurance undertaking which has at least one related insurance undertaking or one related reinsurance undertaking.

Member States may waive calculation of the adjusted solvency of an insurance undertaking or a reinsurance undertaking:

- *if the insurance undertaking or reinsurance undertaking is a related undertaking of another insurance undertaking or a reinsurance undertaking authorised in the same Member State, and that related undertaking is taken into account in the calculation of the adjusted solvency of the participating insurance undertaking or reinsurance undertaking, or*
- *if the insurance undertaking or the reinsurance undertaking is a related undertaking of an insurance holding company which has its registered office in the same Member State as the insurance undertaking or the reinsurance undertaking, and both the holding insurance company and the related insurance undertaking or the related reinsurance undertaking are taken into account in the calculation carried out.*

Member States may also waive calculation of the adjusted solvency of an insurance undertaking or reinsurance undertaking if it is a related insurance undertaking or a related reinsurance undertaking of another insurance undertaking, a reinsurance undertaking or an insurance holding company which has its registered office in another Member State, and if the competent authorities of the Member States concerned have agreed to grant exercise of the supplementary supervision to the competent authority of the latter Member State.

In each case, the waiver may be granted only if the competent authorities are satisfied that the elements eligible for the solvency margins of the insurance undertakings or the reinsurance undertakings included in the calculation are adequately distributed between those undertakings.

Member States may provide that where the related insurance undertaking or the related reinsurance undertaking has its registered office in a Member State other than that of the insurance undertaking or the reinsurance undertaking for which the adjusted solvency calculation is carried out, the calculation shall take account, in respect of the related undertaking, of the solvency situation as assessed by the competent authorities of that other Member State.

2.2. Intermediate insurance holding companies

When calculating the adjusted solvency of an insurance undertaking or a reinsurance undertaking which holds a participation in a related insurance undertaking, a related reinsurance undertaking, a non-member country insurance undertaking or a non-member country reinsurance undertaking, through an insurance holding company, the situation of the intermediate insurance holding company is taken into account. For the sole purpose of that calculation, to be undertaken in accordance with the general principles and methods described in this Annex, this insurance holding company shall be treated as if it were an insurance undertaking or reinsurance undertaking subject to a zero solvency requirement and were subject to the same conditions as are laid down in Article 16 of Directive 73/239/EEC, in Article 27 of Directive 2002/83/EC or in Article 36 of Directive 2005/68/EC, in respect of elements eligible for the solvency margin.

2.3. Related non-member country insurance undertakings and related non-member country reinsurance undertakings

When calculating the adjusted solvency of an insurance undertaking or a reinsurance undertaking which is a participating undertaking in a non-member country insurance undertaking or in a non-member country reinsurance undertaking, the latter shall be treated solely for the purposes of the calculation, by analogy with a related insurance undertaking or a related reinsurance undertaking, by applying the general principles and methods described in this Annex.

However, where the non-member country in which that undertaking has its registered office makes it subject to authorisation and imposes on it a solvency requirement at least comparable to that laid down in Directives 73/239/EEC, 2002/83/EC or 2005/68/EC, taking into account the elements of cover of that requirement, Member States may provide that the calculation shall take into account, as regards that undertaking, the solvency requirement and the elements eligible to satisfy that requirement as laid down by the non-member country in question.

2.4. Related credit institutions, investment firms and financial institutions

When calculating the adjusted solvency of an insurance undertaking or reinsurance undertaking which is a participating undertaking in a credit institution, investment firm or financial institution, the rules laid down in Article 16 of Directive 73/239/EEC, in Article 27 of Directive 2002/83/EC and in Article 36 of Directive 2005/68/EC, on the deduction of such participations shall apply mutatis mutandis, as well as the provisions on the ability of Member States under certain conditions to allow alternative methods and to allow such participations not to be deducted.

2.5. Non-availability of the necessary information

Where information necessary for calculating the adjusted solvency of an insurance undertaking or reinsurance undertaking, concerning a related undertaking with its registered office in a Member State or a non-member country, is not available to the competent authorities, for whatever reason, the book value of that undertaking in the participating insurance undertaking or reinsurance undertaking shall be deducted from the elements eligible for the adjusted solvency margin. In that case, the unrealised gains connected with such participation shall not be allowed as an element eligible for the adjusted solvency margin.

3. **Calculation methods**

Method 1: Deduction and aggregation method

The adjusted solvency situation of the participating insurance undertaking or the participating reinsurance undertaking is the difference between:

- *(i) the sum of:*
  - *(a) the elements eligible for the solvency margin of the participating insurance undertaking or the participating reinsurance undertaking, and*
  - *(b) the proportional share of the participating insurance undertaking or the participating reinsurance undertaking in the elements eligible for the solvency margin of the related insurance undertaking or the related reinsurance undertaking,*

  and
- *(ii) the sum of:*
  - *(a) the book value in the participating insurance undertaking or the participating reinsurance undertaking of the related insurance undertaking or the related reinsurance undertaking, and*
  - *(b) the solvency requirement of the participating insurance undertaking or the participating reinsurance undertaking, and*
  - *(c) the proportional share of the solvency requirement of the related insurance undertaking or the related reinsurance undertaking.*

Where the participation in the related insurance undertaking or the related reinsurance undertaking consists, wholly or in part, of an indirect ownership, then item (ii)(a) shall incorporate the value of such indirect ownership, taking into account the relevant successive interests, and items (i)(b) and (ii)(c) shall include the corresponding proportional shares of the elements eligible for the solvency margin of the related insurance undertaking or the related reinsurance undertaking.

Method 2: Requirement deduction method

The adjusted solvency of the participating insurance undertaking or the participating reinsurance undertaking is the difference between:

- *(i) the sum of the elements eligible for the solvency margin of the participating insurance undertaking or the participating reinsurance undertaking,*

  and
- *(ii) the sum of:*
  - *(a) the solvency requirement of the participating insurance undertaking or the participating reinsurance undertaking, and*
  - *(b) the proportional share of the solvency requirement of the related insurance undertaking or the related reinsurance undertaking.*

When valuing the elements eligible for the solvency margin, participations within the meaning of this Directive are valued by the equity method, in accordance with the option set out in Article 59(2)(b) of Directive 78/660/EEC.

Method 3: Accounting consolidation-based method

The calculation of the adjusted solvency of the participating insurance undertaking or the participating reinsurance undertaking shall be carried out on the basis of the consolidated accounts. The adjusted solvency of the participating insurance undertaking or the participating reinsurance undertaking is the difference between the elements eligible for the solvency margin calculated on the basis of consolidated data, and:

(a) either the sum of the solvency requirement of the participating insurance undertaking or the participating reinsurance undertaking and of the proportional shares of the solvency requirements of the related insurance undertakings or the related reinsurance undertaking, based on the percentages used for the establishment of the consolidated accounts,

(b) or the solvency requirement calculated on the basis of consolidated data.

The provisions of Directives 73/239/EEC, 91/674/EEC, 2002/83/EC and 2005/68/EC shall apply for the calculation of the elements eligible for the solvency margin and of the solvency requirement based on consolidated data.]

NOTES

Substituted, together with Annex II, by European Parliament and Council Directive 2005/68/EC, art 59(9), Annex II.

Repealed as noted at the beginning of this Directive.

[ANNEX II

SUPPLEMENTARY SUPERVISION FOR INSURANCE UNDERTAKINGS AND REINSURANCE UNDERTAKINGS THAT ARE SUBSIDIARIES OF AN INSURANCE HOLDING COMPANY, A NON-MEMBER COUNTRY INSURANCE UNDERTAKING OR A NON-MEMBER COUNTRY REINSURANCE UNDERTAKING

[6124]

1. In the case of two or more insurance undertakings or reinsurance undertakings referred to in Article 2(2) which are the subsidiaries of an insurance holding company, a non-member country insurance undertaking or a non-member country reinsurance undertaking and which are established in different Member States, the competent authorities shall ensure that the method described in this Annex is applied in a consistent manner.

The competent authorities shall exercise the supplementary supervision with the same frequency as that laid down by Directives 73/239/EEC, 91/674/EEC, 2002/83/EC and 2005/68/EC for calculating the solvency margin of insurance undertakings and reinsurance undertakings.

2. Member States may waive the calculation provided for in this Annex with regard to an insurance undertaking or a reinsurance undertaking:

— *if that insurance undertaking or reinsurance undertaking is a related undertaking of another insurance undertaking or reinsurance undertaking and if it is taken into account in the calculation provided for in this Annex carried out for that other undertaking,*

— *if that insurance undertaking or reinsurance undertaking and one or more other insurance undertakings or reinsurance undertakings authorised in the same Member State have as their parent undertaking the same insurance holding company, non-member country insurance undertaking, or non-member country reinsurance undertaking, and the insurance undertaking or reinsurance undertaking is taken into account in the calculation provided for in this Annex carried out for one of these other undertakings,*

— *if that insurance undertaking or reinsurance undertaking and one or more other insurance undertakings or reinsurance undertakings authorised in other Member States have as their parent undertaking the same insurance holding company, non-member country insurance undertaking or non-member country reinsurance undertaking, and an agreement granting exercise of the supplementary supervision covered by this Annex to the supervisory authority of another Member State has been concluded in accordance with Article 4(2).*

In the case of successive participations (for example: an insurance holding company or a non-member country insurance or reinsurance undertaking, which is itself owned by another insurance holding company or a non-member country insurance or reinsurance undertaking), Member States may apply the calculations provided for in this Annex only at the level of the ultimate parent

Part VI European Materials

undertaking of the insurance undertaking or reinsurance undertaking which is an insurance holding company, a non-member country insurance undertaking or a non-member country reinsurance undertaking.

3. The competent authorities shall ensure that calculations analogous to those described in Annex I are carried out at the level of the insurance holding company, non-member country insurance undertaking or non-member country reinsurance undertaking.

The analogy shall consist in applying the general principles and methods described in Annex I at the level of the insurance holding company, non-member country insurance undertaking or non-member country reinsurance undertaking.

For the sole purpose of that calculation, the parent undertaking shall be treated as if it were an insurance undertaking or reinsurance undertaking subject to:

- *a zero solvency requirement where it is an insurance holding company,*
- *a solvency requirement determined in accordance with the principles of Section 2.3 of Annex I, where it is a non-member country insurance undertaking or a non-member country reinsurance undertaking,*

and is subject to the same conditions as laid down in Article 16 of Directive 73/239/EEC, in Article 27 of Directive 2002/83/EC and in Article 36 of Directive 2005/68/EC as regards the elements eligible for the solvency margin.

4. Non-availability of the necessary information

Where information necessary for the calculation provided for in this Annex, concerning a related undertaking with its registered office in a Member State or a non-member country, is not available to the competent authorities, for whatever reason, the book value of that undertaking in the participating undertaking shall be deducted from the elements eligible for the calculation provided for in this Annex. In that case, the unrealised gains connected with such participation shall not be allowed as an element eligible for the calculation.]

NOTES

Substituted as noted to Annex I at **[6123]**.
Repealed as noted at the beginning of this Directive.

DIRECTIVE OF THE EUROPEAN PARLIAMENT AND OF THE COUNCIL

(2002/13/EC)

of 5 March 2002

amending Council Directive 73/239/EEC as regards the solvency margin requirements for non-life insurance undertakings

NOTES

Date of publication in OJ: OJ L77, 20.3.2002, p 17.

[6125]
THE EUROPEAN PARLIAMENT AND THE COUNCIL OF THE EUROPEAN UNION,

Having regard to the Treaty establishing the European Community, and in particular Articles 47(2) and 55 thereof,

Having regard to the proposal from the Commission,[1]

Having regard to the opinion of the Economic and Social Committee,[2]

Acting in accordance with the procedure laid down in Article 251 of the Treaty,[3]

Whereas—

(1) The financial services action plan, as endorsed by the European Council meetings in Cologne on 3 and 4 June 1999 and in Lisbon on 23 and 24 March 2000, recognises the importance of the solvency margin for insurance undertakings to protect policyholders in the single market by ensuring that insurance undertakings have adequate capital requirements in relation to the nature of their risks.

(2) First Council Directive 73/239/EEC of 24 July 1973 on the coordination of laws, regulations and administrative provisions relating to the taking up and pursuit of the business of direct insurance other than life assurance[4] requires insurance undertakings to have solvency margins.

(3) The requirement that insurance undertakings establish, over and above the technical provisions to meet their underwriting liabilities, a solvency margin to act as a buffer against adverse business fluctuations is an important element in the system of prudential supervision for the protection of insured persons and policyholders.

(4) The existing solvency margin rules as established by Directive 73/239/EEC have been substantially unchanged by subsequent Community legislation and Council Directive 92/49/EEC of 18 June 1992 on the coordination of laws, regulations and administrative provisions relating to direct insurance other than life assurance (third non-life insurance Directive)[5] required the Commission to submit a report to the Insurance Committee set up by Council Directive 91/675/EEC,[6] on the need for further harmonisation of the solvency margin.

(5) The Commission has prepared that report in the light of the recommendations of the report on the solvency of insurance undertakings prepared by the Conference of the Insurance Supervisory Authorities of the Member States of the European Union.

(6) While the report concluded that the simple, robust nature of the current system has operated satisfactorily and is based on sound principles benefiting from wide transparency, certain weaknesses have been identified in specific cases, particularly for sensitive risk profiles.

(7) There is a need to simplify and increase the existing minimum guarantee funds, in particular as a result of inflation in claim levels and operational expenses since their original adoption. The thresholds above which the lower percentage rate applies for the determination of the solvency margin requirement on the premiums and claims basis should also be increased accordingly.

(8) To avoid major and sharp increases in the amount of the minimum guarantee funds and the thresholds in the future, a mechanism should be established providing for their increase in line with the European index of consumer prices.

(9) In specific situations where policyholders' rights are threatened, there is a need for the competent authorities to be empowered to intervene at a sufficiently early stage, but in the exercise of those powers, competent authorities should inform the insurance undertakings of the reasons motivating such supervisory action, in accordance with the principles of sound administration and due process. As long as such a situation exists, the competent authorities should be prevented from certifying that the insurance undertaking has a sufficient solvency margin.

(10) In the light of market developments in the nature of reinsurance cover purchased by primary insurers, there is a need for the competent authorities to be empowered to decrease the reduction to the solvency margin requirement in certain circumstances.

(11) Where an insurer substantially reduces or ceases the writing of new business, there is a need to establish an adequate solvency margin in respect of the residual liabilities for existing business as reflected by the level of technical provisions.

(12) For specific classes of non-life business which are subject to a particularly volatile risk profile, the existing solvency margin requirement should be substantially increased so that the required solvency margin is better matched to the true risk profile of the business.

(13) To reflect the impact of differing accounting and actuarial approaches, it is appropriate to make corresponding adjustments to the methodology for the calculation of the solvency margin requirement so that this is calculated in a coherent and consistent manner, thus placing insurance undertakings on an equal footing.

(14) This Directive should lay down minimum standards for the solvency margin requirements and home Member States should be able to lay down stricter rules for insurance undertakings authorised by their own competent authorities.

(15) Directive 73/239/EEC should be amended accordingly,

NOTES

1 OJ C96 E, 27.3.2001, p 129.

2 OJ C193, 10.7.2001, p 16.

3 Opinion of the European Parliament of 4 July 2001 (not yet published in the Official Journal) and Decision of the Council of 14 February 2002.

4 OJ L228, 16.8.1973, p 3. Directive as last amended by Directive 2000/26/EC of the European Parliament and of the Council (OJ L181, 20.7.2000, p 65).

5 OJ L228, 11.8.1992, p 1. Directive as last amended by Directive 2000/64/EC of the European Parliament and of the Council (OJ L290, 17.11.2000, p 27).

6 OJ L374, 31.12.1991, p 32.

HAVE ADOPTED THIS DIRECTIVE—

Article 1 (*Amends Directive 73/239/EEC, arts 3, 20 at* **[6646]**, **[6667]**, *substitutes arts 16, 17 thereof at* **[6660]**, **[6662]**, *and inserts arts 16a, 17a, 20a thereof at* **[6661]**, **[6663]**, **[6668]**.)

[6126]
Article 2
Transitional period

1. Member States may allow insurance undertakings which at the entry into force of this Directive provide insurance in their territories in one or more of classes referred to in the Annex to Directive 73/239/EEC, a period of five years, commencing with the date of entry into force of this Directive, in order to comply with the requirements set out in Article 1 of this Directive.

2. Member States may allow any undertakings referred to in paragraph 1, which upon the expiry of the five-year period have not fully established the required solvency margin, a further period not exceeding two years in which to do so provided that such undertakings have, in accordance with Article 20 of Directive 73/239/EEC, submitted for the approval of the competent authorities the measures which they propose to take for such purpose.

[6127]
Article 3
Transposition

1. Member States shall adopt by 20 September 2003 at the latest the laws, regulations and administrative provisions necessary to comply with this Directive. They shall forthwith inform the Commission thereof.

When Member States adopt these measures, they shall contain a reference to this Directive or be accompanied by such a reference on the occasion of their official publication. The methods of making such a reference shall be laid down by the Member States.

2. Member States shall provide that the measures referred to in paragraph 1 shall first apply to the supervision of accounts for financial years beginning on 1 January 2004 or during that calendar year.

3. Member States shall communicate to the Commission the main provisions of national law which they adopt in the field covered by this Directive.

4. Not later than 1 January 2007 the Commission shall submit to the European Parliament and the Council a report on the application of this Directive and, if necessary, on the need for further harmonisation. The report shall indicate how Member States have made use of the possibilities in this Directive, and, in particular, whether the discretionary powers afforded to the national supervisory authorities have resulted in major supervisory differences in the single market.

[6128]
Article 4
Entry into force

This Directive shall enter into force on the day of its publication in the *Official Journal of the European Communities.*

[6129]
Article 5
Addressees

This Directive is addressed to the Member States.

Done at Brussels, 5 March 2002.

COMMISSION REGULATION

(358/2003/EC)

of 27 February 2003

on the application of Article 81(3) of the Treaty to certain categories of agreements, decisions and concerted practices in the insurance sector

(Text with EEA relevance)

NOTES

Date of publication in OJ: OJ L53, 28.2.2003, p 8.

[6130]

THE COMMISSION OF THE EUROPEAN COMMUNITIES,

Having regard to the Treaty establishing the European Community,

Having regard to Council Regulation (EEC) No 1534/91 of 31 May 1991 on the application of Article 85(3) of the Treaty to certain categories of agreements, decisions and concerted practices in the insurance sector,[1] and in particular Article 1(1)(a), (b), (c) and (e) thereof,

Having published a draft of this Regulation,[2]

Having consulted the Advisory Committee on Restrictive Practices and Dominant Positions,

Whereas:

(1) Regulation (EEC) No 1534/91 empowers the Commission to apply Article 81(3) of the Treaty by regulation to certain categories of agreements, decisions and concerted practices in the insurance sector which have as their object cooperation with respect to—

- the establishment of common risk premium tariffs based on collectively ascertained statistics or the number of claims,
- the establishment of common standard policy conditions,
- the common coverage of certain types of risks,
- the settlement of claims,
- the testing and acceptance of security devices,
- registers of, and information on, aggravated risks.

(2) Pursuant to Council Regulation (EEC) No 1534/91, the Commission adopted Regulation (EEC) No 3932/92 of 21 December 1992 on the application of Article 85(3) of the Treaty to certain categories of agreements, decisions and concerted practices in the insurance sector.[3] Regulation (EEC) No 3932/92, as amended by the Act of Accession of Austria, Finland and Sweden, expires on 31 March 2003.

(3) Regulation (EEC) No 3932/92 does not grant an exemption to agreements concerning the settlement of claims and registers of, and information on, aggravated risks. The Commission considered that it lacked sufficient experience in handling individual cases to make use of the power conferred by Council Regulation (EEC) No 1534/91 in those fields. This situation has not changed.

(4) On 12 May 1999, the Commission adopted a Report[4] to the Council and the European Parliament on the operation of Regulation (EEC) No 3932/92. On 15 December 1999, the Economic and Social Committee adopted an opinion on the Commission's report.[5] On 19 May 2000, the Parliament adopted a Resolution on the Commission's report.[6] On 28 June 2000, the Commission held a consultation meeting with interested parties, including representatives of the insurance sector and national competition authorities, on the Regulation. On 9 July 2002, the Commission published in the Official Journal a draft of the present Regulation, with an invitation to interested parties to submit comments not later than 30 September 2002.

(5) A new Regulation should meet the two requirements of ensuring effective protection of competition and providing adequate legal security for undertakings. The pursuit of these objectives should take account of the need to simplify administrative supervision to as great an extent as possible. Account must also be taken of the Commission's experience in this field since 1992, and the results of the consultations on the 1999 Report and consultations leading up to the adoption of this Regulation.

(6) Regulation (EEC) No 1534/91 requires the exempting regulation of the Commission to define the categories of agreements, decisions and concerted practices to which it applies, to specify the restrictions or clauses which may, or may not, appear in the agreements, decisions and concerted practices, and to specify the clauses which must be contained in the agreements, decisions and concerted practices or the other conditions which must be satisfied.

(7) Nevertheless, it is appropriate to move away from the approach of listing exempted clauses and to place greater emphasis on defining categories of agreements which are exempted up to a certain level of market power and on specifying the restrictions or clauses which are not to be contained in such agreements. This is consistent with an economics based approach which assesses the impact of agreements on the relevant market. However, it should be recognised that in the insurance sector there are certain types of collaboration involving all the undertakings on a relevant insurance market which can be regarded as normally satisfying the conditions laid down in Article 81(3) of the Treaty.

(8) For the application of Article 81(3) of the Treaty by regulation, it is not necessary to define those agreements which are capable of falling within Article 81(1). In the individual assessment of agreements under Article 81(1), account has to be taken of several factors, and in particular the market structure on the relevant market.

(9) The benefit of the block exemption should be limited to those agreements for which it can be assumed with sufficient certainty that they satisfy the conditions of Article 81(3) of the Treaty.

(10) Collaboration between insurance undertakings or within associations of undertakings in the calculation of the average cost of covering a specified risk in the past or, for life insurance, tables of mortality rates or of the frequency of illness, accident and invalidity, makes it possible to improve the knowledge of risks and facilitates the rating of risks for individual companies. This can in turn facilitate market entry and thus benefit consumers. The same applies to joint studies on the probable impact of extraneous circumstances that may influence the frequency or scale of claims, or the yield

of different types of investments. It is, however, necessary to ensure that such collaboration is only exempted to the extent to which it is necessary to attain these objectives. It is therefore appropriate to stipulate that agreements on commercial premiums are not exempted; indeed, commercial premiums may be lower than the amounts indicated by the results of the calculations tables or studies in question, since insurers can use the revenues from their investments in order to reduce their premiums. Moreover, the calculations, tables or studies in question should be non-binding and serve only for reference purposes.

(11) Moreover, the broader the categories into which statistics on the cost of covering a specified risk in the past are grouped, the less leeway insurance undertakings have to calculate premiums on a narrower basis. It is therefore appropriate to exempt joint calculations of the past cost of risks on condition that the available statistics are provided with as much detail and differentiation as is actuarially adequate.

(12) Furthermore, since access to such calculations, tables and studies is necessary both for insurance undertakings active on the geographic or product market in question and also for those considering entering that market, such insurance undertakings must be granted access to such calculations tables and studies on reasonable and non-discriminatory terms, as compared with insurance undertakings already present on that market. Such terms might for example include a commitment from an insurance undertaking not yet present on the market to provide statistical information on claims, should it ever enter the market. They might also include membership of the association of insurers responsible for producing the calculations, as long as access to such membership is itself available on reasonable and non-discriminatory terms to insurance undertakings not yet active on the market in question. However, any fee charged for access to such calculations or related studies to insurance undertakings which have not contributed to them, would not be considered reasonable for this purpose if it were so high as to constitute a barrier to entry on the market.

(13) The reliability of joint calculations, tables and studies becomes greater as the amount of statistics on which they are based is increased. Insurers with high market shares may generate sufficient statistics internally to be able to make reliable calculations, but those with small market shares will not be able to do so, much less new entrants. The inclusion in such joint calculations, tables and studies of information from all insurers on a market, including large ones, promotes competition by helping smaller insurers, and facilitates market entry. Given this specificity of the insurance sector, it is not appropriate to subject any exemption for such joint calculations and joint studies to market share thresholds.

(14) Standard policy conditions or standard individual clauses and standard models illustrating the profits of a life assurance policy can produce benefits. For example, they can bring efficiency gains for insurers; they can facilitate market entry by small or inexperienced insurers; they can help insurers to meet legal obligations; and they can be used by consumer organisations as a benchmark to compare insurance policies offered by different insurers.

(15) However, standard policy conditions must not lead either to the standardisation of products or to the creation of a significant imbalance between the rights and obligations arising from the contract. Accordingly, the exemption should only apply to standard policy conditions on condition that they are not binding, and expressly mention that participating undertakings are free to offer different policy conditions to their customers. Moreover, standard policy conditions may not contain any systematic exclusion of specific types of risk without providing for the express possibility of including that cover by agreement and may not provide for the contractual relationship with the policyholder to be maintained for an excessive period or go beyond the initial object of the policy. This is without prejudice to obligations arising from Community or national law to include certain risks in certain policies.

(16) In addition, it is necessary to stipulate that the common standard policy conditions must be generally available to any interested person, and in particular to the policyholder, so as to ensure that there is real transparency and therefore benefit for consumers.

(17) The inclusion in an insurance policy of risks to which a significant number of policyholders is not simultaneously exposed may hinder innovation, given that the bundling of unrelated risks can be a disincentive for insurers to offer separate and specific insurance cover for them. A clause which imposes such comprehensive cover should therefore not be covered by the block exemption. Where there is a legal requirement on insurers to include in policies cover for risks to which a significant number of policyholders are not simultaneously exposed, then the inclusion in an non-binding model contract of a standard clause reflecting such a legal requirement does not constitute a restriction of competition and falls outside the scope of Article 81(1) of the Treaty.

(18) Co-insurance or co-reinsurance groups (often called "pools"), can allow insurers and reinsurers to provide insurance or reinsurance for risks for which they might only offer insufficient cover in the absence of the pool. They can also help insurance and reinsurance undertakings to acquire experience of risks with which they are unfamiliar. However, such groups can involve restrictions of competition, such as the standardisation of policy conditions and even of amounts of cover and premiums. It is therefore appropriate to lay down the circumstances in which such groups can benefit from exemption.

(19) For genuinely new risks it is not possible to know in advance what subscription capacity is necessary to cover the risk, nor whether two or more such groups could co-exist for the purposes of providing this type of insurance. A pooling arrangement which is for the co-insurance or co-reinsurance exclusively of such new risks (not of a mixture of new risks and existing risks) can therefore be exempted for a limited period of time. Three years should constitute an adequate period for the constitution of sufficient historical information on claims to assess the necessity or otherwise of one single pool. This Regulation therefore grants an exemption to any such group which is newly-created in order to cover a new risk, for the first three years of its existence.

(20) The definition of "new risks" clarifies that only risks which did not exist before are included in the definition, thus excluding for example risks which hitherto existed but were not insured. Moreover, a risk whose nature changes significantly (for example a considerable increase in terrorist activity) falls outside the definition, as the risk itself is not new in that case. A new risk, by its nature, requires an entirely new insurance product, and cannot be covered by additions or modifications to an existing insurance product.

(21) For risks which are not new, it is recognised that such co-insurance and co-reinsurance groups which involve a restriction of competition can also, in certain limited circumstances, involve benefits such as to justify an exemption under Article 81(3) of the Treaty, even if they could be replaced by two or more competing insurance entities. They may for example, allow their members to gain the necessary experience of the sector of insurance involved, they may allow cost savings, or reduction of premiums through joint reinsurance on advantageous terms. However, any exemption for such groups is not justified if the group in question benefits from a significant level of market power, since in those circumstances the restriction of competition deriving from the existence of the pool would normally outweigh any possible advantages.

(22) This Regulation therefore grants an exemption to any such co-insurance or co-reinsurance group which has existed for more than three years, or which is not created in order to cover a new risk, on condition that the insurance products underwritten within the group by its members do not exceed the following thresholds: 25% of the relevant market in the case of co-reinsurance groups, and 20% in the case of co-insurance groups. The threshold for co-insurance groups is lower because the co-insurance pools may involve uniform policy conditions and commercial premiums. These exemptions however only apply if the group in question meets the further conditions laid out in this Regulation, which are intended to keep to a minimum the restrictions of competition between the members of the group.

(23) Pools falling outside the scope of this Regulation may be eligible for an individual exemption, depending on the details of the pool itself and the specific conditions of the market in question. Considering that many insurance markets are constantly evolving, an individual analysis would be necessary in such cases in order to determine whether or not the conditions of Article 81(3) of the Treaty are met.

(24) The adoption by an association or associations of insurance or reinsurance undertakings of technical specifications, rules or codes of practice concerning safety devices, and of procedures for evaluating the compliance of safety devices with those technical specifications, rules or codes of practice, can be beneficial in providing a benchmark to insurers and reinsurers when assessing the extent of the risk they are asked to cover in a specific case, which depends on the quality of security equipment and of its installation and maintenance. However, where there exist Community-level technical specifications, classification systems, rules, procedures or codes of practice harmonised in line with Community legislation covering the free movement of goods, it is not appropriate to exempt by regulation any agreements among insurers on the same subject, since the objective of such harmonisation at European level is to lay down exhaustive and adequate levels of security for security devices which apply uniformly across the Community. Any agreement among insurers on different requirements for safety devices could undermine the achievement of that objective.

(25) As concerns the installation and maintenance of security devices, in so far as no such Community-level harmonisation exists, agreements between insurers laying down technical specifications or approval procedures that are used in one or several Member States can be exempted by regulation; however, the exemption should be subjected to certain conditions, in particular that each insurance undertaking must remain free to accept for insurance, on whatever terms and conditions it wishes, devices and installation and maintenance undertakings not approved jointly.

(26) If individual agreements exempted by this Regulation nevertheless have effects which are incompatible with Article 81(3) of the Treaty, as interpreted by the administrative practice of the Commission and the case-law of the Court of Justice, the Commission may withdraw the benefit of the block exemption. This may occur in particular where studies on the impact of future developments are based on unjustifiable hypotheses; or where recommended standard policy conditions contain clauses which create, to the detriment of the policyholder, a significant imbalance between the rights and obligations arising from the contract; or where groups are used or managed in such a way as to give one or more participating undertakings the means of acquiring or reinforcing a position of significant market power on the relevant market, or if these groups result in market sharing.

(27) In order to facilitate the conclusion of agreements, some of which can involve significant

investment decisions, the period of validity of this Regulation should be fixed at seven years.

(28) This Regulation is without prejudice to the application of Article 82 of the Treaty.

(29) In accordance with the principle of the primacy of Community law, no measure taken pursuant to national laws on competition should prejudice the uniform application throughout the common market of the Community competition rules or the full effect of any measures adopted in implementation of those rules, including this Regulation,

NOTES

1 OJ L143, 7.6.1991, p 1.

2 OJ C163, 9.7.2002, p 7.

3 OJ L398, 31.12.1992, p 7.

4 COM(1999) 192 final.

5 CES 1139/99.

6 PE A5-0104/00.

HAS ADOPTED THIS REGULATION—

CHAPTER I
EXEMPTION AND DEFINITIONS

[6131]
Article 1
Exemption

Pursuant to Article 81(3) of the Treaty and subject to the provisions of this Regulation, it is hereby declared that Article 81(1) of the Treaty shall not apply to agreements entered into between two or more undertakings in the insurance sector (hereinafter referred to as "the parties") with respect to—

(a) the joint establishment and distribution of—
- — calculations of the average cost of covering a specified risk in the past (hereinafter "calculations");
- — in connection with insurance involving an element of capitalisation, mortality tables, and tables showing the frequency of illness, accident and invalidity (hereinafter "tables");

(b) the joint carrying-out of studies on the probable impact of general circumstances external to the interested undertakings, either on the frequency or scale of future claims for a given risk or risk category or on the profitability of different types of investment (hereinafter "studies"), and the distribution of the results of such studies;

(c) the joint establishment and distribution of non-binding standard policy conditions for direct insurance (hereinafter "standard policy conditions");

(d) the joint establishment and distribution of non-binding models illustrating the profits to be realised from an insurance policy involving an element of capitalisation (hereinafter "models");

(e) the setting-up and operation of groups of insurance undertakings or of insurance undertakings and reinsurance undertakings for the common coverage of a specific category of risks in the form of co-insurance or co-reinsurance; and

(f) the establishment, recognition and distribution of—
- — technical specifications, rules or codes of practice concerning those types of security devices for which there do not exist at Community level technical specifications, classification systems, rules, procedures or codes of practice harmonised in line with Community legislation covering the free movement of goods, and procedures for assessing and approving the compliance of security devices with such specifications, rules or codes of practice,
- — technical specifications, rules or codes of practice for the installation and maintenance of security devices, and procedures for assessing and approving the compliance of undertakings which install or maintain security devices with such specifications, rules or codes of practice.

[6132]
Article 2
Definitions

For the purposes of the present Regulation, the following definitions shall apply—

1. "Agreement" means an agreement, a decision of an association of undertakings or a concerted practice.

2. "Participating undertakings" means undertakings party to the agreement and their respective connected undertakings.
3. "Connected undertakings" means:
   (a) undertakings in which a party to the agreement, directly or indirectly:
      (i) has the power to exercise more than half the voting rights, or
      (ii) has the power to appoint more than half the members of the supervisory board, board of management or bodies legally representing the undertaking, or
      (iii) has the right to manage the undertaking's affairs;
   (b) undertakings which directly or indirectly have, over a party to the agreement, the rights or powers listed in (a);
   (c) undertakings in which an undertaking referred to in (b) has, directly or indirectly, the rights or powers listed in (a);
   (d) undertakings in which a party to the agreement together with one or more of the undertakings referred to in (a), (b) or (c), or in which two or more of the latter undertakings, jointly have the rights or powers listed in (a);
   (e) undertakings in which the rights or the powers listed in (a) are jointly held by:
      (i) parties to the agreement or their respective connected undertakings referred to in (a) to (d), or
      (ii) one or more of the parties to the agreement or one or more of their connected undertakings referred to in (a) to (d) and one or more third parties.
4. "Standard policy conditions" refers to any clauses contained in model or reference insurance policies prepared jointly by insurers or by bodies or associations of insurers.
5. "Co-insurance groups" means groups set up by insurance undertakings which:
   (i) agree to underwrite in the name and for the account of all the participants the insurance of a specified risk category; or
   (ii) entrust the underwriting and management of the insurance of a specified risk category in their name and on their behalf to one of the insurance undertakings, to a common broker or to a common body set up for this purpose.
6. "Co-reinsurance groups" means groups set up by insurance undertakings, possibly with the assistance of one or more re-insurance undertakings:
   (i) in order to reinsure mutually all or part of their liabilities in respect of a specified risk category;
   (ii) incidentally, to accept in the name and on behalf of all the participants the re-insurance of the same category of risks;
7. "New risks" means risks which did not exist before, and for which insurance cover requires the development of an entirely new insurance product, not involving an extension, improvement or replacement of an existing insurance product.
8. "Security devices" means components and equipment designed for loss prevention and reduction, and systems formed from such elements.
9. "Commercial premium" means the price which is charged to the purchaser of an insurance policy.

CHAPTER II
JOINT CALCULATIONS, TABLES, AND STUDIES

[6133]
Article 3
Conditions for exemption

1. The exemption provided for in Article 1(a) shall apply on condition that the calculations or tables:
   (a) are based on the assembly of data, spread over a number of risk-years chosen as an observation period, which relate to identical or comparable risks in sufficient number to constitute a base which can be handled statistically and which will yield figures on (inter alia):
      — the number of claims during the said period,
      — the number of individual risks insured in each risk-year of the chosen observation period,
      — the total amounts paid or payable in respect of claims arisen during the said period,

Part VI European Materials

— the total amount of capital insured for each risk-year during the chosen observation period;

(b) include as detailed a breakdown of the available statistics as is actuarially adequate;

(c) do not include in any way elements for contingencies, income deriving from reserves, administrative or commercial costs or fiscal or para-fiscal contributions, and take into account neither revenues from investments nor anticipated profits.

2. The exemptions provided for in both Article 1(a) and Article 1(b) shall apply on condition that the calculations, tables or study results:

(a) do not identify the insurance undertakings concerned or any insured party;

(b) when compiled and distributed, include a statement that they are non-binding;

(c) are made available on reasonable and non-discriminatory terms, to any insurance undertaking which requests a copy of them, including insurance undertakings which are not active on the geographical or product market to which those calculations, tables or study results refer.

[6134]
Article 4
Agreements not covered by the exemption

The exemption provided for in Article 1 shall not apply where participating undertakings enter into an undertaking or commitment among themselves, or oblige other undertakings, not to use calculations or tables that differ from those established pursuant to Article 1(a), or not to depart from the results of the studies referred to in Article 1(b).

CHAPTER III
STANDARD POLICY CONDITIONS AND MODELS

[6135]
Article 5
Conditions for exemption

1. The exemption provided for in Article 1(c) shall apply on condition that the standard policy conditions:

(a) are established and distributed with an explicit statement that they are non-binding and that their use is not in any way recommended;

(b) expressly mention that participating undertakings are free to offer different policy conditions to their customers; and

(c) are accessible to any interested person and provided simply upon request.

2. The exemption provided for in Article 1(d) shall apply on condition that the non-binding models are established and distributed only by way of guidance.

[6136]
Article 6
Agreements not covered by the exemption

1. The exemption provided for in Article 1(c) shall not apply where the standard policy conditions contain clauses which:

(a) contain any indication of the level of commercial premiums;

(b) indicate the amount of the cover or the part which the policyholder must pay himself (the "excess");

(c) impose comprehensive cover including risks to which a significant number of policyholders are not simultaneously exposed;

(d) allow the insurer to maintain the policy in the event that he cancels part of the cover, increases the premium without the risk or the scope of the cover being changed (without prejudice to indexation clauses), or otherwise alters the policy conditions without the express consent of the policyholder;

(e) allow the insurer to modify the term of the policy without the express consent of the policyholder;

(f) impose on the policyholder in the non-life assurance sector a contract period of more than three years;

(g) impose a renewal period of more than one year where the policy is automatically renewed unless notice is given upon the expiry of a given period;

(h) require the policyholder to agree to the reinstatement of a policy which has been suspended on account of the disappearance of the insured risk, if he is once again exposed to a risk of the same nature;

(i) require the policyholder to obtain cover from the same insurer for different risks;

(j) require the policyholder, in the event of disposal of the object of insurance, to make the acquirer take over the insurance policy;

(k) exclude or limit the cover of a risk if the policyholder uses security devices, or installing or maintenance undertakings, which are not approved in accordance with the relevant specifications agreed by an association or associations of insurers in one or several other Member States or at the European level.

2. The exemption provided for in Article 1(c) shall not benefit undertakings or associations of undertakings which agree, or agree to oblige other undertakings, not to apply conditions other than standard policy conditions established pursuant to an agreement between the participating undertakings.

3. Without prejudice to the establishment of specific insurance conditions for particular social or occupational categories of the population, the exemption provided for in Article 1(c) shall not apply to agreements decisions and concerted practices which exclude the coverage of certain risk categories because of the characteristics associated with the policyholder.

4. The exemption provided for in Article 1(d) shall not apply where, withut prejudice to legally imposed obligations, the non-binding models include only specified interest rates or contain figures indicating administrative costs.

5. The exemption provided for in Article 1(d) shall not benefit undertakings or associations of undertakings which concert or undertake among themselves, or oblige other undertakings, not to apply models illustrating the benefits of an insurance policy other than those established pursuant to an agreement between the participating undertakings.

CHAPTER IV
COMMON COVERAGE OF CERTAIN TYPES OF RISKS

[6137]
Article 7
Application of exemption and market share thresholds

1. As concerns co-insurance or co-reinsurance groups which are created after the date of entry into force of the present Regulation in order exclusively to cover new risks, the exemption provided for in Article 1(e) shall apply for a period of three years from the date of the first establishment of the group, regardless of the market share of the group.

2. As concerns co-insurance or co-reinsurance groups which do not fall within the scope of the first paragraph (for the reason that they have been in existence for over three years or have not been created in order to cover a new risk), the exemption provided for in Article 1(e) shall apply as long as the present Regulation remains in force, on condition that the insurance products underwritten within the grouping arrangement by the participating undertakings or on their behalf do not, in any of the markets concerned, represent:

(a) in the case of co-insurance groups, more than 20% of the relevant market;

(b) in the case of co-reinsurance groups, more than 25% of the relevant market.

3. For the purposes of applying the market share threshold provided for in the second paragraph the following rules shall apply:

(a) the market share shall be calculated on the basis of the gross premium income; if gross premium income data are not available, estimates based on other reliable market information, including insurance cover provided or insured risk value, may be used to establish the market share of the undertaking concerned;

(b) the market share shall be calculated on the basis of data relating to the preceding calendar year;

(c) the market share held by the undertakings referred to in Article 2(3)(e) shall be apportioned equally to each undertaking having the rights or the powers listed in Article 2(3)(a).

4. If the market share referred to in point (a) of the second paragraph is initially not more than 20% but subsequently rises above this level without exceeding 22%, the exemption provided for in Article 1(e) shall continue to apply for a period of two consecutive calendar years following the year in which the 20% threshold was first exceeded.

5. If the market share referred to in point (a) of the second paragraph is initially not more than 20% but subsequently rises above 22%, the exemption provided for in Article 1(e) shall continue to apply for one calendar year following the year in which the level of 22% was first exceeded.

6. The benefit of paragraphs 4 and 5 may not be combined so as to exceed a period of two calendar years.

7. If the market share referred to in point (b) of the second paragraph is initially not more than 25% but subsequently rises above this level without exceeding 27%, the exemption provided for in Article 1(e) shall continue to apply for a period of two consecutive calendar years following the year in which the 25% threshold was first exceeded.
8. If the market share referred to in point (b) of the second paragraph is initially not more than 25% but subsequently rises above 27%, the exemption provided for in Article 1(e) shall continue to apply for one calendar year following the year in which the level of 27% was first exceeded.
9. The benefit of paragraphs 7 and 8 may not be combined so as to exceed a period of two calendar years.

[6138]
Article 8
Conditions for exemption
The exemption provided for in Article 1(e) shall apply on condition that:

(a) each participating undertaking has the right to withdraw from the group, subject to a period of notice of not more than one year, without incurring any sanctions;
(b) the rules of the group do not oblige any member of the group to insure or re-insure through the group, in whole or in part, any risk of the type covered by the group;
(c) the rules of the group do not restrict the activity of the group or its members to the insurance or reinsurance of risks located in any particular geographical part of the European Union;
(d) the agreement does not limit output or sales;
(e) the agreement does not allocate markets or customers;
(f) the members of a co-reinsurance group do not agree on the commercial premiums which they charge in direct insurance; and
(g) no member of the group, or undertaking which exercises a determining influence on the commercial policy of the group, is also a member of, or exercises a determining influence on the commercial policy of, a different group active on the same relevant market.

CHAPTER V
SECURITY DEVICES

[6139]
Article 9
Conditions for exemption
The exemption provided for in Article 1(f) shall apply on condition that:

(a) the technical specifications and compliance assessment procedures are precise, technically justified and in proportion to the performance to be attained by the security device concerned;
(b) the rules for the evaluation of installation undertakings and maintenance undertakings are objective, relate to their technical competence and are applied in a non-discriminatory manner;
(c) such specifications and rules are established and distributed with an accompanying statement that insurance undertakings are free to accept for insurance, on whatever terms and conditions they wish, other security devices or installation and maintenance undertakings which do not comply with these technical specifications or rules;
(d) such specifications and rules are provided simply upon request to any interested person;
(e) any lists of security devices and installation and maintenance undertakings compliant with specifications include a classification based on the level of performance obtained;
(f) a request for an assessment may be submitted at any time by any applicant;
(g) the evaluation of conformity does not impose on the applicant any expenses that are disproportionate to the costs of the approval procedure;
(h) the devices and installation undertakings and maintenance undertakings that meet the assessment criteria are certified to this effect in a non-discriminatory manner within a period of six months of the date of application, except where technical considerations justify a reasonable additional period;
(i) the fact of compliance or approval is certified in writing;
(j) the grounds for a refusal to issue the certificate of compliance are given in writing by attaching a duplicate copy of the records of the tests and controls that have been carried out;
(k) the grounds for a refusal to take into account a request for assessment are provided in writing; and

(l) the specifications and rules are applied by bodies accredited to norms in the series EN 45 000 and EN ISO/IEC 17025.

CHAPTER VI
MISCELLANEOUS PROVISIONS

[6140]
Article 10
Withdrawal
The Commission may withdraw the benefit of this Regulation, pursuant to Article 7 of Council Regulation (EEC) No 1534/91, where either on its own initiative or at the request of a Member State or of a natural or legal person claiming a legitimate interest, it finds in a particular case that an agreement to which the exemption provided for in Article 1 applies nevertheless has effects which are incompatible with the conditions laid down in Article 81(3) of the Treaty, and in particular where,

(a) studies to which the exemption in Article 1(b) applies are based on unjustifiable hypotheses;
(b) standard policy conditions to which the exemption in Article 1(c) applies contain clauses which create, to the detriment of the policyholder, a significant imbalance between the rights and obligations arising from the contract;
(c) in relation to the common coverage of certain types of risks to which the exemption in Article 1(e) applies, the setting-up or operation of a group results, through the conditions governing admission, the definition of the risks to be covered, the agreements on retrocession or by any other means, in the sharing of the markets for the insurance products concerned or for neighbouring products.

[6141]
Article 11
Transitional period
The prohibition laid down in Article 81(1) of the Treaty shall not apply during the period from 1 April 2003 to 31 March 2004 in respect of agreements already in force on 31 March 2003 which do not satisfy the conditions for exemption provided for in this Regulation but which satisfy the conditions for exemption provided for in Regulation (EEC) No 3932/92.

[6142]
[Article 11a
The prohibition in Article 81(1) of the Treaty shall not apply to agreements which were in existence at the date of accession of the Czech Republic, Estonia, Cyprus, Latvia, Lithuania, Hungary, Malta, Poland, Slovenia and Slovakia and which, by reason of accession, fall within the scope of Article 81(1) if, within six months from the date of accession, they are so amended that they comply with the conditions laid down in this Regulation.]

NOTES
Inserted by Commission Regulation 886/2004/EC, art 1, Annex.

[6143]
Article 12
Period of validity
This Regulation shall enter into force on 1 April 2003. It shall expire on 31 March 2010.

This Regulation shall be binding in its entirety and directly applicable in all Member States.

Done at Brussels, 27 February 2003.

COMMISSION DECISION

(2009/79/EC)

of 23 January 2009

establishing the Committee of European Insurance and Occupational Pensions Supervisors

(Text with EEA relevance)

NOTES
Date of publication in OJ: OJ L25, 29.1.2009, p 28.

[6144]

THE COMMISSION OF THE EUROPEAN COMMUNITIES,

Having regard to the Treaty establishing the European Community,

Whereas:

(1) As part of the so-called Lamfalussy process, the Commission adopted Decision 2004/6/EC of 5 November 2003 establishing the Committee of European Insurance and Occupational Pensions Supervisors[1] (hereinafter 'the Committee'). The Committee took up its duties on 24 November 2003, serving as an independent body for reflection, debate and advice of the Commission in the insurance, reinsurance and occupational pensions fields.

(2) Fulfilling the provisions of Directive 2005/1/EC of the European Parliament and of the Council of 9 March 2005 amending Council Directives 73/239/EEC, 85/611/EEC, 91/675/EEC, 92/49/EEC and 93/6/EEC and Directives 94/19/EC, 98/78/EC, 2000/12/EC, 2001/34/EC, 2002/83/EC and 2002/87/EC in order to establish a new organisational structure for financial services committees,[2] the Commission carried out a review of the Lamfalussy process in 2007 and presented its assessment in a Communication of 20 November 2007 entitled 'Review of the Lamfalussy process — Strengthening supervisory convergence'.[3]

(3) In the Communication, the Commission pointed out the importance of the Committee of European Securities Regulators, the Committee of European Banking Supervisors and the Committee of European Insurance and Occupational Pensions Supervisors (hereinafter 'the Committees of Supervisors') in an increasingly integrated European financial market. A clear framework for the activities of these Committees in the area of supervisory convergence and cooperation was deemed necessary.

(4) While reviewing the functioning of the Lamfalussy process, the Council invited the Commission to clarify the role of the Committees of Supervisors and consider all different options to strengthen the working of those Committees, without unbalancing the current institutional structure or reducing the accountability of supervisors.[4]

(5) At its meeting of 13 and 14 March 2008, the European Council called for swift improvements to the functioning of the Committees of Supervisors.[5]

(6) On 14 May 2008,[6] the Council invited the Commission to revise the Commission Decisions establishing the Committees of Supervisors so as to ensure coherence and consistency in their mandates and tasks as well as to strengthen their contributions to supervisory cooperation and convergence. The Council noted that specific tasks could be explicitly given to the Committees to foster supervisory cooperation and convergence, and their role in assessing risks to financial stability. Therefore a reinforced legal framework regarding the role and tasks of the Committee in this respect should be provided.

(7) The Committee should serve as an independent advisory group of the Commission in the insurance, reinsurance and occupational pensions fields. However, as regards the occupational pensions field, while the Committee should consider the regulatory and supervisory aspects relating to such arrangements, it should not address labour and social law aspects, such as the organisation of occupational regimes, and in particular, issues relating to compulsory membership (affiliation) or collective agreements.

(8) The Committee's mandate should cover the supervision of financial conglomerates. To avoid duplication of work, to prevent any inconsistencies, to keep the Committee abreast of progress, and to give it the opportunity to exchange information, the collaboration with the Committee of European Banking Supervisors in the supervision of financial conglomerates should be exercised in the Joint Committee on Financial Conglomerates.

(9) The Committee should also contribute to the common and uniform day-to-day implementation of Community legislation and its consistent application by the supervisory authorities.

(10) The Committee does not have any regulatory powers at Community level. It should carry out peer reviews, promote best practices and issue non-binding guidelines, recommendations and standards in order to increase convergence across the Community.

(11) Enhanced bilateral and multilateral supervisory cooperation depends on the mutual understanding and trust between supervisory authorities. The Committee should contribute to the improvement of such cooperation.

(12) The Committee should also foster supervisory convergence across the Community. In order to be more specific about this objective, an indicative and open-ended list of tasks to be carried out by the Committee should be established.

(13) In order to resolve disputes of a cross-border nature between supervisory authorities, in particular within colleges of supervisors, a voluntary and non-binding mediation mechanism should be provided by the Committee.

(14) To benefit from the expertise acquired by the Committee and without prejudice to the powers of supervisory authorities, the supervisory authorities should be able to refer matters to the Committee with a view to obtaining its non-binding opinion.

(15) The exchange of information between the supervisory authorities is fundamental to their

functions. It is central for the efficient supervision of insurance groups and for financial stability. Whilst the insurance legislation imposes clear legal obligations on supervisory authorities to cooperate and exchange information, the Committee should facilitate practical day-to-day exchange of information between them, subject to relevant confidentiality provisions set out in applicable legislation.

(16) In order to reduce the duplication of supervisory tasks and thereby streamline the supervisory process as well as reduce the burden imposed on insurance groups, the Committee should facilitate the delegation of tasks between supervisory authorities, in particular in cases specified in the relevant legislation.

(17) With a view to fostering convergence and consistency across the colleges of supervisors and thereby ensuring a level playing field, the Committee should monitor their functioning without constraining the independence of the members of the college.

(18) Quality, comparability and consistency of supervisory reporting are central to the cost-efficiency of Community supervisory arrangements and the compliance burden on cross-border institutions. The Committee should contribute to ensuring that overlap and duplication is eliminated and that the reporting data is comparable and of appropriate quality.

(19) Financial systems in the Community are closely linked and events in one Member State can have a significant impact on financial institutions and markets in other Member States. The continuing emergence of financial conglomerates and the blurring of distinctions between the activities of firms in the banking, securities and insurance sectors give rise to additional supervisory challenges at national and Community level. In order to safeguard financial stability, a system is needed at the level of the Committee, the Committee of European Banking Supervisors and the Committee of European Securities Regulators in order to identify potential risks, across borders and across sectors, at an early stage and, where necessary, inform the Commission and the other Committees. Furthermore, it is essential that the Committee ensures that finance ministries and national central banks of the Member States are informed. The Committee has its role to play in this respect by identifying risks in the insurance, reinsurance and occupational pension sectors and regularly reporting on the outcome to the Commission. The Council should also be informed of these assessments. The Committee should also cooperate with the European Parliament and provide it with periodic information on the situation in the insurance sector. The Committee should not, in this context, disclose information on individual supervised entities.

(20) In order to adequately deal with cross-sector issues, the activities of the Committee should be coordinated with those of the Committee of European Securities Regulators, the Committee of European Banking Supervisors and the Banking Supervision Committee of the European System of Central Banks. This is of particular importance in addressing possible cross-sectoral risks to financial stability.

(21) Given the globalisation of financial services and the increased importance of international standards, the Committee should also foster dialogue and cooperation with supervisors outside the Community.

(22) The accountability of the Committee towards the Community Institutions is of high importance and should be of a well established standard while respecting the independence of supervisors.

(23) The Committee should draw up its own rules of procedure and fully respect the prerogatives of the institutions and the institutional balance established by the Treaty. The enhanced framework of the activities of the Committee should be accompanied by improved working processes. To this end, if consensus cannot be reached, decisions should be taken by qualified majority corresponding to the rules set out in the Treaty.

(24) For reasons of legal security and clarity Decision 2004/6/EC should be repealed,

NOTES

[1] OJ L3, 7.1.2004, p 30.

[2] OJ L79, 24.3.2005, p 9.

[3] COM(2007) 727 final.

[4] Council Conclusions 15698/07 of 4 December 2007.

[5] Council Conclusions 7652/1/08 Rev 1.

[6] Council Conclusions 8515/3/08 Rev 3.

HAS DECIDED AS FOLLOWS:

[6145]
Article 1
An independent advisory group on insurance and occupational pensions in the Community, called 'the Committee of European Insurance and Occupational Pensions Supervisors' (hereinafter 'the Committee'), is hereby established.

Part VI European Materials

[6146]
Article 2
The Committee shall advise the Commission, in particular as regards the preparation of draft implementing measures in the fields of insurance, reinsurance, occupational pensions and financial conglomerates, on its own initiative or at the request of the Commission.

Where the Commission requests advice from the Committee, it may lay down a time limit within which the Committee shall provide such advice. Such time limit shall be laid down taking into account the urgency of the matter.

[6147]
Article 3
The Committee shall fulfil the tasks assigned to it and contribute to the common and uniform implementation and consistent application of Community legislation by issuing guidelines, recommendations and standards.

[6148]
Article 4
1. The Committee shall enhance cooperation between national supervisory authorities in the insurance, reinsurance and occupational pensions fields and foster the convergence of Member States' supervisory practices and approaches throughout the Community. To this effect, it shall carry out, at least, the following tasks:
 (a) mediate or facilitate mediation between supervisory authorities in cases specified in the relevant legislation or at the request of a supervisory authority;
 (b) provide opinions to supervisory authorities in cases specified in the relevant legislation or at their request;
 (c) promote the effective bilateral and multilateral exchange of information between supervisory authorities subject to applicable confidentiality provisions;
 (d) facilitate the delegation of tasks between supervisory authorities, in particular by identifying tasks which can be delegated and by promoting best practices;
 (e) contribute to ensuring the efficient and consistent functioning of colleges of supervisors in particular through setting guidelines for the operational functioning of colleges, monitoring the coherence of the practices of the different colleges and sharing best practices;
 (f) contribute to developing high quality and common supervisory reporting standards;
 (g) review the practical application of the non-binding guidelines, recommendations and standards issued by the Committee.

2. The Committee shall review the Member States' supervisory practices and assess their convergence on an ongoing basis. The Committee shall report annually on progress achieved and identify the remaining obstacles.
3. The Committee shall develop new practical convergence tools to promote the common supervisory approaches.

[6149]
Article 5
1. The Committee shall monitor and assess developments in the insurance, reinsurance and occupational pensions sector and, where necessary, inform the Committee of European Securities Regulators, the Committee of European Banking Supervisors and the Commission. The Committee shall ensure that the finance ministries and national central banks of the Member States are informed about potential or imminent problems.
2. The Committee shall, at least twice a year, provide to the Commission assessments of micro-prudential trends, potential risks and vulnerabilities in the insurance, reinsurance and occupational pensions sector.

The Committee shall include in these assessments a classification of the main risks and vulnerabilities and indicate to what extent such risks and vulnerabilities pose a threat to financial stability and, where necessary, propose preventative or remedial actions.

The Council shall be informed of these assessments.
3. The Committee shall have in place procedures enabling the supervisory authrities to react promptly. Where appropriate, the Committee shall facilitate a common position within the Community on risks and vulnerabilities which may negatively affect the stability of the financial system of the Community.
4. The Committee shall ensure an adequate coverage of cross-sectoral developments, risks and vulnerabilities by closely cooperating with the Committee of European Securities Regulators, the Committee of European Banking Supervisors and the Banking Supervision Committee of the European System of Central Banks.

[6150]
Article 6

1. The Committee shall contribute to the development of common supervisory prctices in the field of insurance, reinsurance and occupational pensions as well as on a cross-sectoral basis in close cooperation with the Committee of European Securities Regulators and the Committee of European Banking Supervisors.
2. To this effect, it shall in particular establish sectoral and cross-sectoral training programmes, facilitate personnel exchanges and encourage competent authorities to intensify the use of secondment schemes, joint inspection teams and supervisory visits and other tools.
3. The Committee shall, as appropriate, develop new instruments to promote the development of common supervisory practices.
4. The Committee shall enhance cooperation with the supervisory authorities of third countries, in particular by their participation in common training programmes.

[6151]
Article 7

1. The Committee shall be composed of high-level representatives from the national public authorities competent in the field of supervision of insurance, reinsurance and occupational pensions. Each Member State shall designate a high level representative from its competent authorities to participate in the meetings of the Committee.
2. The Commission shall be present at meetings of the Committee and shall designate a high level representative to participate in its debates.
3. The Committee shall elect a chairperson from among its members.
4. The Committee may invite experts and observers to attend its meetings.
5. The Committee shall not address labour and social law aspects such as the organisation of occupational regimes, in particular compulsory membership and collective agreements.

[6152]
Article 8

1. The members of the Committee shall be required not to disclose information covered by the obligation of professional secrecy. All participants in the discussions shall be obliged to comply with the applicable rules of professional secrecy.
2. Whenever discussion of an item on the agenda entails the exchange of confidential information concerning a supervised institution, participation in such discussion may be restricted to members directly involved.

[6152A]
Article 9

1. The Committee shall regularly inform the Commission about the outcome of its activities. It shall have regular contacts with the European Insurance and Occupational Pensions Committee established by Commission Decision 2004/9/EC[1] and the competent Committee of the European Parliament.
2. The Committee shall ensure cross-sectoral consistency of work in the financial services sectors by regularly and closely cooperating with the Committee of European Securities Regulators and the Committee of European Banking Supervisors.
3. The chairperson of the Committee shall have regular contact with the chairpersons of the Committee of European Securities Regulators and of the Committee of European Banking Supervisors, at least once a month.

NOTES

1 OJ L3, 7.1.2004, p 34.

[6152B]
Article 10

The Committee may set up working groups. The Commission shall be invited to the meetings of the working groups as an observer.

[6152C]
Article 11

The Committee shall cooperate in the area of supervision of financial conglomerates with the Committee of European Banking Supervisors in a Joint Committee on Financial Conglomerates.

The Commission and the European Central Bank shall be invited to the meetings of the Joint Committee on Financial Conglomerates as observers.

[6152D]
Article 12
Before transmitting its opinion to the Commission, the Committee shall, at an early stage, consult market participants, consumers and end-users extensively and in an open and transparent manner. The Committee shall publish the results of the consultations, unless the respondent requests otherwise.

[6152E]
Article 13
The Committee shall establish an annual work programme and transmit it to the Council, the European Parliament and the Commission by the end of October each year. The Committee shall periodically and at least annually inform the Council, the European Parliament and the Commission on the achievement of the activities set out in the work programme.

[6152F]
Article 14
The Committee shall work by consensus of its members. If no consensus can be reached, decisions shall be taken by qualified majority. The votes of the representatives of the Members of the Committee shall correspond to the votes of the Member States as laid down in Articles 205(2) and (4) of the Treaty.

Members of the Committee which do not follow the guidelines, recommendations, standards and other measures agreed by the Committee shall be prepared to present the reasons for this choice.

[6152G]
Article 15
The Committee shall adopt its own rules of procedure and organise its own operational arrangements.

With regard to decisions concerning amendments to the rules of the procedure and elections to and dismissals from the Board of the Committee, the rules of procedure may foresee decision-making procedures that are different from those set out in Article 14.

[6152H]
Article 16
Decision 2004/6/EC is repealed.

[6152I]
Article 17
This Decision shall take effect on the day of its publication in the *Official Journal of the European Union.*

Done at Brussels, 23 January 2009.

EUROPEAN PARLIAMENT AND COUNCIL DIRECTIVE

(2009/138/EC)
of 25 November 2009

on the taking-up and pursuit of the business of Insurance and Reinsurance (Solvency II)
(recast)
(Text with EEA relevance)

NOTES
Date of publication in OJ: OJ L335, 17.12.2009, p 1.

[6153]
THE EUROPEAN PARLIAMENT AND THE COUNCIL OF THE EUROPEAN UNION,

Having regard to the Treaty establishing the European Community, and in particular Article 47(2) and Article 55 thereof,

Having regard to the proposal from the Commission,

Having regard to the opinion of the European Economic and Social Committee,[1]

After consulting the Committee of the Regions,

Acting in accordance with the procedure laid down in Article 251 of the Treaty,[2]

Whereas:

(1) A number of substantial changes are to be made to First Council Directive 73/239/EEC of 24 July 1973 on the coordination of laws, regulations and administrative provisions relating to the taking-up and pursuit of the business of direct insurance other than life assurance;[3] Council Directive

78/473/EEC of 30 May 1978 on the coordination of laws, regulations and administrative provisions relating to Community co-insurance;[4] Council Directive 87/344/EEC of 22 June 1987 on the coordination of laws, regulations and administrative provisions relating to legal expenses insurance;[5] Second Council Directive 88/357/EEC of 22 June 1988 on the coordination of laws, regulations and administrative provisions relating to direct insurance other than life assurance and laying down provisions to facilitate the effective exercise of freedom to provide services;[6] Council Directive 92/49/EEC of 18 June 1992 on the coordination of laws, regulations and administrative provisions relating to direct insurance other than life assurance (third non-life insurance Directive);[7] Directive 98/78/EC of the European Parliament and of the Council of 27 October 1998 on the supplementary supervision of insurance undertakings in an insurance group[8] Directive 2001/17/EC of the European Parliament and of the Council of 19 March 2001 on the reorganisation and winding-up of insurance undertakings;[9] Directive 2002/83/EC of the European Parliament and of the Council of 5 November 2002 concerning life assurance;[10] and Directive 2005/68/EC of the European Parliament and of the Council of 16 November 2005 on reinsurance.[11] In the interests of clarity those Directives should be recast.

(2) In order to facilitate the taking-up and pursuit of the activities of insurance and reinsurance, it is necessary to eliminate the most serious differences between the laws of the Member States as regards the rules to which insurance and reinsurance undertakings are subject. A legal framework should therefore be provided for insurance and reinsurance undertakings to conduct insurance business throughout the internal market thus making it easier for insurance and reinsurance undertakings with head offices in the Community to cover risks and commitments situated therein.

(3) It is in the interests of the proper functioning of the internal market that coordinated rules be established relating to the supervision of insurance groups and, with a view to the protection of creditors, to the reorganisation and winding-up proceedings in respect of insurance undertakings.

(4) It is appropriate that certain undertakings which provide insurance services are not covered by the system established by this Directive due to their size, their legal status, their nature — as being closely linked to public insurance systems — or the specific services they offer. It is further desirable to exclude certain institutions in several Member States, the business of which covers only a very limited sector and is restricted by law to a specific territory or to specified persons.

(5) Very small insurance undertakings fulfilling certain conditions, including gross premium income below EUR 5 million, are excluded from the scope of this Directive. However, all insurance and reinsurance undertakings which are already licensed under the current Directives should continue to be licensed when this Directive is implemented. Undertakings that are excluded from the scope of this Directive should be able to make use of the basic freedoms granted by the Treaty. Those undertakings have the option to seek authorisation under this Directive in order to benefit from the single licence provided for in this Directive.

(6) It should be possible for Member States to require undertakings that pursue the business of insurance or reinsurance and which are excluded from the scope of this Directive to register. Member States may also subject those undertakings to prudential and legal supervision.

(7) Council Directive 72/166/EEC of 24 April 1972 on the approximation of the laws of Member States relating to insurance against civil liability in respect of the use of motor vehicles, and to the enforcement of the obligation to insure against such liability;[12] Seventh Council Directive 83/349/EEC of 13 June 1983 based on the Article 54(3)(g) of the Treaty on consolidated accounts;[13] Second Council Directive 84/5/EEC of 30 December 1983 on the approximation of the laws of the Member States relating to insurance against civil liability in respect of the use of motor vehicles;[14] Directive 2004/39/EC of the European Parliament and of the Council of 21 April 2004 on markets in financial instruments;[15] and Directive 2006/48/EC of the European Parliament and of the Council of 14 June 2006 relating to the taking up and pursuit of the business of credit institutions[16] lay down general rules in the fields of accounting, motor insurance liability, financial instruments and credit institutions and provide for definitions in those areas. It is appropriate that certain of the definitions laid down in those directives apply for the purposes of this Directive.

(8) The taking-up of insurance or of reinsurance activities should be subject to prior authorisation. It is therefore necessary to lay down the conditions and the procedure for the granting of that authorisation as well as for any refusal.

(9) The directives repealed by this Directive do not lay down any rules in respect of the scope of reinsurance activities that an insurance undertaking may be authorised to pursue. It is for the Member States to decide to lay down any rules in that regard.

(10) References in this Directive to insurance or reinsurance undertakings should include captive insurance and captive reinsurance undertakings, except where specific provision is made for those undertakings.

(11) Since this Directive constitutes an essential instrument for the achievement of the internal market, insurance and reinsurance undertakings authorised in their home Member States should be allowed to pursue, throughout the Community, any or all of their activities by establishing branches or by providing services. It is therefore appropriate to bring about such harmonisation as is necessary and sufficient to achieve the mutual recognition of authorisations and supervisory systems, and thus a single authorisation which is valid throughout the Community and which allows the supervision

of an undertaking to be carried out by the home Member State.

(12) Directive 2000/26/EC of the European Parliament and of the Council of 16 May 2000 on the approximation of the laws of the Member States relating to insurance against civil liability in respect of the use of motor vehicles (Fourth motor insurance Directive)[17] lays down rules on the appointment of claims representatives. Those rules should apply for the purposes of this Directive.

(13) Reinsurance undertakings should limit their objects to the business of reinsurance and related operations. Such a requirement should not prevent a reinsurance undertaking from pursuing activities such as the provision of statistical or actuarial advice, risk analysis or research for its clients. It may also include a holding company function and activities with respect to financial sector activities within the meaning of Article 2(8) of Directive 2002/87/EC of the European Parliament and of the Council of 16 December 2002 on the supplementary supervision of credit institutions, insurance undertakings and investment firms in a financial conglomerate. [18] In any event, that requirement does not allow the pursuit of unrelated banking and financial activities.

(14) The protection of policy holders presupposes that insurance and reinsurance undertakings are subject to effective solvency requirements that result in an efficient allocation of capital across the European Union. In light of market developments the current system is no longer adequate. It is therefore necessary to introduce a new regulatory framework.

(15) In line with the latest developments in risk management, in the context of the International Association of Insurance Supervisors, the International Accounting Standards Board and the International Actuarial Association and with recent developments in other financial sectors an economic risk-based approach should be adopted which provides incentives for insurance and reinsurance undertakings to properly measure and manage their risks. Harmonisation should be increased by providing specific rules for the valuation of assets and liabilities, including technical provisions.

(16) The main objective of insurance and reinsurance regulation and supervision is the adequate protection of policy holders and beneficiaries. The term beneficiary is intended to cover any natural or legal person who is entitled to a right under an insurance contract. Financial stability and fair and stable markets are other objectives of insurance and reinsurance regulation and supervision which should also be taken into account but should not undermine the main objective.

(17) The solvency regime laid down in this Directive is expected to result in even better protection for policy holders. It will require Member States to provide supervisory authorities with the resources to fulfil their obligations as set out in this Directive. This encompasses all necessary capacities, including financial and human resources.

(18) The supervisory authorities of the Member States should therefore have at their disposal all means necessary to ensure the orderly pursuit of business by insurance and reinsurance undertakings throughout the Community whether pursued under the right of establishment or the freedom to provide services. In order to ensure the effectiveness of the supervision all actions taken by the supervisory authorities should be proportionate to the nature, scale and complexity of the risks inherent in the business of an insurance or reinsurance undertaking, regardless of the importance of the undertaking concerned for the overall financial stability of the market.

(19) This Directive should not be too burdensome for small and medium-sized insurance undertakings. One of the tools by which to achieve that objective is the proper application of the proportionality principle. That principle should apply both to the requirements imposed on the insurance and reinsurance undertakings and to the exercise of supervisory powers.

(20) In particular, this Directive should not be too burdensome for insurance undertakings that specialise in providing specific types of insurance or services to specific customer segments, and it should recognise that specialising in this way can be a valuable tool for efficiently and effectively managing risk. In order to achieve that objective, as well as the proper application of the proportionality principle, provision should also be made specifically to allow undertakings to use their own data to calibrate the parameters in the underwriting risk modules of the standard formula of the Solvency Capital Requirement.

(21) This Directive should also take account of the specific nature of captive insurance and captive reinsurance undertakings. As those undertakings only cover risks associated with the industrial or commercial group to which they belong, appropriate approaches should thus be provided in line with the principle of proportionality to reflect the nature, scale and complexity of their business.

(22) The supervision of reinsurance activity should take account of the special characteristics of reinsurance business, notably its global nature and the fact that the policy holders are themselves insurance or reinsurance undertakings.

(23) Supervisory authorities should be able to obtain from insurance and reinsurance undertakings the information which is necessary for the purposes of supervision, including, where appropriate, information publicly disclosed by an insurance or reinsurance undertaking under financial reporting, listing and other legal or regulatory requirements.

(24) The supervisory authorities of the home Member State should be responsible for monitoring the financial health of insurance and reinsurance undertakings. To that end, they should carry out regular reviews and evaluations.

(25) Supervisory authorities should be able to take account of the effects on risk and asset management of voluntary codes of conduct and transparency complied with by the relevant institutions dealing in unregulated or alternative investment instruments.

(26) The starting point for the adequacy of the quantitative requirements in the insurance sector is the Solvency Capital Requirement. Supervisory authorities should therefore have the power to impose a capital add-on to the Solvency Capital Requirement only under exceptional circumstances, in the cases listed in this Directive, following the supervisory review process. The Solvency Capital Requirement standard formula is intended to reflect the risk profile of most insurance and reinsurance undertakings. However, there may be some cases where the standardised approach does not adequately reflect the very specific risk profile of an undertaking.

(27) The imposition of a capital add-on is exceptional in the sense that it should be used only as a measure of last resort, when other supervisory measures are ineffective or inappropriate. Furthermore, the term exceptional should be understood in the context of the specific situation of each undertaking rather than in relation to the number of capital add-ons imposed in a specific market.

(28) The capital add-on should be retained for as long as the circumstances under which it was imposed are not remedied. In the event of significant deficiencies in the full or partial internal model or significant governance failures the supervisory authorities should ensure that the undertaking concerned makes every effort to remedy the deficiencies that led to the imposition of the capital add-on. However, where the standardised approach does not adequately reflect the very specific risk profile of an undertaking the capital add-on may remain over consecutive years.

(29) Some risks may only be properly addressed through governance requirements rather than through the quantitative requirements reflected in the Solvency Capital Requirement. An effective system of governance is therefore essential for the adequate management of the insurance undertaking and for the regulatory system.

(30) The system of governance includes the risk-management function, the compliance function, the internal audit function and the actuarial function.

(31) A function is an administrative capacity to undertake particular governance tasks. The identification of a particular function does not prevent the undertaking from freely deciding how to organise that function in practice save where otherwise specified in this Directive. This should not lead to unduly burdensome requirements because account should be taken of the nature, scale and complexity of the operations of the undertaking. It should therefore be possible for those functions to be staffed by own staff, to rely on advice from outside experts or to be outsourced to experts within the limits set by this Directive.

(32) Furthermore, save as regards the internal audit function, in smaller and less complex undertakings it should be possible for more than one function to be carried out by a single person or organisational unit.

(33) The functions included in the system of governance are considered to be key functions and consequently also important and critical functions.

(34) All persons that perform key functions should be fit and proper. However, only the key function holders should be subject to notification requirements to the supervisory authority.

(35) For the purpose of assessing the required level of competence, professional qualifications and experience of those who effectively run the undertaking or have other key functions should be taken into consideration as additional factors.

(36) All insurance and reinsurance undertakings should have, as an integrated part of their business strategy, a regular practice of assessing their overall solvency needs with a view to their specific risk profile (own-risk and solvency assessment). That assessment neither requires the development of an internal model nor serves to calculate a capital requirement different from the Solvency Capital Requirement or the Minimum Capital Requirement. The results of each assessment should be reported to the supervisory authority as part of the information to be provided for supervisory purposes.

(37) In order to ensure effective supervision of outsourced functions or activities, it is essential that the supervisory authorities of the outsourcing insurance or reinsurance undertaking have access to all relevant data held by the outsourcing service provider, regardless of whether the latter is a regulated or unregulated entity, as well as the right to conduct on-site inspections. In order to take account of market developments and to ensure that the conditions for outsourcing continue to be complied with, the supervisory authorities should be informed prior to the outsourcing of critical or important functions or activities. Those requirements should take into account the work of the Joint Forum and are consistent with the current rules and practices in the banking sector and Directive 2004/39/EC and its application to credit institutions.

(38) In order to guarantee transparency, insurance and reinsurance undertakings should publicly disclose — that is to say make it available to the public either in printed or electronic form free of charge — at least annually, essential information on their solvency and financial condition. Undertakings should be allowed to disclose publicly additional information on a voluntary basis.

(39) Provision should be made for exchanges of information between the supervisory authorities and authorities or bodies which, by virtue of their function, help to strengthen the stability of the financial system. It is therefore necessary to specify the conditions under which those exchanges of information should be possible. Moreover, where information may be disclosed only with the express agreement of the supervisory authorities, those authorities should be able, where appropriate, to make their agreement subject to compliance with strict conditions.

(40) It is necessary to promote supervisory convergence not only in respect of supervisory tools but also in respect of supervisory practices. The Committee of European Insurance and Occupational Pensions Supervisors (CEIOPS) established by Commission Decision 2009/79/EC[19] should play an important role in this respect and report regularly to the European Parliament and the Commission on the progress made.

(41) The objective of the information and report to be presented in relation to capital add-ons by CEIOPS is not to inhibit their use as permitted under this Directive but to contribute to an ever higher degree of supervisory convergence in the use of capital add-ons between supervisory authorities in the different Member States.

(42) In order to limit the administrative burden and avoid duplication of tasks, supervisory authorities and national statistical authorities should cooperate and exchange information.

(43) For the purposes of strengthening the supervision of insurance and reinsurance undertakings and the protection of policy holders, the statutory auditors within the meaning of Directive 2006/43/EC of the European Parliament and of the Council of 17 May 2006 on statutory audits of annual accounts and consolidated accounts[20] should have a duty to report promptly any facts which are likely to have a serious effect on the financial situation or the administrative organisation of an insurance or a reinsurance undertaking.

(44) Insurance undertakings pursuing both life and non-life activities should manage those activities separately, in order to protect the interests of life policy holders. In particular, those undertakings should be subject to the same capital requirements as those applicable to an equivalent insurance group, made up of a life insurance undertaking and a non-life undertaking, taking into account the increased transferability of capital in the case of composite insurance undertakings.

(45) The assessment of the financial position of insurance and reinsurance undertakings should rely on sound economic principles and make optimal use of the information provided by financial markets, as well as generally available data on insurance technical risks. In particular, solvency requirements should be based on an economic valuation of the whole balance sheet.

(46) Valuation standards for supervisory purposes should be compatible with international accounting developments, to the extent possible, so as to limit the administrative burden on insurance or reinsurance undertakings.

(47) In accordance with that approach, capital requirements should be covered by own funds, irrespective of whether they are on or off the balance-sheet items. Since not all financial resources provide full absorption of losses in the case of winding-up and on a going-concern basis, own-fund items should be classified in accordance with quality criteria into three tiers, and the eligible amount of own funds to cover capital requirements should be limited accordingly. The limits applicable to own-fund items should only apply to determine the solvency standing of insurance and reinsurance undertakings, and should not further restrict the freedom of those undertakings with respect to their internal capital management.

(48) Generally, assets which are free from any foreseeable liabilities are available to absorb losses due to adverse business fluctuations on a going-concern basis and in the case of winding-up. Therefore the vast majority of the excess of assets over liabilities, as valued in accordance with the principles set out in this Directive, should be treated as high-quality capital (Tier 1).

(49) Not all assets within an undertaking are unrestricted. In some Member States, specific products result in ring-fenced fund structures which give one class of policy holders greater rights to assets within their own fund. Although those assets are included in computing the excess of assets over liabilities for own-fund purposes they cannot in fact be made available to meet the risks outside the ring-fenced fund. To be consistent with the economic approach, the assessment of own funds needs to be adjusted to reflect the different nature of assets, which form part of a ring-fenced arrangement. Similarly, the Solvency Capital Requirement calculation should reflect the reduction in pooling or diversification related to those ring-fenced funds.

(50) It is current practice in certain Member States for insurance companies to sell life insurance products in relation to which the policy holders and beneficiaries contribute to the risk capital of the company in exchange for all or part of the return on the contributions. Those accumulated profits are surplus funds, which are the property of the legal entity in which they are generated.

(51) Surplus funds should be valued in line with the economic approach laid down in this Directive. In this respect, a mere reference to the evaluation of surplus funds in the statutory annual accounts should not be sufficient. In line with the requirements on own funds, surplus funds should be subject to the criteria laid down in this Directive on the classification in tiers. This means, inter alia, that only surplus funds which fulfil the requirements for classification in Tier 1 should be considered as Tier 1 capital.

(52) Mutual and mutual-type associations with variable contributions may call for supplementary contributions from their members (supplementary members' calls) in order to increase the amount of financial resources that they hold to absorb losses. Supplementary members' calls may represent a significant source of funding for mutual and mutual-type associations, including when those associations are confronted with adverse business fluctuations. Supplementary members' calls should therefore be recognised as ancillary own-fund items and treated accordingly for solvency purposes. In particular, in the case of mutual or mutual-type associations of shipowners with variable contributions solely insuring maritime risks, the recourse to supplementary members' calls has been a long-established practice, subject to specific recovery arrangements, and the approved amount of those members' calls should be treated as good-quality capital (Tier 2). Similarly, in the case of other mutual and mutual-type associations where supplementary members' calls are of similar quality, the approved amount of those members' calls should also be treated as good-quality capital (Tier 2).

(53) In order to allow insurance and reinsurance undertakings to meet their commitments towards policy holders and beneficiaries, Member States should require those undertakings to establish adequate technical provisions. The principles and actuarial and statistical methodologies underlying the calculation of those technical provisions should be harmonised throughout the Community in order to achieve better comparability and transparency.

(54) The calculation of technical provisions should be consistent with the valuation of assets and other liabilities, market consistent and in line with international developments in accounting and supervision.

(55) The value of technical provisions should therefore correspond to the amount an insurance or reinsurance undertaking would have to pay if it transferred its contractual rights and obligations immediately to another undertaking. Consequently, the value of technical provisions should correspond to the amount which another insurance or reinsurance undertaking (the reference undertaking) would be expected to require to take over and fulfil the underlying insurance and reinsurance obligations. The amount of technical provisions should reflect the characteristics of the underlying insurance portfolio. Undertaking-specific information, such as that regarding claims management and expenses, should therefore be used in their calculation only insofar as that information enables insurance and reinsurance undertakings better to reflect the characteristics of the underlying insurance portfolio.

(56) The assumptions made about the reference undertaking assumed to take over and meet the underlying insurance and reinsurance obligations should be harmonised throughout the Community. In particular, the assumptions made about the reference undertaking that determine whether or not, and if so to what extent, diversification effects should be taken into account in the calculation of the risk margin should be analysed as part of the impact assessment of implementing measures and should then be harmonised at Community level.

(57) For the purpose of calculating technical provisions, it should be possible to apply reasonable interpolations and extrapolations from directly observable market values.

(58) It is necessary that the expected present value of insurance liabilities is calculated on the basis of current and credible information and realistic assumptions, taking account of financial guarantees and options in insurance or reinsurance contracts, to deliver an economic valuation of insurance or reinsurance obligations. The use of effective and harmonised actuarial methodologies should be required.

(59) In order to reflect the specific situation of small and medium-sized undertakings, simplified approaches to the calculation of technical provisions should be provided for.

(60) The supervisory regime should provide for a risk-sensitive requirement, which is based on a prospective calculation to ensure accurate and timely intervention by supervisory authorities (the Solvency Capital Requirement), and a minimum level of security below which the amount of financial resources should not fall (the Minimum Capital Requirement). Both capital requirements should be harmonised throughout the Community in order to achieve a uniform level of protection for policy holders. For the good functioning of this Directive, there should be an adequate ladder of intervention between the Solvency Capital Requirement and the Minimum Capital Requirement.

(61) In order to mitigate undue potential pro-cyclical effects of the financial system and avoid a situation in which insurance and reinsurance undertakings are unduly forced to raise additional capital or sell their investments as a result of unsustained adverse movements in financial markets, the market risk module of the standard formula for the Solvency Capital Requirement should include a symmetric adjustment mechanism with respect to changes in the level of equity prices. In addition, in the event of exceptional falls in financial markets, and where that symmetric adjustment mechanism is not sufficient to enable insurance and reinsurance undertakings to fulfil their Solvency Capital Requirement, provision should be made to allow supervisory authorities to extend the period within which insurance and reinsurance undertakings are required to re-establish the level of eligible own funds covering the Solvency Capital Requirement.

(62) The Solvency Capital Requirement should reflect a level of eligible own funds that enables insurance and reinsurance undertakings to absorb significant losses and that gives reasonable assurance to policy holders and beneficiaries that payments will be made as they fall due.

(63) In order to ensure that insurance and reinsurance undertakings hold eligible own funds that cover the Solvency Capital Requirement on an on-going basis, taking into account any changes in their risk profile, those undertakings should calculate the Solvency Capital Requirement at least annually, monitor it continuously and recalculate it whenever the risk profile alters significantly.

(64) In order to promote good risk management and align regulatory capital requirements with industry practices, the Solvency Capital Requirement should be determined as the economic capital to be held by insurance and reinsurance undertakings in order to ensure that ruin occurs no more often than once in every 200 cases or, alternatively, that those undertakings will still be in a position, with a probability of at least 99,5%, to meet their obligations to policy holders and beneficiaries over the following 12 months. That economic capital should be calculated on the basis of the true risk profile of those undertakings, taking account of the impact of possible risk-mitigation techniques, as well as diversification effects.

(65) Provision should be made to lay down a standard formula for the calculation of the Solvency Capital Requirement, to enable all insurance and reinsurance undertakings to assess their economic capital. For the structure of the standard formula, a modular approach should be adopted, which means that the individual exposure to each risk category should be assessed in a first step and then aggregated in a second step. Where the use of undertaking-specific parameters allows for the true underwriting risk profile of the undertaking to be better reflected, this should be allowed, provided such parameters are derived using a standardised methodology.

(66) In order to reflect the specific situation of small and medium-sized undertakings, simplified approaches to the calculation of the Solvency Capital Requirement in accordance with the standard formula should be provided for.

(67) As a matter of principle, the new risk-based approach does not comprise the concept of quantitative investment limits and asset eligibility criteria. It should however be possible to introduce investment limits and asset eligibility criteria to address risks which are not adequately covered by a sub-module of the standard formula.

(68) In accordance with the risk-oriented approach to the Solvency Capital Requirement, it should be possible, in specific circumstances, to use partial or full internal models for the calculation of that requirement rather than the standard formula. In order to provide policy holders and beneficiaries with an equivalent level of protection, such internal models should be subject to prior supervisory approval on the basis of harmonised processes and standards.

(69) When the amount of eligible basic own funds falls below the Minimum Capital Requirement, the authorisation of insurance and reinsurance undertakings should be withdrawn where those undertakings are unable to re-establish the amount of eligible basic own funds at the level of the Minimum Capital Requirement within a short period of time.

(70) The Minimum Capital Requirement should ensure a minimum level below which the amount of financial resources should not fall. It is necessary that that level be calculated in accordance with a simple formula, which is subject to a defined floor and cap based on the risk-based Solvency Capital Requirement in order to allow for an escalating ladder of supervisory intervention, and that it is based on the data which can be audited.

(71) Insurance and reinsurance undertakings should have assets of sufficient quality to cover their overall financial requirements. All investments held by insurance and reinsurance undertakings should be managed in accordance with the 'prudent person' principle.

(72) Member States should not require insurance or reinsurance undertakings to invest their assets in particular categories of assets, as such a requirement could be incompatible with the liberalisation of capital movements provided for in Article 56 of the Treaty.

(73) It is necessary to prohibit any provisions enabling Member States to require pledging of assets covering the technical provisions of an insurance or reinsurance undertaking, whatever form that requirement might take, when the insurer is reinsured by an insurance or reinsurance undertaking authorised pursuant to this Directive, or by a third-country undertaking where the supervisory regime of that third country has been deemed equivalent.

(74) The legal framework has so far provided neither detailed criteria for a prudential assessment of a proposed acquisition nor a procedure for their application. A clarification of the criteria and the process of prudential assessment is therefore needed to provide the necessary legal certainty, clarity and predictability with regard to the assessment process, as well as to the result thereof. Those criteria and procedures were introduced by provisions in Directive 2007/44/EC. As regards insurance and reinsurance those provisions should therefore be codified and integrated into this Directive.

(75) Maximum harmonisation throughout the Community of those procedures and prudential assessments is therefore critical. However, the provisions on qualifying holdings should not prevent the Member States from requiring that the supervisory authorities are to be informed of acquisitions of holdings below the thresholds laid down in those provisions, so long as a Member State imposes no more than one additional threshold below 10% for that purpose. Nor should those provisions prevent the supervisory authorities from providing general guidance as to when such holdings would be deemed to result in significant influence.

(76) In view of the increasing mobility of citizens of the Union, motor liability insurance is

increasingly being offered on a cross-border basis. To ensure the continued proper functioning of the green card system and the agreements between the national bureaux of motor insurers, it is appropriate that Member States are able to require insurance undertakings providing motor liability insurance in their territory by way of provision of services to join and participate in the financing of the national bureau as well as of the guarantee fund set up in that Member State. The Member State of provision of services should require undertakings which provide motor liability insurance to appoint a representative in its territory to collect all necessary information in relation to claims and to represent the undertaking concerned.

(77) Within the framework of an internal market it is in the interest of policy holders that they should have access to the widest possible range of insurance products available in the Community. The Member State in which the risk is situated or the Member State of the commitment should therefore ensure that there is nothing to prevent the marketing within its territory of all the insurance products offered for sale in the Community as long as they do not conflict with the legal provisions protecting the general good in force in that Member State and in so far as the general good is not safeguarded by the rules of the home Member State.

(78) Provision should be made for a system of sanctions to be imposed when, in the Member State in which the risk is situated or the Member State of the commitment, an insurance undertaking does not comply with any applicable provisions protecting the general good.

(79) In an internal market for insurance, consumers have a wider and more varied choice of contracts. If they are to benefit fully from that diversity and from increased competition, consumers should be provided with whatever information is necessary before the conclusion of the contract and throughout the term of the contract to enable them to choose the contract best suited to their needs.

(80) An insurance undertaking offering assistance contracts should possess the means necessary to provide the benefits in kind which it offers within an appropriate period of time. Special provisions should be laid down for calculating the Solvency Capital Requirement and the absolute floor of the Minimum Capital Requirement which such undertaking should possess.

(81) The effective pursuit of Community co-insurance business for activities which are by reason of their nature or their size likely to be covered by international co-insurance should be facilitated by a minimum of harmonisation in order to prevent distortion of competition and differences in treatment. In that context, the leading insurance undertaking should assess claims and fix the amount of technical provisions. Moreover, special cooperation should be provided for in the Community co-insurance field both between the supervisory authorities of the Member States and between those authorities and the Commission.

(82) In the interest of the protection of insured persons, national law concerning legal expenses insurance should be harmonised. Any conflicts of interest arising, in particular, from the fact that the insurance undertaking is covering another person or is covering a person in respect of both legal expenses and any other class of insurance should be precluded as far as possible or resolved. To that end, a suitable level of protection of policy holders can be achieved by different means. Whichever solution is adopted, the interest of persons having legal expenses cover should be protected by equivalent safeguards.

(83) Conflicts between insured persons and insurance undertakings covering legal expenses should be settled in the fairest and speediest manner possible. It is therefore appropriate that Member States provide for an arbitration procedure or a procedure offering comparable guarantees.

(84) In some Member States, private or voluntary health insurance serves as a partial or complete alternative to health cover provided for by the social security systems. The particular nature of such health insurance distinguishes it from other classes of indemnity insurance and life insurance insofar as it is necessary to ensure that policy holders have effective access to private health cover or health cover taken out on a voluntary basis regardless of their age or risk profile. Given the nature and the social consequences of health insurance contracts, the supervisory authorities of the Member State in which a risk is situated should be able to require systematic notification of the general and special policy conditions in the case of private or voluntary health insurance in order to verify that such contracts are a partial or complete alternative to the health cover provided by the social security system. Such verification should not be a prior condition for the marketing of the products.

(85) To that end, some Member States have adopted specific legal provisions. To protect the general good, it should be possible to adopt or maintain such legal provisions in so far as they do not unduly restrict the right of establishment or the freedom to provide services, it being understood that such provisions should apply in an identical manner. Those legal provisions may differ in nature according to the conditions in each Member State. The objective of protecting the general good may also be achieved by requiring undertakings offering private health cover or health cover taken out on a voluntary basis to offer standard policies in line with the cover provided by statutory social security schemes at a premium rate at or below a prescribed maximum and to participate in loss compensation schemes. As a further possibility, it may be required that the technical basis of private health cover or health cover taken out on a voluntary basis be similar to that of life insurance.

(86) Host Member States should be able to require any insurance undertaking which offers, within their territories, compulsory insurance against accidents at work at its own risk to comply with the specific provisions laid down in their national law on such insurance. However, such a requirement

should not apply to the provisions concerning financial supervision, which should remain the exclusive responsibility of the home Member State.

(87) Some Member States do not subject insurance transactions to any form of indirect taxation, while the majority apply special taxes and other forms of contribution, including surcharges intended for compensation bodies. The structures and rates of such taxes and contributions vary considerably between the Member States in which they are applied. It is desirable to prevent existing differences leading to distortions of competition in insurance services between Member States. Pending subsequent harmonisation, the application of the tax systems and other forms of contribution provided for by the Member States in which the risk is situated or in the Member State of the commitment is likely to remedy that problem and it is for the Member States to make arrangements to ensure that such taxes and contributions are collected.

(88) Those Member States not subject to the application of Regulation (EC) No 593/2008 of the European Parliament and of the Council of 17 June 2008 on the law applicable to contractual obligations (Rome I)[21] should, in accordance with this Directive, apply the provisions of that Regulation in order to determine the law applicable to contracts of insurance falling within the scope of Article 7 of that Regulation.

(89) In order to take account of the international aspects of reinsurance, provision should be made to enable the conclusion of international agreements with a third country aimed at defining the means of supervision over reinsurance entities which conduct business in the territory of each contracting party. Moreover, a flexible procedure should be provided for to make it possible to assess prudential equivalence with third countries on a Community basis, so as to improve liberalisation of reinsurance services in third countries, be it through establishment or cross-border provision of services.

(90) Due to the special nature of finite reinsurance activities, Member States should ensure that insurance and reinsurance undertakings concluding finite reinsurance contracts or pursuing finite reinsurance activities can properly identify, measure and control the risks arising from those contracts or activities.

(91) Appropriate rules should be provided for special purpose vehicles which assume risks from insurance and reinsurance undertakings without being an insurance or reinsurance undertaking. Recoverable amounts from a special purpose vehicle should be considered as amounts deductible under reinsurance or retrocession contracts.

(92) Special purpose vehicles authorised before 31 October 2012 should be subject to the law of the Member State having authorised the special purpose vehicle. However, in order to avoid regulatory arbitrage, any new activity commenced by such a special purpose vehicle after 31 October 2012 should be subject to the provisions of this Directive.

(93) Given the increasing cross-border nature of insurance business, divergences between Member States' regimes on special purpose vehicles, which are subject to the provisions of this Directive, should be reduced to the greatest extent possible, taking account of their supervisory structures.

(94) Further work on special purpose vehicles should be conducted taking into account the work undertaken in other financial sectors.

(95) Measures concerning the supervision of insurance and reinsurance undertakings in a group should enable the authorities supervising an insurance or reinsurance undertaking to form a more soundly based judgment of its financial situation.

(96) Such group supervision should take into account insurance holding companies and mixed-activity insurance holding companies to the extent necessary. However, this Directive should not in any way imply that Member States are required to apply supervision to those undertakings considered individually.

(97) Whilst the supervision of individual insurance and reinsurance undertakings remains the essential principle of insurance supervision it is necessary to determine which undertakings fall under the scope of supervision at group level.

(98) Subject to Community and national law, undertakings, in particular mutual and mutual-type associations, should be able to form concentrations or groups, not through capital ties but through formalised strong and sustainable relationships, based on contractual or other material recognition that guarantees a financial solidarity between those undertakings. Where a dominant influence is exercised through a centralised coordination, those undertakings should be supervised in accordance with the same rules as those provided for groups constituted through capital ties in order to achieve an adequate level of protection for policy holders and a level playing field between groups.

(99) Group supervision should apply in any case at the level of the ultimate parent undertaking which has its head office in the Community. Member States should however be able to allow their supervisory authorities to apply group supervision at a limited number of lower levels, where they deem it necessary.

(100) It is necessary to calculate solvency at group level for insurance and reinsurance undertakings forming part of a group.

(101) The consolidated Solvency Capital Requirement for a group should take into account the global diversification of risks that exist across all the insurance and reinsurance undertakings in that group in order to reflect properly the risk exposures of that group.

(102) Insurance and reinsurance undertakings belonging to a group should be able to apply for the approval of an internal model to be used for the solvency calculation at both group and individual levels.

(103) Some provisions of this Directive expressly provide for a mediatory or a consultative role for CEIOPS, but this should not preclude CEIOPS from also playing a mediatory or a consultative role with regard to other provisions.

(104) This Directive reflects an innovative supervisory model where a key role is assigned to a group supervisor, whilst recognising and maintaining an important role for the solo supervisor. The powers and responsibilities of supervisors are linked with their accountability.

(105) All policy holders and beneficiaries should receive equal treatment regardless of their nationality or place of residence. For this purpose, each Member State should ensure that all measures taken by a supervisory authority on the basis of that supervisory authority's national mandate are not regarded as contrary to the interests of that Member State or of policy holders and beneficiaries in that Member State. In all situations of settling of claims and winding-up, assets should be distributed on an equitable basis to all relevant policy holders, regardless of their nationality or place of residence.

(106) It is necessary to ensure that own funds are appropriately distributed within the group and are available to protect policy holders and beneficiaries where needed. To that end, insurance and reinsurance undertakings within a group should have sufficient own funds to cover their solvency capital requirements.

(107) All supervisors involved in group supervision should be able to understand the decisions made, in particular where those decisions are made by the group supervisor. A soon as it becomes available to one of the supervisors, the relevant information should therefore be shared with the other supervisors, in order for all supervisors to be able to establish an opinion based on the same relevant information. In the event that the supervisors concerned cannot reach an agreement, qualified advice from CEIOPS should be sought to resolve the matter.

(108) The solvency of a subsidiary insurance or reinsurance undertaking of an insurance holding company, third-country insurance or reinsurance undertaking may be affected by the financial resources of the group of which it is part and by the distribution of financial resources within that group. The supervisory authorities should therefore be provided with the means of exercising group supervision and of taking appropriate measures at the level of the insurance or reinsurance undertaking where its solvency is being or may be jeopardised.

(109) Risk concentrations and intra-group transactions could affect the financial position of insurance or reinsurance undertakings. The supervisory authorities should therefore be able to exercise supervision over such risk concentrations and intra-group transactions, taking into account the nature of relationships between regulated entities as well as non-regulated entities, including insurance holding companies and mixed activity insurance holding companies, and take appropriate measures at the level of the insurance or reinsurance undertaking where its solvency is being or may be jeopardised.

(110) Insurance and reinsurance undertakings within a group should have appropriate systems of governance which should be subject to supervisory review.

(111) All insurance and reinsurance groups subject to group supervision should have a group supervisor appointed from among the supervisory authorities involved. The rights and duties of the group supervisor should comprise appropriate coordination and decision-making powers. The authorities involved in the supervision of insurance and reinsurance undertakings belonging to the same group should establish coordination arrangements.

(112) In light of the increasing competences of group supervisors the prevention of arbitrary circumvention of the criteria for choosing the group supervisor should be ensured. In particular in cases where the group supervisor will be designated taking into account the structure of the group and the relative importance of the insurance and reinsurance activities in different markets, internal group transactions as well as group reinsurance should not be double counted when assessing their relative importance within a market.

(113) Supervisors from all Member States in which undertakings of the group are established should be involved in group supervision through a college of supervisors (the College). They should all have access to information available with other supervisory authorities within the College and they should be involved in decision-making actively and on an on-going basis. Cooperation between the authorities responsible for the supervision of insurance and reinsurance undertakings as well as between those authorities and the authorities responsible for the supervision of undertakings active in other financial sectors should be established.

(114) The activities of the College should be proportionate to the nature, scale and complexity of the risks inherent in the business of all undertakings that are part of the group and to the cross-border dimension. The College should be set up to ensure that cooperation, exchange of information and

consultation processes among the supervisory authorities of the College are effectively applied in accordance with this Directive. Supervisory authorities should use the College to promote convergence of their respective decisions and to cooperate closely to carry out their supervisory activities across the group under harmonised criteria.

(115) This Directive should provide a consultative role for CEIOPS. Advice by CEIOPS to the relevant supervisor should not be binding on that supervisor when taking its decision. When taking a decision, the relevant supervisor should, however, take full account of that advice and explain any significant deviation therefrom.

(116) Insurance and reinsurance undertakings which are part of a group, the head of which is outside the Community should be subject to equivalent and appropriate group supervisory arrangements. It is therefore necessary to provide for transparency of rules and exchange of information with third-country authorities in all relevant circumstances. In order to ensure a harmonised approach to the determination and assessment of equivalence of third-country insurance and reinsurance supervision, provision should be made for the Commission to make a binding decision regarding the equivalence of third-country solvency regimes. For third countries regarding which no decision has been made by the Commission the assessment of equivalence should be made by the group supervisor after consulting the other relevant supervisory authorities.

(117) Since national legislation concerning reorganisation measures and winding-up proceedings is not harmonised, it is appropriate, in the framework of the internal market, to ensure the mutual recognition of reorganisation measures and winding-up legislation of the Member States concerning insurance undertakings, as well as the necessary cooperation, taking into account the need for unity, universality, coordination and publicity for such measures and the equivalent treatment and protection of insurance creditors.

(118) It should be ensured that reorganisation measures which were adopted by the competent authority of a Member State in order to preserve or restore the financial soundness of an insurance undertaking and to prevent as far as possible a winding-up situation, produce full effects throughout the Community. However, the effects of any such reorganisation measures as well as winding-up proceedings vis-à-vis third countries should not be affected.

(119) A distinction should be made between the competent authorities for the purposes of reorganisation measures and winding-up proceedings and the supervisory authorities of the insurance undertakings.

(120) The definition of a branch for insolvency purposes, should, in accordance with existing insolvency principles, take account of the single legal personality of the insurance undertaking. However, the legislation of the home Member State should determine the manner in which the assets and liabilities held by independent persons who have a permanent authority to act as agent for an insurance undertaking are to be treated in the winding-up of that insurance undertaking.

(121) Conditions should be laid down under which winding-up proceedings which, without being founded on insolvency, involve a priority order for the payment of insurance claims, fall within the scope of this Directive. Claims by the employees of an insurance undertaking arising from employment contracts and employment relationships should be capable of being subrogated to a national wage guarantee scheme. Such subrogated claims should benefit from the treatment determined by the law of the home Member State (lex concursus).

(122) Reorganisation measures do not preclude the opening of winding-up proceedings. Winding-up proceedings should therefore be able to be opened in the absence of, or following, the adoption of reorganisation measures and they may terminate with composition or other analogous measures, including reorganisation measures.

(123) Only the competent authorities of the home Member State should be empowered to take decisions on winding-up proceedings concerning insurance undertakings. The decisions should produce their effects throughout the Community and should be recognised by all Member States. The decisions should be published in accordance with the procedures of the home Member State and in the Official Journal of the European Union. Information should also be made available to known creditors who are resident in the Community, who should have the right to lodge claims and submit observations.

(124) All the assets and liabilities of the insurance undertaking should be taken into consideration in the winding-up proceedings.

(125) All the conditions for the opening, conduct and closure of winding-up proceedings should be governed by the law of the home Member State.

(126) In order to ensure coordinated action amongst the Member States the supervisory authorities of the home Member State and those of all the other Member States should be informed as a matter of urgency of the opening of winding-up proceedings.

(127) It is of utmost importance that insured persons, policy holders, beneficiaries and any injured party having a direct right of action against the insurance undertaking on a claim arising from insurance operations be protected in winding-up proceedings, it being understood that such protection does not include claims which arise not from obligations under insurance contracts or insurance operations but from civil liability caused by an agent in negotiations for which, according

to the law applicable to the insurance contract or operation, the agent is not responsible under such insurance contract or operation. In order to achieve that objective, Member States should be provided with a choice between equivalent methods to ensure special treatment for insurance creditors, none of those methods impeding a Member State from establishing a ranking between different categories of insurance claim. Furthermore, an appropriate balance should be ensured between the protection of insurance creditors and other privileged creditors protected under the legislation of the Member State concerned.

(128) The opening of winding-up proceedings should involve the withdrawal of the authorisation to conduct business granted to the insurance undertaking unless this has already occurred.

(129) Creditors should have the right to lodge claims or to submit written observations in winding-up proceedings. Claims by creditors resident in a Member State other than the home Member State should be treated in the same way as equivalent claims in the home Member State without discrimination on grounds of nationality or residence.

(130) In order to protect legitimate expectations and the certainty of certain transactions in Member States other than the home Member State, it is necessary to determine the law applicable to the effects of reorganisation measures and winding-up proceedings on pending lawsuits and on individual enforcement actions arising from lawsuits.

(131) The measures necessary for the implementation of this Directive should be adopted in accordance with Council Decision 1999/468/EC of 28 June 1999 laying down the procedures for the exercise of implementing powers conferred on the Commission.[22]

(132) In particular, the Commission should be empowered to adopt measures concerning the adaptation of Annexes and measures specifying in particular the supervisory powers and actions to be taken and laying down more detailed requirements in areas such as the system of governance, public disclosure, assessment criteria in relation to qualifying holdings, calculation of technical provisions and capital requirements, investment rules and group supervision. The Commission should also be empowered to adopt implementing measures granting to third countries the status of equivalence with the provisions of this Directive. Since those measures are of general scope and are designed to amend non-essential elements of this Directive, inter alia, by supplementing it with non-essential elements, they must be adopted in accordance with the regulatory procedure with scrutiny laid down in Article 5a of Decision 1999/468/EC.

(133) Since the objectives of this Directive cannot be sufficiently achieved by the Member States and can therefore, by reason of their scale and effects, be better achieved at Community level, the Community may adopt measures, in accordance with the principle of subsidiarity as set out in Article 5 of the Treaty. In accordance with the principle of proportionality, as set out in that Article, this Directive does not go beyond what is necessary in order to achieve those objectives.

(134) Council Directive 64/225/EEC of 25 February 1964 on the abolition of restrictions on freedom of establishment and freedom to provide services in respect of reinsurance and retrocession;[23] Council Directive 73/240/EEC of 24 July 1973 abolishing restrictions on freedom of establishment in the business of direct insurance other than life insurance;[24] Council Directive 76/580/EEC of 29 June 1976 amending Directive 73/239/EEC on the coordination of laws, regulations and administrative provisions relating to the taking-up and pursuit of the business of direct insurance other than life assurance;[25] and Council Directive 84/641/EEC of 10 December 1984 amending, particularly as regards tourist assistance, First Directive (73/239/EEC) on the coordination of laws, regulations and administrative provisions relating to the taking-up and pursuit of the business of direct insurance other than life[26] have become obsolete and should therefore be repealed.

(135) The obligation to transpose this Directive into national law should be confined to those provisions which represent a substantive change as compared with the earlier Directives. The obligation to transpose the provisions which are unchanged is provided for in the earlier Directives.

(136) This Directive should be without prejudice to the obligations of the Member States relating to the time-limits for transposition into national law of the Directives set out in Annex VI, Part B.

(137) The Commission will review the adequacy of existing guarantee schemes in the insurance sector and make an appropriate legislative proposal.

(138) Article 17(2) of Directive 2003/41/EC of the European Parliament and of the Council of 3 June 2003 on the activities and supervision of institutions for occupational retirement provision[27] refers to the existing legislative provisions on solvency margins. Those references should be retained in order to maintain the status quo. The Commission should conduct its review of Directive 2003/41/EC under Article 21(4) thereof as quickly as possible. The Commission, assisted by CEIOPS, should develop a proper system of solvency rules concerning institutions for occupational retirement provision, whilst fully reflecting the essential distinctiveness of insurance and, therefore, should not prejudge the application of this Directive to be imposed upon those institutions.

(139) Adoption of this Directive changes the risk profile of the insurance company vis-à-vis the policy holder. The Commission should as soon as possible and in any event by the end of 2010 put forward a proposal for the revision of Directive 2002/92/EC of the European Parliament and of

the Council of 9 December 2002 on insurance mediation,[28] taking into account the consequences of this Directive for policy holders.

(140) Further wide-ranging reforms of the regulatory and supervisory model of the EU financial sector are greatly needed and should be put forward swiftly by the Commission with due consideration of the conclusions presented by the group of experts chaired by Jacques de Larosière of 25 February 2009. The Commission should propose legislation needed to tackle the shortcomings identified regarding the provisions related to supervisory coordination and cooperation arrangements.

(141) It is necessary to seek advice from CEIOPS on how best to address the issues of an enhanced group supervision and capital management within a group of insurance or reinsurance undertakings. CEIOPS should be invited to provide advice that will help the Commission to develop its proposals under conditions that are consistent with a high level of policy holder (and beneficiary) protection and the safeguarding of financial stability. In that regard CEIOPS should be invited to advise the Commission on the structure and principles which could guide potential future amendments to this Directive which may be needed to give effect to the changes that may be proposed. The Commission should submit a report followed by appropriate proposals to the European Parliament and the Council for alternative regimes for the prudential supervision of insurance and reinsurance undertakings within groups which enhance the efficient capital management within groups if it is satisfied that an adequate supportive regulatory framework for the introduction of such a regime is in place.

In particular, it is desirable that a group support regime operate on sound foundations based on the existence of harmonised and adequately funded insurance guarantee schemes; a harmonised and legally binding framework for competent authorities, central banks and ministries of finance concerning crisis management, resolution and fiscal burden-sharing which aligns supervisory powers and fiscal responsibilities; a legally binding framework for the mediation of supervisory disputes; a harmonised framework on early intervention; and a harmonised framework on asset transferability, insolvency and winding-up procedures which eliminates the relevant national company or corporate law barriers to asset transferability. In its report, the Commission should also take into account the behaviour of diversification effects over time and risk associated with being part of a group, practices in centralised group risk management, functioning of group internal models as well as supervision of intra-group transactions and risk concentrations.

(142) In accordance with point 34 of the Interinstitutional agreement on better law-making,[29] Member States are encouraged to draw up, for themselves and in the interest of the Community, their own tables illustrating, as far as possible, the correlation between this Directive and the transposition measures, and to make them public,

NOTES

1 OJ C224, 30.8.2008, p 11.

2 Opinion of the European Parliament of 22 April 2009 (not yet published in the Official Journal) and Council Decision of 10 November 2009.

3 OJ L228, 16.8.1973, p 3.

4 OJ L151, 7.6.1978, p 25.

5 OJ L185, 4.7.1987, p 77.

6 OJ L172, 4.7.1988, p 1.

7 OJ L228, 11.8.1992, p 1.

8 OJ L330, 5.12.1998, p 1.

9 OJ L110, 20.4.2001, p 28.

10 OJ L345, 19.12.2002, p 1.

11 OJ L323, 9.12.2005, p 1.

12 OJ L103, 2.5.1972, p 1.

13 OJ L193, 18.7.1983, p 1.

14 OJ L8, 11.1.1984, p 17.

15 OJ L145, 30.4.2004, p 1.

16 OJ L177, 30.6.2006, p 1.

17 OJ L181, 20.7.2000, p 65.

18 OJ L35, 11.2.2003, p 1.

19 OJ L25, 29.1.2009, p 28.

20 OJ L157, 9.6.2006, p 87.

21 OJ L177, 4.7.2008, p 6.

22 OJ L184, 17.7.1999, p 23.

23 OJ 56, 4.4.1964, p 878.

24 OJ L228, 16.8.1973, p 20.
25 OJ L189, 13.7.1976, p 13.
26 OJ L339, 27.12.1984, p 21.
27 OJ L235, 23.9.2003, p 10.
28 OJ L9, 15.1.2003, p 3.
29 OJ C321, 31.12.2003, p 1.

HAVE ADOPTED THIS DIRECTIVE:

TITLE I
GENERAL RULES ON THE TAKING-UP AND PURSUIT OF DIRECT INSURANCE AND REINSURANCE ACTIVITIES

CHAPTER I
SUBJECT MATTER, SCOPE AND DEFINITIONS

SECTION 1
SUBJECT MATTER AND SCOPE

[6154]
Article 1
Subject matter

This Directive lays down rules concerning the following:

(1) the taking-up and pursuit, within the Community, of the self-employed activities of direct insurance and reinsurance;
(2) the supervision of insurance and reinsurance groups;
(3) the reorganisation and winding-up of direct insurance undertakings.

[6155]
Article 2
Scope

1. This Directive shall apply to direct life and non-life insurance undertakings which are established in the territory of a Member State or which wish to become established there.

It shall also apply to reinsurance undertakings which conduct only reinsurance activities and which are established in the territory of a Member State or which wish to become established there with the exception of Title IV.

2. In regard to non-life insurance, this Directive shall apply to activities of the classes set out in Part A of Annex I. For the purposes of the first subparagraph of paragraph 1, non-life insurance shall include the activity which consists of assistance provided for persons who get into difficulties while travelling, while away from their home or their habitual residence. It shall comprise an undertaking, against prior payment of a premium, to make aid immediately available to the beneficiary under an assistance contract where that person is in difficulties following the occurrence of a chance event, in the cases and under the conditions set out in the contract.

The aid may comprise the provision of benefits in cash or in kind. The provision of benefits in kind may also be effected by means of the staff and equipment of the person providing them.

The assistance activity shall not cover servicing, maintenance, after-sales service or the mere indication or provision of aid as an intermediary.

3. In regard to life insurance, this Directive shall apply:

(a) to the following life insurance activities where they are on a contractual basis:
   (i) life insurance which comprises assurance on survival to a stipulated age only, assurance on death only, assurance on survival to a stipulated age or on earlier death, life assurance with return of premiums, marriage assurance, birth assurance;
   (ii) annuities;
   (iii) supplementary insurance underwritten in addition to life insurance, in particular, insurance against personal injury including incapacity for employment, insurance against death resulting from an accident and insurance against disability resulting from an accident or sickness;
   (iv) types of permanent health insurance not subject to cancellation currently existing in Ireland and the United Kingdom;

(b) to the following operations, where they are on a contractual basis, in so far as they are subject to supervision by the authorities responsible for the supervision of private insurance:
  (i) operations whereby associations of subscribers are set up with a view to capitalising their contributions jointly and subsequently distributing the assets thus accumulated among the survivors or among the beneficiaries of the deceased (tontines);
  (ii) capital redemption operations based on actuarial calculation whereby, in return for single or periodic payments agreed in advance, commitments of specified duration and amount are undertaken;
  (iii) management of group pension funds, comprising the management of investments, and in particular the assets representing the reserves of bodies that effect payments on death or survival or in the event of discontinuance or curtailment of activity;
  (iv) the operations referred to in point (iii) where they are accompanied by insurance covering either conservation of capital or payment of a minimum interest;
  (v) the operations carried out by life insurance undertakings such as those referred to in Chapter 1, Title 4 of Book IV of the French 'Code des assurances';

(c) to operations relating to the length of human life which are prescribed by or provided for in social insurance legislation, in so far as they are effected or managed by life insurance undertakings at their own risk in accordance with the laws of a Member State.

SECTION 2
EXCLUSIONS FROM SCOPE

SUBSECTION 1
GENERAL

[6156]
Article 3
Statutory systems

Without prejudice to Article 2(3)(c), this Directive shall not apply to insurance forming part of a statutory system of social security.

[6157]
Article 4
Exclusion from scope due to size

1. Without prejudice to Article 3 and Articles 5 to 10, this Directive shall not apply to an insurance undertaking which fulfils all the following conditions:

(a) the undertaking's annual gross written premium income does not exceed EUR 5 million;
(b) the total of the undertaking's technical provisions, gross of the amounts recoverable from reinsurance contracts and special purpose vehicles, as referred to in Article 76, does not exceed EUR 25 million;
(c) where the undertaking belongs to a group, the total of the technical provisions of the group defined as gross of the amounts recoverable from reinsurance contracts and special purpose vehicles does not exceed EUR 25 million;
(d) the business of the undertaking does not include insurance or reinsurance activities covering liability, credit and suretyship insurance risks, unless they constitute ancillary risks within the meaning of Article 16(1);
(e) the business of the undertaking does not include reinsurance operations exceeding EUR 0,5 million of its gross written premium income or EUR 2,5 million of its technical provisions gross of the amounts recoverable from reinsurance contracts and special purpose vehicles, or more than 10% of its gross written premium income or more than 10% of its technical provisions gross of the amounts recoverable from reinsurance contracts and special purpose vehicles.

2. If any of the amounts set out in paragraph 1 is exceeded for three consecutive years this Directive shall apply as from the fourth year.

3. By way of derogation from paragraph 1, this Directive shall apply to all undertakings seeking authorisation to pursue insurance and reinsurance activities of which the annual gross written premium income or technical provisions gross of the amounts recoverable from reinsurance contracts and special purpose vehicles are expected to exceed any of the amounts set out in paragraph 1 within the following five years.

4. This Directive shall cease to apply to those insurance undertakings for which the supervisory authority has verified that all of the following conditions are met:

(a) none of the thresholds set out in paragraph 1 has been exceeded for the three previous consecutive years; and

(b) none of the thresholds set out in paragraph 1 is expected to be exceeded during the following five years.

For as long as the insurance undertaking concerned pursues activities in accordance with Articles 145 to 149, paragraph 1 of this Article shall not apply.

5. Paragraphs 1 and 4 shall not prevent any undertaking from applying for authorisation or continuing to be authorised under this Directive.

SUBSECTION 2
NON-LIFE

[6158]
Article 5
Operations

In regard to non-life insurance, this Directive shall not apply to the following operations:

(1) capital redemption operations, as defined by the law in each Member State;

(2) operations of provident and mutual benefit institutions whose benefits vary according to the resources available and in which the contributions of the members are determined on a flat-rate basis;

(3) operations carried out by organisations not having a legal personality with the purpose of providing mutual cover for their members without there being any payment of premiums or constitution of technical reserves; or

(4) export credit insurance operations for the account of or guaranteed by the State, or where the State is the insurer.

[6159]
Article 6
Assistance

1. This Directive shall not apply to an assistance activity which fulfils all the following conditions:

(a) the assistance is provided in the event of an accident or breakdown involving a road vehicle when the accident or breakdown occurs in the territory of the Member State of the undertaking providing cover;

(b) the liability for the assistance is limited to the following operations:

   (i) an on-the-spot breakdown service for which the undertaking providing cover uses, in most circumstances, its own staff and equipment;

   (ii) the conveyance of the vehicle to the nearest or the most appropriate location at which repairs may be carried out and the possible accompaniment, normally by the same means of assistance, of the driver and passengers to the nearest location from where they may continue their journey by other means; and

   (iii) where provided for by the home Member State of the undertaking providing cover, the conveyance of the vehicle, possibly accompanied by the driver and passengers, to their home, point of departure or original destination within the same State; and

(c) the assistance is not carried out by an undertaking subject to this Directive.

2. In the cases referred to in points (i) and (ii) of paragraph 1(b), the condition that the accident or breakdown must have happened in the territory of the Member State of the undertaking providing cover shall not apply where the beneficiary is a member of the body providing cover and the breakdown service or conveyance of the vehicle is provided simply on presentation of a membership card, without any additional premium being paid, by a similar body in the country concerned on the basis of a reciprocal agreement, or, in the case of Ireland and the United Kingdom, where the assistance operations are provided by a single body operating in both States.

3. This Directive shall not apply in the case of operations referred to in point (iii) of paragraph 1(b), where the accident or the breakdown has occurred in the territory of Ireland or, in the case of the United Kingdom, in the territory of Northern Ireland and the vehicle, possibly accompanied by the driver and passengers, is conveyed to their home, point of departure or original destination within either territory.

4. This Directive shall not apply to assistance operations carried out by the Automobile Club of the Grand Duchy of Luxembourg where the accident or the breakdown of a road vehicle has occurred outside the territory of the Grand Duchy of Luxembourg and the assistance consists in conveying the vehicle which has been involved in that accident or breakdown, possibly accompanied by the driver and passengers, to their home.

[6160]
Article 7
Mutual undertakings

This Directive shall not apply to mutual undertakings which pursue non-life insurance activities and which have concluded with other mutual undertakings an agreement which provides for the full reinsurance of the insurance policies issued by them or under which the accepting undertaking is to meet the liabilities arising under such policies in the place of the ceding undertaking. In such a case the accepting undertaking shall be subject to the rules of this Directive.

[6161]
Article 8
Institutions

This Directive shall not apply to the following institutions which pursue non-life insurance activities unless their statutes or the applicable law are amended as regards capacity:

(1) in Denmark, Falck Danmark;
(2) in Germany, the following semi-public institutions:
  (a) Postbeamtenkrankenkasse,
  (b) Krankenversorgung der Bundesbahnbeamten;
(3) in Ireland, the Voluntary Health Insurance Board;
(4) in Spain, the Consorcio de Compensación de Seguros.

SUBSECTION 3
LIFE

[6162]
Article 9
Operations and activities

In regard to life insurance, this Directive shall not apply to the following operations and activities:

(1) operations of provident and mutual-benefit institutions whose benefits vary according to the resources available and which require each of their members to contribute at the appropriate flat rate;
(2) operations carried out by organisations, other than undertakings referred to in Article 2, whose object is to provide benefits for employed or self-employed persons belonging to an undertaking or group of undertakings, or a trade or group of trades, in the event of death or survival or of discontinuance or curtailment of activity, whether or not the commitments arising from such operations are fully covered at all times by mathematical provisions;
(3) the pension activities of pension insurance undertakings prescribed in the Employees Pension Act (TyEL) and other related Finnish legislation provided that:
  (a) pension insurance companies which already under Finnish law are obliged to have separate accounting and management systems for their pension activities, as from 1 January 1995, set up separate legal entities for pursuing those activities; and
  (b) the Finnish authorities allow, in a non-discriminatory manner, all nationals and companies of Member States to perform according to Finnish legislation the activities specified in Article 2 related to *that* exemption whether by means of ownership or participation in an existing insurance company or group or by means of creation or participation of new insurance companies or groups, including pension insurance companies.

[6163]
Article 10
Organisations, undertakings and institutions

In regard to life insurance, this Directive shall not apply to the following organisations, undertakings and institutions:

(1) organisations which undertake to provide benefits solely in the event of death, where the amount of such benefits does not exceed the average funeral costs for a single death or where the benefits are provided in kind;
(2) the 'Versorgungsverband deutscher Wirtschaftsorganisationen' in Germany, unless its statutes are amended as regards the scope of its capacity;

(3) the 'Consorcio de Compensación de Seguros' in Spain, unless its statutes are amended as regards the scope of its activities or capacity.

SUBSECTION 4
REINSURANCE

[6164]
Article 11
Reinsurance

In regard to reinsurance, this Directive shall not apply to the activity of reinsurance conducted or fully guaranteed by the government of a Member State when that government is acting, for reasons of substantial public interest, in the capacity of reinsurer of last resort, including in circumstances where such a role is required by a situation in the market in which it is not feasible to obtain adequate commercial cover.

[6165]
Article 12
Reinsurance undertakings closing their activity

1. Reinsurance undertakings which by 10 December 2007 ceased to conduct new reinsurance contracts and exclusively administer their existing portfolio in order to terminate their activity shall not be subject to this Directive.

2. Member States shall draw up a list of the reinsurance undertakings concerned and communicate that list to all the other Member States.

SECTION 3
DEFINITIONS

[6166]
Article 13
Definitions

For the purposes of this Directive, the following definitions shall apply:

(1) 'insurance undertaking' means a direct life or non-life insurance undertaking which has received authorisation in accordance with Article 14;

(2) 'captive insurance undertaking' means an insurance undertaking, owned either by a financial undertaking other than an insurance or reinsurance undertaking or a group of insurance or reinsurance undertakings within the meaning of Article 212(1)(c) or by a non-financial undertaking, the purpose of which is to provide insurance cover exclusively for the risks of the undertaking or undertakings to which it belongs or of an undertaking or undertakings of the group of which it is a member;

(3) 'third-country insurance undertaking' means an undertaking which would require authorisation as an insurance undertaking in accordance with Article 14 if its head office were situated in the Community;

(4) 'reinsurance undertaking' means an undertaking which has received authorisation in accordance with Article 14 to pursue reinsurance activities;

(5) 'captive reinsurance undertaking' means a reinsurance undertaking, owned either by a financial undertaking other than an insurance or reinsurance undertaking or a group of insurance or reinsurance undertakings within the meaning of Article 212(1)(c) or by a non-financial undertaking, the purpose of which is to provide reinsurance cover exclusively for the risks of the undertaking or undertakings to which it belongs or of an undertaking or undertakings of the group of which it is a member;

(6) 'third-country reinsurance undertaking' means an undertaking which would require authorisation as a reinsurance undertaking in accordance with Article 14 if its head office were situated in the Community;

(7) 'reinsurance' means either of the following:

(a) the activity consisting in accepting risks ceded by an insurance undertaking or third-country insurance undertaking, or by another reinsurance undertaking or third-country reinsurance undertaking; or

(b) in the case of the association of underwriters known as Lloyd's, the activity consisting in accepting risks, ceded by any member of Lloyd's, by an insurance or reinsurance undertaking other than the association of underwriters known as Lloyd's;

(8) 'home Member State' means any of the following:

(a) for non-life insurance, the Member State in which the head office of the insurance undertaking covering the risk is situated;

(b) for life insurance, the Member State in which the head office of the insurance undertaking covering the commitment is situated; or

(c) for reinsurance, the Member State in which the head office of the reinsurance undertaking is situated;

(9) 'host Member State' means the Member State, other than the home Member State, in which an insurance or a reinsurance undertaking has a branch or provides services; for life and non-life insurance, the Member State of the provisions of services means, respectively, the Member State of the commitment or the Member State in which the risk is situated, where that commitment or risk is covered by an insurance undertaking or a branch situated in another Member State;

(10) 'supervisory authority' means the national authority or the national authorities empowered by law or regulation to supervise insurance or reinsurance undertakings;

(11) 'branch' means an agency or a branch of an insurance or reinsurance undertaking which is located in the territory of a Member State other than the home Member State;

(12) 'establishment' of an undertaking means its head office or any of its branches;

(13) 'Member State in which the risk is situated' means any of the following:

(a) the Member State in which the property is situated, where the insurance relates either to buildings or to buildings and their contents, in so far as the contents are covered by the same insurance policy;

(b) the Member State of registration, where the insurance relates to vehicles of any type;

(c) the Member State where the policy holder took out the policy in the case of policies of a duration of four months or less covering travel or holiday risks, whatever the class concerned;

(d) in all cases not explicitly covered by points (a), (b) or (c), the Member State in which either of the following is situated:

(i) the habitual residence of the policy holder; or

(ii) if the policy holder is a legal person, that policy holder's establishment to which the contract relates;

(14) 'Member State of the commitment' means the Member State in which either of the following is situated:

(a) the habitual residence of the policy holder;

(b) if the policy holder is a legal person, that policy holder's establishment, to which the contract relates;

(15) 'parent undertaking' means a parent undertaking within the meaning of Article 1 of Directive 83/349/EEC;

(16) 'subsidiary undertaking' means any subsidiary undertaking within the meaning of Article 1 of Directive 83/349/EEC, including subsidiaries thereof;

(17) 'close links' means a situation in which two or more natural or legal persons are linked by control or participation, or a situation in which two or more natural or legal persons are permanently linked to one and the same person by a control relationship;

(18) 'control' means the relationship between a parent undertaking and a subsidiary undertaking, as set out in Article 1 of Directive 83/349/EEC, or a similar relationship between any natural or legal person and an undertaking;

(19) 'intra-group transaction' means any transaction by which an insurance or reinsurance undertaking relies, either directly or indirectly, on other undertakings within the same group or on any natural or legal person linked to the undertakings within that group by close links, for the fulfilment of an obligation, whether or not contractual, and whether or not for payment;

(20) 'participation' means the ownership, direct or by way of control, of 20% or more of the voting rights or capital of an undertaking;

(21) 'qualifying holding' means a direct or indirect holding in an undertaking which represents 10% or more of the capital or of the voting rights or which makes it possible to exercise a significant influence over the management of that undertaking;

(22) 'regulated market' means either of the following:

(a) in the case of a market situated in a Member State, a regulated market as defined in Article 4(1)(14) of Directive 2004/39/EC; or

(b) in the case of a market situated in a third country, a financial market which fulfils the following conditions:

(i) it is recognised by the home Member State of the insurance undertaking and fulfils requirements comparable to those laid down in Directive 2004/39/EC; and

(ii) the financial instruments dealt in on that market are of a quality comparable to that of the instruments dealt in on the regulated market or markets of the home Member State;

(23) 'national bureau' means a national insurers' bureau as defined in Article 1(3) of Directive 72/166/EEC;

(24) 'national guarantee fund' means the body referred to in Article 1(4) of Directive 84/5/EEC;

(25) 'financial undertaking' means any of the following entities:

(a) a credit institution, a financial institution or an ancillary banking services undertaking within the meaning of Article 4(1), (5) and (21) of Directive 2006/48/EC respectively;

(b) an insurance undertaking, or a reinsurance undertaking or an insurance holding company within the meaning of Article 212(1)(f);

(c) an investment firm or a financial institution within the meaning of Article 4(1)(1) of Directive 2004/39/EC; or

(d) a mixed financial holding company within the meaning of Article 2(15) of Directive 2002/87/EC

(26) 'special purpose vehicle' means any undertaking, whether incorporated or not, other than an existing insurance or reinsurance undertaking, which assumes risks from insurance or reinsurance undertakings and which fully funds its exposure to such risks through the proceeds of a debt issuance or any other financing mechanism where the repayment rights of the providers of such debt or financing mechanism are subordinated to the reinsurance obligations of such an undertaking;

(27) 'large risks' means:

(a) risks classified under classes 4, 5, 6, 7, 11 and 12 in Part A of Annex I;

(b) risks classified under classes 14 and 15 in Part A of Annex I, where the policy holder is engaged professionally in an industrial or commercial activity or in one of the liberal professions and the risks relate to such activity;

(c) risks classified under classes 3, 8, 9, 10, 13 and 16 in Part A of Annex I in so far as the policy holder exceeds the limits of at least two of the following criteria:

(i) a balance-sheet total of EUR 6,2 million;

(ii) a net turnover, within the meaning of Fourth Council Directive 78/660/EEC of 25 July 1978 based on Article 54(3)(g) of the Treaty on the annual accounts of certain types of companies,[1] of EUR 12,8 million;

(iii) an average number of 250 employees during the financial year.

If the policy holder belongs to a group of undertakings for which consolidated accounts within the meaning of Directive 83/349/EEC are drawn up, the criteria set out in point (c) of the first subparagraph shall be applied on the basis of the consolidated accounts.

Member States may add to the category referred to in point (c) of the first subparagraph the risks insured by professional associations, joint ventures or temporary groupings;

(28) 'outsourcing' means an arrangement of any form between an insurance or reinsurance undertaking and a service provider, whether a supervised entity or not, by which that service provider performs a process, a service or an activity, whether directly or by sub-outsourcing, which would otherwise be performed by the insurance or reinsurance undertaking itself;

(29) 'function', within a system of governance, means an internal capacity to undertake practical tasks; a system of governance includes the risk-management function, the compliance function, the internal audit function and the actuarial function;

(30) 'underwriting risk' means the risk of loss or of adverse change in the value of insurance liabilities, due to inadequate pricing and provisioning assumptions;

(31) 'market risk' means the risk of loss or of adverse change in the financial situation resulting, directly or indirectly, from fluctuations in the level and in the volatility of market prices of assets, liabilities and financial instruments;

(32) 'credit risk' means the risk of loss or of adverse change in the financial situation, resulting from fluctuations in the credit standing of issuers of securities, counterparties and any debtors to which insurance and reinsurance undertakings are exposed, in the form of counterparty default risk, or spread risk, or market risk concentrations;

(33) 'operational risk' means the risk of loss arising from inadequate or failed internal processes, personnel or systems, or from external events;

(34) 'liquidity risk' means the risk that insurance and reinsurance undertakings are unable to realise investments and other assets in order to settle their financial obligations when they fall due;

(35) 'concentration risk' means all risk exposures with a loss potential which is large enough to threaten the solvency or the financial position of insurance and reinsurance undertakings;

(36) 'risk-mitigation techniques' means all techniques which enable insurance and reinsurance undertakings to transfer part or all of their risks to another party;

(37) 'diversification effects' means the reduction in the risk exposure of insurance and reinsurance undertakings and groups related to the diversification of their business, resulting from the fact that the adverse outcome from one risk can be offset by a more favourable outcome from another risk, where those risks are not fully correlated;

(38) 'probability distribution forecast' means a mathematical function that assigns to an exhaustive set of mutually exclusive future events a probability of realisation;

(39) 'risk measure' means a mathematical function which assigns a monetary amount to a given probability distribution forecast and increases monotonically with the level of risk exposure underlying that probability distribution forecast.

NOTES

[1] OJ L222, 14.8.1978, p 11.

CHAPTER II
TAKING-UP OF BUSINESS

[6167]
Article 14
Principle of authorisation

1. The taking-up of the business of direct insurance or reinsurance covered by this Directive shall be subject to prior authorisation.

2. The authorisation referred to in paragraph 1 shall be sought from the supervisory authorities of the home Member State by the following:

(a) any undertaking which is establishing its head office within the territory of that Member State; or

(b) any insurance undertaking which, having received an authorisation pursuant to paragraph 1, wishes to extend its business to an entire insurance class or to insurance classes other than those already authorised.

[6168]
Article 15
Scope of authorisation

1. An authorisation pursuant to Article 14 shall be valid for the entire Community. It shall permit insurance and reinsurance undertakings to pursue business there, that authorisation covering also the right of establishment and the freedom to provide services.

2. Subject to Article 14, authorisation shall be granted for a particular class of direct insurance as listed in Part A of Annex I or in Annex II. It shall cover the entire class, unless the applicant wishes to cover only some of the risks pertaining to that class.

The risks included in a class shall not be included in any other class except in the cases referred to in Article 16.

Authorisation may be granted for two or more of the classes, where the national law of a Member State permits such classes to be pursued simultaneously.

3. In regard to non-life insurance, Member States may grant authorisation for the groups of classes listed in Part B of Annex I.

The supervisory authorities may limit authorisation requested for one of the classes to the operations set out in the scheme of operations referred to in Article 23.

4. Undertakings subject to this Directive may engage in the assistance activity referred to in Article 6 only if they have received authorisation for class 18 in Part A of Annex I, without prejudice to Article 16(1). In that event this Directive shall apply to the operations in question.

5. In regard to reinsurance, authorisation shall be granted for non-life reinsurance activity, life reinsurance activity or all kinds of reinsurance activity.

The application for authorisation shall be considered in the light of the scheme of operations to be submitted pursuant to Article 18(1)(c) and the fulfilment of the conditions laid down for authorisation by the Member State from which the authorisation is sought.

[6169]
Article 16
Ancillary risks

1. An insurance undertaking which has obtained an authorisation for a principal risk belonging to one class or a group of classes as set out in Annex I may also insure risks included in another class without the need to obtain authorisation in respect of such risks provided that the risks fulfil all the following conditions:

(a) they are connected with the principal risk;
(b) they concern the object which is covered against the principal risk; and
(c) they are covered by the contract insuring the principal risk.

2. By way of derogation from paragraph 1, the risks included in classes 14, 15 and 17 in Part A of Annex I shall not be regarded as risks ancillary to other classes.

However, legal expenses insurance as set out in class 17 may be regarded as a risk ancillary to class 18, where the conditions laid down in paragraph 1 and either of the following conditions are fulfilled:

(a) the main risk relates solely to the assistance provided for persons who fall into difficulties while travelling, while away from their home or their habitual residence; or
(b) the insurance concerns disputes or risks arising out of, or in connection with, the use of sea-going vessels.

[6170]
Article 17
Legal form of the insurance or reinsurance undertaking

1. The home Member State shall require every undertaking for which authorisation is sought under Article 14 to adopt one of the legal forms set out in Annex III.

2. Member States may set up undertakings of a form governed by public law, provided that such bodies have insurance or reinsurance operations as their object, under conditions equivalent to those under which undertakings governed by private law operate.

3. The Commission may adopt implementing measures relating to the extension of the list of forms set out in Annex III.

Those measures, designed to amend non-essential elements of this Directive by supplementing it, shall be adopted in accordance with the regulatory procedure with scrutiny referred to in Article 301(3).

[6171]
Article 18
Conditions for authorisation

1. The home Member State shall require every undertaking for which authorisation is sought:

(a) in regard to insurance undertakings, to limit their objects to the business of insurance and operations arising directly therefrom, to the exclusion of all other commercial business;
(b) in regard to reinsurance undertakings, to limit their objects to the business of reinsurance and related operations; that requirement may include a holding company function and activities with respect to financial sector activities within the meaning of Article 2(8) of Directive 2002/87/EC;
(c) to submit a scheme of operations in accordance with Article 23;
(d) to hold the eligible basic own funds to cover the absolute floor of the Minimum Capital Requirement provided for in Article 129(1)(d);
(e) to show evidence that it will be in a position to hold eligible own funds to cover the Solvency Capital Requirement, as provided for in Article 100, going forward;
(f) to show evidence that it will be in a position to hold eligible basic own funds to cover the Minimum Capital Requirement, as provided for in Article 128, going forward;
(g) to show evidence that it will be in a position to comply with the system of governance referred to in Chapter IV, Section 2;
(h) in regard to non-life insurance, to communicate the name and address of all claims representatives appointed pursuant to Article 4 of Directive 2000/26/EC in each Member State other than the Member State in which the authorisation is sought if the risks to be covered are classified in class 10 of Part A of Annex I to this Directive, other than carrier's liability.

2. An insurance undertaking seeking authorisation to extend its business to other classes or to extend an authorisation covering only some of the risks pertaining to one class shall be required to submit a scheme of operations in accordance with Article 23.

Part VI European Materials

It shall, in addition, be required to show proof that it possesses the eligible own funds to cover the Solvency Capital Requirement and Minimum Capital Requirement provided for in the first paragraph of Article 100 and Article 128.

3. Without prejudice to paragraph 2, an insurance undertaking pursuing life activities, and seeking authorisation to extend its business to the risks listed in classes 1 or 2 in Part A of Annex I as referred to in Article 73, shall demonstrate that it:

(a) possesses the eligible basic own funds to cover the absolute floor of the Minimum Capital Requirement for life insurance undertakings and the absolute floor of the Minimum Capital Requirement for non-life insurance undertakings, as referred to in Article 129(1)(d);

(b) undertakes to cover the minimum financial obligations referred to in Article 74(3), going forward.

4. Without prejudice to paragraph 2, an insurance undertaking pursuing non-life activities for the risks listed in classes 1 or 2 in Part A of Annex I, and seeking authorisation to extend its business to life insurance risks as referred to in Article 73, shall demonstrate that it:

(a) possesses the eligible basic own funds to cover the absolute floor of the Minimum Capital Requirement for life insurance undertakings and the absolute floor of the Minimum Capital Requirement for non-life insurance undertakings, as referred to in Article 129(1)(d);

(b) undertakes to cover the minimum financial obligations referred to in Article 74(3) going forward.

[6172]
Article 19
Close links

Where close links exist between the insurance undertaking or reinsurance undertaking and other natural or legal persons, the supervisory authorities shall grant authorisation only if those links do not prevent the effective exercise of their supervisory functions.

The supervisory authorities shall refuse authorisation if the laws, regulations or administrative provisions of a third country governing one or more natural or legal persons with which the insurance or reinsurance undertaking has close links, or difficulties involved in the enforcement of those measures, prevent the effective exercise of their supervisory functions.

The supervisory authorities shall require insurance and reinsurance undertakings to provide them with the information they require to monitor compliance with the conditions referred to in the first paragraph on a continuous basis.

[6173]
Article 20
Head office of insurance undertakings and reinsurance undertakings

Member States shall require that the head offices of insurance and reinsurance undertakings be situated in the same Member State as their registered offices.

[6174]
Article 21
Policy conditions and scales of premiums

1. Member States shall not require the prior approval or systematic notification of general and special policy conditions, of scales of premiums, of the technical bases, used in particular for calculating scales of premiums and technical provisions, or of forms and other printed documents which an undertaking intends to use in its dealings with policy holders or ceding or retro-ceding undertakings.

However, for life insurance and for the sole purpose of verifying compliance with national provisions concerning actuarial principles, the home Member State may require systematic notification of the technical bases used for calculating scales of premiums and technical provisions. That requirement shall not constitute a prior condition for the authorisation of a life insurance undertaking.

2. Member States shall not retain or introduce prior notification or approval of proposed increases in premium rates except as part of general price-control systems.

3. Member States may subject undertakings seeking or having obtained authorisation for class 18 in Part A of Annex I to checks on their direct or indirect resources in staff and equipment, including the qualification of their medical teams and the quality of the equipment available to such undertakings to meet their commitments arising out of that class.

4. Member States may maintain in force or introduce laws, regulations or administrative provisions requiring approval of the memorandum and articles of association and communication of any other documents necessary for the normal exercise of supervision.

[6175]
Article 22
Economic requirements of the market

Member States shall not require that any application for authorisation be considered in the light of the economic requirements of the market.

[6176]
Article 23
Scheme of operations

1. The scheme of operations referred to in Article 18(1)(c) shall include particulars or evidence of the following:

(a) the nature of the risks or commitments which the insurance or reinsurance undertaking concerned proposes to cover;
(b) the kind of reinsurance arrangements which the reinsurance undertaking proposes to make with ceding undertakings;
(c) the guiding principles as to reinsurance and to retrocession;
(d) the basic own-fund items constituting the absolute floor of the Minimum Capital Requirement;
(e) estimates of the costs of setting up the administrative services and the organisation for securing business; the financial resources intended to meet those costs and, if the risks to be covered are classified in class 18 in Part A of Annex I, the resources at the disposal of the insurance undertaking for the provision of the assistance promised.

2. In addition to the requirements set out in paragraph 1, for the first three financial years the scheme shall include the following:

(a) a forecast balance sheet;
(b) estimates of the future Solvency Capital Requirement, as provided for in Chapter VI, Section 4, Subsection 1, on the basis of the forecast balance sheet referred to in point (a), as well as the calculation method used to derive those estimates;
(c) estimates of the future Minimum Capital Requirement, as provided for in Articles 128 and 129, on the basis of the forecast balance sheet referred to in point (a), as well as the calculation method used to derive those estimates;
(d) estimates of the financial resources intended to cover technical provisions, the Minimum Capital Requirement and the Solvency Capital Requirement;
(e) in regard to non-life insurance and reinsurance, also the following:
    (i) estimates of management expenses other than installation costs, in particular current general expenses and commissions;
    (ii) estimates of premiums or contributions and claims;
(f) in regard to life insurance, also a plan setting out detailed estimates of income and expenditure in respect of direct business, reinsurance acceptances and reinsurance cessions.

[6177]
Article 24
Shareholders and members with qualifying holdings

1. The supervisory authorities of the home Member State shall not grant to an undertaking an authorisation to take up the business of insurance or reinsurance before they have been informed of the identities of the shareholders or members, direct or indirect, whether natural or legal persons, who have qualifying holdings in that undertaking and of the amounts of those holdings.

Those authorities shall refuse authorisation if, taking into account the need to ensure the sound and prudent management of an insurance or reinsurance undertaking, they are not satisfied as to the qualifications of the shareholders or members.

2. For the purposes of paragraph 1, the voting rights referred to in Articles 9 and 10 of Directive 2004/109/EC of the European Parliament and of the Council of 15 December 2004 on the harmonisation of transparency requirements in relation to information about issues whose securities are admitted to trading on a regulated market,[1] as well as the conditions regarding aggregation thereof laid down in Article 12(4) and (5) of that Directive, shall be taken into account.

Member States shall not take into account voting rights or shares which investment firms or credit institutions may hold as a result of providing the underwriting of financial instruments and/or placing of financial instruments on a firm commitment basis included under point (6) of Section A of Annex I to Directive 2004/39/EC, provided that those rights are, on the one hand, not exercised or otherwise used to intervene in the management of the issuer and, on the other, disposed of within one year of the acquisition.

NOTES

[1] OJ L390, 31.12.2004, p 38.

[6178]
Article 25
Refusal of authorisation

Any decision to refuse an authorisation shall state full reasons and shall be notified to the undertaking concerned.

Each Member State shall make provision for a right to apply to the courts where an authorisation is refused.

Such provision shall also be made with regard to cases where the supervisory authorities have not dealt with an application for an authorisation within six months of the date of its receipt.

[6179]
Article 26
Prior consultation of the authorities of other Member States

1. The supervisory authorities of any other Member State concerned shall be consulted prior to the granting of an authorisation to:
   (a) a subsidiary of an insurance or reinsurance undertaking authorised in that Member State;
   (b) a subsidiary of the parent undertaking of an insurance or reinsurance undertaking authorised in that Member State; or
   (c) an undertaking controlled by the same person, whether natural or legal, who controls an insurance or reinsurance undertaking authorised in that Member State.

2. The authorities of a Member State involved which are responsible for the supervision of credit institutions or investment firms shall be consulted prior to the granting of an authorisation to an insurance or reinsurance undertaking which is:
   (a) a subsidiary of a credit institution or investment firm authorised in the Community;
   (b) a subsidiary of the parent undertaking of a credit institution or investment firm authorised in the Community; or
   (c) an undertaking controlled by the same person, whether natural or legal, who controls a credit institution or investment firm authorised in the Community.

3. The relevant authorities referred to in paragraphs 1 and 2 shall in particular consult each other when assessing the suitability of the shareholders and the fit and proper requirements of all persons who effectively run the undertaking or have other key functions involved in the management of another entity of the same group.

They shall inform each other of any information regarding the suitability of shareholders and the fit and proper requirements of all persons who effectively run the undertaking or have other key functions which is of relevance to the other competent authorities concerned for the granting of an authorisation as well as for the ongoing assessment of compliance with operating conditions.

CHAPTER III
SUPERVISORY AUTHORITIES AND GENERAL RULES

[6180]
Article 27
Main objective of supervision

Member States shall ensure that the supervisory authorities are provided with the necessary means, and have the relevant expertise, capacity, and mandate to achieve the main objective of supervision, namely the protection of policy holders and beneficiaries.

[6181]
Article 28
Financial stability and pro-cyclicality

Without prejudice to the main objective of supervision as set out in Article 27, Member States shall ensure that, in the exercise of their general duties, supervisory authorities shall duly consider the potential impact of their decisions on the stability of the financial systems concerned in the European Union, in particular in emergency situations, taking into account the information available at the relevant time.

In times of exceptional movements in the financial markets, supervisory authorities shall take into account the potential pro-cyclical effects of their actions.

[6182]
Article 29
General principles of supervision

1. Supervision shall be based on a prospective and risk-based approach. It shall include the verification on a continuous basis of the proper operation of the insurance or reinsurance business and of the compliance with supervisory provisions by insurance and reinsurance undertakings.

2. Supervision of insurance and reinsurance undertakings shall comprise an appropriate combination of off-site activities and on-site inspections.

3. Member States shall ensure that the requirements laid down in this Directive are applied in a manner which is proportionate to the nature, scale and complexity of the risks inherent in the business of an insurance or reinsurance undertaking.

4. The Commission shall ensure that implementing measures take into account the principle of proportionality, thus ensuring the proportionate application of this Directive, in particular to small insurance undertakings.

[6183]
Article 30
Supervisory authorities and scope of supervision

1. The financial supervision of insurance and reinsurance undertakings, including that of the business they pursue either through branches or under the freedom to provide services, shall be the sole responsibility of the home Member State.

2. Financial supervision pursuant to paragraph 1 shall include verification, with respect to the entire business of the insurance and reinsurance undertaking, of its state of solvency, of the establishment of technical provisions, of its assets and of the eligible own funds, in accordance with the rules laid down or practices followed in the home Member State under provisions adopted at Community level.

Where the insurance undertaking concerned is authorised to cover the risks classified in class 18 in Part A of Annex I, supervision shall extend to monitoring of the technical resources which the insurance undertaking has at its disposal for the purpose of carrying out the assistance operations it has undertaken to perform, where the law of the home Member State provides for the monitoring of such resources.

3. If the supervisory authorities of the Member State in which the risk is situated or the Member State of the commitment or, in case of a reinsurance undertaking, the supervisory authorities of the host Member State, have reason to consider that the activities of an insurance or reinsurance undertaking might affect its financial soundness, they shall inform the supervisory authorities of the home Member State of that undertaking.

The supervisory authorities of the home Member State shall determine whether the undertaking is complying with the prudential principles laid down in this Directive.

[6184]
Article 31
Transparency and accountability

1. The supervisory authorities shall conduct their tasks in a transparent and accountable manner with due respect for the protection of confidential information.

2. Member States shall ensure that the following information is disclosed:

(a) the texts of laws, regulations, administrative rules and general guidance in the field of insurance regulation;
(b) the general criteria and methods, including the tools developed in accordance with Article 34(4), used in the supervisory review process as set out in Article 36;
(c) aggregate statistical data on key aspects of the application of the prudential framework;
(d) the manner of exercise of the options provided for in this Directive;
(e) the objectives of the supervision and its main functions and activities.

The disclosure provided for in the first subparagraph shall be sufficient to enable a comparison of the supervisory approaches adopted by the supervisory authorities of the different Member States.

The disclosure shall be made in a common format and be updated regularly. The information referred to in points (a) to (e) of the first subparagraph shall be accessible at a single electronic location in each Member State.

3. Member States shall provide for transparent procedures regarding the appointment and dismissal of the members of the governing and managing bodies of their supervisory authorities.

4. The Commission shall adopt implementing measures relating to paragraph 2 specifying the key aspects on which aggregate statistical data are to be disclosed, and the format, structure, contents list and publication date of the disclosures.

Those measures, designed to amend non-essential elements of this Directive by supplementing it, shall be adopted in accordance with the regulatory procedure with scrutiny referred to in Article 301(3).

[6185]
Article 32
Prohibition of refusal of reinsurance contracts or retrocession contracts

1. The home Member State of an insurance undertaking shall not refuse a reinsurance contract concluded with a reinsurance undertaking or an insurance undertaking authorised in accordance with Article 14 on grounds directly related to the financial soundness of that reinsurance undertaking or that insurance undertaking.

2. The home Member State of the reinsurance undertaking shall not refuse a retrocession contract concluded by a reinsurance undertaking with a reinsurance undertaking or an insurance undertaking authorised in accordance with Article 14 on grounds directly related to the financial soundness of that reinsurance undertaking or that insurance undertaking.

[6186]
Article 33
Supervision of branches established in another Member State

Member States shall provide that, where an insurance or reinsurance undertaking authorised in another Member State carries on business through a branch, the supervisory authorities of the home Member State may, after having informed the supervisory authorities of the host Member State concerned, carry out themselves, or through the intermediary of persons appointed for that purpose, on-site verifications of the information necessary to ensure the financial supervision of the undertaking.

The authorities of the host Member State concerned may participate in those verifications.

[6187]
Article 34
General supervisory powers

1. Member States shall ensure that the supervisory authorities have the power to take preventive and corrective measures to ensure that insurance and reinsurance undertakings comply with the laws, regulations and administrative provisions with which they have to comply in each Member State.

2. The supervisory authorities shall have the power to take any necessary measures, including where appropriate, those of an administrative or financial nature, with regard to insurance or reinsurance undertakings, and the members of their administrative, management or supervisory body.

3. Member States shall ensure that supervisory authorities have the power to require all information necessary to conduct supervision in accordance with Article 35.

4. Member States shall ensure that supervisory authorities have the power to develop, in addition to the calculation of the Solvency Capital Requirement and where appropriate, necessary quantitative tools under the supervisory review process to assess the ability of the insurance or reinsurance undertakings to cope with possible events or future changes in economic conditions that could have unfavourable effects on their overall financial standing. The supervisory authorities shall have the power to require that corresponding tests are performed by the undertakings.

5. The supervisory authorities shall have the power to carry out on-site investigations at the premises of the insurance and reinsurance undertakings.

6. Supervisory powers shall be applied in a timely and proportionate manner.

7. The powers with regard to insurance and reinsurance undertakings referred to in paragraphs 1 to 5 shall also be available with regard to outsourced activities of insurance and reinsurance undertakings.

8. The powers referred to in paragraphs 1 to 5 and 7 shall be exercised, if need be by enforcement and, where appropriate, through judicial channels.

[6188]
Article 35
Information to be provided for supervisory purposes

1. Member States shall require insurance and reinsurance undertakings to submit to the supervisory authorities the information which is necessary for the purposes of supervision. That information shall include at least the information necessary for the following when performing the process referred to in Article 36:
   (a) to assess the system of governance applied by the undertakings, the business they are pursuing, the valuation principles applied for solvency purposes, the risks faced and the risk-management systems, and their capital structure, needs and management;
   (b) to make any appropriate decisions resulting from the exercise of their supervisory rights and duties.
2. Member States shall ensure that the supervisory authorities have the following powers:
   (a) to determine the nature, the scope and the format of the information referred to in paragraph 1 which they require insurance and reinsurance undertakings to submit at the following points in time:
      (i) at predefined periods;
      (ii) upon occurrence of predefined events;
      (iii) during enquiries regarding the situation of an insurance or reinsurance undertaking;
   (b) to obtain any information regarding contracts which are held by intermediaries or regarding contracts which are entered into with third parties; and
   (c) to require information from external experts, such as auditors and actuaries.
3. The information referred to in paragraphs 1 and 2 shall comprise the following:
   (a) qualitative or quantitative elements, or any appropriate combination thereof;
   (b) historic, current or prospective elements, or any appropriate combination thereof; and
   (c) data from internal or external sources, or any appropriate combination thereof.
4. The information referred to in paragraphs 1 and 2 shall comply with the following principles:
   (a) it must reflect the nature, scale and complexity of the business of the undertaking concerned, and in particular the risks inherent in that business;
   (b) it must be accessible, complete in all material respects, comparable and consistent over time; and
   (c) it must be relevant, reliable and comprehensible.
5. Member States shall require insurance and reinsurance undertakings to have appropriate systems and structures in place to fulfil the requirements laid down in paragraphs 1 to 4 as well as a written policy, approved by the administrative, management or supervisory body of the insurance or reinsurance undertaking, ensuring the ongoing appropriateness of the information submitted.
6. The Commission shall adopt implementing measures specifying the information referred to in paragraphs 1 to 4, with a view to ensuring to the appropriate extent convergence of supervisory reporting.

Those measures, designed to amend non-essential elements of this Directive by supplementing it, shall be adopted in accordance with the regulatory procedure with scrutiny referred to in Article 301(3).

[6189]
Article 36
Supervisory review process

1. Member States shall ensure that the supervisory authorities review and evaluate the strategies, processes and reporting procedures which are established by the insurance and reinsurance undertakings to comply with the laws, regulations and administrative provisions adopted pursuant to this Directive.

That review and evaluation shall comprise the assessment of the qualitative requirements relating to the system of governance, the assessment of the risks which the undertakings concerned face or may face and the assessment of the ability of those undertakings to assess those risks taking into account the environment in which the undertakings are operating.

2. The supervisory authorities shall in particular review and evaluate compliance with the following:
   (a) the system of governance, including the own-risk and solvency assessment, as set out in Chapter IV, Section 2;
   (b) the technical provisions as set out in Chapter VI, Section 2;
   (c) the capital requirements as set out in Chapter VI, Sections 4 and 5;

(d) the investment rules as set out in Chapter VI, Section 6;

(e) the quality and quantity of own funds as set out in Chapter VI, Section 3;

(f) where the insurance or reinsurance undertaking uses a full or partial internal model, on-going compliance with the requirements for full and partial internal models set out in Chapter VI, Section 4, Subsection 3.

3. The supervisory authorities shall have in place appropriate monitoring tools that enable them to identify deteriorating financial conditions in an insurance or reinsurance undertaking and to monitor how that deterioration is remedied.

4. The supervisory authorities shall assess the adequacy of the methods and practices of the insurance and reinsurance undertakings designed to identify possible events or future changes in economic conditions that could have adverse effects on the overall financial standing of the undertaking concerned.

The supervisory authorities shall assess the ability of the undertakings to withstand those possible events or future changes in economic conditions.

5. The supervisory authorities shall have the necessary powers to require insurance and reinsurance undertakings to remedy weaknesses or deficiencies identified in the supervisory review process.

6. The reviews, evaluations and assessments referred to in paragraphs 1, 2 and 4 shall be conducted regularly.

The supervisory authorities shall establish the minimum frequency and the scope of those reviews, evaluations and assessments having regard to the nature, scale and complexity of the activities of the insurance or reinsurance undertaking concerned.

[6190]
Article 37
Capital add-on

1. Following the supervisory review process supervisory authorities may in exceptional circumstances set a capital add-on for an insurance or reinsurance undertaking by a decision stating the reasons. That possibility shall exist only in the following cases:

(a) the supervisory authority concludes that the risk profile of the insurance or reinsurance undertaking deviates significantly from the assumptions underlying the Solvency Capital Requirement, as calculated using the standard formula in accordance with Chapter VI, Section 4, Subsection 2 and:

(i) the requirement to use an internal model under Article 119 is inappropriate or has been ineffective; or

(ii) while a partial or full internal model is being developed in accordance with Article 119;

(b) the supervisory authority concludes that the risk profile of the insurance or reinsurance undertaking deviates significantly from the assumptions underlying the Solvency Capital Requirement, as calculated using an internal model or partial internal model in accordance with Chapter VI, Section 4, Subsection 3, because certain quantifiable risks are captured insufficiently and the adaptation of the model to better reflect the given risk profile has failed within an appropriate timeframe; or

(c) the supervisory authority concludes that the system of governance of an insurance or reinsurance undertaking deviates significantly from the standards laid down in Chapter IV, Section 2, that those deviations prevent it from being able to properly identify, measure, monitor, manage and report the risks that it is or could be exposed to and that the application of other measures is in itself unlikely to improve the deficiencies sufficiently within an appropriate timeframe.

2. In the circumstances set out in points (a) and (b) of paragraph 1 the capital add-on shall be calculated in such a way as to ensure that the undertaking complies with Article 101(3).

In the circumstances set out in paragraph 1(c) the capital add-on shall be proportionate to the material risks arising from the deficiencies which gave rise to the decision of the supervisory authority to set the add-on.

3. In the cases set out in points (b) and (c) of paragraph 1 the supervisory authority shall ensure that the insurance or reinsurance undertaking makes every effort to remedy the deficiencies that led to the imposition of the capital add-on.

4. The capital add-on referred to in paragraph 1 shall be reviewed at least once a year by the supervisory authority and be removed when the undertaking has remedied the deficiencies which led to its imposition.

5. The Solvency Capital Requirement including the capital add-on imposed shall replace the inadequate Solvency Capital Requirement. Notwithstanding the first subparagraph the Solvency Capital Requirement shall not include the capital add-on imposed in accordance with paragraph 1(c) for the purposes of the calculation of the risk margin referred to in Article 77(5).

6. The Commission shall adopt implementing measures laying down further specifications for the circumstances under which a capital add-on may be imposed and the methodologies for the calculation thereof.

Those measures, designed to amend non-essential elements of this Directive by supplementing it, shall be adopted in accordance with the regulatory procedure with scrutiny referred to in Article 301(3).

[6191]
Article 38
Supervision of outsourced functions and activities

1. Without prejudice to Article 49, Member States shall ensure that insurance and reinsurance undertakings which outsource a function or an insurance or reinsurance activity take the necessary steps to ensure that the following conditions are satisfied:
   (a) the service provider must cooperate with the supervisory authorities of the insurance and reinsurance undertaking in connection with the outsourced function or activity;
   (b) the insurance and reinsurance undertakings, their auditors and the supervisory authorities must have effective access to data related to the outsourced functions or activities;
   (c) the supervisory authorities must have effective access to the business premises of the service provider and must be able to exercise those rights of access.

2. The Member State where the service provider is located shall permit the supervisory authorities of the insurance or reinsurance undertaking to carry out themselves, or through the intermediary of persons they appoint for that purpose, on-site inspections at the premises of the service provider. The supervisory authority of the insurance or reinsurance undertaking shall inform the appropriate authority of the Member State of the service provider prior to conducting the on-site inspection. In the case of a non-supervised entity the appropriate authority shall be the supervisory authority.

The supervisory authorities of the Member State of the insurance or reinsurance undertaking may delegate such on-site inspections to the supervisory authorities of the Member State where the service provider is located.

[6192]
Article 39
Transfer of portfolio

1. Under the conditions laid down by national law, Member States shall authorise insurance and reinsurance undertakings with head offices within their territory to transfer all or part of their portfolios of contracts, concluded either under the right of establishment or the freedom to provide services, to an accepting undertaking established within the Community.

Such transfer shall be authorised only if the supervisory authorities of the home Member State of the accepting undertaking certify that after taking the transfer into account the accepting undertaking possesses the necessary eligible own funds to cover the Solvency Capital Requirement referred to in the first paragraph of Article 100.

2. In the case of insurance undertakings paragraphs 3 to 6 shall apply.

3. Where a branch proposes to transfer all or part of its portfolio of contracts, the Member State where that branch is situated shall be consulted.

4. In the circumstances referred to in paragraphs 1 and 3, the supervisory authorities of the home Member State of the transferring insurance undertaking shall authorise the transfer after obtaining the agreement of the authorities of the Member States where the contracts were concluded, either under the right of establishment or the freedom to provide services.

5. The authorities of the Member States consulted shall give their opinion or consent to the authorities of the home Member State of the transferring insurance undertaking within three months of receiving a request for consultation.

The absence of any response within that period from the authorities consulted shall be considered as tacit consent.

6. A transfer of portfolio authorised in accordance with paragraphs 1 to 5 shall be published either prior to or following authorisation, as laid down by the national law of the home Member State, of the Member State in which the risk is situated, or of the Member State of the commitment.

Such transfers shall automatically be valid against policy holders, the insured persons and any other person having rights or obligations arising out of the contracts transferred.

The first and second subparagraphs of this paragraph shall not affect the right of the Member States to give policy holders the option of cancelling contracts within a fixed period after a transfer.

CHAPTER IV
CONDITIONS GOVERNING BUSINESS

SECTION 1
RESPONSIBILITY OF THE ADMINISTRATIVE, MANAGEMENT OR SUPERVISORY BODY

[6193]
Article 40
Responsibility of the administrative, management or supervisory body

Member States shall ensure that the administrative, management or supervisory body of the insurance or reinsurance undertaking has the ultimate responsibility for the compliance, by the undertaking concerned, with the laws, regulations and administrative provisions adopted pursuant to this Directive.

SECTION 2
SYSTEM OF GOVERNANCE

[6194]
Article 41
General governance requirements

1. Member States shall require all insurance and reinsurance undertakings to have in place an effective system of governance which provides for sound and prudent management of the business.

That system shall at least include an adequate transparent organisational structure with a clear allocation and appropriate segregation of responsibilities and an effective system for ensuring the transmission of information. It shall include compliance with the requirements laid down in Articles 42 to 49.

The system of governance shall be subject to regular internal review.

2. The system of governance shall be proportionate to the nature, scale and complexity of the operations of the insurance or reinsurance undertaking.

3. Insurance and reinsurance undertakings shall have written policies in relation to at least risk management, internal control, internal audit and, where relevant, outsourcing. They shall ensure that those policies are implemented.

Those written policies shall be reviewed at least annually. They shall be subject to prior approval by the administrative, management or supervisory body and be adapted in view of any significant change in the system or area concerned.

4. Insurance and reinsurance undertakings shall take reasonable steps to ensure continuity and regularity in the performance of their activities, including the development of contingency plans. To that end, the undertaking shall employ appropriate and proportionate systems, resources and procedures.

5. The supervisory authorities shall have appropriate means, methods and powers for verifying the system of governance of the insurance and reinsurance undertakings and for evaluating emerging risks identified by those undertakings which may affect their financial soundness.

The Member States shall ensure that the supervisory authorities have the powers necessary to require that the system of governance be improved and strengthened to ensure compliance with the requirements set out in Articles 42 to 49.

[6195]
Article 42
Fit and proper requirements for persons who effectively run the undertaking or have other key functions

1. Insurance and reinsurance undertakings shall ensure that all persons who effectively run the undertaking or have other key functions at all times fulfil the following requirements:

(a) their professional qualifications, knowledge and experience are adequate to enable sound and prudent management (fit); and

(b) they are of good repute and integrity (proper).

2. Insurance and reinsurance undertakings shall notify the supervisory authority of any changes to the identity of the persons who effectively run the undertaking or are responsible for other key functions, along with all information needed to assess whether any new persons appointed to manage the undertaking are fit and proper.

3. Insurance and reinsurance undertakings shall notify their supervisory authority if any of the persons referred to in paragraphs 1 and 2 have been replaced because they no longer fulfil the requirements referred to in paragraph 1.

[6196]
Article 43
Proof of good repute

1. Where a Member State requires of its own nationals proof of good repute, proof of no previous bankruptcy, or both, that Member State shall accept as sufficient evidence in respect of nationals of other Member States the production of an extract from the judicial record or, failing this, of an equivalent document issued by a competent judicial or administrative authority in the home Member State or the Member State from which the foreign national comes showing that those requirements have been met.

2. Where the home Member State or the Member State from which the foreign national concerned comes does not issue the document referred to in paragraph 1, it may be replaced by a declaration on oath — or in Member States where there is no provision for declaration on oath by a solemn declaration — made by the foreign national concerned before a competent judicial or administrative authority or, where appropriate, a notary in the home Member State or the Member State from which that foreign national comes.

Such authority or notary shall issue a certificate attesting the authenticity of the declaration on oath or solemn declaration.

The declaration referred to in the first subparagraph in respect of no previous bankruptcy may also be made before a competent professional or trade body in the Member State concerned.

3. The documents and certificates referred to in paragraphs 1 and 2 shall not be presented more than three months after their date of issue.

4. Member States shall designate the authorities and bodies competent to issue the documents referred to in paragraphs 1 and 2 and shall forthwith inform the other Member States and the Commission thereof.

Each Member State shall also inform the other Member States and the Commission of the authorities or bodies to which the documents referred to in paragraphs 1 and 2 are to be submitted in support of an application to pursue in the territory of that Member State the activities referred to in Article 2.

[6197]
Article 44
Risk management

1. Insurance and reinsurance undertakings shall have in place an effective risk-management system comprising strategies, processes and reporting procedures necessary to identify, measure, monitor, manage and report, on a continuous basis the risks, at an individual and at an aggregated level, to which they are or could be exposed, and their interdependencies.

That risk-management system shall be effective and well integrated into the organisational structure and in the decision-making processes of the insurance or reinsurance undertaking with proper consideration of the persons who effectively run the undertaking or have other key functions.

2. The risk-management system shall cover the risks to be included in the calculation of the Solvency Capital Requirement as set out in Article 101(4) as well as the risks which are not or not fully included in the calculation thereof.

The risk-management system shall cover at least the following areas:

(a) underwriting and reserving;
(b) asset-liability management;
(c) investment, in particular derivatives and similar commitments;
(d) liquidity and concentration risk management;
(e) operational risk management;
(f) reinsurance and other risk-mitigation techniques.

The written policy on risk management referred to in Article 41(3) shall comprise policies relating to points (a) to (f) of the second subparagraph of this paragraph.

3. As regards investment risk, insurance and reinsurance undertakings shall demonstrate that they comply with Chapter VI, Section 6.

4. Insurance and reinsurance undertakings shall provide for a risk-management function which shall be structured in such a way as to facilitate the implementation of the risk-management system.

5. For insurance and reinsurance undertakings using a partial or full internal model approved in accordance with Articles 112 and 113 the risk-management function shall cover the following additional tasks:

(a) to design and implement the internal model;

(b) to test and validate the internal model;

(c) to document the internal model and any subsequent changes made to it;

(d) to analyse the performance of the internal model and to produce summary reports thereof;

(e) to inform the administrative, management or supervisory body about the performance of the internal model, suggesting areas needing improvement, and up-dating that body on the status of efforts to improve previously identified weaknesses.

[6198]
Article 45
Own risk and solvency assessment

1. As part of its risk-management system every insurance undertaking and reinsurance undertaking shall conduct its own risk and solvency assessment.

That assessment shall include at least the following:

(a) the overall solvency needs taking into account the specific risk profile, approved risk tolerance limits and the business strategy of the undertaking;

(b) the compliance, on a continuous basis, with the capital requirements, as laid down in Chapter VI, Sections 4 and 5 and with the requirements regarding technical provisions, as laid down in Chapter VI, Section 2;

(c) the significance with which the risk profile of the undertaking concerned deviates from the assumptions underlying the Solvency Capital Requirement as laid down in Article 101(3), calculated with the standard formula in accordance with Chapter VI, Section 4, Subsection 2 or with its partial or full internal model in accordance with Chapter VI, Section 4, Subsection 3.

2. For the purposes of paragraph 1(a), the undertaking concerned shall have in place processes which are proportionate to the nature, scale and complexity of the risks inherent in its business and which enable it to properly identify and assess the risks it faces in the short and long term and to which it is or could be exposed. The undertaking shall demonstrate the methods used in that assessment.

3. In the case referred to in paragraph 1(c), when an internal model is used, the assessment shall be performed together with the recalibration that transforms the internal risk numbers into the Solvency Capital Requirement risk measure and calibration.

4. The own-risk and solvency assessment shall be an integral part of the business strategy and shall be taken into account on an ongoing basis in the strategic decisions of the undertaking.

5. Insurance and reinsurance undertakings shall perform the assessment referred to in paragraph 1 regularly and without any delay following any significant change in their risk profile.

6. The insurance and reinsurance undertakings shall inform the supervisory authorities of the results of each own-risk and solvency assessment as part of the information reported under Article 35.

7. The own-risk and solvency assessment shall not serve to calculate a capital requirement. The Solvency Capital Requirement shall be adjusted only in accordance with Articles 37, 231 to 233 and 238.

[6199]
Article 46
Internal control

1. Insurance and reinsurance undertakings shall have in place an effective internal control system.

That system shall at least include administrative and accounting procedures, an internal control framework, appropriate reporting arrangements at all levels of the undertaking and a compliance function.

2. The compliance function shall include advising the administrative, management or supervisory body on compliance with the laws, regulations and administrative provisions adopted pursuant to this Directive. It shall also include an assessment of the possible impact of any changes in the legal environment on the operations of the undertaking concerned and the identification and assessment of compliance risk.

[6200]
Article 47
Internal audit

1. Insurance and reinsurance undertakings shall provide for an effective internal audit function.

The internal audit function shall include an evaluation of the adequacy and effectiveness of the internal control system and other elements of the system of governance.

2. The internal audit function shall be objective and independent from the operational functions.

3. Any findings and recommendations of the internal audit shall be reported to the administrative, management or supervisory body which shall determine what actions are to be taken with respect to each of the internal audit findings and recommendations and shall ensure that those actions are carried out.

[6201]
Article 48
Actuarial function

1. Insurance and reinsurance undertakings shall provide for an effective actuarial function to:
   (a) coordinate the calculation of technical provisions;
   (b) ensure the appropriateness of the methodologies and underlying models used as well as the assumptions made in the calculation of technical provisions;
   (c) assess the sufficiency and quality of the data used in the calculation of technical provisions;
   (d) compare best estimates against experience;
   (e) inform the administrative, management or supervisory body of the reliability and adequacy of the calculation of technical provisions;
   (f) oversee the calculation of technical provisions in the cases set out in Article 82;
   (g) express an opinion on the overall underwriting policy;
   (h) express an opinion on the adequacy of reinsurance arrangements; and
   (i) contribute to the effective implementation of the risk-management system referred to in Article 44, in particular with respect to the risk modelling underlying the calculation of the capital requirements set out in Chapter VI, Sections 4 and 5, and to the assessment referred to in Article 45.

2. The actuarial function shall be carried out by persons who have knowledge of actuarial and financial mathematics, commensurate with the nature, scale and complexity of the risks inherent in the business of the insurance or reinsurance undertaking, and who are able to demonstrate their relevant experience with applicable professional and other standards.

[6202]
Article 49
Outsourcing

1. Member States shall ensure that insurance and reinsurance undertakings remain fully responsible for discharging all of their obligations under this Directive when they outsource functions or any insurance or reinsurance activities.

2. Outsourcing of critical or important operational functions or activities shall not be undertaken in such a way as to lead to any of the following:
   (a) materially impairing the quality of the system of governance of the undertaking concerned;
   (b) unduly increasing the operational risk;
   (c) impairing the ability of the supervisory authorities to monitor the compliance of the undertaking with its obligations;
   (d) undermining continuous and satisfactory service to policy holders.

3. Insurance and reinsurance undertakings shall, in a timely manner, notify the supervisory authorities prior to the outsourcing of critical or important functions or activities as well as of any subsequent material developments with respect to those functions or activities.

[6203]
Article 50
Implementing measures

1. The Commission shall adopt implementing measures to further specify the following:
   (a) the elements of the systems referred to in Articles 41, 44, 46 and 47, and in particular the areas to be covered by the asset-liability management and investment policy, as referred to in Article 44(2), of insurance and reinsurance undertakings;
   (b) the functions referred to in Articles 44 and 46 to 48;

(c) the requirements set out in Article 42 and the functions subject thereto;
(d) the conditions under which outsourcing, in particular to service providers located in third countries, may be performed.

2. Where necessary to ensure appropriate convergence of the assessment referred to in Article 45(1)(a), the Commission may adopt implementing measures to further specify the elements of that assessment.

3. Those measures, designed to amend non-essential elements of this Directive by supplementing it, shall be adopted in accordance with the regulatory procedure with scrutiny referred to in Article 301(3).

SECTION 3
PUBLIC DISCLOSURE

[6204]
Article 51
Report on solvency and financial condition: contents

1. Member States shall, taking into account the information required in paragraph 3 and the principles set out in paragraph 4 of Article 35, require insurance and reinsurance undertakings to disclose publicly, on an annual basis, a report on their solvency and financial condition.

That report shall contain the following information, either in full or by way of references to equivalent information, both in nature and scope, disclosed publicly under other legal or regulatory requirements:

(a) a description of the business and the performance of the undertaking;
(b) a description of the system of governance and an assessment of its adequacy for the risk profile of the undertaking;
(c) a description, separately for each category of risk, of the risk exposure, concentration, mitigation and sensitivity;
(d) a description, separately for assets, technical provisions, and other liabilities, of the bases and methods used for their valuation, together with an explanation of any major differences in the bases and methods used for their valuation in financial statements;
(e) a description of the capital management, including at least the following:
 (i) the structure and amount of own funds, and their quality;
 (ii) the amounts of the Solvency Capital Requirement and of the Minimum Capital Requirement;
 (iii) the option set out in Article 304 used for the calculation of the Solvency Capital Requirement;
 (iv) information allowing a proper understanding of the main differences between the underlying assumptions of the standard formula and those of any internal model used by the undertaking for the calculation of its Solvency Capital Requirement;
 (v) the amount of any non-compliance with the Minimum Capital Requirement or any significant non-compliance with the Solvency Capital Requirement during the reporting period, even if subsequently resolved, with an explanation of its origin and consequences as well as any remedial measures taken.

2. The description referred to in point (e)(i) of paragraph 1 shall include an analysis of any significant changes as compared to the previous reporting period and an explanation of any major differences in relation to the value of such elements in financial statements, and a brief description of the capital transferability.

The disclosure of the Solvency Capital Requirement referred to in point (e)(ii) of paragraph 1 shall show separately the amount calculated in accordance with Chapter VI, Section 4, Subsections 2 and 3 and any capital add-on imposed in accordance with Article 37 or the impact of the specific parameters the insurance or reinsurance undertaking is required to use in accordance with Article 110, together with concise information on its justification by the supervisory authority concerned.

However, and without prejudice to any disclosure that is mandatory under any other legal or regulatory requirements, Member States may provide that, although the total Solvency Capital Requirement referred to in point (e)(ii) of paragraph 1 is disclosed, the capital add-on or the impact of the specific parameters the insurance or reinsurance undertaking is required to use in accordance with Article 110 need not be separately disclosed during a transitional period ending no later than 31 October 2017.

The disclosure of the Solvency Capital Requirement shall be accompanied, where applicable, by an indication that its final amount is still subject to supervisory assessment.

[6205]
Article 52
Information for and reports by CEIOPS

1. Member States shall require the supervisory authorities to provide the following information to CEIOPS on an annual basis:

(a) the average capital add-on per undertaking and the distribution of capital add-ons imposed by the supervisory authority during the previous year, measured as a percentage of the Solvency Capital Requirement, shown separately as follows:
   (i) for all insurance and reinsurance undertakings;
   (ii) for life insurance undertakings;
   (iii) for non-life insurance undertakings;
   (iv) for insurance undertakings pursuing both life and non-life activities;
   (v) for reinsurance undertakings;

(b) for each of the disclosures set out in point (a), the proportion of capital add-ons imposed under points (a), (b) and (c) of Article 37(1) respectively.

2. CEIOPS shall publicly disclose, on an annual basis, the following information:

(a) for all Member States together, the total distribution of capital add-ons, measured as a percentage of the Solvency Capital Requirement, for each of the following:
   (i) all insurance and reinsurance undertakings;
   (ii) life insurance undertakings;
   (iii) non-life insurance undertakings;
   (iv) insurance undertakings pursuing both life and non-life activities;
   (v) reinsurance undertakings;

(b) for each Member State separately, the distribution of capital add-ons, measured as a percentage of the Solvency Capital Requirement, covering all insurance and reinsurance undertakings in that Member State;

(c) for each of the disclosures referred to in points (a) and (b), the proportion of capital add-ons imposed under points (a), (b) and (c) of Article 37(1) respectively.

3. CEIOPS shall provide the information referred to in paragraph 2 to the European Parliament, the Council and the Commission, together with a report outlining the degree of supervisory convergence in the use of capital add-ons between supervisory authorities in the different Member States.

[6206]
Article 53
Report on solvency and financial condition: applicable principles

1. Supervisory authorities shall permit insurance and reinsurance undertakings not to disclose information where:

(a) by disclosing such information, the competitors of the undertaking would gain significant undue advantage;

(b) there are obligations to policy holders or other counterparty relationships binding an undertaking to secrecy or confidentiality.

2. Where non-disclosure of information is permitted by the supervisory authority, undertakings shall make a statement to this effect in their report on solvency and financial condition and shall state the reasons.

3. Supervisory authorities shall permit insurance and reinsurance undertakings, to make use of — or refer to — public disclosures made under other legal or regulatory requirements, to the extent that those disclosures are equivalent to the information required under Article 51 in both their nature and scope.

4. Paragraphs 1 and 2 shall not apply to the information referred to in Article 51(1)(e).

[6207]
Article 54
Report on solvency and financial condition: updates and additional voluntary information

1. In the event of any major development affecting significantly the relevance of the information disclosed in accordance with Articles 51 and 53, insurance and reinsurance undertakings shall disclose appropriate information on the nature and effects of that major development.

For the purposes of the first subparagraph, at least the following shall be regarded as major developments:

(a) non-compliance with the Minimum Capital Requirement is observed and the supervisory authorities either consider that the undertaking will not be able to submit a realistic short-term finance scheme or do not obtain such a scheme within one month of the date when non-compliance was observed;

(b) significant non-compliance with the Solvency Capital Requirement is observed and the supervisory authorities do not obtain a realistic recovery plan within two months of the date when non-compliance was observed.

In regard to point (a) of the second subparagraph, the supervisory authorities shall require the undertaking concerned to disclose immediately the amount of non-compliance, together with an explanation of its origin and consequences, including any remedial measure taken. Where, in spite of a short-term finance scheme initially considered to be realistic, non-compliance with the Minimum Capital Requirement has not been resolved three months after its observation, it shall be disclosed at the end of that period, together with an explanation of its origin and consequences, including any remedial measures taken as well as any further remedial measures planned.

In regard to point (b) of the second subparagraph, the supervisory authorities shall require the undertaking concerned to disclose immediately the amount of non-compliance, together with an explanation of its origin and consequences, including any remedial measure taken. Where, in spite of the recovery plan initially considered to be realistic, a significant non-compliance with the Solvency Capital Requirement has not been resolved six months after its observation, it shall be disclosed at the end of that period, together with an explanation of its origin and consequences, including any remedial measures taken as well as any further remedial measures planned.

2. Insurance and reinsurance undertakings may disclose, on a voluntary basis, any information or explanation related to their solvency and financial condition which is not already required to be disclosed in accordance with Articles 51 and 53 and paragraph 1 of this Article.

[6208]
Article 55
Report on solvency and financial condition: policy and approval

1. Member States shall require insurance and reinsurance undertakings to have appropriate systems and structures in place to fulfil the requirements laid down in Articles 51 and 53 and Article 54(1), as well as to have a written policy ensuring the ongoing appropriateness of any information disclosed in accordance with Articles 51, 53 and 54.

2. The solvency and financial condition report shall be subject to approval by the administrative, management or supervisory body of the insurance or reinsurance undertaking and be published only after that approval.

[6209]
Article 56
Solvency and financial condition report: implementing measures

The Commission shall adopt implementing measures further specifying the information which must be disclosed and the means by which this is to be achieved.

Those measures, designed to amend non-essential elements of this Directive by supplementing it, shall be adopted in accordance with the regulatory procedure with scrutiny referred to in Article 301(3).

SECTION 4
QUALIFYING HOLDINGS

[6210]
Article 57
Acquisitions

1. Member States shall require any natural or legal person or such persons acting in concert (the proposed acquirer) who have taken a decision either to acquire, directly or indirectly, a qualifying holding in an insurance or reinsurance undertaking or to further increase, directly or indirectly, such a qualifying holding in an insurance or reinsurance undertaking as a result of which the proportion of the voting rights or of the capital held would reach or exceed 20%, 30% or 50% or so that the insurance or reinsurance undertaking would become its subsidiary (the proposed acquisition), first to notify in writing the supervisory authorities of the insurance or reinsurance undertaking in which they are seeking to acquire or increase a qualifying holding, indicating the size of the intended holding and relevant information, as referred to in Article 59(4). Member States need not apply the 30% threshold where, in accordance with Article 9(3)(a) of Directive 2004/109/EC, they apply a threshold of one third.

2. Member States shall require any natural or legal person who has taken a decision to dispose, directly or indirectly, of a qualifying holding in an insurance or reinsurance undertaking first to notify in writing the supervisory authorities of the home Member State, indicating the size of that

person's holding after the intended disposal. Such a person shall likewise notify the supervisory authorities of a decision to reduce that person's qualifying holding so that the proportion of the voting rights or of the capital held would fall below 20%, 30% or 50% or so that the insurance or reinsurance undertaking would cease to be a subsidiary of that person. Member States need not apply the 30% threshold where, in accordance with Article 9(3)(a) of Directive 2004/109/EC, they apply a threshold of one third.

[6211]
Article 58
Assessment period

1. The supervisory authorities shall, promptly and in any event within two working days following receipt of the notification required under Article 57(1), as well as following the possible subsequent receipt of the information referred to in paragraph 2, acknowledge receipt thereof in writing to the proposed acquirer.

The supervisory authorities shall have a maximum of 60 working days as from the date of the written acknowledgement of receipt of the notification and all documents required by the Member State to be attached to the notification on the basis of the list referred to in Article 59(4) (the assessment period), to carry out the assessment provided for in Article 59(1) (the assessment).

The supervisory authorities shall inform the proposed acquirer of the date of the expiry of the assessment period at the time of acknowledging receipt.

2. The supervisory authorities may, during the assessment period, if necessary, and no later than on the fiftieth working day of the assessment period, request any further information that is necessary to complete the assessment. Such request shall be made in writing and shall specify the additional information needed.

For the period between the date of request for information by the supervisory authorities and the receipt of a response thereto by the proposed acquirer, the assessment period shall be interrupted. That interruption shall not exceed 20 working days. Any further requests by the supervisory authorities for completion or clarification of the information shall be at their discretion but shall not result in an interruption of the assessment period.

3. The supervisory authorities may extend the interruption referred to in the second subparagraph of paragraph 2 up to 30 working days if the proposed acquirer is:

(a) situated or regulated outside the Community; or

(b) a natural or legal person not subject to supervision under this Directive, Council Directive 85/611/EEC of 20 December 1985 on the coordination of laws, regulations and administrative provisions relating to undertakings for collective investment in transferable securities (UCITS),[1] Directive 2004/39/EC, or Directive 2006/48/EC.

4. If the supervisory authorities, upon completion of the assessment, decide to oppose the proposed acquisition, they shall, within two working days, and not exceeding the assessment period, inform the proposed acquirer in writing stating the reasons. Subject to national law, an appropriate statement of the reasons for the decision may be made accessible to the public at the request of the proposed acquirer. This shall not prevent a Member State from allowing the supervisory authority to make such disclosure in the absence of a request by the proposed acquirer.

5. If the supervisory authorities do not oppose the proposed acquisition within the assessment period in writing, it shall be deemed to be approved.

6. The supervisory authorities may fix a maximum period for concluding the proposed acquisition and extend it where appropriate.

7. Member States shall not impose requirements for the notification to and approval by the supervisory authorities of direct or indirect acquisitions of voting rights or capital that are more stringent than those set out in this Directive.

8. The Commission shall adopt implementing measures further specifying the adjustments of the criteria set out in Article 59(1), in order to take account of future developments and to ensure the uniform application of Articles 57 to 63.

Those measures, designed to amend non-essential elements of this Directive by supplementing it, shall be adopted in accordance with the regulatory procedure with scrutiny referred to in Article 301(3).

NOTES

[1] OJ L375, 31.12.1985, p 3.

Part VI European Materials

[6212]
Article 59
Assessment

1. In assessing the notification provided for in Article 57(1) and the information referred to in Article 58(2) the supervisory authorities shall, in order to ensure the sound and prudent management of the insurance or reinsurance undertaking in which an acquisition is proposed, and having regard to the likely influence of the proposed acquirer on the insurance or reinsurance undertaking, appraise the suitability of the proposed acquirer and the financial soundness of the proposed acquisition against all of the following criteria:

(a) the reputation of the proposed acquirer;

(b) the reputation and experience of any person who will direct the business of the insurance or reinsurance undertaking as a result of the proposed acquisition;

(c) the financial soundness of the proposed acquirer, in particular in relation to the type of business pursued and envisaged in the insurance or reinsurance undertaking in which the acquisition is proposed;

(d) whether the insurance or reinsurance undertaking will be able to comply and continue to comply with the prudential requirements based on this Directive and, where applicable, other Directives, notably, Directive 2002/87/EC, in particular, whether the group of which it will become part has a structure that makes it possible to exercise effective supervision, effectively exchange information among the supervisory authorities and determine the allocation of responsibilities among the supervisory authorities;

(e) whether there are reasonable grounds to suspect that, in connection with the proposed acquisition, money laundering or terrorist financing within the meaning of Article 1 of Directive 2005/60/EC of the European Parliament and of the Council of 26 October 2005 on the prevention of the use of the financial system for the purpose of money laundering and terrorist financing[1] is being or has been committed or attempted, or that the proposed acquisition could increase the risk thereof.

2. The supervisory authorities may oppose the proposed acquisition only if there are reasonable grounds for doing so on the basis of the criteria set out in paragraph 1 or if the information provided by the proposed acquirer is incomplete.

3. Member States shall neither impose any prior conditions in respect of the level of holding that must be acquired nor allow their supervisory authorities to examine the proposed acquisition in terms of the economic needs of the market.

4. Member States shall make publicly available a list specifying the information that is necessary to carry out the assessment and that must be provided to the supervisory authorities at the time of notification referred to in Article 57(1). The information required shall be proportionate and adapted to the nature of the proposed acquirer and the proposed acquisition. Member States shall not require information that is not relevant for a prudential assessment.

5. Notwithstanding Article 58(1), (2) and (3), where two or more proposals to acquire or increase qualifying holdings in the same insurance or reinsurance undertaking have been notified to the supervisory authority, the latter shall treat the proposed acquirers in a non-discriminatory manner.

NOTES

[1] OJ L309, 25.11.2005, p 15.

[6213]
Article 60
Acquisitions by regulated financial undertakings

1. The relevant supervisory authorities shall work in full consultation with each other when carrying out the assessment if the proposed acquirer is one of the following:

(a) a credit institution, insurance or reinsurance undertaking, investment firm or management company within the meaning of point 2 of Article 1a of Directive 85/611/EEC (the UCITS management company) authorised in another Member State or in a sector other than that in which the acquisition is proposed;

(b) the parent undertaking of a credit institution, insurance or reinsurance undertaking, investment firm or UCITS management company authorised in another Member State or in a sector other than that in which the acquisition is proposed; or

(c) a natural or legal person controlling a credit institution, insurance or reinsurance undertaking, investment firm or UCITS management company authorised in another Member State or in a sector other than that in which the acquisition is proposed.

2. The supervisory authorities shall, without undue delay, provide each other with any information which is essential or relevant for the assessment. In this regard, the supervisory authorities shall communicate to each other upon request all relevant information and shall communicate on their own initiative all essential information. A decision by the supervisory authority that has authorised the insurance or reinsurance undertaking in which the acquisition is proposed shall indicate any views or reservations expressed by the supervisory authority responsible for the proposed acquirer.

[6214]
Article 61
Information to the supervisory authority by the insurance or reinsurance undertaking

On becoming aware of them, the insurance or reinsurance undertaking shall inform the supervisory authority of its home Member State of any acquisitions or disposals of holdings in its capital that cause those holdings to exceed or fall below any of the thresholds referred to in Article 57 and Article 58(1) to (7).

The insurance or reinsurance undertaking shall also, at least once a year, inform the supervisory authority of its home Member State of the names of shareholders and members possessing qualifying holdings and the sizes of such holdings as shown, for example, by the information received at annual general meetings of shareholders or members or as a result of compliance with the regulations relating to companies listed on stock exchanges.

[6215]
Article 62
Qualifying holdings, powers of the supervisory authority

Member States shall require that, where the influence exercised by the persons referred to in Article 57 is likely to operate against the sound and prudent management of an insurance or reinsurance undertaking, the supervisory authority of the home Member State of that undertaking in which a qualifying holding is sought or increased take appropriate measures to put an end to that situation. Such measures may consist, for example, of injunctions, penalties against directors and managers, or suspension of the exercise of the voting rights attaching to the shares held by the shareholders or members in question.

Similar measures shall apply to natural or legal persons failing to comply with the notification obligation established in Article 57.

Where a holding is acquired despite the opposition of the supervisory authorities, the Member States shall, regardless of any other sanctions to be adopted, provide for:

(1) the suspension of the exercise of the corresponding voting rights; or
(2) the nullity of any votes cast or the possibility of their annulment.

[6216]
Article 63
Voting rights

For the purposes of this Section, the voting rights referred to in Articles 9 and 10 of Directive 2004/109/EC, as well as the conditions regarding aggregation thereof laid down in Article 12(4) and (5) of that Directive, shall be taken into account.

Member States shall not take into account voting rights or shares which investment firms or credit institutions may hold as a result of providing the underwriting of financial instruments and/or placing of financial instruments on a firm commitment basis included under point 6 of Section A of Annex I to Directive 2004/39/EC, provided that those rights are, on the one hand, not exercised or otherwise used to intervene in the management of the issuer and, on the other, disposed of within one year of acquisition.

SECTION 5
PROFESSIONAL SECRECY, EXCHANGE OF INFORMATION AND PROMOTION OF SUPERVISORY CONVERGENCE

[6217]
Article 64
Professional secrecy

Member States shall provide that all persons who are working or who have worked for the supervisory authorities, as well as auditors and experts acting on behalf of those authorities, are bound by the obligation of professional secrecy.

Without prejudice to cases covered by criminal law, any confidential information received by such persons whilst performing their duties shall not be divulged to any person or authority whatsoever, except in summary or aggregate form, such that individual insurance and reinsurance undertakings cannot be identified.

However, where an insurance or reinsurance undertaking has been declared bankrupt or is being compulsorily wound up, confidential information which does not concern third parties involved in attempts to rescue that undertaking may be divulged in civil or commercial proceedings.

[6218]
Article 65
Exchange of information between supervisory authorities of Member States

Article 64 shall not preclude the exchange of information between supervisory authorities of different Member States. Such information shall be subject to the obligation of professional secrecy laid down in Article 64.

[6219]
Article 66
Cooperation agreements with third countries

Member States may conclude cooperation agreements providing for the exchange of information with the supervisory authorities of third countries or with authorities or bodies of third countries as defined in Article 68(1) and (2) only if the information to be disclosed is subject to guarantees of professional secrecy at least equivalent to those referred to in this Section. Such exchange of information must be intended for the performance of the supervisory task of those authorities or bodies.

Where the information to be disclosed by a Member State to a third country originates in another Member State, it shall not be disclosed without the express agreement of the supervisory authority of that Member State and, where appropriate, solely for the purposes for which that authority gave its agreement.

[6220]
Article 67
Use of confidential information

Supervisory authorities which receive confidential information under Articles 64 or 65 may use it only in the course of their duties and for the following purposes:

(1) to check that the conditions governing the taking-up of the business of insurance or reinsurance are met and to facilitate the monitoring of the conduct of such business, especially with regard to the monitoring of the technical provisions, the Solvency Capital Requirement, the Minimum Capital Requirement, and the system of governance;
(2) to impose sanctions;
(3) in administrative appeals against decisions of the supervisory authorities;
(4) in court proceedings under this Directive.

[6221]
Article 68
Exchange of information with other authorities

1. Articles 64 and 67 shall not preclude any of the following:
   (a) the exchange of information between several supervisory authorities in the same Member State in the discharge of their supervisory functions;
   (b) the exchange of information, in the discharge of their supervisory functions, between supervisory authorities and any of the following which are situated in the same Member State:
      (i) authorities responsible for the supervision of credit institutions and other financial organisations and the authorities responsible for the supervision of financial markets;
      (ii) bodies involved in the liquidation and bankruptcy of insurance undertakings or reinsurance undertakings and in other similar procedures;
      (iii) persons responsible for carrying out statutory audits of the accounts of insurance undertakings, reinsurance undertakings and other financial institutions;
   (c) the disclosure, to bodies which administer compulsory winding-up proceedings or guarantee funds, of information necessary for the performance of their duties.

The exchanges of information referred to in points (b) and (c) may also take place between different Member States.

The information received by those authorities, bodies and persons shall be subject to the obligation of professional secrecy laid down in Article 64.

2. Articles 64 to 67 shall not preclude Member States from authorising exchanges of information between the supervisory authorities and any of the following:

(a) the authorities responsible for overseeing the bodies involved in the liquidation and bankruptcy of insurance undertakings, reinsurance undertakings and other similar procedures;
(b) the authorities responsible for overseeing the persons charged with carrying out statutory audits of the accounts of insurance undertakings, reinsurance undertakings, credit institutions, investment firms and other financial institutions;
(c) independent actuaries of insurance undertakings or reinsurance undertakings carrying out legal supervision of those undertakings and the bodies responsible for overseeing such actuaries.

Member States which apply the first subparagraph shall require at least that the following conditions are met:

(a) the information must be for the purpose of carrying out the overseeing or legal supervision referred to in the first subparagraph;
(b) the information received must be subject to the obligation of professional secrecy laid down in Article 64;
(c) where the information originates in another Member State, it must not be disclosed without the express agreement of the supervisory authority from which it originates and, where appropriate, solely for the purposes for which that authority gave its agreement.

Member States shall communicate to the Commission and to the other Member States the names of the authorities, persons and bodies which may receive information pursuant to the first and second subparagraphs.

3. Articles 64 to 67 shall not preclude Member States from authorising, with the aim of strengthening the stability, and integrity, of the financial system, the exchange of information between the supervisory authorities and the authorities or bodies responsible for the detection and investigation of breaches of company law.

Member States which apply the first subparagraph shall require that at least the following conditions are met:

(a) the information must be intended for the purpose of detection and investigation as referred to in the first subparagraph;
(b) information received must be subject to the obligation of professional secrecy laid down in Article 64;
(c) where the information originates in another Member State, it shall not be disclosed without the express agreement of the supervisory authority from which it originates and, where appropriate, solely for the purposes for which that authority gave its agreement.

Where, in a Member State, the authorities or bodies referred to in the first subparagraph perform their task of detection or investigation with the aid of persons appointed, in view of their specific competence, for that purpose and not employed in the public sector, the possibility of exchanging information provided for in the first subparagraph may be extended to such persons under the conditions set out in the second subparagraph.

In order to implement point (c) of the second subparagraph, the authorities or bodies referred to in the first subparagraph shall communicate to the supervisory authority from which the information originates the names and precise responsibilities of the persons to whom it is to be sent.

4. Member States shall communicate to the Commission and to the other Member States the names of the authorities, persons or bodies which may receive information pursuant to paragraph 3.

[6222]
Article 69
Disclosure of information to government administrations responsible for financial legislation

Articles 64 and 67 shall not preclude Member States from authorising, under provisions laid down by law, the disclosure of certain information to other departments of their central government administrations responsible for legislation on the supervision of credit institutions, financial institutions, investment services and insurance or reinsurance undertakings and to inspectors acting on behalf of those departments.

Such disclosure shall be made only where necessary for reasons of prudential control. Member States shall, however, provide that information received under Article 65 and Article 68(1), and information obtained by means of on-site verification referred to in Article 32 may only be disclosed with the express consent of the supervisory authority from which the information originated or of the supervisory authority of the Member State in which the on-site verification was carried out.

[6223]
Article 70
Transmission of information to central banks and monetary authorities

Without prejudice to this Section, a supervisory authority may transmit information intended for the performance of their tasks to the following:

(1) central banks and other bodies with a similar function in their capacity as monetary authorities;

(2) where appropriate, other public authorities responsible for overseeing payment systems.

Such authorities or bodies may also communicate to the supervisory authorities such information as they may need for the purposes of Article 67. Information received in this context shall be subject to the provisions on professional secrecy laid down in this Section..

[6224]
Article 71
Supervisory convergence

1. Member States shall ensure that the mandates of supervisory authorities take into account, in an appropriate way, a European Union dimension.

2. Member States shall ensure that in the exercise of their duties supervisory authorities have regard to the convergence in respect of supervisory tools and supervisory practices in the application of the laws, regulations and administrative requirements adopted pursuant to this Directive. For that purpose, Member States shall ensure that the supervisory authorities participate in the activities of CEIOPS pursuant to Decision 2009/79/EC and take duly into account its guidelines and recommendations referred to in paragraph 3 of this Article.

3. CEIOPS shall, where necessary, provide for non-legally binding guidelines and recommendations concerning the implementation of the provisions of this Directive and its implementing measures in order to enhance the convergence of supervisory practices. In addition, CEIOPS shall report regularly and at least every two years to the European Parliament, the Council and the Commission on the progress of the supervisory convergence in the Community.

SECTION 6
DUTIES OF AUDITORS

[6225]
Article 72
Duties of auditors

1. Member States shall provide at least that persons authorised within the meaning of Eighth Council Directive 84/253/EEC of 10 April 1984 based on Article 54(3)(g) of the Treaty on the approval of persons responsible for carrying out the statutory audits of accounting documents[1], who perform in an insurance or reinsurance undertaking the statutory audit referred to in Article 51 of Directive 78/660/EEC, Article 37 of Directive 83/349/EEC or Article 31 of Directive 85/611/EEC or any other statutory task, shall have a duty to report promptly to the supervisory authorities any fact or decision concerning that undertaking of which they have become aware while carrying out that task and which is liable to bring about any of the following:

(a) a material breach of the laws, regulations or administrative provisions which lay down the conditions governing authorisation or which specifically govern pursuit of the activities of insurance and reinsurance undertakings;

(b) the impairment of the continuous functioning of the insurance or reinsurance undertaking;

(c) a refusal to certify the accounts or to the expression of reservations;

(d) non-compliance with the Solvency Capital Requirement;

(e) non-compliance with the Minimum Capital Requirement.

The persons referred to in the first subparagraph shall also report any facts or decisions of which they have become aware in the course of carrying out a task as described in the first subparagraph in an undertaking which has close links resulting from a control relationship with the insurance or reinsurance undertaking within which they are carrying out that task.

2. The disclosure in good faith to the supervisory authorities, by persons authorised within the meaning of Directive 84/253/EEC, of any fact or decision referred to in paragraph 1 shall not constitute a breach of any restriction on disclosure of information imposed by contract or by any legislative, regulatory or administrative provision and shall not involve such persons in liability of any kind.

NOTES

[1] OJ L126, 12.5.1984, p 20.

CHAPTER V
PURSUIT OF LIFE AND NON-LIFE INSURANCE ACTIVITY

[6226]
Article 73
Pursuit of life and non-life insurance activity

1. Insurance undertakings shall not be authorised to pursue life and non-life insurance activities simultaneously.

2. By way of derogation from paragraph 1, Member States may provide that:
   (a) undertakings authorised to pursue life insurance activity may obtain authorisation for non-life insurance activities for the risks listed in classes 1 and 2 in Part A of Annex I;
   (b) undertakings authorised solely for the risks listed in classes 1 and 2 in Part A of Annex I may obtain authorisation to pursue life insurance activity.

However, each activity shall be separately managed in accordance with Article 74.

3. Member States may provide that the undertakings referred to in paragraph 2 shall comply with the accounting rules governing life insurance undertakings for all of their activities. Pending coordination in this respect, Member States may also provide that, with regard to rules on winding-up, activities relating to the risks listed in classes 1 and 2 in Part A of Annex I pursued by those undertakings shall be governed by the rules applicable to life insurance activities.

4. Where a non-life insurance undertaking has financial, commercial or administrative links with a life insurance undertaking, the supervisory authorities of the home Member States shall ensure that the accounts of the undertakings concerned are not distorted by agreements between those undertakings or by any arrangement which could affect the apportionment of expenses and income.

5. Undertakings which on the following dates pursued simultaneously both life and non-life insurance activities covered by this Directive may continue to pursue those activities simultaneously, provided that each activity is separately managed in accordance with Article 74:
   (a) 1 January 1981 for undertakings authorised in Greece;
   (b) 1 January 1986 for undertakings authorised in Spain and Portugal;
   (c) 1 January 1995 for undertakings authorised in Austria, Finland and Sweden;
   (d) 1 May 2004 for undertakings authorised in the Czech Republic, Estonia, Cyprus, Latvia, Lithuania, Hungary, Malta, Poland, Slovakia, and Slovenia;
   (e) 1 January 2007 for undertakings authorised in Bulgaria and Romania;
   (f) 15 March 1979 for all other undertakings.

The home Member State may require insurance undertakings to cease, within a period to be determined by that Member State, the simultaneous pursuit of life and non-life insurance activities in which they were engaged on the dates referred to in the first subparagraph.

[6227]
Article 74
Separation of life and non-life insurance management

1. The separate management referred to in Article 73 shall be organised in such a way that the life insurance activity is distinct from non-life insurance activity.

The respective interests of life and non-life policy holders shall not be prejudiced and, in particular, profits from life insurance shall benefit life policy holders as if the life insurance undertaking only pursued the activity of life insurance.

2. Without prejudice to Articles 100 and 128, the insurance undertakings referred to in Article 73(2) and (5) shall calculate:
   (a) a notional life Minimum Capital Requirement with respect to their life insurance or reinsurance activity, calculated as if the undertaking concerned only pursued that activity, on the basis of the separate accounts referred to in paragraph 6; and
   (b) a notional non-life Minimum Capital Requirement with respect to their non-life insurance or reinsurance activity, calculated as if the undertaking concerned only pursued that activity, on the basis of the separate accounts referred to in paragraph 6.

3. As a minimum, the insurance undertakings referred to in Article 73(2) and (5) shall cover the following by an equivalent amount of eligible basic own-fund items:
   (a) the notional life Minimum Capital Requirement, in respect of the life activity;
   (b) the notional non-life Minimum Capital Requirement, in respect of the non-life activity.

The minimum financial obligations referred to in the first sub-paragraph, in respect of the life insurance activity and the non-life insurance activity, shall not be borne by the other activity.

4. As long as the minimum financial obligations referred to in paragraph 3 are fulfilled and provided the supervisory authority is informed, the undertaking may use to cover the Solvency Capital Requirement referred to in Article 100, the explicit eligible own-fund items which are still available for one or the other activity.

5. The supervisory authorities shall analyse the results in both life and non-life insurance activities so as to ensure that the requirements of paragraphs 1 to 4 are fulfilled.

6. Accounts shall be drawn up so as to show the sources of the results for life and non-life insurance separately. All income, in particular premiums, payments by reinsurers and investment income, and expenditure, in particular insurance settlements, additions to technical provisions, reinsurance premiums and operating expenses in respect of insurance business, shall be broken down according to origin. Items common to both activities shall be entered in the accounts in accordance with methods of apportionment to be accepted by the supervisory authority.

Insurance undertakings shall, on the basis of the accounts, prepare a statement in which the eligible basic own-fund items covering each notional Minimum Capital Requirement as referred to in paragraph 2 are clearly identified, in accordance with Article 98(4).

7. If the amount of eligible basic own-fund items with respect to one of the activities is insufficient to cover the minimum financial obligations referred to in first subparagraph of paragraph 3, the supervisory authorities shall apply to the deficient activity the measures provided for in this Directive, whatever the results in the other activity.

By way of derogation from the second subparagraph of paragraph 3, those measures may involve the authorisation of a transfer of explicit eligible basic own-fund items from one activity to the other.

CHAPTER VI
RULES RELATING TO THE VALUATION OF ASSETS AND LIABILITIES, TECHNICAL PROVISIONS, OWN FUNDS, SOLVENCY CAPITAL REQUIREMENT, MINIMUM CAPITAL REQUIREMENT AND INVESTMENT RULES

SECTION 1
VALUATION OF ASSETS AND LIABILITIES

[6228]
Article 75
Valuation of assets and liabilities

1. Member States shall ensure that, unless otherwise stated, insurance and reinsurance undertakings value assets and liabilities as follows:

(a) assets shall be valued at the amount for which they could be exchanged between knowledgeable willing parties in an arm's length transaction;

(b) liabilities shall be valued at the amount for which they could be transferred, or settled, between knowledgeable willing parties in an arm's length transaction.

When valuing liabilities under point (b), no adjustment to take account of the own credit standing of the insurance or reinsurance undertaking shall be made.

2. The Commission shall adopt implementing measures to set out the methods and assumptions to be used in the valuation of assets and liabilities as laid down in paragraph 1.

Those measures, designed to amend non-essential elements of this Directive by supplementing it, shall be adopted in accordance with the regulatory procedure with scrutiny referred to in Article 301(3).

SECTION 2
RULES RELATING TO TECHNICAL PROVISIONS

[6229]
Article 76
General provisions

1. Member States shall ensure that insurance and reinsurance undertakings establish technical provisions with respect to all of their insurance and reinsurance obligations towards policy holders and beneficiaries of insurance or reinsurance contracts.

2. The value of technical provisions shall correspond to the current amount insurance and reinsurance undertakings would have to pay if they were to transfer their insurance and reinsurance obligations immediately to another insurance or reinsurance undertaking.

3. The calculation of technical provisions shall make use of and be consistent with information provided by the financial markets and generally available data on underwriting risks (market consistency).

4. Technical provisions shall be calculated in a prudent, reliable and objective manner.

5. Following the principles set out in paragraphs 2, 3 and 4 and taking into account the principles set out in Article 75(1), the calculation of technical provisions shall be carried out in accordance with Articles 77 to 82 and 86.

[6230]
Article 77
Calculation of technical provisions

1. The value of technical provisions shall be equal to the sum of a best estimate and a risk margin as set out in paragraphs 2 and 3.

2. The best estimate shall correspond to the probability-weighted average of future cash-flows, taking account of the time value of money (expected present value of future cash-flows), using the relevant risk-free interest rate term structure.

The calculation of the best estimate shall be based upon up-to-date and credible information and realistic assumptions and be performed using adequate, applicable and relevant actuarial and statistical methods.

The cash-flow projection used in the calculation of the best estimate shall take account of all the cash in- and out-flows required to settle the insurance and reinsurance obligations over the lifetime thereof.

The best estimate shall be calculated gross, without deduction of the amounts recoverable from reinsurance contracts and special purpose vehicles. Those amounts shall be calculated separately, in accordance with Article 81.

3. The risk margin shall be such as to ensure that the value of the technical provisions is equivalent to the amount that insurance and reinsurance undertakings would be expected to require in order to take over and meet the insurance and reinsurance obligations.

4. Insurance and reinsurance undertakings shall value the best estimate and the risk margin separately.

However, where future cash flows associated with insurance or reinsurance obligations can be replicated reliably using financial instruments for which a reliable market value is observable, the value of technical provisions associated with those future cash flows shall be determined on the basis of the market value of those financial instruments. In this case, separate calculations of the best estimate and the risk margin shall not be required.

5. Where insurance and reinsurance undertakings value the best estimate and the risk margin separately, the risk margin shall be calculated by determining the cost of providing an amount of eligible own funds equal to the Solvency Capital Requirement necessary to support the insurance and reinsurance obligations over the lifetime thereof.

The rate used in the determination of the cost of providing that amount of eligible own funds (Cost-of-Capital rate) shall be the same for all insurance and reinsurance undertakings and shall be reviewed periodically.

The Cost-of-Capital rate used shall be equal to the additional rate, above the relevant risk-free interest rate, that an insurance or reinsurance undertaking would incur holding an amount of eligible own funds, as set out in Section 3, equal to the Solvency Capital Requirement necessary to support insurance and reinsurance obligations over the lifetime of those obligations.

[6231]
Article 78
Other elements to be taken into account in the calculation of technical provisions

In addition to Article 77, when calculating technical provisions, insurance and reinsurance undertakings shall take account of the following:

(1) all expenses that will be incurred in servicing insurance and reinsurance obligations;

(2) inflation, including expenses and claims inflation;

(3) all payments to policy holders and beneficiaries, including future discretionary bonuses, which insurance and reinsurance undertakings expect to make, whether or not those payments are contractually guaranteed, unless those payments fall under Article 91(2).

[6232]
Article 79
Valuation of financial guarantees and contractual options included in insurance and reinsurance contracts

When calculating technical provisions, insurance and reinsurance undertakings shall take account of the value of financial guarantees and any contractual options included in insurance and reinsurance policies.

Any assumptions made by insurance and reinsurance undertakings with respect to the likelihood that policy holders will exercise contractual options, including lapses and surrenders, shall be realistic and based on current and credible information. The assumptions shall take account, either explicitly or implicitly, of the impact that future changes in financial and non-financial conditions may have on the exercise of those options.

[6233]
Article 80
Segmentation

Insurance and reinsurance undertakings shall segment their insurance and reinsurance obligations into homogeneous risk groups, and as a minimum by lines of business, when calculating their technical provisions.

[6234]
Article 81
Recoverables from reinsurance contracts and special purpose vehicles

The calculation by insurance and reinsurance undertakings of amounts recoverable from reinsurance contracts and special purpose vehicles shall comply with Articles 76 to 80.

When calculating amounts recoverable from reinsurance contracts and special purpose vehicles, insurance and reinsurance undertakings shall take account of the time difference between recoveries and direct payments.

The result from that calculation shall be adjusted to take account of expected losses due to default of the counterparty. That adjustment shall be based on an assessment of the probability of default of the counterparty and the average loss resulting therefrom (loss-given-default).

[6235]
Article 82
Data quality and application of approximations, including case-by-case approaches, for technical provisions

Member States shall ensure that insurance and reinsurance undertakings have internal processes and procedures in place to ensure the appropriateness, completeness and accuracy of the data used in the calculation of their technical provisions.

Where, in specific circumstances, insurance and reinsurance undertakings have insufficient data of appropriate quality to apply a reliable actuarial method to a set or subset of their insurance and reinsurance obligations, or amounts recoverable from reinsurance contracts and special purpose vehicles, appropriate approximations, including case-by-case approaches, may be used in the calculation of the best estimate.

[6236]
Article 83
Comparison against experience

Insurance and reinsurance undertakings shall have processes and procedures in place to ensure that best estimates, and the assumptions underlying the calculation of best estimates, are regularly compared against experience.

Where the comparison identifies systematic deviation between experience and the best estimate calculations of insurance or reinsurance undertakings, the undertaking concerned shall make appropriate adjustments to the actuarial methods being used and/or the assumptions being made.

[6237]
Article 84
Appropriateness of the level of technical provisions

Upon request from the supervisory authorities, insurance and reinsurance undertakings shall demonstrate the appropriateness of the level of their technical provisions, as well as the applicability and relevance of the methods applied, and the adequacy of the underlying statistical data used.

[6238]
Article 85
Increase of technical provisions

To the extent that the calculation of technical provisions of insurance and reinsurance undertakings does not comply with Articles 76 to 83, the supervisory authorities may require insurance and reinsurance undertakings to increase the amount of technical provisions so that they correspond to the level determined pursuant to those Articles.

[6239]
Article 86
Implementing measures

The Commission shall adopt implementing measures laying down the following:

(a) actuarial and statistical methodologies to calculate the best estimate referred to in Article 77(2);
(b) the relevant risk-free interest rate term structure to be used to calculate the best estimate referred to in Article 77(2);
(c) the circumstances in which technical provisions shall be calculated as a whole, or as a sum of a best estimate and a risk margin, and the methods to be used in the case where technical provisions are calculated as a whole;
(d) the methods and assumptions to be used in the calculation of the risk margin including the determination of the amount of eligible own funds necessary to support the insurance and reinsurance obligations and the calibration of the Cost-of-Capital rate;
(e) the lines of business on the basis of which insurance and reinsurance obligations are to be segmented in order to calculate technical provisions;
(f) the standards to be met with respect to ensuring the appropriateness, completeness and accuracy of the data used in the calculation of technical provisions, and the specific circumstances in which it would be appropriate to use approximations, including case-by-case approaches, to calculate the best estimate;
(g) the methodologies to be used when calculating the counterparty default adjustment referred to in Article 81 designed to capture expected losses due to default of the counterparty;
(h) where necessary, simplified methods and techniques to calculate technical provisions, in order to ensure the actuarial and statistical methods referred to in points (a) and (d) are proportionate to the nature, scale and complexity of the risks supported by insurance and reinsurance undertakings including captive insurance and reinsurance undertakings.

Those measures, designed to amend non-essential elements of this Directive by supplementing it, shall be adopted in accordance with the regulatory procedure with scrutiny referred to in Article 301(3).

SECTION 3
OWN FUNDS

SUBSECTION 1
DETERMINATION OF OWN FUNDS

[6240]
Article 87
Own funds

Own funds shall comprise the sum of basic own funds, referred to in Article 88 and ancillary own funds referred to in Article 89.

[6241]
Article 88
Basic own funds

Basic own funds shall consist of the following items:

(1) the excess of assets over liabilities, valued in accordance with Article 75 and Section 2;
(2) subordinated liabilities.

The excess amount referred to in point (1) shall be reduced by the amount of own shares held by the insurance or reinsurance undertaking.

[6242]
Article 89
Ancillary own funds

1. Ancillary own funds shall consist of items other than basic own funds which can be called up to absorb losses.

Ancillary own funds may comprise the following items to the extent that they are not basic own-fund items:

(a) unpaid share capital or initial fund that has not been called up;
(b) letters of credit and guarantees;
(c) any other legally binding commitments received by insurance and reinsurance undertakings.

In the case of a mutual or mutual-type association with variable contributions, ancillary own funds may also comprise any future claims which that association may have against its members by way of a call for supplementary contribution, within the following 12 months.

2. Where an ancillary own-fund item has been paid in or called up, it shall be treated as an asset and cease to form part of ancillary own-fund items.

[6243]
Article 90
Supervisory approval of ancillary own funds

1. The amounts of ancillary own-fund items to be taken into account when determining own funds shall be subject to prior supervisory approval.

2. The amount ascribed to each ancillary own-fund item shall reflect the loss-absorbency of the item and shall be based upon prudent and realistic assumptions. Where an ancillary own-fund item has a fixed nominal value, the amount of that item shall be equal to its nominal value, where it appropriately reflects its loss-absorbency.

3. Supervisory authorities shall approve either of the following:

(a) a monetary amount for each ancillary own-fund item;
(b) a method by which to determine the amount of each ancillary own-fund item, in which case supervisory approval of the amount determined in accordance with that method shall be granted for a specified period of time.

4. For each ancillary own-fund item, supervisory authorities shall base their approval on an assessment of the following:

(a) the status of the counterparties concerned, in relation to their ability and willingness to pay;
(b) the recoverability of the funds, taking account of the legal form of the item, as well as any conditions which would prevent the item from being successfully paid in or called up;
(c) any information on the outcome of past calls which insurance and reinsurance undertakings have made for such ancillary own funds, to the extent that information can be reliably used to assess the expected outcome of future calls.

[6244]
Article 91
Surplus funds

1. Surplus funds shall be deemed to be accumulated profits which have not been made available for distribution to policy holders and beneficiaries.

2. In so far as authorised under national law, surplus funds shall not be considered as insurance and reinsurance liabilities to the extent that they fulfil the criteria set out in Article 94(1).

[6245]
Article 92
Implementing measures

1. The Commission shall adopt implementing measures specifying the following:

(a) the criteria for granting supervisory approval in accordance with Article 90;
(b) the treatment of participations, within the meaning of the third subparagraph of Article 212(2), in financial and credit institutions with respect to the determination of own funds.

Those measures, designed to amend non-essential elements of this Directive by supplementing it, shall be adopted in accordance with the regulatory procedure with scrutiny referred to in Article 301(3).

2. Participations in financial and credit institutions as referred to in paragraph 1(b) shall comprise the following:

(a) participations which insurance and reinsurance undertakings hold in:
   (i) credit institutions and financial institutions within the meaning of Article 4(1) and (5) of Directive 2006/48/EC,

(ii) investment firms within the meaning of point 1 of Article 4(1) of Directive 2004/39/EC;

(b) subordinated claims and instruments referred to in Article 63 and Article 64(3) of Directive 2006/48/EC which insurance and reinsurance undertakings hold in respect of the entities defined in point (a) of this paragraph in which they hold a participation.

SUBSECTION 2
CLASSIFICATION OF OWN FUNDS

[6246]
Article 93
Characteristics and features used to classify own funds into tiers

1. Own-fund items shall be classified into three tiers. The classification of those items shall depend upon whether they are basic own fund or ancillary own-fund items and the extent to which they possess the following characteristics:

(a) the item is available, or can be called up on demand, to fully absorb losses on a going-concern basis, as well as in the case of winding-up (permanent availability);

(b) in the case of winding-up, the total amount of the item is available to absorb losses and the repayment of the item is refused to its holder until all other obligations, including insurance and reinsurance obligations towards policy holders and beneficiaries of insurance and reinsurance contracts, have been met (subordination).

2. When assessing the extent to which own-fund items possess the characteristics set out in points (a) and (b) of paragraph 1, currently and in the future, due consideration shall be given to the duration of the item, in particular whether the item is dated or not. Where an own-fund item is dated, the relative duration of the item as compared to the duration of the insurance and reinsurance obligations of the undertaking shall be considered (sufficient duration).

In addition, the following features shall be considered:

(a) whether the item is free from requirements or incentives to redeem the nominal sum (absence of incentives to redeem);

(b) whether the item is free from mandatory fixed charges (absence of mandatory servicing costs);

(c) whether the item is clear of encumbrances (absence of encumbrances).

[6247]
Article 94
Main criteria for the classification into tiers

1. Basic own-fund items shall be classified in Tier 1 where they substantially possess the characteristics set out in Article 93(1)(a) and (b), taking into consideration the features set out in Article 93(2).

2. Basic own-fund items shall be classified in Tier 2 where they substantially possess the characteristic set out in Article 93(1)(b), taking into consideration the features set out in Article 93(2).

Ancillary own-fund items shall be classified in Tier 2 where they substantially possess the characteristics set out in Article 93(1)(a) and (b), taking into consideration the features set out in Article 93(2).

3. Any basic and ancillary own-fund items which do not fall under paragraphs 1 and 2 shall be classified in Tier 3.

[6248]
Article 95
Classification of own funds into tiers

Member States shall ensure that insurance and reinsurance undertakings classify their own-fund items on the basis of the criteria laid down in Article 94.

For that purpose, insurance and reinsurance undertakings shall refer to the list of own-fund items referred to in Article 97(1)(a), where applicable.

Where an own-fund item is not covered by that list, it shall be assessed and classified by insurance and reinsurance undertakings, in accordance with the first paragraph. That classification shall be subject to approval by the supervisory authority.

[6249]
Article 96
Classification of specific insurance own-fund items

Without prejudice to Article 95 and Article 97(1)(a) for the purposes of this Directive the following classifications shall be applied:

(1) surplus funds falling under Article 91(2) shall be classified in Tier 1;

(2) letters of credit and guarantees which are held in trust for the benefit of insurance creditors by an independent trustee and provided by credit institutions authorised in accordance with Directive 2006/48/EC shall be classified in Tier 2;

(3) any future claims which mutual or mutual-type associations of shipowners with variable contributions solely insuring risks listed in classes 6, 12 and 17 in Part A of Annex I may have against their members by way of a call for supplementary contributions, within the following 12 months, shall be classified in Tier 2.

In accordance with the second subparagraph of Article 94(2), any future claims which mutual or mutual-type associations with variable contributions may have against their members by way of a call for supplementary contributions, within the following 12 months, not falling under point (3) of the first subparagraph shall be classified in Tier 2 where they substantially possess the characteristics set out in Article 93(1)(a) and (b), taking into consideration the features set out in Article 93(2).

[6250]
Article 97
Implementing measures

1. The Commission shall adopt implementing measures laying down the following:

(a) a list of own-fund items, including those referred to in Article 96, deemed to fulfil the criteria, set out in Article 94, which contains for each own-fund item a precise description of the features which determined its classification;

(b) the methods to be used by supervisory authorities, when approving the assessment and classification of own-fund items which are not covered by the list referred to in point (a).

Those measures, designed to amend non-essential elements of this Directive by supplementing it, shall be adopted in accordance with the regulatory procedure with scrutiny referred to in Article 301(3).

2. The Commission shall regularly review and, where appropriate, update the list referred to in paragraph 1(a) in the light of market developments.

SUBSECTION 3
ELIGIBILITY OF OWN FUNDS

[6251]
Article 98
Eligibility and limits applicable to Tiers 1, 2 and 3

1. As far as the compliance with the Solvency Capital Requirement is concerned, the eligible amounts of Tier 2 and Tier 3 items shall be subject to quantitative limits. Those limits shall be such as to ensure that at least the following conditions are met:

(a) the proportion of Tier 1 items in the eligible own funds is higher than one third of the total amount of eligible own funds;

(b) the eligible amount of Tier 3 items is less than one third of the total amount of eligible own funds.

2. As far as compliance with the Minimum Capital Requirement is concerned, the amount of basic own-fund items eligible to cover the Minimum Capital Requirement which are classified in Tier 2 shall be subject to quantitative limits. Those limits shall be such as to ensure, as a minimum, that the proportion of Tier 1 items in the eligible basic own funds is higher than one half of the total amount of eligible basic own funds.

3. The eligible amount of own funds to cover the Solvency Capital Requirement set out in Article 100 shall be equal to the sum of the amount of Tier 1, the eligible amount of Tier 2 and the eligible amount of Tier 3.

4. The eligible amount of basic own funds to cover the Minimum Capital Requirement set out in Article 128 shall be equal to the sum of the amount of Tier 1 and the eligible amount of basic own-fund items classified in Tier 2.

[6252]
Article 99
Implementing measures

The Commission shall adopt implementing measures laying down:

(a) the quantitative limits referred to in Article 98(1) and (2);

(b) the adjustments that should be made to reflect the lack of transferability of those own-fund items that can only be used to cover losses arising from a particular segment of liabilities or from particular risks (ring-fenced funds).

Those measures, designed to amend non-essential elements of this Directive by supplementing it, shall be adopted in accordance with the regulatory procedure with scrutiny referred to in Article 301(3).

SECTION 4
SOLVENCY CAPITAL REQUIREMENT

SUBSECTION 1
GENERAL PROVISIONS FOR THE SOLVENCY CAPITAL REQUIREMENT USING THE STANDARD FORMULA OR AN INTERNAL MODEL

[6253]
Article 100
General provisions

Member States shall require that insurance and reinsurance undertakings hold eligible own funds covering the Solvency Capital Requirement.

The Solvency Capital Requirement shall be calculated, either in accordance with the standard formula in Subsection 2 or using an internal model, as set out in Subsection 3.

[6254]
Article 101
Calculation of the Solvency Capital Requirement

1. The Solvency Capital Requirement shall be calculated in accordance with paragraphs 2 to 5.

2. The Solvency Capital Requirement shall be calculated on the presumption that the undertaking will pursue its business as a going concern.

3. The Solvency Capital Requirement shall be calibrated so as to ensure that all quantifiable risks to which an insurance or reinsurance undertaking is exposed are taken into account. It shall cover existing business, as well as the new business expected to be written over the following 12 months. With respect to existing business, it shall cover only unexpected losses.

It shall correspond to the Value-at-Risk of the basic own funds of an insurance or reinsurance undertaking subject to a confidence level of 99,5% over a one-year period.

4. The Solvency Capital Requirement shall cover at least the following risks:

(a) non-life underwriting risk;
(b) life underwriting risk;
(c) health underwriting risk;
(d) market risk;
(e) credit risk;
(f) operational risk.

Operational risk as referred to in point (f) of the first subparagraph shall include legal risks, and exclude risks arising from strategic decisions, as well as reputation risks.

5. When calculating the Solvency Capital Requirement, insurance and reinsurance undertakings shall take account of the effect of risk-mitigation techniques, provided that credit risk and other risks arising from the use of such techniques are properly reflected in the Solvency Capital Requirement.

[6255]
Article 102
Frequency of calculation

1. Insurance and reinsurance undertakings shall calculate the Solvency Capital Requirement at least once a year and report the result of that calculation to the supervisory authorities.

Insurance and reinsurance undertakings shall hold eligible own funds which cover the last reported Solvency Capital Requirement.

Insurance and reinsurance undertakings shall monitor the amount of eligible own funds and the Solvency Capital Requirement on an ongoing basis.

If the risk profile of an insurance or reinsurance undertaking deviates significantly from the assumptions underlying the last reported Solvency Capital Requirement, the undertaking concerned shall recalculate the Solvency Capital Requirement without delay and report it to the supervisory authorities.

2. Where there is evidence to suggest that the risk profile of the insurance or reinsurance undertaking has altered significantly since the date on which the Solvency Capital Requirement was last reported, the supervisory authorities may require the undertaking concerned to recalculate the Solvency Capital Requirement.

SUBSECTION 2
SOLVENCY CAPITAL REQUIREMENT STANDARD FORMULA

[6256]
Article 103
Structure of the standard formula

The Solvency Capital Requirement calculated on the basis of the standard formula shall be the sum of the following items:

(a) the Basic Solvency Capital Requirement, as laid down in Article 104;
(b) the capital requirement for operational risk, as laid down in Article 107;
(c) the adjustment for the loss-absorbing capacity of technical provisions and deferred taxes, as laid down in Article 108.

[6257]
Article 104
Design of the Basic Solvency Capital Requirement

1. The Basic Solvency Capital Requirement shall comprise individual risk modules, which are aggregated in accordance with point (1) of Annex IV.

It shall consist of at least the following risk modules:

(a) non-life underwriting risk;
(b) life underwriting risk;
(c) health underwriting risk;
(d) market risk;
(e) counterparty default risk.

2. For the purposes of points (a), (b) and (c) of paragraph 1, insurance or reinsurance operations shall be allocated to the underwriting risk module that best reflects the technical nature of the underlying risks.

3. The correlation coefficients for the aggregation of the risk modules referred to in paragraph 1, as well as the calibration of the capital requirements for each risk module, shall result in an overall Solvency Capital Requirement which complies with the principles set out in Article 101.

4. Each of the risk modules referred to in paragraph 1 shall be calibrated using a Value-at-Risk measure, with a 99,5% confidence level, over a one-year period.

Where appropriate, diversification effects shall be taken into account in the design of each risk module.

5. The same design and specifications for the risk modules shall be used for all insurance and reinsurance undertakings, both with respect to the Basic Solvency Capital Requirement and to any simplified calculations as laid down in Article 109.

6. With regard to risks arising from catastrophes, geographical specifications may, where appropriate, be used for the calculation of the life, non-life and health underwriting risk modules.

7. Subject to approval by the supervisory authorities, insurance and reinsurance undertakings may, within the design of the standard formula, replace a subset of its parameters by parameters specific to the undertaking concerned when calculating the life, non-life and health underwriting risk modules.

Such parameters shall be calibrated on the basis of the internal data of the undertaking concerned, or of data which is directly relevant for the operations of that undertaking using standardised methods.

When granting supervisory approval, supervisory authorities shall verify the completeness, accuracy and appropriateness of the data used.

[6258]
Article 105
Calculation of the Basic Solvency Capital Requirement

1. The Basic Solvency Capital Requirement shall be calculated in accordance with paragraphs 2 to 6.

2. The non-life underwriting risk module shall reflect the risk arising from non-life insurance obligations, in relation to the perils covered and the processes used in the conduct of business.

It shall take account of the uncertainty in the results of insurance and reinsurance undertakings related to the existing insurance and reinsurance obligations as well as to the new business expected to be written over the following 12 months.

It shall be calculated, in accordance with point (2) of Annex IV, as a combination of the capital requirements for at least the following sub-modules:

(a) the risk of loss, or of adverse change in the value of insurance liabilities, resulting from fluctuations in the timing, frequency and severity of insured events, and in the timing and amount of claim settlements (non-life premium and reserve risk);

(b) the risk of loss, or of adverse change in the value of insurance liabilities, resulting from significant uncertainty of pricing and provisioning assumptions related to extreme or exceptional events (non-life catastrophe risk).

3. The life underwriting risk module shall reflect the risk arising from life insurance obligations, in relation to the perils covered and the processes used in the conduct of business.

It shall be calculated, in accordance with point (3) of Annex IV, as a combination of the capital requirements for at least the following sub-modules:

(a) the risk of loss, or of adverse change in the value of insurance liabilities, resulting from changes in the level, trend, or volatility of mortality rates, where an increase in the mortality rate leads to an increase in the value of insurance liabilities (mortality risk);

(b) the risk of loss, or of adverse change in the value of insurance liabilities, resulting from changes in the level, trend, or volatility of mortality rates, where a decrease in the mortality rate leads to an increase in the value of insurance liabilities (longevity risk);

(c) the risk of loss, or of adverse change in the value of insurance liabilities, resulting from changes in the level, trend or volatility of disability, sickness and morbidity rates (disability — morbidity risk);

(d) the risk of loss, or of adverse change in the value of insurance liabilities, resulting from changes in the level, trend, or volatility of the expenses incurred in servicing insurance or reinsurance contracts (life-expense risk);

(e) the risk of loss, or of adverse change in the value of insurance liabilities, resulting from fluctuations in the level, trend, or volatility of the revision rates applied to annuities, due to changes in the legal environment or in the state of health of the person insured (revision risk);

(f) the risk of loss, or of adverse change in the value of insurance liabilities, resulting from changes in the level or volatility of the rates of policy lapses, terminations, renewals and surrenders (lapse risk);

(g) the risk of loss, or of adverse change in the value of insurance liabilities, resulting from the significant uncertainty of pricing and provisioning assumptions related to extreme or irregular events (life-catastrophe risk).

4. The health underwriting risk module shall reflect the risk arising from the underwriting of health insurance obligations, whether it is pursued on a similar technical basis to that of life insurance or not, following from both the perils covered and the processes used in the conduct of business.

It shall cover at least the following risks:

(a) the risk of loss, or of adverse change in the value of insurance liabilities, resulting from changes in the level, trend, or volatility of the expenses incurred in servicing insurance or reinsurance contracts;

(b) the risk of loss, or of adverse change in the value of insurance liabilities, resulting from fluctuations in the timing, frequency and severity of insured events, and in the timing and amount of claim settlements at the time of provisioning;

(c) the risk of loss, or of adverse change in the value of insurance liabilities, resulting from the significant uncertainty of pricing and provisioning assumptions related to outbreaks of major epidemics, as well as the unusual accumulation of risks under such extreme circumstances.

5. The market risk module shall reflect the risk arising from the level or volatility of market prices of financial instruments which have an impact upon the value of the assets and liabilities of the undertaking. It shall properly reflect the structural mismatch between assets and liabilities, in particular with respect to the duration thereof.

It shall be calculated, in accordance with point (4) of Annex IV, as a combination of the capital requirements for at least the following sub-modules:

(a) the sensitivity of the values of assets, liabilities and financial instruments to changes in the term structure of interest rates, or in the volatility of interest rates (interest rate risk);
(b) the sensitivity of the values of assets, liabilities and financial instruments to changes in the level or in the volatility of market prices of equities (equity risk);
(c) the sensitivity of the values of assets, liabilities and financial instruments to changes in the level or in the volatility of market prices of real estate (property risk);
(d) the sensitivity of the values of assets, liabilities and financial instruments to changes in the level or in the volatility of credit spreads over the risk-free interest rate term structure (spread risk);
(e) the sensitivity of the values of assets, liabilities and financial instruments to changes in the level or in the volatility of currency exchange rates (currency risk);
(f) additional risks to an insurance or reinsurance undertaking stemming either from lack of diversification in the asset portfolio or from large exposure to default risk by a single issuer of securities or a group of related issuers (market risk concentrations).

6. The counterparty default risk module shall reflect possible losses due to unexpected default, or deterioration in the credit standing, of the counterparties and debtors of insurance and reinsurance undertakings over the following 12 months. The counterparty default risk module shall cover risk-mitigating contracts, such as reinsurance arrangements, securitisations and derivatives, and receivables from intermediaries, as well as any other credit exposures which are not covered in the spread risk sub-module. It shall take appropriate account of collateral or other security held by or for the account of the insurance or reinsurance undertaking and the risks associated therewith.

For each counterparty, the counterparty default risk module shall take account of the overall counterparty risk exposure of the insurance or reinsurance undertaking concerned to that counterparty, irrespective of the legal form of its contractual obligations to that undertaking.

[6259]
Article 106
Calculation of the equity risk sub-module: symmetric adjustment mechanism

1. The equity risk sub-module calculated in accordance with the standard formula shall include a symmetric adjustment to the equity capital charge applied to cover the risk arising from changes in the level of equity prices.

2. The symmetric adjustment made to the standard equity capital charge, calibrated in accordance with Article 104(4), covering the risk arising from changes in the level of equity prices shall be based on a function of the current level of an appropriate equity index and a weighted average level of that index. The weighted average shall be calculated over an appropriate period of time which shall be the same for all insurance and reinsurance undertakings.

3. The symmetric adjustment made to the standard equity capital charge covering the risk arising from changes in the level of equity prices shall not result in an equity capital charge being applied that is more than 10 percentage points lower or 10 percentage points higher than the standard equity capital charge.

[6260]
Article 107
Capital requirement for operational risk

1. The capital requirement for operational risk shall reflect operational risks to the extent they are not already reflected in the risk modules referred to in Article 104. That requirement shall be calibrated in accordance with Article 101(3).

2. With respect to life insurance contracts where the investment risk is borne by the policy holders, the calculation of the capital requirement for operational risk shall take account of the amount of annual expenses incurred in respect of those insurance obligations.

3. With respect to insurance and reinsurance operations other than those referred to in paragraph 2, the calculation of the capital requirement for operational risk shall take account of the volume of those operations, in terms of earned premiums and technical provisions which are held in respect of those insurance and reinsurance obligations. In this case, the capital requirement for operational risks shall not exceed 30% of the Basic Solvency Capital Requirement relating to those insurance and reinsurance operations.

[6261]
Article 108
Adjustment for the loss-absorbing capacity of technical provisions and deferred taxes

The adjustment referred to in Article 103(c) for the loss-absorbing capacity of technical provisions and deferred taxes shall reflect potential compensation of unexpected losses through a simultaneous decrease in technical provisions or deferred taxes or a combination of the two.

That adjustment shall take account of the risk mitigating effect provided by future discretionary benefits of insurance contracts, to the extent insurance and reinsurance undertakings can establish that a reduction in such benefits may be used to cover unexpected losses when they arise. The risk mitigating effect provided by future discretionary benefits shall be no higher than the sum of technical provisions and deferred taxes relating to those future discretionary benefits.

For the purpose of the second paragraph, the value of future discretionary benefits under adverse circumstances shall be compared to the value of such benefits under the underlying assumptions of the best-estimate calculation.

[6262]
Article 109
Simplifications in the standard formula

Insurance and reinsurance undertakings may use a simplified calculation for a specific sub-module or risk module where the nature, scale and complexity of the risks they face justifies it and where it would be disproportionate to require all insurance and reinsurance undertakings to apply the standardised calculation.

Simplified calculations shall be calibrated in accordance with Article 101(3).

[6263]
Article 110
Significant deviations from the assumptions underlying the standard formula calculation

Where it is inappropriate to calculate the Solvency Capital Requirement in accordance with the standard formula, as set out in Subsection 2, because the risk profile of the insurance or reinsurance undertaking concerned deviates significantly from the assumptions underlying the standard formula calculation, the supervisory authorities may, by means of a decision stating the reasons, require the undertaking concerned to replace a subset of the parameters used in the standard formula calculation by parameters specific to that undertaking when calculating the life, non-life and health underwriting risk modules, as set out in Article 104(7). Those specific parameters shall be calculated in such a way to ensure that the undertaking complies with Article 101(3).

[6264]
Article 111
Implementing measures

1. In order to ensure that the same treatment is applied to all insurance and reinsurance undertakings calculating the Solvency Capital Requirement on the basis of the standard formula, or to take account of market developments, the Commission shall adopt implementing measures providing for the following:

(a) a standard formula in accordance with the provisions of Articles 101 and 103 to 109;
(b) any sub-modules necessary or covering more precisely the risks which fall under the respective risk modules referred to in Article 104 as well as any subsequent updates;
(c) the methods, assumptions and standard parameters to be used when calculating each of the risk modules or sub-modules of the Basic Solvency Capital Requirement laid down in Articles 104, 105 and 304, the symmetric adjustment mechanism and the appropriate period of time, expressed in the number of months, as referred to in Article 106, and the appropriate approach for integrating the method referred to in Article 304 in the Solvency Capital Requirement as calculated in accordance with the standard formula;
(d) the correlation parameters, including, if necessary, those set out in Annex IV, and the procedures for the updating of those parameters;
(e) where insurance and reinsurance undertakings use risk-mitigation techniques, the methods and assumptions to be used to assess the changes in the risk profile of the undertaking concerned and to adjust the calculation of the Solvency Capital Requirement;
(f) the qualitative criteria that the risk-mitigation techniques referred to in point (e) must fulfil in order to ensure that the risk has been effectively transferred to a third party;
(g) the methods and parameters to be used when assessing the capital requirement for operational risk set out in Article 107, including the percentage referred to in paragraph 3 of Article 107;
(h) the methods and adjustments to be used to reflect the reduced scope for risk diversification of insurance and reinsurance undertakings related to ring-fenced funds;

(i) the method to be used when calculating the adjustment for the loss-absorbing capacity of technical provisions or deferred taxes, as laid down in Article 108;

(j) the subset of standard parameters in the life, non-life and health underwriting risk modules that may be replaced by undertaking-specific parameters as set out in Article 104(7);

(k) the standardised methods to be used by the insurance or reinsurance undertaking to calculate the undertaking-specific parameters referred to in point (j), and any criteria with respect to the completeness, accuracy, and appropriateness of the data used that must be met before supervisory approval is given;

(l) the simplified calculations provided for specific sub-modules and risk modules, as well as the criteria that insurance and reinsurance undertakings, including captive insurance and reinsurance undertakings, shall be required to fulfil in order to be entitled to use each of those simplifications, as set out in Article 109;

(m) the approach to be used with respect to related undertakings within the meaning of Article 212 in the calculation of the Solvency Capital Requirement, in particular the calculation of the equity risk sub-module referred to in Article 105(5), taking into account the likely reduction in the volatility of the value of those related undertakings arising from the strategic nature of those investments and the influence exercised by the participating undertaking on those related undertakings.

Those measures, designed to amend non-essential elements of this Directive by supplementing it, shall be adopted in accordance with the regulatory procedure with scrutiny referred to in Article 301(3).

2. The Commission may adopt implementing measures laying down quantitative limits and asset eligibility criteria in order to address risks which are not adequately covered by a sub-module. Such implementing measures shall apply to assets covering technical provisions, excluding assets held in respect of life insurance contracts where the investment risk is borne by the policy holders. Those measures shall be reviewed by the Commission in the light of developments in the standard formula and financial markets.

Those measures, designed to amend non-essential elements of this Directive by supplementing it, shall be adopted in accordance with the regulatory procedure with scrutiny referred to in Article 301(3).

SUBSECTION 3

SOLVENCY CAPITAL REQUIREMENT FULL AND PARTIAL INTERNAL MODELS

[6265]

Article 112

General provisions for the approval of full and partial internal models

1. Member States shall ensure that insurance or reinsurance undertakings may calculate the Solvency Capital Requirement using a full or partial internal model as approved by the supervisory authorities.

2. Insurance and reinsurance undertakings may use partial internal models for the calculation of one or more of the following:

(a) one or more risk modules, or sub-modules, of the Basic Solvency Capital Requirement, as set out in Articles 104 and 105;

(b) the capital requirement for operational risk as set out in Article 107;

(c) the adjustment referred to in Article 108.

In addition, partial modelling may be applied to the whole business of insurance and reinsurance undertakings, or only to one or more major business units.

3. In any application for approval, insurance and reinsurance undertakings shall submit, as a minimum, documentary evidence that the internal model fulfils the requirements set out in Articles 120 to 125.

Where the application for that approval relates to a partial internal model, the requirements set out in Articles 120 to 125 shall be adapted to take account of the limited scope of the application of the model.

4. The supervisory authorities shall decide on the application within six months from the receipt of the complete application.

5. Supervisory authorities shall give approval to the application only if they are satisfied that the systems of the insurance or reinsurance undertaking for identifying, measuring, monitoring, managing and reporting risk are adequate and in particular, that the internal model fulfils the requirements referred to in paragraph 3.

6. A decision by the supervisory authorities to reject the application for the use of an internal model shall state the reasons on which it is based.

7. After having received approval from supervisory authorities to use an internal model, insurance and reinsurance undertakings may, by means of a decision stating the reasons, be required to provide supervisory authorities with an estimate of the Solvency Capital Requirement determined in accordance with the standard formula, as set out in Subsection 2.

[6266]
Article 113
Specific provisions for the approval of partial internal models

1. In the case of a partial internal model, supervisory approval shall be given only where that model fulfils the requirements set out in Article 112 and the following additional conditions:

(a) the reason for the limited scope of application of the model is properly justified by the undertaking;

(b) the resulting Solvency Capital Requirement reflects more appropriately the risk profile of the undertaking and in particular complies with the principles set out in Subsection 1;

(c) its design is consistent with the principles set out in Subsection 1 so as to allow the partial internal model to be fully integrated into the Solvency Capital Requirement standard formula.

2. When assessing an application for the use of a partial internal model which only covers certain sub-modules of a specific risk module, or some of the business units of an insurance or reinsurance undertaking with respect to a specific risk module, or parts of both, supervisory authorities may require the insurance and reinsurance undertakings concerned to submit a realistic transitional plan to extend the scope of the model.

The transitional plan shall set out the manner in which insurance and reinsurance undertakings plan to extend the scope of the model to other sub-modules or business units, in order to ensure that the model covers a predominant part of their insurance operations with respect to that specific risk module.

[6267]
Article 114
Implementing measures

The Commission shall adopt implementing measures setting out the following:

(1) the procedure to be followed for the approval of an internal model;

(2) the adaptations to be made to the standards set out in Articles 120 to 125 in order to take account of the limited scope of the application of the partial internal model.

Those measures, designed to amend non-essential elements of this Directive by supplementing it, shall be adopted in accordance with the regulatory procedure with scrutiny referred to in Article 301(3).

[6268]
Article 115
Policy for changing the full and partial internal models

As part of the initial approval process of an internal model, the supervisory authorities shall approve the policy for changing the model of the insurance or reinsurance undertaking. Insurance and reinsurance undertakings may change their internal model in accordance with that policy.

The policy shall include a specification of minor and major changes to the internal model.

Major changes to the internal model, as well as changes to that policy, shall always be subject to prior supervisory approval, as laid down in Article 112.

Minor changes to the internal model shall not be subject to prior supervisory approval, insofar as they are developed in accordance with that policy.

[6269]
Article 116
Responsibilities of the administrative, management or supervisory bodies

The administrative, management or supervisory bodies of the insurance and reinsurance undertakings shall approve the application to the supervisory authorities for approval of the internal model referred to in Article 112, as well as the application for approval of any subsequent major changes made to that model.

The administrative, management or supervisory body shall have responsibility for putting in place systems which ensure that the internal model operates properly on a continuous basis.

[6270]
Article 117
Reversion to the standard formula

After having received approval in accordance with Article 112, insurance and reinsurance undertakings shall not revert to calculating the whole or any part of the Solvency Capital Requirement in accordance with the standard formula, as set out in Subsection 2, except in duly justified circumstances and subject to the approval of the supervisory authorities.

[6271]
Article 118
Non-compliance of the internal model

1. If, after having received approval from the supervisory authorities to use an internal model, insurance and reinsurance undertakings cease to comply with the requirements set out in Articles 120 to 125, they shall, without delay, either present to the supervisory authorities a plan to restore compliance within a reasonable period of time, or demonstrate that the effect of non-compliance is immaterial.

2. In the event that insurance and reinsurance undertakings fail to implement the plan referred to in paragraph 1, the supervisory authorities may require insurance and reinsurance undertakings to revert to calculating the Solvency Capital Requirement in accordance with the standard formula, as set out in Subsection 2.

[6272]
Article 119
Significant deviations from the assumptions underlying the standard formula calculation

Where it is inappropriate to calculate the Solvency Capital Requirement in accordance with the standard formula, as set out in Subsection 2, because the risk profile of the insurance or reinsurance undertaking concerned deviates significantly from the assumptions underlying the standard formula calculation, the supervisory authorities may, by means of a decision stating the reasons, require the undertaking concerned to use an internal model to calculate the Solvency Capital Requirement, or the relevant risk modules thereof.

[6273]
Article 120
Use test

Insurance and reinsurance undertakings shall demonstrate that the internal model is widely used in and plays an important role in their system of governance, referred to in Articles 41 to 50, in particular:

(a) their risk-management system as laid down in Article 44 and their decision-making processes;

(b) their economic and solvency capital assessment and allocation processes, including the assessment referred to in Article 45.

In addition, insurance and reinsurance undertakings shall demonstrate that the frequency of calculation of the Solvency Capital Requirement using the internal model is consistent with the frequency with which they use their internal model for the other purposes covered by the first paragraph.

The administrative, management or supervisory body shall be responsible for ensuring the ongoing appropriateness of the design and operations of the internal model, and that the internal model continues to appropriately reflect the risk profile of the insurance and reinsurance undertakings concerned.

[6274]
Article 121
Statistical quality standards

1. The internal model, and in particular the calculation of the probability distribution forecast underlying it, shall comply with the criteria set out in paragraphs 2 to 9.

2. The methods used to calculate the probability distribution forecast shall be based on adequate, applicable and relevant actuarial and statistical techniques and shall be consistent with the methods used to calculate technical provisions.

The methods used to calculate the probability distribution forecast shall be based upon current and credible information and realistic assumptions.

Insurance and reinsurance undertakings shall be able to justify the assumptions underlying their internal model to the supervisory authorities.

3. Data used for the internal model shall be accurate, complete and appropriate.

Insurance and reinsurance undertakings shall update the data sets used in the calculation of the probability distribution forecast at least annually.

4. No particular method for the calculation of the probability distribution forecast shall be prescribed.

Regardless of the calculation method chosen, the ability of the internal model to rank risk shall be sufficient to ensure that it is widely used in and plays an important role in the system of governance of insurance and reinsurance undertakings, in particular their risk-management system and decision-making processes, and capital allocation in accordance with Article 120.

The internal model shall cover all of the material risks to which insurance and reinsurance undertakings are exposed. Internal models shall cover at least the risks set out in Article 101(4).

5. As regards diversification effects, insurance and reinsurance undertakings may take account in their internal model of dependencies within and across risk categories, provided that supervisory authorities are satisfied that the system used for measuring those diversification effects is adequate.

6. Insurance and reinsurance undertakings may take full account of the effect of risk-mitigation techniques in their internal model, as long as credit risk and other risks arising from the use of risk-mitigation techniques are properly reflected in the internal model.

7. Insurance and reinsurance undertakings shall accurately assess the particular risks associated with financial guarantees and any contractual options in their internal model, where material. They shall also assess the risks associated with both policy holder options and contractual options for insurance and reinsurance undertakings. For that purpose, they shall take account of the impact that future changes in financial and non-financial conditions may have on the exercise of those options.

8. In their internal model, insurance and reinsurance undertakings may take account of future management actions that they would reasonably expect to carry out in specific circumstances.

In the case set out in the first subparagraph, the undertaking concerned shall make allowance for the time necessary to implement such actions.

9. In their internal model, insurance and reinsurance undertakings shall take account of all payments to policy holders and beneficiaries which they expect to make, whether or not those payments are contractually guaranteed.

[6275]
Article 122
Calibration standards

1. Insurance and reinsurance undertakings may use a different time period or risk measure than that set out in Article 101(3) for internal modelling purposes as long as the outputs of the internal model can be used by those undertakings to calculate the Solvency Capital Requirement in a manner that provides policy holders and beneficiaries with a level of protection equivalent to that set out in Article 101.

2. Where practicable, insurance and reinsurance undertakings shall derive the Solvency Capital Requirement directly from the probability distribution forecast generated by the internal model of those undertakings, using the Value-at-Risk measure set out in Article 101(3).

3. Where insurance and reinsurance undertakings cannot derive the Solvency Capital Requirement directly from the probability distribution forecast generated by the internal model, the supervisory authorities may allow approximations to be used in the process to calculate the Solvency Capital Requirement, as long as those undertakings can demonstrate to the supervisory authorities that policy holders are provided with a level of protection equivalent to that provided for in Article 101.

4. Supervisory authorities may require insurance and reinsurance undertakings to run their internal model on relevant benchmark portfolios and using assumptions based on external rather than internal data in order to verify the calibration of the internal model and to check that its specification is in line with generally accepted market practice.

[6276]
Article 123
Profit and loss attribution

Insurance and reinsurance undertakings shall review, at least annually, the causes and sources of profits and losses for each major business unit.

They shall demonstrate how the categorisation of risk chosen in the internal model explains the causes and sources of profits and losses. The categorisation of risk and attribution of profits and losses shall reflect the risk profile of the insurance and reinsurance undertakings.

[6277]
Article 124
Validation standards

Insurance and reinsurance undertakings shall have a regular cycle of model validation which includes monitoring the performance of the internal model, reviewing the ongoing appropriateness of its specification, and testing its results against experience.

The model validation process shall include an effective statistical process for validating the internal model which enables the insurance and reinsurance undertakings to demonstrate to their supervisory authorities that the resulting capital requirements are appropriate.

The statistical methods applied shall test the appropriateness of the probability distribution forecast compared not only to loss experience but also to all material new data and information relating thereto.

The model validation process shall include an analysis of the stability of the internal model and in particular the testing of the sensitivity of the results of the internal model to changes in key underlying assumptions. It shall also include an assessment of the accuracy, completeness and appropriateness of the data used by the internal model.

[6278]
Article 125
Documentation standards

Insurance and reinsurance undertakings shall document the design and operational details of their internal model.

The documentation shall demonstrate compliance with Articles 120 to 124.

The documentation shall provide a detailed outline of the theory, assumptions, and mathematical and empirical bases underlying the internal model.

The documentation shall indicate any circumstances under which the internal model does not work effectively.

Insurance and reinsurance undertakings shall document all major changes to their internal model, as set out in Article 115.

[6279]
Article 126
External models and data

The use of a model or data obtained from a third party shall not be considered to be a justification for exemption from any of the requirements for the internal model set out in Articles 120 to 125.

[6280]
Article 127
Implementing measures

The Commission shall, in order to ensure a harmonised approach to the use of internal models throughout the Community and to enhance the better assessment of the risk profile and management of the business of insurance and reinsurance undertakings, adopt implementing measures with respect to Articles 120 to 126.

Those measures, designed to amend non-essential elements of this Directive by supplementing it, shall be adopted in accordance with the regulatory procedure with scrutiny referred to in Article 301(3).

SECTION 5
MINIMUM CAPITAL REQUIREMENT

[6281]
Article 128
General provisions

Member States shall require that insurance and reinsurance undertakings hold eligible basic own funds, to cover the Minimum Capital Requirement.

[6282]
Article 129
Calculation of the Minimum Capital Requirement

1. The Minimum Capital Requirement shall be calculated in accordance with the following principles:

(a) it shall be calculated in a clear and simple manner, and in such a way as to ensure that the calculation can be audited;

(b) it shall correspond to an amount of eligible basic own funds below which policy holders and beneficiaries are exposed to an unacceptable level of risk were insurance and reinsurance undertakings allowed to continue their operations;

(c) the linear function referred to in paragraph 2 used to calculate the Minimum Capital Requirement shall be calibrated to the Value-at-Risk of the basic own funds of an insurance or reinsurance undertaking subject to a confidence level of 85% over a one-year period;

(d) it shall have an absolute floor of:

(i) EUR 2 200 000 for non-life insurance undertakings, including captive insurance undertakings, save in the case where all or some of the risks included in one of the classes 10 to 15 listed in Part A of Annex 1 are covered, in which case it shall be no less than EUR 3 200 000,

(ii) EUR 3 200 000 for life insurance undertakings, including captive insurance undertakings,

(iii) EUR 3 200 000 for reinsurance undertakings, except in the case of captive reinsurance undertakings, in which case the Minimum Capital Requirement shall be no less than EUR 1 000 000,

(iv) the sum of the amounts set out in points (i) and (ii) for insurance undertakings as referred to in Article 73(5).

2. Subject to paragraph 3, the Minimum Capital Requirement shall be calculated as a linear function of a set or sub-set of the following variables: the undertaking's technical provisions, written premiums, capital-at-risk, deferred tax and administrative expenses. The variables used shall be measured net of reinsurance.

3. Without prejudice to paragraph 1(d), the Minimum Capital Requirement shall neither fall below 25% nor exceed 45% of the undertaking's Solvency Capital Requirement, calculated in accordance with Chapter VI, Section 4, Subsections 2 or 3, and including any capital add-on imposed in accordance with Article 37.

Member States shall allow their supervisory authorities, for a period ending no later than 31 October 2014, to require an insurance or reinsurance undertaking to apply the percentages referred to in the first subparagraph exclusively to the undertaking's Solvency Capital Requirement calculated in accordance with Chapter VI, Section 4, Subsection 2.

4. Insurance and reinsurance undertakings shall calculate the Minimum Capital Requirement at least quarterly and report the results of that calculation to supervisory authorities.

Where either of the limits referred to in paragraph 3 determines an undertaking's Minimum Capital Requirement, the undertaking shall provide to the supervisory authority information allowing a proper understanding of the reasons therefor.

5. The Commission shall submit to the European Parliament and the European Insurance and Occupational Pensions Committee established by Commission Decision 2004/9/EC[1], by 31 October 2017, a report on Member States' rules and supervisory authorities' practices adopted pursuant to paragraphs 1 to 4.

That report shall address, in particular, the use and level of the cap and the floor set out in paragraph 3 as well as any problems faced by supervisory authorities and by undertakings in the application of this Article.

NOTES

[1] OJ L3, 7.1.2004, p 34.

[6283]
Article 130
Implementing measures

The Commission shall adopt implementing measures specifying the calculation of the Minimum Capital Requirement, referred to in Articles 128 and 129.

Those measures, designed to amend non-essential elements of this Directive, by supplementing it, shall be adopted in accordance with the regulatory procedure with scrutiny referred to in Article 301(3).

[6284]
Article 131
Transitional arrangements regarding compliance with the Minimum Capital Requirement

By way of derogation from Articles 139 and 144, where insurance and reinsurance undertakings comply with the Required Solvency Margin referred to in Article 28 of Directive 2002/83/EC, Article 16a of Directive 73/239/EEC or Article 37, 38 or 39 of Directive 2005/68/EC respectively on 31 October 2012 but do not hold sufficient eligible basic own funds to cover the Minimum Capital Requirement, the undertakings concerned shall comply with Article 128 by 31 October 2013.

Where the undertaking concerned fails to comply with Article 128 within the period set out in the first paragraph, the authorisation of the undertaking shall be withdrawn, subject to the applicable processes provided for in the national legislation.

SECTION 6
INVESTMENTS

[6285]
Article 132
Prudent person principle

1. Member States shall ensure that insurance and reinsurance undertakings invest all their assets in accordance with the prudent person principle, as specified in paragraphs 2, 3 and 4.

2. With respect to the whole portfolio of assets, insurance and reinsurance undertakings shall only invest in assets and instruments whose risks the undertaking concerned can properly identify, measure, monitor, manage, control and report, and appropriately take into account in the assessment of its overall solvency needs in accordance with point (a) of the second subparagraph of Article 45(1).

All assets, in particular those covering the Minimum Capital Requirement and the Solvency Capital Requirement, shall be invested in such a manner as to ensure the security, quality, liquidity and profitability of the portfolio as a whole. In addition the localisation of those assets shall be such as to ensure their availability.

Assets held to cover the technical provisions shall also be invested in a manner appropriate to the nature and duration of the insurance and reinsurance liabilities. Those assets shall be invested in the best interest of all policy holders and beneficiaries taking into account any disclosed policy objective.

In the case of a conflict of interest, insurance undertakings, or the entity which manages their asset portfolio, shall ensure that the investment is made in the best interest of policy holders and beneficiaries.

3. Without prejudice to paragraph 2, with respect to assets held in respect of life insurance contracts where the investment risk is borne by the policy holders, the second, third and fourth subparagraphs of this paragraph shall apply.

Where the benefits provided by a contract are directly linked to the value of units in an UCITS as defined in Directive 85/611/EEC, or to the value of assets contained in an internal fund held by the insurance undertakings, usually divided into units, the technical provisions in respect of those benefits must be represented as closely as possible by those units or, in the case where units are not established, by those assets.

Where the benefits provided by a contract are directly linked to a share index or some other reference value other than those referred to in the second subparagraph, the technical provisions in respect of those benefits must be represented as closely as possible either by the units deemed to represent the reference value or, in the case where units are not established, by assets of appropriate security and marketability which correspond as closely as possible with those on which the particular reference value is based.

Where the benefits referred to in the second and third subparagraphs include a guarantee of investment performance or some other guaranteed benefit, the assets held to cover the corresponding additional technical provisions shall be subject to paragraph 4.

4. Without prejudice to paragraph 2, with respect to assets other than those covered by paragraph 3, the second to fifth subparagraphs of this paragraph shall apply.

The use of derivative instruments shall be possible insofar as they contribute to a reduction of risks or facilitate efficient portfolio management.

Investment and assets which are not admitted to trading on a regulated financial market shall be kept to prudent levels.

Assets shall be properly diversified in such a way as to avoid excessive reliance on any particular asset, issuer or group of undertakings, or geographical area and excessive accumulation of risk in the portfolio as a whole.

Investments in assets issued by the same issuer, or by issuers belonging to the same group, shall not expose the insurance undertakings to excessive risk concentration.

[6286]
Article 133
Freedom of investment

1. Member States shall not require insurance and reinsurance undertakings to invest in particular categories of asset.

2. Member States shall not subject the investment decisions of an insurance or reinsurance undertaking or its investment manager to any kind of prior approval or systematic notification requirements.

3. This Article is without prejudice to Member States' requirements restricting the types of assets or reference values to which policy benefits may be linked. Any such rules shall be applied only where the investment risk is borne by a policy holder who is a natural person and shall not be more restrictive than those set out in the Directive 85/611/EEC.

[6287]
Article 134
Localisation of assets and prohibition of pledging of assets

1. With respect to insurance risks situated in the Community, Member States shall not require that the assets held to cover the technical provisions related to those risks are localised within the Community or in any particular Member States.

In addition, with respect to recoverables from reinsurance contracts against undertakings authorised in accordance with this Directive or which have their head office in a third country whose solvency regime is deemed to be equivalent in accordance with Article 172, Member States shall not require the localisation within the Community of the assets representing those recoverables.

2. Member States shall not retain or introduce for the establishment of technical provisions a system with gross reserving which requires pledging of assets to cover unearned premiums and outstanding claims provisions where the reinsurer is an insurance or reinsurance undertaking authorised in accordance with this Directive.

[6288]
Article 135
Implementing measures

1. In order to ensure the uniform application of this Directive, the Commission may adopt implementing measures specifying qualitative requirements in the following areas:

(a) the identification, measurement, monitoring, managing and reporting of risks arising from investments in relation to the first subparagraph of Article 132(2);

(b) the identification, measurement monitoring, managing and reporting of specific risks arising from investment in derivative instruments and assets referred to in the second subparagraph of Article 132(4).

2. In order to ensure cross-sectoral consistency and to remove misalignment between the interests of firms that 'repackage' loans into tradable securities and other financial instruments (originators) and the interests of insurance or reinsurance undertakings that invest in such securities or instruments, the Commission shall adopt implementing measures laying down:

(a) the requirements that need to be met by the originator in order for an insurance or reinsurance undertaking to be allowed to invest in such securities or instruments issued after 1 January 2011, including requirements that ensure that the originator retains a net economic interest of no less than 5%;

(b) qualitative requirements that must be met by insurance or reinsurance undertakings that invest in such securities or instruments.

3. Those measures, designed to amend non-essential elements of this Directive by supplementing it, shall be adopted in accordance with the regulatory procedure with scrutiny referred to in Article 301(3).

CHAPTER VII
INSURANCE AND REINSURANCE UNDERTAKINGS IN DIFFICULTY OR IN AN IRREGULAR SITUATION

[6289]
Article 136
Identification and notification of deteriorating financial conditions by the insurance and reinsurance undertaking

Insurance and reinsurance undertakings shall have procedures in place to identify deteriorating financial conditions and shall immediately notify the supervisory authorities when such

Part VI European Materials

deterioration occurs.

[6290]
Article 137
Non-Compliance with technical provisions

Where an insurance or reinsurance undertaking does not comply with Chapter VI, Section 2, the supervisory authorities of its home Member State may prohibit the free disposal of its assets after having communicated their intentions to the supervisory authorities of the host Member States. The supervisory authorities of the home Member State shall designate the assets to be covered by such measures.

[6291]
Article 138
Non-Compliance with the Solvency Capital Requirement

1. Insurance and reinsurance undertakings shall immediately inform the supervisory authority as soon as they observe that the Solvency Capital Requirement is no longer complied with, or where there is a risk of non-compliance in the following three months.

2. Within two months from the observation of non-compliance with the Solvency Capital Requirement the insurance or reinsurance undertaking concerned shall submit a realistic recovery plan for approval by the supervisory authority.

3. The supervisory authority shall require the insurance or reinsurance undertaking concerned to take the necessary measures to achieve, within six months from the observation of non-compliance with the Solvency Capital Requirement, the re-establishment of the level of eligible own funds covering the Solvency Capital Requirement or the reduction of its risk profile to ensure compliance with the Solvency Capital Requirement.

The supervisory authority may, if appropriate, extend that period by three months.

4. In the event of an exceptional fall in financial markets, the supervisory authority may extend the period set out in the second subparagraph of paragraph 3 by an appropriate period of time taking into account all relevant factors.

The insurance or reinsurance undertaking concerned shall, every three months, submit a progress report to its supervisory authority setting out the measures taken and the progress made to re-establish the level of eligible own funds covering the Solvency Capital Requirement or to reduce the risk profile to ensure compliance with the Solvency Capital Requirement.

The extension referred to in the first subparagraph shall be withdrawn where that progress report shows that there was no significant progress in achieving the re-establishment of the level of eligible own funds covering the Solvency Capital Requirement or the reduction of the risk profile to ensure compliance with the Solvency Capital Requirement between the date of the observation of non-compliance of the Solvency Capital Requirement and the date of the submission of the progress report.

5. In exceptional circumstances, where the supervisory authority is of the opinion that the financial situation of the undertaking concerned will deteriorate further, it may also restrict or prohibit the free disposal of the assets of that undertaking. That supervisory authority shall inform the supervisory authorities of the host Member States of any measures it has taken. Those authorities shall, at the request of the supervisory authority of the home Member State, take the same measures. The supervisory authority of the home Member State shall designate the assets to be covered by such measures.

[6292]
Article 139
Non-Compliance with the Minimum Capital Requirement

1. Insurance and reinsurance undertakings shall inform the supervisory authority immediately where they observe that the Minimum Capital Requirement is no longer complied with or where there is a risk of non-compliance in the following three months.

2. Within one month from the observation of non-compliance with the Minimum Capital Requirement, the insurance or reinsurance undertaking concerned shall submit, for approval by the supervisory authority, a short-term realistic finance scheme to restore, within three months of that observation, the eligible basic own funds, at least to the level of the Minimum Capital Requirement or to reduce its risk profile to ensure compliance with the Minimum Capital Requirement.

3. The supervisory authority of the home Member State may also restrict or prohibit the free disposal of the assets of the insurance or reinsurance undertaking. It shall inform the supervisory authorities of the host Member States accordingly. At the request of the supervisory authority of the home Member State, those authorities shall, take the same measures. The supervisory authority of the home Member State shall designate the assets to be covered by such measures.

[6293]
Article 140
Prohibition of free disposal of assets located within the territory of a Member State

Member States shall take the measures necessary to be able, in accordance with national law, to prohibit the free disposal of assets located within their territory at the request, in the cases provided for in Articles 137 to 139 and Article 144(2) of the undertaking's home Member State, which shall designate the assets to be covered by such measures.

[6294]
Article 141
Supervisory powers in deteriorating financial conditions

Notwithstanding Articles 138 and 139, where the solvency position of the undertaking continues to deteriorate, the supervisory authorities shall have the power to take all measures necessary to safeguard the interests of policy holders in the case of insurance contracts, or the obligations arising out of reinsurance contracts.

Those measures shall be proportionate and thus reflect the level and duration of the deterioration of the solvency position of the insurance or reinsurance undertaking concerned.

[6295]
Article 142
Recovery plan and finance scheme

1. The recovery plan referred to in Article 138(2) and the finance scheme referred to in Article 139(2) shall, at least include particulars or evidence concerning the following:
   (a) estimates of management expenses, in particular current general expenses and commissions;
   (b) estimates of income and expenditure in respect of direct business, reinsurance acceptances and reinsurance cessions;
   (c) a forecast balance sheet;
   (d) estimates of the financial resources intended to cover the technical provisions and the Solvency Capital Requirement and the Minimum Capital Requirement;
   (e) the overall reinsurance policy.

2. Where the supervisory authorities have required a recovery plan referred to in Article 138(2) or a finance scheme referred to in Article 139(2) in accordance with paragraph 1 of this Article, they shall refrain from issuing a certificate in accordance with Article 39 for as long as they consider that the rights of the policy holders, or the contractual obligations of the reinsurance undertaking are threatened.

[6296]
Article 143
Implementing measures

The Commission shall adopt implementing measures specifying the factors to be taken into account for the purpose of the application of Article 138(4) including the maximum appropriate period of time, expressed in total number of months, which shall be the same for all insurance and reinsurance undertakings as referred to in the first subparagraph of Article 138(4).

Where it is necessary to enhance convergence, the Commission may adopt implementing measures laying down further specifications with respect to the recovery plan referred to in Article 138(2), the finance scheme referred to in Article 139(2) and with respect to Article 141, taking due care to avoid pro-cyclical effects.

Those measures, designed to amend non-essential elements of this Directive by supplementing it, shall be adopted in accordance with the regulatory procedure with scrutiny referred to in Article 301(3).

[6297]
Article 144
Withdrawal of authorisation

1. The supervisory authority of the home Member State may withdraw an authorisation granted to an insurance or reinsurance undertaking in the following cases:

(a) the undertaking concerned does not make use of the authorisation within 12 months, expressly renounces it or ceases to pursue business for more than six months, unless the Member State concerned has made provision for authorisation to lapse in such cases;
(b) the undertaking concerned no longer fulfils the conditions for authorisation;
(c) the undertaking concerned fails seriously in its obligations under the regulations to which it is subject.

The supervisory authority of the home Member State shall withdraw an authorisation granted to an insurance or reinsurance undertaking in the event that the undertaking does not comply with the Minimum Capital Requirement and the supervisory authority considers that the finance scheme submitted is manifestly inadequate or the undertaking concerned fails to comply with the approved scheme within three months from the observation of non-compliance with the Minimum Capital Requirement.

2. In the event of the withdrawal or lapse of authorisation, the supervisory authority of the home Member State shall notify the supervisory authorities of the other Member States accordingly, and those authorities shall take appropriate measures to prevent the insurance or reinsurance undertaking from commencing new operations within their territories.

The supervisory authority of the home Member State shall, together with those authorities, take all measures necessary to safeguard the interests of insured persons and, in particular, shall restrict the free disposal of the assets of the insurance undertaking in accordance with Article 140.

3. Any decision to withdraw authorisation shall state the full reasons and shall be communicated to the insurance or reinsurance undertaking concerned.

CHAPTER VIII
RIGHT OF ESTABLISHMENT AND FREEDOM TO PROVIDE SERVICES

SECTION 1
ESTABLISHMENT BY INSURANCE UNDERTAKINGS

[6298]
Article 145
Conditions for branch establishment

1. Member States shall ensure that an insurance undertaking which proposes to establish a branch within the territory of another Member State notifies the supervisory authorities of its home Member State.

Any permanent presence of an undertaking in the territory of a Member State shall be treated in the same way as a branch, even where that presence does not take the form of a branch, but consists merely of an office managed by the own staff of the undertaking or by a person who is independent but has permanent authority to act for the undertaking as an agency would.

2. Member States shall require every insurance undertaking that proposes to establish a branch within the territory of another Member State to provide the following information when effecting the notification provided for in paragraph 1:

(a) the Member State within the territory of which it proposes to establish a branch;
(b) a scheme of operations setting out, at least, the types of business envisaged and the structural organisation of the branch;
(c) the name of a person who possesses sufficient powers to bind, in relation to third parties, the insurance undertaking or, in the case of Lloyd's, the underwriters concerned and to represent it or them in relations with the authorities and courts of the host Member State (the authorised agent);
(d) the address in the host Member State from which documents may be obtained and to which they may be delivered, including all communications to the authorised agent.

With regard to Lloyd's, in the event of any litigation in the host Member State arising out of underwritten commitments, the insured persons shall not be treated less favourably than if the litigation had been brought against businesses of a conventional type.

3. Where a non-life insurance undertaking intends its branch to cover risks in class 10 in Part A of Annex I, not including carrier's liability, it shall produce a declaration that it has become a member of the national bureau and the national guarantee fund of the host Member State.

4. In the event of a change in any of the particulars communicated under point (b), (c) or (d) of paragraph 2, an insurance undertaking shall give written notice of the change to the supervisory authorities of the home Member State and of the Member State where that branch is situated at least one month before making the change so that the supervisory authorities of the home Member State and the supervisory authorities of the Member State where that branch is situated may fulfil their respective obligations under Article 146.

[6299]

Article 146

Communication of information

1. Unless the supervisory authorities of the home Member State have reason to doubt the adequacy of the system of governance or the financial situation of the insurance undertaking or the fit and proper requirements in accordance with Article 42 of the authorised agent, taking into account the business planned, they shall, within three months of receiving all the information referred to in Article 145(2), communicate that information to the supervisory authorities of the host Member State and shall inform the insurance undertaking concerned thereof.

The supervisory authorities of the home Member State shall also attest that the insurance undertaking covers the Solvency Capital Requirement and the Minimum Capital Requirement calculated in accordance with Articles 100 and 129.

2. Where the supervisory authorities of the home Member State refuse to communicate the information referred to in Article 145(2) to the supervisory authorities of the host Member State they shall state the reasons for their refusal to the insurance undertaking concerned within three months of receiving all the information in question.

Such a refusal or failure to act shall be subject to a right to apply to the courts in the home Member State.

3. Before the branch of an insurance undertaking starts business, the supervisory authorities of the host Member State shall, where applicable, within two months of receiving the information referred to in paragraph 1, inform the supervisory authority of the home Member State of the conditions under which, in the interest of the general good, that business must be pursued in the host Member State. The supervisory authority of the home Member State shall communicate this information to the insurance undertaking concerned.

The insurance undertaking may establish the branch and start business as from the date upon which the supervisory authority of the home Member State has received such a communication or, if no communication is received, on expiry of the period provided for in the first subparagraph.

SECTION 2
FREEDOM TO PROVIDE SERVICES: BY INSURANCE UNDERTAKINGS

SUBSECTION 1
GENERAL PROVISIONS

[6300]

Article 147

Prior notification to the home Member State

Any insurance undertaking that intends to pursue business for the first time in one or more Member States under the freedom to provide services shall first notify the supervisory authorities of the home Member State, indicating the nature of the risks or commitments it proposes to cover.

[6301]

Article 148

Notification by the home Member State

1. Within one month of the notification provided for in Article 147, the supervisory authorities of the home Member State shall communicate the following to the Member State or States within the territories of which an insurance undertaking intends to pursue business under the freedom to provide services:

(a) a certificate attesting that the insurance undertaking covers the Solvency Capital Requirement and Minimum Capital Requirement calculated in accordance with Articles 100 and 129;

(b) the classes of insurance which the insurance undertaking has been authorised to offer;

(c) the nature of the risks or commitments which the insurance undertaking proposes to cover in the host Member State.

At the same time, the supervisory authorities of the home Member State shall inform the insurance undertaking concerned of that communication.

2. Member States within the territory of which a non-life insurance undertaking intends, under the freedom to provide services, to cover risks in class 10 in Part A of Annex I other than carrier's liability may require that insurance undertaking to submit the following:

(a) the name and address of the representative referred to in Article 18(1)(h);

(b) a declaration that it has become a member of the national bureau and national guarantee fund of the host Member State.

3. Where the supervisory authorities of the home Member State do not communicate the information referred to in paragraph 1 within the period laid down therein, they shall state the reasons for their refusal to the insurance undertaking within that same period.

Such a refusal or failure to act shall be subject to a right to apply to the courts in the home Member State.

4. The insurance undertaking may start business as from the date on which it is informed of the communication provided for in the first subparagraph of paragraph 1.

[6302]
Article 149
Changes in the nature of the risks or commitments

Any change which an insurance undertaking intends to make to the information referred to in Article 145 shall be subject to the procedure provided for in Articles 147 and 148.

SUBSECTION 2
THIRD PARTY MOTOR VEHICLE LIABILITY

[6303]
Article 150
Compulsory insurance on third party motor vehicle liability

1. Where a non-life insurance undertaking, through an establishment situated in one Member State, covers a risk, other than carrier's liability, classified under class 10 in Part A of Annex I which is situated in another Member State, the host Member State shall require that undertaking to become a member of and participate in the financing of its national bureau and its national guarantee fund.

2. The financial contribution referred to in paragraph 1 shall be made only in relation to risks, other than carrier's liability, classified under class 10 in Part A of Annex I covered by way of provision of services. That contribution shall be calculated on the same basis as for non-life insurance undertakings covering those risks, through an establishment situated in that Member State.

The calculation shall be made by reference to the insurance undertakings' premium income from that class in the host Member State or the number of risks in that class covered there.

3. The host Member State may require an insurance undertaking providing services to comply with the rules in that Member State concerning the cover of aggravated risks, insofar as they apply to non-life insurance undertakings established in that State.

[6304]
Article 151
Non-discrimination of persons pursuing claims

The host Member State shall require the non-life insurance undertaking to ensure that persons pursuing claims arising out of events occurring in its territory are not placed in a less favourable situation as a result of the fact that the undertaking is covering a risk, other than carrier's liability, classified under class 10 in Part A of Annex I by way of provision of services rather than through an establishment situated in that State.

[6305]
Article 152
Representative

1. For the purposes referred to in Article 151, the host Member State shall require the non-life insurance undertaking to appoint a representative resident or established in its territory who shall collect all necessary information in relation to claims, and shall possess sufficient powers to represent the undertaking in relation to persons suffering damage who could pursue claims, including the payment of such claims, and to represent it or, where necessary, to have it represented before the courts and authorities of that Member State in relation to those claims.

That representative may also be required to represent the non-life insurance undertaking before the supervisory authorities of the host Member State with regard to checking the existence and validity of motor vehicle liability insurance policies.

2. The host Member State shall not require that representative to undertake activities on behalf of the non-life insurance undertaking which appointed him other than those set out in paragraph 1.

3. The appointment of the representative shall not in itself constitute the opening of a branch for the purpose of Article 145.

4. Where the insurance undertaking has failed to appoint a representative, Member States may give their approval to the claims representative appointed in accordance with Article 4 of Directive 2000/26/EC to assume the function of the representative referred to in paragraph 1 of this Article.

SECTION 3
COMPETENCIES OF THE SUPERVISORY AUTHORITIES OF THE HOST MEMBER STATE

SUBSECTION 1
INSURANCE

[6306]
Article 153
Language

The supervisory authorities of the host Member State may require the information which they are authorised to request with regard to the business of insurance undertakings operating in the territory of that Member State to be supplied to them in the official language or languages of that State.

[6307]
Article 154
Prior notification and prior approval

1. The host Member State shall not adopt provisions requiring the prior approval or systematic notification of general and special policy conditions, scales of premiums, or, in the case of life insurance, the technical bases used in particular for calculating scales of premiums and technical provisions, or the forms and other documents which an insurance undertaking intends to use in its dealings with policy holders.

2. The host Member State shall only require an insurance undertaking that proposes to pursue insurance business within its territory to effect non-systematic notification of policy conditions and other documents for the purpose of verifying compliance with its national provisions concerning insurance contracts, and that requirement shall not constitute a prior condition for an insurance undertaking to pursue its business.

3. The host Member State shall not retain or introduce a requirement for prior notification or approval of proposed increases in premium rates except as part of general price-control systems.

[6308]
Article 155
Insurance undertakings not complying with the legal provisions

1. Where the supervisory authorities of a host Member State establish that an insurance undertaking with a branch or pursuing business under the freedom to provide services in its territory is not complying with the legal provisions applicable to it in that Member State, they shall require the insurance undertaking concerned to remedy such irregularity.

2. Where the insurance undertaking concerned fails to take the necessary action, the supervisory authorities of the Member State concerned shall inform the supervisory authorities of the home Member State accordingly.

The supervisory authorities of the home Member State shall, at the earliest opportunity, take all appropriate measures to ensure that the insurance undertaking concerned remedies that irregular situation.

The supervisory authorities of the home Member State shall inform the supervisory authorities of the host Member State of the measures taken.

3. Where, despite the measures taken by the home Member State or because those measures prove to be inadequate or are lacking in that Member State, the insurance undertaking persists in violating the legal provisions in force in the host Member State, the supervisory authorities of the host Member State may, after informing the supervisory authorities of the home Member State, take appropriate measures to prevent or penalise further irregularities, including, in so far as is strictly necessary, preventing that undertaking from continuing to conclude new insurance contracts within the territory of the host Member State.

Member States shall ensure that in their territories it is possible to serve the legal documents necessary for such measures on insurance undertakings.

4. Paragraphs 1, 2 and 3 shall not affect the power of the Member States concerned to take appropriate emergency measures to prevent or penalise irregularities within their territories. That power shall include the possibility of preventing insurance undertakings from continuing to conclude new insurance contracts within their territories.

5. Paragraphs 1, 2 and 3 shall not affect the power of the Member States to penalise infringements within their territories.

6. Where an insurance undertaking which has committed an infringement has an establishment or possesses property in the Member State concerned, the supervisory authorities of that Member State may, in accordance with national law, apply the national administrative penalties prescribed for that infringement by way of enforcement against that establishment or property.

7. Any measure adopted under paragraphs 2 to 6 involving restrictions on the conduct of insurance business must be properly reasoned and communicated to the insurance undertaking concerned.

8. Insurance undertakings shall submit to the supervisory authorities of the host Member State at their request all documents requested of them for the purposes of paragraphs 1 to 7 to the extent that insurance undertakings the head office of which is in that Member State are also obliged to do so.

9. Member States shall inform the Commission of the number and types of cases which led to refusals under Articles 146 and 148 in which measures have been taken under paragraph 4 of this Article.

On the basis of that information the Commission shall inform the European Insurance and Occupational Pensions Committee every two years.

[6309]
Article 156
Advertising

Insurance undertakings with head offices in Member States may advertise their services, through all available means of communication, in the host Member State, subject to the rules governing the form and content of such advertising adopted in the interest of the general good.

[6310]
Article 157
Taxes on premiums

1. Without prejudice to any subsequent harmonisation, every insurance contract shall be subject exclusively to the indirect taxes and parafiscal charges on insurance premiums in the Member State in which the risk is situated or the Member State of the commitment

For the purposes of the first subparagraph, movable property contained in a building situated within the territory of a Member State, except for goods in commercial transit, shall be considered as a risk situated in that Member State, even where the building and its contents are not covered by the same insurance policy.

In the case of Spain, an insurance contract shall also be subject to the surcharges legally established in favour of the Spanish 'Consorcio de Compensación de Seguros' for the performance of its functions relating to the compensation of losses arising from extraordinary events occurring in that Member State.

2. The law applicable to the contract under Article 178 of this Directive and under Regulation (EC) No 593/2008 shall not affect the fiscal arrangements applicable.

3. Each Member State shall apply its own national provisions to those insurance undertakings which cover risks or commitments situated within its territory for measures to ensure the collection of indirect taxes and parafiscal charges due under paragraph 1.

SUBSECTION 2
REINSURANCE

[6311]
Article 158
Reinsurance undertakings not complying with the legal provisions

1. Where the supervisory authorities of a Member State establish that a reinsurance undertaking with a branch or pursuing business under the freedom to provide services within its territory is not complying with the legal provisions applicable to it in that Member State, they shall require the reinsurance undertaking concerned to remedy that irregular situation. At the same time, they shall refer those findings to the supervisory authority of the home Member State.

2. Where, despite the measures taken by the home Member State or because such measures prove inadequate, the reinsurance undertaking persists in violating the legal provisions applicable to it in the host Member State, the supervisory authorities of the host Member State may, after informing the supervisory authority of the home Member State, take appropriate measures to prevent or

penalise further irregularities, including, insofar as is strictly necessary, preventing that reinsurance undertaking from continuing to conclude new reinsurance contracts within the territory of the host Member State.

Member States shall ensure that within their territories it is possible to serve the legal documents necessary for such measures on reinsurance undertakings.

3. Any measure adopted under paragraphs 1 and 2 involving sanctions or restrictions on the conduct of reinsurance business shall state the reasons and shall be communicated to the reinsurance undertaking concerned.

SECTION 4
STATISTICAL INFORMATION

[6312]
Article 159
Statistical information on cross-border activities

Every insurance undertaking shall inform the competent supervisory authority of its home Member State, separately in respect of transactions carried out under the right of establishment and those carried out under the freedom to provide services, of the amount of the premiums, claims and commissions, without deduction of reinsurance, by Member State and as follows:

(a) for non-life insurance, by group of classes as set out in Annex V;

(b) for life insurance, by each of classes I to IX, as set out in Annex II.

As regards class 10 in Part A of Annex I, not including carrier's liability, the undertaking concerned shall also inform that supervisory authority of the frequency and average cost of claims.

The supervisory authority of the home Member State shall forward the information referred to in the first and second subparagraphs within a reasonable time and in aggregate form to the supervisory authorities of each of the Member States concerned upon their request.

SECTION 5
TREATMENT OF CONTRACTS OF BRANCHES IN WINDING-UP PROCEEDINGS

[6313]
Article 160
Winding-up of insurance undertakings

Where an insurance undertaking is wound up, commitments arising out of contracts underwritten through a branch or under the freedom to provide services shall be met in the same way as those arising out of the other insurance contracts of that undertaking, without distinction as to nationality as far as the persons insured and the beneficiaries are concerned.

[6314]
Article 161
Winding-up of reinsurance undertakings

Where a reinsurance undertaking is wound up, commitments arising out of contracts underwritten through a branch or under the freedom to provide services shall be met in the same way as those arising out of the other reinsurance contracts of that undertaking.

CHAPTER IX
BRANCHES ESTABLISHED WITHIN THE COMMUNITY AND BELONGING TO INSURANCE OR REINSURANCE UNDERTAKINGS WITH HEAD OFFICES SITUATED OUTSIDE THE COMMUNITY

SECTION 1
TAKING-UP OF BUSINESS

[6315]
Article 162
Principle of authorisation and conditions

1. Member States shall make access to the business referred to in the first subparagraph of Article 2(1) by any undertaking with a head office outside the Community subject to an authorisation.

2. A Member State may grant an authorisation where the undertaking fulfils at least the following conditions:

(a) it is entitled to pursue insurance business under its national law;

(b) it establishes a branch in the territory of the Member State in which authorisation is sought;

(c) it undertakes to set up at the place of management of the branch accounts specific to the business which it pursues there, and to keep there all the records relating to the business transacted;

(d) it designates a general representative, to be approved by the supervisory authorities;

(e) it possesses in the Member State in which authorisation is sought assets of an amount equal to at least one half of the absolute floor prescribed in Article 129(1)(d) in respect of the Minimum Capital Requirement and deposits one fourth of that absolute floor as security;

(f) it undertakes to cover the Solvency Capital Requirement and the Minimum Capital Requirement in accordance with the requirements referred to in Articles 100 and 128;

(g) it communicates the name and address of the claims representative appointed in each Member State other than the Member State in which the authorisation is sought where the risks to be covered are classified under class 10 of Part A of Annex I, other than carrier's liability;

(h) it submits a scheme of operations in accordance with the provisions in Article 163;

(i) it fulfils the governance requirements laid down in Chapter IV, Section 2.

3. For the purposes of this Chapter, 'branch' means a permanent presence in the territory of a Member State of an undertaking referred to in paragraph 1, which receives authorisation in that Member State and which pursues insurance business.

[6316]
Article 163
Scheme of operations of the branch

1. The scheme of operations of the branch referred to in Article 162(2)(h) shall set out the following:

(a) the nature of the risks or commitments which the undertaking proposes to cover;

(b) the guiding principles as to reinsurance;

(c) estimates of the future Solvency Capital Requirement, as laid down in Chapter VI, Section 4, on the basis of a forecast balance sheet, as well as the calculation method used to derive those estimates;

(d) estimates of the future Minimum Capital Requirement, as laid down in Chapter VI, Section 5, on the basis of a forecast balance sheet, as well as the calculation method used to derive those estimates;

(e) the state of the eligible own funds and eligible basic own funds of the undertaking with respect to the Solvency Capital Requirement and Minimum Capital Requirement as referred to in Chapter VI, Sections 4 and 5;

(f) estimates of the cost of setting up the administrative services and the organisation for securing business, the financial resources intended to meet those costs and, where the risks to be covered are classified under class 18 in Part A of Annex I, the resources available for the provision of the assistance;

(g) information on the structure of the system of governance.

2. In addition to the requirements set out in paragraph 1, the scheme of operations shall include the following, for the first three financial years:

(a) a forecast balance sheet;

(b) estimates of the financial resources intended to cover technical provisions, the Minimum Capital Requirement and the Solvency Capital Requirement,

(c) for non-life insurance:

  (i) estimates of management expenses other than installation costs, in particular current general expenses and commissions;

  (ii) estimates of premiums or contributions and claims;

(d) for life insurance, a plan setting out detailed estimates of income and expenditure in respect of direct business, reinsurance acceptances and reinsurance cessions.

3. In regard to life insurance, Member States may require insurance undertakings to submit systematic notification of the technical bases used for calculating scales of premiums and technical provisions, without that requirement constituting a prior condition for a life insurance undertaking to pursue its business.

[6317]
Article 164
Transfer of portfolio

1. Under the conditions laid down by national law, Member States shall authorise branches set up within their territory and covered by this Chapter to transfer all or part of their portfolios of contracts to an accepting undertaking established in the same Member State where the supervisory authorities of that Member State or, where appropriate, of the Member State referred to in Article 167, certify that after taking the transfer into account the accepting undertaking possesses the necessary eligible own funds to cover the Solvency Capital Requirement referred to in the first paragraph of Article 100.

2. Under the conditions laid down by national law, Member States shall authorise branches set up within their territory and covered by this Chapter to transfer all or part of their portfolios of contracts to an insurance undertaking with a head office in another Member State where the supervisory authorities of that Member State certify that after taking the transfer into account the accepting undertaking possesses the necessary eligible own funds to cover the Solvency Capital Requirement referred to in the first paragraph of Article 100.

3. Where under the conditions laid down by national law, a Member State authorises branches set up within its territory and covered by this Chapter to transfer all or part of their portfolios of contracts to a branch covered by this Chapter and set up within the territory of another Member State, it shall ensure that the supervisory authorities of the Member State of the accepting undertaking or, if appropriate, of the Member State referred to in Article 167 certify that:

(a) after taking the transfer into account the accepting undertaking possesses the necessary eligible own funds to cover the Solvency Capital Requirement;

(b) the law of the Member State of the accepting undertaking permits such a transfer; and

(c) that Member State has agreed to the transfer.

4. In the circumstances referred to in paragraphs 1 to 3, the Member State in which the transferring branch is situated shall authorise the transfer after obtaining the agreement of the supervisory authorities of the Member State in which the risks are situated, or the Member State of the commitment, where different from the Member State in which the transferring branch is situated.

5. The supervisory authorities of the Member States consulted shall give their opinion or consent to the supervisory authorities of the home Member State of the transferring branch within three months of receiving a request. The absence of any response from the authorities consulted within that period shall be considered equivalent to a favourable opinion or tacit consent.

6. A transfer authorised in accordance with paragraphs 1 to 5 shall be published as laid down by national law in the Member State in which the risk is situated or the Member State of the commitment.

Such transfers shall automatically be valid against policy holders, insured persons and any other persons having rights or obligations arising out of the contracts transferred.

[6318]
Article 165
Technical provisions

Member States shall require undertakings to establish adequate technical provisions to cover the insurance and reinsurance obligations assumed in their territories calculated in accordance with Chapter VI, Section 2. Member States shall require undertakings to value assets and liabilities in accordance with Chapter VI, Section 1 and determine own funds in accordance with Chapter VI, Section 3.

[6319]
Article 166
Solvency Capital Requirement and Minimum Capital Requirement

1. Each Member State shall require for branches which are set up in its territory an amount of eligible own funds consisting of the items referred to in Article 98(3).

The Solvency Capital Requirement and the Minimum Capital Requirement shall be calculated in accordance with the provisions of Chapter VI, Sections 4 and 5.

However, for the purpose of calculating the Solvency Capital Requirement and the Minimum Capital Requirement, both for life and non-life insurance, account shall be taken only of the operations effected by the branch concerned.

2. The eligible amount of basic own funds required to cover the Minimum Capital Requirement and the absolute floor of that Minimum Capital Requirement shall be constituted in accordance with Article 98(4).

3. The eligible amount of basic own funds shall not be less than half of the absolute floor required under Article 129(1)(d).

The deposit lodged in accordance with Article 162(2)(e) shall be counted towards such eligible basic own funds to cover the Minimum Capital Requirement.

4. The assets representing the Solvency Capital Requirement must be kept within the Member State where the activities are pursued up to the amount of the Minimum Capital Requirement and the excess within the Community.

[6320]
Article 167
Advantages to undertakings authorised in more than one Member State

1. Any undertaking which has requested or obtained authorisation from more than one Member State may apply for the following advantages which may be granted only jointly:

(a) the Solvency Capital Requirement referred to in Article 166 shall be calculated in relation to the entire business which it pursues within the Community;

(b) the deposit required under Article 162(2)(e) shall be lodged in only one of those Member States;

(c) the assets representing the Minimum Capital Requirement shall be localised, in accordance with Article 134, in any one of the Member States in which it pursues its activities.

In the cases referred to in point (a) of the first subparagraph, account shall be taken only of the operations effected by all the branches established within the Community for the purposes of this calculation.

2. Application to benefit from the advantages provided for in paragraph 1 shall be made to the supervisory authorities of the Member States concerned. The application shall state the authority of the Member State which in future is to supervise the solvency of the entire business of the branches established within the Community. Reasons must be given for the choice of authority made by the undertaking.

The deposit referred to in Article 162(2)(e) shall be lodged with that Member State.

3. The advantages provided for in paragraph 1 may be granted only where the supervisory authorities of all Member States in which an application has been made agree to them.

Those advantages shall take effect from the time when the selected supervisory authority informs the other supervisory authorities that it will supervise the state of solvency of the entire business of the branches within the Community.

The supervisory authority selected shall obtain from the other Member States the information necessary for the supervision of the overall solvency of the branches established in their territory.

4. At the request of one or more of the Member States concerned, the advantages granted under paragraphs 1, 2 and 3 shall be withdrawn simultaneously by all Member States concerned.

[6321]
Article 168
Accounting, prudential and statistical information and undertakings in difficulty

For the purposes of this Section, Article 34, Article 139(3) and Articles 140 and 141 shall apply.

As regards the application of Articles 137 to 139, where an undertaking qualifies for the advantages provided for in Article 167(1), (2) and (3), the supervisory authority responsible for verifying the solvency of branches established within the Community with respect to their entire business shall be treated in the same way as the supervisory authority of the Member State in the territory of which the head office of an undertaking established in the Community.

[6322]
Article 169
Separation of non-life and life business

1. Branches referred to in this Section shall not simultaneously pursue life and non-life insurance activities in the same Member State.

2. By way of derogation from paragraph 1 Member States may provide that branches referred to in this Section which, on the relevant date referred to in the first subparagraph of Article 73(5), pursued both activities simultaneously in a Member State may continue to do so there provided that each activity is separately managed in accordance with Article 74.

3. Any Member State which under the second subparagraph of Article 73(5) requires undertakings established in its territory to cease the simultaneous pursuit of the activities in which they were engaged on the relevant date referred to in the first subparagraph of Article 73(5) must also impose this requirement on branches referred to in this Section which are established in its territory and simultaneously pursue both activities there.

Member States may provide that branches referred to in this Section whose head office simultaneously pursues both activities and which on the dates referred to in the first subparagraph of Article 73(5) pursued in the territory of a Member State solely life insurance activity may continue their activity there. Where the undertaking wishes to pursue non-life insurance activity in that territory it may only pursue life insurance activity through a subsidiary.

[6323]
Article 170
Withdrawal of authorisation for undertakings authorised in more than one Member State

In the case of a withdrawal of authorisation by the authority referred to in Article 167(2) that authority shall notify the supervisory authorities of the other Member States where the undertaking operates and those authorities shall take the appropriate measures.

Where the reason for that withdrawal is the inadequacy of the overall state of solvency as fixed by the Member States which agreed to the request referred to in Article 167, the Member States which gave their approval shall also withdraw their authorisations.

[6324]
Article 171
Agreements with third countries

The Community may, by means of agreements concluded pursuant to the Treaty with one or more third countries, agree to the application of provisions different to those provided for in this Section, for the purpose of ensuring, under conditions of reciprocity, adequate protection for policy holders and insured persons in the Member States.

SECTION 2
REINSURANCE

[6325]
Article 172
Equivalence

1. The Commission shall adopt implementing measures specifying the criteria to assess whether the solvency regime of a third country applied to reinsurance activities of undertakings with their head office in that third country is equivalent to that laid down in Title I.

Those measures, designed to amend non-essential elements of this Directive by supplementing it, shall be adopted in accordance with the regulatory procedure with scrutiny referred to in Article 301(3).

2. The Commission may, in accordance with the regulatory procedure referred to in Article 301(2) and taking into account the criteria adopted in accordance with paragraph 1, decide whether the solvency regime of a third country applied to reinsurance activities of undertakings with their head office in that third country is equivalent to that laid down in Title I.

Those decisions shall be regularly reviewed.

3. Where in accordance with paragraph 2 the solvency regime of a third country has been deemed to be equivalent to that laid down in this Directive, reinsurance contracts concluded with undertakings having their head office in that third country shall be treated in the same manner as reinsurance contracts concluded with undertakings authorised in accordance with this Directive.

[6326]
Article 173
Prohibition of pledging of assets

Member States shall not retain or introduce for the establishment of technical provisions a system with gross reserving which requires pledging of assets to cover unearned premiums and outstanding claims provisions where the reinsurer is a third-country insurance or reinsurance undertaking, situated in a country whose solvency regime is deemed to be equivalent to that laid down in this Directive in accordance with Article 172.

[6327]
Article 174
Principle and conditions for conducting reinsurance activity

A Member State shall not apply to third-country reinsurance undertakings taking-up or pursuing reinsurance activity in its territory provisions which result in a more favourable treatment than that

Part VI European Materials

granted to reinsurance undertakings which have their head office in that Member State.

[6328]
Article 175
Agreements with third countries

1. The Commission may submit proposals to the Council for the negotiation of agreements with one or more third countries regarding the means of exercising supervision over the following:

(a) third-country reinsurance undertakings which conduct reinsurance business in the Community;

(b) Community reinsurance undertakings which conduct reinsurance business in the territory of a third country.

2. The agreements referred to in paragraph 1 shall in particular seek to ensure, under conditions of equivalence of prudential regulation, effective market access for reinsurance undertakings in the territory of each contracting party and provide for mutual recognition of supervisory rules and practices on reinsurance. They shall also seek to ensure the following:

(a) that the supervisory authorities of the Member States are able to obtain the information necessary for the supervision of reinsurance undertakings which have their head offices situated in the Community and conduct business in the territory of third countries concerned;

(b) that the supervisory authorities of third countries are able to obtain the information necessary for the supervision of reinsurance undertakings which have their head offices situated within their territories and conduct business in the Community.

3. Without prejudice to Article 300(1) and (2) of the Treaty, the Commission shall with the assistance of the European Insurance and Occupational Pensions Committee examine the outcome of the negotiations referred to in paragraph 1 of this Article and the resulting situation.

CHAPTER X
SUBSIDIARIES OF INSURANCE AND REINSURANCE UNDERTAKINGS GOVERNED BY THE LAWS OF A THIRD COUNTRY AND ACQUISITIONS OF HOLDINGS BY SUCH UNDERTAKINGS

[6329]
Article 176
Information from Member States to the Commission

The supervisory authorities of the Member States shall inform the Commission and the supervisory authorities of the other Member States of any authorisation of a direct or indirect subsidiary, one or more of whose parent undertakings are governed by the laws of a third country.

That information shall also contain an indication of the structure of the group concerned.

Where an undertaking governed by the law of a third country acquires a holding in an insurance or reinsurance undertaking authorised in the Community which would turn that insurance or reinsurance undertaking into a subsidiary of that third country undertaking, the supervisory authorities of the home Member State shall inform the Commission and the supervisory authorities of the other Member States.

[6330]
Article 177
Third-country treatment of Community insurance and reinsurance undertakings

1. Member States shall inform the Commission of any general difficulties encountered by their insurance or reinsurance undertakings in establishing themselves and operating in a third country or pursuing activities in a third country.

2. The Commission shall, periodically, submit a report to the Council examining the treatment accorded, in third countries, to insurance or reinsurance undertakings authorised in the Community, as regards the following:

(a) the establishment in third countries of insurance or reinsurance undertakings authorised in the Community;

(b) the acquisition of holdings in third-country insurance or reinsurance undertakings;

(c) the pursuit of insurance or reinsurance activities by such established undertakings;

(d) the cross-border provision of insurance or reinsurance activities from the Community to third countries.

The Commission shall submit those reports to the Council, together with any appropriate proposals or recommendations.

TITLE II
SPECIFIC PROVISIONS FOR INSURANCE AND REINSURANCE

CHAPTER I
APPLICABLE LAW AND CONDITIONS OF DIRECT INSURANCE CONTRACTS

SECTION 1
APPLICABLE LAW

[6331]
Article 178
Applicable Law

Any Member State not subject to the application of Regulation (EC) No 593/2008 shall apply the provisions of that Regulation in order to determine the law applicable to insurance contracts falling within the scope of Article 7 of that Regulation.

SECTION 2
COMPULSORY INSURANCE

[6332]
Article 179
Related obligations

1. Non-life insurance undertakings may offer and conclude ompulsory insurance contracts under the conditions set out in this Article.

2. Where a Member State imposes an obligation to take out insurance, an insurance contract shall not satisfy that obligation unless it complies with the specific provisions relating to that insurance laid down by that Member State.

3. Where a Member State imposes compulsory insurance and the insurance undertaking is required to notify the supervisory authorities of any cessation of cover, such cessation may be invoked against injured third parties only in the circumstances laid down by that Member State.

4. Each Member State shall communicate to the Commission the risks against which insurance is compulsory under its legislation, stating the following:

(a) the specific legal provisions relating to that insurance;

(b) the particulars which must be given in the certificate which a non-life insurance undertaking must issue to an insured person where that Member State requires proof that the obligation to take out insurance has been complied with.

A Member State may require that the particulars referred to in point (b) of the first subparagraph include a declaration by the insurance undertaking to the effect that the contract complies with the specific provisions relating to that insurance.

The Commission shall publish the particulars referred to in point (b) of the first subparagraph in the Official Journal of the European Union.

SECTION 3
GENERAL GOOD

[6333]
Article 180
General good

Neither the Member State in which a risk is situated nor the Member State of the commitment shall prevent a policy holder from concluding a contract with an insurance undertaking authorised under the conditions of Article 14 as long as that conclusion of contract does not conflict with legal provisions protecting the general good in the Member State in which the risk is situated or in the Member State of the commitment.

SECTION 4
CONDITIONS OF INSURANCE CONTRACTS AND SCALES OF PREMIUMS

[6334]
Article 181
Non-life insurance

1. Member States shall not require the prior approval or systematic notification of general and special policy conditions, scales of premiums, or forms and other printed documents which an insurance undertaking intends to use in its dealings with policy holders.

Member States may require non-systematic notification of those policy conditions and other documents only for the purpose of verifying compliance with national provisions concerning insurance contracts. Those requirements shall not constitute a prior condition for an insurance undertaking to pursue business.

2. A Member State which makes insurance compulsory may require that insurance undertakings communicate to its supervisory authority the general and special conditions of such insurance before circulating them.

3. Member States shall not retain or introduce an obligation of prior notification or approval of proposed increases in premium rates except as part of general price-control systems.

[6335]
Article 182
Life insurance

Member States shall not require the prior approval or systematic notification of general and special policy conditions, scales of premiums, technical bases used in particular for calculating scales of premiums and technical provisions or forms and other printed documents which a life insurance undertaking intends to use in its dealings with policy holders.

However, the home Member State may, for the sole purpose of verifying compliance with national provisions concerning actuarial principles, require systematic communication of the technical bases used in particular for calculating scales of premiums and technical provisions. Those requirements shall not constitute a prior condition for an insurance undertaking to pursue business.

SECTION 5
INFORMATION FOR POLICY HOLDERS

SUBSECTION 1
NON-LIFE INSURANCE

[6336]
Article 183
General Information for policy holders

1. Before a non-life insurance contract is concluded the non-life insurance undertaking shall inform the policy holder of the following:

(a) the law applicable to the contract, where the parties do not have a free choice;

(b) the fact that the parties are free to choose the law applicable and the law the insurer proposes to choose.

The insurance undertaking shall also inform the policy holder of the arrangements for handling complaints of policy holders concerning contracts including, where appropriate, the existence of a complaints body, without prejudice to the right of the policy holder to take legal proceedings.

2. The obligations referred to in paragraph 1 shall apply only where the policy holder is a natural person.

3. The detailed rules for implementing paragraphs 1 and 2 shall be laid down by the Member State in which the risk is situated.

[6337]
Article 184
Additional information in the case of non-life insurance offered under the right of establishment or the freedom to provide services

1. Where non-life insurance is offered under the right of establishment or the freedom to provide services, the policy holder shall, before any commitment is entered into, be informed of the Member State in which the head office or, where appropriate, the branch with which the contract is to be concluded is situated.

Any documents issued to the policy holder shall convey the information referred to in the first subparagraph.

The obligations imposed in the first and second subparagraphs shall not apply to large risks.

2. The contract or any other document granting cover, together with the insurance proposal where it is binding upon the policy holder, shall state the address of the head office or, where appropriate, of the branch of the non-life insurance undertaking which grants the cover.

The Member States may require that the name and address of the representative of the non-life insurance undertaking referred to in Article 148(2)(a) also appear in the documents referred to in the first subparagraph of this paragraph.

SUBSECTION 2
LIFE INSURANCE

[6338]
Article 185
Information for policy holders

1. Before the life insurance contract is concluded, at least the information set out in paragraphs 2 to 4 shall be communicated to the policy holder.

2. The following information about the life insurance undertaking shall be communicated:
   (a) the name of the undertaking and its legal form;
   (b) the name of the Member State in which the head office and, where appropriate, the branch concluding the contract is situated;
   (c) the address of the head office and, where appropriate, of the branch concluding the contract;
   (d) a concrete reference to the report on the solvency and financial condition as laid down in Article 51, allowing the policy holder easy access to this information.

3. The following information relating to the commitment shall be communicated:
   (a) the definition of each benefit and each option;
   (b) the term of the contract;
   (c) the means of terminating the contract;
   (d) the means of payment of premiums and duration of payments;
   (e) the means of calculation and distribution of bonuses;
   (f) an indication of surrender and paid-up values and the extent to which they are guaranteed;
   (g) information on the premiums for each benefit, both main benefits and supplementary benefits, where appropriate;
   (h) for unit-linked policies, the definition of the units to which the benefits are linked;
   (i) an indication of the nature of the underlying assets for unit-linked policies;
   (j) arrangements for application of the cooling-off period;
   (k) general information on the tax arrangements applicable to the type of policy;
   (l) the arrangements for handling complaints concerning contracts by policy holders, lives assured or beneficiaries under contracts including, where appropriate, the existence of a complaints body, without prejudice to the right to take legal proceedings;
   (m) the law applicable to the contract where the parties do not have a free choice or, where the parties are free to choose the law applicable, the law the life insurance undertaking proposes to choose.

4. In addition, specific information shall be supplied in order to provide a proper understanding of the risks underlying the contract which are assumed by the policy holder.

5. The policy holder shall be kept informed throughout the term of the contract of any change concerning the following information:
   (a) the policy conditions, both general and special;
   (b) the name of the life insurance undertaking, its legal form or the address of its head office and, where appropriate, of the branch which concluded the contract;
   (c) all the information listed in points (d) to (j) of paragraph 3 in the event of a change in the policy conditions or amendment of the law applicable to the contract;
   (d) annually, information on the state of bonuses.

Where, in connection with an offer for or conclusion of a life insurance contract, the insurer provides figures relating to the amount of potential payments above and beyond the contractually agreed payments, the insurer shall provide the policy holder with a specimen calculation whereby the potential maturity payment is set out applying the basis for the premium calculation using three different rates of interest. This shall not apply to term insurances and contracts. The insurer shall inform the policy holder in a clear and comprehensible manner that the specimen calculation is only a model of computation based on notional assumptions, and that the policy holder shall not derive any contractual claims from the specimen calculation.

In the case of insurances with profit participation, the insurer shall inform the policy holder annually in writing of the status of the claims of the policy holder, incorporating the profit participation. Furthermore, where the insurer has provided figures about the potential future development of the profit participation, the insurer shall inform the policy holder of differences between the actual development and the initial data.

6. The information referred to in paragraphs 2 to 5 shall be provided in a clear and accurate manner, in writing, in an official language of the Member State of the commitment.

However, such information may be in another language if the policy holder so requests and the law of the Member State so permits or the policy holder is free to choose the law applicable.

7. The Member State of the commitment may require life insurance undertakings to furnish information in addition to that listed in paragraphs 2 to 5 only if it is necessary for a proper understanding by the policy holder of the essential elements of the commitment.

8. The detailed rules for implementing paragraphs 1 to 7 shall be laid down by the Member State of the commitment.

[6339]
Article 186
Cancellation period

1. Member States shall provide for policy holders who conclude individual life insurance contracts to have a period of between 14 and 30 days from the time when they were informed that the contract had been concluded within which to cancel the contract.

The giving of notice of cancellation by the policy holders shall have the effect of releasing them from any future obligation arising from the contract.

The other legal effects and the conditions of cancellation shall be determined by the law applicable to the contract, notably as regards the arrangements for informing the policy holder that the contract has been concluded.

2. The Member States may opt not to apply paragraph 1 in the following cases:

(a) where a contract has a duration of six months or less;

(b) where, because of the status of the policy holder or the circumstances in which the contract is concluded, the policy holder does not need special protection.

Where Member States make use of the option set out in the first subparagraph they shall specify that fact in their law.

CHAPTER II
PROVISIONS SPECIFIC TO NON-LIFE INSURANCE

SECTION 1
GENERAL PROVISIONS

[6340]
Article 187
Policy Conditions

General and special policy conditions shall not include any conditions intended to meet, in an individual case, the particular circumstances of the risk to be covered.

[6341]
Article 188
Abolition of monopolies

Member States shall ensure that monopolies in respect of the taking-up of the business of certain classes of insurance, granted to bodies established within their territories and referred to in Article 8, are abolished.

[6342]
Article 189
Participation in national guarantee schemes

Host Member States may require non-life insurance undertakings to join and participate, on the same terms as non-life insurance undertakings authorised in their territories, in any scheme designed to guarantee the payment of insurance claims to insured persons and injured third parties.

SECTION 2
COMMUNITY CO-INSURANCE

[6343]
Article 190
Community co-insurance operations

1. This Section shall apply to Community co-insurance operations which shall be those co-insurance operations which relate to one or more risks classified under classes 3 to 16 of Part A of Annex I and which fulfil the following conditions:

(a) the risk is a large risk;

(b) the risk is covered by a single contract at an overall premium and for the same period by two or more insurance undertakings each for its own part as co-insurer, one of them being the leading insurance undertaking;

(c) the risk is situated within the Community;

(d) for the purpose of covering the risk, the leading insurance undertaking is treated as if it were the insurance undertaking covering the whole risk;

(e) at least one of the co-insurers participates in the contract through a head office or a branch established in a Member State other than that of the leading insurance undertaking;

(f) the leading insurance undertaking fully assumes the leader's role in co-insurance practice and in particular determines the terms and conditions of insurance and rating.

2. Articles 147 to 152 shall apply only to the leading insurance undertaking.

3. Co-insurance operations which do not satisfy the conditions set out in paragraph 1 shall remain subject to the provisions of this Directive except those of this Section.

[6344]
Article 191
Participation in Community co-insurance

The right of insurance undertakings to participate in Community co-insurance shall not be made subject to any provisions other than those of this Section.

[6345]
Article 192
Technical provisions

The amount of the technical provisions shall be determined by the different co-insurers according to the rules fixed by their home Member State or, in the absence of such rules, according to customary practice in that State.

However, the technical provisions shall be at least equal to those determined by the leading insurer according to the rules of its home Member State.

[6346]
Article 193
Statistical data

Home Member States shall ensure that co-insurers keep statistical data showing the extent of Community co-insurance operations in which they participate and the Member States concerned.

[6347]
Article 194
Treatment of co-insurance contracts in winding-up proceedings

In the event of an insurance undertaking being wound up, liabilities arising from participation in Community co-insurance contracts shall be met in the same way as those arising under the other insurance contracts of that undertaking without distinction as to the nationality of the insured and of the beneficiaries.

[6348]
Article 195
Exchange of information between supervisory authorities

For the purposes of the implementation of this Section the supervisory authorities of the Member States shall, in the framework of the cooperation referred to in Title I, Chapter IV, Section 5, provide each other with all necessary information.

[6349]
Article 196
Cooperation on implementation

The Commission and the supervisory authorities of the Member States shall cooperate closely for the purposes of examining any difficulties which might arise in implementing this Section.

In the course of that cooperation they shall examine in particular any practices which might indicate that the leading insurance undertaking does not assume the role of the leader in co-insurance practice or that the risks clearly do not require the participation of two or more insurers for their coverage.

SECTION 3
ASSISTANCE

[6350]
Article 197
Activities similar to tourist assistance

Member States may make provision *for* assistance to persons who get into difficulties in circumstances other than those referred to in Article 2(2) subject to this Directive.

Where a Member State makes such provision, it shall treat such activity as if it were classified under class 18 in Part A of Annex I.

The second paragraph shall in no way affect the possibilities for classification laid down in Annex I for activities which obviously come under other classes.

SECTION 4
LEGAL EXPENSES INSURANCE

[6351]
Article 198
Scope of this Section

1. This Section shall apply to legal expenses insurance referred to in class 17 in Part A of Annex I whereby an insurance undertaking promises, against the payment of a premium, to bear the costs of legal proceedings and to provide other services directly linked to insurance cover, in particular with a view to the following:

(a) securing compensation for the loss, damage or injury suffered by the insured person, by settlement out of court or through civil or criminal proceedings;

(b) defending or representing the insured person in civil, criminal, administrative or other proceedings or in respect of any claim made against that person.

2. This Section shall not apply to any of the following:

(a) legal expenses insurance where such insurance concerns disputes or risks arising out of, or in connection with, the use of sea-going vessels;

(b) the activity pursued by an insurance undertaking providing civil liability cover for the purpose of defending or representing the insured person in any inquiry or proceedings where that activity is at the same time pursued in the own interest of that insurance undertaking under such cover;

(c) where a Member State so decides, the activity of legal expenses insurance undertaken by an assistance insurer which complies with the following conditions:

(i) the activity is pursued in a Member State other than that in which the insured person is habitually resident;

(ii) the activity forms part of a contract covering solely the assistance provided for persons who fall into difficulties while travelling, while away from their home or their habitual residence.

For the purposes of point (c) of the first subparagraph, the contract shall clearly state that the cover concerned is limited to the circumstances referred to in that point and is ancillary to the assistance.

[6352]
Article 199
Separate contracts

Legal expenses cover shall be the subject of a contract separate from that drawn up for the other classes of insurance or shall be dealt with in a separate section of a single policy in which the nature of the legal expenses cover and, should the Member State so request, the amount of the relevant premium are specified.

[6353]
Article 200
Management of claims

1. The home Member State shall ensure that insurance undertakings adopt, in accordance with the option chosen by the Member State, or at their own choice, where the Member State so agrees, at least one of the methods for the management of claims set out in paragraphs 2, 3 and 4.

Whichever solution is adopted, the interest of persons having legal expenses cover shall be regarded as safeguarded in an equivalent manner under this Section.

2. Insurance undertakings shall ensure that no member of the staff who is concerned with the management of legal expenses claims or with legal advice in respect thereof pursues at the same time a similar activity in another undertaking having financial, commercial or administrative links with the first insurance undertaking and pursuing one or more of the other classes of insurance set out in Annex I.

Composite insurance undertakings shall ensure that no member of the staff who is concerned with the management of legal expenses claims or with legal advice in respect thereof pursues at the same time a similar activity for another class transacted by them.

3. The insurance undertaking shall entrust the management of claims in respect of legal expenses insurance to an undertaking having separate legal personality. That undertaking shall be mentioned in the separate contract or separate section referred to in Article 199.

Where the undertaking having separate legal personality has links to an insurance undertaking which carries on one or more of the classes of insurance referred to in Part A of Annex I, members of the staff of the undertaking having separate legal personality who are concerned with the management of claims or with legal advice connected with such management shall not pursue the same or a similar activity in the other insurance undertaking at the same time. Member States may impose the same requirements on the members of the administrative, management or supervisory body.

4. The contract shall provide that the insured persons may instruct a lawyer of their choice or, to the extent that national law so permits, any other appropriately qualified person, from the moment that those insured persons have a claim under that contract.

[6354]
Article 201
Free choice of lawyer

1. Any contract of legal expenses insurance shall expressly provide that:
   (a) where recourse is had to a lawyer or other person appropriately qualified according to national law in order to defend, represent or serve the interests of the insured person in any inquiry or proceedings, that insured person shall be free to choose such lawyer or other person;
   (b) the insured persons shall be free to choose a lawyer or, where they so prefer and to the extent that national law so permits, any other appropriately qualified person, to serve their interests whenever a conflict of interests arises.

2. For the purposes of this Section 'lawyer' means any person entitled to pursue his professional activities under one of the denominations laid down in Council Directive 77/249/EEC of 22 March 1977 to facilitate the effective exercise by lawyers of freedom to provide services[1].

NOTES

[1] OJ L78, 26.3.1977, p 17.

[6355]
Article 202
Exception to the free choice of lawyer

1. Member States may provide for exemption from Article 201(1) for legal expenses insurance if all the following conditions are met:
   (a) the insurance is limited to cases arising from the use of road vehicles in the territory of the Member State concerned;
   (b) the insurance is connected to a contract to provide assistance in the event of accident or breakdown involving a road vehicle;
   (c) neither the legal expenses insurance undertaking nor the assistance insurer carries out any class of liability insurance;
   (d) measures are taken so that the legal counsel and representation of each of the parties to a dispute is effected by wholly independent lawyers where those parties are insured for legal expenses by the same insurance undertaking.

2. An exemption granted pursuant to paragraph 1 shall not affect the application of Article 200.

[6356]
Article 203
Arbitration

Member States shall, for the settlement of any dispute between the legal expenses insurance undertaking and the insured and without prejudice to any right of appeal to a judicial body which might be provided for by national law, provide for arbitration or other procedures offering comparable guarantees of objectivity.

The insurance contract shall provide for the right of the insured person to have recourse to such procedures.

[6357]
Article 204
Conflict of interest

Whenever a conflict of interests arises or there is disagreement over the settlement of the dispute, the legal expenses insurer or, where appropriate, the claims settlement office shall inform the person

Part VI European Materials

insured of the right referred to in Article 201(1) and of the possibility of having recourse to the procedure referred to in Article 203.

[6358]
Article 205
Abolition of specialisation of legal expenses insurance

Member States shall abolish all provisions which prohibit an insurance undertaking from pursuing within their territory legal expenses insurance and other classes of insurance at the same time.

SECTION 5
HEALTH INSURANCE

[6359]
Article 206
Health insurance as an alternative to social security

1. Member States in which contracts covering the risks under class 2 in Part A of Annex I may serve as a partial or complete alternative to health cover provided by the statutory social security system may require that:

(a) those contracts comply with the specific legal provisions adopted by that Member State to protect the general good in that class of insurance;

(b) the general and special conditions of that insurance be communicated to the supervisory authorities of that Member State before use.

2. Member States may require that the health insurance system referred to in paragraph 1 be operated on a technical basis similar to that of life insurance where all the following conditions are fulfilled:

(a) the premiums paid are calculated on the basis of sickness tables and other statistical data relevant to the Member State in which the risk is situated in accordance with the mathematical methods used in insurance;

(b) a reserve is set up for increasing age;

(c) the insurer may cancel the contract only within a fixed period determined by the Member State in which the risk is situated;

(d) the contract provides that premiums may be increased or payments reduced, even for current contracts;

(e) the contract provides that the policy holders may change their existing contract into a new contract complying with paragraph 1, offered by the same insurance undertaking or the same branch and taking account of their acquired rights.

In the case referred to in point (e) of the first subparagraph, account shall be taken of the reserve for increasing age and a new medical examination may be required only for increased cover.

The supervisory authorities of the Member State concerned shall publish the sickness tables and other relevant statistical data referred to in point (a) of the first subparagraph and transmit them to the supervisory authorities of the home Member State.

The premiums must be sufficient, on reasonable actuarial assumptions, for insurance undertakings to be able to meet all their commitments having regard to all aspects of their financial situation. The home Member State shall require the technical basis for the calculation of premiums to be communicated to its supervisory authorities before the product is circulated.

The third and fourth subparagraphs shall also apply where existing contracts are modified.

SECTION 6
INSURANCE AGAINST ACCIDENTS AT WORK

[6360]
Article 207
Compulsory insurance against accidents at work

Member States may require that any insurance undertaking offering, at its own risk, compulsory insurance against accidents at work within their territories comply with the specific provisions of their national law concerning such insurance, except for the provisions concerning financial supervision, which shall be the exclusive responsibility of the home Member State.

CHAPTER III
PROVISIONS SPECIFIC TO LIFE INSURANCE

[6361]
Article 208
Prohibition on compulsory ceding of part of underwriting

Member States shall not require life insurance undertakings to cede part of their underwriting of activities listed in Article 2(3) to an organisation or organisations designated by national law.

[6362]
Article 209
Premiums for new business

Premiums for new business shall be sufficient, on reasonable actuarial assumptions, to enable life insurance undertakings to meet all their commitments and, in particular, to establish adequate technical provisions.

For that purpose, all aspects of the financial situation of a life insurance undertaking may be taken into account, without the input from resources other than premiums and income earned thereon being systematic and permanent in a way that it may jeopardise the solvency of the undertaking concerned in the long term.

CHAPTER IV
RULES SPECIFIC TO REINSURANCE

[6363]
Article 210
Finite reinsurance

1. Member States shall ensure that insurance and reinsurance undertakings which conclude finite reinsurance contracts or pursue finite reinsurance activities are able to properly identify, measure, monitor, manage, control and report the risks arising from those contracts or activities.

2. In order to ensure that a harmonised approach is adopted with respect to finite reinsurance activities, the Commission may adopt implementing measures specifying the provisions of paragraph 1 with respect to the monitoring, management and control of risks arising from finite reinsurance activities.

Those measures, designed to amend non-essential elements of this Directive, inter alia, by supplementing it, shall be adopted in accordance with the regulatory procedure with scrutiny referred to in Article 301(3).

3. For the purposes of paragraphs 1 and 2 finite reinsurance means reinsurance under which the explicit maximum loss potential, expressed as the maximum economic risk transferred, arising both from a significant underwriting risk and timing risk transfer, exceeds the premium over the lifetime of the contract by a limited but significant amount, together with at least one of the following features:

(a) explicit and material consideration of the time value of money;
(b) contractual provisions to moderate the balance of economic experience between the parties over time to achieve the target risk transfer.

[6364]
Article 211
Special purpose vehicles

1. Member States shall allow the establishment within their territory of special purpose vehicles, subject to prior supervisory approval.

2. In order to ensure a harmonised approach with respect to special purpose vehicles, the Commission shall adopt implementing measures laying down the following:

(a) the scope of authorisation;
(b) mandatory conditions to be included in all contracts issued;
(c) fit and proper requirements as referred to in Article 42 of the persons running the special purpose vehicle;
(d) fit and proper requirements for shareholders or members having a qualifying holding in the special purpose vehicle;
(e) sound administrative and accounting procedures, adequate internal control mechanisms and risk-management requirements;
(f) accounting, prudential and statistical information requirements;
(g) solvency requirements.

Part VI European Materials

Those measures, designed to amend non-essential elements of this Directive, inter alia, by supplementing it, shall be adopted in accordance with the regulatory procedure with scrutiny referred to in Article 301(3).

3. Special purpose vehicles authorised prior to 31 October 2012 shall be subject to the law of the Member State having authorised the special purpose vehicle. However, any new activity commenced by such a special purpose vehicle after that date shall be subject to paragraphs 1 and 2.

TITLE III
SUPERVISION OF INSURANCE AND REINSURANCE UNDERTAKINGS IN A GROUP

CHAPTER I
GROUP SUPERVISION: DEFINITIONS, CASES OF APPLICATION, SCOPE AND LEVELS

SECTION 1
DEFINITIONS

[6365]
Article 212
Definitions

1. For the purposes of this Title, the following definitions shall apply:
   (a) 'participating undertaking' means an undertaking which is either a parent undertaking or other undertaking which holds a participation, or an undertaking linked with another undertaking by a relationship as set out in Article 12(1) of Directive 83/349/EEC;
   (b) 'related undertaking' means either a subsidiary undertaking or other undertaking in which a participation is held, or an undertaking linked with another undertaking by a relationship as set out in Article 12(1) of Directive 83/349/EEC;
   (c) 'group' means a group of undertakings that:
      (i) consists of a participating undertaking, its subsidiaries and the entities in which the participating undertaking or its subsidiaries hold a participation, as well as undertakings linked to each other by a relationship as set out in Article 12(1) of Directive 83/349/EEC; or
      (ii) is based on the establishment, contractually or otherwise, of strong and sustainable financial relationships among those undertakings, and that may include mutual or mutual-type associations, provided that:
         — one of those undertakings effectively exercises, through centralised coordination, a dominant influence over the decisions, including financial decisions, of the other undertakings that are part of the group; and,
         — the establishment and dissolution of such relationships for the purposes of this Title are subject to prior approval by the group supervisor,

   where the undertaking exercising the centralised coordination shall be considered as the parent undertaking, and the other undertakings shall be considered as subsidiaries;
   (d) 'group supervisor' means the supervisory authority responsible for group supervision, determined in accordance with Article 247;
   (e) 'college of supervisors' means a permanent but flexible structure for cooperation and coordination among the supervisory authorities of the Member States concerned;
   (f) 'insurance holding company' means a parent undertaking which is not a mixed financial holding company within the meaning of Directive 2002/87/EC and the main business of which is to acquire and hold participations in subsidiary undertakings, where those subsidiary undertakings are exclusively or mainly insurance or reinsurance undertakings, or third-country insurance or reinsurance undertakings, at least one of such subsidiary undertakings being an insurance or reinsurance undertaking.
   (g) 'mixed-activity insurance holding company' means a parent undertaking, other than an insurance undertaking, a third-country insurance undertaking, a reinsurance undertaking, a third-country reinsurance undertaking, an insurance holding company or a mixed financial holding company within the meaning of Directive 2002/87/EC, which includes at least one insurance or reinsurance undertaking among its subsidiary undertakings.

2. For the purposes of this Title, the supervisory authorities shall also consider as a parent undertaking any undertaking which, in the opinion of the supervisory authorities, effectively exercises a dominant influence over another undertaking.

They shall also consider as a subsidiary undertaking any undertaking over which, in the opinion of the supervisory authorities, a parent undertaking effectively exercises a dominant influence.

They shall also consider as participation the holding, directly or indirectly, of voting rights or capital in an undertaking over which, in the opinion of the supervisory authorities, a significant influence is effectively exercised.

SECTION 2
CASES OF APPLICATION AND SCOPE

[6366]
Article 213
Cases of application of group supervision

1. Member States shall provide for supervision, at the level of the group, of insurance and reinsurance undertakings which are part of a group, in accordance with this Title.

The provisions of this Directive which lay down the rules for the supervision of insurance and reinsurance undertakings taken individually shall continue to apply to such undertakings, except where otherwise provided under this Title.

2. Member States shall ensure that supervision at the level of the group applies as follows:

(a) to insurance or reinsurance undertakings, which are a participating undertaking in at least one insurance undertaking, reinsurance undertaking, third-country insurance undertaking or third-country reinsurance undertaking, in accordance with Articles 218 to 258;

(b) to insurance or reinsurance undertakings, the parent undertaking of which is an insurance holding company which has its head office in the Community, in accordance with Articles 218 to 258;

(c) to insurance or reinsurance undertakings, the parent undertaking of which is an insurance holding company having its head office outside the Community or a third-country insurance or reinsurance undertaking, in accordance with Articles 260 to 263;

(d) to insurance or reinsurance undertakings, the parent undertaking of which is a mixed-activity insurance holding company, in accordance with Article 265.

3. In the cases referred to in points (a) and (b) of paragraph 2, where the participating insurance or reinsurance undertaking or the insurance holding company which has its head office in the Community is a related undertaking of a regulated entity or a mixed financial holding company which is subject to supplementary supervision in accordance with Article 5(2) of Directive 2002/87/EC, the group supervisor may, after consulting the other supervisory authorities concerned, decide not to carry out at the level of that participating insurance or reinsurance undertaking or that insurance holding company the supervision of risk concentration referred to in Article 244 of this Directive, the supervision of intra-group transactions referred to in Article 245 of this Directive, or both.

[6367]
Article 214
Scope of group supervision

1. The exercise of group supervision in accordance with Article 213 shall not imply that the supervisory authorities are required to play a supervisory role in relation to the third-country insurance undertaking, the third-country reinsurance undertaking, the insurance holding company or the mixed-activity insurance holding company taken individually, without prejudice to Article 257 as far as insurance holding companies are concerned.

2. The group supervisor may decide on a case-by-case basis not to include an undertaking in the group supervision referred to in Article 213 where:

(a) the undertaking is situated in a third country where there are legal impediments to the transfer of the necessary information, without prejudice to the provisions of Article 229;

(b) the undertaking which should be included is of negligible interest with respect to the objectives of group supervision; or

(c) the inclusion of the undertaking would be inappropriate or misleading with respect to the objectives of the group supervision.

However, where several undertakings of the same group, taken individually, may be excluded pursuant to point (b) of the first subparagraph, they must nevertheless be included where, collectively, they are of non-negligible interest.

Where the group supervisor is of the opinion that an insurance or reinsurance undertaking should not be included in the group supervision under points (b) or (c) of the first subparagraph, it shall consult the other supervisory authorities concerned before taking a decision.

Where the group supervisor does not include an insurance or reinsurance undertaking in the group supervision under point (b) or (c) of the first subparagraph, the supervisory authorities of the

Member State in which that undertaking is situated may ask the undertaking which is at the head of the group for any information which may facilitate their supervision of the insurance or reinsurance undertaking concerned.

SECTION 3
LEVELS

[6368]
Article 215
Ultimate parent undertaking at Community level

1. Where the participating insurance or reinsurance undertaking or the insurance holding company referred to in Article 213(2)(a) and (b) is itself a subsidiary undertaking of another insurance or reinsurance undertaking or of another insurance holding company which has its head office in the Community, Articles 218 to 258 shall apply only at the level of the ultimate parent insurance or reinsurance undertaking or insurance holding company which has its head office in the Community.

2. Where the ultimate parent insurance or reinsurance undertaking or insurance holding company which has its head office in the Community, referred to in paragraph 1, is a subsidiary undertaking of an undertaking which is subject to supplementary supervision in accordance with Article 5(2) of Directive 2002/87/EC, the group supervisor may, after consulting the other supervisory authorities concerned, decide not to carry out at the level of that ultimate parent undertaking the supervision of risk concentration referred to in Article 244, the supervision of intra-group transactions referred to in Article 245, or both.

[6369]
Article 216
Ultimate parent undertaking at national level

1. Where the participating insurance or reinsurance undertaking or the insurance holding company which has its head office in the Community, referred to in Article 213(2)(a) and (b), does not have its head office in the same Member State as the ultimate parent undertaking at Community level referred to in Article 215, Member States may allow their supervisory authorities to decide, after consulting the group supervisor and that ultimate parent undertaking at Community level, to subject to group supervision the ultimate parent insurance or reinsurance undertaking or insurance holding company at national level.

In such a case, the supervisory authority shall explain its decision to both the group supervisor and the ultimate parent undertaking at Community level.

Articles 218 to 258 shall apply mutatis mutandis, subject to the provisions set out in paragraphs 2 to 6.

2. The supervisory authority may restrict group supervision of the ultimate parent undertaking at national level to one or several sections of Chapter II.

3. Where the supervisory authority decides to apply to the ultimate parent undertaking at national level Chapter II, Section 1, the choice of method made in accordance with Article 220 by the group supervisor in respect of the ultimate parent undertaking at Community level referred to in Article 215 shall be recognised as determinative and applied by the supervisory authority in the Member State concerned.

4. Where the supervisory authority decides to apply to the ultimate parent undertaking at national level Chapter II, Section 1, and where the ultimate parent undertaking at Community level referred to in Article 215 has obtained, in accordance with Article 231 or Article 233(5), permission to calculate the group Solvency Capital Requirement, as well as the Solvency Capital Requirement of insurance and reinsurance undertakings in the group, on the basis of an internal model, that decision shall be recognised as determinative and applied by the supervisory authority in the Member State concerned.

In such a situation, where the supervisory authority considers that the risk profile of the ultimate parent undertaking at national level deviates significantly from the internal model approved at Community level, and as long as that undertaking does not properly address the concerns of the supervisory authority, that supervisory authority may decide to impose a capital add-on to the group Solvency Capital Requirement of that undertaking resulting from the application of such model or, in exceptional circumstances where such capital add-on would not be appropriate, to require that undertaking to calculate its group Solvency Capital Requirement on the basis of the standard formula.

The supervisory authority shall explain such decisions to both the undertaking and the group supervisor.

5. Where the supervisory authority decides to apply Chapter II, Section 1 to the ultimate parent undertaking at national level, that undertaking shall not be permitted to introduce, in accordance with Articles 236 or 243, an application for permission to subject any of its subsidiaries to Articles 238 and 239.

6. Where Member States allow their supervisory authorities to make the decision referred to in paragraph 1, they shall provide that no such decisions can be made or maintained where the ultimate parent undertaking at national level is a subsidiary of the ultimate parent undertaking at Community level referred to in Article 215 and the latter has obtained in accordance with Articles 237 or 243 permission for that subsidiary to be subject to Articles 238 and 239.

7. The Commission may adopt implementing measures specifying the circumstances under which the decision referred to in paragraph 1 can be made.

Those measures, designed to amend non-essential elements of this Directive by supplementing it, shall be adopted in accordance with the regulatory procedure with scrutiny referred to in Article 301(3).

[6370]
Article 217
Parent undertaking covering several Member States

1. Where Member States allow their supervisory authorities to make the decision referred to in Article 216, they shall also allow them to decide to conclude an agreement with supervisory authorities in other Member States where another related ultimate parent undertaking at national level is present, with a view to carrying out group supervision at the level of a subgroup covering several Member States.

Where the supervisory authorities concerned have concluded an agreement as referred to in the first subparagraph, group supervision shall not be carried out at the level of any ultimate parent undertaking referred to in Article 216 present in Member States other than the Member State where the subgroup referred to in the first subparagraph of this paragraph is located.

2. Article 216(2) to (6) shall apply *mutatis mutandis*.

3. The Commission may adopt implementing measures specifying the circumstances under which the decision referred to in paragraph 1 can be made.

Those measures, designed to amend non-essential elements of this Directive by supplementing it, shall be adopted in accordance with the regulatory procedure with scrutiny referred to in Article 301(3).

CHAPTER II
FINANCIAL POSITION

SECTION 1
GROUP SOLVENCY

SUBSECTION 1
GENERAL PROVISIONS

[6371]
Article 218
Supervision of group solvency

1. Supervision of the group solvency shall be exercised in accordance with paragraphs 2 and 3 of this Article, Article 246 and Chapter III.

2. In the case referred to in Article 213(2)(a), Member States shall require the participating insurance or reinsurance undertakings to ensure that eligible own funds are available in the group which are always at least equal to the group Solvency Capital Requirement as calculated in accordance with Subsections 2, 3 and 4.

3. In the case referred to in Article 213(2)(b), Member States shall require insurance and reinsurance undertakings in a group to ensure that eligible own funds are available in the group which are always at least equal to the group Solvency Capital Requirement as calculated in accordance with Subsection 5.

4. The requirements referred to in paragraphs 2 and 3 shall be subject to supervisory review by the group supervisor in accordance with Chapter III. Article 136 and Article 138(1) to (4) shall apply *mutatis mutandis*.

5. As soon as the participating undertaking has observed and informed the group supervisor that the group Solvency Capital Requirement is no longer complied with or that there is a risk of non-compliance in the following three months, the group supervisor shall inform the other supervisory authorities within the college of supervisors, which shall analyse the situation of the group.

[6372]
Article 219
Frequency of calculation

1. The group supervisor shall ensure that the calculations referred to in Article 218(2) and (3) are carried out at least annually, either by the participating insurance or reinsurance undertakings or by the insurance holding company.

The relevant data for and the results of that calculation shall be submitted to the group supervisor by the participating insurance or reinsurance undertaking or, where the group is not headed by an insurance or reinsurance undertaking, by the insurance holding company or by the undertaking in the group identified by the group supervisor after consulting the other supervisory authorities concerned and the group itself.

2. The insurance and reinsurance undertaking and the insurance holding company shall monitor the group Solvency Capital Requirement on an ongoing basis. Where the risk profile of the group deviates significantly from the assumptions underlying the last reported group Solvency Capital Requirement, the group Solvency Capital Requirement shall be recalculated without delay and reported to the group supervisor.

Where there is evidence to suggest that the risk profile of the group has altered significantly since the date on which the group Solvency Capital Requirement was last reported, the group supervisor may require a recalculation of the group Solvency Capital Requirement.

SUBSECTION 2
CHOICE OF CALCULATION METHOD AND GENERAL PRINCIPLES

[6373]
Article 220
Choice of method

1. The calculation of the solvency at the level of the group of the insurance and reinsurance undertakings referred to in Article 213(2)(a) shall be carried out in accordance with the technical principles and one of the methods set out in Articles 221 to 233.

2. Member States shall provide that the calculation of the solvency at the level of the group of insurance and reinsurance undertakings referred to in Article 213(2)(a) shall be carried out in accordance with method 1, which is laid down in Articles 230 to 232.

However, Member States shall allow their supervisory authorities, where they assume the role of group supervisor with regard to a particular group, to decide, after consulting the other supervisory authorities concerned and the group itself, to apply to that group method 2, which is laid down in Articles 233 and 234, or a combination of methods 1 and 2, where the exclusive application of method 1 would not be appropriate.

[6374]
Article 221
Inclusion of proportional share

1. The calculation of the group solvency shall take account of the proportional share held by the participating undertaking in its related undertakings.

For the purposes of the first subparagraph, the proportional share shall comprise either of the following:

(a) where method 1 is used, the percentages used for the establishment of the consolidated accounts; or

(b) where method 2 is used, the proportion of the subscribed capital that is held, directly or indirectly, by the participating undertaking.

However, regardless of the method used, where the related undertaking is a subsidiary undertaking and does not have sufficient eligible own funds to cover its Solvency Capital Requirement, the total solvency deficit of the subsidiary shall be taken into account.

Where in the opinion of the supervisory authorities, the responsibility of the parent undertaking owning a share of the capital is strictly limited to that share of the capital, the group supervisor may nevertheless allow for the solvency deficit of the subsidiary undertaking to be taken into account on a proportional basis.

2. The group supervisor shall determine, after consulting the other supervisory authorities concerned and the group itself, the proportional share which shall be taken into account in the following cases:

(a) where there are no capital ties between some of the undertakings in a group;

(b) where a supervisory authority has determined that the holding, directly or indirectly, of voting rights or capital in an undertaking qualifies as a participation because, in its opinion, a significant influence is effectively exercised over that undertaking;

(c) where a supervisory authority has determined that an undertaking is a parent undertaking of another because, in the opinion of that supervisory authority, it effectively exercises a dominant influence over that other undertaking.

[6375]
Article 222
Elimination of double use of eligible own funds

1. The double use of own funds eligible for the Solvency Capital Requirement among the different insurance or reinsurance undertakings taken into account in that calculation shall not be allowed.

For that purpose, when calculating the group solvency and where the methods described in Subsection 4 do not provide for it, the following amounts shall be excluded:

(a) the value of any asset of the participating insurance or reinsurance undertaking which represents the financing of own funds eligible for the Solvency Capital Requirement of one of its related insurance or reinsurance undertakings;

(b) the value of any asset of a related insurance or reinsurance undertaking of the participating insurance or reinsurance undertaking which represents the financing of own funds eligible for the Solvency Capital Requirement of that participating insurance or reinsurance undertaking;

(c) the value of any asset of a related insurance or reinsurance undertaking of the participating insurance or reinsurance undertaking which represents the financing of own funds eligible for the Solvency Capital Requirement of any other related insurance or reinsurance undertaking of that participating insurance or reinsurance undertaking.

2. Without prejudice to paragraph 1, the following may be included in the calculation only in so far as they are eligible for covering the Solvency Capital Requirement of the related undertaking concerned:

(a) surplus funds falling under Article 91(2) arising in a related life insurance or reinsurance undertaking of the participating insurance or reinsurance undertaking for which the group solvency is calculated;

(b) any subscribed but not paid-up capital of a related insurance or reinsurance undertaking of the participating insurance or reinsurance undertaking for which the group solvency is calculated.

However, the following shall in any event be excluded from the calculation:

(i) subscribed but not paid-up capital which represents a potential obligation on the part of the participating undertaking;

(ii) subscribed but not paid-up capital of the participating insurance or reinsurance undertaking which represents a potential obligation on the part of a related insurance or reinsurance undertaking;

(iii) subscribed but not paid-up capital of a related insurance or reinsurance undertaking which represents a potential obligation on the part of another related insurance or reinsurance undertaking of the same participating insurance or reinsurance undertaking.

3. Where the supervisory authorities consider that certain own funds eligible for the Solvency Capital Requirement of a related insurance or reinsurance undertaking other than those referred to in paragraph 2 cannot effectively be made available to cover the Solvency Capital Requirement of the participating insurance or reinsurance undertaking for which the group solvency is calculated, those own funds may be included in the calculation only in so far as they are eligible for covering the Solvency Capital Requirement of the related undertaking.

4. The sum of the own funds referred to in paragraphs 2 and 3 shall not exceed the Solvency Capital Requirement of the related insurance or reinsurance undertaking.

5. Any eligible own funds of a related insurance or reinsurance undertaking of the participating insurance or reinsurance undertaking for which the group solvency is calculated that are subject to prior authorisation from the supervisory authority in accordance with Article 90 shall be included in the calculation only in so far as they have been duly authorised by the supervisory authority responsible for the supervision of that related undertaking.

[6376]
Article 223
Elimination of the intra-group creation of capital

1. When calculating group solvency, no account shall be taken of any own funds eligible for the Solvency Capital Requirement arising out of reciprocal financing between the participating insurance or reinsurance undertaking and any of the following:

(a) a related undertaking;
(b) a participating undertaking;
(c) another related undertaking of any of its participating undertakings.

2. When calculating group solvency, no account shall be taken of any own funds eligible for the Solvency Capital Requirement of a related insurance or reinsurance undertaking of the participating insurance or reinsurance undertaking for which the group solvency is calculated where the own funds concerned arise out of reciprocal financing with any other related undertaking of that participating insurance or reinsurance undertaking.

3. Reciprocal financing shall be deemed to exist at least where an insurance or reinsurance undertaking, or any of its related undertakings, holds shares in, or makes loans to, another undertaking which, directly or indirectly, holds own funds eligible for the Solvency Capital Requirement of the first undertaking.

[6377]
Article 224
Valuation

The value of the assets and liabilities shall be assessed in accordance with Article 75.

SUBSECTION 3
APPLICATION OF THE CALCULATION METHODS

[6378]
Article 225
Related insurance and reinsurance undertakings

Where the insurance or reinsurance undertaking has more than one related insurance or reinsurance undertaking, the group solvency calculation shall be carried out by including each of those related insurance or reinsurance undertakings.

Member States may provide that where the related insurance or reinsurance undertaking has its head office in a Member State other than that of the insurance or reinsurance undertaking for which the group solvency calculation is carried out, the calculation takes account, in respect of the related undertaking, of the Solvency Capital Requirement and the own funds eligible to satisfy that requirement as laid down in that other Member State.

[6379]
Article 226
Intermediate insurance holding companies

1. When calculating the group solvency of an insurance or reinsurance undertaking which holds a participation in a related insurance undertaking, a related reinsurance undertaking, a third-country insurance undertaking or a third-country reinsurance undertaking, through an insurance holding company, the situation of such an insurance holding company shall be taken into account.

For the sole purpose of that calculation, the intermediate insurance holding company shall be treated as if it were an insurance or reinsurance undertaking subject to the rules laid down in Title I, Chapter VI, Section 4, Subsections 1, 2 and 3 in respect of the Solvency Capital Requirement and were subject to the same conditions as are laid down in Title I, Chapter VI, Section 3, Subsections 1, 2 and 3, in respect of own funds eligible for the Solvency Capital Requirement.

2. In cases where an intermediate insurance holding company holds subordinated debt or other eligible own funds subject to limitation in accordance with Article 98, they shall be recognised as eligible own funds up to the amounts calculated by application of the limits set out in Article 98 to the total eligible own funds outstanding at group level as compared to the Solvency Capital Requirement at group level.

Any eligible own funds of an intermediate insurance holding company, which would require prior authorisation from the supervisory authority in accordance with Article 90 if they were held by an insurance or reinsurance undertaking, may, be included in the calculation of the group solvency only in so far as they have been duly authorised by the group supervisor.

[6380]
Article 227
Related third-country insurance and reinsurance undertakings

1. When calculating, in accordance with Article 233, the group solvency of an insurance or reinsurance undertaking which is a participating undertaking in a third-country insurance or reinsurance undertaking, the latter shall, solely for the purposes of that calculation, be treated as a related insurance or reinsurance undertaking.

However, where the third country in which that undertaking has its head office makes it subject to authorisation and imposes on it a solvency regime at least equivalent to that laid down in Title I, Chapter VI, Member States may provide that the calculation take into account, as regards that undertaking, the Solvency Capital Requirement and the own funds eligible to satisfy that requirement as laid down by the third country concerned.

2. The verification of whether the third-country regime is at least equivalent shall be carried out by the group supervisor, at the request of the participating undertaking or on its own initiative.

In so doing, the group supervisor shall consult the other supervisory authorities concerned and CEIOPS before taking a decision on equivalence.

3. The Commission may adopt implementing measures specifying the criteria to assess whether the solvency regime in a third country is equivalent to that laid down in Title I, Chapter VI.

Those measures, designed to amend non-essential elements of this Directive by supplementing it, shall be adopted in accordance with the regulatory procedure with scrutiny referred to in Article 301(3).

4. The Commission may adopt, after consultation of the European Insurance and Occupational Pensions Committee and in accordance with the regulatory procedure referred to in Article 301(2), and taking into account the criteria adopted in accordance with paragraph 3 of this Article, a decision as to whether the solvency regime in a third country is equivalent to that laid down in Title I, Chapter VI.

Those decisions shall be regularly reviewed to take into account any changes to the solvency regime laid down in Title I, Chapter VI, and to the solvency regime in the third country.

5. Wherein accordance with paragraph 4 the Commission adopts a decision on equivalence of the solvency regime in a third country, paragraph 2 shall not apply.

Where a decision adopted by the Commission in accordance with paragraph 4 concludes that the solvency regime in a third country is not equivalent, the option referred to in the second subparagraph of paragraph 1 to take into account the Solvency Capital Requirement and eligible own funds as laid down by the third country concerned shall not be applicable and the third-country insurance or reinsurance undertaking shall be treated exclusively in accordance with the first subparagraph of paragraph 1.

[6381]
Article 228
Related credit institutions, investment firms and financial institutions

When calculating the group solvency of an insurance or reinsurance undertaking which is a participating undertaking in a credit institution, investment firm or financial institution, Member States shall allow their participating insurance and reinsurance undertakings to apply methods 1 or 2 set out in Annex I to Directive 2002/87/EC *mutatis mutandis*. However, method 1 set out in that Annex shall be applied only where the group supervisor is satisfied as to the level of integrated management and internal control regarding the entities which would be included in the scope of consolidation. The method chosen shall be applied in a consistent manner over time.

Member States shall however allow their supervisory authorities, where they assume the role of group supervisor with regard to a particular group, to decide, at the request of the participating undertaking or on their own initiative, to deduct any participation as referred to in the first paragraph from the own funds eligible for the group solvency of the participating undertaking.

[6382]
Article 229
Non-availability of the necessary information

Where the information necessary for calculating the group solvency of an insurance or reinsurance undertaking, concerning a related undertaking with its head office in a Member State or a third country, is not available to the supervisory authorities concerned, the book value of that undertaking in the participating insurance or reinsurance undertaking shall be deducted from the own funds eligible for the group solvency.

In that case, the unrealised gains connected with such participation shall not be recognised as own funds eligible for the group solvency.

Part VI European Materials

SUBSECTION 4
CALCULATION METHODS

[6383]
Article 230
Method 1 (Default method): Accounting consolidation-based method

1. The calculation of the group solvency of the participating insurance or reinsurance undertaking shall be carried out on the basis of the consolidated accounts.

The group solvency of the participating insurance or reinsurance undertaking is the difference between the following:

(a) the own funds eligible to cover the Solvency Capital Requirement, calculated on the basis of consolidated data;

(b) the Solvency Capital Requirement at group level calculated on the basis of consolidated data.

The rules laid down in Title I, Chapter VI, Section 3, Subsections 1, 2 and 3 and in Title I, Chapter VI, Section 4, Subsections 1, 2 and 3 shall apply for the calculation of the own funds eligible for the Solvency Capital Requirement and of the Solvency Capital Requirement at group level based on consolidated data.

2. The Solvency Capital Requirement at group level based on consolidated data (consolidated group Solvency Capital Requirement) shall be calculated on the basis of either the standard formula or an approved internal model, in a manner consistent with the general principles contained in Title I, Chapter VI, Section 4, Subsections 1 and 2 and Title I, Chapter VI, Section 4, Subsections 1 and 3, respectively.

The consolidated group Solvency Capital Requirement shall have as a minimum the sum of the following:

(a) the Minimum Capital Requirement as referred to in Article 129 of the participating insurance or reinsurance undertaking;

(b) the proportional share of the Minimum Capital Requirement of the related insurance and reinsurance undertakings.

That minimum shall be covered by eligible basic own funds as determined in Article 98(4).

For the purposes of determining whether such eligible own funds qualify to cover the minimum consolidated group Solvency Capital Requirement, the principles set out in Articles 221 to 229 shall apply mutatis mutandis. Article 139(1) and (2) shall apply mutatis mutandis.

[6384]
Article 231
Group internal model

1. In the case of an application for permission to calculate the consolidated group Solvency Capital Requirement, as well as the Solvency Capital Requirement of insurance and reinsurance undertakings in the group, on the basis of an internal model, submitted by an insurance or reinsurance undertaking and its related undertakings, or jointly by the related undertakings of an insurance holding company, the supervisory authorities concerned shall cooperate to decide whether or not to grant that permission and to determine the terms and conditions, if any, to which such permission is subject.

An application as referred to in the first subparagraph shall be submitted to the group supervisor.

The group supervisor shall inform the other supervisory authorities concerned without delay.

2. The supervisory authorities concerned shall do everything within their power to reach a joint decision on the application within six months from the date of receipt of the complete application by the group supervisor.

The group supervisor shall forward the complete application to the other supervisory authorities concerned without delay.

3. During the period referred to in paragraph 2, the group supervisor and any of the other supervisory authorities concerned may consult CEIOPS. CEIOPS shall also be consulted where the participating undertaking so requests.

Where CEIOPS is being consulted, all the supervisory authorities concerned shall be informed and the period referred to in paragraph 2 shall be extended by two months.

4. Where CEIOPS has not been consulted in accordance with the first subparagraph of paragraph 3, and in the absence of a joint decision of the supervisory authorities concerned within six months from the date of receipt of the complete application by the group supervisor, the group supervisor shall request CEIOPS, within a further two months, to deliver advice to all the supervisory authorities concerned. The group supervisor shall take a decision within three weeks of the transmission of that advice, taking full account thereof.

5. Irrespective of whether CEIOPS has been consulted, the group supervisor's decision shall state the full reasons and shall take into account the views expressed by the other supervisory authorities concerned.

The group supervisor shall provide the applicant and the other supervisory authorities concerned with the decision.

The supervisory authorities concerned shall comply with the decision.

6. In the absence of a joint decision within the periods set out in paragraphs 2 and 3 respectively, the group supervisor shall make its own decision on the application.

In making its decision, the group supervisor shall duly take into account the following:

(a) any views and reservations of the other supervisory authorities concerned expressed during the applicable period;

(b) where CEIOPS has been consulted, its advice.

The decision shall state the full reasons and shall contain an explanation of any significant deviation from the positions adopted by CEIOPS.

The group supervisor shall transmit the decision to the applicant and the other supervisory authorities concerned.

That decision shall be recognised as determinative and applied by the supervisory authorities concerned.

7. Where any of the supervisory authorities concerned considers that the risk profile of an insurance or reinsurance undertaking under its supervision deviates significantly from the assumptions underlying the internal model approved at group level, and as long as that undertaking has not properly addressed the concerns of the supervisory authority, that authority may, in accordance with Article 37, impose a capital add-on to the Solvency Capital Requirement of that insurance or reinsurance undertaking resulting from the application of such internal model.

In exceptional circumstances, where such capital add-on would not be appropriate, the supervisory authority may require the undertaking concerned to calculate its Solvency Capital Requirement on the basis of the standard formula referred to in Title I, Chapter VI, Section 4, Subsections 1 and 2. In accordance with Article 37(1)(a) and (c), the supervisory authority may impose a capital add-on to the Solvency Capital Requirement of that insurance or reinsurance undertaking resulting from the application of the standard formula.

The supervisory authority shall explain any decision referred to in the first and second subparagraphs to both the insurance or reinsurance undertaking and the group supervisor.

[6385]
Article 232
Group capital add-on

In determining whether the consolidated group Solvency Capital Requirement appropriately reflects the risk profile of the group, the group supervisor shall pay particular attention to any case where the circumstances referred to in Article 37(1)(a) to (c) may arise at group level, in particular where:

(a) a specific risk existing at group level would not be sufficiently covered by the standard formula or the internal model used, because it is difficult to quantify;

(b) a capital add-on to the Solvency Capital Requirement of the related insurance or reinsurance undertakings is imposed by the supervisory authorities concerned, in accordance with Articles 37 and 231(7).

Where the risk profile of the group is not adequately reflected, a capital add-on to the consolidated group Solvency Capital Requirement may be imposed.

Article 37(1) to (5), together with implementing measures taken in accordance with Article 37(6), shall apply mutatis mutandis.

[6386]
Article 233
***Method 2 (Alternative method)*: Deduction and aggregation method**

1. The group solvency of the participating insurance or reinsurance undertaking shall be the difference between the following:

(a) the aggregated group eligible own funds, as provided for in paragraph 2;

(b) the value in the participating insurance or reinsurance undertaking of the related insurance or reinsurance undertakings and the aggregated group Solvency Capital Requirement, as provided for in paragraph 3.

2. The aggregated group eligible own funds are the sum of the following:

(a) the own funds eligible for the Solvency Capital Requirement of the participating insurance or reinsurance undertaking;

(b) the proportional share of the participating insurance or reinsurance undertaking in the own funds eligible for the Solvency Capital Requirement of the related insurance or reinsurance undertakings.

3. The aggregated group Solvency Capital Requirement is the sum of the following:

(a) the Solvency Capital Requirement of the participating insurance or reinsurance undertaking;

(b) the proportional share of the Solvency Capital Requirement of the related insurance or reinsurance undertakings.

4. Where the participation in the related insurance or reinsurance undertakings consists, wholly or in part, of an indirect ownership, the value in the participating insurance or reinsurance undertaking of the related insurance or reinsurance undertakings shall incorporate the value of such indirect ownership, taking into account the relevant successive interests, and the items referred to in paragraph 2(b) and paragraph 3(b) shall include the corresponding proportional shares, respectively, of the own funds eligible for the Solvency Capital Requirement of the related insurance or reinsurance undertakings and of the Solvency Capital Requirement of the related insurance or reinsurance undertakings.

5. In the case of an application for permission to calculate the Solvency Capital Requirement of insurance and reinsurance undertakings in the group on the basis of an internal model, submitted by an insurance or reinsurance undertaking and its related undertakings, or jointly by the related undertakings of an insurance holding company, Article 231 shall apply *mutatis mutandis*.

6. In determining whether the aggregated group Solvency Capital Requirement, calculated as set out in paragraph 3, appropriately reflects the risk profile of the group, the supervisory authorities concerned shall pay particular attention to any specific risks existing at group level which would not be sufficiently covered, because they are difficult to quantify.

Where the risk profile of the group deviates significantly from the assumptions underlying the aggregated group Solvency Capital Requirement, a capital add-on to the aggregated group Solvency Capital Requirement may be imposed.

Article 37(1) to (5), together with implementing measures taken in accordance with Article 37(6), shall apply mutatis mutandis.

[6387]
Article 234
Implementing measures

The Commission shall adopt implementing measures specifying the technical principles and methods set out in Articles 220 to 229 and the application of Articles 230 to 233 to ensure uniform application within the Community.

Those measures, designed to amend non-essential elements of this Directive by supplementing it, shall be adopted in accordance with the regulatory procedure with scrutiny referred to in Article 301(3).

SUBSECTION 5
SUPERVISION OF GROUP SOLVENCY FOR INSURANCE AND REINSURANCE UNDERTAKINGS THAT ARE SUBSIDIARIES OF AN INSURANCE HOLDING COMPANY

[6388]
Article 235
Group solvency of an insurance holding company

Where insurance and reinsurance undertakings are subsidiaries of an insurance holding company, the group supervisor shall ensure that the calculation of the solvency of the group is carried out at the level of the insurance holding company applying Article 220(2) to Article 233.

For the purpose of that calculation, the parent undertaking shall be treated as if it were an insurance or reinsurance undertaking subject to the rules laid down in Title I, Chapter VI, Section 4, Subsections 1, 2 and 3 as regards the Solvency Capital Requirement and subject to the same conditions as laid down in Title I, Chapter VI, Section 3, Subsections 1, 2 and 3 as regards the own funds eligible for the Solvency Capital Requirement.

SUBSECTION 6
SUPERVISION OF GROUP SOLVENCY FOR GROUPS WITH CENTRALISED RISK MANAGEMENT

[6389]
Article 236
Subsidiaries of an insurance or reinsurance undertaking: conditions

Member States shall provide that the rules laid down in Articles 238 and 239 shall apply to any insurance or reinsurance undertaking which is the subsidiary of an insurance or reinsurance undertaking where all of the following conditions are satisfied:

(a) the subsidiary, in relation to which the group supervisor has not made a decision under Article 214(2), is included in the group supervision carried out by the group supervisor at the level of the parent undertaking in accordance with this Title;

(b) the risk-management processes and internal control mechanisms of the parent undertaking cover the subsidiary and the parent undertaking satisfies the supervisory authorities concerned regarding the prudent management of the subsidiary;

(c) the parent undertaking has received the agreement referred to in the third subparagraph of Article 246(4);

(d) the parent undertaking has received the agreement referred to in Article 256(2);

(e) an application for permission to be subject to Articles 238 and 239 has been submitted by the parent undertaking and a favourable decision has been made on such application in accordance with the procedure set out in Article 237.

[6390]
Article 237
Subsidiaries of an insurance or reinsurance undertaking: decision on the application

1. In the case of applications for permission to be subject to the rules laid down in Articles 238 and 239, the supervisory authorities concerned shall work together within the college of supervisors, in full consultation, to decide whether or not to grant the permission sought and to determine the other terms and conditions, if any, to which such permission should be subject.

An application as referred to in the first subparagraph shall be submitted only to the supervisory authority having authorised the subsidiary. That supervisory authority shall inform and forward the complete application to the other supervisory authorities within the college of supervisors without delay.

2. The supervisory authorities concerned shall do everything within their power to reach a joint decision on the application within three months from the date of receipt of the complete application by all supervisory authorities within the college of supervisors.

3. During the period referred to in paragraph 2, in the case of diverging views concerning the approval of the application referred to in paragraph 1, the group supervisor or any of the other supervisory authorities concerned may consult CEIOPS. Where CEIOPS is being consulted, all supervisory authorities concerned shall be informed and the period referred to in paragraph 2 shall be extended by one month.

Where CEIOPS has been consulted, the supervisory authorities concerned shall duly consider such advice before taking their joint decision.

4. The supervisory authority having authorised the subsidiary shall provide to the applicant the joint decision referred to in paragraphs 2 and 3, shall state the full reasons and shall, where CEIOPS has been consulted, contain an explanation of any significant deviation from the position adopted by CEIOPS. The joint decision shall be recognised as determinative and shall be applied by the supervisory authorities concerned.

5. In the absence of a joint decision of the supervisory authorities concerned within the periods set out in paragraphs 2 and 3, the group supervisor shall take its own decision with regard to the application.

In taking its decision, the group supervisor shall duly consider the following:

(a) any views and reservations of the supervisory authorities concerned expressed during the applicable period;

(b) any reservations of the other supervisory authorities within the college of supervisors expressed during the applicable period;

(c) where CEIOPS has been consulted, its advice.

The decision shall state the full reasons and shall contain an explanation of any significant deviation from the reservations of the other supervisory authorities concerned and the advice of CEIOPS. The group supervisor shall provide the applicant and the other supervisory authorities concerned with a copy of the decision.

[6391]
Article 238
Subsidiaries of an insurance or reinsurance undertaking: determination of the Solvency Capital Requirement

1. Without prejudice to Article 231, the Solvency Capital Requirement of the subsidiary shall be calculated as set out in paragraphs 2, 4, and 5 of this Article.

2. Where the Solvency Capital Requirement of the subsidiary is calculated on the basis of an internal model approved at group level in accordance with Article 231 and the supervisory authority having authorised the subsidiary considers that its risk profile deviates significantly from this internal model, and as long as that undertaking does not properly address the concerns of the supervisory authority, that authority may, in the cases referred to in Article 37, propose to set a capital add-on to the Solvency Capital Requirement of that subsidiary resulting from the application of such model or, in exceptional circumstances where such capital add-on would not be appropriate, to require that undertaking to calculate its Solvency Capital Requirement on the basis of the standard formula. The supervisory authority shall discuss its proposal within the college of supervisors and communicate the grounds for such proposals to both the subsidiary and the college of supervisors.

3. Where the Solvency Capital Requirement of the subsidiary is calculated on the basis of the standard formula and the supervisory authority having authorised the subsidiary considers that its risk profile deviates significantly from the assumptions underlying the standard formula, and as long as that undertaking does not properly address the concerns of the supervisory authority, that authority may, in exceptional circumstances, propose that the undertaking replace a subset of the parameters used in the standard formula calculation by parameters specific to that undertaking when calculating the life, non-life and health underwriting risk modules, as set out in Article 110, or in the cases referred to in Article 37, to set a capital add-on to the Solvency Capital Requirement of that subsidiary.

The supervisory authority shall discuss its proposal within the college of supervisors and communicate the grounds for such proposal to both the subsidiary and the college of supervisors.

4. The college of supervisors shall do everything within its power to reach an agreement on the proposal of the supervisory authority having authorised the subsidiary or on other possible measures.

5. Where the supervisory authority and the group supervisor disagree, the matter shall, within one month from the proposal of the supervisory authority, be referred for consultation to CEIOPS, which shall give its advice within two months of such referral.

The supervisory authority having authorised that subsidiary shall duly consider such advice before taking its final decision.

The decision shall state the full reasons and shall take into account the views including reservations of the other supervisory authorities within the college of supervisors and the advice from CEIOPS.

The decision shall be submitted to the subsidiary and to the college of supervisors.

[6392]
Article 239
Subsidiaries of an insurance or reinsurance undertaking: non-compliance with the Solvency and Minimum Capital Requirements

1. In the event of non-compliance with the Solvency Capital Requirement and without prejudice to Article 138, the supervisory authority having authorised the subsidiary shall, without delay, forward to the college of supervisors the recovery plan submitted by the subsidiary in order to achieve, within six months from the observation of non-compliance with the Solvency Capital Requirement, the reestablishment of the level of eligible own funds or the reduction of its risk profile to ensure compliance with the Solvency Capital Requirement.

The college of supervisors shall do everything within its power to reach an agreement on the proposal of the supervisory authority regarding the approval of the recovery plan within four months from the date on which non-compliance with the Solvency Capital Requirement was first observed.

In the absence of such agreement, the supervisory authority having authorised the subsidiary shall decide whether the recovery plan should be approved, taking due account of the views and reservations of the other supervisory authorities within the college of supervisors.

2. Where the supervisory authority having authorised the subsidiary identifies, in accordance with Article 136, deteriorating financial conditions, it shall notify the college of supervisors without delay of the proposed measures to be taken. Save in emergency situations, the measures to be taken shall be discussed within the college of supervisors.

The college of supervisors shall do everything within its power to reach an agreement on the proposed measures to be taken within one month of notification.

In the absence of such agreement, the supervisory authority having authorised the subsidiary shall decide whether the proposed measures should be approved, taking due account of the views and reservations of the other supervisory authorities within the college of supervisors.

3. In the event of non-compliance with the Minimum Capital Requirement and without prejudice to Article 139, the supervisory authority having authorised the subsidiary shall, without delay, forward to the college of supervisors the short-term finance scheme submitted by the subsidiary in order to achieve, within three months from the date on which non-compliance with the Minimum Capital Requirement was first observed, the reestablishment of the level of eligible own funds covering the Minimum Capital Requirement or the reduction of its risk profile to ensure compliance with the Minimum Capital Requirement. The college of supervisors shall also be informed of any measures taken to enforce the Minimum Capital Requirement at the level of the subsidiary.

[6393]
Article 240
Subsidiaries of an insurance or reinsurance undertaking: end of derogations for a subsidiary

1. The rules provided for in Articles 238 and 239 shall cease to apply where:

(a) the condition referred to in Article 236(a) is no longer complied with;

(b) the condition referred to in Article 236(b) is no longer complied with and the group does not restore compliance with this condition in an appropriate period of time;

(c) the conditions referred to in Article 236(c) and (d) are no longer complied with.

In the case referred to in point (a) of the first subparagraph, where the group supervisor decides, after consulting the college of supervisors, no longer to include the subsidiary in the group supervision it carries out, it shall immediately inform the supervisory authority concerned and the parent undertaking.

For the purposes of Article 236(b), (c) and (d), the parent undertaking shall be responsible for ensuring that the conditions are complied with on an ongoing basis. In the event of non-compliance, it shall inform the group supervisor and the supervisor of the subsidiary concerned without delay. The parent undertaking shall present a plan to restore compliance within an appropriate period of time.

Without prejudice to the third subparagraph, the group supervisor shall verify at least annually, on its own initiative, that the conditions referred to in Article 236(b), (c) and (d) continue to be complied with. The group supervisor shall also perform such verification upon request from the supervisory authority concerned, where the latter has significant concerns related to the ongoing compliance with those conditions.

Where the verification performed identifies weaknesses, the group supervisor shall require the parent undertaking to present a plan to restore compliance within an appropriate period of time.

Where, after consulting the college of supervisors, the group supervisor determines that the plan referred to in the third or fifth subparagraph is insufficient or subsequently that it is not being implemented within the agreed period of time, the group supervisor shall conclude that the conditions referred to in Article 236(b), (c) and (d) are no longer complied with and it shall immediately inform the supervisory authority concerned.

2. The regime provided for in Articles 238 and 239 shall be applicable again where the parent undertaking submits a new application and obtains a favourable decision in accordance with the procedure set out in Article 237.

[6394]
Article 241
Subsidiaries of an insurance or reinsurance undertaking: implementing measures

In order to ensure the uniform application of Articles 236 to 240, the Commission shall adopt implementing measures specifying:

(a) the criteria to be applied when assessing whether the conditions stated in Article 236 are satisfied;

(b) the criteria to be applied when assessing what should be considered an emergency situation under Article 239(2); and

(c) the procedures to be followed by supervisory authorities when exchanging information, exercising their rights and fulfilling their duties in accordance with Articles 237 to 240.

Those measures, designed to amend non-essential elements of this Directive by supplementing it, shall be adopted in accordance with the regulatory procedure with scrutiny referred to in Article 301(3).

[6395]
Article 242
Review

1. By 31 October 2014, the Commission shall make an assessment of the application of Title III, in particular as regards the cooperation of supervisory authorities within, and functionality of, the college of supervisors, the legal status of CEIOPS, and the supervisory practices concerning setting the capital add-ons, and shall present a report to the European Parliament and the Council, accompanied, where appropriate, by proposals for the amendment of this Directive.

2. By 31 October 2015, the Commission shall make an assessment of the benefit of enhancing group supervision and capital management within a group of insurance or reinsurance undertakings including a reference to COM(2008)0119 and the report of the Committee on Economic and Monetary Affairs of the European Parliament on this proposal of 16 October 2008 (A6-0413/2008). That assessment shall include possible measures to enhance a sound cross-border management of insurance groups notably of risks and asset management. In its assessment, the Commission shall, *inter alia*, take into account new developments and progress concerning:

(a) a harmonised framework on early intervention;
(b) practices in centralised group risk management and functioning of group internal models including stress testing;
(c) intra-group transactions and risk concentrations;
(d) the behaviour of diversification and concentration effects over time;
(e) a legally binding framework for the mediation of supervisory disputes;
(f) a harmonised framework on asset transferability, insolvency and winding-up procedures which eliminates the relevant national company or corporate law barriers to asset transferability;
(g) an equivalent level of protection of policy holders and beneficiaries of the undertakings of the same group particularly in crisis situations;
(h) a harmonised and adequately funded EU-wide solution for insurance guarantee schemes;
(i) a harmonised and legally binding framework between competent authorities, central banks and ministries of finance concerning crisis management, resolution and fiscal burden-sharing which aligns supervisory powers with fiscal responsibilities.

The Commission shall present a report to the European Parliament and the Council, accompanied, where appropriate, by proposals for the amendment of this Directive.

[6396]
Article 243
Subsidiaries of an insurance holding company

Articles 236 to 242 shall apply *mutatis mutandis* to insurance and reinsurance undertakings which are the subsidiary of an insurance holding company.

SECTION 2
RISK CONCENTRATION AND INTRA-GROUP TRANSACTIONS

[6397]
Article 244
Supervision of risk concentration

1. Supervision of the risk concentration at group level shall be exercised in accordance with paragraphs 2 and 3 of this Article, Article 246 and Chapter III.

2. The Member States shall require insurance and reinsurance undertakings or insurance holding companies to report on a regular basis and at least annually to the group supervisor any significant risk concentration at the level of the group.

The necessary information shall be submitted to the group supervisor by the insurance or reinsurance undertaking which is at the head of the group or, where the group is not headed by a insurance or reinsurance undertaking, by the insurance holding company or by the insurance or reinsurance undertaking in the group identified by the group supervisor after consulting the other supervisory authorities concerned and the group.

The risk concentrations shall be subject to supervisory review by the group supervisor.

3. The group supervisor, after consulting the other supervisory authorities concerned and the group, shall identify the type of risks insurance and reinsurance undertakings in a particular group shall report in all circumstances.

When defining or giving their opinion about the type of risks, the group supervisor and the other supervisory authorities concerned shall take into account the specific group and risk-management structure of the group.

In order to identify significant risk concentration to be reported, the group supervisor, after consulting the other supervisory authorities concerned and the group, shall impose appropriate thresholds based on solvency capital requirements, technical provisions, or both.

When reviewing the risk concentrations, the group supervisor shall in particular monitor the possible risk of contagion in the group, the risk of a conflict of interests, and the level or volume of risks.

4. The Commission may adopt implementing measures, as regards the definition and identification of a significant risk concentration and the reporting on such a risk concentration, for the purposes of paragraphs 2 and 3.

Those measures, designed to amend non-essential elements of this Directive by supplementing it, shall be adopted in accordance with the regulatory procedure with scrutiny referred to in Article 301(3).

[6398]
Article 245
Supervision of intra-group transactions

1. Supervision of intra-group transactions shall be exercised in accordance with paragraphs 2 and 3 of this Article, Article 246 and Chapter III.

2. The Member States shall require insurance and reinsurance undertakings or insurance holding companies to report on a regular basis and at least annually to the group supervisor all significant intra-group transactions by insurance and reinsurance undertakings within a group, including those performed with a natural person with close links to an undertaking in the group.

In addition, Member States shall require reporting of very significant intra-group transactions as soon as practicable.

The necessary information shall be submitted to the group supervisor by the insurance or reinsurance undertaking which is at the head of the group or, where the group is not headed by an insurance or reinsurance undertaking, by the insurance holding company or by the insurance or reinsurance undertaking in the group identified by the group supervisor after consulting the other supervisory authorities concerned and the group.

The intra-group transactions shall be subject to supervisory review by the group supervisor.

3. The group supervisor, after consulting the other supervisory authorities concerned and the group, shall identify the type of intra-group transactions insurance and reinsurance undertakings in a particular group must report in all circumstances. Article 244(3) shall apply *mutatis mutandis*.

4. The Commission may adopt implementing measures, as regards the definition and identification of a significant intra-group transaction and the reporting on such an intra-group transaction, for the purposes of paragraphs 2 and 3.

Those measures, designed to amend non-essential elements of this Directive by supplementing it, shall be adopted in accordance with the regulatory procedure with scrutiny referred to in Article 301(3).

SECTION 3
RISK MANAGEMENT AND INTERNAL CONTROL

[6399]
Article 246
Supervision of the system of governance

1. The requirements set out in Title I, Chapter IV, Section 2 shall apply *mutatis mutandis* at the level of the group.

Without prejudice to the first subparagraph, the risk management and internal control systems and reporting procedures shall be implemented consistently in all the undertakings included in the scope of group supervision pursuant to Article 213(2)(a) and (b) so that those systems and reporting procedures can be controlled at the level of the group.

2. Without prejudice to paragraph 1, the group internal control mechanisms shall include at least the following:

(a) adequate mechanisms as regards group solvency to identify and measure all material risks incurred and to appropriately relate eligible own funds to risks;

(b) sound reporting and accounting procedures to monitor and manage the intra-group transactions and the risk concentration.

3. The systems and reporting procedures referred to in paragraphs 1 and 2 shall be subject to supervisory review by the group supervisor, in accordance with the rules laid down in Chapter III.

4. Member States shall require the participating insurance or reinsurance undertaking or the insurance holding company to undertake at the level of the group the assessment required by Article 45. The own-risk and solvency assessment conducted at group level shall be subject to supervisory review by the group supervisor in accordance with Chapter III.

Where the calculation of the solvency at the level of the group is carried out in accordance with method 1, as referred to in Article 230, the participating insurance or reinsurance undertaking or the insurance holding company shall provide to the group supervisor a proper understanding of the difference between the sum of the Solvency Capital Requirements of all the related insurance or reinsurance undertakings of the group and the group consolidated Solvency Capital Requirement.

Where the participating insurance or reinsurance undertaking or the insurance holding company so decides, and subject to the agreement of the group supervisor, it may undertake any assessments required by Article 45 at the level of the group and at the level of any subsidiary in the group at the same time, and may produce a single document covering all the assessments.

Before granting an agreement in accordance with the third subparagraph, the group supervisor shall consult the members of the college of supervisors and duly take into account their views or reservations.

Where the group exercises the option provided in the third subparagraph, it shall submit the document to all supervisory authorities concerned at the same time. The exercise of that option shall not exempt the subsidiaries concerned from the obligation to ensure that the requirements of Article 45 are met.

CHAPTER III
MEASURES TO FACILITATE GROUP SUPERVISION

[6400]
Article 247
Group Supervisor

1. A single supervisor, responsible for coordination and exercise of group supervision (group supervisor), shall be designated from among the supervisory authorities of the Member States concerned.

2. Where the same supervisory authority is competent for all insurance and reinsurance undertakings in a group, the task of group supervisor shall be exercised by that supervisory authority.

In all other cases and subject to paragraph 3, the task of group supervisor shall be exercised:

- (a) where a group is headed by an insurance or reinsurance undertaking, by the supervisory authority which has authorised that undertaking;
- (b) where a group is not headed by an insurance or reinsurance undertaking, by the supervisory authority identified in accordance with the following:
  - (i) where the parent of an insurance or reinsurance undertaking is an insurance holding company, by the supervisory authority which has authorised that insurance or reinsurance undertaking;
  - (ii) where more than one insurance or reinsurance undertaking with a head office in the Community have as their parent the same insurance holding company, and one of those undertakings has been authorised in the Member State in which the insurance holding company has its head office, by the supervisory authority of the insurance or reinsurance undertaking authorised in that Member State;
  - (iii) where the group is headed by more than one insurance holding company with a head office in different Member States and there is an insurance or reinsurance undertaking in each of those Member States, by the supervisory authority of the insurance or reinsurance undertaking with the largest balance sheet total;
  - (iv) where more than one insurance or reinsurance undertaking with a head office in the Community have as their parent the same insurance holding company and none of those undertakings has been authorised in the Member State in which the insurance holding company has its head office, by the supervisory authority which authorised the insurance or reinsurance undertaking with the largest balance sheet total; or
  - (v) where the group is a group without a parent undertaking, or in any circumstances not referred to in points (i) to (iv) by the supervisory authority which authorised the insurance or reinsurance undertaking with the largest balance sheet total.

3. In particular cases, the supervisory authorities concerned may, at the request of any of the authorities, take a joint decision to derogate from the criteria set out in paragraph 2 where their application would be inappropriate, taking into account the structure of the group and the relative importance of the insurance and reinsurance undertakings' activities in different countries, and designate a different supervisory authority as group supervisor.

For that purpose, any of the supervisory authorities concerned may request that a discussion be opened on whether the criteria referred to in paragraph 2 are appropriate. Such a discussion shall not take place more often than annually.

The supervisory authorities concerned shall do everything within their power to reach a joint decision on the choice of the group supervisor within three months from the request for discussion. Before taking their decision, the supervisory authorities concerned shall give the group an opportunity to state its opinion.

4. During the three-month period referred to in the third subparagraph of paragraph 3, any of the supervisory authorities concerned may request that CEIOPS be consulted. In the event that CEIOPS is consulted, that period shall be extended by two months.

5. In the event that CEIOPS is consulted, the supervisory authorities concerned shall duly take into account the advice of CEIOPS before taking their joint decision. The joint decision shall state the full reasons and shall contain an explanation of any significant deviation from any advice given by CEIOPS.

6. In the absence of a joint decision derogating from the criteria set out in paragraph 2, the task of group supervisor shall be exercised by the supervisory authority identified in accordance with paragraph 2.

7. CEIOPS shall inform the European Parliament, the Council and the Commission, at least annually, of any major difficulties with the application of paragraphs 2, 3 and 6.

In the event that any major difficulties arise from the application of the criteria set out in paragraphs 2 and 3, the Commission shall adopt implementing measures specifying those criteria.

Those measures, designed to amend non-essential elements of this Directive by supplementing it, shall be adopted in accordance with the regulatory procedure with scrutiny referred to in Article 301(3).

8. Where a Member State has more than one supervisory authority for the prudential supervision of insurance and reinsurance undertakings, such Member State shall take the necessary measures to ensure coordination between those authorities.

[6401]
Article 248
Rights and duties of the group supervisor and the other supervisors College of supervisors

1. The rights and duties assigned to the group supervisor with regard to group supervision shall comprise the following:

(a) coordination of the gathering and dissemination of relevant or essential information for going concern and emergency situations, including the dissemination of information which is of importance for the supervisory task of a supervisory authority;

(b) supervisory review and assessment of the financial situation of the group;

(c) assessment of compliance of the group with the rules on solvency and of risk concentration and intra-group transactions as set out in Articles 218 to 245;

(d) assessment of the system of governance of the group, as set out in Article 246, and of whether the members of the administrative, management or supervisory body of the participating undertaking fulfil the requirements set out in Articles 42 and 257;

(e) planning and coordination, through regular meetings held at least annually or through other appropriate means, of supervisory activities in going-concern as well as in emergency situations, in cooperation with the supervisory authorities concerned and taking into account the nature, scale and complexity of the risks inherent in the business of all undertakings that are part of the group;

(f) other tasks, measures and decisions assigned to the group supervisor by this Directive or deriving from the application of this Directive, in particular leading the process for validation of any internal model at group level as set out in Articles 231 and 233 and leading the process for permitting the application of the regime established in Articles 237 to 240.

2. In order to facilitate the exercise of the group supervision tasks referred to in paragraph 1, a college of supervisors, chaired by the group supervisor, shall be established.

The college of supervisors shall ensure that cooperation, exchange of information and consultation processes among the supervisory authorities that are members of the college of supervisors, are effectively applied in accordance with Title III, with a view to promoting the convergence of their respective decisions and activities.

3. The membership of the college of supervisors shall include the group supervisor and supervisory authorities of all the Member States in which the head office of all subsidiary undertakings is situated.

The supervisory authorities of significant branches and related undertakings shall also be allowed to participate in the college of supervisors. However, their participation shall be limited to achieving the objective of an efficient exchange of information.

The effective functioning of the college of supervisors may require that some activities be carried out by a reduced number of supervisory authorities therein.

4. Without prejudice to any measure adopted pursuant to this Directive, the establishment and functioning of the college of supervisors shall be based on coordination arrangements concluded by the group supervisor and the other supervisory authorities concerned.

In the event of diverging views concerning the coordination arrangements, any member of the college of supervisors may refer the matter to CEIOPS.

After consulting the supervisory authorities concerned, the group supervisor shall duly consider any advice produced by CEIOPS within two months of receipt thereof before taking its final decision. The decision shall state the full reasons and shall contain an explanation of any significant deviation from any advice given by CEIOPS. The group supervisor shall transmit the decision to the other supervisory authorities concerned.

5. Without prejudice to any measure adopted pursuant to this Directive, the coordination arrangements referred to in paragraph 4 shall specify the procedures for:

(a) the decision-making process among the supervisory authorities concerned in accordance with Articles 231, 232 and 247;

(b) consultation under paragraph 4 of this Article and under Article 218(5).

Without prejudice to the rights and duties allocated by this Directive to the group supervisor and to other supervisory authorities, the coordination arrangements may entrust additional tasks to the group supervisor or the other supervisory authorities where this would result in the more efficient supervision of the group and would not impair the supervisory activities of the members of the college of supervisors in respect of their individual responsibilities.

In addition, the coordination arrangements may set out procedures for:

(a) consultation among the supervisory authorities concerned, in particular as referred to in Articles 213 to 217, 219 to 221, 227, 244 to 246, 250, 256, 260 and 262;

(b) cooperation with other supervisory authorities.

6. CEIOPS shall elaborate guidelines for the operational functioning of colleges of supervisors on the basis of comprehensive reviews of their work in order to assess the level of convergence between them. Such reviews shall be carried out at least every three years. Member States shall ensure that the group supervisor transmits to CEIOPS the information on the functioning of the colleges of supervisors and on any difficulties encountered that are relevant for those reviews.

7. The Commission shall adopt implementing measures for the coordination of group supervision for the purposes of paragraphs 1 to 6, including the definition of 'significant branch'.

Those measures, designed to amend non-essential elements of this Directive by supplementing it, shall be adopted in accordance with the regulatory procedure with scrutiny referred to in Article 301(3).

[6402]
Article 249
Cooperation and exchange of information between supervisory authorities

1. The authorities responsible for the supervision of the individual insurance and reinsurance undertakings in a group and the group supervisor shall cooperate closely, in particular in cases where an insurance or reinsurance undertaking encounters financial difficulties.

With the objective of ensuring that the supervisory authorities, including the group supervisor, have the same amount of relevant information available to them, without prejudice to their respective responsibilities, and irrespective of whether they are established in the same Member State, they shall provide one another with such information in order to allow and facilitate the exercise of the supervisory tasks of the other authorities under this Directive. In that regard, the supervisory authorities concerned and the group supervisor shall communicate to one another without delay all relevant information as soon as it becomes available. The information referred to in this subparagraph includes, but is not limited to, information about actions of the group and supervisory authorities, and information provided by the group.

2. The authorities responsible for the supervision of the individual insurance and reinsurance undertakings in a group and the group supervisor shall each call immediately for a meeting of all supervisory authorities involved in group supervision in at least the following circumstances:

(a) where they become aware of a significant breach of the Solvency Capital Requirement or a breach of the Minimum Capital Requirement of an individual insurance or reinsurance undertaking;

(b) where they become aware of a significant breach of the Solvency Capital Requirement at group level calculated on the basis of consolidated data or the aggregated group Solvency Capital Requirement, in accordance with whichever calculation method is used in accordance with Title III, Chapter II, Section 1, Subsection 4;

(c) where other exceptional circumstances are occurring or have occurred.

3. The Commission shall adopt implementing measures determining the items which are, on a systematic basis, to be gathered by the group supervisor and disseminated to other supervisory authorities concerned or to be transmitted to the group supervisor by the other supervisory authorities concerned.

The Commission shall adopt implementing measures specifying the items essential or relevant for supervision at group level with a view to enhancing convergence of supervisory reporting.

The measures referred to in this paragraph, designed to amend non-essential elements of this Directive by supplementing it, shall be adopted in accordance with the regulatory procedure with scrutiny referred to in Article 301(3).

[6403]
Article 250
Consultation between supervisory authorities

1. Without prejudice to Article 248, the supervisory authorities concerned shall, where a decision is of importance for the supervisory tasks of other supervisory authorities, prior to that decision, consult each other in the college of supervisors with regard to the following:

(a) changes in the shareholder structure, organisational or management structure of insurance and reinsurance undertakings in a group, which require the approval or authorisation of supervisory authorities; and

(b) major sanctions or exceptional measures taken by supervisory authorities, including the imposition of a capital add-on to the Solvency Capital Requirement under Article 37 and the imposition of any limitation on the use of an internal model for the calculation of the Solvency Capital Requirement under Title I, Chapter VI, Section 4, Subsection 3.

For the purposes of point (b), the group supervisor shall always be consulted.

In addition, the supervisory authorities concerned shall, where a decision is based on information received from other supervisory authorities, consult each other prior to that decision.

2. Without prejudice to Article 248, a supervisory authority may decide not to consult in cases of urgency or where such consultation may jeopardise the effectiveness of the decision. In that case, the supervisory authority shall, without delay, inform the other supervisory authorities concerned.

[6404]
Article 251
Requests from the group supervisor to other supervisory authorities

The group supervisor may invite the supervisory authorities of the Member State in which a parent undertaking has its head office, and which do not themselves exercise the group supervision pursuant to Article 247, to request from the parent undertaking any information which would be relevant for the exercise of its coordination rights and duties as laid down in Article 248, and to transmit that information to the group supervisor.

The group supervisor shall, when it needs information referred to in Article 254(2) which has already been given to another supervisory authority, contact that authority whenever possible in order to prevent duplication of reporting to the various authorities involved in supervision.

[6405]
Article 252
Cooperation with authorities responsible for credit institutions and investment firms

Where an insurance or reinsurance undertaking and either a credit institution as defined in Directive 2006/48/EC or an investment firm as defined in Directive 2004/39/EC, or both, are directly or indirectly related or have a common participating undertaking, the supervisory authorities concerned and the authorities responsible for the supervision of those other undertakings shall cooperate closely.

Without prejudice to their respective responsibilities, those authorities shall provide one another with any information likely to simplify their task, in particular as set out in this Title.

[6406]
Article 253
Professional secrecy and confidentiality

Member States shall authorise the exchange of information between their supervisory authorities and between their supervisory authorities and other authorities, as referred to in Articles 249 to 252.

Information received in the framework of group supervision, and in particular any exchange of information between supervisory authorities and between supervisory authorities and other authorities which is provided for in this Title, shall be subject to the provisions of Article 295.

[6407]
Article 254
Access to information

1. Member States shall ensure that the natural and legal persons included within the scope of group supervision, and their related undertakings and participating undertakings, are able to exchange any information which could be relevant for the purposes of group supervision.

2. Member States shall provide that their authorities responsible for exercising group supervision shall have access to any information relevant for the purposes of that supervision regardless of the nature of the undertaking concerned. Article 35 shall apply *mutatis mutandis*.

The supervisory authorities concerned may address the undertakings in the group directly to obtain the necessary information, only where such information has been requested from the insurance undertaking or reinsurance undertaking subject to group supervision and has not been supplied by it within a reasonable period of time.

[6408]
Article 255
Verification of information

1. Member States shall ensure that their supervisory authorities may carry out within their territory, either directly or through the intermediary of persons whom they appoint for that purpose, on-site verification of the information referred to in Article 254 on the premises of any of the following:

(a) the insurance or reinsurance undertaking subject to group supervision;
(b) related undertakings of that insurance or reinsurance undertaking;
(c) parent undertakings of that insurance or reinsurance undertaking;
(d) related undertakings of a parent undertaking of that insurance or reinsurance undertaking.

2. Where supervisory authorities wish in specific cases to verify the information concerning an undertaking, whether regulated or not, which is part of a group and is situated in another Member State, they shall ask the supervisory authorities of that other Member State to have the verification carried out.

The authorities which receive such a request shall, within the framework of their competences, act upon that request either by carrying out the verification directly, by allowing an auditor or expert to carry it out, or by allowing the authority which made the request to carry it out itself. The group supervisor shall be informed of the action taken.

The supervisory authority which made the request may, where it so wishes, participate in the verification when it does not carry out the verification directly.

[6409]
Article 256
Group solvency and financial condition report

1. Member States shall require participating insurance and reinsurance undertakings or insurance holding companies to disclose publicly, on an annual basis, a report on the solvency and financial condition at the level of the group. Articles 51 and 53 to 55 shall apply *mutatis mutandis*.

2. Where a participating insurance or reinsurance undertaking or an insurance holding company so decides, and subject to the agreement of the group supervisor, it may provide a single solvency and financial condition report which shall comprise the following:

(a) the information at the level of the group which must be disclosed in accordance with paragraph 1;
(b) the information for any of the subsidiaries within the group which must be individually identifiable and disclosed in accordance with Articles 51 and 53 to 55.

Before granting the agreement in accordance with the first subparagraph, the group supervisor shall consult and duly take into account any views and reservations of the members of the college of supervisors.

3. Where the report referred to in paragraph 2 fails to include information which the supervisory authority having authorised a subsidiary within the group requires comparable undertakings to provide, and where the omission is material, the supervisory authority concerned shall have the power to require the subsidiary concerned to disclose the necessary additional information.

4. The Commission shall adopt implementing measures further specifying the information which must be disclosed and the means by which this is to be achieved as regards the single solvency and financial condition report.

Those measures, designed to amend non-essential elements of this Directive by supplementing it, shall be adopted in accordance with the regulatory procedure with scrutiny referred to in Article 301(3).

[6410]
Article 257
Administrative, management or supervisory body of insurance holding companies

Member States shall require that all persons who effectively run the insurance holding company are fit and proper to perform their duties.

Article 42 shall apply mutatis mutandis.

[6411]
Article 258
Enforcement measures

1. Where the insurance or reinsurance undertakings in a group do not comply with the requirements referred to in Articles 218 to 246 or where the requirements are met but solvency may nevertheless be jeopardised or where the intra-group transactions or the risk concentrations are a threat to the financial position of the insurance or reinsurance undertakings, the following shall require the necessary measures in order to rectify the situation as soon as possible:

(a) the group supervisor with respect to the insurance holding company;

(b) the supervisory authorities with respect to the insurance and reinsurance undertakings.

Where, in the case referred to in point (a) of the first subparagraph, the group supervisor is not one of the supervisory authorities of the Member State in which the insurance holding company has its head office, the group supervisor shall inform those supervisory authorities of its findings with a view to enabling them to take the necessary measures.

Where, in the case referred to in point (b) of the first subparagraph, the group supervisor is not one of the supervisory authorities of the Member State in which the insurance or reinsurance undertaking has its head office, the group supervisor shall inform those supervisory authorities of its findings with a view to enabling them to take the necessary measures.

Without prejudice to paragraph 2, Member States shall determine the measures which may be taken by their supervisory authorities with respect to insurance holding companies.

The supervisory authorities concerned, including the group supervisor, shall where appropriate coordinate their enforcement measures.

2. Without prejudice to their criminal law provisions, Member States shall ensure that sanctions or measures may be imposed on insurance holding companies which infringe laws, regulations or administrative provisions enacted to implement this Title, or on the person effectively managing those companies. The supervisory authorities shall cooperate closely to ensure that such sanctions or measures are effective, especially when the central administration or main establishment of an insurance holding company is not located at its head office.

3. The Commission may adopt implementing measures for the coordination of enforcement measures referred to in paragraphs 1 and 2.

Those measures, designed to amend non-essential elements of this Directive by supplementing it, shall be adopted in accordance with the regulatory procedure with scrutiny referred to in Article 301(3).

[6412]
Article 259
Reporting of CEIOPS

1. CEIOPS shall attend the European Parliament annually for a general parliamentary committee hearing. Where such attendance coincides with the reporting requirement of CEIOPS under Article 71(3), that requirement shall be met, as regards the European Parliament, by the attendance of CEIOPS at that hearing.

2. At the hearing referred to in paragraph 1, CEIOPS shall report, *inter alia*, on all relevant and significant experiences of the supervisory activities and cooperation between supervisors in the framework of Title III, and, in particular:

(a) the process of the nomination of the group supervisor, the number of group supervisors and geographical spread;
(b) the working of the college of supervisors, in particular the involvement and commitment of supervisory authorities where they are not the group supervisor.

3. CEIOPS may, for the purposes of paragraph 1, also report on the main lessons drawn from the reviews referred to in Article 248(6), where appropriate.

CHAPTER IV
THIRD COUNTRIES

[6413]
Article 260
Parent undertakings outside the Community: verification of equivalence

1. In the case referred to in Article 213(2)(c), the supervisory authorities concerned shall verify whether the insurance and reinsurance undertakings, the parent undertaking of which has its head office outside the Community, are subject to supervision, by a third-country supervisory authority, which is equivalent to that provided for by this Title on the supervision at the level of the group of insurance and reinsurance undertakings referred to in Article 213(2)(a) and (b).

The verification shall be carried out by the supervisory authority which would be the group supervisor if the criteria set out in Article 247(2) were to apply, at the request of the parent undertaking or of any of the insurance and reinsurance undertakings authorised in the Community or on its own initiative, unless the Commission had concluded previously in respect of the equivalence of the third country concerned. In so doing, that supervisory authority shall consult the other supervisory authorities concerned and CEIOPS, before taking a decision.

2. The Commission may adopt implementing measures specifying the criteria to assess whether the prudential regime in a third country for the supervision of groups is equivalent to that laid down in this Title. Those measures, designed to amend non-essential elements of this Directive by supplementing it, shall be adopted in accordance with the regulatory procedure with scrutiny referred to in Article 301(3).

3. The Commission may adopt, after consultation of the European Insurance and Occupational Pensions Committee and in accordance with the regulatory procedure referred to in Article 301(2), and taking into account the criteria adopted in accordance with paragraph 2, a decision as to whether the prudential regime for the supervision of groups in a third country is equivalent to that laid down in this Title.

Those decisions shall be regularly reviewed to take into account any changes to the prudential regime for the supervision of groups laid down in this Title and to the prudential regime in the third country for the supervision of groups and to any other change in regulation that may affect the decision on equivalence.

When a decision has been adopted by the Commission, in accordance with the first subparagraph, in respect of a third country, that decision shall be recognised as determinative for the purposes of the verification referred to in paragraph 1.

[6414]
Article 261
Parent undertakings outside the Community: equivalence

1. In the event of equivalent supervision referred to in Article 260, Member States shall rely on the equivalent group supervision exercised by the third-country supervisory authorities, in accordance with paragraph 2.

2. Articles 247 to 258 shall apply *mutatis mutandis* to the cooperation with third-country supervisory authorities.

[6415]
Article 262
Parent undertakings outside the Community: absence of equivalence

1. In the absence of equivalent supervision referred to in Article 260, Member States shall apply to the insurance and reinsurance undertakings either Articles 218 to 258, *mutatis mutandis* and with the exception of Articles 236 to 243, or one of the methods set out in paragraph 2.

The general principles and methods set out in Articles 218 to 258 shall apply at the level of the insurance holding company, third-country insurance undertaking or third-country reinsurance undertaking.

For the sole purpose of the group solvency calculation, the parent undertaking shall be treated as if it were an insurance or reinsurance undertaking subject to the same conditions as laid down in

Title I, Chapter VI, Section 3, Subsections 1, 2 and 3 as regards the own funds eligible for the Solvency Capital Requirement and to either of the following:

(a) a Solvency Capital Requirement determined in accordance with the principles of Article 226 where it is an insurance holding company;

(b) a Solvency Capital Requirement determined in accordance with the principles of Article 227, where it is a third-country insurance undertaking or a third-country reinsurance undertaking.

2. Member States shall allow their supervisory authorities to apply other methods which ensure appropriate supervision of the insurance and reinsurance undertakings in a group. Those methods must be agreed by the group supervisor, after consulting the other supervisory authorities concerned.

The supervisory authorities may in particular require the establishment of an insurance holding company which has its head office in the Community, and apply this Title to the insurance and reinsurance undertakings in the group headed by that insurance holding company.

The methods chosen shall allow the objectives of the group supervision as defined in this Title to be achieved and shall be notified to the other supervisory authorities concerned and the Commission.

[6416]
Article 263
Parent undertakings outside the Community: levels

Where the parent undertaking referred to in Article 260 is itself a subsidiary of an insurance holding company having its head office outside the Community or of a third-country insurance or reinsurance undertaking, Member States shall apply the verification provided for in Article 260 only at the level of the ultimate parent undertaking which is a third-country insurance holding company, a third-country insurance undertaking or a third-country reinsurance undertaking.

However, Member States shall allow their supervisory authorities to decide, in the absence of equivalent supervision referred to in Article 260, to carry out a new verification at a lower level where a parent undertaking of insurance or reinsurance undertakings exists, whether a third-country insurance holding company, a third-country insurance undertaking or a third-country reinsurance undertaking.

In such a case, the supervisory authority referred to in the second subparagraph of Article 260(1) shall explain its decision to the group.

Article 262 shall apply mutatis mutandis.

[6417]
Article 264
Cooperation with third-country supervisory authorities

1. The Commission may submit proposals to the Council for the negotiation of agreements with one or more third countries regarding the means of exercising group supervision over:

(a) insurance or reinsurance undertakings which have, as participating undertakings, undertakings within the meaning of Article 213 which have their head office situated in a third country; and

(b) third-country insurance undertakings or third-country reinsurance undertakings which have, as participating undertakings, undertakings within the meaning of Article 213 which have their head office in the Community.

2. The agreements referred to in paragraph 1 shall, in particular, seek to ensure that:

(a) the supervisory authorities of the Member States are able to obtain the information necessary for the supervision at the level of the group of insurance and reinsurance undertakings which have their head office in the Community and which have subsidiaries or hold participations in undertakings outside the Community; and

(b) the supervisory authorities of third countries are able to obtain the information necessary for the supervision at the level of the group of third-country insurance and reinsurance undertakings which have their head office in their territories and which have subsidiaries or hold participations in undertakings in one or more Member States.

3. Without prejudice to Article 300(1) and (2) of the Treaty, the Commission shall, with the assistance of the European Insurance and Occupational Pensions Committee, examine the outcome of the negotiations referred to in paragraph 1.

CHAPTER V
MIXED-ACTIVITY INSURANCE HOLDING COMPANIES

[6418]
Article 265
Intra-group transactions

1. Member States shall ensure that, where the parent undertaking of one or more insurance or reinsurance undertakings is a mixed-activity insurance holding company, the supervisory authorities responsible for the supervision of those insurance or reinsurance undertakings exercise general supervision over transactions between those insurance or reinsurance undertakings and the mixed-activity holding company and its related undertakings.

2. Articles 245, 249 to 255 and 258 shall apply *mutatis mutandis*.

[6419]
Article 266
Cooperation with third countries

As concerns cooperation with third countries, Article 264 shall apply *mutatis mutandis*.

TITLE IV
REORGANISATION AND WINDING-UP OF INSURANCE UNDERTAKINGS

CHAPTER I
SCOPE AND DEFINITIONS

[6420]
Article 267
Scope of this Title

This Title shall apply to reorganisation measures and winding-up proceedings concerning the following:

(a) insurance undertakings;

(b) branches situated in the territory of the Community of third-country insurance undertakings.

[6421]
Article 268
Definitions

1. For the purpose of this Title the following definitions shall apply:

(a) 'competent authorities' means the administrative or judicial authorities of the Member States which are competent for the purposes of the reorganisation measures or the winding-up proceedings;

(b) 'branch' means a permanent presence of an insurance undertaking in the territory of a Member State other than the home Member State which pursues insurance activities;

(c) 'reorganisation measures' means measures involving any intervention by the competent authorities which are intended to preserve or restore the financial situation of an insurance undertaking and which affect pre-existing rights of parties other than the insurance undertaking itself, including but not limited to measures involving the possibility of a suspension of payments, suspension of enforcement measures or reduction of claims;

(d) 'winding-up proceedings' means collective proceedings involving the realisation of the assets of an insurance undertaking and the distribution of the proceeds among the creditors, shareholders or members as appropriate, which necessarily involve any intervention by the competent authorities, including where the collective proceedings are terminated by a composition or other analogous measure, whether or not they are founded on insolvency or are voluntary or compulsory;

(e) 'administrator' means a person or body appointed by the competent authorities for the purpose of administering reorganisation measures;

(f) 'liquidator' means a person or body appointed by the competent authorities or by the governing bodies of an insurance undertaking for the purpose of administering winding-up proceedings;

(g) 'insurance claim' means an amount which is owed by an insurance undertaking to insured persons, policy holders, beneficiaries or to any injured party having direct right of action against the insurance undertaking and which arises from an insurance contract or from any operation provided for in Article 2(3)(b) and (c) in direct insurance business, including an amount set aside for those persons, when some elements of the debt are not yet known.

The premium owed by an insurance undertaking as a result of the non-conclusion or cancellation of an insurance contract or operation referred to in point (g) of the first subparagraph in accordance with the law applicable to such a contract or operation before the opening of the winding-up proceedings shall also be considered an insurance claim.

2. For the purpose of applying this Title to reorganisation measures and winding-up proceedings concerning a branch situated in a Member State of a third-country insurance undertaking the following definitions shall apply:

(a) 'home Member State' means the Member State in which the branch was granted authorisation in accordance with Articles 145 to 149;
(b) 'supervisory authorities' means the supervisory authorities of the home Member State;
(c) 'competent authorities' means the competent authorities of the home Member State.

CHAPTER II
REORGANISATION MEASURES

[6422]
Article 269
Adoption of reorganisation measures applicable law

1. Only the competent authorities of the home Member State shall be entitled to decide on the reorganisation measures with respect to an insurance undertaking, including its branches.

2. The reorganisation measures shall not preclude the opening of winding-up proceedings by the home Member State.

3. The reorganisation measures shall be governed by the laws, regulations and procedures applicable in the home Member State, unless otherwise provided in Articles 285 to 292.

4. Reorganisation measures taken in accordance with the legislation of the home Member State shall be fully effective throughout the Community without any further formalities, including against third parties in other Member States, even where the legislation of those other Member States does not provide for such reorganisation measures or alternatively makes their implementation subject to conditions which are not fulfilled.

5. The reorganisation measures shall be effective throughout the Community once they become effective in the home Member State.

[6423]
Article 270
Information to the supervisory authorities

The competent authorities of the home Member State shall inform as a matter or urgency the supervisory authorities of that Member State of their decision on any reorganisation measure, where possible before the adoption of such a measure and failing that immediately thereafter.

The supervisory authorities of the home Member State shall inform as a matter of urgency the supervisory authorities of all other Member States of the decision to adopt reorganisation measures including the possible practical effects of such measures.

[6424]
Article 271
Publication of decisions on reorganisation measures

1. Where an appeal is possible in the home Member State against a reorganisation measure, the competent authorities of the home Member State, the administrator or any person entitled to do so in the home Member State shall make public the decision on a reorganisation measure in accordance with the publication procedures provided for in the home Member State and, furthermore, publish in the *Official Journal of the European Union* at the earliest opportunity an extract from the document establishing the reorganisation measure.

The supervisory authorities of the other Member States which have been informed of the decision on a reorganisation measure pursuant to Article 270 may ensure the publication of such decision within their territory in the manner they consider appropriate.

2. The publications provided for in paragraph 1 shall specify the competent authority of the home Member State, the applicable law as provided in Article 269(3) and the administrator appointed, if any. They shall be made in the official language or in one of the official languages of the Member State in which the information is published.

3. The reorganisation measures shall apply regardless of the provisions concerning publication set out in paragraphs 1 and 2 and shall be fully effective as against creditors, unless the competent authorities of the home Member State or the law of that Member State provide otherwise.

4. Where reorganisation measures affect exclusively the rights of shareholders, members or employees of an insurance undertaking, considered in those capacities, paragraphs 1, 2 and 3 shall not apply unless the law applicable to the reorganisation measures provides otherwise.

The competent authorities shall determine the manner in which the parties referred to in the first subparagraph are to be informed in accordance with the applicable law.

[6425]
Article 272
Information to known creditors right to lodge claims

1. Where the law of the home Member State requires a claim to be lodged in order for it to be recognised or provides for compulsory notification of a reorganisation measure to creditors whose habitual residence, domicile or head office is situated in that Member State, the competent authorities of the home Member State or the administrator shall also inform known creditors whose habitual residence, domicile or head office is situated in another Member State, in accordance with Article 281 and Article 283(1).

2. Where the law of the home Member State provides for the right of creditors whose habitual residence, domicile or head office is situated in that Member State to lodge claims or to submit observations concerning their claims, creditors whose habitual residence, domicile or head office is situated in another Member State shall have the same right in accordance with Article 282 and Article 283(2).

CHAPTER III
WINDING-UP PROCEEDINGS

[6426]
Article 273
Opening of winding-up proceedings information to the supervisory authorities

1. Only the competent authorities of the home Member State shall be entitled to take a decision concerning the opening of winding-up proceedings with regard to an insurance undertaking, including its branches in other Member States. This decision may be taken in the absence, or following the adoption, of reorganisation measures.

2. A decision concerning the opening of winding-up proceedings of an insurance undertaking, including its branches in other Member States, adopted in accordance with the legislation of the home Member State shall be recognised without further formality throughout the Community and shall be effective there as soon as the decision is effective in the Member State in which the proceedings are opened.

3. The competent authorities of the home Member State shall inform as a matter of urgency the supervisory authorities of that Member State of the decision to open winding-up proceedings, where possible before the proceedings are opened and failing that immediately thereafter.

The supervisory authorities of the home Member State shall inform as a matter of urgency the supervisory authorities of all other Member States of the decision to open winding-up proceedings including the possible practical effects of such proceedings.

[6427]
Article 274
Applicable law

1. The decision to open winding-up proceedings with regard to an insurance undertaking, the winding-up proceedings and their effects shall be governed by the law applicable in the home Member State unless otherwise provided in Articles 285 to 292.

2. The law of the home Member State shall determine at least the following:

(a) the assets which form part of the estate and the treatment of assets acquired by, or devolving to, the insurance undertaking after the opening of the winding-up proceedings;

(b) the respective powers of the insurance undertaking and the liquidator;

(c) the conditions under which set-off may be invoked;

(d) the effects of the winding-up proceedings on current contracts to which the insurance undertaking is party;

(e) the effects of the winding-up proceedings on proceedings brought by individual creditors, with the exception of lawsuits pending referred to in Article 292;

(f) the claims which are to be lodged against the estate of the insurance undertaking and the treatment of claims arising after the opening of winding-up proceedings;
(g) the rules governing the lodging, verification and admission of claims;
(h) the rules governing the distribution of proceeds from the realisation of assets, the ranking of claims, and the rights of creditors who have obtained partial satisfaction after the opening of winding-up proceedings by virtue of a right in rem or through a set-off;
(i) the conditions for and the effects of closure of winding-up proceedings, in particular by composition;
(j) rights of the creditors after the closure of winding-up proceedings;
(k) the party who is to bear the cost and expenses incurred in the winding-up proceedings; and
(l) the rules relating to the nullity, voidability or unenforceability of legal acts detrimental to all the creditors.

[6428]
Article 275
Treatment of insurance claims

1. Member States shall ensure that insurance claims take precedence over other claims against the insurance undertaking in one or both of the following ways:
(a) with regard to assets representing the technical provisions, insurance claims shall take absolute precedence over any other claim on the insurance undertaking; or
(b) with regard to the whole of the assets of the insurance undertaking, insurance claims shall take precedence over any other claim on the insurance undertaking with the only possible exception of the following:
(i) claims by employees arising from employment contracts and employment relationships;
(ii) claims by public bodies on taxes;
(iii) claims by social security systems;
(iv) claims on assets subject to rights in rem.

2. Without prejudice to paragraph 1, Member States may provide that the whole or part of the expenses arising from the winding-up procedure, as determined by their national law, shall take precedence over insurance claims.

3. Member States which have chosen the option provided for in paragraph 1(a) shall require insurance undertakings to establish and keep up to date a special register in accordance with Article 276.

[6429]
Article 276
Special register

1. Every insurance undertaking shall keep at its head office a special register of the assets used to cover the technical provisions calculated and invested in accordance with the law of the home Member State.

2. Where an insurance undertaking carries on both life and non-life insurance activities, it shall keep at its head office separate registers for each type of business.

However, where a Member State authorises insurance undertakings to cover life and the risks listed in classes 1 and 2 of Part A of Annex I, it may provide that those insurance undertakings must keep a single register for the whole of their activities.

3. The total value of the assets entered, valued in accordance with the law applicable in the home Member State, shall at no time be less than the value of the technical provisions.

4. Where an asset entered in the register is subject to a right in rem in favour of a creditor or a third party, with the result that part of the value of the asset is not available for the purpose of covering commitments, that fact shall be recorded in the register and the amount not available shall not be included in the total value referred to in paragraph 3.

5. The treatment of an asset in the case of the winding-up of the insurance undertaking with respect to the option provided for in Article 275(1)(a) shall be determined by the legislation of the home Member State, except where Articles 286, 287 or 288 apply to that asset where:
(a) the asset used to cover technical provisions is subject to a right in rem in favour of a creditor or a third party, without meeting the conditions set out in paragraph 4;
(b) such an asset is subject to a reservation of title in favour of a creditor or of a third party; or

(c) a creditor has a right to demand the set-off of his claim against the claim of the insurance undertaking.

6. Once winding-up proceedings have been opened, the composition of the assets entered in the register in accordance with paragraphs 1 to 5 shall not be changed and no alteration other than the correction of purely clerical errors shall be made in the registers, except with the authorisation of the competent authority.

However, the liquidators shall add to those assets the yield therefrom and the value of the pure premiums received in respect of the class of insurance concerned between the opening of the winding-up proceedings and the time of payment of the insurance claims or until any transfer of portfolio is effected.

7. Where the product of the realisation of assets is less than their estimated value in the registers, the liquidators shall justify this to the supervisory authorities of the home Member States.

[6430]
Article 277
Subrogation to a guarantee scheme

The home Member State may provide that, where the rights of insurance creditors have been subrogated to a guarantee scheme established in that Member State, claims by that scheme shall not benefit from the provisions of Article 275(1).

[6431]
Article 278
Representation of preferential claims by assets

Member States which choose the option set out in Article 275(1)(b) shall require every insurance undertaking to ensure that the claims which may take precedence over insurance claims pursuant to Article 275(1)(b) and which are registered in the insurance undertaking's accounts are represented, at any moment and independently of a possible winding-up, by assets.

[6432]
Article 279
Withdrawal of the authorisation

1. Where the opening of winding-up proceedings is decided in respect of an insurance undertaking, the authorisation of that undertaking shall be withdrawn in accordance with the procedure laid down in Article 144, except to the extent necessary for the purposes of paragraph 2.

2. The withdrawal of authorisation pursuant to paragraph 1 shall not prevent the liquidator or any other person appointed by the competent authorities from pursuing some of the activities of the insurance undertaking in so far as that is necessary or appropriate for the purposes of winding-up.

The home Member State may provide that such activities shall be pursued with the consent and under the supervision of the supervisory authorities of that Member State.

[6433]
Article 280
Publication of decisions on winding-up proceedings

1. The competent authority, the liquidator or any person appointed for that purpose by the competent authority shall publish the decision to open winding-up proceedings in accordance with the publication procedures provided for in the home Member State and also publish an extract from the winding-up decision in the *Official Journal of the European Union*.

The supervisory authorities of all other Member States which have been informed of the decision to open winding-up proceedings in accordance with Article 273(3) may ensure the publication of such decision within their territories in the manner they consider appropriate.

2. The publication referred to in paragraph 1 shall specify the competent authority of the home Member State, the applicable law and the liquidator appointed. It shall be in the official language or in one of the official languages of the Member State in which the information is published.

[6434]
Article 281
Information to known creditors

1. When winding-up proceedings are opened, the competent authorities of the home Member State, the liquidator or any person appointed for that purpose by the competent authorities shall without delay individually inform by written notice each known creditor whose habitual residence, domicile or head office is situated in another Member State.

2. The notice referred to in paragraph 1 shall cover time-limits, the sanctions laid down with regard to those time-limits, the body or authority empowered to accept the lodging of claims or observations relating to claims and any other measures.

The notice shall also indicate whether creditors whose claims are preferential or secured in rem need to lodge their claims.

In the case of insurance claims, the notice shall further indicate the general effects of the winding-up proceedings on the insurance contracts, in particular, the date on which the insurance contracts or the operations will cease to produce effects and the rights and duties of insured persons with regard to the contract or operation.

[6435]
Article 282
Right to lodge claims

1. Any creditor, including public authorities of Member States, whose habitual residence, domicile or head office is situated in a Member State other than the home Member State shall have the right to lodge claims or to submit written observations relating to claims.

2. The claims of all creditors referred to in paragraph 1 shall be treated in the same way and given the same ranking as claims of an equivalent nature which may be lodged by creditors whose habitual residence, domicile or head office is situated in the home Member State. Competent authorities shall therefore operate without discrimination at Community level.

3. Except in cases where the law of the home Member State otherwise allows, a creditor shall send to the competent authority copies of any supporting documents and shall indicate the following:

(a) the nature and the amount of the claim;
(b) the date on which the claim arose;
(c) whether he alleges preference, security in rem or reservation of title in respect of the claim;
(d) where appropriate, what assets are covered by his security.

The precedence granted to insurance claims by Article 275 need not be indicated.

[6436]
Article 283
Languages and form

1. The information in the notice referred to in Article 281(1) shall be provided in the official language or one of the official languages of the home Member State.

For that purpose a form shall be used bearing either of the following headings in all the official languages of the European Union:

(a) 'Invitation to lodge a claim; time-limits to be observed'; or
(b) where the law of the home Member State provides for the submission of observations relating to claims, 'Invitation to submit observations relating to a claim; time-limits to be observed'.

However, where a known creditor is the holder of an insurance claim, the information in the notice referred to in Article 281(1) shall be provided in the official language or one of the official languages of the Member State in which the habitual residence, domicile or head office of the creditor is situated.

2. Creditors whose habitual residence, domicile or head office is situated in a Member State other than the home Member State may lodge their claims or submit observations relating to claims in the official language or one of the official languages of that other Member State.

However, in that case, the lodging of their claims or the submission of observations on their claims, as appropriate, shall bear the heading 'Lodgement of claim' or 'Submission of observations relating to claims', as appropriate, in the official language or in one of the official languages of the home Member State.

[6437]
Article 284
Regular information to the creditors

1. Liquidators shall, in an appropriate manner, keep creditors regularly informed on the progress of the winding-up.

2. The supervisory authorities of the Member States may request information on developments in the winding-up procedure from the supervisory authorities of the home Member State.

CHAPTER IV
COMMON PROVISIONS

[6438]
Article 285
Effects on certain contracts and rights

By way of derogation from Articles 269 and 274, the effects of the opening of reorganisation measures or of winding-up proceedings shall be governed as follows:

(a) in regard to employment contracts and employment relationships, exclusively by the law of the Member State applicable to the employment contract or employment relationship;

(b) in regard to contracts conferring the right to make use of or acquire immovable property, exclusively by the law of the Member State where the immovable property is situated; and

(c) in regard to rights of the insurance undertaking with respect to immovable property, a ship or an aircraft subject to registration in a public register, exclusively by the law of the Member State under the authority of which the register is kept.

[6439]
Article 286
Rights in rem of third parties

1. The opening of reorganisation measures or winding-up proceedings shall not affect the rights in rem of creditors or third parties in respect of tangible or intangible, movable or immovable assets — both specific assets and collections of indefinite assets as a whole which change from time to time — which belong to the insurance undertaking and which are situated within the territory of another Member State at the time of the opening of such measures or proceedings.

2. The rights referred to in paragraph 1 shall include at least:

(a) the right to dispose of assets or have them disposed of and to obtain satisfaction from the proceeds of or income from those assets, in particular by virtue of a lien or a mortgage;

(b) the exclusive right to have a claim met, in particular a right guaranteed by a lien in respect of the claim or by assignment of the claim by way of a guarantee;

(c) the right to demand the assets from or to require restitution by anyone having possession or use of them contrary to the wishes of the party so entitled;

(d) a right to the beneficial use of assets.

3. The right, recorded in a public register and enforceable against third parties, under which a right in rem within the meaning of paragraph 1 may be obtained, shall be considered to be a right in rem.

4. Paragraph 1 shall not preclude actions for nullity, voidability or unenforceability referred to in Article 274(2)(l).

[6440]
Article 287
Reservation of title

1. The opening of reorganisation measures or winding-up proceedings against an insurance undertaking purchasing an asset shall not affect the rights of a seller which are based on a reservation of title where at the time of the opening of such measures or proceedings the asset is situated within the territory of a Member State other than that in which such measures or proceedings were opened.

2. The opening, after delivery of the asset, of reorganisation measures or winding-up proceedings against an insurance undertaking which is selling an asset shall not constitute grounds for rescinding or terminating the sale and shall not prevent the purchaser from acquiring title where at the time of the opening of such measures or proceedings the asset sold is situated within the territory of a Member State other than that in which such measures or proceedings were opened.

3. Paragraphs 1 and 2 shall not preclude actions for nullity, voidability or unenforceability referred to in Article 274(2)(l).

[6441]
Article 288
Set-off

1. The opening of reorganisation measures or winding-up proceedings shall not affect the right of creditors to demand the set-off of their claims against the claims of the insurance undertaking, where such a set-off is permitted by the law applicable to the claim of the insurance undertaking.

2. Paragraph 1 shall not preclude actions for nullity, voidability or unenforceability referred to in Article 274(2)(l).

[6442]
Article 289
Regulated markets

1. Without prejudice to Article 286 the effects of a reorganisation measure or the opening of winding-up proceedings on the rights and obligations of the parties to a regulated market shall be governed solely by the law applicable to that market.

2. Paragraph 1 shall not preclude actions for nullity, voidability, or unenforceability referred to in Article 274(2)(l) which may be taken to set aside payments or transactions under the law applicable to that market.

[6443]
Article 290
Detrimental acts

Article 274(2)(l) shall not apply where a person who has benefited from a legal act which is detrimental to all the creditors provides proof of that act being subject to the law of a Member State other than the home Member State, and proof that that law does not allow any means of challenging that act in the relevant case.

[6444]
Article 291
Protection of third-party purchasers

The following law shall be applicable where, by an act concluded after the adoption of a reorganisation measure or the opening of winding-up proceedings, an insurance undertaking disposes, for consideration, of any of the following:

(a) in regard to immovable assets, the law of the Member State where the immovable property is situated;

(b) in regard to ships or aircraft subject to registration in a public register, the law of the Member State under the authority of which the register is kept;

(c) in regard to transferable or other securities, the existence or transfer of which presupposes entry in a register or account laid down by law or which are placed in a central deposit system governed by the law of a Member State, the law of the Member State under the authority of which the register, account or system is kept.

[6445]
Article 292
Lawsuits pending

The effects of reorganisation measures or winding-up proceedings on a pending lawsuit concerning an asset or a right of which the insurance undertaking has been divested shall be governed solely by the law of the Member State in which the lawsuit is pending.

[6446]
Article 293
Administrators and liquidators

1. The appointment of the administrator or the liquidator shall be evidenced by a certified copy of the original decision of appointment or by any other certificate issued by the competent authorities of the home Member State.

The Member State in which the administrator or liquidator wishes to act may require a translation into the official language or one of the official languages of that Member State. No formal authentication of that translation or other similar formality shall be required.

2. Administrators and liquidators shall be entitled to exercise within the territory of all the Member States all the powers which they are entitled to exercise within the territory of the home Member State.

Persons to assist or represent administrators and liquidators may be appointed, in accordance with the law of the home Member State, in the course of the reorganisation measure or winding-up proceedings, in particular in host Member States and, specifically, in order to help overcome any difficulties encountered by creditors in that State.

3. In exercising their powers according to the law of the home Member State, administrators or liquidators shall comply with the law of the Member States within which they wish to take action, in particular with regard to procedures for the realisation of assets and the informing of employees.

Those powers shall not include the use of force or the right to rule on legal proceedings or disputes.

[6447]
Article 294
Registration in a public register

1. The administrator, liquidator or any other authority or person duly empowered in the home Member State may request that a reorganisation measure or the decision to open winding-up proceedings be registered in any relevant public register kept in the other Member States.

However, where a Member State provides for mandatory registration, the authority or person referred to in the first subparagraph shall take all the measures necessary to ensure such registration.

2. The costs of registration shall be regarded as costs and expenses incurred in the proceedings.

[6448]
Article 295
Professional secrecy

All persons required to receive or divulge information in connection with the procedures laid down in Articles 270, 273 and 296 shall be bound by the provisions on professional secrecy, as laid down in Articles 64 to 69, with the exception of any judicial authorities to which existing national provisions apply.

[6449]
Article 296
Treatment of branches of third-country insurance undertakings

Where a third-country insurance undertaking has branches established in more than one Member State, each branch shall be treated independently with regard to the application of this Title.

The competent authorities and the supervisory authorities of those Member States shall endeavour to coordinate their actions.

Any administrators or liquidators shall likewise endeavour to coordinate their actions.

TITLE V
OTHER PROVISIONS

[6450]
Article 297
Right to apply to the courts

Member States shall ensure that decisions taken in respect of an insurance or a reinsurance undertaking under laws, regulations and administrative provisions implementing this Directive are subject to the right to apply to the courts.

[6451]
Article 298
Cooperation between the Member States and the Commission

1. The Member States shall cooperate with each other for the purpose of facilitating the supervision of insurance and reinsurance within the Community and the application of this Directive.

2. The Commission and the supervisory authorities of the Member States shall collaborate closely with each other for the purpose of facilitating the supervision of insurance and reinsurance within the Community and of examining any difficulties which may arise in the application of this Directive.

3. Member States shall inform the Commission of any major difficulties to which the application of this Directive gives rise.

The Commission and the supervisory authorities of the Member States concerned shall examine those difficulties as quickly as possible in order to find an appropriate solution.

[6452]
Article 299
Euro

Where this Directive makes reference to the euro, the exchange value in national currencies to be used with effect from 31 December of each year shall be the value which applies on the last day of the preceding October for which exchange values for the euro are available in all Community currencies.

[6453]
Article 300
Revision of amounts expressed in euro

The amounts expressed in euro in this Directive shall be revised every five years, by increasing the base amount in euro by the percentage change in the Harmonised Indices of Consumer Prices of all Member States as published by Eurostat starting from 31 October 2012 until the date of revision and rounded up to a multiple of EUR 100 000.

If the percentage change since the previous revision is less than 5%, the amounts will not be revised.

The Commission shall publish the revised amounts in the Official Journal of the European Union.

The revised amounts shall be implemented by Member States within 12 months of the publication in the Official Journal of the European Union.

[6454]
Article 301
Committee procedure

1. The Commission shall be assisted by the European Insurance and Occupational Pensions Committee.

2. Where reference is made to this paragraph, Articles 5 and 7 of Decision 1999/468/EC shall apply, having regard to the provisions of Article 8 thereof.

3. Where reference is made to this paragraph, Article 5a(1) to (4) and Article 7 of Decision 1999/468/EC shall apply, having regard to the provisions of Article 8 thereof.

[6455]
Article 302
Notifications submitted prior to entry into force of the laws, regulations and administrative provisions necessary to comply with Articles 57 to 63

The assessment procedure applied to proposed acquisitions for which notifications referred to in Article 57 have been submitted to the competent authorities prior to the entry into force of the laws, regulations and administrative provisions necessary to comply with Articles 57 to 63, shall be carried out in accordance with the national law of Member States in force at the time of notification.

Article 303 (*Amends European Parliament and Council Directive 2003/41/EC, art 17 and inserts arts 17a–17d, 21a, 21b thereof.*)

[6456]
Article 304
Duration-based equity risk sub-module

1. Member States may authorise life insurance undertakings providing:

(a) occupational retirement provision business in accordance with Article 4 of Directive 2003/41/EC, or

(b) retirement benefits paid by reference to reaching, or the expectation of reaching, retirement where the premiums paid for those benefits have a tax deduction which is authorised to policy holders in accordance with the national legislation of the Member State that has authorised the undertaking;

where

(i) all assets and liabilities corresponding to the business are ring-fenced, managed and organised separately from the other activities of the insurance undertakings, without any possibility of transfer;

(ii) the activities of the undertaking related to points (a) and (b), in relation to which the approach referred to in this paragraph is applied, are pursued only in the Member State where the undertaking has been authorised; and

(iii) the average duration of the liabilities corresponding to the business held by the undertaking exceeds an average of 12 years;

to apply an equity risk sub-module of the Solvency Capital Requirement, which is calibrated using a Value-at-Risk measure, over a time period, which is consistent with the typical holding period of equity investments for the undertaking concerned, with a confidence level providing the policy holders and beneficiaries with a level of protection equivalent to that set out in Article 101, where the approach provided for in this Article is used only in respect of those assets and liabilities referred in point (i). In the calculation of the Solvency Capital Requirement those assets and liabilities shall be fully considered for the purpose of assessing the diversification effects, without prejudice to the need to safeguard the interests of policy holders and beneficiaries in other Member States.

Subject to the approval of the supervisory authorities, the approach set out in the first subparagraph shall be used only where the solvency and liquidity position as well as the strategies, processes and reporting procedures of the undertaking concerned with respect to asset-liability management are such as to ensure, on an ongoing basis, that it is able to hold equity investments for a period which is consistent with the typical holding period of equity investments for the undertaking concerned. The undertaking shall be able to demonstrate to the supervisory authority that that condition is verified with the level of confidence necessary to provide policy holders and beneficiaries with a level of protection equivalent to that set out in Article 101.

Insurance and reinsurance undertakings shall not revert to applying the approach set out in Article 105, except in duly justified circumstances and subject to the approval of the supervisory authorities.

2. The Commission shall submit to the European Insurance and Occupational Pensions Committee and the European Parliament, by 31 October 2015, a report on the application of the approach set out in paragraph 1 and the supervisory authorities' practices adopted pursuant to paragraph 1, accompanied, where appropriate, by adequate proposals. That report shall address, in particular, cross-border effects of the use of that approach with a view to preventing regulatory arbitrage by insurance and reinsurance undertakings.

TITLE VI
TRANSITIONAL AND FINAL PROVISIONS

CHAPTER I
TRANSITIONAL PROVISIONS

SECTION 1
INSURANCE

[6457]
Article 305
Derogations and abolition of restrictive measures

1. Member States may exempt non-life insurance undertakings which on 31 January 1975 did not comply with the requirements of Articles 16 and 17 of Directive 73/239/EEC whose annual premium or contribution income on 31 July 1978 fell short of six times the amount of the minimum guarantee fund required under Article 17(2) of Directive 73/239/EEC from the requirement to establish such minimum guarantee fund before the end of the financial year in respect of which the premium or contribution income is as much as six times such minimum guarantee fund. After considering the results of the examination provided for under Article 298(2), the Council shall unanimously decide, on a proposal from the Commission, when that exemption is to be abolished by Member States.

2. Non-life insurance undertakings set up in the United Kingdom by Royal Charter or by private Act or by special public Act may continue to pursue their business in the legal form in which they were constituted on 31 July 1973 for an unlimited period.

Life insurance undertakings set up in the United Kingdom by Royal Charter or by private Act or by special Public Act may pursue their activity in the legal form in which they were constituted on 15 March 1979 for an unlimited period.

The United Kingdom shall draw up a list of the undertakings referred to in the first and second subparagraphs and communicate it to the other Member States and the Commission.

3. The societies registered in the United Kingdom under the Friendly Societies Acts may continue the activities of life insurance and savings operations which, in accordance with their objects, they were pursuing as of 15 March 1979.

4. At the request of non-life insurance undertakings which comply with the requirements laid down in Title I, Chapter VI, Sections 2, 4 and 5, Member States shall cease to apply restrictive measures such as those relating to mortgages, deposits and securities.

[6458]
Article 306
Rights acquired by existing branches and insurance undertakings

1. Branches which started business, in accordance with the provisions in force in the Member State where that branch is situated, before 1 July 1994 shall be presumed to have been subject to the procedure laid down in Articles 145 and 146.

2. Articles 147 and 148 shall not affect rights acquired by insurance undertakings carrying on business under the freedom to provide services before 1 July 1994.

SECTION 2
REINSURANCE

[6459]
Article 307
Transitional period for Articles 57(3) and 60(6) of Directive 2005/68/EC

A Member State may postpone the application of the provisions of Article 57(3) of Directive 2005/68/EC amending Article 15(3) of Directive 73/239/EEC and of the provision of Article 60(6) of Directive 2005/68/EC until 10 December 2008.

[6460]
Article 308
Right acquired by existing reinsurance undertakings

1. Reinsurance undertakings subject to this Directive which were authorised or entitled to conduct reinsurance business in accordance with the provisions of the Member States in which they have their head offices before 10 December 2005 shall be deemed to be authorised in accordance with Article 14.

However, they shall be obliged to comply with the provisions of this Directive concerning the pursuit of the business of reinsurance and with the requirements set out in points (b), and (d) to (g) of Article 18(1), Articles 19, 20 and 24 and Title I Chapter VI, Sections 2, 3 and 4.

2. Member States may allow reinsurance undertakings referred to in paragraph 1 which on 10 December 2005 did not comply with Article 18(1)(b), Articles 19 and 20 and Title I Chapter VI, Sections 2, 3 and 4 until 10 December 2008 in order to comply with such requirements.

CHAPTER II
FINAL PROVISIONS

[6461]
Article 309
Transposition

1. Member States shall bring into force the laws, regulations and administrative provisions necessary to comply with Articles 4, 10, 13, 14, 18, 23, 26-32, 34-49, 51-55, 67, 68, 71, 72, 74-85, 87-91, 93-96, 98,100-110, 112, 113, 115-126, 128, 129, 131-134, 136-142, 144, 146, 148, 162-167, 172, 173, 178, 185, 190, 192, 210-233, 235-240, 243-258, 260-263, 265, 266, 303 and 304 and Annexes III and IV by 31 October 2012.

When they are adopted by Member States, those measures shall contain a reference to this Directive or shall be accompanied by such a reference on the occasion of their official publication. They shall also include a statement that references in existing laws, regulations and administrative provisions to the directives repealed by this Directive shall be construed as references to this Directive. Member States shall determine how such reference is to be made and how that statement is to be formulated.

2. Member States shall communicate to the Commission the text of the main provisions of national law which they adopt in the field covered by this Directive.

[6462]
Article 310
Repeal

Directives 64/225/EEC, 73/239/EEC, 73/240/EEC, 76/580/EEC, 78/473/EEC, 84/641/EEC, 87/344/EEC, 88/357/EEC, 92/49/EEC, 98/78/EC, 2001/17/EC, 2002/83/EC and 2005/68/EC, as amended by the acts listed in Part A of Annex VI, are repealed with effect from 1 November 2012, without prejudice to the obligations of the Member States relating to the time-limits for transposition into national law and application of the Directives set out in Part B of Annex VI.

References to the repealed Directives shall be construed as references to this Directive and shall be read in accordance with the correlation table in Annex VII.

[6463]
Article 311
Entry into force

This Directive shall enter into force on the 20th day following its publication in the Official Journal of the European Union.

Articles 1-3, 5-9, 11, 12, 15-17, 19-22, 24, 25, 33, 56-66, 69, 70, 73, 143, 145, 147, 149-161, 168-171, 174-177, 179-184, 186-189, 191, 193-209, 267-300, 302, 305-308 and Annexes I and II, V, VI and VII shall apply from 1 November 2012.

[6464]
Article 312
Addressees

This Directive is addressed to the Member States.

Done at Strasbourg, 25 November 2009

ANNEX I

CLASSES OF NON-LIFE INSURANCE

[6465]

A. Classification of risks according to classes of insurance

1. *Accident* (including industrial injury and occupational diseases):
   — fixed pecuniary benefits,
   — benefits in the nature of indemnity,
   — combinations of the two,
   — injury to passengers,
2. *Sickness:*
   — fixed pecuniary benefits,
   — benefits in the nature of indemnity,
   — combinations of the two,
3. *Land vehicles* (other than railway rolling stock)
   All damage to or loss of:
   — land motor vehicles,
   — land vehicles other than motor vehicles,
4. *Railway rolling* stock
   All damage to or loss of railway rolling stock.
5. *Aircraft*
   All damage to or loss of aircraft.
6. *Ships (sea, lake and river and canal vessels)*
   All damage to or loss of:
   — river and canal vessels,
   — lake vessels,
   — sea vessels,
7. *Goods in transit* (including merchandise, baggage, and all other goods)
   All damage to or loss of goods in transit or baggage, irrespective of the form of transport.
8. *Fire and natural forces*
   All damage to or loss of property (other than property included in classes 3, 4, 5, 6 and 7) due to:
   — fire,
   — explosion,
   — storm,
   — natural forces other than storm,
   — nuclear energy,
   — land subsidence,
9. *Other damage to property*
   All damage to or loss of property (other than property included in classes 3, 4, 5, 6 and 7) due to hail or frost, and any event such as theft, other than that included in class 8.
10. *Motor vehicle liability*
    All liability arising out of the use of motor vehicles operating on the land (including carrier's liability).
11. *Aircraft liability*
    All liability arising out of the use of aircraft (including carrier's liability).
12. *Liability for ships (sea, lake and river and canal vessels)*
    All liability arising out of the use of ships, vessels or boats on the sea, lakes, rivers or canals (including carrier's liability).
13. *General liability*
    All liability other than those referred to in classes 10, 11 and 12.
14. *Credit:*
    — insolvency (general),
    — export credit,

— instalment credit,
— mortgages,
— agricultural credit,

15. *Suretyship:*
— suretyship (direct),
— suretyship (indirect),

16. *Miscellaneous financial loss:*
— employment risks,
— insufficiency of income (general),
— bad weather,
— loss of benefits,
— continuing general expenses,
— unforeseen trading expenses,
— loss of market value,
— loss of rent or revenue,
— other indirect trading loss,
— other non-trading financial loss,
— other forms of financial loss,

17. *Legal expenses*

Legal expenses and costs of litigation.

18. *Assistance*

Assistance for persons who get into difficulties while travelling, while away from their home or their habitual residence.

B. Description of authorisations granted for more than one class of insurance

The following names shall be given to authorisations which simultaneously cover the following classes:

(a) Classes 1 and 2: 'Accident and Health Insurance';
(b) Classes 1 (fourth indent), 3, 7 and 10: 'Motor Insurance';
(c) Classes 1 (fourth indent), 4, 6, 7 and 12: 'Marine and Transport Insurance';
(d) Classes 1 (fourth indent), 5, 7 and 11: 'Aviation Insurance';
(e) Classes 8 and 9: 'Insurance against Fire and other Damage to Property';
(f) Classes 10, 11, 12 and 13: 'Liability Insurance';
(g) Classes 14 and 15: 'Credit and Suretyship Insurance';
(h) All classes, at the choice of the Member States, which shall notify the other Member States and the Commission of their choice.

ANNEX II

CLASSES OF LIFE INSURANCE

[6466]

I. The life insurance referred to in points (a)(i), (ii) and (iii) of Article 2(3) excluding those referred to in II and III;

II. Marriage assurance, birth assurance;

III. The insurance referred to in points (a)(i) and (ii) of Article 2(3), which are linked to investment funds;

IV. Permanent health insurance, referred to in point (a)(iv) of Article 2(3);

V. Tontines, referred to in point (b)(i) of Article 2(3);

VI. Capital redemption operations, referred to in point (b)(ii) of Article 2(3);

VII. Management of group pension funds, referred to in point (b)(iii) and (iv) of Article 2(3);

VIII. The operations referred to in point (b)(v) of Article 2(3);

IX. The operations referred to in Article 2(3)(c).

ANNEX III

LEGAL FORMS OF UNDERTAKINGS

[6467]

A. **Forms of non-life insurance undertaking:**

(1) in the case of the Kingdom of Belgium: 'société anonyme/naamloze vennootschap', 'société en commandite par actions/commanditaire vennootschap op aandelen', 'association d'assurance mutuelle/onderlinge verzekeringsvereniging', 'société coopérative/coöperatieve vennootschap', 'société mutualiste/maatschappij van onderlinge bijstand';

(2) in the case of the Republic of Bulgaria: 'акционерно дружество';

(3) in the case of the Czech Republic: 'akciová spolecnost', 'družstvo';

(4) in the case of the Kingdom of Denmark: 'aktieselskaber', 'gensidige selskaber';

(5) in the case of the Federal Republic of Germany: 'Aktiengesellschaft', 'Versicherungsverein auf Gegenseitigkeit', 'Öffentlich-rechtliches Wettbewerbsversicherungsunternehmen';

(6) in the case of the Republic of Estonia: 'aktsiaselts';

(7) in the case of Ireland: incorporated companies limited by shares or by guarantee or unlimited;

(8) in the case of the Hellenic Republic: 'αν νυμη εταιρ α', 'αλληλασφαλιστικ ς συνεταιρισμ ς';

(9) in the case of the Kingdom of Spain: 'sociedad anónima', 'sociedad mutua', 'sociedad cooperativa';

(10) in the case of the French Republic: 'société anonyme', 'société d'assurance mutuelle', 'institution de prévoyance régie par le code de la sécurité sociale', 'institution de prévoyance régie par le code rural', 'mutuelles régies par le code de la mutualité';

(11) in the case of the Italian Republic: 'società per azioni', 'società cooperativa', 'mutua di assicurazione';

(12) in the case of the Republic of Cyprus: 'εταιρε α περιορισμνης ευθνης με μετοχς', 'εταιρε α περιορισμνης ευθνης χωρ ς μετοχικ κεφ λαιο';

(13) in the case of the Republic of Latvia: 'apdrošinašanas akciju sabiedriba', 'savstarpejas apdrošinašanas kooperativa biedriba';

(14) in the case of the Republic of Lithuania: 'akcine bendrove', 'uždaroji akcine bendrove';

(15) in the case of the Grand Duchy of Luxembourg: 'société anonyme', 'société en commandite par actions', 'association d'assurances mutuelles', 'société coopérative';

(16) in the case of the Republic of Hungary: 'biztosító részvénytársaság', 'biztosító szövetkezet', 'biztosító egyesület','külföldi székhelyu biztosító magyarországi fióktelepe';

(17) in the case of the Republic of Malta: 'limited liability company/kumpannija b' responsabbilta' limitata';

(18) in the case of the Kingdom of the Netherlands: 'naamloze vennootschap', 'onderlinge waarborgmaatschappij';

(19) in the case of the Republic of Austria: 'Aktiengesellschaft', 'Versicherungsverein auf Gegenseitigkeit';

(20) in the case of the Republic of Poland: 'spólka akcyjna', 'towarzystwo ubezpieczen wzajemnych';

(21) in the case of the Portuguese Republic: 'sociedade anónima', 'mútua de seguros';

(22) in the case of Romania: 'societati pe actiuni', 'societati mutuale';

(23) in the case of the Republic of Slovenia: 'delniška družba', 'družba za vzajemno zavarovanje';

(24) in the case of the Slovak Republic: 'akciová spolocnost';

(25) in the case of the Republic of Finland: 'keskinäinen vakuutusyhtiö/ömsesidigt försäkringsbolag','vakuutusosakeyhtiö/försäkringsaktiebolag', 'vakuutusyhdistys/försäkringsförening';

(26) in the case of the Kingdom of Sweden: 'försäkringsaktiebolag', 'ömsesidiga *försäkringsbolag*','understödsföreningar';

(27) in the case of the United Kingdom: companies limited by shares or by guarantee or unlimited, societies registered under the Industrial and Provident Societies Acts, societies registered under the Friendly Societies Acts, the association of underwriters known as Lloyd's;

(28) in any event and as an alternative to the forms of non-life insurance undertaking listed in points (1) to (27), the form of a European Company (SE) as defined in Council Regulation (EC) No 2157/2001[1].

NOTES

[1] OJ L294, 10.11.2001, p 1.

B. **Forms of life insurance undertaking:**

(1) in the case of the Kingdom of Belgium: 'société anonyme/naamloze vennootschap', 'société en commandite par actions/commanditaire vennootschap op aandelen', 'association d'assurance mutuelle/onderlinge verzekeringsvereniging', 'société coopérative/coöperatieve vennootschap';

(2) in the case of the Republic of Bulgaria: 'акционерно дружество', 'взаимозастрахователна кооперации ';

(3) in the case of the Czech Republic: 'akciová spolecnost', 'družstvo';

(4) in the case of the Kingdom of Denmark: 'aktieselskaber', 'gensidige selskaber', 'pensionskasser omfattet af lov om forsikringsvirksomhed (tværgående pensionskasser)';

(5) in the case of the Federal Republic of Germany: 'Aktiengesellschaft', 'Versicherungsverein auf Gegenseitigkeit', 'öffentlich-rechtliches Wettbewerbsversicherungsunternehmen';

(6) in the case of the Republic of Estonia: 'aktsiaselts';

(7) in the case of Ireland: 'incorporated companies limited by shares or by guarantee or unlimited', 'societies registered under the Industrial and Provident Societies Acts', 'societies registered under the Friendly Societies Acts';

(8) in the case of the Hellenic Republic: 'αν νυμη εταιρ α';

(9) in the case of the Kingdom of Spain: 'sociedad anónima', 'sociedad mutua', 'sociedad cooperativa';

(10) in the case of the French Republic: 'société anonyme', 'société d'assurance mutuelle', 'institution de prévoyance régie par le code de la sécurité sociale', 'institution de prévoyance régie par le code rural', 'mutuelles régies par le code de la mutualité';

(11) in the case of the Italian Republic: 'società per azioni', 'società cooperativa', 'mutua di assicurazione';

(12) in the case of the Republic of Cyprus: 'εταιρε α περιορισμνης ευθνης με μετοχς', 'εταιρε α περιορισμνης ευθνης με εγγηση';

(13) in the case of the Republic of the Latvia: 'apdrošinašanas akciju sabiedriba', 'savstarpejas apdrošinašanas kooperativa biedriba';

(14) in the case of the Republic of Lithuania: 'akcine bendrove', 'uždaroji akcine bendrove';

(15) in the case of the Grand Duchy of Luxembourg: 'société anonyme', 'société en commandite par actions', 'association d'assurances mutuelles', 'société coopérative';

(16) in the case of the Republic of Hungary: 'biztosító részvénytársaság', 'biztosító szövetkezet', 'biztosító egyesület','külföldi székhelyu biztosító magyarországi fióktelepe';

(17) in the case of the Republic of Malta: 'limited liability company/kumpannija b' responsabbilta' limitata';

(18) in the case of the Kingdom of the Netherlands: 'naamloze vennootschap', 'onderlinge waarborgmaatschappij';

(19) in the case of the Republic of Austria: 'Aktiengesellschaft', 'Versicherungsverein auf Gegenseitigkeit';

(20) in the case of the Republic of Poland: 'spólka akcyjna', 'towarzystwo ubezpieczen wzajemnych';

(21) in the case of the Portuguese Republic: 'sociedade anónima', 'mútua de seguros';

(22) in the case of Romania: 'societati pe actiuni', 'societati mutuale';

(23) in the case of the Republic of Slovenia: 'delniška družba', 'družba za vzajemno zavarovanje';

(24) in the case of the Slovak Republic: 'akciová spolocnost';

(25) in the case of the Republic of Finland: 'keskinäinen vakuutusyhtiö/ömsesidigt försäkringsbolag','vakuutusosakeyhtiö/försäkringsaktiebolag', 'vakuutusyhdistys/försäkringsförening';

(26) in the case of Kingdom of Sweden: 'försäkringsaktiebolag', 'ömsesidiga försäkringsbolag', 'understödsföreningar';

(27) in the case of the United Kingdom: companies limited by shares or by guarantee or unlimited, societies registered under the Industrial and Provident Societies Acts, societies registered or incorporated under the Friendly Societies Acts, the association of underwriters known as Lloyd's;
(28) in any event and as an alternative to the forms of life insurance undertaking listed in points (1) to (27), the form of a European company (SE) as defined in Regulation (EC) No 2157/2001.

C. **Forms of reinsurance undertaking:**
(1) in the case of the Kingdom of Belgium: 'société anonyme/naamloze vennootschap', 'société en commandite par actions/commanditaire vennootschap op aandelen', 'association d'assurance mutuelle/onderlinge verzekeringsvereniging', 'société coopérative/coöperatieve vennootschap';
(2) in the case of the Republic of Bulgaria 'акционерно дружество';
(3) in the case of the Czech Republic: 'akciová spolecnost';
(4) in the case of the Kingdom of Denmark: 'aktieselskaber', 'gensidige selskaber';
(5) in the case of the Federal Republic of Germany: 'Aktiengesellschaft', 'Versicherungsverein auf Gegenseitigkeit','Öffentlich-rechtliches Wettbewerbsversicherungsunternehmen';
(6) in the case of the Republic of Estonia: 'aktsiaselts';
(7) in the case of Ireland: incorporated companies limited by shares or by guarantee or unlimited;
(8) in the case of the Hellenic Republic: 'αν νυμη εταιρ α', 'αλληλασφαλιστικ ς συνεταιρισμ ς';
(9) in the case of the Kingdom of Spain: 'sociedad anónima';
(10) in the case of the French Republic: 'société anonyme', 'société d'assurance mutuelle', 'institution de prévoyance régie par le code de la sécurité sociale', 'institution de prévoyance régie par le code rural', 'mutuelles régies par le code de la mutualité';
(11) in the case of the Italian Republic: 'società per azioni';
(12) in the case of the Republic of Cyprus: 'εταιρε α περιορισμνης ευθνης με μετοχς', 'εταιρε α περιορισμνης ευθνης με εγγηση';
(13) in the case of the Republic of Latvia: 'akciju sabiedriba', 'sabiedriba ar ierobežotu atbildibu';
(14) in the case of the Republic of Lithuania: 'akcine bendrove', 'uždaroji akcine bendrove';
(15) in the case of the Grand Duchy of Luxembourg: 'société anonyme', 'société en commandite par actions', 'association d'assurances mutuelles', 'société coopérative';
(16) in the case of the Republic of Hungary: 'biztosító részvénytársaság', 'biztosító szövetkezet', 'harmadik országbeli biztosító magyarországi fióktelepe';
(17) in the case of the Republic of Malta: 'limited liability company/kumpannija tà responsabbiltà limitata';
(18) in the case of the Kingdom of the Netherlands: 'naamloze vennootschap', 'onderlinge waarborgmaatschappij';
(19) in the case of the Republic of Austria: 'Aktiengesellschaft', 'Versicherungsverein auf Gegenseitigkeit';
(20) in the case of the Republic of Poland: 'spólka akcyjna', 'towarzystwo ubezpieczen wzajemnych';
(21) in the case of the Portuguese Republic: 'sociedade anónima', 'mútua de seguros';
(22) in the case of Romania 'societate pe actiuni';
(23) in the case of the Republic of Slovenia: 'delniška družba';
(24) in the case of the Slovak Republic: 'akciová spolocnost';
(25) in the case of the Republic of Finland: 'keskinäinen vakuutusyhtiö/ömsesidigt försäkringsbolag','vakuutusosakeyhtiö/försäkringsaktiebolag', 'vakuutusyhdistys/försäkringsförening';
(26) in the case of the Kingdom of Sweden: 'försäkringsaktiebolag', 'ömsesidigt försäkringsbolag';
(27) in the case of the United Kingdom: companies limited by shares or by guarantee or unlimited, societies registered under the Industrial and Provident Societies Acts, societies registered or incorporated under the Friendly Societies Acts, the association of underwriters known as Lloyd's;
(28) in any event and as an alternative to the forms of reinsurance undertaking listed in points (1) to (27), the form of a European Company (SE) as defined in Regulation (EC) No 2157/2001.

ANNEX IV

SOLVENCY CAPITAL REQUIREMENT (SCR) STANDARD FORMULA

[6468]

1. **Calculation of the Basic Solvency Capital Requirement**

The Basic Solvency Capital Requirement set out in Article 104(1) shall be equal to the following:

$$\text{Basic SCR} = \sqrt{\sum_{i,j} \text{Corr}_{i,j} \times \text{SCR}_i \times \text{SCR}_j}$$

where SCR_i denotes the risk module i and SCR_j denotes the risk module j, and where 'i,j' means that the sum of the different terms should cover all possible combinations of i and j. In the calculation, SCR_i and SCR_j are replaced by the following:

— $\text{SCR}_{\text{non-life}}$ denotes the non-life underwriting risk module,
— SCR_{life} denotes the life underwriting risk module,
— $\text{SCR}_{\text{health}}$ denotes the health underwriting risk module,
— $\text{SCR}_{\text{market}}$ denotes the market risk module,
— $\text{SCR}_{\text{default}}$ denotes the counterparty default risk module,

The factor $\text{Corr}_{i,j}$ denotes the item set out in row i and in column j of the following correlation matrix:

j i	Market	Default	Life	Health	Non-life
Market	1	0,25	0,25	0,25	0,25
Default	0,25	1	0,25	0,25	0,5
Life	0,25	0,25	1	0,25	0
Health	0,25	0,25	0,25	1	0
Non-life	0,25	0,5	0	0	1

2. **Calculation of the non-life underwriting risk module**

The non-life underwriting risk module set out in Article 105(2) shall be equal to the following:

$$\text{SCR}_{\text{non-life}} = \sqrt{\sum_{i,j} \text{Corr}_{i,j} \times \text{SCR}_i \times \text{SCR}_j}$$

where SCR_i denotes the sub-module i and SCR_j denotes the sub-module j, and where 'i,j' means that the sum of the different terms should cover all possible combinations of i and j. In the calculation, SCR_i and SCR_j are replaced by the following:

— $\text{SCR}_{\text{nl premium and reserve}}$ denotes the non-life premium and reserve risk sub-module,
— $\text{SCR}_{\text{nl catastrophe}}$ denotes the non-life catastrophe risk sub-module,

3. **Calculation of the life underwriting risk module**

The life underwriting risk module set out in Article 105(3) shall be equal to the following:

$$\text{SCR}_{\text{life}} = \sqrt{\sum_{i,j} \text{Corr}_{i,j} \times \text{SCR}_i \times \text{SCR}_j}$$

where SCR_i denotes the sub-module i and SCR_j denotes the sub-module j, and where 'i,j' means that the sum of the different terms should cover all possible combinations of i and j. In the calculation, SCR_i and SCR_j are replaced by the following:

— $\text{SCR}_{\text{mortality}}$ denotes the mortality risk sub-module,
— $\text{SCR}_{\text{longevity}}$ denotes the longevity risk sub-module,
— $\text{SCR}_{\text{disability}}$ denotes the disability — morbidity risk sub-module,
— $\text{SCR}_{\text{life expense}}$ denotes the life expense risk sub-module,
— $\text{SCR}_{\text{revision}}$ denotes the revision risk sub-module,
— $\text{SCR}_{\text{lapse}}$ denotes the lapse risk sub-module,
— $\text{SCR}_{\text{life catastrophe}}$ denotes the life catastrophe risk sub-module,

4. **Calculation of the market risk module**

Structure of the market risk module

The market risk module, set out in Article 105(5) shall be equal to the following:

$$SCR_{market} = \sqrt{\sum_{i,j} Corr_{i,j} \times SCR_i \times SCR_j}$$

where SCR_i denotes the sub-module i and SCR_j denotes the sub-module j, and where 'i,j' means that the sum of the different terms should cover all possible combinations of i and j. In the calculation, SCR_i and SCR_j are replaced by the following:

— $SCR_{interest\ rate}$ denotes the interest rate risk sub-module,
— SCR_{equity} denotes the equity risk sub-module,
— $SCR_{property}$ denotes the property risk sub-module,
— SCR_{spread} denotes the spread risk sub-module,
— $SCR_{concentration}$ denotes the market risk concentrations sub-module,
— $SCR_{currency}$ denotes the currency risk sub-module,

ANNEX V

GROUPS OF NON-LIFE INSURANCE CLASSES FOR THE PURPOSES OF ARTICLE 159

[6469]

1. Accident and sickness (classes 1 and 2 of Annex I),

2. motor (classes 3, 7 and 10 of Annex I, the figures for class 10, excluding carriers' liability, being given separately),

3. fire and other damage to property (classes 8 and 9 of Annex I),

4. aviation, marine and transport (classes 4, 5, 6, 7, 11 and 12 of Annex I),

5. general liability (class 13 of Annex I),

6. credit and suretyship (classes 14 and 15 of Annex I),

7. other classes (classes 16, 17 and 18 of Annex I).

ANNEX VI

PART A
REPEALED DIRECTIVES WITH LIST OF THEIR SUCCESSIVE AMENDMENTS

[6470]

(referred to in Article 310)

Council Directive 64/225/EEC

(OJ L 56, 4.4.1964, p. 878).

1973 Act of Accession, Article 29, Annex I, Point III(G)(1)

(OJ L 73, 27.3.1972, p. 89).

First Council Directive 73/239/EEC

(OJ L 228, 16.8.1973, p. 3).

1994 Act of Accession, Article 29, Annex I(XI)(B)(II)(1)

(OJ C 241, 29.8.1994, p. 197).

(as substituted by Council Decision 95/1/EC)

(OJ L 1, 1.1.1995, p. 1).

2003 Act of Accession, Article 20, Annex II(3)(1)

(OJ L 236, 23.9.2003, p. 335).

1985 Act of Accession, Article 26, *Annex I(II)(c)(1)(a)*

(OJ L 302, 15.11.1985, p. 156).

Council Directive 76/580/EEC — only Article 1

(OJ L 189, 13.7.1976, p. 13).

Council Directive 84/641/EEC (OJ L 339, 27.12.1984, p. 21).	only Articles 1 to 14
Council Directive 87/343/EEC (OJ L 185, 4.7.1987, p. 72).	only Article 1 and Annex
Council Directive 87/344/EEC (OJ L 185, 4.7.1987, p. 77).	only Article 9
Second Council Directive 88/357/EEC (OJ L 172, 4.7.1988, p. 1).	only Articles 9, 10 and 11
Council Directive 90/618/EEC (OJ L 330, 29.11.1990, p. 44).	only Articles 2, 3 and 4
Council Directive 92/49/EEC (OJ L 228, 11.8.1992, p. 1).	only Articles 4, 5, 6, 7, 9, 10, 11, 13, 14, 17, 18, 24, 32, 33 and 53
European Parliament and Council Directive 95/26/EC (OJ L 168, 18.7.1995, p. 7).	only Article 1, 2(2), third indent, and Article 3(1)
Directive 2000/26/EC of the European Parliament and of the Council (OJ L 181, 20.7.2000, p. 65).	only Article 8
Directive 2002/13/EC of the European Parliament and of the Council (OJ L 77, 20.3.2002, p. 17).	only Article 1
Directive 2002/87/EC of the European Parliament and of the Council (OJ L 35, 11.2.2003, p. 1).	only Article 22
Directive 2005/1/EC of the European Parliament and of the Council (OJ L 79, 24.3.2005, p. 9).	only Article 4
Directive 2005/68/EC of the European Parliament and of the Council (OJ L 323, 9.12.2005, p. 1).	only Article 57
Directive 2006/101/EC of the European Parliament and of the Council (OJ L 363, 20.12.2006, p. 238).	only Article 1 and Annex, Point (1)

Council Directive 73/240/EEC
(OJ L 228, 16.8.1973, p. 20).
Council Directive 76/580/EEC
(OJ L 189, 13.7.1976, p. 13).
Council Directive 78/473/EEC
(OJ L 151, 7.6.1978, p. 25).
Council Directive 84/641/EEC
(OJ L 339, 27.12.1984, p. 21).
Council Directive 87/344/EEC
(OJ L 185, 4.7.1987, p. 77).
Second Council Directive 88/357/EEC
(OJ L 172, 4.7.1988, p. 1).

Council Directive 90/618/EEC (OJ L 330, 29.11.1990, p. 44).	only Articles 5 to 10
Council Directive 92/49/EEC (OJ L 228, 11.8.1992, p. 1).	only Articles 12(1), 19, 23, 27, 30(1), 34, 35, 36, 37, 39(1), 40(1), 42(1), 43(1), 44(1), 45(1) and 46(1)

Directive 2000/26/EC of the European Parliament and of the Council (OJ L 181, 20.7.2000, p. 65).	only Article 9
Directive 2005/14/EC of the European Parliament and of the Council (OJ L 149, 11.6.2005, p. 14).	only Article 3
Council Directive 92/49/EEC (OJ L 228, 11.8.1992, p. 1).	
European Parliament and Council Directive 95/26/EC (OJ L 168, 18.7.1995, p. 7).	only Article 1, second indent, Article 2(1), first indent, Article 4(1), (3) and (5), and Article 5, second indent
Directive 2000/64/EC of the European Parliament and of the Council (OJ L 290, 17.11.2000, p. 27).	only Article 2
Directive 2002/87/EC of the European Parliament and of the Council (OJ L 35, 11.2.2003, p. 1).	only Article 24
Directive 2005/1/EC of the European Parliament and of the Council (OJ L 79, 24.3.2005, p. 9).	only Article 6
Directive 2005/68/EC of the European Parliament and the Council (OJ L 323, 9.12.2005, p. 1).	only Article 58
Directive 2007/44/EC of the European Parliament and of the Council (OJ L 247, 21.9.2007, p. 1).	only Article 1
Directive 98/78/EC of the European Parliament and of the Council (OJ L 330, 5.12.1998, p. 1).	
Directive 2002/87/EC of the European Parliament and of the Council (OJ L 35, 11.2.2003, p. 1).	only Article 28
Directive 2005/1/EC of the European Parliament and of the Council (OJ L 79, 24.3.2005, p. 9).	only Article 7
Directive 2005/68/EC of the European Parliament and of the Council (OJ L 323, 9.12.2005, p. 1).	only Article 59
Directive 2001/17/EC of the European Parliament and of the Council (OJ L 110, 20.4.2001, p. 28).	
Directive 2002/83/EC of the European Parliament and of the Council (OJ L 345, 19.12.2002, p. 1).	
Council Directive 2004/66/EC (OJ L 168, 1.5.2004, p. 35).	only Point II of the Annex
Directive 2005/1/EC of the European Parliament and of the Council (OJ L 79, 24.3.2005, p. 9).	only Article 8
Directive 2005/68/EC of the European Parliament and of the Council *(OJ L 323, 9.12.2005, p. 1).*	only Article 60
Directive 2006/101/EC of the European Parliament and of the Council (OJ L 363, 20.12.2006, p. 238).	only Article 1 and Point 3 of the Annex

Directive 2007/44/EC of the European Parliament and of the Council (OJ L 247, 21.9.2007, p. 1).	only Article 2
Directive 2008/19/EC of the European Parliament and of the Council (OJ L 76, 19.3.2008, p. 44).	only Article 1
Directive 2005/68/EC of the European Parliament and of the Council (OJ L 323, 9.12.2005, p. 1).	
Directive 2007/44/EC of the European Parliament and of the Council (OJ L 247, 21.9.2007, p. 1).	only Article 4
Directive 2008/19/EC of the European Parliament and of the Council (OJ L 76, 19.3.2008, p. 44).	only Article 1
Directive 2008/37/EC of the European Parliament and of the Council (OJ L 81, 20.3.2008, p. 1).	only Article 1

PART B
LIST OF TIME-LIMITS FOR TRANSPOSITION INTO NATIONAL LAW

(referred to in Article 310)

Directive	Time-limit for transposition	Time-limit for application
64/225/EEC	26 August 1965	
73/239/EEC	27 January 1975	27 January 1976
73/240/EEC	27 January 1975	
76/580/EEC	31 December 1976	
78/473/EEC	2 December 1979	2 June 1980
84/641/EEC	30 June 1987	1 January 1988
87/343/EEC	1 January 1990	1 July 1990
87/344/EEC	1 January 1990	1 July 1990
88/357/EEC	30 December 1989	30 June 1990
90/618/EEC	20 May 1992	20 November 1992
92/49/EEC	31 December 1993	1 July 1994
95/26/EC	18 July 1996	18 July 1996
98/78/EC	5 June 2000	
2000/26/EC	20 July 2002	20 January 2003
2000/64/EC	17 November 2002	
2001/17/EC	20 April 2003	
2002/13/EC	20 September 2003	
2002/83/EC	17 November 2002, 20 September 2003, 19 June 2004 (depending upon particular provision)	
2002/87/EC	11 August 2004	
2004/66/EC	1 May 2004	
2005/1/EC	13 May 2005	
2005/14/EC	11 June 2007	
2005/68/EC	10 December 2007	
2006/101/EC	1 January 2007	
2008/19/EC	Not applicable	
2008/37/EC	Not applicable	

[6471]–[6481]

ANNEX VII

CORRELATION TABLE

Directive 73/239/EEC	Directive 78/473/EEC	Directive 87/344/EEC	Directive 88/357/EEC	Directive 92/49/EEC	Directive 98/78/EC	Directive 2001/17/EC	Directive 2002/83/EC	Directive 2005/68/EC	Directive 2007/44/EC	This Directive
Article 1(1)				Article 2		Article 1(1)	Article 2 first sentence	Article 1(1)		Articles 1. 2(2), 2(3) and 267
Article 1(2)										Article 2(2)
Article 1(3)										—
Article 2(1), points (a) to (c)										—
Article 2(1), point (d)							Article 3(4)			Article 3
Article 2(1), point (e)										—
Article 2(2), point (a)										Article 5(1)
Article 2(2), point (b)										Article 5(2)
Article 2(2), polnt (c)										Article 5(3)
Article 2(2), point (d)										Article 5(4)
Article 2(3), first to fourth subparagraphs										Article 6
Article 2(3), fifth subparagraph										Article 15(4)

Directive 73/239/EEC	Directive 78/473/EEC	Directive 87/344/EEC	Directive 88/357/EEC	Directive 92/49/EEC	Directive 98/78/EC	Directive 2001/17/EC	Directive 2002/83/EC	Directive 2005/68/EC	Directive 2007/44/EC	This Directive
Article 3(1), first and second subparagraphs										—
Article 3(1), third subparagraph										Article 4(5)
Article 3(2)										Article 7
Article 4, first sentence										Article 8, first sentence
Article 4, point (a)										Article 8(2)
Article 4, point (b)										—
Article 4, point (c)										Article 8(3)
Article 4, point (e)										—
Article 4, point (f)										Article 8(1)
Article 4, point (g)										Article 8(4)
Article 5, point (a)										—
Article 5, point (b)							Article 1(1), point (o)			—
Article 5, point (c)							Article 1(1), point (p)			Article 134(1)
Article 5, point (d)										—

Directive 73/239/EEC	Directive 78/473/EEC	Directive 87/344/EEC	Directive 88/357/EEC	Directive 92/49/EEC	Directive 98/78/EC	Directive 2001/17/EC	Directive 2002/83/EC	Directive 2005/68/EC	Directive 2007/44/EC	This Directive
Article 6				Article 4			Article 4	Article 3		Article 14(1), (2), points (a) and (b)
Article 7(1) and (2), first subparagraph				Article 5(1) and (2), first subparagraph			Article 5(1) and (2), first subparagraph			Article 15(1) and (2), first subparagraph
Article 7(2), second subparagraph, point (a)				Article 5(2), second subparagraph, point (a)						Article 15(3), first subparagraph
Article 7(2), second subparagraph, point (b)				Article 5(2) second subparagraph, point (b)						—
Article 8(1), point (a)				Article 6(1) point (a)			Article 6(1), point (a)	Annex I		Annex IIIA and B
Article 8(1), point (a), final paragraph								Article 5(2)		Article 17(2)
Article 8(1), point (b)				Article 6(1), point (b)			Article 6(1), point (b)	Article 6, point (a)		Article 18(1), point (a)
								Article 6, point (a)		Article 18(1), point (b)
Article 8(1), point (c)				Article 6(1), point (c)			Article 6(1), point (c)	Article 6, point (b)		Article 18(1), point (c)
Article 8(1), point (d)				Article 6(1), point (d)			Article 6(1), point (d)	Article 6, point (c)		Article 18(1), point (d)
Article 8(1), point (e)				Article 6(1), point (e)			Article 6(1), point (e)	Article 6, point (d)		Article 18, point (g)
Article 8(1), point (f)										Article 18, point (h)

Directive 73/239/EEC	Directive 78/473/EEC	Directive 87/344/EEC	Directive 88/357/EEC	Directive 92/49/EEC	Directive 98/78/EC	Directive 2001/17/EC	Directive 2002/83/EC	Directive 2005/68/EC	Directive 2007/44/EC	This Directive
Article 8(1), second to fourth subparagraphs							Article 6(2)	Article 7		Article 19
Article 8(1a)							Article 6(3)	Article 8		Article 20
Article 8(2)				Article 6(2)			Article 6(4)			Article 18(2)
Article 8(3), first subparagraph				Article 6(3), first subparagraph			Article 6(5), third subparagraph	Article 9(1)		Article 21(4)
Article 8(3), second subparagraph				Article 6(3) second subparagraph and Article 29 first subparagraph, first sentence			Article 6(5), first subparagraph	Article 9(2)		Article 21(1) first subparagraph
Article 8(3), third subparagraph				Article 6(3) third subparagraph and Article 29 second subparagraph						Article 21(2)
Article 8(3), fourth subparagraph				Article 6(3) fourth subparagraph						Article 21(3)
Article 8(4)				Article 6(4)			Article 6(6)	Article 10		Article 22
Article 9, points (a)-(d)				Article 7, points (a)-(d)			Article 7, points (a)-(d)	Article 11(1), points (a), (c), (d) and (e)		Article 23(1), points (a), (c), (d) and (e)

Directive 73/239/EEC	Directive 78/473/EEC	Directive 87/344/EEC	Directive 88/357/EEC	Directive 92/49/EEC	Directive 98/78/EC	Directive 2001/17/EC	Directive 2002/83/EC	Directive 2005/68/EC	Directive 2007/44/EC	This Directive
Article 9, points (e) and (f)				Article 7, points (e) and (f)				Article 11(2), points (a) and (b)		Article 23(2), point (e)
Article 9, points (g) and (h)				Article 7, points (g) and (h)			Article 7(f) and (g)	Article 11(2) (c) and (d)		Article23(2) (a) and (d)
Article 10(1)				Article 32(1)			Article 40(1)			Article 145(1), first subparagraph
Article 10(2), first subparagraph				Article 32(2) first subparagraph			Article 40(2)			Article 145(2)
Article 10(2), second subparagraph				Article 32(2) second subparagraph						Article 145(3)
Article 10(3)				Article 32(3)			Article 40(3)			Article 146(1) and (2)
Article 10(4)				Article 32(4)			Article 40(4)			Article 146(3)
Article 10(5)				Article 32(5)			Article 40(5)			Article 146(3), second subparagraph
Article 10(6)				Article 32(6)			Article 40(6)			Article145(4)
Article 11				Article 33						—
Article 12				Article 56			Article 9	Article 13		Article 25, second subparagraph
Article 12a							Article 9a	Articles 14 and 60(2)		Article 26

Directive 73/239/EEC	Directive 78/473/EEC	Directive 87/344/EEC	Directive 88/357/EEC	Directive 92/49/EEC	Directive 98/78/EC	Directive 2001/17/EC	Directive 2002/83/EC	Directive 2005/68/EC	Directive 2007/44/EC	This Directive
Article 13(1) and (2), first subparagraph				Article 9(1) and (2), first subparagraph			Article 10(1), first sentence and (2), first subparagraph	Article 15(1), first subparagraph and (2)		Article 30(1), (2), first subparagraph
Article 13(2), second subparagraph				Article 9(2), second subparagraph						Article 30(2), second subparagraph
							Article 10(1), second and third sentences	Article 15(1), subparagraph 2		Article 30(3)
Article 13(2), third subparagraph							Article 10(2) second subparagraph	Article 60(3)		Article 32(1)
Article 13(3)				Article 9(3)			Article 10(3)	Article 15(4)		—
Article 14				Article 10			Article 11	Article 16		Article 33
Article 15(1), (2) and (3), second subparagraph				Article 17			Article 20 (1)-(3) and (4) second subparagraph	Article 32(1) and (3)		Articles 76 to 86
Article 15(3), first subparagraph							Article 20(4), first subparagraph	Article 32(2)		Articles 134(2) and 173
Article 15a				Article 18				Article 33		—
Article 16							Article 27	Articles 35, 36, 60(8)		Articles 87-99
Article 16a							Article 28	Articles 37-39, 60(9)		Articles 100-127

Directive 73/239/EEC	Directive 78/473/EEC	Directive 87/344/EEC	Directive 88/357/EEC	Directive 92/49/EEC	Directive 98/78/EC	Directive 2001/17/EC	Directive 2002/83/EC	Directive 2005/68/EC	Directive 2007/44/EC	This Directive
Article 17(1)							Article 29(1)	Article 40(1)		Articles 128 and 129(1) points (a)-(c) and (2)
Article 17(2)							Article 29(2)	Article 40(2)		Article 129(1) point (d)
Article 17a							Article 30	Article 41		—
Article 17b							Articles 28 and 28, point (a)	Article 60(10)		—
Article 18							Article 31			—
Article 14							Article 11	Article 16		Article 33
Article 19(2)				Article 11(2)			Article 13(2)	Article 17(2)		Article 35
Article 19(3), first and second sub-paragraphs, points (a) and (b)			Article 10	Article 11(3) first and second sub-paragraphs, points (a) and (b)			Article 13(3), first and second sub-paragraphs 1 and 2(a) and (b)	Article 17(3) and (4), first subpara-graph, points (a) and (b)		Article 34 (1)-(3), (5), (6) and (7)
Article 19(3), second sub-paragraph, point (c)			Article 10	Article 11(3) second sub-paragraph, point (c)			Article 13(3), second sub-paragraph, point (c)	Article 17(4), first subpara-graph, point (c)		Article 34(8)
Article 19(3), third sub-paragraph			Article 10	Article 11(3) third sub-paragraph			Article 13(3), third sub-paragraph	Article 17(4) second sub-paragraph		Article 35(2), point (b)
Article 20(1)							Article 37(1)	Article 42(1)		Article 137
Article 20(2), first sub-paragraph				Article 13(2) first subpara-graph			Article 37(2), first subpara-graph	Article 42(2), first subpara-graph		—
Article 20(2), second sub-paragraph				Article 13(2) second sub-paragraph			Article 37(2), second sub-paragraph	Article 42(2), second sub-paragraph		Article 138(5)

Directive 73/239/EEC	Directive 78/473/EEC	Directive 87/344/EEC	Directive 88/357/EEC	Directive 92/49/EEC	Directive 98/78/EC	Directive 2001/17/EC	Directive 2002/83/EC	Directive 2005/68/EC	Directive 2007/44/EC	This Directive
Article 20(3), first subparagraph				Article 13(3) first subparagraph			Article 37(3), first subparagraph	Article 42(3), first subparagraph		—
Article 20(3), second subparagraph				Article 13(3) second subparagraph			Article 37(3), second subparagraph	Article 42(3), second subparagraph		Article 39(3)
Article 20(4)				Article 13(4)						—
Article 20(5)				Article 13(2), second subparagraph and (5)			Article 37(2), second subparagraph and (5)	Article 42(2), second subparagraph and (4)		Article 138(5)
Article 20a (1), first subparagraph, first sentence							Article 38(1), first sentence	Article 43(1)		Article 138(2) and article 139(2)
Article 20a (1), first subparagraph, second sentence, points (a)-(e)							Article 38(1), second sentence, points (a)-(e)	Article 43(2), points (a)-(e)		Article 142(1)
Article 20a (2)							Article 38(2)			Article 141
Article 20a (3)							Article 38(3)	Article 43(4)		Article 140(2)
Article 20a (4)							Article 38(4)	Article 43(5)		—
Article 20a (5)							Article 38(5)	Article 43(6)		Article 142(2)
Article 21			Article 11(1)							—

Directive 73/239/EEC	Directive 78/473/EEC	Directive 87/344/EEC	Directive 88/357/EEC	Directive 92/49/EEC	Directive 98/78/EC	Directive 2001/17/EC	Directive 2002/83/EC	Directive 2005/68/EC	Directive 2007/44/EC	This Directive
Article 22(1) first subparagraph, points (a), (b) and (d)				Article 14			Article 39(1) first subparagraph, points (a), (b) and (d)	Article 44(1) first subparagraph, points (a), (b) and (d)		Article144(1), points (a), (b) and (c)
Article 22(1) second subparagraph, first sentence							Article 39(1) second subparagraph, first sentence	Article 44(1) second subparagraph,		Article 144(2), first subparagraph
Article 22(1) second subparagraph, second sentence							Article 39(1) second subparagraph, second sentence			Article 144(2), second subparagraph
Article 22(2)							Article 39(2)	Article 44(2)		Article 144(3)
Article 23(1)							Article 51(1)			Article 162(1)
Article 23 (2)(a)-(g)							Article 51(2)			Article162(2), points (a)-(f) and (h)
Article 23(2), point (h)										Article162(2), point (g)
Article 24 first subparagraph, first sentence							Article 54 first subparagraph, first sentence			Article 165, first sentence
Article 24 first subparagraph, second sentence and third subparagraph							Article 54, first subparagraph, second sentence, third subparagraph			—

Directive 73/239/EEC	Directive 78/473/EEC	Directive 87/344/EEC	Directive 88/357/EEC	Directive 92/49/EEC	Directive 98/78/EC	Directive 2001/17/EC	Directive 2002/83/EC	Directive 2005/68/EC	Directive 2007/44/EC	This Directive
Article 25							Article 55			Article 166
Article 26							Article 56			Article 167
Article 27 first sub-paragraph							Article 52(2), first subparagraph			Article 168, first subparagraph
Article 27 second sub-paragraph							Article 52(2), second sub-paragraph			Article 168, second sub-paragraph
Article 28							Article 52(3)			Article 170
Article 28a				Article 53			Article 53			Article 164
Article 29							Article 57			Article 171
Article 29a							Article 58			Article 176, first to third subparagraphs
Article 29b (1) and (2)							Article 59(1) and (2)	Article 52(1) and (2)		Article 177(1) and (2)
Article 29b (3)-(6)							Article 59(3)-(6)	Article 52(3) and (4)		—
Article 30(1) and (2), point (a)										—
Article 30(2), point (b)										Article 305(1)
Article 30(4)										Article 305(2)
Article 30(5)										Article305(4)
Article 31										—
Article 32										—
Article 33			Article 28				Article 62	Article 54(2)		Article 298(2) and (3)

Directive 73/239/EEC	Directive 78/473/EEC	Directive 87/344/EEC	Directive 88/357/EEC	Directive 92/49/EEC	Directive 98/78/EC	Directive 2001/17/EC	Directive 2002/83/EC	Directive 2005/68/EC	Directive 2007/44/EC	This Directive
Article 34	Article 9		Article 29		Article 11(5)		Article 6(5), fourth subparagraph		Article 6	—
Article 35	Article 10	Article 10	Article 32	Article 57(1)	Article 11(1)-(3)	Article 31(1) and (2)	Article 69(1) to (4)	Article 64(1)	Article 7(1)	Article 309(1)
Article 36	Article 11	Article 11	Article 33	Article 57(2)	Article 11(4)	Article 31(3)	Article 70	Article 64(2)	Article 7(2)	Article 309(2)
Article 37			Article 34							—
Article 38	Article 12	Article 12	Article 35	Article 58	Article 13	Article 33	Article 74	Article 66	Article 9	Article 312
Annex, part A										Article 15(2), second subparagraph and Annex I, Part A
Annex, part A, B										Annex I, Part A and B
Annex, part C										Article 16
Annex, part D										—
	Article 1(1) first subparagraph									Article 190(1)
	Article 1(1) second subparagraph									Article190(2)
	Article 1(2)									—
	Article 2(1)									Article190(1)
	Article 2(2)									Article190(3)
	Article 3									Article 191

Directive 73/239/EEC	Directive 78/473/EEC	Directive 87/344/EEC	Directive 88/357/EEC	Directive 92/49/EEC	Directive 98/78/EC	Directive 2001/17/EC	Directive 2002/83/EC	Directive 2005/68/EC	Directive 2007/44/EC	This Directive
	Article 4(1)									Article 192 first and second subparagraphs
	Article 4(2)									—
	Article 5									Article 193
	Article 6									Article 195
	Article 7									Article 194
	Article 8									Article 196
		Article 1								—
		Article 2								Article 198
		Article 3(1)								Article 199
		Article 3(2) first subparagraph, first sentence								Article 200(1) first subparagraph
		Article 3(2), points (a)-(c)								Article 200(2)-(4)
		Article 3(3)								Article 200(1) second subparagraph
		Article 4								Article 201
		Article 5								Article 202
		Article 6								Article 203
		Article 7								Article 204
		Article 8								Article 205
		Article 9								Article 16(2)
			Article 1							—

Directive 73/239/EEC	Directive 78/473/EEC	Directive 87/344/EEC	Directive 88/357/EEC	Directive 92/49/EEC	Directive 98/78/EC	Directive 2001/17/EC	Directive 2002/83/EC	Directive 2005/68/EC	Directive 2007/44/EC	This Directive
			Article 2, points (a), (b) and (e)							—
			Article 2, point (c)				Article 1(1), point (c)	Article 2(1), point (e)		—
			Article 2, point (d)							Article13(13)
			Article 2, point (f)	Article 1, point (e)			Article 1(1), point (h)			—
			Article 3				Article 1, point (b), second sentence			Article 145(1), second subparagraph
			Article 4							Article 187
			Article 6							—
			Article 7(1), points (a)-(e)							—
			Article 7(1), point (f)	Article 27						—
			Article 7(1), point (g) and (3)							—
			Article 8(1) and (2)							Article 179(1) and (2)
			Article 8(3)							—
			Article 8(4), points (a) and (c)	Article 30(1)						—
			Article 8(4), point (d)							Article 179(3)
			Article 8(5)							Article 179(4)

Directive 73/239/EEC	Directive 78/473/EEC	Directive 87/344/EEC	Directive 88/357/EEC	Directive 92/49/EEC	Directive 98/78/EC	Directive 2001/17/EC	Directive 2002/83/EC	Directive 2005/68/EC	Directive 2007/44/EC	This Directive
			Article 12							—
			Article 12a(1)-(3)							Article 150
			Article 12a (4) first subparagraph							Article 151
			Article 12a (4) second to sixth subparagraphs							Article 152
			Article 14	Article 34			Article 41			Article 147
			Article 16(1), first and second subparagraphs	Article 35			Article 42			Article 148
			Article 16(1) third subparagraph	Article 35						Article 148(2)
			Article 17	Article 36			Article 43			Article 149
			Article 26							—
			Article 27							—
			Article 31							Article 299
			Article 31				Article 68(2)			Article 300
			Annex I	Article 23			Annex II			—
			Annex 2A							—
			Annex 2B							—
			Articles 5, 9, 10, 11							—

Directive 73/239/EEC	Directive 78/473/EEC	Directive 87/344/EEC	Directive 88/357/EEC	Directive 92/49/EEC	Directive 98/78/EC	Directive 2001/17/EC	Directive 2002/83/EC	Directive 2005/68/EC	Directive 2007/44/EC	This Directive
				Article 1, point (a)	Article 1, point (a)	Article 2, point (a)	Article 1(1), point (a)			Article 13(1)
				Article 1, point (b)			Article 1(1), point (b)	Article 2(1), point (d)		Article 13(11)
				Article 1, point (c)		Article 2, point (e)	Article 1(1), point (e)	Article 2(1), point (f)		Article 13(8), point (a)
				Article 1, point (d)			Article 1(1), point (f)	Article 2(1), point (g)		—
				Article 1, point (f)			Article 1(1), point (i)	Article 2(1), point (i)		Article 13(18)
				Article 1, point (g)			Article 1(1), point (j)	Article 2(1), point (j)		Articles 13(21), article 24(2), and Article 63
				Article 1, point (h),	Article 1, point (d)		Article 1(1), point (k)	Article 2(1), point (k)		Article 13(15)
				Article 1, point (i)	Article 1, point (e)		Article 1(1), point (l)	Article 2(1), point (l)		Article 13(16)
				Article 1, point (j)			Article 1(1), point (m)			Article 13(22)
				Article 1, point (k)	Article 1, point (k)	Article 2(h)	Article 1(1), point (n)	Article 2(1), point (m)		Article 13(10)
				Article 1, point (l)			Article 1(1), point (r)	Article 2(1), point (n)		Article 13(17)
				Article 1, point (l)(a)	Article 1, point (f)		Article 1(1), point (r)(i)	Article 2(1), point (n)(i)		Article 13(20)
				Article 1, point (l)(b)			Article 1(1), point (r)(ii)	Article 2(1), point (n)(ii)		Article 13(18)
				Article 3						Article 188
				Article 8				Article 12		Article 24(1)
				Article 12(2)			Article 14(1)	Article 18		Article 39(1)

Directive 73/239/EEC	Directive 78/473/EEC	Directive 87/344/EEC	Directive 88/357/EEC	Directive 92/49/EEC	Directive 98/78/EC	Directive 2001/17/EC	Directive 2002/83/EC	Directive 2005/68/EC	Directive 2007/44/EC	This Directive
				Article 12(3)-(6)			Article 14 (2)-(5)			Article 39(2)-(6)
				Article 15(1) and (2)			Article 15(1) and (2)	Article 19(1)		Article 57
				Article 15(3)			Article 15(3)	Article 22		Article 61
				Article 15(4)			Article 15(4)	Article 23		Article 62
				Articles 15a			Article 15a	Article 19(2)-(8)		Article 58(1)-(7)
				Articles 15b			Article 15b	Article 19a		Article 59
				Articles 15c			Article 15c	Article 20		Article 60
				Article 16(1)			Article 16(1)	Article 24		Article 64
				Article 16(2)			Article 16(2)	Article 25		Article 65
				Article 16(3)			Article 16(3)	Article 26		Article 66
				Article 16(4)			Article 16(4)	Article 27		Article 67
				Article 16(5)			Article 16(5)	Article 28(1)		Article 68(1)
				Article 16 (5b) first to fourth subparagraphs			Article 16(7) first to fourth subparagraphs	Article 28(3) first to fourth subparagraphs		Article 68(3)
				Article 16 (5b) fifth subparagraph			Article 16(7) fifth subparagraph	Article 28(3) fifth subparagraph		Article 68(4)
				Article 16(3)						Article 66
				Article 16 (5c)			Article 16(8)	Article 29		Article 70
				Article 16 (5a)			Article 16(6)	Article 28(2)		Article 68(2)

Directive 73/239/EEC	Directive 78/473/EEC	Directive 87/344/EEC	Directive 88/357/EEC	Directive 92/49/EEC	Directive 98/78/EC	Directive 2001/17/EC	Directive 2002/83/EC	Directive 2005/68/EC	Directive 2007/44/EC	This Directive
				Article 16a (1), point (a)			Article 17(1), point (a)	Article 31(1), first subparagraph		Article 72(1), points (a)-(c)
				Article 16a (1), point (b)			Article 17 (1)(b)	Article 31(1), second subparagraph		Article 72(1) second subparagraph
				Article 16a (2)			Article 17(2)	Article 31(2)		Article 72(2)
				Article 20			Article 22			—
				Article 21			Article 23	Article 34 (1)-(3)		—
				Article 22			Article 24	Article 34(4)		—
				Article 25						—
				Article 28			Article 33			Article 180
				Article 29						Article 181(1) and (3)
				Article 30(2)						Article 181(2)
				Article 31						Article 183
				Article 38			Article 44			Article 153
				Article 39(2) and (3)			Article 45			Article 154
				Article 40(2)			Article 46(1)			Article 155(8)
				Article 40(3)			Article 46(2)			Article 155(1)
				Article 40(4), (6)-(8) and (10)			Article 46(3), (5)-(7) and (9)			Article 155(2), (4)-(6) and (9)
				Article 40(5)			Article 46(4)			Article 155(3)
				Article 40(9)			Article 46(8)			Article 155(7)
				Article 41			Article 47			Article 156
				Article 42(2)			Article 48			Article 160

Directive 73/239/EEC	Directive 78/473/EEC	Directive 87/344/EEC	Directive 88/357/EEC	Directive 92/49/EEC	Directive 98/78/EC	Directive 2001/17/EC	Directive 2002/83/EC	Directive 2005/68/EC	Directive 2007/44/EC	This Directive
				Article 43(2) and (3)						Article 184
				Article 44(2)			Article 49			Article 159 and Annex V
				Article 45(2)						Article 189
				Article 46(2), first and third sub-paragraph.			Article 50(1), first and third sub-paragraphs, and (2)			Article 157
				Ar-ticles 47-50						—
				Article 51			Article 64	Article 56		—
				Article 51, final indent					Article 1(4)	Article 58(8)
				Article 52						—
				Article 54						Article 206
				Article 55						Article 207
				Articles 24 and 26						—
				Articles 12(1), 19, 33, 37, 39(1), 40(1), 42(1), 43(1), 44(1), 45(1), 46(1),						—
					Article 1, point (b)					Article 13(3)
					Article 1, point (c)		Article 1(1), point (s)	Article 2(1), point (c)		Article 13(4)

Directive 73/239/EEC	Directive 78/473/EEC	Directive 87/344/EEC	Directive 88/357/EEC	Directive 92/49/EEC	Directive 98/78/EC	Directive 2001/17/EC	Directive 2002/83/EC	Directive 2005/68/EC	Directive 2007/44/EC	This Directive
					Article 1, point (g)					Article 212(1), point (a)
					Article 1, point (h)					Article 212(1), point (b)
					Article 1, point (i)			Article 59(2), point (a)(i)		Article 210(1), point (f)
					Article 1, point (j)			Article 59(2), point (a)(j)		Article 210(1), point (g)
					Article 1, point (l)			Article 59(2), point (b)		Article 13(6)
					Article 2			Article 59(3)		Article 214(1)
					Article 3			Article 59(3)		Article 214(1) and (2), first and second subparagraphs
					Article 4			Article 59(3)		Article 247(1)
					Article 5(1)			Article 59(4)		Article 246
					Article 5(2)					Article 254(1)
					Article 6			Article 59(5)		Articles 254(2), 255(1) and (2)
					Article 7			Article 59(5)		Articles 249(1), 252, 253
					Article 8			Article 59(5)		Articles 245, 246, 258(1)
					Article 9			Article 59(6)		Articles 218, 219, 258(1)
					Article 10			Article 59(7)		Articles 218, 219, 258(1), 260-263
					Article 10a			Article 59(8)		Articles 264

Directive 73/239/EEC	Directive 78/473/EEC	Directive 87/344/EEC	Directive 88/357/EEC	Directive 92/49/EEC	Directive 98/78/EC	Directive 2001/17/EC	Directive 2002/83/EC	Directive 2005/68/EC	Directive 2007/44/EC	This Directive
					Article 10b					Article 257
					Article 12	Article 32	Article 73	Article 65	Article 8(1)	Article 311
					Annex I			Article 59(9) and Annex II		Articles 213-215, 218-246
					Annex II			Article 59(9) and Annex II		Articles 215-217, 220-243
						Article 1(2)				Article 267
						Article 2, point (b)				Article 268(1), point (b)
						Article 2, point (c)				Article 268(1), point (c)
						Article 2, point (d)				Article 268(1), point (d)
						Article 2, point (f)		Article 2(1), point (h)		Article 13(9)
						Article 2, point (g)				Article 268(1), point (a)
						Article 2, point (i)				Article 268(1), point (e)
						Article 2, point (j)				Article 268(1), point (f)
						Article 2, point (k)				Article 268(1), point (g)
						Article 3				—
						Article 4				Article 269
						Article 5				Article 270
						Article 6				Article 271
						Article 7				Article 272
						Article 8				Article 273

Directive 73/239/EEC	Directive 78/473/EEC	Directive 87/344/EEC	Directive 88/357/EEC	Directive 92/49/EEC	Directive 98/78/EC	Directive 2001/17/EC	Directive 2002/83/EC	Directive 2005/68/EC	Directive 2007/44/EC	This Directive
						Article 9				Article 274
						Article 10				Article 275
						Article 11				Article 277
						Article 12				Article 278
						Article 13				Article 279
						Article 14				Article 280
						Article 15				Article 281
						Article 16				Article 282
						Article 17				Article 283
						Article 18				Article 284
						Article 19				Article 285
						Article 20				Article 286
						Article 21				Article 287
						Article 22				Article 288
						Article 23				Article 289
						Article 24				Article 290
						Article 25				Article 291
						Article 26				Article 292
						Article 27				Article 293
						Article 28				Article 294
						Article 29				Article 295
						Article 30(1)				Article 268(2)
						Article 30(2)				Article 296
						Annex				Article 276
							Article 1(1), point (d)			—
							Article 1(1), point (g)			Article 13(14)

Directive 73/239/EEC	Directive 78/473/EEC	Directive 87/344/EEC	Directive 88/357/EEC	Directive 92/49/EEC	Directive 98/78/EC	Directive 2001/17/EC	Directive 2002/83/EC	Directive 2005/68/EC	Directive 2007/44/EC	This Directive
							Article 1(1), point (q)			—
							Article 1(2)	Article 2(3)		—
							Article 2(1)			Article 2(3)
							Article 3(2), (3) and (8)			Article 9
							Article 3(5), and (7)			Article 10
							Article 3(6)			—
							Article 5(2) second and third sub-paragraphs			Article 15(2) third subpara-graph and (3) second sub-paragraph
							Article 6(5) first and second sub-paragraph			Article 21(1)
							Article 7, point (e)			Article 23(2), point (f)
							Article 8	Article 12		Article 24(1)
							Article 12			Article 208
							Article 16(9)	Article 30		Article 69
							Article 18(1) to (6)			Article 73
							Article 18(7)			—
							Article 19(1), first subpara-graph, first indent			Article 74(1)

Directive 73/239/EEC	Directive 78/473/EEC	Directive 87/344/EEC	Directive 88/357/EEC	Directive 92/49/EEC	Directive 98/78/EC	Directive 2001/17/EC	Directive 2002/83/EC	Directive 2005/68/EC	Directive 2007/44/EC	This Directive
							Article 19(1), second subparagraph, second indent			Article 74(3), second subparagraph
							Article 19(1), second subparagraph, (2) and (3)			Article 74(4)-(7)
							Article 21			Article 209
							Article 25			—
							Article 26			—
							Article 32			—
							Article 34			Article 182
							Article 35			Article 186
							Article 36(1)			Article 185(1)
							Article 36(2)			Article 185(4), first sentence
							Annex III(A)			Article 185(6)
							Article 36(3)			Article 185(7)
							Article 41			Article 147
							Article 42(1)-(3)			Article 148(1), (3) and (4)
							Article 43			Article 149
							Article 45			—
							Article 48			Article 160
							Article 49			Article 159
							Article 51(2), points (a) to (g)			Article 162(2), points (a)-(e), (g) and (h)

Directive 73/239/EEC	Directive 78/473/EEC	Directive 87/344/EEC	Directive 88/357/EEC	Directive 92/49/EEC	Directive 98/78/EC	Directive 2001/17/EC	Directive 2002/83/EC	Directive 2005/68/EC	Directive 2007/44/EC	This Directive
							Article 51(3) and (4)			Article 163
							Article 52(1)			Article 169
							Article 55(1) and (2)			Article 166(1) and (2)
							Article 56			Article 167
							Article 59(1) and (2)	Article 52(1) and (2)		Article 177(1) and (2)
							Article 59(3) and (6)	Article 52(3) and (4)		—
							Article 60(1)			Article 305(2), second and third subparagraphs
							Article 60(2)			Article 305(3)
			Article 31				Article 61			Article 43
							Article 65	Article 55		Article 301(1) and (3)
							Article 66			Article 308
							Article 67	Article 53		Article 297
							Article 68(1)			—
							Article 71			—
							Article 72			Article 310
							Annex I			Annex II
							Annex III			Article 185(2), points (a) -(c), (3), and (5), first subparagraph
							Annex IV			—
							Annex V			Annex VI

Directive 73/239/EEC	Directive 78/473/EEC	Directive 87/344/EEC	Directive 88/357/EEC	Directive 92/49/EEC	Directive 98/78/EC	Directive 2001/17/EC	Directive 2002/83/EC	Directive 2005/68/EC	Directive 2007/44/EC	This Directive
							Annex VI			Annex VII
								Article 1(2), point (d)		Article 11
								Article 2(1), point (a)		Article 13(7)
								Article 2(1), point (b)		—
								Article 2(1), point (h)		Article 13(9)
								Article 2(1), point (o)		Article 13(25)
								Article 2(1), point (p)		Article 13(26)
								Article 2(1), point (q)		Article 210(3)
								Article 2(2)		—
								Article 4(2)		Article 15(5)
								Article 5(1), first subparagraph and (2)		Article 17(1) and (2), Annex IIIC;
								Article 9(1)		Article 21(4)
								Article 11(1), point (b)		Article 23(1), point (b)
								Article 15(3)		Article 32(2)
								Article 21		—
								Article 45		—
								Article 46		Article 211(1) and (2)
								Article 47		Article 158
								Article 48		Article 161

Directive 73/239/EEC	Directive 78/473/EEC	Directive 87/344/EEC	Directive 88/357/EEC	Directive 92/49/EEC	Directive 98/78/EC	Directive 2001/17/EC	Directive 2002/83/EC	Directive 2005/68/EC	Directive 2007/44/EC	This Directive
								Article 50		Article 175
								Article 51		Article 176
								Article 54(1)		Article 298(1)
								Article 61		Article 308
								Article 62		Article 12
								Article 63		Article 307
								Articles 57, 58, 59 and 60, Annex II		—
									Articles 1(4), 2(4) and 4(6)	Article 58(8)
									Article 8(2)	Article 312

Part VI European Materials

C. ACCOUNTING

COUNCIL DIRECTIVE

(91/674/EEC)
of 19 December 1991

on the annual accounts and consolidated accounts of insurance undertakings

NOTES
Date of publication in OJ: OJ L374, 31.12.91, p 7.

[6482]
THE COUNCIL OF THE EUROPEAN COMMUNITIES,

Having regard to the Treaty establishing the European Economic Community, and in particular Article 54 thereof,

Having regard to the proposal from the Commission,[1]

In cooperation with the European Parliament,[2]

Having regard to the opinion of the Economic and Social Committee,[3]

Whereas Article 54(3)(g) of the Treaty requires coordination to the necessary extent of the safeguards which, for the protection of the interests of members and others, are required by Member States of companies and firms within the meaning of the second paragraph of Article 58 of the Treaty, with a view to making such safeguards equivalent throughout the Community;

Whereas Council Directive 78/660/EEC of 25 July 1978 based on Article 54(3)(g) of the Treaty on the annual accounts of certain types of companies,[4] as last amended by Directive 90/605/EEC,[5] need not be applied to insurance companies, hereinafter referred to as "insurance undertakings", pending further coordination; whereas, in view of the major importance of insurance undertakings in the Community, such coordination cannot be delayed any longer following the implementation of Directive 78/660/EEC;

Whereas Council Directive 83/349/EEC of 13 June 1983 based on Article 54(3)(g) of the Treaty on consolidated accounts,[6] as last amended by Directive 90/605/EEC, provides for derogations for insurance undertakings only until the expiry of the deadline imposed for the application of this Directive; whereas this Directive must therefore also include provisions specific to insurance undertakings in respect of consolidated accounts;

Whereas such coordination is also urgently required because insurance undertakings operate across borders; whereas for creditors, debtors, members, policyholders and their advisers and for the general public, improved comparability of the annual accounts and consolidated accounts of such undertakings is of crucial importance;

Whereas in the Member States insurance undertakings of different legal forms are in competition with each other; whereas undertakings engaged in the business of direct insurance customarily engage in the business of reinsurance as well and are therefore in competition with specialist reinsurance undertakings; whereas it is therefore appropriate not to confine coordination to the legal forms covered by Directive 78/660/EEC, but to choose a scope that corresponds to that of Council Directive 73/239/EEC of 24 July 1973 on the coordination of laws, regulations and administrative provisions relating to the taking up and pursuit of the business of direct insurance other than life assurance,[7] as last amended by Directive 90/618/EEC,[8] and to that of Council Directive 79/267/EEC of 5 March 1979 on the coordination of laws, regulations and administrative provisions relating to he taking up and pursuit of the business of direct life assurance,[9] as last amended by Directive 90/619/EEC,[10] but which also includes certain undertakings that are excluded from the scope of those Directives and companies and firms which are reinsurance undertakings;

Whereas, although in view of the specific characteristics of insurance undertakings it would appear appropriate to propose a separate Directive on the annual accounts and consolidated accounts of such undertakings, that does not necessarily require the establishment of a set of standards different from those of Directive 78/660/EEC and 83/349/EEC; whereas such separate standards would be neither appropriate nor consistent with the principles underlying the coordination of company law since, given the important position they occupy in the Community economy, insurance undertakings cannot be excluded from a framework of rules devised for undertakings generally; whereas, for this reason, only the particular characteristics of insurance undertakings have been taken into account and this Directive deals only with derogations from the rules laid down in Directives 78/660/EEC and 83/349/EEC;

Whereas there are major differences in the structure and content of the balance sheets of insurance undertakings in different Member States; whereas this Directive must therefore lay down the same structure and the same item designations for the balance sheets of all Community insurance undertakings;

Whereas, if annual accounts and consolidated accounts are to be comparable, a number of basic questions regarding the disclosure of certain transactions in the balance sheet must be settled;

Whereas, in the interests of greater comparability, it is also necessary that the content of the various balance sheet items be determined precisely;

Whereas it may be useful to distinguish between the commitments of the insurer and those of the reinsurer by showing in the assets the reinsurer's share of technical provisions as an asset;

Whereas the structure of the profit and loss account should also be determined and certain items in it should be defined;

Whereas, given the specific nature of the insurance industry, it may be useful for unrealised gains and losses to be dealt with in the profit and loss account;

Whereas the comparability of figures in the balance sheet and profit and loss account also depends basically on the values at which assets and liabilities are shown in the balance sheet; whereas for a proper understanding of the financial situation of an insurance undertaking the current value of investments as well as their value based upon the principle of purchase price or production cost must be disclosed; whereas, however, the compulsory disclosure of the current value of investments, at least in the notes on the accounts, is prescribed solely for purposes of comparability and transparency and is not intended to lead to changes in the tax treatment of insurance undertakings;

Whereas in the calculation of life assurance provisions use may be made of actuarial methods customarily applied on the market or accepted by the insurance-monitoring authorities; whereas those methods may be implemented by any actuary or expert in accordance with the conditions which may be laid down in national law and with due regard for the actuarial principles recognised in the framework of the present and future coordination of the fundamental rules for the prudential and financial monitoring of direct life assurance business;

Whereas, in the calculation of the provision for claims outstanding, on the one hand, any implicit discounting or deduction should be prohibited, and, on the other hand, precise conditions for recourse to explicit discounting or deduction should be defined, for the sake of prudence and transparency;

Whereas, in view of the special nature of insurance undertakings, certain changes are necessary with regard to the notes on annual accounts and on consolidated accounts;

Whereas, in line with the intention of covering all insurance undertakings that come within the scope of Directive 73/239/EEC and 79/267/EEC as well as certain others, derogations such as those for small and medium-sized insurance undertakings in Directive 78/660/EEC are not provided for, but certain small mutual associations which are excluded from the scope of Directives 73/239/EEC and 79/267/EEC should not be covered;

Whereas for the same reasons the scope allowed Member States pursuant to Directive 83/349 to exempt parent undertakings of groups from compulsory consolidation if the undertakings to be consolidated do not together exceed a certain size has not been extended to insurance undertakings;

Whereas in view of its particular nature special provisions are needed for the association of underwriters known as Lloyd's;

Whereas the provisions of this Directive also apply to the consolidated accounts drawn up by a parent undertaking which is a financial holding company where its subsidiary undertakings are either exclusively or mainly insurance undertakings;

Whereas the examination of problems which arise in connection with this Directive, in particular regarding its application, requires cooperation by representatives of the Member States and the Commission in a contact committee; whereas, in order to avoid the proliferation of such committees, it is desirable that such cooperation take place in the committee provided for in Article 52 of Directive 78/660/EEC; whereas, however, when examining problems concerning insurance undertakings, the committee must be appropriately constituted;

Whereas, in view of the complexity of the matter, the insurance undertakings covered by this Directive must be allowed an appropriate period to implement its provisions; whereas that period must be extended to allow the necessary adjustments to be made concerning, on the one hand, the association of underwriters known as Lloyd's and, on the other, those undertakings which, when this Directive becomes applicable, show their investments at historical cost;

Whereas provision should be made for the review of certain provisions of this Directive after five years' experience of its application, in the light of the aims of greater transparency and harmonisation.

NOTES

1 OJ C131, 18.4.87, p 1.
2 OJ C96, 17.4.89, p 93, and OJ C326, 16.12.91.
3 OJ C319, 30.11.87, p 13.
4 OJ L222, 14.8.78, p 11.
5 OJ L317, 16.11.90, p 60.
6 OJ L193, 18.7.83, p 1.
7 OJ L228, 16.8.73, p 3.
8 OJ L330, 29.11.90, p 44.
9 OJ L63, 13.3.79, p 1.
10 OJ L330, 29.11.90, p 50.

HAS ADOPTED THIS DIRECTIVE—

SECTION 1
PRELIMINARY PROVISIONS AND SCOPE

[6483]
Article 1

[1. [Articles 2, 3, 4(1), (3) to (6), Articles 6, 7, 13, 14, 15(3) and (4), Articles 16 to 21, 29 to 35, 37 to 41, 42, 42a to 42f, 43(1), points 1 to 7b and 9 to 14, 45(1), 46(1) and (2), 46a, 48 to 50, 50a, 50b, 50c, 51(1), 51a, 56 to 59, 60a, 61 and 61a of Directive 78/660/EEC shall apply to the undertakings mentioned in Article 2 of this Directive, except where this Directive provides otherwise.] Articles 46, 47, 48, 51 and 53 of this Directive shall not apply in respect of assets and liabilities that are valued in accordance with Section 7a of Directive 78/660/EEC.

2. Where reference is made in Directives 78/660/EEC and 83/349/EEC to Articles 9, 10 and 10a (balance sheet) or to Articles 22 to 26 (profit and loss account) of Directive 78/660/EEC, such references shall be deemed to be references to Article 6 (balance sheet) or to Article 34 (profit and loss account) of this Directive as appropriate.]

3. References in Directives 78/660/EEC and 83/349/EEC to Articles 31 to 42 of Directive 78/660/EEC shall be deemed to be references to those Articles, taking account of Articles 45 to 62 of this Directive.

4. Where the aforementioned provisions of Directive 78/660/EEC relate to balance-sheet items for which this Directive lays down no equivalent, they shall be deemed to be references to the items in Article 6 of this Directive where the corresponding assets and liabilities items are listed.

NOTES

Para 1: substituted by European Parliament and Council Directive 2003/51/EC, art 4(1); words in square brackets substituted by European Parliament and Council Directive 2006/46/EC, art 4.

Para 2: substituted by European Parliament and Council Directive 2003/51/EC, art 4(1).

[6484]
Article 2

1. The coordination measures prescribed by this Directive shall apply to companies and firms within the meaning of the second paragraph of Article 58 of the Treaty which are—

(a) undertakings within the meaning of Article 1 of Directive 73/239/EEC, excluding those mutual associations which are excluded from the scope of that Directive by virtue of Article 3 thereof but including those bodies referred to in Article 4(a), (b), (c) and (e) thereof except where their activity does not consist wholly or mainly in carrying on insurance business;

(b) undertakings within the meaning of Article 1 of Directive 79/267/EEC, excluding those bodies and mutual associations referred to in Articles 2(2) and (3) and 3 of that Directive; or

(c) undertakings carrying on reinsurance business.

In this Directive, such undertakings shall be referred to as insurance undertakings.

2. Funds of a group pension fund within the meaning of Article 1(2)(c) and (d) of Directive 79/267/EEC which an insurance undertaking administers in its own name but on behalf of third parties must be shown in the balance sheet if the undertaking acquires legal title to the assets concerned. The total amount of such assets and liabilities shall be shown separately or in the notes on the accounts, broken down according to the various assets and liabilities items. However, the

Member States may permit the disclosure of such funds as off-balance-sheet items provided there are special rules whereby such funds can be excluded from the assets available for distribution in the event of the winding up of an insurance undertaking (or similar proceedings).

Assets acquired in the name of and on behalf of third parties must not be shown in the balance sheet.

[6485]
Article 3

Those provisions of this Directive which relate to life assurance shall apply *mutatis mutandis* to insurance undertakings which underwrite only health insurance and which do so exclusively or principally according to the technical principles of life assurance.

Member States may apply the first paragraph to health insurance underwritten by joint undertakings according to the technical principles of life assurance where such activity is significant.

[6486]
[Article 4

1. This Directive shall apply to the association of underwriters known as Lloyd's. For the purpose of this Directive both Lloyd's and Lloyd's syndicates shall be deemed to be insurance undertakings.

2. By way of derogation from Article 65(1), Lloyd's shall prepare aggregate accounts instead of consolidated accounts required by Directive 83/349/EEC. Aggregate accounts shall be prepared by cumulation of all syndicate accounts.]

NOTES

Substituted by European Parliament and Council Directive 2003/51/EC, art 4(2).

SECTION 2
GENERAL PROVISIONS CONCERNING THE BALANCE SHEET AND THE PROFIT AND LOSS ACCOUNT

[6487]
Article 5

The combination of items under the conditions laid down in Article 4(3)(a) or (b) of Directive 78/660/EEC shall be restricted in the case of insurance undertakings,

— as regards the balance sheet, to items preceded by arabic numerals, except for items concerning technical provisions, and
— as regards the profit and loss account, to items preceded by one or more lower-case letters, except for items I(1) and (4) and II(1), (5) and (6).

Combination shall be authorised only under the rules laid down by the Member States.

SECTION 3
LAYOUT OF THE BALANCE SHEET

[6488]
Article 6

The Member States shall prescribe the following layout for balance sheets—

ASSETS

A. *Subscribed capital unpaid*

showing separately called-up capital (unless national law requires called-up capital to be included under liabilities, in which case capital called but not yet paid must be included as an asset either under A or under E(IV)).

B. *Intangible assets*

as described under items B and C(I) of Article 9 of Directive 78/660/EEC, showing separately—

— formation expenses, as defined by national law and in so far as national law permits their being shown as an asset (unless national law requires their disclosure in the notes on the accounts),
— goodwill, to the extent that it was acquired for valuable consideration (unless national law requires its disclosure in the notes on the accounts).

C. *Investments*

I. Land and buildings—
showing separately land and buildings occupied by an insurance undertaking for its own

activities (unless national law requires their disclosure in the notes on the accounts).

II. Investments in affiliated undertakings and participating interests—

1. Shares in affiliated undertakings.
2. Debt securities issued by, and loans to, affiliated undertakings.
3. Participating interests.
4. Debt securities issued by, and loans to, undertakings with which an insurance undertaking is linked by virtue of a participating interest.

III. Other financial investments—

1. Shares and other variable-yield securities and units in unit trusts.
2. Debt securities and other fixed-income securities.
3. Participation in investment pools.
4. Loans guaranteed by mortgages.
5. Other loans.
6. Deposits with credit institutions.
7. Other.

IV. Deposits with ceding undertakings.

D. *Investments for the benefit of life-assurance policyholders who bear the investment risk*

E. *Debtors*

(Amounts owed by—

— affiliated undertakings, and
— undertakings with which an insurance undertaking is linked by virtue of participating interests

shall be shown separately, as sub-items of items I, II and III).

I. Debtors arising out of direct insurance operations

1. policyholders;
2. intermediaries.

II. Debtors arising out of reinsurance operations.

III. Other debtors.

IV. Subscribed capital called but not paid (unless national law requires that capital called but not paid be shown as an asset under A).

F. *Other assets*

I. Tangible assets and stocks as listed under C(II) and D(I) in Article 9 of Directive 78/660/EEC, other than land and buildings, buildings under construction and deposits paid on land and buildings.

II. Cash at bank and in hand.

III. Own shares (with an indication of their nominal value or, in the absence of a nominal value, their accounting par value) to the extent that national law permits their being shown in the balance sheet.

IV. Other.

G. *Prepayments and accrued income*

I. Accrued interest and rent.

II. Deferred acquisition costs (distinguishing those arising in non-life insurance and life-assurance business).

III. Other prepayments and accrued income.

H. *Loss for the financial year*

(unless national law requires it to be shown as a liability under A(VI)).

LIABILITIES

A. *Capital and reserves*

I. Subscribed capital or equivalent funds
(unless national law requires called-up capital to be shown under this item. In that case, the amounts of subscribed capital and paid-up capital must be shown separately).

II. Share premium account.

III. Revaluation reserve.

IV. Reserve.

V. Profit or loss brought forward.

VI. Profit or loss for the financial year

(unless national law requires it to be shown as an asset under H or as a liability under I).

B. *Subordinated liabilities*

C. *Technical provisions*

1. Provision for unearned premiums—
   (a) gross amount . . . .
   (b) reinsurance amount (–) . . . .

2. Life assurance provision—
   (a) gross amount . . . .
   (b) reinsurance amount (–) . . . .

3. Claims outstanding—
   (a) gross amount . . . .
   (b) reinsurance amount (–) . . . .

4. Provision for bonuses and rebates (unless shown under 2)—
   (a) gross amount . . . .
   (b) reinsurance amount (–) . . . .

5. Equalisation provision
6. Other technical provisions—
   (a) gross amount . . . .
   (b) reinsurance amount (–) . . . .

D. *Technical provisions for life-assurance policies where the investment risk is borne by the policyholders—*

(a) gross amount . . . .
(b) reinsurance amount (–) . . . .

E. [*Other provisions*]

1. Provisions for pensions and similar obligations.
2. Provisions for taxation.
3. Other provisions.

F. *Deposits received from reinsurers*

G. *Creditors*

(Amounts owed to—

— affiliated undertakings, and
— undertakings with which an insurance undertaking is linked by virtue of a participating interest

shall be shown separately, as sub-items.)

I. Creditors arising out of direct insurance operations.

II. Creditors arising out of reinsurance operations.
III. Debenture loans, showing convertible loans separately.
IV. Amounts owed to credit institutions.
V. Other creditors, including tax and social security.

H. *Accruals and deferred income*

I. *Profit for the financial year*
(unless national law requires it to be shown as a liability under A(VI)).

NOTES

Under title "Liabilities", words in square brackets in point E, substituted by European Parliament and Council Directive 2003/51/EC, art 4(3).

[6489]
Article 7

Article 14 of Directive 78/660/EEC shall not apply to commitments linked to insurance activities.

SECTION 4
SPECIAL PROVISIONS RELATING TO CERTAIN BALANCE-SHEET ITEMS

[6490]
Article 8

Article 15(3) of Directive 78/660/EEC shall apply only to assets items B and C(I) and (II) as defined in Article 6 of this Directive. Any movements in these items shall be shown on the basis of the balance-sheet value at the beginning of the financial year.

[6491]
Article 9
Assets: item C(III)(2)

Debt securities and other fixed-income securities

1. This item shall comprise negotiable debt securities and other fixed-income securities issued by credit institutions, by other undertakings or by public bodies, in so far as they are not covered by item C(II)(2) or (4).

2. Securities bearing interest the rate of which varies in line with specific factors, for example the interest rate on the inter-bank market or on the Euromarket, shall also be regarded as debt securities and other fixed-income securities.

[6492]
Article 10
Assets: item C(III)(3)

Participation in investment pools

This item shall comprise shares held by an undertaking in joint investments constituted by several undertakings or pension funds, the management of which has been entrusted to one of those undertakings or to one of those pension funds.

[6493]
Article 11
Assets: items C(III)(4) and (5)

Loans guaranteed by mortgages and other loans

Loans to policyholders for which the policy is the main security shall be included under "Other loans" and their amount shall be disclosed in the notes on the accounts. Loans guaranteed by mortgage shall be shown as such even where they are also secured by insurance policies. Where the amount of "Other loans" not secured by policies is material, an appropriate breakdown shall be given in the notes on the accounts.

[6494]
Article 12
Assets: item C(III)(6)

Deposits with credit institutions

This item shall comprise sums the withdrawal of which is subject to a time restriction. Sums deposited with no such restriction shall be shown under F(II) even if they bear interest.

[6495]
Article 13
Assets: item C(III)(7)

Other

This item shall comprise those investments which are not covered by items C(III)(1) to (6). Where the amount of such investments is significant, they must be disclosed in the notes on the accounts.

[6496]
Article 14
Assets: item C(IV)

Deposits with ceding undertakings

In the balance sheet of an undertaking which accepts reinsurance this item shall comprise amounts, owed by the ceding undertakings and corresponding to guarantees, which are deposited with those ceding undertakings or with third parties or which are retained by those undertakings.

These amounts may not be combined with other amounts owed by the ceding insurer to the reinsurer or set off against amounts owed by the reinsurer to the ceding insurer.

Securities deposited with ceding undertakings or third parties which remain the property of the undertaking accepting reinsurance shall be entered in the latter's accounts as an investment, under the appropriate item.

[6497]
Article 15
Assets: item D

Investments for the benefit of life assurance policyholders who bear the investment risk

In respect of life assurance this item shall comprise, on the one hand, investments the value of which is used to determine the value of or the return on policies relating to an investment fund and, on the other hand, investments serving as cover for liabilities which are determined by reference to an index. This item shall also comprise investments which are held on behalf of the members of a tontine and are intended for distribution among them.

[6498]
Article 16
Assets: item F(IV)

Other

This item shall comprise those assets which are not covered by items F(I), (II) and (III). Where such assets are material, they must be disclosed in the notes on the accounts.

[6499]
Article 17
Assets: item G(I)

Accrued interest and rent

This item shall comprise those items that represent interest and rent that have been earned up to the balance-sheet date but have not yet become receivable.

[6500]
Article 18
Assets: item G(II)

Deferred acquisition costs

1. The costs of acquiring insurance policies shall be deferred in accordance with Article 18 of Directive 78/660/EEC in so far as such deferral is not prohibited by Member States.

2. Member States may, however, permit the deduction of acquisition costs from unearned premiums in non-life-insurance business and their deduction by an actuarial method from mathematical reserves in life-assurance business. Where this method is used, the amounts deducted from the provisions must be indicated in the notes on the accounts.

[6501]
Article 19
Liabilities: item A(I)

Subscribed capital or equivalent funds

This item shall comprise all amounts, irrespective of their actual designations, which, in accordance with the legal structure of an insurance undertaking, are regarded under the national law of the Member State concerned as equity capital subscribed by the shareholders or other persons.

[6502]
Article 20
Liabilities: item A(IV)

Reserves

This item shall comprise all the types of reserves listed in Article 9 of Directive 78/660/EEC under liabilities item A(IV), as defined therein. The Member States may also require other types of reserves if necessary for insurance undertakings the legal structures of which are not covered by Directive 78/660/EEC.

Reserves shall be shown separately, as sub-items of liabilities item A(IV), in the balance sheets of the insurance undertakings concerned, except for the revaluation reserve, which shall be shown as a liability under A(III).

[6503]
Article 21
Liabilities: item B

Subordinated liabilities

Where it has been contractually agreed that, in the event of winding up or of bankruptcy, liabilities, whether or not represented by certificates, are to be repaid only after the claims of all other creditors have been met, the liabilities in question shall be shown under this item.

[6504]
Article 22

Where a Member State permits an undertaking's balance sheet to include funds the allocation of which either to policyholders or to shareholders has not been determined by the close of the financial year, those amounts shall be shown as liabilities under an item Ba (Fund for future appropriations).

Variations in this item shall derive from an item II(12a) (Transfers to or from the fund for future appropriations) in the profit and loss account.

[6505]
Article 23
Liabilities: item C

Technical provisions

Article 20 of Directive 78/660/EEC shall apply to technical provisions, subject to Articles 24 to 30 of this Directive.

[6506]
Article 24
Liabilities: items C(1)(b), (2)(b), (3)(b), (4)(b), and (6)(b) and D(b)

Reinsurance amounts

1. The reinsurance amounts shall comprise the actual or estimated amounts which, under contractual reinsurance arrangements, are deducted from the gross amounts of technical provisions.

2. As regards the provision for unearned premiums, the reinsurance amounts shall be calculated according to the methods referred to in Article 57 or in accordance with the terms of the reinsurance policy.

3. Member States may require or permit the reinsurance amounts to be shown as assets. Where this option is exercised, those amounts shall be shown as assets under an item Da (Reinsurers' share of technical provisions), subdivided as follows—

1. Provision for unearned premiums
2. Life assurance provision
3. Claims outstanding
4. Provisions for bonuses and rebates (unless shown under 2)
5. Other technical provisions
6. Technical provisions for life-assurance policies where the investment risk is borne by the policyholders.

Notwithstanding Article 5, these items shall not be combined.

[6507]
Article 25
Liabilities: item C(1)

Provision for unearned premiums

The provision for unearned premiums shall comprise the amount representing that part of gross premiums written which is to be allocated to the following financial year or to subsequent financial years. In the case of life assurance Member States may, pending further harmonisation, require or

Part VI European Materials

permit the provision for unearned premiums to be included in item C(2).

If, pursuant to Article 26, item C(1) also includes the amount of the provision for unexpired risks, the description of the item shall be "Provision for unearned premiums and unexpired risks". Where the amount for unexpired risks is material, it shall be disclosed separately either in the balance sheet or in the notes on the accounts.

[6508]
Article 26
Liabilities: item C(6)
Other technical provisions

This item shall comprise, *inter alia*, the provision for unexpired risks, ie the amount set aside in addition to unearned premiums in respect of risks to be borne by the insurance undertaking after the end of the financial year, in order to provide for all claims and expenses in connection with insurance contracts in force in excess of the related unearned premiums and any premiums receivable on those contracts. However, if national legislation so provides, the provision for unexpired risks may be added to the provision for unearned premiums, as defined in Article 25, and included in the amount shown under item C(1).

Where the amount of unexpired risks is significant, it shall be disclosed separately either in the balance sheet or in the notes on the accounts.

Where the option provided for in the second paragraph of Article 3 is not exercised, this item shall also include the ageing reserves.

[6509]
Article 27
Liabilities: item C(2)
Life assurance provision

The life assurance provision shall comprise the actuarially estimated value of an insurance undertaking's liabilities including bonuses already declared and after deducting the actuarial value of future premiums.

[6510]
Article 28
Liabilities: item C(3)
Claims outstanding

The provision for claims outstanding shall be the total estimated ultimate cost to an insurance undertaking of settling all claims arising from events which have occurred up to the end of the financial year, whether reported or not, less amounts already paid in respect of such claims.

[6511]
Article 29
Liabilities: item C(4)
Provision for bonuses and rebates

The provision for bonuses and rebates shall comprise amounts intended for policyholders or contract beneficiaries by way of bonuses and rebates as defined in Article 39 to the extent that such amounts have not been credited to policyholders or contract beneficiaries or included in an item Ba (Fund for future appropriations), as provided for in Article 22, first paragraph, or in item C(2).

[6512]
Article 30
Liabilities: item C(5)
Equalisation provision

1. The equalisation provision shall comprise any amounts set aside in compliance with legal or administrative requirements to equalise fluctuations in loss ratios in future years or to provide for special risks.

2. Where, in the absence of any such legislative or administrative requirements, reserves within the meaning of Article 20 have been constituted for the same purpose, this shall be disclosed in the notes on the accounts.

[6513]
Article 31
Liabilities: item D
Technical provisions for life-assurance policies where the investment risk is borne by the policyholders.

This item shall comprise technical provisions constituted to cover liabilities relating to investment in the context of life assurance policies the value of or the return on which is determined by reference to investments for which the policyholder bears the risk, or by reference to an index.

Any additional technical provisions constituted to cover death risks, operating expenses or other risks (such as benefits payable at the maturity date or guaranteed surrender values) shall be shown under item C(2).

Item D shall also comprise technical provisions representing the obligations of a tontine's organiser *vis-à-vis* its members.

[6514]
Article 32
Liabilities: item F

Deposits received from reinsurers

In the balance sheet of an undertaking ceding reinsurance this item shall comprise amounts deposited by or withheld from other insurance undertakings under reinsurance contracts. These amounts may not be merged with other amounts owed to or by the other undertakings in question.

Where an undertaking ceding reinsurance has received as a deposit securities which have been transferred to its ownership, this item shall comprise the amount owed by the ceding undertaking by virtue of the deposit.

SECTION 5
LAYOUT OF THE PROFIT AND LOSS ACCOUNT

[6515]
Article 33

1. The Member States shall prescribe the layout shown in Article 34 for profit and loss accounts.

2. The technical account for non-life-insurance business shall be used for those classes of direct insurance which are within the scope of Directive 73/239/EEC and for the corresponding classes of reinsurance business.

3. The technical account for life-assurance business shall be used for those classes of direct insurance which are within the scope of Directive 79/267/EEC and for the corresponding classes of reinsurance business.

4. Member States may require or permit undertakings the activities of which consist wholly of reinsurance to use the technical account for non-life-insurance business for all their business. This shall also apply to undertakings underwriting direct non-life-insurance and also reinsurance.

[6516]
Article 34
Profit and loss account

I. *Technical account—Non-life-insurance business*

1. Earned premiums, net of reinsurance—
   - (a) gross premiums written . . . .
   - (b) outward reinsurance premiums (–) . . . .
   - (c) change in the gross provision for unearned premiums and, in so far as national legislation authorises the inclusion of this provision in liabilities item C(1), in the provision for unexpired risks (+/–) . . . .
   - (d) change in the provision for unearned premiums, reinsurers' share (+/–) . . . .
2. Allocated investment return transferred from the non-technical account (item III(6)) . . . .
3. Other technical income, net of reinsurance . . . .
4. Claims incurred, net of reinsurance—
   - (a) claims paid
     - (aa) gross amount . . . .
     - (bb) reinsurers' share (–) . . . .
   - (b) change in the provision for claims,
     - (aa) gross amount . . . .
     - (bb) reinsurers' share (–) . . . .

5. Changes in other technical provisions, net of reinsurance, not shown under other headings (+/–)

6. Bonuses and rebates, net of reinsurance

7. Net operating expenses—

(a) acquisition costs

(b) change in deferred acquisition costs (+/–)

(c) administrative expenses

(d) reinsurance commissions and profit participation (–)

8. Other technical charges, net of reinsurance

9. Change in the equalisation provision (+/–)

10. Sub-total (balance on the technical account for non-life-insurance business (item III1))

II. *Technical account—Life-assurance business*

1. Earned premiums, net of reinsurance—

(a) gross premiums written

(b) outward reinsurance premiums (–)

(c) change in the provision for unearned premiums, net of reinsurance (+/–)

2. Investment income—

(a) income from participating interests, with a separate indication of that derived from affiliated undertakings

(b) income from other investments, with a separate indication of that derived from affiliated undertakings

(aa) income from land and buildings

(bb) income from other investments

(c) value re-adjustments on investments

(d) gains on the realisation of investments

3. Unrealised gains on investments

4. Other technical income, net of reinsurance

5. Claims incurred, net of reinsurance—

(a) claims paid

(aa) gross amount

(bb) reinsurers' share (–)

(b) change in the provision for claims

(aa) gross amount

(bb) reinsurers' share (–)

6. Change in other technical provisions, net of reinsurance, not shown under other headings (+/–)

(a) life assurance provision, net of reinsurance

(aa) gross amount

(bb) reinsurers' share (–)

(b) other technical provisions, net of reinsurance

7. *Bonuses and rebates*, net of reinsurance

8. Net operating expenses—

(a) acquisition costs,

(b) change in deferred acquisition costs (+/–) . . . .

(c) administrative expenses . . . .

(d) reinsurance commissions and profit participation (–) . . . .

9. Investment charges—

(a) investment management charges, including interest . . . .

(b) value adjustments on investments . . . .

(c) losses on the realisation of investments . . . .

10. Unrealised losses on investments . . . .

11. Other technical charges, net of reinsurance . . . .

12. Allocated investment return transferred to the non-technical account (–) (item III(4)) . . . .

13. Sub-total: (balance on the technical account—life assurance business) (item III(2)) . . . .

III. Non-technical account

1. Balance on the technical account—non-life insurance business (item I(10)) . . . .

2. Balance on the technical account—life-assurance business (item II(13)) . . . .

3. Investment income

(a) income from participating interests, with a separate indication of that derived from affiliated undertakings . . . .

(b) income from other investments, with a separate indication of that derived from affiliated undertakings

(aa) income from land and buildings . . . .

(bb) income from other investments . . . .

(c) value re-adjustments on investments . . . .

(d) gains on the realisation of investments . . . .

4. Allocated investment return transferred from the life-assurance technical account (item II(12)) . . . .

5. Investment charges—

(a) investment management charges, including interest . . . .

(b) value adjustments on investments . . . .

(c) losses on the realisation of investments . . . .

6. Allocated investment return transferred to the non-life insurance technical account (item I(2)) . . . .

7. Other income . . . .

8. Other charges, including value adjustments . . . .

9. Tax on profit or loss on ordinary activities . . . .

10. Profit or loss on ordinary activities after tax . . . .

11. Extraordinary income . . . .

12. Extraordinary charges . . . .

13. Extraordinary profit or loss . . . .

14. Tax on extraordinary profit or loss . . . .

15. Other taxes not shown under the preceding items . . . .

16 Profit or loss for the financial year . . . .

Part VI European Materials

SECTION 6
SPECIAL PROVISIONS RELATING TO CERTAIN PROFIT-AND-LOSS-ACCOUNT ITEMS

[6517]
Article 35

Non-life-insurance technical account: item I(1)(a)

Life-assurance technical account: item II(1)(a)

Gross premiums written

Gross premiums written shall comprise all amounts due during the financial year in respect of insurance contracts regardless of the fact that such amounts may relate in whole or in part to a later financial year, and shall include *inter alia*—

(i) premiums yet to be written, where the premium calculation can be done only at the end of the year—

(ii)

— single premiums, including annuity premiums,

— in life assurance, single premiums resulting from bonus and rebate provisions in so far as they must be considered as premiums on the basis of contracts and where national legislation requires or permits their being shown under premiums;

(iii) additional premiums in the case of half-yearly, quarterly or monthly payments and additional payments from policyholders for expenses borne by the insurance undertaking;

(iv) in the case of coinsurance, the undertaking's portion of total premiums;

(v) reinsurance premiums due from ceding and retroceding insurance undertakings, including portfolio entries,

after deduction of—

— portfolio withdrawals credited to ceding and retroceding insurance undertakings, and

— cancellations.

The above amounts shall not include the amounts of taxes or charges levied with premiums.

[6518]
Article 36

Non-life-insurance technical account: item I(1)(b)

Life-assurance technical account: item II(1)(b)

Outward reinsurance premiums

Outward reinsurance premiums shall comprise all premiums paid or payable in respect of outward reinsurance contracts entered into by an insurance undertaking. Portfolio entries payable on the conclusion or amendment of outward reinsurance contracts shall be added; portfolio withdrawals receivable must be deducted.

[6519]
Article 37

Non-life-insurance technical account: items I(1)(c) and (d)

Life-assurance technical account: item II(1)(c)

Change in the provision for unearned premiums, net of reinsurance

Pending further coordination, Member States may, in the case of life assurance, require or permit the change in unearned premiums to be included in the change in the life assurance provision.

[6520]
Article 38

Non-life-insurance technical account: item I(4)

Life-assurance technical account: item II(5)

Claims incurred, net of reinsurance

1. Claims incurred shall comprise all payments made in respect of the financial year plus the provision for claims but minus the provision for claims for the preceding financial years.

These amounts shall include annuities, surrenders, entries and withdrawals of loss provisions to and from ceding insurance undertakings and reinsurers, external and internal claims management costs and charges for claims incurred but not reported such as referred to in Article 60(1)(b) and (2)(a).

Sums recoverable on the basis of subrogation and salvage within the meaning of Article 60(1)(d) shall be deducted.

2. Where the difference between—

— the loss provision made at the beginning of the year for outstanding claims incurred in previous years, and
— the payments made during the year on account of claims incurred in previous years and the loss provision shown at the end of the year for such outstanding claims is material,

it shall be disclosed in the notes on the accounts, broken down by category and amount.

[6521]
Article 39

Non-life-insurance technical account: item I(6)

Life-assurance technical account: item II(7)

Bonuses and rebates, net of reinsurance

Bonuses shall comprise all amounts chargeable for the financial year which are paid or payable to policyholders and other insured parties or provided for their benefit, including amounts used to increase technical provisions or applied to the reduction of future premiums, to the extent that such amounts represent an allocation of surplus or profit arising on business as a whole or a section of business, after deduction of amounts provided in previous years which are no longer required.

Rebates shall comprise such amounts to the extent that they represent a partial refund of premiums resulting from the experience of individual contracts.

Where material, the amount charged for bonuses and that charged for rebates shall be disclosed separately in the notes on the accounts.

[6522]
Article 40

Non-life-insurance technical account: item I(7)(a)

Life-assurance technical account: item II(8)(a)

Acquisition costs

Acquisition costs shall comprise the costs arising from the conclusion of insurance contracts. They shall cover both direct costs, such as acquisition commissions or the cost of drawing up the insurance document or including the insurance contract in the portfolio, and indirect costs, such as advertising costs or the administrative expenses connected with the processing of proposals and the issuing of policies.

Member States may require policy renewal commissions to be entered in item I(7)(c) or II(8)(c).

[6523]
Article 41

Non-life-insurance technical account: item I(7)(c)

Life-assurance technical account: item II(8)(c)

Administrative expenses

Administrative expenses shall include the costs arising from premium collection, portfolio administration, handling of bonuses and rebates, and inward and outward reinsurance. They shall in particular include staff costs and depreciation provisions in respect of office furniture and equipment in so far as these need not be shown under acquisition costs, claims incurred or investment charges.

[6524]
Article 42

Life-insurance technical account: items II(2) and (9)

Non-technical account: items III(3) and (5)

Investment income and charges

1. All investment income and charges relating to non-life insurance shall be disclosed in the non-technical account.
2. In the case of an undertaking carrying on life-assurance business only, investment income and charges shall be disclosed in the life-assurance technical account.
3. In the case of an undertaking carrying on both life-assurance and non-life-insurance business, investment income and charges shall, to the extent that they are directly connected with the carrying on of the life-assurance business, be disclosed in the life-assurance technical account.
4. Member States may require or permit the disclosure of investment income and charges according to the origin or attribution of the investments, if necessary by providing for further items in the non-life-insurance technical account, by analogy with the corresponding items in the life-assurance technical account.

[6525]
Article 43

Non-life-insurance technical account: item I(2)

Life-assurance technical account: item II(2)

Non-technical account: items III(4) and (6)

Allocated investment return

1. Where part of the investment return is transferred to the non-life-insurance technical account, the transfer from the non-technical account shall be deducted from item III(6) and added to item I(2).
2. Where part of the investment return disclosed in the life-assurance technical account is transferred to the non-technical account, the amount transferred shall be deducted from item II(12) and added to item III(4).
3. Member States may lay down the procedures for and the amounts of transfers of allocated return from one part of the profit and loss account to another. The reasons for such transfers and the bases on which they are made shall be disclosed in the notes on the accounts in either event; where appropriate, a reference to the text of the relevant regulation shall suffice.

[6526]
Article 44

Unrealised gains and losses on investments

Life-assurance technical account: items II(3) and (10)

Unrealised gains and losses on investments

1. In life-assurance business Member States may permit the disclosure in full or in part in items II(3) and (10) in the profit and loss account of variations in the difference between—
   — the valuation of investments at their current value or by means of one of the methods referred to in Article 33(1) of Directive 78/660/EEC, and
   — their valuation at purchase price.

In any event, Member States shall require that the amounts referred to in the first paragraph be disclosed in the afore-mentioned items where they relate to investments shown as assets under D.

2. Member States which require or permit the valuation of the investments shown as assets under C at their current value may, in respect of non-life-insurance, permit the disclosure in full or in part in an item III(3a) and in an item III(5a) in the profit and loss account of the variation in the difference between the valuation of those investments at their current value and their valuation at purchase price.

SECTION 7
VALUATION RULES

[6527]
Article 45

Article 32 of Directive 78/660/EEC, under which the valuation of items shown in the annual accounts must be based on the principle of purchase price or production cost, shall apply to investment subject to Articles 46 to 49 of this Directive.

[6528]
Article 46

1. Member States may require or permit the valuation of investments shown as assets under C on the basis of their current value calculated in accordance with Articles 48 and 49.

2. The investments shown as assets under D shall be shown at their current value.

3. Where investments are shown at their purchase price, their current value shall be disclosed in the notes on the accounts.

However, Member States in which, on the date of the notification of this Directive, investments are shown at their purchase price may give undertakings the option of initially disclosing in the notes on the account the current value of investment shown as assets under C(I) no later than five years after the date referred to in Article 70(1) and the current value of other investments no later than three years after the same date.

4. Where investments are shown at their current value, their purchase price shall be disclosed in the notes on the accounts.

5. The same valuation method shall be applied to all investments included in any item denoted by an arabic numeral or shown as assets under C(I). [Member States may permit derogations from this requirement.]

[6. The method(s) applied to each investment item shall be stated in the notes on the accounts, together with the amounts so determined.]

NOTES

Para 5: words in square brackets added by European Parliament and Council Directive 2003/51/EC, art 4(4)(a).

Para 6: substituted by European Parliament and Council Directive 2003/51/EC, art 4(4)(b).

[6529]
[Article 46a

1. Where assets and liabilities are valued in accordance with Section 7a of Directive 78/660/EEC, paragraphs 2 to 6 of this Article shall apply.

2. The investments shown as assets under D shall be shown at their fair value.

3. Where investments are shown at their purchase price, their fair value shall be disclosed in the notes on the accounts.

4. Where investments are shown at their fair value, their purchase price shall be disclosed in the notes on the accounts.

5. The same valuation method shall be applied to all investments included in any item denoted by an arabic numeral or shown as assets under C(I). Member States may permit derogations from this requirement.

6. The method(s) applied to each investment item shall be stated in the notes on the accounts, together with the amounts so determined.]

NOTES

Inserted by European Parliament and Council Directive 2003/51/EC, art 4(5).

[6530]
Article 47

Where current value is applied to investments, Article 33(2) and (3) of Directive 78/660/EEC shall apply, except as provided in Articles 37 and 44 of this Directive.

[6531]
Article 48

1. In the case of investments other than land and buildings, current value shall mean market value, save as provided in paragraph 5.

2. Where investments are officially listed on an official stock exchange, market value shall mean the value on the balance-sheet date or, when the balance-sheet date is not a stock-exchange trading day, on the last stock-exchange trading day before that date.

3. Where a market exists for investments other than those referred to in paragraph 2, market value shall mean the average price at which such investments were traded on the balance-sheet date or, when the balance-sheet date is not a trading day, on the last trading day before that date.

4. Where on the date on which the accounts are drawn up investments such as referred to in paragraphs 2 or 3 have been sold or are to be sold within the short term, the market value shall be reduced by the actual or estimated realisation costs.

5. Except where the equity method is applied in accordance with Article 59 of Directive 78/660/EEC, all other investments shall be valued on a basis which has prudent regard to the likely realisable value.

6. In all cases the method of valuation shall be precisely described and the reason for adopting it stated in the notes on the accounts.

[6532]
Article 49

1. In the case of land and buildings current value shall mean the market value on the date of valuation, where relevant reduced as provided in paragraphs 4 and 5.

2. Market value shall mean the price at which land and buildings could be sold under private contract between a willing seller and an arm's length buyer on the date of valuation, it being assumed that the property is publicly exposed to the market, that market conditions permit orderly disposal and that a normal period, having regard to the nature of the property, is available for the negotiation of the sale.

3. The market value shall be determined through the separate valuation of each land and buildings item, carried out at least every five years according to methods generally recognised or recognised by the insurance supervisory authorities. Article 35(1)(b) of Directive 78/660/EEC shall not apply.

4. Where the value of any land and buildings item has diminished since the preceding valuation under paragraph 3, an appropriate value adjustment shall be made. The lower value thus arrived at shall not be increased in subsequent balance sheets unless such increase results from a new determination of market value arrived at in accordance with paragraphs 2 and 3.

5. Where on the date on which the accounts are drawn up land and buildings have been sold or are to be sold within the short term, the value arrived at in accordance with paragraphs 2 and 4 shall be reduced by the actual or estimated realisation costs.

6. Where it is impossible to determine the market value of a land and buildings item, the value arrived at on the basis of the principle of purchase price or production cost shall be deemed to be the current value.

7. The method by which the current value of land and buildings has been arrived at and their breakdown by financial year of valuation shall be disclosed in the notes on the accounts.

[6533]
Article 50

Where Article 33 of Directive 78/660/EEC is applied to insurance undertakings, it shall be so in the following manner—

(a) paragraph 1(a) shall apply to assets shown under F(I) as defined in Article 6 of this Directive;

(b) paragraph 1(c) shall apply to assets shown under C(I), (II), (III) and (IV) and F(I) (except for stocks) and (III) as defined in Article 6 of this Directive.

[6534]
Article 51

Article 35 of Directive 78/660/EEC shall apply to insurance undertakings subject to the following provisions—

(a) it shall apply to assets shown under B and C and to fixed assets shown under F(I) as defined in Article 6 of this Directive;

(b) paragraph 1(c)(aa) shall apply to assets shown under C(II), (III) and (IV) and F(III) as defined in Article 6 of this Directive.

Member States may require that value adjustments be made in respect of transferable securities shown as investments, so that they are shown at the lower value to be attributed to them at the balance-sheet date.

[6535]
Article 52

Article 38 of Directive 78/660/EEC shall apply to assets shown under F(I) as defined in Article 6 of this Directive.

[6536]
Article 53

Article 39 of Directive 78/660/EEC shall apply to assets shown under E(I), (II) and (III) and F(II) as defined in Article 6 of this Directive.

[6537]
Article 54

In non-life insurance the amount of any deferred acquisition costs shall be established on a basis compatible with that used for unearned premiums.

In life assurance the calculation of the amount of any acquisition costs to be deferred may be taken into the actuarial calculation referred to in Article 59.

[6538]
Article 55

1.

(a) If they have not been valued at market value, debt securities and other fixed-income securities shown as assets under C(II) and (III) shall be shown in the balance sheet at purchase price. Member States may, however, require or permit such debt securities to be shown in the balance sheet at the amount repayable at maturity.

(b) Where the purchase price of the securities referred to in point (a) exceeds the amount repayable at maturity, the amount of the difference shall be charged to the profit and loss account. Member States may, however, require or permit the amount of the difference to be written off in instalments so that it is completely written off when the securities are repaid. That difference must be shown separately in the balance sheet or in the notes on the accounts.

(c) Where the purchase price of the securities referred to in point (a) is less than the amount repayable at maturity, Member States may require or permit the amount of the difference to be released to income in instalments over the period remaining until repayment. That difference must be shown separately in the balance sheet or in the notes on the accounts.

2. Where debt securities or other fixed-income securities that are not valued at market value are sold before maturity and the proceeds are used to purchase other debt securities or fixed-income securities, Member States may permit the difference between the proceeds of sale and their book value to be spread uniformly over the period remaining until the maturity of the original investment.

[6539]
Article 56
Technical provisions

The amount of technical provisions must at all times be such that an undertaking can meet any liabilities arising out of insurance contracts as far as can reasonably be foreseen.

[6540]
Article 57
Provision for unearned premiums

1. The provision for unearned premiums shall in principle be computed separately for each insurance contract. Member States may, however, permit the use of statistical methods, and in particular proportional and flat-rate methods, where they may be expected to give approximately the same results as individual calculations.

2. In classes of insurance where the assumption of a temporal correlation between risk experience and premium is not appropriate, calculation methods shall be applied that take account of the differing pattern of risk over time.

[6541]
Article 58
Provision for unexpired risks

The provision for unexpired risks referred to in Article 26 shall be computed on the basis of claims and administrative expenses likely to arise after the end of the financial year from contracts concluded before that date, in so far as their estimated value exceeds the provision for unearned premiums and any premiums receivable under those contracts.

[6542]
Article 59
Life assurance provision

1. The life assurance provision shall in principle be computed separately for each life assurance contract. Member States may, however, permit the use of statistical or mathematical methods where they may be expected to give approximately the same results as individual calculations. A summary of the principal assumptions made shall be given in the notes on the accounts.

2. The computation shall be made annually by an actuary or other specialist in this field on the basis of recognised actuarial methods.

[6543]
Article 60
Provisions for claims outstanding

1. Non-life insurance

(a) A provision shall in principle be computed separately for each case on the basis of the costs still expected to arise. Statistical methods may be used if they result in an adequate provision having regard to the nature of the risks; Member States may, however, make the application of such methods subject to prior approval.

(b) This provision shall also allow for claims incurred but not reported by the balance-sheet date; its amount shall be determined having regard to past experience as to the number and magnitude of claims reported after the balance-sheet date.

(c) Claims settlement costs shall be included in the calculation of the provision irrespective of their origin.

(d) Recoverable amounts arising out of the acquisition of the rights of policyholders with respect to third parties (subrogation) or of the legal ownership of insured property (salvage) shall be deducted from the provision for claims outstanding; they shall be estimated on a prudent basis. Where such amounts are material, they shall be disclosed in the notes on the accounts.

(e) By way of derogation from subparagraph (d), Member States may require or permit the disclosure of recoverable amounts as assets.

(f) Where benefits resulting from a claim must be paid in the form of annuity, the amounts to be set aside for that purpose shall be calculated by recognised actuarial methods.

(g) Implicit discounting or deductions, whether resulting from the placing of a present value on a provision for an outstanding claim which is expected to be settled later at a higher figure or otherwise effected, shall be prohibited.

Member States may permit explicit discounting or deductions to take account of investment income. No such discounting or deductions shall be permissible unless—

(i) the expected average date for the settlement of claims is at least four years after the accounting date;

(ii) the discounting or deduction is effected on a recognised prudential basis; the competent authority must be given advance notification of any change in method;

(iii) when calculating the total cost of settling claims, an undertaking takes account of all factors that could cause increases in that cost;

(iv) an undertaking has adequate data at its disposal to construct a reliable model of the rate of claims settlements;

(v) the rate of interest used for the calculation of present values does not exceed a prudent estimate of the investment income from assets invested as a provision for claims during the period necessary for the payment of such claims. Moreover, it must not exceed either of the following—

— the investment income from such assets over the preceding five years,

— the investment income from such assets during the year preceding the balance-sheet date.

When discounting or effecting deductions, an undertaking shall, in the notes on its accounts, disclose the total amount of provisions before discounting or deduction, the categories of claims which are discounted or from which deductions have been made and, for each category of claims, the methods used, in particular the rates used for the estimates referred to in the preceding subparagraph, points (iii) and (v), and the criteria adopted for estimating the period that will elapse before the claims are settled.

2. Life insurance

(a) The amount of the provision for claims shall be equal to the sums due to beneficiaries, plus the costs of settling claims. It shall include the provision for claims incurred but not reported.

(b) Member States may require the disclosure in liabilities item C(2) of the amounts referred to in (a).

[6544]
Article 61

1. Pending further coordination, Member States may require or permit the application of the following methods where, because of the nature of the class or type of insurance in question, information about premiums receivable, claims payable or both for the underwriting years is insufficient when the annual accounts are drawn up for accurate estimates to be made.

Method 1

The excess of the premiums written over the claims and expenses paid in respect of contracts commencing in the underwriting year shall form a technical provision which is included in the technical provision for claims outstanding shown in the balance sheet in liabilities item C(3). The provision may also be computed on the basis of a given percentage of the premiums written where such a method is appropriate for the type of risk insured. Should the need arise, the amount of this technical provision shall be increased to make it sufficient to meet present and future obligations. The technical provision constituted by this method shall be replaced by a provision for claims outstanding estimated in the usual manner as soon as sufficient information has been gathered and not later than the end of the third year following the underwriting year.

Method 2

The figures shown in the technical account or in certain items within it shall relate to a year which wholly or partly precedes the financial year. It must not do so by more than 12 months. The amounts of the technical provisions shown in the annual accounts shall if necessary be increased to make them sufficient to meet present and future obligations.

2. Where one of the methods described in paragraph 1 is adopted, it shall be applied systematically in successive years unless circumstances justify a change. The use of either method shall be disclosed in the notes on the accounts and the reasons given; in the event of a change in the method applied, the effect on the assets, liabilities, financial position and profit or loss shall be indicated in the notes on the accounts. Where Method 1 is used, the length of time that elapses before a provision for claims outstanding is constituted on the usual basis shall be disclosed in the notes on the accounts. Where Method 2 is used, the length of time by which the earlier year to which the figures relate precedes the financial year and the magnitude of the transactions concerned shall be disclosed in the notes on the accounts.

3. For the purposes of this Article, "underwriting year" shall mean the financial year in which the insurance contracts in the class or type of insurance in question commenced.

[6545]
Article 62

Pending further coordination, those Member States which require the constitution of equalisation provisions shall prescribe the valuation rules to be applied to them.

SECTION 8
CONTENTS OF THE NOTES ON THE ACCOUNTS

[6546]
Article 63

In place of the information provided for in Article 43(1)(8) of Directive 78/660/EEC, insurance undertakings shall provide the following particulars—

I. As regards non-life insurance, the notes on the accounts shall disclose—

1. gross premiums written;
2. gross premiums earned;
3. gross claims charges;
4. gross operating expenses;
5. the reinsurance balance.

These amounts shall be shown broken down between direct insurance and reinsurance acceptances, if reinsurance acceptances amount to 10 per cent or more of gross premiums written, and then within direct insurance into the following groups of classes—

— accident and health
— motor, third-party liability
— motor, other classes
— marine, aviation and transport
— fire and other damage to property
— third-party liability
— credit and suretyship
— legal expenses
— assistance
— miscellaneous.

The breakdown into groups of classes within direct insurance shall not be required where the amount of the gross premiums written in direct insurance for the group in question does not exceed ECU 10 million. However, undertakings shall in any case disclose the amounts relating to the three largest groups of classes in their business.

II. As regards life assurance, the notes on the accounts shall disclose—

1. gross premiums written, broken down between direct insurance and reinsurance acceptances, if reinsurance acceptances amount to 10% or more of gross premiums written, and then within direct insurance to indicate—

(a)
(i) individual premiums;
(ii) premiums under group contracts;

(b)
(i) periodic premiums;
(ii) single premiums;

(c)
(i) premiums from non-bonus contracts;
(ii) premiums from bonus contracts;

Part VI European Materials

(iii) premiums from contracts where the investment risk is borne by policyholders.

Disclosure of the figure relating to (a), (b) or (c) shall not be required where it does not exceed 10% of the gross premiums written in direct insurance;

2. the reinsurance balance;

III. In the case covered by Article 33(4), gross premiums broken down between life assurance and non-life insurance.

IV. In all cases, the total gross direct insurance premiums resulting from contracts concluded by the insurance undertaking

— in the Member State of its head office,

— in the other Member States, and

— in other countries,

except that disclosure of the figure relating to the above shall not be required if they do not exceed 5% of total gross premiums.

[6547]
Article 64

In the notes on their accounts insurance undertakings shall disclose the total amount of commissions for direct insurance business taken into the accounts for the financial year. This requirement shall cover commissions of any kind, and in particular acquisition, renewal, collection and portfolio management commissions.

SECTION 9
PROVISIONS RELATING TO CONSOLIDATED ACCOUNTS

[6548]
Article 65

1. Insurance undertakings shall draw up consolidated accounts and consolidated annual reports in accordance with Directive 83/349/EEC, save as otherwise provided in this section.

2. In so far as a Member State does not have recourse to Article 5 of Directive 83/349/EEC, paragraph 1 shall also apply to parent undertakings, the sole or essential object of which is to acquire holdings in subsidiary undertakings and turn them to profit, where those subsidiary undertakings are either exclusively or mainly insurance undertakings.

[6549]
Article 66

Directive 83/349/EEC shall apply subject to the following provisions—

1. Articles 4, 6, and 40 shall not apply;
2. the information referred to in the first and second indents of Article 9(2), namely—
   — the amount of the fixed assets, and
   — the net turnover,

   shall be replaced by particulars of the gross premiums written as defined in Article 35 of this Directive;
3. a Member State may also apply Article 12 of Directive 83/349/EEC to two or more insurance undertakings which are not connected as described in Article 1(1) or (2) of the same Directive but are managed on a unified basis other than pursuant to a contract or provisions of their memoranda or articles of association. Unified management may also consist of important and durable reinsurance links;
4. Member States may permit derogations from Article 26(1)(c) of Directive 83/349/EEC where a transaction has been concluded according to normal market conditions and has established policyholder rights. Any such derogation shall be disclosed and where they have a material effect on the assets, liabilities, financial position and profit or loss of all the undertakings included in the consolidation that fact shall be disclosed in the notes on the consolidated accounts;
5. Article 27(3) of Directive 83/349/EEC shall apply provided that the balance-sheet date of an undertaking included in a consolidation does not precede the consolidated balance-sheet date by more than six months;
6. Article 29 of Directive 83/349/EEC shall not apply to those liabilities items, the valuation of which by the undertakings included in a consolidation is based on the application of provisions specific to insurance undertakings or to those assets items changes in the values of which also affect or establish policyholders' rights. Where recourse is had to this derogation, the fact shall be disclosed in the notes on the consolidated accounts.

[6550]
Article 67

In consolidated accounts alone Member States may require or permit all investment income and charges to be disclosed in the non-technical account, even when such income and charges are connected with life-assurance business.

Furthermore, Member States may in such cases require or permit the allocation of part of the investment return to the life-assurance technical account.

SECTION 10
PUBLICATION

[6551]
Article 68

1. The duly approved annual accounts of insurance undertakings, together with the annual reports and the reports by the persons responsible for auditing the accounts, shall be published as laid down by the laws of each Member State in accordance with Article 3 of Directive 68/151/EEC.[1]

The laws of a Member State may, however, provide that annual reports need not be published as provided in the first subparagraph. In that event, they shall be made available to the public at the undertakings' head offices in the Member State concerned. It must be possible to obtain a copy of all or part of any such report upon request. The price of such a copy shall not exceed its administrative cost.

2. Paragraph 1 shall also apply to the duly approved consolidated accounts, the consolidated annual report and the reports by the persons responsible for auditing the accounts.

3. Where an insurance undertaking which has drawn up annual accounts or consolidated accounts is not established as one of the types of company listed in Article 1(1) of Directive 78/660/EEC and is not required by its national law to publish the documents referred to in paragraph 1 and 2 of this Article as prescribed in Article 3 of Directive 68/151/EEC, it shall at least make them available to the public at its head office. It must be possible to obtain copies of such documents on request. The price of such copies shall not exceed their administrative cost.

4. Member States shall provide for appropriate sanctions for failure to comply with the publication rules laid down in this Article.

NOTES

1 OJ L65, 14.3.68, p 8.

SECTION 11
FINAL PROVISIONS

[6552]
Article 69

The contact committee set up pursuant to Article 52 of Directive 78/660/EEC shall also, when constituted appropriately, have the following functions—

(a) to facilitate, without prejudice to Articles 169 and 170 of the Treaty, harmonised application of this Directive through regular meetings dealing in particular with practical problems arising in connection with its application;

(b) to advise the Commission, if the need arises, on additions or amendments to this Directive.

[6553]
Article 70

1. Member States shall adopt the laws, regulations and administrative provisions necessary for them to comply with this Directive before 1 January 1994. They shall forthwith inform the Commission thereof.

When Member States adopt these measures, they shall include a reference to this Directive or be accompanied by such reference on the occasion of their official publication. The methods of making such a reference shall be laid down by the Member States.

2. Member States may provide that the provisions referred to in paragraph 1 shall first apply to annual accounts and consolidated accounts for financial years beginning on 1 January 1995 or during the calendar year 1995.

3. Member States shall communicate to the Commission the texts of the main provisions of national law which they adopt in the field governed by this Directive.

[6554]
Article 71

Five years after the date referred to in Article 70(2) the Council, acting on a proposal from the Commission, shall examine and if need be revise all those provisions of this Directive which provide for Member State options in the light of the experience acquired in applying this Directive and in particular of the aims of greater transparency and harmonisation of the provisions referred to by this Directive.

[6555]
Article 72

This Directive is addressed to the Member States.

Done at Brussels, 19 December 1991.

(*Annex repealed by European Parliament and Council Directive 2003/51/EC, art 4(6).*)

D. LIFE

DIRECTIVE OF THE EUROPEAN PARLIAMENT AND OF THE COUNCIL

(2002/83/EC)

of 5 November 2002

concerning life assurance

NOTES

Date of publication in OJ: OJ L345, 19.12.2002, p 1.

This Directive is repealed by European Parliament and Council Directive 2009/138/EC on the taking-up and pursuit of the business of Insurance and Reinsurance (Solvency II) at **[6153]** et seq, with effect from 1 November 2012 (see art 310 thereof at **[6462]**).

[6556]

THE EUROPEAN PARLIAMENT AND THE COUNCIL OF THE EUROPEAN UNION,

Having regard to the Treaty establishing the European Community, and in particular Articles 47(2) and Article 55 thereof,

Having regard to the proposal from the Commission,[1]

Having regard to the opinion of the Economic and Social Committee,[2]

Acting in accordance with the procedure laid down in Article 251 of the Treaty,[3]

Whereas:

(1) First Council Directive 79/267/EEC of 5 March 1979 on the coordination of laws, regulations and administrative provisions relating to the taking-up and pursuit of the business of direct life assurance,[4] *the second Council Directive 90/619/EEC of 8 November 1990 on the coordination of laws, regulations and administrative provisions relating to direct life assurance, laying down provisions to facilitate the effective exercise of freedom to provide services and amending Directive 79/267/EEC*[5] *and Council Directive 92/96/EEC of 10 November 1992 on the coordination of laws, regulations and administrative provisions relating to direct life assurance and amending Directives 79/267/EEC and 90/619/EEC (third life assurance Directive)*[6] *have been substantially amended several times. Since further amendments are to be made, the Directives should be recast in the interests of clarity.*

(2) In order to facilitate the taking-up and pursuit of the business of life assurance, it is essential to eliminate certain divergences which exist between national supervisory legislation. In order to achieve this objective and at the same time ensure adequate protection for policy holders and beneficiaries in all Member States, the provisions relating to the financial guarantees required of life assurance undertakings should be coordinated.

(3) It is necessary to complete the internal market in direct life assurance, from the point of view both of the right of establishment and of the freedom to provide services in the Member States, to make it easier for assurance undertakings with head offices in the Community to cover commitments situated within the Community and to make it possible for policy holders to have recourse not only to assurers established in their own country, but also to assurers which have their head office in the Community and are established in other Member States.

(4) Under the Treaty, any discrimination with regard to freedom to provide services based on the fact that an undertaking is not established in the Member State in which the services are provided is prohibited. That prohibition applies to services provided from any establishment in the Community, whether it be the head office of an undertaking or an agency or branch.

(5) This Directive therefore represents an important step in the merging of national markets into an integrated market and that stage must be supplemented by other Community instruments with a view to enabling all policy holders to have recourse to any assurer with a head office in the Community who carries on business there, under the right of establishment or the freedom to provide services, while guaranteeing them adequate protection.

(6) This Directive forms part of the body of Community legislation in the field of life assurance which also includes Council Directive 91/674/EEC of 19 December 1991 on the annual accounts and consolidated accounts of insurance undertakings.[7]

(7) The approach adopted consists in bringing about such harmonisation as is essential, necessary and sufficient to achieve the mutual recognition of authorisations and prudential control systems, thereby making it possible to grant a single authorisation valid throughout the Community and apply the principle of supervision by the home Member State.

(8) As a result, the taking up and the pursuit of the business of assurance are subject to the grant

of a single official authorisation issued by the competent authorities of the Member State in which an assurance undertaking has its head office. Such authorisation enables an undertaking to carry on business throughout the Community, under the right of establishment or the freedom to provide services. The Member State of the branch or of the provision of services may not require assurance undertakings which wish to carry on assurance business there and which have already been authorised in their home Member State to seek fresh authorisation.

(9) The competent authorities should not authorise or continue the authorisation of an assurance undertaking where they are liable to be prevented from effectively exercising their supervisory functions by the close links between that undertaking and other natural or legal persons. Assurance undertakings already authorised must also satisfy the competent authorities in that respect.

(10) The definition of "close links" in this Directive lays down minimum criteria and that does not prevent Member States from applying it to situations other than those envisaged by the definition.

(11) The sole fact of having acquired a significant proportion of a company's capital does not constitute participation, within the meaning of "close links", if that holding has been acquired solely as a temporary investment which does not make it possible to exercise influence over the structure or financial policy of the undertaking.

(12) The principles of mutual recognition and of home Member State supervision require that Member States' competent authorities should not grant or should withdraw authorisation where factors such as the content of programmes of operations or the geographical distribution of the activities actually carried on indicate clearly that an assurance undertaking has opted for the legal system of one Member State for the purpose of evading the stricter standards in force in another Member State within whose territory it carries on or intends to carry on the greater part of its activities. An assurance undertaking must be authorised in the Member State in which it has its registered office. In addition, Member States must require that an assurance undertaking's head office always be situated in its home Member State and that it actually carries on its business there.

(13) For practical reasons, it is desirable to define provision of services taking into account both the assurer's establishment and the place where the commitment is to be covered. Therefore, commitment should also be defined. Moreover, it is desirable to distinguish between activities pursued by way of establishment and activities pursued by way of freedom to provide services.

(14) A classification by class of assurance is necessary in order to determine, in particular, the activities subject to compulsory authorisation.

(15) Certain mutual associations which, by virtue of their legal status, fulfil requirements as to security and other specific financial guarantees should be excluded from the scope of this Directive. Certain organisations whose activity covers only a very restricted sector and is limited by their articles of association should also be excluded.

(16) Life assurance is subject to official authorisation and supervision in each Member State. The conditions for the granting or withdrawal of such authorisation should be defined. Provision must be made for the right to apply to the courts should an authorisation be refused or withdrawn.

(17) It is desirable to clarify the powers and means of supervision vested in the competent authorities. It is also desirable to lay down specific provisions regarding the taking up, pursuit and supervision of activity by way of freedom to provide services.

(18) The competent authorities of home Member States should be responsible for monitoring the financial health of assurance undertakings, including their state of solvency, the establishment of adequate technical provisions and the covering of those provisions by matching assets.

(19) It is appropriate to provide for the possibility of exchanges of information between the competent authorities and authorities or bodies which, by virtue of their function, help to strengthen the stability of the financial system. In order to preserve the confidential nature of the information forwarded, the list of addressees must remain within strict limits.

(20) Certain behaviour, such as fraud and insider offences, is liable to affect the stability, including integrity, of the financial system, even when involving undertakings other than assurance undertakings.

(21) It is necessary to specify the conditions under which the abovementioned exchanges of information are authorised.

(22) Where it is stipulated that information may be disclosed only with the express agreement of the competent authorities, these may, where appropriate, make their agreement subject to compliance with strict conditions.

(23) Member States may conclude agreements on exchange of information with third countries provided that the information disclosed is subject to appropriate guarantees of professional secrecy.

(24) For the purposes of strengthening the prudential supervision of assurance undertakings and protection of clients of assurance undertakings, it should be stipulated that an auditor must have a duty to report promptly to the competent authorities, wherever, as provided for by this Directive, he/she becomes aware, while carrying out his/her tasks, of certain facts which are liable to have a serious effect on the financial situation or the administrative and accounting organisation of an assurance undertaking.

(25) Having regard to the aim in view, it is desirable for Member States to provide that such a duty should apply in all circumstances where such facts are discovered by an auditor during the performance of his/her tasks in an undertaking which has close links with an assurance undertaking.

(26) The duty of auditors to communicate, where appropriate, to the competent authorities certain facts and decisions concerning an assurance undertaking which they discover during the performance of their tasks in a non-assurance undertaking does not in itself change the nature of their tasks in that undertaking nor the manner in which they must perform those tasks in that undertaking.

(27) The performance of the operations of management of group pension funds cannot under any circumstances affect the powers conferred on the respective authorities with regard to the entities holding the assets with which that management is concerned.

(28) Certain provisions of this Directive define minimum standards. A home Member State may lay down stricter rules for assurance undertakings authorised by its own competent authorities.

(29) The competent authorities of the Member States must have at their disposal such means of supervision as are necessary to ensure the orderly pursuit of business by assurance undertakings throughout the Community whether carried on under the right of establishment or the freedom to provide services. In particular, they must be able to introduce appropriate safeguards or impose sanctions aimed at preventing irregularities and infringements of the provisions on assurance supervision.

(30) The provisions on transfers of portfolios should include provisions specifically concerning the transfer to another undertaking of the portfolio of contracts concluded by way of freedom to provide services.

(31) The provisions on transfers of portfolios must be in line with the single legal authorisation system provided for in this Directive.

(32) Undertakings formed after the dates referred to in Article 18(3) should not be authorised to carry on life assurance and non-life insurance activities simultaneously. Member States should be allowed to permit undertakings which, on the relevant dates referred to in Article 18(3), carried on these activities simultaneously to continue to do so provided that separate management is adopted for each of their activities, in order that the respective interests of life policy holders and non-life policy holders are safeguarded and the minimum financial obligations in respect of one of the activities are not borne by the other activity. Member States should be given the option of requiring those existing undertakings established in their territory which carry on life assurance and non-life insurance simultaneously to put an end to this practice. Moreover, specialised undertakings should be subject to special supervision where a non-life undertaking belongs to the same financial group as a life undertaking.

(33) Nothing in this Directive prevents a composite undertaking from dividing itself into two undertakings, one active in the field of life assurance, the other in non-life insurance. In order to allow such division to take place under the best possible conditions, it is desirable to permit Member States, in accordance with Community rules of competition law, to provide for appropriate tax arrangements, in particular with regard to the capital gains such division could entail.

(34) Those Member States which so wish should be able to grant the same undertaking authorisations for the classes referred to in Annex I and the insurance business coming under classes 1 and 2 in the Annex to Council Directive 73/239/EEC of 24 July 1973 on the coordination of laws, regulations and administrative provisions relating to the taking up and pursuit of the business of direct insurance other than life assurance.[8] *That possibility may, however, be subject to certain conditions as regards compliance with accounting rules and rules on winding-up.*

(35) It is necessary from the point of view of the protection of lives assured that every assurance undertaking should establish adequate technical provisions. The calculation of such provisions is based for the most part on actuarial principles. Those principles should be coordinated in order to facilitate mutual recognition of the prudential rules applicable in the various Member States.

(36) It is desirable, in the interests of prudence, to establish a minimum of coordination of rules limiting the rate of interest used in calculating the technical provisions. For the purposes of such limitation, since existing methods are all equally correct, prudential and equivalent, it seems appropriate to leave Member States a free choice as to the method to be used.

(37) The rules governing the calculation of technical provisions and the rules governing the spread, localisation and matching of the assets used to cover technical provisions must be coordinated in order to facilitate the mutual recognition of Member States' rules. That coordination must take account of the liberalisation of capital movements provided for in Article 56 of the Treaty and the progress made by the Community towards economic and monetary union.

(38) The home Member State may not require assurance undertakings to invest the assets covering their technical provisions in particular categories of assets, as such a requirement would be incompatible with the liberalisation of capital movements provided for in Article 56 of the Treaty.

(39) It is necessary that, over and above technical provisions, including mathematical provisions, of sufficient amount to meet their underwriting liabilities, assurance undertakings should possess a

supplementary reserve, known as the solvency margin, represented by free assets and, with the agreement of the competent authority, by other implicit assets, which shall act as a buffer against adverse business fluctuations. This requirement is an important element of prudential supervision for the protection of insured persons and policy holders. In order to ensure that the requirements imposed for such purposes are determined according to objective criteria whereby undertakings of the same size will be placed on an equal footing as regards competition, it is desirable to provide that this margin shall be related to all the commitments of the undertaking and to the nature and gravity of the risks presented by the various activities falling within the scope of this Directive. This margin should therefore vary according to whether the risks are of investment, death or management only. It should accordingly be determined in terms of mathematical provisions and capital at risk underwritten by an undertaking, of premiums or contributions received, of provisions only or of the assets of tontines.

(40) *Directive 92/96/EEC provided for a provisional definition of a regulated market, pending the adoption of a directive on investment services in the securities field, which would harmonise that concept at Community level. Council Directive 93/22/EEC of 10 May 1993 on investment services in the securities field*[9] *provides for a definition of regulated market, although it excludes from its scope life assurance activities. It is appropriate to apply the concept of regulated market also to life assurance activities.*

(41) *The list of items of which the solvency margin required by this Directive may be made up takes account of new financial instruments and of the facilities granted to other financial institutions for the constitution of their own funds. In the light of market developments in the nature of reinsurance cover purchased by primary insurers, there is a need for the competent authorities to be empowered to decrease the reduction to the solvency margin requirement in certain circumstances. In order to improve the quality of the solvency margin, the possibility of including future profits in the available solvency margin should be limited and subject to conditions and should in any case cease after 2009.*

(42) *It is necessary to require a guarantee fund, the amount and composition of which are such as to provide an assurance that the undertakings possess adequate resources when they are set up and that in the subsequent course of business the solvency margin in no event falls below a minimum of security. The whole or a specified part of this guarantee fund must consist of explicit asset items.*

(43) *To avoid major and sharp increases in the amount of the minimum guarantee fund in the future, a mechanism should be established providing for its increase in line with the European index of consumer prices. This Directive should lay down minimum standards for the solvency margin requirements and home Member States should be able to lay down stricter rules for insurance undertakings authorised by their own competent authorities.*

(44) *The provisions in force in the Member States regarding contract law applicable to the activities referred to in this Directive differ. The harmonisation of assurance contract law is not a prior condition for the achievement of the internal market in assurance. Therefore, the opportunity afforded to the Member States of imposing the application of their law to assurance contracts covering commitments within their territories is likely to provide adequate safeguards for policy holders. The freedom to choose, as the law applicable to the contract, a law other than that of the State of the commitment may be granted in certain cases, in accordance with rules which take into account specific circumstances.*

(45) *For life assurance contracts the policy holder should be given the opportunity of cancelling the contract within a period of between 14 and 30 days.*

(46) *Within the framework of an internal market it is in the policy holder's interest that they should have access to the widest possible range of assurance products available in the Community so that they can choose that which is best suited to their needs. It is for the Member State of the commitment to ensure that there is nothing to prevent the marketing within its territory of all the assurance products offered for sale in the Community as long as they do not conflict with the legal provisions protecting the general good in force in the Member State of the commitment and in so far as the general good is not safeguarded by the rules of the home Member State, provided that such provisions must be applied without discrimination to all undertakings operating in that Member State and be objectively necessary and in proportion to the objective pursued.*

(47) *The Member States must be able to ensure that the assurance products and contract documents used, under the right of establishment or the freedom to provide services, to cover commitments within their territories comply with such specific legal provisions protecting the general good as are applicable. The systems of supervision to be employed must meet the requirements of an internal market but their employment may not constitute a prior condition for carrying on assurance business. From this standpoint, systems for the prior approval of policy conditions do not appear to be justified. It is therefore necessary to provide for other systems better suited to the requirements of an internal market which enable every Member State to guarantee policy holders adequate protection.*

(48) *It is necessary to make provision for cooperation between the competent authorities of the Member States and between those authorities and the Commission.*

(49) *Provision should be made for a system of penalties to be imposed when, in the Member State*

in which the commitment is entered into, an assurance undertaking does not comply with those provisions protecting the general good that are applicable to it.

(50) It is necessary to provide for measures in cases where the financial position of the undertaking becomes such that it is difficult for it to meet its underwriting liabilities. In specific situations where policy holders' rights are threatened, there is a need for the competent authorities to be empowered to intervene at a sufficiently early stage, but in the exercise of those powers, competent authorities should inform the insurance undertakings of the reasons motivating such supervisory action, in accordance with the principles of sound administration and due process. As long as such a situation exists, the competent authorities should be prevented from certifying that the insurance undertaking has a sufficient solvency margin.

(51) For the purposes of implementing actuarial principles in conformity with this Directive, the home Member State may require systematic notification of the technical bases used for calculating scales of premiums and technical provisions, with such notification of technical bases excluding notification of the general and special policy conditions and the undertaking's commercial rates.

(52) In an internal market for assurance the consumer will have a wider and more varied choice of contracts. If he/she is to profit fully from this diversity and from increased competition, he/she must be provided with whatever information is necessary to enable him/her to choose the contract best suited to his/her needs. This information requirement is all the more important as the duration of commitments can be very long. The minimum provisions must therefore be coordinated in order for the consumer to receive clear and accurate information on the essential characteristics of the products proposed to him/her as well as the particulars of the bodies to which any complaints of policy holders, assured persons or beneficiaries of contracts may be addressed.

(53) Publicity for assurance products is an essential means of enabling assurance business to be carried on effectively within the Community. It is necessary to leave open to assurance undertakings the use of all normal means of advertising in the Member State of the branch or of provision of services. Member States may nevertheless require compliance with their national rules on the form and content of advertising, whether laid down pursuant to Community legislation on advertising or adopted by Member States for reasons of the general good.

(54) Within the framework of the internal market, no Member State may continue to prohibit the simultaneous carrying on of assurance business within its territory under the right of establishment and the freedom to provide services.

(55) Some Member States do not subject assurance transactions to any form of indirect taxation, while the majority apply special taxes and other forms of contribution. The structures and rates of such taxes and contributions vary considerably between the Member States in which they are applied. It is desirable to prevent existing differences leading to distortions of competition in assurance services between Member States. Pending subsequent harmonisation, application of the tax systems and other forms of contribution provided for by the Member States in which commitments entered into are likely to remedy that problem and it is for the Member States to make arrangements to ensure that such taxes and contributions are collected.

(56) It is important to introduce Community coordination on the winding-up of assurance undertakings. It is henceforth essential to provide, in the event of the winding-up of an assurance undertaking, that the system of protection in place in each Member State must guarantee equality of treatment for all assurance creditors, irrespective of nationality and of the method of entering into the commitment.

(57) The coordinated rules concerning the pursuit of the business of direct insurance within the Community should, in principle, apply to all undertakings operating on the market and, consequently, also to agencies and branches where the head office of the undertaking is situated outside the Community. As regards the methods of supervision this Directive lays down special provisions for such agencies or branches, in view of the fact that the assets of the undertakings to which they belong are situated outside the Community.

(58) It is desirable to provide for the conclusion of reciprocal agreements with one or more third countries in order to permit the relaxation of such special conditions, while observing the principle that such agencies and branches should not obtain more favourable treatment than Community undertakings.

(59) A provision should be made for a flexible procedure to make it possible to assess reciprocity with third countries on a Community basis. The aim of this procedure is not to close the Community's financial markets but rather, as the Community intends to keep its financial markets open to the rest of the world, to improve the liberalisation of the global financial markets in other third countries. To that end, this Directive provides for procedures for negotiating with third countries. As a last resort, the possibility of taking measures involving the suspension of new applications for authorisation or the restriction of new authorisations should be provided for using the regulatory procedure under Article 5 of Council Decision 1999/468/EC.[10]

(60) This Directive should establish provisions concerning proof of good repute and no previous bankruptcy.

(61) In order to clarify the legal regime applicable to life assurance activities covered by this

Directive, some provisions of Directives 79/267/EEC, 90/619/EEC and 92/96/EEC should be adapted. For that purpose some provisions concerning the establishment of the solvency margin and the rights acquired by branches of assurance undertakings established before 1 July 1994 should be amended. The content of the scheme of operation of branches of third-country undertakings to be established in the Community should also be defined.

(62) Technical adjustments to the detailed rules laid down in this Directive may be necessary from time to time to take account of the future development of the assurance industry. The Commission will make such adjustments as and when necessary, after consulting the Insurance Committee set up by Council Directive 91/675/EEC,[11] in the exercise of the implementing powers conferred on it by the Treaty. These measures being measures of general scope within the meaning of Article 2 of Decision 1999/468/EC, they should be adopted by the use of the regulatory procedure provided for in Article 5 of that Decision.

(63) Pursuant to Article 15 of the Treaty, account should be taken of the extent of the effort which must be made by certain economies at different stages of development. Therefore, transitional arrangements should be adopted for the gradual application of this Directive by certain Member States.

(64) Directives 79/267/EEC and 90/619/EEC granted special derogation with regard to some undertakings existing at the time of the adoption of these Directives. Such undertakings have thereafter modified their structure. Therefore they do not need any longer such special derogation.

(65) This Directive should not affect the obligations of Member States concerning the deadlines for transposition and for application of the Directives set out in Annex V(B),

NOTES

Repealed as noted at the beginning of this Directive.

1 OJ C365 E, 19.12.2000, p 1.

2 OJ C123, 25.4.2001, p 24.

3 Opinion of the European Parliament of 15 March 2001 (OJ C343, 5.12.2001, p 202), Council Common Position of 27 May 2002 (OJ C170 E, 16.7.2002, p 45) and decision of the European Parliament of 25 September 2002 (not yet published in the Official Journal).

4 OJ L63, 13.3.1979, p 1. Directive as last amended by Directive 2002/12/EC of the European Parliament and of the Council (OJ L77, 20.3.2002, p 11).

5 OJ L330, 29.11.1990, p 50. Directive as amended by Directive 92/96/EEC (OJ L360, 9.12.1992, p 1).

6 OJ L360, 9.12.1992, p 1. Directive as amended by Directive 2000/64/EC of the European Parliament and of the Council (OJ L290, 17.11.2000, p 27).

7 OJ L374, 31.12.1991, p 7.

8 OJ L228, 16.8.1973, p 3. Directive as last amended by Directive 2002/13/EC of the European Parliament and of the Council (OJ L77, 20.3.2002, p 17).

9 OJ L141, 11.6.1993, p 27. Directive as last amended by Directive 2000/64/EC of the European Parliament and of the Council.

10 OJ L184, 17.7.1999, p 23.

11 OJ L374, 31.12.1991, p 32.

HAVE ADOPTED THIS DIRECTIVE—

TITLE I
DEFINITIONS AND SCOPE

[6557]
Article 1
Definitions

1. For the purposes of this Directive—

(a) "assurance undertaking" shall mean an undertaking which has received official authorisation in accordance with Article 4;

(b) "branch" shall mean an agency or branch of an assurance undertaking;

Any permanent presence of an undertaking in the territory of a Member State shall be treated in the same way as an agency or branch, even if that presence does not take the form of a branch or agency, but consists merely of an office managed by the undertaking's own staff or by a person who is independent but has permanent authority to act for the undertaking as an agency would;

(c) "establishment" shall mean the head office, an agency or a branch of an undertaking;

(d) "commitment" shall mean a commitment represented by one of the kinds of insurance or operations referred to in Article 2;

(e) *"home Member State" shall mean the Member State in which the head office of the assurance undertaking covering the commitment is situated;*

(f) *"Member State of the branch" shall mean the Member State in which the branch covering the commitment is situated;*

(g) *"Member State of the commitment" shall mean the Member State where the policy holder has his/her habitual residence or, if the policy holder is a legal person, the Member State where the latter's establishment, to which the contract relates, is situated;*

(h) *"Member State of the provision of services" shall mean the Member State of the commitment, if the commitment is covered by an assurance undertaking or a branch situated in another Member State;*

(i) *"control" shall mean the relationship between a parent undertaking and a subsidiary, as defined in Article 1 of Council Directive 83/349/EEC,*[1] *or a similar relationship between any natural or legal person and an undertaking;*

(j) *"qualifying holding" shall mean a direct or indirect holding in an undertaking which represents 10% or more of the capital or of the voting rights or which makes it possible to exercise a significant influence over the management of the undertaking in which a holding subsists;*

[For the purposes of this definition, in the context of Articles 8 and 15 and of the other levels of holding referred to in Article 15, the voting rights referred to in Articles 9 and 10 of Directive 2004/109/EC,[2] *as well as the conditions regarding aggregation thereof laid down in Article 12(4) and (5) of that Directive, shall be taken into account.*

Member States shall not take into account voting rights or shares which investment firms or credit institutions may hold as a result of providing the underwriting of financial instruments and/or placing of financial instruments on a firm commitment basis included under point 6 of Section A of Annex I to Directive 2004/39/EC;[3] *provided that those rights are, on the one hand, not exercised or otherwise used to intervene in the management of the issuer and, on the other, disposed of within one year of acquisition.]*

(k) *"parent undertaking" shall mean a parent undertaking as defined in Articles 1 and 2 of Directive 83/349/EEC;*

(l) *"subsidiary" shall mean a subsidiary undertaking as defined in Articles 1 and 2 of Directive 83/349/EEC; any subsidiary of a subsidiary undertaking shall also be regarded as a subsidiary of the undertaking which is those undertakings' ultimate parent undertaking;*

(m) *"regulated market" shall mean—*

— *in the case of a market situated in a Member State, a regulated market as defined in Article 1(13) of Directive 93/22/EEC, and*

— *in the case of a market situated in a third country, a financial market recognised by the home Member State of the assurance undertaking which meets comparable requirements. Any financial instruments dealt in on that market must be of a quality comparable to that of the instruments dealt in on the regulated market or markets of the Member State in question;*

(n) *"competent authorities" shall mean the national authorities which are empowered by law or regulation to supervise assurance undertakings;*

(o) *"matching assets" shall mean the representation of underwriting liabilities which can be required to be met in a particular currency by assets expressed or realisable in the same currency;*

(p) *"localisation of assets" shall mean the existence of assets, whether movable or immovable, within a Member State but shall not be construed as involving a requirement that movable assets be deposited or that immovable assets be subjected to restrictive measures such as the registration of mortgages; assets represented by claims against debtors shall be regarded as situated in the Member State where they are realisable;*

(q) *capital at risk shall mean the amount payable on death less the mathematical provision for the main risk;*

(r) *"close" links shall mean a situation in which two or more natural or legal persons are linked by—*

(i) *participation, which shall mean the ownership, direct or by way of control, of 20% or more of the voting rights or capital of an undertaking; or*

(ii) *control, which shall mean the relationship between a parent undertaking and a subsidiary, in all the cases referred to in Article 1(1) and (2) of Directive 83/349/EEC, or a similar relationship between any natural or legal person and an undertaking; any subsidiary undertaking of a subsidiary undertaking shall also be considered a subsidiary of the parent undertaking which is at the head of those undertakings.*

A situation in which two or more natural or legal persons are permanently linked to one and the same person by a control relationship shall also be regarded as constituting a close link between such persons.

[(s) "reinsurance undertaking" shall mean a reinsurance undertaking within the meaning of Article 2 point (c) of Directive 2005/68/EC of the European Parliament and of the Council of 16 November 2005 on reinsurance.[4]]

2. Wherever this Directive refers to the euro, the conversion value in national currency to be adopted shall as from 31 December of each year be that of the last day of the preceding month of October for which euro conversion values are available in all the relevant Community currencies.

NOTES

Repealed as noted at the beginning of this Directive.

Para 1: words in square brackets in sub-para (j) substituted by European Parliament and Council Directive 2007/44/EC, art 2(1); sub-para (s) added by European Parliament and Council Directive 2005/68/EC, art 60(1).

1 OJ L193, 18.7.1983, p 1. Directive as last amended by Directive 2001/65/EC of the European Parliament and of the Council (OJ L283, 27.10.2001, p 28).

2 Directive 2004/109/EC of the European Parliament and of the Council of 15 December 2004 on the harmonisation of transparency requirements in relation to information about issuers whose securities are admitted to trading on a regulated market (OJ L390, 31.12.2004, p 38).

3 Directive 2004/39/EC of the European Parliament and of the Council of 21 April 2004 on markets in financial instruments (OJ L145, 30.4.2004, p 1). Directive as last amended by Directive 2007/44/EC (OJ L247, 21.9.2007, p 1).

4 OJ L323, 9.12.2005, p 1.

[6558]
Article 2
Scope

This Directive concerns the taking-up and pursuit of the self-employed activity of direct insurance carried on by undertakings which are established in a Member State or wish to become established there in the form of the activities defined below—

1. the following kinds of assurance where they are on a contractual basis—

- *(a) life assurance, that is to say, the class of assurance which comprises, in particular, assurance on survival to a stipulated age only, assurance on death only, assurance on survival to a stipulated age or on earlier death, life assurance with return of premiums, marriage assurance, birth assurance;*
- *(b) annuities;*
- *(c) supplementary insurance carried on by life assurance undertakings, that is to say, in particular, insurance against personal injury including incapacity for employment, insurance against death resulting from an accident and insurance against disability resulting from an accident or sickness, where these various kinds of insurance are underwritten in addition to life assurance;*
- *(d) the type of insurance existing in Ireland and the United Kingdom known as permanent health insurance not subject to cancellation;*

2. the following operations, where they are on a contractual basis, in so far as they are subject to supervision by the administrative authorities responsible for the supervision of private insurance—

- *(a) tontines whereby associations of subscribers are set up with a view to jointly capitalising their contributions and subsequently distributing the assets thus accumulated among the survivors or among the beneficiaries of the deceased;*
- *(b) capital redemption operations based on actuarial calculation whereby, in return for single or periodic payments agreed in advance, commitments of specified duration and amount are undertaken;*
- *(c) management of group pension funds, i.e. operations consisting, for the undertaking concerned, in managing the investments, and in particular the assets representing the reserves of bodies that effect payments on death or survival or in the event of discontinuance or curtailment of activity;*
- *(d) the operations referred to in (c) where they are accompanied by insurance covering either conservation of capital or payment of a minimum interest;*
- *(e) the operations carried out by assurance undertakings such as those referred to in Chapter 1, Title 4 of Book IV of the French "Code des assurances".*

3. Operations relating to the length of human life which are prescribed by or provided for in social insurance legislation, when they are effected or managed at their own risk by assurance undertakings in accordance with the laws of a Member State.

NOTES

Repealed as noted at the beginning of this Directive.

[6559]

Article 3

Activities and bodies excluded

This Directive shall not concern—

1. *subject to the application of Article 2(1)(c), the classes designated in the Annex to Directive 73/239/EEC;*
2. *operations of provident and mutual-benefit institutions whose benefits vary according to the resources available and which require each of their members to contribute at the appropriate flat rate;*
3. *operations carried out by organisations other than undertakings referred to in Article 2, whose object is to provide benefits for employed or self-employed persons belonging to an undertaking or group of undertakings, or a trade or group of trades, in the event of death or survival or of discontinuance or curtailment of activity, whether or not the commitments arising from such operations are fully covered at all times by mathematical provisions;*
4. *subject to the application of Article 2(3), insurance forming part of a statutory system of social security;*
5. *organisations which undertake to provide benefits solely in the event of death, where the amount of such benefits does not exceed the average funeral costs for a single death or where the benefits are provided in kind;*
6. *mutual associations, where—*
   - *the articles of association contain provisions for calling up additional contributions or reducing their benefits or claiming assistance from other persons who have undertaken to provide it, and*
   - *the annual contribution income for the activities covered by this Directive does not exceed EUR 5 million for three consecutive years. If this amount is exceeded for three consecutive years this Directive shall apply with effect from the fourth year.*

   Nevertheless, the provisions of this paragraph shall not prevent a mutual assurance undertaking from applying, or continuing, to be licensed under this Directive;
7. *the "Versorgungsverband deutscher Wirtschaftsorganisationen" in Germany unless its statutes are amended as regards the scope of its activities;*
8. *the pension activities of pension insurance undertakings prescribed in the Employees. Pension Act (TEL) and other related Finnish legislation provided that—*
   (a) *pension insurance companies which already under Finnish law are obliged to have separate accounting and management systems for their pension activities will furthermore, as from the date of accession, set up separate legal entities for carrying out these activities;*
   (b) *the Finnish authorities shall allow in a non-discriminatory manner all nationals and companies of Member States to perform according to Finnish legislation the activities specified in Article 2 related to this exemption whether by means of—*
   - *ownership or participation in an existing insurance company or group,*
   - *creation or participation of new insurance companies or groups, including pension insurance companies;*

   (c) *the Finnish authorities will submit to the Commission for approval a report within three months from the date of accession, stating which measures have been taken to separate TEL activities from normal insurance activities carried out by Finnish insurance companies in order to conform to all the requirements of this Directive.*

NOTES

Repealed as noted at the beginning of this Directive.

TITLE II
THE TAKING UP OF THE BUSINESS OF LIFE INSURANCE

[6560]
Article 4
Principle of authorisation

The taking up of the activities covered by this Directive shall be subject to prior official authorisation.

Such authorisation shall be sought from the authorities of the home Member State by—

(a) *any undertaking which establishes its head office in the territory of that State;*

(b) *any undertaking which, having received the authorisation required in the first subparagraph, extends its business to an entire class or to other classes.*

NOTES

Repealed as noted at the beginning of this Directive.

[6561]
Article 5
Scope of authorisation

1. Authorisation shall be valid for the entire Community. It shall permit an assurance undertaking to carry on business there, under either the right of establishment or freedom to provide services.

2. Authorisation shall be granted for a particular class of assurance as listed in Annex I. It shall cover the entire class, unless the applicant wishes to cover only some of the risks pertaining to that class.

The competent authorities may restrict authorisation requested for one of the classes to the operations set out in the scheme of operations referred to in Article 7.

Each Member State may grant authorisation for two or more of the classes, where its national laws permit such classes to be carried on simultaneously.

NOTES

Repealed as noted at the beginning of this Directive.

[6562]
Article 6
Conditions for obtaining authorisation

1. The home Member State shall require every assurance undertaking for which authorisation is sought to—

(a) *adopt one of the following forms—*

— *in the case of the Kingdom of Belgium: "société anonyme/naamloze vennootschap", "société en commandite par actions/commanditaire vennootschap op aandelen", "association d'assurance mutuelle/onderlinge verzekeringsvereniging", "société coopérative/coöperatieve vennootschap",*

[— *in the case of Bulgaria:* "акционерно дружество", "взаимозастрахователна коопераци ",]

[— *in the case of the Czech Republic: "akciová společnost", "družstvo",]*

— *in the case of the Kingdom of Denmark: "aktieselskaber", "gensidige selskaber", "pensionskasser omfattet af lov om forsikringsvirksomhed (tværgående pensionskasser)",*

— *in the case of the Federal Republic of Germany: "Aktiengesellschaft", "Versicherungsverein auf Gegenseitigkeit", "öffentlich-rechtliches Wettbewerbsversicherungsunternehmen",*

[— *in the case of the Republic of Estonia: "aktsiaselts",]*

— *in the case of the French Republic: "société anonyme", "société d'assurance mutuelle", "institution de prévoyance régie par le code de la sécurité sociale", "institution de prévoyance régie par le code rural" and "mutuelles régies par le code de la mutualité",*

— *in the case of Ireland: "incorporated companies limited by shares or by guarantee or unlimited", "societies registered under the Industrial and Provident Societies Acts" and "societies registered under the Friendly Societies Acts,"*

— *in the case of the Italian Republic: "societá per azioni", "societá cooperativa", "mutua di assicurazione",*

[— *in the case of the Republic of Cyprus:* "Εταιρε α περιορισμνης ευθνης με μετοχς εταιρε α περιορισμνης ευθνης με εγηση",

— *in the case of the Republic of the Latvia: "apdrošināšanas akciju sabiedrība", "savstarpējās apdrošināšanas kooperatīvā biedrība",*
— *in the case of the Republic of Lithuania: "akcins bendrovs", "uždarosios akcins bendrovs",]*
— *in the case of the Grand Duchy of Luxembourg: "société anonyme", "société en commandite par actions", "association d'assurances mutuelles", "société coopérative",*
[— *in the case of the Republic of Hungary: "biztosító részvénytársaság", "biztosító szövetkezet", "biztosító egyesület", "külföldi székhely biztosító magyarországi fióktelepe",*
— *in the case of the Republic of Malta: "kumpanija pubblika", "kumpanija privata", "ferga", "Korp ta' l- Assikurazzjoni Rikonnoxxut",]*
— *in the case of the Kingdom of the Netherlands: "naamloze vennootschap", "onderlinge waarborgmaatschappij",*
— *in the case of the United Kingdom: "incorporated companies limited by shares or by guarantee or unlimited", "societies registered under the Industrial and Provident Societies Acts", "societies registered or incorporated under the Friendly Societies Acts", "the association of underwriters known as Lloyd's",*
— *in the case of the Hellenic Republic: "αν νυμη εταιρ α",*
— *in the case of the Kingdom of Spain: "sociedad anónima", "sociedad mutua", "sociedad cooperativa",*
— *in the case of the Portuguese Republic: "sociedade anónima", "mútua de seguros",*
[— *in the case of Romania: "societăi pe aciuni", "societăi mutuale",]*
[— *in the case of the Republic of Poland: "spółka akcyjna", "towarzystwo ubezpieczeń wzajemnych",]*
— *in the case of the Republic of Austria: "Aktiengesellschaft", "Versicherungsverein auf Gegenseitigkeit",*
[— *in the case of the Republic of Slovenia: "delniška družba", "družba za vzajemno zavarovanje",*
— *in the case of the Slovak Republic: "akciová spoločnost",]*
— *in the case of the Republic of Finland: "keskinäinen vakuutusyhtiö/ömsesidigt försäkringsbolag", "vakuutusosakeyhtiö/försäkringsaktiebolag", "vakuutusyhdistys/försäkringsförening",*
— *in the case of Kingdom of Sweden: "försäkringsaktiebolag", "ömsesidiga försäkringsbolag", "understödsföreningar".*

An assurance undertaking may also adopt the form of a European company when that has been established.

Furthermore, Member States may, where appropriate, set up undertakings in any public-law form provided that such bodies have as their object insurance operations under conditions equivalent to those under which private-law undertakings operate;

(b) *limit its objects to the business provided for in this Directive and operations directly arising therefrom, to the exclusion of all other commercial business;*
(c) *submit a scheme of operations in accordance with Article 7;*
(d) *possess the minimum guarantee fund provided for in Article 29(2);*
(e) *be effectively run by persons of good repute with appropriate professional qualifications or experience.*

2. *Where close links exist between the assurance undertaking and other natural or legal persons, the competent authorities shall grant authorisation only if those links do not prevent the effective exercise of their supervisory functions.*

The competent authorities shall also refuse authorisation if the laws, regulations or administrative provisions of a non-member country governing one or more natural or legal persons with which the assurance undertaking has close links, or difficulties involved in their enforcement, prevent the effective exercise of their supervisory functions.

The competent authorities shall require assurance undertakings to provide them with the information they require to monitor compliance with the conditions referred to in this paragraph on a continuous basis.

3. *Member States shall require that the head offices of insurance undertakings be situated in the same Member State as their registered offices.*

4. An assurance undertaking seeking authorisation to extend its business to other classes or to extend an authorisation covering only some of the risks pertaining to one class shall be required to submit a scheme of operations in accordance with Article 7.

It shall, furthermore, be required to show proof that it possesses the solvency margin provided for in Article 28 and the guarantee fund referred to in Article 29(1) and (2).

5. Member States shall not adopt provisions requiring the prior approval or systematic notification of general and special policy conditions, of scales of premiums, of the technical bases, used in particular for calculating scales of premiums and technical provisions or of forms and other printed documents which an assurance undertaking intends to use in its dealings with policy holders.

Notwithstanding the first subparagraph, for the sole purpose of verifying compliance with national provisions concerning actuarial principles, the home Member State may require systematic notification of the technical bases used for calculating scales of premiums and technical provisions, without that requirement constituting a prior condition for an assurance undertaking to carry on its business.

Nothing in this Directive shall prevent Member States from maintaining in force or introducing laws, regulations or administrative provisions requiring approval of the memorandum and articles of association and the communication of any other documents necessary for the normal exercise of supervision.

Not later than 1 July 1999, the Commission shall submit a report to the Council on the implementation of this paragraph.

6. The provisions referred to in paragraphs 1 to 5 may not require that any application for authorisation be considered in the light of the economic requirements of the market.

NOTES

Repealed as noted at the beginning of this Directive.

Para 1: entries in square brackets relating to Bulgaria and Romania inserted by Council Directive 2006/101/EC, art 1, Annex, para 3(a); other entries in square brackets inserted by Council Directive 2004/66/EC, Annex, Pt II, para (a).

[6563]
Article 7
Scheme of operations

The scheme of operations referred to in Article 6(1)(c) and (4) shall include particulars or evidence of—

- *(a) the nature of the commitments which the assurance undertaking proposes to cover;*
- *(b) the guiding principles as to reassurance;*
- *(c) the items constituting the minimum guarantee fund;*
- *(d) estimates relating to the costs of setting up the administrative services and the organisation for securing business and the financial resources intended to meet those costs;*

in addition, for the first three financial years—

- *(e) a plan setting out detailed estimates of income and expenditure in respect of direct business, reassurance acceptances and reassurance cessions;*
- *(f) a forecast balance sheet;*
- *(g) estimates relating to the financial resources intended to cover underwriting liabilities and the solvency margin.*

NOTES

Repealed as noted at the beginning of this Directive.

[6564]
Article 8
Shareholders and members with qualifying holdings

The competent authorities of the home Member State shall not grant an undertaking authorisation to take up the business of assurance before they have been informed of the identities of the shareholders or members, direct or indirect, whether natural or legal persons, who have qualifying holdings in that undertaking and of the amounts of those holdings.

The same authorities shall refuse authorisation if, taking into account the need to ensure the sound and prudent management of an assurance undertaking, they are not satisfied as to the qualifications of the shareholders or members.

NOTES

Repealed as noted at the beginning of this Directive.

[6565]
Article 9
Refusal of authorisation

Any decision to refuse an authorisation shall be accompanied by the precise grounds for doing so and notified to the undertaking in question.

Each Member State shall make provision for a right to apply to the courts should there be any refusal.

Such provision shall also be made with regard to cases where the competent authorities have not dealt with an application for an authorisation upon the expiry of a period of six months from the date of its receipt.

NOTES

Repealed as noted at the beginning of this Directive.

[6566]
[Article 9a
Prior consultation with the competent authorities of other Member States

1. The competent authorities of the other Member State involved shall be consulted prior to the granting of an authorisation to a life assurance undertaking, which is:

- *(a) a subsidiary of an insurance or reinsurance undertaking authorised in another Member State; or*
- *(b) a subsidiary of the parent undertaking of an insurance or reinsurance undertaking authorised in another Member State; or*
- *(c) controlled by the same person, whether natural or legal, who controls an insurance or reinsurance undertaking authorised in another Member State.*

2. The competent authority of a Member State involved responsible for the supervision of credit institutions or investment firms shall be consulted prior to the granting of an authorisation to a life assurance undertaking which is:

- *(a) a subsidiary of a credit institution or investment firm authorised in the Community; or*
- *(b) a subsidiary of the parent undertaking of a credit institution or investment firm authorised in the Community; or*
- *(c) controlled by the same person, whether natural or legal, who controls a credit institution or investment firm authorised in the Community.*

3. The relevant competent authorities referred to in paragraphs 1 and 2 shall in particular consult each other when assessing the suitability of the shareholders and the reputation and experience of directors involved in the management of another entity of the same group. They shall inform each other of any information regarding the suitability of shareholders and the reputation and experience of directors which is of relevance to the other competent authorities involved for the granting of an authorisation as well as for the ongoing assessment of compliance with operating conditions.]

NOTES

Inserted by European Parliament and Council Directive 2005/68/EC, art 60(2).
Repealed as noted at the beginning of this Directive.

TITLE III
CONDITIONS GOVERNING THE BUSINESS OF ASSURANCE

CHAPTER 1
PRINCIPLES AND METHODS OF FINANCIAL SUPERVISION

[6567]
Article 10
Competent authorities and object of supervision

1. The financial supervision of an assurance undertaking, including that of the business it carries on either through branches or under the freedom to provide services, shall be the sole responsibility of the home Member State. If the competent authorities of the Member State of the commitment have reason to consider that the activities of an assurance undertaking might affect its financial soundness, they shall inform the competent authorities of the undertaking's home Member State. The latter authorities shall determine whether the undertaking is complying with the prudential principles laid down in this Directive.

2. That financial supervision shall include verification, with respect to the assurance undertaking's entire business, of its state of solvency, the establishment of technical provisions, including mathematical provisions, and of the assets covering them, in accordance with the rules laid down or practices followed in the home Member State pursuant to the provisions adopted at Community level.

[The home Member State of the insurance undertaking shall not refuse a reinsurance contract concluded by the insurance undertaking with a reinsurance undertaking authorised in accordance with Directive 2005/68/EC or an insurance undertaking authorised in accordance with Directive 73/239/EEC or this Directive on grounds directly related to the financial soundness of the reinsurance undertaking or the insurance undertaking.]

3. The competent authorities of the home Member State shall require every assurance undertaking to have sound administrative and accounting procedures and adequate internal control mechanisms.

NOTES

Repealed as noted at the beginning of this Directive.

Para 2: words in square brackets inserted by European Parliament and Council Directive 2005/68/EC, art 60(3).

[6568]
Article 11
Supervision of branches established in another Member State

The Member State of the branch shall provide that, where an assurance undertaking authorised in another Member State carries on business through a branch, the competent authorities of the home Member State may, after having first informed the competent authorities of the Member State of the branch, carry out themselves, or through the intermediary of persons they appoint for that purpose, on-the-spot verification of the information necessary to ensure the financial supervision of the undertaking. The authorities of the Member State of the branch may participate in that verification.

NOTES

Repealed as noted at the beginning of this Directive.

[6569]
Article 12
Prohibition on compulsory ceding of part of underwriting

Member States may not require assurance undertakings to cede part of their underwriting of activities listed in Article 2 to an organisation or organisations designated by national regulations.

NOTES

Repealed as noted at the beginning of this Directive.

[6570]
Article 13
Accounting, prudential and statistical information: supervisory powers

1. Each Member State shall require every assurance undertaking whose head office is situated in its territory to produce an annual account, covering all types of operation, of its financial situation and solvency.

2. Member States shall require assurance undertakings with head offices within their territories to render periodically the returns, together with statistical documents, which are necessary for the purposes of supervision. The competent authorities shall provide each other with any documents and information that are useful for the purposes of supervision.

3. Every Member State shall take all steps necessary to ensure that the competent authorities have the powers and means necessary for the supervision of the business of assurance undertakings with head offices within their territories, including business carried on outside those territories, in accordance with the Council directives governing those activities and for the purpose of seeing that they are implemented.

These powers and means must, in particular, enable the competent authorities to—

- *(a) make detailed enquiries regarding the assurance undertaking's situation and the whole of its business, inter alia, by—*
  - *— gathering information or requiring the submission of documents concerning its assurance business,*
  - *— carrying out on-the-spot investigations at the assurance undertaking's premises;*
- *(b) take any measures, with regard to the assurance undertaking, its directors or managers or the persons who control it, that are appropriate and necessary to ensure that the*

undertaking's business continues to comply with the laws, regulations and administrative provisions with which the undertaking must comply in each Member State and in particular with the scheme of operations in so far as it remains mandatory, and to prevent or remedy any irregularities prejudicial to the interests of the assured persons;

(c) *ensure that those measures are carried out, if need be by enforcement, where appropriate through judicial channels.*

Member States may also make provision for the competent authorities to obtain any information regarding contracts which are held by intermediaries.

NOTES

Repealed as noted at the beginning of this Directive.

[6571]
Article 14
Transfer of portfolio

1. Under the conditions laid down by national law, each Member State shall authorise assurance undertakings with head offices within its territory to transfer all or part of their portfolios of contracts, concluded under either the right of establishment or the freedom to provide services, to an accepting office established within the Community, if the competent authorities of the home Member State of the accepting office certify that after taking the transfer into account, the latter possesses the necessary solvency margin.

2. Where a branch proposes to transfer all or part of its portfolio of contracts, concluded under either the right of establishment or the freedom to provide services, the Member State of the branch shall be consulted.

3. In the circumstances referred to in paragraphs 1 and 2, the authorities of the home Member State of the transferring assurance undertaking shall authorise the transfer after obtaining the agreement of the competent authorities of the Member States of the commitment.

4. The competent authorities of the Member States consulted shall give their opinion or consent to the competent authorities of the home Member State of the transferring assurance undertaking within three months of receiving a request; the absence of any response within that period from the authorities consulted shall be considered equivalent to a favourable opinion or tacit consent.

5. A transfer authorised in accordance with this Article shall be published as laid down by national law in the Member State of the commitment. Such transfers shall automatically be valid against policy holders, the assured persons and any other person having rights or obligations arising out of the contracts transferred.

This provision shall not affect the Member States' rights to give policy holders the option of cancelling contracts within a fixed period after a transfer.

NOTES

Repealed as noted at the beginning of this Directive.

[6572]
Article 15
Qualifying holdings

[1. Member States shall require any natural or legal person or such persons acting in concert (hereinafter referred to as the proposed acquirer), who have taken a decision either to acquire, directly or indirectly, a qualifying holding in an assurance undertaking or to further increase, directly or indirectly, such a qualifying holding in an assurance undertaking as a result of which the proportion of the voting rights or of the capital held would reach or exceed 20%, 30% or 50% or so that the assurance undertaking would become its subsidiary (hereinafter referred to as the "proposed acquisition"), first to notify in writing the competent authorities of the assurance undertaking in which they are seeking to acquire or increase a qualifying holding, indicating the size of the intended holding and relevant information, as referred to in Article 15b(4). Member States need not apply the 30% threshold where, in accordance with Article 9(3)(a) of Directive 2004/109/EC, they apply a threshold of one-third.]

[1a. . . .]

[2. Member States shall require any natural or legal person who has taken a decision to dispose, directly or indirectly, of a qualifying holding in an assurance undertaking first to notify in writing the competent authorities of the home Member State, indicating the size of his/her intended holding. Such a person shall likewise notify the competent authorities if he/she has taken a decision to reduce his/her qualifying holding so that the proportion of the voting rights or of the capital held

Part VI European Materials

would fall below 20%, 30% or 50% or so that the assurance undertaking would cease to be his/her subsidiary. Member States need not apply the 30% threshold where, in accordance with Article 9(3)(a) of Directive 2004/109/EC, they apply a threshold of one-third.]

3. On becoming aware of them, assurance undertakings shall inform the competent authorities of their home Member States of any acquisitions or disposals of holdings in their capital that cause holdings to exceed or fall below one of the thresholds referred to in paragraphs 1 and 2.

They shall also, at least once a year, inform them of the names of shareholders and members possessing qualifying holdings and the sizes of such holdings as shown, for example, by the information received at the annual general meetings of shareholders and members or as a result of compliance with the regulations relating to companies listed on stock exchanges.

4. Member States shall require that, if the influence exercised by the persons referred to in paragraph 1 is likely to operate to the detriment of the prudent and sound management of the assurance undertaking, the competent authorities of the home Member State shall take appropriate measures to put an end to that situation. Such measures may consist, for example, in injunctions, sanctions against directors and managers, or the suspension of the exercise of the voting rights attaching to the shares held by the shareholders or members in question.

Similar measures shall apply to natural or legal persons failing to comply with the obligation to provide prior information, as laid down in paragraph 1. If a holding is acquired despite the opposition of the competent authorities, the Member States shall, regardless of any other sanctions to be adopted, provide either for exercise of the corresponding voting rights to be suspended, or for the nullity of votes cast or for the possibility of their annulment.

NOTES

Repealed as noted at the beginning of this Directive.

Para 1: substituted by European Parliament and Council Directive 2007/44/EC, art 2(2)(a).

Para 1a: inserted by European Parliament and Council Directive 2005/68/EC, art 60(4); repealed by European Parliament and Council Directive 2007/44/EC, art 2(2)(b).

Para 2: substituted by European Parliament and Council Directive 2007/44/EC, art 2(2)(c).

[6573]
[Article 15a
Assessment period

1. The competent authorities shall, promptly and in any event within two working days following receipt of the notification required under Article 15(1), as well as following the possible subsequent receipt of the information referred to in paragraph 2 of this Article, acknowledge receipt thereof in writing to the proposed acquirer.

The competent authorities shall have a maximum of 60 working days as from the date of the written acknowledgement of receipt of the notification and all documents required by the Member State to be attached to the notification on the basis of the list referred to in Article 15b(4) (hereinafter referred to as the assessment period), to carry out the assessment provided for in Article 15b(1) (hereinafter referred to as the assessment).

The competent authorities shall inform the proposed acquirer of the date of the expiry of the assessment period at the time of acknowledging receipt.

2. The competent authorities may, during the assessment period, if necessary, and no later than on the fiftieth working day of the assessment period, request any further information that is necessary to complete the assessment. Such request shall be made in writing and shall specify the additional information needed.

For the period between the date of request for information by the competent authorities and the receipt of a response thereto by the proposed acquirer, the assessment period shall be interrupted. The interruption shall not exceed 20 working days. Any further requests by the competent authorities for completion or clarification of the information shall be at their discretion but may not result in an interruption of the assessment period.

3. The competent authorities may extend the interruption referred to in the second subparagraph of paragraph 2 up to 30 working days if the proposed acquirer is:

- *(a) situated or regulated outside the Community; or*
- *(b) a natural or legal person not subject to supervision under this Directive or Directives 85/611/EEC,[1] 92/49/EEC,[2] 2004/39/EC, 2005/68/EC or 2006/48/EC.[3]*

4. If the competent authorities, upon completion of the assessment, decide to oppose the proposed acquisition, they shall, within two working days, and not exceeding the assessment period, inform the proposed acquirer in writing and provide the reasons for that decision. Subject to national law, an appropriate statement of the reasons for the decision may be made accessible to the public at the request by the proposed acquirer. This shall not prevent a Member State from allowing the competent authority to make such disclosure in the absence of a request of the proposed acquirer.

5. If the competent authorities do not oppose the proposed acquisition within the assessment period in writing, it shall be deemed to be approved.

6. The competent authorities may fix a maximum period for concluding the proposed acquisition and extend it where appropriate.

7. Member States may not impose requirements for the notification to and approval by the competent authorities of direct or indirect acquisitions of voting rights or capital that are more stringent than those set out in this Directive.]

NOTES

Inserted, together with arts 15b, 15c, by European Parliament and Council Directive 2007/44/EC, art 2(3).
Repealed as noted at the beginning of this Directive.

1 Council Directive 85/611/EEC of 20 December 1985 on the coordination of laws, regulations and administrative provisions relating to undertakings for collective investment in transferable securities (UCITS) (OJ L375, 31.12.1985, p 3). Directive as last amended by Directive 2005/1/EC of the European Parliament and of the Council (OJ L79, 24.3.2005, p 9).

2 Council Directive 92/49/EEC of 18 June 1992 on the coordination of laws, regulations and administrative provisions relating to direct insurance other than life assurance (third non-life insurance Directive) (OJ L228, 11.8.1992, p 1). Directive as last amended by Directive 2007/44/EC.

3 Directive 2006/48/EC of the European Parliament and of the Council of 14 June 2006 relating to the taking up and pursuit of the business of credit institutions (recast) (OJ L177, 30.6.2006, p 1). Directive as last amended by Directive 2007/44/EC.

[6574]
[Article 15b
Assessment

1. In assessing the notification provided for in Article 15(1) and the information referred to in Article 15a(2), the competent authorities shall, in order to ensure the sound and prudent management of the assurance undertaking in which an acquisition is proposed, and having regard to the likely influence of the proposed acquirer on the assurance undertaking, appraise the suitability of the proposed acquirer and the financial soundness of the proposed acquisition against all of the following criteria:

(a) the reputation of the proposed acquirer;

(b) the reputation and experience of any person who will direct the business of the assurance undertaking as a result of the proposed acquisition;

(c) the financial soundness of the proposed acquirer, in particular in relation to the type of business pursued and envisaged in the assurance undertaking in which the acquisition is proposed;

(d) whether the assurance undertaking will be able to comply and continue to comply with the prudential requirements based on this Directive and, where applicable, other Directives, notably, Directives 98/78/EC[1] and 2002/87/EC,[2] in particular, whether the group of which it will become a part has a structure that makes it possible to exercise effective supervision, effectively exchange information among the competent authorities and determine the allocation of responsibilities among the competent authorities;

(e) whether there are reasonable grounds to suspect that, in connection with the proposed acquisition, money laundering or terrorist financing within the meaning of Article 1 of Directive 2005/60/EC[3] is being or has been committed or attempted, or that the proposed acquisition could increase the risk thereof.

2. The competent authorities may oppose the proposed acquisition only if there are reasonable grounds for doing so on the basis of the criteria set out in paragraph 1 or if the information provided by the proposed acquirer is incomplete.

3. Member States shall neither impose any prior conditions in respect of the level of holding that must be acquired nor allow their competent authorities to examine the proposed acquisition in terms of the economic needs of the market.

4. Member States shall make publicly available a list specifying the information that is necessary to carry out the assessment and that must be provided to the competent authorities at the time of notification referred to in Article 15(1). The information required shall be proportionate and adapted to the nature of the proposed acquirer and proposed acquisition. Member States shall not require information that is not relevant for a prudential assessment.

5. Notwithstanding Article 15a(1), (2) and (3), where two or more proposals to acquire or increase qualifying holdings in the same assurance undertaking have been notified to the competent authority, the latter shall treat the proposed acquirers in a non-discriminatory manner.]

NOTES

Inserted as noted to art 15a at **[6573]**.

Repealed as noted at the beginning of this Directive.

1 Directive 98/78/EC of the European Parliament and of the Council of 27 October 1998 on the supplementary supervision of insurance and reinsurance undertakings in an insurance or reinsurance group (OJ L330, 5.12.1998, p 1). Directive as last amended by Directive 2005/68/EC.

2 Directive 2002/87/EC of the European Parliament and of the Council of 16 December 2002 on the supplementary supervision of credit institutions, insurance undertakings and investment firms in a financial conglomerate (OJ L35, 11.2.2003, p 1). Directive as amended by Directive 2005/1/EC.

3 Directive 2005/60/EC of the European Parliament and of the Council of 26 October 2005 on the prevention of the use of financial system for the purpose of money laundering and terrorist financing (OJ L309, 25.11.2005, p 15).

[6575]
[Article 15c
Acquisitions by regulated financial undertakings

1. The relevant competent authorities shall work in full consultation with each other when carrying out the assessment if the proposed acquirer is one of the following:

(a) a credit institution, assurance undertaking, insurance undertaking, reinsurance undertaking, investment firm or management company within the meaning of Article 1a, point 2 of Directive 85/611/EEC (hereinafter referred to as the UCITS management company) authorised in another Member State or in a sector other than that in which the acquisition is proposed;

(b) the parent undertaking of a credit institution, assurance undertaking, insurance undertaking, reinsurance undertaking, investment firm or UCITS management company authorised in another Member State or in a sector other than that in which the acquisition is proposed; or

(c) a natural or legal person controlling a credit institution, assurance undertaking, insurance undertaking, reinsurance undertaking, investment firm or UCITS management company authorised in another Member State or in a sector other than that in which the acquisition is proposed.

2. The competent authorities shall, without undue delay, provide each other with any information which is essential or relevant for the assessment. In this regard, the competent authorities shall communicate to each other upon request all relevant information and shall communicate on their own initiative all essential information. A decision by the competent authority that has authorised the assurance undertaking in which the acquisition is proposed shall indicate any views or reservations expressed by the competent authority responsible for the proposed acquirer.]

NOTES

Inserted as noted to art 15a at **[6573]**.

Repealed as noted at the beginning of this Directive.

[6576]
Article 16
Professional secrecy

1. Member States shall provide that all persons working or who have worked for the competent authorities, as well as auditors or experts acting on behalf of the competent authorities, shall be bound by the obligation of professional secrecy. This means that no confidential information which they may receive in the course of their duties may be divulged to any person or authority whatsoever, except in summary or aggregate form, such that individual assurance undertakings cannot be identified, without prejudice to cases covered by criminal law.

Nevertheless, where an assurance undertaking has been declared bankrupt or is being compulsorily wound up, confidential information which does not concern third parties involved in attempts to rescue that undertaking may be divulged in civil or commercial proceedings.

2. Paragraph 1 shall not prevent the competent authorities of the different Member States from exchanging information in accordance with the directives applicable to assurance undertakings. That information shall be subject to the conditions of professional secrecy indicated in paragraph 1.

3. Member States may conclude cooperation agreements providing for exchange of information with the competent authorities of third countries or with authorities or bodies of third countries as defined in paragraphs 5 and 6 only if the information disclosed is subject to guarantees of professional secrecy at least equivalent to those referred to in this Article. Such exchange of information must be intended for the performance of the supervisory task of the authorities or bodies mentioned.

Where the information originates in another Member State, it may not be disclosed without the express agreement of the competent authorities which have disclosed it and, where appropriate, solely for the purposes for which those authorities gave their agreement.

[4. Competent authorities receiving confidential information under paragraphs 1 or 2 may use it only in the course of their duties:

- *to check that the conditions governing the taking-up of the business of assurance are met and to facilitate monitoring of the conduct of such business, especially with regard to the monitoring of technical provisions, solvency margins, administrative and accounting procedures and internal control mechanisms, or*
- *to impose penalties, or*
- *in administrative appeals against decisions of the competent authority, or*
- *in court proceedings initiated pursuant to Article 67 or under special provisions provided for in this Directive and other Directives adopted in the field of assurance undertakings and reinsurance undertakings.*

5. Paragraphs 1 and 4 shall not preclude the exchange of information within a Member State, where there are two or more competent authorities in the same Member State, or, between Member States, between competent authorities and:

- *authorities responsible for the official supervision of credit institutions and other financial organisations and the authorities responsible for the supervision of financial markets,*
- *bodies involved in the liquidation and bankruptcy of assurance undertakings, reinsurance undertakings and in other similar procedures, and*
- *persons responsible for carrying out statutory audits of the accounts of assurance undertakings, reinsurance undertakings and other financial institutions,*

in the discharge of their supervisory functions, and the disclosure, to bodies which administer compulsory winding-up proceedings or guarantee funds, of information necessary to the performance of their duties. The information received by those authorities, bodies and persons shall be subject to the obligation of professional secrecy laid down in paragraph 1.

6. Notwithstanding paragraphs 1 to 4, Member States may authorise exchanges of information between the competent authorities and:

- *the authorities responsible for overseeing the bodies involved in the liquidation and bankruptcy of assurance undertakings, reinsurance undertakings and other similar procedures, or*
- *the authorities responsible for overseeing the persons charged with carrying out statutory audits of the accounts of insurance undertakings, reinsurance undertakings, credit institutions, investment firms and other financial institutions, or*
- *independent actuaries of insurance undertakings and reinsurance undertakings carrying out legal supervision of those undertakings and the bodies responsible for overseeing such actuaries.*

Member States which have recourse to the option provided for in the first subparagraph shall require at least that the following conditions are met:

- *this information shall be for the purpose of carrying out the overseeing or legal supervision referred to in the first subparagraph,*
- *information received in this context shall be subject to the conditions of professional secrecy imposed in paragraph 1,*
- *where the information originates in another Member State, it may not be disclosed without the express agreement of the competent authorities which have disclosed it and, where appropriate, solely for the purposes for which those authorities gave their agreement.*

Member States shall communicate to the Commission and to the other Member States the names of the authorities, persons and bodies which may receive information pursuant to this paragraph.]

7. Notwithstanding paragraphs 1 to 4, Member States may, with the aim of strengthening the stability, including integrity, of the financial system, authorise the exchange of information between the competent authorities and the authorities or bodies responsible under the law for the detection and investigation of breaches of company law.

Member States which have recourse to the option provided for in the first subparagraph shall require at least that the following conditions are met—

- *the information shall be for the purpose of performing the task referred to in the first subparagraph,*
- *information received in this context shall be subject to the conditions of professional secrecy imposed in paragraph 1,*
- *where the information originates in another Member State, it may not be disclosed without the express agreement of the competent authorities which have disclosed it and, where appropriate, solely for the purposes for which those authorities gave their agreement.*

Where, in a Member State, the authorities or bodies referred to in the first subparagraph perform their task of detection or investigation with the aid, in view of their specific competence, of persons appointed for that purpose and not employed in the public sector, the possibility of exchanging information provided for in the first subparagraph may be extended to such persons under the conditions stipulated in the second subparagraph.

In order to implement the third indent of the second subparagraph, the authorities or bodies referred to in the first subparagraph shall communicate to the competent authorities which have disclosed the information, the names and precise responsibilities of the persons to whom it is to be sent.

Member States shall communicate to the Commission and to the other Member States the names of the authorities or bodies which may receive information pursuant to this paragraph.

Before 31 December 2000, the Commission shall draw up a report on the application of this paragraph.

[8. Paragraphs 1 to 7 shall not prevent a competent authority from transmitting:

- *to central banks and other bodies with a similar function in their capacity as monetary authorities,*
- *where appropriate, to other public authorities responsible for overseeing payment systems,*

information intended for the performance of their task, nor shall it prevent such authorities or bodies from communicating to the competent authorities such information as they may need for the purposes of paragraphs 4. Information received in this context shall be subject to the conditions of professional secrecy imposed in this Article.]

9. In addition, notwithstanding paragraphs 1 and 4, Member States may, under provisions laid down by law, authorise the disclosure of certain information to other departments of their central government administrations responsible for legislation on the supervision of credit institutions, financial institutions, investment services and assurance undertakings and to inspectors acting on behalf of those departments.

However, such disclosures may be made only where necessary for reasons of prudential control.

However, Member States shall provide that information received under paragraphs 2 and 5 and that obtained by means of the on-the-spot verification referred to in Article 11 may never be disclosed in the cases referred to in this paragraph except with the express consent of the competent authorities which disclosed the information or of the competent authorities of the Member State in which on-the-spot verification was carried out.

NOTES

Repealed as noted at the beginning of this Directive.

Paras 4–6, 8: substituted by European Parliament and Council Directive 2005/68/EC, art 60(5).

[6577]
Article 17
Duties of auditors

1. Member States shall provide at least that—

(a) any person authorised within the meaning of Council Directive 84/253/EEC,[1] performing in an assurance undertaking the task described in Article 51 of Council Directive 78/660/EEC,[2] Article 37 of Directive 83/349/EEC or Article 31 of Council Directive 85/611/EEC[3] or any other statutory task, shall have a duty to report promptly to the competent authorities any fact or decision concerning that undertaking of which he/she has become aware while carrying out that task which is liable to—

- *constitute a material breach of the laws, regulations or administrative provisions which lay down the conditions governing authorisation or which specifically govern pursuit of the activities of assurance undertakings, or*
- *affect the continuous functioning of the assurance undertaking or*
- *lead to refusal to certify the accounts or to the expression of reservations;*

(b) that person shall likewise have a duty to report any facts and decisions of which he/she becomes aware in the course of carrying out a task as described in (a) in an undertaking having close links resulting from a control relationship with the assurance undertaking within which he/she is carrying out the abovementioned task.

2. The disclosure in good faith to the competent authorities, by persons authorised within the meaning of Directive 84/253/EEC, of any fact or decision referred to in paragraph 1 shall not constitute a breach of any restriction on disclosure of information imposed by contract or by any legislative, regulatory or administrative provision and shall not involve such persons in liability of any kind.

NOTES

Repealed as noted at the beginning of this Directive.

[1] OJ L126, 12.5.1984, p 20.

[2] OJ L222, 14.8.1978, p 11. Directive as last amended by Directive 2001/65/EC of the European Parliament and of the Council (OJ L283, 27.10.2001, p 28).

[3] OJ L375, 31.12.1985, p 3. Directive as last amended by Directive 2001/108/EC of the European Parliament and of the Council (OJ L41, 13.2.2002, p 35).

[6578]
Article 18
Pursuit of life assurance and non-life insurance activities

1. Without prejudice to paragraphs 3 and 7, no undertaking may be authorised both pursuant to this Directive and pursuant to Directive 73/239/EEC.

2. By way of derogation from paragraph 1, Member States may provide that—

— undertakings authorised pursuant to this Directive may also obtain authorisation, in accordance with Article 6 of Directive 73/239/EEC for the risks listed in classes 1 and 2 in the Annex to that Directive,

— undertakings authorised pursuant to Article 6 of Directive 73/239/EEC solely for the risks listed in classes 1 and 2 in the Annex to that Directive may obtain authorisation pursuant to this Directive.

3. Subject to paragraph 6, undertakings referred to in paragraph 2 and those which on—

— 1 January 1981 for undertakings authorised in Greece,

— 1 January 1986 for undertakings authorised in Spain and Portugal,

[— 1 January 1995 for undertakings authorised in Austria, Finland and Sweden,]

[— 1 May 2004 for undertakings authorised in the Czech Republic, Estonia, Cyprus, Latvia, Lithuania, Hungary, Malta, Poland, Slovenia and Slovakia,]

[— 1 January 2007 for undertakings authorised in Bulgaria and Romania, and]

— 15 March 1979 for all other undertakings,

carried on simultaneously both the activities covered by this Directive and those covered by Directive 73/239/EEC may continue to carry on those activities simultaneously, provided that each activity is separately managed in accordance with Article 19 of this Directive.

4. Member States may provide that the undertakings referred to in paragraph 2 shall comply with the accounting rules governing assurance undertakings authorised pursuant to this Directive for all of their activities. Pending coordination in this respect, Member States may also provide that, with regard to rules on winding-up, activities relating to the risks listed in classes 1 and 2 in the Annex to Directive 73/239/EEC carried on by the undertakings referred to in paragraph 2 shall be governed by the rules applicable to life assurance activities.

5. Where an undertaking carrying on the activities referred to in the Annex to Directive 73/239/EEC has financial, commercial or administrative links with an assurance undertaking carrying on the activities covered by this Directive, the competent authorities of the Member States within whose territories the head offices of those undertakings are situated shall ensure that the accounts of the undertakings in question are not distorted by agreements between these undertakings or by any arrangement which could affect the apportionment of expenses and income.

6. Any Member State may require assurance undertakings whose head offices are situated in its territory to cease, within a period to be determined by the Member State concerned, the simultaneous pursuit of activities in which they were engaged on the dates referred to in paragraph 3.

7. The provisions of this Article shall be reviewed on the basis of a report from the Commission to the Council in the light of future harmonisation of the rules on winding-up, and in any case before 31 December 1999.

NOTES

Repealed as noted at the beginning of this Directive.

Para 3: third indent substituted by Council Directive 2004/66/EC, Annex, Pt II, para (b); fourth indent (originally inserted by Council Directive 2004/66/EC, Annex, Pt II, para (c)) substituted and fifth indent inserted by Council Directive 2006/101/EC, art 1, Annex, para 3(b), (c).

[6579]
Article 19
Separation of life assurance and non-life insurance management

1. The separate management referred to in Article 18(3) must be organised in such a way that the activities covered by this Directive are distinct from the activities covered by Directive 73/239/EEC in order that—

- *the respective interests of life policy holders and non-life policy holders are not prejudiced and, in particular, that profits from life assurance benefit life policy holders as if the assurance undertaking only carried on the activity of life assurance,*
- *the minimum financial obligations, in particular solvency margins, in respect of one or other of the two activities, namely an activity under this Directive and an activity under Directive 73/239/EEC, are not borne by the other activity.*

However, as long as the minimum financial obligations are fulfilled under the conditions laid down in the second indent of the first subparagraph and, provided the competent authority is informed, the undertaking may use those explicit items of the solvency margin which are still available for one or other activity.

The competent authorities shall analyse the results in both activities so as to ensure that the provisions of this paragraph are complied with.

2.

(a) Accounts shall be drawn up in such a manner as to show the sources of the results for each of the two activities, life assurance and non-life insurance. To this end all income (in particular premiums, payments by re-insurers and investment income) and expenditure (in particular insurance settlements, additions to technical provisions, reinsurance premiums, operating expenses in respect of insurance business) shall be broken down according to origin. Items common to both activities shall be entered in accordance with methods of apportionment to be accepted by the competent authority.

(b) Assurance undertakings must, on the basis of the accounts, prepare a statement clearly identifying the items making up each solvency margin, in accordance with Article 27 of this Directive and Article 16(1) of Directive 73/239/EEC.

3. If one of the solvency margins is insufficient, the competent authorities shall apply to the deficient activity the measures provided for in the relevant Directive, whatever the results in the other activity. By way of derogation from the second indent of the first subparagraph of paragraph 1, these measures may involve the authorisation of a transfer from one activity to the other.

NOTES

Repealed as noted at the beginning of this Directive.

CHAPTER 2
RULES RELATING TO TECHNICAL PROVISIONS AND THEIR REPRESENTATION

[6580]
Article 20
Establishment of technical provisions

1. The home Member State shall require every assurance undertaking to establish sufficient technical provisions, including mathematical provisions, in respect of its entire business.

The amount of such technical provisions shall be determined according to the following principles.

A.

(i) the amount of the technical life-assurance provisions shall be calculated by a sufficiently prudent prospective actuarial valuation, taking account of all future liabilities as determined by the policy conditions for each existing contract, including—

- *all guaranteed benefits, including guaranteed surrender values,*

— *bonuses to which policy holders are already either collectively or individually entitled, however those bonuses are described – vested, declared or allotted,*
— *all options available to the policy holder under the terms of the contract,*
— *expenses, including commissions,*

taking credit for future premiums due;

(ii) *the use of a retrospective method is allowed, if it can be shown that the resulting technical provisions are not lower than would be required under a sufficiently prudent prospective calculation or if a prospective method cannot be used for the type of contract involved;*

(iii) *a prudent valuation is not a "best estimate" valuation, but shall include an appropriate margin for adverse deviation of the relevant factors;*

(iv) *the method of valuation for the technical provisions must not only be prudent in itself, but must also be so having regard to the method of valuation for the assets covering those provisions;*

(v) *technical provisions shall be calculated separately for each contract. The use of appropriate approximations or generalisations is allowed, however, where they are likely to give approximately the same result as individual calculations. The principle of separate calculation shall in no way prevent the establishment of additional provisions for general risks which are not individualised;*

(vi) *where the surrender value of a contract is guaranteed, the amount of the mathematical provisions for the contract at any time shall be at least as great as the value guaranteed at that time;*

B. *the rate of interest used shall be chosen prudently. It shall be determined in accordance with the rules of the competent authority in the home Member State, applying the following principles—*

(a) *for all contracts, the competent authority of the assurance undertaking's home Member State shall fix one or more maximum rates of interest, in particular in accordance with the following rules—*

(i) *when contracts contain an interest rate guarantee, the competent authority in the home Member State shall set a single maximum rate of interest. It may differ according to the currency in which the contract is denominated, provided that it is not more than 60% of the rate on bond issues by the State in whose currency the contract is denominated. If a Member State decides, pursuant to the second sentence of the first subparagraph, to set a maximum rate of interest for contracts denominated in another Member State's currency, it shall first consult the competent authority of the Member State in whose currency the contract is denominated;*

(ii) *however, when the assets of the assurance undertaking are not valued at their purchase price, a Member State may stipulate that one or more maximum rates may be calculated taking into account the yield on the corresponding assets currently held, minus a prudential margin and, in particular for contracts with periodic premiums, furthermore taking into account the anticipated yield on future assets. The prudential margin and the maximum rate or rates of interest applied to the anticipated yield on future assets shall be fixed by the competent authority of the home Member State;*

(b) *the establishment of a maximum rate of interest shall not imply that the assurance undertaking is bound to use a rate as high as that;*

(c) *the home Member State may decide not to apply paragraph (a) to the following categories of contracts—*

— *unit-linked contracts,*
— *single-premium contracts for a period of up to eight years,*
— *without-profits contracts, and annuity contracts with no surrender value.*

In the cases referred to in the second and third indents of the first subparagraph, in choosing a prudent rate of interest, account may be taken of the currency in which the contract is denominated and corresponding assets currently held and where the undertaking's assets are valued at their current value, the anticipated yield on future assets.

Part VI European Materials

Under no circumstances may the rate of interest used be higher than the yield on assets as calculated in accordance with the accounting rules in the home Member State, less an appropriate deduction;

(d) the Member State shall require an assurance undertaking to set aside in its accounts a provision to meet interest-rate commitments vis-à-vis policy holders if the present or foreseeable yield on the undertaking's assets is insufficient to cover those commitments;

(e) the Commission and the competent authorities of the Member States which so request shall be notified of the maximum rates of interest set under (a);

C. the statistical elements of the valuation and the allowance for expenses used shall be chosen prudently, having regard to the State of the commitment, the type of policy and the administrative costs and commissions expected to be incurred;

D. in the case of participating contracts, the method of calculation for technical provisions may take into account, either implicitly or explicitly, future bonuses of all kinds, in a manner consistent with the other assumptions on future experience and with the current method of distribution of bonuses;

E. allowance for future expenses may be made implicitly, for instance by the use of future premiums net of management charges. However, the overall allowance, implicit or explicit, shall be not less than a prudent estimate of the relevant future expenses;

F. the method of calculation of technical provisions shall not be subject to discontinuities from year to year arising from arbitrary changes to the method or the bases of calculation and shall be such as to recognise the distribution of profits in an appropriate way over the duration of each policy.

2. Assurance undertakings shall make available to the public the bases and methods used in the calculation of the technical provisions, including provisions for bonuses.

3. The home Member State shall require every assurance undertaking to cover the technical provisions in respect of its entire business by matching assets, in accordance with Article 26. In respect of business written in the Community, these assets must be localised within the Community. Member States shall not require assurance undertakings to localise their assets in a particular Member State. The home Member State may, however, permit relaxations in the rules on the localisation of assets.

[4. Member States shall not retain or introduce for the establishment of technical provisions a system of gross reserving which requires pledging of assets to cover unearned premiums and outstanding claims provisions by the reinsurer, authorised in accordance with Directive 2005/68/EC when the reinsurer is a reinsurance undertaking or an insurance undertaking authorised in accordance with Directive 73/239/EEC or this Directive.

When the home Member State allows any technical provisions to be covered by claims against a reinsurer which is neither a reinsurance undertaking authorised in accordance with Directive 2005/68/EC nor an insurance undertaking authorised in accordance with Directive 73/239/EEC or this Directive, it shall set the conditions for accepting such claims.]

NOTES

Repealed as noted at the beginning of this Directive.

Para 4: substituted by European Parliament and Council Directive 2005/68/EC, art 60(6).

[6581]

Article 21

Premiums for new business

Premiums for new business shall be sufficient, on reasonable actuarial assumptions, to enable assurance undertakings to meet all their commitments and, in particular, to establish adequate technical provisions.

For this purpose, all aspects of the financial situation of an assurance undertaking may be taken into account, without the input from resources other than premiums and income earned thereon being systematic and permanent in such a way that it may jeopardise the undertaking's solvency in the long term.

NOTES

Repealed as noted at the beginning of this Directive.

[6582]
Article 22
Assets covering technical provisions

The assets covering the technical provisions shall take account of the type of business carried on by an assurance undertaking in such a way as to secure the safety, yield and marketability of its investments, which the undertaking shall ensure are diversified and adequately spread.

NOTES

Repealed as noted at the beginning of this Directive.

[6583]
Article 23
Categories of authorised assets

1. The home Member State may not authorise assurance undertakings to cover their technical provisions with any but the following categories of assets—

A. investments

(a) debt securities, bonds and other money – and capital-market instruments;

(b) loans;

(c) shares and other variable-yield participations;

(d) units in undertakings for collective investment in transferable securities (UCITS) and other investment funds;

(e) land, buildings and immovable-property rights;

B. debts and claims

[(f) debts owed by reinsurers, including reinsurers' shares of technical provisions, and by special purpose vehicles referred to in Article 46 of Directive 2005/68/EC;]

(g) deposits with and debts owed by ceding undertakings;

(h) debts owed by policy holders and intermediaries arising out of direct and reassurance operations;

(i) advances against policies;

(j) tax recoveries;

(k) claims against guarantee funds;

C. others

(l) tangible fixed assets, other than land and buildings, valued on the basis of prudent amortisation;

(m) cash at bank and in hand, deposits with credit institutions and any other body authorised to receive deposits;

(n) deferred acquisition costs;

(o) accrued interest and rent, other accrued income and prepayments;

(p) reversionary interests.

2. In the case of the association of underwriters known as "Lloyd's", asset categories shall also include guarantees and letters of credit issued by credit institutions within the meaning of Directive 2000/12/EC of the European Parliament and of the Council[1] or by assurance undertakings, together with verifiable sums arising out of life assurance policies, to the extent that they represent funds belonging to members.

[3. The inclusion of any asset or category of assets listed in paragraph 1 shall not mean that all these assets should automatically be accepted as cover for technical provisions. The home Member State shall lay down more detailed rules setting the conditions for the use of acceptable assets.]

In determining and applying the rules which it lays down, the home Member State shall, in particular, ensure that the following principles are complied with—

(i) assets covering technical provisions shall be valued net of any debts arising out of their acquisition;

(ii) all assets must be valued on a prudent basis, allowing for the risk of any amounts not being realisable. In particular, tangible fixed assets other than land and buildings may be accepted as cover for technical provisions only if they are valued on the basis of prudent amortisation;

(iii) loans, whether to undertakings, to a State or international organisation, to local or regional authorities or to natural persons, may be accepted as cover for technical provisions only if there are sufficient guarantees as to their security, whether these are based on the status of the borrower, mortgages, bank guarantees or guarantees granted by assurance undertakings or other forms of security;

(iv) *derivative instruments such as options, futures and swaps in connection with assets covering technical provisions may be used in so far as they contribute to a reduction of investment risks or facilitate efficient portfolio management. They must be valued on a prudent basis and may be taken into account in the valuation of the underlying assets;*

(v) *transferable securities which are not dealt in on a regulated market may be accepted as cover for technical provisions only if they can be realised in the short term or if they are holdings in credit institutions, in assurance undertakings, within the limits permitted by Article 6, or in investment undertakings established in a Member State;*

(vi) *debts owed by and claims against a third party may be accepted as cover for the technical provisions only after deduction of all amounts owed to the same third party;*

(vii) *the value of any debts and claims accepted as cover for technical provisions must be calculated on a prudent basis, with due allowance for the risk of any amounts not being realisable. In particular, debts owed by policy holders and intermediaries arising out of assurance and reassurance operations may be accepted only in so far as they have been outstanding for not more than three months;*

(viii) *where the assets held include an investment in a subsidiary undertaking which manages all or part of the assurance undertaking's investments on its behalf, the home Member State must, when applying the rules and principles laid down in this Article, take into account the underlying assets held by the subsidiary undertaking; the home Member State may treat the assets of other subsidiaries in the same way;*

(ix) *deferred acquisition costs may be accepted as cover for technical provisions only to the extent that this is consistent with the calculation of the mathematical provisions.*

4. Notwithstanding paragraphs 1, 2 and 3, in exceptional circumstances and at an assurance undertaking's request, the home Member State may, temporarily and under a properly reasoned decision, accept other categories of assets as cover for technical provisions, subject to Article 22.

NOTES

Repealed as noted at the beginning of this Directive.

Para 1: words in square brackets in sub-para (B) substituted by European Parliament and Council Directive 2005/68/EC, art 60(7)(a).

Para 3: words in square brackets substituted by European Parliament and Council Directive 2005/68/EC, art 60(7)(b).

[1] OJ L126, 26.5.2000, p 1. Directive as amended by Directive 2000/28/EC (OJ L275, 27.10.2000, p 37).

[6584]

Article 24

Rules for investment diversification

1. As regards the assets covering technical provisions, the home Member State shall require every assurance undertaking to invest no more than—

(a) *10% of its total gross technical provisions in any one piece of land or building, or a number of pieces of land or buildings close enough to each other to be considered effectively as one investment;*

(b) *5% of its total gross technical provisions in shares and other negotiable securities treated as shares, bonds, debt securities and other money – and capital-market instruments from the same undertaking, or in loans granted to the same borrower, taken together, the loans being loans other than those granted to a State, regional or local authority or to an international organisation of which one or more Member States are members. This limit may be raised to 10% if an undertaking invests not more than 40% of its gross technical provisions in the loans or securities of issuing bodies and borrowers in each of which it invests more than 5% of its assets;*

(c) *5% of its total gross technical provisions in unsecured loans, including 1% for any single unsecured loan, other than loans granted to credit institutions, assurance undertakings – in so far as Article 6 allows it – and investment undertakings established in a Member State. The limits may be raised to 8% and 2% respectively by a decision taken on a case-by-case basis by the competent authority of the home Member State;*

(d) *3% of its total gross technical provisions in the form of cash in hand;*

(e) *10% of its total gross technical provisions in shares, other securities treated as shares and debt securities which are not dealt in on a regulated market.*

2. The absence of a limit in paragraph 1 on investment in any particular category does not imply that assets in that category should be accepted as cover for technical provisions without limit. The home Member State shall lay down more detailed rules fixing the conditions for the use of acceptable assets. In particular it shall ensure, in the determination and the application of those rules, that the following principles are complied with—

(i) *assets covering technical provisions must be diversified and spread in such a way as to ensure that there is no excessive reliance on any particular category of asset, investment market or investment;*

(ii) *investment in particular types of asset which show high levels of risk, whether because of the nature of the asset or the quality of the issuer, must be restricted to prudent levels;*

(iii) *limitations on particular categories of asset must take account of the treatment of reassurance in the calculation of technical provisions;*

(iv) *where the assets held include an investment in a subsidiary undertaking which manages all or part of the assurance undertaking's investments on its behalf, the home Member State must, when applying the rules and principles laid down in this Article, take into account the underlying assets held by the subsidiary undertaking; the home Member State may treat the assets of other subsidiaries in the same way;*

(v) *the percentage of assets covering technical provisions which are the subject of non-liquid investments must be kept to a prudent level;*

(vi) *where the assets held include loans to or debt securities issued by certain credit institutions, the home Member State may, when applying the rules and principles contained in this Article, take into account the underlying assets held by such credit institutions. This treatment may be applied only where the credit institution has its head office in a Member State, is entirely owned by that Member State and/or that State's local authorities and its business, according to its memorandum and articles of association, consists of extending, through its intermediaries, loans to, or guaranteed by, States or local authorities or of loans to bodies closely linked to the State or to local authorities.*

3. In the context of the detailed rules laying down the conditions for the use of acceptable assets, the Member State shall give more limitative treatment to—

— *any loan unaccompanied by a bank guarantee, a guarantee issued by an assurance undertaking, a mortgage or any other form of security, as compared with loans accompanied by such collateral,*

— *UCITS not coordinated within the meaning of Directive 85/611/EEC and other investment funds, as compared with UCITS coordinated within the meaning of that Directive,*

— *securities which are not dealt in on a regulated market, as compared with those which are,*

— *bonds, debt securities and other money – and capital-market instruments not issued by States, local or regional authorities or undertakings belonging to zone A as defined in Directive 2000/12/EC or the issuers of which are international organisations not numbering at least one Community Member State among their members, as compared with the same financial instruments issued by such bodies.*

4. Member States may raise the limit laid down in paragraph 1(b) to 40% in the case of certain debt securities when these are issued by a credit institution which has its head office in a Member State and is subject by law to special official supervision designed to protect the holders of those debt securities. In particular, sums deriving from the issue of such debt securities must be invested in accordance with the law in assets which, during the whole period of validity of the debt securities, are capable of covering claims attaching to debt securities and which, in the event of failure of the issuer, would be used on a priority basis for the reimbursement of the principal and payment of the accrued interest.

5. Member States shall not require assurance undertakings to invest in particular categories of assets.

6. Notwithstanding paragraph 1, in exceptional circumstances and at the assurance undertaking's request, the home Member State may, temporarily and under a properly reasoned decision, allow exceptions to the rules laid down in paragraph 1(a) to (e), subject to Article 22.

NOTES

Repealed as noted at the beginning of this Directive.

[6585]

Article 25

Contracts linked to UCITS or share index

1. Where the benefits provided by a contract are directly linked to the value of units in an UCITS or to the value of assets contained in an internal fund held by the insurance undertaking, usually divided into units, the technical provisions in respect of those benefits must be represented as closely as possible by those units or, in the case where units are not established, by those assets.

2. Where the benefits provided by a contract are directly linked to a share index or some other reference value other than those referred to in paragraph 1, the technical provisions in respect of those benefits must be represented as closely as possible either by the units deemed to represent the reference value or, in the case where units are not established, by assets of appropriate security and marketability which correspond as closely as possible with those on which the particular reference value is based.

3. Articles 22 and 24 shall not apply to assets held to match liabilities which are directly linked to the benefits referred to in paragraphs 1 and 2. References to the technical provisions in Article 24 shall be to the technical provisions excluding those in respect of such liabilities.

4. Where the benefits referred to in paragraphs 1 and 2 include a guarantee of investment performance or some other guaranteed benefit, the corresponding additional technical provisions shall be subject to Articles 22, 23, and 24.

NOTES

Repealed as noted at the beginning of this Directive.

[6586]
Article 26
Matching rules

1. For the purposes of Articles 20(3) and 54, Member States shall comply with Annex II as regards the matching rules.

2. This Article shall not apply to the commitments referred to in Article 25.

NOTES

Repealed as noted at the beginning of this Directive.

CHAPTER 3
RULES RELATING TO THE SOLVENCY MARGIN AND TO THE GUARANTEE FUND

[6587]
Article 27
Available solvency margin

1. Each Member State shall require of every assurance undertaking whose head office is situated in its territory an adequate available solvency margin in respect of its entire business at all times which is at least equal to the requirements in this Directive.

2. The available solvency margin shall consist of the assets of the assurance undertaking free of any foreseeable liabilities, less any intangible items, including—

- *(a) the paid-up share capital or, in the case of a mutual assurance undertaking, the effective initial fund plus any members' accounts which meet all the following criteria—*
  - *(i) the memorandum and articles of association must stipulate that payments may be made from these accounts to members only in so far as this does not cause the available solvency margin to fall below the required level, or, after the dissolution of the undertaking, if all the undertaking's other debts have been settled;*
  - *(ii) the memorandum and articles of association must stipulate, with respect to any payments referred to in point (i) for reasons other than the individual termination of membership, that the competent authorities must be notified at least one month in advance and can prohibit the payment within that period;*
  - *(iii) the relevant provisions of the memorandum and articles of association may be amended only after the competent authorities have declared that they have no objection to the amendment, without prejudice to the criteria stated in points (i) and (ii);*
- *(b) reserves (statutory and free) not corresponding to underwriting liabilities;*
- *(c) the profit or loss brought forward after deduction of dividends to be paid;*
- *(d) in so far as authorised under national law, profit reserves appearing in the balance sheet where they may be used to cover any losses which may arise and where they have not been made available for distribution to policy holders.*

The available solvency margin shall be reduced by the amount of own shares directly held by the assurance undertaking.

[The available solvency margin shall also be reduced by the following items:

- *(a) participations which the assurance undertaking holds, in:*
  - *— insurance undertakings within the meaning of Article 4 of this Directive, Article 6 of Directive 73/239/EEC, or Article 1(b) of Directive 98/78/EC of the European*

Parliament and of the Council of 27 October 1998 on the supplementary supervision of insurance undertakings in an insurance group,[1]

- *reinsurance undertakings within the meaning of Article 3 of Directive 2005/68/EC or a non-member country reinsurance undertakings within the meaning of Article 1(l) of Directive 98/78/EC,*
- *insurance holding companies within the meaning of Article 1(i) of Directive 98/78/EC,*
- *credit institutions and financial institutions within the meaning of Article 1(1) and (5) of Directive 2000/12/EC of the European Parliament and of the Council of 20 March 2000 relating to the taking up and pursuit of the business of credit institutions,*[2]
- *investment firms and financial institutions within the meaning of Article 1(2) of Council Directive 93/22/EEC of 10 May 1993 on investment services in the securities field*[3] *and of Articles 2(4) and 2(7) of Council Directive 93/6/EEC of 15 March 1993 on the capital adequacy of investments firms and credit institutions;*[4]

(b) *each of the following items which the assurance undertaking holds in respect of the entities defined in point (a) in which it holds a participation:*

- *instruments referred to in paragraph 3,*
- *instruments referred to in Article 16(3) of Directive 73/239/EEC,*
- *subordinated claims and instruments referred to in Article 35 and Article 36(3) of Directive 2000/12/EC.*

Where shares in another credit institution, investment firm, financial institution, insurance or reinsurance undertaking or insurance holding company are held temporarily for the purposes of a financial assistance operation designed to reorganise and save that entity, the competent authority may waive the provisions on deduction referred to in points (a) and (b) of the third subparagraph.

As an alternative to the deduction of the items referred to in (a) and (b) of the third subparagraph which the insurance undertaking holds in credit institutions, investment firms and financial institutions, Member States may allow their insurance undertakings to apply mutatis mutandis methods 1, 2, or 3 of Annex I to Directive 2002/87/EC of the European Parliament and of the Council of 16 December 2002 on the supplementary supervision of credit institutions, insurance undertakings and investment firms in a financial conglomerate.[5] *Method 1 (Accounting consolidation) shall only be applied if the competent authority is confident about the level of integrated management and internal control regarding the entities which would be included in the scope of consolidation. The method chosen shall be applied in a consistent manner over time.*

Member States may provide that, for the calculation of the solvency margin as provided for by this Directive, insurance undertakings subject to supplementary supervision in accordance with Directive 98/78/EC or to supplementary supervision in accordance with Directive 2002/87/EC, need not deduct the items referred to in (a) and (b) of the third subparagraph of this Article which are held in credit institutions, investment firms, financial institutions, insurance or reinsurance undertakings or insurance holding companies which are included in the supplementary supervision. For the purposes of the deduction of participations referred to in this paragraph, participation shall mean a participation within the meaning of Article 1(f) of Directive 98/78/EC.]

3. *The available solvency margin may also consist of—*

(a) *cumulative preferential share capital and subordinated loan capital up to 50% of the lesser of the available solvency margin and the required solvency margin, no more than 25% of which shall consist of subordinated loans with a fixed maturity, or fixed-term cumulative preferential share capital, provided that binding agreements exist under which, in the event of the bankruptcy or liquidation of the assurance undertaking, the subordinated loan capital or preferential share capital ranks after the claims of all other creditors and is not to be repaid until all other debts outstanding at the time have been settled.*

Subordinated loan capital must also fulfil the following conditions—

(i) *only fully paid-up funds may be taken into account;*

(ii) *for loans with a fixed maturity, the original maturity must be at least five years. No later than one year before the repayment date, the assurance undertaking must submit to the competent authorities for their approval a plan showing how the available solvency margin will be kept at or brought to the required level at maturity, unless the extent to which the loan may rank as a component of the available solvency margin is gradually reduced during at least the last five years before the repayment date. The competent authorities may authorise the early repayment of such loans provided application is made by the issuing assurance undertaking and its available solvency margin will not fall below the required level;*

(iii) *loans the maturity of which is not fixed must be repayable only subject to five years' notice unless the loans are no longer considered as a component of the available solvency margin or unless the prior consent of the competent authorities is specifically required for early repayment. In the latter event the assurance undertaking must notify the competent authorities at least six months before the date of the proposed repayment, specifying the available solvency margin and the required solvency margin both before and after that repayment. The competent authorities shall authorise repayment only if the assurance undertaking's available solvency margin will not fall below the required level;*

(iv) *the loan agreement must not include any clause providing that in specified circumstances, other than the winding-up of the assurance undertaking, the debt will become repayable before the agreed repayment dates;*

(v) *the loan agreement may be amended only after the competent authorities have declared that they have no objection to the amendment;*

(b) *securities with no specified maturity date and other instruments, including cumulative preferential shares other than those mentioned in point (a), up to 50% of the lesser of the available solvency margin and the required solvency margin for the total of such securities and the subordinated loan capital referred to in point (a) provided they fulfil the following—*

(i) *they may not be repaid on the initiative of the bearer or without the prior consent of the competent authority;*

(ii) *the contract of issue must enable the assurance undertaking to defer the payment of interest on the loan;*

(iii) *the lender's claims on the assurance undertaking must rank entirely after those of all non-subordinated creditors;*

(iv) *the documents governing the issue of the securities must provide for the loss-absorption capacity of the debt and unpaid interest, while enabling the assurance undertaking to continue its business;*

(v) *only fully paid-up amounts may be taken into account.*

4. *Upon application, with supporting evidence, by the undertaking to the competent authority of the home Member State and with the agreement of that competent authority, the available solvency margin may also consist of—*

(a) *until 31 December 2009 an amount equal to 50% of the undertaking's future profits, but not exceeding 25% of the lesser of the available solvency margin and the required solvency margin. The amount of the future profits shall be obtained by multiplying the estimated annual profit by a factor which represents the average period left to run on policies. The factor used may not exceed six. The estimated annual profit shall not exceed the arithmetical average of the profits made over the last five financial years in the activities listed in Article 2(1).*

Competent authorities may only agree to include such an amount for the available solvency margin—

(i) *when an actuarial report is submitted to the competent authorities substantiating the likelihood of emergence of these profits in the future; and*

(ii) *in so far as that part of future profits emerging from hidden net reserves referred to in point (c) has not already been taken into account;*

(b) *where Zillmerising is not practised or where, if practised, it is less than the loading for acquisition costs included in the premium, the difference between a non-Zillmerised or partially Zillmerised mathematical provision and a mathematical provision Zillmerised at a rate equal to the loading for acquisition costs included in the premium. This figure may not, however, exceed 3,5% of the sum of the differences between the relevant capital sums of life assurance activities and the mathematical provisions for all policies for which Zillmerising is possible. The difference shall be reduced by the amount of any undepreciated acquisition costs entered as an asset;*

(c) *any hidden net reserves arising out of the valuation of assets, in so far as such hidden net reserves are not of an exceptional nature;*

(d) *one half of the unpaid share capital or initial fund, once the paid-up part amounts to 25% of that share capital or fund, up to 50% of the lesser of the available and required solvency margin.*

5. Amendments to paragraphs 2, 3 and 4 to take into account developments that justify a technical adjustment of the elements eligible for the available solvency margin shall be adopted in accordance with the procedure laid down in Article 65(2).

NOTES

Repealed as noted at the beginning of this Directive.

Para 2: words in square brackets inserted by European Parliament and Council Directive 2005/68/EC, art 60(8).

[1] OJ L330, 5.12.1998, p 1. Directive as last amended by Directive 2005/1/EC (OJ L79, 24.3.2005, p 9).

[2] OJ L126, 26.5.2000, p 1. Directive as last amended by Directive 2005/1/EC.

[3] OJ L141, 11.6.1993, p 27. Directive as last amended by Directive 2002/87/EC (OJ L35, 11.2.2003, p 1).

[4] OJ L141, 11.6.1993, p 1. Directive as last amended by Directive 2005/1/EC.

[5] OJ L35, 11.2.2003, p 1. Directive as last amended by Directive 2005/1/EC.

[6588]
Article 28
Required solvency margin

1. Subject to Article 29, the required solvency margin shall be determined as laid down in paragraphs 2 to 7 according to the classes of assurance underwritten.

2. For the kinds of assurance referred to in Article 2(1)(a) and (b) other than assurances linked to investment funds and for the operations referred to in Article 2(3), the required solvency margin shall be equal to the sum of the following two results—

[(a) first result:
a 4% fraction of the mathematical provisions relating to direct business and reinsurance acceptances gross of reinsurance cessions shall be multiplied by the ratio, for the last financial year, of the mathematical provisions net of reinsurance cessions to the gross total mathematical provisions. That ratio may in no case be less than 85%. Upon application, with supporting evidence, by the insurance undertaking to the competent authority of the home Member State and with agreement of that authority, amounts recoverable from the special purpose vehicles referred to in Article 46 of Directive 2005/68/EC may be deducted as reassurance.]

[(b) second result:
for policies on which the capital at risk is not a negative figure, a 0,3% fraction of such capital underwritten by the assurance undertaking shall be multiplied by the ratio, for the last financial year, of the total capital at risk retained as the undertaking's liability after reinsurance cessions and retrocessions to the total capital at risk gross of reinsurance; that ratio may in no case be less than 50%. Upon application, with supporting evidence, by the insurance undertaking to the competent authority of the home Member State and with the agreement of that authority, amounts recoverable from the special purpose vehicles referred to in Article 46 of Directive 2005/68/EC may be deducted as reassurance.]

For temporary assurance on death of a maximum term of three years the fraction shall be 0,1%. For such assurance of a term of more than three years but not more than five years the above fraction shall be 0,15%.

3. For the supplementary insurance referred to in Article 2(1)(c) the required solvency margin shall be equal to the required solvency margin for insurance undertakings as laid down in Article 16a of Directive 73/239/EEC, excluding the provisions of Article 17 of that Directive.

4. For permanent health insurance not subject to cancellation referred to in Article 2(1)(d), the required solvency margin shall be equal to—

(a) a 4% fraction of the mathematical provisions, calculated in compliance with paragraph 2(a) of this Article; plus

(b) the required solvency margin for insurance undertakings as laid down in Article 16a of Directive 73/239/EEC, excluding the provisions of Article 17 of that Directive. However, the condition contained in Article 16a(6)(b) of that Directive that a provision be set up for increasing age may be replaced by a requirement that the business be conducted on a group basis.

5. For capital redemption operations referred to in Article 2(2)(b), the required solvency margin shall be equal to a 4% fraction of the mathematical provisions calculated in compliance with paragraph 2(a) of this Article.

6. For tontines, referred to in Article 2(2)(a), the required solvency margin shall be equal to 1% of their assets.

7. For assurances covered by Article 2(1)(a) and (b) linked to investment funds and for the operations referred to in Article 2(2)(c), (d) and (e), the required solvency margin shall be equal to the sum of the following—

(a) in so far as the assurance undertaking bears an investment risk, a 4% fraction of the technical provisions, calculated in compliance with paragraph 2(a) of this Article;

(b) in so far as the undertaking bears no investment risk but the allocation to cover management expenses is fixed for a period exceeding five years, a 1% fraction of the technical provisions, calculated in compliance with paragraph 2(a) of this Article;

(c) in so far as the undertaking bears no investment risk and the allocation to cover management expenses is not fixed for a period exceeding five years, an amount equivalent to 25% of the last financial year's net administrative expenses pertaining to such business;

(d) in so far as the assurance undertaking covers a death risk, a 0,3% fraction of the capital at risk calculated in compliance with paragraph 2(b) of this Article.

NOTES

Repealed as noted at the beginning of this Directive.

Para 2: words in square brackets substituted by European Parliament and Council Directive 2005/68/EC, art 60(9).

[6589]

[Article 28a

Solvency margin for assurance undertakings conducting reinsurance activities

1. Each Member State shall apply to insurance undertakings whose head office is situated within its territory, the provisions of Articles 35 to 39 of Directive 2005/68/EC in respect of their reinsurance acceptance activities, where one of the following conditions is met:

(a) the reinsurance premiums collected exceed 10% of their total premium;

(b) the reinsurance premiums collected exceed EUR 50 000 000;

(c) the technical provisions resulting from their reinsurance acceptances exceed 10% of their total technical provisions.

2. Each Member State may choose to apply to assurance undertakings referred to in paragraph 1 of this Article and whose head office is situated within its territory the provisions of Article 34 of Directive 2005/68/EC in respect of their reinsurance acceptance activities, where one of the conditions laid down in the said paragraph 1 is met.

In that case, the respective Member State shall require that all assets employed by the assurance undertaking to cover the technical provisions corresponding to its reinsurance acceptances shall be ring-fenced, managed and organised separately from the direct assurance activities of the assurance undertaking, without any possibility of transfer. In such a case, and only as far as their reinsurance acceptance activities are concerned, assurance undertakings shall not be subject to Articles 22 to 26.

Each Member State shall ensure that their competent authorities verify the separation provided for in the second subparagraph.]

NOTES

Inserted by European Parliament and Council Directive 2005/68/EC, art 60(10).

Repealed as noted at the beginning of this Directive.

[6590]

Article 29

Guarantee fund

1. One third of the required solvency margin as specified in Article 28 shall constitute the guarantee fund. This fund shall consist of the items listed in Article 27(2), (3) and, with the agreement of the competent authority of the home Member State, (4)(c).

2. The guarantee fund may not be less than a minimum of EUR 3 million.

Any Member State may provide for a one-fourth reduction of the minimum guarantee fund in the case of mutual associations and mutual-type associations and tontines.

NOTES

Repealed as noted at the beginning of this Directive.

[6591]
Article 30
Review of the amount of the guarantee fund

1. The amount in euro as laid down in Article 29(2) shall be reviewed annually starting on 20 September 2003, in order to take account of changes in the European index of consumer prices comprising all Member States as published by Eurostat.

The amount shall be adapted automatically, by increasing the base amount in euro by the percentage change in that index over the period between 20 March 2002 and the review date and rounded up to a multiple of EUR 100 000.

If the percentage change since the last adaptation is less than 5%, no adaptation shall take place.

2. The Commission shall inform annually the European Parliament and the Council of the review and the adapted amount referred to in paragraph 1.

NOTES

Repealed as noted at the beginning of this Directive.

[6592]
Article 31
Assets not used to cover technical provisions

1. Member States shall not prescribe any rules as to the choice of the assets that need not be used as cover for the technical provisions referred to in Article 20.

2. Subject to Article 20(3), Article 37(1), (2), (3) and (5), and the second subparagraph of Article 39(1), Member States shall not restrain the free disposal of those assets, whether movable or immovable, that form part of the assets of authorised assurance undertakings.

3. Paragraphs 1 and 2 shall not preclude any measures which Member States, while safeguarding the interests of the lives assured, are entitled to take as owners or members of or partners in the assurance undertakings in question.

NOTES

Repealed as noted at the beginning of this Directive.

Part VI European Materials

CHAPTER 4
CONTRACT LAW AND CONDITIONS OF ASSURANCE

[6593]
Article 32
Law applicable

1. The law applicable to contracts relating to the activities referred to in this Directive shall be the law of the Member State of the commitment. However, where the law of that State so allows, the parties may choose the law of another country.

2. Where the policy holder is a natural person and has his/her habitual residence in a Member State other than that of which he/she is a national, the parties may choose the law of the Member State of which he/she is a national.

3. Where a State includes several territorial units, each of which has its own rules of law concerning contractual obligations, each unit shall be considered a country for the purposes of identifying the law applicable under this Directive.

A Member State in which various territorial units have their own rules of law concerning contractual obligations shall not be bound to apply the provisions of this Directive to conflicts which arise between the laws of those units.

4. Nothing in this Article shall restrict the application of the rules of the law of the forum in a situation where they are mandatory, irrespective of the law otherwise applicable to the contract.

If the law of a Member State so stipulates, the mandatory rules of the law of the Member State of the commitment may be applied if and in so far as, under the law of that Member State, those rules must be applied whatever the law applicable to the contract.

5. Subject to paragraphs 1 to 4, the Member States shall apply to the assurance contracts referred to in this Directive their general rules of private international law concerning contractual obligations.

NOTES

Repealed as noted at the beginning of this Directive.

[6594]
Article 33
General good

The Member State of the commitment shall not prevent a policy holder from concluding a contract with an assurance undertaking authorised under the conditions of Article 4 as long as that does not conflict with legal provisions protecting the general good in the Member State of the commitment.

NOTES

Repealed as noted at the beginning of this Directive.

[6595]
Article 34
Rules relating to conditions of assurance and scales of premiums

Member States shall not adopt provisions requiring the prior approval or systematic notification of general and special policy conditions, scales of premiums, technical bases used in particular for calculating scales of premiums and technical provisions or forms and other printed documents which an assurance undertaking intends to use in its dealings with policy holders.

Notwithstanding the first subparagraph, for the sole purpose of verifying compliance with national provisions concerning actuarial principles, the home Member State may require systematic communication of the technical bases used in particular for calculating scales of premiums and technical provisions, without that requirement constituting a prior condition for an assurance undertaking to carry on its business.

Not later than 1 July 1999 the Commission shall submit a report to the Council on the implementation of those provisions.

NOTES

Repealed as noted at the beginning of this Directive.

[6596]
Article 35
Cancellation period

1. Each Member State shall prescribe that a policy holder who concludes an individual life-assurance contract shall have a period of between 14 and 30 days from the time when he/she was informed that the contract had been concluded within which to cancel the contract.

The giving of notice of cancellation by the policy holder shall have the effect of releasing him/her from any future obligation arising from the contract.

The other legal effects and the conditions of cancellation shall be determined by the law applicable to the contract as defined in Article 32, notably as regards the arrangements for informing the policy holder that the contract has been concluded.

2. The Member States need not apply paragraph 1 to contracts of six months' duration or less, nor where, because of the status of the policy holder or the circumstances in which the contract is concluded, the policy holder does not need this special protection. Member States shall specify in their rules where paragraph 1 is not applied.

NOTES

Repealed as noted at the beginning of this Directive.

[6597]
Article 36
Information for policy holders

1. Before the assurance contract is concluded, at least the information listed in Annex III(A) shall be communicated to the policy holder.

2. The policy-holder shall be kept informed throughout the term of the contract of any change concerning the information listed in Annex III(B).

3. The Member State of the commitment may require assurance undertakings to furnish information in addition to that listed in Annex III only if it is necessary for a proper understanding by the policy holder of the essential elements of the commitment.

4. The detailed rules for implementing this Article and Annex III shall be laid down by the Member State of the commitment.

NOTES

Repealed as noted at the beginning of this Directive.

CHAPTER 5
ASSURANCE UNDERTAKINGS IN DIFFICULTY OR IN AN IRREGULAR SITUATION

[6598]
Article 37
Assurance undertakings in difficulty

1. If an assurance undertaking does not comply with Article 20, the competent authority of its home Member State may prohibit the free disposal of its assets after having communicated its intention to the competent authorities of the Member States of commitment.

2. For the purposes of restoring the financial situation of an assurance undertaking, the solvency margin of which has fallen below the minimum required under Article 28, the competent authority of the home Member State shall require that a plan for the restoration of a sound financial position be submitted for its approval.

In exceptional circumstances, if the competent authority is of the opinion that the financial situation of the assurance undertaking will further deteriorate, it may also restrict or prohibit the free disposal of the assurance undertaking's assets. It shall inform the authorities of other Member States within the territories of which the assurance undertaking carries on business of any measures it has taken and the latter shall, at the request of the former, take the same measures.

3. If the solvency margin falls below the guarantee fund as defined in Article 29, the competent authority of the home Member State shall require the assurance undertaking to submit a short-term finance scheme for its approval.

It may also restrict or prohibit the free disposal of the assurance undertaking's assets. It shall inform the authorities of other Member States within the territories of which the assurance undertaking carries on business accordingly and the latter shall, at the request of the former, take the same measures.

[4. Member States shall ensure that the competent authorities have the power to decrease the reduction, based on reinsurance, to the solvency margin as determined in accordance with Article 28 where:

- *(a) the nature or quality of reinsurance contracts has changed significantly since the last financial year;*
- *(b) there is no, or a limited, risk transfer under the reinsurance contracts.]*

5. Each Member State shall take the measures necessary to be able in accordance with its national law to prohibit the free disposal of assets located within its territory at the request, in the cases provided for in paragraphs 1, 2 and 3, of the assurance undertaking's home Member State, which shall designate the assets to be covered by such measures.

NOTES

Repealed as noted at the beginning of this Directive.
Para 4: substituted by European Parliament and Council Directive 2005/68/EC, art 60(11).

[6599]
Article 38
Financial recovery plan

1. Member States shall ensure that the competent authorities have the power to require a financial recovery plan for those insurance undertakings where competent authorities consider that policy holders' rights are threatened. The financial recovery plan must as a minimum include particulars or proof concerning for the next three financial years—

- *(a) estimates of management expenses, in particular current general expenses and commissions;*
- *(b) a plan setting out detailed estimates of income and expenditure in respect of direct business, reinsurance acceptances and reinsurance cessions;*
- *(c) a forecast balance sheet;*
- *(d) estimates of the financial resources intended to cover underwriting liabilities and the required solvency margin;*
- *(e) the overall reinsurance policy.*

2. Where policy holders' rights are threatened because the financial position of the undertaking is deteriorating, Member States shall ensure that the competent authorities have the power to oblige insurance undertakings to have a higher required solvency margin, in order to ensure that the insurance undertaking is able to fulfil the solvency requirements in the near future. The level of this higher required solvency margin shall be based on a financial recovery plan referred to in paragraph 1.

3. Member States shall ensure that the competent authorities have the power to revalue downwards all elements eligible for the available solvency margin, in particular, where there has been a significant change in the market value of these elements since the end of the last financial year.

4. Member States shall ensure that the competent authorities have the powers to decrease the reduction, based on reinsurance, to the solvency margin as determined in accordance with Article 28 where—

(a) the nature or quality of reinsurance contracts has changed significantly since the last financial year;

(b) there is no or an insignificant risk transfer under the reinsurance contracts.

5. If the competent authorities have required a financial recovery plan for the insurance undertaking in accordance with paragraph 1, they shall refrain from issuing a certificate in accordance with Article 14(1), Article 40(3), second subparagraph, and Article 42(1)(a), as long as they consider that policy holders' rights are threatened within the meaning of paragraph 1.

NOTES

Repealed as noted at the beginning of this Directive.

[6600]
Article 39
Withdrawal of authorisation

1. Authorisation granted to an assurance undertaking by the competent authority of its home Member State may be withdrawn by that authority if that undertaking—

(a) does not make use of the authorisation within 12 months, expressly renounces it or ceases to carry on business for more than six months, unless the Member State concerned has made provision for authorisation to lapse in such cases;

(b) no longer fulfils the conditions for admission;

(c) has been unable, within the time allowed, to take the measures specified in the restoration plan or finance scheme referred to in Article 37;

(d) fails seriously in its obligations under the regulations to which it is subject.

In the event of the withdrawal or lapse of the authorisation, the competent authority of the home Member State shall notify the competent authorities of the other Member States accordingly and they shall take appropriate measures to prevent the assurance undertaking from commencing new operations within their territories, under either the freedom of establishment or the freedom to provide services. The home Member State's competent authority shall, in conjunction with those authorities, take all necessary measures to safeguard the interests of the assured persons and shall restrict, in particular, the free disposal of the assets of the assurance undertaking in accordance with Article 37(1), (2), second subparagraph, and (3), second subparagraph.

2. Any decision to withdraw an authorisation shall be supported by precise reasons and notified to the assurance undertaking in question.

NOTES

Repealed as noted at the beginning of this Directive.

TITLE IV
PROVISIONS RELATING TO RIGHT OF ESTABLISHMENT AND FREEDOM TO PROVIDE SERVICES

[6601]
Article 40
Conditions for branch establishment

1. An assurance undertaking that proposes to establish a branch within the territory of another Member State shall notify the competent authorities of its home Member State.

2. The Member States shall require every assurance undertaking that proposes to establish a branch within the territory of another Member State to provide the following information when effecting the notification provided for in paragraph 1—

(a) the Member State within the territory of which it proposes to establish a branch;

(b) a scheme of operations setting out, inter alia, the types of business envisaged and the structural organisation of the branch;

(c) the address in the Member State of the branch from which documents may be obtained and to which they may be delivered, it being understood that that address shall be the one to which all communications to the authorised agent are sent;

(d) *the name of the branch's authorised agent, who must possess sufficient powers to bind the assurance undertaking in relation to third parties and to represent it in relations with the authorities and courts of the Member State of the branch. With regard to Lloyd's, in the event of any litigation in the Member State of the branch arising out of underwritten commitments, the assured persons must not be treated less favourably than if the litigation had been brought against businesses of a conventional type. The authorised agent must, therefore, possess sufficient powers for proceedings to be taken against him and must in that capacity be able to bind the Lloyd's underwriters concerned.*

3. Unless the competent authorities of the home Member State have reason to doubt the adequacy of the administrative structure or the financial situation of the assurance undertaking or the good repute and professional qualification or experience of the directors or managers or the authorised agent, taking into account the business planned, they shall, within three months of receiving all the information referred to in paragraph 2, communicate that information to the competent authorities of the Member State of the branch and shall inform the undertaking concerned accordingly.

The competent authorities of the home Member State shall also attest that the assurance undertaking has the minimum solvency margin calculated in accordance with Articles 28 and 29.

Where the competent authorities of the home Member State refuse to communicate the information referred to in paragraph 2 to the competent authorities of the Member State of the branch, they shall give the reasons for their refusal to the assurance undertaking concerned within three months of receiving all the information in question. That refusal or failure to act shall be subject to a right to apply to the courts in the home Member State.

4. Before the branch of an assurance undertaking starts business, the competent authorities of the Member State of the branch shall, within two months of receiving the information referred to in paragraph 3, inform the competent authority of the home Member State, if appropriate, of the conditions under which, in the interest of the general good, that business must be carried on in the Member State of the branch.

5. On receiving a communication from the competent authorities of the Member State of the branch or, if no communication is received from them, on expiry of the period provided for in paragraph 4, the branch may be established and start business.

6. In the event of a change in any of the particulars communicated under paragraph 2(b), (c) or (d), an assurance undertaking shall give written notice of the change to the competent authorities of the home Member State and of the Member State of the branch at least one month before making the change so that the competent authorities of the home Member State and the competent authorities of the Member State of the branch may fulfil their respective roles under paragraphs 3 and 4.

NOTES

Repealed as noted at the beginning of this Directive.

[6602]
Article 41
Freedom to provide services: prior notification to the home Member State

Any assurance undertaking that intends to carry on business for the first time in one or more Member States under the freedom to provide services shall first inform the competent authorities of the home Member State, indicating the nature of the commitments it proposes to cover.

NOTES

Repealed as noted at the beginning of this Directive.

[6603]
Article 42
Freedom to provide services: notification by the home Member State

1. Within one month of the notification provided for in Article 41, the competent authorities of the home Member State shall communicate to the Member State or Member States within the territory of which the assurance undertaking intends to carry on business by way of the freedom to provide services—

(a) *a certificate attesting that the assurance undertaking has the minimum solvency margin calculated in accordance with Articles 28 and 29;*
(b) *the classes which the assurance undertaking has been authorised to offer;*
(c) *the nature of the commitments which the assurance undertaking proposes to cover in the Member State of the provision of services.*

At the same time, they shall inform the assurance undertaking concerned accordingly.

2. Where the competent authorities of the home Member State do not communicate the information referred to in paragraph 1 within the period laid down, they shall give the reasons for their refusal to the assurance undertaking within that same period. The refusal shall be subject to a right to apply to the courts in the home Member State.

3. The assurance undertaking may start business on the certified date on which it is informed of the communication provided for in the first subparagraph of paragraph 1.

NOTES

Repealed as noted at the beginning of this Directive.

[6604]
Article 43
Freedom to provide services: changes in the nature of commitments

Any change which an assurance undertaking intends to make to the information referred to in Article 41 shall be subject to the procedure provided for in Articles 41 and 42.

NOTES

Repealed as noted at the beginning of this Directive.

[6605]
Article 44
Language

The competent authorities of the Member State of the branch or the Member State of the provision of services may require that the information which they are authorised under this Directive to request with regard to the business of assurance undertakings operating in the territory of that State shall be supplied to them in the official language or languages of that State.

NOTES

Repealed as noted at the beginning of this Directive.

[6606]
Article 45
Rules relating to conditions of assurance and scales of premiums

The Member State of the branch or of the provision of services shall not lay down provisions requiring the prior approval or systematic notification of general and special policy conditions, scales of premiums, technical bases used in particular for calculating scales of premiums and technical provisions, forms and other printed documents which an assurance undertaking intends to use in its dealings with policy holders. For the purpose of verifying compliance with national provisions concerning assurance contracts, it may require an assurance undertaking that proposes to carry on assurance business within its territory, under the right of establishment or the freedom to provide services, to effect only non-systematic notification of those policy conditions and other printed documents without that requirement constituting a prior condition for an assurance undertaking to carry on its business.

NOTES

Repealed as noted at the beginning of this Directive.

[6607]
Article 46
Assurance undertakings not complying with the legal provisions

1. Any assurance undertaking carrying on business under the right of establishment or the freedom to provide services shall submit to the competent authorities of the Member State of the branch and/or of the Member State of the provision of services all documents requested of it for the purposes of this Article in so far as assurance undertakings the head office of which is in those Member States are also obliged to do so.

2. If the competent authorities of a Member State establish that an assurance undertaking with a branch or carrying on business under the freedom to provide services in its territory is not complying with the legal provisions applicable to it in that State, they shall require the assurance undertaking concerned to remedy that irregular situation.

3. If the assurance undertaking in question fails to take the necessary action, the competent authorities of the Member State concerned shall inform the competent authorities of the home Member State accordingly. The latter authorities shall, at the earliest opportunity, take all appropriate measures to ensure that the assurance undertaking concerned remedies that irregular situation. The nature of those measures shall be communicated to the competent authorities of the Member State concerned.

4. If, despite the measures taken by the home Member State or because those measures prove inadequate or are lacking in that State, the assurance undertaking persists in violating the legal provisions in force in the Member State concerned, the latter may, after informing the competent authorities of the home Member State, take appropriate measures to prevent or penalise further irregularities, including, in so far as is strictly necessary, preventing that undertaking from continuing to conclude new assurance contracts within its territory. Member States shall ensure that in their territories it is possible to serve the legal documents necessary for such measures on assurance undertakings.

5. Paragraphs 2, 3 and 4 shall not affect the emergency power of the Member States concerned to take appropriate measures to prevent or penalise irregularities committed within their territories. This shall include the possibility of preventing assurance undertakings from continuing to conclude new assurance contracts within their territories.

6. Paragraphs 2, 3 and 4 shall not affect the power of the Member States to penalise infringements within their territories.

7. If an assurance undertaking which has committed an infringement has an establishment or possesses property in the Member State concerned, the competent authorities of the latter may, in accordance with national law, apply the administrative penalties prescribed for that infringement by way of enforcement against that establishment or property.

8. Any measure adopted under paragraphs 3 to 7 involving penalties or restrictions on the conduct of assurance business must be properly reasoned and communicated to the assurance undertaking concerned.

9. Every two years, [the Commission shall inform the European Insurance and Occupational Pensions Committee of] the number and type of cases in which, in each Member State, authorisation has been refused pursuant to Articles 40 or 42 or measures have been taken under paragraph 4 of this Article. Member States shall cooperate with the Commission by providing it with the information required for that report.

NOTES

Repealed as noted at the beginning of this Directive.

Para 9: words in square brackets substituted by European Parliament and Council Directive 2005/1/EC, art 8(1).

[6608]
Article 47
Advertising

Nothing in this Directive shall prevent assurance undertakings with head offices in other Member States from advertising their services through all available means of communication in the Member State of the branch or Member State of the provision of services, subject to any rules governing the form and content of such advertising adopted in the interest of the general good.

NOTES

Repealed as noted at the beginning of this Directive.

[6609]
Article 48
Winding-up

Should an assurance undertaking be wound up, commitments arising out of contracts underwritten through a branch or under the freedom to provide services shall be met in the same way as those arising out of that undertaking's other assurance contracts, without distinction as to nationality as far as the lives assured and the beneficiaries are concerned.

NOTES

Repealed as noted at the beginning of this Directive.

[6610]
Article 49
Statistical information on cross-border activities

Every assurance undertaking shall inform the competent authority of its home Member State, separately in respect of transactions carried out under the right of establishment and those carried out under the freedom to provide services, of the amount of the premiums, without deduction of reassurance, by Member State and by each of classes I to IX, as defined in Annex I.

The competent authority of the home Member State shall, within a reasonable time and on an aggregate basis forward this information to the competent authorities of each of the Member States concerned which so requests.

NOTES

Repealed as noted at the beginning of this Directive.

[6611]
Article 50
Taxes on premiums

1. Without prejudice to any subsequent harmonisation, every assurance contract shall be subject exclusively to the indirect taxes and parafiscal charges on assurance premiums in the Member State of the commitment, and also, with regard to Spain, to the surcharges legally established in favour of the Spanish "Consorcio de Compensación de Seguros" for the performance of its functions relating to the compensation of losses arising from extraordinary events occurring in that Member State.

2. The law applicable to the contract pursuant to Article 32 shall not affect the fiscal arrangements applicable.

3. Pending future harmonisation, each Member State shall apply to those assurance undertakings which cover commitments situated within its territory its own national provisions for measures to ensure the collection of indirect taxes and parafiscal charges due under paragraph 1.

NOTES

Repealed as noted at the beginning of this Directive.

TITLE V
RULES APPLICABLE TO AGENCIES OR BRANCHES ESTABLISHED WITHIN THE COMMUNITY AND BELONGING TO UNDERTAKINGS WHOSE HEAD OFFICES ARE OUTSIDE THE COMMUNITY

[6612]
Article 51
Principles and conditions of authorisation

1. Each Member State shall make access to the activities referred to in Article 2 by any undertaking whose head office is outside the Community subject to an official authorisation.

2. A Member State may grant an authorisation if the undertaking fulfils at least the following conditions—

(a) it is entitled to undertake insurance activities covered by Article 2 under its national law;

(b) it establishes an agency or branch in the territory of such Member State;

(c) it undertakes to establish at the place of management of the agency or branch accounts specific to the activity which it carries on there and to keep there all the records relating to the business transacted;

(d) it designates a general representative, to be approved by the competent authorities;

(e) it possesses in the Member State where it carries on an activity assets of an amount equal in value to at least one half of the minimum amount prescribed in Article 29(2), first subparagraph, in respect of the guarantee fund and deposits one quarter of the minimum amount as security;

(f) it undertakes to keep a solvency margin complying with Article 55;

(g) it submits a scheme of operations in accordance with the provisions of paragraph 3.

3. The scheme of operations of the agency or branch referred to in paragraph 2(g) shall contain the following particulars or evidence of—

(a) the nature of the commitments which the undertaking proposes to cover;

(b) the guiding principles as to reinsurance;

(c) the state of the undertaking's solvency margin and guarantee fund referred to in Article 55;

(d) estimates relating to the cost of setting up the administrative services and the organisation for securing business and the financial resources intended to meet those costs;

and, in addition shall include, for the first three financial years—

(e) a plan setting out detailed estimates of income and expenditure in respect of direct business, reinsurance acceptances and reinsurance cessions;

(f) a forecast balance sheet;

(g) *estimates relating to the financial resources intended to cover underwriting liabilities and the solvency margin.*

4. A Member State may require systematic notification of the technical bases used for calculating scales of premiums and technical provisions, without that requirement constituting a prior condition for an assurance undertaking to carry on its business.

NOTES

Repealed as noted at the beginning of this Directive.

[6613]
Article 52
Rules applicable to branches of third-country undertakings

1.

(a) *Subject to point (b), agencies and branches referred to in this Title may not simultaneously carry on in a Member State the activities referred to in the Annex to Directive 73/239/EEC and those covered by this Directive.*

(b) *Subject to point (c), Member States may provide that agencies and branches referred to in this Title which on the relevant date referred to in Article 18(3) carried on both activities simultaneously in a Member State may continue to do so there provided that each activity is separately managed in accordance with Article 19.*

(c) *Any Member State which under Article 18(6) requires undertakings established in its territory to cease the simultaneous pursuit of the activities in which they were engaged on the relevant date referred to in Article 18(3) must also impose this requirement on agencies and branches referred to in this Title which are established in its territory and simultaneously carry on both activities there.*

(d) *Member States may provide that agencies and branches referred to in this Title whose head office simultaneously carries on both activities and which on the dates referred to in Article 18(3) carried on in the territory of a Member State solely the activity covered by this Directive may continue their activity there. If the undertaking wishes to carry on the activity referred to in Directive 73/239/EEC in that territory it may only carry on the activity covered by this Directive through a subsidiary.*

2. Articles 13 and 37 shall apply mutatis mutandis to agencies and branches referred to in this title.

For the purposes of applying Article 37, the competent authority which supervises the overall solvency of agencies or branches shall be treated in the same way as the competent authority of the head-office Member State.

3. In the case of a withdrawal of authorisation by the authority referred to in Article 56(2), this authority shall notify the competent authorities of the other Member States where the undertaking operates and the latter authorities shall take the appropriate measures. If the reason for the withdrawal of authorisation is the inadequacy of the solvency margin calculated in accordance with Article 56(1)(a), the competent authorities of the other Member States concerned shall also withdraw their authorisations.

NOTES

Repealed as noted at the beginning of this Directive.

[6614]
Article 53
Transfer of portfolio

1. Under the conditions laid down by national law, each Member State shall authorise agencies and branches set up within its territory and covered by this Title to transfer all or part of their portfolios of contracts to an accepting office established in the same Member State if the competent authorities of that Member State or, if appropriate, those of the Member State referred to in Article 56 certify that after taking the transfer into account the accepting office possesses the necessary solvency margin.

2. Under the conditions laid down by national law, each Member State shall authorise agencies and branches set up within its territory and covered by this Title to transfer all or part of their portfolios of contracts to an assurance undertaking with a head office in another Member State, if the competent authorities of that Member State certify that after taking the transfer into account the accepting office possesses the necessary solvency margin.

3. If under the conditions laid down by national law, a Member State authorises agencies and branches set up within its territory and covered by this Title to transfer all or part of their portfolios of contracts to an agency or branch covered by this Title and set up within the territory of another Member State, it shall ensure that the competent authorities of the Member State of the accepting office or, if appropriate, of the Member State referred to in Article 56 certify that after taking the transfer into account the accepting office possesses the necessary solvency margin, that the law of the Member State of the accepting office permits such a transfer and that the State has agreed to the transfer.

4. In the circumstances referred to in paragraphs 1, 2 and 3 the Member State in which the transferring agency or branch is situated shall authorise the transfer after obtaining the agreement of the competent authorities of the Member State of the commitment, where different from the Member State in which the transferring agency or branch is situated.

5. The competent authorities of the Member States consulted shall give their opinion or consent to the competent authorities of the home Member State of the transferring assurance undertaking within three months of receiving a request; the absence of any response from the authorities consulted within that period shall be considered equivalent to a favourable opinion or tacit consent.

6. A transfer authorised in accordance with this Article shall be published as laid down by national law in the Member State of the commitment. Such transfers shall automatically be valid against policy holders, assured persons and any other persons having rights or obligations arising out of the contracts transferred.

This provision shall not affect the Member States' right to give policy holders the option of cancelling contracts within a fixed period after a transfer.

NOTES

Repealed as noted at the beginning of this Directive.

[6615]
Article 54
Technical provisions

Member States shall require undertakings to establish provisions, referred to in Article 20, adequate to cover the underwriting liabilities assumed in their territories. Member States shall see that the agency or branch covers such provisions by means of assets which are equivalent to such provisions and matching assets in accordance with Annex II.

The law of the Member States shall be applicable to the calculation of such provisions, the determination of categories of investment and the valuation of assets, and, where appropriate, the determination of the extent to which these assets may be used for the purpose of covering such provisions.

The Member State in question shall require that the assets covering these provisions, shall be localised in its territory. Article 20(4) shall, however, apply.

NOTES

Repealed as noted at the beginning of this Directive.

[6616]
Article 55
Solvency margin and guarantee fund

1. Each Member State shall require of agencies or branches set up in its territory a solvency margin consisting of the items listed in Article 27. The minimum solvency margin shall be calculated in accordance with Article 28. However, for the purpose of calculating this margin, account shall be taken only of the operations effected by the agency or branch concerned.

2. One third of the minimum solvency margin shall constitute the guarantee fund.

However, the amount of this fund may not be less than one half of the minimum required under Article 29(2) first subparagraph. The initial deposit lodged in accordance with Article 51(2)(e) shall be counted towards such guarantee fund.

The guarantee fund and the minimum of such fund shall be constituted in accordance with Article 29.

3. The assets representing the minimum solvency margin must be kept within the Member State where activities are carried on up to the amount of the guarantee fund and the excess within the Community.

NOTES

Repealed as noted at the beginning of this Directive.

[6617]
Article 56
Advantages to undertakings authorised in more than one Member State

1. Any undertaking which has requested or obtained authorisation from more than one Member State may apply for the following advantages which may be granted only jointly—

- *(a) the solvency margin referred to in Article 55 shall be calculated in relation to the entire business which it carries on within the Community; in such case, account shall be taken only of the operations effected by all the agencies or branches established within the Community for the purposes of this calculation;*
- *(b) the deposit required under Article 51(2)(e) shall be lodged in only one of those Member States;*
- *(c) the assets representing the guarantee fund shall be localised in any one of the Member States in which it carries on its activities.*

2. Application to benefit from the advantages provided for in paragraph 1 shall be made to the competent authorities of the Member States concerned. The application must state the authority of the Member State which in future is to supervise the solvency of the entire business of the agencies or branches established within the Community. Reasons must be given for the choice of authority made by the undertaking. The deposit shall be lodged with that Member State.

3. The advantages provided for in paragraph 1 may only be granted if the competent authorities of all Member States in which an application has been made agree to them. They shall take effect from the time when the selected competent authority informs the other competent authorities that it will supervise the state of solvency of the entire business of the agencies or branches within the Community.

The competent authority selected shall obtain from the other Member States the information necessary for the supervision of the overall solvency of the agencies and branches established in their territory.

4. At the request of one or more of the Member States concerned, the advantages granted under this Article shall be withdrawn simultaneously by all Member States concerned.

NOTES

Repealed as noted at the beginning of this Directive.

[6618]
Article 57
Agreements with third countries

The Community may, by means of agreements concluded pursuant to the Treaty with one or more third countries, agree to the application of provisions different from those provided for in this Title, for the purpose of ensuring, under conditions of reciprocity, adequate protection for policy holders in the Member States.

NOTES

Repealed as noted at the beginning of this Directive.

TITLE VI
RULES APPLICABLE TO SUBSIDIARIES OF PARENT UNDERTAKINGS GOVERNED BY THE LAWS OF A THIRD COUNTRY AND TO THE ACQUISITIONS OF HOLDINGS BY SUCH PARENT UNDERTAKINGS

[6619]
[Article 58

The competent authorities of the Member States shall inform the Commission and the competent authorities of the other Member States—

- *(a) of any authorisation of a direct or indirect subsidiary, one or more of whose parent undertakings are governed by the laws of a third country;*
- *(b) whenever such a parent undertaking acquires a holding in a Community assurance undertaking which would turn the latter into its subsidiary.*

When the authorisation referred to in point (a) is granted to the direct or indirect subsidiary of one or more parent undertakings governed by the law of third countries, the structure of the group shall be specified in the notification which the competent authorities shall address to the Commission and to the other competent authorities.]

NOTES

Substituted by European Parliament and Council Directive 2005/1/EC, art 8(2).
Repealed as noted at the beginning of this Directive.

[6620]
Article 59
Third-country treatment of Community assurance undertakings

1. The Member States shall inform the Commission of any general difficulties encountered by their assurance undertakings in establishing themselves or carrying on their activities in a third country.

2. Periodically, the Commission shall draw up a report examining the treatment accorded to Community assurance undertakings in third countries, in the terms referred to in paragraphs 3 and 4, as regards establishment and the carrying-on of insurance activities, and the acquisition of holdings in third-country insurance undertakings. The Commission shall submit those reports to the Council, together with any appropriate proposals.

3. Whenever it appears to the Commission, either on the basis of the reports referred to in paragraph 2 or on the basis of other information, that a third country is not granting Community assurance undertakings effective market access comparable to that granted by the Community to insurance undertakings from that third country, the Commission may submit proposals to the Council for the appropriate mandate for negotiation with a view to obtaining comparable competitive opportunities for Community assurance undertakings. The Council shall decide by a qualified majority.

4. Whenever it appears to the Commission, either on the basis of the reports referred to in paragraph 2 or on the basis of other information, that Community assurance undertakings in a third country are not receiving national treatment offering the same competitive opportunities as are available to domestic insurance undertakings and that the conditions of effective market access are not being fulfilled, the Commission may initiate negotiations in order to remedy the situation.

In the circumstances described in the first subparagraph, it may also be decided at any time, and in addition to initiating negotiations, in accordance with the procedure laid down in Article 65(2), that the competent authorities of the Member States must limit or suspend their decisions—

- *regarding requests pending at the moment of the decision or future requests for authorisations, and*
- *regarding the acquisition of holdings by direct or indirect parent undertakings governed by the laws of the third country in question.*

The duration of the measures referred to may not exceed three months.

Before the end of that three-month period, and in the light of the results of the negotiations, the Council may, acting on a proposal from the Commission, decide by a qualified majority whether the measures shall be continued.

Such limitations or suspension may not apply to the setting up of subsidiaries by assurance undertakings or their subsidiaries duly authorised in the Community, or to the acquisition of holdings in Community assurance undertakings by such undertakings or subsidiaries.

5. Whenever it appears to the Commission that one of the situations described in paragraphs 3 and 4 has arisen, the Member States shall inform it at its request—

(a) of any request for the authorisation of a direct or indirect subsidiary one or more parent undertakings of which are governed by the laws of the third country in question;

(b) of any plans for such an undertaking to acquire a holding in a Community assurance undertaking such that the latter would become the subsidiary of the former.

This obligation to provide information shall lapse whenever an agreement is reached with the third country referred to in paragraph 3 or 4 when the measures referred to in the second and third subparagraphs of paragraph 4 cease to apply.

6. Measures taken under this Article shall comply with the Community's obligations under any international agreements, bilateral or multilateral, governing the taking up and pursuit of the business of insurance undertakings.

NOTES

Repealed as noted at the beginning of this Directive.

TITLE VII
TRANSITIONAL AND OTHER PROVISIONS

[6621]
Article 60
Derogations and abolition of restrictive measures

1. Undertakings set up in the United Kingdom by Royal Charter or by private Act or by special Public Act may carry on their activity in the legal form in which they were constituted on 15 March 1979 for an unlimited period.

The United Kingdom shall draw up a list of such undertakings and communicate it to the other Member States and the Commission.

2. The societies registered in the United Kingdom under the Friendly Societies Acts may continue the activities of life assurance and savings operations which, in accordance with their objects, they were carrying on on 15 March 1979.

NOTES

Repealed as noted at the beginning of this Directive.

[6622]
Article 61
Proof of good repute

1. Where a Member State requires of its own nationals proof of good repute and proof of no previous bankruptcy, or proof of either of these, that State shall accept as sufficient evidence in respect of nationals of other Member States the production of an extract from the "judicial record" or, failing this, of an equivalent document issued by a competent judicial or administrative authority in the home Member State or the Member State from which the foreign national comes showing that these requirements have been met.

2. Where the home Member State or the Member State from which the foreign national concerned comes does not issue the document referred to in paragraph 1, it may be replaced by a declaration on oath – or in States where there is no provision for declaration on oath by a solemn declaration – made by the person concerned before a competent judicial or administrative authority or, where appropriate, a notary in the home Member State or the Member State from which that person comes; such authority or notary shall issue a certificate attesting the authenticity of the declaration on oath or solemn declaration. The declaration in respect of no previous bankruptcy may also be made before a competent professional or trade body in the said country.

3. Documents issued in accordance with paragraphs 1 and 2 must not be produced more than three months after their date of issue.

4. Member States shall designate the authorities and bodies competent to issue the documents referred to in paragraphs 1 and 2 and shall forthwith inform the other Member States and the Commission thereof.

Each Member State shall also inform the other Member States and the Commission of the authorities or bodies to which the documents referred to in this Article are to be submitted in support of an application to carry on in the territory of this Member State the activities referred to in Article 2.

NOTES

Repealed as noted at the beginning of this Directive.

TITLE VIII
FINAL PROVISIONS

[6623]
Article 62
Cooperation between the Member States and the Commission

The Commission and the competent authorities of the Member States shall collaborate closely with a view to facilitating the supervision of the kinds of insurance and the operations referred to in this Directive within the Community.

Each Member State shall inform the Commission of any major difficulties to which application of this Directive gives rise, inter alia, any arising if a Member State becomes aware of an abnormal transfer of business referred to in this Directive to the detriment of undertakings established in its territory and to the advantage of agencies and branches located just beyond its borders.

The Commission and the competent authorities of the Member States concerned shall examine such difficulties as quickly as possible in order to find an appropriate solution.

Where necessary, the Commission shall submit appropriate proposals to the Council.

NOTES

Repealed as noted at the beginning of this Directive.

[6624]
Article 63
Reports on the development of the market under the freedom to provide services

The Commission shall forward to the European Parliament and to the Council regular reports, the first on 20 November 1995, on the development of the market in assurance and operations transacted under conditions of freedom to provide services.

NOTES

Repealed as noted at the beginning of this Directive.

[6625]

Article 64

Technical adjustment

[The following technical adjustments, designed to amend non-essential elements of this Directive, shall be adopted in accordance with the regulatory procedure with scrutiny referred to in Article 65(2)]—

— *extension of the legal forms provided for in Article 6(1)(a),*

— *amendments to the list set out in Annex I, or adaptation of the terminology used in that list to take account of the development of assurance markets,*

— *clarification of the items constituting the solvency margin listed in Article 27 to take account of the creation of new financial instruments,*

— *alteration of the minimum guarantee fund provided for in Article 29(2) to take account of economic and financial developments,*

— *amendments, to take account of the creation of new financial instruments, to the list of assets acceptable as cover for technical provisions set out in Article 23 and to the rules on the spreading of investments laid down in Article 24,*

— *changes in the relaxations in the matching rules laid down in Annex II, to take account of the development of new currency-hedging instruments or progress made in economic and monetary union,*

— *clarification of the definitions in order to ensure uniform application of this Directive throughout the Community,*

— *the technical adjustments necessary to the rules for setting the maxima applicable to interest rates, pursuant to Article 20, in particular to take account of progress made in economic and monetary union,*

[— adjustments of the criteria set out in Article 15b(1), in order to take account of future developments and to ensure the uniform application of this Directive.]

NOTES

Repealed as noted at the beginning of this Directive.

Words in first pair of square brackets substituted by European Parliament and Council Directive 2008/19/EC, art 1(1); words in second pair of square brackets added by European Parliament and Council Directive 2007/44/EC, art 2(4).

[6626]

Article 65

Committee procedure

[1. The Commission shall be assisted by the European Insurance and Occupational Pensions Committee established by Commission Decision 2004/9/EC.[1]]

[2. Where reference is made to this paragraph, Article 5a(1) to (4) and Article 7 of Decision 1999/468/EC shall apply, having regard to the provisions of Article 8 thereof.]

3. . . .

NOTES

Repealed as noted at the beginning of this Directive.

Para 1: substituted by European Parliament and Council Directive 2005/1/EC, art 8(3).

Para 2: substituted by European Parliament and Council Directive 2008/19/EC, art 1(2)(a).

Para 3: repealed by European Parliament and Council Directive 2008/19/EC, art 1(2)(b).

[1] OJ L3, 7.1.2004, p 34.

[6627]

Article 66

Rights acquired by existing branches and assurance undertakings

1. Branches which started business, in accordance with the provisions in force in the Member State of the branch, before 1 July 1994 shall be presumed to have been subject to the procedure laid down in Article 40(1) to (5).

They shall be governed, from that date by Articles 13, 20, 37, 39 and 46.

2. Articles 41 and 42 shall not affect rights acquired by assurance undertakings carrying on business under the freedom to provide services before 1 July 1994.

NOTES

Repealed as noted at the beginning of this Directive.

[6628]
Article 67
Right to apply to the courts

Member States shall ensure that decisions taken in respect of an assurance undertaking under laws, regulations and administrative provisions adopted in accordance with this Directive may be subject to the right to apply to the courts.

NOTES

Repealed as noted at the beginning of this Directive.

[6629]
Article 68
Review of amounts expressed in euro

1. The Commission shall submit to the Council before 15 March 1985 a report dealing with the effects of the financial requirements imposed by this Directive on the situation in the insurance markets of the Member States.

2. The Council, acting on a proposal from the Commission, shall every two years examine and, where appropriate, revise the amounts expressed in euro in this Directive, in the light of how the Community's economic and monetary situation has evolved.

NOTES

Repealed as noted at the beginning of this Directive.

[6630]
Article 9
Implementation of new provisions

1. Member States shall bring into force the laws, regulations and administrative provisions necessary to comply with Article 1(1)(m), Article 18(3), Article 51(2)(g), (3) and (4), Article 60(2) and Article 66(1) not later than 19 June 2004. They shall immediately inform the Commission thereof.

2. Member States shall bring into force the laws, regulations and administrative provisions necessary for them to comply with Article 16(3) not later than 17 November 2002. They shall forthwith inform the Commission thereof. Before this date, Member States shall apply the provision referred to in Annex IV(1).

3. Member States shall adopt by 20 September 2003 the laws, regulations and administrative provisions necessary to comply with Articles 3(6), 27, 28, 29, 30 and 38. They shall forthwith inform the Commission thereof.

Member States shall provide that the provisions referred to in the first subparagraph shall first apply to the supervision of accounts for financial years beginning on 1 January 2004 or during that calendar year. Before this date, Member States shall apply the provisions referred to in Annex IV(2) and (3).

4. When Member States adopt the measures mentioned in paragraphs (1), (2) and (3), they shall contain a reference to this Directive or be accompanied by such a reference on the occasion of their official publication. Member States shall determine how such reference is to be made.

5. Not later than 1 January 2007 the Commission shall submit to the European Parliament and to the Council a report on the application of Articles 3(6), 27, 28, 29, 30 and 38 and, if necessary, on the need for further harmonisation. The report shall indicate how Member States have made use of the possibilities under those articles and, in particular, whether the discretionary powers afforded to the national supervisory authorities have resulted in major supervisory differences in the single market.

NOTES

Repealed as noted at the beginning of this Directive.

[6631]
Article 70
Information to the Commission

The Member States shall communicate to the Commission the texts of the main provisions of national law which they adopt in the field covered by this Directive.

NOTES

Repealed as noted at the beginning of this Directive.

[6632]
Article 71
Transitional period for Articles 3(6), 27, 28, 29, 30 and 38

1. Member States may allow assurance undertakings which at 20 March 2002 provided assurance in their territories in one or more of classes referred to in Annex I, a period of five years, commencing on that same date, in order to comply with the requirements set out in Articles 3(6), 27, 28, 29, 30 and 38.

2. Member States may allow any undertakings referred to in paragraph 1, which upon the expiry of the five-year period have not fully established the required solvency margin, a further period not exceeding two years in which to do so provided that such undertakings have, in accordance with Article 37, submitted for the approval of the competent authorities, the measures which they propose to take for such purpose.

NOTES

Repealed as noted at the beginning of this Directive.

[6633]
Article 72
Repealed directives and their correlation with this Directive

1. The Directives listed in Annex V, part A, are hereby repealed, without prejudice to the obligations of the Member States concerning the time limits for transposition and for application of the said Directives listed in Annex V, part B.

2. References to the repealed Directives shall be construed as references to this Directive and shall be read in accordance with the correlation table in Annex VI.

NOTES

Repealed as noted at the beginning of this Directive.

[6634]
Article 73
Entry into force

This Directive shall enter into force on the day of its publication in the Official Journal of the European Communities.

NOTES

Repealed as noted at the beginning of this Directive.

[6635]
Article 74
Addressees

This Directive is addressed to the Member States.

NOTES

Repealed as noted at the beginning of this Directive.

Done at Brussels, 5 November 2002.

ANNEX I

CLASSES OF ASSURANCE

[6636]

I. The assurance referred to in Article 2(1)(a), (b) and (c) excluding those referred to in II and III

II. Marriage assurance, birth assurance

III. The assurance referred to in Article 2(1)(a) and (b), which are linked to investment funds

IV. Permanent health insurance, referred to in Article 2(1)(d)

V. Tontines, referred to in Article 2(2)(a)

VI. Capital redemption operations, referred to in Article 2(2)(b)

VII. Management of group pension funds, referred to in Article 2(2)(c) and (d)

VIII. The operations referred to in Article 2(2)(e)

IX. The operations referred to in Article 2(3)

NOTES

Repealed as noted at the beginning of this Directive.

ANNEX II

MATCHING RULES

[6637]

The currency in which the assurer's commitments are payable shall be determined in accordance with the following rules.

1. Where the cover provided by a contract is expressed in terms of a particular currency, the assurer's commitments are considered to be payable in that currency.

2. Member States may authorise assurance undertakings not to cover their technical provisions, including their mathematical provisions, by matching assets if application of the above procedures would result in the undertaking being obliged, in order to comply with the matching principle, to hold assets in a currency amounting to not more than 7% of the assets existing in other currencies.

3. Member States may choose not to require assurance undertakings to apply the matching principle where commitments are payable in a currency other than the currency of one of the Member States, if investments in that currency are regulated, if the currency is subject to transfer restrictions or if, for similar reasons, it is not suitable for covering technical provisions.

4. Assurance undertakings are authorised not to hold matching assets to cover an amount not exceeding 20% of their commitments in a particular currency.

However, total assets in all currencies combined must be at least equal to total commitments in all currencies combined.

5. Each Member State may provide that, whenever under the preceding procedures a commitment has to be covered by assets expressed in the currency of a Member State, this requirement shall also be considered to be satisfied when the assets are expressed in euro.

NOTES

Repealed as noted at the beginning of this Directive.

ANNEX III

INFORMATION FOR POLICY HOLDERS

[6638]

The following information, which is to be communicated to the policy holder before the contract is concluded (A) or during the term of the contract (B), must be provided in a clear and accurate manner, in writing, in an official language of the Member State of the commitment.

However, such information may be in another language if the policy holder so requests and the law of the Member State so permits or the policy holder is free to choose the law applicable.

A. Before concluding the contract

Information about the insurance undertaking	***Information about the commitment***
(a)1 The name of the undertaking and its legal form	*(a)4 Definition of each benefit and each option*
(a)2 The name of the Member State in which the head office and, where appropriate, the agency or branch concluding the contract is situated	*(a)5 Term of the contract*

Information about the insurance undertaking	Information about the commitment
(a)3 The address of the head office and, where appropriate, of the agency or branch concluding the contract	*(a)6 Means of terminating the contract*
	(a)7 Means of payment of premiums and duration of payments
	(a)8 Means of calculation and distribution of bonuses
	(a)9 Indication of surrender and paid-up values and the extent to which they are guaranteed
	(a)10 Information on the premiums for each benefit, both main benefits and supplementary benefits, where appropriate
	(a)11 For unit-linked policies, definition of the units to which the benefits are linked
	(a)12 Indication of the nature of the underlying assets for unit-linked policies
	(a)13 Arrangements for application of the cooling-off period
	(a)14 General information on the tax arrangements applicable to the type of policy
	(a)15 The arrangements for handling complaints concerning contracts by policy holders, lives assured or beneficiaries under contracts including, where appropriate, the existence of a complaints body, without prejudice to the right to take legal proceedings
	(a)16 Law applicable to the contract where the parties do not have a free choice or, where the parties are free to choose the law applicable, the law the assurer proposes to choose

B. During the term of the contract

In addition to the policy conditions, both general and special, the policy-holder must receive the following information throughout the term of the contract.

Information about the assurance undertaking	Information about the commitment
(b)1 Any change in the name of the undertaking, its legal form or the address of its head office and, where appropriate, of the agency or branch which concluded the contract	*(b)2 All the information listed in points (a)(4) to (a)(12) of A in the event of a change in the policy conditions or amendment of the law applicable to the contract*
	(b)3 Every year, information on the state of bonuses

NOTES

Repealed as noted at the beginning of this Directive.

ANNEX IV

[6639]

1. Professional secrecy

Until 17 November 2002, Member States may conclude cooperation agreements, providing for exchanges of information, with the competent authorities of third countries only if the information disclosed is subject to guarantees of professional secrecy at least equivalent to those referred to in Article 16 of this Directive.

2. Activities and bodies excluded from this Directive

Until 1 January 2004, this Directive shall not concern mutual associations, where—

— *the articles of association contain provisions for calling up additional contributions or reducing their benefits or claiming assistance from other persons who have undertaken to provide it, and*

— *the annual contribution income for the activities covered by this Directive does not exceed EUR 500 000 for three consecutive years. If this amount is exceeded for three consecutive years this Directive shall apply with effect from the fourth year.*

3. **Until 1 January 2004, Member States shall apply the following provisions:**

A. Solvency margin

Each Member State shall require of every assurance undertaking whose head office is situated in its territory an adequate solvency margin in respect of its entire business.

The solvency margin shall consist of—

1. the assets of the assurance undertaking free of any foreseeable liabilities, less any intangible items. In particular the following shall be included—

— *the paid-up share capital or, in the case of a mutual assurance undertaking, the effective initial fund plus any members' accounts which meet all the following criteria:*

(a) the memorandum and articles of association must stipulate that payments may be made from these accounts to members only in so far as this does not cause the solvency margin to fall below the required level, or, after the dissolution of the undertaking, if all the undertaking's other debts have been settled;

(b) the memorandum and articles of association must stipulate, with respect to any such payments for reasons other than the individual termination of membership, that the competent authorities must be notified at least one month in advance and can prohibit the payment within that period;

(c) the relevant provisions of the memorandum and articles of association may be amended only after the competent authorities have declared that they have no objection to the amendment, without prejudice to the criteria stated in (a) and (b),

— *one half of the unpaid share capital or initial fund, once the paid-up part amounts to 25% of that share capital or fund,*

— *reserves (statutory reserves and free reserves) not corresponding to underwriting liabilities,*

— *any profits brought forward,*

— *cumulative preferential share capital and subordinated loan capital may be included but, if so, only up to 50% of the margin, no more than 25% of which shall consist of subordinated loans with a fixed maturity, or fixed-term cumulative preferential share capital, if the following minimum criteria are met:*

(a) in the event of the bankruptcy or liquidation of the assurance undertaking, binding agreements must exist under which the subordinated loan capital or preferential share capital ranks after the claims of all other creditors and is not to be repaid until all other debts outstanding at the time have been settled.

Subordinated loan capital must also fulfil the following conditions—

(b) only fully paid-up funds may be taken into account;

(c) for loans with a fixed maturity, the original maturity must be at least five years. No later than one year before the repayment date, the assurance undertaking must submit to the competent authorities for their approval a plan showing how the solvency margin will be kept at or brought to the required level at maturity, unless the extent to which the loan may rank as a component of the solvency margin is gradually reduced during at least the last five years before the repayment date. The competent authorities may authorise the early repayment of such loans provided application is made by the issuing assurance undertaking and its solvency margin will not fall below the required level;

(d) loans the maturity of which is not fixed must be repayable only subject to five years' notice unless the loans are no longer considered as a component of the solvency margin or unless the prior consent of the competent authorities is specifically required for early repayment. In the latter event the assurance undertaking must notify the competent authorities at least six

months before the date of the proposed repayment, specifying the actual and required solvency margin both before and after that repayment. The competent authorities shall authorise repayment only if the assurance undertaking's solvency margin will not fall below the required level;

(e) *the loan agreement must not include any clause providing that in specified circumstances, other than the winding-up of the assurance undertaking, the debt will become repayable before the agreed repayment dates;*

(f) *the loan agreement may be amended only after the competent authorities have declared that they have no objection to the amendment,*

— *securities with no specified maturity date and other instruments that fulfil the following conditions, including cumulative preferential shares other than those mentioned in the fifth indent, up to 50% of the margin for the total of such securities and the subordinated loan capital referred to in the fifth indent:*

(a) *they may not be repaid on the initiative of the bearer or without the prior consent of the competent authority;*

(b) *the contract of issue must enable the assurance undertaking to defer the payment of interest on the loan;*

(c) *the lender's claims on the assurance undertaking must rank entirely after those of all non-subordinated creditors;*

(d) *the documents governing the issue of the securities must provide for the loss-absorption capacity of the debt and unpaid interest, while enabling the assurance undertaking to continue its business;*

(e) *only fully paid-up amounts may be taken into account.*

2. *in so far as authorised under national law, profit reserves appearing in the balance sheet where they may be used to cover any losses which may arise and where they have not been made available for distribution to policy holders;*

3. *upon application, with supporting evidence, by the undertaking to the competent authority of the Member State in the territory of which its head office is situated and with the agreement of that authority—*

(a) *an amount equal to 50% of the undertaking's future profits; the amount of the future profits shall be obtained by multiplying the estimated annual profit by a factor which represents the average period left to run on policies; the factor used may not exceed 10; the estimated annual profit shall be the arithmetical average of the profits made over the last five years in the activities listed in Article 2 of this Directive.*

The bases for calculating the factor by which the estimated annual profit is to be multiplied and the items comprising the profits made shall be defined by common agreement by the competent authorities of the Member States in collaboration with the Commission. Pending such agreement, those items shall be determined in accordance with the laws of the home Member State.

When the competent authorities have defined the concept of profits made, the Commission shall submit proposals for the harmonisation of this concept by means of a Directive on the harmonisation of the annual accounts of insurance undertakings and providing for the coordination set out in Article 1(2) of Directive 78/660/EEC;

(b) *where Zillmerising is not practised or where, if practised, it is less than the loading for acquisition costs included in the premium, the difference between a non-Zillmerised or partially Zillmerised mathematical provision and a mathematical provision Zillmerised at a rate equal to the loading for acquisition costs included in the premium; this figure may not, however, exceed 3,5% of the sum of the differences between the relevant capital sums of life assurance activities and the mathematical provisions for all policies for which Zillmerising is possible; the difference shall be reduced by the amount of any undepreciated acquisition costs entered as an asset;*

(c) *where approval is given by the competent authorities of the Member States concerned in which the assurance undertaking is carrying on its activities any hidden reserves resulting from the underestimation of assets and overestimation of liabilities other than mathematical provisions in so far as such hidden reserves are not of an exceptional nature.*

B. Minimum solvency margin

Subject to section C, the minimum solvency margin shall be determined as shown below according to the classes of assurance underwritten.

(a) *For the kinds of assurance referred to in Article 2(1)(a) and (b) of this Directive other than assurance linked to investment funds and for the operations referred to in Article 2(3) of this Directive, it must be equal to the sum of the following two results—*

— *first result:*

a 4% fraction of the mathematical provisions relating to direct business gross of reinsurance cessions and to reinsurance acceptances shall be multiplied by the ratio, for the last financial year, of the total mathematical provisions net of reinsurance cessions to the gross total mathematical provisions as specified above; that ratio may in no case be less than 85%,

— *second result:*

for policies on which the capital at risk is not a negative figure, a 0,3% fraction of such capital underwritten by the assurance undertaking shall be multiplied by the ratio, for the last financial year, of the total capital at risk retained as the undertaking's liability after reinsurance cessions and retrocessions to the total capital at risk gross of reinsurance; that ratio may in no case be less than 50%.

For temporary assurance on death of a maximum term of three years the above fraction shall be 0,1%; for such assurance of a term of more than three years but not more than five years the above fraction shall be 0,15%.

(b) *For the supplementary insurance referred to in Article 2(1)(c) of this Directive, it shall be equal to the result of the following calculation—*

— *the premiums or contributions (inclusive of charges ancillary to premiums or contributions) due in respect of direct business in the last financial year in respect of all financial years shall be aggregated,*

— *to this aggregate there shall be added the amount of premiums accepted for all reinsurance in the last financial year,*

— *from this sum shall then be deducted the total amount of premiums or contributions cancelled in the last financial year as well as the total amount of taxes and levies pertaining to the premiums or contributions entering into the aggregate.*

The amount so obtained shall be divided into two portions, the first extending up to EUR 10 million and the second comprising the excess; 18% and 16% of these portions respectively shall be calculated and added together.

The result shall be obtained by multiplying the sum so calculated by the ratio existing in respect of the last financial year between the amount of claims remaining to be borne by the assurance undertaking after deduction of transfers for reinsurance and the gross amount of claims; this ratio may in no case be less than 50%.

In the case of the association of underwriters known as Lloyd's, the calculation of the solvency margin shall be made on the basis of net premiums, which shall be multiplied by flat-rate percentage fixed annually by the competent authority of the head office Member State. This flat-rate percentage must be calculated on the basis of the most recent statistical data on commissions paid. The details together with the relevant calculations shall be sent to the competent authorities of the countries in whose territory Lloyd's is established.

(c) *For permanent health insurance not subject to cancellation referred to in Article 2(1)(d) of this Directive, and for capital redemption operations referred to in Article 2(2)(b) thereof, it shall be equal to a 4% fraction of the mathematical provisions calculated in compliance with the conditions set out in the first result in (a) of this section.*

(d) *For tontines, referred to in Article 2(2)(a) of this Directive, it shall be equal to 1% of their assets.*

(e) *For assurance covered by Article 2(1)(a) and (b) of this Directive linked to investment funds and for the operations referred to in Article 2(2)(c), (d) and (e) of this Directive it shall be equal to—*

— *a 4% fraction of the mathematical provisions, calculated in compliance with the conditions set out in the first result in (a) of this section in so far as the assurance undertaking bears an investment risk, and a 1% fraction of the provisions calculated in the same way, in so far as the undertaking bears no investment risk provided that the term of the contract exceeds five years and the allocation to cover management expenses set out in the contract is fixed for a period exceeding five years, plus*

— *a 0,3% fraction of the capital at risk calculated in compliance with the conditions set out in the first subparagraph of the second result of (a) of this section in so far as the assurance undertaking covers a death risk.*

C. *Guarantee fund*

1. *One third of the required solvency margin as specified in section B shall constitute the guarantee fund. Subject to paragraph 2 of this section, at least 50% of this fund shall consist of the items listed in section A(1) and (2).*

2.

   (a) *The guarantee fund may not, however, be less than a minimum of EUR 800 000.*

   (b) *Any Member State may provide for the minimum of the guarantee fund to be reduced to EUR 600 000 in the case of mutual associations and mutual-type associations and tontines.*

   (c) *For mutual associations referred to in the second sentence of the second indent of Article 3(6) of this Directive, as soon as they come within the scope of this Directive, and for tontines, any Member State may permit the establishment of a minimum of the guarantee fund of EUR 100 000 to be increased progressively to the amount fixed in (b) of this section by successive tranches of EUR 100 000 whenever the contributions increase by EUR 500 000.*

   (d) *The minimum of the guarantee fund referred to in (a), (b) and (c) of this section must consist of the items listed in section A(1) and (2).*

3. *Mutual associations wishing to extend their business within the meaning of Article 6(4) or Article 40 of this Directive may not do so unless they comply immediately with the requirements of paragraph 2(a) and (b) of this section.*

NOTES

Repealed as noted at the beginning of this Directive.

ANNEX V

PART A
REPEALED DIRECTIVES TOGETHER WITH THEIR SUCCESSIVE AMENDMENTS (REFERRED TO IN ARTICLE 72)

[6640]

Council Directive 79/267/EEC

Council Directive 90/619/EEC

Council Directive 92/96/EEC

Directive 95/26/EEC of the European Parliament and of the Council (only Article 1, second indent, Article 2(2), fourth indent, and Article 3(1) as regards the references made to Directive 79/267/EEC)

Directive 2002/12/EC of the European Parliament and of the Council

Second Council Directive 90/619/EEC

Third Council Directive 92/96/EEC

Third Council Directive 92/96/EEC

Directive 95/26/EEC of the European Parliament and of the Council (only Article 1, second indent, Article 2(1), third indent, Article 4(1), (3), (5) and Article 5, third indent, as regards the references made to Directive 92/96/EEC).

Directive 2000/64/EC of the European Parliament and of the Council (Article 2, as regards the references made to Directive 92/96/EEC)

Directive 2002/12/EC of the European Parliament and of the Council (Article 2)

NOTES

Repealed as noted at the beginning of this Directive.

PART B
DEADLINES FOR IMPLEMENTATION

(Referred to in Article 72)

[6641]

Directive	*Time limits for transposition*	*Time limits for application*
79/267/EEC (OJ L63, 13.3.1979, p 1)	*15 September 1980*	*15 September 1981*
90/619/EEC (OJ L330, 29.11.1990, p 50)	*20 November 1992*	*20 May 1993*
92/96/EEC (OJ L360, 9.12.1992, p 1)	*31 December 1993*	*1 July 1994*
95/26/EC (OJ L168, 18.7.1995, p 7)	*18 July 1996*	*18 July 1996*
2000/64/EC (OJ L290, 17.11.2000, p 27)	*17 November 2002*	*17 November 2002*
2002/12/EC (OJ L77, 20.3.2002, p 11)	*20 September 2003*	*1 January 2004*

NOTES

Repealed as noted at the beginning of this Directive.

ANNEX VI

CORRELATION TABLE

[6642]

This Directive	*Directive 79/267/EEC*	*Directive 90/619/EEC*	*Directive 92/96/EEC*	*Directive 95/26/EC*	*Other Acts*
Article 1(1)(a)			*Article 1(a)*		
Article 1(1)(b)		*Article 3*	*Article 1(b)*		
Article 1(1)(c)		*Article 2(c)*			
Article 1(1)(d)			*Article 1(c)*		
Article 1(1)(e)			*Article 1(d)*		
Article 1(1)(f)			*Article 1(e)*		
Article 1(1)(g)		*Article 2(e)*			
Article 1(1)(h) to (l)			*Article 1(f) to (j)*		
Article 1(1)(m)					
Article 1(1)(n)			*Article 1(l)*		
Article 1(1)(o), (p), (q)	*Article 5(b), (c) and (d)*				
Article 1(1)(r)				*Article 2(1)*	
Article	*Article*				

Part VI European Materials

This Directive	*Directive 79/267/EEC*	*Directive 90/619/EEC*	*Directive 92/96/EEC*	*Directive 95/26/EC*	*Other Acts*
1(2)	*5(a), second sentence*				
Article 2	*Article 1*				
Article 3(1) to (4)	*Article 2*				
Article 3(5) and (6)	*Article 3*				
Article 3(7)	*Article 4*				
Article 3(8)					Act of Accession of Austria, Finland and Sweden, adapted by Decision 95/1/EC, Euratom, ECSC
Article 4	*Article 6*				
Article 5	*Article 7*				
Article 6(1)	*Article 8(1)*				
Article 6(2)	*Article 8(1) last three sub-paragraphs*				
Article 6(3)	*Article 8(1)a*				
Article 6(4)	*Article 8(2)*				
Article 6(5)	*Article 8(3)*				
Article 6(6)	*Article 8(4)*				
Article 7	*Article 9*				
Article 8			*Article 7*		
Article 9	*Article 12*				
Article 10	*Article 15*				
Article 11	*Article 16*				
Article 12	*Article 22(1)*				
Article 13	*Article 23*				
Article 14(1) to (5)			*Article 11(2) to (6)*		
Article 15			*Article 14*		
Article 16(1) to (5)			*Article 15(1) to (5)*		
Article 16(6)			*Article 15(5)(a)*		
Article 16(7)			*Article 15(5)(b)*		
Article 16(8)			*Article 15(5)(c)*		
Article 16(9)			*Article 15(6)*		

This Directive	***Directive 79/267/EEC***	***Directive 90/619/EEC***	***Directive 92/96/EEC***	***Directive 95/26/EC***	***Other Acts***
Article 17			*Article 15(a)*		
Article 18(1) and (2)	*Article 13(1) and (2)*				
Article 18(3)					
Article 18(4) to (7)	*Article 13(3) to (7)*				
Article 19	*Article 14*				
Article 20	*Article 17*				
Article 21			*Article 19*		
Article 22			*Article 20*		
Article 23(1)			*Article 21(1) first sub-paragraph*		
Article 23(2)			*Article 21(1) second sub-paragraph*		
Article 23(3) first sub-paragraph			*Article 21(1) third sub-paragraph*		
Article 23(3) second sub-paragraph			*Article 21(1) fourth sub-paragraph*		
Article 23(4)			*Article 21(2)*		
Article 24			*Article 22*		
Article 25			*Article 23*		
Article 26			*Article 24*		
Article 27	*Article 18*				
Article 28	*Article 19*				
Article 29	*Article 20*				
Article 30	*Article 20a*				
Article 31	*Article 21*				
Article 32		*Article 4*			
Article 33			*Article 28*		
Article 34			*Article 29*		
Article 35		*Article 15*			
Article 36			*Article 31*		
Article 37	*Article 24*				
Article 38	*Article 24a*				
Article 39	*Article 26*				
Article 40	*Article 10*				
Article 41		*Article 11*			
Article 42		*Article 14*			
Article 43		*Article 17*			
Article 44			*Article 38*		
Article 45			*Article 39(2)*		
Article 46(1) to (9)			*Article 40(2) to (10)*		

This Directive	*Directive 79/267/EEC*	*Directive 90/619/EEC*	*Directive 92/96/EEC*	*Directive 95/26/EC*	*Other Acts*
Article 47			*Article 41*		
Article 48			*Article 42(2)*		
Article 49			*Article 43(2)*		
Article 50(1)			*Article 44(2) first subparagraph*		
Article 50(2)			*Article 44(2) second subparagraph*		
Article 50(3)			*Article 44(2) third subparagraph*		
Article 51(1) to (2)(f)	*Article 27(1) to (2)(f)*				
Article 51(2)(g)					
Article 51(3) and (4)					
Article 52	*Article 31*				
Article 53	*Article 31a*				
Article 54	*Article 28*				
Article 55	*Article 29*				
Article 56	*Article 30*				
Article 57	*Article 32*				
Article 58	*Article 32a*				
Article 59(1)	*Article 32b(1)*				
Article 59(2)	*Article 32b(2)*				
Article 59(3)	*Article 32b(3)*				
Article 59(4)	*Article 32b(4)*				
Article 59(5)	*Article 32b(5)*				
Article 59(6)	*Article 32b(7)*				
Article 60(1)	*Article 33(4)*				
Article 60(2)					
Article 61	*Article 37*				
Article 62, first subparagraph	*Article 38*	*Article 28, first subparagraph*			
Article 62, second to fourth subparagraphs		*Article 28, second to fourth subparagraphs*			

This Directive	*Directive 79/267/EEC*	*Directive 90/619/EEC*	*Directive 92/96/EEC*	*Directive 95/26/EC*	*Other Acts*
Article 63		*Article 29*			
Article 64			*Article 47*		
Article 65			*Article 47*		
Article 66(1), first sub-paragraph					
Article 66(1) second sub-paragraph			*Article 48(1)*		
Article 66(2)			*Article 48(2)*		
Article 67			*Article 50*		
Article 68(1)	*Article 39(1)*				
Article 68(2)	*Article 39(3)*				
Article 69(1)					
Article 69(2)					*Directive 2000/64/EC, Article 3(1), first sub-paragraph*
Article 69(3)					*Directive 2002/12/EC, Article 3(1), first sub-paragraph, and Directive 2000/64/EC, Article 3(2)*
Article 69(4)					*Directive 2000/64/EC, Article 3(1), second sub-paragraph, and Directive 2002/12/EC, Article 3(1), second sub-paragraph*
Article 69(5)					*Directive 2002/12/EC, Article 3(4)*
Article 70	*Article 41*	*Article 31*	*Article 51(2)*	*Article 6(2)*	*Directive 2000/64/EC, Article 3(2), and Directive 2002/12/EC, Article 3(3)*
Article 71					*Directive 2002/12/EC, Article 2*
Article 72					
Article 73					
Article 74					
Annex I	*Annex*				
Annex II			*Annex I*		

This Directive	***Directive 79/267/EEC***	***Directive 90/619/EEC***	***Directive 92/96/EEC***	***Directive 95/26/EC***	***Other Acts***
Annex III			*Annex II*		
Annex IV					
Annex V					
Annex VI					

NOTES

Repealed as noted at the beginning of this Directive.

E. NON-LIFE

FIRST COUNCIL DIRECTIVE

(73/239/EEC)

of 24 July 1973

on the coordination of laws, Regulations and administrative provisions relating to the taking-up and pursuit of the business of direct insurance other than life assurance

NOTES

Date of publication in OJ: OJ L228, 16.8.73, p 3.

This Directive is repealed by European Parliament and Council Directive 2009/138/EC on the taking-up and pursuit of the business of Insurance and Reinsurance (Solvency II) at **[6153]** et seq, with effect from 1 November 2012 (see art 310 thereof at **[6462]**).

[6643]

THE COUNCIL OF THE EUROPEAN COMMUNITIES,

Having regard to the Treaty establishing the European Economic Community, and in particular Article 57(2) thereof;

Having regard to the General Programme[1] *for the abolition of restrictions on freedom of establishment, and in particular Title IV C thereof;*

Having regard to the proposal from the Commission;

Having regard to the Opinion of the European Parliament;[2]

Having regard to the Opinion of the Economic and Social Committee;[3]

Whereas by virtue of the General Programme the removal of restrictions on the establishment of agencies and branches is, in the case of the direct insurance business, dependent on the coordination of the conditions for the taking-up and pursuit of this business; whereas such coordination should be effected in the first place in respect of direct insurance other than life assurance;

Whereas in order to facilitate the taking-up and pursuit of the business of insurance, it is essential to eliminate certain divergencies which exist between national supervisory legislation; whereas in order to achieve this objective, and at the same time ensure adequate protection for insured and third parties in all the Member States, it is desirable to co-ordinate, in particular, the provisions relating to the financial guarantees required of insurance undertakings;

Whereas a classification of risks in the different classes of insurance is necessary in order to determine, in particular, the activities subject to a compulsory authorisation and the amount of the minimum guarantee fund fixed for the class of insurance concerned;

Whereas it is desirable to exclude from the application of this Directive mutual associations which, by virtue of their legal status, fulfil appropriate conditions as to security and financial guarantees; whereas it is further desirable to exclude certain institutions in several Member States whose business covers a very limited sector only and is restricted by law to a specified territory or to specified persons;

Whereas the various laws contain different rules as to the simultaneous undertaking of health insurance, credit and suretyship insurance and insurance in respect of recourse against third parties and legal defence, whether with one another or with other classes of insurance; whereas continuance of this divergence after the abolition of restrictions on the right of establishment in classes other than life assurance would mean that obstacles to establishment would continue to exist; whereas a solution to this problem must be provided in subsequent coordination to be effected within a relatively short period of time;

Whereas it is necessary to extend supervision in each Member State to all the classes of insurance to which this Directive applies; whereas such supervision is not possible unless the undertaking of such classes of insurance is subject to an official authorisation; whereas it is therefore necessary to define the conditions for the granting or withdrawal of such authorisation; whereas provision must be made for a right to apply to the courts should an authorisation be refused or withdrawn;

Whereas it is desirable to bring the classes of insurance known as transport classes bearing Nos 4, 5, 6, 7 and 12 in Paragraph A of the Annex, and the credit insurance classes bearing Nos 14 and 15 in paragraph A of the Annex, under more flexible rules in view of the continual fluctuations in conditions affecting goods and credit;

Whereas the search for a common method of calculating technical reserves is at present the subject of studies at Community level; whereas it therefore appears to be desirable to reserve the attainment of coordination in this matter, as well as questions relating to the determination of categories of investments and the valuation of assets, for subsequent Directives;

Whereas it is necessary that insurance undertakings should possess, over and above technical reserves of sufficient amount to meet their underwriting liabilities, a supplementary reserve, to be known as the solvency margin, and represented by free assets, in order to provide against business fluctuations; whereas in order to ensure that the requirements imposed for such purposes are determined according to objective criteria, whereby undertakings of the same size are placed on an equal footing as regards competition, it is desirable to provide that such margin shall be related to the overall volume of business of the undertaking and be determined by reference to two indices of security, one based on premiums and the other on claims;

Whereas it is desirable to require a minimum guarantee fund related to the size of the risk in the classes undertaken, in order to ensure that undertakings possess adequate resources when they are set up and that in the subsequent course of business the solvency margin shall in no event fall below a minimum of security;

Whereas it is necessary to make provision for the case where the financial condition of the undertaking becomes such that it is difficult for it to meet its underwriting liabilities;

Whereas the co-ordinated rules concerning the taking-up and pursuit of the business or direct insurance within the Community should, in principle, apply to all undertakings entering the market and, consequently, also to agencies and branches where the head office of the undertaking is situated outside the Community; whereas it is, nevertheless, desirable as regards the methods of supervision to make special provision with respect to such agencies or branches in view of the fact that the assets of the undertakings to which they belong are situated outside the Community;

Whereas it is, however, desirable to permit the relaxation of such special conditions, while observing the principle that such agencies and branches should not obtain more favourable treatment than undertakings within the Community;

Whereas certain transitional provisions are required in order, in particular, to permit small and medium-sized undertakings already in existence to adapt themselves to the requirements which must be imposed by the Member States in pursuance of this Directive, subject to the application of Article 53 of the Treaty;

Whereas it is important to guarantee the uniform application of coordinated rules and to provide, in this respect, for close collaboration between the Commission and the Member States in this field;

NOTES

Repealed as noted at the beginning of this Directive.

1 OJ 2, 15.1.62, p 36/62.

2 OJ C27, 28.3.68, p 15.

3 OJ 158, 18.7.67, p 1.

HAS ADOPTED THIS DIRECTIVE—

TITLE I
GENERAL PROVISIONS

[6644]

[Article 1

1. This Directive concerns the taking-up and pursuit of the self-employed activity of direct insurance, including the provision of assistance referred to in paragraph 2, carried on by undertakings which are established in the territory of a Member State or which wish to become established there.

2. The assistance activity shall be the assistance provided for persons who get into difficulties while travelling, while away from their home or while away from their permanent residence. It shall consist in undertaking, against the prior payment of a premium, to make aid immediately available to the beneficiary under an assistance contract where that person is in difficulties following the occurrence of a chance event, in the cases and under the conditions set out in the contract.

The aid may consist in the provision of benefits in cash or in kind. The provision of benefits in *kind may also be effected by means of the staff and equipment of the person providing them.*

The assistance activity does not cover servicing, maintenance, after-sales service or the mere indication or provision of aid as an intermediary.

3. The classification by classes of the activity referred to in this Article appears in the Annex.]

NOTES

Substituted by Council Directive 84/641/EEC, art 1.

Repealed as noted at the beginning of this Directive.

[6645]

Article 2

This Directive does not apply to—

1. The following kinds of insurance—

(a) Life assurance, that is to say, the branch of insurance which comprises, in particular, assurance on survival to a stipulated age only, assurance on death only, assurance on survival to a stipulated age or an earlier death, life assurance with return of premiums, tontines, marriage assurance, and birth assurance;

(b) Annuities;

(c) Supplementary insurance carried on by life-assurance undertakings, that is to say, insurance against personal injury including incapacity for employment, insurance against death resulting from an accident, and insurance against disability resulting from an accident or sickness, where these various kinds of insurance are underwritten in addition to life assurance;

(d) Insurance forming part of a statutory system of social security;

(e) The type of insurance existing in Ireland and the United Kingdom known as "permanent health insurance not subject to cancellation".

2. The following operations—

(a) Capital redemption operations, as defined by the law in each Member State;

(b) Operations of provident and mutual benefit institutions whose benefits vary according to the resources available and in which the contributions of the members are determined on a flat-rate basis;

(c) Operations carried out by organisations not having a legal personality with the purpose of providing mutual cover for their members without there being any payment of premiums or constitution of technical reserves;

[(d) Pending further coordination, export credit insurance operations for the account of or guaranteed by the State, or where the State is the insurer.]

[3. The assistance activity in which liability is limited to the following operations provided in the event of an accident or breakdown involving a road vehicle which normally occurs in the territory of the Member State of the undertaking providing cover—

— an on-the-spot breakdown service for which the undertaking providing cover uses, in most circumstances, its own staff and equipment,

— the conveyance of the vehicle to the nearest or the most appropriate location at which repairs may be carried out and the possible accompaniment, normally by the same means of assistance, of the driver and passengers to the nearest location from where they may continue their journey by other means,

— if provided for by the Member State of the undertaking providing cover, the conveyance of the vehicle, possibly accompanied by the driver or passengers, to their home, point of departure or original destination within the same State,

unless such operations are carried out by an undertaking subject to this Directive.

In the cases referred to in the first two indents, the condition that the accident or breakdown must have happened in the territory of the Member State of the undertaking providing cover—

(a) shall not apply where the latter is a body of which the beneficiary is a member and the breakdown service or conveyance of the vehicle is provided simply on presentation of a membership card, without any additional premium being paid, by a similar body in the country concerned on the basis of a reciprocal agreement;

(b) shall not preclude the provision of such assistance in Ireland and the United Kingdom by a single body operating in both States.

In the circumstances referred to in the third indent, where the accident or the breakdown has occurred in the territory of Ireland, or in the case of the United Kingdom, in the territory of Northern Ireland, the vehicle, possibly accompanied by the driver and passengers, may be conveyed to their home, point of departure or original destination within either territory.

Moreover, the Directive does not concern assistance operations carried out on the occasion of an accident to or the breakdown of a road vehicle and consisting in conveying the vehicle which has been involved in an accident or has broken down outside the territory of the Grand Duchy of Luxembourg, possibly accompanied by the driver and passengers, to their home, where such operations are carried out by the Automobile Club of the Grand Duchy of Luxembourg.

Undertakings subject to this Directive may engage in the activity referred to under this point only if they have received authorisation for class 18 in point A of the Annex without prejudice to point C of the said Annex. In that event this Directive shall apply to the operations in question.]

NOTES

Repealed as noted at the beginning of this Directive.
Para 2: sub-para (d) substituted by Council Directive 87/343/EEC, art 1(1).
Para 3: added by Council Directive 84/641/EEC, art 2.

[6646]
Article 3

[1. This Directive shall not apply to mutual associations which fulfil all the following conditions—

(a) the articles of association must contain provisions for calling up additional contributions or reducing their benefits;

(b) their business does not cover liability risks unless these constitute ancillary cover within the meaning of point C of the Annex or credit and suretyship risks;

(c) the annual contribution income for the activities covered by this Directive must not exceed EUR 5 million; and

(d) at least half of the contribution income from the activities covered by this Directive must come from persons who are members of the mutual association.

This Directive shall not apply to undertakings which fulfil all the following conditions—

— *the undertaking does not pursue any activity falling within the scope of this Directive other than the one described in class 18 in point A of the Annex,*

— *this activity is carried out exclusively on a local basis and consists only of benefits in kind, and*

— *the total annual income collected in respect of the activity of assistance to persons who get into difficulties does not exceed EUR 200 000.*

Nevertheless, the provisions of this Article shall not prevent a mutual insurance undertaking from applying, or continuing, to be licensed under this Directive.]

2. This Directive shall not, moreover, apply to mutual associations which have concluded with other associations of this nature an agreement which provides for the full reinsurance of the insurance policies issued by them or under which the concessionary undertaking is to meet the liabilities arising under such policies in the place of the ceding undertaking.

In such a case the concessionary undertaking shall be subject to the rules of this Directive.

NOTES

Repealed as noted at the beginning of this Directive.
Para 1: substituted by European Parliament and Council Directive 2002/13/EC, art 1(1); for transitional provisions see art 2 thereof at **[6126]**.

[6647]
Article 4

This Directive shall not apply to the following institutions unless their statutes or the law are amended as regards capacity—

(a) In Germany

The following institutions under public law enjoying a monopoly (Monopolanstalten)—

1. *Badische Gebäudeversicherungsanstalt, Karlsruhe,*
2. *Bayerische Landesbrandversicherungsanstalt, Munich,*
3. *Bayerische Landestierversicherungsanstalt, Schlachtviehversicherung, Munich,*
4. *Braunschweigische Landesbrandversicherungsanstalt, Brunswick,*
5. *Hamburger Feuerkasse, Hamburg,*
6. *Hessische Brandversicherungsanstalt (Hessische Brandversicherungskammer), Darmstadt,*
7. *Hessische Brandversicherungsanstalt, Kassel,*
8. *Hohenzollernsche Feuerversicherungsanstalt, Sigmaringen,*
9. *Lippische Landesbrandversicherungsanstalt, Detmold,*
10. *Nassauische Brandversicherungsanstalt, Wiesbaden,*
11. *Oldenburgische Landesbrandkasse, Oldenburg,*
12. *Ostfriesische Landschaftliche Brandkasse, Aurich,*
13. *Feuersozietät Berlin, Berlin,*
14. *Württembergische Gebäudebrandversicherungsanstalt, Stuttgart.*

However, territorial capacity shall not be regarded as modified in the case of a merger between such institutions which has the effect of maintaining for the benefit of the new institution the territorial capacity of the institutions which have merged, nor shall capacity as to the classes of insurance be regarded as modified if one of these institutions takes over in respect of the same territory one or more of the classes of another such institution.

The following semi-public institutions—

1. *Postbeamtenkrankenkasse,*
2. *Krankenversorgung der Bundesbahnbeamten;*

(b) In France

The following institutions—

1. *Caisse départementale des incendiés des Ardennes,*
2. *Caisse départementale des incendiés de la Côte-d'Or,*
3. *Caisse départementale des incendiés de la Marne,*
4. *Caisse départementale des incendiés de la Meuse,*
5. *Caisse départementale des incendiés de la Somme,*
6. *Caisse départementale grêle du Gers,*
7. *Caisse départementale grêle de l'Hérault;*

(c) In Ireland

Voluntary Health Insurance Board;

(d) In Italy

The Cassa di Previdenza per l'assicurazione degli sportivi (Sportass);

(e) In the United Kingdom

The Crown Agents;

[(f) In Denmark

Falcks Redningskorps A/S, København.]

[(g) In Spain

The following institutions—

1. *Comisaría de Seguro Obligatorio de Viajeros,*
2. *Consorcio de Compensación de Seguros,*
3. *Fondo Nacional de Garantía de Riesgos de la Circulación.]*

NOTES

Repealed as noted at the beginning of this Directive.

Para (f): inserted by Council Directive 84/641/EEC, art 4.

Para (g): inserted by the 1985 Act of Accession of the Kingdom of Spain and the Portuguese Republic.

[6648]

Article 5

For the purposes of this Directive—

[(a) "Unit of account" means the European unit of account (EUA) as defined by Commission Decision 3289/75/ECSC.[1] Wherever this Directive refers to the unit of account, the conversion value in national currency to be adopted shall, as from 31 December of each year, be that of the last day of the preceding month of October for which EUA conversion values are available in all the Community currencies;]

(b) "Matching assets" means the representation of underwriting liabilities expressed in a particular currency by assets expressed or realisable in the same currency;

(c) "Localisation of assets" means the existence of assets, whether movable or immovable, within a Member State but shall not be construed as involving a requirement that movable property be deposited or that immovable property be subjected to restrictive measures such as the registration of mortgages. Assets represented by claims against debtors shall be regarded as situated in the Member State where they are to be liquidated.

[(d) "Large risks" means—

(i) risks classified under classes 4, 5, 6, 7, 11 and 12 of Point A of the Annex;

(ii) risks classified under classes 14 and 15 of point A of the Annex, where the policy-holder is engaged professionally in an industrial or commercial activity or in one of the liberal professions, and the risks relate to such activity;

(iii) [risks classified under classes 3, 8, 9, 10, 13 and 16 of point A of the Annex] in so far as the policy-holder exceeds the limits of at least two of the following three criteria—

first stage: until 31 December 1992—

- *balance-sheet total: 12.4 million ECU,*
- *net turnover: 24 million ECU,*
- *average number of employees during the financial year: 500.*

second stage: from 1 January 1993:

— *balance-sheet total: 6.2 million ECU,*

— *net turnover: 12.8 million ECU,*

— *average number of employees during the financial year: 250.*

If the policy-holder belongs to a group of undertakings for which consolidated accounts within the meaning of Directive 83/349/EEC[2] *are drawn up the criteria mentioned above shall be applied on the basis of the consolidated accounts.*

Each Member State may add to the category mentioned under (iii) risks insured by professional associations, joint ventures or temporary groupings.]

NOTES

Repealed as noted at the beginning of this Directive.

Para (a): substituted by Council Directive 76/580/EEC, art 1.

Para (d): added by Council Directive 88/357/EEC, art 5; words in square brackets in sub-para (iii) substituted by Council Directive 90/618/EEC, art 2.

[1] OJ L327, 19.12.75, p 4.

[2] OJ L193, 18.7.83, p 1.

TITLE II
RULES APPLICABLE TO UNDERTAKINGS WHOSE HEAD OFFICES ARE SITUATED WITHIN THE COMMUNITY

SECTION A:
CONDITIONS OF ADMISSION

[6649]
[Article 6

The taking up of the business of direct insurance shall be subject to prior official authorisation.

Such authorisation shall be sought from the competent authorities of the home Member State by—

(a) *any undertaking which establishes its head office within the territory of that State;*

(b) *any undertaking which, having received the authorisation referred to in the first subparagraph, extends its business to an entire class or to other classes.]*

NOTES

Substituted by Council Directive 92/49/EEC, art 4.

Repealed as noted at the beginning of this Directive.

[6650]
[Article 7

1. Authorisation shall be valid for the entire Community. It shall permit an undertaking to carry on business there, under either the right of establishment or the freedom to provide services.

2. Authorisation shall be granted for a particular class of insurance. It shall cover the entire class, unless the applicant wishes to cover only some of the risks pertaining to that class, as listed in point A of the Annex.

However—

(a) *Member States may grant authorisation for the groups of classes listed in point B of the Annex, attaching to them the appropriate denominations specified therein;*

(b) *authorisation granted for one class or a group of classes shall also be valid for the purpose of covering ancillary risks included in another class if the conditions imposed in point C of the Annex are fulfilled.]*

NOTES

Substituted by Council Directive 92/49/EEC, art 5.

Repealed as noted at the beginning of this Directive.

[6651]
[Article 8

1. The home Member State shall require every insurance undertaking for which authorisation is sought to—

(a) *adopt one of the following forms—*

— *in the case of the Kingdom of Belgium: "société anonyme/naamloze vennootschap", "société en commandite par actions/commanditaire vennootschap op aandelen", "association d'assurance mutuelle/ onderlinge verzekeringsvereniging", "société coopérative/coöperatieve vennootschap";*

— *in the case of the Kingdom of Denmark: "aktieselskaber", "gensidige selskaber"*

— *in the case of the Federal Republic of Germany: "Aktiengesellschaft", "Versicherungsverein auf Gegenseitigkeit", "Öffentlich-rechtliches Wettbewerbsversicherungsunternehmen";*

— *in the case of the French Republic: "société anonyme", "société d'assurance mutuelle", "institution de prévoyance régie par le code de la sécurité sociale", "institution de prévoyance régie par le code rural" and "mutuelles régies par le code de la mutualité";*

— *in the case of Ireland: incorporated companies limited by shares or by guarantee or unlimited;*

— *in the case of the Italian Republic: "società per azioni", "società cooperativa", "mutua di assicurazione";*

— *in the case of the Grand Duchy of Luxembourg: "société anonyme", "société en commandite par actions", "association d'assurances mutuelles", "société coopérative";*

— *in the case of the Kingdom of the Netherlands: "naamloze vennootschap", "onderlinge waarborgmaatschappij";*

— *in the case of the United Kingdom: incorporated companies limited by shares or by guarantee or unlimited, societies registered under the Industrial and Provident Societies Acts, societies registered under the Friendly Societies Acts, the association of underwriters known as Lloyd's;*

— *in the case of the Hellenic Republic:* "ανωνυμη εταιρια" "αλληλασφαλιστικος συνεταιρισμος"

— *in the case of the Kingdom of Spain: "sociedad anónima", "sociedad mutua", "sociedad cooperativa";*

— *in the case of the Portuguese Republic: "sociedade anónima", "mútua de seguros"*

[— *in the case of the Republic of Austria: Aktiengesellschaft, Versicherungsverein auf Gegenseitigkeit*

— *in the case of the Republic of Finland: keskinäinen vakuutusyhtiö/ömsesidigit försäkringsbolag, vakuutusosakeyhtiö/försäkringsaktiebolag, vakuutusyhdistys/ försäkringförening*

— *in the case of the Kingdom of Sweden: "försäkringsaktiebolag," "ömsesidiga försäkringbolag", "understödsföreningar".]*

[— *in the case of the Czech Republic: "akciová společnost", "družstvo";*

— *in the case of the Republic of Estonia: "aktsiaselts";*

— *in the case of the Republic of Cyprus:* "Εταιρε α περιορισμνης ευθνης με μετοχς εταιρε α περιορισμνης ευθνης χωρ ς μετοχικ κεφ λαιο";

— *in the case of the Republic of Latvia: "apdrošināšanas akciju sabiedrība", "savstarpējās apdrošināšanas kooperatīvā biedrība";*

— *in the case of the Republic of Lithuania: "akcins bendrovs", "uždarosios akcins bendrovs";*

— *in the case of the Republic of Hungary: "biztosító részvénytársaság", "biztosító szövetkezet", "biztosító egyesület", "külföldi székhely biztosító magyarországi fióktelepe";*

— *in the case of the Republic of Malta: "kumpanija pubblika", "kumpanija private", "ferga", "Korp ta' l- Assikurazzjoni Rikonnoxxut";*

— *in the case of the Republic of Poland: "spółka akcyjna", "towarzystwo ubezpieczeń wzajemnych";*

— *in the case of the Republic of Slovenia: "delniška družba", "družba za vzajemno zavarovanje";*

— *in the case of the Slovak Republic: "akciová spoločnos';]*

[— *in the case of Bulgaria:* "акционерно дружество"

— *in the case of Romania: "societăi pe aciuni", "societăi mutuale"]*

An insurance undertaking may also adopt the form of a European Company (SE) when that has been established.

Furthermore, Member States may, where appropriate, set up undertakings in any public-law form provided that such bodies have as their objects insurance operations under conditions equivalent to those under which private-law undertakings operate;

(b) *limit its objects to the business of insurance and operations arising directly therefrom, to the exclusion of all other commercial business;*

(c) *submit a scheme of operations in accordance with Article 9;*

(d) *possess the minimum guarantee fund provided for in Article 17(2);*

(e) *be effectively run by persons of good repute with appropriate professional qualifications or experience.*

[(f) *communicate the name and address of the claims representative appointed in each Member State other than the Member State in which the authorisation is sought if the risks to be covered are classified in class 10 of point A of the Annex, other than carrier's liability.]*

[Moreover, where close links exist between the insurance undertaking and other natural or legal persons, the competent authorities shall grant authorisation only if those links do not prevent the effective exercise of their supervisory functions.

The competent authorities shall also refuse authorisation if the laws, regulations or administrative provisions of a non-member country governing one or more natural or legal persons with which the undertaking has close links, or difficulties involved in their enforcement, prevent the effective exercise of their supervisory functions.

The competent authorities shall require insurance undertakings to provide them with the information they require to monitor compliance with the conditions referred to in this paragraph on a continuous basis.]

[1a. Member States shall require that the head offices of insurance undertakings be situated in the same Member State as their registered offices.]

2. An undertaking seeking authorisation to extend its business to other classes or to extend an authorisation covering only some of the risks pertaining to one class shall be required to submit a scheme of operations in accordance with Article 9.

It shall, furthermore, be required to show proof that it possesses the solvency margin provided for in Article 16 and, if with regard to such other classes Article 17(2) requires a higher minimum guarantee fund than before, that is possesses that minimum.

3. Nothing in this Directive shall prevent Member States from maintaining in force or introducing laws, regulations or administrative provisions requiring approval of the memorandum and articles of association and communication of any other documents necessary for the normal exercise of supervision.

Member States shall not, however, adopt provisions requiring the prior approval or systematic notification of general and special policy conditions, scales of premiums and forms and other printed documents which an undertaking intends to use in its dealings with policyholders.

Member States may not retain or introduce prior notification or approval of proposed increases in premium rates except as part of general price-control systems.

Nothing in this Directive shall prevent Member States from subjecting undertakings seeking or having obtained authorisation for class 18 in point A of the Annex to checks on their direct or indirect resources in staff and equipment, including the qualification of their medical teams and the quality of the equipment available to such undertakings to meet their commitments arising out of this class of insurance.

4. The abovementioned provisions may not require that any application for authorisation be considered in the light of the economic requirements of the market.]

NOTES

Substituted by Council Directive 92/49/EEC, art 6.

Repealed as noted at the beginning of this Directive.

Para 1: in sub-para (a), entries relating to Austria, Finland and Sweden in first pair of square brackets inserted by the 1994 Act of Accession of the Kingdom of Norway, the Republic of Austria, the Republic of Finland and the Kingdom of Sweden, Annex I(XI)(B)(II)(1), as adapted by Council Decision 95/1/EC, Annex I(XI)(B)(II)(1), entries in second pair of square brackets inserted by the 2003 Act concerning the conditions of accession of the Czech Republic, the Republic of Estonia, the Republic of Cyprus, the Republic of Latvia, the Republic of Lithuania, the Republic of Hungary, the Republic of Malta, the Republic of Poland, the Republic of Slovenia and the Slovak Republic and the adjustments to the Treaties on which the European Union is founded, and entries relating to Bulgaria and Romania in third pair of square brackets inserted by Council Directive 2006/101/EC, art 1, Annex, para 1; sub-para (f) added by Council Directive 2000/26/EC, art 8(a); words in final pair of square brackets inserted by Council Directive 95/26/EC, art 2(2).

Para 1a: inserted by Council Directive 95/26/EC, art 3(1).

[6652]

[Article 9

The scheme of operations referred to in Article 8(1)(c) shall include particulars or proof concerning—

- (a) *the nature of the risks which the undertaking proposes to cover;*
- (b) *the guiding principles as to reinsurance;*
- (c) *the items constituting the minimum guarantee fund;*
- (d) *estimates of the costs of setting up the administrative services and the organisation for securing business; the financial resources intended to meet those costs and, if the risks to be covered are classified in class 18 in point A of the Annex, the resources at the undertaking's disposal for the provision of the assistance promised*

and, in addition, for the first three financial years—

- (e) *estimates of management expenses other than installation costs, in particular current general expenses and commissions;*
- (f) *estimates of premiums or contributions and claims;*
- (g) *a forecast balance sheet;*
- (h) *estimates of the financial resources intended to cover underwriting liabilities and the solvency margin.]*

NOTES

Substituted by Council Directive 92/49/EEC, art 7.
Repealed as noted at the beginning of this Directive.

[6653]
[Article 10

1. An insurance undertaking that proposes to establish a branch within the territory of another Member State shall notify the competent authorities of its home Member State.

2. The Member States shall require every insurance undertaking that proposes to establish a branch within the territory of another Member State to provide the following information when effecting the notification provided for in paragraph 1—

- (a) *the Member State within the territory of which it proposes to establish a branch;*
- (b) *a scheme of operations setting out, inter alia,* the types of business envisaged and the structural organisation of the branch;
- (c) *the address in the Member State of the branch from which documents may be obtained and to which they may be delivered, it being understood that that address shall be the one to which all communications to the authorised agent are sent;*
- (d) *the name of the branch's authorised agent, who must possess sufficient powers to bind the undertaking in relation to third parties and to represent it in relations with the authorities and courts of the Member State of the branch. With regard to Lloyd's, in the event of any litigation in the Member State of the branch arising out of underwritten commitments, the insured persons must not be treated less favourably than if the litigation had been brought against businesses of a conventional type. The authorised agent must, therefore, possess sufficient powers for proceedings to be taken against him and must in that capacity be able to bind the Lloyd's underwriters concerned.*

Where the undertaking intends its branch to cover risks in class 10 of point A of the Annex, not including carrier's liability, it must produce a declaration that it has become a member of the national bureau and the national guarantee fund of the Member State of the branch.

3. Unless the competent authorities of the home Member State have reason to doubt the adequacy of the administrative structure or the financial situation of the insurance undertaking or the good repute and professional qualifications or experience of the directors or managers or the authorised agent, taking into account the business planned, they shall within three months of receiving all the information referred to in paragraph 2 communicate that information to the competent authorities of the Member State of the branch and shall inform the undertaking concerned accordingly.

The competent authorities of the home Member State shall also attest that the insurance undertaking has the minimum solvency margin calculated in accordance with Articles 16 and 17.

Where the competent authorities of the home Member State refuse to communicate the information referred to in paragraph 2 to the competent authorities of the Member State of the branch they shall give the reasons for their refusal to the undertaking concerned within three months of receiving all the information in question. That refusal or failure to act may be subject to a right to apply to the courts in the home Member State.

4. Before the branch of an insurance undertaking starts business, the competent authorities of the Member State of the branch shall, within two months of receiving the information referred to in paragraph 3, inform the competent authority of the home Member State, if appropriate, of the conditions under which, in the interest of the general good, that business must be carried on in the Member State of the branch.

5. On receiving a communication from the competent authorities of the Member State of the branch or, if no communication is received from them, on expiry of the period provided for in paragraph 4, the branch may be established and start business.

6. In the event of a change in any of the particulars communicated under paragraph 2(b), (c) or (d), an insurance undertaking shall give written notice of the change to the competent authorities of the home Member State and of the Member State of the branch at least one month before making the change so that the competent authorities of the home Member State and the competent authorities of the Member State of the branch may fulfil their respective roles under paragraphs 3 and 4.]

NOTES

Substituted by Council Directive 92/49/EEC, art 32.

Repealed as noted at the beginning of this Directive.

Article 11 (*Repealed by Council Directive 92/49/EEC, art 33.*)

[6654]

Article 12

Any decision to refuse an authorisation shall be accompanied by the precise grounds for doing so and notified to the undertaking in question.

Each Member State shall make provision for a right to apply to the courts should there be any refusal.

Such provision shall also be made with regard to cases where the competent authorities have not dealt with an application for an authorisation upon the expiry of a period of six months from the date of its receipt.

NOTES

Repealed as noted at the beginning of this Directive.

[6655]

[Article 12a

[1. The competent authorities of the other Member State involved shall be consulted prior to the granting of an authorisation to a non-life insurance undertaking, which is:

(a) a subsidiary of an insurance or reinsurance undertaking authorised in another Member State; or

(b) a subsidiary of the parent undertaking of an insurance or reinsurance undertaking authorised in another Member State; or

(c) controlled by the same person, whether natural or legal, who controls an insurance or reinsurance undertaking authorised in another Member State.

2. The competent authority of a Member State involved responsible for the supervision of credit institutions or investment firms shall be consulted prior to the granting of an authorisation to a non-life insurance undertaking which is:

(a) a subsidiary of a credit institution or investment firm authorised in the Community; or

(b) a subsidiary of the parent undertaking of a credit institution or investment firm authorised in the Community; or

(c) controlled by the same person, whether natural or legal, who controls a credit institution or investment firm authorised in the Community.]

3. The relevant competent authorities referred to in paragraphs 1 and 2 shall in particular consult each other when assessing the suitability of the shareholders and the reputation and experience of directors involved in the management of another entity of the same group. They shall inform each other of any information regarding the suitability of shareholders and the reputation and experience of directors which is of relevance to the other competent authorities involved for the granting of an authorisation as well as for the ongoing assessment of compliance with operating conditions.]

NOTES

Inserted by European Parliament and Council Directive 2002/87/EC, art 22(1).

Repealed as noted at the beginning of this Directive.

Paras 1, 2: substituted by European Parliament and Council Directive 2005/68/EC, art 57(1).

SECTION B:
CONDITIONS FOR EXERCISE OF BUSINESS

[6656]
[Article 13

1. The financial supervision of an insurance undertaking, including that of the business it carries on either through branches or under the freedom to provide services, shall be the sole responsibility of the home Member State.

2. That financial supervision shall include verification, with respect to the insurance undertaking's entire business, of its state of solvency, of the establishment of technical provisions and of the assets covering them in accordance with the rules laid down or practices followed in the home Member State under provisions adopted at Community level.

Where the undertaking in question is authorised to cover the risks classified in class 18 in point A of the Annex, supervision shall extend to monitoring of the technical resources which the undertaking has at its disposal for the purpose of carrying out the assistance operations it has undertaken to perform, where the law of the home Member State provides for the monitoring of such resources.

[The home Member State of the insurance undertaking shall not refuse a reinsurance contract concluded by the insurance undertaking with a reinsurance undertaking authorised in accordance with Directive 2005/68/EC of the European Parliament and of the Council of 16 November 2005 on reinsurance[1] or an insurance undertaking authorised in accordance with this Directive or Directive 2002/83/EC of the European Parliament and of the Council of 5 November 2002 concerning life assurance,[2] on grounds directly related to the financial soundness of the reinsurance undertaking or the insurance undertaking.]

3. The competent authorities of the home Member State shall require every insurance undertaking to have sound administrative and accounting procedures and adequate internal control mechanisms.]

NOTES

Substituted by Council Directive 92/49/EEC, art 9.

Repealed as noted at the beginning of this Directive.

Para 2: words in square brackets inserted by European Parliament and Council Directive 2005/68/EC, art 57(2).

1 OJ L323, 9.12.2005, p 1.

2 OJ L345, 19.12.2002, p 1. Directive as last amended by Directive 2005/1/EC (OJ L79, 24.3.2005, p 9).

[6657]
[Article 14

The Member State of the branch shall provide that where an insurance undertaking authorised in another Member State carries on business through a branch the competent authorities of the home Member State may, after having informed the competent authorities of the Member State of the branch, carry out themselves or through the intermediary of persons they appoint for that purpose on-the-spot verification of the information necessary to ensure the financial supervision of the undertaking. The authorities of the Member State of the branch may participate in that verification.]

NOTES

Substituted by Council Directive 92/49/EEC, art 10.

Repealed as noted at the beginning of this Directive.

[6658]
[Article 15

1. The home Member State shall require every insurance undertaking to establish adequate technical provisions in respect of its entire business.

The amount of such technical provisions shall be determined in accordance with the rules laid down in Directive 91/674/EEC.

[2. The home Member State shall require every insurance undertaking to cover the technical provisions and the equalisation reserve referred to in Article 15a of this Directive by matching assets in accordance with Article 6 of Directive 88/357/EEC. In respect of risks situated within the Community, those assets must be localised within the Community. Member States shall not require insurance undertakings to localise their assets in any particular Member State. The home Member State may, however, allow the rules on the localisation of assets to be relaxed.

3. Member States shall not retain or introduce for the establishment of technical provisions a system of gross reserving which requires pledging of assets to cover unearned premiums and outstanding claims provisions by the reinsurer, when the reinsurer is a reinsurance undertaking authorised in accordance with Directive 2005/68/EC or an insurance undertaking authorised in accordance with this Directive or Directive 2002/83/EC.

When the home Member State allows any technical provisions to be covered by claims against a reinsurer which is neither a reinsurance undertaking authorised in accordance with Directive 2005/68/EC nor an insurance undertaking authorised in accordance with this Directive or Directive 2002/83/EC, it shall set the conditions for accepting such claims.]]

NOTES

Substituted by Council Directive 92/49/EEC, art 17.
Repealed as noted at the beginning of this Directive.
Paras 2, 3: substituted by European Parliament and Council Directive 2005/68/EC, art 57(3).

[6659]
[Article 15a

1. Member States shall require every insurance undertaking with a head office within their territories which underwrites risks included in class 14 in point A of the Annex (hereinafter referred to as "credit insurance") to set up an equalisation reserve for the purpose of offsetting any technical deficit or above-average claims ration arising in that class in any financial year.

2. The equalisation reserve shall be calculated in accordance with the rules laid down by the home Member State in accordance with one of the four methods set out in point D of the Annex, which shall be regarded as equivalent.

3. Up to the amount calculated in accordance with the methods set out in point D of the Annex, the equalisation reserve shall be disregarded for the purpose of calculating the solvency margin.

4. Member States may exempt insurance undertakings with head offices within their territories from the obligation to set up equalisation reserves for credit insurance business where the premiums or contributions receivable in respect of credit insurance are less than 4% of the total premiums or contributions receivable by them and less than ECU 2 500 000.]

NOTES

Inserted by Council Directive 87/343/EEC, art 1(3); substituted by Council Directive 92/49/EEC, art 18.
Repealed as noted at the beginning of this Directive.

[6660]
[Article 16

1. Each Member State shall require of every insurance undertaking whose head office is situated in its territory an adequate available solvency margin in respect of its entire business at all times, which is at least equal to the requirements in this Directive.

2. The available solvency margin shall consist of the assets of the insurance undertaking free of any foreseeable liabilities, less any intangible items, including—

- *(a) the paid-up share capital or, in the case of a mutual insurance undertaking, the effective initial fund plus any members' accounts which meet all the following criteria—*
  - *(i) the memorandum and articles of association must stipulate that payments may be made from these accounts to members only in so far as this does not cause the available solvency margin to fall below the required level, or, after the dissolution of the undertaking, if all the undertaking's other debts have been settled;*
  - *(ii) the memorandum and articles of association must stipulate, with respect to any payments referred to in point (i) for reasons other than the individual termination of membership, that the competent authorities must be notified at least one month in advance and can prohibit the payment within that period;*
  - *(iii) the relevant provisions of the memorandum and articles of association may be amended only after the competent authorities have declared that they have no objection to the amendment, without prejudice to the criteria stated in points (i) and (ii);*
- *[(b) reserves (statutory and free reserves) which neither correspond to underwriting liabilities nor are classified as equalisation reserves;]*
- *(c) the profit or loss brought forward after deduction of dividends to be paid.*

The available solvency margin shall be reduced by the amount of own shares directly held by the insurance undertaking.

For those insurance undertakings which discount or reduce their technical provisions for claims outstanding to take account of investment income as permitted by Article 60(1)(g) of Council

Directive 91/674/EEC of 19 December 1991 on the annual accounts and consolidated accounts of insurance undertakings,[1] the available solvency margin shall be reduced by the difference between the undiscounted technical provisions or technical provisions before deductions as disclosed in the notes on the accounts, and the discounted or technical provisions after deductions. This adjustment shall be made for all risks listed in point A of the Annex, except for risks listed under classes 1 and 2. For classes other than 1 and 2, no adjustment need be made in respect of the discounting of annuities included in technical provisions.

[[The available solvency margin shall also be reduced by the following items:

(a) participations which the insurance undertaking holds in:

- *insurance undertakings within the meaning of Article 6 of this Directive, Article 4 of Directive 2002/83/EC, or Article 1(b) of Directive 98/78/EC of the European Parliament and of the Council,*
- *reinsurance undertakings within the meaning of Article 3 of Directive 2005/68/EC or non-member country reinsurance undertakings within the meaning of Article 1(l) of Directive 98/78/EC,*
- *insurance holding companies within the meaning of Article 1(i) of Directive 98/78/EC,*
- *credit institutions and financial institutions within the meaning of Article 1(1) and (5) of Directive 2000/12/EC of the European Parliament and of the Council,*
- *investment firms and financial institutions within the meaning of Article 1(2) of Council Directive 93/22/EEC and of Article 2(4) and (7) of Council Directive 93/6/EEC.]*

(b) each of the following items which the insurance undertaking holds in respect of the entities defined in (a) in which it holds a participation:

- *instruments referred to in paragraph 3,*
- *instruments referred to in Article 18(3) of Directive 79/267/EEC,*
- *subordinated claims and instruments referred to in Article 35 and Article 36(3) of Directive 2000/12/EC.*

Where shares in another credit institution, investment firm, financial institution, insurance or reinsurance undertaking or insurance holding company are held temporarily for the purposes of a financial assistance operation designed to reorganise and save that entity, the competent authority may waive the provisions on deduction referred to under (a) and (b) of the fourth subparagraph.

As an alternative to the deduction of the items referred to in (a) and (b) of the fourth subparagraph which the insurance undertaking holds in credit institutions, investment firms and financial institutions, Member States may allow their insurance undertakings to apply mutatis mutandis methods 1, 2, or 3 of Annex I to Directive 2002/87/EC of the European Parliament and of the Council of 16 December 2002 on the supplementary supervision of credit institutions, insurance undertakings and investment firms in a financial conglomerate.[2] Method 1 (Accounting consolidation) shall only be applied if the competent authority is confident about the level of integrated management and internal control regarding the entities which would be included in the scope of consolidation. The method chosen shall be applied in a consistent manner overtime.

Member States may provide that, for the calculation of the solvency margin as provided for by this Directive, insurance undertakings subject to supplementary supervision in accordance with Directive 98/78/EC or to supplementary supervision in accordance with Directive 2002/87/EC, need not deduct the items referred to in (a) and (b) of the fourth subparagraph which are held in credit institutions, investment firms, financial institutions, insurance or reinsurance undertakings or insurance holding companies which are included in the supplementary supervision.

For the purposes of the deduction of participations referred to in this paragraph, participation shall mean a participation within the meaning of Article 1(f) of Directive 98/78/EC.]

3. The available solvency margin may also consist of—

(a) cumulative preferential share capital and subordinated loan capital up to 50% of the lesser of the available solvency margin and the required solvency margin, no more than 25% of which shall consist of subordinated loans with a fixed maturity, or fixed-term cumulative preferential share capital, provided in the event of the bankruptcy or liquidation of the insurance undertaking, binding agreements exist under which the subordinated loan capital or preferential share capital ranks after the claims of all other creditors and is not to be repaid until all other debts outstanding at the time have been settled.

Subordinated loan capital must also fulfil the following conditions—

(i) only fully paid-up funds may be taken into account;

(ii) for loans with a fixed maturity, the original maturity must be at least five years. No later than one year before the repayment date the insurance undertaking must submit to the competent authorities for their approval a plan showing how the available solvency margin will be kept at or brought to the required level at maturity, unless the extent to which the loan may rank as a component of the available solvency margin is gradually reduced during at least the last five years before the repayment date. The competent authorities may authorise the early repayment of such loans provided application is made by the issuing insurance undertaking and its available solvency margin will not fall below the required level;

(iii) loans the maturity of which is not fixed must be repayable only subject to five years' notice unless the loans are no longer considered as a component of the available solvency margin or unless the prior consent of the competent authorities is specifically required for early repayment. In the latter event the insurance undertaking must notify the competent authorities at least six months before the date of the proposed repayment, specifying the available solvency margin and the required solvency margin both before and after that repayment. The competent authorities shall authorise repayment only if the insurance undertaking's available solvency margin will not fall below the required level;

(iv) the loan agreement must not include any clause providing that in specified circumstances, other than the winding-up of the insurance undertaking, the debt will become repayable before the agreed repayment dates;

(v) the loan agreement may be amended only after the competent authorities have declared that they have no objection to the amendment;

(b) securities with no specified maturity date and other instruments, including cumulative preferential shares other than those mentioned in point (a), up to 50% of the lesser of the available solvency margin and the required solvency margin for the total of such securities and the subordinated loan capital referred to in point (a) provided they fulfil the following—

(i) they may not be repaid on the initiative of the bearer or without the prior consent of the competent authority;

(ii) the contract of issue must enable the insurance undertaking to defer the payment of interest on the loan;

(iii) the lender's claims on the insurance undertaking must rank entirely after those of all non-subordinated creditors;

(iv) the documents governing the issue of the securities must provide for the loss-absorption capacity of the debt and unpaid interest, while enabling the insurance undertaking to continue its business;

(v) only fully paid-up amounts may be taken into account.

4. Upon application, with supporting evidence, by the undertaking to the competent authority of the home Member State and with the agreement of that competent authority, the available solvency margin may also consist of—

(a) one half of the unpaid share capital or initial fund, once the paid-up part amounts to 25% of that share capital or fund, up to 50% of the lesser of the available solvency margin and the required solvency margin;

(b) in the case of mutual or mutual-type association with variable contributions, any claim which it has against its members by way of a call for supplementary contribution, within the financial year, up to one half of the difference between the maximum contributions and the contributions actually called in, and subject to a limit of 50% of the lesser of the available solvency margin and the required solvency margin. The competent national authorities shall establish guidelines laying down the conditions under which supplementary contributions may be accepted;

(c) any hidden net reserves arising out of the valuation of assets, in so far as such hidden net reserves are not of an exceptional nature.

5. Amendments to paragraphs 2, 3 and 4 to take into account developments that justify a technical adjustment of the elements eligible for the available solvency margin, shall be adopted in accordance with the procedure laid down in Article 2 of Council Directive 91/675/EEC.[3]]

NOTES

Substituted by European Parliament and Council Directive 2002/13/EC, art 1(2); for transitional provisions see art 2 thereof at **[6126]**.

Repealed as noted at the beginning of this Directive.

Para 2: words in first and third (inner) pairs of square brackets substituted by European Parliament and Council Directive 2005/68/EC, art 57(4); words in second (outer) pair of square brackets substituted by European Parliament and Council Directive 2002/87/EC, art 22(2).

[1] OJ L374, 31.12.1991, p 7.

[2] OJ L35, 11.2.2003.

[3] OJ L374, 31.12.1991, p 32.

[6661]
[Article 16a

1. The required solvency margin shall be determined on the basis either of the annual amount of premiums or contributions, or of the average burden of claims for the past three financial years.

In the case, however, of insurance undertakings which essentially underwrite only one or more of the risks of credit, storm, hail or frost, the last seven financial years shall be taken as the reference period for the average burden of claims.

2. Subject to Article 17, the amount of the required solvency margin shall be equal to the higher of the two results as set out in paragraphs 3 and 4.

3. The premium basis shall be calculated using the higher of gross written premiums or contributions as calculated below, and gross earned premiums or contributions.

Premiums or contributions in respect of the classes 11, 12 and 13 listed in point A of the Annex shall be increased by 50%.

The premiums or contributions (inclusive of charges ancillary to premiums or contributions) due in respect of direct business in the last financial year shall be aggregated.

To this sum there shall be added the amount of premiums accepted for all reinsurance in the last financial year.

From this sum there shall then be deducted the total amount of premiums or contributions cancelled in the last financial year, as well as the total amount of taxes and levies pertaining to the premiums or contributions entering into the aggregate.

The amount so obtained shall be divided into two portions, the first portion extending up to EUR 50 million, the second comprising the excess; 18% and 16% of these portions respectively shall be calculated and added together.

[The sum so obtained shall be multiplied by the ratio existing in respect of the sum of the last three financial years between the amount of claims remaining to be borne by the undertaking after deduction of amounts recoverable under reinsurance and the gross amount of claims; that ratio may in no case be less than 50%. Upon application, with supporting evidence, by the insurance undertaking to the competent authority of the home Member State and with the agreement of that authority, amounts recoverable from special purpose vehicles referred to in Article 46 of Directive 2005/68/EC may be deducted as reinsurance.]

With the approval of the competent authorities, statistical methods may be used to allocate the premiums or contributions in respect of the classes 11, 12 and 13.

4. The claims basis shall be calculated, as follows, using in respect of the classes 11, 12 and 13 listed in point A of the Annex, claims, provisions and recoveries increased by 50%.

The amounts of claims paid in respect of direct business (without any deduction of claims borne by reinsurers and retrocessionaires) in the periods specified in paragraph 1 shall be aggregated.

To this sum there shall be added the amount of claims paid in respect of reinsurances or retrocessions accepted during the same periods and the amount of provisions for claims outstanding established at the end of the last financial year both for direct business and for reinsurance acceptances.

From this sum there shall be deducted the amount of recoveries effected during the periods specified in paragraph 1.

From the sum then remaining, there shall be deducted the amount of provisions for claims outstanding established at the commencement of the second financial year preceding the last financial year for which there are accounts, both for direct business and for reinsurance acceptances. If the period of reference established in paragraph 1 equals seven years, the amount of provisions for claims outstanding established at the commencement of the sixth financial year preceding the last financial year for which there are accounts shall be deducted.

One-third, or one-seventh, of the amount so obtained, according to the period of reference established in paragraph 1, shall be divided into two portions, the first extending up to EUR 35 million and the second comprising the excess; 26% and 23% of these portions respectively shall be calculated and added together.

[The sum so obtained shall be multiplied by the ratio existing in respect of the sum of the last three financial years between the amount of claims remaining to be borne by the undertaking after

deduction of amounts recoverable under reinsurance and the gross amount of claims; that ratio may in no case be less than 50%. Upon application, with supporting evidence, by the insurance undertaking to the competent authority of the home Member State and with the agreement of that authority, amounts recoverable from special purpose vehicles referred to in Article 46 of Directive 2005/68/EC may be deducted as reinsurance.]

With the approval of the competent authorities, statistical methods may be used to allocate the claims, provisions and recoveries in respect of the classes 11, 12 and 13. In the case of the risks listed under class 18 in point A of the Annex, the amount of claims paid used to calculate the claims basis shall be the costs borne by the insurance undertaking in respect of assistance given. Such costs shall be calculated in accordance with the national provisions of the home Member State.

5. If the required solvency margin as calculated in paragraphs 2, 3 and 4 is lower than the required solvency margin of the year before, the required solvency margin shall be at least equal to the required solvency margin of the year before multiplied by the ratio of the amount of the technical provisions for claims outstanding at the end of the last financial year and the amount of the technical provisions for claims outstanding at the beginning of the last financial year. In these calculations technical provisions shall be calculated net of reinsurance but the ratio may in no case be higher than 1.

6. The fractions applicable to the portions referred to in the sixth subparagraph of paragraph 3 and the sixth subparagraph of paragraph 4 shall each be reduced to a third in the case of health insurance practised on a similar technical basis to that of life assurance, if—

- *(a) the premiums paid are calculated on the basis of sickness tables according to the mathematical method applied in insurance;*
- *(b) a provision is set up for increasing age;*
- *(c) an additional premium is collected in order to set up a safety margin of an appropriate amount;*
- *(d) the insurance undertaking may cancel the contract before the end of the third year of insurance at the latest;*
- *(e) the contract provides for the possibility of increasing premiums or reducing payments even for current contracts.]*

NOTES

Inserted by European Parliament and Council Directive 2002/13/EC, art 1(3); for transitional provisions see art 2 thereof at **[6126]**.

Repealed as noted at the beginning of this Directive.

Paras 3, 4: words in square brackets substituted by European Parliament and Council Directive 2005/68/EC, art 57(5).

[6662]
[Article 17

1. One third of the required solvency margin as specified in Article 16a shall constitute the guarantee fund. This fund shall consist of the items listed in Article 16(2), (3) and, with the agreement of the competent authority of the home Member State, (4)(c).

2. The guarantee fund may not be less than EUR 2 million. Where, however, all or some of the risks included in one of the classes 10 to 15 listed in point A of the Annex are covered, it shall be EUR 3 million.

Any Member State may provide for a one-fourth reduction of the minimum guarantee fund in the case of mutual associations and mutual-type associations.]

NOTES

Substituted by European Parliament and Council Directive 2002/13/EC, art 1(4); for transitional provisions see art 2 thereof at **[6126]**.

Repealed as noted at the beginning of this Directive.

[6663]
[Article 17a

1. The amounts in euro as laid down in Article 16a(3) and (4) and Article 17(2) shall be reviewed annually starting 20 September 2003 in order to take account of changes in the European index of consumer prices comprising all Member States as published by Eurostat.

The amounts shall be adapted automatically by increasing the base amount in euro by the percentage change in that index over the period between the entry into force of this Directive and the review date and rounded up to a multiple of EUR 100 000.

If the percentage change since the last adaptation is less than 5%, no adaptation shall take place.

2. The Commission shall inform annually the European Parliament and the Council of the review and the adapted amounts referred to in paragraph 1.]

NOTES

Inserted by European Parliament and Council Directive 2002/13/EC, art 1(5); for transitional provisions see art 2 thereof at **[6126]**.

Repealed as noted at the beginning of this Directive.

[6664]
[Article 17b

1. Each Member State shall require that an insurance undertaking whose head office is situated within its territory and which conducts reinsurance activities establishes, in respect of its entire business, a minimum guarantee fund in accordance with Article 40 of Directive 2005/68/EC, where one of the following conditions is met:

- *(a) the reinsurance premiums collected exceed 10% of its total premium;*
- *(b) the reinsurance premiums collected exceed EUR 50 000 000;*
- *(c) the technical provisions resulting from its reinsurance acceptances exceed 10% of its total technical provisions.*

2. Each Member State may choose to apply to such insurance undertakings as are referred to in paragraph 1 of this Article and whose head office is situated within its territory the provisions of Article 34 of Directive 2005/68/EC in respect of their reinsurance acceptance activities, where one of the conditions laid down in the said paragraph 1 is met.

In that case, the relevant Member State shall require that all assets employed by the insurance undertaking to cover the technical provisions corresponding to its reinsurance acceptances shall be ring-fenced, managed and organised separately from the direct insurance activities of the insurance undertaking, without any possibility of transfer. In such a case, and only as far as their reinsurance acceptance activities are concerned, insurance undertakings shall not be subject to Articles 20, 21 and 22 of Directive 92/49/EEC[1] and Annex I to Directive 88/357/EEC.

Each Member State shall ensure that their competent authorities verify the separation provided for in the second subparagraph.

3. If the Commission decides, pursuant to Article 56(c) of Directive 2005/68/EC to increase the amounts used for the calculation of the required solvency margin provided for in Article 37(3) and (4) of that Directive, each Member State shall apply to such insurance undertakings as are referred to in paragraph 1 of this Article the provisions of Articles 35 to 39 of that Directive in respect of their reinsurance acceptance activities.]

NOTES

Inserted by European Parliament and Council Directive 2005/68/EC, art 57(6).

Repealed as noted at the beginning of this Directive.

1 Council Directive 92/49/EEC of 18 June 1992 on the coordination of laws, regulations and administrative provisions relating to direct insurance other than life assurance (third non-life insurance Directive) (OJ L228, 11.8.1992, p 1). Directive as last amended by Directive 2005/1/EC.

[6665]
[Article 18

1. Member States shall not prescribe any rules as to the choice of the assets that need not be used as cover for the technical provisions referred to in Article 15.

2. Subject to Article 15(2), Article 20(1), (2), (3) and (5) and the last subparagraph of Article 22(1), Member States shall not restrain the free disposal of those assets, whether movable or immovable, that form part of the assets of authorised insurance undertakings.

3. Paragraphs 1 and 2 shall not preclude any measures which Member States, while safeguarding the interests of the insured persons, are entitled to take as owners or members of or partners to the undertakings in question.]

NOTES

Substituted by Council Directive 92/49/EEC, art 26.

Repealed as noted at the beginning of this Directive.

[6666]
[Article 19

1. Each Member State shall require every undertaking whose head office is situated in its territory to produce an annual account, covering all types of operation, of its financial situation, solvency and, as regards cover for risks listed under No 18 in point A of the Annex, other resources available to them for meeting their liabilities, where its laws provide for supervision of such resources.

Part VI European Materials

[1a. In respect of credit insurance, the undertaking shall make available to the supervisory authority accounts showing both the technical results and the technical reserves relating to that business.]

[2. Member States shall require insurance undertakings with head offices within their territories to render periodically the returns, together with statistical documents, which are necessary for the purposes of supervision. The competent authorities shall provide each other with any documents and information that are useful for the purposes of supervision.

3. Every Member State shall take all steps necessary to ensure that the competent authorities have the powers and means necessary for the supervision of the business of insurance undertakings with head offices within their territories, including business carried on outwith those territories, in accordance with the Council Directives governing such business and for the purpose of seeing that they are implemented.

These powers and means must, in particular, enable the competent authorities to—

(a) make detailed enquiries regarding an undertaking's situation and the whole of its business, inter alia, by—
- *gathering information or requiring the submission of documents concerning insurance business,*
- *carrying out on-the-spot investigations at the undertaking's premises;*

(b) take any measures with regard to an undertaking, its directors or managers or the persons who control it, that are appropriate and necessary to ensure that that undertaking's business continues to comply with the laws, regulations and administrative provisions with which the undertaking must comply in each Member State and in particular with the scheme of operations insofar as it remains mandatory, and to prevent or remedy any irregularities prejudicial to the interests of insured persons;

(c) ensure that those measures are carried out, if need be by enforcement and where appropriate through judicial channels.

Member States may also make provision for the competent authorities to obtain any information regarding contracts which are held by intermediaries.]

NOTES

Substituted by Council Directive 84/641/EEC, art 11.

Repealed as noted at the beginning of this Directive.

Para 1a: inserted by Council Directive 87/343/EEC, art 1(7).

Para 2: substituted, together with para 3, by Council Directive 92/49/EEC, art 11.

Para 3: added by Second Council Directive 88/357/EEC, art 10; substituted, together with para 2, by Council Directive 92/49/EEC, art 11.

[6667]
[Article 20

1. If an undertaking does not comply with Article 15, the competent authority of its home Member State may prohibit the free disposal of its assets after having communicated its intention to the competent authorities of the Member States in which the risks are situated.

2. For the purposes of restoring the financial situation of an undertaking the solvency margin of which has fallen below the minimum required under [Article 16a], the competent authority of the home Member State shall require that a plan for the restoration of a sound financial situation be submitted for its approval.

In exceptional circumstances, if the competent authority is of the opinion that the financial situation of the undertaking will deteriorate further, it may also restrict or prohibit the free disposal of the undertaking's assets. It shall inform the authorities of other Member States within the territories of which the undertaking carries on business of any measures it has taken and the latter shall, at the request of the former, take the same measures.

3. If the solvency margin falls below the guarantee fund as defined in Article 17, the competent authority of the home Member State shall require the undertaking to submit a short-term finance scheme for its approval.

It may also restrict or prohibit the free disposal of the undertaking's assets. It shall inform the authorities of other Member States within the territories of which the undertaking carries on business accordingly and the latter shall, at the request of the former, take the same measures.

4. The competent authorities may further take all measures necessary to safeguard the interests of insured persons in the cases provided for in paragraphs 1, 2 and 3.

5. Each Member State shall take the measures necessary to be able, in accordance with its national law, to prohibit the free disposal of assets located within its territory at the request, in the cases provided for in paragraphs 1, 2 and 3, of the undertaking's home Member State, which shall designate the assets to be covered by such measures.]

NOTES

Substituted by Council Directive 92/49/EEC, art 13(1).

Repealed as noted at the beginning of this Directive.

Para 2: words in square brackets substituted by European Parliament and Council Directive 2002/13/EC, art 1(6); for transitional provisions see art 2 thereof at **[6126]**.

[6668]
[Article 20a

1. Member States shall ensure that the competent authorities have the power to require a financial recovery plan for those insurance undertakings where competent authorities consider that policyholders' rights are threatened. The financial recovery plan shall as a minimum include particulars or proof concerning for the next three financial years—

(a) estimates of management expenses, in particular current general expenses and commissions;

(b) a plan setting out detailed estimates of income and expenditure in respect of direct business, reinsurance acceptances and reinsurance cessions;

(c) a forecast balance sheet;

(d) estimates of the financial resources intended to cover underwriting liabilities and the required solvency margin;

(e) the overall reinsurance policy.

2. Where policyholders' rights are threatened because the financial position of the undertaking is deteriorating, Member States shall ensure that the competent authorities have the power to oblige insurance undertakings to have a higher required solvency margin, in order to ensure that the insurance undertaking is able to fulfil the solvency requirements in the near future. The level of this higher required solvency margin shall be based on the financial recovery plan referred to in paragraph 1.

3. Member States shall ensure that the competent authorities have the power to revalue downwards all elements eligible for the available solvency margin, in particular, where there has been a significant change in the market value of these elements since the end of the last financial year.

[4. Member States shall ensure that the competent authorities have the power to decrease the reduction, based on reinsurance, to the solvency margin as determined in accordance with Article 16a where:

(a) the nature or quality of reinsurance contracts has changed significantly since the last financial year;

(b) there is no, or a limited, risk transfer under the reinsurance contracts.]

5. If the competent authorities have required a financial recovery plan for the insurance undertaking in accordance with paragraph 1, they shall refrain from issuing a certificate in accordance with Article 10(3), second subparagraph of this Directive, Article 16(1)(a) of Council Directive 88/357/EEC (second non-life insurance Directive)[1] *and Article 12(2) of Council Directive 92/49/EEC (third non-life insurance Directive),*[2] *as long as they consider that policyholders' rights are threatened within the meaning of paragraph 1.]*

NOTES

Inserted by European Parliament and Council Directive 2002/13/EC, art 1(7); for transitional provisions see art 2 thereof at **[6126]**.

Repealed as noted at the beginning of this Directive.

Para 4: substituted by European Parliament and Council Directive 2005/68/EC, art 57(7).

[1] OJ L172, 4.7.1988, p 1. Directive as last amended by Directive 2000/26/EC of the European Parliament and of the Council (OJ L181, 20.7.2000, p 65).

[2] OJ L228, 11.8.1992, p 1. Directive as last amended by Directive 2000/64/EC of the European Parliament and of the Council (OJ L290, 17.11.2000, p 27).

Article 21 (*Repealed by Second Council Directive 88/357/EEC, art 11(1).*)

[6669]
[Article 22

1. Authorisation granted to an insurance undertaking by the competent authority of its home Member State may be withdrawn by that authority if that undertaking—

Part VI European Materials

(a) *does not make use of that authorisation within 12 months, expressly renounces it or ceases to carry on business for more than six months, unless the Member State concerned has made provision for authorisation to lapse in such cases;*

(b) *no longer fulfils the conditions for admission;*

(c) *has been unable, within the time allowed, to take the measures specified in the restoration plan or finance scheme referred to in Article 20;*

(d) *fails seriously in its obligation under the regulations to which it is subject.*

In the event of the withdrawal or lapse of authorisation, the competent authority of the home Member State shall notify the competent authorities of the other Member States accordingly, and they shall take appropriate measures to prevent the undertaking from commencing new operations within their territories, under either the right of establishment or the freedom to provide services. The home Member State's competent authority shall, in conjunction with those authorities, take all measures necessary to safeguard the interests of insured persons and, in particular, shall restrict the free disposal of the undertaking's assets in accordance with Article 20(1), (2), second subparagraph, or (3), second subparagraph.

2. Any decision to withdraw authorisation shall be supported by precise reasons and communicated to the undertaking in question.]

NOTES

Substituted by Council Directive 92/49/EEC, art 14.
Repealed as noted at the beginning of this Directive.

[TITLE IIIA
RULES APPLICABLE TO AGENCIES OR BRANCHES ESTABLISHED WITHIN THE COMMUNITY AND BELONGING TO UNDERTAKINGS WHOSE HEAD OFFICES ARE OUTSIDE THE COMMUNITY]

NOTES

Title heading substituted by Council Directive 90/618/EEC, art 3(1).

[6670]
Article 23

1. Each Member State shall make access to the business referred to in Article 1 by any undertaking whose head office is outside the Community subject to an official authorisation.

2. A Member State may grant an authorisation if the undertaking fulfils at least the following conditions—

(a) *It is entitled to undertake insurance business under its national law;*

(b) *It establishes an agency or branch in the territory of such Member State;*

(c) *It undertakes to establish at the place of management of the agency or branch accounts specific to the business which it undertakes there, and to keep there all the records relating to the business transacted;*

(d) *It designates an authorised agent, to be approved by the competent authorities;*

(e) *It possesses in the country where it carries on its business assets of an amount equal to at least one-half of the minimum amount prescribed in Article 17(2), in respect of the guarantee fund, and deposits one-fourth of the minimum amount as security;*

(f) *It undertakes to keep a margin of solvency in accordance with the requirements referred to in Article 25;*

(g) *It submits a scheme of operations in accordance with the provisions of Article 11(1) and (2).*

[(h) *Communicate the name and address of the claims representative appointed in each Member State other than the Member State in which the authorisation is sought if the risks to be covered are classified in class 10 of point A of the Annex, other than carrier's liability.]*

NOTES

Repealed as noted at the beginning of this Directive.
Para 2: sub-para (h) added by Council Directive 2000/26/EC, art 8(b).

[6671]
Article 24

Member States shall require undertakings to establish adequate technical reserves to cover the underwriting liabilities assumed in their territories. Member States shall see that the agency or branch covers such technical reserves by means of assets which are equivalent to such reserves and are, to the extent fixed by the State in question, matching assets.

The law of the Member States shall be applicable to the calculation of technical reserves, the determination of categories of investments, and the valuation of assets.

The Member State in question shall require that the assets representing the technical reserves shall be localised in its territory. Article 15(3) shall, however, be applicable.

NOTES

Repealed as noted at the beginning of this Directive.

[6672]

Article 25

1. Each Member State shall require for agencies or branches established in its territory a solvency margin consisting of assets free of all foreseeable liabilities, less any intangible items. The solvency margin shall be calculated in accordance with the provisions of Article 16(3). However, for the purpose of calculating this margin, account shall be taken only of the premiums or contributions and claims pertaining to the business effected by the agency or branch concerned.

2. One-third of the solvency margin shall constitute the guarantee fund. The guarantee fund may not be less than one-half of the minimum required under Article 17(2). The initial deposit lodged in accordance with Article 23(2)(e) shall be counted towards such guarantee fund.

3. The assets representing the solvency margin must be kept within the country where the business is carried on up to the amount of the guarantee fund and the excess, within the Community.

NOTES

Repealed as noted at the beginning of this Directive.

[6673]

[Article 26

1. Any undertaking which has requested or obtained authorisation from more than one Member State may apply for the following advantages which may be granted only jointly—

(a) the solvency margin referred to in Article 25 shall be calculated in relation to the entire business which it carries on within the Community; in such case, account shall be taken only of the operations effected by all the agencies or branches established within the Community for the purposes of this calculation;

(b) the deposit required under Article 23(2)(e) shall be lodged in only one of those Member States;

(c) the assets representing the guarantee fund shall be localised in any one of the Member States in which it carries on its activities.

2. Application to benefit from the advantages provided for in paragraph 1 shall be made to the competent authorities of the Member States concerned. The application must state the authority of the Member State which in future is to supervise the solvency of the entire business of the agencies or branches established within the Community. Reasons must be given for the choice of authority made by the undertaking. The deposit shall be lodged with that Member State.

3. The advantages provided for in paragraph 1 may only be granted if the competent authorities of all Member States in which an application has been made agree to them. They shall take effect from the time when the selected supervisory authority informs the other supervisory authorities that it will supervise the state of solvency of the entire business of the agencies or branches within the Community.

The supervisory authority selected shall obtain from the other Member States the information necessary for the supervision of the overall solvency of the agencies and branches established in their territory.

4. At the request of one or more of the Member States concerned, the advantages granted under this Article shall be withdrawn simultaneously by all Member States concerned.]

NOTES

Substituted by Council Directive 84/641/EEC, art 12.
Repealed as noted at the beginning of this Directive.

[6674]

Article 27

The provisions of Articles 19 and 20 shall also apply in relation to agencies and branches of undertakings to which this Title applies.

[As regards the application of Article 20, where an undertaking qualifies for the advantages provided for in Article 26(1), the authority responsible for verifying the solvency of agencies or

Part VI European Materials

branches established within the Community with respect to their entire business shall be treated in the same way as the authority of the State in the territory of which the head office of a Community undertaking is situated.]

NOTES

Repealed as noted at the beginning of this Directive.
Words in square brackets substituted by Council Directive 84/641/EEC, art 13.

[6675]
Article 28

In the case of a withdrawal of authorisation by the authority referred to in Article 26(2), this authority shall notify the authorities of the other Member States where the undertaking operates and the latter supervisory authorities shall take the appropriate measures. If the reason for the withdrawal of the authorisation is the inadequacy of the overall state of solvency as fixed by the Member States which agreed to the request referred to in Article 26, the Member States which gave their approval shall also withdraw their authorisations.

NOTES

Repealed as noted at the beginning of this Directive.

[6676]
[Article 28a

1. Under the conditions laid down by national law, each Member State shall authorise agencies and branches set up within its territory and covered by this Title to transfer all or part of their portfolios of contracts to an accepting office established in the same Member State if the competent authorities of that Member State or, if appropriate, of the Member State referred to in Article 26 certify that after taking the transfer into account the accepting office possesses the necessary solvency margin.

2. Under the conditions laid down by national law, each Member State shall authorise agencies and branches set up within its territory and covered by this Title to transfer all or part of their portfolios of contracts to an insurance undertaking with a head office in another Member State if the competent authorities of that Member State certify that after taking the transfer into account the accepting office possesses the necessary solvency margin.

3. If under the conditions laid down by national law a Member State authorises agencies and branches set up their portfolios of contracts to an agency or branch covered by this Title and set up within the territory of another Member State it shall ensure that the competent authorities of the Member State of the accepting office or, if appropriate, of the Member State referred to in Article 26 certify that after taking the transfer into account the accepting office possesses the necessary solvency margin, that the law of the Member State of the accepting office permits such a transfer and that that State has agreed to the transfer.

4. In the circumstances referred to in paragraphs 1, 2 and 3 the Member State in which the transferring agency or branch is situated shall authorise the transfer after obtaining the agreement of the competent authorities of the Member State in which the risks are situated, where different from the Member State in which the transferring agency or branch is situated.

5. The competent authorities of the Member States consulted shall give their opinion or consent to the competent authorities of the home Member State of the transferring insurance undertaking within three months of receiving a request; the absence of any response from the authorities consulted within that period shall be considered equivalent to a favourable opinion or tacit consent.

6. A transfer authorised in accordance with this Article shall be published as laid down by national law in the Member State in which the risk is situated. Such transfers shall automatically be valid against policy-holders, insured persons and any other persons having rights or obligations arising out of the contracts transferred.

This provision shall not affect the Member States' right to give policy-holders the option of cancelling contracts within a fixed period after a transfer.]

NOTES

Inserted by Council Directive 92/49/EEC, art 53.
Repealed as noted at the beginning of this Directive.

[6677]
Article 29

The Community may, by means of agreements concluded pursuant to the Treaty with one or more third countries, agree to the application of provisions different to those provided for in this Title, for the purpose of ensuring, under conditions of reciprocity, adequate protection for insured persons in the Member States.

NOTES

Repealed as noted at the beginning of this Directive.

[TITLE IIIB
RULES APPLICABLE TO SUBSIDIARIES OF PARENT UNDERTAKINGS GOVERNED BY THE LAWS OF A THIRD COUNTRY AND TO ACQUISITIONS OF HOLDINGS BY SUCH PARENT UNDERTAKINGS]

NOTES

Title heading inserted by Council Directive 90/618/EEC, art 3(2).

[6678]
[Article 29a

1. The competent authorities of the Member States shall inform the Commission and the competent authorities of the other Member States—

(a) of any authorisation of a direct or indirect subsidiary, one or more of whose parent undertakings are governed by the law of a third country;

(b) whenever such a parent undertaking acquires a holding in a Community insurance undertaking which would turn the latter into its subsidiary.

2. When the authorisation referred to in paragraph 1(a) is granted to the direct or indirect subsidiary of one or more parent undertakings governed by the law of a third country, the structure of the group shall be specified in the notification which the competent authorities shall address to the Commission.]

NOTES

Inserted, together with art 29b, by Council Directive 90/618/EEC, art 4.
Substituted by European Parliament and Council Directive 2005/1/EC, art 4(1).
Repealed as noted at the beginning of this Directive.

[6679]
[Article 29b

1. Member States shall inform the Commission of any general difficulties encountered by their insurance undertakings in establishing themselves or carrying on their activities in a third country.

2. Initially not later than six months before the application of this Directive, and thereafter periodically, the Commission shall draw up a report examining the treatment accorded to Community insurance undertakings in third countries, in the terms referred to in paragraphs 3 and 4, as regards establishment and the carrying on of insurance activities, and the acquisition of holdings in third-country insurance undertakings. The Commission shall submit those reports to the Council, together with any appropriate proposals.

3. Whenever it appears to the Commission, either on the basis of the reports referred to in paragraph 2 or on the basis of other information, that a third country is not granting Community insurance undertakings effective market access comparable to that granted by the Community to insurance undertakings from that third country, the Commission may submit proposals to the Council for the appropriate mandate for negotiation with a view to obtaining comparable competitive opportunities for Community insurance undertakings. The Council shall decide by a qualified majority.

4. Whenever it appears to the Commission, either on the basis of the reports referred to in paragraph 2 or on the basis of other information, that Community insurance undertakings in a third country are not receiving national treatment offering the same competitive opportunities as are available to domestic insurance undertakings and that the conditions of effective market access are not being fulfilled, the Commission may initiate negotiations in order to remedy the situation.

[In the circumstances described in the first subparagraph, it may also be decided at any time, and in addition to initiating negotiations, in accordance with the procedure referred to in Article 5 of Decision 1999/468/EC[1] *and in compliance with Article 7(3) and Article 8 thereof that the competent authorities of the Member States must limit or suspend their decisions regarding the following—*

(a) requests for authorisation, whether pending at the moment of the decision or submitted thereafter;

(b) the acquisition of holdings by direct or indirect parent undertakings governed by the law of the third country in question.]

Part VI European Materials

The duration of the measures referred to may not exceed three months.

Before the end of that three-month period, and in the light of the results of the negotiations, the Council may, acting on a proposal from the Commission, decide by a qualified majority that the measures shall be continued.

Such limitations or suspension may not apply to the setting up of subsidiaries by insurance undertakings or their subsidiaries duly authorised in the Community, or to the acquisition of holdings in Community insurance undertakings by such undertakings or subsidiaries.

5. Whenever it appears to the Commission that one of the situations described in paragraphs 3 and 4 has arisen, the Member States shall inform it at its request—

- *(a) of any request for the authorisation of a direct or indirect subsidiary, one or more parent undertakings of which are governed by the laws of the third country in question;*
- *(b) of any plans for such an undertaking to acquire a holding in a Community insurance undertaking such that the latter would become the subsidiary of the former.*

This obligation to provide information shall lapse once an agreement is concluded with the third country referred to in paragraph 3 or 4 or when the measures referred to in the second and third subparagraphs of paragraph 4 cease to apply.

6. Measures taken under this Article shall comply with the Community's obligations under any international agreements, bilateral or multilateral, governing the taking-up and pursuit of the business of insurance undertakings.]

NOTES

Inserted, together with art 29a, by Council Directive 90/618/EEC, art 4.

Repealed as noted at the beginning of this Directive.

Para 4: words in square brackets substituted by European Parliament and Council Directive 2005/1/EC, art 4(2).

[1] OJ L184, 17.7.1999, p 23.

TITLE IV
TRANSITIONAL AND OTHER PROVISIONS

[6680]
Article 30

1. Member States shall allow undertakings referred to in Title II which at the entry into force of the implementing measures to this Directive provide insurance in their territories in one or more of the classes referred to in Article 1 a period of five years, commencing with the date of notification of this Directive, in order to comply with the requirements of Articles 16 and 17.

2. Furthermore, Member States may—

- *(a) allow any undertakings referred to in (1), which upon the expiry of the five-year period have not fully established the margin of solvency, a further period not exceeding two years in which to do so provided that such undertakings have, in accordance with Article 20, submitted for the approval of the supervisory authority the measures which they propose to take for such purpose;*
- *(b) exempt undertakings referred to in (1) whose annual premium or contribution income upon the expiry of the period of five years falls short of six times the amount of the minimum guarantee fund required under Article 17(2) from the requirement to establish such minimum guarantee fund before the end of the financial year in respect of which the premium or contribution income is as much as six times such minimum guarantee fund. After considering the results of the examination provided for under Article 33, the Council shall unanimously decide, on a proposal from the Commission, when this exemption is to be abolished by Member States.*

3. Undertakings desiring to extend their operations within the meaning of Article 8(2) or Article 10 may not do so unless they comply immediately with the rules of this Directive. However, the undertakings referred to in paragraph (2)(b) which within the national territory extend their business to other classes of insurance or to other parts of such territory may be exempted for a period of ten years from the date of notification of the Directive from the requirement to constitute the minimum guarantee fund referred to in Article 17(2).

4. An undertaking having a structure different from any of those listed in Article 8 may continue, for a period of three years from the notification of the Directive, to carry on their present business in the legal form in which they are constituted at the time of such notification. Undertakings set up in the United Kingdom "by Royal Charter" or "by private Act" or "by special public Act" may continue to carry on their business in their present form for an unlimited period.

Undertakings in Belgium which, in accordance with their objects, carry on the business of intervention mortgage loans or savings operations in accordance with No 4 of Article 15 of the provisions relating to the supervision of private savings banks, coordinated by the "arrête royal" of 23 June 1967, may continue to undertake such business for a period of three years from the date of notification of this Directive.

The Member States in question shall draw up a list of such undertakings and communicate it to the other Member States and the Commission.

5. At the request of undertakings which comply with the requirements of Articles 15, 16 and 17, Member States shall cease to apply restrictive measures such as those relating to mortgages, deposits and securities established under present regulations.

NOTES

Repealed as noted at the beginning of this Directive.

[6681]
Article 31

Member States shall allow agencies or branches referred to in Title III which, at the entry into force of the implementing measures to this Directive, are undertaking one or more classes referred to in Article 1 and do not extend their business within the meaning of Article 10(2) a maximum period of five years, from the date of notification of this Directive, in order to comply with the conditions of Article 25.

NOTES

Repealed as noted at the beginning of this Directive.

[6682]
Article 32

During a period which terminates at the time of the entry into force of an agreement concluded with a third country pursuant to Article 29 and at the latest upon the expiry of a period of four years after the notification of the Directive, each Member State may retain in favour of undertakings of that country established in its territory the rules applied to them on 1 January 1973 in respect of matching assets and the localisation of technical reserves, provided that notification is given to the other Member States and the Commission and that the limits of relaxations granted pursuant to Article 15(2) in favour of the undertakings of Member States established in its territory are not exceeded.

NOTES

Repealed as noted at the beginning of this Directive.

TITLE V
FINAL PROVISIONS

[6683]
Article 33

The Commission and the competent authorities of the Member States shall collaborate closely for the purpose of facilitating the supervision of direct insurance within the Community and of examining any difficulties which may arise in the application of this Directive.

NOTES

Repealed as noted at the beginning of this Directive.

[6684]
Article 34

1. The Commission shall submit to the Council, within six years from the date of notification of this Directive, a report on the effects of the financial requirements imposed by this Directive on the situation on the insurance markets of the Member States.

2. The Commission shall, as and when necessary, submit interim reports to the Council before the end of the transitional period provided for in Article 30(1).

NOTES

Repealed as noted at the beginning of this Directive.

[6685]
Article 35

Member States shall amend their national provisions to comply with this Directive within 18 months of its notification and shall forthwith inform the Commission thereof.

The provisions thus amended shall, subject to Articles 30, 31 and 32, be applied within 30 months from the date of notification.

NOTES

Repealed as noted at the beginning of this Directive.

[6686]
Article 36

Upon notification of this Directive, Member States shall ensure that the texts of the main provisions of a legislative, regulatory or administrative nature which they adopt in the field covered by this Directive are communicated to the Commission.

NOTES

Repealed as noted at the beginning of this Directive.

[6687]
Article 37

The Annex shall form an integral part of this Directive.

NOTES

Repealed as noted at the beginning of this Directive.

[6688]
Article 38

This Directive is addressed to the Member States.

NOTES

Repealed as noted at the beginning of this Directive.

Done at Brussels, 24 July 1973.

ANNEX

[6689]

A. Classification of risks according to classes of insurance

1. *Accident* (including industrial injury and occupational diseases)
   - *fixed pecuniary benefits*
   - *benefits in the nature of indemnity*
   - *combinations of the two*
   - *injury to passengers*
2. *Sickness*
   - *fixed pecuniary benefits*
   - *benefits in the nature of indemnity*
   - *combinations of the two*
3. *Land vehicles (other than railway rolling stock)*
   All damage to or loss of
   - *land motor vehicles*
   - *land vehicles other than motor vehicles*
4. *Railway rolling stock*
   All damage to or loss of railway rolling stock
5. *Aircraft*
   All damage to or loss of aircraft
6. *Ships (sea, lake and river and canal vessels)*
   All damage to or loss of
   - *river and canal vessels*
   - *lake vessels*
   - *sea vessels*
7. *Goods in transit* (including merchandise, baggage, and all other goods)
   All damage to or loss of goods in transit or baggage, irrespective of the form of transport
8. *Fire and natural forces*
   All damage to or loss of property (other than property included in classes 3, 4, 5, 6 and 7) due to
   - *fire*
   - *explosion*

— *storm*
— *natural forces other than storm*
— *nuclear energy*
— *land subsidence*

9. Other damage to property

All damage to or loss of property (other than property included in classes 3, 4, 5, 6 and 7) due to hail or frost, and any event such as theft, other than those mentioned under 8

10. Motor vehicle liability

All liability arising out of the use of motor vehicles operating on the land (including carrier's liability)

11. Aircraft liability

All liability arising out of the use of aircraft (including carrier's liability)

12. Liability for ships (sea, lake and river and canal vessels)

All liability arising out of the use of ships, vessels or boats on the sea, lakes, rivers or canals (including carrier's liability)

13. General liability

All liability other than those forms mentioned under Nos 10, 11 and 12

14. Credit

— *insolvency (general)*
— *export credit*
— *instalment credit*
— *mortgages*
— *agricultural credit*

15. Suretyship

— *suretyship (direct)*
— *suretyship (indirect)*

16. Miscellaneous financial loss

— *employment risks*
— *insufficiency of income (general)*
— *bad weather*
— *loss of benefits*
— *continuing general expenses*
— *unforeseen trading expenses*
— *loss of market value*
— *loss of rent or revenue*
— *indirect trading losses other than those mentioned above*
— *other financial loss (non-trading)*
— *other forms of financial loss*

17. Legal expenses

Legal expenses and costs of litigation

[18. Assistance

Assistance for persons who get into difficulties while travelling, while away from home or while away from their permanent residence.]

The risks included in a class may not be included in any other class except in the cases referred to in point C.

NOTES

Repealed as noted at the beginning of this Directive.
Para 18: inserted by Council Directive 84/641/EEC, art 14.

[6690]

B. Description of authorisations granted for more than one class of insurance

Where the authorisation simultaneously covers—

(a) Classes Nos 1 and 2, it shall be named "Accident and Health Insurance";
(b) Classes Nos 1 (fourth indent), 3, 7 and 10, it shall be named "Motor Insurance";
(c) Classes Nos 1 (fourth indent), 4, 6, 7 and 12, it shall be named "Marine and Transport Insurance";
(d) Classes Nos 1 (fourth indent), 5, 7 and 11, it shall be named "Aviation Insurance";
(e) Classes Nos 8 and 9, it shall be named "Insurance against Fire and other Damage to Property";

(f) *Classes Nos 10, 11, 12 and 13, it shall be named "Liability Insurance";*
(g) *Classes Nos 14 and 15, it shall be named "Credit and Suretyship Insurance";*
(h) *All classes, it shall be named at the choice of the Member State in question, which shall notify the other Member States and the Commission of its choice.*

NOTES

Repealed as noted at the beginning of this Directive.

[6691]

C. Ancillary risks

An undertaking obtaining an authorisation for a principal risk belonging to one class or a group of classes may also insure risks included in another class without an authorisation being necessary for them if they—

— *are connected with the principal risk,*
— *concern the object which is covered against the principal risk, and*
— *are covered by the contract insuring the principal risk.*

[However, the risks included in classes 14, 15 and 17 in point A may not be regarded as risks ancillary to other classes.

Nonetheless, the risk included in class 17 (legal expenses insurance) may be regarded as an ancillary risk of class 18 where the conditions laid down in the first subparagraph are fulfilled, where the main risk relates solely to the assistance provided for persons who fall into difficulties while travelling, while away from home or while away from their permanent residence.

Legal expenses insurance may also be regarded as an ancillary risk under the conditions set out in the first subparagraph where it concerns disputes or risks arising out of, or in connection with, the use of sea-going vessels.]

NOTES

Words in square brackets substituted by Council Directive 87/344/EEC, art 9.
Repealed as noted at the beginning of this Directive.

[6692]

[D. Methods of calculating the equalisation reserve for the credit insurance class

Method No 1

1. In respect of the risks included in the class of insurance in point A No 14 (hereinafter referred to as "credit insurance"), the undertaking shall set up an equalisation reserve to which shall be charged any technical deficit arising in that class for a financial year.

2. Such reserve shall in each financial year receive 75% of any technical surplus arising on credit insurance business, subject to a limit of 12% of the net premiums or contributions until the reserve has reached 150% of the highest annual amount of net premiums or contributions received during the previous five financial years.

Method No 2

1. In respect of the risks included in the class of insurance listed in point A No 14 (hereinafter referred to as "credit insurance") the undertaking shall set up an equalisation reserve to which shall be charged any technical deficit arising in that class for a financial year.

2. The minimum amount of the equalisation reserve shall be 134% of the average of the premiums or contributions received annually during the previous five financial years after subtraction of the cessions and addition of the reinsurance acceptances.

3. Such reserve shall in each of the successive financial years receive 75% of any technical surplus arising in that class until the reserve is at least equal to the minimum calculated in accordance with paragraph 2.

4. Member States may lay down special rules for the calculation of the amount of the reserve and/or the amount of the annual levy in excess of the minimum amounts laid down in this Directive.

Method No 3

1. An equalisation reserve shall be formed for class 14 in point A (hereinafter referred to as "credit insurance") for the purpose of offsetting any above-average claims ratio for a financial year in that class of insurance.

2. The equalisation reserve shall be calculated on the basis of the method set out below.

All calculations shall relate to income and expenditure for the insurer's own account.

An amount in respect of any claims shortfall for each financial year shall be placed to the equalisation reserve until it has reached, or is restored to, the required amount.

There shall be deemed to be a claims shortfall if the claims ratio for a financial year is lower than the average claims ratio for the reference period. The amount in respect of the claims shortfall shall be arrived at by multiplying the difference between the two ratios by the earned premiums for the financial year.

The required amount shall be equal to six times the standard deviation of the claims ratios in the reference period from the average claims ratio, multiplied by the earned premiums for the financial year.

Where claims for any financial year are in excess, an amount in respect thereof shall be taken from the equalisation reserve. Claims shall be deemed to be in excess if the claims ratio for the financial year is higher than the average claims ratio. The amount in respect of the excess claims shall be arrived at by multiplying the difference between the two ratios by the earned premiums for the financial year.

Irrespective of claims experience, 3.5% of the required amount of the equalisation reserve shall be first placed to that reserve each financial year until its required amount has been reached or restored.

The length of the reference period shall be not less than 15 years and not more than 30 years. No equalisation reserve need be formed if no underwriting loss has been noted during the reference period.

The required amount of the equalisation reserve and the amount to be taken from it may be reduced if the average claims ratio for the reference period in conjunction with the expenses ratio show that the premiums include a safety margin.

Method No 4

1. An equalisation reserve shall be formed for class 14 in point A (hereinafter referred to as "credit insurance") for the purpose of offsetting any above-average claims ratio for a financial year in that class of insurance.

2. The equalisation reserve shall be calculated on the basis of the method set out below.

All calculations shall relate to income and expenditure for the insurer's own account.

An amount in respect of any claims shortfall for each financial year shall be placed to the equalisation reserve until it has reached the maximum required amount.

There shall be deemed to be a claims shortfall if the claims ratio for a financial year is lower than the average claims ratio for the reference period. The amount in respect of the claims shortfall shall be arrived at by multiplying the difference between the two ratios by the earned premiums for the financial year.

The maximum required amount shall be equal to six times the standard deviation of the claims ratio in the reference period from the average claims ratio, multiplied by the earned premiums for the financial year.

Where claims for any financial year are in excess, an amount in respect thereof shall be taken from the equalisation reserve until it has reached the minimum required amount. Claims shall be deemed to be in excess if the claims ratio for the financial year is higher than the average claims ratio. The amount in respect of the excess claims shall be arrived at by multiplying the difference between the two ratios by the earned premiums for the financial year.

The minimum required amount shall be equal to three times the standard deviation of the claims ratio in the reference from the average claims ratio multiplied by the earned premiums for the financial year.

The length of the reference period shall be not less than 15 years and not more than 30 years. No equalisation reserve need be formed if no underwriting loss has been noted during the reference period.

Both required amounts of the equalisation reserve and the amount to be placed to it or the amount to be taken from it may be reduced if the average claims ratio for the reference period in conjunction with the expenses ratio show that the premiums include a safety margin and that safety margin is more than one-and-a-half times the standard deviation of the claims ratio in the reference period. In such a case the amounts in question shall be multiplied by the quotient or one-and-a-half times the standard deviation and the safety margin.]

NOTES

Repealed as noted at the beginning of this Directive.

Point D added by Council Directive 87/343/EEC, art 1(8), Annex.

Part VI European Materials

COUNCIL DIRECTIVE

(73/240/EEC)

of 24 July 1973

abolishing restrictions on freedom of establishment in the business of direct insurance other than life assurance

NOTES

Date of publication in OJ: OJ L228, 16.8.73, p 20.

This Directive is repealed by European Parliament and Council Directive 2009/138/EC on the taking-up and pursuit of the business of Insurance and Reinsurance (Solvency II) at **[6153]** et seq, with effect from 1 November 2012 (see art 310 thereof at **[6462]**).

[6693]

THE COUNCIL OF THE EUROPEAN COMMUNITIES,

Having regard to the Treaty establishing the European Economic Community, and in particular Article 54(2) and (3) thereof;

Having regard to the General Programme for the abolition of restrictions on freedom of establishment,[1] and in particular Title IV C thereof;

Having regard to the proposal from the Commission;

Having regard to the Opinion of the European Parliament;[2]

Having regard to the Opinion of the Economic and Social Committee;[3]

Whereas the General Programme referred to above provides for the abolition of all discriminatory treatment of the nationals of the other Member States as regards establishment in the business of direct insurance other than life assurance;

Whereas, in accordance with this General Programme, the lifting of restrictions on the setting-up of agencies and branches is, as regards direct insurance undertakings, dependent upon the coordination of conditions of taking up and pursuit of the business; whereas this coordination has been achieved for direct insurance other than life assurance, by the First Council Directive of 24 July 1973;

Whereas the scope of this Directive is in all respects the same as that defined in item A of the Annex to the First Directive on coordination; whereas it appeared reasonable in the circumstances to exclude, for purposes of coordination, credit-insurance for exports;

Whereas, in accordance with the General Programme referred to above, the restrictions on the right to join professional organisations must be abolished where the professional activities of the persons concerned involve the exercise of this right;

NOTES

Repealed as noted at the beginning of this Directive.

1 OJ 2, 15.1.62, p 36/62.

2 OJ C27, 28.3.68, p 15.

3 OJ 118, 20.6.67, p 2323/67.

HAS ADOPTED THIS DIRECTIVE—

[6694]

Article 1

Member States shall abolish, in respect of the natural persons and undertakings covered by Title I of the General Programme for the abolition of restrictions on freedom of establishment, hereinafter called "beneficiaries", the restrictions referred to in Title III of this programme affecting the right to take up and pursue self-employed activities in the classes of insurance specified in Article 1 of the First Coordination Directive.

By "First Coordination Directive" is meant the First Council Directive of 24 July 1973 on coordination of the laws, regulations and administrative provisions relating to the taking-up and pursuit of the business of direct insurance other than life assurance.

However, as regards credit-insurance for exports, these restrictions shall be maintained until the coordination programme laid down in Article 2(2)(d), of the First Coordination Directive *has been carried out.*

NOTES

Repealed as noted at the beginning of this Directive.

[6695]
Article 2

1. Member States shall in particular abolish the following restrictions—

(a) those which prevent beneficiaries from establishing themselves in the host country under the same conditions and with the same rights as nationals of that country;

(b) those existing by reason of administrative practices which result in treatment being applied to beneficiaries that is discriminatory by comparison with that applied to nationals.

2. The restrictions to be abolished shall include in particular those arising out of measures which prevent or limit the establishment of beneficiaries by the following means—

(a) In Germany—

the provisions granting the Federal Ministry of Economic Affairs the discretionary right to impose its own conditions of access to this business on foreign nationals and to prevent them from pursuing this business within the Federal Republic (Law of 6 June 1931 (VAG), Article 106(2), No 1, in conjunction with Article 8(1), No 3, Article 106(2), last sentence, and Article 111(2));

(b) In Belgium—

the obligation to hold a "carte professionelle" (Article 1 of the Law of 19 February 1965);

(c) In France—

— *the need to obtain special consent (Law of 15 February 1917, as amended and supplemented by the "décret-loi" of 30 October 1935, Article 2(2)—"décret" of 19 August 1941, as amended, Articles 1 and 2—"décret" of 13 August 1947, as amended, Articles 2 and 10);*

— *the obligation to provide a surety-bond or special guarantees as a reciprocal requirement (Law of 15 February 1917, amended and supplemented by the "décret-loi" of 30 October 1935, Article 2(2)—"décret-loi" of 14 June 1938, Article 42—"décret" of 30 December 1938, as amended, Article 143— "décret" of 14 December 1966, Articles 9, 10 and 11);*

— *the obligation to deposit technical reserves ("décret" of 30 December 1938, amended Article 179—"décret" of 13 August 1947, as amended, Articles 8 and 13—"décret" of 14 December 1966, Title I).*

(d) In Ireland—

the provision that, to be eligible for an insurance licence, a company must be registered under the Irish Companies Acts, two-thirds of its shares must be owned by Irish citizens and the majority of the directors (other than a full-time managing director) must be Irish citizens (Insurance Act, 1936, Section 12; Insurance Act, 1964, Section 7).

3. The laws, regulations or administrative provisions that involve beneficiaries in the obligation to provide a deposit or special surety-bond shall not be abolished, as long as the undertakings do not fulfil the financial conditions under Articles 16 and 17 of the First Coordination Directive in accordance with the provisions of Article 30(1) and (2) of the same Directive.

NOTES

Repealed as noted at the beginning of this Directive.

[6696]
Article 3

1. Where a host Member State requires of its own nationals wishing to take up any activity referred to in Article 1 proof of good repute and proof of no previous bankruptcy, or proof of either of these, that State shall accept as sufficient evidence, in respect of nationals of other Member States, the production of an extract from the "judicial record" or, failing this, of an equivalent document issued by a competent judicial or administrative authority in the country of origin or the country whence the foreign national comes, showing that these requirements have been met.

2. Where the country of origin or the country whence the foreign national comes does not issue such documentary proof of good repute or documentary proof of no previous bankruptcy, such proof may be replaced by a declaration on oath—or in States where there is no provision for declaration on oath, by a solemn declaration—made by the person concerned before a competent judicial or administrative authority, or where appropriate a notary, in the country of origin or in the country whence that person comes; such authority or notary will issue a certificate attesting the authenticity of the declaration on oath or solemn declaration. A declaration in respect of no previous bankruptcy may also be made before a competent professional or trade body in the said country.

3. Documents issued in accordance with paragraph 1 or with paragraph 2 may not be produced more than three months after their date of issue.

4. Member States shall, within the time limit laid down in Article 6, designate the authorities and bodies competent to issue these documents and shall forthwith inform the other Member States and the Commission thereof.

NOTES

Repealed as noted at the beginning of this Directive.

[6697]
Article 4

1. Member States shall ensure that beneficiaries have the right to join professional or trade organisations under the same conditions and with the same rights and obligations as their own nationals.

2. The right to join professional or trade organisations shall, in the case of establishment, entail eligibility for election or appointment to high office in such organisations. However, such posts may be reserved for nationals where, in pursuance of any provision laid down by law or regulation, the organisation concerned is involved in the exercise of official authority.

3. In the Grand Duchy of Luxembourg, membership of the "Chambre de commerce" shall not give beneficiaries the right to take part in the election of the administrative organs of that Chamber.

NOTES

Repealed as noted at the beginning of this Directive.

[6698]
Article 5

No Member State shall grant to any of its nationals who go to another Member State for the purpose of pursuing any activity referred to in Article 1 any aid liable to distort the conditions of establishment.

NOTES

Repealed as noted at the beginning of this Directive.

[6699]
Article 6

Member States shall amend their national regulations in accordance with this Directive and within 18 months of the notification of the First Coordination Directive and shall forthwith inform the Commission thereof. The regulations thus amended shall be implemented at the same time as the laws, regulations and administrative provisions set up in pursuance of the First Directive.

NOTES

Repealed as noted at the beginning of this Directive.

[6700]
Article 7

This Directive is addressed to the Member States.

NOTES

Repealed as noted at the beginning of this Directive.

Done at Brussels, 24 July 1973.

COUNCIL DIRECTIVE

(78/473/EEC)

of 30 May 1978

on the coordination of laws, regulations and administrative provisions relating to Community co-insurance

NOTES

Date of publication in OJ: OJ L151, 7.6.78, p 25.

This Directive is repealed by European Parliament and Council Directive 2009/138/EC on the taking-up and pursuit of the business of Insurance and Reinsurance (Solvency II) at **[6153]** et seq, with effect from 1 November 2012 (see art 310 thereof at **[6462]**).

[6701]

THE COUNCIL OF THE EUROPEAN COMMUNITIES,

Having regard to the Treaty establishing the European Economic Community, and in particular Articles 57(2) and 66 thereof,

Having regard to the proposal from the Commission,

Having regard to the Opinion of the European Parliament,[1]

Having regard to the Opinion of the Economic and Social Committee,[2]

Whereas the effective pursuit of Community co-insurance business should be facilitated by a minimum of coordination in order to prevent distortion of competition and inequality of treatment, without affecting the freedom existing in several Member States;

Whereas such coordination covers only those co-insurance operations which are economically the most important, ie those which by reason of their nature or their size are liable to be covered by international co-insurance;

Whereas this Directive thus constitutes a first step towards the coordination of all operations which may be carried out by virtue of the freedom to provide services; whereas this coordination, in fact, is the object of the Proposal for a Second Council Directive on the coordination of laws, regulations and administrative provisions relating to direct insurance other than life assurance and laying down provisions to facilitate the effective exercise of freedom to provide services, which the Commission forwarded to the Council on 30 December 1975;[3]

Whereas the leading insurer is better placed than the other co-insurers to assess claims and to fix the minimum amount of reserves for outstanding claims;

Whereas work is in progress on the winding-up of insurance undertakings; whereas provision must be made at this stage to ensure that, in the event of winding-up, beneficiaries under Community co-insurance contracts enjoy equality of treatment with beneficiaries in respect of the other insurance business, irrespective of the nationality of such persons;

Whereas special cooperation should be provided for in the Community co-insurance field both between the competent supervisory authorities of the Member States and between those authorities and the Commission; whereas any practices which might indicate a misuse of the purpose of the Directive are to be examined in the course of such cooperation,

NOTES

Repealed as noted at the beginning of this Directive.

1 OJ C60, 13.3.75, p 16.

2 OJ C47, 27.2.95, p 40.

3 OJ C32, 12.2.95, p 2.

HAS ADOPTED THIS DIRECTIVE—

TITLE I
GENERAL PROVISIONS

[6702]

Article 1

1. This Directive shall apply to Community co-insurance operations referred to in Article 2 which relate to risks classified under point A. 4, 5, 6, 7, 8, 9, 11, 12, 13 and 16 of the Annex to the First Council Directive of 24 July 1973 on the coordination of laws, regulations and administrative provisions relating to the taking-up and pursuit of the business of direct insurance other than life assurance,[1] *hereinafter called the "First Coordination Directive".*

It shall not apply, however, to Community co-insurance operations covering risks classified under point A. 13 which concern damage arising from nuclear sources or from medicinal products. The exclusion of insurance against damage arising from medicinal products shall be examined by the Council within five years of the notification of this Directive.

2. This Directive shall apply to risks referred to in the first subparagraph of paragraph 1 which by reason of their nature or size call for the participation of several insured for their coverage.

Any difficulties which may arise in implementing this principle shall be examined pursuant to Article 8.

NOTES

Repealed as noted at the beginning of this Directive.

[1] OJ L228, 16.8.93, p 3.

[6703]
Article 2

1. This Directive shall apply only to those Community co-insurance operations which satisfy the following conditions—

(a) the risk, within the meaning of Article 1(1), is covered by a single contract at an overall premium and for the same period by two or more insurance undertakings, hereinafter referred to as "co-insurers", each for its own part; one of these undertakings shall be the leading insurer;

(b) the risk is situated within the Community;

(c) for the purpose of covering this risk, the leading insurer is authorised in accordance with the conditions laid down in the First Coordination Directive, ie he is treated as if he were the insurer covering the whole risk;

(d) at least one of the co-insurers participates in the contract by means of a head office, agency or branch established in a Member State other than that of the leading insurer;

(e) the leading insurer fully assumes the leader's role in co-insurance practice and in particular determines the terms and conditions of insurance and rating.

2. Those co-insurance operations which do not satisfy the conditions set out in paragraph 1 or which cover risks other than those specified in Article 1 shall remain subject to the national laws operative at the time when this Directive comes into force.

NOTES

Repealed as noted at the beginning of this Directive.

[6704]
Article 3

The right of undertakings which have their head office in a Member State and which are subject to and satisfy the requirements of the First Coordination Directive to participate in Community co-insurance may not be made subject to any provisions other than those of this Directive.

NOTES

Repealed as noted at the beginning of this Directive.

TITLE II
CONDITIONS AND PROCEDURES FOR COMMUNITY CO-INSURANCE

[6705]
Article 4

1. The amount of the technical reserves shall be determined by the different co-insurers according to the rules fixed by the Member State where they are established or, in the absence of such rules, according to customary practice in that State. However, the reserve for outstanding claims shall be at least equal to that determined by the leading insurer according to the rules or practice of the State where such insurer is established.

2. The technical reserves established by the different co-insurers shall be represented by matching assets. However, relaxation of the matching assets rule may be granted by the Member States in which the co-insurers are established in order to take account of the requirements of sound management of insurance undertakings. Such assets shall be localised either in the Member States in which the co-insurers are established or in the Member State in which the leading insurer is established, whichever the insurer chooses.

NOTES

Repealed as noted at the beginning of this Directive.

[6706]
Article 5

The Member States shall ensure that co-insurers established in their territory keep statistical data showing the extent of Community co-insurance operations and the countries concerned.

NOTES

Repealed as noted at the beginning of this Directive.

[6707]
Article 6

The supervisory authorities of the Member States shall cooperate closely in the implementation of this Directive and shall provide each other with all the information necessary to this end.

NOTES

Repealed as noted at the beginning of this Directive.

[6708]
Article 7

In the event of an insurance undertaking being wound up, liabilities arising from participation in Community co-insurance contracts shall be met in the same way as those arising under that undertaking's other insurance contracts without distinction as to the nationality of the insured and of the beneficiaries.

NOTES

Repealed as noted at the beginning of this Directive.

TITLE III
FINAL PROVISIONS

[6709]
Article 8

The Commission and the competent authorities of the Member States shall cooperate closely for the purposes of examining any difficulties which might arise in implementing this Directive.

In the course of this cooperation they shall examine in particular any practices which might indicate that the purpose of the provisions of this Directive and in particular of Article 1(2) and Article 2 are being misused either in that the leading insurer does not assume the leader's role in co-insurance practice or that the risks clearly do not require the participation of two or more insurers for their coverage.

NOTES

Repealed as noted at the beginning of this Directive.

[6710]
Article 9

The Commission shall submit to the Council within six years of the notification of this Directive a report on the development of Community co-insurance.

NOTES

Repealed as noted at the beginning of this Directive.

[6711]
Article 10

Member States shall amend their national provisions so as to comply with this Directive within 18 months of its notification and shall immediately inform the Commission thereof.

The provisions thereby amended shall be applied within 24 months of such notification.

NOTES

Repealed as noted at the beginning of this Directive.

[6712]
Article 11

Upon notification of this Directive Member States shall ensure that the texts of the main provisions of laws, regulations or administrative measures which they adopt in the field covered by this Directive are communicated to the Commission.

NOTES

Repealed as noted at the beginning of this Directive.

[6713]
Article 12

This Directive is addressed to the Member States.

NOTES

Repealed as noted at the beginning of this Directive.

Done at Brussels, 30 May 1978.

Part VI European Materials

COUNCIL DIRECTIVE

(84/641/EEC)

of 10 December 1984

amending, particularly as regards tourist assistance, the First Directive (73/239/EEC) on the coordination of laws, regulations and administrative provisions relating to the taking-up and pursuit of the business of direct insurance other than life assurance

NOTES

Date of publication in OJ: OJ L339, 27.12.84, p 21.

This Directive is repealed by European Parliament and Council Directive 2009/138/EC on the taking-up and pursuit of the business of Insurance and Reinsurance (Solvency II) at **[6153]** et seq, with effect from 1 November 2012 (see art 310 thereof at **[6462]**).

[6714]

THE COUNCIL OF THE EUROPEAN COMMUNITIES,

Having regard to the Treaty establishing the European Economic Community, and in particular Article 57(2) thereof,

Having regard to the proposal from the Commission,[1]

Having regard to the opinion of the European Parliament,[2]

Having regard to the opinion of the Economic and Social Committee,[3]

Whereas the First Council Directive (73/239/EEC) of 4 July 1973 on the co-ordination of laws, regulations and administrative provisions relating to the taking-up and pursuit of the business of direct insurance other than life assurance,[4] *hereinafter referred to as the "First Directive", as amended by Directive 76/580/EEC,*[5] *eliminated certain differences between the laws of Member States in order to facilitate the taking-up and pursuit of the above business;*

Whereas considerable progress has been achieved in that area of business involving the provision of benefits in kind; whereas such benefits are governed by provisions which differ from one Member State to another; whereas those differences constitute a barrier to the exercise of the right of establishment;

Whereas, in order to eliminate that barrier to the right of establishment, it should be specified that an activity is not excluded from the application of the First Directive for the simple reason that it constitutes a benefit solely in kind or one for which the person providing it uses his own staff or equipment only; whereas, therefore such provision of assistance consisting in the promise of aid on the occurrence of a chance event should be covered by the above Directive, taking into account the special characteristics of such assistance;

Whereas the purpose of the inclusion, for reasons of supervision, of assistance operations in the scope of the First Directive, which does not involve the definition of these operations, is not to affect the fiscal rules applicable to them;

Whereas the sole fact of providing certain forms of assistance on the occasion of an accident or breakdown involving a road vehicle normally occurring in the territory of the Member State of the undertaking providing cover is not a reason for any person or undertaking that is not an insurance undertaking to be subject to the arrangements of the First Directive;

Whereas provision should be made for certain relaxations to the condition that the accident or breakdown must occur in the territory of the Member State of the undertaking providing cover in order to take into account either the existence of reciprocal agreements or of certain specific circumstances relating to the geographical situation or to the structure of the organisations concerned, or to the very limited economic importance of the operations referred to;

Whereas an organisation of a Member State whose main activity is to provide services on behalf of the public authorities should be excluded from the scope of the First Directive;

Whereas an undertaking offering assistance contracts must possess the means necessary for it to provide the benefits in kind which it offers within an appropriate period of time; whereas special provisions should be laid down for calculating the solvency margin and the minimum amount of the guarantee fund which such undertaking must possess;

Whereas certain transitional provisions are necessary in order to permit undertakings providing only assistance to adapt themselves to the application of the First Directive;

Whereas, having regard to special structural and geographical difficulties, it is necessary to allow a transitional period to the automobile club of a Member State for bringing itself into line with the said Directive concerning repatriation of the vehicle, possibly accompanied by the driver and passengers;

Whereas it is necessary to keep up-to-date the provisions of the First Directive concerning the legal forms which insurance undertakings may assume; whereas certain provisions of the said Directive concerning the rules applicable to agencies or branches established within the Community and belonging to undertakings whose head offices are situated outside the Community should be amended in order to make them consistent with the provisions of Directive 79/267/EEC;[6]

NOTES

Repealed as noted at the beginning of this Directive.

1 OJ C51, 10.3.81, p 5; OJ C30, 4.2.83, p 6.

2 OJ C149, 14.6.82, p 129.

3 OJ C343, 31.12.81, p 9.

4 OJ L228, 16.8.73, p 3.

5 OJ L189, 13.7.76, p 13.

6 OJ L63, 13.3.79, p 1.

HAS ADOPTED THIS DIRECTIVE—

Articles 1–14 (*Art 1 substitutes First Council Directive 73/239/EEC, art 1 at* **[6644]***; art 2 inserts art 2(3) thereof at* **[6645]***; art 4 inserts art 4(f) thereof at* **[6647]***; arts 11, 12 substitute arts 19, 26 thereof at* **[6666]**, **[6673]***; art 13 amends art 27 thereof at* **[6674]***; art 14 amends the Annex thereto at* **[6689]** *; arts 3, 9, 10 contain amendments which have now been superseded by provisions contained in European Parliament and Council Directive 2002/13/EC; arts 5–8 contain amendments which have now been superseded by provisions contained in Council Directive 92/49/EEC.*)

[6715]

Article 15

Any Member State may, in its territory, make the provision of assistance to persons who get into difficulties in circumstances other than those referred to in Article 1 subject to the arrangements introduced by the First Directive. If a Member State makes use of this possibility it shall, for the purposes of applying these arrangements, treat such activity as if it were listed in class 18 in point A of the Annex to the First Directive without prejudice to point C thereof.

The preceding paragraph shall in no way affect the possibilities for classification laid down in the Annex to the First Directive for activities which obviously come under other classes.

It shall not be possible to refuse authorisation to an agency or branch solely on the grounds that the activity covered by this Article is classified differently in the Member State in the territory of which the head office of the undertaking is situated.

NOTES

Repealed as noted at the beginning of this Directive.

[6716]

Article 16

1. Member States may allow undertakings which, on the date of notification of this Directive, provide only assistance in their territories, a period of five years from that date in order to comply with the requirements set out in Articles 16 and 17 of the First Directive.

2. Member States may allow any undertakings referred to in paragraph 1 which, upon expiry of the five-year period, have not fully established the solvency margin, a further period not exceeding two years in which to do so provided that such undertakings have, in accordance with Article 20 of the First Directive, submitted for the approval of the supervisory authority the measures which they propose to take for that purpose.

3. Any undertaking referred to in paragraph 1 which wishes to extend its business within the meaning of Article 8(2) or Article 10 of the First Directive may do so only on condition that it complies forthwith with that Directive.

4. Any undertaking referred to in paragraph 1 which has a form different to those referred to in Article 8 of the First Directive may continue for a period of three years from the date of notification of this Directive to carry on its existing business in the form in which it exists on that date.

5. This Article shall apply mutatis mutandis to undertakings formed after the date of notification of this Directive which take over business already conducted on that date by a legally distinct body.

NOTES

Repealed as noted at the beginning of this Directive.

[6717]
Article 17

Member States may allow agencies and branches referred to in Title III of the First Directive which provide only assistance in the territories of those Member States a maximum period of five years commencing on the date of notification of this Directive in order to comply with Article 25 of the First Directive, provided such agencies or branches do not extend their business within the meaning of Article 10(2) of the First Directive.

NOTES

Repealed as noted at the beginning of this Directive.

[6718]
Article 18

During a period of eight years from the date of notification of this Directive, the condition that the accident or breakdown must have happened in the territory of the Member State of the undertaking providing cover shall not apply to the operations referred to in the third indent of the first subparagraph of Article 2(3) of the First Directive where these operations are carried out by the ELPA (Automobile and Touring Club of Greece).

NOTES

Repealed as noted at the beginning of this Directive.

[6719]
Article 19

1. Member States shall amend their national provisions in order to comply with this Directive not later than 30 June 1987. They shall forthwith inform the Commission thereof. The provisions thus amended shall, subject to Articles 16, 17 and 18 of this Directive apply at the latest beginning on 1 January 1988.

2. Member States shall communicate to the Commission the texts of the main provisions laid down by law, regulation or administrative action which they adopt in the field governed by this Directive.

NOTES

Repealed as noted at the beginning of this Directive.

[6720]
Article 20

The Commission shall report to the Council, within six years of notification of this Directive, on the difficulties arising from the application thereof, and in particular Article 15 thereof. It shall, if appropriate, submit proposals to put an end to them.

NOTES

Repealed as noted at the beginning of this Directive.

[6721]
Article 21

This Directive is addressed to the Member States.

NOTES

Repealed as noted at the beginning of this Directive.

Done at Brussels, 10 December 1984.

COUNCIL DIRECTIVE

(87/344/EEC)

of 22 June 1987

on the coordination of laws, regulations and administrative provisions relating to legal expenses insurance

NOTES

Date of publication in OJ: OJ L185, 4.7.87, p 77.

This Directive is repealed by European Parliament and Council Directive 2009/138/EC on the taking-up and pursuit of the business of Insurance and Reinsurance (Solvency II) at **[6153]** et seq, with effect from 1 November 2012 (see art 310 thereof at **[6462]**).

[6722]
THE COUNCIL OF THE EUROPEAN COMMUNITIES,

Having regard to the Treaty establishing the European Economic Community, and in particular Article 57(2) thereof,

Having regard to the proposal from the Commission,[1]

Having regard to the Opinion of the European Parliament,[2]

Having regard to the Opinion of the Economic and Social Committee,[3]

Whereas Council Directive 73/239/EEC of 24 July 1973 on the coordination of laws, regulations and administrative provisions relating to the taking-up and pursuit of the business of direct insurance other than life assurance,[4] *as last amended by Directive 87/343/EEC,*[5] *eliminated, in order to facilitate the taking-up and pursuit of such activities, certain differences existing between national laws;*

Whereas, however, Article 7(2)(c) of Directive 73/239/EEC provides that "pending further coordination, which must be implemented within four years of notification of this Directive, the Federal Republic of Germany may maintain the provision prohibiting the simultaneous undertaking in its territory of health insurance, credit and suretyship insurance or insurance in respect of recourse against third parties and legal defence, either with one another or with other classes";

Whereas the present Directive provides for the coordination of legal expenses insurance as envisaged in Article 7(2)(c) of Directive 73/239/EEC;

Whereas, in order to protect insured persons, steps should be taken to preclude, as far as possible, any conflict of interests between a person with legal expenses cover and his insurer arising out of the fact that the latter is covering him in respect of any other class of insurance referred to in the Annex to Directive 73/239/EEC or is covering another person and, should such a conflict arise, to enable it to be resolved;

Whereas legal expenses insurance in respect of disputes or risks arising out of, or in connection with, the use of sea-going vessels should, in view of its specific nature, be excluded from the scope of this Directive;

Whereas the activity of an insurer who provides services or bears the cost of defending the insured person in connection with a civil liability contract should also be excluded from the scope of this Directive if that activity is at the same time pursued in the insurer's own interest under such cover;

Whereas Member States should be given the option of excluding from the scope of this Directive the activity of legal expenses insurance undertaken by an assistance insurer where this activity is carried out in a Member State other than the one in which the insured person normally resides and where it forms part of a contract covering solely the assistance provided for persons who fall into difficulties while travelling, while away from home or while away from their permanent residence;

Whereas the system of compulsory specialisation at present applied by one Member State, namely the Federal Republic of Germany, precludes the majority of conflicts; whereas, however, it does not appear necessary, in order to obtain this result, to extend that system to the entire Community, which would require the splitting-up of composite undertakings;

Whereas the desired result can also be achieved by requiring undertakings to provide for a separate contract or a separate section of a single policy for legal expenses insurance and by obliging them either to have separate management for legal expenses insurance, or to entrust the management of claims in respect of legal expenses insurance to an undertaking having separate legal personality, or to afford the person having legal expenses cover the right to choose his lawyer from the moment that he has the right to claim from his insurer;

Whereas, whichever solution is adopted, the interest of persons having legal expenses cover shall be protected by equivalent safeguards;

Whereas the interest of persons having legal expenses cover means that the insured person must be able to choose a lawyer or other person appropriately qualified according to national law in any inquiry or proceedings and whenever a conflict of interests arises;

Whereas Member States should be given the option of exempting undertakings from the obligation to give the insured person this free choice of lawyer if the legal expenses insurance is limited to cases arising from the use of road vehicles on their territory and if other restrictive conditions are met;

Whereas, if a conflict arises between insurer and insured, it is important that it be settled in the fairest and speediest manner possible; whereas it is therefore appropriate that provision be made in legal expenses insurance policies for an arbitration procedure or a procedure offering comparable guarantees;

Whereas the second paragraph of point C of the Annex to Directive 73/239/EEC provides that the risks included in classes 14 and 15 in point A may not be regarded as risks ancillary to other

Part VI European Materials

classes; whereas an insurance undertaking should not be able to cover legal expenses as a risk ancillary to another risk without having obtained an authorisation in respect of the legal expenses risk; whereas, however, Member States should be given the option of regarding class 17 as a risk ancillary to class 18 in specific cases; whereas, therefore, point C of the said Annex should be amended accordingly;

NOTES

Repealed as noted at the beginning of this Directive.

[1] OJ C198, 7.8.79, p 2.

[2] OJ C260, 12.10.81, p 78.

[3] OJ C348, 31.12.80, p 22.

[4] OJ L228, 16.8.73, p 3.

[5] OJ L185, 4.7.87, p 72.

HAS ADOPTED THIS DIRECTIVE—

[6723]
Article 1

The purpose of this Directive is to coordinate the provisions laid down by law, regulation or administrative action concerning legal expenses insurance as referred to in paragraph 17 of point A of the Annex to Council Directive 73/239/EEC in order to facilitate the effective exercise of freedom of establishment and preclude as far as possible any conflict of interest arising in particular out of the fact that the insurer is covering another person or is covering a person in respect of both legal expenses and any other class in that Annex and, should such a conflict arise, to enable it to be resolved.

NOTES

Repealed as noted at the beginning of this Directive.

[6724]
Article 2

1. This Directive shall apply to legal expenses insurance. Such consists in undertaking, against the payment of a premium, to bear the costs of legal proceedings and to provide other services directly linked to insurance cover, in particular with a view to—

- *securing compensation for the loss, damage or injury suffered by the insured person, by settlement out of court or through civil or criminal proceedings;*
- *defending or representing the insured person in civil, criminal, administrative or other proceedings or in respect of any claim made against him.*

2. This Directive shall not, however, apply to—

- *legal expenses insurance where such insurance concerns disputes or risks arising out of, or in connection with, the use of sea-going vessels,*
- *the activity pursued by the insurer providing civil liability cover for the purpose of defending or representing the insured person in any inquiry or proceedings if that activity is at the same time pursued in the insurer's own interest under such cover,*
- *where a Member State so chooses, the activity of legal expenses insurance undertaken by an assistance insurer where this activity is carried out in a Member State other than the one in which the insured person normally resides, where it forms part of a contract covering solely the assistance provided for persons who fall into difficulties while travelling, while away from home or while away from their permanent residence. In this event the contract must clearly state that the cover in question is limited to the circumstances referred to in the foregoing sentence and is ancillary to the assistance.*

NOTES

Repealed as noted at the beginning of this Directive.

[6725]
Article 3

1. Legal expenses cover shall be the subject of a contract separate from that drawn up for the other classes of insurance or shall be dealt with in a separate section of a single policy in which the nature of the legal expenses cover and, should the Member State so request, the amount of the relevant premium are specified.

2. Each Member State shall take the necessary measures to ensure that the undertakings established within its territory adopt, in accordance with the option imposed by the Member State, or at their own choice, if the Member State so agrees, at least one of the following solutions, which are alternatives—

- *(a) the undertaking shall ensure that no member of the staff who is concerned with the management of legal expenses claims or with legal advice in respect thereof carries on at the same time a similar activity*
  - *— if the undertaking is a composite one, for another class transacted by it,*
  - *— irrespective of whether the undertaking is a composite or a specialised one, in another having financial, commercial or administrative links with the first undertaking and carrying on one or more of the other classes of insurance set out in Directive 73/239/EEC;*
- *(b) the undertaking shall entrust the management of claims in respect of legal expenses insurance to an undertaking having separate legal personality. That undertaking shall be mentioned in the separate contract or separate section referred to in paragraph 1. If the undertaking having separate legal personality has links with an undertaking which carries on one or more of the other classes of insurance referred to in point A of the Annex to Directive 73/239/EEC, members of the staff of the undertaking who are concerned with the processing of claims or with legal advice connected with such processing may not pursue the same or a similar activity in the other undertaking at the same time. In addition, Member States may impose the same requirements on the members of the management body;*
- *(c) the undertaking shall, in the contract, afford the insured person the right to entrust the defence of his interests, from the moment that he has the right to claim from his insurer under the policy, to a lawyer of his choice or, to the extent that national law so permits, any other appropriately qualified person.*

3. Whichever solution is adopted, the interest of persons having legal expenses cover shall be regarded as safeguarded in an equivalent manner under this Directive.

Part VI European Materials

NOTES

Repealed as noted at the beginning of this Directive.

[6726]
Article 4

1. Any contract of legal expenses insurance shall expressly recognise that—

- *(a) where recourse is had to a lawyer or other person appropriately qualified according to national law in order to defend, represent or serve the interests of the insured person in any inquiry or proceedings, that insured person shall be free to choose such lawyer or other person;*
- *(b) the insured person shall be free to choose a lawyer or, if he so prefers and to the extent that national law so permits, any other appropriately qualified person, to serve his interests whenever a conflict of interests arises.*

2. Lawyer means any person entitled to pursue his professional activities under one of the denominations laid down in Council Directive 77/249/EEC of 22 March 1977 to facilitate the effective exercise by lawyers of freedom to provide services.[1]

NOTES

Repealed as noted at the beginning of this Directive.

[1] OJ L78, 26.3.77, p 17.

[6727]
Article 5

1. Each Member State may provide exemption from the application of Article 4(1) for legal expenses insurance if all the following conditions are fulfilled—

- *(a) the insurance is limited to cases arising from the use of road vehicles in the territory of the Member State concerned;*
- *(b) the insurance is connected to a contract to provide assistance in the event of accident or breakdown involving a road vehicle;*
- *(c) neither the legal expenses insurer nor the assistance insurer carries out any class of liability insurance;*

(d) *measures are taken so that the legal counsel and representation of each of the parties to a dispute is effected by completely independent lawyers when these parties are insured for legal expenses by the same insurer.*

2. *The exemption granted by a Member State to an undertaking pursuant to paragraph 1 shall not affect the application of Article 3(2).*

NOTES

Repealed as noted at the beginning of this Directive.

[6728]
Article 6

Member States shall adopt all appropriate measures to ensure that, without prejudice to any right of appeal to a judicial body which might be provided for by national law, an arbitration or other procedure offering comparable guarantees of objectivity is provided for whereby, in the event of a difference of opinion between a legal expenses insurer and his insured, a decision can be taken on the attitude to be adopted in order to settle the dispute.

The insurance contract must mention the right of the insured person to have recourse to such a procedure.

NOTES

Repealed as noted at the beginning of this Directive.

[6729]
Article 7

Whenever a conflict of interests arises or there is disagreement over the settlement of the dispute, the legal expenses insurer or, where appropriate, the claims settlement office shall inform the person insured of

— *the right referred to in Article 4,*
— *the possibility of having recourse to the procedure referred to in Article 6.*

NOTES

Repealed as noted at the beginning of this Directive.

[6730]
Article 8

Member States shall abolish all provisions which prohibit an insurer from carrying out within their territory legal expenses insurance and other classes of insurance at the same time.

NOTES

Repealed as noted at the beginning of this Directive.

Article 9 (*Amends the Annex to First Council Directive 73/239/EEC at* **[6691]**.)

[6731]
Article 10

Member States shall take the measures necessary to comply with this Directive by 1 January 1990. They shall forthwith inform the Commission thereof.

They shall apply these measures from 1 July 1990 at the latest.

NOTES

Repealed as noted at the beginning of this Directive.

[6732]
Article 11

Following notification[1] of this Directive, Member States shall communicate to the Commission the texts of the main provisions of national law which they adopt in the field governed by this Directive.

NOTES

Repealed as noted at the beginning of this Directive.

1 This Directive was notified to the Member States on 25 June 1987.

[6733]
Article 12

This Directive is addressed to the Member States.

NOTES

Repealed as noted at the beginning of this Directive.

Done at Luxembourg, 22 June 1987.

SECOND COUNCIL DIRECTIVE

(88/357/EEC)

of 22 June 1988

on the coordination of laws, regulations and administrative provisions relating to direct insurance other than life assurance and laying down provisions to facilitate the effective exercise of freedom to provide services and amending Directive 73/239/EEC

NOTES

Date of publication in OJ: OJ L172, 4.7.88, p 1.

This Directive is repealed by European Parliament and Council Directive 2009/138/EC on the taking-up and pursuit of the business of Insurance and Reinsurance (Solvency II) at **[6153]** et seq, with effect from 1 November 2012 (see art 310 thereof at **[6462]**).

[6734]

THE COUNCIL OF THE EUROPEAN COMMUNITIES,

Having regard to the Treaty establishing the European Economic Community, and in particular Articles 57(2) and 66 thereof,

Having regard to the proposal from the Commission,[1]

In cooperation with the European Parliament,[2]

Having regard to the Opinion of the Economic and Social Committee,[3]

Whereas it is necessary to develop the internal insurance market and, to achieve this objective, it is desirable to make it easier for insurance undertakings having their head office in the Community to provide services in the Member States, thus making it possible for policy-holders to have recourse not only to insurers established in their own country, but also to insurers which have their head office in the Community and are established in other Member States;

Whereas, pursuant to the Treaty, any discrimination with regard to freedom to provide services based on the fact that an undertaking is not established in the Member State in which the services are provided has been prohibited since the end of the transitional period; whereas this prohibition applies to services provided from any establishment in the Community, whether it is the head office of an undertaking or an agency or branch;

Whereas, for practical reasons, it is desirable to define the provision of services taking into account both the insurer's establishment and the place where the risk is situated; whereas therefore a definition of the situation of the risk should also be adopted; whereas, moreover, it is desirable to distinguish between the activity pursued by way of establishment and the activity pursued by way of freedom to provide services;

Whereas it is desirable to supplement the First Council Directive 73/239/EEC of 24 July 1973 on the coordination of laws, regulations and administrative provisions relating to the taking-up and pursuit of the business of direct insurance other than life assurance,[4] *hereinafter referred to as the "First Directive", as last amended by Directive 87/343/EEC,*[5] *in order particularly to clarify the powers and means of supervision vested in the supervisory authorities; whereas it is also desirable to lay down specific provisions regarding the taking-up, pursuit and supervision of activity by way of freedom to provide services;*

Whereas policy-holders who, by virtue of their status, their size or the nature of the risk to be insured, do not require special protection in the State in which the risk is situated should be granted complete freedom to avail themselves of the widest possible insurance market; whereas, moreover, it is desirable to guarantee other policy-holders adequate protection;

Whereas the concern to protect policy-holders and to avoid any disturbance of competition justifies coordinating the relaxation of the matching assets rules, provided for by the First Directive;

Whereas the provisions in force in the Member States regarding insurance contract law continue to differ; whereas the freedom to choose, as the law applicable to the contract, a law other than that of the State in which the risk is situated may be granted in certain cases, in accordance with rules taking into account specific circumstances;

Whereas the scope of this Directive should include compulsory insurance but should require the contract covering such insurance to be in conformity with the specific provisions relating to such insurance, as provided by the Member State imposing the insurance obligation;

Part VI European Materials

Whereas the provisions of the First Directive on the transfer of portfolio should be reinforced and supplemented by provisions specifically covering the transfer of the portfolio of contracts concluded for the provision of services to another undertaking;

Whereas the scope of the provisions specifically concerning freedom to provide services should exclude certain risks, the application to which of the said provisions is rendered inappropriate at this stage by the specific rules adopted by the Member States' authorities, owing to the nature and social implications of such provisions; whereas, therefore, these exclusions should be re-examined after this Directive has been in force for a certain period;

Whereas, in the interests of protecting policy-holders, Member States should, at the present stage in coordination, be allowed the option of limiting the simultaneous pursuit of activity by way of freedom to provide services and activity by way of establishment; whereas no such limitation can be provided for where policy-holders do not require this protection;

Whereas the taking-up and pursuit of freedom to provide services should be subject to procedures guaranteeing the insurance undertaking's compliance with the provisions regarding both financial guarantees and conditions of insurance; whereas these procedures may be relaxed in cases where the activity by way of provision of services covers policy-holders who, by virtue of their status, their size or the nature of the risk to be insured, do not require special protection in the State in which the risk is situated;

Whereas it is necessary to initiate special cooperation with regard to freedom to provide services between the competent supervisory authorities of the Member States and between these authorities and the Commission; whereas provision should also be made for a system of penalties to apply where the undertaking providing the service fails to comply with the provisions of the Member State of provision of service;

Whereas, pending future coordination, the technical reserves should be subject to the rules and supervision of the Member State of provision of services where such provision of services involves risks in respect of which the State receiving the service wishes to provide special protection for policy-holders; whereas, however, if such concern to protect the policy-holders is unjustified, the technical reserves continue to be subject to the rules and supervision of the Member State in which the insurer is established;

Whereas some Member States do not subject insurance transactions to any form of indirect taxation, while the majority apply special taxes and other forms of contribution, including surcharges intended for compensation bodies; whereas the structure and rate of these taxes and contributions vary considerably between the Member States in which they are applied; whereas it is desirable to avoid a situation where existing differences lead to disturbances of competition in insurance services between Member States; whereas, pending future harmonisation, the application of the tax system and of other forms of contributions provided for by the Member State in which the risk is situated is likely to remedy such mischief and whereas it is for the Member States to establish a method of ensuring that such taxes and contributions are collected;

Whereas it is desirable to prevent the uncoordinated application of this Directive and of Council Directive 78/473/EEC of 30 May 1978 on the coordination of laws, regulations and administrative provisions relating to Community co-insurance[6] *from leading to the existence of three different systems in every Member State; whereas, therefore, the criteria defining "large risks" in this Directive should also define risks likely to be covered under Community co-insurance arrangements;*

Whereas it is desirable to take into account, within the meaning of Article 8C of the Treaty, the extent of the effort which needs to be made by certain economies showing differences in development; whereas, therefore, it is desirable to grant certain Member States transitional arrangements for the gradual application of the specific provisions of this Directive relating to freedom to provide services;

NOTES

Repealed as noted at the beginning of this Directive.

1 OJ C32, 12.2.76, p 2.

2 OJ C36, 13.2.78, p 14, OJ C167, 27.6.88 and Decision of 15 June 1988 (not yet published in the Official Journal).

3 OJ C204, 30.8.76, p 13.

4 OJ L228, 16.8.73, p 3.

5 OJ L185, 4.7.87, p 72.

6 OJ L151, 7.6.78, p 25.

HAS ADOPTED THIS DIRECTIVE—

TITLE I
GENERAL PROVISIONS

[6735]
Article 1

The object of this Directive is—

(a) *to supplement the First Directive 73/239/EEC;*

(b) *to lay down special provisions relating to freedom to provide services for the undertakings and in respect of the classes of insurance covered by that First Directive.*

NOTES

Repealed as noted at the beginning of this Directive.

[6736]
Article 2

For the purposes of this Directive—

(a) *"First Directive" means—*
Directive 73/239/EEC;

(b) *"undertaking"—*
— *for the purposes of applying Titles I and II, means— any undertaking which has received official authorisation under Article 6 or 23 of the First Directive;*
— *for the purposes of applying Title III and Title V, means— any undertaking which has received official authorisation under Article 6 of the First Directive;*

(c) *"establishment"—*
means the head office, agency or branch of an undertaking, account being taken of Article 3;

(d) *"Member State where the risk is situated" means—*
— *the Member State in which the property is situated, where the insurance relates either to buildings or to buildings and their contents, in so far as the contents are covered by the same insurance policy,*
— *the Member State of registration, where the insurance relates to vehicles of any type,*
— *the Member State where the policy-holder took out the policy in the case of policies of a duration of four months or less covering travel or holiday risks, whatever the class concerned,*
— *the Member State where the policy-holder has his habitual residence or, if the policy-holder is a legal person, the Member State where the latter's establishment, to which the contract relates, is situated, in all cases not explicitly covered by the foregoing indents;*

(e) *"Member State of establishment" means—*
the Member State in which the establishment covering the risk is situated;

(f) *"Member State of provision of services" means—*
the Member State in which the risk is situated when it is covered by an establishment situated in another Member State.

NOTES

Repealed as noted at the beginning of this Directive.

[6737]
Article 3

For the purposes of the First Directive and of this Directive, any permanent presence of an undertaking in the territory of a Member State shall be treated in the same way as an agency or branch, even if that presence does not take the form of a branch or agency, but consists merely of an office managed by the undertaking's own staff or by a person who is independent but has permanent authority to act for the undertaking as an agency would.

NOTES

Repealed as noted at the beginning of this Directive.

[6738]
Article 4

For the purposes of this Directive and the First Directive, general and special policy conditions shall not include specific conditions intended to meet, in an individual case, the particular circumstances of the risk to be covered.

NOTES

Repealed as noted at the beginning of this Directive.

TITLE II
PROVISIONS SUPPLEMENTARY TO THE FIRST DIRECTIVE

Article 5 (*Inserts First Council Directive 73/239/EEC, art 5(d) at* **[6648]**.)

[6739]
Article 6

For the purposes of applying the first subparagraph of Article 15(2) and Article 24 of the First Directive, the Member States shall comply with Annex 1 to this Directive as regards the matching rules.

NOTES

Repealed as noted at the beginning of this Directive.

[6740]
Article 7

1. The law applicable to contracts of insurance referred to by this Directive and covering risks situated within the Member States is determined in accordance with the following provisions—

(a) Where a policy-holder has his habitual residence or central administration within the territory of the Member State in which the risk is situated, the law applicable to the insurance contract shall be the law of that Member State. However, where the law of that Member State so allows, the parties may choose the law of another country.

(b) Where a policy-holder does not have his habitual residence or central administration in the Member State in which the risk is situated, the parties to the contract of insurance may choose to apply either the law of the Member State in which the risk is situated or the law of the country in which the policy-holder has his habitual residence or central administration.

(c) Where a policy-holder pursues a commercial or industrial activity or a liberal profession and where the contract covers two or more risks relating to these activities and situated in different Member States, the freedom of choice of the law applicable to the contract shall extend to the laws of those Member States and of the country in which the policy-holder has his habitual residence or central administration.

(d) Notwithstanding subparagraphs (b) and (c), where the Member States referred to in those subparagraphs grant greater freedom of choice of the law applicable to the contract, the parties may take advantage of this freedom.

(e) Notwithstanding subparagraphs (a), (b) and (c), when the risks covered by the contract are limited to events occurring in one Member State other than the Member State where the risk is situated, as defined in Article 2(d), the parties may always choose the law of the former State.

[(f) in the case of the risks referred to in Article 5(d) of Directive 73/239/EEC, the parties to the contract may choose any law.]

(g) The fact that, in the cases referred to in subparagraph (a) or (f), the parties have chosen a law shall not, where all the other elements relevant to the situation at the time of the choice are connected with one Member State only, prejudice the application of the mandatory rules of the law of that Member State, which means the rules from which the law of that Member State allows no derogation by means of a contract.

(h) The choice referred to in the preceding subparagraphs must be expressed or demonstrated with reasonable certainty by the terms of the contract or the circumstances of the case. If this is not so, or if no choice has been made, the contract shall be governed by the law of the country, from amongst those considered in the relevant subparagraphs above, with which it is most closely connected. Nevertheless, a severable part of the contract which has a closer connection with another country, from amongst those considered in the relevant subparagraphs, may by way of exception be governed by the law of that other country. The contract shall be rebuttably presumed to be most closely connected with the Member State in which the risk is situated.

(i) Where a State includes several territorial units, each of which has its own rules of law concerning contractual obligations, each unit shall be considered as a country for the purposes of identifying the law applicable under this Directive.

A Member State in which various territorial units have their own rules of law concerning contractual obligations shall not be bound to apply the provisions of this Directive to conflicts which arise between the laws of those units.

2. Nothing in this Article shall restrict the application of the rules of the law of the forum in a situation where they are mandatory, irrespective of the law otherwise applicable to the contract.

If the law of a Member State so stipulates, the mandatory rules of the law of the Member State in which the risk is situated or of the Member State imposing the obligation to take out insurance may be applied if and in so far as, under the law of those States, those rules must be applied whatever the law applicable to the contract.

Where the contract covers risks situated in more than one Member State, the contract is considered for the purposes of applying this paragraph as constituting several contracts each relating to only one Member State.

3. Subject to the preceding paragraphs, the Member States shall apply to the insurance contracts referred to by this Directive their general rules of private international law concerning contractual obligations.

NOTES

Repealed as noted at the beginning of this Directive.

Para 1: sub-para (f) substituted by Council Directive 92/49/EEC, art 27.

[6741]

Article 8

1. Under the conditions set out in this Article, insurance undertakings may offer and conclude compulsory insurance contracts in accordance with the rules of this Directive and of the First Directive.

2. When a Member State imposes an obligation to take out insurance, the contract shall not satisfy that obligation unless it is in accordance with the specific provisions relating to that insurance laid down by that Member State.

3. When, in the case of compulsory insurance, the law of the Member State in which the risk is situated and the law of the Member State imposing the obligation to take out insurance contradict each other, the latter shall prevail.

4.

[(a) Subject to subparagraph (c), the third subparagraph of Article 7(2) shall apply where the insurance contract provides cover in two or more Member States, at least one of which makes insurance compulsory.]

(b) . . .

(c) A Member State may, by way of derogation from Article 7, lay down that the law applicable to a compulsory insurance contract is the law of the State which imposes the obligation to take out insurance.

(d) Where a Member State imposes compulsory insurance and the insurer must notify the competent authorities of any cessation of cover, such cessation may be invoked against injured third parties only in the circumstances laid down in the legislation of that State.

5.

(a) Each Member State shall communicate to the Commission the risks against which insurance is compulsory under its legislation, stating—

— the specific legal provisions relating to that insurance,

— the particulars which must be given in the certificate which an insurer must issue to an insured person where that State requires proof that the obligation to take out insurance has been complied with. A Member State may require that those particulars include a declaration by the insurer to the effect that the contract complies with the specific provisions relating to that insurance.

(b) The Commission shall publish the particulars referred to in subparagraph (a) in the Official Journal of the European Communities.

(c) A Member State shall accept, as proof that the insurance obligation has been fulfilled, a certificate, the content of which is in conformity with the second indent of subparagraph (a).

NOTES

Repealed as noted at the beginning of this Directive.

Para 4: sub-para (a) substituted and sub-para (b) repealed by Council Directive 92/49/EEC, art 30(1).

Articles 9–11 (*Arts 9, 10 contain amendments to First Council Directive 73/239/EEC, which have been superseded by provisions contained in Council Directive 92/49/EEC; art 11(1) repeals First Council Directive 73/239/EEC, art 21; art 11(2)–(7) repealed by Council Directive 92/49/EEC, art 2(1).*)

TITLE III
PROVISIONS PECULIAR TO THE FREEDOM TO PROVIDE SERVICES

[6742]
Article 12

1. This Title shall apply where an undertaking, through an establishment situated in a Member State, covers a risk situated, within the meaning of Article 2(d), in another Member State; the latter shall be the Member State of provision of services for the purposes of this Title.

2. This Title shall not apply to the transactions, undertakings and institutions to which the First Directive does not apply, nor to the risks to be covered by the institutions under public law referred to in Article 4 of that Directive.

. . .

3. . . .

NOTES

Repealed as noted at the beginning of this Directive.
Para 2: words omitted repealed by Council Directive 92/49/EEC, art 37.
Para 3: repealed by Council Directive 92/49/EEC, art 37.

[6743]
[Article 12a

1. This Article shall apply where an undertaking, through an establishment situated in a Member State, covers a risk, other than carrier's liability, classified under class 10 of point A of the Annex to Directive 73/239/EEC which is situated in another Member State.

2. The Member State of provision of services shall require the undertaking to become a member of and participate in the financing of its national bureau and its national guarantee fund.

The undertaking shall not, however, be required to make any payment or contribution to the bureau and fund of the Member State of provision of services in respect of risks covered by way of provision of services other than one calculated on the same basis as for undertakings covering risks, other than carrier's liability, in class 10 through an establishment situated in that Member State, by reference to its premium income from that class in that Member State or the number of risks in that class covered there.

3. This Directive shall not prevent an insurance undertaking providing services from being required to comply with the rules in the Member State of provision of services concerning the cover of aggravated risks, insofar as they apply to established undertakings.

4. The Member State of provision of services shall require the undertaking to ensure that persons pursuing claims arising out of events occurring in its territory are not placed in a less favourable situation as a result of the fact that the undertaking is covering a risk, other than carrier's liability, in class 10 by way of provision of services rather than through an establishment situated in that State.

For this purpose, the Member State of provision of services shall require the undertaking to appoint a representative resident or established in its territory who shall collect all necessary information in relation to claims and shall possess sufficient powers to represent the undertaking in relation to persons suffering damage who could pursue claims, including the payment of such claims, and to represent it or, where necessary, to have it represented before the courts and authorities of that Member State in relation to these claims.

The representative may also be required to represent the undertaking before the competent authorities of the State of provision of services with regard to checking the existence and validity of motor vehicle liability insurance policies.

The Member State of provision of services may not require that appointee to undertake activities on behalf of the undertaking which appointed him other than those set out in the second and third subparagraphs.

. . .

The appointment of the representative shall not in itself constitute the opening of a branch or agency for the purpose of Article 6(2)(b) of Directive 73/239/EEC and the representative shall not be an establishment within the meaning of Article 2(c) of this Directive.

[If the insurance undertaking has failed to appoint a representative, Member States may give their approval to the claims representative appointed in accordance with Article 4 of Directive 2000/26/EC[1] *assuming the function of the representative appointed according to this paragraph.]]*

NOTES

Inserted by Council Directive 90/618/EEC, art 6.

Repealed as noted at the beginning of this Directive.

Para 4: words omitted repealed by European Parliament and Council Directive 2005/14/EC, art 3; final sub-paragraph added by Council Directive 2000/26/EC, art 9.

[1] Directive 2000/26/EC of the European Parliament and of the Council of 16 May 2000 on the approximation of the laws of the Member States relating to insurance against civil liability in respect of the use of motor vehicles and amending Council Directives 73/239/EEC and 88/357/EEC (OJ L181, 20.7.2000, p 65).

Article 13 (*Repealed by Council Directive 92/49/EEC, art 37.*)

[6744]
[Article 14

Any undertaking that intends to carry on business for the first time in one or more Member States under the freedom to provide services shall first inform the competent authorities of the home Member State, indicating the nature of the risks it proposes to cover.]

NOTES

Substituted by Council Directive 92/49/EEC, art 34.

Repealed as noted at the beginning of this Directive.

Article 15 (*Repealed by Council Directive 92/49/EEC, art 37.*)

[6745]
[Article 16

1. Within one month of the notification provided for in Article 14, the competent authorities of the home Member State shall communicate to the Member State or Member States within the territories of which an undertaking intends to carry on business under the freedom to provide services—

(a) a certificate attesting that the undertaking has the minimum solvency margin calculated in accordance with Articles 16 and 17 of Directive 73/239;

(b) the classes of insurance which the undertaking has been authorised to offer;

(c) the nature of the risks which the undertaking proposes to cover in the Member State of the provision of services.

At the same time, they shall inform the undertaking concerned accordingly.

Each Member State within the territory of which an undertaking intends, under the freedom to provide services, to cover risks in class 10 of point A of the Annex to Directive 73/239 other than carrier's liability may require that the undertaking—

— *communicate the name and address of the representative referred to in Article 12a(4) of this Directive;*

— *produce a declaration that the undertaking has become a member of the national bureau and national guarantee fund of the Member State of the provision of services.*

2. Where the competent authorities of the home Member State do not communicate the information referred to in paragraph 1 within the period laid down, they shall give the reasons for their refusal to the undertaking within that same period. That refusal shall be subject to a right to apply to the courts in the home Member State.

3. The undertaking may start business on the certified date on which it is informed of the communication provided for in the first subparagraph of paragraph 1.]

NOTES

Substituted by Council Directive 92/49/EEC, art 35.

Repealed as noted at the beginning of this Directive.

[6746]
[Article 17

Any change which an undertaking intends in make to the information referred to in Article 14 shall be subject to the procedure provided for in Articles 14 and 16.]

NOTES

Substituted by Council Directive 92/49/EEC, art 36.

Repealed as noted at the beginning of this Directive.

Articles 18–25 (*Repealed by Council Directive 92/49/EEC, arts 19, 39(1), 40(1), 42(1), 43(1), 44(1), 45(1), 46(1).*)

[6747]
Article 26

1. The risks which may be covered by way of Community co-insurance within the meaning of Directive 78/473/EEC shall be those defined in Article 5(d) of the First Directive.

2. The provisions of this Directive regarding the risks defined in Article 5(d) of the First Directive shall apply to the leading insurer.

NOTES

Repealed as noted at the beginning of this Directive.

TITLE IV
TRANSITIONAL ARRANGEMENTS

[6748]
Article 27

1. Greece, Ireland, Spain and Portugal may apply the following transitional arrangements—

(i) until 31 December 1992, they may apply, to all risks, the regime other than that for risks referred to in Article 5(d) of the First Directive,

(ii) from 1 January 1993 to 31 December 1994, the regime for large risks shall apply to risks referred to under (i) and (ii) of Article 5(d) of the First Directive; for risks referred to under (iii) of the abovementioned Article 5(d), these Member States shall fix the thresholds to apply therefor;

(iii) Spain

— *from 1 January 1995 to 31 December 1996, the thresholds of the first stage described in Article 5(d)(iii) of the First Directive shall apply,*

— *from 1 January 1997, the thresholds of the second stage shall apply.*

Portugal, Ireland and Greece

— *from 1 January 1995 to 31 December 1998 the thresholds of the first stage described in Article 5(d)(iii) of the First Directive shall apply,*

— *from 1 January 1999 the thresholds of the second stage shall apply.*

[The derogation allowed from 1 January 1995 shall only apply to contracts covering risks classified under classes 3, 8, 9, 10, 13 and 16 situated exclusively in one of the four Member States benefiting from the transitional arrangements.]

2. Until 31 December 1994, Article 26(1) of this Directive shall not apply to risks situated in the four Member States listed in this Article. For the transitional period from 1 January 1995, the risks defined under Article 5(d) (iii) of the First Directive situated in these Member States and capable of being covered by Community co-insurance within the meaning of Directive 78/473/EEC shall be those which exceed the thresholds referred to in paragraph 1(iii) of this Article.

NOTES

Repealed as noted at the beginning of this Directive.
Para (1): words in square brackets substituted by Council Directive 90/618/EEC, art 10.

TITLE V
FINAL PROVISIONS

[6749]
Article 28

The Commission and the competent authorities of the Member States shall collaborate closely for the purpose of facilitating the supervision of direct insurance within the Community.

Every Member State shall inform the Commission of any major difficulties to which application of this Directive gives rise, inter alia, any arising if a Member State becomes aware of an abnormal transfer of insurance business to the detriment of undertakings established in its territory and to the advantage of branches and agencies located just beyond its borders.

The Commission and the competent authorities of the Member States concerned shall examine these difficulties as quickly as possible in order to find an appropriate solution.

Where necessary, the Commission shall submit appropriate proposals to the Council.

NOTES

Repealed as noted at the beginning of this Directive.

[6750]
Article 29

The Commission shall forward to the Council regular reports, the first on 1 July 1993, on the development of the market in insurance transacted under conditions of freedom to provide services.

NOTES

Repealed as noted at the beginning of this Directive.

[6751]
Article 30

Where this Directive makes reference to the ECU, the exchange value in national currencies to be used with effect from 31 December of each year shall be the value which applies on the last day of the preceding October for which exchange values for the ECU are available in all Community currencies.

Article 2 of Directive 76/580/EEC[1] *shall apply only to Articles 3, 16 and 17 of the First Directive.*

NOTES

Repealed as noted at the beginning of this Directive.

[1] OJ L189, 13.9.76, p 13.

[6752]
Article 31

Every five years, the Council, acting on a proposal from the Commission, shall review and if necessary amend any amounts expressed in ECU in this Directive, taking into account changes in the economic and monetary situation of the Community.

NOTES

Repealed as noted at the beginning of this Directive.

[6753]
Article 32

Member States shall amend their national provisions to comply with this Directive within 18 months of the date of its notification[1] *and shall forthwith inform the Commission thereof.*

The provisions amended in accordance with this Article shall be applied within 24 months of the date of the notification of the Directive.

NOTES

Repealed as noted at the beginning of this Directive.

[1] This Directive was notified to Member States in 30 June 1988.

[6754]
Article 33

Upon notification of this Directive, Member States shall ensure that the texts of the main laws, regulations or administrative provisions which they adopt in the field covered by this Directive are communicated to the Commission.

NOTES

Repealed as noted at the beginning of this Directive.

[6755]
Article 34

The Annexes shall form an integral part of this Directive.

NOTES

Repealed as noted at the beginning of this Directive.

[6756]
Article 35

This Directive is addressed to the Member States.

NOTES

Repealed as noted at the beginning of this Directive.

Done at Luxembourg, 22 June 1988.

ANNEX 1

MATCHING RULES

[6757]

The currency in which the insurer's commitments are payable shall be determined in accordance with the following rules—

1. *Where the cover provided by a contract is expressed in terms of a particular currency, the insurer's commitments are considered to be payable in that currency.*
2. *Where the cover provided by a contract is not expressed in terms of any currency, the insurer's commitments are considered to be payable in the currency of the country in which the risk is situated. However, the insurer may choose the currency in which the premium is expressed if there are justifiable grounds for exercising such a choice.*

This could be the case if, from the time the contract is entered into, it appears likely that a claim will be paid in the currency of the premium and not in the currency of the country in which the risk is situated.

3. *The Member States may authorise the insurer to consider that the currency in which he must provide cover will be either that which he will use in accordance with experience acquired or, in the absence of such experience, the currency of the country in which he is established—*
    - *for contracts covering risks classified under classes 4, 5, 6, 11, 12 and 13 (producers' liability only), and*
    - *for contracts covering the risks classified under other classes where, in accordance with the nature of the risks, the cover is to be provided in a currency other than that which would result from the application of the above procedures.*
4. *Where a claim has been reported to an insurer and is payable in a specified currency other than the currency resulting from application of the above procedures, the insurer's commitments shall be considered to be payable in that currency, and in particular the currency in which the compensation to be paid by the insurer has been determined by a court judgment or by agreement between the insurer and the insured.*
5. *Where a claim is assessed in a currency which is known to the insurer in advance but which is different from the currency resulting from application of the above procedures, the insurers may consider their commitments to be payable in that currency.*
6. *The Member States may authorise undertakings not to cover their technical reserves by matching assets if application of the above procedures would result in the undertaking—whether head office or branch—being obliged, in order to comply with the matching principle, to hold assets in a currency amounting to not more than 7% of the assets existing in other currencies.*

However—

(a) *in the case of technical reserve assets to be matched in Greek drachmas, Irish pounds and Portuguese escudos, this amount shall not exceed—*

- *1 million ECU during a transitional period ending 31 December 1992;*
- *2 million ECU from 1 January 1993 to 31 December 1998;*

(b) *in the case of technical reserve assets to be matched in Belgian francs, Luxembourg francs and Spanish pesetas, this amount shall not exceed 2 million ECU during a transitional period ending 31 December 1996.*

From the end of the transitional periods defined under (a) and (b), the general regime shall apply for these currencies, unless the Council decides otherwise.

7. *The Member States may choose not to require undertakings—whether head offices or branches—to apply the matching principle where commitments are payable in a currency other than the currency of one of the Community Member States, if investments in that currency are regulated, if the currency is subject to transfer restrictions or if, for similar reasons, it is not suitable for covering technical reserves.*

[8. *Insurance undertakings may hold non-matching assets to cover an amount not exceeding 20% of their commitments in a particular currency.*

9. *A Member State may provide that when under the preceding procedures a commitment must be covered by assets expressed in a Member State's currency that requirement shall also be considered as satisfied when the assets are expressed in ecus.]*

NOTES

Repealed as noted at the beginning of this Directive.

Points 8, 9: substituted by Council Directive 92/49/EEC, art 23.

ANNEX 2A

UNDERWRITING ACCOUNT

[6758]

1. Total gross premiums earned

2. Total cost of claims

3. Commission costs

4. Gross underwriting result

NOTES

Repealed as noted at the beginning of this Directive.

ANNEX 2B

UNDERWRITING ACCOUNT

[6759]

1. Gross premiums for the last underwriting year

2. Gross claims in the last underwriting year (including reserve at the end of underwriting year)

3. Commission costs

4. Gross underwriting result

NOTES

Repealed as noted at the beginning of this Directive.

COUNCIL DIRECTIVE

(92/49/EEC)

of 18 June 1992

on the coordination of laws, regulations and administrative provisions relating to direct insurance other than life assurance and amending Directives 73/239/EEC and 88/357/EEC (third non-life insurance Directive)

NOTES

Date of publication in OJ: OJ L228, 11.8.92, p 1.

This Directive is repealed by European Parliament and Council Directive 2009/138/EC on the taking-up and pursuit of the business of Insurance and Reinsurance (Solvency II) at **[6153]** et seq, with effect from 1 November 2012 (see art 310 thereof at **[6462]**).

[6760]

THE COUNCIL OF THE EUROPEAN COMMUNITIES,

Having regard to the Treaty establishing the European Economic Community, and in particular Articles 57(2) and 66 thereof,

Having regard to the proposal from the Commission,[1]

In cooperation with the European Parliament,[2]

Having regard to the opinion of the Economic and Social Committee,[3]

(1) Whereas it is necessary to complete the internal market in direct insurance other than life assurance from the point of view both of the right of establishment and of the freedom to provide services, to make it easier for insurance undertakings with head offices in the Community to cover risks situated within the Community;

(2) Whereas the Second Council Directive of 22 June 1988 on the coordination of laws, regulations and administrative provisions relating to direct insurance other than life assurance and laying down provisions to facilitate the effective exercise of freedom to provide services and amending Directive 73/239/EEC (88/357/EEC)[4] has already contributed substantially to the achievement of the internal market in direct insurance other than life assurance by granting policyholders who, by virtue of their status, their size or the nature of the risks to be insured, do not

require special protection in the Member State in which a risk is situated complete freedom to avail themselves of the widest possible insurance market;

(3) Whereas Directive 88/357/EEC therefore represents an important stage in the merging of national markets into an integrated market and that stage must be supplemented by other Community instruments with a view to enabling all policyholders, irrespective of their status, their size or the nature of the risks to be insured, to have recourse to any insurer with a head office in the Community who carries on business there, under the right of establishment or the freedom to provide services, while guaranteeing them adequate protection;

(4) Whereas this Directive forms part of the body of Community legislation already enacted which includes the First Council Directive of 24 July 1973 on the coordination of laws, regulations and administrative provisions relating to the taking up and pursuit of the business of direct insurance other than life assurance (73/239/EEC)[5] and the Council Directive of 19 December 1991 on the annual accounts and consolidated accounts of insurance undertakings (91/674/EEC);[6]

(5) Whereas the approach adopted consists in bringing about such harmonisation as is essential, necessary and sufficient to achieve the mutual recognition of authorisations and prudential control systems, thereby making it possible to grant a single authorisation valid throughout the Community and apply the principle of supervision by the home Member State;

(6) Whereas, as a result, the taking up and the pursuit of the business of insurance are henceforth to be subject to the grant of a single official authorisation issued by the competent authorities of the Member State in which an insurance undertaking has its head office; whereas such authorisation enables an undertaking to carry on business throughout the Community, under the right of establishment or the freedom to provide services; whereas the Member State of the branch or of the provision of services may no longer require insurance undertakings which wish to carry on insurance business there and which have already been authorised in their home Member State to seek fresh authorisation; whereas Directives 73/239/EEC and 88/357/EEC should therefore be amended along those lines;

(7) Whereas the competent authorities of home Member States will henceforth be responsible for monitoring the financial health of insurance undertakings, including their state of solvency, the establishment of adequate technical provisions and the covering of those provisions by matching assets;

(8) Whereas certain provisions of this Directive define minimum standards; whereas a home Member State may lay down stricter rules for insurance undertakings authorised by its own competent authorities;

(9) Whereas the competent authorities of the Member States must have at their disposal such means of supervision as are necessary to ensure the orderly pursuit of business by insurance undertakings throughout the Community whether carried on under the right of establishment or the freedom to provide services; whereas, in particular, they must be able to introduce appropriate safeguards or impose sanctions aimed at preventing irregularities and infringements of the provisions on insurance supervision;

(10) Whereas the internal market comprises an area without internal frontiers and involves access to all insurance business other than life assurance throughout the Community and, hence, the possibility for any duly authorised insurer to cover any of the risks referred to in the Annex to Directive 73/239/EEC; whereas, to that end, the monopoly enjoyed by certain bodies in certain Member States in respect of the coverage of certain risks must be abolished;

(11) Whereas the provisions on transfers of portfolios must be adapted to bring them into line with the single authorisation system introduced by this Directive;

(12) Whereas Directive 91/674/EEC has already effected the necessary harmonisation of the Member States' rules on the technical provisions which insurers are required to establish to cover their commitments, and that harmonisation makes it possible to grant mutual recognition of those provisions;

(13) Whereas the rules governing the spread, localisation and matching of the assets used to cover technical provisions must be coordinated in order to facilitate the mutual recognition of Member States' rules; whereas that coordination must take account of the measures on the liberalisation of capital movements provided for in the Council Directive of 24 June 1988 for the implementation of Article 67 of the Treaty (88/361/EEC)[7] and the progress made by the Community towards economic and monetary union;

(14) Whereas, however, the home Member State may not require insurance undertakings to invest the assets covering their technical provisions in particular categories of assets, as such a requirement would be incompatible with the measures on the liberalisation of capital movements provided for in Directive 88/361/EEC;

(15) Whereas, pending the adoption of a Directive on investment services harmonising inter alia the definition of the concept of regulated market, for the purposes of this Directive and without prejudice to such future harmonisation that concept must be defined provisionally; whereas that definition will be replaced by that harmonised at Community level which will give the home Member State of the market the responsibilities for these matters which this Directive transitionally

gives to the insurance undertaking's home Member State;

(16) Whereas the list of items of which the solvency margin required by Directive 73/239/EEC may be made up must be supplemented to take account of new financial instruments and of the facilities granted to other financial institutions for the constitution of their own funds;

(17) Whereas within the framework of an integrated insurance market policyholders who, by virtue of their status, their size or the nature of the risks to be insured, do not require special protection in the Member State in which a risk is situated should be granted complete freedom to choose the law applicable to their insurance contracts;

(18) Whereas the harmonisation of insurance contract law is not a prior condition for the achievement of the internal market in insurance; whereas, therefore, the opportunity afforded to the Member States of imposing the application of their law to insurance contracts covering risks situated within their territories is likely to provide adequate safeguards for policyholders who require special protection;

(19) Whereas within the framework of an internal market it is in the policyholder's interest that he should have access to the widest possible range of insurance products available in the Community so that he can choose that which is best suited to his needs; whereas it is for the Member State in which the risk is situated to ensure that there is nothing to prevent the marketing within its territory of all the insurance products offered for sale in the Community as long as they do not conflict with the legal provisions protecting the general good in force in the Member State in which the risk is situated, and insofar as the general good is not safeguarded by the rules of the home Member State, provided that such provisions must be applied without discrimination to all undertakings operating in that Member State and be objectively necessary and in proportion to the objective pursued;

(20) Whereas the Member States must be able to ensure that the insurance products and contract documents used, under the right of establishment or the freedom to provide services, to cover risks situated within their territories comply with such specific legal provisions protecting the general good as are applicable; whereas the systems of supervision to be employed must meet the requirements of an integrated market but their employment may not constitute a prior condition for carrying on insurance business; whereas from this standpoint systems for the prior approval of policy conditions do not appear to be justified; whereas it is therefore necessary to provide for other systems better suited to the requirements of an internal market which enable every Member State to guarantee policyholders adequate protection;

(21) Whereas if a policyholder is a natural person, he should be informed by the insurance undertaking of the law which will apply to the contract and of the arrangements for handling policyholders' complaints concerning contracts;

(22) Whereas in some Member States private or voluntary health insurance serves as a partial or complete alternative to health cover provided for by the social security systems;

(23) Whereas the nature and social consequences of health insurance contracts justify the competent authorities of the Member State in which a risk is situated in requiring systematic notification of the general and special policy conditions in order to verify that such contracts are a partial or complete alternative to the health cover provided by the social security system; whereas such verification must not be a prior condition for the marketing of the products; whereas the particular nature of health insurance, serving as a partial or complete alternative to the health cover provided by the social security system, distinguishes it from other classes of indemnity insurance and life assurance insofar as it is necessary to ensure that policyholders have effective access to private health cover or health cover taken out on a voluntary basis regardless of their age or risk profile;

(24) Whereas to this end some Member States have adopted specific legal provisions; whereas, to protect the general good, it is possible to adopt or maintain such legal provisions insofar as they do not unduly restrict the right of establishment or the freedom to provide services, it being understood that such provisions must apply in an identical manner whatever the home Member State of the undertaking may be; whereas these legal provisions may differ in nature according to the conditions in each Member State; whereas these measures may provide for open enrolment, rating on a uniform basis according to the type of policy and lifetime cover; whereas that objective may also be achieved by requiring undertakings offering private health cover or health cover taken out on a voluntary basis to offer standard policies in line with the cover provided by statutory social security schemes at a premium rate at or below a prescribed maximum and to participate in loss compensation schemes; whereas, as a further possibility, it may be required that the technical basis of private health cover or health cover taken out on a voluntary basis be similar to that of life assurance;

(25) Whereas, because of the coordination effected by Directive 73/239/EEC as amended by this Directive, the possibility, afforded to the Federal Republic of Germany under Article 7(2)(c) of the same Directive, of prohibiting the simultaneous transaction of health insurance and other classes is no longer justified and must therefore be abolished;

(26) Whereas Member States may require any insurance undertakings offering compulsory insurance against accidents at work at their own risk within their territories to comply with the specific provisions laid down in their national law on such insurance; whereas, however, this

requirement may not apply to the provisions concerning financial supervision, which are the exclusive responsibility of the home Member State;

(27) Whereas exercise of the right of establishment requires an undertaking to maintain a permanent presence in the Member State of the branch; whereas responsibility for the specific interests of insured persons and victims in the case of third-party liability motor insurance requires adequate structures in the Member State of the branch for the collection of all the necessary information on compensation claims relating to that risk, with sufficient powers to represent the undertaking vis-à-vis injured parties who could claim compensation, including powers to pay such compensation, and to represent the undertaking or, if necessary, to arrange for it to be represented in the courts and before the competent authorities of that Member State in connection with claims for compensation;

(28) Whereas within the framework of the internal market no Member State may continue to prohibit the simultaneous carrying on of insurance business within its territory under the right of establishment and the freedom to provide services; whereas the option granted to Member States in this connection by Directive 88/357/EEC should therefore be abolished;

(29) Whereas provision should be made for a system of penalties to be imposed when, in the Member State in which a risk is situated, an insurance undertaking does not comply with those provisions protecting the general good that are applicable to it;

(30) Whereas some Member States do not subject insurance transactions to any form of indirect taxation, while the majority apply special taxes and other forms of contribution, including surcharges intended for compensation bodies; whereas the structures and rates of such taxes and contributions vary considerably between the Member States in which they are applied; whereas it is desirable to prevent existing differences leading to distortions of competition in insurance services between Member States; whereas, pending subsequent harmonisation, application of the tax systems and other forms of contribution provided for by the Member States in which risks are situated is likely to remedy that problem and it is for the Member States to make arrangements to ensure that such taxes and contributions are collected;

(31) Whereas technical adjustments to the detailed rules laid down in this Directive may be necessary from time to time to take account of the future development of the insurance industry; whereas the Commission will make such adjustments as and when necessary, after consulting the Insurance Committee set up by Directive 91/675/EEC,[8] *in the exercise of the implementing powers conferred on it by the Treaty;*

(32) Whereas it is necessary to adopt specific provisions intended to ensure smooth transition from the legal regime in existence when this Directive becomes applicable to the regime that it introduces, taking care not to place an additional workload on Member States' competent authorities;

(33) Whereas under Article 8c of the Treaty account should be taken of the extent of the effort which must be made by certain economies at different stages of development; whereas, therefore, transitional arrangements should be adopted for the gradual application of this Directive by certain Member States,

NOTES

Repealed as noted at the beginning of this Directive.

1 OJ C244, 28.9.90, p 28 and OJ C93, 13.4.92, p 1.

2 OJ C67, 16.3.92, p 98 and OJ C150, 15.6.92.

3 OJ C102, 18.4.91, p 7.

4 OJ L172, 4.7.88, p 1. Last amended by Directive 90/618/EEC (OJ L330, 29.11.90, p 44).

5 OJ L228, 16.8.73, p 3. Last amended by Directive 88/357/EEC (OJ L172, 4.7.88, p 1).

6 OJ L374, 31.12.91, p 7.

7 OJ L178, 8.7.88, p 5.

8 OJ L374, 31.12.91, p 32.

HAS ADOPTED THIS DIRECTIVE—

TITLE I
DEFINITIONS AND SCOPE

[6761]
Article 1

For the purposes of this Directive—

(a) insurance undertaking shall mean an undertaking which has received official authorisation in accordance with Article 6 of Directive 73/239/EEC;

(b) *branch* shall mean an agency or branch of an insurance undertaking, having regard to Article 3 of Directive 88/357/EEC;

(c) *home Member State* shall mean the Member State in which the head office of the insurance undertaking covering a risk is situated;

(d) *Member State of the branch* shall mean the Member State in which the branch covering a risk is situated;

(e) *Member State of the provision of services* shall mean the Member State in which a risk is situated, as defined in Article 2(d) of Directive 88/357/EEC, if it is covered by an insurance undertaking or a branch situated in another Member State;

(f) *control* shall mean the relationship between a parent undertaking and a subsidiary, as defined in Article 1 of Directive 83/349/EEC,[1] or a similar relationship between any natural or legal person and an undertaking;

(g) *qualifying holding* shall mean a direct or indirect holding in an undertaking which represents 10% or more of the capital or of the voting rights or which makes it possible to exercise a significant influence over the management of the undertaking in which a holding subsists.

[For the purposes of this definition, in the context of Articles 8 and 15 and of the other levels of holding referred to in Article 15, the voting rights referred to in Articles 9 and 10 of Directive 2004/109/EC,[2] as well as the conditions regarding aggregation thereof laid down in Article 12(4) and (5) of that Directive, shall be taken into account.

Member States shall not take into account voting rights or shares which investment firms or credit institutions may hold as a result of providing the underwriting of financial instruments and/or placing of financial instruments on a firm commitment basis included under point 6 of Section A of Annex I to Directive 2004/39/EC,[3] provided that those rights are, on the one hand, not exercised or otherwise used to intervene in the management of the issuer and, on the other, disposed of within one year of acquisition.]

(h) *parent undertaking* shall mean a parent undertaking as defined in Articles 1 and 2 of Directive 83/349/EEC;

(i) *subsidiary* shall mean a subsidiary undertaking as defined in Articles 1 and 2 of Directive 83/349/EEC; any subsidiary of a subsidiary undertaking shall also be regarded as a subsidiary of the undertaking which is those undertakings' ultimate parent undertaking;

(j) *regulated market* shall mean a financial market regarded by an undertaking's home Member State as a regulated market pending the adoption of a definition in a Directive on investment services and characterised by—

— regular operation; and

— the fact that regulations issued or approved by the appropriate authorities define the conditions for the operation of the market, the conditions for access to the market and, where the Council Directive of 5 March 1979 coordinating the conditions for the admission of securities to official stock-exchange listing (79/279/EEC)[4] applies, the conditions for admission to listing imposed in that Directive or, where that Directive does not apply, the conditions to be satisfied by a financial instrument in order to be effectively dealt in on the market.

For the purposes of this Directive, a regulated market may be situated in a Member State or in a third country. In the latter event, the market must be recognised by the home Member State and meet comparable requirements. Any financial instruments dealt in on that market must be of a quality comparable to that of the instruments dealt in on the regulated market or markets of the Member State in question;

(k) *competent authorities* shall mean the national authorities which are empowered by law or regulation to supervise insurance undertakings.

[(l) *close links* shall mean a situation in which two or more natural or legal persons are linked by—

(a) "participation", which shall mean the ownership, direct or by way of control, of 20% or more of the voting rights or capital of an undertaking, or

(b) "control", which shall mean the relationship between a parent undertaking and a subsidiary, in all the cases referred to in Article 1(1) and (2) of Directive 83/349/EEC,[5] or a similar relationship between any natural or legal person and an undertaking; any subsidiary undertaking of a subsidiary undertaking shall also be considered a subsidiary of the parent undertaking which is at the head of those undertakings.

A situation in which two or more natural or legal persons are permanently linked to one and the same person by a control relationship shall also be regarded as constituting a close link between such persons.]

NOTES

Repealed as noted at the beginning of this Directive.

Point (g): words in square brackets substituted by European Parliament and Council Directive 2007/44/EC, art 1(1).

Point (l): added by Council Directive 95/26/EC, art 2(1).

1 OJ L193, 18.7.83, p 1.

2 Directive 2004/109/EC of the European Parliament and of the Council of 15 December 2004 on the harmonisation of transparency requirements in relation to information about issuers whose securities are admitted to trading on a regulated market (OJ L390, 31.12.2004, p 38).

3 Directive 2004/39/EC of the European Parliament and of the Council of 21 April 2004 on markets in financial instruments (OJ L145, 30.4.2004, p 1). Directive as last amended by Directive 2007/44/EC (OJ L247, 21.9.2007, p 1).

4 OJ L66, 13.3.79, p 21. Last amended by Directive 82/148/EEC (OJ L62, 5.3.83, p 22).

5 OJ L193, 18.7.83, p 1. Directive as last amended by Directive 90/605/EEC (OJ L317, 16.11.90, p 60).

[6762]
Article 2

1. This Directive shall apply to the types of insurance and undertakings referred to in Article 1 of Directive 73/239/EEC.

2. This Directive shall apply neither to the types of insurance or operations, nor to undertakings or institutions to which Directive 73/239/EEC does not apply, nor to the bodies referred to in Article 4 of that Directive.

NOTES

Repealed as noted at the beginning of this Directive.

[6763]
Article 3

Notwithstanding Article 2(2), Member States shall take every step to ensure that monopolies in respect of the taking up of the business of certain classes of insurance, granted to bodies established within their territories and referred to in Article 4 of Directive 73/239/EEC, are abolished by 1 July 1994.

NOTES

Repealed as noted at the beginning of this Directive.

TITLE II
THE TAKING UP OF THE BUSINESS OF INSURANCE

Articles 4–7 (*Substitute First Council Directive 73/239/EEC, arts 6–9 at* **[6649]–[6652]**.)

[6764]
Article 8

The competent authorities of the home Member State shall not grant an undertaking authorisation to take up the business of insurance before they have been informed of the identities of the shareholders or members, direct or indirect, whether natural or legal persons, who have qualifying holdings in that undertaking and of the amounts of those holdings.

The same authorities shall refuse authorisation if, taking into account the need to ensure the sound and prudent management of an insurance undertaking, they are not satisfied as to the qualifications of the shareholders or members.

NOTES

Repealed as noted at the beginning of this Directive.

TITLE III
HARMONISATION OF THE CONDITIONS GOVERNING THE BUSINESS OF INSURANCE

CHAPTER 1

Articles 9–11 (*Substitute First Council Directive 73/239/EEC, arts 13, 14, 19(2), (3) at* **[6656]**, **[6657]**, **[6666]**.)

[6765]

Article 12

1. . . .

2. Under the conditions laid down by national law, each Member State shall authorise insurance undertakings with head offices within its territory to transfer all or part of their portfolios of contracts, concluded either under the right of establishment or the freedom to provide services, to an accepting office established within the Community, if the competent authorities of the home Member State of the accepting office certify that after taking the transfer into account the latter possesses the necessary solvency margin.

3. Where a branch proposes to transfer all or part of its portfolio of contracts, concluded either under the right of establishment or the freedom to provide services, the Member State of the branch shall be consulted.

4. In the circumstances referred to in paragraphs 2 and 3, the competent authorities of the home Member State of the transferring undertaking shall authorise the transfer after obtaining the agreement of the competent authorities of the Member States in which the risks are situated.

5. The competent authorities of the Member States consulted shall give their opinion or consent to the competent authorities of the home Member State of the transferring insurance undertaking within three months of receiving a request; the absence of any response within that period from the authorities consulted shall be considered equivalent to a favourable opinion or tacit consent.

6. A transfer authorised in accordance with this Article shall be published as laid down by national law in the Member State in which the risk is situated. Such transfers shall automatically be valid against policy-holders, insured persons and any other persons having rights or obligations arising out of the contracts transferred.

This provision shall not affect the Member States' rights to give policy-holders the option of cancelling contracts within a fixed period after a transfer.

NOTES

Repealed as noted at the beginning of this Directive.

Para 1: repeals Second Council Directive 88/357/EEC, art 11(2)–(7).

Articles 13, 14 (*Substitute First Council Directive 73/239/EEC, arts 20, 22 at* **[6667]**, **[6669]**.)

[6766]

Article 15

[1. Member States shall require any natural or legal person or such persons acting in concert (hereinafter referred to as the proposed acquirer), who have taken a decision either to acquire, directly or indirectly, a qualifying holding in an insurance undertaking or to further increase, directly or indirectly, such a qualifying holding in an insurance undertaking as a result of which the proportion of the voting rights or of the capital held would reach or exceed 20%, 30% or 50% or so that the insurance undertaking would become its subsidiary (hereinafter referred to as the proposed acquisition), first to notify in writing the competent authorities of the insurance undertaking in which they are seeking to acquire or increase a qualifying holding, indicating the size of the intended holding and relevant information, as referred to in Article 15b(4). Member States need not apply the 30% threshold where, in accordance with Article 9(3)(a) of Directive 2004/109/EC, they apply a threshold of one-third.]

[1a. . . .]

[2. Member States shall require any natural or legal person who has taken a decision to dispose, directly or indirectly, of a qualifying holding in an insurance undertaking first to notify in writing the competent authorities of the home Member State, indicating the size of his intended holding. Such a person shall likewise notify the competent authorities if he has taken a decision to reduce his qualifying holding so that the proportion of the voting rights or of the capital held would fall below 20%, 30% or 50% or so that the insurance undertaking would cease to be his subsidiary. Member States need not apply the 30% threshold where, in accordance with Article 9(3)(a) of Directive 2004/109/EC, they apply a threshold of one-third.]

3. On becoming aware of them, insurance undertakings shall inform the competent authorities of their home Member States of any acquisitions or disposals of holdings in their capital that cause holdings to exceed or fall below any of the thresholds referred to in paragraphs 1 and 2.

They shall also, at least once a year, inform them of the names of shareholders and members possessing qualifying holdings and the sizes of such holdings as shown, for example, by the information received at annual general meetings of shareholders or members or as a result of compliance with the regulations relating to companies listed on stock exchanges.

4. Member States shall require that, where the influence exercised by the persons referred to in paragraph 1 is likely to operate against the prudent and sound management of an insurance undertaking, the competent authorities of the home Member State shall take appropriate measures to put an end to that situation. Such measures may consist, for example, in injunctions, sanctions against directors and managers, or suspension of the exercise of the voting rights attaching to the shares held by the shareholders or members in question.

Similar measures shall apply to natural or legal persons failing to comply with the obligation to provide prior information imposed in paragraph 1. If a holding is acquired despite the opposition of the competent authorities, the Member States shall, regardless of any other sanctions to be adopted, provide either for exercise of the corresponding voting rights to be suspended, or for the nullity of votes cast or for the possibility of their annulment.

NOTES

Repealed as noted at the beginning of this Directive.

Para 1: substituted by European Parliament and Council Directive 2007/44/EC, art 1(2)(a).

Para 1a: inserted by European Parliament and Council Directive 2002/87/EC, art 24(1); repealed by European Parliament and Council Directive 2007/44/EC, art 1(2)(b).

Para 2: substituted by European Parliament and Council Directive 2007/44/EC, art 1(2)(c).

[6767]
[Article 15a

1. The competent authorities shall, promptly and in any event within two working days following receipt of the notification required under Article 15(1), as well as following the possible subsequent receipt of the information referred to in paragraph 2 of this Article, acknowledge receipt thereof in writing to the proposed acquirer.

The competent authorities shall have a maximum of 60 working days as from the date of the written acknowledgement of receipt of the notification and all documents required by the Member State to be attached to the notification on the basis of the list referred to in Article 15b(4) (hereinafter referred to as the assessment period), to carry out the assessment provided for in Article 15b(1) (hereinafter referred to as the assessment).

The competent authorities shall inform the proposed acquirer of the date of the expiry of the assessment period at the time of acknowledging receipt.

2. The competent authorities may, during the assessment period, if necessary, and no later than on the 50th working day of the assessment period, request any further information that is necessary to complete the assessment. Such request shall be made in writing and shall specify the additional information needed.

For the period between the date of request for information by the competent authorities and the receipt of a response thereto by the proposed acquirer, the assessment period shall be interrupted. The interruption shall not exceed 20 working days. Any further requests by the competent authorities for completion or clarification of the information shall be at their discretion but may not result in an interruption of the assessment period.

3. The competent authorities may extend the interruption referred to in the second subparagraph of paragraph 2 up to 30 working days if the proposed acquirer is:

(a) situated or regulated outside the Community; or

(b) a natural or legal person not subject to supervision under this Directive or Directives 85/611/EEC,[1] 2002/83/EC,[2] 2004/39/EC, 2005/68/EC[3] or 2006/48/EC.[4]

4. If the competent authorities, upon completion of the assessment, decide to oppose the proposed acquisition, they shall, within two working days, and not exceeding the assessment period, inform the proposed acquirer in writing and provide the reasons for that decision. Subject to national law, an appropriate statement of the reasons for the decision may be made accessible to the public at the request of the proposed acquirer. This shall not prevent a Member State from allowing the competent authority to make such disclosure in the absence of a request by the proposed acquirer.

5. If the competent authorities do not oppose the proposed acquisition within the assessment period in writing, it shall be deemed to be approved.

6. The competent authorities may fix a maximum period for concluding the proposed acquisition and extend it where appropriate.

7. Member States may not impose requirements for the notification to and approval by the competent authorities of direct or indirect acquisitions of voting rights or capital that are more stringent than those set out in this Directive.]

NOTES

Inserted, together with arts 15b, 15c by European Parliament and Council Directive 2007/44/EC, art 1(3).
Repealed as noted at the beginning of this Directive.

1 Council Directive 85/611/EEC of 20 December 1985 on the coordination of laws, regulations and administrative provisions relating to undertakings for collective investment in transferable securities (UCITS) (OJ L375, 31.12.1985, p 3). Directive as last amended by Directive 2005/1/EC of the European Parliament and of the Council (OJ L79, 24.3.2005, p 9).

2 Directive 2002/83/EC of the European Parliament and of the Council of 5 November 2002 concerning life assurance (OJ L345, 19.12.2002, p 1). Directive as last amended by Directive 2007/44/EC.

3 Directive 2005/68/EC of the European Parliament and of the Council of 16 November 2005 on reinsurance (OJ L323, 9.12.2005, p 1). Directive as amended by Directive 2007/44/EC.

4 Directive 2006/48/EC of the European Parliament and of the Council of 14 June 2006 relating to the taking up and pursuit of the business of credit institutions (recast) (OJ L177, 30.6.2006, p 1). Directive as last amended by Directive 2007/44/EC.

[6768]
[Article 15b

1. In assessing the notification provided for in Article 15(1) and the information referred to in Article 15a(2), the competent authorities shall, in order to ensure the sound and prudent management of the insurance undertaking in which an acquisition is proposed, and having regard to the likely influence of the proposed acquirer on the insurance undertaking, appraise the suitability of the proposed acquirer and the financial soundness of the proposed acquisition against all of the following criteria:

(a) the reputation of the proposed acquirer;

(b) the reputation and experience of any person who will direct the business of the insurance undertaking as a result of the proposed acquisition;

(c) the financial soundness of the proposed acquirer, in particular in relation to the type of business pursued and envisaged in the insurance undertaking in which the acquisition is proposed;

(d) whether the insurance undertaking will be able to comply and continue to comply with the prudential requirements based on this Directive and, where applicable, other Directives, notably, Directives 73/239/EEC, 98/78/EC,[1] 2002/13/EC[2] and 2002/87/EC,[3] in particular, whether the group of which it will become a part has a structure that makes it possible to exercise effective supervision, effectively exchange information among the competent authorities and determine the allocation of responsibilities among the competent authorities;

(e) whether there are reasonable grounds to suspect that, in connection with the proposed acquisition, money laundering or terrorist financing within the meaning of Article 1 of Directive 2005/60/EC[4] is being or has been committed or attempted, or that the proposed acquisition could increase the risk thereof.

2. The competent authorities may oppose the proposed acquisition only if there are reasonable grounds for doing so on the basis of the criteria set out in paragraph 1 or if the information provided by the proposed acquirer is incomplete.

3. Member States shall neither impose any prior conditions in respect of the level of holding that must be acquired nor allow their competent authorities to examine the proposed acquisition in terms of the economic needs of the market.

4. Member States shall make publicly available a list specifying the information that is necessary to carry out the assessment and that must be provided to the competent authorities at the time of notification referred to in Article 15(1). The information required shall be proportionate and adapted to the nature of the proposed acquirer and the proposed acquisition. Member States shall not require information that is not relevant for a prudential assessment.

5. Notwithstanding Article 15a(1), (2) and (3), where two or more proposals to acquire or increase qualifying holdings in the same insurance undertaking have been notified to the competent authority, the latter shall treat the proposed acquirers in a non-discriminatory manner.]

NOTES

Inserted as noted to art 15a at **[6767]**.

Repealed as noted at the beginning of this Directive.

1 Directive 98/78/EC of the European Parliament and of the Council of 27 October 1998 on the supplementary supervision of insurance and reinsurance undertakings in an insurance or reinsurance group (OJ L330, 5.12.1998, p 1). Directive as last amended by Directive 2005/68/EC.

2 Directive 2002/13/EC of the European Parliament and of the Council of 5 March 2002 amending Council Directive 73/239/EEC as regards the solvency margin requirements for non-life insurance undertakings (OJ L77, 20.3.2002, p 17).

3 Directive 2002/87/EC of the European Parliament and of the Council of 16 December 2002 on the supplementary supervision of credit institutions, insurance undertakings and investment firms in a

financial conglomerate (OJ L35, 11.2.2003, p 1). Directive as amended by Directive 2005/1/EC.

4 Directive 2005/60/EC of the European Parliament and of the Council of 26 October 2005 on the prevention of the use of financial system for the purpose of money laundering and terrorist financing (OJ L309, 25.11.2005, p 15).

[6769]
[Article 15c

1. The relevant competent authorities shall work in full consultation with each other when carrying out the assessment if the proposed acquirer is one of the following:

- *(a) a credit institution, assurance undertaking, insurance undertaking, reinsurance undertaking, investment firm or management company within the meaning of Article 1a, point 2 of Directive 85/611/EEC (hereinafter referred to as the "UCITS management company") authorised in another Member State or in a sector other than that in which the acquisition is proposed;*
- *(b) the parent undertaking of a credit institution, assurance undertaking, insurance undertaking, reinsurance undertaking, investment firm or UCITS management company authorised in another Member State or in a sector other than that in which the acquisition is proposed; or*
- *(c) a natural or legal person controlling a credit institution, assurance undertaking, insurance undertaking, reinsurance undertaking, investment firm or UCITS management company authorised in another Member State or in a sector other than that in which the acquisition is proposed.*

2. The competent authorities shall, without undue delay, provide each other with any information which is essential or relevant for the assessment. In this regard, the competent authorities shall communicate to each other upon request all relevant information and shall communicate on their own initiative all essential information. A decision by the competent authority that has authorised the insurance undertaking in which the acquisition is proposed shall indicate any views or reservations expressed by the competent authority responsible for the proposed acquirer.]

NOTES

Inserted as noted to art 15a at **[6767]**.

Repealed as noted at the beginning of this Directive.

[6770]
Article 16

1. The Member States shall provide that all persons working or who have worked for the competent authorities, as well as auditors and experts acting on behalf of the competent authorities, shall be bound by the obligation of professional secrecy. This means that no confidential information which they may receive while performing their duties may be divulged to any person or authority whatsoever, except in summary or aggregate form, such that individual insurance undertakings cannot be identified, without prejudice to cases covered by criminal law.

Nevertheless, where an insurance undertaking has been declared bankrupt or is being compulsorily wound up, confidential information which does not concern third parties involved in attempts to rescue that undertaking may be divulged in civil or commercial proceedings.

2. Paragraph 1 shall not prevent the competent authorities of different Member States from exchanging information in accordance with the Directives applicable to insurance undertakings. Such information shall be subject to the conditions of professional secrecy laid down in paragraph 1.

[3. Member States may conclude cooperation agreements providing for exchange of information with the competent authorities of third countries or with authorities or bodies of third countries as defined in paragraphs 5 and 5a only if the information disclosed is subject to guarantees of professional secrecy at least equivalent to those referred to in this Article. such exchange of information must be intended for the performance of the supervisory task of the authorities or bodies mentioned.

Where the information originates in another Member State, it may not be disclosed without the express agreement of the competent authorities which have disclosed it and, where appropriate, solely for the purposes for which those authorities gave their agreement.]

[4. Competent authorities receiving confidential information under paragraph 1 or 2 may use it only in the course of their duties:

- *to check that the conditions governing the taking up of the business of insurance are met and to facilitate monitoring of the conduct of such business, especially with regard to the monitoring of technical provisions, solvency margins, administrative and accounting procedures and internal control mechanisms,*

— *to impose penalties,*

— *in administrative appeals against decisions of the competent authorities, or*

— *in court proceedings initiated under Article 53 or under special provisions provided for in this Directive and other Directives adopted in the field of insurance undertakings and reinsurance undertakings.*

5. Paragraphs 1 and 4 shall not preclude the exchange of information within a Member State, where there are two or more competent authorities in the same Member State, or, between Member States, between competent authorities and:

— *authorities responsible for the official supervision of credit institutions and other financial organisations and the authorities responsible for the supervision of financial markets,*

— *bodies involved in the liquidation and bankruptcy of insurance undertakings, reinsurance undertakings and in other similar procedures, and*

— *persons responsible for carrying out statutory audits of the accounts of insurance undertakings, reinsurance undertakings and other financial institutions,*

in the discharge of their supervisory functions, and the disclosure, to bodies which administer compulsory winding-up proceedings or guarantee funds, of information necessary to the performance of their duties. The information received by those authorities, bodies and persons shall be subject to the obligation of professional secrecy laid down in paragraph 1.

6. Notwithstanding paragraphs 1 to 4, Member States may authorise exchanges of information between the competent authorities and:

— *the authorities responsible for overseeing the bodies involved in the liquidation and bankruptcy of assurance undertakings, reinsurance undertakings and other similar procedures, or*

— *the authorities responsible for overseeing the persons charged with carrying out statutory audits of the accounts of insurance undertakings, reinsurance undertakings, credit institutions, investment firms and other financial institutions, or*

— *independent actuaries of insurance undertakings or reinsurance undertakings carrying out legal supervision of those undertakings and the bodies responsible for overseeing such actuaries.*

Member States which have recourse to the option provided for in the first subparagraph shall require at least that the following conditions are met:

— *this information shall be for the purpose of carrying out the overseeing or legal supervision referred to in the first subparagraph,*

— *information received in this context shall be subject to the conditions of professional secrecy imposed in paragraph 1,*

— *where the information originates in another Member State, it may not be disclosed without the express agreement of the competent authorities which have disclosed it and, where appropriate, solely for the purposes for which those authorities gave their agreement.*

Member States shall communicate to the Commission and to the other Member States the names of the authorities, persons and bodies which may receive information pursuant to this paragraph.]

NOTES

Repealed as noted at the beginning of this Directive.

Para 3: substituted by European Parliament and Council Directive 2000/64/EC, art 2.

Paras 4–6: substituted for paras 4, 5, 5a–5c (originally inserted by Council Directive 95/26/EC, art 4(1), (3), (5)), 6, by European Parliament and Council Directive 2005/68/EC, art 58(2).

[6771]

[Article 16a

1. Member States shall provide at least that—

(a) any person authorised within the meaning of Directive 84/253/EEC,[1] performing in a insurance undertaking the task described in Article 51 of Directive 78/660/EEC,[2] Article 37 of Directive 83/349/EEC or Article 31 of Directive 85/611/EEC or any other statutory task, shall have a duty to report promptly to the competent authorities any fact or decision concerning that undertaking of which he has become aware while carrying out that task which is liable to—

— *constitute a material breach of the laws, regulations or administrative provisions which lay down the conditions governing authorisation or which specifically govern pursuit of the activities of insurance undertakings, or*

Part VI European Materials

— *affect the continuous functioning of the insurance undertaking, or*
— *lead to refusal to certify the accounts or to the expression of reservations;*

(b) that person shall likewise have a duty to report any facts and decisions of which he becomes aware in the course of carrying out a task as described in (a) in an undertaking having close links resulting from a control relationship with the insurance undertaking within which he is carrying out the abovementioned task.]

2. The disclosure in good faith to the competent authorities, by persons authorised within the meaning of Directive 84/253/EEC, of any fact or decision referred to in paragraph 1 shall not constitute a breach of any restriction on disclosure of information imposed by contract of by any legislative, regulatory or administrative provision and shall not involve such persons in liability of any kind.]

NOTES

Inserted by Council Directive 95/26/EC, art 5.
Repealed as noted at the beginning of this Directive.

1 OJ L126, 12.5.84, p 20.

2 OJ L222, 14.8.78, p 11. Directive as last amended by Directive 90/605/EEC (OJ L317, 16.11.90, p 60).

CHAPTER 2

Articles 17–19 (*Arts 17, 18 substitute First Council Directive 73/239/EEC, arts 15, 15a at* **[6658]**, **[6659]***; art 19 repeals Second Council Directive 88/357/EEC, art 23.)*

[6772]
Article 20

The assets covering the technical provisions shall take account of the type of business carried on by an undertaking in such a way as to secure the safety, yield and marketability of its investments, which the undertaking shall ensure are diversified and adequately spread.

NOTES

Repealed as noted at the beginning of this Directive.

[6773]
Article 21

[1. The home Member State may not authorise insurance undertakings to cover their technical provisions and equalisation reserves with any assets other than those in the following categories—]

A ***Investments***

(a) debt securities, bonds and other money and capital market instruments;
(b) loans;
(c) shares and other variable yield participations;
(d) units in undertakings for collective investment in transferable securities and other investment funds;
(e) land, buildings and immovable property rights;

B ***Debts and claims***

[(f) debts owed by reinsurers, including reinsurers shares of technical provisions, and by the special purpose vehicles referred to in Article 46 of Directive 2005/68/EC of the European Parliament and of the Council of 16 November 2005 on reinsurance.[1]]
(g) deposits with and debts owed by ceding undertakings;
(h) debts owed by policyholders and intermediaries arising out of direct and reinsurance operations;
(i) claims arising out of salvage and subrogation;
(j) tax recoveries;
(k) claims against guarantee funds;

C ***Others***

(l) tangible fixed assets, other than land and buildings, valued on the basis of prudent amortisation;
(m) cash at bank and in hand, deposits with credit institutions and any other bodies authorised to receive deposits;
(n) deferred acquisition costs;
(o) accrued interest and rent, other accrued income and prepayments;

In the case of the association of underwriters known as Lloyd's, asset categories shall also include guarantees and letters of credit issued by credit institutions within the meaning of

Directive 77/780/EEC[2] *or by assurance undertakings, together with verifiable sums arising out of life assurance policies, to the extent that they represent funds belonging to members.*

[The inclusion of any asset or category of assets listed in the first subparagraph shall not mean that all those assets should automatically be accepted as cover for technical provisions. The home Member State shall lay down more detailed rules setting the conditions for the use of acceptable assets.]

In the determination and the application of the rules which it lays down, the home Member State shall, in particular, ensure that the following principles are complied with—

- *(i) assets covering technical provisions shall be valued net of any debts arising out of their acquisition;*
- *(ii) all assets must be valued on a prudent basis, allowing for the risk of any amounts not being realisable. In particular, tangible fixed assets other than land and buildings may be accepted as cover for technical provisions only if they are valued on the basis of prudent amortisation;*
- *(iii) loans, whether to undertakings, to State authorities or international organisations, to local or regional authorities or to natural persons, may be accepted as cover for technical provisions only if there are sufficient guarantees as to their security, whether these are based on the status of the borrower, mortgages, bank guarantees or guarantees granted by insurance undertakings or other forms of security;*
- *(iv) derivative instruments such as options, futures and swaps in connection with assets covering technical provisions may be used insofar as they contribute to a reduction of investment risks or facilitate efficient portfolio management. They must be valued on a prudent basis and may be taken into account in the valuation of the underlying assets;*
- *(v) transferable securities which are not dealt in on a regulated market may be accepted as cover for technical provisions only if they can be realised in the short term;*
- *(vi) debts owed by and claims against a third party may be accepted as cover for technical provisions only after deduction of all amounts owed to the same third party;*
- *(vii) the value of any debts and claims accepted as cover for technical provisions must be calculated on a prudent basis, with due allowance for the risk of any amounts not being realisable. In particular, debts owed by policyholders and intermediaries arising out of insurance and reinsurance operations may be accepted only insofar as they have been outstanding for not more than three months;*
- *(viii) where the assets held include an investment in a subsidiary undertaking which manages all or part of the insurance undertaking's investments on its behalf, the home Member State must, when applying the rules and principles laid down in this Article, take into account the underlying assets held by the subsidiary undertaking; the home Member State may treat the assets of other subsidiaries in the same way;*
- *(ix) deferred acquisition costs may be accepted as cover for technical provisions only to the extent that that is consistent with the calculation of the technical provision for unearned premiums.*

2. Notwithstanding paragraph 1, in exceptional circumstances and at an insurance undertaking's request, the home Member State may, temporarily and under a properly reasoned decision, accept other categories of assets as cover for technical provisions, subject to Article 20.

NOTES

Repealed as noted at the beginning of this Directive.

Para 1: words in square brackets substituted by European Parliament and Council Directive 2005/68/EC, art 58(3).

1 OJ L323, 9.12.2005, p 1.

2 OJ L322, 17.2.77, p 30. Last amended by Directive 89/646/EEC (OJ L386, 30.12.89, p 1).

[6774]

Article 22

[1. As regards the assets covering technical provisions and equalisation reserves, the home Member State shall require every insurance undertaking to invest no more than—]

Part VI European Materials

(a) *10% of its total gross technical provisions in any one piece of land or building, or a number of pieces of land or buildings close enough to each other to be considered effectively as one investment;*

(b) *5% of its total gross technical provisions in shares and other negotiable securities treated as shares, bonds, debt securities and other money and capital market instruments from the same undertaking, or in loans granted to the same borrower, taken together, the loans being loans other than those granted to a State, regional or local authority or to an international organisation of which one or more Member States are members. This limit may be raised to 10% if an undertaking does not invest more than 40% of its gross technical provisions in the loans or securities of issuing bodies and borrowers in each of which it invests more than 5% of its assets;*

(c) *5% of its total gross technical provisions in unsecured loans, including 1% for any single unsecured loan, other than loans granted to credit institutions, assurance undertaking—in so far as Article 8 of Directive 73/239/EEC allows it—and investment undertakings established in a Member State;*

(d) *3% of its total gross technical provisions in the form of cash in hand;*

(e) *10% of its total gross technical provisions in shares, other securities treated as shares and debt securities, which are not dealt in on a regulated market.*

2. The absence of a limit in paragraph 1 on investment in any particular category does not imply that assets in that category should be accepted as cover for technical provisions without limit. The home Member State shall lay down more detailed rules fixing the conditions for the use of acceptable assets. In particular it shall ensure, in the determination and the application of those rules, that the following principles are complied with—

(i) *assets covering technical provisions must be diversified and spread in such a way as to ensure that there is no excessive reliance on any particular category of asset, investment market or investment;*

(ii) *investment in particular types of asset which show high levels of risk, whether because of the nature of the asset or the quality of the issuer, must be restricted to prudent levels;*

(iii) *limitations on particular categories of asset must take account of the treatment of reinsurance in the calculation of technical provisions;*

(iv) *where the assets held include an investment in a subsidiary undertaking which manages all or part of the insurance undertaking's investments on its behalf, the home Member State must, when applying the rules and principles laid down in this Article, take into account the underlying assets held by the subsidiary undertaking; the home Member State may treat the assets of other subsidiaries in the same way;*

(v) *the percentage of assets covering technical provisions which are the subject of non-liquid investments must be kept to a prudent level;*

(vi) *where the assets held include loans to or debt securities issued by certain credit institutions, the home Member State may, when applying the rules and principles laid down in this Article, take into account the underlying assets held by such credit institutions. This treatment may be applied only where the credit institution has its head office in a Member State, is entirely owned by that Member State and/or that State's local authorities and its business, according to its memorandum and articles of association, consists of extending, through its intermediary, loans to or guaranteed by the State or local authorities or loans to bodies closely linked to the State or to local authorities.*

3. In the context of the detailed rules laying down the conditions for the use of acceptable assets, the Member State shall give more limitative treatment to—

— *any loan unaccompanied by a bank guarantee, a guarantee issued by an insurance undertaking, a mortgage or any other form of security, as compared with loans accompanied by such collateral;*

— *UCITS not coordinated within the meaning of Directive 85/611/EEC*[1] *and other investment funds, as compared with UCITS coordinated within the meaning of that Directive;*

— *securities which are not dealt in on a regulated market, as compared with those which are;*

— *bonds, debt securities and other money and capital-market instruments not issued by States, local or regional authorities or undertakings belonging to Zone A as defined in Directive 89/647/EEC,*[2] *or the issuers of which are international organisations not numbering at least one Community Member State among their member, as compared with the same financial instruments issued by such bodies.*

4. Member States may raise the limit laid down in paragraph 1(b) to 40% in the case of certain debt securities when these are issued by a credit institution which has its head office in a Member State and is subject by law to special official supervision designed to protect the holders of those debt securities. In particular, sums deriving from the issue of such debt securities must be invested in accordance with the law in assets which, during the whole period of validity of the debt securities, are capable of covering claims attaching to the debt securities and which, in the event of failure of the issues, would be used on a priority basis for the reimbursement of the principal and payment of the accrued interest.

5. Member States shall not require insurance undertakings to invest in particular categories of assets.

6. Notwithstanding paragraph 1, in exceptional circumstances and at an insurance undertaking's request, the home Member State may, temporarily and under a properly reasoned decision, allow exceptions to the rules laid down in paragraph 1(a) to (e), subject to Article 20.

NOTES

Repealed as noted at the beginning of this Directive.

Para 1: words in square brackets substituted by European Parliament and Council Directive 2005/68/EC, art 58(4).

[1] OJ L375, 31.12.85, p 3. Amended by Directive 88/220/EEC (OJ L100, 19.4.88, p 31).

[2] OJ L386, 30.12.89, p 14.

Articles 23, 24 (*Art 23 substitutes Annex 1, points 8, 9 to Second Council Directive 88/357/EEC at* **[6757]**; *art 24 contains amendments which have now been superseded by provisions contained in European Parliament and Council Directive 2002/13/EC.*)

[6775]
Article 25

No more than three years after the date of application of this Directive the Commission shall submit a report to the Insurance Committee on the need for further harmonisation of the solvency margin.

NOTES

Repealed as noted at the beginning of this Directive.

Article 26 (*Substitutes First Council Directive 73/239/EEC, art 18 at* **[6665]**.)

CHAPTER 3

Article 27 (*Substitutes Second Council Directive 88/357/EEC, art 7(1)(f) at* **[6740]**.)

[6776]
Article 28

The Member State in which a risk is situated shall not prevent a policyholder from concluding a contract with an insurance undertaking authorised under the conditions of Article 6 of Directive 73/239/EEC, as long as that does not conflict with legal provisions protecting the general good in the Member State in which the risk is situated.

NOTES

Repealed as noted at the beginning of this Directive.

[6777]
Article 29

Member States shall not adopt provisions requiring the prior approval or systematic notification of general and special policy conditions, scales of premiums, or forms and other printed documents which an insurance undertaking intends to use in its dealings with policyholders. They may only require non-systematic notification of those policy conditions and other documents for the purpose of verifying compliance with national provisions concerning insurance contracts, and that requirement may not constitute a prior condition for an undertaking's carrying on its business.

Member States may not retain or introduce prior notification or approval of proposed increases in premium rates except as part of general price-control systems.

[6778]
Article 30

1. . . .

2. Notwithstanding any provision to the contrary, a Member State which makes insurance compulsory may require that the general and special conditions of the compulsory insurance be communicated to its competent authority before being circulated.

NOTES

Para 1: amends Second Council Directive 88/357/EEC, art 8 at **[6741]**.

Repealed as noted at the beginning of this Directive.

[6779]

Article 31

1. Before an insurance contract is concluded the insurance undertaking shall inform the policyholder of—

- *the law applicable to the contract where the parties do not have a free choice, or the fact that the parties are free to choose the law applicable and, in the latter case, the law the insurer proposes to choose;*
- *the arrangements for handling policyholders' complaints concerning contracts including, where appropriate, the existence of a complaints body, without prejudice to the policyholders' right to take legal proceedings.*

2. The obligation referred to in paragraph 1 shall apply only where the policyholder is a natural person.

3. The rules for implementing this Article shall be determined in accordance with the law of the Member State in which the risk is situated.

NOTES

Repealed as noted at the beginning of this Directive.

TITLE IV

PROVISIONS RELATING TO RIGHT OF ESTABLISHMENT AND THE FREEDOM TO PROVIDE SERVICES

Articles 32–37 (*Art 32 substitutes First Council Directive 73/239/EEC, art 10 at* **[6653]***; art 33 repeals art 11 thereof; arts 34–36 substitute Second Council Directive 88/357/EEC, arts 14, 16, 17 at* **[6744]**, **[6745]**, **[6746]***; art 37 repeals art 12 (in part), arts 13, 15 thereof.)*

[6780]

Article 38

The competent authorities of the Member State of the branch or the Member State of the provision of services may require that the information which they are authorised under this Directive to request with regard to the business of insurance undertakings operating in the territory of that State shall be supplied to them in the official language or languages of that State.

NOTES

Repealed as noted at the beginning of this Directive.

[6781]

Article 39

1. . . .

2. The Member State of the branch or of the provision of services shall not adopt provisions requiring the prior approval or systematic notification of general and special policy conditions, scales of premiums, or forms and other printed documents which an undertaking intends to use in its dealings with policyholders. It may only require an undertaking that proposes to carry on insurance business within its territory, under the right of establishment or the freedom to provide services, to effect non-systematic notification of those policy conditions and other documents for the purpose of verifying compliance with its national provisions concerning insurance contracts, and that requirement may not constitute a prior condition for an undertaking's carrying on its business.

3. The Member State of the branch or of the provision of services may not retain or introduce prior notification or approval of proposed increases in premium rates except as part of general price-control systems.

NOTES

Repealed as noted at the beginning of this Directive.

Para 1: repeals Second Council Directive 88/357/EEC, art 18.

[6782]

Article 40

1. . . .

2. Any undertaking carrying on business under the right of establishment or the freedom to provide services shall submit to the competent authorities of the Member State of the branch and/or of the Member State of the provision of services all documents requested of it for the purposes of this Article insofar as undertakings with head offices in those Member States are also obliged to do so.

3. If the competent authorities of a Member State establish that an undertaking with a branch or carrying on business under the freedom to provide services within its territory is not complying with the legal provisions applicable to it in that State, they shall require the undertaking concerned to remedy that irregular situation.

4. If the undertaking in question fails to take the necessary action, the competent authorities of the Member State concerned shall inform the competent authorities of the home Member State accordingly. The latter authorities shall, at the earliest opportunity, take all appropriate measures to ensure that the undertaking concerned remedies that irregular situation. The nature of those measures shall be communicated to the competent authorities of the Member State concerned.

5. If, despite the measures taken by the home Member State or because those measures prove inadequate or are lacking in that State, the undertaking persists in infringing the legal provisions in force in the Member State concerned, the latter may, after informing the competent authorities of the home Member State, take appropriate measures to prevent or penalise further infringements, including, insofar as is strictly necessary, preventing that undertaking from continuing to conclude new insurance contracts within its territory. Member States shall ensure that within their territories it is possible to serve the legal documents necessary for such measures on insurance undertakings.

6. Paragraphs 3, 4 and 5 shall not affect the emergency power of the Member States concerned to take appropriate measures to prevent irregularities within their territories. This shall include the possibility of preventing insurance undertakings from continuing to conclude new insurance contracts within their territories.

7. Paragraphs 3, 4 and 5 shall not affect the powers of the Member States to penalise infringements within their territories.

8. If an undertaking which has committed an infringement has an establishment or possesses property in the Member State concerned, the competent authorities of the latter may, in accordance with national law, apply the administrative penalties prescribed for that infringement by way of enforcement against that establishment or property.

9. Any measure adopted under paragraphs 4 to 8 involving penalties or restrictions on the conduct of insurance business must be properly reasoned and communicated to the undertaking concerned.

10. Every two years, the Commission shall [inform the European Insurance and Occupational Pensions Committee of] the number and types of cases in which, in each Member State, authorisation has been refused under Article 10 of Directive 73/239/EEC or Article 16 of Directive 88/357/EEC as amended by this Directive or measures have been taken under paragraph 5. Member States shall cooperate with the Commission by providing it with the information required for that report.

NOTES

Repealed as noted at the beginning of this Directive.

Para 1: repeals Second Council Directive 88/357/EEC, art 19.

Para 10: words in square brackets substituted by European Parliament and Council Directive 2005/1/EC, art 6.

[6783]
Article 41

Nothing in this Directive shall prevent insurance undertakings with head offices in Member States from advertising their services, through all available means of communication, in the Member State of the branch or the Member State of the provision of services, subject to any rules governing the form and content of such advertising adopted in the interest of the general good.

NOTES

Repealed as noted at the beginning of this Directive.

[6784]
Article 42

1. . . .

Part VI European Materials

2. In the event of an insurance undertaking's being wound up, commitments arising out of contracts underwritten through a branch or under the freedom to provide services shall be met in the same way as those arising out of that undertaking's other insurance contracts, without distinction as to nationality as far as the persons insured and the beneficiaries are concerned.

NOTES

Repealed as noted at the beginning of this Directive.

Para 1: repeals Second Council Directive 88/357/EEC, art 20.

[6785]
Article 43

1. . . .

2. Where insurance is offered under the right of establishment or the freedom to provide services, the policyholder shall, before any commitment is entered into, be informed of the Member State in which the head office or, where appropriate, the branch with which the contract is to be concluded is situated.

Any documents issued to the policyholder must convey the information referred to in the first subparagraph.

The obligations imposed in the first two subparagraphs shall not apply to the risks referred to in Article 5(d) of Directive 73/239/EEC.

3. The contract or any other document granting cover, together with the insurance proposal where it is binding upon the policyholder, must state the address of the head office, or, where appropriate, of the branch of the insurance undertaking which grants the cover.

Each Member State may require that the name and address of the representative of the insurance undertaking referred to in Article 12a(4) of Directive 88/357/EEC also appear in the documents referred to in the first subparagraph.

NOTES

Repealed as noted at the beginning of this Directive.

Para 1: repeals Second Council Directive 88/357/EEC, art 21.

[6786]
Article 44

1. . . .

2. Every insurance undertaking shall inform the competent authority of its home Member State, separately in respect of transactions carried out under the right of establishment and those carried out under the freedom to provide services, of the amount of the premiums, claims and commissions, without deduction of reinsurance, by Member State and by group of classes, and also as regards class 10 of point A of the Annex to Directive 73/239/EEC, not including carrier's liability, the frequency and average cost of claims.

The groups of classes are hereby defined as follows—

- *accident and sickness (classes 1 and 2);*
- *motor (classes 3, 7 and 10, the figures for class 10, excluding carriers' liability, being given separately);*
- *fire and other damage to property (classes 8 and 9);*
- *aviation, marine and transport (classes 4, 5, 6, 7, 11 and 12);*
- *general liability (class 13);*
- *credit and suretyship (classes 14 and 15);*
- *other classes (classes 16, 17 and 18).*

The competent authority of the home Member State shall forward that information within a reasonable time and in aggregate form to the competent authorities of each of the Member States concerned which so request.

NOTES

Repealed as noted at the beginning of this Directive.

Para 1: repeals Second Council Directive 88/357/EEC, art 22.

[6787]
Article 45

1. . . .

2. Nothing in this Directive shall affect the Member States' right to require undertakings carrying on business within their territories under the right of establishment or the freedom to provide services to join and participate, on the same terms as undertakings authorised there, in any scheme designed to guarantee the payment of insurance claims to insured persons and injured third parties.

NOTES

Repealed as noted at the beginning of this Directive.
Para 1: repeals Second Council Directive 88/357/EEC, art 24.

[6788]
Article 46

1. . . .

2. Without prejudice to any subsequent harmonisation, every insurance contract shall be subject exclusively to the indirect taxes and parafiscal charges on insurance premiums in the Member State in which the risk is situated as defined in Article 2(d) of Directive 88/357/ EEC, and also, in the case of Spain, to the surcharges legally established in favour of the Spanish "Consorcio de Compensación de Seguros" for the performance of its functions relating to the compensation of losses arising from extraordinary events occurring in that Member State.

In derogation from the first indent of Article 2(d) of Directive 88/357/EEC, and for the purposes of this paragraph, moveable property contained in a building situated within the territory of a Member State, except for goods in commercial transit, shall be a risk situated in that Member State, even if the building and its contents are not covered by the same insurance policy.

The law applicable to the contract under Article 7 of Directive 88/357/EEC shall not affect the fiscal arrangements applicable.

Pending future harmonisation, each Member State shall apply to those undertakings which cover risks situated within its territory its own national provisions to ensure the collection of indirect taxes and parafiscal charges due under the first subparagraph.

NOTES

Repealed as noted at the beginning of this Directive.
Para 1: repeals Second Council Directive 88/357/EEC, art 25.

TITLE V
TRANSITIONAL PROVISIONS

[6789]
Article 47

The Federal Republic of Germany may postpone until 1 January 1996 the application of the first sentence of the second subparagraph of Article 54(2). During that period, the provisions of the following subparagraph shall apply in the situation referred to in Article 54(2).

When the technical basis for the calculation of premiums has been communicated to the competent authorities of the home Member State in accordance with the third sentence of the second subparagraph of Article 54(2), those authorities shall without delay forward that information to the competent authorities of the Member State in which the risk is situated so that they may comment. If the competent authorities of the home Member State take no account of those comments, they shall inform the competent authorities of the Member State in which the risk is situated accordingly in detail and state their reasons.

NOTES

Repealed as noted at the beginning of this Directive.

[6790]
Article 48

Member States may allow insurance undertakings with head offices in their territories, the buildings and land of which that cover their technical provisions exceed, at the time of the notification of this Directive, the percentage laid down in Article 22(1)(a), a period expiring no later than 31 December 1998 within which to comply with that provision.

NOTES

Repealed as noted at the beginning of this Directive.

[6791]
Article 49

The Kingdom of Denmark may postpone until 1 January 1999 the application of this Directive to compulsory insurance against accidents at work. During that period the exclusion provided for in

Article 12(2) of Directive 88/357/EEC for accidents at work shall continue to apply in the Kingdom of Denmark.

NOTES

Repealed as noted at the beginning of this Directive.

[6792]
Article 50

Spain, until 31 December 1996, and Greece and Portugal, until 31 December 1998, may operate the following transitional arrangements for contracts covering risks situated exclusively in one of those Member States other than those defined in Article 5(d) of Directive 73/239/EEC—

(a) *in derogation from Article 8(3) of Directive 73/239/EEC and from Articles 29 and 39 of this Directive, the competent authorities of the Member States in question may require the communication, before use, of general and special insurance policy conditions;*

(b) *the amount of the technical provisions relating to the contracts referred to in this Article shall be determined under the supervision of the Member State concerned in accordance with its own rules, or, failing that, in accordance with the procedures established within its territory in accordance with this Directive. Cover of those technical provisions by equivalent and matching assets and the localisation of those assets shall be effected under the supervision of that Member State in accordance with its rules and practices adopted in accordance with this Directive.*

NOTES

Repealed as noted at the beginning of this Directive.

TITLE VI
FINAL PROVISIONS

[6793]
Article 51

[The following technical adjustments designed to amend nonessential elements of Directives 73/239/EEC and 88/357/EEC and of this Directive, inter alia, by supplementing them, shall be adopted in accordance with the regulatory procedure with scrutiny referred to in Article 2 of Directive 91/675/EEC]—

— *extension of the legal forms provided for in Article 8(1)(a) of Directive 73/239/EEC;*

— *amendments to the list set out in the Annex to Directive 73/239/EEC, or adaptation of the terminology used in that list to take account of the development of insurance markets;*

— *clarification of the items constituting the solvency margin listed in Article 16(1) of Directive 73/239/EEC to take account of the creation of new financial instruments;*

— *alteration of the minimum guarantee fund provided for in Article 17(2) of Directive 73/239/EEC to take account of economic and financial developments;*

— *amendments, to take account of the creation of new financial instruments, to the list of assets acceptable as cover for technical provisions set out in Article 21 of this Directive and to the rules on the spreading of investments laid down in Article 22;*

— *changes in the relaxations in the matching rules laid down in Annex 1 to Directive 88/357/EEC, to take account of the development of new currency-hedging instruments or progress made towards economic and monetary union;*

— *clarification of the definitions in order to ensure uniform application of Directives 73/239/EEC and 88/357/EEC and of this Directive throughout the Community.*

[— *adjustments of the criteria set out in Article 15b(1), in order to take account of future developments and to ensure the uniform application of this Directive.]*

NOTES

Repealed as noted at the beginning of this Directive.

Words in first pair of square brackets substituted by European Parliament and Council Directive 2008/36/EC, art 1; words in second pair of square brackets added by European Parliament and Council Directive 2007/44/EC, art 1(4).

[6794]
Article 52

1. Branches which have started business, in accordance with the provisions in force in their Member State of establishment, before the entry into force of the provisions adopted in implementation of this Directive shall be presumed to have been subject to the procedure laid down in Article 10(1) to (5) of Directive 73/239/EEC. They shall be governed, from the date of that entry into force, by Articles 15, 19, 20 and 22 of Directive 73/239/EEC and by Article 40 of this Directive.

2. Articles 34 and 35 shall not affect rights acquired by insurance undertakings carrying on business under the freedom to provide services before the entry into force of the provisions adopted in implementation of this Directive.

NOTES

Repealed as noted at the beginning of this Directive.

Article 53 (*Inserts First Council Directive 73/239/EEC, art 28a at* **[6676]**.)

[6795]
Article 54

1. Notwithstanding any provision to the contrary, a Member State in which contracts covering the risks in class 2 of point A of the Annex to Directive 73/239/EEC may serve as a partial or complete alternative to health cover provided by the statutory social security system may require that those contracts comply with the specific legal provisions adopted by that Member State to protect the general good in that class of insurance, and that the general and special conditions of that insurance be communicated to the competent authorities of that Member State before use.

2. Member States may require that the health insurance system referred to in paragraph 1 be operated on a technical basis similar to that of life assurance where—

- *the premiums paid are calculated on the basis of sickness tables and other statistical data relevant to the Member State in which the risk is situated in accordance with the mathematical methods used in insurance;*
- *a reserve is set up for increasing age;*
- *the insurer may cancel the contract only within a fixed period determined by the Member State in which the risk is situated;*
- *the contract provides that premiums may be increased or payments reduced, even for current contract;*
- *the contract provides that the policyholder may change his existing contract into a new contract complying with paragraph 1, offered by the same insurance undertaking or the same branch and taking account of his acquired rights. In particular, account must be taken of the reserve for increasing age and a new medical examination may be required only for increased cover.*

In that event, the competent authorities of the Member State concerned shall publish the sickness tables and other relevant statistical data referred to in the first subparagraph and transmit them to the competent authorities of the home Member State. The premiums must be sufficient, on reasonable actuarial assumptions, for undertakings to be able to meet all their commitments having regard to all aspects of their financial situation. The home Member State shall require that the technical basis for the calculation of premiums be communicated to its competent authorities before the product is circulated. This paragraph shall also apply where existing contracts are modified.

NOTES

Repealed as noted at the beginning of this Directive.

[6796]
Article 55

Member States may require that any insurance undertaking offering, at its own risk, compulsory insurance against accidents at work within their territories comply with the specific provisions of their national law concerning such insurance, except for the provisions concerning financial supervision, which shall be the exclusive responsibility of the home Member State.

NOTES

Repealed as noted at the beginning of this Directive.

[6797]
Article 56

Member States shall ensure that decisions taken in respect of an insurance undertaking under laws, regulations and administrative provisions adopted in accordance with this Directive may be subject

Part VI European Materials

to the right to apply to the courts.

NOTES

Repealed as noted at the beginning of this Directive.

[6798]
Article 57

1. The Member States shall adopt the laws, regulations and administrative provisions necessary for their compliance with this Directive not later than 31 December 1993 and bring them into force no later than 1 July 1994. They shall forthwith inform the Commission thereof.

When they adopt such measures the Member States shall include references to this Directive or shall make such references when they effect official publication. The manner in which such references are to be made shall be laid down by the Member States.

2. The Member States shall communicate to the Commission the texts of the main provisions of national law which they adopt in the field covered by this Directive.

NOTES

Repealed as noted at the beginning of this Directive.

[6799]
Article 58

This Directive is addressed to the Member States.

NOTES

Repealed as noted at the beginning of this Directive.

Done at Luxembourg, 18 June 1992.

F. INSURANCE MEDIATION

DIRECTIVE OF THE EUROPEAN PARLIAMENT AND OF THE COUNCIL

(2002/92/EC)

of 9 December 2002

on insurance mediation

NOTES

Date of publication in OJ: OJ L9, 15.1.2003, p 3.

[6800]

THE EUROPEAN PARLIAMENT AND THE COUNCIL OF THE EUROPEAN UNION,

Having regard to the Treaty establishing the European Community, and in particular Article 47(2) and Article 55 thereof,

Having regard to the proposal from the Commission,[1]

Having regard to the opinion of the Economic and Social Committee,[2]

Acting in accordance with the procedure laid down in Article 251 of the Treaty,[3]

Whereas:

(1) Insurance and reinsurance intermediaries play a central role in the distribution of insurance and reinsurance products in the Community.

(2) A first step to facilitate the exercise of freedom of establishment and freedom to provide services for insurance agents and brokers was made by Council Directive 77/92/EEC of 13 December 1976 on measures to facilitate the effective exercise of freedom of establishment and freedom to provide services in respect of the activities of insurance agents and brokers (ex ISIC Group 630) and, in particular, transitional measures in respect of those activities.[4]

(3) Directive 77/92/EEC was to remain applicable until the entry into force of provisions coordinating national rules concerning the taking-up and pursuit of the activities of insurance agents and brokers.

(4) Commission Recommendation 92/48/EEC of 18 December 1991 on insurance intermediaries[5] was largely followed by Member States and helped to bring closer together national provisions on the professional requirements and registration of insurance intermediaries.

(5) However, there are still substantial differences between national provisions which create barriers to the taking-up and pursuit of the activities of insurance and reinsurance intermediaries in the internal market. It is therefore appropriate to replace Directive 77/92/EEC with a new directive.

(6) Insurance and reinsurance intermediaries should be able to avail themselves of the freedom of establishment and the freedom to provide services which are enshrined in the Treaty.

(7) The inability of insurance intermediaries to operate freely throughout the Community hinders the proper functioning of the single market in insurance.

(8) The coordination of national provisions on professional requirements and registration of persons taking up and pursuing the activity of insurance mediation can therefore contribute both to the completion of the single market for financial services and to the enhancement of customer protection in this field.

(9) Various types of persons or institutions, such as agents, brokers and "bancassurance" operators, can distribute insurance products. Equality of treatment between operators and customer protection requires that all these persons or institutions be covered by this Directive.

(10) This Directive contains a definition of "tied insurance intermediary" which takes into account the characteristics of certain Member States' markets and whose purpose is to establish the conditions for registration applicable to such intermediaries. This definition is not intended to preclude Member States from having similar concepts in respect of insurance intermediaries who, while acting for and on behalf of an insurance undertaking and under the full responsibility of that undertaking, are entitled to collect premiums or amounts intended for the customer in accordance with the financial guarantees laid down by this Directive.

(11) This Directive should apply to persons whose activity consists in providing insurance mediation services to third parties for remuneration, which may be pecuniary or take some other form of agreed economic benefit tied to performance.

(12) This Directive should not apply to persons with another professional activity, such as tax experts or accountants, who provide advice on insurance cover on an incidental basis in the course of that other professional activity, neither should it apply to the mere provision of information of a

general nature on insurance products, provided that the purpose of that activity is not to help the customer conclude or fulfil an insurance or reinsurance contract, nor the professional management of claims for an insurance or reinsurance undertaking, nor the loss adjusting and expert appraisal of claims.

(13) This Directive should not apply to persons practising insurance mediation as an ancillary activity under certain strict conditions.

(14) Insurance and reinsurance intermediaries should be registered with the competent authority of the Member State where they have their residence or their head office, provided that they meet strict professional requirements in relation to their competence, good repute, professional indemnity cover and financial capacity.

(15) Such registration should allow insurance and reinsurance intermediaries to operate in other Member States in accordance with the principles of freedom of establishment and freedom to provide services, provided that an appropriate notification procedure has been followed between the competent authorities.

(16) Appropriate sanctions are needed against persons exercising the activity of insurance or reinsurance mediation without being registered, against insurance or reinsurance undertakings using the services of unregistered intermediaries and against intermediaries not complying with national provisions adopted pursuant to this Directive.

(17) Cooperation and exchange of information between competent authorities are essential in order to protect customers and ensure the soundness of insurance and reinsurance business in the single market.

(18) It is essential for the customer to know whether he is dealing with an intermediary who is advising him on products from a broad range of insurance undertakings or on products provided by a specific number of insurance undertakings.

(19) This Directive should specify the obligations which insurance intermediaries should have in providing information to customers. A Member State may in this area maintain or adopt more stringent provisions which may be imposed on insurance intermediaries independently of their place of residence where they are pursuing mediation activities on its territory provided that any such more stringent provisions comply with Community law, including Directive 2000/31/EC of the European Parliament and of the Council of 8 June 2000 on certain legal aspects of information society services, in particular electronic commerce, in the Internal Market (Directive on electronic commerce).[6]

(20) If the intermediary declares that he is giving advice on products from a broad range of insurance undertakings, he should carry out a fair and sufficiently wide-ranging analysis of the products available on the market. In addition, all intermediaries should explain the reasons underpinning their advice.

(21) There is less of a need to require that such information be disclosed when the customer is a company seeking reinsurance or insurance cover for commercial and industrial risks.

(22) There is a need for suitable and effective complaint and redress procedures in the Member States in order to settle disputes between insurance intermediaries and customers, using, where appropriate, existing procedures.

(23) Without prejudice to the right of customers to bring their action before the courts, Member States should encourage public or private bodies established with a view to settling disputes out-of-court, to cooperate in resolving cross-border disputes. Such cooperation could for example be aimed at enabling customers to contact extra-judicial bodies established in their Member State of residence about complaints concerning insurance intermediaries established in other Member States. The setting up of the FIN-NET network provides increased assistance to consumers when they use cross-border services. The provisions on procedures should take into account Commission Recommendation 98/257/EC of 30 March 1998 on the principles applicable to the bodies responsible for out-of-court settlement of consumer disputes.[7]

(24) Directive 77/92/EEC should accordingly be repealed,

NOTES

1 OJ C29 E, 30.1.2001, p 245.

2 OJ C221, 7.8.2001, p 121.

3 Opinion of the European Parliament of 14 November 2001 (OJ C140 E, 13.6.2002, p 167), Council Common Position of 18 March 2002 (OJ C145 E, 18.6.2002, p 1) and Decision of the European Parliament of 13 June 2002 (not yet published in the Official Journal). Council Decision of 28 June 2002.

4 OJ L26, 31.1.1977, p 14. Directive as last amended by the Act of Accession of 1994.

5 OJ L19, 28.1.1992, p 32.

6 OJ L178, 17.7.2000, p 1.

7 OJ L115, 17.4.1998, p 31.

HAVE ADOPTED THIS DIRECTIVE—

CHAPTER I
SCOPE AND DEFINITIONS

[6801]
Article 1
Scope

1. This Directive lays down rules for the taking-up and pursuit of the activities of insurance and reinsurance mediation by natural and legal persons which are established in a Member State or which wish to become established there.

2. This Directive shall not apply to persons providing mediation services for insurance contracts if all the following conditions are met—

(a) the insurance contract only requires knowledge of the insurance cover that is provided;
(b) the insurance contract is not a life assurance contract;
(c) the insurance contract does not cover any liability risks;
(d) the principal professional activity of the person is other than insurance mediation;
(e) the insurance is complementary to the product or service supplied by any provider, where such insurance covers—
  (i) the risk of breakdown, loss of or damage to goods supplied by that provider, or
  (ii) damage to or loss of baggage and other risks linked to the travel booked with that provider, even if the insurance covers life assurance or liability risks, provided that the cover is ancillary to the main cover for the risks linked to that travel;
(f) the amount of the annual premium does not exceed EUR 500 and the total duration of the insurance contract, including any renewals, does not exceed five years.

3. This Directive shall not apply to insurance and reinsurance mediation services provided in relation to risks and commitments located outside the Community.

This Directive shall not affect a Member State's law in respect of insurance mediation business pursued by insurance and reinsurance intermediaries established in a third country and operating on its territory under the principle of freedom to provide services, provided that equal treatment is guaranteed to all persons carrying out or authorised to carry out insurance mediation activities on that market.

This Directive shall not regulate insurance mediation activities carried out in third countries nor activities of Community insurance or reinsurance undertakings, as defined in First Council Directive 73/239/EEC of 24 July 1973 on the coordination of laws, regulations and administrative provisions relating to the taking-up and pursuit of the business of direct insurance other than life assurance[1] and First Council Directive 79/267/EEC of 5 March 1979 on the coordination of laws, regulations and administrative provisions relating to the taking-up and pursuit of the business of direct life assurance,[2] carried out through insurance intermediaries in third countries.

NOTES

[1] OJ L228, 16.8.1973, p 3. Directive as last amended by Directive 2002/13/EC of the European Parliament and of the Council (OJ L77, 20.3.2002, p 17).

[2] OJ L63, 13.3.1979, p 1. Directive as last amended by Directive 2002/12/EC of the European Parliament and of the Council (OJ L77, 20.3.2002, p 11).

[6802]
Article 2
Definitions

For the purpose of this Directive—

1. "insurance undertaking" means an undertaking which has received official authorisation in accordance with Article 6 of Directive 73/239/EEC or Article 6 of Directive 79/267/EEC;
2. "reinsurance undertaking" means an undertaking, other than an insurance undertaking or a non-member-country insurance undertaking, the main business of which consists in accepting risks ceded by an insurance undertaking, a non-member-country insurance undertaking or other reinsurance undertakings;
3. "insurance mediation" means the activities of introducing, proposing or carrying out other work preparatory to the conclusion of contracts of insurance, or of concluding such contracts, or of assisting in the administration and performance of such contracts, in particular in the event of a claim.

These activities when undertaken by an insurance undertaking or an employee of an insurance undertaking who is acting under the responsibility of the insurance undertaking shall not be considered as insurance mediation.

The provision of information on an incidental basis in the context of another professional activity provided that the purpose of that activity is not to assist the customer in concluding or performing an insurance contract, the management of claims of an insurance undertaking on a professional basis, and loss adjusting and expert appraisal of claims shall also not be considered as insurance mediation;

4. "reinsurance mediation" means the activities of introducing, proposing or carrying out other work preparatory to the conclusion of contracts of reinsurance, or of concluding such contracts, or of assisting in the administration and performance of such contracts, in particular in the event of a claim.

These activities when undertaken by a reinsurance undertaking or an employee of a reinsurance undertaking who is acting under the responsibility of the reinsurance undertaking are not considered as reinsurance mediation.

The provision of information on an incidental basis in the context of another professional activity provided that the purpose of that activity is not to assist the customer in concluding or performing a reinsurance contract, the management of claims of a reinsurance undertaking on a professional basis, and loss adjusting and expert appraisal of claims shall also not be considered as reinsurance mediation;

5. "insurance intermediary" means any natural or legal person who, for remuneration, takes up or pursues insurance mediation;
6. "reinsurance intermediary" means any natural or legal person who, for remuneration, takes up or pursues reinsurance mediation;
7. "tied insurance intermediary" means any person who carries on the activity of insurance mediation for and on behalf of one or more insurance undertakings in the case of insurance products which are not in competition but does not collect premiums or amounts intended for the customer and who acts under the full responsibility of those insurance undertakings for the products which concern them respectively.

Any person who carries on the activity of insurance mediation in addition to his principal professional activity is also considered as a tied insurance intermediary acting under the responsibility of one or several insurance undertakings for the products which concern them respectively if the insurance is complementary to the goods or services supplied in the framework of this principal professional activity and the person does not collect premiums or amounts intended for the customer;

8. "large risks" shall be as defined by Article 5(d) of Directive 73/239/EEC;
9. "home Member State" means—
   (a) where the intermediary is a natural person, the Member State in which his residence is situated and in which he carries on business;
   (b) where the intermediary is a legal person, the Member State in which its registered office is situated or, if under its national law it has no registered office, the Member State in which its head office is situated;
10. "host Member State" means the Member State in which an insurance or reinsurance intermediary has a branch or provides services;
11. "competent authorities" means the authorities which each Member State designates under Article 7;
12. "durable medium" means any instrument which enables the customer to store information addressed personally to him in a way accessible for future reference for a period of time adequate to the purposes of the information and which allows the unchanged reproduction of the information stored.

In particular, durable medium covers floppy disks, CD-ROMs, DVDs and hard drives of personal computers on which electronic mail is stored, but it excludes Internet sites, unless such sites meet the criteria specified in the first paragraph.

CHAPTER II
REGISTRATION REQUIREMENTS

[6803]
Article 3
Registration

1. Insurance and reinsurance intermediaries shall be registered with a competent authority as defined in Article 7(2), in their home Member State.

Without prejudice to the first subparagraph, Member States may stipulate that insurance and reinsurance undertakings and other bodies may collaborate with the competent authorities in registering insurance and reinsurance intermediaries and in the application of the requirements of Article 4 to such intermediaries. In particular, in the case of tied insurance intermediaries, they may be registered by an insurance undertaking or by an association of insurance undertakings under the supervision of a competent authority.

Member States need not apply the requirement referred to in the first and second subparagraphs to all the natural persons who work in an undertaking and pursue the activity of insurance or reinsurance mediation.

As regards legal persons, Member States shall register such persons and shall also specify in the register the names of the natural persons within the management who are responsible for the mediation business.

2. Member States may establish more than one register for insurance and reinsurance intermediaries provided that they lay down the criteria according to which intermediaries are to be registered.

Member States shall see to it that a single information point is established allowing quick and easy access to information from these various registers, which shall be compiled electronically and kept constantly updated. This information point shall also provide the identification details of the competent authorities of each Member State referred to in paragraph 1, first subparagraph. The register shall indicate further the country or countries in which the intermediary conducts business under the rules on the freedom of establishment or on the freedom to provide services.

3. Member States shall ensure that registration of insurance intermediaries – including tied ones – and reinsurance intermediaries is made subject to the fulfilment of the professional requirements laid down in Article 4.

Member States shall also ensure that insurance intermediaries – including tied ones – and reinsurance intermediaries who cease to fulfil these requirements are removed from the register. The validity of the registration shall be subject to a regular review by the competent authority. If necessary, the home Member State shall inform the host Member State of such removal, by any appropriate means.

4. The competent authorities may provide the insurance and reinsurance intermediaries with a document enabling any interested party by consultation of the register(s) referred to in paragraph 2 to verify that they are duly registered.

That document shall at least provide the information specified in Article 12(1)(a) and (b), and, in the case of a legal person, the name(s) of the natural person(s) referred to in the fourth subparagraph of paragraph 1 of this Article.

The Member State shall require the return of the document to the competent authority which issued it when the insurance or reinsurance intermediary concerned ceases to be registered.

5. Registered insurance and reinsurance intermediaries shall be allowed to take up and pursue the activity of insurance and reinsurance mediation in the Community by means of both freedom of establishment and freedom to provide services.

6. Member States shall ensure that insurance undertakings use the insurance and reinsurance mediation services only of registered insurance and reinsurance intermediaries and of the persons referred to in Article 1(2).

[6804]
Article 4
Professional requirements

1. Insurance and reinsurance intermediaries shall possess appropriate knowledge and ability, as determined by the home Member State of the intermediary.

Home Member States may adjust the required conditions with regard to knowledge and ability in line with the activity of insurance or reinsurance mediation and the products distributed, particularly if the principal professional activity of the intermediary is other than insurance mediation. In such cases, that intermediary may pursue an activity of insurance mediation only if an insurance intermediary fulfilling the conditions of this Article or an insurance undertaking assumes full responsibility for his actions.

Member States may provide that for the cases referred to in the second subparagraph of Article 3(1), the insurance undertaking shall verify that the knowledge and ability of the intermediaries are in conformity with the obligations set out in the first subparagraph of this paragraph and, if need be, shall provide such intermediaries with training which corresponds to the requirements concerning the products sold by the intermediaries.

Member States need not apply the requirement referred to in the first subparagraph of this paragraph to all the natural persons working in an undertaking who pursue the activity of insurance or reinsurance mediation. Member States shall ensure that a reasonable proportion of the persons within the management structure of such undertakings who are responsible for mediation in respect of insurance products and all other persons directly involved in insurance or reinsurance mediation demonstrate the knowledge and ability necessary for the performance of their duties.

2. Insurance and reinsurance intermediaries shall be of good repute. As a minimum, they shall have a clean police record or any other national equivalent in relation to serious criminal offences linked to crimes against property or other crimes related to financial activities and they should not have previously been declared bankrupt, unless they have been rehabilitated in accordance with national law.

Member States may, in accordance with the provisions of the second subparagraph of Article 3(1), allow the insurance undertaking to check the good repute of insurance intermediaries.

Member States need not apply the requirement referred to in the first subparagraph of this paragraph to all the natural persons who work in an undertaking and who pursue the activity of insurance and reinsurance mediation. Member States shall ensure that the management structure of such undertakings and any staff directly involved in insurance or reinsurance mediation fulfil that requirement.

3. Insurance and reinsurance intermediaries shall hold professional indemnity insurance covering the whole territory of the Community or some other comparable guarantee against liability arising from professional negligence, for at least EUR 1 000 000 applying to each claim and in aggregate EUR 1 500 000 per year for all claims, unless such insurance or comparable guarantee is already provided by an insurance undertaking, reinsurance undertaking or other undertaking on whose behalf the insurance or reinsurance intermediary is acting or for which the insurance or reinsurance intermediary is empowered to act or such undertaking has taken on full responsibility for the intermediary's actions.

4. Member States shall take all necessary measures to protect customers against the inability of the insurance intermediary to transfer the premium to the insurance undertaking or to transfer the amount of claim or return premium to the insured.

Such measures shall take any one or more of the following forms—

(a) provisions laid down by law or contract whereby monies paid by the customer to the intermediary are treated as having been paid to the undertaking, whereas monies paid by the undertaking to the intermediary are not treated as having been paid to the customer until the customer actually receives them;

(b) a requirement for insurance intermediaries to have financial capacity amounting, on a permanent basis, to 4% of the sum of annual premiums received, subject to a minimum of EUR 15 000;

(c) a requirement that customers' monies shall be transferred via strictly segregated client accounts and that these accounts shall not be used to reimburse other creditors in the event of bankruptcy;

(d) a requirement that a guarantee fund be set up.

5. Pursuit of the activities of insurance and reinsurance mediation shall require that the professional requirements set out in this Article be fulfilled on permanent basis.

6. Member States may reinforce the requirements set out in this Article or add other requirements for insurance and reinsurance intermediaries registered within their jurisdiction.

7. The amounts referred to in paragraphs 3 and 4 shall be reviewed regularly in order to take account of changes in the European Index of Consumer Prices as published by Eurostat. The first review shall take place five years after the entry into force of this Directive and the successive reviews every five years after the previous review date.

The amounts shall be adapted automatically by increasing the base amount in euro by the percentage change in that Index over the period between the entry into force of this Directive and the first review date or between the last review date and the new review date and rounded up to the nearest euro.

[6805]
Article 5
Retention of acquired rights

Member States may provide that those persons who exercised a mediation activity before 1 September 2000, who were entered in a register and who had a level of training and experience similar to that required by this Directive, shall be automatically entered in the register to be created, once the requirements set down in Article 4(3) and (4) are complied with.

[6806]
Article 6
Notification of establishment and services in other Member States

1. Any insurance or reinsurance intermediary intending to carry on business for the first time in one or more Member States under the freedom to provide services or the freedom of establishment shall inform the competent authorities of the home Member State.

Within a period of one month after such notification, those competent authorities shall inform the competent authorities of any host Member States wishing to know, of the intention of the insurance or reinsurance intermediary and shall at the same time inform the intermediary concerned.

The insurance or reinsurance intermediary may start business one month after the date on which he was informed by the competent authorities of the home Member State of the notification referred to in the second subparagraph. However, that intermediary may start business immediately if the host Member State does not wish to be informed of the fact.

2. Member States shall notify the Commission of their wish to be informed in accordance with paragraph 1. The Commission shall in turn notify all the Member States of this.

3. The competent authorities of the host Member State may take the necessary steps to ensure appropriate publication of the conditions under which, in the interest of the general good, the business concerned must be carried on in their territories.

[6807]
Article 7
Competent authorities

1. Member States shall designate the competent authorities empowered to ensure implementation of this Directive. They shall inform the Commission thereof, indicating any division of those duties.

2. The authorities referred to in paragraph 1 shall be either public authorities or bodies recognised by national law or by public authorities expressly empowered for that purpose by national law. They shall not be insurance or reinsurance undertakings.

3. The competent authorities shall possess all the powers necessary for the performance of their duties. Where there is more than one competent authority on its territory, a Member State shall ensure that those authorities collaborate closely so that they can discharge their respective duties effectively.

[6808]
Article 8
Sanctions

1. Member States shall provide for appropriate sanctions in the event that a person exercising the activity of insurance or reinsurance mediation is not registered in a Member State and is not referred to in Article 1(2).

2. Member States shall provide for appropriate sanctions against insurance or reinsurance undertakings which use the insurance or reinsurance mediation services of persons who are not registered in a Member State and who are not referred to in Article 1(2).

3. Member States shall provide for appropriate sanctions in the event of an insurance or reinsurance intermediary's failure to comply with national provisions adopted pursuant to this Directive.

4. This Directive shall not affect the power of the host Member States to take appropriate measures to prevent or to penalise irregularities committed within their territories which are contrary to legal or regulatory provisions adopted in the interest of the general good. This shall include the possibility of preventing offending insurance or reinsurance intermediaries from initiating any further activities within their territories.

5. Any measure adopted involving sanctions or restrictions on the activities of an insurance or reinsurance intermediary must be properly justified and communicated to the intermediary concerned. Every such measure shall be subject to the right to apply to the courts in the Member State which adopted it.

[6809]
Article 9
Exchange of information between Member States

1. The competent authorities of the various Member States shall cooperate in order to ensure the proper application of the provisions of this Directive.

2. The competent authorities shall exchange information on insurance and reinsurance intermediaries if they have been subject to a sanction referred to in Article 8(3) or a measure referred to in Article 8(4) and such information is likely to lead to removal from the register of such intermediaries. The competent authorities may also exchange any relevant information at the request of an authority.

3. All persons required to receive or divulge information in connection with this Directive shall be bound by professional secrecy, in the same manner as is laid down in Article 16 of Council Directive 92/49/EEC of 18 June 1992 on the coordination of laws, regulations and administrative provisions relating to direct insurance other than life assurance and amending Directives 73/239/EEC and 88/357/EEC (third non-life insurance Directive)[1] and Article 15 of Council Directive 92/96/EEC of 10 November 1992 on the coordination of laws, regulations and administrative provisions relating to direct life assurance and amending Directives 79/267/EEC and 90/619/EEC (third life assurance Directive).[2]

NOTES

1 OJ L228, 11.8.1992, p 1. Directive as last amended by Directive 2000/64/EC of the European Parliament and of the Council (OJ L290, 17.11.2000, p 27).

2 OJ L360, 9.12.1992, p 1. Directive as last amended by Directive 2000/64/EC of the European Parliament and of the Council.

[6810]
Article 10
Complaints

Member States shall ensure that procedures are set up which allow customers and other interested parties, especially consumer associations, to register complaints about insurance and reinsurance intermediaries. In all cases complaints shall receive replies.

[6811]
Article 11
Out-of-court redress

1. Member States shall encourage the setting-up of appropriate and effective complaints and redress procedures for the out-of-court settlement of disputes between insurance intermediaries and customers, using existing bodies where appropriate.

2. Member States shall encourage these bodies to cooperate in the resolution of cross-border disputes.

CHAPTER III
INFORMATION REQUIREMENTS FOR INTERMEDIARIES

[6812]
Article 12
Information provided by the insurance intermediary

1. Prior to the conclusion of any initial insurance contract, and, if necessary, upon amendment or renewal thereof, an insurance intermediary shall provide the customer with at least the following information—

(a) his identity and address;
(b) the register in which he has been included and the means for verifying that he has been registered;
(c) whether he has a holding, direct or indirect, representing more than 10% of the voting rights or of the capital in a given insurance undertaking;
(d) whether a given insurance undertaking or parent undertaking of a given insurance undertaking has a holding, direct or indirect, representing more than 10% of the voting rights or of the capital in the insurance intermediary;
(e) the procedures referred to in Article 10 allowing customers and other interested parties to register complaints about insurance and reinsurance intermediaries and, if appropriate, about the out-of-court complaint and redress procedures referred to in Article 11.

In addition, an insurance intermediary shall inform the customer, concerning the contract that is provided, whether—

(i) he gives advice based on the obligation in paragraph 2 to provide a fair analysis, or
(ii) he is under a contractual obligation to conduct insurance mediation business exclusively with one or more insurance undertakings. In that case, he shall, at the customer's request provide the names of those insurance undertakings, or

(iii) he is not under a contractual obligation to conduct insurance mediation business exclusively with one or more insurance undertakings and does not give advice based on the obligation in paragraph 2 to provide a fair analysis. In that case, he shall, at the customer's request provide the names of the insurance undertakings with which he may and does conduct business.

In those cases where information is to be provided solely at the customer's request, the customer shall be informed that he has the right to request such information.

2. When the insurance intermediary informs the customer that he gives his advice on the basis of a fair analysis, he is obliged to give that advice on the basis of an analysis of a sufficiently large number of insurance contracts available on the market, to enable him to make a recommendation, in accordance with professional criteria, regarding which insurance contract would be adequate to meet the customer's needs.

3. Prior to the conclusion of any specific contract, the insurance intermediary shall at least specify, in particular on the basis of information provided by the customer, the demands and the needs of that customer as well as the underlying reasons for any advice given to the customer on a given insurance product. These details shall be modulated according to the complexity of the insurance contract being proposed.

4. The information referred to in paragraphs 1, 2 and 3 need not be given when the insurance intermediary mediates in the insurance of large risks, nor in the case of mediation by reinsurance intermediaries.

5. Member States may maintain or adopt stricter provisions regarding the information requirements referred to in paragraph 1, provided that such provisions comply with Community law.

Member States shall communicate to the Commission the national provisions set out in the first subparagraph.

In order to establish a high level of transparency by all appropriate means, the Commission shall ensure that the information it receives relating to national provisions is also communicated to consumers and insurance intermediaries.

[6813]
Article 13
Information conditions

1. All information to be provided to customers in accordance with Article 12 shall be communicated—

(a) on paper or on any other durable medium available and accessible to the customer;
(b) in a clear and accurate manner, comprehensible to the customer;
(c) in an official language of the Member State of the commitment or in any other language agreed by the parties.

2. By way of derogation from paragraph 1(a), the information referred to in Article 12 may be provided orally where the customer requests it, or where immediate cover is necessary. In those cases, the information shall be provided to the customer in accordance with paragraph 1 immediately after the conclusion of the insurance contract.

3. In the case of telephone selling, the prior information given to the customer shall be in accordance with Community rules applicable to the distance marketing of consumer financial services. Moreover, information shall be provided to the customer in accordance with paragraph 1 immediately after the conclusion of the insurance contract.

CHAPTER IV
FINAL PROVISIONS

[6814]
Article 14
Right to apply to the courts

Member States shall ensure that decisions taken in respect of an insurance intermediary, reinsurance intermediary or an insurance undertaking under the laws, regulations and administrative provisions adopted in accordance with this Directive may be subject to the right to apply to the courts.

Article 15 (*Repeals Directive 77/92/EEC.*)

[6815]
Article 16
Transposition

1. Member States shall bring into force the laws, regulations and administrative provisions necessary to comply with this Directive before 15 January 2005. They shall forthwith inform the Commission thereof.

These measures shall contain a reference to this Directive or shall be accompanied by such reference on the occasion of their official publication. The methods of making such reference shall be laid down by the Member States.

2. Member States shall communicate to the Commission the text of the laws, regulations and administrative provisions which they adopt in the field governed by this Directive. In that communication they shall provide a table indicating the national provisions corresponding to this Directive.

[6816]
Article 17
Entry into force

This Directive shall enter into force on the day of its publication in the *Official Journal of the European Communities*.

[6817]–[6847]
Article 18
Addressees

This Directive is addressed to the Member States.

Done at Brussels, 9 December 2002.

G. MOTOR INSURANCE

COUNCIL DIRECTIVE

(90/618/EEC)

of 8 November 1990

amending, particularly as regards motor vehicle liability insurance, Directive 73/239/EEC and Directive 88/357/EEC which concern the coordination of laws, regulations and administrative provisions relating to direct insurance other than life assurance (Directive on Freedom of Motor Insurance Services)

NOTES

Date of publication in OJ: OJ L330, 29.11.90, p 44.

[6848]

THE COUNCIL OF THE EUROPEAN COMMUNITIES,

Having regard to the Treaty establishing the European Economic Community, and in particular Articles 57(2) and 66 thereof,

Having regard to the proposal from the Commission,[1]

In cooperation with the European Parliament,[2]

Having regard to the Opinion of the Economic and Social Committee,[3]

Whereas in order to develop the internal insurance market, the Council adopted on 24 July 1973 Directive 73/239/EEC on the coordination of laws, regulations and administrative provisions relating to the taking-up and pursuit of the business of direct insurance other than life assurance[4] (also referred to as the "First Directive") and on 22 June 1988 Directive 88/357/EEC on the coordination of laws, regulations and administrative provisions relating to direct insurance other than life assurance and laying down provisions to facilitate the effective exercise of freedom to provide services and amending Directive 73/239/EEC[5] (also referred to as the "Second Directive");

Whereas Directive 88/357/EEC made it easier for insurance undertakings having their head office in the Community to provide services in the Member States, thus making it possible for policyholders to have recourse not only to insurers established in their own country, but also to insurers who have their head office in the Community and are established in other Member States;

Whereas the scope of the provisions of Directive 88/357/EEC specifically concerning freedom to provide services excluded certain risks, the application to which of the said provisions was rendered inappropriate at that stage by the specific rules adopted by the Member States' authorities, owing to the nature and social implications of such provisions; whereas those exclusions were to be re-examined after that Directive had been implemented for a certain period;

Whereas one of the exclusions concerned motor vehicle liability insurance, other than carrier's liability;

Whereas, however, when the abovementioned Directive was adopted the Commission gave an undertaking to present to the Council as soon as possible a proposal concerning freedom to provide services in the area of insurance against civil liability in respect of the use of motor vehicles (other than carrier's liability);

Whereas, subject to the provisions of the said Directive concerning compulsory insurance, it is appropriate to provide for the possibility of large risk treatment, within the meaning of Article 5 of the said Directive, for the said insurance class of motor vehicle liability;

Whereas large risk treatment should also be envisaged for insurance covering damage to or loss of land motor vehicles and land vehicles other than motor vehicles;

Whereas Directive 88/357/EEC laid down that the risks which may be covered by way of Community co-insurance within the meaning of Council Directive 78/473/EEC of 30 May 1978 on the coordination of laws, regulations and administrative provisions relating to Community co-insurance[6] were to be large risks as defined in Directive 88/357/EEC whereas the inclusion by the present Directive of the motor insurance classes in the large risks definition of Directive 88/357/EEC will have the effect of including those classes in the list of classes which may be covered by way of Community co-insurance;

Whereas Council Directive 72/166/EEC of 24 April 1972 on the approximation of the laws of the Member States relating to insurance against civil liability in respect of the use of motor vehicles, and to the enforcement of the obligation to insure against such liability,[7] as last amended by Directive 90/232/EEC,[8] built on the green card system and the agreements between the national motor insurers' bureaux in order to enable green card checks to be abolished;

Part VI European Materials

Whereas it is desirable, however, to grant Member States transitional arrangements for the gradual application of the specific provisions of this Directive relating to large risk treatment for the said insurance classes, including where risks are covered by coinsurance;

Whereas to ensure the continued proper functioning of the green card system and the agreements between the national motor insurers' bureaux it is appropriate to require insurance undertakings providing motor liability insurance in a Member State by way of provision of services to join and participate in the financing of the bureau of that Member State;

Whereas Council Directive 84/5/EEC of 30 December 1983 on the approximation of the laws of the Member States relating to insurance against civil liability in respect of the use of motor vehicles,[9] as last amended by Directive 90/232/EEC, required the Member States to set up or authorise a body (guarantee fund) with the task of providing compensation to victims of accidents caused by uninsured or unidentified vehicles;

Whereas it is also appropriate to require insurance undertakings providing motor liability insurance in a Member State by way of provision of services to join and participate in the financing of the guarantee fund set up in that Member State;

Whereas the rules in force in some Member States concerning the cover of aggravated risks apply to all undertakings covering risks through an establishment situated there; whereas the purpose of those rules is to ensure that the compulsory nature of motor liability insurance is balanced by the possibility for motorists to obtain such insurance; whereas Member States should be permitted to apply those rules to undertakings providing services in their territories to the extent that the rules are justified in the public interest and do not exceed what is necessary to achieve the abovementioned purpose;

Whereas in the field of motor liability insurance the protection of the interests of persons suffering damage who could pursue claims in fact concerns each and everyone and that it is therefore advisable to ensure that these persons are not prejudiced or put to greater inconvenience where the motor liability insurer is operating by way of provision of services rather than by way of establishment; whereas for this purpose, and insofar as the interests of these persons are not sufficiently safeguarded by the rules applying to the supplier of services in the Member State in which it is established, it should be provided that the Member State of provision of services shall require the undertaking to appoint a representative resident or established in its territory to collect all necessary information in relation to claims and shall possess sufficient powers to represent the undertaking in relation to persons suffering damage who could pursue claims, including the payment of such claims, and to represent it or, where necessary, to have it represented before the courts and authorities of that Member State in relation to these claims;

Whereas this representative may also be required to represent the undertaking before the competent authorities of the Member State of provision of services in relation to the control of the existence and validity of motor vehicle liability insurance policies;

Whereas provision should be made for a flexible procedure to make it possible to assess reciprocity with third countries on a Community basis; whereas the aim of this procedure is not to close the Community's financial markets but rather, as the Community intends to keep its financial markets open to the rest of the world, to improve the liberalisation of the global financial markets in third countries; whereas, to that end, this Directive provided for procedures for negotiating with third countries and, as a last resort, for the possibility of taking measures involving the suspension of new applications for authorisation or the restriction of new authorisations,

NOTES

1 OJ C65, 15.3.89 p 6 and OJ C180, 20.7.90, p 6.
2 OJ C68, 19.3.90, p 85 and Decision of 10 October 1990 (not yet published in the Official Journal).
3 OJ C194, 31.7.89, p 3.
4 OJ L228, 16.8.73, p 3.
5 OJ L172, 4.7.88, p 1.
6 OJ L151, 7.6.78, p 25.
7 OJ L103, 2.5.72, p 1.
8 OJ L129, 19.5.90, p 33.
9 OJ L8, 11.1.84, p 17.

HAS ADOPTED THIS DIRECTIVE—

[6849]
Article 1
For the purposes of this Directive—

(a) "vehicle" means a vehicle as defined in Article 1(1) of Directive 72/166/EEC;
(b) "bureau" means a national insurers' bureau as defined in Article 1(3) of Directive 72/166/EEC;
(c) "guarantee fund" means the body referred to in Article 1(4) of Directive 84/5/EEC;
(d) "parent undertaking" means a parent undertaking as defined in Articles 1 and 2 of Directive 83/349/EEC;[1]
(e) "subsidiary" means a subsidiary undertaking as defined in Articles 1 and 2 of Directive 83/349/EEC; any subsidiary undertaking of a subsidiary undertaking shall also be regarded as a subsidiary of the parent undertaking which is at the head of those undertakings.

NOTES

1 OJ No C65, 15.3.1989, p 6, and OJ No C180, 20.7.1990, p 6.

Articles 2–10 (*Art 2 amends First Council Directive 73/239/EEC, art 5(d) at* **[6648]***; art 3 substitutes Title heading III by Title heading IIIA and inserts Title heading IIIB of that Directive; art 4 inserts arts 29a, 29b thereof at* **[6678]**, **[6679]***; arts 5, 7–9 contain amendments to Council Directive 88/357/EEC and these amendments have now been superseded by provisions contained in Council Directive 92/49/EEC; art 6 inserts Council Directive 88/357/EEC, art 12a at* **[6743]***; art 10 amends art 27(1) thereof at* **[6748]**.)

[6850]
Article 11

Notwithstanding Article 23(2) of Directive 88/357/EEC, in the case of a large risk within the meaning of Article 5(d) of Directive 73/239/EEC, classified under class 10, other than carrier's liability, the Member State of provision of services may provide that—

— the amount of the technical reserves relating to the contract concerned shall be determined, under the supervision of the authorities of that Member State, in accordance with its rules or, failing such rules, in accordance with established practice in that Member State, until the date by which the Member States must comply with a Directive coordinating the annual accounts of insurance undertakings,
— the covering of these reserves by equivalent and matching assets shall be under the supervision of the authorities of that Member State in accordance with its rules or practice, until the notification of a Third Directive on non-life insurance,
— the localisation of the assets referred to in the second indent shall be under the supervision of the authorities of that Member State in accordance with its rules or practice until the date by which the Member States must comply with a Third Directive on non-life insurance.

[6851]
Article 12

Member States shall amend their national provisions to comply with this Directive within 18 months of the date of its notification[1] and shall forthwith inform the Commission thereof.

The provisions amended pursuant to the first subparagraph shall be applied within 24 months of the date of the notification of this Directive.

NOTES

1 This Directive was notified to the Member States on 20 November 1990.

[6852]
Article 13

This Directive is addressed to the Member States.

Done at Brussels, 8 November 1990.

Part VI European Materials

EUROPEAN PARLIAMENT AND COUNCIL DIRECTIVE

(2009/103/EC)

of 16 September 2009

relating to insurance against civil liability in respect of the use of motor vehicles, and the enforcement of the obligation to insure against such liability

(codified version)

(Text with EEA relevance)

NOTES

Date of publication in OJ: OJ L263, 7.10.2009, p 11.

[6853]

THE EUROPEAN PARLIAMENT AND THE COUNCIL OF THE EUROPEAN UNION,

Having regard to the Treaty establishing the European Community, and in particular Article 95(1) thereof,

Having regard to the proposal from the Commission,

Having regard to the opinion of the European Economic and Social Committee[1],

Acting in accordance with the procedure laid down in Article 251 of the Treaty[2],

Whereas:

(1) Council Directive 72/166/EEC of 24 April 1972 on the approximation of the laws of Member States relating to insurance against civil liability in respect of the use of motor vehicles, and to the enforcement of the obligation to insure against such liability[3], Second Council Directive 84/5/EEC of 30 December 1983 on the approximation of the laws of the Member States relating to insurance against civil liability in respect of the use of motor vehicles[4], Third Council Directive 90/232/EEC of 14 May 1990 on the approximation of the laws of the Member States relating to insurance against civil liability in respect of the use of motor vehicles[5] and Directive 2000/26/EC of the European Parliament and of the Council of 16 May 2000 on the approximation of the laws of the Member States relating to insurance against civil liability in respect of the use of motor vehicles (Fourth motor insurance Directive)[6] have been substantially amended several times[7]. In the interests of clarity and rationality those four Directives should be codified, as well as Directive 2005/14/EC of the European Parliament and of the Council of 11 May 2005 amending Council Directives 72/166/EEC, 84/5/EEC, 88/357/EEC and 90/232/EEC and Directive 2000/26/EC of the European Parliament and of the Council relating to insurance against civil liability in respect of the use of motor vehicles[8].

(2) Insurance against civil liability in respect of the use of motor vehicles (motor insurance) is of special importance for European citizens, whether they are policyholders or victims of an accident. It is also a major concern for insurance undertakings as it constitutes an important part of non-life insurance business in the Community. Motor insurance also has an impact on the free movement of persons and vehicles. It should therefore be a key objective of Community action in the field of financial services to reinforce and consolidate the internal market in motor insurance.

(3) Each Member State must take all appropriate measures to ensure that civil liability in respect of the use of vehicles normally based in its territory is covered by insurance. The extent of the liability covered and the terms and conditions of the insurance cover are to be determined on the basis of those measures.

(4) In order to exclude any possible misinterpretation of this Directive and to make it easier to obtain insurance cover for vehicles bearing temporary plates, the definition of the territory in which the vehicle is normally based should refer to the territory of the State of which the vehicle bears a registration plate, irrespective of whether such a plate is permanent or temporary.

(5) While respecting the general criterion of the registration plate to determine the territory in which the vehicle is normally based, a special rule should be laid down for accidents caused by vehicles without a registration plate or bearing a registration plate which does not correspond or no longer corresponds to the vehicle. In this case and for the sole purpose of settling the claim, the territory in which the vehicle is normally based should be deemed to be the territory in which the accident took place.

(6) A prohibition of systematic checks on motor insurance should apply to vehicles normally based in the territory of another Member State as well as to vehicles normally based in the territory of a third country but entering from the territory of another Member State. Only non-systematic checks which are not discriminatory and are carried out as part of a control not aimed exclusively at insurance verification may be permitted.

(7) The abolition of checks on green cards for vehicles normally based in a Member State which

enter the territory of another Member State can be effected by means of an agreement between the national insurers' bureaux, whereby each national bureau would guarantee compensation in accordance with the provisions of national law in respect of any loss or injury giving entitlement to compensation caused in its territory by one of those vehicles, whether or not insured.

(8) Such a guarantee agreement presupposes that all Community motor vehicles travelling in Community territory are covered by insurance. The national law of each Member State should, therefore, provide for the compulsory insurance of vehicles against civil liability, such insurance to be valid throughout Community territory.

(9) The system provided for in this Directive could be extended to vehicles normally based in the territory of any third country in respect of which the national bureaux of the Member States have concluded a similar agreement.

(10) Each Member State should be able to act in derogation from the general obligation to take out compulsory insurance in respect of vehicles belonging to certain natural or legal persons, public or private. For accidents caused by such vehicles, the Member State so derogating should designate an authority or body to compensate for the damage to victims of accidents caused in another Member State. Steps should be taken to ensure that due compensation is paid not only to the victims of accidents caused by these vehicles abroad but also the victims of accidents occurring in the Member State in which the vehicle is normally based, whether or not they are resident in its territory. Furthermore, Member States should ensure that the list of persons exempt from compulsory insurance and the authorities or bodies responsible for compensation of victims of accidents caused by such vehicles is communicated to the Commission for publication.

(11) Each Member State should be able to act in derogation from the general obligation to take out compulsory insurance in respect of certain types of vehicles or certain vehicles having a special plate. In that case, the other Member States are allowed to require, at the entry into their territory, a valid green card or a frontier insurance contract, in order to ensure the provision of compensation to victims of any accident which may be caused by those vehicles in their territories. However, since the elimination of border controls within the Community means that it is not possible to ensure that vehicles crossing frontiers are covered by insurance, compensation for victims of accidents caused abroad cannot be guaranteed. Steps should also be taken to ensure that due compensation is awarded to the victims of accidents caused by those vehicles not only abroad but also in the Member State in which the vehicle is normally based. For this purpose, Member States should treat the victims of accidents caused by those vehicles in the same way as victims of accidents caused by uninsured vehicles. Indeed, compensation to victims of accidents caused by uninsured vehicles should be paid by the compensation body of the Member State in which the accident took place. Where payments are made to victims of accidents caused by vehicles subject to the derogation, the compensation body should have a claim against the body of the Member State in which the vehicle is normally based. After a certain period to allow for the implementation and application of this possibility of derogation, and taking into account the lessons drawn therefrom, the Commission should, when appropriate, submit proposals for its replacement or repeal.

(12) Member States' obligations to guarantee insurance cover at least in respect of certain minimum amounts constitute an important element in ensuring the protection of victims. The minimum amount of cover for personal injury should be calculated so as to compensate fully and fairly all victims who have suffered very serious injuries, while taking into account the low frequency of accidents involving several victims and the small number of accidents in which several victims suffer very serious injuries in the course of one and the same event. A minimum amount of cover per victim or per claim should be provided for. With a view to facilitating the introduction of these minimum amounts, a transitional period should be established. However, a period shorter than the transitional period should be provided for, in which Member States should increase these amounts to at least half the levels provided for.

(13) In order to ensure that the minimum amount of cover is not eroded over time, a periodic review clause should be provided using as a benchmark the European Index of Consumer Prices (EICP) published by Eurostat, as provided for in Council Regulation (EC) No 2494/95 of 23 October 1995 concerning harmonised indices of consumer prices[9]. Procedural rules governing such a review should also be laid down.

(14) It is necessary to make provision for a body to guarantee that the victim will not remain without compensation where the vehicle which caused the accident is uninsured or unidentified. It is important to provide that the victim of such an accident should be able to apply directly to that body as a first point of contact. However, Member States should be given the possibility of applying certain limited exclusions as regards the payment of compensation by that body and of providing that compensation for damage to property caused by an unidentified vehicle may be limited or excluded in view of the danger of fraud.

(15) It is in the interest of victims that the effects of certain exclusion clauses be limited to the relationship between the insurer and the person responsible for the accident. However, in the case of vehicles stolen or obtained by violence, Member States may specify that compensation will be payable by the abovementioned body.

(16) In order to alleviate the financial burden on that body, Member States may make provision

for the application of certain excesses where the body provides compensation for damage to property caused by uninsured vehicles or, as the case may be, vehicles stolen or obtained by violence.

(17) The option of limiting or excluding legitimate compensation for victims on the basis that the vehicle is unidentified should not apply where the body has paid compensation for significant personal injuries to any victim of the accident in which damage to property was caused. Member States may provide for an excess, up to the limit prescribed in this Directive, to be borne by the victim of the damage to property. The conditions in which personal injuries are to be considered significant should be determined by the national legislation or administrative provisions of the Member State where the accident takes place. In establishing those conditions, the Member State may take into account, inter alia, whether the injury has required hospital care.

(18) In the case of an accident caused by an uninsured vehicle, the body which compensates victims of accidents caused by uninsured or unidentified vehicles is better placed than the victim to bring an action against the party liable. Therefore, it should be provided that that body cannot require that victim, if he is to be compensated, to establish that the party liable is unable or refuses to pay.

(19) In the event of a dispute between the body referred to above and a civil liability insurer as to which of them should compensate the victim of an accident, Member States, to avoid any delay in the payment of compensation to the victim, should ensure that one of those parties is designated as being responsible in the first instance for paying compensation pending resolution of the dispute.

(20) Motor vehicle accident victims should be guaranteed comparable treatment irrespective of where in the Community accidents occur.

(21) The members of the family of the policyholder, driver or any other person liable should be afforded protection comparable to that of other third parties, in any event in respect of their personal injuries.

(22) Personal injuries and damage to property suffered by pedestrians, cyclists and other non-motorised road users, who are usually the weakest party in an accident, should be covered by the compulsory insurance of the vehicle involved in the accident where they are entitled to compensation under national civil law. This provision does not prejudge the issue of civil liability, or the level of awards of damages in respect of a given accident, under national legislation.

(23) The inclusion within the insurance cover of any passenger in the vehicle is a major achievement of the existing legislation. This objective would be placed in jeopardy if national legislation or any contractual clause contained in an insurance policy excluded passengers from insurance cover because they knew or should have known that the driver of the vehicle was under the influence of alcohol or of any other intoxicating agent at the time of the accident. The passenger is not usually in a position to assess properly the level of intoxication of the driver. The objective of discouraging persons from driving while under the influence of intoxicating agents is not achieved by reducing the insurance cover for passengers who are victims of motor vehicle accidents. Cover of such passengers under the vehicle's compulsory motor insurance does not prejudge any liability they might incur pursuant to the applicable national legislation, nor the level of any award of damages in a specific accident.

(24) All compulsory motor insurance policies should cover the entire territory of the Community.

(25) Some insurance undertakings insert into insurance policies clauses to the effect that the contract will be cancelled if the vehicle remains outside the Member State of registration for longer than a specified period. This practice is in conflict with the principle set out in this Directive, according to which compulsory motor insurance should cover, on the basis of a single premium, the entire territory of the Community. It should therefore be specified that the insurance cover is to remain valid during the whole term of the contract, irrespective of whether the vehicle remains in another Member State for a particular period, without prejudice to the obligations under Member States' national legislation with respect to the registration of vehicles.

(26) In the interests of the party insured, every insurance policy should guarantee for a single premium, in each Member State, the cover required by its law or the cover required by the law of the Member State where the vehicle is normally based, when that cover is higher.

(27) Steps should be taken to make it easier to obtain insurance cover for vehicles imported from one Member State into another, even though the vehicle is not yet registered in the Member State of destination. A temporary derogation from the general rule determining the Member State where the risk is situated should be made available. For a period of 30 days from the date when the vehicle is delivered, made available or dispatched to the purchaser, the Member State of destination should be considered to be the Member State where the risk is situated.

(28) Any person wishing to take out a new motor insurance contract with another insurer should be in a position to justify his accident and claims record under the old contract. The policyholder should have the right to request at any time a statement concerning the claims, or the absence of claims, involving the vehicle or vehicles covered by the insurance contract at least during the preceding five years of the contractual relationship. The insurance undertaking, or any body which may have been appointed by a Member State to provide compulsory insurance or to supply such statements, should provide this statement to the policyholder within 15 days of the request.

(29) In order to ensure due protection for victims of motor vehicle accidents, Member States

should not permit insurance undertakings to rely on excesses against an injured party.

(30) The right to invoke the insurance contract and to claim against the insurance undertaking directly is of great importance for the protection of victims of motor vehicle accidents. In order to facilitate an efficient and speedy settlement of claims and to avoid as far as possible costly legal proceedings, a right of direct action against the insurance undertaking covering the person responsible against civil liability should be provided for victims of any motor vehicle accident.

(31) In order to obtain an adequate level of protection for victims of motor vehicle accidents, a 'reasoned offer' procedure should be extended to any kind of motor vehicle accident. This same procedure should also apply *mutatis mutandis* where the accident is settled by the system of national insurers' bureaux.

(32) Under Article 11(2) read in conjunction with Article 9(1)(b) of Council Regulation (EC) No 44/2001 of 22 December 2000 on jurisdiction and the recognition and enforcement of judgments in civil and commercial matters[10], injured parties may bring legal proceedings against the civil liability insurance provider in the Member State in which they are domiciled.

(33) The green card bureau system ensures the ready settlement of claims in the injured party's country of residence even where the other party comes from a different European country.

(34) Parties injured as a result of a motor vehicle accident falling within the scope of this Directive and occurring in a State other than that of their residence should be entitled to claim in their Member State of residence against a claims representative appointed there by the insurance undertaking of the responsible party. This solution would enable damage suffered by injured parties outside their Member State of residence to be dealt with under procedures which are familiar to them.

(35) This system of having claims representatives in the injured party's Member State of residence affects neither the substantive law to be applied in each individual case nor the matter of jurisdiction.

(36) The existence of a direct right of action for the injured party against the insurance undertaking is a logical supplement to the appointment of such representatives and moreover improves the legal position of parties injured as a result of motor vehicle accidents occurring outside their Member State of residence.

(37) It should be provided that the Member State where the insurance undertaking is authorised should require that undertaking to appoint claims representatives resident or established in the other Member States to collect all necessary information in relation to claims resulting from such accidents and to take appropriate action to settle the claims on behalf and for the account of the insurance undertaking, including the payment of compensation. Claims representatives should have sufficient powers to represent the insurance undertaking in relation to persons suffering damage from such accidents, and also to represent the insurance undertaking before national authorities including, where necessary, before the courts, in so far as this is compatible with the rules of private international law on the conferral of jurisdiction.

(38) The activities of the claims representative are not sufficient in order to confer jurisdiction on the courts in the injured party's Member State of residence if the rules of private international law on the conferral of jurisdiction do not so provide.

(39) The appointment of representatives responsible for settling claims should be one of the conditions for access to and carrying on the activity of insurance listed in class 10 of point A of the Annex to First Council Directive 73/239/EEC of 24 July 1973 on the coordination of laws, regulations and administrative provisions relating to the taking-up and pursuit of the business of direct insurance other than life assurance[11], except for carriers' liability. That condition should therefore be covered by the single official authorisation issued by the authorities of the Member State where the insurance undertaking establishes its head office, as specified in Title II of Council Directive 92/49/EEC of 18 June 1992 on the coordination of laws, regulations and administrative provisions relating to direct insurance other than life assurance and amending Directives 73/239/EEC and 88/357/EEC (third non-life insurance Directive)[12]. That condition should also apply to insurance undertakings having their head office outside the Community which have secured an authorisation granting them access to the activity of insurance in a Member State of the Community.

(40) In addition to ensuring that the insurance undertaking has a representative in the State where the injured party resides, it is appropriate to guarantee the specific right of the injured party to have the claim settled promptly. It is therefore necessary to include in national law appropriate effective and systematic financial or equivalent administrative penalties — such as injunctions combined with administrative fines, reporting to supervisory authorities on a regular basis, on-the-spot checks, publications in the national official journal and in the press, suspension of the activities of the company (prohibition on the conclusion of new contracts for a certain period), designation of a special representative of the supervisory authorities responsible for verifying that the business is run in line with insurance laws, withdrawal of the authorisation for this business line, sanctions to be imposed on directors and management staff — in the event that the insurance undertaking or its representative fails to fulfil its obligation to make an offer of compensation within a reasonable

period of time. This should not prejudice the application of any other measure, especially under the law applicable to supervisory matters, which may be considered appropriate. However, it is a condition that liability and the damage and injury sustained should not be in dispute, so that the insurance undertaking is able to make a reasoned offer within the prescribed period of time. The reasoned offer of compensation should be in writing and should contain the grounds on the basis of which liability and damages have been assessed.

(41) In addition to those sanctions, it is appropriate to provide that interest should be payable on the amount of compensation offered by the insurance undertaking or awarded by the court to the injured party when the offer has not been made within the prescribed time limit. If Member States have existing national rules which cover the requirement for late-payment interest, this provision could be implemented by a reference to those rules.

(42) Injured parties suffering loss or injury as a result of motor vehicle accidents sometimes have difficulty in establishing the name of the insurance undertaking providing insurance against civil liability in respect of the use of motor vehicles involved in an accident.

(43) In the interests of such injured parties, Member States should set up information centres to ensure that such information concerning any accident involving a motor vehicle is made available promptly. Those information centres should also make available to injured parties information concerning claims representatives. It is necessary that such centres should cooperate with each other and respond rapidly to requests for information about claims representatives made by centres in other Member States. It seems appropriate that such centres should collect information about the actual termination date of the insurance cover but not about the expiry of the original validity of the policy if the duration of the contract is extended owing to non-cancellation.

(44) Specific provision should be made with respect to vehicles (for example, government or military vehicles) which fall within the exemptions from the obligation to be insured against civil liability.

(45) The injured party may have a legitimate interest in being informed about the identity of the owner or usual driver or the registered keeper of the vehicle, for example if he can obtain compensation only from those persons because the vehicle is not duly insured or the damage exceeds the sum insured, in which event this information should also be provided.

(46) Certain information provided, such as the name and address of the owner or usual driver of the vehicle and the number of the insurance policy or the registration number of the vehicle, constitutes personal data within the meaning of Directive 95/46/EC of the European Parliament and of the Council of 24 October 1995 on the protection of individuals with regard to the processing of personal data and on the free movement of such data[13]. The processing of such data which is required for the purposes of this Directive should therefore comply with the national measures taken pursuant to Directive 95/46/EC. The name and address of the usual driver should be communicated only if national legislation provides for such communication.

(47) In order to ensure that the injured party will not remain without the compensation to which he is entitled, it is necessary to make provision for a compensation body to which the injured party may apply where the insurance undertaking has failed to appoint a representative or is manifestly dilatory in settling a claim or where the insurance undertaking cannot be identified. The intervention of the compensation body should be limited to rare individual cases where the insurance undertaking has failed to comply with its duties in spite of the deterrent effect of the potential imposition of penalties.

(48) The role played by the compensation body is that of settling the claim in respect of any loss or injury suffered by the injured party only in cases which are capable of objective determination and therefore the compensation body should limit its activity to verifying that an offer of compensation has been made in accordance with the time limits and procedures laid down, without any assessment of the merits.

(49) Legal persons who are subrogated by law to the injured party in his claims against the person responsible for the accident or the latter's insurance undertaking (such as, for example, other insurance undertakings or social security bodies) should not be entitled to present the corresponding claim to the compensation body.

(50) The compensation body should have a right of subrogation in so far as it has compensated the injured party. In order to facilitate enforcement of the compensation body's claim against the insurance undertaking where the latter has failed to appoint a claims representative or is manifestly dilatory in settling a claim, the body providing compensation in the injured party's State should also enjoy an automatic right of reimbursement with subrogation to the rights of the injured party on the part of the corresponding body in the State where the insurance undertaking is established. This body is the best placed to institute proceedings for recourse against the insurance undertaking.

(51) Even though Member States may provide that the claim against the compensation body is to be subsidiary, the injured person should not be obliged to present his claim to the person responsible for the accident before presenting it to the compensation body. In such a case the injured party should be in at least the same position as in the case of a claim against the guarantee fund.

(52) This system can be made to function by means of an agreement between the compensation

bodies established or approved by the Member States, defining their functions and obligations and the procedures for reimbursement.

(53) Where it is impossible to identify the insurer of a vehicle, it should be provided that the ultimate debtor in respect of the damages to be paid to the injured party is the guarantee fund provided for this purpose situated in the Member State where the uninsured vehicle, the use of which has caused the accident, is normally based. Where it is impossible to identify the vehicle, it should be provided that the ultimate debtor is the guarantee fund provided for this purpose situated in the Member State in which the accident occurred.

(54) This Directive should be without prejudice to the obligations of the Member States relating to the time limits for transposition into national law and application of the Directives set out in Annex I, Part B,

NOTES

1 OJ C224, 30.8.2008, p 39.

2 Opinion of the European Parliament of 21 October 2008 (not yet published in the Official Journal) and Council Decision of 13 July 2009.

3 OJ L103, 2.5.1972, p 1.

4 OJ L8, 11.1.1984, p 17.

5 OJ L129, 19.5.1990, p 33.

6 OJ L181, 20.7.2000, p 65.

7 See Annex I, Part A.

8 OJ L149, 11.6.2005, p 14.

9 OJ L257, 27.10.1995, p 1.

10 OJ L12, 16.1.2001, p 1.

11 OJ L228, 16.8.1973, p 3.

12 OJ L228, 11.8.1992, p 1.

13 OJ L281, 23.11.1995, p 31.

HAVE ADOPTED THIS DIRECTIVE:

CHAPTER 1
GENERAL PROVISIONS

[6854]
Article 1
Definitions

For the purposes of this Directive:

1. 'vehicle' means any motor vehicle intended for travel on land and propelled by mechanical power, but not running on rails, and any trailer, whether or not coupled;

2. 'injured party' means any person entitled to compensation in respect of any loss or injury caused by vehicles;

3. 'national insurers' bureau' means a professional organisation which is constituted in accordance with Recommendation No 5 adopted on 25 January 1949 by the Road Transport Sub-committee of the Inland Transport Committee of the United Nations Economic Commission for Europe and which groups together insurance undertakings which, in a State, are authorised to conduct the business of motor vehicle insurance against civil liability;

4. 'territory in which the vehicle is normally based' means:
   (a) the territory of the State of which the vehicle bears a registration plate, irrespective of whether the plate is permanent or temporary; or
   (b) in cases where no registration is required for a type of vehicle but the vehicle bears an insurance plate, or a distinguishing sign analogous to the registration plate, the territory of the State in which the insurance plate or the sign is issued; or
   (c) in cases where neither a registration plate nor an insurance plate nor a distinguishing sign is required for certain types of vehicle, the territory of the State in which the person who has custody of the vehicle is permanently resident; or
   (d) in cases where the vehicle does not bear any registration plate or bears a registration plate which does not correspond or no longer corresponds to the vehicle and has been involved in an accident, the territory of the State in which the accident took place, for the purpose of settling the claim as provided for in the first indent of Article 2(a) or in Article 10;

Part VI European Materials

5. 'green card' means an international certificate of insurance issued on behalf of a national bureau in accordance with Recommendation No 5 adopted on 25 January 1949 by the Road Transport Sub-committee of the Inland Transport Committee of the United Nations Economic Commission for Europe;

6. 'insurance undertaking' means an undertaking which has received its official authorisation in accordance with Article 6 or Article 23(2) of Directive 73/239/EEC;

7. 'establishment' means the head office, agency or branch of an insurance undertaking as defined in Article 2(c) of Second Council Directive 88/357/EEC of 22 June 1988 on the coordination of laws, regulations and administrative provisions relating to direct insurance other than life assurance and laying down provisions to facilitate the effective exercise of freedom to provide services[1].

NOTES

[1] OJ L172, 4.7.1988, p 1.

[6855]
Article 2
Scope

The provisions of Articles 4, 6, 7 and 8 shall apply to vehicles normally based on the territory of one of the Member States:

(a) after an agreement has been concluded between the national insurers' bureaux under the terms of which each national bureau guarantees the settlement, in accordance with the provisions of national law on compulsory insurance, of claims in respect of accidents occurring in its territory, caused by vehicles normally based in the territory of another Member State, whether or not such vehicles are insured;

(b) from the date fixed by the Commission, upon its having ascertained in close cooperation with the Member States that such an agreement has been concluded;

(c) for the duration of that agreement.

[6856]
Article 3
Compulsory insurance of vehicles

Each Member State shall, subject to Article 5, take all appropriate measures to ensure that civil liability in respect of the use of vehicles normally based in its territory is covered by insurance.

The extent of the liability covered and the terms and conditions of the cover shall be determined on the basis of the measures referred to in the first paragraph.

Each Member State shall take all appropriate measures to ensure that the contract of insurance also covers:

(a) according to the law in force in other Member States, any loss or injury which is caused in the territory of those States;

(b) any loss or injury suffered by nationals of Member States during a direct journey between two territories in which the Treaty is in force, if there is no national insurers' bureau responsible for the territory which is being crossed; in such a case, the loss or injury shall be covered in accordance with the national laws on compulsory insurance in force in the Member State in whose territory the vehicle is normally based.

The insurance referred to in the first paragraph shall cover compulsorily both damage to property and personal injuries.

[6857]
Article 4
Checks on insurance

Member States shall refrain from making checks on insurance against civil liability in respect of vehicles normally based in the territory of another Member State and in respect of vehicles normally based in the territory of a third country entering their territory from the territory of another Member State. However, they may carry out non-systematic checks on insurance provided that those checks are not discriminatory and are carried out as part of a control which is not aimed exclusively at insurance verification.

[6858]
Article 5
Derogation from the obligation in respect of compulsory insurance of vehicles

1. A Member State may derogate from Article 3 in respect of certain natural or legal persons, public or private; a list of such persons shall be drawn up by the State concerned and communicated to the other Member States and to the Commission.

A Member State so derogating shall take the appropriate measures to ensure that compensation is paid in respect of any loss or injury caused in its territory and in the territory of other Member States by vehicles belonging to such persons.

It shall in particular designate an authority or body in the country where the loss or injury occurs responsible for compensating injured parties in accordance with the laws of that State in cases where Article 2(a) is not applicable.

It shall communicate to the Commission the list of persons exempt from compulsory insurance and the authorities or bodies responsible for compensation.

The Commission shall publish that list.

2. A Member State may derogate from Article 3 in respect of certain types of vehicle or certain vehicles having a special plate; the list of such types or of such vehicles shall be drawn up by the State concerned and communicated to the other Member States and to the Commission.

Any Member State so derogating shall ensure that vehicles referred to in the first subparagraph are treated in the same way as vehicles for which the insurance obligation provided for in Article 3 has not been satisfied.

The guarantee fund of the Member State in which the accident has taken place shall then have a claim against the guarantee fund in the Member State where the vehicle is normally based.

From 11 June 2010 Member States shall report to the Commission on the implementation and practical application of this paragraph.

The Commission, after examining those reports, shall, if appropriate, submit proposals for the replacement or repeal of this derogation.

[6859]
Article 6
National insurers' bureaux

Each Member State shall ensure that, where an accident is caused in its territory by a vehicle normally based in the territory of another Member State, the national insurers' bureau shall, without prejudice to the obligation referred to in Article 2(a), obtain information:

(a) as to the territory in which the vehicle is normally based, and as to its registration mark, if any;

(b) in so far as is possible, as to the details of the insurance of the vehicle, as they normally appear on the green card, which are in the possession of the person having custody of the vehicle, to the extent that those details are required by the Member State in whose territory the vehicle is normally based.

Each Member State shall also ensure that the bureau communicates the information referred to in points (a) and (b) to the national insurers' bureau of the State in whose territory the vehicle referred to in the first paragraph is normally based.

CHAPTER 2

PROVISIONS CONCERNING VEHICLES NORMALLY BASED IN THE TERRITORY OF THIRD COUNTRIES

[6860]
Article 7
National measures concerning vehicles normally based on the territory of third countries

Each Member State shall take all appropriate measures to ensure that vehicles normally based in the territory of a third country which enter the territory in which the Treaty is in force shall not be used in its territory unless any loss or injury caused by those vehicles is covered, in accordance with the requirements of the laws of the various Member States on compulsory insurance against civil liability in respect of the use of vehicles, throughout the territory in which the Treaty is in force.

[6861]
Article 8
Documentation concerning vehicles normally based in the territory of third countries

1. Every vehicle normally based in the territory of a third country must, before entering the territory in which the Treaty is in force, be provided either with a valid green card or with a certificate of frontier insurance establishing that the vehicle is insured in accordance with Article 7.

However, vehicles normally based in a third country shall be treated as vehicles normally based in the Community if the national bureaux of all the Member States severally guarantee, each in accordance with the provisions of its own national law on compulsory insurance, settlement of claims in respect of accidents occurring in their territory caused by such vehicles.

Part VI European Materials

2. Having ascertained, in close cooperation with the Member States, that the obligations referred to in the second subparagraph of paragraph 1 have been assumed, the Commission shall fix the date from which and the types of vehicles for which Member States shall no longer require production of the documents referred to in the firs subparagraph of paragraph 1.

CHAPTER 3
MINIMUM AMOUNTS COVERED BY COMPULSORY INSURANCE

[6862]
Article 9
Minimum amounts

1. Without prejudice to any higher guarantees which Member States may prescribe, each Member State shall require the insurance referred to in Article 3 to be compulsory at least in respect of the following amounts:

(a) in the case of personal injury, a minimum amount of cover of EUR 1 000 000 per victim or EUR 5 000 000 per claim, whatever the number of victims;

(b) in the case of damage to property, EUR 1 000 000 per claim, whatever the number of victims.

If necessary, Member States may establish a transitional period extending until 11 June 2012 at the latest within which to adapt their minimum amounts of cover to the amounts provided for in the first subparagraph.

Member States establishing such a transitional period shall inform the Commission thereof and indicate the duration of the transitional period.

However, until 11 December 2009 at the latest, Member States shall increase guarantees to at least a half of the levels provided for in the first subparagraph.

2. Every five years after 11 June 2005 or the end of any transitional period as referred to in the second subparagraph of paragraph 1, the amounts referred to in that paragraph shall be reviewed in line with the European Index of Consumer Prices (EICP) established pursuant to Regulation (EC) No 2494/95.

The amounts shall be adjusted automatically. Such amounts shall be increased by the percentage change indicated by the EICP for the relevant period, that is to say, the five years immediately preceding the review referred to in the first subparagraph, and rounded up to a multiple of EUR 10 000.

The Commission shall communicate the adjusted amounts to the European Parliament and to the Council and shall ensure their publication in the *Official Journal of the European Union.*

CHAPTER 4
COMPENSATION FOR DAMAGE CAUSED BY AN UNIDENTIFIED VEHICLE OR A VEHICLE FOR WHICH THE INSURANCE OBLIGATION PROVIDED FOR IN ARTICLE 3 HAS NOT BEEN SATISFIED

[6863]
Article 10
Body responsible for compensation

1. Each Member State shall set up or authorise a body with the task of providing compensation, at least up to the limits of the insurance obligation for damage to property or personal injuries caused by an unidentified vehicle or a vehicle for which the insurance obligation provided for in Article 3 has not been satisfied.

The first subparagraph shall be without prejudice to the right of the Member States to regard compensation by the body as subsidiary or non-subsidiary and the right to make provision for the settlement of claims between the body and the person or persons responsible for the accident and other insurers or social security bodies required to compensate the victim in respect of the same accident. However, Member States may not allow the body to make the payment of compensation conditional on the victim establishing in any way that the person liable is unable or refuses to pay.

2. The victim may in any event apply directly to the body which, on the basis of information provided at its request by the victim, shall be obliged to give him a reasoned reply regarding the payment of any compensation.

Member States may, however, exclude the payment of compensation by that body in respect of persons who voluntarily entered the vehicle which caused the damage or injury when the body can prove that they knew it was uninsured.

3. Member States may limit or exclude the payment of compensation by the body in the event of damage to property by an unidentified vehicle.

However, where the body has paid compensation for significant personal injuries to any victim of the same accident in which damage to property was caused by an unidentified vehicle, Member States may not exclude the payment of compensation for damage to property on the basis that the vehicle is unidentified. Nevertheless, Member States may provide for an excess of not more than EUR 500 to be borne by the victim of such damage to property.

The conditions in which personal injuries are to be regarded as significant shall be determined in accordance with the legislation or administrative provisions of the Member State in which the accident takes place. In this regard, Member States may take into account, inter alia, whether the injury required hospital care.

4. Each Member State shall apply its laws, regulations and administrative provisions to the payment of compensation by the body, without prejudice to any other practice which is more favourable to the victim.

[6864]
Article 11
Disputes

In the event of a dispute between the body referred to in Article 10(1) and the civil liability insurer as to which must compensate the victim, the Member States shall take the appropriate measures so that one of those parties is designated to be responsible in the first instance for paying compensation to the victim without delay.

If it is ultimately decided that the other party should have paid all or part of the compensation, that other party shall reimburse accordingly the party which has paid.

CHAPTER 5
SPECIAL CATEGORIES OF VICTIM, EXCLUSION CLAUSES, SINGLE PREMIUM, VEHICLES DISPATCHED FROM ONE MEMBER STATE TO ANOTHER

[6865]
Article 12
Special categories of victim

1. Without prejudice to the second subparagraph of Article 13(1), the insurance referred to in Article 3 shall cover liability for personal injuries to all passengers, other than the driver, arising out of the use of a vehicle.

2. The members of the family of the policyholder, driver or any other person who is liable under civil law in the event of an accident, and whose liability is covered by the insurance referred to in Article 3, shall not be excluded from insurance in respect of their personal injuries by virtue of that relationship.

3. The insurance referred to in Article 3 shall cover personal injuries and damage to property suffered by pedestrians, cyclists and other non-motorised users of the roads who, as a consequence of an accident in which a motor vehicle is involved, are entitled to compensation in accordance with national civil law.

This Article shall be without prejudice either to civil liability or to the quantum of damages.

[6865A]
Article 13
Exclusion clauses

1. Each Member State shall take all appropriate measures to ensure that any statutory provision or any contractual clause contained in an insurance policy issued in accordance with Article 3 shall be deemed to be void in respect of claims by third parties who have been victims of an accident where that statutory provision or contractual clause excludes from insurance the use or driving of vehicles by:

(a) persons who do not have express or implied authorisation to do so;
(b) persons who do not hold a licence permitting them to drive the vehicle concerned;
(c) persons who are in breach of the statutory technical requirements concerning the condition and safety of the vehicle concerned.

However, the provision or clause referred to in point (a) of the first subparagraph may be invoked against persons who voluntarily entered the vehicle which caused the damage or injury, when the insurer can prove that they knew the vehicle was stolen.

Member States shall have the option — in the case of accidents occurring on their territory — of not applying the provision in the first subparagraph if and in so far as the victim may obtain compensation for the damage suffered from a social security body.

2. In the case of vehicles stolen or obtained by violence, Member States may provide that the body specified in Article 10(1) is to pay compensation instead of the insurer under the conditions set out in paragraph 1 of this Article. Where the vehicle is normally based in another Member State, that body can make no claim against any body in that Member State.

Member States which, in the case of vehicles stolen or obtained by violence, provide that the body referred to in Article 10(1) is to pay compensation may fix in respect of damage to property an excess of not more than EUR 250 to be borne by the victim.

3. Member States shall take the necessary measures to ensure that any statutory provision or any contractual clause contained in an insurance policy which excludes a passenger from such cover on the basis that he knew or should have known that the driver of the vehicle was under the influence of alcohol or of any other intoxicating agent at the time of an accident, shall be deemed to be void in respect of the claims of such passenger.

[6865B]
Article 14
Single premium

Member States shall take the necessary steps to ensure that all compulsory policies of insurance against civil liability arising out of the use of vehicles:

(a) cover, on the basis of a single premium and during the whole term of the contract, the entire territory of the Community, including for any period in which the vehicle remains in other Member States during the term of the contract; and

(b) guarantee, on the basis of that single premium, in each Member State, the cover required by its law or the cover required by the law of the Member State where the vehicle is normally based when that cover is higher.

[6865C]
Article 15
Vehicles dispatched from one Member State to another

1. By way of derogation from the second indent of Article 2(d) of Directive 88/357/EEC, where a vehicle is dispatched from one Member State to another, the Member State where the risk is situated shall be considered to be the Member State of destination, immediately upon acceptance of delivery by the purchaser, for a period of 30 days, even though the vehicle has not formally been registered in the Member State of destination.

2. In the event that the vehicle is involved in an accident during the period mentioned in paragraph 1 of this Article while being uninsured, the body referred to in Article 10(1) in the Member State of destination shall be liable for the compensation provided for in Article 9.

CHAPTER 6
STATEMENT, EXCESS, DIRECT ACTION

[6865D]
Article 16
Statement relating to the third party liability claims

Member States shall ensure that the policyholder has the right to request at any time a statement relating to the third party liability claims involving the vehicle or vehicles covered by the insurance contract at least during the preceding five years of the contractual relationship, or to the absence of such claims.

The insurance undertaking, or a body which may have been appointed by a Member State to provide compulsory insurance or to supply such statements, shall provide that statement to the policyholder within 15 days of the request.

[6865E]
Article 17
Excess

Insurance undertakings shall not require any party injured as a result of an accident to bear any excess as far as the insurance referred to in Article 3 is concerned.

[6865F]
Article 18
Direct right of action

Member States shall ensure that any party injured as a result of an accident caused by a vehicle covered by insurance as referred to in Article 3 enjoys a direct right of action against the insurance undertaking covering the person responsible against civil liability.

CHAPTER 7
SETTLEMENT OF CLAIMS ARISING FROM ANY ACCIDENT CAUSED BY A VEHICLE COVERED BY INSURANCE AS REFERRED TO IN ARTICLE 3

[6865G]
Article 19
Procedure for the settlement of claims

Member States shall establish the procedure referred to in Article 22 for the settlement of claims arising from any accident caused by a vehicle covered by insurance as referred to in Article 3.

In the case of claims which may be settled by the system of national insurers' bureaux provided for in Article 2 Member States shall establish the same procedure as in Article 22.

For the purpose of applying this procedure, any reference to an insurance undertaking shall be understood as a reference to national insurers' bureaux.

[6865H]
Article 20
Special provisions concerning compensation for injured parties following an accident in a Member State other than that of their residence

1. The object of Articles 20 to 26 is to lay down special provisions applicable to injured parties entitled to compensation in respect of any loss or injury resulting from accidents occurring in a Member State other than the Member State of residence of the injured party which are caused by the use of vehicles insured and normally based in a Member State.

Without prejudice to the legislation of third countries on civil liability and private international law, these provisions shall also apply to injured parties resident in a Member State and entitled to compensation in respect of any loss or injury resulting from accidents occurring in third countries whose national insurer's bureaux have joined the green card system whenever such accidents are caused by the use of vehicles insured and normally based in a Member State.

2. Articles 21 and 24 shall apply only in the case of accidents caused by the use of a vehicle:
   (a) insured through an establishment in a Member State other than the State of residence of the injured party; and
   (b) normally based in a Member State other than the State of residence of the injured party.

[6865I]
Article 21
Claims representatives

1. Each Member State shall take all measures necessary to ensure that all insurance undertakings covering the risks classified in class 10 of point A of the Annex to Directive 73/239/EEC, other than carrier's liability, appoint a claims representative in each Member State other than that in which they have received their official authorisation.

The claims representative shall be responsible for handling and settling claims arising from an accident in the cases referred to in Article 20(1).

The claims representative shall be resident or established in the Member State where he is appointed.

2. The choice of its claims representative shall be at the discretion of the insurance undertaking.

The Member States may not restrict this freedom of choice.

3. The claims representative may act for one or more insurance undertakings.

4. The claims representative shall, in relation to such claims, collect all information necessary in connection with the settlement of the claims and shall take the measures necessary to negotiate a settlement of claims.

The requirement of appointing a claims representative shall not preclude the right of the injured party or his insurance undertaking to institute proceedings directly against the person who caused the accident or his insurance undertaking.

5. Claims representatives shall possess sufficient powers to represent the insurance undertaking in relation to injured parties in the cases referred to in Article 20(1) and to meet their claims in full.

They must be capable of examining cases in the official language(s) of the Member State of residence of the injured party.

6. The appointment of a claims representative shall not in itself constitute the opening of a branch within the meaning of Article 1(b) of Directive 92/49/EEC and the claims representative shall not be regarded as an establishment within the meaning of Article 2(c) of Directive 88/357/EEC or an establishment within the meaning of Regulation (EC) No 44/2001.

[6865J]
Article 22
Compensation procedure

The Member States shall create a duty, backed by appropriate, effective and systematic financial or equivalent administrative penalties, whereby, within three months of the date when the injured party presented his claim for compensation either directly to the insurance undertaking of the person who caused the accident or to its claims representative,

(a) the insurance undertaking of the person who caused the accident or its claims representative is required to make a reasoned offer of compensation in cases where liability is not contested and the damages have been quantified; or

(b) the insurance undertaking to whom the claim for compensation has been addressed or its claims representative is required to provide a reasoned reply to the points made in the claim in cases where liability is denied or has not been clearly determined or the damages have not been fully quantified.

Member States shall adopt provisions to ensure that, where the offer is not made within the three-month time limit, interest shall be payable on the amount of compensation offered by the insurance undertaking or awarded by the court to the injured party.

[6865K]
Article 23
Information centres

1. In order to enable the injured party to seek compensation, each Member State shall establish or approve an information centre responsible:

(a) for keeping a register containing the following information:

(i) the registration numbers of motor vehicles normally based in the territory of the State in question;

(ii) the numbers of the insurance policies covering the use of those vehicles for the risks classified in class 10 of point A of the Annex to Directive 73/239/EEC, other than carrier's liability and, where the period of validity of the policy has expired, the date of termination of the insurance cover;

(iii) insurance undertakings covering the use of vehicles for the risks classified in class 10 of point A of the Annex to Directive 73/239/EEC, other than carrier's liability, and claims representatives appointed by such insurance undertakings in accordance with Article 21 of this Directive whose names are to be notified to the information centre in accordance with paragraph 2 of this Article;

(iv) the list of vehicles which, in each Member State, benefit from the derogation from the requirement for civil liability insurance cover in accordance with Article 5(1) and (2);

(v) as regards the vehicles provided for in point (iv):

— the name of the authority or body designated in accordance with the third subparagraph of Article 5(1) as responsible for compensating injured parties in the cases where the procedure provided for in Article 2(2)(a) is not applicable, if the vehicle benefits from the derogation provided for in the first subparagraph of Article 5(1),

— the name of the body covering the vehicle in the Member State where it is normally based if the vehicle benefits from the derogation provided for in Article 5(2);

(b) or for coordinating the compilation and dissemination of that information; and

(c) for assisting entitled persons to be apprised of the information mentioned in points (a)(i) to (v).

The information under points (a)(i), (ii) and (iii) must be preserved for a period of seven years after the termination of the registration of the vehicle or the termination of the insurance contract.

2. Insurance undertakings referred to in point (a)(iii) of paragraph 1 shall notify to the information centres of all Member States the name and address of the claims representative appointed by them in accordance with Article 21 in each of the Member States.

3. Member States shall ensure that the injured party is entitled for a period of seven years after the accident to obtain without delay from the information centre of the Member State where he resides, the Member State where the vehicle is normally based or the Member State where the accident occurred the following information:

(a) the name and address of the insurance undertaking;

(b) the number of the insurance policy; and

(c) the name and address of the insurance undertaking's claims representative in the State of residence of the injured party.

Information centres shall cooperate with each other.

4. The information centre shall provide the injured party with the name and address of the owner or usual driver or registered keeper of the vehicle if the injured party has a legitimate interest in obtaining this information. For the purposes of this provision, the information centre shall address itself in particular:

(a) to the insurance undertaking; or

(b) to the vehicle registration agency.

If the vehicle benefits from the derogation provided for in the first subparagraph of Article 5(1) the information centre shall inform the injured party of the name of the authority or body designated in accordance with the third subparagraph of Article 5(1) as responsible for compensating injured parties in cases where the procedure provided for in Article 2(a) is not applicable.

If the vehicle benefits from the derogation provided for in Article 5(2) the information centre shall inform the injured party of the name of the body covering the vehicle in the country where it is normally based.

5. Member States shall ensure that, without prejudice to their obligations under paragraphs 1 and 4, the information centres provide the information specified in these paragraphs to any party involved in any traffic accident caused by a vehicle covered by insurance as referred to in Article 3.

6. The processing of personal data resulting from paragraphs 1 to 5 must be carried out in accordance with national measures taken pursuant to Directive 95/46/EC.

[6865L]
Article 24
Compensation bodies

1. Each Member State shall establish or approve a compensation body responsible for providing compensation to injured parties in the cases referred to in Article 20(1).

Such injured parties may present a claim to the compensation body in their Member State of residence:

(a) if, within three months of the date when the injured party presented his claim for compensation to the insurance undertaking of the vehicle the use of which caused the accident or to its claims representative, the insurance undertaking or its claims representative has not provided a reasoned reply to the points made in the claim; or

(b) if the insurance undertaking has failed to appoint a claims representative in the Member State of residence of the injured party in accordance with Article 20(1); in such a case, injured parties may not present a claim to the compensation body if they have presented a claim for compensation directly to the insurance undertaking of the vehicle the use of which caused the accident and if they have received a reasoned reply within three months of presenting the claim.

Injured parties may not however present a claim to the compensation body if they have taken legal action directly against the insurance undertaking.

The compensation body shall take action within two months of the date when the injured party presents a claim for compensation to it but shall terminate its action if the insurance undertaking, or its claims representative, subsequently makes a reasoned reply to the claim.

The compensation body shall immediately inform:

(a) the insurance undertaking of the vehicle the use of which caused the accident or the claims representative;

(b) the compensation body in the Member State in which the insurance undertaking which issued the policy is established;

(c) if known, the person who caused the accident;

that it has received a claim from the injured party and that it will respond to that claim within two months of the presentation of that claim.

This provision shall be without prejudice to the right of the Member States to regard compensation by that body as subsidiary or non-subsidiary and the right to make provision for the settlement of claims between that body and the person or persons who caused the accident and other insurance undertakings or social security bodies required to compensate the injured party in respect of the same accident. However, Member States may not allow the body to make the payment of compensation subject to any conditions other than those laid down in this Directive, in particular the injured party's establishing in any way that the person liable is unable or refuses to pay.

2. The compensation body which has compensated the injured party in his Member State of residence shall be entitled to claim reimbursement of the sum paid by way of compensation from the compensation body in the Member State in which the insurance undertaking which issued the policy is established.

The latter body shall be subrogated to the injured party in his rights against the person who caused the accident or his insurance undertaking in so far as the compensation body in the Member State of residence of the injured party has provided compensation for the loss or injury suffered.

Each Member State shall be obliged to acknowledge this subrogation as provided for by any other Member State.

3. This Article shall take effect:

(a) after an agreement has been concluded between the compensation bodies established or approved by the Member States relating to their functions and obligations and the procedures for reimbursement;

(b) from the date fixed by the Commission upon its having ascertained in close cooperation with the Member States that such an agreement has been concluded.

[6865M]
Article 25
Compensation

1. If it is impossible to identify the vehicle or if, within two months of the date of the accident, it is impossible to identify the insurance undertaking, the injured party may apply for compensation from the compensation body in the Member State where he resides. The compensation shall be provided in accordance with the provisions of Articles 9 and 10. The compensation body shall then have a claim, on the conditions laid down in Article 24(2):

(a) where the insurance undertaking cannot be identified: against the guarantee fund in the Member State where the vehicle is normally based;

(b) in the case of an unidentified vehicle: against the guarantee fund in the Member State in which the accident took place;

(c) in the case of a third-country vehicle: against the guarantee fund in the Member State in which the accident took place.

2. This Article shall apply to accidents caused by third-country vehicles covered by Articles 7 and 8.

[6865N]
Article 26
Central body

Member States shall take all appropriate measures to facilitate the timely provision to the victims, their insurers or their legal representatives of the basic data necessary for the settlement of claims.

Those basic data shall, where appropriate, be made available in electronic form in a central repository in each Member State, and be accessible by parties involved in the case at their express request.

[6865O]
Article 27
Penalties

Member States shall fix penalties for breaches of the national provisions which they adopt in implementation of this Directive and shall take the steps necessary to secure the application thereof. The penalties shall be effective, proportional and dissuasive. The Member States shall notify to the Commission as soon as possible any amendments concerning provisions adopted pursuant to this Article.

CHAPTER 8
FINAL PROVISIONS

[6865P]
Article 28
National provisions

1. Member States may, in accordance with the Treaty, maintain or bring into force provisions which are more favourable to injured parties than the provisions needed to comply with this Directive.

2. Member States shall communicate to the Commission the text of the main provisions of domestic law which they adopt in the field governed by this Directive.

[6865Q]
Article 29
Repeal

Directives 72/166/EEC, 84/5/EEC, 90/232/EEC, 2000/26/EC and 2005/14/EC, as amended by the Directives listed in Annex I, Part A, are hereby repealed, without prejudice to the obligations of the Member States relating to the time limits for transposition into national law and application of the Directives set out in Annex I, Part B.

References to the repealed Directives shall be construed as references to this Directive and shall be read in accordance with the correlation table in Annex II.

[6865R]
Article 30
Entry into force

This Directive shall enter into force on the 20th day following its publication in the *Official Journal of the European Union.*

[6865S]
Article 31
Addressees

This Directive is addressed to the Member States.

Done at Strasbourg, 16 September 2009

ANNEX I

PART A
REPEALED DIRECTIVE WITH LIST OF ITS SUCCESSIVE AMENDMENTS

[6865T]
(referred to in Article 29)

Council Directive 72/166/EEC (OJ L 103, 2.5.1972, p. 1)	
Council Directive 72/430/EEC (OJ L 291, 28.12.1972, p. 162)	
Council Directive 84/5/EEC (OJ L 8, 11.1.1984, p. 17)	Only Article 4
Directive 2005/14/EC of the European Parliament and Council (OJ L 149, 11.6.2005, p. 14)	Only Article 1
Council Directive 84/5/EEC (OJ L 8, 11.1.1984, p. 17)	
Annex I, point IX.F of the 1985 Act of Accession (OJ L 302, 15.11.1985, p. 218)	
Council Directive 90/232/EEC (OJ L 129, 19.5.1990, p. 33)	Only Article 4
Directive 2005/14/EC of the European Parliament and Council (OJ L 149, 11.6.2005, p. 14)	Only Article 2
Council Directive 90/232/EEC (OJ L 129, 19.5.1990, p. 33)	
Directive 2005/14/EC of the European Parliament and Council (OJ L 149, 11.6.2005, p. 14)	Only Article 4
Directive 2000/26/EC of the European Parliament and Council (OJ L 181, 20.7.2000, p. 65)	
Directive 2005/14/EC of the European Parliament and Council (OJ L 149, 11.6.2005, p. 14)	Only Article 5
Directive 2005/14/EC of the European Parliament and Council (OJ L 149, 11.6.2005, p. 14)	

PART B
LIST OF TIME LIMITS FOR TRANSPOSITION INTO NATIONAL LAW AND APPLICATION

(referred to in Article 29)

Directive	Time limit for transposition	Date of application
72/166/EEC	31 December 1973	—
72/430/EEC	—	1 January 1973
84/5/EEC	31 December 1987	31 December 1988
90/232/EEC	31 December 1992	—
2000/26/EC	19 July 2002	19 January 2003
2005/14/EC	11 June 2007	—

ANNEX II

CORRELATION TABLE

[6865U]

Directive 72/166/EEC	Directive 84/5/EEC	Directive 90/232/EEC	Directive 2000/26/EC	This Directive
Article 1, points (1) to (3)				Article 1, points (1) to (3)
Article 1, point (4), first indent				Article 1, point (4)(a)
Article 1, point (4), second indent				Article 1, point (4)(b)
Article 1, point (4), third indent				Article 1, point (4)(c)
Article 1, point (4), fourth indent				Article 1, point (4)(d)
Article 1, point (5)				Article 1, point (5)
Article 2(1)				Article 4
Article 2(2), introductory wording				Article 2, introductory wording
Article 2(2), first indent				Article 2, point (a)
Article 2(2), second indent				Article 2, point (b)
Article 2(2), third indent				Article 2, point (c)
Article 3(1), first sentence				Article 3, first paragraph
Article 3(1), second sentence				Article 3, second paragraph
Article 3(2), introductory wording				Article 3, third paragraph, introductory wording
Article 3(2), first indent				Article 3, third paragraph, point (a)
Article 3(2), second indent				Article 3, third paragraph, point (b)
Article 4, introductory wording				Article 5(1), first subparagraph
Article 4, point (a), *first subparagraph*				Article 5(1), first subparagraph
Article 4, point (a), second subparagraph, first sentence				Article 5(1), second subparagraph

Directive 72/166/EEC	Directive 84/5/EEC	Directive 90/232/EEC	Directive 2000/26/EC	This Directive
Article 4, point (a), second subparagraph, second sentence				Article 5(1), third subparagraph
Article 4, point (a), second subparagraph, third sentence				Article 5(1), fourth subparagraph
Article 4, point (a), second subparagraph, fourth sentence				Article 5(1), fifth subparagraph
Article 4, point (b), first subparagraph				Article 5(2), first subparagraph
Article 4, point (b), second subparagraph, first sentence				Article 5(2), second subparagraph
Article 4, point (b), second subparagraph, second sentence				Article 5(2), third subparagraph
Article 4, point (b), third subparagraph, first sentence				Article 5(2), fourth subparagraph
Article 4, point (b), third subparagraph, second sentence				Article 5(2), fifth subparagraph
Article 5, introductory wording				Article 6, first subparagraph, introductory wording
Article 5, first indent				Article 6, first paragraph, point (a)
Article 5, second indent				Article 6, first paragraph, point (b)
Article 5, final wording				Article 6, second paragraph
Article 6				Article 7
Article 7(1)				Article 8(1), first subparagraph
Article 7(2)				Article 8(1), second subparagraph
Article 7(3)				Article 8(2)
Article 8				—
	Article 1(1)			Article 3, fourth paragraph
	Article 1(2)			Article 9(1)
	Article 1(3)			Article 9(2)
	Article 1(4)			Article 10(1)
	Article 1(5)			Article 10(2)
	Article 1(6)			Article 10(3)
	Article 1(7)			Article 10(4)
	Article 2(1), first subparagraph, introductory wording			Article 13(1), first subparagraph, introductory wording

Part VI European Materials

Directive 72/166/EEC	Directive 84/5/EEC	Directive 90/232/EEC	Directive 2000/26/EC	This Directive
	Article 2(1), first indent			Article 13(1), first subparagraph, point (a)
	Article 2(1), second indent			Article 13(1), first subparagraph, point (b)
	Article 2(1), third indent			Article 13(1), first subparagraph, point (c)
	Article 2(1), first subparagraph, final wording			Article 13(1), first subparagraph, introductory wording
	Article 2(1), second and third subparagraphs			Article 13(1), second and third subparagraphs
	Article 2(2)			Article 13(2)
	Article 3			Article 12(2)
	Article 4			—
	Article 5			—
	Article 6			—
		Article 1, first paragraph		Article 12(1)
		Article 1, second paragraph		Article 13(3)
		Article 1, third paragraph		—
		Article 1a, first sentence		Article 12(3), first subparagraph
		Article 1a, second sentence		Article 12(3), second subparagraph
		Article 2, introductory wording		Article 14, introductory wording
		Article 2, first indent		Article 14, point (a)
		Article 2, second indent		Article 14, point (b)
		Article 3		—
		Article 4		Article 11
		Article 4a		Article 15
		Article 4b, first sentence		Article 16, first paragraph
		Article 4b, second sentence		Article 16, second paragraph
		Article 4c		Article 17
		Article 4d	Article 3	Article 18
		Article 4e, first paragraph		Article 19, first paragraph
		Article 4e, second paragraph, first sentence		Article 19, second paragraph
		Article 4e, second paragraph, second sentence		Article 19, third paragraph
		Article 5(1)		Article 23(5)

Directive 72/166/EEC	Directive 84/5/EEC	Directive 90/232/EEC	Directive 2000/26/EC	This Directive
		Article 5(2)		—
		Article 6		—
			Article 1(1)	Article 20(1)
			Article 1(2)	Article 20(2)
			Article 1(3)	Article 25(2)
			Article 2, introductory wording	—
			Article 2, point (a)	Article 1, point (6)
			Article 2, point (b)	Article 1, point (7)
			Article 2, points (c), (d) and (e)	—
			Article 4(1), first sentence	Article 21(1), first subparagraph
			Article 4(1), second sentence	Article 21(1), second subparagraph
			Article 4(1), third sentence	Article 21(1), third subparagraph
			Article 4(2), first sentence	Article 21(2), first subparagraph
			Article 4(2), second sentence	Article 21(2), second subparagraph
			Article 4(3)	Article 21(3)
			Article 4(4), first sentence	Article 21(4), first subparagraph
			Article 4(4), second sentence	Article 21(4), second subparagraph
			Article 4(5), first sentence	Article 21(5), first subparagraph
			Article 4(5), second sentence	Article 21(5), second subparagraph
			Article 4(6)	Article 22
			Article 4(7)	—
			Article 4(8)	Article 21(6)
			Article 5(1), first subparagraph, introductory wording	Article 23(1), first subparagraph, introductory wording
			Article 5(1), first subparagraph, point (a), introductory wording	Article 23(1), first subparagraph, point (a), introductory wording
			Article 5(1), first subparagraph, point (a)(1)	Article 23(1), first subparagraph, point (a)(i)

Part VI European Materials

Directive 72/166/EEC	Directive 84/5/EEC	Directive 90/232/EEC	Directive 2000/26/EC	This Directive
			Article 5(1), first subparagraph, point (a)(2)	Article 23(1), first subparagraph, point (a)(ii)
			Article 5(1), first subparagraph, point (a)(3)	Article 23(1), first subparagraph, point (a)(iii)
			Article 5(1), first subparagraph, point (a)(4)	Article 23(1), first subparagraph, point (a)(iv)
			Article 5(1), first subparagraph, point (a)(5), introductory wording	Article 23(1), first subparagraph, point (a)(v), introductory wording
			Article 5(1), first subparagraph, point (a)(5)(i)	Article 23(1), first subparagraph, point (a)(v), first indent
			Article 5(1), first subparagraph, point (a)(5)(ii)	Article 23(1), first subparagraph, point (a)(v), second indent
			Article 5(1), second subparagraph	Article 23(1), second subparagraph
			Article 5(2), (3) and (4)	Article 23(2), (3) and (4)
			Article 5(5)	Article 23(6)
			Article 6(1)	Article 24(1)
			Article 6(2), first subparagraph	Article 24(2), first subparagraph
			Article 6(2), second subparagraph, first sentence	Article 24(2), second subparagraph
			Article 6(2), second subparagraph, second sentence	Article 24(2), third subparagraph
			Article 6(3), first subparagraph	Article 24(3)
			Article 6(3), second subparagraph	—
			Article 6a	Article 26
			Article 7, introductory wording	Article 25(1), introductory wording
			Article 7, point (a)	Article 25(1), point (a)
			Article 7, point (b)	Article 25(1), point (b)
			Article 7, point (c)	Article 25(1), point (c)

Directive 72/166/EEC	**Directive 84/5/EEC**	**Directive 90/232/EEC**	**Directive 2000/26/EC**	**This Directive**
			Article 8	—
			Article 9	—
			Article 10(1) to (3)	—
			Article 10(4)	Article 28(1)
			Article 10(5)	Article 28(2)
				Article 29
			Article 11	Article 30
			Article 12	Article 27
Article 9	Article 7	Article 7	Article 13	Article 31
				Annex I
				Annex II

H. REINSURANCE

COUNCIL DIRECTIVE

(64/225/EEC)
of 25 February 1964

on the abolition of restrictions on freedom of establishment and freedom to provide services in respect of reinsurance and retrocession

NOTES

Date of publication in OJ: OJ L56, 3.4.64, p 878 (S edn 1963–64, p 131).

This Directive is repealed by European Parliament and Council Directive 2009/138/EC on the taking-up and pursuit of the business of Insurance and Reinsurance (Solvency II) at **[6153]** et seq, with effect from 1 November 2012 (see art 310 thereof at **[6462]**).

[6866]

THE COUNCIL OF THE EUROPEAN ECONOMIC COMMUNITY,

Having regard to the Treaty establishing the European Economic Community, and in particular Articles 54(2) and (3) and 63(2) thereof;

Having regard to the General Programme for the abolition of restrictions on freedom of establishment,[1] *and in particular Title IV A thereof;*

Having regard to the General Programme for the abolition of restrictions on freedom to provide services,[2] *and in particular Title V C thereof;*

Having regard to the proposal from the Commission;

Having regard to the Opinion of the European Parliament;[3]

Having regard to the Opinion of the Economic and Social Committee;[4]

Whereas the General Programmes provide that all branches of reinsurance must, without distinction, be liberalised before the end of 1963 as regards both right of establishment and provision of services;

Whereas reinsurance is effected not only by undertakings specialising in reinsurance but also by so-called "mixed" undertakings, which deal both in direct insurance and in reinsurance and which should therefore be covered by measures taken in implementation of this Directive in respect of that part of their business which is concerned with reinsurance and retrocession;

Whereas, for the purposes of applying measures concerning right of establishment and freedom to provide services, companies and firms are to be treated in the same way as natural persons who are nationals of Member States, subject only to the conditions laid down in Article 58 and, where necessary, to the condition that there should exist a real and continuous link with the economy of a Member State; whereas therefore no company or firm may be required, in order to obtain the benefit of such measures, to fulfil any additional condition, and in particular no company or firm may be required to obtain any special authorisation not required of a domestic company or firm wishing to pursue a particular economic activity; whereas, however, such uniformity of treatment should not prevent Member States from requiring that a company having a share capital should operate in their countries under the description by which it is known in the law of the Member State under which it is constituted, and that it should indicate the amount of its subscribed capital on the business papers which it uses in the host Member State;

NOTES

Repealed as noted at the beginning of this Directive.

[1] OJ 2, 15.1.62, p 36/62.

[2] OJ 2, 15.1.62, p 36/62.

[3] OJ 33, 4.3.63, p 482/63.

[4] OJ 56, 4.4.63, p 882/64.

HAS ADOPTED THIS DIRECTIVE—

[6867]

Article 1

Member States shall abolish, in respect of the natural persons and companies or firms covered by Title I of the General Programmes for the abolition of restrictions on freedom of establishment and freedom to provide services the restrictions referred to in Title III of those General Programmes

Part VI European Materials

affecting the right to take up and pursue the activities specified in Article 2 of this Directive.

NOTES

Repealed as noted at the beginning of this Directive.

[6868]

Article 2

The provisions of this Directive shall apply—

1. *to activities of self-employed persons in reinsurance and retrocession falling within Group ex 630 in Annex I to the General Programme for the abolition of restrictions on freedom of establishment;*
2. *in the special case of natural persons, companies or firms referred to in Article 1 which deal both in direct insurance and in reinsurance and retrocession, to that part of their activities which is concerned with reinsurance and retrocession.*

NOTES

Repealed as noted at the beginning of this Directive.

[6869]

Article 3

Article 1 shall apply in particular to restrictions arising out of the following provisions—

(a) with regard to freedom of establishment—

— in the Federal Republic of Germany

(1) Versicherungsaufsichtsgesetz of 6 June 1931, last sentence of Article 106(2), and Article 111(2), whereby the Federal Minister of Economic Affairs is given discretionary powers to impose on foreign nationals conditions for taking up activities in insurance and to prohibit such nationals from pursuing such activities in the territory of the Federal Republic;

(2) Gewerbeordnung, paragraph 12, and Law of 30 January 1937, Article 292, whereby foreign companies and firms are required to obtain prior authorisation;

— in the Kingdom of Belgium

Arrêté royal No 62 of 16 November 1939 and Arrêté ministériel of 17 December 1945, which require the possession of a carte professionelle;

— in the French Republic

(1) Décret-loi of 12 November 1938 and Décret of 2 February 1939, both as amended by the Law of 8 October 1940, which require the possession of a carte d'identité de commerçant;

(2) Second paragraph of Article 2 of the Law of 15 February 1917, as amended and supplemented by Décret-loi of 30 October 1935, which requires that special authorisation be obtained;

— in the Grand Duchy of Luxembourg

Law of 2 June 1962, Articles 19 and 21 (Mémorial A No 31 of 19 June 1962).

[— in the Kingdom of Denmark

Law of 23 December 1959 on the acquisition of immovable property.]

(b) with regard to freedom to provide services—

— in the French Republic

Law of 15 February 1917, as amended by Décret-loi of 30 October 1935, namely—

(1) The second paragraph of Article 1, which empowers the Minister of Finance to draw up a list of specified undertakings, or of undertakings of a specified country, with which no contract for reinsurance or retrocession of any risk in respect of any person, property or liability in France may be concluded;

(2) the last paragraph of Article 1, which prohibits the acceptance of reinsurance or of retrocession risks insured by the undertakings referred to in (b)(1) above;

(3) the first paragraph of Article 2, which requires that the name of the person referred to in that Article must be submitted to the Minister of Finance for approval;

— in the Republic of Italy

The second paragraph of Article 73 of the consolidated text approved by Decreto No 449 of 13 February 1959, which empowers the Minister of Industry and Commerce to prohibit the transfer of reinsurance or retrocession risks to specified foreign undertakings which have not established legal representation in Italian territory.

[— in the Kingdom of Denmark

Law of 23 December 1959 on the acquisition of immovable property.]

NOTES

Repealed as noted at the beginning of this Directive.

Words in square brackets in sub-paras (a), (b) added by the 1972 Act of Accession of Denmark, Ireland and the United Kingdom.

[6870]

Article 4

Member States shall adopt the measures necessary to comply with this Directive within six months of its notification and shall forthwith inform the Commission thereof.

NOTES

Repealed as noted at the beginning of this Directive.

[6871]

Article 5

This Directive is addressed to the Member States.

NOTES

Repealed as noted at the beginning of this Directive.

Done at Brussels, 25 February 1964.

DIRECTIVE OF THE EUROPEAN PARLIAMENT AND OF THE COUNCIL

(2005/68/EC)

of 16 November 2005

on reinsurance and amending Council Directives 73/239/EEC, 92/49/EEC as well as Directives 98/78/EC and 2002/83/EC

(Text with EEA relevance)

NOTES

Date of publication in OJ: OJ L323, 9.12.2005, p 1.

This Directive is repealed by European Parliament and Council Directive 2009/138/EC on the taking-up and pursuit of the business of Insurance and Reinsurance (Solvency II) at **[6153]** et seq, with effect from 1 November 2012 (see art 310 thereof at **[6462]**).

[6872]

THE EUROPEAN PARLIAMENT AND THE COUNCIL OF THE EUROPEAN UNION,

Having regard to the Treaty establishing the European Community, and in particular Articles 47(2) and 55 thereof,

Having regard to the proposal from the Commission,

Having regard to the opinion of the European Economic and Social Committee,[1]

After consulting the Committee of the Regions,

Acting in accordance with the procedure laid down in Article 251 of the Treaty,[2]

Whereas:

(1) Council Directive 73/239/EEC of 24 July 1973 on the coordination of laws, regulations and administrative provisions relating to the taking-up and pursuit of the business of direct insurance other than life assurance,[3] *Council Directive 92/49/EEC of 18 June 1992 on the coordination of laws, regulations and administrative provisions relating to direct insurance other than life assurance*[4] *and Directive 2002/83/EC of the European Parliament and of the Council of 5 November 2002 concerning life assurance*[5] *have laid down the provisions relating to the taking-up and pursuit of direct insurance in the Community.*

(2) Those Directives provide for the legal framework for insurance undertakings to conduct insurance business in the internal market, from the point of view both of the right of establishment and of the freedom to provide services, in order to make it easier for insurance undertakings with head offices in the Community to cover commitments situated within the Community and to make it

Part VI European Materials

possible for policy holders to have recourse not only to insurers established in their own country, but also to insurers which have their head office in the Community and are established in other Member States.

(3) The regime laid down by those Directives applies to direct insurance undertakings in respect of their entire business carried on, both direct insurance activities as well as reinsurance activities by way of acceptances; however reinsurance activities conducted by specialised reinsurance undertakings are neither subject to that regime nor any other regime provided for by Community law.

(4) Reinsurance is a major financial activity as it allows direct insurance undertakings, by facilitating a wider distribution of risks at worldwide level, to have a higher underwriting capacity to engage in insurance business and provide insurance cover and also to reduce their capital costs; furthermore, reinsurance plays a fundamental role in financial stability, since it is an essential element in ensuring the financial soundness and the stability of direct insurance markets as well as the financial system as a whole, because it involves major financial intermediaries and institutional investors.

(5) Council Directive 64/225/EEC of 25 February 1964 on the abolition of restrictions on freedom of establishment and freedom to provide services in respect of reinsurance and retrocession[6] *has removed the restrictions on the right of establishment and the freedom to provide services related to the nationality or residence of the provider of reinsurance. It has not however removed restrictions caused by divergences between national provisions as regards prudential regulation of reinsurance. This situation has resulted in significant differences in the level of supervision of reinsurance undertakings in the Community, which create barriers to the pursuit of reinsurance business, such as the obligation for the reinsurance undertaking to pledge assets in order to cover its part of the technical provisions of the direct insurance undertaking, as well as the compliance by reinsurance undertakings with different supervisory rules in the various Member States in which they conduct business or an indirect supervision of the various aspects of a reinsurance undertaking by the competent authorities of direct insurance undertakings.*

(6) The Action Plan for Financial Services has identified reinsurance as a sector which requires action at Community level in order to complete the internal market for financial services. Moreover, major financial fora, such as the International Monetary Fund and the International Association of Insurance Supervisors (IAIS) have highlighted the lack of harmonised reinsurance supervision rules at Community level as an important gap in the financial services regulatory framework that should be filled.

(7) This Directive aims at establishing a prudential regulatory framework for reinsurance activities in the Community. It forms part of the body of Community legislation in the field of insurance aimed at establishing the Internal Market in the insurance sector.

(8) This Directive is consistent with major international work carried out on reinsurance prudential rules, in particular the IAIS.

(9) This Directive follows the approach of Community legislation adopted in respect of direct insurance by carrying out the harmonisation which is essential, necessary and sufficient to ensure the mutual recognition of authorisations and prudential control systems, thereby making it possible to grant a single authorisation valid throughout the Community and apply the principle of supervision by the home Member State.

(10) As a result, the taking up and the pursuit of the business of reinsurance are subject to the grant of a single official authorisation issued by the competent authorities of the Member State in which a reinsurance undertaking has its head office. Such authorisation enables an undertaking to carry on business throughout the Community, under the right of establishment or the freedom to provide services. The Member State of the branch or of the provision of services may not require a reinsurance undertaking which wishes to carry on reinsurance business in its territory and which has already been authorised in its home Member State to seek fresh authorisation. Furthermore a reinsurance undertaking which has already been authorised in its home Member State should not be subject to additional supervision or checks related to its financial soundness performed by the competent authorities of an insurance undertaking which is reinsured by that reinsurance undertaking. In addition, Member States should not be allowed to require a reinsurance undertaking authorised in the Community to pledge assets in order to cover its part of the cedant's technical provisions. The conditions for the granting or withdrawal of such authorisation should be defined. The competent authorities should not authorise or continue the authorisation of a reinsurance undertaking which does not fulfil the conditions laid down in this Directive.

(11) This Directive should apply to reinsurance undertakings which conduct exclusively reinsurance business and do not engage in direct insurance business; it should also apply to the so-called "captive" reinsurance undertakings created or owned by either a financial undertaking other than an insurance or reinsurance undertaking or a group of insurance or reinsurance undertakings to which Directive 98/78/EC of the European Parliament and of the Council of 27 October 1998 on the supplementary supervision of insurance undertakings in an insurance group[7] *applies, or by one or several non-financial undertakings, the purpose of which is to provide reinsurance cover exclusively for the risks of the undertakings to which they belong. When in this Directive reference is made to*

reinsurance undertakings, it should include captive reinsurance undertakings, except where special provision is made for captive reinsurance undertakings. Captive reinsurance undertakings do not cover risks deriving from the external direct insurance or reinsurance business of an insurance or reinsurance undertaking belonging to the group. Furthermore, insurance or reinsurance undertakings belonging to a financial conglomerate may not own a captive undertaking.

(12) This Directive should however not apply to insurance undertakings which are already subject to Directives 73/239/EEC or 2002/83/EC; however, in order to ensure the financial soundness of insurance undertakings which also carry on reinsurance business and that the specific characteristics of those activities is duly taken into account by the capital requirements of those insurance undertakings, the provisions relating to the solvency margin of reinsurance undertakings contained in this Directive should apply to reinsurance business of those insurance undertakings, if the volume of their reinsurance activities represents a significant part of their entire business.

(13) This Directive should not apply to the provision of reinsurance cover carried out or fully guaranteed by a Member State for reasons of substantial public interest, in the capacity of reinsurer of last resort, in particular where because of a specific situation in a market, it is not feasible to obtain adequate commercial cover; in this regard, a lack of "adequate commercial cover" should mainly mean a market failure which is characterised by an evident lack of a sufficient range of insurance offers, although excessive premiums should not per se imply inadequacy of that commercial cover. Article 1(2)(d) of this Directive also applies to arrangements between insurance undertakings to which Directives 73/239/EEC or 2002/83/EC apply and which aim to pool financial claims ensuing from major risks such as terrorism.

(14) Reinsurance undertakings are to limit their objects to the business of reinsurance and related operations. This requirement may allow a reinsurance undertaking to carry on, for instance, activities, such as provision of statistical or actuarial advice, risk analysis or research for its clients. It may also include a holding company function and activities with respect to financial sector activities within the meaning of Article 2, point 8, of Directive 2002/87/EC of the European Parliament and of the Council of 16 December 2002 on the supplementary supervision of credit institutions, insurance undertakings and investment firms in a financial conglomerate.[8] *In any case, this requirement does not allow the carrying on of unrelated banking and financial activities.*

(15) This Directive should clarify the powers and means of supervision vested in the competent authorities. The competent authorities of the reinsurance undertaking's home Member State should be responsible for monitoring the financial health of reinsurance undertakings, including their state of solvency, the establishment of adequate technical provisions and equalisation reserves and the covering of those provisions and reserves by quality assets.

(16) The competent authorities of the Member States should have at their disposal such means of supervision as are necessary to ensure the orderly pursuit of business by reinsurance undertakings throughout the Community whether carried on under the right of establishment or the freedom to provide services. In particular, they should be able to introduce appropriate safeguards or impose penalties aimed at preventing irregularities and infringements of the provisions on reinsurance supervision.

(17) The provisions governing transfers of portfolios should be in line with the single authorisation provided for in this Directive. They should apply to the various kinds of transfers of portfolios between reinsurance undertakings, such as transfers of portfolios resulting from mergers between reinsurance undertakings or other instruments of company law or transfers of portfolios of outstanding losses in run-off to another reinsurance undertaking. Moreover, the provisions governing transfers of portfolios should include provisions specifically concerning the transfer to another reinsurance undertaking of the portfolio of contracts concluded under the right of establishment or the freedom to provide services.

(18) Provision should be made for the exchange of information between the competent authorities and authorities or bodies which, by virtue of their function, help to strengthen the stability of the financial system. In order to preserve the confidential nature of the information forwarded, the list of addressees should remain within strict limits. It is therefore necessary to specify the conditions under which the abovementioned exchanges of information are authorised; moreover, where it is laid down that information may be disclosed only with the express agreement of the competent authorities, these may, where appropriate, make their agreement subject to compliance with strict conditions. In this regard, and with a view to ensuring the proper supervision of reinsurance undertakings by the competent authorities, this Directive should provide for rules enabling Member States to conclude agreements on exchange of information with third countries provided that the information disclosed is subject to appropriate guarantees of professional secrecy.

(19) For the purposes of strengthening the prudential supervision of reinsurance undertakings, it should be laid down that an auditor has a duty to report promptly to the competent authorities, wherever, as provided for by this Directive, he/she becomes aware, while carrying out his/her tasks, of certain facts which are liable to have a serious effect on the financial situation or the administrative and accounting organisation of a reinsurance undertaking. Having regard to the aim in view, it is desirable for Member States to provide that such a duty should apply in all circumstances where such facts are discovered by an auditor during the performance of his/her tasks

in an undertaking which has close links with a reinsurance undertaking. The duty of auditors to communicate, where appropriate, to the competent authorities certain facts and decisions concerning a reinsurance undertaking which they discover during the performance of their tasks in a non-reinsurance undertaking does not in itself change the nature of their tasks in that undertaking nor the manner in which they must perform those tasks in that undertaking.

(20) Provision should be made to define the application of this Directive to existing reinsurance undertakings which were already authorised or entitled to conduct reinsurance business in accordance with the provisions of the Member States before the application of this Directive.

(21) In order to allow a reinsurance undertaking to meet its commitments, the home Member State should require a reinsurance undertaking to establish adequate technical provisions. The amount of such technical provisions should be determined in accordance with Council Directive 91/674/EEC of 19 December 1991 on the annual accounts and consolidated accounts of insurance undertakings[9] *and, in respect of life reinsurance activities, the home Member State should also be allowed to lay down more specific rules in accordance with Directive 2002/83/EC.*

(22) A reinsurance undertaking conducting reinsurance business in respect of credit insurance, whose credit reinsurance business amounts to more than a small proportion of its total business, should be required to set up an equalisation reserve which does not form part of the solvency margin; that reserve should be calculated according to one of the methods laid down in Directive 73/239/EEC and which are recognised as equivalent; furthermore, this Directive should allow the home Member State also to require reinsurance undertakings whose head office is situated within its territory to set up equalisation reserves for classes of risks other than credit reinsurance, following the rules laid down by that home Member State. Following the introduction of the International Financial Reporting Standards (IFRS 4), this Directive should clarify the prudential treatment of equalisation reserves established in accordance with this Directive. However, since supervision of reinsurance needs to be reassessed under the Solvency II project, this Directive does not pre-empt any future reinsurance supervision under Solvency II.

(23) A reinsurance undertaking should have assets to cover technical provisions and equalisation reserves which should take account of the type of business that it carries out in particular the nature, amount and duration of the expected claims payments, in such a way as to secure the sufficiency, liquidity, security, quality, profitability and matching of its investments, which the undertaking should ensure are diversified and adequately spread and which gives the undertaking the possibility of responding adequately to changing economic circumstances, in particular developments in the financial markets and real estate markets or major catastrophic events.

(24) It is necessary that, over and above technical provisions, reinsurance undertakings should possess a supplementary reserve, known as the solvency margin, represented by free assets and, with the agreement of the competent authority, by other implicit assets, which is to act as a buffer against adverse business fluctuations. This requirement is an important element of prudential supervision. Pending the revision of the existing solvency margin regime, which the Commission is carrying on under the so-called "Solvency II project", in order to determine the required solvency margin of reinsurance undertakings, the rules provided for in existing legislation in the field of direct insurance should be applicable.

(25) In the light of the similarities between life reassurance covering mortality risk and non-life reinsurance, in particular the cover of insurance risks and the duration of the life reassurance contracts, the required solvency margin for life reassurance should be determined in accordance with the provisions laid down in this Directive for the calculation of the required solvency margin for non-life reinsurance; the home Member State should however be allowed to apply the rules provided for in Directive 2002/83/EC for the establishment of the required solvency margin in respect of life reassurance activities which are linked to investment funds or participating contracts.

(26) In order to take account of the particular nature of some types of reinsurance contracts or specific lines of business, provision should be made to make adjustments to the calculation of the required solvency margin; these adjustments should be made by the Commission, after consulting the European Insurance and Occupational Pensions Committee, set up by Commission Decision 2004/9/EC[10] *in the exercise of its implementing powers conferred by the Treaty.*

(27) These measures should be adopted by the use of the regulatory procedure provided for in Article 5 of Council Decision 1999/468/EC of 28 June 1999 laying down the procedures for the exercise of implementing powers conferred on the Commission.[11]

(28) The list of items eligible to represent the available solvency margin laid down by this Directive should be that provided for in Directives 73/239/EEC and 2002/83/EC.

(29) Reinsurance undertakings should also possess a guarantee fund in order to ensure that they possess adequate resources when they are set up and that in the subsequent course of business the solvency margin in no event falls below a minimum of security; however, in order to take account of the specificities of captive reinsurance undertakings, provision should be made to allow the home Member State to set the minimum guarantee fund required for captive reinsurance undertakings at a lower amount.

(30) Certain provisions of this Directive define minimum standards. A home Member State should

be able to lay down stricter rules for reinsurance undertakings authorised by its own competent authorities, in particular with respect to solvency margin requirements.

(31) This Directive should be applicable to finite reinsurance activities; therefore, a definition of finite reinsurance for the purposes of this Directive is necessary; owing to the special nature of this line of reinsurance activity, the home Member State should be given the option of laying down specific provisions for the pursuit of finite reinsurance activities. These provisions could differ from the general regime laid down in this Directive on a number of specific points.

(32) This Directive should provide for rules concerning those special purpose vehicles that assume risks from insurance and reinsurance undertakings. The special nature of such special purpose vehicles, which are not insurance or reinsurance undertakings, calls for the establishment of specific provisions in Member States. Furthermore, this Directive should provide that the home Member State should lay down more detailed rules in order to set the conditions under which outstanding amounts from a special purpose vehicle can be used as assets covering technical provisions by an insurance or a reinsurance undertaking. This Directive should also provide that recoverable amounts from a special purpose vehicle may be considered as amounts deductible under reinsurance or retrocession contracts within the limits set out in this Directive, subject to an application by the insurance undertaking or reinsurance undertaking to the competent authority and after agreement by that authority.

(33) It is necessary to provide for measures in cases where the financial position of the reinsurance undertaking becomes such that it is difficult for it to meet its underwriting liabilities. In specific situations, there is also a need for the competent authorities to be empowered to intervene at a sufficiently early stage, but in the exercise of those powers, competent authorities should inform the reinsurance undertakings of the reasons motivating such supervisory action, in accordance with the principles of sound administration and due process. As long as such a situation exists, the competent authorities should be prevented from certifying that the reinsurance undertaking has a sufficient solvency margin.

(34) It is necessary to make provision for cooperation between the competent authorities of the Member States in order to ensure that a reinsurance undertaking carrying on its activities under the right of establishment and the freedom to provide services complies with the provisions applicable to it in the host Member State.

(35) Provision should be made for the right to apply to the courts should an authorisation be refused or withdrawn.

(36) It is important to provide that reinsurance undertakings whose head office is situated outside the Community and which conduct reinsurance business in the Community should not be subject to provisions which result in treatment more favourable than that provided to reinsurance undertakings having their head office in a Member State.

(37) In order to take account of the international aspects of reinsurance, provision should be made to enable the conclusion of international agreements with a third country aimed at defining the means of supervision over reinsurance entities which conduct business in the territory of each contracting party.

(38) Provision should be made for a flexible procedure to make it possible to assess prudential equivalence with third countries on a Community basis, so as to improve liberalisation of reinsurance services in third countries, be it through establishment or cross-border provision of services. To that end, this Directive should provide for procedures for negotiating with third countries.

(39) The Commission should be empowered to adopt implementing measures provided that these do not modify the essential elements of this Directive. These implementing measures should enable the Community to take account of the future development of reinsurance. The measures necessary for implementation of this Directive should be adopted in accordance with Decision 1999/468/EC.

(40) The existing Community legal framework for insurance should be adapted in order to take account of the new supervisory regime for reinsurance undertakings laid down by this Directive and in order to ensure a consistent regulatory framework for the whole insurance sector. In particular, the existing provisions which permit "indirect supervision" of reinsurance undertakings by the authorities competent for the supervision of direct insurance undertakings should be adapted. Furthermore, it is necessary to abolish the current provisions enabling Member States to require pledging of assets covering the technical provisions of an insurance undertaking, whatever form this requirement might take, when the insurer is reinsured by a reinsurance undertaking authorised pursuant to this Directive or by an insurance undertaking. Finally, provision should be made for the solvency margin required for insurance undertakings conducting reinsurance activities, when such activities represent a significant part of their business, to be subject to the solvency rules provided for reinsurance undertakings in this Directive. Directives 73/239/EEC, 92/49/EEC and 2002/83/EC should therefore be amended accordingly.

(41) Directive 98/78/EC should be amended in order to guarantee that reinsurance undertakings in an insurance or a reinsurance group are subject to supplementary supervision in the same manner as insurance undertakings which are currently part of an insurance group.

(42) The Council, in accordance with paragraph 34 of the Interinstitutional agreement on better law-making,[12] should encourage Member States to draw up, for themselves and in the interest of the Community, their own tables, illustrating, as far as possible, the correlation between this Directive and the transposition measures, and to make them public.

(43) Since the objective of this Directive, namely the establishment of a legal framework for the taking up and pursuit of reinsurance activities, cannot be sufficiently achieved by the Member States and can therefore, by reason of the scale and effects of the action, be better achieved at Community level, the Community may adopt measures, in accordance with the principle of subsidiarity as set out in Article 5 of the Treaty. In accordance with the principle of proportionality, as set out in that Article, this Directive does not go beyond what is necessary in order to achieve this objective.

(44) Since this Directive defines minimum standards, Member States may lay down stricter rules,

NOTES

Repealed as noted at the beginning of this Directive.

[1] OJ C120, 20.5.2005, p 1

[2] Opinion of the European Parliament of 7 June 2005 (not yet published in the Official Journal) and Decision of the Council of 17 October 2005.

[3] OJ L228, 16.8.1973, p 3. Directive as last amended by Directive 2005/1/EC of the European Parliament and of the Council (OJ L79, 24.3.2005, p 9).

[4] OJ L228, 11.8.1992, p 1. Directive as last amended by Directive 2005/1/EC.

[5] OJ L345, 19.12.2002, p 1. Directive as last amended by Directive 2005/1/EC.

[6] OJ 56, 4.4.1964, p 878.

[7] OJ L330, 5.12.1998, p 1. Directive as last amended by Directive 2005/1/EC.

[8] OJ L35, 11.2.2003, p 1. Directive as amended by Directive 2005/1/EC.

[9] OJ L374, 31.12.1991, p 7. Directive as amended by Directive 2003/51/EC of the European Parliament and of the Council (OJ L178, 17.7.2003, p 16).

[10] OJ L3, 7.1.2004, p 34.

[11] OJ L184, 17.7.1999, p 23.

[12] OJ C321, 31.12.2003, p 1.

HAVE ADOPTED THIS DIRECTIVE—

TITLE I
SCOPE AND DEFINITIONS

[6873]
Article 1
Scope

1. This Directive lays down rules for the taking up and pursuit of the self-employed activity of reinsurance carried on by reinsurance undertakings, which conduct only reinsurance activities, and which are established in a Member State or wish to become established therein.

2. This Directive shall not apply to the following:

- *(a) insurance undertakings to which Directives 73/239/EEC or 2002/83/EC apply;*
- *(b) activities and bodies referred to in Articles 2 and 3 of Directive 73/239/EEC;*
- *(c) activities and bodies referred to in Article 3 of Directive 2002/83/EC;*
- *(d) the activity of reinsurance conducted or fully guaranteed by the government of a Member State when this is acting, for reasons of substantial public interest, in the capacity of reinsurer of last resort, including in circumstances where such a role is required by a situation in the market in which it is not feasible to obtain adequate commercial cover.*

NOTES

Repealed as noted at the beginning of this Directive.

[6874]
Article 2
Definitions

1. For the purposes of this Directive, the following definitions shall apply:

- *(a) "reinsurance" means the activity consisting in accepting risks ceded by an insurance undertaking or by another reinsurance undertaking. In the case of the association of underwriters known as Lloyd's, reinsurance also means the activity consisting in accepting risks, ceded by any member of Lloyd's, by an insurance or reinsurance undertaking other than the association of underwriters known as Lloyd's;*

(b) "captive reinsurance undertaking" means a reinsurance undertaking owned either by a financial undertaking other than an insurance or a reinsurance undertaking or a group of insurance or reinsurance undertakings to which Directive 98/78/EC applies, or by a non-financial undertaking, the purpose of which is to provide reinsurance cover exclusively for the risks of the undertaking or undertakings to which it belongs or of an undertaking or undertakings of the group of which the captive reinsurance undertaking is a member;

(c) "reinsurance undertaking" means an undertaking which has received official authorisation in accordance with Article 3;

(d) "branch" means an agency or a branch of a reinsurance undertaking;

(e) "establishment" means the head office or a branch of a reinsurance undertaking, account being taken of point (d);

(f) "home Member State" means the Member State in which the head office of the reinsurance undertaking is situated;

(g) "Member State of the branch" means the Member State in which the branch of a reinsurance undertaking is situated;

(h) "host Member State" means the Member State in which a reinsurance undertaking has a branch or provides services;

(i) "control" means the relationship between a parent undertaking and a subsidiary, as defined in Article 1 of Directive 83/349/EEC,[1] or a similar relationship between any natural or legal person and an undertaking;

(j) "qualifying holding" means a direct or indirect holding in an undertaking which represents 10% or more of the capital or of the voting rights or which makes it possible to exercise a significant influence over the management of the undertaking in which a holding subsists;

(k) "parent undertaking" means a parent undertaking as defined in Articles 1 and 2 of Directive 83/349/EEC;

(l) "subsidiary" means a subsidiary undertaking as defined in Articles 1 and 2 of Directive 83/349/EEC;

(m) "competent authorities" means the national authorities which are empowered by law or regulation to supervise reinsurance undertakings;

(n) "close links" means a situation in which two or more natural or legal persons are linked by:

(i) participation, which shall mean the ownership, direct or by way of control, of 20% or more of the voting rights or capital of an undertaking, or

(ii) control, in all the cases referred to in Article 1(1) and (2) of Directive 83/349/EEC or a similar relationship between any natural or legal person and an undertaking;

(o) "financial undertaking" means one of the following entities:

(i) a credit institution, a financial institution or an ancillary banking services undertaking within the meaning of Article 1(5) and (23) of Directive 2000/12/EC,[2]

(ii) an insurance undertaking, a reinsurance undertaking or an insurance holding company within the meaning of Article 1(i) of Directive 98/78/EC,

(iii) an investment firm or a financial institution within the meaning of point 1 of Article 4(1) of Directive 2004/39/EC,[3]

(iv) a mixed financial holding company within the meaning of Article 2(15) of Directive 2002/87/EC;

(p) "special purpose vehicle" means any undertaking, whether incorporated or not, other than an existing insurance or reinsurance undertaking, which assumes risks from insurance or reinsurance undertakings and which fully funds its exposure to such risks through the proceeds of a debt issuance or some other financing mechanism where the repayment rights of the providers of such debt or other financing mechanism are subordinated to the reinsurance obligations of such a vehicle;

(q) "finite reinsurance" means reinsurance under which the explicit maximum loss potential, expressed as the maximum economic risk transferred, arising both from a significant underwriting risk and timing risk transfer, exceeds the premium over the lifetime of the contract by a limited but significant amount, together with at least one of the following two features:

(i) explicit and material consideration of the time value of money,

(ii) contractual provisions to moderate the balance of economic experience between the parties over time to achieve the target risk transfer.

2. For the purposes of paragraph 1(a) of this Article, the provision of cover by a reinsurance undertaking to an institution for occupational retirement provision falling under the scope of Directive 2003/41/EC[4] *where the law of the institution's home Member State permits such provision, shall also be considered as an activity falling under the scope of this Directive.*

For the purposes of paragraph 1(d), any permanent presence of a reinsurance undertaking in the territory of a Member State shall be treated in the same way as an agency or branch, even if that presence does not take the form of a branch or agency, but consists merely of an office managed by the undertaking's own staff or by a person who is independent but has permanent authority to act for the undertaking as an agency would.

[For the purposes of paragraph 1(j), in the context of Articles 12 and 19 to 23 and of the other levels of holding referred to in Article 19 to 23, the voting rights referred to in Articles 9 and 10 of Directive 2004/109/EC,[5] *as well as the conditions regarding aggregation thereof laid down in Article 12(4) and (5) of that Directive shall be taken into account.*

Member States shall not take into account voting rights or shares which investment firms or credit institutions may hold as a result of providing the underwriting of financial instruments and/or placing of financial instruments on a firm commitment basis included under point 6 of Section A of Annex I to Directive 2004/39/EC, provided that those rights are, on the one hand, not exercised or otherwise used to intervene in the management of the issuer and, on the other, disposed of within one year of acquisition.]

For the purposes of paragraph 1(l), any subsidiary of a subsidiary undertaking shall also be regarded as a subsidiary of the undertaking which is those undertakings' ultimate parent undertaking.

For the purposes of paragraph 1(n):

- *any subsidiary undertaking of a subsidiary undertaking shall be considered a subsidiary of the parent undertaking which is at the head of those undertakings;*
- *a situation in which two or more natural or legal persons are permanently linked to one and the same person by a control relationship shall also be regarded as constituting a close link between such persons.*

3. Wherever this Directive refers to the euro, the conversion value in national currency to be adopted shall, as from 31 December of each year, be that of the last day of the preceding month of October for which euro conversion values are available in all the Community currencies.

NOTES

Repealed as noted at the beginning of this Directive.

Para 2: words in square brackets substituted by European Parliament and Council Directive 2007/44/EC, art 4(1).

1 Seventh Council Directive 83/349/EEC of 13 June 1983 based on the Article 54(3)(g) of the Treaty on consolidated accounts (OJ L193, 18.7.1983, p 1). Directive as last amended by Directive 2003/51/EC.

2 Directive 2000/12/EC of the European Parliament and of the Council of 20 March 2000 relating to the taking up and pursuit of the business of credit institutions (OJ L126, 26.5.2000, p 1). Directive as last amended by Directive 2005/1/EC.

3 Directive 2004/39/EC of the European Parliament and of the Council of 21 April 2004 on markets in financial instruments (OJ L145, 30.4.2004, p 1).

4 Directive 2003/41/EC of the European Parliament and of the Council of 3 June 2003 on the activities and supervision of institutions for occupational retirement provision (OJ L235, 23.9.2003, p 10).

5 Directive 2004/109/EC of the European Parliament and of the Council of 15 December 2004 on the harmonisation of transparency requirements in relation to information about issuers whose securities are admitted to trading on a regulated market (OJ L390, 31.12.2004, p 38).

TITLE II
THE TAKING-UP OF THE BUSINESS OF REINSURANCE AND AUTHORISATION OF THE REINSURANCE UNDERTAKING

[6875]
Article 3
Principle of authorisation

The taking up of the business of reinsurance shall be subject to prior official authorisation.

Such authorisation shall be sought from the competent authorities of the home Member State by:

(a) any undertaking which establishes its head office in the territory of that State;

(b) any reinsurance undertaking which, having received the authorisation, extends its business to reinsurance activities other than those already authorised.

NOTES

Repealed as noted at the beginning of this Directive.

[6876]
Article 4
Scope of authorisation

1. An authorisation pursuant to Article 3 shall be valid for the entire Community. It shall permit a reinsurance undertaking to carry on business there, under either the right of establishment or the freedom to provide services.

2. Authorisation shall be granted for non-life reinsurance activities, life reassurance activities or all kinds of reinsurance activities, according to the request made by the applicant.

It shall be considered in the light of the scheme of operations to be submitted pursuant to Articles 6(b) and 11 and the fulfilment of the conditions laid down for authorisation by the Member State from which the authorisation is sought.

NOTES

Repealed as noted at the beginning of this Directive.

[6877]
Article 5
Form of the reinsurance undertaking

1. The home Member State shall require every reinsurance undertaking for which authorisation is sought to adopt one of the forms set out in Annex I.

A reinsurance undertaking may also adopt the form of a European Company (SE), as defined in Regulation (EC) No 2157/2001.[1]

2. Member States may, where appropriate, set up undertakings in any public-law form provided that such bodies have as their objects reinsurance operations under conditions equivalent to those under which private-law undertakings operate.

NOTES

Repealed as noted at the beginning of this Directive.

[1] Council Regulation (EC) No 2157/2001 of 8 October 2001 on the Statute for a European company (SE) (OJ L294, 10.11.2001, p 1). Regulation as amended by Regulation (EC) No 885/2004 (OJ L168, 1.5.2004, p 1).

[6878]
Article 6
Conditions

The home Member State shall require every reinsurance undertaking for which authorisation is sought to:

- *(a) limit its objects to the business of reinsurance and related operations; this requirement may include a holding company function and activities with respect to financial sector activities within the meaning of Article 2, point (8), of Directive 2002/87/EC;*
- *(b) submit a scheme of operations in accordance with Article 11;*
- *(c) possess the minimum guarantee fund provided for in Article 40(2);*
- *(d) be effectively run by persons of good repute with appropriate professional qualifications or experience.*

NOTES

Repealed as noted at the beginning of this Directive.

[6879]
Article 7
Close links

1. Where close links exist between the reinsurance undertaking and other natural or legal persons, the competent authorities shall grant authorisation only if those links do not prevent the effective exercise of their supervisory functions.

2. The competent authorities shall refuse authorisation if the laws, regulations or administrative provisions of a non-member country governing one or more natural or legal persons with which the reinsurance undertaking has close links, or difficulties involved in their enforcement, prevent the effective exercise of their supervisory functions.

3. The competent authorities shall require reinsurance undertakings to provide them with the information they require to monitor compliance with the conditions referred to in paragraph 1 on a continuous basis.

NOTES

Repealed as noted at the beginning of this Directive.

[6880]
Article 8
Head office of the reinsurance undertaking

Member States shall require that the head offices of reinsurance undertakings be situated in the same Member State as their registered offices.

NOTES

Repealed as noted at the beginning of this Directive.

[6881]
Article 9
Policy conditions and scales of premiums

1. This Directive shall not prevent Member States from maintaining in force or introducing laws, regulations or administrative provisions requiring approval of the memorandum and articles of association and communication of any other documents necessary for the normal exercise of supervision.

2. However, Member States may not adopt provisions requiring the prior approval or systematic notification of general and special policy conditions, scales of premiums and forms and other printed documents which a reinsurance undertaking intends to use in its dealings with ceding or retroceding undertakings.

NOTES

Repealed as noted at the beginning of this Directive.

[6882]
Article 10
Economic requirements of the market

Member States may not require that any application for authorisation be considered in the light of the economic requirements of the market.

NOTES

Repealed as noted at the beginning of this Directive.

[6883]
Article 11
Scheme of operations

1. The scheme of operations referred to in Article 6(b) shall include particulars or evidence of:

- *(a) the nature of the risks which the reinsurance undertaking proposes to cover;*
- *(b) the kinds of reinsurance arrangements which the reinsurance undertaking proposes to make with ceding undertakings;*
- *(c) the guiding principles as to retrocession;*
- *(d) the items constituting the minimum guarantee fund;*
- *(e) estimates of the costs of setting up the administrative services and the organisation for securing business and the financial resources intended to meet those costs.*

2. In addition to the requirements in paragraph 1, the scheme of operations shall for the first three financial years contain:

- *(a) estimates of management expenses other than installation costs, in particular current general expenses and commissions;*
- *(b) estimates of premiums or contributions and claims;*
- *(c) a forecast balance sheet;*
- *(d) estimates of the financial resources intended to cover underwriting liabilities and the solvency margin.*

NOTES

Repealed as noted at the beginning of this Directive.

[6884]
Article 12
Shareholders and members with qualifying holdings

The competent authorities of the home Member State shall not grant to an undertaking an authorisation to take up the business of reinsurance before they have been informed of the identities of the shareholders or members, direct or indirect, whether natural or legal persons, who have qualifying holdings in that undertaking and of the amounts of those holdings.

The same authorities shall refuse authorisation if, taking into account the need to ensure the sound and prudent management of a reinsurance undertaking, they are not satisfied as to the qualifications of the shareholders or members.

NOTES

Repealed as noted at the beginning of this Directive.

[6885]
Article 13
Refusal of authorisation

Any decision to refuse an authorisation shall be accompanied by the precise grounds for doing so and notified to the undertaking in question.

Each Member State shall make provision for a right to apply to the courts, pursuant to Article 53, should there be any refusal.

Such provision shall also be made with regard to cases where the competent authorities have not dealt with an application for an authorisation upon the expiry of a period of six months from the date of its receipt.

NOTES

Repealed as noted at the beginning of this Directive.

[6886]
Article 14
Prior consultation with the competent authorities of other Member States

1. The competent authorities of the other Member State involved shall be consulted prior to the granting of an authorisation to a reinsurance undertaking, which is:

- *(a) a subsidiary of an insurance or reinsurance undertaking authorised in another Member State; or*
- *(b) a subsidiary of the parent undertaking of an insurance or reinsurance undertaking authorised in another Member State; or*
- *(c) controlled by the same person, whether natural or legal, who controls an insurance or reinsurance undertaking authorised in another Member State.*

2. The competent authority of a Member State involved, which is responsible for the supervision of credit institutions or investment firms, shall be consulted prior to the granting of an authorisation to a reinsurance undertaking which is:

- *(a) a subsidiary of a credit institution or investment firm authorised in the Community; or*
- *(b) a subsidiary of the parent undertaking of a credit institution or investment firm authorised in the Community; or*
- *(c) controlled by the same person, whether natural or legal, who controls a credit institution or investment firm authorised in the Community.*

3. The relevant competent authorities referred to in paragraphs 1 and 2 shall in particular consult each other when assessing the suitability of the shareholders and the reputation and experience of directors involved in the management of another entity of the same group. They shall inform each other of any information regarding the suitability of shareholders and the reputation and experience of directors which is of relevance to the other competent authorities involved for the granting of an authorisation as well as for the ongoing assessment of compliance with operating conditions.

NOTES

Repealed as noted at the beginning of this Directive.

TITLE III
CONDITIONS GOVERNING THE BUSINESS OF REINSURANCE

CHAPTER 1
PRINCIPLES AND METHODS OF FINANCIAL SUPERVISION

SECTION 1
COMPETENT AUTHORITIES AND GENERAL RULES

[6887]
Article 15
Competent authorities and object of supervision

1. The financial supervision of a reinsurance undertaking, including that of the business it carries on either through branches or under the freedom to provide services, shall be the sole responsibility of the home Member State.

If the competent authorities of the host Member State have reason to consider that the activities of a reinsurance undertaking might affect its financial soundness, they shall inform the competent authorities of the reinsurance undertaking's home Member State. The latter authorities shall determine whether the reinsurance undertaking is complying with the prudential rules laid down in this Directive.

2. The financial supervision pursuant to paragraph 1 shall include verification, with respect to the reinsurance undertaking's entire business, of its state of solvency, of the establishment of technical provisions and of the assets covering them in accordance with the rules laid down or practices followed in the home Member State under provisions adopted at Community level.

3. The home Member State of the reinsurance undertaking shall not refuse a retrocession contract concluded by the reinsurance undertaking with a reinsurance undertaking authorised in accordance with this Directive or an insurance undertaking authorised in accordance with Directives 73/239/EEC or 2002/83/EC on grounds directly related to the financial soundness of that reinsurance undertaking or that insurance undertaking.

4. The competent authorities of the home Member State shall require every reinsurance undertaking to have sound administrative and accounting procedures and adequate internal control mechanisms.

NOTES

Repealed as noted at the beginning of this Directive.

[6888]
Article 16
Supervision of branches established in another Member State

The Member State of the branch shall provide that, where a reinsurance undertaking authorised in another Member State carries on business through a branch, the competent authorities of the home Member State may, after having first informed the competent authorities of the Member State of the branch, carry out themselves or through the intermediary of persons they appoint for that purpose, on-the-spot verification of the information necessary to ensure the financial supervision of the undertaking. The authorities of the Member State of the branch may participate in that verification.

NOTES

Repealed as noted at the beginning of this Directive.

[6889]
Article 17
Accounting, prudential and statistical information: supervisory powers

1. Each Member State shall require every reinsurance undertaking whose head office is situated in its territory to produce an annual account, covering all types of operation, of its financial situation and of its solvency.

2. Member States shall require reinsurance undertakings with head offices within their territories to render periodically the returns, together with statistical documents, which are necessary for the purposes of supervision. The competent authorities shall provide each other with any documents and information that are useful for the purposes of supervision.

3. Every Member State shall take all steps necessary to ensure that the competent authorities have the powers and means necessary for the supervision of the business of reinsurance undertakings with head offices within their territories, including business carried on outside those territories.

4. In particular, the competent authorities shall be enabled to:

(a) make detailed enquiries regarding a reinsurance undertaking's situation and the whole of its business, inter alia, by gathering information or requiring the submission of documents concerning its reinsurance and retrocession business, and by carrying out on-the-spot investigations at the reinsurance undertaking's premises;

(b) take any measures with regard to a reinsurance undertaking, its directors or managers or the persons who control it, that are appropriate and necessary to ensure that that reinsurance undertaking's business continues to comply with the laws, regulations and administrative provisions with which the reinsurance undertaking must comply in each Member State;

(c) ensure that those measures are carried out, if need be, by enforcement and where appropriate through judicial channels.

Member States may also make provision for the competent authorities to obtain any information regarding contracts which are held by intermediaries.

NOTES

Repealed as noted at the beginning of this Directive.

[6890]
Article 18
Transfer of portfolio

Under the conditions laid down by national law, each Member State shall authorise reinsurance undertakings with head offices within its territory to transfer all or part of their portfolios of contracts, including those concluded either under the right of establishment or the freedom to provide services, to an accepting office established within the Community, if the competent authorities of the home Member State of the accepting office certify that, after taking the transfer into account, the latter possesses the necessary solvency margin referred to in Chapter 3.

NOTES

Repealed as noted at the beginning of this Directive.

Part VI European Materials

SECTION 2
QUALIFYING HOLDINGS

[6891]
[Article 19
Acquisitions

1. Member States shall require any natural or legal person or such persons acting in concert (hereinafter referred to as the proposed acquirer), who have taken a decision either to acquire, directly or indirectly, a qualifying holding in a reinsurance undertaking or to further increase, directly or indirectly, such a qualifying holding in a reinsurance undertaking as a result of which the proportion of the voting rights or of the capital held would reach or exceed 20%, 30% or 50% or so that the reinsurance undertaking would become its subsidiary (hereinafter referred to as the proposed acquisition), first to notify in writing the competent authorities of the reinsurance undertaking in which they are seeking to acquire or increase a qualifying holding, indicating the size of the intended holding and relevant information, as referred to in Article 19a(4). Member States need not apply the 30% threshold where, in accordance with Article 9(3)(a) of Directive 2004/109/EC, they apply a threshold of one-third.

2. The competent authorities shall, promptly and in any event within two working days following receipt of the notification, as well as following the possible subsequent receipt of the information referred to in paragraph 3, acknowledge receipt thereof in writing to the proposed acquirer.

The competent authorities shall have a maximum of 60 working days as from the date of the written acknowledgement of receipt of the notification and all documents required by the Member State to be attached to the notification on the basis of the list referred to in Article 19a(4) (hereinafter referred to as the assessment period), to carry out the assessment provided for in Article 19a(1) (hereinafter referred to as the assessment).

The competent authorities shall inform the proposed acquirer of the date of the expiry of the assessment period at the time of acknowledging receipt.

3. The competent authorities may, during the assessment period, if necessary, and no later than on the 50th working day of the assessment period, request any further information that is necessary to complete the assessment. Such request shall be made in writing and shall specify the additional information needed.

For the period between the date of request for information by the competent authorities and the receipt of a response thereto by the proposed acquirer, the assessment period shall be interrupted. The interruption shall not exceed 20 working days. Any further requests by the competent authorities for completion or clarification of the information shall be at their discretion but may not result in an interruption of the assessment period.

4. The competent authorities may extend the interruption referred to in the second subparagraph of paragraph 3 up to 30 working days if the proposed acquirer is:

(a) situated or regulated outside the Community; or

(b) a natural or legal person not subject to supervision under this Directive or Directives 85/611/EEC,[1] 92/49/EEC, 2002/83/EC, 2004/39/EC or 2006/48/EC.[2]

5. If the competent authorities, upon completion of the assessment, decide to oppose the proposed acquisition, they shall, within two working days, and not exceeding the assessment period, inform the proposed acquirer in writing and provide the reasons for that decision. Subject to national law, an appropriate statement of the reasons for the decision may be made accessible to the public at the request of the proposed acquirer. This shall not prevent a Member State from allowing the competent authority to make such disclosure in the absence of a request by the proposed acquirer.

6. If the competent authorities do not oppose the proposed acquisition within the assessment period in writing, it shall be deemed to be approved.

7. The competent authorities may fix a maximum period for concluding the proposed acquisition and extend it where appropriate.

8. Member States may not impose requirements for notification to and approval by the competent authorities of direct or indirect acquisitions of voting rights or capital that are more stringent than those set out in this Directive.]

NOTES

Substituted by European Parliament and Council Directive 2007/44/EC, art 4(2).

Repealed as noted at the beginning of this Directive.

1 Council Directive 85/611/EEC of 20 December 1985 on the coordination of laws, regulations and administrative provisions relating to undertakings for collective investment in transferable securities (UCITS) (OJ L375, 31.12.1985, p 3). Directive as last amended by Directive 2005/1/EC of the European Parliament and of the Council (OJ L79, 24.3.2005, p 9).

2 Directive 2006/48/EC of the European Parliament and of the Council of 14 June 2006 relating to the taking up and pursuit of the business of credit institutions (recast) (OJ L177, 30.6.2006, p 1). Directive as last amended by Directive 2007/44/EC.

[6892]
[Article 19a
Assessment

1. In assessing the notification provided for in Article 19(1) and the information referred to in Article 19(3), the competent authorities shall, in order to ensure the sound and prudent management of the reinsurance undertaking in which an acquisition is proposed, and having regard to the likely influence of the proposed acquirer on the reinsurance undertaking, appraise the suitability of the proposed acquirer and the financial soundness of the proposed acquisition against all of the following criteria:

(a) the reputation of the proposed acquirer;

(b) the reputation and experience of any person who will direct the business of the reinsurance undertaking as a result of the proposed acquisition;

(c) the financial soundness of the proposed acquirer, in particular in relation to the type of business pursued and envisaged in the reinsurance undertaking in which the acquisition is proposed;

(d) whether the reinsurance undertaking will be able to comply and continue to comply with the prudential requirements based on this Directive and, where applicable, other Directives, notably, Directives 98/78/EC and 2002/87/EC, in particular, whether the group of which it will become a part has a structure that makes it possible to exercise effective supervision, effectively exchange information among the competent authorities and determine the allocation of responsibilities among the competent authorities;

(e) whether there are reasonable grounds to suspect that, in connection with the proposed acquisition, money laundering or terrorist financing within the meaning of Article 1 of Directive 2005/60/EC[1] is being or has been committed or attempted, or that the proposed acquisition could increase the risk thereof.

2. The competent authorities may oppose the proposed acquisition only if there are reasonable grounds for doing so on the basis of the criteria set out in paragraph 1 or if the information provided by the proposed acquirer is incomplete.

3. Member States shall neither impose any prior conditions in respect of the level of holding that must be acquired nor allow their competent authorities to examine the proposed acquisition in terms of the economic needs of the market.

4. Member States shall make publicly available a list specifying the information that is necessary to carry out the assessment and that must be provided to the competent authorities at the time of notification referred to in Article 19(1). The information required shall be proportionate and adapted to the nature of the proposed acquirer and the proposed acquisition. Member States shall not require information that is not relevant for a prudential assessment.

5. Notwithstanding Article 19(2), (3) and (4), where two or more proposals to acquire or increase qualifying holdings in the same reinsurance undertaking have been notified to the competent authority, the latter shall treat the proposed acquirers in a non-discriminatory manner.]

NOTES

Inserted by European Parliament and Council Directive 2007/44/EC, art 4(3).
Repealed as noted at the beginning of this Directive.

1 Directive 2005/60/EC of the European Parliament and of the Council of 26 October 2005 on the prevention of the use of financial system for the purpose of money laundering and terrorist financing (OJ L309, 25.11.2005, p 15).

[6893]
[Article 20
Acquisitions by regulated financial undertakings

1. The relevant competent authorities shall work in full consultation with each other when carrying out the assessment if the proposed acquirer is one of the following:

(a) a credit institution, assurance undertaking, insurance undertaking, reinsurance undertaking, investment firm or management company within the meaning of Article 1a, point 2 of Directive 85/611/EEC (hereinafter referred to as the UCITS management company) authorised in another Member State or in a sector other than that in which the acquisition is proposed;

(b) the parent undertaking of a credit institution, assurance undertaking, insurance undertaking, reinsurance undertaking, investment firm or UCITS management company authorised in another Member State or in a sector other than that in which the acquisition is proposed; or

(c) a natural or legal person controlling a credit institution, assurance undertaking, insurance undertaking, reinsurance undertaking, investment firm or UCITS management company authorised in another Member State or in a sector other than that in which the acquisition is proposed.

2. The competent authorities shall, without undue delay, provide each other with any information which is essential or relevant for the assessment. In this regard, the competent authorities shall communicate to each other upon request all relevant information and shall communicate on their own initiative all essential information. A decision by the competent authority that has authorised the reinsurance undertaking in which the acquisition is proposed shall indicate any views or reservations expressed by the competent authority responsible for the proposed acquirer.]

NOTES

Substituted by European Parliament and Council Directive 2007/44/EC, art 4(4).
Repealed as noted at the beginning of this Directive.

[6894]
Article 21
Disposals

Member States shall require any natural or legal person who proposes to dispose, directly or indirectly, of a qualifying holding in a reinsurance undertaking first to inform the competent authorities of the home Member State, indicating the size of his intended holding.

[Such a person shall likewise notify the competent authorities if he has taken a decision to reduce his qualifying holding so that the proportion of the voting rights or of the capital held would fall below 20%, 30% or 50% or so that the reinsurance undertaking would cease to be his subsidiary. Member States need not apply the 30% threshold where, in accordance with Article 9(3)(a) of Directive 2004/109/EC, they apply a threshold of one-third.]

NOTES

Repealed as noted at the beginning of this Directive.
Words in square brackets substituted by European Parliament and Council Directive 2007/44/EC, art 4(5).

[6895]
Article 22
Information to the competent authority by the reinsurance undertaking

On becoming aware of them, reinsurance undertakings shall inform the competent authorities of their home Member States of any acquisitions or disposals of holdings in their capital that cause holdings to exceed or fall below any of the thresholds referred to in Articles 19 and 21.

They shall also, at least once a year, inform them of the names of shareholders and members possessing qualifying holdings and the sizes of such holdings as shown, for example, by the information received at annual general meetings of shareholders or members or as a result of compliance with the regulations relating to companies listed on stock exchanges.

NOTES

Repealed as noted at the beginning of this Directive.

[6896]
Article 23
Qualifying holdings: powers of the competent authority

Member States shall require that, where the influence exercised by the persons referred to in Article 19 is likely to operate against the prudent and sound management of a reinsurance undertaking, the competent authorities of the home Member State shall take appropriate measures to put an end to that situation. Such measures may consist, for example, in injunctions, penalties against directors and managers, or suspension of the exercise of the voting rights attaching to the shares held by the shareholders or members in question.

Similar measures shall apply to natural or legal persons failing to comply with the obligation to provide prior information imposed pursuant to Article 19. If a holding is acquired despite the opposition of the competent authorities, the Member States shall, regardless of any other penalties to be adopted, provide either for exercise of the corresponding voting rights to be suspended, or for the nullity of votes cast or for the possibility of their annulment.

NOTES

Repealed as noted at the beginning of this Directive.

SECTION 3
PROFESSIONAL SECRECY AND EXCHANGES OF INFORMATION

[6897]
Article 24
Obligation

1. Member States shall provide that all persons working or who have worked for the competent authorities, as well as auditors and experts acting on behalf of the competent authorities, are bound by an obligation of professional secrecy.

Pursuant to that obligation, and without prejudice to cases covered by criminal law, no confidential information which they may receive while performing their duties may be divulged to any person or authority whatsoever, except in summary or aggregate form, such that individual reinsurance undertakings cannot be identified.

2. However, where a reinsurance undertaking has been declared bankrupt or is being compulsorily wound up, confidential information which does not concern third parties involved in attempts to rescue that undertaking may be divulged in civil or commercial proceedings.

NOTES

Repealed as noted at the beginning of this Directive.

[6898]
Article 25
Exchange of information between competent authorities of Member States

Article 24 shall not prevent the competent authorities of different Member States from exchanging information in accordance with the Directives applicable to reinsurance undertakings. Such information shall be subject to the conditions of professional secrecy laid down in Article 24.

NOTES

Repealed as noted at the beginning of this Directive.

[6899]
Article 26
Cooperation agreements with third countries

Member States may conclude cooperation agreements providing for exchange of information with the competent authorities of third countries or with authorities or bodies of third countries as defined in Article 28(1) and (2) only if the information disclosed is subject to guarantees of professional secrecy at least equivalent to those referred to in this Section. Such exchange of information shall be intended for the performance of the supervisory task of the authorities or bodies mentioned.

Where the information originates in another Member State, it may not be disclosed without the express agreement of the competent authorities which have disclosed it and, where appropriate, solely for the purposes for which those authorities gave their agreement.

NOTES

Repealed as noted at the beginning of this Directive.

[6900]
Article 27
Use of confidential information

Competent authorities receiving confidential information under Articles 24 and 25 may use it only in the course of their duties:

- *(a) to check that the conditions governing the taking up of the business of reinsurance are met and to facilitate monitoring of the conduct of such business, especially with regard to the monitoring of technical provisions, solvency margins, administrative and accounting procedures and internal control mechanisms,*
- *(b) to impose penalties,*
- *(c) in administrative appeals against decisions of the competent authorities, or*
- *(d) in court proceedings initiated under Article 53 or under special provisions provided for in this Directive and other Directives adopted in the field of insurance and reinsurance undertakings.*

NOTES

Repealed as noted at the beginning of this Directive.

[6901]
Article 28
Exchange of information with other authorities

1. Articles 24 and 27 shall not preclude the exchange of information within a Member State, where there are two or more competent authorities in the same Member State, or, between Member States, between competent authorities and:

- *(a) authorities responsible for the official supervision of credit institutions and other financial organisations and the authorities responsible for the supervision of financial markets,*
- *(b) bodies involved in the liquidation and bankruptcy of insurance and reinsurance undertakings and in other similar procedures, and*
- *(c) persons responsible for carrying out statutory audits of the accounts of insurance undertakings, reinsurance undertakings and other financial institutions,*

in the discharge of their supervisory functions, or the disclosure to bodies which administer compulsory winding-up proceedings or guarantee schemes of information necessary to the performance of their duties. The information received by those authorities, bodies and persons shall be subject to the conditions of professional secrecy laid down in Article 24.

2. Notwithstanding Articles 24 to 27, Member States may authorise exchanges of information between the competent authorities and:

- *(a) the authorities responsible for overseeing the bodies involved in the liquidation and bankruptcy of insurance or reinsurance undertakings and other similar procedures, or*
- *(b) the authorities responsible for overseeing the persons charged with carrying out statutory audits of the accounts of insurance or reinsurance undertakings, credit institutions, investment firms and other financial institutions, or*
- *(c) independent actuaries of insurance or reinsurance undertakings carrying out legal supervision of those undertakings and the bodies responsible for overseeing such actuaries.*

Member States which have recourse to the option provided for in the first subparagraph shall require at least that the following conditions are met:

(a) *this exchange of information shall be for the purpose of carrying out the overseeing or legal supervision referred to in the first subparagraph;*

(b) *information received in this context shall be subject to the conditions of professional secrecy imposed in Article 24;*

(c) *where the information originates in another Member State, it may not be disclosed without the express agreement of the competent authorities which have disclosed it and, where appropriate, may only be disclosed for the purposes for which those authorities gave their agreement.*

Member States shall communicate to the Commission and to the other Member States the names of the authorities, persons and bodies which may receive information pursuant to this paragraph.

3. Notwithstanding Articles 24 to 27, Member States may, with the aim of strengthening the stability, including the integrity, of the financial system, authorise the exchange of information between the competent authorities and the authorities or bodies responsible under the law for the detection and investigation of breaches of company law.

Member States which have recourse to the option provided for in the first subparagraph shall require at least that the following conditions are met:

(a) *the information shall be for the purpose of performing the task referred to in the first subparagraph;*

(b) *information received in this context shall be subject to the conditions of professional secrecy imposed in Article 24;*

(c) *where the information originates in another Member State, it may not be disclosed without the express agreement of the competent authorities which have disclosed it and, where appropriate, solely for the purposes for which those authorities gave their agreement.*

Where, in a Member State, the authorities or bodies referred to in the first subparagraph perform their task of detection or investigation with the aid, in view of their specific competence, of persons appointed for that purpose and not employed in the public sector, the possibility of exchanging information provided for in the first subparagraph may be extended to such persons under the conditions laid down in the second subparagraph.

In order to implement point (c) of the second subparagraph, the authorities or bodies referred to in the first subparagraph shall communicate to the competent authorities which have disclosed the information the names and precise responsibilities of the persons to whom it is to be sent.

Member States shall communicate to the Commission and to the other Member States the names of the authorities or bodies which may receive information pursuant to this paragraph.

NOTES

Repealed as noted at the beginning of this Directive.

[6902]
Article 29
Transmission of information to central banks and monetary authorities

This Section shall not prevent a competent authority from transmitting to central banks and other bodies with a similar function in their capacity as monetary authorities, and where appropriate, to other public authorities responsible for overseeing payment systems, information intended for the performance of their task. Nor shall it prevent such authorities or bodies from communicating to the competent authorities such information as they may need for the purposes of Article 27.

Information received in this context shall be subject to the conditions of professional secrecy imposed in this Section.

NOTES

Repealed as noted at the beginning of this Directive.

[6903]
Article 30
Disclosure of information to government administrations responsible for financial legislation

Notwithstanding Articles 24 and 27, Member States may, under provisions laid down by law, authorise the disclosure of certain information to other departments of their central government administrations responsible for legislation on the supervision of credit institutions, financial institutions, investment services and insurance or reinsurance undertakings and to inspectors acting on behalf of those departments.

However, such disclosures may be made only where necessary for reasons of prudential control.

Member States shall, however, provide that information received under Articles 25 and 28(1) and that obtained by means of the on-the-spot verification referred to in Article 16 may never be disclosed in the cases referred to in this Article except with the express consent of the competent authorities which disclosed the information or of the competent authorities of the Member State in which on-the-spot verification was carried out.

NOTES

Repealed as noted at the beginning of this Directive.

SECTION 4
DUTIES OF AUDITORS

[6904]
Article 31
Duties of auditors

1. Member States shall provide at least that any person authorised in accordance with Directive 84/253/EEC,[1] performing in a reinsurance undertaking the task described in Article 51 of Directive 78/660/EEC,[2] Article 37 of Directive 83/349/EEC or Article 31 of Directive 85/611/EEC[3] or any other statutory task, shall have a duty to report promptly to the competent authorities any fact or decision concerning that undertaking of which he/she has become aware while carrying out that task which is liable to:

(a) constitute a material breach of the laws, regulations or administrative provisions which lay down the conditions governing authorisation or which specifically govern pursuit of the activities of insurance or reinsurance undertakings, or

(b) affect the continuous functioning of the reinsurance undertaking, or

(c) lead to refusal to certify the accounts or to the expression of reservations.

That person shall also have a duty to report any facts and decisions of which he/she becomes aware in the course of carrying out a task as described in the first subparagraph in an undertaking having close links resulting from a control relationship with the reinsurance undertaking within which he/she is carrying out the abovementioned task.

2. The disclosure to the competent authorities, by persons authorised in accordance with Directive 84/253/EEC, of any relevant fact or decision referred to in paragraph 1 of this Article shall not constitute a breach of any restriction on disclosure of information imposed by contract or by any legislative, regulatory or administrative provision and shall not involve such persons in liability of any kind.

NOTES

Repealed as noted at the beginning of this Directive.

1 Eighth Council Directive 84/253/EEC of 10 April 1984 based on Article 54(3)(g) of the Treaty on the approval of persons responsible for carrying out the statutory audits of accounting documents (OJ L126, 12.5.1984, p 20).

2 Fourth Council Directive 78/660/EEC of 25 July 1978 based on Article 54(3)(g) of the Treaty on the annual accounts of certain types of companies (OJ L222, 14.8.1978, p 11). Directive as last amended by Directive 2003/51/EC.

3 Council Directive 85/611/EEC of 20 December 1985 on the coordination of laws, regulations and administrative provisions relating to undertakings for collective investment in transferable securities (UCITS) (OJ L375, 31.12.1985, p 3). Directive as last amended by Directive 2005/1/EC.

CHAPTER 2
RULES RELATING TO TECHNICAL PROVISIONS

[6905]
Article 32
Establishment of technical provisions

1. The home Member State shall require every reinsurance undertaking to establish adequate technical provisions in respect of its entire business.

The amount of such technical provisions shall be determined in accordance with the rules laid down in Directive 91/674/EEC. Where applicable, the home Member State may lay down more specific rules in accordance with Article 20 of Directive 2002/83/EC.

2. Member States shall not retain or introduce a system with gross reserving which requires pledging of assets to cover unearned premiums and outstanding claims provisions if the reinsurer is a reinsurance undertaking authorised in accordance with this Directive or an insurance undertaking authorised in accordance with Directives 73/239/EEC or 2002/83/EC.

Part VI European Materials

3. When the home Member State allows any technical provisions to be covered by claims against reinsurers who are not authorised in accordance with this Directive or insurance undertakings which are not authorised in accordance with Directives 73/239/EEC or 2002/83/EC, it shall set the conditions for accepting such claims.

NOTES

Repealed as noted at the beginning of this Directive.

[6906]
Article 33
Equalisation reserves

1. The home Member State shall require every reinsurance undertaking which reinsures risks included in class 14 listed in point A of the Annex to Directive 73/239/EEC to set up an equalisation reserve for the purpose of offsetting any technical deficit or above-average claims ratio arising in that class in any financial year.

2. The equalisation reserve for credit reinsurance shall be calculated in accordance with the rules laid down by the home Member State in accordance with one of the four methods set out in point D of the Annex to Directive 73/239/EEC, which shall be regarded as equivalent.

3. The home Member State may exempt reinsurance undertakings from the obligation to set up equalisation reserves for reinsurance of credit insurance business where the premiums or contributions receivable in respect of reinsurance of credit insurance are less than 4% of the total premiums or contributions receivable by them and less than EUR 2 500 000.

4. The home Member State may require every reinsurance undertaking to set up equalisation reserves for classes of risks other than credit reinsurance. The equalisation reserves shall be calculated according to the rules laid down by the home Member State.

NOTES

Repealed as noted at the beginning of this Directive.

[6907]
Article 34
Assets covering technical provisions

1. The home Member State shall require every reinsurance undertaking to invest the assets covering the technical provisions and the equalisation reserve referred to in Article 33 in accordance with the following rules:

- *(a) the assets shall take account of the type of business carried out by a reinsurance undertaking, in particular the nature, amount and duration of the expected claims payments, in such a way as to secure the sufficiency, liquidity, security, quality, profitability and matching of its investments;*
- *(b) the reinsurance undertaking shall ensure that the assets are diversified and adequately spread and allow the undertaking to respond adequately to changing economic circumstances, in particular developments in the financial markets and real estate markets or major catastrophic events. The undertaking shall assess the impact of irregular market circumstances on its assets and shall diversify the assets in such a way as to reduce such impact;*
- *(c) investment in assets which are not admitted to trading on a regulated financial market shall in any event be kept to prudent levels;*
- *(d) investment in derivative instruments shall be possible insofar as they contribute to a reduction of investment risks or facilitate efficient portfolio management. They shall be valued on a prudent basis, taking into account the underlying assets, and included in the valuation of the institution's assets. The institution shall also avoid excessive risk exposure to a single counterparty and to other derivative operations;*
- *(e) the assets shall be properly diversified in such a way as to avoid excessive reliance on any one particular asset, issuer or group of undertakings and accumulations of risk in the portfolio as a whole. Investments in assets issued by the same issuer or by issuers belonging to the same group shall not expose the undertaking to excessive risk concentration.*

Member States may decide not to apply the requirements referred to in point (e) to investment in government bonds.

2. Member States shall not require reinsurance undertakings situated in their territory to invest in particular categories of assets.

3. Member States shall not subject the investment decisions of a reinsurance undertaking situated in their territory or its investment manager to any kind of prior approval or systematic notification requirements.

4. Notwithstanding paragraphs 1 to 3, the home Member State may, for every reinsurance undertaking whose head office is situated in its territory, lay down the following quantitative rules, provided that they are prudentially justified:

- *(a) investments of gross technical provisions in currencies other than those in which technical provisions are set should be limited to 30%;*
- *(b) investments of gross technical provisions in shares and other negotiable securities treated as shares, bonds and debt securities which are not admitted to trading on a regulated market should be limited to 30%;*
- *(c) the home Member State may require every reinsurance undertaking to invest no more than 5% of its gross technical provisions in shares and other negotiable securities treated as shares, bonds, debt securities and other money and capital market instruments from the same undertaking, and no more than 10% of its total gross technical provisions in shares and other negotiable securities treated as shares, bonds, debt securities and other money and capital market instruments from undertakings which are members of the same group.*

5. Furthermore, the home Member State shall lay down more detailed rules setting the conditions for the use of amounts outstanding from a special purpose vehicle as assets covering technical provisions pursuant to this Article.

NOTES

Repealed as noted at the beginning of this Directive.

CHAPTER 3
RULES RELATING TO THE SOLVENCY MARGIN AND TO THE GUARANTEE FUND

SECTION 1
AVAILABLE SOLVENCY MARGIN

[6908]
Article 35
General rule

Each Member State shall require of every reinsurance undertaking whose head office is situated in its territory an adequate available solvency margin in respect of its entire business at all times, which is at least equal to the requirements of this Directive.

NOTES

Repealed as noted at the beginning of this Directive.

[6909]
Article 36
Eligible items

1. The available solvency margin shall consist of the assets of the reinsurance undertaking free of any foreseeable liabilities, less any intangible items, including:

- *(a) the paid-up share capital or, in the case of a mutual reinsurance undertaking, the effective initial fund plus any members' accounts which meet all the following criteria:*
  - *(i) the memorandum and articles of association shall stipulate that payments may be made from those accounts to members only in so far as this does not cause the available solvency margin to fall below the required level, or, after the dissolution of the undertaking, if all the undertaking's other debts have been settled;*
  - *(ii) the memorandum and articles of association shall stipulate, with respect to any payments referred to in point (i) for reasons other than the individual termination of membership, that the competent authorities must be notified at least one month in advance and can prohibit the payment within that period;*
  - *(iii) the relevant provisions of the memorandum and articles of association may be amended only after the competent authorities have declared that they have no objection to the amendment, without prejudice to the criteria stated in points (i) and (ii);*
- *(b) statutory and free reserves which neither correspond to underwriting liabilities nor are classified as equalisation reserves;*
- *(c) the profit or loss brought forward after deduction of dividends to be paid.*

2. *The available solvency margin shall be reduced by the amount of own shares directly held by the reinsurance undertaking.*

For those reinsurance undertakings which discount or reduce their non-life technical provisions for claims outstanding to take account of investment income as permitted by Article 60(1)(g) of Directive 91/674/EEC, the available solvency margin shall be reduced by the difference between the undiscounted technical provisions or technical provisions before deductions as disclosed in the notes on the accounts, and the discounted or technical provisions after deductions. This adjustment shall be made for all risks listed in point A of the Annex to Directive 73/239/EEC, except for risks listed under classes 1 and 2 of point A of that Annex. For classes other than 1 and 2 listed in point A of that Annex, no adjustment need be made in respect of the discounting of annuities included in technical provisions.

In addition to the deductions in the first and second subparagraphs, the available solvency margin shall be reduced by the following items:

(a) *participations which the reinsurance undertaking holds in the following entities:*
  (i) *insurance undertakings within the meaning of Article 6 of Directive 73/239/EEC, Article 4 of Directive 2002/83/EC, or Article 1(b) of Directive 98/78/EC,*
  (ii) *reinsurance undertakings within the meaning of Article 3 of this Directive or non-member country reinsurance undertakings within the meaning of Article 1(l) of Directive 98/78/EC,*
  (iii) *insurance holding companies within the meaning of Article 1(i) of Directive 98/78/EC,*
  (iv) *credit institutions and financial institutions within the meaning of Article 1(1) and (5) of Directive 2000/12/EC,*
  (v) *investment firms and financial institutions within the meaning of Article 1(2) of Directive 93/22/EEC*[1] *and of Article 2(4) and (7) of Directive 93/6/EEC;*[2]
(b) *each of the following items which the reinsurance undertaking holds in respect of the entities defined in (a) in which it holds a participation:*
  (i) *instruments referred to in paragraph 4,*
  (ii) *instruments referred to in Article 27(3) of Directive 2002/83/EC,*
  (iii) *subordinated claims and instruments referred to in Article 35 and Article 36(3) of Directive 2000/12/EC.*

Where shares in another credit institution, investment firm, financial institution, insurance or reinsurance undertaking or insurance holding company are held temporarily for the purposes of a financial assistance operation designed to reorganise and save that entity, the competent authority may waive the provisions on deduction referred to under (a) and (b) of the third subparagraph.

As an alternative to the deduction of the items referred to in (a) and (b) of the third subparagraph which the reinsurance undertaking holds in credit institutions, investment firms and financial institutions, Member States may allow their reinsurance undertakings to apply mutatis mutandis methods 1, 2, or 3 of Annex I to Directive 2002/87/EC. Method 1 (Accounting consolidation) shall only be applied if the competent authority is confident about the level of integrated management and internal control regarding the entities which would be included in the scope of consolidation. The method chosen shall be applied in a consistent manner over time.

Member States may provide that, for the calculation of the solvency margin as provided for by this Directive, reinsurance undertakings subject to supplementary supervision in accordance with Directive 98/78/EC or to supplementary supervision in accordance with Directive 2002/87/EC need not deduct the items referred to in (a) and (b) of the third subparagraph which are held in credit institutions, investment firms, financial institutions, insurance or reinsurance undertakings or insurance holding companies which are included in the supplementary supervision.

For the purposes of the deduction of participations referred to in this paragraph, participation shall mean a participation within the meaning of Article 1(f) of Directive 98/78/EC.

3. *The available solvency margin may also consist of:*

(a) *cumulative preferential share capital and subordinated loan capital up to 50% of the available solvency margin or the required solvency margin, whichever is the smaller, no more than 25% of which shall consist of subordinated loans with a fixed maturity, or fixed-term cumulative preferential share capital, provided that, in the event of the bankruptcy or liquidation of the reinsurance undertaking, binding agreements exist under which the subordinated loan capital or preferential share capital ranks after the claims of all other creditors and is not to be repaid until all other debts outstanding at the time have been settled.*

Subordinated loan capital shall also fulfil the following conditions:
  (i) *only fully paid-up funds may be taken into account;*

(ii) *for loans with a fixed maturity, the original maturity shall be at least five years. No later than one year before the repayment date the reinsurance undertaking shall submit to the competent authorities for their approval a plan showing how the available solvency margin will be kept at or brought to the required level at maturity, unless the extent to which the loan may rank as a component of the available solvency margin is gradually reduced during at least the last five years before the repayment date. The competent authorities may authorise the early repayment of such loans provided that application is made by the issuing reinsurance undertaking and that its available solvency margin will not fall below the required level;*

(iii) *loans the maturity of which is not fixed shall be repayable only subject to five years' notice unless the loans are no longer considered as a component of the available solvency margin or unless the prior consent of the competent authorities is specifically required for early repayment. In the latter event the reinsurance undertaking shall notify the competent authorities at least six months before the date of the proposed repayment, specifying the available solvency margin and the required solvency margin both before and after that repayment. The competent authorities shall authorise repayment only if the reinsurance undertaking's available solvency margin will not fall below the required level;*

(iv) *the loan agreement shall not include any clause providing that in specified circumstances, other than the winding-up of the reinsurance undertaking, the debt will become repayable before the agreed repayment dates;*

(v) *the loan agreement may be amended only after the competent authorities have declared that they have no objection to the amendment;*

(b) *securities with no specified maturity date and other instruments, including cumulative preferential shares other than those referred to in point (a), up to 50% of the available solvency margin or the required solvency margin, whichever is the smaller, for the total of such securities and the subordinated loan capital referred to in point (a) provided that they fulfil the following:*

(i) *they may not be repaid on the initiative of the bearer or without the prior consent of the competent authority;*

(ii) *the contract of issue shall enable the reinsurance undertaking to defer the payment of interest on the loan;*

(iii) *the lender's claims on the reinsurance undertaking shall rank entirely after those of all non-subordinated creditors;*

(iv) *the documents governing the issue of the securities shall provide for the loss-absorption capacity of the debt and unpaid interest, while enabling the reinsurance undertaking to continue its business;*

(v) *only fully paid-up amounts may be taken into account.*

4. Upon application, with supporting evidence, by the reinsurance undertaking to the competent authority of the home Member State and with the agreement of that competent authority, the available solvency margin may also consist of:

(a) *one half of the unpaid share capital or initial fund, once the paid-up part amounts to 25% of that share capital or fund, up to 50% of the available solvency margin or the required solvency margin, whichever is the smaller;*

(b) *in the case of a non-life mutual or mutual-type association with variable contributions, any claim which it has against its members by way of a call for supplementary contribution, within the financial year, up to one half of the difference between the maximum contributions and the contributions actually called in, and subject to a limit of 50% of the available solvency margin or the required solvency margin, whichever is the smaller. The competent national authorities shall establish guidelines laying down the conditions under which supplementary contributions may be accepted;*

(c) *any hidden net reserves arising out of the valuation of assets, in so far as such hidden net reserves are not of an exceptional nature.*

5. In addition, with respect to life reassurance activities, the available solvency margin may, upon application, with supporting evidence, by the reinsurance undertaking to the competent authority of the home Member State and with the agreement of that competent authority, consist of:

(a) *until 31 December 2009, an amount equal to 50% of the undertaking's future profits, but not exceeding 25% of the available solvency margin or the required solvency margin, whichever is the smaller; the amount of the future profits shall be obtained by multiplying the estimated annual profit by a factor which represents the average period*

Part VI European Materials

left to run on policies; the factor used may not exceed six; the estimated annual profit shall not exceed the arithmetical average of the profits made over the last five financial years in the activities listed in Article 2(1) of Directive 2002/83/EC.

Competent authorities may only agree to include such an amount for the available solvency margin:

- *(i) when an actuarial report is submitted to the competent authorities substantiating the likelihood of emergence of these profits in the future; and*
- *(ii) insofar as that part of future profits emerging from hidden net reserves referred to in paragraph 4(c) has not already been taken into account;*

(b) where Zillmerising is not practised or where, if practised, it is less than the loading for acquisition costs included in the premium, the difference between a non-Zillmerised or partially Zillmerised mathematical provision and a mathematical provision Zillmerised at a rate equal to the loading for acquisition costs included in the premium; this figure may not, however, exceed 3,5% of the sum of the differences between the relevant capital sums of life reassurance activities and the mathematical provisions for all policies for which Zillmerising is possible; the difference shall be reduced by the amount of any undepreciated acquisition costs entered as an asset.

6. Amendments to paragraphs 1 to 5 of this Article to take into account developments that justify a technical adjustment of the elements eligible for the available solvency margin shall be adopted in accordance with the procedure laid down in Article 55(2).

NOTES

Repealed as noted at the beginning of this Directive.

[1] Council Directive 93/22/EEC of 10 May 1993 on investment services in the securities field (OJ L141, 11.6.1993, p 27). Directive as last amended by Directive 2002/87/EC of the European Parliament and of the Council (OJ L35, 11.2.2003, p 1).

[2] Council Directive 93/6/EEC of 15 March 1993 on the capital adequacy of investments firms and credit institutions (OJ L141, 11.6.1993, p 1). Directive as last amended by Directive 2005/1/EC.

SECTION 2
REQUIRED SOLVENCY MARGIN

[6910]

Article 37
Required solvency margin for non-life reinsurance activities

1. The required solvency margin shall be determined on the basis either of the annual amount of premiums or contributions, or of the average burden of claims for the past three financial years.

However, in the case of reinsurance undertakings which essentially underwrite only one or more of the risks of credit, storm, hail or frost, the last seven financial years shall be taken as the reference period for the average burden of claims.

2. Subject to Article 40, the amount of the required solvency margin shall be equal to the higher of the two results as set out in paragraphs 3 and 4 of this Article.

3. The premium basis shall be calculated using the higher of gross written premiums or contributions as calculated below, and gross earned premiums or contributions.

Premiums or contributions in respect of the classes 11, 12 and 13 listed in point A of the Annex to Directive 73/239/EEC shall be increased by 50%.

Premiums or contributions in respect of classes other than classes 11, 12 and 13 listed in point A of the Annex to Directive 73/239/EEC may be increased by up to 50%, for specific reinsurance activities or contract types, in order to take account of the specificities of these activities or contracts, in accordance with the procedure referred to in Article 55(2) of this Directive. The premiums or contributions, inclusive of charges ancillary to premiums or contributions, due in respect of reinsurance business in the last financial year shall be aggregated.

From that sum there shall then be deducted the total amount of premiums or contributions cancelled in the last financial year, as well as the total amount of taxes and levies pertaining to the premiums or contributions entering into the aggregate.

The amount so obtained shall be divided into two portions, the first portion extending up to EUR 50 000 000, the second comprising the excess; 18% and 16% of these portions respectively shall be calculated and added together.

The sum so obtained shall be multiplied by the ratio existing in respect of the sum of the last three financial years between the amount of claims remaining to be borne by the reinsurance undertaking after deduction of amounts recoverable under retrocession and the gross amount of claims; that ratio may in no case be less than 50%. Upon application, with supporting evidence, by the reinsurance undertaking to the competent authority of the home Member State and with the agreement of that authority, amounts recoverable from special purpose vehicles as referred to in Article 46 may also be deducted as retrocession.

With the approval of the competent authorities, statistical methods may be used to allocate the premiums or contributions.

4. The claims basis shall be calculated, as follows, using in respect of the classes 11, 12 and 13 listed in point A of the Annex to Directive 73/239/EEC, claims, provisions and recoveries increased by 50%.

Claims, provisions and recoveries in respect of classes other than classes 11, 12 and 13 listed in point A of the Annex to Directive 73/239/EEC, may be increased by up to 50%, for specific reinsurance activities or contract types, in order to take account of the specificities of those activities or contracts, in accordance with the procedure referred to in Article 55(2) of this Directive.

The amounts of claims paid, without any deduction of claims borne by retrocessionaires, in the periods specified in paragraph 1 shall be aggregated.

To that sum there shall be added the amount of provisions for claims outstanding established at the end of the last financial year.

From that sum there shall be deducted the amount of recoveries effected during the periods specified in paragraph 1.

From the sum then remaining, there shall be deducted the amount of provisions for claims outstanding established at the commencement of the second financial year preceding the last financial year for which there are accounts. If the reference period established in paragraph 1 equals seven years, the amount of provisions for claims outstanding established at the commencement of the sixth financial year preceding the last financial year for which there are accounts shall be deducted.

One third, or one seventh, of the amount so obtained, according to the reference period established in paragraph 1, shall be divided into two portions, the first extending up to EUR 35 000 000 and the second comprising the excess; 26% and 23% of these portions respectively shall be calculated and added together.

The sum so obtained shall be multiplied by the ratio existing in respect of the sum of the last three financial years between the amount of claims remaining to be borne by the undertaking after deduction of amounts recoverable under retrocession and the gross amount of claims; that ratio may in no case be less than 50%. Upon application, with supporting evidence, by the reinsurance undertaking to the competent authority of the home Member State and with the agreement of that authority, amounts recoverable from special purpose vehicles as referred to in Article 46 may also be deducted as retrocession.

With the approval of the competent authorities, statistical methods may be used to allocate claims, provisions and recoveries.

5. If the required solvency margin as calculated in paragraphs 2, 3 and 4 is lower than the required solvency margin of the year before, the required solvency margin shall be at least equal to the required solvency margin of the year before multiplied by the ratio between the amount of the technical provisions for claims outstanding at the end of the last financial year and the amount of the technical provisions for claims outstanding at the beginning of the last financial year. In these calculations technical provisions shall be calculated net of retrocession but the ratio may in no case be higher than 1.

6. The fractions applicable to the portions referred to in the fifth subparagraph of paragraph 3 and the seventh subparagraph of paragraph 4 shall each be reduced to a third in the case of reinsurance of health insurance practised on a similar technical basis to that of life assurance, if:

- *(a) the premiums paid are calculated on the basis of sickness tables according to the mathematical method applied in insurance;*
- *(b) a provision is set up for increasing age;*
- *(c) an additional premium is collected in order to set up a safety margin of an appropriate amount;*
- *(d) the insurance undertaking may cancel the contract before the end of the third year of insurance at the latest;*
- *(e) the contract provides for the possibility of increasing premiums or reducing payments even for current contracts.*

NOTES

Repealed as noted at the beginning of this Directive.

[6911]
Article 38
Required solvency margin for life reassurance activities

1. The required solvency margin for life reassurance activities shall be determined in accordance with Article 37.

2. Notwithstanding paragraph 1 of this Article, the home Member State may provide that for reinsurance classes of assurance business covered by Article 2(1)(a) of Directive 2002/83/EC linked to investment funds or participating contracts and for the operations referred to in Article 2(1)(b), 2(2)(b), (c), (d) and (e) of Directive 2002/83/EC, the required solvency margin is to be determined in accordance with Article 28 of Directive 2002/83/EC.

NOTES

Repealed as noted at the beginning of this Directive.

[6912]
Article 39
Required solvency margin for a reinsurance undertaking simultaneously conducting non-life and life reinsurance

1. The home Member State shall require every reinsurance undertaking conducting both non-life and life reinsurance business to have an available solvency margin to cover the total sum of required solvency margins in respect of both non-life and life reinsurance activities which shall be determined in accordance with Articles 37 and 38 respectively.

2. If the available solvency margin does not reach the level required in paragraph 1 of this Article, the competent authorities shall apply the measures provided for in Articles 42 and 43.

NOTES

Repealed as noted at the beginning of this Directive.

SECTION 3
GUARANTEE FUND

[6913]
Article 40
Amount of the guarantee fund

1. One third of the required solvency margin as specified in Articles 37, 38 and 39 shall constitute the guarantee fund. This fund shall consist of the items listed in Article 36(1), (2) and (3) and, with the agreement of the competent authority of the home Member State, in Article 36(4)(c).

2. The guarantee fund shall not be less than a minimum of EUR 3 000 000.

Any Member State may provide that as regards captive reinsurance undertakings, the minimum guarantee fund shall not be not less than EUR 1 000 000.

NOTES

Repealed as noted at the beginning of this Directive.

[6914]
Article 41
Review of the amount of the guarantee fund

1. The amounts in euro as laid down in Article 40(2) shall be reviewed annually as from 10 December 2007 in order to take account of changes in the European index of consumer prices comprising all Member States as published by Eurostat.

The amounts shall be adapted automatically by increasing the base amount in euro by the percentage change in that index over the period between the entry into force of this Directive and the review date and rounded up to a multiple of EUR 100 000.

If the percentage change since the last adaptation is less than 5%, no adaptation shall take place.

2. The Commission shall inform the European Parliament and the Council annually of the review and the adapted amounts referred to in paragraph 1.

NOTES

Repealed as noted at the beginning of this Directive.

CHAPTER 4
REINSURANCE UNDERTAKINGS IN DIFFICULTY OR IN AN IRREGULAR SITUATION AND WITHDRAWAL OF AUTHORISATION

[6915]
Article 42
Reinsurance undertakings in difficulty

1. If a reinsurance undertaking does not comply with Article 32, the competent authority of its home Member State may prohibit the free disposal of its assets after having communicated its intention to the competent authorities of the host Member States.

2. For the purposes of restoring the financial situation of a reinsurance undertaking the solvency margin of which has fallen below the minimum required under Articles 37, 38 and 39, the competent authority of the home Member State shall require that a plan for the restoration of a sound financial situation be submitted for its approval.

In exceptional circumstances, if the competent authority is of the opinion that the financial situation of the reinsurance undertaking will deteriorate further, it may also restrict or prohibit the free disposal of the reinsurance undertaking's assets. It shall inform the authorities of other Member States within the territories of which the reinsurance undertaking carries on business of any measures it has taken and the latter shall, at the request of the former, take the same measures.

3. If the solvency margin falls below the guarantee fund as defined in Article 40, the competent authority of the home Member State shall require the reinsurance undertaking to submit a short-term finance scheme for its approval.

It may also restrict or prohibit the free disposal of the reinsurance undertaking's assets. It shall inform the authorities of all other Member States and the latter shall, at the request of the former, take the same measures.

4. Each Member State shall take the measures necessary to be able, in accordance with its national law, to prohibit the free disposal of assets located within its territory at the request, in the cases provided for in paragraphs 1, 2 and 3, of the reinsurance undertaking's home Member State, which shall designate the assets to be covered by such measures.

NOTES
Repealed as noted at the beginning of this Directive.

[6916]
Article 43
Financial recovery plan

1. Member States shall ensure that the competent authorities have the power to require a financial recovery plan for those reinsurance undertakings where competent authorities consider that their obligations arising out of reinsurance contracts are threatened.

2. The financial recovery plan shall, as a minimum, include particulars or proof for the next three financial years concerning:

- *(a) estimates of management expenses, in particular current general expenses and commissions;*
- *(b) a plan setting out detailed estimates of income and expenditure in respect of reinsurance acceptances and reinsurance cessions;*
- *(c) a forecast balance sheet;*
- *(d) estimates of the financial resources intended to cover underwriting liabilities and the required solvency margin;*
- *(e) the overall retrocession policy.*

3. Where the financial position of the reinsurance undertaking is deteriorating and the contractual obligations of the reinsurance undertaking are threatened, Member States shall ensure that the competent authorities have the power to oblige reinsurance undertakings to have a higher required solvency margin, in order to ensure that the reinsurance undertaking is able to fulfil the solvency requirements in the near future. The level of this higher required solvency margin shall be based on a financial recovery plan referred to in paragraph 1.

4. Member States shall ensure that the competent authorities have the power to revalue downwards all elements eligible for the available solvency margin, in particular, where there has been a significant change in the market value of those elements since the end of the last financial year.

5. Member States shall ensure that the competent authorities have the power to decrease the reduction, based on retrocession, to the solvency margin as determined in accordance with Articles 37, 38 and 39 where:

Part VI European Materials

(a) the nature or quality of retrocession contracts has changed significantly since the last financial year;

(b) there is no or a limited risk transfer under the retrocession contracts.

6. If the competent authorities have required a financial recovery plan for the reinsurance undertaking in accordance with paragraph 1 of this Article, they shall refrain from issuing a certificate in accordance with Article 18, as long as they consider that its obligations arising out of reinsurance contracts are threatened within the meaning of the said paragraph 1.

NOTES

Repealed as noted at the beginning of this Directive.

[6917]
Article 44
Withdrawal of authorisation

1. Authorisation granted to a reinsurance undertaking by the competent authority of its home Member State may be withdrawn by that authority if that undertaking:

(a) does not make use of that authorisation within 12 months, expressly renounces it or ceases to carry on business for more than 6 months, unless the Member State concerned has made provision for authorisation to lapse in such cases;

(b) no longer fulfils the conditions for admission;

(c) has been unable, within the time allowed, to take the measures specified in the restoration plan or finance scheme referred to in Article 42;

(d) fails seriously in its obligations under the regulations to which it is subject.

In the event of the withdrawal or lapse of authorisation, the competent authority of the home Member State shall notify the competent authorities of the other Member States accordingly, and they shall take appropriate measures to prevent the reinsurance undertaking from commencing new operations within their territories, under either the right of establishment or the freedom to provide services.

2. Any decision to withdraw an authorisation shall be supported by precise reasons and communicated to the reinsurance undertaking in question.

NOTES

Repealed as noted at the beginning of this Directive.

TITLE IV
PROVISIONS RELATING TO FINITE REINSURANCE AND SPECIAL PURPOSE VEHICLES

[6918]
Article 45
Finite reinsurance

1. The home Member State may lay down specific provisions concerning the pursuit of finite reinsurance activities regarding:

— *mandatory conditions for inclusion in all contracts issued;*

— *sound administrative and accounting procedures, adequate internal control mechanisms and risk management requirements;*

— *accounting, prudential and statistical information requirements;*

— *the establishment of technical provisions to ensure that they are adequate, reliable and objective;*

— *investment of assets covering technical provisions in order to ensure that they take account of the type of business carried on by the reinsurance undertaking, in particular the nature, amount and duration of the expected claims payments, in such a way as to secure the sufficiency, liquidity, security, profitability and matching of its assets;*

— *rules relating to the available solvency margin, required solvency margin and the minimum guarantee fund that the reinsurance undertaking shall maintain in respect of finite reinsurance activities.*

2. In the interests of transparency, Member States shall communicate the text of any measures laid down by their national law for the purposes of paragraph 1 to the Commission without delay.

NOTES

Repealed as noted at the beginning of this Directive.

[6919]
Article 46
Special purpose vehicles

1. Where a Member State decides to allow the establishment within its territory of special purpose vehicles within the meaning of this Directive, it shall require prior official authorisation thereof.

2. The Member State where the special purpose vehicle is established shall lay down the conditions under which the activities of such an undertaking shall be carried on. In particular, that Member State shall lay down rules regarding:

- *scope of authorisation;*
- *mandatory conditions for inclusion in all contracts issued;*
- *the good repute and appropriate professional qualifications of persons running the special purpose vehicle;*
- *fit and proper requirements for shareholders or members having a qualifying holding in the special purpose vehicle;*
- *sound administrative and accounting procedures, adequate internal control mechanisms and risk management requirements;*
- *accounting, prudential and statistical information requirements;*
- *the solvency requirements of special purpose vehicles.*

3. In the interests of transparency, Member States shall communicate the text of any measures laid down by their national law for the purposes of paragraph 2, to the Commission without delay.

NOTES

Repealed as noted at the beginning of this Directive.

TITLE V
PROVISIONS RELATING TO RIGHT OF ESTABLISHMENT AND FREEDOM TO PROVIDE SERVICES

[6920]
Article 47
Reinsurance undertakings not complying with the legal provisions

1. If the competent authorities of the host Member State establish that a reinsurance undertaking with a branch or carrying on business under the freedom to provide services within its territory is not complying with the legal provisions applicable to it in that State, they shall require the reinsurance undertaking concerned to remedy that irregular situation. At the same time, they shall refer those findings to the competent authority of the home Member State.

If, despite the measures taken by the competent authority of the home Member State or because such measures prove inadequate, the reinsurance undertaking persists in infringing the legal provisions applicable to it in the host Member State, the latter may, after informing the competent authority of the home Member State, take appropriate measures to prevent or penalise further infringements, including, insofar as is strictly necessary, preventing that reinsurance undertaking from continuing to conclude new reinsurance contracts within its territory. Member States shall ensure that within their territories it is possible to serve the legal documents necessary for such measures on reinsurance undertakings.

2. Any measure adopted under paragraph 1 involving penalties or restrictions on the conduct of reinsurance business shall be properly reasoned and communicated to the reinsurance undertaking concerned.

NOTES

Repealed as noted at the beginning of this Directive.

[6921]
Article 48
Winding-up

In the event of a reinsurance undertaking's being wound up, commitments arising out of contracts underwritten through a branch or under the freedom to provide services shall be met in the same way as those arising out of that undertaking's other reinsurance contracts.

NOTES

Repealed as noted at the beginning of this Directive.

TITLE VI
REINSURANCE UNDERTAKINGS WHOSE HEAD OFFICES ARE OUTSIDE THE COMMUNITY AND CONDUCTING REINSURANCE ACTIVITIES IN THE COMMUNITY

[6922]
Article 49
Principle and conditions for conducting reinsurance business

A Member State shall not apply to reinsurance undertakings having their head offices outside the Community and commencing or carrying out reinsurance activities in its territory provisions which result in a treatment more favourable than that accorded to reinsurance undertakings having their head office in that Member State.

NOTES

Repealed as noted at the beginning of this Directive.

[6923]
Article 50
Agreements with third countries

1. The Commission may submit proposals to the Council for the negotiation of agreements with one or more third countries regarding the means of exercising supervision over:

(a) reinsurance undertakings which have their head offices situated in a third country, and conduct reinsurance business in the Community,

(b) reinsurance undertakings which have their head offices in the Community and conduct reinsurance business in the territory of a third country.

2. The agreements referred to in paragraph 1 shall in particular seek to ensure under conditions of equivalence of prudential regulation, effective market access for reinsurance undertakings in the territory of each contracting party and provide for mutual recognition of supervisory rules and practices on reinsurance. They shall also seek to ensure that:

(a) the competent authorities of the Member States are able to obtain the information necessary for the supervision of reinsurance undertakings which have their head offices situated in the Community and conduct business in the territory of third countries concerned,

(b) the competent authorities of third countries are able to obtain the information necessary for the supervision of reinsurance undertakings which have their head offices situated within their territories and conduct business in the Community.

3. Without prejudice to Articles 300(1) and (2) of the Treaty, the Commission shall with the assistance of the European Insurance and Occupational Pensions Committee examine the outcome of the negotiations referred to in paragraph 1 of this Article and the resulting situation.

NOTES

Repealed as noted at the beginning of this Directive.

TITLE VII
SUBSIDIARIES OF PARENT UNDERTAKINGS GOVERNED BY THE LAWS OF A THIRD COUNTRY AND ACQUISITIONS OF HOLDINGS BY SUCH PARENT UNDERTAKINGS

[6924]
Article 51
Information from Member States to the Commission

The competent authorities of the Member States shall inform the Commission and the competent authorities of the other Member States:

(a) of any authorisation of a direct or indirect subsidiary, one or more parent undertakings of which are governed by the laws of a third country;

(b) whenever such a parent undertaking acquires a holding in a Community reinsurance undertaking which would turn the latter into its subsidiary.

When an authorisation as referred to in point (a) is granted to the direct or indirect subsidiary of one or more parent undertakings governed by the laws of a third country, the structure of the group shall be specified in the notification which the competent authorities shall address to the Commission.

NOTES

Repealed as noted at the beginning of this Directive.

[6925]
Article 52
Third country treatment of Community reinsurance undertakings

1. Member States shall inform the Commission of any general difficulties encountered by their reinsurance undertakings in establishing themselves and operating in a third country or carrying on activities in a third country.

2. The Commission shall, periodically, draw up a report examining the treatment accorded to Community reinsurance undertakings in third countries, in the terms referred to in paragraph 3, as regards the establishment of Community reinsurance undertakings in third countries, the acquisition of holdings in third-country reinsurance undertakings, the carrying on of reinsurance activities by such established undertakings and the cross-border provision of reinsurance activities from the Community to third countries. The Commission shall submit those reports to the Council, together with any appropriate proposals or recommendations.

3. Whenever it appears to the Commission, either on the basis of the reports referred to in paragraph 2 or on the basis of other information, that a third country is not granting Community reinsurance undertakings effective market access, the Commission may submit recommendations to the Council for the appropriate mandate for negotiation with a view to obtaining improved market access for Community reinsurance undertakings.

4. Measures taken under this Article shall comply with the Community's obligations under any international agreements, in particular in the World Trade Organisation.

NOTES
Repealed as noted at the beginning of this Directive.

TITLE VIII
OTHER PROVISIONS

[6926]
Article 53
Right to apply to the courts

Member States shall ensure that decisions taken in respect of a reinsurance undertaking under laws, regulations and administrative provisions implementing this Directive are subject to the right to apply to the courts.

NOTES
Repealed as noted at the beginning of this Directive.

[6927]
Article 54
Cooperation between the Member States and the Commission

1. Member States shall cooperate with each other for the purpose of facilitating the supervision of reinsurance within the Community and the application of this Directive.

2. The Commission and the competent authorities of the Member States shall collaborate closely for the purpose of facilitating the supervision of reinsurance within the Community and of examining any difficulties which may arise in the application of this Directive.

NOTES
Repealed as noted at the beginning of this Directive.

[6928]
Article 55
Committee procedure

1. The Commission shall be assisted by the European Insurance and Occupational Pensions Committee.

[2. Where reference is made to this paragraph, Article 5a(1) to (4) and Article 7 of Decision 1999/468/EC shall apply, having regard to the provisions of Article 8 thereof.]

3. . . .

NOTES
Repealed as noted at the beginning of this Directive.
Para 2: substituted by European Parliament and Council Directive 2008/37/EC, art 1(1)(a).
Para 3: repealed by European Parliament and Council Directive 2008/37/EC, art 1(1)(b).

[6929]
Article 56
Implementing measures

[The following implementing measures designed to amend non-essential elements of this Directive, inter alia, by supplementing it, shall be adopted in accordance with the regulatory procedure with scrutiny referred to in Article 55(2):]

(a) extension of the legal forms provided for in Annex I,

(b) clarification of the items constituting the solvency margin listed in Article 36 to take account of the creation of new financial instruments,

(c) increase by up to 50% of the premiums or claims amounts used for the calculation of the required solvency margin provided for in Article 37(3) and (4), in classes other than classes 11, 12 and 13 listed in point A of the Annex to Directive 73/239/EEC, for specific reinsurance activities or contract types, to take account of the specificities of those activities or contracts,

(d) alteration of the minimum guarantee fund provided for in Article 40(2) to take account of economic and financial developments,

(e) clarification of the definitions in Article 2 in order to ensure uniform application of this Directive throughout the Community,

[(f) adjustments of the criteria set out in Article 19a(1), in order to take account of future developments and to ensure the uniform application of this Directive.]

NOTES

Repealed as noted at the beginning of this Directive.

Words in first pair of square brackets substituted by European Parliament and Council Directive 2008/37/EC, art 1(2).

Para (f): added by European Parliament and Council Directive 2007/44/EC, art 4(6).

Articles 57–60 *((Title IX) Art 57 amends Directive 73/239/EEC, arts 12a, 13, 15, 16, 16a, 20a at* **[6655]**, **[6656]**, **[6658]**, **[6660]**, **[6661]**, **[6668]**, *and inserts art 17b thereof at* **[6664]** *; art 58 amends Directive 92/49/EEC, arts 15, 16, 21, 22 at* **[6766]**, **[6770]**, **[6773]**, **[6774]**; *art 59 amends Directive 98/78/EC, Title, arts 1, 5, 9, 10, 10a* **[6108]**, **[6112]**, **[6116]**, **[6117]**, **[6118]**, *and substitutes arts 2–4, 6–8 thereof, Annexes I, II thereto at* **[6109]–[6111]**, **[6113]–[6115]**, **[6123]**, **[6124]**; *art 60 amends Directive 2002/83/EC, arts 1, 10, 15, 16, 20, 23, 27, 28, 37 at* **[6557]**, **[6567]**, **[6572]**, **[6576]**, **[6580]**, **[6583]**, **[6587]**, **[6588]**, **[6598]** *and inserts arts 9a, 28a thereof at* **[6566]**, **[6589]**.)

TITLE X
TRANSITIONAL AND FINAL PROVISIONS

[6930]
Article 61
Right acquired by existing reinsurance undertakings

1. Reinsurance undertakings subject to this Directive which were authorised or entitled to conduct reinsurance business in accordance with the provisions of the Member States in which they have their head offices before 10 December 2005 shall be deemed to be authorised in accordance with Article 3.

However, they shall be obliged to comply with the provisions of this Directive concerning the carrying on of the business of reinsurance and with the requirements set out in Article 6(a), (c), (d), Articles 7, 8 and 12 and Articles 32 to 41 as from 10 December 2007.

2. Member States may allow reinsurance undertakings referred to in paragraph 1 which at 10 December 2005 do not comply with Articles 6(a), 7, 8 and Articles 32 to 40 a period until 10 December 2008 in order to comply with such requirements.

NOTES

Repealed as noted at the beginning of this Directive.

[6931]
Article 62
Reinsurance undertakings closing their activity

1. Reinsurance undertakings which by 10 December 2007 have ceased to conduct new reinsurance contracts and exclusively administer their existing portfolio in order to terminate their activity shall not be subject to this Directive.

2. Member States shall draw up the list of the reinsurance undertakings concerned and they shall communicate that list to all the other Member States.

NOTES

Repealed as noted at the beginning of this Directive.

[6932]
Article 63
Transitional period for Articles 57(3) and 60(6)

A Member State may postpone the application of the provisions of Article 57(3) of this Directive amending Article 15(3) of Directive 73/239/EEC and of the provision of Article 60(6) of this Directive until 10 December 2008.

NOTES

Repealed as noted at the beginning of this Directive.

[6933]
Article 64
Transposition

1. Member States shall bring into force the laws, regulations and administrative provisions necessary to comply with this Directive by 10 December 2007. They shall forthwith communicate to the Commission the texts of those measures.

When Member States adopt those measures, they shall contain a reference to this Directive or be accompanied by such a reference on the occasion of their official publication. Member States shall determine how such reference is to be made.

2. Member States shall communicate to the Commission the text of the main provisions of national law which they adopt in the field covered by this Directive.

NOTES

Repealed as noted at the beginning of this Directive.

[6934]
Article 65
Entry into force

This Directive shall enter into force on the day following its publication in the Official Journal of the European Union.

NOTES

Repealed as noted at the beginning of this Directive.

[6935]
Article 66
Addressees

This Directive is addressed to the Member States.

NOTES

Repealed as noted at the beginning of this Directive.

Done at Strasbourg, 16 November 2005

ANNEX I

[6936]

Forms of reinsurance undertakings:

- *in the case of the Kingdom of Belgium: "société anonyme/naamloze vennootschap", "société en commandite par actions/commanditaire vennootschap op aandelen", "association d'assurance mutuelle/onderlinge verzekeringsvereniging", "société coopérative/coöperatieve vennootschap";*
- *in the case of the Czech Republic: "akciová společnost";*
- *in the case of the Kingdom of Denmark: "aktieselskaber", "gensidige selskaber";*
- *in the case of the Federal Republic of Germany: "Aktiengesellschaft", "Versicherungsverein auf Gegenseitigkeit", "Öffentlich-rechtliches Wettbewerbsversicherungsunternehmen";*
- *in the case of the Republic of Estonia: "aktsiaselts";*
- *in the case of the Hellenic Republic: "αν νυμη εταιρ α", "αληλασφαλιστικ ς συνεταιρισμ ς";*
- *in the case of the Kingdom of Spain: "sociedad anónima";*

— *in the case of the French Republic: "société anonyme", "société d'assurance mutuelle", "institution de prévoyance régie par le code de la sécurité sociale", "institution de prévoyance régie par le code rural" and "mutuelles régies par le code de la mutualité";*
— *in the case of Ireland: incorporated companies limited by shares or by guarantee or unlimited;*
— *in the case of the Italian Republic: "società per azioni";*
— *in the case of the Republic of Cyprus: "Εταιρε α Περιορισμνης Ευθνης με μετοχς" "Εταιρε α Περιορισμνης Ευθνης με εγηση";*
— *in the case of the Republic of Latvia: "akciju sabiedrība", "sabiedrība ar ierobežotu atbildību";*
— *in the case of the Republic of Lithuania: "akcin bendrov", "uždaroji akcin bendrov";*
— *in the case of the Grand Duchy of Luxembourg: "société anonyme", "société en commandite par actions", "association d'assurances mutuelles", "société coopérative";*
— *in the case of the Republic of Hungary: "biztosító részvénytársaság", "biztosító szövetkezet", "harmadik országbeli biztosító magyarországi fióktelepe";*
— *in the case of the Republic of Malta: "limited liability company/kumpannija tà responsabbiltà limitata";*
— *in the case of the Kingdom of the Netherlands: "naamloze vennootschap", "onderlinge waarborgmaatschappij";*
— *in the case of the Republic of Austria: "Aktiengesellschaft", "Versicherungsverein auf Gegenseitigkeit";*
— *in the case of the Republic of Poland: "spółka akcyjna", "towarzystwo ubezpieczeń wzajemnych";*
— *in the case of the Portuguese Republic: "sociedade anónima", "mútua de seguros";*
— *in the case of the Republic of Slovenia: "delniška družba";*
— *in the case of the Slovak Republic: "akciová spoločnost";*
— *in the case of the Republic of Finland: "keskinäinen vakuutusyhtiö/ömsesidigt försäkringsbolag", "vakuutusosakeyhtiö/försäkringsaktiebolag", "vakuutusyhdistys/försäkringsförening";*
— *in the case of the Kingdom of Sweden: "försäkringsaktiebolag", "ömsesidigt försäkringsbolag";*
— *in the case of the United Kingdom: incorporated companies limited by shares or by guarantee or unlimited, societies registered under the Industrial and Provident Societies Acts, societies registered or incorporated under the Friendly Societies Acts, "the association of underwriters known as Lloyd's".*

NOTES

Repealed as noted at the beginning of this Directive.

(*Annex II substitutes Directive 98/78/EC, Annexes I, II at* **[6123]**, **[6124]**.)

I. WINDING UP

COUNCIL DIRECTIVE

(2001/17/EC)

of 19 March 2001

on the reorganisation and winding-up of insurance undertakings

NOTES

Date of publication in OJ: OJ L110, 20.4.2001, p 28.

This Directive is repealed by European Parliament and Council Directive 2009/138/EC on the taking-up and pursuit of the business of Insurance and Reinsurance (Solvency II) at **[6153]** et seq, with effect from 1 November 2012 (see art 310 thereof at **[6462]**).

[6937]

THE EUROPEAN PARLIAMENT AND THE COUNCIL OF THE EUROPEAN UNION,

Having regard to the Treaty establishing the European Community, and in particular Articles 47(2) and 55 thereof,

Having regard to the proposal from the Commission,[1]

Having regard to the opinion of the Economic and Social Committee,[2]

Acting in accordance with the procedure laid down in Article 251 of the Treaty,[3]

Whereas:

(1) First Council Directive 73/239/EEC of 24 July 1973 on the coordination of laws, regulations and administrative provisions relating to the taking up and pursuit of the business of direct insurance other than life assurance,[4] *as supplemented by Directive 92/49/EEC,*[5] *and the First Council Directive 79/267/EEC of 5 March 1979 on the coordination of laws, regulations and administrative provisions relating to the taking up and pursuit of the business of direct life assurance,*[6] *as supplemented by Directive 92/96/EEC,*[7] *provide for a single authorisation of the insurance undertakings granted by the home Member State supervisory authority. This single authorisation allows the insurance undertaking to carry out its activities in the Community by means of establishment or free provision of services without any further authorisation by the host Member State and under the sole prudential supervision of the home Member State supervisory authorities.*

(2) The insurance directives providing a single authorisation with a Community scope for the insurance undertakings do not contain coordination rules in the event of winding-up proceedings. Insurance undertakings as well as other financial institutions are expressly excluded from the scope of Council Regulation (EC) No 1346/2000 of 29 May 2000 on insolvency proceedings.[8] *It is in the interest of the proper functioning of the internal market and of the protection of creditors that coordinated rules are established at Community level for winding-up proceedings in respect of insurance undertakings.*

(3) Coordination rules should also be established to ensure that the reorganisation measures, adopted by the competent authority of a Member State in order to preserve or restore the financial soundness of an insurance undertaking and to prevent as much as possible a winding-up situation, produce full effects throughout the Community. The reorganisation measures covered by this Directive are those affecting pre-existing rights of parties other than the insurance undertaking itself. The measures provided for in Article 20 of Directive 73/239/EEC and Article 24 of Directive 79/267/EEC should be included within the scope of this Directive provided that they comply with the conditions contained in the definition of reorganisation measures.

(4) This Directive has a Community scope which affects insurance undertakings as defined in Directives 73/239/EEC and 79/267/EEC which have their head office in the Community, Community branches of insurance undertakings which have their head office in third countries and creditors resident in the Community. This Directive should not regulate the effects of the reorganisation measures and winding-up proceedings vis-à-vis third countries.

(5) This Directive should concern winding-up proceedings whether or not they are founded on insolvency and whether they are voluntary or compulsory. It should apply to collective proceedings as defined by the home Member State's legislation in accordance with Article 9 involving the realisation of the assets of an insurance undertaking and the distribution of their proceeds. Winding-up proceedings which, without being founded on insolvency, involve for the payment of insurance claims a priority order in accordance with Article 10 should also be included in the scope of this Directive. Claims by the employees of an insurance undertaking arising from employment contracts and employment relationships should be capable of being subrogated to a national wage guarantee scheme; such subrogated claims should benefit from the treatment determined by the

home Member State's law (lex concursus) according to the principles of this Directive. The provisions of this Directive should apply to the different cases of winding-up proceedings as appropriate.

(6) The adoption of reorganisation measures does not preclude the opening of winding-up proceedings. Winding-up proceedings may be opened in the absence of, or following, the adoption of reorganisation measures and they may terminate with composition or other analogous measures, including reorganisation measures.

(7) The definition of branch, in accordance with existing insolvency principles, should take account of the single legal personality of the insurance undertaking. The home Member State's legislation should determine the way in which the assets and liabilities held by independent persons who have a permanent authority to act as agent for an insurance undertaking should be treated in the winding-up of an insurance undertaking.

(8) A distinction should be made between the competent authorities for the purposes of reorganisation measures and winding-up proceedings and the supervisory authorities of the insurance undertakings. The competent authorities may be administrative or judicial authorities depending on the Member State's legislation. This Directive does not purport to harmonise national legislation concerning the allocation of competences between such authorities.

(9) This Directive does not seek to harmonise national legislation concerning reorganisation measures and winding-up proceedings but aims at ensuring mutual recognition of Member States' reorganisation measures and winding-up legislation concerning insurance undertakings as well as the necessary cooperation. Such mutual recognition is implemented in this Directive through the principles of unity, universality, coordination, publicity, equivalent treatment and protection of insurance creditors.

(10) Only the competent authorities of the home Member State should be empowered to take decisions on winding-up proceedings concerning insurance undertakings (principle of unity). These proceedings should produce their effects throughout the Community and should be recognised by all Member States. All the assets and liabilities of the insurance undertaking should, as a general rule, be taken into consideration in the winding-up proceedings (principle of universality).

(11) The home Member State's law should govern the winding-up decision concerning an insurance undertaking, the winding-up proceedings themselves and their effects, both substantive and procedural, on the persons and legal relations concerned, except where this Directive provides otherwise. Therefore all the conditions for the opening, conduct and closure of winding-up proceedings should in general be governed by the home Member State's law. In order to facilitate its application this Directive should include a non-exhaustive list of aspects which, in particular, are subject to the general rule of the home Member State's legislation.

(12) The supervisory authorities of the home Member State and those of all the other Member States should be informed as a matter of urgency of the opening of winding-up proceedings (principle of coordination).

(13) It is of utmost importance that insured persons, policy-holders, beneficiaries and any injured party having a direct right of action against the insurance undertaking on a claim arising from insurance operations be protected in winding-up proceedings. Such protection should not include claims which arise not from obligations under insurance contracts or insurance operations but from civil liability caused by an agent in negotiations for which, according to the law applicable to the insurance contract or operation, the agent himself is not responsible under such insurance contract or operation. In order to achieve this objective Member States should ensure special treatment for insurance creditors according to one of two optional methods provided for in this Directive. Member States may choose between granting insurance claims absolute precedence over any other claim with respect to assets representing the technical provisions or granting insurance claims a special rank which may only be preceded by claims on salaries, social security, taxes and rights in rem over the whole assets of the insurance undertaking. Neither of the two methods provided for in this Directive impedes a Member State from establishing a ranking between different categories of insurance claims.

(14) This Directive should ensure an appropriate balance between the protection of insurance creditors and other privileged creditors protected by the Member State's legislation and not harmonise the different systems of privileged creditors existing in the Member States.

(15) The two optional methods for treatment of insurance claims are considered substantially equivalent. The first method ensures the affectation of assets representing the technical provisions to insurance claims, the second method ensures insurance claims a position in the ranking of creditors which not only affects the assets representing the technical provisions but all the assets of the insurance undertaking.

(16) Member States which, in order to protect insurance creditors, opt for the method of granting insurance claims absolute precedence with respect to the assets representing the technical provisions should require their insurance undertakings to establish and keep up to date a special register of such assets. Such a register is a useful instrument for identifying the assets affected to such claims.

(17) In order to strengthen equivalence between both methods of treatment of insurance claims,

this Directive should oblige the Member States which apply the method set out in Article 10(1)(b) to require every insurance undertaking to represent, at any moment and independently of a possible winding-up, claims, which according to that method may have precedence over insurance claims and which are registered in the insurance undertaking's accounts, by assets allowed by the insurance directives in force to represent the technical provisions.

(18) The home Member State should be able to provide that, where the rights of insurance creditors have been subrogated to a guarantee scheme established in such home Member State, claims by that scheme should not benefit from the treatment of insurance claims under this Directive.

(19) The opening of winding-up proceedings should involve the withdrawal of the authorisation to conduct business granted to the insurance undertaking unless such authorisation has previously been withdrawn.

(20) The decision to open winding-up proceedings, which may produce effects throughout the Community according to the principle of universality, should have appropriate publicity within the Community. In order to protect interested parties, the decision should be published in accordance with the home Member State's procedures and in the Official Journal of the European Communities and, further, by any other means decided by the other Member States' supervisory authorities within their respective territories. In addition to publication of the decision, known creditors who are resident in the Community should be individually informed of the decision and this information should contain at least the elements specified in this Directive. Liquidators should also keep creditors regularly informed of the progress of the winding-up proceedings.

(21) Creditors should have the right to lodge claims or to submit written observations in winding-up proceedings. Claims by creditors resident in a Member State other than the home Member State should be treated in the same way as equivalent claims in the home Member State without any discrimination on the grounds of nationality or residence (principle of equivalent treatment).

(22) This Directive should apply to reorganisation measures adopted by a competent authority of a Member State principles which are similar mutatis mutandis to those provided for in winding-up proceedings. The publication of such reorganisation measures should be limited to the case in which an appeal in the home Member State is possible by parties other than the insurance undertaking itself. When reorganisation measures affect exclusively the rights of shareholders, members or employees of the insurance undertaking considered in those capacities, the competent authorities should determine the manner in which the parties affected should be informed in accordance with relevant legislation.

(23) This Directive provides for coordinated rules to determine the law applicable to reorganisation measures and winding-up proceedings of insurance undertakings. This Directive does not seek to establish rules of private international law determining the law applicable to contracts and other legal relations. In particular, this Directive does not seek to govern the applicable rules on the existence of a contract, the rights and obligations of parties and the evaluation of debts.

(24) The general rule of this Directive, according to which reorganisation measures and the winding-up proceedings are governed by the law of the home Member State, should have a series of exceptions in order to protect legitimate expectations and the certainty of certain transactions in Member States other than the home Member State. Such exceptions should concern the effects of such reorganisation measures or winding-up proceedings on certain contracts and rights, third parties' rights in rem, reservations of title, set-off, regulated markets, detrimental acts, third party purchasers and lawsuits pending.

(25) The exception concerning the effects of reorganisation measures and winding-up proceedings on certain contracts and rights provided for in Article 19 should be limited to the effects specified therein and should not include any other issues related to reorganisation measures and winding-up proceedings such as the lodging, verification, admission and ranking of claims regarding such contracts and rights, which should be governed by the home Member State's legislation.

(26) The effects of reorganisation measures or winding-up proceedings on a lawsuit pending should be governed by the law of the Member States in which the lawsuit is pending concerning an asset or a right of which the insurance undertaking has been divested as an exception to the application of the law of the home Member State. The effects of such measures and proceedings on individual enforcement actions arising from these lawsuits should be governed by the home Member State's legislation, according to the general rule of this Directive.

(27) All persons required to receive or divulge information connected with the procedures of communication provided for in this Directive should be bound by professional secrecy in the same manner as that established in Article 16 of Directive 92/49/EEC and Article 15 of Directive 92/96/EEC, with the exception of any judicial authority to which specific national legislation applies.

(28) For the sole purpose of applying the provisions of this Directive to reorganisation measures and winding-up proceedings concerning branches situated in the Community of an insurance undertaking whose head office is located in a third country the home Member State should be defined as the Member State in which the branch is located and the supervisory authorities and competent

authorities as the authorities of that Member State.

(29) Where there are branches in more than one Member State of an insurance undertaking whose head office is located outside the Community, each branch should be treated independently with regard to the application of this Directive. In that case the competent authorities, supervisory authorities, administrators and liquidators should endeavour to coordinate their actions,

NOTES

Repealed as noted at the beginning of this Directive.

1 OJ C71, 19.3.1987, p 5, and OJ C253, 6.10.1989, p 3.

2 OJ C319, 30.11.1987, p 10.

3 Opinion of the European Parliament of 15 March 1989 (OJ C96, 17.4.1989, p 99), confirmed on 27 October 1999, Council Common Position of 9 October 2000 (OJ C344, 1.12.2000, p 23) and Decision of the European Parliament of 15 February 2001.

4 OJ L228, 16.8.1973, p 3. Directive as last amended by European Parliament and Council Directive 95/26/EC (OJ L168, 18.7.1995, p 7).

5 Council Directive 92/49/EEC of 18 June 1992 on the coordination of laws, regulations and administrative provisions relating to direct insurance other than life assurance and amending Directives 73/239/EEC and 88/357/EEC (third non-life insurance directive) (OJ L228, 11.8.1992, p 1).

6 OJ L63, 13.3.1979, p 1. Directive as last amended by Directive 95/26/EC.

7 Council Directive 92/96/EEC of 10 November 1992 on the coordination of laws, regulations and administrative provisions relating to direct life assurance and amending Directives 79/267/EEC and 90/619/EEC (third life assurance directive) (OJ L360, 9.12.1992, p 1).

8 OJ L160, 30.6.2000, p 1.

HAVE ADOPTED THIS DIRECTIVE—

TITLE I
SCOPE AND DEFINITIONS

[6938]
Article 1
Scope

1. This Directive applies to reorganisation measures and winding-up proceedings concerning insurance undertakings.

2. This Directive also applies, to the extent provided for in Article 30, to reorganisation measures and winding-up proceedings concerning branches in the territory of the Community of insurance undertakings having their head office outside the Community.

NOTES

Repealed as noted at the beginning of this Directive.

[6939]
Article 2
Definitions

For the purpose of this Directive—

(a) "insurance undertaking" means an undertaking which has received official authorisation in accordance with Article 6 of Directive 73/239/EEC or Article 6 of Directive 79/267/EEC;

(b) "branch" means any permanent presence of an insurance undertaking in the territory of a Member State other than the home Member State which carries out insurance business;

(c) "reorganisation measures" means measures involving any intervention by administrative bodies or judicial authorities which are intended to preserve or restore the financial situation of an insurance undertaking and which affect pre-existing rights of parties other than the insurance undertaking itself, including but not limited to measures involving the possibility of a suspension of payments, suspension of enforcement measures or reduction of claims;

(d) "winding-up proceedings" means collective proceedings involving realising the assets of an insurance undertaking and distributing the proceeds among the creditors, shareholders or members as appropriate, which necessarily involve any intervention by the administrative or the judicial authorities of a Member State, including where the collective proceedings are terminated by a composition or other analogous measure, whether or not they are founded on insolvency or are voluntary or compulsory;

(e) *"home Member State" means the Member State in which an insurance undertaking has been authorised in accordance with Article 6 of Directive 73/239/EEC or Article 6 of Directive 79/267/EEC;*

(f) *"host Member State" means the Member State other than the home Member State in which an insurance undertaking has a branch;*

(g) *"competent authorities" means the administrative or judicial authorities of the Member States which are competent for the purposes of the reorganisation measures or the winding-up proceedings;*

(h) *"supervisory authorities" means the competent authorities within the meaning of Article 1(k) of Directive 92/49/EEC and of Article 1(l) of Directive 92/96/EEC;*

(i) *"administrator" means any person or body appointed by the competent authorities for the purpose of administering reorganisation measures;*

(j) *"liquidator" means any person or body appointed by the competent authorities or by the governing bodies of an insurance undertaking, as appropriate, for the purpose of administering winding-up proceedings;*

(k) *"insurance claims" means any amount which is owed by an insurance undertaking to insured persons, policy holders, beneficiaries or to any injured party having direct right of action against the insurance undertaking and which arises from an insurance contract or from any operation provided for in Article 1(2) and (3), of Directive 79/267/EEC in direct insurance business, including amounts set aside for the aforementioned persons, when some elements of the debt are not yet known. The premiums owed by an insurance undertaking as a result of the non-conclusion or cancellation of these insurance contracts and operations in accordance with the law applicable to such contracts or operations before the opening of the winding-up proceedings shall also be considered insurance claims.*

NOTES

Repealed as noted at the beginning of this Directive.

Part VI European Materials

TITLE II
REORGANISATION MEASURES

[6940]
Article 3
Scope

This Title applies to the reorganisation measures defined in Article 2(c).

NOTES

Repealed as noted at the beginning of this Directive.

[6941]
Article 4
Adoption of reorganisation measures—applicable law

1. Only the competent authorities of the home Member State shall be entitled to decide on the reorganisation measures with respect to an insurance undertaking, including its branches in other Member States. The reorganisation measures shall not preclude the opening of winding-up proceedings by the home Member State.

2. The reorganisation measures shall be governed by the laws, regulations and procedures applicable in the home Member State, unless otherwise provided in Articles 19 to 26.

3. The reorganisation measures shall be fully effective throughout the Community in accordance with the legislation of the home Member State without any further formalities, including against third parties in other Member States, even if the legislation of those other Member States does not provide for such reorganisation measures or alternatively makes their implementation subject to conditions which are not fulfilled.

4. The reorganisation measures shall be effective throughout the Community once they become effective in the Member State where they have been taken.

NOTES

Repealed as noted at the beginning of this Directive.

[6942]
Article 5
Information to the supervisory authorities

The competent authorities of the home Member State shall inform as a matter of urgency the home Member State's supervisory authorities of their decision on any reorganisation measure, where possible before the adoption of such a measure and failing that immediately thereafter. The supervisory authorities of the home Member State shall inform as a matter of urgency the supervisory authorities of all other Member States of the decision to adopt reorganisation measures including the possible practical effects of such measures.

NOTES

Repealed as noted at the beginning of this Directive.

[6943]
Article 6
Publication

1. Where an appeal is possible in the home Member State against a reorganisation measure, the competent authorities of the home Member State, the administrator or any person entitled to do so in the home Member State shall make public its decision on a reorganisation measure in accordance with the publication procedures provided for in the home Member State and, furthermore, publish in the Official Journal of the European Communities at the earliest opportunity an extract from the document establishing the reorganisation measure. The supervisory authorities of all the other Member States which have been informed of the decision on a reorganisation measure pursuant to Article 5 may ensure the publication of such decision within their territory in the manner they consider appropriate.

2. The publications provided for in paragraph 1 shall also specify the competent authority of the home Member State, the applicable law as provided in Article 4(2) and the administrator appointed, if any. They shall be carried out in the official language or in one of the official languages of the Member State in which the information is published.

3. The reorganisation measures shall apply regardless of the provisions concerning publication set out in paragraphs 1 and 2 and shall be fully effective as against creditors, unless the competent authorities of the home Member State or the law of that State provide otherwise.

4. When reorganisation measures affect exclusively the rights of shareholders, members or employees of an insurance undertaking, considered in those capacities, this Article shall not apply unless the law applicable to these reorganisation measures provides otherwise. The competent authorities shall determine the manner in which the interested parties affected by such reorganisation measures shall be informed in accordance with the relevant legislation.

NOTES

Repealed as noted at the beginning of this Directive.

[6944]
Article 7
Information to known creditors—right to lodge claims

1. Where the legislation of the home Member State requires lodgement of a claim with a view to its recognition or provides for compulsory notification of a reorganisation measure to creditors who have their normal place of residence, domicile or head office in that State, the competent authorities of the home Member State or the administrator shall also inform known creditors who have their normal place of residence, domicile or head office in another Member State, in accordance with the procedures laid down in Articles 15 and 17(1).

2. Where the legislation of the home Member State provides for the right of creditors who have their normal place of residence, domicile or head office in that State to lodge claims or to submit observations concerning their claims, creditors who have their normal place of residence, domicile or head office in another Member State shall have the same right to lodge claims or submit observations in accordance with the procedures laid down in Articles 16 and 17(2).

NOTES

Repealed as noted at the beginning of this Directive.

TITLE III
WINDING-UP PROCEEDINGS

[6945]
Article 8
Opening of winding-up proceedings—information to the supervisory authorities

1. Only the competent authorities of the home Member State shall be entitled to take a decision concerning the opening of winding-up proceedings with regard to an insurance undertaking, including its branches in other Member States. This decision may be taken in the absence, or following the adoption, of reorganisation measures.

2. A decision adopted according to the home Member State's legislation concerning the opening of winding-up proceedings of an insurance undertaking, including its branches in other Member States, shall be recognised without further formality within the territory of all other Member States and shall be effective there as soon as the decision is effective in the Member State in which the proceedings are opened.

3. The supervisory authorities of the home Member State shall be informed as a matter of urgency of the decision to open winding-up proceedings, if possible before the proceedings are opened and failing that immediately thereafter. The supervisory authorities of the home Member State shall inform as a matter of urgency the supervisory authorities of all other Member States of the decision to open winding-up proceedings including the possible practical effects of such proceedings.

NOTES
Repealed as noted at the beginning of this Directive.

[6946]
Article 9
Applicable law

1. The decision to open winding-up proceedings with regard to an insurance undertaking, the winding-up proceedings and their effects shall be governed by the laws, regulations and administrative provisions applicable in its home Member State unless otherwise provided in Articles 19 to 26.

2. The law of the home Member State shall determine in particular—

- *(a) the assets which form part of the estate and the treatment of assets acquired by, or devolving on, the insurance undertaking after the opening of the winding-up proceedings;*
- *(b) the respective powers of the insurance undertaking and the liquidator;*
- *(c) the conditions under which set-off may be invoked;*
- *(d) the effects of the winding-up proceedings on current contracts to which the insurance undertaking is party;*
- *(e) the effects of the winding-up proceedings on proceedings brought by individual creditors, with the exception of lawsuits pending as provided for in Article 26;*
- *(f) the claims which are to be lodged against the insurance undertaking's estate and the treatment of claims arising after the opening of winding-up proceedings;*
- *(g) the rules governing the lodging, verification and admission of claims;*
- *(h) the rules governing the distribution of proceeds from the realisation of assets, the ranking of claims, and the rights of creditors who have obtained partial satisfaction after the opening of winding-up proceedings by virtue of a right in rem or through a set-off;*
- *(i) the conditions for and the effects of closure of winding-up proceedings, in particular by composition;*
- *(j) creditors' rights after the closure of winding-up proceedings;*
- *(k) who is to bear the cost and expenses incurred in the winding-up proceedings;*
- *(l) the rules relating to the voidness, voidability or unenforceability of legal acts detrimental to all the creditors.*

NOTES
Repealed as noted at the beginning of this Directive.

[6947]
Article 10
Treatment of insurance claims

1. Member States shall ensure that insurance claims take precedence over other claims on the insurance undertaking according to one or both of the following methods—

(a) *insurance claims shall, with respect to assets representing the technical provisions, take absolute precedence over any other claim on the insurance undertaking;*

(b) *insurance claims shall, with respect to the whole of the insurance undertaking's assets, take precedence over any other claim on the insurance undertaking with the only possible exception of—*

(i) *claims by employees arising from employment contracts and employment relationships,*

(ii) *claims by public bodies on taxes,*

(iii) *claims by social security systems,*

(iv) *claims on assets subject to rights in rem.*

2. *Without prejudice to paragraph 1, Member States may provide that the whole or a part of the expenses arising from the winding-up procedure, as defined by their national legislation, shall take precedence over insurance claims.*

3. *Member States which have opted for the method provided for in paragraph 1(a) shall require that insurance undertakings establish and keep up to date a special register in line with the provisions set out in the Annex.*

NOTES

Repealed as noted at the beginning of this Directive.

[6948]
Article 11
Subrogation to a guarantee scheme

The home Member State may provide that, where the rights of insurance creditors have been subrogated to a guarantee scheme established in that Member State, claims by that scheme shall not benefit from the provisions of Article 10(1).

NOTES

Repealed as noted at the beginning of this Directive.

[6949]
Article 12
Representation of preferential claims by assets

By way of derogation from Article 18 of Directive 73/239/EEC and Article 21 of Directive 79/267/EEC, Member States which apply the method set out in Article 10(1)(b) of this Directive shall require every insurance undertaking to represent, at any moment and independently from a possible winding-up, the claims which may take precedence over insurance claims pursuant to Article 10(1)(b) and which are registered in the insurance undertaking's accounts, by assets mentioned in Article 21 of Directive 92/49/EEC and Article 21 of Directive 92/96/EEC.

NOTES

Repealed as noted at the beginning of this Directive.

[6950]
Article 13
Withdrawal of the authorisation

1. *Where the opening of winding-up proceedings is decided in respect of an insurance undertaking, the authorisation of the insurance undertaking shall be withdrawn, except to the extent necessary for the purposes of paragraph 2, in accordance with the procedure laid down in Article 22 of Directive 73/239/EEC and Article 26 of Directive 79/267/EEC, if the authorisation has not been previously withdrawn.*

2. *The withdrawal of authorisation pursuant to paragraph 1 shall not prevent the liquidator or any other person entrusted by the competent authorities from carrying on some of the insurance undertakings' activities in so far as that is necessary or appropriate for the purposes of winding-up. The home Member State may provide that such activities shall be carried on with the consent and under the supervision of the supervisory authorities of the home Member State.*

NOTES

Repealed as noted at the beginning of this Directive.

[6951]
Article 14
Publication

1. The competent authority, the liquidator or any person appointed for that purpose by the competent authority shall publish the decision to open winding-up proceedings in accordance with the publication procedures provided for in the home Member State and also publish an extract from the winding-up decision in the Official Journal of the European Communities. The supervisory authorities of all the other Member States which have been informed of the decision to open winding-up proceedings in accordance with Article 8(3) may ensure the publication of such decision within their territories in the manner they consider appropriate.

2. The publication of the decision to open winding-up proceedings provided for in paragraph 1 shall also specify the competent authority of the home Member State, the applicable law and the liquidator appointed. It shall be in the official language or in one of the official languages of the Member State in which the information is published.

NOTES
Repealed as noted at the beginning of this Directive.

[6952]
Article 15
Information to known creditors

1. When winding-up proceedings are opened, the competent authorities of the home Member State, the liquidator or any person appointed for that purpose by the competent authorities shall without delay individually inform by written notice each known creditor who has his normal place of residence, domicile or head office in another Member State thereof.

2. The notice referred to in paragraph 1 shall in particular deal with time limits, the penalties laid down with regard to those time limits, the body or authority empowered to accept the lodgement of claims or observations relating to claims and the other measures laid down. The notice shall also indicate whether creditors whose claims are preferential or secured in rem need to lodge their claims. In the case of insurance claims, the notice shall further indicate the general effects of the winding-up proceedings on the insurance contracts, in particular, the date on which the insurance contracts or the operations will cease to produce effects and the rights and duties of insured persons with regard to the contract or operation.

NOTES
Repealed as noted at the beginning of this Directive.

[6953]
Article 16
Right to lodge claims

1. Any creditor who has his normal place of residence, domicile or head office in a Member State other than the home Member State, including Member States' public authorities, shall have the right to lodge claims or to submit written observations relating to claims.

2. The claims of all creditors who have their normal place of residence, domicile or head office in a Member State other than the home Member State, including the aforementioned authorities, shall be treated in the same way and accorded the same ranking as claims of an equivalent nature lodgeable by creditors who have their normal place of residence, domicile or head office in the home Member State.

3. Except in cases where the law of the home Member State allows otherwise, a creditor shall send copies of supporting documents, if any, and shall indicate the nature of the claim, the date on which it arose and the amount, whether he alleges preference, security in rem or reservation of title in respect of the claim and what assets are covered by his security. The precedence granted to insurance claims by Article 10 need not be indicated.

NOTES
Repealed as noted at the beginning of this Directive.

[6954]
Article 17
Languages and form

1. The information in the notice referred to in Article 15 shall be provided in the official language or one of the official languages of the home Member State. For that purpose a form shall be used bearing the heading "Invitation to lodge a claim; time limits to be observed" or, where the law of

Part VI European Materials

the home Member State provides for the submission of observations relating to claims, "Invitation to submit observations relating to a claim; time limits to be observed", in all the official languages of the European Union.

However, where a known creditor is a holder of an insurance claim, the information in the notice referred to in Article 15 shall be provided in the official language or one of the official languages of the Member State in which the creditor has his normal place of residence, domicile or head office.

2. Any creditor who has his normal place of residence, domicile or head office in a Member State other than the home Member State may lodge his claim or submit observations relating to his claim in the official language or one of the official languages of that other Member State. However, in that event the lodgement of his claim or the submission of observations on his claim, as appropriate, shall bear the heading "Lodgement of claim" or "Submission of observations relating to claims", as appropriate, in the official language or one of the official languages of the home Member State.

NOTES

Repealed as noted at the beginning of this Directive.

[6955]
Article 18
Regular information to the creditors

1. Liquidators shall keep creditors regularly informed, in an appropriate manner, in particular regarding the progress of the winding-up.

2. The supervisory authorities of the Member States may request information on developments in the winding-up procedure from the supervisory authorities of the home Member State.

NOTES

Repealed as noted at the beginning of this Directive.

TITLE IV
PROVISIONS COMMON TO REORGANISATION MEASURES AND WINDING-UP PROCEEDINGS

[6956]
Article 19
Effects on certain contracts and rights

By way of derogation from Articles 4 and 9, the effects of the opening of reorganisation measures or of winding-up proceedings on the contracts and rights specified below shall be governed by the following rules—

- *(a) employment contracts and employment relationships shall be governed solely by the law of the Member State applicable to the employment contract or employment relationship;*
- *(b) a contract conferring the right to make use of or acquire immovable property shall be governed solely by the law of the Member State in whose territory the immovable property is situated;*
- *(c) rights of the insurance undertaking with respect to immovable property, a ship or an aircraft subject to registration in a public register shall be governed by the law of the Member State under whose authority the register is kept.*

NOTES

Repealed as noted at the beginning of this Directive.

[6957]
Article 20
Third parties' rights in rem

1. The opening of reorganisation measures or winding-up proceedings shall not affect the rights in rem of creditors or third parties in respect of tangible or intangible, movable or immovable assets—both specific assets and collections of indefinite assets as a whole which change from time to time—belonging to the insurance undertaking which are situated within the territory of another Member State at the time of the opening of such measures or proceedings.

2. The rights referred to in paragraph 1 shall in particular mean—

- *(a) the right to dispose of assets or have them disposed of and to obtain satisfaction from the proceeds of or income from those assets, in particular by virtue of a lien or a mortgage;*

(b) *the exclusive right to have a claim met, in particular a right guaranteed by a lien in respect of the claim or by assignment of the claim by way of a guarantee;*
(c) *the right to demand the assets from, and/or to require restitution by, anyone having possession or use of them contrary to the wishes of the party so entitled;*
(d) *a right in rem to the beneficial use of assets.*

3. The right, recorded in a public register and enforceable against third parties, under which a right in rem within the meaning of paragraph 1 may be obtained, shall be considered a right in rem.

4. Paragraph 1 shall not preclude actions for voidness, voidability or unenforceability referred to in Article 9(2)(l).

NOTES

Repealed as noted at the beginning of this Directive.

[6958]
Article 21
Reservation of title

1. The opening of reorganisation measures or winding-up proceedings against an insurance undertaking purchasing an asset shall not affect the seller's rights based on a reservation of title where at the time of the opening of such measures or proceedings the asset is situated within the territory of a Member State other than the State in which such measures or proceedings were opened.

2. The opening of reorganisation measures or winding-up proceedings against an insurance undertaking selling an asset, after delivery of the asset, shall not constitute grounds for rescinding or terminating the sale and shall not prevent the purchaser from acquiring title where at the time of the opening of such measures or proceedings the asset sold is situated within the territory of a Member State other than the State in which such measures or proceedings were opened.

3. Paragraphs 1 and 2 shall not preclude actions for voidness, voidability or unenforceability referred to in Article 9(2)(l).

NOTES

Repealed as noted at the beginning of this Directive.

[6959]
Article 22
Set-off

1. The opening of reorganisation measures or winding-up proceedings shall not affect the right of creditors to demand the set-off of their claims against the claims of the insurance undertaking, where such a set-off is permitted by the law applicable to the insurance undertaking's claim.

2. Paragraph 1 shall not preclude actions for voidness, voidability or unenforceability referred to in Article 9(2)(l).

NOTES

Repealed as noted at the beginning of this Directive.

[6960]
Article 23
Regulated markets

1. Without prejudice to Article 20 the effects of a reorganisation measure or the opening of winding-up proceedings on the rights and obligations of the parties to a regulated market shall be governed solely by the law applicable to that market.

2. Paragraph 1 shall not preclude any action for voidness, voidability, or unenforceability referred to in Article 9(2)(l) which may be taken to set aside payments or transactions under the law applicable to that market.

NOTES

Repealed as noted at the beginning of this Directive.

[6961]
Article 24
Detrimental acts

Article 9(2)(l) shall not apply, where a person who has benefited from a legal act detrimental to all the creditors provides proof that—

(a) *the said act is subject to the law of a Member State other than the home Member State, and*

(b) *that law does not allow any means of challenging that act in the relevant case.*

NOTES

Repealed as noted at the beginning of this Directive.

[6962]

Article 25

Protection of third-party purchasers

Where, by an act concluded after the adoption of a reorganisation measure or the opening of winding-up proceedings, an insurance undertaking disposes, for a consideration, of—

(a) *an immovable asset,*

(b) *a ship or an aircraft subject to registration in a public register, or*

(c) *transferable or other securities whose existence or transfer presupposes entry in a register or account laid down by law or which are placed in a central deposit system governed by the law of a Member State,*

the validity of that act shall be governed by the law of the Member State within whose territory the immovable asset is situated or under whose authority the register, account or system is kept.

NOTES

Repealed as noted at the beginning of this Directive.

[6963]

Article 26

Lawsuits pending

The effects of reorganisation measures or winding-up proceedings on a pending lawsuit concerning an asset or a right of which the insurance undertaking has been divested shall be governed solely by the law of the Member State in which the lawsuit is pending.

NOTES

Repealed as noted at the beginning of this Directive.

[6964]

Article 27

Administrators and liquidators

1. The administrator's or liquidator's appointment shall be evidenced by a certified copy of the original decision appointing him or by any other certificate issued by the competent authorities of the home Member State.

A translation into the official language or one of the official languages of the Member State within the territory of which the administrator or liquidator wishes to act may be required. No legalisation or other similar formality shall be required.

2. Administrators and liquidators shall be entitled to exercise within the territory of all the Member States all the powers which they are entitled to exercise within the territory of the home Member State. Persons to assist or, where appropriate, represent administrators and liquidators may be appointed, according to the home Member State's legislation, in the course of the reorganisation measure or winding-up proceedings, in particular in host Member States and, specifically, in order to help overcome any difficulties encountered by creditors in the host Member State.

3. In exercising his powers according to the home Member State's legislation, an administrator or liquidator shall comply with the law of the Member States within whose territory he wishes to take action, in particular with regard to procedures for the realisation of assets and the informing of employees. Those powers may not include the use of force or the right to rule on legal proceedings or disputes.

NOTES

Repealed as noted at the beginning of this Directive.

[6965]

Article 28

Registration in a public register

1. The administrator, liquidator or any other authority or person duly empowered in the home Member State may request that a reorganisation measure or the decision to open winding-up proceedings be registered in the land register, the trade register and any other public register kept in the other Member States.

However, if a Member State prescribes mandatory registration, the authority or person referred to in subparagraph 1 shall take all the measures necessary to ensure such registration.

2. The costs of registration shall be regarded as costs and expenses incurred in the proceedings.

NOTES

Repealed as noted at the beginning of this Directive.

[6966]
Article 29
Professional secrecy

All persons required to receive or divulge information in connection with the procedures of communication laid down in Articles 5, 8 and 30 shall be bound by professional secrecy, in the same manner as laid down in Article 16 of Directive 92/49/EEC and Article 15 of Directive 92/96/EEC, with the exception of any judicial authorities to which existing national provisions apply.

NOTES

Repealed as noted at the beginning of this Directive.

[6967]
Article 30
Branches of third country insurance undertakings

1. Notwithstanding the definitions laid down in Article 2(e), (f) and (g) and for the purpose of applying the provisions of this Directive to the reorganisation measures and winding-up proceedings concerning a branch situated in a Member State of an insurance undertaking whose head office is located outside the Community—

- *(a) "home Member State" means the Member State in which the branch has been granted authorisation according to Article 23 of Directive 73/239/EEC and Article 27 of Directive 79/267/EEC, and*
- *(b) "supervisory authorities" and "competent authorities" mean such authorities of the Member State in which the branch was authorised.*

2. When an insurance undertaking whose head office is outside the Community has branches established in more than one Member State, each branch shall be treated independently with regard to the application of this Directive. The competent authorities and the supervisory authorities of these Member States shall endeavour to coordinate their actions. Any administrators or liquidators shall likewise endeavour to coordinate their actions.

NOTES

Repealed as noted at the beginning of this Directive.

[6968]
Article 31
Implementation of this Directive

1. Member States shall bring into force the laws, regulations and administrative provisions necessary to comply with this Directive before 20 April 2003. They shall forthwith inform the Commission thereof.

When Member States adopt these measures, they shall contain a reference to this Directive or shall be accompanied by such reference on the occasion of their official publication. The methods of making such reference shall be laid down by Member States.

2. National provisions adopted in application of this Directive shall apply only to reorganisation measures or winding-up proceedings adopted or opened after the date referred to in paragraph 1. Reorganisation measures adopted or winding-up proceedings opened before that date shall continue to be governed by the law that was applicable to them at the time of adoption or opening.

3. Member States shall communicate to the Commission the text of the main provisions of domestic law which they adopt in the field governed by this Directive.

NOTES

Repealed as noted at the beginning of this Directive.

[6969]
Article 32
Entry into force

This Directive shall enter into force on the day of its publication in the Official Journal of the European Communities.

NOTES

Repealed as noted at the beginning of this Directive.

[6970]
Article 33
Addressees

This Directive is addressed to the Member States.

NOTES

Repealed as noted at the beginning of this Directive.

Done at Brussels, 19 March 2001

ANNEX

SPECIAL REGISTER REFERRED TO IN ARTICLE 10(3)

[6971]
1. Every insurance undertaking must keep at its head office a special register of the assets used to cover the technical provisions calculated and invested in accordance with the home Member State's rules.

2. Where an insurance undertaking transacts both non-life and life business, it must keep at its head office separate registers for each type of business. However, where a Member State authorises insurance undertakings to cover life and the risks listed in points 1 and 2 of Annex A to Directive 73/239/EEC, it may provide that those insurance undertakings must keep a single register for the whole of their activities.

3. The total value of the assets entered, valued in accordance with the rules applicable in the home Member State, must at no time be less than the value of the technical provisions.

4. Where an asset entered in the register is subject to a right in rem in favour of a creditor or a third party, with the result that part of the value of the asset is not available for the purpose of covering commitments, that fact is recorded in the register and the amount not available is not included in the total value referred to in point 3.

5. Where an asset employed to cover technical provisions is subject to a right in rem in favour of a creditor or a third party, without meeting the conditions of point 4, or where such an asset is subject to a reservation of title in favour of a creditor or of a third party or where a creditor has a right to demand the set-off of his claim against the claim of the insurance undertaking, the treatment of such asset in case of the winding-up of the insurance undertaking with respect to the method provided for in Article 10(1)(a) shall be determined by the legislation of the home Member State except where Articles 20, 21 or 22 apply to that asset.

6. The composition of the assets entered in the register in accordance with points 1 to 5, at the time when winding-up proceedings are opened, must not thereafter be changed and no alteration other than the correction of purely clerical errors must be made in the registers, except with the authorisation of the competent authority.

7. Notwithstanding point 6, the liquidators must add to the said assets the yield therefrom and the value of the pure premiums received in respect of the class of business concerned between the opening of the winding-up proceedings and the time of payment of the insurance claims or until any transfer of portfolio is effected.

8. If the product of the realisation of assets is less than their estimated value in the registers, the liquidators must be required to justify this to the home Member States' competent authorities.

9. The supervisory authorities of the Member States must take appropriate measures to ensure full application by the insurance undertakings of the provisions of this Annex.

NOTES

Repealed as noted at the beginning of this Directive.

Index

A

ACCOUNTS
banking and insurance companies, preparation and modifications, **[3390]**
Companies Act 1985 provisions, **[3376]**
consolidated, **[6548]–[6550]**
EC Directive
annual and consolidated, **[6482]–[6555]**
individual, banking and insurance companies
balance sheet format, **[6488]–[6514]**
notes to accounts, **[6546]**, **[6547]**
preparation generally, **[3376]**
profit and loss account format, **[6487]**, **[6515]–[6526]**
valuation, EC Directive rules, **[6527]–[6545]**
Insurance Accounts Directive (Miscellaneous Insurance Undertakings) Regulations 1993, **[4067]–[4074]**
insurance business, ABI Statement of Recommended Practice on Accounting for, **[5126]–[5134]**
insurance company
general interpretation, **[4458]**
group accounts, **[4454]**
modifications, **[4455]**
individual accounts, **[4449]**, **[4450]**
accounting principles and rules, **[4451]**
interpretation, **[4453]**
notes to, **[4452]**
provisions, interpretation, **[4456]**, **[4457]**
insurance premium tax
periods/returns etc, **[3558]**, **[4088]–[4092]**
schemes, special, **[3575]**, **[4104]–[4112]**
insurance undertakings
industrial and provident societies, provisions applying, **[4472]**, **[4474]**
interpretation, **[4460]**
non-compliance, penalties for, **[4463]**
preparation of, **[4461]**
publication, **[4462]**
summary proceedings, **[4471]**
Interim Prudential Sourcebook: Insurers (IPRU(INS))
financial reporting, accounts and statements, **[2097]**

ACCOUNTS – *cont.*
Interim Prudential Sourcebook: Insurers (IPRU(INS)) – *cont.*
Lloyd's, Insurance Accounts Directive (Lloyd's Syndicate and Aggregate Accounts) Regulations 2004, **[4347]–[4364]**
reference date, change, **[2170]**
summary financial statements
Companies (Summary Financial Statement) Regulations 1995, **[4132]–[4133A]**
Companies (Summary Financial Statement) Regulations 2008, **[4446]–[4448]**
winding up, **[4229]**
ACTUARY
access to books etc, **[228]**
actuarial investigation, meaning, **[3382]**
appointment, authorised person, **[227]**
approved person, required function, appointed actuary (CF12), **[2163]**
business transfer scheme, banking/insurance, reduction of benefits when order made, **[81]**
disqualification, **[232]**, **[2219O]**
distribution of profits, investigation of insurance company with long term business, **[3382]**
FSA rules, modification/waiver, **[121]**
information to FSA
good faith etc, **[229]**
persons with close links, **[230]**
requirements, **[859]**, **[860]**
Lloyd's
approved person, required function (CF12B), **[2163]**
supervision, FSA Handbook, **[2157]**
misleading information, provision to, **[233]**
resignation, notice, **[231]**
supervision, FSA Handbook, **[2157]**
winding up, actuarial advice, **[4223]**
ADMINISTRATION ORDER
administrator
appointment by company/directors, **[250]**
duty, report to FSA, **[248]**
FSA participation
application, **[246]**
powers generally, **[246]–[250]**

ADMINISTRATION ORDER – *cont.*
insurers, legislation applicable
modifications, Insolvency Act/Rules 1986, **[852]–[856]**
mutual credit/set-off, **[855]**
Treasury, power to order, **[247]**
Northern Ireland. *See* NORTHERN IRELAND
publication, **[4280]**
ADVERTISEMENT
war risks, restriction on insurance against, **[3161]–[3166]**
AGENT
investments, dealing as, **[518]–[521]**
See also INVESTMENTS
AGREEMENTS
insurance business. *See* INSURANCE BUSINESS
regulated activity, in course. *See* REGULATED ACTIVITY
APPEALS
insurance tax premium, to Tribunal, **[3564]**, **[3565]**
Tribunal decision, from on point of law, **[110]**
Tribunal, reference to from Court of Appeal decision, leave required, **[110]**
APPOINTED REPRESENTATIVE
activities, exemption as regulated activities
generally, **[596]–[598A]**, **[2220]**
list, business to which applicable, **[597]**
annual report, **[2170]**
approved person, **[2163]**
contracts by authorised person, **[598]**, **[598A]**
FSA supervision, **[2165]**
insurance mediation, **[2221]**
APPROVED PERSONS
fit and proper test for approved persons (FIT), **[2045]–[2053]**
See also FIT AND PROPER TEST FOR APPROVED PERSONS (FIT): FSA HANDBOOK
regulated activity
authorisation not required, **[2220]**
conduct, statement/code, FSA
principles, **[64]**, **[65]**
publication, **[68]**
controlled functions, approval, FSA
application
determination, **[61]**
procedure, **[60]**, **[62]**
Tribunal, reference to, **[62]**
withdrawal, **[63]**
disciplinary powers, FSA
extent, **[66]**
policy statement, **[69]**, **[70]**
procedure, **[67]**
Tribunal, reference to, **[67]**
statements of principle and code of practice for approved persons (APER), **[2034]–[2044]**
See also STATEMENTS OF PRINCIPLE AND CODE OF PRACTICE FOR APPROVED PERSONS (APER): FSA HANDBOOK
supervision, FSA Handbook, **[2163]**
variation of Part IV permission, supervision, **[2159]**
ASSOCIATION OF BRITISH INSURERS
Codes of Practice and guidance, **[5041]–[5147]**
AUDITOR
access to books etc, **[228]**
appointment, authorised person, **[227]**
communications, **[649]**, **[650]**
disqualification, **[232]**, **[2219O]**
FSA rules re, modification/waiver, **[121]**
information to FSA
good faith etc, **[229]**
persons with close links, **[230]**
insurance undertaking, of
appointment, **[4464]**
audit authority, duty to notify
auditor, of, **[4468]**
non-compliance, penalties for, **[4470]**
undertaking, of, **[4469]**
functions, **[4465]**
industrial and provident societies, provisions applying, **[4472]**, **[4474]**
removal on improper grounds, **[4467]**
reports, signature, **[4466]**
summary proceedings, **[4471]**
internal audit, systems and control functions of approved person (CF15), **[2033]**
Lloyd's Return, examination, **[2176]**
misleading information, provision to, **[233]**
resignation, notice, **[231]**
supervision, FSA Handbook, **[2156]**
winding up, audit, **[4229]**
AUTHORISED PERSON
acting otherwise than in accordance, permission rights of action, **[621]**
actuary, appointment etc, **[227]–[233]**
See also ACTUARY
appointed representative and, contract, **[598]**, **[598A]**
auditor, appointment etc, **[227]–[233]**
See also AUDITOR
clients' money, handling by
constructive trustee, institution holding liability, when arises, **[112]**
FSA, rule-making power, **[112]**
collective investment scheme, permission to act as manager
FSA, powers to prohibit/restrict, **[113]**
control over
acquisition
acquirer, meaning, **[146]**
approval, **[151]**, **[152]**
list, circumstances, **[146]**
objection, **[153]**
control, meaning, **[146]**, **[159]**
improperly acquired shares
FSA powers, **[156]**
increase
controller, meaning, **[147]**
list, circumstances, **[147]**
interpretation, **[158G]**
notification, proposal to FSA
FSA, duty re, **[150]**
obligation, **[145]**

AUTHORISED PERSON – *cont.*
control over – *cont.*
notification, proposal to FSA – *cont.*
procedure, **[149]**
objection
acquisition, to, **[153]**
existing control, to, **[154]**
FSA, by, **[158A]**
notices, procedure, **[155]**
offences, **[158], [158F]**
reduction
controller, meaning, **[148]**
list, circumstances, **[148]**
notices, requirements for, **[158E]**
notification, procedure, **[157]**
obligation to notify FSA, **[158D]**
restriction notices, **[158B]**
sale of shares, order for, **[158C]**
controlled functions, approval, FSA
application
determination, **[61]**
procedure, **[60]**, **[62]**
Tribunal, reference to, **[62]**
withdrawal, **[63]**
reasonable care, duty, **[59]**
damages, right of action
principles for businesses (PRIN), **[2010]**
disciplinary measures, FSA
decision notice, **[175]**
financial penalties, **[173]**
policy statements, **[177]**, **[178]**
proposed, **[174]**
public censure, **[172]**, **[176]**
exempt from general prohibition, carrying on regulated activity, **[19]**
false claim, **[24]**
financial promotion, **[21]**
information re, public record
FSA, duty to maintain, **[234]**
list, persons classified as, **[31]**
Lloyd's as, **[202]**
See also LLOYD'S
permission to act as
acting without, effect, **[20]**
interim, **[20]**
notice, scope, **[848]–[851]**
requirement, **[20]**
sale of shares, order for, **[158C]**
See also PART IV PERMISSION; REGULATED ACTIVITY
AVIATION INSURANCE
commercial aircraft contracts, insurance premium tax not payable, **[3592]**
war risks, Marine and Aviation Insurance (War Risks) Act 1952, **[3173]–[3181]**

B

BANKING BUSINESS
financial reports, **[2170]**
BANKING BUSINESS – *cont.*
group and individual accounts, preparation, **[3376]**
transfers. *See* BUSINESS TRANSFERS
BANKRUPTCY
debt avoidance, provisions against, right of FSA to apply for order, **[263]**
FSA, petitioner, conditions, **[260]**
insurance, long-term contracts, treatment of assets on winding up, **[266]**
continuation, insurer in liquidation, **[264]**
liabilities, insurer, determination, **[267]**
reduction in value of contracts as alternative to winding up, **[265]**
rules, list, **[267]**
insurance premium tax liability, effect, **[3566]**
Lloyd's member, **[3361]**
motor vehicle insurance, third party liabilities
bankruptcy of insured or secured persons not to affect third party claims, **[3407]**
person other than FSA, petitioner
re individual carrying on regulated activity contravening general prohibition
FSA participation, proceedings, powers, **[262]**
insolvency practitioner, immediate report to FSA, **[261]**
See also WINDING UP
BODY CORPORATE
transactions excluded from regulated activity, conditions, **[2220]**
BUILDING SOCIETIES
Building Societies Commission
Chief Registrar, transferred functions, **[664]**
dissolution, **[659]**
FSMA 2000, application to transferred functions, **[667]**
transferred functions, **[653]–[658]**, **[666]**
Treasury, power to order transfer, function to FSA, **[223]**, **[226]**
controller, exemption, **[1030]**
financial reports, **[2170]**
Investor Protection Board
dissolution, **[661]**
Treasury, power to terminate, **[224]**
other mutual society, transfer to
application of provisions, **[4536]**
confirmation of, **[4542]**
distribution of funds, **[4540]**
regulated term, **[4541]**
distributions, application of provisions, **[4543]**
EEA mutual society, **[4552]**
false declarations, **[4546]**
holding mutual, membership of, **[4544]**
interpretation, **[4537]**
members, issue of statement or summary to, **[4547]–[4551]**
share rights, application of provisions, **[4543]**
successor company, formation of, **[4539]**
transfer resolution, **[4538]**
transfer statements, **[4548]**, **[4549]**
transfer summaries, **[4550]**

BUILDING SOCIETIES – *cont.*
other mutual society, transfer to – *cont.*
trustee account holders, protection of interests, **[4546]**
BUSINESS ANGEL-LED ENTERPRISE CAPITAL FUNDS
activities excluded as regulated activities, **[575]**
meaning, **[576]**
See also COLLECTIVE INVESTMENT SCHEME
BUSINESS TRANSFERS
banking business
FSMA 2000 order
applicants, requirements, **[76]**, **[824]**, **[825]**
application, **[75]**
effect, **[80]**
persons entitled to be heard, **[78]**
reduction, benefits
actuary, appointment, court, **[81]**
requirement, **[72]**
sanctions, court, **[79]**
outside UK, certification, **[337]**
reclaim fund scheme
activities of, **[325A]**
Authority, service of petition on, **[257]**
financial resources, certificate as to, **[337A]**
meaning, **[74A]**
scheme within definition, banking business transfer scheme, **[74]**
FSA supervision, **[2172]**
insurance business
FSA supervision, **[2172]**
FSMA 2000 order
applicants, requirements, **[76]**, **[820]–[823]**
application, **[75]**
effect, **[80]**
persons entitled to be heard, **[78]**
policyholders to whom rights apply, **[82]**
reduction, benefits
actuary, appointment, court, **[81]**
reinsurance contracts, notice of transfer, **[82A]**
requirement, **[72]**
right to terminate, **[81A]**
sanctions, court, **[79]**
outside UK
certification, **[83]**, **[336]**
effect, authorisation, other EEA States, **[84]**, **[338]**
FSA supervision, **[2172]**
Treasury, powers, **[85]**
scheme
reports, **[77]**
within definition, insurance business transfer scheme, **[73]**
insurance premium tax liability, **[3566]**

C

CHANNEL TUNNEL
contracts re, insurance tax premium not payable, **[3592]**
CIVIL PROCEEDINGS
jurisdiction, FSMA 2000, **[302]**
CLEARING HOUSE
recognised, authorisation unnecessary to carry on regulated activity, **[2220]**
CLIENT ASSETS (CASS)
application, **[2126]**
client money and mandates, insurance mediation activity, **[2130]**
client money distribution, **[2132A]**
client money: MIFID business, **[2132]**
collateral, **[2128]**
custody, MIFID business, **[2131]**
damages, action for, **[2139]**
fees and payments, **[2137]**
general provisions, **[2126]**
mandates, **[2133]**
powers exercised, **[2138]**
record keeping requirements, **[2136]**
rules that can be waived, **[2140]**
transitional provisions, **[2134]**, **[2135]**
CLOSE LINKS
annual report, **[2170]**
controllers, FSA supervision, **[2164]**
threshold conditions, **[2026]**, **[2170]**
CODES
employers' liability, tracing insurance policies, Code of Practice, DETR, **[5148]–[5151]**
genetic testing, ABI Code of Practice, **[5092]–[5096]**
market identifier, transaction reporting, **[2171]**
mortgage endowment policy reviews, ABI Code of Practice, **[5044]**
CO-INSURANCE, COMMUNITY
EC Directive, coordination laws and administrative provisions, **[6701]–[6713]**
COLLECTIVE INVESTMENT SCHEME
authorisation, **[331]**
authorised person, manage
FSA, restrictive powers, **[113]**
enforcement, FSA powers, **[2219N]**
establishment etc, **[2220]**
inquiry, independent, Treasury, powers, **[14]**
See also BUSINESS ANGEL-LED ENTERPRISE CAPITAL FUNDS
COMMISSION
insurers' commission clawback, notification to FSA, **[2169]**
COMMITTEE OF EUROPEAN INSURANCE AND OCCUPATIONAL PENSIONS SUPERVISORS
establishment of, **[6144]–[6152I]**

COMPENSATION
FSA scheme, **[179]–[191]**, **[611]–[614]**
See also FINANCIAL SERVICES COMPENSATION SCHEME
guidance. *See* COMPENSATION SOURCEBOOK (COMP)
International Oil Pollution Compensation Fund, **[3603]**
Motor Insurers' Bureau
victims, untraced/uninsured drivers, **[5021]–[5036]**
See also MOTOR VEHICLE INSURANCE
unenforceable agreement in course, regulated activity, **[28]**
COMPENSATION SOURCEBOOK (COMP)
assignment of rights, **[2190]**
calculation of, **[2195]**
damages, actions for, **[2203]**
EEA firms, participation by, **[2197]**
eligible claimants, **[2188]**
fees and required payments, **[2201]**
firms accepting deposits, disclosure requirements, **[2197B]**
FSCS, **[2185]**
funding, **[2196]**
introduction and overview, **[2184]**
limit on amount, **[2193]**
notification requirements, **[2200]**
payment, **[2194]**
time limits and postponement, **[2192]**
persons in default, relevant, **[2189]**
powers exercised, **[2202]**
protected claims, **[2188]**
qualifying conditions, **[2186]**
record keeping requirements, **[2199]**
rejection of application and withdrawal of offer, **[2191]**
rules that can be waived, **[2204]**
special situations, **[2197A]**
transitional provisions, **[2198]**
COMPETITION
Competition Commission, role, **[343]**
Treaty on functioning of European Union, rules applicable to undertakings, **[6013]**
COMPLAINTS
distance marketing, as to, **[4338]**
transitional provisions FSMA 2000
after commencement about acts/omissions before commencement, **[915]**
determination, **[918]**
exemption, liability, damages, **[920]**
fees, **[919]**
funding, **[919]**
generally, **[914]–[924]**
information held by person operating former scheme, **[923]**
privilege, **[921]**
procedure, **[916]**
records, **[922]**
reporting, **[922]**
scheme rules, **[917]**
CONSUMER CREDIT
Ombudsman scheme
funding, **[200A]**
jurisdiction, **[193A]**, **[348A]**
CONSUMER PANEL
establishment, FSA, **[10]**
FSA, duty to consider representations, **[11]**
purpose, **[10]**
CONSUMER PROTECTION
consumer, meaning, **[5]**, **[14]**, **[111]**
EEA firm, Consumer Credit Act business
Office of Fair Trading, powers to
prohibit, **[170]**
restrict, **[171]**
FSA regulatory objective, **[5]**
Treaty firm, Consumer Credit Act business
Office of Fair Trading, powers to
prohibit, **[170]**
restrict, **[171]**
unfair contract terms
breach of contract, effect, **[3324]**
choice of law clauses, **[3342]**
dealing as consumer, **[3327]**
evasion by means, secondary contract, **[3325]**
exemption clauses, **[3328]**
'guarantee', consumer goods, **[3321]**
international supply contracts, **[3341]**
liability arising in contract, **[3319]**
negligence
liability, **[3318]**
meaning, **[3317]**
reasonableness, test, **[3326]**, **[3348]**
sale/supply, goods, liability arising, **[3321]–[3323]**
sea carriage, passengers, temporary provision, **[3343]**
Unfair Contract Terms Act 1977, **[3317]–[3348]**
Unfair Terms in Consumer Contracts Regulations 1999, **[4193]–[4210]**
unreasonable indemnity clauses, **[3320]**
unfair trading, protection from
interpretation, **[4476]**
offences
aggressive commercial practices, **[4485]**
bodies of persons, committed by, **[4489]**
default of other person, due to, **[4490]**
due diligence defence, **[4491]**
innocent publication of advertisement defence, **[4492]**
misleading omissions, **[4484]**
misleading practices, **[4483]**
penalty for, **[4487]**
time limit for prosecutions, **[4488]**
unfair commercial practices, **[4482]**, **[4486]**, **[4493]**
prohibitions
aggressive commercial practices, **[4481]**
misleading omissions, **[4480]**
misleading practices, **[4479]**
promotion of unfair commercial practices, **[4478]**

CONSUMER PROTECTION – *cont.*
unfair trading, protection from – *cont.*
prohibitions – *cont.*
unfair commercial practices, **[4477]**, **[4493]**
See also DISTANCE MARKETING
CONTRACT OF INSURANCE. *SEE* INSURANCE BUSINESS
CONTRACTUAL OBLIGATIONS
law applying to
absence of choice, in, **[6098AE]**
burden of proof, **[6098AS]**
carriage, contracts of, **[6098AF]**
consent and material validity, **[6098AK]**
consumer contracts, **[6098AG]**
contractual subrogation, **[6098AO]**
formal validity, **[6098AL]**
freedom of choice, **[6098AD]**
habitual residence, place of, **[6098AT]**
incapacity, in case of, **[6098AN]**
individual employment contracts, **[6098AI]**
insurance contracts, **[6098AH]**
legal subrogation, **[6098AP]**
multiple liability, **[6098AQ]**
overriding mandatory provisions, **[6098AJ]**
public policy of forum, **[6098AV]**
scope of, **[6098AM]**
set-off, **[6098AR]**
states with more than one legal system, **[6098AW]**
voluntary assignment, **[6098AO]**
Rome I Regulation
contract of insurance, application to, **[1033]**
existing international conventions, relationship with, **[6098AZ]**, **[6098BA]**
final provisions, **[6098BD]**
habitual residence, place of, **[6098AT]**
other law, relationship with, **[6098AX]**
preamble, **[6098AA]**
public policy of forum, **[6098AV]**
renvoi, exclusion of, **[6098AU]**
review clause, **[6098BB]**
Rome Convention, relationship with, **[6098AY]**
scope, **[6098AB]**, **[6098AC]**
states with more than one legal system, **[6098AW]**
uniform rules, **[6098AD]–[6098AS]**
CONTROLLERS
annual report, **[2170]**
close links, FSA supervision, **[2164]**
exemption
authorised building societies, **[1030]**
calculations matters affecting, **[1028]**
friendly societies, **[1031]**
interpretation, **[1027]**
non-directive firms, **[1029]**
CREDIT
contracts re
insurance tax premium not payable, **[3592]**
insurance tax premium, **[3559]**, **[4093]–[4095]**
CREDIT UNIONS
financial report to FSA, **[2170]**
regulated activities, transitional exemption, **[595F]**
CREDIT UNIONS – *cont.*
transfer of functions to FSA, Treasury powers, **[225]**, **[226]**
CRIME. *SEE* FINANCIAL CRIME; OFFENCES; PROCEEDS OF CRIME
CRITICAL ILLNESS COVER
ABI statement of best practice, **[5078]–[5087]**
managing claims, ABI Code of Practice, **[5124]**, **[5125]**

D

DAMAGES
FSA, exemption, liability, **[324]**, **[335]**
FSA rules, contravention
actionable, private person, **[123]**
misrepresentation, for, **[3185]**
Ombudsman scheme, exemption, liability, **[347]**
professional firms, **[2217]**
regulated activity, prohibition order, breach, statutory duty
actionable, private person, **[71]**
rights of action re regulated activity
authorised person acting otherwise than in accordance, permission, **[621]**
incoming firms, **[624]**
private person
meaning, **[620]**, **[623]**
prohibition orders and performance, controlled function, **[622]**
DATA PROTECTION
accessible record, meaning, **[3642BN]**
application of Act, **[3619]**
assessment notice
code of practice, **[3642AKC]**
limitations, **[3642AKB]**
service of, **[3642AKA]**
data controller
duty to make information available, **[3637]**
failure to comply with requirements, compensation for, **[3626]**
meaning, **[3615]**
notification by, **[3631]**
changes, duty as to, **[3633]**
offences, **[3634]**
preliminary assessment, **[3635]**
register of notifications, **[3632]**
registrable particulars, meaning, **[3629]**
data, meaning, **[3615]**
data processor, meaning, **[3615]**
data subject, meaning, **[3615]**
definitions, **[3615]**, **[3642BO]**, **[3642BP]**
electronic means, transmission of notices by, **[3642BJ]**
enforcement notice
appeals, **[3642AR]**, **[3642AS]**
cancellation, **[3642AK]**
contravention, in respect of, **[3642AJ]**
failure to comply with, **[3642AQ]**
service of, **[3642AJ]**
fees regulations, **[3639]**

DATA PROTECTION – *cont.*
Information Commissioner. *See* INFORMATION COMMISSIONER
information notice
appeals, **[3642AR]**, **[3642AS]**
failure to comply with, **[3642AQ]**
service of, **[3642AM]**
special, **[3642AN]**
Information Tribunal. *See* INFORMATION TRIBUNAL
jurisdiction and procedure, **[3628]**
monetary penalty notices
enforcement, **[3642BC]**
further provision, **[3642BD]**
guidance as to, **[3642BB]**
meaning, **[3642AZ]**
procedural rights, **[3642BA]**
services, power of, **[3642AZ]**
offences
directors, liability of, **[3642BI]**
entry and inspection, powers of, **[3642CG]**
prosecutions and penalties, **[3642BH]**
orders, regulations and rules, **[3642BM]**
personal data
assessment, request for, **[3642AL]**
exemptions
confidential references, **[3642CB]**
corporate finance, **[3642CB]**
crime and taxation, **[3642]**
domestic purposes, **[3642AF]**
further, power to make, **[3642AH]**
information available by or under enactment, **[3642AC]**
law, disclosures required by, **[3642AD]**
legal proceedings, disclosures made in connection with, **[3642AD]**
legal professional privilege, **[3642CB]**
management forecasts, **[3642CB]**
national security purposes, **[3641]**
negotiations, **[3642CB]**
Parliamentary privilege, **[3642AE]**
preliminary provisions, **[3640]**
regulatory activity, **[3642AA]**
research, history and statistics, **[3642AB]**
self-incrimination, **[3642CB]**
health records, **[3642BF]**
meaning, **[3615]**
processing, conditions, **[3642BW]**
rectification, blocking, erasure and destruction, **[3627]**
right of access to, **[3621]**, **[3622]**
production of certain records, prohibition of requirement, **[3642BE]**
sensitive personal
meaning, **[3616]**
processing, conditions, **[3642BX]**
special purposes
determination as to, **[3642AO]**
restrictions on enforcement, **[3642AP]**
transfer outside EU, **[3642BY]**
transitional relief, **[3642CC]–[4642CF]**
unlawful obtaining of, **[3642AY]**

DATA PROTECTION – *cont.*
principles
first, relevant conditions, **[3642BW]**, **[3642BX]**
interpretation, **[3642BV]**
list of, **[3642BU]**
references to, **[3617]**
processing
assessable, **[3635]**
automated decision making, rights in relation to, **[3625]**
direct marketing, right to prevent for purposes of, **[3624]**
likely to cause damage or distress, right to prevent, **[3623]**
meaning, **[3615]**
registration, without, **[3630]**
relevant conditions, **[3642BW]**, **[3642BX]**
Scotland, exercise of rights by children in, **[3642BL]**
special purposes, meaning, **[3617]**
supervisors, power to make provision for appointment, **[3636]**
transitional provisions and savings, **[3642CI]**
DEPOSIT
acceptance
in breach, general prohibition, regulated activity, **[29]**
specified activity, **[2220]**
whether doing so as regulated activity by way of business, **[592]**
specified investment, **[2220]**
DIRECTOR, COMPANY
liability, protection, **[3384]**
DISABILITY DISCRIMINATION
Disability Discrimination Act 1995, **[3607]–[3609]**
employment, **[3607]**
goods/facilities/services, **[3608]**
insurance services, **[3607]**
DISCLOSURE
competition information, **[238]**
confidential information, by FSA
exceptions to restrictions, **[236]**
restrictions, **[235]**
FSA control of information rules, **[120]**, **[121]**
Inland Revenue, by, **[237]**
market abuse, protected, **[104]**
medical information, **[5109]–[5123]**
offences, **[239]**
privilege
complaints procedure, transitional provisions FSMA 2000, **[921]**
professional firms, **[2208]**
protected items
meaning, **[300]**
no requirement to produce/ disclose/permit inspection, FSMA 2000, **[300]**
third party, qualifying indemnity provisions, **[3386]**
Treasury, power to remove restrictions, **[240]**
winding up proceedings
EEA regulator, confidential information from, **[4285]**

DISCLOSURE – *cont.*
winding up proceedings – *cont.*
third country insurer, confidential information, **[4319]**
DISHONESTY
financial crime, **[6]**
DISTANCE MARKETING
cancellation, contract
automatic
attached distance contract, **[4332]**
exceptions to right, **[4331]**
period, **[4330]**
right, **[4329]**
complaints, consideration, **[4338]**
contracting-out, prevention, **[4336]**
enforcement authorities, **[4337]**
FSA, function, **[4343]**
financial services marketed by intermediary, **[4326]**
generally, **[4321]–[4346]**
information
publication, **[4341]**
required prior to conclusion, contract, **[4327]**, **[4345]**
voice telephone communications, **[4346]**
written and additional, **[4328]**
injunction to secure compliance with regulations, **[4339]**
offences, **[4342]**
payment, services provided before cancellation, **[4333]**
professional firms, **[2209]**
undertakings and orders, notification to OFT, **[4340]**
unsolicited services, **[4335]**
DISTRIBUTION, PROFITS AND ASSETS
assets, company, restriction, **[3378]**
banking/insurance companies, by, **[3383]**
insurance company with long term business
actuarial investigation, **[3382]**
realised profits, **[3382]**
investment companies, **[3379]**, **[3380]**

E

ELECTRONIC COMMERCE
Electronic Communications Act 2000, **[3655]–[3662]**
electronic signature etc, **[3655]**
facilitation, **[3655]–[3659]**
financial promotion
exempt communications, all controlled activities
incoming, **[989]**
mere conduits/caching/hosting, **[985]**
incoming ECA providers, transactions not regulated activities, conditions, **[2220]**
insurance mediation activities, E-Commerce Directive, **[2221]**
key escrow requirements, prohibition, **[3660]**
ELECTRONIC MONEY
dematerialised instructions re investments, **[2220]**
ELMI, financial report to FSA, **[2170]**
issue
specified activity, **[2220]**
specified investment, **[2220]**
EMPLOYMENT
disability discrimination, **[3607]**
employee share schemes
exemption as regulated activity, **[2220]**
employers' liability
Employers' Liability (Compulsory Insurance) Act 1969, **[3189]–[3195]**
Employers' Liability (Compulsory Insurance) Regulations 1998, **[4180]–[4191]**
tracing insurance policies, DETR Code of Practice, **[5148]–[5151]**
Employment Rights Act 1996, **[3610]**, **[3611]**
winding up of UK insurer, effect on EEA employment contract, **[4307]**
ENERGY MARKET PARTICIPANTS
waiver, form, **[2174]**
EC COMPANIES. *SEE* TRANSITIONAL PROVISIONS FSMA 2000
EC DIRECTIVES. *SEE* EUROPEAN MATERIALS
EEA FIRM
authorisation, **[333]**, **[334]**
qualification for, **[2167]**
compensation scheme, participation in, **[2197]**
Consumer Credit Act business
Office of Fair Trading, powers to
prohibit, **[170]**
restrict, **[171]**
EEA passport rights, exercise, generally. *See* EEA PASSPORT RIGHTS
financial reports, **[2170]**
home state regulator, meaning, **[312]**
incoming, FSA supervision, **[2168]**
intervention by FSA
additional procedure, certain cases, **[166]**
contravention, requirement imposed by FSA, **[169]**
generally, **[160]–[169]**
incoming firm, as, **[160]**, **[2168]**
injunction, application, court, FSA
certain overseas insurance companies, **[165]**
power of intervention, FSA
general grounds, exercise, **[161]**
in support, overseas regulator, **[162]**
meaning, **[163]**
procedure on exercise, **[164]**
rescission, requirements, **[167]**
variation, requirements, **[167]**
regulated activity, authorisation, termination, **[34]**
reinsurers, **[2177]**
winding up, court
FSA, no power to petition, **[256]**
generally. *See* WINDING UP
EEA PASSPORT RIGHTS
definitions, **[328]**, **[633]**
e-commerce, **[2177]**, **[2221]**

EEA PASSPORT RIGHTS – *cont.*
exercise by
EEA firms
approval, controlled functions, **[639]**
cessation, regulated activities, UK
cancellation, qualification for authorisation, **[638]**
changes, insurance firms
branch details, **[636]**
services, **[637]**
consent notice, establishment, branch, **[634]**
generally, **[329]**, **[634]**–**[639]**
regulator's notice, provision, services, **[635]**
UK firms, outside UK
branch, establishment
partly completed procedures, **[2166]**
changes, insurance firms
branch details, **[640]**–**[642]**, **[2166]**
failure to notify, offences, **[645]**
services, **[643]**, **[644]**, **[2166]**
FSA supervision, **[2166]**
generally, **[37]**, **[330]**, **[640]**–**[646]**, **[2166]**, **[2177]**
scope, outward passport, **[646]**
services, provision, **[2166]**
FSA guidance, **[2177]**
freedom to provide services, **[2177]**
generally, **[633]**–**[648]**, **[2166]**, **[2177]**
insurance mediation, **[2221]**
interpretative communications, **[2177]**
EEA STATES
insurance business transfer from UK to, **[84]**
EFTA FIRMS
FSA implementation of third country decisions, Treasury directions, **[296]**
EUROPEAN MATERIALS
Committee of European Insurance and Occupational Pensions Supervisors, establishment, **[6144]**–**[6152]**
EC Directives
accounts of insurance undertakings, annual and consolidated, **[6482]**–**[6555]**
agreements, decisions and concerted practices, insurance sector
application of Article 81(3) of the Treaty, Commission Regulation, **[6130]**–**[6143]**
application of Article 85(3) of the Treaty, **[6099]**–**[6106]**
co-insurance, coordination of laws and administrative provisions, **[6701]**–**[6713]**
direct insurance other than life assurance business
administrative provisions re taking-up/pursuit
coordination, laws etc, **[6643]**–**[6692]**, **[6714]**–**[6721]**, **[6760]**–**[6799]**, **[6872]**–**[6936]**
Directive. *See* SOLVENCY II DIRECTIVE
freedom of establishment
restrictions, abolition, **[6693]**–**[6700]**
freedom to provide services
coordination, laws etc, **[6734]**–**[6759]**

EUROPEAN MATERIALS – *cont.*
EC Directives – *cont.*
direct insurance other than life assurance business – *cont.*
reinsurance
amendments and proposals, **[6872]**–**[6936]**
supplementary supervision, **[6107]**–**[6124]**
solvency margin requirements, **[6125]**–**[6129]**
supplementary supervision, **[6107]**–**[6124]**
Swiss Confederation and EEC, agreement, terms etc, **[6021]**–**[6024]**, **[6025]**–**[6090]**, **[6091]**–**[6094]**
European Insurance and Occupational Pensions Committee, **[6095]**–**[6098]**
freedom of establishment, abolition of restrictions, **[6866]**–**[6871]**, **[6693]**–**[6700]**
freedom to provide services
direct insurance business, **[6734]**–**[6759]**
reinsurance/retrocession
restrictions, abolition, **[6866]**–**[6871]**
guarantees, short-term transactions (political risks) with public/private buyers
harmonisation, basic provisions, **[6014]**–**[6020]**
insurance group, insurance undertakings, supplementary supervision, **[6107]**–**[6124]**
insurance mediation, **[6800]**–**[6817]**
legal expenses insurance, coordination of laws etc, **[6722]**–**[6733]**
life assurance, taking up business of, **[6556]**–**[6642]**
motor vehicle insurance, approximation of laws, **[6848]**–**[6852]**, **[6853]**–**[6865U]**
reinsurance
amendments, **[6872]**–**[6936]**
supplementary supervision, **[6107]**–**[6124]**
reorganisation, insurance undertakings, **[6936]**–**[6971]**
tourist assistance, direct insurance business, **[6714]**–**[6721]**
EC Regulation, application of Article 81(3) to insurance agreements, **[6130]**–**[6143]**
proposed EC Directives
reinsurance, **[6872]**–**[6936]**
Treaty on functioning of European Union
competition rules applicable to undertakings, **[6013]**
free movement
capital and payments, **[6008]**–**[6011]**
services, **[6001]**–**[6007]**
EXCHANGE LOSSES
contracts, insurance tax premium not payable, **[3592]**

F

FINANCIAL CONGLOMERATE
financial report, member, to FSA, **[2170]**

FINANCIAL CRIME
financial promotion, contravention, restrictions, **[25]**
meaning, **[6]**
offence, meaning, **[6]**
reduction, financial crime
FSA regulatory objective, **[6]**
regulated activity, contravention, general prohibition, offence, **[23]**
regulated person, meaning, **[6]**
FINANCIAL MARKET
information re
misconduct/misuse
financial crime, **[6]**
FINANCIAL PROMOTION
contravention, restrictions, offence, **[25]**
controlled activities
exempt communications
all, **[977]–[989]**
certain, **[994]–[1020]**
meaning, **[968]**, **[1021]**
controlled investments, meaning, **[968]**, **[1022]**
exempt communications, all controlled activities
company director etc, promotion broadcast, **[988]**
customers/potential customers, from, **[978]**
electronic commerce
incoming, **[989]**
mere conduits/caching/hosting, **[985]**
exempt persons, **[981]**
follow-up non-real time communications/solicited real time communications, **[979]**
generally, **[977]–[989]**
generic promotions, **[982]**
introductions, **[980]**
investment professionals, **[986]**
journalists, by, **[987]**
mere conduits, **[984]**, **[985]**
overseas recipients, to, **[977]**
unauthorised persons, caused to be made/directed by, **[983]**
exempt communications, certain controlled activities
advice centres, **[1020]**
associations of high net worth/sophisticated investors, **[1015]**
central banks etc, by, **[1003]**
certified high net worth individuals, **[1011]**, **[1024]**
common interest group of a company, **[1016]**
EEA States other than UK, nationals, **[1005]**
financial markets, **[1006]**
generally, **[994]–[1020]**
governments, by, **[1003]**
group companies, **[1009]**
high net worth companies, **[1012]**
industrial and provident societies, **[1004]**
joint enterprises, **[1008]**
one off non-real time, **[995]**
one off unsolicited real time, **[996]**
FINANCIAL PROMOTION – *cont.*
exempt communications, certain controlled activities – *cont.*
overseas communicators
non-real time to previously overseas customers, **[1000]**
solicited real time, **[999]**
unsolicited real time to
knowledgeable customers, **[1002]**
previously overseas customers, **[1001]**
pension products offered by employers, **[1019]**
persons in business of
disseminating information, **[1010]**
placing promotional material, **[1007]**
persons placing promotional material in particular publications, **[1017]**
real time
introductions re qualifying credit, **[997]**
required/authorised by enactments, **[998]**
sale of goods, **[1018]**
self-certified sophisticated investors, **[1014]**
solicited real time, **[995]**, **[999]**
sophisticated investors, **[1013]**
supply of services, **[1018]**
unincorporated associations etc, **[1012]**
exempt communications, deposits/insurance
relevant insurance activity
interpretation, **[990]**
non-real time, **[991]**
non-real time, reinsurance/large risks, **[992]**
real time, **[993]**
exemptions, application etc
combination, different exemptions, **[976]**
degree of prominence to be given to required indications, **[974]**
interpretation
communications, **[970]**
outgoing electronic commerce communications, **[973]**
real time communications, **[971]**
solicited/unsolicited real time communications, **[972]**
qualifying contracts of insurance, **[975]**
FSA, powers, **[118]**
generally, **[966]–[1024]**
investments
acting/not acting in the course of business
Treasury, power to specify circumstances, **[21]**
controlled activity, meaning, **[21]**
offence, contravention, restrictions, **[25]**
outside UK, originating, **[21]**
restrictions generally, **[21]**
PERG, **[2223]**
principles for businesses (PRIN), FSA Handbook
application to communications/approval, **[2004]**
generally. *See* PRINCIPLES FOR BUSINESSES (PRIN): FSA HANDBOOK

FINANCIAL SERVICES AND MARKETS TRIBUNAL
appeal
Court of Appeal decision, from, leave required, **[110]**
Tribunal decision, from on point of law, **[110]**
decisions, **[106A]**
establishment, **[105]**
functions, **[105]**
legal assistance scheme
funding, **[109]**
Lord Chancellor, powers to establish, **[107]**
provisions, **[108]**
market abuse, penalty
reference by person given decision notice, **[98]**
membership, **[341]**
panels, **[340]**
president, appointment/function, **[340]**
procedure, **[342]**
proceedings before, **[106A]**
offences, **[106B]**
reference to, procedure, **[106]**
regulated activity
approved person, disciplinary measure
reference, right, **[67]**
authorised person, controlled function, approval, FSA
reference, right, **[62]**
permission to carry on
aggrieved applicant, right to refer, **[55]**
prohibition order, challenge, **[57]**, **[58]**
rules generally, **[339]**–**[342]**
staff, **[340]**
supervisory notices, **[106A]**
FINANCIAL SERVICES AUTHORITY (FSA)
annual public meeting/report, **[321]**
authorised persons
control over, notification etc to, **[145]**–**[159]**
disciplinary measures against, **[172]**–**[178]**
See also AUTHORISED PERSON
clients' money, handling by authorised person
rule-making power, **[112]**
collective investment schemes
authorisation, **[331]**
authorised person, manager
power to restrict, **[113]**
compensation scheme, **[179]**–**[191]**
See also FINANCIAL SERVICES COMPENSATION SCHEME
complaints, investigation, **[321]**
constitution, **[321]**
consultation
draft rules, pre-requisites, **[128]**
practitioners/consumers
Consumer Panel, **[10]**
general duty, **[8]**
Practitioner Panel, **[9]**
representations by Panels, duty to consider, **[11]**
contravention, rules
damages, action for, **[123]**
evidential provisions, **[122]**

FINANCIAL SERVICES AUTHORITY (FSA) – *cont.*
contravention, rules – *cont.*
limitations on effect, **[123]**
control of information rules, **[120]**
damages, exemption, liability, **[324]**, **[335]**
distance marketing, function, **[4343]**
enforcement, **[321]**
approach to, **[2219B]**
approval as sponsor, cancellation of, **[2219Q]**
approval, withdrawal of, **[2219I]**
auditors and actuaries, disqualification of, **[2219O]**
collective investment schemes, **[2219N]**
conduct of investigations, **[2219D]**
criminal offences, prosecution of, **[2219L]**
financial penalties, **[2219G]**
Handbook, **[2219A]**–**[2219T]**
incoming firms, intervention against, **[2219H]**
information gathering and investigation powers, **[2219C]**
injunctions, **[2219J]**
insolvency, **[2219M]**
investigation guidelines, **[2219S]**
members of professions, disapplication orders against, **[2219P]**
non-FSMA powers, **[2219R]**
permission, variation and cancellation of, **[2219H]**
prohibition orders, **[2219I]**
public censures, **[2219G]**
publicity, **[2219F]**
restitution and redress, **[2219K]**
settlement, **[2219E]**
transitional provisions, **[2219T]**
fees, **[323]**
financial promotion rules, powers, **[118]**
functions, FSMA 2000, **[1]**
general duties, **[2]**
general rule-making power, **[111]**
good governance, duty, **[7]**
guidance re rules etc
notification to Treasury, **[131]**
powers, **[130]**
Handbook. *See* FINANCIAL SERVICES AUTHORITY HANDBOOK
incoming firms, intervention by FSA, **[160]**–**[169]**
See also EEA FIRM; TREATY FIRM
information gathering, **[132]**, **[133]**
See also INFORMATION
Information, power to require, **[185A]**
injunction application, **[165]**, **[268]**, **[269]**, **[2219J]**
See also INJUNCTIONS
insolvency, powers generally, **[242]**–**[267]**
See also INSOLVENCY
insurance business rules, powers to prohibit authorised person effecting or carrying out contracts, **[114]**
insurance mediation, unauthorised person, powers, **[581]**–**[585]**

FINANCIAL SERVICES AUTHORITY (FSA) – *cont.*
international obligations, proposed action, Treasury powers, **[298]**
investigative powers, **[134]–[144]**, **[321]**, **[2219C]**, **[2219S]**
See also INVESTIGATIONS
Lloyds's, duties re, **[201]–[211]**
See also LLOYD'S
modification, rules, powers
rules to which applicable, **[121]**
money laundering, rules, powers, **[119]**
monitoring, **[321]**
mutual societies, transfers re, **[221]–[226]**
See also BUILDING SOCIETIES; CREDIT UNIONS; FRIENDLY SOCIETIES; INDUSTRIAL AND PROVIDENT SOCIETIES
non-executive committee, **[321]**
non-executive members, **[321]**
notices generally, **[275]–[284]**
See also NOTICES
overseas regulator, exercise of own-initiative power re permission for regulated activity in support, **[47]**
penalties which may impose, **[323]**
price stabilising rules, powers, **[117]**
professions, financial services, provision, members, **[212]–[220]**
See also PROFESSIONS, MEMBERS
records, **[321]**
regulated activity
generally. *See* REGULATED ACTIVITY
permission to carry on
generally. *See* REGULATED ACTIVITY
own-initiative power, exercise, **[45]**, **[47]**, **[53]**
variation
overseas regulator, in support, **[47]**
own initiative, **[45]**
regulatory objectives, **[3]–[6]**
restitution order, **[270]–[274]**
See also RESTITUTION ORDER
review of efficiency etc
documents/information, reviewer, right, access, **[13]**
Treasury, appointment independent person, **[12]**
written report, **[12]**
rule-making powers
generally, **[111]–[129]**
instruments, writing, requirement, **[126]**
scheme order by Treasury, **[292]**
status, **[1]**, **[322]**
third country decision, implementation
direction by Treasury
consequences, **[295]**
EFTA firms, **[296]**
Gibraltar, **[297]**
terms, **[293]**, **[294]**
Treasury, notification, FSA rules, **[125]**
verification of rules, **[127]**

FINANCIAL SERVICES AUTHORITY (FSA) – *cont.*
waiver, rules, powers
rules to which applicable, **[121]**, **[2011]**
FINANCIAL SERVICES AUTHORITY HANDBOOK
client assets, **[2126]–[2140]**
See also CLIENT ASSETS (CASS)
compensation, **[2184]–[2204]**
See also COMPENSATION SOURCEBOOK (COMP)
financial penalties, insurance against, **[2054]**
fit and proper test for approved persons (FIT), **[2045]–[2053]**
See also FIT AND PROPER TEST FOR APPROVED PERSONS (FIT): FSA HANDBOOK
general prudential sourcebook (GENPRU), **[2055]–[2064]**
See also GENERAL PRUDENTIAL SOURCEBOOK (GENPRU)
glossary, **[2001]**
insurance: new conduct of business sourcebook, **[2111]–[2125]**
See also INSURANCE: NEW CONDUCT OF BUSINESS SOURCEBOOK (ICOBS)
interim prudential sourcebook: insurers (IPRU(INS)), **[2093]–[2109]**
See also INTERIM PRUDENTIAL SOURCEBOOK: INSURERS (IPRU(INS))
perimeter guidance manual, **[2220]–[2223]**
See also PERIMETER GUIDANCE MANUAL (PERG)
principles for businesses (PRIN), **[2002]–[2011]**
See also PRINCIPLES FOR BUSINESSES (PRIN): FSA HANDBOOK
professional firms, **[2205]–[2218]**
See also PROFESSIONAL FIRMS (PROF)
prudential sourcebook for insurers (INSPRU), **[2064]–[2080]**
See also PRUDENTIAL SOURCEBOOK FOR INSURERS (INSPRU)
prudential sourcebook for mortgage and home finance firms, and insurance intermediaries (MIPRU), **[2081]–[2092]**
See also PRUDENTIAL SOURCEBOOK FOR MORTGAGE AND HOME FINANCE FIRMS, AND INSURANCE INTERMEDIARIES (MIPRU)
responsibilities of providers and distributors for fair treatment of customer, **[2224]**
senior management arrangements, systems and controls (SYSC), **[2012]–[2024]**
See also SENIOR MANAGEMENT ARRANGEMENTS, SYSTEMS AND CONTROLS (SYSC): FSA HANDBOOK
service companies, **[2019]**
statements of principle and code of practice for approved persons (APER), **[2034]–[2044]**
See also STATEMENTS OF PRINCIPLE AND CODE OF PRACTICE FOR APPROVED PERSONS (APER): FSA HANDBOOK
supervision, **[2154]–[2182]**
See also SUPERVISION (SUP)

FINANCIAL SERVICES AUTHORITY HANDBOOK – *cont.*
threshold conditions (COND), **[2025]–[2033]**
See also THRESHOLD CONDITIONS (COND): FSA HANDBOOK
training and competence, **[2141]–[2153]**
See also TRAINING AND COMPETENCE SOURCEBOOK
unfair contract terms regulatory guide, **[2225]**, **[2226]**
FINANCIAL SERVICES COMPENSATION SCHEME
duties of, **[2185]**
electing participants, **[611]–[614]**
FSA, establishment
body corporate to exercise functions, scheme manager, **[179]**
scheme, **[180]**
guidance. *See* COMPENSATION SOURCEBOOK (COMP)
immunity, statutory, to whom applicable, **[189]**
information required, powers
authorised person, from, **[185A]**
court, **[188]**
scheme manager
inspection, documents held by liquidator, **[187]**
to require, **[186]**
relevant persons, persons not to be regarded as, **[612]**
scheme
contingency funding, **[181A]**
insolvency, relevant person, recovery, rights, **[182]**
insurance policies
long-term, continuity, **[183]**
safeguard, policy holder in financial difficulties, **[184]**
National Loans Fund
borrowing from, **[190B]**
investing in, **[190A]**
provisions, list, **[181]**
rules, **[180]**
scheme manager, requirements re, **[180]**
special resolution regime, contribution to costs of, **[181B]**
scheme agent, **[188A]**
scheme manager
annual report, **[185]**
Banking Act functions, **[191]**
body corporate, **[179]**
constitution, **[179]**
delegation of functions, **[188A]**
expenses, **[190]**
function, **[179]**, **[180]**
information, powers
inspection, documents held by liquidator, **[187]**
to require, **[186]**
inspection, documents held, Official Receiver, **[191]**
payments in error, **[190C]**
powers generally, **[181]**

FINANCIAL SERVICES COMPENSATION SCHEME – *cont.*
subrogated claims in winding up, priority, **[4301]**
FIRE
accidental
no action against person where accidentally begins, **[3006]**
Fires Prevention (Metropolis) Act 1774, **[3005]**, **[3006]**
money insured on house, how to be applied, **[3005]**
FIT AND PROPER TEST FOR APPROVED PERSONS (FIT): FSA HANDBOOK
assessment of fitness/propriety, **[2045]**
damages, action for, no rules, **[2052]**
fees etc, no requirements, **[2050]**
generally, **[2045]–[2053]**
main criteria
competence/capability, **[2046]**
financial soundness, **[2046]**
honesty/integrity/reputation, **[2046]**
notification, no requirements, **[2048]**
persons to whom applicable, **[2045]**
powers exercised, FSA, **[2051]**
purpose, **[2045]**
record keeping, no requirements, **[2048]**
transitional provisions, none directly applicable, **[2047]**
waiver, no rules, **[2053]**
FLOOD INSURANCE
ABI/Government statement for England, **[5141]–[5144]**
ABI/Government statement for Scotland, **[5145]**, **[5146]**
ABI Statement on provision of, **[5147]**
FOREIGN AND INTERNATIONAL TRANSIT, GOODS
contracts re
insurance tax premium not payable, **[3592]**
FRAUD
financial crime, **[6]**
FRIENDLY SOCIETIES
Friendly Societies Commission
Chief Registrar
report after dissolution, Commission, **[662]**
transferred functions, **[654]**, **[664]**
dissolution, **[660]**
FSMA 2000, application to transferred functions, **[667]**
transferred functions, **[654]–[658]**, **[665]**
Treasury, power to order transfer, function to FSA, **[221]**, **[226]**
insurance policy, contract by, **[3016]**
Interim Prudential Sourcebook: Insurers (IPRU(INS)) inapplicable, **[2070]**
manager, meaning, **[310]**
operation generally, **[350]**, **[351]**
Registry, power of Treasury to order transfer of function to FSA, **[222]**
self-regulating organisations for, **[351]**
transfers or amalgamations
FSA supervision, **[2172]**
Schedule 15 statement to members, **[2172]**

FUNERAL PLAN CONTRACT
information society services
exclusion from regulated activity, **[563]**
insurance/trust arrangement, covered by
exclusion from regulated activity, **[562]**
regulated activity, **[502]**, **[503]**, **[561]**, **[2220]**
rights under, **[2220]**
FUTURES
specified investment, **[2220]**

G

GAMING CONTRACT
Gaming Act 1845, **[3007]**, **[3008]**
enforceability, **[299]**
false pretences, obtaining money by
acts constituting, **[3007]**
marine insurance, void, **[3051]**
specified regulated activity, **[631]**, **[632]**
void, **[3008]**, **[3051]**
GENERAL PRUDENTIAL SOURCEBOOK (GENPRU)
application, **[2055]**
capital resources, **[2056]**
classification of groups, **[2057]**
cross sector groups, **[2057]**
damages, right of action for, **[2055]**, **[2063]**
fees and payment requirements, **[2061]**
financial resources, adequacy of, **[2055]**
Lloyd's, application to, **[2055]**, **[2072]**
notification and reporting requirements, **[2060]**
powers exercised, **[2062]**
record keeping requirements, **[2059]**
rules that can be waived, **[2064]**
scope, **[2055]**
third country groups, **[2057]**
transitional provisions, **[2058]**
valuation, **[2055]**
GENETIC TESTING
ABI Code of Practice, **[5092]–[5096]**
ABI genetics adviser's responsibilities, **[5039]**
arbitration scheme, **[5096]**
Chief Medical Officer of insurance company, duties, **[5094]**
Concordat and Moratorium on Genetics and Insurance, **[5077]**
confidentiality guidelines, **[5095]**
legal and ethical framework, **[5042]**
nominated genetics underwriter, responsibilities, **[5093]**
GIBRALTAR
FSA, third country decisions, implementation
Treasury, directions, **[297]**
UK firm, branch/cross-border services in
EEA passport rights, **[2166]**
GROUP
insurance tax premium, **[3567]**
insurance undertakings, supplementary supervision, **[6107]–[6124]**
meaning, **[308]**
GROUP – *cont.*
participating interest, meaning, **[308]**
policies, validation, **[3201]**
reports from, **[2170]**
GROUP AND JOINT ENTERPRISES
transaction not constituting regulated activity, **[569]**, **[2220]**
GUARANTEE
EC Directive on short-term transactions with public o private buyers, harmonisation, **[6014]–[6020]**
Lloyd's, powers, **[3152]**
unfair contract terms, guarantee of consumer goods, **[3321]**

H

HIV AND INSURANCE
ABI statement of best practice, **[5097]–[5108]**

I

INCOME PROTECTION INSURANCE
ABI statement of best practice, **[5060]–[5076]**
managing claims, ABI Code of Practice, **[5124]**, **[5125]**
INDIVIDUAL CAPITAL ASSESSMENT
Guide to process for insurers, **[5050]–[5054]**
INDUSTRIAL AND PROVIDENT SOCIETIES
transfer, functions to FSA
Treasury, powers, **[225]**, **[226]**
INDUSTRIAL ASSURANCE
Industrial Assurance (Individual Transfer) Regulations 1928, **[4001]–[4005]**
Industrial Assurance (Premium Receipt Books) Regulations 1948, **[4006]–[4011]**
repealed legislation, **[303]**
INFORMATION. *SEE ALSO* DISCLOSURE; INVESTIGATIONS
cancellation of Part IV permission, supply to FSA, **[2159]**
competition information, disclosure, **[238]**
confidential, disclosure by FSA
exceptions to restrictions, **[236]**, **[2170]**
restrictions, **[235]**
core requirements, notification to FSA, **[2169]**
distance marketing
publication, **[4341]**
required prior to conclusion, contract, **[4327]**, **[4345]**
voice telephone communications, **[4346]**
written and additional, **[4328]**
FSA powers to require
authorised persons, from, **[185A]**
notice in writing to authorised person, **[132]**
reports by skilled persons, **[133]**
supervision, **[2169]**

INFORMATION. *SEE ALSO* DISCLOSURE; INVESTIGATIONS – *cont.*
Financial Services Compensation Scheme powers
court, **[188]**
scheme agent, **[188A]**
scheme manager
delegation of functions, **[188A]**
inspection, documents held by liquidator, **[187]**
to require, **[186]**
incidental basis, provision re insurance/investments
exclusion from regulated activity, **[573]**
information society services
exclusion as regulated activity
agreement to carry on specified kinds of activity, **[565]**
EEA State other than UK, from, **[571]**
funeral plan contract, **[563]**
Lloyd's, **[560]**
stakeholder pension scheme, **[550]**
Inland Revenue, disclosure by, **[237]**
medical information, **[5109]–[5123]**
See also MEDICAL INFORMATION
Ombudsman scheme powers to require
court, **[199]**
Ombudsman, **[198]**
variation of Part IV permission, supply to FSA, **[2159]**
INFORMATION COMMISSIONER
appointment, **[3620]**
assessment notice
code of practice, **[3642AKC]**
limitations, **[3642AKB]**
service of, **[3642AKA]**
assessment, request to for, **[3642AL]**
authenticity of documents, **[3642BZ]**
codes of practice, **[3642AV]**
data sharing code
alteration or replacement, **[3642AVC]**
effect of, **[3642AVE]**
preparation of, **[3642AVA]**
procedure, **[3642AVB]**
publication, **[3642AVD]**
disclosure of information to, **[3642BG]**
duties of, **[3642AU]**
enforcement notice
cancellation, **[3642AK]**
service of, **[3642AJ]**
information notice
service of, **[3642AM]**
special, **[3642AN]**
international co-operation, **[3642AX]**
monetary penalty notices
enforcement, **[3642BC]**
further provision, **[3642BD]**
guidance as to, **[3642BB]**
meaning, **[3642AZ]**
procedural rights, **[3642BA]**
services, power of, **[3642AZ]**
INFORMATION COMMISSIONER – *cont.*
notification regulations, functions in relation to, **[3638]**
officers and staff, **[3642BZ]**
preliminary assessment by, **[3635]**
reports, **[3642AV]**
seal, **[3642BZ]**
service of notices by, **[3642BK]**
special purposes
assistance in cases involving, **[3642AW], [3642CH]**
determination as to, **[3642AO]**
restrictions on enforcement, **[3642AP]**
INFORMATION TRIBUNAL
appeals, hearing, **[3642CA]**
disclosure of information to, **[3642BG]**
establishment of, **[3620]**
members of, **[3620]**
INJUNCTIONS
distance marketing regulations, to secure compliance, **[4339]**
FSA application
relevant requirements, **[268]**
market abuse, FSA application, **[269]**
overseas insurance firm, FSA intervention powers, **[165]**
INLAND WATERWAYS
British Waterways Act 1995, **[3597]–[3599]**
certificates, **[3598]**
insurance policies, vessels, **[3599]**
licences, **[3598]**
INQUIRIES
Treasury, independent, FSMA 2000
appointed person, powers, **[16]**
appointment, person to hold, **[15]**
non-compliance as contempt of court, **[18]**
procedure, **[16]**
relevant cases, **[14]**
terms, discretion, **[15]**
written report, publication, discretion, **[17]**
INSIDER TRADING. *SEE ALSO* MARKET ABUSE
inside information, meaning, **[89]**
insider, meaning, **[88]**
INSOLVENCY
administration order, **[246]–[250]**
See also ADMINISTRATION ORDER
bankruptcy, **[260]–[267]**
See also BANKRUPTCY
FSA powers generally, **[242]–[267]**
Financial Services Compensation scheme, rights recovery against relevant person, **[182]**
insurer, meaning, **[669]**
Lloyd's, modification, law
notification, **[4319]–[4326]**
publication, **[4319]–[4326]**
receivership, **[251]**, **[252]**
See also RECEIVERSHIP
voluntary arrangements, FSA participation, powers
company, **[243]**
individual, **[244]**

INSOLVENCY – *cont.*
winding up, **[253]–[259]**
See also BANKRUPTCY; WINDING UP
INSURANCE BUSINESS
accounting for, ABI Statement of Recommended Practice, **[5126]–[5123]**
administration order, legislation applicable
modifications, Insolvency Act/Rules 1986, **[852]–[856]**
mutual credit/set-off, **[855]**
Treasury, powers, **[247]**
agreements/decisions/concerted practices, insurance sector
application, Article 81(3) of the Treaty
EC Regulation, **[6130]–[6143]**
application, Article 85(3) of the Treaty
EC Directive, **[6099]–[6106]**
authorised person
FSA, powers to prohibit from effecting/carrying out contracts etc, **[114]**
bankruptcy
insurer, long-term contracts
assets, insurer on winding up
treatment, Treasury, powers, **[266]**
continuation
insurer in liquidation, **[264]**
liabilities, insurer, determination, **[267]**
reduction, value, contracts
alternative to winding up, **[265]**
rules, list, **[267]**
See also WINDING UP
breakdown insurance
exclusion from regulated activity, **[507]**
claims management on behalf, insurer
not a regulated activity, **[542]**
community co-insurers
exclusion from regulated activity, **[506]**
connected contract of insurance
exclusion from regulated activity, **[572]**
meaning, **[572]**
contract of insurance
applicable law generally, **[670]–[679]**, **[1032]–[1035]**
assistance, administration/performance
exclusions from regulated activity, **[542]**, **[543]**
regulated activity, **[541]**
general
applicable law, **[673]**
choice of law, **[675]**
list, **[586]**
mandatory rules, **[674]**
1990 Act, **[676]**
governing law, **[6098AH]**
identification, PERG, **[2222]**
long-term
applicable law, **[677]**
list, **[587]**
mandatory rules, **[678]**
1990 Act, **[679]**
principal, as, **[2220]**

INSURANCE BUSINESS – *cont.*
contract of insurance – *cont.*
rights under
specified investment, **[578]**, **[2220]**
risks larger than large risks, choice of law, **[1034]**
Rome I Regulation, application of, **[1033]**
taxable insurance contract, **[3577]**
definitions, **[311]**, **[503]**
EC Directives
direct insurance other than life assurance business
administrative provisions re taking-up and pursuit
coordination, laws etc, **[6643]–[6692]**, **[6714]–[6721]**, **[6760]–[6799]**, **[6872]–[6936]**
Directive. *See* SOLVENCY II DIRECTIVE
freedom of establishment, abolition of restrictions, **[6693]–[6700]**
freedom to provide services, coordination of laws etc, **[6734]–[6759]**
reinsurance
amendments, **[6872]–[6936]**
supplementary supervision, **[6107]–[6124]**
solvency margin requirements, **[6125]–[6129]**
supplementary supervision, **[6107]–[6124]**
Swiss Confederation and EEC, agreement, terms etc, **[6021]–[6024]**, **[6025]–[6090]**, **[6091]–[6094]**
EEA passport rights
EEA firms
changes
branch details, **[636]**
services, **[637]**
UK firms, outside UK
changes
branch details, **[640]–[642]**, **[2166]**
failure to notify, offences, **[645]**
services, **[643]**, **[644]**, **[2166]**
FSA Handbook, insurance: conduct of business. *See* INSURANCE: NEW CONDUCT OF BUSINESS SOURCEBOOK (ICOBS)
incoming firm, FSA
intervention powers, certain overseas insurance companies, **[165]**
information, provision on incidental basis, exclusion from regulated activity, **[573]**
information society services, exclusion from regulated activity, **[508]**
insolvency. *See* INSOLVENCY
long term business contracts, insurance premium tax not payable, **[3592]**
motor insurance
compensation claims, interest, when payable, relevant authorised person, **[857]**, **[858]**
generally. *See* MOTOR VEHICLE INSURANCE
non-EEA insurers carrying on business in UK, variation of threshold conditions, **[629]**
persistency reports, insurers, **[2170]**

INSURANCE BUSINESS – *cont.*
profits, company, distribution
long term business, with
actuarial investigation, **[3382]**
realised profits, **[3382]**
regulated activity
contracts of insurance/effecting/carrying out, **[505]**
exclusions, **[506]–[508]**
general prohibition, exemptions from, **[509]**
reinsurance
EC Directives
amendments, **[6872]–[6936]**
supplementary supervision, **[6107]–[6124]**
insurance premium tax not payable, **[3592]**
reorganisation of insurance undertakings, EC Directive, **[6936]–[6971]**
rights of action against insurers,
European Communities (Rights Against Insurers) Regulations 2002, **[4248]**, **[4249]**
run-off plans, **[2176]**
scheme of operations, **[2176]**
Swiss general insurance companies carrying on business in UK, variation of threshold conditions, **[630]**
transfers. *See* BUSINESS TRANSFERS
transitional provisions FSMA 2000. *See* TRANSITIONAL PROVISIONS FSMA 2000
Treasury, restrictive powers re certain persons not authorised persons
asset identification rules, lessening effectiveness, **[115]**
variation of Part IV permission, effect, **[2159]**
winding up. *See* WINDING UP
See also INSURANCE: NEW CONDUCT OF BUSINESS SOURCEBOOK (ICOBS)
INSURANCE: CONDUCT OF BUSINESS SOURCEBOOK (COBS)
insurance mediation, **[2110A]**
permitted links, **[2110C]**
with-profits business, **[2110B]**
INSURANCE: NEW CONDUCT OF BUSINESS SOURCEBOOK (ICOBS)
application, **[2111]**
cancellation, **[2117]**
claims handling, **[2118]**
client categorisation, **[2112]**
client needs, identification and advising, **[2115]**
communications, **[2112]**
damages, action for, **[2124]**
distance communications, **[2113]**
fees and required payments, **[2122]**
firm, services and remuneration, information about, **[2114]**
general matters, **[2112]**
inducements, **[2112]**
notification requirements, **[2121]**
powers exercised, **[2123]**
product information, **[2116]**
product sales, data reporting, **[2170]**
record keeping requirements, **[2112]**, **[2120]**
rules that can be waived, **[2125]**
INSURANCE: NEW CONDUCT OF BUSINESS SOURCEBOOK (ICOBS) – *cont.*
transitional provisions, **[2119]**
INSURANCE MEDIATION
appointed representative, **[2165]**
designated professional body, duty to notify FSA in writing of particulars of unauthorised member, **[583]**
EC Directive, **[588]–[590]**, **[6800]–[6817]**
PERG, **[2221]**
professional firms, **[2211]**
principles for businesses (PRIN), FSA Handbook
application to ancillary activities, **[2004]**
generally. *See* PRINCIPLES FOR BUSINESSES (PRIN): FSA HANDBOOK
regulated activity, activities to which exclusion applies, **[2220]**
unauthorised person carrying on
designated professional body, member, **[583]**, **[585]**
exclusion, person not fit and proper
FSA, powers, **[584]**
generally, **[581]–[585]**
record of unauthorised persons
FSA, duty to maintain, **[582]**, **[585]**
INSURANCE POLICY
assignees, power to sue, **[3009]**
assignment
mode, **[3013]**
notice of, **[3011]**
receipt, notice, **[3014]**
defences to action on
equitable grounds, **[3010]**
definition, **[626]**
friendly society contracts, **[3016]**
lending on security of policy, arranging transactions not regulated activity arranging investment deals, **[530]**
long-term, continuity, role of Financial Services Compensation scheme, **[183]**
Policies of Assurance Act 1867, **[3009]–[3018]**
policyholder, definition, **[627]**
premium, failure to pay, winding up, **[4232]**
principal place of business, specification, **[3012]**
records, **[4158]–[4166]**
safeguard for policy holder in financial difficulties
role of Financial Services Compensation scheme, **[184]**
INSURANCE PREMIUM TAX
accounting
returns etc, **[3558]**, **[4088]–[4092]**
schemes, special, **[3575]**, **[4104]–[4112]**
administration
accounting for tax, **[3558]**
register, information required to keep up to date, **[3557]**
registration
insurers, **[3555]**, **[4079]–[4082]**
taxable intermediaries, **[3556]**
amounts of premiums, directions, **[3570]**
appeals, **[3564]**, **[3565]**
assessment, **[3560]**, **[3591]**

INSURANCE PREMIUM TAX – *cont.*
bankruptcy, effect, **[3566]**
charge to tax, **[3549]**
chargeable amount, **[3550]**
Commissioner's decisions, review, **[3563]–[3563G]**, **[3565]**
contract of insurance as taxable insurance contract, **[3577]**
contracts not taxable, **[3592]**
credit, **[3559]**, **[4093]–[4095]**
deemed date, receipt, certain premiums, **[3571]**
definition, **[3548]**
different rates applicable, charge to tax, **[3576]**
entry to premises etc, authorised person, **[3587]**
fees to be treated as premiums, higher rate contracts, **[3554]**
generally, **[3548]–[3581]**
groups of companies, **[3567]**
higher rate
fees to be treated as premiums, **[3554]**
premiums liable, **[3552]**, **[3582]–[3585]**
increase, rate, announcement
apportionment, **[3574]**
contracts treated as made, date, increase, **[3573]**
exceptions, **[3574]**
premiums treated as received, date, increase, **[3572]**
information, provision, **[3568]**, **[3587]**, **[3591]**
Insurance Premium Tax Regulations 1994, **[4075]–[4128]**
interest on, **[3590]**
liability of insured, **[3569]**, **[4116]–[4125]**
liability to pay, **[3553]**
offences, **[3589]**
overpaid, recovery, **[3588]**
partnerships, **[3566]**
penalties, **[3568]**, **[3589]**
rate, **[3551]**, **[3612]**
records, **[3586]**, **[4100]**, **[4101]**
recovery, **[3588]**
reimbursement arrangements, **[4096]–[4098]**
security for, **[3591]**
taxable insurance contract
contract of insurance as, **[3577]**
definition, power to change, **[3578]**
premium, meaning, **[3579]**
taxable intermediaries/fees, **[3613]**
time for payment, **[3558]**
transfer, business, effect, **[3566]**
INTERIM PRUDENTIAL SOURCEBOOK: INSURERS (IPRU(INS))
definitions, **[2104]**, **[2105]**
financial reporting
accounts and statements, **[2097]**
marine mutual, for, **[2098]**
enhanced capital requirement, **[2102]**
*group capital adequacy, **[2101]***
Lloyd's, requirements for, **[2103]**
marine mutual, accounts/statements for, **[2098]**
material connected-party transactions, **[2100]**
statistical rules, **[2099]**
INTERIM PRUDENTIAL SOURCEBOOK: INSURERS (IPRU(INS)) – *cont.*
general insurance business
classes/groups of classes, **[2107]**
reporting categories, **[2108]**
long-term insurance business
classes, **[2106]**
identification and application of assets and liabilities, **[2094]**
non-UK insurers, rules applicable to branches, **[2096]**
transitional arrangements, **[2109]**
INVESTIGATIONS
FSA, by
admissibility, statements, **[141]**
appointment, persons to conduct
general investigation, **[134]**
particular cases, **[135]**
powers, **[138]–[140]**
conduct, generally, **[137]–[143]**
connected person, **[344]**, **[345]**
entry, premises, warrant, **[143]**
non-compliance, offences, **[144]**
overseas regulators, assistance in support, **[136]**
production, documents, **[142]**
INVESTMENT EXCHANGE
recognised
authorisation unnecessary to carry on regulated activity, **[2220]**
INVESTMENTS
absence of holding out
not regulated activity dealing as principal, **[511]**
acceptance, instruments creating/acknowledging indebtedness
not regulated activity dealing as principal, **[513]**
administration/safeguard
administration of assets which not regulated activity, **[547]**
regulated activity, **[544]**
advising on
advice in course, administration by authorised person
exclusion, regulated activity, **[555]**
advice in newspapers etc
exclusion, regulated activity, **[554]**
approved person, customer function, **[2163]**
regulated activity, **[552]**, **[2220]**
agent, dealing as
exclusions, **[519]–[521]**
regulated activity, **[518]**, **[2220]**
approved person, customer function, **[2163]**
arrangements
in course, administration by authorised persons
not regulated activity arranging deals, **[529]**
not causing a deal
not regulated activity arranging deals, **[524]**
arranging acceptance, debentures in connection, loans
not regulated activity arranging deals, **[531]**

INVESTMENTS – *cont.*
arranging contracts to which arranger party
not regulated activity arranging deals, **[527]**
arranging deals with/through authorised persons
not regulated activity arranging deals, **[528]**
arranging transactions
in connection, lending on security, insurance policy
not regulated activity arranging deals, **[530]**
to which arranger party
not regulated activity arranging deals, **[526]**
attorney managing
not regulated activity managing investments, **[539]**
carrying on by way of business
regulated activity, conditions, **[593]**
collective. *See* COLLECTIVE INVESTMENT SCHEME
contracts for differences, **[2220]**
contractually based, dealing in
not regulated activity dealing as principal, **[512]**
controlled
meaning, **[30]**
rights conferred by
exercise consequential to unlawful communication
obligations unenforceable, **[30]**
deals with/through authorised persons
not regulated activity dealing as agent, **[519]**
designated
principles for businesses (PRIN), FSA Handbook
application to ancillary activities, **[2004]**
generally. *See* PRINCIPLES FOR BUSINESSES (PRIN): FSA HANDBOOK
enabling parties to communicate, not regulated activity, **[525]**
finance provision as sole purpose of arrangement, not regulated activity, **[532]**
information provision on incidental basis, exclusion from regulated activity, **[573]**
insurance contract, assistance, administration/performance
exclusions from regulated activity, **[542]**, **[543]**
regulated activity, **[541]**
international securities self-regulating organisations, not regulated activity arranging deal, **[536]**
introductions not regulated activity
arranging deal, **[533]**, **[534]**
qualifying customers, to, **[546]**
management
financial report, **[2170]**
regulated activity, **[538]**, **[2220]**
mortgage contracts, regulated, arrangement
regulated activity, **[523]**

INVESTMENTS – *cont.*
own shares, issue, company
not regulated activity
arranging deal, **[535]**
dealing as principal, **[515]**
principal, dealing as
exclusions, **[511]**–**[517]**
regulated activity, **[510]**, **[2220]**
profits, investment company, distribution, **[3379]**, **[3380]**
promotion
acting/not acting in the course of business
Treasury, power to specify circumstances, **[21]**
controlled activity, meaning, **[21]**
FSA, powers, **[118]**, **[326]**, **[327]**
offence, contravention, restrictions, **[25]**
outside UK, originating, **[21]**
restrictions generally, **[21]**
regulated activity
advising
exclusions, **[554]**–**[556]**
specified activity, **[552]**, **[2220]**
arranging deals
exclusions, **[524]**–**[537]**
specified activities, **[522]**, **[523]**, **[2220]**
dealing as agent
exclusions, **[519]**–**[521]**
specified activity, **[518]**, **[2220]**
dealing as principal
exclusions, **[511]**–**[517]**
specified activity, **[510]**, **[2220]**
insurance contract, assistance, administration/performance
exclusions from regulated activity, **[542]**, **[543]**
specified activity, **[541]**, **[2220]**
management
exclusions, **[539]**, **[540]**
specified activity, **[538]**, **[2220]**
multilateral trading facility, operating, **[523A]**
PERG, **[2220]**
safeguarding/administration
exclusions, **[545]**–**[548]**
specified activity, **[544]**, **[2220]**
specified, general, **[577]**, **[2220]**
rights to, **[2220]**
risk management
not regulated activity
agent, dealing as, **[520]**
principal, dealing as, **[516]**
specified, **[577]**–**[580]**, **[2220]**
third party, acceptance, responsibility, administration etc, **[545]**
not a regulated activity, **[545]**

J

JOINT ENTERPRISE. *SEE* GROUP AND JOINT ENTERPRISES

L

LEGAL ASSISTANCE
Access to Justice Act 1999, **[3643]–[3645]**
EC Directive
legal expenses insurance
coordination laws etc, **[6722]–[6733]**
funding
insurance premiums, recovery by way of costs, **[3643]**
recovery where body undertakes to meet costs liabilities, **[3644]**
Tribunal, proceedings before
funding, **[109]**
Lord Chancellor, powers to establish scheme, **[107]**
provisions, **[108]**
LIFE ASSURANCE
amount recoverable, **[3003]**
EC Directive
taking up business of, **[6556]–[6642]**
Life Assurance Act 1774, **[3001]–[3004]**
Life Assurance and Other Policies (Keeping of Information and Duties of Insurers) Regulations 1997, **[4158]–[4166]**
married woman
Married Women's Property Act 1882
moneys payable not to form part, estate of the insured, **[3040]**
names, persons interested to be on policy, **[3002]**
payment into court
Life Assurance Companies (Payment into Court) Act 1896, **[3044]–[3047]**
person with no interest in life to be assured
prohibition, **[3001]**
records, **[4158]–[4166]**
ships/goods etc ineligible, **[3004]**
LIFEBOATS/EQUIPMENT
contracts re
insurance premium tax not payable, **[3592]**
LISTED SECURITIES
inquiry, independent, Treasury, powers, **[14]**
meaning, **[14]**
LLOYD'S
accounts
aggregate. *See* aggregate accounts, *below*
euros, delivery and publication in, **[4509]**
Insurance Accounts Directive (Lloyd's Syndicate and Aggregate Accounts) Regulations 2004, **[4347]–[4364]**
statutory, publication requirements, **[4508]**
syndicate. *See* syndicate accounts, *below*
LLOYD'S – *cont.*
actuaries, **[2157]**
approved person, required function (CF12B), **[2163]**
aggregate accounts
approval and signing, **[4512]**
auditor, appointment and removal, **[4530]**
auditor's report
duties as to, **[4519]**
names stated in, **[4517]**
omission of names, **[4518]**
requirement to obtain, **[4515]**
signature, **[4516]**
Council, publication by, **[4511]**
delivery and publication, **[4520]**
disclosure, **[4529]**
non-compliance, penalties for, **[4521]**
annual report
approval and signing, **[4514]**
Council, preparation by, **[4513]**
delivery and publication, **[4520]**
requirements, **[4528]**
Appeal Tribunal, **[3359]**
arrangement, deals in contracts of insurance written at
regulated activity, **[559]**
authorised person, as, **[202]**
bankruptcy, member, **[3361]**
borrowing powers, **[3170]**
business transfers, FSA supervision, **[2172]**
byelaws
Lloyd's Act 1871, **[3030]**
Lloyd's Act 1982, **[3368]**, **[3372]**
capital stock
purposes for which to be held, **[3150]**
transfer to Society by Trustees, **[3149]**
Chairman and Deputy Chairmen, **[3356]**
Committee
meaning, **[4533]**
powers, **[3358]**
Companies Act 1948, provisions applicable, **[3365]**
Companies Clauses Act, parts applicable, **[3031]**
contracts
Lloyd's Act 1871 provisions, **[3024]**
member, party, contract of insurance, **[3360]**
Council
membership etc, **[3355]**, **[3374]**
powers, **[3358]**
debts to be paid/received, **[3026]**
Disciplinary Committee, **[3359]**
FSA
general duty
information re, **[201]**
review, whether to exercise powers, **[201]**
power to apply FSMA 2000 to underwriting
consultation before direction, **[206]**
core provisions applicable, **[204]**

LLOYD'S – *cont.*
FSA – *cont.*
power to apply FSMA 2000 to underwriting – *cont.*
direction (insurance market direction), **[203]**, **[205]**
exercise through Council, **[205]**
regulation by, **[4522]**
former underwriting members
authorised/unauthorised person
permission to carry out contract already underwritten, **[207]**, **[208]**
meaning, **[211]**
rules applicable to, **[209]**
GENPRU, application of, **[2055]**, **[2072]**
guarantees, powers, **[3152]**
incorporation, **[3022]**
information society services
exclusion as regulated activity, **[560]**
insolvency law, modification
notification, **[4319]–[4326]**
publication, **[4319]–[4326]**
INSPRU, application of, **[2072]**
Interim Prudential Sourcebook: Insurers (IPRU(INS))
limited application to, **[2103]**, **[2076]**
statistical rules, financial reporting, **[2099]**
investments, **[2220]**
liabilities
generally, **[3366]**
members, saving for, Lloyd's Act 1871, **[3036]**
Lloyd's Act 1871, **[3019]–[3041]**
Lloyd's Act 1911, **[3143]–[3154]**
Lloyd's Act 1951, **[3167]–[3172]**
Lloyd's Act 1982, **[3352]–[3375]**
Lutine, salvage operations, **[3034]**
management, underwriting capacity of a Lloyd's syndicate
regulated activity, **[558]**
managing agent
meaning, **[4495]**
report, **[4526]**
members' advisers, financial report to FSA, **[2170]**
membership
cessation on bankruptcy, **[3361]**
classification, **[3371]**
exclusion, violation, fundamental rules etc, **[3038]**
notices to members, **[3153]**
objects of Society, **[3146]**, **[3147]**
other societies, incorporation, agreements, **[3035]**
property vested in, **[3023]**
recovery of wreck etc, power to undertake, **[3033]**
regulated activities permitted
cancellation, **[2159]**
to carry out, **[202]**, **[557]–[559]**, **[2220]**
variation, **[2159]**
reorganisation
Insurers (Reorganisation and Winding Up) (Lloyd's) Regulations 2005, **[4398]–[4445]**

LLOYD'S – *cont.*
reorganisation – *cont.*
Lloyd's Market Reorganisation Order, **[4400]–[4428]**
reporting by, to FSA
requirement, **[2170]**
reporting to, underwriting agents, **[2170]**
senior statutory auditor, **[4496]**
stamp or mark, penalty for imitation, **[3032]**
syndicate accounts
annual, preparation, **[4498]**
approval and signing, **[4500]**
contents, **[4525]**
managing agent's report, **[4526]**
non-compliance, penalties for, **[4510]**
persons to whom sent, **[4501]**
publication, **[4502]**
requirements, **[4525]**
underwriting year, preparation, **[4499]**
syndicate auditor
appointment and removal of, **[4527]**
remuneration, **[4528]**
syndicate auditor's report
duties, **[4504]**
names stated in, **[4505]**
omission of names, **[4506]**
requirement of, **[4503]**
signature, **[4504]**
syndicate capacity, specified investment, **[580]**
syndicate membership
insurance premium tax, registration, **[4084]**, **[4085]**
specified investment, **[580]**
syndicate participation at, advice
approved person, customer function, adviser (CF25), **[2163]**
regulated activity, **[557]**
transfer schemes, **[210]**, **[826]–[830]**
trustee, as, **[3151]**, **[3171]**
winding up, Insurers (Reorganisation and Winding Up) (Lloyd's) Regulations 2005, **[4398]–[4445]**
LOANS
acceptance of debentures in connection with arrangement, not regulated activity, **[531]**
LOCAL GOVERNMENT
local authority
accident insurance, members, **[3196]**
probation committees, voluntary assistants, insurance, **[3198]**
voluntary assistants, insurance, **[3197]**
Local Government Act 1972, **[3196]–[3200]**

M

MARINE INSURANCE
abandonment
effect, **[3110]**
notice, **[3109]**
advance freight, **[3059]**

MARINE INSURANCE – *cont.*
assignment, interest, **[3062]**
bottomry, **[3057]**
charges of insurance, **[3060]**
contingent interest, **[3054]**
contract
deemed to be concluded, time, **[3068]**
embodied in policy, **[3069]**
rectification by assured, **[3133]**
defeasable interest, **[3054]**
definition, **[3048]**
disclosure
agent effecting insurance, **[3066]**
assured, by, **[3065]**
double insurance, **[3079]**
gambling on loss by maritime perils, prohibition, **[3141]**
implied obligations
variation, agreement/usage, **[3134]**
indemnity, measure
general average contributions, **[3120]**
general provision, **[3122]**
liability, insurer for loss, extent, **[3114]**
partial loss
freight, **[3117]**
goods etc, **[3118]**
ship, **[3116]**
particular average warranties, **[3123]**
salvage charges, **[3120]**
successive losses, **[3124]**
suing and labouring clause, **[3125]**
third parties, liabilities to, **[3121]**
total loss, **[3115]**
valuation, apportionment, **[3119]**
insurable interest
definition, **[3052]**
generally, **[3051]–[3062]**
insurable value, **[3063]**
loss
actual total loss, **[3104]**
constructive total loss, **[3107]**, **[3108]**
general average loss, **[3113]**
included/excluded losses, **[3102]**
missing ship, **[3105]**
partial/total loss, **[3103]**
particular average loss, **[3111]**
salvage charges, **[3112]**
transhipment, effect, **[3106]**
see also 'indemnity, measure' *above*
marine adventure, definition, **[3050]**
Marine and Aviation Insurance (War Risks) Act 1952, **[3173]–[3181]**
Marine Insurance Act 1906, **[3048]–[3140]**
Marine Insurance (Gambling Policies) Act 1909, **[3141]**, **[3142]**
maritime peril, definition, **[3050]**
mixed sea/land risks, **[3049]**
mutual insurance, **[3132]**
partial interest, **[3055]**
policy
assignment, **[3097]**, **[3098]**
contract to be embodied, **[3069]**

MARINE INSURANCE – *cont.*
policy – *cont.*
evidence of, **[3136]**
floating policy by ship/s, **[3076]**
form, **[3140]**
signature, insurer, **[3071]**
specified matters, **[3070]**
subject matter, designation, **[3073]**
terms, construction, **[3077]**
unvalued, **[3075]**
valued, **[3074]**
voyage and time policies, **[3072]**
premium
generally, **[3078]**, **[3099]–[3101]**
return, **[3129]–[3131]**
quantum, interest, **[3061]**
reasonable time, meaning, **[3135]**
reinsurance, **[3056]**
rights of insurer on payment
contribution, **[3127]**
subrogation, **[3126]**
under insurance, effect, **[3128]**
representations pending negotiation, contract, **[3067]**
salvage charges, **[3112]**, **[3120]**
uberrimae fidei, **[3064]**
voyage
alteration, port of departure, **[3090]**
change, **[3092]**
commencement, risk
implied conditions, **[3089]**
delay, **[3095]**, **[3096]**
deviation, **[3093]**, **[3096]**
different destination, **[3091]**
several ports of discharge, **[3094]**
wagering/gaming contract, avoidance, **[3051]**
wages, master/seamen, **[3058]**
war risks
Marine and Aviation Insurance (War Risks) Act 1952, **[3173]–[3181]**
warranties etc, **[3080]–[3088]**, **[3123]**
when interest must attach, **[3053]**
See also SHIPPING
MARKET ABUSE
code
City Code, FSA powers to provide conformity, **[91]**
cost benefit analysis
meaning, **[92]**
to accompany, **[92]**
draft, requirement, **[92]**
effect on decision whether market abuse has occurred, **[93]**
FSA, powers to alter/replace, **[90]**
matters which may be specified, **[90]**
representations, FSA to consider, **[92]**
decision notice, FSA, **[98]**
disclosures, protected, **[104]**
injunction, FSA application, **[269]**
inside information, meaning, **[89]**
insider, meaning, **[88]**

MARKET ABUSE – *cont.*
investigation, FSA power to suspend/terminate, **[99]**
meaning, **[86]**
notification to FSA, **[2169]**
penalties
generally, **[86]–[99A]**
imposition
court, powers, **[100]**
FSA powers, **[94]**
policy statement, FSA
preparation, requirement, **[95]**
procedure before issue, **[96]**
transactions not void/unenforceable by imposition, **[103]**
place where behaviour constituting occurs, **[87]**
restitution order, FSA application, **[271]**
Treasury
guidance, **[101]**
prescribed markets, powers to specify, **[102]**
Tribunal, reference to
person to whom decision notice re penalty given, **[98]**
warning notice, proposed action, FSA, **[97]**
MARKET CONFIDENCE, FINANCIAL SYSTEM
FSA regulatory objective, **[3]**
financial system, meaning, **[3]**
See also FINANCIAL MARKET
MEDICAL INFORMATION
ABI and BMA joint guidelines, **[5109]–[5123]**
adults lacking capacity, **[5117]**
confidentiality of reports, **[5123]**
content of reports, **[5114]**
deceased people, **[5118]**
explanations, **[5115]**
fees, **[5119]**
further information, **[5121]**
general practitioner reports, **[5112]**
independent medical reports, **[5113]**
medical factors in insurance, **[5110]**
medical reports, **[5111]**
release of information to verify claims, **[5116]**
return and quality of reports, **[5120]**
risk assessment, in, **[5122]**
MISCONDUCT
information re financial market, financial crime, **[6]**
MISLEADING INFORMATION/STATEMENT
actuary, provision to, **[233]**
auditor, provision to, **[233]**
misleading FSA
FSA supervisory powers, **[2169]**
offence, **[285]**
residual cases, **[286]**
specified activities, list, **[840]**
MISREPRESENTATION
damages for, **[3185]**
innocent, removal of certain bars to rescission for, **[3184]**
liability for, provision excluding avoidance, **[3186]**
past transactions, **[3187]**
MONEY LAUNDERING
bureau de change, notification by firm establishing or ceasing business, **[2169]**
FSA, powers
notification requirements, **[2169]**
to make rules, **[119]**
to modify/waive rules, **[121]**
MORTGAGE
mortgage endowment policy reviews
ABI Code of Practice, **[5044]**
Guidance for insurers complying with ABI Code of Practice, **[5045]**
regulated mortgage contract
advising on, regulated activity, **[553]**, **[594]**, **[2220]**
arrangement, regulated activity, **[594]**, **[2220]**
principles for businesses (PRIN), FSA Handbook
application to ancillary activities, **[2004]**
generally. *See* PRINCIPLES FOR BUSINESSES (PRIN): FSA HANDBOOK
regulated activity, **[502]**, **[503]**, **[523]**, **[594]**
rights under, **[2220]**
MOTOR VEHICLE INSURANCE
compensation
body, **[4250]–[4269]**
claims, interest, when payable, relevant authorised person, **[857]**, **[858]**
Motor Insurers' Bureau
victims, untraced/uninsured drivers, **[5021]–[5036]**
see also 'Motor Insurers' Bureau' *below*
compulsory, **[4034]–[4039]**, **[4250]–[4269]**
insurance against civil liability, **[6848]–[6852]**, **[6853]–[6865U]**
handicapped person, insurance premium tax not payable, **[3592]**
information requirements, **[4250]–[4269]**
Motor Insurers' Bureau
compensation, victims, uninsured drivers
agents, **[5035]**
apportionment, damages, **[5035]**
assignment of judgment and undertakings, **[5033]**
claimants not of full age/capacity, **[5030]**
conditions precedent to MIB's obligation, **[5033]**
decisions, MIB, notification, **[5035]**
disputes, reference to Secretary of State, **[5035]**
duration, agreement, **[5031]**
exceptions to agreement, **[5032]**
interpretation, **[5030]**
limitation, liability, MIB, **[5034]**
notice of
intention to apply for judgment, **[5033]**
relevant proceedings, **[5033]**
service, proceedings, **[5033]**
obligation, MIB, **[5031]**
recoveries, **[5035]**
service, notices, **[5033]**

MOTOR VEHICLE INSURANCE – *cont.*
Motor Insurers' Bureau – *cont.*
compensation, victims, untraced drivers
accelerated procedure, **[5027]**
agreement
conditions, **[5023]**
duration, **[5022]**
exclusions, **[5022]**
limitation, **[5022]**
scope, **[5022]**
terms, **[5023]**
appeals against MIB's decision, **[5026]**
applicants' representatives, **[5021]**
arbitration procedure, **[5026]**, **[5028]**
conditions precedent to MIB's obligations, **[5023]**
contribution
applicant to legal costs, **[5023]**
MIB to applicant's legal costs, **[5029]**
enforcement against MIB, **[5028]**
generally, **[5021]–[5036]**
interest on compensation, **[5023]**
interpretation, **[5021]**
guidance notes, victims, road traffic accidents, **[5036]**
investigation, claims, **[5023]**
joint and several liability, **[5024]**
notification, decision, **[5025]**
payment, award, **[5025]**
service, notices on MIB, **[5028]**
Motor Vehicles (Compulsory Insurance) (No 2) Regulations 1973, **[4034]–[4039]**
Motor Vehicles (Compulsory Insurance) (Information Centre and Compensation Body) Regulations 2003, **[4250]–[4269]**
Motor Vehicles (International Motor Insurance Card) Regulations 1971, **[4012]–[4019]**
Motor Vehicles (Third Party Risks) Regulations 1972, **[4020]–[4033]**
Motor Vehicles (Third-party Risks Deposits) Regulations 1992, **[4042]–[4048]**
premiums, higher rate, **[3585]**
prudential sourcebook. *See* PRUDENTIAL SOURCEBOOK FOR MORTGAGE AND HOME FINANCE FIRMS, AND INSURANCE INTERMEDIARIES (MIPRU)
Road Traffic Act 1988, **[3397]–[3415]**
third party liabilities
bankruptcy, insured/secured persons
not to affect third party claims, **[3407]**
car-sharing arrangements
private use, vehicle, **[3404]**
compulsory insurance/security
certificates of insurance
avoidance, certain exceptions, **[3402]**
issue, **[3401]**
surrender, **[3401]**
exceptions from requirement, **[3398]**
policy, contents, **[3399]**
securities, requirements, **[3400]**
users, motor vehicles to be insured/secured, **[3397]**

MOTOR VEHICLE INSURANCE – *cont.*
third party liabilities – *cont.*
emergency treatment, traffic casualties
payment, **[3410]**, **[3411]**
hospital treatment, traffic casualties
payment, **[3409]**, **[3411]**
information as to insurance/security, duty where claim made, **[3408]**
insurers/persons giving security, duty
duty to satisfy judgment against person insure/secured against third party risks, **[3405]**, **[3406]**
passengers, liability towards
avoidance, certain agreements, **[3403]**

N

NHS CHARGES
recovery, liability of insurers, **[3663]**
NOMINEE
transactions not regulated activity, conditions, **[566]**, **[2220]**
NON-INVESTMENT BUSINESS
activities in course of
not regulated activities, conditions, **[567]**
NORTHERN IRELAND
insurers, winding-up rules 2005, **[4365]–[4397]**
Unfair Contract Terms Act 1977, provisions applicable, **[3317]–[3328]**, **[3341]–[3348]**
See also CONSUMER PROTECTION
NOTICES
decision notice
disciplinary measures, FSA, **[175]**
procedure, **[283]**
publication prohibited, **[279]**
requirements, **[98]**, **[276]**, **[2154]**
restitution order, **[274]**
third party
access to FSA material, **[282]**
rights, **[280]**, **[281]**
discontinuance, of
publication, **[279]**
requirements, **[277]**
final, **[278]**
FSA, to
supervision requirements, **[2169]**, **[2180]**
permission notice, scope, **[848]–[851]**
procedure, statement of, FSA
consultation, **[284]**
requirements, **[283]**
service, notices by FSA
method, **[301]**, **[2170]**
supervisory
procedure, **[283]**
publication, **[279]**
market abuse
proposed action, FSA, **[97]**
restitution order, FSA application, **[271]**
procedure, **[283]**
publication prohibited, **[279]**

NOTICES – *cont.*
requirements, **[275]**
third party
access to FSA material, **[282]**
rights, **[280]**, **[281]**
winding up, service, **[4284]**
NUCLEAR INSTALLATIONS
Nuclear Installations Act 1965, **[3181]–[3183]**

O

OFFENCES
body corporate, **[288]**
control over authorised person, **[158]**
disclosure, confidential information, **[239]**
distance marketing, **[4342]**
financial promotion, contravention, restrictions, **[25]**
Financial Services and Markets Tribunal, proceedings before, **[106B]**
FSA investigation, non-compliance, **[144]**
institution, proceedings
by whom permitted, **[289]**
consent, when required, **[289]**
FSA powers, **[289]**, **[290]**
Insurance premium tax, re, **[3589]**
jurisdiction, **[291]**
meaning, **[6]**, **[289]**
misleading FSA, residual cases, **[286]**
misleading information, provision to actuary/auditor, **[233]**
misleading statements/practices, **[285]**
partnership, **[288]**
procedure, **[291]**
regulated activity
contravention, general prohibition, offence, **[23]**
prohibition order, FSA, breach, **[56]**
OFFICE OF FAIR TRADING (OFT)
distance marketing, notification of undertakings and orders to, **[4340]**
EEA firm, powers as to Consumer Credit Act business
prohibition, **[170]**
restriction, **[171]**
Treaty firm, powers as to Consumer Credit Act business
prohibition, **[170]**
restriction, **[171]**
OFFICIAL RECEIVER
inspection, documents held
Financial Services Compensation Scheme manager, powers, **[191]**
OIL POLLUTION. *SEE* SHIPPING
ONLINE
insurance bought on, ABI Guide, **[5042]**
OMBUDSMAN SCHEME
administration, **[192]**
compulsory jurisdiction
awards, **[196]**
conditions, **[193]**
OMBUDSMAN SCHEME – *cont.*
compulsory jurisdiction – *cont.*
consumer credit, **[193A]**, **[348A]**
costs, **[197]**
determination, **[195]**
procedure generally, **[348]**
damages, exemption, liability, **[347]**
establishment, **[347]**
funding
consumer credit licensees, **[200A]**
industry, **[200]**
information, powers to require
court, **[199]**
Ombudsman, **[198]**
operation generally, **[346]–[349]**
panel, **[347]**
privilege, **[347]**
status, **[347]**
voluntary jurisdiction, **[194]**, **[349]**
OPTIONS
specified investment, **[2220]**
OUTER SPACE ACT 1986
activities to which applicable, **[3391]**
licence
grant, **[3394]**
terms, **[3395]**
persons to whom applicable, **[3392]**
unlicensed activities, prohibition, **[3393]**
OVERSEAS PERSON
transactions not treated as regulated activities, **[565]**, **[570]**, **[2220]**
OVERSEAS REGULATOR
FSA
exercise, own-initiative power in support, **[47]**
intervention, power re incoming firm exercise in support, **[162]**
investigation in support, **[136]**

P

PARENT UNDERTAKING
controller, meaning, **[309]**
disregarded holdings, **[309A]**
group, meaning, **[308]**
meaning, **[307]**
PART IV PERMISSION
regulated activity, to carry on
additional
FSA
duty to consider, **[50]**
supervision, **[2159]**
application, **[40]**, **[51]**
cancellation, **[54]**, **[2159]**
connected person, **[49]**
determination, application, **[62]**
FSA own-initiative power, exercise
Procedure, **[53]**
variation, permission, **[45]**
grant, procedure, **[42]**
Lloyd's, **[202]**

PART IV PERMISSION – *cont.*
regulated activity, to carry on – *cont.*
See also LLOYD'S
notice, scope, **[848]–[851]**
PERG, **[2220]**
prohibitions, **[48]**
requirements which may be imposed, **[43]**
restrictions, **[48]**
threshold conditions, **[41]**, **[332]**, **[628]–[630]**
Tribunal, reference to, **[55]**
variation
acquisition, control over UK authorised person, on, **[46]**
authorised person, request, **[44]**
FSA
criteria, **[2160]**
own initiative, **[45]**
supervision, **[2159]**, **[2160]**
PARTNERSHIP
insurance premium tax, **[3566]**
meaning, **[304]**
offences, commission, **[288]**
regulated activity, authorisation as firm, **[32]**
PASSPORT RIGHTS. *SEE* EEA PASSPORT RIGHTS
PENSION SCHEMES
individual pension accounts
notification to FSA, **[2169]**
occupational
assets, management
notification to FSA, **[2169]**
EC Decision
Committee of European Insurance and Occupational Pensions Supervisors establishment, **[6144]–[6152]**
EC Directive
European Insurance and Occupational Pensions Committee, **[6095]–[6098]**
managing investments
carrying on business as regulated activity, **[595]**
pension transfer specialist
approved person, customer function (CF24), **[2163]**
stakeholder
basic advice
regulated activity, **[551]**, **[2220]**
characteristics, **[956]**
conditions, **[956]**, **[957]**
data reports, **[2170]**
establishment etc
regulated activity, **[549]**, **[2220]**
information society services
exclusion from regulated activity, **[550]**
linked long-term contracts
rights under, **[955]**
reductions permitted,
investor's rights/investment property, **[958]**
rights under
specified investment, **[579]**, **[2220]**
PENSION SCHEMES – *cont.*
stakeholder – *cont.*
smooth linked long-term contracts, conditions, **[957]**
stakeholder product, meaning, **[953]**
units, certain collective investment schemes, **[954]**
PERIMETER GUIDANCE MANUAL (PERG)
authorisation, **[2220]**
contracts of insurance, identification, **[2222]**
financial promotion, **[2223]**
insurance mediation activities, **[2221]**
regulated activity, **[2220]**
PERSONAL REPRESENTATIVE
transactions not regulated activity, conditions, **[566]**, **[2220]**
PRACTITIONER PANEL
establishment, FSA, **[9]**
FSA, duty to consider representations, **[11]**
membership, **[9]**
purpose, **[9]**
PREMIUM TAX. *SEE* INSURANCE PREMIUM TAX
PRICE STABILISING
FSA, rules, powers, **[117]**, **[121]**
Treasury, power to limit FSA rules, **[117]**
PRINCIPLES FOR BUSINESSES (PRIN): FSA HANDBOOK
activities to which applicable, **[2004]**
application
incoming EEA/Treaty firms, modification, **[2002]**, **[2004]**
rules generally, **[2004]**
UCITS qualifiers, modification, **[2002]**, **[2004]**
whole/part, every firm, **[2002]**, **[2004]**
breach, consequences, **[2002]**
classification, activities, generally, **[2002]**
clients
characteristics, **[2002]**
classification, **[2002]**, **[2004]**
damages, action for contravention, rules
authorised person, list, **[2010]**
private person, no right of action, **[2004]**
deposits, acceptance, **[2002]**
designated investment business, classification, **[2002]**
electronic money, issue, **[2002]**
fees etc, **[2008]**
fit and proper standard in threshold conditions, link, **[2002]**
group activities, **[2002]**
list, **[2003]**
notification requirements, **[2007]**
outside UK, markets, standards, **[2002]**
powers exercised, list, **[2009]**
purpose, **[2002]**
record keeping requirements, none, **[2006]**
regulators, meaning, **[2004]**
territorial application, **[2004]**
transitional provisions, none, **[2005]**
waiver, rules, **[2011]**

PRIVATE INVESTIGATORS
instruction and use of, ABI Guidelines, **[5135]–[5140]**
PRIVATE MEDICAL INSURANCE COVER
selling, ABI statement of best practice, **[5088]–[5091]**
PRIVILEGE. *SEE* DISCLOSURE
PROCEEDS OF CRIME
handling, financial crime, **[6]**
PROFESSIONAL FIRMS (PROF)
damages, rights of action, **[2217]**
disclosure, **[2208]**
distance marketing regulations, **[2209]**
exempt firm, status, **[2206]**
fees payable, **[2210]**, **[2215]**
FSA
duties and powers, **[2207]**
powers exercised, list, **[2216]**
firms and bodies to which applicable, **[2205]**
ICOB, when applicable, **[2084]**, **[2209]**
insurance mediation activity, **[2211]**
non-mainstream regulated activities, **[2209]**
notification requirements, **[2214]**
purpose, **[2205]**
record keeping requirements, **[2213]**
transitional provisions, **[2212]**
waiver of rules, **[2218]**
PROFESSIONAL INDEMNITY INSURANCE
solicitors, **[3315]**, **[5009]–[5019]**
See also SOLICITORS
PROFESSIONS, MEMBERS
activities in course of profession
authorisation as regulated activities not required, **[2220]**
not regulated activities, conditions, **[567]**, **[2220]**
financial services, provision
FSA, general duty, **[212]**
general prohibition
activities to which exemption inapplicable, **[601]–[610]**
consultation before direction FSA, **[217]**
directions, **[215]**
exemption from, **[214]**
orders
FSA powers, **[216]**
procedure, **[218]**
variation, **[218]**
persons to whom inapplicable
false claim to be, **[220]**
rules, **[219]**
generally, **[212]–[220]**, **[600]–[610]**
insurance mediation, **[2221]**
professional firms, FSA Handbook, **[2205]–[2218]**
See also PROFESSIONAL FIRMS (PROF)
Treasury, power to designate bodies, **[213]**
PROFITS
distribution
banking/insurance companies, by, **[3383]**
insurance company
long term business, with
actuarial investigation, **[3382]**
PROFITS – *cont.*
distribution – *cont.*
insurance company – *cont.*
long term business, with – *cont.*
realised profits, **[3382]**
investment companies, **[3379]**, **[3380]**
PROPERTY
immovable
winding up, UK insurer
property in EEA State, effect, **[4308]**
PRUDENTIAL SOURCEBOOK FOR INSURERS (INSPRU)
asset-related capital requirement, **[2066]**
capital resources requirements, **[2065]**
credit risk insurance, **[2066]**
damages, actions for, **[2073]**, **[2079]**
derivatives in insurance, **[2067]**
equalisation provisions, **[2065]**
fees and payments requirements, **[2077]**
group risk: insurance groups, **[2070]**
individual capital assessment, **[2071]**
insurance special purpose vehicles, **[2065]**
internal-contagion risk, **[2065]**
liquidity risk management, **[2068]**
Lloyd's, application to, **[2072]**
market risk in insurance, **[2067]**
mathematical reserves, **[2065]**
notification and reporting requirements, **[2076]**
operational risk management, **[2069]**
powers exercised, **[2078]**
premiums amounts, **[2065]**
record keeping requirements, **[2075]**
rules that can be waived, **[2080]**
technical provisions for insurance business, **[2065]**
transitional provisions, **[2074]**
with-profits insurance capital, **[2065]**
PRUDENTIAL SOURCEBOOK FOR MORTGAGE AND HOME FINANCE FIRMS, AND INSURANCE INTERMEDIARIES (MIPRU)
annual income, calculation of, **[2084]**
application, **[2081]**
capital resources, **[2084]**
damages, actions for, **[2091]**
fees and payments requirements, **[2089]**
general provisions, **[2081]**
insurance mediation activity, **[2082]**
insurance undertakings and mortgage lenders using, **[2085]**
knowledge, ability and good repute, **[2082]**
notification requirements, **[2088]**
powers exercised, **[2090]**
professional indemnity insurance, **[2083]**
record keeping requirements, **[2077]**
rules that can be waived, **[2092]**
transitional provisions, **[2086]**
PUBLIC AWARENESS, FINANCIAL SYSTEM
FSA regulatory objective, **[4]**
financial system, meaning, **[4]**

R

RAILWAY SAFETY
railway operator etc, direction to
Secretary of State, powers re insurance, **[3541]**
RECEIVERSHIP
FSA participation, proceedings, powers, **[251]**
receiver, duty, report to FSA, **[252]**
REGULATED ACTIVITY
agreement in course, carrying on
controlled
meaning, **[30]**
unlawful communications, resulting from enforceability, **[30]**
unenforceable
compensation, amount recoverable, **[28]**
unauthorised person
contravening general prohibition, by, **[26]**
not contravening general prohibition, through, **[27]**
agreement to carry on specified kinds of activity as, **[564]**
exclusions, **[565]**
approved persons
conduct, statement/code, FSA
principles, **[64]**, **[65]**
publication, **[68]**
controlled functions, approval, FSA
application
determination, **[61]**
procedure, **[60]**, **[62]**
Tribunal, reference to, **[62]**
withdrawal, **[63]**
disciplinary powers, FSA
extent, **[66]**
policy statement, **[69]**, **[70]**
procedure, **[67]**
Tribunal, reference to, **[67]**
authorised person generally. *See* AUTHORISED PERSON
authorisation, firm
change, membership does not affect, **[32]**
dissolution, effect, **[32]**
EEA firm ceasing to qualify, **[34]**
firm, meaning, **[32]**
Treaty firm
Cancellation, **[35]**
ceasing to qualify, **[35]**
withdrawal/cancellation, **[33]**–**[35]**
carrying on regulated activity by way of business
PERG, **[2220]**
Treasury, powers, **[306]**
2001 Order, text, **[591]**–**[595]**
carrying on regulated activity in UK, meaning, **[305]**
credit unions, transitional provisions, **[595F]**
deposit, acceptance
breach, general prohibition, [29]
exemption, **[595D]**, **[595H]**
exempt person
deposits, accepting, **[595D]**, **[595H]**
false claim, **[24]**

REGULATED ACTIVITY – *cont.*
exempt person – *cont.*
general prohibition, exemption, **[19]**
interpretation, **[595B]**
particular regulated activities, in respect of, **[595E]**, **[595I]**, **[595J]**
regulated activity other than insurance business, **[595C]**, **[595G]**
financial promotion, investment
offence, contravention, restrictions, **[25]**
restrictions, **[21]**
See also INVESTMENTS; TREASURY
inquiry, independent, Treasury, powers, **[14]**
insurance generally. *See* INSURANCE BUSINESS; INSURANCE POLICY
investments generally. *See* INVESTMENTS
meaning, **[22]**, **[325]**
permission to carry on
additional
FSA, duty to consider, **[50]**
supervision, **[2159]**
application, **[40]**, **[51]**
cancellation, **[54]**, **[2159]**
connected person, **[49]**
determination, application, **[62]**
FSA own-initiative power, exercise
Procedure, **[53]**
variation, permission, **[45]**
grant, procedure, **[42]**
Lloyd's, **[202]**
See also LLOYD'S
notice, scope, **[848]**–**[851]**
prohibitions, **[48]**
requirements which may be imposed, **[43]**
restrictions, **[48]**
threshold conditions, **[41]**, **[332]**, **[628]**–**[630]**
Tribunal, reference to, **[55]**
variation
acquisition, control over UK authorised person, on, **[46]**
authorised person, request, **[44]**
FSA
criteria, **[2160]**
own initiative, **[45]**
supervision, **[2159]**, **[2160]**
See also PART IV PERMISSION
persons carrying on but not needing authorisation, **[2220]**
principles for businesses (PRIN), FSA Handbook
application, **[2004]**
generally. *See* PRINCIPLES FOR BUSINESSES (PRIN): FSA HANDBOOK
prohibition, general, carrying on
contravention
agreement unenforceable, **[26]**
offence, **[23]**
PERG, **[2220]**
deposit, acceptance in breach, **[29]**
exemption
appointed representative, **[39]**
authorised/exempt person, **[19]**

REGULATED ACTIVITY – *cont.*
prohibition, general, carrying on – *cont.*
exemption – *cont.*
specified persons/persons within specified class
exemption order, Treasury, **[38]**
prohibition order, FSA
action for damages, breach, statutory duty, **[71]**
breach, offence, **[56]**
contents, **[56]**
procedure, **[57]**
revocation application, **[58]**
Tribunal, reference to, right, **[57]**, **[58]**
variation application, **[58]**
self-regulating organisations, transitional provisions, **[351]**
specified activities generally, **[504]–[576]**, **[2220]**
stakeholder pension scheme, arrangement/advice etc, **[549]**, **[550]**
See also PENSION SCHEMES
unauthorised person, agreement
by contravening general prohibition
unenforceable against other party, **[26]**
through not contravening general prohibition
unenforceable against other party, **[27]**
UK link, requirement, PERG, **[2220]**
See also PART IV PERMISSION
REGULATED PERSON
financial crime by, reduction
FSA regulatory objective, **[6]**
meaning, **[6]**
REINSURANCE
EC Directives
amendments, **[6872]–[6936]**
Solvency II. *See* SOLVENCY II DIRECTIVE
supplementary supervision, **[6107]–[6124]**
insurance premium tax not payable, **[3592]**
terrorism, financing o reinsurance obligation, **[3543]**, **[3544]**
transfer of contracts, notice of, **[82A]**
REPORTING REQUIREMENTS
FSA supervision, **[2170]**
transaction reporting, FSA supervision, **[2171]**
REPRESENTATIVES
appointed. *See* APPOINTED REPRESENTATIVE
personal. *See* PERSONAL REPRESENTATIVE
RESERVATION OF TITLE
winding up, UK insurer
agreements re assets, effect in EEA State, **[4311]**
RESTITUTION ORDER
FSA
application, conditions, **[270]**
power to require
decision notice, **[274]**
relevant requirements, **[272]**
warning notice, **[273]**
market abuse, FSA application, **[271]**
RETIREMENT
ABI Good Practice Guide, **[5055]–[5059]**
RETIREMENT – *cont.*
four or six month wake-up letter, **[5059]**
key pre-retirement events, **[5056]**, **[5057]**
pre-retirement wake-up packs, guidance on, **[5058]**
RIGHTS OF ACTION. *SEE* DAMAGES
RISK MANAGEMENT
investment business, not regulated activity dealing as principal, **[516]**
RISKS CONTRACTS
large risk situated outside EEA, exclusion as regulated activity, **[574]**

S

SALE OF GOODS
activities connected
not regulated activities
conditions, **[568]**, **[2220]**
relevant goods or services, meaning, **[572]**
product sales, data reporting, **[2170]**
unfair contract terms, liability arising, **[3321]–[3323]**
See also CONSUMER PROTECTION
SCHEME OF ARRANGEMENT
publication, qualifying decisions etc, **[4280]**
SCOTLAND
Building Societies Commission, transferred functions. *See* BUILDING SOCIETIES
Friendly Societies Commission, transferred functions. *See* FRIENDLY SOCIETIES
inquiries, independent, Treasury, powers, **[16]**
See also INQUIRIES
insolvency, trust deeds for creditors, FSA participation, **[245]**
insurance tax premium, diligence, **[4127]**
interdict, FSA, application, **[268]**
nominee for another person, transactions as not regulated activity, **[566]**
solicitors, professional indemnity, **[5001]**
third parties, rights against insurers, **[3159]**
unfair contract terms
breach of contract, consequences, **[3337]**
breach of duty, liability, **[3331]**
evasion by means, secondary contract, **[3338]**
'guarantee of consumer goods', **[3334]**
reasonableness, test, **[3339]**
sale/hire purchase contracts, implied obligations, **[3335]**
supply of goods, implied obligations, **[3336]**
Unfair Contract Terms Act 1977, provisions applicable, **[3330]–[3340]**
unreasonable exemptions, consumer/standard form contracts, control, **[3332]**
unreasonable indemnity clauses, consumer contracts, **[3333]**
See also CONSUMER PROTECTION
SECURITIES AND FUTURES FIRMS
financial report according to category, **[2170]**

SENIOR MANAGEMENT ARRANGEMENTS, SYSTEMS AND CONTROLS (SYSC): FSA HANDBOOK
application
activities to which SYSC2/SYSC3 applicable, **[2012]**
to whom applicable, SYSC2/SYSC3, **[2012]**
Chinese Walls, **[2016E]**
conflicts of interest, **[2016E]**
credit risk management systems and controls, **[2016J]**
damages, action for, SYSC2/SYSC3
authorised person, **[2023]**
private person, no right, **[2012]**
employees, gents and relevant persons, **[2016A]**
fees etc, no requirement, **[2021]**
group risk systems and controls, **[2016G]**
insurance risk systems and controls, **[2016L]**
liquidity risk systems and controls, **[2016F]**
market risk management systems and controls, **[2016K]**
notification/reporting, no requirements, **[2020]**
operational risk systems and controls, **[2016H]**
organisational requirements, **[2015]**
outsourcing, **[2016C]**
powers exercised, list, **[2022]**
prudential risk management, **[2016I]**
public interest disclosure act (PIDA), **[2016]**
purpose, **[2012]**
record-keeping, **[2016D]**
remuneration code, **[2016N]**
risk control, **[2016B]**
senior management arrangements, responsibilities, **[2013]**
systems and controls, **[2014]**
territorial extent, **[2012]**
transitional provisions, none, **[2018]**
waiver, rules, **[2024]**
whistleblowing, **[2016M]**
SERVICE COMPANIES
Handbook requirements, **[2219]**
SERVICE OF PROCESS. *SEE* NOTICES
SET-OFF
administration order
legislation applicable, **[855]**
winding up, UK insurer
creditors' right when permitted, applicable EEA State, **[4312]**
SHIPPING
commercial ships
contracts re
insurance premium tax not payable, **[3592]**
hazardous/noxious substances, carriage
International Convention on Liability/Compensation for Damage in Connection with the Carriage of Hazardous and Noxious Substances By Sea, **[3606]**
Merchant Shipping Act 1995, **[3600]–[3606]**
Merchant Shipping (Compulsory Insurance: Ships Receiving Trans-shipped Fish) Regulations 1998, **[4170]–[4178]**

SHIPPING – *cont.*
pollution
oil
International Oil Pollution Compensation Fund, **[3603]**
liability
compulsory insurance, **[3600]**, **[4167]–[4169]**
third parties, rights against insurers, **[3602]**
Oil Pollution (Compulsory Insurance) Regulations 1997, **[4167]–[4169]**
shipowners
compulsory insurance/security, **[3604]**
trans-shipped fish, ships receiving
compulsory insurance, **[4170]–[4178]**
See also INLAND WATERWAYS; MARINE INSURANCE
SKILLED PERSON
report by,
supervision, FSA Handbook, **[2158]**
See also SUPERVISION (SUP)
SOLICITORS
professional indemnity
disclosure guidelines, **[5009A]**
requirements generally, **[3315]**
Solicitors' Indemnity (Enactment) Rules 2007
contributions, **[5005]**
fund
maintenance and termination, **[5007]**
management and administration, **[5006]**
general provisions/definitions, **[5003]**, **[5008]**
indemnity cover, **[5004]**
indemnity periods, **[5003]**
making of, **[5002]**
Solicitors' Indemnity Insurance Rules 2008
accountants' reports, **[5016]**
assigned risks pool, **[5012]**
Council, general powers, **[5015]**
definitions and interpretation, **[5010]**
disciplinary offences and reporting, **[5014]**
firms in default, **[5013]**
minimum terms and conditions, **[5017]**
rating schedule 2009/2010, **[5018]**
registered European lawyers, **[5019]**
responsibility and monitoring, **[5011]**
Solicitors' (Scotland) Professional Indemnity Insurance Contingency Fund Rules 2007, **[5009]**
Solicitors Act 1974, **[3315]**, **[3316]**
SOLVENCY II DIRECTIVE
assets and liabilities, valuation of, **[6228]**
branches in Community belonging to undertakings with head offices outside Community
reinsurance, **[6325]–[6328]**
taking up of business, **[6315]–[6324]**
conditions governing business
administrative, management or supervisory body, responsibility of, **[6193]**
auditors, duties of, **[6225]**
confidential information, use of, **[6220]**

SOLVENCY II DIRECTIVE – *cont.*
conditions governing business – *cont.*
cooperation agreements, **[6219]**
exchange of information, **[6218]–[6223]**
professional secrecy, **[6217]**
public disclosure, **[6204]–[6209]**
qualifying holdings, **[6210]–[6216]**
supervisory convergence, **[6224]**
system of governance, **[6167]–[6203]**
definitions, **[6166]**
difficulty or irregular situation, undertakings in, **[6289]–[6297]**
direct insurance contracts
applicable law, **[6331]**
compulsory insurance, **[6332]**
conditions and scale of premiums, **[6334, [6335]**
general good, **[6333]**
policy holders, information for, **[6336]–[6339]**
duration-based equity risk sub-module, **[6456]**
freedom to provide services, **[6300]–[6305]**
group, supervision of undertakings in
application, cases of, **[6366]**
definitions, **[6365]**
group solvency, **[6371]–[6396]**
internal control, **[6399]**
intra-group, transactions, **[6398]**
levels, **[6368]–[6370]**
measures to facilitate, **[6400]–[6412]**
mixed-activity insurance holding companies, **[6418], [6419]**
risk concentration, **[6397]**
risk management, **[6399]**
scope, **[6367]**
third countries, **[6413]–[6417]**
insurance undertakings, establishment by, **[6298], [6299]**
investments, **[6285]–[6288]**
legal forms of undertakings, **[6467]**
life and non-life insurance activity, pursuit of, **[6226], [6227]**
life insurance
classes of, **[6466]**
provisions specific to, **[6361], [6361]**
minimum capital requirement, **[6281]–[6284]**
non-life insurance
accidents at work, against, **[6360]**
assistance, **[6350]**
classes of, **[6465], [6469]**
Community co-insurance, **[6343]–[6349]**
general provisions, **[6340]–[6342]**
health insurance, **[6359]**
legal expenses insurance, **[6351]–[6356]**
own funds, **[6240]–[6252]**
preamble, **[6153]**
reinsurance rules, **[6363], [6364]**
reorganisation and winding up
administrators and liquidators, **[6446]**
contracts and rights, effect on, **[6438]**
definitions, **[421]**
detrimental acts, **[6443]**
lawsuits pending, **[6445]**

SOLVENCY II DIRECTIVE – *cont.*
reorganisation and winding up – *cont.*
registration, **[6447]**
regulated markets, **[6442]**
reorganisation measures, **[6422]–[6425]**
reservation of title, **[6440]**
scope, **[6420]**
set-off, **[6441]**
third country undertakings, treatment of branches of, **[6449]**
third parties, rights in rem, **[6439]**
third-party purchasers, protection of, **[6444]**
winding-up proceedings, **[6426]–[6437]**
right to apply to courts, **[6450]**
scope, **[6155]**
exclusions from, **[6156]–[6165]**
solvency capital requirements, **[6253]–[6280], [6468]**
statistical information, **[6312]**
subject matter, **[6154]**
subsidiaries governed by laws of third country, **[6329], [6330]**
supervisory authorities, **[6180]–[6192]**
host member state, competencies, **[6306]–[6311]**
taking up of business, **[6167]–[6179]**
technical provisions, **[6229]–[6239]**
transitional provisions, **[6457]–[6460]**
winding-up proceedings, treatment of branches in, **[6313], [6314]**
STAKEHOLDER PENSION. *SEE* PENSION SCHEMES
STATEMENTS OF PRINCIPLE AND CODE OF PRACTICE FOR APPROVED PERSONS (APER): FSA HANDBOOK
code of practice
authorisation levels/job descriptions, **[2037]**
breaches, possible, regulatory requirements, **[2037]**
control systems, **[2037]**
delegation/continuing responsibilities, **[2037]**
factors relating to
all statements of principle, **[2036]**
principles 5 to 7, **[2036]**
general, **[2036]**
knowledge about business, **[2037]**
reporting lines, **[2037]**
responsibilities, apportionment, **[2037]**
specific, **[2037]**
suitability, individuals, **[2037]**
systems and procedures, review/improvement, **[2037]**
temporary vacancies, **[2037]**
damages, right of action, no rules, **[2043]**
fees etc, no requirements, **[2041]**
generally, **[2034]–[2044]**
notification/reporting requirements, **[2040]**
powers exercised, FSA, list, **[2042]**
purpose, **[2034]**
record keeping requirements, none, **[2039]**
transitional provisions, none directly applicable, **[2038]**

SUBSIDIARY UNDERTAKING
controller, meaning, **[309]**
group, meaning, **[308]**
meaning, **[307]**
SUPERVISION (SUP)
actuaries, **[2157]**
appointed representatives, **[2165]**
approved persons, **[2163]**
auditors, **[2156]**
authorisation, qualifying for, **[2167]**
controllers and close links, **[2164]**
damages, rights of action, **[2182]**
EEA passport rights
issues, guidance, **[2177]**
UK firm, exercise by, **[2166]**
fee, **[2173]**
FSA approach, **[2154]**
incoming EEA firm
cancellation, qualification for authorisation, **[2168]**
change, details, **[2168]**
individual guidance, **[2162]**
individual requirements
FSA, power to set on own initiative, **[2160]**
variation of firm's permission, criteria, **[2160]**
information gathering by FSA on own initiative, **[2155]**
modification rules. *See* 'waiver/modification, rules' *below*
notifications to FSA, requirements, **[2169]**, **[2180]**
Part IV permission
cancellation, **[2159]**
variation, **[2159]**, **[2160]**
powers exercised by FSA, list, **[2181]**
prudential categories and sub-categories, **[2175]**
record keeping requirements, **[2179]**
reporting requirements, **[2170]**
scheme of operation and run-off plans, insurers, **[2176]**
skilled person, reports by, **[2158]**
transaction reporting, **[2171]**
transfers of business, **[2172]**
See also BUSINESS TRANSFERS
transitional provisions, **[2178]**
waiver and modification of rules, **[2161]**
energy market participants, **[2174]**
rules which can be waived, list, **[2161]**
SUPPLY OF SERVICES
activities connected
not regulated activities
conditions, **[568]**, **[2220]**
relevant goods or services, meaning, **[572]**
EEA passport rights, **[2177]**
EU, free movement within, Treaty on functioning of European Union, **[6001]–[6007]**
service company, financial reports, **[2170]**
unfair contract terms, liability arising, **[3321]–[3323]**
See also CONSUMER PROTECTION
SWITZERLAND
EC Directive
direct insurance
Swiss Confederation and EEC, agreement, terms etc, **[6021]–[6024]**, **[6025]–[6090]**, **[6091]–[6094]**

T

TAXATION
insurance premium tax, **[3548]–[3581]**
See also INSURANCE PREMIUM TAX
TERRORISM
Reinsurance (Acts of Terrorism) Act 1993, **[3543]–[3545]**
reinsurance obligation, financing
Treasury, obligations, **[3543]**, **[3544]**
THIRD PARTY
arbitration, dispute re rights, **[3653]**
Contracts (Rights of Third Parties) Act 1999, **[3646]–[3654]**
contractual term, right to enforce, **[3646]**
decision/warning notices by FSA
access to FSA material, **[282]**
rights, **[280]**, **[281]**
indemnity provisions, qualifying
description, **[3385]**
disclosure, **[3386]**
individual guidance given by FSA, effect on rights of third parties, **[2162]**
investments, acceptance, responsibility, administration etc, **[545]**
not a regulated activity, **[545]**
marine insurance, liability to, **[3121]**
motor vehicle insurance, **[3397]–[3408]**
Motor Vehicles (Third Party Risks) Regulations 1972, **[4020]–[4033]**
Motor Vehicles (Third-party Risks Deposits) Regulations 1992, **[4042]–[4048]**
See also MOTOR VEHICLE INSURANCE
oil pollution, shipping, rights against insurers, **[3602]**
promisee, enforcement, contract, **[3649]**
promisor
defences, **[3648]**
party promisor, protection from double liability, **[3650]**
rescission, contract, right, **[3647]**
rights against insurers
Third Parties (Rights Against Insurers) Act 1930, **[3155]–[3160]**
variation, contract, right, **[3647]**
winding up, UK insurer
purchasers, protection in EEA State, **[4315]**
rights in rem, effect in EEA State, **[4310]**
THRESHOLD CONDITIONS (COND): FSA HANDBOOK
adequate resources, **[2026]**

THRESHOLD CONDITIONS (COND): FSA HANDBOOK – *cont.*
approval, acquisitions, **[2025]**
Banking Act 2009, assessment of conditions, **[2026A]**
business integrity, **[2026]**
claims representatives, appointment, **[2026]**
close links, **[2026]**, **[2170]**
competent/prudent management, **[2026]**
compliance, proper standards, **[2026]**
disclosure, guidance, **[2029]**
due diligence/care/skill, **[2026]**
FSA, own-initiative power, exercise, **[2025]**
fees etc, no requirements, **[2030]**
firms to which applicable, **[2025]**
generally, **[2025]–[2033]**
increases of control, **[2025]**
legal status, **[2026]**
location, offices, **[2026]**
notification requirements, none, **[2029]**
overview, **[2025]**
parent undertaking, meaning, **[2026]**
Part IV permission
application for, **[2025]**
generally. *See* PART IV PERMISSION
variation, **[2025]**
powers exercised, **[2031]**
purpose, **[2025]**
record keeping, no requirements, **[2028]**
regulated activities to which applicable, **[2025]**
subsidiary undertaking, meaning, **[2026]**
suitability, **[2026]**
transitional provisions, none, **[2027]**
TOURIST ASSISTANCE
EC Directive
direct insurance business
coordination, laws/regulations/administrative provisions, **[6714]–[6721]**
TRACING AGENTS
instruction and use of, ABI Guidelines, **[5135]–[5140]**
TRADE CREDIT INSURANCE
ABI Statement of Principles, **[5041]**
TRAINING AND COMPETENCE SOURCEBOOK
activities and products/sectors to which applying, **[2144]**
application and purpose, **[2141]**
circumstances in which not applying, **[2146]**
competence, **[2142]**
damages, action for, **[2152]**
fees and payments, **[2150]**
notification requirements, **[2149]**
powers exercised, **[2151]**
record keeping, **[2143]**, **[2148]**
rules that can be waived, **[2153]**
territorial scope, **[2145]**
transitional provisions, **[2147]**
TRANSFER OF BUSINESS. *SEE* BUSINESS TRANSFERS
TRANSITIONAL PROVISIONS FSMA 2000
complaints, **[914]–[924]**
See also COMPLAINTS
TRANSITIONAL PROVISIONS FSMA 2000 – *cont.*
principles for businesses (PRIN), FSA Handbook, **[2005]**
TRAVEL INSURANCE
premiums, higher rate, **[3585]**
TREASURY
administration order, legislation applicable, insurers
power to order, **[247]**
bankruptcy, insurer with long-term contracts
assets, insurer on winding up
treatment, powers, **[266]**
building societies
Building Societies Commission, power to order transfer of function to FSA, **[223]**
Investor Protection Board, power to terminate, **[224]**
business transfers, banking/insurance outside UK, powers, **[85]**
carrying on regulated activities by way of business, powers, **[306]**
credit unions, powers as to transfer of functions to FSA, **[225]**, **[226]**
disclosure of confidential information, power to remove restrictions, **[240]**
financial promotion, restrictions, **[21]**
FSA review of effectiveness, appointment of Independent person, **[12]**
friendly societies
Friendly Societies Commission, power to order transfer of function to FSA, **[221]**, **[226]**
Registry, power to order transfer of function to FSA, **[222]**
industrial and provident societies, powers of transfer of functions to FSA, **[225]**, **[226]**
inquiries, independent, FSMA 2000
appointed person, powers, **[16]**
appointment, person to hold, **[15]**
non-compliance as contempt of court, **[18]**
procedure, **[16]**
relevant cases, **[14]**
written report, publication, discretion, **[17]**
insurance business, restrictive powers as to certain persons not authorised persons, **[115]**
international obligations, meaning of relevant person, **[298]**
market abuse
guidance, **[101]**
prescribed markets, power to specify, **[102]**
notification by FSA of its
guidance re rules, **[131]**
rules, **[125]**
price stabilising rules, FSA
power to limit, **[117]**
professions, members providing financial services
power to designate, **[213]**
regulated activity, carrying on, general prohibition
exemption order, provisions
specified persons/persons within specified class, **[38]**

TREASURY – *cont.*
scheme order by
authorisation, FSA to operate scheme conditions, **[292]**
terrorism, legislation
reinsurance obligations, financing, **[3543]**, **[3544]**
third country decisions, implementation, FSA, directions
consequences, **[295]**
EFTA firms, **[296]**
Gibraltar, **[297]**
terms, **[293]**, **[294]**
TREATY FIRM
Consumer Credit Act business
Office of Fair Trading, powers to
prohibit, **[170]**
restrict, **[171]**
home state regulator, meaning, **[312]**
intervention by FSA
contravention, requirement imposed by FSA, **[169]**
generally, **[160]–[169]**
incoming firm, as, **[160]**
injunction, application, court, FSA
certain overseas insurance companies, **[165]**
power of intervention, FSA
general grounds, exercise, **[161]**
in support, overseas regulator, **[162]**
meaning, **[163]**
procedure on exercise, **[164]**
rescission, requirements, **[167]**
variation, requirements, **[167]**
regulated activity, authorisation, termination, **[35]**
winding up by court, no power of FSA to petition, **[256]**
TRIBUNALS
Financial Services and Markets. *See* FINANCIAL SERVICES AND MARKETS TRIBUNAL
Lloyd's Appeal Tribunal, **[3359]**
TRUSTEE
bare, transactions as not regulated activity, **[566]**, **[2220]**

U

UCITS MANAGEMENT COMPANY
financial report to FSA, **[2170]**
UNFAIR CONTRACTS. *SEE ALSO* CONSUMER PROTECTION
Regulatory Guide, **[2225]**, **[2226]**
statements of good practice, **[2226]**
Unfair Contract Terms Act 1977, **[3317]–[3348]**
UNINCORPORATED ASSOCIATION
regulated activity, authorisation as firm, **[32]**
UNIT LINKED FUNDS
ABI Guide of Good Practice for, **[5046]–[5049]**
UNIT TRUST SCHEME
manager, **[310]**
meaning, **[304]**

W

WALES
Electronic Communications Act 2000, modifications, **[3658]**
WAR RISKS
insurance against
advertisement, restriction, **[3161]–[3166]**
Marine and Aviation Insurance (War Risks) Act 1952, **[3173]–[3181]**
WINDING UP
accounts, **[4229]**
actuarial advice, **[4223]**
assets
attribution, company's long-term business, **[4221]**
costs payable out of
apportionment, **[4237]**
custody, **[4225]**
excess, long-term business assets, **[4222]**
audit, **[4229]**
court
FSA, petition, power to present
bodies to which applicable, **[255]**
bodies to which inapplicable
EEA/Treaty firms, **[256]**
person other than FSA, petition re authorised person permitted to carry out insurance contracts
copy, petition to be served on FSA, **[257]**
FSA participation, proceedings, powers, **[259]**
report to FSA
liquidator's duty, **[258]**
publication, order, **[4280]**
creditors
dividends to, **[4234]**
EEC creditors, submission of claims, **[4282]**
meetings, **[4235]**
notification to, **[4281]**
reports to, **[4283]**
disclosure of confidential information from EEA regulator, **[4285]**
EEA insurers
prohibition against winding up etc in UK, **[4273]**
schemes of arrangement, **[4274]**
reorganisation and winding up proceedings effective in UK, **[4275]**
failure to pay premiums, **[4232]**
insurers
EEA insurers. *See* 'EEA insurers' *above*
generally, **[4270]–[4320]**
jurisdiction, **[4273]–[4276]**
modifications, law re UK insurers, **[4277]–[4285]**
UK insurers. *See* 'UK insurers' *below*
Insurers (Winding Up) Rules 2001, **[4212]–[4244]**
liabilities
attribution, company's long-term business, **[4220]**

WINDING UP – *cont.*
Lloyd's
Insurers (Reorganisation and Winding Up) (Lloyd's) Regulations 2005, **[4398]–[4445]**
long-term business
powers, **[4221]**, **[4222]**, **[4228]**
remuneration, liquidator carrying on, **[4236]**
Northern Ireland, insurers in, **[4365]–[4397]**
notification
creditors, to, **[4281]**
forms, **[4244]**
relevant decisions
EEA regulators, to, **[4279]**
FSA, to, **[4278]**
preferential debts
composite insurers
application of other assets, **[4296]**
apportionment of costs payable out of assets, **[4299]**
attributable to long-term and general business, **[4291]**
excess, long term and general business assets, **[4295]**
general business, **[4293]**
general meetings of creditors, **[4298]**
proof of debts, **[4297]**
long-term and general insurers, **[4290]**
non-transferring composite insurer
insufficiency of long-term and business assets, **[4294]**
long-term business, **[4292]**
priority
payment of insurance claims, **[4286]–[4302]**
See also 'preferential debts' *above*
subrogated claims, Financial Services Compensation Scheme, **[4301]**

WINDING UP – *cont.*
proof of debts, **[4231]**
records
accounting/valuation etc, **[4227]**
financial, separate for long-term and other business, **[4216]**
security by liquidator/special manager, **[4230]**
service of notices and documents, **[4284]**
stop order
notice, **[4238]**
valuation, long-term policies when made, **[4243]**
summary remedy against liquidators, **[4300]**
third country insurers, disclosure of confidential information, **[4319]**
UK insurers, recognition of EEA rights, **[4303]–[4316]**
valuation
general business policies, **[4217]**, **[4239]**
linked life/deferred annuity policies, **[4241]**
long-term policies, **[4218]**, **[4242]**, **[4243]**
non-linked life/deferred annuity policies etc, **[4240]**
policy, of
notice, **[4233]**
voluntary
court, confirmation, **[4276]**
FSA participation, proceedings, powers, **[253]**
insurance debts, treatment, **[4302]**
insurers effecting/carrying out long-term insurance contracts
consent, FSA, requirement, **[254]**
publication, **[4280]**
See also BANKRUPTCY; INSOLVENCY
WITH-PROFITS BONDS
promotional material, industry best practice, **[5043]**